CHAMBERS

BIOGRAPHICAL
DICTIONARY

Editor
Melanie Parry

CHAMBERS

CHAMBERS

An Imprint of Chambers Harrap Publishers Ltd
7 Hopetoun Crescent, Edinburgh EH7 4AY
Larousse Kingfisher Chambers Inc., 95 Madison Avenue, New York, New York 10016

Copyright © Chambers Harrap Publishers Ltd 1997
Reprinted 1998 (twice), 1999

First edition 1897
Second edition 1929
Third edition 1935
Fourth edition 1961
Fifth edition 1990
Sixth edition 1997

British Library Cataloguing in Publication Data for this book is available from the British
Library.

Library of Congress Catalog Card Number 97-67756

ISBN 0-550-16060-4 Hardback
     0-550-14220-7 Paperback

Cover painting: *Sunday Afternoon on the Island of La Grande Jatte* by Georges Seurat
courtesy of The Bridgeman Art Library

Cover designed by Button Design Company

Typeset by Chambers Harrap Publishers Ltd, Edinburgh, and BPC Digital Techset Ltd, Exeter
Printed and bound in France by Partenaires

CHAMBERS

BIOGRAPHICAL
DICTIONARY

Editor
Melanie Parry

CHAMBERS

CHAMBERS

An Imprint of Chambers Harrap Publishers Ltd
7 Hopetoun Crescent, Edinburgh EH7 4AY
Larousse Kingfisher Chambers Inc., 95 Madison Avenue, New York, New York 10016

British Library Cataloguing in Publication Data for this book is available from the British
Library.

Library of Congress Catalog Card Number 97-67756

ISBN 0-550-16060-4 Hardback
      0-550-14220-7 Paperback

Cover painting: *Sunday Afternoon on the Island of La Grande Jatte* by Georges Seurat
courtesy of The Bridgeman Art Library

Cover designed by Button Design Company

Typeset by Chambers Harrap Publishers Ltd, Edinburgh, and BPC Digital Techset Ltd, Exeter
Printed and bound in France by Partenaires

PREFACE

The *Chambers Biographical Dictionary* was first published in 1897, the year of Queen Victoria's Diamond Jubilee; but this first edition would read strangely to a modern reader. A great deal has changed over the last century, both in societal attitudes and in society itself, and biography as a genre has changed to reflect these developments. Less deferential and moralistic, it has become more critical and objective, attempting to offer a balanced assessment of a person's achievement and lasting significance, and its language is now in consequence more concise, less rhetorical and more accessible.

Building on the extensive work undertaken for the fifth edition in 1990, the sixth edition reflects these developments while retaining the traditional breadth of information and detail which users have come to expect from the Chambers name. Given the diversity of people now in the public arena, not to mention the differing viewpoints of readers, editors and consultants, to impose a strict law of retention or selection on the biographies would undoubtedly mean limiting the book's potential to satisfy. Although entries had to be deleted to make space for new ones, the original criteria for inclusion—achievement and recognition—were adhered to as far as possible; it now contains a broader range of entries than ever before, and has unrivalled coverage—in a single volume—of fields such as science, literature, art, sport, politics, film and television, in an attempt to reflect the ever-changing nature of greatness and fame, and to meet the demands of contemporary readers.

No single-volume dictionary can ever be truly complete, but the *Chambers Biographical Dictionary* is more complete, and more reflective of changing times and changing attitudes than most. Its aim is both to inform, by providing up-to-date and readable entries, and to please, by including all who may reasonably be the subject of inquiry. A century old, but always evolving, it is an indispensable tool for the general reader looking for a clear, authoritative assessment of the personalities who, for better or worse, have shaped our world.

Melanie Parry
May 1997

CONTRIBUTORS

Editor
Melanie Parry

Editorial Assistant
Helen Cox
Research Assistant
Jocasta Whittingham

North American consultant
David Replogle and Associates

New Zealand and Australian consultant
James G Orton

Other consultants and authors
Robert Allen (panels and miscellaneous) Trevor Anderson (anthropology)
Neville Garden (classical music) Elspeth Harrison (biblical characters)
Anthony Hayward (television) Anna Howes (art)
Allan Hunter (cinema) Kenny Mathieson (folk, jazz and pop music)
Basil Morgan (rulers and nobility) Trevor Royle (military and politics)
Peter Small (sport) Alice Stoakley (miscellaneous)
Alison Twaddle (religion) Ruth Winstone (politics)

Publishing Manager
Elaine Higgleton

Readers of non-English entries
George Davidson (Chinese) Michel Vercambre (French)
Martin Mellor (Russian)

External copy-editors and proofreaders
Michael Ayton Helen Bleck
Lesley Cameron Angela Cran
Kate Eden Amanda Farquhar
Jennifer Gibb Garry Griffin
Anne Horscroft Betty Kirkpatrick
Stephanie Pickering Jane Pollock
Catherine Schwarz Nicola Wood

Keyers
Trevor Anderson Anne Benson
Robin McMorran Nicholas Shearing
David Thomson Isabelle Vitale

Data processors
Siri Hansen Dave Sparks

Prepress department
Ilona Bellos-Morison
Elaine McAdam Louise McGinnity

ACKNOWLEDGEMENTS

I would like to extend particular thanks to the following people for their contribution to this book: Min Lee, who organized the project in its early stages and spent much time analysing headword lists; Angela Cran, who was also instrumental in the early stages and thereafter provided much editorial back-up and encouragement; Robert Allen, who recrafted the majority of the panels from existing material, and wrote further original entries at short notice; Steve Gill of The Point for help with design and layout; Ilona Bellos-Morison for her management of the prepress process; Helen Cox and Jocasta Whittingham for their hard work and good humour; and Mark Parry, for many months of unfailing forbearance and support.

NOTE ON THE TEXT

LAYOUT
This new edition departs dramatically from the former style of the *Chambers Biographical Dictionary*, with the use of italicized 'identifiers' denoting the nationality and occupation of each person making it easier than ever before for the reader to find information and to browse.

ORDER OF ENTRIES
The entries are sorted into an alphabetical order that disregards spaces or hyphens between words in the surname (or in the entire name if there is no comma). Saints tend to precede rulers, who in turn precede popes and other people with the same name. Rulers are sorted into chronological sequences within countries, which are themselves sorted alphabetically. However, the rules are not set in stone, and have been disregarded in cases where it is thought that the reader would instinctively look for a person in a different order.

FOREIGN NAMES
The Pinyin transliteration of Chinese names has been used in most cases, accompanied by the Wade–Giles version in parentheses. Exceptions to this rule occur when the subject is better known under his or her Wade–Giles spelling, eg Chiang Kai-shek, and the order is reversed. Arabic names containing the particle al- or ibn- will normally be found under the element following the particle. Names of kings will often be found under their original spelling, eg Henri, Karl and Kristian instead of Henry, Charles and Christian. Cross references will assist the reader who tries to find the entry under the anglicized or alternative spelling.

FOREIGN TITLES OF WORKS
Titles of books, films, musical works, paintings and suchlike which appear in a foreign language have mainly been translated into English. Italicized translations imply that the work has been published or presented (in the case of films) under that English title, whereas the use of quotation marks implies the inclusion of a literal translation to assist the reader in understanding the reference.

BIBLIOGRAPHICAL INFORMATION
In addition to the bibliographies contained in the panels, about a quarter of the general entries have extra bibliographical information. Occasionally this is an autobiography, distinguishable by the absence of an author preceding the title, but usually an actual biography is cited, with its author and date.

ACCURACY
Every attempt is made to provide accurate information, but it is inevitable in a reference book of this size that mistakes and inconsistencies slip through the net, for which the publisher apologizes. This edition incorporates many of the suggestions and corrections brought to the attention of the reference department by helpful readers over the years, and the publisher continues to request notification of inaccuracies so that the process of improving the *Chambers Biographical Dictionary* may continue.

Abbreviations

To help the reader, the use of abbreviations and acronyms has been kept to a minimum in this new edition. Many abbreviations that are used are explained in the text, and others are explained below:

ABA	Amateur Boxing Association	Lt	Lieutenant
ABC	Australian Broadcasting Corporation	m.	married
		MA	Master of Arts
AIDS	acquired immune deficiency syndrome	MARS	Modern Architectural Research Society
BA	Bachelor of Arts	MBE	Member, Order of the British Empire
BAFTA	British Academy of Film and Television Arts	MC	Military Cross
BBC	British Broadcasting Corporation	MCC	Marylebone Cricket Club
BP	British Petroleum	MGM	Metro-Goldwyn-Mayer
CBE	Commander, Order of the British Empire	MEP	Member of the European Parliament
CBS	Columbia Broadcasting System	MP	Member of Parliament
CD-Rom	compact disk read-only memory	NATO	North Atlantic Treaty Organization
CIA	Central Intelligence Agency	OBE	Officer, Order of the British Empire
CND	Campaign for Nuclear Disarmament	OEEC	Organization for European Economic Cooperation
DBE	Dame Commander, Order of the British Empire	OM	Order of Merit
		POW	prisoner of war
DFC	Distinguished Flying Cross	QC	Queen's Counsel
DNA	deoxyribonucleic acid	RADA	Royal Academy of Dramatic Art
DSO	Companion of the Distinguished Service Order	RAF	Royal Air Force
		RCA	Radio Corporation of America
EC	European Community	RIBA	Royal Institute of British Architects
EEC	European Economic Community	RNA	ribonucleic acid
FA	Football Association	SAS	Special Air Service
fl.	*floruit* (Latin), flourished	SNP	Scottish National Party
FRS	Fellow of the Royal Society	TUC	Trades Union Congress
GPO	General Post Office	UCLA	University of California at Los Angeles
HQ	headquarters		
IBM	International Business Machines	UK	United Kingdom
ICI	Imperial Chemical Industries	UN	United Nations
IRA	Irish Republican Army	UNESCO	United Nations Educational, Scientific and Cultural Organization
ITN	Independent Television News		
KBE	Knight Commander, Order of the British Empire	US	United States ('American')
KC	King's Counsel	USA	United States of America
KG	Knight, Order of the Garter	USSR	Union of Soviet Socialist Republics
LCC	London County Council (now GLC)	VC	Victoria Cross
Legco	Legislative Council	VE Day	Victory in Europe Day
LLB	*Legum baccalaureus* (Latin), Bachelor of Laws	WASP	White Anglo-Saxon Protestant
		WBA	World Boxing Association
LP	long-playing record	WBC	World Boxing Council
LSE	London School of Economics	YMCA	Young Men's Christian Association

Aalto, (Hugo Henrik) Alvar
1898–1976
Finnish architect and designer

Born in Kuortane, he studied at Helsinki Polytechnic and evolved a unique architectural style based on irregular and asymmetric forms and the imaginative use of natural materials. Regarded as the father of Modernism in Scandinavia, Aalto designed numerous public and industrial buildings in Finland, including the sanatorium at Paimio, the library at Viipuri and the Sunila pulp mill at Kotka and the Finlandia concert hall in Helsinki. In the USA he built the Baker House hall of residence at the Massachusetts Institute of Technology and in Iceland he designed the Nordic Centre in Reykjavík (1968). In the 1930s he also pioneered the use of factory-made laminated birchwood for a distinctive style of Finnish furniture. ⊞ Karl Fleig, *Alvar Aalto* (1963); *Alvar Aalto 1963–1970* (1971)

Aaltonen, Wäinö (Valdemar) 1894–1966
Finnish sculptor

He was born in St Mårtens, and studied at Helsinki. One of the leading Finnish sculptors, he was the most versatile, combining classical form with individual characterization. His best-known works are the bust of **Sibelius** (1928, in the Gothenburg Museum) and the bronze statue of the Olympic runner **Paavo Nurmi** (commissioned by the Finnish government in 1924).

Aaron 15th–13th century BC
Biblical patriarch

He was the first high priest of the Israelites and said to be the founder of the priesthood. He was spokesman to the Egyptian pharaoh for his elder brother **Moses** in his attempts to lead their people out of Egypt, and performed a number of miracles. Later he gave in to the demands of the rebellious Israelites in the desert and organized the making of a Golden Calf for idolatrous worship, in Moses' absence. He and his sons were ordained as priests after the construction of the Ark of the Covenant and the Tabernacle, and Aaron was confirmed as hereditary high priest by the miracle of his rod blossoming into an almond tree (hence various plants nicknamed 'Aaron's Rod'). He is said to have died at the age of 123. ⊞ Harold H Rowley, *Worship in Ancient Israel* (1967)

Aaron, Hank (Henry Lewis) 1934–
US baseball player

Born in Mobile, Alabama, he is regarded as one of the greatest batters ever. A right-handed batting outfielder, he set almost every batting record in his 23-season career with the Milwaukee Braves and the Milwaukee Brewers: 2,297 runs batted in, 1,477 extra-base hits, and 755 home runs (he broke **Babe Ruth**'s long-standing record of 714 in 1974). In 1957 he was named the Most Valuable Player (MVP), leading the Braves (later the Atlanta Braves) to the World Series Championship. ⊞ Henry Aaron and Lonnie Wheeler, *I Had a Hammer: The Hank Aaron Story* (1991)

Aasen, Ivar Andreas 1813–96
Norwegian philologist, lexicographer and writer

Born in Sunmøre, the son of a peasant, he was a fervent nationalist, and created the national language called *Landsmål* (later known as *Nynorsk*, New Norwegian), based on western Norwegian dialects. He announced in 1836 that he planned 'an independent and national language' based on a synthesis of rural dialects descended from Old Norse, to replace the official Dano-Norwegian *Riksmål* (language of the realm). It eventually achieved recognition alongside *Riksmål* in 1885. He published a *Grammar of the Norwegian Dialects* (1848), followed by a *Dictionary of the Norwegian Dialects* (1850).

Abailard, Peter See Abelard, Peter (panel)

Abakanowicz, Magdalena
1930–
Polish artist

She was born in Falenty, near Warsaw, and her privileged upbringing was cut short by the Nazi invasion of Poland and the subsequent Russian 'liberation'. Educated at the Warsaw Academy of Fine Arts (1950–55) during the repressive period of Socialist Realism, she sought to escape from conventional art forms through weaving. In the 1960s she achieved international recognition with her monumental woven fibre installations, the 'Abakans'. Her later works include primitive and disturbing figurative groups made from burlap sacking. Her sisal *Black Garment* (1968) is in the Stedelijk Museum, Amsterdam. In 1978 she took part in the pioneering exhibition 'Soft Art' in Zurich, and in 1980 represented Poland at the Venice Biennale. From 1965 she taught at the State College of Arts, Poznan, becoming professor in 1979 until 1990. Since 1992 she has been a member of the Presidential Council for Culture.

Abalkin, Leonid Ivanovich 1930–
Soviet economist

Born in Moscow, he was director of the Institute of Economics of the USSR Academy of Sciences (1986–) and a member of the Supreme Soviet of the USSR with special responsibility for economic affairs. His published works centre on the theoretical problems of political economy under socialism. He is an advisor to President **Yeltsin**.

Abb, St See Ebba, St

Abbado, Claudio 1933–
Italian conductor

Born in Milan, he studied piano and composition at the Verdi Academy there. He made his debut as an opera conductor at La Scala Milan in 1960, and went on to be musical director there (1968–86). His tenure was marked occasionally by controversy, but mostly by acclaim, and he established his standing as one of the leading conductors in the world. While at La Scala, he was also the principal conductor of the London Symphony Orchestra (1979–88), and worked regularly with the Vienna Philharmonic. He quit the Milan house to become musical director of the Vienna State Opera (1986–91). He accepted a new challenge when he became **Herbert von Karajan**'s successor as the fifth chief conductor of the Berlin Philharmonic Orchestra, a post he has held with distinction since 1989. In 1994 he was artistic director of the Salzburg Easter Festival.

Abbas I, the Great 1571–1629
Fifth Safavid Shah of Persia

After his accession (1587) he established a counterweight to the Turkmen tribal chiefs by creating a standing army. From 1598 he recovered Azerbaijan and parts of Armenia from the Ottomans, and Khurasan from the Uzbeks. He transferred his capital from Qazvin to Isfahan, which he developed with a programme of public works, and established diplomatic and economic relations with western Europe. During his reign Persian artistic development reached its zenith.

'Abbas, al- c.565–c.653
Merchant and Islamic apostle

He was the founder of the 'Abbasid dynasty of the Islamic Empire who ruled as caliphs of Baghdad (750–1258). The maternal uncle of the Prophet Muhammad and a rich merchant of Mecca, he was at first hostile to his nephew, but ultimately became one of the chief apostles of Islam and gave his name to the dynasty.

Abbas, Ferhat 1899–1985
Algerian nationalist leader

Born in Taher in the Kabylie country, he founded a Muslim Students' Association in 1924, before becoming a chemist. He served as a volunteer in the French army in 1939, but after France's defeat he produced in 1942 a 'Manifesto of the Algerian People'. In 1955 he joined the Front de Libération Nationale (FLN), the main Algerian resistance organization, and worked with Ahmed Ben Bella in Cairo, before founding in 1958 a 'Provisional Government of the Algerian Republic' in Tunis. He headed the Algerian government-in-exile before independence from France in 1962 when he became President of the National Constituent Assembly. He fell out of favour and was exiled but was restored to favour shortly before his death.

Abbas Hilmi Pasha 1874–1944
Last Khedive of Egypt

Born in Alexandria, he succeeded his father, Tewfik Pasha (1892), and attempted to rule independently of British influence. At the outbreak of war in 1914 he sided with Turkey and was deposed later that year when the British made Egypt a protectorate. He spent the remainder of his life in exile, largely in Switzerland.

Abbate or Abati, Niccolò dell' c.1512–1571
Italian fresco painter

Born in Modena, he spent much of his life in France and executed frescoes for the Palace of Fontainebleau near Paris. Few of his frescoes survive, but the Louvre, Paris, has a collection of his drawings. He influenced French landscape painting.

Abbe, Cleveland 1838–1916
US meteorologist

Born in New York City, he published work on the atmosphere and climate, and was responsible for the introduction of the US system of Standard Time.

Abbe, Ernst 1840–1905
German physicist

Born in Eisenach, he became professor at the University of Jena in 1870, and in 1878 director of the astronomical and meteorological observatories there. Consulted by the Jena optical instrument-maker Carl Zeiss in the 1860s, Abbe studied the resolution limit and manufacturing process of microscopes. He developed instruments for measuring refractive indices of glass and a focometer to control the performance of the optical workshop. Zeiss took Abbe into partnership, and following Zeiss's death in 1888 Abbe became owner of the company. He invented the arrangement later known as 'Abbe's homogeneous immersion', and arising out of his work on the microscope, he founded the diffraction theory of optical imaging, from which modern optical imaging techniques have developed.

Abbot, Charles See Colchester, 1st Baron

Abbot, Charles Greely 1872–1973
US astrophysicist

He was born in Wilton, New Hampshire. As director of the Astrophysical Observatory at the Smithsonian Institution (1907–44), he carried out important research on solar radiation. He became the 'grand old man' of US solar physics, published many books and devised an apparatus for converting solar energy to power just before his hundredth birthday.

Abbot, Ezra 1819–94
US biblical scholar

He was born in Jackson, Maine, and as a professor at Harvard, was on the committee for the revision of the English text of the Bible.

Abbot, George 1562–1633
English prelate

Born in Guildford, Surrey, he was educated at Balliol College, Oxford, obtaining a fellowship in 1583. Through Thomas Sackville's influence he rose to be Master of University College (1597), Dean of Winchester (1600), and Vice-Chancellor of Oxford University (1600–05). He owed his promotion to the sees of Lichfield (1609), London (1610), and finally Canterbury (1611) to the Earl of Dunbar. In 1619 he founded a hospital in Guildford. A sincere but narrow-minded Calvinist, he was equally opposed to Catholics and to heretics. His brother Robert (1560–1617), from 1615 Bishop of Salisbury, was a learned theologian.

Abbott, Berenice 1898–1991
US photographer

Born in Springfield, Ohio, she studied at Ohio State University with the intention of becoming a journalist, then moved to New York (1918), and to Europe (1921), where she studied sculpture. She worked in Paris as assistant to Man Ray (1923–25) and in 1926 opened her own portrait studio there. Her work was first shown at the Au Sacre du Printemps gallery, Paris (1926). In 1929 she returned to work in New York, where from 1934 she also taught photography. From the early 1930s she became the companion of art historian and critic Elizabeth McCausland and in 1968 settled in Maine. Abbott is well known for her innovative documentation of town- and cityscape, for example her project *Changing New York* (1929–39, also the title of a book, 1939, with text by McCausland), and her pioneering illustrations of the laws and processes of physics. Her other publications include, as editor, *The World of Atget* (1964) and as photographer, *The Attractive Universe* (1969, text by E G Valens).

Abbott, Bud (William) 1898–1974
US comedian

Born in Asbury Park, New Jersey, the son of a circus bareback rider, he led a life on the fringes of show business until 1931, when he teamed up with Lou Costello, originally Louis Francis Cristillo (1908–50), born in Paterson, New Jersey. They began performing as a comedy team in Vaudeville, with the tall, thin Abbott as the sour-tempered straight man, and the short, chubby Costello as the bumbling clown. They later brought their routines to films, radio, and television. Their films include *Buck Privates* (1941), *Lost in a Harem* (1944), and *The Naughty Nineties* (1945), in which they performed their famous 'Who's on First' routine.

Abbott, Diane Julie 1953–
English politician

Educated at Harrow City Girls' School and Newnham College, Cambridge, she worked for the National Council for Civil Liberties, the Greater London Council (GLC) and Lambeth Borough Council. She joined the Labour Party in 1971 and served on the Westminster City Council (1982–86). Elected to parliament as MP for Hackney North and Stoke Newington in 1987, she became the first black woman member of the House of Commons, and has been referred to as one of the Labour 'rebels'.

Abbott, George Francis 1887–1995
US dramatist, director, producer and actor

He was born in Forestville, New York State, and began his career in 1913 as an actor. He wrote his first play, *The Head of the Family* (1912), for the Harvard Dramatic Club, and continued his career in New York, establishing himself with *The Fall Guy* (with James Gleason, 1925). He subsequently wrote and co-wrote almost 50 plays and musicals, among them *Love 'em and Leave 'em* (1925); *Three Men on a Horse* (1935); *On Your Toes* (with Richard Rodgers and Lorenz Hart, 1936); *The Boys from Syracuse* (based on *The Comedy of Errors*, 1938); *The Pajama Game* (with Richard Bissell, 1954); and *Damn Yankees* (1955). In addition to an illustrious career as a producer, he directed over 100 theatrical pieces, among them Rodgers and Hart's *Pal Joey* and *On Your Toes*, and Irving Berlin's *Call Me Madam*. He was awarded the Pulitzer Prize for drama (1960) for the hit musical *Fiorello!* (1959), along with co-writer Jerome Weidman (1913–98), lyricist Sheldon Harnick (1924–) and composer Jerry Bock (1928–). He also won six Tony awards for his work. He directed a revival of *Broadway* at 100 years of age and collaborated on a Broadway revival of *Damn Yankees* shortly before his death at the age of 107.

Abbott, Grace 1878–1939
US social reformer, writer and director
Born in Grand Island, Nebraska, she studied at Grand Island College and Nebraska and Chicago universities. In 1908 she started work at Jane Addams's Hull House, and headed the Immigrants' Protective League (1908–17). She worked at the US Children's Bureau (1917–19), and became its director from 1921 to 1934. She was responsible for administering the Maternity and Infancy Act. She was also president of the National Conference of Social Workers (1923–24), the unofficial US representative to the League of Nations Advisory Committee on Traffic in Women and Children (1922–34), Professor of Public Welfare at the University of Chicago (1934) and editor of *Social Service Review*. She wrote many articles and full-length works about child-labour laws and the exploitation of immigrants, including *Women in Industry* (1910), *The Immigrant in Massachusetts* (1915), *The Child and the State* (1938) and *Public Assistance* (1939).

Abbott, Jacob 1803–79
US clergyman
Born in Hallowell, Maine, he was educated at Bowdoin College, Maine and at Andover Newton Theological School. He founded Mount Vernon School for Girls in Boston (1829) and was the author of *The Young Christian* (1832) and many other works. His son Lyman Abbott (1835–1922), born in Roxbury, Massachusetts, succeeded Henry Ward Beecher at Plymouth Congregational Church, Brooklyn, in 1890, edited *The Outlook*, and wrote *Christianity and Social Problems* (1897), *The Spirit of Democracy* (1910), *Reminiscences* (1915), *Silhouettes of my Contemporaries* (1922) and other books.

Abbott, Sir John Joseph Caldwell 1821–93
Canadian politician
Born in Saint Andrews (now St-André-Est), Quebec, he became a lawyer and began his political career in the House of Commons (1860–74, 1880–87). He held many government positions as a member of the Conservative Party, and served as the first Canadian-born Prime Minister (1891–92).

Abbott, Robert Sengstacke 1868–1940
US newspaper publisher and editor
Born at St Simons Island, Georgia, the son of former slaves, he trained as a printer at the Hampton Institute in Virginia. He founded and edited (1905–40) the *Chicago Defender*, which spoke out against racial prejudice and campaigned against the unjust treatment of black Americans.

Abboud, Ibrahim 1900–83
Sudanese soldier
Commander-in-Chief of the Sudanese army from the time of attainment of independence (1956), he was the leader of the military regime which took over after Abdullah Khalil surrendered his leadership to the army in 1958. Abboud's regime was unable either politically or economically to maintain effective rule over the country, and was overthrown in 1964. He resigned and retired into private life.

Abd al-Hadi, Awni 1889–1970
Palestinian politician
Active in the Arab nationalist movement against the Turks before World War I, he helped to organize the 1st Arab Congress in Paris (1913). He became a member of King Abdullah ibn Hussein's staff after the so-called 'liberation' of Palestine in the latter years of the war, and subsequently became involved in the pan-Arab movement. He was a member of the Arab Higher Committee in 1936 and was also behind the Arab 'Rebellion' of the same year. Exiled by the British (1937–41), he later helped to found the Arab League (1945). He was Jordanian ambassador to Britain (1951–55). Despite holding government posts in Jordan, he spent the later years of his life in Egypt.

Abd-ar-Rahman I 731–88
Emir of Muslim Spain
A member of the Umayyad dynasty, he survived the massacre of his family by the 'Abbasids (750), and conquered most of Muslim Spain, founding the emirate of al-Andalus (756) with its capital at Córdoba. Allying with the Christian Basques, he defeated Frankish incursions under Charlemagne.

Abd-ar-Rahman II 792–852
Emir of Córdoba
He ruled from 822 and was a patron of the arts and of architecture.

Abd-ar-Rahman III 891–961
Emir of Córdoba
He ruled from 912 and proclaimed himself caliph in 929. Under him the Umayyad emirate reached the peak of its power, extending its boundaries in successful campaigns against the Fatimids and the kings of León and Navarre. A great builder, he created a new city, Madimat az-Zahra, for his court and government.

Abd-ar-Rahman d.732
Saracen leader
He was defeated and killed by Charles Martel at the Battle of Tours.

Abd-ar-Rahman 1778–1859
Sultan of Fez and Morocco
He succeeded his uncle (1822), and was involved in Abd-el-Kader's war against the French in Algeria. His subjects' piracy brought risk of war with more than one European state. At home, although he faced tribal challenges, he was a capable administrator and actively advanced public works.

Abd-ar-Rahman c.1840–1901
Emir of Afghanistan
The grandson of Dost Mohammed Khan, he was driven into exile in Russia (1869), but was brought back and proclaimed emir with British support (1880). He consolidated his power and arranged for the withdrawal of British troops, leaving Great Britain in control of foreign affairs, and in 1893 subscribed to the Durand Line (named after Sir Henry Durand, 1812–71) as the India–Afghanistan border.

Abd-el-Kader 1807–83
Algerian soldier, nationalist and emir

Born in Mascara, after the French conquest of Algiers he was elected emir by the Arab tribes of Oran, and waged a long struggle with the French (1832–47). In 1835 he defeated a large French army at Makta. Eventually crushed by overpowering force, he took refuge in Morocco and began a crusade against the enemies of Islam, but was defeated at Isly in 1844. He surrendered in 1847, was sent to France, and afterwards lived in Brusa and Damascus.

Abd-el-Krim 1880–1963
Moroccan Berber chief

Born in Ajdir, he began a career in the Spanish colonial government in Morocco before leading unsuccessful revolts against Spain and France (1921, 1924–25) and becoming known as the 'Wolf of the Rif Mountains'. He formed the Republic of the Rif and served as its President (1921–26), but was made to surrender by a large Franco-Spanish army under Marshal **Pétain** and was exiled to the island of Réunion. Granted amnesty in 1947, he went to Egypt where he formed the North African Liberation Committee.

Abduh, Muhammad 1849–1905
Egyptian reformer

An initiator of the reform movement in late 19th century Egypt, he became convinced of the need for educational reorganization and a reappraisal of Islam's position in the modern world. Exiled after the suppression of the Urabi Revolt, he went eventually to Paris, where he renewed his acquaintance with Jamal al-Din al-Afghani. Permitted to return to Cairo, by 1889 he had been appointed the state Mufti, the highest (clerical) post. He was fervently patriotic and was thus opposed to Egyptian control being vested in either European or Oriental despots. He was, however, primarily a theologian and the maintenance of the true religion of Islam, shorn of falsifying abuses, was his prime motivation.

Abd-ul-Aziz 1830–76
Sultan of Turkey

Born in Constantinople (now Istanbul), he succeeded (1861) his brother **Abd-ul-Medjid**, whose liberal and westernizing reforms he continued, promulgating the first Ottoman civil code, and visiting western Europe (1871). Thereafter he became more autocratic, and after revolts in Bosnia, Herzegovina and Bulgaria, he was forced to abdicate.

Abd-ul-Hamid II *known as* the Great Assassin
1842–1918
Last Sultan of Turkey

Born in Constantinople (now Istanbul), he was the second son of Sultan **Abd-ul-Medjid** and successor to his brother Murad V. He promulgated the first Ottoman constitution (1876), but suspended it (1878) and ruled autocratically. He was intelligent and industrious, but intensely suspicious and his reign was notable for his cruel suppression of revolts in the Balkans, which led to wars with Russia (1877–78), and especially for appalling Armenian massacres (1894–96). Revolts in Crete (1896–97) led to war with Greece. Later a reform movement by the revolutionary Young Turks forced him to restore the constitution and summon a parliament (1908), but when he attempted a counter-revolution, he was deposed (1909) and exiled.

Abdul-Jabbar, Kareem, *originally* Lewis Ferdinand Alcindor, Jnr, *known as* Lew 1947–
US basketball player

Born in New York City, he led the University of California at Los Angeles team to three national championships. He became a professional player who holds the all-time record for games played (1,560) and points scored (38,387). In his career with the National Basketball

Association, he played with the Milwaukee Bucks and Los Angeles Lakers. He took the name Abdul-Jabbar when he converted to Islam in 1969. He retired in 1989.

Abdullah ibn Buhaina See Blakey, Art

Abdullah ibn Hussein 1882–1951
First King of Jordan

Born in Mecca, the second son of **Hussein ibn Ali**, he took a prominent part in the Arab revolt against Turkey (1916–18), becoming emir of the British mandated territory of Transjordan (1921). He became king when the mandate ended (1946), and was proclaimed King of Palestine (1948); but, with the formal establishment of the state of Israel, he had to be satisfied with sovereignty over the Hashemite Kingdom of Jordan (1949). He aroused opposition from Arab nationalists, and was assassinated in the presence of his grandson, who succeeded him. He was the grandfather of King **Hussein**.

Abdullah, Sheikh Muhammad 1905–82
Kashmiri politician

Born in Soura, near Srinagar, he was a leading figure in the struggle for India's independence and the fight for the rights of Kashmir. Known as the 'Lion of Kashmir', he participated actively in the Muslim struggle to overthrow the Hindu maharajah and substitute constitutional government, for which he was imprisoned several times. He was the founder of the Kashmir Muslim (later, National) Conference, and then the Quit Kashmir movement in 1946, when he was again detained. A year later, he was released by the emergency administration and in 1948 was appointed Prime Minister of Kashmir. However, for his championing of the cause of an independent Kashmir, and his subsequent treasonable refusal to pledge his loyalty to India, he was again imprisoned for most of the period 1953–68. He contested the 1972 elections at the head of his Plebiscite Front, but lost to the Congress Party. As Chief Minister of Jammu and Kashmir from 1975 until his death, he was instrumental in persuading **Indira Gandhi** to grant Kashmir a degree of autonomy.

Abdüllhak Hamid Tarhan 1852–1937
Turkish dramatist

Born in Bebek, he belonged to the Tanzimat (Transformation) school of writers, who sought to bring Turkey into Europe, and was influenced by **Racine** and **Shakespeare**. His bold verse plays, usually on themes from Islamic history, are genuinely stirring as well as intelligently conceived. His influence on the Turkish theatre cannot be over-estimated.

Abd-ul-Medjid 1823–61
Sultan of Turkey

The successor to his father **Mahmud II** (1839), he was well educated, and continued the liberal reforms of the previous reign, reorganizing the court system and education, and granting various rights to citizens, including Christians. In 1850 he refused to give up the Hungarian political refugee **Lajos Kossuth** to the **Habsburgs** and in 1854 he secured an alliance with Great Britain and France to resist Russian demands, thus precipitating the Crimean War (1854–56). The Ottoman Empire was subsequently increasingly weakened by financial difficulties and internal nationalist problems.

Abdul Rahman, Tunka Putra 1903–90
Malaysian statesman

Born in Alor Star, Kedah, the son of the Sultan of Kedah, he trained as a lawyer at Cambridge and joined the Civil Service in his home state of Kedah in 1931, becoming a public prosecutor in 1949, after passing his Bar exams in London. In 1945 he founded the United Malays' National Organisation (UMNO) and in 1952 was nominated to the executive and legislative councils of the Federation of Malaya, becoming Chief Minister in 1955 and Prime Minister on independence in 1957. He negotiated the formation of the Federation of Malaysia, embracing Singapore, Sarawak and Sabah (1961–62) and remained Prime Minister of the enlarged entity when it was established in 1963. After the outbreak of violent anti-Chinese riots in Kuala Lumpur, he withdrew from active politics in 1970.

À Beckett or A'Beckett, Gilbert Abbott
1811–56
English humorist
Born in London, he was educated at Westminster and in 1841 was called to the Bar. In 1849 he became a metropolitan police magistrate. As well as writing for *Punch* and *The Times*, he was the author of *The Comic Blackstone* (1846), and comic histories of England and Rome. 📖 A A'Beckett, *The A'Becketts of Punch: memoirs of fathers and sons* (1903)

Abegg, Richard 1869–1910
German chemist
He was born in Danzig (now Gdańsk, Poland). While a professor at Breslau (now Wrocław, Poland), he was one of the first chemists to perceive the chemical significance of the newly discovered (1897) electron and his 'rule of eight' (1904) concerning the electric basis of linkages between atoms was an important stage in the development of modern valency theory. He did significant work on osmotic pressures, the freezing point of dilute solutions, and the dielectric constant of ice. He died in a ballooning accident.

Abe Kobo 1924–93
Japanese novelist and playwright
Born in Tokyo, he trained as a doctor, but turned to literature. Recognition in Japan came with the award of the Akutagawa prize for *The Wall* in 1951. His international reputation is often linked with that of writers like Junichiro Tanizaki, Yasunari Kawabata and Yukio Mishima, but unlike them he stands outside the great tradition of Japanese literature. His predominant theme of alienation is explored in a series of novels and plays. His novels include *Daiyon Kampyoki* (1959, Eng trans *Inter Ice Age Four*, 1971), *Suna no onna* (1962, Eng trans *The Woman in the Dunes*, 1965) and *Mikkai* (1977, Eng trans *Secret Rendezvous*, 1980). 📖 H Yamaanouchi, *The Search for Authenticity in Modern Japanese Literature* (1978)

Abel
Biblical character
The brother of Cain and second son of Adam and Eve, he was a shepherd, whose gift was accepted by God. He was murdered by his brother, Cain, whose gift God did not accept (Genesis 4.2–16).

Abel, Sir Frederick Augustus 1827–1902
English chemist and inventor
He was born in London, and studied at the Royal Polytechnic Institution and the Royal College of Chemistry, where he was appointed an assistant in 1846. In 1852 he moved to the Royal Military Academy, Woolwich, where he lectured in chemistry before being appointed ordnance chemist in 1854 and chemist to the War Department in 1858. During his long and distinguished career at Woolwich, which lasted more than 30 years, he developed high explosives and smokeless gunpowder. In 1889, he and Sir James Dewar invented cordite, which quickly became the standard propellant used by the British army. Abel also devised a new method to manufacture guncotton which prevented it from exploding spontaneously, and invented the 'Abel tester', a device for determining the flash point of petroleum. He was elected FRS in 1860.

Abel, John Jacob 1857–1938
US biochemist
Born in Cleveland, Ohio, he studied at Johns Hopkins University and widely in Europe before returning to Johns Hopkins as its first Professor of Pharmacology (1893–1932). He was the first to determine the molecular weight of cholesterol and its derivative, cholic acid, and in 1897 isolated the hormone adrenaline from the adrenal gland. In 1892 he discovered carbonic acid in horse urine and associated it with urea production, and in 1914 he joined a cellophane sac to an artery, using this technique of dialysis to show that blood contains amino acids, thereby pioneering dialysis for the treatment of kidney disease. In 1927 his research team crystallized insulin, showed it to be a protein and demonstrated that its hypoglycaemic action was not caused by contaminants.

Abel, Niels Henrik 1802–29
Norwegian mathematician
Born in Finnøy, he showed mathematical genius by the age of 15, entered Oslo University in 1821, and in 1823 proved that there is no algebraic formula for the solution of a general polynomial equation of the 5th degree. Such a formula had been sought ever since the cubic and quartic equations had been solved in the 16th century by Girolamo Cardano and others. He developed the concept of elliptic functions independently of Carl Gustav Jacobi, and pioneered its extension to the theory of Abelian integrals and functions, which became a central theme of later 19th-century analysis, although his work was not fully understood in his lifetime. Abel emphasized the analogy of the elliptic functions with the familiar trigonometric functions, and the new functions became influential in the development of complex analysis. 📖 Eric T Bell, *Men of Mathematics* (1937)

Abelard, Peter See panel p6

Abell, Kjeld 1901–61
Danish playwright
Born in Ribe, he graduated in politics, then worked as a scene painter and dress designer at theatres in Paris and London. His breakthrough as a playwright came in Copenhagen with *Melodien der blev væk* (1935, 'The Melody that got Lost'). The leading modernizer of 20th-century Danish drama, he broke emphatically from naturalistic drama in the tradition of Ibsen. He placed actors among the audience, used innovative stage designs, and blended speech and song. Subsequent plays include *Anna Sophie Hedvig* (1939), *Silkeborg* (written during World War II, but first performed in 1946), *Den blå pekingeser* (1954, 'The Blue Pekinese') and *Skriget* (1961, 'The Scream'). 📖 Fodnoten i støvet (1951); F J Marker, *Kjeld Abell* (1976)

Abelson, Philip Hauge 1913–
US physical chemist
Born in Tacoma, Washington, he was educated at Washington State College and the University of California at Berkeley, and played a major part in the development of the atomic bomb. He worked at the Carnegie Institution, Washington DC, from 1939 to 1941. In 1940 Abelson assisted Edwin Mattison McMillan to bombard uranium with neutrons, which led to the creation of a new element, neptunium, the first element discovered to be heavier than uranium and the first to be made synthetically. In 1941 he transferred to the Naval Research Laboratory in Washington DC. From 1941 he worked on the Manhattan atomic bomb project, devising a cheap method for making uranium hexafluoride and then developing the gas diffusion process for obtaining the enriched uranium required for the atomic bomb. In 1946 he moved back to the Carnegie Institution, where he was appointed director of the Geophysics Laboratory in 1953, then president (1971–78), then trustee (1978–). He

---

Abelard or Abailard, Peter 1079–1142
French philosopher and scholar

Peter Abelard was born near Nantes in Brittany, the eldest son of a noble Breton house. He studied under Johannes Roscellinus at Tours and William of Champeaux in Paris, and enjoyed great success as a teacher and educator. In 1115 he was appointed lecturer in the cathedral school of Notre Dame in Paris, where his pupils included **John of Salisbury**. There he became tutor to **Héloïse**, the beautiful and talented 17-year-old niece of the canon Fulbert with whom he was lodging. They fell passionately in love, but when their affair was discovered, Fulbert threw Abelard out of the house. The couple fled to Brittany, where Héloïse gave birth to a son, Astrolabe. They returned to Paris, and were secretly married. Héloïse's outraged relatives took their revenge on Abelard by breaking into his bedroom one night and castrating him. Abelard fled in shame to the abbey of St Denis to become a monk, and Héloïse took the veil at Argenteuil as a nun.

In 1121, the Church condemned him for heresy, and he became a hermit at Nogent-sur-Seine. There his pupils helped him to build a monastic school which he named the Paraclete. In 1125 he was elected abbot of St Gildas-de-Rhuys in Brittany, and the Paraclete was given to Héloïse and a sisterhood.

In his final years Abelard was again accused of numerous heresies and he retired to the monastery of Cluny. He died at the priory of St Marcel, near Chalon; his remains were taken to the Paraclete at the request of Héloïse, and when she died in 1164 she was laid in the same tomb. In 1800 their ashes were taken to Paris, and in 1817 they were buried in one sepulchre at Père Lachaise.

📖 Abelard and Héloïse are renowned for the collection of their correspondence. His other works include *Sic et non* (a key text in the 12th-century movement from faith to reason), *Nosce te ipsum* (an account of his ethical system) and *Historia Calamitatum Mearum* (c.1132, 'The Story of my Troubles').

📖 J G Sikes, *Peter Abailard* (1932). **Alexander Pope** wrote a poem about them called *Eloisa to Abelard* (1717).

> *Non enim facile de his, quos plurimum diligimus, turpitudinem suspicamur.*
> 'We do not easily suspect evil of those whom we love most.' From *Historia Calamitatum Mearum*, ch.6.

---

worked on the development of nuclear submarines and also promoted the peaceful uses of radioactive isotopes. He used the method to identify amino acids in fossils of various ages and fatty acids in rocks more than 1,000 million years old.

Abencerrages
Noble Moorish family

They went to Spain in the 8th century, and were legendary for their feud with another Moorish family (the Zegris) which led to their massacre in the Alhambra by the King of Granada, Abu al-Hasan or his son, **Boabdil**, in the 1480s. The massacre was the theme of a romance by **René de Chateaubriand, Dryden**'s *Conquest of Granada*, and an opera by **Cherubini**. Their names comes from the Arabic for 'saddler's son'.

Abercrombie, Lascelles 1881–1938
English poet and critic

Born in Ashton-on-Mersey, Cheshire, he was educated at Malvern College and Victoria University, Manchester. He became Professor of English at Leeds (1922) and London (1929), and Reader at Oxford (1935). His works include *Romanticism* (1926), *Principles of Literary Criticism* (1932) and several volumes of Georgian-style poetry, collected as *The Poems of Lascelles Abercrombie* (1930). A posthumous collection of *Lyrics and Unfinished Poems* appeared in 1940. He was the brother of Sir **Patrick Abercrombie**. 📖 O Ellon, *Lascelles Abercrombie, 1881–1938* (1939)

Abercrombie, Sir (Leslie) Patrick 1879–1957
English architect and pioneer of town-planning in Great Britain

He was Professor of Town Planning at Liverpool (1915–35) and University College London (1935–46). His major work was the replanning of London (*County of London Plan*, 1943, and *Greater London Plan*, 1944), and he was consultant for the replanning of many other cities, including Bath, Doncaster, Dublin, Edinburgh, Hull, Plymouth and Sheffield. He was also much involved in the policy of creating postwar new towns. He was the brother of **Lascelles Abercrombie**.

Abercromby, Sir Ralph 1734–1801
Scottish general

Born in Menstrie in Clackmannanshire, he served in Europe in the Seven Years War (1756–63). He was MP for Clackmannanshire from 1774 to 1780. Rejoining the army in 1793 he distinguished himself as a major-general in Flanders under **Frederick, Duke of York**, and led successful operations against the French in St Lucia and Trinidad (1795–96). He held commands in Ireland and Scotland (1797–99), and in 1800 was in command in the Mediterranean to deal with the French army left by **Napoleon I** in Egypt. He led the Anglo-Turkish forces against the French at Aboukir Bay in 1801, but was mortally wounded.

Aberdare, Henry Austin Bruce, 1st Baron
1815–95
Welsh politician

Born in Duffryn, Glamorganshire, he was called to the Bar in 1837, entered parliament in the same year, and was Liberal MP for Merthyr Tydfil from 1852 to 1873. Home Secretary under **Gladstone** (1868–73), he was Lord President of the Council from 1873 to 1874. He was closely interested in education and chaired the committee whose report led to the Welsh Intermediate Education Act of 1889. He was influential in the movement for the establishment of the University of Wales and became the first chancellor in 1895.

Aberdeen, George Hamilton Gordon, 4th Earl of 1784–1860
Scottish statesman and Prime Minister

Born in Edinburgh and educated at Harrow, he inherited a peerage at the age of seven. His joint guardians were **William Pitt** the Younger and **Henry Dundas**. He succeeded his grandfather as earl in 1801, was elected a Scottish representative peer in 1806, and in 1813 was sent as special ambassador to Vienna to negotiate the Treaty of Töplitz that created the alliance of Great Powers against Napoleon I. He was Foreign Secretary twice, under the Duke of **Wellington** (1828–30) and under Sir **Robert Peel** (1841–46), and brought to an end the Chinese War, established an entente cordiale with France, and cemented relations with the USA. A confirmed free-trader, he resigned with Peel over the repeal of the Corn Laws in 1846. In 1852, on the resignation of Lord **Derby**, he was made Prime Minister of a coalition government that was immensely popular until he committed Great Britain to an alliance with France and Turkey in the Crimean War in 1854. The gross mismanagement of the war aroused popular discontent, and he was forced to resign in 1855. 📖 Muriel E Chamberlain, *Lord Aberdeen: A Political Biography* (1983)

Aberdeen, James Campbell Hamilton Gordon, 7th Earl of, and 1st Marquis
1847–1934
Scottish politician

He was laird of Haddo House in Aberdeenshire for 64 years, appointed Viceroy of Ireland twice (1886, 1905–15), Governor of Canada (1893–98), and made a marquis in 1915. In 1877 he married Ishbel-Maria Marjoribanks (1857–1939), youngest daughter of the 1st Lord Tweedmouth, with whom he turned Haddo House into a model estate for the local community, and published a book of reminiscences, *We twa'* (1925).

Aberhart, William 1878–1943
Canadian politician

Born in Huron County, Ontario, he was educated at Queen's University in Kingston. In 1935, after a career as a clergyman and teacher, he became a member of the Alberta legislature, forming the Canadian Social Credit Party and becoming premier in the same year. In 1937 the federal government thwarted his ambition to give each Albertan a monthly $5 dividend from the province's natural resources, but he was returned to power in 1940 and remained in office until his death. His evangelical style of speech-making earned him the nickname 'Bible Bill'.

Abernathy, Ralph David 1926–90
US civil rights leader

Born in Linden, Alabama, he became a Baptist minister in Montgomery where he was befriended by **Martin Luther King, Jnr**. Together they organized a successful bus boycott to protest at segregation (1955) and took part in many other civil rights demonstrations. Abernathy served as an officer of the Southern Christian Leadership Conference (SCLC), becoming president (1968–77) after King was assassinated, and led the Poor People's March on Washington DC. An advocate of non-violence, he wrote in his autobiography, *And the Walls Came Tumbling Down* (1989), about his role in the civil rights movement.

Abernethy, John 1764–1831
English surgeon

Born in London, he was apprenticed to the assistant surgeon at St Bartholomew's Hospital in 1779. He was himself elected assistant surgeon (1787), and soon after began to lecture. After initial diffidence as a lecturer, his lectures soon attracted large crowds. In 1813 he was appointed surgeon to Christ's Hospital, in 1814 Professor of Anatomy and Surgery to the College of Surgeons, and in 1815 full surgeon to St Bartholomew's, a post which he resigned in 1829. His practice increased with his celebrity, which the eccentricity and rudeness of his manners helped to heighten. Of his works the most important is his *Constitutional Origin and Treatment of Local Diseases* (1809).

Abington, Frances, *née* Barton 1737–1815
English actress

Of obscure origins, she was a flower-girl, street singer, milliner and kitchen-maid before making her first appearance on the London stage at the Haymarket (1755). She rose to fame in Dublin (after 1759) and returned to Drury Lane on the invitation of **David Garrick**. A versatile performer, she excelled not only in **Shakespeare** but also in a variety of comedy roles (Lady Teazle, Polly Peachum, Lucy Lockit). Sir **Joshua Reynolds** painted her portrait as Miss Prue in *Love for Love*.

Abiola, Moshood Kastumawo 1937–98
Nigerian politician

Born at Abeokuta in Ogun state, he was educated at the local Baptist Boys High School and the University of Glasgow. After graduating he pursued a career in accountancy, mainly in public and private publishing companies. In 1979 he was elected to parliament as a member of the National Party and continued to pursue his interests in publishing and telecommunications. As a member of the Social Democratic Party he contested successfully the 1993 presidential elections but was arrested and charged with treason following a military coup. He spent the rest of his life in prison and died shortly before his scheduled release.

Abney, Sir William de Wiveleslie 1844–1920
English chemist and educationist

Born in Derby, he was educated at the Royal Military Academy at Woolwich and joined the Royal Engineers in 1861. He later became an instructor and then head at the School of Military Engineering. In 1877 he moved to the department of science and art in South Kensington and became assistant secretary to the Board of Education in 1899 and, after his retirement in 1903, its principal scientific adviser. He invented a gelatine emulsion which made instantaneous photography viable and an emulsion-coated paper from which modern photographic papers were developed. A pioneer of stellar photography, he discovered how to make photographic plates that were sensitive to red and infrared light. In 1885 he co-authored a seminal paper on the infrared spectra of organic substances. He was elected FRS in 1876.

About, Edmond François Valentin 1828–85
French journalist and novelist

Born in Dieuze, Lorraine, he went to school in Paris and studied archaeology in Athens. On returning to Paris, he devoted himself to a literary career. He was a sceptical, crusading journalist, and founded the journal *Le XIX Siècle* ('The Nineteenth Century'). His fiction includes *Le Roi des montagnes* (1856, 'The King of the Mountains'), *Madelon* (1863), *Alsace* (1872), which cost him a week's imprisonment at the hands of the Germans, and *Le Roman d'un brave homme* (1880, 'The Story of a Good Man').

Abraham or Abram c.2000–1650BC
Old Testament father of the Hebrew people

Born, according to Genesis, in the Sumerian town of Ur of the Chaldees (Ur, Iraq), he migrated with his family and flocks via the ancient city of Mari on the Euphrates (Haran) to the Promised Land of Canaan, where he settled at Shechem (Nablus). After a period in Egypt, he is said to have lived to be 175 years old, and was buried with his first wife Sarah in the cave of Machpelah in Hebron. By Sarah he was the father of Isaac (whom he was prepared to sacrifice for God) and grandfather of **Jacob** ('Israel'). By his second wife Hagar (Sarah's Egyptian handmaiden) he was the father of **Ishmael**, the ancestor of twelve clans. By his third wife Keturah he had six sons who became the ancestors of the Arab tribes. He was also the uncle of Lot. Abraham is traditionally regarded as the father of the three great monotheistic religions: Judaism, Christianity and Islam. 📖 André Parrot, *Abraham and His Times* (1968)

Abraham, Sir Edward Penley 1913–
English biochemist

Born in Southampton and educated at Queen's College, Oxford, he received a Rockefeller Foundation travelling fellowship (1938–39) and worked in Stockholm before joining the Sir William Dunn School of Pathology at Oxford to study wound shock and the purification of penicillin. Sir **Ernst Chain** had previously isolated penicillin as a powder, and Abraham found that it readily crystallized as the sodium salt, thereby providing the crucially sought confirmation of its purity. During 1950–60 he isolated the antibiotic cephalosporin C which has properties similar to penicillin. Cephalosporin antibiotics are used against a variety of bacteria, particularly for patients allergic to penicillin, but unfortunately possess undesirable side-effects. He was elected FRS in 1958, and served as Professor of Chemical Pathology at Oxford from 1964 to 1980 when he became an honorary Fellow. He was knighted in 1980.

Abraham, William, *nicknamed* Mabon 1842–1922
Welsh trade unionist and politician
He was born in Cwmavon, Glamorganshire, and became a leading figure in the miners' union in South Wales. He was a strong advocate of sliding-scale agreements whereby wages were regulated by the selling price of coal, and also a believer in compromise with the coal-owners. His influence declined with the miners' strike in 1898 and the replacement of the sliding-scale agreements by collective bargaining. He was elected as MP for the Rhondda from 1885 to 1918 and for the West Rhondda division, 1918–20, and devoted himself to mining legislation.

Abrams, Creighton Williams 1914–74
US soldier
Born in Springfield, Massachusetts, he graduated from West Point, and commanded a tank battalion in World War II. After service in the Korean War (1950–53), he commanded the federal troops during the race riots in Mississippi and Alabama (1962–63). Vice-chief of the US army from 1964 to 1967, he succeeded William C Westmoreland as commander of the US forces in Vietnam (1968–72), and supervised the gradual withdrawal of troops. He was army Chief of Staff from 1972 to 1974.

Absalom 11th century BC
Biblical figure
He was the third and favourite son of King **David** of Israel in the Old Testament. A handsome, vain young man, he rebelled against his father and drove him out of Jerusalem. In an ensuing battle he was defeated, and as he was fleeing on a mule his hair was caught in the branch of an oak tree, leaving him dangling in the air, where he was killed by Joab (Samuel 2 18).

Absalon or Axel 1128–1201
Danish prelate and statesman
The foster-brother of Valdemar I, the Great (1131–82) whom he helped to the throne in 1157, he was appointed Bishop of Roskilde in 1158 and elected Archbishop of Lund in 1177. As Chief Minister to Valdemar, he led an army against the Wends in 1169 and extended Danish territories in the Baltic by capturing Rügen. In 1169 he built a fortress at Havn which became the nucleus of Copenhagen. As Chief Minister to Knut VI he led an expedition in 1184 that captured Mecklenburg and Pomerania. As Archbishop of Lund, he was largely responsible for the systematization of Danish ecclesiastical law.

Abse, Dannie 1923–
Welsh writer and physician
Born in Cardiff, he was educated at the Welsh National School of Medicine, King's College London and Westminster Hospital, and has been the senior specialist in the chest clinic at the Central Medical Establishment, London, since 1954. His literary output includes nine volumes of poetry, two novels and half a dozen plays. Autobiographical volumes are *A Poet in the Family* (1974), *A Strong Dose of Myself* (1982), and the novel *Ash on a Young Man's Sleeve* (1954). He has recently been involved in an academic debate regarding the question of anti-Semitism in the work of **T S Eliot**.

Abu al-Faraj See **Bar Hebraeus**

Abu al-Faraj al-Isfahani 897–967
Arabic scholar and literary historian
He worked in Baghdad and his greatest work, *Al-Aghani*, is a treasury of Arabic song and poetry.

Abu al-Fida, *also called* Abulfeda 1273–1331
Muslim prince and historian
Born in Damascus, he ruled from 1310 over Hama in Syria. He was a generous patron of literature and science, and his *Annals* were one of the earliest Arabic historical sources to be made available to western scholars. His *Geography* was also widely known.

Abu 'Ali al-Hasan ibn al-Haytham See **Alhazen**

Abu Bakr c.570–634
First Muslim caliph
He was one of the earliest converts to Islam. He became chief adviser to the Prophet **Muhammad** who married his daughter Aïshah, and on the death of the Prophet in 632 was elected leader of the Muslim community, with the title 'khalifat Rasubul Allah', ('successor of the messenger of God'). In his short reign of two years he put down the 'Apostasy', a religious and political revolt directed against the government at Medina, and set in motion the great wave of Arab conquests over Persia, Iraq and the Middle East.

Abulfeda See **Abu al-Fida**

Abu-Mashar See **Albumazar**

Abu Nuwas c.760–c.814
Arab poet
He was a favourite at the court of the caliph **Harun al-Raschïd** in Baghdad, and figures in the *Arabian Nights*. He abandoned older, traditional forms for erotic and witty lyrics and was considered one of the greatest poets of the 'Abbasid period. ⌷ W H Ingrams, *Abu Nuwas in Life and Legend* (1933)

Abu Tammam, *in full* Abu Tamman Habib ibn Aws 807–c.850
Arab poet
Born near Lake Tiberias, he was the son of a Christian. He rose to favour under caliphs al-Ma'mūn and al-Mutasim as a composer of panegyrics. He travelled extensively and towards the end of his life discovered a private library of desert poetry at Hamadhan. From this he compiled a celebrated anthology of early Arab poetry, the *Hamasu*. ⌷ F Ruckert, *Hamasa oder des altesten arabischen Volkslieder gesammelt von Abu Tammam* (1846)

Abzug, Bella, *originally* Bella Savitzky 1920–98
US feminist, lawyer and politician
Born in the Bronx, New York City, she was educated at Hunter College, New York and Columbia University and practised as a lawyer in New York (1944–70). She became noted for defending those accused of un-American activities as a prominent peace campaigner, founding Women Strike for Peace (1961) and the National Women's Political Caucus. Winning a seat in Congress (1971), she vigorously championed welfare issues, and became known as 'Battling Bella'. She ran unsuccessfully for a Senate seat (1976) and for appointment as Mayor of New York (1977). She returned to her lawyer's practice in 1980, but continued her involvement in political issues. Her publications include *Gender Gap: Bella Abzug's Guide to Political Power for American Women* (1984).

Accum, Friedrich 1769–1838
German chemist
Born in Bückeburg, Lower Saxony, he went to London in 1793, where he lived for nearly 30 years. He pioneered the introduction of gas lighting and his *Treatise on Adulteration*

of Food and Culinary Poisons (1820) did much to arouse public opinion against unclean food and dishonest trading.

Achard, Franz Karl 1753–1821
Swiss chemist
He was born in Berlin. He took up **Andreas Marggraf's** discovery of sugar in beet and perfected a process for its extraction on a commercial scale, after which he opened (1801) the first beet sugar factory, in Silesia. Later he was commissioned by **Frederick II the Great** to improve the way in which tobacco was processed. He also worked on boiling points and on the effect of heat on thermal conductivity.

Acheampong, Ignatius Katu 1931–79
Ghanaian soldier and politician
He taught in commercial colleges before joining the army in 1953. Trained in Great Britain and the USA, he served with the UN in the Congo and, following the 1966 military overthrow of **Kwame Nkrumah**, was chairman of the Western Region's administration for the National Liberation Council. Acting head of the 1st Brigade when he led the coup overthrowing **Kofi Busia** (1972), he became chairman of the National Redemption Council, then chairman of the Supreme Military Council and head of state (1972–78), until he was deposed and later executed.

Achebe, Chinua, *originally* Albert Chinualumogo 1930–
Nigerian novelist, poet and essayist
Born in Ogidi, the son of a mission teacher, he was educated at the University College of Ibadan. His early career was in broadcasting, but the publication of his first novel *Things Fall Apart* (1958) at once heralded the emergence of a unique voice in African literature. Set in the second half of the 19th century and presenting an unsentimentalized picture of the Ibo people, it has since been translated into over 40 languages. Writing exclusively in English, he confirmed his early promise with four more novels, *No Longer At Ease* (1960), *Arrow of God* (1964), *A Man of the People* (1966) and *Anthills of the Savanna* (1987), which was shortlisted for the Booker Prize. An overtly political writer, he has taught at the universities of Massachusetts and Connecticut in the USA, and at the University of Nigeria at Nsukka. ▢ D Carroll, *Chinua Achebe* (1970); G D Skillan, *The Novels of Chinua Achebe* (1969)

Achenbach, Andreas 1815–1910
German landscape and marine painter
Born in Cassel, he studied at St Petersburg and travelled extensively in Holland, Scandinavia and Italy, where he produced many watercolours. His paintings of the North Sea coasts of Europe had considerable influence in Germany, and he was regarded as the father of 19th-century German landscape painting. His brother and pupil Oswald (1827–1905) was also a landscape painter.

Acheson, Dean Gooderham 1893–1971
US politician and lawyer
Born in Middletown, Connecticut, he was educated at Yale and Harvard, and joined the department of state in 1941, where he was Under-Secretary (1945–47) and Secretary of State in the Truman administration (1949–53). He developed US policy for the containment of Communism, helped to formulate the Marshall Plan (1947–48) and participated in the establishment of NATO (1949). He wrote *Power and Diplomacy* (1958), *Morning and Noon* (1965), and *Present at the Creation* (1969), for which he was awarded the Pulitzer Prize. ▢ Douglas Brinkley, *Dean Acheson: The Cold War Years 1953–1971* (1992)

Acheson, Edward Goodrich 1856–1931
US chemist and inventor
He was born in Washington, Pennsylvania, and from 1880 to 1881 did research on electric lamps as an assistant to **Thomas Edison**. After 1884 he worked independently to develop the electric furnace for the conversion of carbon into diamonds, without success. In 1891 he developed the manufacture of silicon carbide (carborundum), an extremely useful abrasive, and in 1896 devised a new way of making lubricants based on colloidal graphite.

Achilles See **Albert III**

Achterberg, Gerrit 1905–62
Dutch poet
He was born in Langbroek. He had already published two collections of poetry whose major theme had been his desire to be united with a beloved in death, when in 1937 he shot and killed his landlady; he also shot at her young daughter, who was not killed. He then spent six years in a psychiatric hospital. His poetry opposes a close observance of traditional form to an extreme, and deliberately psychotic, violence of content. His most famous poem is *De ballade van de gasfitter* (1953, Eng trans in *A Tourist Does Golgotha*, 1972), a series of 14 strict sonnets about a confused gas worker whose job is to fill holes (*dichter* in Dutch, means 'poet', 'closer of holes', and 'closer to'). A unique poet of great power, he is the key figure in Netherlandic poetry. ▢ *Odyssey*, 1 (1961)

Achurch, Janet 1864–1916
English actress
Born in Lancashire, she made her London debut in 1883, and subsequently toured with the actor-manager **Frank Benson**, playing various Shakespearean roles. She is best known for her pioneering association with the works of **Ibsen**. She took the role of Nora in *The Doll's House* (1889), and both produced and starred in *Little Eyolf* (1896). After playing the title role in **George Bernard Shaw's** *Candida* (1900), which he wrote for her, she was described by the playwright as a tragic actress of genius. She also toured extensively with her actor-husband Charles Carrington, until she retired in 1913.

Acker, Kathy, *pseudonym* Black Tarantula 1944–97
US novelist, short-story writer and performance artist
She was born in New York. Her work is visceral in approach and influenced by the drug imagery of **William Burroughs**. *I Dreamt I Was a Nymphomaniac: Imagining* (1974) also draws on rock music lyrics and pornography. Her first novel, *The Childlike Life of the Black Tarantula* (1975), was published under the pseudonym Black Tarantula. *Great Expectations* (1982) and *Don Quixote* (1986) recall **Jorge Luis Borges's** 'intertextual' adaptations of literary classics. Later works, which reflect her fascination with sex and violence, include *Blood and Guts in High School* (1984), *In Memoriam to Identity* (1990) and *My Mother: demonology* (1993).

Ackerley, J(oseph) R(andolph) 1896–1967
English writer
He was born in Herne Hill, Kent, educated at Rossall School, Lancashire, and studied law at Cambridge. His friendship with **E M Forster** resulted in his appointment as private secretary to the Maharajah of Chhokrapur, from which experience he wrote *Hindoo Holiday* (1932), an intelligent and amusing log of his five months in India. From 1935 to 1959 he was literary editor of *The Listener*. His books include *My Dog Tulip* (1956), eulogized by **Christopher Isherwood** as 'one of the greatest masterpieces of animal literature'; *We Think the World of You* (1960), his only novel; and the autobiographical *My Father and Myself* (1968) and *My Sister and Myself; The Diaries of J R Ackerley* (1982), which were published posthumously. ▢ N Braybrooke (ed), *The Letters of J.R. Ackerley* (1975)

Ackermann, Rudolph 1764–1834
German art publisher

He was born in Saxony. In 1795 he opened a print shop in London and published a well-known set of coloured engravings of London. He is said to have introduced lithography as a fine art into England, and originated the 'Annuals' with his *Forget-me-not* (1825).

Ackroyd, Peter 1949–
English novelist, biographer and critic

He was born in London and educated at Clare College, Cambridge, and at Yale. He was literary editor of the *Spectator* (1973–77), and later (from 1986) television critic of *The Times*. The author of 14 books, he has published two volumes of poetry (*London Lickpenny*, 1973, and *Country Life*, 1978), as well as critical and biographical works, including *Notes for a New Culture* (1976), *Ezra Pound and His World* (1981) and *T S Eliot* (1984). His novels are erudite, playful, and complex, and draw on literary and historical sources. Later works include *English Music* (1992), *Blake* (1995) and *Milton in America* (1996).

Acland, Sir Arthur Herbert Dyke 1847–1926
English politician and educational reformer

Born in Holnicote, near Porlock, Somerset, he was educated at Rugby and Christ Church, Oxford, and became Liberal MP for Rotherham (1885–99). As vice-president of the Committee of Council on Education (1892–95), he secured the raising of the school leaving age to 11. He wrote several history textbooks, notably *A Handbook of the Political History of England* with C Ransome (1882).

Acland, Sir Richard Thomas Dyke 1906–90
English politician

Educated at Rugby and Balliol College, Oxford, he entered Parliament in 1931, and resigned from the Liberals to found, with J B Priestley, the Common Wealth Party (1942). In keeping with its advocacy of public ownership on moral grounds, he gave away his Devon family estate to the National Trust. With the exclipse of his party, he became a Labour MP in 1945, but resigned in 1955 in protest against Labour's support for Great Britain's nuclear defence policy. His books include *Unser Kampf* (1940), *What it Will be Like* (1943), *Nothing Left to Believe* (1949), *Waging Peace* (1958), and *The Next Step* (1974).

Aconzio, Jacopo, *also called* Jacobus Acontius 1492–1566
Italian engineer, courtier and writer

Born in Trent, Tirol, he went to Basle, Switzerland (1557), and to England (c.1559), after repudiating Catholicism. His best-known work, the antidogmatic *Stratagemata Satanae* (1565), offers a very early advocacy of toleration. As an engineer in England he advised on the refortification of Berwick upon Tweed and on land reclamation in Kent.

Acosta, Gabriel or Uriel d' c.1591–1640
Portuguese Jewish theologian

Born in Oporto, he studied canon law. Although brought up a Catholic, he adopted the faith of his fathers when fairly young, and went to Amsterdam where he took the name Uriel, only to find how little modern Judaism accorded with the Mosaic Law. For his *Examination of Pharisaic Traditions* (1624), a charge of atheism was brought against him by Jews, before a Christian magistracy. Having lost all his property, twice been excommunicated, and submitted to humiliating penance, he at last shot himself. His autobiographical *Exemplar Humanae Vitae* was published in 1640.

Acton, Sir Harold Mario 1904–94
English writer

Born in Florence, he lived most of his life there. He was educated at Eton, and at Christ Church, Oxford, where he wrote his first published poetry, collected in *Aquarium* (1923). He travelled widely, especially in China, his love for which led him to publish several books on its literature and theatre, as well as a novel with a Chinese setting, *Peonies and Ponies* (1941). During World War II he served in the RAF, and afterwards began an autobiography, *Memoirs of an Aesthete* (1948); a second volume called *More Memoirs of an Aesthete* followed in 1970. He lived extensively at 'La Pietra', a villa overlooking Florence, where he wrote *Great Houses of Italy: The Tuscan Villas* (1973), *Nancy Mitford: A Memoir* (1975), and *The Soul's Gymnasium and Other Stories* (1982), based on his Florentine friends. He was knighted in 1974.

Acton (of Aldenham), John Emerich Edward Dalberg Acton, 1st Baron 1834–1902
English historian and editor

Born in Naples, he was educated at St Mary's College at Oscott, Ireland, under Cardinal Wiseman, and at Munich University by Professor Johann Döllinger. He sat as a Liberal MP (1859–64), and was created baron by Gladstone in 1869. As a leader of the Liberal Roman Catholics in England, he opposed the doctrine of papal infallibility. In 1895 he was appointed Professor of Modern History at Cambridge and was founder-editor of the *Cambridge Modern History*, but died after editing the first two volumes.

Acton, Sir John Francis Edward 1736–1811
English naval officer

Born in Besançon, France, he served in the French navy then moved to the Tuscan navy and rose to command a Tuscan squadron against Algeria in 1774. In Naples he became admiral, reorganized and commanded the Neapolitan forces, then became Prime Minister (under Ferdinand IV, later Ferdinand I of the Two Sicilies) in charge of the entire Neapolitan administration. He fell from power when the French entered Naples in 1806, and fled with the royal family to Palermo, Sicily.

Adair, John c.1655–c.1722
Scottish surveyor and cartographer

He did notable work in mapping Scotland and its coast and islands. Little is known of him until 1683 when he was commissioned 'to survey the shires'. He prepared maps of counties in the central belt of Scotland (1680–86), and in 1703 published *Description of the Sea-Coast and Islands of Scotland* (Part 1). He was elected FRS in 1688, and his work was paid for (inadequately) by a tonnage act of 1686. His maps and charts set new standards of quality and accuracy.

Adair, John Eric 1934–
British leadership development consultant and writer

Educated at Cambridge, London and Oxford, he developed his 'Action-Centred Leadership' model while involved with leadership training as a senior lecturer at Sandhurst (1963–69) and as an associate director of the Industrial Society (1969–73). The model, which has been used widely in industry and in the armed services, states that the leader of a group of people has to ensure that needs are met in three inter-related areas—getting the task done, maintaining the team and the personal requirements of individual members.

Adalbert, St, *known as* the Apostle of the Prussians c.956–97
Bohemian prelate

Born in Prague, he was appointed the first native Bishop of Prague in 982, but the hostility of the corrupt clergy whom he tried to reform obliged him to go to Rome in

990. He then took the gospel to the Hungarians, the Poles, and then the Prussians, by whom he was murdered. His feast day is 23 April.

Adalbert, St d.981
German Benedictine missionary
He was sent by Emperor Otto I the Great at the request of St Olga, Princess of Kiev, to convert the Russians (961). He became the first Bishop of Magdeburg in 968 His feast day is 20 June.

Adalbert c.1000–72
German prelate
Born of a noble Saxon family, he was appointed Archbishop of Bremen and Hamburg in 1043. As Papal Legate to the North (1053), he extended his spiritual influence over Scandinavia, and carried Christianity to the Slavonic Wends. In 1063 he became tutor to the young Henry IV (of the Germans) and ruled over the whole kingdom for three years until he was deposed by enemy princes in 1066. He never regained his earlier authority and even lost Bremen, from which he was banished for three years.

Adam
Biblical character, the first man
The Book of Genesis describes God's creation of Adam from the dust of the earth, and of Eve from Adam's rib. In the biblical accounts Adam and Eve lived in the Garden of Eden until their disobedience by eating an apple from the tree of knowledge led to their banishment. Afterwards they had three sons, Cain, Abel and Seth. In the New Testament, Adam is seen as a precursor of Jesus Christ, who is a second Adam (1 Corinthians 15.45 and elsewhere).

Adam of Bremen d.c.1085
German ecclesiastical historian
As a canon at Bremen Cathedral from c.1066, he compiled the *Gesta Hammaburgensis ecclesiae pontificum* (c.1075, 'History of the Archbishopric of Hamburg'), based on church archives and interviews with learned men. It is the most important source for the history, geography and politics of northern Europe between the 8th and 11th centuries, and contains the first written reference to the discovery of *Vinland* (North America) by the Norse explorer, Leif the Lucky, around the year 1000.

Adam, Adolphe Charles 1803–56
French composer
Born in Paris, he was the son of the pianist Louis Adam (1758–1848). He wrote successful operas, such as *Le postillon de Longjumeau* (1835, 'The Postilion of Longjumeau') and *Si j'étais roi* (1852, 'If I were King'), but is chiefly remembered for the ballet *Giselle* (1841), from a story by Théophile Gautier.

Adam, James 1730–94
Scottish architect
Born in Kirkcaldy, Fife, he was the brother and partner of Robert Adam and son of the architect William Adam of Maryburgh (1689–1748). He studied in Rome and joined the family partnership in 1763. In 1769 he succeeded his brother as architect of the king's works. He designed a few buildings independently, notably the Glasgow Infirmary (1792). His fame has been overshadowed by that of his elder brother, though their names are linked inextricably in their work and cemented by their publication of *The Works in Architecture of Robert and James Adam* (3 vols, 1773, 1779, 1822).

Adam, Juliette, *née* Lamber 1836–1936
French writer

Born in Verberie, Oise, she married the journalist and senator Edmond Adam (1816–77), and during the Empire her salon brought together wits, artists, and politicians. She produced stories and books on social and political questions, but is remembered as the founder and editor of *La Nouvelle Revue* (1879–1926), a periodical of great general interest. She published her *Mémoires* from 1895 to 1905.

Adam, Lambert Sigisbert 1700–59, **Nicolas Sébastien** 1705–78, **François Gaspard** 1710–61
French sculptors
Born in Nancy, they lived in Lorraine, and all three produced sculpture which, although described as French Rococo, was influenced by the 17th-century Roman Baroque style, especially that of Gian Lorenzo Bernini. Each was successful and received important commissions: Lambert Sigisbert (Adam the Elder) produced the Neptune fountain at Versailles, Nicolas Sébastien (Adam the Younger) the monument of Queen Catherine Opalinska, at Nancy (1749), and François Gaspard did work for Frederick II the Great.

Adam, Leonhard 1891–1960
Australian anthropologist
He was born in Berlin, Germany, and studied ethnology and Sinology at the university there. He first practised as a lawyer but, being a Jew, was stripped of his posts in 1933. In 1938 he fled to England and taught at the University of London. His major work, *Primitive Art*, was published in 1940. Interned as an enemy alien, he was deported to Australia but eventually released on parole to the University of Melbourne, where he worked on Aboriginal cultures as a research scholar. He became an Australian citizen in 1956; his position was never regularized by the university but he attended an international congress in Paris as a delegate in 1960. He died suddenly in Bonn that year.

Adam, Paul Auguste Marie 1862–1920
French novelist and essayist
He was born in Paris. Among his numerous novels are *Chair Molle* (1885, 'Weak Flesh'), *Le Mystère des foules* (1895, 'The Mystery of the Masses'), *Lettres de Malaisie* (1879, 'Letters from Malaysia'), and *La Force* (1899, 'The Power'). He was co-founder of *Symboliste* and other French literary periodicals. 📖 F Jean-Desthieux, *Paul Adam: le dernier des encyclopédistes* (1928)

Adam, Robert 1728–92
Scottish architect
Born in Kirkcaldy, Fife, the brother of James Adam, he studied at Edinburgh and in Italy (1754–58). From 1761 to 1769 he was architect of the king's works, jointly with Sir William Chambers. He established a practice in London in 1758 and during the next 40 years he and his brother James succeeded in transforming the prevailing Palladian fashion in architecture by a series of romantically elegant variations on diverse classical originals. Their style of interior decoration was based on ancient Greek and Roman characterized by the use of the oval, and lines of decoration in hard plaster, enlivened by painted panels in low relief. One of their greatest projects was the Adelphi (demolished 1936), off the Strand in London, a residential block built as a speculative venture, which damaged the brothers' finances, and was eventually disposed of by a lottery. Surviving examples of their work are Home House in London's Portland Square, Lansdowne House, Derby House, Register House in Edinburgh, the Old Quad of Edinburgh University, and the oval staircase in Culzean Castle, Ayrshire. 📖 John Fleming, *Robert Adam and His Circle, in Edinburgh and Rome* (1962)

Adam, Stephen 1848–1910
Scottish stained-glass artist

Born in Bonnington, near Edinburgh, he was educated at Cannonmills School and apprenticed to the Edinburgh firm of Ballantine and Allan. He studied part-time at the Haldane Academy, where he won a silver medal for the best stained-glass window design (1865). He moved to Glasgow in 1870 and set up his own studio in partnership with David Small. Over the next 40 years he received ecclesiastic and domestic commissions for work all over the west of Scotland, and developed a distinct modern style, influenced by **Daniel Cottier** and **Edward Burne-Jones**. He used new types of glass in unusual mixtures of colour, and he outlined his approach to stained-glass design in a pamphlet entitled *Stained Glass—its History and Development* (1877). A further pamphlet, *The Truth in Decorative Art—Stained Glass Medieval and Modern*, was published in 1896. Examples of his work can be seen in Paisley Abbey and at New Kilpatrick Church, Bearsden, in Glasgow, where a four-light window depicts episodes from the life of Christ. Other examples of domestic work can be seen in the People's Palace, Glasgow.

Adamic, Louis 1899–1951
US writer

He was born in Blato, Dalmatia, Yugoslavia, the son of Slovene peasants, and emigrated to the USA in 1913. He served in the US army, and became naturalized in 1918. He began writing short stories in the early 1920s, utilizing his experiences and personal observations in his books—as in *Laughing in the Jungle* (1932), about an immigrant. Other works include *Dynamite: the Story of Class Violence in America* (1931), *My America 1928–38* (1938, an autobiographical survey), *From Many Lands* (1940), *Dinner at the White House* (1946) and *The Eagle and the Root* (1950). ◻ H A Christian, *Louis Adamic: a checklist* (1971)

Adamnan, St See Adomnan, St

Adamov, Arthur 1908–70
French dramatist

He was born in Kislovodsk in the Caucasus, Russia, brought up in France and educated in Switzerland and Germany. Before turning to drama he wrote *L'Aveu* ('The Confession'), about his despair at life's meaninglessness. His earlier plays belong to the Theatre of the Absurd which gave dramatic expression to the philosophical notion of the ultimately baffling nature of the world and man's existence. His works include *L'Invasion* (1950, 'The Invasion') and *Le ProfesseurTaranne* (1951), on the themes of bad communication and loss of identity, and his best-known play *Ping-Pong* (1955). With *Paolo Paoli* (1957) he abandoned the Absurd, and his distinctive talent, for Brechtian Epic Theatre. Later plays include *Le printemps '71* (1961), about the Paris Commune, and *La Politique des Restes* (1963). His death from overdosing was probably suicide. ◻ M Esslin, 'Arthur Adamov: The Curable and the Incurable', in *The Theatre of the Absurd* (1983)

Adams, Abigail, *née* Smith 1744–1818
US letter writer and First Lady

She was born in Weymouth, Massachusetts, and educated at home. After marrying **John Adams** in 1764, she managed his farm and maintained a strong interest in politics, often travelling with him. As the wife of the Vice-President then 2nd President of the new republic, she made observations in her letters that were lively and astute. She is considered to have been a strong political influence, and her letters, published in 1840 by her grandson, paint a vivid picture of the times and reflect her strong views on women's rights.

Adams, Ansel Easton 1902–84
US photographer

Born in San Francisco, he initially trained as a musician but became a professional photographer in 1927. His work is notable for his broad landscapes of the western USA, especially of Yosemite National Park, California, in the 1930s. A devotee of straight, clear photography and print perfection, he was one of the founders with **Edward Weston** of the Group f/64 (1932) and helped to set up the department of photography at the New York Museum of Modern Art (1940). He established the photographic department of the California School of Fine Art in San Francisco and was a prolific writer and lecturer, always stressing the importance of image quality at every stage of a photographer's work. He was also a conservationist and a director of the Sierra Club (from 1936). His publications included *Taos Pueblo* (1930) and *Born Free and Equal* (1944).

Adams, Brooks 1848–1927
US geopolitical historian

Born in Quincy, Massachusetts, he was the son of **Charles Francis Adams**. He graduated from Harvard, spent a year at Harvard Law School, and acted as secretary to his father in Geneva when the former US ambassador to the UK was helping arbitrate US claims against Great Britain for its failure to prevent the launch of the Confederate raider *Alabama* during the Civil War. Admitted to the Massachusetts Bar, he practised in Boston and later lectured in Boston University school of law (1904–11). His major work was *The Law of Civilization and Decay* (1896). He was an impassioned racialist and prophet of American doom, regarding immigrants as nationally corrupting. He was the brother of **Henry Brooks Adams**.

Adams, Bryan Guy 1959–
Canadian rock singer and guitarist

Born in Kingston, Ontario, he played in bands in Canada, then in 1978 began his solo career as a songwriter, with writing partner Jim Vallance. He began recording in 1979, but had his first major success with his third album, *Cuts Like a Knife* (1983). His first number one single, 'Heaven' (1985), was backed with a song about **Diana**, Princess of Wales. He does much work for charity, and supports Amnesty International, a political facet of his work reflected on his *Into The Fire* (1987) album. His original hard rock credentials began to fade after the global success of '(Everything I Do) I Do For You', and he has taken a more commercial approach in the 1990s. He remains a consistent bestseller. ◻ H Gregory, *Bryan Adams: The Inside Story* (1992)

Adams, Charles Francis 1807–86
US diplomat and author

Born in Boston, he was the son of **John Quincy Adams**, 6th President of the USA, grandson of **John Adams**, 2nd President, and father of **Henry Brooks Adams**. He was admitted to the Bar in 1828. He was a member of the US House of Representatives as the congressman for Massachusetts (1858–61). During the Civil War he was Minister to Great Britain (1861–68), and from 1871 to 1872 was one of the US arbitrators on the *Alabama* claims. He published the life and works of his grandfather (*Works of John Adams*, 1850–56) and father (*Memoirs of John Quincy Adams*, 1874–77), and edited the *Letters* of his grandmother, **Abigail Adams**.

Adams, Douglas Noel 1952–
English novelist and scriptwriter

He was born and educated in Cambridge. He worked as script editor on the popular television series *Doctor Who* (1978–80). Adams is best known for his humorous radio series, *The Hitch-Hiker's Guide to the Galaxy*, which he also wrote as a sequence of novels: *The Hitch-Hiker's Guide to the Galaxy* (1979), *The Restaurant at the End of the*

Universe (1980), *Life, The Universe and Everything* (1982) and *So Long, and Thanks for All The Fish* (1984). A further novel, *Mostly Harmless*, was added in 1992.

Adams, Gerry (Gerald) 1948–
Northern Ireland politician

Born in Belfast, he became politically active at an early age, joining the Irish Nationalist Party, Sinn Féin (We ourselves), the political wing of the IRA (Irish Republican Army). During the 1970s he was successively interned and then released because of his connections with the IRA, and in 1978 was elected vice-president of Sinn Féin and later president. In 1982 he was elected to the Northern Ireland Assembly and in the following year to the UK parliament as member for Belfast West. He declined to take up his seat at Westminster and in the 1992 general election lost it to Joe Hendron of the Social Democratic and Labour Party. Due to government censorship, his voice was one of several banned in 1988 from being broadcast by the media, although, in accordance with electoral legislation, this ban was temporarily lifted during the 1992 election. It was lifted again in 1995 as part of the peace process formed with the aim of ending sectarian violence. Since 1995, Adams has been permitted entry to the USA and has had a degree of success there in raising funds for Sinn Féin. 📖 *Before the Dawn* (1996); *Cage Eleven* (1990).

Adams, Sir Grantley Herbert 1898–1971
Barbadian politician

After studying classics at Oxford he was called to the English Bar in 1924 and returned to the West Indies to practise. He was a prominent figure in Caribbean politics and became premier of Barbados (1954–58) before being elected the first Prime Minister of the short-lived West Indies Federation (1958–62), which would have united seven former British colonies into a single state.

Adams, Hannah 1755–1831
US historian and memoirist

She was born in Medfield, Massachusetts. She grew up during the pre-independence era and published her first important book, the *Alphabetical Compendium of the Various Sects* (1784), at the age of 29. Her range of scholarship was also visible in *A Summary History of New England* (1799), one of the best available accounts of the pre- and post-Revolutionary north-eastern states. Often described as the first professional female author to emerge in the USA, her autobiography (published posthumously in 1832) is a vital document in the history of the young republic.

Adams, Henry Brooks 1838–1918
US historian

He was born in Boston, the son of **Charles Francis Adams** (1807–86) and grandson of **John Quincy Adams**, 6th President of the USA. Educated at Harvard, he acted as his father's secretary in Washington (1860–61) and England (1861–68), then worked as a journalist in Washington (1868–70) before teaching medieval and American history at Harvard (1870–77). He edited the *North American Review* (1870–76) and wrote two novels, *Democracy* (1880) and *Esther* (1884). He also wrote historical works, including the monumental *History of the United States during the Administrations of Jefferson and Madison* (9 vols, 1870–77), and *Mont Saint Michel and Chartres* (1904), a study of the unity of art and religion in the Middle Ages, and an autobiography, *The Education of Henry Adams* (1907), which was awarded the Pulitzer Prize in 1919. 📖 L Auchincloss, *Adams* (1971); E Samuels, *The Young Adams, Adams: The Middle Years, Adams: The Major Phase* (1948–64).

Adams, Herbert Baxter 1850–1901
US historian and educator

Born in Shutesbury, Massachusetts, he was educated at Amherst College and Heidelberg, and in 1876 joined the newly-formed Johns Hopkins University in Baltimore, Maryland, as Professor of History. His pupils included the future President **Woodrow Wilson** and the historian **Frederick Jackson Turner**. Adams established the American Historical Association *Reports* and inaugurated the *Johns Hopkins Studies in Historical and Political Science* series. His major publication was the *Life and Writings of Jared Sparks* (1893), the subject being a popular but unreliable historian of revolutionary America.

Adams, James Truslow 1878–1949
US historian

Born in Brooklyn, New York, he made his fortune as a stockbroker by 1912, then devoted himself to a life of scholarship. He wrote numerous popular and critically well-received books on US history, including *The Founding of New England* (1921, Pulitzer Prize), *The Adams Family* (1930), and *The Epic of America* (1931). Editor-in-chief of the six-volume *Dictionary of American History* (1940), he also was a contributor to the *Dictionary of American Biography* and a member of the Pulitzer Prize history jury.

Adams, John 1735–1826
2nd President of the USA

Born in Braintree (now Quincy), Massachusetts, the son of a farmer, he studied at Harvard, was admitted to the Bar in 1758, and settled in Boston in 1768. Of strongly colonial sympathies, he declined the post of advocate-general in the Court of Admiralty, and led the protest against the Stamp Act (1765). Despite failing health, he was sent as a delegate from Massachusetts to the first Continental Congress. He proposed the election of **George Washington** as Commander-in-Chief, and was the 'colossus' of the debate that resulted in the Declaration of Independence. President of the Board of War, and a member of around 90 committees (and chairman of 25 of them), he worked incessantly. He retired from Congress in 1777, only to be sent to France and Holland as commissioner from the new republic. One of the commissioners who in 1783 negotiated and signed the Treaty of Paris, he was Minister to Great Britain in 1785–88. While in London, he published his *Defence of the Constitution of the United States* (3 vols, 1787). In 1789 he became Vice-President of the USA under Washington. They were re-elected in 1792, and in 1796 Adams succeeded Washington as President, with **Thomas Jefferson** as Vice-President. Although a leader of the Federalist Party, he resisted **Alexander Hamilton** and other Federalists who called for war with France after the bribery scandal known as the XYZ affair, instead defusing the crisis through diplomacy. This and his signing of the Alien and Sedition Acts (1798) eroded his popularity, and on being defeated by Jefferson in the election of 1800, he retired to his home in Quincy. He was for many years estranged from Jefferson, but in old age they were reconciled and carried on a correspondence that became a classic of American historical literature; they died on the same day—4 July 1826, the 50th anniversary of the Declaration of Independence. 📖 Page Smith, *John Adams* (2 vols, 1962)

Adams, John, *alias* Alexander Smith c.1760–1829
English seaman

He took part in the mutiny against Captain **William Bligh** on the *Bounty* in 1789. With **Fletcher Christian** and seven other mutineers he founded a colony on Pitcairn Island. When the island was first visited in 1809 by the US sealer *Topaz*, Adams was the sole European survivor (most of the mutineers had been killed by their Tahitian companions in 1794). Revered as the patriarch of the Pitcairn settlement, he was given a royal pardon for his part in the mutiny.

Adams, Sir John 1920–84

English nuclear physicist

Educated at Eltham School, London, he went from school into the Siemens Research Laboratory at Woolwich before working on wartime radar development. His work on short wavelength systems took him to Harwell, where he engineered the world's first major postwar accelerator (the 180MeV cyclotron) in 1949. At CERN (Conseil Européen pour la Recherche Nucléaire) at Geneva, he engineered the 25 GeV proton synchroton (1954) and he became director-general in 1960. In 1961 he was recalled to Great Britain to establish the laboratory at Culham, Oxford, for research on controlled nuclear fusion. He was later appointed controller of the new Ministry of Technology in 1964, and in 1966 Member for Research at the UK Atomic Energy Authority. From 1969 to 1976 he returned to Geneva to oversee the building of the 450 GeV super-proton-synchrotron. He was director-general of CERN for a second time from 1976 to 1980.

Adams, John Bodkin 1899–1983

Suspected British murderer

Born in Northern Ireland, he became a doctor in Eastbourne. He was tried in 1957 for the murder of one of his patients, Edith Alice Morrell. She, like other patients before her, had died in mysterious circumstances, following long courses of heroin and morphine prescribed by Adams. He was a beneficiary of her will, despite the fact that she added a codicil cutting him out just before she died. At his trial, his defence counsel was able to exploit the inconsistent evidence provided by the prosecution and he was found not guilty. He subsequently resigned from the National Health Service and was later struck off the Medical Register. He continued to treat a few private patients in Eastbourne and was reinstated by the General Medical Council in 1961. While some believed he had killed nine or ten patients for personal gain during his years as a practitioner, others have argued that he merely practised a form of euthanasia.

Adams, John Coolidge 1947–

US composer

Born in Worcester, Massachusetts, he studied the clarinet as a boy. While still a music student at Harvard, he conducted the Boston Symphony Orchestra and the Boston Opera. Later he moved to San Francisco and became head of the department of composition at the Conservatory. His music is sometimes described as Minimalist—a style involving much repetition of melodies and phrases—but is actually more imaginative. His major works are the opera *Nixon in China* (1987, about the presidential visit), *Harmonium* (1980) for chorus and orchestra, and the *Grand Pianola Music* (1981–82). He has also written for films, including *Matter of Heart*.

Adams, John Couch 1819–92

English astronomer

Born in Lidcot, Cornwall, he graduated as Senior Wrangler and first Smith's Prizeman (1843) at St John's College, Cambridge, and was elected to a fellowship there. He studied the unexplained irregularities in the motion of the planet Uranus, assuming that these were due to an unknown perturbing body in the space beyond Uranus, and by 1845 he had derived elements for the orbit of such a body, named Neptune. His prediction of Neptune occurred almost simultaneously with that of the French astronomer Urbain Jean Joseph Leverrier, while the German astronomer Johann Galle, working on these calculations, actually observed Neptune in 1846. In 1848 Adams was awarded the Copley Medal of the Royal Society. In 1858 he was appointed Lowndean Professor of Astronomy and Geometry at Cambridge, where he spent the rest of his life pursuing problems in mathematical astronomy; his work on the motion of the Moon earned

him the Gold Medal of the Royal Astronomical Society (1866). Three years after his death a portrait medallion of Adams was placed in Westminster Abbey, London, near the grave of Isaac Newton. 📖 H M Harrison, *Voyager in Space and Time: the life of John Couch Adams, Cambridge Astronomer* (1994)

Adams, John Quincy 1767–1848

6th President of the USA

Born in Braintree (now Quincy), Massachusetts, the son of John Adams, the 2nd President of the USA, at the age of 14 he became private secretary to the US envoy in St Petersburg. After accompanying his father in Paris for the peace negotiations with Great Britain, he began to study at Harvard in 1785 and was admitted to the Bar in 1790. Successively Minister to The Hague, London, Lisbon and Berlin, he was elected to the US Senate from Massachusetts in 1803. He was nominally a Federalist, but he angered his party by supporting Jeffersonian policies such as the 1807 embargo, and in 1808 he was forced to resign his seat. In 1809 he was Minister to St Petersburg; in 1814 a member of the commission to negotiate peace between Great Britain and the USA; and from 1815 to 1817 Minister at the court of St James's, London. As Secretary of State under President James Monroe, he negotiated with Spain the treaty for the acquisition of Florida (1819), and was the principal author of the Monroe Doctrine. He ran for president against Andrew Jackson and others in 1824, and when none of the candidates gained a majority of electoral votes, Adams was chosen as President (1825) by the House of Representatives and was accused by the Jacksonians of having gained the deciding block of votes by making a corrupt bargain with Henry Clay. Plagued by partisan attacks, his administration accomplished nothing of importance. He was defeated by Jackson in 1828 and retired to his home at Quincy, depressed and impoverished. In 1830 he was elected to the House of Representatives, where he became noted as a promoter of antislavery views. 📖 Bennett Champ Clark, *John Quincy Adams, Old Man Eloquent* (1932)

Adams, Marcus Algernon 1875–1959

English portrait photographer

Born in Southampton, he was educated at Reading University and at Paris. He was apprenticed to his father, Walton Adams, also a professional photographer, and in 1919 established his own studio in London, specializing in formal children's portraits with a romantic style. From 1926 until his retirement in 1957 members of three generations of the British royal family were frequent sitters, and his portraits of them were published all over the world.

Adams, Maude, *originally* Maude Kiskadden 1872–1953

US actress

Born in Salt Lake City, Utah, she was a child star before making her New York debut in 1888, having taken her actress-mother's maiden name. After achieving fame as Lady Babbie in J M Barrie's *The Little Minister* (1897), she starred in several more of his plays, and is said to have inspired his most famous character, Peter Pan, a role she took in New York in 1905. She retired in 1918, but returned to the stage in Shakespearean roles (1931, 1934), and taught theatre in Missouri from 1937 to 1950.

Adams, Richard George 1920–

English novelist

Born in Berkshire, he was educated at Worcester College, Oxford, and after wartime service in the army worked as a civil servant with the Department of the Environment (1948–74). He made his name as a writer with the best-selling *Watership Down* (1972), an epic tale of a community of rabbits. Later books have included *Shardik* (1974), *The*

Plague Dogs (1977), *The Iron Wolf* (1980), *The Girl in a Swing* (1980), *Maia* (1984), *The Bureaucats* (1985) and *Traveller* (1989). 📖 *The Day Gone By* (1990)

Adams, Samuel 1722–1803
American revolutionary politician

Born in Boston, the second cousin of **John Adams**, 2nd President of the USA, he was chief agitator at the so-called Boston Tea Party (1773). He became a tax collector and then a member of the Massachusetts legislature (1765–74). He organized opposition to the Stamp Act (1765), and organized the Non-Importation Association (1798) and the Boston Committee of Correspondence (1772). After the Boston Tea Party he was a delegate to the First and Second Continental Congresses (1774–75), and signed the Declaration of Independence (1776). He anticipated **Napoleon I** by calling the English 'a nation of shopkeepers' in 1776. He was Lieutenant-Governor of Massachusetts from 1789 to 1794, and Governor from 1794 to 1797. 📖 Stewart Beach, *Samuel Adams: The Fateful Years, 1764–1776* (1965)

Adams, Truda (Gertrude), *later known as* Truda Carter, *née* Sharp 1890–1958
English ceramicist

Educated at the Royal Academy Schools, London, she moved to Durban, South Africa (1914) after meeting John Adams, who was on the staff at the Royal College of Art. Returning to England in 1920–21, they were persuaded to move to Dorset and help set up Carter, Stabler and Adams (Poole Pottery) with **Harold Stabler** and Cyril Carter. Truda Adams became resident designer there, providing the majority of the trademark 'Poole' designs, and her range of brush-stroke floral patterns with restrained colouring were extremely popular throughout the 1920s and 1930s. Having divorced John Adams, Truda married Cyril Carter in 1931, and continued to design for the company until 1950. Her work was purchased for many museum collections, and she exhibited in the Royal Academy's Ceramic Exhibition (1935), and the International Exhibition in Paris (1937).

Adams, Walter Sydney 1876–1956
US astronomer

Born in Antioch, Syria, of US parents, he studied at Dartmouth College, Massachusetts, the University of Chicago and the Yerkes Observatory. In 1904 he went with **George Hale** to help establish the Mount Wilson Observatory, near Pasadena, California, where he became deputy director and then director (1923–46). He was responsible for the design and installation of the 2.54 and 5.08 m telescopes at Mount Wilson and Palomar. He developed spectroscopic methods to relate stellar spectra to luminosity and used this to measure the distance to 6,000 stars. He also used spectroscopic methods to measure the temperature, pressure and density of the light-emitting material in sunspots. In 1915 he obtained the first spectrum of the white dwarf star Sirius B, showed that it was hotter than the Sun, contrary to expectations, and that it had a density 40,000 times that of water. In 1925 he measured the gravitational red shift induced in the light leaving the surface of Sirius B, adding yet further support to **Albert Einstein**'s general theory of relativity. Adams's 1934 observations of Mars showed that the atmosphere had less than 0.1 per cent oxygen. In 1941 he discovered spectral lines introduced by interstellar cyanogen molecules, giving an early clue to the existence of the microwave background radiation in the universe.

Adams, Will(iam) 1564–1620
English navigator

Born in Gillingham, Kent, he served with the Dutch in 1598 as pilot major of a fleet bound for the Indies. As pilot of the Dutch vessel *de Liefde* he reached the Japanese port of Oita in April 1600. The first Englishman to visit Japan, he was thrown into prison as a pirate at the instigation of jealous Portuguese traders, but was freed after building two ships for the shogun **Tokugawa** Ieyasu (1543–1616, shogun 1603–05), and received a pension and the rank of samurai (1600–20). He also served as the agent of the Dutch East India Company. 📖 Richard James, *Will Adams: An Illustrated Life of Will Adams, 1564–1620* (1973)

Adams, William Bridges 1797–1872
English engineer and inventor

Born in Madeley, Staffordshire, he built some of the first steam rail-cars, and in 1847 patented the fish-plate which is universally used for jointing rails. He took out 32 patents in all, relating to locomotives, wheel-carriages, roads, bridges and buildings, but made little or no money out of any of them. He is said to have suggested in 1850 the idea of the Crystal Palace that was designed for the 1851 Great Exhibition by **Joseph Paxton**.

Adamson, Joy Friederike Victoria, *née* Gessner 1910–80
British naturalist and writer

She was born in Austria. She moved to Kenya in 1937, where she married her third husband, British game warden George Adamson (1906–89), in 1943. She studied and painted wildlife, and made her name with a series of books about the lioness Elsa: *Born Free* (1960), *Elsa* (1961), *Forever Free* (1962), and *Elsa and Her Cubs* (1965). She was murdered in her home by tribesmen. 📖 Adrian House, *The Great Safari: the lives of George & Joy Adamson* (1993)

Adamson, Robert 1821–48
Scottish chemist

He was born in St Andrews, Fife. He helped the artist **David Octavius Hill** to apply the calotype process of making photographic prints on silver chloride paper, newly invented by **William Henry Fox Talbot**, for a commission to portray the founders of the Scottish Free Church in 1843. Working together, Hill providing the artistic direction and Adamson the technical skill, they produced some 2,500 calotypes, mainly portraits but also landscapes, between 1843 and 1848.

Adanson, Michel 1727–1806
French botanist

He was born in Aix-en-Provence and grew up in Paris, where he studied theology, classics and philosophy attending classes in the Jardin du Roi, taught by **Bernard Jussieu**, who influenced his approach to plant classification. During six years in Senegal he collected thousands of botanical and zoological specimens, and on his return published *Histoire naturelle du Sénégal* (1757, 'Natural History of Senegal') and *Les Familles naturelles des plantes* (1763–64). In the latter work he analysed the theoretical basis for the classification of plants in natural order, criticising **Linnaeus**'s reliance on a single character as the basis, suggesting instead that trial and experience should determine how plants should be grouped. His detailed descriptions of each family anticipated the modern multi-character approach in taxonomy. The baobab genus of African savannah trees, *Adansonia*, is named after him.

Adcock, (Kareen) Fleur 1934–
New Zealand poet

Born in Papakura, Auckland, she was educated in the UK and became resident there from 1963, working with the Foreign and Commonwealth Office (1963–79). Writing in a lucid, mostly narrative manner, and preferring invented situations to autobiographical matter, she is most successful when writing about apparently marginal or peripheral locations, such as New Zealand, Ulster, or the English Lakes. Her first collection was *The Eye of the Hurricane* (1964), and was followed by *In Focus* (1977), and the Wordsworthian *Below Loughrigg* (1977). She was editor of the influential *Oxford Book of Contemporary New Zealand Poetry* (1982), which re-affirmed links with her origins, and her *Selected Poems* appeared in 1983. She was married to the Maori poet Alistair Te Ariki Campbell and her sister is the novelist Marilyn Duckworth.

Addams, Charles Samuel 1912–88
US cartoonist
Born in Westfield, New Jersey, he was a regular contributor to the *New Yorker* magazine from 1935 onwards, specializing in macabre humour and a ghoulish group which was immortalized on television in the 1960s as *The Addams Family*.

Addams, Jane 1860–1935
US social reformer and feminist and Nobel Prize winner
She was born in Cedarville, Illinois, and attended Rockford College, Illinois. In 1899 she founded the first US settlement house, Hull House in Chicago, dedicated to settlement work among the immigrant poor, where she made her home. Addams worked to secure social justice by sponsoring legislation relating to housing, factory inspection, female suffrage and pacifism. She also campaigned for the abolition of child labour and the recognition of labour unions. Many of these reforms were adopted by the Progressive Party as part of its platform in 1912; she seconded **Theodore Roosevelt**'s nomination for President and was an active campaigner on his behalf. She was the first woman president of the National Conference of Social Work (1910), the founder and president of the national Federation of Settlements (1911–35), the vice-president of the National American Woman Suffrage Association (1911–14), and also helped to found the American Civil Liberties Union in 1920. President of the Women's International League for Peace and Freedom (1919–35), she shared the 1931 Nobel Peace Prize, awarded in recognition of her efforts to end hostilities in World War I. Her many books include *Democracy and Social Ethics* (1902) and *Peace and Bread in Time of War* (1922).

Addin, Muslih See **Sádi**

Addington, Henry See **Sidmouth, 1st Viscount**

Addison, Christopher Addison, 1st Viscount
1869–1951
English politician
Born in Hogsthorpe, Lincolnshire, and educated at Trinity College School, Harrogate, he qualified at St Bartholomew's Hospital, London, and became Professor of Anatomy at Sheffield University. In 1910 he was elected Liberal MP for Hoxton, representing the constituency until 1922. He became Parliamentary Secretary to the Board of Education (1914), Minister of Munitions (1916), and Great Britain's first Minister of Health (1919). Difficulties with **Lloyd George** led to his resignation in 1921 and to his joining the Labour Party. Elected MP for Swindon, he became Minister of Agriculture in 1929. Created a baron in 1937, he assumed leadership of the Labour peers in 1940. In 1945 he became Leader of the House of Lords and Dominions Secretary. His publications include *Politics From Within 1911–18* (1925), and *Four And a Half Years* (1934).

Addison, Joseph 1672–1719
English essayist and politician
Born in Milston, Wiltshire, he was educated at Charterhouse and Queen's College and Magdalen College, Oxford, of which he became a Fellow. A distinguished classical scholar, he began his literary career in 1693 with a poetical address to **John Dryden** and an *Account of the Greatest English Poets* (1694). In 1699 he obtained a pension to train for the diplomatic service and spent four years in France, Italy, Austria, Germany, and Holland. The *Campaign*, a poem commissioned by Charles Montagu, 1st Earl of **Halifax** to celebrate the victory of Blenheim (1704), brought him a commissionership of Excise. Elected MP for Malmesbury in 1708, he kept the seat for life. A prominent member of the Kit-Kat Club, and a friend of **Jonathan Swift** and **Richard Steele**, he contributed to Steele's periodical *The Tatler*, and in March 1711 he and Steele founded the *Spectator*, 274 numbers of which were the work of Addison. His essay 'On the Pleasures of the Imagination' explored new ground in aesthetics, and laid the basis for the idea of 'sensibility' that became so influential later in the century. He also wrote an opera, *Rosamond* (1706), and the blank-verse tragedy *Cato* (1713) as well as other articles and a prose comedy, *The Drummer* (1715). After the accession of **George I** (1714), he became secretary to the Earl of **Sunderland** as Lord-Lieutenant of Ireland, and in 1716 he was appointed a lord commissioner of trade. In the Hanoverian cause, he issued (1715–16) a political newspaper, the *Freeholder*, which cost him many of his old friends, and he was satirized by **Pope** as 'Atticus'. He became Secretary of State under Sunderland in 1717, but resigned his post a year later, owing to failing health. Almost his last literary undertaking was a paper war on the Peerage Bill of 1719. 📖 P Smithers, *The Life of Joseph Addison* (1954); N Ogle, *The Life of Addison* (1826).

Addison, Thomas 1793–1860
English physician
Born near Newcastle upon Tyne, he graduated in medicine at Edinburgh in 1815. He then settled in London, and became assistant physician (1824), and physician (1837) to Guy's Hospital. His chief researches were on pneumonia, tuberculosis and especially on the disease of the suprarenal capsules, known as Addison's disease (first described 1849). 📖 George Pallister, *Thomas Addison MD, FRCP (1795–1860)* (1975)

Ade, George 1866–1944
US humorist and playwright
Born in Kentland, Indiana, he graduated from Purdue University and became a columnist for a Chicago newspaper, writing humorous fables depicting common folk (*Fables in Slang*, 1899). He also wrote popular plays, including *The Sultan of Sulu*, (1902), *The College Widow* (1904), and *Father and the Boys* (1907), and scripts for early films.

Adela c.1062–1137
French noblewoman
She was the youngest daughter of **William the Conqueror**. In 1080 she married Stephen, later (1090) Count of Blois; King **Stephen** of England was the third of her nine children. She had a flair for administration and was cultured and pious.

Adelaide, St, *German* Adelheid 931–99
Holy Roman Empress
The daughter of **Rudolf II** of Burgundy, she married Lothair, son of Hugh of Italy, in 947. After his death (950) she was imprisoned by his successor, **Berengar II**, but was rescued by King **Otto I, the Great**, of Germany, who married her in 951. They became emperor and empress in 962. Their son was **Otto II**, over whom Adelaide exercised considerable influence when he succeeded his father (973). She became joint regent with the Empress **Theophano** for her grandson **Otto III**, and sole regent from 991 to 996. A prominent supporter of the Cluniac reform movement, she retired to a convent she had founded at Seltz in Alsace. Her feast day is 16 December.

Adelaide, Queen 1792–1849
Consort of William IV of Great Britain
She was the eldest daughter of George, Duke of Saxe-Meiningen. In 1818 she married William, Duke of Clarence, who succeeded his brother, **George IV**, as **William IV** (1830–37). She acquired some unpopularity

through her alleged political interference during the agitation (1831–32) preceding the 1832 Reform Act. Their two children, both daughters, died in infancy, and William was succeeded by his niece, Queen **Victoria**.

Adelard, *known as* Adelard of Bath 12th century
English philosopher
Born in England, he studied at Tours, France, travelled widely in Italy and the Near East, and is known to have been in Bath in 1130. His philosophical and scientific writings include many important translations from Arabic into Latin, as well as his best known work, *De Eodem et Diverso* ('On Identity and Difference', manuscript only) and *Perdifficiles Quaestiones Naturales*.

Adenauer, Konrad 1876–1967
German statesman
Born in Cologne, he studied at Freiburg, Munich and Bonn, before practising law in Cologne, where he became Lord Mayor in 1917. A member of the Centre Party under the Weimar Republic, he was a member of the Provincial Diet and president of the Prussian State Council (1920–33). In 1933 he was dismissed from all his offices by the Nazis, and imprisoned in 1934 and 1944. In 1945, under Allied occupation, he became Lord Mayor again, and helped to found the Christian Democratic Union (CDU). As the first Chancellor of the Federal Republic of Germany (1949–63), he established closer links with the French, and aimed to rebuild West Germany on a basis of partnership with other West European nations through NATO and the EEC. Although relations were restored with the USSR, relations with other countries in Eastern Europe remained frigid. His restraint during the Berlin crisis (1961–62) as well as his great age caused a decline in the fortunes of his parties at the polls (1961), necessitating a coalition with the Free Democrats, who pressed him for an early retirement. He complied in October 1963. ⊞ Paul Weymar, *Konrad Adenauer* (1955)

Ader, Clément 1841–1926
French engineer and pioneer of aviation
Born in Muret, he built a steam-powered bat-winged aeroplane, the *Eole*, in 1890. It made the first powered take-off in history, but could not be steered and flew for no more than 50 metres.

Adie, Kate (Kathryn) 1945–
English television reporter
Born in Sunderland, she took a degree in Scandinavian studies at Newcastle University, joined BBC Radio in 1969 as a technician and then producer, and moved to television in 1977, when she began a two-year spell with BBC South. A reporter on the BBC's national news since 1979, she has reported from troublespots around the world and has been chief news correspondent since 1989. She has twice been the winner of the Monte Carlo International TV News award (1981, 1990), won the BAFTA Richard Dimbleby award in 1989 and was voted 1992 Reporter of the Year.

Adjani, Isabelle Jasmine 1955–
French actress
Born in Paris to an Algerian father and German mother, she was an artistic child and ran her own theatre group before making her film debut in *Le Petit Bougnat* (1969, 'The Little Coalman'). She subsequently appeared in a number of film and television roles before being offered a contract with the Comédie-Française in Paris (1972). Hailed as 'the phenomenon of her generation' by *Le Figaro*, she went on to pursue a film career, winning acclaim for her performances in *L'Histoire d'Adèle H* (1975, *The Story of Adèle H*), *L'Été Meurtrier* (1983, *One Deadly Summer*) and *Camille Claudel* (1988). A major star in France, she has also recorded an album and is an active human rights campaigner. She has increasingly limited her screen appearances but after a lengthy absence returned in *Toxic Affair* (1993), *La Reine Margot* (1994) and *Diabolique* (1996).

Adler, Alfred 1870–1937
Austrian psychiatrist
He was born and trained in Vienna. He first practised as an ophthalmologist but later turned to mental disease and became a prominent member of the psychoanalytical group that formed around **Sigmund Freud** in 1900. His best-known work was *Studie über Minderwertigkeit von Organen* (1907, 'Study of Organ Inferiority and its Psychical Compensation'), which aroused great controversy. In 1911 he broke with Freud and developed his own 'Individual Psychology', investigating the psychology of the individual considered as different from others. His main contributions to psychology include the concept of the inferiority complex, and his special treatment of neurosis as the exploitation of shock. He opened the first child-guidance clinic in Vienna in 1921. In 1932 he moved to the USA to teach. His other published works include *The Practice and Theory of Individual Psychology* (trans 1923) and *Understanding Human Nature* (trans 1927). ⊞ Hertha Orgler, *Alfred Adler* (4th edn, 1973)

Adler, Cyrus 1863–1940
US religious leader and educator
Born in Van Buren, Arkansas, he attended a yeshiva in Philadelphia and studied at the University of Pennsylvania before earning a PhD in Semitics at Johns Hopkins University in 1887. He became an important lay leader of US Jews and a major figure in conservative Judaism, helping to found such organizations as the Jewish Historical Society, American Jewish Committee, and Jewish Welfare Board. He also served as president of Dropsie College in Philadelphia (1908–40) and the Jewish Theological Seminary in New York City (1924–40).

Adler, Dankmar 1844–1900
US architect
Born in Stadtlengsfeld, Prussia, he emigrated to the USA with his father in 1854 and studied architecture in Detroit and Chicago. He designed the Central Music Hall in Chicago, and in 1881 he entered into a partnership with **Louis Sullivan**, in which Sullivan's speciality proved to be aesthetics and Adler's engineering. Their work profoundly influenced 20th-century architecture, serving as a bridge between the classical revival of the 19th century and the simple, functional style of modern architecture. Among their designs were the Wainwright Building in St Louis (1890), considered the first true skyscraper, and the Transportation Building at the world's Columbia Exposition in Chicago (1893). The partnership dissolved in 1895.

Adler, Felix 1851–1933
US educator
Born in Alzey, Germany, he was taken to New York City at the age of six and graduated from Columbia University. After earning a PhD at Heidelberg and teaching at Cornell University, he founded the Society for Ethical Culture (1876), a non-sectarian organization devoted to achieving high moral potential through practical deeds as well as religious teachings. He also established the Manhattan Trade School for Girls and the Workingmen's School, which gave moral instruction and manual training. He was active in reform movements affecting tenement housing and child labour, and taught political and social ethics at Columbia from 1902. His writings include *Creed and Deed* (1877), *The Religion of Duty* (1905), and *An Ethical Philosophy of Life* (1918).

Adler, Jankel 1895–1949
Polish painter

He was born near Łódź. A Jewish upbringing along with early memories of ritualistic symbols and decorative folk motifs form the basis of his work. Although he is sometimes compared to **Marc Chagall**, stylistically his work owes more to Cubism and **Picasso**. Forced by Nazi persecution to wander throughout Europe, he worked in Berlin then Düsseldorf (where he met and admired **Paul Klee**), and on being labelled a 'degenerate' artist in Germany moved to Paris in 1933, where he worked briefly in **Stanley William Hayter**'s Atelier 17 (1937). He subsequently joined the Polish army in France but was evacuated to Scotland in 1941. He never wholeheartedly embraced abstraction, believing 'abstract painting can very easily become ornamental'. His idiosyncratic style had a certain influence on British artists, notably **Robert Colquhoun** and **Robert MacBryde**.

Adler, Larry (Lawrence Cecil) 1914–
US musician and self-taught harmonica virtuoso

Educated at Baltimore City College, he won the Maryland Harmonica Championship at the age of 13 and began his show business career in New York the following year. He has played as a soloist with some of the world's leading symphony orchestras, and has had pieces composed for him by **Ralph Vaughan Williams**, **Malcolm Arnold**, **Darius Milhaud** and others. He wrote the music for several films, including *Genevieve* (1954). He emigrated to the UK after being blacklisted in the USA for alleged pro-Communist leanings. 📖 *It Ain't Necessarily So* (1985)

Adler, Stella 1903–92
US actress and teacher

She was born in New York City, the daughter of the Yiddish actor Jacob Adler. She worked as an actress in both Yiddish theatre and on Broadway, including notable roles in **Clifford Odets**'s *Awake and Sing* and *Paradise Lost* (1935) for the Group Theatre (founded by her husband, **Harold Clurman**). She also directed plays, but is best known for her work as a teacher. She founded the Stella Adler Conservatory of Acting (1949), where she encouraged students to use imagination and the play itself as their inspiration, in opposition to the self-absorbed Method acting of **Lee Strasberg**.

Adolf Fredrik 1710–71
King of Sweden

Born in Gottorp, Schleswig, the son of Christian Augustus, Duke of Schleswig-Holstein-Gottorp, he was descended on his mother's side from King **Karl XI**, and was the first king of the House of Holstein-Gottorp. A favourite of the Empress **Elizabeth Petrovna** of Russia, he was adopted as successor designate to King **Fredrik I** (1743). In 1744 he married Louisa Ulrika, sister of King **Frederick II, the Great** of Prussia, and was appointed Commander-in-Chief of the Swedish forces (1747). As king from 1751, his powers were limited by the Riksdag (parliament) during the so-called Era of Liberty, but this came to an end when he was succeeded by his son, **Gustav III**.

Adomnan or Adamnan, St c.625–704
Irish monk

Born and educated in Donegal, Ireland, he joined the Columban brotherhood of Iona at the age of 27, of which, in 679, he was chosen abbot. In 686 he visited Aldfrid, King of Northumbria, to procure the release of some Irish captives, and was converted to Roman views as to the celebration of Easter and the shape of the tonsure. He failed to impose those views in Iona. He left a treatise *De Locis Sanctis*, one of our earliest descriptions of Palestine. *Adomnan's Vision*, a professed account of his visit to heaven and hell, is a work of the 10th or 11th century, but the *Vita*

Sancti Columbae is undoubtedly his, and reveals a great deal concerning the remarkable community of Iona. His feast day is 23 September.

Adorno, Theodor 1903–69
German social philosopher and musicologist

Born in Frankfurt, he studied there and became an associate of the Institute for Social Research and a member of the movement known as the 'Frankfurt School', which also included **Max Horkheimer** and **Herbert Marcuse**. In 1934 he emigrated to the USA to teach at the institute in exile at the New School of Social Research in New York; in 1960 he returned with the school to Frankfurt. His philosophy is most fully presented in *Negative Dialectics* (1966), a difficult and obscure work. He argues that the task of 'critical theory' is to dissolve all conceptual distinctions so that they cannot deform the true nature of reality. His sociological writings on music, mass-culture and art are generally much more accessible, and include *Philosophie der neuen Musik* (1949), *Versuch über Wagner* (1952), *Dissonanzen* (1956) and *Mahler* (1960).

Adrian IV or Hadrian, *originally* Nicolas Breakspear 1100–59
English cleric and pope

Born in Abbots Langley, near St Albans, Hertfordshire, he was educated at Merton Priory and Avignon. He became a monk himself in the monastery of St Rufus, near Avignon, and in 1137 was elected its abbot. Complaints about his strictness led to a summons to Rome, where the pope, **Eugenius III**, recognized his qualities and appointed him Cardinal-Bishop of Albano in 1146. In 1152 he was sent as Papal Legate to Scandinavia to reorganize the Church, where he earned fame as the 'Apostle of the North'. He was elected pope in 1154, the only Englishman to attain the title. One of his early acts is said to have been the issue of a controversial Bull granting Ireland to **Henry II**. Faced with rebellion in Rome fomented by **Arnold of Breschia**, he excommunicated the whole city until Arnold was expelled (he was later executed). He also excommunicated the powerful William I, the Bad, of Sicily, but was later glad to accept him as an ally. In 1155 he crowned **Frederick I**, **Barbarossa** as Holy Roman Emperor in front of his massed army in a show of strength in support of the papacy, but their relationship quickly deteriorated when Adrian tried to impose feudal power over him. For the rest of his papacy Adrian was engaged in a bitter struggle with Frederick for supremacy in Europe.

Adrian VI, *originally* Adrian Dedel 1459–1523
Dutch pope

Born in Utrecht, he studied in Louvain, and was made a doctor of theology (1491). He was appointed tutor in 1507 to the seven-year-old Charles (later Charles I of Spain and the Emperor **Charles V**), who when he became king in 1516 made Adrian Inquisitor-General of Aragon and effective co-regent with the dying **Ferdinand, the Catholic**'s choice **Ximenes**. On Ximenes's death, Charles worked closely with Adrian and made him regent in his absence from 1520, but in 1522 on the death of **Leo X**, Adrian was almost unanimously elected pope (1522). He tried in vain to attack the sale of indulgences which had prompted **Martin Luther**'s first revolt, and demanded Luther's punishment for heresy. He allied with the emperor, England and Venice against France, thus failing to unite Christendom against the Ottoman Turks, who captured Rhodes.

Adrian (of Cambridge), Edgar Douglas Adrian, 1st Baron 1889–1977
English physiologist and Nobel Prize winner

Born in London, he trained in the Physiological Laboratory, Cambridge, where he became a lecturer, and also a Fellow of Trinity College, Cambridge. Devoting his career to the study of the nervous system, he recorded the electrical activity of nerve fibres, and showed that neural information is conveyed by variations in the frequency at which nervous impulses are transmitted. In an examination of sensory systems in different animals, he investigated the response mechanisms of receptors and sense organs, and then studied the recording and analysing of information in the central nervous system. He also developed techniques to study and understand the gross electrical activity of the brain, electroencephalography (EEG), used clinically for the study of epilepsy and other brain disorders. For his work on the function of neurons he shared the 1932 Nobel Prize for physiology or medicine with Sir **Charles Sherrington**. Adrian was appointed Professor of Physiology at Cambridge (1937–51), Master of Trinity College, Cambridge (1951–65), and Chancellor of the university (1968–75). He also served in many other capacities, including those of Foreign Secretary (1945–50) and president (1950–55) of the Royal Society.

Ady, Endre 1877–1919
Hungarian poet and journalist
He went to Paris in the wake of his mistress, and was there stimulated by Symbolist procedures (as he understood them) to break away from the prevailing Hungarian conservative poetics. His *Új versek* (1906, 'New Verses'), was the most incisive collection of poetry ever published in Hungary, and around it and Ady himself there coalesced a group of eager young radical writers. By the end of the war, and of the short-lived **Béla Kun** government, Ady was fatally ill with syphilis and alcoholism; but he had changed the direction of Hungarian poetry and remains influential in the literature of his country.

AE or A. E. See Russell, George, William

Aegidius, St See Giles, St

Ælfric, *known as* Grammaticus ('the Grammarian') c.955–c.1020
Anglo-Saxon churchman and writer of vernacular prose
He was a pupil of Bishop Æthelwold of Winchester, became a monk and later abbot at the new monastery of Cerne Abbas in Dorset, and subsequently the first abbot of Eynsham in Oxfordshire. He composed two books of 80 *Homilies* (990–92) in Old English, a paraphrase of the first seven books of the Bible, and a book of *Lives of the Saints* (993–98). He also wrote a widely-used Latin grammar and Latin–English glossary, accompanied by a Latin *Colloquium* between a master, his pupil, and various craftsmen (including a ploughman, a shepherd and a merchant), which gives a vivid picture of social conditions in England. He was the greatest vernacular prose writer of his time.

Aelian, *in full* Claudius Aelianus, *called* the Sophist c.170–c.235AD
Roman rhetorician who wrote in Greek
He was born in Praeneste, and taught rhetoric in Rome (c.220BC). His *Variae Historiae* (*Historical Miscellanies*) and *De Natura Animalium* (*On the Characteristics of Animals*) are copious and valuable collections of curiosities, mostly taken from earlier writings now lost.

Aenesidemus 1st century BC
Greek philosopher
Born in Knossos, Crete, he broke away from the Athenian Academy to revive the Sceptical tradition of **Pyrrho**. His works, which include *An Outline of Pyrrhonism* and *Pyrrhonian Discourses*, are now lost, but he is credited with defining the 10 Sceptical 'modes' or 'tropes' of suspending judgement.

Aertsen, Pieter 1508/9–1579
Dutch painter
Born in Amsterdam, the first of a family dynasty of painters, from 1535 to c.1555 he worked in Antwerp. Few of his religious altarpieces survived the Reformation, and he is best known for paintings of everyday life and contemporary domestic interiors, which frequently include some religious reference. Such a treatment of religious subject matter continued a trend begun in early Netherlandish painting of the 15th century and can also be seen in the work of Aertsen's contemporary **Pieter Brueghel**. His still-life painting was less dependent on tradition and had a considerable influence on later Dutch art.

Aeschines c.389–c.322BC
Athenian orator
He was born in Athens, and was a soldier, actor and clerk before starting his public career. He became prominent in Athenian politics between 348 and 330BC, and his advocacy of peace with Macedonia brought him frequently into bitter conflict with **Demosthenes**, his chief opponent. Defeated in his attempt to undermine Demosthenes in 330, he went into voluntary exile in Rhodes, where he taught rhetoric. Of his speeches, only three survive. ▢ Edward M Harris, *Aeschines and Athenian Politics* (1995)

Aeschylus c.525–c.456BC
Greek tragic dramatist
Born in Eleusis, he served in the Athenian army in the Persian Wars, was wounded at Marathon (490BC) and probably fought at Salamis (480). His first victory as a poet was gained in the dramatic competitions of 484 and he won 13 first prizes in tragic competitions before losing to **Sophocles** in 468. Out of some 60 plays ascribed to him, only seven are extant: *The Persians*, the *Seven against Thebes*, the *Prometheus Bound*, the *Suppliants*, and the *Oresteia*, which comprises three plays about the murder of Agamemnon and its consequences (the *Agamemnon*, the *Choephoroe* and the *Eumenides*) and was his last great success on the Athenian stage (458). He was the first great writer of tragedy and must be credited with devising its classical form and presentation. His verse is marked by the grandeur of its diction, and by the great scope of its themes (the conflict between human and divine law, free will and fate, retribution and forgiveness). He was regarded in antiquity as the exemplar of his two great successors, Sophocles and **Euripides**. A story says that he died in Sicily when an eagle dropped a tortoise on his bald head. ▢ T Rosenmeyer, *The Art of Aeschylus* (1982); G Murray, *Aeschylus: the Inventor of Tragedy* (1940)

Aesop or Esop 6th century BC
Semi-legendary Greek author of fables
Tradition represents him as a slave in Samos, and as a confidant of King **Croesus** of Lydia, for whom he undertook various unlikely missions. The fables attributed to him are simple tales, often of animals, devised to illustrate moral lessons, and are probably derived from many sources. They were first popularized by the Roman poet **Phaedrus** in the 1st century AD. **Erasmus** published an edition in Latin in 1513 which was widely used in schools. They also served as models for the verse fables of **Jean de La Fontaine** (1668–94). ▢ B E Perry, *The Text Tradition of the Greek Life of Aesop* (1970)

Æthelred or Ailred of Rievaulx 1109–66
English chronicler
Born in Hexham, Northumberland, he was a page to Prince Henry of Scotland, and became a Cistercian monk at Rievaulx Abbey. He was a friend and adviser to both King **David I** of Scotland and King **Stephen** of England, and wrote *Relatio de Standardo*, a vivid account of the Battle

of the Standard between them at Northallerton, Yorkshire, in 1138. He also wrote spiritual works, and biographies of Edward the Confessor and St Ninian.

Æthelthryth, St See Etheldreda, St

Æthelbert See Ethelbert

Æthelflaed See Ethelflæd

Æthelred See Ethelred

Aethelstan See Athelstan

Aëtius, Flavius c.390–454AD
Roman general

He was born in Moesia. In 433AD he became patrician, consul, and general-in-chief, and as such maintained the empire for 20 years. His main achievements were the destruction of the Burgundian Kingdom in eastern Gaul, and the defeat of Attila the Hun in 451. Three years later the jealous Emperor Valentinian III stabbed him to death.

Aflaq, Michel 1910–89
Syrian politician

He was born in Damascus and educated at the University of Paris. A schoolteacher and then journalist in Damascus, he was, with Salah al-Din Bitar, the founder of the Ba'ath Socialist Party (1943). The ideology behind the party was essentially socialist, with an emphasis on Arab unity. It was also anti-Zionist and instrumental in the foundation with Gamal Abd al-Nasser of the United Arab Republic (1958–61). Ousted from Syria in 1966 and settling in Baghdad, Aflaq's political influence declined, but even today (hostile) Arab presses are inclined to refer to the Ba'ath Party as being Aflaqi.

Africanus, Leo See Leo Africanus

Africanus, Sextus Julius c.160–c.240AD
Roman traveller and historian

Born in Libya, he wrote *Chronologia*, a history of the world from the creation to AD221. His chronology, which antedates Jesus Christ's birth by three years, was accepted by Byzantine churches.

Aga Khan III *in full* Aga Sultan Sir Mohammed Shah 1877–1957
Imam (leader) of the Ismaili sect of Muslims

Born in Karachi, India (now in Pakistan), he succeeded to the title in 1885. He founded Aligarh University (1910). He worked for the British cause in both World Wars, and in 1937 was president of the League of Nations assembly. He welcomed the creation of Pakistan (1947), and hoped for a blending of European and Ismaili culture. A keen racecourse enthusiast, he owned several Derby winners. He was succeeded as 49th Imam by his grandson Karim, the son of Aly Khan, as Aga Khan IV. ▢ Anne Edwards, *Throne of Gold: The Lives of the Aga Khans* (1995)

Aga Khan IV, Karim 1936–
Imam (leader) of the Ismaili sect of Muslims

Born in Geneva, Switzerland, the grandson of Aga Khan III and son of the late Aly Khan, he succeeded his grandfather as 49th Imam (1957). He was educated at Le Rosey in Switzerland, and later read oriental history at Harvard. He married an English woman, Sarah Croker Poole (1969).

Aganbegyan, Abel Gazevich 1932–
Soviet economist

Born in Tbilisi, Georgia, he was educated at the Moscow State Economic Institute. As Professor of Economics at Novosibirsk State University, and Director of the Institute of Economics and Industrial Engineering, with his colleagues he developed the models for managing the national economy which the Soviet government started

to apply in the late 1980s. He was the chairman of several national committees and councils and personal adviser to President Mikhail Gorbachev on economic affairs.

Agassi, Andre 1970–
US tennis player

Born in Las Vegas, Nevada, he defeated Stefan Edberg to win the inaugural ATP world championship in 1991, and went on to win the men's singles at Wimbledon in 1992. In 1990 he was a member of the victorious US Davis Cup team. He won the US Open in 1994 and though knocked out of Wimbledon in the first round in 1996, he went on to win the gold medal at the Atlanta Olympics the same year.

Agassiz, Alexander Emmanuel Rodolphe 1835–1910
US oceanographer and marine zoologist

He was born in Neuchâtel, Switzerland, the son of Louis Agassiz, and went to the USA in 1849 to join his father, studying engineering and zoology at Harvard. He used his engineering skills to speed up dredging and deep soundings, and also invented mechanical strain equalizers, a new double-edged dredge and a closing tow net for mid-depth sampling. Between 1877 and 1880 he sailed the Atlantic and the Pacific oceans, studying the Gulf Stream, the plankton abundance and the dependence of the bottom fauna upon it. He resurrected and became the chairman of copper mines in Michigan which financed his scientific travels, particularly his searches for evidence on reef theory. From 1873 to 1885 he was curator of the Harvard Museum of Comparative Zoology founded by his father, which contains both their collections.

Agassiz, Elizabeth Cabot Cary, *née* Cary 1822–1907
US naturalist and educator

Born in Boston, Massachusetts, she married the widowed glaciologist Louis Agassiz in 1850 and with him established the pioneering Agassiz School for Girls in Boston (1856). They also conducted a young ladies' school in Cambridge, Massachusetts. She accompanied her husband on his expeditions to Brazil (1865–66), which inspired them to write *A Journey in Brazil* (1868), and she also travelled along the Pacific and Atlantic coasts of the Americas (1871–72). She then served as president of the Society for Collegiate Instruction of Women and was a founder and president of Radcliffe College for Women (1894–1902), which was founded in 1879 and chartered in 1894. Her other publications include *Seaside Studies in Natural History* (1865).

Agassiz, (Jean) Louis (Rodolphe) 1807–73
US naturalist and glaciologist

Born in Môtier-en-Vully, Switzerland, he studied at the medical school of Zurich and at the universities of Heidelberg and Munich. His main interest was zoology and while still a student he published *The Fishes of Brazil* (1829) which brought him to the attention of Georges Cuvier. In 1832 he was appointed Professor of Natural History at the University of Neuchâtel, where he became interested in glaciers. He examined evidence for the glacial transportation of rock material and proved that glaciers are mobile. Tracing their previous extents in the Alps, he developed the theory of ice ages, with global cooling and the past effects on flora and fauna. He can be considered the father of glacial theory for having given credibility to the previously unacceptable ideas of Horace Bénédict de Saussure and James Hutton. Following a successful Lowell lecture tour in Boston in 1846, he was appointed Professor of Natural History at the Lawrence Scientific School at Harvard. In 1859 Agassiz founded the Museum for Comparative Zoology at Harvard, to which he donated his collections. He became an oceanographer in 1851, taking an interest in coral reefs. His publications include *Études sur les glaciers* (1840) and *Système Glacière* (1847). ▭ Edward Lurie, *Louis Agassiz: A Life in Science* (1960)

Agate, James Evershed 1877–1947
English critic and essayist

Born in Manchester, and educated at Manchester Grammar School, he wrote dramatic criticism for several newspapers including the *Manchester Guardian*, and for the BBC, before becoming drama critic of the *Sunday Times* (1923). He wrote also on literature and films, and was the author of essays, novels and, notably, a nine-part autobiography in the form of a diary, *Ego* (1935–48), describing literary London and the personalities of his day. ▭ James Harding, *Agate* (1986)

Agatha, St d.251AD
Christian martyr

Born in Catania, Sicily, she is said to have dedicated herself and her virginity to God, rejected the love of the Roman consul Quintinian, and suffered a cruel martyrdom. Tortured and mutilated by having her breasts removed (though her wounds were healed during a vision of St **Peter**), she may have been killed by being rolled over burning coals. She is the patron saint of Catania, and is invoked against fire and lightning; she is also the patron saint of bell-founders. Her feast day is 5 February.

Agatharcos 5th century BC
Athenian artist

Living during the time of **Pericles**, when the arts flourished, he was named by the Roman architect **Marcus Vitruvius Pollio** as the founder of scene painting and a pioneer of perspective.

Agathocles 369–289BC
Tyrant of Syracuse

He fought the Carthaginians and invaded Tunisia, and took on the royal title (305BC) in imitation of the Macedonian generals who succeeded **Alexander the Great**. A ruthless tyrant according to the hostile tradition, he nevertheless enjoyed popular support, and under him Sicily achieved her last period of independent power before the Roman conquest.

Agee, James 1909–55
US novelist, poet, film critic and screen writer

He was born in Knoxville, Tennessee, and educated at Harvard. He worked for several magazines before being commissioned to rove the southern states during the Depression with the photographer Walker Evans, an assignment that produced the documentary *Let Us Now Praise Famous Men* (1941). He became a literary celebrity and was wooed by Hollywood for which he wrote classic film scripts including *The African Queen* (1951) and *The Night of the Hunter* (1955). Other works include his only novel, the unfinished semi-autobiographical *A Death in the Family* (1955), which was awarded a posthumous Pulitzer Prize, and *Agee on Film* (1958). ▭ L Bergreen, *Agee: a Life* (1984)

Agesilaus 444–360BC
King of Sparta

He ruled Sparta from 399BC, and was called on by the Ionians to assist them against **Artaxerxes II** (397). He launched an ambitious campaign in Asia, but the Corinthian War (395–387) recalled him to Greece. At Coronea (394) he defeated the Greek allied forces, and arranged a peace in favour of Sparta (387). However, his narrow view of Spartan interests probably contributed to Sparta's conquest by Thebes in 371. His biography was written by **Cornelius Nepos**, and an encomium was written by his friend **Xenophon**.

Aggesen, Sven 12th century
Danish historian

He was the author of *Compendiosa Historia Regnum Daniae*, the earliest known Latin history of the kings of Denmark, spanning the years from 300 to 1185.

Agis IV c.263–241BC
King of Sparta

Of the Eurypontid dynasty, he reigned from 244 to 241BC. He sought to revive Sparta's military power by a programme of cancellation of debts and redistribution of land, but was opposed by powerful reactionary interests and executed. His aims were revived successfully by **Cleomenes III**. Plutarch's *Life of Agis* is the principal source for his reign.

Agnelli, Giovanni 1866–1945
Italian manufacturer

Born in Villa Perosa, Piedmont, he was educated at a military academy and became a cavalry officer. In 1899 he founded Fiat (Fabbrica Italiana Automobili Torino). He was appointed a senator in 1923, and mobilized Italian industry in World War II. His grandson, named Giovanni Agnelli in his honour (b. 1921), became chairman of Fiat in 1966.

Agnes, St c.292–c.304AD
Roman Christian

She was probably martyred in Rome during the persecutions of **Diocletian**. The patron saint of virgins, she is said to have refused to consider marriage, and consecrated her maidenhood to God. Her emblem is a lamb, and her feast day is 21 January.

Agnes of Assisi, St 1197–1253
Italian Christian

The daughter of Count Favorino Scifi, she joined her sister, who became St **Clare**, in a convent in 1211, in the face of violent parental opposition. They became co-founders of the order of the Poor Ladies of San Damiano (Poor Clares, formerly called Minoresses). In 1219 she became abbess of a newly established community of the order at Monticelli.

Agnesi, Maria Gaetana 1718–99
Italian mathematician and scholar

Born in Milan and educated privately, she was a child prodigy, speaking six languages by the age of 11. She published books on philosophy and mathematics, and her mathematical textbook *Istituzioni analitiche* (1784) became famous throughout Italy. One of the few women mathematicians to gain a reputation before the 20th century, she assimilated the work of many different authors and developed new mathematical techniques. She is mainly remembered for her description of a versed sine curve, which following an early mistranslation of Italian, became known as the 'witch of Agnesi'.

Agnew, Spiro T(heodore) 1918–96
US politician

Born in Baltimore, Maryland, the son of a Greek immigrant, he served in World War II and studied law at the University of Maryland. In 1966 he was elected Governor of Maryland on a liberal platform, supporting anti-discrimination and anti-poverty legislation, but by 1968 he had become considerably more conservative. As a compromise figure acceptable to many in the Republican Party, he became **Richard Nixon**'s running mate in the 1968 election, and took office as Vice-President in 1969. He resigned in 1973 after charges of corruption during his years in Maryland politics were brought against him. After pleading no contest to income tax evasion, he was sentenced to probation and fined. He published *Go*

Quietly ... or Else in 1980. ⊞ Richard M Cohen, *A Heartbeat Away: The Investigation and Resignation of Vice-President Spiro T Agnew* (1974)

Agnon, Shmuel Yosef, *originally* Shmuel Josef Czaczkes 1888–1970
Israeli novelist and Nobel Prize winner

Born in Buczacz, Galicia (now Poland), he went to Palestine in 1907, studied in Berlin (1913–24), then settled in Jerusalem and changed his surname to Agnon. He wrote an epic trilogy of novels on Eastern Jewry in the early 20th century: *Hakhnasath Kallah* (1931, Eng trans *The Bridal Canopy*, 1937), *Ore-ah Nata Lalun* (1939, Eng trans *A Guest for the Night*, 1968) and *Tmol Shilshom* (1945, 'The Day Before Yesterday') as well as several volumes of short stories. He is considered the greatest writer in modern Hebrew, and became the first Israeli to win the Nobel Prize for literature, jointly with the Swedish author Nelly Sachs, in 1966. ⊞ S Sneh, *Schmuel Iosef Agnon* (1970); A J Band, *Nostalgia and Nightmare: a study in the fiction of Agnon* (1968)

Agostini, Giacomo 1943–
Italian motorcyclist

Born in Lovere, Bergamo, he won a record 15 world titles between 1966 and 1975, including the 500cc title a record eight times (1966–72, 1975). Thirteen of these titles were on an MV Agusta, the others on a Yamaha. He won 10 Isle of Man TT Races (1966–75), including the Senior TT five times (1968–72). After retirement in 1975 he became manager of the Yamaha racing team.

Agostino di Duccio 1418–81
Italian sculptor

He was born in Florence, and his best and most original work is the relief decoration for the Tempio Malatestiano at Rimini, a church designed by Leon Battista Alberti. His style is characterized by a strong emphasis on line and, in its essentially decorative quality, differs from the more powerful naturalism of his greatest contemporary, Donatello. Although compelled to leave Florence—due, it was said, to being accused of stealing from a church— he returned for sufficient time to begin working on a large piece of marble which, left unfinished, was later used by Michelangelo to produce the famous statue of *David*.

Agoult, Marie de Flavigny, Comtesse d', *pseudonym* Daniel Stern 1805–76
French writer

Born in Frankfurt am Main, Germany, of French parentage, and educated at a convent in Paris, and a notable beauty, she married the Comte d'Agoult in 1827, but in 1834 left him for Franz Liszt. She wrote novels such as *Nélida* (1845) under the pseudonym Daniel Stern. A close friend of George Sand, she held a salon in Paris and wrote on numerous subjects, including *Esquisses morales* (1849), *Histoire de la révolution de 1848* (1850), *Dante et Gœthe* (1866), and a play, *Jeanne d'Arc* (1857). Their daughter Cosima married Richard Wagner.

Agricola, Georgius, *Latin name of* Georg Bauer 1494–1555
German mineralogist and metallurgist

He was born in Glauchau, Saxony, and became Rector of the school at Zwickau (1518–22). Later, he practised as a physician in Chemnitz and followed his interest in minerals to study mining. He was among the first to recognize the erosive power of rivers in forming landscapes, but his ideas about the ability of exhausted mines to regenerate themselves did not stand the test of time. He was author of *De Natura Fossilum* (1546), in which a systematic classification of minerals was attempted, and his *De Re Metallica* (1555, translated by US President Herbert Hoover in 1912), is a detailed record of 16th century mining, ore-smelting and metal working which remained a standard work for almost four centuries.

Agricola, Gnaeus Julius AD40–93
Roman general

He was born in Forum Julii (now Fréjus, Provence). Rome's longest-serving and most successful governor in Britain (AD78–84), he skilfully implemented a two-pronged policy, of conquest in the north and Romanization in the south. He subdued northern England and Lowland Scotland, and actively encouraged the development of Roman-style towns in the south. He failed to conquer the extreme north of Scotland and Ireland, but the circumnavigation of Britain by his fleet greatly impressed contemporaries. Recalled about 84 by Emperor Domitian, probably out of jealousy, he lived quietly in retirement in Rome until his death. His son-in-law Tacitus wrote his biography. ⊞ D E Soulsby, *Selections From Tacitus: Agricola Handbook* (1982)

Agricola, Johann, *originally* Johann Schneider or Schnitter, *also called* Magister Islebius 1492–1566
German reformer

Born in Eisleben, he studied at Wittenberg and Leipzig, and was sent (1525) by Martin Luther to Frankfurt, to institute Protestant worship. One of the most zealous founders of Protestantism, he preached in Eisleben until 1536, when he was appointed to a chair at Wittenberg. He had to resign, however, in 1540 for his opposition to Luther in the great Antinomian controversy. He wrote many theological books, but his collection of German proverbs (1528–29) is his most important work. ⊞ Gustav Kawerau, *Johann Agricola von Eislebene, Bietr zur Reformationsgeschichte* (1881)

Agricola, Rudolphus, *properly* Roelof Huysman 1443–85
Dutch humanist

Born near Groningen, in Friesland, he studied in Italy (1473–80), alternately at Heidelberg and Worms, dividing his time between private studies and public lectures. He was the foremost scholar of the Renaissance 'new learning' in Germany and his writings had a profound influence on Erasmus and other northern scholars. He was also a distinguished musician and painter.

Agrippa, Marcus Vipsanius c.63–12BC
Roman general and politician

He played an important role in various of Augustus's military campaigns, including his victory over Sextus, the son of Pompey in 36BC, and over Mark Antony at Actium (31). He was responsible for the administration of several parts of the new Roman Empire, including the improvement of the public amenities of Rome. The Emperors Caligula and Nero were descendants of his marriage with Augustus's daughter, Julia.

Agrippa von Nettesheim, Henricus Cornelius 1486–1535
German occultist philosopher

Born in Cologne, he travelled widely and had a varied, if insecure, career as physician, diplomat, teacher and soldier. He acted as agent to Maximilian I on missions to Paris (1506) and London (1510), where he was the guest of John Colet. He was with the army in Italy (1511) and subsequently lectured at Pavia (1515) and was made doctor both of law and medicine. In 1518 he became town orator at Metz but in 1520 was back in Cologne where he aroused the hostility of the Inquisition through defending a witch. He later served as doctor and astrologer to Louise of Savoy, the Queen Mother of France, in Lyons (1524) and as historian to Margaret of Austria at Antwerp (1528–30), but neither position brought him prosperity. His major and influential work, a treatise on magic, *De occulta philosophia*, was completed in 1510 and published in an enlarged edition in 1533. In his sceptical work, *De incertitudine et vanitate scientarum atque artium declamatio* (1526), he rejected all human knowledge and advocated faith in divine revelation.

Agrippina, the Elder c.14BC–AD33
Roman noblewoman
She was the daughter of **Marcus Vipsanius Agrippa** and granddaughter of the Emperor **Augustus**. She married **Germanicus Caesar**, and was the mother of **Caligula** and Agrippina, the Younger. Regarded as a model of heroic womanhood, she accompanied her husband on his campaigns, and took his ashes home when he was murdered (AD19). Her popularity led the jealous **Tiberius** to banish her (AD30) to the island of Pandataria, where she died of starvation in suspicious circumstances. A portrait of her survives in the Capitoline Museum, Rome.

Agrippina, the Younger AD15–59
Roman empress
She was the daughter of **Agrippina, the Elder** and **Germanicus**. She married first Cnaeus Domitius Ahenobarbus, by whom she had a son, the future Emperor **Nero**. Her third husband was her uncle, the Emperor **Claudius**, who subsequently made Nero his successor, ousting **Britannicus**, his own son by his former wife, **Messalina**. Agrippina then proceeded to poison all her son's rivals and enemies, and finally (allegedly) the emperor himself. She ruled as virtual co-regent with Nero, but he had her put to death.

Aguesseau, Henri François d' 1668–1751
French jurist
Born in Limoges, and pronounced by **Voltaire** the most learned magistrate that France had ever possessed, he was a steady defender of the rights of the people and of the Gallican Church. He was Advocate General and Attorney-General to the Parlement of Paris, and three times Chancellor of France, under **Louis XV** (1717–18, 1720–22, 1737–50). He secured the adoption of important reforms and attempted in vain a codification of French law.

Aguilera Malta, Demetrio 1909–81
Ecuadorean novelist, dramatist, poet, journalist and film director
Born in Guayaquil into a middle-class family, he contributed in 1930 to a story anthology by the so-called Grupo de Guayaquil. He was a reporter in the Spanish Civil War, and wrote two books about it, severely critical of General **Franco**. He also wrote plays and stories, but he is best known for the novels *Siete lunas y siete serpientes* (1970, Eng trans *Seven Serpents and Seven Moons*, 1979) and *El sequestro del general* (1973, Eng trans *Babelandia*, 1985), both of which have been classified as 'magic realist'. For a long period he was forbidden to enter the USA on account of his description of its policies in Panama in the novel *Canal Zone* (1935). □ V Carrabino (ed), *The Power of Myth in Literature and Film* (1981)

Aguilo i Fuster, Marian 1825–97
Spanish writer and philologist
Born in Valencia, he worked as librarian there and at Barcelona. He was a powerful influence in the renaissance of the Catalan language and the poetic tradition of Catalonia. He published *Romancer popular de la terra catalana* (1893), and a dictionary of Catalan was published posthumously.

Aguinaldo, Emilio 1870–1964
Filipino revolutionary
He led the rising against Spain in the Philippines (1896–98), and against the USA (1899–1901), but after capture in 1901 took an oath of allegiance to the USA.

Aguirre, José Antonio 1904–60
Basque politician
Born into a middle-class, Carlist family, he became leader of the conservative Basque Nationalist Party (PNV), the main Basque party of the 1930s. He was elected as the first President (Lendakari) of the Basque country (Euzkadi) after the Second Spanish Republic passed the Autonomy Statute in 1936. After the fall of Bilbao (1937), he took the government into exile in France. Following the outbreak of World War II, he was denied passage to England, and so undertook an extraordinary journey via Nazi Germany (complete with artificial moustache and glasses), Sweden, and Brazil to Uruguay. After the war, he headed the government-in-exile in France.

Aguiyi-Ironsi, Johnson 1925–66
Nigerian soldier and politician
He joined the colonial army in 1942 and was trained in the UK before commanding the Nigerian contingent in the UN involvement in the Congo. Appointed Commander-in-Chief in 1965, he assumed power following the officers' coup of January 1966, but was killed in the counter-coup, led by **Yakubu Gowon** (July 1966).

Agutter, Jenny (Jennifer Anne) 1952–
English actress
Born in Taunton, Somerset, she made her film debut at the age of 11 in *East of Sudan* (1964), following it with *Ballerina* (1965) and the role of Bobbie in *The Railway Children* (1970), which she had already played in a BBC television serial (1968). Hollywood success followed, with appearances in *Logan's Run* (1976), *The Eagle Has Landed* (1976), *Amy* (1981) and *An American Werewolf in London* (1981). She won a BAFTA award for *Equus* (1977) and, on television, an Emmy for *The Snow Goose* (1971). She has guest-starred in television series such as *Murder, She Wrote*, *The Equalizer*, *Boon*, *Love Hurts* and *Heartbeat*.

Ahab 9th century BC
King of Israel
A warrior king (c.889–850BC) and builder, he extended his capital city of Samaria and refortified Megiddo and Hazor. He fought against the Assyrians at the Battle of Karkar (853). To extend his alliances in the north he married **Jezebel**, daughter of the King of Tyre and Sidon, who introduced Phoenician customs and the worship of the Phoenician god, Baal. This aroused the furious hostility of the prophet **Elijah**. Ahab was killed in battle against the Syrians at Ramoth Gilead.

Ahidjo, Ahmadou 1924–89
Cameroonian politician
Born in Garoua, and educated at the École Supérieure d'Administration, Yaoundé, he was a radio operator in the post office before entering politics in 1947, being elected to the Territorial Assembly. He represented Cameroon in the Assembly of French Union (1953–57). From 1957 to 1960 he held senior positions in the Territorial Assembly of Cameroon. In 1960, when most of the British Cameroons was amalgamated with the French Cameroons, he became President and was re-elected to that post in 1972, 1975 and 1980. He resigned in 1982 and went into voluntary exile in France. His one-party state, although severe on the rival, but outlawed, Union des Populations Camerounaises (UPC), was relatively successful economically and less repressive than many West African states.

Ahlquist, Raymond Perry 1914–83
US pharmacologist
Born in Missoula, Montana, he studied pharmaceutical chemistry at the University of Washington, Seattle, became an assistant professor at South Dakota State College (1940–44) and then moved to the Medical College of Georgia, becoming Professor of Pharmacology (1948–

77), and Charbonnier Professor (1977–83). Ahlquist's major contribution was published in 1948, a paper that described the role played by different populations of cell receptors in diverse biological actions. This dual receptor concept provided an explanation for effects that had long been observed, but it contradicted another widely accepted theory postulated by many others, including Walter Cannon, and took many years to gain acceptance. The potential applications of the concept were recognized by Sir James Black in his development of beta-blockers.

Ahmad ibn Ibrahim al-Ghazi, also known as Ahmad Gran c.1506–1543
Sultan of Adal, Somalia

He declared a jihad against Christian Ethiopia in the 1530s, and with assistance from the Ottomans, dominated the empire until his defeat and death in battle against the Emperor Galawdewos in 1543.

Ahmad Khan, Sir Sayyid 1817–98
Indian lawyer and educator

One of the most influential Indian Muslims of the 19th century, he was an employee of the British East India Company and later a judge. He worked to further the Muslim cause in India within the British system by embracing this system and European civilization. An opponent of Muslim participation in the Indian National Congress, following the Indian Uprising (1857–58), he wrote a widely read book and a pamphlet denying that the Muslims were responsible or involved in the rebellion. He held progressive views on the issue of the social position of women, which brought him into conflict with orthodox Islamic leaders. His greatest legacy was his establishment of the Mohammedan Anglo-Oriental College (now Aligarh Muslim University) in 1875 and the development of the Muslim Educational Conference, which eventually spread across India.

Ahmad Shah Durrani c.1722–73
Founder and first monarch of Afghanistan

Born in Multan, Punjab, a chieftain of the Sadozai clan of the Abdali tribe, and a cavalry general under the Persian Emperor Nadir Shah, he was elected king of the Afghan provinces when the emperor was assassinated (1745). He established his capital at Kandahar, and made nine successful invasions of the Punjab and plundered Lahore (1752) and Delhi (1757). He defeated the Marathas at Panipat (1761), and the Sikhs near Lahore (1762), when he razed the Temple of Amritsar. He appointed his son Viceroy of the Punjab, but eventually acknowledged Sikh power there. After his death the great Afghan empire he had founded soon disintegrated.

Ahmed Arabi, also called Arabi Pasha 1839–1911
Egyptian soldier and nationalist leader

An officer in the Egyptian army, he fought in the Egyptian–Ethiopian War (1875–79), took part in the officers' revolt that deposed Ismail Pasha (1879), and was the leader of a rebellion against the new khedive, Tewfik Pasha, in 1881 that led to the setting up of a nationalist government, with Ahmed Arabi as War Minister. The British intervened to protect their interests in the Suez Canal, and he was defeated at Tel-el-Kebir (1882). He was sentenced to death, but exiled to Ceylon instead and pardoned (1901), being allowed to return to Cairo.

Ahmet I 1590–1617
Sultan of Turkey

The son of Mehmet III, he was born in Manisa, and succeeded in 1603. He waged an unsuccessful war with Persia (Iran) from 1602 to 1612 and internal rebellion weakened Ottoman authority. He built the Blue Mosque in Constantinople (Istanbul).

Ahmet II 1642–95
Sultan of Turkey

The son of Ibrahim, he was born in Edirne and succeeded in 1691. A disastrous defeat at Slankamen (1691) by the Austrians lost him Hungary and his Arab provinces were plagued by unrest.

Ahmet III 1673–1736
Sultan of Turkey

He was the son of Mehmet IV, and in 1703 succeeded his brother Mustafa II. He sheltered Karl XII of Sweden after Poltava (1709), thus annoying Peter I, the Great, with whom he waged a successful war terminated by the Treaty of Adrianople (1713), by which he regained Azov. He defeated the Venetians (1715), gaining the Morea, but soon after was defeated by the Austrians, losing territories around the Danube, especially Belgrade. He was deposed by the janissaries (1730) and died in prison. His reign was known as the Tulip Period because of the luxurious court life and the popularity of the flower in Constantinople (Istanbul).

Ahmose I 16th century BC
King of ancient Egypt

He founded the 18th dynasty and freed Egypt from the alien Shepherd Kings (Hyksos).

Ahmose II 6th century BC
King of ancient Egypt

He ruled from 569 to 525BC, cultivated the friendship of the Greeks, and greatly promoted the prosperity of Egypt. He built the temple of Isis at Memphis.

Ahrweiler, Hélène, née Glykatzi 1926–
French academic

She was born in Athens, Greece, where she studied and later taught middle eastern history and archaeology, specializing in Byzantine studies. She moved to France in 1950 as a researcher for the Centre National de la Recherche Scientifique, becoming the first woman head of the history department at the Sorbonne in 1967. As a vice-president of the Sorbonne in 1970, she was much involved in establishing the schools of humanities and social science as separate entities. She became the first woman president of the Sorbonne in 1976, and on her retirement became Chancellor of the Universities of Paris (1982–89). Her other prestigious appointments include the presidency of the Centre National d'Art et de Culture Georges Pompidou (1989–91).

Ai Ch'ing See Ai Qing

Aidan, St, known as the Apostle of Northumbria d.651
Christian monk

Born in Ireland, he became a monk in the Celtic monastery on the island of Iona. In 635, he was summoned by King Oswald of Northumbria to evangelize the north. He established a church and monastery on the island of Lindisfarne, of which he was appointed the first Bishop, and from there travelled throughout Northumbria founding churches. His feast day is 31 August. ▣ Henry Kelsey, *St Aidan & St Cuthbert* (1959)

Aidid, Mohamed Farah c.1930–1996
Somali soldier and politician

Born in a country area of Italian Somaliland, he served in the colonial police force and transferred to the Somali army following the country's independence in 1960. During the war with Ethiopia over the possession of Ogaden province he was promoted general by President Siad Barre. In the early 1970s he lost that support and was imprisoned. Freed, following Barre's overthrow, he was appointed ambassador to India. In 1993 he was elected leader of the Hebr Gader clan during a civil war which ruined Somalia and led to intervention by United Nations forces. He was reported dead in 1996 and his son assumed control of the country.

Aiken, Conrad Potter 1889–1973
US poet and novelist
Born in Savannah, Georgia, he was educated at Harvard, where his room mate was T S Eliot, and his contemporaries were Robert Benchley and Walter Lippmann. He made his name with his first collection of verse, *Earth Triumphant* (1914), followed by other volumes, including *Turns and Intervals* (1917), *Punch, the Immortal Liar* (1921) and *Senlin* (1925). His *Selected Poems* won the 1930 Pulitzer Prize. He also wrote short stories and novels, including *Blue Voyage* (1927), the autobiographical *Great Circle* (1933), *King Coffin*, and another autobiographical novel, *Ushant* (1952). ⌨ J Martin, *Conrad Aiken: a life of his art* (1962)

Aiken, Howard Hathaway 1900–73
US mathematician and computer engineer
Born in Hoboken, New Jersey, he grew up in Indianapolis, Indiana, and was educated at the universities of Wisconsin and Chicago, before moving to Harvard (1939–61). He succeeded in persuading IBM to sponsor the building of a calculating machine, resulting in the Automatic Sequence-Controlled Calculator (ASCC), or Harvard Mark I. Completed in 1943 and weighing 35 tons, this was the world's first program-controlled calculator, which Aiken regarded as the realization of Charles Babbage's dream. A Mark II was built in 1947, but by then Aiken's design was being overtaken by the development of the stored-program computer. He later became professor at Miami University (1961–73).

Ailey, Alvin, Jnr 1931–89
US dancer and choreographer
Born in Texas, he became a member of Lester Horton's company in 1950, assuming directorship after Horton's death in 1953. In New York he trained with Martha Graham, Charles Weidman and Hanya Holm, while dancing and acting on Broadway and elsewhere. He retired from the stage in 1965 to devote himself to the Alvin Ailey American Dance Theater, a popular, multiracial modern dance ensemble he had formed in 1958. Ailey's work has been widely performed; direct and often topical, it is influenced by his observations of black urban body language and the contrasting rhythms of rural life. His most famous dance is *Revelations* (1960), an alternately mournful and celebratory study of religious spirit. His other works include *Creation of the World* (1961) and *At the Edge of the Precipice* (1983).

Ailly, Pierre d', *also called* Petrus de Alliaco 1350–1420
French theologian and Nominalist philosopher
Born in Compiègne, he became Chancellor of the University of Paris, and Bishop of Compiègne, and was appointed a cardinal (1411), and a papal legate (1413) in Germany by the antipope John XXIII. At the Council of Constance (1414–18) he headed the reform party, but agreed to the sentence on Jan Huss and Jerome of Prague. He was prominent in the election of Pope Martin V in 1417 that ended the Great Schism.

Ailred of Rievaulx See Æthelred of Rievaulx

Aimard, Gustave, *pseudonym of* Olivier Gloux 1818–83
French adventurer and novelist
Born in Paris, he sailed as a cabin boy to the USA and spent 10 adventurous years in Arkansas and Mexico. He travelled also in Spain, Turkey, and the Caucasus. In Paris, he served as an officer of the Garde Mobile (1848) and organized the Francs-tireurs de la Presse (1870–71). He became known as the French James Fenimore Cooper and his numerous adventure stories include *La grande Filibuste* (1860, 'The Great Piracy') and *La Forêt vierge* (1873, 'The Virgin Forest').

Ainmiller or Ainmüller, Max Emanuel 1807–70
German stained-glass artist
Born in Munich, he executed windows for many European cathedrals, including Cologne, Basle, Glasgow and St Paul's in London.

Ainsworth, William Harrison 1805–82
English historical novelist
Born in Manchester, he studied for the law but married a publisher's daughter and began a literary career instead. He is chiefly remembered for popularizing the story of the highwayman Dick Turpin in *Rookwood* (1834) and the legend of Herne the Hunter in *Windsor Castle* (1843). He edited *Bentley's Miscellany* (1840–42), *Ainsworth's Magazine* (1842–54) and sometimes the *New Monthly Magazine*. *Rookwood* was his first major success, but he wrote no fewer than 39 popular historical romances, seven of which were illustrated by the cartoonist George Cruikshank.

Ai Qing (Ai Ch'ing), *originally* Jiang Haicheng 1910–96
Chinese poet
Born in Jinhua County, Zhejiang (Chekiang) Province, he studied painting in France (1928–31), but returned to China when the Japanese invaded, and was arrested for leftist activities and imprisoned (1932–35). His first published poem, 'Dayanhe' (1934), named after his wet-nurse, and his collection of poetry, also *Dayanhe* (1936), brought him fame. In 1941 he joined the Communists at Yan'an (Yen-an). After the Communist take-over in 1949 he became associate editor, with Mao Dun, of the *People's Literature* journal. He was an active propagandist for Communist-controlled literature, but at the time of the Hundred Flowers Campaign (1956–57) he was accused of revisionism and stripped of his party membership. In 1959 he was exiled to a remote district in the desert area of Xinjiang (Sinkiang) for 17 years but was allowed to publish again from 1978. He held numerous positions, among them vice-president of the China International Cultural Exchange Centre from 1984 and honorary president of the Poetry Society from 1991.

Airy, Anna 1882–1964
English artist, etcher and writer
Born in Greenwich, London, she studied at the Slade School of Art in London under Henry Tonks and Philip Wilson Steer, winning the Melville–Nettleship prize for three consecutive years. Her subject matter, such as cockfighting, gambling and boxing, was drawn from criminal haunts along the banks of the Thames. In 1918 she was commissioned by the Imperial War Museum to paint munitions factories. An occasional Inspector in Art to the Board of Education, she was elected to many societies, including the Royal Society of Painters and Etchers and the Royal Institute of Oil Painters. She wrote *The Art of Pastel*.

Airy, Sir George Biddell 1801–92
English astronomer and geophysicist
Born in Alnwick, Northumberland, he graduated as Senior Wrangler and Smith's Prizeman (1823) from Trinity College, Cambridge, and was elected a Fellow. He became Lucasian Professor of Mathematics in 1826, and Plumian Professor of Astronomy and director of the Cambridge Observatory in 1828. His research on optics earned him the Copley Medal of the Royal Society (1831), and his investigations in planetary theory earned him the Royal Astronomical Society's Gold Medal (1833). Two years later he was appointed Astronomer Royal and director of the Greenwich Observatory, which he completely reorganized, and he later achieved worldwide acceptance

of the Greenwich zero meridian. He pioneered the transmission of telegraphic time signals for the railways and determined the mean density of the Earth through pendulum experiments in mines. He was a member of the commission which in 1846 selected the standard railway track gauge, rejecting the wider **Brunel** gauge used on the Great Western Railway. He was president of the Royal Society in 1871, four times president of the Royal Astronomical Society and received the Prussian *Pour le Mérite* and membership of the French Legion of Honour. He was knighted in 1872. ⌺ *Autobiography of Sir George Airy* (1896)

Airy Shaw, Herbert Kenneth 1902–85
English botanist
Born in Woodbridge, Suffolk, he graduated in botany from Cambridge, where he developed a special interest in plant classification. From 1925 he worked at Kew Gardens, Surrey, studying European and oriental plants, but during the 1930s becoming increasingly interested in tropical Asian botany. He became a leading authority on tropical plants, and was also an expert on nomenclatural matters. He published more than 250 papers, together with regional treatments of the flora of Siam (Thailand) (1972), Borneo (1975) and New Guinea (1980), amongst others. He also edited the 7th and 8th editions (1966, 1973) of John Willis's *Dictionary of the Flowering Plants and Ferns*. He had a lifelong interest in entomology and wrote many papers on the subject.

Aïshah or Ayeshah, *known as* the Mother of Believers c.613–678
Wife of the prophet Muhammad
The daughter of **Abu Bakr**, the first caliph, she married the prophet **Muhammad** at the age of nine, and became the third and favourite of his nine wives, but had no children. When Muhammad died (632) she resisted the claims to the caliphate of **Ali**, Muhammad's son-in-law (who had accused her of infidelity), in favour of her father. She fomented opposition against the 3rd caliph, 'Uthman (which led to his death), and when Ali became the 4th caliph (656) she led a revolt against him, but was defeated and captured at the Battle of the Camel at Basra, and was exiled to Medina.

Aitken, John 1839–1919
Scottish physicist
Born in Falkirk, he studied marine engineering at Glasgow University, but ill health cut short his engineering career and his interests shifted towards research in the physical sciences. His largest and most significant body of work related to the processes involved in the boiling of liquids and the condensation of vapours. He showed that for clouds to form, atmospheric water vapour needs a solid or liquid nucleus to condense upon. This highlighted the importance of dust to the formation of rain and mist. A skilled designer and maker of experimental equipment, he developed the dust counter, which he used to investigate the meteorological and industrial influences on the production of dust. He also showed that the dew on cold surfaces comes mainly from the ground and not from the air. The Royal Society of Edinburgh published his *Collected Scientific Papers* (1923).

Aitken, Sir Max (John William Maxwell) 1910–85
British newspaper publisher
He was born in Montreal, Canada, and educated at Westminster School and Pembroke College, Cambridge. He was the son of the 1st Lord **Beaverbrook**. He established a reputation as a playboy and socialite before the war, but served with great distinction as a fighter pilot, ending the war as a group captain. He became a Conservative MP briefly, for Holborn (1945–50), before joining his father in running Beaverbrook Newspapers (*Daily Express* and *Sunday Express*). They had frequent disagreements and when his father died, he renounced his claim to the barony but retained his father's baronetcy. The newspapers were already in decline, and in 1977 they were sold to Trafalgar House. A yachting enthusiast, he became a leading ocean-racing skipper, launched the annual Boat Show, promoted the sport of offshore powerboat racing and promoted British motor racing after the war by establishing the sport at Silverstone.

Aitken, Robert Grant 1864–1951
US astronomer
Born in Jackson, California, he took his degree at Williams College and in 1895 joined the Lick Observatory, where he was director from 1930 to 1935. He undertook (assisted by William Hussey) a massive survey of double stars between 1899 and 1915, discovering more than 4,500 new ones, and concentrating on determining their motions and orbits. His discoveries gained him the Gold Medal of the Royal Astronomical Society in 1932. He published *Binary Stars* (1918) and the *New General Catalogue of Double Stars* (1932).

Akahito Yamabe no early 8th century
Japanese poet
He seems to have kept his position as a minor official at the imperial court largely through his poetic ability. His impression of snow-capped Mount Fuji is a famous example of his work. He is known as one of the 'twin stars'—Hitomaro being the other—of the great anthology of classical Japanese poetry known as the *Man'yōshū* (759, 'Collection of a Myriad Leaves', Eng trans 1929–49).

Akbar the Great, *originally* Jalal-ud-Din-Muhammad Akbar 1542–1605
Mughal Emperor of India
Born in Umarkot, Sind, he succeeded his father, Humayun (1556), and took over from his regent in 1560. The start of his reign was marred by civil war and rebellion, but he soon gained control of the whole of India north of the Vindhya Mountains. He constructed roads, promoted commerce and was responsible for extensive reforms of the tax system. He was unusually tolerant towards non-Muslims and the Jesuits established a permanent mission at his court, where he encouraged science, literature and the arts. He abolished slavery (1582), put a stop to the practice of forced *sati* (the burning of a widow along with her dead husband), legalized the remarriage of widows and forbade polygamy except in cases of barrenness. Though himself illiterate, his enlightened, original mind presided, from his new palace-capital of Iatchpur Sikri, near Delhi, over a government that was to be a model for the future Mughal Empire. ⌺ Muni Lal, *Akbar* (1980)

Akeley, Carl Ethan 1864–1926
US naturalist and sculptor
Born in Clarendon, New York State, he trained as a taxidermist and sought to bring a new realism to the discipline. He invented a cement gun, which he used for applying skin to a sculpted model of the animal. As a sculptor he modelled lions and elephants for the Field Museum in Chicago and the American Museum of Natural History in New York City. Akeley made frequent trips to Africa to study wildlife and in 1916 designed a motion-picture camera, with which he took the first films of gorillas in their habitat.

Akenside, Mark 1721–70
English poet and physician
He was born in Newcastle upon Tyne and studied theology at Edinburgh University, but abandoned it for medicine, and practised at Northampton and later in

---

Akhenaten and Nefertiti 14th century BC
Egyptian king and queen of the 18th dynasty

Akhenaten (also spelt Akhenaton) was the assumed name of Amenhotep IV. He was the son of **Amenhotep III** (with whom he may have ruled jointly for a time) and his wife Tiy. Six years into his reign (1379–1362BC) he renounced the worship of the old gods, introduced a purified and monotheistic solar cult of the sun-disc (Aten), and changed his name. For these actions he became known as the 'Heretic Pharaoh'.

He built a new capital at Amarna (Akhetaten), where the excavations of the royal archive have yielded many royal letters and other historical documents. The arts flourished, and the period is noted for a fine sensuous realism in art that was in contrast to the stylized art of previous and succeeding reigns.

He was married to Nefertiti (Nofretete), who is thought to have been an Asian princess born in Mitanni. She is immortalized in the beautiful sculptured head found at Amarna in 1912 and now on display in Berlin. Two of their six daughters were married to Akhenaten's successors Smenkhare and **Tut'ankhamun**.

📖 Philipp Vanderberg, *Nefertiti: An Archaeological Biography* (1978); C Aldred, *Akhenaten, Pharaoh of Egypt* (1968); Evelyn Wells, *Nefertiti* (1964).

'I shall build Akhetaten in this place for Aten, my Father. … I shall build in this place a mansion of Aten for Aten my Father. In the Isle of Aten I shall build a sanctuary of the Great Royal Wife Nefertiti for Aten my Father. I shall build the Palace of Pharaoh. I shall build a palace for the Queen.'
From a letter of the Amarna archive, quoted in J H Breasted, *Ancient Records of Egypt* (vol 2, 949).

London. His haughty manner was caricatured in Tobias Smollett's *Adventures of Peregrine Pickle* (1751). In 1761 he was appointed one of the physicians to the queen. He contributed verses to the *Gentleman's Magazine*, and in 1744 published *The Pleasures of Imagination*, a didactic poem begun when he was 17.

Akerman, Chantal 1950–
Belgian film director, screenwriter and actress

Born in Brussels, she studied film in Brussels and Paris, and began making short films, inspired by **Jean-Luc Godard**. Her experimental visual style was sparse and her narratives minimal, but strongly defined. She worked with other experimentalists in New York in 1972, and since then has divided her time between Europe and the USA. Her demanding and often controversial films seek to reverse traditional male perspectives, and include *Jeanne Dielman* (1975), *Les Rendez-vous d'Anna* (1978, *Rendezvous with Anna*), and her first English language film, *Histoires d'Amérique* (1989, *American Stories*).

Akers, Benjamin Paul 1825–61
US sculptor

He was born in Saccarappa, Maine, and is remembered especially for his *Dead Pearl Diver*.

Akhenaten See panel above

Akhmatova, Anna, *pseudonym of* Anna Andreyevna Gorenko 1888–1966
Russian poet

Born in Odessa, she studied in Kiev before moving to St Petersburg. In 1910 she married **Nikolai Gumilev**, who at first influenced her style, and with him and **Osip Mandelstam** started the neoclassicist Acmeist movement. She was divorced from Gumilev in 1918. After her early collections of terse but lyrical poems, including *Vecher* (1912, 'Evening'), *Chokti* (1913, 'The Rosary') and *Belaya Staya* (1917, 'The White Flock'), she developed an impressionist technique. She remained as far as possible neutral to the Revolution. After the publication of *Anno Domini MCMXXI* (1922), she was officially silenced until 1940 when she published *Iz shesti knig* ('From Six Books'), but in 1946 her verse was banned. She was reinstated in the 1950s. Her later works include *Poema bez geroya* (1940–62, published 1976, 'Poem without a Hero') and the banned *Rekviem* (Munich, 1963, 'Requiem'), a moving cycle of poems on the **Stalin** purges, during which her only son was arrested. *The Complete Poems of Anna Akhmatova* was published in 1993. 📖 S Driver, *Anna Akhmatova* (1972)

Akhromeyev, Sergei Fyodorovich 1923–91
Soviet World War II commander

He joined the Red Army in 1940 and was in command of a tank battalion by 1945. He then rose steadily to be first Deputy-Chief of the General Staff by 1979 and marshal by 1981. Opposed to escalating military expenditure, he was called in to replace **Nikolai Ogarkov** as Chief of the General Staff in 1984 and aided **Mikhail Gorbachev** in his post-1985 arms control talks. He tried, but failed, to accommodate fully to the Gorbachev era, and resigned in 1988 in disgust at Gorbachev's unilateral troop cuts. He committed suicide in the aftermath of the attempted coup in 1991, in apparent dismay at perestroika's results.

Aki, Keiiti 1930–
US seismologist

Born in Yokohama, Japan, he studied geophysics at the University of Tokyo, was a Research Fellow at the California Institute of Technology, and moved permanently to the USA in 1966, becoming a US citizen in 1976. He was Professor of Geophysics and then R R Shrock Professor at the Massachusetts Institute of Technology (1966–84), and is now W M Keck Professor of Geological Sciences (1984–) and Science Director at the Southern California Earthquake Center (1991–). In 1966 he introduced the concept of seismic moment, pioneered strong motion seismology in 1968, and in 1969 discovered coda waves, which describe the ground vibrations as waves spread out from an earthquake source. He also developed seismic modelling techniques (1974), produced the first quantitative analysis of the volcanic tremors, and his Aki–Larner method allowed the theoretical calculation of seismic motion. He co-authored the popular *Quantitative Seismology: Theory and Methods* (2 vols) in 1980.

Akiba ben Joseph See Akiva ben Joseph

Akihito 1933–
Emperor of Japan

Born in Tokyo, the eldest son of **Hirohito** (Showa), he was educated among commoners at the élite Gakushuin school, unlike previous princes. In 1959 he married Michiko Shoda (1934–), the daughter of a flour company president, who thus became the first non-aristocrat to enter the imperial family. In another break with tradition, his three children, the Oxford-educated Crown Prince Hiro, Prince Aya and Princess Nori, were raised at Akihito's home, instead of by tutors and chamberlains in a separate imperial dormitory. An amateur marine biologist, like his late father, he has written several monographs on the goby (a spiny fish of the Gobiidae family). On his becoming emperor (1989), the new Heisei

(Achievement of Universal Peace) era commenced. 📖 Charlie May Simon, *The Sun and the Birch: The Story of Crown Prince Akihito and Crown Princess Michiko* (1960)

Akins, Zoë 1886–1958
US dramatist, novelist and poet

Born in Humansville, Montana, she trained as an actress in New York, and in 1912 published *Interpretations*, a collection of poetry. Later, she concentrated on writing plays. Her most popular were *Déclassée* (1919), a society melodrama, followed by *Daddy's Gone A-Hunting* (1921), a sentimental portrayal of a failing marriage, and *The Greeks had a Word for It* (1930), a comedy about the Ziegfeld showgirls. Her best plays are witty and light, but not without irony, and contain wise observations on middle-class women. In 1935, Akins was awarded the Pulitzer Prize for her dramatization of **Edith Wharton**'s novel, *The Old Maid*. Among her other works are a contribution to the screen adaptation of the musical, *Showboat*, and two novels, *Forever Young* (1941) and *Cake upon the Water* (1951).

Akiva or Akiba ben Joseph c.50–135AD
Jewish rabbi, scholar and teacher in Palestine

A pupil of Rabbi Eliezer, he founded a rabbinical school at Jaffna. He is credited with extensive exegetical attempts to relate Jewish legal traditions to scriptural texts, and with providing the basis for the Mishnah by his systematic grouping and codification of the *halakhoth* (legal traditions). He apparently supported the revolt against Rome under **Simon Bar Kokhba** in 132 against the Emperor **Hadrian**, and was martyred by the Romans soon afterwards, by being flayed alive.

Akong Tulku Rinpoche, *also known as* Shetrup Akong Tarap 1940–
Tibetan Buddhist doctor and lama

Born in Riwoche, eastern Tibet, he escaped to India following the 1959 uprising and went to the UK in 1963. In 1967 he established Samye Ling, a centre for the preservation of Tibetan culture, in Eskdalemuir, Scotland. This first Tibetan monastery in the West specializes in the Kagyu tradition, renowned for its instruction in meditation. A doctor of Tibetan medicine, he published *Taming the Tiger* (1987), a textbook on the principles of Tara Rokpa therapy, and is director of the worldwide Rokpa Trust, a network of charitable centres offering 'help where help is needed'. He has been instrumental in developing the Holy Island Project as a centre for peace and interfaith dialogue.

Aksakov, Sergei Timofeyevich 1791–1859
Russian novelist

Born in Ufa, the son of a wealthy landowner, he held government posts in St Petersburg and Moscow before a meeting with **Nikolai Gogol** in 1832 turned him to literature. His house became the centre of a Gogol cult. He wrote *Metel* (1834, 'The Blizzard'), *Semeinaya Khronika* (1846–56, 'A Family Chronicle'), and *Detskie gody Bagrovnuka* (1858, 'Childhood Years of Bagrov-grandchild'). His writing shows his love of country sports and deep feeling for nature, and conveys a vivid impression of the rural, serf-owning society of the period. 📖 S I Mashinsky, *Sergei Timofeyevich Aksakov* (1973)

Alacoque, St Marguerite Marie 1647–90
French nun

Born in Janots, Burgundy, she took orders at Paray-le-Monial, and was a member of the Visitation Order. She was the founder of the devotion to the Sacred Heart. She was canonized in 1920, and her feast day is 17 October.

Alain-Fournier, *pseudonym of* Henri-Alban Fournier 1886–1914
French writer

Born in La Chapelle d'Angillon, the son of a country schoolmaster, he became a literary journalist in Paris, but was killed at St Rémy, Haute Meuse, soon after the outbreak of World War I. He left a semi-autobiographical fantasy novel, one of the outstanding French novels of the 20th century, *Le Grand Meaulnes* (first published in the *Nouvelle Revue Française*, 1913, Eng trans in the USA *The Wanderer*, 1958, in UK *The Lost Domain*, 1966), and a few short stories, collected in *Miracles* (1924). His voluminous family correspondence was published posthumously. 📖 R D D Gibson, *The Quest of Alain-Fournier* (1953)

Alamán, Lucas 1792–1853
Mexican politician and historian

Born in Guanajuato, as a boy he witnessed its siege by **Miguel Hidalgo**'s forces (1810), and grew up to be an ardent Conservative. A Creole aristocrat, he trained as a mining engineer, and once faced the Inquisition for possessing banned books. As a deputy to the Spanish Cortes (1820–21) summoned by **Ferdinand VII** in the wake of the Riego Revolt (1820), he spoke out for Mexican independence and in favour of monarchy. After independence in 1821, he negotiated with the Vatican and France to set up a Mexican royal house. Mexico's most influential Conservative, Minister of State to Emperor **Itúrbide** (1822), Foreign Minister and Minister of State for **Antonio Bustamante** and President **Santa Anna**, he founded the National Museum and died shortly after completing his monumental *Historia de Mexico* (1842–52, 'History of Mexico').

Alanbrooke (of Brookeborough), Alan Francis Brooke, 1st Viscount 1883–1963
British field marshal and master of strategy in World War II

Born in Bagnères-de-Bigorre, France, he trained at the Royal Military Academy, Woolwich, joined the Royal Field Artillery in 1902, and in World War I rose to General Staff Officer. In World War II he commanded the 2nd Corps of the British Expeditionary Force (1939–40), covering the evacuation from Dunkirk in France. He became Commander-in-Chief Home Forces (1940–41), and Chief of the Imperial General Staff (CIGS) from 1941 to 1946, working on the strategy which led to the defeat of Germany. As principal strategic adviser to **Churchill** he accompanied him to the conferences with **Franklin D Roosevelt** and **Stalin**. He became a field marshal in 1944, and was created baron in 1945 and viscount in 1946. The book *Triumph in the West* (1959), based on his war diaries, presented a controversial view of Churchill and General **Eisenhower**. 📖 Sir David Fraser, *Alanbrooke* (1982)

Alarcón, Juan Ruiz de, *in full* Juan Ruiz de Alarcón y Mendoza c.1580–1639
Spanish dramatist

Born in Taxco, Mexico, he was a lawyer, and became a member of the Council of the Indies in Madrid in 1626. He was neglected for generations, except by plagiarists, but is now considered a leading playwright of the Golden Age of Spanish drama. He was a master of both heroic tragedies and, notably, character comedies, and his *La verdad sospechosa* ('The Suspicious Truth') was the model for **Corneille**'s *Le Menteur*.

Alarcón, Pedro Antonio de 1833–91
Spanish writer

Born in Guadic, he served with distinction in the African campaign of 1859–60, and became a radical journalist. At the Restoration in 1874, however, he became a Conservative, and served as minister to Stockholm, and councillor of state. He published a vivid war diary, travel notes and poems, but is best known for his novels, particularly *Sombrero de tres picos* (1874, Eng trans *The Three-*

Cornered Hat), on which **Manuel de Falla** based his ballet, *The Three-Cornered Hat*. 📖 R Carrasco, *Pedro Antonio de Alarcón autor dramatico* (1933)

Alaric I *also called* Alaric the Goth c.AD370–410
King of the Visigoths

Born in Dacia, he led the Gothic auxiliaries of the eastern Roman Emperor **Theodosius I, the Great** in AD394. He was elected King of the Visigoths (395) and invaded Greece, but was eventually driven from the Peloponnese by **Flavius Stilicho** and the troops of the Roman western empire. He was appointed Governor of Illyria by the eastern Emperor **Arcadius**, but in 401 he invaded Italy where Stilicho defeated him again (402). He agreed to join the western Emperor **Honorius** in an attack on Arcadius, but when Honorius failed to pay the promised subsidy Alaric laid siege to Rome (408). In 410 he entered the city, which his troops looted for three days, though he prohibited rape or the destruction of religious buildings. The sack of Rome, the first capture of the city by foreigners in 800 years, is vividly described by **Edward Gibbon**. Both contemporaries and later historians consider 410 as the end of the Roman Empire. Alaric set off to invade Sicily, but died at Cosenza. 📖 Colin D Gordon, *The Age of Attila* (1960)

Alaric II AD450–507
King of the Visigoths

He reigned (from AD485) over Gaul south of the Loire, and most of Spain. In 506 he issued a code of laws known as the Breviary of Alaric (*Breviarum Alaricianum*). An Arian Christian, he was routed and killed at the Battle of Vouillé, near Poitiers, by the Orthodox **Clovis**, King of the Franks.

Alas, Leopoldo, *pseudonym* Clarin ('bugle')
1852–1901
Spanish writer

Born in Zamora, he was Professor of Law at Oviedo, but is better known as a literary figure, in particular for the great 19th-century novel *La Regenta* (1884–85, 'The Regent's Wife', 1984). He also wrote one other novel, short stories (*Cuentos morales*, 1896, 'Moral Stories'), the social drama *Teresa* (1895), and treatises on law and economics.

Alava, Don Miguel Ricardo de 1771–1843
Spanish soldier and politician

He served under the Duke of **Wellington** in the Peninsular War from 1811, and was ambassador to the Netherlands for King **Ferdinand VII**. However, as President of the Cortes in 1822 he aided in the deposition of the monarch. He fled when the French reinstated Ferdinand in 1823, but later served Queen María Cristina (1806–78, regent for **Isabella II**) as ambassador to London and Paris. Having refused to take the oath to the Constitution of 1837, he went into exile in France.

Alba, Ferdinand Alvarez de Toledo See Alva, Ferdinand Alvarez de Toledo

---

Alban, St 3rd century AD
Roman soldier and first Christian martyr in Britain

He was, according to **Bede** and some earlier writers, a pagan Romano-Briton living in the town of Verulamium (now St Albans), who was scourged and beheaded, around 300AD, for helping a fugitive Christian priest who had converted him. King **Offa** of Mercia founded a monastery on the site of his execution in 793, and the place was renamed St Albans. His feast day is 22 June.

Albani, Francesco 1578–1660
Italian painter of the Bolognese school

He studied, along with **Guido Reni**, first under **Denys Calvaert**, and afterwards under **Ludovico Carracci**. He painted about 45 altarpieces, although he was more interested in mythological or pastoral subjects.

Albanie, Count d'
Title assumed by two brothers

John Sobieski Stolberg Stuart (1795–1872) and Charles Stolberg Stuart (1799–1880) were the sons of a Royal Navy lieutenant, Thomas Allen, who claimed to be the son of Prince **Charles Edward Stuart**. Handsome and plausible, they were celebrated by Edinburgh society, and produced a Latin history of clan tartans called *Vestiarum Scoticum* whose manuscript they claimed to have discovered in a monastery in Cadiz.

Albany, Duke of
Royal Scottish title

It was first conferred in 1398 on Robert (c.1340–1420), brother of **Robert III** of Scotland, who was succeeded by his son Murdoch (d.1425). Queen **Victoria** made her youngest son Leopold (1853–84) Duke of Albany in 1881. His son Leopold (1884–1918), Duke of Saxe-Coburg (1905–18), forfeited his British titles in 1917.

Albany, Louisa Caroline, Countess of
1752–1824
Princess of Stolberg

The daughter of Prince Gustav Adolf of Stolberg (d.1757), she secretly married the ageing Prince **Charles Edward Stuart** in Florence in 1772. She left him (1780) and the marriage was dissolved (1784), whereupon she took up with the Italian dramatist, Count **Vittorio Alfieri**. After his death (1803) she lived with a French painter, François Fabre. Her ashes are buried with those of Alfieri in Florence.

Albee, Edward Franklin, III 1928–
US dramatist

Born in Virginia, he was adopted by a rich theatre-owning family, and educated in Connecticut. His play *The Zoo Story* (1958) was influenced by the Theatre of the Absurd and began his attack on the complacency of the US middle class. He continued this in further one-act plays, such as *The American Dream* (1960). He had an enormous success with *Who's Afraid of Virginia Woolf?* (1962, filmed 1966), which, with caustic wit, exposes a marriage built on illusions. The bizarrely plotted *Tiny Alice* (1964) was denounced as obscure by many US theatre critics—of whom Albee has a famously low opinion. Other works include *A Delicate Balance* (1966, Pulitzer Prize), *Box* and *Quotations from Chairman Mao Tse-Tung* (both 1968). His later plays, such as the brilliant allegory *The Man Who Had Three Arms* (1982), again displayed great poetic intelligence and masterly dialogue, but were not commercially successful. His dramatizations include *Malcolm* (1965) and *Lolita* (1981). He had little success with his later plays until *Three Tall Women* (1991, Pulitzer Prize) revived his career. 📖 G McCarthy, *Edward Albee* (1987); C W E Bigsby, *Albee* (1969).

Albéniz, Isaac Manuel Francisco 1860–1909
Spanish composer and pianist

Born in Camprodón, Catalonia, he studied under **Franz Liszt** and became known especially for his picturesque piano works based on Spanish folk music. He also wrote several operas.

Alberdi, Juan Bautista 1810–84
Argentine political thinker

A creole of Basque inheritance, he studied law in Buenos Aires. Persecuted by the dictator **Juan Manuel de Rosas**, he was exiled to Montevideo in 1839, travelled in Europe and then lived in Valparaíso, Chile, for 10 years. Author of a treatise which profoundly influenced the Constituent Congress of Santa Fé, which drew up the Argentinian federal constitution of 1853, he is regarded as its intellectual godfather. He argued that a democratic future for Argentina could only be guaranteed by the attainment of economic and educational equality: to achieve this, European immigration should be encouraged and the economy opened up to foreign investment by a strong federal government. He coined the phrase 'To govern is to populate' which had an enduring, if equivocal, impact on modern Argentina. Appointed Minister to France and England in 1854 by General Justo José de Urquiza, Alberdi spent most of the remainder of his life in Europe.

Alberoni, Guilio 1664–1752
Spanish-Italian cardinal and politician

Born in Firenzuola, near Piacenza, he became a priest and in 1713 was agent for the Duke of Parma in Madrid, where he quickly gained the favour of Philip V. Rising rapidly, he became Prime Minister of Spain and was made a cardinal in 1717. Though he was wise in home affairs, his foreign policy was often impetuous and irresponsible. He violated the Treaty of Utrecht by invading Sardinia, and was subsequently confronted by the 'Quadruple Alliance' of England, France, Austria and Holland, resulting in the destruction of the Spanish fleet. He later tried to provoke a war between Austria and Turkey, an insurrection in Hungary and the downfall of the regent in France. In 1719, in the face of international pressure, Philip dismissed him and ordered him to leave Spain. He returned to Italy and spent most of his remaining years in a monastery, until Pope Innocent XIII befriended him in 1721.

Albers, Josef 1888–1976
US painter and designer

Born in Bottrop, Westphalia, Germany, he trained in Berlin, Essen and Munich, and from 1920 was involved with the Bauhaus, where he studied and later taught. There he worked on glass pictures, typography and furniture design. In 1933 he emigrated to the USA where he spread the Bauhaus ideas, teaching at the experimental Black Mountain College in North Carolina (1934–50) and later at Yale (1950–58). He became a US citizen in 1939. As a painter he was interested chiefly in colour relationships, and from 1950 he produced a series of wholly abstract canvases, *Homage to the Square*, exploring this theme. His colour theories are expounded in *The Interaction of Colour* (1963).

Albert I c.1255–1308
King of Germany

The son of Rudolf I of Habsburg, he was elected King of Germany in opposition to the deposed Adolf of Nassau, whom he then defeated and killed at Göllheim (1298). He proceeded energetically to restore the power of the monarchy and reduce that of the electoral princes, but was murdered by his disaffected nephew, John, while moving to check unrest in Swabia.

Albert I 1875–1934
King of the Belgians

Born in Brussels, the younger son of Philip, Count of Flanders, he succeeded his uncle, Leopold II, in 1909. At the outbreak of World War I he refused a German demand for the free passage of their troops, and after a heroic resistance led the Belgian army in retreat to Flanders. He commanded the Belgian and French army in the final offensive on the Belgian coast (1918), and re-entered Brussels in triumph. After the war he modernized the electoral system and took an active part in the industrial reconstruction of the country; the Albert Canal, linking Liège with Antwerp, is named after him. He was killed in a climbing accident in the Ardennes, and was succeeded by his son, Leopold III. 📖 Marie Rose Thielemans, *Le Roi Albert, au travers de ses lettres inedites, 1882–1916* (1982)

Albert II *called* Alcibiades 1522–57
Margrave of Brandenburg-Kulmbach

He entered military service under Emperor Charles V and was commissioned to raise a force against the Protestant Schmalkaldic League (1546). His relationships with the emperor and with the German states, both Catholic and Protestant, were turbulent and resulted in his defeat at Sievershausen and temporary outlawry to France (1553–56) as a threat to public order, and gave him his nickname Alcibiades, after the wayward Athenian statesman and pupil of Socrates.

Albert III *called* Achilles 1414–86
Elector of Brandenburg

Born in Tangermünde, Brandenburg, he was the third son of the Elector Frederick I. He inherited Ansbach from his father (1440), and succeeded (1470) his brother, Frederick II who had abdicated. He increased control over bandit nobles and his salaried officials. His most important legacy to Brandenburg was the *Dispositio Achillea* (1473), which did much to establish the rule of primogeniture, so that when he died Brandenburg remained undivided.

Albert V 1528–79
Duke of Bavaria

Educated at the Jesuit college at Ingolstadt, he succeeded to the dukedom in 1550. He was a devout Catholic and established the pattern of Wittelsbach absolutism in Bavaria based upon the suppression of Protestantism, aided by the Jesuits, and the centralization of ducal authority. A patron of the arts, he founded a state library.

Albert VII *known as* the Pious 1559–1621
Archduke of Austria

He was the third son of the Emperor Maximilian II. In 1577 he was made cardinal, and in 1584 Archbishop of Toledo. From 1585 to 1595 he was Viceroy of Portugal. In 1596 he was appointed stadtholder of the Netherlands, where he displayed a moderation unusual among the proconsuls of Spain. He relinquished his orders, and in 1598 married the infanta Isabella, daughter of Philip II of Spain.

Albert, *called* the Bear c.1100–1170
Count of Ballenstëdt

Count of Ballenstëdt from 1123, he founded the House of Ascania which ruled in Brandenburg for 200 years. In 1134, in return for service in Italy, Emperor Lothar III granted him extensive lands between the Elbe and the Oder. He obtained Brandenburg itself (1150) by a treaty formerly made with Count Pribislav, and took the title margrave.

Albert 1490–1568
1st Duke of Prussia

Born in Ansbach, he was the younger son of the Margrave of Ansbach, and was elected the last Grand Master of the Teutonic Order in 1511. He embraced the Reformation, and, on the advice of Martin Luther, declared himself secular Duke of Prussia (1519). He cultivated Protestant Denmark and Sweden against the Emperor Charles V, but had to surrender privileges to the nobles to sustain his finances.

Albert, Prince 1819–61
Prince consort to Queen Victoria of Great Britain

Born at Schloss Rosenau, near Coburg, he was the younger son of the Duke of Saxe-Coburg-Gotha and Louisa, daughter of the Duke of Saxe-Gotha-Altenburg. Studious and earnest by nature, he was educated in Brussels and Bonn, and in 1840 married his first cousin, Queen Victoria—a marriage that became a lifelong love-match. He was given the title Prince Consort (1857) and throughout their marriage he was, in effect, the Queen's private secretary. Ministerial distrust and public misgivings because of his German connections limited his political influence, although his advice was usually judicious and far-sighted. He was interested in the encouragement of the arts and the promotion of social and industrial reforms. He designed Osborne House on the Isle of Wight, was a patron of **Franz Winterhalter** and Sir **Edwin Landseer**, and he planned and managed the Great Exhibition of 1851, whose profits enabled the building of museum sites in South Kensington (including the Victoria and Albert Museum, the Science Museum, and the Natural History Museum) and the Royal Albert Hall (1871). His death, possibly from cancer rather than typhoid, led to a long period of seclusion by his widow. The Albert Memorial in Kensington Gardens, designed by Sir **George Gilbert Scott**, was erected in his memory (1871). ⬜ Daphne Bennet, *King Without a Crown: Albert Prince Consort of England 1819–1861* (1977)

Albert, Carl Bert 1908–
US politician
Born in McAlester, Oklahoma, he studied law as a Rhodes scholar at Oxford. He was a Democratic congressman from Oklahoma (1946–77) and a supporter of President **Lyndon B Johnson**'s domestic and civil rights programmes. Chairman of the Democratic National Convention in 1968, he also served as Speaker of the House of Representatives (1971–77).

Albert, Eugen Francis Charles d' 1864–1932
German pianist and composer
Born in Glasgow, Scotland, he was the son of a French musician and Italian mother. He studied in London and with **Liszt** (from 1881), and composed operas (*Tiefland*), a suite, a symphony, many songs, and much music for the piano.

Alberti, Leon Battista 1404–72
Italian architect
Born in Genoa, he worked in Florence from 1428 and became one of the best-known figures of the Renaissance. His *Della Pittura* (1436) contains the first description of perspective construction. Influenced by **Marcus Vitruvius Pollio**, he wrote *De re aedificatoria* (10 vols, 1485), which stimulated interest in antique Roman architecture. His own designs, which include the churches of San Francesco in Rimini and Santa Maria Novella in Florence, are among the best examples of the pure classical style. He was skilled also as a musician, painter, poet and philosopher. ⬜ Franco Borsi, *Leon Battista Alberti* (1977)

Alberti, Rafael 1902–
Spanish poet and dramatist
A member of the great 'Generation of '27', which included **Federico García Lorca**, **Luis Cernuda** and Pedro Salinas, he began as a painter. He fought against General **Franco** and in 1939 went into exile to Argentina, then Rome, only to return home after Franco's death. His best poetry is considered to be his fifth collection *Sobre los ángeles* (1929, English version, *Concerning the Angels*, 1967), showing the influences of Surrealism and the Spanish critic **José Ortega y Gasset**. He subsequently retreated into more simplistic communist verse, but in the bitterness of exile, his poetry reverted to its old and less certain self. His *Selected Poems* (1966) and *The Owl's Insomnia* (1973) have also been translated into English.

Albertus Magnus, St, Graf von Bollstädt,
known as **Doctor Universalis** c.1200–80
German philosopher and cleric
Born in Lauingen, he studied in Padua, and, entering the newly-founded Dominican order, taught theology in the schools of Hildesheim, Ratisbon, and Cologne, where St **Thomas Aquinas** was his pupil. He lectured in Paris for nine years until 1254, when he became provincial of the Dominicans in Germany, and in 1260 was named Bishop

of Ratisbon. In 1262 he retired to his convent in Cologne to write. Noted for the breadth of his learning, in legend he appears as a magician. He was a faithful follower of **Aristotle** as presented by Jewish, Arabian and Western commentators, and comprehensively documented 13th-century European knowledge of the natural sciences, mathematics and philosophy. He was also an alchemist, although his works express doubts about the possibility of transmutation of the elements, and he gave a detailed description of the element arsenic. Of his works the most notable are the *Summa theologiae* and the *Summa de creaturis*. He was canonized in 1931 and named Doctor of the Church by Pope **Pius XI**. His feast day is 15 November. ⬜ F J Kovach and R W Shahan (eds), *Albert the Great* (1980)

Albin, Eleazar d.1759
English naturalist and watercolourist
Working from a pub called The Dog and Duck in Tottenham Court Road, London (at that time in open country), he published *The History of Insects* (1720), illustrated with his own metal engravings, *A Natural History of Spiders* (1735), and *A Natural History of British Birds* (3 vols, 1731–38), the first book on British birds with coloured plates.

Albinoni, Tomasso Giovanni 1671–1751
Italian composer
Born in Venice, he wrote 48 operas, and a number of concertos which have been revived in recent times. The popular Adagio in G minor attributed to him is spurious.

Albinus See **Alcuin**

Alboin d.c.572
King of the Lombards in Pannonia
King from 565, he fought against the Ostrogoths, and killed Cunimund, King of the Gepidae (566), marrying his daughter Rosamund. In 568 he invaded Italy, which he conquered as far as the Tiber, and made his capital at Pavia. He extended his Italian dominions, but at a feast at Verona he made Rosamund drink from her father's skull, and she incited her lover to murder him (c.572).

Albrechtsberger, Johann Georg 1736–1809
Austrian composer and writer on musical theory
Born in Klosterneuburg, he became first court organist at Vienna (1792) and kapellmeister of St Stephen's from 1793 until his death. **Johann Hummel** and **Beethoven** were among his pupils.

Albright, Ivan Le Lorraine 1897–1983
US painter
Born in North Harvey, Illinois, he began as an architectural student but turned to painting after World War I, in which he served as a medical draughtsman in France. The clinical studies he made then of surgical operations laid the foundations of the meticulous technique he perfected later (he often took 10 years to paint a picture), as well as stimulating an obsession with morbid subject matter. After the war he studied at the Art Institute of Chicago (1919–23), the Pennsylvania Academy of Fine Arts (1923) and the National Academy of Design, New York (1924). His style has been called 'Magic Realism', and had obvious links with Surrealism, but he remained one of the most idiosyncratic of 20th-century painters.

Albright, Madeleine Korbel, *née* Korbel 1937–
US diplomat
Born in Czechoslovakia, she was educated at Wellesley College and Columbia University. She was a staff member of the National Security Council during the administration of President **Carter**, and has been a senior adviser to prominent Democrats. Now head of the Center for National Policy, she has been the USA's permanent representative to the United Nations since 1993, and was

---

Alcibiades c.450–404BC
Athenian statesman, a member of the powerful Alcmaeonid family

After the death of his father Clinias in 447, Alcibiades was brought up in the house of **Pericles**. **Socrates** also exercised a considerable influence over him. Alcibiades was the principal mover in sending an expedition against Syracuse in 415BC, which he jointly commanded. While the fleet was preparing to sail, all the 'Herms' or small statues of Hermes in Athens were mutilated in a single night. Alcibiades' enemies contrived to blame him for this, and he was recalled to stand trial for sacrilege. He fled to Sparta and advised the Spartans to send help to Syracuse, which contributed substantially to the Athenians' defeat in 413 and caused them economic problems at home. He fell out with the Spartans in 412 and rejoined the Athenian side, directing Athenian operations in the eastern Aegean, where he won several notable victories. He was unjustly blamed for the Athenian defeat off Notium (406), and went into voluntary exile, where he actively intrigued with the Persians. He was assassinated in 404BC.

📖 **Thucydides** is the principal source. There is a life by **Plutarch**, and Alcibiades appears in **Plato's** *Symposium*.

Aristophanes, in the *Frogs* (405), makes **Aeschylus** say of Alcibiades: 'It is wiser not to rear a lion's whelp, but if you do, you must accept its ways.'

---

appointed Secretary of State in President **Clinton's** Cabinet in 1996. The first US ambassador to the UN to have been born outside the USA, she is also Professor of International Affairs at Georgetown University.

Albright, William Foxwell 1891–1971
US archaeologist and biblical scholar
Born in Coquimbo, Chile, of US missionary parents, he studied at Johns Hopkins University and taught there from 1929 to 1958. He was also director of the American School of Oriental Research in Jerusalem (1921–29, 1933–36), and excavated many notable sites in Palestine, including Gibeah. He wrote several authoritative books, including *From the Stone Age to Christianity* (1940), *The Bible and the Ancient Near East* (1961) and *Yahweh and the Gods of Canaan* (1968).

Albumazar or Abu-Mashar 787–885
Arab astronomer and astrologer
Born in Balkh, Afghanistan, he spent much of his life in Baghdad, where he became the leading astrologer of his day, and his books were widely circulated. Despite his fantastic theories about the beginning and end of the world, he did valuable work on the nature of the tides. He was cast as a rascally wizard in the play *Albumazar*, by Thomas Tomkis (1615), which was revived, with a prologue by **John Dryden**, in 1668.

Albuquerque, Affonso d', *called* the Great
1453–1515
Portuguese Viceroy of the Indies
Born near Lisbon, he landed on the Malabar Coast, India in 1502, conquered Goa and established what was to become, with Ceylon, Malacca and the island of Ormuz, the Portuguese East Indies. He established a reputation as a wise and fair man. In 1515 he was replaced peremptorily by the king, and died shortly afterwards. His commentaries were translated by Birch for the **Hakluyt** Society (4 vols, 1875–84). 📖 E Prestage, *Alfonso de Albuquerque, Governor of India* (1929)

Alcaeus c.620–after 580BC
Greek lyric poet
He was born and lived in Mytilene on the island of Lesbos, where he was a contemporary of **Sappho**. He wrote in a variety of metres, including the four-line Alcaic stanza named after him and used notably (in Latin) by **Horace**. He composed drinking songs, hymns, political odes and love songs, of which only fragments now remain.

Alcalá Zamora, Niceto 1877–1949
Spanish politician
A lawyer and landowner from Andalucia, he was Liberal Minister of Development (1917) and Minister of War (1922). In opposing the dictatorship of **Miguel Primo de Rivera** (1923–30), he joined the Republican cause and, with the establishment of the Second Republic (1931), headed both the provisional government and the Constituent Cortes's first administration. He resigned in October of that year over the new constitution's anticlerical clauses, but accepted the presidency in December. A florid orator, he proved a highly conscientious if conservative and interventionist president. He was removed in 1936 after a decisive vote of the Cortes against him (238–5), and died in exile in Buenos Aires.

Alcamenes 5th century BC
Greek sculptor
He was the pupil and rival of **Phidias** in Athens. A Roman copy of his *Aphrodite* is in the Louvre, Paris, and his marble *Procne with Itys* has been restored to the Acropolis at Athens.

Alcester, Frederick Beauchamp Paget Seymour, 1st Baron 1821–95
English naval commander
Educated at Eton, he joined the navy in 1834, and served in Burma. He commanded the floating battery, *Meteor*, in the Baltic Sea (1855–56) during the Crimean War, and commanded the naval brigade in New Zealand during the Maori War (1860–61). He was Commander-in-Chief in the Mediterranean (1880–83), and bombarded Alexandria in 1882.

Alciatus, Andrea Alciato 1492–1550
Italian jurist
Born in Milan, he was professor at several universities, and with **Budaeus** and Zasius was a leader of legal humanism. A correspondent of **Thomas More** and **Erasmus**, he wrote *Annotationes* to the last 10 books of **Justinian** I's *Code* containing references to classical history and literature, as well as *Dispunctiones*, *Paradoxa* and other works.

Alcibiades See panel above

Alcindor, Lew See Abdul-Jabbar, Kareem

Alciphron fl.180AD
Greek writer
He wrote 118 fictitious letters from ordinary people, such as farmers and fishermen, affording glimpses into everyday life in 4th century BC Athens.

Alcmaeon fl.520BC
Greek physician and philosopher, the first recorded anatomist
Born in Crotona, Italy, he advanced the Pythagorean doctrine that health depends on the equal balance of opposites (such as dry and wet, hot and cold). He also founded original medical theories based on empirical surgical practice. He was the true discoverer of the Eustachian tubes, and the pioneer of embryology through anatomical dissection.

Alcman fl.c.630BC
Greek lyric poet

Born, according to one tradition, in Asia Minor, he lived in Sparta. He wrote six books of poems. Of one, a choral hymn, about half survives, otherwise there are only short fragments, mostly written in the Doric dialect. His subjects include animals, food, night and sleep.

Alcock, Sir John William 1892–1919
English aviator

Born in Manchester, he served as a captain in the Royal Naval Air Service in World War I. He made a bombing raid on Constantinople (Istanbul) and was captured by the Turks in 1917. After the war he became a test pilot for Vickers Aircraft, and with **Arthur Whitten Brown** as navigator, he was the first to fly the Atlantic Ocean nonstop (14 June 1919). The journey, in a Vickers-Vimy biplane from Newfoundland to Ireland, took 16 hours and 27 minutes. Both men were knighted after the flight. Soon afterwards Alcock was killed in an aeroplane accident in France.

Alcott, (Amos) Bronson 1799–1888
US teacher and Transcendentalist

Born near Wolcott, Connecticut, he was the father of **Louisa M Alcott**. He started as a pedlar, became an itinerant teacher, then opened an unorthodox, unsuccessful school in Boston, a vegetarian co-operative farming community (called Fruitlands), which also failed, and published books on the principles of education. An ardent Transcendentalist, and a brilliant teacher and educationist, he was eventually appointed Superintendent of Schools in Concord, Massachusetts in 1859. The family fortunes were saved by the success of his daughter's *Little Women* (1868), and in 1879 he established the Concord Summer School of Philosophy and Literature.

Alcott, Louisa M (ay) 1832–88
US writer

Born in Germantown, Philadelphia, the daughter of the Transcendentalist **Bronson Alcott**, she was a nurse in a Union hospital during the Civil War, and published her letters from this period as *Hospital Sketches* in 1864. In 1868 she achieved enormous success with *Little Women*, which drew on her own home experiences, and became a children's classic. A second volume, *Good Wives*, appeared in 1869, followed by *An Old Fashioned Girl* (1870), *Little Men* (1871) and *Jo's Boys* (1886). She also wrote adult novels and was involved in women's suffrage and other reform movements. 📖 M Saxton, *Louisa May: a modern biography of Alcott* (1977)

Alcover, Joan 1854–1926
Spanish poet

Born in Palma, Majorca, he is chiefly known as a poet in Catalan, although his first writings were in the Castilian language. He presided over a literary salon in Majorca, where he was known as a precise literary critic and skilled conversationalist. His poetry reflects the tragedy of his life (his wife and four children died in rapid succession) and a deep feeling for his native landscape. He published *Poesias* (1887), *Metereos* (1901) and *Poèmes Biblics* (1919). 📖 J Arus, *Tres poetas: Maragall, Alcover, Guesch* (1970)

Alcuin, *Anglo-Saxon name* Ealhwine, *known as* Albinus c.737–804
Northumbrian scholar, and adviser to the Emperor Charlemagne

Born in York, he was educated at the cloister school, of which in 778 he became master. In 781, returning from Rome, he met **Charlemagne** at Parma, and joined the court at Aix-la-Chapelle (now Aachen). Here he devoted himself first to the education of the royal family, but through his influence the court became a school of culture for the Frankish empire, inspiring the Carolingian Renaissance. In 796 he settled in Tours as abbot and the school there soon became one of the most important in the empire. He continued to correspond with Charlemagne until his death. His works comprise poems, works on grammar, rhetoric, and dialectics, theological and ethical treatises, lives of several saints, and over 200 letters. 📖 E M W Buxton, *Alcuin* (1922)

Alda, Alan, *originally* Alphonso Joseph d'Abruzzo 1936–
US actor and director

Born in New York City, the son of actor Robert Alda (1914–86), he performed with his father at the Hollywood Canteen (1945) and progressed, via summer stock and small television appearances, to his Broadway debut in *Only in America* (1959). Subsequent theatre work included *Purlie Victorious* (1961–62), *The Owl and the Pussycat* (1964–65) and *The Apple Tree* (1966–67). He made his film debut in *Gone Are the Days* (1963), but it was his role as Captain 'Hawkeye' Pierce in the Korean War comedy series *M*A*S*H* (1972–83), which he also wrote and directed at times, that brought him his greatest popularity. The television film *Kill Me If You Can* (1977) allowed him a change of pace as a condemned murderer. His acerbic sense of humour has been highlighted in films such as *The Four Seasons* (1980), *Sweet Liberty* (1986) and *A New Life* (1988). He also appeared in the **Woody Allen** films *Crimes and Misdemeanors* (1989) and *Manhattan Murder Mystery* (1993), and in *Flirting with Disaster* (1996).

Alden, John c.1599–1687
Pilgrim leader

Born in England, he travelled to America with the Pilgrims as a cooper on the *Mayflower* and became a leader of the Plymouth Colony, serving as assistant to the governor. **Henry Wadsworth Longfellow**'s poem *The Courtship of Miles Standish* gives a fictional account of the marriage of John Alden and Priscilla Mullins.

Alder, Kurt 1902–58
German organic chemist and Nobel Prize winner

Born in Königshütte (now Chorzów, Poland), he studied chemistry at the universities of Berlin and Kiel and became a professor at Kiel in 1934. In 1928, in collaboration with **Otto Diels**, he reported a facile reaction between a diene and a compound with an activated double bond to give a cyclic product (the Diels–Alder reaction), a reaction valuable in synthetic organic chemistry. For its discovery, Alder and Diels were jointly awarded the Nobel Prize for chemistry in 1950. In 1936 Alder joined I G Farbenindustrie, but returned to academic life in 1940 as professor in Cologne, where he remained until his death.

Aldhelm or Ealdhelm, St c.640–709
Anglo-Saxon scholar and prelate

He was educated at Malmesbury and Canterbury. He became first abbot of Malmesbury about 675, and first Bishop of Sherbourne in 705. He wrote Latin treatises, letters and verses, as well as some English poems that have disappeared. A skilled architect, he built a little church still standing, it is claimed, at Bradford-on-Avon.

Aldington, Richard, *originally* Edward Godfree 1892–1962
English poet, novelist, editor and biographer

Born in Hampshire, he was educated at London University, and in 1913 became editor of *The Egoist*, the periodical of the Imagist school, to which he belonged. His first volume of poetry was called *Images 1910–1915* (1915). His experiences in World War I left him ill and bitter, and this led to his best-known novel *Death of a Hero* (1929). As well as other novels, such as *The Colonel's Daughter* (1931), he published further volumes of poetry, including *A Fool i' the Forest* (1925). At the beginning of World War II he went to the USA, where he published his *Poetry of the English-*

Speaking World (1941) and many biographies, including *Wellington* (1946), which was awarded the James Tait Black Memorial Prize, a study of **D H Lawrence** (1950), and a controversial portrait of *Lawrence of Arabia* (1955). He married **Hilda Doolittle**, also a poet, in 1913 (they divorced in 1937). He published his autobiography, *Life for Life's Sake*, in 1940, and his correspondence with **Lawrence Durrell**, *Literary Lifelines*, appeared in 1981. A Kershaw and F J Temple, *Richard Aldington: an intimate portrait* (1965)

Aldiss, Brian Wilson 1925–
English science-fiction writer and novelist

He was born in Dereham, Norfolk, and educated at Framlingham College. After working in bookselling, he embarked on a prolific career of writing with his first novel, *The Brightfount Diaries*, in 1955. He was literary editor of the *Oxford Mail* (1958–69), and had considerable success with *The Hand-Reared Boy* (1970) and *A Soldier Erect* (1971). He is best known, however, as a writer of science fiction, such as *Non-Stop* (1958, entitled *Starship* in the USA), *The Saliva Tree* (1966), *Frankenstein Unbound* (1973), *Helliconia Spring* (1982), *Helliconia Summer* (1983), *Helliconia Winter* (1985) and *Dracula Unbound* (1991). His more experimental works in the genre include *Report on Probability A* (1964) and *Barefoot in the Head* (1969). He also writes graphic novels, has edited many books of short stories, and produced histories of science fiction such as *Billion Year Spree* (1973) and *Trillion Year Spree* (1986). In 1995 he published *The Detatched Retina* and *At the Caligula Hotel*. Bury My Heart at W. H. Smith's (1990)

Aldred or Ealdred or Alred d.1069
Anglo-Saxon prelate

He was appointed abbot of Tavistock (1027), Bishop of Worcester (1044), and Archbishop of York (1060). He undertook several diplomatic missions to the Continent, and was the first English bishop to visit Jerusalem (1058). It is said that he crowned **Harold II** in 1066; he certainly crowned **William the Conqueror**, and proved a faithful servant to the Norman king. He was active and courageous, but ambitious, greedy and self-seeking.

Aldrich, Nelson Wilmarth 1841–1915
US politician

Born in Foster, Rhode Island, of poor origins, he began his political career in 1869 as a Republican member of the Providence Common Council and served in the Rhode Island legislature (1875–78). He was elected to the US House of Representatives in 1878, after which the Rhode Island legislature chose him for a seat in the US Senate (1881–1911). By the turn of the century he controlled the Senate for the Republicans on domestic issues and ruthlessly defended big business and a high protective tariff. He became known as an authority on fiscal policy, and his recommendations on monetary reform were influential in the subsequent creation of the Federal Reserve System. Uneasy with President **Theodore Roosevelt**, who was careful not to alienate him but anxious not to seem subservient to him, he crudely paraded domination of President **William Howard Taft** in 1909–10. He refused to face the ordeal of meeting the voters when it was made mandatory by constitutional amendment, and retired in 1911. His daughter married John D Rockefeller, Jnr (1874–1960), and **Nelson Aldrich Rockefeller**, who became Governor of New York, was his grandson.

Aldrich, Thomas Bailey 1836–1907
US writer

Born in Portsmouth, New Hampshire, he worked in New York City as a merchant's clerk from the age of 13, before writing freelance articles and becoming editor of the *Atlantic Monthly* (1881–90). He was the author of many short stories and novels, and several volumes of poetry,

and his most successful book, *The Story of a Bad Boy* (1870), was an autobiographical novel about his boyhood. *Prudence Palfrey* (1874) and *The Queen of Sheba* (1877) were more romantic. *The Stillwater Tragedy* (1880) is a detective story. C Samuels, *Thomas Bailey Aldrich* (1965)

Aldridge, (Harold Edward) James 1918–
British journalist and writer

Born in White Hills, Victoria, Australia, he moved to England before World War II, during which he served as a war correspondent in Europe. His first books, *Signed with Their Honour* (1942), *The Sea Eagle* (1944) and *Of Many Men* (1946), all draw on his war experiences. He later turned to the political turmoil in Europe and the Near East in such books as *The Diplomat* (1950) and *The Last Exile* (1961). A follower of the **Hemingway** school, he makes reference to Hemingway, Zelda and **F Scott Fitzgerald** and other real-life characters of the period in his novel *One Last Glimpse* (1977). He is also the author of several children's books including *The True Story of Lilli Stubek* (1984) and *The True Story of Spit MacPhee* (1986).

Aldrin, Buzz (Edwin Eugene) 1930–
US astronaut

Born in Montclair, New Jersey, he was educated at West Point and the Massachusetts Institute of Technology. He was an air force pilot in the Korean War and became an astronaut in 1963. He set up a space-walking record in 1966 during the flight of Gemini 12, and during the 1969 expedition in Apollo 11 with **Neil Armstrong** and **Michael Collins** he became the second man to set foot on the Moon. He published *Men From Earth* in 1989.

Aldrovandi, Ulisse 1522–1605
Italian naturalist

He was born in Bologna, was imprisoned at Rome in 1549 as a heretic, and graduated in medicine at the University of Bologna (1553), where he occupied successively its chairs of botany and natural history, and established its botanical garden in 1567. He published many handsomely illustrated books on birds, fishes and insects.

Aldus Manutius, *also called* Aldo Manucci or Manuzio c.1450–1515
Italian scholar and printer

He was born in Bassiano and was the founder of the Aldine Press, which produced the first printed editions of many Greek and Roman classics. He had beautiful founts of Greek type and Latin type made, and first used italics on a large scale. In all, 908 works were issued, of which the rarest and most valuable are those from 1490 to 1497, the *Virgil* of 1501, and the *Rhetores Graeci*.

Aleardi, Aleardo, Count 1812–78
Italian poet and patriot

Born in Verona, he took part in the rising against Austria in 1848, and became a deputy in the Italian parliament (1866) and later senator. He was popular in his time as a writer of patriotic lyrics.

Alebua, Ezekiel 1947–
Solomon Islands politician

He rose from the ranks of the right-of-centre Solomon Islands United Party (SIUPA) to become deputy Prime Minister in the 1984–86 government led by Sir **Peter Kenilorea**. After Kenilorea's resignation in 1986, he was narrowly elected by the national parliament to take over as Prime Minister and held this position until SIUPA was defeated in the general election of 1989. Under his premiership the Solomon Islands joined Papua New Guinea and Vanuatu to form the 'Spearhead Group' (1988), which is dedicated to preserving Melanesian cultural traditions.

Aleichem, Sholem or Sholom or Shalom,
pen-name of **Solomon J Rabinowitz** 1859–1916
Russian Jewish writer

Born in Pereyaslev in the Ukraine, the son of Russian Jewish shopkeepers, he spent much of his youth in and around the neighbouring town of Voronkov, which was to feature as Krasilevke, the setting of many of his stories. He worked for some years as a rabbi, then devoted himself to writing and Yiddish culture, contributing to the Hebrew magazine *Hamelitz* and the first Yiddish newspaper (established 1883). In 1893 he moved to Kiev, but the pogroms of 1905 drove him to the USA, where he attempted to establish himself as a playwright for the Yiddish theatre, which was flourishing in New York at the time. He travelled widely, giving readings of his work in many European cities, and from 1908 to 1914 spent most of his time in Italy to improve his health. He returned to settle in New York in 1914. His short stories and plays portray Jewish life in Russia in the late 19th century with vividness, humour and sympathy. They were first widely introduced to a non-Jewish public in 1943 in Maurice Samuel's *The World of Sholom Aleichem*. His other work includes *Jewish Children* (Eng trans 1920), *Stories and Satires* (Eng trans 1959) and *Old Country Tales* (Eng trans 1966). The popular musical *Fiddler on the Roof* is based on his stories.

Aleixandre, Vicente 1898–1984
Spanish poet and Nobel Prize winner

Born in Seville, he suffered from renal tuberculosis in his youth, which forced him to remain in Spain after the Civil War despite his Republican sympathies. Among his early works were *Ambito* (1928, 'Ambit'), *La Destrucción o el amor* (1935, 'Destruction or Love') and *Pasión de la Tierra* (1935, 'Passion of the World'), but it was his collected poems, *Mis Poemas Mejores* (1937), that established his reputation as a major poet. His later publications include *En un vasto dominio* (1962, 'In a Vast Domain'), *Presencias* (1965, 'Presences') and *Antologia Total* (1976, 'Complete Works'). He was awarded the Nobel Prize for literature in 1977. ⌨ K Schwartz, *Vicente Aleixandre* (1970)

Alekhine, Alexander Alexandrovich 1892–1946
French chess player

Born in Moscow, Russia, he became addicted to chess from the age of 11 and gained his Master title at St Petersburg in 1909. The Russian Revolution left him without his legacy and he worked as a magistrate before taking up French citizenship. Having prepared more thoroughly than his opponent, he defeated **José Capablanca** in 1927 to win the world championship. Married four times to older women, and an alcoholic, he was successful in defences of his title until he faced **Max Euwe** in 1935. Adopting a new regimen of rigid self-discipline, he regained his title by beating Euwe in a return match of 1937. During World War II he played in tournaments organized in Nazi Germany and contributed anti-Semitic articles to the Nazi press. Ostracized by most of the chess world after the war, he died, destitute, in Estoril, Portugal.

Aleksandrov, Pavel Sergeyevich 1896–1982
Russian mathematician

Born in Bogorodsk, he studied at Moscow University and became professor there in 1929. The leader of the Soviet school of topologists, he developed many of the methods of combinatorial or algebraic topology. Following hints dropped by **Emmy Noether** he was able to define the Betti numbers in terms of suitable homology groups. He was a life-long friend of the German topologist **Heinz Hopf**, and their book *Topologie* (1935) was a landmark in the development of the subject.

Alekseyev, Mikhail Vasilevich 1857–1918
Russian general

He fought in the Russo–Japanese War (1904–05) and was promoted general. In World War I he was appointed Chief of the Imperial General Staff in 1915, and directed the retreat from Warsaw after the crushing German invasion. After the Russian Revolution in 1917 he organized the volunteer army against the Bolsheviks.

Alekseyev, Vasily 1942–
Soviet weightlifter

Born in Pokrovo-Shishkino, he set 80 world records (1970–77), more than any other athlete in any sport. He was Olympic super-heavyweight champion in 1972 and 1976, and won eight world titles and nine European titles.

Alekseyevich, Pyotr See **Kropotkin, Peter**

Alemán, Mateo 1547–1610 or 1620
Spanish novelist

Born in Seville, he led a disorderly, poverty-stricken life in Spain, and ultimately emigrated to Mexico in 1608. His great work is the important picaresque novel *Guzmán de Alfarache* (1599, second part 1604, Eng trans *The Spanish Rogue*, 1622, 1924), in which the decline and ultimate repentance of a runaway boy mirrors the sinful and corrupt state of Spain. ⌨ E Cros, *Mateo Alemán: introducción a su vida y su obras* (1971)

Alembert, Jean le Rond d' 1717–83
French philosopher and mathematician

He was born in Paris and studied law, medicine and mathematics at the Collège Mazarin. In 1743 he published *Traité de dynamique*, developing the mathematical theory of Newtonian dynamics, including the principle named after him. Later he worked on fluid motion, partial differential equations, the motion of vibrating strings, and celestial mechanics. Until 1758 he was **Diderot's** principal collaborator on the *Encyclopédie*, of which he was scientific editor, and wrote the *Discours préliminaire*, proclaiming the philosophy of the French Enlightenment. ⌨ Thomas L Hankins, *Jean d'Alembert: Science and Enlightenment* (1970)

Alençon
French ducal family

A branch of the House of Valois, representatives of which fell at Crécy and Agincourt, they held high command at Pavia (1525). Subsequently the title was given to a brother of **Charles IX**, who fought against the Huguenots, to a brother of **Louis XIII**, to the grandson of **Louis XIV**, and to a grandson of **Louis Philippe**.

Alepoudelis, Odysseus See **Elytis, Odysseus**

Alessandri Palma, Arturo 1868–1950
Chilean politician

He was born in Longaví, in Linares province. He became a member of the Chamber of Deputies (1897–1915), then senator (1915–18, 1944–50) and Minister of the Interior (1918–20). Elected President on a reform platform in 1920, he was ousted, but was soon recalled by the armed forces (1924–25). In 1932–38 he served a second, more conservative, term.

Alessi, Galeazzo 1512–72
Italian architect

Born in Perugia, he studied ancient architecture, and gained a European reputation by his designs for palaces and churches in Genoa and elsewhere. He was a pupil of Caporali and a friend of **Michelangelo**.

Alexander I c.1077–1124
King of Scotland

He was the fourth son of **Malcolm III** Canmore and Queen **Margaret**. In 1107 he succeeded his brother, Edgar, but only to the area north of the Forth (see **David I**). He married Sibylla, a natural daughter of **Henry I** of England. He initiated a shift towards a more diocesan-based episcopacy.

Alexander II 1198–1249
King of Scotland

Born in Haddington, East Lothian, the son of **William I**, he succeeded to the throne in 1214. By 1215 he was demonstrating an independent approach towards England, allying himself with the disaffected English barons. The accession of **Henry III** of England eased relations, which his marriage (1221) to Henry's sister, Princess Joan cemented, leading to the settlement of the frontier question by the Treaty of York (1237). Relations with England were weakened when he married a French noblewoman and had a son (the future **Alexander III**) after Joan's death (1238). He vigorously asserted royal authority in the western Highlands and the south-west, and died while attempting to extend his rule, at the expense of Norway, to the Western Isles.

Alexander III 1241–86
King of Scotland

In 1249 he succeeded his father, **Alexander II**, and in 1251 he married Princess Margaret (1240–75), eldest daughter of **Henry III** of England. He annexed the Hebrides and the Isle of Man after his defeat of King **Haakon IV** of Norway at Largs (1263) and the Treaty of Perth (1266). Scotland emerged as a European kingdom as a result of judicious marriage alliances with Norway and Flanders. The period between 1266 and the death of Queen Margaret (1275) has often been seen as a golden age for Scotland: factional politics had almost disappeared, the kingdom had been consolidated, the king's authority was unquestioned, and there was a considerable, favourable balance of trade. Alexander's lack of heirs prompted his marriage to Yolande, daughter of the Count of Dreux (1285), but he died shortly afterwards, leaving a disputed succession and causing renewed interference by England in Scottish affairs.

Alexander I 1777–1825
Emperor of Russia

Born in St Petersburg, the grandson of **Catherine the Great**, he became emperor in 1801 and instituted a wide range of reforms, notably in administration, education, science, and the system of serfdom. In 1805 Russia joined the coalition against **Napoleon I**, but after a series of military defeats was forced to conclude the Treaty of Tilsit (1807) with France. With French encouragement Alexander attacked Sweden in order to secure possession of Finland (1808), and renewed hostilities against Turkey which were continued until the Peace of Bucharest (1812). When Napoleon broke the Treaty by invading Russia in 1812, Alexander pursued the French back to Paris. He took an active part in the destruction of Napoleon's retreating army at Dresden and Leipzig in 1813 and entered Paris with the Allies in 1814. He claimed and received Poland at the Congress of Vienna (1814–15). During the last years of his reign his increased religious mysticism, influenced by the cosmopolitan religious mystic Madame von **Krüdener**, contributed to his founding of the Holy Alliance (1815), a document delineating Christian principles, and intended to exclude the House of **Bonaparte** from power in France, which was signed by Emperor Francis I (see **Francis II**), **Frederick William III**, and other European leaders. His mysterious death at Taganrog caused a succession crisis which led to the attempted revolutionary coup of the Decembrists. ⨌ Henri Troyat, *Alexander of Russia* (1986)

Alexander II *known as* the Liberator 1818–81
Tsar of Russia

Born in St Petersburg, he was educated by his father **Nicholas I** and subjected to rigorous military training that affected his health. In 1841 he married Princess Marie of Hesse-Darmstadt (1824–80). He succeeded to the throne (1855) during the Crimean War, and signed the Treaty of Paris that ended it (1856). The great achievement of his reign was the emancipation of the serfs in 1861 (hence his nickname), followed by judicial and social reforms, including the building of railways and schools, and the establishment of jury-based public trials and elected assemblies (*Zemstva*) in the provinces. He maintained friendly relations with Prussia, especially in the Franco-Prussian War (1870–71), and married his only daughter Marie to Alfred, second son of Queen **Victoria**. Although he sold Alaska to the USA (1867), he extended the Russian Empire in the Caucasus and central Asia, and successfully fought against Turkey (1877–78), winning the liberation of Bulgaria. In 1880, soon after the death of his first wife, he married his mistress, Katharina Dolgorukova (1847–1922). Despite his liberal views, his government was severe in repressing peasant unrest and revolutionary movements. After several assassination attempts he was mortally injured by a bomb thrown at him in St Petersburg. ⨌ Martha E Almedingen, *The Emperor Alexander II* (1962)

Alexander III 1845–94
Tsar of Russia

Born in St Petersburg, he was the younger son and successor of **Alexander II** (1881). In 1866 he married Princess Marie Dagmar (1847–1928), daughter of King **Kristian IX** of Denmark and sister of Queen **Alexandra** of Great Britain. A massively impressive figure, with huge self-confidence, he was openly critical of his father's reforming policies before his accession. He followed a repressive domestic policy, especially in the persecution of Jews, and promoted Russian language and traditions and the Orthodox Church. Abroad, his policy was cautious, and he consolidated Russia's hold on central Asia to the frontier of Afghanistan, provoking a crisis with Great Britain (1885). In the last years of his reign he discouraged the triple alliance of Russia, Germany and Austria and became a virtual ally of France. Despite several assassination attempts, he died a natural death and was succeeded by his son **Nicholas II**.

Alexander I 1888–1934
King of the Serbs, Croats and Slovenes, and King of Yugoslavia

Born in Cetinje, the second son of **Peter I**, he distinguished himself in the Balkan War (1912–13), was Commander-in-Chief of the Serbian army in World War I, and acted as regent for his father (1914–21). He was King of the Serbs, Croats and Slovenes (1921–29), and tried to build up a strong and unified Yugoslavia, imposing a royal dictatorship (1929). In 1934 he set out on a state visit to France but was assassinated in Marseilles by a Macedonian terrorist in the pay of Croatian nationalists.

Alexander III *originally* **Orlando Bardinelli** c.1105–81
Italian pope

Born in Siena, he studied the principles of law and administration under **K P Pobedonostev**. He taught law at Bologna, and became adviser to Pope **Adrian IV**. As pope (1159–81), he was engaged in a struggle with the Emperor **Frederick I**, **Barbarossa** who supported antipopes against him. The Emperor was finally defeated at the Battle of Legnano (1176) and peace was concluded by the Treaty of Venice (1177). The other notable conflict of church and state in which he was involved was that between **Henry II**

Alexander the Great 356–323BC
King of Macedonia

Alexander was born in Pella, the son of **Philip II**, King of Macedonia, and **Olympias**. He was educated by eminent Greek teachers including **Aristotle**, and there are several accounts of his assertiveness and strength of character at an early age. He was only 16 when Philip appointed him regent in his absence on a campaign against Byzantium, and at the battle fought against an alliance of Greek cities at Chaeronea (338BC), Alexander commanded the left wing of the Macedonian army and took a decisive part in the action. Philip, now master of the Greek mainland, was appointed general of the Greeks for an invasion of Achaemenid Persia, but was assassinated at his daughter's wedding in 336. It is possible that Alexander himself was implicated in or privy to the plot.

Alexander, not yet 20, became king, and ruthlessly crushed rebellions in Illyria and on the Greek mainland; Thebes was razed to the ground as a warning to the Greeks (335). He took up Philip's plans for a Greek crusade against Persia, crossed the Hellespont and won a major victory over the Persians at Granicus (334), which opened the way to the Greek cities of Asia Minor. At a pass near Issus, in Cilicia, he met **Darius III** in battle and completely defeated him (333). The family of Darius, as well as his treasure, fell into Alexander's hands, and were treated by him with great clemency and magnanimity.

Alexander proceeded to occupy Damascus, and took and destroyed Tyre after a long and hard siege (332). He marched on to Palestine, and was welcomed in Egypt as a liberator from the Persians. At this point there occurred a key event in Alexander's life: at the cost of six weeks' loss of progress in his campaign, he marched into the Libyan desert to consult the oracle of Ammon at Siwa. Great mystery surrounds the oracle's reply, and it became the subject of much fantasy in the medieval Alexander Romance; whatever it was, Alexander exploited it as a basis for later divine honours in the Greek and Persian worlds. He founded Alexandria, the first and most famous of his new cities, in 331. He again set out to meet Darius, and at Gaugamela near Arbela he won another decisive victory over an even greater army than at Issus. Darius fled, and was eventually murdered by one of his satraps (330).

The great cities of Babylon, Susa and the Persian capital Persepolis opened their gates to Alexander. During his stay in Persepolis, the royal palace was burned down; according to some accounts, this was the work of Alexander himself in a fit of drunkenness. In 329 he overthrew the Scythians and in 328–327 subdued Sogdiana, where he was married to Princess Roxana. Meanwhile, relations with his followers became increasingly difficult: in 330 he

executed Philotas and his father Parmenion, in 328 he murdered his friend Cleitus the Black during a drunken brawl, and in 327 the court historian Callisthenes fell out of favour and may have been executed.

In 326 Alexander proceeded to the conquest of India, and at the Hydaspes (Jhelum) overthrew the local king Porus in a hard-fought and costly battle. At the River Hyphasis (Beas), his army refused to go on any further and he was forced to begin the return march. He sent **Nearchus** downstream to the Persian Gulf, while he himself marched through Gedrosia (Baluchistan), suffering heavy losses on the way (325). At Susa, he held mass marriages of himself and the Macedonian leaders with women of the Persian aristocracy (324). At Babylon he was planning further ambitious conquests, of Arabia and to the west, when he was taken ill after a banquet, and died 11 days later.

Alexander's body was appropriated by **Ptolemy I Soter** and entombed in Alexandria. An unclear succession resulted in a long power-struggle for parts of the empire between Alexander's leading generals. Eventually it was divided into several kingdoms, principally the Ptolemies in Egypt, the Seleucids in Asia and the Antigonids in Macedonia.

In later antiquity, Alexander was viewed variously as a ruthless conqueror and destroyer at one extreme, and as a far-sighted statesman pursuing a civilizing mission for the world at the other. Modern scholarship continues to fluctuate between these opposing views. Two issues that caused great offence in the Greek world are still the subject of much discussion: his adoption of Persian customs, and his wish that he be honoured as a god in his lifetime, for which there was no precedent on this scale outside the oriental kingdoms. Alexander's early death, the lack of unambiguous evidence about his ultimate intentions, and the legends that grew up around him in his lifetime and after his death, preclude any definitive conclusion.

📖 There has been more written about Alexander over many centuries than any other figure in history. Contemporary accounts of his life have not survived, but those by **Ptolemy I Soter** and Aristobulus (a Greek engineer on the expedition) were used as principal sources by Arrian of Nicomedia, who wrote an account of Alexander's life in the 2nd century AD. The medieval Alexander Romance developed many fantastic and imaginary stories about him, including a visit to China. Alexander is the subject of much modern historical fiction, most notably by Mary Renault (1905–83) in the novels *Fire from Heaven* (1969), *The Persian Boy* (1972) and *Funeral Games* (1981).

---

of England and **Thomas à Becket**. He also called the third Lateran Council (1179). 📖 Marshall W Baldwin, *Alexander III and the Twelfth Century* (1968)

Alexander VI *originally* Rodrigo Borgia 1431–1503
Spanish pope

He was born in Játiva, Spain, and studied law at Bologna University. The beautiful Giovanna Catanei, known as Vanozza, bore him **Cesare Borgia**, **Lucrezia Borgia**, and other children. In 1455 he was made a cardinal by his uncle, Pope Calixtus III (1378–1458, pope from 1455), and in 1492, on the death of Innocent VIII, was elevated to the papal chair, which he had previously secured by flagrant bribery. The long absence of the popes from Italy had weakened their authority and curtailed their revenues. To compensate for this loss, Alexander endeavoured to break the power of the Italian princes, and ruthlessly to appropriate their possessions for the benefit of his own

family. He died most likely of fever, but there is some evidence for the tradition that he was accidentally poisoned by wine intended for Cardinal da Corneto, his host. He apportioned the New World between Spain and Portugal and introduced the censorship of books. Under his pontificate **Savonarola** was executed as a heretic. 📖 Michael de la Bedoyere, *The Meddlesome Friar and the Wayward Pope: The Story of the Conflict Between Savonarola and Alexander VI* (1958)

Alexander VII *originally* Fabio Chigi 1599–1667
Italian pope

He was born in Siena. As nuncio in Cologne, he had protested against the Treaty of Westphalia (1648), which ended the Thirty Years War. His papal election (1655) was said to have been settled by belief in his opposition to nepotism, to which he later succumbed. He supported the Jesuits against the Jansenists and forbade the translation of the Roman Missal into French. He was also responsible for the construction of the colonnade in the piazza at St Peter's, Rome, and wrote some Latin poems which were published.

Alexander VIII *originally* Pietro Vito Ottoboni
1610–91
Italian pope
Born in Venice, he was an aristocrat who was elected (1689) in succession to the anti-French **Innocent XI** with the help of the French ambassador. Alexander, however, continued Innocent's policy of hostility to **Louis XIV's** policy of Gallicanism, condemning the 1682 declaration by the French clergy in its favour. He was hostile to the Jesuits and was pleased at the defeat of Louis XIV's ally, the ousted **James VII and II** of Scotland, England and Ireland, at the Battle of the Boyne (1689).

Alexander Nevsky c.1220–1263
Russian Grand Prince, hero and saint
Born in Vladimir, he received his surname from his victory over the Swedes on the River Neva (1240). He later defeated the Teutonic Knights (1242) and the Lithuanians (1245), and also helped maintain Novgorod's independence from the Mongol Empire. He was canonized by the Russian Orthodox Church in 1547, and is the subject of a film by **Sergei Eisenstein**. ⌨ V Pashuto, *Aleksandr Nevskii* (1974)

Alexander of Battenberg See Battenberg, Prince Alexander of

Alexander of Hales, *known as the* Irrefragable Doctor c.1170–1245
English scholastic philosopher
Born in Hales, Gloucestershire, he studied in Paris and became Professor of Philosophy and Theology there, later entering the Franciscan order. His chief work was the *Summa Universae Theologiae*, a system of instruction for the schools of Christendom.

Alexander of Tralles 6th century
Greek physician
Born in Tralles, Huydra, he practised in Rome, and was the author of *Twelve Books on Medicine*, a major work on pathology which was current for several centuries in Latin, Greek and Arabic.

Alexander Severus AD208–35
Roman emperor
He was the cousin and adopted son of **Heliogabalus**, whom he succeeded in AD222. A weak ruler, under the influence of others, especially his mother, he failed to control the military. Though successful against the Sassanid Artaxerxes (233), he and his mother were murdered by mutinous troops during a campaign against the Germans. Fifty years of political and military instability in the Roman Empire followed his death.

Alexander the Great See panel p37

Alexander, Bill, *originally* William Alexander Paterson 1948–
English stage director
He was born in Hunstanton, Norfolk, and worked at the Bristol Old Vic (1971–73) and the Royal Court Theatre, London, before joining the Royal Shakespeare Company (RSC) in 1977 as an assistant to **John Barton** and **Trevor Nunn**. He became resident (later associate 1984–91, and honorary associate) director at the RSC, directing new plays such as **Howard Barker's** *The Hang of the Gaol* (1978), *Crimes in Hot Countries* (1985), and *Country Dancing* (1986). His Shakespearean productions include *RichardIII* (1984), *The Merry Wives of Windsor* (1985), *A Midsummer Night's Dream* (1986), *Twelfth Night*, *The Merchant of Venice* (both 1987), *Cymbeline* (1987, 1989), *The Taming of the Shrew* (1990)

and *Much Ado About Nothing* (1990). He became artistic director of the Birmingham Repertory Theatre in 1993.

Alexander, Cecil Frances, *née* Humphreys
1818–95
Irish poet and hymn writer
Born in County Wicklow, she became the wife of Bishop William Alexander (1824–1911). She published *Verses for Holy Seasons* (1846) and her popular *Hymns for Little Children* (1848), which included the well-known 'All things bright and beautiful', 'Once in Royal David's city' and 'There is a green hill far away'. She also wrote some ballads on Irish history.

Alexander, Franz Gabriel 1891–1964
US psychoanalyst
He was born in Budapest, Hungary, where his father was Professor of Philosophy, and received his MD from Budapest University. During World War I he was a medical officer, after which he studied and then worked at the Institute for Psychoanalysis in Berlin. He settled permanently in the USA in 1932, where he founded the Chicago Institute for Psychoanalysis. Although he wrote widely on psychoanalytic and cultural issues, his work on psychosomatic disorders, among which he included peptic ulcer, essential hypertension, and rheumatic arthritis, was especially influential.

Alexander, Grover Cleveland 1887–1950
US baseball player
Born in Elba, Nebraska, he was one of the greatest right-handed pitchers in the history of the game. In a long and brilliant career, he played for the Philadelphia Phillies (1911–17), Chicago Cubs (1918–26) and St Louis Cardinals (1926–29). He shared (with Christy Mathewson, 1880–1925) a record of 373 wins. In 1926 he led the St Louis Cardinals to a sensational victory over the New York Yankees and in 1938 he was elected to the National Baseball Hall of Fame.

Alexander (of Tunis), Sir Harold Rupert Leofric George Alexander, 1st Earl 1891–1969
Anglo-Irish field marshal and politician
Born in Caledon, County Tyrone, in World War I he commanded a battalion of the Irish Guards on the Western Front and led it through the battles of Passchendaele, Cambrai (1917) and Hazebrouck (1918). Between 1932 and 1939 he was a staff officer with the Northern Command and in India. In 1940 he commanded the rearguard at the Dunkirk evacuation, and was the last man to leave France. His North Africa command (1942–43) brought one of the most complete victories in World War II. He commanded the invasions of Sicily and Italy (1943), was appointed field marshal on the capture of Rome in June 1944 and became Supreme Allied Commander in the Mediterranean for the rest of the war. From 1946 to 1952 he was Governor-General of Canada and from 1952 to 1954 Minister of Defence in the Conservative government.

Alexander, Jean 1925–
English actress
She was born in Liverpool, and after working as a library assistant, she joined the Adelphi Guild Theatre in Macclesfield (1949) and toured for two years. She spent the next 11 years with a variety of repertory companies, starting as a stage manager and often doubling as a wardrobe mistress. Moving to London, she appeared in television plays like *Jacks and Knaves* (1961) before being cast in the long-running *Coronation Street* (1964–87). Her character of the dowdy, tactless gossip Hilda Ogden, a cleaner renowned for her shabby raincoat, hair curlers and ever-dangling cigarette, won her the Royal Television Society's Best Performance award (1984–85). Since she

retired from the series, she has been seen in such programmes as *Boon* (1988), *Last of the Summer Wine* (1988) and the film *Scandal* (1989). Her autobiography, *The Other Side of the Street*, was published in 1989.

Alexander, John White 1856–1915
US painter

Born in Allegheny, Pennsylvania, he worked as an illustrator for Harper's magazine, and as a portrait painter, owning studios in Paris and New York. He painted portraits of Auguste Rodin, Mark Twain, Thomas Hardy, Grover Cleveland, Andrew Carnegie, Alphonse Daudet, Walt Whitman, Maude Adams and Robert Louis Stevenson. Other paintings include *The Pot of Basil*, *The Green Bow*, *Study in Black and Green*, and *The Engagement Ring*.

Alexander, Sir Kenneth John Wilson 1922–
Scottish economist and educationist

Born in Edinburgh, he was educated at George Heriot's School, Edinburgh and the School of Economics, Dundee. After holding university posts in Leeds, Sheffield and Aberdeen he became Professor of Economics at Strathclyde University (1963–80). From 1981 to 1986 he was Principal and Vice-Chancellor of Stirling University, and since 1986 he has been Chancellor of Aberdeen University. His many public services include the chairmanship of the Highlands and Islands Development Board (1976–80), and he chaired the committee on adult education which produced what is always referred to as 'the Alexander Report' (1975). His publications include *The Economist in Business* (1967) and *The Political Economy of Change* (1975).

Alexander, Samuel 1859–1938
Australian philosopher

Born of Jewish parents in Sydney, he moved to England and studied at Balliol College, Oxford (1877). He was made a Fellow of Lincoln College, Oxford, where he was tutor in philosophy until 1893, when he was appointed Professor of Philosophy at Manchester University. His growing concern for the situation of European Jewry led him to introduce his colleague Chaim Weizmann (later to become leader of the Zionist movement) to Arthur James Balfour, a meeting which led to the Balfour Declaration (1917), establishing the principle of a Jewish national home, and eventually to the establishment of the state of Israel. Alexander retired in 1924, and was awarded the Order of Merit in 1930.

Alexander, William See Stirling, 1st Earl of

Alexanderson, Ernst Frederick Werner 1878–1975
US electrical engineer and inventor

Born in Uppsala, Sweden, he went to the USA in 1901 and the following year joined the General Electric Company in Schenectady, New York, where he worked with Charles Steinmetz. He invented the 'Alexanderson alternator' for transoceanic communication, and also antenna structures, and radio receiving and transmitting systems. By 1930 he had perfected a complete television system, and by 1955 a colour television receiver. He has 300 patents to his credit.

Alexandra, Queen 1844–1925
Queen consort of Edward VII of Great Britain and Northern Ireland

Born in Copenhagen, the eldest daughter of King Kristian IX of Denmark, she married Edward (1863) when he was Prince of Wales. She engaged in much charity work: she founded the Imperial (Royal) Military Nursing Service (1902), and instituted the annual Alexandra Rose Day in aid of hospitals (1912).

Alexandra, Princess, the Hon Mrs Angus Ogilvy 1936–
British princess

The daughter of George, Duke of Kent and Princess Marina of Greece, she married (1963) the Hon Angus Ogilvy (1928–). They have a son, James (1964–), and a daughter, Marina (1966–).

Alexandra (Alix) Fyodorovna 1872–1918
German princess, and Empress of Russia as the wife of Nicholas II

Born in Darmstadt, the daughter of Grand Duke Louis of Hesse-Darmstadt and Alice Maud Mary (the daughter of Queen Victoria), she married Nicholas in 1894 and tended to dominate him. Deeply pious and superstitious, she came under the evil influence of the fanatical Rasputin in her concern for her haemophiliac son, Alexis. During World War I, while Nicholas was away at the front, she meddled disastrously in politics and was (erroneously) thought to be a German agent. When the revolution broke out, she was imprisoned by the Bolsheviks with the rest of the royal family (1917), and later shot in a cellar at Yekaterinberg.

Alexis or Aleksei I Mikhailovich 1629–76
Second Romanov Tsar of Russia

He was born in Moscow, and succeeded his father Michael Romanov in 1645. Personally abstemious and benevolent, he had great interest in western culture and technology. Abroad, he waged war against Poland (1654–67), regaining Smolensk and Kiev, while at home his attempts to place the Orthodox Church under secular authority brought him into conflict with the patriarch, Nikon. His new code of laws (1649) legitimized peasant serfdom in Russia and he generally strengthened the centralizing autocracy. He suppressed a great peasant revolt led by Stenka Razin (1670–71). His son became Peter I, the Great.

Alexis or Aleksei Petrovich 1690–1718
Russian prince

The eldest son of Peter I, the Great, he was born in Moscow. A heavy drinker, having opposed the tsar's reforms, he was excluded from the succession, and escaped to Vienna and then to Naples. Induced to return to Russia, he was condemned to death, but pardoned, only to die in prison a few days after. His son became tsar, as Peter II.

Alexis or Aleksei, *originally* Sergei Vladimirovich Simansky 1877–1970
Russian Orthodox ecclesiastic

He accommodated to the Soviet regime to save Orthodoxy. First elected to a bishopric in 1913, he was made Metropolitan of Leningrad (now St Petersburg) in 1933 and, despite one spell of exile, was able to survive to earn a reputation for his courage during the Siege of Leningrad. He was then elected Patriarch of Moscow and All Russia in 1944, in succession to Patriarch Sergei. He generally supported Soviet attitudes to the world at large in order to protect his Christian flock at home, in which he had some success.

Alexis, Willibald See Häring, Georg Wilhelm Heinrich

Alexius I Comnenus 1048–1118
Byzantine emperor

Born in Constantinople (Istanbul), he was founder of the Comnenian dynasty (see Comnenus). The nephew of the Emperor Isaac I, Comnenus, he was commander of the western Byzantine armies when he was brought to the throne by a military coup, succeeding Nicephorus III Botaneiates (1081). By making strategic alliances, he was able to defeat invasions by the Normans of Sicily under Robert Guiscard and Bohemond I (1107), and later the

Pechenegs, who had threatened Constantinople (1091). He built a new fleet and co-operated with the First Crusade (1096–1100) to recover Crete, Cyprus, and the western coast of Anatolia, but was unable to regain the interior, or Syria. Although unwilling to limit the power of the Byzantine nobles, he reformed the army and administration but undermined the financial stability of the empire by debasing the coinage. His reign is well known from the *Alexiad*, the biography written by his daughter Anna Comnena.

Alfarabius See **Farabi, Abu Nasr al-**

Alfieri, Vittorio, Count 1749–1803
Italian poet and dramatist
He was born in Asti, near Piedmont, inherited a vast fortune at the age of 14, and travelled throughout Europe before turning his hand to writing, achieving great success with his first play, *Cleopatra*, in 1775. In Florence in 1777 he met the Countess of Albany, the estranged wife of Prince Charles Edward Stuart, and after separating from her husband, she became his mistress. He wrote more than a score of tragedies, six comedies, and *Abele*, a 'tramelogedia', or mixture of opera and tragedy. He also wrote an autobiography, *Vita* (1803). His political writings identify him as a precursor of the Risorgimento. □ G Megaro, *Alfieri: Forerunner of Italian Nationalism* (1930)

Alfonsin (Foulkes), Raul 1927–
Argentine politician
Born in Chascomas and educated at military and law schools, he joined the Radical Civil Union (UCR) in 1945. He served in local government (1951–62) but was imprisoned by the Perón government for his political activities in 1953. During two brief periods of civilian rule, between 1963 and 1976, he was a member of the Chamber of Deputies, at other times practising as a lawyer. When constitutional government returned in 1983 he was elected President and ensured that several leading military figures were brought to trial for human rights abuses. In 1986 he was joint winner of the Council of Europe's human rights prize. He was replaced as president by Carlos Menem in 1989 but remained leader of the UCR.

Alfonso I also called **Affonso or Afonso Henriques** 1110–85
Earliest King of Portugal
He was born in Guimarães. His mother, Theresa of Castile, ruled until 1128 in his name after his father, Henry of Burgundy, first Count of Portugal, had died. He attacked the Moors, defeated them at Ourique (1139), and proclaimed himself king, so securing Portuguese independence from León. He took Lisbon (1147), and later, all Galicia, Estremadura and Elvas.

Alfonso V also known as **Affonso o Africano** 1432–81
King of Portugal
Born in Sintra, he succeeded his father, Duarte (1438), ruling at first under the regency of his uncle Pedro. The surname Africano was given in recognition of his campaigns in Morocco, where he captured Tangier (1471). He tried without success to unite Castile with Portugal, was defeated at Toro (1476), and gave up his claims in the Treaty of Alcáçovas (1479), after which Portugal's interests were directed towards expansion in Africa.

Alfonso I called **el Batallador ('the Battler')** 1073–1134
King of Aragon and Navarre
Deeply religious, he succeeded to the throne in 1104 and became involved in a conflict with Castile and León, ruling the latter when he married its queen, Urraca. He liberated Saragossa from Moorish rule (1118), but was forced to surrender his claims to León (1126).

Alfonso III called **the Great** c.838–910
King of León, Asturias and Galicia
He ruled from 866 until his death. Helped by civil war in the Muslim eminate of Córdoba, he fought over 30 campaigns and gained numerous victories over the Moors, occupied Coimbra, and extended his territory as far as Portugal and Old Castile. He made Santiago de Compostela the religious centre of his kingdom. His three sons conspired against him and eventually dethroned him.

Alfonso V, called **the Magnanimous** 1396–1458
King of León, Castile and Sicily
He succeeded his father, Ferdinand I, in 1416. At home he faced a jealous aristocracy and a restless Catalonian peasantry. Abroad, after a series of campaigns against Corsica, Sardinia and Naples, he made himself King of Naples (1442), never returning to Spain.

Alfonso VIII 1155–1214
King of Castile
The son of Sancho III, he was King of Castile from 1158. His anarchic minority ended in 1169, but his reign suffered continual disputes with Alfonso IX of León, until an alliance with Aragon and Navarre and papal support enabled him to win the decisive victory of Las Navas de Tolosa (1212). This severely weakened Muslim power and paved the way for the reconquest of southern Spain. He married a daughter of Henry II of England and founded Spain's first university.

Alfonso X, called **the Astronomer or the Wise** 1221–84
King of León and Castile
Born in Burgos, Spain, he succeeded his father, Ferdinand III, in 1252. He captured Cadiz and Algarve from the Moors, and thus united Murcia with Castile. In 1271 he crushed an insurrection headed by his son Philip, but was defeated in a second rising under another son, Sancho (1282). Alfonso was the founder of a Castilian national literature. He initiated the first general history of Spain written in Castilian, as well as a translation of the Old Testament by Toledo Jews. His great code of laws (*Siete Partidas*) and his planetary tables (adapted from Arabic models) were of major importance, and he wrote several long poems, besides works on chemistry and philosophy.

Alfonso XII 1857–85
King of Spain
The son of Isabella II, he was born in Madrid and educated in Vienna and England. After a period of republican rule following the overthrow of his mother (1868), he was formally proclaimed king (1874) and in 1876 he suppressed the last opposition of the Carlists (supporters of the Spanish pretender Don Carlos de Bourbon, 1788–1855, and his successors). Tactful and judicious, if politically inexperienced, he summoned the Cortes (parliament) to provide a new constitution, and under the influence of his Prime Minister, Antonio Cánovas del Castillo, his reign was a time of peace and relative prosperity. In 1879 he married Maria Christina (1858–1929), daughter of Archduke Charles Ferdinand of Austria. His premature death from tuberculosis dashed the hopes of those supporters of a developing constitutional monarchy. He was succeeded by his posthumously-born son, Alfonso XIII.

Alfonso XIII 1886–1941
King of Spain
He was born in Madrid, the posthumous son of Alfonso XII, and his mother, Maria Christina of Austria, acted as regent until 1902, when he assumed full power. In 1906 he married Princess Ena of Battenberg, granddaughter of Queen Victoria. His reign was increasingly autocratic and

unpopular. After neutrality during World War I, he was blamed for the Spanish defeat in the Moroccan War (1921), and from 1923 he associated himself with the military dictatorship of Miguel Primo de Rivera (1923–30). In 1931 Alfonso agreed to elections, which voted overwhelmingly for a republic. He refused to abdicate, but left Spain, and died in exile.

Alford, Henry 1810–71
English clergyman

Born in London, he was a Fellow of Trinity College, Cambridge (1834), and Dean of Canterbury (1857). He was first editor of the *Contemporary Review* (1866–70), wrote on the classics and published poems and hymns, including 'Come ye thankful people, come'.

Alford, Kenneth, *pseudonym of* Frederick J Ricketts
1881–1945
English composer

One of the world's best-known composers of military music, he was born in London and first proved his musical prowess as an organist. His gifts as a composer were first shown, however, at the military academy Kneller Hall. His best-known march 'Colonel Bogey', written in 1914, was later used to great effect in the film *The Bridge on the River Kwai* (1957). Alford was a bandmaster for most of his life, including being bandmaster of the Royal Marines (1928–44). Several of his marches reflect the drama and the bitterness of military life, rather than its pomp and glory.

Alfred, *called* the Great 849–99
Anglo-Saxon King of Wessex

Born in Wantage, Berkshire, he was the youngest son of King Æthelwulf. As a child he travelled to Rome and the Frankish court of Charles I, the Bald. He succeeded his brother Ethelred I as king (871), when Viking invaders were occupying the north and east of England, and Wessex was under constant attack. Early in 878 the Danish army led by Guthrum invaded Wessex but Alfred defeated them at Edington, Wiltshire (878). He repelled another invasion (885), captured London (886), and made a treaty formalizing the partition of England, with the Danelaw under Viking rule. Modelling his kingship on Charlemagne and his Frankish successors, he created a ring of fortified strongholds (*burhs*) around his kingdom and built a fleet (hence his reputation as the 'father of the English navy'). His strategy enabled his successors to reconquer the Danelaw. He promoted education in the vernacular, fostered all the arts, and inspired the production of the *Anglo-Saxon Chronicle*. He himself translated Latin books into Anglo-Saxon, including the *Pastoral Care* of Pope Gregory I, the Great, the *Consolations of Philosophy* by Boethius, and the works of St Augustine, the Venerable Bede and Orosius. He was buried in Winchester.

Alfvén, Hannes Olof Gösta 1908–96
Swedish theoretical physicist and Nobel Prize winner

Born in Norrköping and educated at Uppsala University, he joined the Royal Institute of Technology, Stockholm in 1940, becoming Professor of Electronics in 1945 and Professor of Plasma Physics in 1964. He moved to the University of California in 1967. He did pioneering work on plasmas (ionized gases) and their behaviour in magnetic and electric fields. In 1942 he predicted the existence of waves in plasmas (Alfvén waves), which were later observed. His theories have been applied to the motion of particles in the Earth's magnetic field, to plasmas in stars and to experimental nuclear fusion reactors. He shared the Nobel Prize for physics with Louis Néel in 1970 and retired in 1989. He is the author of *Cosmical Electro-*

dynamics (1950), *Structure and Evolutionary History of the Solar System* (1975, with Gustaf Arrhenius) and a science-fiction novel written under a pseudonym.

Alfvén, Hugo Emil 1872–1960
Swedish composer and violinist

Born in Stockholm, he was a composer in the late Romantic tradition, and wrote five symphonies and the ballet *Prodigal Son* (1957) amongst many other works. He made much use of folk melodies and his best-known piece is *Midsommarvaka* (1904, 'Midsummer Vigil', better known as the *Swedish Rhapsody*). He was director of music at Uppsala University from 1910 to 1939.

Algardi, Alessandro 1598–1654
Italian sculptor

He was born in Bologna, but worked in Rome from 1625, superseding Gian Lorenzo Bernini at the papal court. His chief work is a colossal Baroque relief, in St Peter's, Rome, of Pope Leo I restraining Attila from marching on Rome (1650).

Alger, Horatio 1832–99
US writer and clergyman

Born in Revere, Massachusetts, he was educated at Harvard. He became a Unitarian minister, and wrote boys' adventure stories on the 'poor boy makes good' theme, such as *Ragged Dick* (1867) and *From Canal Boy to President* (1881).

Algren, Nelson 1909–81
US novelist

Born in Detroit, he moved early to Chicago, where he trained as a journalist at the University of Illinois, before becoming a migrant worker during the Depression. In Chicago again from 1935, he became a leading member of the 'Chicago school of realism'. He produced a series of uncompromising novels, including *Somebody in Boots* (1935), *Never Come Morning* (1942) and *The Man with the Golden Arm* (1949), a novel about drug addiction regarded by some as his best work. He had a transatlantic affair with Simone de Beauvoir, which is described in her novel *Les Mandarins* (1954) and in her autobiography. 📖 M Cox and W Chatterton, *Nelson Algren* (1975)

Alhazen, *Latinized name of* Abu 'Ali al-Hasan ibn al-Haytham c.965–c.1040
Arab mathematician

Born in Basra, Iraq, he wrote a work on optics (known in Europe in Latin translation from the 13th century) giving the first account of atmospheric refraction and reflection from curved surfaces, and the construction of the eye. He constructed spherical and parabolic mirrors, and it was said that he spent a period of his life feigning madness to escape a boast he had made that he could prevent the flooding of the Nile. In later life he turned to mathematics and wrote on Euclid's treatment of parallels and on Apollonius of Perga's theory of conics.

Ali, *properly* 'Alī ibn Abī Ṭālib d.661
Fourth Islamic caliph

The cousin and son-in-law of the prophet Muhammad, he converted to Islam while still a boy, and later married the prophet's daughter Fatima. He withdrew, or was excluded from, government during the caliphates of Abu-Bakr and Omar, and disagreed with 'Uthman in the interpretation of the Koran and application of the law. Although not involved in the death of 'Uthman he was elected caliph soon after, but encountered opposition, led by Mu'awiya, Governor of Syria, which was the beginning of a major Sunni–Shiite division within Islam that has persisted to the present day. The issue was still undecided when he was murdered in the mosque in Kufa, his capital, by a member of a third Muslim party, the Kharijites.

Ali, Maulana Muhammad 1878–1931 and Ali, Maulana Shaukat 1873–1938
Muslim Indian political activists

Both brothers were closely associated with the internal politics of Aligarh College prior to World War I. In 1911 Muhammad Ali founded *Comrade*, an English-language weekly paper espousing pan-Islamic views. Shortly afterwards he moved the paper to Delhi, and also bought an Urdu paper, *Hamdard*, which he used to set forth his political views. In 1913 Shaukat Ali organized *Anjuman-i-Khuddam-i-Kaaba* to provide Indian support for Muslim causes in the Middle East. The continued activities of this movement after the outbreak of World War I resulted in the detention of both brothers between 1915 and 1919. On their release, they joined the Khilafat Conference, to protest against British policy towards the Sultan of Turkey, who was also Caliph of Islam. Muhammad soon became the leader. Because of Mahatma Gandhi's support of the Khilafat Movement, the brothers allied with the Indian National Congress and Muhammad persuaded the Khilafat Conference to adopt Gandhi's strategy of Satyagraha (literally, 'truth-force'—a philosophy of non-violent resistance to evil). The brothers were again arrested in 1921. In 1923, Muhammad Ali was elected president of the Congress. Kemal Atatürk's 1924 abolition of the Caliphate undermined the Khilafat movement, which continued on with dwindling support and influence. During the late 1920s both brothers broke with Congress and afterwards concentrated on affairs concerning the Muslim community, although they remained highly influential national political leaders.

Ali, Muhammad See Mehemet 'Ali

Ali, (Chaudri) Muhammad 1905–80
Pakistani politician

Born in Jullundur, India, he was educated at Punjab University. In 1928 he left a chemistry lectureship at Islamia College, Lahore, for the Indian Civil Service. Four years later, when he was made Accountant-General of Bahawalpur State, he re-established its finances. In 1936 he became Private Secretary to the Indian Finance Minister and in 1945 was the first Indian ever to be appointed Financial Advisor of War and Supply. In 1947, on the partition of India, he became the first Secretary-General of the Pakistan government, in 1951 Finance Minister, and in 1955 Prime Minister. He resigned in 1956, because of lack of support from members of his own party, the Muslim League. A man of powerful intellect, he was often described in Pakistan as the 'brains trust' of the post-partition governments.

Ali, Muhammad, *formerly* Cassius Marcellus Clay 1942–
US boxer

Born in Louisville, Kentucky, he won the Olympic amateur light-heavyweight title in Rome in 1960. After turning professional, he won the world heavyweight title in 1964 by defeating Sonny Liston in seven rounds at Miami Beach (and subsequently in a rematch at Lewiston, Maine). He joined the Black Muslim sect in 1964, changed his name to Muhammad Ali, and refused military service on religious grounds. For this he was sentenced to prison and stripped of his title in 1967, but he was able to return to professional boxing in 1970 when the Supreme Court quashed his conviction. He lost to Joe Frazier in 1971, but defeated him in January 1974 and regained his title by beating George Foreman in October of that year in Zaire. He lost it again (to Leon Spinks) in February 1978 but regained it in a rematch in September of that year. He thus made history by regaining the world heavyweight title twice. He retired in 1981. In 1996, Ali, showing visible signs of the Parkinson's Disease which now afflicts him, made an emotionally-charged public appearance at the Olympic Games in Atlanta, Georgia, when he lit the Olympic torch. He was also awarded a gold medal to replace the 1960 Rome medal which he had thrown into a river. 📖 M Hassan, *Muhammad Ali* (1982)

Alia, Ramiz 1925–
Albanian communist leader

Born into a poor Muslim family in Shkoder in north-west Albania, he fought for the National Liberation Army during World War II. A former president of the youth wing of the ruling Communist Party of Labour of Albania (APL), he was inducted into the party's central committee in 1954 and made Minister of Education in 1955 and head of Agitprop in 1958. He entered the APL's secretariat (1960) and politburo (1961) and in 1982 became head of state. On the death of Enver Hoxha (1985), he took over as APL, and thus national, leader. In 1992 he was placed under house arrest and later sentenced to nine years' imprisonment for abuse of power and violation of citizens' rights.

Ali Bey 1728–73
Egyptian ruler

Born a slave in Akkhasia in the Caucasus, he distinguished himself in the service of Ibrahim Katkhuda and became chief of the Mamluks. On the death of Ibrahim (1754), he gradually established in Egypt an adminstration independent of Ottoman overlordship. He gained control of Mecca and Syria. Defeated by Ottoman forces (1772), he took refuge in Syria. An attempt to regain power (1773) led to defeat at Salahiya where he was mortally wounded. He was an excellent administrator, and under him Egypt briefly achieved independence for the first time in over 200 years, but after his death lapsed into virtual anarchy.

Alice Maud Mary 1843–78
British princess

Born at Buckingham Palace, London, she was the second daughter of Queen Victoria. In 1862 she married Prince Louis of Hesse-Darmstadt, who succeeded his uncle as Grand Duke (1877). They had four daughters: the eldest became the mother of Louis, Earl Mountbatten; the youngest, Alexandra (Alix) Feodorovna married Nicholas II of Russia.

Ali Pasha, *surnamed* Arslan, *also known as* the Lion of Janina c.1741–1822
Turkish leader

An Albanian brigand and assassin, he was born in Tepelene and became Pasha of Trikala (1787) and Janina, Greece (1788), and governor of Rumili (1803). At Janina he maintained a barbarous but cultured court which was visited by Lord Byron and other European travellers. He intrigued with France and Great Britain, but he was deposed in 1820 by Sultan Mahmud II, and was put to death in 1822.

Alkan, *pseudonym of* Charles Henri Valentin Morhange 1813–88
French composer and pianist

A brilliant eccentric who lived all his life in Paris, he was giving piano recitals from an early age. When only 25, he shared the concert platform with Frédéric Chopin, then did not play again in public for 10 years. All of his music, such as the 12 Studies in Minor Keys, requires the utmost brilliance from a pianist, and often reflects Alkan's off-beat interests. His style is forward-looking and the *Allegro barbaro* is plainly the model for Béla Bartók's piece of the same name (1911). His piano piece *Le Chemin de fer* is the first known music to describe the railway. Alkan died as strangely as he lived when his bookcase fell on him. 📖 Ronald Smith, *Alkan* (2 vols: *The Enigma* and *The Music*, 1976)

Allais, Maurice 1911–
French economist, engineer and Nobel prize winner
Born in Paris, and educated at the École Polytechnique and the École Nationale Supérieure des Mines, he was appointed Professor of Economic Analysis at the latter institution (1944–88). He was Professor of Economic Theory at the Institute of Statistics in Paris (1947–68) and also director of the Centre for Economic Analysis (1954–80). His primary contributions have been in the re-formulation of the theories of general economic equilibrium and maximum efficiency and in the development of new concepts, particularly in relation to capital and consumer choice. In 1977 he was named an officer of the Legion of Honour and in 1988 he was awarded the Nobel Prize for economics.

Allan, David, *known as the* **Scottish Hogarth** 1744–96
Scottish genre and portrait painter
Born in Alloa, Clackmannanshire, he studied in Glasgow and at the Academy of St Luke in Rome, where he trained under **Gavin Hamilton** and won the gold medal. He went to London for a time (1777–80) to paint portraits, then moved to Edinburgh as a master at the Edinburgh Academy of Arts, of which he became director in 1786. He illustrated **Allan Ramsay**'s *Gentle Shepherd* and some of **Robert Burns**'s poems.

Allan, Sir Hugh 1810–82
Canadian entrepreneur
Born in Saltcoats, Ayrshire in Scotland, he emigrated to Montreal in 1826 and became a partner in the Allan line, an ocean-going shipping line. By 1859 he was one of the wealthiest men in the province. His relationship with Conservative politicians enabled him to win back the contract to deepen the St Lawrence in 1854. In 1862 the British Secretary for War accused him of charging excessive fares, and causing the death of many immigrants. He was also charged with bribery in the Pacific Scandal of 1873 which brought down the Conservative government. In return for donating campaign funds to the party, he had hoped to receive the charter for building the Canadian Pacific Railway.

Allan, Robert Marshall 1886–1946
Australian obstetrician
Born in Brisbane, he was educated at Edinburgh University, and after war service with the Royal Army Medical Corps, he returned to Australia. His later career was much taken up with the risks of childbirth and of infant morbidity. His appointment as director of Melbourne University's Obstetrical Research Committee led to many other appointments and awards and in 1944 he chaired a Federal enquiry into Australia's declining birth rate.

Allan, Sir William 1782–1850
Scottish historical painter
Born in Edinburgh, he was a fellow pupil with **David Wilkie** at the Trustees Academy, then studied at the Royal Academy schools in London. From 1805 he spent several years in Russia and Turkey, painting scenes of Russian life. In 1835 he was elected Royal Academician, and in 1835 president of the Royal Scottish Academy. In 1841 he succeeded Wilkie as Queen's Limner (painter) in Scotland. His Scottish historical paintings include scenes from the novels of Sir **Walter Scott**.

Allan-Shetter, Liz (Elizabeth), *née* Allan 1947–
US water-skier
She has won the overall world championship three times (1965, 1969, 1973), as well as eight individual titles: one tricks, three slalom and four jumps. Her total of 11 world titles is also a world record, as is her feat of winning all four titles for an unique Grand Slam in 1969. Widely considered the sport's all-time best female competitor, she has also taken 42 US national titles, nine Masters Cup for Women titles and the Olympic title when water-skiing was a demonstration sport in 1972.

Allardice, Robert Barclay See **Barclay-Allardice, Robert**

Allbutt, Sir Thomas Clifford 1836–1925
English physician
He was born in Dewsbury, West Yorkshire. Educated at Cambridge, he studied medicine in London and Paris, practised at Leeds, and became Regius Professor of Medicine at Cambridge in 1892. In 1867 he introduced the short clinical thermometer, a great advance on the old model, which was a foot (c.30cm) long and had to be kept in position for 20 minutes. He wrote many medical works and books on the history of medicine.

Allen, Betty 1936–
Scottish chef and restaurateur
Born in Bathgate, West Lothian, she is self-taught like many other successful chefs of her generation. Her first hotel was in Largo, Fife (1973–78), which she ran with her husband, and in 1978 they moved to Port Appin, Argyll, opening the Airds Hotel. There, with her son and fellow-chef Graeme (1966–) and her husband, she has won wide acclaim with her imaginative but simple presentation of excellent local produce. National recognition has been followed by international appreciation, and in 1990 she and **Hilary Brown** became the first women in Scotland to receive a Michelin star.

Allen, Ethan 1738–89
American soldier, Revolutionary leader, and writer
He was born in Litchfield, Connecticut. Allen distinguished himself early in the Revolutionary War when he led Vermont's Green Mountain Boys with **Benedict Arnold** in the capture of Fort Ticonderoga from the British (10 May 1775). He then assisted in an effort to capture Montreal, but was himself captured. He returned to Vermont and continued to campaign for its independence from New York. He wrote *The Narrative of Colonel Ethan's Captivity* (1779) and the deistical *Reason, the Only Oracle of Man* (1784). ▣ Charles A Jellison, *Ethan Allen: Frontier Rebel* (1969)

Allen, Florence Ellinwood 1884–1966
US judge and feminist
Born in Salt Lake City, Utah, she was educated at Western Reserve University in Cleveland, Ohio. She became involved in the New York League for the Protection of Immigrants (1910) and the College Equal Suffrage League. Graduating from New York University Law School in 1913, she was admitted to the Ohio Bar in 1914, and worked assiduously for women's rights. She became the first woman to sit on a general federal bench and first on a court of last resort. She won great respect both as a judge and as a feminist and retired in 1959. In 1965 she published the autobiographical *To Do Justly*.

Allen, Sir Geoffrey 1928–
English chemical physicist and industrial chemist
He received his PhD from the University of Leeds, studied for two years at the National Research Council in Ottawa, Canada, and eventually became Professor of Chemical Physics at the University of Manchester. He then moved to professorships at Imperial College of Science and Technology. After years of researching the chemistry and physics of polymers, in 1981 he joined Unilever, and since then has held various industrial appointments, including director of Unilever and Courtaulds, and executive adviser to Kobe Steel Ltd. Through the Society of Chemical Industry he is known as a spokesman for the subject of chemistry to the general public. He was chairman of the Science Research Council

in 1977. Knighted in 1979, he is a vice-president of the Royal Society and a senior vice-president of the Institute of Materials. Since 1994 he has been Chancellor of the University of East Anglia.

Allen, George 1832–1907
English publisher and engraver

Born in Newark-on-Trent, Nothinghamshire, he was a pupil of John Ruskin, for whom he engraved many plates, and whose publisher he subsequently became. He started a business in Bell Yard, Fleet Street, which ultimately merged with others and became the well-known house of Allen and Unwin.

Allen, Gubby, *properly* Sir George Oswald Browning Allen 1902–89
English cricketer

Born in Sydney, Australia, he was educated at Eton and Trinity College, Cambridge, where he got a cricket Blue. He played for England in 25 Tests. He was captain in the tests against India in 1936, and on the tour of Australia that followed the controversial 'Bodyline' series of 1932–33 under D R Jardine, in which he disapproved of his captain's tactics. He is the only player to have taken all 10 wickets in an innings at Lord's (10–49 v Lancashire, 1929), and with L E G Ames he holds the all-time Test eighth-wicket record with a partnership of 246 against New Zealand in 1931. A member of the London Stock Exchange, he returned briefly to Test cricket on the MCC tour of West Indies in 1947. He was chairman of the England Cricket Selection Committee from 1955 to 1961.

Allen, Gracie (Grace Ethel Rosalie) 1895–1964
US comedy actress

Born in San Francisco, California, to a showbusiness family, she made her stage debut as a child and was a regular vaudeville performer from her teenage years onwards. She met her future husband George Burns in 1922 and they subsequently formed a double-act under the title 'Sixty-Forty'. Her chic, scatter-brained persona earned the laughs whilst Burns played the incredulous straight man. Their own radio show, *The Adventures of Gracie*, began in 1932 and they eventually transferred to television in the long running *The Burns and Allen Show* (1950–57). She also appeared in a number of films, often with Burns, including *We're Not Dressing* (1934), *A Damsel in Distress* (1937) and *The Gracie Allen Murder Case* (1939), and they remained a beloved institution of US showbusiness until her retirement through ill health in 1958.

Allen, Sir Harry Brookes 1854–1926
Australian pathologist

Born in Geelong, Victoria, and educated at Melbourne University, in 1906 he became its Foundation Professor of Pathology, a position he held until 1924. He pioneered the wider recognition of colonial academic qualifications, and was also influential in the merging of the Medical Society of Victoria with the British Medical Association, in the establishment at his old university of the Walter and Eliza Hall Institute of Medical Research, and of the Institute of Tropical Medicine at Townsville, Queensland. His stature as a medical administrator was recognized with an LLD (Doctor of Laws) from Edinburgh University in 1912, and a knighthood in 1914.

Allen, (William) Hervey 1889–1949
US writer

Born in Pittsburg, he trained for the US navy, in which he became a midshipman. In World War I, however, he fought with distinction as a lieutenant in the army, and later published his war diary, *Towards the Flame* (1926). His best-known novel, *Anthony Adverse* (1933), sold a million and a half copies. It was followed by *Action at Aquila* (1938), *The Forest and the Fort* (1943), *Bedford Village* (1945)

and *The City of the Dawn*, which was unfinished at his death. Allen also wrote a study of Edgar Allan Poe under the title *Israfel* (1926).

Allen, James Alfred van *See* Van Allen, James Alfred

Allen, Ralph, *also called* the Man of Bath c.1694–1764
English philanthropist

A deputy postmaster at Bath, he made a fortune by improving postal routes in England. He built the mansion of Prior Park, near Bath, and was a friend of Pope, Henry Fielding and the Earl of Chatham.

Allen, Richard 1760–1831
US clergyman

Born to slave parents in Philadelphia, he bought his freedom, became an itinerant preacher, and at the age of 27 founded the Free African Society of Philadelphia, the first organization of free African-Americans. He was spiritual leader of the first African Methodist Episcopal Church, and served as its bishop from 1816 to 1831. Throughout his life in Philadelphia, Allen worked as a leader in many African-American institutions to improve the lives of newly freed slaves.

Allen, Walter Ernest 1911–
English novelist and critic

Born in Birmingham, he worked as a schoolmaster and university lecturer in the USA, then became a journalist. His first novel was *Innocence is Drowned* (1938), and he had considerable success with *Dead Man Over All* in 1950. His other novels include *Rogue Elephant* (1946) and *All In A Lifetime* (1959). He has written several critical works, including *The English Novel—A short critical history* (1954) and *Tradition and Dream* (1964).

Allen, William 1532–94
English prelate

Born in Rossall, Lancashire, he studied at Oxford and was elected Fellow of Oriel College, and in 1556 during the reign of Mary I, he became Principal of St Mary's Hall, Oxford. After the accession of Elizabeth I in 1558 he eventually went into exile in Flanders (1561) rather than take the Oath of Supremacy. After a three-year visit to England in 1562, he returned permanently to the Low Countries. He received priest's orders in Mechlin, in 1568 founded the English college at Douai to train missionary priests for the reconversion of England to Catholicism, and later founded similar establishments in Rome (1575–78) and Valladolid (1589). In 1587 he was created a cardinal. He inspired and helped to translate the Douai–Rheims Bible (1582, 1609), which was for many years the traditional Catholic vernacular Bible.

Allen, Woody, *originally* Allen Stewart Konigsberg 1935–
US screenwriter, actor, director, short-story writer and occasional jazz clarinettist

He was born in Brooklyn, New York City, and launched his career as a comedian in clubs and on television, developing the self-deprecating neurosis and 'genetic dissatisfaction with everything' that were to become his stock-in-trade. He made his film debut scripting and acting in *What's New, Pussycat?* (1965). *Take the Money and Run* (1969) was the first of his own films, which are mainly comedies centred on modern US city life. His first movie projects—often co-scripted with Marshall Brickman—were more obviously vehicles for his stand-up routines: *Bananas* (1971), *Everything You Always Wanted to Know About Sex … But Were Afraid to Ask* (1972), *Sleeper* (1973) and *Love and Death* (1975). After *Annie Hall* (1977, three Academy Awards for Best Director, Best Script and Best Picture) and *Manhattan* (1979), his films took on a more fictive and structured aspect (in the eyes of detractors, they were simply less funny), as in *Stardust Memories* (1980), *Broadway Danny Rose* (1984), *Hannah and Her Sisters* (1986, Academy Award for Best Original Screenplay), *Crimes and Misdemeanours* (1989), *Alice* (1990), *Bullets Over Broadway* (1994), *Mighty Aphrodite* (1995) and *Everyone Says I Love You* (1996). A frequent magazine contributor, he has also written plays, notably *Play it Again, Sam* (1969) which was successfully filmed in 1972, and books of stories and sketches, including *Getting Even* (1971), *Without Feathers* (1975), *Side Effects* (1980) and *The Floating Light Bulb* (1982). 📖 E Lax, *Woody Allen* (1991)

Allenby, Edmund Henry Hynman, 1st Viscount 1861–1936
English field marshal
Educated at Haileybury and Sandhurst, he joined the Inniskilling Dragoons. He served in South Africa (1884–85, 1888), and in the Second Boer War (1899–1902). In World War I his command in France (1915–17) captured the Vimy Ridge, after which he was appointed Commander-in-Chief of the Egyptian expeditionary force against the Turks, took Beersheba and Gaza, and entered Jerusalem (1917). In the following year he routed the Turks in the great cavalry Battle of Megiddo. Promoted field marshal, he was High Commissioner in Egypt (1919–25), and granted independence to Ethiopia in 1922. 📖 Lawrence James, *Imperial Warrior: the life and times of Field Marshal Viscount Allenby, 1861–1936* (1993)

Allende, Isabel 1942–
Chilean novelist
She was born in Lima, Peru, the niece and goddaughter of former Chilean President Salvador Allende. Several months after the overthrow of Chile's coalition government in 1973 by the forces of a junta headed by General Pinochet, she and her family fled Chile. She sought sanctuary in Venezuela, and her first novel, *Casa de los espíritus* (Eng trans *The House of the Spirits*, 1985), arose directly out of her exile and her estrangement from her family, in particular her aged grandfather, who remained in Chile. It became a worldwide bestseller and achieved critical success, and Allende was heralded as the most exciting talent to emerge from Latin America since Gabriel García Márquez. In 1987 she published *De Amor y de Sombra* (Eng trans *Of Love and Shadows*, 1987) and *Eva Luna*, and in 1993 *El Plan infinito* (Eng trans *The Infinite Plan*, 1993). Her first non fiction work, *Paula* (1994, Eng trans, 1995), was written as a letter to her daughter.

Allende (Gossens), Salvador 1908–73
Chilean politician
Born in Valparaíso, he took an early interest in politics and was arrested several times, while a medical student, for his radical activities. He helped found the Chilean Socialist Party (1933), a Marxist organization which stayed clear of the Soviet-orientated Communist Party. He was elected to the Chamber of Deputies (1937–41), served as Minister of Health (1939–41) and was a senator (1945–70). He sought, and failed to win, the presidency in 1952, 1958 and 1964 but was narrowly successful in 1970. He tried to build a socialist society within the framework of a parliamentary democracy but met widespread opposition from business interests, supported by the US CIA. He was overthrown, in September 1973, by a military junta, led by General Pinochet, and died in the fighting in the presidential palace in Santiago. 📖 Lester A Sobel, *Chile and Allende* (1975)

Alley, Rewi 1897–1987
New Zealand poet
Born in Springfield, Canterbury, he spent most of his working life in China. After service in World War I he returned to New Zealand but, after a failed sheep-farming venture, went to Shanghai (1927). There he be-

came involved in flood and famine relief work and later organized industrial co-operatives. He published 16 volumes of poetry from *Gung Ho!* (1948) to *Today and Tomorrow* (1975), mainly set in China, though one, *Poems for Aotearoa* (1972), looks back to his homeland. He also translated and published over 30 volumes of Maoist verse and a book on western imperialism.

Alleyn, Edward 1566–1626
English actor
Born in London, he was a contemporary of Shakespeare, and acted in many of Christopher Marlowe's plays. He founded Dulwich College (1619) and deposited in its library documents relating to his career (including the *Diary* of Philip Henslowe, whose stepdaughter he married), which give a unique insight into the financial aspects of Elizabethan theatre. 📖 G L Hosking, *Life and Times of Edward Alleyn* (1970)

Allgood, Sara 1883–1950
US actress
She was born in Dublin, Ireland, and first appeared at the opening night of the Abbey Theatre there (1904) in Lady Gregory's *Spreading the News*. She also played the Widow Quinn in J M Synge's *Playboy of the Western World*, Isabella in *Measure for Measure* when Annie Horniman opened her Manchester company with it (1908), and toured Australia with *Peg O' My Heart* (1915). Returning to the Abbey, she created the parts of Juno Boyle and Bessie Burgess in Sean O'Casey's *Juno and the Paycock* (1924) and *The Plough and the Stars* (1926) respectively. Her performance of Juno in the Alfred Hitchcock film (1930, US title *The Shame of Mary Boyle*) gives a glimpse of the dignity and realism she brought to the part. In 1940 she settled in Hollywood, and became a US citizen in 1945. She appeared in over 30 films, including *Jane Eyre* (1943), *The Lodger* (1944) and *Between Two Worlds* (1944), but was seldom offered parts suited to her talent, and died penniless.

Alliaco, Petrus de See Ailly, Pierre d'

Allingham, Margery Louise 1904–66
English detective-story writer
Born in London, she was the creator of the fictional detective Albert Campion, and wrote a string of elegant and witty novels, including *Crime at Black Dudley* (1928), *Police at the Funeral* (1931), *Flowers for the Judge* (1936), *More Work for the Undertaker* (1949), *The Tiger in the Smoke* (1952), *The China Governess* (1963) and *The Mind Readers* (1965). 📖 Julia Thorogood, *Margery Allingham: a biography* (1991)

Allingham, William 1824–89
Irish poet
Born in Ballyshannon, County Donegal, he worked in the Irish Customs (1846–70), and in 1874 succeeded James Froude as editor of *Fraser's Magazine*. In 1874 he married Helen Paterson (1848–1926), who made a name by her book illustrations and water colours, and edited his *Diary* (1907), a rich recollection of Victorian literary life. His works include *Day and Night Songs* (1855), illustrated by Dante Gabriel Rossetti and Sir John Everett Millais, *Laurence Bloomfield in Ireland* (1864), *Irish Songs and Poems* (1887) and *Collected Poems* (1888–93). 📖 H Kropf, *William Allingham und seine Dichtung* (1928)

Allon, Yigal 1918–80
Israeli military commander and politician
After Israeli independence in 1948, he attended university in Jerusalem and Oxford. Under the British Mandate, he was prominent in the Haganah (the Israel Defence Force, or official Israeli army) and Palmach (the army's striking force), involved both in the allied occupation of Syria and Lebanon and in military activities against the British administration in Palestine. Having played a vital role in the War of Independence in 1948,

Allon helped to formulate Israeli policy in the Six-Day War (5–10 June 1967), became deputy Prime Minister (1968) and Foreign Minister (1974–77). A keen archaeologist, he was responsible for excavating the ruins at Masada.

Allori, Alessandro 1535–1607
Italian Mannerist painter

He was adopted and trained by **Bronzino**, whose name he and his son, Cristofano (1577–1621), later adopted. They both were portrait painters at the Medici court and executed religious works for the churches of Florence.

Allsopp, Samuel 1780–1838
English philanthropist

He was a member of the brewing firm of Allsopp & Sons, Burton-on-Trent, Staffordshire, and was noted for his contribution to charities in his public and private life. The youngest of his three sons, Henry (1811–1887), to whom the development of the firm was largely due, represented Worcestershire in parliament (1874–1880), and in 1886 was created Lord Hindlip.

Allston, Washington 1779–1843
US artist and writer

Born in Waccamaw, South Carolina, he studied at Harvard and the Royal Academy in London before going on to Paris and Rome, where he formed close friendships with **Coleridge** and **Bertel Thorvaldsen**. He worked for a time in London, but returned to the USA in 1820, and eventually settled at Cambridgeport, Massachusetts, in 1830. The earliest American Romantic painter, he painted large canvases, such as *The Rising of a Thunderstorm at Sea* (1804), and religious scenes, such as *Belshazzar's Feast* (1817–43). He also published a book of poems, *The Sylphs of the Seasons with other Poems* (1813), and a gothic art novel, *Monaldi* (1842).

Almack, William, *possibly originally* McCall d.1781
English clubman

Of either Yorkshire or Scottish origin, he went at an early age to London where he was successively valet and innkeeper. He opened a gaming club in Pall Mall in 1763, and Almack's Assembly Rooms in King Street, St James's, in 1765. These became centres of London society. The club was acquired by Brooks in 1778, and the rooms on his death passed to his niece, Mrs Willis, whose name they bore for many years.

Almagro, Diego de 1475–1538
Spanish conquistador

Born in Almagro, Castile, he was on the first exploratory expedition from Peru against the Incas led by **Francisco Pizarro** (1524–28). In the second expedition (from 1532), he joined Pizarro in 1533 at Cajamarca, where the Inca chieftain **Atahualpa** was executed, and occupied the Inca capital of Cuzco. In 1535–36 he led the conquest of Chile, but came back to Cuzco in 1537, and after a dispute with Pizarro occupied it by force, thus beginning a civil war among the Spaniards. Early in 1538 he was defeated by an army led by Pizarro's brother, Hernando, and was captured and executed. 📖 Manuel Ballesteros Gaibrois, *Diego de Almagro* (1977)

Alma-Tadema, Sir Lawrence 1836–1912
British painter

Born in Dronryp, Friesland, the Netherlands, he had planned to become a doctor but studied at the Antwerp Academy of Art instead. He moved to England in 1870 and became naturalized in 1873. He specialized in subjects from Greek, Roman and Egyptian antiquity and achieved great popularity with classical idyllic scenes such as *Tarquinius superbus* (1867), *Pyrrhic Dance* (1869), *Roses of Heliogabalus* (1888) and *The Conversion of Paula* (1898).

Almeida, Brites de fl.1385
Portuguese heroine

She was born in Aljubarrota, and is said to have been a baker. About 1385, during the war between John I and the King of Cadiz, she led her townspeople against the Spanish forces attacking her village and killed seven of them with her baker's shovel. The incident was celebrated by **Luis de Camoëns** in a poem. The shovel is believed to have been preserved as a relic in Aljubarrota for several generations.

Almeida, Francisco de c.1450–1510
Portuguese soldier and Viceroy of the Indies

He was 1st Viceroy of the Portuguese Indies (1505–09) until he was superseded by **Affonso d'Albuquerque**. He was killed in South Africa on his voyage home in a skirmish with Hottentots at Table Bay, and buried where Cape Town now stands.

Almeida-Garrett, João Baptista da Silva Leitão 1799–1854
Portuguese writer and politician

Born in Oporto, he was brought up in the Azores, and was exiled after the 1820 revolt. He returned and supported **Pedro I** and became Minister of the Interior. A pioneer of the Romantic movement and of modern Portuguese drama, he wrote the historical play *Gil Vicente* (1838), the epic *Camões* (1825), and many ballads.

Almirante, Giorgio c.1915–88
Italian politician

Born near Parma, a journalist and teacher by profession, he helped to found the neo-Fascist movement after the war and was first elected to parliament in 1948. He became national secretary of the Movimento Sociale Italiano (MIS) in 1969. In the 1972 general election, at the peak of his influence, his party won nine per cent of the votes and 56 parliamentary seats. He retired owing to ill health in 1987.

Almodóvar, Pedro 1951–
Spanish film director

He was born in Calzada de Calatrava. He moved to Madrid in 1967, where he worked for a telephone company. He began making films in the mid-1970s and took full advantage of the post-**Franco** cultural freedom to develop a recognizable personal style, combining provocative, often shocking, subject matters, iconoclastic attitudes, flamboyant use of colour and a playful perspective on the clichés of popular culture. His first film to attain worldwide success was the frenetic farce *Mujeres al Borde de un Ataque de Nervios* (1988, *Women on the Verge of a Nervous Breakdown*). Later films include *Tie Me Up, Tie Me Down!* (1990), *High Heels* (1991), and *Kika* (1993).

Almohads, *Arabic* al-Muwahhidun ('the Unitarians') 12th–13th century
Arabic religious movement

Founded around the year 1124 in the High Atlas mountains by the Berber Ibn Tumart (1091–1130), its principal tenets were the belief in the essential unity of God, an allegorical interpretation of the Koran, and moral reform. The movement gained rapid support among the Berber peasantry of Morocco, and proclaiming himself Mahdi, or divinely appointed leader, Ibn Tumart took the offensive against the perceived corruption and literalism of the **Almoravids**. His successor Abd al-Mu'min (d.1163) gradually conquered Morocco and extended his rule as far as Tunisia and into Spain, establishing a hereditary monarchy with the succession of his own son Abu Ya'qub Yusuf (d.1184). Art, architecture and the sciences flourished under Almohad rule, but the original faith rapidly declined, and disputes broke out. After the defeat of al-Nasir (d.1214) by the Christians at Las Navas de Tolosa

(1212), the empire disintegrated under the pressure of local dynasties, its last remnant being finally extinguished in 1276.

Almond, Hely Hutchinson 1832–1903
Scottish educationist and author
Born in Glasgow and precociously clever as a child, he was educated in Glasgow and at Balliol College, Oxford. He became a tutor at Loretto School, Musselburgh (then a preparatory school) in 1857, then a master at Merchiston School, Edinburgh, in 1858, and acquired Loretto School in 1862, making it a public school. He sought to rule by persuasion, not force, and believed passionately 'that the laws of physical well-being are the laws of God'. He insisted on open windows, shorts, shirt-sleeves, compulsory cold baths all year, and long runs in wet weather. He epitomized the late 19th-century cult of athleticism in public schools and published *Health Lectures* (1884) and a number of volumes of sermons.

Almoravids, *Arabic* al-Murabatun, *also known as* al-mulaththamun ('the veiled ones') 11th–12th century
Nomadic Berber people of the western Sahara
In the mid-11th century they were converted to a puritanical form of orthodox Islam by the Malikite jurist and missionary 'Abd Allah ibn Yasin (d.1059). Assisted by their domination of the gold trade between West Africa and the Iberian peninsula, and an efficient military organization, they invaded Morocco in 1058 under the tribal chief Abu Bakr ibn Umar (d.1088), founding a new capital at Marrakesh (c.1070). His cousin Yusuf ibn Tashufin (1061–1106) conquered the rest of Morocco and Algeria, and crossed into Spain in response to the Iberian Muslims' appeals for assistance against the Christians. After defeating Alfonso VI of Castile (1086) he, and then his son Ali ibn Yusuf (d.1143), annexed the Muslim kingdoms which had arisen after the collapse of the Umayyad caliphate in Spain, and took the offensive against the Christians. This vast, but politically unstable, empire barely survived Ali's death, however, unable to withstand the twin threat of an invigorated Reconquista under El Cid and Alfonso VII in Spain, and a new religious and political rival in Morocco, the Almohads.

Almquist or Almqvist, Carl Jonas Love 1793–1866
Swedish writer
He was born in Stockholm, and became a clergyman and teacher, but was accused of forgery and attempted murder, and fled to the USA. Returning to Europe, he spent the last year of his life in Bremen under the assumed name 'Professor Carl Westermann'. A prolific essayist and philosopher, he produced a body of work ranging from Swedenborgian mysticism to Social Realism, and including novels, plays, poems and essays. The 17-volume series *Törnrosenbok* (1833–40, 'The Book of the Wild Rose') is an eclectic summation of his earlier vision. 🕮 G Balgård, *Carl Jonas Love Almqvist: samhallsvisignaren* (1973)

al-Murabatun See Almoravids

al-Muwahhidun See Almohads

al-Nasser, Gamal Abd See Bar Hebraeus

Alonso, Alicia, *originally* Alicia de la Caridad del Cobre Martínez Hoyo 1921–
Cuban dancer and choreographer
Born in Havana, she launched her career in the USA where she studied and performed with the School of American Ballet and George Balanchine. During that time she made several trips back home to make guest appearances with the Cuban company Pro Arte. In 1948 she returned permanently to form the Alicia Alonso Company which grew into the Ballet de Cuba, a national ballet company for Cuba, making many successful tours

of the world. She remained as director when **Castro's** regime was established in 1959. Though best remembered for the development of her company, as a dancer she was famed for several roles, particularly the title role in *Giselle* (1943). Alonso had roles created for her in many works, including **Antony Tudor's** *Undertow* (1945) and *Goya Pastorale* (1940), and Balanchine's *Themes and Variations* (1947).

Alonso, Dámaso 1898–1990
Spanish poet and philologist
He was born in Madrid, where he studied under the Spanish philologist and critic Ramon Menéndez Pidal (1869–1968) before travelling widely in Europe and the USA as teacher and lecturer. He became Professor of Romance Philology at Madrid University, and established his reputation as an authority on **Luis de Góngora y Argote**. He also published poetry, of which *Hijos de la ira* (1970, Eng trans *Children of Wrath*, 1970) is the best known. It is religious in inspiration, powerful and emotional in expression. 🕮 E Alvarado de Ricord, *La Obra poetica di Dámaso Alonso* (1968)

Alonso, Mateo 1878–1955
Argentine sculptor
He is best known for his statue of *Christ the Redeemer*, erected in 1904 at the top of the Uspallata Pass, in the Andes.

Aloysius, St See Gonzaga, Luigi

Alp Arslan, *literally* 'hero lion' c.1030–72
Seljuk sultan
He succeeded his uncle, **Muhammad Tüghrül Beg** (c.990–1063), in 1063. He concentrated on extending the frontiers of the Seljuk Empire, conquering Georgia, Armenia and much of Asia Minor. He entrusted the central administration to his capable vizier Nizam al-Mulk. He restored good relations with the 'Abbasid caliph and was about to launch a major offensive against the caliphate's rivals the Fatimids, when he was recalled to meet a Byzantine offensive in Armenia. At Manzikert (1071) he defeated and captured the Emperor Romanus IV, opening up the interior of Anatolia to the nomadic Turkmen tribes. Killed in a struggle with a prisoner while on campaign in Persia (Iran), he was succeeded by his son Malik-Shah.

Alpher, Ralph Asher 1921–
US physicist
Born in Washington DC, he studied at George Washington University, spent World War II as a civilian physicist and later worked at Johns Hopkins University, Baltimore, and in industry. Together with **Hans Bethe** and **George Gamow**, he proposed in 1948 the 'alpha, beta, gamma' theory which suggests that the abundances of chemical elements are the result of thermonuclear processes in the early universe. These ideas later became part of the 'Big Bang' model of the universe. Also in 1948, he predicted that a hot Big Bang must have produced intense electromagnetic radiation, and this background radiation was in fact observed in 1964 by **Arno Penzias** and **Robert Wilson**.

Alpino, Prospero, *Latin* Prosper Alpinus 1553–1616
Italian botanist and physician
He was born in Marostica in the republic of Venice, and spent three years as physician to the Venetian consul in Cairo. During this period he observed the sexual fertilization of the date palm, in which male and female flowers are on different trees, and described 57 species, wild or cultivated, in Egypt. He wrote *De plantis Aegypti liber* (1592), an early example of a Flora—a description of the plants found in a particular area. In this and his *De medecina Egyptorum* (1591) he brought the coffee plant and the

banana to European attention for the first time. In 1594 he became lecturer in botany at the University of Padua, and director of the botanic garden there (1603).

Alred See Aldred

Alston, Richard John William 1948–
English choreographer

Born in Stoughton, Sussex, he was educated at Eton and Croydon College of Art (1965–67), also studying at the London School of Contemporary Dance (1967–70). His first piece of choreography was performed at The Place, London, in 1968. In 1969, *Something to Do* became the first in a series of nine dances made for London Contemporary Dance Theatre. With the aim of experimenting and developing his work, he co-founded Strider in 1972 (disbanded 1975), the forerunner of the contemporary dance company Second Stride. From 1975 to 1977 he studied in New York with Merce Cunningham, who greatly influenced his technique. Returning to Great Britain, he spent three years as a freelance choreographer before joining Ballet Rambert as resident choreographer in 1980, becoming director (1986–92). He renamed the company Rambert Dance Company in 1987. Noted for its lyricism, his work often employs the talents of other artists—in 1991 the US composer Steve Reich set Alston's *Roughcut* to the music of live guitar and clarinet and pre-recorded tape. Alston is currently artistic director of The Place and the Richard Alston Dance Company (1994–   ).

Alstyne, Mrs Van See Crosby, Fanny

Altdorfer, Albrecht c.1480–1538
German painter, engraver and architect

He was born in Regensburg and his most outstanding works are biblical and historical subjects set against highly imaginative and atmospheric landscapes. His *Landscape with a Footbridge*, in the National Gallery, London, is one of a pair of paintings which mark him out as the first painter of pure landscape. He was a leading member of the Danube School of German painting, and also a pioneer of copperplate etching. From 1526 he was town architect of Regensburg.

Alter, David 1807–81
US physicist

Born in Westmoreland, Pennsylvania, he was one of the earliest investigators of the spectrum, and pioneered the use of the spectroscope in determining the chemical constitution of a gas or vaporized solid.

Altgeld, John Peter 1847–1902
US politician and social reformer

Born in Nassau, Germany, he was taken to the USA in infancy. He served in the Union army during the Civil War, was a judge of the Superior Court in Illinois (1886–91), and Governor of Illinois (1893–97). He created controversy when he pardoned three men convicted of complicity in the 1886 Chicago Haymarket Riots (in which a bomb had been thrown and seven policemen killed) because he considered their convictions unjust. He also protested to the President against the use of federal troops to break the Pullman strike of 1894. The first Democratic governor of Illinois, he showed his liberal ideas in his advocacy of prison reform.

Althusser, Louis 1918–90
French philosopher

Born in Birmandreis, Algeria, he was educated in Algiers and in France, and imprisoned in concentration camps during World War II. From 1948 he taught in Paris, and joined the Communist Party. He wrote influential works on the interpretation of Marxist theory, including *Pour Marx* (1965, 'For Marx') and *Lénin et la philosophie* (1969,

'Lenin and Philosophy'). In 1980 he murdered his wife, following which he was confined in an asylum. 📖 Yann Moulier Boutang, *Louis Althusser: une biographie* (1992)

Altizer, Thomas Jonathan Jackson 1927–
US theologian

Born in Cambridge, Massachusetts, he studied the history of religions at Chicago, and taught religion, and later English, at Emory University (1956–68) and the State University of New York (from 1968). As a proponent of one strand of the 1960s 'Death of God' theology, and under the influence of Nietzsche, William Blake, and Hegel's view of *kenosis* as the self-negation of being, he held that in the Incarnation God became fully human and lost his divine attributes and existence. His writings include *The Gospel of Christian Atheism* (1966), *Radical Theology and the Death of God* (1966, essays), *Descent into Hell* (1970), and *The Self-Embodiment of God* (1977).

Altman, Robert 1925–
US film director

Born in Kansas City, Missouri, he worked on industrial documentaries before directing his first feature film *The Delinquents* (1957). He became active in television, and the critical and commercial success of *M*A*S*H* (1970) in particular established him in the cinema. Noted for his use of multi-track sound, overlapping dialogue and kaleidoscopic narratives, he has constantly explored the unheroic reality of cherished American myths. His films include *McCabe And Mrs Miller* (1971), *The Long Goodbye* (1973) and *Nashville* (1975). A neglected figure in the 1980s, he returned to favour with the television drama *Tanner* (1988) and the Hollywood satire *The Player* (1992). Subsequent films include *Short Cuts* (1993) and *Kansas City* (1995).

Altman, Sidney 1939–
Canadian biologist and Nobel Prize winner

Born in Montreal, he was educated at the Massachusetts Institute of Technology and the University of Colorado, Boulder. He became assistant then associate professor (1971–80) at Yale University, where since 1980 he has been Professor of Biology. He also acted as Dean of Yale College (1985–89). In the early 1970s, Altman studied the process by which transfer RNA, the amino acid carrier in protein synthesis, is formed. He found that the initial form of RNA was split by the enzyme ribonuclease P, and after parallel studies by Thomas Cech he discovered in 1983 that it is the enzyme's RNA component alone which catalyses the formation of transfer RNA. Other such examples of RNA catalysis have further confirmed the predictions of Francis Crick, and have suggested a possible route for the emergence of a pre-evolutionary living system. For his pioneering research, Altman shared the 1989 Nobel Prize for chemistry with Cech. He became a US citizen in 1984 while retaining his Canadian citizenship.

Altounyan, Roger Edward Collingwood 1922–87
British physician and medical pioneer

Born in Syria of Armenian–English extraction, he spent his summer holidays with his four sisters in the Lake District, England, where they met the author Arthur Ransome and became the real-life models of the children in his *Swallows and Amazons* series of adventure books. After qualifying as a doctor at the Middlesex Hospital in London, he practised at his grandfather's Armenian Hospital in Aleppo, Syria. He returned to England in 1956 to join a pharmaceutical company, where he worked in his own time to develop the drug Intal to combat asthma, from which he himself suffered. A pilot and flying instructor during World War II, he developed the spinhaler device to inhale the drug, based on the aerodynamic principles of aircraft propellers.

Alva or Alba, Ferdinand Alvarez de Toledo, Duke of 1508–82
Spanish general

Born in Piedrahita, he was made Governor of Feuenterrabia at the age of 17, and he fought so well in the Battle of Pavia (1525), in Hungary against the Turks, in Charles V's expedition to Tunis and Algiers, and in Provence, that he became general at 26, and Commander-in-Chief at 30. He defended Navarre and Catalonia (1542), and in 1547 contributed greatly to Charles V's victory at Mühlberg over the Elector of Saxony. After the abdication of Charles V in 1556, Alva overran the States of the Church, but was obliged by Philip II to conclude a peace and restore all his conquests. On the revolt of the Netherlands, he was sent as lieutenant-general in 1567 to enforce Spanish control there. He established the so-called 'Bloody Council', which drove thousands of Huguenot artisans to emigrate to England. He executed Counts Egmont and Horn, then defeated William of Orange, and entered Brussels in 1568. Holland and Zeeland renewed their efforts against him, and succeeded in destroying his fleet, until he was recalled by his own wish in 1573. He later commanded the successful invasion of Portugal in 1581.

Alvarado, Pedro de c.1485–1541
Spanish conquistador

Companion of Hernán Cortés during the conquest of Mexico (1519–21), he became Governor of Tenochtitlán, where the harshness of his rule incited an Aztec revolt which drove the Spaniards out. In the following year Tenochtitlán was recaptured and razed, and Mexico City built in its place. From 1523 to 1527 he was sent by Cortés on an expedition to Guatemala, which also conquered parts of El Salvador. He returned to Spain, and in 1529 was appointed Governor of Guatemala. He embarked on an expedition to conquer Quito, Ecuador, in 1534, but was bought off by Francisco Pizarro. 📖 John E Kelly, *Pedro de Alvarado, Conquistador* (1932)

Álvarez (Cubero), José 1768–1827
Spanish sculptor

He was imprisoned in Rome for refusing to recognize Joseph Bonaparte as King of Spain, but was later released and employed by Napoleon I to decorate the Quirinal Palace. In 1816 he became court sculptor to Ferdinand VII in Madrid, where he executed, in the classical style, *Antilochus and Memnon* (Royal Museum) and portraits and busts of the nobility and of Gioacchino Rossini.

Alvarez, Luis Walter 1911–88
US experimental physicist and Nobel Prize winner

Born in San Francisco, he studied physics at the University of Chicago where he worked together with Arthur Compton in the study of cosmic rays. He joined Ernest Lawrence at Berkeley University in 1936 where he worked on nuclear physics. During World War II he invented a radar guidance system for landing aircraft in conditions of poor visibility. After the war he returned to Berkeley where he became Professor of Physics in 1945. There he developed Donald Glaser's bubble chamber technique in order to carry out a range of experiments in which a large number of sub-atomic particles were identified. These results ultimately led to the quark model invented by Murray Gell-Mann and George Zweig. In 1968 Alvarez was awarded the Nobel Prize for physics for this work. He applied physics and ingenuity to a variety of problems, ranging from the pyramids of Egypt to the assassination of President Kennedy, and he founded two companies to make optical devices. With his geologist son Walter (1940–) he studied the catastrophe which killed the dinosaurs, deducing that its cause was the impact on Earth of an asteroid or comet. He was a scientist of exceptionally wide-ranging talents.

Álvarez (Quintero), Serafín 1871–1938 and Joaquín 1873–1944
Spanish playwrights

Brothers, they were born in Utrera, and were the joint authors of well over a hundred modern Spanish plays, all displaying a characteristic gaiety and sentiment. Some are well known in the translations of Helen and Harley Granville-Barker: *Fortunato*, *The Lady from Alfaqueque*, and *A Hundred Years Old* (all produced in 1928), and *Don Abel Writes a Tragedy* (1933). Other titles include *Las flores* (1901, 'The Flowers'), *El genio alegre* (1906, 'The Happy Spirit/Genius'), and *Pueblo de mujeres* (1912, 'Nation of Women'). 📖 D Diaz Hierro, *Huelva y los hermanos Alvarez Quintero* (1972); J Losada de la Torre, *Perfil de los hermanos Alvarez Quintero* (1945).

Alvaro, Corrado 1895–1956
Italian novelist and journalist

Born in Reggio, he was the sometime editor of *Il Mondo*, and the author of several novels and collections of essays. His best novels are *I maestri del diluvio* (1935, 'The Masters of the Flood') and *L'Uomo è forte* (1934, 'The Strong Man'), both set in Soviet Russia, though he declared that his criticisms were of fascist and not communist society. The deeply-felt disparity between town and country, his own sophisticated life as a cultivated man and his idealized memory of his native south are recurring themes in his work. 📖 L Alessandrini, *Corrado Alvaro* (1968)

Alypius fl.c.360BC
Greek writer on music

His surviving work, published in 1652, consists of a list of symbols for the notation of the Greek modes and scales.

Alzheimer, Alois 1864–1915
German psychiatrist and neuropathologist

He was born in Markbreit, and studied medicine in Würzburg and Berlin. After posts in a couple of psychiatric hospitals, he became head of the anatomical laboratories of Emil Kraepelin's psychiatric clinic in Munich and, in 1912, Professor of Psychiatry and Neurology at the University of Breslau (now Wrocław, Poland). He made important contributions to the preparation of microscopical sections of brain tissue and left some clinical studies, but is best remembered for his full clinical and pathological description, in 1907, of presenile dementia (Alzheimer's disease).

Amadeus See Hoffman, Ernst Theodor Wilhelm

Amadeus VI called the Green Count 1334–83
Ruler of Savoy

Born in Chambéry, Savoy, he succeeded in 1343. He founded the Order of the Annunziata and added Vaud to the possessions of Savoy. Abroad, he successfully arbitrated in Italian power struggles, fought the Turks and Bulgarians, and restored his cousin, John V Palaeologus, to the Byzantine throne.

Amadeus VIII, the Peaceful, also known as Felix V 1383–1451
Antipope and ruler of Saxony

Born in Chambéry, Savoy, he became Count (1391) and Duke (1416) of Savoy, and ruler of Piedmont (1419). In 1434 he retired to the monastery of Ripaille, beside Lake Geneva, but was elected pope (1439) as Felix V (an antipope, in opposition to Eugenius IV). He resigned in 1449.

Amado, Jorge 1912–
Brazilian novelist

Born on a cocoa plantation near Ilhéus, Bahia, he was imprisoned for his political beliefs in 1935 and latterly spent several years in exile, though he was briefly a Communist deputy of the Brazilian parliament (1946–47). His first novel, *O país do carnaval* (1932, 'The Country of the Carnival'), follows a youthful member of the intelligentsia seeking political answers in the wake of the revolution of 1930. Amado's next few novels outlined his personal manifesto and highlighted the cause of various exploited groups in society. *Gabriela, cravo e canela* (1952, Eng trans *Gabriela, Clove and Cinnamon*, 1962) marked a change in style and emphasis. Subsequent books, like *Dona Flor e seus dois maridos: História moral e de amor* (1966, Eng trans *Dona Flor and Her Two Husbands*, 1969) and *O gato malhado e a andorinha sinha* (1976, Eng trans *The Swallow and the Tom Cat*, 1982) show equal social awareness and compassion, but are more subtle, and use irony to good effect. Amado is regarded by many as Brazil's greatest living novelist.

Amagatsu, Yushio 1948–
Japanese choreographer, performer and director
Born in Yokosuka City, near Tokyo, he became artistic director of the Butoh dance-theatre troupe Sankai Juku (Studio of the Mountain and Sea). His company, based partly in Paris, was formed in 1975 out of intensive physical and psychological workshops. Their repertory is small but intriguing, consisting of only a handful of full-length productions including the signature piece *Kinkan Shonen* (1978, 'The Kumquat Seed'), *Jomon Sho* (1982, 'Homage to Prehistory') and *Unetsu* (1985, 'Eggs Standing Out of Curiosity').

Amanullah Khan 1892–1960
Ruler of Afghanistan 1919–29
He was born in Paghman, and as Governor of Kabul he assumed the throne on the assassination of his father, Habibullah Khan (ruler 1901–19). After an inconclusive religious war against the British in India (1919–22), independence for Afghanistan was recognized by Great Britain by the Treaty of Rawalpindi (1919). He assumed the title of king in 1926. Although he was patriotic and charming, his impulsive tactlessness and zeal for westernizing reforms provoked rebellion (1928). He abdicated (1929) and went into exile in Rome. He was succeeded by **Mohammed Nadir Shah**.

Amarasimha probably 6th century
Sanskrit lexicographer
He wrote the *Amara-kosha*, a dictionary of synonyms in verse.

Amati
Italian family of violin makers in Cremona
Andrea (c.1520–1580) whose earliest known label dates from 1564, was the founder who developed the standard violin. Others were his younger brother Nicola (1530–1600), Andrea's two sons, Antonio (1550–1638) and Geronimo (1551–1635), and the latter's son, Niccolo (1596–1684), the master of **Guarnieri** and **Stradivari**. Geronimo (1649–1740) was the last important Amati.

Ambartsumian, Viktor Amazaspovich 1908–96
Soviet–Armenian astrophysicist
Born in Tiflis (now, Tbilisi), Georgia, he was educated at the University of Leningrad (now St Petersburg). He was Professor of Astrophysics there (1934–44) and from 1944 at Yerevan, where he founded the Byurakan Astronomical Observatory which became one of the USSR's most important observatories. He devised theories of young star clusters and methods for computing the mass ejected from nova stars. In 1955 he proposed that enormous explosions occur within the cores of galaxies, of the same form as those producing supernovae, but on a galactic scale. In 1939 he wrote *Theoretical Astrophysics* (Eng trans 1958), which was widely influential. He was a very politically active member of the Communist Party of the Soviet Union, winning many awards, and after the collapse of the country was awarded the National Hero of Armenia medal.

Ambedkar, Bhimrao Ranji 1893–1956
Indian politician and champion of the depressed classes
Born in a Ratnagiri village on the Konkan coast of Bombay, the son of an Indian soldier, he was educated at Elphinstone College, Bombay, Columbia University, and the London School of Economics. He became a London barrister and later a member of the Bombay Legislative Assembly and the leader of 60 million untouchables (members of the lowest caste). In 1941 he became a member of the Governor-General's council. Appointed Law Minister in 1947, he was the principal author of the Indian Constitution. He resigned in 1951 and with some thousands of his followers he publicly embraced the Buddhist faith not long before his death. His dedicated work for the untouchables helped to secure a better life for them. His publications include *Annihilation of Caste* (1937).

Ambler, Eric 1909–98
English novelist and playwright
Born in London, he was educated at Colfe's Grammar School and London University, then served an apprenticeship in engineering and worked as an advertising copywriter before turning to writing thrillers, invariably with an espionage background. Considered by **Graham Greene** to be Great Britain's best thriller writer, he published his first novel, *The Dark Frontier*, in 1936. His best-known books are *Epitaph for a Spy* (1938), *The Mask of Dimitrios* (1939), *Dirty Story* (1967) and *The Intercom Conspiracy* (1970). He co-authored novels with Charles Rodda under the pseudonym Eliot Reed and received the Crime Writers' Association award four times, and the **Edgar Allan Poe** award (1964). In 1993 he published *The Story So Far*. He also wrote a number of screenplays. 📖 *Here Lies: An Autobiography* (1985)

Amboise, Georges d' 1460–1510
French prelate and statesman
Born in Chaumont-sur-Loire, he was made Bishop of Montauban at the age of 14 and Archbishop of Rouen in 1493. He became a cardinal and Prime Minister under **Louis XII** in 1498. In an attempt to secure his election as pope he encouraged a schism between the French Church and Rome, and convened a separate council, first in Pisa, then in Milan and Lyons. An able minister, he effected the Treaty of Blois in 1505 that brought about an alliance between France and Spain.

Ambrogini, Angelo See **Politian**

Ambrose, St c.339–97AD
Italian bishop, writer and Doctor of the Church
Born in Trier, Germany, the son of the prefect of Gaul, he practised law in Rome and in AD369 was appointed consular prefect of Upper Italy. Though he was an unbaptized layman, his fairness in dealing with the Arian/Catholic controversy led to his appointment as Bishop of Milan in 374. One of the four Latin Doctors of the Church (with St **Augustine**, St **Jerome**, and **Gregory I, the Great**), he is remembered for his preaching, for his introduction of the use of hymns, for his literary works, and for many improvements in the service—the Ambrosian ritual and Ambrosian chant. His feast day is 7 December. 📖 F Homes-Dudden, *The Life and Times of St Ambrose* (2 vols, 1935)

Amdahl, Gene Myron 1922–
US computer scientist and entrepreneur

Born in Flandreau, South Dakota, he studied electrical engineering at South Dakota State University and later became project manager at an IBM plant in 1952, the year in which he was awarded a PhD in physics at the University of Wisconsin. From 1960 he managed the company's advanced data processing systems and led the design of several IBM computers, most notably the extremely successful System/360. In 1970 he founded the Amdahl Corporation for producing computers compatible with IBM machines. Although he was successful, he resigned as chairman of the company and in 1980 set up Trilogy Ltd to compete with both the Amdahl Corporation and IBM.

Amenhotep II 15th century BC
King of Egypt of the 18th dynasty
The son of **Tuthmosis III** and Queen **Hatshepsut**, he ruled from 1450 to 1425BC, and fought successful campaigns in Palestine and on the Euphrates. His mummy was discovered at Thebes in a well-preserved tomb.

Amenhotep III c.1411–c.1375BC
King of Egypt of the 18th dynasty
The son of **Tuthmosis IV**, he ruled from 1417 to 1379 BC and consolidated Egyptian supremacy in Babylonia and Assyria. In a reign of spectacular wealth and magnificence, he built his great capital city, Thebes, and its finest monuments, including the Luxor temple, the great pylon at Karnak, and the colossi of Memnon.

Amenhotep IV See **Akhenaten**

Amery, John 1912–45
English pro-Nazi adventurer
He was the elder son (later disowned) of the Conservative politician **L S Amery**. He was declared bankrupt in 1936, and was a gun-runner for General **Franco** in the Spanish Civil War and liaison officer with French Cagoulards. Recruited by the Nazis in France, where he had been living since the outbreak of World War II, he began pro-**Hitler** broadcasts from Berlin in 1942. He tried to raise an anti-Bolshevik free corps in the British internee camp at St Denis to fight for the Nazis on the Russian front (1943), and made speeches for Hitler in Norway, France, Belgium and Yugoslavia (1944). Captured by Italian partisans in 1945 and handed over to the British authorities, he was tried in London for high treason and pleaded guilty after an attempt to prove Spanish citizenship. He was hanged in December 1945.

Amery, L(eopold Charles Maurice) S(tennett) 1873–1955
English Conservative politician
Born in Gorakpur, India, he was educated at Harrow and Oxford. After 10 years on the staff of *The Times* he became MP for Sparkbrook, Birmingham, a seat which he held for 34 years. He served as Colonial Under-Secretary, First Lord of the Admiralty and Colonial Secretary between 1919 and 1929 and then returned to office in **Churchill's** wartime administration as Secretary of State for India and Burma. He became famous for his exhortation to **Neville Chamberlain**, in May 1940, adapting **Cromwell's** words, 'In the name of God, go!' His publications include *My Political Life* (3 vols, 1953–55).

Ames, James Barr 1846–1910
US jurist
Born in Boston, he was educated at Harvard, and was appointed to the Harvard Law School faculty in 1873 where he became Dean from 1895. He adopted the case method of instruction pioneered by **Christopher Langdell** and published numerous casebooks. He took part in founding the *Harvard Law Review* and published *Lectures on Legal History* (1913).

Ames, Joseph 1689–1759
English bibliographer and antiquary
Born in Yarmouth on the Isle of Wight, he became an ironmonger or ship-chandler in London, and at the suggestion of friends compiled *Typographical Antiquities* (1749), the foundation of English bibliography.

Ames, Leslie Ethelbert George 1905–90
English cricketer
Born in Eltham, Kent, he was educated at Harvey Grammar School, Folkestone, and played cricket there, but only took up the wicket-keeping at which he excelled when he joined the Kent team. He was also a formidable batsman, and scored 37,245 runs in his career. He served in the RAF during World War II, achieving the rank of squadron leader, and played again for Kent after the war. Retiring from the game in 1951, he continued with Kent as coach and manager. From 1950 to 1958 he was an England selector and took three MCC sides on tour as manager.

Ames, William, *Latin* Amesius 1576–1633
English Puritan theologian
Born in Ipswich, Suffolk, he wrote mostly in Latin, and spent the later half of his life in Holland, where he became a professor of theology. He is famous for his exposition of Calvinist doctrine.

Amesius See **Ames, William**

Amherst, Jeffrey Amherst, 1st Baron 1717–97
English soldier
He was born in Riverhead, Kent, and joined the army at the age of 14. He played an important part in the North American phase of the Seven Years War (1756–63), and was in command of the expedition against the French in Canada and captured Louisburg (1758). Appointed Commander-in-Chief of North America in 1759, he captured Montreal in 1760. He was Governor-General of British North America from 1760 to 1763, and was Commander-in-Chief of the British army from 1772 to 1796. Amherst College was named after him.

Amherst (of Arakan), William Pitt, 1st Earl 1773–1857
English colonialist
Born in Bath, the nephew and adopted son of Jeffrey, 1st Baron **Amherst**, in 1800 he married the widowed Countess Dowager of Plymouth (*née* Sarah Archer, 1762–1838), a keen naturalist. In 1816 he was sent as ambassador to China, but his mission failed when he refused to kowtow to the emperor as was the custom at the time. In 1823 he was appointed Governor-General of India, where he survived the first Burmese War and was rewarded with an earldom (1826). The Amhersts returned to England in 1828, bringing a pair of rare Burmese pheasants, which were later named Lady Amherst's pheasants in her honour. Soon after his wife's death, Lord Amherst married another Dowager Duchess of Plymouth, the widow of his eldest stepson.

Amici, Giovanni Battista 1784–1863
Italian optician, astronomer and natural philosopher
He was born in Modena. He constructed optical instruments, perfecting his own alloy for telescope mirrors and, in 1827, produced the dioptric, achromatic microscope that bears his name. He became director of the Florence Observatory in 1835.

Amicis, Edmondo de 1846–1908
Italian novelist
Born in Oneglia, he became director of the Italia Militare, Florence, in 1867, but turned to literature, recording his experiences as a soldier in *La vita militare* (1868, 'The Military Life'). He is chiefly remembered for

his alliance with **Alessandro Manzoni** in an attempt to 'purify' the Italian language. *L'Idioma gentile* (1905, 'The Gentle Language') presents his views on this subject. His most popular work is the sentimental *Il Cuore* (1886), translated into English as *An Italian Schoolboy's Journal*, 1887, then into *The Heart of a Boy*, 1960, and into more than 25 other languages. He also travelled widely, producing books about his adventures. 📖 V Chialant, *Edmondo de Amicis, educatore e artista* (1911)

Amiel, Henri Frédéric 1821–81
Swiss philosopher and writer
Born in Geneva, he became Professor of Aesthetics (1849) and of Moral Philosophy (1853–81) at the Academy of Geneva. He published some essays and poems, but his fame as an intellectual and critic rests on his diaries (1847 onwards), published posthumously as *Journal intime* (1883, 'Private Journal').

Amies, Sir (Edwin) Hardy 1909–
English couturier and dressmaker by appointment to Queen Elizabeth II
After studying languages in France and Germany, he worked as a trainee in Birmingham before becoming a managing designer in London in 1934, where he made a name for himself especially with his tailored suits for women. He founded his own fashion house in 1946, was awarded a royal warrant in 1955, started designing for men in 1959 and is now known chiefly for his menswear. His publications include *The Englishman's Suit* (1994).

Amin (Dada), Idi 1925–
Ugandan soldier and politician
Born in Koboko of a peasant family, after a rudimentary education he rose rapidly to become Commander-in-Chief of the army and air force (1966). Originally a friend of Prime Minister **Milton Obote**, in 1971 he staged a coup, dissolving parliament and establishing a military dictatorship. He expelled 500 Israeli citizens, all Ugandan Asians with British passports, and the British High Commissioner, seized foreign-owned businesses and estates and ordered the killing of thousands of his opponents. His attempt to annex the Kagera area of Tanzania (1978) gave President **Nyerere** the opportunity to send his troops into Uganda. Amin was deposed within six months (1979). He fled to Libya and after expulsion from several countries settled in Saudi Arabia (1980–88). In 1993 his latest wife bore him his 43rd child.

Amiot, Jacques See Amyot, Jacques

Amis, Sir Kingsley 1922–95
English novelist and poet
Born in London, he was educated at the City of London School and at St John's College, Oxford, and was a lecturer in English Literature at University College, Swansea (1948–61) and Fellow of Peterhouse, Cambridge (1961–63). He achieved huge success with his first novel, *Lucky Jim* (1954), the story of a comic anti-hero in a provincial university. 'Jim' appeared again as a small-town librarian in *That Uncertain Feeling* (1956), and as a provincial author abroad in *I Like It Here* (1958). After the death of **Ian Fleming**, he wrote a James Bond novel, *Colonel Sun* (1968), under the pseudonym of Robert Markham, as well as *The James Bond Dossier* (1965). His later novels include *I Want It Now* (1968), *Ending Up* (1974), *Jake's Thing* (1978), *Stanley and the Women* (1984), *The Old Devils* (1986, Booker Prize), *The Folks That Live On The Hill* (1990), and *The Russian Girl* (1992). He also published four books of poetry, and wrote non-fiction works, including one on the history of science fiction. He was married (1965–83) to the novelist Elizabeth Jane Howard (1923–). His son is **Martin Amis**. 📖 *Memoirs* (1991); R Rabinowitz, *The Reaction Against Experiment in the English Novel* (1967)

Amis, Martin Louis 1949–
English novelist and journalist
Born in Oxford, the son of **Kingsley Amis**, he was educated at Exeter College, Oxford, and acted in the film *A High Wind in Jamaica* (1965). He worked for the *Times Literary Supplement* and *New Statesman*, but has been a full-time writer since 1979. He began precociously with his first novel, *The Rachel Papers* (1973), and followed it with two more witty satires, *Dead Babies* (1975) and *Success* (1978). Subsequent novels include *Money* (1984), *Einstein's Monsters* (1986), a short-story collection on the theme of nuclear destruction, *London Fields* (1989), *Time's Arrow* (1991), which plays with concepts of time and history, and *The Information* (1995). He has also written a great deal of literary journalism.

Amman, Jakob c.1645–c.1730
Swiss religious
He was a Mennonite bishop, whose followers founded the Amish sect in the 1690s. Its members still practise an exclusively rural and simple way of life in various parts of the USA and Canada.

Ammanati, Bartolommeo 1511–92
Italian architect and sculptor
Born in Settignano, he executed the ducal palace in Lucca, working in the late Renaissance style. He also designed part of the Pitti Palace and the Ponte S Trinità (destroyed in World War II) in Florence, and made the Neptune fountain in the Piazza della Signoria there.

Ammann, Othmar Hermann 1879–1965
US structural engineer
Born in Schaffhausen, Switzerland, he emigrated to the USA in 1904 to work with the Pennsylvania Steel Company. He became a US citizen in 1924. Later he designed some of the USA's greatest suspension bridges, including the George Washington Bridge (3,500ft/1,060m) in New York (1931), Golden Gate Bridge (4,200ft/1,260m) in San Francisco (1937) and Verrazano Narrows Bridge (4,260ft/1,280m) in New York (1965), each in its day the longest span in the world.

Ammianus Marcellinus c.330–390AD
Roman historian
Born of Greek parents in Antioch, he fought in Gaul, Germany and the East, then settled in Rome and devoted himself to literature. He wrote in Latin a history of the Roman empire from AD98 (the death of **Domitian**). It comprised 31 books, of which only the last 18 are extant; these cover the years 353 to 378, the events of his own lifetime.

Ammonius, surnamed Saccas c.160–242AD
Greek philosopher
A sack-carrier in Alexandria, Egypt, as a young man, he was the founder of Neoplatonic philosophy, and was the teacher of **Plotinus**, **Origen** and **Longinus**, but left no writings.

Amontons, Guillaume 1663–1705
French instrument-maker and physicist
Born in Paris, he was incurably deaf from adolescence and studied geometry, mechanics and physical science in order to qualify himself for employment in public works. He designed many instruments, including a hygrometer (1687), a 'folded' barometer (1688), a conical nautical barometer (1695), and various air thermometers. Between 1699 and 1702 he discovered the interdependence of volume, temperature and pressure of gases, later demonstrated explicitly by **Joseph Gay-Lussac** and **Jacques Charles**. In 1703 Amontons defined the 'extreme cold' of his thermometric apparatus as that point at which the air would exert no pressure, hinting at an absolute zero of

temperature. Daniel Fahrenheit owed much to his investigation of the thermal expansion of mercury (1704). Amontons died as a result of gangrene.

Amory, Derick Heathcoat Amory, 1st Viscount 1899–1981
English Conservative politician
Born in Tiverton, Devon, and educated at Eton and Christ Church, Oxford, he entered parliament in 1945. He was Minister of Pensions (1951–53), at the Board of Trade (1953–54), Minister of Agriculture (1954–58) and was made viscount while he was Chancellor of the Exchequer (1958–60).

Amory, Thomas c.1691–1788
Irish writer
He was born in Dublin, and studied medicine there at Trinity College, but was wealthy enough to adopt the life of a gentleman of leisure in London, where he lived a very secluded life. His chief works include *Memoirs of Several Ladies of Great Britain* (1755), *A History of Antiquities, Productions of Nature* (1755), and the *Life of John Buncle* (2 vols, 1756–66), an odd combination of autobiography, fantastic descriptions of scenery, deistical theology, and sentimental rhapsody. 📖 *Memoirs of the Life, Character and Writings of the Author* (1764)

Amos 835–765BC
Old Testament prophet
Born in Tekoa, near Bethlehem, he was the earliest prophet in the Bible to have a book named after him. He worked as a herdsman, and was an outspoken critic of the unjust acts of the northern kingdom of Israel.

Amour, Elizabeth Isabel 1885–1945
Scottish ceramic artist
Born in Manchester, England, she studied design and decorative art at Glasgow School of Art. She founded the Bough Pottery in Edinburgh (c.1921–42) which specialized in decorative pottery, and was assisted by her three brothers and her sister. The studio collaborated with the artist Robert Burns (1869–1941) to make tableware for Crawford's Hanover Street Tearooms. A professional member of the Scottish Society of Artists, she was a founder-member of the Scottish Society of Women Artists. Her younger brother, Richard Amour (1899–1949), was also a ceramic decorator.

Ampère, André Marie 1775–1836
French mathematician and physicist
He was born in Lyons, where his father was a wealthy merchant. The family then moved to the nearby village of Poleymieux, where their house is now a national museum. Ampère educated himself by means of his father's library. He gained a lectureship in mathematics at the École Polytechnique in Paris in 1803, was appointed Inspector-General of the Imperial University in 1808 and was elected to the chair of experimental physics at the Collège de France in 1824. Although he contributed to a number of fields, he is best known for laying the foundations of the science of electrodynamics through his theoretical and experimental work, following Hans Christian Oersted's discovery in 1820 of the magnetic effects of electric currents, in *Observations électro-dynamiques* (1822, 'Electrodynamic Observations') and *Théories des phénomènes électro-dynamiques* (1830, 'Theory of Electrodynamic Phenomena'). Ampère was elected FRS, and his name is given to the basic SI unit of electric current (ampere, amp). 📖 James R Hofmann, *André-Marie Ampère* (1995)

Amr ibn al-'As d.664
Arab soldier

A convert to Islam, he joined the prophet Muhammad in 629, and took part in the conquest of Palestine in 638. In 639 he undertook the conquest of Egypt; in 642 he captured Alexandria after a 14-month siege and accepted the capitulation of Egypt. He became the first Muslim governor of Egypt (642–44), where he founded the first city on the site of Cairo. He helped Mu'awiyah, founder of the Umayyad dynasty, to seize the caliphate from Ali by capturing Alexandria again in 658, and was Governor of Egypt again from 661 to 663.

Amundsen, Roald Engelbreth Gravning 1872–1928
Norwegian explorer, the first man to navigate the Northwest Passage and to reach the South Pole
Born in Borge, he abandoned his medical studies in favour of a life at sea. In 1897 he served with the Belgian Antarctic expedition as first mate of the *Belgica*, the first vessel to overwinter in Antarctica. From 1902 to 1906 he sailed the Northwest Passage from east to west in the smack *Gjöa* (the first person to navigate the waterway in both directions) and located the Magnetic North Pole. In 1910 he set sail in the *Fram* in an attempt to reach the North Pole, but hearing that Robert Peary had apparently beaten him to it, he switched to the Antarctic and reached the South Pole in December 1911, one month ahead of Captain Scott. He built a new ship, the *Maud*, and sailed her through the Northeast Passage in 1918. In 1926 he flew the airship *Norge* from Spitsbergen to Alaska across the North Pole with Lincoln Ellsworth and Umberto Nobile, circling the Pole twice. In 1928 he disappeared when searching by plane for Nobile, whose airship, *Italia*, had gone missing on another flight to the Pole. He wrote several books, including *My Life as an Explorer* (1927). 📖 Charles Turley, *Roald Amundsen, Explorer* (1935)

Amyot or Amiot, Jacques 1513–93
French humanist
He was born in Melun. One of the most lucid of French prose writers, he translated many classical texts, the most important being his French version of Plutarch's *Lives*, which was the basis of Sir Thomas North's translation into English, and of some of Shakespeare's history plays. He was appointed Bishop of Auxerre (1570).

Anacharsis 6th century BC
Scythian prince
According to Herodotus, he travelled widely in quest of knowledge, and visited Athens in Solon's time. Tradition maintains that he despised all Greeks except Spartans.

Anacreon c.570–c.475BC
Greek lyric poet
From Teos, Asia Minor, he helped to found the Greek colony of Abdera in Thrace (c.540BC) despite threatened attack by the Persians. He was invited to Samos by Polycrates to tutor his son. After the tyrant's downfall, he was brought to Athens by Hipparchus, son of the tyrant Pisistratus, and later went to Thessaly. His work, which survives only in fragments, includes poems of love and wine, satires, dedications and epitaphs. A model for the Latin lyric poets, it was also widely imitated by French and English poets of the Renaissance. 📖 V Martin, *Quatre Figures de la Poésie Grecque* (1931)

Anand, Mulk Raj 1905–
Indian novelist and critic
He was born in Peshawar (now in Pakistan), and his early life was fraught with tragedy and family problems. He left India for Great Britain, where he was beaten up for blacklegging during the General Strike (1926). His first novel, *Untouchable* (1935), was rejected by 19 publishers, the 20th agreeing to take it on if E M Forster would write a preface. This he did, sparking off a remarkable career for Anand. His humanist novels, such as *The Coolie* (1936), *Two*

Leaves and a Bud (1937) and *The Village* (1939, the first of a trilogy), depict life in the poverty-stricken Punjab. He later began an ambitious seven-volume autobiographical work of fiction, *The Seven Ages of Man*, which began with *Seven Summers: The Story of an Indian Childhood* (1951). 📖 M Berry, *Mulk Raj Anand: the man and the novelist* (1971)

Anastasia, *in full* **Grand Duchess Anastasia Nikolayevna Romanov** 1901–?1918
Russian duchess
Born in Peterhof, the youngest daughter of Tsar **Nicholas II**, she is believed to have perished when the **Romanov** family were executed by the Bolsheviks in a cellar in Yekaterinburg on 19 July 1918. Various people have claimed to be Anastasia, especially Mrs 'Anna Anderson' Manahan, who died in Virginia, USA (1984) at the age of 82. She had been rescued from a suicide attempt in a Berlin canal (1918), and for more than 30 years fought unsuccessfully to establish her identity as Anastasia, living under the name of Anna Anderson. Most of the surviving members and friends of the Romanov family were sceptical or downright hostile. Her story inspired two films (*Anastasia*, with **Ingrid Bergman**, and *Is Anna Anderson Anastasia?* with Lilli Palmer), and several books. In 1968 she went to the USA and married a former history professor, Dr John Manahan. 📖 John Klier and Helen Mingay, *The Search for Anastasia* (1995)

Anaxagoras 500–428BC
Ionian philosopher
Born in Clazomenae, Asia Minor, he taught for 30 years in Athens, where his many illustrious pupils included **Pericles** and **Euripides**. His explanations of physical phenomena by natural causes brought accusations of impiety, and he was banished from Athens. He withdrew to Lampsacus, on the Hellespont, and died there. He held that matter is infinitely divisible (ie that any piece of matter, regardless of how small it is, contains portions of all kinds of matter), and that order is produced from chaos by an intelligent principle.

Anaximander 611–547BC
Ionian philosopher
Born in Miletus, Asia Minor, he was successor and perhaps pupil of **Thales**. He posited that the first principle was not a particular substance like water or air but the 'Boundless' (*apeiron*), which he conceived of in both physical and theological terms. He is believed to have used the gnomon (a sundial with a vertical rod) to measure the lengths of the seasons, by fixing the times of the equinoxes and solstices, and he is also thought to have drawn the first map of the inhabited world (he recognized that the Earth's surface must be curved, though he visualized it as a cylinder rather than a sphere). No trace of his scientific writings has been found, but he is credited with many imaginative scientific speculations, for example that the Earth is unsupported and at the centre of the universe, that living creatures first existed in the waters of the Earth, and that human beings must have developed from some lower species that more quickly matured into self-sufficiency. He is sometimes called the father of astronomy.

Anaximenes d.c.500BC
Greek philosopher
Born in Miletus, Asia Minor, he became the third of the three great Milesian thinkers, succeeding **Thales** and **Anaximander**. No biographical details are known about him. He proposed that the first principle and basic form of matter was air, which could be transformed into other substances by a process of condensation and expansion. He also believed that the Earth and the heavenly bodies were flat and floated on the air like leaves.

Ancel, Paul See **Celan, Paul**

Anckarström, Johan Jakob 1762–92
Swedish army officer and assassin
He was a page in the court, served in the royal bodyguard, and after settling on his estates in 1783 was tried for high treason, but released for lack of evidence. Soon afterwards he conspired with a ring of disaffected nobles to murder King **Gustav III** of Sweden, and after drawing the short straw, wounded the king mortally with a pistol at a masked ball at the Royal Opera House. He was publicly flogged for three days, and then executed.

Ancre, Baron de Lussigny, Marquis d', *originally* **Concino Concini** d.1617
French adventurer
Born in Florence, Italy, he went to the French court in 1600, in the train of **Marie de Medicis**, the wife of **Henri IV**. After Henri's assassination in 1610 he became chief favourite of the queen-regent during the minority of **Louis XIII**, and was made a marquis, and, in 1614, Marshal of France, though he had never seen war. Prodigiously extravagant, he squandered vast sums on the decoration of his palaces. Hated alike by nobility and populace, he put down one rebellion in 1616, but was assassinated in the Louvre, Paris, during a second rebellion.

Ancus Marcius 640–616BC
Traditionally the fourth King of Rome
He is said by historians like **Livy** to have founded the port of Ostia, and to have conquered the neighbouring Latin tribes, settling them on the Aventine.

Andel, Tjeerd Hendrik van See **Van Andel, Tjeerd Hendrik**

Anders, Władysław 1892–1970
Polish general
Born in Blonie, he served in the Polish Corps in World War I (1914–17), and in the Russo-Polish War (1919–20) he commanded the 15th Lancers. At the outbreak of World War II he commanded the Nowogrodek Cavalry Brigade, fighting both Germans and Russians, but was captured by the Russians and harshly treated (1939–41). On his release he became Commander-in-Chief of the Polish forces in the Middle East and Italy. After the war, deprived of his nationality by the Polish Communist government in 1946, he was a leading figure in the 140,000-strong Free Polish Community in Great Britain, and Inspector-General of the Polish forces-in-exile. He wrote *An Army in Exile* (1949). 📖 Zdzislaw Stahl, *General Anders: 2 Korpus* (1985)

Andersen, Hans Christian 1805–75
Danish writer
Born in Odense, Fünen, the son of a shoemaker and a washerwoman, he had a talent for poetry, and at 14 went to Copenhagen to seek a job in the theatre. He failed, but his writing attracted the attention of influential men and, application having been made to the king, he was given place at an advanced school. In 1829 he established his reputation with 'A Walk from the Holmen Canal to the Easternmost Point of Amager', a literary satire in the form of a humorous narrative. He received a travelling pension from the king in 1833 and toured widely in Europe, writing poetry, travel books, novels and plays. In 1835 he began publishing the tiny pamphlets of fairy tales which are his greatest work (translated into English in 1846). There are more than 150 of them, including 'The Tin Soldier', 'The Emperor's New Clothes', 'The Tinderbox', 'The Snow Queen', 'The Little Mermaid' and 'The Ugly Duckling'. He also wrote an autobiography *Mit Livs Eventyr* (1855, rev edn 1870), translated by **Mary Howitt** as *The True Story of My Life* (1847). He is considered to be one of the world's greatest storytellers. 📖 R Bain, *Hans Christian Andersen: a biography* (1895)

Anderson, Carl David 1905–91
US physicist and Nobel Prize winner

Born in New York City, he studied at the California Institute of Technology (Caltech) under **Robert Millikan**, and in 1932 discovered the positron, the positively charged electron-type particle, thus confirming the existence of antimatter predicted by **Paul Dirac**. He did notable work on gamma and cosmic rays, and was awarded the 1936 Nobel Prize for physics (jointly with **Victor Hess**). Later he confirmed the existence of intermediate-mass particles known as mesons or muons. He spent his entire career at Caltech and was named professor emeritus in 1976.

Anderson, Elizabeth Garrett, *née* Garrett 1836–1917
English physician, the first English woman doctor

Born in London, she was brought up at Aldeburgh in Suffolk. In 1860 she began studying medicine, in the face of prejudiced opposition to the admission of women, and eventually (1865) qualified as a medical practitioner by passing the Apothecaries' Hall examination. In 1866 she established a dispensary for women in London (later renamed the Elizabeth Garrett Anderson Hospital, where she instituted medical courses for women. In 1870 she was appointed a visiting physician to the East London Hospital, and headed the poll for the London School Board. She was given the degree of MD by the University of Paris in the same year. In 1908 she was elected Mayor of Aldeburgh—the first woman mayor in England. Her sister was the suffragette **Millicent Fawcett**. ⚏ Jo Manton, *Elizabeth Garrett Anderson* (1965)

Anderson, Ethel 1883–1958
Australian writer

Born in Leamington Spa, Warwickshire, England, she was a friend of **John Maynard Keynes, Charles Darwin**, and of the poet Frances Cornford. She married an army officer and lived for some time in India. She wrote two books of verse, *Squatter's Luck* (1942) and *Sunday at Yarralumla* (1947), some essays, and two books of short stories, *Indian Tales* (1948) and *The Little Ghosts* (1959), delicate tales based on her Indian experiences. Her best-known book, *At Parramatta* (1956), turns vignettes of Australian middle-class life in the 1850s into a microcosm of the Seven Deadly Sins. She also wrote an oratorio, *The Song of Hagar* (1958), set to music by the composer **John Antill**.

Anderson, Gerry 1929–
British creator of television programmes

He entered the British film industry as a trainee with the Colonial Film Unit and later worked as an assistant editor on such films as *The Wicked Lady* (1945) before co-founding Pentagon Films (1955). Initially intending to make commercials, he co-produced and directed such television series as *The Adventures of Twizzle* (1956) and *Torchy, the Battery Boy* (1957). He enjoyed his greatest success with a number of adventure series that combined puppet characters with technologically advanced hardware and special effects, the best known being *Fireball XL-5* (1962–63), *Thunderbirds* (1965–66) and *Captain Scarlet and the Mysterons* (1967–68). He later branched out into live action shows (with human actors) like *The Protectors* (1972–74) and *Space 1999* (1975–77) before returning to the use of increasingly sophisticated puppetry in *Terrahawks* (1983–84). He switched back to live action for *Space Precinct* (1995–).

Anderson, James 1662–1728
Scottish antiquary and lawyer

He was born in Edinburgh. In 1705 he published a treatise vindicating the independence of Scotland and in 1727 a valuable collection of historical documents. He spent the rest of his life working on his *Selectus Diplomatum et Numismatum Scotiae Thesaurus* (1739).

Anderson, James 1739–1808
Scottish agricultural economist

Born in Hermiston, near Edinburgh, he had a farm in Aberdeenshire, where he invented the 'Scotch plough' (a two horse plough without wheels). He edited *The Bee* at Edinburgh (1790–93), and moved to London in 1797. His *Recreations of Agriculture* anticipated **David Ricardo's** theory of rent.

Anderson, Sir James Norman Dalrymple 1908–94
English Anglican scholar and lay reader

He was born in London and, after graduating from Cambridge, he became a missionary in Egypt. In World War II he rose to be intelligence colonel and Cairo-based Chief Secretary for Arab Affairs. By 1954 he was Professor of Oriental Law at London University. A strong evangelical, he was the first chairman of the Church of England's House of Laity (1970). His publications include *Islamic Law in Africa* (1955), *God's Law and God's Love* (1980), *Christianity and the World Religions* (1985), and the autobiographical *An Adopted Son* (1985).

Anderson, John See **Waverley, 1st Viscount**

Anderson, John 1726–96
Scottish scientist

Born in Roseneath, Dunbartonshire, he studied at Glasgow University, where from 1756 to 1760 he was Professor of Oriental Languages, and then of Natural Philosophy. He established a bi-weekly class for mechanics, and at his death left all he had to found Anderson's College in Glasgow. The author of *Institutes of Physics* (1786), he also invented the balloon post, and a gun which he presented to the French National Convention in 1791.

Anderson, John 1893–1962
Australian philosopher

Born in Scotland, he was Professor of Philosophy at Sydney, from 1927. He can be regarded as the founder and main exponent of an Australian school of philosophy, espousing a distinctive blend of realism, empiricism and materialism.

Anderson, John Stuart 1908–90
English chemist

Born in London, he studied there at Imperial College. At Heidelberg University his research opened up the chemistry of the metal nitrosyl complexes, and at Melbourne University in 1938 he developed a method for recovering the element protactinium from the Springfields nuclear separation process. His studies of metal halides and the partition of minor lanthanide elements led naturally to an interest in solids, and in later years his major discoveries were in the areas of solid-state and high-temperature chemistry. During a spell at the Atomic Energy Research Establishment at Harwell he worked on uranium oxides. At Oxford, where he was the first Professor of Inorganic Chemistry (1963–75), he worked on lanthanide carbides at extremely high temperatures, and also developed electron microscopy to determine crystalline structures. With Harry Eméleus (1903–93) he wrote the influential textbook *Modern Aspects of Inorganic Chemistry* (1938). He was elected Fellow of the Royal Society in 1953, and received the Davy Medal of the Royal Society in 1973. He won the Royal Society of Chemistry solid-state award in 1974 and the Longstaff Medal in 1976.

Anderson, Dame Judith, *originally* Frances
Margaret Anderson 1898–1992
Australian actress
Born in Adelaide, South Australia, she made her Sydney
stage debut in *A Royal Divorce* (1915) and first appeared in
New York in 1918. She toured the USA throughout the
1920s, enjoying successes with *Cobra* (1924) and *Strange
Interlude* (1928–29). She made her film debut in *Madame of
the Jury* (1930) but preferred the stage, appearing in productions like *Mourning Becomes Electra* (1932), *The Old Maid*
(1935), *Hamlet* (1936, with John Gielgud), and *Macbeth*
(1937) at the Old Vic in London. Her chilling performance as the sinister Mrs Danvers in Alfred Hitchcock's
Rebecca (1940) earned her a cinema career portraying cruel
and domineering women in films like *Laura* (1944) and
Diary of a Chambermaid (1946). Her many theatre credits
include the title part in Robinson Jeffers's adaptation of
Medea (1947, 1982), *The Seagull* (1960) and *Hamlet* (1970–71)
in the title role. Her later film appearances comprise *Cat on
a Hot Tin Roof* (1958), *A Man Called Horse* (1970), *Inn of the
Damned* (1974) and *Star Trek III* (1984). A Broadway theatre
was named in her honour in 1984. The same year, she
joined the cast of the television soap opera *Santa Barbara*.

Anderson, Sir Kenneth Arthur Noel 1891–1959
British general
Born in India, he was educated at Charterhouse and
Sandhurst and commissioned into the Seaforth High-
landers. In World War I he served in France (1914–16), and
fought under Viscount Allenby in Palestine in 1917–18.
Between the wars he served in India. In World War II he
fought at Dunkirk (1940), and was Commander of the 1st
British Army in North Africa (1942–43) and captured
Tunis (1943). He was Governor-General of Gibraltar from
1947 to 1952.

Anderson, Lindsay Gordon 1923–94
British stage and film director
Born in Bangalore, India, he was educated at Oxford,
became a film critic, and was co-founder and editor of
Sequence (1949–51). He made his directorial debut with the
documentary *Meeting the Pioneers* (1948) and was a key figure in the 'Free Cinema' movement of the 1950s, winning
an Academy Award for *Thursday's Children* (1953). His subsequent feature films often took an abrasive or iconoclastic stance towards the state of the nation and include
This Sporting Life (1963), *If...* (1968) and *Britannia Hospital* (1982). A director at the Royal Court Theatre from
1957, he also directed for television, acted, and wrote
About John Ford (1981).

Anderson, Margaret C(aroline) 1886–1973
US author, editor and publisher
Born in Indianapolis, Indiana, she was a founder in 1914
of the famous literary magazine the *Little Review*, which
published pieces by, among others, Carl Sandburg,
Sherwood Anderson, Amy Lowell, Wallace Stevens, W B
Yeats, Ernest Hemingway and Ezra Pound. Its extracts of
James Joyce's *Ulysses* (published in book form in Paris, in
1922) which appeared between 1917 and 1920 were considered to contain indecent material and several editions
of the magazine were burned by the US Post Office and in
1920, Anderson and her colleague Jane Heap were convicted of publishing obscene material. In 1923 she moved
to Paris where the *Little Review* appeared from 1924 to
1929.

Anderson, Marian 1902–93
US contralto
She was born into a poor black family in Philadelphia,
and had her training financed by members of the church
where she sang in the gospel choir. She studied in New
York and spent most of her career as a concert singer. She
made several trips to Europe (1925–33), and overcame

racial discrimination to sing at Carnegie Hall in 1929.
However, in 1939 she was prevented from performing at
Constitution Hall in Washington DC, but there was such a
protest that Eleanor Roosevelt and others arranged for
her to appear in concert at the Lincoln Memorial, and
she performed triumphantly to an audience of 75,000.
Renowned for the range and rich tone of her voice, she
became the first black singer at the White House and at
the Metropolitan Opera. President Eisenhower made her
a delegate to the United Nations in 1958, and she received
many honours and international awards. She published
her autobiography, *My Lord, What a Morning*, in 1956.

Anderson, Maxwell 1888–1959
US historical dramatist
Born in Atlantic, Pennsylvania, he attended the
University of North Dakota and Stanford University. He
became a verse playwright, and was in vogue in the late
1920s to the early 1940s with numerous plays, including
Elizabeth the Queen (1930), *Mary of Scotland* (1933), *Key Largo*
(1939) and *The Eve of St Mark* (1942). Commercially successful, his plays had strong, simple themes, most of
which suggest a firm commitment to democratic humanism. He also wrote screenplays, most notably that
from Erich Maria Remarque's novel *All Quiet on the Western
Front* (1930). He won a Pulitzer Prize for *Both Your Houses* in
1933. ▫ M D Bailey, *Maxwell Anderson: the playwright as
prophet* (1957)

Anderson, Philip Warren 1923–
US physicist and Nobel Prize winner
Born in Indianapolis, Indiana, he studied antenna engineering at the Naval Research Laboratories during
World War II and then at Harvard, where he received his
PhD. As a student under John H Van Vleck he worked on
pressure broadening in microwave and infrared spectra.
He joined Bell Telephone Laboratories in 1949, where he
demonstrated that it is possible for an electron in disordered materials to be trapped in a small region (1958).
This process, later known as 'Anderson localization',
furthered our understanding of disordered materials and
contributed to their extensive exploitation in modern
applications such as solar cells, thin film transistors and
xerography. His work also included theoretical studies of
superfluidity and magnetism, and he clarified the meaning of the Josephson effect. He was appointed assistant
director of Bell Telephone Laboratories in 1974, moving
the following year to Princeton University to become
Professor of Physics. For his theoretical work on the
electronic structure of magnetic and disordered systems
he shared the 1977 Nobel Prize for physics with Sir Nevill
Mott and Van Vleck.

Anderson, Robert 1806–71
US soldier
Born near Louisville, Kentucky, he served in the Black
Hawk War, the Mexican War (1846–48), and the begin-
ning of the American Civil War (1861–65), when he de-
fended Fort Sumter against the Confederate attack in
July 1861.

Anderson, Sir Robert Rowand 1834–1921
Scottish architect and military engineer
Born in Edinburgh, he was educated there then trained at
the Royal Institution, and gained experience with Sir
George Gilbert Scott in London. He studied on the
Continent and published *Examples of the Municipal,
Commercial and Street Architecture* (1868). From 1860 he
worked for the Royal Engineers, starting an independent
practice in 1868. His passion was for gothic styles, and his
versatility is seen in the Byzantine design for Santa
Sophia, Galston (1882), and classical additions to Pollock
House, Glasgow (1901). His design for the University
Medical School in Edinburgh (1874) was extremely

popular and in domestic architecture he was among the pioneers of the 17th century Scottish revival. He executed a series of conservative restorations, such as Dunblane Cathedral (1890–93). He was knighted in 1902 and received the Royal Institute of British Architects Gold Medal in 1916.

Anderson, Sherwood 1876–1941
US fiction writer

Born in Camden, Ohio, the son of an itinerant harness maker, he had an uncertain childhood and irregular schooling, and at 17 enlisted to fight in the Spanish-American War. He later returned to Ohio and married, but in 1912 left his family and his lucrative position as head of a paint factory to devote all his time to writing. Settling in Chicago, he joined a literary circle that included **Carl Sandburg, Theodore Dreiser** and **Edgar Lee Masters**. His first novel was *Windy McPherson's Son* (1916), but his best-known work is *Winesburg, Ohio* (1919), a collection of interrelated short stories which portray the 'secret lives' of marginal characters and the sensibilities of the young artist who observes them and then escapes. Subsequent books include *Poor White* (1920) and *The Triumph of the Egg* (1921). His *Memoirs* (1942) and *Letters* (1953) were published posthumously. 📖 Howe, *Sherwood Anderson: A Biography* (1951)

Anderson, Thomas 1819–74
Scottish organic chemist

He studied at Edinburgh and Stockholm, became Professor of Chemistry at Glasgow, and discovered pyridine.

Andersson, Bibi (Birgitta) 1935–
Swedish actress

Born in Stockholm, she studied at the Kungliga Dramatiska Teatern there. She began her career in 1949 as a film extra and is best known for her roles in many **Ingmar Bergman** films such as *Sjunde inseglet* (1956, *The Seventh Seal*), *Persona* (1966) and *The Touch* (1971). As a theatre actress she has been attached to both the Malmö Municipal Theatre and the Royal Dramatic Theatre, Stockholm. In the 1970s she took many stage roles in the USA. She has been the recipient of numerous awards, including the British Academy Award for Best Foreign Actress (1971) for her part in *The Touch*.

Andersson, Dan(iel) 1888–1920
Swedish poet and novelist

One of Sweden's foremost writers in his time, he dealt with religious and metaphysical themes in his novels, as in the autobiographical *De tre hemlösa* (1918, 'Three Homeless Ones'). His poems about traditional charcoal-burners in *Kolarhistorier* (1914) and *Kolvakterens visor* (1915) turned them into national folk-figures. 📖 G Agren, *Dan Anderssons vag* (1970)

Andersson, Johan Gunnar 1874–1960
Swedish archaeologist, pioneer of the study of prehistoric China

Born in Knista, he trained as a geologist, and went to China in 1914 as technical adviser to the government on coalfields and oil resources, but became fascinated by fossil remains and soon took up archaeology. He was the first to identify prehistoric pottery in China, at Yang-shao-ts'un, Hunan, in 1921, and over the next year discovered numerous settlements with comparable ceramics across a vast stretch of the middle Yellow River Valley. Soon he was able to characterize the first Neolithic or farming culture of north China, dated c.5000–3000BC and named Yang-shao after his initial find. From 1921 to 1926 he also initiated excavations in the limestone caves at Chou-k'ou-tien near Peking, finding important fossils of *Homo erectus* alongside stone tools, charcoal, and charred bones in deposits 400,000–800,000 years old. Popularly known as 'Peking Man', these fossils were lost during the Japanese invasion of China in 1941. He wrote an autobiographical study, *Children of the Yellow Earth: Studies in Prehistoric China* (1934), and *Research into the Prehistory of China* (1943).

Andersson, Karl Johan 1827–67
Swedish explorer

In 1850 he went with the scientist **Francis Galton** to southwest Africa, going on to travel alone there in 1853–54, and publishing *Lake Ngami, or Discoveries in South Africa* in 1856. He explored the Okavango River in 1858, and in 1866 set out for the Cunene. He came within sight of the stream, but had to retrace his steps, and died on the homeward journey.

Andrade, Edward Neville da Costa 1887–1971
English physicist

He was born in London and studied there before receiving his PhD from Heidelberg University. He continued his studies at Cambridge and Manchester, and became Professor of Physics at the Artillery College in Woolwich (1920–28) and University College London (1928–50). For part of World War II he was scientific adviser to the director of scientific research at the Ministry of Supply. He was known for his work on grain growth in metals and the viscosity of liquids. From 1950 until his retirement in 1952 he was director of the Royal Institution and the **Davy–Faraday** Laboratory.

Andrassy, Julius, Count 1823–90
Hungarian politician

Born in Volosca, he was a supporter of **Lajos Kossuth** and he was prominent in the struggle for independence (1848–49), after which he remained in exile until 1858. When the Dual Monarchy was formed in 1867 he became Prime Minister of Hungary.

Andre, Carl 1935–
US sculptor

He was born in Massachusetts, and trained briefly at Phillips Art College, Andover, before gravitating to New York City, where he became close friends with **Frank Stella**. His initial experiments, with wood-cutting, were inspired by **Constantine Brancusi**, then a job on the Pennsylvania Railroad in the 1960s led him to experiment with mass-produced materials. This was a reaction against the gestural aspects of American Abstract Expressionism, intended to focus the viewer's mind on the materials themselves, and he is now best known for his Minimalist sculptures of that period, such as *Equivalents*, a floor piece consisting of 120 bricks stacked in two layers to form a rectangle (Tate Gallery, London). An interest in mathematics and the philosophy of **Laozi** are evident in his work. His *144 Magnesium Square* (1969, Tate Gallery) can be walked on, evidence of his increasing concern with the site itself as sculpture. In the 1970s his work is characterized by the use of flat metal plates enriched with colour, as in *Twelfth Copper Corner* (1975). In the 1980s he returned to working in wood, for example *Bloody Angle* (1985, Stedelijk Museum, Amsterdam).

André, John 1751–80
English soldier

Born in London, he was of French-Swiss descent. In 1774 he joined the army in Canada, and became aide-de-camp to Sir **Henry Clinton**, and adjutant-general. When **Benedict Arnold** obtained the command of West Point in 1780, André was selected to negotiate with him for its betrayal. As he approached the British lines he was captured and handed over to the American military authorities. He was tried as a spy, and hanged at Tappantown.

Andrea da Firenze, *originally* **Andrea Bonaiuti**
fl.c.1343–1377
Italian painter

His most famous work is the monumental fresco cycle in the Spanish Chapel of the Dominican church of S Maria Novella in Florence, painted c.1366–68. These paintings, an elaborate celebration of the Dominican doctrine, form a highly distinctive mural scheme, the whole interior of the building being covered with descriptive scenes painted in a meticulously detailed but severe style. Many panel paintings of varying quality are attributed to him, but his only other documented work is the *Life of St Ranieri*, frescoes in the Camposanto in Pisa, completed in 1377.

Andrea del Sarto See **Sarto, Andrea del**

Andreä, Johann Valentin 1586–1654
German theologian

Born near Tübingen, he was Protestant court-chaplain at Stuttgart, and was long regarded as the founder or restorer of the Rosicrucians. He wrote *Chymische Hochzeit Christiani Rosenkreuz* (1616).

Andreas-Salomé, Lou 1861–1937
German novelist and thinker

Born in Russia, Lou, as she is always called, became a lay analyst after studying with **Sigmund Freud**. Loved by **Nietzsche** and the lover of **Rilke**, she was responsible for releasing much poetry in Rilke, whom she understood better than any other woman in his life. Her *Die Erotik* (1910) is a key text, although it has been ignored by latter-day feminists. Her *Rainer Maria Rilke* (1928) remains a seminal work on the poet. ☐ H F Peters, *My Sister, My Spouse* (1962); L Binion, *Frau Lou* (1968)

Andreev, Leonid Nikolayevich See **Andreyev, Leonid Nikolayevich**

Andreotti, Giulio 1919–
Italian Christian Democrat politician

Born in Rome and educated at the University of Rome he was elected to the first post-war Constituent Assembly in 1945 and to parliament in 1947. He was appointed Minister of the Interior in 1954 and served as Minister of Finance (1955–58), as Minister of the Treasury (1958) and as Minister of Defence (1959–66). Of particular interest to him was the economic development of the poorer southern areas of Italy. He was first appointed Prime Minister in 1972 and served two further terms (1976–79, 1989–92).

Andretti, Mario Gabriele 1940–
US racing driver

Born in Montona, Italy, he emigrated with his family to Nazareth, Pennsylvania, in the USA in 1955 and began his career in stock car and midget car racing, then progressed to the US Auto Club circuit, in which he was champion three times (1965, 1966, 1969). In a Formula One career stretching from 1968 to 1982, he competed in 128 Grand Prix, winning 16. His most successful year was 1978, when he won the racing drivers' world championship. He won the Indianapolis 500 in 1969 and was placed second, after a contested decision, in 1981.

Andrew, St 1st century AD
One of the 12 Apostles of Jesus Christ

He was a fisherman who had previously followed **John the Baptist**. According to tradition he preached the Gospel in Asia Minor and Scythia, and was crucified in Achaia (Greece) by order of the Roman governor. The belief that his cross was X-shaped dates only from the 14th century. He was the brother of Simon Peter (St **Peter**), and is the patron saint of Scotland and of Greece and Russia. His feast day is 30 November. ☐ Ursula Hall, *St Andrew and Scotland* (1994)

Andrew, Agnellus Matthew 1908–87
Roman Catholic bishop and broadcaster

Born near Glasgow, he was ordained in 1932 and engaged in parish work in Manchester until he became assistant to the head of religious broadcasting at the BBC (1955–67). He was then adviser to the Independent Broadcasting Authority (1968–75). A well-known TV commentator for many papal and national events, he was founder and director of the National Catholic Radio and TV Centre in Hatch End, Middlesex (1955–80). Having been made titular Bishop of Numana he became from 1980 external head of the Vatican commission for communication.

Andrew, John Albion 1818–67
US abolitionist politician

Born in Windham, Maine, he was Governor of Massachusetts (1860–66) and mobilized the state during the Civil War.

Andrew, Prince See **York, Duke of**

Andrew, (Christopher) Rob(ert) 1963–
English rugby union player

Born in Richmond, Yorkshire, he is the world record holder, with 22, for international dropped goals (20 for England, 2 for Lions). As England's most capped fly-half he played 69 times between 1985 and 1995 and scored a record 396 points. He made an English record of 30 points against Canada in 1994 when he kicked 12 out of 12 (6 penalties, 6 conversions). He was one of the first to embrace union's professionalism when he left his club Wasps and signed for Sir **John Hall**'s Newcastle Rugby Club. Having retired from international rugby in 1995, he was appointed Newcastle's development director and attracted many leading players to the club.

Andrewes, Lancelot 1555–1626
English prelate and scholar

Born in Barking, Essex, he was educated at Ratcliffe, Merchant Taylors' School, and at Pembroke Hall, Cambridge. He took orders in 1580 and in 1589, through Sir **Francis Walsingham**'s influence, was appointed a prebendary of St Paul's and Master of Pembroke Hall. In 1597 **Elizabeth I** made him a prebendary, and in 1601 Dean of Westminster. He rose still higher under **James VI and I**, and took part in the translation of the Authorized Version of the Bible (1607). He became successively Bishop of Chichester (1605), Ely (1609), and Winchester (1618). A powerful preacher and defender of Anglican doctrines, he is considered one of the most learned theologians of his time. His *Private Prayers* were published posthumously, and his *Works* (11 vols) were published between 1841 and 1854.

Andrews, Anthony 1948–
English actor

Born in North London, the son of a BBC music arranger, he acted in costume dramas such as *The Pallisers* (1974), *The Duchess of Duke Street* (1976–77) and *Upstairs, Downstairs* (1975), before starring as Brian Ash in *Danger U.X.B.* (1979). He became known worldwide in the role of Sebastian Flyte in *Brideshead Revisited* (1981), which won him a BAFTA Best Actor award. Television movies and mini-series followed, including *Mistress of Paradise* (1981), *Ivanhoe* (1982), *The Scarlet Pimpernel* (1983), *Sparkling Cyanide* (1983), *A.D.* (1985), *The Woman He Loved* (1988), *The War Lord* (1991) and *Danielle Steel's Jewels* (1993).

Andrews, Charles Freer 1871–1940
English Anglican missionary to India

Born in Newcastle upon Tyne, the son of a minister of the Catholic Apostolic Church, he graduated from Cambridge and went to India in 1904. Going to South Africa in 1913 to help the oppressed Indian labourers there, he began a lifelong friendship with **Mahatma Gandhi**, and contributed towards the **Smuts-Gandhi** agreement. Back in India he gave up western ways of living and joined **Rabindranath Tagore's** settlement at Santiniketan, intent on living as one of the poor. He recorded his experiences in *What I Owe to Christ* (1932).

Andrews, Eamon 1922–87
Irish broadcaster

Born in Dublin, he was an All-Ireland amateur juvenile middleweight boxing champion. He began sports commentating for Radio Éireann in 1939 and subsequently worked on various programmes for BBC Radio, including *Sports Report* (1950–62). On television he hosted the parlour game *What's My Line?* (1951–63) and *This is Your Life* (1955–87). Active as a chat show host, children's presenter, as well as being a keen businessman, he later returned to *What's My Line?* (1984–87). His books include *This Is My Life* (1963) and *Surprises of Your Life* (1978).

Andrews, Ernest Clayton 1870–1948
Australian geologist

Born in Sydney, he was educated at Sydney University. Specializing in physiography, he studied the evolution of the Pacific Rim coastlines, in particular those of eastern Australia and the western USA, and the glaciers of New Zealand. He also published papers on the flora of these areas, and studied the coral reef formations of Fiji and Tonga. He held many offices in the scientific bodies of the USA, New Zealand and Australia, and was president of the Australasian Association for the Advancement of Science from 1930 to 1932.

Andrews, Frank M(axwell) 1884–1943
US air force officer

Born in Nashville, he trained at West Point, and served in the aviation section of the signal corps in World War I. Between the wars he became the first commander of the general-headquarters air force (1935–39), and helped develop the B-17 bomber. In World War II he was head of the US Caribbean Defense Command (1941–42) and the Middle East Command (1942–43), before succeeding **Dwight D Eisenhower** as commander of the US forces in Europe. He was killed in a plane crash. Andrews Airforce Base in Washington is named after him.

Andrews, Julie, *originally* Julia Elizabeth Wells 1935–
English singer and actress

She was born in Walton-on-Thames, Surrey, into a showbusiness family. Trained as a singer, she made her London debut in the 1947 revue *Starlight Roof*. Radio and stage successes led to a role in the New York production of *The Boyfriend* (1954) and several long-running Broadway musicals, notably *My Fair Lady* (1956) and *Camelot* (1960), as well as the very successful film musicals *Mary Poppins* (1964, Academy Award for Best Actress), and *The Sound of Music* (1965). Voted the world's most popular star, she made strenuous efforts to change her rather prim image by portraying a breast-baring movie-star in *S.O.B.* (1981), and a transvestite in *Victor/Victoria* (1982). Active for some time in television, since 1970 she has appeared almost exclusively in films directed by her second husband, Blake Edwards. A return to Broadway in the stage version of *Victor/Victoria* (1995–97) proved a personal triumph. ▢ Robert Windeler, *Julie Andrews, A Biography* (1970)

Andrews, Roy Chapman 1884–1960
US naturalist and explorer

He was born in Beloit, Wisconsin, and after graduating from Beloit College, he joined the staff of the American Museum of Natural History, New York, later becoming director there (1935–42). He is chiefly remembered as the discoverer of fossil dinosaur eggs and fossil mammals in Mongolia, but also made many valuable contributions to palaeontology, archaeology, botany, zoology, geology and topography. He explored Alaska before World War I, and took part in several expeditions to Central Asia sponsored by the Museum of Natural History. His published works included *Across Mongolian Plains* (1921), *The Ends of the Earth* (1929), *Meet Your Ancestors* (1945), *Heart of Asia* (1951) and *In the Days of the Dinosaur* (1959). ▢ *Under a Lucky Star* (1943)

Andrews, Thomas 1813–85
Irish physical chemist

Born in Belfast, he studied medicine at Edinburgh University, and he practised as a physician in Belfast, where he was Professor of Chemistry at Queen's College (1849–79). He is noted for his discovery of the critical temperature of gases, above which they cannot be liquefied, however great the pressure applied.

Andrews Sisters, The
US vocal harmony trio

LaVerne (1915–67), Maxene (1918–) and Patti (1920–) Andrews were born and raised in Minneapolis, and began to work on the RKO circuit when in their early teens, with the youngest sister Patti singing lead lines, and Maxene and LaVerne singing soprano and contralto harmonies. Their breakthrough record was *Bei Mir Bist Du Schön* (1939), a huge wartime success; others include 'Pistol Packin' Mama' (1943) with **Bing Crosby**, and 'Boogie Woogie Bugle Boy'. They retired as a group in the late 1950s, but Maxene continued to perform into the 1980s. Their records have continued to outsell every female act in history, accounting for nearly 60 million discs worldwide.

Andreyev or Andreev, Leonid Nikolayevich 1871–1919
Russian writer and artist

Born in Oryel, he suffered from poverty and ill health as a student at St Petersburg University, and attempted suicide, before taking to writing and portrait painting. He enjoyed a period of fame after the success of *Zhili-byli* (1901, 'Once Upon a Time'). His best works include *Gubernator* (1906, Eng trans *His Excellency the Governor*, 1921). He is most famous, however, for his terrifyingly effective drama, *Tot, kto poluchaet poshchochiny* (1915, Eng trans, *He Who Gets Slapped*, 1915). He died in exile after fleeing the 1917 Revolution. ▢ L N Afonin, *Leonid Andreyev* (1959)

Andrianov, Nikolai Yefimovich, *nicknamed* Old One-Leg 1952–
Soviet gymnast

Born in Vladimir, he won 15 Olympic medals (seven gold) between 1972 and 1980. In addition, he won 12 world championship medals, including the overall individual title in 1978.

Andrić, Ivo 1892–1975
Serbian author and diplomat and Nobel Prize winner

Born near Travnik (now in Bosnia-Herzegovina), he was interned by the Austrian government as a Yugoslav nationalist during World War I. He later joined the diplomatic service and was minister in Berlin at the outbreak of World War II. His chief works *Na Drini Ćuprija* (1945, Eng trans *The Bridge on the Drina*, 1959) and *Travnička hronika* (1945, Eng trans *Bosnian Story*, 1958), earned him the 1961 Nobel Prize for literature and the nickname 'the Yugoslav

Tolstoy'. His house in Travnik is now a museum. ☐ E C Hawkesworth, *Andrić: a bridge between East and West* (1984)

Andronicus, *called* Cyrrhestes 1st century BC
Greek architect
Born in Cyrrhus, he constructed the Tower of the Winds in Athens, known in the Middle Ages as the Lantern of Demosthenes.

Andronicus I Comnenus c.1122–1185
Byzantine emperor
Born in Constantinople (Istanbul), the grandson of Alexius I Comnenus, he acted treasonably and created scandal until the death of Manuel (1182), when he became first guardian, then colleague, of the young Emperor Alexius II. Emperor from 1183, he massacred the westerners in Constantinople, and caused first the dowager empress to be strangled, then Alexius himself, and married his youthful widow. His reign was vigorous, and restored prosperity to the provinces, but tyranny and murder were its characteristics in the capital, leading to a popular uprising in which he was overthrown and killed.

Andronicus II Palaeologus 1260–1332
Byzantine emperor
He was born in Constantinople (Istanbul), and during his reign (1282–1328), he withdrew from the negotiations for the union of the Greek and Roman communions, and restored the Greek ritual in full. An intellectual theologian rather than a warrior, he presided over the golden age of the Mount Athos monasteries. The empire suffered much from Catalan mercenaries, hired for the wars with the Turks, and declined to the status of a minor state.

Andronicus III Palaeologus 1296–1341
Byzantine Emperor
Born in Constantinople (Istanbul), the grandson of Andronicus II Palaeologus, he was excluded from the succession for the accidental murder of his brother, but compelled his grandfather to make him his colleague in the empire and then to abdicate (1328). During his reign (1328–41), which saw almost constant warfare, the Turks occupied the southern shores of the Bosphorus, and the Serbians conquered Bulgaria, Epirus and Macedonia. He relied on Cantacuzenus, a future emperor, to reform the law courts and rebuild the imperial navy.

Andronicus of Rhodes fl.70–50BC
Greek Aristotelian philosopher
He lived in Rome in Cicero's time and edited the writings of Aristotle.

Andronicus, Livius See Livius Andronicus

Andropov, Yuri 1914–84
Soviet politician
Born in the village of Nagutskoye in Stavropol province of the North Caucasus region of southern Russia, the son of a railway official, he trained as a water transport engineer and began work in the shipyards of the upper Volga, at Rybinsk (renamed Andropov from 1984 to 1991), in 1930. Here he became politically active and in 1940 was given the task of 'sovietizing' the newly ceded Karelian peninsula, but, within a year, after its occupation by Germany, he was engaged in organizing a partisan resistance movement. After World War II he made rapid progress, being promoted to the post of Second Party Secretary in Karelia, and was then brought to Moscow to work for the Communist Party central committee. He was ambassador in Budapest, 1954–57, where he came to the notice of the strict ideologist, Mikhail Suslov, for his part in crushing the Hungarian uprising of 1956. He was appointed head of the KGB (1967–82) and, in 1973, became a full member of the politburo. His firm handling of dissident movements while he was at the KGB enhanced his reputation, enabling him to be chosen as General Secretary Leonid Brezhnev's successor in 1973. In this post he proved to be more radical and reformist than his previous record would have suggested, but he died after less than 15 months in office. During that time he had successfully groomed a group of potential successors, one of whom was Mikhail Gorbachev. ☐ Zhores Medvedev, *Andropov* (1983)

Andros, Sir Edmund 1637–1714
British colonial official
Born in London to an aristocratic family, he began life as a royal page and did military service in the West Indies. He became British colonial Governor of New York (1674–81), then was named Governor (1686) of the Dominion of New England. He was resented because of his effete manner, enforcement of unpopular laws, and efforts to impose Anglicanism on Congregational Boston, and in 1689 he was deposed by rebellious Boston colonists, including Cotton Mather, and sent to England. He later returned to become Governor of Virginia (1692–97).

Andrzejewski, Jerzy 1909–83
Polish novelist
He began as a somewhat right-wing Catholic writer in the tradition of François Mauriac. He became internationally famous with *Popiol i diament* (1948, Eng trans *Ashes and Diamonds*, 1968), memorably filmed by Andrzej Wajda (1958). An analysis of an unnamed Polish town and its sufferings under the Nazis, it is likely to be judged his finest novel. Having tried to accommodate himself to the communist regime as a social realist, he became critical of the regime in modernist novels such as *Ciemnósci kryja ziemie* (1957, Eng trans *The Inquisitors*, 1960).

Aneurin or Aneirin fl.6th–7th century
Ancient British poet
The creator of the oldest surviving poetry composed in Scotland, his principal work, *Y Gododdin*, celebrates the British heroes who were annihilated by the Saxons in the bloody Battle of Cattraeth (Catterick, Yorkshire) c.600. It contains one of the earliest mentions of King Arthur. The poem's language, metrical forms and general technique suggest a long tradition of praise poetry in the Brythonic language, the form of primitive Welsh which was current in Cumbria and southern Scotland. ☐ S Turner, *A Vindication of the Genuineness of the Ancient British Poems of Aneurin, etc* (1803)

Anfinsen, Christian B(oehmer) 1916–95
US biochemist and Nobel Prize winner
Born in Monessen, Pennsylvania, he was educated at Harvard, and from 1939 to 1944 worked at the Carlsberg Laboratory, a leading institute of protein chemistry. During 1947–48 he worked with Hugo Theorell at the Medical Nobel Institute before moving to the National Institutes of Health in Bethesda, Maryland (1950–82). He applied enzymic and chemical hydrolysis in the preliminary fragmentation of the protein insulin, eventually deducing the structure of the amino acids of the enzyme ribonuclease (RNA). The final primary sequence of ribonuclease reflected the combined research of several workers including Stanford Moore and William Stein, with whom he shared the Nobel Prize for chemistry in 1972. From 1955 Anfinsen studied the secondary and tertiary structures of ribonuclease. He related his observations to molecular biology and evolution in *The Molecular Basis of Evolution* (1959). From 1958 he was a co-editor of the important review series *Advances in Protein Chemistry* and was the author of some 200 original scientific articles.

Angas, George Fife 1789–1879
English shipowner

Born in Newcastle upon Tyne, he is regarded as a founder of South Australia. He was appointed commissioner for the formation of the colony in 1834, and emigrated to Adelaide in 1851.

Angela of Brescia See **Angela Merici, St**

Angela Merici, St, *also called* Angela of Brescia
1474–1540
Italian founder
Born in Desenzano, near Lake Garda, she became a Franciscan tertiary after her husband died, founding girls' schools and caring for the sick. During a pilgrimage to the Holy Land (1524–25) she became blind for a while. She declined a papal invitation (1525) to work in Rome, but founded the Ursulines, the oldest teaching order of women in the Catholic Church, in Brescia in 1535. The order was, in her lifetime, an uncloistered and informal order dedicated to Christian education in their own homes, and confirmed a vision received 29 years earlier. She was canonized in 1807 and her feast day is 1 June.

Angeles, Victoria de los See **de los Angeles, Victoria**

Angelico, Fra, *real name* Guido di Pietro, *monastic name* Giovanni da Fiesole c.1387–1455
Italian painter
Born in Vicchio, Tuscany, as a young man he entered the Dominican monastery of San Domenico at Fiesole, near Florence, making his vows in 1408. The community was obliged to leave Fiesole (1409), and some time after its return in 1418 Fra Angelico began to paint. In 1436 he was transferred to Florence, where he worked for **Cosimo de' Medici**, and in 1445 he was summoned by the pope to Rome where he worked until his death. His most important frescoes are in the Florentine convent of San Marco, which is now a museum. These 'aids to contemplation' are characterized by pale colours, crisp delineation of form, and the use of local landscape as background. His altarpiece there is an early example of the *sacra conversazione*. In 1447 he began a Last Judgment at Orvieto, which was finished by **Luca Signorelli**. In Rome only the frescoes in the chapel of Nicholas V survive. Of his easel pictures, a *Coronation of the Virgin* is held by the Louvre, Paris, and a *Glory* by the London National Gallery, both of which were originally at Fiesole. There are other notable examples in the Uffizi, Florence.

Angélique, Mère See **Arnauld, Marie-Angélique**

Angell, Sir Norman, *originally* Ralph Norman Angell Lane 1872–1967
English writer, pacifist and Nobel Prize winner
Born in Holbeach, Lincolnshire, he wrote *The Great Illusion* (1910) and *The Great Illusion 1933* (1933) to prove the economic futility of war even for the victors. He won the Nobel Peace Prize in 1933. He was a Labour MP from 1929 until 1931. 📖 Albert Marrin, *Sir Norman Angell* (1979)

Angelou, Maya 1928–
US writer
She was born in St Louis, Missouri, and after the breakup of her parents' marriage, she and her brother lived with their grandmother in Stamps, Arkansas. She was raped by her mother's boyfriend when she was eight and for the next five years was mute. In her teens she moved to California to live with her mother, and at 16 gave birth to her son, Guy. She has had a variety of occupations in what she describes as 'a roller-coaster life'. In her twenties she toured Europe and Africa in the musical *Porgy and Bess*. In New York she joined the Harlem Writers Guild and continued to earn her living singing in night-clubs and performing in **Jean Genet**'s *The Blacks*. In the 1960s she was involved in Black struggles and then spent several years in Ghana as editor of *African Review*. Her multi-volume autobiography, commencing with *I Know Why the Caged Bird Sings* (1970), is imbued with optimism, humour and homespun philosophy, and was a critical and popular success. She has published several volumes of verse, including *And Still I Rise* (1978), and is the Reynolds Professor of American Studies at Wake Forest University in North Carolina. In 1993 she published a collection of personal reflections, *Wouldn't take nothing for my journey now*, and in the same year she read her poem 'On the Pulse of Morning' at President **Clinton**'s inauguration.

Angerstein, John Julius 1735–1823
English financier and underwriter
Of Russian origin, his collection of 38 paintings bought by the nation in 1824 for £57,000, formed the nucleus of the National Gallery, London.

Angerville, Richard See **Aungerville, Richard**

Anglesey, Henry William Paget, 1st Marquis of 1768–1854
English field marshal
Born in London, he sat in parliament at various times between 1790 and 1810, in 1812 succeeding his father as Earl of Uxbridge. He served in the army in Flanders (1794), Holland (1799), and the Peninsular War (1808), and for his services as commander of the British cavalry at the Battle of Waterloo (1815), where he lost a leg, he was made Marquis of Anglesey (1815). He served as Lord Lieutenant of Ireland (1828–29, 1830–33), where he advocated Catholic emancipation, but lost his popularity through coercive measures against **Daniel O'Connell**. Appointed field marshal in 1846, he was Master General of the Ordnance (1846–52) and is credited with establishing Ireland's board of education.

Angliss, Sir William Charles 1865–1957
Australian businessman
Born in Dudley, Worcestershire, England, he entered the butchering trade when he was young. He emigrated to Australia in 1884, eventually opening a butcher's shop in Melbourne. From this small beginning grew a chain of meat stores across the country and he was a pioneer of the Australian meat exporting industry. In 1934, when the company was sold to the Vestey family, it had become the largest meat exporter in Australia. Sir William retained many other industrial and business interests, was a member of the Legislative Council of Victoria for 40 years, and was knighted in 1939. On his death he left £1 million to charity.

Angoulême, Louis Antoine de Bourbon, Duc d' 1775–1844
French soldier and aristocrat
Born at Versailles, the eldest son of **Charles X** of France, he fled from France with his father after the Revolution of 1789, and lived in various places, including Holyroodhouse in Edinburgh. In 1799 he married his cousin, Marie Thérèse (1778–1851), only daughter of **Louis XVI**. After the Restoration (1814), he made an unsuccessful effort, as lieutenant-general of France, to oppose **Napoleon I** on his return from Elba (1815). In 1823 he led the French army of invasion into Spain to restore **Ferdinand VII** to his throne. After the July revolution (1830), he renounced his claim to the throne and accompanied his father into exile.

Ångström, Anders Jonas 1814–74
Swedish physicist
Born in Lödgö, he became Professor of Physics at the University of Uppsala in 1858, and from 1867 he was secretary to the Royal Society at Uppsala. He wrote on heat, magnetism, and especially optics; the angstrom unit, for measuring wavelengths of light, is named after him. He studied the solar spectrum, measured the wavelengths of

around 1,000 **Fraunhofer** lines, and implied that he believed hydrogen to be present in the Sun. His son, Knut J Ångström (1857–1910), was also a noted Uppsala physicist, and made important studies of solar radiation.

Aniello, Tommaso See **Masaniello**
Ann, Mother See **Lee, Ann**

Anna Comnena 1083–1148
Byzantine princess
The daughter of Emperor **Alexius I Comnenus**, she tried in vain to secure the imperial crown, and failed in her attempt to overthrow or poison her brother (1118). Disappointed and ashamed, she withdrew from the court, and sought solace in literature. On the death of her husband (1137), she wrote a life of her father, the *Alexiad*, which contains an account of the First Crusade.

Anna Ivanovna 1693–1740
Empress of Russia
Born in Moscow, she was the younger daughter of Ivan V and niece of **Peter I, the Great**. In 1710 she married the Duke of Courland, who died the following year. After the early death of **Peter II** she was elected to the throne by the Supreme Privy Council (1730), with conditions that severely limited her authority. Uninterested in government, she abolished the council and ruled as an autocrat with her German favourite, **Ernst Johann Biron**, who assumed the title of Duke of Courland and became the real power behind the throne. They established a reign of terror and financial extortion, in which 20,000 people are said to have been banished to Siberia. Abroad Russia won control of Poland (1733–35) but only gained Azov in an expensive war against Turkey (1735–39).

Annan, James Craig 1864–1946
Scottish photographer
The son of **Thomas Annan**, he studied chemistry and natural philosophy, joined the family firm of T and R Annan, which he ran until his death, and became a member of the artistic community in Glasgow in the 1890s. He went to Vienna and studied the art of photogravure, a photographic etching process, with its inventor, **Karl Klic**, and was to become a master of this medium. Among his friends was **David Young Cameron**; together they travelled to the Low Countries (1892) and Italy (1894), producing work complementary in character and subject. Annan gained an international reputation during his lifetime, exhibiting in Europe and the USA. He exhibited with the pictorialist photographers of the 'Linked Ring Brotherhood', who promoted photography as Art. The US photographer **Alfred Stieglitz** admired his work and published examples in his influential magazine *Camera Work* (1903–17).

Annan, Thomas 1829–87
Scottish photographer
He was born in Fife, the son of a farmer and flax-spinner. After apprenticeship as a lithographer, he jointly set up a photographic studio in 1855 and opened his own printing works in 1859. Much encouraged and influenced by **David Octavius Hill**, Annan was known in his own day for the accurate reproduction of paintings, including Hill's enormous *Signing of the Deed of Demission*.... He took a particular interest in the question of permanence and purchased the Scottish rights to the carbon process in 1866 and the British rights to Karl Klic's photogravure process in the 1880s. In the late 1850s and 1860s, he took a number of lyrical landscape photographs. These have been overshadowed by his series *The Old Closes and Streets of Glasgow* (1868–71), a curiously moving group of photographs of the derelict areas condemned to destruction by the Glasgow Improvement Act of 1866. His son was the photographer **James Craig Annan**.

Annas 1st century AD
Israeli high priest
He was appointed in AD6 and deposed by the Romans in AD15, but was still described later by this title in the New Testament. He apparently questioned **Jesus** after his arrest (John 18) and Peter after his detention (Acts 4). His other activities are described in the works of **Flavius Josephus**.

Anne, St 50BC–AD50
Mother of the Virgin Mary
She is first mentioned in the *Protevangelium* of James, in the 2nd century. She is said to have been born in Nazareth or in Bethlehem, and to have lived with her husband Joachim from the age of 20. Bemoaning her barrenness, and her loneliness, for Joachim had retreated into the wilderness to pray about his apparent sterility, she promised God that any child of theirs would be dedicated to his service. The couple were reconciled and **Mary** was born. Later tradition tells of Joachim's death and Anne's remarriages, which led to her being named as the grandmother not only of **Jesus Christ**, but also of several of the Apostles. She is the patron saint of Brittany and of Canada, and her feast day is 26 July.

Anne, Queen See panel p63

Anne, Princess, *in full* Anne Elizabeth Alice Louise, *also called* the Princess Royal 1950–
British princess
The only daughter of Queen **Elizabeth II** of Great Britain and Northern Ireland, and Prince **Philip**, she married (1973) Lieutenant (now Captain) **Mark Phillips** of the Queen's Dragoon Guards. They have two children: Peter Mark Andrew (1977–) and Zara Anne Elizabeth (1981–). The couple separated in 1989 and divorced in 1992. In December 1992 Anne married Commander Timothy Laurence. An accomplished horsewoman, Anne has ridden in the British equestrian team, and was European cross-country champion (1972). She is a keen supporter of charities and overseas relief work, and as president of Save the Children Fund she has travelled widely promoting its activities. 📖 Brian Hoey, *Anne: The Private Princess Revealed (1997)*

Anne Boleyn 1501–36
English queen
The daughter of Sir Thomas Boleyn and Elizabeth Howard, daughter of the Duke of Norfolk, she was at the French court from 1519 to 1521. On her return her suitors included Henry Percy, the heir to the Earl of Northumberland, and King **Henry VIII**, who began to shower favours upon her father, having already had an affair with her sister. Anne did not apparently respond until negotiations for Henry's divorce from **Catherine of Aragon** began (1527), but, as these dragged on, their association became more open and they were secretly married in January 1533. **Thomas Cranmer** soon declared the marriage legal (May 1533) and Anne was crowned with great splendour in Westminster Hall on Whitsunday. Within three months Henry's passion had cooled. It was not revived by the birth (September 1533) of a princess (later **Elizabeth I**), still less by that of a stillborn son (1536). On May Day that year the King rode off abruptly from a tournament held at Greenwich, leaving Anne behind, and the next day she was arrested and taken to the Tower of London. A secret commission investigated charges of Anne's supposed adultery with her brother, Lord Rochford, and four others. Her uncle, **Thomas Howard**, 3rd Duke of Norfolk, presided at her trial, and pronounced her guilty of treason. She was beheaded on Tower Green on 19 May. Eleven days later Henry was married to **Jane Seymour**. Anne actively favoured religious

Anne 1665–1714
Queen of Great Britain and Ireland from 1702

Anne was born at St James's Palace in London, the second daughter of the Duke of York (later **James VII and II**) and his first wife, Anne Hyde. She was the younger sister of **Mary II** (wife of **William III**). Although her father became a Catholic and married the Catholic **Mary of Modena** in 1773, Anne was brought up a staunch Protestant. In 1683 she married Prince George of Denmark (1653–1708); she bore him 17 children, only one of whom survived infancy but died at the age of 12.

For much of her life she was greatly influenced by her close friend and confidante, **Sarah Churchill**, the future Duchess of Marlborough. During her father's reign, Anne took no part in politics. When he was overthrown in the Glorious Revolution of 1688, she supported the accession of her sister Mary and her brother-in-law William, and was placed in the succession; but after quarrelling with Mary she was drawn by the Marlboroughs into Jacobite intrigues for the restoration of her father or to secure the succession of his son, **James Stuart**, the Old Pretender. In 1701, however, after the death of her own son, she signed the Act of Settlement designating the Hanoverian descendants of **James VI and I** as her successors, and in 1702 she succeeded William III on the throne.

Queen Anne's reign was marked by a concern for national unity under the Crown, which was achieved with the union of the parliaments of Scotland and England in 1707. The other major event was the War of the Spanish Succession (1701–13) with Marlborough's victories over the French at Blenheim, (1704), Ramillies (1706), Oudenarde (1708) and Malplaquet (1709). Anne finally broke with the Marlboroughs in 1710–11, when Sarah was supplanted by a new favourite, Sarah's cousin, Mrs **Abigail Masham**, and the Whigs were replaced by a Tory administration led by **Robert Harley**, 1st Earl of Oxford, and Lord **Bolingbroke**. Anne was the last Stuart monarch, and on her death in August 1714, she was succeeded by **George I**.

📖 Edward Gregg, *Queen Anne* (1984); David B Green, *Queen Anne* (1970).

Notable figures of Queen Anne's reign: John Churchill, 1st Duke of **Marlborough**; Sir **George Rooke**, English admiral who captured Gibraltar in 1704; Sir **Cloudesley Shovel**, who rose to the rank of admiral from being a cabin boy; the scientist Sir **Isaac Newton**; and the literary figures **Alexander Pope**, Jonathan Swift and Joseph Addison.

'I have changed my Ministers but I have not changed my measures. I am still for moderation, and I will govern by it.' From an address to her new Tory administration, January 1711.

---

reformers during the 1530s and used her political influence to advance her family and friends. 📖 Marie Louise Bruce, *Anne Boleyn* (1972)

Anne of Austria 1601–66
Queen of France
Born in Valladolid, Spain, she was the eldest daughter of **Philip III** of Spain and wife of **Louis XIII** of France, whom she married in 1615. The marriage was unhappy, and much of it was spent in virtual separation, due to the influence of the king's Chief Minister Cardinal **Richelieu**, who aimed to restrict her influence. In 1638, however, they had their first son, Louis, who succeeded his father (1643) as **Louis XIV**. Anne was appointed regent (1643–51), and with Richelieu having died in 1642 she wielded power with her favourite, Cardinal **Mazarin**, whom she may have secretly married, as Prime Minister. They ruled France during the Frondes, and after Louis technically came of age (1651) she retired to the convent of Val de Grâce, and Louis XIV became absolute monarch. 📖 Ruth Kleinman, *Anne of Austria* (1986)

Anne of Bohemia 1366–94
Queen of England
The daughter of the Emperor **Charles IV**, she married **Richard II** as his first wife in 1382. Richard was devoted to her but the expenses of her household soured relations between king and parliament. She died of the plague, childless.

Anne of Brittany 1476–1514
Duchess of Brittany and twice Queen of France
The daughter of Duke Francis II of Brittany, she succeeded her father in 1488. She struggled to maintain Breton independence, but was forced to marry **Charles VIII** of France (1491), thus uniting Brittany with the French Crown. After his death, she married his successor, **Louis XII** in 1499. She was also a noted patron of the arts.

Anne of Cleves 1515–57
German princess and Queen of England
She was the daughter of John, Duke of Cleves, a noted champion of Protestantism in Germany. Plain and ill-educated, she was selected for purely political reasons after the death of **Jane Seymour**, and was married in 1540 to **Henry VIII**, as his fourth wife. Henry, who claimed to have been deluded by the portrait by **Hans Holbein**, the Younger, had the marriage annulled by parliament six months later. She was granted a pension and lived the rest of her life quietly in England. If Henry privately referred to her as the 'Flanders mare', he was publicly courteous towards her. 📖 Julia Watson, *Anne of Cleves* (1972)

Anne of Denmark 1574–1619
Danish princess, and Queen of Scotland and England
The daughter of King **Frederik II** of Denmark, she married (1589) **James VI** of Scotland, the future **James I** of England. A convert to Roman Catholicism, she was empty-headed, high-spirited and extravagant, but encouraged the arts and architecture, and appeared in dramatic roles in court masques by **Ben Jonson**. In her later years she lived apart from her husband.

Annesley, James 1715–60
Irish claimant to the earldom of Anglesea
Born in Dunmaine, County Wexford, he was the alleged son of Mary Sheffield, Lady Altham. At the instance of his uncle, he was allegedly kidnapped and shipped to the American plantations (1728) and was reported sold as a slave. His uncle later became Earl of Anglesea. James returned to Ireland (1741) and in 1744 his uncle was tried and convicted for assaulting James the previous year. But, because of lack of funds, he was unable to take his probably valid claim to the House of Lords. Annesley was the inspiration for **R L Stevenson's** *Kidnapped*.

Annigoni, Pietro 1910–88
Italian painter
Born in Milan, he worked in England during the 1950s, and held a London exhibition in 1954. He was one of the few 20th-century artists to put into practice the technical methods of the old masters, and his most usual medium was tempera, although there are frescoes by him in the Convent of St Mark in Florence (1937). His Renaissance manner is shown at its best in his portraits, for example of Queen **Elizabeth II** (1955, 1970) and President **Kennedy** (1961). 📖 *An Artist's Life* (1977)

Anning, Mary 1799–1847
English fossil collector

Born in Lyme Regis, Dorset, she was the daughter of a carpenter and vendor of fossil specimens who died in 1810, leaving her to make her own living. In 1811 she discovered in a local cliff the fossil skeleton of an ichthyosaur, now in the Natural History Museum, London. She also discovered the first plesiosaur (1821) and the first pterodactyl, *Dimorphodon* (1828). She did much to advance knowledge by her diligence and aptitude in collecting specimens.

Anno, Mitsumas 1926–
Japanese children's author and illustrator

Born in Tsuwano, he is renowned for his visual puzzles, and his best work can be seen in *Topsy-Turvies: Pictures to Stretch the Imagination* (1970), *Dr Anno's Magical Midnight Circus* (1972) and *Anno's Alphabet: An Adventure in Imagination* (1975).

Annunzio, Gabriele d' See D'Annunzio, Gabriele

Anouilh, Jean 1910–87
French dramatist

He was born in Bordeaux, of French and Basque parentage, and after studying law in Paris began his career as a copywriter and as a gag-man in films. His first play, *L'Hermine* (1931, Eng trans *The Ermine*, 1955), was not a success, but his steady output soon earned him recognition. He was influenced by the neoclassical fashion inspired by **Jean Giraudoux**, but his very personal approach to the re-interpretation of Greek myths was less poetic, and more in tune with the contemporary taste for artifice and stylization. Among his many successful plays are *Antigone* (1946, prod in English, New York 1946, London 1949), *Médée* (1946, Eng trans *Medea*, 1956), *L'Alouette* (1953, Eng trans *The Lark*, 1955), *Becket* (1959, first performed in London, 1961), *Cher Antoine* (1969, Eng trans *Dear Antoine*, 1971), *L'Arrestation* (1974, Eng trans *The Arrest*, 1974) and *La Culotte* (1978, 'The Breeches'). ⬚ A D Fazia, *Jean Anouilh* (1972); J Harvey, *Jean Anouilh: a study in theatrics* (1964)

Anquotil, Jacques 1934–87
French racing cyclist

Born in Normandy, he was the foremost of the second wave of French cyclists to emerge after World War II. He won the Tour de France five times, including four successes in a row (1961–64). Excelling in time-trial stages, he could make ferocious attacks, or suddenly distance the field on a conventional stretch of road. He won the Tours of France and Spain in 1963 and those of France and Italy the following year. He retired in 1969.

Anschütz, Ottomar 1846–1907
German photographer

Born in Yugoslavia, he was a pioneer of instant photography. He also made an early series of pictures of moving animals and people, so making a substantial contribution to the invention of the cinematograph.

Anselm, St 1033–1109
Italian theologian and philosopher

He was born near Aosta, Piedmont. He left Italy in 1056, and in 1078 he became abbot of the Abbey of Bec, in Normandy, then was appointed Archbishop of Canterbury in 1093. Frequently in conflict over Church rights, first with **William II** (William Rufus), then with **Henry I**, his resoluteness led to his being exiled by both kings, but in 1107 he threatened excommunication, and a compromise was reached. A follower of **Augustine**, Anselm was a major figure in early scholastic philosophy, remembered especially for his theory of atonement and his ontological proof for the existence of God. He defined God as 'something than which nothing greater can be conceived'. Since anything that exists in reality is by nature greater than anything that exists only in the mind, God must exist in reality, for otherwise he would not be 'the greatest conceivable being'. He was possibly canonized in 1163 and his feast day is 21 April.

Ansermet, Ernest Alexandre 1883–1969
Swiss conductor and musical theorist

Born in Vevey, he read physics and mathematics at Lausanne University, and studied music privately. He gave up teaching mathematics in 1910 to devote his time to music. He was conductor of the Montreux Kursaal in 1912 and of **Sergei Diaghilev's** Ballets Russes (1915–23). In 1918 he founded the Orchestre de la Suisse Romande, whose conductor he remained till 1967. Known for his interpretations of modern French and Russian composers, his compositions include a symphonic poem *Feuilles de printemps*, piano pieces and songs.

Ansett, Sir Reginald Myles 1909–81
Australian businessman

Born in Inglewood, Victoria, the son of a garage proprietor, he was educated at Inglewood state school and Swinburne Technical College, and he started a local road passenger service with a secondhand car. When new legislation hindered expansion of this he opened a regular air service to Melbourne in 1936 becoming a pioneer of passenger flight. Stiff postwar competition brought about diversification, but in 1957 Ansett Transport Industries took over one rival, ANA (Australian National Airways), thus forming the largest private transport system in the southern hemisphere, with a country-wide network of air and coach services. Through pressure from Ansett, the Australian Federal Government was forced to introduce its 'two airlines' policy and give him parity with his rival, the state-owned TAA (Trans Australian Airlines). In 1996 Ansett's group became partly owned by Air New Zealand.

Anskar or Ansgar, St, German St Scharies, known as the Apostle of the North 801–65
Frankish prelate

Born in Picardy, he became a Benedictine monk. In 826 he was sent to preach the gospel in Denmark, but was soon driven out. In 829 he survived a dangerous seavoyage to Birka, the chief mart in Sweden, and was allowed to build the first church in Sweden there. He was consecrated Archbishop of the newly founded archdiocese of Hamburg in 831, and named as papal legate to all the northern peoples. In 845 the Danes attacked Hamburg and burned it to the ground, and Anskar narrowly escaped death. He returned to Scandinavia in 849, and built a church at Hedeby, in Denmark, and at neighbouring Ribe. After his death, however, despite all his missionary work, Scandinavia lapsed into paganism for a century or more. He is the patron saint of Scandinavia, and his feast day is 3 February.

Anson, George Anson, Baron 1697–1762
English naval commander

Born in Shugborough Park, Staffordshire, he joined the navy in 1712, and was made a captain in 1724. In 1739, on the outbreak of war with Spain (the War of Jenkins' Ear, 1739–48), he received the command of a Pacific squadron of six vessels, and sailed from England in 1740. With one ship and less than 200 men, but with £500,000 of Spanish treasure, he returned to Spithead in 1744, having circumnavigated the globe. He defeated the French off Cape Finisterre (1747), and captured £300,000, and was made First Lord of the Admiralty (1751). In 1761 he was appointed Admiral of the Fleet. He wrote *Voyage Round the World* (1748).

Anson-Dyer, Ernest See **Dyer, Anson**

Anstey, Christopher 1724–1805
English writer
Born in Brinkley, Cambridgeshire, he was educated at Eton and King's College, Cambridge, of which he was a Fellow (1745–54). In 1766 he wrote the *New Bath Guide*, an epistolary novel in verse, setting out the exploits of Squire Blunderhead and his family, which achieved great popularity. 📖 W C Powell, *Christopher Anstey: Bath Laureate* (1944)

Anstey, F, *pseudonym of* **Thomas Anstey Guthrie**
1856–1934
English writer
Born in London, he studied at Trinity Hall, Cambridge, and in 1880 was called to the Bar. A whimsical humorist, he wrote *Vice Versa* (1882), *The Tinted Venus* (1885), *The Brass Bottle* (1900), and many other novels and dialogues. He was on the staff of *Punch* from 1887 to 1930. 📖 M J Turner, *A Bibliography of the Writings of F. Anstey, T.A. Guthrie, etc* (1931)

Antalcidas 4th century BC
Spartan politician and naval commander
He is chiefly known by the treaty concluded by him with Persia at the close of the Corinthian War in 386BC. As a result of this treaty Asia Minor accepted the overlordship of Persia, while various other Greek cities had their independence confirmed.

Antar, *properly* **I'Antarah Ibn Shaddad Al-'Absi**
6th century
Arab poet and warrior
He was born of a Bedouin chieftain and a black slave in the desert near Medina, Arabia. The author of one of the seven Golden Odes of Arabic literature, and the subject of the 10th-century *Romance of Antar*, he is regarded as the model of Bedouin heroism and chivalry. 📖 V E Menil, *Disputatio philologica de Antar ejusque poemate arabico Moallakah* (1814)

Antenor 6th century BC
Greek sculptor
He worked in Athens, and is known to have executed bronze statues of *Harmodius* and *Aristogiton*, and a majestic marble of *Kore* from the Acropolis (now in the Acropolis Museum).

Anthony of Padua See **Antony of Padua, St**

Anthony, C L See **Smith, Dodie**

Anthony, Susan B(rownell) 1820–1906
US social reformer and women's suffrage leader
Born in Adams, Massachusetts, she attended schools in Battensville, New York and Philadelphia. Her feminist activities began at 17 when she campaigned for equal pay for women teachers, and she was also an early supporter of the temperance and antislavery movements, founding the Woman's State Temperance Society of New York (1852). In 1869 she founded the National American Woman Suffrage Association with **Elizabeth Stanton**. She organized the 1888 International Council of Women and the 1904 International Woman Suffrage Alliance in Berlin, and with Stanton and **Matilda Joslyn Gage** produced the four-volume *History of Woman Suffrage* (1881–1902). In 1978, in recognition of her services to the cause of worldwide sexual equality, her face was depicted on the silver dollar, the first woman to appear on US currency. 📖 Kathleen Barry, *Susan B Anthony: a biography of a singular feminist* (1988)

Antigonus, *also called* **Monophthalmos ('the one-eyed')** d.301BC
Macedonian general
He was one of the generals of **Alexander the Great**. After Alexander's death, he received the provinces of Phrygia Major, Lycia and Pamphylia. On the regent Antipater's death in 319BC, aiming to rule all Asia, he waged incessant wars against the other generals, making himself master of all Asia Minor and Syria. In 306 he assumed the title of king together with his son Demetrius Poliorcetes, but was defeated and slain by **Lysimachus** and his son, **Cassander**, and **Seleucus I** at Ipsus in Phrygia. 📖 C Wehrli, *Antigone et Demetrios* (1968)

Antigonus II Gonatas c.319–239BC
King of Macedonia
He succeeded to the throne in 276BC, seven years after the death of his father, Demetrius Poliorcetes. **Pyrrhus of Epirus** overran Macedonia in 274, but Antigonus soon recovered his kingdom, and consolidated it despite incessant wars. Personally unostentatious, he was strict in observing his kingly duties. 📖 W W Tarn, *Antigonus Gonatas* (1913)

Antill, John Henry 1904–86
Australian composer
Born in Ashfield, New South Wales, he sang in the choir of St Andrew's Cathedral, Sydney, but was trained as a mechanical draughtsman and apprenticed on the railway. Entering the New South Wales Conservatorium of Music at the age of 21, he studied composition with **Alfred Hill**, becoming a member of the Conservatorium orchestra and later of the ABC (now Sydney) Symphony Orchestra. He worked for the Australian Broadcasting Commission where he became Federal Music Editor. His major work, the ballet *Corroboree* (1946), blends Aboriginal and western themes. The suite was premiered in 1944 and the ballet itself in 1950. His compositions include operas and choral works, ballet suites and a symphony.

Antinous d.130AD
Bithynian youth of matchless beauty
A native of Claudiopolis, he was a favourite of the Emperor **Hadrian**, and his companion on all his journeys. He was drowned in the Nile, near Besa, perhaps through suicide. The emperor founded the city of Antinopolis on the banks of the Nile in his memory, and enrolled him among the gods.

Antiochus I *called* **Soter** c.323–c.261BC
Seleucid King of Syria
He was the son of **Seleucus I**, one of **Alexander the Great's** generals, whose murder (280BC) gave him the whole Syrian Empire, but left him too weak to assert his right to Macedonia. He gained the name of Soter ('Saviour') for a victory over the Gauls (275BC).

Antiochus II *called* **Theos ('God')** c.286–246BC
Seleucid King of Syria
The son and successor (261BC) of **Antiochus I**, he married **Berenice Syra**, daughter of **Ptolemy II**, exiling his first wife, Laodice, and her children. On his death there followed a struggle between the rival queens; Berenice and her son were murdered and Laodice's son, **Seleucus II**, succeeded.

Antiochus III *called* **the Great** 242–187BC
Seleucid King of Syria
The grandson of **Antiochus II**, he succeeded his brother in 223BC. He waged war against **Ptolemy IV, Philopator**, obtained Palestine and Coele-Syria (198), and married his daughter Cleopatra to the young King **Ptolemy V** of Egypt, which became almost a Seleucid protectorate. He afterwards became involved in war with the Romans, but refused to invade Italy at **Hannibal's** request. He entered Greece, but was defeated at Thermopylae (191), and by **Scipio the Elder** at Magnesia (190/189). Peace was granted him only on condition of his yielding all his dominions

west of Mount Taurus, and paying a heavy tribute. To raise the money, he attacked a rich temple in Elymais, when the people rose against him, and killed him. ◻ Edwin Robert Bevan, *The House of Seleucus* (2 vols, 1902)

Antiochus IV, *called* Epiphanes ('God Manifest') c.215–163BC
Seleucid King of Syria

The son of **Antiochus III**, he succeeded his brother (175BC), fought against Egypt and conquered a great part of it. He twice took Jerusalem, where his attempt to stamp out Judaism and establish the worship of Greek gods provoked the Jews to a successful insurrection under Mattathias and his sons, the **Maccabees**. Eccentric and munificent, he encouraged the foundation of Greek cities, especially in the East.

Antipater d.4BC
Judean prince

He was a son of **Herod, the Great** by his first wife. He conspired against his half-brothers and had them executed, then plotted against his father and was himself executed five days before Herod died.

Antiphon 5th century BC
Greek philosopher and Sophist

Nothing is known of his life or even his identity but he is generally distinguished from Antiphon the orator. He is important as the author of two works, *On Truth* and *On Concord*, which survive in fragmentary form and deal with themes characteristic of the Sophistic movement such as the relation of 'nature' and 'convention', and the nature of language.

Antisthenes c.455–c.360BC
Greek philosopher

He is thought to be co-founder, with his pupil **Diogenes of Sinope**, of the Cynic school. He was a rhetorician and a disciple of **Gorgias**, and later became a close friend of **Socrates** whose asceticism and lack of interest in worldly goods he admired. He was one of the few intimates who were with Socrates in prison in the last hours of his life. Only fragments of his many works survive.

Antokolski, Mark Matveyevich 1843–1902
Russian sculptor

He was born at Wilno (now Vilnius, Lithuania), of Jewish parentage, and from 1880 lived and worked in Paris, but most of his works are in the Alexander III Museum in St Petersburg. *Ivan the Terrible* and *Turgenev* are the most famous of his portrait statues.

Antommarchi, Francesco 1780–1838
Corsican physician

He was born in Corsica and became **Napoleon I**'s physician on St Helena in 1818. Napoleon ultimately gave him his full confidence, and left him 100,000 francs. In 1822 he exhibited Napoleon's death mask, and the following year he published *Les Derniers Moments de Napoléon*. During the Polish revolution he served Warsaw as director of military hospitals. Afterwards he went to the West Indies. He died in Cuba.

Antonelli, Giacomo 1806–76
Italian prelate

Born in Sonnino, he went to Rome after his birthplace had been demolished by bandits in 1819, and he entered the Grand Seminary there, where he gained the favour of Pope **Gregory XVI**. In 1847 he was made cardinal-deacon by **Pius IX**, and in 1848 was premier and Minister of Foreign Affairs in a Liberal cabinet, which framed the famous *Statuto* or Constitution. He accompanied the pope in his flight to Gaeta in 1848, and, returning with him to Rome, became Foreign Secretary in 1850, and supported the reactionary policy of absolute papal administrative power. In the Vatican Council of 1869–70 he showed great tact and ability.

Antonello da Messina c.1430–1479
Italian painter

Born in Messina, he was the only major 15th-century Italian artist to come from Sicily. An accomplished master of oil painting, he helped popularize the medium, although **Giorgio Vasari**'s claim that he brought his tutor **Jan van Eyck**'s oil-painting technique to Italy is incorrect (he did not know van Eyck and is unlikely to have visited northern Europe). His style is a delicate synthesis of the northern and Italian styles. In 1475 he was working in Venice, where his work influenced **Giovanni Bellini**'s portraits. There are fragments of his Venetian San Cassiano altarpiece in Vienna. His first dated work, the *Salvator Mundi* (1465), and a self-portrait are in the National Gallery, London.

Antonescu, Ion 1882–1946
Romanian general and dictator

Born into an aristocratic family in Pitesti, he served as military attaché in Rome and London, and became Chief of Staff and Minister of Defence in 1937. Imprisoned in 1938 for plotting a right-wing revolt, he was a supporter of **Hitler**. In September 1940 he assumed dictatorial powers and forced the abdication of King **Carol II**. He headed a Fascist government allied to Nazi Germany until 1944 when he was overthrown after the Russian victory, and then executed for war crimes. ◻ Larry Watts, *Romanian Cassandra: Ion Antonescu and the struggle for reform, 1916–1941* (1993)

Antoninus Pius, *originally* Titus Aurelius Fulvus Boionius Arrius Antoninus, *after adoption* Titus Aelius Hadrianus Antoninus AD86–161
Roman emperor

Born in Lanuvium, the son of a consul, he was sent as proconsul into Asia by the Emperor **Hadrian**, was adopted by him (AD138) and the same year came to the throne. His reign was proverbially peaceful and happy, as a result of his integrity and benevolence. The persecution of Christians was restrained by his progressive measures. In his reign the empire was extended, and the Antonine Wall, named after him, was built between the Forth and Clyde rivers in North Britain. The epithet *Pius* was conferred on him for his defence of Hadrian's memory. By his wife Faustina he had four children, one of whom married **Marcus Aurelius**, his adopted son and successor. ◻ Mason Hammond, *The Antonine Monarchy* (1959)

Antonioni, Michelangelo 1912–
Italian film director

He was born in Ferrara, Italy, and after taking a degree in political economy at Bologna University, began as a film critic before becoming an assistant director (1942). He made several documentaries (1945–50) before turning to feature films, often scripted by himself, and noted for character study rather than plot. They include *Cronaca di un Amore* (1950, *Story of a Love Affair*), *Le Amiche* (1955, *The Girl Friends*) and *Il Grido* (1957, *The Outcry*). He gained an international reputation with *L'Avventura* (1959, *The Adventure*), a long, slow-moving study of its two main characters. Later films include *La Notte* (1961, *The Night*), *L'Eclisse* (1962, *The Eclipse*), *Blow-up* (1967), *Zabriskie Point* (1970), *The Passenger* (1974) and *The Oberwald Mystery* (1980). Recovering from a stroke, he returned to filmmaking with *Beyond the Clouds* (1996).

Antonov, Oleg Konstantinovich 1906–84
Soviet aircraft designer

Born in Troitskoe, Moscow region, he graduated from the Leningrad (now St Petersburg) Polytechnic Institute in 1930 and became a member of the Communist Party in

Antony, Mark, *also known as* Marcus Antonius c.83–30BC
Roman politician and soldier

Mark Antony was related on his mother's side to **Julius Caesar**, and after assisting Caesar in Gaul (53–50BC), Antony went to Rome to become tribune of the plebs (49) and defend Caesar's cause. He was expelled from the senate and fled to Caesar, who made this a pretext for his war against **Pompey**. Caesar left him in charge in Italy, and at Pharsalia (48) Antony led the left wing of Caesar's army. In 47 he was made master of the horse, and was left to govern Italy during Caesar's absence in Africa. He held no further post until 44, when he was consul with Caesar.

After Caesar's assassination, the conspirators fled, leaving Antony with almost absolute power. In the young Octavianus **Augustus** (named as heir in Caesar's will), he encountered a more ruthless and astute politician than himself. He was besieged and defeated at Mutina (43), and fled to Gaul. There he found support in the army of **Lepidus**, and returned to Rome at the head of 17 legions and 10,000 cavalry. Augustus held a consultation with Antony and Lepidus near Bononia, where it was decided that the three should share control of the Roman world as triumvirs. In Rome, a reign of terror began; among their first victims was **Cicero**, who had attacked Antony in the series of speeches called the Philippics.

After securing Italy and raising money, Antony and Augustus led their troops into Macedonia, and defeated **Brutus** and **Cassius** at Philippi (42). Antony went on to Athens, and then passed over to Asia, where he met and was captivated by **Cleopatra**. He followed her to Egypt (winter 41–40), until called back by news of a dispute with Augustus. A new division of the Roman world was now arranged, Antony taking the east, and Augustus the west, while Lepidus had to be content with Africa; Antony also married Augustus's sister **Octavia** (40). Differences grew up between Antony and Augustus, and in 37 Antony separated from Octavia and rejoined Cleopatra. His position in the east, his relations with Cleopatra, and his unsuccessful campaigns against the Parthians (36 and 34), were seized upon by Augustus and misrepresented for propaganda purposes. Eventually Augustus declared war on Cleopatra (32) and in the naval engagement of Actium (31), Antony and Cleopatra were defeated. Antony returned to Egypt where, deserted by the navy and army and deceived by a false report of Cleopatra's death, he committed suicide.

📖 **Shakespeare** used Lord North's translation of **Plutarch** as his source for the plays *Julius Caesar* and *Antony and Cleopatra*.

> Plutarch's description of the events after the assassination of Caesar includes the following episode, which corresponds to the speech beginning 'Friends, Romans, countrymen': 'It so happened that when Caesar's body was carried out for burial, Antony delivered the customary eulogy over it in the Forum. When he saw that his oratory had cast a spell over the people and that they were deeply stirred by his words, he began to introduce into his praise a note of pity and of indignation at Caesar's fate. Finally, at the close of his speech, he snatched up the dead man's robe and brandished it aloft, all bloodstained as it was and stabbed through in many places, and called those who had done the deed murderers and villains.'
> From *Antony*, 14 (translated by I Scott-Kilvert, 1965).

1945. He was the head of the experimental design department in 1946, and became designer-general for the aircraft industry in 1962. His well-known designs include the AN-2, AN-10, AN-12, AN-14, AN-22 (Antei) and AN-24. He was a Deputy to the Supreme Soviet of the USSR from 1958 to 1966. He received the Lenin Prize in 1962 and the Order of Lenin twice. After World War II he became senior designer with the Ministry of Aviation (until 1963). The author of over 50 books on glider and aircraft design, his name is perpetuated in the AN-225 aircraft which carried the Soviet shuttle orbiter *Buran* above its fuselage.

Antony or Anthony, St, *also called* Antony of Egypt or Antony the Great c.251–356AD
Egyptian ascetic and the father of Christian monasticism

Born in Koman, Upper Egypt, he sold his possessions for the poor at 20, then spent 20 years in the desert, where he withstood a famous series of temptations, often represented in later art. In AD305 he left his retreat and founded a monastery near Memphis and Arsinoë. Aged over 100, he made a journey to Alexandria in c.355 to dispute with the Arians, but soon returned to his desert home. St **Athanasius** wrote his biography. His feast day is 17 January.

Antony or Anthony of Padua, St 1195–1231
Portuguese friar

He was born in Lisbon. At first an Augustinian monk, in 1220 he joined the Franciscan order, and, noted for his preaching, became one of its most active proponents. Canonized in 1232 by **Gregory IX**, he is the patron saint of Portugal, the lower animals (legend has it that he preached to fishes when men refused to listen), and lost property. His feast day is 13 June.

Antony, Mark See panel above

Antraigues, Emanuel Delaunay, Comte d'
1755–1812
French politician

Born in Villeneuve de Berg, he provided, with his *Mémoires sur les États-généraux* (1788, 'Reports on the States General'), one of the first sparks of the French Revolution, but in 1789, when he was chosen a deputy, he defended the hereditary privileges and the kingly veto, and opposed the union of the three Estates. After 1790 he was employed in diplomacy in St Petersburg, Vienna and Dresden. In England he acquired great influence with **George Canning**. He was murdered, with his wife, near London, by an Italian servant.

Antschel, Paul See Celan, Paul

Anza, Juan Bautista de 1735–88
Spanish explorer

Born in Fronteras, Mexico, he made an expedition with the Spanish army from Sonora over the Colorado Desert to Spanish missions in California (1774), becoming the first to establish a land route to Spain's northern possessions, which were normally reached by sea. He founded San Francisco in 1776 and was later Governor of New Mexico (1777–88).

Anzengrüber, Ludwig 1839–89
Austrian playwright and novelist

Born in Vienna, he worked as a bookshop assistant, a touring actor and a police clerk before the success of his play *Der Pfarrer von Kirchfeld* (1870, 'The Pastor of Kirchfeld'), enabled him to devote the rest of his life to writing. He was the author of several novels, of which the best is *Der Sternsteinhof* (1885, 'The Sternstein Farm'), and about 20 plays, mostly about Austrian peasant life.

Anzilotti, Dionisio 1867–1950
Italian judge and jurist

Born in Pistoia, he was educated at Pisa. Professor of Law at Rome University (1911–37), he was a founder of the positive school of international law; this derived the law from international precedent rather than from theory. He was a founder of the *Rivista di diritto internazionale* (1906) and author of *Corso di diritto internazionale* (1912). Later he became a judge of the Permanent Court of International Justice (1921–30), and its president (1928–30).

Aouita, Said 1960–
Moroccan track athlete
Born in Rabat, he set world records at 1,500m and 5,000m in 1985, becoming the first man for 30 years to hold both records. He has since broken world records at 2 miles, 2,000m, and 3,000m. He was the 1984 Olympic champion, 1986 overall Grand Prix winner, and 1987 world 5,000m champion.

Apelles 4th century BC
Greek painter
Probably born in Colophon, on the Ionian coast of Asia Minor, he was trained at Ephesus and Sicyon and visited Macedon, where he became the friend of **Alexander the Great**. He is said to have accompanied Alexander on his expedition to Asia and to have settled at Ephesus. None of his work has survived, but his fame is apparent from ancient writings.

Apicius, Marcus Gavius 1st century AD
Roman nobleman and gourmet
He was prominent during the reign of the Emperor Tiberius in the 1st century AD, and his name is associated with one of the world's first books of recipes, known as *Of Culinary Matters*.

Apollinaire, Guillaume, *pseudonym of* Wilhelm Apollinaris de Kostrowitzky 1880–1918
French poet
Born in Rome of Polish descent, he settled in Paris in 1900, and became a leader of the movement rejecting poetic traditions in outlook, rhythm and language. The bizarre, Symbolist and fantastic elements of his work have affinities with the Cubist school in painting. His poetry includes *L'Enchanteur pourrissant* (1909, 'The Decaying Magician'), *Le Bestiaire* (1911, Eng trans 1977), *Alcools* (1913, Eng trans 1964) and *Calligrammes* (1918). He was wounded in World War I, and during his convalescence wrote the play *Les Mamelles de Tirésias* (1918, 'The Breasts of Tiresias'), for which he coined the term 'surrealist', and the Modernist manifesto *L'Esprit nouveau et les poètes* (1946, 'The New Spirit and the Poets'). 📖 S Bates, *Guillaume Apollinaire* (1967); P M Adema, *Guillaume Apollinaire: le mal-aimé* (1952)

Apollinaris, *called* the Younger c.310–c.390AD
Syrian prelate
Bishop of Laodicea from AD360, he was one of the sternest opponents of Arianism. He supported a doctrine (Apollinarianism) condemned by the Council of Constantinople (381) as denying the true human nature of **Jesus Christ**. He should not be confused with Claudius Apollinaris, known as 'the Apologist', Bishop of Hierapolis in Phrygia in the 2nd century, who wrote an *Apology* for the Christian faith, and several other works, all lost.

Apollodorus 5th century BC
Greek painter
An Athenian, he is said to have introduced the technique of chiaroscuro (light and shade).

Apollodorus fl.c.140BC
Athenian scholar
He was the author of a work on mythology and one on etymology, and best known for his verse *Chronicle* of Greek history from the fall of Troy.

Apollonius, *called* Dyskolos ('bad-tempered')
2nd century AD
Alexandrian grammarian
He was the first to reduce Greek syntax to a system. He wrote a treatise *On Syntax* and shorter works on pronouns, conjunctions and adverbs.

Apollonius of Perga fl.250–220BC
Greek mathematician
Known as 'the Great Geometer', he was the author of the definitive ancient work on conic sections which laid the foundations of later teaching on the subject. Apollonius also wrote on various geometrical problems, including that of finding a circle touching three given circles, and put forward two descriptions of planetary motion.

Apollonius of Tyana c.3–c.97AD
Greek philosopher and seer
Born in Tyana, Cappadocia, Asia Minor, he was said to be a zealous neo-Pythagorean teacher, who travelled to India, meeting the Magi at Babylon on his way. When he returned, he was hailed as a sage, and a worker of miracles. The Emperor **Vespasian** was his patron. After travelling widely in Spain, Italy and Greece, Apollonius seems to have settled at Ephesus in Asia Minor, where he opened a school. He was worshipped after his death, and a century later **Philostratus** wrote a colourful, and largely apocryphal, history presenting him as a sort of saviour or rival to **Jesus Christ**.

Apollonius Rhodius b.c.295BC
Greek poet and literary scholar
Born in Alexandria, Egypt, he was a pupil of **Callimachus** and became head of the Alexandrian library c.260–247BC, before retiring to Rhodes. His great (and only surviving) work is the *Argonautica*, an epic poem on the Homeric model describing the voyage of Jason and the *Argo* to recover the Golden Fleece. Its narrative of the love of Jason and Medea was used by **Virgil** as a model for the story of Aeneas and Dido in Book IV of the *Aeneid*.

Appel, Karel Christian 1921–
Dutch painter and sculptor
Born in Amsterdam, he studied at the Royal College of Art there. He began his artistic career in 1938, and was one of an influential group of Dutch, Belgian and Danish Expressionists known as 'Cobra'. His work, containing swirls of brilliant colour and aggressively contorted figures, has affinities with American Abstract Expressionism, and he is considered one of the most powerful exponents of this style. He has had many exhibitions in Europe and the USA and has won many prizes, including the UNESCO prize, the Venice Biennale (1953) and the Guggenheim International prize (1961).

Appert, Nicolas François 1749–1841
French chef and inventor
He was born in Châlons-sur-Marne. A chef and confectioner to trade, in 1795 he began experiments in preserving food in hermetically sealed containers, in response to a call from the French government for a solution to the problem of feeding the greatly expanded army and navy. His success, which earned him a French government prize of 12,000 francs in 1810, was due to his use of an autoclave for sterilization. He opened the world's first commercial canning factory in 1812. Initially he used glass jars and bottles, changing to tin-plated metal cans in 1822. At the time the scientific principles of food preservation were unknown, awaiting the bacteriological discoveries of **Louis Pasteur** in the 1860s.

Appia, Adolphe 1862–1928
Swiss scene designer and theatrical producer
He was born in Geneva, and was one of the first to replace the usual rich stage settings of his day with simple planes. He pioneered the symbolic use of lighting, particularly in the presentation of opera, and wrote *Die Musik und die Inscenierung* (1899, 'Music and Staging') and *La Mise-en-scène du drame Wagnérien* (1895, 'The Staging of the Wagnerian Drama').

Appian of Alexandria, *Greek* Appianos
2nd century AD
Roman historian and lawyer
A native of Alexandria, he flourished during the reigns of Trajan, Hadrian and Antoninus Pius. He compiled 24 books of Roman conquests down to Vespasian, written in Greek. Nine books survive complete, with fragments of others.

Appiani, Andrea, *known as* the Painter of the Graces 1754–1817
Italian artist
Born in Milan, he was court painter to Napoleon I. His best-known work is the set of frescoes depicting *Psyche* in the Monza Palace in Milan.

Appianos See Appian of Alexandria

Appius Claudius Caecus fl.312–308BC
Roman politician and general
His fame rests primarily on his great reforming censorship (312–308BC), during which he opened up the political process to the lower orders, made the Senate less exclusive and launched a number of projects to improve the quality of life in Rome, including the building of the city's first aqueduct, the Aqua Appia, as well as the first great Roman road, the Via Appia (Appian Way). A fervent expansionist, he actively participated in Rome's wars against the Etruscans, Sabines and Samnites. Despite blindness in old age (giving him the nickname 'caecus'), he continued to be active in politics, especially during the war against Pyrrhus of Epirus (280–279). A skilled orator, as well as a writer, he was regarded by the Romans as the father of Latin oratory and prose-writing.

Applegath, Augustus 1788–1871
English inventor
Born in London, he was a printer who made a number of improvements to the steam-powered flat-bed press of Friedrich König (1813). A rotary printing press had been patented by William Nicholson in 1790, but his and others' attempts to construct one all failed, and it was not until 1848 that the first workable vertical-drum rotary printing press was built by Applegath for *The Times* newspaper in London. It was, however, soon eclipsed by the horizontal rotary press developed at about the same time in the USA by Richard Hoe.

Appleseed, Johnny See Chapman, John

Appleton, Sir Edward Victor 1892–1965
English physicist and Nobel Prize winner
Born in Bradford, he studied at St John's College, Cambridge, and was appointed assistant demonstrator in experimental physics at the Cavendish Laboratory in 1920. His researches on the propagation of wireless waves led to his appointment as Wheatstone Professor of Physics at London University (1924). In 1936 he returned to Cambridge as Jacksonian Professor of Natural Philosophy. In 1939 he became Secretary of the Department of Scientific and Industrial Research, and in 1949 was appointed Principal and Vice-Chancellor of Edinburgh University. In 1947 he won the Nobel Prize for physics for his contribution towards exploring the ionosphere. His work revealed the existence of a layer of electrically charged particles in the upper atmosphere (the Appleton layer) which plays an essential part in making wireless communication possible between distant stations, and was also fundamental to the development of radar. 📖 Ronald Clark, *Sir Edward Appleton* (1972)

Apponyi, Albert Georg, Count 1846–1933
Hungarian statesman
Born in Vienna, he entered the Hungarian Diet in 1872, and showing himself to be a brilliant orator, soon became leader of the moderate opposition which became the National Party in 1891. In 1899 he and his supporters went over to the Liberal government party, and from 1901 to 1903 he was President of the Diet. From 1906 to 1910 he was Minister of Culture and, a devout Catholic, he gave asylum to expelled French Jesuits. He introduced free public education. In 1920 he led the Hungarian peace delegation, protested bitterly against the terms imposed under the Treaty of Trianon, which reduced Hungary to about a third of its pre-war size, and resigned. He frequently represented his country at the League of Nations.

Apraxin or Apraksin, Fyodor Matveyevich, Count 1671–1728
Russian naval commander
Having served Peter I, the Great, from 1682, he was appointed admiral in 1707 and built the navy into a powerful fighting force. In the Great Northern War (1700–21) he fought off the Swedes at St Petersburg (1708), captured Viborg, Åbo and Helsinki, and routed the Swedish fleet in 1713, thus taking control of the Baltic Sea. Later he commanded successful engagements against Turkey and Persia. He is often referred to as the 'father of the Russian navy'.

Apraxin or Apraksin, Stepan Fyodorovich, Count 1702–58
Russian soldier
He served in the war against the Turks (1736–39), and at the outbreak of the Seven Years War (1756–63) was appointed marshal. He commanded the Russian forces invading East Prussia in 1757, and defeated the Prussians at the Battle of Gross-Jägersdorf, but fell from favour and died in prison. His uncle was Count Fyodor Apraxin.

Apuleius, Lucius 2nd century AD
Roman writer, satirist and rhetorician
Born in Madaura, in Numidia, Africa, he was educated at Carthage and Athens. He used the fortune bequeathed to him by his father to travel, visiting Italy and Egypt, where it is likely that he was initiated into the mysterious religion of Isis and Osiris. His knowledge of priestly fraternities is reflected in his novel, the *Metamorphoses* (Eng trans *The Golden Ass*, 1566), a tale of adventure containing elements of magic, satire and romance, notably the story of Cupid and Psyche. Having married a wealthy, middle-aged widow, Aemilia Pudentilla, who nursed him in Alexandria, he was charged by her relations with having employed magic to gain her affections. His *Apologia*, still extant, was an eloquent speech in his defence. He later settled in Carthage, where he devoted himself to literature, philosophy and rhetoric. 📖 E H Haight, *Apuleius and his Influence* (1927)

Aquaviva, Claudius 1543–1615
Italian prelate and Jesuit
Born in Naples, he entered the Society of Jesus in 1567, and was appointed fifth general of the Jesuit Order in 1581. A noted educator and organizer, his book, *Ratio atque institutio studiorum* (1586, 'The Reason and Establishment of Studies'), laid the basis for later Jesuit education.

Aquila, *known as* Ponticus fl.130
Translator of the Old Testament into Greek

Aquinas, St Thomas 1225–74
Italian scholastic philosopher and theologian

Thomas Aquinas was born in the castle of Roccasecca, near Aquino, and was a descendant of the family of the Counts of Aquino. He was educated by the Benedictines of Monte Cassino, and at the University of Naples. In 1244, bitterly opposed by his family, he entered the Dominican order of mendicant friars. His brothers kidnapped him and kept him a prisoner in the family castle for over a year; in the end he made his way to Cologne to become a pupil of the great Dominican luminary, **Albertus Magnus**. In 1252 he went to Paris, and taught there, with growing reputation, until in 1258 he was summoned by the pope to teach successively in Anagni, Orvieto, Rome and Viterbo. He died at Fossanuova on his way to defend the papal cause at the Council of Lyons, and was canonized in 1323.

Aquinas's prolific writings have exercised enormous intellectual authority throughout the Church. He was the first among the metaphysicians of the 13th century to stress the importance of sense perception and the experimental foundation of human knowledge. Through his commentaries he made **Aristotle**'s thought available and acceptable in the Christian West, and in his philosophical writings he tried to combine and reconcile Aristotle's scientific rationalism with the Christian doctrines of faith and revelation.

His influence on the theological thought of succeeding ages was immense. Aquinas was known as the 'Doctor Angelicus' and the only other scholastic theologian who rivalled him was the 'Doctor Subtilis', **Duns Scotus**. The Franciscans followed Scotus, and the Dominicans Thomas, with the result that medieval theologians were divided into two schools, Scotists and Thomists, whose divergencies penetrate more or less every branch of doctrine.

📖 Aquinas's best-known writings are two large encyclopedic syntheses: the *Summa contra Gentiles* (1259–64), which deals chiefly with the principles of natural religion, and the *Summa Theologiae* (1266–73), which was still uncompleted at his death but contains his mature thought in systematic form and includes the famous 'five ways' or proofs of the existence of God.

> *Solus homo delectatur in ipsa pulchitrudine sensibilium secundum seipsam.*
> 'Only man delights in the beauty of sense objects for their own sake.'
> From *Summa Theologiae*, bk 1.

A native of Sinope, he is said to have been first a pagan, then a Christian, and finally a Jew.

Aquin, Louis Claude d' See **Daquin, Louis Claude**

Aquinas, St Thomas See panel above

Aquino, Benigno, *nicknamed* Ninoy 1932–83
Filipino politician

Born into a political family, he rose rapidly through provincial politics to become a senator at the age of 35. He was the principal opposition leader during the period of martial law, declared by President **Ferdinand Marcos** in 1972; it is generally accepted that if martial law had not been declared then, and the 1973 presidential election thereby abandoned, he would have succeeded Marcos as President. However, Aquino was arrested and sentenced to death on charges of murder and subversion (1977). In 1980, suffering from a heart condition, he was allowed to leave for the USA for surgery (and exile). On his return to the Philippines (1983), he was assassinated by a military guard at Manila airport. His death unleashed mass demonstrations against the Marcos order, which were to lead, in 1986, to the collapse of the Marcos presidency and the succession of Benigno's widow, **Cory Aquino**.

Aquino, Cory (Maria Corazón) *née* Cojuango 1933–
Filipino politician

The daughter of a wealthy sugar baron in Tarlac province, she studied in the USA where she gained a degree in mathematics at Mount St Vincent College, New York. In 1956 she married **Benigno Aquino**, and after his imprisonment in 1972 by President **Ferdinand Marcos** kept him in touch with the outside world. She lived in exile with Benigno in the USA until 1983, when he returned to the Philippines and was assassinated at Manila airport. She took up her husband's cause, and with widespread support claimed victory in the 1986 presidential elections, accusing President Marcos of ballot-rigging. The nonviolent 'people's power' movement which followed brought the overthrow of Marcos and Aquino's installation as President. Her presidency was, however, much troubled by internal opposition. In 1989 the sixth, and most serious, attempted coup against her was resisted

with assistance from the USA. In 1992 she did not run for the presidency again, but instead supported the successful bid of General **Fidel Ramos**.

Arabi Pasha See **Ahmed Arabi**

Arafat, Yasser See panel p71

Arago, (Dominique) François (Jean) 1786–1853
French scientist and politician

Born in Estagel, in the Pyrénées Orientales region, he went to the École Polytechnique, Paris, at the age of 17. In 1804 he became secretary to the Observatory and in 1830 its chief director. He took a prominent part in the July Revolution (1830) and as a member of the Chamber of Deputies voted with the extreme left. In 1848 he became a member of the provisional government, but refused to take the oath of allegiance to **Napoleon III** after the events of 1851–52. His achievements were mainly in the fields of astronomy, magnetism and optics. He developed a polarimeter, which he used to observe the polarization of cometary light, concluding that comets are not self-luminous, but simply reflect sunlight. Arago encouraged **Urbain Jean Joseph Leverrier** in his mathematical studies to discover Neptune. He is especially remembered for his great compendium of astronomy, *Astronomie populaire* ('Popular Astronomy'), which did much to extend the scientific enlightenment of the European middle classes. In studies of magnetism he gave an early demonstration of the magnetic field produced by the flow of an electric current round a conducting coil. He also speculated on the nature of light, propounding first the particle theory and later the wave theory of **Augustin Fresnel**.

Aragon, Catherine of See **Catherine of Aragon**

Aragon, Louis 1897–1983
French writer and political activist

Born in Paris, he became one of the most brilliant of the Surrealist group and co-founded the journal *Littérature* with **André Breton** in 1919. He published two volumes of poetry, *Feu de joie* (1920, 'Bonfire') and *Le Mouvement perpétuel* (1925, 'Perpetual Motion'), and a Surrealist novel, *Le Paysan de Paris* (1926, 'The Peasant of Paris'). After a visit to the USSR in 1930 he became a convert to communism. Thereafter he wrote social-realistic novels in a series

Arafat, Yasser, *real name* Mohammed Abed Ar'ouf Arafat 1929–
Palestinian resistance leader

Yasser Arafat was born in Jerusalem. He was educated at Cairo University (1952–56), where he was leader of the Palestinian Students' Union. He co-founded the Al Fatah resistance group in 1956 and began work as an engineer in Kuwait. Three years later he began contributing to a new Beirut magazine, *Filastinuna* ('Our Palestine'), which expressed the anger and frustration of Palestinian refugees, who felt betrayed and neglected by the Arab regimes.

In 1964 the Arab states founded the Palestine Liberation Organization (PLO), a body consisting of many factions that were often in disagreement with one another. Within five years, Arafat's Al Fatah group had gained control of the organization, and he became its acknowledged (though not universally popular) leader. He skilfully managed the uneasy juxtaposition of militancy and diplomacy, and gradually gained world acceptance of the PLO; the organization was formally recognized by the United Nations in 1974, and Arafat addressed its General Assembly in the same year. Under his leadership, the PLO's original aim—to create a secular democratic state over the whole of the pre-war Palestine—was modified to one of establishing an independent Palestinian state in any part of Palestine from which Israel would agree to withdraw.

In the 1980s the growth of factions within the PLO reduced his power and, in 1983, he was forced to leave Lebanon, while members of the organization dispersed widely to Tunisia, the Yemen, Syria, Jordan and other Arab states. Arafat, however, remained leader of the majority of the PLO. In 1985 he agreed with King **Hussein** of Jordan to recognize the state of Israel, provided that territory which had been seized was restored. This initiative failed but, in July 1988, Hussein surrendered his right to administer the West Bank, indicating that the PLO might take over the responsibility. Arafat, to the surprise of many Western politicians, persuaded the majority of his colleagues to acknowledge the right of Israel to co-exist with an independent state of Palestine.

In 1993 Arafat and the Prime Minister of Israel **Yitzhak Rabin** negotiated a peace agreement at the White House (signed in Cairo in 1994), by which Israel agreed to withdraw from Jericho and the Gaza Strip. Arafat and Rabin, together with Israel's Foreign Minister **Shimon Peres**, were jointly awarded the Nobel Prize for peace in 1994. The same year, Arafat returned to the occupied territories as head of a Palestinian state, and reached agreement following year on further Israeli withdrawals from the West Bank. In January 1995 he signed a further agreement of co-operartion with King Hussein of Jordan. The following month he met Hussein, together with Rabin and President **Mubarak**, in an attempt to revitalize the peace process. Events later in the year, the encroachment of Israelis into new settlements on the West Bank, suicide attacks by Hamas terrorists, and above all the assassination of Rabin in November, did little to encourage peace.

Having invited the terrorist group Hamas to talks on the future of Palestine (1995), he was elected president of the Palestinian National Council, with 88 per cent of the vote, in January 1996. In May, Shimon Peres was narrowly defeated in the elections in Israel, and was replaced as Prime Minister by the conservative hard-liner **Binyamin Netanyahu**.

📖 A Hart, *Arafat* (1994); A Gowers and T Walker, *Behind the Myth: Yasir Arafat and the Palestinian Revolution* (1992).

'The castor oil of the Palestinian peace movement.'
Said of Arafat in an American radio broadcast, 4 July 1994.

---

entitled *Le Monde réel* (1933–51, 'The Real World'), and war poems, including *Le Crève-Cœur* (1941, 'Heartbreak') and *Les Yeux d'Elsa* (1942, 'Elsa's Eyes'), about his lifelong partner, the writer Elsa Triolet. The novel *La Semaine sainte* (1958, 'Holy Week') attempted a Marxist analysis of the events of 1815. He was an important editor of left-wing publications, and an influential essayist. 📖 A Hurant, *Louis Aragon: prisonnier politique* (1970)

Araki, Sadao 1877–1966
Japanese soldier and politician

An ultra-nationalist, he was a leader of the right-wing Kodaha (Imperial Way) faction of the army. He was Minister for War (1931–33) and Minister for Education (1938–40). After World War II he was convicted as a war criminal and sentenced to life imprisonment, but released in 1965.

Aram, Eugene 1704–59
English scholar and murderer

Born in Ramsgill, Yorkshire, he was a gardener's son and, self-taught, became a schoolmaster, first at Ramsgill, and in 1734 at Knaresborough. In 1745 he was tried for the murder of a wealthy shoemaker, but acquitted for want of evidence. Following this he was a schoolmaster at various places in England, gathering a considerable amount of data for a comparative lexicon and discussing a possible relationship between Celtic and Indo-European languages. In 1759, on fresh evidence being discovered concerning the murder charge, he was tried at York, and hanged. At the trial he conducted his own defence, attacking the doctrine of circumstantial evidence. After his condemnation he confessed his guilt. His story was the subject of a romance by **Bulwer Lytton** and a ballad by **Thomas Hood**.

Arana Goiri, Sabino de 1865–1903
Basque nationalist

From a well-to-do Carlist family, he created much of the language and symbolism of Basque nationalism. Not only did he revive the Basque language, by publishing grammars, textbooks, histories, newspapers and magazines, but he also created the word Euzkadi for the Basque ethnic nation, designed the first Basque flag (the ikurriña), founded the first Basque cultural club, and coined many of its key political slogans. He founded the Basque Nationalist Party (PNV) in 1895. He was also the first Basque nationalist to win public office.

Aranda, Pedro Pablo Abarca y Bolea, Conde de 1718–99
Spanish general and statesman

He was born in Siétamo. He was made ambassador to Poland in 1760, but in 1766 was recalled to Madrid and made Prime Minister to restore order after the Esquilache riots. He expelled the Jesuits, blamed for the insurrection, from Spain in 1767, but in 1773 fell from power and was sent to France as ambassador. Returning in 1787, he became Prime Minister again in 1792, but antagonized **Manuel de Godoy**, and died in Aragon in enforced retirement.

Arany, János 1817–82
Hungarian poet

Born in Nagy-Szalonta, he was a leader with **Sándor Petőfi** of the popular national school, and is regarded as one of the greatest Hungarian poets. He was chief secretary of the Hungarian Academy from 1870 to 1879. His works include the satire *The Lost Constitution* (1845), which won the Kisfaludy Society Prize, and the *Toldi* trilogy (1847–54), the story of the adventures of a young peasant in the 14th-century Hungarian court. He also published successful translations of **Aristophanes** and **Shakespeare**.
📖 D Keveroztury, *Arany János* (1971)

Arason, Jón c.1484–1550
Icelandic prelate
Born in Eyjafjörður, in the north of Iceland, he was consecrated bishop of the northern see of Hólar in 1524. He fiercely resisted the imposition of Lutheranism from Denmark by the Crown, and when he was declared an outlaw raised a small army of adherents and seized the southern see of Skálholt, which had accepted Lutheranism by then. Eventually he and two of his sons were captured in an ambush, and beheaded. Since his execution, Jón Arason has been regarded as a national hero. He was a turbulent, charismatic figure, and a fine poet of both religious and satirical verse. He introduced a printing press to Hólar, the first in Iceland, but none of the books he printed has survived.

Aratus of Sicyon c.271–213BC
Leading politician of 3rd-century BC Greece
He joined Sicyon to the hitherto small Achaean League in 251BC, which he then gradually built up as a major power, seizing the Acrocorinth from Macedonian control in 243BC, and bringing new Peloponnesian cities into membership of the League. However, the revival of Spartan power under **Cleomenes III** caused him to turn for support to Antigonus Doson of Macedonia, and so undo the achievements of the earlier part of his career. Aratus's memoirs have not been preserved, but they were used by **Plutarch** in his *Life of Aratus*.

Arber, Agnes, *née* Robertson 1879–1960
English botanist
She was born in London and educated at University College London (UCL), and Newnham College, Cambridge, beginning her career as research assistant to the plant anatomist Ethel Sargant. From 1903 to 1909 she worked at UCL, and in 1909 married Edward Arber, demonstrator in palaeobotany at Cambridge. Her study of early printed herbals led to her first and most widely read book, *Herbals, Their Origin and Evolution* (1912), which became the standard work. Also interested in the philosophy of biology, she published *Goethe's Botany* (1946), *The Natural History of Plant Form* (1950), *The Mind and the Eye* (1954) and *The Manifold and the One* (1957). Her main contributions, however, were to comparative plant anatomy, on which she published three books: *Water Plants: a Study of Aquatic Angiosperms* (1920), *Monocotyledons: A Morphological Study* (1925), and *The Gramineae: A Study of Cereal, Bamboo and Grass* (1934). She was the third woman to be elected FRS (1948).

Arber, Werner 1929–
Swiss microbiologist and Nobel Prize winner
Born in Gränichen, he studied at the Swiss Federal Institute of Technology, Geneva University, and the University of Southern California, returning to Geneva and then to Basle University as Professor of Molecular Biology from 1970. In the 1960s he proposed that when bacteria defend themselves against phages (the viruses which attack bacteria) they use selective enzymes which cut the phage DNA at specific points in the DNA chain. Such 'restriction enzymes' clearly gave the option of securing short lengths of DNA, which could then be joined in specific ways to secure an 'un-natural DNA', and

provide an opening to the new field of so-called genetic engineering. Through the efforts of many groups, especially in the USA, this was brought to full fruition in the 1970s, with valuable results such as the preparation of monoclonal antibodies for use in clinical diagnosis and treatment of disease. He shared the Nobel Prize for physiology or medicine in 1978 with **Hamilton Smith** and **Daniel Nathams**.

Arbus, Diane, *née* Nemerov 1923–71
US photographer
Born in New York City, she rebelled against the social norms of her privileged background and her work in conventional fashion photography. Her aim was to portray people 'without their masks', and she became famous in the 1960s for her ironic studies of both the wealthy and the deprived classes. She married fellow photographer Allan Arbus in 1941, but they were divorced in 1969. After years of increasing depression, she committed suicide.

Arbuthnot, John 1667–1735
Scottish physician and writer
Born in Inverbervie, Kincardineshire, he studied at Aberdeen, Oxford and St Andrews universities. He became a close friend of **Jonathan Swift** and all the literary celebrities of the day, as well as a physician-in-ordinary to Queen **Anne** (1705), and in London was much admired for his good humour, wit and erudition. In 1712 he published five satirical pamphlets against the Duke of **Marlborough**, called *The History of John Bull*, which was the origin of the popular image of John Bull as the typical Englishman. With Swift, **Pope**, **John Gay** and others he founded the Scriblerus Club, and he was the chief contributor to the *Memoirs of Martin Scriblerus* (1741). As a physician he was ahead of his time, writing *An Essay Concerning the Nature of Ailments* (1731) which stressed the value of suitable diet in the treatment of disease. 📖 Lester Middlesworth Beattie, *John Arbuthnot, mathematician and satirist* (1935)

Arbuzov, Aleksei Nikolayevich 1908–86
Soviet dramatist
He was born in Moscow, and educated at the Leningrad (now St Petersburg) Theatre School. From 1930 onwards he was a prolific and successful playwright, starting with *Class* (1930). His most notable works were *Tanya* (1939), which has been described as a Soviet version of Ibsen's *A Doll's House*, *The Promise* (1965), and *Cruel Games* (1978).

Arcadius AD377–408
First Roman emperor of the East alone
He was born in Spain, and ruled with his father, the Emperor **Theodosius I, the Great** (AD383–95). On Theodosius's death Arcadius received the eastern half of the Roman Empire, the western falling to his brother **Honorius**. Arcadius's dominion extended from the Adriatic to the Tigris, and from Scythia to Ethiopia, but the real rulers over this vast empire were the Gaul Rufinus, the eunuch Eutropius, and his wife, Empress Eudoxia, who persecuted and banished St **John Chrysostom** (404).

Arcaro, Eddie (George Edward) 1916–97
US jockey
Born in Cincinnati, Ohio, he was five-times winner of the Kentucky Derby, the top horse race in the USA (first run in 1875). He won 4,799 races in a career spanning 30 years, from 1931 to 1961, and was six times leading money-winner in the USA. He also won the triple crown twice, in 1941 and 1948 (Kentucky Derby, Preakness and Belmont Stakes). His career winnings totalled more than $30 million.

Arcesilaus or Arcesilas c.316–c.241BC
Greek philosopher

Archimedes c.287–212BC
Greek mathematician, the most celebrated of antiquity, and one of its greatest creative geniuses

Archimedes was born in Syracuse, the son of an astronomer called Phidias, and probably studied at Alexandria. He lived for part of his life at the court of Hieron II of Syracuse. It was during the Roman capture of the city under **Marcellus** that Archimedes was killed, supposedly by a Roman soldier whose challenge Archimedes ignored while immersed in a mathematical problem. In **Plutarch's** Life of Marcellus, various devices invented by Archimedes are described which are said to have delayed the fall of Syracuse. He is also remembered in popular tradition for inventing the Archimedean screw (which is still used for raising water), and for the story that he discovered 'Archimedes' principle' while in the bath and ran into the street with a cry of *Eureka!* ('I have found it!'); the principle states that a body immersed in a fluid displaces a volume of fluid equal to its own volume. He also demonstrated the powers of levers in moving large weights, and in this context made his famous declaration: 'Give me a firm spot on which to stand, and I shall move the Earth'.

His major importance in mathematics, however, lies in his discovery of formulae for the areas and volumes of spheres, cylinders, parabolas, and other plane and solid figures, in which the methods he used anticipated the theories of integration to be developed 1800 years later. He also used mechanical arguments involving infinitesimals as a heuristic tool for obtaining the results prior to rigorous proof. He founded the science of hydrostatics, studying the equilibrium positions of floating bodies of various shapes. His work combines an extraordinary freedom of approach with enormous technical skill in the details of his proofs. His astronomical work is lost, and other works have only survived in Arabic translation.

📖 G E R Lloyd, *Greek Science after Aristotle* (1973); B Farrington, *Greek Science* (1953).

> **Cicero**, as Quaestor of Sicily in 75BC, came across the neglected tomb of Archimedes in Syracuse. It was marked by a column on which a cylinder circumscribed a sphere, in remembrance of Archimedes' discovery of the ratio between the volumes of solids.

He was born in Pitane, Aeolia, Asia Minor, and became the sixth head of the Athenian Academy founded by **Plato**. He modelled his philosophy on the critical dialectic of Plato's earlier dialogues but gave it a sharply Sceptical turn, directed particularly against Stoic doctrines. Under his leadership the school became known as the 'Middle Academy' to distinguish it from the 'Old Academy'.

Arch, Joseph 1826–1919
English preacher and reformer

He was born in Barford, Warwickshire, and while still a farm labourer became a Primitive Methodist preacher. In 1872 he founded the National Agricultural Labourers' Union, and he was later MP for Northwest Norfolk.

Archbold, John Frederick 1785–1870
English lawyer

A prolific author of practical legal textbooks, he is best remembered for *Criminal Pleading, Evidence and Practice* (1822) a work which, repeatedly revised, is an essential handbook for lawyers in the English criminal courts.

Archelaus fl.c.450BC
Greek philosopher and cosmologist

Reputed to have been the pupil of **Anaxagoras** and the teacher of **Socrates**, he made some limited modifications to the physical theories of Anaxagoras and others.

Archelaus d.399BC
King of Macedonia

He ruled from 413 to 399BC, and was a great patron of the arts. He was portrayed by **Plato** in the *Gorgias* as a cruel monster.

Archelaus 1st century AD
Ethnarch of Judaea

He was the son of **Herod, the Great**, and succeeded his father in AD1, when he maintained his position against an insurrection raised by the Pharisees. His heirship being disputed by his brother **Herod Antipas**, Archelaus went to Rome, where his authority was confirmed by **Augustus**, who made him Ethnarch of Judaea, Samaria, and Idumaea, while his brothers, Antipas and Philip, were made tetrarchs over the other half of Herod's dominions. After a nine-year reign, he was deposed by Augustus for his tyranny, and banished to Vienne, in Gaul, where he died.

Archer (of Weston-Super-Mare), Jeffrey Howard Archer, Baron 1940–
British writer and former politician

Educated at Brasenose College, Oxford, he sat as Conservative MP for the constituency of Louth (1969–74), but resigned from the House of Commons after a financial disaster that led to bankruptcy. In order to pay his debts he turned to writing fiction. His first book, *Not a Penny More, Not a Penny Less* (1975), based on his own unfortunate experiences in the financial world, was an instant bestseller, which he followed up with other blockbusters like *Shall We Tell the President?* (1976), *Kane and Abel* (1979), which was dramatized on television, and *First Among Equals* (1984, also televised). Despite critical reservations about their literary merits, his books continue to sell in vast numbers. Recent titles include *Honour Among Thieves* (1993), *Twelve Red Herrings* (1994) and *The Proprietors* (1996). He has also written two plays, *Beyond Reasonable Doubt* (1987) and *Exclusive* (1990), and in 1988 he capped his lifelong interest in the theatre by buying one outright—the Playhouse, London. He was Deputy Chairman of the Conservative Party (1985–86), but resigned following allegations over which he later cleared his name in a successful libel action against the *Daily Star*. He was made a life peer in 1992. In 1996 he proposed a Bill in parliament which would give male and female royals equal rights in succession.

Archer, Robyn 1948–
Australian singer and actress

She was born in Adelaide, South Australia, and after graduating from Adelaide University, worked in Sydney night-clubs before returning to her studies and teaching English for three years. In 1974 she sang Annie I in Brecht/Weill's *The Seven Deadly Sins* which led to a contract with New Opera South Australia, and in 1975 she played Jenny in Weill's *Threepenny Opera*. Since then her name has been linked with the German cabaret songs of Weill, **Hanns Eisler** and **Paul Dessau**, and she was invited by the National Theatre, London, to perform in a Brecht compilation, *To Those Born Later* (1977). She returned to Sydney (1978) to write and star in a series of one-woman and political cabaret shows, one of which, *A Star is Torn* (1979), ran for two seasons in London's West End (1982–83). Thereafter she concentrated on writing and producing and she also appeared on the BBC television series *Cabaret*.

Archer, Thomas c.1668–1743
English Baroque architect
Born in Tamworth-in-Arden, Warwickshire, he studied abroad, and designed the churches of St John's, Westminster (1714–28), and St Paul's, Deptford (1712–30). He also designed Roehampton House in Surrey and the North Front of Chatsworth in Derbyshire.

Archilochus of Paros fl.714–676BC
Greek poet
From the island of Paros, he is regarded as the first of the lyric poets, and also wrote elegies and hymns. His work was highly regarded by the ancients, who placed him on a level with **Homer, Pindar** and **Sophocles**. **Plato** called him 'the very wise', but much of his renown is for vituperative satire. Only fragments of his work survive. He is said to have died in a battle between Paros and Naxos. 🕮 T Bretenstein, *Hésiode et Archiloque* (1971)

Archimedes See panel p73

Archipenko, Alexander 1880–1964
US sculptor
He was born in Kiev, Ukraine, and studied there and in Moscow and Paris. In France he took an active part in the Cubist movement, and introduced holes and voids into sculpture, as in *Walking Woman* (1912, Benveo Art Museum). He was in Berlin between 1921 and 1923. After 1923 he lived in the USA, based in New York, except when he taught in the new Bauhaus in Chicago (1937–39). His work is characterized by extreme economy of form, and shows the influence of **Constantin Brancusi.** From c.1946 he experimented with new materials, such as Plexiglas, lit from within. As **Guillaume Apollinaire** said, he was one of the most important originators of 'sculpture pure'.

Arcimboldo, Giuseppe c.1530–1593
Italian painter
Born in Milan, where he began his career as a designer of stained-glass windows for the cathedral, he later moved to Prague and became a court painter to the **Habsburgs. Rudolf II** admired his work enough to make him a Count Palatine. It was while he was court painter that he executed the work for which he is best known, fantastic heads composed of fragmented landscape, animals, vegetables, flowers and other non-human objects, brightly coloured and showing great attention to detail. While the artistic importance of these caricatures has always been considered debatable, they have been greatly admired by 20th-century Surrealists such as **Salvador Dalí.**

Ardashir I, *also called* Artaxerxes d.241AD
Founder of the Persian dynasty of the Sassanids
He overthrew Ardavan (Artabanus), the last of the Parthian kings (c.226AD). He next conquered Media and a large part of the Iranian highlands, and created the biggest threat faced by Rome in the East, but was defeated by **Alexander Severus** (233). He made Zoroastrianism the state religion.

Arden, Elizabeth, *née* Florence Nightingale Graham c.1880–1966
US beautician and businesswoman
Born in Woodbridge, Ontario in Canada, and a nurse by training, she went to New York City in 1908 and opened a beauty salon on Fifth Avenue in 1910, adopting the personal and business name of 'Elizabeth Arden'. She produced and advertised cosmetics on a large scale, and developed a worldwide chain of salons. With her rival, **Helena Rubinstein,** she helped to make cosmetics 're-spectable', introducing tinted lipstick, mascara and eye-shadow, to match different outfits.

Arden, John 1930–
British playwright
He was born in Barnsley, Yorkshire, and educated at Sedbergh School, King's College, Cambridge, and the Edinburgh College of Art. The college dramatic society produced his first play, a romantic comedy entitled *All Fall Down*, in 1955. *Live Like Pigs* (1958), with its Rabelaisian realism and humour, broke new ground in theatrical presentation. It was followed by *Serjeant Musgrave's Dance* (1959), staged in the Brechtian tradition, *The Workhouse Donkey* (1963), a caricature of local politics in the north of England, and *Armstrong's Last Goodnight* (1964). Arden has continually experimented with dramatic form and theatrical technique, both in the plays he has written alone and in the many pieces in which he has collaborated with his wife, Margaretta D'Arcy. *The Happy Haven* (1961) followed the commedia dell'arte tradition, the nativity play *The Business of Good Government* (1960) uses medieval stage techniques, and *The Ballygombeen Bequest* (1972) uses vaudeville on the theme of the political and class conflict in Ireland. He has also written television scripts, a volume of essays, and a novel, *Silence Among the Weapons* (1982), and since 1972 has written increasingly for radio, including a nine-part series, *Whose Is the Kingdom?* (1988). A second novel, *The Book of Bale*, appeared the same year, and continues Arden's theme of using early history to look closely at timeless moral issues. In 1991 he published a volume of novellas entitled *Cogs Tyrannicus*, followed by the novel *Jack Juggler and the Emperor's Whore* in 1995. 🕮 J R Brown, *Theatre Language: a study of Arden, Osborne, Pinter and Wesker* (1972)

Ardizzone, Edward Jeffrey Irving 1900–79
British illustrator and author
Born in Haiphong, Vietnam, to an Italian father and a Scottish mother, he attended evening classes at the Westminster School of Art, London (1920–21), and worked as a freelance illustrator from 1926. His first children's book, *Little Tim and the Brave Sea Captain* (1936), made his name. He was an official war artist in World War II, after which he taught at Camberwell School of Art (1948–52), and at the Royal College of Art (1953–61). From 1952 to 1953 he worked for UNESCO in India. An accomplished draughtsman in watercolour, pen-and-ink, and pencil, he illustrated over 170 books, including **Graham Greene's** children's stories, and several books by James Reeves, in a deceptively casual style based on simplified forms shadowed with loosely hatched lines.

Areios See Arius

Arenas, Reinaldo 1943–90
Cuban novelist
Born in a small rural town in the province of Oriente, he moved to Havana, studied briefly at the university there, and took a job at the National Library. His book *Celestino antes del Alba* (1967, 'Celestino Before Dawn') is the first of five semi-autobiographical novels which describe his fantastic poetic vision of Cuba after the Revolution. Because of the disenchantment with the Revolution expressed in his novels, and also because of his homosexuality, he was placed in a re-education camp, imprisoned, and his works banned. In 1980, he left Cuba for the USA. Though mainly a novelist, he also wrote short stories, articles and a number of experimental theatre pieces.

Arendt, Hannah 1906–75
US philosopher and political theorist
Born in Hanover, Germany, she was educated at Marburg, Freiburg and Heidelberg universities. She moved to the USA in 1940 as a refugee from the Nazis and worked for various Jewish organizations and became chief editor at Schocken Books (1946–48). She became naturalized in 1950, and after the publication of her first major work, *The Origins of Totalitarianism* (1951), she

held academic posts at Princeton, Chicago and in New York. Focusing on the moral issues raised by the cataclysmic history of the 20th century, she often touched a political nerve and had an effect and a readership far beyond the academic world. Among her books are *The Human Condition* (1958), *Eichmann in Jerusalem* (1963) and *The Life of the Mind* (published posthumously, 1978).

Arens, Moshe 1925–
Israeli politician

He was born in Lithuania and educated at Massachusetts and California Institutes of Technology. He lectured in aeronautical engineering at the Israel Institute of Technology, Haifa, and was deputy director of Israel Aircraft Industries before entering the Knesset in 1973. He served as ambassador to the USA (1982–83), and then Minister of Defence (1983–84). He was then a Minister without portfolio until 1987, being appointed Foreign Minister until 1990, when he returned to his former role of Minister of Defence (1990–92).

Arensky, Anton Stepanovich 1861–1906
Russian composer

Born in Novgorod, he studied under **Rimsky-Korsakov**, and from 1895 conducted the court choir at St Petersburg. His compositions, which show the influence of **Tchaikovsky**, include five operas, two symphonies, and vocal and instrumental pieces.

Aretaeus fl.100AD
Greek physician

Born in Cappadocia, he was considered to rank next to **Hippocrates**. The first four books of his great work, preserved nearly complete, discuss the causes and symptoms of diseases, the other four, the cure.

Arete of Cyrene 5th–4th century BC
Greek philosopher

Born probably in Cyrene, Libya, she was educated by her father, the philosopher **Aristippus**, who is sometimes held to be the founder of Cyreniac or Hedonistic philosophy, though it seems likely that it was Arete's son, also called Aristippus, who formalized this philosophy. Arete taught philosophy (consequently nicknamed 'Mother-taught'). It would seem, therefore, that she was an important link in the evolution and transmission of Hedonistic ideas. Though some authorities credit her with over 40 works, none of these survive, and the authenticity of the single surviving letter from her father to Arete has also been challenged.

Aretino, Pietro 1492–1556
Italian poet

Born in Arezzo, Tuscany, he was banished from his native town and went to Perugia, where he worked as a bookbinder, and afterwards wandered through Italy in the service of various noblemen. In Rome (1517–27) he won the friendship of Giovanni de' Medici (Pope **Leo X**) which he subsequently lost by writing his *Sonetti Lussuriosi* (1524, 'Lewd Sonnets'), and ingratiated himself with **Francis I** at Milan in 1524. He also acquired powerful friends when he settled in Venice. His poetical works include five comedies and a tragedy. 📖 F Berni, *La Vita di Pietro Aretino* (1939)

Arfe, Henrique de 16th century
Spanish silversmith

With his son he carved in silver many of the finest Gothic altarpieces and crucifixes in the Spanish cathedrals and monasteries.

Arfe, Juan de, y Villafane 1535–c.1603
Spanish metal engraver

Born in León, he made altarpieces for the cathedrals at Avial, Burgos and Seville.

Argand, Aimé 1755–1803
Swiss physicist and chemist

Born in Geneva, he lived for a time in England. In 1784 he invented the Argand lamp for use in lighthouses.

Argand, Jean-Robert 1768–1822
Swiss mathematician

Born in Geneva, he gave his name to the Argand diagram, in which complex numbers are represented by points in the plane. By profession a book-keeper, his work was largely independent of that of the more famous mathematicians of his time.

Argelander, Friedrich Wilhelm August 1799–1875
German astronomer

Born in Memel, East Prussia, he plotted (1852–1861) the position of all the stars of the northern hemisphere above the ninth magnitude.

Argensola, Bartolomé Leonardo de 1562–1631 and Lupercio de 1559–1613
Spanish poets

Born in Barbastro, both were educated at Huesca University and both entered the service of Maria of Austria. Their poems led them to be called the 'Spanish Horaces', but they were also official historians of Aragon. Lupercio wrote some tragedies. 📖 J A Molina, *Los Argensola* (1939)

Argenson, René Louis Voyer, Marquis d' 1694–1757
French statesman

The son of the Marquis d'Argenson (1652–1721), who created the secret police and established the *lettres de cachet*, he became Councillor to the Parlement of Paris in 1716, and Foreign Minister (1744–47). His *Mémoires* are an important source of information on the period. He fell a victim in 1747 to the machinations of Madame de **Pompadour**, as, 10 years later, did his brother, Marc Pierre, Comte d'Argenson (1696–1764), who had become War Minister in 1743.

Argentina, La, originally Antonia Mercé 1890–1936
Spanish dancer

Born in Buenos Aires, Argentina, she moved to Spain with her parents, both Spanish dancers, when she was two, making her debut as a classical dancer when she was six and becoming a dancer with Madrid Opera at the age of 11. She gave up classical dance at 14 to study Spanish dance with her mother. Her first foreign tour, at the age of 18, was a success and the blueprint for the rest of her life. She became well-known internationally and earned Spanish dance a new popularity. She is often said to be the greatest female Spanish dancer in history.

Argyll
Title of the Campbell chiefs

The Campbells were a powerful West Highland clan, who had achieved knighthood in the 13th century and obtained the barony of Lochow in 1315. From 1445 the chief was styled Lord Campbell until the earldom of Argyll was conferred upon Colin, 2nd Lord Campbell in 1457.

Argyll, Archibald, 1st Duke of c.1651–1703
Son of the 9th Earl of Argyll

He was an active promoter of the Glorious Revolution, organized the massacre of the Macdonalds of Glencoe (1692), and was created Duke of Argyll in 1701.

Argyll, Archibald Campbell, 2nd Earl of d.1513
Scottish nobleman

The son of Colin, 1st Earl, he was Lord High Chancellor of Scotland (1494). He was killed at the Battle of Flodden.

Argyll, Archibald Campbell, 5th Earl of
1530–73
Scottish nobleman
The son of the 4th Earl, he was a Protestant follower of Mary, Queen of Scots. He succeeded to the earldom in 1558 and was involved in the assassination of her huband, Lord Darnley (1567). He later supported King James VI and I and became Lord High Chancellor of Scotland in 1572.

Argyll, Archibald Campbell, 7th Earl of
c.1576–1638
Scottish noble
He succeeded to the title in 1584, and as King's Lieutenant was defeated by the rebel army led by the earls of Errol and Huntly at Glenlivet in 1594. In 1607 he was granted rich Crown lands in Kintyre that had been forfeited by the Macdonalds of Islay, and he suppressed risings by the Macdonalds in 1614 and 1615 in order to plant Lowland settlers in Inverary. He also helped in the extermination of the MacGregor clan from 1610 onwards. He later became a convert to Catholicism and served the King of Spain.

Argyll, Archibald Campbell, Marquis and 8th Earl of, *known as* the Covenanting Marquis *or* Cross-Eyed Archibald 1607–61
Scottish noble
Son of Archibald, 7th Earl of Argyll, he became a member of Charles I's Privy Council in 1626, but in 1638 joined the Covenanters in support of Scottish Presbyterianism. In 1641 he was reconciled with Charles and created Marquis of Argyll. In the English Civil War he joined the Parliamentary side, and after being defeated by the Marquis of Montrose at Inverlochy in 1645 took part in the defeat of Montrose and his Royalists at Philiphaugh in 1645. He formed a Scottish government under Cromwell's patronage, but after the execution of the king he repudiated Cromwell, accepted the proclamation of Charles II as King in Scotland (1649), and crowned him at Scone in 1651. After the defeat of the Scottish army at Worcester that autumn, however, he submitted to Cromwell again. At the Restoration of Charles II in 1660 he was arrested, found guilty of complying with the English occupation, and executed.

Argyll, Archibald Campbell, 9th Earl of
1629–85
Scottish noble
Son of Archibald, 8th Earl of Argyll, he was imprisoned by Cromwell for a suspected royalist plot (1657–60). After the Restoration of Charles II in 1660, he came into favour, but his efforts on behalf of his father led to him being imprisoned again until 1663, when the titles and lands forfeited at his father's execution in 1661 were restored to him. In 1681 he refused to sign the Test Act that forced all public office holders to declare their belief in Protestantism, and was sentenced to death for treason. He escaped to Holland. In 1685, after the accession of James VII and II, he conspired with the Duke of Monmouth to overthrow the King. Monmouth's invasion of England was delayed; Argyll landed in Scotland, but failed to rouse the Covenanters to his cause and was captured and executed.

Argyll, John Campbell, 2nd Duke of 1678–1743
Scottish politician
He succeeded Archibald, 1st Duke of Argyll in 1703. A committed Unionist, he was a high commissioner to the Scottish parliament of 1704 and one of the strongest supporters of the Act of Union of 1707. An outstanding soldier, he took part in the War of the Spanish Succession (1701–14), and fought under the Duke of Marlborough at Oudenarde (1708) and Malplaquet (1709). At the time of the Jacobite Rising in Scotland (1715–16) he commanded the Hanoverian forces that dispersed the Jacobite troops without a battle. He was created Duke of Greenwich in 1719.

Argyll, John Douglas Sutherland Campbell, 9th Duke of 1845–1914
British nobleman
Born in London, he married Queen Victoria's fourth daughter, Princess Louise (1871), and was Governor-General of Canada (1878–83).

Argyropoulos, Joannes 1416–c.1486
Greek scholar
He was born in Constantinople (Istanbul) and became a professor at Florence under the Medici. He was one of the earliest teachers of Greek learning in the West, and translated Aristotle into Latin.

Arias, Benito, *also called* Montano 1527–98
Spanish theologian and linguist
Born in Fregenal de la Sierra, he became a Benedictine monk and was a delegate to the Council of Trent (1562–64). For Philip II he edited the famous Antwerp Polyglot edition of the Bible (1568–73).

Arias Navarro, Carlos 1908–89
Spanish politician
Notorious as the 'Butcher of Malaga' for being state prosecutor there during the Nationalists' savage repression during the Spanish Civil War (1936–39), he became the Director-General of Security (1957–65) and the Mayor of Madrid (1965–73). Named Minister of the Interior (June 1973), he became Prime Minister after the assassination of Luis Carrero Blanco in December of that year. Following General Franco's death (1975), he was confirmed as the first Prime Minister of the monarchy. He resigned in 1976 under King Juan Carlos I, having proven too hardline to effect the transition to democracy.

Arias Sanchez, Oscar 1940–
Costa Rican politician and Nobel Prize winner
Born in Heredia, Costa Rica, he was educated in England at Essex University and the London School of Economics, then returned to Costa Rica, where he started a law practice. He entered politics, joining the left-wing National Liberation Party (PLN) and later became its secretary-general. Elected President of Costa Rica in 1986, on a neutralist platform, he was the major author of a Central American Peace Agreement aimed at securing peace in the region, and particularly in Nicaragua. He completed his term as President in 1990, and although enormously popular in Costa Rica was barred by the constitution from seeking re-election. He won the 1987 Nobel Peace Prize.

Aribau, Bonaventura Carles 1798–1862
Spanish economist and writer
Born in Barcelona, he became a banker in Madrid, and was appointed director of the Mint and of the Spanish Treasury (1847). He was also decorated by Prince Albert for his work on the industrial section of the Great Exhibition of 1851. He was editor of the *Biblioteca de autores españoles* ('Library of Spanish Writers'), and was the author of the *Oda a la Patria* (1833, 'Ode to the Motherland'), one of the earliest and best modern poems in Catalan, which greatly influenced contemporary Catalan writers. ▢ M de Montoliu, *Los grans personalitats de la litteratura catalana* (1936)

Ariosto, Ludovico 1474–1533
Italian poet
Born in Reggio nell'Emilia, he abandoned law for poetry. At the court of Cardinal Ippolito d'Este, at Ferrara, he produced, over a period of 10 years, his great poem,

Aristotle 384–322BC
Greek philosopher and scientist, a highly important and influential figure in the history of Western thought

Aristotle was born at Stagira, a Greek colony on the peninsula of Chalcidice. His father was court physician to Amyntas III of Macedon (grandfather of **Alexander the Great**). In 367 he went to Athens and was first a pupil then a teacher at **Plato**'s Academy, where he stayed for 20 years until Plato's death in 347. **Speusippus** succeeded Plato as head of the Academy, and Aristotle left Athens for 12 years. He spent time at Atarneus in Asia Minor (where he married), at Mytilene, and in about 342 was appointed by **Philip II**, King of Macedon, to act as tutor to his 13-year-old son Alexander.

Aristotle finally returned to Athens in 335 to found his own school (called the Lyceum from its proximity to the temple of Apollo Lyceius), where he taught for the next 12 years. His followers became known as 'peripatetics', supposedly from his restless habit of walking up and down while lecturing. When Alexander the Great died in 323 there was a strong anti-Macedonian reaction in Athens; Aristotle was accused of impiety and, perhaps with the fate of **Socrates** in mind, he took refuge at Chalcis in Euboea, where he died the next year.

Aristotle's writings represent a vast output covering many fields of knowledge: logic, metaphysics, ethics, politics, rhetoric, poetry, biology, zoology, physics and psychology. He believed that sense perception is the only means of human knowledge. In ethics, he believed that human happiness is achieved by living in conformity with nature. In natural philosophy, he saw that the Earth is the centre of the eternal universe. He taught that everything beneath the orbit of the Moon was composed of earth, air, fire and water; everything above the orbit of the Moon was composed of ether. All material things could be analysed in terms of their matter and their form, and form constituted their essence.

📖 Most of the extant work consists of unpublished material in the form of lecture notes or students' textbooks, which were edited and published by **Andronicus of Rhodes** in the middle of the 1st century BC. His work exerted an enormous influence on medieval philosophy (especially through St **Thomas Aquinas**), Islamic philosophy (especially through **Averroës**), and on the whole western intellectual and scientific tradition. The works most read today include the *Metaphysics* (the book written 'after the *Physics*'), *Nicomachean Ethics*, *Politics*, *Poetics*, the *De Anima* and the *Organon* (treatises on logic).

> 'Nature, as we say, does nothing without some purpose; and for the purpose of making man a political animal she has endowed him alone among the animals with the power of reasoned speech.' *Politics*, bk 1, ch.2, 1253a (trans by T A Sinclair).

Orlando Furioso (1516, 'Orlando Enraged', enlarged 3rd edition, 1532), which takes up the epic tale of **Roland** (as Orlando) from the French *chansons de geste* and forms a continuation of **Matteo Boiardo**'s *Orlando Innamorato* ('Orlando in Love'). He also wrote comedies, satires, sonnets, and a number of Latin poems. 📖 C P Brand, *Ludovico Ariosto: an introduction to the Orlando Furioso* (1974)

Aristarchos or Aristarchus of Samos fl.270BC
Greek astronomer

He worked in Alexandria, Egypt, and is famous for his theory of the motion of the Earth, maintaining not only that the Earth revolves on its axis but that it travels in a circle around the Sun, anticipating the theory of **Copernicus**. He was also a practical astronomer and developed a method for determining the relative distances of the Sun and Moon. His result, though greatly in error due to the crudeness of his method, was the first attempt to make this important observation. He inferred correctly that as the Sun and Moon are almost of the same apparent size, their dimensions are in proportion to their distances.

Aristarchus of Samothrace c.215–143BC
Alexandrian grammarian and critic

Best known for his edition of **Homer**, he also wrote many commentaries and treatises, edited **Hesiod**, **Pindar**, **Sophocles**, **Aeschylus** and other authors, and was the founder of a school of philologists. He was the head of the Alexandrian Library from c.180 to c.145BC.

Aristide, Jean Bertrand 1953–
Haitian political leader

Born in Port-Salut, Haiti, he was ordained a Roman Catholic priest in 1982 and assigned to a small parish in the slums of Port-au-Prince. He became one of the leading critics of the **Duvalier** regime and was exiled (1982–85), but he returned and was elected President of Haiti in 1990. He was almost immediately forced into exile by the military, and began a three-year effort to regain the presidency with the backing of the US government, which recognized Aristide as the democratic alternative in Haiti despite its discomfort with his socialist rhetoric. In a last-minute effort before a planned US invasion, a US diplomatic team led by **Jimmy Carter** negotiated a peaceful occupation and transfer of power in 1994, and Aristide returned to serve out the final year of his presidency. Barred by the Haitian constitution from seeking a second consecutive term, he gave his backing to former premier Rene Preval, who was elected to succeed him as President in 1996. He has left the priesthood to marry and is expected to run for the presidency again in the year 2000.

Aristides c.550–c.467BC
Athenian general and politician

A respected general in the Graeco-Persian Wars, he held command under **Miltiades**, the younger at the Battle of Marathon (490BC). However, he was banished to Aegina (c.483) as a result of his opposition to **Themistocles**' naval policy until the Persians invaded again (480) under **Xerxes I**. Aristides served at Salamis (c.480) and, with **Pausanias**, at Plataea (479). He altered the constitution so that all citizens were admitted to the archonship, and organized the Delian League after the defeat of the Persians.

Aristides 2nd century AD
Greek Christian apologist

He wrote an early *Apology for the Christian Faith*, mentioned by **Eusebius of Caesarea** and St **Jerome**. It only came to light late in the 19th century.

Aristippus 410–350BC
Greek philosopher

He was born in Cyrene, North Africa, and founded the Cyrenaic school of hedonism, which was influential in the late 4th and early 3rd centuries BC, and which argued that pleasure was the highest good. He became a pupil of **Socrates** in Athens, and taught philosophy both at Athens and Aegina, the first of the pupils of Socrates to charge fees for instruction. Much of his life was spent in Syracuse, at the court of **Dionysius** the tyrant, where he seems to have practised what he preached in a very wholehearted fashion. He also lived in Corinth with the famous courtesan **Laïs**, but retired later to Cyrene, where his daughter **Arete** and his grandson Aristippus the Younger developed his views and formed a new school.

Aristophanes c.448–c.385BC
Greek comic dramatist

He wrote some 50 plays, but only 11 are extant. The best-known of his earlier works, in which the satire is largely political, are *Hippeis* (424, 'Knights'), *Nephelai* (423, 'Clouds') and *Sphekes* (422, 'Wasps') (named from their respective choruses), and *Eirene* (421, 'Peace'). These were followed by *Ornithes* (414, 'Birds'), *Lysistrata* (411, 'Destroyer of Armies'), *Thesmophoriazusae* (411, 'The Women attending the Thesmophoria') and *Batrachoi* (405, 'Frogs', which contains a burlesque poetic contest between **Aeschylus** and **Euripides**). Later come *Ecclesiazusae* (392, 'Women in Parliament') and *Plutus* (388). In the last, the themes are personal, and the chorus plays only a marginal role. Aristophanes is the only writer of Old Comedy of whom complete plays survive. The objects of his often savage satire are social and intellectual pretension. The plots of his plays show a genius for comic and often outrageous invention, and the verse in his choruses marks him as a notable poet. ⌑ L E Lord, *Aristophanes: his plays and influence* (1925)

Aristotle See panel p77

Aristoxenus of Tarentum 4th century BC
Greek philosopher and musical theorist

A pupil of **Aristotle**, he wrote influential works on rhythm and harmonics, parts of which survive.

Arius, *Greek* Areios c.250–336AD
Libyan theologian, founder of the heresy 'Arianism'

Trained in Antioch, he became a presbyter in Alexandria and c.319AD maintained, against his bishop, that in the doctrine of the Trinity the Son was not co-equal or co-eternal with the Father, but only the first and highest of all finite beings, created out of nothing by an act of God's free will. He secured the support of clergy and laity in Egypt, Syria, and Asia Minor, but was deposed and excommunicated in 321 by a synod of bishops at Alexandria. **Eusebius of Nicomedia** absolved him, and in 323 convened another synod in Bithynia, which pronounced in his favour. At Nicomedia, Arius wrote a theological work in verse and prose, called *Thaleida*, some fragments of which remain. To settle the controversy the Emperor **Constantine I, the Great** called the Council of Nicaea (Nice), in Bithynia (325) with 318 bishops present, besides priests, deacons and acolytes. Arius boldly expounded and defended his opinions but the reasoning of **Athanasius** greatly influenced the Council to define the absolute unity of the divine essence, and the absolute equality of the three persons. Two dissenting bishops were banished along with Arius, who was recalled in 334, but was refused admission to church communion, fuelling the controversy in the East. In 336 Arius went to Constantinople (Istanbul), where he died suddenly, before he could be admitted to the sacrament. After his death the strife spread more widely abroad. The West was mainly orthodox, the East largely Arian or semi-Arian. There was a good deal of persecution on both sides and Arianism was at last virtually suppressed in the Roman Empire under **Theodosius I, the Great** in the East (379–95), and **Valentinian II** in the West. Among the Germanic nations, however, it continued to spread through missionary efforts and was revived in England by the philosophers **Samuel Clarke** and **William Whiston**, only to be superseded by Unitarianism.

Arkwright, Sir Richard 1732–92
English industrialist and inventor of mechanical spinning

Born in Preston, Lancashire, he settled about 1750 as a barber in Bolton, and developed a profitable process for dyeing hair. In 1767 he moved to Preston, where he patented his celebrated spinning frame—the first machine that could produce cotton-thread of sufficient tenuity and strength to be used as warp. He entered into partnership with Jedidiah Strutt of Derby, and set up a large, water-powered, factory at Cromford, Derbyshire (1771), and in 1775 took out a fresh patent for various additional improvements to machinery. His success stimulated rival cotton spinners to use his designs, and in 1781 he prosecuted nine different manufacturers—the outcome, however, was that in 1785 his letters patent were cancelled. His inventions diminished the demand for labour, and in 1779 his large mill near Chorley was destroyed by a mob. In 1787 he became High-Sheriff of Derbyshire, and in 1790 he introduced the steam engine into his works at Nottingham.

Arlen, Harold, *originally* Hyman Arluck 1905–86
US composer

Born in Buffalo, New York, the son of a cantor, he began his career as a singer and pianist. He was one of the busiest composers in show business during the 1930s and 1940s, writing songs for Harlem's Cotton Club ('I've Got the World on a String', 'Stormy Weather') and Broadway shows and working with lyricists such as E Y Harburg, **Ira Gershwin**, and Johnny Mercer. His numerous songs for films include 'Over the Rainbow', 'That Old Black Magic' and 'One for My Baby'. His popular compositions were included in Broadway's *Harold Arlen Songbook* (1967).

Arlen, Michael, *originally* Dikran Kouyoumdjian 1895–1956
British novelist

Born in Ruschuk, Bulgaria, of Armenian descent, he was educated at Malvern College, England, and Edinburgh University. He became a naturalized British citizen in 1922, but lived in France from 1928 until World War II, and settled in the USA after the war. He began by writing novels and short stories on stylish London life, and made his reputation with *Piracy* (1922), and notably, *The Green Hat* (1924). Among his short-story collections are *The Romantic Lady* (1921) and *These Charming People* (1923). His last novel was *The Flying Dutchman* (1939). ⌑ M J Arlen, *Exiles* (1971)

Arletty, *originally* Léonie Bathiat 1898–1992
French film and stage actress

Born in Courbevoie, she worked in a munitions factory and as a secretary before her beauty brought her modelling assignments and stage work in revues like *Si Que je serais roi* (1922, 'If I were but King'). She made her film debut in *La Douceur d'Aimer* ('Sweetness of Love') in 1930 but continued to star on stage in *L'École Des Veuves* (1936, 'The School for Widows') and *Fric-Frac* (1936) until such roles as a droll Queen of Ethiopia in *Les perles de la couronne* (1937, *The Pearls of the Crown*) brought her renown on screen. She became associated with director **Marcel Carné**, starring in *Hôtel du Nord* (1938), *Le Jour se Lève* (1939, *Daybreak*) and *Les Visiteurs du soir* (1942, 'Evening Visitors'), but her most famous role was in his 1944 film, *Les Enfants du Paradis* ('The Children of Paradise'). Following a period of wartime imprisonment due to accusations of collaboration, she resumed her career successfully with the thriller *Portrait d'un assassin* (1949, 'Portrait of a Murderer'). Later films include *Huis clos* (1955, *No Exit*), *The Longest Day* (1962), her sole appearance in a US production, and *Le Voyage à Biarritz* (1963), her last screen appearance.

Arlington, Henry Bennet, 1st Earl of 1618–85
English statesman

He was born in Arlington, Middlesex. Following a period in Spain after the English Civil War, he returned to England with the Restoration and was created Lord Arlington in 1663 and Earl of Arlington in 1672. A member of the cabal ministry under Charles II, he was Secretary of State (1662–74), negotiated the Triple Alliance against France (1668), and helped to develop the English party system. In 1674 he was cleared of an embezzlement charge, but resigned and became Lord Chamberlain.

Arliss, George, originally Augustus George Andrews 1868–1946
English actor

He was born in London and first appeared on the stage at the Elephant and Castle (1887), but made his reputation as an actor in the USA, where he lived for 22 years from 1901, in plays like *The Second Mrs Tanqueray* (1901) and *Disraeli* (1911). He returned to London to play the raja in *The Green Goddess* (1923). His film career began in the USA in 1920. He is remembered for his portrayals of famous historical characters, such as the Duke of Wellington, Cardinal Richelieu and Voltaire, which were always coloured by his own individual personality. He won an Academy Award for *Disraeli* (1929). His autobiography, *Up the Years from Bloomsbury*, was published in 1940.

Arlott, (Leslie Thomas) John 1914–91
English writer and broadcaster

Born in Basingstoke, Hampshire, he was a clerk in a mental hospital then became a detective in Southampton Borough Police (1934–45) before joining the BBC. He went on to gain popularity as a top cricket commentator, retiring eventually in 1980. He wrote numerous books about cricket, including *Arlotton Cricket* (1984).

Arlt, Roberto 1900–42
Argentine novelist and dramatist

Born in Buenos Aires of a German emigrant father and a Swiss–Italian mother, he was initially reproached for his poor syntax. He then became one of the most poetic of the 20th century urban realist Latin-American novelists. His father mocked Arlt throughout his childhood. He rose above this and taught himself to write, composing 'crime spots' in the newspapers. His major work, four novels, and about 50 short stories followed and in the 1930s, he devoted himself to theatre. Of his work only *Los siete locos* (1929, Eng trans *The Seven Madmen*, 1984) has ever been translated. The phantasmagorical world this and its sequel *Los lanzallamas* (1931, 'The Flame Throwers') conjure up can only be matched in blackness by the Argentinian political scene which formed their background. His last novel however, *El Amor Brujo* (1932, 'Love the Magician'), tells of frustrated love. His pieces for the newspaper *El Mundo* have been collected as *Aguafuertes* in two volumes (1950–53) and his daughter Mirta edited his complete novels and stories (1963). 📖 K Schwartz, *A New History of Spanish–American Fiction* (1971)

Armand, Inessa 1875–1920
Russian politician

Born in Paris, France, where her French father lived, she was brought up in Russia by a rich family after her parents died. Her intellectual interests and travels brought her into contact with Lenin and she joined his party in 1905. She was twice exiled, but she returned to Russia in 1917. One of the most active women Bolsheviks, she was a champion of Soviet women's causes. She also founded Zhenotdel (1919), the women's section of the Communist Party, and organized branches everywhere until she died of overwork and cholera. Zhenotdel, however, continued at least until 1930.

Armani, Giorgio 1935–
Italian fashion designer

Born in Piacenza, he studied medicine in Milan, and after military service worked in a department store until he became a designer for Nino Cerruti in 1961. He also freelanced before setting up the Giorgio Armani company in 1975. He designed first for men, then women, including loose-fitting blazers and jackets, and has won numerous awards.

Armatrading, Joan 1950–
British singer and songwriter

Born in St Christopher-Nevis in the Caribbean, she moved to Great Britain at the age of eight. Gaining a reputation as an amateur performer around Birmingham, she began writing songs with a friend, Pam Nester, and moved to London in 1971. They made one album, *Whatever's For Us*, before breaking up acrimoniously. Armatrading then signed to A&M and recorded *Back to the Night* (1975), a well-crafted album that caught a new feminist consciousness. She had great success with the often-reissued 'Love and Affection' (1976), but she was essentially an album artist with only sporadic chart appeal. *Me, Myself, I* (1980) was a personal declaration of independence, and shortly afterwards she was an honoured guest at her native island's independence celebrations. Since her album, *The Key* (1983), she has been less prominent (despite persuading Princess Margaret to guest in a video, the first member of the British Royal Family to do such a thing).

Armfelt, Gustaf Mauritz 1757–1814
Swedish soldier and politician

Born in Finland, he was a favourite of King Gustav III towards the end of his reign. He fought in Gustav's war against Russia (1788–90) and helped to negotiate the Peace of Värälä. He was a member of the regency council during the minority of Gustav IV Adolf and Swedish ambassador in Vienna in 1802–04. He commanded the Swedish army against Napoleon I in Pomerania. After the deposition of Gustav IV Adolf in 1809, he was exiled by his successor, Karl XIII, and entered Russian service. He became Governor-General of Finland, by then a grand duchy under the Russian tsar.

Ármín See Vámbéry, Arminius

Arminius d.19AD
Chief of the German Cherusci

He served as an officer in the Roman army and acquired Roman citizenship. However, in AD9 he allied with other German tribes against the Romans, and in the Teutoburg Forest ambushed and annihilated an entire Roman army of three legions commanded by Publius Quintilius Varus. As a result the Emperor Augustus abandoned the attempt to extend the Roman frontier from the Rhine to the Elbe. Arminius continued to resist the Romans and the Marcomanni, but was murdered by some of his own kinsmen. Tacitus praised him as the 'liberator of Germany'.

Arminius, Jacobus, properly Jakob Hermandszoon, also called Jacob Harmensen 1560–1609
Dutch theologian

Born in Oudewater, he studied at Utrecht, Leyden, Geneva and Basle, and was ordained in 1588. Despite his opposition to the doctrine of predestination he was made Professor of Theology at Leyden in 1603. In 1604 his colleague Francis Gomarus attacked his doctrines and from this time he was engaged in a series of bitter controversies. In 1608 Arminius asked the Netherlands States General to hold a synod to settle the argument, but he died before it took place. His followers continued the dispute for many years and influenced the development of religious thought all over Europe. In England Laudians and Latitudinarians were Arminian in tendency, and Wesleyans and many Baptists and Congregationalists are distinctly anti-Calvinist. ⌨ Kaspar Brandt, *Historiae vitae Jacobi Arminii* (1724)

Armitage, Edward 1817–96
English painter

Born in London, he studied under **Paul Delaroche** and became professor at the Royal Academy schools in 1875. He produced paintings on historical and biblical subjects, including the frescoes *Death of Marmion*, and *Personification of the Thames* in the House of Lords.

Armitage, Karole 1954–
US dancer and choreographer

Born in Madison, Wisconsin, she trained in classical ballet, and moved from the Ballets de Genève, Switzerland (1972–74) to the **Merce Cunningham** Dance Company in New York (1976–81), where her unique style began to take shape. Cunningham created several roles for her in several works, including *Squaregame* (1976) and *Channels/Inserts* (1981). During this period she became interested in choreography and with *Drastic Classicism* began a choreographic career which took her to Paris, where she worked with dancers such as **Michael Clark** and created pieces for Paris Opera Ballet. Her work has been described as a 'molotov cocktail', a controversial blend of wit, high heels and invention.

Armitage, Kenneth 1916–
English sculptor

Born in Leeds, he studied at Leeds College of Art and at the Slade School in London (1937–39), and in 1952 he gained international recognition when he exhibited at the Venice Biennale. His bronzes are usually of semi-abstract figures, united into a group by stylized clothing, such as *People in a Wind* (1951, Tate Gallery, London). In 1956 he won first prize in an international competition for a war memorial at Krefeld. At the 1958 Venice Biennale he won the David E Bright Foundation Prize for the best sculptor under 45, with his exhibition including *Sprawling Woman* and *Two Seated Figures*. In the 1970s he combined sculpture and painting in figures of wood, plaster and paper, as in *Figure and Clouds* (1972), but returned to bronze by the 1980s. From 1971 he was visiting tutor at the Royal College of Art in London. He became a member of the Royal Academy in 1994.

Armour, Mary Nicol Neill, *née* Steel 1902–
Scottish painter

Born in Blantyre, Strathclyde, she won a scholarship to Hamilton Academy, then studied at Glasgow School of Art. In 1927 she married the artist William Armour. She executed a mural commission for the Royal Navy and was elected associate member of the Royal Scottish Academy (RSA) in 1941. She also taught at Glasgow School of Art (1951–62) and her customary landscape and flower studies became more free in handling and brighter in colour. She was elected to both the Royal Scottish Water Colour Society (1956) and the RSA (1958).

Armstead, Henry Hugh 1828–1905
English sculptor

He was born in London, the son of a heraldic chaser, and worked at first in gold and silver, but from 1863 he turned to sculpture. His best-known works are the marble reliefs and bronze statues of Astronomy, Chemistry, Rhetoric and Medicine for the **Albert** Memorial in London, the fountain at King's College, Cambridge, the oak panels of the legend of King **Arthur** in the House of Lords (1866–70), the reredorse at Westminster Abbey, London (1871), and the statues on the Government offices in Whitehall (1875).

Armstrong, Archy d.1672
Scottish court jester

He was employed in the courts of **James VI and I** and **Charles I**. He gained much wealth and influence, but was dismissed in 1637 for insolence to Archbishop **Laud**, and withdrew in 1641 to Arthuret in Cumberland.

Armstrong, Edwin Howard 1890–1954
US electrical engineer and inventor

Born in New York City, he graduated from Columbia University, having already discovered the principle of the feedback circuit, although the Supreme Court later awarded the patent priority to **Lee De Forest**. During World War I his interest in methods of detecting aircraft led him to devise the superheterodyne circuit, which became the basis for amplitude-modulation radio receivers. By 1939, as Professor of Electrical Engineering at Columbia University (1935–54), he had perfected the frequency-modulation system of radio transmission that virtually eliminated the problem of interference from static, and after World War II he developed a technique which allowed several different signals to use the same carrier-wave frequency. These and many other inventions were universally adopted and could have brought him great satisfaction, but he engaged in many lawsuits, and in the end he took his own life. ⌨ Lawrence Lessing, *Man of High Fidelity: Edwin Howard Armstrong* (1956)

Armstrong, Gillian May 1952–
Australian film director

Born in Melbourne, she studied theatre design and film, and won a scholarship to the Film and Television School in Sydney where she directed three short films, including *Gretel* (1974). After her graduation she made documentaries and the drama *The Singer and the Dancer* (1976) which won the Australian Film Institute (AFI) award for Best Short. Her first feature film, *My Brilliant Career* (1979), was the first Australian feature directed by a woman since the 1930s and won 11 AFI awards, including Best Film and Best Director, earning Armstrong an international reputation of great promise. She enjoyed a change of pace in the breezy musical comedy *Starstruck* (1982), and continued to focus attention on the difficulties facing independent women in *Mrs Soffel* (1984), *High Tide* (1987), and *The Last Days of Chez Nous* (1993). In 1995 her dramatization of **Louisa M Alcott's** *Little Women* was highly acclaimed, and in 1996 she began filming **Peter Carey's** novel *Oscar and Lucinda*.

Armstrong, Henry, *originally* Henry Jackson 1912–88
US boxer and Baptist minister

Born in Columbus, Mississippi, he was the only man to hold world titles at three weights simultaneously. In August 1938 he held the feather-weight, light-weight, and welter-weight titles. In 1940 he fought a draw with Cerefino Garcia for the middle-weight title. He had the last of his 175 fights in 1945 and in 1951 he was ordained.

Armstrong, Henry Edward 1848–1937
English chemist

Born in London, he studied chemistry at the Royal College of Chemistry and began research with Sir **Edward Frankland**, but received his PhD from Leipzig in 1870 for work with **Hermann Kolbe**. He returned to the UK to become professor at the London institutions which later became Imperial College, and remained there until his retirement in 1911. He did pioneering work in a number of areas of organic chemistry, particularly the structure and reactions of benzene and naphthalene compounds. He also speculated on the state of ions in aqueous solution. However, he is best remembered for the inspirational nature of his teaching. He was elected FRS in 1876.

Armstrong, John c.1709–1779
Scottish physician and poet

Born in the manse at Liddesdale, Roxburghshire, he studied at Edinburgh University, and went into practice in London. He published a sex manual in blank verse for newly-weds called *The Oeconomy of Love* (1736), followed in 1744 by another didactic medical work in the same style. In 1746 he was appointed physician to the London Soldiers' Hospital, and from 1760 to 1763 physician to the forces in Germany.

Armstrong, Johnnie d.1530
Scottish Border freebooter and cattle rustler ('reiver')

He was either John Armstrong of Gilnockie, near Langholm, who was seized by King James V at a parley at Caerlanrig chapel and summarily hanged with several of his followers in 1529, or John Armstrong ('Black Jock'), brother of Thomas Armstrong of Mangerton, executed in 1530. He was the hero of many Border ballads.

Armstrong, Louis, *popularly known as* Satchmo (from Satchelmouth) *or* Pops 1901–71
US jazz trumpeter and singer

He was born in New Orleans and brought up by his mother in extreme poverty. While serving a sentence for delinquency in the city's 'home for coloured waifs', he learned to play the cornet, and from that humble start developed into the first major jazz virtuoso. Released from the institution in 1914, he worked as a musician in local bars, getting encouragement from King Oliver, the city's leading cornettist. In 1919, Armstrong replaced Oliver in the band led by Edward 'Kid' Ory, and also played on Mississippi riverboats. In 1922, he joined Oliver's band in Chicago, and recordings by the Creole Jazz Band, featuring the cornet partnership, set new standards of musicianship in early jazz. These standards were surpassed by Armstrong himself a few years later, recording with his 'Hot Five' and 'Hot Seven' studio groups, when his playing moved beyond the constraints of New Orleans-style collective improvisation towards the virtuoso delivery for which he later gained world renown. A 1926 recording of his use of 'Scat singing' (imitating an instrument with the voice using abstract vocables) started a vogue in jazz, of which he became the most celebrated exponent. The group included his then wife, Lilian Armstrong (*née* Hardin, 1898–1971), who went on to a successful career as a jazz pianist after their divorce in 1931, leading her own all-women band, and died on stage during a tribute concert to Louis. From the late 1920s Armstrong, then playing trumpet, began two decades as a star soloist and singer with various big bands, sometimes in commercial settings not worthy of his great talent. In 1947, the formation of his first All Stars group marked a return to small-group jazz. Armstrong made the first of many overseas tours in 1933. He appeared in more than 50 films as a musician and entertainer. 📖 J L Collier, *Louis Armstrong* (1983)

Armstrong, Neil Alden 1930–
US astronaut

Born in Wapakoneta, Ohio, he was educated there and at Purdue University. A fighter pilot in Korea and later a civilian test pilot, in 1962 he was chosen as an astronaut and in 1966 he commanded Gemini 8. With Buzz Aldrin and Michael Collins he set out in Apollo 11 on a successful Moon-landing expedition. On 20 July 1969 Armstrong and Aldrin became, in that order, the first men to set foot on the Moon, Collins remaining in the command module. Armstrong published *First on the Moon* in (1970) and taught aerospace engineering at Cincinnati University (1971–79). 📖 Andrew Langley, *Journey into Space* (1994)

Armstrong (of Ilminster), Robert Armstrong, Baron 1927–
English civil servant

Educated at Eton and Christ Church, Oxford, he entered the Civil Service in 1950 and rose rapidly to become deputy head of the Home Office and the Treasury. In 1970 he became Principal Private Secretary to the Prime Minister, Edward Heath and, under Margaret Thatcher, Cabinet Secretary and head of the Civil Service (1983–87). He would have remained relatively anonymous had it not been for his testimony during the British Government's disastrous attempt in the Australian courts in 1986 to halt publication of Peter Wright's book *Spycatcher*, when Armstrong made the famous remark that he had perhaps been 'economical with the truth'. He retired shortly afterwards, and was given a life peerage in 1988. Since 1994 he has been Chancellor of the University of Hull.

Armstrong, Samuel Chapman 1839–93
US educator

He was born in Wailuku, on Maui Island, Hawaii, the son of US missionaries. After serving in the Civil War as Union colonel of a unit of black troops, he became an agent of the Freedmen's Bureau. Seeing a need for educating newly freed slaves, he established the Hampton Institute in Virginia (1868) to provide both academic and vocational training, and served as its director until 1893.

Armstrong, Sir Walter 1850–1918
Scottish writer on art

Born in Roxburghshire, in the Scottish Borders, he wrote works on Velázquez, Thomas Gainsborough, Sir Joshua Reynolds, Sir Henry Raeburn and Sir Thomas Lawrence. He was director of the National Gallery of Ireland from 1892 to 1914.

Armstrong, William George Armstrong, Baron 1810–1900
English inventor and industrialist

He was born in Newcastle upon Tyne. Articled to a solicitor, he became a partner, but turned to engineering, and in 1840 produced a much improved hydraulic engine, in 1842 an apparatus for producing electricity from steam, and in 1845 the hydraulic crane. In 1847 he founded the Elswick Engine-Works, Newcastle, which produced hydraulic cranes, engines, accumulators, and bridges at first, but was soon to be famous for its ordnance, and especially the 'Armstrong' breech-loading gun, whose barrel was built up of successive coils of wrought iron. From 1882 shipbuilding was included. In 1897 the firm amalgamated with Joseph Whitworth & Co, and in 1927 merged into Vickers Armstrong Ltd.

Arnarson, Ingólfur late 9th century
Norwegian Viking

Originally from Hördaland, south-west Norway, he is honoured as the first settler of Iceland in 874. According to early historical tradition in *Landnámabók*, the Icelandic 'Book of Settlements', he left Norway after some local disputes and settled on a farm he named Reykjavík (Steamy Bay) because of its hot springs. This later became the country's capital, and his descendants held the hereditary and honorary post of supreme chieftain (*alsherjargoði*) of the Icelandic parliament (Althing) after its foundation in 930.

Árnason, Jón, *known as* the Grimm of Iceland 1819–88
Icelandic collector of folk-tales

Born in northern Iceland, he became national librarian in Reykjavík. He collected and published a huge collection of Icelandic folk-tales and fairy-tales (*Íslenskar Þjóðsögur og ævintýri*, 2 vols, 1862–64), translated as *Legends of Iceland* by Eiríkur Magnússon (1864–66).

Arnaud, Henri 1641–1721
French pastor

Military leader of the Waldenses, he wrote in exile at Schönberg his famous *Histoire de la glorieuse rentrée des Vaudois dans leurs vallées* (1710, 'History of the Glorious Return of the Waldensians in their Valleys').

Arnaud, Yvonne Germaine 1892–1958
French actress

Born in Bordeaux, and educated in Paris, she trained as a concert pianist and toured Europe as a child prodigy. With no previous acting experience, she took the role of Princess Mathilde in the musical comedy *The Quaker Girl* (1911), and was an instant success. Further success on the British stage followed with *The Girl in the Taxi* (1912) and many musicals and farces including *Tons of Money* (1922), *A Cuckoo in the Nest* (1925), *The Improper Duchess* (1931) and *Love for Love* (1943). She was thought to be miscast in Jean Anouilh's *Colombe* (1951) but was praised for her performance in *Dear Charles* (1952) and was noted for her charm, vivacity and musical accent. She made her film debut in *Desire* (1920) and made several film adaptations of her stage successes as well as films like *On Approval* (1931), *The Ghosts of Berkeley Square* (1947) and *Mon oncle* (1958, *My Uncle*). She lived for many years near Guildford, Surrey, where a theatre was opened in her honour (1965).

Arnauld, Angélique, *known as* Mère Angélique de Saint Jean 1624–84
French Jansenist nun

She was the daughter of Robert Arnauld (1588–1674). She entered the convent of Port-Royal des Champs in Paris and was successively subprioress and abbess (1678). During the persecution of the Port-Royalists she is said to have been very courageous.

Arnauld, Antoine, *known as* the Great Arnauld
1612–94
French Jansenist philosopher, lawyer, mathematician and priest

His attacks on the Jesuits and his activities as head of the Jansenist sect in France led to his expulsion from the Sorbonne, persecution, and ultimate refuge in Belgium. While at Port Royal, where there was a Jansenist community, he collaborated with Blaise Pascal and Pierre Nicole (1625–95) on the work known as the *Port-Royal Logic* (1662).

Arnauld, Marie-Angélique, *known as* Mère Angélique 1591–1661
French Jansenist nun

She was made abbess of Port-Royal at the age of 11, and reformed the convent by the severity of her discipline. She resigned in 1630, but returned to be prioress under her sister Agnes (1593–1671). She was also the sister of Antoine Arnauld.

Arndt, Ernst Moritz, *known as* Father Arndt
1769–1860
German poet and patriot

Born in the then Swedish island of Rügen, the son of a former serf, he was educated at Stralsund, Greifswald and Jena with a view to the ministry, but in 1805, after travelling extensively in Europe, became Professor of History at Greifswald. His *Geschichte der Leibeigenschaft in Pommern und Rügen* (1803) led to the abolition of serfdom, and in his *Geist der Zeit* (1806, Eng trans *Spirit of the Times*, 1808) he attacked Napoleon I so boldly that after the Battle of Jena (1806) he had to take refuge in Stockholm (1806–09). 'Was ist des deutschen Vaterland?' and others of his patriotic songs helped to rouse the spirit of Germany. In 1817 he married a sister of Friedrich Schleiermacher and in 1818 became Professor of History in the new University of Bonn. Aiming steadily at constitutional reforms, he was suspended in 1819 for participation in so-called 'demagogic movements', and was not restored till 1840. He was elected a member of the German national assembly in 1848, but retired from it in 1849. He was revered by the whole German people as 'Father Arndt'. His works comprise an account of the Shetland and Orkney Islands (1826), numerous political addresses, some volumes of reminiscences, two volumes of letters (1878–92) and poems.

Arne, Thomas Augustine 1710–78
English composer

Born in London and educated at Eton, he began his musical career as a violinist, forming his style chiefly on Corelli. He produced his first opera, *Rosamond* in 1733, which was followed by his comic operetta, *Tom Thumb*, and then *Comus* (1738). His best-known opera was *Artaxerxes* (1762). He was composer to Drury Lane Theatre during the 1740s, for which he composed his famous settings of Shakespearean songs, including 'Under the Greenwood Tree', 'Where the Bee Sucks', and 'Blow, Blow, thou Winter Wind'. His best-known piece is 'Rule, Britannia', originally written for *The Masque of Alfred* (1740). His son Michael (1740–86) was also a musician and composer, remembered for his song 'Lass with the delicate air'.

Arniches y Barrera, Carlos 1866–1943
Spanish playwright

Born in Alicante, he moved while young to Madrid and became so entrenched in the life of the capital that he was inextricably identified with it. He started off in journalism, then turned to writing plays and excelled in the 'sainete', a short comedy or one-act farce reflecting everyday life. Originally it was an entr'acte made famous by Ramón de la Cruz. This kind of popular, comic work was at first rather scorned by critics but popular with audiences, who found the characters instantly recognizable. His output numbered over 300 pieces, the best-known of which include *El Santo de la Isidra* (1898, 'The Saint of Isidra') and *El Puñao de Rosas* (1902, 'The Bunch of Roses'), which were comedies, and *Los Caciques* (1919), a social criticism which finally won him critical acclaim. While never patronizing his audience, he maintained a common code of morality in his well-constructed slices of 'madrileño' life.

Arnim, Achim von, *real name* Karl Joachim Friedrich Ludwig von Arnim 1781–1831
German writer

Born in Berlin, he was the author of fantastic but original romances. He stirred up a warm sympathy for old popular poetry and folk-tales, and published over 20 volumes, mainly tales and novels, including the folk-song collection *Des Knaben Wunderhorn* (1806, 'The Boy's Magic Horn') with Clemens von Brentano. His writing is overtly moralistic and his most ambitious work is the unfinished novel *Die Kronenwächter* (1817, 'The Crown Minder'). His wife, Bettina (1785–1859), Brentano's sister, was as a girl infatuated with Goethe, and afterwards published a (largely fictitious) *Correspondence* with him, as well as 10 volumes of tales and essays. ▥ H Liedke, *Literary Criticism and Romantic Theory in the Works of Achim von Arnim* (1927)

Arnim, Hans Georg von 1581–1641
German soldier and diplomat

Born in Brandenburg, he served in the Swedish army under Gustaf II Adolf in the war with Russia (1613–17), and with the Poles against Sweden in 1621. During the Thirty Years War (1618–48) he served with the Imperial armies under Wallenstein (1625–28). In 1631, however, leading the Saxon army in alliance with the Swedes against the Imperial army, he took Prague, but was soon driven out by Wallenstein.

Arnim, Jürgen, Baron von 1891–1971
German soldier
Born of an old Silesian military family, he served in World War I, and in World War II was given command of a Panzer Division in the Russian campaign. He took over the 5th Panzer Army in Tunisia in 1943 and succeeded Erwin Rommel in command of the Afrika Corps. In May 1943 he surrendered his troops to the Allies, and was interned in Great Britain and later the USA.

Arnim, Karl Joachim Friedrich Ludwig von
See **Arnim, Achim von**

Arnim, Mary Annette, Countess von,
pseudonym **Elizabeth**, *née* Mary Annette Beauchamp
1866–1941
New Zealand writer
She was born in New Zealand and travelled to England with her family in 1871. She attended Queen's College School in London and won a prize for her organ-playing at the Royal School of Music. Following her marriage in 1891 to the Prussian Count von Arnim-Schlagenthin, she went to live on his Pomeranian estate which provided the inspiration for her best-known work, *Elizabeth and her German Garden* (1898), written under her pseudonym Elizabeth. On her death she tried to settle in England, Switzerland and France, and her experiences at this time are described in *All the Dogs of My Life* (1936). Her other books include *Enchanted April* (1922) and *Mr Skeffington* (1940). She was courted by the writer **H G Wells**, but eventually married Francis, 2nd Earl Russell (1865–1931), the elder brother of the philosopher **Bertrand Russell**, but they separated in 1919. She was the cousin of **Katherine Mansfield**.

Arno, Peter, *pseudonym of* Curtis Arnoux Peters
1904–68
US cartoonist
Born in New York, he was one of the first contributors to the *New Yorker* magazine, from 1925, with satirical drawings of New York café society. He also wrote musical revues, including *Here Comes the Bride* (1931).

Arnobius the Elder d.330AD
Teacher of rhetoric
He taught at Sicca, in Numidia, Africa, and became a Christian about 300AD. He wrote a vigorous defence of Christianity, *Adversus Nationes*, translated in volume xix of the *Ante-Nicene Library*.

Arnold of Brescia c.1100–55
Italian churchman and politician
Born at Brescia, he was possibly educated in France under **Peter Abelard**. He became a monk, but his preaching against the wealth and power of the Church led to his banishment from Italy (1139). He returned to Rome in 1145 and became involved in an insurrection against the papal government, which continued for some 10 years. When this movement failed, he fled, but was captured by the forces of Emperor **Frederick I, Barbarossa**, brought to Rome, condemned for heresy, and hanged. 🕮 G W Greenaway, *Arnold of Brescia* (1931)

Arnold, Aberhard 1883–1935
German pacifist, founder of the Bruderhof movement in Nazi Germany
Born in Breslau, he studied theology at Halle, but disqualified himself from the degree through his insistence on being baptized on profession of faith (he later obtained a doctorate with a dissertation on **Nietzsche**). A convinced pacifist associated with the Student Christian Movement, he linked spiritual authenticity with an awareness of economic injustice. He visited Bruderhof colonies in Canada, and incurred the hostility of the Gestapo which saw allegiance to the state as the highest

priority. He died of complications following a leg injury. A selection of his writings and addresses, *God's Revolution*, was published in 1984.

Arnold, Benedict 1741–1801
American general and turncoat
Born in Norwich, Connecticut, at the age of 14 he ran away from home and joined the provincial troops, but soon deserted, and became a merchant in New Haven. In the American Revolution he joined the colonial forces, and for his gallantry at the Siege of Quebec (1775) was made a brigadier-general. He also fought with distinction at the Battles of Ridgefield and Saratoga, and in 1778 was placed in command of Philadelphia. His resentment at being passed over for promotion, followed by his marriage to a woman of loyalist sympathies, led him to conspire with **John André** to deliver West Point to the British. When the plan was detected and André was captured, Arnold fled behind British lines, and was given a command in the royal army. He moved to England in 1781, and lived the rest of his life in obscurity in London. 🕮 James T Flexner, *The Traitor and the Spy* (1953)

Arnold, Sir Edwin 1832–1904
English poet and journalist
Born in Gravesend, Kent, he won the Newdigate Prize for poetry at Oxford in 1852, taught at King Edward's School, Birmingham, and in 1856 became principal of Deccan College, Poona (Pune), India. Returning in 1861, he joined the staff of the *Daily Telegraph*, of which he became editor in 1863. He wrote *The Light of Asia* (1879) on Buddhism, and other poems coloured by his experience of the East.

Arnold, Eve 1913–
US photojournalist
Born in Philadelphia to Russian immigrant parents, she originally studied medicine but changed to photography studies at the New School for Social Research, New York (1947–48). The first woman to photograph for Magnum Photos (1951), she became a full member of the group in 1957. She moved to London in 1961, and travelled to the USSR five times from 1965, to Afghanistan and Egypt (1967–71), and to China (1979). Her photo-essays have appeared in publications like *Life*, *Look* and the *Sunday Times*. The exhibition 'Eve Arnold in Britain' was shown at the National Portrait Gallery, London, in 1991. Well known for her photography of women, the poor and the elderly as well as celebrities such as **Marilyn Monroe**, she published *The Un-retouched Woman* (1976), *In China* (1980) and *All in a Day's Work* (1989), among other books. She also made the film *Behind the Veil* (1973).

Arnold, Henry Harley, *known as* Hap Arnold
1886–1950
US air force officer
Born in Gladwyne, Pennsylvania, he was educated at the US Military Academy, West Point, and was commissioned into the infantry in 1907. He learned to fly with the **Wright** brothers and served with the air section of signal corps. He commanded 1st Air Wing, GHQ Air Force (1931), and became commanding general US Army Air Corps (1938) and chief of US Army Air Forces (1941). He was a general of the army (1944) and of the air force (1947). He wrote several books, including *This Flying Game* (1936) and *Global Mission* (1949).

Arnold, Joseph 1782–1818
English botanist
Born in Beccles, Suffolk, he studied medicine at Edinburgh University, graduating in 1807, and in 1808 he entered service with the British navy. He visited Java with Sir **Stamford Raffles**, who later invited Arnold to accompany him to Sumatra as naturalist. In 1818 at Pulau Lebar,

Sumatra, Arnold discovered the largest flower known, measuring a yard across and weighing 15 lb. This was later named *Rafflesia arnoldii* by Robert Brown.

Arnold, Sir Malcolm Henry 1921–
English composer
Born in Northampton, Northamptonshire, he studied composition with Gordon Jacob at the Royal College of Music (1938–40) and was principal trumpet player with the London Philharmonic Orchestra until 1948. A prolific writer, his work is inventive and colourful, and makes adventurous and dramatic use of traditional tonality and form. He has composed eight symphonies and other orchestral music including the overture *Tam O'Shanter* (1955), 18 concertos, five ballets, two one-act operas, and vocal, choral and chamber music. Of his film scores, *Bridge over the River Kwai* received an Academy Award (1957). He was knighted in 1993.

Arnold, Matthew 1822–88
English poet and critic
Born in Laleham, Middlesex, the eldest son of Thomas Arnold of Rugby, he was educated at Winchester, Rugby, and Balliol College, Oxford. He won the Newdigate prize with a poem on Cromwell (1843), and in 1845 was elected a Fellow of Oriel College. He was private secretary to Lord Lansdowne (1847–51), then was appointed one of the lay inspectors of schools (1851–86), and from 1857 to 1867 he was Professor of Poetry at Oxford. He was frequently sent by the government to inquire into the state of education on the Continent, especially in France, Germany and Holland, and his reports of English deficiencies attracted much attention in England, as did his application to scripture of the methods of literary criticism. He made his mark with *Poems: A New Edition* (1853–54), which contained 'The Scholar Gipsy' and 'Sohrab and Rustum', and with *New Poems* (1867), which contained 'Dover Beach' and 'Thyrsis'. He published several distinguished works of criticism including *On the Study of Celtic Literature* (1867), *Culture and Anarchy* and *Literature and Dogma* (1872). 📖 M Thorpe, *Matthew Arnold* (1969); L Trilling, *Matthew Arnold* (1939)

Arnold, Thomas 1795–1842
English educationist and scholar
Born in East Cowes, Isle of Wight, he was the father of Matthew Arnold, and was educated at Winchester and Corpus Christi College, Oxford, where he was a brilliant Classical scholar. He took deacon's orders in 1818 and settled at Laleham, near Staines, as a private 'crammer' of students, and married Mary Penrose. In 1828 he was appointed headmaster of Rugby, charged with the task of regenerating the school. He reformed the school, introduced mathematics, modern history and modern languages to the curriculum, and instituted the form system and also introduced the prefect system to keep discipline. He had a profound and lasting effect on the development of public school education in England. In 1841 he was appointed Regius Professor of Modern History at Oxford. He was the author of six volumes of sermons, an edition of Thucydides, and a *History of Rome* (3 vols, 1838–43). His second son, Thomas (1823–1900), was a literary scholar, and his daughter, Mary Augusta, was the novelist Mrs (Mary Augusta) Ward. 📖 Michael McCrum, *Thomas Arnold, headmaster: a reassessment* (1989); David Newsome, *Godliness and Good Learning: Four Studies in a Victorian Ideal* (1961)

Arnolfo di Cambio 1232–1302
Italian sculptor and architect
Born in Colle di Val d'Elsa, he was a pupil of Nicola Pisano and worked on his master's shrine of S Dominic, Bologna and the pulpit at Siena before going to Rome in 1277 where he executed a portrait of Charles of Anjou,

one of the first modern portrait statues. His tomb of Cardinal de Braye at Orvieto, now much altered, set the style for wall-tombs for more than a century. The famous bronze statue of Saint Peter in Saint Peter's, Rome, is attributed to him. He was the designer of Florence Cathedral and the remains of his sculptural decoration for it are in the cathedral museum.

Arnulf See Ernulf

Arp, Halton Christian 1927–
US astronomer
Born in New York City, he studied at Harvard and the California Institute of Technology before spending most of his scientific life at the Mount Wilson and Palomar Observatory. In 1956 he was the first to establish the relationship between the maximum luminosity of novae and the rate at which this luminosity declines. In 1966 he produced an *Atlas of Peculiar Galaxies*. Arp has done much to relate radio galaxies to their optical counterparts, and is known for his work on high-luminosity variable stars found in globular clusters.

Arp, Hans or Jean 1887–1966
Alsatian sculptor and poet
He was born in Strasbourg, and had a command of three languages: French, German and Alsatian. He was the outstanding poet of the Dada movement, which he helped to found (1916) with Hugo Ball in Zurich, and illustrated some of their publications. Later poetry includes the collection *Le Siège de l'Air* (1946). As a sculptor he began by producing abstract reliefs in wood, such as *Madame Torso in a Wavy Hat* (1916, Berne) and *Forest* (1916, Penrose Collection, London), but after 1928 he worked increasingly in three dimensions, and he was second only to Constantin Brancusi in his influence on organic abstract sculpture. Examples of later three-dimensional work include *Landmark* (1938) and *Ptolemy I* (1953, both in Paris). In 1922 he married and worked closely with the constructivist artist, Sophie Taeuber(-Arp). From 1949 he visited the USA, where he executed a monumental wood relief for Harvard (1950), in 1954 he won the International prize for sculpture at the Venice Biennale, and in 1958 he created a mural for the UNESCO building in Paris. 📖 R W Last, *Hans Arp* (1969)

Árpád d. c.907
National hero of Hungary
A Magyar chieftain in the Caucasus, he led the Magyars from the Black Sea into the Valley of the Danube after defeat by the Pechenegs (c.896) and occupied modern Hungary. He founded the Árpád dynasty of Hungary, from St Stephen (997) to 1301. Under him the Magyars first gained a footing in that country about 884.

Arrabal, Fernando 1932–
Spanish dramatist and novelist
Born in Melilla, Spanish Morocco, he studied law in Madrid and drama in Paris, and then settled permanently in France. His first play, *Pique-nique en campagne* (1959, Eng trans *Picnic on the Battlefield*, 1964), established him in the tradition of the Theatre of the Absurd, greatly influenced by Samuel Beckett. He coined the term 'Panic theatre', intended to shock the senses, employing sadism and blasphemy to accomplish its aims. In *Le Cimetière des voitures* (1958, Eng trans *The Car Cemetery*, 1969) life is seen as a used car dump, and in *Cérémonie pour un noir assassiné* (1965, Eng trans *Ceremony for a Murdered Black*, 1972), ceremonial rites are used to play out sadistic fantasies. He writes in Spanish, his work being translated into French by his wife. In 1967 he was charged by a Spanish court with blasphemy and anti-patriotism, and his *Et ils passèrent des menottes aux fleurs* (1969, Eng trans *And They Put Handcuffs on the Flowers*, 1971), based on conversations with Spanish

political prisoners, was eventually banned in France and Sweden while becoming his first major success in the USA in 1971. As well as several plays, he has published poetry and novels including *Baal Babylone* (1959, Eng trans 1961). 🕮 A Schifres, *Entretiens avec Arrabal* (1969)

Arrau, Claudio 1903–91
Chilean pianist
Born in Chillan, he gave his first recital in Santiago aged five. His musical education was sponsored by the Chilean government, and he studied at the Stern Conservatory, Berlin (1912–18), with the Liszt pupil Martin Krause (1853–1918). Arrau himself taught there from 1924 to 1940. He has appeared at all major concert halls and festivals throughout the world and is renowned as an interpreter of Bach, Beethoven, Chopin, Schumann, Liszt and Brahms. His musical thoughts were collected in *Conversations with Arrau* by Joseph Horowitz (1982).

Arrhenius, Svante August 1859–1927
Swedish physical chemist and Nobel Prize winner
Born in Wijk, near Uppsala, he went to the University of Uppsala in 1876, where he studied both chemistry and physics, and in 1881 he moved to Stockholm. His doctoral thesis on the experimental determination and theoretical interpretation of the electrical conductivities of dilute solutions of electrolytes was barely accepted by the University of Uppsala, whose scientific establishment was outraged by its novel ideas. Arrhenius was fortunately already highly regarded by Wilhelm Ostwald, Jacobus van't Hoff and other prominent physical chemists, and was awarded a travelling scholarship by the Academy of Sciences. In 1891 he became a lecturer in the Stockholm Högskola and was promoted to professor in 1895. In 1902 he received the Davy Medal of the Royal Society and was elected a Foreign Member of the Society in 1911. He was awarded the Nobel Prize for chemistry in 1903. He became director of the Nobel Institute of Physical Chemistry in Stockholm in 1905, a post he held until a few months before his death. His other main contribution to physical chemistry was his formulation in 1889 of the dependence of the rate coefficient of a chemical reaction on temperature (the Arrhenius equation). In later life he applied the methods of physical chemistry to the chemistry of living matter, and he was also interested in astrophysics, particularly the origins and destinies of stars and planets.

Arriaga, Juan Crisóstomo 1806–26
Spanish composer
Born near Bilbao, he was a child prodigy, producing his first opera, *Los esclavos felices* ('The Happy Slaves') in 1820. He became an assistant professor at the Paris Conservatoire in 1824, and although he died at the age of 19, his compositions show remarkable maturity, with the Symphony in D being reminiscent of Beethoven.

Arriaga, Manoel José de 1840–1917
Portuguese statesman
He took part in the revolution of 1910 which overthrew King Manuel II (1889–1932, ruled 1908–10), and from 1911 to 1915 was the first elected President of the Republic of Portugal.

Arrian, *Latin* Flavius Arrianus c.95–180AD
Greek historian
A native of Nicomedia, Bithynia, he became an officer in the Roman army, and was appointed Governor of Cappadocia by Hadrian. He edited the *Encheiridion* ('Manual of Philosophy') of his friend and mentor Epictetus, whose *Diatribai* ('Lectures') he wrote out in eight books, of which four have been preserved. His chief work is the *Anabasis Alexandrou*, a history of the campaigns of Alexander the Great, which has survived almost entire. His accounts of the people of India, and of a voyage round the Euxine, are valuable for ancient geography.

Arrianus, Flavius See Arrian

Arrol, Sir William 1839–1913
Scottish engineer
Born in Houston, Renfrewshire, he got his first job in a thread mill as a cotton boy at the age of 10 by lying about his age. He became an apprentice blacksmith at the age of 14, studied mechanics and hydraulics at night school, and started his own engineering business at the age of 29. He made a railway viaduct at Greenock in 1865, constructed the second Tay Railway Bridge (1882–87) to replace the ill-fated bridge that collapsed in 1879, the Forth Railway Bridge (1883–90), and Tower Bridge in London (1886–94). He was an MP for South Ayrshire from 1892 to 1906.

Arrom, Cecilia Francesca de See Caballero, Fernán

Arrow, Kenneth Joseph 1921–
US economist and Nobel Prize winner
Born in New York City, he graduated at Columbia University and was professor at Stanford University (1949–68) and Harvard (1968–79). In 1962 he served on the Council of Economic Advisers in the John F Kennedy administration. His primary field is the study of collective choice based on uncertainty and risk. His books include *Social Choices and Individual Values* (1951) and *The Future and the Present in Economic Life* (1978). He shared the 1972 Nobel Prize for economics with Sir John Hicks.

Arrowsmith, Aaron 1750–1823
English cartographer
Born in Winston, Durham, he went to London about 1770, and by 1790 had established a great map-making business. His nephew, John Arrowsmith (1790–1873), was also an eminent cartographer.

Arsinoë c.316–270BC
Macedonian princess
She was the daughter of Ptolemy I, Soter and one of the most conspicuous of Hellenistic queens. She married first (c.300BC) the aged Lysimachus, King of Thrace, secondly (and briefly) her stepbrother, Ptolemy Ceraunus, and finally (c.276) her own brother, Ptolemy II, Philadelphus, so becoming queen of Egypt. Several cities were named after her.

Arsonval, (Jacques-)Arsène d' 1851–1940
French physicist
He was born in Borie into an ancient French noble family, and followed family tradition by choosing a medical career. He attended the lectures of Claude Bernard, became his assistant (1873–78) and was director of the Laboratory of Biological Physics at the Collège de France from 1882, and professor from 1894. Arsonval invented the reflecting galvanometer named after him, the first electrically controlled constant-temperature incubator, and also experimented with high-frequency oscillating currents for electromedical purposes. Created a knight of the Legion of Honour in 1884, he received the Grand Cross when he retired in 1931.

Artachaies fl.c.500BC
Persian engineer
He built military roads and bridges in the service of Xerxes I, and supervised the construction of a canal, wide enough for two warships to be rowed abreast, across the one and a half miles of the Athos peninsula in northern Greece.

Artaud, Antonin Marie Joseph 1896–1948
French dramatist, actor, director and theorist of the Surrealist movement

He was born in Marseilles and became an active member of the Surrealist movement (1924–26). He published a volume of verse *L'Ombilic des limbes* (1925, 'The Umbilicus of Limbo'), and co-founded the Théâtre **Alfred Jarry** (1927). The theatre that he proposed dispensed with narrative and psychological realism, and returned to theatre as a primitive rite, and the mythology of the human mind as expressed in dreams and interior obsessions. The function of drama was to give expression, through movement and gesture, to the inexpressible locked within the conciousness. His main theoretical work is the book, *LeThéâtre et son Double* (1938, Eng trans *TheTheatre and its Double*, 1958). As the creator of what has been termed the Theatre of Cruelty, his influence on post-war theatre was profound. A manic-depressive, his last years were spent in a mental institution, from where he continued to write. His *Collected Works* appeared in English in 1968–74 (4 vols). ▣ Martin Esslin, *Antonin Artaud* (1976)

Artaxerxes See **Ardashir I**

Artaxerxes I *called* Longimanus ('Long-Handed') d.425BC
King of Persia

The second son of **Xerxes I**, he reigned from c.464 to 425BC. In a long and peaceful reign, he sanctioned the Jewish religion in Jerusalem, and appointed **Nehemiah** governor of Judea (445BC).

Artaxerxes II *called* Mnemon ('Mindful') d.c.358BC
King of Persia

The son of **Darius II**, he reigned from 404 to c.358BC. He lost control of Egypt, but became the arbiter of Greece. He rebuilt the royal palace at Susa.

Artaxerxes III *originally* Ochus d.338BC
King of Persia

The son and successor of **Artaxerxes II**, he found the empire disintegrating at his accession (358BC), but his cruel energy did much to build it up again. He was poisoned by his favourite eunuch, Bagoas.

Artedi, Peter 1705–35
Swedish ichthyologist and botanist

Known as 'the father of ichthyology', he wrote *Ichthyologia*, a very important systematic study of fishes; it was edited by **Linnaeus**, his closest friend, and was published in 1738, after Artedi had drowned in an Amsterdam canal. He inspired Linnaeus in classification of animals and plants.

Artemisia II d.c.350BC
Queen of Caria

She was the sister and wife of Mausolus, ruler of Caria. She succeeded Mausolus (353–352BC) and erected the magnificent Mausoleum at Halicarnassus (now Bodrum, Turkey) to his memory. It was one of the traditional Seven Wonders of the Ancient World. She was also a botanist and gave her name to the plant genus *Artemisia*.

Art Ensemble of Chicago
US experimental jazz group

The Art Ensemble of Chicago provided a crucial focal point for the developments growing out of the experimental AACM (Association for the Advancement of Creative Musicians) movement in Chicago. The band was formed as a co-operative in 1968 by Lester Bowie (trumpet), Roscoe Mitchell (saxophones), Joseph Jarman (saxophones) and Malachi Favors (bass), with Famadou Don Moye (drums) joining in 1969. Their ritualistic free-form jazz explorations embraced elements of many musical traditions, including all forms of jazz, blues, soul, funk and a wide variety of ethnic music, which they

dubbed Great Black Music. Both the Art Ensemble, which is still performing, and its many offshoots have been significant forces in contemporary American jazz.

Artevelde, Jacob van 1290–1345
Flemish statesman

A wealthy and highborn brewer of Ghent, he organized an anti-French alliance of Flemish towns in the conflict between France and England at the outbreak of the Hundred Years War (1337–1453). He concluded a treaty with **Edward III** (1340), and was effectively Governor of Flanders, but when he proposed that **Edward**, 'the **Black Prince**', should be elected Count of Flanders, he was killed in a popular insurrection. His son, Philip van Artevelde (1340–82) headed a Ghent revolt against the Count of Flanders in 1382, but was defeated and killed at the Battle of Roosebeke.

Arthur fl.early 6th century
Semi-legendary King of the Britons

He may have been a Romano-British war leader in the west of England called Arturus, but he is represented as having united the British tribes against the invading Saxons, and as having been the champion of Christendom. His most famous victory was supposedly at Mount Badon (c.518) and a 10th-century source associates his death with a battle at Camlan (c.539), after which he was buried at Glastonbury. The *Anglo-Saxon Chronicle* makes no mention of him, however, and he first appears in the 9th century Welsh chronicle, **Nennius's** *Historia Britonum*. Other works in which he appears include the *Annales Cambriae* (10th century), and *The Black Book of Camarthen* (12th century). He also figures in the Welsh romance *Kilhwch and Olwen*, and in the *Gesta Regum Anglorum* of **William of Malmesbury**. The story of Arthur became interwoven with legends of the Holy Grail and the Knights of the Round Table at Camelot, told by such writers as **Geoffrey of Monmouth, Chrétien de Troyes, Layamon**, and **Sir Thomas Malory.**

Arthur, Prince 1187–1203
Duke of Brittany

Born in Nantes, he was the posthumous son of Geoffrey, Duke of Brittany, and grandson of **Henry II**. On the death of his uncle, **Richard I** (1199), he claimed the English throne. Although Richard had made him his heir, there was no established English custom as to whether the Crown should pass to Arthur or to Richard's brother, **John** (Lackland), but the French king, **Philip II**, upheld Arthur's claim until John came to terms with Philip in the Treaty of Le Goulet. Arthur was captured and imprisoned by John (1202), and died, possibly on John's orders. Rumours about his death helped to undermine John's authority in Anjou, Maine and Normandy.

Arthur, Prince 1486–1502
English prince

Born in Winchester, he was the eldest son of **Henry VII**. When he was less than two years old a marriage was arranged between him and **Catherine of Aragon** in order to provide an alliance between England and Spain. The wedding took place in November 1501, but Arthur, a sickly young man, died six months later at Ludlow before the marriage was consummated.

Arthur, Chester Alan 1830–86
21st President of the USA

Born in Fairfield, Vermont, the son of an Irish Baptist minister, he became the head of an eminent law firm and leader of the Republican Party in New York State. He was appointed Collector of Customs for the port of New York in 1871, and his removal in 1878 by President **Rutherford B Hayes**, who was determined to carry out Civil Service reform, outraged New York Republicans. To placate the 'stalwart' faction of the party, he was chosen as the Republican vice-presidential nominee in 1880 and was elected with **James A Garfield** as President. On Garfield's assassination in 1881 Arthur became President, and although it was expected that he would use the office to champion the spoils systems, he instead supported the Civil Service Reform Act of 1883. His administration (1881–85) was known for its efficiency and integrity, but by 1884 ill health had sapped his energy, and he failed to win his party's presidential nomination.

Arthur, Sir George 1785–1854
British diplomat
Born near Plymouth, he was Governor of British Honduras (1814–22), Van Diemen's Land (1823–36), Upper Canada (1837–41) and Bombay (1842–46).

Arthur, Jean, *originally* Gladys Georgianna Greene 1905–91
US actress
Born in New York City, the daughter of a photographer, she left school at the age of 15 to become a model, and later an actress. She made her film debut in *Cameo Kirby* (1923) followed by several unremarkable roles. Being a husky-voiced, vivacious actress, she survived the transition to sound, became adept at comedy and co-starred with some of Hollywood's most prominent actors. Her best films include *Mr Deeds Goes to Town* (1936), *Mr Smith Goes to Washington* (1939) and *The More The Merrier* (1943, Academy Award nomination). She retired from the screen after *Shane* (1953) and later taught drama at Vassar College. Her infrequent stage appearances include a highly regarded *Peter Pan* (1950) and *The First Monday in October* (1975), and she was the star of the television series *The Jean Arthur Show*.

Artigas, José Gervasio 1764–1850
Uruguayan national hero
Born in Montevideo, he was a gaucho in his youth, then an army officer in Spanish service. He became the most important local patriot leader in the wars of independence against Spain, and also resisted the centralizing pretensions of Buenos Aires. The last 30 years of his life were spent in exile in Paraguay.

Artin, Emil 1898–1962
Austrian mathematician
Born in Vienna, he studied in Leipzig, Germany, and taught at the universities of Göttingen and Hamburg before emigrating to the USA in 1937, where he held posts at Indiana and Princeton before returning to Hamburg in 1958. His work was mainly in algebraic number theory and class field theory, and has had great influence on modern algebra. On the basis of earlier work by Takagi, Artin solved **David Hilbert**'s problem concerning the existence of a general reciprocity law, thus completing a line of inquiry begun by **Carl Friedrich Gauss** which was central to the theory of numbers. Recently Artin's work on braids (a part of knot theory) caught the attention of particle physicists.

Artzybashev, Boris 1899–1965
US artist
Born in Kharkov, Russia, he was the son of the author Mikhail Artzybashev (1878–1927). He went to the USA in 1919, and illustrated books and magazine covers. His illustrations had a vivid and repetitive brilliance of pattern, reminiscent of the early Ballets Russes décors. He also wrote stories for children, based on Russian folklore.

Arundel, Thomas 1353–1414
English prelate and statesman
The third son of Richard Fitzalan, Earl of Arundel, he was Chancellor of England five times (1386–89, 1391–96, 1399, 1407–10, 1412–13). He became archdeacon of

Taunton and Bishop of Ely (1374), then Archbishop of York (1388), and finally of Canterbury (1396). He supported the nobles opposed to **Richard II**, who banished him (1397), but he returned to help seat Henry of Lancaster (**Henry IV**) on the throne (1399). He was a vigorous opponent of the Lollards.

Arup, Sir Ove Nyquist 1895–1988
English civil engineer
Born in Newcastle upon Tyne, of Danish parentage, he studied philosophy and engineering in Denmark before moving to London in 1923. He became increasingly concerned with the solution of structural problems in Modernist architecture, for example the Highpoint flats (1936–38) and the spiral reinforced concrete ramps of the penguin pool at Regent's Park Zoo (1934), both in London. He was responsible for the structural design of Coventry Cathedral (designed by Sir **Basil Spence**, 1962) and St Catherine's College, Oxford (by **Arne Jacobsen**, 1964). With his partner Jack Zunz, he evolved the structural design which permitted the realization of **Jørn Utzon**'s unique architectural conception of the Sydney Opera House (1956–73).

Arzner, Dorothy 1900–79
US film director
Born in San Francisco, she studied medicine at the University of Southern California and became a volunteer ambulance driver during World War I. She began her film career as a script typist in 1919, then, diligently learning the craft of filmmaking, she progressed from script supervisor to editor on such important silent features as *Blood and Sand* (1922). Encouraged by director James Cruze (1884–1942), she edited several of his westerns including *The Covered Wagon* (1923) and *Old Ironsides* (1926) which she also wrote. After making her directorial debut with *Fashions for Women* (1927), she directed Paramount's first sound feature *Wild Party* (1929). Her best-known films include *Merrily We Go To Hell* (1932), *Christopher Strong* (1933) and *Dance, Girl Dance* (1940). The only major woman director in Hollywood in the 1930s, she worked with many of the top female stars of the era, such as Clara Bow, Claudette Colbert and Katharine Hepburn.

Asad, Hafez al- See **Assad, Hafez al-**

Asada Goryu 1734–99
Japanese astronomer
Born in Kizuki, Kanagawa, he did much to turn Japanese astronomy and calendrical science away from Asiatic and towards Western models. He was self-taught in astronomy and medicine, but achieved recognition in both, and made a living from the latter. He improved astronomical instruments, but his best work was on the numerology of planetary distances and on the calendar.

Asam, Cosmas Damian 1686–1739 and Egid Quirin 1692–1750
Bavarian architects and decorators
Sons of the fresco painter Hans Georg Asam (1649–1711), they worked together, Cosmas as a fresco painter and Egid as a sculptor. After training in Rome under **Carlo Fontana**, they developed to spectacular heights the Baroque idea of combining architecture, sculpture, painting and lighting effects in church interiors to produce highly emotive decoration and melodramatic *tableau vivant* high altars. The most fantastic of these altars is that of the Abbey Church in Weltenburg, which depicts the story of St George and the dragon. Another of their well-known churches is St John Nepomuk, Munich (1732–46).

Asbjørnsen, Peter Christian 1812–85
Norwegian folklorist

Born in Christiania (now Oslo), he studied at the university there, then for four years was a tutor in the country. On long journeys on foot he collected popular poetry and folklore, and, with his friend **Jørgen Moe**, Bishop of Christiansand, published the famous *Norske Folkeeventyr* (1841–44, Eng trans *Norwegian Folk Stories*, 1859), followed by *Norske Huldreeventyr og Folkesagn* (1945–48) which he published alone.

Asbury, Francis 1745–1816
US churchman

Born in Handsworth, Staffordshire, England, he was sent as a Methodist missionary to America in 1771. He was a key figure in the foundation of the Methodist Episcopal Church (1770–84), and in 1784 was consecrated as superintendent. In 1785 he became the first Methodist bishop in the USA.

Asch, Sholem 1880–1957
US writer

Born in Kutno, Poland, he was educated at the Hebrew school there. He went to Warsaw in 1899 and in 1900 he had his first story in Hebrew published. He emigrated to the USA in 1914 and became naturalized in 1920. His prolific output of novels and short stories, most of them originally in Yiddish but many since translated, includes *The Mother* (1930), *The War Goes On* (1936), *Der man fun Netseres* (1943, Eng trans *The Nazarene*), *The Apostle* (1943), *East River* (1946) and *Moses* (1951), mostly concerned with the fate of modern Jewry. His early work includes the plays *Mottke Gânef* (1916, Eng trans *Mottke the Thief*,1917) and *Got fun Nekomeh* (1907, Eng trans *The God of Vengeance*, 1918). ▢ C Lieberman, *The Christianity of Sholem Asch* (1953)

Ascham, Roger 1515–68
English humanist and scholar

Born in Kirby Wiske near Thirsk, Yorkshire, he was educated at St John's College, Cambridge. He became Reader in Greek there, despite his avowed leaning to the Reformed doctrines (c.1538). In defence of archery he published, in 1545, *Toxophilus* ('Lover of the Bow'), the pure English style of which ranks it among English classics. It provided the model for many later books, including Izaak Walton's *Compleat Angler*. In 1546 he was appointed University Orator. From 1548 to 1550 he was tutor to the Princess Elizabeth (the future **Elizabeth I**), and later became Latin secretary to **Mary I** (1554). His moderation prevented him from offending by his Protestantism and after Mary's death Elizabeth retained him at court as secretary and tutor. His principal work was *The Scholemaster*, an influential treatise on education, published posthumously by his widow in 1570. ▢ LV Ryan, *Roger Ascham* (1963)

Asclepiades fl.1st century BC
Greek physician

Born in Pruss, Bithynia, he seems to have been a peripatetic teacher of rhetoric before settling in Rome as a physician. There he advanced the doctrine that disease results from discord in the corpuscles of the body, and recommended good diet and exercise as a cure.

Ascoli, Graziadio Isaia 1829–1907
Italian philologist

Born of Jewish parentage in Görz (now Gorizio, in north Italy), he was appointed Professor of Philology in Milan in 1860. He is known mainly for his work on Italian dialectology, although he also made contributions to the fields of Indo-European, Celtic and Romance linguistics, in particular the 'substratum' theory, according to which certain features of the pronunciation of French, Provençal, and northern Italian dialects are attributable

to Celtic speech habits causing modifications to the Latin spoken in these regions. He founded the *Archivio glottologico italiano* in 1873. He was created a senator in 1888.

Aselli, Gasparo 1582–1626
Italian physician

Born in Cremona, he studied medicine at the University of Pavia before practising in Milan. Famed for his surgical skills, he served from 1612 to 1620 as the head surgeon of the Spanish army in Italy. His surgical experience clearly re-established an interest in anatomical investigation that had initially been sparked by his teacher, Giambattista Carcano-Leone, himself the pupil of the pre-eminent **Gabriele Fallopius**. Aselli's most notable work was the discovery of the lacteal vessels of the intestine.

Ash'arī, al-, *in full* Abū al-Ḥasan al-Ash'arī 873/874–935/936
Islamic theologian and philosopher

Born in Basra, he studied with the sect of Mutazilites, with whom he broke at the age of 40. In 915 he moved to Baghdad and associated with disciples of Ibn Hanbal, but gradually evolved his own theology and gathered around him his own school of followers. His major work is *Maqalat*, and his major thesis was to defend the idea of God's omnipotence and to reaffirm traditional interpretations of religious authority within Islam.

Ashbee, Charles Robert 1863–1942
English designer, architect and writer

Born in Isleworth, Surrey, he was educated at King's College, Cambridge, and was much influenced by the work and thinking of **William Morris** and **John Ruskin**. He founded the Essex House Press and the London Survey, and was founder and director of the Guild of Handicraft (1888–1908) in London's East End (later in Gloucestershire), employing over 100 craftworkers, the largest-scale attempt to put into practice the ideals of the Arts and Crafts movement. As an architect he specialized in church restoration, and his publications include *The Book of Cottages and Little Houses* (1906). He was also a noted silversmith.

Ashbery, John Lawrence 1927–
US poet, critic and novelist

Born in New York City, he attended Harvard, where he became close friends with the poets Kenneth Koch and Frank O'Hara, and he has been associated with the highly visual, almost Abstract Expressionist language of the New York school. He published his first volume, a chapbook, *Turandot and Other Poems*, in 1953, but did not attract critical attention until the publication of *Some Trees* in 1956. Influenced by **W H Auden**, he inspires both admiration and antipathy. In 1976 his twelfth collection, *Self-Portrait in a Convex Mirror*, won the National Book Critics Circle Prize, the National Book Award for poetry, and the Pulitzer Prize for poetry. Other volumes include *The Tennis Court Oath* (1962), *Rivers and Mountains* (1966), *Houseboat Days* (1977) and *Shadow Train* (1982). His only novel is *A Nest of Ninnies* (1969), co-authored with James Schuyler. He has also published several volumes of non-fiction including *April Galleons* (1987). ▢ D Shapiro, *John Ashbery: An Introduction to the Poetry* (1979)

Ashburner, Michael 1942–
English geneticist

He studied at Cambridge, where he remained as a research assistant from 1966 to 1968, when he received his PhD. He then became a university demonstrator (1968–73), lecturer (1973–80), Reader in Developmental Genetics (1980–91) and Senior Research Fellow at Churchill College (1980–90). Elected FRS in 1990, he has been Professor of Biology at Cambridge since 1991, and has held research fellowships and visiting professorships in many countries. Ashburner is best known for his work on the heat shock genes of the fruit fly. These genes are activated by a short burst of increased temperature, and are thus useful in the study of gene control.

Ashburton, 1st Baron See Baring, Alexander

Ashby (of Brandon, Suffolk), Eric Ashby, Baron 1904–92
Australian botanist and educator
Born in London, England, educated at London and Chicago universities, he was appointed Professor of Botany at Sydney University in 1938. From 1947 to 1950 he held the chair of botany at Manchester University, where he was also director of the botanical laboratories. He became president and Vice-Chancellor of Queen's University, Belfast (1950–59), and Vice-Chancellor of Cambridge (1967–69). He was deeply involved in experimental biology and environmental matters, and published numerous books and papers on these subjects. He chaired the Royal Commission on Environmental Pollution (1970–73) and was knighted in 1956. He was created a life peer in 1973. Ashby was also a member of the University Grants Commission (1959–67), and president of the British Association for the Advancement of Science in 1963.

Ashby, Dame Margery Irene, *née* Corbett
1882–1981
English feminist
The daughter of the Liberal MP for East Grinstead, she was educated at home and studied classics at Newnham College, Cambridge. She attended the first International Women's Suffrage Congress in Berlin (1904) and subsequently worked with various women's organizations, travelling widely throughout the world and becoming president of the International Alliance of Women for 23 years (1923–46). In recognition of her international work she was awarded an honarary degree by Mount Holyoke College, USA. Married to Arthur Ashby from 1910, she stood as Liberal candidate seven times between 1918 and 1944. She was also co-founder of the Townswomen's Guilds with Eva Hubback.

Ashby, Winifred 1879–1975
US immunologist
Educated at Northwestern and Washington universities, and gaining a PhD at the University of Minnesota (1921), she joined the scientific staff of the St Elizabeth's Hospital in Washington in 1924, remaining there until 1949. Her pioneering work was first published in 1919 and her observations on patients receiving transfusions during the next few years provided fundamental information about the life-span of red blood cells. She devised the Ashby technique, a method of determining survival rates of red blood cells in the human body. Her work was little recognized at the time, however, and did not achieve widespread usage until World War II.

Ashcroft, Dame Peggy (Edith Margaret Emily) 1907–91
English actress
She was born in Croydon, Greater London, and first appeared on the stage with the Birmingham Repertory Company in 1926. She scored a great success in London in *Jew Süss* (1929), played Desdemona to Paul Robeson's Othello (1930), and acted leading parts at the Old Vic in the season of 1932–33. Other great roles included a memorable Juliet in John Gielgud's production of *Romeo and Juliet* (1935), *Cleopatra* (1935), and *Hedda Gabler* (1954). She worked both in films, such as *A Passage to India* (1984, Academy Award for Best Supporting Actress), and on the British and US stage, and in 1991 received the Olivier award for outstanding service to the theatre. She was

created DBE in 1956. 📖 Garry O'Connor, *The Secret Woman: The Life of Peggy Ashcroft* (1997)

Ashdown, Paddy, *properly* Jeremy John Durham Ashdown 1941–
English politician
Born in India, he spent his childhood and youth in India and Ulster, and joined the Royal Marines when his parents emigrated to Australia. Serving in the Special Boat Squadron (the navy's equivalent of the SAS), in Malaysia and Northern Ireland, he also acquired a first class degree in Mandarin at Hong Kong University. After five years in the diplomatic service, in 1976 he moved to south-west England, and overturned a large Conservative majority to become Liberal MP for Yeovil in 1983. In 1988 he won election as leader of the new Liberal and Social Democratic Party (the Liberal Democrats). In the 1997 general election his party won 46 seats compared to 20 in 1992. His publications include *Citizen's Britain* (1989) and *Making Change Our Ally* (1994).

Ashe, Arthur Robert, Jnr 1943–93
US tennis player
He was born in Richmond, Virginia. After studying at the University of California at Los Angeles on a tennis scholarship he was selected for the US Davis Cup side in 1963. He won the US national singles championship in 1968 and the first US Open championship later the same year. He was a professional tennis player from 1969 to 1979 and pursued a highly successful career, winning the men's singles at the Australian Open (1970) and at Wimbledon (1975) when he defeated Jimmy Connors. In his retirement (from 1980), he became a campaigner for AIDS (Acquired Immune Deficiency Syndrome) Awareness, having become a sufferer himself, allegedly after a blood transfusion during his second heart bypass operation in 1983. He was the first male black tennis player to achieve world ranking. 📖 Ed Weissberg, *Arthur Ashe* (1991)

Asher, Jane 1946–
English actress and writer
Born in London, she made her film debut at the age of five in *Mandy* (1952) and continued acting as a child. Other notable film appearances include *The Greengage Summer* (1961), *The Prince and the Pauper* (1962), *Alfie* (1966), *The Winter's Tale* (1968), *Henry VIII and His Six Wives* (1972) and *Paris by Night* (1989). On television, she played Celia Ryder in *Brideshead Revisited*, Faith Ashley in *Wish Me Luck* (1988–90) and Felicity Troy in *The Choir* (1995). Her stage plays include *The Philanthropist* (West End and Broadway). She also runs Jane Asher Party Cakes and has written many books mainly on cookery. She is married to Gerald Scarfe.

Ashford, Daisy (Margaret Mary), *married name* Mrs George Norman 1881–1972
English author
She was born in Petersham, Surrey. As an adult, she was apparently content to run a market garden with her husband, whom she married in 1920. Her fame rests on a story written in 1890, when she was nine years old: *The Young Visiters, or Mr Salteena's Plan*, in which Bernard Clark and Mr Salteena ('not quite a gentleman') vie for the hand of 17-year-old Ethel Monticue. Ashford discovered her imperfectly-spelled manuscript in 1919, and on its publication, with an introduction by J M Barrie, it became a bestseller. *The Young Visiters* subsequently became a successful play (1920) and provided the basis of musical (1968), and remains a popular success. Other juvenile Ashford writings appeared in *DA: Her Book* (1920). 📖 R M Malcolmson, *Daisy Ashford* (1984)

Ashkenazy, Vladimir 1937–
Icelandic pianist and conductor

Born in Gorky (now Nizhny Novgorod), USSR, he was joint winner (with **John Ogdon**) of the Tchaikovsky Piano Competition in Moscow (1962) and earned an international reputation as a concert pianist before concentrating more on conducting. He took Icelandic nationality in 1972, and became director of the Royal Philharmonic Orchestra, London, in 1987.

Ashley, Laura, *née* Mountney 1925–85
Welsh fashion designer

Born in Merthyr Tydfil, south Wales, she married Bernard Ashley in 1949 and they started up a business manufacturing furnishing materials and wallpapers with patterns and motifs based upon document sources mainly from the 19th century. When she gave up work to have a baby she experimented with designing and making clothes, and this transformed the business from one small shop to an international chain selling clothes, furnishing fabrics and wallpapers. Ashley Mountney Ltd became Laura Ashley Ltd in 1968, and her work continued to be characterized by a romantic style and the use of natural fabrics, especially cotton. 📖 Anne M Sebba, *Laura Ashley: A Life by Design* (1990)

Ashmole, Elias 1617–92
English antiquary

Born in Lichfield, Staffordshire, he qualified as a lawyer in 1638 and subsequently combined work for the Royalist cause with the study of mathematics, natural philosophy, astronomy, astrology and alchemy, entering Brasenose College, Oxford. In 1646 he became acquainted with **William Lilly** and other famous astrologers, and in 1650 he edited a work of the astrologer **John Dee** to which he added a treatise of his own. In 1652 he issued his *Theatrum Chymicum*, and in 1672 his major work, a *History of the Order of the Garter*. After the Restoration he mainly devoted himself to heraldic and antiquarian studies. In 1677 he presented to the University of Oxford a fine collection of rarities, bequeathed him by his friend **John Tradescant**, the Younger, thus founding the Ashmolean Museum (built in 1682). Among his other friends were **John Selden** and **William Dugdale**, whose daughter became Ashmole's third wife.

Ashmun, Jehudi 1794–1828
US philanthropist

Born in Champlain, New York, he was the founder in 1822 of the colony of Liberia as a homeland for freed US slaves on the west coast of Africa.

Ashoka See Aśocka

Ashton, Sir Frederick William Mallandaine 1904–88
English dancer and choreographer

Born in Guayaquil, Ecuador, he was brought up in Peru where he saw **Anna Pavlova** dance. Following education at an English public school, he had a brief business career in the City of London, during which time he took ballet classes with **Léonide Massine** in secret. He continued his studies with **Marie Rambert** who commissioned his first piece, *A Tragedy of Fashion* (1926). After a year dancing under the direction of **Bronislava Nijinska** in the USA, he returned to Britain to help found the Ballet Club, which later became Ballet Rambert (now Rambert Dance Company). During this time he partnered and created roles for dancers like **Alicia Markova**. He joined the Sadler's Wells Ballet in 1935 as a dancer/choreographer, and despite frequent trips abroad to the New York City Ballet, the Royal Danish Ballet company, and other companies, he remained at Sadler's Wells as the company developed into the Royal Ballet. In 1948 he became one of the company's artistic directors and in 1963 succeeded Dame **Ninette de Valois** as director, a post he held for seven years. His work includes *Façade* (1931), *Ondine* (1958),

La Fille Mal gardee (1960), *Marguérite and Armand* (1963, for which he teamed **Rudolf Nureyev** and **Margot Fonteyn**), *The Dream* (1964), *A Month in the Country* (1979), *Monotones* (1965), *Five Brahms Waltzes in the Manner of Isadora Duncan* (1979, created for **Lynn Seymour**) and *Rhapsody* (1980). He also worked in film, for *The Tales of Beatrix Potter* (1971), and opera—creating the dances in **Benjamin Britten**'s *Death in Venice* (1973). He was knighted in 1962, and given many other honours around the world. 📖 David Vaughan, *Frederick Ashton and his Ballets* (1977)

Ashton, Sir John William, *known as* Will 1881–1963
Australian landscape painter

Born in York, England, he moved with his family to Adelaide, South Australia, at the age of three. In 1899 he returned to England and studied in the artists' colony at St Ives, Cornwall, notably under Talmadge. He exhibited widely in London, at the Royal Academy and in private galleries, and at the Paris Salon. He quickly gained a reputation as a landscape artist, known especially for his bridges of the Seine and other French and Mediterranean subjects. He was a leading opponent of modern trends in painting.

Ashton, Julian Rossi 1851–1942
Australian painter and teacher

Born in Alderstone, Surrey, England, he studied art part time while working in the engineers' office of the Great Eastern Railway. In 1878 he emigrated to Australia and, while working as an illustrator for the Melbourne newspaper *The Age*, covered the capture of the **Ned Kelly** gang. He later moved to Sydney and in 1896 founded the Sydney Art School. He is best known for his influence on later Australian artists including **George Lambert**, Sydney Long, **Elioth Gruner** and **William Dobell**. He organized the Grafton Gallery (London) exhibition of Australian art in 1898, and worked strenuously for the recognition of Australian artists.

Ashton-Warner, Sylvia Constance 1908–84
New Zealand novelist and schoolteacher

Born in Stratford, she became a teacher and taught in several schools containing large numbers of Maori pupils. She developed an innovative method of teaching them to read and became interested in educational theory. She began her writing career with an autobiographical account of her teaching life, *Teacher*, which was at first rejected. She recast it as fiction and it appeared to considerable acclaim as *Spinster* (1958), through the success of which *Teacher* finally appeared in 1963. Other novels include *Incense to Idols* (1960), *Bell Call* (1964), *Greenstone* (1966) and *Three* (1971). Her autobiographical *I Passed This Way* (1979) highlights a sense of alienation from her homeland.

Ashurbanipal or Assurbanipal, *also called* Sardanapalus 7th century BC
King of Assyria

The eldest son of **Esarhaddon** and grandson of Sennacherib, he was the last of the great Assyrian kings and his reign (668–627BC) marks the zenith of Assyrian splendour. He extended his rule from Elam to Egypt, but the revolt of Babylon shook the empire. A generous patron of the arts, he founded in Nineveh the first systematically gathered and organized library in the ancient Middle East. The name Sardanapalus is also used for a legendary king whose story seems to draw from the lives of Ashurbanipal, his brother Shamash-shum-ukin, and Sin-shar-ishkun, the last Assyrian king.

Asimov, Isaac 1920–92
US novelist, critic and popular scientist

Born in Petrovichi, Russia, he was taken to the USA when he was three. He took a PhD in chemistry at Columbia University and led a distinguished career as an academic biochemist. As a science-fiction writer, he produced a prodigious body of work including *Foundation* (1951), *Foundation and Empire* (1952), *Second Foundation* (1953), *The Caves of Steel* (1954), *The Naked Sun* (1957), and the short stories which form the collection *I, Robot* (1950). A leading spokesman for science fiction, he became ubiquitous on television and on the lecturing circuit and was an untiring contributor to newspapers and magazines. Increasingly regarded as a scientific seer, he added the term 'robotics' to the English language. ◻ N Goble, *Asimov Analyzed* (1972)

Aske, Robert d.1537
English rebel
Originally from Yorkshire he became an attorney at Gray's Inn, London. He headed the Catholic rising known as the Pilgrimage of Grace in protest at **Henry VIII**'s dissolution of the monasteries, and was subsequently hanged in York for treason.

Askew, Anne 1521–46
English Protestant martyr
Born near Grimsby, Humberside, she was an early convert to the Reformed doctrines. Rejected because of this by her husband, she went to London to sue for a separation, but in 1545 was arrested on a charge of heresy. After examination and torture on the rack, she was burned in Smithfield, London.

Askey, Arthur 1900–82
English comedian
Born in Liverpool, he made his professional debut in 1924. A small man (he stood only 5ft 2in high), he became principal comedian in summer seasons at British seaside resorts. He achieved wide recognition on radio with *Band Wagon* (1938), and became known as 'Big-hearted Arthur'. He had a button-holing style, a cheery manner, a harmless humour, and made a catchphrase of 'I thank you!' He appeared regularly on television, and in several films.

Aśoka or Ashoka 3rd century BC
Ruler of India
The last major Mauryan emperor (c.269–232BC), and conqueror of Kalinga, he was a convert to Buddhism, and organized it as the state religion, while giving freedom to other religous sects. He gave up armed conquest in favour of disseminating *dharma* (broadly, moral principles), and inscribed his pronouncements on rocks and pillars. He founded hospitals, dug wells and planted roadside trees.

Aspasia 5th century BC
Greek adventuress
She was born in Miletus, Anatolia. Intellectual and vivacious, she was lampooned in Greek comedy and satire, but was held in high regard by **Socrates** and his followers. She was a great inspiration to **Pericles**, who successfully defended her against a charge of impiety, and became his mistress after his separation from his Athenian wife.

Aspdin, Joseph 1779–1855
English bricklayer and inventor
He was born in Leeds. A stonemason to trade, like many others he engaged in the search for an artificial cement in an effort to reduce the building industry's dependence on increasingly scarce and expensive timber. In 1824 he patented what he called 'Portland cement', manufactured from clay and limestone, a hydraulic cement which would set hard even under water.

Aspinall, Sir John Audley Frederick 1851–1937
English mechanical engineer

Born in Liverpool, he rose from locomotive fireman to be chief mechanical engineer and general manager of the Lancashire and Yorkshire Railway (1899–1919). He designed many types of locomotives and completed one of the first main-line railway electrification schemes in Great Britain from Liverpool to Southport (1904).

Asplund, Erik Gunnar 1885–1940
Swedish architect
Born in Stockholm, he designed the Stockholm City Library (1924–27), and he was responsible for most of the buildings in the Stockholm Exhibition of 1930. Their design was acclaimed for the new gaiety and imagination with which the architect used simple modern forms and methods, such as the cantilever and glass walls. His other works in Stockholm include the Woodland Chapel, Skandia Cinema, City Library and Woodland Crematorium, and the law courts in Gothenburg (1934–37).

Asquith, H(erbert) H(enry), 1st Earl of Oxford and Asquith 1852–1928
English statesman
He was born in Morley, Yorkshire, and educated at City of London School and Balliol College, Oxford. Called to the Bar in 1876, he became a QC in 1890 and was Liberal MP for East Fife (1886–1918). He became Home Secretary (1892–95) and, despite upsetting many of his fellow Liberals by his support for the anti-Boer imperialists during the South African War (1899–1902), Chancellor of the Exchequer (1905–08), succeeding Sir **Henry Campbell-Bannerman** as Prime Minister in April 1908. The social reforms in the early years of his administration (which included the introduction of old-age pensions) were overshadowed by a clash with the House of Lords over the 'People's Budget' of 1909, resulting in a restriction of their powers in the Parliament Act 1911. Asquith was also confronted by the suffragette movement, industrial strife, the threat of civil war over Home Rule for Ireland and the international crises which led to World War I. In May 1915 he formed and headed a war coalition but was ousted in December 1916 by supporters of **Lloyd George** and some Conservatives who thought his conduct of the war was not sufficiently vigorous. He lost his East Fife seat in 1918, led the Independent Liberals who rejected Lloyd George's continuing coalition with the Conservatives, and returned to the Commons as MP for Paisley in 1920. His disagreements with Lloyd George weakened the Liberal party and, although he was recognized as leader again between 1923 and 1926, the Liberals failed to regain their earlier position as the main opposition to the Conservatives. He was created an earl in 1925. He wrote his *Memories and Reflections* (1928) and his second wife **Margot Asquith** wrote a lively *Autobiography* (1922; revised edition 1962). ◻ J A Spender and Cyril Asquith, *Life of Herbert Henry Asquith, Lord Oxford and Asquith* (2 vols, 1932)

Asquith, Margot (Emma Alice Margaret), née Tennant 1864–1945
Scottish society figure
She was born in Peeblesshire, the daughter of Sir Charles Tennant, and received little formal education but possessed unusual literary, artistic and musical talents. Clever and sharp-tongued, she became a brilliantly witty hostess who led a group of young intellectuals and aesthetes called the 'Souls' who advocated greater freedom for women. In 1894 she married H H Asquith who became Prime Minister in 1908. Extremely influential in society, she continued her extravagant lifestyle unabashed during World War I. When Asquith was forced to resign in 1916, she wrote two famously indiscreet autobiographies.

Assad or Asad, Hafez al- 1928–
Syrian general and statesman

He was born in Qardaha, near Latakia in north-west Syria, into a peasant family of nine children, and changed his family name of Wahsh (boar in Arabic), to Assad (lion). After local schooling he joined the Ba'ath party at 16 and embarked on a military career, training as an airman and was then sent to the USSR for further studies. On his return to what was then the United Arab Republic of Egypt and Syria he commanded a night fighter squadron based in Cairo from 1958 to 1961, when the union with Egypt was dissolved and Syria became an independent republic. In 1966 Salah Jadid, secretary of the Ba'ath party, seized power and Assad was made Minister of Defence and Commander of the Air Force (1966–70), from which positions he built up a strong personal power base. When Jadid ordered Syrian forces into Jordan to fight King Hussein, Assad refused to commit his aircraft, saying he would never fight another Arab country. The army returned in defeat, Jadid was disgraced and Assad assumed ultimate power in a bloodless coup. As Prime Minister and then President (1971–), he has held power with a determined ruthlessness, despite suffering a heart attack in 1983. He belongs to the minority Alawi sect of Islam and has followed a policy of strengthening his nation and relentlessly opposing Israel, supporting the Palestinian radicals against Yasser Arafat's mainstream PLO (Palestine Liberation Organization). After the 1973 Arab–Israeli War, he negotiated a partial withdrawal of Israeli troops from Syria. In 1976 he sent Syrian troops into Lebanon, and did so again in early 1987. By 1989 he had imposed Syrian control over the greater part of Lebanon. He enjoyed Soviet support, and was one of the few Arab leaders to support Iran in its war with Iraq (1980–88). An austere, private man, he has few close contacts outside his family, of wife, daughter and four sons, his only extravagance reputedly being a liking for large, luxurious cars. He is generally regarded as the most skilful politician in the Middle East but his relations with the West have been damaged by a difference of views concerning terrorist activity. Relationships were, however, partially mended in 1987 when, following a meeting with former US President Jimmy Carter, Assad worked actively to secure the release of Western hostages. During the Gulf War of 1991 he pursued a policy of non-involvement and after it ended he entered discussions with US Secretary of State James Baker over the future of Lebanon, Israel and the PLO. Following the 1995 peace accord between Israel and the PLO, hopes are high that agreement can be reached over Lebanon, and that Syria will enter into a lasting peace with Israel. ▢ Moshe Ma'oz, *Asad* (1988)

Asselyn, Jan, *nicknamed* Crabbetje ('Little Crab') 1610–52
Dutch painter

Born in Amsterdam, he travelled to Italy and became a successful painter of Italianate landscapes which depicted imaginary Arcadian vistas inspired by the Roman countryside, often including Roman ruins. In this, and in his interest in subtle lighting effects, he was influenced by the major landscape painter of his day, Claude Lorrain. He is the subject of an etching by his friend Rembrandt.

Asser 9th century
Welsh scholar and bishop

He spent his youth in the monastic community at St David's. Gaining a reputation for scholarship, he was enlisted into the royal service as counsellor to Alfred the Great, King of Wessex and from c.885 divided his year between the court and St David's. The king's growing reliance on him resulted in Asser being made Bishop of Sherborne in 901 shortly before the king died. He is best known for his unfinished Latin biography of Alfred, first published in 1572.

Asser, Tobias Michael Carel 1838–1913
Dutch jurist and Nobel Prize winner

He was born in Amsterdam and became a Professor of Law at Amsterdam University. He founded the *Revue de droit International et de Législation comparée* ('Review of International Law and of Comparative Legislation') in 1869 and was a founder of the Institute of International Law in 1873. He persuaded the Dutch government to call the first Hague Conference for the unification of International Private Law in 1893, and was awarded, jointly with the Austrian pacifist Alfred Fried (1864–1921), the Nobel Peace Prize in 1911 for his work in creating the Permanent Court of Arbitration at the Hague Peace Conference of 1899.

Assurbanipal See Ashurbanipal

Astaire, Adele, *professional name of* Adele Austerlitz 1898–1981
US dancer, actress and singer

Born in Omaha, Nebraska, she was the older sister of Fred Astaire. Her career began in her teens, partnering her brother in a song-and-dance act that reached Broadway in 1917. Their post-war show *For Goodness Sake* (1922, known in the UK as *Stop Flirting*) was a big success, and they went on to further success in 1924 in Gershwin shows, including *Lady, Be Good* and *Funny Face*—both now inextricably associated with Fred's name. Adele's contribution to Fred Astaire's success was arguably greater than that of any of his other partners, including Ginger Rogers, but her activities decreased following her marriage to Lord Charles Cavendish (1932). *Smiles* (1930) was one of her last big successes.

Astaire, Fred, *professional name of* Frederick Austerlitz 1899–1987
US actor, dancer and singer

He was born in Omaha, Nebraska, and began his career teamed with his sister Adele Astaire as a touring vaudeville act (1916), rising to stardom with her on Broadway in specially written shows like *Lady Be Good* (1924) and *Funny Face* (1927). When Adele married (1932), Fred went to Hollywood and continued with various partners, notably Ginger Rogers, and choreographer Hermes Pan. His many films include *The Gay Divorcée* (1934), *Top Hat* (1935) and *Swing Time* (1936). He announced his retirement in 1946, but returned to create further classic musicals like *Easter Parade* (1948) and *The Bandwaggon* (1953), then turned to straight acting, winning an Academy Award nomination for *The Towering Inferno* (1974) and an Emmy for *A Family Upside Down* (1978). He received a special Academy Award in 1949 for his 'unique artistry and contributions to the technique of musical pictures'. A hard-working perfectionist who made his dancing appear effortless, he revolutionized the film musical with a succession of original and innovative tap-dance routines. He was described as the world's greatest dancer by both George Balanchine and Rudolf Nureyev. He published his autobiography, *Steps in Time*, in 1960. ▢ Bill Adler, *Fred Astaire: A Wonderful Life* (1987)

Astaire, Mrs Fred See Smith, Robyn

Astbury, William Thomas 1889–1961
English X-ray crystallographer

Born in Longton, Stoke-on-Trent, Staffordshire, he studied at Cambridge and with Sir William Bragg's team at University College London (1920–21) before becoming a lecturer in textile physics at the University of Leeds (1928), where he held the new chair of biomolecular structure from 1945. In 1926 he began taking X-ray diffraction photographs using natural protein fibres such as those of hair, wool and horn. Using the photographic techniques he had helped to develop, he showed that diffraction patterns could be obtained which changed when the fibre was stretched or wet. On this basis he classified fibrous proteins, and although his interpretation of their molecular structures proved incorrect, his pioneer work laid the basis for important work which followed, most notably by **Linus Pauling**. Astbury probably coined the phase 'molecular biology' and, with Florence Bell he attempted (wrongly) the first hypothetical structure for the key genetic material DNA (1938).

Astell, Mary 1668–1731
English religious writer
She was born in Newcastle upon Tyne, and later settled in Chelsea, London. In 1694 she proposed an Anglican academic sisterhood, but it was strongly criticized by Bishop **Gilbert Burnet** and did not materialize.

Astley, Philip 1742–1814
English theatrical manager and equestrian
Born in Newcastle under Lyme, Staffordshire, he started a circus at Lambeth in 1770, and also built Astley's Amphitheatre (1798), once one of the sights of London. He also established amphitheatres in Paris and several other venues in Europe. He was considered the best horse-tamer of his time.

Aston, Francis William 1877–1945
English physicist and Nobel Prize winner
Born in Birmingham and educated at Malvern, Birmingham and Cambridge, he was noted for his work on isotopes. He invented the mass spectrograph in 1919, with which he investigated the isotopic structures of elements and for which he won the Nobel Prize for chemistry in 1922. The Aston dark space, in electronic discharges, is named after him.

Astor, John Jacob 1763–1848
US financier
Born in Waldorf, Germany, the son of a butcher, he went to London at the age of 16 and worked with his brother, a maker of musical instruments. He emigrated to the USA in 1783 and invested his small capital in a fur business in New York. He built up a fur trading empire, first in Canada and then in the Far West, combining his holdings in the American Fur Company in 1808. He also prospered in the China trade, and he invested shrewdly in New York real estate. Astor used his friendship with **Thomas Jefferson** to advantage, in one instance gaining permission for one of his ships to sail to Canton during the 1807 embargo. He founded the settlement of Astoria in 1811. Astor helped the government finance the war of 1812 by lending them money at exorbitant rates of interest. He also used his influence to ease through Congress the Act establishing the Second Bank of United States. His major philanthropic act was the endowment of the Astor Library, now the New York Public Library. The Astor family became one of the leading clans in the USA's wealthy aristocracy.

Astor, John Jacob 1864–1912
US financier
A great-grandson of **John Jacob Astor** (1763–1848), he served in the Spanish-American war, and built part of the Waldorf-Astoria hotel in New York. He was drowned with the *Titanic*.

Astor (of Hever), John Jacob Astor, Baron 1886–1971
British newspaper proprietor
Born in New York, he was the son of William Waldorf, 1st Viscount **Astor**. Educated at Eton and New College, Oxford, he was aide-de-camp to the Viceroy of India (1911–14), was elected MP for Dover in 1922, and became chairman of the Times Publishing Company after the death of Lord Northcliffe (**Alfred Harmsworth**), resigning his directorship in 1962. ⌨ Derek Wilson, *The Astors, 1763–1992* (1993)

Astor, Mary, *originally* Lucille Langhanke 1906–87
US film actress
Born in Quincy, Illinois, she made her film debut in *The Beggar Maid* (1921) and was cast as beautiful ingénues in historical dramas like *Beau Brummell* (1924) and *Don Juan* (1926). She carved a special niche playing bitchy women of the world, winning an Academy Award for *The Great Lie* (1941), but her range also included the treacherous femme fatale of *The Maltese Falcon* (1941), comedy in *The Palm Beach Story* (1942) and tender drama in *Dodsworth* (1936). Despite press revelations of a scandalous private life and alcoholism, she moved into a phase playing warm-hearted matriarchs, most memorably in *Meet Me in St. Louis* (1944). She also appeared in films like *Act of Violence* (1948) and *Return to Peyton Place* (1961). Active on stage and television, she retired after *Hush, Hush Sweet Charlotte* (1964) and began to write novels and autobiography, including *A Life on Film* (1971).

Astor, Nancy Witcher Astor, Viscountess, *née* Langhorne 1879–1964
British politician
Born in Danville, Virginia, USA, the daughter of a wealthy tobacco auctioneer, she married **Waldorf Astor**, 2nd Viscount Astor, whom she succeeded as Conservative MP for Plymouth in 1919, becoming the first woman MP to sit in the House of Commons. She was known for her interest in social problems, especially women's rights and temperance.

Astor, Waldorf Astor, 2nd Viscount 1879–1952
British politician
He was born in New York City, USA, the son of **William Waldorf Astor**, 1st Viscount Astor. He moved to England with his family in 1889, was educated at Eton and New College, Oxford, and elected MP for Plymouth in 1910. On passing to the House of Lords in 1919 he became parliamentary secretary to the local government board (subsequently Ministry of Health) and his wife, **Nancy Astor**, succeeded him in the House of Commons. He was proprietor of the *Observer* (1919–45).

Astor, William Backhouse 1792–1875
US financier
The elder son of **John Jacob Astor** (1763–1848), he was born in New York. He augmented his inherited wealth and is said to have left $50 million. He added to his father's library bequest, and on account of his great property interests was known as the 'landlord of New York'.

Astor, William Waldorf Astor, 1st Viscount 1848–1919
British newspaper proprietor
Born in New York, he was the great-grandson of the fur magnate **John Jacob Astor** (1763–1848). Defeated in the election for governor of New York State (1881), he was US minister to Italy (1882–85). He emigrated to Great Britain in 1892 and bought the *Pall Mall Gazette* and *Pall Mall Magazine*. Naturalized in 1899, he bought the *Observer* in 1911, and was made a viscount in 1917.

Astorga, Nora 1949–88
Nicaraguan revolutionary and diplomat
Born in Managua, she studied sociology at the University of Washington DC then transferred to study law at the Universidad of Centroamericana in Managua. She started working covertly with the Sandinistas as a student. Later, as lawyer and head of personnel for a Nicaraguan construction company, she was involved in luring the National Guard general Perez Varga to her house where he

was ambushed and killed by rebels. Astorga was subsequently named ambassador to the USA. Although this appointment was vetoed by the CIA, she represented Daniel Ortega's regime at the United Nations and was successful in obtaining a World Court Decision which declared US support for the Contra guerillas illegal.

Astruc, Jean 1684–1766
French physician and biblical scholar
Born in Sauve, he wrote a work on Moses which laid the foundations for modern criticism of the Pentateuch, as well as volumes on the diseases of women and on venereal disease. He was employed as medical consultant to King Louis XV.

Asturias, Miguel Angel 1899–1974
Guatemalan fiction writer, poet and Nobel Prize winner
A law graduate from the National University, he spent many years in exile, particularly in Paris, where he studied anthropology and translated the Mayan sacred book *Popul Vuh*, written in the Quiche language, into Spanish. This was to have an enduring influence on his fiction. His most successful novel, *El Señor Presidente* was published in 1946 (Eng trans *The President*, 1963). Other books include *Hombres de maiz* (1949, Eng trans *Men of Maize*, 1975) and a trilogy on the foreign exploitation of the banana trade. A difficult, experimental and ambitious writer, he flirted with 'automatic writing' as a route into the unconscious. He was awarded the Nobel Prize for literature in 1967. In the Guatemalan Civil Service from 1946, he was ambassador to France (1966–70). 🕮 R J Callan, *Miguel Angel Asturias* (1970)

Atahualpa c.1502–1533
Last Emperor of the Incas
On the death of his father Huayna-Capac (c.1527) he ruled the northern half of the Inca Empire, the Kingdom of Quito, and in 1532 overthrew his elder brother, Huascar, who ruled Peru from Cuzco. Brave, ambitious, and popular with his troops, he was captured (1532) by the Spaniards led by Francisco Pizarro, who invaded and conquered Peru. Although a vast ransom was paid for his release, Atahualpa was found guilty of treason and strangled to death.

Atanasoff, John Vincent 1903–95
US physicist and computer pioneer
Of Bulgarian extraction, he was born in Hamilton, New York, and was educated at the University of Florida, Iowa State College and the University of Wisconsin, where he received a PhD in physics. In 1942,. with the help of Clifford Berry, he built an electronic calculating machine—the ABC (Atanasoff–Berry-Computer)—one of the first calculating devices utilizing vacuum tubes. Atanasoff failed to appreciate the importance of his work and he let the project drop and dismantled the ABC in 1948. His ideas entered the mainstream of computer development through John W Mauchly, who was influenced by Atanasoff in constructing the ENIAC (Electronic Numerical Integrator and Calculator). In 1972 a landmark court case ruled that Atanasoff—not John Presper Eckert and Mauchly—was the true originator of the electronic digital computer. In 1981 he received the Computer Pioneer Medal and in 1990 was awarded the National Medal of Technology.

Atatürk, Mustapha Kemal, *originally* Mustafa Kemal 1881–1938
Turkish general and statesman
He was born in Salonika and led the Turkish nationalist movement from 1909. During World War I he became a general and fought against the British in the Dardanelles, earning the title *pasha*. He drove the Greeks from Anatolia (1919–22), raising a nationalist rebellion in protest against the postwar division of Turkey, and in 1921 he established a provisional government in Ankara. The following year the Ottoman Sultanate was formally abolished, and in 1923 Turkey was declared a secular republic, with Kemal as President (1923–38). The focus of a strong personality cult, Kemal launched a programme of revolutionary social and political reform intended to transform Turkey from a feudal absolute monarchy into a modern republic. His reforms included the political emancipation of women (1934) and the introduction of the Latin alphabet to replace Arabic script, as well as increased educational opportunities and the suppression of traditional Islamic loyalties in favour of a secular Turkish nationalism. In 1935, upon the introduction of surnames into Turkey, he took the name Atatürk (Father of the Turks).

Atget, (Jean) Eugène (Auguste) 1857–1927
French photographer
He was born in Libourne, near Bordeaux, and worked as a sailor and actor before turning to photography, in which he was self-taught. Shunning modern methods, he continued to use gelatin dry-plate negatives and printing-out paper in order to achieve the extreme contrasts in light and dark that characterize his powerful, poetic photographs of Parisian scenes. He sold his work (he took over 10,000 photographs) cheaply to artists for use as source material, and to historical societies as records of Paris. Shortly before his death he was 'discovered' and rescued from obscurity by Berenice Abbott, who later published his work. He is regarded as one of the most influential documentary photographers of the 20th century. 🕮 Berenice Abbott, *The World of Atget* (1964)

Athaliah d.837 BC
Biblical character
She was the daughter of Ahab and Jezebel, and wife of Jehoram, King of Judah. She ruled Judah herself after her son, Ahaziah, was killed by Jehu (843 BC), slaughtering all the royal children except Ahaziah's son Joash. Her support of Baal worship led, after six years, to an insurrection headed by the priests. Joash was made king, and Athaliah put to death. Her fate is the subject of a play by Racine, to which Felix Mendelssohn added incidental music.

Athanaric d.381 AD
Visigothic chieftain
As chieftain (from AD364) he fought three campaigns against the Emperor Valens (b.c.328, ruled 364–378), brother of Emperor Valentinian I, and was a fierce persecutor of the Christians in Dacia (Romania). Finally defeated by the Huns in 376, he was driven from the north of the Danube, and died at Constantinople (Istanbul).

Athanasius, St c.296–373 AD
Greek Christian theologian and prelate
He was born in Alexandria. In his youth he often visited the celebrated hermit St Antony, and himself for a time embraced an anchorite's life. As a deacon, he was distinguished participant at the great Council of Nicaea (Nice) in AD325. In 326 he was chosen Patriarch of Alexandria and primate of Egypt, and was newly installed when Arius, banished on the condemnation of his doctrine at Nicaea, was recalled, and recanted. In opposition to the wishes of Emperor Constantine, Athanasius refused to restore Arius to communion. For this, and on other charges brought by the Arians, he was deposed by the Synod of Tyre in 335. The sentence was confirmed by the Synod of Jerusalem in 336, when he was banished to Trèves. In 338 he was restored until 341, when he was condemned by a council of 97 (mainly Arian) bishops in Antioch. Orthodox synods in Alexandria and in Sardica declared their support for him, and he was again restored to office (349). Under the Arian Emperor Constantius, he was again condemned and expelled, and went to a remote

desert in Upper Egypt. Under **Julian** 'the Apostate', toleration was proclaimed to all religions, and he became once more Patriarch of Alexandria (361). His next controversy was with the heathen subjects of Julian, who forced him to flee from Alexandria, and hide in the Theban desert until 363, when Emperor Jovian (c.331–364) ascended the throne. After holding office for a short time he was expelled again by the Arians under the Emperor Valens (364–378) who, after petitions from the orthodox Alexandrians, restored him to his See, in which he continued until his death. A great leader during the most trying period in the history of the early Christian church, Athanasius' conscientiousness, wisdom, courage and intellect distinguish him in his age. His writings, polemical, historical, and moral, are simple, cogent and clear. The polemical works treat chiefly of the Trinity, the Incarnation and the divinity of the Holy Spirit. The so-called *Athanasian Creed* (representing Athanasian beliefs) was little heard of until the 7th century. His feast day is 2 May. ▫ F L Cross, *The Study of St Athanasius* (1945)

Athelstan or Aethelstan c.895–939
Anglo-Saxon king
The grandson of **Alfred the Great**, he was the son of **Edward, the Elder**, whom he succeeded as King of Wessex and Mercia (924). A warrior king, he extended his rule over parts of Cornwall and Wales, and kept Norse-held Northumbria under control. In 937 he defeated a confederation of Scots, Welsh and Vikings from Ireland in a major battle at Brunanburh. He fostered Haakon (the future **Haakon I, Haraldsson**), the son of King **Harald Halfdanarson** of Norway. One of his sisters married the Emperor **Otto I, the Great**, another married Hugh the White, Duke of the Franks, father of **Hugo Capet**, King of France. These marriages showed Athelstan's European standing, and he was presented with the Emperor **Constantine**'s sword and **Charlemagne**'s lance by the Duke of the Franks. At home, Athelstan improved the laws, built monasteries, and promoted commerce. He died unmarried and was succeeded by his half-brother, **Edmund I**.

Athenaeus 2nd century AD
Greek writer
Born in Naucratis, Egypt, he lived first in Alexandria, and later, towards the close of the 2nd century AD, in Rome. He wrote the *Deipnosophistae* ('Banquet of the Learned'), a collection of anecdotes and excerpts from ancient authors arranged as scholarly dinner-table conversation. Thirteen of its 15 books survive more or less complete, together with a summary of the other two.

Athenais See Eudocia

Atherton, Gertrude Franklin, *née* Horn
1857–1948
US novelist
She was born in San Francisco. Left a widow in 1887, she travelled extensively, living in Europe most of her life, and the settings for her novels range from Ancient Greece to California and the West Indies. She was made Chevalier of the Legion of Honour for her relief work in France during World War I, and in 1934 became president of the American National Academy of Literature. The most popular of her many novels are *The Conqueror* (1902), a fictional biography of **Alexander Hamilton**, and *Black Oxen* (1923), which is concerned with the possibility of rejuvenation. ▫ J H Jackson, *Gertrude Atherton* (1940)

Athlone, 1st Earl of See Ginckell, Godert de

Atholl, Katharine Marjory Stewart-Murray, Duchess of, *née* Ramsay 1874–1960
Scottish Conservative politician
Born in Bamff, Perthshire, daughter of historian Sir James Ramsay, she studied at Wimbledon High School and the Royal College of Music and was an accomplished pianist and composer. In 1899 she married John George Stewart-Murray, Marquess of Tullibardine, the future 8th Duke of Atholl, becoming Duchess of Atholl in 1917. During the Boer War and World War I she organized concerts for the troops abroad and helped in hospital work. Though an early opponent of women's suffrage, she became MP for Kinross and Perthshire in 1923 and was the first Conservative woman minister as Parliamentary Secretary to the Board of Education (1924–29). She successfully resisted changes in policy which would have adversely affected the education of poorer children, and from 1929 to 1939 campaigned against ill-treatment of women and children in the British Empire. She was responsible for translating an unexpurgated edition of *Mein Kampf* to warn of **Hitler**'s intentions. On principle she opposed Britain's policy of imagining a collective European policy of non-intervention in the Spanish Civil War, while not advocating British assistance to the Spanish Republic. She published the best-selling *Searchlight on Spain* (1938). She opposed the Munich Agreement, and was dropped as Tory candidate, resigned her seat in parliament and was defeated in the resultant by-election where she was lampooned as the 'Red Duchess'. From 1939 to 1960 she worked to aid refugees from totalitarianism. Other publications include *Women and Politics* (1931).

Atiyah, Sir Michael Francis 1929–
English mathematician
Born in London and educated in Egypt and at Manchester Grammar School, he graduated from Trinity College, Cambridge. After lecturing in Cambridge and Oxford he became Savilian professor at Oxford (1963–69), and in 1966 was awarded the Fields Medal (the mathematical equivalent of the Nobel Prize). After three years at Princeton University he returned to Oxford as Royal Society research professor in 1973. He became Master of Trinity College and president of the Royal Society in 1990. He has worked on algebraic geometry, algebraic topology, index theory of differential operators, and most recently on the mathematics of quantum field theory, where he has been particularly concerned with bridging the gap between mathematicians and physicists. One of the most distinguished British mathematicians of his time, he was appointed to the Order of Merit in 1992. His *Collected Works* (5 vols) were published in 1988.

Atkins, Anna, *née* Children 1799–1871
English photographer and illustrator
Born in Tonbridge, she was the daughter of the scientist John George Children who had an early interest in the processes of photography, and was also a friend of Sir **John Herschel**, the originator of the cyanotype (blueprint) process. In 1825 she married John Pelly Atkins, a Jamaican coffee-plantation owner and railway promoter. She is best known for scientific illustration and particularly for her books of original cyanotype illustrations of plants, the first of which was the privately published and pioneering *British Algae: Cyanotype Impressions* (12 parts, 1843–53). She was the first person to produce a photographically illustrated book, pre-dating the *Pencil of Nature* (1844–46) of **William Henry Fox Talbot**, and was the first to use it as part of an extensive scientific study of the natural world.

Atkins, Chet (Chester Burton) 1924–
US country music guitarist, producer and record executive
Born in Luttrell, Tennessee, he began to play guitar as a child, and developed a distinctive style, influenced by Merle Travis's finger-picking, but encompassing jazz, blues, and other colourings. He worked with the **Carter**

Family and Hank Williams before signing with RCA. He took over the label's country roster in 1952, and brought in many important artists, including Dolly Parton, Willie Nelson, Waylon Jennings and Charley Pride. His smooth, pop-based production approach, later dubbed 'country-politan', laid the foundations of country music's modern commercial success. He is a virtuoso guitarist, and has recorded many albums since his debut in 1953 with *Gallopin' Guitar*.

Atkinson, Rowan Sebastian 1955–
English actor, writer and comic

Born in Newcastle upon Tyne, he first appeared in Oxford University revues at the Edinburgh Festival Fringe, and in 1981 became the youngest performer to have had a one-man show in the London's West End. His subsequent appearances include *The Nerd* (1984), *The New Revue* (1986) and *The Sneeze* (1988). On television he has starred in *Not the Nine O'Clock News* (1979–82), *Blackadder*, a comedy series set in various historical periods (1983–89), and the silent comedy series *Mr Bean* (1990–) where much of the entertainment lies in his facial elasticity. Feature films he has appeared in include *The Tall Guy* (1989), *The Witches* (1990) and *Four Weddings and a Funeral* (1994), and he had a voice part in *The Lion King* (1994).

Atkinson, Thomas Wittlam 1799–1861
English architect and travel-writer

He was born in Cawthorne, Yorkshire, and worked as a quarryman, stonemason, then architect. Between 1848 and 1853, he travelled some 40,000 miles (64,360km) in Asiatic Russia with his wife Lucy, painting and keeping journals which formed the basis of several works on that part of the world.

Atlas, Charles, *originally* Angelo Siciliano 1894–1972
US physical culturist

He was born in Acri, Italy, and emigrated to the USA with his family in 1904. A '97-pound weakling' as a youth, he developed a system of muscle exercises that improved his physique until he resembled the statue of a Greek god (Atlas). Billing himself as 'the World's Most Perfectly Developed Man', he taught his bodybuilding system through a successful worldwide mail-order business.

Atta, Hakim ben See Mokanna, al-

Attenborough, Sir David Frederick 1926–
English naturalist and broadcaster

Born in London, he is the younger brother of filmmaker Richard Attenborough. After service in the Royal Navy (1947–49) and three years as an editorial assistant in an educational publishing house, he joined the BBC in 1952 as a trainee producer. For the series *Zoo Quest* (1954–64) he made zoological and ethnographic expeditions to remote parts of the globe to capture intimate footage of rare wildlife in its natural habitat. From 1965 to 1968 he was Controller of BBC 2 and subsequently director of programmes (1969–72) before returning to documentary-making, with such series as *Life on Earth* (1979), *The Living Planet* (1984), *The First Eden* (1987), *Lost Worlds, Vanished Lives* (1989), *The Trials of Life* (1990), *Life in the Freezer* (1993) and *The Private Life of Plants* (1995). His books include *Zoo Quest to Guiana* (1956), *The Tribal Eye* (1976), *The Living Planet* (1984), *The Trials of Life* (1990) and *The Private Life of Plants* (1994).

Attenborough, Richard Attenborough, Baron 1923–
English film actor, producer and director

He was born in Cambridge and trained at RADA before making his first professional appearance in *Ah, Wilderness* (1941) and film debut in *In Which We Serve* (1942). At first typecast as weak and cowardly youths, he played the thug Pinkie in *Brighton Rock* on stage (1943) and on film (1947).

He developed into a conscientious character actor, winning British Academy Awards as the kidnapper in *Séance on a Wet Afternoon* (1964) and the bombastic sergeant major in *Guns at Batasi* (1964). He was actor–producer of several feature films in the 1960s before turning director on *O What a Lovely War!* (1969). A 20-year crusade to film the life of Mahatma Gandhi led to *Gandhi* (1982) which won eight Academy Awards. His other directorial credits include *Cry Freedom* (1987), *Shadowlands* (1993) and *In Love and War* (1996). After a lengthy absence, he returned to acting in *Jurassic Park* (1993). The Richard Attenborough Centre for Disability and the Arts was opened in 1997 at Leicester University. A tireless ambassador for the British film industry, he married actress Sheila Sim (1922–) in 1944 and is the brother of Sir David Attenborough.

Atterbury, Francis 1663–1732
English prelate

Born in Milton Keynes, Buckinghamshire, he was educated at Westminster and Christ Church, Oxford. In c.1687 he took orders and won such a reputation as a preacher that he was appointed lecturer of St Bride's (1691), a royal chaplain, and minister to Bridewell Hospital. He then became successively dean of Carlisle (1704), Prolocutor of Convocation (1710), dean of Christ Church (1712), and Bishop of Rochester and dean of Westminster (1713). In 1715 he refused to sign the bishops' Declaration of Fidelity, and in 1722 he was committed to the Tower for conspiring to restore the Stuarts. Atterbury, who defended himself with great ability, was deprived of all his offices, and for ever banished from the kingdom. In 1723 he left England, and settled in Paris. His works comprise sermons, and letters to Pope, Jonathan Swift, Henry Bolingbroke, and others of his friends. Charles Boyle's *Examination of Bentley's Dissertations on the Epistle of Phalaris* (1698), a clever but shallow performance, satirized by Swift in his *Battle of the Books* (1704), was really by Atterbury who had been the young earl's tutor at Christ Church.

Atticus, Titus Pomponius 110–32BC
Roman intellectual, businessman and writer

He was born in Rome, of a wealthy family, and educated with Cicero and Gaius Marius the Younger. He acquired the surname Atticus because of his long residence in Athens (85–65BC) to avoid the civil war. In 32 he was informed that a disorder he suffered from was terminal, and he died after five days of voluntary starvation. He was a wealthy and highly cultivated man who espoused the Epicurean philosophy and combined his literary activities with a successful business career. He amassed a large library, wrote histories of Greece and Rome (now lost), and was an intimate friend of Cicero, who used him as an editor and consultant. Cicero's *Letters to Atticus* form a famous and prolific correspondence.

Attila c.406–453AD
King of the Huns

Called the Scourge of God, he was the legendary king who appears as Etzel in the German *Nibelungenlied* and Atli in the Old Icelandic *Völsunga Saga* and the heroic poems of the *Edda*. In AD434 he became king (jointly at first with a brother) of the Huns from Asia, who ranged from the north of the Caspian to the Danube. He soon had dominion over Vandals, Ostrogoths, Gepidae and Franks, so that his rule extended over Germany and Scythia from the Rhine to the frontiers of China. Having murdered his brother he devastated all the countries between the Black Sea and the Mediterranean (447). The Emperor Theodosius was defeated, and Constantinople (Istanbul) survived only because the Huns knew nothing of siege warfare. Thrace, Macedonia and Greece were overrun, but when Attila invaded Gaul (451), Aëtius, the Roman commander, and Theodoric I, the King of the

Visigoths, finally defeated him. He retreated to Hungary, but invaded Italy (452), Rome itself being saved only by huge bribes from Pope Leo I. Attila died the night after his marriage to a Burgundian princess, Ildeco, and the Hunnish Empire decayed. His death, in a pool of blood in bed, led to stories of vengeance and murder by his bride, graphically described by Edward Gibbon. 🕮 E A Thompson, *A History of Attila and the Huns* (1948)

Attlee (of Walthamstow), Clement Richard Attlee, 1st Earl 1883–1967
English Labour statesman

Born in Putney, near London, he was educated at University College, Oxford, and was called to the Bar in 1905. Through Haileybury House, a boy's club in the Stepney slums, he developed a practical interest in social problems which, alongside the works of John Ruskin and William Morris converted him to socialism, and in 1910 he became secretary of Toynbee Hall in east London. A lectureship at the newly founded London School of Economics (1913–23) was interrupted by service in World War I, in which he was wounded, and attained the rank of major. In 1919 he became the first Labour Mayor of Stepney, and in 1922 he entered parliament and became Ramsay MacDonald's parliamentary secretary (1922–24), Under-Secretary of State for War (1924), served on the Simon Commission on India (1927–30) and was Postmaster-General (1931) but did not become a member of the coalition government. One of the few Labour MPs to retain his parliamentary seat in the following election, he became Deputy Leader of the Opposition (1931–35) under George Lansbury, whom he succeeded as Leader in 1935, and paved the way for Churchill's wartime premiership by refusing to commit his party to a coalition under Neville Chamberlain. He was Dominions Secretary (1942–43) and Deputy Prime Minister (1942–45) in Churchill's War Cabinet. As Leader of the Opposition he accompanied Sir Anthony Eden to the San Francisco and Potsdam conferences (1945), and returned to the latter as Prime Minister after the 1945 Labour victory. Despite severe economic problems during his six years in office, he carried through a vigorous programme of nationalization and reform—the National Health Service was introduced and independence was granted to India (1947) and Burma (1948). Labour's foreign policy of support for NATO in the face of Russian intransigence, particularly the necessity for re-arming the Germans and the manufacture of British atom bombs, precipitated continuing party strife which at times taxed even Attlee's competent chairmanship. He earned affection and respect by his sheer lack of dogma, oratorical gifts or showmanship and by his balanced judgment, and quiet yet unmistakable authority which belied the public image of 'Little Clem'. He was Leader of the Opposition from 1951 to 1955 when he resigned and accepted an earldom. His many books include *The Labour Party in Perspective* (1937), with supplement *Twelve Years Later* (1949), and an autobiography, *As It Happened* (1954).

Attucks, Crispus c.1723–1770
American Revolutionary patriot

Nothing is known with certainty of his early life, but some historians identify him as the Massachusetts-born son of an African slave and a Natick Indian, who escaped from slavery and found work as a sailor on whaling ships. Accounts of the Boston Massacre (5 March 1770) describe him as a huge man, one of the foremost in the crowd of colonists that gathered to taunt a small group of British soldiers and the first to fall when the soldiers opened fire. He and the other four Americans killed in the massacre were hailed as martyrs by the independence movement and were buried in a common grave. His patriotism is honoured by a statue on Boston Common (erected 1888).

Attwell, Mabel Lucie 1879–1964
English artist and writer

Born in London, she studied at Heatherley's and other art schools, and married cartoonist Harold Earnshaw (1908). When her husband lost an arm in World War I, she worked to support him and their three children, at first illustrating children's classics such as the *Water Babies* (1915) and *Peter Pan* (1921). She was noted for her studies of children, both humorous and serious, with which she illustrated her own and others' stories for children. Her popular 'cherubic' dimpled tots were continued in annuals and children's books by her daughter, working under her mother's name. 🕮 Chris Beetles, *Mabel Lucie Attwell* (1988)

Attwood, Thomas 1765–1838
English musician and composer

Born in Halesowen, Worcestershire, he was a pupil of Mozart. He was organist of St Paul's from 1796 until his death.

Attwell, Winifred 1914–83
Trinidadian pianist and entertainer

Born in Trinidad, she was a piano-player from early childhood, and turned from a career in pharmacy to become a pop cabaret performer. This led to a lucrative contract with the British Decca record label and a string of 'ragtime' hits, featuring a jangly, public-bar piano sound, including 'Black and White Rag', 'Coronation Rag', and 'Let's Have a Party'. She enjoyed success later with concerts and records, but faded from view in the 1960s and emigrated to Australia.

Atwood, Margaret Eleanor 1939–
Canadian writer, poet and critic

Born in Ottawa, she spent her early years in northern Ontario and Quebec bush country. After graduating from the University of Toronto and Radcliffe College, she held a variety of jobs ranging from waitress and summer-camp counsellor to lecturer in English literature and writer-in-residence. Her first published work, a collection of poems entitled *The Circle Game* (1966), won the Governor-General's award. Since then she has published several volumes of poetry, collections of short stories— *Dancing Girls* (1977) and *Bluebeard's Egg* (1987)—and *Survival* (1972), an acclaimed study of Canadian literature. She is best known, however, as a novelist. *The Edible Woman* (1969) deals with emotional cannibalism and provoked considerable controversy within and beyond the women's movement. It was followed by *Surfacing* (1972), *Lady Oracle* (1976), *Life Before Man* (1979) and *Bodily Harm* (1982). In 1985, *The Handmaid's Tale* was shortlisted for the Booker Prize, as was *Cat's Eye* in 1989 and *Alias Grace* in 1996. Recent works include *The Robber Bride* (1993) and a collection of poems, *Morning in the Burned House* (1995). She has been described by one commentator as 'a staunch moralist' who insists 'that modern man must reinvent himself' and she is also a tireless campaigner for social justice. 🕮 J H Rosenberg, *Margaret Atwood* (1984); S Grace, *A Violent Duality* (1979)

Auber, Daniel-François-Esprit 1782–1871
French composer of operas

Born in Caen, he was a pupil of Cherubini. His best-known works are *La Muette de Portici* (1828, 'Mute Girl of Portici'), usually entitled *Masaniello*, and *Fra Diavolo* (1830, 'Brother Devil').

Aublet, Jean Baptiste Christophe Fusée 1723–78
French botanist, explorer and humanist

Born near Arles, Provence, he spent nine years establishing a garden of medicinal plants in Mauritius (1753–61), and then spent two years in Guyana (then French Guiana), where his studies of the tropical forest formed the basis for his *Histoire des plantes de la Guiane française* (4 vols, 1775, 'History of the Plants of French Guyana') and laid the foundation of tropical American forest botany. He later became the first secular slavery abolitionist, and his interest in racial and ethnic problems led Oliver Fuller Cook to give the name *Ethnora maripa* to the famous Maripa palm, which Aublet had discovered.

Aubrey, John 1626–97
English antiquary, biographer and folklorist
Born in Easton Piercy, Wiltshire, he was educated at Malmesbury, Blandford, and Trinity College, Oxford. He studied law but was never called to the Bar. In 1648 he discovered the remains of Avebury, and carried out archeological research there and elsewhere. He was nominated as one of the original Fellows of the Royal Society (1622). In 1652 he succeeded to several estates, but was forced through lawsuits to part with the last of them in 1670, and to part with his books in 1677. His last years were passed, in 'danger of arrests', under the protection of **Thomas Hobbes, Elias Ashmole**, and others. Only *Miscellanies* (1696), containing stories and folklore, was printed in his lifetime, but he left a mass of material. His biographical and anecdotal material on celebrities of his time like Hobbes, **Milton**, and **Francis Bacon**, collected for the antiquary Anthony à Wood (1632–95), was published in *Letters by Eminent Persons* (1813), better known as *Brief Lives*.

Aubriet, Claude 1665–1742
French flower and animal painter
He accompanied Joseph Tournefort on his Levant journey (1700–02). The much-cultivated plant, aubrietia, with its purple trailing plants, is named after him.

Aubusson, Pierre d' 1423–1503
French soldier and prelate
Grand Master of the Knights Hospitallers from 1476, his outstanding achievement was his defence of Rhodes (1480) against a besieging army of 100,000 Turks under Sultan **Mohammed II, the Conqueror**. In 1481 he made a treaty with the Turks under the new sultan, **Bayezit II**, by agreeing to imprison the Sultan's rebellious brother, Djem. In 1489 he was created cardinal for handing Djem over to Pope Innocent VIII. ▢ Gilles Rossignol, *Pierre d'Aubusson* (1991)

Auchincloss, Louis Stanton 1917–
US novelist, short-story writer and critic
Born in Lawrence, New York, he trained as a lawyer and was admitted to the New York Bar in 1941. He is a novelist of manners, at home with old money and a highly codified, traditional society, but also has a fine sense of intrigue. His first novel was *The Indifferent Children* (1947), written under the pseudonym Andrew Lee. The best of his subsequent books are *Pursuit of the Prodigal* (1959), *Portrait in Brownstone* (1962), *The Embezzler* (1966) and *A World of Profit* (1968). His later novels have attracted less critical acclaim. ▢ C C Dahl, *Louis Auchincloss* (1986)

Auchinleck, Sir Claude John Eyre 1884–1981
English field marshal
In World War I he served in Egypt and Mesopotamia, and in World War II he served in northern Norway and commanded an unsuccessful raid on Narvik (1940). He became Commander-in-Chief in India (1941) and succeeded **Archibald Wavell** in North Africa in July 1941. He made a successful advance into Cyrenaica, but was later thrown back by **Erwin Rommel**. His regrouping of the 8th Army on El Alamein paved the way for ultimate victory, but at the time Auchinleck was made a scapegoat for the retreat and replaced by General **Alexander** in 1942. In 1943 he returned to India as Commander-in-Chief, and subsequently served as Supreme Commander India and Pakistan (1947). He was promoted field marshal in 1946. ▢ Philip Warner, *Auchinleck the Lonely Soldier* (1982)

Auchterlonie, Willie 1872–1963
Scottish golf club maker
Born in St Andrews, Fife, he won the Open Golf Championship at the age of 21, using only seven homemade clubs. In 1935 he was appointed professional to the Royal and Ancient at St Andrews, where his workshop and store became venerated by golfers.

Auden, W(ystan) H(ugh) 1907–73
US poet and essayist
Born in York, England, he was educated at Gresham's School, Holt, and Christ Church, Oxford. His first volume of *Poems* (1930) was accepted for publication by T S Eliot at Faber and Faber. In the 1930s he wrote passionately on social problems of the 1930s from a far-left standpoint, especially in his collection of poems *Look, Stranger!* (1936). He paid many visits to Berlin and in 1935 he married Erika Mann, the daughter of **Thomas Mann**, in order to provide her with a passport out of Nazi Germany. He went to Spain as a civilian in support of the Republican side and reported on it in *Spain* (1937), followed by a verse commentary (with prose reports by **Christopher Isherwood**) on the Sino-Japanese war in *Journey to a War* (1939). He also collaborated with Isherwood in three plays—*The Dog Beneath the Skin* (1935), *The Ascent of F6* (1936) and *On the Frontier* (1938)—and with **Louis MacNeice** in *Letters from Iceland* (1937), and wrote the libretto for *Ballad of Heroes* by **Benjamin Britten** in 1939. He emigrated to New York in 1939 and was naturalized in 1946. *Another Time* (1940) contains some of his best-known poems. He was appointed associate professor at Michigan University, but returned to live in England when he was Professor of Poetry at Oxford (1956–61). In the USA he converted to Anglicanism, tracing this in *The Sea and the Mirror* (1944) and *For the Time Being* (1944). His later works include *Nones* (1951), *The Shield of Achilles* (1955), *Homage to Clio* (1960) and *City Without Walls* (1969). He edited many anthologies and collections, wrote much literary criticism and several librettos. A master of verse form, using fresh and accessible language, his influence as a poet has been immense. ▢ H Carpenter, *W H Auden: A Biography* (1981)

Audley, Sir James c.1316–1386
English knight
One of the original Knights of the Garter (1344), in 1350 he fought at Sluys, and in 1354 attended **Edward, the Black Prince**, who declared him the bravest knight on his side at Poitiers. In 1267 he was Governor of Aquitaine, in 1369 Great Seneschal of Poitou.

Audley (of Walden), Thomas Audley, Baron 1488–1544
English politician
Educated for the law, he became attorney for the Duchy of Lancaster in 1530 and King's Sergeant in 1531. Active in furthering **Henry VIII**'s designs, he profited greatly by ecclesiastical confiscations. In 1529 he was appointed Speaker of the House of Commons and in 1532 Lord Chancellor. He was named in the Commission for the trial of **Anne Boleyn**, and for the examination of **Catherine Howard**. He was made a baron in 1538.

Audouin, Jean Victor 1797–1841
French entomologist and naturalist
Born in Paris, he trained as a doctor, made a study of the blister beetle (Spanish Fly), then much used for medicinal purposes, and in 1833 was appointed Professor of Entomology at the Jardin des Plantes in Paris. He also studied silkworms and vine parasites, and was co-author of the *Dictionnaire classique d'histoire naturelle* (1822, 'Classical Dictionary of Natural History'). He also compiled the

Audubon, John James 1785–1851
US ornithologist and bird artist

Audubon was born in Les Cayes, Haiti, the illegitimate son of a French sea captain named Jean Audubon and a Creole woman. He was taken to France and adopted by Audubon and his wife, who died young. In 1803 he was sent to the USA to look after his father's property near Philadelphia, where he spent time hunting and drawing birds, but in 1807 he sold up. The following year he married Lucy Bakewell, who was later to provide much of their income through tutoring, and moved to Kentucky. There he had some unsuccessful business ventures, meanwhile devoting himself to his 'Great Idea'—an ambitious project to make a comprehensive catalogue of every species of bird in America. In order to paint the birds in lifelike poses, he would either trap them, or shoot them and thread wires into their bodies to make them stand up. He painted in pastel, watercolour and oils.

Around 1819, declared bankrupt, he explored the Ohio and Mississippi rivers in search of different subjects, stopping at the various towns to earn money painting portraits, and all the while adding to his vast collection of bird illustrations. In 1821 he and his wife moved to New Orleans.

In 1826 he took his work to Europe in search of a publisher, holding exhibitions in Paris, London, Liverpool and Edinburgh. A born showman, he cultivated a rugged backwoodsman image that appealed to fashionable society. In London he sought out the engraver and painter Robert Havell (1793–1878) to make the copperplate engravings of 'double-elephant' plates, and 1827 saw the publication in England of the first of the 87 portfolios of his massive *Birds of America* (1827–38). It eventually comprised coloured life-size plates of 1,065 birds, and cost $115,000. He also published, with the Scottish ornithologist William MacGillivray (1796–1852), an accompanying text, *Ornithological Biography* (1831–39). Between 1840 and 1844 he produced a 'miniature' edition in seven volumes which became a bestseller.

He eventually returned to the USA to settle; his spacious country house on the Hudson River is now Audubon Park, in New York City. There he prepared drawings for *The Viviparous Quadrupeds of North America* (3 vols, 1845–53, with **John Bachman**), which was completed by his two sons. The National Audubon Society, dedicated to the conservation of birds in the USA, was founded in his honour in 1866.
📖 Mary Durant and Michael Harwood, *On the Road with John James Audubon* (1980); A B Adams, *John James Audubon, A Biography* (1976).

---

ornithological section of the compendious *Description de l'Égypte* (1826, 'Description of Egypt'). Audouin's Gull was named after him.

Audrey, St See Etheldreda, St

Audubon, John James See panel above

Aue, Hartmann von See Hartmann von Aue

Auenbrugger, Leopold 1722–1809
Austrian physician
He was born in Graz, the son of an innkeeper. As a boy he learned that by tapping on the sides of winebarrels he could determine the fluid level, at the point where the sound changed character, and when he became a physician in Vienna, he introduced the use of percussion for medical diagnosis. His short book describing the technique, *Inventum novum* (1761, 'New Invention'), made little impact on medical practice until its value was appreciated by French physicians in the early 19th century. Also interested in the arts, he wrote the libretto for one of **Antonio Salieri**'s operas.

Auer, Karl, Baron von Welsbach 1858–1929
Austrian chemist
Born in Vienna, he invented the gas mantle which bears his name and carried out important work on the rare metals, isolating the elements neodymium and praseodymium. Finding that a mixture of thorium nitrate and cerium nitrate becomes incandescent when heated, he used this mixture to impregnate gas mantles, thereby making gas lighting cheaper and more efficient. His mantle is still used in kerosene lamps. He also made osmium filaments for use in electric light bulbs, the forerunners of the cheaper tungsten filaments used today, and developed the cerium–iron alloy known as 'Auer metal' or 'mischmetal'. The first improvement over the flint and steel in use since medieval times, it is still used to strike sparks in cigarette lighters and gas appliances.

Auerbach, Berthold, *originally* Moses Baruch Auerbacher 1812–82
German novelist
Born in Nordstetten in the Black Forest, he studied at the universities of Tübingen, Munich, and Heidelberg, and in 1836 was imprisoned as a member of the students' Burschenschaft, a nationalist youth movement. Destined for the Synagogue, he abandoned theology for law, then law for history and philosophy, especially that of **Spinoza**, on whose life he based a novel of that name (1837), and whose works he translated (1841). However, his fame chiefly rests on his *Schwarzwälder Dorfgeschichten* (1843, 'Black Forest Village Tales'). Of his longer works the best known are *Barfüssele* (1856, 'Little Barefoot') and *Auf der Höhe* (1865, 'On the Summit'). 📖 L Stein, *Berthold Auerbach und das Judenthum* (1882)

Auerbach, Charlotte 1899–1994
German geneticist
Born in Crefel, she attended university courses in Berlin, Würzburg and Freiburg, where she graduated in 1925. She started her PhD course at the Kaiser Wilhelm Institute, but in 1933 anti-Semitism forced her to move to Edinburgh, where she completed her thesis at the Institute of Animal Genetics. In 1938 she worked with the US geneticist **Hermann Müller**. Her studies of the effects of nitrogen mustard and mustard gas on the fruit fly led her to discover chemical mutagenesis, which thereafter became her main research. She was appointed lecturer in genetics at Edinburgh University (1947), reader (1957) and professor (1967–69). She was one of the very first to work out how chemical compounds cause mutations and to compare the differences between the actions of chemical mutagens and X-rays. She was elected Fellow of the Royal Society in 1957, and was their Darwin Medallist in 1976.

Auerbach, Frank 1931–
British artist
Born in Germany, he came to Great Britain in 1939. He studied in London at St Martin's School of Art (1948–52) and the Royal College of Art (1952–55), but his most important formative influence was **David Bomberg**, who taught him briefly at the Borough Polytechnic, London. He works with oil paint of predominantly earth colours, thickly applied in layers, allowing the image to emerge mysteriously through the raised impasto. His works on

paper in charcoal are similarly reworked. His subject matter is figurative, portraits of a few close friends and familiar views of Primrose Hill and Camden Town in London.

Auersperg, Anton Alexander, Graf von
pseudonym **Anastasius Grün** 1806–76
Austrian poet
He was distinguished by his liberalism and ultra-German sympathies, and was one of the best-known epic and lyrical poets in the German language. His works include a volume of love poetry, *Blätter der Liebe* (1830, 'Leaves of Love'), a collection of political poetry, *Spaziergänge eines Wiener Poeten* (1831, 'A Viennese Poet's Walks'), and *Gedichte* (1837, 'Poems'), a volume of lyrical poems. ⌑ E Schatzmayer, *Anastasius Grüns Dichtungen* (1865)

Auger, Pierre Victor 1899–1993
French physicist
Born in Paris, he was educated at the École Normale Supérieure and later became professor at the University of Paris. He discovered that an atom can de-excite from a state of high energy non-radiatively, by losing one of its own electrons rather than emitting a photon. Electrons emitted in this way are known as Auger electrons, used in the calibration of nuclear detectors. He later investigated the properties of the neutron and worked on cosmic-ray physics, discovering extended air showers (also known as Auger showers) where the interaction of cosmic rays with Earth's upper atmosphere produces cascades of large numbers of secondary particles.

Augereau, Pierre François Charles, Duc de Castiglione 1757–1816
French soldier
Of humble origins, he achieved rapid promotion under Napoleon I in Italy, where he fought at Lodi and Castiglione (1796). In 1797 he defeated a royalist coup against the Directory. He opposed Napoleon's assumption of power as First Consul in 1799, but was reconciled, and promoted to marshal in 1804 and created Duke of Castiglione in 1808. On Napoleon's fall in 1814 he declared for the monarchy, but was forced to retire.

Augier, (Guillaume Victor) Émile 1820–89
French dramatist
He was born in Valence. A leader of the school that reacted against the excesses of Romantic drama, his *Théâtre complet* (1890, 'Complete Plays') fills seven volumes, and includes several fine social comedies, such as *Le Gendre de M. Poirier* (1854, with Jules Sandeau, 'Mr Poirier's Son-in-Law') and *Les Fourchambault* (1878). ⌑ A Denoist, *Essais de critique dramatique* (1898)

Augspurg *or* Augsburg, Anita Johanna Theodora Sophie 1857–1943
German feminist, pacifist and writer
Born in Verden an der Aller, she trained as a teacher, then worked as an actor and photographer before involvement with women's rights led her to study law in Zurich (1893–97). She became a leading figure in the Bund Deutscher Frauenvereine (Federation of German Women's Associations) in Berlin, alongside Lida Heymann, Minna Cauer and Marie Stritt (1856–1928). In 1902, the four founded the Deutscher Verband für Frauenstimmrecht to campaign for women's suffrage. Subsequently Augspurg became increasingly identified with the more militant elements in the suffrage movement. After German women gained the vote in 1919, Augspurg, Heymann and Cauer worked for civil rights, producing the newspaper *Die Frau im Staat* (1919–33). When Hitler came to power in 1933, Augspurg and Heymann moved to Zurich where they compiled their memoirs, *Erlebtes-Erschautes*.

August, Bille 1948–
Danish film director
He was born in Lundtofte, he studied photogaphy in Stockholm before attending the Danish Film School, qualifying as a cinematographer in 1971. Active in television from 1973, he made his feature debut with *Honning Måne* (1979, *In My Life*). His international breakthrough came with a version of **Martin Andersen Nexö's** novel *Pelle Erobreren* (1987, *Pelle the Conqueror*) which won the Palme D'Or at Cannes and an Academy Award for Best Foreign Film. *Den Goda Viljan* (1992, 'The Best Intentions') also won the Palme D'Or. His recent films include *The House of the Spirits* (1993), *Jerusalem* (1996) and *Miss Smilla's Feeling for Snow* (1996).

Augusta, Julia See Livia, Drusilla

Augustine of Canterbury, St d.604
Italian prelate and the first Archbishop of Canterbury
Born probably in Rome, he was prior of a Benedictine monastery there, when in 596 Pope **Gregory I, the Great** sent him with 40 other monks to convert the Anglo-Saxons to Christianity. He was kindly received by **Ethelbert**, King of Kent, whose wife was a Christian, and the conversion and baptism of the king contributed greatly to his success. It is recorded that Augustine baptized 1,000 people in the River Swale in one day. Augustine was made Bishop of the English in 597, and established his church at Canterbury. His efforts to extend his authority over the native Celtic Christianity were less successful. He died at Canterbury, and in 612 his body was transferred to the Abbey of Saints Peter and Paul, now the site of St Augustine's Missionary College (1848). His feast day is 26 May. ⌑ Margaret Deanesly, *Augustine of Canterbury* (1964)

Augustine of Hippo, St, *originally* Aurelius Augustinus AD354–430
Numidian Christian, one of the four Latin Doctors of the Church
Born in Tagaste (now Souk-Ahras), Numidia, he was brought up a Christian by his devout mother, Monica (who became St Monica). He went to Carthage to study and had a son, Adeodatus (AD372), by a mistress there. He became deeply involved in Manicheanism, which seemed to offer a solution to the problem of evil, a theme which was to preoccupy him throughout his life. In 383 he moved to teach in Rome, then in Milan, and became influenced by Scepticism and then by Neoplatonism. He finally became converted to Christianity and was baptized (together with his son) by St Ambrose in 387. Ordained a priest in 391, he returned to North Africa and became Bishop of Hippo in 396, where he was a relentless antagonist of the heretical schools of Donatists, Pelagians and Manicheans. He was an unusually productive writer and much of his work is marked by personal spiritual struggle. His *Confessions* (397) is a classic of world literature and a spiritual autobiography as well as an original work of philosophy (with a famous discussion on the nature of time). *De Civitate Dei* (413–26, 'The City of God'), a work of 22 books, is an influential and important vindication of Christianity, and *De Trinitate* ('The Trinity') is a weighty exposition of the doctrine of the Trinity. The central tenets of his creed were the corruption of human nature through the fall of Man, the consequent slavery of the human will, predestination and the perseverance of the Saints. His feast day is 28 August.

Augustus II, the Strong 1670–1733
Elector of Saxony and twice King of Poland
Born in Dresden, which he was later to beautify, he succeeded to the electorship as Frederick Augustus I (1694) on the death of his brother, John George IV. After fighting against France and the Turks, he renounced his Lutheranism and became a Roman Catholic (1696), to

Augustus, (Gaius Julius Caesar) Octavianus 63BC–14AD
The first Roman emperor

Augustus was the son of the senator and praetor Gaius Octavius, and Atia, **Julius Caesar**'s niece. Originally known as Gaius Octavius, he became Gaius Julius Caesar Octavianus through adoption by Caesar in his will (44BC), and later received the name Augustus ('sacred', 'venerable') in recognition of his services and position (27). At the time of Caesar's assassination (March 44), Augustus was a student at Apollonia in Illyricum, but he returned at once to Italy to claim his inheritance. **Mark Antony** refused at first to surrender Caesar's property, but Augustus outmanoeuvred him in the campaign of Mutina, gained the consulship and carried out Caesar's will (43). When Antony returned from Gaul with **Lepidus**, Augustus joined them in forming a triumvirate. He received Africa, Sardinia and Sicily; Antony received Gaul; and Lepidus received Spain. Their power was soon made absolute by their reign of terror in Italy, and by their victory at Philippi over the republicans under **Brutus** and **Cassius** (42).

Difficulties between Augustus and Antony caused by Antony's wife Fulvia were removed by Fulvia's death and by Antony's marriage with **Octavia**, sister of Augustus. The Roman world was divided again, Augustus taking the western half and Antony the eastern, while Lepidus had to be content with Africa. Augustus gradually built up his position in Italy and the West, ingratiating himself with the Roman people and misrepresenting the actions of Antony in the East. War was declared against **Cleopatra**, whom Antony had joined in 37, and after his naval victory at Actium (31) Augustus became the sole ruler of the Roman world. Antony and Cleopatra committed suicide.

In 29, after settling affairs in Egypt, Greece and the East, Augustus returned to Rome in triumph, and proclaimed universal peace. Augustus was now in all but name the sole ruler of the Roman Empire, although his rule had tobe based on republican forms; this was achieved by means of several settlements (in 27, 23 and 19BC).

At home and abroad the declared policy of Augustus was one of national revival and restoration of traditional Roman values. He legislated to mould the fabric of Roman society, and beautified the city of Rome; it was his proud boast that 'he had found the city built of brick, and left it built of marble'. Abroad, he pursued a policy of calculated imperial conquest, and considerably extended the territory of the Roman Empire in central and northern Europe, although his policy had to be brought to a halt when disaster struck in his later years, with the revolt of Pannonia (AD6) and the loss of three entire legions in Germany under **Varus** (AD9).

His domestic life was clouded with setbacks and disasters, although he eventually achieved an acceptable succession with his stepson **Tiberius**, whom he adopted in AD4.

A statesman of exceptional skill, Augustus brought about the difficult transition from republic to empire and provided the Roman world with effective institutions and a lasting period of peace.

📖 Augustus' *Autobiography* is lost, but a record of his public achievements, the *Res Gestae Divi Augusti*, written by himself and originally inscribed on bronze pillars in front of his Mausoleum in Rome, survives in several copies in Greek and Latin from Asia Minor.

The Augustan Age was a period of great cultural achievement, especially in literature through the patronage of **Maecenas** and the work of **Horace**, **Virgil**, **Ovid**, **Propertius**, **Tibullus** and **Livy**.

Acta est fabula.
'The play is over.'
Last words (attributed).

---

secure his election to the Polish throne as Augustus II (1697–1704). With **Peter I, the Great** of Russia and Frederik IV of Denmark, he planned the partition of Sweden, invading Livonia in 1700. Defeated by **Karl XII** of Sweden, Augustus was deposed (1704) and replaced by **Stanisław Leszczyński**. Although he recovered the throne in 1709, by the end of his reign Poland was little more than a Russian protectorate. He was succeeded, as elector and king, by his son, Frederick Augustus.

Augustus, Octavianus See panel above

Augustus, Romulus See **Romulus Augustulus**

Aukrust, Olav Lom 1883–1929
Norwegian poet

He was a schoolmaster who wrote large quantities of religious and patriotic verse. *Himmelvarden* (1916), in New Norwegian, contains many passages of great lyric power, and *Hamar i Hellom* (1926), of which the chief poem is *Emme*, summons the people of Norway to use the power of their traditions to achieve security and progress. His final collection of poems, *Solrenning*, is incomplete and was published posthumously in 1930. 📖 I Krokann, *Olav Aukrust* (1933)

Aulén, Gustaf Emmanuel Hildebrand 1879–1977
Swedish Lutheran theologian and composer

He was born in Ljungby, Kalmar. Professor of Systematic Theology at Lund (1913–33), and Bishop of Strängnäs (1933–52), he was a leading representative of the Scandinavian school of theology that sought Christian truth behind doctrines rather than in the form in which they were presented. He wrote several books, including *The Faith of the Christian Church* (1954) and *Jesus in Contemporary Historical Research* (1976). His most famous study, *Christus Victor* (1931), presented the death of Christ as a triumph over the powers of evil, following the approach of **Irenaeus** and **Martin Luther**. He also wrote a commentary and explanation on **Dag Hammarskjöld**'s famous *Markings* in 1969. Aulén's second love was music: he played the piano and organ, and was president of the Royal Swedish Academy of Music (1944–50).

Aulenti, Gae(tana) 1927–
Italian architect

Born in Aulenti, she trained at Milan Polytechnic and in 1954 set up a practice involved with architecture, furniture design, stage design, interiors and product design. She taught at Venice and Milan in the 1960s before spending three years researching with Luca Roncini in Florence. Since 1974 she has been on the board of directors of Lotus International, and her name has also been associated with the giant business concerns Fiat and Olivetti. Her works include the Palazzo Grassi, Venice (1985), Museo de l'Arte Catalana, Barcelona (1985), the Pirelli Offices, Rome (1986), and the redesign of the Musée d'Orsay in Paris (1980–86), which was nominated by the International Union of Architects as one of the 10 most important works in the previous three years.

Aulnoy, Marie Catherine Jumelle de Barneville, Comtesse d' c.1650–1705
French writer

Aung San Suu Kyi 1945–
Burmese political leader and founder of the National League for Democracy

Aung San Suu Kyi was born in Rangoon, the daughter of Burmese nationalist hero General **Aung San**, who founded the Anti-Fascist People's Freedom League and led Burma's fight for independence from British rule until his assassination a few months before it was achieved. Her mother was Daw Khin Kyi, who was appointed Burma's ambassador to India in 1961. Suu Kyi went with her to India, and her circle of friends there included Sanjay and **Rajiv Gandhi**. Later, she went to Oxford University to read Politics, Philosophy and Economics, and in 1969 worked for the United Nations in New York. In 1972 she married Michael Aris, an academic specializing in Tibetan studies. After a period in Bhutan, she went to Kyoto University in Japan, and later they were reunited in Oxford to pursue their academic careers and bring up their two sons.

In 1988 Suu Kyi returned to Burma to visit her mother, who was recovering from a stroke. She found the country in a state of extreme political unrest under a new military junta which succeeded years of military rule. After appeals to the government for more open consultation on the country's future, she co-founded the National League for Democracy (NLD) and became its General Secretary. The government had established its State Law and Order Restoration Council (SLORC), introduced martial law and imprisonment without trial, and banned public meetings, forbidding Suu Kyi to hold her office. Nonetheless, she toured the country and addressed supporters, who attended in large numbers. As a result, she was held under house arrest by the military junta (1989–95), allowed only two visits from her husband and one from her sons; and to survive she needed all her considerable resources of determination and self-discipline.

Despite this imprisonment of its leader, the National League for Democracy won an overwhelming victory in the elections of 1990, amounting to 80 per cent of the popular vote, although the result was ignored and many newly elected MPs were jailed. Her release in July 1995 did not change her long-standing conviction that the military had no place in politics, but she was careful not to provoke violent reactions, emphasizing the need for dialogue and reconciliation and appealing to exiled Burmese opposition groups to practise patience. She was reappointed General Secretary of the NLD in October 1995, but is continually vilified by the pro-government newspapers. Since her release she has continued to address supporters at the gates of her compound, some of whom have been arrested, to work towards the framing of a new constitution; she urges them to call on the outside world, especially the West, to support her cause by withholding investment capital which, rather than encourage freedom, only serves to strengthen and underpin the military regime.

Aung San Suu Kyi was awarded the Sakharov Prize for Freedom of Thought (1990), the Simón Bolívar Prize (1992) and the Nobel Peace Prize (1991).

📖 Aung San Suu Kyi has written a biography of her father, *Aung San* (1984). See also her *Freedom From Fear* (1991), *Towards a True Refuge* (1993) and *Freedom From Fear and Other Writings* (1995).

> 'I am not a martyr. I have suffered, but there are many more in my country who have suffered much more than me.'
> From an interview in *The Times Magazine* (2 March 1996).

Born near Honfleur, she wrote romances of court life, but is mainly remembered for her charming fairytales, *Contes de Fées* (1698, 'Fairy Tales').

Aulus Gellius See **Gellius, Aulus**

Aumale, Henri-Eugène-Philippe-Louis d'Orléans, Duc d' 1822–97
French soldier

Born in Paris, the fourth son of King **Louis Philippe**, he distinguished himself in the campaigns in Algeria, where in 1847 he succeeded Marshal **Bugeaud** as Governor-General. With the onset of the Revolution of 1848 he retired to England, where he became known by his contributions to the *Revue de deux mondes*, his incisive pamphlets against **Napoleon III**, and his important works, *Histoire des princes de Condé* (1869–97, 'History of the Princes de Condé') and *Les Institutions militaires de la France* (1867, 'French Military Institutions'). Elected to the Assembly in 1871, in 1886 he bequeathed his magnificent château at Chantilly to the nation.

Aungerville or **Angerville, Richard**, *also called* **Richard de Bury** 1287–1345
English churchman

Born in Bury St Edmunds, Suffolk, he studied at Oxford and became a Benedictine monk at Durham. Having been tutor to **Edward III**, he was made successively Dean of Wells and Bishop of Durham. He also acted for a time as High Chancellor, as ambassador to the pope and to France and Germany, and as commissioner for a truce with Scotland. He collected manuscripts and books, and his own principal work, *Philobyblon*, intended to serve as a handbook to the library which he founded in connection with Durham College at Oxford (afterwards suppressed), describes the state of learning in England and France.

Aung San 1915–47
Burmese nationalist

He was the dominant figure in the nationalist movement during and after the Pacific War. At the beginning of the 1940s, Aung San, working with Japanese agents, formed the anti-British Burma Independence Army, which entered Burma with the invading Japanese in January 1942. He rapidly became disillusioned with the Japanese, however, and, as a leading figure in the Anti-Fascist People's Freedom League (AFPFL), turned his troops against them (1945). In the immediate post-war period he became president of the AFPFL and, in 1946, was effectively Prime Minister in the Governor's Executive Council. In January 1947 he travelled to London to negotiate, with success, Burma's independence. On 19 July, however, he was assassinated by a political rival. His death removed the one figure who might have held together Burma's warring political interests as the country achieved independence (1948). His daughter is Aung San Suu Kyi.

Aung San Suu Kyi See panel above

Aurangzeb 1618–1707
Mughal Emperor of India

Born in Dhod, Malwa, he was the third son of Emperor **Shah Jahan**. When Shah Jahan became seriously ill (1657), the throne was seized by his eldest son, Dara, but his three brothers, Shuja, Murad and Aurangzeb combined to oust him. Dara's army was defeated at Samugarh (1658), Shah Jahan and Murad were imprisoned in Delhi, Shuja fled the country and Dara was executed (1659). During Aurangzeb's reign (1659–1707), the empire remained outwardly prosperous, but his puritanical and narrow outlook alienated the various communities of the empire, particularly the Hindus. Opposed by his own rebellious sons and by the Mahratha Empire in the south, he died a fugitive.

Aurelian, *properly* Lucius Domitius Aurelianus
c.215–275AD
Roman emperor
He was born of humble origins in Dacia or Pannonia. He rose through the army and on the death of Claudius II (AD270), was elected emperor by the army, with whom he was very popular. He repulsed the Alemanni and Marcomanni, and erected new walls around Rome. He resigned Dacia to the Goths, and made the Danube the frontier of the empire. He defeated **Zenobia**, Regent of Palmyra, and destroyed the city (273). He quelled a rebellion in Egypt, and recovered Gaul from Tetricus, his rival emperor. By restoring good discipline in the army, order in domestic affairs, and political unity to the Roman dominions, he was entitled Restitutor Orbis— 'Restorer of the World'. Although a harsh disciplinarian, he increased the distribution of free food in Rome. He was assassinated by his own officers near Byzantium during a campaign against the Persians.

Aurelius, Marcus See **Marcus Aurelius**

Auric, Georges 1899–1983
French composer
Born in Lodève, Hérault, he studied under **Vincent d'Indy** and became one of the group of young French composers known as Les Six. Inspired by both **Erik Satie** and **Igor Stravinsky**, his music exemplifies the modern return to counterpoint, and his compositions range from orchestral pieces to ballets, songs and film scores, including **Jean Cocteau's** *La Belle et la Bête* (1946) and several British films, including *Passport to Pimlico* (1949). He was director of the Paris Opera and Opéra Comique (1962–68), then resigned to compose.

Auriol, Jacqueline 1917–
French aviator
The daughter-in-law of **Vincent Auriol**, she broke the women's jet speed record in 1955 by flying at 715 miles per hour in a French *Mystère*. She published *I Live To Fly* in 1970.

Auriol, Vincent 1884–1966
French socialist statesman
He studied law, and was a Deputy (1914–40, 1945–47), Minister of Finance in the Popular Front government (1936–37) and Minister of Justice (1937–38). He opposed the granting of power to Marshal **Philippe Pétain** in 1940, and joined the French Resistance, escaping to Algeria in 1943, where he became president of the Foreign Affairs Committee of the Consultative Assembly. He represented France at the first meeting of the UN, was elected president of the Constituent Assembly in 1946, and was first President of the Fourth Republic (1947–53).

Aurobindo, Sri, *originally* Sri Aurobindo Ghose
1872–1950
Indian philosopher, poet and mystic
Born in Calcutta into a high-caste Bengali family, he was educated in England at Cambridge. A proficient linguist, he returned to India in 1892 and became a professor in Baroda and Calcutta. In 1908 he was imprisoned by the British authorities in India for sedition, and studied yoga in jail. Renouncing nationalism and politics for yoga and Hindu philosophy, he founded an ashram in 1910 at Pondicherry, then French territory. An experiment in community living, the ashram, known as Auroville, continued to attract Western visitors long after Aurobindo's death, even if many did not grasp the underlying philosophy: salvation of society by the influence of the individual attainment of supermind or higher consciousness through integral yoga, as expressed in *The Life Divine* (1940), *The Synthesis of Yoga* (1948), *Aurobindo on Himself* (1953) and many other books.

Ausonius, Decius Magnus c.309–392AD
Latin poet
Born in Burdigala (Bordeaux), he taught rhetoric there for 30 years, and was then appointed by Emperor **Valentinian I** tutor to his son **Gratian**. He held the offices of quaestor, prefect of Latium and consul of Gaul. On the death of Gratian, Ausonius retired to his estate in Bordeaux, where he occupied himself with literature and rural pursuits. His works include epigrams, poems on his deceased relatives and on his colleagues, epistles in verse and prose, and idylls. 📖 C Aymonier, *Ausone et ses amis* (1935)

Austen, Jane See panel p104

Austen, Winifred 1876–1964
English wildlife artist
Born in Ramsgate, the daughter of a naval surgeon, she took up painting professionally at an early age, and after a brief marriage moved to the village of Orford in East Suffolk in 1926. She illustrated Patrick Chalmers's *Birds Ashore and Aforeshore* (1935) and painted postcards under the signature 'Spink'.

Auster, Paul, *pseudonym* Paul Benjamin 1947–
US novelist and poet
Born in Newark, New Jersey, he has worked as a merchant seaman, census-taker, and teacher of creative writing. He wrote his first novel, *Squeeze Play*, in 1982, by which time he had already produced several volumes of poetry, a selection of which appeared with some essays in *Ground Work* (1990). The cerebral mystery novels which make up *The New York Trilogy* (1985–87) were followed by *In the Country of Last Things* (1987), a nightmarish vision of a society trapped in terminal social disintegration. Other novels include the evocative *The Music of Chance* (1991).

Austin, Alfred 1835–1913
English poet
Born of Catholic parents in Leeds, he was educated at Stonyhurst and Oscott College, and graduated from London University. He was called to the Bar in 1857, but abandoned law for literature. He was a strong supporter of **Disraeli**, and an ardent imperialist. He published *The Season: a Satire* (1861), *The Human Tragedy* (1862), *The Conversion of Winckelmann* (1862) and a dozen more volumes of poems of little merit, and an autobiography (1911). From 1883 to 1893 he edited the *National Review*. His appointment as Poet Laureate (1896) brought public derision. He was much parodied as a poet.

Austin (of Longbridge), Herbert Austin, 1st Baron 1866–1941
English car manufacturer
Born in Buckinghamshire and educated at Rotherham Grammar School and Brampton College, he went to Australia in 1884 and worked in engineering shops there. He went back to England in 1893 and joined the Wolseley Sheep-Shearing Company in Birmingham. In 1895, with the Wolseley Company, he produced his first three-wheel car, and in 1905 he opened his own works near Birmingham, which rapidly developed and whose considerable output included, in 1921, the popular 'Baby' Austin 7. He was Conservative MP for King's Norton (1918–24).

Austin, John 1790–1859
English jurist
He was born in Creeting Mill, Suffolk, was called to the Bar in 1818, and in 1826 was appointed Professor of Jurisprudence at the newly-founded University of

Austen, Jane 1775–1817
English novelist

Jane Austen was born in Steventon, Hampshire, the sixth of seven children of a country rector; her father was an able scholar and served as her tutor. She spent the first 25 years of her life in Steventon, and the last eight in nearby Chawton (moving to Winchester just a few months before her death), and did almost all of her writing in those two places. During the intervening years in Bath, which appears to have been an unsettled time in her otherwise ordered and rather uneventful life, her writing was more sporadic, and she abandoned an early novel, *The Watsons*, following the death of her father in 1805. She never married, although she had a number of suitors, and wrote percipiently on the subjects of courtship and marriage in her novels.

She began to write at an early age to amuse her family. By 1790 she had completed a burlesque on popular fiction in the manner of **Samuel Richardson**, entitled *Love and Friendship*, and ridiculed the taste for Gothic fiction in her novel *Northanger Abbey*, which was written at this time, but not published until 1818.

Her characteristic subject was the closely observed and often ironically depicted morals and mores of country life, which she rendered with genius. Her best-known works in this vein are *Sense and Sensibility* (1811), *Pride and Prejudice* (1813), *Emma* (1816), and the posthumously published *Persuasion* (1817). *Mansfield Park* (1814) is a darker and more serious dissection of her chosen fictional territory, and although never as popular, it is arguably her masterpiece.

Modern research has seen the publication of the fragment of an unfinished novel, *Sanditon*, which she was writing when she died, and some very early pieces, including *Lady Susan*, a juvenile work in epistolary form. Her own letters, although carefully filleted by her sister Cassandra after her death, are one of the few revealing documentary sources on her life.

Her greatness has been clearer to subsequent generations than to her own, although Sir **Walter Scott** praised the delicate observation and fine judgement in her work, which she herself characterized as 'the little bit (two inches wide) of ivory on which I work with so fine a brush, as produces little effect after much labour'. If she chose a small canvas for her labours, however, she worked upon it with exquisite understanding.

📖 D Le Faye (ed), *Jane Austen's Letters* (1995); P Honan, *Jane Austen: her life* (1987); J R Liddell, *The Novels of Jane Austen* (1974); E Jenkins, *Jane Austen: a biography* (1938).

> 'Three or four families in a country village is the very thing to work on.' From a letter to Anna Austen, 9 September 1814. Quoted in R W Chapman (ed), *Jane Austen's Letters* (1952).

> 'That young lady had a talent for describing the involvements and feelings and characters of ordinary life, which is to me the most wonderful I ever met with. The Big Bow-wow strain I can do myself like any now going; but the exquisite touch, which renders ordinary commonplace things and characters interesting, from the truth of the description and the sentiment, is denied to me.' Walter Scott, *Journal*, 14 March 1826.

London (now University College). The subject was not recognized as a necessary branch of legal study, and from lack of students he resigned the chair (1832). His *Province of Jurisprudence Determined* (1832), defining (on a utilitarian basis) the field of ethics and law in time had a great influence on English views of the subject, introducing a precise terminology previously unknown, and inspired the English analytical school of jurists, which concentrated on examination of terminology and concepts. His *Lectures on Jurisprudence* were published in 1863.

Austin, J(ohn) L(angshaw) 1911–60
English philosopher

Born in Lancaster, Lancashire, he was educated at Balliol College, Oxford. He taught in Oxford (from 1945), where he was a leading figure in the 'Oxford Philosophy' movement and became professor (1952). His distinctive contribution was the meticulous examination of ordinary linguistic usage to resolve philosophical questions. He pioneered the analysis of speech acts, and his best-known works are *Philosophical Papers* (1961), *Sense and Sensibilia* (1962) and *How to do Things with Words* (1962). All his work is characterized by great precision and refinement.

Austin, Robert Sargent 1895–1973
English etcher

Born in Leicester, he trained at the Royal College of Art, London, and became an artist and teacher with knowledge of all techniques of printmaking. He worked almost exclusively with a burin to execute detailed line engravings which bear a stylistic comparison to those of **Dürer**. His mature work from 1930 to 1940 includes some of the finest prints of the period. He taught at the Royal College of Art and most of his life was spent refining the traditional art of line engraving. He retired in 1955 and made no more prints until 1963, when he executed another three impressive works.

Austin, Stephen Fuller, *known as* the Father of Texas 1793–1836
US colonizer

He was born in Austinville, Virginia. He established the first settlement of Americans in Texas on the Brazos river in 1822. Leader of the colony, he was also influential with the Mexican government but was unsuccessful in convincing Mexico that Texas should have a separate state government. After the Texas Revolution (1836) he served briefly as Secretary of State of the Texas Republic.

Austral, Florence, *originally* Florence Wilson 1894–1968
Australian soprano

Born in Richmond, Victoria, she adopted the name of her country as a stage name prior to her debut in 1922 at Covent Garden, London. She toured the USA and Canada in the 1920s, and appeared in the complete cycles of *The Ring* at Covent Garden, London and at the Berlin State Opera, which she joined as a principal in 1930. Also appearing frequently in the concert hall, often with Sir **Henry Wood** and his BBC Symphony Orchestra, she made many recordings with other leading singers of her day. She returned to Australia after World War II where she taught until her retirement in 1959.

Avebury, 1st Baron See Lubbock, Sir John

Avedon, Richard 1923–
US photographer

Born in New York City, the son of Russian–Jewish immigrants, he studied at Columbia University and the Design Laboratory of the New School for Social Research, New York, before becoming a staff photographer on *Harper's Bazaar* (1945–65). In 1966 he moved to *Vogue*, under **Diana Vreeland**. He established his own studio in 1946 and has contributed to several other magazines on a freelance basis since 1950, including the *New*

Yorker since 1992. Famous for his photographs of fashion models and celebrities, he originally concentrated on dramatic, motion photographs out of doors, and later developed an uncompromisingly realistic and stark style which has great emotional impact. His publications include *Nothing Personal* (1964), *Avedon: Photographs 1947–77* (1978, text by Rosamond Bernier) and an autobiography (1993). 📖 John Szarkowski, *The Photographer's Eye* (1965)

Aventinus, *Latin name of* **Johannes Thurmayr** 1477–1534
German humanist scholar and historian
Born in Abensberg (Latin *Aventinum*), Bavaria, he taught Greek and mathematics at Kraków, and wrote a history of Bavaria. He was known as the 'Bavarian Herodotus'.

Avenzoar, *Arabic name* **Ibn Zohr** c.1072–1162
Arab physician
Born in Seville, he published influential medical works describing such conditions as kidney stones and pericarditis, and was considered the greatest clinician in the western caliphate.

Averlino, Antonio de Pietro See **Filarete, Antonio**

Averroës or **Averrhoës**, *also called* **Ibn Rushd**, *Arabic in full* **Abū al-Walīd Muḥammad ibn Aḥmad ibn Muḥammad ibn Rushd** 1126–98
Islamic philosopher and physician
Born in Córdoba, Spain, the son of a distinguished family of jurists, he served as kadi (judge) and physician in Córdoba and Seville, and in Morocco. He also wrote on jurisprudence and medicine at this time as well as beginning his extensive philosophical output. In 1182 he became court physician to Caliph Abu Yusuf, but in 1185 was banished in disgrace (for reasons now unknown) by the caliph's son and successor. Many of his works were burnt, but after a brief period in exile he was restored to grace and lived in retirement in Marrakesh until his death. The most numerous and the most important of his works were the *Commentaries* on **Aristotle**, many of them known only through their Latin (or Hebrew) translations. Both influential and controversial in the development of scholastic philosophy in the Middle Ages, they offered a partial synthesis of Greek and Arabic philosophical traditions. He was the most famous of the medieval Islamic philosophers. 📖 Barry S Cogan, *Averroës and the Metaphysics of Causation* (1985)

Avery, Milton Clark 1893–1965
US painter
He was born in Sand Bank, New York. A figurative painter who worked with bold, flat masses of colour, he was influenced by **Henri Matisse**. His major works, reflecting his interest in people, beaches, and landscapes, include *Sea and Sand Dunes* (1955), *Moon Path* (1958), *Beach Blankets* (1960) and *Dunes and Sea II* (1960).

Avery, Oswald Theodore 1877–1955
US bacteriologist
Born in Halifax, Nova Scotia in Canada, he studied medicine at Colgate University and spent his career at the Rockefeller Institute Hospital, New York (1913–48). He became an expert on pneumococci, and in 1928 investigated a claim that a non-virulent, rough-coated strain could be transformed into the virulent smooth strain, by the mere presence of some of the dead smooth bacteria. Avery confirmed this result, and went on in 1944 to show that the transformation is caused by the presence of DNA in the dead bacteria, although he did not suggest that the molecules which carry the whole reproductive pattern of any living species (the genes) are simply DNA, a concept which was to emerge only later.

Avery, Tex, *originally* **Frederick Bean** 1908–80
US animated cartoon director
He was born in Texas and after failing to achieve his ambition to create a newspaper strip, joined the **Walter Lantz** animation studio (1929). Moving to Warner Brothers to direct his first cartoon, Porky Pig in *Goldiggers of '49* (1935), he soon was noticed for his zany comedy, creating Daffy Duck in *Porky's Duck Hunt* (1937), and developing Bugs Bunny in *A Wild Hare* (1940). Moving to MGM he created Droopy (*Dumb Hounded*, 1943), Screwy Squirrel (*Screwball Squirrel*, 1944), George and Junior (*Henpecked Hoboes*, 1946), and the classics, *King Size Canary* (1947) and *Bad Luck Blackie* (1949). In 1955 he moved into television commercials and later joined **Hanna–Barbera** for the television series *The Flintstones* (1979).

Avicebrón, *Arabic name* **Solomon ben Yehuda ibn Gabirol** c.1020–c.1070
Jewish poet and philosopher
He was born in Malaga, Spain. Most of his prose work is lost, but there survives an ethical treatise in Arabic and a Latin translation of his most famous work, *Fons vitae* ('The Fountain of Life'). Neoplatonist in character, it was very influential among later Christian scholastics. His poetry became part of the mystical tradition of the Kabbalah. 📖 F Brunner, *Platonisme et Aristotelisme* (1965)

Avicenna, *Arabic name* **Abū ʿAlī al-Ḥusayn ibn ʿAbd Allāh ibn Sīnā** 980–1037
Persian philosopher and physician
Born near Bokhara, Persia (Iran), he was renowned for his precocious and prodigious learning, becoming physician to several sultans, and for some time vizier in Hamadan. He was one of the main interpreters of **Aristotle** to the Islamic world, and was the author of some 200 works on science, religion and philosophy. His medical textbook, *al-Qānūn fī at-tibb* ('Canon of Medicine'), long remained a standard work. 📖 S M Afnan, *Avicenna: His Life and Works* (1958)

Ávila, St Teresa of See **Teresa of Ávila, St**

Ávila Camacho, Manuel 1897–1955
Mexican soldier and politician
Born in Tezuitlán, Mexico, he studied accounting, then joined the revolutionary army of **Venustiano Carranza**, rising to become a general and Minister of National Defense (1937–39). As President of Mexico from 1940 to 1946, he brought stability to the country, pursuing a policy of moderate social reform, expanding the school system, and sponsoring social security legislation. He cooperated with the USA in World War II, supplying labour and raw materials for the war effort and sending pilots to the Pacific.

Avison, Charles c.1710–1770
English composer
Born in Newcastle, he wrote an *Essay on Musical Expression* (1752), and he is mentioned in **Robert Browning's** *Parleyings* (1887). He was also known as a critic.

Avogadro, (Lorenzo Romano) Amedeo Carlo 1776–1856
Italian physicist and chemist
Born in Turin, Piedmont region, he trained as a lawyer, graduating as doctor of ecclesiastical law in 1796. From 1806 he abandoned his official positions to concentrate on science, and soon became Professor of Mathematics and Physics at the College of Vercelli (1809). In 1819 he was elected to the Turin Academy of Sciences. He was appointed to the first Italian chair of mathematical physics, established at Turin, from 1820–1822 and again from 1834 until his retirement in 1850. He published widely on physics and chemistry and, in 1811, seeking to explain **Joseph Gay-Lussac's** law of combining gaseous volumes

(1809), he formulated the famous hypothesis that equal volumes of all gases contain equal numbers of molecules when at the same temperature and pressure (Avogadro's law). The hypothesis was practically ignored for around 50 years, a neglect partially explained by Avogadro's social, intellectual and geographical isolation. In 1860 at the Karlsruhe Chemical Congress, **Stanislao Cannizzaro** circulated a work which attempted to systematize inorganic chemistry using a re-statement of Avogadro's hypothesis in contemporary terms. Universal acceptance did not come until the 1880s. ⊞ Mario Morselli, *Amadeo Avogadro* (1984)

Awdry, W(ilbert) V(ere) 1911–97
English author and Church of England clergyman
He was born in Ampfield, Hampshire. His railway stories for young people, especially those featuring Thomas the Tank Engine, delighted generations of small children. The first, *The Three Railway Engines*, appeared in 1945, and *Thomas, the Tank Engine*, a year later. Over 25 books followed, each based on a real experience, until *Tramway Engines* appeared in 1972, following which Awdry's son, Christopher, succeeded to the authorship.

Awolowo, Chief Obafemi 1909–87
Nigerian politician
Educated in Protestant schools, he was a teacher, trader, trade union organizer and journalist, before being an external student of law at London University and becoming a solicitor and advocate of the Nigerian Supreme Court. He helped found and then led the Action Group, a party based on the Yoruba of Western Nigeria, from 1951 to 1966, when the party was banned. He was premier of the Western Region (1954–59) and then Leader of the Opposition in the federal parliament from 1960 to 1962, when he was imprisoned. Released after the 1966 coup, he was Federal Commissioner for Finance and Vice-President, Federal Executive Council of Nigeria (1967–71), when he returned to private practice. He returned to politics in 1979 as the unsuccessful presidential candidate for the Unity Party of Nigeria.

Axel See Absalon

Axel, Gabriel Mørch 1918–
Danish film director
He was born in Denmark, lived as a child in France, and trained as an actor at Copenhagen Royal Theatre. He began directing films in the 1950s, and his Danish films include *Den røde Kappe* (1966, 'The Red Cape'). In 1987 he made his international breakthrough with *Babette's Feast* (*Babettes Gæstebud*), an adaptation of a short story by **Karen Blixen**, which in 1988 won the Academy Award in the Best Foreign Language Film category. He has directed several films for French television including *Un crime de notre temps* (1977), *La ronde de nuit* (1978) and *Le curé de Tours* (1980). His other Danish films include, *Christian* (1989), describing a young man's journey through Europe in search of his identity.

Axel, Richard 1946–
US molecular biologist
Born in New York City, he graduated in medicine from Johns Hopkins University in 1970. At Columbia University he has been a Visiting Fellow at the Department of Pathology (1971–72), Assistant Professor of Pathology at the Institute for Cancer Research (1972–78), and is now both Professor of Pathology and Biochemistry and a member of the Institute of Cancer Research there. In 1975 he showed that when DNA is combined with cellular proteins as chromatin it can be split at specific regions, regions later shown to contain genes which are transcriptionally active. This was an essential step in understanding gene activation and regulation. In 1979 he was responsible for developing the technique which made it possible to mutate cloned genes in specific ways, reintroduce the mutated genes into cells and then determine the effect of mutations on gene activity. This technology has been the basis for our understanding of gene regulation, and it may be used therapeutically to cure certain genetic diseases.

Axelrod, Julius 1912–
US pharmacologist and Nobel Prize winner
Born in New York City, he qualified in biology and chemistry, and worked for some years as a laboratory analyst before entering research; he obtained his PhD at the age of 45. In 1949 he joined the section of heart chemistry of the National Institutes of Health and then moved as chief of the pharmacological section of the Clinical Sciences Laboratory at the National Institutes for Mental Health (1955–84). His research focused on the chemistry and pharmacology of the nervous system, especially the role of the catecholamines, adrenaline and noradrenaline. His work accelerated investigations into the links between brain chemistry and psychiatric disease, and in the search for psychoactive drugs. He jointly won the 1970 Nobel Prize for physiology or medicine with **Ulf von Euler** and **Bernard Katz**.

Ayckbourn, Sir Alan 1939–
English playwright
Born in London and educated at Haileybury School, Hertfordshire, he was an acting stage manager in repertory before joining Stephen Joseph's Theatre-in-the-Round company at Scarborough. A founder-member of the Victoria Theatre, Stoke-on-Trent in 1962, he returned in 1964 as producer to Scarborough, where most of his plays have been premiered. The first of a torrent of west-end successes was *Relatively Speaking* in 1967, and he was quickly established as a master of farce. His plays often shrewdly observe the English class-structure, but it is in sheer mechanical ingenuity that he excels. He has made considerable experiments with staging and dramatic structure: *Way Upstream* (1982), for example, necessitates the flooding of the stage. Among his most successful farces are *Time and Time Again* (1972), *Bedroom Farce* (1977) and *Joking Apart* (1979). He has written two musicals, *Jeeves* (with **Andrew Lloyd Webber**, 1975) and *Making Tracks* (with Paul Todd, 1981), and was a BBC radio drama producer (1964–70). Later plays, including *Woman in Mind* (1985) and *Henceforward* (1987), reflect an increasingly bleak vision of society, and he has revealed himself to be a savage social commentator. In 1996, Ayckbourn staged a revised version of one of his less successful plays, *It Could Be Any One of Us*, and the same year, he and the Stephen Joseph's Theatre moved to a new location in Scarborough. He is also recognized as a distinguished director, not only of his own work, but of plays by such authors as **Arthur Miller**.

Ayer, Sir A(lfred) J(ules) 1910–89
English philosopher
Born in London and educated at Eton and Oxford, he was a pupil of **Gilbert Ryle**. In World War II he served with the Welsh Guards and subsequently as attaché at the British Embassy in Paris (1945). He became Grote Professor at University College London (1947) and was later Wykeham Professor of Logic at Oxford (1959–78). His first and most important book, *Language, Truth and Logic* (1936), was a lucid, concise and forceful account of the antimetaphysical doctrines of the Vienna Circle of philosophers, whom he visited in 1932. This 'young man's book' with its iconoclastic dismissal of moral and religious discourse as not, in a literal sense, significant, aroused great hostility. His later publications include *The Problem of Knowledge* (1956) and *The Central Questions of Philosophy* (1972). He was knighted in 1970. ⊞ John Foster, *Ayer* (1985)

Ayers, Sir Henry 1821–97
Australian politician

Born in Portsea, Hampshire, England, he emigrated to South Australia in 1841 and took up a post with the South Australia Mining Association, with which he was associated for 50 years. Elected in 1863 to the first Legislative Council for the state under responsible government, he was a member of the Council for 36 years. He was premier four times in the next 10 years. During his last ministry, the overland telegraph to Darwin was completed, linking Australia with overseas telegraph networks, and Ayers received the KCMG. He was elected President of the Legislative Council in 1881, and was appointed GCMG upon his retirement in 1894. Ayers Rock, a giant monolith in the south of the (then) Northern Territories of South Australia, was named after him by **William Gosse** in 1873.

Ayeshah See **Aïshah**

Ayliffe, John 1676–1732
English scholar in Roman law

He was born in Winchester, Hampshire. Educated at Winchester School and New College, Oxford, he wrote *Parergon Juris Canonici Anglicani* (1726), a compendium of Anglican ecclesiastical law with a historical introduction, and *A New Pandect of the Roman Civil Law* (1734), an extremely erudite work including a long history of the civil law down to his own time.

Aylmer, Sir Felix Edward, *originally* Felix Edward Aylmer-Jones 1889–1979
English actor

He was born into a military family and educated at Magdalen College School and Exeter College, Oxford. He made his first stage appearance in London with Seymour Hicks (1871–1949) at the Coliseum (1911), after which he went to Birmingham Repertory Theatre. After service in World War I, he enjoyed a series of steady successes on stage and screen. Although termed a 'character actor', his range was extensive, whether typifying the folly of age as Polonius in **Olivier's** *Hamlet* or the wisdom of experience as Sir Patrick Cullen in Anthony Asquith's *The Doctor's Dilemma*. He was president of British Actors' Equity (1949–69). He was also a keen **Dickens** scholar, publishing *Dickens Incognito* (1959) and *The Drood Case* (1964).

Aylmer, John 1521–94
English prelate

Born probably at Aylmer Hall, Norfolk, he graduated from Cambridge in 1541, and became tutor to Lady **Jane Grey**. In 1553 he was installed as archdeacon of Stow, but fled to the Continent to escape persecution during the reign of **Mary I**. He returned to become archdeacon of Lincoln (1562), and in 1577 was consecrated Bishop of London. Equally disciplinarian to both Catholics and Puritans, he was pilloried as 'Morrell', the 'proude and ambitious pastoure', in **Edmund Spenser's** *Shephard's Calendar* (1579).

Aylward, Gladys 1902–70
English missionary in China

Born in London, she left school at 14 to be a parlourmaid, but her ambition was to go as a missionary to China. In 1930, she spent all her savings on a railway ticket to Tientsin in northern China, and with a Scottish missionary, Mrs Jeannie Lawson, founded the Inn of the Sixth Happiness in Yangcheng. From there in 1938 she made a great trek across the mountains leading over 100 children to safety during the war with Japan. After nine years with the Nationalists caring for the wounded, she returned to England in 1948, preached for five years, then in 1953 settled in Taiwan as head of an orphanage. The 1958 film *The Inn of the Sixth Happiness*, starring **Ingrid Bergman**, was based on her life.

Aylwin, (Azòcar) Patricio 1919–
Chilean lawyer and politician

Born in Santiago, after a successful early legal career, he was elected president of the Christian Democratic Party in 1973, and as leader of the opposition coalition triggered the national plebiscite of October 1989 that brought down General **Pinochet** in the 1988 elections. Power was formally transferred from the military regime to Aylwin in 1990, but his inability to secure the two-thirds majority in Congress necessary to amend the 1980 constitution allowed the outgoing junta to nominate almost one-fifth of the Senate's membership and thus to thwart Aylwin's efforts to lift press censorship and to abolish the death penalty. Continuing revelations about the previous regime's record on human rights triggered violent demonstrations, but Pinochet still resisted attempts to remove him as military Commander-in-Chief, which post he has vowed to retain until 1997.

Ayrer, Jacob c.1540–1625
German dramatist

Born in Franconia, he was a citizen of Nuremberg in 1594, and procurator in the courts of law. One of the most prolific playwrights of the 16th century, he produced over a hundred plays of all kinds, including several *Singspiele*, or musical plays. 📖 W Kozumplik, *The Phonology of Jacob Ayrer's Language* (1942)

Ayres, Gillian 1930–
English painter

Born in Barnes, London, she trained at Camberwell School of Art, and first exhibited in 1952. In 1957 she was commissioned to paint a series of 80 panels (since destroyed by fire) for South Hampstead School, London. Her free, abstract style, with its emphasis on colour and the active properties of paint, was influenced by seeing photographs of **Jackson Pollock** at work. In 1981 she went to live in North Wales, moving in 1987 to the West Country. During the 1980s she introduced gold into her pictures and turned from acrylics to oils, the titles of her paintings expressing the essential literary Britishness of her inspiration—*Green Grow the Rushes, O!* (1990), *May Day Games* (1990), *Go and Catch a Falling Star* (1990). Exhibitons include Glasgow's Great British Art Show in 1990. Her selection as the only artist representing Britain at the Indian Triennial of 1991 brought fresh inspiration, as she had rarely been out of her native country. Still playing with words, she painted for the event, among other works, *Indian Summer; A Midsummer Night* and *A Great While Ago The World Began.*

Ayrton, Hertha, *originally* Phoebe Sarah Marks 1854–1923
English physicist

Born in Portsea, near Portsmouth, and educated in mathematics at Cambridge, she is best known for her work on wave motion, the formation of sand ripples, and the behaviour of the electric arc. She performed extensive research on arc lamps (with her husband **William Ayrton**), including cinema projector lamps and search lights, and her improvements to search light technology were put into practice in aircraft detection during both world wars. During World War I she invented the Ayrton fan for dispersing poison gases—this invention was later adapted to various other applications, including improvement of ventilation in mines. Nominated for fellowship of the Royal Society in 1902, she received the society's Hughes Medal in 1906.

Ayrton, Michael 1921–75
English painter, sculptor, illustrator, art critic, translator and novelist

He was born in London and derived his many varied gifts in part from a cultured family which included scientists and engineers, writers and politicians. His early painting falls into the wartime English Neo-Romantic movement along with that of Graham Sutherland, John Minton and John Craxton. His sculpture dates from 1954, when he began treating subjects from classical mythology, in particular the tale of Daedalus and Icarus, which led to his building of a maze in brick and stone in the Catskill Mountains, New York State. He produced a huge number of now highly prized book illustrations, including Thomas Nashe's *The Unfortunate Traveller*. His book *British Drawings* (1946) had an impact on the reception of the Neo-Romantics. *Tittivulus, the Verbiage Collector* (1953) was a satire on bureaucracy and the critical establishment. *The Maze Maker* (1967) was a novel based on the Daedalus story, which he had also explored in the prose *Testament of Daedalus* (1962). A second novel, *The Midas Consequence*, was published in 1974. He translated and illustrated the work of Archilochos of Paros, wrote a study of the sculptor Giovanni Pisano, and published collections of essays, including *Fabrications* (1972). ▣ M Yorke, in *The Spirit of Place* (1988)

Ayrton, William Edward 1847–1908
English engineer and inventor
Born in London, he studied mathematics at University College London, and electricity at Glasgow under William Kelvin. He joined the Indian telegraph service (1868), and was appointed to the chair of natural philosophy and telegraphy at the new Imperial Engineering College in Tokyo, where he established laboratories for the teaching of applied electricity, the first of their kind. Returning to London in 1879 he became Professor of Physics and Electrical Engineering successively at the City and Guilds of London Institute, Finsbury Technical College (1881) and the Central Technical College (1884). With his colleague John Perry (1850–1920) he invented the first absolute block system for electric railways (1881) and many electrical measuring instruments, and published some 70 scientific and technical papers between 1876 and 1891.

Ayton, Sir Robert 1570–1638
Scottish poet and courtier
Born in Kinaldie, near St Andrews, he was educated at St Andrews University and studied law in Paris. He became a courtier of James VI and I in London, and was a friend of Ben Jonson and Thomas Hobbes. He wrote lyrics in English and Latin, and is credited with the prototype of 'Auld Lang Syne'. ▣ A Johnson, *Delitiae poetarum scotorum* (1637)

Aytoun, William Edmonstoune 1818–65
Scottish poet and humorist
Born in Edinburgh, he was educated at the Edinburgh Academy and Edinburgh University, and was called to the Bar in 1840. He published a collection of romantic pastiches, *Poland, Homer and Other Poems* (1832), and in 1836 began a lifelong connection with *Blackwood's Magazine*, to which he contributed countless parodies and burlesque reviews. In 1845 he was appointed Professor of Rhetoric and Belles-Lettres at Edinburgh University, and in five years quintupled the number of his students. In 1849 he married a daughter of John Wilson ('Christopher North'), and he was made Sheriff of Orkney in 1852. His works include *Bon Gaultier Ballads* (1845), *Lays of the Scottish Cavaliers* (1848), *Firmilian, a Spasmodic Tragedy* (1854), *Poems of Goethe* (1858, with Theodore Martin) and *Norman Sinclair* (1861), a semi-autobiographical novel. ▣ M E Weinstein, *William Aytoun and the Spasmodic Controversy* (1968)

Ayub Khan, Mohammed 1907–74
Pakistani field marshal and politician

He was born in Abbottabad and educated at Aligarh Moslem University and at Sandhurst. He served in World War II, became first Commander-in-Chief of Pakistan's army (1951) and later field marshal (1959). He became President of Pakistan in 1958 after a bloodless army coup, and established a stable economy and political autocracy. In March 1969, after widespread civil disorder and violent opposition from both the right and left wings, he relinquished power and martial law was re-established. He published his autobiography, *Friends, Not Masters*, in 1967.

Azaña (y Díaz), Manuel 1880–1940
Spanish politician and intellectual
Born in Alcalá de Henares, he qualified as a lawyer, served as a bureaucrat, but became eminent in the literary and political world. In 1925 he founded a political party, *Acción Republicana*. With the advent of the Second Republic (1931), he became Minister of War and then Prime Minister (1931–33) of a reforming government. An outstanding orator and thinker, he himself was closely identified with army reform and anticlericalism. During a period of opposition (1933–36) when he was the chief architect of the Popular Front coalition which triumphed in the general election of February 1936, he resumed the premiership. In May of that year he became President, and remained throughout the Spanish Civil War until February 1939, when General Franco forced him into exile in France, where he died. Azaña was the leading politician of the Second Republic and the greatest embodiment of its liberal, reformist vision.

Azariah, Vedanayakam Samuel 1874–1945
Indian prelate, and first Indian bishop of the Anglican Church of India, Burma and Ceylon
He was born in Vellalanvillai, Madras State. A firm believer in co-operation between foreign and Indian church workers (on which topic he addressed the Edinburgh World Missionary Conference in 1910), and in the development of indigenous leadership in a united Indian Church, he was appointed bishop of Dornakal, Andhra Pradesh, in 1912. Bringing to his post experience gained with the Tinnevelly and National missionary societies, and the YMCA, he took a leading role in the Tranquebar (1919) and Nagpur (1931) conferences for church union, and was chairman of the National Christian Council of India, Burma and Ceylon from 1929.

Azcona del Hoyo, José Simon 1927–
Honduran politician
Born in La Ceiba, he trained as a civil engineer in Honduras and Mexico, developing a particular interest in urban development and low-cost housing. As a student he became interested in politics and fought the 1963 general election as a candidate for the Liberal Party of Honduras (PLH) but his career was interrupted by a series of military coups. He served in the governments of Roberto Suazo and Walter Lopez (1982–86), which were ostensibly civilian administrations but, in reality, controlled by the army commander-in-chief, General Gustavo Alvarez. The latter was removed by junior officers in 1984 and in 1986 Azcona narrowly won the presidential election. A moderate conservative, he served as President of Honduras until 1990, signing the Central American Peace Accord of 1987 despite his government's quiet acceptance of the presence in Honduras of Nicaraguan Contras backed by the USA. He was barred by law from seeking a second term.

Azeglio, Massimo Taparelli, Marquese d' 1798–1866
Italian politician, painter and novelist
Born in Piedmont, he was influenced by his friend Cesare Balbo and the exiled Vincenzo Gioberti, and he developed a moderate, patriotic programme with his

famous *Degli ultimi casi di Romagna* (1846). As well as developing Balbo and Gioberti's ideas, he succeeded them as Piedmontese Prime Minister, replacing the latter in 1849 and retaining the post until 1852. During his period of office, extensive anticlerical legislation was initiated which was to continue under his successor, **Camillo, Conte di Cavour**. In 1860 d'Azeglio was made Governor of Milan after its acquisition from the Austrians, but he remained unenthusiastic about the annexation of the south of Italy.

Azhari, Ismail al- 1900–69
Sudanese politician

He was the leader of the Sudanese Unionist Party which, to the surprise and indeed disappointment of the British, was the victor of the first Sudanese parliamentary elections in 1953. He formed the first government in 1954. Opposed by the Mahdists, he was nonetheless able to guide the Sudan towards independence 1956. He became President of the Supreme Council of the Sudan in 1964, but a military coup in 1969 resulted in his being placed under house arrest and he died during this confinement.

Azikiwe, Nnamdi, *known as* Zik of Africa 1904–96
Nigerian journalist and politician

Born in Zungeri, in north Nigeria, he spent four years as a government clerk before going to the USA, where he studied at Storer College, Lincoln University and Howard University. He then taught at Lincoln, where he obtained two further degrees. He returned to Africa in 1934 and edited the *African Morning Post* (1934–37) in Accra before going back to Nigeria to take up the editorship of the *West African Pilot* (1937–45). He was a member of the executive of the Nigerian Youth Movement (1934–41) and helped found the National Council of Nigeria and the Cameroons (NCNC) of which he was Secretary (1944–46) and President (1946–60). A member of the Nigerian Legco (1947–51), he became Prime Minister of the Eastern Region (1954–59) after two years as Leader of the Opposition. In 1960 Nigeria became independent from Great Britain, and Azikiwe became the first black Governor-General and Commander-in-Chief (1960–63) and the first President of the Nigerian Republic (1963–66). He was in Britain at the time of the 1966 military uprising, but returned as a private citizen to Nigeria soon afterwards. He returned to politics in 1979 as leader of the Nigerian People's Party (1979–96), which came third in the 1979 election. He allied his Party for a few years with that of President **Shagari**, and was a member of the Council of State (1979–83). 📖 *My Odyssey: an autobiography* (1970)

Azorín, *pseudonym of* José Martinez Ruiz 1873–1967
Spanish novelist and critic

Born in Monóvar, and educated at Valencia, he belongs to the generation of **Baroja** and **Unamuno**, and his early novel *La voluntad* (1902, 'Willpower') reflects their pessimism. His lucid essays rebelled against the prevailing florid manner, but they are uneven in their insights. His other novels include *Don Juan* (1922) and *Dona Inés* (1925). 📖 L A LaJohn, *Azorín and the Spanish Stage* (1961)

Ba Da Shan See **Zhu Da**

Baade, (Wilhelm Heinrich) Walter 1893–1960
US astronomer
Born in Schröttinghausen, Germany, he studied at the universities of Münster and Göttingen, and from 1919 to 1931 worked at the Hamburg Observatory, Bergedorf. In 1931 he moved to the Mount Wilson Observatory (now part of Hale Observatories) in California. Baade's major interest was the stellar content of various systems of stars. He discovered two discrete stellar types or 'populations', which are characterized by blue stars in spiral galaxies and fainter red stars in elliptical galaxies. In 1944, helped by the wartime blackout in the Pasedena area, he resolved the centre of the Andromeda galaxy and its two companions into stars. In the 1950s he began a systematic survey of the positions of the recently discovered radio sources which led to a number of optical identifications. He was awarded the Gold Medal of the Royal Astronomical Society in 1954. After retirement he became Gauss Professor at the University of Göttingen (1959).

Baader, Andreas 1943–77
West German terrorist
Born in Munich, into a middle-class family, he became associated with the student protest movement of the later 1960s and was imprisoned for setting fire to department stores in Frankfurt in 1968. Critical of Germany's postwar materialism and military dominance by the USA, he formed, with **Ulrike Meinhof**, the underground guerilla group Rote Armee Fraktion (Red Army Faction). The Faction 'sprang' Baader from prison in 1970 and carried out a series of political assassinations and terrorist outrages. He was captured and sentenced to life imprisonment in 1977 and, after the Red Army Faction failed to secure his release by hi-jacking a Lufthansa passenger plane at Mogadishu, Somalia, he committed suicide.

Baader, Franz Xaver von 1765–1841
German Roman Catholic theologian and mystical philosopher
Born in Munich, he was a follower of **Jakob Böhme**. He regarded **David Hume's** philosophy as atheistic and opposed **Immanuel Kant** by maintaining that the true ethical end is not obedience to a moral law, but a realization of the divine life.

Baal-Shem-Tov, *properly* **Israel ben Eliezer** 1699–1760
Polish Jewish teacher and healer
He was born probably in Thiste, Podolia, but little is known of his humble origins. He became the founder of modern Hasidism.

Babangida, Ibrahim 1941–
Nigerian politician and soldier
He was born in Minna, Niger state. Educated at military schools in Nigeria, he was commissioned in 1963 and, after training in the UK, became an instructor at the Nigerian Defence Academy. After further training in the USA he became a major-general (1983). He took part in the overthrow of the government of **Shehu Shagari** in 1983 and was made Commander-in-Chief of the army. In 1985 he led a coup against President **Muhammadu Buhari** and assumed the presidency himself. In 1993 he was replaced by General Sani Abacha (1943–98) following military intervention in the general elections.

Babbage, Charles 1791–1871
English mathematician

Born in Teignmouth, Devon, and educated at Trinity and Peterhouse colleges, Cambridge, he spent most of his life attempting to build two calculating machines. The first, the 'difference engine', was designed to calculate tables of logarithms and similar functions by repeated addition performed by trains of gear wheels. A small prototype model described to the Astronomical Society in 1822 won the Society's first gold medal, and Babbage received government funding to build a full-sized machine. However, by 1842 he had spent large amounts of money without any substantial result, and government support was withdrawn. Meanwhile he had conceived the plan for a much more ambitious machine, the 'analytical engine', which could be programmed by punched cards to perform many different computations. The cards were to store not only the numbers but also the sequence of operations to be performed, an idea too ambitious to be realized by the mechanical devices available at the time. The idea can now be seen to be the essential germ of today's electronic computer, with Babbage regarded as the pioneer of modern computers. He held the Lucasian chair of mathematics at Cambridge from 1828 to 1839. 📖 Daniel Halacy, *Charles Babbage: Father of the Computer* (1970)

Babbitt, Irving 1865–1933
US critic and writer
Born in Dayton, Ohio, he became Professor of French at Harvard (1894–1933). Primarily a moralist and teacher, he was a leader of the 'new selective humanism' which flourished in the USA in the 1920s. His books include *Literature and the American College* (1908), *The New Laokoön* (1910), *Rousseau and Romanticism* (1919), and *On Being Creative* (1932). 📖 S C Brennan, *Irving Babbitt* (1987)

Babbitt, Isaac 1799–1862
US goldsmith and inventor
Born in Taunton, Massachusetts, he manufactured the first Britannia metal tableware in 1824, using an alloy of copper, tin and antimony. In 1839, after further experimentation with the same ingredients, he invented a journal box lined with a soft, silver-white alloy now called Babbitt metal, and still used to reduce friction in metal.

Babbitt, Milton Byron 1916–
US composer
Born in Philadelphia, he studied music and mathematics at the universities of New York and Princeton. His teachers included **Roger Sessions**, later a colleague in the music school at Princeton, where he taught from 1938. He used his flair for mathematical reasoning in formulating his musical theories and helped to evolve a 'Princeton school' of Modernist composition; this applied the principles of twelve-note music, not only to melody and harmony, but to other musical parameters such as rhythm. His work stresses the rhythmic problems of serial composition and the organizing principles underlying large structures using that system. He advanced that method into a rigorously delineated serial system by the 1960s, and made extensive use of electronic instruments in realising his theoretical concepts. Babbitt was director of the Columbia–Princeton Electronic Music Center in New York City from 1959. His work includes *Three Compositions* for piano (1947), *Philomel* for voice and magnetic tape (1964) and *Triad* for clarinet, viola and piano (1994).

Babcock, Harold Delos 1882–1968
US physicist and astronomer

Born in Edgerton, Wisconsin, he was educated at the University of California and joined the staff of the Mount Wilson Observatory (now part of Hale Observatories) in California in 1909. He became best known for his studies on the magnetic fields of the Sun and other stars. With his son, Horace Welcome Babcock (1912–), he invented the solar magnetograph (1951), which made possible detailed observations of the Sun's magnetic field, and resulted in the discovery of magnetically variable stars. His investigations of the magnetic field of the star 78 Virginis provided a link between the electromagnetic and the relativity theories. His son became director of the Hale Observatories in 1964, and as well as investigating stellar magnetism, studied the glow of the night sky and the rotation of galaxies.

Babcock, Stephen Moulton 1843–1931
US agricultural chemist
Born near Bridgewater, New York, he studied at Tufts College, the University of Göttingen and Cornell. He then taught at Cornell, moving to become chief chemist at the New York Experimental Station at Geneva (1882). In 1887 he was appointed Professor of Agricultural Chemistry at the University of Wisconsin and chief chemist to the Wisconsin Agricultural Experiment Station. He became the station's assistant director in 1901. He devised the 'Babcock test' for measuring fat in milk. Because this test could be carried out by unskilled operatives, it was soon widely used and much improved the quality of dairy produce. From 1907 onwards he studied the effect of selective diets on cattle. The importance of accessory food factors ('vitamins') emerged from this work and was developed more fully by Sir Frederick Gowland Hopkins. Babcock also invented an instrument to measure viscosity in liquids and carried out research on milk, sugar and fat solvents. He is sometimes called the 'father of scientific dairying'.

Bâb-ed-Din, *literally* 'Gate of Righteousness', *originally* Mirza Ali Mohammed 1819–50
Persian religious leader
He was born in Shiraz. In 1844 he declared himself the Bab ('Gateway') to the prophesied 12th Imam; he then claimed to be the Imam himself. He was imprisoned in 1847 and later executed at Tabriz. The religion he founded (Babism) was the forerunner of the Bahai faith (see Baha-Allah).

Babel, Isaak Emmanuilovich 1894–c.1941
Russian short-story writer
Born in the Jewish ghetto of Odessa, he worked as a journalist in St Petersburg, served in the Tsar's army on the Romanian front and, after the Revolution, in various Bolshevik campaigns as a Cossack supply officer. A protégé of Maxim Gorky, he is remembered for his stories of the Jews in Odessa in *Odesskie rasskazy* (1916, Eng trans *Odessa Tales*, 1924), and stories of war in *Konarmiya* (1926, Eng trans *Red Cavalry*, 1929), but also wrote plays, albeit less successfully. He was exiled to Siberia in the mid-1930s, and died in a concentration camp there. 📖 R W Hallett, *Isaac Babel* (1973)

Babeuf, François-Noël 1760–97
French politician
He was born in St Quentin. During the French Revolution (as 'Gracchus Babeuf'), he advocated a rigorous system of communism (Babouvism). His conspiracy to destroy the Directory (1796) and establish an extreme democratic and communist system (a 'Republic of Equals') was discovered, and he was guillotined. 📖 R B Rose, *Gracchus Babeuf, the First Revolutionary Communist* (1978)

Babilée, Jean, *originally* Jean Gutman 1923–
French dancer and choreographer

Born in Paris, he began performing and devising dances in the early 1940s and studied at the Paris Opera Ballet School. He was very successful as a member of the Ballets de Champs-Élysées and the Ballets de Paris, appearing in Janine Charrat's *Jeu de cartes* (1945, 'Game of Cards'), as the suicidal artist in Roland Petit's *Le Jeune homme et la mort* (1946, 'The Young Man and Death'), in *Spectre de la Rose*, and as the Bluebird in *Sleeping Beauty*. In the 1950s he was a guest of the Paris Opera Ballet and American Ballet Theater before forming his own eponymous company. From 1972 to 1973 he was director of Ballet du Rhin in Strasbourg. In the early 1980s Maurice Béjart created a solo for Babilée called *Life*, that showed he had lost little of his charisma and dynamic ability. He has also been a stage and film actor.

Babinet, Jacques 1794–1872
French physicist
Born in Lusignan, he standardized light measurement by using the red cadmium line's wavelength as the standard for the angstrom unit. Babinet's principle, that similar diffraction patterns are produced by two complementary screens, is named after him. He also invented an elegant instrument for measuring the polarization of light, the Babinet compensator (1849).

Babington, Antony 1561–86
English conspirator
Born into a wealthy Catholic family in Dethick, Derbyshire, he served as a page to Mary, Queen of Scots during her imprisonment at Sheffield. In 1586 he was induced by John Ballard and other Catholic emissaries to lead a conspiracy aiming to murder Elizabeth I and release Mary (the Babington Plot). Coded messages in which Mary approved the plot were intercepted by Francis Walsingham, and were later used against her. Babington fled but was captured at Harrow and executed with the others.

Babinski, Joseph François Felix 1857–1932
French neurologist
Born in Paris, he described a reflex of the foot symptomatic of upper motor neurone disease. Independently of Alfred Frölich (1871–1953), a Viennese pharmacologist, he investigated an endocrinal disorder, adiposogenital dystrophy, known as Babinski–Frölich disease.

Babits, Mihály 1883–1941
Hungarian poet
He was a schoolmaster, but devoted himself to writing from 1917. He became a novelist and essayist, and a distinguished translator of Dante, Shakespeare, and the Greek classics. 📖 M Becedek, *Babits Mihály* (1969)

Babrius fl.c.2nd century AD
Greek writer
Little is known of him except that he collected Aesopic fables, which he turned into popular verse. Almost all of these were thought to have been lost, but in 1844 a Greek discovered 123 of them at Mount Athos. A translation of these and those by Phaedrus was made by Ben Edwin Perry and was published in 1965. 📖 J Werner, *Questiones Babrianae* (1892)

Babur 1483–1530
First Mughal Emperor of India
Born in Fergana, Central Asia, a descendant of Genghis Khan and nephew of Sultan Mahmud Mirza of Samarkand, he attempted unsuccessfully as a young man to establish himself as ruler there. He had greater success in Afghanistan, entering Kabul in 1504, but later again failed to win Samarkand (1511–12). The death of Sikandir Lodi (1517) brought civil war to the Afghan Lodi Empire in India and Babur took advantage of this to invade. He defeated Ibrahim Lodi decisively at Panipat, north of

Delhi (1526) and founded the Mughal Empire. The following year he defeated the Hindu Rajput confederacy and, despite continuing resistance from the Hindus and from the Afghans, the military strength of the Mughals enabled him to consolidate his gains. As well as being a distinguished soldier, he was also a poet and diarist, with interests in architecture, gardens and music. His memoirs depict a sensitive, magnanimous and convivial ruler. Himself a Muslim, he initiated the policy of toleration towards non-Muslims that became a hallmark of the Mughal Empire at its height. ⚏ Muni Lal, *Babar: Life and Times* (1977)

Bacall, Lauren, *originally* Betty Perske 1924–
US film actress
Born in New York City, she became a student at the American Academy of Dramatic Arts and made her stage debut in *Johnny Two-by-Four* (1942). She also worked as a model. Seen on the cover of *Harper's Bazaar*, she was signed to a contract by director Howard Hawks and launched as 'Slinky! Sultry! Sensational!' in the film *To Have and Have Not* (1944). Husky-voiced and with a feline grace, she appeared as tough, sophisticated and cynical as her co-star Humphrey Bogart, whom she married in 1945. They co-starred in such thrillers as *The Big Sleep* (1946), *Dark Passage* (1947) and *Key Largo* (1948), and she displayed a gift for light comedy in *How To Marry a Millionaire* (1953). After Bogart's death in 1957, she turned increasingly to the theatre, enjoying Broadway successes in *Goodbye Charlie* (1959), *The Cactus Flower* (1965–67), *Applause* (1970–72, Tony award) and *Woman Of The Year* (1981, Tony award). Later film appearances include *Harper* (1966), *Murder On The Orient Express* (1974), *The Shootist* (1976) and *The Mirror Has Two Faces* (1996). She was married to the actor Jason Robards, Jnr (1961–69) and has written two volumes of autobiography: *By Myself* (1979) and *Now* (1994).

Bacchelli, Riccardo 1891–1985
Italian novelist
Born in Bologna, he studied at the university there until 1912, when he began to write articles for literary journals. He wrote works in a large number of different genres and mediums, but is best known for his historical novels. His works include *Il diavolo al Pontelungo* (1927, 'The Devil at Pontelungo'), a humorous tale of Mikhail Bakunin's efforts to introduce socialism into Italy, the three-volume family chronicle of the Risorgimento, *Il mulino del Po* (1938–40, 'The Mill on the Po'), and *Bellezza e Unamità* (1972, 'Beauty and Humanity'). ⚏ M Saccenti, *Riccardo Bacchelli* (1973)

Bacchylides 5th century BC
Greek lyric poet
He was born on the island of Ceos and was a nephew of the poet Simonides. Little of his poetry survived until the end of the nineteenth century, when papyri containing substantial victory odes were acquired by the British Museum. He was a rival of Pindar and wrote odes celebrating patrons' victories in the Olympic and other games, including Hieron of Syracuse. He also wrote choral dithyrambs in narrative form, one of which is a dialogue between Aegeus and his son Theseus. He lived in Athens and for a time in Syracuse, and is thought to have spent the years from 460 to 452 in political exile in the Peloponnese, where according to Plutarch he wrote some of his best work.

Bacciochi, Maria Anna Elisa, *née* Bonaparte 1777–1820
Corsican princess
She was born in Ajaccio, Corsica, the eldest of Napoleon I's sisters. She married Felice Bacciochi, and was created a princess (1805) and Grand Duchess of Tuscany (1809) by her brother.

Bach, Alexander, Baron von 1813–93
Austrian politician
A prominent supporter of the 1848 revolution in Vienna, he became Minister of Justice in the revolutionary government of Wessenberg-Doblhof. He resigned in 1848, but his rapid personal conversion from liberalism to neo-absolutism brought him high office in the counter-revolutionary government led by Felix Schwarzenberg. Here he served as Interior Minister and achieved reforms in the system of provincial government which influence Austria to this day.

Bach, C(arl) P(hilipp) E(manuel), *known as the* Berlin or Hamburg Bach 1714–88
German composer
Born in Weimar, he was educated at the Thomasschule, Leipzig, where his father, J S Bach, was cantor, and at Frankfurt University. In 1740 he became cembalist (a cembalo is an instrument like a harpsichord) to the future Frederick II, the Great. Later, he was kapellmeister at Hamburg (1767). He was left-handed and therefore found it easiest to play the organ and clavier, for which his most accomplished pieces were composed. He introduced the sonata form, wrote numerous concertos, keyboard sonatas, church and chamber music, and bridged the transitional period between his father and Franz Haydn, by his homophonic, formal, yet delicate, compositions. In 1753 he published *Die wahre Art das Klavier zu spielen* (Eng trans *The True Art of Playing Keyboard Instruments*, 1949), the first methodical treatment of the subject.

Bach, Johann Christian, *known as the* London Bach 1735–82
German composer
Born in Leipzig, he was the 11th and youngest son of J S Bach, and studied under his brother C P E Bach in Berlin and, from 1754, in Italy. After becoming a Catholic, he was appointed organist at Milan (1760) where he composed ecclesiastical music, including two masses, a requiem and a Te Deum, as well as operas. In 1762 he settled in London and was appointed composer to the London Italian opera. He became musician to Queen Charlotte Sophia (1763) and later collaborated with Karl Friedrich Abel (1723–87). The young Mozart on his London visit (1764) took to him and was influenced by his style. Bach developed symphonic form, and was twice painted by Thomas Gainsborough.

Bach, Johann Christoph Friedrich, *known as the* Bückeburg Bach 1732–95
German composer
Born in Leipzig, he was the ninth son of J S Bach. Educated in Leipzig at the Thomasschule and at the university, he became kapellmeister at Bückeburg in 1750. He was an industrious but undistinguished composer of church music.

Bach, Johann Sebastian See panel p113

Bach, Wilhelm Friedemann, *known as the* Halle Bach 1710–84
German composer
Born in Weimar, he was the eldest and most gifted son of J S Bach. Educated in Leipzig at the Thomasschule and the university, he became organist at Dresden (1733) and Halle (1747). However, his way of life became increasingly dissolute and from 1764 he lived without fixed occupation at Brunswick, Göttingen and Berlin. He was a very distinguished organist, but few of his compositions, which include church cantatas and several instrumental pieces, were published, since he rarely wrote them down.

Bache, Alexander Dallas 1806–67
US geophysicist

Bach, Johann Sebastian 1685–1750
German composer

Johann Sebastian Bach was born in Eisenach. Orphaned before he was 10, he was placed in the care of his elder brother, Johann Christoph Bach (1671–1721), organist at Ohrdruf, who taught him to play the organ and clavier. Bach was forbidden to use his brother's music library, and resorted to copying out scores at night, a habit which remained with him throughout his life and eventually ruined his eyesight. In 1700 he became a church chorister at St Michael's church, Lüneberg. When his voice broke, he served as a violinist and harpsichord accompanist.

In 1704, after a year at the court of Weimar, he was appointed organist at Arnstadt, where he wrote many of his early church cantatas, including the colourful 'Easter' cantata, BWV15. He found his official duties as choirmaster increasingly tedious, and in 1705 he took a month's leave, which he exceeded, to journey on foot to Lübeck to hear the organist **Diderik Buxtehude**. This and his innovations in the chorale accompaniments infuriated the authorities at Arnstadt. In 1707, now married to his cousin Maria Barbara Bach, he left to become organist at Mühlhausen. The prevailing Calvinism there meant disapproval of his more elaborate anthems, but his imposing inaugural cantata, 'God is my King', was approved for publication.

In 1708 he moved to the ducal court at Weimar and remained there nine years. The two toccatas and fugues in D minor, the fantasia and fugue in G minor, the preludes and fugues in C and G, and the *Little Organ Book* of short preludes, all belong to this period. In 1716 the duke gave the senior post of kapellmeister to a musician who was greatly inferior to Bach, who promptly resigned, to take up shortly afterwards the post of kapellmeister to Prince Leopold of Anhalt-Cöthen.

During his time at Cöthen, Bach wrote four overtures, the six French and six English suites, several concertos for one and two violins, and others for various groups of instruments. Six of these were written in 1721 as a commission for the margrave of Brandenburg, who has given his name to them ever since. In *The Well-tempered Clavier* (1722), which profoundly influenced **Mozart**, Bach transformed the conventional structure of preludes and fugues written in each major and minor key.

In 1720 Maria died suddenly. Of their seven children, four had survived. In 1722 Bach married Anna Magdalena Wilken, an accomplished singer, harpsichordist and copyist, for whom he wrote a collection of keyboard pieces. For his six surviving children by her, Bach wrote a keyboard instruction book, and with Anna he completed a second *Notebook*. In 1723 he was appointed cantor of the Thomasschule in Leipzig, a post which he retained for the remainder of his life, despite acrimonious disagreements with the authorities and his colleagues. To make it more difficult for them to overrule his decisions, Bach solicited the title of court composer to the Elector of Saxony (**Augustus II**), and for his sponsor he wrote the 30 'Goldberg Variations'. Goldberg was a pupil of his, and of his son **Wilhelm Friedemann Bach**.

Bach's house in Leipzig became a centre of musical pilgrimage, and many eminent musicians, including several relations, became his pupils. He became conductor of the Collegium Musicum, a society composed mainly of students, in 1729, but in 1743 refused to join the newly sponsored concert society, from which originated the famous *Gewandhaus* concerts. At Leipzig he wrote nearly 300 church cantatas, of which 200 survive, mainly choral in character but including many fine arias for solo voices. His greatest works from this period are usually reckoned to be the two passions (*St John Passion* and *St Matthew Passion*), the *Mass in B Minor* (begun in 1733), and the *Christmas Oratorio*.

In 1747 Bach visited Berlin and was unexpectedly invited to Potsdam by **Frederick the Great**, who asked him to try his latest Silbermann pianofortes. After much improvisation, Bach departed with a subject given to him by Frederick which he developed into a trio for flute, violin, and clavier, entitled *The Musical Offering*. He died two years later, almost totally blind, of apoplexy. At the time of his death he was engaged on a masterly series of fugues for keyboard, *The Art of Fugue*. His work stands midway between the old and the new, his main achievement being his remarkable development of polyphony. To his contemporaries he was known mainly as an organist, and a century was to pass before he was to achieve due recognition as a composer.

📖 T Dowley, *Bach His Life and Times* (1985); M Boyd, *Bach* (1983); H T David and A Mendel, *The Bach Reader* (1966).

> Bach's definition of music: 'An agreeable harmony for the honour of God and the premissible delights of the soul.' Quoted in Derek Watson, *Music Quotations* (1991).
>
> Beethoven described Bach as 'The immortal god of harmony.' Quoted in a letter to Christoph Breitkopf (1801).
>
> 'There is nothing to it. You only have to hit the right notes at the right time and the instrument plays itself.' Of the organ. Quoted in K Geiringer, *The Bach Family* (1954).

Born in Philadelphia, he was the great-grandson of **Benjamin Franklin**. He became Professor of Natural Philosophy at Pennsylvania University (1828–41) and as superintendent of the US Coast Survey had the entire coastline mapped in his lifetime.

Bachelard, Gaston 1884–1962
French philosopher

Born in Bar-sur-Aube, he had an unusual range of interests and influence in the history of science, psychoanalysis, and literary criticism, which were connected in such works as *La Psychoanalyse du feu* (1937, 'Psychoanalysis of Fire') and *La Flamme d'une chandelle* (1961, 'The Flame of a Candle').

Bachman, John 1790–1874
US clergyman and naturalist

Born in Rhinebeck, New York, he was a Lutheran pastor in Charleston, South Carolina, from 1815. He was co-author with **John James Audubon** of *The Viviparous Quadrupeds of North America* (1845–49).

Bachofen, Johann Jakob 1815–87
Swiss jurist and historian

Professor of Roman Law at Basle from 1841, he is known for his work on the theory of matriarchy, *Das Mutterrecht* (1841).

Baciccia, *originally* Giovanni Battista Gaulli
1639–1709
Italian painter

Born in Genoa, he is best known for his spectacular Baroque illusionistic ceiling frescoes. Their illusionism is enhanced by the combination of painted figures and stucco work which breaks down the barrier between two- and three-dimensional representation. His flamboyant

Bacon, Francis, Baron Verulam of Verulam and Viscount St Albans 1561–1626
English philosopher and statesman

Francis Bacon was born in London, the younger son of Sir **Nicholas Bacon**, and nephew of **William Cecil**, Lord Burghley. He studied at Trinity College, Cambridge, and at Gray's Inn, being called to the Bar in 1582. He became an MP in 1584 and courted the favour of the 2nd Earl of **Essex**, from whom he accepted a gift of land at Twickenham. However, when Essex was tried for treason Bacon helped to secure his conviction. He was knighted by **James I** (1603), to whom he had professed his loyalty and whom he supported in parliament. Among his schemes was one for the union of England and Scotland, as a result of which he was made a commissioner for the union.

In 1607 he was appointed Solicitor-General, and in 1613, Attorney-General. In 1616 he prosecuted the Scottish courtier Robert Carr, Earl of Somerset (c.1590–1645), with whom he was intimate, for the murder of Sir Thomas Overbury (1581–1613), who had been poisoned in the Tower. In the same year Bacon became a privy councillor, in 1617 Lord Keeper, and in 1618 Lord Chancellor. He was raised to the peerage as Lord Verulam, and created viscount in 1621. However, complaints were made that he accepted bribes from suitors in his court, and he was publicly accused before his fellow peers, fined, imprisoned, and banished from parliament and the court. Although soon released, and later pardoned, he never returned to public office, and died deeply in debt. He earned a reputation for obsequiousness, which was often justified. In March 1626 he caught cold while stuffing a fowl with snow, in order to observe the effect of cold on the preservation of flesh, and died. He was buried in St Michael's Church, St Albans.

Bacon's philosophy may be studied in *The Advancement of Learning* (1605), a review of the state of knowledge in his own time, and its chief defects, in *De Augmentis Scientiarum* (1623), a Latin expansion of the *Advancement*, and in *Novum Organum* (1620). He stressed the importance of experiment in interpreting nature and the necessity for proper regard for any possible evidence which might run counter to any held thesis; his creation of the method of scientific induction gave an impetus to future scientific investigation.

As a writer of English prose and a student of human nature, he is seen to best advantage in his essays. His *History of Henry VII* (1622) shows scholarly research. His religious works include prayers and verse translations of seven Psalms (1625). His legal and constitutional works include *Maxims of the Law* (1630), *Reading on the Statute of Uses* (1642), and *Elements of the Common Laws of England* (1630).

'The wisest, brightest, meanest of mankind.'

and colourful style is indebted to **Rubens** and **Correggio**, but the most forceful qualities of his work, best seen in the ceiling of the Jesuit church of The Gesò in Rome, were probably encouraged by his friend **Gian Bernini** who similarly promoted a sensual and ecstatic art in the service of the Church. Baciccia also painted portraits of the papal court which are of a quieter mood.

Back, Sir George 1796–1878
English explorer

Born in Stockport, Greater Manchester, he sailed with Sir **John Franklin** on three Polar expeditions—to the Spitsbergen Seas (1819), the Coppermine River (1819–25) and the Mackenzie River (1822–27). In 1833–35 he went in search of the Arctic explorer Sir **John Ross**, who was erroneously supposed to be lost, and discovered Artillery Lake and the Great Fish River, or Back's River, which he traced to the Frozen Ocean. In 1836–37 he further explored the Arctic shores. He was knighted in 1839, and made admiral in 1857.

Backhuysen or Backhuizen, Ludolf 1631–1708
Dutch marine painter

Born in Emden, he is best known for his *Rough Sea at the Mouth of the Maas* (Louvre, Paris) and several seascapes in London, Amsterdam and The Hague.

Backus, John 1924–
US computer programmer

He studied mathematics at Columbia University, before joining IBM in 1950 as a computer programmer. After developing an assembly language for IBM's 701 computer, Backus then suggested the development of a compiler and higher level language for the IBM 704. This was approved as the FORTRAN (FORmula TRANslation) project, which was not completed until 1957. FORTRAN was a landmark programming language which opened the computer up to the non-specialist, allowed computers to talk to each other, and paved the way for other computer languages such as COBOL, ALGOL and BASIC. Backus joined IBM Research (1963–91) and was awarded the 1994 Charles Stark Draper Award by the National Academy of Engineering.

Bacon, Delia Salter 1811–59
US writer

She was born in Tallmadge, Ohio, and spent the years 1853–58 in England trying to prove the theory that Shakespeare's plays were written by **Francis Bacon**, Sir **Walter Raleigh**, **Edmund Spenser**, and others. She did not originate the idea herself, but was the first to give it currency in her *Philosophy of the Plays of Shakspeare Unfolded* (1857, with a preface by **Nathaniel Hawthorne**). She was the sister of **Leonard Bacon**. V C Hopkins, *Prodigal Puritan: a life of Delia Bacon* (1959)

Bacon, Francis See panel above

Bacon, Francis 1909–92
British artist

Born in Dublin of English parents, he settled permanently in England in 1928. After working as an interior designer he began painting in about 1930 without any formal training. He first made a major impact in 1945 with his *Three Figures at the Base of a Crucifixion*. Although the initial inspiration for his work was Surrealism he made frequent use of imagery annexed from old masters such as **Velasquez**, and **Eadweard Muybridge's** photographs of figures in motion. These are usually translated into blurred and gory figures imprisoned in unspecific, architectural settings. His pictures frequently evoke atmospheres of terror and angst. A technical perfectionist, Bacon destroyed a great deal of his prolific output. His works are in all major collections, including that of the Vatican. He is widely regarded as Great Britain's most important postwar artist. John Russell, *Francis Bacon* (1985)

Bacon, John 1740–99
English sculptor

He was born in London, and became one of the first students of the Royal Academy Schools. His style was Rococo rather than Neoclassical. Among his works in

London are the monuments to **Chatham** (William Pitt, the Elder) in Westminster Abbey (1779–83), and the statue of Dr **Johnson** in St Paul's Cathedral (1796). Others include **Thomas Guy** (1779, Guy's Hospital, London), Sir **William Blackstone** (1784, All Souls, Oxford) and **Samuel Whitbread** (1799, Cardington, Bedfordshire).

Bacon, John See **Baconthorpe, John**

Bacon, Leonard 1801–81
US Congregationalist clergyman
Born in Detroit, he was Professor of Theology at Yale (1866–71), and wrote a history of Congregationalism in the USA. He was an early leader in the antislavery movement, and was founder-editor (1848) of the free-soil paper, *The Independent*. He was the brother of **Delia Salter Bacon**.

Bacon, Nathaniel c.1642–1676
American colonialist
Born in Suffolk, he emigrated to Virginia in 1673, and made a name for himself with his raids against the Native Indians. His activities prompted the English governor Sir William Berkeley (1606–77) to declare him a rebel in 1676, whereupon Bacon captured and burned Jamestown. He briefly controlled most of Virginia, but died suddenly.

Bacon, Sir Nicholas 1509–79
English statesman
He attained high legal office which, as a Protestant, he lost under **Mary I, Tudor**. However, on the accession of **Elizabeth I** (1558) he was made Lord Keeper of the Great Seal, and with **William Cecil** was left to manage Church affairs. A staunch anti-Catholic, he was an implacable enemy of **Mary, Queen of Scots**.

Bacon, Roger c.1214–1292
English philosopher and scientist
Born probably in Ilchester, Somerset, he studied at Oxford and Paris. He wrote commentaries on **Aristotle's** physics and metaphysics, and began to gain a reputation for unconventional learning in philosophy, magic and alchemy, becoming known as *Doctor Mirabilis* ('Wonderful Teacher'). In 1247 he began to devote himself to experimental science and also joined the Franciscan Order, returning to Oxford in 1250. Again in Paris, he compiled (1266–67) his *Opus Majus* ('Great Work') along with two other works, a summary of all his learning. In 1277 his writings were condemned by the Franciscans for 'suspected novelties', and he was imprisoned. He died in Oxford soon after his eventual release. He has been (mistakenly) credited with scientific inventions like the magnifying glass and gunpowder, but he published some remarkable speculations about lighter-than-air flying machines, mechanical transport on land and sea, the circumnavigation of the globe, and the construction of microscopes and telescopes. His views on the primacy of mathematical proof and on experimentalism have often seemed strikingly modern, and despite surveillance and censorship from the Franciscans he published many works on mathematics, philosophy and logic whose importance was only recognized in later centuries. 📖 Andrew G Little (ed), *Roger Bacon Essays* (1914)

Baconthorpe or **Bacon, John**, *called* the Resolute Doctor c.1290–1346
English scholar
Born in Baconthorpe, Norfolk, he was a Carmelite by training. He taught at Cambridge, and wrote commentaries on the Arab philosopher, **Ibn Averroës**. He anticipated **John Wycliffe's** teaching that priests should be subordinate to kings. He was the great-nephew of **Roger Bacon**.

Bacovia, George, *pseudonym of* G Vasiliu 1881–1957
Romanian poet
His poetry, beautifully translated into English in the bilingual *Plumb* (1980), is elegant and melancholy. A manic-depressive and an alcoholic, he captured the sad but excited nature of his fugitive and poverty-stricken existence. He exercised a great influence upon his younger contemporaries. He was married to the poet Agatha Grigorescu. 📖 M Seymour-Smith, *Who's Who in Twentieth Century Literature* (1976)

Badarayana
Indian philosopher
This unknown Indian philosopher is the reputed author of the *Vedanta* (or *Brahama*) *Sutra*, and is sometimes identified with the 5th-century sage Vyasa, who is traditionally credited with compiling the *Mahabharata*. Nothing is known of Badarayana apart from his connection with the *Vedanta Sutra*, which cannot be dated with certainty. He may simply be a personification of an anonymous process of editing. The *Vedanta Sutra* is the foundation text of *Vedanta*, one of the six classic systems of Hindu philosophy. Its varied interpretation is the basis of the schools founded by **Śankara**, **Ramanuja** and **Madhva**.

Baddeley, Sophia, *née* Snow 1745–86
English actress and singer
Born probably in London, she eloped in 1763 with the actor Robert Baddeley (1732–94), but the marriage was brief and unhappy. She played Ophelia at Drury Lane (1765), and was a noted singer but squandered her money and became addicted to laudanum. She escaped her creditors by fleeing to Edinburgh, where she continued to perform until her death.

Baden-Powell, Robert Stephenson Smyth Baden-Powell, 1st Baron 1857–1941
English soldier and founder of the Boy Scouts
He was born in London and educated at Charterhouse. He joined the army in 1876, served in India and Afghanistan, was on the staff in Ashanti and Matabeleland, and won fame as the defender of Mafeking (1899–1900) in the Boer War. He was promoted lieutenant-general in 1907. He is best known, however, as the founder of the Boy Scouts (1908) and, with his sister Agnes (1858–1945), of the Girl Guides (1910). He published *Scouting for Boys* (1908), founded the Wolf Cubs (1916), and was acclaimed World Chief Scout in 1920. 📖 Tim Jeal, *The Boy-Man: The Life of Lord Baden-Powell* (1990)

Bader, Sir Douglas Robert Stuart 1910–82
English aviator
Born in London, he lost both legs in a flying accident in 1931 and was invalided out of the RAF, but overcame his disability and returned in 1939. He commanded the first RAF Canadian Fighter Squadron, evolving tactics that contributed to victory in the Battle of Britain, but was captured in 1941 after a collision with an enemy aircraft over Béthune. He received many honours, and he was knighted in 1976. 📖 Robert Jackson, *Douglas Bader: A Biography* (1983)

Badía-y-Leblich, Domingo 1766–1818
Spanish traveller
Born in Barcelona, he studied Arabic and, disguised as a Muslim, visited (1803–07) Morocco, Tripoli, Cyprus, Egypt, and Mecca (the first Christian to be there since the spread of the Islamic faith). He also travelled to Syria and Constantinople (Istanbul).

Badoglio, Pietro 1871–1956
Italian general

He was born in Piedmont. As Governor of Libya (1929–34), he achieved the pacification of the Sanusi tribesmen by 1932. In 1935 he replaced **Emilio De Bono** at the head of the conquest of Abyssinia and became Viceroy of the new colony in May 1936. On Italy's entry into World War II (1940) he was made Commander-in-Chief, but resigned after humiliating defeats in Greece and Albania (December 1940). In 1943 he was asked by **Victor Emmanuel III** to form an anti-fascist government after the arrest of **Mussolini**. He signed an armistice with the Allies at Malta and declared war on Germany. Badoglio formed a broad coalition government including **Palmira Togliatti**, **Benedetto Croce** and **Carlo Sforza** in April 1944, but after the liberation of Rome in June he was obliged to resign under pressure from the Americans and politicians with better anti-fascist credentials. He was replaced by **Ivanoe Bonomi**.

Baeck, Leo 1873–1956
German Jewish religious leader

Born in Lissa, Prussia, he was rabbi in Berlin (1912–42), and when the Nazis came to power became the political leader of German Jewry. He spent three years in the Theresienstadt concentration camp (1942–45). After the war he lectured in Great Britain. His chief publications were *Das Wesen des Judentums* (1905, Eng trans *The Essence of Judaism*, 1948) and *The Pharisees and Other Essays* (1947).

Baeda, St See Bede, St

Baedeker, Karl 1801–59
German publisher

He was born in Essen and started his own publishing business in Coblenz in 1827. He is best known for the authoritative guidebooks which still bear his name.

Baekeland, Leo Hendrik 1863–1944
US chemist

He was born in Ghent, Belgium, and studied there and at other Belgian universities, before becoming Professor of Physics and Chemistry at Bruges in 1885. He emigrated to the USA in 1889 and founded a chemical company to manufacture one of his inventions: photographic printing paper which could be used with artificial light. Subsequently he made the first synthetic phenolic resin, known as Bakelite, which replaced hard rubber and amber as an insulator. Its success led to the founding of the Bakelite Corporation in 1910. Baekeland wrote on many topics in organic chemistry and electrochemistry and on the reform of patent law. He was elected president of the American Chemical Society in 1924 and received many academic honours at home and abroad.

Baer, Karl Ernst Ritter von 1792–1876
German naturalist and pioneer in embryology

Born in Piep, Estonia, he graduated in medicine from Dorpat University and later studied at the universities of Berlin, Vienna and Würzburg. He was appointed professor at Königsberg University (1817–34), and from 1834 taught at St Petersburg University. From 1826 he investigated the mammalian ovary, research which finally established that reproduction necessarily involved an egg (ovum). Investigating embryo development, he was the first to differentiate the notochord, the gelatinous cord that in vertebrates becomes the backbone and skull. He also drew attention to the neural folds which develop into the central nervous system, and formulated the 'biogenetic law', which states that in embryonic development, general characters appear before special ones. In the development process his ideas proved important to comparative anatomy, embryology and evolutionary theory.

Baeyer, Johann Friedrich Wilhelm Adolf von 1835–1917
German organic chemist and Nobel Prize winner

Born in Berlin, he discovered a new double salt of copper and sodium at the age of 12. At Heidelberg he studied under **Robert Wilhelm Bunsen** and **August Kekule von Stradonitz**, and he became Professor of Chemistry at Strassburg (1872) and Munich (1875–1915). His research covered many aspects of chemistry, notably the synthesis of the dye indigo and the elucidation of its structure, and the mechanism of photosynthesis. He studied the condensation of phenols and aldehydes, the polyacetylenes, the stability of polymethylene rings, the terpenes and the basicity of organic oxygen compounds. He was awarded the 1905 Nobel Prize for chemistry.

Baez, Joan 1941–
US folk-singer and civil rights campaigner

She was born in Staten Island, New York. Her strong, pure soprano was one of the major voices of the folk revival of the 1960s. She broadened her traditional and ballad repertoire to include songs by contemporary writers like **Bob Dylan** (with whom she had a much-publicized relationship), Phil Ochs and Tim Hardin, and was writing her own songs by the end of the decade. A Quaker, she was active in the civil rights and peace movements, and she has continued to combine humanitarian work with music. Her later recordings were aimed at a more mainstream rock market, and have often included distinguished guests, like **Paul Simon** on *Speaking With Dreams* (1990), or the diverse collaborations which made up *Ring Them Bells* (1995). 💿 *And A Voice To Sing With* (1990)

Baffin, William c.1584–1622
English navigator

He was born probably in London, and from 1612 to 1616 was the pilot on several expeditions in search of the Northwest Passage. The most significant of these were the voyages under the command of Robert Bylot on the *Discovery*, during which they examined Hudson Strait (1615), discovered Baffin Bay (1616), and discovered Lancaster, Smith and Jones sounds (1616) which were later shown to lead to the Arctic Ocean and the Pacific Ocean. These were to be the most important explorations of the Passage for nearly two centuries and were largely ignored by future Arctic explorers until confirmed by Sir **John Ross** in 1818. Baffin sailed as far north as latitude 77° 45′ N, and was possibly the first person to determine a degree of longitude at sea by lunar observation. He later carried out extensive surveys of the Red Sea (1616–21), and was killed at the Siege of Ormuz.

Bagaza, Jean-Baptiste 1946–
Burundian politician and soldier

Born in Rutovu, Bururi Province, he attended military schools in Belgium then returned to Burundi to become assistant to the head of the armed forces, with the rank of lieutenant-colonel. In 1976 he led a coup to overthrow President Micombero and was appointed President by a Supreme Revolutionary Council. In 1984 the post of Prime Minister was abolished and Bagaza was elected head of state and government. In 1987 he was himself ousted in a coup led by Major Pierre Buyoya. During the civil war in Burundi in 1996 he was a leading supporter of the Tutsis' demands to control the country.

Bagehot, Walter 1826–77
English economist and journalist

Born in Langport, Somerset, he graduated in mathematics at University College London, and was called to the Bar in 1852. After a spell as banker in his father's firm at Langport, he succeeded his father-in-law **James Wilson** as editor of *The Economist* in 1860. His *English*

Constitution (1867) became a standard work. He followed Thomas Hill Green (1836–82) and others in applying the theory of evolution to politics, as in *Physics and Politics* (1872). Other works include *Lombard Street* (1875), *Literary Studies* (1878) and *Economic Studies* (1880). He advocated many constitutional reforms, including the introduction of life peers. 📖 Alastair Buchan, *The Spare Chancellor: The Life of Walter Bagehot* (1959)

Bagford, John 1650–1716
English antiquary
Born in London, he was originally a shoemaker. He made a scrapbook collection of English broadside ditties and verses in 64 volumes for **Robert Harley**, known as *The Bagford Ballads*.

Baha-Allah, *literally* 'Glory of God', *originally* Mirza Huseyn Ali 1817–92
Persian religious leader and founder of the Islamic Bahai movement
Born in Teheran, he became a follower of the Shiraz merchant Mirza Ali Mohammed (see **Bâb-ed-din**), founder of the Persian Babi sect. Persecuted and imprisoned in 1852, he was exiled to Baghdad, Constantinople (Istanbul) and Acre. In 1863 he proclaimed himself as the prophet that Bâb-ed-din had foretold, and became the leader of the new Bahai faith.

Bahr, Hermann 1863–1934
Austrian dramatist, novelist and critic
Born in Linz, he studied in Vienna and Berlin, and took a leading part in the successive literary movements of Naturalism, Neo-Romanticism and Expressionism. His 'decadent' novel *Die gute Schule* (1890, 'The Good School') is highly regarded. He published social novels such as *Die schöne Frau* (1899, 'The Beautiful Woman') and comedies such as *Die gelbe Nachtigall* (1907, 'The Yellow Nightingale') and the theatrical farce *Das Konzert* (1909, 'The Concert'). He was appointed manager of the Deutsches Theater, Berlin (1903), and the Burgtheater, Vienna (1918). 📖 E Widder, *Hermann Bahr: sein Weg zum Glauben* (1963)

Baïf, Jean Antoine de 1532–89
French poet
Born in Venice, he was a member of the Pléiade, a group of seven poets gathered around **Pierre de Ronsard**. His works include *Amours* (1552, 'Love Poems') and 'Passe Temps' ('Pastime', in *Œuvres en rime*, 1573), as well as translations from the Greek. He attempted to introduce blank verse into French poetry, and experimented with combinations of poetry and music. 📖 M Auge-Chignet, *La vie, les idées et l'œuvre de Jean Antoine de Baïf* (1909)

Baikie, William Balfour 1825–64
Scottish explorer, naturalist and linguist
Born in Kirkwall, Orkney, he studied medicine at Edinburgh, and in 1848 became a naval surgeon. On the Niger expedition of 1854, he succeeded through the captain's death to the command of the *Pleiad*, and penetrated 250 miles (402.5km) higher than any previous traveller. In a second expedition in 1857 the *Pleiad* was wrecked, and he was left to continue his work single-handed from Lukoja. Within five years he had opened the navigation of the Niger, constructed roads, collected a native vocabulary, translated parts of the Bible and prayer book into Hausa, and founded a city state, Lokoja, on the Niger.

Bailey, David Royston 1938–
English photographer
Born and educated in London, he originally specialized in freelance fashion photography from 1959. His work soon extended to portraits expressing the free spirit of the 1960s and he made some impressive nude studies. He has written extensively on photography, including a biography of **Andy Warhol** (1974), *Black and White Memories* (1983) and *The Lady Is a Tramp* (1995, also filmed in 1995). He has been a director of television commercials and documentaries since the 1970s, and made *Who Dealt?* (1993), a film for television.

Bailey, Sir Donald Coleman 1901–85
English engineer
Born in Rotherham, South Yorkshire, he graduated from Sheffield University. During World War II he designed the prefabricated, mobile, rapidly-erected bridge which bears his name. He was knighted in 1946.

Bailey, Francis Lee 1933–
US criminal lawyer
Born in Waltham, Massachusetts, he studied at Harvard and Boston University. Whilst at law school he founded a detective agency to conduct his own case research. He had a highly successful career as a defence attorney, defending **Albert Desalvo** (the Boston Strangler) and the kidnapped heiress Patty Hearst (1954–), who was convicted of bank robbery with her left-wing terrorist abductors. His books include *The Defense Never Rests* (1971) and *For the Defense* (1975).

Bailey, Liberty Hyde 1858–1954
US horticulturist and botanist
Born in South Haven, Michigan, he was Professor of Horticulture at Michigan State (1885) and Cornell (1888) universities, and he founded a laboratory, the Bailey Hortorium in New York State College, in 1920. He edited various works such as the *Standard Cyclopedia of Horticulture* (1914–17), and coined the term 'cultivar'.

Bailey, Nathan or Nathaniel d.1742
English lexicographer
He was the compiler of *An Universal Etymological English Dictionary* (1721; supplementary volume 1727), used by Dr **Johnson** as the basis of his own dictionary. Apart from this, all that is known about him is that he was a Seventh-Day Baptist, and that he kept a boarding-school in Stepney, near London, where he died.

Bailey, Pearl Mae 1918–90
US singer and actress
Born in Newport News, Virginia, she began her career as a nightclub singer and dancer in Washington DC. She continued to work in jazz throughout her career, notably with arranger **Don Redman** and drummer Louie Bellson (1924–), whom she married in 1952. Her principal reputation was made on the musical stage, in films, and on television, beginning with *St Louis Woman* on Broadway in 1946. Her greatest success came in the all-black production of *Hello, Dolly!* in 1967. Her autobiography, *The Raw Pearl*, was published in 1968.

Baillie, Lady Grizel, *née* Hume 1665–1746
Scottish poet
She was the daughter of the Covenanter Sir Patrick Hume (1641–1724). In 1684 she supplied him with food during his concealment in the vault beneath Polwarth Church, and helped shelter another Covenanter, **Robert Baillie**, whose son, George, she married in 1692. She is remembered by her songs, particularly 'And werena my heart licht I wad dee'. In 1911 her domestic notebook was published as *The Household Book*, giving an interesting insight into the minutiae of daily household management. 📖 Countess Ashburnham, *Lady Grisell Baillie: a sketch of her life* (1893)

Baillie, Dame Isobel 1895–1983
Scottish soprano
Born in Hawick, in the Scottish Borders, she moved with her family to Manchester. She had singing lessons from the age of nine, and made her debut with the Hallé

Orchestra under Sir Hamilton Harty in 1921. After studies in Milan, she won immediate success in her opening season in London in 1923. Regarded as one of the 20th century's most distinguished oratorio singers, she regularly performed with such conductors as Sir Thomas Beecham, Arturo Toscanini and Bruno Walter, and gave over 1,000 performances of the *Messiah*. ⌨ *Never Sing Louder Than Lovely* (1982)

Baillie, John 1886–1960
Scottish theologian
Born in Gairloch, Ross-shire, he studied philosophy at Edinburgh, and trained for the ministry at New College, Edinburgh, Marburg and Jena. During World War I he served with the YMCA in France. After the war he went to the USA, where he taught Christian and systematic theology in New York (1920–35). Back in Scotland he was Professor of Divinity at New College from 1935 to 1936. His theological works include the modern devotional classic *Diary of Private Prayer* (1937), and he was chairman of the influential church committee that produced the report *God's Will for Church and Nation* (1946) in favour of the Welfare State and state intervention in the economy.

Baillie, Matthew 1761–1823
Scottish physician and anatomist
He was born in Shotts, Lanarkshire. After seven years at Glasgow University and Oxford (1773–80) he studied anatomy under William Hunter, his uncle, and in 1783 succeeded to Hunter's anatomy school in Great Windmill Street, London. He was the author of the first treatise in English on morbid anatomy: *Morbid Anatomy of Some of the Most Important Parts of the Human Body* (1793).

Baillie (of Jerviswood), Robert d.1684
Scottish conspirator
He was a native of Lanarkshire, who in 1683 entered into correspondence with, and subsequently joined, the Duke of Monmouth's supporters in London. On the discovery of the Rye House Plot he was arrested and sent to Scotland. He was tried at Edinburgh, condemned to death (on insufficient evidence), and hanged. His son married Lady Grizel Baillie.

Baillieu, William Lawrence 1859–1936
Australian businessman
Born in Queenscliff, Victoria, he had various business interests before buying into the London Bank of Australia, which later joined with the English, Scottish & Australian Bank. The profits from this were invested in lead and zinc extraction at Broken Hill, New South Wales, and founded the family fortunes. A member of the Legislative Council of Victoria from 1901 to 1922, he was involved in most of the significant business developments of the period and was a founder of the Melbourne newspaper *The Herald*. His son, Clive Latham Baillieu (1889–1967), represented Australia on many international committees, and became 1st Baron Baillieu of Sefton in 1953.

Bailly, Jean Sylvain 1736–93
French astronomer and politician
Born in Paris, he wrote the *Histoire de l'astronomie* (1775–87, 'History of Astronomy'). As president of the National Assembly and Mayor of Paris during the Revolution of 1789, he had great integrity, but lost his popularity by allowing the National Guard to fire on anti-royalist crowds. He withdrew from public affairs but was arrested and taken to Paris, where he was guillotined.

Baily, Edward Hodges 1788–1867
English sculptor
He was born in Bristol, and trained at the Royal Academy Schools, London. His *Eve at the Fountain* (1818, Bristol) established his reputation, and he executed many of the well-known London statues, including that of Nelson in Trafalgar Square (1839–43), Fox and Mansfield (1856) in St Stephen's Hall, Palace of Westminster, the gilt *Athene* (1829) on the Athenaeum, Pall Mall, the marble statue of George Stephenson (1852) at Euston Station, and the reliefs on the south side of the Marble Arch (1828).

Baily, Francis 1774–1844
English astronomer
Born in Newbury, Berkshire, he made a large fortune as a stockbroker. On his retirement in 1825 he devoted himself to astronomy and was president of the Royal Astronomical Society when he died. He detected the phenomenon known as 'Baily's beads' during an eclipse of the Sun in 1836 and calculated the mean density of the Earth.

Bain, Alexander 1818–1903
Scottish empirical philosopher and psychologist
He was born in Aberdeen, where he later became Professor of Logic (1860–81). He was one of a circle which included John Stuart Mill and George Grote and he wrote books about both the former and his father, James Mill. However, Bain's most important works are *The Senses and the Intellect* (1855), *The Emotions and the Will* (1859) and *Mental and Moral Science* (1868). He also founded the famous journal, *Mind*, in 1876. His psychology was firmly based on physiology and he sought to explain mind through a physical theory of the association of ideas.

Bain, Aly 1945–
Shetland fiddler
Born in Lerwick, Shetland, he studied with the great fiddler Tom Anderson before leaving Shetland in 1968 to play traditional music professionally. His extraordinary gifts emerged initially with singer/guitarist Mike Whellans. In 1972, they joined Cathal McConnell and Robin Morton in The Boys of the Lough, a group which remains a vital force, albeit with several changes of personnel. He has greatly expanded his stylistic repertoire, and has recorded solo, with accordion player Phil Cunningham, and with the Scottish Ensemble, a classical string group. His television work includes *Aly Meets The Cajuns* (1988) and *The Transatlantic Sessions* (1996). ⌨ A Clark, *Fiddler On The Loose* (1993)

Bainbridge, Beryl Margaret 1934–
English novelist and actress
Born in Liverpool, she attended ballet school in Tring, Hertfordshire, and was a repertory actress (1949–60), then a clerk for her eventual publisher, Duckworth (1961–73). Her novels, beginning with *A Weekend with Claude* (1967, revised 1981), are marked by concision, caustic wit, and carefully turned prose. She has also written short stories, essays and a number of television plays. Her novel, *An Awfully Big Adventure* (1985), was adapted for the stage in 1992 and for the big screen in 1995, and her 1996 novel *Every Man For Himself* reached the Booker Prize shortlist and won the Whitbread Novel award.

Bainton, Edgar Leslie 1880–1956
English composer, teacher and conductor
Born in London, he studied at the Royal College of Music there before being appointed a professor, and later Principal, of the Conservatorium of Music, Newcastle upon Tyne (1912–34). In 1938 he was appointed director of the New South Wales Conservatorium in Sydney, and there, apart from his work as administrator and educator, he conducted the State Symphony Orchestra (now the Sydney Symphony Orchestra). In 1938 he conducted an open-air concert for Australia's 150th anniversary, with a choir of 5,000 and massed brass bands. A prolific though conservative composer, he wrote three operas, chamber

music, song settings and piano pieces. He came out of retirement in 1950 to conduct the National Orchestra of New Zealand in a series of concerts and festivals there.

Bainton, Roland 1894–1984
US Congregational minister and Reformation scholar
Born in Ilkeston, Derbyshire, England, he was taken to Canada by his father in 1898. He was educated at Whitman College and at Yale. He taught church history at Yale Divinity School (1920–62), and was probably the best-known scholar of the Protestant Reformation in America, his works being translated into a dozen languages. His books include *The Church of Our Fathers* (1950), *Here I Stand* (1950), *The Reformation of the Sixteenth Century* (1952), *Christian Attitudes Toward War and Peace* (1960), *Early and Medieval Christianity* (1962), and *Erasmus of Christendom* (1969).

Bairakdar, Mustafa 1755–1808
Turkish Grand Vizier, Pasha of Rustchuk
After the revolt of the janissaries (1807) by which Selim III was deposed in favour of Mustapha IV, he marched his troops in 1808 to Constantinople (Istanbul), but found Selim already dead. He executed the murderers, deposed Mustapha, and proclaimed his brother, Mahmud II, sultan. He endeavoured to carry out Selim's reforms and to annihilate the janissaries, who, however, rebelled and demanded the restoration of Mustapha. Mustafa Bairakdar defended himself bravely until, strangling Mustapha, he threw his head to the besiegers, and then blew himself up.

Baird, John Logie 1888–1946
Scottish electrical engineer and television pioneer
Born in Helensburgh, Strathclyde, he studied electrical engineering in Glasgow at the Royal Technical College (now the University of Strathclyde) and at Glasgow University. Poor health compelled him to give up the post of engineer to the Clyde Valley electric power company, and he finally settled in Hastings, East Sussex (1922), and began research into the possibilities of television. Hampered by continuing ill health and lack of financial support, he nevertheless succeeded in building a television apparatus, almost entirely from scrap materials, and in 1926 gave the first demonstration of a television image. His 30-line mechanically scanned system was adopted by the BBC in 1929, being superseded in 1936 by his 240-line system. In the following year the BBC chose a rival 405-line system with electronic scanning made by Marconi–EMI. Other areas of research initiated by Baird in the 1920s included radar and infrared television ('Noctovision'). He continued his research up to the time of his death and succeeded in producing three-dimensional and coloured images (1944), as well as projection onto a screen and stereophonic sound. ▢ Geoff Hutchinson, *Baird: The Story of John Logie Baird, 1888–1946* (1985)

Baird, Spencer Fullerton 1823–87
US naturalist
Born in Reading, Pennsylvania, of Scottish descent, he was educated at Dickinson College, Carlisle, and studied medicine in New York. However, he turned to ornithology, encouraged by John Audubon and others. In 1846 he was appointed Professor of Natural History at Dickinson College, and built up a vast collection of North American fauna. In 1850 he was appointed assistant secretary to Joseph Henry at the Smithsonian Institution in Washington DC (secretary from 1878), and published *Catalogue of North American Mammals* (1857) and *Catalogue of North American Birds* (1858). He was also co-author of *A History of North American Birds* (1874–84). From 1871 he was the first US commissioner of fish and fisheries. Baird's Sandpiper and Baird's Sparrow are named in his honour.

Bairnsfather, (Charles) Bruce 1888–1959
British cartoonist
Born in Murree, India, he served in France during World War I, and became famous for his war cartoons featuring the character 'Old Bill'. During World War II, he was an official war cartoonist attached to the US army in Europe. His drawings appeared in various periodicals, war books, in his *Fragments from France* (6 vols, 1916), and in *Jeeps and Jests* (1943). ▢ Tonie Holt, *In Search of the Better Ole: The Life, Works and Collectables of Bruce Bairnsfather* (1985)

Ba Jin (Pa Chin), *pseudonym of* Li Feigan (Li Fei-kan) 1904–
Chinese writer
He was born into a wealthy family in Chengdu, Sichuan (Szechwan). Educated in the traditional classical style in Shanghai and Nanjing (Nanking), he also studied in France (1927–29), and became an enthusiastic anarchist. His major trilogy—*Jia* (1931, 'The Family'), *Chun* (1938, 'Spring') and *Qiu* (1940, 'Autumn')—attacked the traditional family system, and was immensely popular with the younger generation. Several other novels confirmed his standing as one of China's foremost patriotic writers. Although never a member of the Communist Party, he held important literary positions in the Communist regime after renouncing his earlier anarchism, but during the Cultural Revolution (1966–76) he was purged and compelled to do manual work. He re-emerged in 1977, and published a collection of essays about his experience, entitled *Random Thoughts* (1979).

Bakatin, Vadim Viktorovich 1937–
Soviet politician
Educated as an engineer in Novosibirsk, he worked in the construction industry before being selected for political work in the Communist Party of the USSR. With further training in social sciences he worked his way up from First Secretary in Kirov (1985–87) and in Kemerovo (1987–88) to the Central Secretariat in Moscow. In search of new blood, Mikhail Gorbachev appointed him Minister of the Interior (1988) but dismissed him under right-wing pressure (1990) as too liberal, particularly on the nationalities question. In 1991 he ran against Boris Yeltsin and others for election as President of the Russian Federation, allegedly as Gorbachev's candidate, but he came bottom of the poll. After the failure of the August coup of the same year, Gorbachev appointed him head of the KGB with instructions to convert it into a normal police force but he left at the end of the year. In 1992 he published *The Deliverance from the KGB*.

Baker, Sir Benjamin 1840–1907
English civil engineer
Born in Frome, Somerset, he entered into a long association with John Fowler in 1861, as consulting engineer. Together they designed the London Metropolitan railway, Victoria station, and many bridges. Their greatest achievement was the Forth Rail Bridge (1883–90), built on the cantilever principle. Baker was also consulting engineer for the Aswan Dam in Egypt and its subsequent heightening, and the Hudson River Tunnel in New York (1888–91). He also designed the vessel which carried Cleopatra's Needle to London, and many miles of the London underground railways.

Baker, Chet (Chesney Henry) 1929–88
US jazz trumpet player
He was born in Yale, Oklahoma. His good looks and sweet trumpet style helped make him an icon of the 'cool' jazz school in the 1950s. He first came to wide attention in Gerry Mulligan's famous pianoless quartet in 1953, but drug addiction severely interrupted his career at many points. Nonetheless, his limpid horn tone and fragile singing won him a following at all points in his career,

and he continued to perform in his highly distinctive style until his death in a fall from a hotel window in Amsterdam. His life was chronicled in a moving documentary film, *Let's Get Lost* (1989).

Baker, George See Divine, Father

Baker, Sir Herbert 1862–1946
English architect
Born in Kent, he designed Groote Schuur, near Cape Town, for **Cecil Rhodes**, the Union Government buildings at Pretoria, and, with **Edwin Lutyens**, Viceroy's House in New Delhi, India. He was also the designer in Oxford of Rhodes House and in London, of the new Bank of England, South Africa House, and others.

Baker, Howard Henry, Jnr 1925–
US politician
Born in Huntsville, Tennessee, the son of a congressman, he studied law at the University of Tennessee and represented his native state in the Senate from 1967 to 1985. A Republican, he was vice-chairman of the committee investigating the Watergate scandal (1973), and served as Senate minority leader (1977–81) and majority leader (1981–85). He was White House Chief of Staff (1987–88) during the **Reagan** administration.

Baker, James Addison III 1930–
US politician
Born in Houston, Texas, into a wealthy patrician legal family, he studied at Princeton and the University of Texas Law School, served in the US Marines, and became a successful corporate lawyer. After the death of his first wife, he entered politics as a Republican county manager of the unsuccessful 1970 campaign for the Senate by his close friend, **George Bush**. Later, at Bush's suggestion, he was appointed Under-Secretary of Commerce (1975–76) in the **Gerald Ford** administration and managed Ford's 1976 presidential and Bush's 1979 Republican Party nomination campaigns. President **Ronald Reagan** made him his White House Chief of Staff in 1981 and Secretary of the Treasury in 1985. After directing Bush's victorious presidential campaign in 1988, he was Secretary of State (1989–92). In the final year of the Bush administration he was once again Chief of Staff, and he ran Bush's unsuccessful re-election campaign.

Baker, Dame Janet Abbott 1933–
English mezzo-soprano
Born in Hatfield, Yorkshire, she sang in various local choirs before going to study music in London (1953). She made her debut in 1956 as Roza in **Bedřich Smetana**'s *The Secret* at Glyndebourne. During the 1960s she worked as a soloist for **Sir John Barbirolli**, after which she had an extensive operatic career, specializing in early Italian opera and the works of **Benjamin Britten**. Also a concert performer, she was a noted interpreter of **Mahler** and **Elgar**. In 1982 she retired from the operatic stage and published her autobiography, *Full Circle*. She was created DBE in 1976 and Companion of Honour in 1994. ▣ Alan Blyth, *Janet Baker* (1973)

Baker, Josephine, *originally* Freda Josephine McDonald 1906–75
French entertainer and campaigner
Born in St Louis, Missouri, USA, she ran away from home at the age of 13 and joined a vaudeville company. In 1925 she went to Paris with La Revue Nègre, where her natural singing and dancing ability captured the attention of the French as an example of the African-American jazz scene. She became a French citizen in 1937, and during World War II worked for the Red Cross and the French Résistance, for which she was awarded the Croix de Guerre, the Rosette de la Résistance and was appointed a Chevalier of the Legion of Honour. After the war, she

campaigned for civil rights in the USA and worked to achieve a Global Village, but the expenses required for this impoverished her. She was NAACP (National Association for the Advancement of Colored People) Woman of the Year in 1951.

Baker, Kenneth Wilfred Baker, Baron 1934–
English Conservative politician
He was born in Newport, Monmouth, and read history at Magdalen College, Oxford, entering local politics in 1962 as a Conservative councillor in Twickenham. In 1968 he was elected to the House of Commons, representing Acton, then St Marylebone, and later Mole Valley (1983–97). After holding junior posts (1970–74) he became Parliamentary Private Secretary to **Edward Heath** when he was Leader of the Opposition. In the **Thatcher** administration he rose from Minister of State in the Department of Trade to become Secretary of State for the Environment (1985) and for Education (1986), responsible for introducing a controversial education reform bill. He was appointed Chairman of the Conservative Party in 1989, retaining his seat in the Cabinet. Under **John Major** he became Home Secretary (1990) but was succeeded by **Kenneth Clarke** two years later. He declined the position of Secretary of State for Wales, and turned his attention to writing. He was made a life peer in 1997.

Baker, Sir Samuel White 1821–93
English explorer
Born in London, he went in 1845 to Ceylon (Sri Lanka), where he established an agricultural settlement at Nuwara Eliya, and afterwards supervised the construction of a railway across the Dobrudja. In 1860 he undertook the exploration of the Nile sources. At Gondokoro (1863), he met the explorers **John Speke** and **James Grant**, who told Baker of a great lake, Luta Nzige, described to them by the local people. In 1864 Baker reached this inland sea into which the Nile flows and named it Albert Nyanza. He was knighted in 1866, joined the Prince of Wales in Egypt for the opening of the Suez Canal (1869), and was subsequently invited to command an expedition, organized by the Pasha of Egypt, for the suppression of slavery and the annexation of the equatorial regions of the Nile Basin. He returned to Europe in 1873 and later travelled in Cyprus, Syria, India, Japan and the USA.

Baker, Sir Stanley 1928–76
Welsh actor
Born in Ferndale, Rhondda Valley, the son of a miner, he made a youthful screen debut in *Undercover* (1943). He then worked with repertory companies in Birmingham and London before completing military service with the Royal Army Service Corps. Often cast in ruthlessly villainous supporting roles, he gained renown for roles as a working-class anti-hero in adult dramas and historical epics like *Zulu* (1963), *Sands of the Kalahari* (1965) and *Robbery* (1967), which he also co-produced. Critically admired for his role as a petulant Oxford don in *Accident* (1967), he spent the last years of his cinema career involved in a variety of undistinguished European features. A director of Harlech Television from 1968, he frequently appeared in television roles, including *How Green Was My Valley* (1975). He was knighted in 1976.

Bakewell, Robert 1725–95
English agriculturist
Born in Dishley, Leicestershire, he improved the standard and methods of the management of sheep, cattle, and draught horses by selection and inbreeding. He established the Leicester breed of sheep and the Dishley breed of longhorn cattle, and aroused a wide interest in breeding methods. ▣ S Dunkerley, *Robert Bakewell* (1988)

Balanchine, George, *originally* Georgi Melitonovich Balanchivadze 1904–83
US choreographer, a major figure in 20th-century dance

George Balanchine was born in St Petersburg, the son of a Georgian folk musician. After graduating in 1921 he enrolled at the Petrograd Conservatory to study composition, but he turned to ballet and formed his own small company whose innovations were frowned on by the theatre authorities. During a European tour in 1924, he defected with a group of dancers who performed for a time in London as the Soviet State Dancers. Eventually they were taken into **Sergei Diaghilev**'s Ballets Russes in Paris, and at this point he changed his name to Balanchine. In 1925 he succeeded **Bronislava Nijinska** as choreographer and ballet-master. His ballets *Apollo* (1928) and *The Prodigal Son* (1929) are regarded as his masterpieces of that period.

After Diaghilev's death in 1929 and his own serious illness, he worked for various companies, including that of the 1930 Cochran Revue in London, then helped to found Les Ballets Russes de Monte Carlo in 1932 and Les Ballets the following year. He opened the School of American Ballet in New York in 1934.

After World War II and the break-up of the American Ballet, Balanchine directed a private company, the Ballet Society, which in 1948 emerged as the New York City Ballet. With that company he created over 90 works of great variety, ranging from the theatrical *Nutcracker* (1954) to the abstract *Agon* (1957). Other important works include *Don Quixote* (1966), *Coppelia* (1974), *Symphony in C, Episodes* (1959), *Kammermusik No. 2* (1978) and **Schumann's** *Davidsbündlertänze* (1980). In addition to his prolific output Balanchine is noted for his range of styles and controlled technique. He was also a successful musical comedy and film choreographer. His musicals include *Ziegfeld Follies* (1935) and *On Your Toes* (1936), and his films include *The Goldwyn Follies* (1938) and *Star Spangled Rythms* (1942).

📖 S Caras, *Balanchine* (1985); L Kirstein, *Portrait of Mr Balanchine* (1984); Bernard Taper, *Balanchine* (1963, rev edn 1974).

'In my ballets, woman is first. Men are consorts. God made men to sing the praises of women. They are not equal to men: they are better.' Quoted in *Time*, 15 September 1980.

Bakey, Michael Ellis De See DeBakey, Michael Ellis

Bakst, Leon 1866–1924
Russian painter
Born in St Petersburg, he painted religious and genre works in Moscow, then turned to scenery design at Hermitage Court Theatre in St Petersburg. In 1908 he went to Paris, where he was associated with Sergei Diaghilev from the beginnings of the Russian ballet, designing the décor and costumes for numerous productions (1909–21). His rich, exuberant colours, seemingly uncontrolled, in reality produced a powerful theatrical effect which revolutionized fashion and decoration generally. 📖 Irina Pruzhan, *Leon Bakst* (1988)

Bakunin, Mikhail Aleksandrovich 1814–76
Russian revolutionary
Born near Moscow, of aristocratic descent, he took part in the German revolutionary movement (1848–49) and was condemned to death. Sent to Siberia in 1855, he escaped to Japan, and arrived in England in 1861. In 1870 he attempted an abortive rising at Lyons. As a leading anarchist he was the opponent of **Karl Marx** in the Communist International, but at the Hague Congress in 1872 he was outvoted and expelled. He believed that Communism, with its theoretical 'withering away of the state', was an essential step towards anarchism. 📖 E H Carr, *Mikhail Bakunin* (1937)

Balaguer, Joaquim 1907–
Dominican Republic politician
He was Professor of Law at Santo Domingo University from 1938, and ambassador to Colombia and Mexico in the 1940s before entering politics. He served in the dictatorial regime of Rafael Trujillo, after whose assassination in 1961 he fled to the USA (1962). Returning in 1965, he won the presidency as leader of the Christian Social Reform Party (PRSC) in 1966. He was re-elected in 1970 and 1974. The failure of the economic policies of the Dominican Revolutionary Party (PRD) brought the PRSC and Balaguer back to power in 1986, at the age of 79.

Balakirev, Mili Alekseyevich 1836–1910
Russian composer
Born in Nizhny Novgorod, he turned to composing after an early career as a concert pianist, and became the leader of the national Russian school of music. **César Cui**, Mussorgsky, Rimsky-Korsakov, Aleksandr Borodin, and Tchaikovsky were all influenced by him. He founded the Petersburg Free School of Music (1862), and was director of the Imperial Capella (from 1883). His compositions include two symphonies, a symphonic poem *Tamara* (1867–82), and the oriental fantasy for piano, *Islamey* (1869).

Balanchine, George See panel above

Balard, Antoine Jérôme 1802–76
French chemist
Born in Montpellier, he became an apothecary there. His investigations into sea water and marine life led him to devise a test for iodine, which he discovered turns blue in the presence of starch. This very simple and sensitive test is still used today. The same investigations led to the isolation of bromine, which he recognized as an element, around 1825. Such success by a young apothecary caused a stir in scientific circles, not least because the similarities between iodine, bromine and chlorine showed clearly that there are 'families' of elements. Balard taught for a while at the University of Montpellier, where in 1834 he identified hypochlorous acid and chlorine monoxide while working on the chemistry of bleaching. He also studied bleaching powder and methods of extracting soda and potash from sea water. He was appointed to the chair of chemistry at the Sorbonne (1842) and at the Collège de France (1851). He was known for his generosity to colleagues and students, and was the mentor of **Louis Pasteur**.

Balas, Iolanda 1936–
Romanian athlete
She was born in Timorsauru, and her achievement in the high jump was unprecedented in the history of athletics. Unbeaten from 1956 to 1967, she was twice Olympic champion (1960, 1964) and twice European champion (1958, 1962), the first Romanian to win an athletics European and Olympic medal. She won the high jump eight times at the world Student Games and the gold at the first European Indoor games (1966). She won 16 consecutive national titles from the age of 14, and set 14 world records at high jump between 1956 and 1961.

Balassi or Balassa, Bálint 1554–94
Hungarian knight, adventurer and lyric poet

Born in Kékkö, he died fighting the Turkish invaders. His poetry was inspired by military heroism, his love for the idealized figure of beauty and happiness he named 'Julia', and religion. He also experimented in drama (*Credulus and Julia*), and wrote *Little Garden for Diseased Minds* (1572). One of his verse forms is still known as the 'Balassi stanza'. ◫S Eckhardt, *Balassa Bálint* (1941)

Balbo, Cesare 1789–1853
Italian statesman and political writer

He wrote widely on political problems and Italian history, his most important work, *Delle Speranze d'Italia* ('Of the Hopes of Italy'), appearing in 1844. Echoing Vincenzo Gioberti, to whom it was dedicated, it called for the creation of an Italian Confederation. It also demanded the end of Austrian rule in Lombardy-Venetia and that the Habsburgs seek compensation by expansion into the Balkans. In 1847, in a growing climate of reform, Balbo accepted the invitation of King Charles Albert (1798–1849) to enter a moderate government and the following year fleetingly held office as Piedmont's first constitutional Prime Minister. In his final years he supported the policies of the Marchese D'Azeglio and Conte di Cavour despite reservations about their anticlericalism.

Balbo, Italo, Count 1896–1940
Italian politician

An early supporter of Italian intervention in World War I, he served from 1915 as an officer in the Alpini. From 1920 he played a key part in the Fascist movement and was one of the leaders in the March on Rome. In 1926 he became Secretary of State for Aviation. He was made Governor of Libya in 1934 but was killed when his plane was accidentally brought down by Italian anti-aircraft fire at Tobruk (1940). He was one of several Fascist leaders who disliked Mussolini's move towards Hitler and who spoke out in defence of the Jews.

Balboa, Vasco Núñez de 1475–1519
Spanish explorer

He was born in Jerez-de-Los-Caballeros, and in 1511 joined an expedition to Darién (Central America) as a stowaway. Taking advantage of an insurrection, he took command, founded a colony at Darién and extended Spanish influence into neighbouring areas. On one of these expeditions he climbed a peak and sighted the Pacific Ocean, the first European to do so, and took possession for Spain. The governorship was granted in 1514 to Pedro Arias de Ávila, for whom Balboa undertook many successful expeditions and whose daughter he married. However, after a disagreement in 1519 Balboa was beheaded. ◫ Kathleen Romoli, *Balboa: A Political Biography* (1973)

Balbuena, Bernardo de 1568–1627
Spanish poet and prelate

Born in Valdepeñas, he spent his working life in Central America, where he wrote all his poetry. He became Bishop of Puerto Rico in 1620, and wrote an epic on the national hero, Bernardo del Capio, in *El Bernardo o la victoria de Roncesvalles* (1624, 'Bernardo, or the Victory of Roncesvalles'), which contains much allegory. ◫ J Roja Garciduenas, *Bernardo de Balbuena* (1958)

Balch, Emily Greene 1867–1961
US social reformer, pacifist and Nobel Prize winner

She was born in Jamaica Plain, Massachusetts, and educated at Bryn Mawr College. She studied political economy at the Sorbonne (1890–91) and published *Public Assistance of the Poor in France* (1893). From 1896 to 1918 she taught economics at Wellesley College, becoming Professor of Economics and Sociology from 1913, and her innovative courses included coverage of Karl Marx and women's place in the economy. In 1906 she became a socialist. An active pacifist, she openly opposed World War I

and was viewed by the authorities with increasing suspicion. In 1919 her academic appointment was not renewed. She helped establish the Women's International League for Peace and Freedom (1919) and subsequently proved an indefatigable administrator, writer and promoter for peace. She shared the 1946 Nobel Peace Prize with John Mott. Her works include *Our Slavic Fellow Citizens* (1910) and *Toward Human Unity* (1952).

Balchen, Bernt 1899–1973
US aviator and explorer

He was born in Tveit Topdal, Norway. In 1924 he was commissioned as a flight lieutenant in the Royal Norwegian Naval Air Force and flew rescue missions over the Arctic, as well as assisting the explorers Roald Amundsen and Lincoln Ellsworth in planning flights over the North Pole. He was chief pilot to Richard Byrd's first Antarctic expedition (1928–30) and to the Ellsworth Antarctic expedition (1932–35). He became a US citizen in 1931. In 1935 he returned to Norway as manager of DNL (Norwegian Air Lines), and after wartime service in the US air force resumed this post in 1946. He returned to active US duty in 1948, commanding an Arctic Rescue Unit, and as adviser to the Pentagon.

Balcon, Sir Michael Elias 1896–1977
English film producer

Born in Birmingham, he was rejected for military service because of a flaw in his left eye and spent World War I empoyed by the Dunlop Rubber Company. He subsequently formed a modest distribution company, moved into film production with advertising films and documentaries, and in 1921 helped to found Gainsborough Pictures. In 1931 he took charge of production at Gaumont British and backed British films that could compete in the international market, among them *Rome Express* (1932) and *The Thirty Nine Steps* (1935). After a brief spell as head of British production for the Hollywood studio MGM, he became head of production at Ealing Studios (1938–58). Among the many classic films created under his control are *Whisky Galkore* (1948), *The Blue Lamp* (1949), *The Lavender Hill Mob* (1951) and *The Cruel Sea* (1953). Subsequently chairman of British Lion (1964–68) and of the Bryanston Company (1959–75), he also served as a director of Border Television and as a governor of the British Film Institute. He was knighted in 1948. ◫ *A Lifetime Of Films* (1969)

Balczerowicz, Leszek 1947–
Polish economist and politician

A talented economic researcher at the Central School of Planning in Warsaw, he was also a strong supporter and adviser of Solidarity. In 1989 he was appointed Finance Minister after the Wałesa revolution and achieved something of an economic miracle in stabilizing the currency and introducing the first stage of marketization. Following the 1991 elections, Wałesa judged his economic stringency too unpopular and engineered his dismissal in 1992. His achievement, nonetheless, won wide international praise and he won the 1992 Ludwig Erhard prize.

Baldini, Antonio 1889–1962
Italian writer

Born in Rome, he recounted his war experiences in *Nostro purgatorio* (1918, 'Our Purgatory'), but his most characteristic works are *Michelaccio* (1924, 'Michael'), *La dolce calamità* (1929, 'Sweet Calamity'), and *Amici allo spiedo* (1932, 'Friends on the Spit'). He was a founder of *La Ronde*, a journal dedicated to high artistic taste and stylistic refinement, and in 1931 he became editor of the *Nuova Antologia*. ◫C di Bicse, *Antonio Baldini* (1973)

Baldinucci, Filippo 1624–96
Italian art historian

Born in Florence, he was entrusted by Cardinal Leopoldo Medici with the arrangement of the Medici collection. He wrote six volumes on Italian artists since **Giovanni Cimabué**.

Baldovinetti, Alesso 1427–99
Italian painter
He worked in Florence and was a representative of the late 15th century Florentine school. His frescoes, noted for their landscape backgrounds, are mostly poorly preserved as a result of his experiments in technique, but he also executed mosaics of great beauty and worked on stained glass.

Baldung, Hans, *also called* Hans Grien or Grün
c.1476–1545
German painter and engraver
Born in Weiersheim, near Strasbourg, he may have been a pupil of **Albrecht Dürer**. His mature works display deliberate exaggeration of late Gothic styles to obtain often morbid quasi-Expressionist effects in the manner of **Matthias Grünewald**, as in *Die Frau und den Tod* (Basle) and *Die Eitelkeit* ('Vanity', Vienna).

Baldwin I c.1171–c.1205
Emperor of Constantinople
Born in Valenciennes, he succeeded his parents as Count of Hainault and Flanders in 1195. In 1202 he joined the Fourth Crusade, and in 1204 was made the first Latin Emperor of Constantinople (Istanbul). The Greeks, with the aid of the Bulgarians, rose and took Adrianople. Baldwin laid siege to the town, but was defeated and executed.

Baldwin II 1217–73
Emperor of Constantinople
Born in Constantinople (Istanbul), the nephew of **Baldwin I**, he succeeded his brother Robert as emperor in 1228. To raise money he sold alleged relics, including **Jesus Christ**'s crown of thorns and part of the True Cross, to **Louis IX** of France. The Greeks, under **Michael VIII Palaeologus**, took Constantinople in 1261, extinguishing the Latin Empire. Thereafter Baldwin lived as a fugitive, having sold his rights to **Charles of Anjou**.

Baldwin II, *known as* Baldwin du Bourg d.1131
King of Jerusalem
He was a son of Count Hugh of Rethel. He succeeded his cousin Baldwin I as Count of Edessa (1100) and King of Jerusalem (1118). He expanded his territory and attacked Muslim Damascus, with assistance from the Templars and Hospitallers.

Baldwin III c.1130–62
King of Jerusalem
The grandson of **Baldwin II of Bourg**, he succeeded his father, Fulk of Anjou, in 1143, but enjoyed sole authority (1152) only after long disputes and civil war with his mother Melisende. His main achievement was the capture of Ascalon, the last Fatimid stronghold in Palestine, in 1153.

Baldwin d.1190
English prelate
Born in Exeter, Devon, he became Bishop of Worcester in 1180 and Archbishop of Canterbury in 1184. He crowned **Richard I**, and made a tour of Wales preaching in favour of the Crusades. He died on a Crusade.

Baldwin, James Arthur 1924–87
US writer
Born in Harlem, New York City, into a strongly religious African-American family, he was preaching in churches at the age of 14, an experience that inspired his novel *Go Tell it on the Mountain* (1954). He moved to Europe, living mainly in Paris from 1948 to 1957, in a conscious rejection of US society and its racism, before returning to the USA as a civil rights activist. His novels are often strongly autobiographical but marked by a **Flaubert**ian attention to form. *Giovanni's Room* (1957) is a study of gay relationships, and *Another Country* (1963) examines the sexual dynamics of US racism. He also wrote *Tell Me How Long The Train's Been Gone* (1968) and *Just Above My Head* (1979). His journalism has been extremely influential and controversial. *Notes of a Native Son* (1955) is an ironic response to cultural and racial politics. Other works include *The Fire Next Time* (1963), and the plays *The Amen Corner* (1955), *Blues for Mr Charlie* (1964) and *The Women at the Well* (1972). 🕮 J Campbell, *Talking at the Gates: a life of James Baldwin* (1991); W J Weatherby, *James Baldwin: artist on fire* (1989)

Baldwin, James Mark 1861–1934
US psychologist
He was born in Columbia, South Carolina, and studied at Berlin and Leipzig, where he met **Wilhelm Wundt**. A specialist in child psychology and social psychology, he was professor at Toronto (1889), Princeton (1893), Johns Hopkins (1903), the University of Mexico (1909) and Paris (1918). An influential figure in the early stages of psychology, he was the founder-editor of the *Psychological Review* (1894–1909) and editor of the *Dictionary of Philosophy and Psychology* (1901–06).

Baldwin, Matthias William 1795–1866
US locomotive engineer and industrialist
Born in Elizabethtown, New Jersey, he was a jeweller up to the age of 30, but abandoned that trade in favour of tool-making. He then began to make hydraulic presses and printing machinery, and by 1827 was manufacturing steam engines. His first locomotive, *Old Ironsides*, was completed in 1832 and remained in service for 20 years. He developed accurately fitted steam joints which allowed the use of pressures up to 120 lb (54kg) per square inch, twice that used in British locomotives at the time. The Baldwin locomotive works built over 1,000 engines by 1861, and remained for many years the world's largest manufacturer of locomotives.

Baldwin, Robert 1804–58
Canadian lawyer and politician
He was the leader of the Canada West reforming clique who formed a coalition with **Louis Lafontaine** to establish a reform party, which became a precursor of the Liberal Party. With his father, William Baldwin, he devised the theory of 'responsible government'. This was rejected initially by the British government and governors such as Sir Charles Metcalfe (1785–1846), although Sir Charles Bagot (1781–1843) accepted a level of participation by the Executive Council in government. Metcalfe's autocratic government led both Baldwin and Lafontaine to resign. In 1848 Baldwin regained power as a partner with Lafontaine in the 'Great Ministry', during the period of transition from colonial rule to self-government.

Baldwin, Roger Nash 1884–1981
US reformer
He was born in Wellesley, Massachusetts. A civil rights activist, he was a founder of the American Civil Liberties Union (1920) and its director until 1950. He also taught at the New School for Social Research in New York City (1938–42).

Baldwin (of Bewdley), Stanley Baldwin, 1st Earl 1867–1947
English Conservative politician and Prime Minister
Born in Bewdley, Worcestershire, he was educated at Harrow and Trinity College, Cambridge, and became vice-chairman of the family iron and steel business. An MP in 1906, he became president of the Board of Trade (1921), and he unexpectedly succeeded **Bonar Law** as premier in 1923, being preferred to **George Curzon**.

Shortly afterwards he brought down the Liberal coalition with a speech that revealed his distrust of David Lloyd-George, despite criticism of his handling, as Chancellor of the Exchequer, of the US debt. His period of office included the General Strike (1926) and was interrupted by the Ramsay MacDonald Coalition (1931–35), in which he served as Lord President of the Council. He skilfully avoided a party split by his India Act (1935), but his disavowal of the Hoare–Laval pact ceding Ethiopian territory to Italy, and the policy of non-intervention in Spain (1936) came to be regarded as betrayals of the League of Nations. He was noted for his reluctance to re-arm Great Britain's defences and for his tact and resolution during the constitutional crisis culminating in Edward VIII's abdication (1936). Criticism of his failure to recognize the threat from Nazi Germany brought his resignation in 1937. Although Baldwin's competence as an international politician is questionable, he was one of the party's best-ever electoral assets, with a combination of patriotism, social consciousness, and readiness always to govern by consensus.

Bale, John, known as Bilious Bale 1495–1563
English cleric and dramatist

Born near Dunwich, Suffolk, he was a Carmelite by training. Turning Protestant in 1533, he obtained the Suffolk living of Thorndon. In 1540 he was obliged to flee to Germany but, recalled by Edward VI, he was made Bishop of Ossory in Leinster. Here he so outraged Catholics with his polemical writings that they attacked his house and killed five servants. On Queen Elizabeth I's accession (1533) he was made a prebendary of Canterbury. He wrote a Latin history of 'British' authors (from Adam and Seth onwards!) and a drama, *King John*, which is considered the first English historical play.

Balenciaga, Cristóbal 1895–1972
Spanish couturier

He was born in Guetaria in the Basque country, the son of a seamstress. Helped by a local aristocrat, he trained as a tailor, and in 1915 opened dressmaking and tailoring shops of his own in Madrid and Barcelona. He left Spain for Paris in 1937 because of the Spanish Civil War, and became a couturier. A perfectionist, he designed clothes that were noted for their dramatic simplicity and elegant design. He retired in 1968. 📖 Lesley Ellis Miller, *Cristóbal Balenciaga* (1993)

Balewa, Sir Abubakar Tafawa 1912–66
Nigerian politician

Born in Bauchi, he worked as a teacher and education officer before entering the Nigerian Legco and was a founder-member of the Northern People's Congress. He entered the Federal Assembly in 1947 and was appointed consecutively Federal Minister of Works (1952–54), Minister of Trade (1954–57), Chief Minister (1957–59) and Prime Minister (1959–66). Essentially sympathetic to Western priorities, he was seen within Nigeria as a supporter of northern interests in the first years of independence. He was overthrown and assassinated in the 1966 coup.

Balfa, Dewey 1927–92
Cajun musician and teacher

Born in Mamou, Louisiana, he was the leading figure in a Cajun family who made an enormous contribution to the preservation and dissemination of the authentic music of the French-based Louisiana Cajun community. Taught by their father Charles, the Balfa Brothers band also featured his brothers Rodney and Will, both killed in a road accident (1979), as well as the great accordionist Nathan Abshire. Dewey continued to play fiddle, make recordings, teach and proselytize for the music, and received numerous honours. His daughter Christine now main-

tains the family tradition in Balfa Toujours, with her husband, Dirk Powell. Her sister, Nelda, is also an occasional member.

Balfe, Michael William 1808–70
English composer

Born in Dublin, Ireland, of English parents, he made his debut as a violinist at the age of eight, having begun to compose two years earlier. During a year in Italy (1825–26) under Rossini, he was inspired to become an opera singer, which he did with considerable success. In 1833 he went to England, and in 1846 was appointed conductor of the London Italian Opera. Of his numerous operas, operettas and other compositions, the most enduring success was *The Bohemian Girl* (1843).

Balfour, Arthur James Balfour, 1st Earl of 1848–1930
Scottish statesman and philosopher

Born into an ancient Scottish family, he succeeded to the family estate in East Lothian in 1856. Educated at Eton and Trinity College, Cambridge, he entered parliament in 1874, becoming Secretary for Scotland (1886) and Chief Secretary for Ireland (1887–91), where his policy of suppression earned him the name of 'Bloody Balfour'. A Conservative, he succeeded his uncle Robert Cecil (3rd Marquis of Salisbury) as Prime Minister (1902–05), and later served as First Lord of the Admiralty (1915–16). As Foreign Secretary (1916–19), he was responsible for the Balfour Declaration (1917), which promised Zionists a national home in Palestine. He resigned in 1922, was created an earl, but served again as Lord President (1925–29). 📖 S H Zebel, *Balfour: A Political Biography* (1973)

Balfour, Lady Frances 1858–1931
Scottish suffragist, churchwoman and author

Born in London, she had political ambitions that were stifled by the role of women at that time, but she had strong connections with both the Whig and Tory parties, the former through her own family, and the latter through her marriage to Eustace Balfour, the brother of Arthur James Balfour. A tireless worker for women's rights, she lectured on behalf of the National Union of Woman's Suffrage Societies. She also spoke out on such issues as Irish Home Rule and free trade. Working for the Church of Scotland, she fought for the re-union of 1929, just as her father had opposed the Disruption in 1843. She wrote a number of memoirs, including those of her sister, Lady Victoria Campbell (1911), and Dr Elsie Inglis (1918). 📖 *Ne Obliviscaris* (1930)

Balfour, Francis Maitland 1851–82
Scottish embryologist

He was born in Edinburgh, the brother of Arthur James Balfour, and showed precocious promise in natural history while still at Harrow. He graduated in natural science from Cambridge in 1871, and embarked upon physiological research under Sir Michael Foster, producing notable work on elasmobranch development in 1878. In the same year he was elected FRS. He published *Treatise on Comparative Embryology* (2 vols, 1880), was awarded a medal by the Royal Society in 1881, and he took up a new chair in animal morphology at Cambridge in 1882. Continuing the work of Karl Baer and Charles Darwin, Balfour was distinguished by painstaking microscopic accounts of the development process in the embryo.

Balfour, George 1872–1941
Scottish electrical engineer and pioneering contractor

Born in Portsmouth, he served an apprenticeship in a foundry in Dundee and qualified as a journeyman engineer. After working for a New York company specializing in electric tramways and power plants, he founded his own construction company, Balfour Beatty Ltd, in 1909 with an accountant, Andrew Beatty. They built and operated the tramway systems for Dunfermline, Llanelli, and many towns in the Midlands, and designed the first major hydro-electrical schemes in Scotland, as well as pioneering the National Grid in the 1930s. Balfour also built the giant Kut Barrage on the Tigris for Iraq. He was Unionist MP for Hampstead, London, from 1918.

Balfour (of Pittendreich), Sir James d.1583
Scottish jurist and politician
After the murder of Cardinal David Beaton in 1547 he was taken prisoner with John Knox and sent to France. Released in 1549, he returned to Scotland and 'served with all parties, deserted all, and yet profited by all'. He was involved in the murder of Lord Darnley, and was commissioned to compile the *Practicks or a System of the More Ancient Law of Scotland* (published 1754), an invaluable repertory of ancient statutes and decisions. He became Lord President of the Court of Session in 1567, and withdrew to France in 1580.

Balfour, John Hutton 1808–84 and Sir Isaac Bayley 1853–1922
Scottish botanists
They were born in Edinburgh. John Hutton Balfour studied medicine at the university there and in Paris. He was appointed Professor of Botany at the universities of Edinburgh and Glasgow and became Regius Keeper of the Royal Botanic Garden in Edinburgh. He was instrumental in the establishment of the Botanical Society of Edinburgh (now the Botanical Society of Scotland), was an inspiring teacher and field worker, and wrote several textbooks. He retired in 1879. His son Isaac Bayley Balfour studied botany in Edinburgh and in Germany, became Sherardian Professor of Botany at Oxford, and in 1888 succeeded his father in both the Edinburgh posts. The naturalist on the expedition to Rodriguez Island in 1880, he brought back and introduced to cultivation *Begonia socotrana*, one of the parents of many of today's *Begonia* hybrids. He founded the journal *Annals of Botany*, and transformed the Royal Botanic Garden of Edinburgh into one of the world's great gardens. He was knighted in 1920.

Baliol See Balliol

Ball, John d.1381
English rebel
Born in St Albans, Hertfordshire, he was an excommunicated priest who was executed as one of the leaders in the Peasants' Revolt of 1381, led by Wat Tyler.

Ball, John 1818–89
Irish botanist and alpinist
Born in Dublin, he was taken to Switzerland at the age of seven, and was profoundly affected by the view of the Alps from the Jura Mountains. The following year, at Ems, he spent much time trying to measure the height of the hills with a mountain barometer. After a period at Cambridge, Ball visited Sicily and published a valuable paper on its botany. In 1852 he became Liberal MP for Carlow and advocated many measures which later became law, including the disestablishment of the Church of Ireland. As Colonial Under-Secretary (1855–57), he influenced the government in its decision to prepare a series of Floras of the British colonies and possessions. He was the first president of the Alpine Club (1857), wrote the *Alpine Guide* (1863–68), and in 1871 accompanied Sir Joseph Dalton Hooker and George Frederick Maw to Morocco to investigate the flora of the Great Atlas Mountains. His *Spicilegium Florae Maroccanae* (1877–78) is the earliest work on the Moroccan flora. In 1882 he visited South America. He proposed one theory on the antiquity of the alpine flora, and another claiming that most endemic South American plants originated on a hypothetical ancient mountain range in Brazil.

Ball, Lucille Desirée 1910–89
US comedienne
Born in Celoron, New York, she was an amateur performer as a child. After a spell as a model and chorus girl she moved to Hollywood where she spent several years in bit parts and B-movies before more substantial roles were offered. A lively redhead with a rasping voice and infallible timing, she began working in television in 1951 and became one of its best-loved characters, starring in situation comedies such as *I Love Lucy* (1951–55), *The Lucy Show* (1962–68) and *Here's Lucy* (1968–73). She bought her own studio with her first husband, Desi Arnaz, and also became a successful production executive, making the occasional film, including comedies such as *The Facts of Life* (1960) and *Yours, Mine and Ours* (1968).

Balla, Giacomo 1871–1958
Italian artist
Born in Turin, he was one of the founders of Futurism and a signatory to the 1910 Futurist Manifesto. After a visit to Paris in 1900 he was strongly influenced by Impressionism and Divisionism, which he introduced to his pupils Umberto Boccioni and Gino Severini. Primarily concerned with conveying movement and speed in painterly terms, he achieved this by imitating time-lapse photography; *Dog on a Leash* (1912) exemplifies this technique. Although Futurism outlived World War I, by 1930 Balla was painting in a more conventional style.

Balladur, Edouard 1929–
French politician
Born in Smyrna, Turkey, he was educated in France at Marseilles, Aix-en-Provence and Paris. In 1966 he became technical adviser to Prime Minister Georges Pompidou and quickly established a reputation as a technocrat. His many public schemes included the construction of a road under Mont Blanc. As a politician he became Minister of Economy in 1986 and Prime Minister in 1993. Following the death of President Mitterrand he contested the French presidential election in 1995 but lost to Jacques Chirac. 📖 Nicolas Bazire, *Edouard Balladur* (1995)

Ballantine, James 1808–77
Scottish artist and poet
Born in Edinburgh, he was originally a house-painter. He learned drawing under Sir William Allan, and was one of the first to revive the art of glass-painting. Two of his volumes of prose and verse, *The Gaberlunzie's Wallet* (1843) and *Miller of Deanhaugh* (1845), contain some of his best-known songs and ballads. He also wrote *Lilias Lee* (1871), a tale after the manner of Edmund Spenser.

Ballantrae, Baron see Fergusson, Bernard Edward

Ballantyne, James 1772–1833 and John 1774–1821
Scottish printers
They were born in Kelso and were both at Kelso Grammar School with Sir Walter Scott. James was trained for the law, but in 1797 started the Tory *Kelso Mail*. In 1802, having already printed some ballads for Scott, he produced the first two volumes of the *Border Minstrelsy*. At Scott's suggestion he moved the firm to Edinburgh, and in 1805 Scott became a secret partner in the business, which in 1808 expanded into the printing, publishing and bookselling firm of John Ballantyne & Co, Scott having one-half share, and each of the brothers a quarter. As early as 1813 bankruptcy threatened the firm, and it was deeply involved in Archibald Constable's ruin (1826). John had died bankrupt five years earlier, and James was employed by the creditors' trustees in editing the *Weekly Journal* and in the literary management of the printing office.

Ballantyne, John See **Bellenden, John**

Ballantyne, Robert Michael 1825–94
Scottish children's writer
He was born in Edinburgh, a nephew of John and James Ballantyne, the printer and publisher of Sir Walter Scott. Educated at The Edinburgh Academy, he joined the Hudson's Bay Company in 1841, and worked as a clerk at the Red River Settlement in northern Canada until 1847, returning to Edinburgh in 1848. His adventure stories include *The Young Fur Traders* (1856), about his experiences in Canada, *Coral Island* (1858), his most famous work, and *Martin Rattler* (1859), *The Dog Crusoe* (1861) and *The Rover of the Andes* (1885). He also published an autobiography, *Personal Reminiscences in Book-Making* (1893). ⊞ E Quayle, *Ballantyne the Brave* (1967)

Ballard, J(ames) G(raham) 1930–
British fiction writer
Born in Shanghai, China, he was educated at Cambridge. Until recently he was better known for his science fiction, fashioning a series of novels at once inventive, experimental and, in several cases, bizarre. He has commented that 'science fiction is the authentic literature of the 20th century, the only fiction to respond to the transforming nature of science and technology'. His early novels, including his first, *The Drowned World* (1962), offer a view of the world beset by elemental catastrophe, a theme also taken up in *The Drought* (1965) and *The Day of Creation* (1985). The more experimental side of his fiction is seen in the 'fragmented novels', like *The Atrocity Exhibition* (1970) and *Crash* (1973, filmed 1996). He has been admired for his short stories, particularly those included in such collections as *The Terminal Beach* (1964), *The Disaster Area* (1967), *Vermilion Sands* (1973) and *War Fever* (1990). *Empire of the Sun* (1984), a mainstream novel which is portentously autobiographical, was shortlisted for the Booker Prize. Its sequel, *The Kindness of Women* (1991), is also autobiographical. He won the Guardian Fiction prize in 1984 and the James Tait Black Memorial Prize in 1985. Most recently, he published *Rushing to Paradise* (1994). ⊞ Peter Brigg, *J G Ballard* (1985)

Ballesteros, Seve(riano) 1957–
Spanish golfer
Born in Santander, he started as a caddy for foreigners and became one of the world's leading golfers. A highly combative, adventurous player, he has continually set records, and has an uncanny ability to produce recovery shots. When he won the British Open championship in 1979 he was the youngest player in the 20th century to do so, and he took the title again in 1984 and 1988. He was the youngest player ever to win the US Masters in 1980 (a position usurped by Tiger Woods in 1997), and only the second European winner. In 1997 he was made captain of the European side for the Ryder Cup, the first to be held in Spain. ⊞ Lauren St John, *Seve* (1993)

Balliol or **Baliol**
Anglo-Norman family
The founder, Guido or Guy, held Bailleul, Harcourt, and other fiefs in Normandy, and received large possessions in Durham and Northumberland from William II, Rufus. Bernard, Guy's son (d.c.1167), built the fortress of Barnard Castle, and Bernard's great-grandson, John de Balliol, founded Balliol College, Oxford (c.1263). His wife, Devorguilla, the great-great-granddaughter of David I, founded Sweetheart Abbey, Kirkcudbrightshire (1275). Their third son, John, became King of Scotland (1292–96).

Balliol or **Baliol, Edward de** c.1283–1364
King of Scotland
The elder son of John de Balliol, he landed with 3,400 followers at Kinghorn, Fife (1332), accompanied by the barons displaced by Robert Bruce, who were bent on recovering their forfeited Scottish estates. At Dupplin Moor, Perthshire, they surprised and routed the Scottish army under the new regent, the Earl of Mar, and in September he was crowned King of Scotland at Scone. Less than three months later, he was himself surprised at Annan and fled across the Border on an unsaddled horse. Two attempts to regain Scotland (1334–35) were unsuccessful and he eventually resigned his claims to the Scottish throne to Edward III (1356) in return for a pension of £2,000. He died without heirs.

Balliol or **Baliol, John de**, *also known as* **Toom Tabard** c.1250–1315
King of Scotland
The son of the founder of Balliol College, Oxford, he succeeded to his mother's estates and her right to the lordship of Galloway, as well as to his father's vast possessions in England and Normandy. On the death of Margaret, the Maid of Norway (1290), he became a claimant to the Crown of Scotland. His claim was pronounced superior to that of Robert Bruce, Lord of Annandale, by Edward I of England. Balliol swore allegiance to Edward before and after his investiture at Scone (1292) and was forced to repudiate the Treaty of Bingham (1290), which guaranteed Scottish liberties. By 1295 a council of 12 magnates had taken control of government out of Balliol's hands and concluded an alliance with France, then at war with England. Edward invaded Scotland, took Balliol prisoner, stripped him of his royal insignia (hence the name Toom Tabard or Empty Jacket) and forced him to surrender his crown (1296). Imprisoned for three years, first at Hertford and then in the Tower of London, he was eventually allowed to retire to his estates in France (1302), where he died.

Ballou, Hosea 1771–1852
US clergyman
Born in Richmond, New Hampshire, he was brought up in the Baptist Church, but his belief that salvation was open to all people led to his excommunication in 1791. He became a teacher and an itinerant preacher, expounding his own brand of theology, which denied the Trinity and original sin, and in 1794 he was ordained a minister in the nascent Universalist Church. He became the leading figure in the Universalist movement, serving as a pastor and circuit rider in Vermont, New Hampshire, and Massachusetts, editing Universalist magazines and publishing theological works such as *A Treatise on the Atonement* (1805).

Balmaceda, José Manuel 1840–91
Chilean politician
A Liberal, he was elected to Congress in 1870, and served in the Cabinet of President Santa María (1881–86). Balmaceda's strong presidency (1886–91) provoked resistance from Congress and he was defeated in the resulting civil war (1891). His suicide mythologized his rule as a struggle against the dominion of foreign, principally British, interests.

Balmain, Pierre Alexandre 1914–82
French couturier
Born in St Jean-de-Maurienne, he was the son of a draper. He studied architecture in Paris, then turned to dress design, working for Edward Molyneux and other designers, and opening his own fashion house in 1945. His designs were famous for elegant simplicity and included evening dresses, sportswear and stoles. He also designed for the theatre and cinema.

Balmer, Johann Jakob 1825–98
Swiss physicist

Born in Lausanne, he was self-educated and spent most of his life teaching in a girls' school, but late in life became interested in spectra. In 1855 he produced a simple formula for the frequencies of hydrogen lines in the visible spectrum. A full explanation of the relation later became clear through **Niels Bohr**'s theory of atomic structure. The Balmer Series describes the visible and near ultraviolet atomic spectrum of hydrogen.

Balmerino, Arthur Elphinstone, 6th Baron
1688–1746
Scottish Jacobite

He fought with the Jacobites in the Rising of 1715, escaped to the Continent, and was pardoned in 1733. He was one of the first to join Prince **Charles Edward Stuart** in the 1745 Rising, was captured at Culloden in 1746 and beheaded at Tower Hill, London.

Balmont, Konstantin Dmitriyevich 1867–1943
Russian poet, translator and essayist

He was born in Gumnishchi, Vladimir province, and his work was coloured by his extensive travelling during his periodic exiles. He translated many works by English authors into Russian, especially those of **Shelley**. He was one of the greatest Russian Symbolists and his best-known verse collection is *Budemkak Solntse* (1903, 'Let Us Be As The Sun'). 📖 L L Kobuilinksy, *Russian Symbolists* (1972)

Balnaves, Henry c.1512–1579
Scottish reformer

Born in Kirkcaldy, Fife, he was made a Lord of Session by **James V** in 1538, and in 1543 was appointed Secretary of State by the Regent **James Hamilton**, Earl of Arran. Shortly after, however, he was imprisoned, with **John Knox**, in Blackness Castle for his Protestantism. When the castle was captured by the French (1547), Balnaves, with Knox and others, was sent to Rouen. While in prison there, he wrote a treatise on Justification which, with notes and a preface by Knox, was published in 1584 as *The Confession of Faith*. In 1566 he was allowed to return to Scotland and took an active part on the side of the Lords of the Congregation.

Balthasar, Hans Urs von 1905–88
Swiss Catholic theologian

He was born in Lucerne. The author of some 60 books on theology, philosophy and spirituality, he was remarkable for drawing considerable inspiration for his theology from the religious experiences of the mystic Adrienne von Speyr (1902–67), with whom he formed a secular institute after leaving the Jesuits. His chief work, *Herrlichkeit* (1961–69, Eng trans *The Glory of the Lord: A Theological Aesthetics*, 1983–), is a 20th-century statement of a theology of the beautiful, the good, and the true, holding that in the incarnation of **Jesus Christ** God transformed the meaning of culture.

Balthus, Count Balthasar Klossowski de Rola 1908–
French painter

Born in Paris, of Polish descent, he had no formal training, but received early encouragement from **Pierre Bonnard** and **André Derain**. His work includes landscapes and portraits, but he is chiefly known for his interiors with adolescent girls, languidly erotic scenes painted in a highly distinctive naturalist style with a hint of Surrealism. He has grown in fame and popularity in recent years, despite the fact that he has lived for many years as a virtual recluse.

Baltimore, David 1938–
US microbiologist and Nobel Prize winner

Born in New York City, he studied chemistry at Swarthmore College, the Massachusetts Institute of Technology (MIT) and Rockefeller University. He conducted research into virology at the Salk Institute (1965–68), became Professor of Biology at MIT (1972), and was later director of the Whitehead Institute at Cambridge, Massachusetts. In 1970 he discovered the 'reverse transcriptase' enzyme which can transcribe DNA into RNA, and which allows scientists to manipulate the genetic code. His research into the connection between viruses and cancer earned him the 1975 Nobel Prize for physiology or medicine, jointly with **Renato Dulbecco** and **Howard Temin**. In the 1980s he chaired a US National Academy of Sciences committee on AIDS, a 'retrovirus' which has RNA as its genetic code.

Baltimore, George Calvert, 1st Baron
c.1580–1632
English aristocrat and colonialist

Born in Kiplin, North Yorkshire, he entered parliament in 1609, was knighted in 1617, and was Secretary of State (1619–25). In 1625 he declared himself a Catholic, was created Baron Baltimore in the Irish peerage, and retired to his Irish estates. In 1621 he had dispatched colonists to a small settlement at Ferryland in Newfoundland, which he visited in 1627. His subsequent attempts to settle in Virginia led to disputes, and he returned home to obtain a fresh charter. He died before the grant was made final and the patent passed to his son, Cecil, (c.1605–1675). The territory was called Maryland, in honour of **Charles I**'s queen. Cecil's younger brother, Leonard (c.1610–c.1660), became first governor (1634–47).

Balzac, Honoré de 1799–1850
French novelist

Born in Tours, he was educated at the Collège de Vendôme, and studied law at the Sorbonne, Paris. His father wished him to become a notary, but he left Tours in 1819 to seek his fortune as an author in Paris. His first success was with *Le Dernier Chouan* in 1829 (Eng trans *The Chouans*, 1893), followed in the same year by *La Peau de chagrin* (Eng trans *The Magic Skin*, 1888). After writing several other novels, he conceived the idea of the *Comédie humaine* (1842–53, 'The Human Comedy'), a complete picture of modern civilization. Among the masterpieces which form part of Balzac's vast scheme are *Le Père Goriot* (1835, Eng trans *Père Goriot*, 1886), *Illusions perdues* (1837–43, 3 vols, Eng trans *Lost Illusions*, 1893), *Les Paysans* (1855, completed by his wife, Eng trans *Sons of the Soil*, 1890), *La Femme de trente ans* (1831–34, 'The Thirty-year-old Woman') and *Eugénie Grandet* (1833, Eng trans 1859). The *Contes drolatiques* (1832–37, 'Droll Tales'), a series of **Rabelaisian** stories, stand by themselves. He worked regularly for up to 18 hours a day, and wrote 85 novels in 20 years. However, as a young man he had incurred a heavy burden of debt and his work failed to bring him wealth, which may help account for his obsession with the workings of money in the novels. During his later years he lived principally in his villa at Sèvres. In 1850, only three months before his death, he married Eveline Hanska, a rich Polish lady with whom he had corresponded for more than 15 years. 📖 G Robb, *Balzac* (1994); A Maurois, *Prométhée, ou La vie de Balzac* (1965)

Banach, Stefan 1892–1945
Polish mathematician

Born in Kraków, he studied at Lvov University, where he became a lecturer (1919), then professor (1927). During World War II he was forced to work in a German research institute where his health was ruined, and he died soon after the war. He is regarded as one of the founders of functional analysis, and his book *Théorie des opérations linéaires* (1932) remains a classic. He founded an important school of Polish mathematicians which emphasized the importance of topology and real analysis, and his name is attached to a class of infinite dimensional linear spaces which are important in the study of analysis, and are increasingly applied to problems in physics, especially in particle physics.

Banco, Nanni di c.1384–1421
Italian sculptor

He was recorded as a member of the Stonemasons' Guild in 1405, and was working with his father shortly thereafter on the Porta della Mandorla of Florence Cathedral. In his early years he shared two cathedral commissions, for pairs of free-standing figures, with his contemporary Donatello. Later he contributed statues to three of the niches on the guild hall in Or San Michele. His best work there was the group of *Four Crowned Saints*, which shows strong classical influence, but in his most important later commission, the relief of the *Assumption of the Virgin* above the Porta della Mandorla (1414–21), he returned to a more Gothic manner. He is regarded as one of the major artists of the early Renaissance.

Bancroft, Anne, *originally* Anna Maria Louisa Italiano 1931–
US actress

Born in New York City, she was a child actress and dancer, and made her television debut in 1950 under the name Anna Marno. Her film debut, as Anne Bancroft, followed in 1952. She won a Tony award for her performance in *Two For a Season* on Broadway (1958), and another for *The Miracle Worker* (1959), gaining an Academy Award for the film version in 1962. Her major films include *The Pumpkin Eater* (1964), *The Graduate* (1967), *The Turning Point* (1977), *The Elephant Man* (1980), *Agnes of God* (1985) and *84 Charing Cross Road* (1987). She has been married to Mel Brooks since 1964 and has appeared in a number of his films, including *To Be Or Not To Be* (1983) and *Dracula—Dead and Loving It* (1995).

Bancroft, George 1800–91
US historian and politician

Born in Worcester, Massachusetts, he studied divinity at Harvard and history at Göttingen. He lectured in Greek at Harvard, preached, and established a school using advanced European methods. He wrote both poetry and prose; his major work was a monumental *History of the United States* (10 vols, 1834–40, 1852–74). A Democrat, he was Secretary to the Navy (1845–46) and established the Naval Academy at Annapolis. He was US Minister in Great Britain (1846–49) and Germany (1876–74).

Bancroft, Hubert Howe 1832–1918
US historian

Born in Granville, Ohio, he settled in San Francisco in 1852, started a bookshop, and amassed a fortune. In 1905 he collected and transferred 60,000 volumes to the University of California, mainly on American history and ethnography, and edited and published *The Native Races of the Pacific States* (1875–76) as one of 39 volumes of a *History of the Pacific States of America* (1875–90). He also wrote the autobiographical *Literary Industries* (1891) and *Retrospection* (1912).

Bancroft, Richard 1544–1610
English prelate

Born in Farnworth, Lancashire, he graduated from Cambridge in 1567, and after a series of preferments was consecrated Bishop of London in 1597. He attended Queen Elizabeth I during her last illness, and took the lead at the Hampton Court Conference. Succeeding John Whitgift as Archbishop of Canterbury in 1604, he worked hard to make the Roman Catholics faithful to the Crown by supporting the secular clergy rather than the Jesuits, and assisted in re-establishing episcopacy in Scotland.

Bancroft, Sir Squire 1841–1926
English actor-manager

He was born in London and made his debut at Birmingham (1861) and in London (1865). In 1867 he married Marie Wilton (1840–1921), a distinguished actress born in Doncaster. From 1865 to 1880 the Prince of Wales's Theatre witnessed their triumphs in T W Robertson's comedies, and in plays such as *School for Scandal* and *Masks and Faces*. In 1880 they leased the Haymarket Theatre, where they continued their success, and retired in 1885.

Band, The
North American rock band

The Band were among the most influential groups ever to emerge from US rock music, although four of its members were Canadian. The original line-up featured Robbie Robertson (guitar), Garth Hudson (organ), Richard Manuel (piano), Rick Danko (bass) and Arkansas-born Levon Helm (drums), the only US member of the group. They backed singer Ronnie Hawkins in the early 1960s, then became Bob Dylan's first electric band in 1965. Their debut album as The Band was *Music From Big Pink* (1968), a classic they immediately topped with *The Band* (1969). The potent mix of Americana embedded in their music produced several more albums, before the group finally split up with the spectacular *The Last Waltz* concert and film in 1976. Manuel died in 1986, and Robertson has never joined any reunions, but the remaining members re-emerged as The Band in the 1990s. 🕮 B Hoskyns, *Across The Great Divide* (1993)

Banda, Hastings Kamuzu 1898–1997
Malawian politician and physician

Born near Kasungu, Nyasaland, he achieved an education by self-help in South Africa, graduating in philosophy and in medicine in the USA and obtaining further honours at Glasgow and Edinburgh universities. He practised medicine in Liverpool during the whole of World War II and then ran a successful London practice before returning to his homeland in 1958 to lead the Malawi African Congress. He was jailed for a year in 1959 but, given an unconditional pardon, became Minister of National Resources (1961), then Prime Minister (1963), President of the Malawi (formerly Nyasaland) Republic (1966), and Life President (1971). He established a strong, one-party control of Malawi, brooking little opposition while at the same time following a pragmatic foreign policy line, recognizing both the white regime in South Africa and the socialist government in Angola. Banda lost his presidency in 1994 in the first all-party elections and was later placed under house arrest, charged and put on trial, following the murder of three Cabinet members and one MP in 1995; however, in December 1995 he was found not guilty and acquitted. 🕮 John Lloyd Lwanda, *Kamuzu Banda of Malawi: a Study in Promise, Power and Paralysis* (1993)

Bandaranaike, Sirimavo Ratwatte Dias 1916–
Sri Lankan politician

She was born in Ratnapura. The widow of S W R D Bandaranaike, who was assassinated in 1959, she became the leader of the Sri Lanka Freedom Party (SLFP) and the first woman Prime Minister in the world when she was elected in 1960. She held office from 1960 to 1965, and again from 1970 to 1977. Her second term was especially turbulent, with the 1971 People's Liberation Front (JVP) insurrection followed by the introduction of a new republican constitution in 1972 and a period of severe economic shortages. The United National Party (UNP) government of Junius Jayawardene stripped her of her civil rights in 1980, forcing her to relinquish temporarily the leadership of the SLFP to her son, Anura. In 1994 she was re-elected as Prime Minister.

Bandaranaike, S(olomon) W(est) R(idgeway) D(ias) 1899–1959
Ceylonese politician

Born in Colombo, and educated there and at Oxford, he was called to the Bar in 1925. He became president of the Ceylon National Congress, and helped to found the United National Party (UNP). He was Leader of the House in Ceylon's first parliament, and Minister of Health. In 1951 he resigned from the government and organized the Sri Lanka Freedom Party (SLFP). In 1956 he was the main partner in a populist coalition which defeated the UNP in an election dominated by the issue of national language and the spirit of Buddhist revivalism, and became Prime Minister. Bandaranaike's Sinhala-only proposals were opposed by representatives of the Tamil minority and Sinhala–Tamil violence swiftly followed. When he was assassinated by a Buddhist monk, he was succeeded by his wife, **Sirimavo Bandaranaike**. ⚏ James Manor, *The Expedient Utopian: Bandaranaike and Ceylon* (1989)

Bandelier, Adolf Francis Alphonse 1840–1914
US archaeologist and anthropologist

He was born in Berne, Switzerland. A disciple of **Lewis Henry Morgan**, he worked from 1880 principally on the pueblos of Arizona and New Mexico, using a mixture of documentary research, ethnography, and archaeological survey to investigate the lives of their earliest inhabitants and to establish a chronology for the region. A long sojourn in Peru and Bolivia followed (1892–1903), its results published as *The Islands of Titicaca and Koati* (1910). He then held museum and teaching posts in New York and Washington DC, departing in 1913 for Spain to study colonial records of the Pueblo Indians. He pioneered the study of the pre-Columbian Indian cultures in Southwestern USA, Peru and Bolivia, and Bandelier National Monument, a gorge near Santa Fe, New Mexico, was established in his memory in 1916.

Bandello, Matteo c.1485–1561
Italian cleric and writer

Born in Castelnuovo, Piedmont, he was educated in Milan then attended the University of Pavia. For a while a Dominican, he was driven from Milan by the Spaniards after the Battle of Pavia (1525), and, settling in France, was in 1550 made Bishop of Agen. His 214 tales (1554–73), collected as *Novelliere*, have no over-all narrative framework, but were used as source material by **Shakespeare**, **Philip Massinger**, and others, and are valuable (if perhaps a little unreliable) for the social history of the period. ⚏ K H Hartley, *Bandello and the Heptameron* (1960)

Bandiera, Attilio c.1810–44 and Emilio 1819–44
Italian revolutionaries

The sons of a Venetian admiral, they were lieutenants in the Habsburg navy. In 1840 they founded a nationalist secret society and planned to seize an Austrian frigate and launch a mutiny. When their plans were discovered they deserted ship in Corfu and travelled to the Kingdom of the Two Sicilies with the intention of launching an insurrection. Captured by Neapolitan troops, they were tried and executed.

Bandinelli, Baccio 1493–1560
Italian sculptor

He was born in Florence, the son of a famous goldsmith. A rival of **Michelangelo**, he executed the statues of *Hercules and Cacus* (1534) outside the Vecchio Palace, and *Adam and Eve* (1547, National Museum, Florence). His best works are the bas-reliefs in Florence Cathedral (1555).

Banerjea, Sir Surendranath 1848–1925
Indian politician and journalist

Born in Calcutta, the son of a doctor, he was a fervent nationalist and founded the Calcutta Indian Association in 1876. He was editor of *The Bengali* newspaper from 1879 to 1921. Initially regarded as 'extremist' by the British, but later as a moderate, he was important in the Indian National Congress (of which he was president in 1902) and a member of the Calcutta Corporation, and was twice returned to the Central Legislature. He welcomed the Montagu–**Chelmsford** reforms for the government of India, and subsequently broke with Congress over the question of non-co-operation. He published an autobiography, *A Nation in the Making* (1925).

Banerjee, Satyendranath 1897–
Indian artist

Born in West Bengal, he subsequently lived in Calcutta. Talented as a child, he became a protégé of **Rabindranath Tagore** and a teacher at the Calcutta College of Arts. Examples of his work may be found in galleries throughout India and in private collections.

Banerji, Bibhuti Bhusan 1894–1950
Indian (Bengali) author

He is best known for his novel *Pather Panchali* (1928–99, Eng trans *Chronicle of the Street*, 1969), made famous by **Satyajit Ray**'s great trilogy of films under the same title. It is essentially the story of the author's own childhood in rural Bengal, and the films reflect it with an authenticity almost unique in the history of the translation of books to cinema.

Bánffy, Dezsö Bánffy, Baron 1843–1911
Hungarian politician

He was born into an aristocratic family in Transylvania, where the population was ethnically mixed. In 1876 he became Lord Lieutenant of the county of Szolnok-Doboka, acquiring a reputation for denying the rights of nationalities other than his fellow Magyars. In 1892 he became Speaker of the Hungarian parliament, and from 1895 to 1899 he was Prime Minister. In these capacities he was much concerned with developing the ruthless policy of enforced Magyarization as an antidote to the emerging nationalism of the subject peoples of the Hungarian half of the Austro-Hungarian Empire.

Bang, Bernhard 1848–1932
Danish veterinary surgeon

Born in Sorö, Zeeland, he studied medicine but later became interested in the healing of animals, and in 1880 was appointed Professor of Veterinary Surgery at Copenhagen University, where he investigated bacillary diseases, mainly of cattle. He is known particularly for his work on bovine brucellosis, known as Bang's disease.

Ban Gu (Pan Ku) AD32–92
Chinese historian

He initiated a tradition of dynastic histories under imperial patronage unparalleled in other civilizations. In AD82 he completed a history of the Western Han Dynasty (202BC–AD9). The tradition pioneered by Ban Gu served a crucial political and moral role in imperial China. The history of a preceding dynasty highlighted its shortcomings in providing wise and benevolent government, thus serving as lessons for the future and enhancing the legitimacy of the current ruling dynasty.

Banim, John 1798–1842 and Michael 1796–1874
Irish novelists

They were brothers, both born in County Kilkenny. John studied art at Dublin and became a painter of miniatures. Michael was a postmaster. John achieved some success as a playwright when a tragedy was produced at Covent Garden in 1821, and subsequently collaborated with Michael to write such novels as the *Tales of the O'Hara Family* (1826), characterized by a faithful portrayal of humble

Irish people. John's illness, due to a spinal disorder, and poverty were alleviated by a state pension. Michael's other novels include *The Croppy* (1828) and *The Town of the Cascades* (1864). 📖 P J Murray, *The Life of John Banim* (1857)

Bani-Sadr, Abolhassan 1935–
Iranian politician

The son of a preacher and landowner, he was associated with **Ayatollah Khomeini** from 1966. He studied economics and sociology at the Sorbonne in Paris, having fled there in 1963 after a brief imprisonment in Iran. He was an important figure in the Iranian Revolution of 1978–79 and was elected first President of the Islamic Republic of Iran in 1980. He was soon criticized, however, by the fundamentalists and was eventually dismissed (1981) by Ayatollah Khomeini for failing to establish a 'truly Islamic country'. He fled to France where he was granted political asylum. The same year, he formed the National Council of Resistance to oppose the Iranian government and was chairman until 1984.

Bankes, Lady Mary, *née* Hawtrey d.1661
English royalist

She was married to Sir John Bankes (1589–1644). She defended Corfe Castle (1643, 1645–46) against the Parliamentarians, but was betrayed by one of her own men and was forced to surrender the castle to the Roundheads. The castle was sacked and destroyed, but she and her children were allowed to leave in safety.

Bankhead, Tallulah 1903–68
US actress

She was born in Huntsville, Alabama. She made her stage debut in 1918, and appeared in many plays and films, her two most famous stage roles being Regina in *The Little Foxes* (1939) and Sabina in *The Skin of our Teeth* (1942). Her best film performance was in *Lifeboat* (1944). She also performed on radio and television.

Banks, Don 1923–80
Australian composer

He was born in Melbourne, and studied at the Melbourne Conservatorium (1947–49), and then with **Mátyás Seiber** and **Luigi Nono**, amongst others. Having settled in England, he founded the Australian Musical Association in London, and was chairman of the Society for the Promotion of New Music (1967–68). From 1969 to 1971 he was music director of Goldsmith's College, London, and in 1973 he returned to Australia to become chairman of the Australian Council for the Arts Music Board. In 1974 he was appointed head of Composition and Electronic Music Studies at Canberra School of Music, and became head of the School of Composition Music Studies at the Sydney Conservatorium (1978). Banks's work was particularly influenced by **Milton Babbitt**, and jazz played a crucial part in his musical development. His compositions include a sonata for violin and piano (1953), a trio for horn, violin and piano, *Equations 1, 2 and 3* (1963–64, 1969, 1972) for jazz group, a four-track tape composition, *Shadows of Space* (1972), a trilogy for orchestra (1977) and *An Australian Entertainment* (1979), as well as many film and television scores.

Banks, Gordon 1937–
English footballer

Born in Sheffield, he started his career as a goalkeeper with Chesterfield and Leicester City but was transferred to Stoke City because Peter Shilton (1949–) was also on the Leicester staff. His performances in the 1966 and 1970 World Cups were outstanding and England might well have retained the trophy in Mexico had he been able to play in the crucial match against West Germany. An eye injury from a car crash in 1972 effectively ended his career.

Banks, Iain Menzies 1954–
Scottish novelist and science-fiction writer

Born in Dunfermline, Fife, he was educated at Gourock and Greenock high schools and the University of Stirling. He made a major impact with his controversial first novel, *The Wasp Factory* (1984), a study of insanity which shifted between psychological acuity and grotesque fantasy. Subsequent novels drew more directly on science fiction and fantasy in multi-layered narratives. *The Crow Road* (1992) incorporated familiar motifs and themes of Scottish writing, viewed from a slightly displaced perspective. He writes science-fiction novels using the name Iain M Banks, including *The State of the Art* (1989, rev edn 1991) and *Against a Dark Background* (1993). His other works include *Cleaning Up* (1987), *Complicity* (1993) and *Whit* (1995).

Banks, Sir Joseph 1744–1820
English botanist

He was born in London, and educated at Harrow, Eton, and Christ Church, Oxford. In 1766 he made a voyage to Newfoundland collecting plants, and between 1768 and 1771 accompanied Captain **James Cook**'s expedition round the world in a vessel, the *Endeavour*, equipped at his own expense. In 1778 he was elected president of the Royal Society, an office which he held for 41 years. His significance lies in his far-reaching influence, rather than through any single personal contribution to science. He founded the African Association, and the colony of New South Wales owed its origin mainly to him. Through him the bread-fruit was transferred from Tahiti to the West Indies, the mango from Bengal, and many fruits of Ceylon and Persia. He was made a baronet in 1781, and his name is commemorated in the genus *Banksia*. 📖 Hector C Cameron, *Sir Joseph Banks* (1952)

Banks, Lynne Reid 1929–
English novelist

Born in London, she trained at RADA and worked as an actress and journalist before turning to writing. She was widely acclaimed for the novel *The L-Shaped Room* (1960). *The Backward Shadow* (1970) and *Two Is Lonely* (1974) complete the trilogy. The first added a female perspective to other novels being published at the time, which similarly dealt with young working- and lower-middle-class people coming to terms with sexuality and family life in a grim postwar Great Britain. She has also widely published plays, biographical fiction and children's books, most recently *Broken Bridge* (1994).

Banks, Nathaniel Prentiss 1816–94
US politician and soldier

Born in Waltham, Massachusetts, he studied law, and became successively a member of the state and national legislatures. He was Speaker of Congress in 1856, and in 1857, 1859 and 1861 was elected Governor of Massachusetts. In the Civil War he commanded on the Potomac River and captured Fort Hudson (1863).

Banks, Thomas 1735–1805
English sculptor

Born in Lambeth, London, he was apprenticed to an ornament carver, and married into wealth. From 1772 to 1779 he lived in Rome, and he visited Russia in 1781. He produced many accomplished works in the neoclassical manner, the best-known being his monument the sleeping child, *Penelope Boothby* (1793, Ashbourne, Derbyshire), and those to Captains Burgess and Westcott in St Paul's Cathedral, London (1802 and 1805). He also executed some effective portrait busts, such as that of **Warren Hastings** (1799, National Portrait Gallery, London).

Bannatyne, George 1545–1608
Scottish antiquary and collector of poems

He was born in Edinburgh but was a native of Forfarshire (Tayside). He became a wealthy merchant and burgess in Edinburgh, but his claim to fame was his 800-page manuscript of 15th- and 16th-century Scottish poetry (the Bannatyne Manuscript), compiled during an outbreak of plague in Edinburgh when he withdrew to his father's estate at Kirktown or Newtyle in Forfarshire. The Bannatyne Club was founded in his honour in 1823 to encourage the study of Scottish history and literature.

Banneker, Benjamin 1731–1806
US mathematician and astronomer

Born in Ellicott, Maryland, the son of a slave father and free mother, he was interested in mathematics and science, and as a young man constructed an entirely wooden clock that kept perfect time. He was recommended by **Thomas Jefferson** to assist with surveying the site of the District of Columbia and the city of Washington, and in his correspondence with Jefferson he defended the intellectual equality of African-Americans. Banneker also published an almanac containing astronomical and tide calculations.

Bannen, Ian 1928–
Scottish actor

Born in Airdrie, near Glasgow, he made his stage debut in *Armlet of Jade* (1947) at the Gate Theatre, Dublin. His many stage appearances include *A View from the Bridge* (1956), *Serjeant Musgrave's Dance* (1959), *Hedda Gabler* (1977) and *Moon for the Misbegotten* (1983). He made his film debut in *Private's Progress* (1956) and proved himself an incisive character actor across a wide range of comic and abrasive roles. His many notable films include *The Hill* (1965), *The Flight of the Phoenix* (1965, Academy Award nomination), *The Offence* (1972) and *Hope and Glory* (1987). His prolific television credits include *Jesus of Nazareth* (1977), *Tinker, Tailor, Soldier, Spy* (1979) and the series *Doctor Finlay* (1993–96).

Bannerman, Helen Brodie, *née* Boog Watson 1862–1946
Scottish children's writer and illustrator

Born in Edinburgh, she married a doctor in the Indian Medical Service and spent much of her life in India. It was there that she wrote the children's classic *The Story of Little Black Sambo* (1899), the tale of a black boy and his adventures with the tigers, based on illustrated letters she had written to her children. Phenomenally popular when it first appeared, it was judged by some after her death to be racist and demeaning to blacks. She wrote several other illustrated books for children.

Bannister, Sir Roger Gilbert 1929–
English athlete and neurologist

Born in Harrow, he was the first man to break the 'four-minute mile'. He was educated at University College School, Exeter, and Merton College, Oxford, and completed his medical training at St Mary's Hospital, London. He won the mile event in the Oxford v Cambridge match four times (1947–50), and was a finalist in the 1,500 metres in the 1952 Olympic Games in Helsinki. At an athletics meeting at Iffley Road, Oxford, in 1954, he ran the mile in under four minutes (3 minutes 59.4 seconds). After a distinguished medical career, he was appointed Master of Pembroke College, Oxford (1985–93). Since 1994 he has been chairman of the Medical Commission on Accident Prevention. He was knighted in 1975.

Banting, Sir Frederick Grant 1891–1941
Canadian physiologist and Nobel Prize winner

Born in Alliston, Ontario, he studied medicine at Toronto University and later became professor there (1923). Working under **John Macleod** on pancreatic secretions, in 1921 he discovered (with his assistant **Charles H Best**) the hormone insulin, still the principal remedy for diabetes. For this discovery he was jointly awarded the Nobel Prize for physiology or medicine in 1923 with Macleod; he shared the award with Best. He established the Banting Research Foundation in 1924, and the Banting Institute at Toronto in 1930. He was knighted in 1934. ▢ Lloyd Stevenson, *Sir Frederick Banting* (2nd edn, 1947)

Bantock, Sir Granville 1868–1946
English composer

He was born in London, and was Professor of Music at Birmingham University (1908–34). His inspiration was often drawn from oriental life, as in his *Omar Khayyám* (in three parts, 1906, 1907, 1909). His works include the choral work *Atalanta in Calydon* (1912) and the *Hebridean Symphony* (1916).

Banville, (Étienne Claude Jean Baptiste) Théodore (Faullain) de 1823–91
French poet and dramatist

Born in Moulins, he was well known for his lyrics and parodies in *Les Cariatides* (1841, 'The Caryatids') and *Dans la fournaise* (1892, 'In the Furnace'). He was given the title 'roi des rimes' for his ingenuity in handling the medieval ballades and rondels. His comedy *Gringoire* (1866) holds an established place in French repertory. ▢ A Carel, *Histoire anecdotique des contemporains* (1885)

Ban Zhao (Pan Chao) AD45–c.114
Chinese historian and moralist

Born in Anling, Gufang (now called Xianyang, Shaanxi (Shensi) province), the sister of the military commander, **Ban Chao (Pan Ch'ao)**, and **Ban Gu**, she helped complete Ban Gu's history of the former Han dynasty and became a tutor to empresses and court ladies. Ban Zhao compiled a book of moral admonitions for women, emphasizing the virtues of deference and modesty, which exerted a lasting influence on attitudes towards women in China. A crucial assumption underpinning these moral admonitions was that women should not play any public role.

Bao Dai, *originally* Nguyen Vinh Thuy 1913–97
Indo-Chinese ruler

Born in Hue, the son of Emperor Khai Dai (d. 1925), he succeeded as Emperor of Annam on his father's death, and ascended the throne in 1932. In 1945 he was forced to abdicate by the Viet Minh under **Ho Chi Minh**. In 1949, having renounced his hereditary title, he returned to Saigon as head of the state of Vietnam within the French Union. After the French Indo-China War he was deposed in 1955 by **Ngo Dinh Diem**. South Vietnam then became a republic, and Bao Dai went to live in France.

Barabbas 1st century AD
Biblical rebel and murderer

As described in Mark 15 and Luke 23, he was arrested but apparently released by popular acclaim in preference to **Pontius Pilate**'s offer to release **Jesus Christ**. He was possibly also called 'Jesus Barabbas' (in some manuscripts of Matthew 27.16–17).

Baraka, Amiri, *adopted name of* LeRoi (Everett LeRoy) Jones 1934–
US poet, playwright, prose writer and essayist

Born in Newark, New Jersey, into a middle-class African-American family, he removed himself from his bourgeois roots into black nationalism (he took the name 'Amiri Baraka' in 1967) and later Marxism–Leninism. A prolific poet and dramatist with over 50 titles to his name, he is best known for work dating from the early 1960s, when his cultural and racial anger spilled out in poetry collections like *Preface to a Twenty Volume Suicide Note* (1961), *The Dead Lecturer* (1964), *Black Magic* (1967), and in plays like *The Toilet*, *Dutchman* and *The Slave* (all 1964). His other works include a volume of stories, *Tales* (1967), and a seminal study of the social significance of African-American music, *Blues People* (1963). 📖 *The Autobiography of LeRoi Jones/Amiri Baraka* (1984)

Bárány, Robert 1876–1936
Austrian physician, otologist and Nobel Prize winner
Born in Vienna, he graduated from the University of Vienna, then undertook further studies in internal medicine, psychiatric neurology, neurology and surgery in Frankfurt, Heidelberg, Freiburg and Vienna. In 1903 he joined the staff of the University of Vienna ear clinic. He pioneered the study in humans of the inner ear's balancing apparatus, proving the connection between this apparatus and the brain, and thus making it possible for equilibrium disturbances and vertigo to be investigated systematically. He volunteered for service during World War I. In 1915, while in a Russian POW camp in Siberia, news reached him that he had been awarded the 1914 Nobel Prize for physiology or medicine. He was released and in 1917 was appointed director of the oto-rhino-laryngology clinic at the University of Uppsala, Sweden.

Barat, St Madeleine Sophie 1779–1865
French nun
Born into a peasant family in Joigny, Burgundy, she was educated by her highly religious brother Louis. She intended to become a Carmelite nun but in 1800 she was persuaded by Louis and his superior, Abbé Joseph Varin, to form the Society of the Sacred Heart of Jesus, a new educational institute which would promote educational work among all classes. The first Convent of the Sacred Heart opened at Amiens in 1801, with Barat as superior from 1802. The convent received papal approval in 1826, and during her 63-year rule the convent grew and established 100 further foundations in Europe, North Africa and in the USA under Sister **Rose Philippine Duchesne**, the Society's first missionary. Barat's work was so highly valued that instead of allowing her to retire at 85, the Order gave her an assistant for her remaining year of life. She was canonized in 1925 and her feast day is 25 May.

Barba Jacob, Porfirio, *pseudonym of* Miguel Angel Osorio Benítez 1883–1942
Colombian poet
Born in Santa Rose de Osos, Antioquia, he was a legendary wandering figure in Latin American literature, not unlike Baron Corvo (**Frederick William Rolfe**). His lyrical poetry uses as a framework the *modernista* style established by **Rubén Darío**, although he was never a *modernista* poet. He modelled his conduct on that of various European *poètes maudits*, and was often involved in scandal. His most famous line is: 'En nada creo, en nada' ('I believe in nothing, nothing'), from 'La reina'. He published *Poesías completas* in 1960, and his complete works of 1962 contains his untruthful and entertaining autobiography, *La divina tragedia* ('The Divine Tragedy').

Barbara, St d.c.200AD
Christian virgin martyr
According to legend, she was a maiden of great beauty whose father immured her in a tower to discourage any suitors. On discovering that she had become a Christian, she was beheaded by her father, for which he was instantly struck by lightning. Her emblem is a tower. Her feast day, 4 December, was deleted from the Roman calendar in 1969.

Barbari, Jacopo de' c.1475–c.1516
Venetian painter and engraver
He worked from 1500 in Germany (where he was known as Jakob Walch) and the Netherlands. From 1510 he was court painter in Brussels. He is chiefly noted for his engravings, mainly of mythological figures, which were influential in the development of northern European graphic art, in particular in the treatment of the nude. His painting *The Dead Bird* (1504) is one of the earliest examples of still life.

Barbarossa, Khair-ed-din, *known as* Redbeard d.1546
Barbary pirate
Born in Mitylene, he became a Turkish corsair along with his brother, attacking shipping in the Mediterranean. After the execution of his brother Horuk (1518), Barbarossa captured Algiers (1529) and was made admiral of the Homan fleet (1533). 📖 Ernle Bradford, *The Sultan's Admiral: The Life of Barbarossa* (1969)

Barber, Chris (Donald Christopher) 1930–
English jazz trombonist and bandleader
Born in Welwyn Garden City, Hertfordshire, he was a leading figure in the trad movement, having taken over the Ken Colyer band in 1953. He replaced Colyer's purism with a flexible and responsive repertoire grounded on good musicianship and an eye to the market. His successes include 'Rock Island Line' (1956) and 'Petite Fleur' (1959), which feature skiffle pioneer Lonnie Donegan (1931–) and clarinettist Monty Sunshine (1928–) respectively, rather than his own characteristic trombone sound. Recent work with New Orleans vocalist Dr John (born Malcolm Rebennack, 1941–) underlined his ability to synthesize and package styles, and he is also a fine musicologist.

Barber, Samuel 1910–81
US composer
Born in West Chester, Pennsylvania, he studied at the Curtis Institute, Philadelphia, and won two Pulitzer travelling scholarships (1935, 1936) as well as the US Prix de Rome. His early music, which includes the setting for voice and string quartet of **Matthew Arnold's** *Dover Beach* (1931), the overture to *The School for Scandal* (1931), the First Symphony (1936) and the well-known *Adagio for Strings* (an arrangement of the slow movement of his string quartet Op 11, 1936) is traditionally neo-Romantic. However, after 1939 his work became increasingly individual, with more emphasis on chromaticism and dissonance and some experimentation with atonality, as in the piano sonata of 1949. Among the works of this period are the *Capricorn Concerto* (1944), the ballet *Medea* (1946), and several vocal pieces, including *Nuvoletta* (1947) from **James Joyce's** *Finnegan's Wake*, and *Hermit Songs* (1952–53). His first full-length opera, *Vanessa*, was performed at the Salzburg Festival (1958), followed by *Antony and Cleopatra* at the Metropolitan Opera in New York (1966).

Barbera, Joseph Roland 1911–
US animated cartoonist
Born in New York City, he studied accounting, but turned to cartooning and worked as a writer/animator on a series entitled *Tom and Jerry* about two boys, one tall and one short. In 1937 he moved to the new MGM animation studio in Hollywood, where he teamed up with **William Denby Hanna**. Together they made *Puss Gets the Boot* (1939), featuring a cat and a mouse; they went on to make over 200 film shorts of the immortal cat and mouse duo, *Tom and Jerry*. In 1957 they formed Hanna-Barbera Productions and turned to television with dozens of popular series such as *Huckleberry Hound*, *Yogi Bear* and *The Flintstones*.

Barbey D'Aurevilly, Jules 1808–89
French writer
Born in St Sauveur-le-Vicomte, he was a Romantic, and was extreme in his rejection of 18th-century values. His best-known novels are *La Vieille maîtresse* (1851, 'The Old Mistress') and *L'Ensorcelée* (1854, 'The Bewitched Woman'). He also published poetry and literary criticism. 📖 J Canu, *Barbey D'Aurevilly* (1965)

Barbier, Henri Auguste 1805–82
French poet

Born in Paris, he was famous for satirizing prominent social types for their efforts to procure favour after the July Revolution. He wrote a number of collections of poems, including *Iambes* (1831), *Il pianto* (1833) and *Lazare* (1837), and he influenced **Victor Hugo**.

Barbier, (Paul) Jules 1825–1901
French dramatist

He was born in Paris. Together with Michel Carré (1819–72), he made often sentimental versions of texts by such authors as **Shakespeare** and **Goethe**. Among their libretti are those for **Charles Gounod's** *Faust* (1859), **Ambroise Thomas's** *Hamlet* (1868) and **Jacques Offenbach's** *Les Contes d'Hoffmann* (1880, 'The Tales of Hoffmann'). 📖 M Carré, *L'amour mouille, comédie vaudeville* (1849)

Barbirolli, Sir John 1899–1970
British conductor and cellist

Born in London of Franco-Italian origin, he served in World War I, and played in several leading string quartets (1920–24). He succeeded **Arturo Toscanini** as conductor of the New York Philharmonic Orchestra (1937), and returned to England as permanent conductor (1943–58) of the Hallé Orchestra in Manchester which, under his direction and with his promotion of the works of modern composers, regained its place among the world's finest. He married the oboist Evelyn Rothwell (1911–) in 1939. He was awarded the Gold Medal of the Royal Philharmonic Society in 1950 and given the Freedom of Manchester in 1958, when he became the Hallé's principal conductor. 📖 Charles Reid, *John Barbirolli* (1971)

Barbon, Praise-God See Barebone, Praise-God

Barbou
French family of printers

Their founder, Jean Barbou (1490–1543) of Lyons, issued a beautiful edition of the works of **Clément Marot** in 1539. His son Hugues (1538–1603) moved to Limoges, where his edition of *Cicero's Letters to Atticus* appeared in 1580. Joseph Gérard (1715–1813) settled in Paris, and continued in 1755 the series of Latin duodecimo classics—rivals to the earliest **Elzevirs**—which had been begun in 1743. The House continued until 1824.

Barbusse, Henri 1873–1935
French novelist

He was born in Asnières of an English mother. He fought as a volunteer in World War I, which inspired his masterpiece, *Le Feu* (1916, Eng trans *Under Fire*, 1917), in which a powerful realism is accompanied by a deep feeling for all human suffering. Other works include *Le Couteau entre les dents* (1921, 'Knife Between the Teeth') and *Le Judas de Jésus* (1927, 'Jesus's Judas'). A noted pacifist, and an increasingly militant communist, he later settled in the USSR. 📖 J Duclos and J Freville, *Henri Barbusse* (1946)

Barca See Hamilcar

Barclay, Alexander c.1475–1552
Scottish poet and author

Born probably in Scotland, he may have studied at universities in England, France and Italy, and in 1508 he became chaplain of Ottery St Mary, Devon. He became a monk at the Benedictine monastery of Ely (c.1511), and later became a Franciscan at Canterbury. His famous poem, *The Shyp of Folys of the Worlde* (1509), is partly a translation and partly an imitation of the German *Narrenschiff* (1494) by **Sebastian Brant**. He also published *Egloges* ('Eclogues'), an early example of English pastoral verse,

and a number of translations, including **Sallust's** *Jugurthine War*. 📖 A Koelbing, in *Cambridge History of English History*, Volume 3 (1909)

Barclay, John 1582–1621
Scottish satirist

Born in Pont-à-Mousson, Lorraine, France, the son of a Scots father and a French mother, he lived in London and Rome, and wrote mostly in Latin. His principal works are *Euphormionis Satyricon* (1603–07), a picaresque satire on the Jesuits, and *Argenis* (1621), an allegorical romance set in his own time. 📖 E Bensby, in *Cambridge History of English Literature*, Volume 4 (1909)

Barclay, Robert 1648–90
Scottish Quaker

Born in Gordonstoun, he was educated at the Scots College in Paris, where his uncle was Rector. He refused to stay in France and embrace Roman Catholicism as heir to his uncle's estates. In 1664 he returned to Scotland, and became a Quaker in 1667. He married a fellow Quaker in Aberdeen in 1670, the first Quaker wedding in Scotland, and took over his father's estate at Ury. In 1672 he startled Aberdeen by walking through its streets in sackcloth and ashes. Frequently imprisoned for attending illegal meetings, he at last found a protector in the Duke of York (the future **James VII and II**), because of distant family connections. He made several journeys to Holland and Germany, the latter with **William Penn** of Pennsylvania and **George Fox**. He became one of the proprietors of East New Jersey in 1682, and was appointed its nominal non-resident governor. The writer of many scholarly and lucid tracts in defence of Quakerism, he endeavoured to harmonize it with the great religious concepts of his day, especially in his classic *Apology for the True Christian Divinity* (1678).

Barclay, Robert 1843–1913
English banker

Under him, the merger of 20 banks took place to form Barclay and Company Limited (1896). In 1917 the name was changed to Barclay's Bank Limited.

Barclay, William 1907–78
Scottish theologian, religious writer and broadcaster

Born in Wick, Caithness, and educated at the universities of Glasgow and Marburg, he was ordained in the Church of Scotland in 1933. After 13 years as a parish minister in Renfrew, he became a lecturer at Trinity College, Glasgow, specializing in Hellenistic Greek, and in 1963 he was appointed Professor of Divinity and Biblical Criticism (retired 1974). He wrote many academic studies, but it is for his popular writings and broadcasts, in which he spoke plainly about Christian teaching and beliefs, that he is best remembered. He was a prolific writer, producing well over 60 books, among them *A New Testament Wordbook* (1955) and his *New People's Life of Jesus* (1965). His *Daily Study Bible* (New Testament) won international acclaim, and in 1968 he published his own translation of the New Testament.

Barclay-Allardice, Robert, *known as* Captain Barclay 1779–1854
Scottish soldier and sportsman

He succeeded to the estate of Urie, near Stonehaven, in 1797, and joined the army in 1805, taking part in the Walcheren expedition of 1809 before retiring to take up management of his estates. His celebrated feat of walking 1,000 miles (1,609km) in 1,000 consecutive hours was performed at Newmarket from June to July 1809.

Barclay de Tolly, Mikhail Bogdanovich, Prince 1761–1818
Russian field marshal

Born in Luhde-Grosshof, Livonia, of Scottish descent, he joined the Russian army in 1786, and served in Turkey, Sweden, and Poland, losing an arm at the Battle of Eylau (1807). He was appointed Minister of War in 1810. Defeated by Napoleon I at Smolensk (1812) and replaced, he later served again as Commander-in-Chief, and took part in the invasion of France and the capture of Paris (1814). He was made a prince and a field marshal in 1815. Statues of him were erected at St Petersburg and Dorpat.

Barcroft, Sir Joseph 1872–1947
Irish physiologist

Born in Newry, County Down, he read natural sciences at King's College, Cambridge, graduated in 1897, and stayed at the Physiological Laboratory in Cambridge for his entire career. He retired in 1937 and was appointed head of the newly created Animal Physiology Unit of the Agricultural Research Council in 1942. During World War I he worked in chemical warfare, but his academic work concentrated on understanding respiratory function, including whole animal physiological experiments, observations on humans at extremes of altitude on expeditions in the Andes, and important biochemical work on haemoglobin and its interaction with oxygen. In the final years of his life he focused on the physiology of the developing foetus, measuring foetal blood volume and placental blood flow, the transfer of gases across the placental membrane, and the control of the respiration, movement and growth parameters of the foetus. He was elected FRS in 1910 and knighted in 1935.

Bardeen, John 1908–91
US physicist and double Nobel Prize winner

Born in Madison, Wisconsin, he studied electrical engineering at the University of Wisconsin, worked as a geophysicist at the Gulf Research Laboratories for three years, then obtained his PhD in mathematical physics at Harvard (1936). He joined a new solid-state physics group at Bell Telephone Laboratories in 1945. Together with Walter Brattain and William Shockley he developed the point-contact transistor (1947), for which they shared the Nobel Prize for physics in 1956. Bardeen was professor at Illinois University (1951–75), and with Leon Cooper and John Schrieffer he won the Nobel Prize for physics again in 1972 for the first satisfactory theory of superconductivity (the Bardeen–Cooper–Schrieffer, or BCS, theory); this incorporated Bardeen's ideas on the involvement of electron–phonon interactions and Cooper's discovery that two electrons could form a resonant state.

Bardot, Brigitte, *originally* Camille Javal 1934–
French film actress

Born in Paris, the daughter of an industrialist, she was a ballet student and model and her appearance on the cover of *Elle* magazine led to her film debut in *Le Trou normand* (1952, *Crazy for Love*). A succession of small roles followed, but it was *Et Dieu créa la femme* (1956, *And God Created Woman*), made with the director Roger Vadim (1928–), later her husband, that established her reputation as an international sex symbol. Her professional image of petulant sexuality was reinforced by a much publicized off-camera love life. Her many screen credits include *La Vérité* (1960, *The Truth*), *Le Mépris* (1963, *Contempt*) and *Viva Maria* (1965), whilst *Vie Privée* (1962, *A Very Private Affair*) was an autobiographical depiction of a young woman trapped by the demands of her stardom. Her last major film was *Si Don Juan était une femme* (1973, 'If Don Juan were a Woman'). Since then she has become closely concerned with animal welfare and the cause of endangered animal species, forming the Foundation for the Protection of Distressed Animals in 1976. In 1996 she published a controversial autobiography, *Initiales B. B.* 📖 Simone de Beauvoir, *Brigitte Bardot and the Lolita Syndrome* (1960)

Barebone or Barbon, Praise-God c.1596–1679
English leather merchant and controversial Anabaptist preacher

A Londoner, he was nominated by Oliver Cromwell to sit in the 'Short Parliament' of 1653, which consequently nicknamed the 'Barebones Parliament'. His fiery preaching attracted huge crowds and often occasioned riots. He was fiercely opposed to the Restoration of Charles II, and was imprisoned in the Tower of London from 1661 to 1662.

Barenboim, Daniel 1942–
Israeli pianist and conductor

Born in Buenos Aires, Argentina, he made his debut there at the age of seven. His family moved to Austria then to Israel in 1952. He studied with Igor Markevich (1912–83) and Nadia Boulanger, and has performed regularly in Europe since 1954. A noted exponent of Mozart and Beethoven, he gained his reputation as pianist/conductor with the English Chamber Orchestra, then became musical director of the Orchestre de Paris (1975–89) and of the Chicago Symphony Orchestra (1991–), and musical and artistic director of the Deutsche Staatsoper, Berlin (1992–). He married the cellist Jacqueline du Pré in 1967, and became an Israeli citizen.

Barents, Willem d.1597
Dutch navigator

He was pilot to several Dutch expeditions in search of the Northeast Passage, and died off Novaya Zemlya. His winter quarters were found undisturbed in 1871, and in 1875 part of his journal was recovered by another expedition. 📖 Rayner Unwin, *A Writer Away From Home: William Barents and the North-East Passage* (1995)

Barère (de Vieuzac), Bertrand 1755–1841
French revolutionary

Originally a monarchist, he was later a supporter of Robespierre, becoming a member of the Committee of Public Safety. He was later imprisoned (1794), but escaped into exile, not returning to Paris until 1830.

Baretti, Giuseppe Marc Antonio 1719–89
Italian critic

Born in Turin, he established himself as a teacher of Italian in London in 1751. He returned to the Continent (1760–66), where he published a book of travels, and in Venice started the *Frusta Letteraria*, or 'literary scourge', in which he criticized many Italian literary fashions. In 1769 he stabbed a Haymarket bully in self-defence, and was tried for murder, but was acquitted—Dr Johnson, Edmund Burke, and David Garrick testifying to his character. His 36 works included an Italian and English Dictionary (1760), and a pamphlet in French defending Shakespeare against Voltaire's criticisms.

Barham, Richard Harris 1788–1845
English humorist

He was born in Canterbury, and had a near-fatal coach accident in 1802 which partially crippled his right arm for life. He entered Brasenose College, Oxford (1807), was ordained (1813), and in 1821 received a minor canonry of St Paul's Cathedral, London. After unsuccessful attempts at novel writing, he began a series of burlesque metrical tales in 1837 under the pen name 'Thomas Ingoldsby'. Collected under the title *The Ingoldsby Legends* (3 vols, 1840–47), they at once became popular for their droll humour, irony and esoteric learning. His lyrics were published in 1881. 📖 W G Lane, *Richard Harris Barham* (1968)

Bar Hebraeus, *Arabic* Abu al-Faraj 1226–86
Syrian historian

He was born in Armenia of a Jewish convert to Christianity. Proficient in Syriac, Arabic and Greek, he was equally learned in philosophy, theology and medicine. At the age of 20, he was made a bishop, and by 1264 he was assistant patriarch of the Eastern Jacobite (Monophysite) Church. Of his numerous writings, the best known is a Syriac universal history.

Baring
English family of financiers

John (1730–1816) and Francis (1740–1810) Baring were the sons of John Baring (1697–1748), a German cloth manufacturer who in 1717 had started a small business at Larkbear, near Honiton, Devon. In 1770 they established the financial and commercial house Baring Brothers & Co., now known as Barings. Francis was created a baronet by **William Pitt, the Younger** in 1793, and by the time of his death had amassed a huge fortune. In February 1995 Nick Leeson, a 28-year-old derivatives trader based in Singapore, lost over £600 million trading on the Tokyo stockmarket and caused the collapse of what had become a 200-year-old merchant banking empire. He was sentenced to six and a half years' imprisonment in Singapore and Barings was bought by the Dutch bank ING.

Baring, Alexander, 1st Baron Ashburton
1774–1848
English politician

The second son of **Francis Baring**, he succeeded him in 1810 as head of Baring Brothers & Co., having previously been MP for Taunton. He represented Taunton, Callington and Thetford as a Liberal until 1832, and in 1833 was returned for north Essex as a Conservative. In Sir **Robert Peel**'s brief administration (1834–35) he was President of the Board of Trade, and was created Baron Ashburton in 1835. In 1842, as special ambassador to the USA, he concluded the Washington, or Ashburton, Treaty defining the frontier line between Maine and Canada. He opposed free trade, but strongly supported the penny postage system when it was proposed in 1837.

Baring, Evelyn, Baron Howick of Glendale
1903–73
British administrator

Educated at Winchester and Oxford, he joined the Indian Civil Service in 1926. In 1942 he became Governor of Southern Rhodesia (Zimbabwe) and from 1944 to 1951 was UK High Commissioner and Governor of the High Commission territories of Bechuanaland, Basutoland, and Swaziland. In 1952 he became Governor of Kenya, quelling the Mau-Mau rebellion by 1956. He retired in 1959. Knighted in 1942, he was made a peer in 1960.

Baring, Maurice 1874–1946
English journalist and author

Born in London, he was the fifth son of Edward Charles Baring (Baron Revelstoke). He was educated at Eton and Trinity College, Cambridge, then held diplomatic posts, and was foreign correspondent for *The Times* (1904–14). During World War I he was an officer in the Royal Flying Corps (1914–18). He wrote novels, such as *Passing By* (1921) and *Cat's Cradle* (1925), a novella *The Lonely Lady of Dulwich* (1934), plays, including *The Black Prince* (1902), and books on Russia, such as *Landmarks in Russian Literature* (1910). He published an autobiography, *The Puppet Show of Memory*, in 1922.

Baring-Gould, Sabine 1834–1924
English writer and clergyman

Born in Exeter, of an old Devon family, he was educated at Clare College, Cambridge, and became rector of Lew Trenchard in Devon in 1881. He wrote novels, topographical, mythological, theological studies, and hymns, among them 'Onward, Christian Soldiers'.

Barke, James 1905–58
Scottish novelist

Born at Torwoodlee, near Galashiels, in the Borders, he retired from his position as chief cost accountant with a shipbuilding company to devote himself to writing. His novels include *The World his Pillow* (1933), *Major Operation* (1936) and *The Land of the Leal* (1939), but he is chiefly remarkable for his devoted research on the life of **Robert Burns**, resulting in a five-volume cycle of novels (1946–54) collected as *The Immortal Memory*, an edition of *Poems and Songs of Robert Burns* (1955) and the posthumous *Bonnie Jean*, about Burns and Jean Armour. 📖 Moira Burgess, *The Glasgow Novel, 1870–1970* (1972)

Barker, Sir Ernest 1874–1960
English political scientist

Born in Cheshire, he studied at Manchester Grammar School and Balliol College, Oxford, and was Fellow of several Oxford colleges before becoming Principal of King's College London (1920–27). He then became Professor of Political Science and Fellow of Peterhouse, Cambridge (1928–39). His earliest work was *The Political Thought of Plato and Aristotle* (1906) and 40 years later he produced his revered translation of **Aristotle**'s *Politics*. His second work was *Political Thought in England from Herbert Spencer to To-Day* (1915). He edited a great enquiry into English culture entitled *The Character of England* (1947) and produced a masterly brief compassionate sketch of Irish history, in the light of which he introduced **Naomi Mitchison**'s novel about Vercingetorix's Gaul, *The Conquered* (1923). He opened up theoretical questions in his *National Character* (1927), *Reflections on Government* (1942) and *Principles of Social and Political Theory* (1951). He emerged from retirement to be Professor of Political Science in war-ravaged Cologne (1947–48), later producing the autobiography *Age and Youth* (1953). He mingled the love of classical learning with a fascination with the changing ideas of society in his own time.

Barker, George Granville 1913–91
English poet, novelist, playwright and scriptwriter

Born in Loughton, Essex, he lived much of his life in the USA and Italy and enjoyed a long, prolific career. However from 1933 he suffered due to an association with **Dylan Thomas**, and from the inference that he was a member of the pre-war New Apocalyptics. He was an energetic and eloquent writer, whose publications culminated in *Collected Poems* (1987). *Street Ballads* was published posthumously in 1992. 📖 M H Fodaski, *George Barker* (1969)

Barker, Harley Granville See **Granville-Barker, Harley**

Barker, Howard 1946–
English dramatist

Born in London, he studied history at the University of Sussex. His first play, *Cheek*, was produced at the Royal Court Theatre, London, in 1970. He has written over 20 plays, on ambitious themes such as the nature of history, the degradation of political morality and the need to reshape society according to finer values. They include *Stripwell* (1975), *The Hang of the Gaol* (1978), *Crimes in Hot Countries* (1983), *The Castle*, *Downchild* (both 1985), *Possibilities* (1988) and *Golgo* (1990). Some, such as *Scenes from an Execution* (1984, staged 1990) and *A Hard Heart* (1992), were written for radio and then adapted for stage. His poetry includes *The Ascent of Monte Grappa* (1991). He formed The Wrestling School in 1989, a company which performed only his own works.

Barker, Robert 1739–1806
Irish portrait painter

He was born in Kells and settled in Edinburgh. In 1788 he exhibited the earliest known panorama of Edinburgh.

Barker, Ronnie (Ronald William George)
1929–
English comic actor

Born in Bedford, Bedfordshire, he made his professional debut at Aylesbury Repertory Theatre in *Quality Street* (1948). His London debut came in *Mourning Becomes Electra* (1955) and later theatrical appearances include *Camino Real* (1957), *Irma La Douce* (1958), *Platonov* (1960) and *A Midsummer Night's Dream* (1962). An affable figure, adept at precisely detailed characterizations, tongue-twisting comic lyrics and saucy humour, he made many television appearances including *The Frost Report* (1966–67), *Frost Over England*, and the sitcoms *Hark at Barker* (1969–70), *His Lordship Entertains* (1972), *Open All Hours* (1976, 1981–85), the hugely popular *Porridge* (1974–77), *Going Straight* (1978) and *Clarence* (1988). With **Ronnie Corbett**, he made the long-running *The Two Ronnies* (1971–87). His films include *Wonderful Things* (1958), *Robin and Marian* (1976) and *Porridge* (1979). A keen collector of Victoriana, he has written light-hearted books on the subject, including *Book of Boudoir Beauties* (1975) and *Ooh-la-la!* (1983).

Barker (of Bath), Thomas 1769–1847
English painter

Born near Pontypool, Wales, he moved with his family to Bath and spent most of his life there. He taught himself to paint and became known for his rural scenes. His eldest son, Thomas Jones Barker (1815–82), was born in Bath and became a painter of battle scenes, later styled the 'English **Horace Vernet**'.

Barker Family, *also called* the Bloody Barkers
1872–c.1935
US gangsters, bankrobbers and kidnappers

Arizona Donnie Clark (1872–1935, known as 'Ma'), who was born in Springfield, Missouri, was the leader of a notorious gang known as the Bloody Barkers. She and her husband George Barker and their four sons Herman (b.1894), Lloyd (b.1896), Arthur (b.1899, known as 'Doc') and Fred (b.1902), roamed through the American Mid-West, robbing, killing and kidnapping. The gang accumulated $3 million from their raids, and large rewards were offered for their bodies. In 1927 Herman committed suicide to avoid capture. In 1939 Fred was killed trying to escape from Alcatraz. Lloyd was killed by his wife in 1949 and in 1935 Doc and Ma were killed at Lake Weir in Florida in a 45-minute gun battle with the FBI. George Barker buried them in Welch, Oklahoma.

Barkhausen, Heinrich Georg 1881–1956
German physicist

He was born in Bremen, and in 1911 was appointed Professor of Low-Current Technology in the Technische Hochschule, Dresden, the first chair ever devoted to the field of electrical communications. He carried out fundamental research on electron tubes and electrical oscillations, developed with Karl Kurz the Barkhausen–Kurz oscillator (a forerunner of the present-day microwave tubes), and wrote comprehensive books on both subjects. In 1919 he discovered that the magnetization of iron proceeds in discrete steps and he devised a loudspeaker system to render this discontinuity audible. This phenomenon is now known as the Barkhausen effect. He was awarded the Heinrich Hertz Medal in 1928, and the Morris Liebmann Memorial prize of the Institute of Radio Engineers (1933), of which he was vice-president in 1935.

Barkla, Charles Glover 1877–1944
English physicist and Nobel Prize winner

Born in Widnes, Lancashire, he studied at the universities of Liverpool and Cambridge. He left his early work on electromagnetic waves to study X-rays, which he researched for 40 years, becoming Professor of Physics at London University (1909–13) and Professor of Natural Philosophy at Edinburgh University (1913–44). Barkla deduced from the scattering of X-rays by gases that more massive atoms contain more electrons, thus taking the first steps towards the concept of the atomic number. In 1904 he demonstrated that X-rays could be polarized and established that they are transverse waves. Much of his work concerned secondary X-rays, which he found to consist of X-rays scattered from the incident beam and a fluorescent radiation characteristic of the scattering substance. By 1911 he was recognized as a world leader in the field and in 1917 was awarded the Nobel Prize for physics.

Bar Kokhba, Simon, *also spelt* Cochba or Kochbas d.135AD
Jewish leader in Palestine

He led, with the rabbi **Akiba ben Joseph**, a rebellion of Jews in Judea from AD132, in response to the founding of a Roman colony (Aelia Capitolina) in Jerusalem, with a temple of Jupiter on the ruins of their own temple. It was suppressed by the Emperor **Hadrian** with ruthless severity, and Simon Bar Kokhba was killed at the Battle of Bethar. In 1960 some of his letters were found in caves near the Dead Sea. ▢Yigael Yadin, *Bar-Kokhba* (1971)

Barlach, Ernst 1870–1938
German sculptor, playwright and poet

He was born in Wedel, and was identified with the German Expressionist school of both art and drama. While he was best known as a sculptor in wood (his work in this medium being influenced by Gothic sculpture and Russian folk-carving), his greatest achievement was his war memorial at Güstrow Cathedral, a great bronze *Angel of Death*, which was removed by **Hitler** as 'degenerate'. Barlach's plays include *Der tote Tag* (1912, 'The Dead Day'), *Der arme Vetter* (1918, 'The Poor Cousin') and *Die Sündflut* (1924, 'The Flood'), and he also wrote some fiction. ▢E M Chick, *Ernst Barlach* (1967)

Barlow, Joel 1754–1812
US poet and politician

Born in Redding, Connecticut, he served as military chaplain during the American Revolution, and spent 16 years abroad, mostly in France, in political, literary and mercantile pursuits. He was US consul at Algiers and ambassador to France in 1811. His *Columbiad* (1807) is a history from the time of **Christopher Columbus** to the French Revolution. His other works include the poem 'Hasty Pudding' (1796). ▢ J Woodress, *A Yankee's Odyssey: the life of Barlow* (1958)

Barlow, Mrs See **Walter, Lucy**

Barlow, Peter 1776–1862
English natural philosopher

Born in Norwich, Norfolk, and largely self-educated, he obtained a post as a teacher of mathematics at the Royal Military Academy, Woolwich, in 1801. For the next 15 years he devoted himself to pure science, devised mathematical tables and made useful studies in applied physics. His *New Mathematical Tables* (1814) were reprinted as late as 1947 as *Barlow's Tables*. He became interested in the strength of construction materials, and carried out extensive series of tests on timber, cast and wrought iron, and other materials. He also worked on the strength of ships' timbers, on tidal engineering, and on ships' magnetism and its correction (for which he received the Copley Medal of the Royal Society in 1825). The Barlow lens is used both as an astronomical eyepiece and in photography.

Barlow, Thomas 1607–91
English bishop

Born in Orton, Westmorland, he was educated at Appleby and Queen's College, Oxford, of which he became provost in 1657. Throughout the ecclesiastical controversies of the time, he secured his advancement by casuistry, always modifying his arguments so as to be on the winning side. This earned him the name of 'the Trimmer'. His advancement to the bishopric of Lincoln (1675) was so unpopular that he avoided the cathedral. He was, if anything, a Calvinist and an opponent of **Jeremy Taylor**.

Barna, Viktor, *originally* Gyözö Braun 1911–72
British table tennis player

Born in Budapest, Hungary, he won a record 20 English titles between 1931 and 1953, including five singles titles (1933–35, 1937–38), and also won 15 world titles, including five singles (1930, 1932–35). One of the game's greatest players, he emigrated to France before becoming a British citizen in 1938. After retirement, he played exhibitions and formed the Swaythling Club, a social club for ex-table tennis internationals.

Barna da Siena fl.c.1350
Italian painter

He was born in Siena, the only information on his career being contained in the writings of **Lorenzo Ghiberti**. He was a follower of the great Sienese painter, **Simone Martini**, but unlike that of previous Sienese painting which is characterized by graceful line, his style displays a sense of solidity and physical power more typical of Florentine art, especially that of **Giotto**. A series of frescoes in San Gimignano remained unfinished because, according to Ghiberti, he died as a result of a fall from the scaffolding.

Barnard, Christiaan Neethling 1922–
South African surgeon

Born in Beaufort West, he graduated from Cape Town Medical School. After a period of research in the USA he returned to Cape Town in 1958 to work on open-heart surgery and organ transplantation. In December 1967 at Groote Schuur Hospital he performed the first successful human heart transplant. The recipient, Louis Washkansky, died of pneumonia 18 days later, drugs given to prevent tissue rejection having heightened the risk of infection. A second patient, Philip Blaiberg, operated on in January 1968, survived for 594 days. 📖 L E Leopold, *Christiaan Barnard: The Man with the Golden Hands* (1971)

Barnard, Edward Emerson 1857–1923
US astronomer

Born in Nashville, Tennessee, into a poor family, he had little education in his early years, but became experienced in photographic techniques during work in a portrait studio and developed a strong amateur interest in astronomy. After discovering a number of comets and becoming skilled in astronomical work, he became both a teacher and a student at the observatory of Vanderbilt University. He moved to Lick Observatory in 1887 and was appointed professor at Yerkes Observatory of the University of Chicago in 1895. Following a systematic photographic survey of the sky, he correctly concluded with **Maximilian Wolf** that those areas of the Milky Way which appear to be devoid of stars, or 'black nebulae', are in fact clouds of obscuring matter. His wide-ranging research included studies of novae, binary stars and variable stars. He discovered the fifth satellite of Jupiter (1892), later named Amalthea, and identified (1916) the star with the greatest known apparent motion across the sky, now known as Barnard's star. 📖 William Sheehan, *The Immortal Fire Within: The Life and Works of Edward Emerson Barnard* (1995)

Barnard, Frederick Augustus Porter 1809–89
US educator

Born in Sheffield, Massachusetts, he graduated from Yale then taught at the universities of Alabama and Mississippi. However, as an ardent Unionist he felt obliged to leave the South during the Civil War, and in 1864 he became president of Columbia College in New York City. During his 25 years there, he improved and expanded the school, making it into a major university. He believed in the importance of higher education for women, and Barnard College (Columbia's women's college) was named after him.

Barnard, Henry 1811–1900
US educationist

Born in Hartford, Connecticut, and educated at Yale, he became the first US Commissioner of Education (1867). He advocated centralization of school control and teacher training at the universities.

Barnard, Marjorie Faith 1897–1987
Australian novelist, critic, historian and biographer

Born in Sydney, she wrote many books in conjunction with Flora Eldershaw as 'M Barnard Eldershaw'. Best known are *A House is Built* (1929) and the anti-Utopian novel *Tomorrow and Tomorrow* (1947, eventually published in unexpurgated form as *Tomorrow and Tomorrow and Tomorrow*, 1983). Her historical writing includes *Macquarie's World* (1941) and the impressive and scholarly one-volume *A History of Australia* (1962). Her subsequent writings include two collections of short stories, biographies of convict-architect Francis Greenaway and Governor Lachlan Macquarie, and a critical study of her friend **Miles Franklin**. She won many prizes, including the **Patrick White** Literary Award in 1983. 📖 L E Rorabacher, *Marjorie Barnard and M. Barnard Eldershaw* (1973)

Barnardo, Thomas John 1845–1905
Irish doctor and philanthropist

Born in Dublin, he was the founder of homes for destitute children. A clerk by profession, he was converted to Christianity in 1862, and after a spell of preaching in the Dublin slums went to London (1866) to study medicine with the aim of becoming a medical missionary. Instead, he founded, while still a student, the East End Mission for destitute children in Stepney (1867) and a number of homes in Greater London, which came to be known as the 'Dr Barnardo's Homes'. The organization now flourishes under the name of Barnardos, and is the largest child-care charity working in the UK. 📖 Gillian Wagner, *Barnardo* (1979)

Barnato, Barney, *originally* Isaacs 1852–97
South African speculator

Born in London, England, he worked in Vaudeville and, following his brother, went out to Kimberley with a small circus in 1873. He made a fortune in diamonds there, but after engineering the Kaffir boom in mining stocks (1895) committed suicide at sea.

Barnave, Antoine 1761–93
French revolutionary

Born in Grenoble, he became a member of the new National Assembly (1789), and helped to carry through the Civil Constitution of the Clergy. He brought back the royal family from their abortive flight to Varennes (1791), but subsequently developed Royalist sympathies, advocated a constitutional monarchy, and was guillotined.

Barnes, Djuna 1892–1982
US novelist, poet and illustrator

Born in Cornwall-on-Hudson, New York, she began her career as a reporter and illustrator for magazines, then became a writer of one-act plays and short stories, published in a variety of magazines and anthologies. Her works, many of which she illustrated, range from the outstanding novel *Nightwood* (1936) to her verse play *The*

Antiphon (1958), both included in *Selected Works* (1962). Her literary style has been acclaimed by many critics, including T S Eliot. 📖 A Field, *The Formidable Miss Barnes* (1973)

Barnes, Dame (Alice) Josephine (Mary Taylor) 1912–
English obstetrician and gynaecologist

Born in Shorlingham, Norfolk, she read physiology at Lady Margaret Hall, Oxford, before completing her clinical training at University College Hospital, London (1937). After various obstetrics, gynaecology and surgery appointments in London and Oxford, she became deputy academic head of the Obstetric Unit of University College Hospital (1947–52), and surgeon to the Marie Curie Hospital (1947–67). She has served in many medical positions, such as in the Royal Society of Medicine, the British Medical Association (first woman president, 1979–80), the Royal College of Obstetricians and Gynaecologists, and the National Association of Family Planning Doctors. She has also served on many national and international committees, including the Royal Commission on Medical Education (1965–68), the Committee on the Working of the Abortion Act (1971–73), and the Advertising Standards Authority (1980–93). She has published extensively on obstetrics, gynaecology and family planning, and was created DBE in 1974.

Barnes, Julian Patrick 1946–
English novelist

He was born in Leicester. The crisp precision of his prose is partly explained by his having worked both as a journalist and as a lexicographer on the *Oxford English Dictionary Supplement*. His intellect, wit and love of France are reflected in his third novel, *Flaubert's Parrot* (1984), in which a retired English doctor discovers in the Museum of Rouen the stuffed parrot which was said to have stood upon Gustave Flaubert's desk during the writing of *Un Cœur Simple* in 1877. Later novels include *A History of the World in 10 Chapters* (1989), a confection of fictional narrative, philosophical deliberation and art criticism, *Talking It Over* (1991), and *The Porcupine* (1992). In 1996 he published his first collection of short stories, *Cross Channel*.

Barnes, Juliana See Berners, Juliana

Barnes, Peter 1931–
English dramatist and screenwriter

His only major commercial success has been *The Ruling Class* (1968), a play in which a madman inherits an earldom, believes he is God, and is only assumed to have been successfully rehabilitated when he delivers a rampagingly right-wing speech in a decrepit House of Lords. His other plays have not shared its success. They include *Sclerosis* (1965), *The Bewitched* (1974), *Laughter* (1978), *Red Noses* (1985), *Sunsets and Glories* (1990) and the screenplays *Enchanted April* (1991) and *Bye Bye Columbus* (1992).

Barnes, Thomas 1785–1841
English editor and journalist

Born in London, he was educated at Christ's Hospital and Pembroke College, Cambridge. In 1809 he became drama critic of *The Times*, and in 1817 he became the editor, a post which he held for 24 years. His leading principle was that a newspaper should not be a servant of the state but an independent means of its best development. He made *The Times* one of the most popular and respected newspapers in Great Britain.

Barnes, William 1801–86
English pastoral poet

Born in Rushay, near Sturminster Newton, Dorset, he worked in a solicitor's office, then founded his own school, first in Wiltshire and then in Dorchester. He went to St John's College, Cambridge, to take holy orders, then became curate of Whitcombe (1847) and rector of

Winterborne Came, Dorset (1862). Meanwhile he had become widely known and greatly admired for his idyllic poetry in the Dorset dialect. His three volumes of poetry were collected in 1879 as *Poems of Rural Life in the Dorset Dialect*. He also wrote several philological works, and some poetry in standard English. 📖 W D Jacobs, *William Barnes: Linguist* (1952)

Barnett, Samuel Augustus 1844–1913
English clergyman and social reformer

Born in Bristol and educated at Wadham College, Oxford, he went in 1873 to a Whitechapel parish where his interest in and sympathy with the poor of London were aroused. Discussions with Arnold Toynbee led Barnett to found (1884) Toynbee Hall in Whitechapel, London, in his memory. It became the first university settlement, for university men to live in close contact with their East End neighbours. He also took part in advocating other educational reforms, poor relief measures, and universal pensions. In 1894 he became canon of Bristol, and from 1906 was canon of Westminster.

Barneveldt, Jan van Olden 1547–1619
Dutch statesman and lawyer

He was born in Amersfoort. As adviser to Prince Maurice, he opposed his warlike schemes and in 1609 concluded a truce with Spain, which eventually resulted in his being considered as a secret ally of Spain. He was illegally arrested, condemned as a traitor, and executed.

Barney, Natalie Clifford 1876–1972
US poet, playwright, novelist, essayist, memoirist and epigrammatist

Born in Bar Harbor, Maine, she inherited vast wealth from her parents and, attracted by the artistic ambience and climate of moral freedom, relocated to Paris in 1902. She remained there until her death, setting up and presiding over a salon which became one of the most respected and influential of the day, frequented by Ezra Pound and other prominent artistic and literary figures. She is better known for her active and outspoken lesbianism than for her literary work, which is characteristically inaccessible. Her infrequent publications, mostly written in French, were printed by small publishing houses in limited editions, now out of print. She is now receiving more attention from feminist critics, in the light of her continual artistic struggle with the question of female experience. Among her published works is *The One Who is Legion, or AD's After-Life* (1930), an attempt to explore the western concept of the feminine.

Barns-Graham, Wilhelmina 1912–
Scottish painter

Born in St Andrews, Fife, and trained at Edinburgh College of Art, she moved to Cornwall in 1940, where she became involved with Penwith Society of Arts, working with Ben Nicholson and Barbara Hepworth. She also met the younger group of 'St Ives' artists, including Roger Hilton and the writer David Lewis, whom she married in 1949. Her work in the 1960s and 1970s branched from the figurative to the abstract, with the square becoming the predominant motif. In 1973 she returned to St Andrews, and in later years generally painted large watercolours and gouaches in brilliant colour.

Barnsley, Edward 1900–87
English furniture designer

Born in Pinbury, Gloucestershire, he was the son of Sidney Barnsley (1865–1926) who formed Kenton & Co with Ernest Gimson in 1890. He took over the furniture workshops of Geoffrey Lupton in Foxfield, Hampshire, in 1919 and made furniture in the same manner as his father and Gimson. In 1937 he succeeded Peter Waals as design adviser to Loughborough Training College, and in 1945 he was appointed consultant to the Rural Industries Bureau.

Barnum, Phineas Taylor 1810–91
US showman

Born in Bethel, Connecticut, he began his career of entertaining and deluding an eager public with the exhibition of an elderly former slave billed as the 160-year-old nurse of **George Washington**. From 1841 he ran Barnum's American Museum in New York City, exhibiting such curiosities as the Fiji mermaid and the dwarf 'General Tom Thumb' (**Charles Stratton**) and promoting them with flamboyant publicity. He managed the US tour of Swedish singer **Jenny Lind** (1850), and after dabbling in Connecticut politics he opened in 1871 a three-ring touring circus that he called the 'Greatest Show on Earth'. In 1881 he joined with his rival James Anthony Bailey (1847–1906) to found the famous Barnum and Bailey Circus. ▭ Neil Harris, *Humbug: The Art of P T Barnum* (1973)

Barocci or Baroccio, Federico 1528–1612
Italian painter

Born in Urbino, he went to Rome in 1548 and was influenced by **Correggio**. He later developed a very personal colour scheme of vivid reds and yellows, and his fluent pictorial style influenced **Rubens** and his school. His *Madonna del Popolo* (1575–79) is in the Uffizi Gallery, Florence, and his *Christ Crucified* in Genoa Cathedral.

Baroja y Nessi, Pío 1872–1956
Spanish writer

Born in San Sebastian, he studied medicine and practised in a northern Spanish village before working in the family bakery in Madrid. His work is distinguished by an often violent humour and a vivid style in part derived from 19th-century Russian and French writers. He wrote more than 70 volumes of novels and essays, including *La Lucha por la vida* (1904, Eng trans *The Struggle for Life*, 1922–24), a trilogy, and *Memorias de un hombre de acción* (1913–28, 'Memories of a Man of Action'), a set of 14 novels. He exercised a substantial influence upon his successors, in particular **Camilo José Cela**. ▭ B P Patt, *Pió Baroja* (1971)

Baron, Salo Wittmayer 1895–1989
US educator and historian

Born in Tarnow, Galicia (now in Austria), he was the first Professor of Jewish History in the USA, and taught at Columbia University from 1930 to 1963. Among his works are *The Jewish Community* (3 vols, 1942) and *A Social and Religious History of the Jews* (27 vols, 1952–80).

Barr, Archibald 1855–1931
Scottish engineer

Born near Paisley, Renfrewshire, he graduated from Glasgow University as an engineering apprentice. He was Professor of Civil and Mechanical Engineering at Leeds (1884–89), then succeeded his teacher, **James Thomson**, in the regius chair of civil engineering at Glasgow. He set up the James Watt research laboratories in 1900 and with **William Stroud** founded the firm of scientific instrument makers who were pioneers of naval range-finding, later inventing height finders for anti-aircraft artillery.

Barr, Roseanne See Roseanne

Barras, Paul François Jean Nicolas, Comte de 1755–1829
French revolutionary

He was born in Fox-Amphoux. An original member of the Jacobin Club, he was chiefly responsible for the overthrow of **Robespierre**, and was given dictatorial powers by the National Convention. In 1795, acting against a Royalist uprising, he was aided by his young friend Napoleon Bonaparte (later **Napoleon I**), who fired on the rebels (the historical 'whiff of grapeshot'). Barras became

one of the five members of the Directory (1795). Once more dictator in 1797, he guided the state almost alone, until his hedonism and corruption made him so unpopular that Napoleon overthrew him easily (1799). ▭ J Vivent, *Barras, Le Roi de la République* (1938)

Barrault, Jean-Louis 1910–94
French actor and producer

Born in Le Vesinet, he made his Paris stage debut in *Volpone* (1931). A member of the Comédie-Française (1940–46), he formed the Compagnie Renaud-Barrault with his actress wife Madeleine Renaud (1903–94). Director of the Théâtre de France (1959–68), Théâtre des Nations (1965–67, 1972–74) and the Théâtre d'Orsay (1974–81), he was renowned for a sensitive, poetic style of acting that included a fluidity born of his training in mime with Étienne Decroux. He made his film debut in *Les Beaux jours* (1935) and gave significant performances in *Drole de drame* (1937), *Les Enfants du Paradis* (1945, 'The Children of Paradise'), *La Ronde* (1950) and *La Nuit de Varennes* (1981). The actress Marie-Christine Barrault (1944–) is his niece. He published an autobiography, *Reflections on Theatre*, in 1951, and a volume of memoirs in 1974 entitled *Memories for Tommorrow*. ▭ Anne Germain, *Renaud-Barrault: les feux de la rampe et de l'amour* (1992)

Barre, Mohamed Siad 1919–
Somali soldier and politician

Educated locally and at an Italian military academy, he was a police officer in Somaliland, under both Italian and British trusteeship, before joining the Somali army in 1960. He led a successful coup in 1969. Using a KGB-trained secret service and manipulating the clan divisions of the Somalis, he was backed first by the USSR and then by the USA. When uprisings took place in 1989, he used the air force and army in an attempt to stamp out the opposition, but was unsuccessful. Forced to leave Mogadishu in 1991, he left behind an impoverished country divided into competing warring factions. In 1992 US troops attempted to restore order in Somalia; however two years later they were forced to pull out, leaving the country in chaos.

Barre, Raymond 1924–
French conservative politician

Born in St Denis on the French dependency of Réunion, he made his reputation as an influential neo-liberal economist at the Sorbonne and as vice-president of the European Commission (1967–72). He was Minister of Foreign Trade under President **Giscard d'Estaing** and was appointed Prime Minister (1976–81) after the resignation of **Jacques Chirac** in 1976. Holding concurrently the Finance Ministry portfolio, he concentrated on economic affairs, gaining a reputation as a determined budget-cutter. With unemployment mounting between 1976 and 1981, he became deeply unpopular, but his term as Prime Minister was later favourably reassessed after the failure of the 1981–83 socialist administration's reflationary experiment. During the 1980s he built up a firm political base in the Lyons region, representing the centre-right Union for French Democracy (UDF). He contested the 1988 presidential election but was eliminated in the first ballot. ▭ Henri Amouroux, *Monsieur Barre* (1986)

Barrès, (Auguste) Maurice 1862–1923
French novelist and politician

He was born in Charmes-sur-Moselle. A member of the Chamber of Deputies (1889–93), he was an apostle of nationalism, individualism, provincial patriotism and national energy. He wrote a trilogy on his own self-analysis (*Le Culte du Moi*, 1888–91, 'The Cult of the Self'), a nationalistic trilogy that included *L'Appel au soldat* (1906,

'The Call to the Soldier'), and many other works, including *Colette Baudoche* (1909, Eng trans 1918). ⌑ F Mauriac, *La rencontre avec Barrès* (1945)

Barrie, J M, *properly* Sir James Matthew Barrie
1860–1937
Scottish novelist and dramatist

Born in Kirriemuir, Angus, the son of a weaver, he graduated from Edinburgh University in 1882, then settled in London and became a regular contributor to the *St James's Gazette* and *British Weekly* (as 'Gavin Ogilvy'). He wrote a series of autobiographical prose works, including *The Little Minister* (1891, dramatized 1897), set in his native village disguised as 'Thrums'. From 1890 he wrote for the theatre. Works like the successful *Walker, London* (1892), and *The Admirable Crichton* (1902), a good-humoured social satire, established his reputation, but it is as the creator of *Peter Pan* (1904) that he will be chiefly remembered. Aware of the popular demand for dramatic sentimentality on the London stage, Barrie provided surface romance within dramatic structures which indirectly suggested a bleaker vision of life. He continued his excursions into fairyland in later plays such as *Dear Brutus* (1917) and *Mary Rose* (1920). His last play, *The Boy David* (1936), tried a biblical theme, but despite containing some of his finest writing won no laurels in the theatre. ⌑ Harry Geduld, *J M Barrie* (1971); J Dunbar, *Barrie: the man behind the image* (1970)

Barrington, George, *originally* George Waldron
1755–1804
Irish writer and adventurer

He was born in Maynooth, County Kildare, the son of a silversmith. In London he turned to pickpocketing, and in 1790 he was transported to Botany Bay, Australia. He was set free in 1792, and rose to the position of High Constable of Parramatta, New South Wales. He wrote historical works on Australia.

Barrington, Sir Jonah 1760–1834
Irish judge, politician and writer

Born in Abbeyleix into the Protestant episcopalian ascendancy, and educated at Trinity College, Dublin, he was called to the Irish Bar in 1788. He became MP for various constituencies, obtained an Admiralty Court judgeship in 1798, and refused to vote for the union of Irish and British parliaments despite the tempting offer of a lucrative job. He became involved in intricate political manoeuvres and was gradually overwhelmed by debts for which he pilfered court funds (1805–10), which resulted in his disgrace and dismissal in 1830. Settling in France, he produced *The Rise and Fall of the Irish Nation* (1833), largely based on his earlier *Historic Anecdotes and Secret Memoirs of the Legislative Union between Great Britain and Ireland* (1809), and *Personal Sketches of his own Time* (3 vols, 1827–32).

Barrios, Edourdo 1884–1963
Chilean novelist and dramatist

Born in Valparaíso, of a Chilean father and a Peruvian mother, he worked variously as a weight-lifter, officer cadet, nitrate company accountant, academic and acrobat, and served as Minister of Education during the dictatorship of Ibáñez del Campo. He was one of the earliest psychological novelists of South America, and his *El niño que enloqueció de amor* (1915, 'The Boy Who Went Mad for Love') is often cited as the first novel of this kind. *El hermano asno* (1922, Eng trans as *Brother Ass* in *Fiesta in November*, 1942) is often taken to be his best novel, while his attempt at a major novel, *Gran señor y rajadiablos* (1948, 'Gentleman and Hell Raiser'), has not outlasted its initial popularity. ⌑ N J Davison, *Edourdo Barrios* (1970)

Barron, Clarence Walker 1855–1928
US editor and publisher

Born in Boston, he began his career in journalism with the *Boston Evening Transcript*. He founded the Boston News Bureau (1887) and the Philadelphia News Bureau (1897) to give businessmen reliable financial information. In 1901, when he bought Dow Jones and Co, he became publisher of the *Wall Street Journal*, which he augmented with *Barron's National Business and Financial Weekly* (1921).

Barros, João de 1496–1570
Portuguese historian

Born in Viseu, he became Governor of Portuguese Guinea and is known for his monumental *Decades* (1552–1615), the history of the Portuguese in the East Indies.

Barrow, Clyde 1909–34
US thief and murderer

Born in Texas, he was the partner of **Bonnie Parker**. Despite their popular romantic image, they and their gang were responsible for a number of murders. The pair met in 1932. When Barrow first visited Parker's house, he was arrested on seven counts of burglary and car theft. He was convicted and sentenced to two years in jail. Parker smuggled a gun to him and he escaped. Recaptured a few days later after robbing a railway office, he was sentenced to 14 years imprisonment. He persuaded a fellow-prisoner to chop off two of his toes and was subsequently released. With their gang, Parker and Barrow continued to rob and murder until they were shot dead at a police roadblock in Louisiana in May 1934. Their end was predicted by Parker in a poem, variously called *The Story of Bonnie and Clyde* and *The Story of Suicide Sal*.

Barrow, Errol Walton 1920–87
Barbadian politician

Born in Barbados, he flew in the RAF (1940–47), then studied at London University and Lincoln's Inn. Returning to Barbados, he became active in the Barbados Labour Party (BLP) and was elected to the House of Assembly in 1951. In 1955 he left the BLP and co-founded the Democratic Labour Party (DLP), becoming its chairman in 1958. In the elections following independence in 1961 the DLP was victorious and Barrow became the first Prime Minister. His unbroken tenure was ended in 1976 by the BLP, led by 'Tom' Adams. In 1986, a year after Adams's death, Barrow returned to power with a decisive majority but he died the following year and was succeeded by Erskine Lloyd Sandiford.

Barrow, Isaac 1630–77
English mathematician and divine

Born in London, he was educated at Charterhouse and Trinity College, Cambridge, where he was elected a Fellow in 1649. He travelled abroad (1655–59), became Professor of Geometry at Gresham College, London (1662), and the first Lucasian Professor of Mathematics at Cambridge (1663), but he resigned in 1669 to become royal chaplain. He founded the library of Trinity College, Cambridge, when he became Master in 1673. Barrow published Latin versions of **Euclid** and **Archimedes**, and lectures on optics, as well as extensive theological works and sermons. In his original work in mathematics he anticipated aspects of the theories of differential calculus, which began to develop at the end of the 17th century.

Barrow, Sir John 1764–1848
English naval administrator and traveller

Born in Dragley Beck, Morecambe Bay, Lancashire, he was educated at Ulverston school, worked at a Liverpool iron-foundry, and worked on a whaler in Greenland waters (1781). He then taught mathematics at a school in Greenwich, and in 1792 was appointed private secretary to Lord **Macartney**, the British envoy to China, accompanying him to Cape Colony, South Africa in 1797. Barrow wrote about his experiences in these countries in *Travels in China* (1804) and *Account of Travels into the Interior of*

Southern Africa (2 vols, 1801–04). He was appointed second secretary to the Admiralty (1804–45), he promoted Arctic expeditions by Sir John Ross, Sir James Clark Ross and Sir John Franklin, and was a founder and vice-president of the (Royal) Geographical Society (1830). Barrow Strait and Point Barrow in the Arctic, and Cape Barrow in the Antarctic, were named in his honour, as was the northern duck, Barrow's Goldeneye.

Barr Smith, Robert 1824–1915
Australian businessman

Born in Renfrewshire, Scotland, and educated at Glasgow University, he settled in South Australia in 1854. There he joined the company established by a fellow Scot, Thomas Elder, whose sister Joanna he later married. The two men went into partnership as Elder, Smith & Co and became one of the world's largest woolbrokers with extensive pastoral holdings. Barr Smith, as well as being a woolbroking pioneer, built up considerable interests in mining, shipping and finance, and helped found the Bank of Adelaide. Closely involved for many years with Adelaide University, he established the library there which bears his name, and made philanthropic gifts to State and Church. The pastoral interests established by the company are still maintained, after many mergers, in the name of Elders IXL, the brewing giant.

Barry, Sir Charles 1795–1860
English architect

Born in London and educated privately, he was apprenticed to a firm of surveyors before going to Italy (1817–20). On his return, he designed the Travellers' Club (1831), the Manchester Athenaeum (1836), the Reform Club (1837), and the new Palace of Westminster (1840), completed after his death by his son Edward Middleton Barry (1830–80). His work showed the influence of the Italian Renaissance. His fifth son, Sir John Wolfe-Barry (1836–1918), was engineer of the Tower Bridge and Barry Docks.

Barry, Elizabeth 1658–1713
English actress

Her patron was the Earl of Rochester and her many roles included the chief characters in the plays of Thomas Otway and William Congreve.

Barry, James 1741–1806
Irish historical painter

Born in Cork, he was the son of a shipmaster. A protégé of Edmund Burke, he studied in Italy (1766–70), and in 1782 he was appointed Professor of Painting at the Royal Academy, from which his irritable temper brought about his expulsion (1799). His most celebrated paintings are *Adam and Eve* (1771) and *Venus Rising from the Waves* (1772). He decorated the Great Room of the Society of Arts with a series of pictures illustrating human progress.

Barry, Marie Jeanne, Comtesse du, *née* Bécu 1741–93
French courtesan

Born in Vaucouleurs, the illegitimate daughter of a dressmaker, she was introduced to society as Mademoiselle Lange by her lover, Jean du Barry. She married Jean's brother, Comte Guillaume du Barry, and became the official mistress of Louis XV. She wielded much influence, helped to bring about the downfall of the Finance Minister, the Duc de Choiseul (1770), and was notorious for her extravagance, though she was a generous patron of the arts. She was banished from court after Louis's death (1774), and was guillotined during the French Revolution.

Barry, Philip 1896–1949
US dramatist

Born in Rochester, New York, he enjoyed success with his first professional production, *You and I* (1923). He is now remembered for such plays as *The Philadelphia Story* (1939), a bright comedy of manners which was a hit for the actress Katharine Hepburn. *Holiday* (1929) and *The Animal Kingdom* (1932) contain sharper satire but are still, at heart, affectionate comedies. His genuinely more serious work, including the psychological dramas, *Hotel Universe* (1930) and *Here Come the Clowns* (1938), were not as successful.

Barry, Spranger 1719–77
Irish actor

He was born in Dublin, where he made his debut (1744). He moved to London (1746) and became a great rival of David Garrick. In 1768 he married the actress Mrs Ann Dancer (*née* Street, 1734–1801).

Barrymore, Ethel 1879–1959
US actress

She was born in Philadelphia, the daughter of the actor-playwright Maurice Barrymore and the actress Georgiana Drew Barrymore. In 1897–98 she scored a great success in London with Sir Henry Irving in *The Bells*. Other noteworthy appearances were in *Trelawney of the Wells* (1911), *The Second Mrs Tanqueray* (1924), *Whiteoaks* (1938) and *The Corn is Green* (1942). Her film appearances include *Rasputin and the Empress* (1932), the only production in which she and her brothers, Lionel Barrymore and John Barrymore, appeared together, and *None But the Lonely Heart* (1944, Academy Award, Best Supporting Actress). She also appeared on radio and television. ▢ Hollis Alpert, *The Barrymores* (1964)

Barrymore, John 1882–1942
US actor

He was born in Philadelphia. He spent some time studying art, but eventually returned to the family profession, making his name in Shakespearean roles, his *Hamlet* being particularly famous. He also appeared in many films. His classical nose and distinguished features won for him the nickname of 'The Great Profile', the name of the last film in which he appeared (1940), but his screen appearances never fully reflected his talents. John was the younger brother of Ethel Barrymore and Lionel Barrymore. ▢ Hollis Alpert, *The Barrymores* (1964)

Barrymore, Lionel 1878–1954
US actor

He was born in Philadelphia. He appeared in small parts in the early films of D W Griffith before making his name in Gerald du Maurier's *Peter Ibbetson* (1917) and in *The Copperhead* (1918). He subsequently took many roles in films and radio plays, notably *A Free Soul* (1931, Academy Award for Best Actor), *Grand Hotel*, *David Copperfield*, *Dinner at Eight*, *Captains Courageous* and *Duel in the Sun*. For a short time he was a director with MGM. After twice accidentally breaking a hip he was confined to a wheelchair, but continued to act, playing Dr Gillespie in the original *Dr Kildare* film series with great success. He also had etchings exhibited and was a talented musician, musical arranger and composer. The elder brother of Ethel Barrymore and John Barrymore, he wrote *We Barrymores* (1951). ▢ Hollis Alpert, *The Barrymores* (1964)

Barsanti, Francesco 1690–1775
Italian composer and performer

Born in Lucca, he went in 1714 to London, where he played flute then oboe with the Italian Opera. In Edinburgh from 1742, he became prominent both as a performer and composer, and published *A Collection of Old Scots Tunes* (1742). He wrote flute and violin sonatas, concerti grossi, an overture and other chamber works.

Barstow, Stan(ley) 1928–
English novelist

Born in Yorkshire into a mining community that provided much material for his fiction, he achieved a major success with his first novel, *A Kind of Loving* (1960), which later grew into a trilogy about its working-class protagonist, with *The Watchers on the Shore* (1966) and *The Right True End* (1976). His novels, which are firmly based on the difficulties of everyday experience, include *Joby* (1964), a delicate evocation of childhood trauma, *A Raging Calm* (1968), *Just You Wait and See* (1986), *Give Us This Day* (1989), *Next of Kin* (1991) and *In My Own Good Time* (1996). He has also written short novels, stories, and plays for theatre, radio and television.

Bart, Jean See Barth, Jean

Bart, Lionel 1930–
English composer and lyricist
He was born in London. In 1959 his *Lock Up Your Daughters*, a musical based upon **Henry Fielding**'s 1730 play, *Rape upon Rape*, ended the US domination of the musical theatre in London. He followed it with *Fings Ain't Wot They Used T'be* (1959), *Oliver* (1960, adapted from **Dickens**'s *Oliver Twist*) and *Blitz!* (1962), a cavalcade of East End life during World War II. *Maggie May*, a between-the-wars story of a Liverpool prostitute, followed in 1964, but his Robin Hood musical, *Twang!* (1965), was a flop, as was *La Strada* (1969). 📖 David Roper, *Bart!: The Unauthorized Life and Times Ins and Outs Ups and Downs of Lionel Bart* (1994)

Barth, Heinrich 1821–65
German explorer
He was born in Hamburg, and after studying archaeology at Berlin, was appointed by the British government to a mission to central Africa to suppress slavery (1849). He continued his explorations on his own, which extended to Adamáwa in the south, and from Bagirmi in the east to Timbuktu in the west, nearly 12,000 miles (19,320km), which he described in *Travels and Discoveries in Central Africa* (5 vols, 1857–58). He was later appointed Professor of Geography at Berlin University.

Barth or Bart, Jean 1651–1702
French privateer
Born in Dunkirk, he served first in the Dutch navy under **Michiel de Ruyter**, but on the outbreak of war with Holland (1672) joined the French service. In 1691, in command of a small squadron in the North Sea, he destroyed many English vessels. In 1694, after a desperate struggle with a superior Dutch fleet, he recaptured a convoy of 96 ships and took them to Dunkirk. Soon after he was taken prisoner but escaped from Plymouth to France where **Louis XIV** received him at Versailles, and in 1697 appointed him to the command of a squadron. 📖 Jacques Duquesne, *Jean Bart* (1986)

Barth, John Simmons 1930–
US novelist and short-story writer
Born in Cambridge, Maryland, he was educated at Johns Hopkins University, and was a professional drummer before turning to literature and teaching. His earliest novels—*The Floating Opera* (1956), *End of the Road* (1958), *The Sot-Weed Factor* (1960) and *Giles Goat-Boy* (1966)—combined realism, formidable learning and fantastic humour in an attempt to make 'a transcension of the antithesis between the modern and the pre-modern which would revitalize fiction'. His later novels, *Letters* (1979), *Sabbatical* (1982), *Tidewater Tales* (1988) and *The Last Voyage of Somebody the Sailor* (1991), are prolix and less assured. Since 1991, he has been professor emeritus at Johns Hopkins University. 📖 C B Harris, *Passionate Virtuosity: the fiction of Barth* (1983)

Barth, Karl 1886–1968
Swiss theologian

He was born in Basle, and studied at Berne, Berlin, Tübingen and Marburg. Whilst pastor at Safenwil, Aargau, he wrote a commentary of St Paul's epistle to the Romans (1919) which established his theological reputation. He became professor at Göttingen (1921), Münster (1925) and Bonn (1930), refused to take an unconditional oath to **Hitler**, was dismissed and became professor at Basle (1935–62). He played a leading role in the German Confessing Church and Barmen Declaration (1934). His theology begins with the realization of human wickedness, the principal sin being man's endeavour to make himself, rather than God, the centre of the world, and re-emphasized God's unquestionable authority and 'otherness'. However Barth was criticized on the grounds that his own reasoned exposition of antiphilosophical theology itself constitutes philosophy and that he prescribed belief in a divinity which failed to explain the nature of humanity. His many works include *Knowledge of God and the Service of God* (1938) and the monumental *Church Dogmatics* (1932–67). 📖 J S Bowden, *Karl Barth* (1971)

Barthélemy Saint-Hilaire, Jules 1805–95
French scholar and politician
Born in Paris, he was co-founder of the journal *Le Bon sens* (1830), became professor at the Collège de France, and produced a 35-volume translation of **Aristotle** (1833–95), as well as various writings on Indian philosophy. He became a member of the Chamber of Deputies in 1848, and was Foreign Minister from 1880 to 1881.

Barthelme, Donald 1931–89
US novelist and short-story writer
Born in Philadelphia, Pennsylvania, he worked as a journalist and magazine editor before turning to fiction. An experimentalist who rejected the traditions of the conventional novel form and was inventive in his use of language, he was associated with the mid-1960s avant-garde. The short stories in *Come Back, Dr Caligari* (1964) and *Unspeakable Practices, Unnatural Acts* (1968) are regarded as his most characteristic work. Other collections include *City Life* (1970) and *Sadness* (1972), and share the broader humour of his novels *Snow White* (1967) and *The Dead Father* (1975). He won the National Book award in 1972. He was the brother of the novelist Frederick Barthelme (1943–). 📖 M Couturier and R Durand, *Barthelme* (1982)

Barthes, Roland 1915–80
French writer, critic and teacher
He was born in Cherbourg, and after researching and teaching he began to write. His collection of essays entitled *Le Degré zéro de l'écriture* (1953, Eng trans *Writing Degree Zero*, 1967) immediately established him as France's leading critic of Modernist literature. His literary criticism avoided the traditional value judgements and investigation of the author's intentions, addressing itself instead to analysis of the text as a system of signs or symbols whose underlying structure and interconnections form the 'meaning' of the work as a whole. Despite criticism from more traditional scholars he continued with this method and produced *Mythologies* (1957), a semiological exploration of such diverse cultural phenomena as wrestling, children's toys and film stars' faces. Though influenced by Marxism, **Sigmund Freud**, Existentialism and Structuralism, he remained a versatile individualist and a fierce critic of what he saw as stale and oppressive bourgeois thinking. For 16 years he was a member of the faculty of the École Pratique des Hautes Études in Paris, and from 1976 he was Professor of Literary Semiology at the Collège de France. He continued to produce witty and thought-provoking books, including an imaginative autobiography, *Roland Barthes by Roland Barthes*. He gained international recognition as a developer of semiology and Structuralism.

Bartholdi, (Frédéric) Auguste 1834–1904
French sculptor

He was born in Colmar, Alsace, and specialized in enormous monuments, such as the red sandstone *Lion of Belfort* (1880, Belfort) and the colossal bronze *Statue of Liberty* on Bedloe's Island, New York Harbour. Unveiled in 1886, it was a present to the USA from the French Republic.

Bartholin, Caspar, the Elder, *Latin* Bartholinus, *originally* Caspar Berthelsen 1585–1629
Danish physician

Born in Malmö, Sweden, he studied at Copenhagen, Basle and at Padua, refused professorships in philosophy, anatomy, and Greek, but accepted one in medicine at Copenhagen University (1613) and in theology there (1624). He was the first to describe the functions of the olfactory nerve, and was the author of *Anatomicae Institutiones Corporis Humani* (1611, 'Textbook of Human Anatomy'), for long the received textbook of anatomy. He was the father of Thomas Bartholin, the Elder, and Erasmus Bartholin.

Bartholin, Caspar, the Younger 1655–1738
Danish anatomist

Born in Copenhagen, the son of Thomas Bartholin, the Elder, he studied medicine in Holland and France, and became an expert anatomist. He was the first to describe the greater vestibular glands in the female reproductive system ('Bartholin's glands') and the larger salivatory duct of the sublingual gland ('Bartholin's duct').

Bartholin, Erasmus 1625–98
Danish physician, physicist and mathematician

The son of Caspar Bartholin, the Elder, and brother of Thomas Bartholin, the Elder, he studied medicine at the universities of Leyden in the Netherlands and Padua in Italy. He was appointed Professor of Medicine and Mathematics at Copenhagen University in 1656. In 1669 he discovered that when an object is viewed through Iceland feldspar (calcite), a double image is produced, but he was unable to explain this. Christiaan Huygens, Isaac Newton and Augustin Fresnel all contributed to the explanation of the phenomenon of double refraction, which is basic to the understanding of polarization.

Bartholin, Thomas, the Elder, *Latin* Bartholinus 1616–80
Danish physician and mathematician

He was the son of Caspar Bartholin, the Elder, and father of Caspar Bartholin, the Younger and Thomas Bartholin, the Younger. A fine mathematician and experimental physiologist, he was the first to describe the human lymphatic system, which he studied independently of Olof Rudbeck, and he defended the theory of blood circulation introduced by William Harvey. He was Professor of Mathematics at Copenhagen University (1646–48), then of Anatomy (1648–61). As personal physician to King Kristian V of Denmark, Bartholin was of great importance in the reform of the Danish medical system and medical education. He produced the first Danish pharmacopoeia, established the first Danish scientific journal, and wrote numerous literary, philosophical and historical works.

Bartholin, Thomas, the Younger 1659–90
Danish antiquary

The son of Thomas Bartholin, the Elder, he became professor designatus at the age of only 18, and was appointed royal antiquary in 1684 at the age of 25, his task being to seek out and study old manuscripts in Iceland for the Royal Library. In 1688, with the help of his young assistant, the Icelandic antiquary and manuscript-collector

Árni Magnússon (1663–1730), he published a notable work on early Nordic history, *Danicarum...libri tres* ('Three Books...of Danish Antiquities').

Bartholomé, Paul Albert 1848–1928
French sculptor

He was born in Thiverval, and is best known for the group of statuary inspired by his wife's death, *Aux morts* (1895, Père Lachaise Cemetery), and for the monument to Jean Jacques Rousseau in the Panthéon, Paris. His work was academic in style.

Bartholomew 1st century AD
One of the 12 Apostles of Jesus Christ

Little is known of his family, but his name is linked with St Philip's in all but one list of the Apostles in the Gospels. He is often considered identical with Nathaniel of Cana. If this is correct, Jesus Christ described him as 'a true Israelite in whom there is nothing false'. According to Erebius in his *Church History*, Bartholomew had left behind the Hebrew Gospel according to St Matthew in India. He is reported to have worked as a missionary in Ethiopia and in Mesopotamia, where traditional holds that he was martyred. His feast day is 24 August.

Bartholomew, John George 1860–1920
Scottish cartographer

Born in Edinburgh, he was the son of John Bartholomew (1831–93), map engraver and publisher. After graduating from Edinburgh University he joined his father's firm, and published the *Survey Atlas of Scotland* (1895–1912), followed by a similar atlas of England and Wales, a *Physical Atlas of the World* (2 vols, 1889–1911), and *The Times Survey Atlas of the World*, which appeared (1921) after his death. He is best known for his system of layer colouring of contours.

Barthou, Jean Louis 1862–1934
French politician

Born in Oloron-Sainte-Marie, he practised law and after several ministerial appointments became Prime Minister in 1913, when he introduced three-year conscription. He held several Cabinet posts during World War I, was Minister of Justice (1922, 1926, 1928) and president of the Reparations Committee. As Foreign Minister in 1934, he attempted to negotiate an Eastern 'Locarno' Treaty, to strengthen French links with the states of Eastern Europe against the threat from Germany. He invited King Alexander I of Yugoslavia to France, and was assassinated with him in Marseilles by Croatian terrorists.

Bartlett, Sir Frederic C(harles) 1886–1969
English psychologist

He was born in Stow-on-the-Wold, Gloucestershire. Professor of Experimental Psychology at Cambridge (1931–52), he wrote on practical (ergonomic) problems in applied psychology, and devised tests for servicemen in World War II. He is perhaps best known for his pioneering 'cognitive' approach to understanding human memory, which emphasized 'meaning' rather than the formation of simple associations. His chief works were *Psychology and Primitive Culture* (1923), *Remembering: A Study in Experimental and Social Psychology* (1932), *The Problem of Noise* (1934) and *Thinking* (1958).

Bartlett, John 1820–1905
US bookseller

Born in Plymouth, Massachusetts, he was for many years the owner of the University Book Store at Harvard (1849–63). He compiled *Bartlett's Familiar Quotations* (1855) and also published a *Complete Concordance to Shakespeare's Dramatic Works and Poems* (1894).

Bartlett, Neil 1932–
English chemist

Bartók, Béla 1881–1945
Hungarian composer

Béla Bartók was born in Nagyszentmiklós (now Sînnicolau Mare, Romania). He learned to play the piano mainly from his mother and first appeared in public in 1892. Among his teachers was István Thomán, a former pupil of **Liszt**. He toured widely as a pianist. His early compositions display the influence of Liszt and **Robert Wagner** and later of **Strauss** and **Claude Debussy**. He was inspired most of all, however, by Hungarian folksongs, which he collected and studied widely from 1904, later in association with his fellow musician **Zoltán Kodály**; their researches were extended to Slovak, Romanian, Balkan and Near-Eastern melodies. Bartók was Professor of Piano at the Budapest Academy from 1907 to 1934.

The spread of Fascism and the events of the 1930s made it impossible for him to remain in central Europe. After his mother's death in 1939, he left Hungary and settled in the USA. He worked at the classification of Yugoslav folk music held at Harvard, and on his collection of Romanian melodies. His health declined from 1942 and, although he recovered to achieve a number of major works and had hopes of returning home at the end of World War II, he died in New York three years later.

♫ Bartók was one of the foremost composers of the first half of the 20th century. His principal works are the opera *Duke Bluebeard's Castle*; the ballets *The Wooden Prince* and *The Miraculous Mandarin*; two violin concertos and three piano concertos; orchestral music including the *Concerto for Orchestra*; chamber music including six string quartets and the *Sonata for 2 pianos and percussion*; works for violin and piano; an important corpus of piano music; and some songs, choruses and folk-song arrangements.

📖 Elliot Antokoletz, *The Music of Béla Bartók* (1984); Halsey Stevens, *The Life and Music of Béla Bartók* (rev edn 1964).

> 'I cannot conceive of music that expresses absolutely nothing.' Quoted in Machlis, *Introduction to Contemporary Music* (1963).

Born in Newcastle upon Tyne, he was educated at the University of Durham before taking up an academic appointment at the University of British Columbia in Canada in 1958. From 1966 to 1969 he worked at the Bell Telephone Laboratories, New Jersey, became Professor of Chemistry at the University of California at Berkeley (1969–94), then emeritus. He is famous for his discovery in 1962 of the first chemical compound of the noble gas xenon, thus disproving the supposition that noble gas compounds do not exist. He was elected FRS in 1973, and won the Chemical Society Corday–Morgan Medal (1962) and the American Chemical Society award for Distinguished Service to Inorganic Chemistry (1989).

Bartók, Béla See panel above

Bartolini, Lorenzo 1777–1850
Italian sculptor
He was born in Vernio, Tuscany. The best of his works, in the Neoclassical manner, are *Charity*, *Machiavelli*, and the Demidov monument, and his busts of Madame de Staël, **Byron** and **Franz Liszt**.

Bartolommeo, Fra, *real name* **Baccio della Porta**
1475–1517
Italian painter
Born near Florence, he was a pupil of Cosimo di Rosselli (1439–1507), in whose studio he met Mariotto Albertinelli (1474–1515), with whom he later often collaborated. Under the influence of **Savonarola** he publicly burned many of his paintings and in 1500 became a Dominican novice, but **Raphael's** visit to Florence in 1504 encouraged him to take up painting again, and they became close friends, helping one another with their work. He worked in Venice (1507) and then in Florence (c.1509–1512) before going to Rome. Overwhelmed by the work of Raphael in the Vatican apartments and **Michelangelo** in the Sistine Chapel, he refused all entreaties to collaborate with them. His work is distinguished by controlled composition and delicate drawing and use of colour. His later work is inferior. Most of his work is still in Florence, but there is a notable *Annunciation* by him in the Louvre.

Bartolozzi, Francesco 1727–1815
Italian engraver
Born in Florence, he settled in London to become engraver to **George III**. There he produced exquisite line engravings such as *The Silence* and *Clytie*. In 1769, on the formation of the Royal Academy in London, he was nominated a member, and from a design by his friend **Giambattista Cipriani**, executed the diploma that is still in use. In 1802 he became superintendent of the Royal Academy of Engravers in Lisbon. His prints, said to be more numerous than those of any engraver, include line engravings and stippled works, printed in brown and 'Bartolozzi red'.

Bartolus, *also called* **Bartolo di Sassoferrato**
c.1314–1357
Italian judge and jurist
Born in Venatura, Sassoferrato, near Ancona, he studied law at the universities of Perugia and Bologna. A professor at Pisa and Perugia, he was the leader of the school of commentators on the Roman law whose aim was to isolate general principles which could be used to solve contemporary problems. His opinion as an expert on Roman laws was highly regarded, and he was also a founder of international private law, distinguishing 'real' statutes which applied to foreigners from 'personal' statutes which did not. His extensive writings include *Commentarius in Tria Digesta*, *Commentarius in libros IX Codicis priores*, *Commentarius super libris III posterioribus Codicis*, *Lectura super Authenticis*, and opinions given on particular cases.

Barton, Clara (Clarissa Harlowe) 1821–1912
US founder of the US Red Cross
Born in Oxford, Massachusetts, she was a schoolteacher from 1836 to 1854, worked in the Patent Office in Washington DC (1854–57), and during the Civil War (1861–65) helped to obtain and distribute supplies and comforts for the wounded. In Europe for health reasons (1869–73), she worked for the International Red Cross in the Franco-Prussian War (1870–71). Back in the USA she established the US branch of the Red Cross in 1881 and became its first president (1881–1904). As a result of her campaigning, the USA signed the Geneva Convention in 1882.

Barton, Sir Derek Harold Richard 1918–98
English chemist and Nobel Prize winner
Born in Gravesend, Kent, he received his undergraduate and postgraduate training at Imperial College, London, obtaining his PhD in 1942. After two years in military intelligence and a year with Albright and Wilson, he returned to Imperial College as assistant lecturer and then ICI Fellow. In 1949 he spent a year at Harvard while **Robert Woodward** was on sabbatical, and produced a

seminal paper on the relationship between conformation and chemical reactivity for which he shared the 1969 Nobel Prize for chemistry with **Odd Hassel**. In 1950 he moved to Birkbeck College, then to the chair of organic chemistry in Glasgow in 1955 and back to Imperial College in 1957. By 1960, X-ray crystallography had largely replaced degradative studies in the determination of structure, and Barton turned his attention to synthetic and biosynthetic work. He also pioneered the use of photochemical reactions in synthesis. In 1977 he was appointed director of the French National Centre for Scientific Research (CNRS) Institute for the Chemistry of Natural Substances in Gif-sur-Yvette. After 11 very productive years in France, he was appointed distinguished professor at Texas Agricultural and Mechanical University (1986–95), where his research continued unabated. He received many honours, including election to the Royal Society in 1954. He was knighted in 1972 and made an Officer of the French Legion of Honour in 1985.

Barton, Sir Edmund 1849–1920
Australian jurist and statesman

Born in Sydney, he was elected to the New South Wales legislature in 1879. He was leader of the Federation movement from 1896, headed the committee that drafted the Commonwealth Constitution Bill and led the delegation that presented it to the British parliament in 1900. He was the first Prime Minister of the Australian Commonwealth (1901–03). From 1903 until his death he served as a high court judge.

Barton, Elizabeth, *known as* the Maid of Kent or the Nun of Kent c.1506–1534
English prophet

Born in Kent, she was a domestic servant at Aldington. After an illness in 1525, she began to go into trances and make prophecies against the authorities. Archbishop **Warham** sent two monks to examine her, and one of these, Edward Bocking, convinced that she was directly inspired by the Virgin **Mary**, became her confessor at the Priory of St Sepulchre at Canterbury. She denounced **Henry VIII**'s divorce and marriage to **Anne Boleyn**, and was hanged for treason at Tyburn with Bocking.

Barton, Glenys 1944–
English sculptor

Born in Stoke-on-Trent, Staffordshire, she was trained at the Royal College of Art and began exhibiting in 1973. Whilst artist-in-residence at the Wedgwood factory (1976–77), she experimented with clay and ceramic figure design techniques. Her work shows a particular interest in the shape of the skull, and many of her heads are portraits, but she gives them a timeless quality by removing hair and avoiding facial details. She uses a large variety of glazes to obtain different effects on the smooth clay surfaces, both in the complete heads and her more recent relief profiles.

Barton, John Bernard Adie 1928–
English stage director

He was born in London and educated at King's College, Cambridge, where he was a Fellow (1954–60). He joined the newly created Royal Shakespeare Company at Stratford-upon-Avon in 1960 and was associate director there from 1964 to 1991, when he became advisory director. He wrote and directed *The Hollow Crown* (1961), an anthology about English monarchs, and adapted the three parts of *Henry VI* into two plays, *Henry VI* and *Edward VI*, for the monumental Wars of the Roses sequence (1963–64). He also adapted and directed a series of 10 plays based on the *Oresteia* legend as *The Greeks* (1980). He is the author of *Playing Shakespeare* (1984), based on his television series (1982). His writing for television includes *The War That Never Ends* (1990).

Bartram, John 1699–1777
American botanist

Born near Darby, Pennsylvania, and educated locally, he became a successful farmer and also built up an unrivalled collection of North American plants, which he sold to European botanists and horticulturists. This successful business allowed Bartram to travel extensively in search of plants. In 1743 the British Crown commissioned him to visit the Indian tribes of the 'League of Six Nations', the results of which were published, and in 1765 he was named King's Botanist. He was considered to be the 'father of American botany', and **Carolus Linnaeus** called him 'the greatest natural botanist in the world'. His son William Bartram (1759–1823) was also a botanist, whose bestselling *Travels* (1791) strongly influenced English Romanticism. 📖 Ernest Earnest, *John and William Bartram, Botanists and Explorers* (1940)

Baruch 7th–6th century BC
Biblical character

Described as the companion and secretary of the prophet **Jeremiah** (see Jeremiah 36), he was possibly of a wealthy family. His name became attached to several Jewish works of a much later date, known as 1 Baruch (the Book of Baruch), 2 (the Syriac Apocalypse of) Baruch, and 3 (the Greek Apocalypse of) Baruch. There is also a Christian Apocalypse of Baruch in Ethiopic.

Baruch See **Spinoza, Benedict de**

Baruch, Bernard Mannes 1870–1965
US financier and statesman

Born in Camden, South Carolina, and educated in New York City, he began life as an office boy, but made a fortune by speculation and was one of the few speculators who anticipated the Wall Street Crash. He helped to coordinate US industries in World War I and draft the economic sections of the Treaty of Versailles (1919). He became a powerful political influence, 'the adviser of presidents' and of **Winston Churchill** in World War II. He served on many commissions, particularly the American Atomic Energy Commission.

Barwick, Sir Garfield Edward John 1903–97
Australian judge

Born in Sydney, he was Attorney-General of Australia (1958–64), and Minister for External Affairs (1962–64) during a critical period of the Vietnam War. From 1964 to 1981 he was Chief Justice of Australia, and in 1975 gave crucial advice to the Governor-General Sir **John Kerr** which resulted in the subsequent dismissal of the **Whitlam** administration.

Bary, Heinrich Anton de 1831–88
German botanist

Born in Frankfurt am Main, he was successively Professor of Botany at the universities of Freiburg, Halle and Strassburg. He studied the morphology and physiology of the fungi, discovering many of the complexities of their life cycles. He described the plasmodium of slime moulds (mobile masses of living matter resulting from the fusion of individual cells), and he noted that the plasmodium possesses nuclei and a differentiated external layer, the plasmalemma. He established the principal features of plant anatomy, and the systematic terminology he used is, in most respects, still in use. He is sometimes described as the founder of modern mycology.

Barye, Antoine Louis 1796–1875
French sculptor

He was born in Paris and was distinguished for his bronze statues of animals (Louvre, Paris). His style was vigorous, in the spirit of the Romantic movement. He created the pediment *Napoleon dominating History and the Arts* at the Louvre, and the equestrian statue of **Napoleon I** at Ajaccio.

Baryshnikov, Mikhail Nikolayevich 1948–
US dancer and choreographer
Born in Riga, Latvia, of Russian parents, he was first trained at the Riga Choreography School and then with the Kirov Ballet in Leningrad (now St Petersburg). He created roles in *Vestris* (1969) and *Creation of the World* (1971). In 1974 he defected to the West while on tour in Canada and then went to the USA. His new career began at the American Ballet Theater, where he partnered **Gelsey Kirkland**, moving to New York City Ballet, where he worked with **George Balanchine**. Roles were created for him by Balanchine and others, including **Jerome Robbins** (1979, *Opus 19 / The Dreamer*) and **Frederick Ashton** (1980, *Rhapsody*). In 1980, he returned to the American Ballet Theater, taking over as artistic director. He has always maintained an interest in ballet as a popular art form and has taken part in several Hollywood films, including *The Turning Point* (1977), in which he starred as a seductive young principal dancer. *White Knights*, with choreography by **Twyla Tharp**, followed in 1985, and *Dancers* in 1987. In 1990 he founded the White Oak Dance Project, a touring modern-dance company. Gennady Smakov, *Baryshnikov: From Russia to the West* (1981)

Barzini, Luigi 1874–1947
Italian journalist and author
Born in Orvieto, he had a notable career as a foreign correspondent, travelling widely and covering the international expedition against the Boxers in China (1900), the outbreak of the Russo-Japanese War (1904) and the San Francisco earthquake. He was present at the early attempts to fly, and interviewed the **Wright** brothers, Orville and Wilbur. His book *Peking to Paris* (1908), describing a motor-car race in 1907 across two continents, is considered a classic.

Basaldella, Mirko 1910–69
Italian sculptor and painter
Born in Udine, he studied in Venice, Florence and Milan, and first exhibited in Rome in 1936. Best known for the bronze memorial doors he designed for the Ardeatine caves near Rome, he won second prize in the international Unknown Political Prisoner competition (1953). He was influenced by primitive and prehistoric forms. His brother Afro Basaldella (1912–) is also a sculptor.

Baselitz, Georg 1938–
German avant-garde artist
Born in Deutschbaselitz, Saxony, he studied art in East Berlin (1956–57) before emigrating to the West in 1957. He had his first one-man show in Berlin in 1961. His violent subject matter and his 'wild Expressionist' style show affinities with **Edvard Munch** and **Oskar Kokoschka**. Although he often paints sets, such as the *Strassenbild* cycle (1979–80), with a shouting or gesticulating figure at a window repeated from canvas to canvas, his real forte is painting figures, trees, animals, and other objects, upside down.

Basevi, George 1794–1845
English architect
Born in London, he became a pupil of Sir **John Soane**. He travelled in Greece and Italy (1816–19), designed in classic revivalist style the Fitzwilliam Museum in Cambridge, laid out part of London's Belgravia, and designed country mansions and Gothic churches. He fell to his death while surveying Ely Cathedral.

Bashkirtseva, Marya Konstantinovna 1860–84
Russian artist and diarist
She was born near Poltava, southern Russia, into a noble family, and travelled in Germany and France with her mother before they settled in Paris. From the age of 12 she kept a diary in French, selections of which were published posthumously as *Journal de Marie Bashkirtseff, avec un portrait* (1887), which candidly plots the psychological progress of a growing artist's mind. She studied painting in Paris and became a painter of some promise, exhibiting in the Salon of 1880, but died young of tuberculosis.

Basho, Matsuo, *pseudonym of* Matsuo Munefusa 1644–94
Japanese poet
He was born in Ueno. He took his pen name from the banana tree, after settling down in his hermitage near Tokyo. He was responsible for turning the 17-syllable haiku from a light-hearted diversion into a serious art form. After being apprenticed to a samurai, he led a wandering life, partly documented in his book of travels, *Oku no hosomichi* (1689, 'The Narrow Road to the Deep North', Eng trans *Noboyuki Yuasa*, 1966), written in a mixture of poetic prose and haiku. As well as formal elegance, Basho's verse has a modern and almost existential quality, which influenced **Ezra Pound** and the Imagists. M Ueda, *Basho* (1970)

Basie, Count (William) 1904–84
US jazz pianist, organist and bandleader
Born in Red Bank, New Jersey, he became one of the most significant big-band leaders of the swing era and beyond. He started by playing drums in a children's band, and then became a piano accompanist for silent films. He drifted away from his studies to take casual jobs as a musician and was given some coaching by **Fats Waller** in New York. After several years touring the vaudeville circuit as a soloist and accompanist to blues singers, in 1927 he reached Kansas City, then emerging as the centre of a distinct style of orchestral jazz to which Basie was to remain true during his half-century as a bandleader. In 1929 he began a five-year involvement as pianist and co-arranger with the Bennie Moten band. When Moten died in 1935 the band was largely re-formed under Basie's leadership, at first being called the Barons of Rhythm, and including the important tenor saxophone stylist **Lester Young** as a featured soloist. A radio broadcast was heard by record producer John Hammond, who organized a major tour for the band, which led to recording and booking contracts. Now called the Count Basie Orchestra and established in New York, the band quickly achieved national fame and worked to heavy touring schedules—as well as making film and television appearances—until 1950 when big bands appeared to be no longer viable. However after two years of leading an octet, Basie re-formed a 16-piece orchestra and continued to lead it until his death. During his 50-year career he employed some of the most eminent swing musicians. Among his most popular pieces are his compositions 'One O'Clock Jump' and 'Jumpin' at the Woodside'. Stanley Dance, *The World of Count Basie* (1980)

Basil I, the Macedonian c.812–886
Byzantine emperor
Born in Thrace, he rose in the imperial service from obscure origins to become co-ruler (866) with Michael III, whom he murdered in 867. He recovered parts of Calabria, developed the navy and revised **Justinian I**'s law code. The dynasty he founded ruled Constantinople (Istanbul) until 1056.

Basil II, Bulgaroctonus c.958–1025
Byzantine emperor
He came to the throne as sole ruler in 976. A revolt (989), involving the army and aristocracy, was quelled with the support of **Vladimir I**, who married Basil's sister Anna and

converted to Christianity. Vladimir's Russian troops became the core of the future Varangian Guard, the élite unit of the Byzantine army. Thereafter Basil supported the peasantry at the expense of the great landowners. His 15-year war against the Bulgarians culminated in victory in the Belasica Mountains. Fourteen thousand prisoners were blinded and in groups of a hundred, each led by a one-eyed man, sent back to their tsar, Samuel, who died of shock (1015). Bulgaria was annexed to the empire by 1018, while the eastern frontier was extended to Lake Van in Armenia. Austere and irascible, he died unmarried, and left no leader to consolidate his work.

Basil the Great, St c.329–379AD
Bishop of Caesarea and Doctor of the Church
Born in Caesarea, Cappadocia, he studied at Byzantium and Athens. He lived for a time as a hermit, and in AD 370 succeeded **Eusebius of Caesarea** as bishop of his native city. Along with his brother, St **Gregory of Nyssa** and St **Gregory of Nazianzus**, he defended Christian philosophy against Arianism. He is regarded as one of the greatest of the Greek Fathers. His feast day is 1 or 2 January. ⏚ Paul Fedwick, *The Church and the Charisma of Leadership of Basil of Caesarea* (1979)

Basil, Colonel W(assili) de, *originally* Vasili Grigorevich Voskresensky 1881–1951
Russian ballet impresario, personality and publicist
Born in Kaunas, and originally an army officer, he began his theatrical career in Paris as assistant to Prince Zeretelli, director of an itinerant Russian opera company. In 1932 he and **René Blum** co-founded the Ballets Russes de Monte Carlo, heir to **Sergei Diaghilev**'s Ballets Russes. The company gained an international reputation for its high calibre dancers.

Basilides fl.c.125AD
Syrian Gnostic philosopher
He founded a sect in Alexandria, Egypt, and his esoteric doctrines seem to have blended Christian thought with elements from **Zoroaster**, Indian philosophy and magic. His disciples (Basilidians) were active in Egypt, Syria, Italy and even Gaul into the 4th century.

Basilius, John See Bessarion, John

Basire, James 1730–1802
English engraver
From a notable family of London engravers, he was the teacher of **William Blake**. His father Isaac (1704–68), son James (1769–1822) and grandson James (1796–1869) were also engravers.

Baskerville, John 1706–75
English printer
Born at Sion Hill, Wolverley, Worcestershire, he began as a footman, became a writing master in Birmingham, and from 1740 carried on a successful japanning business there. Around 1750, following experiments in letter founding, he produced several types, one of which bears his name, and manufactured his own paper and ink. His works include editions of **Virgil**, **Milton** and the Bible. In 1758 he became printer to Cambridge University. Unaffected by superstition, he chose to be buried in his own garden, but his remains were exhumed. ⏚ Philip Gaskell, *John Baskerville: A Bibliography* (rev edn, 1973)

Baskin, Leonard 1922–
US artist
Born in New Brunswick, New Jersey, he studied the Talmud with the intent of becoming a rabbi but turned to sculpture and graphic art instead. His strongly moulded figures and black-and-white engravings convey a concern for the vulnerability and mortality of humans and the threat of spiritual decay; he often uses birds of prey to symbolize evil and death. He taught at Smith College (1953–73) and founded and operated the Gehenna Press, publishing illustrated books. His work has been exhibited in many major US museums and galleries.

Basov, Nikolai Gennadevich 1922–
Soviet physicist, inventor and Nobel Prize winner
Born in Voronezh, he served in the Red Army during World War II, and studied in Moscow. He joined the Lebedev Physics Institute, Moscow, as a laboratory assistant in 1948, became deputy director (1958–73), and was appointed director in 1973. His work in quantum electronics provided the theoretical basis for the development of the maser (Microwave Amplification by Stimulated Emission of Radiation) in 1955. In 1958 he proposed the use of semiconductors for the creation of lasers (Light Amplification by Stimulated Emission of Radiation), subsequently successfully producing numerous types of these devices (1960–65). In 1968 he used powerful lasers to produce thermonuclear reactions. For his work on amplifiers and oscillators used to produce laser beams he was awarded the 1964 Nobel Prize for physics jointly with his colleague **Aleksandr Prokhorov** and the US physicist **Charles Townes**.

Bass, George 1771–1803/12
English naval surgeon
He was born at Aswarby, Lincolnshire, and joined the navy. With **Matthew Flinders** he explored (1795–1800) the strait between Tasmania and Australia that bears his name. He died at sea either on the journey to South America or while mining there.

Bass, Michael Thomas 1799–1884
English brewer
Born in Burton-on-Trent, Staffordshire, he joined the family business (founded by his grandfather, William Bass, in 1777), which he expanded considerably. He helped to improve the lot of workers both as employer and as Liberal MP (1848–83). His son, Michael Arthur Bass (1837–1909), became Baron Burton in 1886.

Bassani, Giorgio 1916–
Italian novelist and poet
Born in Bologna, he lived until 1943 in Ferrara, where much of his fiction is set. *Cinque storie ferraresi* ('Five Stories of Ferrara') appeared in 1956, most of them composed in the aftermath of World War II. A sensitive chronicler of Italian Jews and their suffering under fascism, he is a realist who writes elegiacally. One of the outstanding Italian novelists of the 20th century, he is at his most exquisite in *Gli Occhiali d'Oro* (1960, 'The Gold-Rimmed Spectacles') and *Il Giardino dei Finzi-Contini* (1965, 'The Garden of the Finzi-Continis'). ⏚ G Varanini, *Bassani* (1970)

Bassano, Jacopo da, *properly* Giacomo da Ponte 1510–92
Venetian painter
Born in Bassano, he is regarded as the founder of genre painting in Europe. His best paintings are of peasant life and biblical scenes, and include the altarpiece of the Nativity at Bassano, *Jacob's Return to Canaan* and *Portrait of a Gentleman*. His four sons also became painters, notably Francesco (1549–92) and Leandro (1557–1662), who, like their father, anticipated the Mannerist style.

Bassi, Agostino Maria 1773–1856
Italian biologist and pioneer bacteriologist
Born in Lodi, he was educated at Pavia University. His work on animal diseases was partly anticipated by **Louis Pasteur** and **Robert Koch**. As early as 1835 he showed after many years' work that a disease of silkworms (muscardine)

is fungal in origin, that it is contagious, and that it can be controlled, and he proposed that some other diseases are transmitted by micro-organisms.

Bassompierre, François de 1579–1646
French soldier and politician
Born in Haroué, Lorraine, he was promoted to the rank of Marshal of France in 1622, and took an active part in the siege of La Rochelle. He served as ambassador to Switzerland, Spain and England, but was imprisoned by Cardinal Richelieu in the Bastille from 1631 to 1643. He was an accomplished courtier, excessively devoted to gallantries and luxury. His *Memoirs* (1665), written in the Bastille, contain interesting sidelights on his sojourn in London as ambassador.

Bastian, Adolf 1826–1905
German ethnologist
Born in Bremen, he studied at Berlin, Heidelberg, Prague, Jena and Würzburg. He travelled widely, collecting material for his ethnological studies in most continents. He is best known for his theory that variations in folk cultures could be traced back to the effects of local geographical conditions on a basic set of elementary ideas (*Elementargedanken*) common to humankind.

Bastian, Henry Charlton 1837–1915
English biologist
Born in Truro, Cornwall, and privately educated, he studied medicine at University College London. After serving at St Mary's Hospital, London, as an assistant physician, he was elected Professor of Pathological Anatomy at University College in 1867, rising to become Hospital Physician (1871), and Professor of Clinical Medicine (1887–95). He developed a large private practice, held an appointment at the National Hospital, Queen Square (1868–1902), and was awarded numerous honours. Bastian's lasting fame derives from his pioneering researches in clinical neurology, and, from 1869, he published a series of papers on the brain centres controlling speech, investigating the neurological basis of such pathological forms as word blindness (alexia) and word deafness. He also championed the doctrine of spontaneous generation.

Bastien-Lepage, Jules 1848–84
French painter
He was born in Damvillers, Meuse, Lorraine, and studied under the academic artist Alexandre Cabanel. His pictures are mostly of rustic scenes, such as *Les Foins (The Hayfield*, 1878, Musée d'Orsay, Paris), which influenced the Naturalist school throughout Europe and the USA, but he also painted portraits of Sarah Bernhardt and the Prince of Wales (later Edward VII).

Bastos, Augustos Roa 1917–
Paraguayan novelist
He has lived in exile since 1947, and is the author of several works of fiction. He has also worked as a journalist, screenwriter and teacher. Until his retirement in 1985 he was a professor at the University of Toulouse. *I The Supreme* (1947, Eng trans 1986) is his masterpiece.

Bata, Tomas 1876–1932
Czechoslovakian industrialist
He was born in Zlin, Moravia. From a small shoemaking business, he built up the largest leather factory in Europe, producing 75,000 pairs of shoes a day by 1928. He was killed when an aircraft struck one of his factory chimneys.

Batchelor, Joy 1914–1991
English animated cartoon producer
Born in Watford, Hertfordshire, she became a fashion artist for *Harper's Bazaar* magazine. She tried animation with *Robin Hood* (1935), and in 1941 married fellow-producer John Halas, and formed the Halas–Batchelor animation unit. In World War II they made propaganda films for the Ministry of Information, followed by the first British feature-length cartoon, *Handling Ships*, in 1945, and the *Charley* series (1947). In 1952 they made the first British stereoscopic cartoon, *The Owl and the Pussycat*. Other films have included George Orwell's *Animal Farm* (1954) and the television series *Tales of Hoffnung* (1965).

Bateman, Henry Mayo 1887–1970
Australian cartoonist
Born in Sutton Forest, New South Wales, he lived in England from infancy. From 1906, influenced by the French cartoonist Caran d'Ache, he developed a purely visual style of comic strip for *Punch* and other periodicals. He is best known for a series of humorous drawings depicting embarrassing 'The Man Who...' situations such as *The Guardsman Who Dropped His Rifle*. He wrote *The Art of Drawing* (1926) and *Himself* (1937).

Bateman, Kate Josephine, *also known as* Mrs Crowe 1842–1917
US actress
Born in Baltimore, Maryland, she was the daughter of Hezekiah Linthicum Bateman (1812–75), the theatrical manager. She began acting at the age of four, and after successful tours in the USA, acted in London with Henry Irving in Shakespearean plays (1875–77). She married Dr George Crowe in 1866. Her sisters, Isabel (1854–1934) and Virginia (1853–1940), were both distinguished actresses. The latter married Edward Compton (1854–1918) and was the mother of Fay Compton and Sir Compton Mackenzie.

Bates, Alan, *originally* Arthur Bates 1934–
English actor
He was born in Allestree, Derbyshire, and after national service in the RAF, he studied at RADA. He made his stage debut in *You and Your Wife* (1955) at Coventry. Following his London debut in *The Mulberry Bush* (1956) he appeared in *Look Back in Anger* (1956), *Long Day's Journey Into Night* (1958) and *The Caretaker* (1960). His first film was *The Entertainer* (1960) and he was then seen in some of the most popular British films of the decade, including *A Kind of Loving* (1962), *Georgy Girl* (1966), *Far From the Madding Crowd* (1967) and *Women in Love* (1969). His stage career has combined the classics with contemporary roles in *In Celebration* (1969), *Butley* (1971, Tony award), *Otherwise Engaged* (1975), *Melon* (1987) and David Storey's *Stages* (1992). His films include *The Fixer* (1968), *The Go-Between* (1971), *An Unmarried Woman* (1978), *We Think the World of You* (1988), *Hamlet* (1990) and *Secret Friends* (1992). His television work includes the series *The Mayor of Casterbridge* (1978), *An Englishman Abroad* (1982, BAFTA award), *Pack of Lies* (1987), Alan Bennett's *Boulevard Haussman* (1991), *Hard Times* (1994) and *Oliver's Travels* (1995).

Bates, Daisy May, *née* O'Dwyer 1863–1951
Australian anthropologist
Born in Tipperary, Ireland, she arrived in Australia in 1884, and the same year married Harry Morant. After a period in England as a London journalist she was commissioned by *The Times* to investigate the condition of Aboriginals. She returned to Australia in 1899, and from that time spent most of her life in the north and west of the country with remote tribes, by whom she was known as Kabbarli (grandmother). In 1910–11 she was a member of the Radcliffe-Brown anthropological expedition. Her own work included making detailed notes of Aboriginal life and customs, and working for Aboriginal welfare, setting up camps for the aged. She published an account of her life in 1938. When over 80 she returned to live with a tribe in South Australia, but illness forced her return to Adelaide and her retirement in 1945.

Bates, H(erbert) E(rnest) 1905–74
English novelist, playwright, and short-story writer
Born in Rushden, Northamptonshire, he began his working life as a solicitor's clerk, provincial journalist and warehouse clerk. His first play, *The Last Bread*, and his first novel, *The Two Sisters*, both appeared in 1926. In his early days he benefited from the advice of **Edward Garnett** and was later influenced by **Stephen Crane**. He is one of the greatest exponents of the short-story form. His essay in literary criticism, *The Modern Short Story*, is regarded as a classic. His best-known works are *Fair Stood the Wind for France* (1944), *The Jacaranda Tree* (1949) and *The Darling Buds of May* (1958). ▢ *An Autobiography* (1969–72)

Bates, Henry Walter 1825–92
English naturalist
Born in Leicester, with his friend **Alfred Wallace** he left to explore the Amazon in 1848, and continued until 1859, when he returned with 14,700 specimens, including almost 8,000 species of insect new to science. In 1861 his *Contributions to an Insect Fauna of the Amazon Valley* described the phenomenon now known as Batesian mimicry, in which harmless, edible species of animal resemble others which are distasteful or poisonous, and thus gain protection from predators. This discovery provided strong evidence in favour of natural selection. In 1864 he became assistant secretary of the Royal Geographical Society. ▢ H P Moon, *Henry Walker Bates FRS, 1825–1892: Explorer, Scientist and Darwinian* (1976)

Bateson, Gregory 1904–80
US anthropologist
Born in Grantchester, Cambridgeshire, England, the son of geneticist **William Bateson**, he studied physical anthropology at Cambridge, but made his career in the USA. His first major monograph, *Naven* (1936), based on fieldwork in New Guinea, was an innovative work introducing many themes that have since become central to the anthropological study of ritual and symbolism. With **Margaret Mead** he was involved with the culture-and-personality movement, publishing *Balinese Character* in 1942. Influenced by the theory of cybernetics, he went on to study problems of communication and learning among aquatic mammals and human schizophrenics, and developed a distinctive interpretation of schizophrenia based on the notion of the 'double-bind'. The anthology *Steps to an Ecology of Mind* (1973), and his book *Mind and Nature* (1978), indicate the extraordinary range of his interests.

Bateson, William 1861–1926
English geneticist
He was born in Whitby, Yorkshire, and studied natural sciences at Cambridge. He introduced the term 'genetics' in 1909, and became the UK's first Professor of Genetics at Cambridge (1908–10). He left to become director of the new John Innes Horticultural Institution (1910–26). He went on to produce the first English translation of **Gregor Mendel**'s work on heredity. Bateson showed that some genes are inherited together, a process now known as 'linkage', and he played a dominant part in establishing Mendelian ideas, but was a major opponent of chromosome theory. Although an ardent evolutionist, he was opposed to **Charles Darwin**'s theory of natural selection, as the small changes demanded by the theory seemed insufficient to account for the evolutionary process.

Bathori, Elizabeth d.1614
Polish murderess
In 1610 she was discovered to have murdered 650 young girls, so that she could keep her youth by bathing in their warm blood. Her accomplices were burnt; but she was imprisoned for life in the walls of her fortress of Csej. She was the niece of Stephen Bathori, King of Poland, and wife of the Hungarian Count Nádasdy.

Bathsheba b.c.970BC
Biblical character
She was the daughter of Eliam and the wife of Uriah the Hittite, an army officer. After King **David** had committed adultery with Bathsheba, Uriah was sent to his death, in order to hide the king's crime, enabling him to take the beautiful Bathsheba for himself. Nathan the prophet forced David to condemn his own action, and prophesied the death of their first child. Their second child was **Solomon**, David's successor. Jewish tradition holds that the song in praise of a good wife in Proverbs 31 was written by Solomon in memory of his mother.

Batista y Zaldivar, Fulgencio 1901–73
Cuban dictator
Born in Oriente province, a labourer's son, he rose from sergeant-major to colonel in the army coup against President Machado (1931–33) and himself became President (1940–44). In 1952 he overthrew President Prio, and, with himself as sole candidate, was re-elected President (1954). He ruled as a ruthless, embezzling dictator until his overthrow by **Fidel Castro** in 1959, when he found refuge in the Dominican Republic.

Batman, John 1801–39
Australian pioneer
Born in Rose Hill, New South Wales, he settled in Tasmania but in 1835 sailed to the mainland looking for grazing land. He explored the area where Melbourne now stands and said: 'This will be the place for a village'. With **John Pascoe Fawkner** he is regarded as the founder of Melbourne.

Batoni or Battoni, Pompeo Girolamo 1708–87
Italian painter
Born in Lucca, he trained in Rome and settled there. He was a learned man, whose style was influenced by his study of **Raphael** and classical antiquity. From 1735 he received many important commissions for religious, mythological and historical paintings, but it is for his portraits, particularly of distinguished foreign visitors, that he is most famous. After **Anton Raphael Mengs** left Rome in 1761 he was virtually unchallenged in this field. He painted three popes, and became curator for the papal collections.

Batten, Jean 1909–82
New Zealand pioneer aviator
Born in Rotorua, she abandoned a possible career in music, went to England in 1929 and at 21 took her pilot's and ground engineer licences. In 1934, in a Gypsy Moth, she broke **Amy Johnson**'s record for the flight from England to Australia by nearly five days. She became the first woman to complete the return journey and in 1935 flew over the South Atlantic Ocean to Argentina. Her autobiography was republished as *Alone in the Sky* in 1979.

Battenberg, Prince Alexander of 1857–93
First Prince of Bulgaria
Born in Verona, Austria (now in Italy), he was the second son of Prince Alexander of Hesse, and his morganatic wife, the Polish Countess von Hauke. He was also uncle of Louis, 1st Earl **Mountbatten**, and nephew of Tsar **Alexander II** of Russia. He was elected prince of the new principality of Bulgaria (1879). In 1885 he annexed eastern Romania after an uprising there, provoking the hostility of Serbia, whose army he defeated in two weeks. In 1886 he was overpowered by pro-Russian army conspirators in his Sofia palace and forced to abdicate. Although he was freed, he could not overcome the hostility of Tsar **Alexander III**, and retired to Darmstadt in Austria as Count Hartenau.

Battenberg, Prince Henry of 1858–96
German prince
The third son of Prince Alexander of Hesse, he married in 1885 Princess Beatrice (1857–1944), youngest daughter of Queen Victoria, and died at sea of fever caught in the Ashanti campaign.

Battenberg, Prince Louis Alexander See Mountbatten

Battenberg
Family of German origin
The name is derived from a family of German counts who died out in the 14th century. The title was revived (1851) for the Polish countess Julia Theresa von Hauke (1825–95), the morganatic wife of Prince Alexander of Hesse.

Battlefield Band
Scottish folk group
The Battlefield Band were the first Scottish folk group to incorporate both electric instruments and musical influences from rock, pop and country into their music. The band formed in 1972 in Glasgow, and if their pioneering role has been usurped by the likes of Runrig and Capercaillie, they retain a large worldwide following. Singer and keyboard player Alan Reid (1950–) is the only founder-member still in the current line-up, with singer and guitarist Alastair Russell (1951–), and two virtuoso instrumentalists, piper Iain MacDonald (1960–), and fiddler John McCusker (1973–). Former members include fiddler Brian McNeill (1950–), a key figure in both the band's development and the Scottish folk scene.

Battoni, Pompeo Girolamo See Batoni, Pompeo Girolamo

Battutah, Ibn See Ibn Battutah

Batyushkov, Konstantin Nikolayevich
1787–1855
Russian poet
Born in Vologda, he served in the Napoleonic Wars, but became insane in 1821 and was confined in an asylum for the remaining 34 years of his life. Profoundly influenced by French and Italian writers, his work was much admired by Alexander Pushkin. His most impressive work was *Ymerayushi Tass* ('The Death of Tasso'). ☐ I Serman, *Konstantin Batyushkov* (1974)

Baudelaire, Charles Pierre 1821–67
French Symbolist poet
Born in Paris, he had an unhappy childhood quarrelling with his stepfather, and was sent on a voyage to India. He stopped off at Mauritius, where Jeanne Duval became his mistress and inspiration. On his return to Paris in 1843 he spent much of his time in the studios of Eugène Delacroix and Honoré Daumier, and wrote art criticisms in *Le Salon de 1845* and *Le Salon de 1846*. In 1847 he published an autobiographical novel, *La Fanfarlo*. His major work is an influential collection of poems, *Les Fleurs du mal* (1857, Eng trans *Flowers of Evil*, 1909), for which author, printer and publisher were prosecuted for impropriety in 1864. Later works include *Les Paradis artificiels* (1860, 'Artificial Paradises') and *Petits Poèmes en prose* (1869, 'Little Poems in Prose'). He translated (1856–65) the works of Thomas De Quincey and Edgar Allan Poe. Having written a critical work on his literary associates Honoré de Balzac, Théophile Gautier and Gérard de Nerval, published posthumously in 1880, he took to drink and opium, became paralysed, and died in poverty. ☐ E Starkie, *Baudelaire* (1957); H Peyre, *Connaissance de Baudelaire* (1951)

Baudouin I 1930–93
King of the Belgians
Born near Brussels, the elder son of Leopold III and his first wife, Queen Astrid, he succeeded to the throne (1951) on the abdication of his father over the controversy of the latter's conduct during World War II. In 1960 he married the Spanish Doña Fabiola de Mora y Aragon. He was succeeded by his brother, Albert II (1934–).

Baudry, Paul Jacques Aimé 1828–86
French painter
Born in La Roche-sur-Yon, he is chiefly known for the 30 large panels, illustrative of music and dancing, executed for the foyer of the Paris Opera (1866–76).

Bauer, Ferdinand Lucas 1760–1826 and Franz Andreas 1758–1840
Austrian natural historians
Born in Feldsberg, Austria (now in Moravia), they were two of three illustrious brothers, the other being Josef Anton Bauer (b.1756). All three specialized in natural history subjects, particularly plants. In 1780 Franz and Ferdinand began working for Baron Nicolaus von Jacquin, director of the university's botanic garden in Vienna, and they jointly illustrated Jacquin's *Icones Plantarum Rariorum* (1753–91). Ferdinand accompanied John Sibthorp (1758–96) as a botanical illustrator on a Mediterranean voyage, and he illustrated *Flora Graeca* (1806–40) by Sibthorp and James Edward Smith (1759–1828). He went on the Flinders expedition to Australia (1801–06), working under Robert Brown, and returned with many illustrations of new plants and animals. Some of his paintings were published in *Illustrationes Florae Novae-Hollandiae* (1813). Franz became botanical painter to King George III at Kew, where he remained for 50 years, producing hundreds of illustrations, some of which are in *Illustrations of Orchidaceous Plants* (1830–38).

Bauer, Georg See Agricola, Georgius

Bauer, Gustav 1870–1944
German politician
A senior trade unionist before World War I, he became a Social Democratic Party (SPD) member of the Reichstag in 1912. He was appointed a junior Minister of Labour (1918) and became Minister of Labour (1919). He succeeded Philipp Scheidemann as Chancellor and in 1919 headed the government which signed the Treaty of Versailles under protest. He resigned as Chancellor during the Kapp Putsch (1920) and, after holding various further ministerial posts, eventually resigned from parliament in 1928 on becoming involved in a corruption trial.

Bauhin, Caspar or Gaspard 1560–1624
Swiss botanist and physician
He was born in Basle and studied at the universities of Basle, Padua, Montpellier, Paris and Tübingen. He was appointed Professor of Anatomy and Botany at Basle and compiled a medical textbook, the *Theatrum Anatomicum* (1605). His more important work *Pinax Theatri Botanici* (1623) was much used by Carolus Linnaeus and is still important today as a comprehensive compendium of the plants of the 17th century, although the arrangement of the plants within the book has been criticized, as it conforms to no single organizing principle.

Baum, L(yman) Frank 1856–1919
US writer
Born in Chittenango, New York, he worked as a magazine editor until the publication and tremendous success of his second children's book, *The Wonderful Wizard of Oz* (1900), which was staged as a musical in 1901. (The classic movie version, starring Judy Garland, Bert Lahr, and Ray Bolger, was made in 1939.) Baum travelled in Europe, then settled in California, where he continued to write stories about the land of Oz, a total of 14 books in all.

Baum, Vicki, *originally* Vicki Hedvig 1888–1960
US novelist
She was born in Vienna, Austria, and studied music at the Vienna Conservatory, then moved to Berlin to write for a magazine. After writing several novels and short stories in German, she made her name with *Menschen im Hotel* (1930, Eng trans *Grand Hotel*), which became a bestseller and a popular film. She emigrated to the USA in 1931, where she published her later novels, including *Falling Star* (1934), *Headless Angel* (1948) and *The Mustard Seed* (1953). She was naturalized in 1938.

Baumé, Antoine 1728–1804
French chemist
Born in Senlis, he invented the 'Baumé' hydrometer, and many dyeing processes.

Baumeister, Willi 1889–1955
German painter
Born in Stuttgart, he was for some years a professor at the Frankfurt School of Art, but the Hitler regime prohibited him from teaching and he turned to scientific research on colour and to prehistoric archaeology. These interests are reflected in work such as *African Histories*, a series of paintings depicting strange organic forms, and his illustrations for the Bible stories and the *Epic of Gilgamesh* (1942–53). His series of paintings, from the *Mauerbilder* murals, through *Painter with his Palette* to the *Montaru* and *Monturi* experiments, show a wide variety of theme and style and continuously novel treatment.

Baumer, Gertrude 1873–1954
German feminist
Born in Hohenlimburg, Westphalia, she became involved in feminist politics while studying at Berlin University. Considered the leader of the German feminist movement, from 1910 to 1919 she was president of the League of German Women's Associations, and in 1917 founded a socialist school for women. She edited the newspaper *Die Frau* (1893–1944, 'Woman'), and was a member of the Reichstag from 1920 to 1933. When the Nazis came to power she lost this position and was interrogated by the Gestapo. After World War II she founded the Christian Social Union but was soon forced by ill health to retire from public life.

Baumgarten, Alexander Gottlieb 1714–62
German philosopher
Born in Berlin, he became Professor of Philosophy at Frankfurt an der Oder in 1740. His main works are *Metaphysica* (1739), a systematic rendering of the rationalistic philosophy of Christian von Wolff, to whose school he belonged, and *Aesthetica* (1750–58), a long unfinished treatise which pioneered this field and helped establish the modern term 'aesthetics'.

Baur, Ferdinand Christian 1792–1860
German Protestant theologian and New Testament critic
Born in Schmiden, near Stuttgart, he studied at the Seminary of Blaubeuren and the University of Tübingen. He held the Tübingen chair of theology from 1826, and founded the Tübingen School, the first to use strict historical research methods in the study of early Christianity.

Bausch, Pina 1940–
German dancer and choreographer
Born in Solingen, West Germany (Germany), she trained first with Kurt Jooss at the Essen Folkwangschule from 1955, and then with José Limón and Antony Tudor in New York in 1959. After a season with the Metropolitan Opera Ballet Company (1960–61) and another with US choreographer Paul Taylor, she returned to Essen where she staged several operas for the Wuppertal Theatre. Her success led to an invitation to found her own company. After staging Stravinsky's *Le Sacre du printemps* (1975, *The Rite of Spring*) and the Brecht and Weill *Seven Deadly Sins*, she began to produce her own work in the late 1970s. Her choreography and particularly her unusual stagings mark a turning point in contemporary dance and have remained a powerful influence. Stages are strewn with dead leaves (1977, *Bluebeard*), pink and white carnations (15,000 of them in *Carnations*, 1982) or chairs (1978, *Café Muller*).

Bawden, Nina 1925–
English writer
Born in London, she writes primarily on the domestic issues of the middle-classes, such as friendships, marriages, divorces and family life. *Anna Apparent* (1972) is a study of an illegitimate child evacuee, while the middle-aged narrator of *Afternoon of a Good Woman* (1976) reflects on a life of disappointment and emotional betrayal before turning to face her future with renewed resilience. *The Ice House* (1983) casts a discriminating eye on a 30-year female friendship, with all its confidences and rivalries. She also writes children's books, including *Carrie's War* (1973), the story of a child being evacuated to Wales during World War II. Her autobiography, *In My Own Time*, was published in 1994.

Bax, Sir Arnold Edward Trevor 1883–1953
English composer
Born in London, he studied piano at the Royal Academy of Music there. A visit to Russia in 1910 directly inspired such piano pieces as *Gopak* (1911) and *In a Vodka Shop* (1915), but much more influential on Bax was the Celtic revival. He wrote several Irish short stories (under the name of Dermot O'Byrne), and composed orchestral pieces (1912–13), and many songs set to the words of revival poets (eg, 1923–24, *St Patrick's Breastplate*, and 1917, *An Irish Elegy*, for English horn, harp and strings). Between 1921 and 1939 he wrote seven symphonies in widely diverse moods, and his *Mater Ora Filium* (1921) is a highly accomplished English choral work. He was prolific in many other areas, encompassing tone poems, such as *In the Faery Hills* (1909) and *Tintagel* (1917), chamber music, piano solos and concertos, and in 1942 he was appointed Master of the King's Musick. He published an autobiograpy, *Farewell my Youth* (1943). His brother Clifford (1886–1962) was a playwright and author. 📖 Colin Scott-Sutherland, *Arnold Bax* (1973)

Bax, Ernest Belfort 1854–1926
English writer and reformer
Born in Leamington, Warwickshire, he became a founder of English socialism. A barrister, he founded with William Morris the Socialist League, and wrote much on socialism, history and philosophy.

Baxendale, Leo 1930–
English strip cartoonist
Born in Lancashire, he first worked as a label designer, and later joined the *Lancashire Evening Post* (1950), drawing sports cartoons, and writing and illustrating articles. He began to freelance strips to the *Beano* comic beginning with *Little Plum* (1953), followed by *Minnie the Minx* (1953) as a female version of *Dennis the Menace*. A large cartoon series, *When The Bell Rings* (1954), evolved into *The Bash Street Kids*, a riotous gang of juvenile delinquents. He designed the new weekly comic *Wham* (1964), and despite leaving the field in 1974 remains the most imitated artist in British comics.

Baxter, George 1804–67
English engraver and printmaker
The son of John Baxter, he was born in Lewes, Sussex. He developed a method of printing in oil colours, using copper or steel plates for his outlines, with neutral tones on the same plate obtained by aquatint or stipple. His

process, patented in 1835, required a combination of between 10 and 20 wood and metal blocks for each reproduction.

Baxter, James Keir 1926–72
New Zealand poet, dramatist and critic

Born in Dunedin, he worked as a labourer, journalist and teacher, and led a bohemian life until he was converted to Roman Catholicism. Subsequently he founded a religious community on the Wanganui River. He published more than 30 books of poetry, his first volume, *Beyond the Palisade* (1944), appearing when he was 18. The poems he wrote before his conversion are collected in *In Fires of No Return* (1958). Latterly he was less productive but his appointment to the Burns Fellowship at the University of Otago in 1966 inspired him, and *Howrah Bridge and Other Poems* (1961) and *Autumn Testament* (1972) are among his best work. His *Collected Poems* (1979) was edited by J E Weir who, since Baxter's death, has produced editions of previously unpublished verse. His plays include *The Band Rotunda* (1967), *The Sore-Footed Man* (1967) and *The Temptation of Oedipus* (1967). ◫ J E Weir, *The Poetry of James Keir Baxter* (1970)

Baxter, John 1781–1858
English printer

Born in Surrey, he settled in Lewes and published the illustrated 'Baxter's Bible' and the first book of cricket rules. He was the first to use an ink-roller.

Baxter, Richard 1615–91
English nonconformist churchman

Born in Rowton, Shropshire, he acquired great knowledge by private study, and in 1638 was made a deacon. He adopted nonconformist views, and during the English Civil War was army chaplain for the Puritans. At the Restoration he was appointed a royal chaplain, but the Act of Uniformity (1662) drove him out of the English Church. He returned to London in 1672, where he preached and wrote, arguing for the toleration of dissent within the Church. His controversial opinions led him in 1685 to be brought before Judge Jeffreys for alleged sedition, and he was imprisoned for 18 months.

Baxter, Stanley 1926–
Scottish comic actor

Born in Glasgow, he made his professional debut as Correction's Varlet at the Edinburgh Festival production of *The Thrie Estates* in 1948. His stage appearances include *The Amorous Prawn* (1959), *Chase Me, Comrade* (1965) and *What The Butler Saw* (1969). He made his television debut in *Shop Window* (1951) and his film debut in *Geordie* (1956), following with pictures such as *Crooks Anonymous* (1962) and *The Fast Lady* (1962). A firm favourite on the small screen, his many television series include *On the Bright Side* (1959), *Baxter On...* (1964), and *The Stanley Baxter Show* (1968–71). He subsequently created glittering comic extravaganzas such as *The Stanley Baxter Picture Show* (1972), *The Stanley Baxter Moving Picture Show* (1974), *Stanley Baxter's Christmas Box* (1976) and *Stanley Baxter on Television* (1979).

Bayard, James Asheton 1767–1815
US politician

A lawyer, he was elected to Congress in 1796, and became a conspicuous member of the Federal Party. He was in the Senate from 1804 to 1813, opposed the war of 1812, and was one of the negotiators appointed by President Madison to conclude the peace treaty with Great Britain which followed.

Bayard, James Asheton 1799–1880
US politician

The son of James Bayard, he was also a distinguished Democratic senator.

Bayard, Pierre du Terrail, Chevalier de
1476–1524
French soldier

Born in the Château Bayard, near Grenoble, he accompanied Charles VIII to Italy in 1494–95 and was knighted after the Battle of Fornovo. In the service of Louis XII he fought with legendary bravery at Milan (1501) and Barletta (1502), and campaigned in Spain and against the Genoese and Venetians, taking Brescia by storm in 1512. At Marignano he won a brilliant victory for Francis I, and when Charles V invaded Champagne with a large army in 1521, Bayard defended Mézières, saving France from invasion. While defending the passage of the River Sesia in Italy, he was mortally wounded and died facing the foe, reciting the *Miserere*. A brilliant commander, he was known as *le Chevalier sans peur et sans reproche* ('the knight without fear and without reproach').

Bayard, Richard Henry 1796–1868
US politician

The son of James Bayard (1767–1815), and brother of James Bayard (1799–1880) he was a long-serving senator, and represented the USA in Belgium.

Bayard, Thomas Francis 1828–98
US politician

The son of James Bayard (1799–1880), he qualified for the Bar and, entering the Senate (1869), acted with the Democrats. After being Secretary of State (1885–89), he was ambassador to Great Britain from 1893 to 1897.

Bayer, Johann 1572–1625
German astronomer and celestial map-maker

Born in Rhain, Bavaria, he was by profession a lawyer, but had a keen interest in astronomy. He published a celestial atlas, *Uranometria* (1603), in which the positions of nearly 1,000 stars are depicted in addition to a similar number recorded in Tycho Brahe's famous catalogue. Bayer added 12 new constellations to the 48 defined by Ptolemy in the 2nd century; this part of the atlas incorporated observations of the Dutch navigator Petrus Theodori (d.1596). Bayer also introduced the mode of designating stars in each constellation in order of magnitude by letters of the Greek alphabet, a system which remains in use for stars visible with the naked eye. The *Uranometria* distinguished some non-stellar objects, for example the star cluster Praesepe which Galileo later resolved with his telescope.

Bayes, Thomas 1702–61
English mathematician

He was born in London, and in 1731 became Presbyterian minister in Tunbridge Wells. He is principally remembered for his posthumously published *Essay towards solving a problem in the doctrine of chances* (1763), in which he was the first to study the idea of statistical inference, and to estimate the probability of an event from the frequency of its previous occurrences. Although his mathematical results are now a standard part of statistical theory, there is still controversy about how and when they may be applied.

Bayezit I *also spelt* Bayezid *or* Bajazet c.1360–c.1403
Sultan of the Ottoman Empire

In 1389 he succeeded his father, Murat I, who was killed at the Battle of Kossovo, and swiftly conquered Bulgaria, parts of Serbia, Macedonia and Thessaly, and most of Asia Minor, earning him the name of Yildirim ('Thunderbolt'). For 10 years he blockaded Constantinople (Istanbul), and inflicted a crushing defeat on King Sigismund of Hungary at Nicopolis, on the Danube (1396). Bayezit would have entirely destroyed the Greek Empire if he had not in turn been completely defeated by Timur near Ankara in 1402. Bayezit himself fell into the hands of the conqueror, who treated him with great generosity (his incarceration in an iron cage being a myth), and in whose camp he died. He was succeeded by his son Süleyman I.

Bayezit II 1448–1512
Sultan of the Ottoman Empire
Born in Thrace, he succeeded his father, **Mehmet II**, the conqueror of Constantinople (Istanbul), in 1481. During his reign a succession of wars against Hungary, Poland, Venice, Egypt and Persia (Iran) served, on the whole, to establish Ottoman power in the Balkans, Asia Minor and the eastern Mediterranean.

Bayle, Pierre 1647–1706
French Protestant philosopher and critic
Born in Carlat, Languedoc, he studied under the Jesuits at Toulouse. He turned Catholic for a while, but reconverted to Calvinism and became Professor of Philosophy at Sedan in 1675. Forced into exile, he became a professor at the University of Rotterdam (1681), and he started a popular journal of literary criticism, *Nouvelles de la république des lettres* (1684, 'News from the Republic of Letters'). He wrote a strong defence of liberalism and religious toleration, but was dismissed from the university in 1693, attacked by the theologian Jurieu as an agent of France and an enemy of Protestantism. He then concentrated on his major work, the encyclopedic *Dictionnaire historique et critique* (1697, 'Historical and Critical Dictionary'). He was further persecuted for the work's alleged profanity, and for the claim in it that morality was independent of religion, but his writings later influenced the 18th-century Enlightenment, **Voltaire** and others. 🕮E Labrousse, *Bayle* (1983)

Baylis, Lilian Mary 1874–1937
English theatrical manager
She was born in London, the daughter of musicians. In 1890 the family emigrated to South Africa, where she became a music teacher in Johannesburg. Returning to London in 1898, she helped with the management of the Royal Victoria Hall (the Old Vic), becoming sole manager in 1912 and establishing its reputation for Shakespearean theatre. In 1931 she reopened Sadler's Wells Theatre for the exclusive presentation of opera and ballet, founding the companies that were to become the English National Opera and the Royal Ballet. 🕮 Richard Findlater, *Lilian Baylis: The Lady of the Old Vic* (1975)

Bayliss, Sir William Maddock 1860–1924
English physiologist
Born in Wednesbury, West Midlands, he studied science at University College London (UCL) and received a BSc in 1882, but failed his second MB in anatomy, after which he concentrated on physiological studies. He went to Oxford in 1885 and received a degree in physiology in 1888 before returning to UCL, where he remained for the rest of his life, from 1912 as Professor of General Physiology. Much of his research was conducted in collaboration with **Ernest Starling**, with whom he studied electrophysiology, the vascular system and intestinal motility. In studies of pancreatic secretion they showed that the discharge is induced by a chemical substance which they called secretin, the first known hormone. During World War I Bayliss worked on wound shock. His celebrated book *Principles of General Physiology* first appeared in 1914 and is considered a classic. In 1903 he took out an action for libel against the secretary of the National Antivivisection Society, who had accused Bayliss of carrying out experiments on unanaesthetized animals, and he donated the damages he won to the furtherance of research in physiology. He was elected FRS in 1903, and knighted in 1922.

Baynton, Barbara Janet Ainsleigh 1857–1929
Australian writer and socialite
Born in Scone, New South Wales, of Irish stock, she was the daughter of a carpenter. While working as a governess she married a son of the house who later left her for one of her servants. She then married a retired surgeon, Thomas Baynton, and, entering a life of leisure and culture, began to write stories for *The Bulletin*. Her husband died in 1904, and she moved to London, becoming wealthy from investments on the stock exchange. She travelled frequently between England and Australia, and in 1921 married the fifth Lord Headley, from whom she soon separated. She wrote one novel, *HumanToll* (1907), and a number of short stories first collected in *Bush Studies* (1902) and, with two more stories, as *Cobbers* (1917). Her writing, which describes the grime and squalor of the real bush, as endured by women and the underprivileged, contrasts with the romanticized male 'mateship' of **Henry Lawson** and his followers.

Bazaine, Achille François 1811–88
French soldier
Born in Versailles, he served in Algeria, Spain and the Crimean War (1854–56). In the war with Austria of 1859 he captured Solferino in Italy, and in the Mexican expedition of 1861–67 commanded the army in 1862. He was made Marshal of France in 1864. In the Franco-Prussian War of 1870–71, after the abdication of **Napoleon III**, he failed to support his subordinate commanders at the battles of Spicheren and St Privat la Montagne, and in September 1870 was trapped by the Prussians at Metz, eventually surrendering his whole army of 173,000 men. For this he was court-martialled in 1873 and sentenced to death for treason. The sentence was commuted to 20 years' imprisonment, but in 1874 he escaped to Spain from the fortress of the Île Ste Marguerite, near Cannes. 🕮Maurice Baumont, *Bazaine, les secrets d'un maréchal (1811–1888)* (1978)

Bazaine, Jean René 1904–75
French painter and designer
He was born in Paris. His style developed through Cubism to abstract art, as in *Shadows on the Hill* (1961, Galerie Maeght, Paris), and he produced a number of very successful tapestry designs, as well as stained glass, as in the church of Assy (1944–46), and mosaics (UNESCO, Paris, 1958).

Bazalgette, Sir Joseph William 1819–91
English engineer
Born in Enfield, Middlesex, he constructed London's drainage system and the Thames embankment, and was a notable pioneer of public health engineering.

Bazán, Emilia Pardo See **Pardo Bazán, Emilia**

Bazin, René 1853–1932
French novelist
Born in Angers, he became a professor of law at Angers University, after studying there and in Paris. He depicted with charm and colour the life of peasant people in the various French provinces. Some of his novels, such as *Les Oberlé* (1901, 'The Oberlé Family'), also deal with the social problems of his time. 🕮 G Duhamelet, *René Bazin, romancier catholique* (1935)

Baziotes, William 1912–63
US painter
Born in Pittsburgh, Pennsylvania, he studied at the National Academy of Design in New York from 1933 to 1936. His early work was influenced by **Picasso**, but in the 1940s he was one of a number of US painters, including **Jackson Pollock**, **Arshile Gorky** and **Robert Motherwell**, whose art developed from European Surrealism. Baziotes's work stemmed from the ideal of intuitive, auto-

matic expression through abstraction, permitting the subconscious to dictate colour and line. His dream-like images often contain suggestions of animal forms.

Beach, Amy Marcy See Beach, Mrs H H A

Beach, Frank Ambrose 1911–
US comparative psychologist and endocrinologist
Born in Emporia, Kansas, he studied at Kansas State University and at the University of Chicago, then later at Harvard (1935–36). He worked at the American Museum of Natural History in New York in its department of Experimental Biology, which under his direction became the department of Animal Behavior (1936–46), and he subsequently became Professor of Psychology first at Yale (1946–58) and then at the University of California at Berkeley (1958–78). One of the first US biologists to appreciate the work of European ethologists, in his research he has been concerned with the hormonal regulation of reproductive behaviour. He demonstrated how sensory and experiential factors affect the hormonal regulation of behaviour, and developed the concept of 'gender role' to account for aspects of human sexuality. He wrote *Hormones and Behavior* (1948) and *Sex and Behavior* (1965).

Beach, Mrs H H A, *professional name of* Amy Marcy Beach, *née* Cheney 1867–1944
US concert pianist and composer
Born in Henniker, New Hampshire, she made her professional concert debut at the age of 16 in Boston, where she met and married a local surgeon, Henry Harris Aubrey Beach in 1885. She then devoted herself to composition, in which she was mostly self-taught. Her *Mass* (1892) was an important work, but it was her Symphony in E-minor Op.32 that established her romantic style, reminiscent of folk. The first symphony written by a US woman, it was performed by the Boston Symphony Orchestra in 1896. Like Olivier Messiaen, Beach transcribed and made use of birdsong in her work. She had become an established composer by the time of her husband's death (1910), and she performed successfully in Europe, returning to the USA just before World War I.

Beach, Moses Yale 1800–68
US journalist and inventor
Born in Wallingford, Connecticut, he experimented with engines and invented, but failed to patent, a rag-cutting machine widely used in paper mills. After beginning his career in journalism with the *New York Sun* in 1834, he bought the paper in 1838, and it flourished under his editorship. Famously preoccupied with speed, he introduced ingenious ways to get news (such as boats meeting ships from Europe, carrier pigeons, and pony express riders). He also originated syndicated news stories, established the first European edition of a US paper (*American Sun*, 1848), and organized the New York Associated Press to reduce costs and competition.

Beach Boys, The See Wilson, Brian

Beadle, George Wells 1903–89
US biochemical geneticist and Nobel Prize winner
Born in Wahoo, Nebraska, he became interested in agricultural genetics, studying the genetics of maize, the fruit fly (*Drosophila*) and the bread mould *Neurospora*. At Stanford University (1937–46), in association with Edward Tatum, he developed the idea that specific genes control the production of specific enzymes. Beadle and Tatum shared the Nobel Prize for physiology or medicine in 1958 with Joshua Lederberg. As president of the American Association for the Advancement of Science (AAAS), Beadle worked in the 1950s for more openness in scientific research. He was a professor at the California Institute of Technology (Caltech, 1946–61), and president of Chicago University from 1961 to 1968.

Beaglehole, John Cawte 1901–71
New Zealand historian of Australasian exploration
Born in Wellington, he graduated from Victoria University College (later Victoria University), to which he returned in 1936 as lecturer in history, later becoming Professor of British Commonwealth History (1963–66). His PhD was obtained after some years at University College London, and on his return to New Zealand he suffered from academic prejudice against his left-wing opinions. He produced major works such as *The Exploration of the Pacific* (1934), *New Zealand, A Short History* (1936) and *The Discovery of New Zealand* (1939). His life's work was the Hakluyt Society edition of *The Journals of Captain James Cook on his Voyages of Discovery* (1955–67), associated with which was his *The Endeavour Journal of Sir Joseph Banks* (1962). His biography of Cook was published posthumously.

Beale, Dorothea 1831–1906
English pioneer of women's education
Born in London, she was educated at Queen's College, London, and taught there from 1849. In 1857 she was appointed head teacher of Clergy Daughters' School in Westmoreland, and from 1858 to 1906 was principal of Cheltenham Ladies' College. In 1885 she founded St Hilda's College, Cheltenham, the first English training college for women teachers, and sponsored St Hilda's Hall in Oxford for women teachers in 1893. An ardent suffragette, she was immortalized in verse with Frances Mary Buss: 'Miss Buss and Miss Beale, Cupid's darts do not feel'.

Beale, Lionel Smith 1828–1906
English physiologist and microscopist
He was born in London and entered King's College London to study medicine. He graduated in 1851, established a private laboratory and became a teacher of microscopy. Just two years later, he was elected Professor of Physiology and Morbid Anatomy at King's College, becoming Professor of Pathological Anatomy in 1869, and Professor of the Principles and Practice of Medicine in 1876. He won many honours, including presidency of the Microscopical Society (1879–80). A master of the techniques of vital staining and a fine investigator of cellular tissue, 'Beale's cells' (the pyriform nerve ganglion cells) commemorate his researches. He attracted greatest notice, however, for his opposition to the theories of T H Huxley and Charles Darwin.

Beale, Mary, *née* Cradock 1632–99
English painter
Born in Barrow, Suffolk, the daughter of a clergyman, she married in 1651 by which time she was already a practising portrait painter and a devoted follower of the most celebrated portraitist of her day, Sir Peter Lely. Very little is known of her work before about 1670, but several of her husband's diaries record her painting commissions which include a number of portraits of clerics. She also produced copies of Lely's work.

Beals, Jessie Tarbox, *née* Tarbox 1870–1942
US photographer
Born in Hamilton, Canada, a daughter of the inventor Nathaniel Tarbox, she became a teacher in Massachusetts in 1887, carrying out portrait photography in the summers of the 1890s. She married machinist Alfred T Beals in 1897, and after she had taught him photography, they became itinerant photographers (1900). She became a journalist in upstate New York (1902), then established a studio in New York City (1905). In 1910–12 she made documentary photographs of children of the New York slums. Although she and Alfred continued to work together, she left him in 1917 and they divorced. Their work was published in the journals *Harper's Bazaar* and *Vogue*,

among others. In 1928–29 she visited southern California, photographing mainly celebrities and gardens. She and **Frances Benjamin Johnston** are considered to be among the very first women press photographers.

Beamon, Bob (Robert) 1946–
US athlete

Born in New York City, he became a noted long jumper. He smashed the world record at the 1968 Olympic Games in Mexico City, with a jump of 8.90m (29ft 2ins)—55cm (21ins) further than the previous record. The high altitude increased the difficulty of the jump and made the achievement all the more impressive. The record stood until 1991, when it was broken by Mike Powell in Tokyo.

Bean, Charles Edwin Woodrow 1879–1968
Australian journalist and war historian

Born in Bathurst, New South Wales, he was educated at Oxford. He became London correspondent for the *Sydney Morning Herald* and became official correspondent to the Australian Imperial Forces in World War I. Landing at Gallipoli in 1915, he stayed at the front throughout, and on being appointed Australia's official war historian, he returned to Gallipoli in 1919 to research the campaign. His major work is the 12-volume *Official History of Australia in the War of 1914–18* (1921–42), in which he takes much credit for the creation of the ANZAC legend. He wrote six of the 12 volumes and edited the others, and in 1946 published his own single-volume abridgement, *Anzac to Amiens*. 📖 K Fewster, *The Frontline Diary of C. E. W. Bean* (1983); D McCarthy, *Gallipoli to the Somme* (1983)

Bean, Roy c.1825–1903
US frontiersman

Born in Mason County, Kentucky, he served with Confederate irregulars in New Mexico during the Civil War and was a blockade runner in San Antonio, Texas. In 1882 he moved to the sparsely populated region west of the Pecos River and opened a saloon to serve workmen building the Southern Pacific Railroad. Doubling as a justice of the peace, he styled himself the 'law west of the Pecos' and presided over a bar-room court, often interrupting the proceedings to serve liquor. His arbitrary and sometimes bigoted rulings made him a legend in a state that admired the unconventional. After falling in love with a picture of the British actress **Lillie Langtry**, he named his Texas settlement for her.

Beane, Sawney fl.c.1600
Scottish mass murderer and cannibal

Born near Edinburgh during the reign of **James VI and I**, he moved to Galloway as a young man, taking with him a woman of evil reputation. For 25 years Beane and his rapidly expanding family lived like savages in a huge cave, terrorizing travellers within the area. Hundreds of people vanished. He and his 48-strong family, who are thought to have killed up to 1,000 people, were finally tracked down and executed in Edinburgh with particular brutality.

Beard, Charles Austin 1874–1948
US historian

Born in Knightstown, Indiana, he studied at DePauw University, Oxford and Columbia, where he taught from 1907 until 1917. After work on European history, he produced *An Economic Interpretation of the Constitution of the United States* (1913), arguing for personal and group economic interests as explanation of the framing of the Constitution in 1787, the first effectual popular demolition of a 'Golden Age' origin of the USA. He also wrote *The Economic Origins of Jeffersonian Democracy* (1915), and *The Rise of American Civilization* (1927), in which his wife, **Mary Ritter Beard**, was his collaborator, as with its sequels,

America in Midpassage (1939) and *The American Spirit* (1942). Their conclusions were summed up in *A Basic History of the United States* (1944), which was influential for a time.

Beard, James 1903–85
US chef

He was born in Portland, Oregon. An influential teacher of cooking, he wrote numerous cookbooks on American cuisine, including *The James Beard Cookbook* (1959), *American Cookery* (1972), and *Beard on Bread* (1973), as well as an autobiography of his early years, *Delights and Prejudices* (1964).

Beard, Mary Ritter 1876–1958
US feminist and historian

She was born in Indianapolis, Indiana, and educated at DePauw University. In 1900 she married **Charles Austin Beard** and became involved in women's suffrage, first in Oxford, England, where her husband was a student, then in New York (from 1902) where they both enrolled at Columbia University. After the birth of her son (1907) she joined the National Women's Trade Union League, helping to run strikes and protests. She became a member of the Woman Suffrage movement (1910), and after a period of editing *The Woman Voter* became involved with the Wage Earners' League. She worked assiduously (1913–17) for the Congressional Union (later the National Women's Party) under **Alice Paul**'s leadership, but gradually became more interested in teaching and writing. Her publications include *Woman's Work in Municipalities* (1915), *On Understanding Women* (1931) and, most famously, *Women as a Force in History* (1946). With her husband she wrote several influential works on American history, including *The Rise of American Civilization* (1927). A polemical, perceptive commentator, she is best remembered for illuminating women's history.

Bearden, Romare 1914–88
US artist

He was born in Charlotte, North Carolina, and raised in Harlem, New York City. A painter whose vibrant works express the theme of the experience of African-Americans in the USA, he is represented in numerous US museums. In the 1960s he was a founder of the Cinque Gallery, for young artists, and the Spiral Group to aid African-American artists.

Beardsley, Aubrey Vincent 1872–98
English illustrator

Born in Brighton, Sussex, he worked in an architect's and fire-insurance offices. He became famous by his fantastic posters and illustrations for *Morte d'Arthur*, **Oscar Wilde**'s *Salome*, **Pope**'s *Rape of the Lock*, *Mlle de Maupin*, *Volpone*, as well as for the *Yellow Book* magazine (1894–96) and his own *Book of Fifty Drawings*, mostly executed in black and white, in a highly individualistic asymmetrical style. With Wilde he is regarded as leader of the Decadents of the 1890s. He died of tuberculosis at Menton, having become a Roman Catholic. 📖 Brigid Brophy, *Black & White: A Portrait of Aubrey Beardsley* (1970)

Beatles, The See panel p156

Beaton, Sir Cecil Walter Hardy 1904–80
English photographer and designer

He was born in London, and educated at Harrow and Cambridge. In the 1920s, as a staff photographer for *Vanity Fair* and *Vogue*, he became famous for his society portraits, including those of royalty. After World War II, he designed scenery and costumes for many ballet, operatic, theatrical and film productions, including *My Fair Lady* (1964) and *Gigi* (1958). His publications include *The Book of Beauty* (1930), *My Royal Past* (1939), *The Glass of Fashion*

The Beatles
English pop band

The Beatles became the best-known group in popular music in the 1960s. They formed in Liverpool in 1960; three of the founder-members, **John Lennon**, **Paul McCartney** and George Harrison (1943–), were later joined by Ringo Starr, (originally Richard Starkey, 1940–), who replaced the original drummer, Pete Best, before their breakthrough. The group learned their trade through gruelling engagements at the city's Cavern Club and at venues in Hamburg, West Germany. Under the management of Brian Epstein, a local record-shop owner, they signed a recording contract in 1962 and their regional popularity quickly spread across the country with such records as 'Love Me Do', 'She Loves You' and 'I Want to Hold Your Hand'. In 1964 the last two titles were released in the USA, and 'Beatlemania' spread rapidly around the world, with the group consistently surpassing all previous figures for concert attendances and record sales.

They provoked hysteria wherever they played as teen idols in the first half of the decade, then became the first mature rock icons in the second. The early songs of Lennon and McCartney involved simple but effective harmonies which nevertheless won acclaim from serious musicians and critics; William Mann, then England's leading classical music critic, described them in *The Times* as the most important songwriters since **Schubert**. The pair showed a remarkable ability to assimilate various styles and their compositional technique, enhanced by producer George Martin, developed quickly. Their decision to record their own songs had the effect, in the UK, of ending the dominance of 'Tin Pan Alley' and was widely imitated by other performers. Their music ranged from the lyrically beautiful 'Yesterday' to the complex rhythms of 'Paperback Writer', the nostalgia of 'Penny Lane', and the surrealism of 'Strawberry Fields Forever'.

Controversially created MBE in 1965 (Lennon later returned his insignia in protest against the Vietnam War), the group were involved for a while with Indian mysticism and 'transcendental' meditation, and the use of hallucinogenic drugs. The latter flirtation had a major influence on the recording of *Sergeant Pepper's Lonely Hearts Club Band* (1967), an album which, with its long musically and thematically linked songs, achieved a new maturity for pop and became perhaps the most influential recording since the advent of **Elvis Presley**. Their eponymous double album of 1968 included 'Helter-Skelter', a song claimed as an inspiration by Charles Manson. After a long period of inactivity and a patchy final album, the group dissolved in 1970 amid complex legal wranglings.

After the group parted, Paul McCartney recorded alone and with the highly-successful group Wings. John Lennon wrote and recorded in the USA with his wife, **Yoko Ono**, and was murdered in New York (1980). George Harrison recorded intermittently and became a successful film producer. The band 're-united' to add their singing and playing to 'Free as A Bird' (1995), a previously unreleased demo tape sung by Lennon. It was a disappointment, but provided much valuable publicity for the launch of an *Anthology* series of their recordings.

♫ Major recordings: *Please Please Me* (1963), *Beatles For Sale* (1964), *Rubber Soul* (1965), *Revolver* (1966), *Sergeant Pepper's Lonely Hearts Club Band* (1967), *The Beatles* (1968, also known as *The White Album*), *Abbey Road* (1969) and *Let It Be* (1970). They also made the films *A Hard Day's Night* (1964), *Help!* (1965) and *Magical Mystery Tour* (1967).

📖 See biography by P Norman, *Shout!* (1981) and Pete Best's *The Best Years of the Beatles* (1996).

John Lennon, ever the agent provocateur, prompted a massive furore in the USA in 1966 when he suggested that the Beatles were 'more popular than Christ now. I don't know which will go first. Rock and roll or Christianity'.

(1959) and *The Magic Image* (1975), and he provided the drawings and illustrations for many other books. He also wrote several volumes of autobiography (1961–78).

Beaton or Bethune, David 1494–1546
Scottish statesman and Roman Catholic prelate

Born in Balfour, Fife, he was educated at St Andrews, Glasgow and Paris universities. He was Scottish 'resident' at the French court (1519) and was appointed Bishop of Mirepoix by **Francis I** (1537). In 1525 he took his seat in the Scots parliament as abbot of Arbroath and became Privy Seal. Elevated to cardinal (1538), he was made Archbishop of St Andrews in 1539. On James V's death, he produced a forged will, appointing himself and three others regents of the kingdom during the minority of the infant **Mary, Queen of Scots**. The nobility, however, elected the Protestant James Hamilton, 2nd Earl of Arran, regent. Beaton was arrested, but soon regained favour and was made Chancellor (1543). A persecutor of the Scottish Protestants, he had the reformer **George Wishart** burnt at St Andrews (1546), but was murdered in revenge three months later by a group of Protestant conspirators. He was the nephew of **James Beaton**. 📖 Sir John Herkless, *Cardinal Beaton: Priest and Politician* (1891)

Beaton or Bethune, James 1470–1539
Scottish prelate and statesman

He graduated from St Andrews in 1493, and rose rapidly to be Archbishop of Glasgow (1509), and of St Andrews (1522). One of the regents during **James V**'s minority, he upheld the **Hamilton** against the **Douglas** faction, and in 1526 had 'to keep sheep in Balgrumo', while the Douglases plundered his castle. He was soon, however, reinstated in his see, and was a zealous supporter of France. An opponent of the Reformation, he initiated persecution of Protestants: **Patrick Hamilton** and three other Protestants were burnt at the stake during his primacy. He was the uncle of Cardinal **David Beaton**.

Beatrix, *in full* Beatrix Wilhelmina Armgard 1938–
Queen of the Netherlands

Born in Soestdk, the eldest daughter of Queen **Juliana** and Prince **Bernhard Leopold**, she married (1966) a West-German diplomat, Claus-Georg von Amsberg (1926–). Their son, Prince Willem-Alexander (1967–) is the first male heir to the Dutch throne in over a century; their other sons are Johan Friso (1968–) and Constantijn (1969–). She acceded to the throne on her mother's abdication in 1980.

Beatty, David Beatty, 1st Earl 1871–1936
English naval commander

Born in Nantwich, Cheshire, he joined the navy in 1884 and served in the Sudan (1896–98). As commander of a battleship he took part in the China War (1900) and in 1912 was appointed to command the 1st Battle Cruiser Squadron. At the outbreak of World War I he steamed into Heligoland Bight, and destroyed three German cruisers. In January 1915 he pursued German battle cruisers near the Dogger Bank, sinking the *Blücher*, and took part in the Battle of Jutland (1916). He succeeded Lord Jellicoe as Commander-in-Chief of the Grand Fleet in

1916 and became First Sea Lord in 1919. 📖 Charles Beatty, *Our Admiral: A Biography of Admiral of the Fleet Earl Beatty* (1980)

Beatty, Warren, *originally* Warren Beaty 1937–
US film actor, director and producer

Born in Richmond, Virginia, the brother of actress Shirley MacLaine, he studied at the Stella Adler Acting School. He was first seen in the television series *The Many Loves of Dobie Gillis* (1955–59) before making his Broadway debut in *A Loss of Roses* (1959) and his film debut in *Splendor in the Grass* (1961). He appeared as a broodingly handsome leading man in several comedies as well as portraying more complex combinations of naivety and cynicism in films like *Lilith* (1964) and *Mickey One* (1965). He acted in and produced *Bonnie and Clyde* (1967), co-wrote *Shampoo* (1975) and co-directed *Heaven Can Wait* (1978). He was the producer, co-writer and star of *Reds* (1981) which won him an Academy Award as Best Director. Recent films include *Dick Tracy* (1990) and *Bugsy* (1991). His enduring Casanova image has often detracted from his many political interests and consistent efforts to expand the scope of his talents. In 1992 he married the actress Annette Bening (1958–), his co-star in *Bugsy* (1991). He subsequently made *Bulworth* (1997).

Beau Brummell See Brummell, George Bryan

Beauchamp, Pierre 1636–1705
French dancer, choreographer and ballet-master

Born in Versailles, he trained in music and dance, and made his debut in 1650. Later he became Superintendent of the Court Ballet of Louis XIV, with which he also performed. In 1671 he was appointed Director of the Académie Royale de Danse. He choreographed many ballets, including those for operas and comedies by Jean Baptiste Lully and Molière, all now lost. He was known as a dancer of dignity and virtuosity able to execute remarkable pirouettes and *tours en l'air*. Some credit him with the invention of classical ballet's five positions. He also created his own notation system.

Beaufort, Duke of
English title

It was conferred in 1682 on Henry Somerset, 3rd Marquis of Worcester. Henry, the 7th Duke (1792–1853), and his son Henry, the 8th Duke (1824–1899), were famous sportsmen, the latter an editor of the *Badminton Library*, Badminton House in Gloucestershire being the family residence. The 8th duke's second son, Lord Henry (1849–1932), was a songwriter.

Beaufort, Sir Francis 1774–1857
British naval officer and hydrographer

Born in Navan, County Meath, Ireland, he joined the Royal Navy in 1787, fought in the retreat of Cornwallis (1795), and was severely wounded near Malaga. After a period working on shore telegraphs in Ireland he held three commands, and was dangerously wounded while surveying the coast of Asia Minor and suppressing piracy. From 1829 to 1855 he was hydrographer to the navy, devising the Beaufort scale of wind force and a tabulated system of weather registration. He was promoted rear admiral in 1846. 📖 Alfred Friendly, *Beaufort of the Admiralty: The Life of Sir Francis Beaufort, 1774–1857* (1977)

Beaufort, Henry 1377–1447
English cardinal and politician

He studied at Oxford and Aix-la-Chapelle, was consecrated Bishop of Lincoln (1398) and Winchester (1405), and became a cardinal in 1426. He was Lord Chancellor on three occasions (1403–05, 1413–17, 1424–26). He strongly opposed Henry V's proposition to levy a new impost on the clergy for the war against France, but he

lent the King (1416–21), out of his own private purse, £28,000—a sum which justifies the belief that he was the wealthiest subject in England. In 1427 the pope sent him as legate into Germany, to organize a crusade against the Hussites. This undertaking failed, and he fell from papal favour. During the 1430s he controlled the government of the young King Henry VI of England. 📖 L B Radford, *Henry Beaufort* (1908)

Beaufort, Lady Margaret, Countess of Richmond 1443–1509
English noblewoman

The daughter of John Beaufort, 1st Duke of Somerset, she married Edmund Tudor, Earl of Richmond in 1455. The Lancastrian claim to the English Crown was transferred to her when the male line died out, and it was because of her descent from John of Gaunt that her son Henry (Henry VII) ascended the throne after the defeat of Richard III (1485). During the Wars of the Roses she married Henry Stafford, son of the Duke of Buckingham (1464), and in 1473, Thomas Stanley, 1st Earl of Derby, who was instrumental in helping Henry VII assume the Crown. She was a benefactress of Oxford and Cambridge universities, where she endowed two divinity professorships. She also founded Christ's College and St John's College, Cambridge, and was a patron of William Caxton. She translated Thomas à Kempis into English. 📖 Michael K Jones, *The King's Mother: Lady Margaret Beaufort, Countess of Richmond and Derby* (1992)

Beauharnais, Alexandre Beauharnais, Vicomte de 1760–94
French soldier

He served in Louis XVI's army in the American Revolution (1775–83) under the Comte de Rochambeau, but in 1789 embraced the French Revolution. He was made Secretary of the National Assembly, but was guillotined for his failure to relieve Metz. In 1779 he had married Joséphine de Beauharnais, later wife of Napoleon I, and in 1802 his daughter Hortense married Napoleon's brother Louis. Beauharnais was thus the grandfather of Napoleon III.

Beauharnais, Eugène de 1781–1824
French general

After the marriage of his mother, Joséphine, to Napoleon I, he served with his stepfather in Italy and Egypt, and rapidly rose to the highest military rank. In 1805 he was made a prince of France, and from 1805 to 1814 was Viceroy of Italy. As viceroy he established his court at Milan but was allowed little rein by his stepfather in running the affairs of the kingdom. In 1806 he married Augusta, daughter of Maximilian of Bavaria. In 1813–14 he tried to resist the Austrian invasion of Italy but eventually fled to Munich, where he was offered protection by his father-in-law and created Duke of Leuchtenberg.

Beauharnais, Hortense Eugénie Cécile 1783–1837
Queen of Holland

She was born in Paris, the daughter of Alexandre, Vicomte de Beauharnais. As a child she was a great favourite of her stepfather, Napoleon I, and in 1802 married his brother Louis, King of Holland (1806–10); the youngest of their three children became Napoleon III. In 1810–11 she was the mistress of Comte Auguste de Flahaut, their son becoming Duc de Morny. She was created Duchesse de St Leu by Louis XVIII (1814) at Tsar Alexander I's request. She was a gifted artist and a composer, whose marching song, *Partant pour la Syrie* ('Onward to Syria'), became the national anthem of France's Second Empire.

Beauvoir, Simone de 1908–86
French socialist, feminist and writer

Simone de Beauvoir was born in Paris and educated at the Sorbonne, where she later lectured. She will probably be remembered chiefly for the enormous impact made by *Le Deuxième sexe* (1949, Eng trans *The Second Sex*, 1953), a study of women's social situation and historical predicament; it was one of the first feminist tracts which, despite its alleged shortcomings, remains authoritative for its intelligence and the forcefulness of the case it presents. It inspired many women to salutary writings and actions and led several to refer to its author as 'the mother of us all'. She was also a notable novelist and autobiographer. The lifelong companion of **Jean-Paul Sartre**, she contributed with him to the Existentialist movement of the mid-20th-century.

Her more autobiographical writings and novels include *Les Mandarins* (1954), a winner of the Prix Goncourt;

Mémoires d'une jeune fille rangée (1958, Eng trans *Memoirs of a Dutiful Daughter*, 1959); *La Force de l'âge* (1960, Eng trans *The Prime of Life*, 1963); *La Force des choses* (1963, Eng trans *The Force of Circumstance*, 1965); *Une Mort très douce* (1964, Eng trans *A Very Easy Death*, 1972); *Toute compte fait* (1972, Eng trans *All Said and Done*, 1974); and *La Cérémonie des adieux* (1981, Eng trans *Adieux: A Farewell to Sartre*).

📖 D Bair, *Simone de Beauvoir* (1990); R D Cottrell, *Simone de Beauvoir* (1975).

> *On ne naît pas femme: on le devient.* ('One is not born a woman: one becomes a woman.') From *Le deuxième sexe*, ch.1 (1949).

Beauharnais, Joséphine de, *née* Marie Josèphe Rose Tascher de la Pagerie 1763–1814
French empress

She was born in Martinique and married (1779) the Vicomte de **Beauharnais**, who was executed in 1794. Two years later, she married **Napoleon I**. She accompanied him on his Italian campaign, but soon returned to Paris. At Malmaison, the Palais du Luxembourg and the Tuileries, she attracted the most brilliant society of France, and contributed considerably to the establishment of her husband's power. Their marriage, being childless, was dissolved (1809), but she retained the title of empress. Her children from her first marriage were **Eugène** and **Hortense de Beauharnais**. 📖 R M Wilson, *Josephine* (1984)

Beaumarchais, Pierre Augustin Caron de 1732–99
French playwright

Born in Paris, the son of a watchmaker, he was brought up in his father's trade, and invented, at 21, a new escapement which was pirated by a rival. The affair brought him to notice at court, where his good looks and fine speech and manners quickly procured him advancement. He was engaged to teach the harp to **Louis XV**'s daughters, and made a fortune through two judicious marriages and profitable speculation with Duverney, a rich Parisian banker. His first plays, *Eugénie* (1767, Eng trans *The School for Rakes*, 1769) and *Les Deux Amis* (1770, Eng trans *The Two Friends*, 1800), were only moderately successful, and he made his reputation with *Mémoires du Sieur Beaumarchais par lui-même* (1774–78, 'Autobiography'), a work which united the bitterest satire with the sharpest logic. The same brilliant satire burns in his two famous comedies, *Le Barbier de Séville* (1775, Eng trans *The Barber of Seville*, 1776) and *La Folle journée ou le mariage de Figaro* (1784, Eng trans *The Follies of a Day; or, The Marriage of Figaro*, 1785). The latter had a most unprecedented success, but the Revolution cost Beaumarchais his vast fortune, and, suspected of an attempt to sell arms to the émigrés, he had to take refuge in Holland and England (1793). 📖 R Pomeau, *Beaumarchais, l'homme et l'œuvre* (1956)

Beaumont, Agnes 1652–1720
English religious autobiographer

Born in Edworth, Bedfordshire, the daughter of a widowed yeoman farmer, she joined one of **John Bunyan**'s congregations at Gamlingay at the age of 20, and became his friend. Two years later (1674), her father forbade her to attend a meeting, and when she defied him he locked her out of the house for two days. They were soon reconciled, but the strain of the incident killed him. It took a coroner's jury to clear the accusation that she and Bunyan had conspired to poison him. The story is related in her auto-

biography, the 'Narrative of the Persecution of Agnes Beaumont', which still survives in manuscript form and was published in a collection called *An Abstract of the Gracious Dealings of God with Several Eminent Christians* (1760).

Beaumont, Francis c.1584–1616
English Elizabethan dramatist

Born in Gracedieu, Leicestershire, the brother of Sir **John Beaumont**, he was educated at Broadgates Hall (now Pembroke College), Oxford, and entered the Inner Temple in 1600. He soon became a friend of **Ben Jonson** and **John Fletcher**. With the latter, Beaumont was to be associated closely until he married Ursula Isley (1613) and retired from the theatre. He and Fletcher are said to have shared everything: work, lodgings, and even clothes. Their dramatic works, compiled in 1647, contained 35 pieces, and another folio, published in 1679, 52 works. Modern research finds Beaumont's hand in only about 10 plays, which include, however, the masterpieces. *The Woman Hater* (1607) is attributed solely to Beaumont, and he had the major share in *The Knight of the Burning Pestle* (1609), a burlesque of knight errantry and a parody of **John Heywood**'s *Four Prentices of London*. *Philaster* (1610), *The Maid's Tragedy* (1611) and *A King and No King* (1611) established their joint popularity. Other works include *The Masque of the Inner Temple*, written by Beaumont in honour of the marriage of the Elector Palatinate **Frederick V** and the princess **Elizabeth** (1613). 📖 W W Appleton, *Beaumont and Fletcher: a critical study* (1956)

Beaumont, Sir John 1582–1627
English poet

He is best known for his work *Bosworth Field*, in which the heroic couplet makes its first appearance in English poetry. He was the elder brother of **Francis Beaumont**. 📖 A Chalmers, in *The Works of Early English Poets* (1910)

Beaumont, William 1785–1853
US surgeon

He was born in Lebanon, Connecticut, and became a surgeon in the US army. His study on human digestion occuring in the stomach was based on experiments with a young French–Canadian patient, Alexis St Martin, who was suffering from a gunshot wound which had left a permanent opening in his stomach, and which Beaumont treated. He wrote the pioneering work *Experiments and Observations on the Gastric Juice and the Physiology of Digestion* (1833).

Beau Nash See Nash, Richard

Beauregard, Pierre Gustave Toutant 1818–93
US general

He graduated from the US Military Academy at West Point (1838), served in the Mexican War (1846–48), and was appointed by the Confederate government to the command at Charleston, where he commenced the war by the bombardment of Fort Sumter (12 April 1861). He fought at Bull Run (1861), then took command at Shiloh (1862), and later defended Charleston and Richmond. 📖 T Harry Williams, *P G T Beauregard: Napoleon in Gray* (1954)

Beauvoir, Simone de See panel p158

Beaverbrook, Max (William Maxwell Aitken), 1st Baron 1879–1964
British newspaper magnate and politician

Born in Maple, Ontario, Canada, the son of a Presbyterian minister, he was educated in Newcastle, New Brunswick. He was a stockbroker in 1907 and by 1910 had made a fortune out of the amalgamation of Canadian cement mills. He went to Great Britain in 1910, entered parliament (1911–16), and became private secretary to Bonar Law. He was an observer at the Western Front early in World War I and wrote *Canada in Flanders* (1917). When Lloyd George became premier, he was made Minister of Information (1918). In 1919 he plunged into journalism and took Fleet Street by storm by taking over the *Daily Express* and making it into the most widely read daily newspaper in the world. He founded the *Sunday Express* (1921) and bought the *Evening Standard* (1929). The 'Beaverbrook press' fully expressed the ebullient, relentless, and crusading personality of its owner. In World War II Churchill successfully harnessed Beaverbrook's dynamic administrative powers to the production of much-needed aircraft. He was made Minister of Supply (1941–42), Lord Privy Seal, and lend-lease administrator in the USA. He became Chancellor of the University of New Brunswick in 1947. He wrote *Politicians and the Press* (1925), *Politicians and the War* (1928–32), *Men and Power* (new edn 1956), and *The Decline and Fall of Lloyd George* (1963). 📖 A J P Taylor, *Beaverbrook* (1956)

Bebel, Ferdinand August 1840–1913
German socialist

Born in Cologne, he became a master turner. By 1871 he had become a leader of the German Social Democrat movement and its chief spokesman in the Reichstag. Occasional imprisonment added to his popularity. He wrote widely on socialism, on the Peasants' War, on the status of women, and published an autobiography, *My Life* (trans 1912).

Beccafumi, Domenico, *originally* di Pace
c.1486–1551
Italian painter

Born in Siena, he was influenced by High Renaissance artists such as Michelangelo and Raphael without forsaking the traditionally Sienese qualities of decorative colour and sinuous line. His paintings are characterized by unusual perspective, complicated figure poses and complex colour effects, and are considered an early manifestation of the post-Renaissance style known as Mannerism. He also produced Old Testament designs for the marble floor of Siena cathedral as well as frescoes for the city hall. Much of his best work remains in the Pinacoteca, Siena.

Beccaria, Cesare, Marchese de 1738–94
Italian jurist and philosopher

He was born in Milan and studied at a Jesuit school in Parma. In 1764 he published anonymously *Dei delitti e delle pene* ('On Crimes and Punishments'). Denouncing capital punishment and torture, and advocating prevention of crime by education, the work had a widespread influence on the punishment and prevention of crime. He was

appointed Professor of Political Philosophy at Milan in 1768 and a member of the board for reform of the judicial code in 1791.

Beche, Sir Henry Thomas de la See De la Beche, Sir Henry Thomas

Becher, Johann Joachim 1635–82
German chemist and physician

Born in Speyer, the Palatinate, he had little formal education, but was appointed Professor of Medicine at Mainz in 1666. He was subsequently physician to the Elector of Bavaria in Munich, where he was also involved in commercial projects. He later spent some time in Vienna, but in 1678 he fell into disgrace with his patrons; he fled to Holland and in 1680 to England, where he died shortly after. In 1667 he published a classification of substances, particularly minerals, under the title *Physicae subterraneae*, in which he expounded a three 'element' theory of matter. This was later elaborated into the phlogiston theory by Georg Stahl. Becher published many other works, including *Tripus hermeticus* (1680), which contained a catalogue of chemical apparatus, and he also practised alchemy, undertaking experiments designed to transmute sand into gold.

Bechet, Sidney Joseph 1897–1959
US jazz musician

Born in New Orleans, he was already an outstanding jazz clarinettist as a teenager. He took up the soprano saxophone in 1919, his forceful style making him the first significant saxophone voice in jazz. Touring Europe after World War I with Will Marion Cook's Southern Syncopated Orchestra, Bechet was recognized as 'an artist of genius' by Swiss conductor Ernest Ansermet. As the New Orleans style declined in popularity, Bechet spent much of the 1930s in obscurity, emerging in 1940 as a figurehead of the traditional jazz revival. The warmth of his reception during many tours in Europe led him to make his permanent home in Paris, where he was an influential and honoured father-figure of his music. 📖 John Chilton, *Sidney Bechet the Wizard of Jazz* (1987)

Bechstein, Karl 1826–1900
German manufacturer

He was born in Gotha. In 1856 he founded his famous piano factory in Berlin. His grand pianos were of a very high standard, and were produced in large quantities.

Beck, Jozef 1894–1944
Polish colonel

He helped Marshal Józef Piłsudski to seize control in his 1926 coup, became Deputy Foreign Minister in 1930 and was finally Foreign Minister from 1932 to 1939. Following Hitler's rise to power, he tried to maintain first an equilibrium between Nazi Germany and the USSR, and then a policy of partial co-operation with Hitler to expand and defend his country. He assisted in the dismemberment of Czechoslovakia in 1938, and defeated the Anglo-French bid to form an alliance with the USSR in 1939. In August 1939, he had to face the consequences when Hitler invaded a Poland that was virtually defenceless, and he escaped abroad.

Beckenbauer, Franz 1945–
German footballer

Born in Munich, he has been a dynamic force in West German football over the last quarter of a century as player, coach, manager and administrator. He captained the West German national side to European Nations Cup success in 1972 and to the World Cup triumph of 1974. He was European Footballer of the Year in 1972, and won three successive European Cup winner's medals with Bayern Munich (1974–76). He retired from playing in 1983, and in 1984 was appointed coach to the West

German national team, a post he held until their victory in the 1990 World Cup. His masterful style led to his being nicknamed 'Kaiser Franz'. Appointed manager of West Germany in 1986, he took them to consecutive World Cup finals, as runners up in 1986 and then as winners (for Germany) in 1990.

Becker, Boris 1967–
German tennis player

Born in Leimen, he first came to prominence in 1984 when he finished runner-up in the US Open. In 1985 he became the youngest-ever winner of the men's singles at Wimbledon, as well as the first unseeded winner. A big serve and diving volleys made him the best grass court player of the 1980s. He successfully defended his title in 1986, won it for a third time in 1989, and was a beaten finalist in 1988, 1990 and 1991. He also won the US Open in 1989, the Australian Open in 1991 and the Grand Slam Cup in 1996, and with Michael Stich won a gold medal for Germany in the 1992 Olympic doubles. 📖 Johnny Waller and Marianne Lassen, *Boris Becker Wunderkind* (1986)

Becker, Carl Lotus 1873–1945
US historian

Born near Waterloo, Iowa, he was a graduate of Wisconsin University. He taught at Columbia, Pennsylvania State College, Dartmouth and Kansas (1902–16), and became Professor of European History at Cornell University (1917–41). He was influenced by his Wisconsin teacher, Frederick Jackson Turner. He wrote *The Declaration of Independence* (1922, 1942), an essay on Benjamin Franklin for the *Dictionary of American Biography*, which was published as a separate book, and *The Heavenly City of the Eighteenth Century Philosophers* (1932). His other works included *Beginnings of the American People* (1915), *The Eve of Revolution* (1918), *Modern History* (1931) and *Progress and Power* (1936).

Becker, Wilhelm 1907–
Swiss astronomer

Born in Münster, he studied at the university there (1927) and in Berlin (1932). Between 1932 and 1953 he was an astronomer at the observatories of Munich, Potsdam, Vienna and Hamburg before being appointed Professor of Astronomy and Director of the Astronomical Institute at Basle (1953–77). Becker's chief field of activity has been stellar photographic photometry. He was a pioneer of the three-colour system used to compare stellar brightnesses and to determine the stellar distances of young star clusters. Studies of such clusters have contributed substantially to the mapping of the Milky Way.

Becket, Isaac 1653–1719
English mezzotint engraver

Born in Kent, he took an apprenticeship in calico printing and learned from Edward Lutterel the art of mezzotint engraving. He executed many plates from the portraits of Sir Godfrey Kneller, including that of Charles II and Kneller's self-portrait.

Becket, Thomas (à) 1118–70
English saint and martyr, Archbishop of Canterbury

He was born in London, the son of a wealthy Norman merchant. Educated at Merton Priory and in London, he trained in knightly exercises at Pevensey Castle, studied theology in Paris, and became a notary. About 1142 he entered the household of Theobald, Archbishop of Canterbury, who sent him to study canon law at Bologna and Auxerre. At the papal court in 1152 he prevented the recognition of King Stephen's son Eustace as heir to the throne; and in 1155 he became Chancellor, the first Englishman since the Norman Conquest who had filled any high office. A brilliant figure at court, he showed his knightly prowess in the Toulouse campaign (1159) and was also a skilled diplomat. He changed dramatically when he was created Archbishop of Canterbury in 1162.

He resigned the chancellorship, turned a rigid ascetic, showed his liberality only in charities, and became a zealous servant of the Church. He soon championed its rights against the king and had courtiers, several nobles and other laymen excommunicated for their alienation of Church property. Henry II, who, like all the Norman kings, endeavoured to keep the clergy in subordination to the state, in 1164 convoked the Council of Clarendon, which adopted the so-called 'Constitutions', or laws relating to the respective powers of Church and State. Initially Becket refused to consent, but afterwards was induced to give his unwilling approval. Henry now began to perceive that Becket's notions and his own were utterly antagonistic, and exhibited his hostility to Becket, who tried to leave the country. For this offence Henry confiscated his goods, and sequestered the revenues of his see. A claim was also made on him for 44,000 marks, as the balance due by him to the Crown when he ceased to be Chancellor. Becket appealed to Pope Alexander III and escaped to France. He spent two years at the Cistercian abbey of Pontigny in Burgundy; and then went to Rome, and pleaded personally before the pope, who reinstated him in the see of Canterbury. Becket returned to France, and wrote angry letters to the English bishops, threatening them with excommunication. Several futile efforts were made to reconcile him with Henry, but in 1170 an agreement was reached and Becket returned to England, entering Canterbury amid the rejoicings of the people, who regarded him as a shield from the oppressions of the nobility. Fresh quarrels soon broke out and excommunications were renewed. Henry's impetuously voiced wish to be rid of 'this turbulent priest' led to Becket's murder in Canterbury cathedral in 1170, by four knights, Hugh de Merville, William de Tracy, Reginald Fitzurse, and Richard le Breton. Becket's martyrdom forced confessions from the king; he was canonized in 1173 and Henry did public penance at his tomb in 1174. In 1220 his bones were transferred to a shrine in the Trinity chapel, until it was destroyed during the Reformation in 1538. It was the place of pilgrimage described by Chaucer in the Prologue to the *Canterbury Tales*. His feast day is 29 December. 📖 D Knowles, *Thomas Becket* (1970)

Beckett, Gilbert Abbott À See À Beckett, Gilbert Abbott

Beckett, Margaret Mary, *née* Jackson 1943–
English Labour politician

Born in Ashton-under-Lyne, she trained as an engineer at Manchester College of Science and Technology, and worked as a metallurgist before entering parliament as Labour MP of Lincoln (1974–79). During this time she was Parliamentary Under-Secretary of State for the Department of Education and Science (1976–79). In 1979 she joined Granada Television as chief researcher until 1983, when she was elected MP for Derby South. A fiercely pragmatic politician, she rose through the ranks to serve as Opposition front bench spokesperson on health and social security (1984–89), shadow chief secretary to the Treasury (1989–92), shadow Leader of the House and campaigns co-ordinator (1992–94) and deputy Leader (1992–94). After the sudden death of Labour leader John Smith (1994), she was acting Leader for a few months until Tony Blair took over and she was given the shadow health portfolio again. She was shadow front bench spokesperson for trade and industry (1995–97), and after Labour's landslide win in the 1997 general election, entered the Cabinet as President of the Board of Trade.

Beckett, Samuel Barclay 1906–89
Irish writer, playwright and Nobel Prize winner

Born in Dublin and educated at Portora Royal School, Enniskillen, and Trinity College, Dublin, he became a lecturer in English at the École Normale Supérieure in

Paris and later in French at Trinity College, Dublin. From 1932 he lived mostly in France and was, for a time, secretary to **James Joyce**, with whom he shared the same tantalizing preoccupation with language, with the failure of human beings to communicate successfully mirroring the pointlessness of life which they strive to make purposeful. His early poetry and first two novels, *Murphy* (1938) and *Watt* (1953), were written in English, but many subsequent works first appeared in French: the trilogy *Molloy, Malone Meurt* and *L'Innommable* (translated in 1955, 1956 and 1958), and the plays *En attendant Godot* (1953, Eng trans *Waiting for Godot*, 1956), which took London by storm, and *Fin de partie* (1957, Eng trans *End Game*, 1958), for example. *Godot* best exemplifies the Beckettian view of the human predicament, the poignant bankruptcy of all hopes, philosophies, and endeavours. His later works include *Happy Days* (1961), *Not I* (1973) and *Ill Seen Ill Said* (1981). He was awarded the 1969 Nobel Prize for literature. Although there were one or two increasingly short pieces in later years—*Breath* (1970) shows a heap of rubbish on the stage and has a soundtrack which consists of a single breath—he wrote very infrequently towards the end of his life. ⌨ Deirdre Bair, *Samuel Beckett: A Biography* (1978); A Alvarez, *Beckett* (1973); R Hayman, *Samuel Beckett* (1968)

Beckford, William Thomas 1759–1844
English writer and art collector
He was born in Fonthill, Wiltshire, and at 16 revealed remarkable intellectual precocity in his satirical *Memoirs of Extraordinary Painters*. From 1777 he spent much time on the Continent, meeting **Voltaire** in 1778. He entered parliament (1784), but became involved in a scandal and was excluded from society. He wrote, in French, *Vathek*, an Arabian tale of gloomy imaginative splendour modelled on Voltaire's style, which was published in France in 1787 and in an unauthorized English version in 1786. After spending three years in Portugal (1793–96) he returned to England and erected Fonthill Abbey, designed by **James Wyatt**. Its chief feature was a tower (276ft, 83.6m high), in which Beckford lived in mysterious seclusion until 1822. In 1834 he published *Italy, with Sketches of Spain and Portugal* (which incorporated, in modified form, *Dreams, Waking Thoughts*, and *Incident*, suppressed in 1783), and in 1835 another volume of *Recollections* of travel. ⌨ G Chapman, *Beckford* (1952)

Beckmann, Ernst Otto 1853–1923
German chemist
Born in Solingen, North Rhine-Westphalia, he went to the University of Leipzig in 1875 and on graduation became an assistant at the Technische Hochschule in Brunswick. In 1883 he returned to Leipzig and, after appointments in Giessen and Erlangen, became director of the newly founded Kaiser Wilhelm Institute in 1912. He is best known for his discovery of a reaction by which ketoximes are converted into amides, and for the accurate thermometer, used to determine molecular weights by freezing point depression or boiling point elevation, which bears his name.

Beckmann, Max 1884–1950
German painter, draughtsman and printmaker
Born in Leipzig, he moved to Berlin in 1904, where he began painting large-scale, dramatic works. The suffering he experienced as a hospital orderly in World War I led him to develop a highly individual, distorted, expressive style influenced by Gothic art, which he used to convey the disillusionment he saw around him in postwar Germany. A series of self-portraits reflects the anguish caused by contemporary events, and nine monumental triptychs painted between 1932 and his death form a moral commentary on the relationship between public aggression and the role of the individual. On learning that his work was to be included in an exhibition of Degenerate Art to be mounted by the Nazis in 1937 he fled to Holland, where he lived until finally emigrating to the USA in 1947. He taught at various US universities until his death.

Becque, Henry 1837–99
French dramatist
Born in Neuilly, he is known for two naturalistic plays, *Les Corbeaux* (1882, Eng trans *The Vultures*, 1913) and *La Parisienne* (1885, Eng trans *Parisienne*, 1943), both dramatic portrayals of bourgeois life and character. ⌨ L B Hyslop, *Henry Becque* (1972)

Bécquer, Gustavo Adolfo 1836–70
Spanish romance writer and lyric poet
He was born in Seville. His *Legends* are written in a type of musical prose, but he is best known for his troubadour love verses, although his poems in *Rimas* (1871) have been seen as crucial precursors of modern Spanish poetry. ⌨ R Benitez, *Bécquer, traditionalista* (1971)

Becquerel, Alexandre-Edmond 1820–91
French physicist
Born in Paris, he was the son and assistant of **Antoine César Becquerel**. At 18 he decided to join his father at the Natural History Museum of Paris. In 1852 he was appointed to the chair of physics at the Conservatoire des Arts et Métiers, taught chemistry at the Société Chimique de Paris (1860–63), and eventually succeeded his father at the Museum in 1878. His research covered electricity, magnetism and optics. He demonstrated in 1843 that **James Joule's** law governing heat and electric current applied not only to solids, but also to liquids. He also investigated diamagnetism, the magnetic properties of oxygen, and solar radiation, and constructed the 'actinometer' (an instrument that determined light intensity by measuring electric current) and a phosphoroscope.

Becquerel, Antoine César 1788–1878
French physicist
He was born in Châtillon-Coligny on the River Loing and chose a military career, joining the Corps of Engineers after graduating from the École Polytechnique. He left military service after the fall of **Napoleon I** (1815), and devoted himself to science. Becquerel investigated the electrical properties of minerals, and was the first to use electrolysis to isolate metals from their ores. In 1837 he was awarded the Copley Medal of the Royal Society, and the following year became professor at the Natural History Museum of Paris (1838). He wrote a great number of scientific papers, many with his son, but also with **André Ampère** and **Jean-Baptiste Biot**, and corresponded with **Michael Faraday** on the topic of diamagnetism. He invented several laboratory instruments, such as an electromagnetic balance and a differential galvanometer.

Becquerel, Antoine Henri 1852–1908
French physicist and Nobel Prize winner
Born in Paris, he studied at the École Polytechnique and the School of Bridges and Highways, and later succeeded his father **Alexandre-Edmond Becquerel** to the chair of physics at the Natural History Museum. He was an expert in fluorescence and phosphorescence, continuing the work of his father and grandfather. During his study of fluorescent uranium salt, pitchblende, he accidentally left a sample that had not been exposed to light on top of a photographic plate, and noticed later that the plate had a faint image of the pitchblende. He concluded that these 'Becquerel rays' were a property of atoms, thus discovering radioactivity and prompting the beginning of the nuclear age. His work led to the discovery of radium by **Marie** and **Pierre Curie** and he subsequently shared with them the 1903 Nobel Prize for physics.

Bedard, Myriam 1969–
Canadian biathlete
She is the most successful female biathlete. Her sport is regarded by many as the most demanding in the world, since the combination of cross-country skiing and then controlling the heartbeat sufficiently to shoot a rifle with accuracy requires a level of fitness unimagined by most other sportspeople. The winner of two Olympic gold medals, she shares the record for most Olympic medals with Antje Miserky and Anfisa Restzova. In 1980 she won an Olympic bronze medal in the women's events, and when the biathlon was introduced as an Olympic sport for women in 1992, she won a bronze in the 15,000 metres event. In 1994 she won Olympic golds in 7,500 metres and 15,000 metres.

Bedaux, Charles Eugène 1886–1944
US industrialist
Born in Charenton-le-Pont, France, he emigrated to the USA in 1906, where he originated an efficiency system which provoked much controversy, and became controller of companies providing efficiency surveys throughout the world. He returned to live in France, and the Duke and Duchess of Windsor were married at his home in 1937. Under German occupation he acted as intermediary between Vichy and Berlin, but he was arrested on suspicion of treason by US troops in N Africa after the liberation there, and committed suicide.

Beddoes, Thomas 1760–1808
English physician and writer
Born in Shifnal, he studied medicine and became Reader in Chemistry at Oxford, but his sympathies with the French Revolution led to his resignation (1792). From 1798 to 1801 he developed at Clifton (near Bristol) a 'pneumatic institute' for the cure of diseases by the inhalation of gases, with Humphry Davy his assistant. He wrote on political, social, and medical subjects and edited the works of John Brown, founder of the Brunonian movement.

Beddoes, Thomas Lovell 1803–49
English poet and physiologist
Born in Clifton, near Bristol, the eldest son of Thomas Beddoes, he was educated at Charterhouse and Oxford. In 1822 he published *The Bride's Tragedy*, a sombre murder drama. He went to Göttingen (1825) to study medicine, and then led a wandering life as doctor and democrat, in Germany and Switzerland, with occasional visits to England. From 1825 he was engaged in the composition of a Gothic–Romantic drama in blank verse, *Death's Jestbook*, which appeared in 1850, a year after his suicide.
📖 H W Donner, *Thomas Lovell Beddoes: the making of a poet* (1935); *The Letters of Thomas Lovell Beddoes* (1894)

Bede or **Baeda, St**. *also called* the **Venerable Bede**
c.673–735
Anglo-Saxon scholar, theologian and historian
Born near Monkwearmouth, Durham, he studied at the Benedictine monastery there from the age of seven. In 682 he moved to the new monastery of Jarrow, Tyne and Wear, where he was ordained priest in 703 and remained a monk for the rest of his life, studying and teaching. Besides Latin and Greek, classical as well as patristic, literature, he studied Hebrew, medicine, astronomy and prosody. He wrote homilies, lives of saints, lives of abbots, hymns, epigrams, works on chronology, grammar and physical science, commentaries on the Old and New Testaments, and translated the Gospel of St John into Anglo-Saxon just before his death. His greatest work was his Latin *Historia Ecclesiastica Gentis Anglorum* ('Ecclesiastical History of the English People'), which he finished in 731, and is the single most valuable source for early English history. It was later translated into Anglo-Saxon

by, or under, King **Alfred**. He was buried at Jarrow, and his bones were moved to Durham in the 11th century. He was canonized in 1899 and his feast day is 27 May. 📖 P H Blair, *The World of Bede* (1970)

Bede, Cuthbert See **Bradley, Edward**

Bedford, John of Lancaster, Duke of
1389–1435
English soldier, statesman and prince
The third son of **Henry IV**, he was made Governor of Berwick-upon-Tweed and Warden of the East Marches (1403). His brother, **Henry V**, created him Duke of Bedford (1414), and during the war with France he was appointed Lieutenant of the Kingdom. After Henry's death (1422), Bedford became Guardian of England and virtual Regent of France during the minority of his nephew, **Henry VI**. In the Hundred Years War, helped by alliance with Burgundy, he defeated the French in several battles including Cravant (1423) and Verneuil (1424), but in 1428–29 he failed to capture Orleans. He had **Joan of Arc** burned at the stake in Rouen (1431), and had Henry VI crowned King of France (1431), but in 1435 a treaty was negotiated between **Charles VII** and the Duke of Burgundy, which, together with English insolvency, was to ruin English interests in France. Yet, single-minded, consistent and clear-sighted, at his death he presided over more French territory than Henry V had possessed.

Bédier, Charles Marie Joseph 1864–1938
French scholar and medievalist
Born in Paris, he was appointed Professor of Medieval French Language and Literature at the Collège de France in 1893, and received his doctorate for *Les Fabliaux* (1893). His *Roman de Tristan et Iseult* (1900, 'The Romance of Tristan and Isolde') gained him a European reputation, and *Les Légendes épiques* (1908–13) developed in exquisite French his theory of the origin of the great cycles of romance.

Bedmar, Alfonso de Cueva, Marqués de
1572–1655
Spanish conspirator
He was sent in 1607 as ambassador to Venice, and in 1618 plotted the overthrow of the republic. One of the conspirators betrayed the plot, which forms the theme of Thomas Otway's *Venice Preserved*. Bedmar was dismissed, and went to Flanders, where he became president of the Council. In 1622 he was made a cardinal, and finally Bishop of Oviedo.

Bednorz, (Johannes) Georg 1950–
German physicist and Nobel Prize winner
Born in West Germany, he studied at Münster University and at the Swiss Federal Institute of Technology in Zurich. He then joined the IBM Zurich research laboratory (1982–) and investigated, with **Alex Müller**, a new range of material types based on oxides, a departure from the more conventional intermetallic compounds. In 1986 they observed superconductivity at a temperature 12 kelvin higher than the previous record of 23 kelvin, revealing at a stroke a whole new family of superconducting compounds. Within two years superconductivity at temperatures as high as 90 kelvin had been achieved, and with superconductors now able to operate using inexpensive and plentiful coolants, the practical applications of superconducting devices multiplied enormously. Bednorz was awarded the 1987 Nobel Prize for physics jointly with Müller only one year after the announcement of their discovery.

Bee or **Begh** or **Bega, St** 7th century
Irish princess
She took the veil from **St Aidan** and founded the nunnery of St Bees in Cumberland.

Beebe, (Charles) William 1877–1962
US naturalist and explorer

Born in Brooklyn, New York, he was curator of ornithology for the New York Zoological Society from 1899, wrote many widely read books, including *Galapagos* (1923) and *The Arcturus Adventure* (1925), and explored ocean depths down to almost 1,000 metres in a bathysphere (1934). 📖 Robert Henry Walker, *Natural Man: The Life of William Beebe* (1975)

Beecham, Sir Thomas 1879–1961
English conductor and impresario

Born in St Helens, Lancashire, he was educated at Rossall School and Wadham College, Oxford. He began his career as a conductor with the New Symphony Orchestra at the Wigmore Hall in 1906 and, as impresario and producer of opera, later introduced 60 works unknown to British audiences, as well as **Sergei Diaghilev's** Ballets Russes. He was principal conductor (1932) and artistic director (1933) of Covent Garden, and in 1943 conducted at the Metropolitan Opera, New York. In 1946 he founded the Royal Philharmonic Orchestra, and conducted at Glyndebourne from 1948 to 1949. Beecham did much to champion the works of **Frederick Delius, Jean Sibelius** and **Richard Strauss**, and was noted for his candid pronouncements on musical matters, for his 'Lollipop' encores (of popular works of classical music), and for his after-concert speeches. He was the son of the famous 'pill millionaire', Sir Joseph Beecham (1848–1916).

Beecher, Catharine Esther 1800–78
US educationist

Born in East Hampton, New York, she was the eldest daughter of **Lyman Beecher**. She became principal of a Hartford seminary, and wrote on female higher education and the duties of women.

Beecher, Henry Ward 1813–87
US Congregationalist clergyman and writer

Born in Litchfield, Connecticut, he was the son of **Lyman Beecher**. Educated at Amherst College, Massachusetts, he preached at Indianapolis, and in 1847 became the first pastor of Plymouth Congregational Church, in Brooklyn, New York City, where he preached temperance and denounced slavery. He favoured the free-soil party in 1852, and the Republican candidates in 1856 and 1860, and on the outbreak of the Civil War in 1861 his church raised and equipped a volunteer regiment. At the end of the war in 1865 he became an earnest advocate of reconciliation. For many years he wrote for *The Independent*, and after 1870 edited *The Christian Union* (later *Outlook*). His many writings included *Seven Lectures to Young Men* (1844), *Summer in the Soul* (1858), *Yale Lectures on Preaching* (1874) and *Evolution and Religion* (1885). He was the brother of **Harriet Beecher Stowe**.

Beecher, Lyman 1775–1863
US Presbyterian minister

Born in New Haven, Connecticut, he studied at Yale, and was minister at East Hampton, New York (1799–1810), Litchfield, Connecticut (1810–26), and Hanover St Church, Boston (1826–32). His evangelical preaching aroused opposition amongst conservative Presbyterians, and he was charged with heresy but acquitted. He then became leader of the New School Presbyterians. He was the father of 13 children, including **Catherine Beecher, Harriet Beecher Stowe**, and **Henry Ward Beecher**.

Beechey, Sir William 1753–1839
English portrait painter

Born in Burford, Oxfordshire, he entered the Royal Academy as a student in 1772, became a painter in the **Reynolds** tradition and was appointed court painter to Queen **Charlotte** in 1793.

Beeching, Richard Beeching, Baron 1913–85
English engineer and administrator

Born in Maidstone, Kent, and educated at Imperial College, London, he became chairman of the British Railways Board (1963–65) and deputy chairman of ICI (1966–68). He is best known for the scheme devised and approved under his chairmanship (the Beeching Plan) for the substantial contraction of the rail network of the UK. He identified 5,000 miles of track and 2,000 stations for closure, and this had a tremendous effect on the future of the railways. He was created a life peer in 1965.

Beer, Esmond de See De Beer, Esmond

Beer, Sir Gavin Rylands de See de Beer, Sir Gavin Rylands

Beer, Michael c.1605–1666
German architect

He was born in Au, where he founded the influential Auer Zunft (Guild of Au) in 1657. The guild provided a structured theoretical architectural training in a series of family workshops. His major work was his designs for the residence and church of St Lawrence in Kempten (1651–53) and for Abbot Roman Giel von Gielsburg, the first ecclesiastical building started after the Thirty Years War. Stressing simple cubic forms, he reduced applied decoration to a minimum. The design was influential in the forming of the Vorarlberger Münsterschema's work at Ellwangen and Obermarchthal.

Beerbohm, Sir (Henry) Max(imilian), called the Incomparable Max 1872–1956
English writer and caricaturist

Born in London, the son of a Lithuanian corn merchant, and half-brother of Sir **Herbert Beerbohm Tree**, he was educated at Charterhouse and Merton College, Oxford. He published his first volume of essays (some of which had appeared in the *Yellow Book*) under the ironic title *The Works of Max Beerbohm* (1896). He succeeded **George Bernard Shaw** as drama critic of *The Saturday Review*, until 1910, when he married a US actress, Florence Kahn (d.1951), and went to live, except during the two World Wars, in Rapallo, Italy. His delicate, unerring, aptly-captioned caricatures were collected in various volumes beginning with *Twenty-five Gentlemen* (1896) and *Poet's Corner* (1904). Further volumes of parodies and stories were *Happy Hypocrite* (1897) and *A Christmas Garland* (1912), full of gentle humour, elegance, and rare wit, and ending with *And Even Now* (1920). His best-known work was his only novel, *Zuleika Dobson* (1912), an ironic romance of Oxford undergraduate life. His broadcast talks from 1935 were another of his singularly brilliant stylistic accomplishments. A month before his death he married Elizabeth Jungmann, his late wife's greatest friend. 📖 Lord Edward C D G Cecil, *Max: a biography* (1964)

Beerbohm Tree, Sir Herbert See Tree, Sir Herbert Beerbohm

Beernaert, Auguste 1829–1912
Belgian politician and Nobel Prize winner

He trained as a lawyer, entered politics and was appointed Minister for Public Works in 1873. He became a member of the Belgian parliament in 1874, opposing the ruling liberal governments of the day. He was appointed Minister of Agriculture, Trade and Industry in 1884, and took over the leadership of the government later the same year. He was responsible for introducing multiple-vote universal suffrage to Belgium in 1893, and for important reforms in labour law; he was also a supporter of King Leopold II's colonial policies in the Congo. He left the government in 1894, and became chairman of the

Beethoven, Ludwig van 1770–1827
German composer

Beethoven was born in Bonn, where his father was a tenor in the service of the Elector of Cologne, and his grandfather a bass singer and kapellmeister. He had his first music lessons from his father, who was ambitious on his behalf and saw him as a second Mozart. He first appeared as a keyboard prodigy at Cologne in 1778. In 1787 he visited Vienna, where he is thought to have received lessons from Mozart, but he hurried back to Bonn on his mother's death. Two years later he was allotted half his father's salary to act as head of the family, and at this time he was playing viola in the opera orchestra.

Beethoven came into contact with Haydn in 1790, and two years later Haydn agreed to teach him in Vienna, which Beethoven made his permanent home. He was also taught by Johann Albrechtsberger and Antonio Salieri, and was befriended by Prince Karl Lichnowsky, to whom Beethoven dedicated several works including the Opus 1 piano trios. In 1795 he played in Vienna for the first time with the B flat piano concerto, and published his Opus 1 trios and Opus 2 piano sonatas. He went on to perform in Prague, Dresden and Berlin, and earned a growing reputation as a pianist and improvisor.

Beethoven's creative output is traditionally divided into three periods. By 1802 he had composed three piano concertos, two symphonies, the String Quartet Op.29, and Op.31, but already suffered deeply from depression caused by his increasing deafness—a condition movingly described in a document later known as the 'Heiligenstadt Testament' written that year when he stayed at a village near Vienna; it was discovered only after Beethoven's death. The first works of his 'middle period' show him as the heroic, unbounded optimist, determined to strive creatively in the face of despair.

His third symphony, a much longer work than was usual at the time, was originally dedicated to Napoleon Bonaparte, but on learning that he had proclaimed himself emperor, Beethoven defaced the title page and called the work Eroica (1804). In the opera Fidelio the themes of fidelity, personal liberation, and symbolic passage from darkness to light dominate; in association with this work he composed the three Leonora overtures. The first version of Fidelio was produced in 1814, by which time the rich corpus of the middle years was complete: piano sonatas including the Waldstein, Appassionata and Lebewohl; the Symphonies 4–8; the Rasumovsky Quartets; the 4th and 5th piano concertos; incidental music to Goethe's Egmont, and the Archduke Trio (dedicated to his pupil the Archduke Rudolph of Austria). These middle period years were also characterized by unhappy romantic affairs, including the still unidentified 'Immortal Beloved', referred to in a letter which was again discovered only after his death.

His domestic life declined: according to the accounts of contemporaries he was ill-kempt, unhygienic, argumentative, and arrogant; and he was disordered in business dealings, quarrelsome with friends, and tormented more and more by illness. A dispute that arose in 1815 over the guardianship of his nephew Karl, the son of his late brother, began an intense and protracted personal and legal anxiety that lasted until his death. Yet the last decade of Beethoven's life saw the most extraordinary and supremely great achievements: the Diabelli Variations, the last piano sonatas, the last six string quartets, the Mass in D (Missa Solemnis) and the Choral Symphony (No.9).

On his deathbed he was so pleased with the gift of £100 from the London Philharmonic Society that he promised them his 10th Symphony. The motto of the finale of Beethoven's last quartet (Op.135)—'Must it be?—It must be!'—with its dark questioning and exuberant, confident affirmation, encapsulates much of his philosophy. His musical sketchbooks show a mind of indefatigable logic and striving for perfection. The Romantics embraced him as their supreme precursor; and his influence on succeeding generations of musicians has been immense.

📖 The earliest biography of Beethoven (1866–79) is by the American A W Thayer, who interviewed acquaintances and researched the documentary evidence. It was revised by Eliot Forbes and reissued in 1964 and 1973. Later works include Alessandri Comini, The Changing Image of Beethoven (1987); Beethoven (1977) by Maynard Solomon (who identifies the 'Immortal Beloved' as Antonie Brentano, the wife of a Frankfurt businessman and the dedicatee of the Diabelli Variations); and George R Marek, Beethoven, Biography of a Genius (1969).

'I shall hear in heaven.'
Attributed last words, quoted in Ian Crofton and Donald Fraser, A Dictionary of Musical Quotations (1985).

Belgian Senate for five years until 1899. His work on weapons reduction and international law earned him the Nobel Peace Prize in 1909.

Beethoven, Ludwig van See panel above

Beeton, Mrs Isabella Mary, née Mayson 1836–65
English cookery writer

She was educated in Heidelberg and became an accomplished pianist. In 1856 she married Samuel Orchard Beeton, a publisher, and her *Book of Household Management*, first published in parts (1859–60) in a cookery and domestic science magazine founded by her husband, made her name a household word. She died after the birth of her fourth son. 📖 Sarah Freeman, *Isabella and Sam: The Story of Mrs Beeton* (1977)

Bega, St See Bee, St

Beggarstaff, J See Nicholson, Sir William Newzam Prior

Begh, St See Bee, St

Begin, Menachem See panel p165

Behaim, Martin 1440–1507
German navigator and geographer

Born in Nuremberg, he settled in Portugal about 1484 and was associated with the later Portuguese discoveries along the coast of Africa. He revisited Nuremberg in 1490 and there constructed the oldest extant terrestrial globe.

Beham, Barthel 1502–40
German painter and engraver

Born in Nuremberg, he was the younger brother and pupil of Hans Sebald Beham, and one of Dürer's seven followers known as the 'Little Masters'. He became a court painter in Munich and made numerous engravings and paintings of Bavarian aristocracy.

Beham, Hans Sebald 1500–50
German painter and engraver

Born in Nuremberg, he was one of Dürer's seven followers known as the 'Little Masters'. Working in Frankfurt am Main, he produced hundreds of woodcuts and copper engravings as illustrations for books.

Behan, Brendan 1923–64
Irish author

Begin, Menachem 1913–92
Israeli statesman and Nobel Prize winner

Menachem Begin was born in Brest-Litovsk, Poland. He studied law at Warsaw University, and as an active Zionist became head of the Betar Zionist movement in Poland in 1931. On the invasion of Poland in 1939 he fled to Lithuania, where he was arrested by the Russians. He was released in 1941, enlisted in the Free Polish Army, and was sent to British-mandated Palestine in 1942. After being discharged from the army the following year, he became Commander-in-Chief of the Irgun Zvai Leumi resistance group in Israel and gained a reputation as a terrorist.

He founded the right-wing Herut Freedom Movement in 1948, became chairman of the Herut Party, and was a member of the first, second and third Knessets. In 1973 three parties combined to form the Likud Front, a right-of-centre nationalist party with Begin as its leader; in the 1977 elections it ousted the Israel Labour Party and Begin formed a coalition government. He was re-elected Prime Minister in the national elections of 1981.

Throughout his life he was a man of hard-line views concerning the Arabs, but in the late 1970s he sought a peaceful settlement with the Egyptians and attended peace conferences in Jerusalem (1977) and at Camp David (1978) at the invitation of President **Jimmy Carter**. In 1978 he and President **Sādāt** of Egypt were jointly awarded the Nobel Prize for peace. He resigned the premiership in 1983.

📖 S Sofer, *Begin* (1988); A Perlmutter, *The Life and Times of Menachem Begin* (1987); E Sliver, *Begin* (1984).

> The PLO charter led Begin to comment to the press: 'Israel is still the only country in the world against which there is a written document to the effect that it must disappear.' (22 March 1978).

Born in Dublin, he left school at 14 to become a house painter, and soon joined the IRA. In 1939 he was sentenced to three years in Borstal for attempting to blow up a Liverpool shipyard, and soon after his release was given 14 years by a Dublin military court for the attempted murder of two detectives. He was released by a general amnesty (1946), but was in prison again in Manchester (1947) and was deported in 1952. In prison he had learned to speak Irish from fellow IRA detainees, and read voraciously. His first play, *The Quare Fellow* (1954; filmed 1962), starkly dramatized the prison atmosphere prior to a hanging. His exuberant Irish wit, spiced with balladry and bawdry and a talent for fantastic caricature, found scope in his next play, *The Hostage* (1958, first produced in Irish as *An Giall*). It is also evident in the autobiographical novel, *Borstal Boy* (1958), and in *Brendan Behan's Island* (1963). He was the brother of **Dominic Behan**. 📖 D Behan, *My Brother Bernard* (1965)

Behan, Dominic 1928–89
Irish novelist and folklorist
Born in Dublin, the brother of **Brendan Behan**, he adapted old airs and poems into contemporary Irish Republican material, notably in *The Patriot Game*. Resentfully overshadowed for much of his life by the legend of his brother, he lived largely outside Ireland from 1947 as a journalist and singer. He ultimately settled in Scotland, where for the first time he won acceptance in his own right as a writer, and as an Irish and Scottish nationalist. His only novel, *The Public Life of Parable Jones*, was published just before his death. 📖 *Teems of Times and Happy Returns* (1961)

Behn, Aphra, *née* Johnson 1640–89
English writer and adventuress
Born in Wye, Kent, she was brought up in Surinam, where she made the acquaintance of the enslaved Negro prince Oroonoko, the subject afterwards of one of her novels, in which she anticipated **Jean Jacques Rousseau's** 'noble savage'. Returning to England in 1663, she married a merchant called Behn, who died within three years. She then turned professional spy at Antwerp, sent back political and naval information, but received little thanks, and on her return was imprisoned for debt. She turned to writing, as perhaps the first professional woman author in England, and wrote many coarse but popular Restoration plays, especially *The Forced Marriage* (1670), *The Rover* (1678), and *The Feigned Courtizans* (1678), and later published *Oroonoko* (1688). 📖 G Woodcock, *The Incomparable Aphra* (1948)

Behrens, Peter 1868–1940
Pioneering German architect and designer
Born in Hamburg, he trained as a painter, and was appointed director of the Düsseldorf Art and Craft School (1903–07). In 1907 he became artistic adviser to **Walther Rathenau** at the AEG electrical company in Berlin, for whom he designed a turbine assembly works (1909) of glass and steel, a landmark in industrial architectural style. For AEG he designed everything from factory complexes to industrial brochures, and he also designed workers' apartment houses in Vienna and Stuttgart, and the German embassy in St Petersburg (1912). He was professor at Düsseldorf and Vienna, and trained several notable modern architects, including **Le Corbusier, Ludwig Mies van der Rohe** and **Walter Gropius**. 📖 Alan Windsor, *Peter Behrens: Architect and Designer* (1981)

Behring, Emil von 1854–1917
German bacteriologist, pioneer in immunology and Nobel Prize winner
Born in Hansdorf, West Prussia, he enrolled in the Army Medical College in Berlin in 1874, obtaining his medical degree in 1878. In 1888 he went to join **Ludwig Koch's** Institute of Hygiene in Berlin, where his major contribution was the development of a serum therapy against tetanus and diphtheria (1890), which became instrumental in counteracting these diseases. Behring's recommendations for reducing the occurrence of tuberculosis in animals and for disinfecting milk were important public health measures. He later became Professor of Hygiene at Halle University (1894–95) and at Marburg University (from 1895), and was awarded the first Nobel Prize for physiology or medicine in 1901. During World War I, the tetanus vaccine developed by him helped to save so many lives that he received the Iron Cross, very rarely awarded to a civilian.

Behrman, S(amuel) N(athaniel) 1893–1973
US playwright, screenwriter and journalist
Born in Worcester, Massachusetts, he was educated at Harvard and Columbia universities, and became famous after the production of his sophisticated comedy, *The Second Man* (1927). He was described as the US **Noël Coward**, but his comedies of manners soon foundered on the harsh realities of Depression and war. However, his anecdotal portrait of the great art collector *Duveen* (1952), and *The Worcester Account* (1954), about his boyhood, retain their freshness and contain some of his best work. He co-wrote the screenplays *Queen Christina* (1933) and *Anna Karenina* (1935), both for **Greta Garbo**. 📖 *Tribulations and Laughter: a memoir* (1972)

Beiderbecke, (Leon) Bix 1903–31
US cornettist

The archetypal white youngster smitten by early jazz (and the posthumous subject of Dorothy Baker's novel *Young Man With a Horn*, 1938), he was born to musical parents in Davenport, Iowa, and was largely self-taught on piano and cornet. He played in local bands as a teenager and quickly progressed to working with established professionals. On being expelled from military academy at the age of 19, he began the short career that made him one of the most celebrated jazz performers of the 1920s. His bell-like tone and lyrical solo improvisations were heard to best effect in various small groups; but despite being an indifferent reader of music, he also transformed the commercial sound of such big bands as the **Paul Whiteman** and Jean Goldkette orchestras. His later career was ravaged by alcoholism, and he died of pneumonia at the age of 28.

Beilby, Sir George Thomas 1850–1924
Scottish industrial chemist
Born in Edinburgh and educated at Edinburgh University, he worked as a chemist with oil shale, gold and chemical companies. In 1881 he designed a continuous retort which increased the yield of paraffin and ammonia from shale. He discovered an economical way of producing potassium cyanide, which is needed to extract gold from low grade ores, and the first factory was established at Leith. He also studied flow in solids and explained why metals harden with cold working. He founded the Fuel Research Station at East Greenwich and was a member of many government committees. He was knighted in 1916.

Beilstein, Friedrich Konrad 1838–1906
German–Russian chemist
Born in St Petersburg of German parentage, he studied in Heidelberg, Göttingen and Paris, and in 1860 became assistant to **Friedrich Wöhler** in Göttingen. From 1866 until his retirement he was professor at the Technical Institute in St Petersburg. His name is synonymous with his *Handbuch der organischen Chemie* ('Handbook of Organic Chemistry'), first published in 1880, which aims to be a complete catalogue of all organic compounds. It is a work of great importance to all organic chemists, although the cost of each volume has become a substantial barrier to its wide use.

Béjart, Maurice, *originally* Maurice Jean Berger 1928–
French dancer and choreographer
Born in Marseilles, he trained at the Marseilles Opera Ballet and then in Paris and London. He moved to the Royal Swedish Ballet (then under **Roland Petit**) where he both performed and choreographed. In 1954 he founded the Mudra School and his own company, which was invited to remain as the Ballet of the 20th Century in Brussels after a major success there. He has developed a physical style, which displays the talents of the male dancer; and was the first to present a ballet in a sports arena. His works include *The Firebird* (1970), in which a ballerina becomes the leader of the partisans, *Notre Faust* (1975, 'Our Faust'), a black mass set to **J S Bach** and tango music, *Choreographic Offering* (1971) and *Kabuki* (1986). In 1988 the company moved to Lausanne, Switzerland.

Bek, Antony d.1311
English prelate
Bishop of Durham from 1283, he took a prominent part in the Scottish wars of **Edward I**, and from 1300 was involved in ecclesiastical disputes. His brother, Thomas (d.1293), was Bishop of St Davids from 1280.

Beke, Charles Tilstone 1800–74
English explorer and biblical critic
Born in London, he became a scholar of ancient history, philology and ethnography, and wrote *Origines Biblicae* (1834). From 1840 until 1843 he explored Abyssinia

(Ethiopia), where he fixed the latitude of over 70 stations, mapped 70,000 square miles (182,000km^2), and collected 14 vocabularies, and in 1874 he explored the region at the head of the Red Sea.

Békésy, Georg von 1899–1972
US physicist, physiologist and Nobel Prize winner
Born in Budapest, Hungary, he studied chemistry in Berne, Switzerland, studied optics at the University of Budapest for his doctoral degree, and worked as a telephone research engineer in Hungary (1924–46). In 1932 he was given a concurrent appointment at Budapest University and in 1940 was created Professor of Experimental Physics. In 1946 the Swedish neurophysiologist Yvnge Zotterman (1898–1982) invited him to Stockholm, and the following year he moved to Harvard. He won the 1961 Nobel Prize for physiology or medicine, for his discoveries about the physical mechanisms of the ear, which explained how people distinguished sounds. He was also interested in developing instrumentation, and his work contributed techniques for measuring deafness, improving surgery of the ear and in working towards restoring hearing.

Bekhterev, Vladimir Mikhailovich 1857–1927
Russian neuropathologist
He was born in Viatka province, and as professor at Kazan University he researched into neural electricity and founded the psychoneurological institute in Leningrad (now St Petersburg).

Bel, Joseph Achille Le See **Le Bel, Joseph Achille**

Belafonte, Harry 1927–
US singer and actor
Born in New York City, he spent part of his childhood in Jamaica, returning to New York in 1940. His lilting calypso songs of the 1950s brought him superstar status, and his album *Calypso*, with the popular 'Banana Boat Song', was the first to sell over a million copies. An award-winning performer on TV and in films, he has worked for civil rights in the USA as a director of the Southern Christian Leadership Conference (SCLC), in South Africa, and as a UNICEF goodwill ambassador.

Belasco, David 1853–1931
US playwright, director and theatre-manager
Born in San Francisco and one of the most powerful figures on Broadway, he owned the Belasco Theatre where, from 1906 until his death, he directed numerous plays; these were usually heroic melodramas, often incorporating sensational stage effects. Belasco, nicknamed the 'Bishop of Broadway', also found time to write over 50 plays, both alone and in collaboration, most of them sentimental domestic and historical dramas. He also wrote *Hearts of Oak* (1879, with James A Herne) and *The Heart of Maryland* (1895). As an author, though, he is chiefly remembered for writing *Madame Butterfly* (1900, with John L Long) and *The Girl of the Golden West* (1905). Both were transformed into operas by **Puccini**, the former becoming one of the composer's most celebrated works.
📖 L L Marker, *David Belasco* (1975)

Belaúnde Terry, Fernando 1913–
Peruvian statesman
Born in Lima, the son of a Prime Minister, he was an architect before entering politics and becoming leader of the Popular Action Party (AP) in 1956. He campaigned for the presidency in 1956 and 1962, eventually winning it in 1963, but was deposed by the army in a bloodless coup in 1968. He fled to the USA where he lectured at Harvard. He returned to Peru two years later but was deported and did

Bell, Alexander Graham 1847–1922
US inventor

Alexander Graham Bell was born in Edinburgh, Scotland, the son of **Alexander Melville Bell**. Educated there and in London, he first worked as an assistant to his father in teaching elocution (1868–70). In 1872 he opened a school in Boston for training teachers of the deaf, and in 1873 he was appointed Professor of Vocal Physiology at Boston, where he devoted himself to the teaching of deaf-mutes and to spreading his father's system of 'visible speech'.

After experimenting with various acoustical devices he produced the first intelligible telephonic transmission with a message to his assistant on 5 June 1875. He patented the telephone in 1876, defended the patent against **Elisha Gray**, and formed the Bell Telephone Company in 1877. In 1880 he established the Volta Laboratory, and invented the photophone (1880) and the graphophone (1887). He also founded the journal *Science* (1883). After 1897 his principal interest was in aeronautics.

📖 D Eber, *Genius at Work: Images of Alexander Graham Bell* (1982); R V Bruce, *Alexander Graham Bell and the Conquest of Solitude* (1973).

'Yes, Alec, it is I, your father, speaking.' The words of Alexander Melville Bell to his son—some of the earliest words to be spoken and heard on a long-distance telephone call (1876).

not re-establish himself until 1976. He won the presidency again in 1980, and was the first civilian to hand over to another constitutionally elected civilian (1985).

Belcher, Sir Edward 1799–1877
English naval commander

He joined the navy in 1812, and from 1836 to 1842 explored the western coast of the USA. In 1852 he commanded a fruitless expedition in search of Sir **John Franklin**. He became rear admiral in 1872.

Belidor, Bernard Forest de 1698–c.1761
French engineer

Born in Catalonia, Spain, he was the son of a French army officer. As Professor of Artillery at La Fère Military Academy, Belidor wrote some of the best-known and most comprehensive engineering handbooks in pre-revolutionary France, covering military engineering (ballistics and fortifications) in his *Science des Ingénieurs* (1729–49, 'The Science of Engineers') and civil engineering in his *Architecture Hydraulique* (4 vols, 1737–53, 'Hydraulic Architecture'), both of which influenced engineering practice in France and other European countries for a century after their publication.

Belinksy, Vissarion Grigorevich 1811–48
Russian literary critic and journalist

Born in Fribourg, Switzerland, he edited the *Moscow Observer* (1838–39), and afterwards became principal critic of *The Annals of the Fatherland*, and of *Sovremennik* in 1846. The foremost Russian critic of his day, he had a profound influence on subsequent critics in his country. His *Survey of Russian Literature since the 18th Century* was published in 1834, and a complete edition of his works between 1859 and 1862 (12 vols).

Belisarius 505–65
Byzantine general

Born in Germania, Illyria, he served Emperor **Justinian I**. He defeated a great Persian army at Dara in 530, and in 532 suppressed a dangerous insurrection in Constantinople (Istanbul) by the destruction of 30,000 of the 'Green' faction. In Africa he twice defeated the Vandals (534–35), conquered the Ostrogoths in Italy (535), conquered Sicily (536), and occupied Rome, which he defended for a year (537–38). In 540 he captured the Ostrogothic capital, Ravenna, but in 542 he was campaigning against the Persians, and from 544 to 548 he was again sent to Italy to deal with the resurgent Ostrogoths. In 562 he was falsely accused of conspiracy against the emperor, but in 563 he was restored to honour. 📖 Robert Graves, *Count Belisarius* (1938)

Bell, Alexander Graham See panel above

Bell, Alexander Melville 1819–1905
US educationist

He was born in Edinburgh, Scotland, and was the father of **Alexander Graham Bell**. A teacher of elocution at Edinburgh University and University College London, he moved to Canada in 1870 and settled in Washington. In 1882 he published his system of 'visible speech', showing the position of the vocal chords for each sound.

Bell, Andrew 1753–1832
Scottish educationist and founder of the 'Madras System' of education

Born in St Andrews, Fife, he took Episcopal orders, and went to India in 1787, and in 1789 became superintendent of the Madras military orphanage. Finding it impossible to obtain teaching staff, he taught with the aid of the pupils themselves by introducing the monitorial system. His pamphlet entitled *An Experiment in Education* (1797) had attracted little attention in Great Britain until in 1803 **Joseph Lancaster** also published a tract recommending the monitorial system. Lancasterian schools began to spread over the country and in 1811 the National Society for the Education of the Poor was founded, of which Bell became superintendent, and whose schools soon numbered 12,000.

Bell, Sir Charles 1774–1842
Scottish anatomist, surgeon and neurophysiological pioneer

Born in Edinburgh, he studied at Edinburgh University, moving to London in 1804, where he became proprietor of an anatomy school and rose to prominence as a surgeon. In 1812 he was appointed surgeon to the Middlesex Hospital and in 1828 he became one of the co-founders of the Middlesex Hospital Medical School. An interest in gunshot wounds led him to treat the wounded from the Battle of Corunna (1809), and after Waterloo he organized a hospital in Brussels. He was knighted in 1831, and in 1836 he was appointed Professor of Surgery at Edinburgh. Today he is remembered for his pioneering neurophysiological researches, first set out in his *Idea of a New Anatomy of the Brain* (1811). Bell demonstrated that nerves consist of separate fibres sheathed together and that fibres convey either sensory or motor stimuli but never both. His work on the functions of the spinal nerves triggered disputes with **François Magendie**. Bell's experimental work led to the discovery of the long thoracic nerve ('Bell's nerve'), and the type of facial paralysis known as 'Bell's palsy' is named after him. He was distantly related to the Edinburgh surgeon Joseph Bell (1837–1911), said to have been the inspiration for **Arthur Conan Doyle's** Sherlock Holmes.

Bell, (Arthur) Clive Heward 1881–1964
English art and literary critic

He studied at Trinity College, Cambridge, and stated his aesthetic theory of *Significant Form* in *Art* (1914). Another version of this was formulated in 1920 by Roger Fry, a fellow-member of the Bloomsbury Group, described in his *Old Friends* (1956). His critical essays include *Since Cézanne* (1922), *Civilization* (1928), *Proust* (1929) and *An Account of French Painting* (1931). In 1907 he married Vanessa Bell, sister of Virginia Woolf and daughter of Sir Leslie Stephen. Their son Julian (1908–37), also a writer, was killed in the Spanish Civil War.

Bell, George Kennedy Allen 1883–1958
English prelate and ecumenist

Born on Hayling Island, Hampshire, and educated at Oxford, he was ordained in 1907, and became chaplain to Archbishop Randall Davidson (1914–24), dean of Canterbury (1924–29), and Bishop of Chichester (1929–58). A strong supporter of the ecumenical movement, and friend of Martin Niemöller and Dietrich Bonhoeffer, German Lutheran opponents of Nazism, he risked misunderstanding during World War II by his efforts towards peace with Germany and his condemnation of the policy of saturation bombing. His published works included *Randall Davidson* (1935), *Christianity and World Order* (1940), *Christian Unity: The Anglican Position* (1948) and *The Kingship of Christ* (1954).

Bell, Gertrude Margaret Lowthian 1868–1926
English archaeologist and traveller

Born at Washington Hall, she studied at Lady Margaret Hall, Oxford, and travelled much in the Middle East, learning to speak Persian and Arabic. During World War I she was appointed to the Arab Bureau in Cairo and seconded to the Mesopotamia Expeditionary Force in Basra and Baghdad, and subsequently became Oriental Secretary to the British High Commission in Iraq. First director of antiquities in Iraq, on her death she left money to fund the British Institute of Archaeology in Iraq.

Bell, (Chester) Gordon 1934–
US computer scientist and designer

He was born in Kirlesville, Missouri. He studied electrical engineering at the Massachusetts Institute of Technology (MIT), and worked at the Engineering Speech Communication Laboratory there (1959–60), before joining Kenneth Olsen's Digital Equipment Corporation (DEC) in 1960. At DEC he was vice-president of engineering (1972–83), and became chiefly known for his design of the VAX (Virtual Address Extension) range of superminicomputers, all of which shared the same software and could transfer data over networks. They were the basis of DEC's fortunes in the early 1980s. Professor of Computer Science at Carnegie Mellon University from 1966 to 1972, he was also assistant director of the National Science Foundation from 1986, co-founder of the Stardent Computer Company, and co-founder of the Boston Computer Museum, of which he became a director.

Bell, Henry 1767–1830
Scottish engineer and pioneer of steam navigation

Born at Torphichen Mill, Linlithgow, he successfully launched the 30-ton *Comet* on the Clyde in 1812. Plying regularly between Greenock and Glasgow, it was the first passenger-carrying steamboat in European waters.

Bell, J(ohn) J(oy) 1871–1934
Scottish journalist and humorous writer

He is best known for his *Wee MacGreegor* (1902), an amusing, poignant evocation of boyhood in Glasgow in the days before World War I. Dramatized in 1911, it has been described as Scotland's equivalent of *Huckleberry Finn* and *Just William*. 📖 *Do You Remember?* (1934)

Bell, John 1797–1869
US politician

Born in Tennessee, he was Speaker of the House of Representatives (1836) and a senator (1847–59). Moderate in his views, he was nominated for the presidency in 1860 by the newly formed Constitutional Union Party, but received only 39 electoral votes, losing to Abraham Lincoln.

Bell, John 1811–95
English sculptor

Born in Hopton, Suffolk, he produced the Guards' Crimean War Memorial (1858) in Waterloo Place, London, and the *America* group on the Albert Memorial, London (1873).

Bell, John Stewart 1928–90
Irish nuclear physicist

Born in Belfast, he studied physics at Queen's University there, then went to the University of Birmingham to study under Sir Rudolf Peierls. In his PhD thesis, he proved the powerful 'CPT theorem', which states that to ensure that particles and antiparticles have the same mass and lifetime, a theory must be symmetric under the combination of three separate symmetries: C-charge conjugation symmetry, P-parity, and T-time invariance. After completing his PhD he joined the theory division of CERN (Conseil Européen pour la Recherche Nucléaire) in Geneva, where he worked on accelerator physics, and with Jack Steinberger studied the relationship between the observation of CP violation and implications for the CPT theorem. He also made important contributions to the foundations of quantum mechanics, showing that predictions of certain hidden variable theories were bounded by inequalities. Work done by experimenters used these inequalities, leading ultimately to the proof that the world we live in is truly quantum mechanical. Bell's work was honoured by the award of the Dirac Medal of the Institute of Physics and the Heineman Prize of the American Physical Society, and he was elected FRS in 1972.

Bell, John Zephaniah 1794–1883
Scottish painter

Born in Dundee, he was educated at the Royal High School in Edinburgh. Originally trained for a career in law, he studied at the Royal Academy Schools in London, then went to Paris and studied under Antoine Gros. He also travelled to Rome (1825) where he came into contact with the Nazarenes, a group of painters including Peter von Cornelius and Johann Overbeck, who were interested in early Italian art. Bell was best known for his portraiture, although his long and varied career brought him neither popular nor professional recognition. He was one of the earliest members of the Royal Scottish Academy.

Bell, Lawrence Dale 1894–1956
US aircraft designer and constructor

Born in Mentone, Indiana, he began his career as a mechanic to two exhibition pilots in 1913. He made rapid progress, becoming superintendent of the Glenn L Martin aircraft factory in 1915 and vice-president and general manager of the Consolidated Aircraft Corporation in 1929. In 1935 he formed the Bell Aircraft Corporation and among its more notable aircraft were the Airacuda, Airacobra, Kingcobra and, in 1942, the P-59 Airacomet, the first US jet-propelled aircraft. From 1941 he produced a famous line of helicopters, and in 1947 he created the first rocket-propelled aeroplane, the Bell X-1, the first manned aircraft to exceed the speed of sound.

Bell, Patrick 1799–1869
Scottish clergyman and inventor

Born in Auchterhouse, near Dundee, the son of a farmer, he worked on the development of a mechanical reaper, the prototype of which earned a £50 premium from the

Highland and Agricultural Society in 1827. Its adoption by British farmers was very slow, however, and when four of his reapers were sent to the USA they enabled **Cyrus McCormick** and others to realize their full potential. By 1843 he had abandoned his active interest in agricultural machinery and had entered the church as minister of Carmylie, Arbroath. Belatedly, in 1868, he was awarded £1,000 in appreciation of his invention of the first efficient 'reaping machine'.

Bell, Robert Anning 1863–1933
English painter, designer, illustrator and decorator

Born in London, he was articled to an architect, but studied painting from 1881 at the Royal Academy Schools, Westminster School of Art, and in Paris, where he studied under Morot. In London he studied with Sir **George Frampton**. He executed mosaics in the Houses of Parliament and Westminster Cathedral, London, and held successive posts at Liverpool University (from 1894), Glasgow School of Art (1911) and the Royal College of Art, London, where he was Professor of Design (1918–24).

Bell, Thomas 1792–1880
English naturalist and dental surgeon

Born in Poole, Dorset, he became a dental surgeon at Guy's Hospital (1817–61), then lectured in and became Professor of Zoology at King's College London in 1836. He was secretary of the Royal Society, president of the Linnean Society (1853–61) and first president of the Ray Society (1844). In 1858 he apparently recorded in the Annual Zoology Report of the Linnean Society that the year had produced nothing of any particular interest, despite the seminal report by **Alfred Wallace** and **Charles Darwin** that led to the theory of evolution by means of natural selection. Bell's *British Stalk-eyed Crustacea* (1853) remains a standard work on British crabs and lobsters. In 1877 he edited the *Natural History of Selborne*, by **Gilbert White**, whose house he purchased.

Bell, Vanessa, *née* Stephen 1879–1961
English painter and decorative designer

Born in Kensington, London, she was the daughter of Sir **Leslie Stephen** and elder sister of **Virginia Woolf**, and a leading member of the Bloomsbury Group. She married the critic **Clive Bell** in 1907, but left him in 1916 to live with **Duncan Grant**, a fellow-contributor to **Roger Fry's** Omega Workshops (1913–20). She exhibited four pictures in her decorative style (influenced by **Henri Matisse**) in the second Post-Impressionist Exhibition in 1912. Elected to the London Group in 1919, she exhibited with them regularly from 1920.

Bella, Stefano Della 1610–64
Italian engraver

Born in Florence, he worked for Cardinal **Richelieu** and for the Grand Duke of Tuscany. His work was in the manner of **Jacques Callot** and his large output consisted of battle scenes and sieges, landscapes, and animal and masque designs. Many of his works can be found in the Royal Library at Windsor, England.

Bellamy, David James 1933–
English botanist, writer and broadcaster

Born in London, he took a doctorate in botany and was senior lecturer in the department of botany at Durham University (1960–80). He is a director of the Conservation Foundation, president of Population Concern (since 1988) and of the National Association for Environmental Education (since 1989), and has been a visiting professor at Nottingham University since 1987. His television career began with *Life in Our Sea* in 1970 and he became widely known as a presenter of the popular science series *Don't Ask Me* (1974–78). His own series have included *Bellamy on Botany* (1972), *Bellamy's Britain* (1974), *Bellamy's Europe* (1976), *Discovery* (1985), *Bellamy's Bugle*

(1986–88), *Bellamy Rides Again* (1991–92) and *Bellamy's Border Raids: The Peak District* (1994). His books include *Bellamy's New World* (1983), *The Queen's Hidden Garden* (1984), *Bellamy's Changing Countryside* (4 vols, 1989) and *Blooming Bellamy* (1993).

Bellamy, Edward 1850–98
US novelist

Born in Chicopee Falls, Massachusetts, he studied law and was called to the Bar (1871), but instead took a career in journalism. He achieved immense popularity with his Utopian romance *Looking Backward 2000–1887* (1888), a work which predicted a new social order and influenced economic thinking in the USA and Europe. The sequel *Equality* (1897) was much less acclaimed. ☐ A E Morgan, *Edward Bellamy* (1944)

Bellamy, George Anne c.1727–1788
English actress

She was the illegitimate daughter of a Quaker schoolgirl and Lord Tyrawley, and first appeared at Covent Garden, London, in 1742. Despite a brilliant theatrical career, through profligacy and extravagance she spent her last years in poverty. She published an autobiographical *Apology* (1785).

Bellany, John 1942–
Scottish painter and etcher

Born in Port Seton, he studied at Edinburgh College of Art (1960–65) and at the Royal College of Art (1965–68). Like many Scots of his generation, he adopted an expressive form of realism in the 1970s inspired by **Fernand Léger** and by German art. A retrospective of his work was held at the Scottish National Gallery of Modern Art and at the Serpentine Gallery, London, in 1986. He was elected an RA in 1991.

Bellarmine, St Francis, *properly* San Roberto Francesco Romolo Bellarmino 1542–1621
Italian Jesuit theologian

Born in Montepulciano, near Siena, he joined the Jesuits at Rome in 1560, and studied theology at Padua and Louvain in the Spanish Netherlands. In 1570 he was appointed Professor of Theology at Louvain, but returned to Rome in 1576, becoming Rector of the Roman College in 1592. He was made a cardinal in 1599 against his own inclination, and in 1602 Archbishop of Capua. After the death of Clement VIII, he evaded the papal chair, but was induced by **Paul V** to hold an important place in the Vatican from 1605 till his death. In the 17th century, stone beer jugs with a caricature of his likeness, called bellarmines, were produced by Flemish Protestants to ridicule him. He was canonized in 1930, and his feast day is 17 May. ☐ James Brodrick, *Robert Bellarmine, Saint and Scholar* (1961)

Bellay, Joachim du 1522–60
French poet and prose writer

Born in Liré, he was, after his friend and fellow-student **Pierre de Ronsard**, the most important member of the Pléiade. His *Défense et illustration de la langue française* (1549, 'Defence and Illustration of the French Language'), the manifesto of the Pléiade, advocating the rejection of medieval linguistic traditions and a return to classical and Italian models, had a considerable influence at the time. It was accompanied by an example in the form of a set of Petrarchan sonnets, *l'Olive*, dedicated to an unknown lady. A visit to Rome in 1533 inspired more sonnets, including the collections *Les Antiquités de Rome* ('Roman Antiquities') and *Les Regrets* (1558). ☐ L Clark Keating, *Joachim du Bellay* (1976)

Bell Burnell, (Susan) Jocelyn, *née* Bell 1943–
English radio astronomer

Born in York, she was educated at the universities of Glasgow and Cambridge, where she received her PhD (1968). She was co-discoverer with **Antony Hewish** of the first pulsar in 1967. She later joined the staff of the Royal Observatory, Edinburgh, and became the manager of their **James Clerk Maxwell** Telescope on Hawaii. She was awarded the Herschel Medal of the Royal Astronomical Society in 1989 and since 1991 has been Professor of Physics at the Open University.

Belleau, Rémy 1528–77
French poet
Born in Nogent le Rotrou, he was a member of the Pléiade and published in 1556 a translation of **Anacreon** that was at first believed to be an original imitation. *Bergerie* (1565, 'Pastoral', 2nd edn 1572) is a medley of delicately descriptive prose and verse, of which *Avril* ('April') still appears in anthologies. *Amours* (1576, 'Love Poems') is a collection of poems concerned with the appearance and arcane powers of precious stones. ⌨ S Eckhardt, *Rémy Belleau, sa vie, sa 'Bergerie'* (1917)

Bellenden or Ballantyne, John d.1587
Scottish ecclesiastic and writer
Born towards the close of the 15th century, he matriculated from St Andrews in 1508 and completed his theological studies at the Sorbonne, Paris. He enjoyed great favour at the court of **James V**, at whose request he made translations (1533) of **Hector Boece**'s *Historiae Gentis Scotorum* (1526), and of the first five books of **Livy**. These are interesting as vigorous examples of early Scottish prose: the *Croniklis of Scotland* is a very free translation of *Historiae*, and contains numerous passages not found in Boece, so that it is in some respects almost an original work. As a reward, Bellenden received considerable grants from the Treasury, and was made Archdeacon of Moray and Canon of Ross. He later became involved in ecclesiastical controversy, and went to Rome. ⌨ R W Chambers and W W Seton, *Bellenden's Translation of the History of Hector Boece* (1919)

Bellingshausen, Fabian Gottlieb Benjamin, von 1778–1852
Russian explorer
He was born in Oesel and joined the Russian navy at the age of 10. In 1819–21 he led an expedition around the world which made several discoveries in the Pacific Ocean, and sailed as far south as 70° in the Antarctic. The Bellingshausen Sea there is named after him.

Bellini, Gentile See **Bellini, Giovanni**

Bellini, Giovanni c.1430–1516
Venetian painter
One of a family of painters, he became the greatest Venetian artist of his time and was instrumental in making Venice an artistic centre to rival Florence. His father Jacopo Bellini (c.1400–70) had studied under **Gentile da Fabriano** and painted a wide range of subjects, of which a few Madonnas in Italy and drawings in the Louvre, Paris, and the British Museum, London, remain, showing Jacopo's interest in architectural and landscape setting. Giovanni's style progressed from the sharp and stylized manner inherited from his father to the more sensuous, painterly one for which he is famous. His sense of design was learned from the severe classical style of his brother-in-law **Andrea Mantegna** and his fluid, oil technique from **Antonello da Messina**. His art is essentially calm and contemplative; one of his chief contributions to Italian art was his successful integration of figures with landscape background. Another is his naturalistic treatment of light. Almost all his pictures are religious and he remains best known for a long series of Madonnas to which he brought a humanistic sensibility. All the most talented younger painters of his day, including **Titian**, came to his

studio and through them his innovations were perpetuated. His own style continued to develop to the end, and his later work is influenced by the youthful genius **Giorgione**. Giovanni's brother Gentile (c.1429–1507) worked in Jacopo's studio and was chosen to paint the portrait of Sultan Muhammad II in Constantinople (Istanbul). This portrait, together with his *Adoration of the Kings*, is in the National Gallery, London. ⌨ Giles Robertson, *Giovanni Bellini* (1968)

Bellini, Jacopo See **Bellini, Giovanni**

Bellini, Vincenzo 1801–35
Italian operatic composer
Born in Catania, Sicily, he was an organist's son, and was sent by a Sicilian nobleman to the San Sebastians Conservatorio in Naples. He wrote many operas, but international success came with *Il Pirata* (1827, 'The Pirate'), and was followed by *I Capuleti ed i Montecchi* (1830, 'The Capulets and the Montagues', based on *Romeo and Juliet*) and his two great works of lyrical expression, *La Sonnambula* (1831, 'The Sleepwalking Girl') and *Norma* (1831). *I Puritani* (1834, 'The Puritans') shows the influence of the French school. ⌨ Leslie Orrey, *Bellini* (1978)

Bellmann, Carl Michael 1740–95
Swedish poet and writer of popular songs
Born in Stockholm, he entered banking in 1757, but had to flee to Norway six years later to escape his creditors. In 1776 he was brought back as a protégé of King **Gustav III**, who gave him a sinecure as secretary of the national lottery. He founded a drinking club, the *Bacci orden* or 'Knights of Bacchus', and put in verse his impressions of his friends and others. His collections include the *Songs of Fredman* (1790) and *Epistles of Fredman* (1791), which combine burlesque with biblical parody and minute observation of Swedish life. There is a long-standing Bellmann Society in Sweden devoted to his memory. ⌨ P B Austin, *Life and Songs of Carl Michael Bellmann* (1967)

Bello, Sir Ahmadu 1910–66
Nigerian statesman
Educated at Katsina College, he started his career as a teacher but became a major political figure following his appointment as Saudana of Sokoto (1938). He led the Northern People's Congress (NPC) from 1951, reaching the post of Prime Minister in 1954. He was a major figure in national politics, exercising his power through the NPC from his base in the Hausa-dominated north of the country. He was assassinated in the coup of 1966.

Bello, Andrés 1781–1865
Venezuelan writer and polymath
He was born and educated in Caracas. He lived in London (1810–29) before settling in Chile, where he became a senior public servant, senator, and first Rector of the university (1843). Considered the most remarkable Latin American intellectual of the 19th century, his writings embrace language, law, education, history, philosophy, poetry, drama and science. ⌨ E R Monmegal, *Este otro Andrés Bello* (1969)

Belloc, (Joseph) Hilaire P(ierre) 1870–1953
British writer and poet
He was born in St Cloud, near Paris. His family moved to England during the Franco-Prussian War, and settled there in 1872. He was educated at the Oratory School, Birmingham, under **John Newman**, and Balliol College, Oxford, but did military service in the French army. He became a naturalized British subject (1902) and a Liberal MP (1906–10). Disapproving of modern industrial society and socialism, he wrote *The Servile State* (1912), advocating a return to the system of medieval guilds. He was a close friend of **G K Chesterton**, who illustrated many of his books. He is best known for his nonsensical

verse for children, *The Bad Child's Book of Beasts* (1896) and the *Cautionary Tales* (1907); his numerous travel books, including *The Path to Rome* (1902) and *The Old Road* (1910); his historical studies, including *Robespierre* (1901), *Richelieu* (1929) and *Napoleon* (1932); and his religious books, including *Europe and the Faith* (1920) and *The Great Heresies* (1938). He was an energetic Roman Catholic apologist. His sister Marie Belloc (1868–1947) was a novelist and playwright. 📖 A N Wilson, *Hilaire Belloc* (1984)

Bellotto, Bernardo 1720–80
Italian painter
A nephew and pupil of **Canaletto**, he achieved prominence as a painter, and also as an engraver on copper. He worked in Venice, Rome, Verona, Brescia, Milan, England, Dresden where he was court painter (1747–57), and Warsaw, where he was court painter from 1767.

Bellovacensius, Vincentius See Vincent de Beauvais

Bellow, Saul 1915–
US writer and Nobel Prize winner
He was born in Lachine, Quebec, Canada, the son of immigrant Russian parents, and spent his childhood in Montreal. In 1924 his family moved to Chicago, a city that was to figure largely in his fiction, and he attended university there and at Northwestern in Evanston, Illinois. He abandoned his post-graduate studies at Wisconsin University to become a writer, and his first novel, *The Dangling Man*, a study of a man in pre-draft limbo, appeared in 1944. He became an associate professor at Minnesota University, and after being awarded a Guggenheim Fellowship in 1948 travelled to Paris and Rome. Other works include *The Victim* (1947), *The Adventures of Augie March* (1953), *Henderson the Rain King* (1959), *Herzog* (1964), *Mr Sammler's Planet* (1970), *Humboldt's Gift* (1975), *The Dean's December* (1982) and *More Die of Heartbreak* (1986). Most are concerned with the fate of liberal humanism in a violent and absurd environment which has severed the present from an intellectually and emotionally nourishing past. In 1962 he was appointed a professor at the University of Chicago, and in 1976 was awarded the Nobel Prize for literature. His recent publications include a volume of three tales, *Something to Remember Me By* (1991) and a collection of essays, *It All Adds Up* (1994). 📖 J Braham, *A Sort of Columbus: The American Voyages of Bellow's Fiction* (1984); M Bradbury, *Bellow* (1982)

Bellows, George Wesley 1882–1925
US painter and lithographer
Born in Columbus, Ohio, he was a leading figure in the movement which sought to break away from Post-Impressionism into the vivid harshness of Social Realism. He delighted in prize fights, festivals and the teeming life of the cities. Probably his most famous work is *Firpo and Dempsey*, which hangs in the Museum of Modern Art, New York. His work has a bold freshness which, coupled with the crude vigour of his subject matter, places him among the leaders of American Realism.

Belloy, Dormont de, *properly* Pierre Laurent Buyrette 1727–75
French dramatist
He was one of the first to introduce on the French stage native instead of classical heroes. His first success, *Zelmire* (1762), was followed by *Le Siège de Calais* (1765), *Gaston et Bayard* (1771) and *Pierre le cruel* (1772, 'Peter the Cruel').

Belmont, Alva Erstkin, *née* Smith 1853–1933
US reformer
Born in Mobile, Alabama, into a well-established Southern family, she was a committed socialite, who cleverly worked her way into the New York social élite as the wife of William Henry Vanderbilt (married 1875, divorced 1895), and married her daughter to the Duke of Marlborough. After the death of her second husband (1908), she developed an interest in women's rights, and became involved with militant feminism, inviting **Christabel Pankhurst** to the USA to speak in 1914, and donating generously to the cause. From 1921 to 1933 she was president of the National Woman's Party.

Belmonte, Juan 1894–1962
Spanish bullfighter
In a career that spanned 25 years he was renowned for his noble style of preparing the bull for its death. A small, ugly man, comical in appearance, it was said he underwent a transformation once in front of the bull. He would wait before it, standing still with his hands held low, thus risking much. He was gored many times, and his body carried the scars. Respected by other revered bullfighters such as **Dominguin**, at a time when bullfighting was less about money and more about respect, he was regarded as a prince among matadors.

Belon, Pierre 1517–64
French naturalist
From 1546 to 1549 he travelled in Asia Minor, Egypt and Arabia, writing valuable treatises on trees, herbs, birds and fishes. He was one of the first to establish the homologies between the skeletons of different vertebrates. He planted the first cedar in France and formed two early botanical gardens.

Belteshazzar See Daniel

Bely, Andrei, *pseudonym of* Boris Nikolayevich Bugayev 1880–1934
Russian novelist, poet and critic
He was born in Moscow. A leading Symbolist writer, he early met **Vladimir Soloviev**, the religious philosopher, and fell under his influence. While at Moscow University Bely wrote Decadent poetry, which he published in *Simfoniya (2-aya, dramaticheskaya)* (1902, 'Symphony (Second, Dramatic)'). His reputation, however, rests on his prose. *Serebryany golub* (1909, Eng trans *The Silver Dove*, 1974), his first and most accessible novel, was followed by his masterpiece, *Peterburg* (1916, Eng trans *St Petersburg*, 1959), in which the action centres on a bomb camouflaged as a tin of sardines. The autobiographical *Kotik Letayev* (1922, Eng trans *Kotik Letaev*, 1971) is his most original work, a stream-of-consciousness attempt to show how children become aware of what is going on in the world. His later novels, written after a sojourn in Berlin (1921–23), are more overtly satirical of the pre-revolutionary Russian scene but are still highly experimental. He is regarded as one of the most important Russian writers of the 1920s. 📖 J D Elsworth, *Andrei Bely* (1972)

Belzoni, Giovanni Battista 1778–1823
Italian explorer and antiquity hunter
He was born in Padua, and in 1803 went to England, where he earned a living performing as a strong man in circuses as he was 6 feet 7 inches tall (2m). In 1815 he went to Egypt, and turned to tomb-robbing and the exploration of Egyptian antiquities, removing from Thebes the colossal bust of **Rameses II**, which, together with finds from the tomb of Sethos I which he had opened up in 1817, he sent to the British Museum, London. He explored the temple of Edfu, cleared the temple of Abu Simbel, opened the pyramid of Khephren at Giza and discovered the ruins of the city of Berenice near Benghazi. He returned to Europe in 1819, publishing his discoveries as *Narrative of the Operations and Recent Discoveries within the Pyramids, Temples, Tombs and Excavations in Egypt and Nubia* (1820). He died of dysentery in Benin, Africa, while searching for the source of the River Niger.

Beman, Deane R 1938–
US golf administrator

Born in Washington DC, he was a member of the US Walker Cup team (1959–65) and the Eisenhower trophy team (1960–66), and became a moderately successful professional golfer in the early 1970s. As commissioner of the US Professional Golfers' Association Tour (1974–94), he steered it through the boom and trough of the 1970s and 1980s and is responsible for its current structure. His success has been due partly to combining the US Tour with both corporate America and with television. His supporters claim he has generated a huge increase in prize money for the players, but some critics argue that in the process he has sold golf's soul. He resigned in June 1994.

Bembo, Pietro 1470–1547
Italian scholar and ecclesiastic

Born in Venice, he was educated mainly by his father who was an eminent figure in the Republic. In 1513 he was made secretary to Pope Leo X, and in 1539 a cardinal by Paul III, who appointed him to the dioceses of Gubbio and Bergamo. Bembo was the restorer of good style in both Latin and Italian literature, especially with his *Prose della volgar lingua* (1525, 'Discussions of the Vernacular Language'), which marked an era in Italian grammar. He also published a book of his own Italian poetry, *Rime* (1530, 'Verses').

Benacerraf, Baruj 1920–
US immunologist and Nobel Prize winner

He was born in Caracas, Venezuela. His family moved to the USA (1940) and he entered the Medical College of Virginia. In 1949 he was a research director at the Broussais Hospital, Paris, and in 1956 he returned to the USA to a post at the New York University School of Medicine, where he became Professor of Pathology in 1960. In New York, his research concentrated upon the cells involved in the body's defence against foreign substances, or antigens. He showed that response to antigens was genetically determined, and named the determining genes as the immune-response genes. He later clarified how genetically determined structures on cell surfaces regulate responses to diseased cells and in organ transplants. For this work he shared the 1980 Nobel Prize for physiology or medicine with Jean Dausset and George Snell. Benacerraf moved to the National Institutes of Health in 1968 and to Harvard Medical School in 1970. In 1990 he was awarded the National Medal of Science.

Ben Ali, Zine el Abidine 1936–
Tunisian politician

After studying electronics at military schools in France and the USA, he began a career in military security, rising to the position of Director-General of National Security. He became Minister of the Interior and then Prime Minister under 'President-for-Life' Habib Bourguiba, who had been in power since 1956. In 1987 he forced Bourguiba to retire and assumed the presidency himself; he immediately embarked on constitutional reforms, promising a greater degree of democracy.

Benavente, Jacinto 1866–1954
Spanish dramatist

Born in Madrid, he intended to enter the legal profession but turned instead to literature. After publishing some poems and short stories he won recognition as a playwright with his *El nido ajeno* (1893, 'The Other Nest'), which was followed by some brilliantly satirical society comedies. His masterpiece is *Los intereses creados* (1907, 'Human Concerns'), an allegorical play in the commedia dell'arte style. He also wrote several plays for children. 📖 M Penuelas, translated by K Englev, *Jacinto Benavente* (1968)

Ben Bella, Ahmed 1918–
Algerian politician

Born in Maghnia, on the Moroccan border, he served with distinction in the French army in World War II. In 1949 he became leader of the extremist independence movement, the Organisation Spéciale (Special Organization), the paramilitary wing of the Algerian nationalist Parti du Peuple Algérien (Party of the Algerian People). In 1950 he was imprisoned, but he escaped to Cairo, where he founded the National Liberation Front (FLN). The FLN then embarked on a long war (1954–62) which led to independence and Ben Bella's election in 1963 as President. He was deposed in 1965 in a coup led by General Houari Boumédienne and kept under house arrest until 1979. Between 1981 and 1990, he went into exile, but afterwards he returned to Algeria, promoting himself as a symbol of revolutionary spirit.

Benbow, John 1653–1702
English naval commander

Born in Shrewsbury, Shropshire, he joined the navy in 1678, transferred to the merchant services after a court martial and rejoined the navy in 1689. He was Master of the Fleet at Beachy Head (1690), Barfleur and La Hogue (1692), and commanded squadrons off Dunkirk (1693–95). As rear admiral he was Commander-in-Chief West Indies from 1698. In the West Indies, on 19 August 1702, he came up against a superior French force and for four days he kept up a running fight until he was wounded and forced to return to Jamaica, where he died.

Bench, Johnny Lee 1947–
US baseball player

Born in Oklahoma City, he played in the National League with Cincinnati Reds and was the outstanding catcher of the 1970s. He had great ability with the bat, hit over 200 home runs, and led the league three times in seven years for runs batted in. He was the National League's Most Valuable Player (MVP) on several occasions and almost monopolized the Golden Glove award for his particular position.

Benchley, Robert Charles 1889–1945
US humorist, critic and parodist

He was born in Worcester, Massachusetts, and studied at Harvard where he edited the *Lampoon* and starred in the Hasty Pudding shows. While working for *Vanity Fair* he met Dorothy Parker and together with Robert Sherwood, James Thurber, George Kaufman and Franklin P Adams, they formed the notorious Algonquin Round Table. Subsequently Benchley worked as a drama critic for *Life* (1920–29) and the *New Yorker* (1929–40) but he was fired for excessive drinking. He was at his most brilliant in the sketches collected in *20,000 Leagues under the Sea, or, David Copperfield* (1928), *From Bed to Worse* (1934) and *My Ten Years in a Quandary, and How They Grew* (1936). His humour derives from the predicament of the 'Little Man', himself writ large, beset on all sides by the complexity of existence in the modern world. E B White and Thurber thought him a finer humorist even than Mark Twain, and Parker described him as a 'kind of saint'. He appeared in cameo roles in many films. 📖 N W Yates, *Robert Benchley* (1968)

Benda, Georg Anton 1722–95
Bohemian musician

Born in Alt-Benatek, he became kapellmeister to the Duke of Gotha (1748–78). He composed operettas, cantatas and melodramas, and introduced music drama with spoken text. His brothers, Franz (1709–86) and Joseph (1724–1804), were both in turn konzertmeister of Frederick II, the Great of Prussia.

Benda, Julien 1867–1956
French philosopher and essayist

Born in Paris and educated at the university there, he found fame writing in opposition to **Henri Bergson**, just before World War I. He then caused a sensation in 1927 with *La Trahison des clercs* ('The Treachery of the Intellectuals') in which he accuses modern thinkers of abandoning philosophical neutrality to support doctrines of class and race hatred, such as Marxism and Fascism, going on to attempt to 'restore the primacy of the spiritual'. He published little during the German occupation of France but much afterwards, including *Tradition de l'existentialisme* (1947, 'Tradition of Existentialism') and *La Dialectique Materialiste* (1948, 'Materialist Dialectique'). He wrote two novels, *L'Ordination* (1911, 'The Ordination') and *Les Amorandes* (1922). 📖 *La Jeunesse d'un clerc* (1936)

Beneden, Edouard Joseph Louis-Marie van
1846–1910
Belgian cytologist and embryologist
Born in Liège, he travelled to Brazil in 1872 and returned with a number of specimens. In 1877 he proposed the creation of the phylum Mesozoa, to cater for the transition between single-celled and multi-celled organisms, and in 1887 demonstrated the constancy of the number of chromosomes in the cells of an organism, decreasing during maturation and restored at fertilization.

Benedetti, Mario 1920–
Uruguayan novelist, short-story writer and poet
He was born in Paso de los Toros. His early stories, included in *Esta Mañana* (1949, 'This Morning') and *El Último Viaje y otros cuentos* (1951, 'The Last Journey and other stories'), tell of the frustrations of mass existence in the cities. His novels, like *Quién de Nosotros* (1955, 'Which One of Us'), expand on that theme, but his poetry, such as the collection *Noción de la Patria* (1963, 'Concept of the Homeland'), though often political, can also engage in more abstract notions. He has also written several volumes of lively literary criticism, including *Literatura Uruguayo siglo XX* (1963, rev edn 1969).

Benedetto, Anthony Dominick See Bennett, Tony

Benedict VIII d.1024
First of the Tusculan popes
Born probably in the county of Tusculum, Italy, he was elected in 1012. He was temporarily driven from Rome by the antipope Gregory VI, of the Crescenti family, but was restored to the papal chair by the Emperor **Henry II**, whom he crowned in 1014. Later he defeated the Saracens and the Greeks in northern Italy, and introduced clerical and monastic reforms. The uncle of Pope **Benedict IX**, he was succeeded by his brother, John XIX.

Benedict IX d.c.1065
Last of the Tusculan popes
He succeeded his uncle, John XIX, in 1032, obtaining the papal throne by simony. In 1036 the Romans banished him on account of his licentiousness. Several times reinstalled, he was as often deposed.

Benedict XIII
Title assumed by two popes
Pedro de Luna (c.1328–1423), born in Illneca, Kingdom of Aragon, Spain, was elected as antipope by the French cardinals in 1394 in succession to the antipope Clement VII at Avignon after the Great Western Schism of 1378; and Pietro Francesco Orsini (1649–1730), an Italian Dominican cardinal, was elected pope in 1724. A learned man of simple habits and pure morals, he placed himself under the guidance of the unscrupulous Cardinal Niccolo Coscia.

Benedict XIV, *originally* Prospero Lambertini
1675–1758
Italian pope
Born in Bologna, he studied theology and law at Rome, and became pope in 1740. He tried to stimulate the economy through liberal commercial policies, the reduction of taxes and agricultural improvement, and was similarly far-sighted and realistic in the conciliatory approach he adopted towards the monarchs of his day. He urged that restraint be exercised by those responsible for compiling the index of prohibited literature, and was also keen to avoid too open a breach with Jansenism. However, he was not merely a doctrinal pragmatist: in the *Ex quo singulari* (1742) and the *Omnium sollicitudinum* (1744) he denounced, and prohibited, the various traditional practices which Jesuits had tolerated among converts in India and China, saying they were incompatible with the Catholic faith. Distinguished by his learning and ability, he founded chairs of physics, chemistry and mathematics in Rome, revived the academy of Bologna, rebuilt some churches, and encouraged literature and science.

Benedict XV, *originally* Giacomo Della Chiesa
1854–1922
Italian pope
Born of a noble Italian family, he was ordained at 24, became secretary to the papal embassy in Spain (1883) then secretary to Cardinal Rampolla, bishop (1900), Archbishop of Bologna (1907), and cardinal (May 1914). Although a junior cardinal, he was elected to succeed **Pius X** in September 1914, soon after the outbreak of World War I. He made repeated efforts to end the war, and organized war relief on a munificent scale.

Benedict Biscop, St c.628–689
Anglo-Saxon churchman
Born in Northumbria, he became a monk in 653, journeyed to Rome five times and from 669 to 671 was abbot of St Peter's, Canterbury. In 674 he founded a monastery at Wearmouth, endowing it generously with books, and in 682 founded a second monastery at Jarrow. He is said to have introduced stone edifices and glass windows to England. One of his pupils was the Venerable **Bede**. His feast day is usually celebrated on 12 January.

Benedict of Nursia, St c.480–c.547AD
Italian founder of Western monasticism
Born in Nursia, near Spoleto, he was educated at Rome, and as a boy of 14 lived alone for three years in a cave near Subiaco, praying and meditating. Appointed the abbot of a neighbouring monastery at Vicovaro, he soon left it to found 12 small highly disciplined monastic communities. He ultimately established a monastery on Monte Cassino, near Naples, later one of the richest and most famous in Italy. In 515 he is said to have composed his *Regula Monachorum*, which became the common rule of all Western monasticism. He was declared the patron saint of all Europe by Pope **Paul VI** in 1964. His feast day is 11 July.

Benedict, Sir Julius 1804–85
German composer
Born in Stuttgart, he studied under **Johann Hummel** and **Carl Weber**, and was conductor at a Vienna opera house at 20 years of age. In 1836 he settled in London, achieving considerable success with *Lily of Killarney* (1862).

Benedict, Ruth, *née* Fulton 1887–1948
US anthropologist
Born in New York City, she studied philosophy and English literature at Vassar before going on to study anthropology under Alexander Goldenweiser and **Franz Boas** at Columbia University. She became a leading member of the culture-and-personality movement in US anthropology during the 1930s and 1940s. Her most important contribution lay in her 'configurational' approach to entire cultures, according to which each culture tends to predispose its individual members to adopt an ideal type of personality. Thus every culture, she believed,

could be characterized in terms of its own distinctive ethos. Her best-known works include *Patterns of Culture* (1934), *Race: Science and Politics* (1940), a book against racism, and *The Chrysanthemum and the Sword: Patterns of Japanese Culture* (1946). In 1948, the year of her death, she became professor at Columbia University.

Benediktsson, Einar 1864–1940
Icelandic poet and entrepreneur
Born in Ellíavatan, near Reykjavík, he became a country magistrate, but toured Europe for many years, seeking capital (unsuccessfully) for ambitious industrial schemes to exploit Iceland's natural resources, notably fishing and hydroelectric power. His literary output reflected his patriotic concerns. He published five volumes of ornate poetry that resembled the skaldic tradition of intricate metaphor and vocabulary, but which he modernized considerably. ⌾ S J Nordal, *Einar Benediktsson* (1971)

Benelli, Sem 1877–1949
Italian dramatist
He was born in Prato, Tuscany, and wrote plays in prose and verse. His outstanding successes were *Tignola* (1908, 'The Bookworm'), a light comedy, and *La cena della beffe* (1909, Eng trans *The Jest*, 1919), a powerful tragedy in verse. ⌾ C Lavi, *Sem Benelli, il suo teatro e la sua compagnia* (1928)

Beneš, Eduard 1884–1948
Czechoslovak statesman
Born in Kožlany, a farmer's son, he studied law and became Professor of Sociology at Prague. As an émigré during World War I he worked in Paris with **Tomáš Masaryk** for Czech independence, becoming Foreign Minister of the new state (1918–35), and for a while premier (1921–22). In 1935 he succeeded Masaryk as President, but resigned in 1938 following the Munich Agreement. He then left the country, setting up a government in exile, first in France, then in Great Britain. Returning to Czechoslovakia in 1945, he was re-elected President the following year, but resigned after the Communist takeover in 1948.

Benesh, Rudolph 1916–75 and Joan Benesh, *née* Rothwell 1920–
English dance notators
Born in London and Liverpool respectively, Rudolph was first a painter and Joan a member of the Sadler's Wells Ballet. Together they copyrighted (1955) a dance notation system, called choreology, that has been included in the syllabus of London's Royal Academy of Dancing and is used to document all important Royal Ballet productions. They opened their own Institute in 1962 and their influence on a great number of notators and educators has been incalculable.

Benet, Juan 1927–93
Spanish novelist, dramatist and civil engineer
His complex, 'hermetic' work is most influenced by **William Faulkner** and alludes to many other writers, and for that reason has not been widely read outside Spain, except by its devoted critics. His successful novel, *Una Meditación* (1970), however, was translated as *A Meditation* in 1982, and whilst his 'baroque' prose is generally considered problematic, his journalistic work is noted for its lucidity. ⌾ D K Herzberger, *The Novelistic World of Juan Benet* (1977)

Benét, Stephen Vincent 1898–1943
US poet and novelist
Born in Bethlehem, Pennsylvania, the brother of **William Rose Benét**, he published his first volume of verse in 1915 while still a student at Yale. His work was often inspired by American history and folklore, and he is best known for his long poems *John Brown's Body* (1928), on the Civil

War, and *Western Star* (1943). He wrote several volumes of evocative poems in traditional form, including the collection *Ballads and Poems 1915–30* (1931) and *Burning City* (1936). His other writings include four more novels, short stories such as 'The Devil and Daniel Webster', and two one-act folk operas. He was awarded the 1929 and the 1943 Pulitzer prizes. ⌾ C Fenton, *Stephen Vincent Benét* (1958)

Benét, William Rose 1886–1950
US poet, editor, novelist and playwright
Born in Fort Hamilton, New York, he was the brother of **Stephen Benét**. He published many collections of poetry, among them *Merchants from Cathay* (1913), *Moons of Grandeur* (1920) and *The Stairway of Surprise* (1947), but his career was largely eclipsed by the success of his wife, **Elinor Wylie**, and of his brother. ⌾ *My Brother Steve* (1943)

Benfey, Theodor 1809–81
German–Jewish philologist
Born near Göttingen, his interest in philology was aroused by the Hebrew lessons he received from his father, and his early work was in the fields of classical and Hebrew philology. His *Lexicon of Greek Roots* was published between 1839 and 1842. Having learned Sanskrit in a few weeks to win a bet, he later turned his attention to Sanskrit philology. He was professor at Göttingen from 1848, and published an edition of the Sama-veda (1848), a *Manual of Sanskrit* (1852–54), and his best-known work, the *Sanskrit-English Dictionary* (1866). Benfey died in Göttingen while working on a grammar of Vedic Sanskrit.

Bengel, Johann Albrecht 1687–1752
German theologian
Born in Winnenden, Württemberg, he studied at the University of Tübingen. He was the first Protestant author (1734) to treat the exegesis of the New Testament critically.

Ben-Gurion, David, *originally* David Gruen 1886–1973
Israeli statesman
Born in Plonsk, Poland, he emigrated to Palestine in 1906. Expelled by the Turks during World War I, he recruited Jews to the British Army in North America. In Palestine in 1919 he founded a socialist party and became Secretary to the Histadrut in 1921. He led the Mapai (Labour) Party from its formation in 1930 and headed the Jewish Agency in 1935. Ben-Gurion moulded the Mapai into the main party of the Yishuv during British rule and became Prime Minister after independence (1948–53), when he was responsible for Israel absorbing large numbers of refugees from Europe and Arab countries. He was Prime Minister again from 1955 to 1963. ⌾ Michel Bar-Zohar, *Ben Gurion: The Armed Prophet* (1967)

Benigni, Roberto 1952–
Italian comic actor
Born in Misericordia, he moved swiftly from local cabaret to national television in programmes like *Onda Libera* and *L'Altra Domenica* where he won notoriety for his fearless assault on such taboo topics as sex, God, the Church and politics and earned the description 'dung-heap **Woody Allen**'. His tousled hair and angelic demeanour conceal an aggressive and often anarchic sense of mischief. He made his film debut in *Berlinguer, Ti Voglio Bene* (1977) and made his directorial debut with *Tu Mi Turbi* (1983). Subsequent films like *Il Piccolo Diavolo* (1985, *The Little Devil*), *Johnny Stecchino* (1991) and *Il Mostro* (1994, *The Monster*) broke box-office records across Europe and established him as one of Italy's favourite film comics. His English-language films include *Down By Law* (1986), *Night on Earth* (1991) and *Son of The Pink Panther* (1993). His rare performances for other Italian directors

include *La Luna* (1979) for **Bernardo Bertolucci** and *La Voce Della Luna* (1990, *The Voice of The Moon*) for **Federico Fellini**.

Benincasa, Caterina See **Catherine of Siena, St**

Benioff, Victor Hugo 1899–1968
US geophysicist
Born in Los Angeles, he was educated in physics and astronomy, first worked at Lick Observatory (1923–24) and in 1924 moved to the Carnegie Institution in Washington, where he developed a system of seismic recording drums which produced measurements of unprecedented accuracy. He went on to invent other instruments which enabled the precise determination of seismic traveltime, improved the recording of distant seismic events and enabled first motion determinations, which give the directions of the fault breaks caused by earthquakes. When the Seismological Laboratory moved from Carnegie to the California Institute of Technology in 1937, Benioff became assistant Professor of Seismology and Professor from 1950, and collaborated with **Beno Gutenberg** and **Charles Richter**. From about 1950 he worked on general problems in earthquake mechanisms and global tectonics, developed several new analytical techniques and amassed evidence of earthquakes around the Pacific, in 1954 publishing his records of seismically active crustal slabs beneath ocean trenches, now known as **Wadati–Benioff** zones.

Benítez, Miguel Angel Osorio See **Barba Jacob, Porfirio**

Benjamin
Biblical character
He was the youngest son of **Jacob** and Jacob's favourite wife **Rachel**, who died soon after Benjamin was born. He was held in great affection by his father and his brother **Joseph**; his story is told in Genesis 37–50. He gave his name to the smallest of the 12 tribes of Israel, the Benjamites, to which King **David** and St **Paul** belonged.

Benjamin of Tudela d.1173
Spanish rabbi and traveller
He was born in Navarre, and from 1159 to 1173 made a journey from Saragossa through Italy and Greece, to Palestine, Persia (Iran), and the borders of China, returning by way of Egypt and Sicily. He was the first European traveller to describe the Far East.

Benjamin, Judah Philip 1811–84
US lawyer
Born in St Croix, West Indies, of Jewish parents, he studied law at Yale University. He practised as a lawyer in New Orleans, becoming active in politics and serving first with the Whigs, and afterwards with the Democrats. He sat in the US Senate (1852–1860) and in 1861, when the Civil War broke out, joined **Jefferson Davis**'s Cabinet as Attorney-General. He was briefly Secretary of War, and then Secretary of State until Davis's capture in 1865, when he escaped to England. Called to the English Bar in 1866, he became a QC in 1872 and wrote a legal classic, *The Sale of Personal Property* (1868).

Benjamin, Paul See **Auster, Paul**

Benjamin, Walter 1892–1940
German literary and Marxist critic
Born in Berlin, he was educated at the Kaiser Friedrich School, and at the Friedrich-Wilhelm Gymnasium in Thuringia. He was influenced initially by the Cabbalistic tradition. His early work includes the 1925 study *Trauerspiel* (Eng trans *The Origin of German Tragic Drama*, 1977), an attempt to understand the 17th century from a German standpoint, and the so-called 'Arcades Project', which focused upon post-Napoleonic France. Towards the end of the 1920s, Benjamin, encouraged by his encounter with **Bertolt Brecht**, turned towards Marxian materialism, producing essays like 'The Work of Art in an Age of Mechanical Reproduction' (1936), and 'Theses on the Philosophy of History', both of which are included in the posthumous 1969 collection, *Illuminations* (ed Hannah Arendt). Benjamin's reputation was revived by these and the aphoristic and autobiographical *Reflections* (published first in English, 1978), making him a central figure in neo-Marxist and materialist criticism, and an icon of heroic resistance against totalitarianism. He committed suicide. 📖 P Wolin, *Walter Benjamin: An Aesthetic of Redemption* (1982)

Benn, Gottfried 1886–1956
German poet
Born in Mansfeld, West Prussia, he embraced the philosophy of nihilism as a young man, and became one of the few intellectuals to favour Nazi doctrines, although his poems were banned by the Nazis in 1938. (Ironically, they were banned again by the Allies in 1945 for his earlier pro-Nazi sympathies.) Trained in medicine as a venereologist, he began writing Expressionist verse that dealt with the uglier aspects of his profession, such as *Morgue* (1912). Later his work became more versatile, though still pessimistic, and his postwar poetry won him a place among the leading poets of the century. 📖 E Buddeburg, *Gottfried Benn* (1961)

Benn, Tony (Anthony Neil Wedgwood) 1925–
English Labour politician
Born in London, the son of Viscount Stansgate, he was educated at Westminister School and New College, Oxford. A Labour MP from 1950 to 1960, he was debarred from the House of Commons on succeeding to his father's title, but was able to renounce it in 1963 and was re-elected to parliament the same year. He was Postmaster-General (1964–66), Minister of Technology (1966–70), and assumed responsibility for the Ministry of Aviation in 1967 and Ministry of Power in 1969. From 1970 to 1974 he was Opposition Spokesman on Trade and Industry, and on Labour's return to government he was made Secretary of State for Industry, and Minister for Posts and Telecommunications, the following year becoming Secretary of State for Energy, a position he held until the Conservative victory in the 1979 elections. Representing the left wing of Labour opinion he unsuccessfully stood for the deputy leadership of the party in 1981. He lost his seat in the general election of 1983, but returned to represent Chesterfield from 1984. He was the main focus for the left-wing challenge to the Labour leadership in the late 1970s and 1980s which ultimately failed but which led some on the right to leave and form the Social Democratic Party. Among his publications are *Arguments for Socialism* (1979), *Arguments for Democracy* (1981) and *Years of Hope* (1994). 📖 Jad Adams, *Tony Benn* (1992)

Bennet, Abraham 1750–99
English physicist
Born in Taxal, Cheshire, he was ordained in London in 1775, and appointed to curacies first at Tideswell and then in Wirksworth, Derbyshire, where he remained for the rest of his life. His main interest was in atmospheric electricity, which he tried to relate to the weather. During his investigations of small electric charges he invented in 1786 the gold-leaf electroscope, which was based on the 'portable electrometer' of Tiberius Cavallo (1749–1809). He also invented a 'doubling process' which allowed him to measure atmospheric charges. These experiments were described in his *New Experiments on Electricity*, published in 1789, the year in which he was elected FRS.

Bennet, Henry See Arlington, 1st Earl of

Bennett, Alan 1934–
English dramatist, actor and director
Born in Leeds, he was educated at Leeds Modern School and Oxford, where he studied Modern History. He came to prominence as a writer and performer in *Beyond the Fringe*, a revue performed at the Edinburgh Festival in 1960, and wrote a television series, *On The Margin* (1966), before his first stage play, *Forty Years On* (1968). He is essentially a humanist, noted for his wry, self-deprecating humour, which combines a comic-tragic view of life, and later plays include *Getting On* (1971, about a Labour MP), *Habeas Corpus* (1973), *The Old Country* (1977), a double bill, *Single Spies* (1988) and *The Madness of George III* (1991). The latter was rewritten as a screenplay entitled *The Madness of King George* in 1995 then made into an award-winning film starring Nigel Hawthorne and Helen Mirren. He has also written much for television, including *An Englishman Abroad* (1983), *The Insurance Man* (1986), and a series of six monologues, *Talking Heads* (1988). His memoirs were published in 1994 entitled *Writing Home*.

Bennett, (Enoch) Arnold 1867–1931
English novelist
Born near Hanley, Staffordshire, the son of a solicitor, he was educated locally and at London University. He became a solicitor's clerk in London, but soon took up journalism, and in 1893 became assistant editor (editor in 1896) of the journal *Woman*. He published his first novel, *The Man from the North*, in 1898. In 1902 he moved to Paris, where he lived for 10 years, and from then on was engaged exclusively in journalistic and creative writing. His claims to recognition as a novelist rest mainly on the early *Anna of the Five Towns* (1902), the more celebrated *The Old Wives' Tale* (1908), and the *Clayhanger* series—*Clayhanger* (1910), *Hilda Lessways* (1911), *These Twain* (1916), subsequently issued (1925) as *The Clayhanger Family*—in all of which novels the 'Five Towns', centres of the pottery industry, feature not only as background, but almost as dramatis personae. He excelled again with *Riceyman Steps* (1923), a picture of drab life in London, and his genial, humorous streak shows in works like *The Card* (1911), *The Grand Babylon Hotel* (1902), *Imperial Palace* (1930), and the play *The Great Adventure* (1913). *Lord Raingo* (1926) is a political novel. The play *Milestones* (1912), written in collaboration with Edward Knoblock, was much performed. He was a sound and influential critic, and as 'Jacob Tonson' on *The New Age* he was a discerning reviewer. His *Journals*, written in the manner of the brothers Edmond and Jules de Goncourt, were published posthumously. 📖 M Drabble, *Arnold Bennett: a biography* (1974)

Bennett, Floyd 1890–1928
US aviator
Born near Warrensburg, New York, he became a naval pilot during World War I. He accompanied Richard Evelyn Byrd on an expedition to Greenland (1925). In May 1926 he piloted Byrd on the first aeroplane flight over the North Pole, and received the Congressional Medal of Honour. He died while planning Byrd's flight over the South Pole in 1929.

Bennett, James Gordon 1795–1872
US journalist
Born in Keith, Banffshire, Scotland, he emigrated to Nova Scotia in 1819, and became a journalist for the *New York Enquirer* (1826–28) and the *Morning Courier and New York Enquirer* (1829–32). In 1835 he started the *New York Herald*, which he edited until 1867, pioneering many journalistic innovations, such as the use of European correspondents. He was the father of James Gordon Bennett. 📖 Oliver Carlson, *The Man who Made the News: James Gordon Bennett* (1942)

Bennett, James Gordon 1841–1918
US journalist
Born in New York, he was the son and successor of James Gordon Bennett. In 1870 he sent Henry Morton Stanley to find David Livingstone, and with the *Daily Telegraph* financed Stanley's journey to central Africa (1874–77). He also promoted polar exploration, storm warnings, motoring and yachting.

Bennett, Jill 1931–90
English actress
Born in London, she made her debut at Stratford in 1949, and in London in 1950. She scored her first major success in Jean Anouilh's *Dinner With The Family* (1957), and went on to establish a considerable reputation as an elegant, sharp-witted actress, both in classical and contemporary drama. She married the playwright John Osborne in 1968, and played in a number of his works, including *Time Present* (1968), *West of Suez* (1971), *Watch It Come Down* (1976), as well as an acclaimed title role in his version of Ibsen's classic drama *Hedda Gabler* (1972).

Bennett, Louise Simone, *also known as* Miss Hou 1919–
Jamaican poet
Born in Kingston, and educated at Excelsior High School, she studied journalism by correspondence course before going to the Royal Academy of Dramatic Art in London in 1945. After graduating she taught drama in Jamaica, performed in theatres in Great Britain and the USA, and lectured widely on Jamaican folklore and music. In 1954 she married the Jamaican actor and impresario, Eric Coverley. Her numerous books include retellings of Jamaican folk stories, collections of her own ballads and *Jamaican Labrish* (1966), a poetry collection, of which she was the editor. Her use of Jamaican dialect and speech rhythms, humour and satirical wit for the purposes of social and political comment have made her one of the outstanding performance poets of the 20th century. 📖 M Morris, in *Fifty Caribbean Writers*, (ed D C Dance, 1986)

Bennett, Michael 1943–87
US dancer, choreographer, director and producer
Born in Buffalo, New York, he began his career as a chorus boy before turning to Broadway show choreography. His first hit, *Promises, Promises* (1968) was followed by *Coco* (1970), *Company* (1970), *Follies* (co-director, 1971), *Seesaw* (1973) and the popular masterpiece *A Chorus Line* (1975), the success of which was unequalled by such later shows as *Ballroom* (1978) and *Dreamgirls* (1981).

Bennett, Richard Bedford, 1st Viscount 1870–1947
Canadian statesman
Born in New Brunswick and educated in Nova Scotia, he was a lawyer by training and was elected to parliament in 1911. He became Conservative leader from 1927, and Prime Minister from 1930 to 1935. He convened the Empire Economic Conference in Ottawa in 1932, out of which came a system of Empire trade preference known as the Ottawa Agreements. He retired to Great Britain in 1938 and was made a peer in 1941.

Bennett, Sir Richard Rodney 1936–
English composer
Born in Broadstairs, Kent, he was educated at the Royal Academy of Music in London (1953–56), and in Paris under Pierre Boulez and Olivier Messiaen. From 1963 to 1965 he was Professor of Composition at the Royal Academy of Music, and in 1970–71 was a visiting professor at the Peabody Institute in Baltimore. Well known for his music for films (1963, *Billy Liar*, 1973, *Murder on the Orient Express*), he has also composed operas, orchestral works, chamber music, and experimental works for one

and two pianos. Some of his music uses the twelve-note scale, and his interest in jazz has prompted such works as *Jazz Calendar* (1963) and *Jazz Pastoral* (1969). His more recent work shows a growing emphasis on internal rhythmic structure. Among his other pieces are *The Approaches of Sleep* (1959); *Winter Music* (1960); *The Music That Her Echo Is* (1967); *The House of Sleeps* (1971); the two operas commissioned by Sadler's Wells: *The Mines of Sulphur* (1965) and *A Penny for a Song* (1968); the opera commissioned by Covent Garden: *Victory* (1970); the choral work: *Spells* (1975); and a birthday present for pianist Susan Bradshaw entitled *A Book of Hours* (1991).

Bennett, Tony, *stage name of* Anthony Dominick Benedetto 1926–
US jazz and popular singer
Born in New York, he began performing under the name 'Joe Bari', but changed to Tony Bennett at the suggestion of Bob Hope in 1950. He had a series of hit singles during the 1950s and early 1960s which established his reputation as a powerful interpreter of sophisticated popular songs, including his signature tune, 'I Left My Heart in San Francisco' (1962). He worked in more jazz-oriented settings in the 1960s with Count Basie, Duke Ellington and Woody Herman, among others, and recorded two fine albums with pianist Bill Evans in the mid-1970s. Bennett's career took an unexpected late turn with a highly successful MTV *Unplugged* show in 1994, which brought him to a much younger audience. 🕮 T Jasper, *Tony Bennett* (1984)

Bennett, Sir William Sterndale 1816–75
English pianist and composer
Born in Sheffield, he studied at the Royal Academy of Music, London, and at Leipzig, and attracted Felix Mendelssohn's attention at the Düsseldorf Musical Festival (1833). In 1849 he founded the Bach Society, becoming Professor of Music at Cambridge (1856), and in 1868 Principal of the Royal Academy of Music. His earlier compositions, piano pieces, songs, and the cantatas *The May Queen* (1858) and *The Women of Samaria* (1867), are his most popular works.

Bennigsen, Levin August Theophil, Count 1745–1826
German soldier
Born in Brunswick, he joined the Russian army in 1773, and took part in the assassination of the emperor Paul. In the Napoleonic Wars (1800–15) he fought at Pultusk (1806) and commanded at Eylau (1807). At the Battle of Borodino (1812) he commanded the Russian centre, and defeated Joachim Murat at Tarutino (1812). He fought at the Battle of Leipzig (1813) and was created count by Alexander I in the field. His son, Alexander Levin (1809–93), was a distinguished Hanoverian statesman.

Benny, Jack, *originally* Benjamin Kubelsky 1894–1974
US comedian
Born in Waukegan, Illinois, he was a child prodigy violinist, performing as part of a vaudeville double-act, 'Salisbury and Benny', and also appearing as 'Ben Benny, the Fiddlin' Kid'. After naval service during World War I, he returned to the stage and toured extensively before making his film debut in the short *Bright Moments* (1928). Following his Broadway success in *The Earl Carroll Vanities* (1930) and his radio debut in the *Ed Sullivan Show* (1932), he earned his own radio series which, combined with its subsequent television incarnation, *The Jack Benny Show* (1950–65), won him the loyalty and warm affection of a mass audience. A gentle, bemused, self-effacing figure, his humour lacked malice, relying for its effect on his grasp of timing and an act based on his ineptitude as a fiddler, his perennial youth and an unfounded reputation

as the world's meanest man. A sporadic film career also provided him with an opportunity for self-deprecation but did include *Charley's Aunt* (1941), *To Be or Not To Be* (1942) and *It's in the Bag* (1945). He continued to appear regularly in television specials until his death.

Benois, Alexandre Nikolayevich 1870–1960
Russian painter
Of Italian, French and German origins, he was the founder of the *Mir Iskusstva* ('World of Art') movement in St Petersburg in 1899 and was intimately connected with the rise of Sergei Diaghilev's Ballets Russes, designing many of the sets. After the Revolution he became curator of paintings at the Hermitage Museum, but in 1928 settled in Paris. From 1938 he designed for La Scala, Milan. Benois was the great-uncle of Peter Ustinov.

Benois, Nadia (Nadezhda Leontievna) 1896–1975
Russian painter and designer
She was born in St Petersburg, the daughter of a court architect and professor of architecture, and studied first with her uncle and then at a private academy in St Petersburg. She married in 1920 and moved to England. Her travels in Scotland, France, Wales and Ireland inspired her landscape paintings which were Impressionist in style. She exhibited in London, Paris, Pittsburgh and Canada, and from 1932 designed sets and costumes for several ballet companies, including the Ballet Rambert. She also designed the set for her son Peter Ustinov's play, *House of Regrets* (1942). She has worked closely with the French avant-garde theatre company, Compagnie des Quinze.

Benoît de Sainte-Maure fl.c.1150
French poet
Born in either Sainte-Maure, near Poitiers, or Sainte-More, near Tours, he wrote a vast romance, *Roman de Troie* ('Tale of Troy'); it became a source book to many later writers, notably Boccaccio, who in turn inspired Chaucer and Shakespeare to use Benoît's episode of Troilus and Cressida.

Benserade, Isaac de 1613–91
French poet and dramatist
He was born in Paris, and is remembered as the librettist for Jean Baptiste Lully's ballets and as the author of a sonnet, *Job* (c.1649). 🕮 C I Silin, *Benserade and his Ballets de cour* (1940)

Benson, Arthur Christopher 1862–1925
English writer
He was master of Magdalene College, Cambridge, and wrote studies of Dante Gabriel Rossetti, Edward Fitzgerald, Walter Pater, Lord Tennyson and John Ruskin, a memoir of his brother Robert Hugh Benson, and a biography of his father Edward White Benson. His poems include *Land of Hope and Glory* (1902). 🕮 *The Diary* (1926)

Benson, Sir Frank Robert 1858–1939
English Shakespearean actor-manager
He was born in Alresford, Hampshire, and first appeared on the London stage in Henry Irving's production of *Romeo and Juliet* (1882) at the Lyceum. He was knighted (1916) by King George V on the stage of Drury Lane during a Shakespeare tercentenary matinee.

Benson, Frank Weston 1862–1951
US artist
Born in Salem, Massachusetts, he became a teacher at the Museum of Fine Arts in Boston. He painted women and children, sensitive etchings and wash drawings of wildfowl, and murals in the Library of Congress.

Benson, Sidney William 1918–
US physical chemist

Born in New York City, he was educated at the universities of Columbia, New York and Harvard. Later he moved to the University of Southern California (USC), where he became Professor of Chemistry, and from 1963 to 1976 was chairman of the department of kinetics and thermochemistry at Stanford Research Institute. From 1977 to 1990 he was director of the Hydrocarbon Research Institute, becoming professor emeritus in 1991. Benson has received many international awards, including the Langmuir Award of the American Chemical Society (1986) and the Polanyi Medal of the Royal Society of Chemistry (1986). His wide-ranging contributions to physical chemistry include kinetics, photochemistry, theory of liquid structure, and thermochemistry. He is best known for work in the area covered by his book *Thermochemical Kinetics* (1968).

Benson, William Arthur Smith 1854–1924
English architect, designer and metalworker
Born in London, he was educated at Winchester and Oxford, where he met William Morris and Edward Burne-Jones. In 1880 he opened a small workshop in Hammersmith specializing in metalwork, later moving to larger premises in Chiswick and opening showrooms in Bond Street in 1887. Apart from designing lamps and light fittings, silver mounts and hinges, he designed wallpapers and furniture for Morris & Co and J S Henry. He was a founder-member of the Art Workers Guild and supported the formation of the Arts and Crafts Exhibition Society. He was managing director of Morris & Co from 1896 to 1920.

Bentham, George 1800–84
English botanist
He was born in Stoke, Plymouth, but during 1805–07 lived in St Petersburg, acquiring a knowledge of Russian and Scandinavian languages. He spent much of his youth in France, studying at the universities of Tours and Montpellier. From 1826 to 1832 he was secretary to his uncle, Jeremy Bentham, and partly rewrote Jeremy's work on naval administration. From 1829 to 1840 he was secretary of the Royal Horticultural Society. From 1832 he published many important botanical works, most notably the *Genera Plantarum* (3 vols, 1862–83), which remains a standard work.

Bentham, Jeremy 1748–1832
English philosopher, writer on jurisprudence and social reformer
Born in London, he went to Queen's College, Oxford, at the age of 12 and was called to the Bar at the age of 15. He was more interested in the theory of the law, and is best known as a pioneer of utilitarianism in his works *A Fragment on Government* (1776) and *Introduction to the Principles of Morals and Legislation* (1789), which argued that the aim of all actions and legislation should be 'the greatest happiness of the greatest number'. He held that laws should be socially useful and not just reflect the status quo, and developed a 'hedonic calculus' to estimate the effects of different actions. He travelled widely in Europe and Russia, was made an honorary citizen of the French Republic (1792), and wrote on penal and social reform, economics and politics. He planned a special prison (the Panopticon) and a special school (the Chrestomathia), and helped start the *Westminster Review* (1823). He also founded University College London, where his clothed skeleton can still be seen. 📖 Ross Harrison, *Bentham* (1983)

Bentham, Sir Samuel 1757–1831
English inventor and naval architect
He was born in London, and apprenticed as a shipwright. Unable to find work at home, he went to Russia (1783) where he introduced some revolutionary heavy naval armaments that enabled a much smaller Russian force to defeat the Turks in 1788. For nearly 20 years after 1795 he

devoted his energies to building up Great Britain's naval strength during the critical period of the Napoleonic Wars, introducing advances in naval architecture, ship-building, large-calibre non-recoil carronades, the use of steam dredgers, and dockyard administration. His campaign against corruption and maladministration in the Admiralty dockyards aroused such bitterness that in 1812 he was forced to resign, though not before many of his reforms had been put into effect. He was the brother of Jeremy Bentham.

Bentinck, Lord George 1802–48
English politician
Born at Welbeck Abbey, Nottinghamshire, the son of the 4th Duke of Portland, he joined the army in 1819 and from 1822 to 1825 was private secretary to his uncle, George Canning, then Foreign Secretary. He entered parliament in 1828, supported Catholic emancipation and the Reform Bill, but left the Whigs in 1834 to form a separate parliamentary group with Lord Stanley (Edward, 14th Earl of Derby). On Robert Peel's third betrayal of his party in introducing free-trade measures, Bentinck, supported by Disraeli who idolized him, led the Tory opposition to Peel. A great lover of racing and field sports, he stamped out many dishonest turf practices.

Bentinck, William, 1st Earl of Portland
1649–1709
English soldier and courtier
He was born in Holland. The boyhood friend of William III, he was entrusted with the secrets of his foreign policy, and after the revolution was created an English peer, and given large estates.

Bentinck, William Henry Cavendish, 3rd Duke of Portland 1738–1809
English statesman
He became an MP in 1761, succeeding to the dukedom in 1762. His first Cabinet post was as Lord Chamberlain of the Household under the Marquis of Rockingham (1765–66). Along with other aristocratic Whigs, he maintained connection with Rockingham which kept him in opposition until 1782, when he was Lord Lieutenant of Ireland. He was nominal head of the ministry usually known as the Fox–North coalition (1783) which George III hated and rapidly dismissed. He led the Whigs in opposition to William Pitt, the Younger until 1794, when he agreed to join him in a coalition government to provide order and stability and to meet the challenge of the French Revolutionary Wars. Some have seen the Pitt–Portland coalition as the foundation of the Tory (later called Conservative) Party. He served as Home Secretary (1794–1801) during a period of considerable radical disturbance in England and rebellion in Ireland (1798), and as Lord President of the Council under Henry Addington (Viscount Sidmouth) in 1801–03. In Pitt's last ministry he was successively Lord President (1804–05) and Minister without Portfolio (1805–06). He was summoned by George III in 1807 to head an administration of Pittites after the fall of the 'Ministry of all the Talents'; by now old, frail and gouty, he was little more than titular leader until his death in office.

Bentinck, Lord William Henry Cavendish
1774–1839
British soldier
Appointed Governor of Madras in 1803, he was recalled from India following a mutiny of native troops, and fought during the Napoleonic Wars (1800–15) in Spain and Sicily. Elected to parliament, he became Governor-General of India (1828–35), where he introduced some important administrative reforms. 📖 John Rosselli, *Lord William Bentinck: The Making of a Liberal Imperialist, 1774–1839* (1974)

Bentine, Michael 1921–96
English comedy performer

Born in Watford, Hertfordshire, of Peruvian parentage, he made his stage debut in *Sweet Lavender* at Cardiff in 1941 and, after wartime service in the RAF, worked at the Windmill Theatre (1946) and in the show *Starlight Roof* (1947). One of the early members of The Goons (1951–52), he left the popular radio series to pursue a solo career and on television made the animated children's series *The Bumblies* (1954), before appearing in *After Hours* (1959–60), *It's A Square World* (1960–64) and *All Square* (1966–67), which allowed him to indulge his penchant for surreal humour, mechanical jokes and illustrated lectures in which anything could happen. Later television series, often for children, included *The Golden Silents* (1965), *Potty Time* (1973–80) and *Mad About It* (1981). He also co-wrote and appeared in the films *The Sandwich Man* (1966) and *Bachelor of Arts* (1969), and wrote numerous novels and autobiographies, including *The Long Banana Skin* (1975) and *A Shy Person's Guide to Life* (1984). 📖 *The Reluctant Jester* (1992)

Bentley, Charles Raymond 1929–
US geophysicist and glaciologist

Born in Rochester, New York, he studied physics at Yale and geophysics at Columbia, where he became research geophysicist (1952–56). He spent two years in Antarctica and participated in the scientific effort for the International Geophysical Year (1957–58). He has since worked at the University of Wisconsin-Madison, becoming A P Crary Professor in 1968. In west Antarctica he discovered that the ice rests on a floor far below sea-level, which means that the region would be open ocean if the ice melted. He has pioneered the application of geophysical techniques such as radioglaciology, the use of electromagnetic waves to measure the thickness and properties of the ice. He has contributed to the understanding of the Antarctic crust, and in the 1980s his research group investigated the soft sediment beneath an Antarctic ice stream that is now believed to be a critical factor in the movement of the ice surface.

Bentley, Derek William c.1933–1953
English alleged murderer

Born in south London, he was a man of low intelligence, who worked variously as a furniture remover, a dustman and a road-sweeper. On Sunday 2 November 1952, when he was 19 and his friend Christopher Craig was 16, they broke into a confectionery warehouse in Croydon. They were seen climbing over the fence, and the police were alerted. Bentley, who was carrying a knife and a knuckle-duster, and Craig, who was armed with a gun, were approached by the police. Bentley was quickly caught, but Craig fired several shots, initially wounding one policeman and then killing another. Both were arrested and charged and Bentley, who reputedly had the mental age of a child of 10 or 11, was found guilty and was given the death sentence. Craig, who was too young to receive the death penalty, was detained indefinitely. Despite a series of appeals to the government and to the Queen, all of which received vigorous public support, Bentley was hanged on 28 January 1953. Craig was released in 1963 and Bentley was granted a posthumous limited pardon by the Home Secretary in 1993.

Bentley, Edmund Clerihew 1875–1956
English journalist and novelist

Born in London, he worked on the *Daily News* (1901–12) and *The Daily Telegraph* (1912–34). He is chiefly remembered as the author of *Trent's Last Case* (1913; US, *The Woman in Black*, 1912), which is regarded as a milestone in the transformation of the detective novel. A close friend of G K Chesterton, he originated and gave his name to the type of humorous verse-form known as the 'clerihew'. 📖 *Those Days* (1940)

Bentley, Richard 1662–1742
English Classical scholar

Born in Oulton, Yorkshire, he was educated at Wakefield Grammar School and St John's College, Cambridge. Originally a teacher, he resigned to become private tutor to the son of the influential Dr Edward Stillingfleet (1635–99), then dean of St Paul's, who rewarded him with the post of archdeacon of Ely and Keeper of the Royal Libraries (1694). He had made his mark as a Classical scholar with a Latin treatise on the Greek chronicler John Malalas, addressed to the New Testament critic John Mill (1645–1707) (*Epistola ad Joannem Millium*, 1691), and delivered the first Robert Boyle lectures in Oxford, *A Confutation of Atheism* (1692). He established an international reputation with his dispute with Charles Boyle, 4th Earl of Orrery (1697–99), in which he proved that the so-called *Epistles of Phalaris* were spurious (a controversy that was satirized by Jonathan Swift in his *Battle of the Books*, 1704). He was appointed Master of Trinity College, Cambridge, in 1700, and Regius Professor of Divinity in 1717. He published critical texts of many classical authors, including the Greek New Testament. One of his daughters was the mother of the dramatist and novelist, Richard Cumberland.

Benton, Thomas Hart, *known as* Old Bullion 1782–1858
US politician

Born near Hillsborough, North Carolina, he was admitted to the Bar in 1806, served as a colonel of volunteers in the War of 1812, and settled in the frontier town of St Louis in 1815. Elected as a Missouri senator in 1820, he remained in the US Senate for 30 years and became a leader of the Democratic Party. He acquired his nickname because of his opposition to paper currency. He was an ally of President Andrew Jackson in his battle against the Bank of the United States. In his later years he adopted an antislavery position that finally lost him his seat in the Senate.

Bentsen, Lloyd Millard, Jnr 1921–
US Democrat politician

Born in Mission, Texas, into a rich landholding family, he studied law at Texas University, Austin, and served as a combat pilot during World War II. After briefly working as a county judge, he was a member of the House of Representatives (1948–54), and then built up a substantial fortune as president of the Lincoln Consolidated insurance company in Houston. He returned to congress as a senator for Texas in 1971, became chairman of the influential Finance Committee, and was vice-presidential running-mate to Michael Dukakis in the Democrats' 1988 presidential challenge. Although Dukakis was defeated, the patrician Bentsen, an enlightened conservative Democrat, enhanced his reputation with an impressive campaign. He was Secretary of the Treasury for Bill Clinton from 1992 to 1994.

Bentzon, Niels Viggo 1919–
Danish composer and pianist

Born in Copenhagen, he was educated at the Royal Danish Academy of Music. He made his debut in 1943 and has been a reader at the Academy since 1960. His compositions include an opera, symphonies, ballets, piano concertos and chamber music. He was awarded the Ove Christensen Honorary prize in 1962 and the Carl Nielsen prize in 1965.

Benz, Karl Friedrich 1844–1929
German engineer and car manufacturer

Born in Karlsruhe, he developed a two-stroke engine from 1877 to 1879, and founded a factory for its manufacture, leaving in 1883 when his backers refused to finance a mobile engine. He then founded his second company, Benz & Co, Rheinische Gasmotorenfabrik, at Mannheim. His first car—one of the earliest petrol-driven vehicles—was completed in 1885 and sold to a French manufacturer. In 1926 the firm was merged with the Daimler-Motoren-Gesellschaft to form Daimler-Benz and Co. ◻ Brian Williams, *Karl Benz* (1991)

Benzer, Seymour 1921–
US geneticist
Born in New York City, he studied physics at Purdue University, Indiana, and taught biophysics there until 1965, when he moved to the California Institute of Technology (Caltech). He was appointed Professor of Biology (1967–75), then Boswell Professor of Neuroscience (1975–). A member of the Phage Group set up by Max Delbrück, A D Hershey and Salvador Luria, he showed that genes and proteins were co-linear, ie that a change in a gene led to a change in the protein it coded for. In 1961 he discovered 'hot spots', sections of the DNA strand more susceptible to mutations than would be expected by chance. Since the 1960s, Benzer has moved away from bacterial genetics to research the genetics underlying the behaviour of the fruit fly, *Drosophila*.

Ben-Zvi, Itzhak 1884–1963
Israeli statesman
Born in Poltava, Ukraine, he migrated to Palestine in 1907, where he became a prominent Zionist, and was a founder of the Jewish Labour Party. He was elected President of Israel on the death of Dr Chaim Weizmann in 1952. A prominent scholar and archaeologist, he wrote on the history of the Middle East.

Beolco, Angelo See Ruzzante

Beran, Josef 1888–1969
Czech Catholic priest and archbishop
Imprisoned in Dachau concentration camp in World War II, he was made Archbishop of Prague in 1946. Although the Catholic Church was anxious to avoid too close an involvement in politics, he spoke out in favour of democracy during the Communist seizure of power in February 1948. Within a year the Church was persecuted, and Beran and most churchmen were cut off from contact with Rome. It was 1965 before the situation eased sufficiently for him to leave for Rome, where he was appointed cardinal.

Béranger, Pierre Jean de 1780–1857
French poet
He was born in Paris, and after a scanty education left regular employment as a clerk at the University of Paris (1798) for an impecunious literary life. His lyrics were coloured by his politics, a curious compound of republicanism and Bonapartism, and led to spells of imprisonment in 1821 and 1828, but their vivacity, satire and wit endeared them to the masses. ◻ E de Pompery, *Béranger: sa biographie* (1865)

Bérard, Christian 1902–49
French painter and designer
He designed ballet sets and costumes for many of the great choreographers and décor for the theatrical productions of Louis Jouvet and others. As a painter he was a reluctant exhibitor who disliked having his work reproduced, and when designing for the theatre last minute repaintings were not uncommon. His fame rests mainly on his stage décor, especially for the productions of Molière by Jean-Louis Barrault.

Berberian, Cathy (Catherine) 1925–83
US soprano and composer
Born in Attleboro, Massachusetts, of Armenian extraction, she studied music and drama at Columbia and at New York universities. She was married to the composer Luciano Berio from 1950 to 1966, who wrote many works for her, including *Circles* (1960), which she performed on her US debut, *Sequenza III* (1963) and *Recital I* (1971). Other composers, including Igor Stravinsky and Henri Pousseur, wrote pieces for her and she performed work as diverse as Claudio Monteverdi and John Lennon and Paul McCartney. Her own compositions include *Stripsody* (1966), an unaccompanied 'cartoon' for vocalist, and *Morsicat(h)y* (1971) for piano.

Berceo, Gonzalo de c.1180–c.1246
Spanish poet
Born in Verceo, he was the earliest known Castilian poet. He became a deacon and wrote more than 13,000 verses on devotional subjects, of which the best is a biography of St Oria. He was also the author of *Milagros de la Virgen*, a collection of legends of the Virgin's appearances on Earth. His poems were not discovered and published until the late 18th century. ◻ J E Keller, *Gonzalo de Berceo* (1972)

Berchem or Berghem, Nicholas 1620–83
Dutch landscape painter
He was born in Haarlem and worked mainly there. His early training was by his father, the still-life painter Pieter Claesz (c.1596–1661), but he developed a very different style. On visiting Italy in his twenties he made landscape studies for which, when he painted them, he was to become famous and influential. His work is represented in most European collections.

Berchet, Giovanni 1783–1851
Italian poet
Born in Milan, he translated foreign, especially English, literature, and through his translation of *The Vicar of Wakefield* (1809) became interested in ballads. In 1816 he published a pamphlet, *Lettera semiseria di Grisostomo* ('Grisostomo's Semi-serious Letter'), which became a manifesto of the Romantic movement in Italy. In 1821 he left Italy to avoid arrest, and lived in exile, mainly in England, until the abortive Revolution of 1848. He was received in Milan with enthusiasm and made director of education, but had to flee again to Piedmont. His best-known works are *I Profughi di Parga* (1821, 'The Refugees of Parga'), *Il Romito del Cenisio* ('The Hermit of Cenisio') and *Il Trovatore* ('The Troubadour'). ◻ C Rosa, *Giovanni Berchet: Studio critico biografico* (1872)

Berdyaev, Nikolai Aleksandrovich 1874–1948
Russian religious philosopher
Born into an aristocratic family in Kiev, he developed strong revolutionary sympathies as a student at Kiev University and supported the Russian Revolution of 1917. He secured a professorship at Moscow but his unorthodox spiritual and libertarian ideals led to his dismissal in 1922. He moved to Berlin, where he founded an Academy of the Philosophy of Religion which he later transferred to Clamart, near Paris. He described himself as a 'believing freethinker' and his fierce commitment to freedom and individualism brought him into conflict with both ecclesiastical and political powers. His main ideas are developed in his journal *The Path* and his books *Dukh i realnost* (1927, 'Freedom and the Spirit'), *O naznacheni cheloveka* (1931, 'The Destiny of Man') and *Samopoznaniye* (1949, 'Dreams and Reality').

Berengar I d.924
King of Italy and Emperor of the Romans
He succeeded his father Eberhard, a count of Frankish origin, as Margrave of Friuli. He was King of Italy from 888 and Emperor of the Romans from 915. He died at the hands of his own men.

Berengar II c.900–966
King of Italy
He was the grandson of Berengar I. He succeeded his father as Margrave of Ivrea in 928 and became king in 950. In 951/2 he was dethroned by the Emperor Otto I and later, after three years' refuge in a mountain fortress, was sent as a prisoner to Bavaria (963) where he died.

Berengar of Tours 999–1088
French scholastic theologian
Born probably in Tours, Touraine (now in France), he studied under Fulbert at Chartres. In 1031 he was appointed Preceptor of the Cathedral school in Tours, and c.1040 archdeacon of Angers. An opponent of the doctrine of transubstantiation, he was excommunicated by Pope Leo IX in 1050. Finally, in 1078, he was cited to appear at Rome, where he repeatedly renounced, but apparently never abandoned, his 'error'. He spent his last years in a cell on an island in the Loire, near Tours.

Berenice, known as Berenice Syra c.280BC–c.246BC
Queen of Syria as the wife of Antiochus II
The daughter of Ptolemy II, Philadelphus, she married Antiochus II of Syria in 252BC, which brought about a hiatus in the fighting between the Egyptians and the Seleucids. When Antiochus died however, Antiochus's divorced wife Laodice (who had been exiled with her children on his marriage to Berenice) plotted the death of the queen and her young son, enabling her own son to succeed as Seleucus II. Berenice's brother Ptolemy III, Euergetes came from Egypt to Syria to avenge his sister's death, an act which resulted in the Third Syrian War.

Berenice 1st century BC
Princess of the Jewish Idumean dynasty
She was the daughter of Costobarus and Salome, who was a sister of Herod the Great. She was married to her cousin Aristobulus from c.17BC and their children were Herod of Chalcis, Herod Agrippa I (father of the Jewish Berenice), Aristobulus, Herodias and Mariamne. She allegedly set in motion the plot to murder her husband by her uncle Herod, whose brother-in-law Theudion she later married. Her third husband was Archelaus, whom she married when Theudion was executed for scheming against Herod.

Berenice, known as the Jewish Berenice
c.28AD–c.79AD
Princess of the Jewish Idumean dynasty
She was the daughter of Herod Agrippa I and Cypros. Her first husband died before consummating their marriage, so she was married again, this time to her uncle Herod of Chalcis. After she had given birth to two sons, he died (AD48) and Berenice moved to the court of her brother, Herod Agrippa II, with whom she allegedly had an incestuous relationship. To quell such rumours she married a Cilician priest-king, but soon returned to Agrippa, with whom she vainly tried to prevent a Jewish rebellion. After the recapture of Jerusalem by Rome (AD70), she became the mistress of Flavius Titus, who had noticed her some years earlier during a visit to Judea. They made no secret of living together in Rome, but Titus was advised, on account of Berenice's race, to send her away. The love affair continued but never culminated in marriage, even when Berenice returned to Rome around 79, the year Titus became emperor. She is the model for the tragic heroine of Racine's *Berenice* (1670) and Pierre Corneille's *Tite et Bérénice* (1670).

Berenice I fl.c.317BC–c.275BC
Macedonian princess and Queen of Egypt
Born in Macedonia, she went to Egypt as a lady-in-waiting to Eurydice, who became the second wife of Ptolemy I, Soter. Ptolemy married Berenice as his third wife (c.317BC) and made her Queen of Egypt in 290.

Their son became Ptolemy II, Philadelphus when he succeeded his father in 283, and their daughter Arsinoë married Ptolemy II as his second wife.

Berenice II c.269BC–221BC
Princess of Cyrene
The daughter of Magas, King of Cyrene, she was urged by her mother to marry a Macedonian prince, Demetrius the Fair, but she arranged for Demetrius to be murdered and married Ptolemy III, Eurgetes (247BC) instead, thus uniting Cyrene (in modern Libya) with Egypt. When her husband went to fight in the Third Syrian War to avenge the murder of his sister (Berenice Syra), Berenice dedicated a lock of her hair to Aphrodite for his safe return. According to the court astronomer, the hair ended up in heaven and became the constellation Coma Berenices ('Hair of Berenice'). Berenice's son Ptolemy IV, Philopator succeeded his father and began his reign by having her poisoned; he married his sister Arsinoë III.

Berenice III d.c.80BC
Egyptian princess
The daughter of Ptolemy IX and either Cleopatra Selene or Cleopatra IV, she first married her uncle, Ptolemy X, and became queen after the death (101BC) of the dowager queen Cleopatra III, Ptolemy VIII's widow. The people of Alexandria, thinking that Ptolemy had murdered Cleopatra, rebelled and expelled him in 87, so he raised an army in Syria and returned to Egypt, where he plundered the tomb of Alexander the Great to pay his soldiers. Expelled again, he fled to Asia Minor, taking Berenice with him. She returned to Egypt after his death (80) and became sole ruler of Egypt. With the help of the Roman dictator Lucius Cornelius Sulla, Ptolemy Alexander, the son of Ptolemy X, went to Egypt to marry Berenice, but when she refused to marry and surrender her authority, he had her murdered.

Berenice IV d.55BC
Egyptian princess
She was the daughter of Ptolemy XII, Auletes and the elder sister of Cleopatra. While her father was forced by impending insurrection away from Egypt (58–55BC), his wife died and Berenice was proclaimed queen. Towards the end of her reign, Alexandria was attacked by Aulus Gabinius, the Roman proconsul of Syria. Ptolemy XII was recalled in 55, whereupon he had his daughter murdered.

Berenson, Bernard 1865–1959
US art critic
Born in Vilnius, Lithuania, he moved to the USA in 1875, studied at Harvard University, and became a leading authority on Italian Renaissance art. In 1900 he moved to Italy, where he lived in an 18th-century villa, I Tatti, outside Florence. He produced a vast amount of critical literature which, apart from standard works on each of the Italian schools, includes *Italian Painters of the Renaissance* (1894–1907), *The Study and Criticism of Italian Art* (1901–16), *Aesthetics and History* (1950) and the autobiographical *Sketch for a Self Portrait* (1949). He bequeathed his villa and art collection to Harvard University, which turned it into a Centre for Italian Renaissance Culture.

Berenson, Senda 1868–1954
US physical education instructor
Born in Lithuania, she was a physical education teacher at Smith College, Massachusetts, and introduced the game of basketball to her students in 1893, having read about it in the YMCA publication *Physical Education*. The game had been conceived two years before by Dr James Naismith, a PE instructor at the YMCA Training School in Springfield, Massachusetts. Berenson established the first official rules for girls in 1899, and chaired the American Association for the Advancement of Physical

Education Committee on Basketball for Girls for 12 years. In 1901 she wrote *Line Basket Ball for Women*, the first published rules for women's basketball. She was posthumously inducted into the Naismith Memorial Basketball Hall of Fame and the International Women's Sports Hall of Fame for her contribution to women's basketball.

Beresford, Charles William de la Poer, 1st Baron 1846–1919
Irish naval commander
Born in Philipstown, Offaly, the son of the 4th Marquis of Waterford, he joined the navy in 1859, and was promoted captain in 1882 for his services at the bombardment of Alexandria. He also served in the Nile expedition (1884). He was Lord of the Admiralty (1886–88), but resigned, sat in parliament as a Conservative, and commanded the Mediterranean fleet (1905–07) and Channel fleet (1907–09). He clashed with Admiral John Fisher over naval policy and reforms.

Beresford, Jack 1899–1977
English oarsman
Educated at Bedford School, he served in the army during World War I. He competed for Great Britain at five Olympics (1920–36) as sculler and oarsman, winning three gold and two silver medals, and received the Olympic Diploma of Merit in 1949. He won the Diamond Sculls at Henley four times, and was elected president of the Thames Rowing Club in 1971.

Beresford, William Carr Beresford, 1st Viscount 1768–1854
British soldier
He joined the army in 1785 and served in Nova Scotia and Egypt. He distinguished himself at the taking of the Cape of Good Hope (1806) and at the capture and loss of Buenos Aires (1807). In the Peninsular War (1808–14) he took the command (1809) of the Portuguese army, and defeated Marshal Soult at Albuera (1811). He was present at the capture of Badajoz (1812), and at Salamanca was severely wounded. He left Portugal in 1822, and in the Wellington administration (1828–30) was Master-General of the Ordnance.

Berg, Alban 1885–1935
Austrian composer
Born in Vienna, he studied under Arnold Schoenberg, and allied the twelve-note technique to a traditional style. He is best known for his opera *Wozzeck* (first performed 1925), his Violin Concerto (1935), and the *Lyric Suite* for string quartet (1926). His unfinished opera *Lulu* was posthumously produced from 1978 to 1979.

Berg, David Brandt See David, Moses

Berg, Patty (Patricia Jane) 1918–
US golfer
Born in Minneapolis, Minnesota, she began playing in amateur competitions in 1933, and won the Minnesota State championships in 1935, 1936 and 1938. Considered the foremost female golfer in the USA, she won the US amateur title in 10 of the 13 tournaments she entered in 1938. She was named Outstanding Female Athlete by the Associated Press for 1938, 1943 and 1955. She co-founded the Ladies Professional Golf Association (LPGA), officially chartered in 1950, serving as its president (1949—when discussions began—to 1952). She has earned a place in the Halls of Fame of the LPGA (1951) and the International Women's Sports (1980), among others.

Berg, Paul 1926–
US molecular biologist and Nobel Prize winner

Born in Brooklyn, New York City, he was educated at Pennsylvania State and Western Reserve universities, although his studies were interrupted by World War II, which he spent in the US navy. He later became Professor of Biochemistry at Stanford (from 1959) and at Washington (from 1970), and then was appointed director of the Beckman Center of Molecular and Genetic Medicine (1985–) and Cahill Professor of Biochemistry (1994–) at Stanford. In the 1960s, he purified several transfer RNA molecules (tRNAs). In the 1970s he developed techniques to cut and splice genes from one organism into another. Concerned about the effects of mixing genes from different organisms, he organized a year-long moratorium on genetic engineering experiments, and in 1975 chaired an international committee to draft guidelines for such studies. These techniques are now widely used in biological research. In 1978 Berg enabled gene transfer between cells from different mammalian species for the first time. He shared the 1980 Nobel Prize for chemistry with Frederick Sanger and Walter Gilbert.

Berganza, Teresa 1935–
Spanish mezzo-soprano
Born in Madrid, she made her debut there in 1955. Especially noted for Mozart and Rossini roles, she first sang in England at Glyndebourne (1958), then at Covent Garden, London (1959), and subsequently in concert and opera in Vienna, Milan, Edinburgh, in Israel, the USA and elsewhere. In 1994 she became the first woman member of the Spanish Royal Academy of Arts.

Bergelson, David 1884–1952
Russian novelist and story writer
He was born in the Ukraine into a prosperous family of timber merchants, but their fortunes declined, and he experienced poverty at first hand. A Yiddish writer, he emphasized the social decline of the period through which he lived. *Nokh alemen* (1913, Eng trans *When All is Said and Done*, 1977), features the 'first authentic heroine of Yiddish fiction'. Bergelson lived in Berlin for a while, and struggled against communist dictation of artistic creation, but eventually he returned to Russia and became a socialist realist. Yet even his fiction of that period, such as *Midas hadin* (1925, 'Full Severity of the Law'), has its power and attraction. After he turned back, as well as he could, to Jewish themes, he was executed by Stalin on a trumped-up charge. *Baym Dnieper* (1932–40, 'Along the Dnieper'), is one of the most remarkable novels written under Stalinist oppression. ▢ C A Madison, *Yiddish Literature* (1968)

Bergen, Candice 1946–
US actress
Born in Beverly Hills, California, the daughter of Edgar Bergen, she attended school in Switzerland but dropped out to become an actress. After making her film debut in *The Group* (1966), she became a leading lady of 1970s cinema. Other films include *Carnal Knowledge* (1971), *The Wind and the Lion* (1975), *Starting Over* (1979) and *Gandhi* (1982). She is best known for playing a single mother in the television series *Murphy Brown* (1988–) but also acted in the mini-series *Hollywood Wives* (1985). She made her Broadway debut in *Hurlyburly* (1985). She was married to French film director Louis Malle from 1980 until his death, and published an autobiography, *Knock Wood*, in 1984.

Bergen, Edgar John, originally Bergren 1903–78
US ventriloquist
Born in Chicago, he had a natural talent for projecting his voice and began to perform as a ventriloquist while still in high school. His first dummy, Charlie McCarthy, was caustic, short-tempered, and often insulting, in contrast to Bergen's own unobjectionable persona and Midwestern rectitude. They appeared in vaudeville and short

films but won their greatest success on the radio in the 1930s and 1940s, a somewhat baffling phenomenon since the listening audience could not know whether Bergen was moving his lips. Their film appearances included *A Letter of Introduction* (1938), which won a special wooden Academy Award, and *You Can't Cheat an Honest Man* (1939). In the 1940s Bergen expanded the act by introducing two new dummies, the dimwitted Mortimer Snerd and the spinster Effie Klinker.

Berger, Hans 1873–1941
German psychiatrist, inventor of electroencephalography
Born in Neuses bei Coburg, he studied medicine at Jena University, where he remained for the rest of his career, becoming Professor of Psychiatry in 1919. His research attempted (mostly unsuccessfully) to establish relationships between psychological states and various physiological parameters, such as heartbeat, respiration and the temperature of the brain itself. In the course of this work, he placed electrical recording equipment on the surface of the skull, and from the mid-1920s, he recorded what became known as 'brain waves'. Although precise correlations between electrical brain activity and psychic processes has not emerged, Berger's electroencephalograph, particularly after the work of individuals such as **Edgar Douglas Adrian**, has become a useful tool of research and diagnosis into brain functions and diseases.

Berger, John Peter 1926–
English novelist, playwright and art critic
Born in London, he studied at the Central and Chelsea Schools of Art and began his working life as a painter and a drawing teacher, but soon turned to writing. His novels reflect his Marxism and artistic background, and have been well-received. Titles include *A Painter of Our Time* (1958), *The Foot of Clive* (1962) and *Corker's Freedom* (1964). His fame was enhanced with the publication of *G* (1972), a story of migrant workers in Europe, which won the Booker Prize. In his acceptance speech, Berger denounced the sponsors and announced that he would donate half of the prize money to the militant Black Panthers Party. Among his other writings the best known are *Ways of Seeing* (1972), on the visual arts, and *Pig Earth* (1979), a collection of short stories of French peasant life, and the first of the *Into Their Labours* trilogy, completed with *Once in Europa* (1989) and *Lilac and Flag* (1991). In 1992 he published *Keeping a Rendezvous*, a collection of essays and poems. Since 1990 he has been Visiting Fellow at the British Film Institute, London.

Berger, Maurice Jean See Béjart, Maurice

Berger, Victor Louis 1860–1929
US Socialist leader and editor
Born in Nieder-Rehbach, Transylvania (now in Romania), he grew up in Hungary and emigrated to the USA in 1878. With **Eugene V Debs** he founded the Social Democratic Party, and he campaigned throughout his life for socialism in the USA. The first Socialist elected to Congress (1910), he was excluded after his re-election in 1918 because of his opposition to US involvement in World War I. He was convicted of sedition in 1918, but his sentence was reversed by the Supreme Court in 1923.

Bergerac, Savinien Cyrano de See Cyrano de Bergerac, Savinien

Bergeron, Tor Harold Percival 1891–1977
Swedish meteorologist
Born near London, England, of Swedish parents, he graduated from Stockholm University in 1916, joined the Bergen School under **Vilhelm Bjerknes** (1922) and obtained his doctorate at Oslo University (1928). He researched the occlusion process whereby air in the warm sector of a depression is forced upwards, and he also explained different types of weather fronts by studying surface and upper air observations in detail. After promoting the Bergen School ideas internationally, he returned to the Swedish Meteorological and Hydrological Institute in 1936 and later became professor at Uppsala University (1947–61). He proposed the currently accepted theory that rain is initiated by the coexistence of ice crystals and water vapour in clouds, and later studied the effects of topography on precipitation, and the precipitation mechanism in hurricanes. He received the International Meteorological Organization prize (1966) and was awarded the Symons gold medal of the Royal Meteorological Society.

Berggrav, Eivind 1884–1959
Norwegian Lutheran bishop
He was born in Stavanger, and after some years spent as a teacher, pastor and prison chaplain, he became Bishop of Troms and then Bishop of Oslo and primate of the Norwegian Church (1937–50). Following the Nazi occupation of 1940, he led the Church's opposition to the **Quisling** government (*With God in the Darkness*, 1943), refusing to endorse the war against Russia as a fight against atheism, and opposing Nazi attempts to monopolize the education of young people. For this he was imprisoned (1941–45). He wrote some 30 books and was a strong supporter of the ecumenical movement, becoming a president of the World Council of Churches (1950–54).

Berghem, Nicholas See Berchem, Nicholas

Berghmans, Ingrid 1961–
Belgian judo player
Born in Hasselt, she is a tall woman who prefers an upright style of play and is well known for her grace, strength and femininity. A fourth dan who married fellow player Marc Vallot in 1990, she has won a record six world titles, and an additional four silvers and a bronze. She was Olympic champion in 1988, when judo was a demonstration sport, and was European champion three times at the 72kg level and three times at Open level. She has won the British Open numerous times, as well as Japan's Fukuoka title and the Canadian Open title.

Bergius, Friedrich 1884–1949
German chemist and Nobel Prize winner
Born in Goldschmieden, near Breslau (Wrocław, Poland). After studying chemistry at Leipzig, he received his doctorate in 1907. He was appointed assistant lecturer at Hanover in 1909 and began examining the conversion of wood into coal. He also developed a process for the conversion of coal into oil. He continued this work when he became head of the research laboratory of the Goldschmidt company in Essen in 1914. Finding himself unable to continue these studies after World War I, he turned his attention to the acidic hydrolysis of wood to sugar. After World War II he founded a company in Madrid and in 1947 he became scientific adviser to the government of Argentina. He shared the 1931 Nobel Prize for chemistry with **Carl Bosch** for his work on coal.

Bergman, Bo Hjalmar 1869–1967
Swedish lyric poet
Born in Stockholm, he studied law at Uppsala and later became a literary critic. The pessimism of his early poetry, as in *Marionetterna* (1903, 'Puppets'), gradually gave way to the optimistic humanism of *En människa* (1908, 'A Member of the Race'), which was frequently in opposition to the growing totalitarianism of modern society. His varied output includes novels, short stories, and two volumes of memoirs. 📖 K Asplund, *Bo Bergman: Manniskan och diktaren* (1970)

Bergman, Ingrid 1915–82
Swedish film and stage actress

Ingrid Bergman was born in Stockholm. After studying at the Royal Dramatic Theatre, she was offered a contract by Svenskfilmindustri and made her film debut in *Munkbrogreven* (1934, 'The Count of Monk's Bridge'). Unaffected and vivacious, she was signed by **David O Selznick** to appear in an English-language remake of *Intermezzo* (1939, with **Leslie Howard**), the story of a tragic romance between a concert pianist and a married violinist, and became an immensely popular romantic star in such films as *Casablanca* (1942), *For Whom the Bell Tolls* (1943), *Gaslight* (1944), which won her a first Oscar for best actress, *Spellbound* (1945) and *Notorious* (1946, with **Cary Grant**). Despite attempts at unsympathetic parts, the characteristics she most compellingly conveyed were goodness and stoicism in the face of suffering.

In 1950 she gave birth to the illegitimate child of director **Roberto Rossellini**. The ensuing scandal led to her being ostracized from the US film industry. She continued her career in Europe, making films with Rossellini that included *Stromboli* (1950) and *Viaggio in Italia* (1954, 'Journey to Italy'). After separating from Rossellini she was welcomed back by Hollywood in 1956, won an Academy Award for her part in *Anastasia*, and played missionary **Gladys Aylward** in *The Inn of the Sixth Happiness* (1958). In later years she worked on stage and television, notably in *Hedda Gabler* (1963), *A Month In The Country* (1965) and *Waters of the Moon* (1978).

Her last film was **Ingmar Bergman**'s *Autumn Sonata* (1978), a deeply felt exploration of a mother–daughter relationship. She was nominated seven times for an Academy Award, and won a third Award for best supporting actress in *Murder on the Orient Express* (1974). In 1982 she played Israeli Prime Minister **Golda Meir** in a television production *A Woman Called Golda*, for which she won an Emmy award.

📖 Ingrid Bergman, *My Story* (1980); L J Quirk, *Films of Ingrid Bergman* (1970).

'How dare he make love to me and not be a married man?' Line spoken by Ingrid Bergman in *Indiscreet*, 1958.

Bergman, Hjalmar Fredrik Elgérus 1883–1931
Swedish novelist, poet and playwright

He was born in Örebro, a place he frequently satirized in later life, taking revenge for the humiliation he had suffered as a stout and painfully shy youth. His work ranges from the dark psychology of *En döds memoarer* (1918–19, 'The Memoirs of a Dead Man'), to an almost Symbolist interpretation of conventional Realism, as in *Markurells i Wadköping* (1919, Eng trans *God's Orchid*, 1924), and to the lighter comic touch of plays like *Swedenhielms* (1925, 'The Swedenhielms') and *Patrasket* (1928, 'The Rabble'). 📖 E Linder, trans by Catherine Djurklou, *Hjalmar Bergman* (1975).

Bergman, (Ernst) Ingmar 1918–
Swedish film and stage director and writer

He was born in Uppsala, and became a trainee theatre director in Stockholm. He began his film career in the script department of Svensk Filmindustri (1943) and continued to alternate between stage and screen, making his film debut with *Crisis* (1945). His films include the elegiac *Sommernattens Leende* (1955, *Smiles of a Summer Night*), the sombre *Det Sjunde Inseglet* (1957, *The Seventh Seal*), *Smultronstället* (1957, *Wild Strawberries*) and *Ansiktet* (1958, *The Face*). They became a cult for art-cinema audiences, winning many international prizes. Preoccupied with guilt, emotional repression and death, he created a succession of bleak masterpieces, outstanding for their photographic artistry and haunting imagery, including *Skammen* (1968, *Shame*), *Viskningar ock Rop* (1972, *Cries and Whispers*) and the British-Norwegian co-production *Autumn Sonata* (1978). His last film, *Fanny and Alexander* (1982), was an unexpectedly life-affirming evocation of autobiographical elements from his own childhood. Still active in the theatre, he has continued to write screenplays, including *The Best Intentions* (1992), winner of the Palme D'Or at the Cannes Film Festival. He returned to direction with the television drama *Making Noises And Throwing Himself Around* (1997). He has published an autobiography, *The Magic Lantern* (1988), and a number of novels, including *Private Confessions* (1994).

Bergman, Ingrid See panel above

Bergman, Torbern Olof 1735–84
Swedish chemist and physicist

Born in Catherineberg, West Gothland, he studied at the University of Uppsala, first theology and law, and then natural science. After graduating in 1758 he began to teach mathematics and physics at the university, where he became Professor of Chemistry and Mineralogy in 1767. His earliest publications were in physics and he seems largely to have been self-taught in chemistry. He was a pioneer in analytical chemistry, particularly of minerals. His most important paper was his *Essay on Elective Attractions* (1775). From 1775 to 1783 he compiled extensive affinity tables for acids and bases. His failing health led to the work being abandoned in an incomplete state, but it stimulated much later work on chemical affinity.

Bergner, Elisabeth 1900–86
Austrian actress

Born in Vienna, she made her stage debut in Zurich, but earned her reputation in Berlin in the 1920s, where she was particularly associated with the Expressionist dramas of **Frank Wedekind**, and had an international success in the title role of **George Bernard Shaw**'s *St Joan* in 1924. She moved to London, where her boyish figure and elfin looks so captivated **J M Barrie** that he wrote *The Boy David* (1936) for her. She fled to Switzerland after its humiliating failure, and spent the war years in the USA, before returning to Europe in 1951. She was awarded the Schiller prize for her contribution to German culture in 1963.

Bergognone, Ambrogio See Borgognone, Ambrogio

Bergson, Henri 1859–1941
French philosopher and Nobel Prize winner

Born in Paris, the son of a Polish Jewish musician and an English mother, he was educated in Paris at the Lycée Condorcet and the École Normale Supérieure (1878–81). He became professor at the Collège de France (1900–24), and was an original thinker who became something of a cult figure. He contrasted the fundamental reality of the dynamic flux of consciousness with the inert physical world of discrete objects, which was a convenient fiction for the mechanistic descriptions of science. The *élan vital*, or 'creative impulse', not a deterministic natural selection, is at the heart of evolution, and intuition, not analysis, reveals the real world of process and change. His own writings are literary, suggestive and analogical rather than philosophical in the modern sense, and he greatly influenced such writers as **Marcel Proust** (to whom he was connected by marriage), **Georges Sorel** and **Samuel**

Butler. His most important works were *Essai sur les données immédiates de la conscience* (1889, Eng trans *Time and Freewill*, 1910), *Matière et Mémoire* (1896, Eng trans *Matter and Memory*, 1911) and *L'Évolution Créatrice* (1907, Eng trans *Creative Evolution*, 1911). He was awarded the Nobel Prize for literature in 1927.

Bergström, Sune Karl 1916–
Swedish biochemist and Nobel Prize winner

Born in Stockholm, he studied medicine and chemistry at the Karolinska Institute in Stockholm, and taught chemistry at Lund University (1948–58) before returning to the Karolinska Institute as professor (1958–81). He studied the formation of bile acids from cholesterol and made major contributions towards solving the metabolic pathway involved. He also isolated and purified the prostaglandins, complex fatty acids produced by nearly all mammalian cells, which promote contraction of the intestinal and uterine muscle, and thus are employed in foetal abortion. Together with his former student **Bengt Samuelsson** and **John Vane**, Bergström was awarded the 1982 Nobel Prize for physiology or medicine for his work on prostaglandins.

Beria, Lavrenti Pavlovich 1899–1953
Soviet secret police chief

Born near Sukhumi, Georgia, into a peasant family, he became organizer of a Bolshevik group at a Baku college in 1917. From 1921 to 1931 he served as a member of the OGPU (a forerunner of the KGB) in the Caucasus, before becoming First Secretary of the Georgian Communist Party in 1931. In 1938 he was appointed Soviet Commissar for Internal Affairs by his patron, **Stalin**, and was active in purging Stalin's opponents as vice-president of the State Committee for Defence during World War II. He gained the title of Marshal in 1945. On Stalin's death in 1953, he attempted to seize power, but the coup was foiled by fearful military and party leaders. Following arrest by Marshal **Georgi Zhukov**, he was tried for treason and executed. Described as the 'Himmler of Russia', he was a plotter of ruthless ambition and a notoriously skilled organizer of forced labour, terror and espionage. 📖 Tadeusz Wittlin, *Commisar: The Life and Death of Lavrenti Pavlovich Beria* (1972)

Bering, Vitus Jonassen 1681–1741
Danish navigator

Born in Horsens, he joined the navy of **Peter I, the Great** in 1703. For his bravery in the wars with Sweden he was appointed to lead an expedition of discovery in the Sea of Kamchatka to determine whether the continents of Asia and America were joined. Sailing in 1728 from a port on the east of Kamchatka, he followed the coast northwards until, from its westward trend, he believed he had reached the north-east point of Asia. However, he failed to see land to the east and sought permission for a return voyage. In 1733 he was given command of the 600-strong Great Northern expedition to explore the Siberian coast and Kuril Islands, then in 1741 he sailed from Okhotsk towards the American continent, and sighting land, followed the coast northwards. However, sickness and storms forced him to return, and he was wrecked on the island of Avatcha (Bering Island), where he died of scurvy. Bering Sea and Bering Strait are also named after him. His discoveries were confirmed by Captain **James Cook.** 📖 Raymond H Fisher, *Bering's Voyages: Whither and Why* (1977)

Berio, Luciano 1925–
Italian composer and teacher of music

Born in Oreglia, he studied at the Music Academy in Milan, and then with **Luigi Dallapiccola** at Tanglewood, USA. He and **Bruno Maderna** founded an electronic studio in Milan (1954–61), and in 1962 Berio moved to

the USA. He taught composition at the Juilliard School in New York then returned to Italy in 1972 to continue his musical work. He is particularly interested in the combining of live and pre-recorded sound, and the use of tapes and electronic music, as in his compositions *Mutazioni* (1954, 'Mutations'), *Omaggio a James Joyce* (1958, 'Homage to James Joyce') and *Questo vuol dire che…* (1969–70, 'This Means That…'). His *Sequenza* series for solo instruments (1958–75) are striking virtuoso pieces. *Visage* (1961) was written specially for radio, and consists of a single word pronounced and repeated in varying ways. Pieces such as *Passaggio* (1963), for one female performer and two choruses, one in the pit and one in the audience, show the same pleasure in the dramatic tension of musical expression as his larger-scale stage works, *Laborintus II* (1965) and *Opera* (1969–70, revised in three acts in 1977). Between 1950 and 1966 he was married to the US soprano **Cathy Berberian**, for whom he wrote many works. *Continuo* (1991) is one of his more recent compositions.

Berkeley, Busby, *originally* William Berkeley Enos 1895–1976
US choreographer and director

He was born in Los Angeles, and served in the US army. Choosing a career in the theatre, he worked as an actor, stage manager and dance director. He directed his first Broadway show, *A Night in Venice*, in 1928 and was subsequently hired by **Samuel Goldwyn** to devise the musical number for the film *Whoopee* (1930). He stayed in Hollywood to become one of the cinema's most innovative choreographers, noted for his mobile camera-work and kaleidoscopic routines involving great numbers of chorus girls and much sexual innuendo. His work enhanced films like *42nd Street* (1933), *Gold Diggers of 1933* (1933), *Dames* (1934) and *Lady Be Good* (1941). In later years, ill health restricted his opportunities, but he directed *Take Me Out to the Ball Game* (1948), contributed imaginatively to *Small Town Girl* (1953) and enjoyed a Broadway success as the supervising producer of the 1971 revival of *No, No, Nanette*. 📖 Dave Martin and Bob Pike, *The Genius of Busby Berkeley* (1973)

Berkeley, George 1685–1753
Irish Anglican Bishop and philosopher

Born at Dysert Castle, Kilkenny, he was educated at Kilkenny College and Trinity College, Dublin (where he remained, as Fellow and tutor, until 1713). In 1724 he became dean of Derry, but became obsessed with a romantic scheme to found a college in the Bermudas which he gave up only after years of lobbying for support. In 1734 he became Bishop of Cloyne, and in 1752 moved to Oxford. His most important books were published in his early years: *Essay towards a New Theory of Vision* (1709), *A Treatise concerning the Principles of Human Knowledge* (1710) and *Three Dialogues between Hylas and Philonous* (1713). His remaining literary work was divided between questions of social reform and of religious reflection. 📖 A C Grayling, *Berkeley, the Central Arguments* (1986)

Berkeley, Sir Lennox Randall Francis 1903–89
English composer

Born in Oxford, he was a pupil of **Nadia Boulanger**. His early compositions, the largest of which is the oratorio *Jonah* (1935), show the influence of his French training in their conciseness and lucidity. Later works, notably the *Stabat Mater* (1946), the operas *Nelson* (1953) and *Ruth* (1956), and the orchestral *Windsor Variations* (1969) and *Voices of the Night* (1973), have won him wide recognition for their combination of technical refinement and emotional appeal. He was knighted in 1974.

Berkeley, Michael Fitzhardinge 1948–
English composer

Born in London, the son of Lennox Berkeley, he studied at the Royal Academy of Music and with **Richard Rodney Bennett**. He has composed concertos, and orchestral, chamber and choral works, including a powerful plea for peace in a nuclear age, the oratorio *Or Shall We Die?* (1983, text by **Ian McEwan**). He is well known for his introductions to music on radio and television.

Berkman, Alexander 1870–1936
US anarchist

Born in Vilna, Russia (now Vilnius, Lithuania), he emigrated to the USA in 1887 and became involved with radical labour groups in New York City. In 1889 he met fellow anarchist **Emma Goldman**, who was to be his lover for many years. In retaliation for the deaths of strikers during the Homestead Strike of 1892, he attempted to kill Carnegie Steel Co chairman **Henry Clay Frick**, and was jailed for 14 years, a period he chronicled after his release in his *Prison Memoirs of an Anarchist* (1912). He was imprisoned again (1917–19) for obstructing the draft in World War I. Deported to Russia along with Goldman in 1919, he was initially sympathetic to the Russian Revolution but became disenchanted. He committed suicide in France.

Berkoff, Steven 1937–
English dramatist, actor and director

He was born in London, and after studying at the École Jacques Lecoq in Paris, he founded the London Theatre Group, for whom he directed his own adaptations from the classics, including **Franz Kafka**'s *Metamorphosis* (1969), in which he himself played the role of the young man who finds himself transformed into a beetle. His own plays include *Greek* (1979, a variant of the Oedipal myth transferred to contemporary London) and *West* (1983, an adaptation of the Beowulf legend); *Decadence* (1981) counterpoints the sexual and social activities of an upper-class couple with that of a working-class woman and a private detective, and in *Kvetch* (1987) the anxieties of a group of West End Jews are metamorphosed into a comic dinner party. He has also played film villains, as in *Beverly Hills Cop* (1984). Other plays and adaptations include *Agamemnon* (1977), *The Fall of the House of Usher* (1977), *The Trial* (1981), *Sink the Belgrano* (1986), *In the Penal Colony* (1988) and *Brighton Beach Scumbags* (1991). His books include *I am Hamlet* (1989) and *Coriolanus in Deutschland* (1992).

Berkowitz, David, *also known as* Son of Sam
c.1953–
US murderer

He dubbed himself 'Son of Sam' in a note to the New York Police Department. He terrorized the city for a year between 1976 and 1977, preying on courting couples and women. He shot dead six people and wounded another seven. A special squad of 200 detectives was set up to trace him, but he avoided detection. At one time he was thought to have been a policeman. He was finally caught because of a parking ticket: he watched as it was stuck on his car, and then tore it to pieces. A woman witnessed this, noticed a strange smile on his face and reported him to the police. Berkowitz's car was traced and he was arrested. Pleading insanity, he claimed at his trial that Satanic voices told him to kill. Pronounced sane, he received a prison sentence of 365 years in August 1977.

Berlage, Hendrick Petrus 1856–1934
Dutch architect and town planner

He was born in Amsterdam. He designed the Amsterdam Bourse (1903) in a neo-Romanesque style, but he was later influenced by **Frank Lloyd Wright**, and was largely responsible for the spread of his theories in Holland. He became architectural adviser to the authorities of Amsterdam, The Hague and Rotterdam. His other buildings include Holland House, London (1914) and the Gemeente museum in The Hague (1934).

Berle, Milton, *originally* Milton Berlinger 1908–
US entertainer

Born in New York City, he began his career as a child performer in vaudeville, and later appeared as a comic actor in silent films and on Broadway. His zany but accessible style of comedy won him a loyal following, and he was a regular on several radio programmes. Because his variety show *Texaco Star Theater* (1948–56) made the new medium of television popular, he was nicknamed 'Mr Television'.

Berlichingen, Götz von See Götz von Berlichingen

Berlin, Irving, *originally* Israel Baline 1888–1989
US composer

Born in Temun, Siberia, he was taken to the USA as a child. He worked for a time as a singing waiter in a Bowery beer-hall, introducing some of his own songs like 'Alexander's Ragtime Band' and 'Everybody's Doin It'. A 'soldier show' in 1918 led to musical comedy and films in the 1920s and 1930s. In 1939 he wrote 'God Bless America', which achieved worldwide popularity in World War II and has become America's unofficial national anthem. The 1940s saw him at the peak of his career, with the hit musical *Annie Get Your Gun* (1946) and a stream of songs like 'Anything You Can Do', 'Doin' What Comes Naturally', 'There's No Business Like Show Business', 'We're a Couple of Swells', and the enduring 'White Christmas'. 'Call Me Madam' came in 1950, and in 1954 he received a special presidential citation as a composer of patriotic songs. In all, he wrote the words and music for more than 900 songs.

Berlin, Sir Isaiah 1907–97
British philosopher and historian of ideas

Born in Riga, Latvia, he emigrated to England with his Russian-speaking Jewish family in 1921 and was educated at St Paul's School, London, and Corpus Christi College, Oxford. Most of his academic career was spent at Oxford, where he became a Fellow of All Souls (1932), Chichele Professor of Social and Political Theory (1957–67) and President of Wolfson College (1966–75). He also served as a diplomat in the British embassies in Moscow and in Washington. His works include *Karl Marx* (1939), *Historical Inevitability* (1954), *The Age of Enlightenment* (1956), *Two Concepts of Liberty* (1959), *Vico and Herder* (1976), *Magnus of the North* (1993), four volumes of essays (1978–80) and translations of **Ivan Turgenev**. Considered one of the leading liberal thinkers of the century, he was knighted in 1957 and appointed to the Order of Merit in 1971. ⊞ John Gray, *Isaiah Berlin* (1995)

Berliner, Émile 1851–1929
US inventor

Born in Hanover, Germany, he worked as an apprentice printer until he emigrated to the USA in 1870, and he later became chief inspector for the Bell Telephone Company. In the years after 1876 he patented several improvements to **Alexander Graham Bell**'s telephone, and lost a 15-year battle with **Thomas Edison** for the rights to a new mouthpiece which both men claimed to have invented. He scored a notable victory over Edison in 1888 when he first demonstrated the flat disc gramophone record whose performance was in every way superior to Edison's original cylinders. By 1895 he had also developed a method of making several copies of a record in shellac from a single master disc. In 1915 he invented the first acoustic tiles.

Berlinguer, Enrico 1922–84
Italian politician

Born in Sardinia into a wealthy landowning family, he devoted himself from his early twenties to making the Italian Communist Party (PCI), which had been created following a split in the Socialist Party in 1921, a major force in Italian politics, and became Secretary-General in 1972. In 1976, under his leadership, it won more than a third of the Chamber of Deputies' seats, prompting Berlinguer to propose the 'historic compromise' with the Christian Democrat Party (DC) by which, in return for social reforms and an increased say on policy formation, the PCI agreed to respect the Church and constitutional institutions and discourage labour militancy. Under Berlinguer's influence, Italian communism flourished in the 1970s but the coalition was undermined by the traditional DC suspicion of the left, the anti-communist attitude of Pope John Paul II and the anti-Soviet feeling which was caused by the invasion of Afghanistan. By 1979 Berlinguer was once again in opposition although he continued to pursue his vision of 'Eurocommunism' which rejected the rigid Stalinist doctrines of the USSR.

Berlioz, (Louis) Hector 1803–69
French composer

Born in Côte-Saint-André, he first studied medicine, but produced some large-scale works before entering the Paris Conservatoire in 1826. He fell in love with the Irish Shakespearean actress Harriet Smithson (1800–54) and wrote the *Symphonie fantastique* (1830) for her; they married in 1833. After winning the Prix de Rome (1830), he spent two years in Italy. His other works include his symphony *Harold en Italie* (1834, 'Harold in Italy', written for Paganini), the *Grande messe des morts* (1837, 'High Mass for the Dead'), the dramatic symphony *Roméo et Juliette* (1839, 'Romeo and Juliet'), the cantata *La Damnation de Faust* (1846, 'The Damnation of Faust'), and his operas *Les Troyens* (1856–58, 'The Trojans') and *Béatrice et Bénédict* (1860–62). One of the founders of 19th-century programme music, Berlioz also wrote several books, including a treatise on orchestration and an autobiography. Despite a considerable reputation in Germany, Prussia and Great Britain, he failed to win respect in France, and that, together with the deaths of his second wife and his son, and his own ill health, overshadowed his later years.

Berlitz, Charles Frambach 1914–
US educationist

He was born in New York City, the grandson of Maximilian Delphinus Berlitz, who had founded the Berlitz School in 1878 as a German émigré to the USA and developed what became known as 'the Method'. This consists of demonstrations and the identification of objects, with the instructors speaking only in the language being taught. By 1914 there were over 300 schools throughout the world, but large financial losses caused by World War I led to the sale of all the schools outside North and Central America in 1921. Charles graduated from Yale *magna cum laude* in 1936 and went on to restore the Berlitz company's fortunes through commissions for the services in World War II and business courses for employees going overseas afterwards.

Berlusconi, Silvio 1936–
Italian businessman and politician

He was born in Milan. He has interests in television stations, housing, financial services, a cinema chain, and Milan AC football club. He is leader of the right-wing Forza Italia Party, which won more seats (155) in the 1994 election than any other (though not an absolute majority). He formed a government which included neo-Fascist ministers but resigned at the end of that year having received a vote of no-confidence. He did, however, remain at the head of a caretaker government.

Bernadette, St, *originally* Marie Bernarde Soubirous 1844–79
French nun and visionary

Born in Lourdes, she claimed to have received 18 apparitions of the Blessed Virgin in 1858 at the Massabielle Rock, near Lourdes, which has since become a well-known place of pilgrimage. Attending a local school run by the Sisters of Charity of Nevers, she became a nun in 1866, and was beatified in 1925 and canonized in 1933. Her feast day is 18 February or 16 April.

Bernadotte
Swedish royal dynasty

The House was founded in 1818 by Jean Baptiste Jules Bernadotte who became King Karl XIV Johan of Sweden. On his death he was succeeded by his son, Oskar I, and the reigning monarchs of Sweden, Norway, Denmark and Belgium are his direct descendants. In 1794 Bernadotte's future wife Désirée met Napoleon I, who later described her as his 'first love', and her elder sister, Julie, married Joseph Bonaparte. Désirée's eventual marriage to Bernadotte (1798) eased his strained relations with Bonaparte. Count Folke (1895–1948), great-great-grandson of Jean Bernadotte and nephew of King Gustav V, acted as mediator in both World Wars. He was appointed by the United Nations to mediate in Palestine and produced a partition plan, but was then assassinated by Jewish terrorists.

Bernal, John Desmond, *nicknamed* Sage 1901–71
Irish crystallographer

Born in Nenagh, County Tipperary, he was educated by the Jesuits at Stonyhurst, Lancashire, won a scholarship to Emmanuel College, Cambridge, and from the first showed himself a polymath. He developed modern crystallography and was a founder of molecular biology, pioneering work on the structure of water. He progressed from a lectureship at Cambridge to a professorship of physics and then crystallography at Birkbeck College, London (1937–68), and included among his major works *The Origin of Life* (1967). His wartime service involved abortive attempts at creating artificial icebergs to act as aircraft carriers, as well as working on bomb tests and the scientific underpinning of the invasion of the European Continent. A communist from his student days, he was involved in international peace activity during the Cold War and supported Trofim Denisovich Lysenko in the USSR when his destruction of Soviet genetics drove J B S Haldane out of the British Communist Party. Bernal's hopes for communism's possibilities for science were first shown in his *The Social Function of Science* (1939) and *Marx and Science* (1952).

Bernard of Clairvaux, St, *also known as* the Mellifluous Doctor 1090–1153
French theologian and reformer

Born near Dijon, he entered the Cistercian monastery of Citeaux in 1113. In 1115 he became the first abbot of the newly founded monastery of Clairvaux, in Champagne. He led a studious, ascetic life and founded more than 70 monasteries. Known for his eloquence, an antidote to the dry scholasticism of the age, he drew up the statutes of the Knights Templars in 1128, secured the recognition of Pope Innocent II, and spoke (1146) in favour of France taking part in the Second Crusade. His writings comprise more than 400 epistles, 340 sermons, a Life of St Malachy, and several theological treatises. The monks of his reformed branch of the Cistercians are often called Bernardines. He was canonized in 1174, and his feast day is 20 August. 📖 Bruno Scott James, *St Bernard of Clairvaux* (1957)

Bernard of Menthon, St, *also called* the Apostle of the Alps 923–1008
Italian churchman
Born in Savoy, he founded, as archdeacon of Aosta, the hospices in the Alpine passes that were named after him, as were St Bernard dogs, trained by the monks to go to the aid of travellers. He was canonized in 1115 and his feast day is 28 May or 15 June.

Bernard of Morval or Morlaix 12th century
French Benedictine monk of Cluny
Said to have been born of English parents in Morval, he is the author of a fine Latin poem, *De Contemptu Mundi*, in 3,000 'leonine-dactylic' hexameters. Some of these were translated by John Mason Neale into hymns, among them 'Jerusalem the Golden' and 'The World is Very Evil'.

Bernard, Claude 1813–78
French physiologist
Born near Villefranche, he studied medicine at the University of Paris, and in 1841 became assistant at the Collège de France to François Magendie, with whom he worked until his own appointment in 1854 to the chair of general physiology. In 1855 he succeeded Magendie as Professor of Experimental Physiology. His earliest researches were on the action of the secretions of the alimentary canal, the pancreatic juice, and the connection between the liver and nervous system, for which he received three prizes from the Academy (1851–53). However, his greatest contribution to physiological theory was the concept that life requires a constant internal environment (*milieu intérieur*), with cells functioning best within a narrow range of osmotic pressure and temperature. Later researches were on the changes of temperature of the blood, the oxygen in arterial and in venous blood, the opium alkaloids, curare, and the sympathetic nerves. His *Introduction to the Study of Experimental Medicine* (1865) is a classic account of the new biology. Bernard stands as one of the founders of modern physiological research, combining experimental skill with an aptitude for theory. 🕮
J M D Olmsted, *Claude Bernard: Physiologist* (1938)

Bernard, Émile 1868–1941
French painter and writer
Born in Lille, a fellow student with Vincent Van Gogh and Toulouse-Lautrec at the Académie of Fernand Cormon, he later worked with Paul Gauguin at Pont Aven. In Paris in 1889 he joined the Group Synthétiste and in 1890 launched a magazine, *La Rénovation esthétique*. He travelled for several years in Egypt and the Middle East, returning to Paris in 1901. From 1921 to 1928 he lived in Venice. He is credited with founding the so-called Cloisonnist style.

Bernard, Jessie Shirley, *née* Ravitch 1903–96
US sociologist and writer
Born in Minneapolis, Minnesota, she studied at the University of Minnesota where she met Luther Lee Bernard, whom she married in 1925. She worked alongside him, and together they produced works which included *Origins of American Sociology* (1943). In 1947 the couple moved to Pennsylvania State University, where she wrote *American Community Behaviour* (1949), three years before her husband's death and her subsequent trip to Europe. She resigned from Pennsylvania State University in 1964, and pursued a career as an influential and ground-breaking feminist writer. Her pertinent analyses include *The Sex Game* (1968), *Women, Wives and Mothers* (1975) and *The Female World from a Global Perspective* (1987).

Bernard, Tristan, *originally* Paul Bernard 1866–1947
French novelist and dramatist
He was born in Besançon, and his first success came with the novel *Les Mémoires d'un jeune homme rangé* (1899, 'Memoirs of a Dutiful Young Man'). In the same year he wrote a comedy, *L'Anglais tel qu'on le parle* ('English as it is Spoken'),

and from then on produced a number of popular, light-hearted pieces with stock comic situations, including *Daisy* (1902), *Triplepatte* (1905), *Le Petit café* (1911, 'The Small Café') and *Le Prince Charmant* (1921, 'Prince Charming'). 🕮
J J Bernard, *Mon père Tristan Bernard* (1955)

Bernardino of Siena, St 1380–1444
Italian monk
Born in Massa di Carrara, he entered the Franciscan order in 1404, and in 1438 was appointed its vicar-general for Italy, becoming famous by his rigid restoration of the rule. He founded the *Fratres de Observantia*, a branch of the Franciscan order, which already numbered over 300 monasteries in Italy during his day. He was canonized in 1450 and his feast day is 20 May.

Berners, Gerald Hugh Tyrwhitt-Wilson, 14th Baron 1883–1950
English composer
Born in Bridgnorth, Shropshire, his early works appeared under the name of Gerald Tyrwhitt. His total output was small, but includes an orchestral fugue and several ballets, of which the best-known are *The Triumph of Neptune* (1926) and *A Wedding Bouquet* (1937, after a play by Gertrude Stein). All his work is distinguished by a delicate and witty sense of pastiche. He was a noted eccentric and dabbled in fiction and painting.

Berners or Barnes, Juliana b.c.1388
English prioress and writer
She was either the daughter of Sir James Berners (one of Richard II's favourites who was beheaded soon after his daughter's birth), or the wife of the lord of the manor of Julians Barns near St Albans, Hertfordshire, which would explain her other name, Dame Julyans Barnes. Some traditions hold that after 1430 she was the prioress of Sopwell nunnery in St Albans, but this seems unlikely. She was a woman of great beauty and learning, and like other fashionable noblewomen of her day, took part in several different fieldsports, which provided material for her writings, such as her the *Treatyse perteynynge to Hawkynge, Huntynge, Fysshynge, and Coote Armiris*, which formed part of *The Book of St Albans* (1486).

Berneville, Comtesse d' See Aulnoy, Marie Catherine

Bernhard Leopold 1911–
Prince of the Netherlands
Born in Jena, the son of Prince Bernhard Casimir of Lippe-Biesterfeld, he married in 1937 Juliana, the only daughter of Wilhelmina, Queen of the Netherlands, and the title of Prince of the Netherlands was conferred on him. During World War II he escaped to England, where he helped to organize the Dutch Resistance. After Juliana's accession to the throne (1948), he was influential in encouraging cultural and trading activities. He was involved (1976) in a controversy over the activities of Lockheed Aircraft Corporation, and this produced a constitutional crisis that harmed the monarchy.

Bernhardt, Sarah, *originally* Sarah-Marie-Henriette Rosine Bernard 1844–1923
French actress
She was born in Paris and entered the Paris Conservatoire in 1859. She made her debut as Iphigénie at the Comédie-Française (1862), but attracted little notice and moved to the Odéon, where she played minor parts (1867), and won fame as Zanetto in François Coppée's *Le Passant* (1869), and as the Queen of Spain in Victor Hugo's *Ruy Blas* (1872). She was recalled to the Comédie Française and after 1876 she made frequent visits to London, the USA and Europe. Her most famous roles include *Phèdre* (1877) and Marguerite in *La Dame aux camélias* (1884). In 1882 she married Jacques Daria or Damala (d.1889), a Greek actor,

from whom she was divorced shortly afterwards. Her French nationality was restored in 1916. She founded the Théâtre Sarah Bernhardt in 1899. In 1915 she had a leg amputated, but did not abandon the stage. A legendary figure in the theatre world, she was considered to be the greatest *tragédienne* of her day. 📖 E Pronier, *Une vie au théâtre: Sarah Bernhardt* (1942)

Berni or Bernia, Francesco c.1497–1535
Italian poet

Born in Lamporecchio, Tuscany, he went in 1517 from Florence to Rome, where he entered the service of his uncle, Cardinal Bibbiena, of Ghiberti, Chancellor to Clement VII, and in 1532 of Cardinal Ippolito de' Medici. A year later he went to Florence, where, refusing to poison Cardinal Salviati, he was himself poisoned. His recast or *rifacimento* of Matteo Boiardo's *Orlando Innamorato* (1542) is still read in Italy in preference to the original. He played a large part in establishing Italian as a literary language. 📖 A Virgil, *Francesco Berni* (1981)

Bernini, Gian Lorenzo 1598–1680
Italian sculptor, architect and painter

Born in Naples, the son of a sculptor, he went to Rome at an early age, and there attracted the attention of Cardinal Scipione Borghese, who became his patron. For him he sculpted a series of life-size marble statues which established his reputation as the leading sculptor of his day (1618–25, Borghese Gallery, Rome). Under Pope Urban VIII, he designed the famous baldacchino for St Peter's, and there is much other sculptural and architectural work by him still in the Vatican. However, under the next pope, Innocent X, he fell out of favour, partly because of the structurally unsound towers on the facade of St Peter's for which he was responsible. In 1647 he designed the fountain of the four river gods in the middle of the Piazza Navona. Superseded in papal favour by the sculptor Alessandro Algardi, Bernini concentrated on private commissions, the most famous of which is the Cornaro Chapel in the Church of Santa Maria della Vittoria. The central element of the design, the sculpture depicting *The Ecstasy of Saint Theresa*, is one of the great works of the Baroque period. In 1665 he travelled to Paris to design the east front of the Louvre for Louis XIV, but his designs were never executed and he returned to Rome having only completed a portrait bust of the king. The dominant figure of the Baroque period in Rome, he did his last work on the tomb of Alexander VII in St Peter's and the small Jesuit Church of San Andrea della Quirinale. 📖 Filippo Baldinucci, *Vita del cavaliere Gio Lorenzo Bernino* (1682, Eng trans *The Life of Bernini*, 1966)

Bernoulli, Daniel 1700–82
Swiss mathematician

Born in Groningen, the Netherlands, the son of Jean Bernoulli, he studied medicine and mathematics at the universities of Basle, Strasbourg and Heidelberg, and became Professor of Mathematics at St Petersburg University (1725). In 1732 he returned to Basle to become Professor of Anatomy, then was appointed to a professorship in botany, and finally physics. He worked on trigonometric series, mechanics and vibrating systems, and pioneered the modern field of hydrodynamics. His *Hydrodynamica* (1738) explored the physical properties of flowing fluids, and anticipated the kinetic theory of gases, pointing out that pressure would increase with increasing temperature. He solved a differential equation proposed by Jacopo Riccati, now known as Bernoulli's equation.

Bernoulli, Jacques or Jakob 1654–1705
Swiss mathematician

He was born in Basle, the brother of Jean Bernoulli. He studied theology and travelled in Europe before returning to Basle (1682), where he became professor in 1687. He investigated infinite series, the cycloid, transcendental curves, logarithmic spiral and the catenary. In 1690 he applied Gottfried Leibniz's newly discovered differential calculus to a problem in geometry, and introduced the term 'integral'. His *Ars conjectandi* (1713), an important contribution to probability theory, included his 'law of large numbers', his permutation theory and the 'Bernoulli numbers', coefficients found in exponential series.

Bernoulli, Jean or Johann 1667–1748
Swiss mathematician

He was born in Basle, the younger brother of Jacques Bernoulli, graduated in medicine but turned to mathematics, and became professor at the universities of Groningen (1695) and Basle (1705). He wrote on differential equations, both in general and with respect to the length and area of curves, isochronous curves and curves of quickest descent. He founded a dynasty of mathematicians which continued for two generations, and was employed by the Marquis de l'Hospital to help him write the first textbook on the differential calculus.

Bernstein, Carl 1944–
US journalist and author

He was born in Washington, DC. With journalist Bob Woodward (1943–) he was responsible for unmasking the Watergate cover-up (1972), which resulted in a constitutional crisis and the resignation of President Richard Nixon (9 August 1974). For their coverage, Bernstein and Woodward earned virtually every major journalism award, including the Sigma Delta Chi Award for distinguished service in the field of Washington correspondence and the George Polk Memorial Award, and won for the *Washington Post* the 1973 Pulitzer Prize for public service. Together they wrote the bestseller *All the President's Men* (1974), which became a successful film, and *The Final Days* (1976), an almost hour-by-hour account of President Nixon's last months in office. In 1989 he published *Loyalties: a son's memoirs*.

Bernstein, Eduard 1850–1932
German socialist leader

Born in Berlin, he was an associate of Friedrich Engels, and played a major part in unifying the German socialist movement in 1875. As a leading intellectual in the Social Democratic Party (SPD), he was prominent in establishing its Marxist ideology. Later he was an advocate of revisionism, an evolutionary form of Marxism, and a member of the Reichstag periodically (1902–28). He was exiled for his beliefs (1888–1901), during which time he lived in London, where he influenced, and was in turn influenced by, the British Fabians and other socialists.

Bernstein, Leonard 1918–90
US conductor, pianist and composer

Born in Lawrence, Massachusetts, he was educated at Harvard and the Curtis Institute of Music. He achieved fame suddenly in 1943, when he conducted the New York Philharmonic Orchestra as a substitute for Bruno Walter. His compositions include three symphonies, a television opera, a mass, a ballet, and many choral works and songs, but he is best known for his two musical comedies *On the Town* (1944) and *West Side Story* (1957), and for his concerts for young people. Later works include the ballet, *The Dybbuk* (1974), *Songfest* (1977), *Halil* (1981), and a revision of his operetta *Candide* (1956, 1988).

Bernstein, Richard Barry 1923–90
US physical chemist

Born in Long Island, New York, he was educated at Columbia University, New York, and from 1944 to 1946 he worked on the Manhattan (atomic bomb) Project to separate uranium-235. From 1948 to 1963 he held appointments at Illinois Institute of Technology, Chicago, and the University of Michigan, and subsequently was professor in succession at the universities of Wisconsin (Madison), Texas (Austin), Columbia, and finally at the University of California (Los Angeles). Bernstein received many awards, including the Hinshelwood lectureship at Oxford (1980), the Debye Award of the American Chemical Society (1981), and a National Medal of Science (1989). His researches were in chemical kinetics using molecular beam scattering and laser techniques to elucidate much of what occurs when molecules react. He co-authored *Molecular Reaction Dynamics* (1974), and also wrote *Chemical Dynamics via Molecular Beam and Laser Techniques* (1982). In 1955 he was the pioneer of 'femtochemistry', the study of reactions which take place on extremely small timescales.

Bernstein, Sidney Lewis Bernstein, Baron
1899–1993
English businessman
Born in Ilford, London, he left school at the age of 15 to work in the family property development business. He had an interest in entertainment and began his career by buying the derelict music hall, the Empire Theatre, in Edmonton (1922) and turning it into a cinema. He built the first new cinema in 1929 in Dover, the design of which was copied across the country. After World War II, during which he served as Films Adviser to the Ministry of Information, he went to Hollywood for five years, but returned to the UK and in 1954 met the challenge of starting up a commercial television franchise. Under his leadership Granada Television became renowned for its drama and current affairs programmes, with the long-running *World in Action* and drama series like *Brideshead Revisited* (1981) and *Jewel in the Crown* (1984). The Granada empire also embraced television rental, theatres and motorway services.

Berosus or Berossus fl.c.260BC
Babylonian priest
He wrote in Greek three books of Babylonian–Chaldean history, in which he made use of the archives in the temple of Bel at Babylon, and of which only a few fragments have been preserved by Josephus, Eusebius and Syncellus.

Berra, Yogi (Lawrence Peter) 1925–
US baseball player and coach
Born in St Louis, Missouri, he played with the New York Yankees from 1946 to 1963, including 14 World Series (a record). He also set the record for most home runs by a catcher in the American League (313). He went on to manage and coach the Yankees and then did the same for their arch-rivals, the New York Mets. In 1986 he went on to coach the Houston Astros. His most famous quote was 'It ain't over 'til it's over'.

Berri, Nabih 1939–
Lebanese politician and soldier
Born in Freetown, Sierra Leone, he studied law at Beirut University. In 1978 he became leader of Amal ('Hope'), a branch of the Shiite nationalist movement founded by Iman Musa Sadr. Backed by Syria, it became the main Shiite military force in West Beirut and Southern Lebanon during the country's civil wars, but in 1988 its Beirut branch was heavily defeated by the Iranian-backed Hezbollah ('Children of God') and was disbanded. Berri joined the Lebanese parliament in 1984 as Minister of Justice and from 1990 to 1992 he held the post of Speaker.

Berruguete, Alonso c.1489–1561
Spanish painter and sculptor
Born in Paredes de Nava, Valladolid, he studied under his father, Pedro Berruguete. He became the major Spanish sculptor of the 16th century and an important figure in the introduction of the Italian Mannerist style into Spain. The Italian artist and historian Giorgio Vasari mentions him several times in his *Lives of the Artists*. In Italy from 1504 to 1517 he copied work by Michelangelo—in whose letters his name appears—and completed an altarpiece begun by Filippino Lippi. He was appointed court painter to Charles V on his return to Spain, and was later ennobled. In his home country he was most successful as a sculptor and his best-known work is the wood and alabaster carvings for the choir of Toledo cathedral.

Berruguete, Pedro c.1450–1504
Spanish painter
He was born in Valladolid, Castile. He is thought to have spent time in Italy, and is probably the 'Pietro spagnuolo' who worked in 1477 on a series of paintings of famous men for the decoration of the palace library at Urbino, alongside Melozzo di Forli and Joos van Gent. He was painter to the court of Ferdinand, the Catholic and Isabella of Castile, and his later work, at the cathedrals of Toledo and Avila, helped to introduce Italian Renaissance style to Spain. He was the father of Alonso Berruguete.

Berry, Charles Ferdinand de Bourbon, Duc de 1778–1820
French aristocrat
He was born at Versailles, the second son of Charles X. During the Revolution and Empire he lived in exile in Russia and England. In 1814 he returned to France, was appointed commander of the troops in and around Paris (1815), and in 1816 married Caroline (1798–1870), eldest daughter of Francis, afterwards King of the Two Sicilies. Assassinated by the Bonapartist fanatic Pierre Louis Louvel in front of the Paris Opéra, he left only a daughter; but the same year the widowed duchess gave birth to Henri, Comte de Chambord.

Berry, Chuck (Charles Edward Anderson)
1926–
US pop singer
The biggest influence on pre-Beatles rock, he was born in St Louis, Missouri, and learned to play the guitar at high school. He served three years in a reform school for armed robbery (1944–47), then worked in a factory and trained as a hairdresser before moving to Chicago in 1955 and launching his professional career. Introduced to Chess Records by Muddy Waters, he had his first success with 'Maybellene' (1955). With songs such as 'School Days' (1957), 'Rock And Roll Music' (1957) and 'Johnny B Goode' (1958), he appealed to teenagers of all races. Jailed in 1962 for two years on a charge (1959) of transporting a minor over state lines for immoral purposes, he never fully recovered his creativity thereafter, although 'My Ding A Ling' (1972) was the most successful single of his career. His influence was pivotal to the British pop renaissance of the early 1960s and is evident in much of the Beatles' and the Rolling Stones' work. He was awarded a Grammy in 1984 for lifetime achievement. 📖 *Chuck Berry: The Autobiography* (1987)

Berry, James Gomer See Kemsley, 1st Viscount

Berry, Wendell 1934–
US poet, novelist and essayist
Raised in Henry County, Kentucky, he quickly grasped the economic, cultural and racial contradictions of middle America, and these form the substance of his finest writing, including the novel *A Place on Earth* (1967, rev edn 1983), and of his verse, notably in *The Broken Ground* (1964), *Farming: A Handbook* (1970), *The Country of Marriage* (1973), the significantly titled *A Part* (1980) and *The Wheel* (1982). All of his verse up to that point was published in a *Collected Poems* (1985). *Nathan Coulter* (1960) established the retrospective style of his fiction, also evident in *The*

Memory of Old Jack (1974) and *Remembering* (1988). *The Unsettling of America* (1977) gives a straightforward account of the status of US agriculture, while avoiding bland discursiveness or reactionary pastoralism. ☐ *The Hidden Wound* (1970)

Berry, William Ewert See Camrose, 1st Viscount

Berryman, John, *originally* John Allyn Smith
1914–72
US poet, biographer, novelist and academic
Born in McAlester, Oklahoma, he adopted his step-father's name at the age of 12. Educated at Columbia University and Clare College, Cambridge, he taught at several US universities including the University of Minnesota, where he became Regents Professor of Humanities (1955–72). His biography of Stephen Crane (1950) is rated highly but his reputation rests on his poetry. His first collection, *Poems*, appeared in 1942, and was followed by *The Dispossessed* (1948) and *Homage to Mistress Bradstreet* (1956, inspired by the first New England poet, Anne Bradstreet), which established his reputation. His major work is his *Dream Songs*, begun in 1955: *77 Dream Songs* (1964) won the Pulitzer Prize in 1965, and *His Toy, His Dream, His Rest: 308 Dream Songs* (1968) received the National Book award in 1969. The complete sequence was published in 1969. His other books include the novel *Recovery* (1973), concerning alcoholism. Unable to overcome his own drink problem and mental illness, he committed suicide. ☐ J Haffenden, *John Berryman* (1982)

Bert, Paul 1833–86
French physiologist and politician
Born in Auxerre, he studied in Paris from 1853, obtaining licentiates in law and in natural sciences, and after short periods as professor at the University of Bordeaux and at the Museum of Natural History, he succeeded Claude Bernard as Professor of Physiology at the Sorbonne in 1869. Later he joined the Liberal Republican Party, was elected in 1872 to the Chamber of Deputies, and as Minister of Public Instruction fought for free, compulsory and secular elementary education. He worked on the effect of changes in atmospheric pressure, altitude and the composition of the air upon blood gases, and his studies of the oxygen content of the air and barometric pressure had important implications for deep-sea diving and acclimatization at high altitudes. His *La Pression barométrique* (1878, 'Barometric Pressure') was translated in 1943 because of its importance for aviation medicine.

Berthelot, (Pierre-Eugène) Marcellin
1827–1907
French chemist and politician
Born in Paris, he became the first Professor of Organic Chemistry at the Collège de France (1865). He was put in charge of Paris defences in the Franco-Prussian War (1870–71), and was Foreign Minister (1895–96) and an Academician (1900). He helped to found thermochemistry, introduced a standard method for determining the latent heat of steam, and discovered many of the derivatives of coal tar. His syntheses of many fundamental organic compounds helped to destroy the classical division between organic and inorganic compounds. He studied the mechanism of explosion, wrote many scholarly works on the history of early chemistry and did much to initiate the chemical analyses of archaeological objects. He received the Legion of Honour in 1861 and succeeded Louis Pasteur as secretary of the French Academy of Sciences in 1889. ☐ Jean Jacques, *Berthelot, 1827–1907: autopsie d'un mythe*

Berthelot, Sabin 1794–1880
French naturalist

Born in Marseilles, he joined the navy and served in the Napoleonic Wars, then joined the merchant fleet. In 1820 he went to the Canaries, where he did some teaching and became an expert botanist. He lived in the Canaries for 44 years, studying the fauna and flora and early history of the islands. With the English botanist Philip Barker-Webb he compiled a massive *L'Histoire Naturelle des Îles Canaries* (1830–50, 'Natural History of the Canary Islands'). He was later appointed French consul there (1847). Berthelot's Pipit was named in his honour.

Berthier, Alexandre 1753–1815
Prince of Neuchâtel and Wagram and Marshal of the French Empire
Born at Versailles, he joined the army (1770) and fought with the Marquis de Lafayette in the American Revolution. In the French Revolution he rose to be Chief of Staff in the Army of Italy (1795), and in 1798 proclaimed the Republic in Rome. He became Chief of Staff to Napoleon I, on whose fall he had to surrender the principality of Neuchâtel, but was allowed to keep his rank as peer and marshal. He retired to Bamberg and, at the sight of a Russian division marching towards the French frontier, he fell from a window and died.

Berthollet, Claude Louis, Comte de 1749–1822
French chemist
Born in Talloires, Savoy, he studied medicine at Turin and Paris. He helped Antoine Lavoisier with his research on gunpowder and also with the creation of a new system of chemical nomenclature which is still in use today. He accepted Lavoisier's antiphlogistic doctrines, but disproved his theory that all acids contain oxygen. He was the first chemist to realize that there is a connection between the manner in which a chemical reaction proceeds and the mass of the reagents; this insight led others to formulate the law of definite proportions later stated by Joseph Louis Proust. He also demonstrated that chemical affinities are affected by the temperature and concentration of the reagents. Following Joseph Priestley's discovery that ammonia is composed of hydrogen and nitrogen, Berthollet made the first accurate analysis of their proportions. He was elected to the Academy of Sciences in 1781 and was active during the French Revolution. After accompanying Napoleon I to Egypt he remained there for two years, helping to reorganize the educational system. He voted for Napoleon's deposition in 1814, and on the restoration of the Bourbons was created a count.

Berthoud, Ferdinand 1727–1807
Swiss horological craftsman and inventor
Born in Neuchâtel, he began as an apprentice to his brother in Placemont, then worked in Paris from 1748. He sought to improve the accuracy of the measurement of longitude at sea by improving the design of spring-driven chronometers, of which he made about 70 during his lifetime. By 1780 he had developed a spring detent escapement, bimetallic strips for temperature compensation and other refinements, some of which were still in use a century later. He is also remembered as a prolific writer on horology and the application of machine tools to precision craftsmanship.

Bertillon, Alphonse 1853–1914
French police officer
He was born in Paris. As chief of the identification bureau in Paris, in 1880 he devised a system of identifying criminals by anthropometric measurements (later superseded by fingerprints).

Bertolucci, Bernardo 1940–
Italian film director
He was born in Parma, and was an amateur filmmaker and poet. He became an assistant to Pier Paolo Pasolini on *Accattone!* (1961, 'Beggar!'). His collection of poetry, *In*

Cerca del Mistero (1962, 'In Search of Mystery'), won the Premio Viareggio prize and he made his directorial debut the same year with *La Commare Secca* (*The Grim Reaper*). A member of the Italian Communist Party, he makes films which depict the tension between conventionality and rebellion, exploring the complex relationships between politics, sex and violence with visual élan and dramatic intensity. The success of *Il Conformista* (1970, *The Conformist*) and *Ultimo Tango a Parigi* (1972, *Last Tango in Paris*) allowed him to make the Marxist epic *Novecento* (1976, *1900*). He won a Best Director Academy Award for the epic *The Last Emperor* (1987). Other films include *The Sheltering Sky* (1990), *Little Buddha* (1993) and *Stealing Beauty* (1996), which marked his return to Italy. 📖 Robert P Kolker, *Bernardo Bertolucci* (1985)

Bertrand, Aloysius, *properly* Jacques-Louis Napoléon Bertrand 1807–41
French poet
He was born in Ceva, Italy, of a French father and an Italian mother, but his family later settled in France, in Dijon (1815). He moved to Paris in 1829. His fame is due to his *Gaspard de la Nuit* written around 1830 and published posthumously in 1842. This early example of a prose poem was to influence Baudelaire, Stéphane Mallarmé, Arthur Rimbaud and Guillaume Apollinaire. Elaborately rhythmical, it deals with such quintessentially Romantic themes as heightened sensibility, the medieval and the Gothic, and the opposition of the sentimental and the grotesque. Bertrand also edited and directed various periodicals and published a volume of poetry, *La Volupté* (1834). He died of tuberculosis.

Bertrand, Henri Gratien, Comte 1773–1844
French soldier and military engineer
Born in Châteauroux, he fought in Italy and Egypt before becoming Napoleon I's aide-de-camp (1804) and Grand Marshal (1813). He shared Napoleon's banishment to St Helena, and when the Emperor died returned to France, where he was appointed commandant of the École Polytechnique (1830). His shorthand diary provided a detailed account of Napoleon's life in exile.

Bertrand, Louis Marie Émile 1866–1941
French writer
Born in Spincourt, he spent some years in Algeria, which provides a setting for *Sang des races* (1898, 'Blood of the People'). He also wrote *La Cina* (1900, 'China'), other realistic novels and travel books, historical novels, and biographical studies of Gustave Flaubert and Louis XIV.

Bérulle, Pierre de 1575–1629
French prelate and theologian
Born near Troyes, he was educated by Jesuits and studied theology at the Sorbonne, becoming ordained in 1599. A leader of the Catholic reaction against Calvinism, he founded the French Congregation of the Oratory (1611) and introduced the Carmelite Order into France. He was Ambassador to Spain in 1626, Minister of State until dismissed by Cardinal Richelieu, and was made a cardinal in 1627. Many of his pupils became famous, and he widely influenced French religious teaching. He was dubbed 'Apostolus Verbi Incarnati' by Pope Urban VIII.

Berwald, Franz Adolf 1796–1868
Swedish composer
Born in Stockholm, into a musical family, he played the violin and viola in the Swedish Court Orchestra, until he won a scholarship to Berlin in 1828. A friend of several composers, including Mendelssohn and Hector Berlioz, he made his reputation with four symphonies he composed, the *Sérieuse* and *Capricieuse* in 1842 and the *Singulière* and *Eb* in 1845. In 1847 Jenny Lind's appearance in his *Ein Ländlisches Verlobungsfest in Schweden* ('A Swedish Country Betrothal') in Vienna brought him great acclaim. He returned to Sweden in 1849 and divided his time between music, business concerns and increasing involvement in social issues until 1867, when he was made Professor of Composition at the Swedish Royal Academy. His fiery expression and original inspiration made him the most impressive Swedish composer of the 19th century.

Berwick, James Fitzjames, 1st Duke of 1670–1734
French and Jacobite general
He was the illegitimate son of James VII and II. Educated in France as a Catholic, he was created Duke of Berwick (1687), but fled from England at the Glorious Revolution of 1688. He fought in his father's Irish campaign (1689–91), and then in Flanders and against the Camisards. In 1706 he was created a Marshal of France, and in Spain established the throne of Philip V by the decisive victory of Almanza (1707) in the War of the Spanish Succession. Appointed Commander-in-Chief of the French forces (1733), he was killed while besieging Phillippsburg.

Berwick, Mary See Procter, Adelaide Ann

Berzelius, Jöns Jacob 1779–1848
Swedish chemist
Born in Väfversunda, East Götland, he studied medicine at Uppsala and worked as an unpaid assistant in the College of Medicine at Stockholm before succeeding to the chair of medicine and pharmacy in 1807. In 1815 he was appointed Professor of Chemistry at the Royal Caroline Medico-Chirurgical Institute in Stockholm, retiring in 1832. Soon after Alessandro Volta's invention of the electric battery, Berzelius began in 1802 to experiment with the voltaic pile. Working with Wilhelm Hisinger he discovered that all salts are decomposed by electricity. He went on to suggest that all compounds are made up of positive and negative components, a theory which laid the foundations for our understanding of radicals. In 1803 he and Hisinger discovered cerium; Berzelius also discovered selenium and thorium and was the first person to isolate silicon, zirconium and titanium. His greatest achievement, however, was his contribution to atomic theory. Matching the idea of constant proportions with John Dalton's atomic theory, and persuaded of the central importance of oxygen from his studies of Antoine Lavoisier's work, he drew up a table of atomic weights using oxygen as a base, devising the modern system of chemical symbols. He also made significant contributions to organic chemistry. A pioneer of gravimetric analysis, he has had few rivals as an experimenter. As a result of the poverty of his early years, he had to improvise much of his apparatus and some of his innovations are still standard laboratory equipment, eg wash bottles, filter paper and rubber tubing. He was elected to the Stockholm Royal Academy of Sciences in 1808 and became its secretary in 1818. He was awarded the Gold Medal of the Royal Society of London, and in 1835 he was created a baron by Charles XIV. 📖 Hans Krook, *Jacob Berzelius* (1979)

Berzsenyi, Daniel 1776–1836
Hungarian lyric poet
Born in Heteny, he was educated by his father. He won fame as a patriotic poet with his *Ode to Magyarokhoz*, inspired by the Magyar nobility's successful opposition to Napoleon I on the Styrian Alps. Collections of his verse were published in 1813 and 1830. 📖 O Merenyi, *Berzsenyi Daniel* (1966)

Besant, Annie, *née* Wood 1847–1933
English theosophist
She was born in London of Irish parentage. After her separation in 1873 from her husband, the Reverend Frank Besant (brother of Sir Walter Besant), she became in 1874

vice-president of the National Secular Society. A close associate of **Charles Bradlaugh**, she was an ardent proponent of birth control and socialism. In 1889, after meeting Madame **Blavatsky**, she developed an interest in theosophy, and went to India, where she became involved in politics, being elected president of the Indian National Congress from 1917 to 1923. Her publications include *The Gospel of Atheism* (1877) and *Theosophy and the New Psychology* (1904). 📖 Arthur Nethercot, *The First Five Lives of Annie Besant* (1960); *The Last Four Lives of Annie Besant* (1963)

Besant, Sir Walter 1836–1901
English novelist and social reformer

Born in Portsmouth, he studied at King's College London and at Christ's College, Cambridge, and after a few years as a professor in Mauritius, devoted himself to literature. In 1871 he entered into a literary partnership with **James Rice**, and together they produced many novels, including *Ready-Money Mortiboy* (1872) and *The Steamy Side* (1881). Besant himself wrote *All Sorts and Conditions of Men* (1882) and *Children of Gibeon* (1886), describing conditions in the slums of the East End of London, and other novels advocating social reform, resulting in the establishment of the People's Palace, London (1887), for popular recreation. He was secretary of the Palestine Exploration Fund and first chairman of the Incorporated Society of Authors (1884). He was the brother-in-law of **Annie Besant**. 📖 F W Sage, *Sir Walter Besant, novelist* (1956)

Bessarion or Basilius, John 1403–72
Byzantine theologian

Born in Trebizond (Trabzon), he was educated in Constantinople (Istanbul). As Archbishop of Nicaea (Iznik) from 1437, he accompanied the Greek Emperor, John Palaeologus, to the Councils of Ferrara and Florence in Italy, to bring about union between the Byzantine and Latin Churches (1438). He joined the Roman Church, was made a cardinal by Pope **Eugenius IV** (1439), served as Papal Governor of Bologna (1450–55), and was twice nearly elected pope. He was one of the earliest scholars to transplant Greek literature and philosophy into the West.

Bessel, Friedrich Wilhelm 1784–1846
German mathematician and astronomer

Born in Minden, Westphalia, he started as a ship's clerk but in 1810 was appointed director of the observatory and professor at Königsberg. He catalogued stars and was the first to identify the nearest stars and determine their distances. He predicted the existence of a planet beyond Uranus as well as the existence of dark stars. In the course of this work he systematized the mathematical functions involved, which today bear his name, although **Joseph Fourier** had worked on them earlier. 📖 Henry S Williams, *The Great Astronomers* (1930)

Bessemer, Sir Henry 1813–98
English metallurgist and inventor

Born in Charlton, Hertfordshire, he learned metallurgy in his father's type foundry, and at the age of 17 set up his own business in London to produce small castings and art work. In 1840 he developed a method for the production of bronze powder and 'gold' paint, at a fraction of the cost of the long-established German process. The profits from this enterprise enabled him to set up his own small iron-works at St Pancras in London. In 1855, as a result of his efforts to find a method of manufacturing stronger gun-barrels for use in the Crimean War (1853–56), he patented an economical process by which molten pig-iron can be turned directly into steel by blowing air through it in a 'Bessemer converter'. Bessemer established a steelworks at Sheffield in 1859, which expanded from armaments to meet the worldwide demand for steel rails,

locomotives and bridges. He was elected FRS in 1877 and knighted in 1879. Other English steelmasters were reluctant to accept Bessemer's process, but in the USA entrepreneurs like **Andrew Carnegie** made a fortune from it. 📖 *An Autobiography* (1905)

Bessmertnova, Natalia 1941–
Soviet ballerina

Born in Moscow, she trained at the Bolshoi Ballet School (1952–61), joining the company on graduation. She has become famous for her interpretation of all the major roles of the classical repertory. She has also taken important roles in ballets devised by her husband **Yuri Grigorovich**, particularly *Ivan the Terrible* (1975). She was awarded the Lenin prize in 1986.

Besson, Jacques c.1535–c.1575
French mathematician, engineer and inventor

Born in Grenoble, he is remembered for his *Théâtre des Instruments mathématiques et méchaniques* (1578), which anticipated similar works by **Agostino Ramelli** and Vittorio Zonca (1568–1603), Italian engineers who reflected the growing interest in machines, practical and impractical, at the end of the 16th century. His plates illustrate devices ranging from an already well-known type of dredging vessel, through improved designs for screw-cutting lathes and fire-engines, to sketches in the realms of fantasy such as a ship that would speed up as the strength of the wind dropped.

Besson, Luc 1959–
French film director

Born in Paris, he worked as an unpaid assistant on international productions like *Moonraker* (1979), and directed a number of short films and commercials before his feature debut *Le Dernier combat* (1983, 'The Last Battle'). He enjoyed great popular success with the thriller *Subway* (1985) and the globe-trotting saga *The Big Blue* (1988). Telling original stories with remarkable visual flair and technical virtuosity, his subsequent feature films include *Nikita* (1990), *Leon* (1994) and *The Fifth Element* (1997). He has also directed documentaries and pop videos.

Best, Charles Herbert 1899–1978
Canadian physiologist

He was born in West Pembroke, Maine, and graduated in physiology and biochemistry from the University of Toronto. As a research student there in 1921 he helped **Frederick Banting** to isolate the hormone insulin, used in the treatment of diabetes. (Banting gave him a share of his 1923 Nobel Prize for physiology or medicine.) In 1929 Best succeeded **John Macleod** as Professor of Physiology at Toronto, and on Banting's death in 1941 he became director of the Banting and Best department of medical research. He enjoyed considerable success during his later career. He discovered choline (a vitamin that prevents liver damage) and histaminase (the enzyme that breaks down histamine), introduced the use of the anticoagulant, heparin, and continued to work on insulin, showing in 1936 that the administration of zinc with insulin can prolong its activity.

Best, George 1946–
Northern Irish footballer

Born in Belfast, he is considered the greatest individual footballing talent ever produced by Northern Ireland. He was the leading scorer for Manchester United in the Football League First Division in 1967–68, and in 1968 won a European Cup medal and the title of European Footballer of the Year. However, he became increasingly unable to cope with the pressure of top-class football, and was virtually finished by the time he was 25 years old. His attempted come-backs with smaller clubs in

England, the USA and Scotland were unsuccessful, but in his short time as a player he had made himself one of the game's immortals. ☐ Michael Parkinson, *Best* (1975)

Bestall, A(lfred) E(dmeades) 1892–1986
English illustrator and author

He was born in Manderlay, Burma. Although his drawings appeared in many books, including four volumes of the *Boys and Girls Annual* (1935–36), and several issues of the *Tatler* and *Punch*, he is mainly remembered for having illustrated and written the Rupert Bear picture strip in the *Daily Express* newspaper for 30 years (1935–65), taking over from Rupert's creator, Mary Tourtel. He also illustrated and wrote 41 volumes of the *Rupert Bear Annual* (1936–76). Rupert's inquisitive, white furry face, red pull-over and yellow check trousers and scarf are known to millions through Bestall's drawings. ☐ A Bestall and G Perry, *Rupert: A Bear's Life* (1985)

Betancourt, Rómulo 1908–81
Venezuelan statesman and reformer

He was born in Guatire, Miranda. One of the founders of the Acción Democrática Party, he held power from 1945 to 1947. On the fall of the Pérez Jiménez dictatorship (1950–58), he was elected President (1959–64) of the new Venezuelan democracy. He chose a moderate course, adopting an agrarian law (1960), and ambitious economic development plans which provided for a transition from the dictatorship.

Bethe, Hans Albrecht 1906–
US physicist and Nobel Prize winner

Born in Strassburg, Germany (now Strasbourg, France), he was educated at the universities of Frankfurt and Munich. He taught in Germany until 1933 when he moved first to England and then to the USA, where he held the chair of physics at Cornell University until his retirement (1935–75, now emeritus). During World War II he was director of theoretical physics for the Manhattan atomic bomb project based at Los Alamos. In 1939 he proposed the first detailed theory for the generation of energy by stars through a series of nuclear reactions. He also contributed with Ralph Alpher and George Gamow to the 'alpha, beta, gamma' theory of the origin of the chemical elements during the early development of the universe. He was awarded the 1967 Nobel Prize for physics. ☐ Jeremy Bernstein, *Hans Bethe, Prophet of Energy* (1980)

Bethlen, István (Stephen), Count 1874–1951
Hungarian statesman

Born in Gernyeszeg (Cornesti), Transylvania, he was a leader of the counter-revolutionary movement after World War I, and as Prime Minister (1921–31) promoted Hungary's economic reconstruction.

Bethlen, Gábor or Gabriel 1580–1629
King of Hungary

Born into a Hungarian Calvinist family, he was elected Prince of Transylvania (1613). Fierce, unscrupulous, yet astute, in 1619 he invaded Hungary and, although he soon lost the royal title, he forced Emperor Ferdinand II to grant religious freedom to the Hungarian Protestants and to recognize his authority in several Hungarian provinces, making him titular king (1620–21). Gábor resumed hostilities against the empire (1623, 1626), but his declining health precluded further success.

Bethmann Hollweg, Theobald von 1856–1921
German statesman

Born in Hohenfinow, Brandenburg, he qualified in law, then rose in the service of Prussia and the German Empire, becoming Imperial Chancellor in 1909. Although not identified with the German élite's most bellicose elements, and fearing the effects of war upon German society, he nevertheless played an important part in the events which brought about general war in 1914. Anxious for a negotiated peace in 1917, he was forced from office. He wrote *Reflections on the World War* (1920).

Bethune, David See Beaton, David

Bethune, James See Beaton, James

Bethune, Jennie Louise, *née* Blanchard 1856–1913
US architect

Born in Waterloo, New York, she was educated by her parents. She expressed an interest in buildings and prepared to attend Cornell University to study architecture, but instead took an apprenticeship with Richard Waite in an established architectural practice. She soon became his assistant and received what was considered a man's training in a male profession. When she was 25 she opened her own office in Buffalo, where she had moved with her family. She married a colleague from Waite's office, Robert Bethune, and set up a partnership with him. Her reputation gained an enthusiastic reception when she was admitted to the Western Association of Architects in 1885. In 1888 she was granted a fellowship to the American Institute of Architects, the first woman to be so honoured.

Bethune, Mary McLeod, *née* McLeod 1875–1955
US educator and administrator

Born in Mayesville, South Carolina, to parents who had been slaves before the American Civil War, she began her career by teaching in Southern schools. In 1904 she opened the Daytona Normal and Industrial Institute for Girls, which merged in 1923 with the Cookman Institute to become the co-educational Bethune–Cookman College, of which Bethune was president until 1942, then again from 1946 to 1947. She was also founder-president of the National Council of Negro Women (1935–49). She was director of the division of Negro Affairs within the National Youth Administration, and insisted that the number of blacks enrolled in the programme be increased despite the reluctance of state administrators (there was a 40 per cent unemployment rate among black youths). She also administered the Special Negro Fund which assisted many black college students, and was sent by the State Department to attend the San Francisco Conference to establish the United Nations (1945).

Bethune, Norman 1899–1939
Canadian surgeon

He was born in Gravenhurst, Ontario, the son of a clergyman. He interrupted his medical studies at Toronto University to enlist in the Canadian Expeditionary Force in 1914, but, invalided home the following year, he completed his medical education and rejoined the war effort as a surgeon-lieutenant. In the 1920s he contracted tuberculosis which drew him into chest surgery, especially the surgical treatment of tuberculosis. He worked as a surgeon in the Spanish Civil War in 1936–37, and in 1938–39 he was in China with the Eight Route Army, during the war with Japan. He died of septicaemia following a cut acquired while operating on a wounded Chinese soldier, and became a national hero in China.

Béthune, Quesnes de See Conon de Béthune

Betjeman, Sir John See panel p195

Bettelheim, Bruno 1903–90
US psychologist and educator

Born in Vienna, Austria, he was incarcerated in the Nazi concentration camps Dachau and Buchenwald the same year he was awarded his PhD from the University of Vienna (1938), and on his release in 1939 he emigrated to the USA. His article 'Individual and Mass Behavior in

---

Betjeman, Sir John 1906–84
English poet, broadcaster and writer on architecture

John Betjeman was born in Highgate, London. His father, who was of Dutch descent, was a manufacturer of household objects. He was educated at Highgate Junior School (where T S Eliot was one of his teachers), Marlborough School and Magdalen College, Oxford (where he met and got to know W H Auden and Louis MacNeice). The early period of his life is dealt with in his blank-verse autobiography, *Summoned by Bells* (1960). He left university without a degree, and marked time as a cricket master in a preparatory school. He was sacked as the *Evening Standard*'s film critic, but went on to write for the *Architectural Review* and became general editor of the *Shell Guides* in 1934.

He wrote the bleak 'Death in Leamington' for the *London Mercury* in 1930 and a year later his first collection of verse, *Mount Zion; or In Touch with the Infinite* was published. Other collections include *Continual Dew; A Little Book of Bourgeois Verse* (1937), *Old Lights for New Chancels* (1940), *New Bats in Old Belfries* (1945), *A Few Late Chrysanthemums* (1954) and *Collected Poems* (1958), of which 100,000 copies were sold of the first edition; a larger second edition appeared in 1962. Later (but lesser) volumes are *A Nip in the Air* (1972) and *High and Low* (1976).

Betjeman's passionate interest in architecture (especially of Victorian churches) and topography led to the publication of a number of books, including *Ghastly Good Taste* (1933, subtitled 'a depressing story of the rise and fall of English architecture'), *Vintage London* (1942) and *Cornwall* (1965), and is also reflected in his poetry.

He was the quintessential poet of the suburbs, particular, jolly, nostalgic and wary of change, preferring the countryside to the city. Inveterately self-deprecatory, he described himself as 'the Ella Wheeler Wilcox de nos jours', and in *Who's Who* as a 'poet and hack'. He was an astute and sensitive social critic, impassioned in his abhorrence of modern architecture and town planning ('Come, friendly bombs, and fall on Slough. It isn't fit for humans now'), and beneath the froth lies a poet undeniably melancholic and serious. He frequently broadcast on radio and television, and wrote *Metro-land*, a script for television, in 1973. He was knighted in 1969 and won the Duff Cooper Memorial prize. He succeeded Cecil Day Lewis as Poet Laureate in 1972. He is buried in the churchyard at St Endellion in Cornwall.

📖 P Denton, *Betjeman's London* (1989); B Hillier, *Young Betjeman* (1988, the first volume of an authorized biography); D Stanford, *John Betjeman: A Study* (1961); J Guest, *The Best of Betjeman* (an anthology).

'Think of what our Nation stands for,
Books from Boots' and country lanes,
Free speech, free passes, class distinction,
Democracy and proper drains.
Lord, put beneath Thy special care
One-eighty-nine Cadogan Square.'
Old Lights for New Chancels, 'In Westminster Abbey' (1940).

Extreme Situations' was based on his experiences in the camps. As a professor at the University of Chicago (1944–73), he directed a school for emotionally disturbed and autistic children and wrote numerous works, including *Love Is Not Enough* (1950), *The Informed Heart* (1960) and *The Uses of Enchantment: The Meaning and Importance of Fairy Tales* (1976, National Book award).

Betterton, Thomas c.1635–1710
English actor, theatre manager and adapter of dramas

Born in London, he joined the acting company which reopened the Cockpit theatre in Drury Lane in 1660, and the following year joined Sir William D'Avenant's company at Lincoln's Inn Fields Theatre. After D'Avenant's death in 1671, Betterton moved to the Dorset Garden Theatre, and then the Theatre Royal, Drury Lane, when the two companies amalgamated (1682). In 1695 he reopened the Lincoln's Inn Fields Theatre. A fine actor and a shrewd manager, he tailored many of Shakespeare's plays to suit the audiences of the times. He also wrote plays of his own, including *The Amorous Widow* (1667), and adapted a text for Henry Purcell's semi-opera *The Prophetess, or The History of Dioclesian* (1690). He is considered one of the most outstanding personalities of the Restoration era. His wife, Mary Sanderson (d.1712), was one of the first English actresses and shared his stage triumphs.

Betti, Ugo 1892–1953
Italian dramatist and poet

Born in Camerino, he studied law, and became a judge in Rome (1930–44) and librarian of the Ministry of Justice (1944–53). His poetry includes the verses in *Re pensieroso* (1922, 'The Meditative King'), and among his short-story collections are *Caino* (1929, 'Cain') and *Le Case* (1937, 'Houses'). In his best play, *La Padrona* (1929), life appears symbolically in the person of a cynical, masterful and attractive woman. *Corruzione al Palazzo di Giustizia* (1944,

Eng trans *Corruption in the Palace of Justice*, 1957) and *La fuggitiva* (1953, 'The Fugitive') deal mercilessly with his own profession. 📖 G Moro, *Il teatro di Ugo Betti* (1973)

Betty, William Henry West, *known as* Young Roscius 1791–1874
English actor

He was born in Shrewsbury, Shropshire, and made his debut at the age of 11. He met with considerable success as a child prodigy but retired from the stage in 1808. After studying for two years at Cambridge, he returned to acting (1812) and retired finally in 1824.

Beuckelaer or Bueckelaer, Joachim c.1530–1573
Flemish painter

He worked in Antwerp. He was very much influenced by his uncle and teacher Pieter Aertsen. Like Aertsen, he painted still lifes and market pieces, and he was the first painter to specialize in depicting fish stalls.

Beust, Friedrich Ferdinand, Count von 1809–86
Saxon and Austrian politician

Born in Dresden, he was appointed Foreign Secretary (1866–71) and Imperial Chancellor (1867–71), then ambassador in London (1871–78) and Paris (1878–82). His chief achievement was the reconciliation of Hungary to Austria (the Ausgleich, 1867).

Beuys, Joseph 1921–86
German avant-garde artist

Born in Kleve, he served as a pilot in the Luftwaffe in World War II, during which he was shot down, and he then studied art at the Düsseldorf Academy, where he later became Professor of Sculpture (1961–71). His sculpture consisted mainly of assemblages of bits and pieces of rubbish, which were also included as elements of 'happenings' which he organized. His work, which had links with the Italian movement known as Arte Povera, flouted the conventions even of modern art, being deliberately anti-formal and banal. An exhibition of his unconventional drawings toured Great Britain and Ireland in 1974. He was also a prominent political activist and crusader for direct democracy, and helped to found the Green Party in Germany.

Bevan, Aneurin 1897–1960
Welsh Labour politician

Born in Tredegar, Monmouthshire, he was one of 13 children of a miner. He began work in the pits at the age of 13. Six years later he was chairman of a Miners' Lodge of more than 4,000 members. Active in trade unionism in the South Wales coalfield, he led the Welsh miners in the 1926 General Strike. Elected as the Independent Labour Party (ILP) MP for Ebbw Vale (1929), he joined the more moderate Labour Party in 1931, establishing a reputation as a brilliant, irreverent and often tempestuous orator. In 1934 he married **Jennie Lee**. During World War II he was frequently a 'one-man Opposition' against **Churchill**. Appointed Minister of Health in the 1945 Labour government, he introduced the revolutionary National Health Service in 1948. He became Minister of Labour in 1951, but resigned the same year over the National Health charges proposed in the Budget. From this period dated 'Bevanism', the left-wing movement aimed at making the Labour Party more socialist and less 'reformist'. It made Bevan the centre of prolonged and often bitter disputes with his party leaders, but the movement began to wither late in 1956 when he became Shadow Foreign Secretary. He ceased to be a 'Bevanite' at the 1957 Brighton party conference when he opposed a one-sided renunciation of the hydrogen bomb by Great Britain. The most publicized Labour politician of his time, he brought to the Commons radical fervour, iconoclastic restlessness and an acute intellect. He published *In Place of Fear* (1952). 🕮 Michael Foot, *Aneurin Bevan* (2 vols, 1975)

Bevan, Edward John 1856–1921
English industrial chemist

Born in Birkenhead, he studied chemistry at Owens College, Manchester, and became a consulting chemist. In 1892, with Charles Cross, he patented the viscose process of rayon manufacture. The process uses cellulose (wood pulp) which is dissolved and then regenerated, forming either yarn (rayon) or film (cellophane). This process laid the foundations of the synthetic textile industry. Cross and Bevan also initiated many improvements in paper-making.

Beveridge, William Henry Beveridge, 1st Baron 1879–1963
British economist, administrator and social reformer

Born of Scottish descent in Rangpur, Bengal, he was educated at Charterhouse and Balliol College, Oxford. As leader writer on the *Morning Post*, he made himself the leading authority on unemployment insurance, and compiled his notable report, *Unemployment* (1909, revised 1930). He entered the Board of Trade in 1908 and became director of Labour Exchanges (1909–16). He was director of the London School of Economics (1919–37) and Master of University College, Oxford (1937–45). From 1934 he served on several commissions and committees and was the author of the *Report on Social Insurance and Allied Services* (1942), known as 'The Beveridge Report'. This was a comprehensive scheme of social insurance, covering the whole community without income limit. Published at the height of World War II, it was a remarkable testimony to Great Britain's hopes for the future, and provided the basis for the creation of the welfare state. He was elected as a Liberal MP in 1944, but defeated in 1945. He was made a baron in 1946. He wrote the autobiographical *Power*

and Influence (1953), and books on unemployment and social security. 🕮 John Williams and Tony Keynes, *Beveridge, and Beyond* (1987)

Beverton, Raymond John Heaphy 1922–95
English marine biologist

Born in London, he graduated from Cambridge (1947), and began his career as research officer at the Fisheries Laboratory, Lowestoft (1947–59), subsequently becoming deputy director there (1959–65). He was later appointed secretary and chief executive of the Natural Environment Research Council (1965–80) and Professor of Fisheries Ecology at the University of Wales Institute of Science and Technology (1984–87). In early studies of the North Sea plaice population he noted its remarkable constancy, despite the high natural mortality rates of the early stages of fish. His studies of the mechanisms which control the early life-history stages helped him to resolve the problem of how to allow smaller fish to reach full growth before harvesting them. In Beverton's classic text *On the Dynamics of Exploited Fish Populations* (1957) his 'yield per recruit' and subsequent 'stock and recruitment' models provided fisheries scientists with a convenient and elegant means of predicting the commercial fishing pressure that natural stocks could withstand. He was elected FRS in 1975.

Bevin, Ernest 1881–1951
English Labour politician

He was born in Winsford, Somerset, and orphaned by the age of seven. In 1894 he moved to Bristol to earn his living as a van boy and later a van driver. Self-educated, he came early under the influence of trade unionism and the Baptists, and was for a time a lay preacher. At the age of 30 he was a paid official of the dockers' union and in 1920 he earned himself a national reputation by his mostly successful handling of his union's claims before a wage tribunal at which he was opposed by an eminent barrister. This won him the title 'the dockers' KC'. He built up the gigantic National Transport and General Workers' Union from 32 separate unions and became its general secretary (1921–40). He was one of the leaders in the General Strike (1926), served on the Macmillan Committee on finance, and furthered the work of the International Labour Organization. In 1940 he became Minister of Labour and National Service in **Churchill**'s coalition government, successfully attained complete mobilization of Great Britain's manpower by 1943 and was a significant member of the War Cabinet. He began to take a keen interest in foreign affairs and became Foreign Secretary in **Clement Atlee**'s Labour government (1945–51). In this office he was responsible for the satisfactory conclusion of peace treaties with south-east European countries and with Italy, despite growing Soviet disinclination to co-operate. He accepted the necessity for the Western powers to establish a federal government in Western Germany and by the Berlin air lift (June 1948–May 1949) accepted and met the Soviet challenge for the control of that city. He was largely responsible for the successful conclusion of mutual assistance (1948) and defence agreements (1949) with other European powers and the USA, but opposed total integration of European states, believing that Great Britain had special Commonwealth obligations, acquiescing reluctantly in the formation of a Council of Europe. He failed to settle the difficult problem of Palestine, which he handed over to the United Nations. He concluded a new treaty with Egypt (1946) and arranged on his own initiative the meeting of the Commonwealth Foreign Ministers (1950) out of which emerged the 'Colombo Plan'. Ill health made him relinquish office in March 1951, and he died a month later. His wife, Florence Anne (d.1968), was made DBE in 1952, largely as a recognition of her husband's services. The pioneer of modern trade unionism, Bevin was essentially a skilled and moderate negotiator, robust, down-to-earth, a 'John Bull' of trade unionists. He believed that he might be able to achieve world peace and conciliation in the manner he had successfully applied in union affairs, but he was essentially a realist, and his realism earned him the censure of the more left-wing elements in his party as well as the esteem of many of his political opponents. He wrote *The Job to be Done* (1942). 📖 Alan Bullock, *The Life and Times of Ernest Bevin* (3 vols, 1960–83)

Bewick, Thomas 1753–1828
English wood-engraver
Born in Ovingham, Northumberland, he was apprenticed aged 14 to Ralph Beilby (1744–1817), a Newcastle engraver; he became his partner in 1776 and, taking his brother John (1760–95) as an apprentice, consolidated his reputation with his woodcuts for *Gay's Fables* (1779). His other works include *History of Quadrupeds* (1790), *Chillingham Bull* (1789) and *History of British Birds* (1797–1804), which included decorative arrangements in black and white, and renderings of landscape and rustic life. He later produced *Aesop's Fables* (1818), in which he was assisted by his son, Robert Elliott (1788–1849), who became his partner in 1812 and also took part in the cuts for an unfinished *History of British Fishes*. Bewick's Swan was named in his honour shortly after his death. 📖 Basil Anderson, *Thomas Bewick, the Tyneside Engraver* (1928)

Beyatli, Yahya Kemal 1884–1958
Turkish poet and critic
He was born in Skopje, Macedonia. A diplomat and member of parliament, he was also a neoclassical poet of great technical excellence. He remained active in Turkish literature until his death, when he was given a massive state funeral. 📖 A H Tanipar, *Yayha Kemal* (1962)

Beza, Theodorus, *also called* Théodore de Bèze 1519–1605
French reformer
Born of a noble family at Vézelay, Burgundy, he studied Greek and law at Orleans. He became well known as a writer of witty (but indecent) verses in *Juvenilia* (1548), and settled in Paris where he became part of fashionable society. Eventually taking a more mature view of life, he married his mistress, and in 1548 went with her to Geneva, where he joined John Calvin. From 1549 to 1554 he was Professor of Greek at Lausanne, and in 1559, with Calvin, he founded the academy at Geneva and became Professor of Theology and first Rector there. On Calvin's death (1564) Beza took over responsibility for the Genevese church. He presided over the synods of French reformers held at La Rochelle in 1571 and at Nîmes in 1572. His best-known work is the Latin New Testament, and his only important literary work is a drama on *The Sacrifice of Abraham*. 📖 P F Geisendorf, *Théodore de Bèze* (1949)

Bèze, Théodore de See Beza, Theodorus

Bhabha, Homi Jehangir 1909–66
Indian physicist
He was born and educated in Bombay before entering Cambridge in 1927, where his tutor was **Paul Dirac**. He became professor at the Indian Institute of Science in Bangalore in 1941, the same year that he was elected Fellow of the Royal Society. In 1945 he became director of the Tata Institute for Fundamental Research in Bombay, and then director of the Indian Atomic Energy Commission. In 1948 he was appointed director of the Atomic Energy Research Centre, posthumously renamed the Bhabha Atomic Research Centre. In his early career he derived a correct expression for the probability of scattering positrons by electrons, a process now known as Bhabha scattering. His classic paper on cosmic-ray showers (1937) described how primary cosmic rays from space interact with the upper atmosphere to produce particles observed at ground level. This paper also demonstrated the existence of muons, 'fast, unstable cosmic-ray particles'. In 1938 Bhabha was the first to conclude that observations of the properties of such particles would lead to the straightforward experimental verification of **Albert Einstein**'s special relativity theory.

Bharati, C Subramania, *pseudonym of* C Subramania Iyer 1882–1921
Indian (Tamil) writer, translator and poet
He was the sole Tamil poet of the 20th century to understand that the earlier traditions of Tamil literature must be preserved, but that mere imitation was inadequate, and the first to enrich his language with the vernacular idiom without violating its essence. His work includes the long poems *Kannan pattu* (1917, 'The Krishna Songs'), *Pancali capatam* (1912, 'Panchali's Vow') and *Kuyil pattu* (1912, 'Kuyil's Song'), this last being the lyrical dream of a poet who listens to stories told to him by a cuckoo. He translated some of **Rabindranath Tagore** into Tamil. He spent the last years of his life virtually in exile in Pondicherry because of his activities on behalf of the Congress Party.

Bhartrihari fl.7th century
Hindu poet and philosopher
He was the author of three *satakas* (centuries) of stanzas on practical conduct, love, and renunciation of the world, and a Sanskrit grammarian. 📖 *The Proverbial Philosophy of Bhartrihari* (1890)

Bhasa fl.3rd century AD
Sanskrit dramatist
He was the author of plays on religious and legendary themes. 📖 A D Pusalkar, *Bhasa: a study* (1940)

Bhattacharya, Narendranath See Roy Manabendra Nath

Bhattari, Krishna Prasad 1925–
Nepalese statesman
As an opponent of absolute monarchy, he was in hiding for 12 years until 1990, when, as leader of the centrist Nepali Congress Party, he became Prime Minister in the wake of the revolution that year, which ended the uncontested rule of King **Birendra**. However, in Nepal's first multi-party elections in three decades (1991), he offered his resignation to the king after losing his own seat in the 205-member House of Representatives to the Marxist leader of the United Communist Party, Madan Bhandari.

Bhavabhûti, *surnamed* Srî-Kantha fl.8th century
Indian dramatist
He flourished in 730, and is regarded as one of the great Indian dramatists. 📖 Vimla Gera, *The Mind and Art of Bhavabhûti* (1973)

Bhave, Vinoba 1895–1982
Indian land reformer
Born in a Maharashtra village, he was taken into the care of **Mahatma Gandhi** as a young scholar, an event which changed his life. Distressed by the land hunger riots in Telengana, Hyderabad (1951), he began a walking mission throughout India to persuade landlords to give land to the peasants. A barefoot, ascetic saint, his silent revolution led to 4,000,000 acres of land being redistributed in four years. He was claimed to be the most notable spiritual figure in India after the death of Gandhi, whose ardent disciple he was.

Bhindranwale, Sant Jarnail Singh 1947–84
Indian politician and Sikh extremist leader
Born into a poor Punjabi Jat farming family, he trained at the orthodox Damdani Taksal Sikh missionary school, becoming its head priest in 1971 and assuming the name Bhindranwale. Initially encouraged by Sanjay Gandhi

Bhutto, Benazir 1953–
Pakistani politician, the first modern-day woman leader of a Muslim nation

Benazir Bhutto was born in Karachi, the daughter of the former Prime Minister **Zulfikar Ali Bhutto**, and of Begum Nusrat Bhutto, also a politician. She was educated at Oxford University, where she became president of the Union. She returned to Pakistan in 1977; after the military coup led by General **Mohammed Zia ul-Haq**, in which her father was executed (1979), she was placed under house arrest at frequent intervals until 1984.

Between 1984 and 1986, she and her mother lived in England, and she became the joint leader in exile of the opposition Pakistan People's Party (PPP). Martial law was lifted in Pakistan in December 1985, and she returned the following April to launch a nationwide campaign for open elections. In 1988 she was elected Prime Minister, after the death of Zia in mysterious circumstances. Only three months before, she had given birth to her first child, having married Asif Ali Zardari, a wealthy landowner, in 1987. (She appointed him Minister of Investments in 1996.)

In her first term, she achieved an uneasy compromise with the army and improved relations with India; and she led Pakistan back into the Commonwealth in 1989. She also became, in 1990, the first head of government to bear a child while in office. That year her government was removed from office by presidential decree, and she was accused of corruption. She was later defeated in the elections, but was returned to power in the elections of 1993. In September 1995 the armed forces were discovered to have hatched a plot to remove her; and a year later her brother Murtaza was killed during a gun battle with police. Defeated in the 1997 election, she continues to live under the threat of constant political abuse and personal violence.

📖 Her autobiography is *Daughter of the East* (1988). See also *Trial of Benazir Bhutto: An Insight into the Status of Women in Islam* (1990).

> 'When I had my last meeting with my father in jail, he said: I leave the choice to you. You don't have to continue the struggle. You've suffered enough. I said, No, Papa, I'll never leave the struggle. At that moment I realised that I could not leave it. Too many people had lost their lives.'
> Quoted in *The Independent*, 28 September 1996.

(1946–80), the son and political adviser of **Indira Gandhi**, who sought to divide the Sikh Akali Dal movement, he campaigned violently against the heretical activities of Nirankari Sikhs during the later 1970s. His campaign broadened into a demand for a separate state of 'Khalistan' during the early 1980s, precipitating a bloody Hindu–Sikh conflict in Punjab. After taking refuge in the Golden Temple complex at Amritsar and building up an arms cache for terrorist activities, with about 500 devoted followers, he died at the hands of the Indian Security Forces who stormed the temple in 'Operation Blue Star'.

Bhumibol Adulyadej 1927–
King of Thailand

Born in Cambridge, Massachusetts, USA, he is the second son of Prince Mahidol of Songkhla and grandson of King **Chulalongkorn** (Rama V). He was educated in Bangkok and Switzerland, and became monarch as King Rama IX (1946) after the assassination of his elder brother, King Ananda Mahidol. He married Queen Sirikit in 1950 and has one son, Crown Prince Vajiralongkorn (1952–), and three daughters. As king, he has been the focus of unity and a stabilizing influence in a country noted for its political turbulence, and he was active, with popular support, in helping to overthrow the military government of Field Marshal Thanom Kittikachorn (1973). During his reign, Thailand has undergone 10 successful military coups and that of General Suchinda Kraprayoon in 1991 was reverted the following year when Bhumibol intervened, bringing about Suchinda's subsequent resignation. Now the longest reigning monarch in Thailand's history, he is a highly respected figure, viewed in some quarters as semi-divine, and he wields considerable political influence.

Bhutto, Benazir See panel above

Bhutto, Zulfikar Ali 1928–79
Pakistani statesman

Born in Larkana in the province of Sind in British-ruled India, he was the son of a landed aristocrat. A graduate of the universities of California and Oxford, he began a career in law and joined the Pakistani Cabinet in 1958 as Minister of Commerce, and became Foreign Minister in 1963. Dropped from the Cabinet, he founded the Pakistan People's Party (PPP) in 1967. After the secession of East Pakistan (Bangladesh) in 1971, he became President (1971–73) and Prime Minister (1973–77). He introduced social and economic reforms, but opposition to his policies, especially from right-wing Islamic parties, led to the army (under General Zia ul-Haq) seizing control after the 1977 elections. Tried for corruption and murder, he was sentenced to death in 1978. In spite of worldwide appeals for clemency, the sentence was carried out in 1979. His elder daughter, **Benazir Bhutto**, became PPP leader. 📖 Salmaan Taseer, *Bhutto: A Political Biography* (1979)

Bialik, Chaim Nachman 1873–1934
Hebrew poet

He was born in the Ukraine. After studying the Talmud in Odessa, he returned to his home near Zhitomir and became a wood merchant, at which he failed disastrously. **Maxim Gorky** helped him to emigrate in 1921 to Berlin, where he established the Devir publishing house. When he went to Palestine in 1924 he took this with him. His poetry is always cast in a personal form, and is often uninhibitedly erotic. His works include an influential anthology of the *Aggadah* (folk poetry). 📖 M Waxman, *A History of Jewish Literature* (1947)

Bianchi, Kenneth Alessio, *known as* the Hillside Strangler 1950–
US murderer

He was born in Rochester, New York, and adopted by a couple named Bianchi. He married in 1971, but was soon deserted by his wife and moved to Los Angeles to stay with his cousin, Angelo Buono. There he enjoyed a life of drug-taking and promiscuity, and found a job and his own accommodation. In 1977 a series of 10 murders began; all the victims were women who had been stripped naked and strangled. In 1978, after splitting up with his girlfriend and the mother of his child, he moved to Bellingham, Washington, where he again found work. In January 1979 two more women were found strangled and Bianchi was arrested. Questioned under hypnosis, he claimed to be a man called Steve who was indeed the 'Hillside Strangler'. Buono too was implicated and charged with one murder. After a trial lasting five years, Bianchi was sentenced to five life sentences, but he always claimed it was Steve and not he who had committed the crimes.

Biandrata, Giorgio See **Blandrata, Giorgio**

Bias 6th century BC
Greek orator
A native of Priene, Ionia, he became famous for his pithy
sayings, and was one of the 'Seven Wise Men' of Greece (the
others were Chilon, Cleobulus, Periander, Pittacus of
Mitylene, Solon and Thales).

Bichat, Marie François Xavier 1771–1802
French physician
Born in Thoirette, Jura, he studied medicine, first in
Lyons, but his education was interrupted by military service during the Revolution. He settled in Paris in 1793 at
the height of the Terror, and from 1797 taught medicine,
from 1801 working at the Hôtel-Dieu, Paris's huge hospital for the poor. Performing his researches with great
fervour during the last years of his short life, he carried
out over 600 post-mortems. His lasting importance lay in
simplifying anatomy and physiology, by showing how the
complex structures of organs could be grasped in terms of
their elementary tissues.

Bickerstaffe, Isaac c.1735–c.1812
Irish playwright
Born in Dublin, he became page to Lord Chesterfield,
the Lord Lieutenant. Later he was an officer of marines,
but was dismissed from the service on the suspicion of
committing a capital offence, and in 1772 had to flee the
country. Of his numerous pieces, produced between 1760
and 1771, the best known is *The Maid of the Mill*, and he is
credited with establishing the comic opera in the English
theatre. Among his musical collaborators were Thomas
Arne and Samuel Arnold (1740–1802). ▣ P A Tasch, *The
Dramatic Cobbler* (1971)

Bickford, William 1774–1834
English inventor
He was born in Bickington, near Ashburton in Devon,
and set up as a leather merchant in Tuckingmill, near
Camborne in Cornwall. Though unconnected with
mining, he was distressed by the frequent accidents
caused by premature detonation of explosive charges in
mines. After several attempts he was successful in combining gunpowder and flax yarn into a reliable slow-
burning fuse, which he patented in 1831.

Bidault, Georges 1899–1983
French statesman
He was born and educated in Paris, where he became a
professor of history and edited the Catholic newspaper
L'Aube. He served in both world wars, was taken prisoner in
World War II, was released, and took part in the French
Resistance movement. He then became leader of the
Mouvement Républicain Populaire (MRP) and was Prime
Minister (1946, 1949–50), deputy Prime Minister (1950,
1951), and Foreign Minister (1944, 1947, 1953–54).
Although devoted to French interests, he supported many
measures of European co-operation. Prime Minister again
in 1958, he opposed General de Gaulle over the Algerian
War, and was charged with plotting against the security of
the state. He was in exile from 1962 to 1968.

Bidder, George Parker 1806–78
English engineer and mathematician
Born in Moreton-Hampstead, Devon, he showed an early
gift for arithmetical calculations, giving public demonstrations as the 'Calculating Boy'. He was educated at
Camberwell and Edinburgh, and became a civil engineer, inventing the railway swing bridge and designing
the Royal Victoria Docks, London, which were opened in
1856. He was also a parliamentary adviser.

Biddle, John 1615–62
English preacher and the founder of English Unitarianism

Born in Wotton-under-Edge, Gloucestershire, he studied
at Magdalen Hall, Oxford. In 1641 he was elected Master of
the Gloucester Free School, but in 1645 was put
in prison for rejecting in his preaching the deity of the Holy
Ghost. After years of controversy, during which time a
work by him (1647) was burnt by the hangman as blasphemous, he was finally banished to the Scilly Isles in 1655.
On his release in 1658, he continued to preach in London
until after the Restoration. Arrested again in 1662, he could
not pay his fine of £100, and was sent to jail where he died.

Biela, Wilhelm von 1782–1856
Austrian army officer and astronomer
Born in Russia, he observed in 1826 the periodic comet
named after him, although it had already been seen in 1772
by Jacques Leibax Montaigne and by Jean-Louis Pons in
1825. Carl Friedrich Gauss computed the orbit and the
period eventually turned out to be 6.75 years.

Bierce, Ambrose Gwinnett 1842–1914
US short-story writer and journalist
Born in Meigs County, Ohio, he grew up in Indiana and
fought for the Union in the Civil War. In the UK from
1872 to 1875, he wrote copy for *Fun* and other magazines,
and in 1887 joined the *San Francisco Examiner*. He wrote
Tales of Soldiers and Civilians (1892) and his most celebrated
story, 'An Occurrence at Owl Creek Bridge', which is a
haunted, near-death fantasy of escape, influenced by
Edgar Allan Poe and in turn influencing Stephen Crane
and Ernest Hemingway. He compiled the much-quoted
Cynic's Word Book (published in book form 1906), now
better known as *The Devil's Dictionary*. He moved to
Washington DC, and in 1913 went to Mexico to report on
Pancho Villa's army and disappeared. ▣ R O'Connor,
Bierce: A Biography (1967)

Biermann, Aenne, *née* Anna Sibilla Sternefeld
1898–1933
German photographer
She was born in Goch am Niederrhein and took up
photography seriously after a meeting in 1929 with the
geologist Rudolf Hundt, with whom she later collaborated on photographing minerals. Her best-known work
comprises sensitive studies of childhood and photographs of buildings, animals, plants, and natural and artificial objects. These were innovative in the manner of
the Neue Sachlichkeit, or 'new objectivity', in which
modernist artists adopted strategies which rendered familiar subject matter in an unfamiliar way. Her photographs were included in important group exhibitions
such as *Film und Foto* (1929, Stuttgart) and *Die neue
Fotographie* (1930, Basle), and a book of her work with
text by Franz Roh, *Fototek 2: Aenne Biermann*, appeared
in 1930.

Biermann, Ludwig 1907–86
German astronomer
Born in Hamm, he was educated at the University of
Berlin, where he graduated in 1932 and was later a lecturer
(1938–45). He led the astrophysics division of the Max
Planck Institute for Physics and Astrophysics, first at
Göttingen University (1947–58) and as the Institute's director at Munich (1958–75). He was a theoretician and his
early work on stellar atmospheres led to studies of magnetic phenomena in sunspots and the solar corona, but
his greatest achievement was his theoretical prediction
(1951) of the existence of a continuous stream of high-
speed particles flowing from the Sun, which acted as the
driving force behind the ionic tails of comets. The existence of this 'solar wind' was confirmed in 1959.
Biermann was awarded the gold medal of the Royal
Astronomical Society in 1974.

Biermann, Wolf 1936–
German poet, singer and playwright

He grew up in Hamburg and emigrated with his family to East Germany in 1953. Biermann attended Humboldt University in Berlin and joined the **Brecht**ian Berliner Ensemble. His early verse reflected Brecht's militant aesthetics, and in 1965 he was censured by the East German authorities and forbidden to either publish or perform in public, which guaranteed him a sympathetic audience in the West. His best-known books are *The Wire Harp* (Eng trans 1968) and *Poems and Ballads* (trans 1977).

Bierstadt, Albert 1830–1902
US painter

He was born near Düsseldorf, Germany, and he studied there. In the USA he became associated with the Hudson River school, and like his contemporary **Frederick Church** painted vast panoramic landscapes in which truth to topographical detail is secondary to dramatic and awe-inspiring effect. His paintings of the Rocky Mountains gained him great popularity.

Biffen, (William) John Biffen, Baron 1930–
English Conservative politician

After graduating from Jesus College, Cambridge (1953), he went into industry as a management trainee and seven years later moved to the Economist Intelligence Unit. In 1961 he entered the House of Commons and after the 1979 general election was made Chief Secretary to the Treasury. A monetarist in economic policy, he favoured a more pragmatic approach in social matters than the Prime Minister, **Margaret Thatcher**, and, although he was promoted and became a very successful leader of the Commons, he was removed from the Cabinet after the 1987 general election. As a backbencher he continued to express his disapproval of European economic and monetary union. The only member of the 1979 Cabinet to stand in the 1992 general election, he stood down in 1997 and gained a life peerage. He is the author of *Inside the House of Commons* (1989).

Biffen, Sir Rowland Harry 1874–1949
English botanist and geneticist

Born in Cheltenham, Gloucestershire, and educated at Cambridge, he travelled in Brazil and the West Indies studying natural sources for rubber. He was appointed as a demonstrator in botany at Cambridge in 1898 and in 1908 became the first Professor of Agricultural Botany there, a post which he retained until 1931. He was also director of the Plant Breeding Institute at Cambridge from 1912 to 1931. Using **Mendel**ian genetic principles, he pioneered the breeding of hybrid rust-resistant strains of wheat. He wrote *The Auricula*, published posthumously in 1951, and was knighted in 1925.

Bigelow, Erastus Brigham 1814–79
US inventor

Born in West Boylston, Massachusetts, he went to work at the age of 10. He invented looms for various kinds of material, a carpet loom, and a machine for making knotted counterpanes. In 1861 he founded the Massachusetts Institute of Technology.

Bigelow, Jacob 1787–1879
US physician and botanist

Born in Sudbury, Massachusetts, he was educated at the universities of Harvard and Pennsylvania, and practised medicine in Boston. He held several professorships at Harvard, and helped to compile the single-word nomenclature of the American Pharmacopoeia of 1820, subsequently adopted in England. He published a study of all of the plants growing within the Boston area, and with Francis Booth he later extended the range of his work, this enlarged work becoming a standard manual of botany for many years. The genus *Bigelovia* is named after him.

Bigelow, John 1817–1911
US writer and diplomat

Born in Malden, New York, he was co-owner and managing editor of the New York *Evening Post* from 1850 to 1861, when he went as consul to Paris. From 1865 to 1866 he was US Minister in France, and in 1875 he was elected Secretary of State for New York. He published a biography of **Benjamin Franklin** (1874) and edited his works. His son, Poultney (1855–1954), was an international journalist and traveller, and friend of Kaiser **Wilhelm II**.
📖 M A Clapp, *Forgotten First Citizen* (1968)

Bigelow, Kathryn 1952–
US film director

She began her career as a painter, but switched to filmmaking after enrolling at Columbia University graduate film school in New York. She worked initially as a script supervisor and as an actress before co-directing *The Loveless* (1984). Her first commercial success arrived with the contemporary horror film *Near Dark* (1987). Her stylish direction earned her attention, and her reputation was enhanced by her best film, the tense police thriller *Blue Steel* (1990). Her other films include *Point Break* (1991) and *Strange Days* (1995).

Biggers, Earl Derr 1884–1933
US novelist and playwright

Born in Warren, Ohio, he was educated at Harvard, and entered journalism as a staff writer on the Boston *Traveller*. He introduced the famous character 'Charlie Chan' in a series of detective novels starting with *The House without a Key* (1925) and finishing with *Keeper of the Keys*, which appeared a year before his death.

Biggs, Ronald 1929–
English thief

He was a member of the gang who carried out the Great Train Robbery. On 8 August 1963, the night mail train from Glasgow to London was stopped at Sears Crossing in Buckinghamshire. The robbers escaped with 120 mailbags, containing over £2.5 million. Biggs was among the first five to be arrested for the theft. He had been traced by fingerprints left on a ketchup bottle and on a Monopoly board at the gang's farm hideout. He was convicted and sentenced to 25 years for conspiracy and 30 years (to run concurrently) for armed robbery. He escaped from Wandsworth Prison on 8 July 1965 and fled to Australia. Pursued by the police, he eventually settled in Brazil. There, saved from extradition because his girlfriend was pregnant (under Brazilian law, fathers of Brazilian children cannot be extradited), he continued to live, supported by an income generated largely by press interviews. 📖 Colin Mackenzie, *The Most Wanted Man: The Story of Ronald Biggs* (1979)

Bigordi, Domenico di Tommaso See Ghirlandaio, Domenico

Bihzad, Ustad Kamal al-Din b.c.1440BC
Persian painter

Born in Herat, he was the most famous Persian painter of the end of the 15th century (the Timurid period), known as 'the Marvel of the Age'. He worked under the patronage of Shah Baisunkur Mirza at his academy for painters, calligraphers, illuminators and bookbinders; only a few of his works remain. Bihzad lost the stiffness and detail of the paintings of the earlier 15th century and his works are masterpieces of composition, full of action and realism, and introducing entirely new colour combinations.

Bikila, Abebe 1932–73
Ethiopian athlete

Born in Ethiopia, he was the first black athlete to win a gold in an Olympics marathon when he ran barefoot in Rome in 1960 and set a new world record of 2 hours, 15 minutes and 16.2 seconds. He went on to run in the 1964 Tokyo Olympics and, this time wearing socks and shoes, won again and beat his own Olympic record by three minutes. He had undergone an appendicectomy only 40 days before. A car crash in 1969 paralysed him and he was confined to a wheelchair for the rest of his life.

Biko, Steve (Stephen) 1946–77
South African black activist
Born in King William's Town, Cape Province, he became involved in politics while studying medicine at Natal University, and was one of the founders (and the first president) of the all-black South African Students Organization (1969). His encouragement of black self-reliance and his support of black institutions made him a popular figure, and in 1972 he became honorary president of the Black People's Convention, a coalition of over 70 black organizations. The following year he was served with a banning order severely restricting his movements and freedom of speech and association, and in 1975 the restrictions were increased. He was detained four times in the last few years of his life, and died in police custody as a result of beatings received. His story was the basis for **Richard Attenborough's** 1987 film *Cry Freedom*. In 1997 five former security policemen confessed to having been involved in his murder. 📖 Donald Woods, *Biko* (1979)

Bill, Max 1908–94
Swiss artist and teacher
Born in Winterthur, he trained at the Zurich School of Arts and Crafts (1924–27), and was a fellow-student with **László Moholy-Nagy** and **Josef Albers** at the Bauhaus in Dessau (1927–29). Working as an architect as well as a painter, sculptor and product designer, he developed the essential Bauhaus principles of co-operative design along abstract (or 'concrete') and purely functionalist lines; he designed typewriters, tables, chairs, lamps and electric wall-plugs. He was a delegate to the Swiss parliament (1967–71).

Billaud-Varenne, Jean Nicolas 1756–1819
French revolutionary
He became secretary, then vice-president, of the Jacobin Club (1792) and was one of those responsible for the September Massacres (1792) in which the mob seized and murdered innocent victims from Paris prisons. He attacked the Girondins, was elected to the Convention and became a member of the Committee of Public Safety (1793). He supported **Robespierre**, but deserted him at the time of Thermidor. He was nevertheless transported to Cayenne, Guiana, where he lived until 1815. He then fled to Haiti.

Billiere, Sir Peter de la 1935–
English general
The son of a prominent navy surgeon, he was educated at Harrow and joined the army in 1952. He spent most of his early career in anonymity as an SAS commander, and showed great courage when under fire. After active service in Malaya, Aden, Oman and Northern Ireland, he showed his brilliance as a strategist in the 1991 Gulf War, where he commanded a 45,000 to 60,000-strong British task force. Following the war, he was promoted to general, making him equal in rank to General **Norman Schwarzkopf**, and was appointed personal adviser on the Middle East to Defence Secretary Tom King. During the 20 years he spent in the Gulf, he learned to speak Arabic and became popular with many leading figures in the region. Following his retirement from the army he wrote *Storm Command* (1992), an account of his service in the Gulf, and *Looking for Trouble* (1994), an autobiography.

Billings, John Shaw 1838–1913
US physician and librarian
Born in Switzerland County, Indiana, he was an army surgeon during the Civil War and in 1864 was put in charge of the surgeon-general's library in Washington, DC. From this collection he created the National Library of Medicine, one of the finest medical library systems in the world, and he served as its librarian until 1895. He produced (with Dr Robert Fletcher) the *Index Catalogue* and *Index Medicus* of medical publications, valuable contributions to the medical profession, and in 1896 he became the first director of the New York Public Library.

Billings, Josh, *pseudonym of* Henry Wheeler Shaw 1818–85
US humorist
He was born in Lanesboro, Massachusetts, and worked as a land agent in Poughkeepsie, New York. He published facetious almanacs and collections of witticisms, relying heavily on deliberate misspelling. The first of these was *Josh Billings, His Sayings* (1866). 📖 C Clemens, *Josh Billings, Yankee Humorist* (1932)

Billington-Greig, Teresa, *née* Billington 1877–1964
English suffragette, socialist and writer
Born in Blackburn, Lancashire, she was educated at a convent school then undertook Manchester University extension classes. A teacher and a member of the Independent Labour Party, she was secretary of the Manchester Equal Pay League, and first met **Emmeline Pankhurst** when her job was threatened for refusing to teach religious instruction. A friend of the Pankhursts and **Annie Kenney**, Billington-Greig joined the Women's Social and Political Union in 1903 and became its London organizer (1907). However in 1907, in dispute with the Pankhursts, she founded the Women's Freedom League with **Charlotte Despard** and **Edith How-Martyn**. Though an ardent suffragette, twice imprisoned for her activities, she became a critic of the more militant suffragists, as she indicates in *The Militant Suffrage Movement* (1911).

Billroth, (Christian Albert) Theodor 1829–94
Austrian surgeon
Born in Bergen auf Rügen, Prussia (now in Germany), he became Professor of Surgery at Zurich (1860–67) and Vienna (1867–94). A pioneer of modern abdominal surgery, he performed the first successful excision of the larynx (1874) and the first resection of the intestine (1881). A brilliant musician, he was a friend of **Brahms**.

Billy the Kid See Bonney, William H

Bilney, Thomas c.1495–1531
English clergyman
Educated at Trinity Hall, Cambridge, and ordained in 1519, he was opposed to the formal 'good works' of the schoolmen, and denounced saint and relic worship, influencing **Hugh Latimer** and other young Cambridge men with his reforming views. He was cautioned by **Thomas Wolsey** (1526), made to recant by Cuthbert Tunstall (1474–1559) in 1527, but imprisoned in the Tower for a year. When he eventually resumed his preaching, he was burned in Norwich.

Binchy, Maeve 1940–
Irish novelist, playwright and short-story writer
Born in Dublin and educated at University College, Dublin, she worked as a teacher and part-time travel writer before joining the *Irish Times* in 1969, later becoming the paper's London correspondent. She has had plays staged in Dublin and won awards in Ireland and Prague for her television play *Deeply Regretted By* (1979). Her collections of short stories include *Victoria Line, Central Line* (1987) and *Dublin 4* (1982), and her novels include *Light a*

Penny Candle (1982), *Firefly Summer* (1987), *Circle of Friends* (1990, film version 1995) *The Copper Beech* (1992), *The Glass Lake* (1994) and *Evening Class* (1996).

Bindoff, Tim (Stanley Thomas) 1908–80
English historian
Born in Brighton, Sussex, he was a graduate of London University, where he taught throughout his life, and he was professor at Queen Mary College from 1951 to 1975. He wrote several important works on British and western European diplomatic history, including *Tudor England* (1950), which (as a Pelican paperback) launched the first academic paperback history series.

Binet, Alfred 1857–1911
French psychologist, the founder of 'Intelligence Tests'
Born in Nice, he abandoned his law studies after developing an interest in Jean Charot's work at the Salpêtrière Hospital in Paris, and moved there (1878–91). Director of physiological psychology at the Sorbonne from 1892, his first tests were used on his children. Later, with Théodore Simon, he expanded the tests (1905) to encompass the measurement of relative intelligence amongst deprived children (the Binet–Simon tests). These were later developed further by Lewis Terman. ☐ Theta Holmes Wolf, *Alfred Binet* (1973)

Binford, Lewis Roberts 1930–
US archaeologist, pioneer of the 'processual' school ('New Archaeology')
Trained originally in forestry and wildlife conservation, he studied anthropology at Michigan University and taught at Ann Arbor, Chicago, Santa Barbara, and Los Angeles before becoming Professor of Anthropology at the University of New Mexico, Albuquerque. An ethno-archaeologist rather than an excavator, he has worked to striking effect among the Navajo, the Nunamiut Inuit, and the Alyawara Aboriginals of Australia. He directs particular attention to the systemic nature of human culture and the ever-changing interaction between the technological, social and ideological subsystems of all societies, ancient and modern, and his work has powerfully influenced the intellectual development of archaeology. His original manifesto *New Perspectives in Archaeology* (1968, with Sally R Binford) has subsequently been elaborated in the autobiographical *An Archaeological Perspective* (1972), *Bones* (1981) and *In Pursuit of the Past* (1983).

Bing, Ilse 1899–1998
German photojournalist
Born in Frankfurt am Main, she trained in music and art and attended the university there from 1920. Studying for a PhD in history of art, she began photographing in 1928 to illustrate her dissertation on the architect Friedrich Gilly. She abandoned her academic studies in 1929 and went to Paris (1930) where her photographic work was widely published, featuring in *Vu* and *Le Monde Illustré*. She first went to New York City in 1936, refused the offer of a staff position on *Life* magazine, and thereafter saw her work included in important exhibitions in the USA. In 1937 she married pianist and musicologist Konrad Wolff; they emigrated to New York in 1941. She gave up photography in 1959, but her work was 're-discovered' in 1976 when it was included in two major exhibitions in New York at the Museum of Modern Art and the Witkin Gallery. Her publications include *Words as Visions* (1974).

Bingham, George Caleb 1811–79
US painter
He was born in Augusta County, Virginia, but lived in Missouri after 1819. A painter of frontier scenes along the Missouri River valley, he produced genre paintings such as *Jolly Flatboatmen*, *Raftsmen Playing Cards*, *Emigration of Daniel Boone*, *County Election* and *Fur Traders Descending the*

Missouri. He was also involved in politics, serving in the Missouri legislature and winning election to the posts of state treasurer (1862) and adjutant general (1875).

Bingham, Hiram 1875–1956
US archaeologist and politician
Born in Honolulu, Hawaii, the son and grandson of Congregationalist missionaries, he earned a PhD in history from Harvard in 1905 and taught at Yale from 1907 to 1924. He was an expert mountaineer, and he buttressed his research into South American history with arduous journeys, retracing Simón Bolívar's 1819 march across the northern coast of the continent in 1906–07. He organized and directed the Yale expedition in search of the lost Inca capital and discovered Machu Picchu high in the Peruvian Andes in 1911. He wrote several books on the Incas and on his explorations, and he· later served as Governor of Connecticut and US senator (1924–33).

Bingzhi, Jiang See Ding Ling

Binh, Nguyen Thi See Nguyen Thi Binh

Binnig, Gerd Karl 1947–
German physicist and Nobel Prize winner
Born in Frankfurt am Main, he was educated at Goethe University there, and then joined IBM's Zurich research laboratories (1978), where he became a group leader in 1984. There he started work with Heinrich Rohrer on a new form of high-resolution electron microscope which used the tunnelling electron current between a scanning needle, whose tip measured just one atom wide, and the surface of a sample to profile the sample's surface. For this work Binnig and Rohrer shared the 1986 Nobel Prize for physics with Ernst Ruska, who had invented the electron microscope some 55 years earlier. The scanning tunnelling electron microscope, an important piece of research equipment, allows atom by atom inspection of surfaces and has been particularly useful in the development of electronic circuits. Since 1987 he has been Honorary Professor of Physics at the University of Munich.

Binyon, (Robert) Laurence 1869–1943
English poet and art critic
Born in Lancaster, he was educated at Oxford, where he won the Newdigate prize for poetry. He worked in the British Museum, and was in charge of Oriental prints and paintings (1913–33), and was Norton Professor of Poetry at Harvard (1933–34). His study *Painting in the Far East* (1908) was the first European treatise on the subject, and *Japanese Art* (1909), *Botticelli* (1913) and *Drawings and Engravings of William Blake* (1922) followed. Meanwhile he had achieved a reputation as a poet in the tradition of Wordsworth and Matthew Arnold. His poetry includes *Lyric Poems* (1894), *Odes* (1901), containing some of his best work, especially 'The Sirens' and 'The Idols', and *Collected Poems* (1931). He also wrote plays—*Paris and Oenone*, *Attila*, *Arthur*—and translated Dante's *Divine Comedy* into terza rima (1933–43). Extracts from his elegy 'For the Fallen' (set to music by Elgar) adorn war memorials throughout the British Commonwealth. ☐ *A Laurence Binyon Anthology* (1927)

Biondi, Matt(hew) 1965–
US swimmer
Born in Morego, California, he won a record seven medals at the 1986 world championships, including three golds, and at the 1988 Olympics won seven medals, including five golds. He set the 100 metres freestyle world record of 48.74 seconds in Orlando, Florida, in 1986. He won silver in the 50 metres freestyle at the 1992 Olympics, and announced his retirement in 1993.

Biot, Jean Baptiste 1774–1862
French physicist and astronomer

Born in Paris, he became Professor of Physics at the Collège de France. He made a balloon ascent with **Joseph Louis Gay-Lussac** to study magnetism at high altitudes in 1804. He travelled to Spain with **François Arago** in 1806 to determine the length of a degree of longitude. He invented a polariscope and established the fundamental laws of the rotation of the plane of polarization of light by optically active substances. His son, Édouard Constant (1803–50), was a Chinese scholar.

Birch, Arthur John 1915–
Australian chemist
Born in Sydney, he graduated from the University of Sydney in 1936 and obtained a scholarship to work with Sir **Robert Robinson** at Oxford. After research fellowships at Oxford, he worked at Cambridge until his appointment as professor at the University of Sydney in 1952. In 1955 he was appointed professor at the University of Manchester, but he returned to Australia in 1967 to the National University in Canberra, becoming its Foundation Professor of Organic Chemistry. He is most famous for the Birch reduction using metal-ammonia solutions, a technique of great value in the synthesis of a number of natural products. A member of several important Australian and Commonwealth scientific committees, he was elected FRS in 1958. Since 1980 he has been Professorial Fellow at Lincoln College, Oxford. He published *How Chemistry Works* in 1950.

Birchall, (James) Derek 1930–
English industrial chemist
Born in Leigh, Lancashire, he joined ICI in 1957. After early discoveries concerning the ferricyanide ion, at ICI he has pioneered numerous innovations including novel inorganic fire-extinguishing agents, inorganic fibres and new phosphate complexes. He has also worked on the toxic effects of aluminium and silicon. Elected Fellow of the Royal Society in 1982, he received an OBE in 1990. Other awards include the Royal Society of Chemistry awards for Solids and Materials Processing (1990) and Materials Science (1991), and the Royal Society of Chemistry Industrial Lectureship (1991–92). Since 1992 he has been Professor of Inorganic Chemistry at Keele University.

Bird, Bonnie 1914–95
US dancer and teacher
Born in Portland, Oregon, she was head of dance at the Cornish School of Fine Arts (1937–40), where her students included **Merce Cunningham** and Jane Dudley. She married Ralph Gundlach in 1938. After World War II she founded the dance company, the Merry-Go Rounders, chaired the American Dance Guild (1965–67), and was partly responsible for founding the Congress on Research in Dance. Together with Marion North, she reshaped the Laban Centre for Movement and Dance from 1974, introducing professional training for dancers and Great Britain's first degree course in Dance Studies (1977). Bird also provided the inspiration for the *Dance Theatre Journal*, of which she was an editorial adviser from its creation in 1983. Also in 1983 she formed the Transitions Dance Company, designed to provide student dancers with experience in new choreography; a year later she founded the New Choreography Fund, which has both sponsored works and undertaken research.

Bird, Larry (Joe) 1956–
US basketball player
Born in French Lick, Indiana, he starred on the basketball team at Indiana State University, demonstrating his excellence in both passing and shooting. In 1979 he became a professional with the Boston Celtics, leading the team to a National Basketball Association (NBA) championship (1980–81 season). He was most valuable player

(MVP) in the 1984 and 1986 NBA championship finals and MVP for the NBA three times (1984–86). He retired from the game in 1992.

Bird, Vere Cornwall 1910–
Antiguan statesman
He was a founder-member of the Antigua Trades and Labour Union (1939) and then leader of the Antigua Labour Party (ALP). In the pre-independence period he was elected to the Legislative Council and became Chief Minister (1960–67) and then premier (1967–71, 1976–81). When full independence, as Antigua and Barbuda, was achieved in 1981 he became Prime Minister, and he and his party were re-elected in 1984 and 1989.

Birde, William See Byrd, William

Birdseye, Clarence 1886–1956
US businessman and inventor
Born in Brooklyn, New York City, he became a fur trader in Labrador, where he observed that food kept well in the freezing winter conditions. On his return to the USA he developed a process for freezing food in small packages suitable for retailing, and in 1924 he helped found the General Seafoods Company, marketing quick frozen foods. He sold the company in 1929. He was president of Birdseye Frosted Foods (1930–34) and of Birdseye Electric Company (1935–38). Some 300 patents are credited to him. Among his other inventions were infrared heat lamps, the recoilless harpoon gun and a method of removing water from food.

Birdwood, William Riddell 1865–1951
British field marshal
He was born in Kirkee, India, where his father was an official of the government of Bombay. Trained at Sandhurst, in 1914 he was put in command of the Australian and New Zealand contingents then arriving in Egypt for the Dardanelles offensive. He planned the landing at Gallipoli, on Anzac Cove as it was subsequently known. Upon evacuation from the Peninsula, he took his troops to the Western Front, through the battles of the Somme and Ypres in 1916 and 1917. After the war he returned to India to command the Northern Army, becoming Commander-in-Chief in 1925, and retiring in 1930.

Birendra, Bir Bikram Shah Dev 1945–
King of Nepal
The son of King Mahendra, he was born in Kathmandu, and educated at St Joseph's College, Darjeeling, Eton, and Tokyo and Harvard universities. He married Queen Aishwarya Rajya Laxmi Devi Rana (1970), and has two sons and one daughter. Appointed Grand Master and Colonel-in-Chief of the Royal Nepalese Army (1964), he became king on his father's death (1972). During his reign there has been gradual progress towards political reform, but Nepal remained essentially an absolute monarchy, with political activity banned, until 1990, when Birendra was forced to concede much of his power.

Birgitta or Bridget, St c.1303–1373
Swedish visionary and author
Born in Finsta, Uppland, she was married at the age of 13, gave birth to eight children, and gained considerable political insight through travel and service at the Swedish court. She undertook several pilgrimages—to Trondheim (1338), Santiago de Compostela (1341) and Palestine (1372). Widowed in 1344, she subsequently moved to Rome. Her monastery at Vadstena in Sweden was founded towards the end of her life. Her numerous revelations were recorded by her confessors and very widely published in Latin after her death as *Revelationes coelestes* (there is also a 14th-century translation into Swedish). They are characterized by vivid realistic detail and abundant

imagery, frequently inspired by her experiences as a mother. She was canonized in 1391. ▣ Johannes Jørgensen, *Saint Bridget of Sweden* (2 vols, 1954)

Biringuccio, Vannoccio Vincenzio Agustino Luca 1480–1539
Italian metallurgical engineer

He was born in Siena. His *De la Pirotechnia* (1540, 'Concerning Pyrotechnics') was the earliest printed work covering the whole of mining and metallurgy as well as other important industrial processes, and pre-dated **Georgius Agricola**'s better-known *De Re Metallica* (1555). He himself worked as a manager of iron mines, an armourer and gunfounder and a military engineer, before taking up his final post as director of the Papal foundry and munitions in Rome.

Birkbeck, George 1776–1841
English physician and educationist

He was born in Settle, Yorkshire, and in 1799 became Professor of Natural Philosophy at Anderson's College, Glasgow, where he delivered his first free lectures to the working classes. In 1804 he became a physician in London. He was the founder and first president of the London Mechanics' or Birkbeck Institute (1824)—the first in the UK, which developed into Birkbeck College, a constituent college of London University.

Birkeland, Kristian Olaf Bernhard 1867–1917
Norwegian physicist

Born in Christiania (Oslo), he studied physics at the universities of Paris and Geneva, and briefly under **Heinrich Hertz** in Bonn, Germany. In 1898 he was appointed to the chair of physics at the University of Christiania. Later he moved to Cairo, partly for health reasons, but also to resume his astronomical observations. Birkeland demonstrated the electromagnetic nature of the aurora borealis, and in 1903 developed a method for obtaining nitrogen from the air with Samuel Eyde (1866–1940). This led to increased production of nitric acid, a key ingredient in fertilizers and the explosives industry, which could be obtained by 'fixing' atmospheric nitrogen. The Birkeland–Eyde process was the first large-scale process which exploited the cheap electricity generated by the Norwegian hydroelectric plants.

Birkenhead, Frederick Edwin Smith, 1st Earl of 1872–1930
English lawyer and statesman

Born in Birkenhead, Cheshire, he attended Birkenhead Grammar School, studied at Wadham College, Oxford (Fellow of Merton, 1896), and was called to the Bar in 1899. He entered parliament as a Conservative in 1906 and by his provocative maiden speech established himself as a considerable orator and wit. In the Irish crisis (1914) he vigorously supported **Edward Carson**'s organized resistance to Home Rule. He became Attorney-General (1915–19), and Lord Chancellor (1919–22). His extraordinary ability was seen at its best in the trial of **Roger Casement** (1916), when he appeared for the Crown. Despite his earlier convictions, he played a major part in the Irish settlement of 1921 and was created earl in 1922. **Stanley Baldwin** appointed him Secretary of State for India (1924–28), but his conduct caused much criticism and he resigned to devote himself to a City directorship. His greatest achievements as a lawyer were the preparation of the series of Acts reforming land law, and a textbook on international law. He also wrote *Famous Trials* (1925). ▣ John Campbell, *F E Smith, First Earl of Birkenhead* (1983)

Birkett (of Ulverston), William Norman Birkett, 1st Baron 1883–1962
English lawyer and politician

Born in Ulverston, Cumbria, he studied at Emmanuel College, Cambridge, was called to the Bar (1913) and earned his considerable reputation as counsel in notable murder trials. He was a Liberal MP (1923–24, 1929–31). A judge of the King's Bench Division (1941–50), he was chairman of the advisory committee on the famous Defence Regulation 18B during World War II and figured prominently in the summing up of the Nuremberg Trials (1945–46), in which he was the British alternate judge to Lord Justice **Geoffrey Lawrence**. A Lord Justice of Appeal (1950–57), he was made a baron in 1958.

Birkhoff, George David 1884–1944
US mathematician

Born in Overisel, Michigan, he studied at the universities of Harvard and Chicago, and was professor at the universities of Wisconsin (1902–09), Princeton (1909–12) and Harvard (1912–39). In 1913 he proved '**Poincaré**'s last theorem', which Jules Poincaré had left unproven at his death. This was a crucial step in the analysis of motions determined by differential equations, and opened the way to modern topological dynamics. Later he extended Poincaré's work and developed ergodic theory, where the methods of probability theory are applied to particle motion. He is regarded as the leading US mathematician of the early part of the 20th century.

Birley, Eric 1906–95
English historian and archaeologist

Born in Swinton, Manchester, he was educated at Clifton College and Brasenose College, Oxford, and he became a lecturer at Durham University in 1931, specializing in the archaeology of **Hadrian**'s Wall. During World War II he served in military intelligence. He founded the Congress of Roman Frontier Studies in 1949, and was Professor of Roman-British History and Archaeology at Durham (1956–71), and became founder-chairman of the Vindolanda Trust in 1970. His many publications include *Roman Britain and the Roman Army* (1953).

Birley, Sir Robert 1903–82
English educationist and scholar

Born in Midnapore, Bengal, and educated at Rugby and Balliol College, Oxford, he taught history at Eton from 1926. He became headmaster of Charterhouse in 1935, was adviser on education to the deputy military governor, British Zone, Germany, in 1947, and was headmaster of Eton (1949–62). He was appointed visiting Professor of Education at Witwatersrand (1962–67) and Professor of Social Science, City University (1967). Essentially a traditionalist, his early reputation as a radical led to the nickname 'Red Robert'.

Birmingham Six
Alleged IRA terrorists unjustly imprisoned

This is the familiar collective name for the six men found guilty of the IRA bombing of the Mulberry Bush and Tavern in the Town pubs in Birmingham in 1974, in which 21 people were killed and 160 injured; each was sentenced to 21 life sentences. However the prosecution case at their 1975 trial was based mainly on confessions, which the defence claimed had been extracted after severe beatings, and one of which was shown to have been forged. Also, the forensic evidence relied on the now discredited Geiss test for determining whether an individual had recently handled explosive substances. In February 1991, following their second appeal in three years, the Director of Public Prosecutions announced that he could no longer argue that the convictions were safe and satisfactory, and the following month the Birmingham Six were set free after 16 years of wrongful imprisonment. Their names are Hugh Callaghan (1931–), Patrick Hill (1944–), Gerard

Hunter (1949–), Richard McIlkenny (1934–), William Power (1947–) and John Walker (1936–). ▣ Paddy Joe Hill, *Forever Lost, Forever Gone* (1995)

Birney, James Gillespie 1792–1857
US abolitionist

Born in Danville, Kentucky, he settled on a plantation in Alabama in 1818 but eventually came to realize that slavery was morally unjustifiable. After freeing his own slaves (1834), he founded the Kentucky Anti-Slavery Society (1835) and published the antislavery newspaper *Philanthropist* (1836–37). As secretary of the American Anti-Slavery Society, he advocated the advancement of the abolitionist cause through political action and ran for US President as a Liberty Party candidate (1840 and 1844).

Biron or Bühren, Ernst Johann 1690–1772
Duke of Courland

Born in Kalnciems, Courland (now Latvia), he assumed the name and arms of the French Ducs de Biron, when, as favourite of Anna Ivanovna, he became the real ruler of Russia on her accession to the throne (1730). He was blamed for most of the misfortunes of the time, especially exploitation of the nation's resources for personal gain, but greatly improved the country's administration. In 1737 Anna made him Duke of Courland, and on her death (1740) he assumed the regency, but was arrested and banished to Siberia. Peter III allowed him to return in 1762 and he was eventually given back his titles.

Birrell, Augustine 1850–1933
English politician and writer

Born in Wavertree, Liverpool, and educated in Amersham and at Trinity Hall, Cambridge, he was called to the Bar in 1875 and was Liberal MP for West Fife (1889–1900) and Bristol North (1906–18). He was president of the Board of Education (1905–07) and put through the 1906 Education Act, was Chief Secretary for Ireland (1907–16), and founded the National University of Ireland (1908), resigning after the Easter Rising of 1916. He was the author of volumes of essays, *Obiter Dicta* (1884–87) and *More Obiter Dicta* (1924), whose charm and unobtrusive scholarship inspired the verb 'to birrell', meaning to comment on life gently and allusively, mixing good nature with irony. He also wrote Lives of Charlotte Brontë (1887), William Hazlitt (1902) and Andrew Marvell (1905) for the *English Men of Letters* series. ▣ *Things Past Redress* (1937)

Birt, Sir John 1944–
English television executive and controller

Born in Bootle, Merseyside, he attended St Mary's College, Liverpool, then studied engineering at St Catherine's College, Oxford. He trained with Granada Television, working on *World in Action*, then started to successfully produce programmes. Moving to London Weekend Television, he became head of current affairs (1974–77), controller of features and current affairs (1977–81) and director of programmes (1982–87). He joined the BBC in 1987 as deputy director-general, and created controversy with his criticism of the news and current affairs programmes. He became director-general of the BBC in 1993, which caused controversy when it was revealed that he had been working as a freelance for the BBC and not as a member of staff, a situation which various newspapers claimed gave him certain tax benefits, so he became a member of staff immediately. He was knighted in 1998.

Birtwistle, Sir Harrison 1934–
English composer

Born in Accrington, Lancashire, he began his career as a clarinettist, studying at the Royal Manchester College of Music and the Royal Academy of Music in London. While in Manchester he formed, with other young musicians including Peter Maxwell Davies and John Ogdon, the New Manchester Group for the performance of modern

music. He was director of music at Cranborne Chase School (1962–65) and then spent two years studying in the USA. In 1967 he formed the Pierrot Players, again with Maxwell Davies, and much of his work was written for them and for the English Opera Group. His early work was influenced by Igor Stravinsky and by the medieval and Renaissance masters. His first composition, *Refrains and Choruses*, was written in 1957, but it was two works of 1965, the instrumental *Tragoedia* and the vocal/instrumental *Ring a Dumb Carillon*, that established him as a leading composer. He was an associate director of the National Theatre (1975–88), became the composer-in-residence at the London Philharmonic Orchestra in 1993, and Henry Purcell Professor of Composition at King's College London in 1994. Among his later works are the operas *Punch and Judy* (1966–67) and *The Masque of Orpheus* (1974–82), the 'dramatic pastoral' *Down by the Greenwood Side* (1969), *The Fields of Sorrow* (1971), *On The Sheer Threshold of the Night* (1980), *Pulse Sampler* (1981), *Earth Dances* (1986) and the opera *Gawain* (1990). He was knighted in 1988. ▣ Michael Hall, *Harrison Birtwistle* (1984)

Biryukova, Aleksandra Pavlovna 1929–
Soviet politician

She was trained and worked as a textile engineer until 1968. She had earlier taken official jobs, and in 1968 she became secretary of the Trade Union Presidium and in 1985 deputy chairman. In 1986 Mikhail Gorbachev selected her for the Secretariat of the Central Committee of the Communist Party and in 1988 appointed her deputy Prime Minister responsible for Social Development. She was also made a candidate member of the politburo, the first woman since Yekaterina Furtseva to achieve this distinction. One of the few Soviet women to reach positions of political importance, she was, however, pushed aside in the turmoil of 1990–91.

Biscop, Simon See Episcopius, Simon

Bishop, Elizabeth 1911–79
US poet

Born in Worcester, Massachusetts, she grew up in New England and Nova Scotia, and graduated from Vassar College. She lived in Brazil from 1952 to 1967, published several travel books, including *Brazil* (1967), and taught at Harvard from 1970. She was noted for her verse, which often evokes images of nature. Her first collection, *North and South* (1946), was reprinted with additions as *Poems: North and South—A Cold Spring* (1955) and received the 1956 Pulitzer Prize for poetry. A *Complete Poems* was published in 1979. ▣ A Stevenson, *Elizabeth Bishop* (1966)

Bishop, Sir Henry R(owley) 1786–1855
English composer

Born in London, he was musical director at Covent Garden (1810–24), held professorships at Edinburgh and Oxford, and in 1842 received the first knighthood conferred upon a musician. Few of his many, and popular, glees and operas have survived, but he is remembered for 'Home, Sweet Home' (1821).

Bishop, Isabella, née Bird 1831–1904
English writer and traveller

She was born in Boroughbridge, Yorkshire, and from 1854 visited Canada and the USA, the Sandwich Islands (Hawaii), the Rocky Mountains, Yezo, Persia (Iran) and Kurdistan, Tibet, and Korea. She wrote *Englishwoman in America* (1856) and many other travel books. In 1892 she was elected the first woman Fellow of the Royal Geographical Society.

Bishop, John Peale 1892–1944
US poet, fiction writer and essayist

Born in Charles Town, West Virginia, he was managing editor of *Vanity Fair* after World War I but joined the exodus of US literati to Paris in 1922. In debt to the 17th-century metaphysical poets, his collections include *Green Fruit* (1917), *Now with His Love* (1933) and *Minute Particulars* (1936). His *Collected Poems* was published in 1948. A year before he died he was appointed consultant in comparative literature at the Library of Congress. ⌨ E C Spindler, *John Peale Bishop: a biography* (1980)

Bishop, Maurice 1946–83
Grenadian politician

He was the leader of the New Jewel Movement which overthrew the government of Eric Gairy in 1979 and set up a Marxist People's Revolutionary Government. Disagreements over policy led to Bishop's overthrow and murder by his deputy, Bernard Coard, and the Commander of the Armed Forces, General Austin (1983), and the creation of a Revolutionary Military Council (RMC). The USA and moderate Caribbean governments, shocked by the bloody coup and fearful of imagined Cuban influence, instigated military intervention to depose the RMC and arrest the coup leaders. Coard, Austin and 12 others were sentenced to death, but these sentences were commuted to life imprisonment in 1991.

Bishop, (John) Michael 1936–
US molecular biologist, virologist and Nobel Prize winner

Born in York, Pennsylvania, he was educated at Gettysburg College and at Harvard Medical School, where he graduated in medicine in 1962. He was resident in general medicine at Massachusetts General Hospital (1962–64), became a research associate in virology at the National Institutes of Health in Washington, DC (1964–66), and remained in Washington as assistant then associate professor. He moved to San Francisco in 1972 to become Professor of Microbiology and Immunology at the University of California Medical Centre, and was appointed the director of the G W Cooper Research Foundation in 1981. He has received many major awards, including the Nobel Prize for physiology or medicine in 1989 (jointly with Harold Varmus) for his discovery of oncogenes, normal cellular genes involved in the normal growth and development of all mammalian cells. Certain faults in oncogene regulation can severely damage the growth of the affected cell type and cause cancer. An understanding of the function of oncogenes is therefore a crucial step in combating all types of cancer.

Bishop, William Avery 1894–1956
Canadian airman

He was born in Owen Sound, Ontario. A member of the Canadian Expeditionary Force in 1914, he joined the Royal Flying Corps in 1915, and became the most successful Allied 'ace' of World War I, officially credited with the destruction of 72 enemy aircraft. In 1917 he was awarded the VC for single-handedly downing seven German planes. He was appointed the first Canadian air marshal in 1939, and was director of the Royal Canadian Air Force throughout World War II.

Bismarck, Prince Otto Edward Leopold von, Duke of Lauenburg 1815–98
Prusso-German statesman, the first Chancellor of the German Empire

He was born in Schönhausen, Brandenburg, and studied law and agriculture at Göttingen, Berlin and Greifswald. In 1847 he became known in the new Prussian parliament as an ultra-royalist, and opposed equally the constitutional demands of 1848 and the scheme of a German empire, as proposed by the Frankfurt parliament of 1849. In 1851, as Prussian member of the resuscitated German diet of Frankfurt, he resented the predominance of

Austria, and demanded equal rights for Prussia. He was sent as Minister to St Petersburg in 1859, and in 1862 to Paris, the same year he became Prime Minister. The death of the King of Denmark (1863) fuelled the Schleswig-Holstein question, and excited a fever of German nationalism, which led to the defeat of Denmark by Austria and Prussia, and the annexation of the duchies. This provoked the 'Seven Weeks' War' between Prussia and Austria, which ended in the defeat of Austria at the Battle of Königgratz (1866), and the reorganization of Germany under the leadership of Prussia. During this Bismarck was an influential figure, and, from being universally disliked, became highly popular and a national hero. He further unified German feeling during the Franco-Prussian War (1870–71), which he deliberately provoked, when he acted as spokesman of Germany, and in 1871 he dictated the terms of peace to France. Created a count in 1866, he was then made a prince and became the first Chancellor of the new German Empire (1871–90). After the Peace of Frankfurt (1871) the sole aim of his policy was to consolidate and protect the young empire. His long and bitter struggle with the Vatican, called the *Kulturkampf*, was a failure, but apart from this his domestic policy was marked by universal suffrage, reformed coinage, codification of the law, nationalization of the Prussian railways, repeated increase of the army, a protective tariff (1879), and various attempts to combat socialism and to establish government monopolies. To counteract Russia and France, in 1879 he formed the Austro-German Treaty of Alliance (published in 1888), which Italy joined in 1886, and he presided over the Berlin Congress in 1878. The phrase 'man of blood and iron' was used by the 'Iron Chancellor' in a speech in 1862. Two attempts were made on his life (1866, 1874). Disapproving the initially liberal policy of the Emperor Wilhelm II, along with his son Herbert (1849–1904), the Foreign Secretary, he resigned the chancellorship in March 1890, becoming Duke of Lauenburg. He was finally reconciled with Wilhelm in 1894. ⌨ Lothar Gall, *Bismarck* (2 vols, 1986)

Bissière, Roger 1886–1964
French painter

Born in Villeréal, Lot-et-Garonne, he moved to Bordeaux in 1901, where he attended the École des Beaux-Arts before going to Paris in 1910. A friend of Georges Braque and Juan Gris, he transformed natural appearances into glowing tapestry-like patches of colour, as in *Black Venus* (1945, Musée National d'Art Moderne, Paris) and *Noir et Rouge* (Museum of Modern Art, New York), and described his painting as a 'desire for poetry'. A successful eye operation in 1948 transformed his work and resulted in it receiving international acclaim. He exhibited at the Venice Biennale in 1954 and in 1964, when he won a special mention. From 1958 he designed windows for churches, including Metz Cathedral (1960–61).

Bitar, Salah al-Din Dates unavailable
Syrian politician

Co-founder in 1943 with Michel Aflaq of the Ba'ath Socialist Party, he played a considerable part in the founding of the short-lived United Arab Republic (UAR), a union of Egypt and Syria established in 1958, from which Syria seceded in 1961. Despite a broad influence through its essentially socialist and pan-Arab ideology, the failure of the UAR dealt a considerable blow to the Ba'ath as originally conceived by Bitar and Aflaq, and paved the way for the separate development of one-party Ba'athist rule in Syria and Iraq.

Bitzius, Albert, *pseudonym of* Jeremias Gotthelf 1797–1854
Swiss writer

Born in Morat, in Freiburg canton, he studied at Berne, and in 1832 became pastor of Lützelfluh, Emmenthal. He wrote many novels of Swiss village life, including *Käthi* (1847) and *Uli der Knecht* (1841, Eng trans *Ulric, the Farm Servant*, 1885). ▭ C Guggisberg, *Albert Bitzius* (1935)

Bixio, Girolamo, *known as* Nino 1821–73
Italian soldier
Born in Chiaveri, near Genoa, he was a merchant captain by training, and became one of Garibaldi's most trusted followers. Bixio fought in several campaigns, and was elected a deputy in the Italian parliament in 1861 and a senator in 1870.

Biya, Paul 1933–
Cameroonian statesman
Born in Muomeka'a, he graduated with a law degree from Paris University and entered politics under the aegis of Ahmadou Ahidjo. He was a Junior Minister in 1962, a Minister of State in 1968 and Prime Minister in 1975. When Ahidjo unexpectedly retired in 1982, he became President and reconstituted the government with his own supporters. He survived a coup attempt in 1984 (almost certainly instigated by Ahidjo) and was re-elected President in 1988 with more than 98 per cent of the vote.

Bizet, Georges, *originally* Alexandre Césare Léopold 1838–75
French composer
Born in Paris, he studied at the Conservatoire there under Ludovic Halévy, whose daughter he married in 1869, and in Italy. Although he won the Prix de Rome in 1857 with *Le Docteur Miracle* ('Doctor Miracle'), his efforts to achieve a reputation as an operatic composer with such works as *Les Pêcheurs de Perles* (1863, 'The Pearl-Fishers') and *La Jolie fille de Perth* (1867, 'The Fair Maid of Perth') were largely unsuccessful. His charming incidental music to Daudet's play *L'Arlésienne* (1872, 'The Maid of Arles') was successful and survived in the form of two orchestral suites. Bizet's reputation is based on these and on the four-act opera *Carmen*, completed just before his death of heart disease, although *Les Pêcheurs* and *La Jolie fille* have enjoyed recent revivals. *Carmen* proved too robust at first for French taste, but its delicate orchestration and operatic intensity have ensured its current popularity.

Bjelke-Petersen, Sir Joh(annes) 1911–
Australian politician
He was born in New Zealand of Danish parents, his father being pastor of the village of Dannevirke, North Island. In 1913 they moved to Kingaroy, Queensland, Australia. He entered state politics in 1947 as a Country Party (later National Party) member of the Legislative Assembly, becoming a Minister in 1963. In 1968, as a result of his firm stand on law and order, he was made Police Minister, then Deputy Leader and, following the sudden death of Jack Pizzey, became premier of Queensland. A vocal supporter of states' rights as against federal intervention, he controlled a strongly right-wing government, first in coalition with the Liberal Party and after 1983 in his own right. He was knighted in 1982 and retired from the premiership in 1987.

Bjelke-Petersen, Marie Caroline 1874–1969
Australian writer
Born in Jagtvejen, Copenhagen, Denmark, she went to Tasmania with her parents in 1891. She received attention for her romantic novels *The Captive Singer* (1917), *The Immortal Flame* (1919) and *Jewelled Nights* (1924), and many others. The latter title was filmed in 1925, starring the Australian actress Louise Lovely, with location scenes shot in Tasmania. Subsequently Bjelke-Petersen's florid romances became very popular in the USA.

Bjerknes, Jacob Aall Bonnevie 1897–1975
US meteorologist
Born in Stockholm, Sweden, he was the son of the Norwegian physicist Vilhelm Bjerknes. He became Professor of the Geophysical Institute at Bergen, and with his father he formulated the theory of cyclones on which modern weather forecasting is based. In 1940 he formed the meteorological school for US air force weather officers at the University of California and was made the first Professor of Meteorology at the University of California at Los Angeles. He began research into problems of ocean–atmosphere interaction in 1959, discovering that changes in wind stress could cause changes in ocean currents and conversely, that unusual sea temperature anomalies would result in atmospheric changes. He was active internationally and was awarded the Symons Gold Medal of the Royal Meteorological Society (1940) and the International Meteorological Organization prize (1959).

Bjerknes, Vilhelm F(riman) K(oren) 1862–1951
Norwegian mathematician, meteorologist and geophysicist
Born in Christiania (Oslo), he graduated from the University of Christiania in 1888, then worked in Bonn for two years as assistant and collaborator to Heinrich Hertz, before returning to Norway where he received his PhD in 1892. He was appointed lecturer (1893), then Professor of Applied Mechanics and Mathematical Physics (1895) at the University of Stockholm. He initially collaborated with his father (a mathematics professor) on theories of hydrodynamical forces. While continuing this work at Stockholm, he produced his famous circulation theorem (1898) and applied his thorough knowledge of hydrodynamics to a study of atmospheric and ocean processes. He devised equations which enabled both the thermal energy and that due to baroclinicity to be calculated for a developing cyclone. In 1907 he returned to Norway, and collaborated with Harald Sverdrup on dynamic meteorology. In 1912 he and Sverdrup moved to Leipzig where Bjerknes became Professor of Geophysics, though soon after Fridtjof Nansen persuaded him to set up a geophysical institute in Bergen, where, until 1926, he spent the most productive years of his life.

Bjorken, James David 1934–
US theoretical physicist
Born in Chicago, and educated at the Massachusetts Institute of Technology and Stanford University, he has held posts at the Stanford Linear Accelerator Center (1959–79; 1991–) and at the Fermi National Accelerator Laboratory (1979–90). His best-known work has been in deep inelastic scattering theory, which describes the scattering of high-energy leptons (eg electrons) by nucleons (protons and neutrons). He predicted in the early 1960s that for large momentum transfers, ie close collisions, the deep inelastic cross-section would 'scale', in other words would only depend on dimensionless variables, in direct contrast with elastic scattering where cross-section falls dramatically at high momentum transfers. In 1990 these predictions were verified by Jerome Friedman, Henry Kendall and Richard Taylor's Nobel Prize-winning research, and Richard Feynman incorporated this cross-section data into his theory of partons, now known as quarks.

Björling, Jussi, *properly* Johan Jonaton 1911–60
Swedish tenor
Born in Stora Tuna, he toured as a treble from 1916 with his tenor father, David, and two brothers as the Björling Male Voice Quartet. From 1928 he studied at the Stockholm Conservatory under Joseph Hislop and John Forsell. His debut as a principal with the Royal Swedish Opera was as Don Ottavio (1930) and he sang regularly

with the company until 1938. By then he was in international demand, making successful debuts at Chicago (1937), New York (1938), London (1939) and San Francisco (1940). Although his repertoire was mainly Italian he sang rarely in Italy, but became a favourite in the USA, especially at the Metropolitan, New York, and as a recording artist. His qualities were purity of tone, warm evenness throughout his register, and great power, seemingly effortless and unstrained, on high notes. Vocal beauty and fine musicianship compensated for his rather basic skills as an actor.

Bjørnson, Bjørnstjerne Martinius 1832–1910
Norwegian writer, politician and Nobel Prize winner

Born in Kvikne, Österdalen, the son of a pastor, and educated at Molde, Christiania (Oslo) and Copenhagen, he was a playwright and novelist of wide-ranging interests, a lifelong champion of liberal causes and constantly active politically as a Home Ruler and republican. His first successful drama was *Mellem Slagene* (1856, 'Between Blows'), about the Norwegian civil wars. An ardent patriot, he sought to free the Norwegian theatre from Danish influence and revive Norwegian as a literary language. He worked as a newspaper editor simultaneously with being director of Bergen's Ole Bull Theatre (1857–59) and of the Oslo Theatre (1863–67), where he recreated Norway's epic past in saga-inspired dramas such as *Kong Sverre* (1861) and his trilogy about the pretender *Sigurd Slembe* (1862). He was named Norway's national poet, and his poem, *Ja, vi elsker dette landet* (1870, 'Yes, We Love This Land of Ours') became the national anthem. His other major works include the novel *Fiskerjenten* (1868, 'The Fisher Girl'), the epic poem *Arnljot Gelline* (1870), and his greatest plays, *Over Evne I* and *II* (1893, 1895, 'Beyond One's Powers'), about a clergyman capable of working miracles but incapable of responding to his wife's love. He was awarded the 1903 Nobel Prize for literature. ▢ O Anker, *Bjørnstjerne Bjørnson: the man and his work* (1955)

Bjornson, Maria 1949–
British stage designer

She was born in Paris of Norwegian and Romanian parents. She has designed sets and costumes for both straight drama and opera in many British theatres such as the Glasgow Citizens' Theatre. Her work for the Royal Shakespeare Company includes *A Midsummer Night's Dream* (1981), *The Tempest* (1982), *Hamlet* and *Camille* (both 1984). She also designed Hal Prince's production of Andrew Lloyd Webber's *The Phantom of the Opera* (1986) and Trevor Nunn's production of Lloyd Webber's *Aspects of Love* (1989), as well as Nunn's production of *Così Fan Tutti*, and the cobbled streets of Hamburg for his production of Pam Gems's *The Blue Angel* (both 1991). She has a painter's eye both for detail and overall effect, and uses fabrics expressively. She has also worked for Houston Opera, Netherlands Opera, the Royal Opera House, English National Opera and Welsh National Opera.

Björnsson, Sveinn 1881–1952
Icelandic diplomat and statesman

Born in Copenhagen, Denmark, the son of an Icelandic newspaper editor, he studied law in Copenhagen and was elected a member of the Icelandic parliament (Althing) in 1914–16 and 1920. During World War I he was envoy to the USA and Great Britain, and was ambassador to Denmark (1920–24, 1926–41). During the German occupation of Denmark he was elected Regent of Iceland and, when Iceland declared its independence of Denmark in 1944, he was elected the new republic's first President. Re-elected in 1948, he died in office.

Black, Adam 1784–1874
Scottish publisher

He was born in Edinburgh, the son of a master builder. Educated at the High School of Edinburgh, he was apprenticed at 15 to an Edinburgh bookseller. He set up his own bookshop in 1807, and started publishing in 1817. In 1826 he bought the *Encyclopaedia Britannica* after Archibald Constable's failure and in 1854 he bought the rights to Walter Scott's novels from Cadell (1788–1849). He was Lord Provost between 1843 and 1848, and Liberal MP for the burgh (1856–65).

Black, Cilla, *originally* Priscilla Maria Veronica White 1943–
English singer and television presenter

Born in Liverpool, she made her debut at the city's legendary Cavern Club and had No 1 singles with 'Anyone Who Had a Heart' (1964) and 'You're My World' (1964). Subsequent chart hits included 'You've Lost That Lovin' Feelin'' (1965), 'Alfie' (1966), 'Step Inside Love' (1968) and 'Surround Yourself with Sorrow' (1969). She also appeared in the films *Ferry Cross the Mersey* and *Work is a Four-Letter Word* (1967). Turning to television presenting, she became the host of *Surprise, Surprise* (1984–   ) and *Blind Date* (1985–   ), and marked her 30 years in show business with *Cilla's Celebration* (1993). Her publications include *Step Inside* (1985) and *Through the Years—My Life in Pictures* (1993).

Black, Clementina Maria 1853–1922
English suffragist, trade unionist and novelist

Born in Brighton, East Sussex, she was educated at home. On her mother's death she moved to London, where she conducted research for her novels and lectured on 18th-century literature. After serving as secretary of the Women's Provident and Protective League, she set up the more militant Women's Trade Union Association (1889). This merged with the Women's Industrial Council (1897) and she became its president, playing an important part in collecting data on women's work and campaigning against sweated industries. Her publications include *Sweated Industry and the Minimum Wage* (1907), *A Case for Trade Boards* (1909), and her best-known book, *Married Women's Work* (1915), as well as a number of novels. She was the sister of Constance Garnett (1862–1946), who was a distinguished translator of Russian literature and the wife of Edward Garnett.

Black, Hugo la Fayette 1886–1971
US judge

Born in Clay County, Alabama, he studied and practised law in Alabama and became a police court judge. In 1926 he entered the US Senate and as a liberal leader promoted the Tennessee Valley Authority and federal wages and hours laws. Appointed to the Supreme Court of the US Senate in 1937, he frequently dissented, holding firm views on individual freedoms against restrictions. He held that the Fourteenth Amendment made the Bill of Rights generally applicable to the states and that the First Amendment's guarantees of freedoms were absolute.

Black, Sir James Whyte 1924–
Scottish pharmacologist and Nobel Prize winner

Born in Uddington, Strathclyde, he graduated in medicine at St Andrews University and became an assistant lecturer in physiology there (1946–47), a lecturer at the University of Malaya and then senior lecturer at Glasgow Veterinary School (1950–58). Following appointments at ICI Pharmaceuticals (1958–64) and the Wellcome Research Laboratories (1978–84) as director of therapeutic research, he was appointed Professor of Pharmacology and departmental head at University College London (1973–77). Since 1984 he has held similar posts at King's College Medical School in London. In 1962 while at ICI, he discovered the drug netherlide (Alderlin), the first beta-blocking drug, which opened the way to new treatments for certain types of heart disease (angina, tachycardia), and led to his development of safer, more effective drugs. At the Wellcome Laboratories he produced burimamide and cimetidine, new drugs with which he distinguished classes of histamine receptor, used in the treatment of ulcers. He was elected FRS in 1976 and knighted in 1981, and shared with **Gertrude Elion** and **George Hitchings** the 1988 Nobel Prize for physiology or medicine. He became Chancellor of Dundee University in 1992.

Black, Joseph 1728–99
Scottish chemist
Born in Bordeaux, France, the son of a wine merchant, he was educated at Belfast, Glasgow and Edinburgh. In his MD thesis of 1754 he showed that the causticity of lime and the alkalis is due to the absence of the 'fixed air' (carbon dioxide) present in limestone and the carbonates of the alkalis. With this discovery he was the first person to realize that there are gases other than air, and his experimental method laid the foundations of quantitative analysis. In 1756 he succeeded **William Cullen** as Professor of Anatomy and Chemistry at Glasgow, but soon after exchanged duties with the professor of the Institutes of Medicine, practising also as a physician. Between 1756 and 1761 he evolved the theory of 'latent heat' on which his scientific fame chiefly rests. In 1766 he succeeded Cullen in the chair of medicine and chemistry at Edinburgh. Black was also a successful industrial consultant and was widely consulted on problems such as bleaching and dyeing, iron-making, ore analysis, fertilizers and water supplies. Famed as a teacher, his chemistry classes drew students from all over the UK, Europe and America. ⊞ William Ramsay, *Life and Letters of Joseph Black* (1918)

Black, Sir Misha 1910–77
British designer
Born in Russia, he trained as an architect, his early work being mainly in commercial exhibition design. He designed the famous pre-war cafés for the firm Kardomah, for which he was consultant from 1936 to 1950. Very much a team designer, he was a founder of one of the earliest design consultancies, the Industrial Design Partnership (1935), and later of the Design Research Unit (1945), both with **Milner Gray**. He contributed to the 'Britain Can Make It' exhibition in 1946 and to the 'Festival of Britain' in 1951. His outstanding postwar design work was for British Rail, London Transport and P & O. He became a royal designer for industry in 1957, and was Professor of Industrial Design at the Royal College of Art, London (1959–75).

Black, William 1841–98
Scottish novelist
Born in Glasgow, and educated at the Glasgow School of Art, he moved to London as a journalist and was a war correspondent during the Austro-Prussian War (1866) and the Franco-Prussian War of 1870–71. An early member of the 'kailyard school', his first success was *A Daughter of Heth* (1871), followed by a succession of colourfully overwritten novels, usually set in the Highlands and involving an outsider marrying into the community. ⊞ Sir Thomas Reid, *William Black, novelist* (1902)

Blackadder, Elizabeth 1931–
Scottish painter
Born in Falkirk, Stirlingshire, she studied at Edinburgh University and Edinburgh College of Art, where she later taught (1962–86). Her early work was mainly landscape, but from the 1970s she began to concentrate on still life, for which she is now best known. In both oil and water colour she paints recognizable objects with apparently random associations (eg cats, fans, ribbons, flowers and plants) on an abstract empty background. Her interest in calligraphic gesture and the space between motifs shows considerable Japanese influence. She was the first Scottish woman painter to be elected to full membership of both the Royal Academy (1976) and the Royal Scottish Academy (1972).

Blackbeard See Teach, Edward

Blackburn, Helen 1842–1903
Irish social reformer
Born in Knightstown, County Kerry, she was the daughter of a civil engineer and inventor, and in 1859 she moved with her family to London. A staunch believer in the vote as the key to women's equality, she was Secretary of the National Society for Women's Suffrage from 1874 to 1895. Her many publications include a *Handbook for Women engaged in Social and Political Work* (1881) and *Women's Suffrage: a Record of the Movement in the British Isles* (1902). In 1899, with Jessie Boucherett (owner of *The Englishwoman's Review* which Blackburn edited, 1881–90), she founded the Freedom of Labour Defence League, aimed at maintaining women's freedom and their powers of earning. In 1903 (with Nora Vynne) she published *Women under the Factory Act*.

Blackburn, Jemima 1823–1909
Scottish painter
She was born in Edinburgh, the youngest child of James Wedderburn, the Solicitor-General for Scotland. She showed a precocious talent from an early age and her animal drawings greatly impressed Sir **Edwin Landseer**, whom she met in 1843. One of the most popular illustrators in Victorian Britain, she illustrated 27 books, the most important being *Birds from Nature* (1862, 1868), which demonstrates her great skill with brush and lithographic crayon. Her most enduring works are the albums containing hundreds of watercolours depicting the day-to-day events of late-19th-century family life in the Scottish Highlands.

Blackburn, Robert 1885–1955
British aircraft designer
Born in Leeds, he designed his first plane in 1910, and founded the Blackburn Aircraft Company in 1914 under contract to build military biplanes.

Blacket, Edmund Thomas 1817–83
Australian architect
Born in Southwark, London, England, he arrived in Sydney in 1842. One year later he had designed his first church and was appointed chief architect for the diocese by **William Broughton**, first (and only) Anglican Bishop of Australia. He quickly built up a steady practice but in 1849 became government architect for New South Wales, returning to private practice in 1854 to design the new University of New South Wales, whose Great Hall is generally considered the finest building of its style in the southern hemisphere. His academic and ecclesiastical work, including cathedrals in Sydney and Perth, was Victorian Gothic in style, but in commercial designs for banks and hotels, he adopted classical forms.

Blackett, Patrick Maynard Stuart, Baron 1897–1974
English physicist and Nobel Prize winner
Born in London and educated at Dartmouth College, he served in the Royal Navy during World War I. He then went to Magdalene College, Cambridge, and studied physics at the Cavendish Laboratory. He was the first to photograph, in 1925, nuclear collisions involving transmutation. He was professor at London University (1933–37) and Manchester University (1937–53), and subsequently returned to London as professor at the Imperial College of Science and Technology (1953–65). Blackett was awarded the Nobel Prize for physics in 1948 for developing the Wilson cloud chamber, using it to confirm

the existence of the positron (the antiparticle of the electron). He pioneered research on cosmic radiation and, in World War II, operational research. He also contributed to the theories of particle pair production, and the discovery of 'strange' particles. ⊞ Bernard Lovell, *P M S Blackett* (1976)

Black Hawk 1767–1838
Native American leader

Born in Saukenuk, a village of the Sauk people in Illinois, he became a Sauk chief and opposed US expansion into his people's ancestral lands, though he was unable to prevent members of the Sauk and Fox tribes from signing a treaty that ceded all of their lands east of the Mississippi to the USA. He sided with the British in the War of 1812 and fought US forces until 1815. In the ensuing decade he and his people were forced to move westward, but they kept revisiting their homeland. Their effort to plant crops there in 1832 led to a conflict with federal troops and began the Black Hawk War, which lasted from April to August of that year. Black Hawk and his followers were finally defeated at Bad Axe River in Wisconsin, and he was captured and imprisoned. After his death his bones were displayed in an Iowa museum.

Blackman, Frederick Frost 1866–1947
English botanist

Born in Lambeth, London, and educated at Mill Hill School, he studied medicine at St Bartholomew's Hospital, but then studied natural sciences at St John's College, Cambridge. Thereafter he worked at the Cambridge Botany School (1891–1936). He was renowned for his fundamental research both on the respiration of plants, showing conclusively for the first time that the bulk of the exchange of CO_2 between leaves and air was via the stomata, and on the limiting factors affecting plants' growth.

Blackmore, Richard Doddridge 1825–1900
English novelist

Born in Longworth, Berkshire, he was educated at Blundell's School, Tiverton, and Exeter College, Oxford. He was called to the Bar at the Middle Temple in 1852, and practised for a while, but poor health made him take to market gardening and literature in Teddington. After publishing several collections of poetry, he found his real niche in fiction. *Clara Vaughan* (1864) was the first of 15 novels, mostly with a Devonshire background, of which *Lorna Doone* (1869) is his masterpiece and an accepted classic of the West Country. Other novels include *The Maid of Sker* (1872), *Alice Lorraine* (1875) and *Tommy Upmore* (1884). ⊞ K G Budd, *The Last Victorian* (1960)

Blackmun, Harry Andrew 1908–
US jurist

Born in Nashville, Illinois, he graduated from Harvard in mathematics (1929) and law (1932), and was called to the Minnesota Bar in 1932. He served as clerk to the presiding judge of the US 8th District Court of Appeals (1932–33), building up a law practice and teaching at the St Paul College of Law (1935–41) and the University of Minnesota Law School (1945–47). He became resident counsel for the Mayo Clinic at Rochester (1950–59) and Judge of the 8th Circuit of US Court of Appeals (1959–70). He was nominated by President Richard Nixon to the US Supreme Court (1970–94). He has been a quiet but effective influence in moderating the views of his more conservative colleagues.

Blackstone, Tessa Ann Vosper Evans, Baroness, *née* Blackstone 1942–
English sociologist

Born in Bures, Suffolk, she was educated at the London School of Economics. She lectured in sociology at Enfield College of Technology (1965–66), and in social administration at the London School of Economics for nine years, then became adviser to the Central Policy Review Staff in the Cabinet Office (1975–78). After being Professor of Educational Administration at the University of London Institute of Education (1978–83), she was director of education at the Inner London Education Authority, then was Master of London University's Birkbeck College (1987). Awarded a life peerage in 1987, she has served in the House of Lords as Opposition front bench spokesperson on education and science (1988–92) and on foreign affairs (1992–). Her books on education and social issues include *Prisons and Penal Reform* (1990).

Blackstone, Sir William 1723–80
English judge and jurist

Born in London, he obtained a scholarship in 1738 from Charterhouse to Pembroke College, Oxford. In 1741 he entered the Inner Temple and was elected a Fellow of All Souls (1744). After an unsuccessful period at the Bar, he was appointed a Professor of English Law at Oxford. He was made a King's Counsel in 1761, and became MP for Hindon, Wiltshire (1761–70) and Principal of New Inn Hall, Oxford. In 1763, he was made Solicitor-General to the Queen, and from 1770 to 1780 was a judge of the Court of Common Pleas. He published his celebrated *Commentaries on the Laws of England* (1765–69) which became a highly influential work, setting out the structure of English law and explaining its major principles.

Blackwell, Sir Basil Henry 1889–1984
English publisher and bookseller

Born in Oxford, he was the son of the chairman of the famous Oxford bookshop (founded in 1846). He was educated at Magdalen College School and Merton College, and joined the family business in 1913, but also published independently, founding the Shakespeare Head Press (1921). He succeeded to the chairmanship in 1924 and from that time joined the family bookselling interest with that of publishing, mostly on academic subjects.

Blackwell, Elizabeth 1821–1910
US physician, the first woman doctor in the USA

She was born in Bristol, England, the sister of Emily Blackwell. Her family emigrated to the USA in 1832, where her father died six years later, leaving a widow and nine children. Elizabeth helped to support the family by teaching, devoting her leisure to the study of medical books. After fruitless applications for admission to various medical schools, she entered that of Geneva, in New York State, and graduated in 1849. She next visited Europe and, after much difficulty, was admitted into La Maternité in Paris, and St Bartholomew's Hospital in London. In 1851 she returned to New York City where she established a dispensary, The New York Infirmary for Indigent Women and Children. After 1868 she lived in England until her death. She was responsible for opening the field of medicine to women. ⊞ Dorothy C Wilson, *Lone Woman: The Story of Elizabeth Blackwell, the First Woman Doctor* (1970)

Blackwell, Emily 1826–1910
US physician

She was born in Bristol, England, the sister of Elizabeth Blackwell. Her family emigrated to the USA in 1832, and she was educated at Cleveland (Western Reserve) University, followed by work in Europe where she was assistant to Sir James Simpson. In 1856 she helped open her sister's dispensary in New York City (The New York Infirmary for Indigent Women and Children). From 1869 to 1910 she ran the dispensary, and from 1869 to 1899 was Dean and Professor of Obstetrics and Diseases of Women at the Women's Medical College which was attached to the infirmary. She was the first woman doctor to undertake major surgery on a considerable scale.

Blackwood, Algernon Henry 1869–1951
English novelist
Born in Shooters Hill, Kent, he was educated at Edinburgh University before working his way through Canada and the USA, as related in his *Episodes before Thirty* (1923). His novels, which reflect his taste for the supernatural and the occult, include *The Human Chord* (1910) and *The Wave* (1916). He also published the collections of short stories, *Tales of the Uncanny and Supernatural* (1949), *John Silence* (1908) and *Tongues of Fire* (1924).

Blackwood, Lord (Ian) Basil Gawaine Temple 1870–1917
English artist
The son of the 1st Marquess of Dufferin and Ava, he was educated at Harrow and at Balliol College, Oxford. He made his reputation as illustrator for **Hilaire Belloc's** *The Bad Child's Book of Beasts*, *More Beasts for Worse Children*, *Cautionary Tales for Children*, *More Peers*, *A Moral Alphabet* and *The Modern Traveller*. He held posts in the colonial service in South Africa and Barbados, was private secretary to the Irish viceroy, and died in World War I.

Blackwood, William 1776–1834
Scottish publisher
Born in Edinburgh, he was apprenticed to a bookseller at the age of 14 and established himself as a bookseller in Edinburgh—principally of antiquarian books—in 1804. In 1817 he started *Blackwood's Magazine* as a Tory rival to the Whig *Edinburgh Review*, and from the seventh number assumed the editorship himself with **John Wilson** ('Christopher North'), **John Gibson Lockhart**, **James Hogg**, and others as contributors.

Blaeu, Latin Coesius, Willem Janszoon 1571–1638
Dutch map-maker, mathematician and astronomer
Born in Alkmaar, he founded a publishing firm in Amsterdam, specializing in globes. His son Jan (d.1673) started his own business, but later entered into partnership with his brother Cornelis (d.1650). His *Atlas Major* (11 vols) is valuable and shows local history. The volume on Scotland contains 49 maps, prepared by Timothy Pont (c.1560–1630), and local details by Sir John Scot. Jan also published topographical plates and views of towns. Two of his sons carried on the business until 1700.

Blaine, James Gillespie 1830–93
US journalist and politician
Born in West Brownsville, Pennsylvania, he settled in Maine, where he edited the Kennebec Journal (1854–60) and served in the state legislature. He then became a member of the US House of Representatives (1863–76), serving as Speaker from 1869 to 1875, before becoming a senator (1876–81) and Secretary of State (1881). He was the Republican candidate for President in 1884 but lost the election by a narrow margin to **Grover Cleveland**, a loss that might perhaps have been avoided if one of his supporters had not alienated the Catholic vote in New York by assailing the Democrats as the party of 'Rum, Romanism, and Rebellion'. As Secretary of State once again (1889–92), in the **Harrison** administration, he organized the first Pan-American Conference (1889).

Blainey, Geoffrey Norman 1930–
Australian social historian
Born in Melbourne, he attended Melbourne University, and was Professor of Economic History there for 20 years. In 1966 his *The Tyranny of Distance* showed how geographical isolation had shaped the history and the people of Australia. *Triumph of the Nomads* (1975) and *A Land Half Won* (1980) completed his trilogy, *A Vision of Australian*

History. Other books include *The Rush that Never Ended* (1963), on Australian mining, *The Steel Master* (1971), a life of Essington Lewis, and *Jumping Over the Wheel* (1993). He reached a wide popular audience through his books and *The Blainey View* on television. He is inaugural Chancellor of the University of Ballarat, Victoria (1994–).

Blair, Bonnie 1964–
US speedskater
She was born in Cornwall, New York. She is the most decorated female Olympian after **Lidiya Skoblikova** with six medals, all for speedskating, as well as being the first US speedskater to win in more than one Olympic Games. Her five gold medals were for the 500 metres in 1988, 1992 and 1994, and for the 1,000 metres in 1992 and 1994. In 1994 she became a professional speedskater and motivational speaker and in 1995 she set the 500 metres world record at Calgary.

Blair, Catherine 1872–1946
Scottish painter and reformer
She was born in Bathgate, Midlothian, and from her late thirties she was at the forefront of both the Women's Suffrage Movement and the Scottish Women's Rural Institute. In 1920 she founded the Mak' Merry Pottery in Macmerry, East Lothian, which specialized in painting pottery blanks to a high standard in a colourful and decorative manner. Throughout her life she was an outspoken champion of the ordinary cottar woman.

Blair, Francis Preston 1791–1876
US journalist and politician
Born in Abingdon, Virginia, he was a supporter of President **Andrew Jackson**, whom he advised as a member of the Kitchen Cabinet. In 1830 he founded the Jacksonian Democratic newspaper, the *Globe*, serving as its editor until 1845. A political sage who wielded great influence behind the scenes, he balked at the growing Southern bias in the Democratic Party and was instrumental in founding the Republican Party in 1856. He served as an adviser to President **Abraham Lincoln** and organized the Hampton Roads Peace Conference (1865) in an unsuccessful effort to end the Civil War.

Blair, Robert 1699–1746
Scottish poet and preacher
Born in Edinburgh and educated at Edinburgh University, he was ordained minister of Athelstaneford, East Lothian, in 1731. He is best known as the author of *The Grave* (1743), a blank-verse poem which heralded the 'churchyard school' of poetry. The 1808 edition was illustrated by **William Blake**. 📖 W Row, *The Life of Mr Robert Blair* (1848, ed T McCrie)

Blair, Tony (Anthony Charles Lynton) 1953–
British Labour politician
Born in Edinburgh, he was educated at Fettes College and St John's College, Oxford. After graduating he became a barrister specializing in trade union and employment law. He was elected to parliament as Labour MP for Sedgefield in 1983 and achieved success as opposition Home Affairs spokesman in 1992 by promoting law and order, traditionally a Conservative interest. In 1994 he succeeded **John Smith** as Leader of the Labour Party and instituted a series of reforms to streamline and modernize the Labour Party. In 1997 Labour's landslide win in the general election made Blair Prime Minister, the third-youngest, after Pitt, the Younger, and Lord Liverpool, to take office. He has published *New Britain: My Vision for a Young Country* (1996). 📖 Jon Sopel, *Tony Blair: The Moderniser* (1995)

Blaise or Blasius, St d.c.316AD
Armenian churchman and martyr

Born in Sebastea in Cappadocia, Asia Minor, he became Bishop of Sebastea and is said to have suffered martyrdom during a period of persecution. He is the patron saint of woolcombers, and is invoked in cases of throat trouble and cattle diseases. His feast day is 3 February.

Blaize, Herbert Augustus 1918–89
Grenadian statesman

After qualifying and practising as a solicitor, he entered politics and helped to found the centrist Grenada National Party (GNP), being elected to parliament in 1957. He held ministerial posts before becoming premier in 1967. After full independence, in 1974, he led the official opposition and then went into hiding (1979–83) following the left-wing coup by Maurice Bishop. After the US invasion of 1983, when normal political activity had resumed, he returned to lead a reconstituted New National Party (NNP) and win the 1984 general election.

Blake, Eubie (James Hubert) 1883–1983
US pianist and composer

He was born in Baltimore, Maryland, and began working with bandleader Noble Sissle in 1915. They scored a significant success with *Shuffle Along* (1921), one of the earliest African-American Broadway productions. He contributed to numerous musicals, notably *Chocolate Dandies* (1929, with Sissle), and was the subject of the Broadway musical *Eubie* (1978). His most important legacy lay in his mastery of ragtime piano, and he was increasingly recognized as a major practitioner. During his long career he wrote, recorded and performed numerous songs, such as 'I'm Just Wild About Harry' and 'Memories of You'. He marked his hundredth birthday with the wry observation: 'If I'd known I was gonna to live this long I would have taken better care of myself'. 📖 R Kimball and W Bolcom, *Reminiscing with Sissle and Blake* (1972)

Blake, Eugene Carson 1906–85
US Presbyterian clergyman and ecumenist

Born in St Louis, Missouri, and educated at Princeton, he served pastorates in New York and California before becoming stated clerk of the Presbyterian Church, USA. In 1967 he was appointed general secretary of the World Council of Churches, a demanding post he held for five years, during which time Pope Paul VI paid his historic visit to the Geneva offices. His dream was the formation of a church that would be 'truly reformed, truly catholic, and truly evangelical'.

Blake, Peter 1932–
English painter

He was born in Dartford, Kent. From the mid-1950s, while still a student at the Royal College of Art, he was a pioneer of the Pop Art movement in Great Britain, using media imagery from sources such as comics, advertisements and popular magazines. His most widely-known work is the cover design for the Beatles' album *Sergeant Pepper's Lonely Hearts Club Band* (1967). In 1975 he was a founder-member of the Brotherhood of Ruralists, a community of painters living in the West Country dedicated to a nostalgic view of country life.

Blake, Sir Peter James 1948–
New Zealand yachtsman

He was born in Auckland. In 1994 he was co-skipper with Robin Knox-Johnston on a record-breaking circumnavigation, and in 1995, for only the second time in its 144-year history, he took the America's Cup away from America with a non-US crew in his boat, *Black Magic*. Denis Conner's *Young America* was defeated 5–0 in the finals by *Black Magic*, which had an average winning margin of just under three minutes—a huge distance on water. Blake ran the Team New Zealand operation and sold 100,000 pairs of 'lucky' red socks to finance it. He was knighted in 1995.

Blake, Robert 1599–1657
English naval commander

Born in Bridgwater, Somerset, he was educated at Wadham College, Oxford. He led the life of a quiet country gentleman until 1640, when he became MP for Bridgwater in the Short Parliament, later serving in the Long Parliament (1645–53). In the Civil War he took part in the defence of Bristol (1643), Lyme Regis (1644) and Taunton (1644–45). Appointed admiral in 1649, he blockaded Lisbon, destroyed Prince Rupert's fleet, and captured the Scilly Isles and Jersey. In the first Dutch War (1652–54) he defeated Maarten Tromp at the Battle of Portland (1653) and shattered Dutch supremacy at sea. His greatest victory was in 1657 at Santa Cruz off Tenerife, where he destroyed a Spanish treasure fleet. He is considered one of the greatest English admirals.

Blake, William See panel p213

Blakemore, Colin Brian 1944–
British physiologist

After a period at Cambridge (1968–79), he was appointed Waynflete Professor of Physiology at Oxford University in 1979. He has worked on the physiology of the brain, and published *Mechanics of the Mind* in 1977. He gave the BBC Reith Lectures in 1976, and received the Michael Faraday award of the Royal Society in 1989. He became the object of fierce criticism by animal-rights acitivists and in 1994 won an injunction to prevent them from publishing his home address and telephone number.

Blakeslee, Albert Francis 1874–1954
US botanist

Born in Genesco, New York, he was educated at the East Greenwich (Rhode Island) Academy, Wesleyan University and Harvard University. At Harvard, he studied *Mucor* (bread mould) reproduction, and continued this work in Germany, before returning to Harvard for a year and then working as Professor of Botany at Connecticut Agricultural College, Storrs. From 1915 to 1942 he worked at Cold Spring Harbor, teaching genetics and experimenting with the genus *Datura*, discovering the first *Datura* haploid, the first sectorial chimaera, and the first species hybrid. In 1937 he established that treatment with colchicine can bring about polyploidy in plants. From 1936 he was director of the Carnegie Station for Experimental Evolution, and in 1942 he moved to Smith College Genetics Experiment Station, Northampton, Massachusetts, as its first director.

Blakey, Art(hur), *also known as* Abdullah ibn Buhaina 1919–90
US jazz drummer and bandleader

Born in Pittsburgh, Pennsylvania, he began as a pianist, but switched to drums. His early engagements included work with the Billy Eckstine Orchestra (1944–47), which featured many of the emerging bebop musicians. Blakey adopted the new style, and recorded with the first of his many versions of The Jazz Messengers in 1947. The group, initially co-led with Horace Silver, became the most important band in the development of the influential hard bop style of the 1950s, and its ex-members constitute a virtual 'who's who' of the form. Blakey's own fervent, driving drum style (with its trademark press rolls) lay at the heart of their music, and he was a hugely influential teacher and mentor to young musicians throughout his life.

Blalock, Alfred 1899–1964
US surgeon

Born in Culloden, Georgia, he received his medical education at Johns Hopkins University, and his postgraduate training there and at Vanderbilt University Hospital. He joined the staff at Vanderbilt (1925–41) and at Johns Hopkins (1941–64), where he pioneered the

Blake, William 1757–1827
English poet, painter, engraver and mystic

William Blake was born in London, the son of an Irish hosier. He did not go to school, but was apprenticed in 1771 to the engraver **James Basire**. After studying at the Royal Academy School he began to produce watercolour figure subjects and to engrave illustrations for magazines. His first book of poems, *Poetical Sketches*, appeared in 1783.

He went on to produce many 'illuminated books', in which the text is interwoven with his imaginative designs. These were printed from engraved copper plates and then either hand-coloured or printed in colour by himself or his wife, Catherine Boucher. Such books include *Songs of Innocence* (1789) and *Songs of Experience* (1794), collections of delicate lyrics which express his ardent belief in the freedom of the imagination and his hatred of rationalism and materialism; and mystical and prophetical works such as the *Book of Thel* (1789) and *The Marriage of Heaven and Hell* (1793). Epic poems include *The Four Zoas* (1795–1804, begun as *Vala*), *Milton* (1804–08) and *Jerusalem* (1804–20).

His figure designs include a highly acclaimed series of 537 coloured illustrations to **Edward Young**'s *Night Thoughts* (1797) and 12 to **Robert Blair**'s *The Grave* (1808). His finest artistic work is to be found in the 21 *Illustrations to the Book of Job* (1826), completed when he was almost 70, and unequalled in modern religious art for imaginative force and visionary power. At his death he was employed on the illustrations to the *Divina Commedia* of **Dante**. He is also known as a wood engraver.

Among the most important of his paintings are *The Canterbury Pilgrims*, which the artist himself engraved; *The Spiritual Form of Pitt guiding Behemoth* (now in the National Gallery, London); *Jacob's Dream*; and *The Last Judgement*.

During his life he met with little encouragement from the public, but he was supported by the friendship of **William Hayley**, **John Flaxman** and **Samuel Palmer**, and by the financial generosity of **John Linnell**. He was upheld by the most real and vivid faith in the unseen, guided and encouraged—as he believed—by perpetual visitations from the spiritual world.

♫ Blake's poetry was used as a basis for many musical compositions. Notable among these are: *Ghost of Abel* (Dennis Arundell), *Songs and Proverbs* (**Benjamin Britten**), *Seasons* (Eric Fogg), *Job* (**Ralph Vaughan Williams**), *Jerusalem* (**Hubert Parry**), *Song of Liberty* (**Michael Tippett**). Other songs have been set by William Busch, Phyllis Tate, and others.

📖 Steward Crehan, *Blake in Context* (1984); Jack Lindsay, *William Blake: His Life and Work* (1978); David Bindman, *Blake as an Artist* (1977).

> 'A truth that's told with bad intent
> Beats all the lies you can invent
> It is right it should be so
> Man was made for joy and woe
> And when this we rightly know
> Thro' the world we safely go
> Joy and woe are woven fine
> A clothing for the soul divine.'
> 'Auguries of Innocence' (c.1803).

---

surgical treatment of various congenital defects of the heart and its associated blood vessels, many of which could be recognized by the presence of cyanosis in infants, and performed the first 'blue baby' operation, co-operating with the paediatrician **Helen Taussig**. He also did important experimental work on the pathophysiology of surgical shock and its treatment by transfusion of whole blood or blood plasma, and was the first to treat *myasthenia gravis* by removal of the thymus gland. His collected scientific papers were published in 1966.

Blamey, Sir Thomas 1884–1951
Australian field marshal

He was born near Wagga Wagga, New South Wales. He joined the regular army in 1906 and played an important part in the evacuation of Gallipoli. He became Chief of Staff of the Australian Corps in 1918. At the outbreak of World War II he commanded the Australian Imperial Forces in the Middle East. He served as deputy Commander-in-Chief to **Archibald Wavell** and had command of Commonwealth operations in Greece (1941). He became Commander-in-Chief of Allied land forces in Australia (1942) and received the Japanese surrender in 1945. In 1950 he was made a field marshal, the first Australian soldier to hold this rank.

Blampied, Edmund 1886–1966
British artist

Born in Jersey, he is best known for his etchings which depict everyday farming life, in particular horses and peasants. Apart from his lithographs and watercolours, he produced some 115 etchings, and is considered one of the most talented British etchers. During the German occupation he designed the Jersey occupation stamps.

Blanc, (Jean Joseph) Louis 1811–82
French politician and historian

Born in Madrid, he studied in Paris, where in 1839 he founded the *Revue du Progrès* and wrote his chief work on socialism, *L'Organisation du travail* (1839, Eng trans *The Organization of Work*, 1911), proposing the establishment of co-operative workshops subsidized by the state. After the February Revolution (1848) he became a member of the provisional government, which had no power and achieved nothing. Charged with fomenting the June Days rising of Parisian workers, he fled in 1848 to Belgium, moving to London in 1851. On the fall of the Second Empire he returned to France, and was elected to the National Assembly in 1871. He opposed the Paris Commune (1871), but led the extreme left in the first parliaments of the Third Republic.

Blanc, Raymond René 1949–
French chef and restaurateur

He was born near Besançon, and after training as a waiter he went to England in 1972 to manage a pub on the River Thames, the Rose Revived, where he began to cook in 1975. He opened a small restaurant in Oxford in 1977, Les Quat' Saisons, and progressed through more elaborate premises before opening Le Manoir aux Quat' Saisons in 1984. He is a popular broadcaster whose publications include *Recipes from Le Manoir aux Quat' Saisons* (1988), *Cooking for Friends* (1991) and *Blanc Mange* (1994).

Blanchard, Jean Pierre François 1753–1809
French balloonist, inventor of the parachute

He was born in Les Andelys. With **John Jeffries** he was the first to cross the English Channel by balloon, from Dover to Calais, in 1785. He was killed at La Haye during practice parachute jumps from a balloon.

Blanchflower, Danny (Robert Dennis) 1926–93
Northern Irish footballer and broadcaster

Born in Belfast, he was a powerful influence in the Northern Ireland side which reached the World Cup quarter-finals in 1958. Transferring from Aston Villa to Tottenham Hotspur, he master-minded the London club's double success of 1960–61 in the League and the FA Cup, the first time the double had been achieved this century. He was British Footballer of the Year in 1960–61, and won a European Cupwinners' Cup medal with Tottenham. On his retiral he was much in demand as a newspaper columnist and television commentator. His influence on the game was immortalized in the British film *The Glory, Glory Days*.

Blanco, Serge 1958–
French rugby union player
Born in Venezuela, he represented Biarritz at club level. He played 93 times for France and became the second most capped international player behind **Philippe Sella**. His position as full-back allowed him to score 38 international tries. Pacy and glamorous, he was a charismatic player and personality who brought an exciting expectation to every game in which he played and was revered as a national figure. He retired in 1991.

Blanda, (George) Frederick 1927–
US footballer
Born in Youngwood, Pennsylvania, he holds the record for the most points (2,002) in any National Football League (NFL) career. He played for the Chicago Bears, Baltimore Colts, Houston Oilers and Oakland Raiders (1949–75).

Blandrata or Biandrata, Giorgio c.1515–c.1590
Italian physician, theologian and founder of Unitarianism in Poland and Transylvania
Born in Saluzzo, Piedmont, he was compelled to flee to Geneva in 1556 due to the freedom of his religious opinions, but in 1558 **John Calvin's** displeasure at his anti-Trinitarianism drove him to Poland. Finally, in 1563, he became physician to John Sigismund, Prince of Transylvania. He is said to have been strangled in his sleep by his nephew.

Blane, Sir Gilbert 1749–1834
Scottish physician
He was born in Blanefield, Ayrshire. In 1779 he sailed with Admiral **George Rodney** to the West Indies. As head of the Navy Medical Board, he introduced the compulsory use of lemon juice on board navy ships to prevent scurvy. He also pioneered the use of statistics in clinical medicine.

Blankers-Koen, Fanny (Francina) 1918–
Dutch athlete
She was born in Amsterdam and achieved success at the comparatively late age of 30, when she dominated women's events in the London Olympics of 1948. She won four gold medals: the 100 metres (11.9 seconds), 200 metres (24.4 seconds), 80 metres hurdles (11.2 seconds) and the 4 × 100 metres relay, and earned the nickname 'the flying Dutch housewife'. Unequalled among women as an all-round athlete, though primarily a sprinter, she at various times also held world records for both high and long jumps.

Blanqui, (Louis) Auguste 1805–81
French revolutionary
Born in Puget-Théniers, he worked from 1830 at building up a network of secret societies committed to violent revolution. He spent 37 years in prison, and was in prison in 1871 when he was elected president of the revolutionary Commune of Paris. He was released in 1879. In 1881 his followers, known as Blanquists, joined the Marxists.

Blashford-Snell, Colonel John 1936–
English explorer and youth leader
Born in Hereford, he was educated at Victoria College, Jersey, and the Royal Military Academy, Sandhurst, and was commissioned into the Royal Engineers in 1957. He participated in over 40 expeditions, and led the Blue Nile (1968), British Trans-Americas (1972) and Zaire River (1975/84) expeditions under the aegis of the Scientific Exploration Society (SES), of which he is chairman. He then went on to lead two major youth projects: Operation Drake (1978–80) and Operation Raleigh, which involved over 4,000 young people in adventurous, scientific and community projects in over 73 countries (1984–88) before being established as the Raleigh Trust. He has written several books on his adventures and projects, including (with Ann Tweedy) *Operation Raleigh, Adventure Unlimited* (1990) and *Something Lost Behind the Ranges* (1994).

Blasis, Carlo 1797–1878
Italian dancer, choreographer and teacher
Born in Naples, he danced in France, Italy, London and Russia, and became director of the Dance Academy in Milan in 1837. The author of noted treatises on the codification of ballet technique (1820, 1840, 1857), he is regarded as the most important ballet teacher of the 19th century.

Blasius, St See Blaise, St

Blatch, Harriot (Eaton) Stanton, *née* Stanton 1856–1940
US suffrage leader
Born in Seneca Falls, New York, the daughter of **Elizabeth Cady Stanton**, she was educated at Vassar College, where she studied mathematics. She moved to Basingstoke, England, on her marriage (1882) to William Blatch, and was impressed by the work of the Women's Franchise League. After her return to the USA she founded the Equality League of Self-Supporting Women (1907) and became an activist for women's rights, founding the Women's Political Union in 1908. Her published works include *Mobilizing Woman-Power* (1918) and *A Woman's Point of View* (1920).

Blavatsky, Helena Petrovna, *known as* Madame Blavatsky, *née* Hahn 1831–91
US theosophist
Born in Yekaterinoslav, Russia (now Dnipopetrovsk, Ukraine), she travelled widely in the East, including Tibet, and went to the USA in 1873. In 1875, with **Henry Steel Olcott**, she founded the Theosophical Society in New York City and later carried on her work in India. Her psychic powers were widely acclaimed but did not survive investigation by the Society for Psychical Research, although this did not deter her large following, which included **Annie Besant**. Her writings include *Isis Unveiled* (1877). 🕮 Marion Meade, *Madame Blavatsky* (1980)

Bleasdale, Alan 1946–
English dramatist
He was born in Liverpool and was educated at Wade Deacon Grammar School, Widnes, and Padgate Teacher Training College. His television play *The Blackstuff* (1980), and the ensuing television series *The Boys From the Blackstuff* (1982), about a group of unemployed Liverpudlians, were an enormous success, and established his reputation for hard-hitting social dramas. *The Monocled Mutineer*, a television series set during World War I, followed in 1986 but was less well received. He enjoyed another success with *GBH* (1990), a television drama about corruption in local politics. His stage plays include *Are You Lonesome Tonight?* (1985), a musical about **Elvis Presley**, and *On The Ledge* (1993), a savage social drama about life in high-rise flats in Liverpool.

Blériot, Louis 1872–1936
French aviator

Born in Cambrai, he made the first flight across the English Channel (25 July 1909) from Baraques to Dover in a small 24-hp monoplane. He later became an aircraft manufacturer.

Bles, Herri Met de, nicknamed Herri Patenier ('with the white forelock') c.1500–1550
Flemish painter
Probably a relation of **Joachim Patenier**, who was clearly an influence on him, he was a member of the Antwerp guild of painters and specialized in landscapes with figures. Few details are known about him or his life, except that he was known to Italian collectors, with whom his work was popular, as Civetta ('owl'), as owls often appear in his work.

Blessed, Brian 1936–
English actor
Born in Mexborough, South Yorkshire, he made his name on television as PC Fancy Smith in *Z Cars* (1962–65) and later played King Guthrum in *Churchill's People* (1975), Emperor Augustus in *I, Claudius* (1976) and Long John Silver in *Return to Treasure Island* (1989). His film roles include Prince Vultan in *Flash Gordon* (1980), the Duke of Exeter in *Henry V* (1989), Lord Locksley in *Robin Hood: Prince of Thieves* (1991) and Antonio in *Much Ado About Nothing* (1993). He climbed 25,400 feet (7,700m) without oxygen for the BBC documentary *Galahad of Everest* in 1990 and returned to climb Everest three years later, reaching 28,000 feet (8,500m) without oxygen, the oldest man to do so.

Blessington, Marguerite Gardiner, Countess of, née Marguerite Power 1789–1849
Irish literary hostess, memoirist and novelist
She was born in Knockbrit, near Clonmel, County Tipperary. Sold into marriage at 14 by her dissolute father, she abandoned her husband, and when her spouse fell to his death from a window, she married the Earl of Blessington, with whom she had been living for some time. After his death from apoplexy in 1829, she became one of London's most vivacious hostesses, a prolific author, and a dreadful debtor. Travels in Europe with her husband and Count Alfred d'Orsay provided material for her entertaining and important *Journal of Conversations with Lord Byron* (1832), and for two travel books, *The Idler in Italy* (1839) and *The Idler in France* (1841). Her other writings include a number of three-volume novels concerning upper middle-class manners.

Bleuler, Eugen 1857–1939
Swiss psychiatrist who coined the word 'schizophrenia'
He was born in Zollikon, near Zurich, studied medicine at the University of Bern, and became Professor of Psychiatry at Zurich (1898–1927). He carried out research on epilepsy and other physiological conditions, then turned to psychiatry, and in 1911 published an important study on what he called schizophrenia or 'splitting of the mind'. One of his pupils was **Carl Gustav Jung**.

Bley, Carla, née Borg 1938–
US jazz composer, bandleader and pianist
Born in Oakland, California, she moved to New York City as a teenager and worked as a cigarette girl to supplement her occasional income from music. She founded the Jazz Composers Orchestra with Michael Mantler in 1964, which she subsequently developed into a distribution network for commercially difficult music. Composition was always her major artistic concern, and she has produced significant works for important jazz musicians like Gary Burton and Charlie Haden, as well as many pieces for her own ensembles. One of the most distinctive figures in contemporary jazz, she has made a major impact in a traditionally male-dominated field.

Blicher, Steen Steensen 1782–1848
Danish poet and novelist
He was born in Jutland near Viborg, which forms the background of much of his work. He became a teacher and clergyman, and took a great interest in the social and spiritual problems of his day. His collection *Traekfuglene* (1838, 'The Migratory Birds'), ranks among the purest of Danish lyrical poetry, and his short stories, often in dialect, such as 'E Bindstouw', are among the masterpieces of Danish literature. 📖 H P B Poulsen, *Steen Steensen Blicher* (1952)

Bligh, William 1754–c.1817
English naval officer
Born in Plymouth, he went to sea at the age of 15 and was picked by Captain **James Cook** as sailing master of the *Resolution* on his third voyage (1776–80). In 1787 he was chosen by Sir **Joseph Banks** to command the *Bounty* on a voyage to Tahiti to collect plants of the bread-fruit tree and introduce them to the West Indies. On the return voyage, on 28 April 1789, **Fletcher Christian** led a mutiny, and Bligh and 18 men were cast adrift in an open boat without charts. In June they reached Timor, in the East Indies, having travelled nearly 4,000 miles. Bligh served under Lord **Nelson** in command of the *Glatton* at the Battle of Copenhagen in 1801. In 1805 he was appointed Governor of New South Wales and was imprisoned (1808–10) by mutinous soldiers during the so-called 'Rum Rebellion' inspired by **John MacArthur**. Bligh was exonerated of all blame, and promoted admiral on his retirement in 1811. 📖 Gavin Kennedy, *Bligh* (1978)

Blind Harry See **Harry, Blind**

Blind Jack of Knaresborough See **Metcalf, John**

Bliss, Sir Arthur (Drummond) 1891–1975
English composer
Born in London, he studied under **Gustav Holst**, **Charles Stanford** and **Ralph Vaughan Williams** at the Royal College of Music, and in 1921 became Professor of Composition there. After a year, he resigned to devote himself to composition, including music for the film *Things to Come* (1935), based on the 1933 novel by **H G Wells**; the ballets *Checkmate* (1937) and *Miracle in the Gorbals* (1944); the opera *The Olympians* (1949); chamber music; and piano and violin works. He was music director of the BBC (1942–44), and in 1953 succeeded Sir **Arnold Bax** as Master of the Queen's Musick.

Bliss, Philip Paul 1838–76
US evangelist and hymnwriter
Co-author with Ira Sankey (1840–1908) of *Gospel Songs* (1874), he was best known for such favourites as 'Hold the Fort', 'Down Life's Dark Vale We Wander', 'Jesus Loves Me', 'Let the Lower Lights Be Burning' and 'Pull for the Shore', all contained in *Gospel Songs*. He was killed in the Ashtabula train disaster.

Blixen, Karen, Baroness, pseudonym Isak Dinesen 1885–1962
Danish storyteller and novelist
Born in Rungsted, she was educated at home and in France, Switzerland and England, and adopted English as her main literary language, translating some of her most important works back into Danish. In 1914 she married her cousin, Baron Bror Blixen Finecke, from whom she contracted syphilis. Their life on an unproductive coffee plantation in Kenya is recounted in *Den Afrikanske Farm* (1937, Eng trans *Out of Africa*, 1938), which was also the basis of a Hollywood film. After her divorce and the death of her lover Denys Finch-Hatton in a plane crash, she returned to Denmark and began writing the brooding, existential tales for which she is best

known. Like the singer in 'The Wide-Travelling Lioness' (*Seven Gothic Tales*, 1934, Danish trans 1935) they are usually concerned with identity and personal destiny, and are markedly aristocratic in spirit. This is confirmed in *Winter's Tales* (1942), *Last Tales* (1957) and *Anecdotes of Destiny* (1958). 'Babett's Feast' (1950), also successfully filmed, shows a lighter side to her artistic nature. ◻ J Thurman, *Isak Dinesen: the Life of a Storyteller* (1982)

Bloch, Ernest 1880–1959
US composer

Born in Geneva, Switzerland, of Jewish descent, he studied in Brussels, Frankfurt, and Munich and lived in Paris until 1904. His first notable success came with the production of his opera *Macbeth* in Paris in 1910, and from 1911 he taught composition and aesthetics at the Geneva Conservatory. In 1916 he went to the USA, where he held several teaching posts, becoming a US citizen in 1924. His reputation grew, and rapidly spread to Europe, where he returned for eight years in 1930. His compositions include *Trois Poèmes juifs* (1913, 'Three Jewish Poems'), the Hebrew *Sacred Service* (1930–33) for baritone, chorus, and orchestra, and numerous other chamber and orchestral works. His symphonies include the *Israel* (1912–16), and the 'epic rhapsody' *America* (1926).

Bloch, Felix 1905–83
US physicist and Nobel Prize winner

Born in Zurich, Switzerland, he was educated at the University of Leipzig in Germany, where he obtained his PhD in 1928. For his PhD, he solved **Erwin Schrödinger's** equation to explain the conduction of metals, giving rise to the band model of solids which forms the basis of much of solid-state physics. He left Germany for the USA in 1933 and became Professor of Theoretical Physics at Stanford University (1934–71). During World War II he worked on radar, and after the war he developed the technique of nuclear magnetic resonance (NMR). This method has several important applications and has become a useful tool in chemistry and biology. He was awarded the 1952 Nobel Prize for physics jointly with **Edward Mills Purcell** for this work. Bloch was the first director-general of CERN (Conseil Européen pour la Recherche Nucléaire) in Geneva (1954–55).

Bloch, Jean-Richard 1884–1947
French novelist, playwright and critic

A polemicist for communism, his reputation is based on his novel *Et compagnie* (1918, '& Co'), which belongs to the school of realistic writing derived from **Émile Zola** and Pierre Hamp (1876–1962). ◻ P Abraham, *Les trois frères* (1971)

Bloch, Konrad Emil 1912–
US biochemist and Nobel Prize winner

Born in Neisse, Germany (Nysa in Poland), he was educated at the Technische Hochschule, Munich, and at Columbia University, and emigrated to the USA in 1936. In 1954 he was appointed Professor of Biochemistry at Harvard University. Bloch's findings on glucose underlie our present-day understanding that, in animals, fatty acids cannot be converted into sugars. In 1943 he revealed the direct metabolic relationship between cholesterol and bile acids, and in the 1950s his discovery that the mould *Neurospora* required acetate for growth resulted in the recognition of mevalonic acid as the first-formed building block. For his work on cholesterol, Bloch shared the 1964 Nobel Prize for physiology or medicine with **Feodor Lynen**. He was awarded the US National Medal of Science in 1988.

Bloch, Marc 1886–1944
French historian

Born in Lyons, he studied in Paris, Leipzig and Berlin, taught at Montpellier and Amiens, and was called up at the beginning of World War I. Professor of Medieval History at Strasbourg from 1919, he was co-founder of the periodical *Annales d'histoire économique et sociale*, which transformed historians' view of their subject. Later he became Professor of Economic History at the Sorbonne (1936). He rejoined the army in 1939, and, after teaching in Vichy France, joined the Resistance in 1943 to be captured, tortured and shot by the Germans. His work has been extensively translated since his death, notably his last major work *La société féodale* (1939, Eng trans *Feudal Society*, 1961), his memoir of France in 1939–40 (*Strange Defeat*), and his unfinished *Apologie pour l'histoire*, translated as *The Historian's Craft*.

Bloch, Martin 1883–1954
British painter

Born in Neisse in Silesia, Germany, he was forced to leave Germany by the Nazis in 1934, and went to Denmark, and later to England, where he opened a school of painting with Roy de Maistre. He interpreted the English landscape through his brilliant colours and expressionist technique.

Block, Herbert Lawrence, *pen name* Herblock 1909–
US cartoonist

He was born in Chicago, and his first job as an editorial cartoonist was with the *Chicago Daily News* (1929–33). He joined the *Washington Post* in 1946 and syndicated his cartoons to more than 200 other newspapers. He satirized McCarthyism, the Vietnam War, and the arms race, winning Pulitzer Prizes in 1942, 1954, and 1979, and he was awarded the Presidential Medal of Freedom in 1994. His work has been collected in numerous volumes, including *The Herblock Book* (1952), *Straight Herblock* (1964), and *Herblock's State of the Union* (1972).

Bloemaert, Abraham 1564–1651
Dutch landscape painter

Born in Gorinchem, he settled in Utrecht in 1593, and taught **Albert Cuyp**, Gerard van Honthorst and Hendrik Terbrugghen. He was the father of the copper engraver, Cornelius Bloemaert (1603–88).

Bloembergen, Nicolaas 1920–
US physicist and Nobel Prize winner

Born in Dordrecht, the Netherlands, and educated at the universities of Utrecht and Leyden, he received his PhD in 1946 and then moved to the USA to join the staff of Harvard, where he was appointed Gordon McKay Professor of Applied Physics in 1957 then Rumford Professor of Physics in 1974. He then became Gerhard Gade University Professor (1980–90, now emeritus). His early interest was in nuclear magnetic resonance which he studied under Nobel laureate **Edward Mills Purcell**. He later pioneered pumping methods to energize masers and introduced a modification to **Charles Townes's** early design, enabling the maser to work continuously rather than intermittently. His work on interactions of radiation with matter remains fundamental to modern research, and he also investigated methods of using laser light to selectively excite and break a single bond in a molecule. For his contributions to the development of the laser, he shared the 1981 Nobel Prize for physics with **Arthur Schawlow** and **Kai Siegbahn**.

Blois, Natalie de 1921–
US architect

Graduating from Columbia University School of Architecture in 1944, she started working for Skidmore, Owings and Merrill (SOM), a firm at that stage known for reliability and competence rather than originality. By 1948 she was working with Louis Skidmore as a design coordinator for the Terrace Plaza Hotel, Cincinnati. In 1952 SOM asked her to be senior designer on a series of US consulates in Germany. On returning to the USA she continued as a senior designer, working on some of SOM's most famous buildings, including the General Life Insurance Company Building in Bloomfield, Connecticut (1957), the Pepsi-Cola Building in Park Avenue, New York (1959), and the Union Carbide Building, New York (1960). In 1968 she was made a design associate and worked on the Boots Building in Nottingham, England. In 1974 she left SOM to become a senior project designer with Neuhaus and Taylor in Texas.

Blok, Aleksandr Aleksandrovich 1880–1921
Russian poet
Born in St Petersburg, he married (1903) the daughter of the famous chemist Dmitri Mendeleyev. His poetry collections include *Stikhi o Prekrasnoy Dame* (1904, 'Songs about the Lady Fair') and *Nochnye Chasy* (1911, 'Nocturnal Hours'). He welcomed the 1917 Revolution and wrote two poems, *Dvenadtsat* (1918, Eng trans *The Twelve*, 1920), a symbolic sequence of revolutionary themes, and *Skify* (1918, 'The Scythians'), an ode inciting Europe to follow Russia. Soon disillusioned, however, he suffered greatly in the hard times which followed the Revolution. Other works include the romantic verse drama *Roza i Krest* (1922, 'The Rose and the Cross'). ▢ A Ashukin, *Aleksandr Blok* (1923)

Blomdahl, Karl-Birger 1916–68
Swedish composer
Born in Stockholm, he was Professor of Composition there from 1960 to 1964 and head of music at Radio Sweden from 1965. Inspired by Paul Hindemith, he composed symphonies, concertos, chamber and electronic music. His two completed operas are based on texts from Swedish literature: *Aniara* (1957–58) on the space epic by Harry Martinson, and *Herr von Hancken* (1962–63, 'Mr von Hancken') on the novel by Bo Hjalmar Bergman.

Blomfield, Sir Reginald 1856–1942
English architect
He designed the Menin Gate and Lambeth Bridge, and wrote books on architecture and garden designs. He was the grandson of the Classical scholar, Charles James Blomfield (1786–1857).

Blondel, *also called* Blondel de Nesle fl.12th century
French troubadour
According to legend, he accompanied Richard I, Cœur de Lion, to Palestine on the Crusades, and located him when imprisoned in the Austrian castle of Dürrenstein (1193) by means of the song they had jointly composed. He is featured in Sir Walter Scott's *The Talisman* (1825).

Blondel, Nicolas François 1618–86
French military engineer and architect
Born in Ribemont, he was equally successful as a naval engineer and ship's captain, as a diplomat and intelligence officer, and as tutor to the son of the French Secretary of State. In the 1660s he fortified the Channel ports of Dunkirk and Le Havre, and planned the major naval base at Rochefort on the Charente river which was fortified by Sébastien Vauban. In architecture his principal surviving work is the triumphal arch at Porte St Denis in Paris, built in 1674 to celebrate French victories on the Rhine.

Blondin, Charles, *properly* Jean François Gravelet 1824–97
French acrobat and tightrope walker
He was born in Hesdin, near Calais, and trained at Lyons. In 1859 he crossed Niagara Falls on a tightrope. He later performed several variations on his feat, making crossings blindfolded, with a wheelbarrow, with a man on his back, and on stilts.

Blood, Thomas c.1618–1680
Irish adventurer
A Parliamentarian during the Civil War, he was deprived of his estate at the Restoration. In 1663 he put himself at the head of a plot to seize Dublin Castle and James Butler Ormonde, the Lord Lieutenant. The plot was discovered and his chief accomplices executed. On 9 May 1671, together with three others, he broke into the Tower of London and stole the crown, while one of his associates took the orb. They were pursued and captured, but Blood was later pardoned by King Charles II, who also restored his estate.

Bloom, Claire, *originally* Patricia Claire Blume 1931–
English actress
Born in London, she formed the Shakespeare Memorial Theatre in Stratford-upon-Avon in 1948 and moved to the Old Vic in 1952, establishing a reputation as a distinguished Shakespearean actress. Her stage roles include Cordelia opposite John Gielgud in a West End production of *King Lear* (1955) and Blanche du Bois in Tennessee Williams's *A Streetcar Named Desire* (1974). Her many film appearances include *Limelight* (1952), *Richard III* (1955), *Look Back in Anger* (1959) and *Crimes and Misdemeanors* (1989). On television, she has played many classical roles, as well as Edith Galt Wilson in *Backstairs at the White House* (1979), Lady Marchmain in *Brideshead Revisited* (1981) and Cecily Jordan in *A Village Affair* (1995). She published her memoirs, *Leaving a Doll's House,* in 1996.

Bloomer, Amelia, *née* Jenks 1818–94
US champion of women's rights and dress reform
Born in Homer, New York, she founded and edited the feminist paper *The Lily* (1849–55), and worked closely with Susan Anthony. In her pursuit of dress equality she wore her own version of trousers for women which came to be called 'bloomers'.

Bloomfield, Leonard 1887–1949
US linguist
He was born in Chicago and after holding several university posts, he was appointed Professor of German and Linguistics at Ohio State University (1921), becoming Professor of Germanic Philology at Chicago University in 1927, and Sterling Professor of Linguistics at Yale in 1940. His early interest was in Indo-European, especially Germanic, phonology and morphology, but he later made studies of Malayo-Polynesian languages (especially Tagalog) and of the languages of Native Americans (particularly Menomini and Cree). He played a major part in making linguistics an independent scientific discipline, understanding by the word 'scientific' the rejection of all data that could not be directly observed or physically measured. Although he had in his *Introduction to the Study of Language* (1914) indicated his adherence to Wilhelm Wundt's mentalistic psychology, in his major work on linguistic theory, *Language* (1933), he advocated and himself adopted behaviourism as the theoretical framework for linguistic analysis and description. This led to the almost total neglect of the study of meaning within the 'Bloomfieldian' school of linguistics, and a concentration on phonology, morphology and syntax.

Bloor, Ella, *known as* Mother Bloor, *née* Reeve 1862–1951
US radical and feminist
Born on Staten Island, New York, she married at the age of 19, and was a mother of four by 1892. She became interested in women's rights and the labour movement, and her political interests led to her divorce in 1896. In 1901 she joined the Socialist Party. She first wrote under the name Ella Bloor in 1906, reporting for Upton Sinclair. She was the party organizer for Connecticut for many years,

attracting support for various labour causes. In 1919 she helped found the American Communist Party. Arrested more than 30 times during her career, she became a distinguished Party speaker and was a member of the Party's central committee (1932–48). Her works include *Women of the Soviet Union* (1930) and *We Are Many* (1940).

Blore, Edward 1787–1879
English artist and architect of the Gothic revival
Born in Derby, the son of Thomas Blore (1764–1818), the topographer, he was the architect of Sir Walter Scott's Abbotsford (c.1816).

Blouet, Paul, *pseudonym of* Max O'Rell 1848–1903
French writer
He was born in Brittany, served in the Franco-Prussian War and fought against the Commune, and was severely wounded. In 1873 he went to England as a newspaper correspondent, and he later became French master at St Paul's School, London (1876–84). From 1887 he lectured in Great Britain, the USA, and the British colonies. His works include *John Bull et son île* (1883, Eng trans *John Bull and his Island*, 1884) and *Un Français en Amérique* (1891, Eng trans *A Frenchman in America*, 1891)—both translations published under his pseudonym.

Blount, Charles, 8th Lord Mountjoy and Earl of Devonshire 1563–1606
English soldier
He came from a declining family whose fortunes he was determined to revive. He served in the Low Countries, in Brittany, and in the Azores (1597). In 1600 he accepted the Irish command against the rebellion of Hugh O'Neill, Earl of Tyrone, winning a decisive victory at Kinsale (1601), laying Munster waste and ultimately receiving Tyrone's surrender at Mellifont, in 1603, concealing Queen Elizabeth I's death six days previously, thus enabling him to exact more stringent terms. Made Lord Lieutenant of Ireland, he reduced disaffected towns, and returned to England where he was rewarded by King James VI and I with an earldom, mastership of the ordnance, and lands, and by King Philip III of Spain with a pension.

Blount, Thomas 1618–79
English lexicographer and antiquary
Born in Bordesley, Worcestershire, he wrote miscellaneous legal and historical works, including a history of Charles II's escape after the Battle of Worcester (*Boscobel*, 1660). He was also the author of *Glossographia*, a dictionary of the 'hard words of whatsoever language' used in English (1656), a dictionary of obscure legal terms (*A Law Dictionary*, 1670), and the *Fragmenta Antiquitatis: Ancient Tenures of Land, and Jocular Customs of some Manors* (1679).

Blow, John 1649–1708
English composer
Born in Newark-on-Trent, Nottinghamshire, he sang in the Chapel Royal choir, was appointed organist at Westminster Abbey (1668), Master of the Children at the Chapel Royal (1674) and subsequently organist there, and Master of the Children at St Paul's (1687). Much of his large output of anthems and church services is uninspired, but the best, eg, the Ode for St Cecilia's Day, 'Begin the Song', has a grandeur which enhances his reputation. He wrote a small amount of instrumental music and a masque, *Vénus and Adonis* (1687), which was performed before Charles II.

Bloy, Léon Marie 1846–1917
French writer
He was born in Périgeux, and wrote novels, essays, and religious and critical studies with a strong Roman Catholic bias, containing bitter castigation of political and social institutions. This made him unpopular in his day but has contributed to the revival of interest in his

works in the second half of the 20th century. His *Le Désespéré* (1886, 'The Desperate Man') and *La Femme pauvre* (1897, 'The Poor Woman') are autobiographical. Other books include *Le Pèlerin de l'absolu* (1914, 'On a Pilgrimage to the Absolute'). His journal, which relates the spiritual and mystical conversions of his later life, was published in 1924. 📖 R Heppenstall, *Léon Bloy* (1953)

Blücher, Gebbard Leberecht von, Prince of Wahlstadt, *known as* Marshal Forward 1742–1819
Prussian field marshal
Born in Rostock, Mecklenburg, after two years in the Swedish service (1756–58), he fought with the Prussian cavalry (1760–70), but was discharged for dissipation and insubordination, and for 15 years farmed his own estates. He fought against the French in 1793 on the Rhine and in 1806 at Auerstädt, and fought also at Lübeck and Stralsund. When the Prussians rose against France in 1813 Blücher took chief command in Silesia. At the Katzbach he repulsed the enemy, and at Leipzig (1813) won important successes. In January 1814 he crossed the Rhine, and though once routed by Napoleon I won several battles, and on 31 March entered Paris. After Napoleon's return in 1815, Blücher assumed the general command; he suffered a severe defeat at Ligny, but completed Wellington's victory at the Battle of Waterloo (1815) by his timely appearance on the field, where his Prussians pursued the fleeing enemy all through the night. At the second taking of Paris, he wanted to inflict on Paris what other capitals had suffered, but was restrained by Wellington. 📖 Roger Parkinson, *The Hussar General: The Life of Blücher, Man of Waterloo* (1975)

Blum, Léon 1872–1950
French Socialist statesman
He was born in Paris into a Jewish family. A lawyer, he was radicalized by the Dreyfus Affair (1899), and was elected to the chamber in 1919, becoming one of the leaders of the Socialist Party. In 1924 he lent his support to Édouard Herriot, a policy which resulted in great electoral advances by the Left and as a consequence the elections of 1936 gave France its first socialist Prime Minister since 1870. In 1938 Blum formed a second 'popular front' government which had a stormy existence. During World War II he was interned in Germany. On his return in 1946 he was elected Prime Minister of the six-week caretaker government and originated the Anglo-French treaty of alliance and methods to deal with the rise of prices. As a writer he worked on magazines with Marcel Proust and most of the other leading authors of his day, wrote a play, *La Colère* (1902, 'Anger'), and theatrical criticism. After World War I he turned to political writings. His importance lay in his transmission, to French writers, of the humanist ideas of Lucien Herr (librarian at the École Normale), who had helped convert Blum's mentor Jean Jaurès to socialism.

Blum, René 1878–1942
French impresario and critic
Born in Paris, he became critic and editor of the literary journal *Gil Blas*. While he was director of the Theatre of the Monte Carlo Casino he took over the administration of the Ballets Russes immediately after Sergei Diaghilev's death in 1929, renaming it the Ballets Russes de Monte Carlo, with Léonide Massine as director. During World War II he was arrested in France while the company was on tour in the USA, and he died within a week of being sent to Auschwitz.

Blumberg, Baruch Samuel 1925–
US biochemist and Nobel Prize winner
Born in New York City, he studied at Columbia University and at Oxford, and became Professor of Biochemistry at the University of Pennsylvania in 1964. Blumberg

discovered the 'Australia antigen' in 1964 and reported its association with hepatitis B (known as the HBV virus). The finding was very rapidly applied to screening blood donors. His study of the distribution of the HBV virus in the population revealed that apparently healthy people could carry and transmit the live virus, and led to ethical and employment problems associated with screening medical and welfare employees. In 1969 Blumberg introduced a protective vaccine, now widely used. He shared the 1976 Nobel Prize for physiology or medicine with **Daniel Gajdusek**. In 1989 he became the Fox Chase Distinguished Professor and Senior Advisor to the President at the Fox Chase Cancer Center.

Blume, Judy Sussman 1938–
US writer for teenagers
She was born in New Jersey, and educated at New York University. Her first published book was *The One in the Middle is the Green Kangaroo* (1969). Her third book, *Are You There, God It's Me, Margaret* (1970), brought acclaim for her candid approach to the onset of puberty and for her natural, if unsubtle, style. As with subsequent books, attempts were made to restrict its circulation. Her explicitness brought her into conflict with parents, but she has a remarkable rapport with her readers and confronts subjects which previously were ignored. Her other books include *Then Again, Maybe I Won't* (1971), *It's not the End of the World* (1972), *Deenie* (1973), *Blubber* (1974), *Forever* (1975), *Superfudge* (1980), and *Here's to You, Rachel Robinson* (1993).

Blume, Karel Lodewijk 1796–1862
German botanist and physician
Born in Brunswick, he was appointed as head of the vaccination programme in Java in 1818, where he collected specimens of flora. Returning to the Netherlands in 1829, he was the founder and first director of the Rijksherbarium, first in Brussels and then in Leyden. With Philipp Franz von Siebold he founded the Royal Dutch Society for the Advancement of Horticulture (1842). He was the author of many important works on the flora of Java, including the four-volume *Rumphia* (1835–48). His name is commemorated in the genus *Blumea*. His work was an essential basis for later studies of the plant geography of this botanically important region.

Blumenbach, Johann Friedrich 1752–1840
German anthropologist
Born in Gotha, he studied at Jena and Göttingen, where he became Extraordinary Professor of Medicine in 1776. On the basis of his study of comparative skull measurements, he established a quantitative basis for racial classification.

Blunck, Hans Friedrich 1888–1961
German novelist, poet and folklorist
He was born in Altona, and after studying law became a propagandist, then a university official, and farmer. Steeped in the folklore of the North German plain, his writings lent colour to the racial theories of National Socialism. His poetical works include *Sturm überm Land* (1915, 'Storm Over the Land'), *Der Wanderer* (1925, 'The Wanderer'), *Erwartung* (1936, 'Expectation'), and among his novels are *Werdendes Volk* (1933) and *Die Urvätersaga* (1934, 'Saga of the Forefathers'). He published the autobiographical *Unwegsame Zeiten* ('Pathless Times') in 1953. 📖 C Jenssen, *Hans Friedrich Blunck* (1935)

Blundell, Sir Michael 1907–
Kenyan farmer and politician
Born in London, he emigrated to Kenya in 1925 to farm, and served throughout World War II. He then involved himself in settler politics, being a member of Legco (1948–63) and leader of the European members (1952–54) and then Minister of Agriculture (1955–59, 1961–63). He broke with the dominant white group to espouse political

change involving black Kenyans in national politics and was much vilified for this. However, he was an essential bridge between the white-dominated colonial years and the black majority rule of independent Kenya.

Blunden, Edmund Charles 1896–1974
English poet and critic
Born in Yalding, Kent, he was educated at Christ's Hospital and Queen's College, Oxford. He served in France in World War I and won the MC. He was Professor of English Literature at Tokyo (1924–27), Fellow of Merton College, Oxford, from 1931, joined the staff of the *Times Literary Supplement* in 1943, returned to the Far East and from 1953 lectured at the University of Hong Kong. He was professor at Oxford from 1966 to 1968. A lover of the English countryside, he is essentially a nature poet, as is evident in *Pastorals* (1916) and *The Waggoner and Other Poems* (1920), but his prose work *Undertones of War* (1928) is perhaps his best. Other works include *The Bonadventure* (1922), on his visit to the USA, a biography of **Leigh Hunt**, and books on **Charles Lamb** and **Keats**. He also edited John Clare, Smart, Shelley, Keats and Wilkie Collins.

Blunkett, David 1947–
English Labour politician
He was born in Sheffield and, blind from birth, attended the Royal Normal College for the Blind in Shrewsbury; he joined the Labour Party at the age of 16. After gaining qualifications at night school he studied politics at Sheffield University under Professor Bernard Crick (1929–), who has described him as a realist with the 'conscience of the old Left'. Blunkett became a member of Sheffield City Council in 1970 and was its leader by 1978, having trained as a further education teacher. In 1983 he won a place on the Labour Party's national executive committee (NEC), the first non-MP to do so since **Harold Laski** in 1943. As NEC chairman in 1993–94, he announced the first one-member-one-vote election for the Labour leadership. MP for Sheffield (Brightside) since 1987, he was front bench spokesman for the environment (1988–92), then entered the Shadow Cabinet as spokesman for health (1992–94), education (1994–95) and education and employment (1995–97). Following Labour's general election victory in 1997, he became Secretary of State for Education and Employment. His publications include *On a Clear Day* (1995).

Blunt, Anthony Frederick 1907–83
English art historian and Soviet spy
Born in Bournemouth, Hampshire, he was educated at Marlborough School and Trinity College, Cambridge, where he was made a Fellow in 1932. At Cambridge he became a Communist and met **Guy Burgess, Kim Philby** and **Donald Maclean**. He acted as a 'talent-spotter' for Burgess, supplying names of likely recruits to the Russian Communist cause, and while serving in British Intelligence during World War II he passed on information to the Russian government. He assisted the defection of Burgess and Maclean in 1951. In 1964, after the defection of Philby, Blunt confessed in return for his immunity, and he continued as Surveyor of the Queen's Pictures (1945–72). His full involvement in espionage was made public only in 1979 after the publication of *The Climate of Treason* by Andrew Boyle. Blunt had been Director of the Courtauld Institute of Art (1947–1974) and among his publications were *Art and Architecture in France 1500–1700* (1953) and his study of **Poussin** (1966–67). His knighthood awarded in 1956 was annulled in 1979. 📖 Barrie Penrose, *Conspiracy of Silence: The Secret Life of Anthony Blunt* (rev edn, 1987)

Blunt, Wilfrid Scawen 1840–1922
English poet and traveller

Born in Petworth, Sussex, and educated at Stonyhurst and Oscott, he served in the diplomatic service (1859–70). His first published volume of poems was *Sonnets and Songs by Proteus* (1875). He travelled in the Near and Middle East, espoused the cause of Arabi Pasha (Ahmed Arabi) and Egyptian nationalism (1882), stood for parliament and was imprisoned in 1888 for activity in the Irish Land League. In prison, he wrote the sonnet sequence *In Vinculis* (1899). He also wrote political verse and love poems, and bred Arab horses. ▣ M J Reinehr, *The Writings of Wilfrid Scawen Blunt* (1940)

Bly, Nellie See Seaman, Elizabeth Cochrane

Bly, Robert Elwood 1926–
US poet, critic, translator and editor
He was born in Madison, Minnesota, and was educated at Harvard and the University of Iowa. As a critic he is caustic, and as a poet, for a man so aware of foreign literature (he has translated Pablo Neruda and Selma Lagerlöf, among others), his poetry is surprisingly American in tone and locale, often dealing with the space and silences of his home state. His first collection was *Silence in the Snowy Fields* (1962), followed by such volumes as *The Shadow-Mothers* (1970), *Sleepers Joining Hands* (1972), *Talking All Morning* (1980), *In the Month of May* (1985) and *The Apple Found in the Plowing* (1989). In 1991 he published *Iron John*, a controversial study of maleness and its frustrations, and he became a leading figure in the 'men's movement'. *The Sibling Society* (1997) examines adolescence. ▣ H Nelson, *Robert Bly: An Introduction to the Poetry* (1984)

Blyth, Sir Chay (Charles) 1940–
British yachtsman
He was educated in Hawick before joining the Parachute Regiment (1958–67). In 1966 he rowed across the North Atlantic with John Ridgeway, and in 1970–71 became the first person to sail solo round the world in the difficult westwards direction. He circumnavigated the globe again in the 1973–74 Round the World Yacht Race, this time sailing eastwards with a crew of paratroopers, and won the Elapsed Time prize. As well as winning other races, he has sailed the Atlantic from Cape Verde to Antigua in record-breaking time (1977), and organized the British Steel Challenge Round World Yacht Race (1992–93). He was knighted in 1997.

Blyth, Edward 1810–73
English naturalist and zoologist
He was born in London, where he became a pharmacist, but spent so much time on ornithology that his business failed. His many articles on survival and natural selection of bird species anticipated Charles Darwin. He was curator of the museum of the Asiatic Society in Bengal (1841–62). Several birds are named after him, including Blyth's Kingfisher, Blyth's Pipit and Blyth's Warbler.

Blyton, Enid Mary 1897–1968
English children's writer
Born in London, she trained as a Froebel kindergarten teacher, then became a journalist, specializing in educational and children's publications. In 1922 she published her first book, *Child Whispers*, a collection of verse, but it was in the late 1930s that she began writing her many children's stories featuring such characters as Noddy, the Famous Five, and the Secret Seven. She edited various magazines, including *Sunny Stories* and *Pictorial Knowledge* for children, and *Modern Teaching*. She identified closely with children, and always considered her stories highly educational and moral in tone, but has recently been criticized for racism, sexism and snobbishness, as well as stylistic inelegance and over-simplicity. She published over 600 books, and is one of the most translated British authors.

Her works also include school readers and books on nature and religious study. ▣ B Stoney, *Enid Blyton: a biography* (1974)

Boabdil, *properly* Abu Abdallah Muhammad
d.c.1493
Last Moorish King of Granada
He dethroned his father, Abu-al-Hasan (1482), but while he continued to struggle for power against his father and uncle the Christians gradually conquered the kingdom. Malaga fell in 1487, and after a two-year siege Granada itself capitulated to Ferdinand, the Catholic and Isabella of Castile (1492). He was granted a small lordship in the Alpujarras, but sold his rights to the Spanish Crown (1493) and retired to Morocco where he died.

Boadicea See Boudicca

Boas, Franz 1858–1942
US anthropologist
He was born in Minden, Germany, and studied at the universities of Heidelberg, Bonn and Kiel. His expeditions to the Arctic and to British Columbia shifted his interest to the tribes there and thence to ethnology and anthropology, and prompted his emigration to the USA in 1886, where he made his career, ultimately as Professor of Anthropology at Columbia from 1899. A specialist in studies of Native American tribes of the Pacific Northwest, he was also Curator of Anthropology at the American Museum of Natural History (1901–05). He sought to bring together ethnology, physical anthropology, archaeology and linguistics, and rejected the simple determinism and eugenic theories of the time. He and his pupils established new and less simple concepts of culture and of race, as outlined in his collection of papers, *Race, Language and Culture* (1940). His other books include *The Mind of Primitive Man* (1911) and *Anthropology and Modern Life* (1928). He was the dominant figure in establishing modern anthropology in the USA.

Boateng, Paul Yaw 1951–
British Labour politician
He began his education in the international school at Accra, Ghana, and completed it in England, graduating in law and qualifying as a solicitor. Displaying an intense interest in race relations and civil liberties, he operated the Paddington Law Centre (1976–79) before joining a practice. He became politically active as a member of the Greater London Council (GLC) in 1981 and entered the House of Commons, representing Brent South, in 1987. In 1989 he became the first black member of the Labour Shadow Cabinet as Treasury and Economic Affairs Spokesman (1989–92) then was appointed Legal Affairs Spokesman (1992–97), but was not given a Cabinet post when Labour came to power in 1997.

Bocage, Manoel Barbosa du 1765–1805
Portuguese lyric poet
Born in Setubal, he served in the army and the navy. He sailed in 1786 to India and China, returning to Lisbon in 1790, where, recognized as a poet, he joined the literary circle Nova Arcadia, but was expelled in 1794 for his unorthodox views. He was jailed for anti-clericalism in 1797, and released two years later after torture at the hands of the Inquisition. He is essentially a romantic, but his sonnets are classical in form. He often satirizes, as in *Pina de Talião* ('Talião's Pine Cone'). ▣ R Correia, *Bocage: cronica dramatica e grotesca* (1965)

Boccaccio, Giovanni 1313–75
Italian writer
Born in Tuscany or Paris, he abandoned commerce and the study of canon law, and in Naples (1328) he turned to story-writing in verse and prose. Until 1350 he lived alternately in Florence and Naples, producing prose tales, pastorals and poems. The *Teseide* ('Book of Theseus') is a

graceful version in ottava rima of the medieval romance of Palamon and Arcite, which was partly translated by Chaucer in the *Knight's Tale*. The *Filostrato*, also in ottava rima, deals with the loves of Troilus and Cressida, also in great part translated by Chaucer. After 1350 he became a diplomat and a scholar, formed a lasting friendship with Petrarch, and visited Rome, Ravenna, Avignon and Brandenburg as Florentine ambassador. In 1358 he completed his major work, the *Decameron*, begun some 10 years before, with medieval subject matter and classical form. For some time he held a chair founded to expound the works of Dante, and produced a commentary on the *Divina Commedia*. He wrote in Latin an elaborate work on mythology, *De genealogia deorum gentilium* ('The Genealogies of the Gentile Gods'), and treatises, for example *De claris mulieribus* ('Famous Women') and *De Montibus* ('On Mountains'). ▭V Branca, *Boccaccio: the man and his works* (1976)

Boccherini, Luigi, *nicknamed* Haydn's wife 1743–1805
Italian composer

Born in Lucca, he was a cellist and composer at the courts of the Infante Don Luis in Madrid and Frederick II of Prussia. He is best known for his chamber music (the minuet which is among the most popular of classical tunes is from his string quintet in E), and for his cello concertos and sonatas. The similarity of his work to that of his greater contemporary earned his nickname.

Boccioni, Umberto 1882–1916
Italian artist and sculptor

Born in Reggio, he was the most original artist of the Futurist school, and its principal theorist. After working with Giacomo Balla, Gino Severini, and Emilio Marinetti in Rome and Paris from 1898 to 1914, he wrote a comprehensive survey of the movement, *Pittura, scultura futuriste* (1914, 'Futurist Painting and Sculpture'). An important bronze sculpture, *Unique Forms of Continuity in Space* (1913), is in the Museum of Modern Art, New York.

Bock, Fedor von 1880–1945
German field marshal

Born in Küstrin, he was educated at Potsdam Military School. He served with distinction as a staff officer in World War I and later commanded the German armies invading Austria (1938), Poland (1939) and the Lower Somme, France (1940). Promoted field marshal in 1940, he participated in the invasion of the USSR with remarkable success (1941), but was dismissed by Hitler for failing to capture Moscow (1942). He was killed with his wife and daughter in an air-raid.

Böcklin, Arnold 1827–1901
Swiss painter

Born in Basle, he combined classical themes involving nymphs and satyrs and mythological subjects with the dark romantic landscapes, rocks and castles characteristic of 19th-century German painting.

Bode, Johann Elert 1747–1826
German astronomer

Born in Hamburg, he founded the *Astronomisches Jahrbuch* ('Astronomy Yearbook') in 1774. He became director of the Berlin Observatory (1786), where he remained until a year before his death. He is best known for the empirical rule known as Bode's law, which expresses the proportionate distances of the planets from the Sun. The rule, alternatively called the Titius–Bode law, was first discovered in 1766 by Johann Daniel Titius and was brought into use by Bode. It does not hold for the most distant planet, Pluto, and has no theoretical foundation. It proved useful in stimulating a search for a missing planet between Mars and Jupiter where the asteroids were found to lie. Bode proposed the name Uranus for the planet discovered by William Herschel in 1781.

Bodenstedt, Friedrich Martin von 1819–92
German writer

Born in Peine, Hanover, he lived for a while in Moscow, travelled in the Middle East, and was a professor at Munich University (from 1854) and director of the Meiningen court theatre (1867–73). He translated into German many Russian, English, and Persian texts, and published poetry. His best-known work is *Lieder des Mirza Schaffy* (1851, 'Songs of Mirza Schaffy'), alleged to be a translation from the Tartar.

Bodenstein, Ernst August Max 1871–1942
German physical chemist

Born in Magdeburg, he studied under Viktor Meyer at Heidelberg and Walther Nernst at Göttingen, and later worked with Wilhelm Ostwald in Leipzig, becoming Titular Professor there in 1904. In 1908 he was appointed Professor of Physical Chemistry at the Technische Hochschule in Hanover, and in 1923 was appointed Professor and Director of the Institute for Physical Chemistry in Berlin. Bodenstein may be regarded as a founder of gas kinetics, in which he developed great experimental skill. The results of his research on the reactions between hydrogen and the halogens were not understood until the concept of chain reactions was developed by Jens Christiansen and David Chapman. These and related studies laid the foundations for the researches of Sir Cyril Hinshelwood, and Nikolai Semenov and many others.

Bodhidharma 6th century
Indian monk and founder of the Ch'an (or Zen) sect of Buddhism

Born near Madras, he travelled to China in 520, where he had a famous audience with the emperor. He argued that merit leading to salvation could not be accumulated through good deeds, and taught meditation as the means of return to Buddha's spiritual precepts.

Bodichon, Barbara, *née* Leigh Smith 1827–90
English champion of women's rights

Born in London, the daughter of a radical MP who believed strongly in women's rights, she studied at Bedford College there, and in 1852 opened a primary school in London. She wrote *Women at Work* (1857) and with Bessie Rayner Parkes was a founder of the feminist magazine *The Englishwoman's Journal* (1858). She helped to found the college for women that became Girton College, Cambridge, and was also a landscape watercolourist.

Bo Diddley, *stagename of* Elias Bates, *later* McDaniel 1928–
US rock and roll singer and guitarist

Born in McComb, Mississippi, he was a boxer for a time, where he picked up his stage name. He began singing blues in Chicago clubs in the early 1950s, but established his trademark style with his first single, 'Bo Diddley', in 1955. His chugging rhythms and custom-made guitar, with its rectangular sound box and distorted amplification, gave him a distinctive if limited style, and he had a number of hits in the rock and roll era, notably with his version of 'Who Do You Love'. He never really adapted to changing fashions, but remained popular on revival packages, and was a highly influential figure for later rock artists. ▭E Kierch, *Where Are You Now, Bo Diddley* (1986)

Bodin, Jean c.1530–96
French political philosopher

He was born and educated in Angers, where he pursued a successful legal career and was also active politically. He visited Great Britain (1581) as secretary to the Duke of Alençon, who sought the hand of Queen Elizabeth I of England. His major work, *Les Six Livres de la République* (1576, *The Six Bookes of a Commonweale*, 1606), expounds the belief that property and the family form the basis of society, and that a limited monarchy is the best possible form of government. His *Colloquium Heptaplomeres* (1587) presented a plea for religious tolerance through the device of a conversation between a Jew, a Muslim, a Lutheran, a Zwinglian, a Roman Catholic, an Epicurean and a Theist. Despite his enlightened views he shared the general belief of the time in sorcery and witchcraft, which he propounded in his influential *Démonomanie des sorciers* (1580, 'Demonomania of Sorcerers'). He died of the plague. ▣ Julian Franklin, *Jean Bodin and the Rise of Absolutist Theory* (1973)

Bodley, Sir Thomas 1545–1613
English scholar and diplomat

Born in Exeter, he studied languages and divinity at Geneva, where his Protestant family had been forced to take refuge during the persecutions of Queen Mary I, but in 1558 he went to Magdalen College, Oxford, and was appointed Greek lecturer at Merton College in 1564. He studied Hebrew, and travelled extensively in Europe (1576–80) to master modern languages. In the service of Queen Elizabeth I of England he was ambassador to Denmark, France and Holland. In 1597 he retired from court and settled in Oxford. In 1587 he married a wealthy widow, and then spent huge sums on the repair and extension of the university library originally established by Humphrey, Duke of Gloucester, and collected books from all over Europe. The library, renamed the Bodleian, was opened in 1602. He was knighted by King James VI and I in 1604.

Bodmer, Johann Georg 1786–1864
Swiss inventor

He was born in Zurich, and became a skilled mechanical engineer. His many inventions reflected the wide range of his interests in textile machinery, machine tools, screw propellers, armaments, steam engines, furnaces, boilers, and locomotives. Many of his most revolutionary innovations met with determined resistance from those unwilling to accept changes in established practice. Among his most successful inventions were a percussion shell (1805), a cotton carding and spinning machine which he manufactured in a factory he established in England (1824), and an opposed-piston steam engine (1834).

Bodmer, Sir Walter Fred 1936–
English geneticist

Born in Frankfurt, Germany, and educated at Clare College, Cambridge, he remained at Cambridge as a demonstrator in the genetics department during 1960–61. He then moved to Stanford University, and later became Professor of Genetics at the University of Oxford (1970–79). He was appointed director of research at the Imperial Cancer Research Fund in 1979, and became director-general there (1991–96). He has also served as chairman of the BBC Science Consultative Group (1981–87), president of the Royal Statistical Society (1984–85) and vice-president of the Royal Institution (1981–82). He was elected FRS in 1974 and knighted in 1986. Bodmer has published extensively on the genetics of the HLA histocompatibility system, which distinguishes foreign cells in the animal body and is a vital factor in transplant surgery. He has also published on somatic cell genetics, cancer genetics and human population genetics. In 1996 he was appointed Principal of Hertford College, Oxford.

Bodoni, Giambattista 1740–1813
Italian printer

Born in Saluzzo, he designed (1790) a modern typeface still widely used today. His press in Parma published editions of the classics widely admired for their elegance. ▣ Hermann Falk, *Giambattista Bodonis Typenkunst* (1915)

Boece or Boyis or Boethius, Hector c.1465–1536
Scottish historian

Born in Dundee, he studied at Montaigu College, Paris, where c.1492 to 1498 he was a regent or Professor of Philosophy, and where he became a friend of Erasmus. Bishop Elphinstone then invited him to preside over his newly founded university of Aberdeen, and he was at the same time made a canon of the cathedral. In 1522 he published his biographies, in Latin, of the bishops of Mortlach and Aberdeen, and in 1527 the Latin *History of Scotland*, which contained a large amount of fiction. The king awarded him a pension until he was promoted to a benefice in 1534.

Boehm, Sir Joseph Edgar 1834–90
British sculptor

Born in Vienna, Austria, he was educated in England, and finally settled there in 1862. The queen's effigy on the coinage issued in 1887 was from his designs, and he executed two of London's best-known monuments: the seated statue of Thomas Carlyle (1875, Chelsea Embankment), and the Duke of Wellington astride his horse Copenhagen (1888, Hyde Park Corner).

Boehm or Böhm, Theobald 1794–1881
German flautist and inventor

Born in Munich, he became a member of the Bavarian Court Orchestra in 1818 while working in the family trade as a goldsmith. In 1828 he opened a flute factory in Munich, and in 1831 determined to make a flute which would be acoustically perfect. As this involved making holes in places where they could not be fingered, he devised a key mechanism to overcome the problem, and in 1847 produced the model on which the modern flute is based. Attempts to use his key system on the oboe and bassoon have been largely unsuccessful, though certain features have been applied to the clarinet.

Boeing, William Edward 1881–1956
US aircraft manufacturer

He was born in Detroit, Michigan and studied at Yale's Sheffield Scientific School. Having learned to fly in Los Angeles in 1915, he formed the Pacific Aero Products Co in 1916 to build seaplanes he had designed with Conrad Westerfelt. Renamed as Boeing Airplane Company in 1917, it eventually became the largest manufacturer of military and civilian aircraft in the world. In 1927 he formed the Boeing Air Transport Company which introduced many novelties, including flying passengers by night, having two pilots and a stewardess, and the use of constant two-way radio telephone. He retired in 1934, when his air transport company became United Air Lines.

Boerhaave, Hermann 1668–1738
Dutch physician and botanist

He was born in Voorhout, near Leyden. In 1682 he went to Leyden, where he studied theology and oriental languages, and took his degree in philosophy in 1689. However, in 1690 he began the study of medicine, and in 1701 was appointed lecturer on the theory of medicine, and in 1709 Professor of Medicine and Botany. The two works on which his medical fame chiefly rests, *Institutiones Medicae* (1708, 'Medical Principles') and *Aphorismi de Cognoscendis et Curandis Morbis* (1709, 'Aphorisms on the Recognition and Treatment of Diseases'), were translated into various European languages, and even into Arabic. He pointed out that both plants and animals show the

Bogart, Humphrey DeForest 1899–1957
US film actor

Humphrey Bogart was born in New York City, the son of a doctor. After serving briefly with the US navy he became a stage manager and walk-on actor, graduating to juvenile leads before making his film debut in *Broadway's Like That* in 1930. Alternating between stage and screen, he was frequently cast as a vicious hoodlum, most memorably in *The Petrified Forest* (1936), on the strength of which he was given a long-term contract with Warner Brothers. After further gangster roles, notably in *Angels With Dirty Faces* (1938), he achieved stardom with his roles in *High Sierra* (1941), playing the part of an ageing mobster, *The Maltese Falcon* (1941), *Casablanca* (1942, with **Ingrid Bergman**), playing the cynical nightclub owner Rick, which won him his first Oscar nomination for best actor, and *To Have and Have Not* (1944), which also marked the début of **Lauren Bacall**, who became his fourth wife in 1945.

Over the next 15 years he created an indelible and enduring screen persona of the lone wolf; cynical but heroic, abrasive, romantic and stubbornly faithful to his own code of ethics, as in *The Big Sleep* (1946), in which he memorably played **Raymond Chandler**'s private detective Philip Marlowe, and in *Key Largo* (1948, with **Edward G Robinson**). His considerable acting prowess was also displayed when he played the selfish prospector in *The Treasure of the Sierra Madre* (1948), the gin-sodden boatman in *The African Queen* (1951), which won him an Oscar for Best Actor, and the psychopathic captain in *The Caine Mutiny* (1954). He died after a long struggle with cancer.

📖 A Eyles, *Humphrey Bogart* (1990).

'If she can stand it, I can. Play it!' Line spoken by Humphrey Bogart as Rick in *Casablanca*. The line is commonly rendered 'Play it again, Sam', a conflation with an earlier line of Ingrid Bergman, 'Play it, Sam. Play *As Time Goes By*.'

---

same law of generation, and by 1718 he was teaching sex in plants, his international stature ensuring widespread acceptance of these ideas. In 1724 he also became Professor of Chemistry, and his *Elementa Chemiae* (1724, 'Elements of Chemistry') is a classic. Meanwhile patients came from all parts of Europe to consult him, earning him a fortune. 📖 G A Lindeboom, *Hermann Boerhaave: The Man and his Work* (1968)

Boesak, Allan Aubrey 1945–
South African churchman

He was born in Kakamas, north-western Cape Province. Lecturer and student chaplain at Western Cape University, president of the alliance of Black Reformed Christians in South Africa (1981), and president of the World Alliance of Reformed Churches (1982–91), he sees the Christian gospel in terms of liberation of the oppressed. He was an outspoken opponent of apartheid, and leader of the coloured, or mixed-race, community in South Africa. *Farewell to Innocence* (1977), his study of Black theology, has been followed by several collections of sermons and addresses, including *The Finger of God* (1982), *Black and Reformed* (1984), *Walking on Thorns* (1984), and *If this is Treason, I am Guilty* (1987). Publicity surrounding his personal life led to his withdrawal from politics just as his dream of a democratically elected government in South Africa became a reality.

Boethius, Anicius Manlius Severinus
c.475–524AD
Roman philosopher and politician

Born of a patrician Roman family, he studied in Athens and later produced the translations of and commentaries on **Aristotle** and **Porphyry** that became the standard textbooks on logic in medieval Europe. He was made consul in 510AD during the Gothic occupation of Rome and later Chief Minister to the ruler **Theodoric**, but in 523 he was accused of treason and imprisoned in Pavia, and was executed the following year. It was during his imprisonment that he wrote the famous *De Consolatione Philosophiae* ('The Consolation of Philosophy'), in which Philosophy personified solaces the distraught author by explaining the mutability of all earthly fortune and the insecurity of everything except virtue. The *Consolation* was for the next thousand years probably the most widely read book after the Bible. He is sometimes described as 'the last of the Roman philosophers, the first of the scholastic theologians'. 📖 H H Patch, *The Tradition of Boethius* (1935)

Boethius, Hector See **Boece, Hector**

Böex, Joseph and Séraphin See **Rosny**

Boff, Leonardo 1938–
Brazilian Franciscan liberation theologian

He was born of Italian descent in Concordia, Santa Catarina. Ordained in Brazil in 1964, he studied at Würzburg, Louvain, Oxford and Munich, and became Professor of Systematic Theology in Petrópolis, Rio. His best-known work, *Jesus-Christ Liberator* (1972, Eng trans, 1978), offers hope and justice for the oppressed rather than religious support of the status quo in church and society. He has written several books on reforming church structures from grass-roots 'basic communities', including *Church: Charism and Power* (1984), which provoked official ecclesiastical censure. Besides collaborating with his brother Clodovis on introductions to liberation theology, he has written widely on other themes, including *St Francis: A Model for Human Liberation* (1985), *The Maternal Face of God* (1988) and *Ecology and Spirituality* (1991).

Bogan, Louise 1897–1970
US poet and short-story writer

Born in Livermore, Maine, she began writing in high school and first published a collection of verse, *Body of this Death*, in 1923. Her writing is a sometimes erotic celebration of, and often disillusioned lament for, romantic love, and her two marriages and other relationships with men led her to believe that love almost always ends in acrimony and betrayal. While editions of her collected poetry were published in 1941 and 1954, *The Blue Estuaries* (1968) is the definitive volume, all 105 poems having been selected by the author herself. 📖 *Journey Around My Room* (ed R Limmer, 1980)

Bogarde, Sir Dirk, *originally* Derek Niven Van Den Bogaerde 1921–
English actor and novelist

Born in Hampstead, London, he was originally a scene designer and commercial artist, before he began acting in repertory theatre and made his film debut as an extra in *Come On George* (1940). After service in World War II, he was signed to a long-term contract with Rank Films, spending many years playing small-time crooks, military heroes and romantic or light comedy roles, as in *Doctor in the House* (1954), until he was voted Britain's top box-office star (1955 and 1957). Ambitious to tackle more challenging material, he played Sidney Carton in *A Tale of Two Cities* (1958), a blackmailed homosexual in *Victim* (1961) and a sinisterly manipulative valet in *The Servant* (1963).

Subsequently favouring European cinema, he has created a series of distinguished characterizations, subtly portraying decadence, enigma and ambiguity, notably in *The Damned* (1969), *Death in Venice* (1971), *The Night Porter* (1973) and *Providence* (1977). After a break of 13 years from the big screen he appeared as a dying father in *Daddy Nostalgie* (1990, *These Foolish Things*). Knighted in 1991, he has published seven volumes of autobiography and a number of novels, including *Voices in the the Garden* (1981), *West of Sunset* (1984) and *Jericho* (1992). ◻ Robert Tanitch, *Dirk Bogarde: The Complete Career Illustrated* (1988)

Bogardus, James 1800–74
US inventor
He was born in Catskill, New York. Apprenticed to a watchmaker, he made improvements in eight-day clocks, and invented a delicate engraving machine, the dry gas meter, the transfer machine for producing banknote plates from separate dies, a pyrometer, a deep-sea sounding machine, a dynamometer, and in 1839 a method of engraving postage stamps, which was adopted by the British government. He also erected the first cast-iron building in the USA at his own factory in New York City in 1848.

Bogart, Humphrey DeForest See panel p223

Bogdanov, Michael 1938–
English stage director
He was born in London and educated at the universities of Dublin, Munich and the Sorbonne. At the Royal Shakespeare Company he directed *The Taming of the Shrew* (1978), *Romeo and Juliet* (1986) and Sean O'Casey's *Shadow of a Gunman* (1980). His National Theatre productions include Howard Brenton's *The Romans in Britain* (1980), Pedro Calderón's *The Mayor of Zalamea* (1981), Chekhov's *Uncle Vanya* (1982), and Thomas Kyd's *The Spanish Tragedy* (1982). In 1986, with actor Michael Pennington, he became co-founder and artistic director of the touring English Shakespeare Company. He was also artistic director of the Deutsche Schauspielhaus in Hamburg (1989–92).

Bogilyubov, Nikolai Nikolaevich 1909–92
Soviet mathematical physicist
Born in Nizhny Novgorod, he was educated at the Academy of Sciences in the Ukraine, and subsequently worked there and at the Soviet Academy of Sciences in Moscow. Later he became director of the Joint Institute for Nuclear Research in Dubna (1965). He developed the technique of changing variables in quantum field theory known as the Bogilyubov transformation, which has since been used in many areas of research. He has also contributed to the theory of superconductivity, where a material loses all resistance to electrical flow when cooled to very low temperatures.

Bogomolov, Oleg Timofeyevich 1927–
Soviet economist and official
He was educated at the Moscow Institute of Foreign Trade then worked at the Soviet Ministry of Foreign Trade, and afterward at Comecon (Council for Mutual Economic Assistance). Serving on the State Planning Commission and the Communist Party Central Committee, he became director of the Institute of the Economics of the World Socialist System in 1969. There he was involved in attempts to improve Comecon output in Leonid Brezhnev's time, and he became a reformist adviser to both Yuri Andropov and Mikhail Gorbachev. In 1990 he was elected to the Soviet Congress of Deputies, but his influence appeared to decline as more radical ideas came to the fore.

Bogue, David 1750–1825
Scottish Congregational minister

Born in Coldingham, Berwickshire, he became an Independent minister and tutor at a Gosport seminary, out of which grew the London Missionary Society. He was also a founder of the British and Foreign Bible Society and the Religious Tract Society and (with Dr James Bennet) wrote a *History of Dissenters* (1809).

Bohemond I c.1056–1111
Prince of Antioch
The eldest son of Robert Guiscard, he distinguished himself in his father's war against the Byzantine Emperor, Alexius I Comnenus (1081–85). His brother Roger took the Apulian throne, and Bohemond joined the First Crusade (1096). While the other crusaders advanced to storm Jerusalem, he established himself as first Latin prince in Antioch (1098). He was taken prisoner by the Turks (1100–03), then returned to Europe to collect troops, and after defeating Alexius (1107) was acknowledged by him as Prince of Antioch in return for his vassalage.

Bohemond II c.1108–31
Prince of Antioch
The younger son of Bohemond I, he assumed the government of Antioch in 1119 (succeeding de facto 1126), and was killed in battle with the Turks.

Bohm, David Joseph 1917–92
US theoretical physicist
Born in Wilkes-Barre, Pennsylvania, he graduated from Pennsylvania State College and studied under Robert Oppenheimer at the University of California at Berkeley. After participating in the Manhattan Project to develop the atomic bomb, he became assistant professor at Princeton University in 1947, but in 1951 was dismissed for political reasons. He moved to Brazil as professor at the University of São Paulo (1951–55), and later to the UK as a Research Fellow at Bristol University (1957–61) and Professor of Theoretical Physics at Birkbeck College, London (1961–83). On the Manhattan Project Bohm developed important techniques to describe oscillations in plasmas (high-temperature ionized gases), and he later applied these techniques to greatly enhance our understanding of electron behaviour in metals. He also had a great interest in quantum mechanics, writing *Quantum Theory* (1951), one of the clearest expositions of the subject ever written, and proposing radical new approaches to the field, notably the 'pilot-wave' theory (which assumes that particles can exert an instantaneous influence on each other across huge distances). In later work Bohm investigated many of the philosophical problems associated with modern physics, and the nature of thought and consciousness. He was elected FRS in 1990.

Böhm, Theobald See Boehm, Theobald

Böhme, Jakob 1575–1624
German mystical writer and alchemical thinker
He was born near Görlitz, and for many years worked as a cobbler. He was persecuted for the profoundly gnostic elements in his wild but seminal thinking, and from 1618 was forbidden to circulate his writings. He is the chief heir of Meister Eckhart, and of Paracelsus. He regarded God as possessing both love and anger, and therefore as containing the seeds of both good and evil. His writing is, because he dealt in paradoxes, obscure and even confused, but nonetheless vigorous and spiritually provocative. He influenced the work of Angelus Silesius and Goethe, Romantic thinkers such as Johann Hamann, Hegel, Friedrich Schelling and, later, Carl Gustav Jung, and his writings were studied by Isaac Newton. ◻ S Hobhouse, *Jakob Böhme, His Life and Teaching* (1950)

Bohr, (Aage) Niels 1922–
Danish physicist and Nobel Prize winner

Born in Copenhagen, he was the son of the Nobel prize-winning physicist **Niels Bohr**. Educated at the universities of Copenhagen and London, he worked from 1946 at his father's Institute of Theoretical Physics in Copenhagen where he became Professor of Physics (1956–92). From 1963 to 1970 he was also director there and from 1975 to 1981 he was director of Nordita (the Nordic Institute for Theoretical Atomic Physics). Together with **Benjamin Roy Mottelson** he developed the collective model of the nucleus, which combined the quantum-mechanical shell model of the nucleus and the classical liquid drop model developed by Niels Bohr, **Hans Bethe** and Baron **Carl von Weizsäcker** to support the work of **James Rainwater**. This model has been developed and explains the properties of nuclei well. Aage Bohr shared the 1975 Nobel Prize for physics with Mottelson and Rainwater for this work.

Bohr, Niels Henrik David 1885–1962
Danish physicist and Nobel Prize winner
Born in Copenhagen and educated at Copenhagen University, he went to England to work with Sir **J J Thomson** at Cambridge and **Ernest Rutherford** at Manchester University, and returned to Copenhagen University as professor (1916). He greatly extended the theory of atomic structure when he explained the spectrum of hydrogen by means of Rutherford's atomic model and the quantum theories of **Albert Einstein** and **Max Planck** (1913). Bohr's model was later shown to be a solution of **Erwin Schrödinger**'s equation. During World War II he escaped from German-occupied Denmark and assisted atom bomb research in the USA, returning to Copenhagen in 1945. He later worked on nuclear physics and developed the liquid drop model of the nucleus used by **Hans Bethe** and Baron **Carl von Weizsäcker**. He was founder and director of the Institute of Theoretical Physics at Copenhagen, (1920–22), and was awarded the Nobel Prize for physics in 1922. His son, **Aage Niels Bohr**, won the 1975 Nobel Prize for physics. 🕮 Ruth E Moore, *Niels Bohr: The Man, His Science, and the World They Changed* (1966)

Bohun
English family
The family was founded by the Norman Humphrey de Bohun. The fourth descendant, Henry, was made Earl of Hereford in 1199. Humphrey, fourth Earl of Hereford (1276–1322), was taken prisoner at Bannockburn (1314), and fell at Boroughbridge. In 1380 the heiress of the earldoms of Hereford, Essex and Northampton married Henry Bolingbroke (**Henry IV**).

Boiardo, Matteo Maria, Count of Scandiano
?1441–1494
Italian poet
Born in Scandiano, he studied at Ferrara, lived at the court there and was appointed Governor of Modena (1481), and of Reggio (1487). Because of his clemency and opposition to capital punishment, he has been called the 'Flower of Chivalry'. His early lyric poems in *Canzioniere* were inspired by a woman, Antonia Caprara, whom he met in 1469, but his fame rests on the unfinished *Orlando Innamorato* (1486), a long narrative poem in which the **Charlemagne** romances are recast into ottava rima. His other works comprise Latin eclogues, a versification of **Lucian**'s *Timon*, translations of **Herodotus**, the *Ass* of Lucian, and the *Golden Ass* of **Apuleius**, and a series of sonnets and *Canzoni* (1499). 🕮 G Reichenbach, *Matteo Maria Boiardo* (1929)

Boïeldieu, François Adrien 1775–1834
French composer
Born in Rouen, his opera *Le Calife de Bagdad* (1800, 'The Calife of Bagdad'), which was performed in Paris, brought him acclaim. He conducted at St Petersburg (1803–10) and on his return produced his two major works, *Jean de Paris* (1812) and *La Dame blanche* (1825, 'The White Lady'), notable for their bright and graceful melodies. His son Adrien (1816–83) also composed operas.

Boileau, Nicolas, *known as* Boileau Despréaux
1636–1711
French poet and critic
Born in Paris, he studied law and theology at Beauvais, before devoting himself to literature. In 1677 the king appointed him, along with **Racine**, official royal historian. His first publications (1660–66) were satires, some of which got him into trouble. *L'Art poétique* ('The Art of Poetry'), imitated by **Pope** in the *Essay on Criticism*, was published in 1674, along with the first part of the serio-comic *Lutrin* ('Lectern'). Between 1669 and 1677 he published nine epistles, written, like his satires, on the Horatian model. His works include several critical dissertations, a collection of epigrams, a translation of **Longinus**'s *On the Sublime*, a *Dialogue des héros de roman* ('A Conversation between the Heroes of Novels'), and a series of letters (many to Racine). His influence as a critic has been profound. 🕮 J E White, *Nicolas Boileau* (1969)

Bois, Franz de la Boë See Sylvius, Franciscus

Boisbaudran, Paul Émile Lecoq de 1838–1912
French chemist
Born in Cognac, he received no formal education but studied course books of the École Polytechnique, carrying out experimental work in a home laboratory. He was awarded the Cross of the Legion of Honour and (in 1879) the Davy Medal of the Royal Society. He is best known for his work in spectroscopic analysis. In *Spectres lumineux* (1874, 'Luminous Spectra'), he presented studies of the spectra of 35 elements. In 1875 he discovered a new element, gallium, and recognized it as the eka-aluminium predicted by **Dmitri Mendeleyev**. From 1879 he studied the rare earth elements and was involved in the discoveries of samarium, dysprosium, terbium, europium and gadolinium.

Bois-Reymond, Emil du 1818–96
German physiologist
Born in Berlin of French parentage, he became Professor of Physiology at Berlin in 1855. He investigated the physiology of muscles and nerves, and discovered the electricity in the nerves of animals. His brother Paul (1831–89), a mathematician, wrote on the theory of functions.

Boissier, Pierre-Edmond 1810–85
Swiss botanist and traveller
Born in Geneva, he studied at Geneva Academy, and after a six-month journey to Italy (1833) spent studying plants and shells, he decided to make botany his vocation. In 1834–36 he discovered many new species in Spain, later publishing the results. From 1842 to 1846 he travelled in Greece, Turkey, Syria and Egypt, and the many new plants discovered were described in *Diagnoses Plantarum Orientalium Novarum* (3 vols, 1843–59). He accumulated one of his period's best collections of Middle Eastern plants and compiled a complete *Flora Orientalis* (5 vols, 1867–84). This was the first Flora covering the entire Middle East and remains a standard work, although it has since been superseded by other works.

Boissy d'Anglas, François Antoine de
1756–1826
French politician
A member of the Estates General (1789), he joined the successful conspiracy against **Robespierre**. He was elected secretary of the Convention, and a member of the Committee of Public Safety. He was later called to the Senate by **Napoleon I** and made a peer by **Louis XVIII**.

Boito, Arrigo 1842–1918
Italian composer and poet
Born in Padua, he studied at the Milan Conservatorio. His first important work was the opera *Mefistofele* (1868), which survived its initial failure and later grew in popularity. Thereafter he concentrated mainly on writing libretti, the best-known of which are those for Verdi's *Otello* (1884–86) and *Falstaff* (1889–92). Another opera, *Nerone*, written in 1916, was not produced till 1924. ◫ P Nardi, *Vita di Arrigo Boito* (1944)

Bo Juyi (Po Chü-i) 772–846
Chinese poet of the Tang dynasty
He was born in Shaanxi (Shensi) province, of which he became Governor in 831. He was so admired as a lyric poet that his poems were collected by imperial order and engraved on stone tablets. ◫ A Waley, *The Life and Times of Po Chü-i* (1949)

Bok, Bart Jan 1906–83
US astronomer
Born in Hoorn, the Netherlands, and educated at the universities of Leyden and Groningen, he went to Harvard in 1929 and spent 25 years there, becoming associate director of the Harvard College Observatory and in 1947 Robert Wheeler Willson Professor of Astronomy. In 1957 he became director of the Mount Stromlo Observatory in Australia, and he was responsible for siting a major southern hemisphere observatory on Siding Springs Mountain in New South Wales. He returned to the USA in 1966 as director of the Stewart Observatory in Tucson, Arizona. His lifelong interest, pursued largely in collaboration with his wife Priscilla Fairfield Bok (1896–1975), was in the structure of our galaxy, in particular in the distribution of stars and interstellar matter in regions of potential star formation. His study of small dark clouds, the Bok globules, showed they contain enough material for future condensations into star clusters.

Bok, Edward William 1863–1930
US editor
He was born in Den Helder, the Netherlands, and emigrated to the USA at the age of six. He worked as a stenographer in his youth and became editor of the *Brooklyn Magazine* at 19. He ran the Bok Syndicate Press from 1886 to 1891 and was editor-in-chief of *The Ladies' Home Journal* from 1889 to 1919. He published several books in celebration of the American gospel of business success, and a highly influential autobiography, *The Americanization of Edward Bok* (1920). He created the 100,000 American Peace award, and the Harvard Advertising awards in 1923.

Bokassa, Jean Bédel 1921–96
Central African Republic soldier and politician
He was born in Bobangui, Lobay, and joined the French army in 1939. After independence he was made army Commander-in-Chief, with the rank of colonel. On 1 January 1966 he led the coup which overthrew his cousin President David Dacko and steadily increased his personal power, making himself Life President and, in 1977, crowning himself Emperor Bokassa I of the renamed Central African Empire. His rule was noted for its gratuitous violence and in September 1979 he was overthrown and exiled. Sentenced to death (in absentia) in 1980, he returned to the Central African Republic in 1986, was retried and, found guilty of murder and other crimes, was again sentenced to death. His sentence was commuted to life imprisonment and he was freed in 1993.

Boker, George Henry 1823–90
US poet, playwright, and diplomat
Born in Philadelphia, he won belated recognition for his 400 sonnets and for *Francesca da Rimini* (1855), a romantic verse tragedy and the best US play before the Civil War.

His propaganda for the North secured him the post of Minister to Turkey (1871–75) and Russia (1875–78). ◫ E S Bradley, *George Henry Boker: poet and patriot* (1927)

Bol, Ferdinand c.1616–1680
Dutch painter
He studied under **Rembrandt** in the 1630s and was one of his most talented followers. Working in Amsterdam, for many years he painted in a style so close to his master's that some of his portraits have been mistaken for his. After c.1650, when the Rembrandtesque style was no longer fashionable, Bol's work became more elegant and courtly. After marrying a wealthy widow in 1669, he appears to have stopped painting.

Bolam, James 1938–
English actor
Born in Sunderland, he starred as Terry Collier in the television sitcom *The Likely Lads* (1964–66), alongside Rodney Bewes as Bob Ferris in its sequel, *Whatever Happened to the Likely Lads?* (1973–74) and in a cinema version (1976), before playing strong-willed Jack Ford in the gritty Northern drama *When the Boat Comes In* (1976–81). He has since starred in *Only When I Laugh* (1979–81), the *Beiderbecke* trilogy (1985–88), *Room at the Bottom* (1986–88), *Andy Capp* (1988) and *Second Thoughts* (1991–94). He was in the films *A Kind of Loving* (1962), *The Loneliness of the Long Distance Runner* (1962) and *O Lucky Man!* (1973). His West End stage plays include *Arms and the Man*, *Run for Your Wife* and *Jeffrey Bernard is Unwell*.

Bold, Alan 1943–
Scottish poet, biographer, critic and editor
Born in Edinburgh, he was educated at Broughton High School and Edinburgh University. After a variety of jobs, including journalism, he became a full-time writer in 1967. A prolific writer and anthologizer, he has been a particularly influential commentator on the work of **Hugh MacDiarmid**, and his biography of the poet won the McVitie Scottish Writer of the Year Award in 1989. He has published several volumes of poetry in both English and Scots, including *In this Corner: Selected Poems 1963–83*. He is a trenchant and combative literary commentator.

Boldrewood, Rolf, *pseudonym of* Thomas Alexander Browne 1826–1915
Australian novelist
He was born in London, but his family emigrated to Australia in 1830, and he was educated in Sydney, then became a squatter in Victoria. After a series of misadventures and some years as an inspector of goldfields, he started writing serials for Australian periodicals to pay his debts. 'The Squatter's Dream' (1875) echoed Boldrewood's own misfortunes and was subsequently published as *Ups and Downs* (1878, rev edn *The Squatter's Dream*, 1890). His success was confirmed by *Robbery Under Arms*, a bush adventure, first published as a serial in the *Sydney Morning Herald* in 1882. Over the next 20 years he wrote many novels in a similar vein, among them *A Colonial Reformer* (1890) and *A Romance of Canvas Town* (1898). ◫ A Brissenden, *Rolf Boldrewood* (1972)

Bolet, Jorge 1914–90
US pianist
Born in Havana, Cuba, he studied at the Curtis Institute of Music, Philadelphia, from the age of 12, and was head of piano studies there. He also had lessons from **Leopold Godowsky**, Rosenthal and **Rudolf Serkin**. His career was interrupted during World War II by service in the Cuban and, later, US armies (he became a US citizen in 1944). He is renowned for his interpretation of **Liszt**, the German, Spanish and Russian Romantics and the repertoire of virtuosi-composers such as Godowsky, **Anton Rubinstein** and Carl Tausig.

Boleyn, Anne See Anne Boleyn

Bolger, James 1935–
New Zealand National Party politician
Born on a farm at Taranaki, he became a National Party MP in 1972. His farming interests led to his appointment as Minister of Agriculture in 1977; he became Minister of Finance in 1981 and Leader of the National Party in 1990. In 1994 he was elected Prime Minister and introduced a number of free market reforms and cuts in public spending. He was defeated in the 1996 general election and resigned as party leader in 1997.

Bolingbroke, Henry St John, 1st Viscount
1678–1751
English statesman and writer
He was born in Battersea, London, and became the Tory MP for Wootton Bassett in 1701. He was successively Secretary for War (1704–08) and Foreign Secretary (1710), and he shared the leadership of the party with Robert Harley. He was made a peer and in 1713 he negotiated the Treaty of Utrecht. After engineering Harley's downfall, he was plotting a Jacobite restoration when Queen Anne died, and George I succeeded. He fled to France, where he served James Edward Stuart, the Old Pretender as Secretary of State and wrote *Reflections on Exile*. In 1723 he obtained permission to return to England, where he became the associate of Pope, Jonathan Swift, and other men of letters. A series of letters attacking Robert Walpole in the *Craftsman* were reprinted as *A Dissertation of Parties*. Unable to return to political life, he went back to France, where he remained from 1735 to 1742 and wrote his *Letters on the Study and Use of History* (1752). His last years were spent in Battersea, where he wrote his *Letters on the Spirit of Patriotism* and *Idea of a Patriot King* (1749), which had a profound political influence. He also wrote *Reflections Concerning Innate Moral Principles* (1752), and he was much admired as an orator. ⌨ Jeffrey Hart, *Bolingbroke: Tory Humanist* (1965)

Bolitho, Henry Hector 1898–1977
New Zealand biographer, journalist, novelist and historian
Born in Auckland, he accompanied the Prince of Wales (later Edward VIII) on his 1920 tour and subsequently published *With the Prince in New Zealand*. He moved to Sydney in 1921 and then to Europe as a representative for Australian and New Zealand journals. He settled in London at the age of 24 and, renewing his acquaintance with the royal family, became an unofficial court biographer, who wrote many polite accounts of royalty. His books include three books on the reign of Queen Victoria; *Edward VIII: His Life and Reign* and *King George VI: a character study* (both 1937); *The Romance of Windsor Castle* (1946); and *A Century of British Monarchy* (1951). His novels include *Solemn Boy* (1927) and he also wrote memoirs of Arthur Stanley, Dame Marie Tempest and Alfred Mond. ⌨ *A Biographer's Notebook* (1950)

Bolívar, Simón, *known as* the Liberator 1783–1830
South American revolutionary leader
Born in Caracas, Venezuela, of a noble family, he studied law in Madrid. After the declaration of independence by Venezuela in 1811, he fled to New Granada and raised an army. In 1813, he entered Caracas as conqueror and proclaimed himself dictator of western Venezuela. Driven out in 1814, he made repeated descents on Venezuela from the West Indies, and in 1817 began to make headway against the Spaniards, but it was only in 1821 that the victory of Carabobo virtually ended the war; and it was not until 1824 that the royalist troops were finally driven out. In 1819 Bolívar became President of the new republic of Colombia (comprising modern Venezuela, Colombia and, from 1822, Ecuador). In 1824 he joined with other rebel leaders including Antonio de Sucre and José de San Martin to drive the Spaniards out of Peru, and made himself dictator there for a time. Upper Peru was made a separate state, and called Bolivia in his honour, while he was named perpetual protector, but his Bolivian constitution provoked political dissension, and led to the expulsion of the Colombian troops. His assumption of supreme power, after his return to Colombia in 1828, roused the apprehension of the republicans there, and in 1829 Venezuela separated itself from Colombia. Bolívar resigned in 1830. Although his life ended in dictatorship, his ideal of a federation of all Spanish-speaking South American states continued to exert a lively influence.

Bolkiah, Sir Hassanal 1946–
Sultan of Brunei
The son of Sultan Sir Omar Ali Saifuddin, he was educated at the Victoria Institute in Kuala Lumpur, Malaysia, and Sandhurst. Appointed crown prince (1961), he became sultan (1967) on his father's abdication. On independence (1984), Sultan Bolkiah also became Prime Minister and Defence Minister, governing in a personalized, familial manner. As head of an oil- and gas-rich micro-state, he is reputed to be the richest individual in the world, with an estimated wealth of $25 billion. A moderate Muslim, he has two wives, Princess Saleha (m.1965), and Mariam Bell (m.1981), who is a former air stewardess.

Böll, Heinrich 1917–85
German writer and Nobel Prize winner
Born in Cologne, he served as an infantryman in World War II before becoming a full-time writer. His first novel, *Der Zug war pünktlich* (Eng trans *The Train was on Time*, 1956), was published in 1949. A trilogy, *Und sagte kein einziges Wort* (1953, Eng trans *Acquainted with the Night*, 1954), *Haus ohne Hüter* (1954, Eng trans *The Unguarded House*, 1957) and *Das Brot der frühen Jahre* (1955, Eng trans *The Bread of our Early Years*, 1957), depicting life in Germany during and after the Nazi regime, gained him a worldwide reputation. His later novels, characteristically satirizing modern German society, included *Gruppenbild mit Dame* (1971, Eng trans *Group Portrait with Lady*, 1973) and *Die verlorene Ehre der Katharina Blum* (1974, Eng trans *The Lost Honour of Katharina Blum*, 1975). He also wrote a number of plays, and a volume of poems. He was awarded the 1972 Nobel Prize for literature. ⌨ Charlotte W Ghurye, *The Writer and Society: studies in the fiction of Günter Grass and Heinrich Böll* (1976); J H Reid, *Heinrich Böll: withdrawal and re-emergence* (1973)

Bolm, Adolph 1884–1951
Russian dancer, choreographer and teacher
Born in St Petersburg, he studied with Nikolai Legat and others at the Imperial Ballet School, graduating into the Maryinsky Theatre in 1903 and eventually becoming a soloist. He organized and danced in Anna Pavlova's first tours (1908–09), and at the same time joined Serge Diaghilev's Ballets Russes. From 1911 he travelled the world with the company, remaining in the USA after the 1916 tour. One of the USA's ballet pioneers, he became widely known as a dancer, teacher and choreographer. He was closely associated with the Chicago Civic Opera and the companies now known as American Ballet Theater and San Francisco Ballet. His choreography can be seen in the films *The Mad Genius* (1931), *The Men in Her Life* (1941) and *Affairs of Cellini* (1934).

Bologna, Giovanni 1524–1608
Flemish sculptor and architect
Born in Douai, France, he went to Italy in 1551, where he won great popularity and executed much work in Florence for the Medici, including the *Flying Mercury* (1564) and various fountains in the Boboli gardens, the

Rape of the Sabines (1580), and *Hercules and the Centaur* (1599). Several of his bronzes are in the Wallace Collection, London.

Bolt, Robert Oxton 1924–95
English playwright

Born in Manchester, he was educated at Manchester University, and worked as a schoolmaster until the success of his first play, *Flowering Cherry* (1957), a domestic drama about a frustrated insurance salesman. He achieved success with the Academy Award-winning *A Man for All Seasons* (1960), about the moral courage of Sir Thomas More. His later plays include *The Tiger and the Horse* (1960) and *State of Revolution* (1977), and among his screenplays are *Lawrence of Arabia* (1962), *Dr Zhivago* (1965, Academy Award), *Ryan's Daughter* (1970) and *The Mission* (1986).

Bolton, Geoffrey Curgenven 1931–
Australian historian and writer

He was born in Perth, Western Australia (WA). He was Foundation Professor of the Menzies Centre for Australian Studies, University of London (1982–85), and held chairs in history at the University of Western Australia, Murdoch University, WA (1973–89), University of Queensland, and Edith Cowen University, WA, from 1993. As general editor of the *Oxford History of Australia*, he wrote *The Middle Way* (vol 5, revised edition 1996), and delivered the ABC's Boyer Lectures in 1992. His many books include biographies of the West Australian pioneer Alexander Forrest (1849–1901), and of the postwar ABC chairman Sir Richard Boyer.

Boltwood, Bertram Borden 1870–1927
US radiochemist

Born in Amherst, Massachusetts, he was educated at Yale, Munich and Leipzig. He was an instructor at Yale from 1897 to 1900, and later established himself as a consulting chemist with his own laboratory. From 1904 onwards he concentrated on radiochemistry, becoming the leading American in this field and laying the foundations for the study of isotopes. In 1906 he returned to Yale and became Professor of Radiochemistry in 1910. By showing that there is a constant ratio of radium to uranium in unaltered minerals, he confirmed the work of Ernest Rutherford and Frederick Soddy which suggested that radioactive elements decay and transmute into other elements. He introduced Pb:U ratios as a method for dating rocks in 1907 and this, together with other radiometric dating methods developed from his work, eventually revolutionized geology and archaeology. In 1907 he discovered the element ionium, since renamed thorium 230. He committed suicide.

Boltzmann, Ludwig 1844–1906
Austrian physicist

Born in Vienna, he studied at the University of Vienna where he obtained his PhD in 1867. From 1869 he held professorships in mathematics and physics at the universities of Graz, Vienna, Munich and Leipzig, numbering Walther Nernst amongst his many students. Although his interests were diverse he is most celebrated for the application of statistical methods to physics and the relation of kinetic theory to thermodynamics. In 1868 he extended James Clerk Maxwell's theory of the velocity distribution for colliding gas molecules to derive the 'Maxwell–Boltzmann distribution'. In 1877 he presented the famous 'Boltzmann equation' which showed how increasing entropy corresponded to increasing molecular randomness. Other work dealt with electromagnetism, viscosity, and diffusion, and in 1884 he derived the law for black-body radiation found experimentally by Josef Stefan, his teacher in Vienna. Boltzmann's work came under attack from

positivists in Vienna, and partly because of the unpopularity of his views, he suffered severe depression from 1900 and committed suicide.

Bolyai, János 1802–60
Hungarian mathematician

Born in Kolozsvár, he took up a military career, but retired due to ill health in 1833. After attempting to prove Euclid's parallel postulate, that the straight line which passes through a given point and is parallel to another given line is unique, he realized that it was possible to have a consistent system of geometry in which this postulate did not hold, and so became one of the founders of non-Euclidean geometry, together with Nikolai Lobachevski. His work continued that of his father Farkas (or Wolfgang, 1775–1856), but its poor reception inclined him not to publish again, and credit for his discovery was largely posthumous.

Bolzano, Bernard 1781–1848
Czech theologian, philosopher and mathematician

Born in Prague of Italian ancestry, he was ordained as a priest in 1804 and appointed Professor of the Philosophy of Religion in 1805, but was deprived of his chair in 1819 for non-conformity. Despite his poor health, he left a large body of writing that is only now being published. In mathematics, he pioneered the theory of functions of a real variable, and investigated the concept of the infinite. He discovered, but did not publish, the first example of a function that is continuous everywhere it is defined, but nowhere differentiable.

Bombard, Alain Louis 1924–
French physician and marine biologist

He was born in Paris, and in 1952 set out across the Atlantic alone in his rubber dinghy *L'Hérétique* to prove his claim that shipwreck castaways could sustain life on nothing more than fish and plankton. He landed at Barbados 62 days later on 24 December 1952, emaciated, but vindicated in his theories. He started a marine laboratory—'La Coryphene'—at Saint-Malo, for the study of the physiopathology of the sea.

Bomberg, David 1890–1957
English painter

Born in Birmingham, he trained as a lithographer before studying painting in London at the City and Guilds School, at the Westminster School of Art (1908–10) under Walter Sickert, and at the Slade (1911–13). He was a founder member of the London Group (1913). In Paris he met avant-garde artists including Amedeo Modigliani, André Derain and Picasso, and their influence is clear in such large compositions as *The Mud Bath* and *In the Hold* (1913–14), which combine abstract and Vorticist influences. He later travelled widely.

Bombois, Camille 1883–1970
French primitive painter

Born in Venarey-les-Laumes, Côte d'Or, the son of a bargeman, he had no academic training, and worked in a travelling circus, then as a porter on the Paris Métro, as a navvy and a docker, painting as a hobby. By 1923 he had been discovered by collectors and was able to devote all his time to painting his very personal landscapes (eg, of the *Sacré Cœur*) and pictures of wrestlers and acrobats. They are uncompromisingly realistic, with a childlike frankness and simplicity of technique.

Bonald, Louis Gabriel Ambroise, Vicomte de 1754–1840
French writer

Born in Le Monna, near Millau, he emigrated to Heidelberg, Germany, during the French Revolution. He wrote *Théorie du pouvoir politique et religieux* (1796, 'Theory of Political and Religious Power'), advocating the system of monarchy and prophesying the return of the **Bourbons**. He was appointed Minister of Instruction by **Napoleon I** in 1808, and in 1815 ennobled by **Louis XVIII**. 📖 M H Quinlan, *The Historical Thought of the Vicomte de Bonald* (1953)

Bonaparte
Influential Corsican family
They were active from the 16th century. The name was spelt Buonaparte until 1768.

Bonaparte, (Maria Annunciata) Caroline
1782–1839
Queen of Naples
Born in Ajaccio, Corsica, the youngest surviving daughter of **Charles** and **Marie Bonaparte**, she married **Joachim Murat** (1800), becoming Queen of Naples in 1808. She brought a brilliant court life to the Neapolitan palaces of Caserta and Portici. After her husband's execution she lived, under surveillance, at Frohsdorf in Austria (1815–24) and Trieste (1824–31) before settling in Florence for the last seven years of her life.

Bonaparte, Charles Louis Napoléon See Napoleon III

Bonaparte, Charles Marie 1746–85
Corsican lawyer
He was born in Ajaccio, and in 1773 was appointed Royal Counsellor and Assessor to **Louis XVI** in Ajaccio. Married to **Marie Bonaparte**, he was father of **Napoleon I**.

Bonaparte, (Marie-Anne) Élisa 1777–1820
Grand Duchess of Tuscany
Born in Ajaccio, Corsica, the eldest surviving daughter of **Charles** and **Marie Bonaparte**, she married Felix Baciocchi in 1797. As Duchess of Lucca (from 1806), she managed the economy of her small state so profitably that in 1809 **Napoleon I** made her Grand Duchess of Tuscany, where she revived the court glories of the Pitti Palace. Towards the end of her life she called herself Countess of Compignano.

Bonaparte, François Charles Joseph See Napoleon II

Bonaparte, Jérôme 1784–1860
King of Westphalia
Born in Ajaccio, Corsica, he was the son of **Charles** and **Marie Bonaparte**, and brother of **Napoleon I**. He served in the navy (1800–02) and lived in New York (1803–05). His marriage to Elizabeth Patterson (1785–1879) at Baltimore (1803) was declared null and void by Napoleon. He was given a high military command in the Prussian campaign (1806), led an army corps at Wagram (1809), incurred his brother's displeasure during the invasion of Russia (1812), but fought with tenacity at Waterloo (1815). He became sovereign of Westphalia (1807–13) and married Princess Catherine of Württemberg in 1807. After exile in Rome, Florence and Switzerland, he returned to Paris (1847). His nephew **Napoleon III** appointed him Governor of the Invalides, created him a Marshal of France, and consulted him over the strategy of the Crimean War, where his son Prince Napoleon Joseph Charles Paul (1822–91) fought at the Alma and Inkerman. His great-grandson Louis, Prince Napoleon, (b.1914), became head of the House of Bonaparte in 1926.

Bonaparte, Joseph 1768–1844
King of Naples and Sicily, and King of Spain
Born in Corte, Corsica, he was the eldest surviving son of **Charles** and **Marie Bonaparte**, and brother of **Napoleon I**. He married (1794) Julie Clary (1771–1845), elder sister of Desirée **Bernadotte**. He served Napoleon on diplomatic missions and was a humane sovereign in southern Italy, where he finally abolished feudalism, and reorganized

justice, finance and education. In Spain he faced continuous rebellion and in 1813 his army was defeated by **Wellington** at Vittoria. He spent much of his later life in exile in New Jersey but settled in Florence for his last years. 📖 Michael Ross, *The Reluctant King: Joseph Bonaparte, King of the Two Sicilies and Spain* (1976)

Bonaparte, Louis 1778–1846
King of Holland
Born in Ajaccio, Corsica, he was the son of **Charles** and **Marie Bonaparte**, and the brother of **Napoleon I**. He was a soldier, serving originally in the artillery but later in the cavalry. He married Napoleon's stepdaughter, **Hortense de Beauharnais** in 1802. After becoming Governor of Paris (1805), he ruled Holland as King Lodewijk I (1806–10) but abdicated because Napoleon had complained that he was too attached to the interests of the Dutch. He became Count of Saint-Leu, settled in Austria, Switzerland, and later in Florence, and mainly pursued literary interests. He was the father of **Napoleon III**.

Bonaparte, Lucien 1775–1840
Prince of Canino
A younger brother of **Napoleon I**, he was born in Ajaccio, Corsica. He was made a member of the Council of Five Hundred (1798), and was later elected its president, saving his brother's career (1799) by refusing his outlawry. He was Minister of the Interior, and ambassador to Madrid (1800). He was offered the crowns of Italy and Spain on condition that he divorce his second wife, but he refused them, and lived on his state of Canino, in the papal states. Essentially a republican, he denounced the arrogant policy of his brother towards the court of Rome, and was 'advised' to leave Roman territory. In 1810, on his way to the USA, he was captured by the English and kept a prisoner at Ludlow and Thorngrove, Worcestershire, till 1814. He spent the rest of his life in Italy.

Bonaparte, Marie Letizia, *née* Ramolino
c.1749–1836
Corsican noblewoman
Born in Ajaccio, the daughter of a French army captain, she married **Charles Marie Bonaparte** in 1764. Of her 12 children, five died in infancy; the fourth child became **Napoleon I**. She was accorded official status as 'Madame Mère de l'Empereur' (1804) and encouraged her son to seek reconciliation with the Church. Her half-brother Cardinal Fesch (1763–1839) became Archbishop of Lyons. She supported the fallen Napoleon on Elba (1814) but spent the last 18 years of her life in dignified retirement in Rome.

Bonaparte, Napoléon Joseph Charles Paul,
nicknamed **Plon-Plon** 1822–91
French politician
The son of **Jérôme Bonaparte** and nephew of **Napoleon I**. He was born in Trieste, Italy, and grew up in Italy. He entered military service in Württemberg (1837), and was expelled from France (1845) for republicanism. In 1848, having taken the name Jérôme on his elder brother's death, he was elected to the legislative national assembly. In 1851 he was named as the successor to **Napoleon III**. He fought in the Crimean War (1854), but was recalled by the emperor, and made Minister for the Colonies and Algeria (1858). In 1859 he married Princess Clotilda, daughter of **Victor Emmanuel II** of Sardinia, by whom he had two sons and a daughter. After the fall of the Second Empire he took up residence in England, but returned to France (1872) and sat in the Chamber of Deputies. The death of the Prince Imperial (1879) made him head of the family, and in 1886, as pretender to the throne, he was exiled from France with his eldest son, Victor (1862–1926).

Bonaparte, (Marie) Pauline 1780–1825
Princess Borghese

Born in Ajaccio, Corsica, she was the daughter of **Charles** and **Marie Bonaparte**, and was **Napoleon I**'s favourite sister. She married General Leclerc (1772–1802) in 1797 and accompanied him on an expedition to Haiti (1802) on which he contracted yellow fever and died. In 1803 she married Prince Camillo Borghese; her private life soon shocked the patrician family into which she married, not least because of her willingness to pose as a nude Venus for the sculptor **Antonio Canova**. She loyally supported Napoleon in his exile on Elba.

Bonaventure or Bonaventura, St, *originally* Giovanni di Fidanza, *known as* Doctor Seraphicus
1221–74
Italian theologian and Doctor of the Church
Born near Orvieto, Tuscany, he became a Franciscan in 1243, a professor of theology at Paris in 1253, the General of his order in 1257, and Cardinal Bishop of Albano in 1273. He died during the Council of Lyons from ascetic exhaustion. His most important works are the *Breviloquium* (a dogmatic); the *Itinerarium Mentis in Deum*; *De Reductione Artium ad Theologiam*, a commentary on **Peter Lombard**; and his *Biblia Pauperum*, ('Poor Man's Bible'). His feast day is 14 July. ▢ J G Bougerol, *Introduction à l'étude de Saint Bonaventure* (1961, Eng trans 1964)

Bond, Edward 1934–
English dramatist and director
He was born in London. His work uses a variety of metaphors for the corruption of the capitalist society. His first play, *The Pope's Wedding*, was given a Sunday night reading at the Royal Court Theatre, London, in 1962 and aroused great controversy. *Saved* (1965) achieved notoriety through a scene in which a baby in a pram is stoned to death. Both these plays were set in contemporary England, although later plays, such as *Narrow Road to the Deep North* (1968), use historical themes to look at broad contemporary issues. Other plays include *Lear* (1972), a reworking of **Shakespeare**'s play, *The Fool* (1976), based on the life of the 'peasant poet', John Clare, *The Woman* (1978), in which the characters are drawn from Greek tragedy, *The Worlds* (1979), a trilogy, *The War Plays* (1985), for television, *Olly's Prison* (1992) and *Tuesday* (1993), and *Coffee: a tragedy* (1995).

Bond, (Thomas) Michael 1926–
English children's author
He was born in Newbury, Berkshire, and worked for many years as a BBC cameraman. The creator of several fictional animal characters, he is best known for his most popular creation, Paddington Bear, a small bear so named because he was discovered at Paddington Station in London. Paddington wears a sou'wester, wellington boots and a duffle-coat, from a toggle of which hangs a luggage label bearing the words, 'Please look after this bear'. Hapless, vulnerable and good-natured, Paddington has so far been the hero of almost 40 stories since his first appearance in *A Bear Called Paddington* (1958); his enormous popularity shows no sign of waning. His other creation is Monsieur Pamplemousse, about whom he has written a series of books for adults (1983–93).

Bond, William Cranch 1789–1859
US astronomer
Born in Portland, Maine, he started work in the family shop as a watchmaker, and turned to astronomy after witnessing the solar eclipse of 1806. His home observatory became the best US observatory of the day. In 1839 he moved it to Harvard, and was awarded an honorary MA and the title of Observer. He became the observatory's first director. Together with his son George Phillips Bond (1825–65), director of the Harvard Observatory 1858–65) and simultaneously with **William Lassell**, he discovered Hyperion, a satellite of Saturn.

They also discovered Saturn's crêpe ring, but erroneously concluded that all Saturn's rings are liquid. He collaborated with his son in the field of celestial photography, exhibiting a daguerreotype photograph of the Moon at the Great Exhibition in London in 1851. In 1850 they photographed the planet Jupiter and the star Vega, and in 1857 the double star Mizar.

Bondfield, Margaret Grace 1873–1953
English Labour politician and trade unionist
Born in Somerset, she became chairman of the Trades Union Congress (TUC) in 1923 and as Minister of Labour (1929–31) was the first woman to be a British Cabinet Minister.

Bondi, Sir Hermann 1919–
British mathematical physicist
Born in Vienna, he moved to England in 1937 to study at Trinity College, Cambridge, where he later became a Fellow (1943–49). He became a British citizen in 1947 and in 1954 moved to King's College London as Professor of Applied Mathematics (emeritus, 1985). Bondi served with great distinction as director-general of the European Space Research Organization (1967–71), as chief scientific advisor to the Ministry of Defence and as chairman of the National Environmental Research Council (1980–84). Scientifically he is best known for his seminal book on cosmology, published in 1952, and for his proposal, with **Sir Fred Hoyle** and **Thomas Gold**, that the universe was in a steady state, matter being continuously created to fill the gaps left by the expansion. This theory fell out of favour when it was discovered that in the past the universe was more dense, and with the discovery by **Arno Penzias** and **Robert Wilson**, of the microwave background radiation (1965). In 1962 Bondi wrote a keynote paper showing how the emission of gravitational waves is a necessary consequence of **Albert Einstein**'s general theory of relativity. He was Master of Churchill College, Cambridge from 1989, becoming Fellow in 1990. He was knighted in 1973.

Bone, Sir Muirhead 1876–1953
Scottish artist
Born in Glasgow, he studied architecture, but became a self-taught artist. He married Gertrude Dodd, author of *Days in Old Spain* which, along with others, he illustrated, and as a draughtsman he exhibited extensively from 1902. Generally accepted as one of the greatest etchers of the 20th century, he was trustee of both the National Gallery and the Imperial War Museum, London. His work, which has been likened, technically, to that of **Giambattista Piranesi**, combines meticulous realism with a strong sense of composition, and his subject matters range from the architectural to portraiture and landscape. He made over 500 etchings, drypoints and lithographs besides many thousands of drawings and watercolours. He travelled to the USA, Spain, Italy, Holland, France, Turkey and Sweden. His son Stephen (1904–58) was an artist and critic.

Bone, Phyllis Mary 1896–1972
Scottish animal sculptor
Born in Hornby, Lancashire, she studied at Edinburgh College of Art, in Italy and in Paris, and exhibited at the Royal Academy, Royal Scottish Academy, Paris Salon, British Empire Exhibition and the Royal Glasgow Institute. Her many commissions include a Scottish National War Memorial granite sculpture on Inchcape Monument, a carving for St Winifred's Church, Welbeck, and works for St John's Church, Perth, and Edinburgh's Zoological Building. Her works can be seen in Aberdeen Art Gallery and Glasgow Museum and Art Gallery. She was the first woman to be elected to the Royal Scottish Academy.

Boner, Ulrich 1300–49
Swiss fable writer

He was a Dominican friar in Bern from 1324, and his *Edelstein* ('Precious Stone'), a collection of fables and jokes, was one of the first German books printed (1461).
📖 J J Oberlin, *Bonerii gemma* (1782)

Bongo, Omar, *originally* Albert-Bernard Bongo 1935–
Gabonese statesman

Born in Lewai, Franceville, and educated in Brazzaville, he joined the French Civil Service in 1957, becoming head of the Ministry of Information and Tourism (1963), and then Minister of National Defence (1964–65). He was made Vice-President in 1967. When President M'ba died in 1967, he took over the interlocking posts of President, Prime Minister and Secretary-General of the *Parti Democratique Gabonais* (PDG), establishing a one-party state in 1968. He converted to Islam in 1973, and has presided over the exploitation of Gabon's rich mineral resources (it has the highest per capita income of any African country) without notably diminishing inequalities. In 1986 he was re-elected for the third time and has since remained in power, though as President only from 1995.

Bonham-Carter, Lady Violet, Baroness Asquith (of Yarnbury) 1887–1969
English Liberal politician and publicist

Daughter of H H Asquith by his first marriage, she married in 1915 Sir Maurice Bonham-Carter (d.1960), a scientist and civil servant. She was prominent in cultural and political movements, serving as President of the Liberal Party Organization (1944–45) and as a governor of the BBC (1941–46). She was created a life peeress in 1964, and published *Winston Churchill as I Knew Him* in 1965. Jo Grimond was her son-in-law. Her eldest son Mark (1922–) stood unsuccessfully as a Liberal candidate in 1945 and 1964 and was Liberal MP for Torrington (1958–59). He became director of the Royal Opera House, Covent Garden (1958–82), and first chairman of the Race Relations Board (1966–70).

Bonheur, Rosa 1822–99
French animal painter and sculptor

Born in Bordeaux, she exhibited at the Salon in 1841. Known for her detailed depictions of animals, particularly horses, she led an unconventional lifestyle, wearing trousers and smoking. In 1865 she became the first woman to be awarded the Grand Cross of the Légion d'Honneur. Her paintings include *Ploughing with Oxen* (1849, Luxembourg), and her famous *Horse Fair* (1853 in the Metropolitan Museum of Modern Art, New York).

Bonhoeffer, Dietrich 1906–45
German Lutheran pastor and opponent of Nazism

He was born in Breslau (Wrocław, Poland), the son of an eminent psychiatrist. He was educated at Tübingen and Berlin, where he was influenced by Karl Barth. He left Germany in 1933 in protest against the Nazi enforcement of anti-Jewish legislation, and worked in German parishes in London until 1935, when he returned to Germany, to become head of a pastoral seminary of the German Confessing Church until its closure by the Nazis in 1937. He became deeply involved in the German resistance movement and in 1943 was arrested and imprisoned until 1945, when he was hanged at Flossenbürg. His controversial writings, of increasing importance in modern theology, include *Sanctorum Communio* (1927) and *Akt und Sein* (1931, 'Act and Being'), on the nature of the Church, and the best-known and most-interpreted, *Ethik* (1949, 'Ethics') and *Widerstand und Ergebung* (1951, Eng trans *Letters and Papers from Prison*, 1953), on the place of Christian belief and the concept of Christ in the modern world.

Boniface, St See Bruno, St

Boniface, St, *originally* Wynfrith, *also known as* the Apostle of Germany c.680–c.754
Anglo-Saxon missionary

Born in Wessex (probably in Crediton in Devon), he became a Benedictine monk in Exeter as a child, and taught in the monastery of Nursling near Romsey, where he was elected abbot in 717. He declined this offer in order to spread Christianity among the Frisians, but a war curtailed his immediate plans. He returned to Nursling, but set out again in 718 with a commission from Pope Gregory II to preach the gospel to all the tribes of Germany. He met with great success and was consecrated Bishop (723), Archbishop and Primate of Germany (732). His goal was to impose Roman Catholic order on the whole Frankish kingdom and to suppress the irregularities of Irish or Columban Christianity. He had resumed his missionary work among the Frisians when he was killed at Dokkum, near Leeuwarden, by pagans. His feast day is 5 June.

Boniface VIII, *originally* Benedetto Gaetani c.1235–1303
Italian pope

Born in Anagni, he studied law in Bologna and was elected pope in 1294. His reign was marked by the strong assertion of papal authority, claiming supreme power in temporal affairs in the Bull *Unam Sanctam* (1302, 'One Holy'). His authority was challenged, most notably by Philip IV, the Fair, of France, who had Boniface taken prisoner at Anagni in 1303. He died soon after and the papacy took up residence at Avignon.

Bonington, Chris(tian John Storey) 1934–
English mountaineer and photo-journalist

Born in Hampstead, London, he was educated at University College School, London, and the Royal Military Academy, Sandhurst, before joining the Tank Regiment (1956–1961). He started climbing at Harrison's Rocks in Kent before progressing to climbs in Scotland and Wales. His early mountaineering ascents include Annapurna II (1960), Nuptse (1961), Central Pillar of Freney, Mont Blanc (1961), Central Tower of Paine (1963), Brammah (1973), Changabang (1974), Mount Kongur, China (1981), Shivling West (1983) and the first British ascents of the North Wall of the Eiger (1962) and Mt Vinson in Antarctica (1983). He led or co-led many successful expeditions, including Annapurna South Face (1970) and Everest 1972 and 1975 (the south-west face), and reached the summit of Everest himself in 1985. He has written several books including the autobiographical *I Chose to Climb* (1966), *The Next Horizon* (1973) and *Mountaineer* (1989). 📖 Rob Hunter, *Chris Bonington* (1983)

Bonington, Richard Parkes 1801–28
English painter

Born near Nottingham, he moved to Calais around 1817, and there and at Paris he studied art and began a friendship with Eugène Delacroix, who introduced him to oriental art. His first works were exhibited in the Salon in 1822. He also began to work in lithography, illustrating Baron Taylor's *Voyages*. From 1824 he experimented increasingly in romantic subjects taken from history and studied armour. His best-known works followed: *Francis I and Marguerite of Navarre*, *Henry IV receiving the Spanish Ambassador*, *Entrance to the Grand Canal*, and *Ducal Palace*. His work forms an important link between French and English art. He excelled in light effects achieved by the use of a large expanse of sky, broad areas of pure colour and the silhouetting of dark and light masses, as well as his rich colouring of heavy draperies and brocades.

Bonivard or Bonnivard, François de 1493–1570
Swiss monk and politician

Born in Seyssel, Savoy, he was prior of the abbey of St Victor, and opposed the Duke of Savoy. His imprisonment in the dungeons of Chillon Castle (1532–36) was the subject of many popular folk-songs and of Byron's legendary poem, *Prisoner of Chillon* (1816). A convert to the Protestant faith, Bonivard, after his liberation by the Bernese, wrote an important *Chronicle*, begun in 1542 and amended by John Calvin in 1551, but unpublished until 1831.

Bon Jovi, Jon, *originally* John Francis Bongiovi, Jnr 1962–
US rock singer, bandleader and actor

Born in Perth Amboy, New Jersey, he is the singer and charismatic frontman of Bon Jovi, one of the most commercially successful rock bands of the 1980s. He played in bands in New Jersey before moving to New York, where he worked in a menial capacity at the Power Station studios. He formed Bon Jovi in the early 1980s, and was the focal point of the band's subsequent success, although guitarist Ritchie Sambuca was also a major factor. *Slippery When Wet* (1986) established them as major players on the rock scene. He attempted to concentrate on a solo career from 1990, and made his delayed acting debut in Young Guns II, but has continued to tour and record with Bon Jovi. 📖 M Dome, *Faith and Glory* (1994)

Bonnard, Abel 1883–1968
French poet, novelist, and essayist

Born in Poitiers, he won the National Poetry Prize with his first collection of poems, *Les Familiers* (1906, 'The Familiars'). He wrote the psychological novel, *La Vie et l'amour* (1913, 'Life and Love'), and later published travel books and collections of essays. He was Minister of Education in the Vichy government (1942–44), fled to Spain and was sentenced to death in his absence (1945). He returned to France (1958) and was banished (1960). 📖 R Brasillach, *Abel Bonnard* (1971)

Bonnard, Pierre 1867–1947
French painter and lithographer

Born in Paris, he joined the group called 'Les Nabis', which included Maurice Denis and Édouard Vuillard, with whom he formed the Intimist group. His style was formed under the influence of Impressionism, Japanese prints and the works of Paul Gauguin and Toulouse-Lautrec. Ignoring the movement towards abstraction, he continued to paint interiors and landscapes, in which everything is subordinated to the subtlest rendering of light and colour effects.

Bonnat, Léon Joseph Florentin 1833–1922
French painter

Born in Bayonne, he was well known as a painter of religious subjects, and as a portraitist of notable contemporaries, eg *Madame Pasca* (1874, Musée d'Orsay, Paris). He taught Toulouse-Lautrec and Georges Braque. He used his earnings from painting to collect old masters, which he donated to form the nucleus of the Musée Bonnat at Bayonne, while his studio and personal effects are in the Musée Basque, Bayonne.

Bonner, Edmund c.1500–1569
English prelate

The reputation he gained at Oxford recommended him to Thomas Wolsey, who made him his chaplain. After Wolsey's fall, he continued in King Henry VIII's service, and in 1540 was made Bishop of London. Imprisoned, however, from 1549 to 1553 for refusing to recognize royal supremacy during the minority of Edward VI, he was restored to office later, under Mary I, and pronounced sentence on several Protestant martyrs. On Elizabeth I's accession (1558), he went with his episcopal colleagues to pay homage at Highgate, but was excepted from the honour of kissing her hand. In May 1559 he refused the Oath of Supremacy, so was deposed and imprisoned in the Marshalsea, where he died.

Bonner, Yelena 1923–
Soviet civil rights campaigner

She was born in Moscow. After the arrest of her parents in Stalin's 'great purge' of 1937, she was brought up in Leningrad (St Petersburg) by her grandmother. During World War II she served in the army, but suffered serious eye injuries. In 1965 she joined the Communist Party (CPSU), but became disillusioned after the Soviet invasion of Czechoslovakia (1968). She married Andrei Sakharov in 1971 and resigned from the CPSU a year later. During the next 14 years she and her husband led the Soviet dissident movement. Following a KGB crackdown, Sakharov was banished to Gorky (now Nizhny Novgorod) in 1980 and Bonner followed in 1984. After hunger strikes, she was permitted to travel to Italy for specialist eye treatment in 1981 and 1984. The couple were finally released from Gorky in 1986, as part of a new 'liberalization' policy by the Gorbachev administration, and remained prominent campaigners for greater democratization. Following Sakharov's death in 1989 she remained a critic of the post-Soviet governments of Presidents Gorbachev and Yeltsin.

Bonnet, Charles Étienne 1720–93
Swiss naturalist and philosopher

Born in Geneva, he distinguished himself by researches on parthenogenesis, polypi, the tapeworm, the respiration of insects, the use of leaves, etc. Failing sight made him abandon his experiments and turn to philosophy. He was critical of vitalistic theories and pointed out that the nonexistence of the soul can never be proved. He held a catastrophic theory of evolution.

Bonneville, Nicholas de 1760–1828
French writer

He was appointed president of a Paris district during the French Revolution (1789). A student of English and German literature, he translated Shakespeare, founded several newspapers, and wrote a history of modern Europe (1792).

Bonney, William H, *also known as* Billy the Kid 1859–81
US outlaw

Born in New York City, he grew up in bad company in Kansas, Colorado and New Mexico, and killed his first man at the age of 12. In 1876 he began a series of crimes and killings in the Southwest and Mexico, and two years later he gathered a band of followers and began rustling cattle. He had killed 21 men, one for each year of his life, when he was finally tracked down and shot in Fort Sumner, New Mexico. 📖 Pat Garrett, *The Life of Billy the Kid* (1882)

Bonnie and Clyde See Parker, Bonnie

Bonnier, Albert 1820–1900
Swedish publisher

He founded the prestigious Bonnier publishing house in Stockholm in 1837. His liberal beliefs and his support of, for instance, August Strindberg, brought him into conflict with the prevailing censorship laws. Under him and successive generations of the family, the company has developed and diversified, becoming the largest publisher in Sweden and one of the country's largest companies.

Bonnivard, François de See **Bonivard, François de**

Bonny Dundee See **Dundee, 1st Viscount**

Bono, Edward de See **de Bono, Edward Francis Charles Publius**

Bono, Emilio de See **De Bono, Emilio**

Bonomi, Ivanoe 1873–1952
Italian politician
A graduate in natural sciences and law, he took up journalism in 1898, writing for *Avanti!* and *Critica socialista*. In 1909 he was elected to parliament. Expelled from the Italian Socialist Party in 1912, he founded a reformist socialist movement. In 1916–21 he was a minister on a number of occasions, serving under **Vittorio Orlando**, Francesco Nitti and **Giovanni Giolitti**, and was briefly premier himself (1921–22). He opposed **Mussolini's** seizure of power but left politics in 1924. From 1942, he was a leading figure in the anti-Fascist struggle, replacing **Pietro Badoglio** as Prime Minister (1944) and establishing a broad, anti-Fascist coalition government. In 1945 he was forced to resign in favour of the more radical Ferruccio Parri. He became president of the Senate in 1948.

Bononcini or **Buononcini, Giovanni Maria**
1642–78
Italian composer
Born near Modena, he became a violinist in the court orchestra there in 1671, and subsequently maestro di cappella of the cathedral. From 1666 he published a great quantity of chamber and vocal music, together with a treatise, the *Musico prattico*, which was influential in its day. His sons Giovanni Battista (1670–1755) and Marc Antonio (1675–1726) were notable composers, the former specially remembered for his rivalry with **Handel**.

Bonpland, Aimé Jacques Alexandre 1773–1858
French botanist
Born in La Rochelle, he travelled with Baron von **Humboldt** in South America (1799–1804), and collected and described (but did not publish) 6,000 new species of plants. Named Professor of Natural History at Buenos Aires University in 1816, he undertook a journey up the Parana, but **José Francia**, dictator of Paraguay, arrested him, and kept him prisoner for nine years.

Bontempelli, Massimo 1878–1960
Italian novelist, playwright and journalist
He was born in Como, Lombardy. His novel *La scacchiera davanti allo specchio* (1922, 'The Chess Board Before the Mirror'), may be regarded as one of the first novels of magical realism, although that term (coined independently by Bontempelli in his critical work of 1938, *L'avventura novecentista*, 'Twentieth Century Adventure') is, outside painting, often employed as applying only to Latin-American or German novels. Subsequent novels include the majestic *Il figlio di due madri* (1929, 'The Son of Two Mothers') and *Vita e morte do Adria e suoi figli* (1930, 'The Life and Death of Adria and Her Two Sons'), both again in the 'magical realist' mode. He initially, although unhappily, acted as a propagandist for fascism, but he was suspended from the party for two years from 1938. He refused to accept a university chair offered to him after its occupier had been deprived of it because he was a Jew. However, when he was elected a senator on a Communist ticket after World War II, he was not able to take it up owing to his past. His most notable play is the Pirandellian *Nostra Dea* (1925, 'Our Goddess'). F Tempesti, *Bontempelli* (1974, in Italian)

Bontemps, Arna Wendell 1902–73
US writer

Born in Alexandria, Louisiana, he became a leading figure in the Harlem Renaissance of the 1920s and 1930s. He wrote poems such as 'Southern Mansion' and 'A Black Man Talks of Reaping' and the novels *God Sends Sunday* (1931), *Black Thunder* (1936), and *Drums at Dusk* (1939). His anthologies of African-American verse and folklore and his non-fiction historical works helped establish a much wider appreciation of the richness and validity of black culture. R A Bone, *The Negro Novel in America* (1958)

Bonvicino, Alessandro See **Moretto da Brescia**

Boole, George 1815–64
English mathematician and logician
Born in Lincoln, Lincolnshire, he was largely self-taught, and although he did not receive a degree, he was appointed Professor of Mathematics at Cork University in 1849. He was one of the first to direct attention to the theory of invariants, expressions in several variables that do not change when the coordinates change. His algebraic treatment of differential operators gradually led him to consider the operations of logic algebraically also, resulting in the work for which he is best remembered, his *Mathematical Analysis of Logic* (1847) and *Laws of Thought* (1854). In these he employed mathematical symbolism to express logical relations, thus becoming an outstanding pioneer of modern symbolic logic. Boolean algebra is a generalization of the familiar operations of arithmetic, and it is particularly useful in the design of circuits and computers. E T Bell, *Men of Mathematics* (1937)

Boom, Corrie ten See **ten Boom, Corrie**

Boone, Daniel 1735–1820
US frontiersman
He was born in Pennsylvania to Quaker parents and moved with them to western North Carolina. He had little formal education but learned to hunt and trap. After working as a blacksmith in North Carolina he travelled to Kentucky in 1767–68 through the Cumberland Gap in the Appalachian Mountains (1769–71), becoming one of the first to explore the area. In 1775 he marked out the Wilderness Road and founded Boonesborough on the Kentucky River. Twice captured by Native Americans, he repeatedly (1775–78) repelled their attacks and became famed for his heroism. He was a successful surveyor, trapper and landowner, and ushered new settlers into Kentucky, but he lost his large landholdings to debt and legal mismanagement and moved further west into Missouri. He played a crucial role in extending US settlement beyond the Allegheny Mountains and many legends have grown up around his life. He features in **Byron's** *Don Juan*. John Bakeless, *Daniel Boone* (1939)

Boorde or **Borde, Andrew** c.1490–1549
English Carthusian monk, physician and writer
Born near Cuckfield, Sussex, he studied medicine at Orleans, Toulouse, Montpellier, and Wittenberg from 1527. He visited Rome and Santiago de Compostela, and for **Thomas Cromwell** went on a confidential mission in France and Spain. He practised medicine in Glasgow (1536), and travelled through Europe to Jerusalem. His chief works are his *Dyetary* and the *Fyrst Boke of the Introduction of Knowledge* (1548), a guidebook to the Continent, which contains the first known specimen of gypsy language, and also his *Itinerary of England* (1735).

Boorman, John 1933–
English film director
Born in Shepperton, Middlesex, he was a film critic before becoming an assistant director for television (1955). He worked for Southern Television and, in 1962, became head of the BBC documentary unit. His first feature film,

Catch Us If You Can (1965), was followed by the stylish US thriller *Point Blank* (1967). Heavily influenced by the Arthurian legends, his films show a subtle use of colour and often include mythological resonances or involve some form of quest, as in *Deliverance* (1972) and *Excalibur* (1981). *Hope and Glory* (1987), an affectionate recreation of his wartime childhood, was both a critical and commercial success. He has contributed to various periodicals, launched an annual magazine in book form, *Projections: A Forum For Film-Makers* (1992–), and written *Money into Light* (1985), an autobiographical account of the compromises and exigencies inherent in international film production. Recent films include *Where The Heart Is* (1990) and *Beyond Rangoon* (1995).

Boorstin, Daniel Joseph 1914–
US academic and librarian

Born in Atlanta, Georgia, he attended Harvard, then won a Rhodes scholarship to Oxford, where he studied jurisprudence and civil laws. He was admitted to the English Bar in 1937. He became senior historian of the Smithsonian Institution, Washington DC, director of the National Museum of History and Technology, Washington DC (1969–73), and Professor of American History at the University of Chicago (1944–69). He has also spent much time outside the USA and has written many works which explore and explicate his native land, including *A History of the United States* (1980), *The Americans* trilogy (1965, 1968, 1973) and *The Discoverers* (1983). He was librarian of Congress (1975–87).

Boot (of Trent), Jesse Boot, 1st Baron
1850–1931
English drug manufacturer

Born in Nottingham, he inherited his father's herbalist's shop at 13 and studied pharmacy in his leisure hours. In 1877 he opened his first chemist's shop in Nottingham and, by mass selling at reduced prices, introduced the modern chain store. In 1892 he began large-scale drug manufacture and by the early 1900s was controlling the largest pharmaceutical retail trade in the world, with over 1,000 branches in 1931. Knighted in 1909, he was created a peer in 1929. ◻Christopher Weir, *Jesse Boot of Nottingham: Founder of the Boots Company* (1994)

Booth, Barton 1681–1733
English actor

He was born in Lancashire, the son of a squire, and educated at Westminster School. He became an actor and played with success for two seasons at Dublin, and in 1700 joined Thomas Betterton's company in London. His performance as Cato in Joseph Addison's tragedy in 1713 brought him wealth and fame.

Booth, Catherine, *née* Mumford 1829–90
English co-founder of the Salvation Army

Born in Derbyshire, the daughter of a Wesleyan preacher, she met William Booth at Brixton Wesleyan Church, from which they were both expelled for religious zeal, and they married in 1855. She became a gifted preacher herself, and shared in her husband's evangelistic work. Following preaching tours round the country, they returned to London (1864) to start the work that became the Salvation Army. Their eight children all became active in the Salvation Army movement, and she also started the Army's women's work. Her funeral was attended by 36,000 people. Her belief in woman preachers is outlined in the pamphlet *Female Ministry* (1859).

Booth, Charles 1840–1916
English shipowner, statistician, and social reformer

Born in Liverpool, he joined his brother Alfred in founding the Booth Steamship Company and the allied leather factories of Alfred Booth & Co. An ardent radical in his youth, he settled in London in 1875 and devoted 18 years to the preparation of his great *Life and Labour of the People in London* (1903), the prototype of the modern social survey, based on organized on-the-spot investigation. He was also a pioneer of old-age pensions. He became President of the Royal Statistical Society (1892–94) and was made a Privy Councillor (1904).

Booth, Edwin Thomas 1833–93
US actor

He was born in Harford County, Maryland, the son of Junius Brutus Booth (1796–1852) and brother of John Wilkes Booth. He played Tressel at the age of 16 to his father's Richard III and quickly rose to the top of his profession. He visited England (1861–62), and produced *Hamlet* in New York for a record run (1864). Ruined by opening a theatre in New York in 1869, he was able to settle his debts by 1877. He visited Germany and Great Britain (1880–82) and played Othello to Henry Irving's Iago.

Booth, John Wilkes 1839–65
US assassin

Born in Baltimore, he became a successful actor in Washington DC. In 1865 he entered into a conspiracy to avenge the defeat of the Confederates, and shot President Lincoln at Ford's Theatre, Washington DC, on 14 April. He managed to escape to Virginia, but was tracked down and, refusing to surrender, was shot dead. He was the son of the actor Junius Booth and brother of Edwin Thomas Booth. ◻ Gene Smith, *American Gothic: The Story of America's Legendary Theatrical Family—Junius, Edwin, and John Wilkes Booth* (1992)

Booth, Margaret 1898–
US film editor

Born in Los Angeles, she began cutting film for D W Griffith, and in 1921 moved to the Mayer studio, which became MGM in 1924. She was one of their leading film editors, and was supervising film editor at MGM from 1939 to 1968. She returned to more hands-on editing assignments after leaving MGM, working with various independent filmmakers. The first woman to achieve success in her field, her film credits include *The Mutiny on the Bounty* (1935) and *The Way We Were* (1973). She received an Academy Award for overall career achievement in 1977.

Booth, William 1829–1912
English religious leader, founder and 'general' of the Salvation Army

Born in Nottingham, he married Catherine Mumford (1829–90) in 1855 and became a Methodist New Connexion minister on Tyneside (1855–61). The couple went on preaching tours abroad and returned in 1864 to begin The Christian Mission in London's East End (1865) which in 1878 became the Salvation Army. Though often imprisoned for preaching in the open air, his men and women waged war on such evils as sweated labour and child prostitution, and a worldwide network of social and regenerative agencies was established. Opinion changed, and Booth was made freeman of London, honorary doctor of Oxford, was a guest at Edward VII's coronation, and opened the US Senate with prayer. His book, *In Darkest England and the Way Out* (1890), describes his philosophy and motivation. He and Catherine had eight children who all became active in the Salvation Army movement. They included William Branwell Booth (1856–1929), Chief of Staff from 1880 and general from 1912; Ballington Booth (1857–1940), commander in Australia (1883–85) and the USA (1887–96); and Evangeline Cora Booth (1865–1950), commander in Canada (1896–1904) and the USA (1904–34), and general (1934–39).

Boothby (of Buchan and Rattray Head), Robert John Graham Boothby, 1st Baron
1900–86
Scottish Conservative politician
Born in Edinburgh, he was educated at Eton and Oxford and in 1924 was elected MP for East Aberdeenshire, the seat he held until 1958. 'Discovered' in 1926 by **Churchill**, he was his Parliamentary Private Secretary until 1929. From 1940 to 1941 he was Parliamentary Secretary to the Ministry of Food and later served in the RAF. He became in 1948 an original member of the Council of United Europe and was a British delegate to its consultative assembly (1949–54). He was knighted in 1953 and raised to the peerage in 1958. An outstanding commentator on public affairs on radio and TV, he brought to political argument a refreshing candour and a robust independence. He wrote *The New Economy* (1943), *I Fight To Live* (1947) and *My Yesterday, Your Tomorrow* (1962)

Boothe, Clare 1903–87
US writer
Born in New York, she was on the editorial staff of *Vogue* and other periodicals. She wrote *European Spring* (1940), and other books, but was most successful with her plays, which include *The Women* (1936) and *Kiss the Boys Goodbye* (1938). She was elected to the House of Representatives as a Republican in 1942, and was US ambassador to Italy (1953–57). She married (1935) **Henry R Luce**.

Boothroyd, Betty 1929–
English Labour politician
Born in Dewsbury, Yorkshire, she was a member of the dance troupe the Tiller Girls, and a political assistant before becoming a Hammersmith borough councillor in 1965. She had first stood for parliament in 1957, and was finally elected as MP for West Bromwich in 1973 (West Bromwich West since 1974). Becoming Deputy Speaker of the House of Commons in 1987, she commanded wide respect by her magisterial, even-handed performances. After the 1992 general election she became the first woman Speaker of the House of Commons. She has been Chancellor of the Open University since 1994.

Bopp, Franz 1791–1867
German philologist
Born in Mainz, after four years' study in Paris, paid for by the Bavarian government, he produced his first study of Indo-European grammar, *Über das Conjugationssystem der Sanskritsprache ...* (1816, 'On the System of Conjugation in Sanskrit'), in which he traced the common origin of the grammatical forms of these languages. In 1821 he was appointed Professor of Sanskrit and Comparative Grammar in Berlin. His greatest work is *A Comparative Grammar of Sanskrit, Zend, Greek, Latin, Lithuanian, Old Slavonic, Gothic and German* (6 vols, 1833–52; trans 1856), a revised edition of which (publ 1856–61) included Old Armenian.

Bór, Tadeusz Komorowski See Komorowski-Bór

Bora, Katherine von 1499–1552
German nun
Having adopted Lutheran doctrines, she ran away from the Cistercian convent of Nimptschen, near Grimma, in 1523, and married **Martin Luther** in 1525. They had several children, both their own and adopted.

Borah, William Edgar 1865–1940
US Republican politician
Born in Illinois, he was elected senator for Idaho in 1907. He advocated disarmament and, being a convinced isolationist, was instrumental in blocking the USA's entry into the League of Nations in 1919.

Borchgrevink, Carsten Egeberg 1864–1934
Norwegian explorer
He was born in Oslo. After emigrating to Australia, he was the leading member of the first party to set foot on the Antarctic continent (1894), and was the first to winter there (1898–99).

Borda, Jean Charles de 1733–99
French mathematician and astronomer
Born in Dax, Landes, he helped to measure the arc of the meridian and to establish the metric system, and he was noted also for his work on fluid mechanics.

Borde, Andrew See Boorde, Andrew

Borden, Lizzie Andrew 1860–1927
US alleged murderess
Born in Fall River, Massachusetts, she was accused of murdering her wealthy father and hated stepmother with an axe, in August 1892. In one of the most highly publicized murder trials in US history, she claimed to have been outside in the barn at the time of the murder, and despite a great deal of circumstantial evidence, was acquitted. She lived out her life in Fall River and was buried alongside her father and stepmother. The case is immortalized in a children's nursery rhyme.

Borden, Sir Robert Laird 1854–1937
Canadian statesman
Born in Grand Pré, Nova Scotia, he practised as barrister and became leader of the Conservative Party in 1901. In 1911 he overthrew Sir **Wilfrid Laurier**'s ministry over the question of reciprocity with the USA and was Prime Minister of the Dominion until 1920. He organized Canada for war, and was the first overseas premier to attend a Cabinet meeting in London (1915). An architect of postwar peace, he was Canada's delegate at the Paris Peace Conference (1919) where he insisted on Canada having separate membership of the League of Nations, and remained premier until 1920.

Border, Allan 1955–
Australian cricketer
Born in Cremorne, Sydney, he made his Test debut for Australia in 1978, and captained the team from 1984 to 1994. He established a world record of most Test match and one-day international appearances, and in 1993 set a new world record for runs scored in Test matches when his career total reached 10,161. He has played county cricket in England for Gloucestershire and Essex. He retired from Test cricket in 1995 and from Sheffield Shield cricket in 1996.

Bordet, Jules Jean Baptiste Vincent 1870–1961
Belgian physiologist and Nobel Prize winner
Born in Soignies, he graduated from the University of Brussels in 1892, and in 1894 went to Paris to work at the Pasteur Institute. In 1901 he became director of the Pasteur Institute in Brussels. He explained the mechanics of bacteriolysis as being due to the action of two substances: a specific antibody present only in immunized animals, and a non-specific, heat-labile substance which he identified as **Hans Buchner**'s 'alexin'. This work made possible new techniques for the diagnosis and control of infectious diseases. He went on to discover the whooping cough bacillus, extracted an endotoxin, and prepared a vaccine (1906). An authority on serology, he was awarded the 1919 Nobel Prize for physiology or medicine.

Bordone, Paris 1500–71
Italian painter of the Venetian school
Born in Treviso, he worked there and in Vicenza, Venice and Paris. He was strongly influenced by **Titian**, his most celebrated work being the *Fisherman Presenting the Ring of St Mark to the Doge* in the Venice Accademia.

Borel, Émile Félix Édouard Justin 1871–1956
French mathematician and politician

Born in Saint Affrique, he studied and then taught at the École Normale Supérieure, and became professor at the Sorbonne in 1909. In addition to his prolific mathematical work, he was active in politics, scientific popularization and journalism, became a member of the Chamber of Deputies (1924–36), and was Minister for the Navy (1925–40). His mathematical work was first in complex analysis, applying ideas in Cantorian set theory to the classical theory of functions, and subsequently he worked on measure theory and probability. He also wrote on the theory of games (1921–27), independently of the work of **John Neumann** on this subject.

Borelli, Giovanni Alfonso 1608–79
Italian mathematician and physiologist

Born in Naples, he probably received a mathematical training at the University of Naples, and acquired a reputation as a fine mathematics lecturer, rising to hold chairs at the universities of Naples, Pisa and Messina, and pursuing studies in mathematics, geometry and observational astronomy. Impressed by the thinking of **William Harvey** and **Descartes**, he became one of the most articulate advocates of the iatrophysical school of medicine, which sought to explain all bodily functions by physical laws.

Borg, Björn Rune 1956–
Swedish tennis player

A talented all-round sportsman in his youth, he left school aged 14 to concentrate on tennis, and at 15 was selected for the Swedish Davis Cup team. He was Wimbledon junior champion at 16, and became the dominant player in world tennis in the 1970s. In 1976 he won the first of his record five consecutive Wimbledon singles titles (1976–80). He also won the Italian championship twice and the French Open six times between 1974 and 1981. His Wimbledon reign ended in 1981 when he lost in the final to **John McEnroe**. He retired in 1983 and turned to business interests, but had little success and returned twice to professional tennis in the early 1990s, before entering the Seniors' Tour for the over-35s. His autobiography is *My Life and Games* (1980). 📖 Larry Audette, *Björn Borg* (1979)

Borge, Victor 1909–
US entertainer and pianist

Born in Denmark, he was educated at the Royal Danish Academy of Music, Copenhagen, and in Vienna and Berlin. He made his debut as a pianist in 1926 and as a revue actor in 1933. Since 1940 he has worked in the USA for radio, television and theatre, and has performed with leading symphony orchestras on worldwide tours since 1956. He became a US citizen in 1948.

Borges, Jorge Luis 1899–1986
Argentine writer

Born in Buenos Aires, he was educated there and at Geneva and Cambridge. From 1918 he was in Spain, where he was a member of the avant-garde Ultraist literary group, returning to Argentina in 1921. From 1923, he published poems and essays, and in 1941 appeared the first collection of the intricate and fantasy-woven short stories for which he is famous. Later collections include *Ficciónes* (1944 and 1956, Eng trans in US *Ficciones*, 1962, Eng trans in UK *Fictions*, 1965), *El Aleph* (1949, Eng trans *The Aleph and Other Stories 1933–1969*, 1970 (US); 1973 (UK)), *La Muerta y la Brújula* ('Death and the Compass', 1951) and the verse collection *El Hacedor* (1960, Eng trans *Dreamtigers*, 1963). Some stories from *El Aleph* appear in the collection of translations, *Labyrinths* (1962). He became director of the National Library in 1955, after losing his sight. His last book was *Atlas* (1986), written with

his companion, Maria Kodama, whom he married a month before his death. 📖 J Sturrock, *The Ideal Fictions of Jorge Luis Borges* (1977);J M Cohen, *Jorge Luis Borges* (1973)

Borgia, *Italian form of* Borja
Ancient Spanish family in the province of Valencia

Alfonso de Borgia (1378–1458), bishop, accompanied Alfonso of Aragon to Naples, and was elected pope as Calixtus III (1455). His nephew Rodrigo Borgia (1431–1503) ascended the papal throne (1492) as **Alexander VI**. Before this, he had had a number of children by a Roman girl, Giovanna Catanei, known as Vanozza. Two of these children, **Cesare** and **Lucrezia Borgia**, became especially notorious as ambitious, murderous public figures.

Borgia, Cesare c.1476–1507
Italian soldier

He was the illegitimate son of Rodrigo Borgia (later Pope **Alexander VI**) and brother of **Lucrezia Borgia**. He was appointed Archbishop of Valencia (1492) and a cardinal (1493) after his father's election to the papacy (1492). He relinquished his cardinal's hat to marry Princess Charlotte d'Albret, sister of the King of Navarre (1498), and succeeded his elder brother Juan (whom he may have murdered) as Captain-General of the papal army (1499). In two campaigns, with French help (1499–1501), he became master of the Romagna, taking Perugia, Siena, Piombini and Urbino, and was made Duke of Romagna by his father. His ambitious plans for a Kingdom of Central Italy spread terror in an atmosphere of constant treachery and cruelty. In 1502, on the eve of a third campaign, he and his father were mysteriously taken ill at a banquet, believed to have been poisoned. Though his father died, Cesare survived, but his enemies, led by Pope **Julius II** (elected 1503), forced him to relinquish the Romagna. He surrendered at Naples (1504), under promise of safe conduct, but was imprisoned in Spain. He escaped (1506) and fled to the court of Navarre, but was killed at the siege of Viana. Despite attempts to rehabilitate his reputation, he remains a monster in the public perception. He was praised by **Machiavelli** in *Il Principe* as a model prince and the saviour of Italy: opportunistic, aggressive and ruthless. He encouraged art, and was the friend of **Pinturicchio** and the protector of **Leonardo da Vinci**. 📖 W H Woodward, *Cesare Borgia* (1913)

Borgia, Lucrezia 1480–1519
Italian noblewoman

Born in Rome, the illegitimate daughter of Rodrigo Borgia (later Pope **Alexander VI**), she was married off three times by her father for political reasons: first, at the age of 12 to Giovanni Sforza, Lord of Pesaro (1493), but this marriage was annulled by her father (1497); second, to Alfonso of Aragon, nephew of the King of Naples (1498), but this marriage was ended (1500) when Alfonso was murdered by her brother **Cesare Borgia**; and third (1501), to Alfonso d'Este (1486–1534). The son of the Duke of Este, Alfonso inherited the duchy of Ferrara, where Lucrezia established a brilliant court of artists and men of letters, including **Ariosto** and **Titian**. A patroness of art and education, in legend she has become notorious, quite unfairly, for wantonness, vice and crime (including incest with her brother and father).

Borglum, (John) Gutzon (de la Mothe) 1867–1941
US sculptor

He was born in Idaho, of Danish descent, and won renown for works of vast proportions such as the famous Mount Rushmore National Memorial portraying **George Washington**, **Abraham Lincoln**, **Thomas Jefferson**, and **Theodore Roosevelt**, hewn out of the solid rock of the mountainside (completed in 1939). His other monumental works include the head of Lincoln in the US

Capitol Rotunda, and the *Twelve Apostles* in the Cathedral of St John the Divine in New York.

Borgognone or Bergognone, Ambrogio
c.1445–1523

Italian painter

His work is in the native Milanese tradition, characterized by a gracefulness which conveys a feeling of genuine piety. *Virgin Crowned*, in the Brera Gallery in Milan, and the frescoes at the Certosa di Pavia are good examples of his work.

Boris Godunov c.1551–1605

Tsar of Russia

Of Tatar stock, he became a close friend of Ivan IV, and during the reign of Ivan's feeble son Fyodor (1584–98), Godunov was virtual ruler of the country; he colonized western Siberia and created the patriarchate (1589). He became tsar on Fyodor's death (1598), and continued the expansionist policies of Ivan, going to war against both Poland and Sweden. At home, he disposed of the Tatar threat but was involved in the last years of his reign in a civil war against a pretender, claiming to be Dmitri, younger son of Ivan IV. A disputed succession inaugurated the Time of Troubles, during which the country lapsed into chaos (until 1613).

Borja See Borgia

Borlaug, Norman Ernest 1914–

US plant pathologist and geneticist

He was born in Cresco, Iowa. As director of the Wheat Programme at the International Center for Maize and Wheat Improvement, he developed 'dwarf' wheats which dramatically increased yields and made possible the 'green revolution'. He was awarded the 1970 Nobel Peace Prize.

Bormann, Martin 1900–45

German Nazi politician

Born in Halberstadt, he participated in the abortive Munich putsch of 1923 and became one of Hitler's closest advisers. After Rudolf Hess's flight to Scotland, he was appointed Reichsminister ('party chancellor') in May 1941 and was with Hitler to the last. His own fate was uncertain for a time, but he is now known to have committed suicide by a poison capsule during the breakout by Hitler's staff from the Chancellory (1 May 1945). He was sentenced to death in absentia by the Nuremberg Court (1946).

Born, Max 1882–1970

German physicist and Nobel Prize winner

Born in Breslau (Wrocław, Poland) and educated at the universities of Breslau, Heidelberg, Zurich and Göttingen, he was appointed Professor of Theoretical Physics at Göttingen University (1921–33), lecturer at Cambridge (1933–36) and Professor of Natural Philosophy at Edinburgh University (1936–53). In 1925, with his assistant Pascual Jordan, he built upon the earlier work of Werner Heisenberg to produce a systematic quantum theory. He used Erwin Schrödinger's wave equation to show that the state of a particle (eg its energy or position) could only be predicted in terms of probabilities, deducing from this the existence of quantum jumps between discrete states. This led to a statistical approach to quantum mechanics. He shared the 1954 Nobel Prize for physics with Walther Bothe for their work in the field of quantum physics. ⌨ *My Life and Views* (1968)

Börne, Ludwig, *originally* Löb Baruch 1786–1838

German political writer and satirist

He was born in Frankfurt, of Jewish descent, and edited various journals (1812–21), establishing his reputation as a vigorous opponent of the Prussian government, and inciting the German people to revolution and social reform. The French revolution of July 1830 drew him to Paris, where he finally settled in 1832. He and Heinrich Heine who wrote critical articles on his political views, became bitterly hostile to each other.

Borodin, Aleksandr Porfirevich 1833–87

Russian composer and scientist

Born in St Petersburg, he was an illegitimate son of Prince Gedeanov, who registered him as the child of a serf. Borodin trained in medicine and distinguished himself as a chemist, then in 1862 began to study music, under Mili Alekseyevich Balakirev. His works include the unfinished opera *Prince Igor* (1869–70, 1874–87), which contains the Polovtsian Dances), three symphonies, and the symphonic sketch *In the Steppes of Central Asia* (1880). From 1872, he lectured in chemistry at the St Petersburg School of Medicine for Women.

Borodin, Mikhail Markovich, *originally* Mikhail Markovich Grusenberg 1884–1951

Russian and Soviet politician and political adviser

He participated in the Jewish worker movement in his native Russia and met Lenin in 1904. After 1905 he lived in exile in Great Britain and the USA. When the United Front was formed between the Guomindang (Kuomintang) and the Chinese Communist Party in 1923 Borodin, as the representative of both the Comintern and the Soviet Communist Party, became a personal adviser to Sun Yat-sen. He helped transform the Guomindang into a disciplined and centrally-controlled revolutionary party, as well as convincing Sun of the necessity of creating mass-based organizations. When the United Front broke down in 1927 Borodin was compelled to leave China. Made the scapegoat for the failure of Stalin's policy in China, Borodin was henceforth given only minor posts. He died in a Siberian prison camp.

Borotra, Jean, *nicknamed* the Bounding Basque 1898–94

French tennis player

Born near Biarritz, he was the most famous of the so-called Four Musketeers (with Lacoste, Cochet and Brugnon) who emerged in the 1920s to make France one of the leading tennis nations. He won the men's singles title at Wimbledon in 1924, and his extraordinary fitness enabled him to compete in veterans' events at that same venue when he was almost 80. He also won the French and Australian championships, as well as several Davis Cup medals between 1927 and 1932. He was secretary of Physical Education in the Vichy government (1940–42), but was imprisoned by the Nazis from 1943 to 1945.

Borough, Steven 1525–84

English navigator

He was born in Northam, Devon. In 1553 he commanded the *Searchthrift*, the first English ship to reach northern Russia via North Cape, and became chief pilot to the newly founded Muscovy Company. He discovered the entrance to the Kara Sea.

Borough, William 1536–99

English navigator

He became controller of the navy, and drew up charts of the Northern Ocean (1560) and the north Atlantic (1576). He was vice-admiral in Francis Drake's Cadiz adventure, and commanded a ship against the Armada in 1588.

Borovansky, Edouard 1902–59

Czech dancer, choreographer and ballet director

Born in Přerov, Czech Republic, he studied and took roles at Prague's National Theatre and School, prior to dancing with **Anna Pavlova**'s company. A soloist of character roles in Colonel de Basil's Ballets Russes de Monte Carlo (1932–39), he stayed on in Melbourne during one of the troupe's Australian tours, opening a ballet school and club with his wife Xenia Nikolaeva in 1940. Out of this grew the Borovansky Ballet (1942) which became professional in 1944. He staged both classics and original works for this financially unstable company. The Australian Ballet, formed in 1962, drew many of its members and much of its impetus from Borovansky's company and pioneering efforts, and his influence on Australian classical dance was considerable.

Borromeo, St Carlo 1538–84
Italian prelate
Born in his father's castle of Arona, on Lake Maggiore, he gained a PhD in canon and civil law from the University of Padua in 1559. At the age of 22, he was appointed a cardinal and Archbishop of Milan by his uncle, Pope **Pius IV**. He did much to bring the Council of Trent (1545–63) to a successful conclusion, and had the principal part in drawing up the famous *Catechismus Romanus* (1566). He was renowned for his determined efforts to maintain ecclesiastical discipline and for his poor relief during the famine of 1570 and the plague of 1576. He founded in 1570 the Helvetic College at Milan, and he brought about an alliance of the seven Swiss Catholic cantons for the defence of the faith. In 1578 he founded the community later known as the Oblates of St Ambrose. He was canonized in 1610 and his feast day is 4 November. His nephew, Count Frederico Borromeo (1564–1631), from 1595 Archbishop of Milan, founded the Ambrosian Library.

Borromini, Francesco 1599–1667
Italian Baroque architect and sculptor
Born in northern Italy, he spent all his working life in Rome, where he was associated with his great rival **Gian Bernini** in the Palazzo Berberini (1620–31) and the Baldacchino in St Peter's (1631–33). His own chief buildings were the S Carlo alle Quattro Fontane (1641), S Ivo della Sapienza (1660), S Andrea delle Fratte (1653–65), and the oratorio of S Philippo Neri (1650). He is particularly noted for his command of spatial effects. Although now considered one of the great Baroque architects, he had limited influence during his lifetime.

Borrow, George Henry 1803–81
English writer
Born in East Dereham, Norfolk, he was educated at the High School, Edinburgh and at Norwich Grammar School (1816–18). For the next five years he was articled to a firm of solicitors, but he turned to literature, editing six volumes of *Celebrated Trials and Remarkable Cases of Criminal Jurisprudence* (1825). He was an accomplished linguist and travelled widely as an agent for the Bible Society, visiting St Petersburg (1833–35), Portugal, Spain, and Morocco (1835–39) and touring south-eastern Europe (1844), and Wales (1854). He wrote numerous books in which romantic fiction and autobiography often overlapped: *The Zincali or an Account of the Gypsies of Spain* (1840), *The Bible in Spain* (1843), which was an instant success as a travel book, *Lavengro* (1851) and its sequel, *The Romany Rye* (1857), both novels about his own gypsy life, *Wild Wales* (1862), and *Romano Lavo-Lil*, or *Word-book of the English-Gypsy Language* (1874). 🕮 M D Armstrong, *George Borrow* (1950)

Bosanquet, Bernard 1848–1923
English philosopher
Born near Alnwick, Tyne and Wear, he taught at the universities of Oxford (1871–81) and St Andrews (1903–08). He was one of the school of British idealists, much influenced by **Hegel**, whose other members included **F H**

Bradley, **T H Green**, Edward Caird and James Ferrier. His main philosophical works are *Knowledge and Reality* (1885), *Logic* (1888), *History of Aesthetic* (1892), *The Philosophical Theory of the State* (1899) and *The Principle of Individuality and Value* (1912).

Boscawen, Edward, *known as* Old Dreadnought 1711–61
English naval commander
He distinguished himself at the sieges of Porto Bello (1739) and Cartagena (1741), and in command of the *Dreadnought* in 1744, he captured the French *Médée*. He had an important part in the victory off Cape Finisterre (1747), and, in command of the East Indian expedition, displayed great military skill in the retreat from Pondicherry. In 1755 he intercepted the French fleet off Newfoundland, capturing two ships and 1,500 men. He was appointed Commander-in-Chief of the successful expedition against Cape Breton (1758) and also gained victory over the French Toulon fleet in Lagos Bay (1759).

Bosch, Carl 1874–1940
German industrial chemist and Nobel Prize winner
Born in Cologne, he studied organic chemistry at Leipzig but also showed an early talent for engineering. He worked for Badische Anilin und Soda Fabrik, becoming its general manager in 1910. In 1909 he began work to adapt the laboratory process developed by his brother-in-law, Fritz Haber, for synthesizing ammonia to commercial production. The industrial production of ammonia was of enormous importance to agriculture as it was made into nitrates for fertilizers; it also affected the manufacture of explosives. Bosch invented the process which bears his name, in which hydrogen is produced on an industrial scale by passing steam and water gas over a catalyst at high temperatures. He became president of I G Farbenindustrie. In 1931 he shared the Nobel Prize for chemistry with **Friedrich Bergius** for his part in the invention and development of chemical high-pressure methods, and in 1935 succeeded **Max Planck** as director of the Kaiser Wilhelm Institute.

Bosch, Hieronymus, *real name* Jerome van Aken c.1450–1516
Dutch painter
Named after the town in which he was born, 's Hertogenbosch in northern Brabant, he probably spent the whole of his life there. It is difficult to trace the development of his work because none of it is dated, but there are some quite conventional pictures which contrast with the depictions of a bizarre, nightmarish world for which he is famous. Although the roots of his work can be traced to devotional woodcuts of the period, the extravagance of his vision is hard to explain, as is its acceptance by local churches for which he worked. After his death, **Philip II** of Spain avidly collected his works and the majority of them are now in the Prado, Madrid, including his masterpiece, *The Garden of Earthly Delights*. He had many imitators in his lifetime but only **Pieter Brueghel**, the Elder, had the ability to incorporate the imagery of Bosch into his own art. Bosch was adopted in the 20th century as the precursor of the Surrealist movement.

Bosch, Johannes van den 1780–1844
Dutch reformer and politician
He joined the Dutch East Indian Army, rapidly reaching the rank of colonel. Returning to the Netherlands in 1815 he was put in charge of East Indies military affairs. He produced two important political essays which shaped his further career and to some extent the Dutch state as well. One was on poor-relief, resulting in the foundation of the Society for Charity (1818), which tried to take urban paupers and compel them to be agricultural labourers in a number of 'colonies' in the east of the country. The other

was on the 'Culture System', a plan to make the Dutch colonies earn money for the mother country. Launched in 1834, the plan was eventually highly successful in financial terms, if not in human ones. Popular with King William I, Van den Bosch served as Governor-General of the Dutch East Indies (1828–33), and as Minister of Colonies (1834–39).

Bosch, Juan 1909–
Dominican Republic politician and writer
The founder of the Dominican Revolutionary Party, he lived in exile in Cuba and Costa Rica during the Trujillo dictatorship. Bosch became President in 1963 but his reformist government lasted only six months before it was overthrown by the army and he was again exiled. He has been the losing candidate in every presidential election since 1966 and, although by 1990 he had moderated his Marxism, his party again lost the election of that year, despite having appeared to be the front runner.

Boscovich, Roger Joseph 1711–87
Croatian mathematician and astronomer
Born in Ragusa (Dubrovnik), he was educated in physics and mathematics at the Collegium Romanum in Rome, where he was later appointed to the chair in mathematics (1740). He became Professor of Mathematics at Pavia in 1764. He devised new methods for determining the orbits and rotation axes of planets, and investigated the shape of the Earth. As a leading proponent of Isaac Newton's theory of gravitation, he wrote prolifically on gravity, astronomy, optics and trigonometry.

Bose, Sir Jagadis Chandra 1858–1937
Indian physicist and botanist
He was born in Mymensingh, Bengal (now in east Pakistan), attended St Xavier's, a Jesuit College in Calcutta, and went to London to study medicine, but transferred to Cambridge when he was awarded a scholarship and graduated in natural science in 1884. He returned to Calcutta where he was appointed Professor of Physics at Presidency College. Bose became known for his study of electric waves, their polarization and reflection, and for his experiments demonstrating the sensitivity and growth of plants. In some of his ideas he foreshadowed Norbert Wiener's cybernetics. He founded the Bose Research Institute in Calcutta for physical and biological sciences in 1917, was knighted in the same year and became the first Indian physicist to be elected FRS (1920).
📖 Ashis Nandy, *Alternative Sciences: Creativity and Authenticity in Two Indian Scientists* (2nd edn, 1995)

Bose, Satyendra Nath 1894–1974
Indian physicist
Born in Calcutta and educated at Presidency College there, he became professor at Dacca University before being appointed to another chair at Calcutta University in 1952. Later he was appointed National Professor by the Indian government (1959) and president of the National Institute of Sciences of India (1949–50). In 1924 he succeeded in deriving the Planck black-body radiation law, without reference to classical electrodynamics. Albert Einstein generalized his method to develop a system of statistical quantum mechanics, now called Bose–Einstein statistics, for integral spin particles which Paul Dirac named 'bosons'. Bose also contributed to the studies of X-ray diffraction and the interaction of electromagnetic waves with the ionosphere.

Bose, Subhas Chandra 1897–1945
Indian nationalist leader
A successful candidate for the Indian Civil Service in 1920, he did not take up his appointment, returning instead to Calcutta to work in the Non-Co-operation Movement and the Swaraj Party. He also managed the Calcutta newspaper *Forward*, and became the Chief Executive Officer of the Calcutta Corporation when Congress won its control in 1924. He spent the years 1925–27 under detention in Mandalay. In 1928 Bose formed an Independence League with Jawaharlal Nehru in opposition to Congress's objective of dominion status. Throughout the 1930s Bose took part in the civil disobedience movement, but became increasingly dissatisfied with the non-violent methods of Mahatma Gandhi and increasingly radical in his beliefs. Bose felt that a disciplined mass revolutionary movement was the fastest and best path toward Indian statehood. He was twice in succession President of the Indian National Congress (1938). Having resigned from the organization (1939), he formed Forward Bloc, a militant nationalist party. With the outbreak of World War II, he supported the Axis Powers. Escaping from detention, he fled to Nazi Germany, then (1943) sailed to Singapore to take command of the Indian National Army (INA), a force formed of prisoners of war of the Japanese army. This force fought against the British in Burma and participated in the disastrous Japanese attempt to invade India from Burma. In 1943 he announced the formation of the Provisional Government of Free India. He was reported killed in an aircrash in Formosa (Taiwan). For many years, however, his most devoted followers still refused to believe that he was dead, and many still cherish his ideas, attitudes and beliefs.

Bosio, François Joseph, Baron 1769–1845
French sculptor
He was born in Monaco. For Napoleon I he carved the bas-reliefs for the Column of the Place Vendôme in Paris, and he also sculpted the Quadriga of the Arc de Triomphe du Carrousel and other well-known Paris statues. He was director of the Académie des Beaux-Arts in Paris until his death.

Bosman, (Jean-)Marc c.1964–
Belgian footballer
He is responsible for a court case, the outcome of which in December 1995 enabled footballers to move freely within the EC. When he tried to leave FC Liège because they had offered him a new contract with a 60 per cent cut in pay, he tried to move to the French club Dunkerque. Liège bargained for £250,000 and Dunkerque refused. Bosman was suspended; he took the Belgian football authorities to the European Court of Justice (because if Belgian clubs failed to agree on a footballer's transfer fee, the selling club could retain the footballer against his will and cut his wages). However, the price Bosman has paid is high: he had to live in a lock-up garage during the legal proceedings; both his marriage and playing career came to an end; he became an alcoholic; and he was not allowed any unemployment benefit by Belgium. He subsequently went on to run a clothes shop.

Bossuet, Jacques Bénigne 1627–1704
French churchman and pulpit orator
Born in Dijon, he was educated in the Jesuits' School there and at the Collège de Navarre in Paris. He received a canonry at Metz in 1652, in 1661 preached before Louis XIV, and in 1669 delivered the funeral oration for Henrietta Maria. His reputation as an orator spread over France, and he became a very influential figure at court. As Bishop of Meaux (1681) he took a leading part in settling the Gallican controversy, between Louis XIV and the pope (1682). His greatest works are the *Histoire Universelle*, regarded by many as the first attempt at a philosophy of history, the *Oraisons funèbres* (1669, 'Funeral Orations') and the *Histoire des variations des Églises protestantes* (1688, 'History of the Variations in Protestant Churches'). His *Politique tirée de l'écriture sainte* (1709, 'Statecraft Drawn from the Holy Scriptures') upholds the divine right of kings.

Boswell, James 1740–95
Scottish writer and biographer of Dr Johnson

James Boswell was born in Edinburgh, the eldest son of a judge called Lord Auchinleck. He was educated privately and at the University of Edinburgh. He studied civil law at Glasgow, but his true goal was literary fame and the friendship of the famous. At the age of 18 he began to keep an astonishingly frank and self-probing journal. In the spring of 1760 he ran away to London, where he hobnobbed with the young Duke of York and with **Richard Brinsley Sheridan**'s father, made plans to join the army, and skilfully resisted all attempts to lure him into matrimony.

He first met Dr **Samuel Johnson** on his second visit to London, on 16 May 1763, at Tom Davies's bookshop in Russell Street. By the following year they were on such cordial terms that Johnson accompanied him as far as Harwich. Boswell was on his way to Utrecht to continue his legal studies, but stayed only for the winter and then toured Germany, France, Switzerland, and Italy. By an astounding process of literary gatecrashing he introduced himself to **Voltaire** and **Jean Jacques Rousseau**. From Rousseau he procured an introduction to the hero of Corsica **Pasquale de Paoli**, whom he 'Boswellized' in *Account of Corsica* (1768), which had an immediate success and was translated into several languages.

Boswell had many love affairs. There was the serious and high-minded affair with 'Zélide' of Utrecht, and liaisons with the Irish Mary Anne Montgomery, and with numerous others in London, Rome and elsewhere, including a disreputable episode with Rousseau's mistress, Thérèse Le Vasseur. Finally, in 1769, he married a cousin, Margaret Montgomerie, a prudent, amiable woman who put up with his shortcomings.

In 1773 Boswell was elected to Johnson's famous literary club, and took the great doctor on a memorable journey to the Hebrides. He was called to the English Bar in 1786, but he hardly practised. Boswell's wife died in 1789, leaving him six children, and thereafter his drinking habits got the better of him.

▢ The discoveries of Boswell's manuscripts, at Malahide Castle in Ireland in 1927 and at Fettercairn House in Scotland in 1930, which have been assembled by Yale University, are proof of his literary industry and integrity. A major literary enterprise (1777–83) was a series of 70 monthly contributions to the *London Magazine* under the pseudonym 'The Hypochondriak'. After Johnson's death the *The Journal of the Tour of the Hebrides* (1785) appeared. Its great success made Boswell plan his masterpiece, the *Life of Samuel Johnson* (1791), of which *The Journal* served as a first instalment.

▢ I Finlayson, *The Moth and the Candle: a life of James Boswell* (1985).

'A man, indeed, is not genteel when he gets drunk; but most vices may be committed very genteelly; a man may debauch his friend's wife genteelly: he may cheat at cards genteelly.' From *The Life of Samuel Johnson* (vol 2, entry for 6 April 1775).

Boston, Ralph 1939–
US athlete

Born in Laurel, Mississippi, he was a leading high-jumper of the 1960s. He established an unusual treble by winning the gold medal at the 1960 Rome Olympics, a silver at Tokyo in 1964 and a bronze at Mexico City in 1968. He spent much time coaching **Bob Beamon** before the latter's record-breaking long-jump in Mexico City.

Boston Strangler See **Desalvo, Albert**

Boswell, Alexander Boswell, 1st Baronet
1775–1822
Scottish songwriter and printer

The son of **James Boswell**, he was educated at Westminster and Oxford. He set up a private press at Auchinleck, Ayrshire, where he printed many books of early English and Scottish literature, and a volume of poems in the Ayrshire dialect (1803). He contributed 12 songs to **George Thomson**'s *Select Collection* (1817), of which 'Good night, and joy be wi' ye a', 'Jenny's Bawbee', and 'Jenny dang the Weaver' were very popular. He was created a baronet in 1821, and died of a wound received in a duel with James Stuart of Dunearn, who had challenged him as the author of anonymous political lampoons.

Boswell, James See panel above

Bosworth, Joseph 1789–1876
English philologist

Born in Derbyshire, he was Professor of Anglo-Saxon at Oxford from 1858. He compiled *An Anglo Saxon Dictionary* (1838), and in 1867 gave £10,000 for a chair of Anglo-Saxon at Cambridge.

Both, Andries c.1612–1641
Dutch painter

Born in Utrecht, he was traditionally thought to have collaborated with his brother **Jan Both** by painting the figures in his landscapes, but he is now recognized as the author of paintings and drawings of scenes more akin to the work of **Adriaen Brouwer**. With his brother he travelled to Italy where, returning home from a party in Venice, he fell into a canal and was drowned.

Both, Jan c.1618–1652
Dutch painter

Born in Utrecht, he lived in Italy from 1638 to 1641 and there perfected his style of painting views of the Roman countryside bathed in a golden light and populated by picturesque peasants. He became a leading exponent of 'Italianate' landscape, and his style shows the influence of **Claude** Lorrain. Back in Utrecht Both became a prominent member of the painters' guild, and his idyllic style was adapted by other Dutch painters to their views of Dutch landscape. He was the brother of **Andries Both**.

Botha, Louis 1862–1919
South African statesman and soldier

He was born in Greytown, Natal. A member of the Transvaal Volksraad, he succeeded **Piet Joubert** (1900) as Commander-in-Chief of the Boer forces during the war, and in 1907 became Prime Minister of the Transvaal colony under the new constitution. In 1907 and 1911 he attended imperial conferences in London; in 1910 he became the first premier of the Union of South Africa. He suppressed **Christian De Wet**'s rebellion in 1914, and conquered German Southwest Africa in 1914–15. ▢ Earl Buxton, *General Botha* (1924)

Botha, P(ieter) W(illem) 1916–
South African statesman

The son of an internee in the Anglo-Boer War, he was steeped in politics. An advocate of apartheid before the National Party gained power, he entered parliament in 1948 and became Deputy Minister of the Interior (1958–61), Minister of Community Development, Public Works and Coloured Affairs (1961–66), Minister of Defence (1966–78) and Prime Minister (1978–89). Leader of the

Cape section of the National Party, in 1966 he was chosen as leader of the Party on **John Vorster**'s resignation on the second ballot only because the Transvaal Nationalists were divided. He thus became Prime Minister. Having built up the defence forces and supported the invasion of Angola in 1975, he now sought constitutional changes, but his ideas, although too progressive for some of his Party (some members defected in 1982 to form the Conservative Party), were too cautious to appeal to the Black opposition. He suffered a stroke in 1989 and resigned later that year.

Botha, Pik (Roelof Frederik) 1932–
South African politician

After a career in the diplomatic service (1953–70), he entered politics and was elected to parliament. He forsook national politics in 1974 to become South Africa's permanent representative at the United Nations and then ambassador to the USA. He returned to domestic politics in 1977 and became Foreign Minister in the government of State President **P W Botha** and that of **F W De Klerk**. He brought his influence as a sounding board of international opinion strongly to bear in supporting the notable reforms that were introduced at the end of the 1980s. In 1992 he became leader of the Transvaal National Party and since 1994 has been Minister of Energy.

Botham, Ian Terence 1955–
English cricketer

Born in Heswall, Merseyside, he is regarded as an extremely talented all-rounder. He played for England in 102 Test matches, took 383 wickets, and scored 5,200 runs. He held the record number of Test wickets (373 wickets at an average of 27.86 runs until overtaken by **Richard Hadlee**), and has four times taken 10 wickets in a match. His performance in 1981 won the Test series against Australia almost single-handed. His spells as captain of Somerset and England were, however, notably unsuccessful. He played for Worcestershire (1987–91) and Durham (1992–93), before his retirement in 1993. Off-the-field brushes with authority alternated with successful charity fund-raising campaigns such as his walk from John o' Groats to Land's End and his re-enactment of **Hannibal**'s crossing of the Alps. In 1996 he and team-mate Allan Lamb lost a libel suit brought against **Imran Khan** who had accused them of ball-tampering. *Botham: my autobiography* was published in 1994.

Bothe, Walther Wilhelm Georg 1891–1957
German physicist and Nobel Prize winner

Born in Oranienburg, Brandenburg, he was educated under **Max Planck** at the University of Berlin, where he received his PhD in 1914. From 1934 he was head of the Max Planck Institute for Medical Research at Heidelberg. He developed an electric circuit to replace the laborious process of counting scintillations by eye used by **Hans Geiger** and **Ernest Marsden**. He also developed the co-incidence technique which allowed two particles to be associated with each other, and used this to study cosmic rays and nuclear physics, showing that the recoil electron and scattered photon appear simultaneously in **Compton** scattering. His work on the development of the coincidence technique in counting processes brought him the Nobel Prize for physics in 1954, shared with **Max Born**.

Bothwell, James Hepburn, 4th Earl of
c.1535–78
Scottish nobleman

One of the greatest nobles in 16th-century Scotland, he succeeded his father as earl and hereditary Lord High Admiral (1556). A professed Protestant, he nevertheless was a staunch supporter of **Mary of Guise**, regent for her daughter **Mary, Queen of Scots** (whom he later married), and was appointed warden of the Border Marches (1558).

In France in 1560, he met the young Mary, shortly before the death of her first husband, **Francis II** of France, and on her return to Scotland (1561) she appointed him a Privy Councillor. In the following year he was accused of plotting to kidnap her, and imprisoned, but she recalled him (1565), shortly after her marriage to Lord **Darnley**. In February 1566 Bothwell married, in a Protestant ceremony, the Catholic sister of the Earl of Huntly. Shortly afterwards (March 1566), Mary's secretary, **David Rizzio**, was murdered by Darnley, and Bothwell became her protector and chief adviser. The year 1567 was to be a year of high drama. Darnley himself was murdered in an explosion in Edinburgh (9 February), the chief suspect being Bothwell, who underwent a rigged trial and was acquitted (12 April). He then made a show of abducting Mary (23 April), who was pregnant (probably by him) and carried her off to Dunbar. After his divorce was finalized, he was made Duke of Orkney, and married Mary as her third husband at the Palace of Holyroodhouse, Edinburgh, with Protestant rites (15 May), but the marriage did not last long. Bothwell was self-confident, arrogant and ruthless, and his effective usurpation of the government of Scotland was never accepted by the Scottish lords. Mary was forced to surrender to an army of rebellious Scottish noblemen at Carberry Hill (20 June), and he fled to Norway, where he was arrested on a trumped-up charge and imprisoned. On 24 July, Mary miscarried (twins), and on the same day was forced to abdicate in favour of her infant son, **James VI**. The marriage was annulled in 1570. By then, Bothwell was imprisoned, first at Malmö in Sweden and subsequently at Dragsholm (1573) in Zeeland, Denmark, where he died, apparently insane. 🕮 Humphrey Drummond, *The Queen's Man: James Hepburn, Earl of Bothwell and Duke of Orkney, 1536–1578* (1975)

Botolph or Botulph, St d.c.680
Saxon abbot

Born in East Anglia, he founded a monastery in 654 in Icanhoe (Ox Island); it is usually identified as Boston ('Botolph's Stone') in Lincolnshire or Iken in Suffolk.

Bottai, Giuseppe 1895–1959
Italian politician

One of the founders of the Fascist Party, Bottai took an active part in the March on Rome. He was one of the Fascist Grand Council members who demanded **Mussolini**'s resignation in July 1943. Sentenced to death by the Republic of Salò and to life imprisonment by the Italian authorities after World War II, he escaped and joined the French Foreign Legion. He returned to Italy on being amnestied.

Bottesini, Giovanni 1823–89
Italian musician

Born in Crema, Lombardy, he was a highly skilled double bass player. He was also successful as a conductor and composer, and his works include symphonies, overtures and several operas, such as *Cristoforo Colombo* (1847) and *Ali Babà* (1871).

Böttger, Johann Friedrich 1682–1719
German ceramicist

He established and perfected the manufacture of porcelain at Dresden and, later, at Meissen.

Botticelli, Sandro, *originally* Alessandro Filipepi
1445–1510
Florentine painter

Born in Florence, he learned his distinctive linear style from **Fra Filippo Lippi**, with whom he studied, but added to it something very personal and graceful. By 1480 he had his own workshop and was responsible for frescoes which form part of the 1482 scheme of decoration of the Sistine Chapel. He produced mostly religious works but is best known for his treatment of mythological subjects, *The Birth of Venus* (c.1482–84) and the *Primavera* (c.1478), both of which are in the Uffizi, Florence. During the last decade of the 15th century, under the influence of Girolamo Savonarola, his style became more severe and emotional, eg his *Mystic Nativity* (1500, National Gallery, London). His work includes the illustrations for Dante's *Divina Commedia*, which he executed in pen and ink and silverpoint. By the time of his death, his linear style was out of fashion, but during the Victorian period it became a source of inspiration for the Pre-Raphaelite movement and Art Nouveau. 📖 C J Argan, *Botticelli* (1957)

Bottomley, Gordon 1874–1948
English poet and playwright

Born in Keighley, Yorkshire, he began his working life as a bank clerk before turning to poetry. His interest in Celtic folklore emerged in much of his work, including his first collection of verse, *The Mickle Drede* (1896). He is best remembered for his *Poems of Thirty Years* (1925) and his collections of plays, including *King Lear's Wife and Other Plays* (1920), which, although they mostly constituted an uneasy blend of poetry and rhetoric, won critical approval. His poetry anticipated Imagism. 📖 *Poet and Painter: the correspondence of Gordon Bottomley and Paul Nash* (1955)

Bottomley, Horatio William 1860–1933
English journalist, financier and politician

Born in Bethnal Green, London and raised in an orphanage, he became, successively, an errand boy, a solicitor's clerk and a shorthand writer in the Supreme Court. In 1884 he started a local paper, *The Hackney Hansard*. He was a brilliant journalist and a persuasive speaker, with a consuming desire for a life of luxury. By 1900 he had promoted nearly 50 companies with a total capital of £20 million. In 1891 and 1909 he was charged with fraud and acquitted, and between 1901 and 1905 had 67 bankruptcy petitions and writs filed against him. Meanwhile he had founded the weekly *John Bull* (1906) and become MP for South Hackney (1906–12). In 1911 he presented a petition in bankruptcy and applied for the Chiltern Hundreds. During World War I he received subscriptions worth nearly £900,000 for various enterprises. In 1918 he was discharged from his bankruptcy and became an MP again (1918–22), but in 1922 was found guilty of fraudulent conversion and sent to prison. He died in poverty.

Bottomley, Virginia Hilda Brunette Maxwell 1948–
English Conservative politician

Born in Scotland, she was educated at Essex University and the London School of Economics. She worked as a researcher for a child poverty action group, and as a lecturer in a college of further education and psychiatric social worker before unsuccessfully contesting her first seat, the Isle of Wight, in 1983. She became MP for Surrey South-West in 1984. Appointed Minister at the Department of the Environment (1988–89), she tackled such issues as the dumping of toxic waste, lead-free petrol and litter. She became Secretary of State for Health in 1992 and was involved in the controversial closure of several hospitals, part of the lengthy reform of the health service. In 1995–97 she was Secretary of State for National Heritage, with responsibilities including the newly launched National Lottery.

Botulph, St See Botolph, St

Botvinnik, Mikhail Moiseyevich 1911–95
Soviet chess player

Born in Leningrad (now St Petersburg), he was an electrical engineer by training. He won the 1948 tournament organized by FIDE (Fédération Internationale des Échecs) to fill the world championship, vacant after the

death of Alexander Alekhine, and was world champion 1948–57, 1958–60 and 1961–63. He led Soviet domination of world chess for most of the remainder of the 20th century, contested only by the US player Bobby Fischer. After regaining his title twice, from Vasili Smyslov and Mikhail Tal, he lost in 1963 to Tigran Petrosian and devoted most of his remaining career to training Soviet players and to the development of chess computers.

Botzaris, Marcos See Bozzaris, Marcos

Boubat, Édouard 1923–
French photographer

Born in Paris, he trained at the École Estienne there and worked as a photogravure printer before taking his first photograph, *Little Girl in the Dead Leaves*, in 1946. He worked as a staff photographer for *Réalités* magazine from 1951 to 1965, when he went freelance. He developed a unique, recognizable style that followed neither the documentary style of the photojournalists nor the storytelling style of the humanists, seeming to capture a specific moment within a situation that would speak of another time and place. His publications include *Préférées* (1980). 📖 Bernard George, *Édouard Boubat* (1973)

Bouch, Sir Thomas 1822–80
English civil engineer

Born in Thursby, Cumbria, he was the designer of the first Tay Railway Bridge, opened in 1877. The centre spans were blown down while a train was crossing in a severe gale two years later, with the loss of over 70 lives. The inquiry blamed Bouch's design and supervision of construction, and he died less than a year later.

Boucher, François 1703–70
French painter

Born in Paris, he was the purest Rococo painter at the court of Louis XV. As a young man he engraved the work of Antoine Watteau. From 1727 to 1731 he was in Italy, and he was received into the Academy in 1734. He worked on a range of material from stage design to tapestry, and from 1755 was director of the famous Gobelins factory. A refined portrait painter also, he produced several portraits of the king's most famous mistress, Madame de Pompadour, and it was she who bought his greatest pictures, *The Rising* and *The Setting of the Sun*. In 1765 he became *premier peintre du Roi*, but by this time his style was under attack from Diderot, and when Sir Joshua Reynolds visited his studio he was scandalized to find Boucher working without a model. His work is usually considered, along with that of his pupil, Jean Fragonard, to be wholly representative of the frivolous spirit of his age. Some of it can be seen in the London Wallace Collection.

Boucher (de Crèvecœur) de Perthes, Jacques 1788–1868
French archaeologist

He was born in Rethel. From 1837 at Moulin-Quignon in the Somme Valley he discovered flint hand-axes in association with the bones of extinct animals, from which he drew conclusions about the great age of the human race. His views were at first greeted with incredulity but came to be upheld 20 years later. An autobiography, *Sur dix rois: Souvenirs de 1796 à 1860*, appeared in 1863–66.

Boucicault, Dion(ysius Lardner), *also called* Lee Morton 1820–90
Irish dramatist and actor

Born in Dublin, and educated at University College School, London, he had an early success on the London stage with *London Assurance* (1841), a comedy written under the pseudonym 'Lee Morton'. He adapted a number of French plays into English, then went to the USA in

1853, where his successful melodramas included *The Colleen Bawn* (1860) and *The Octoroon, or Life in Louisiana* (1859). 📖 R G Hogan, *Dion Boucicault* (1969)

Boucicault, Nina 1867–1950
English actress

Born in London, the daughter of the distinguished playwright **Dion Boucicault** and the Scottish actress Agnes Robertson, she made her acting debut in her father's company in the USA in 1885. It was the beginning of a long and successful career which ended with her retirement from the stage in 1936. Although she played many different roles and styles, she is chiefly remembered as the actress who first played Peter Pan in the London première of **J M Barrie**'s immensely popular play in 1904.

Boudicca, *incorrectly called* Boadicea d.61AD
British warrior-queen

She was queen of the native tribe of Iceni (Norfolk, Suffolk and part of Cambridgeshire). Her husband, Prasutagus, an ally of Rome, had made the Emperor **Nero** his co-heir, but when he died (AD60) the Romans annexed and pillaged all the Iceni territory. According to **Tacitus**, Boudicca was flogged and her daughters raped. The Iceni rebelled, led by Boudicca, and destroyed Camulodunum (Colchester), Londinium (London) and Verulamium (St Albans), killing up to 70,000 Romans. The Roman governor of Britain, Suetonius Paulinus, who had been absent in Mona (Angelsey), overwhelmed the Iceni in a bloody battle. Some 80,000 of the tribesmen were slaughtered, against only 400 Roman dead, and Boudicca herself is said to have taken poison.

Boudin, (Louis) Eugène 1824–98
French painter

Born in Honfleur, he was a precursor of Impressionism, and is noted for his seascapes, which include *Deauville* (Tate Gallery, London), *Harbour of Trouville* (National Gallery, London), and *Corvette Russe* (Luxembourg, Paris).

Boufflers, Stanislas, Marquis de, *known as* the Chevalier de Boufflers 1737–1815
French writer and soldier

He was born in Lunéville, near Nancy, the son of the witty Marquise de Boufflers, who played an important part at the court of **Stanislas Leszczynski**, the exiled King of Poland. He joined the Knights of Malta, rose to be maréchal de camp, became governor of Senegal (1785), entered the Académie Française (1788), and corresponded with and married Mme de Sabran. He was a poet and literary man much admired in French salons, especially for his picaresque romance, *Aline*.

Bougainville, Louis Antoine de 1729–1811
French navigator, mathematician and soldier

Born in Paris, he studied law and then mathematics, publishing an important treatise on integral calculus, and was elected FRS. In 1756 he served with distinction in Canada as Marquis de **Montcalm**'s aide-de-camp. Joining the French navy in 1763, he was responsible for colonizing the Falkland Islands for France, and for their transfer to Spain. In command of the ships *La Boudeuse* and *L'Étoile*, he accomplished the first French circumnavigation of the world (1766–69), which he described in his valuable *Voyage autour du monde* (1771, Eng trans *A Voyage Round the World*, 1772). The largest of the Solomon Islands is named after him, as is the plant *Bougainvillaea*. In the American Revolution he commanded several ships of the line, and was made a field marshal in 1780 and a vice-admiral in 1791. After the outbreak of the French Revolution he devoted himself solely to scientific pursuits. **Napoleon I** made him a senator, count of the Empire, and member of the Légion d'Honneur. 📖 Michael Ross, *Bougainville* (1978)

Boughton, Rutland 1878–1960
English composer

Born in Aylesbury, Buckinghamshire, he was strongly influenced by **Richard Wagner**'s principles of music drama and also by socialist ideas. Attempting to develop an English style, with a strong choral element, he used subjects based on British legend, and founded the Glastonbury Festival (1914–26). He wrote the successful opera *The Immortal Hour* (1913), a choral drama *Bethlehem* (1915), *The Queen of Cornwall* (1924), five music dramas (1908–45), and other stage, choral and instrumental works, including an Arthurian cycle which was never performed complete. His failure at Glastonbury was due not to musical reasons, but to financial difficulties, to his insufficient dramatic gifts, and to general disapproval of his private life and of his communist ideals. A strong individualist, he expressed his ideas in his writings, notably *The Reality of Music* (1934).

Bouguer, Pierre 1698–1758
French physicist

Born in Le Croisic, Brittany, he succeeded his father as hydrographer royal in 1713 at the age of 15. In 1735 he was sent on the famous **Lacondamine** expedition to Peru to measure the length of a degree of the meridian near the equator. There, from 1735 to 1742, he investigated the length of the seconds pendulum at great elevations, the deviation of a plumbline through the attraction of a mountain, the altitude limit of perpetual snow, the obliquity of the ecliptic, and other scientific topics. His views on the intensity of light laid the foundations of photometry, and one of his most important discoveries was the law of absorption, also known as **Lambert**'s law. In 1748 he invented a heliometer, to measure the light of the Sun and other luminous bodies.

Bouguereau, William Adolphe 1825–1905
French painter

Born in La Rochelle, he studied art while engaged in business at Bordeaux and in 1850 won the Prix de Rome. He returned from Italy in 1855 and became very successful in France, characteristically depicting mildly erotic historical and mythological scenes. His works include *The Body of St Cecilia borne to the Catacombs* (1854) and *Mater Afflctorum* (1876).

Bouillé, François Claude Amour, Marquis de 1739–1800
French general

Born at the castle of Cluzel in Auvergne, he entered the army at the age of 14, and served during the Seven Years War (1756–63). In 1768 he was appointed Governor of Guadeloupe, and afterwards Commander-in-Chief in the West Indies. In the American Revolution (1775–83) he took from the British Dominica, Tobago, St Eustache, Saba, St Martin, St Christopher and Nevis. **Louis XVI** nominated him a member of the Assembly of Notables in 1787–88; in 1790 he was made Commander-in-Chief of the army of the Meuse, Saar and Moselle. Forced to flee from France for his part in the attempted escape of Louis XVI, in 1791 he entered the service of **Gustav III** of Sweden. In 1793 he went to England, where he wrote his *Mémoires sur la Révolution* ('Report on the Revolution').

Bouillon, Godfrey of See Godfrey of Bouillon

Boulanger, Georges Ernest Jean Marie 1837–91
French general and politician

Born in Rennes, he served in Italy, China, and in the Franco-Prussian War (1870–71), and helped suppress the Paris Commune (1871). In 1886, as the protégé of **Clemenceau**, he was appointed Minister of War. He introduced many reforms in soldiers' pay and living conditions and became a popular national figure among the Parisians, often appearing among them on horseback. When he lost office in 1887, 'Boulanger fever' only increased. He was 'exiled' by the army to a command at Clermont-Ferrand, and although deprived of his command in 1888 was immediately elected Deputy for Dordogne and Nord, and demanded a revision of the constitution. In the same year he was wounded in a duel with the Président du Conseil Floquet. Boulangism became most influential in 1889, and was supported with large sums of money by leading royalists for their own ends. Fearing a coup d'état, the government prosecuted Boulanger, who lost courage and fled the country in 1889. He was condemned in his absence, and eventually shot himself on his mistress's grave in Brussels.

Boulanger, Lili 1893–1918
French composer

Born in Paris, and encouraged and supervised by her elder sister Nadia Boulanger, she studied at the Paris Conservatoire. In 1913, she was the first woman to win the Prix de Rome, with her cantata *Faust et Hélène*. She returned from Rome to look after the families of musicians fighting in World War I but died, leaving unfinished an opera based on Maurice Maeterlinck's *La princesse Maleine* (1918). Among the many pieces she composed are *Pour les funérailles d'un soldat* (1912, 'For the Funeral of a Soldier'), *Du fond de l'abîme* (1914–17, 'From the Bottom of the Abyss') and *Vieille prière bouddhique* (1917, 'Old Buddhistic Prayer').

Boulanger, Nadia 1887–1979
French musician

Born in Paris, she studied at the Conservatoire there (1879–1904), where she won several prizes. She went on to write many vocal and instrumental works, winning second prize at the Prix de Rome in 1908 for her cantata, *La Sirène* ('The Siren'). After 1918 she devoted herself to teaching, first at home, and later at the Conservatoire and at the École Normale de Musique. She was also a noted organist and conductor.

Boule, Pierre Marcellin 1861–1942
French palaeontologist

Born in Montsalvy (Cantal), he became Professor at the Musée National d'Histoire Naturelle, and worked on the geology of the mountains of central France, and on human fossils. He made the first complete reconstruction of a Neanderthal skeleton, and published *Les Hommes fossiles* (1921, Eng trans *Fossil Men* 1957).

Boulez, Pierre 1925–
French conductor and composer

Born in Montbrison, he studied at the Paris Conservatoire (1943–45) under Olivier Messiaen, and in 1948 became musical director of Jean-Louis Barrault's Théâtre Marigny, where he established his reputation as an interpreter of contemporary music. His early work, notably the sonatine for flute and piano (1946), and two piano sonatas (1946, 1948), rebelled against what he saw as the conservatism of such composers as Igor Stravinsky and Arnold Schoenberg. In later compositions he has developed the very individual view of music already apparent in the sonatine, namely that whereas tonal music of the past can be seen as a straightforward progression from a point of departure, contemporary music describes a fluid and infinite universe out of which it is the composer's task to make a coherent work of art. Such works as *Le Marteau sans maître* (1955, 'The Hammer without a Master') established his reputation worldwide. He was conductor of the BBC Symphony Orchestra (1971–75) and of the New York Philharmonic (1971–77), then became director of the Institut de Recherche et de Co-ordination Acoustique/Musique at the Pompidou Centre in Paris (1977–91). In the early 1990s he became a regular guest

conductor with the Cleveland (Ohio) and Chicago Symphony orchestras and in 1992 participated in the 150th anniversary concert of the New York Philharmonic.

Boulle, Charles André See Buhl, Charles André

Boullée, Étienne-Louis 1728–99
French architect

Born in Paris, he was elected to the Académie in 1762, and became architect to the King of Prussia. He is of interest not so much for his neoclassical work before the French Revolution (such as the Hôtel de Brunoy, Paris, 1772), but for his later, more original and visionary designs for ambitious projects of an austerely formal and geometric nature, such as the design (1784) for a colossal spherical monument to Isaac Newton. He remained a figure of influence during the French Revolution and, through his pupils, was an influence on the architecture of the Napoleonic period.

Boult, Sir Adrian Cedric 1889–1983
English conductor

Born in Chester, he studied at Oxford and Leipzig. He conducted the City of Birmingham Orchestra from 1924 to 1930, when he was appointed musical director of the BBC and conductor of the newly formed BBC Symphony Orchestra. Extensive tours in Europe and the USA won him a high reputation as a champion of English music, and this had a great influence upon the musical policy of the BBC. After his retirement from broadcasting in 1950, he was conductor-in-chief of the London Philharmonic Orchestra until 1957 and its president from 1965. He continued to conduct regularly until 1981. In 1973 he published his autobiography, *My Own Trumpet*. 📖 Michael Kennedy, *Adrian Boult* (1987)

Boulting Brothers
English film directors and producers

John Edward (1913–85) and Roy (1913–) Boulting were twins, born in Bray, Berkshire. Together they produced and directed a series of films for Charter Films, which they had founded in 1937, and later for British Lion. Among the most notable are *Lucky Jim* (1957, based on the novel by Kingsley Amis) and several comedies of postwar English life, including *I'm All Right, Jack* (1959), *Heavens Above* (1963) and *The Family Way* (1966). Roy Boulting has been married six times, once (1971–76) to the actress Hayley Mills (1946–).

Boulton, Matthew 1728–1809
English engineer

He was born in Birmingham, where his father was a silver-stamper. He extended the business by the purchase of a piece of barren heath at Soho, near Birmingham, and his works opened there in 1762. He entered into partnership with James Watt, and in 1774 they established a manufactory of steam engines. They also improved coining machinery, and it was only in 1882 that a Boulton press at the Mint was finally discarded. 📖 Eric Delieb, *The Great Silver Manufactory: Matthew Boulton and the Birmingham Silversmiths, 1760–1790* (1971)

Boumédienne, Houari, *originally* Mohammed Bou Kharrouba 1927–78
Algerian soldier and statesman

Born in Guelma in eastern Algeria, he was educated in Cairo and became a teacher. In 1954 he joined the FLN (Algerian National Liberation Front) to conduct guerrilla operations against the French. When Algeria gained independence in 1962, he became Minister of National Defence. In 1965 he led a military coup against President Ben Bella and established an Islamic socialist government, presiding over the Council of Revolution as effective head of state until he formally accepted election as president in 1976. He directed a four-year plan which increased industrial output and revolutionized agricultural production. Shortly before his death, he tried to establish a North African socialist federation.

Bourassa, (Joseph-Napoléon) Henri
1868–1952
French–Canadian politician and journalist
Born in Montreal, a grandson of **Louis Joseph Papineau**, he became a leader of the Nationalist Party and the Canadian nationalist movement, serving in the House of Commons (1896–1907, 1925–35) and the Quebec legislature (1908–12). He was an advocate of Canadian autonomy within the British Empire and biculturalism within Canada. In 1910 he founded the French–Canadian nationalist newspaper *Le Devoir* in Montreal, and edited it until 1932.

Bourassa, Robert 1933–96
French–Canadian politician
He was born in Montreal, studied law, and was admitted to the Quebec bar in 1957. He was leader of the Quebec Liberal Party when it won an emphatic election victory in 1970, secured by means of its refusal to give prominence to the constitutional and language controversies and its promise to help the unemployment crisis by generating 100,000 jobs. During the 'October crisis' he was accused of being too ready to hand over power to Ottawa by those who suspected that he hoped to undermine his nationalist and left-wing opponents. He responded by reinforcing his demands for a special status for Quebec within the Confederation. He resigned as party leader when the Liberals lost the 1976 provincial elections to the Péquistes (Parti Québecois), but was re-elected in 1983 and led the party to victory in 1985, serving as Prime Minister until 1993.

Bourbaki, Charles Denis Sauter 1816–97
French soldier
Born in Pau, he fought in the Crimea and Italy, and during the Franco-Prussian War of 1870–71 he commanded the Imperial Guard at Metz. Under **Léon Gambetta** he organized the Army of the North and commanded the Army of the Loire. His attempt to break the Prussian line at Belfort in 1871 ended in disaster, and in the retreat to Switzerland that followed he attempted suicide.

Bourbon
French royal house
For generations it occupied the thrones of France and Naples, and until 1931 that of Spain. Adhémar, sire of Bourbon in the 10th century, traced his descent from **Charles Martel**. In 1272 the Bourbon heiress married the sixth son of **Louis IX** of France. The family divided, the elder branch ended with the Constable de Bourbon (**Charles Bourbon**) in 1527. His son, Antoine (1518–62), obtained by marriage the throne of Navarre, and Antoine's son was Henri of Navarre (**Henri IV**), who became heir to the Crown of France in 1589 (see **Louis XIII-XVIII**, **Charles X** and the Comte de Chambord). The Orléans branch descends from a younger son of **Louis XIII** (Philippe, 1640–1701). From **Louis XIV** descend also the branches that formerly held the thrones of Spain, Parma and Naples. A younger brother of Antoine de Bourbon (Henri IV's father) founded the houses of Condé and Conti. The sons and grandsons of **Louis Philippe** held titles derived from Paris, Chartres, Nemours, Eu, Joinville, Aumale and Montpensier.

Bourbon, Charles, *known as* Conestable or Constable de Bourbon 1490–1527
French soldier
The son of the Count of Montpensier and the only daughter of the Duke of Bourbon, he thus united the vast estates of both these branches of the Bourbon family. For his bravery at the Battle of Marignano in 1515 he was made Conestable of France by **Francis I**. Having lost royal favour, he renounced the service of France, and concluded a private alliance with the Emperor **Charles V** (1523), and with **Henry VIII** of England. In 1524 he was chief commander at the great victory of Pavia, in which Francis I was taken prisoner. But Charles V distrusted him, though he made him Duke of Milan and Spanish commander in Northern Italy. Along with **Georg von Frundsberg**, he led the mixed army of Spanish and German mercenaries that stormed and plundered Rome in 1527, but was struck down in the fierce struggle—by a bullet fired by **Benvenuto Cellini**, as the latter asserted. ⌨ Desmond Seward, *The Bourbon Kings of France* (1976)

Bourdelle, Émile Antoine 1861–1929
French sculptor, painter and teacher
Born in Montauban, he studied at the École des Beaux-Arts, Paris, and under **Auguste Rodin**. He found inspiration in Greek art, relating its style to his own time. He illustrated a number of books, and his teaching had considerable influence.

Bourdon, Eugène 1808–84
French inventor and industrialist
Born in Paris, he became an instrument-maker to trade, and in 1835 founded a machine shop in Paris to manufacture model steam engines for educational and demonstration purposes. Aware of the need for an accurate means of measuring the pressure of the steam in high-pressure steam engines and boilers, in 1849 he patented a simple but ingenious device which is still in widespread use today for measuring the pressure of steam and many other fluids. The 'Bourdon gauge' makes use of the fact that a curved length of metal tube, closed at one end, will tend to straighten out as the pressure of the fluid in it is increased. A system of levers and ratchets converts this movement into the rotation of a pointer on a dial.

Bourdonnais, Bertrand de la See La Bourdonnais, Bertrand François Mahé de

Bourgelat, Claude 1712–99
French veterinary surgeon
Born in Lyons, he founded there in 1761 the first veterinary school in Europe.

Bourgeois, Jeanne Marie See Mistinguett

Bourgeois, Léon Victor Auguste 1851–1925
French socialist statesman and Nobel Prize winner
Born in Paris, he studied law and served as Minister of Public Instruction (1890–92, 1898), Minister of Labour (1912–13, 1917) and as Prime Minister (1895–96). A delegate to The Hague Conference (1907), he was one of the founders of the League of Nations and in 1920 was awarded the Nobel Peace Prize. He advocated a form of socialism (called solidarism) which stressed the respon and obligations of individuals as members of society.

Bourgeois, Louise 1911–
US sculptor
Born in Paris, she studied at the École du Louvre, the Académie des Beaux-Arts and at private art schools before emigrating to the USA in 1938. She began painting, and had a one-woman show at the Bertha Schaefer Gallery in New York in 1945. In the late 1940s she turned to wood-carving, and in the 1960s to stone and metal, creating abstract sculptures which suggest figures, or parts of figures, such as *Labyrinthine Tower* (1963). Her forms became increasingly fantastical in the 1970s, and included weirdly coloured totem forests or cave-like environments, like *Destruction of the Father* (1974). Her work of the 1980s and 1990s, filled with potent sexual imagery, celebrated femininity without sentiment or polemicism, as in her *Spiders* (1995), a collection of large metal spiders

---

Bourke-White, Margaret, *originally* Margaret White 1906–71
US photojournalist who pioneered the photo-essay

Margaret Bourke-White was born in New York City, the daughter of a print designer, and studied photography at Columbia University. She started her career in 1927 as an industrial and architectural photographer, but was engaged by *Fortune* magazine in 1929 and became a staff photographer and associate editor on *Life* magazine when it started publication in 1936. Her 70 photographs for the study by **Erskine Caldwell** of rural poverty in the southern USA, *You Have Seen Their Faces* (1937), were highly individual, in contrast to the more dispassionate records of the US government FSA (Farm Security Administration) workers. She was married to Caldwell from 1939 to 1942.

She covered World War II for *Life* and was the first woman photographer to be attached to the US armed forces, producing outstanding reports of the Siege of

Moscow (1941) and the opening of the concentration camps (1944). After the war, she recorded the troubles in India, Pakistan and South Africa, and was an official UN war correspondent during the Korean War.

From 1952 she suffered from Parkinson's Disease, but she continued to produce many photo-journalistic essays until her retirement from *Life* in 1969. Her books include *Eyes on Russia* (1931), *Halfway to Freedom* (1946) and an autobiography, *Portrait of Myself* (1963).

📖 V Goldberg, *Margaret Bourke-White* (1986).

'The beauty of the past belongs to the past.' On modern photojournalism. Quoted in *Christian Science Monitor* (5 December 1986).

---

spiked with knitting needles. A one-woman show at the Museum of Modern Art in New York City in 1982 and a retrospective at La Musée d'Art Moderne, Paris, in 1995 gained her recognition as a major 20th-century artist.

Bourget, Paul 1852–1935
French poet, essayist and novelist

He was born in Amiens, and began by writing verse: *La Vie inquiète* (1875, 'The Anxious Life'), *Edel* (1878), and *Les Aveux* (1881, 'Confessions'). His *Essais* (1883) indicated his true strength however. The second series, *Nouveaux Essais de psychologie contemporaine* (1886, 'New Essays on Contemporary Psychology'), was a subtle inquiry into the causes of pessimism in France. His first novel, *L'Irréparable* (1884, 'Beyond Repair'), was followed by a steady stream of works which placed him in the front rank of modern French novelists. *L'Étape* (1902, 'The Halting-Place') marked the crystallization of his talent. His works after 1892 showed a marked reaction moving from realism and scepticism towards mysticism. 📖 G Bennoville, *Paul Bourget* (1936)

Bourguiba, Habib ibn Ali 1903–
Tunisian statesman

Born in Monastir, Tunisia, he studied law in Paris and became a radical Tunisian nationalist in 1934. Over the next 20 years he served three prison sentences imposed by the French authorities. In 1956, however, the government of **Pierre Mendès-France** in Paris recognized that, in contrast to other Arab leaders, Bourguiba was moderate in his demands and he was accepted as Tunisia's first Prime Minister, becoming President in 1957. By 1962 he had secured the withdrawal of the French from their Tunisian military bases and thereafter he was able to improve trading contacts with the former imperial power. In 1975 he was declared President for Life. His authority, however, was threatened by riots instigated by Islamic fundamentalists in 1983 and 1984, and subsequently he exercised little influence on policy. In 1987 he was deposed by his Prime Minister, General **Ben Ali**, on the grounds of senility.

Bourignon, Antoinette 1616–80
French religious

Born in Lille, she believed herself called to restore the pure spirit of the gospel, and fleeing from home entered a convent. She was in charge of a hospital in Lille, and in Amsterdam (1667) she gathered followers and published works. Driven out, she founded a hospital in East Friesland. Bourignonism so prevailed in Scotland about 1720 that till 1889 a solemn renunciation was demanded from every entrant into the ministry.

Bourke-White, Margaret See panel above

Bourmont, Louis de Ghaisnes, Comte de 1773–1846
French general

Born in the castle of Bourmont, in Anjou, he went into exile at the Revolution, but from 1794 to 1799 was engaged in the struggle in La Vendée. Subsequently he obtained the favour of **Napoleon I**, and for services in 1813–14 was made general. In 1814 he declared for the **Bourbons** but, on Napoleon's return from Elba went over to him, only to desert once more on the eve of Ligny. His evidence helped to bring about **Michel Ney**'s execution. He was appointed Minister of War in 1829, and in 1830 received command of the expedition that conquered Algiers. His rapid success won him the marshal's baton, but at the July Revolution of 1830 he was superseded and went to England to share the exile of **Charles X**.

Bourne, Francis Alphonsus 1861–1935
English prelate

Born in Clapham, London, he was ordained a priest in 1884, became Bishop of Southwark in 1897, and in 1903 he succeeded **Herbert Vaughan** as Archbishop of Westminster. He was created a cardinal in 1911. He travelled widely, and is best remembered for his zeal for education, and his organization of the International Eucharistic Congress in 1908. His chief works are *Ecclesiastical Training* (1926) and *Occasional Sermons* (1930).

Bourne, Hugh 1772–1852
English founder of the Primitive Methodists

He was born in Fordhays, Staffordshire, and his zeal as a Wesleyan preacher for large open-air meetings, carried on once from 6am till 8pm, received no approbation from the leaders of the denomination, and in 1808 he was cut off from the Wesleyan connection. But he quickly gathered round him many devoted followers, and in 1810 a committee of ten members was formed at Standley, near Bemersley. The title of Primitive Methodists was adopted in 1812; colloquially, they were sometimes also called Ranters. Bourne and his brother founded the first chapel of the body in Tunstall in 1811. For the greater part of his life he worked as a carpenter and builder, but found time to visit Scotland, Ireland and the USA. Amongst his writings is a *History of the Primitive Methodists* (1823).

Bournonville, August 1805–79
Danish dancer and choreographer

Born in Copenhagen, he was the son of a French dancer. After training with the Royal Danish Ballet, he moved to Paris (1926) to study under the great teacher, **Auguste Vestris**, at the Paris Opera. He spent the rest of his career (from 1828) with the Royal Danish Ballet, first as a dancer and, from 1830, as director, though he continued to dance in lead roles for another 20 years. He staged over 60 known works, a dozen of which survive today, the most popular being *La Sylphide* (1836) and *Napoli* (1842). His choreography is busy and makes much use of pointe work. Very influential and described as a great believer in bourgeois values, he moved away from the emotional heights of French Romanticism towards a style where equality of the sexes was more important. He was a close friend of **Hans Christian Andersen.**

Bourrienne, Louis Antoine Fauvelet de
1769–1834
French politician
Born in Sens, he studied at the military school of Brienne, where he met the young **Napoleon I.** In 1797 he became Napoleon's secretary and accompanied him to Egypt (1798), but he was dismissed in 1802 for being implicated in the dishonourable bankruptcy of the house of Coulon (army contractors) and appointed to a post in Hamburg until 1813. Recalled and fined for embezzlement, he joined the supporters of the **Bourbons**, after whose restoration he was elected a deputy and figured as an antiliberal. His *Mémoires* (1829–31, Eng trans 1893) are not always reliable.

Boussingault, Jean Baptiste Joseph Dieudonné 1802–87
French agricultural chemist
Born in Paris, he studied at the School of Mines at St Étienne and then served under **Simón Bolívar** in the South American War of Independence, remaining in South America until 1832. He then became Professor of Chemistry at Lyons and finally Professor of Agriculture at the Conservatoire des Arts et Métiers, Paris (1839–87). He was elected to the Academy of Sciences in 1839. He demonstrated that legumes increase nitrogen in soil by fixing atmospheric nitrogen, but that all other plants have to absorb nitrogen from the soil. He further showed that all green plants absorb carbon from the atmosphere in the form of carbon dioxide. His work laid the basis for modern advances in microbiology.

Boutros-Ghali, Boutros 1922–
Egyptian politician and diplomat
Born in Cairo, he received a doctorate in international law from the University of Paris. He travelled with President **Anwar Sādāt** to Jerusalem on the diplomatic mission that resulted in the Camp David Accords (1978), and was appointed Minister of State for Foreign Affairs (1977–91). In 1992 he became Secretary-General of the United Nations, the first Arab and first African to do so, but he failed to be re-elected in 1996.

Bouts, Dierick or Dirk or Thierry c.1415–1475
Dutch painter
Born in Haarlem, but usually placed with the Flemish school, he worked at Louvain and Brussels, coming under the influence of **Roger van der Weyden.** He produced austere religious paintings, with rich, gem-like colour. His *Resurrection* is in the Munich Pinakothek.

Boveri, Theodor Heinrich 1862–1915
German biologist and pioneer of cytology
Born in Bamberg, he studied history and philosophy at Munich University, but soon changed to science, and graduated in medicine in 1885. From 1893 he taught zoology and anatomy at the University of Würzburg. Continuing **Edouard Beneden's** work on cell chromosomes, Boveri studied cell-division in the roundworm *Ascaris*, demonstrating the individuality of chromosomes, and in his research on sea-urchin eggs showed that normal development requires an appropriate number of chromosomes for the species, with chromosome deficiency leading to abnormality. By 1910 it was widely accepted that chromosomes are the actual vehicles of heredity. Later, it was seen that they are composed of smaller genetic elements, genes, which, later still, were seen to be, themselves, composed of DNA. 📖 Fritz Baltzer, *Theodor Boveri: Life and Work of a Great Biologist 1862–1915* (1967)

Bovet, Daniel 1907–92
Italian pharmacologist and Nobel Prize winner
Born in Neuchâtel, Switzerland, he studied chemistry at Geneva and worked in the Department of Chemical Therapeutics at the Pasteur Institute, Paris (1929–47) before being invited, with his wife and collaborator Philomena Nitti, to establish the Laboratory of Chemotherapeutics at the Superior Institute of Health in Rome. He discovered the first antihistamine drugs in 1939. His second major study involved drugs blocking the action of adrenaline and noradrenaline, thereby preventing hypertension (high blood pressure), one of the most common medical disorders, and vasoconstriction. Visiting Brazil he became interested in the Indian neuromuscular poison curare, of which he later made synthetic analogues, which have been much used as muscle relaxants in anaesthesia since 1950. He was awarded the 1957 Nobel Prize for physiology or medicine.

Bowditch, Henry Pickering 1840–1911
US physiologist
Born in Boston, he went to Harvard in 1857, graduating in 1868, and spent three years in Europe studying experimental physiology and microscopy with such teachers as **Emil Ludwig.** Returning to the USA, he obtained a teaching post at Harvard in physiology. Bowditch went on to produce important experimental work on cardiac contraction, on the innervation of the heart, on the vascular system, and on the reflexes. He later emphasized the importance of nutrition and environment (rather than heredity) in child growth. He helped build up the Harvard physiology department as Dean of the Harvard Medical School (1883–93), instituting important reforms in medical education, and was a founder of the American Physiological Society (1887).

Bowdler, Thomas 1754–1825
English doctor and man of letters
Born in Ashley, Bath, he retired from medical practice and settled in the Isle of Wight to devote himself to literary pursuits. He is immortalized as the editor of the 'Family Shakespeare' (10 vols, 1818), in which 'those words and expressions are omitted which cannot with propriety be read aloud in a family'. 'Bowdlerizing' has become a synonym for prudish expurgation. 📖 Noel Perrin, *Dr Bowdler's Legacy* (1969)

Bowe, Riddick, *nicknamed* Big Daddy 1967–
US boxer
Born in Brooklyn, New York, he became a high earner, and is considered to be the world's best heavyweight after **Mike Tyson,** whom he never fought through management disagreements. He fought **Evander Holyfield** three times, and won twice. His only loss, in a career total of 38 fights, was to Holyfield in 1993, when the hard bout was interrupted by a paraglider crashing into Caesar's Palace ring. Since he was reputedly a hamburger junkie, Bowe's defeat was attributed by the press to a fast-food overdose. However he beat Herbie Hide to win the World Boxing Organization heavyweight title in 1995.

Bowen, Elizabeth Dorothea Cole 1899–1973
Irish novelist and short-story writer
She was born in County Cork, the daughter of a wealthy barrister and landowner, and was brought up in Dublin. Educated in England at Downe House School in Kent,

she married in 1923 and in the same year published her first collection of short stories, *Encounters*, followed by *Anne Lee's* (1926). Her first novel, *The Hotel* (1927), began a string of delicately-written explorations of personal relationships, of which *The Death of the Heart* (1938) and *The Heat of the Day* (1949), a war story, are the best known. She was also a perceptive literary critic, and published *English Novelists* (1942) and *Collected Impressions* (1950). 📖Hermione Lee, *Elizabeth Bowen: An Estimation* (1981)

Bowen, Norman Levi 1887–1956
US geologist
He was born in Kingston, Ontario, Canada, the son of English immigrants. He studied at Queen's University, Ontario, and became professor there (1919–21) and at Chicago (1937–47); he was also associated with the Geophysical Laboratory at Washington DC. He was a pioneer in the field of experimental petrology, particularly the study of silicates and igneous rocks. His work is summarized in his book, *The Evolution of Igneous Rocks* (1928).

Bower, Frederick Orpen 1855–1948
English botanist
Born in Ripon, Yorkshire, he went to Trinity College, Cambridge, learned laboratory methods from **Julius von Sachs** at Würzburg University and went on to Strasbourg in 1879. In 1882 he became lecturer in botany at South Kensington, and from 1885 to 1925 he was Regius Professor of Botany at the University of Glasgow. He devoted himself to research in plant morphology and built up a worldwide reputation, from 1890 concentrating on the evolutionary morphology of pteridophytes and publishing three major works, *The Origin of A Land Flora* (1908), *The Ferns* (3 vols, 1923–28) and *Primitive Land Plants* (1935). He played a major part in the introduction of the 'new botany' into British education.

Bower or Bowmaker, Walter 1385–1449
Scottish chronicler
Born in Haddington, he was abbot of Inchcolm in the Firth of Forth from 1417. He is believed to have been among the first Bachelors of Arts at St Andrews University, whose foundation he records in 1410. He was one of two commissioners appointed to collect ransom money for King **James I** on his return to Scotland in 1424, and he acted as diplomat at the negotiations at Perth in 1432 for peace with the English, when he vigorously defended the needs of the Franco-Scottish 'auld' alliance. From about 1440 he continued the Latin *Scotichronicon* of **John of Fordun** from 1153 until 1437, the first connected history of Scotland.

Bowes-Lyon, Lady Elizabeth See Elizabeth

Bowie, David, *real name* David Robert Jones 1947–
English rock singer
He was born in Brixton, London. His early career was undistinguished, and he came close to becoming a Buddhist monk before the success of 'Space Oddity' (1969), a song based on the **Stanley Kubrick** film *2001: A Space Odyssey*. His career blossomed throughout the 1970s as he adopted a range of extreme stage images to suit a variety of musical styles and concepts. His albums have included *Hunky Dory* (1971), *The Rise And Fall Of Ziggy Stardust And The Spiders From Mars* (1972), *Diamond Dogs* (1974) (originally a musical adaptation of **George Orwell's** *1984*, changed after pressure from the author's estate), *Low* (1977) and *Heroes* (1977). He has also acted on Broadway in *The Elephant Man* (1980) and in films, including *The Man Who Fell To Earth* (1976), *Merry Christmas Mr Lawrence* (1983) and *Labyrinth* (1986). *Black Tie White Noise* (1993) was his most successful record in some years.

He then signed a new major recording contract, the first fruit of which reunited him with a former collaborator, Brian Eno, on *Outside* (1995). 📖 J Hopkins, *Bowie* (1986)

Bowie, James 1790–1836
Mexican pioneer
Born in Kentucky, USA, he went to Texas in 1828 and settled in San Antonio. Although he became a naturalized Mexican citizen (c.1831), he joined the agitation for Texas independence and became a colonel in the Texan army (1835–36). He fell ill during the siege of the Alomo and was found dead in his cot when the Mexicans stormed the citadel. He is sometimes said to be the inventor of the curved dagger or sheath-knife named after him.

Bowlby, (Edward) John (Mostyn) 1907–90
English psychiatrist
The son of an eminent surgeon, he was educated at the Royal Naval College, Dartmouth, and Trinity College, Cambridge, then became psychologist at the London Child Guidance Clinic (1937–40). After World War II he moved to the Tavistock Clinic (1946–72), to become chairman of the department for children and parents (1946–68). His early research concerned crime and juvenile delinquency, but he is best known for his work on the effects of maternal deprivation upon the mental health and emotional development of children. His work led to theories that were based upon psychoanalytic ideas, but bolstered by analogies with the parent–infant interactions seen in certain animal species. He argued that it was essential for the mother to be present during a critical formative period in order for emotional bonds to be formed. He was a consultant in mental health for the World Health Organization and honorary consultant psychiatrist to the Tavistock Clinic from 1972 to 1990.

Bowles, Jane, *née* Auer 1918–73
US fiction writer and playwright
For many years she suffered from acute ill health and her literary output was consequently slim. An original writer, she has been linked with **Gertrude Stein** whose influence is apparent. *In the Summer House* (1953), a play, is her most accessible work. Her *Collected Works* appeared in 1967. She married **Paul Bowles** in 1938. 📖 I Finlayson, in *Tangier: the city of the dream* (1991)

Bowles, Paul Frederick 1910–
US novelist, composer, poet, travel writer and translator
He was born in New York City. After studying at the University of Virginia, he went to Europe in 1931 to study music with **Aaron Copland** in Paris, and became a composer and music critic. He did not devote himself to writing until after World War II. His first novel, *The Sheltering Sky*, set in Morocco, appeared in 1949 and was immediately influential, sparking off a US literary exodus to Tangier, of which he became a resident in 1952. He wrote three other novels, *Let It Come Down* (1952), *The Spider's House* (1955) and *Up Above the World* (1966), as well as several collections of short stories, including *Pages from Cold Point* (1968) and *Midnight Mass* (1981), and a collection of poems, *Scenes* (1968). He has also translated and taped original stories of indigenous lives, including *M'Hashish* (1964) by Mohammed Mrabet. He was married to the writer **Jane Bowles**. 📖 *Without Stopping* (1972)

Bowles, William Lisle 1762–1850
English clergyman and poet
Born in King's Sutton vicarage, Northamptonshire, and educated at Trinity College, Oxford, he became vicar of Bremhill in Yorkshire and prebendary of Salisbury in 1804, and later chaplain to the prince regent (1818). He was a forerunner of the Romantic movement in English poetry, his *Fourteen Sonnets, written chiefly on Picturesque Spots during a Journey* (1789, published anonymously), had **S T Coleridge**, **Wordsworth** and **Robert Southey** among their

enthusiastic admirers. His best poetical work is *The Missionary of the Andes*. In 1806 he published an edition of **Pope**, and an opinion which he expressed on Pope's poetical merits led to a memorable controversy (1809–25) in which **Thomas Campbell** and **Byron** were his antagonists. 📖 G Gilfillan, *A Critical Dissertation by the Rev. Geo Gilfillan* (1855)

Bowmaker, Walter See Bower, Walter

Bowman, Isaiah 1878–1950
US geographer
Born in Waterloo, Canada, he was educated at Harvard and Yale, and became assistant professor at Yale (1909–15) during which time he joined three important expeditions to the Andes. This was influential in his development of regional diagrams and the concept of topographic types. He became director of the American Geographical Society (1915–35), and his significant work on the boundaries during 1914 to 1918 led to his appointment as chief territorial specialist at the Versailles Peace Conference. He was president of Johns Hopkins University from 1935 to 1948. He published *The New World: Problems of Political Geography* (1921), *Forest Physiography* (1911), *South America* (1915) and *International Relations* (1930).

Bowman, Sir William 1816–92
English physician and ophthalmic surgeon
He was born in Nantwich, Cheshire. In 1840 he joined King's College Hospital in London, and there, with Richard B Todd (1809–60), he researched and published *Physiological Anatomy and Physiology of Man* (1845–56). Their most significant discoveries concerned the function of the kidney, part of which is now called Bowman's Capsule, in particular the fact that urine is a by-product. He also gained a high reputation by his *Lectures on Operations on the Eye* (1849), describing the ciliary muscle. His *Collected Papers* appeared in 1892.

Bowring, Sir John 1792–1872
British diplomat
Born in Exeter, on leaving school he entered a merchant's office, and acquired a knowledge of 200 languages. In 1821 he formed a close friendship with **Jeremy Bentham**, and in 1824 became the first editor of his radical *Westminster Review*. He visited Switzerland, Italy, Egypt, Syria, and the states of Germany, and prepared valuable government reports on their commerce. He sat in parliament from 1835 to 1849, actively promoting free trade. From 1849 he was British consul in Hong Kong, and in 1854 he was knighted and made Governor. In 1856, in retaliation for an insult to the British by a Chinese pirate ship, he ordered the bombardment of Canton, an event which almost caused the downfall of the **Palmerston** ministry. In 1855 he concluded a commercial treaty with Siam, and in 1858 made a tour through the Philippines. He published his autobiography in 1877.

Bowyer, William 1699–1777
English printer and classical scholar
He studied at St John's College, Cambridge, and in 1722 went into partnership with his father, William Bowyer. Known as the 'learned printer', in 1767 he was nominated printer to the Houses of Parliament. He published several philological tracts, translated **Julius Caesar**'s *Commentaries* (1750) and **Jean Jacques Rousseau**'s paradoxical *Discourse* (1751), and wrote two essays on the *Origin of Printing* (1774). His chief production was a Greek New Testament.

Box, (Violette) Muriel, *née* Baker 1905–91
English screenwriter
Born in Tolworth, Surrey, she began her career as a script girl, and made her writing debut with *Alibi Inn* (1935). She married Sydney Box (1907–83) in 1935, with whom she

established a very successful writing partnership until 1958. They shared an Oscar for *The Seventh Veil* (1945), and collaborated on many films for Sydney Box's production company, Verity Films, before being signed to major studios within the Rank Organization. Sidney's sister, the film producer Betty Box (1920–), also became part of the creative team before taking charge of Islington Studios in 1947, and oversaw many films, including *The 39 Steps* (1960) and *Deadlier Than The Male* (1966). An active women's rights campaigner during the 1960s, Muriel Box founded the feminist press Femina Books in 1966. Her marriage to Sydney Box ended in 1969, and following her remarriage in 1970 to the Lord Chancellor, **Gerald Gardiner**, she turned her attention to political causes.

Boyce, William 1711–79
English composer
Born in London, he was appointed composer (1736) and organist (1758) to the Chapel Royal, and in 1757 became Master of the King's Musick. A leading composer of church music, his works include the song 'Hearts of Oak' and the serenata *Solomon* (1743), and he compiled a valuable collection of *Cathedral Music* (1760).

Boycott, Charles Cunningham 1832–97
English soldier
Born in Burgh St Peter, Norfolk, as land agent for Lord Erne in County Mayo he was one of the first victims in 1880 of **Charles Stewart Parnell**'s system of social excommunication: on his refusal to lower rents, his tenants were advised to stop communicating with him. He thus gave, in the verb 'to boycott', a new word to most European languages.

Boycott, Geoffrey 1940–
English cricketer
Born in Fitzwilliam, Yorkshire, he is the most celebrated batsman in postwar English cricket. He gained his county cap for Yorkshire (1963) and was capped for England in 1964. He played 108 times for England between 1964 and 1982, and scored more than 150 centuries, but there was controversy over his value as a player. He was elected a member of the general committee in 1984. He scored his 100th first-class century in a Test match against Australia on his home ground, Headingley, in 1977. His publications include *Boycott, The Autobiography* (1987) and *Boycott on Cricket* (1990). 📖 Don Mosey, *Boycott* (1985)

Boyd, Anne 1946–
Australian composer and flautist
Born in Sydney, she studied composition there under **Peter Sculthorpe** and **Richard Meale**, and later under Wilfrid Mellers at the University of York, England. After some years teaching in England and Australia, she became founding head of the department of music at Hong Kong University (1981). Her interest in ethno-musicology, in Australian Aboriginal music and that of Japan and Java, is reflected in her compositions, many of which have been recorded, such as *As I Crossed the Bridge of Dreams* and her children's opera, *The Little Mermaid*.

Boyd, Arthur Merric 1862–1940
Australian painter
He was born in Opoho, New Zealand. He arrived in Australia in 1886 and in that year married Emma Minnie à Beckett, granddaughter of Sir William à Beckett, first chief justice of Victoria (1852–57). He is particularly known for his watercolours.

Boyd, Arthur Merric Bloomfield 1920–
Australian painter, sculptor and potter
Born in Murrumbeena, Victoria, the son of **Merric Boyd** and brother of **Guy Boyd**, he studied briefly at the National Gallery of Victoria Art School and, after 1936, with his grandfather **Arthur Merric Boyd** at Rosebud,

Victoria. After the war he exhibited with the Contemporary Arts Society in Melbourne, then returned to Murrumbeena and the pottery established by his father, where he worked with his brother-in-law John Perceval. He moved to London in 1959, where he exhibited at the Zwemmer Galleries the following year and was represented in the Whitechapel and Tate exhibitions of 1961 and 1962. These established his position as a painter of international significance. He took up a fellowship in creative arts at the Australian National University, Canberra, in 1972, and later presented a large collection of his drawings to the Australian National Gallery in Canberra. He designed a tapestry for the new Parliament House in Canberra which was installed in 1988. He is also noted as an etcher and as a theatre and ballet designer.

Boyd, Benjamin c.1796–1851
Australian colonist
Born in Merton Hall, Wigtownshire, Scotland, he was a Scottish trader and stockbroker before he arrived in Hobson's Bay in his yacht *Wanderer* in 1842 and moved to Port Jackson. He became one of the largest and most powerful squatters in south-eastern New South Wales, and spent a fortune trying to found 'Boyd Town' as a commercial port. When the enterprise failed, he sailed off to join the Gold Rush in California in 1849. He disappeared, in mysterious circumstances, during a journey amongst the Solomon Islands.

Boyd, Guy Martin à Beckett 1925–
Australian sculptor
He was born in Murrumbeena, Victoria, the son of Merric Boyd and brother of Arthur Merric Bloomfield Boyd. Starting as a potter, he moved on to sculpture in 1964, quickly making a name for himself. He has exhibited in London, and was commissioned to produce mural reliefs for Tullamarine (Melbourne) and Kingsford Smith (Sydney) airports. He lived in Canada from 1976 to 1981.

Boyd, Martin à Beckett 1893–1972
Australian novelist and poet
Born in Lucerne, Switzerland, the son of Arthur Merric Boyd, he was brought up in Melbourne, and lived for much of his life in Great Britain. After World War I he tried journalism for a time. His first three novels appeared under a pseudonym, 'Martin Mills', as did his fourth, *Dearest Idol* (1929), for which he adopted the name 'Walter Beckett'. Thereafter he acknowledged his authorship, and produced his best work, to be seen in what is now referred to as the 'Langton tetralogy': *The Cardboard Crown* (1952), *A Difficult Young Man* (1955), *Outbreak of Love* (1957) and *When Blackbirds Sing* (1962). He wrote two autobiographies: the earlier, *A Single Flame* (1938) was superceded by *Day of My Delight: An Anglo-Australian Memoir* (1965) in which he casts light on his fiction and its characters, and on the multi-talented Boyd family. ▢ B Niall, *Martin Boyd* (1974)

Boyd, (William) Merric 1888–1959
Australian ceramic artist
Born in St Kilda, Victoria, he was the son of Arthur Merric Boyd. He studied at the pioneering porcelain works at Yarraville, Victoria, and then served with the Royal Flying Corps in World War I, at Wedgwood, Stoke-on-Trent, England. He returned to Australia in the early 1920s, founded a famous studio at Murrumbeena, outside Melbourne, and experimented with new ceramic techniques. His pottery is sought after by collectors.

Boyd, (Theodore) Penleigh 1890–1923
Australian landscape artist and dry-point etcher
He was born in Westbury, Wiltshire, the son of Arthur Merric Boyd, and studied under Frederick McCubbin. He exhibited at the Royal Academy, London in 1922.

Boyd, Robin Gerard Penleigh 1919–71
Australian architect, critic and writer
Born in Melbourne, he reached a wide and popular audience with his books *Australia's Home* (1952), *The Australian Ugliness* (1960) and *The Great Australian Dream* (1972). He delivered the Australian Broadcasting Corporation's Boyer Lecture, 'Artificial Australia', in 1967, and was a member of the judging panel for the new Parliament House at Canberra. His critical work shaped the future direction of Australian architecture and was acknowledged with several awards.

Boyd, William Clouser 1903–
US biochemist
Born in Dearborn, Mississippi, and educated at Harvard, from 1948 he taught at the Boston Medical School, as Professor of Immunochemistry. From the early 1930s, Boyd studied the nature of antigen–antibody interactions, identifying the groups important for eliciting an antibody response, and the quantitative relationship between antigen and antibody in forming a precipitate. He later used Karl Landsteiner's discovery of blood groups to examine racial differences and the distribution and migration of racial groups, systematically collecting and classifying blood samples on a worldwide basis. By 1950, in his book *Genetics and the Races of Man*, he was able to present evidence for the existence of 13 human races, distinguishable by blood type. Racial distinction is now seen as more complex, but the study of blood groups remains the richest source of information on inherited traits related to race.

Boydell, John 1719–1804
English illustrator
Born in Dorrington, Shropshire, he travelled to London in 1741, where he learned engraving, started a print shop, and in 1790 was Lord Mayor. From his 'Shakespeare Gallery' of 162 pictures by John Opie, Joshua Reynolds, James Northcote (1746–1831), Benjamin West, and others, a volume of plates was engraved (1803) to accompany an edition of Shakespeare's works (9 vols, 1792–1801). The large sums of money he spent on these illustrations resulted in financial problems.

Boyd Orr, John Boyd Orr, 1st Baron 1880–1971
Scottish biologist and Nobel Prize winner
Born in Kilmaurs, Ayrshire, and educated at Glasgow University, he served with distinction in World War I, became director of the Rowett Research Institute and Professor of Agriculture at Aberdeen University (1942–45), and was the first director of the United Nations Food and Agriculture Organization (1945–48). Despite his pessimism about the world food situation, his great services in improving that situation brought him the Nobel Peace Prize in 1949, the year he was made a peer.

Boye, Karin Maria 1900–41
Swedish poet and novelist
Born in Gothenburg, she studied at Uppsala University and worked as a teacher and journalist. In 1925 she abandoned Christianity in favour of the socialist Clarté group, but she was more directly affected by psychoanalytic ideas than by Marxism, becoming interested in the relationship between instinct and social convention. Much of her poetry appeared in the modernist journal *Spektrum* which she founded and edited from 1931, and in which she also published translations of T S Eliot. Her collections include *Moln* (1922, 'Cloud'), *För trädets skull* (1935, 'For the Tree's Sake') and the posthumous *De sju dödssynderna* (1941, 'The Seven Deadly Sins'), published after her suicide. She had been depressed about the rise of totalitarianism, a concern she explored in her novels *Kris* (1934, 'Crisis') and *Kallocain* (1940). ▢ M Adenius and O G H Lagercrantz, *Karin Boye* (1942)

Boyer, Alexis, Baron de 1757–1833
French surgeon
He was born in Uzerches, Limousin, the son of a tailor. In 1805 he was imperial surgeon to **Napoleon I**, whom he accompanied on his campaigns. Subsequently he was consultant surgeon to **Louis XVIII, Charles X**, and **Louis Philippe**.

Boyer, Charles 1897–1978
French actor
Born in Figeac, he was educated at the Sorbonne and studied drama at the Paris Conservatoire before making his stage debut in *Les Jardins de Murcie* (1920, 'The Gardens of Murcie') and his film debut in *L'Homme du large* (1920, 'The Seafarer'). A popular matinee idol, he moved to Hollywood where his handsome looks, bass voice and expressive eyes made him the world's ideal Frenchman. Adept at comedy and drama, he appeared in such films as *Algiers* (1938), *Love Affair* (1939) and *Gaslight* (1944). He developed into an urbane, scene-stealing character actor of great charm in films like *Barefoot in the Park* (1967) and *Stavisky* (1974). A performer on television and the stage, he received a special Academy Award in 1943 for his efforts in promoting Franco-American cultural relations. He committed suicide two days after the death of his wife of 44 years.

Boyer, Herbert Wayne 1936–
US biochemist
Born in Pittsburgh, Pennsylvania, he studied there and worked at the University of California at San Francisco from 1966. A pioneer of genetic engineering, he showed in the 1970s that these methods could be used to make insulin and other costly biochemicals commercially, and in 1976 formed Genentech, Inc, for this purpose.

Boyer, Jean Pierre 1776–1850
Haitian politician
Born a mulatto in Port-au-Prince, he was sent to France when young, and in 1792 joined the army. He fought against the British on their invasion of Haiti, and established an independent republic in the western part of the island. President Pétion, on his deathbed, recommended him as his successor (1818). After the death of **Henri Christophe**, he united the negro district with the mulatto (1820). The following year he also added the eastern district, hitherto Spanish, and in 1825, for 150,000,000 francs, obtained recognition of independence from France. He governed Haiti well for 15 years, but his partiality to the mulattos made the negroes rise in 1843, and he fled.

Boyer, Sir Richard James Fildes 1891–1961
Australian broadcasting administrator
Born in Taree, New South Wales, he served with the Australian Imperial Force during World War I, at Gallipoli and in France. He was a member of the Australian delegation to the League of Nations in 1939 and was appointed to the Australian Broadcasting Commission (ABC) in 1940. After Prime Minister **John Curtin** affirmed the independence of the ABC, Boyer accepted the chairmanship in 1945. He greatly extended the educational influence of the ABC, particularly with the establishment on television of the University of the Air. He also encouraged the expansion of the ABC's orchestras. The ABC Lectures were renamed the 'Boyer Lectures' in his honour after his death.

Boyis, Hector See Boece, Hector

Boyle, Charles, 4th Earl of Orrery 1676–1731
Irish Jacobite soldier and writer
He edited the spurious *Letters of Phalaris*, satirized by **Jonathan Swift** in his *Battle of the Books* (1704). He fought at the Battle of Malplaquet (1709), helped to negotiate the Treaty of Utrecht (1713), and was imprisoned in the Tower of London as a Jacobite (1721). The 'orrery', a kind of planetarium, was named in his honour by the inventor, George Graham. His grandfather was **Roger Boyle**.

Boyle (of Handsworth), Sir Edward Charles Gurney, Baron 1923–81
English politician and educational administrator
Educated at Eton and Christ Church, Oxford, he was MP for the Handsworth Division of Birmingham (1950–70), Parliamentary Secretary at the Ministry of Education (1957–59) and Minister of Education (1962–64). He was Vice-Chancellor of Leeds University from 1970 to 1981. A humane pragmatist, he won great affection and held the development of personality to be the first concern of education. Under his influence, the Conservative Party moved from an intransigent defence of the grammar schools to a more pragmatic approach to secondary educational organization. A great enthusiast for the work of further education, he was a notably successful vice-chancellor. His period as minister for education came at the end of two decades of expansion of educational provision and expectation.

Boyle, Jimmy 1944–
Scottish murderer
Born in the Gorbals, then a notorious slum area of Glasgow, he was involved in shop-lifting, street-fighting and vandalism from a very early age. In his early teens he was sent to Larchgrove Remand Home for theft. This was followed by a spell in Borstal. Later charges of serious assault led to two years in prison. A member of a powerful gang in Glasgow, Boyle was subsequently twice charged with murder and cleared, and was eventually imprisoned for serious assault. In 1967, he was convicted for the murder of Babs Rooney and given a life sentence. In 1973 he became one of the first offenders to participate in Barlinnie Prison Special Unit's rehabilitation programme. He went on to produce many sculptures, which were exhibited in several countries, and to write his autobiography, *A Sense of Freedom* (1977). After his release in 1982, he published his prison diaries, *The Pain of Confinement* (1984), and worked with young offenders. He has become Scotland's most celebrated reformed criminal.

Boyle, John, 5th Earl of Cork and 5th Earl of Orrery 1707–62
Irish writer
He was an intimate of **Jonathan Swift, Pope** and Dr **Johnson**, and is remembered more for his rancorous *Remarks on the Life and Writings of Dr Jonathan Swift* (1751). He also made an excellent translation of the *Letters of Pliny* (1751).

Boyle, Kay 1902–92
US novelist, short-story writer, poet and essayist
Born in St Paul, Minnesota, she was brought up and educated in the USA, studying music and architecture, then lived in Europe for 30 years as part of the literary expatriate fraternity of Paris's Left Bank in the 1920s and latterly as the *New Yorker's* foreign correspondent (1945–53). Influenced by **Henry James**, she used her experience of expatriation most effectively in *Plagued by the Nightingale* (1931) and *Generation Without Farewell* (1960), but her novels are generally inferior to her stories, which are amassed in several volumes including *The Smoking Mountain* (1951). Her poems, indebted to **William Carlos Williams** and **Pádraic Colum**, were collected in 1962. 🕮 S W Spanier, *Kay Boyle: Artist and Activist* (1986)

Boyle, Mark 1934–
Scottish artist

Born in Glasgow, he began as a law student at Glasgow University, at the same time writing poems and painting. In 1964 he organized an event called 'Street', in which a group of people looked out through an ordinary shop-window into an ordinary street. His *London Study* of 1969 was a piece of fibreglass pavement left lying for 17 years to gather real dust. His ongoing project, *Journey to the Surface of the Earth*, began in 1969 with 1,000 darts thrown at a map of the world by blindfolded people. Boyle visits each site in turn, selects a six-foot square and makes a cast of it. He represented Great Britain at the 1978 Venice Biennale. Later work conveys a sense of urban aggression in its use of concrete, broken glass and rusting metal. He works with his partner Joan Hills and their two children, all artists; they exhibit as The Boyle Family.

Boyle, Richard, 1st Earl of Cork, *known as* the Great Earl 1566–1643
Anglo-Irish administrator
Born in Canterbury, England, he studied at Cambridge and the Middle Temple, then went to Ireland (1588) to make his fortune. He married an heiress, purchased large estates in Munster, promoted the immigration of English Protestants, and won the favour of Queen Elizabeth I. He built roads, bridges, harbours, towns and castles, and acquired wealth from his ironworks. In 1620 he became Earl of Cork, and was made hereditary Lord High Treasurer in 1631. Although sidelined by Lord Deputy Wentworth (from 1633), he helped to secure his execution, and defended Munster against the Irish rebels (1641).

Boyle, Robert 1627–91
Irish physicist and chemist
The seventh son of Richard Boyle, 1st Earl of Cork, he was born at Lismore Castle, Munster. He studied at Eton and travelled in Europe for six years. On his return, he settled on the family estates at Stalbridge, Dorset, and devoted himself to science. He was one of the first members of the anti-scholastic 'invisible college', an association of Oxford intellectuals opposed to the prevalent doctrines of scholasticism, which became the Royal Society in 1645. Settling at Oxford in 1654, with Robert Hooke as his assistant, he carried out experiments on air, vacuum, combustion and respiration. In 1661 he published his *Sceptical Chymist*, in which he criticized the current theories of matter and defined the chemical element as the practical limit of chemical analysis. In 1662 he arrived at Boyle's law, which states that the pressure and volume of gas are inversely proportional. He also researched the calcination of metals, properties of acids and alkalis, specific gravity, crystallography and refraction, and first prepared phosphorus. As a director of the East India Company (for which he had procured the Charter) he worked for the propagation of Christianity in the East, circulated at his own expense translations of the Scriptures, and by bequest founded the 'Boyle Lectures' in defence of Christianity. In 1668 he took up residence in London with his sister, Lady Ranelagh, and gave much of his time to the Royal Society. He was, surprisingly, an alchemist, but his alchemy was a logical outcome of his atomism. If every substance is merely a rearrangement of the same basic elements, transmutations should be possible. Modern atomic physics has proved him right. 📖 Marie Boas, *Robert Boyle and Seventeenth-Century Chemistry* (1968)

Boyle, Roger, Baron Broghill and 1st Earl of Orrery 1621–79
Irish soldier and politician
He was the third son of Richard Boyle, 1st Earl of Cork. In the Civil War he first took the Royalist side, but after the death of Charles I he came under the personal influence of Cromwell, and distinguished himself in the Irish campaign. He became one of Cromwell's special council and

a member of his House of Lords. On Cromwell's death, he tried to support Richard Cromwell, but after his abdication crossed to Ireland, and secured it for King Charles II. Four months after the Restoration he was made Earl of Orrery. He wrote poems, eight heroic plays, two comedies, a romance, *Parthenissa* (1654–65), and a *Treatise on the Art of War* (1677).

Boys, Sir Charles Vernon 1855–1944
English physicist
He was born in Rutland, Leicestershire. His many inventions include an improved torsion balance, the radio-micrometer, a calorimeter, and a camera with moving lens, with which he photographed lightning flashes.

Bozzaris or Botzaris, Marcos 1788–1823
Greek patriot
Born in Suli, Epirus, he was forced in 1803 to retreat to the Ionian Isles by Ali Pasha. In 1820, at the head of 800 expatriated Suliotes, he gained several victories for Ali against the Sultan. In 1822 he defended Missolonghi, but was killed in an attack on the Turkish-Albanian army at Karpenisi.

Brabazon (of Tara), John Theodore Cuthbert Moore-Brabazon, 1st Baron 1884–1964
English aviator and politician
He was educated at Harrow and Cambridge. The first holder of a flying licence, during World War I he served with the Royal Flying Corps (RFC), reaching the rank of lieutenant-colonel and winning the MC. He was responsible for several innovations in aerial photography. In 1918 he entered parliament and became Private Parliamentary Secretary to Churchill at the War Office. Between 1923 and 1927 he was twice Parliamentary Secretary to the Ministry of Transport. He was a prominent member of the enquiry into the R101 airship disaster. In 1940 he became Minister of Transport, and in 1941 Minister of Aircraft Production, but resigned due to public displeasure at his outspoken criticism of the ally, Russia.

Brabham, Sir Jack (John Arthur) 1926–
Australian racing-driver
Born in Sydney, after service with the Royal Australian Air Force he started his racing career in 1947, in 'midget' cars. He won the Australian Grand Prix in 1955 (and again in 1963 and 1964), then went to the UK where he joined the successful Cooper team. He won his first Formula 1 World Drivers' championship at Sebring, Florida, in 1959 by pushing his car over the finishing-line and won the title again in 1960. In 1966 he won his third world title, and also the Constructor's championship, with a car of his own design, the Repco-Brabham. A string of successes followed, and three BARC (British Automobile Racing Club) gold medals in 1959, 1966 and 1967. He retired from the circuits in 1970, but has remained active in the motor-racing field, though he no longer owns Brabham cars. He was knighted in 1979.

Brace, Charles Loring 1826–90
US philanthropist and social reformer
Born in Litchfield, Connecticut, he founded the Children's Aid Society in 1853, and pioneered philanthropic methods based on self-help.

Bracegirdle, Anne c.1663–1748
English actress
She was renowned for her beauty, and for her performances (1688–1707) at Drury Lane and Lincoln's Inn Fields under Thomas Betterton, particularly in the plays of William Congreve.

Bracton, Henry de c.1210–1268
English ecclesiastic and jurist

He was born possibly in Exeter. In 1264 he became Archdeacon of Barnstaple and Chancellor of Exeter Cathedral. *De Legibus et Consuetudinibus Angliae*, the earliest attempt at a systematic treatment of English law, based on decided cases and the practice of royal courts, is attributed to him. It was first printed in its entirety in 1569. In 1887 *Bracton's Note Book* was published, with proof, later doubted, that this was the actual collection on which Bracton's treatise was founded.

Bradbury, John Swanwick Bradbury, 1st Baron 1872–1950
English government official
He was born in Winsford, Cheshire. As Secretary to the Treasury (1913–19) he was responsible for the substitution of £1 and 10 shilling notes for gold coins. Treasury bills bearing his signature are often called 'Bradburys'.

Bradbury, Malcolm Stanley 1932–
English novelist and critic
Born in Sheffield, he graduated from University College, Leicester, before taking undergraduate courses in London and the USA. With Angus Wilson, he co-founded a creative writing programme at the University of East Anglia and was later appointed Professor of American Studies (1970–). He is the author of numerous critical works embracing Modernist and post-Modernist ideas, and his own novels, many of them inspired by academia, include *Eating People is Wrong* (1959), *Stepping Westward* (1965), *The History Man* (1975), *Rates of Exchange* (1982), and *Dr Criminale* (1992). He has written short-stories and television plays, and made several television productions, including the Emmy-award winning *Porterhouse Blue*. He also writes regularly for *The Independent*. 📖 J Haffenden, *Novelists in Interview* (1985)

Bradbury, Ray(mond Douglas) 1920–
US science-fiction writer
He was born in Waukegan, Illinois. An avid reader of sensational fiction and comics, he began early to contribute to pulp magazines, graduating to more literary magazines and short-story anthologies. He has written such notable novels as *Fahrenheit 451* (1953), *Dandelion Wine* (1957), *Death is a Lonely Business* (1985) and most recently, *A Graveyard for Lunatics* (1990). However, he is primarily a short-story writer, creating some of the finest examples in the genre, among them 'The Day It Rained Forever', 'R Is for Rocket' and those included in *The Martian Chronicles* (1950). A prolific and wide-ranging writer, he has been the recipient of numerous awards. 📖 J L Garci, *Ray Bradbury humanista del futuro* (1971)

Braddock, Edward 1695–1755
Scottish soldier
He was born in Perthshire. Commissioned in the Coldstream Guards in 1710, in 1755 he was appointed to command against the French in the French and Indian Wars in America. He was mortally wounded when ambushed on his way to attack Fort Duquesne (Pittsburgh), on 9 July 1755. His force was decimated and of his staff only George Washington escaped unhurt.

Braddon, Mary Elizabeth 1835–1915
English novelist
Born in London, she attained fame with a Victorian thriller, *Lady Audley's Secret* (1862), the story of a golden-haired murderess. Of some 75 popular novels, perhaps the best is *Ishmael* (1884). Her *The Doctor's Wife* (1864) is an adaptation of the theme of Gustave Flaubert's *Madame Bovary*.

Braddon, Russell Reading 1921–95
Australian author and scriptwriter

He was born in Sydney, the great-grandson of Sir Edward Braddon, premier of Tasmania (1894–99), and educated at Sydney University. During World War II he was a prisoner of the Japanese for four years, at the notorious Changi Jail, Singapore, and worked on the Burma Railway. His experiences were published as *The Naked Island* (1952, dramatized 1961) and *End of a Hate* (1958). A string of popular novels followed, including *End Play* (1972, filmed 1976) and *The Year of the Angry Rabbit* (1964, filmed as *Night of the Lepus*, 1972), but he is perhaps best known for his biographies, such as those of wartime hero Leonard Cheshire, *Cheshire VC* (1954) and the Resistance heroine *Nancy Wake* (1956).

Bradfield, John Job Crew 1867–1943
Australian civil engineer and designer
Born in Sandgate, Queensland, he was educated at Sydney University. In 1913 his original plan for a bridge across Sydney Harbour was adopted but, because of World War I, work did not begin until 1923. The widest and heaviest bridge of this type, it was opened in 1932. He also planned an underground electric railway system for Sydney, and designed many other bridges, dams, and highways. He drew up plans to dam the Burdekin and other Queensland rivers, drive the waters back through tunnels to the western side of the Great Dividing Range and so irrigate the dry inland plains.

Bradford, Barbara Taylor 1933–
English novelist
Born in Leeds, she worked as a journalist specializing in interior design, then left for the USA, where she now lives. Her early publications, books of domestic advice such as *How to Solve Your Decorating Problems* and three volumes of *How to be a Perfect Wife*, appeared during the 1960s and 1970s. She is internationally known, though, for her bestselling romantic trilogy, *A Woman of Substance* (1979), *Hold the Dream* (1985), and *To Be the Best* (1988). Bradford writes about strong, adaptable women triumphing in a man's world due to their intellect and indomitable spirit.

Bradford, William 1590–1657
American colonist and religious leader, one of the Pilgrim Fathers
Born in Austerfield, Yorkshire, England, he was a non-conformist from boyhood, and went to Holland with a separatist group in 1609, seeking freedom of worship. In Leyden he became a tradesman and read widely. One of the moving spirits in the Pilgrim Fathers' expedition to the New World in 1620, he sailed on the *Mayflower*, and in 1621 took over from John Carver as elected governor of Plymouth colony. He was re-elected 30 times between 1622 and 1656, and was perceived as a fair, but firm leader. He wrote a *History of Plimmoth Plantation* (completed c.1651, printed in 1856), a long descriptive poem (1654), a letter-book (1624–30) and a *Dialogue between some young men born in New England and sundry ancient men that came out of Holland*. 📖 B Smith, *Bradford of Plymouth* (1951)

Bradford, William 1663–1752
American printer
He was born in Barnwell, Leicestershire, England. A Quaker, he emigrated to the USA in 1685 and founded the country's first paper-mill, in Philadelphia in 1690. After moving to New York in 1693, he printed official papers, money, books, plays, and the first New York newspaper (*New York Gazette*, 1725).

Bradlaugh, Charles 1833–91
English social reformer
Born in London, he was in turn errand boy, coal-merchant, and trooper in Dublin. He returned to London in 1853, and became a busy secularist lecturer, pamphleteering under the name of 'Iconoclast'. From 1860 he was editor, and from 1862 proprietor, of the

National Reformer. In 1880 he was elected MP for Northampton but as an unbeliever refused to take the oath, and was expelled and re-elected regularly until 1886 when he took the oath and his seat. In 1886 he was prosecuted, with Annie Besant, for republishing a pamphlet advocating birth control (*The Fruits of Philosophy*); the conviction was subsequently quashed on appeal. ⌻ David Tribe, *President Charles Bradlaugh MP* (1971)

Bradlee, Benjamin Crowninshield 1921–
US journalist and author

Born in Boston, he was a founder of the *New Hampshire Sunday News*. He subsequently joined the *Washington Post* (1948) as a police and federal courts reporter, and worked for *Newsweek* where, because of a close friendship with President John F Kennedy, he regularly filed scoops. In 1965 he became managing editor of the *Washington Post* and encouraged the investigative journalism which reached apotheosis in the Watergate scandal. His *Conversations with Kennedy* was published in 1975, and he announced his retirement in 1991.

Bradley, Andrew Cecil 1851–1935
English critic

Born in Cheltenham, Gloucestershire, the brother of Francis Herbert Bradley, he was educated at Cheltenham College and Balliol College, Oxford, where he became a Fellow in 1874. The most influential commentator of his generation, he was Professor of Literature and History at Liverpool (1822), of English Language and Literature at Glasgow (1890), and of Poetry at Oxford from 1901 to 1906. He published *Poetry for Poetry's Sake* (1901), and *Commentary on 'In Memoriam'* (1901), but made his name with his magisterial *Shakespearean Tragedy* (1904). He also published *Oxford Lectures on Poetry* (1909).

Bradley, Edward, *pseudonym* Cuthbert Bede 1827–89
English writer and clergyman

He was born in Kidderminster, Worcestershire, and was educated at Durham University. His facetious description of Oxford undergraduate life in *Adventures of Mr Verdant Green* (1853–57) was the first and most popular of his 26 works. He was also an illustrator, and drew for *Punch* as well as his own works.

Bradley, Francis Herbert 1846–1924
Welsh philosopher

Born in Glasbury, Brecknockshire (Powys), he became a Fellow of Merton College, Oxford in 1870 but lived as a semi-invalid most of his life. He was probably the most important figure in the British idealist movement of this period and was much influenced by Immanuel Kant and Hegel. His most important works are *Ethical Studies* (1876), *Principles of Logic* (1883), and the highly original and influential *Appearance and Reality* (1893). He was the brother of Andrew Cecil Bradley.

Bradley, Henry 1845–1923
English philologist and lexicographer

In 1886 he became joint editor of the *Oxford English Dictionary* with Sir James Murray, and senior editor in 1915. He wrote *The Making of English* (1904) and *English Place-Names* (1910).

Bradley, James 1693–1762
English astronomer

Born in Sherborne, Gloucestershire, he was educated at Northleach Grammar School and Balliol College, Oxford. His genius for mathematics and astronomy won him the friendship of Edmond Halley and Isaac Newton. He was Savilian Professor of Astronomy at Oxford (1721) and in 1742 succeeded Halley as Regius Professor of Astronomy at Greenwich. In 1729 he published his discovery of the aberration of light, providing the first

observational proof of the Copernican hypothesis. In 1748 he discovered that the inclination of the Earth's axis to the ecliptic is not constant. He was appointed Astronomer Royal in 1742.

Bradley, Omar N(elson) 1893–1981
US general

He was born in Clark, Missouri. Trained at West Point, he entered the army in 1915 and served in World War I. He commanded the II Corps in Tunisia and Sicily (1943), and in 1944 he commanded the US forces at the Normandy invasion, and later the US 12th Army Group through France. He became the first permanent chairman of the US Joint Chiefs of Staff (1949–53), and in 1950 was promoted to a five-star general of the army. He published his war memoirs, *A Soldier's Story*, in 1951, and an autobiography, *General's Life*, in 1983.

Bradley, Tom (Thomas) 1917–98
US politician

Born on a cotton plantation in Calvert, Texas, the child of sharecroppers, he moved to Los Angeles with his family at the age of seven. He joined the Los Angeles police department in 1940, retiring from the force in 1961 to become a lawyer. After serving on the city council (1963–73), he became the first black mayor of Los Angeles (1973–93), presiding over 20 years of rapid urban growth and struggling to deal with divisions caused by racial tensions and extremes of wealth and poverty.

Bradman, Don (Sir Donald George) 1908–
Australian cricketer

Born in Cootamundra, New South Wales, he is regarded as one of the greatest batsmen in the history of the game. He played for Australia from 1928 to 1948 (captain 1936–48). A prodigious scorer, he made the highest aggregate and largest number of centuries in Tests against England, and holds the record for the highest Australian Test score against England (334 at Leeds in 1930). His batting average in Test matches was an astonishing 99.94 runs per innings. The first Australian cricketer to be knighted (1949), he was chairman of the Australian Cricket Board (1960–63, 1969–72). ⌻ Irving Rosewater, *Sir Donald Bradman: A Biography* (1978)

Bradshaw, George 1801–53
English printer and Quaker

Born in Salford, Greater Manchester, he was educated locally then was apprenticed to an engraver. A Manchester mapmaker, he is best remembered for the series of railway guides (Bradshaws) which he originated in 1839. He died of cholera in Christiania (now Oslo).

Bradshaw, John 1602–59
English judge

Born near Stockport, Cheshire, he was called to the Bar in 1627. He was president at the trial of Charles I (1649), and on that occasion, he was said to be both short-tempered and long-winded. As a reward, he was made Permanent President of the Council of State and Chancellor of the Duchy of Lancaster, with a grant of estates worth £2,000 per annum. His 'stiff republicanism' estranged him from Oliver Cromwell. He was buried in Westminster Abbey, but at the Restoration (1660) his body was dug up and hanged as a regicide, as were those of Cromwell and Henry Ireton.

Bradshaw, Robert 1916–78
St Kitts-Nevis politician

He took St Kitts-Nevis to associated statehood in 1967. The founder and leader of the St Kitts-Nevis Labour Party (1940) and Federal Minister of Finance (1958–62), he briefly made the world press in 1969, when his dispute with Anguilla forced that island to declare its independence of St Kitts; this action resulted in a farcical British military intervention.

Bradstreet, Anne, *née* Dudley 1612–72
American Puritan poet
Born in Northampton, England, in 1628 she married a Nonconformist minister, Simon Bradstreet (1603–97), who later became Governor of Massachusetts. She emigrated with her husband to New England in 1630. Her first volume of poems, *The Tenth Muse lately sprung up in America*, written in the style of Phineas Fletcher, was published by her brother-in-law in London in 1650 without her knowledge. She is considered the first English poet in America. Wendy Martin, *An American Triptych: Anne Bradstreet, Emily Dickinson, Adrienne Rich* (1986); E W White, *Anne Bradstreet: the tenth muse* (1971)

Bradwell, Myra R, *née* Colby 1831–94
US lawyer and campaigner for women's rights
Born in Manchester, Vermont, and educated at Portage and at the Ladies' Seminary, Elgin, near Chicago, she became a school teacher as universities were closed to women. Following her marriage in 1852 to lawyer James B Bradwell, she studied law to assist him. Despite passing her legal examinations in 1869, she was debarred from practising until 1892 on grounds of gender. She argued her case in both state and national supreme courts, procuring state legislation in 1882 which granted all persons, irrespective of sex, the right to select a profession. In 1868 she established, managed and edited the *Chicago Legal News* and in 1869 summoned the first Women's Suffrage Convention in Chicago.

Brady, Ian 1938–
Scottish murderer
Born in Glasgow, he was a clerk with a fascination for Nazi memorabilia. He was found guilty of the murder of two children, John Kilbride and Lesley Ann Downey, and a 17-year-old boy, Edward Evans, on 6 May 1966. The harrowing case details revealed that Brady, with his lover Myra Hindley, lured young children into their home in Manchester and tortured them before killing them. Brady and Hindley recorded their crimes with photographs and a tape, which was played in court. The lovers were described as the 'Moors Murderers' because they buried most of their victims on Saddleworth Moor in the Pennines. Hindley made a private confession to two other murders in 1986, and the body of Pauline Reade was found in August 1987, 24 years after her disappearance. The body of 12-year-old Keith Bennett has never been found.

Brady, James Buchanan, *nicknamed* Diamond Jim 1856–1917
US financier
Born in New York City, he began as a hotel bellhop, then worked for the New York Central Railroad, and later amassed a fortune as a salesman of railroad equipment, becoming famous for his extravagant tastes and display of diamond jewellery. His endowment to Johns Hopkins Hospital established the Brady Urological Institute.

Brady, Mathew B 1823–96
US photographer
Born near Lake George, New York, he operated a portrait studio in New York City, first using daguerrotype and then switching to wet-plate photography in 1855. He built up a thriving business, photographing numerous public figures such as Abraham Lincoln, but gave this up to take on a major project to record the American Civil War with the Union armies. In 1862 he organized a team which covered all the major engagements and camp life. Though widely acclaimed, this effort ruined him financially and, despite a belated government grant, he died in poverty in a New York almshouse. Now in the Library of Congress, his photographs form a unique and invaluable pictorial history of the Civil War.

Brady, Matthew 1799–1826
Australian thief and bushranger
Born in Manchester, England, of Irish descent, he was convicted in 1820 of stealing a basket of groceries. Transported for seven years to New South Wales, he was sent in 1823 to the penal colony of Macquarie Harbour in Van Diemen's Land (now Tasmania). Brady escaped with a small group in the following year, and they terrorized the island. After many exploits, including capturing an entire township, when the senior citizens and the local army garrison were all locked up in the town jail, some of his gang turned informers. He was eventually captured and hanged in Hobart.

Brady, Nicholas 1659–1726
Irish Anglican clergyman and poet
Born in Bandon, County Cork, and educated at Christ Church, Oxford, and Dublin, he took holy orders and was rector at Stratford-upon-Avon from 1702 to 1705. With Nahum Tate he produced a metrical version of the Psalms (1696), which met with strong opposition from many of the Tory clergy. He also wrote a tragedy, *The Rape*, and translated Virgil's *Aeneid*.

Bragg, Braxton 1817–76
US Confederate general
Born in Warrenton, North Carolina, he graduated from West Point Military Academy in 1837 and fought in the Seminole Wars and the Mexican War. After resigning from the US army in 1856, he lived on a plantation in Louisiana. At the outbreak of the Civil War he became a general in the Confederate army, and in 1862 he was given command of the army of Tennessee. He won a notable victory at Chickamauga (1863), the hardest-fought battle in the war, but was badly beaten by General Ulysses S Grant at Chattanooga later the same year. He was often criticized for indecisiveness and lack of resolution, and at the end of 1863 he surrendered his command, becoming military adviser to Jefferson Davis.

Bragg, Sir (William) Lawrence 1890–1971
British physicist and Nobel Prize winner
Born in Adelaide, Australia, the son of Sir William Bragg, he was educated at Adelaide University from the age of 15, and Trinity College, Cambridge, where he discovered the Bragg law (1912), which describes the conditions for X-ray diffraction by crystals. He later collaborated with his father in the study of crystals by X-ray diffraction and continued it as professor at Manchester University and then at Cambridge (from 1938). Like his father, he became director of the Royal Institution (1954–65) and did much to popularize science. He shared the 1915 Nobel Prize for physics with his father, became Professor of Physics at Victoria University, Manchester (1919–37), and then succeeded Ernest Rutherford as head of the Cavendish Laboratory in Cambridge (1938–53). There he supported Francis Crick and James Watson in their work, using X-ray crystal studies to deduce the helical structure of DNA, so creating molecular biology and revolutionizing biological science. He was knighted in 1941.

Bragg, Melvyn Bragg, Baron 1939–
English novelist and television arts presenter
Born in Lovell, near Carlisle, he produced the television programme *Monitor* (1963) and presented *Second House* (1973–77) and the books programme *Read All About It* (1976–77), before becoming presenter and editor of the arts series *The South Bank Show* (1978–). He was head of arts at London Weekend Television from 1982 to 1990,

when he became controller of arts there and chairman of Border Television. He has presented BBC Radio 4's *Start the Week* since 1988. He co-wrote the films *Isadora* (1969), *Jesus Christ Superstar* (1973) and *Clouds of Glory*, as well as the stage musical *The Hired Man* (1984), adapted from his novel. His other novels include *Without a City Wall* (1968), *The Nerve* (1971), *The Silken Net* (1974), *A Time to Dance* (1990, adapted for television, 1992), *Crystal Rooms* (1992) and *Credo* (1996).

Bragg, Sir William Henry 1862–1942
English physicist and Nobel Prize winner

He was born in Westward, Cumberland. He was educated at Trinity College, Cambridge, and achieved Third Wrangler in the Mathematical Tripos, Part I (1884). He was appointed Professor of Mathematics at Adelaide, Australia (1886), but his extraordinary scientific career only really began when in 1904 he gave a lecture on radioactivity which inspired him to research into this area. He became professor at Leeds in 1909 and from 1912 worked in conjunction with his son, **Lawrence Bragg**, on determining the atomic structure of crystals from their X-ray diffraction patterns. Their efforts won them a joint Nobel Prize for physics in 1915, the only father–son partnership to share this honour. William Bragg moved to University College London the same year and became director of the Royal Institution in 1923. His works include *Studies in Radioactivity* (1912), *X-rays and Crystal Structure* (1915, with his son) and *The Universe of Light* (1933). During World War I he directed research on submarine detection for the Admiralty. He was knighted in 1920, probably both as recognition for his war work and his scientific eminence. He was elected a Fellow of the Royal Society in 1907, was awarded its Rumford Medal in 1916 and served as the society's president from 1935 to 1940. ▣ G M Caroe, *William Henry Bragg, 1862–1942: Man and Scientist* (1978)

Braham, John 1774–1856
British tenor

Born in London of German-Jewish parents, he had his first great success at Drury Lane (1796), and for 50 years held a reputation as one of the finest tenors of his time. He spent most of his fortune on the purchase of the Colosseum in Regent's Park and on building the St James's Theatre in Picadilly (opened 1835).

Brahe, Tycho or Tyge 1546–1601
Danish astronomer

Born into a noble family in Knudstrup, South Sweden (then under Danish rule), he studied mathematics and astronomy at the University of Copenhagen, and then at Leipzig, Wittenberg, Rostock and Augsburg (1562–69). From the age of 14, when he saw the partial solar eclipse of 1560, he was obsessed by astronomy. In 1563 he discovered serious errors in the existing astronomical tables, and in 1572 carefully observed a new star in Cassiopeia (the supernova now known as Tycho's star), a significant observation which made his name. In 1576, with royal aid, he established his Uraniborg (Castle of the Heavens) Observatory on the island of Ven (formerly Hven), in The Sound (between Zealand Island and Sweden). There, for 20 years, he successfully carried out his observations, measuring the positions of 777 stars and creating a catalogue of them with such accuracy that it provided a vital source of information for later astronomers. In 1596, on the succession of Kristian IV, he was forced to leave the country; after travelling for three years he accepted an invitation from the Emperor Rudolf II to Benatky, near Prague, where he assisted Johannes Kepler. Brahe did not subscribe to Copernicus's theory of a sun-centered planetary system, but his data allowed Kepler to prove that Copernicus was essentially correct. Gifted but hot-tempered, Brahe lost most of his nose in a duel at the age of 19, and wore a false silver nose for the rest of his life. He is considered the greatest pre-telescope observer. ▣ J L E Dreyer, *Tycho Brahe* (1890)

Brahms, Johannes See panel p257

Braid, James ?1795–1860
Scottish surgeon and hypnotist

Born in Rylawhouse, Fife, he was educated at Edinburgh University, and spent most of his life practising surgery in Manchester, where his operation for club-foot was famous. In 1841, however, he attended a popular demonstration of 'Mesmerism' and devoted much of the rest of his working life to investigating the phenomena associated with what he himself first called 'neurohypnotism', later shortened to 'hypnotism'. His papers and books on the subject helped keep serious concerns with hypnotism alive and Braid was looked upon as an important pioneer in the field by Jean Charcot and others who, from the 1880s, systematically incorporated hypnotism in their treatment of nervous disorders.

Braid, James 1870–1950
Scottish golfer

Born in Earlsferry, Fife, he trained as a joiner and went to work in St Andrews, where he became an impressive player. In 1893 he moved to London as a club-maker at the Army & Navy Stores, before becoming a professional golfer at Romford later that year, and at Walton Heath from 1904 until his death. He won the Open championship five times between 1901 and 1910 (when he became the first player to break 300 for 72 holes at St Andrews), four *News of the World* matchplay championships between 1903 and 1911, and the French Championship in 1910. With Harry Vardon and John Henry Taylor he formed the so-called 'Great Triumvirate' of British golf in the Edwardian era. He was a fine teacher, and became a celebrated designer of golf courses.

Braidwood, Thomas 1715–1806
Scottish teacher

After studying at Edinburgh University he opened a school there, in 1760, the first school in Great Britain for people who could neither hear nor speak. The school, which was visited by Dr Johnson in 1773, was transferred 10 years later to Hackney, London.

Braille, Louis 1809–52
French educationist

Born in Coupvray, near Paris, he was blind from the age of three, and at 10 entered the Institution des Jeunes Aveugles in Paris. He studied organ playing, and became professor of the Institution in 1826. In 1829 he devised a system of raised-point writing which the blind could both read and write. ▣ Stephen Keeler, *Louis Braille* (1986)

Brailsford, Henry Noel 1873–1958
English socialist author and political journalist

Born in Yorkshire and educated at Glasgow University, he became assistant Professor of Logic there, leaving to join the Greek Foreign Legion in the war with Turkey in 1897. He described his experiences in *The Broom of the War God* (1898). His socialism was pre-eminently international in outlook and was the key to everything he did (see *The War of Steel and Gold*, 1914). He joined the Independent Labour Party in 1907 and edited (1922–26) its weekly organ, the *New Leader*. He was a leader-writer to several influential papers, including the *Manchester Guardian* and the *Daily Herald*. His literary work includes *Shelley, Godwin and their Circle* (1913), *Socialism for Today* (1925), *Voltaire* (1935), and *Subject India* (1943).

Brain, Aubrey Harold 1893–1955
English horn player

Brahms, Johannes 1833–97
German composer

Johannes Brahms was born in Hamburg, the son of a poor orchestral musician. He showed early talent as a pianist, and as a young boy was compelled by family poverty to earn his living playing in the dockside inns of Hamburg. Although his reputation spread rapidly, it was not until 1853 that he was able to concentrate on composition. This was after he had met the flamboyant Hungarian refugee violinist Ede Reményi (1828–98), with whom he went on tour, and from whom he probably absorbed much of the spirit which went into the *Hungarian Dances* (1868–80) and *Zigeunerlieder* (1888). During the tour he met the violinist **Joseph Joachim**, who became a lifelong friend and supporter, as did the composer **Franz Liszt**.

Brahms was introduced by Joachim to **Clara** and **Robert Schumann**, whose enthusiasm for Brahms's early works, especially his assistance in publishing the piano sonatas, helped to establish his reputation; Brahms's devotion to Schumann expressed itself in his lifelong care for Schumann's widow and children. His relationship to Clara was particularly close, and its exact nature has caused much interest and speculation. However, he never married, and after 1863, when he settled in Vienna, his life was uneventful except for occasional public appearances in Austria and Germany at which he played his own works. He was adopted by the anti-Wagnerian faction as the leader of traditional principles aginst 'modern' iconoclasm, and his fame as a composer spread rapidly.

Firmly based on classical foundations, his works contain hardly any programme music apart from a few pieces such as the *Tragic Overture* (1886) and the C minor quartet (1855–75, inspired by **Goethe**'s *Werther*). He waited many years before venturing into great orchestral works: the first, *Variations on a Theme of Haydn*, appeared when he was 40, and his first symphony when he was 43. The *Academic Festival Overture* (1880), also dating from this period, was composed in honour of his honorary doctorate at Breslau University. His greatest choral work is the *German Requiem*, which had its first full performance in 1869. He wrote much chamber music, some of it inspired by the German clarinettist Richard Mühlfeld (1856–1907), whom he heard playing at Meiningen, and many songs. He was prolific in all fields except opera, and the quality of his work is extraordinarily even, largely because of his ruthless destruction of early efforts and his refusal to publish any work which failed to measure up to his self-imposed standards of excellence.

📖 I Keys, *Johannes Brahms* (1989); M Musgrave, *The Music of Brahms* (1985); P Latham, *Brahms* (rev edn, 1975).

'When I feel the urge to compose, I begin by appealing directly to my Maker and I first ask Him the three most important questions pertaining to our life here in this world—whence, wherefore, whither.' Quoted in *A Hopkins, Music All Around Me* (1967).

Born in London, he studied at the Royal College of Music and became chief horn player in the New Symphony Orchestra (1911) and London Symphony Orchestra (1912). In 1923 he became professor at the Royal Academy of Music, and from 1930 to 1945 was principal horn of the BBC Symphony Orchestra. He was the father of **Dennis Brain**, and another son, Leonard (1915–75), was an oboist.

Brain, Dennis 1921–57
English horn player

Born in London, he studied under his father, **Aubrey Brain**, at the Royal Academy of Music, also becoming a fine organist. Chief horn player with the Royal Philharmonic and Philharmonia Orchestras, his skill won him fame throughout Europe. Amongst the composers who wrote works specially for him are **Benjamin Britten**, **Paul Hindemith** and **Malcolm Arnold**.

Braine, John Gerard 1922–86
English novelist

Born in Bradford, he was educated at St Bede's Grammar School and had various jobs, including service in the Royal Navy, before following his mother's profession of librarian. In 1951 he went to London to become a full-time writer, but returned north the same year, after his mother's death in a road accident. He then spent 18 months in hospital suffering from tuberculosis, and it was during this period of enforced rest that he began to write his first successful novel, *Room at the Top*. He went back to library work until 1957 when the book was published and its success enabled him to embark again on a full-time career as a novelist. The theme of aggressive ambition and determination to break through rigid social barriers identified him with the 'angry young men' of the 1950s. His other novels include *The Vodi* (1959), *Life at the Top* (1962, a sequel to *Room at the Top*), *The Jealous God* (1964), *The Crying Game* (1964), *Stay with Me Till Morning* (1968), *The Queen of a Distant Country* (1972), *Finger of Fire* (1977) and *One and Last Love* (1981). 📖 J W Lee, *John Braine* (1973)

Brainerd, David 1718–47
American missionary

He was born in Haddam, Connecticut, and studied at Yale College, where his opinions caused doctrinal disputes and his expulsion. He worked successfully among the Native Americans from 1742, and recorded his experiences in his *Journal*, published posthumously in 1749.

Braithwaite, (Florence) Lilian 1873–1948
English actress

Born in Croydon, she made her professional debut in 1897 as a member of a Shakespearean company touring to South Africa, run by her husband Gerald Lawrence. She then joined the celebrated company run by actor-manager Sir **Frank Benson** in London, where she made an early impression in both Shakespearean roles and in contemporary plays. She enjoyed a lengthy and successful stage career, reserving some of her most famous performances for its latter stages, which included a three-year run in *Arsenic and Old Lace* from 1942. She was made a DBE in 1943. Her daughter, the actress Joyce Carey, followed her onto the stage.

Bramah, Joseph 1748–1814
English inventor

Born in Stainborough, Yorkshire, the son of a farmer, he was lamed at 16, so was apprenticed to the village carpenter, and later became a cabinetmaker in London. He made numerous inventions, including a beer machine for use at the bar of public houses, a safety lock (patented 1788) which he manufactured in partnership with **Henry Maudslay**, a hydraulic press (1795), and a very ingenious machine for printing bank-notes (1806). He was one of the first to propose the application of the screw-propeller.

Bramante, Donato or Donino, *originally* Donato di Pasuccio d'Antonio or Donato d'Agnolo or D'Angelo 1444–1514
Italian High Renaissance architect

Born near Urbino, he started as a painter, and from 1477 to 1499 worked in Milan, where he executed his first building projects, such as S Maria delle Grazie (1488–99). He spent the last 15 years of his life, from 1499, in Rome, where he was employed by popes Alexander VI and Julius II and where his most important work was done. He designed the new Basilica of St Peter's (begun in 1506), the Belvedere courtyard, the Tempietto di S Pietro in Montorio (1502), the Palazzo dei Tribunali (1508) and the Palazzo Caprini (c.1510). ⨆ Constantino Baroni, *Bramante* (1944)

Branagh, Kenneth Charles 1960–
Northern Irish actor and director

He was born in Belfast and moved to England with his family when young. He studied at RADA and went straight to the West End, playing the communist public schoolboy, Judd, in *Another Country* (1981). In 1984 he joined the Royal Shakespeare Company, appearing in the title role of *Henry V*, as Laertes in *Hamlet*, and the King of Navarre in *Love's Labour's Lost*. In 1987 he co-founded and became co-director of the Renaissance Theatre Company, directing the company's productions of *Romeo and Juliet* (in which he also starred), and *Twelfth Night*. He starred in successful tours (1988, 1989), and his other appearances include the title roles in *Coriolanus* (1992) and *Hamlet* (1992) for the RSC. He has appeared in television drama, written two plays produced on the Edinburgh Fringe, and both appeared in and directed several films, including *Henry V* (1989), *Dead Again* (1991), *Peter's Friends* (1992), *Much Ado About Nothing* (1993), *Mary Shelley's Frankenstein* (1994) and *Hamlet* (1996). He published his autobiography, *Beginning*, in 1989. ⨆ Ian Shuttleworth, *Ken & Em: A Biography of Kenneth Branagh and Emma Thompson* (1994)

Brancusi, Constantin 1876–1957
Romanian sculptor

He was born in Hobiţa and moved to Tîrgu Jiu, near Pestisani, as a boy. After several different jobs, he won a scholarship to the Bucharest Academy, and went to Paris in 1904, where he refused to work with Auguste Rodin, saying no one could flourish under a 'big tree', and developed his highly individual style. Brancusi's *The Kiss* (1901–21, various versions) was the most abstract sculpture of the period, representing two block-like figures. His *Sleeping Muse* (1910, Pompidou Centre, Paris) shows Rodin's influence, but is the first of his many characteristic, highly-polished egg-shaped carvings. *The Prodigal Son* (1925) shows the influence of African sculpture. His aim was simplification, to identify the essence, which he saw as being objective, and he was therefore outside the subjective Expressionist schools of the day. Other works include several versions of *Mademoiselle Pogany* (1913–31), *Bird in Space* (1925) and *The Sea-Lions* (1943). On his death he bequeathed his Paris studio and its contents to the French nation, and it has been re-erected in front of the Pompidou Centre.

Brand, Dollar See Ibrahim, Abdullah

Brand, Hennig 17th century
German alchemist

He was born in Hamburg and was active in the second half of the century. He began his career as a military officer and subsequently practised as a physician. Around 1669 he discovered in urine a white waxy substance which glowed in the dark and which he named phosphorus ('light bearer'). He is the first scientist known to have discovered an element, the names of earlier discoverers being lost. He did not publicize his discovery, and phosphorus was discovered independently by Robert Boyle in 1680.

Brand, Sir Jan Hendrik 1823–88
South African statesman

Born in Capetown, he was President of the Orange Free State from 1864 until his death. He defeated the Basutos (1865–69), and favoured friendship with Great Britain.

Brand, Max, *pseudonym of* Frederick Schiller Faust 1892–1944
US novelist and short-story writer

Born in Seattle, he was orphaned at the age of 13, but after leading a nomadic lifestyle as an agricultural worker, he paid his own way through university. In 1918 he became a Western writer, contributing stories to around 24 pulp magazines using many pseudonyms. His first novel, *The Untamed*, appeared under the Brand name in 1919. Other novels include *Trailin'* (1919) and *Destry Rides Again* (1930). He spent more than a decade (1926–37) in a Florentine villa, and died in Italy, where he was serving as a war correspondent with the US 88th Infantry Division. ⨆ R Easton, *Max Brand: The Big Westerner* (1970)

Brandan, St See Brendan, St

Brandeis, Louis Dembitz 1856–1941
US judge

Born in Louisville, Kentucky, he was educated there and at Dresden and Harvard, and practised in Boston. He conducted many labour arbitrations, and was frequently involved in cases challenging the power of monopolies and cartels, and in cases concerning the constitutionality of maximum hours and minimum wages legislation. He formulated the economic doctrine of the New Freedom adopted by Woodrow Wilson for his 1912 presidential campaign. Appointed to the US Supreme Court in 1916, he favoured governmental intervention to control the economy where public interest required it, but was also a strong defender of the rights of private property. He was generally a supporter of Franklin D Roosevelt's New Deal legislation, and is remembered as a perceptive and thoughtful judge. Brandeis University at Waltham in Massachusetts is named after him.

Brando, Marlon 1924–
US film and stage actor

Born in Omaha, Nebraska, he trained in Method acting at the New York Actors Studio, which emphasized the principles of Stanislavsky. He made his New York debut in 1943 and appeared in several plays before achieving fame as the inarticulate and brutal Stanley Kowalski in Tennessee Williams's *A Streetcar Named Desire* on stage (1947) and on film (1951). His varied film parts include the original motorcycle rebel in *The Wild One* (1953), Mark Antony in *Julius Caesar* (1953), the singing gambler Sky Masterson in *Guys and Dolls* (1955), a Western outlaw in *One-Eyed Jacks*, which he also directed (1961), a convincingly English Fletcher Christian in *Mutiny on the Bounty* (1962) and the US widower in the controversial *Last Tango in Paris* (1972). He won an Academy Award for *On the Waterfront* (1954) but refused to accept a second for *The Godfather* (1972), in protest against the film industry's treatment of Native Americans. He has been a prominent campaigner for the Civil Rights movement. Following *Apocalypse Now* (1977) he grew reclusive, but ended an eight-year absence from the screen with the anti-apartheid drama *A Dry White Season* (1989). Other recent films include *The Freshman* (1990), *Don Juan De Marco* (1995) and *The Island of Dr Moreau* (1996). He has published an autobiography: *Songs My Mother Taught Me* (1994). ⨆ David Shipman, *Brando* (1974)

Brandon, Charles, 1st Duke of Suffolk 1484–1545
English soldier and courtier

The son of **Henry VII**'s standard-bearer who was killed at Bosworth (1485), he served as squire to **Henry VIII**, and was created Duke of Suffolk (1514). The next year he secretly married the King's sister Mary, widow of Louis XII of France, and so was the grandfather of Lady **Jane Grey**. He commanded the unsuccessful invasion of France (1523) and captured Boulogne (1544).

Brandt, Bill (William) 1904–83
British photographer

Born in Germany, he studied with **Man Ray** in Paris in 1929, and went to London in 1931. During the 1930s he made a series of striking social records, contrasting the lives of the rich and the poor, and during World War II he worked for the Ministry of Information recording conditions in London during the Blitz. Although he later produced some lyrical and dramatic landscapes, his greatest creative work was his treatment of the nude, in which his essays on pure form, as published in *Perspective of Nudes* (1961) and *Shadows of Light* (1966), approached the Surreal. He was still working shortly before his death. His collections include *The English At Home* (1936) and *A Night in London* (1938).

Brandt, Georg 1694–1768
Swedish chemist

Born in Riddarhyttan, he studied medicine and chemistry at Leyden under **Hermann Boerhaave** and received his MD at Rheims in 1726. The following year he was made director of the chemical laboratory at the Bureau of Mines, Stockholm, and in 1730 he became Assay Master of the Swedish Mint. Around 1730 he discovered cobalt. He systematically investigated arsenic and its compounds, publishing the results in 1733, and he discovered the difference between potash and soda. He was also one of the first chemists to decry alchemy and to expose its fraudulent practices.

Brandt, Willy, *originally* Karl Herbert Frahm 1913–92
German statesman and Nobel Prize winner

Born in Lübeck and educated there, he joined the Social Democrats at 17 and, as a fervent anti-Nazi, fled in 1933 to Norway, where he changed his name, took Norwegian citizenship, attended Oslo University, and worked as a journalist. On the occupation of Norway in 1940, he went to Sweden, continuing as a journalist in support of the German and Norwegian resistance movements. In 1945 he returned to Germany, in 1948 regained German citizenship and from 1949 to 1957 was a member of the Bundestag, being president of the Bundesrat (1955–57). Notably a pro-West, anti-Communist leader, he became Mayor of West Berlin (1957–66), achieving international renown during the Berlin Wall crisis (1961). He was Chairman of the Sozialdemokratische Partei Deutschlands (SPD) in 1964, playing a key role in the party's remoulding as a more moderate and popular force. In 1966 he led the SPD into a 'Grand Coalition' government with the Christian Democrats under **Kurt Kiesinger**'s chancellorship and, as Foreign Minister, instituted the new policy of *Ostpolitik* (reconciliation between eastern and western Europe). This policy was continued when Brandt was elected Chancellor in 1969, culminating in the signing of the Basic Treaty with East Germany in September 1972. Brandt was awarded the Nobel Peace Prize in 1971, but was forced to resign the chancellorship in April 1974, following the discovery that his close aide, Gunther Guillaume, had been an East German spy. He continued to serve, however, as SPD chairman until 1987, and headed an influential international commission (the Brandt Commission) on economic development between 1977 and 1983. The commission's main report, entitled *North-South: A Programme for Survival*

(1980), advocated urgent action by the rich north to improve conditions in the poorer southern hemisphere. ⌨ Alma and Edward Homze, *Willy Brandt: A Biography* (1974)

Brangwyn, Sir Frank William 1867–1956
British artist

Born in Bruges, of Welsh parentage, he was apprenticed to **William Morris** (1882–84), then went to sea and travelled widely. He was an official war artist in World War I. Although he excelled in many media, particularly etching, he was most famous for his vigorously-coloured murals, such as the *British Empire Panels* (1925). Intended for the House of Lords, these were rejected and are now in the Swansea Guildhall. In 1936 a Brangwyn Museum was opened in Bruges.

Branly, Edouard 1844–1940
French physicist

Born in Amiens, he was awarded degrees in mathematics and natural sciences, a doctorate from the Sorbonne, and a medical degree from the Catholic University, both in Paris. He investigated electric waves, the effects of ultraviolet light waves and the electrical conductivity of gases. He invented the coherer for the reception of wireless telegraphic (radio) waves in 1890, thereby establishing the principles later developed by **Guglielmo Marconi**, and evolved the forerunner of receiving antennae.

Branner, H(ans) C(hristian) 1903–66
Danish novelist, short-story writer and playwright

He was born in Ordrup. A former actor and publisher, he wrote a number of psychologically realistic novels, beginning with *Legetøj* (1936, 'Toys'), which expressed his fears about fascism. Later works bear the mark of French Existentialism: *Drømmen om en kvinde* (1949, 'A Woman's Dream'), and the later *Ingen kender Natten* (1955, 'Nobody Knows the Night'), which returns to the Nazi occupation for its material. His ability to capture the inner life was also evident in the Joycean short stories of *To Minutters Stilhed* (1944, 'Two Minutes of Silence'), and his remarkable plays for radio. ⌨ T L Markey, *Hans Christian Branner* (1973)

Brannigan, Owen 1908–73
English bass baritone

Born in Annitsford, Northumberland, he studied at the Guildhall School of Music in London. His gifts as an actor signalled for him a career in opera. He regularly sang at Sadler's Wells between 1943 and 1958, and had a distinguished career in oratorio. **Benjamin Britten**'s operas found in him an ideal interpreter and he sang the principal roles in premières of *Peter Grimes, Rape of Lucretia, Noye's Fludde* and *A Midsummer Night's Dream*. Brannigan also enjoyed light opera—he recorded almost all of the **Gilbert** and **Sullivan** operettas—and he often included North Country folksongs in his recitals.

Branson, Richard See panel p260

Brant, Joseph, *Mohawk name* Thayendanegea 1742–1807
Mohawk chief

The brother-in-law of the Irish fur trader, Sir **William Johnson**, he learned English and converted to Anglicanism. He served the British in the French and Indian War (1754–63), and during the rising led by the Hawa chief **Pontiac** (1763–66). In the American Revolution (1775–83), he commanded the Mohawks on the British side, fought in the Cherry Valley Massacre, New York (1778) and ravaged Mohawk Valley (now in New York State). After the Revolution he was assigned land in Canada by the British, and in 1785 went to England to persuade the British government to indemnify the Indians for their losses in the war. He translated St Mark's Gospel and

Branson, Richard Charles Nicholas 1950–
English entrepreneur and businessman

Richard Branson was born in London, the son of Ted Branson, a lawyer, and Eve Branson, a former ballet teacher who seems to have encouraged her son's tendency to seek unorthodox challenges. He was educated at Stowe School, but left at the age of 16 to devote himself to his first enterprise, a magazine called *Student*. This was at first successful (the first issue is said to have sold 50,000 copies), but in the end proved unprofitable and was discontinued. In 1969 Branson began the Virgin mail-order business; two years later he opened the first branch of his record chain; and in 1973 he founded the Virgin record label. The success of these ventures, combined with some shrewd commercial judgements (he signed a contract with **The Sex Pistols** in 1977), soon gained him a reputation in youth culture as the acceptable face of capitalism.

He founded Virgin Atlantic Airlines in 1984, and, with his business continuing to grow, floated the company in 1986 (and bought it back two years later). He later took legal action against British Airways for an alleged 'dirty tricks' campaign' designed to put him out of business. The High Court eventually ruled in his favour, and he was awarded damages of around $1 million. When Virgin Music was sold for £560 million to Thorn EMI in 1992, Branson was able to put more capital into the airline, and the same year he made plans to start a luxury train service between London and Edinburgh, although these had to be

shelved pending the privatization of British Rail. His activities diversified still further in 1993 when, with TV-am, he launched Virgin FM, the UK's second independent national radio station. In 1995 Virgin bought the MGM UK chain of 116 high-street cinemas, with the intention of developing them in new ways.

Branson now runs the second-largest private company in Britain. The motto of all this acitivity has been 'organic expansion' into areas where there is a perceived need. A grinning, outwardly informal and ebullient man, he has proved himself to be an astute self-publicist. In 1986 he won the Blue Riband title for the fastest sea-crossing of the Atlantic. The following year, he became, with Per Lindstrand, the first to cross the Atlantic in a hot air balloon, and he repeated the feat across the Pacific in 1991. His attempt to circumnavigate the world in 1997 was unsuccessful.

📖 Rupert Saunders and Anthony Smith, *Virgin Global Challenger the Last Great Adventure* (1997); Tim Jackson, *Virgin King: Inside Richard Branson's Business Empire* (1994).

> 'I chose *Virgin* because it reflected an inexperience in business ... and also a freshness and slight outrageousness.' Branson commenting on the name, in an interview published in the *New York Times* (28 February 1993).

---

the Prayer Book into Mohawk, and founded the first Episcopal church in Upper Canada. A statue of him was unveiled at Brantford, Ontario (1886). 📖 Harvey Chalmers and Ethel B Monture, *Joseph Brant: Mohawk* (1955)

Brant, Sebastian 1458–1521
German poet and humanist

Born in Strasbourg, he studied and lectured at Basle. His *Narrenschiff* (1494, 'Ship of Fools'), a popular vernacular satire on the follies and vices of his times, is not very poetical, but is full of sound sense and moral teaching. In 1509 it was translated into English by both **Alexander Barclay** and Henry Watson. His other writings include biographies of the Saints and translations from Latin texts. 📖 E H Teydal, *Sebastian Brant* (1967)

Branting, Karl Hjalmar 1860–1925
Swedish politician and Nobel Prize winner

Born in Stockholm, he was co-founder of the Social Democratic Party of Sweden in 1889 and was its first parliamentary representative in 1896. He became chairman of the party in 1907 and helped to lead it away from revolutionary Marxism towards a more moderate 're-visionist' programme. He was Prime Minister in 1920, and again from 1921 to 23 and 1924 to 25. In 1921 he shared the Nobel Peace Prize for his work in international diplomacy, and was Sweden's first representative at the League of Nations (1922–25).

Brantôme, Pierre de Bourdeilles, Seigneur de c.1540–1614
French soldier and writer

Born in Périgord, he was educated at Paris and Poitiers, and at 16 was given the abbacy of Brantôme, from which he took his name, but he never took orders, and spent most of his life as a courtier and soldier. In 1561 he accompanied **Mary, Queen of Scots** to Scotland, and in 1565 he joined the expedition sent to Malta to assist the Knights of St John against the sultan. He also served in Italy, Africa and Hungary, and was made chamberlain to **Charles IX** and **Henri III**, and fought against the Huguenots. About 1594 he was injured after a fall from a

horse and retired to write his memoirs. His works, first published posthumously in 1665–66, comprise *Vies des grands capitaines* ('Lives of the Great Captains'), *Vies des dames galantes* ('Lives of the Courtesans') and *Vies des dames illustres* ('Lives of the Illustrious Ladies'). They provide a vivid, often scandalous, picture of the Valois court, and their literary merit and historical interest are considerable. 📖 R D Cottrell, *Brantôme: the writer as portraitist of his age* (1970)

Braque, Georges 1882–1963
French painter

Born in Argenteuil, the son of a house painter, he spent his boyhood in Le Havre. In Paris (from 1900), he studied at the École des Beaux-Arts, and became one of the founders of classical Cubism, working with **Picasso** from 1908 to 1914. After World War I (in which he was wounded) he developed a personal, non-geometric, semi-abstract style. In 1924 and 1925 he designed scenes for two **Diaghilev** ballets, *Les Fâcheux* and *Zéphyr et Flore*. His paintings are mainly of still life, the subject being transformed into a two-dimensional pattern. They are among the outstanding decorative achievements of the 20th century and have had a pervasive influence on other painters. He was made a Commander of the Legion of Honour in 1951. 📖 Raymond Cogniac, *Georges Braque* (1980)

Brasch, Charles Orwell 1909–73
New Zealand poet, critic and editor

Born in Dunedin, he established *Landfall*, a periodical of art, literature and politics, in 1947, and was its editor for 20 years, exercising great influence on the form and direction of contemporary New Zealand poets. In 1962 he edited a selection of verse, *Landfall Country: Work from Landfall, 1947–1961*. His own verse includes *The Land and the People* (1939), *Disputed Ground: Poems 1939–1945* (1948), *Not Far Off* (1969) and the posthumous *Home Ground* (1974, edited by Alan Roddick). His *Collected Poems* were published posthumously in 1984. 📖 *Indirections: A Memoir 1909–1947* (1980), ed J Bertram

Brassaï, *properly* **Gyula Halasz** 1899–1984
French painter and photographer
Born in Brasso, Hungary, and trained as an artist, he went
to Paris in 1923 and worked as a journalist. From 1930 he
made candid photographic records of the underworld
and nightlife of 1930s Paris. His first collection, *Paris de
Nuit* (1933, 'Paris at Night'), caused a sensation. He refused to photograph during the German occupation but
worked in **Picasso**'s studio. His photographic work after
the war retained its Parisian ethos. He became a French
citizen in 1948.

Brassey, Thomas 1805–70
English engineer
Born in Buerton, Cheshire, he was articled to a land
surveyor, and in 1834 obtained contracts for a viaduct
through **George Stephenson**. In 1836 he settled in
London as a railway contractor. His operations soon extended to all parts of the world and for his contract of the
Great Northern Railway (1847–51) he employed between
5,000 and 6,000 men.

Bratby, John Randall 1928–92
English artist and writer
Born in Wimbledon, London, he was a leading protagonist of the English New Realist school, with a reputation
for being the enfant terrible of the artistic establishment.
In the 1950s he was associated with the 'kitchen sink'
school because of his preoccupation with working-class
domestic interiors and he is considered to be a precursor
of Pop Art. He was a prolific painter with a bold, colourful and vigorous style which often had distinctive
white overdrawing. He represented Great Britain at the
Venice Biennale in 1956, and many of his works are in
public collections. He wrote several novels, including the
autobiographical *Breakdown* (1960), with his own illustrations. Notable paintings are *Baby in Pram* (Liverpool),
Still Life with Chip-Frier (1956), the mural *The Feeding of the
Five Thousand* (1963) and the paintings he did for the 1958
film of **Joyce Cary**'s novel *The Horse's Mouth*.

Brathwaite, Edward Kamau, *originally* **Lawson
Edward Brathwaite** 1930–
West Indian poet and historian
Born in Bridgetown, Barbados, he made his reputation
with the three long poems reprinted together in 1973 as
The Arrivants: A New World Trilogy. Each one of *Rights of
Passage* (1967), *Masks* (1968) and *Islands* (1969) analyses a
different aspect of West Indian blacks' dispossession and
their attempts to reconstitute an African-cum-Caribbean
culture. His historical researches, for works such as *The
Folk Culture of the Slaves of Jamaica* (1970), have comple-
mented his creative output, which has continued with
Mother Poem (1977) and *Sun Poem* (1982), both celebrations
of his native island. 📖 L Brown, 'The Cyclical Vision of
Brathwaite' in *West Indian Poetry* (1978)

Brattain, Walter Houser 1902–87
US physicist and Nobel Prize winner
Born in Amoy, China, of US parents, he grew up on a
cattle ranch in Washington, and was educated at the
University of Oregon and at Minnesota. He then joined
Bell Telephone Laboratories where he worked as a research physicist until his retirement in 1967, working on
the surface properties of semiconductors. With **John
Bardeen** and **William Shockley** he developed the point-
contact transistor, using a thin germanium crystal. Soon,
the junction transistor devised by Shockley, in the form of
the silicon microchip, took the dominant place it has held
in electronics ever since. He shared the Nobel Prize for
physics with Bardeen and Shockley in 1956.

Brauchitsch, Walther von 1881–1948
German field marshal
Born in Berlin, he was commissioned into the 3rd Guards
Regiment of Foot in 1900. After studying at the War
Academy he was promoted captain and served on the
General Staff during World War I. Between 1939 and 1941
he was Commander-in-Chief of the Germany army, a
period of spectacular triumphs, but was dismissed by
Hitler following the failure of the attack on Moscow.
Suffering from ill health, he was allowed to retire and
played no further part in the German war effort. After the
war he gave perjured evidence at the Nuremburg War
Crimes trials but died before his own case was brought to
court. 📖 Corelli Barnett (ed), *Hitler's Generals* (1989)

Braudel, Fernand 1902–85
French historian
Born in Lorraine, he studied at the Sorbonne, and taught
in Algerian schools (1923–32), in Paris (1932–35) and at
São Paulo University, Brazil (1935–38). He wrote, from
memory, his great work *La Mediteranée et le monde mediter-
ranéen à l'époque de Philippe II* (published 1949, Eng trans *The
Mediterranean and the Mediterranean World in the Age of Phillip
II*, 1972–73) in a German prison camp in Lübeck
throughout World War II, after which it won a doctorate.
He became professor at the Collège de France (1949–72),
was editor of the professional journal *Annales d'histoire
économique et sociale*, wrote the first volume of *Civilisation
matérielle et capitalisme* (1967, Eng trans *Civilization and
Capitalism*) as well as its *Afterthoughts*, and a study of Italian
achievements outside Italy, following the ideas of **Marc
Bloch**. His final work, *The Identity of France*, continued his
ideas on the study of environment and human behaviour
and his utilization of geography and sociology.

Brauer, Adriaen See **Brouwer, Adriaen**

Braun, Emma Lucy 1889–1971
US botanist
Born in Cincinnati, Ohio, she graduated in geology from
the University of Cincinnati and gained a PhD in botany.
She remained in academic positions at the university,
becoming Professor of Plant Ecology in 1946, until taking early retirement in 1948. Her ecological work focused
on detailed case studies of the vegetation in a variety of
habitats in Ohio and Kentucky, and her analyses of regional variations over a period of time became very important. She contributed to the growing conservation
movement, stressing the importance of preserving natural habitats, and became the first woman to be elected
president of the Ecological Society of America.

Braun, Eva 1912–45
German mistress of Adolf Hitler
Born in Munich, she was secretary to **Hitler**'s staff photographer, became Hitler's mistress in the 1930s and is said
to have married him before they committed suicide together in the air-raid shelter of the Chancellery during the
fall of Berlin. 📖 Glenn B Infield, *Eva and Adolf* (1974)

Braun, (Karl) Ferdinand 1850–1918
German physicist and Nobel Prize winner
Born in Fulda, Hessen, he studied at the universities of
Marburg and Berlin, held posts at the universities of
Würzburg, Leipzig, Marburg, Karlsruhe, Tübingen and
Strasbourg and then returned to Tübingen as Professor of
Physics and director of the Physical Institute which he
had founded. Although his main contributions were in
pure science, he is best known for the first cathode-ray
(the 'Braun tube') oscilloscope introduced in 1897, providing a basic component of the television. In 1909 he
shared with **Gugliemo Marconi** the Nobel Prize for physics for his practical contribution to wireless telegraphy.

Braun, Lili, *née* **von Kretschmann** 1865–1916
German socialist author and feminist

Born in Halberstadt, she married the socialist writer and politician Heinrich Braun (1854–1927) in 1895 and became a member of the Social Democrat Party in 1896. Her best-known book is *Im Schatten der Titanen* (1908, 'In the Shadow of the Titans'), and she is known for her novel *Liebesbriefe der Marquise* (1912, 'Love Letters of the Marquis'), and her *Memoiren einer Sozialistin* (1909–11, 'Memoirs of a Woman Socialist').

Braun, Wernher von 1912–77
US rocket pioneer

Born in Wirsitz, Germany, he studied engineering at the universities of Berlin and Zurich and founded in 1930 a society for space travel which maintained a rocket-launching site near Berlin. The German army authorities became interested in rockets, and by 1936, with Hitler's backing, von Braun was director of the German rocket research station at Peenemünde, on the Baltic coast, where he perfected and launched the famous V-2 rockets against Great Britain in September 1944. At the end of the war he surrendered, with his entire development team, to the USA. He became a US citizen in 1955, was director of the US army's Ballistic Missile Agency at Huntsville, Alabama, and was chiefly responsible for the manufacture and successful launching of the first US artificial earth satellite, *Explorer I*, in 1958. He was also director of the Marshal Space Flight Center (1960–70), where he developed the Saturn rocket for the *Apollo 8* moon landing (1969). His books include *Conquest of the Moon* (1953) and *Space Frontier* (1967).

Braxfield, Robert MacQueen, Lord 1722–99
Scottish judge

Born near Lanark, he was admitted advocate in 1744, and became highly respected, particularly in the field of feudal law. He was appointed Lord of Session as Lord Braxfield (1776) and Lord Justice Clerk of Scotland in 1788. As a judge, he was noted for his harshness towards political prisoners. He was the judge at the trial of Deacon Brodie. Hard-headed, hard-hearted and hard-drinking, he was the model for Lord Weir of R L Stevenson's unfinished novel, *Weir of Hermiston* (1896).

Bray, Thomas 1656–1730
English clergyman and philanthropist

Born in Marton, Shropshire, he was educated at All Souls' College, and became rector of Sheldon in 1690. He established a system of parochial libraries in England, and also in Maryland, where he was sent as commissary from 1699 to 1706. Out of his library scheme grew the Society for Promoting Christian Knowledge (SPCK). He published *Catechetical Lectures* and other works.

Brazil, Angela 1868–1947
English children's writer

Born in Preston, Lancashire, she was a governess for some years before beginning to write. She never married, and lived with her brother and sister, describing her adult self as 'an absolute schoolgirl'. She wrote a series of stories of school life, all heavily moralistic, and notable for their healthy realism. Among the best of them are *The New Girl at St Chad's*, *A Fourth Form Friendship* and *Captain Peggie*.

Brazza, Pierre Savorgnan de 1852–1905
French explorer

Born in Rio de Janeiro, Brazil, of Italian extraction, he joined the French navy in 1870, served in Gabon, West Africa, where he explored the Ogowe River (1876–78). He became a French citizen in 1874, and in 1878 the French government gave him 100,000 francs for exploring the country north of the Congo, where he secured vast grants of land for France, and founded stations, including that of Brazzaville on the north shore of Stanley Pool.

Bréal, Michel 1832–1915
French comparative philologist and mythologist

Born in Rhenish Bavaria, in 1858 he settled in Paris, and in 1866 became Professor of Comparative Grammar at the Collège de France. He founded the science of semantics with his *Essai de Sémantique* (1897. 'Essay on Semantics'), an exposition of principles for the study of the meaning of words.

Bream, Julian Alexander 1933–
English guitarist and lutenist

Born in London, he made his debut there in 1950. A protégé of Andrés Segovia, he has edited much music for guitar and lute, and has an international reputation. He formed the Julian Bream Consort in 1961. Many works have been specially written for him, by Benjamin Britten, Hans Werner Henze, Michael Tippett, William Walton and others. ⊞ Tony Palmer, *Julian Bream: A Life on the Road* (1982)

Breasted, James Henry 1865–1935
US archaeologist and historian, the founder of US Egyptology

Born in Rockford, Illinois, he studied at Yale and Berlin before joining the faculty at Chicago in 1894. His five-volume *Ancient Records of Egypt* (1906) transcribed every hieroglyphic inscription then known, and he then led expeditions to Egypt and Nubia (1905–07) to copy inscriptions that were perishing or had hitherto been inaccessible. With funding from John D Rockefeller, he set up his own Oriental Institute at Chicago University (1919), to promote research on ancient Egypt and western Asia, establishing a field station, Chicago House, at Luxor five years later. Under his directorship, the Institute undertook notable excavations in the 1920s and 1930s in northern Palestine, at Khorsabad and Tell Asmar in Iraq, and (from 1931) at Persepolis, the Achaemenid capital of Iran. His other books include *Ancient Times* (1916) and *The Dawn of Conscience* (1933).

Brecht, Bertolt See panel p263

Breckinridge, John 1760–1806
American politician

Born near Staunton, Virginia, he became a member of Congress in 1792 and, as Attorney-General of Kentucky (1795–97), was largely responsible for the state's reformed penal code. He was a staunch supporter of Thomas Jefferson, who made him Attorney-General of the USA in 1805.

Breckinridge, John Cabell 1821–75
US politician

Born near Lexington, Kentucky, he practised law there until 1847, when he was appointed major of a volunteer regiment for the Mexican War. He sat in Congress from 1851 to 1855, and in 1856 was elected Vice-President, with James Buchanan as President. In 1860 he was the pro-slavery candidate for the presidency, but was defeated by Abraham Lincoln. A senator from March to December 1861, he was appointed a Confederate major-general in 1862, was Secretary of War in Jefferson Davis's Cabinet, and escaped to Europe, returning in 1868.

Brehm, Alfred Edmund 1829–84
German naturalist

Born in Renthendorf, he travelled in Africa, Spain, Norway, Lapland, Siberia, and Turkestan, and became keeper of the Hamburg Zoological Garden in 1863. He was the founder and director of the Berlin Aquarium in 1867. His greatest work is the *IllustriertesThierleben* on which many other natural histories are largely based.

Bremer, Fredrika 1801–65
Swedish novelist

Brecht, (Eugen) Bertolt Friedrich 1898–1956
German playwright and poet

Bertolt Brecht, who is considered by many to be Germany's greatest dramatist, was born in Augsburg. He studied medicine and philosophy at Munich and Berlin universities, and served briefly as a medical orderly in 1918.

He won the Kleist drama prize in 1922 for his first two Expressionist plays, *Trommeln in der Nacht* (1918, Eng trans *Drums in the Night*, 1966) and *Baal* (1918, Eng trans 1964); these were followed by *Mann ist Mann* (1926, Eng trans *A Man's a Man*, 1964) with its clownish, inhuman soldiery.

He was keenly interested in the effects produced by combining drama and music, and consequently collaborated with **Kurt Weill**, **Hanns Eisler** and **Paul Dessau** in his major works. His reputation was established by the *Dreigroschenoper* (1928, Eng trans *The Threepenny Opera*, 1958), an adaptation of **John Gay**'s *Beggar's Opera* in a sham Victorian London setting, with music by Weill.

A Marxist, Brecht regarded his plays as social experiments, requiring critical detachment, not emotional involvement, from the observing audience. He began to experiment with Verfremdungseffekt ('alienation effects') and introduced 'epic' theatre, requiring the audience to see the stage as a stage, actors as actors, and not to adhere to the traditional make-believe of the theatre. Thus, to prevent the audience from identifying themselves with a principal actor, the camp-following title character in *Mutter Courage und ihre Kinder* (1941, Eng trans *Mother Courage and her Children*, 1961) is deliberately made to muff her lines, and *Puntilla* (1940) is given an increasingly ugly make-up.

With Hitler's rise to power in 1933, Brecht sought asylum in Denmark, Sweden and Finland, journeyed across Russia and Persia (Iran), and in 1941 settled in Hollywood.

His abiding hatred of Nazi Germany found expression in a series of short, episodic plays and poems collected under the title of *Furcht und Elend des dritten Reiches* (1945, 'Fear and Loathing under the Third Reich'), and in *Der aufhaltsame Aufstieg des Arturo Ui* (1957, Eng trans *The Resistible Rise of Arturo Ui*, 1976).

He denied membership of the Communist Party before a Senate sub-committee on un-American activities in 1946, and in 1948 accepted the East German government's offer of a theatre in East Berlin. The *Berliner Ensemble* was founded, producing under his direction his later plays, such as *Der gute Mensch von Sezuan* (1943, Eng trans *The Good Person of Setzuan*, 1948) and *Der kaukasische Kreidekreis* (1947, Eng trans *The Caucasian Chalk Circle*, 1948). The company toured in western Europe, and visited London shortly after Brecht's death, with Helene Weigel, his widow, as the leading actress.

Although he was apparently unsympathetic towards the East German anti-Communist uprising in 1953 and was a recipient of the Stalin Peace Prize (1954), Brecht proved as artist and thinker to be an embarrassment to the East German authorities. His opera *Lukullus* (1932–51), in which the Roman general has to account for his deeds before a tribunal-of-the-shadows, was withdrawn by order after the first night. *Galileo* (1938) underlined the moral that, however much the intellect may be oppressed, truth will out.

📖 M Esslin, *Bertolt Brecht* (1969); K Volker, *Bertolt Brecht: A Biography* (1979).

'One observes, they have gone too long without a war here. Where is morality to come from in such a case, I ask? Peace is nothing but slovenliness, only war creates order.'
From *Mutter Courage*, sc.1 (1930)

She was born near Åbo in Finland, and brought up near Stockholm. Her *Teckningar utur hvardagslifvet* (1828, 'Scenes from Everyday Life') were successful stories which helped introduce realistic family fiction into Swedish literature. *Familjen H* (1831, 'The H Family'), and *Hemmet* (1839, 'The Home') considerably developed the genre. Novels like *Hertha* (1856) and *Fader och dotter* (1858, 'Father and Daughter') reflect her interest in female education and political emancipation, acquired during her visits to Great Britain and the USA. She travelled widely elsewhere in Europe and the Levant and published two volumes of impressions. 📖 E Ehrnach, *Fredrika Bremer* (1955)

Brenan, Gerald, originally Edward Fitz-Gerald Brenan 1894–1987
English travel writer, Hispanophile and novelist

He was born in Malta, the son of an officer in an Irish regiment, and after an itinerant boyhood he set off with a donkey, travelling across Europe to the Balkans and back again. He then went to Spain and settled in Yegen, the isolated village which became the focus of his classic *South from Granada* (1957). This was preceded by his best-known book, *The Spanish Labyrinth* (1943), still regarded as one of the most profound and perceptive studies of modern Spain. Other books include two volumes of memoirs, *A Life of One's Own* (1962) and *Personal Record* (1974), *The Literature of the Spanish People* (1951) and a novel, *Thoughts in a Dry Season* (1978).

Brendan or Brandan, St 484–577
Irish abbot and traveller

Born in Tralee, now in County Kerry, he is traditionally the founder of the monastery of Clonfert in County Galway (561), and other monasteries in Ireland and Scotland. The *Navigation of St Brendan* (c.1050) recounts his legendary voyage to a land of saints far to the west and north, possibly the Hebrides and the Northern Isles, or even Iceland. In old maps 'St Brendan's country' is placed west of the Cape Verde Islands. His feast day is 16 May.

Brendel, Alfred 1931–
Austrian pianist

Born in Wiesenberg, Moravia, he made his debut in Graz (1948), and is a distinguished interpreter of **Mozart**, **Beethoven**, **Schubert**, **Liszt** and **Schoenberg**. He tours internationally, giving master-classes and making frequent television appearances, and has written many perceptive essays on music.

Brennan, Christopher John 1870–1932
Australian poet, academic and critic

Born in Sydney of a Catholic family, he was intended for the priesthood, but studied the classics and philosophy at Sydney University. Going to Berlin University in 1892 to read philosophy, he was distracted by French Symbolist poetry, which influenced his future writing. He returned to Sydney University (1894), and was appointed Associate Professor of German Literature in 1920, but his intemperate and iconoclastic nature led to his dismissal five years later. He published a few volumes of verse, notably *Poems 1913* (1914); compositions such as 'The Wanderer' voiced the torment of Brennan's own life. A later collection was *A Chant of Doom and Other Verses* (1918), and some of his poetry was published posthumously. His criticism appeared mainly in journals, but he is also known for his co-editing of the standard college anthology *From Blake to Arnold* (1900), which contains much of his critical work. 📖 J P McAuley, *Christopher Brennan* (1973)

Brennan, William J(oseph), Jnr 1906–97
US jurist
Born in Newark, New Jersey, he was educated at the University of Pennsylvania and Harvard, and after practising law he rose in the New Jersey court system to the state supreme court. Named to the US Supreme Court in 1956, he took an active role in the liberal decisions handed down under Chief Justice Earl Warren. He retired from the Court in 1990 and was awarded the US Medal of Freedom in 1992.

Brenner, Sydney 1927–
British molecular biologist
He was born in Germiston, South Africa, and educated at Witwatersrand University and Oxford. He joined the staff of the Medical Research Council (MRC) in 1957, served as director of the MRC Molecular Biology Laboratory in Cambridge (1979–86), then became director of the MRC Molecular Genetics Unit there (1986–92). With Francis Crick, Brenner worked to unravel the genetic code, working out the nucleotide codes for the 20 amino acids in 1961. He went on to research the embryology of the nematode worm, with the objective of relating the anatomy of an animal to the genetic basis of its structure. Since 1992 Brenner has been a member of the Scripps Research Center at La Jolla, California. He was elected FRS in 1965.

Brentano, Clemens von 1778–1842
German poet, novelist and dramatist
Born in Ehrenbreitstein, he led a somewhat irresponsible early life, before becoming a Roman Catholic in 1818 and withdrawing to the monastery of Dülmen, near Münster (1818–24), where he recorded the revelations of the nun, Anna Katharina Emmerich. In his earliest poems the peculiarities of the Romantic school are carried to excess. His writing for the stage, which includes the notable *Die Gründung Prags* (1815, Eng trans 'The Founding of Prague'), is characterized by great dramatic power, and a wonderful humour. He was mostly successful in his novellas, particularly in the *Geschichte vom braven Kasperl* (1817, Eng trans 'Tale of Honest Kasper'), and with his brother-in-law Achim von Arnim he edited *Des Knaben Wunderhorn* ('The Boy's Magic Horn'), a collection of folk songs. 📖 J B Heinreise, *Clemens von Brentano* (1878)

Brentano, Franz Clemens 1838–1917
German psychologist and philosopher
He was born in Marienberg, the nephew of Clemens von Brentano and brother of Lujo Brentano. He became a Catholic priest in 1864 and taught philosophy at Würzburg until 1873 when he abandoned the priesthood, rejecting papal infallibility, and moved to teach at Vienna until retirement in 1895. He spent his later years in Florence and Zurich. He stressed the connection between psychology and philosophy and in his most important work, *Psychologie vom empirischen Standpunkte* (1874, 'Psychology from an Empirical Standpoint'), developed the important doctrine of 'intentionality', characterizing mental events as involving the 'direction of the mind to an object'. Among his students were Edmund Husserl, Alexius von Meinong and Tomáš Masaryk.

Brentano, Heinrich von 1904–64
German statesman
Born in Offenbach, he became a successful lawyer and one of the founders of the Christian Democratic Party. He went into politics in Hesse in 1945 and was elected in 1949 to the Federal Diet at Bonn, where he played a prominent part in drafting the Constitution. He became Foreign Minister in 1955, aligning West Germany closely with the policies of the Atlantic Alliance, but resigned in 1961 to facilitate the formation of a coalition government of Dr Konrad Adenauer's parties with the Free Democrats.

Brentano, Lujo (Ludwig Josef) 1844–1931
German political economist and Nobel Prize winner
He was born in Aschaffenburg, Bavaria, the brother of Franz Brentano. In 1868 he went to England to study the condition of the working classes, and especially trade associations and unions. The outcome of this was his *English Guilds* (1870) and *Die Arbeitergilden der Gegenwart* (2 vols, 1871–72, 'Workers' Guilds of the Present'). He became Professor of Economics in five universities and wrote on wages, labour in relation to land, compulsory insurance for workmen, and an *Economic History of England* (1929). A prominent pacifist, he was awarded the Nobel Peace Prize in 1927. He was the nephew of Clemens von Brentano.

Brent-Dyer, Elinor M(ary) 1894–1969
English children's writer
Born in South Shields, Tyne and Wear, she was educated at Leeds University, and then became headmistress of the Margaret Roper Girls' School in Hereford. The first of her 98 schoolgirl novels, *Gerry Goes to School*, appeared in 1922. Her fourth book, *The School at the Chalet* (1925), established her famous 'Chalet School' series, set in an English school in the Austrian Tyrol. Centred on Jo Bettany, the series sought to evangelize against English parochialism and xenophobia. Perhaps the best single title was *The Chalet School in Exile* (1940), a judicious account of the school's flight from Nazi rule with a grim depiction of persecution of Jews. The final book in the series, *Prefects of the Chalet School*, was published posthumously in 1970.

Brent of Bin See Franklin, (Stella Marian Sarah) Miles

Brenton, Howard 1942–
English dramatist
Born in Portsmouth, he wrote for fringe theatre companies during the late 1960s, and was resident dramatist at the Royal Court Theatre, London, from 1972 to 1973, where his play *Magnificence*, dealing with urban terrorism, was staged. *The Churchill Play* (1974) takes a bleak look at a future Great Britain governed by hardliners using troops to brutalize trade unionists. It was followed by *Weapons of Happiness* (1976, the first new play to be produced at the National Theatre's South Bank building), *The Romans in Britain* (premiered 1980), and *The Genius*, on the nuclear arms race (premiered 1983). He has also collaborated with David Hare on a number of projects, the most outstanding being *Pravda* (1985), a furiously ebullient satire on the craveness of the national press. He has also written a political thriller, *Diving for Pearls* (1989) and translations of the work of Brecht, Goethe and Büchner. In 1995 he published a volume of diaries and essays, *Hot Irons*.

Brenz, Johann 1499–1570
German Lutheran reformer
Born in Weil, Swabia, he studied at Heidelberg University, and was ordained in 1520. He was co-author of the Württemberg Confession of Faith, and his Catechism (1551) stands next to Martin Luther's in Protestant Germany.

Breshko-Breshkovskaya, Yekaterina Konstantinovna 1844–1934
Russian revolutionary
She was the daughter of a Polish landowner and a Russian aristocrat, and associated with various liberal and revolutionary groups in the more open society of St Petersburg under Alexander II. In the 1870s she worked with the Narodniki revolutionaries (Russian populists who pinned their hopes for political and social change on

the peasantry, whom they tried to stir into action) and was arrested and sent to Siberia (1874–96). In 1901 she helped to found the Socialist Revolutionaries but in 1908 she was again exiled to Siberia, from which she was able to return only in 1917. Colourful and independent-minded, though dubbed the 'Grandmother of the Revolution', she fell out with the Bolsheviks after their victory in October 1917, and died in Prague a firm anti-communist.

Bresson, Robert 1907–
French film director
Born in Bromont-Lamothe, he pursued a career as a painter before turning to the cinema. He made his directorial debut with *Les Affaires publiques* (1934, 'Public Affairs'). A prisoner of war in Germany, he subsequently directed *Les Anges du péché* (1943, *Angels of the Streets*) and *Les Dames du Bois de Boulogne* (1946, *Ladies of the Park*). His distinctive style emerged during the 1950s, when his use of non-professional actors, natural sound and restrained emotions created austere narratives dealing with redemption and salvation that were dominated by a strong Catholic sensibility. His notable films include *Journal d' un Curé de Campagne* (1950, *Diary of a Country Priest*) and *Pickpocket* (1959). Later, equally rigorous films explored the concept of saintliness, the attraction of suicide and humankind's innate sense of greed. These include *Au hasard Balthazar* (1966, *Balthazar*), *Une Femme douce* (1969, 'A Gentle Woman') and *L'Argent* (1983, 'Money').

Breton, André 1896–1966
French poet, essayist and critic, founder and theorist of the Surrealist movement
Born in Tinchebray, Normandy, he joined the Dadaist group in 1916 and was co-founder of the Dada magazine *Littérature* (1919). In 1930 he joined the Communist Party for a time, and spent the war years in the USA. He collaborated with Philippe Soupault to write *Les Champs magnétiques* (1920, 'Magnetic Fields'), one of the first experiments in automatic writing. In 1922 he turned to Surrealism, and in 1924 he published *Manifeste du surréalisme – Poisson soluble* ('Solublefish'), and became editor of *La Révolution surréaliste* (1924–30). He later wrote two further Surrealist manifestos (1930), and *Qu'est-ce que le surréalisme?* (1934, Eng trans *What is Surrealism?* 1936). His major novel was *Nadja* (1928, Eng trans 1960), which mingles the irrational and the everyday. 📖 M A Caws, *André Breton* (1971)

Breton, Nicholas c.1555–c.1626
English poet
Born in London, the son of a merchant, and stepson of George Gascoigne, he was educated at Oxford and became a prolific writer of all kinds of verse, prose and pamphlets. His best-known poem is *The Passionate Shepheard* (1604). His prose work *Wits Trenchmour* (1597) is a fishing idyll on which Izaak Walton drew for *The Compleat Angler*. He also wrote a prose romance, *The Strange Fortune of Two Excellent Princes* (1600), and a collection of character observations, *Fantasticks* (1626). 📖 G A Tannenbaum, *Elizabethan Bibliographies* (1937)

Bretón de los Herreros, Manuel 1796–1873
Spanish dramatist
Born in Quel, he was educated in Madrid, then served in the army from 1812 to 1822. He is the author of some 150 plays, most of which are social comedies concerned with middle-class manners and mores, in which caricature rather than character is portrayed. His first play, *A la vejez, viruelas* (1824, 'In Old Age, Chickenpox') gained him immediate popularity. Many of his works were translations and adaptations. He also wrote poetry, and was a prominent figure in his day. 📖 G le Gentil, *La poète Manuel Bretón de los Herreros* (1903)

Bretonneau, Pierre(-Fidèle) 1778–1862
French physician
Born in Tours, he studied in Paris and became chief physician in Tours hospital in 1816. He was the first to perform a tracheotomy as well as the first to name diphtheria and describe typhoid fever.

Brett, Jeremy, *originally* Jeremy Huggins 1933–95
English actor
Born in Berkswell, Warwickshire, he won acclaim for his classical performances with the Old Vic in the 1950s and appeared on Broadway as the Duke of Aumerle in *Richard II* (1956). On television, he played D'Artagnan in *The Three Musketeers* (1966–67), Maxim de Winter in *Rebecca* (1979) and poet Robert Browning in *The Barretts of Wimpole Street* (1982), before his definitive portrayal of Sir Arthur Conan Doyle's Victorian sleuth in *The Adventures of Sherlock Holmes* (1984–85), *The Return of Sherlock Holmes* (1986–88), *The Casebook of Sherlock Holmes* (1991) and *The Memoirs of Sherlock Holmes* (1994), as well as several specials. He once acted Dr Watson, to Charlton Heston's Holmes, in a Los Angeles stage production entitled *The Crucifer of Blood* (1981). His films include *War and Peace* (1956) and *My Fair Lady* (1964).

Breuer, Marcel Lajos 1902–81
US architect and designer
Born in Pécs, Hungary, he was a student at the Bauhaus in Germany from 1920, and by 1924 had taken charge of the furniture workshop. He designed probably the first modern tubular steel chair, the 'Wassily' (1925), and the well-known 'Cesca' cantilevered chair (1928). In England from 1935 to 1937, he was in partnership with the architect F R S Yorke, during which time he designed the laminated wood 'Isokon' long chair for Jack Pritchard (1936). In 1937 he joined Walter Gropius in the USA as Associate Professor of Architecture at Harvard University (1937–46) and in architectural practice. Working independently after 1947, he designed the majority of his architectural projects, including the UNESCO building in Paris (with Bernard Zehrfuss and Pier Luigi Nervi in 1958) and the Whitney Museum in New York City (1966). He was a significant figure in the Modern movement, and his classic furniture designs, in particular, represented major developments in materials and techniques.

Breughel See Brueghel

Breuil, Henri Édouard Prosper 1877–1961
French archaeologist
Born in Mortain, he trained as a priest, became interested in cave art in 1900, and was responsible the following year for the discovery of the famous decorated caves at Combarelles and Font-de-Gaume in the Dordogne. Noted for his studies of artistic technique and the detailed copying of hundreds of paintings in Europe, Africa, and elsewhere, he later became professor at the Collège de France (1929–47). His work marked the beginning of the study of Palaeolithic art, as shown by his *Quatre cents siècles de l'art pariétal* (1952, 'Four Hundred Centuries of Cave Art'). 📖 Alan Brodick, *Father of Prehistory* (1963)

Brewer, Ebenezer Cobham 1810–97
English clergyman
Born in London, he took a first-class degree in law at Trinity Hall, Cambridge in 1835, one year after receiving orders. He then became a London schoolmaster. His most enduring work is his *Dictionary of Phrase and Fable* (1870), still a standard work of reference.

Brewster, Sir David 1781–1868
Scottish physicist
Born in Jedburgh, Roxburghshire, and educated for the Church, he became editor of the *Edinburgh Magazine* (later the *Edinburgh Philosophical Journal*) in 1802, and of the *Edinburgh Encyclopaedia* in 1808. He was interested in the

study of optics, and in 1815 he observed that measurement of the angle at which reflected light is polarized enables the calculation of the refractive index of a glass surface (Brewster's law). In the same year he showed that stress on transparent materials can alter the way in which they transmit light. In 1816 he invented the kaleidoscope, and later improved Sir Charles Wheatstone's stereoscope by fitting refracting lenses. In 1818 he was awarded the Rumford gold and silver medals for his discoveries on the polarization of light. He was one of the chief originators of the British Association for the Advancement of Science (1831), and was knighted in 1832. He was appointed Principal of St Salvator and St Leonard's at St Andrews University (1838) and was later Principal of Edinburgh University from 1859. 📖 Roy Campbell, *Sir David Brewster (1781–1868)* (1982)

Brezhnev, Leonid Ilyich 1906–82
Soviet statesman

Born in Kamenskoye (then called Dneprodzerzhinsk), Ukraine, the son of a steelworker, he joined the Komsomol (Communist Youth League) in 1923 and, having trained as an agricultural surveyor, worked on the collectivization programmes in Belorussia and the Urals region during the 1920s. He was accepted into the Communist Party (CPSU) in 1931, studied at the Dneprodzerzhinsk Metallurgical Institute until 1935, and in 1938 was appointed party propaganda chief at Dnepropetrovsk where he impressed the new Ukrainian party chief, Nikita Khrushchev, with his organizational skills. Between 1941 and 1945 he served as a political commissar to the Southern Army and after the war was sent to Moldavia as party chief (1950–52) to 'sovietize' the newly-ceded republic. The CPSU leader, Joseph Stalin, inducted Brezhnev into the secretariat and the politburo, as a 'candidate' member (1952). Brezhnev was removed from these posts following Stalin's death in 1953, but, with Khrushchev's patronage, returned to favour in 1954, being sent to Kazakhstan to oversee implementation of the new 'virgin lands' agricultural programme. From 1956–57, he returned to the politburo and secretariat, was removed in 1960, but returned and was elected the new CPSU General Secretary in 1964, when Khrushchev was ousted. He emerged as an international statesman during the early 1970s and in May 1977 gained the additional title of State President, becoming the first person to hold simultaneously the position of General Secretary and President of the Supreme Soviet. During the later 1970s, however, as his health deteriorated, policy-making became paralysed and economic difficulties mounted. The Brezhnev era saw the Soviet Union establish itself as a military and political superpower, extending its influence in Africa and Asia. At home, however, it was a period of caution and, during the 1970s, of economic stagnation, which was criticized by the Gorbachev administration.

Březina, Otakar, *properly* Václav Jebavý 1868–1929
Czech poet

Born in Pocatky, he was a leading exponent of Symbolism in Czech poetry in his collections *Polar Winds* (1897), *Temple Builders* (1899), *The Hands* (1901) and others.

Brian c.926–1014
King of Ireland

The 'Brian Boroimhe' or 'Boru' ('Brian of the tribute') of the annalists, he became chief of Dál Cais in 976, and after much fighting he made himself King of Leinster (984). After further campaigns in all parts of the country, his rule was acknowledged over the whole of Ireland (1002). He was killed after defeating the Vikings at Clontarf.

Brian, (William) Havergal 1876–1972
English composer and writer on music

Born in Dresden, Staffordshire, and championed by such figures as Thomas Beecham, Henry Wood, Donald Tovey and Granville Bantock, his success seemed secure, but after 1918, his work was largely neglected. The great scale of certain works, his unfashionable style of expansive post-Romanticism, the sheer number of his works, and an immoderate private life all contributed to this. A revival of interest in his music occurred in the last decade or so of his life. He wrote 32 symphonies (including No. 1, 'The Gothic', 1919–27, and No. 32, 1968), a monumental setting of Shelley's *Prometheus Unbound*, a violin concerto and five operas (including *The Tigers*, 1916–19, and *Faust*, 1955–56). His musical criticism (1904–49) was distinguished by his broad outlook.

Briand, Aristide 1862–1932
French Socialist statesman and Nobel Prize winner

Born in Nantes, he began his political career on the extreme left, advocating a revolutionary general strike, but soon moved to the centre as a 'republican socialist', refusing to join the United Socialist Party (SFIO, Section Française de l'Internationale Ouvrière), which did not allow its members to participate in 'bourgeois' governments. He held ministerial office almost continuously from 1906, being a Cabinet Minister 25 times, and Prime Minister 11 times. Apart from his periods as Prime Minister (1909–11, 1913, 1915–17, 1921–22, 1925–26, 1929), his most important offices were as Minister of Public Instruction and Minister of Religion (1906–08), during which he implemented the Separation of Church and State (voted 1905), and as Foreign Minister (1925–32), when he became known as the 'apostle of peace'. With Jean Jaurès he founded the socialist paper *L'Humanité* (1904). He was a fervent advocate of the League of Nations, and of Franco-German reconciliation. He shared the 1926 Nobel Peace Prize with Gustav Stresemann, concluded the Kellogg–Briand Pact which proscribed war as a means of solving disputes (1928), and launched the idea of a United States of Europe (1929). 📖 Valentine Thompson, *Briand, Man of Peace* (1930)

Brice, Fanny, *originally* Fanny Borach 1891–1951
US singer and actress

Born in New York, she sang as a child in her parents' saloon, then won a singing contest at 13. She toured in the comedy *College Girls*, and was signed by Florenz Ziegfeld for the *Follies of 1910*, where her vivacious style made her a star. She performed in many other shows and revues, and was adept at both comic and torch songs. She married a well-known gangster, Nicky Arnstein, and her life story provided the basis of the hit musical *Funny Girl* (1964).

Brickhill, Paul Chester Jerome 1916–91
Australian writer

Born in Melbourne, and educated at Sydney University, he worked in journalism before serving with the Royal Australian Air Force during World War II. Shot down in North Africa, he was for two years a prisoner-of-war in Germany, in Stalag Luft III from which the intrepid escape was made, later described by him in *The Great Escape* (1951, filmed 1963). His first published book, *Escape to Danger* (1946), collected many stories of prison-camp life. He went on to become one of the most successful nonfiction writers of the postwar period, with *The Dam Busters* (1951, filmed 1956), *Escape—or Die* (1952), and the story of the amputee air ace Douglas Bader, *Reach for the Sky* (1954, filmed 1956).

Bridge, Frank 1879–1941
English composer and conductor

Born in Brighton, Sussex, he studied under Sir **Charles Stanford**, as **Benjamin Britten** was later to study under him. He played the viola in leading quartets and conducted the New Symphony Orchestra from its inception at Covent Garden (1905) and often at the London Promenade Concerts. He is best known for his string quartets, but his full orchestral works were less successful, except perhaps his 'Sea' suite.

Bridger, James, *usually known as* Jim 1804–81
US frontiersman and scout

Born in Richmond, Virginia, he was apprenticed to a blacksmith but abandoned the trade to become a fur trapper in the frontier wilderness of the 1820s. A famous mountain man and the first white man to see the Great Salt Lake (1824), he operated the Rocky Mountain Fur Co until the fur trade began to decline in the 1830s. Using Fort Bridger on the Oregon Trail as his home base, he later served as scout and guide for exploring and surveying expeditions.

Bridges, Harry, *in full* Alfred Bryant Renton Bridges 1901–90
US labour leader

Born in Melbourne, Australia, he shipped out as a merchant seaman and arrived in the USA in 1920, eventually settling in San Francisco as a longshoreman. A political radical and union activist, he organized the International Longshoremen's and Warehousemen's Union (1937), and served as its president until 1977. The US government tried many times to deport him as a communist, and after he became a US citizen (1945), he was found guilty of denying membership of the Communist Party but appealed his conviction and was cleared by the US Supreme Court.

Bridges, Jeff 1949–
US actor

Born in Los Angeles, the son of actor Lloyd Bridges (1913–98), he made his film debut as an infant in *The Company She Keeps* (1950) and his adult film debut in *Halls of Anger* (1970). He received Academy Award nominations for *The Last Picture Show* (1971), *Thunderbolt and Lightfoot* (1974) and *Starman* (1984) and has proved himself as a versatile actor, mixing populist mainstream fare with more offbeat character roles. His many films include *Jagged Edge* (1985), *The Fabulous Baker Boys* (1989), in which he co-starred with his brother Beau (1941–), *The Fisher King* (1991) and *The Mirror Has Two Faces* (1996).

Bridges, Robert Seymour 1844–1930
English poet and critic

Born in Walmer, Kent, he was educated at Eton and Corpus Christi College, Oxford, then studied medicine at St Bartholomew's Hospital and practised until 1881. At university he met **Gerard Manley Hopkins** and arranged for the posthumous publication of his poems in 1918. Bridges's first collection, *Poems*, appeared in 1873, and was followed by *The Growth of Love* (1876), a sequence of sonnets. He then wrote two long poems, *Prometheus the Firegiver* (1883) and *Eros and Psyche* (1885), but for the next decade he concentrated on eight plays, only one of which was performed in his lifetime. He contributed to criticism with studies of **Milton** (1893) and **Keats** (1895) and wrote poems set to music by **Hubert Parry**, as well as *A Practical Discourse on Hymn Singing* (1901). In 1912 he published his *Collected Poems* and in 1913 was appointed Poet Laureate, and produced *The Spirit of Man* (1916). After World War I, he published *October and Other Poems* (1920) and the long poem *The Testament of Beauty* (1929). 📖 L P Smith, *Robert Bridges: recollections* (1931)

Bridget, St, *also called* St Brigid *or* St Bride
c.453–523
Irish abbess

Born (according to tradition) in Fochart, County Louth, she is said to be the daughter of a peasant woman and an Ulster prince. She entered a convent at Meath at 13, and founded four monasteries for women, the chief at Kildare (c.470), where she was buried. Her legendary history includes many miracles, some of which were apparently transferred to her from the Celtic goddess, Ceridwen. One of the three great saints of Ireland (with **St Patrick** and **St Columba**), she is patron saint of Leinster and was also revered in Scotland (as St Bride). Her feast day is 1 February.

Bridget, St See also Birgitta, St

Bridgman, Laura Dewey 1829–89
US teacher, devoid of sight, hearing and speech

Born in Hanover, New Hampshire, at the age of two a violent fever destroyed her sight, hearing, smell, and in some degree taste. **Dr Samuel Howe** educated her systematically using a kind of raised alphabet at his Perkins School for the Blind, and she became a skilful teacher of others with the same disabilities. She is referred to in **Charles Dickens**'s *American Notes* (1842).

Bridgman, P(ercy) W(illiams) 1882–1961
US physicist and Nobel Prize winner

Born in Cambridge, Massachusetts, he went to Harvard in 1900 and remained there, becoming Hollis Professor of Mathematics and Natural Philosophy (1926), Higgins Professor (1950) and, on his retirement, professor emeritus (1954–61). Soon after completing his PhD in 1908 he initiated experiments on the properties of solids and liquids under high pressure, research for which he was awarded the Nobel Prize for physics in 1946. Studying the physical properties of liquids and solids under extreme conditions, he obtained a new form of phosphorus and demonstrated that at high pressures, viscosity increases with pressure for most liquids. He became deeply concerned with the foundations of his subject and developed the 'operationalist' approach, with which he hoped to influence the scientific and social thinking of the time. In 1961 he became increasingly debilitated and incurably ill with cancer, and took his own life.

Bridie, James, *pseudonym of* Osborne Henry Mavor 1888–1951
Scottish dramatist

Born in Glasgow, the son of an engineer, he qualified as a doctor at Glasgow University and became a successful general practitioner and consultant. Always interested in theatre, he seized his chance when the Scottish National Players produced his *Sunlight Sonata* in 1928 under the pseudonym of Mary Henderson. After that, he wrote a stream of plays, among them *The Anatomist* (1931), *A Sleeping Clergyman* (1933), *Mr Bolfry* (1943) and *Dr Angelus* (1947). He served in both world wars in the Royal Army Medical Corps and after the second became head of the Scottish Committee of The Council for the Encouragement of Music and the Arts. He founded the Citizens' Theatre in Glasgow in 1943. 📖 H Luyben, *James Bridie: clown and philosopher* (1965)

Bridport, 1st Viscount See Hood, Alexander

Brierley, Sir Ron(ald Alfred) 1937–
New Zealand entrepreneur

Born in Wellington and educated at Wellington College, he founded what was to become Brierley Investments Limited in 1961 (chairman to 1989; founder-president 1989–) and moved his operations to Sydney in the early 1970s. He sold his Industrial Equities conglomerate just before the 1987 crash and later became chairman of the UK-based Guinness Peat Group (1990–). He is also president of the New Zealand Cricket Foundation and on the Board of Trustees of Sydney Cricket Ground Trust. He was knighted in 1988.

Brieux, Eugène 1858–1932
French dramatist

Born in Paris, of poor parents, he experienced many of the social evils which his witty, didactic plays expose. His works include *L'Engrenage* (1894, Eng trans *The Evasion*, 1896) and *Maternité* (1903, Eng trans *Maternity*, 1907). His attack on the judiciary in *La Robe Rouge* (1900, 'The Red Robe'), and his use of the effects of syphilis in *Les Avariés* (1901, Eng trans *Damaged Goods*, 1914), both aroused public controversies. ⌨ W H Scheifley, *Brieux and Contemporary French Society* (1917)

Briggs, Barry 1934–
New Zealand speedway rider

Born in Christchurch, he appeared in a record 17 consecutive world championship finals (1954–70), during which he scored a record 201 points and took part in 87 races, winning the title in 1957–58, 1964, and 1966. He won the British League Riders' championship six times (1965–70). His career started with Wimbledon (1952), and he also rode for New Cross, Southampton, Swindon, and Hull. After retiring in 1976, he ran a motorcycle business in Southampton, and was a co-promoter of the 1982 world championships in Los Angeles.

Briggs, Henry 1561–1630
English mathematician

Born in Warley Wood, Halifax, he graduated from St John's College, Cambridge, and became a Fellow in 1588. In 1596 he became the first Professor of Geometry at Gresham College, London, and in 1619 first Savilian Professor of Geometry at Oxford. He visited John Napier in 1616 and 1617 and, with Napier's agreement, proposed the use of the base 10 for logarithms. This was an important simplification for the practical use of logarithms in calculation. He calculated and published logarithmic and trigonometric tables to 14 decimal places.

Briggs, Raymond Redvers 1934–
English children's illustrator and writer

He was born in London, and went on to study at art college, before becoming a successful children's illustrator. His early publications, such as *Midnight Adventure* (1961), were conventional, but his *Mother Goose Treasury* (1966) with over 900 illustrations, established his reputation for eccentric comedy, and won him the Kate Greenaway Medal. He was awarded a second Greenaway Medal for *Father Christmas* (1973), which uses the comic-strip format, and features a grumpy, expletory Santa, who reluctantly braves the wintry elements. *Fungus the Bogeyman* (1977) brought Briggs love and loathing, and *The Snowman* (1979) enchanted adults and children alike. A provocative as well as an entertaining artist, he expressed his anxiety for the future well-being of the planet in *When the Wind Blows* (1982), and attacked the political manipulation of the Falklands War in *The Tin Pot Foreign General and the Old Iron Woman* (1983). In 1992 he was awarded the Kurt Maschler award for *The Man* and in 1994 he published *The Bear*.

Brighouse, Harold 1882–1958
English playwright

He was born near Manchester, one of the first 20th-century English authors to write plays that were both popular and set beyond the metropolitan and country-house world of the fashionable and wealthy. Between 1909 and his death he completed over 70 plays, many of them amiably folksy one-act comedies set in Lancashire. Some of the full-length plays, such as *Lonesome-Like* (1911) and *The Odd Man Out* (1912), are overlooked, and his

reputation depends on only one play, *Hobson's Choice* (1915). It was highly popular at the time, and is frequently revived.

Bright, John 1811–89
English orator and radical politician

Born in Rochdale, Lancashire, he was the son of a Quaker cotton-spinner. When the Anti-Corn Law League was formed in 1839 he was a leading member, and, with Richard Cobden, engaged in free-trade agitation. He became MP for Durham (1843) and strongly opposed the Corn Laws until they were repealed. He was elected MP for Manchester in 1847. Like Cobden, he was a member of the Peace Society and energetically denounced the Crimean War (1854). Elected in 1857 for Birmingham, he seconded the motion against the Conspiracy Bill that led to the overthrow of Lord Palmerston's government. His name was closely associated with the Reform Act of 1867. In 1868 he accepted office as President of the Board of Trade but retired through illness in 1870, returning in 1881 as Chancellor of the Duchy of Lancaster. He retired from the Gladstone ministry in 1882, opposing his Home Rule policy (1886–88). ⌨ G M Trevelyan, *John Bright* (2nd edn, 1925)

Bright, Richard 1789–1858
English physician

Born in Bristol, he studied medicine in Edinburgh, London, Berlin and Vienna. His *Travels from Vienna through Lower Hungary* (1818) recorded interesting observations on gypsies and diplomacy in Vienna at the close of the Napoleonic period. From 1820 he was on the staff at Guy's Hospital, London, where he made many careful clinical and pathological observations. (Bright's disease of the kidneys is named after him.) He also left important observations on diseases of the nervous system, lungs and abdomen, and was much sought after as a consultant physician, becoming physician extraordinary to Queen Victoria. ⌨ Pamela Bright, *Dr Richard Bright (1789–1858)* (1983)

Bright, Timothy c.1551–1615
English inventor, doctor and clergyman

Born in Yorkshire, he abandoned medicine for the church, and in 1588 was granted a teaching patent for a system of shorthand he had invented.

Brigid, St See Bridget, St

Bril, Mattys or Mattheus II 1550–84
Flemish landscape painter

Born in Antwerp, he painted frescoes in the Vatican. He was the brother of Paul Bril.

Bril, Paul 1556–1626
Flemish painter

Born in Antwerp, he worked in Rome, and raised the prestige of landscape painting by his frescoes. He was the brother of Mattys Bril.

Brillat-Savarin, (Jean) Anthelme 1755–1826
French lawyer, gastronome and writer

Born in Belley, he was became a deputy there in 1789, and mayor in 1793. During the French Revolution he took refuge in Switzerland, and afterwards in the USA, where he played in the orchestra of a New York theatre. From 1796 until his death he was a member of the Court of Cassation, the French high court. His *Physiologie du goût* (1825, 'The Physiology of Taste'), an elegant and witty compendium on the art of dining, has appeared in numerous editions and translations, including *A Handbook of Gastronomy*, with 52 etchings by Lalauze (1884). ⌨ Giles MacDonogh, *Brillat-Savarin: The Judge and His Stomach* (1992)

Brindley, James 1716–72
English engineer and canal builder

Born in Thornsett, Derbyshire, he was apprenticed to a millwright. He became an engineer, and in 1752 contrived a water engine for draining a coalmine. A silk mill and several others of his works brought him to the notice of Francis Egerton, 3rd Duke of Bridgewater, who employed him (1759) to execute the canal between Worsley and Manchester, a difficult enterprise completed in 1772. He also commenced the Grand Trunk Canal, and completed the Birmingham, Chesterfield, and other canals, in all constructing 365 miles (584km) of canals. He was illiterate all his life. ⌨ Cyril T G Boucher, *James Brindley, Engineer 1716–1772* (1968)

Brinell, Johann August 1849–1925
Swedish engineer and metallurgist

Born in Brungetofta, he started working at the Lesjöfers Ironworks in 1875 and was chief engineer at the Fagersta Ironworks from 1882. He invented the Brinell machine for measuring the hardness of alloys and metals.

Brink, André 1935–
South African writer, critic and translator

He was born in Vrede, Orange Free State, was educated in both South Africa and France, and became Professor of Afrikaans and Dutch Literature at Rhodes University, Grahamstown (1980–90), before going on to become Professor of English at the University of Cape Town. An Afrikaner dissident, he emerged as a writer in the 1950s but it was not until his seventh novel, *Kennis van die aand* (1973)—which he later translated into English as *Looking on Darkness* (1974)—was banned by the South African authorities that he began to attract international attention. Relating the story of a coloured actor who makes good in London and returns to South Africa to confront the apartheid regime, it won the author admiration, though more for his courage than his style. Subsequent books have been criticized for their sentimentality and sensationalism but the best, such as *Rumours of Rain* (1978), *A Chain of Voices* (1982) and *States of Emergency* (1988), are powerful narratives which highlighted conditions in South Africa without resorting to propaganda. He received the Martin Luther King Memorial prize and the French Prix Medicis Étranger in 1980, has thrice won the CNA Award, South Africa's most prestigious commendation, and has twice been runner-up for the Booker Prize. ⌨ *Pot Pourri: Skatse uit parys* (1962)

Brinkley, David McClure 1920–
US news commentator

Born in Wilmington, North Carolina, he began his career as a reporter for his hometown newspaper. In 1943 he became a news writer and television broadcaster for NBC in Washington. From 1951 to 1981 he was the network's Washington correspondent, and from 1956 to 1970 he co-anchored a popular NBC nightly news programme, the *Huntley-Brinkley Report*, with Chet Huntley (1911–74). Since 1981 he has hosted *ABC This Week*, a weekly news programme. He is the recipient of numerous journalism awards, including the Presidential Medal of Freedom (1992).

Brinster, Ralph Lawrence 1932–
US molecular biologist

Born in Montclair, New Jersey, he was educated at Rutgers University and at the University of Pennsylvania. Since 1960 he has taught at the School of Veterinary Medicine at the University of Pennsylvania, where he became Rich King Mellon Professor of Reproductive Physiology. With Richard Palmiter, he was the first to successfully inject the human growth hormone gene into a mouse embryo and replace the embryo into the mother's uterus. These mice proved to be significantly larger than their normal counterparts, indicating that the human growth hormone gene had been active. This technique is now a vital tool in the investigation of regulatory mechanisms controlling gene expression, and it is hoped that the technique can be extended to replace faulty genes in human genetic diseases such as cystic fibrosis.

Brisbane, Sir Thomas Makdougall 1773–1860
Scottish general and astronomer

Born in Largs, Ayrshire, he joined the army at the age of 16, served in Flanders, the West Indies, Spain, and North America, and was promoted major-general in 1813. From 1821 to 1825 he was Governor of New South Wales. He improved the disorganized system of land grants, reformed the currency and improved the efficiency of several government projects. In 1822 he set up an observatory at Paramatta, near Sydney. He catalogued 7,385 stars in Australia, and received the Copley Medal from the Royal Society. Brisbane, the capital of Queensland, was named after him.

Briscoe, Arthur John Trevor 1873–1943
English etcher

Born in Birkenhead, Merseyside, he studied at the Slade School of Art in London, and later in Paris. He served in World War I and on his return from Paris he purchased a boat and explored the French and British coasts and Dutch canals. Almost his entire output of some 189 etchings are of seafaring subjects, executed over a period of 10 years.

Brisley, Stuart 1933–
English sculptor and performance artist

Born at Grayswood, near Haslemere, Surrey, he studied at Guildford School of Art and the Royal College of Art, then the universities of Munich and Florida. From 1963 he began constructing light mobiles but, under the influence of Joseph Beuys, he came to public notice with his ritualistic performances; in 1972 he lay in a bath while meat rotted on the floor—until after 10 days his fellow artists begged him to stop. In 1973 he performed *Ten Days* over the Christmas period in Berlin, refusing *haute cuisine* food and leaving it to rot, as a comment on over-consumption in the West. Other shows include *Survival in Alien Circumstances*, in which he dug a hole and lived in it for two weeks. In 1985 his sound installation on the subject of nuclear attack, *Normal Activities may be Resumed*, was held at the Institute of Contemporary Arts, London, and in 1986–87 his *Georgiana Collection*, which included sculpture, toured Glasgow, Londonderry, Belfast and the Serpentine Gallery, London. His 1996 exhibition *Black* at the South London Gallery focused upon the marital split of Charles and Diana, the Prince and Princess of Wales.

Brissot (de Warville), Jacques Pierre 1754–93
French revolutionary

Born near Chartres, he was a lawyer and journalist who wrote on criminal law (*Théorie des lois criminelles* (1780) and *Bibliothèque des lois criminelles* (1782–86)). After a brief imprisonment in the Bastille, he retired in 1787 to London, and the following year visited North America as representative of the *Société des amis des noirs*. In 1789 he was present at the storming of the Bastille, and was elected Representative for Paris in the National Assembly, where he influenced the early movements of the Revolution. He established *Le Patriote français*, which became the organ of the earliest Republicans, and became leader of the Girondins (or Brissotins). He contributed to the fall of the monarchy, but in the Convention his moderation made him suspect to Robespierre, and, with 20 other Girondins, he was guillotined.

Britannicus, in full Claudius Tiberius Britannicus Caesar AD 41–55
Emperor's son

He was the son of the Emperor **Claudius** and **Messalina**, and was surnamed in honour of his father's triumph in Britain (AD43). Claudius's fourth wife, **Agrippina, the Younger**, caused her husband to adopt her son **Nero**, and treat Britannicus as an imbecile. Nero, after his accession, had his step-brother poisoned, claiming he was subject to epileptic fits. He is the subject of a tragedy by **Racine**.

Brittain, Vera Mary 1893–1970
English writer, feminist and pacifist

She was born in Newcastle-under-Lyme, Staffordshire. After studying at Oxford she served as a nurse in World War I, recording her experiences in her best known book, *Testament of Youth* (1933, republished 1978). As well as writing a number of novels, she made several lecture tours in the USA, promoting feminism and pacifism. In 1925 she married George Catlin, Professor of Politics at Cornell, and wrote the sequels, *Testament of Friendship* (1940) and *Testament of Experience* (1957). Her daughter is the English politician **Shirley Williams**. ☐V Brittain and J S Reid (eds), *Selected Letters of Winifred Holtby and Vera Brittain* (1960)

Brittan, Sir Leon 1939–
English Conservative politician

Born in London and educated at Trinity College, Cambridge, and Harvard, he qualified as a barrister. He was chairman of the Conservative Bow Group (1964–65), editor of *Crossbow* magazine (1966–68), and elected as an MP in 1974. From 1979 he held ministerial posts under **Margaret Thatcher**, including Chief Secretary to the Treasury (1981–83), Home Secretary (1983–85) and Secretary for Trade and Industry (1985–86). He resigned from the Cabinet in 1986 after a conflict with **Michael Heseltine** (Secretary for Defence) over the takeover of Westland Helicopters. In 1989 he became vice-president of the European Commission with special responsibility for competition policy. He is also an MEP, and Chancellor of the University of Teeside (1993–).

Britten, Benjamin, Baron Britten of Aldeburgh See panel p271

Britten, Roy John 1919–
US molecular biologist

Born in Washington DC, he graduated from the University of Virginia in 1941 and studied further at the University of Princeton. He then joined the department of terrestrial magnetism at the Carnegie Institution of Washington (1951–71). From 1973 to 1981 he was senior research associate at the California Institute of Technology, and was appointed Distinguished Carnegie Senior Research Associate in Biology in 1981. He is a Fellow of the American Academy of Arts and Sciences, and a member of the US National Academy of Sciences. He studied with **Eric Davidson** the genomes of higher organisms, which they showed to contain DNA strands organized into unique, single-copy DNA sequences (coding for single genes), moderately repetitive DNA (coding for gene families), and highly repetitive sequences which are repeated hundreds of thousands of times in the genome. The role of this highly repetitive DNA remains unknown.

Britton, Alison 1948–
English potter

Born in Harrow, Middlesex, she was trained at Leeds School of Art, the Central School of Art and Design and the Royal College of Art. Her unique handbuilt, high-fired earthenware, often with hand-painted and inlaid patterns, broke new ground in an era when many of the traditional values of wheelmade pottery gave way to a more expressive generation of potters. Her work can be seen in public collections throughout the world and she

has also written many articles. She is a member of the Crafts Council and was awarded the OBE for services to pottery in 1990.

Britton, John 1771–1857
English topographer and antiquary

Born in Kingston St Michael, near Chippenham, at 16 he went to London, and was in turn cellarman, clerk, and compiler of a song book and a dramatic miscellany. He was employed with Edward Wedlake Brayley (1773–1854) to compile *The Beauties of Wiltshire*, its success leading to *The Beauties of England and Wales* (15 vols, 1803–14). He also compiled *Architectural Beauties of Great Britain* (1805–14), and *Cathedral Antiquities of England* (14 vols, 1814–35)

Britton, Nathaniel Lord 1859–1934
US botanist

Born in Staten Island, New York, he was originally a geologist, having trained at the School of Mines at Columbia College, but later became Professor of Botany at Columbia in 1891, where he reorganized the herbarium and library on taxonomic principles, and was the initiator and first director of the New York Botanical Garden (1896–1921). He published *Flora of Richmond County* in 1879, and wrote *Illustrated Flora of the Northern United States, Canada and the British Possessions* (1896–98), and *Flora of Bermuda* (1918). He was also co-author of the four-volume monographic work *The Cactaceae* (1919–23).

Brizeux, Julien Auguste Pélage 1803–58
French poet

He was born in Lorient. Much of his work, including a translation of **Dante's** *Divina Commedia*, was influenced by Italian styles, but his verse also incorporated the folklore and dialect of Brittany. ☐C Levigne, *Brizeux et ses œuvres* (1898)

Brizola, Leonel de Moura 1922–
Brazilian politician

He became a state deputy in 1947 on a **Vargas** ticket, and went on to become leader of the Partido Trabalhista Brasileiro (PTB, Brazilian Workers' Party) a decade later. As Governor of Rio Grande do Sul, his support for his brother-in-law, **João Goulart**, Getúlio Vargas's heir, enabled Goulart to assume office as President in 1961 and proved crucial once more in 1964 when, as Popular Deputy for Guanabara, he urged the left to take to the streets in defence of the President. Exiled in 1964, he advocated armed opposition to the new regime, and by the 1970s had become the standard-bearer of the exiled Social Democrats. Amnestied in 1979, he founded the Partido Democratico Trabalhista (Democratic Workers' Party). He became Governor of Rio de Janeiro in the first direct elections in 1982 and led the successful campaign in 1985 which ended the military government. Narrowly defeated by Lula in 1989 for the left-wing candidacy for the presidency, he was again elected Governor of Rio de Janeiro in 1990.

Broad, Charlie Dunbar 1887–1971
English philosopher

Born in London, he was educated at Dulwich College, London, and Trinity College, Cambridge. He was Professor of Moral Philosophy at Cambridge (1933–53). His work is characterized by thorough analysis and appraisal, as in *Scientific Thought* (1930) and the two-volume *Examination of McTaggart's Philosophy* (1933, 1938), which contains most of his own original thought. He also had a strong interest in parapsychology and served as president of the Society for Psychical Research.

Broadbent, Donald Eric 1926–93
English psychologist

Britten, (Edward) Benjamin, Baron Britten of Aldeburgh 1913–76
English composer

Benjamin Britten was born in Lowestoft. He studied the piano under Harold Samuel (1879–1937) and composition under **Frank Bridge**. Awarded a scholarship to the Royal College of Music, he worked there under **John Ireland**; he was already a prolific composer, and some of his student works have survived to stand beside more mature compositions: notable among these is the set of choral variations, *A Boy was Born* (1933). During the 1930s Britten wrote a great deal of incidental music for plays and documentary films, collaborating at times with **W H Auden**, whose poetry provided texts for the song cycles *Our Hunting Fathers* (1936) and *On This Island* (1937).

From 1939 to 1942 Britten worked in the USA, producing his large-scale instrumental works, the Violin Concerto (1939) and the *Sinfonia da Requiem* (1940). After his return to the UK, his works were mostly vocal and choral; significant exceptions are the Variations and Fugue on a Theme of Purcell (*The Young Person's Guide to the Orchestra*, 1946), the String Quartets No.1 (1941) and No.3 (1945), the Cello Symphony (1963), the Cello Sonata (1961) and three suites for solo cello (1964, 1967, 1972); the last group of these works was all for the cellist **Mstislav Rostropovich**.

After 1945, in addition to his choral and vocal works, notably the 'Spring' Symphony (1949), Britten's reputation was due largely to his achievement in opera. His first work, *Peter Grimes* (1945), was an immediate success, and is generally regarded as the first great English opera since **Henry Purcell**. Britten wrote two further operas on a large scale, *Billy Budd* (1951) and *Gloriana* (1953), the latter for the coronation of Queen **Elizabeth II**, and five 'chamber operas', including *The Turn of the Screw* (1954, based on the **Henry James** novella), which are on a smaller scale and employ a basic orchestra of 12 players.

Britten displays to great effect a special genius in writing with a simplicity that attracts amateur performers while retaining artistic and dramatic effectiveness; this quality is especially marked in the 'children's operas' *The Little Sweep*, incorporated in *Let's Make an Opera!* (1949), and *Noye's Fludde* (1958), which is a musical rendering of a 14th-century miracle play. His later operas include *A Midsummer Night's Dream* (1960), *Owen Wingrave* (1970) and *Death in Venice* (1973). In addition to his enormous activity as a composer, Britten was an accomplished pianist, usually heard as an accompanist, particularly with **Peter Pears**, with whom he and Eric Crozier founded in 1948 the annual Aldeburgh Festival. Several of his own works had their first performances there. He was awarded a life peerage in 1976.

In recent years, Britten's personal life and in particular his homosexuality have been more openly considered in the context of his musical achievement, where the role of the outsider in society is a crucial element (notably in the operas). In 1996, discussion of a possible memorial to Britten in Aldeburgh gave rise to some quite astonishingly disparaging remarks in the press about him, especially by **Malcolm Williamson**.

📖 There are good biographies of Britten by H Carpenter (1992) and M Kennedy, written from a mainly personal and a mainly musical viewpoint respectively. See also D Mitchell and P Reed, *Letters from a Life: Selected Letters and Diaries of Benjamin Britten* (2 vols, 1991); P Evans, *The Music of Benjamin Britten* (1989); A Blyth, *Remembering Britten* (1981); A Gishford (ed), *Tribute to Benjamin Britten on His Fiftieth Birthday* (1963).

> 'I remember the first time I tried the result looked rather like the Forth Bridge.' Of his first attempts at composition. Quoted in the *Sunday Telegraph* (1964).

Born in Birmingham and educated at Winchester College and (after three years in the RAF) at Cambridge, he joined the scientific staff of the Medical Research Council's Applied Psychology Research Unit in Cambridge after World War II (director, 1949–58). A major figure in postwar experimental psychology, he was the most influential British psychologist in the movement to import ideas from communication theory and cybernetics into cognitive psychology. His first book, *Perception and Communication* (1958), was a milestone in the development of this field, and his work at the Applied Psychology Unit did much to advance the reputation of experimental psychology as an applied science. From 1974 he was a member of the external staff of the Medical Research Council, based in Oxford. He was awarded the American Psychological Association's Distinguished Scientist award (1975).

Broadwood, John 1732–1812
Scottish piano manufacturer

Born in Cockburnspath, Berwickshire, he walked to London to become a cabinet maker, married the daughter of the Swiss-born harpsichord-maker, Burkhardt Tschudi, and in 1770 founded with him the great London pianoforte house. His grandson, Henry Fowler Broadwood (1811–93), was also a great improver of the piano.

Broca, (Pierre) Paul 1824–80
French surgeon and anthropologist

Born in Sainte-Foy-la-Grande, Gironde, he was educated at the University of Paris, where he received his MD in 1849, and became assistant professor at the faculty of medicine in 1853. He first located the motor speech centre in the brain (1861), since known as the convolution of Broca or Broca's gyrus, and did research on prehistoric surgical operations. His anthropological investigations gave strong support to **Charles Darwin**'s theory of the evolutionary descent of man. 📖 Francis Schiller, *Paul Broca, Founder of French Anthropology, Explorer of the Brain* (1979)

Broch, Hermann 1886–1951
Austrian novelist and essayist

Born in Vienna, he spent his early adult life working in his father's textile business and was over 40 when he went to Vienna University to study philosophy and mathematics. When the Nazis invaded Austria in 1938 he was imprisoned, but influential friends, including **James Joyce**, obtained his release and facilitated his emigration to the USA in 1940. His masterpiece is *Der Tod des Virgil* (1945, Eng trans *The Death of Virgil*,1946). Other notable books include *Die Schlafwandler* (3 vols, 1931–32, Eng trans *The Sleepwalkers*), *Die unbekannte Grösse* (1933, Eng trans *The Unknown Quantity*) and *Der Versucher* (Eng trans *The Spell*) published posthumously in 1953 and first translated into English in 1987. 📖 D C Cohn, *The Sleepwalkers: elucidations* (1966)

Brockhaus, Friedrich Arnold 1772–1823
German publisher

He was founder of the firm of Brockhaus in Leipzig and publisher of the famous *Konversations-Lexikon*, begun by R G Löbel in 1796 and completed in 1811. An improved edition, which he edited, was begun in 1812. The business was carried on by his descendants. The first illustrated edition of the *Lexikon* was published in 1892–97.

Brockhurst, Gerald Leslie 1891–1979
English artist and etcher
Born in Birmingham, he studied at the Birmingham School of Art, and at the age of 22 won the Royal Academy's Gold Medal and scholarship which took him to France and Italy. His etchings and lithographs are mainly concerned with the themes of young womanhood and portraiture. He was influenced by the early Italian Renaissance painters and his masterpiece, *Adolescence*, was exhibited at the Royal Academy, London, in 1933.

Brockway, (Archibald) Fenner Brockway, Baron 1888–1988
English politician, pacifist and a founder of the Campaign for Nuclear Disarmament
He was born in Calcutta, India, into a missionary family, and educated at the School for the Sons of Missionaries (now Eltham College) at Blackheath in England. As a young journalist he was converted to socialism by an interview with Keir Hardie. He joined the Independent Labour Party and became a militant pacifist, and was imprisoned during World War I. In the 1930s he claimed to have been the last socialist to speak publicly in Germany before Hitler came to power (1933). He was elected to parliament for the first time in 1929–31, and again in 1950–64. He was made a life peer in 1964, and wrote more than 20 books, including his autobiographical volumes *Inside the Left*, *Outside the Right*, *Towards Tomorrow* and (in 1986), *98 not out*. He died six months before his hundredth birthday.

Brod, Max 1884–1968
Austrian novelist, biographer, essayist, poet and dramatist
Born in Prague, he became a Zionist and emigrated to Palestine in 1939, where he became the literary director of the Habimah Theatre in Tel Aviv. Although he is known in the English-speaking world as the long-time friend, editor and biographer of Franz Kafka, he was a versatile and prolific writer in his own right, publishing, among others, *Die Frau, nach der man sich sehnt* (1927, Eng trans *Three Loves*) and *Zauberreich der Liebe* (1928, 'The Magic Realm of Love'). His work includes novels on religious and social themes, such as *Tycho Brahes Weg Zu Gott* (1916, Eng trans *The Redemption of Tycho Brahe*), plays, autobiographical writings, and literary criticism. 📖 M Pazi, *Max Brod, Werk und Persönlichkeit* (1970)

Brodie, Deacon See Brodie, William

Brodie, William, *known as* Deacon Brodie 1741–88
Scottish cabinetmaker and burglar
Born in Edinburgh, the son of a wealthy wright (carpenter) and cabinetmaker, he followed his father in business and also became a deacon on the town council. Though highly regarded in society, his private life, which included two mistresses and five children, and a predilection for gambling, put him under financial pressure. By 1785 he had squandered his inheritance and so turned to burgling the homes of his acquaintances. In 1786 he enlisted the help of three professional criminals. Together they carried out a number of thefts, including that of the silver mace from the University of Edinburgh. In 1788 the gang were unsuccessful in their attempt to break into the Excise Office of Scotland and Brodie fled to Holland. He was brought back to Edinburgh, stood trial and was hanged outside St Giles High Kirk, on a new gallows which he himself had designed.

Brodsky, Iosif Aleksandrovich 1940–96
US–Russian poet, translator and critic, and Nobel Prize winner
Born in Leningrad (now St Petersburg), he was tried as a 'social parasite' in 1964, and sent into exile. Although not known generally, he had poetry circulated in *samizdat* form, and various critics and poets interceded on his behalf. His cause was taken up in the USA, but in 1972 he was expelled from Russia. In 1977 he became a US citizen, and in 1987 he was awarded the Nobel Prize for literature. Some of his later work was written in English and he also translated his own Russian poems into English. A scholarly poet, he introduced English metaphysical influences into Russian poetry, as well as aspects of W B Yeats, T S Eliot, and W H Auden. His many collections include *Stikhotvoreniia i Poemy* (1965, 'Longer and Shorter Poems'), *Uraniia: Novaia Kniga Stikhov* (1985, 'Urania: A New Book of Poems', published in English as *To Urania: Selected Poems 1965–1985*, 1988) and *Pereschyonnaya mesnost* (1995, 'Broken Country'). His translations of John Donne and Andrew Marvell into Russian are particularly prized. English translations of his work are in *Selected Poems* (1973) and *Less Than One* (prose essays, 1980). He became US Poet Laureate in 1991 and in 1992 published *Watermark*, a prose work on Venice. 📖 *A Part of Speech* (1979)

Broecker, Wallace 1931–
US chemical oceanographer and climatologist
Born in Chicago, he was educated at Columbia University and has remained there throughout his career, becoming assistant professor in 1959, associate professor in 1961, and professor in 1964. Since 1977 he has been Newberry Professor of Geology. His work has been broad-ranging, involving measurements of chemical elements in the oceans, salinities, upwelling and radiocarbon dating. He has pioneered techniques to track chemical isotopes over vast distances and back thousands of years in time. He formulated simple 'box' models of the ocean system, both for the present and back to glacial times, which more recently (1991) have been used to provide an overview of an oceanic 'global conveyor' which may fluctuate with time, changing the Earth's climate.

Broederlam, Melchior fl.1381–1409
Dutch painter
Born in Ypres, he became court painter to Philip, the Bold, Duke of Burgundy, in 1387, and was in Paris in 1390. For the Chartreuse de Champmol, Philip's main religious foundation, he was commissioned in 1392 to paint a pair of shutters for an altarpiece. Now held in Dijon, these are his only known surviving works. They are among the earliest examples of the elegant, refined, richly decorative style known as International Gothic. He was also a goldsmith and stained-glass designer.

Brogan, Sir Denis William 1900–74
Scottish historian
Born in Rutherglen, Glasgow, of Irish descent, he was educated at Glasgow, Oxford and Harvard. He became a Fellow of Corpus Christi College, Oxford (1934) and Professor of Political Science at Cambridge (1939). He is known for his books on historical and modern USA, such as *The American Political System* (1933) and *Introduction to American Politics* (1954), as well as more general works, such as *The English People* (1943) and *The French Nation* (1957).

Broglie, Louis-Victor Pierre Raymond, 7th Duc de 1892–1987
French physicist and Nobel Prize winner
Born in Dieppe, he studied history, but service at the Eiffel Tower radio station during World War I initiated his interest in science, and he took a doctorate at the Sorbonne (1924). Influenced by Einstein's work on the photoelectric effect which he interpreted as showing that waves can behave as particles, Broglie put forward the converse idea—that particles can behave as waves. The

waves were detected experimentally by Clinton Davisson and Lester Germer in 1927, and separately by Sir George Thomson, and the idea of wave-particle duality was used by Erwin Schrödinger in his development of quantum mechanics. Broglie was awarded the ⁻Nobel Prize for physics in 1929.

Broke, Sir Philip Bowes Vere 1776–1841
English naval commander
Born in Broke Hall, Ipswich, he joined the navy in 1792, and was appointed to the frigate *Shannon* in 1806. In her he fought a duel with the US frigate *Chesapeake*, off Boston, on 1 June 1813, which made 'brave Broke'a hero in popular song. He captured the *Chesapeake*, but was wounded so severely that he retired from active service.

Brome, Richard c.1590–1652
English dramatist
Little is known of him except that a note in the Biographica Dramatica of 1764 records he had 'originally been no better than a menial servant to the celebrated Ben Jonson'. He picked up some literary tips from his employer, however, as scholars have detected Jonsonian influences in his plays. He was certainly writing in 1635, as he put his name to a contract signed on 20 July that year, to write plays for the Salisbury Court Theatre. Although the original document is lost (the information comes from a subsequent lawsuit), it is thought to be the earliest instance of an English dramatist signing a contract. Broome specialized in satirical comedies, and his works include *The Northern Lass* (1629), *The City Wit* (1630), about a man taking revenge on his mother-in-law and his wife's suitors, and *A Jovial Crew* (1641). 📖 R J Kaufman, *Richard Brome, Caroline playwright* (1961)

Bromfield, Louis 1896–1956
US novelist
Born in Mansfield, Ohio, he was educated at Cornell Agricultural College and Columbia University, then served in the French army (from 1914), winning the Croix de Guerre. He returned to the USA to work as a journalist, and subsequently published a number of novels on US life, including *Early Autumn* (1926, Pulitzer Prize), *The Rains Came* (1937), *Colorado* (1947), and *Mr Smith* (1951). His short stories include *Awake and Rehearse* (1929), and his plays *The House of Women* (1927). 📖 D D Anderson, *Louis Bromfield* (1964)

Brongniart, Alexandre 1770–1847
French naturalist, chemist and geologist
Born in Paris, early in his career he attempted to improve the art of enamelling and subsequently became director of the porcelain factory at Sèvres (1800). From 1808, he was professor at the Sorbonne and in 1822 he succeeded René Just Haüy as Professor of Mineralogy at the Natural History Museum in Paris. He was a close associate of Georges Cuvier, and together they undertook classical studies of the geological strata of the Paris Basin using the nature of fossils within the beds to map out the sequence. They thereby deduced the fundamental stratigraphic principle whereby the changing fossil record can be related to the relative age of rock strata, published in *Essai sur la géographie minéralogique des environs de Paris* (1808, 'Essay on the Mineralogical Geography of the Environs of Paris'). They noted the alternation of freshwater and marine strata in the Tertiary rocks around Paris, and interpreted this as being the result of catastrophic processes. Brongniart's zoological interests led him to elucidate the zoological and geological relations of trilobites. He introduced the term Jurassic for the limestones and clays of the Cotswolds. His son Adolphe Théodore (1801–76) was a noted palaeobotanist.

Bronhill, June, *originally* June Gough 1929–
Australian soprano
Born in Broken Hill, New South Wales, she adapted her stage name from this. After she came third to Joan Sutherland in the Sydney *Sun* Aria competition (1949), and winning it the following year, her home town raised funds to send her to London for further study. In 1954 she made an immediate success at Sadler's Wells in musicals such as *Robert and Elizabeth* and *The Sound of Music*, and in operetta, particularly as *The Merry Widow* (*Die lustige Witwe*). Later, she took the lead in *The Bride of Lammermoor* (*Lucia di Lammermoor*) at Covent Garden, London (1959). More recently she has appeared in speaking roles, especially in comedy, such as in *Arsenic and Old Lace* (1991).

Bronk, Detlev Wulf 1887–1975
US neurophysiologist
Born in New York City, he served in World War I then studied both electrical engineering and physics at the University of Michigan. He worked with Edgar Adrian at Cambridge (1927–28) on the biophysical properties of the motor nerve fibre which they succeeded in isolating, and with A V Hill in London on temperature changes in muscles during activity. In 1930 he became director of the Eldridge Reeves Johnson Foundation for Medical Physics at the University of Pennsylvania. He was president of Johns Hopkins University from 1949 and of the Rockefeller Institute (later University) from 1953 to 1968. His research contributed significantly to the study of the autonomic nervous system, especially the mechanisms controlling cardiac function, and also helped to promote a biophysical approach to medical research.

Bronowski, Jacob 1908–74
Polish mathematician, poet and humanist
Born in Łódź, Poland, he spent World War I with his grandparents in Germany, and went with them to live in England in 1920. He was educated at Jesus College, Cambridge and became a lecturer at University College, Hull (1934–42), then left to develop operations research methods for the government. He became director of the Coal Research Establishment of the National Coal Board, and oversaw the development of smokeless fuel. He was a popular broadcaster, particularly in the BBC's *Brains Trust* and *The Ascent of Man* (1973).

Brønsted, Johannes Nicolaus 1879–1947
Danish physical chemist
Born in Varde, Jutland, he trained initially as a chemical engineer at the Technical University of Denmark, then studied chemistry at the University of Copenhagen. After graduating, he spent a period in industry before becoming an assistant at the University of Copenhagen (1905). In 1908 he was appointed to the new chair of physical chemistry at the University of Copenhagen. In 1930 he became director of a new Physico-Chemical Institute in Copenhagen. Most of his contributions to physical chemistry concerned the behaviour of solutions. His studies of the effect of ionic strength on the solubilities of sparingly soluble salts provided strong experimental support for the Debye–Hückel theory (1923) and his analogous studies of rates of reaction involving ions were also interpreted in terms of the same theory (1920–24). He is known for a novel and valuable definition of acids and bases, the Brønsted–Lowry definition, which defines an acid as a substance with a tendency to lose a proton, and a base as a substance that tends to gain a proton.

Brontë, Anne See panel p275

Brontë, Charlotte See panel p275

Brontë, Emily See panel p275

Bronterre See O'Brien, James

Bronzino, Agnolo, *also called* Il Bronzino, *properly* Agnolo Tori di Cosimo di Moriano 1503–72
Italian Mannerist painter

Born in Monticelli, he was a pupil of **Jacopo da Pontormo**, who then adopted him. He decorated the chapel of the Palazzo Vecchio in Florence, and painted the *Christ in Limbo* (1552) in the Uffizi, Florence. His *Venus, Folly, Cupid and Time* (1542–45) is in the National Gallery, London, and his portraits include most of the **Medici** family, **Dante**, **Boccaccio** and **Petrarch**. His nephew, **Alessandro Allori**, and nephew's son, both Florentine painters, adopted his name.

Brook, Peter Stephen Paul 1925–
English theatre and film director

He was born in London and educated at Westminster, Greshams and Magdalen College, Oxford. His theatrical involvement began while at university—his first work as director was a production of **Christopher Marlowe's** *Dr Faustus* presented in London in 1943. In 1944 he joined a film company but left the following year to direct **Jean Cocteau's** *The Infernal Machine*, after which he directed many classical plays at the Birmingham Repertory Theatre, including a notable production of *King John* by **Shakespeare**. In Brook's first season at Stratford (1947), his highly original production of *Romeo and Juliet* did not meet with wide critical acclaim. From 1947 to 1950 he was also director of productions at the Royal Opera House, Covent Garden, London, directing a memorable **Dali**-designed *Salome*. During the 1950s he worked on many productions in Great Britain, Europe and the USA, including a French version of **Arthur Miller's** *Death of a Salesman* at the Belgian National Theatre in 1951, and the 1953 revival of **Thomas Otway's** *Venice Preserved*. In 1962 he returned to Stratford to join the newly established Royal Shakespeare Company for which he directed, among other productions, the legendary **Paul Scofield's** *King Lear* (1963), **Peter Weiss's** *Marat/Sade* (1964), *U.S.* (1966), and in 1970 his greatly acclaimed *Midsummer Night's Dream*. Most of his work in the 1970s was done with the Paris-based Centre for Theatre Research, which he helped to set up in 1970 and with which he has travelled widely in Africa and Asia; in 1978 he again returned to Stratford to direct *Antony and Cleopatra*. Among his films are *The Beggar's Opera* (1952), *Lord of the Flies* (1962), *The Marat/Sade* (1967), *King Lear* (1969) and *Meetings With Remarkable Men* (1979). In 1988 he directed a production of *The Mahabharata* in Glasgow. Later Paris productions include a nine-hour adaptation of *The Mahabharata*, which subsequently toured the world, and *L'Homme Qui* which was staged in Paris (1993) then later, in English as *The Man Who*, at the National Theatre (1994) and in New York (1995). Brook's work is difficult to categorize and difficult to assess, although he is acknowledged to be 'the director's director'. His publications include his autobiography *The Shifting Point* (1988) and *There Are No Secrets* (1993). 📖 J C Trewin, *Peter Brook* (1971)

Brook, 1st Baron See Greville, Sir Fulke

Brooke, Sir Basil Stanlake See Brookeborough, 1st Viscount

Brooke, Edward William 1919–
US politician

He was born in Washington, DC. After serving with distinction as Attorney-General of Massachusetts, where he worked to expose corruption in state government, he became the first African-American elected to the US Senate since Reconstruction. A Republican, he served from 1967 to 1979. Brooke was awarded the NAACP (National Association for the Advancement of Colored People) Spingarn Medal in 1967.

Brooke, Sir James 1803–68
English soldier, and Raja of Sarawak

He was born in Benares, India, and educated in Norwich, Norfolk. In 1838 he sailed in a schooner-yacht from London for Sarawak, a province on the north-west coast of Borneo, with the aim of defeating piracy. Made Raja of Sarawak (1841) for assisting the local sultan against Dayak rebel tribes, he instituted free trade, framed a new code of laws, declared the Dayak custom of head-hunting a capital crime, and vigorously set about suppressing piracy. In 1857 Brooke repelled, with native forces, a series of attacks by a large body of Chinese, who had been irritated by his efforts to prevent opium smuggling. He was succeeded as raja (1868) by his nephew, Sir Charles Johnson, who changed his name to Brooke. He was succeeded in turn in 1917 by his son, Sir Charles Vyner, who in 1946 ceded Sarawak to the British Crown.

Brooke, (Bernard) Jocelyn 1908–66
English novelist, poet and amateur botanist

He was born in Kent, ran away from boarding school twice, then studied at Worcester College, Oxford, and tried various occupations before joining the family wine firm. During World War II he enlisted in the Royal Army Medical Corps, but following the critical success of his autobiographical novel *The Military Orchid* (1948), he bought himself out and thereafter devoted himself to writing. *A Mine of Serpents* (1949) and *The Goose Cathedral* (1950), the former drawing heavily on his obsession with pyrotechnics, completed what became known as *The Orchid Trilogy*. His other works include two volumes of poetry, *December Spring* (1946) and *The Elements of Death* (1952), a **Kafka**esque novel called *The Image of a Drawn Sword* (1950), and botanical books.

Brooke, Peter Leonard 1934–
English Conservative politician

He was born in London and educated at Marlborough and Balliol College, Oxford. After briefly serving on Camden Borough Council in the late 1960s, he entered the House of Commons as MP for the City of London and Westminster South in 1977. He advanced quickly, becoming an Assistant Whip (1979–81), Government Whip (1981–83), Under-Secretary of State for Education and Science (1983–85), and Minister of State at the Treasury (1985–87). Briefly Paymaster General in 1987, he succeeded **Norman Tebbit** that same year as chairman of the Conservative Party. Appointed Secretary of State for Northern Ireland in 1989, he resigned from the Cabinet in 1992, stood unsuccessfully for the Speakership of the House of Commons, and was reappointed to the Cabinet as Secretary of State for National Heritage (1992–94).

Brooke, Rupert Chawner 1887–1915
English poet

He was born at Rugby school, where his father was a master, and educated at King's College, Cambridge. In 1909 he settled in Granchester, and began to publish his poetry in journals, and also travelled in Germany, later visiting the USA and Tahiti. His *Poems* appeared in 1911, and he also contributed to the first and second volumes of *Georgian Poetry*. Five war sonnets were published in 1915 and brought him great public recognition, which was increased by *1914 and Other Poems*, published in 1915, after his death. He died a commissioned officer on Skyros on his way to the Dardanelles and was buried there. 📖 C Hassall, *Rupert Brooke, a biography* (1972)

Brookeborough, Sir Basil Stanlake Brooke, 1st Viscount 1888–1973
Northern Irish statesman

Born in Fermanagh, he was elected to the Northern Ireland parliament in 1929. He became Minister of Agriculture in 1933, Minister of Commerce in 1941, and Prime Minister from 1943 until his resignation in 1963. A

Brontë, *originally* Brunty or Prunty
The name of three sisters who hold a remarkable place in English literary history

Anne, Charlotte and Emily Brontë were born in Thornton, Yorkshire, the daughters of Patrick Brontë (1777–1861), a clergyman of Irish descent, and his Cornish wife Maria (1783–1821). There were two other sisters, Maria and Elizabeth, who both died in childhood, and a brother, Branwell (1817–48).

In 1820 the family moved to Haworth, now part of Keighley, when their father became rector there, and four of the daughters—Maria, Elizabeth, Charlotte and Emily—were sent in 1824 to the Clergy Daughters' School at Cowan Bridge, which was later to become the model for Lowood in *Jane Eyre*. After their mother's death from cancer, an aunt came to look after the children. Their childhood was spent in the sole companionship of one another on the wild Yorkshire moors, and Branwell's 12 toy soldiers inspired them to construct two fantasy worlds of their own, *Gondal* and *Angria*, which contained all the exotic places and were peopled by all the great figures they had read about. Incidents in these were described by the children in verse and prose in rival collections of notebooks. In 1846 the sisters published a volume of poems under three pseudonyms, Currer Bell (Charlotte), Ellis Bell (Emily) and Acton Bell (Anne).

Brontë, Anne, *pseudonym* Acton Bell 1820–49

Anne worked as a governess, but had to leave her second post because of her brother's infatuation with her employer. As well as sharing in the poems of 1846, she wrote two novels, *Agnes Grey* (1845) and *The Tenant of Wildfell Hall* (1848); these are generally regarded as lesser works than those of her sisters, although *Wildfell Hall*, with its controversial subject-matter and questioning of the status of married women, had a certain success.

Brontë, Charlotte, *pseudonym* Currer Bell 1816–55

Charlotte worked for a time as a teacher and governess. In Brussels (1843–44), she formed an attachment to a married man, M Constantin Heger, who rejected her; she later scornfully satirized him in *Villette* (1852). Charlotte wrote four complete novels. *The Professor*, which was not published until after her death, dwells on the theme of moral madness, possibly inspired by Branwell's degeneration. It was rejected by her publisher, but with sufficient encouragement for her to complete her masterpiece, *Jane*

Eyre (1847). This in essence, through the master-pupil love relationship between Rochester and Jane, constituted a magnificent plea for feminine equality with men in the avowal of their passions. It was followed in 1849 by *Shirley*, a novel set against the background of the Luddite riots.

By now her brother and two sisters were dead, and she was left alone at Haworth with her father. *Villette*, founded on her memories of Brussels, was published in 1853. In 1850 she met and formed a friendship with Mrs **Gaskell**, who wrote a memoir of her. She married her father's curate, Arthur Bell Nicholls, in 1854 but died in pregnancy the following year, leaving the fragment of another novel, *Emma*. Two stories, *The Secret* and *Lily Hart*, were published for the first time in 1978.

Brontë, Emily Jane, *pseudonym* Ellis Bell 1818–48

Emily worked as a governess in Halifax. She went to Brussels with Charlotte and in 1845 embarked on a joint publication of poems after Charlotte's discovery of her *Gondal* verse, including such fine items as 'To Imagination', 'Plead for Me' and 'Last Lines'. Her single novel, *Wuthering Heights* (1847), is an intense and powerful tale of love and revenge set in the remote wilds of 18th-century Yorkshire; it has much in common with Greek tragedy, and no real counterpart in English literature.

📖 W Gerin, *The Brontës* (1973–74), *Anne Brontë* (1959), *Charlotte Brontë* (1967), *Emily Brontë* (1971); E Gaskell, *The Life of Charlotte Brontë* (1860).

'All true histories contain instruction; though in some, the treasure may be hard to find, and when found, so trivial in quantity that the dry, shrivelled kernel scarcely compensates for the trouble of cracking the nut.'
Anne Brontë, *Agnes Grey*, ch.1.

'Reader, I married him.'
Charlotte Brontë, *Jane Eyre*, ch.38.

'No coward soul is mine,
No trembler in the world's storm-troubled sphere:
I see Heaven's glories shine,
And faith shines equal, arming me from fear.'
Emily Brontë, 'No coward soul is mine' (1846).

staunch supporter of Unionist policy, he exhibited an unswerving determination to preserve the ties between Northern Ireland and Great Britain. He retired from politics in 1968.

Brookes, Sir Norman Everard 1877–1968
Australian tennis player

Born in Melbourne, he went to Wimbledon in 1905, winning the all-comers' singles title, and returned the following year to win the singles, doubles, and mixed doubles titles. In the same year, he and Anthony Wilding achieved Australasia's first victory in the Davis Cup. He won again at Wimbledon in 1914 and, after service in World War I, played Davis Cup tennis until 1921, and captained six winning teams. He was also a national golf champion. He was appointed Chevalier of the Legion of Honour, and was knighted in 1939.

Brookner, Anita 1928–
English novelist and art historian

She was born in London. An authority on 18th-century painting, she was the first woman Slade Professor at Cambridge (1967–68), and was a Reader at the Courtauld

Institute of Art (1977–88). She is the author of *Watteau* (1968), *The Genius of the Future* (1971) and *Jacques-Louis David* (1981). As a novelist she was a late starter, but in 12 years (1981–92) she published as many novels, elegant, witty and imbued with cosmopolitan melancholy. Invariably, her main characters are women, self-sufficient in all but love. By winning the Booker Prize, *Hôtel du Lac* (1984) has become her best-known novel, and it is regarded by many as her most accomplished. Other titles include *Friends from England* (1987), *Brief Lives* (1990), *A Closed Eye* (1991), *Fraud* (1992), *A Family Romance* (1993), *A Private View* (1994) and *Incidents in the Rue Laugier* (1995).

Brooks, Cleanth 1906–
US academic and critic

A Rhodes scholar at Exeter College, Oxford, he then became a teacher at the Louisiana State University (1932–47), before moving on to Yale University, where later he became Gray Professor of Rhetoric (1960–75). He was crucial in establishing New Criticism as an academic method, in part by jointly editing, with Robert Penn Warren, *The Southern Review* (1935–42). Also influential were his works, which included *Understanding Poetry* (1938;

written with Warren), *The Well Wrought Urn* (1947), and *Literary Criticism: A Short History* (1957; written with William K Wimsatt, Jnr).

Brooks, (Troyal) Garth 1962–
US country music singer

He was born in Yukon, Oklahoma, and his mother, Colleen Carroll, was a country singer. He has achieved astonishing success, and in 1996 his combined record sales surpassed 60 million, making him the biggest-selling artist in any genre in that decade. He served an apprenticeship on the club circuit before making a traditional country debut album in 1989. *No Fences* (1990) and *Ropin' The Wind* (1991) smashed all previous sales records for country music, and put him alongside the biggest rock and pop acts. His genuine sincerity, spectacular rock-style stage shows and subsequent albums have served to confirm that eminence. 📖 R Mitchell, *One Of A Kind* (1994)

Brooks, Gwendolyn Elizabeth 1917–
US poet and novelist

Born in Topeka, Kansas, and brought up in the slums of Chicago, she wrote actively from an early age, and her first poem was published at the age of 13. She has taught English in a number of colleges, and was Publicity Director of the NAACP (National Association for the Advancement of Colored People) for a time in the 1930s. Her first collection, *A Street in Bronzeville* (1945), established the central theme of her work, chronicling the cares of city-dwelling black Americans and her novel *Annie Allen* (1949) made her the first African-American to win the Pulitzer Prize. Subsequent works in both poetry and prose have been increasingly radical in tone, as in *Riot* (1969) and *Blacks* (1987). Other works include the novel *Maud Martha* (1953), an autobiography, *Report From Part One* (1972), *Winnie* (1988) and *Children Coming Home* (1991). 📖 G E Kent, *A Life of Gwendolyn Brooks* (1990)

Brooks, Louise 1906–85
US actress

Born in Cherryvale, Kansas, she became a member of the Denishawn Dancers troupe in 1922, then moved to New York and joined the cast of, among others, the *Ziegfeld Follies* (1925–26). She made her film debut in *Street of Forgotten Men* (1925) and signed a contract with Paramount that led to roles in such comedies as *It's The Old Army Game* (1926), *Just Another Blonde* (1927) and *Rolled Stockings* (1927). She then went to Germany to work for G W Pabst (1885–1967) in *Die Büchse von Pandora* (1928, *Pandora's Box*) and *Das Tagebüch einer Verlorenen* (1929, *Diary of a Lost Girl*). Brooks returned to Hollywood but was given only supporting roles and retired after playing opposite John Wayne in the B western *Overland Stage Raiders* (1938). She later ran a dance studio, worked in radio soap opera, and became a writer on film, publishing an autobiography, *Lulu in Hollywood*, in 1982.

Brooks, Mel, originally Melvin Kaminsky 1926–
US film actor and director

Born in New York City, after service with the US Army, he performed as a comic in nightclubs and secured employment as a writer for radio and television. He wrote for the comic Sid Caesar on such television programmes as *Your Show of Shows* (1950–54) and *Caesar's Hour* (1954–57), won an Academy Award for the short film *The Critic* (1963) and devised the popular series *Get Smart* (1965–70). He made his feature-length cinema debut with *The Producers* (1968) and has proven adept at comedies that spoof the major cinematic genres and skirt the boundaries of good taste. His films include *Blazing Saddles* (1974), *Young Frankenstein* (1974), *High Anxiety* (1977) and *Dracula—Dead and Loving It* (1995). His company Brooksfilms has also been

responsible for such offbeat fare as *The Elephant Man* (1980) and *The Fly* (1986). He has been married to Anne Bancroft since 1964.

Brooks, Phillips 1835–93
US Protestant Episcopal preacher

Born in Boston, he studied at Harvard, and after serving curacies in Philadelphia and Boston, was consecrated Bishop of Massachusetts in 1891. A keen thinker and powerful preacher, he opposed the theory of apostolic succession, but is best known for his Yale *Lectures on Preaching* (1877).

Brooks, Van Wyck 1886–1963
US author and critic

He was born in Plainfield, New Jersey, and graduated from Harvard. He spent much of his life as a writer in tracing the cultural and literary history of the USA, and in early works such as *The Wine of the Puritans* (1909) he attacked the narrow-mindedness and materialism in US society that he regarded as the legacy of the Puritans. He also wrote biographical studies of Mark Twain (1920), Henry James (1925), Ralph Waldo Emerson (1932) and Washington Irving (1944), and won the Pulitzer Prize with his *Flowering of New England* (1936), which chronicled the birth of a national literature in the early and mid-19th century. 📖 W Wasserstrom, *Van Wyck Brooks* (1968)

Broom, Robert 1866–1951
South African palaeontologist

Born in Paisley, Strathclyde, Scotland, he graduated in medicine from Glasgow and practised in Australia before moving to South Africa in 1897 as a general physician. He was appointed Professor of Zoology and Geology at Victoria College (1903–10) and in 1934 became palaeontologist at the Transvaal Museum, Pretoria. In 1936 he began to study fossil hominids and concluded that Raymond Dart was correct in his view that *Australopithecus africanus* is an ancestor of modern-day humans. In 1947 he found a partial skeleton of this hominid, including the pelvis, which proved that he had walked upright about 1–2 million years ago. His studies on human ancestry are given in his book *Finding the Missing Link* (1950). He also wrote *The Coming of Man* (1933).

Broonzy, Big Bill, real name William Lee Conley Broonzy 1893–1958
US blues singer, composer and musician

Born in Scott, Mississippi, he began his musical life as a fiddler, but switched to guitar when he moved to Chicago in 1920. One of the most eclectic stylists among the great blues performers, he encompassed American folk-song and jazz as well as rural and urban blues. For much of his career his appearances were confined to small clubs and bars throughout the USA, but in the 1950s the folk-music revival and international interest in traditional jazz and blues brought him a wider audience, and he toured extensively, performing in Europe, Africa and South America.

Brophy, Brigid Antonia 1929–95
English writer and critic

She was born in London and educated at St Paul's Girls' School and at Oxford. Her novels include *Hackenfeller's Ape* (1953), dealing with ethical and philosophical concerns to do with vivisection, *The Finishing Touch* (1963), *In Transit* (1969), and *Palace Without Chairs* (1978), on themes of lesbianism and transsexuality, and *The Snow Ball* (1964), in which the characters dress up for a ball as characters from Mozart's *Don Giovanni*. Her critical works include *Mozart the Dramatist* (1964), the controversial *Fifty Works of English Literature We Could Do Without* (1967, jointly with her husband Sir Michael Levey and Charles Osborne), a study of Aubrey Beardsley (1968), and *Prancing Novelist* (1973), a defence of Ronald Firbank's work. She campaigned vigorously against vivisection and in 1972 began a successful campaign for the establishment of a Public Lending Right. In the early 1980s she was afflicted with multiple sclerosis; she wrote about her illness in a collection of essays called *Baroque 'n' Roll* (1985).

Broschi, Carlo, *stage name* Farinelli 1705–82
Italian singer

Born in Naples, he became the most famous of castrato singers. He visited London in 1734, and in Spain was made a grandee, with a pension of £2,000 a year.

Brosse, Salomon de 1565–1626
French architect

Born in Verneuil, he was architect to Marie de Médicis. He designed the Luxembourg Palace in Paris (1615–20), and Louis XIII's hunting lodge (1624–26), the nucleus of the Palace of Versailles.

Brothers, Richard 1757–1824
English religious fanatic

He was born in Newfoundland, of English parents. In 1793 he declared himself to be the 'nephew of the Almighty', an apostle of a new religion, the Anglo-Israelites. In 1795, for prophesying the destruction of the monarchy, he was sent to Newgate prison, London, and subsequently to an asylum, but not before he had acquired a number of disciples, some of them men of influence and standing.

Brougham and Vaux, Henry Peter Brougham, 1st Baron 1778–1868
Scottish jurist and politician

Born in Edinburgh, he went Edinburgh University aged 14, and in 1802 co-founded the influential *Edinburgh Review*, to which he was a prolific contributor. Aware that his Liberal views were ahead of their time for Scotland, he moved to London, was called to the Bar in 1808, and entered Parliament in 1810. As a barrister, his greatest triumph was the successful defence of Queen Caroline of Brunswick in 1820, and, as Lord Chancellor from 1830, he was one of the greatest reformers of the courts, establishing the judicial committee of the Privy Council and the Central Criminal Court, though he was unsuccessful in his efforts to establish what is now the county-court system. In 1834 he enraged King William IV by taking the Great Seal with him on a tour and using it as the centrepiece of a house party game. His three-volume *Life and Times*, written in old age and published posthumously in 1871, is unreliable. The brougham carriage was named after him.

Broughton, 1st Baron See Hobhouse, John Cam

Broughton, William Grant 1788–1853
Australian prelate

Born in Westminster, London, he worked as a clerk in East India House for five years before going to Cambridge. Ordained in 1818, he ministered in Hampshire before he accepted an invitation from the Duke of Wellington to become the second archdeacon of New South Wales. He arrived in Sydney in 1829 to supervise a large territory which extended over all of Australia and some regions beyond. When the post was elevated to a See in 1836 he became Bishop of Australia. With the division in 1847 into more manageable dioceses he was restyled Bishop of Sydney and Metropolitan of Australia. A high churchman with Tractarian sympathies, he had to counter Anglicans of liberal and (to a lesser extent) of evangelical traditions.

Brouncker (of Castle Lyons), William Brouncker, 2nd Viscount 1620–84
Irish mathematician

Educated at Oxford, he was a founder-member and first president of the Royal Society. He expressed *pi* as a continued fraction, and found expressions for the logarithm as an infinite series. With John Wallis he solved Pierre de Fermat's questions about Pell's equation, giving a general method for their solution.

Broun-Ramsay, James Andrew See Dalhousie, Marquis of

Brouwer or Brauer, Adriaen c.1605–1638
Flemish painter

Born in Oudenarde, he studied at Haarlem under Frans Hals, and about 1630 settled at Antwerp. His favourite subjects were scenes from tavern life, country merry-makings, card players and smoking and drinking groups. He was also a notable landscape painter

Brouwer, Luitzen Egbertus Jan 1881–1966
Dutch mathematician

Born in Overschie, he entered Amsterdam University at the age of 16, where he was professor from 1912 to 1951. His doctoral thesis was on the foundations of mathematics, an area in which worked throughout his life. He founded the intuitionist or constructivist school of mathematical logic, in which the existence of a mathematical object can only be proved by giving an explicit method for its construction. He also made fundamental advances in topology, introducing the concept of simplicial approximation, the degree of a mapping, and proving the invariance of dimension, and the fixed point theorem named after him.

Browder, Earl Russell 1871–1973
US politician

Born in Wichita, Kansas, he was a member of the US Communist Party from 1921, becoming its secretary general from 1936. He was also a nominee for US President in 1940. He advocated reconciliation between socialism and capitalism, a stance that caused his expulsion by the Communists in 1946.

Brown, Sir Arthur Whitten 1886–1948
British aviator

He was born in Glasgow of US parents. As navigator with Sir John William Alcock he made the first non-stop crossing of the Atlantic, in a Vickers-Vimy biplane on 14 June 1919, and shared a £10,000 prize given by the London *Daily Mail*. Both men were knighted after the flight. 📖 G Wallace, *The Flight of Alcock & Brown* (1955)

Brown, Capability See Brown, Lancelot

Brown, Charles Brockden 1771–1810
US novelist

Born in Philadelphia, he was the first professional US writer. He made use of the English style of Gothic romance, and was much admired by Sir Walter Scott, Keats, and Shelley. *Wieland* (1798), *Ormund* (1799) and *Jane Talbot* (1804), among many others, are full of incident and subtle analysis, but extravagant in style. 📖 A Axelrod, *Charles Brockden Brown: an American tale* (1983)

Brown, David 1951– and Hilary 1952–
Scottish husband and wife team of restaurateurs

Hilary was born in Glasgow and graduated in food and nutrition from Glasgow College of Domestic Science. She taught home economics for two years before she and her husband David, also born in Glasgow, decided to start their own restaurant. He attends to the front of house and the celebrated wine list, while she is the chef. In 1975 the couple opened La Potinière in Gullane, East Lothian. The restaurant soon earned acclaim and in 1990 Hilary Brown and Betty Allen became the first women in Scotland to receive a Michelin star.

Brown, Ford Madox 1821–93
British historical painter

Born in Calais, France, he studied art at Bruges, Ghent, and Antwerp. In Paris he produced his *Manfred on the Jungfrau* (1841), a work intensely dramatic in feeling, but sombre in colouring. A visit to Italy (1845) led him to seek a greater variety and richness of colouring, as in *Chaucer reciting his Poetry* (1851). He settled in England in 1846. He contributed verse, prose, and design to the Pre-Raphaelite *Germ*, and in his youth Dante Gabriel Rossetti worked in his studio. He was a close associate of William Morris, and in 1861 was a founder-member of Morris, Marshall, Faulkner & Company (later Morris & Company) for which he produced some designs for furniture and stained glass. Among his more mature works are *Christ washing Peter's Feet*, *The Entombment* and his best-known painting, *The Last of England* (1855). He completed 12 frescoes for Manchester Town Hall, just before his death. He was the grandson of the physician John Brown.

Brown, George 1818–80
Canadian politician and journalist

Born in Alloa, Scotland, he emigrated to New York City in 1837 and to Canada in 1843. A supporter of Responsible Government in 1848, he became a member of the Canadian legislative assembly in 1851. As editor of the *Toronto Globe* he used his considerable influence to speak for the Clear Grits, pressing the case for representation by population ('rep by pop'), to give Canada West a majority of seats in the legislature. After the Liberal-Conservatives took over government in 1854, Brown reorganized the party, and won the 1857 elections by advocating the acquisition of the North West from the Hudson's Bay Company. In 1858, in alliance with A A Dorion, the leader of the Liberals of Canada East, he formed a government which survived only a few days. He played a major role with Sir Alexander Galt, Sir John Macdonald, and Sir Georges Étienne Cartier, in a coalition government established to devise the constitutional reforms required for confederation. This he continued to support even after resigning (1865). Brown was also an anti-slavery activist, involved in the settlement of fugitive slaves during the 1850s. He was shot and killed by an employee sacked from the *Globe*.

Brown, George Alfred See George-Brown, Baron

Brown, George Douglas, *pseudonym* George Douglas 1869–1902
Scottish writer

Born in Ochiltree, Ayrshire, the illegitimate son of a farmer, he was educated at the village school and Ayr Academy, then at Glasgow University and Balliol College, Oxford, on a scholarship. He settled in London as a journalist, published a boys' adventure book, *Love and Sword* (1899), but made his name, under the pseudonym George Douglas, with *The House with the Green Shutters* (1901), a powerfully realistic novel and an antidote to the 'Kailyard School'. He died of pneumonia before he was able to complete two other novels. ◫ F R Hart, *The Scottish Novel* (1978)

Brown, George Mackay 1921–96
Scottish poet, novelist and short-story writer

Born in Stromness, Orkney, the 'Hamnavoe' of his stories and poems, he suffered early from tuberculosis and was unable to work when he left school. In 1957 he went to Newbattle Abbey College, where Edwin Muir was warden, then did postgraduate work on Gerard Manley Hopkins at Edinburgh University. He published his first collection, *The Storm*, in 1954, and it was followed by *Loaves and Fishes* (1959). His work draws on old sea yarns, myths, Scandinavian sagas and the folklore of Orkney, and his conversion to Catholicism in 1961 brought his concern with religion into relief. His works include the short story collections *A Calendar of Love* (1967) and *A Time to Keep* (1969), and the novels *Greenvoe* (1972), *Magnus* (1973), and *Beside the Ocean of Time* (1994), which was shortlisted for the Booker Prize. His *Selected Poems* were published in 1991. ◫ R Fulton, *Contemporary Scottish Poetry* (1974)

Brown, (James) Gordon 1951–
Scottish Labour politician

He was born in Kirkcaldy, Fife, the son of a Church of Scotland minister, and educated at Kirkcaldy High School and Edinburgh University. While still a student he was elected Rector of Edinburgh University (1972–75). After working as a lecturer and television journalist, he entered the House of Commons in 1983, as Labour MP for Dunfermline East. He rose rapidly in the parliamentary party's hierarchy, becoming its senior Front Bench Spokesman on Treasury affairs under John Smith in 1987. He became Opposition Spokesman for Trade and Industry (1989–92) and the Treasury (1992–97), and Chancellor of the Exchequer in 1997 when Labour came to power. His publications include *John Smith: Life and Soul of the Party* (1994, with J Naughtie).

Brown, Helen Gurley, *née* Gurley 1922–
US journalist and commentator on gender affairs

Born in Green Forest, Arkansas, she studied at Texas State College and Woodbury College, and after working in junior management for three years embarked upon a career in advertising. In 1965 she was appointed editor-in-chief of the ailing *Cosmopolitan* magazine which she transformed into an international success, remaining at *Cosmopolitan* until she retired in 1996 at the age of 73. Brown is the recipient of many awards, including the Distinguished Achievement award in journalism of Stanford University (1977) and the New York Women in Communications award (1985). Her first book was the bestseller *Sex and the Single Girl* (1962) which reflected a new mood of female independence. Other works include *Outrageous Opinions* (1966), *Sex and the New Single Girl* (1970) and *Having it All* (1982).

Brown, Herbert Charles, *originally* Herbert Brovarnik 1912–
US chemist and Nobel Prize winner

Born to Russian émigrés in London, England, his family moved to Chicago when he was two years old. Despite acute financial difficulty, he eventually attended the University of Chicago for graduate work, where he first encountered the chemistry of boron. Apart from some excursions into physical organic chemistry, the use of boron compounds in organic synthesis has been the dominating theme of his work and it was for this that he was awarded the Nobel Prize for chemistry in 1979. He spent most of his professional life at Purdue University where he was professor (1947–60), R B Wetherill Research Professor (1960–78, emeritus 1978–). He continued his work after his retirement and in 1987 received the Priestley Medal of the American Chemical Society.

Brown, James 1928–
US soul singer, songwriter and producer

He was born in Barnwell, South Carolina. He began his professional career backed by a former gospel group, The Famous Flames, with whom he recorded his first 'cry' ballads, 'Please, Please, Please' and 'Try Me' (1958). Mixing gospel and blues roots with his own aggressive energy, he put together a band and roadshow which by 1962 had made him America's leading rhythm and blues star and earned him the nickname 'Soul Brother Number One'.

'Out Of Sight' (1964) brought him his first international success. During the late 1960s he courted controversy with what was perceived as an ambiguous stance on racial politics, recording both 'America Is My Home' and 'Say It Loud, I'm Black and I'm Proud'. An enduring influence on pop music, he was one of the first entertainers to assume complete control of his own career. His songs have included 'Papa's Got A Brand New Bag' (1965), 'It's A Man's Man's Man's World' (1966), 'Ain't It Funky Now' (1969), 'Sex Machine' (1970) and 'Get Up Offa That Thing' (1976), and his work has provided countless samples for the new generation of rap and hip hop artists. In 1988 he was jailed for six years on charges that included aggravated assault, but resumed his career on his early release. 📖 G Brown *James Brown* (1996)

Brown, Janet 1924–
Scottish actress, comedienne and impressionist
Born in Rutherglen, Glasgow, she made her first appearance at the Savoy Cinema, Glasgow, at the age of 13, followed by her broadcasting debut on Radio Scotland the same year. After her first London stage appearance (1945), she appeared in many radio variety series (*Music Hall*, *Variety Bandbox*), finally achieving her own series on BBC Radio Scotland (1949). Early television appearances include *Rooftop Rendezvous* and a star role in the sitcom *Friends and Neighbours* (1954) with her husband Peter Butterworth. She made her film debut in *Floodtide* (1949) and her stage debut as actress in James Bridie's *Mr Gillie*, at the King's Theatre, Glasgow (1950). She later attained national fame with her impression of Prime Minister Thatcher on television and radio during the 1980s. Her other television appearances include *Mike Yarwood in Persons*, *Meet Janet Brown* and *Janet and Company*.

Brown, Joe (Joseph) 1930–
English mountaineer
Born in Manchester, he is one of the finest British rock-climbers of the post-war period. In the 1950s, he formed a partnership with Don Whillans, and together they set new standards, putting up many original routes on rock faces in the Peak District and most notably on the huge face of Clogwyn Du'r Arddu in North Wales. In 1954 they made the first British ascent of the west face of the Petit Dru in the Alps, reducing the recorded ascension time from six days to 25 hours. With George Band, Brown reached the summit of Kangchenjunga, the world's third-highest mountain (1955). In 1966 he pioneered a series of extremely difficult routes on the sea cliffs of Gogarth in Anglesey, the most famous of them being Spider's Web. His many expeditions have taken him to the world's major mountain ranges. He published his autobiography *The Hard Years* in 1967.

Brown, John c.1735–1788
Scottish physician
Born in Bunkle parish, Berwickshire, he taught at Duns and Edinburgh, and after studying medicine became assistant to Professor William Cullen. Thinking himself slighted by Cullen, he began to give lectures himself on a new system of medicine, the Brunonian system, according to which all diseases are divided into the sthenic, depending on an excess of excitement, and the asthenic. The former were to be cured by debilitating medicines, and the latter by stimulants. He also condemned the practice of bloodletting.

Brown, John 1800–59
US abolitionist
Born in Torrington, Connecticut, of Pilgrim descent, he was successively tanner and land surveyor, shepherd and farmer. A strong abolitionist, he wandered through the country on antislavery enterprises. He was twice married and had 20 children. In 1854, five of his sons moved to

Kansas, and, joining them after the border conflict had begun, he became a leader in the strife. His home was burned in 1856 and one of his sons killed. When the war in Kansas ended, Brown began to drill men in Iowa. His next scheme was to establish a stronghold in the mountains of Virginia as a refuge for runaway slaves, and in 1859 he seized the Federal arsenal at Harpers Ferry in Virginia, intending to launch a slave insurrection, and took several citizens prisoner. The arsenal was stormed by Colonel Robert E Lee with a company of marines. Brown and six men, barricading themselves in an engine-house, continued to fight until two of Brown's sons were killed and he was severely wounded. Tried by a Virginia court for insurrection, treason and murder, he was convicted and hanged at Charlestown, Virginia. The song 'John Brown's body lies a-mouldering in the grave' (attributed to Thomas B Bishop (1835–1905)), commemorating the Harpers Ferry raid, was highly popular with Republican soldiers as a marching song in the Civil War. Provided with more fitting words by Julia Ward Howe, it became 'The Battle Hymn of the Republic'. 📖 Stephen B Oates, *To Purge This Land With Blood: A Biography of John Brown* (1970)

Brown, Sir John 1816–96
English industrialist
Founder of the Atlas Steel Works at Sheffield, employing 4,500 workers, he invented the process of rolling armour-plate, and was one of the first to make rolled steel rails.

Brown, John 1826–83
Scottish retainer
He was born in Craithenaird, Balmoral, Aberdeenshire, the son of a crofter, and for 34 years was Queen Victoria's personal attendant at Balmoral.

Brown, Lancelot, *also known as* Capability Brown 1715–83
English landscape gardener
Born in Kirkharle, Northumberland, he established a purely English style of garden layout, using simple means to produce natural effects, as in the gardens of Blenheim, Kew, Stowe, Warwick Castle, Chatsworth, and others. He got his nickname from telling clients that their gardens had great 'capabilities'. 📖 Dorothy Stroud, *Capability Brown* (rev edn, 1975)

Brown, Michael Stuart 1941–
US molecular geneticist and Nobel Prize winner
Born in New York City, he was educated at the University of Pennsylvania, and since 1977 has been Paul J Thomas Professor of Genetics at the University of Texas and director of the Centre for Genetic Diseases. With Joseph Goldstein, he began to work on cholesterol metabolism, studying how cholesterol is carried in the bloodstream by proteins called LDLs (low-density lipoproteins). Working on the genetic disease hypocholesterolemia, which results in abnormally high levels of cholesterol in the bloodstream, Brown found that sufferers from the disease lack a receptor to which the LDLs bind, thereby stopping cholesterol production. In 1984 Brown and Goldstein elucidated the gene sequence which codes for the LDL receptor, opening up the possibility of synthesizing drugs to control cholesterol metabolism. They were jointly awarded the 1985 Nobel Prize for physiology or medicine.

Brown, Olympia 1835–1926
US Universalist minister and woman suffragist
Born in Prairie Ronde, Michigan, she was educated at Antioch College and at St Lawrence University theological school. In 1863 she became the first US woman to be ordained by full denominational authority when she was ordained by the Northern Universalist Association in Malone, New York. As a supporter of women's rights, she

served as president of the Woman Suffrage Association (1884–1912) and was also vice-president of the National Woman Suffrage Association in 1892.

Brown, Rachel Fuller 1898–1980
US biochemist

Born in Springfield, Massachusetts, she was educated at the University of Chicago, and began her career as a chemist at the New York State Department of Health in 1926. She made important studies of the causes of pneumonia and the bacteria involved. Shortly after the end of World War II, when methods of controlling bacterial forms of disease had been introduced, she isolated the first antifungal antibiotic, nystatin (1949). She received the Pioneer Chemist award of the American Institute of Chemists in 1975.

Brown, Robert 1773–1858
Scottish botanist

He was born in Montrose and educated at Aberdeen and Edinburgh. In 1798 he visited London, where his ability so impressed Sir **Joseph Banks** that he was appointed naturalist to **Matthew Flinders**'s coastal survey of Australia in 1801–05. He brought back nearly 4,000 species of plants for classification. Appointed librarian to the Linnaean Society, he published *Prodromus Florae Novae Hollandiae et insulae Van-diemen* (1810). In 1810 he received charge of Banks' library and collections, and when they were transferred to the British Museum in 1827 he became botanical keeper there. He is renowned for his investigation on the impregnation of plants and for being the first to note that, in general, living cells contain a nucleus. In 1827 he first observed the movement of fine particles in a liquid, which was named the 'Brownian movement'.

Brown, Thomas 1663–1704
English satirist

He was born in Shifnal, Shropshire. As a student at Christ Church, Oxford, he produced his famous extempore adaptation of **Martial**'s 32nd epigram, 'Non amo te, Sabi-di', at the demand of Dr **John Fell**, the Dean: 'I do not love thee, Dr Fell'. After teaching at Kingston-on-Thames, he settled in London, where he made an uncertain living by writing scurrilous satirical poems and pamphlets, and published *Amusements Serious and Comical* (1700). He was a friend of Mrs **Aphra Behn**.

Brown, Tina 1953–
English writer and editor

Born in Maidenhead, Berkshire, and educated at Oxford, she began her career in 1978 as a columnist for *Punch* magazine, won the 1978 Young Journalist of the Year award, and became editor-in-chief of *Tatler* magazine in 1979. She married the English journalist and *Sunday Times* editor **Harold Evans** in 1981. After leaving *Tatler* in 1983, she moved with Evans to New York City, where she became editor-in-chief of Condé–Nast's *Vanity Fair* magazine in 1984. From 1992 to 1998 she was the fourth editor of the *New Yorker* (founded 1925), a part of the USA's heritage and traditionally the publisher of the best of US writing. Brown immediately implemented changes that brought censure and praise, enlivening the magazine through the use of more colour and increased focus on current events, and improving its circulation by over 25 per cent. Her books include the play *Under the Bamboo Tree* (1973), *Loose Talk* (1979) and *Life as A Party* (1983).

Brown, Trisha 1936–
US choreographer

She was born in Aberdeen, Washington. A meeting with the dancer **Yvonne Rainer** at a West Coast summer school, under the direction of the experimental choreographer and dancer Anna Halprin, led her to New York in 1961. There, along with Rainer and others, Brown founded the experimental Judson Dance Company in 1962. Throughout the 1960s and 1970s she created a series of daringly original 'equipment pieces' where dancers were rigged in block and tackle harness to allow them to walk on walls or down the trunks of trees. *Walking of the Walls*, *Man Walking Down the Side of a Building* and *Spiral* are from this period, along with *Roof Piece* (1973), which dotted dancers across Manhattan roofs, signalling to one another. Between 1970 and 1976 she ran an improvisational group, Grand Union. In the late 1970s she began to work in traditional theatres, adding design and music to her pieces for the first time. **Robert Rauschenberg**, the US painter, created elements such as costumes, sets and electrical scores for several of her works, including *Glacial Decoy* (1979), *Set and Reset* (1983), *Astral Convertible* (1989) and *If You Couldn't See Me* (1994).

Brown, William Wells c.1816–1884
US writer

Born into slavery in Kentucky, he was raised in St Louis, but after gaining his freedom, helped runaway slaves in Ohio. He achieved fame with his autobiographical *Narrative of William W Brown, a Fugitive Slave* (1847), and became a leading advocate of abolition. He published a collection of poems, *The Anti-Slavery Harp* (1848), and an account of his travels in Europe, but is best known for his novel *Clotelle; or, The President's Daughter* (1853), the story of an illegitimate mulatto girl born to President **Jefferson**'s housekeeper. It was published in London, and subsequently appeared in the USA (1864) with all references to the president omitted. His other works were a play, *The Escape* (1858), and an account of the history and culture of *The Black Man* (1863), later expanded as *The Rising Son* (1874).

Browne, Charles Farrar, *pseudonym* Artemus Ward 1834–67
US humorist

He was born in Waterford, Maine, and from 1858 wrote for the *Cleveland Plaindealer* a series of letters combining business platitudes and shrewd satire. In 1861, as Artemus Ward, he entered the lecture field, and in 1866 he went to London, where he contributed to *Punch*, and was very popular as 'the genial showman', exhibiting an amusing Panorama at the Egyptian Hall. His publications include *Artemus Ward, His Book* (1862).

Browne, Coral Edith 1913–91
Australian actress

Born in Melbourne, she made her stage debut there in 1931 after studying painting and costume design. She acted in Australia for three years, then moved to London and worked in experimental theatre until she was offered the lead in *The Man who came to Dinner* in 1941. She then appeared in various popular plays, including *The Last of Mrs Cheyney* (1944), *Lady Frederick* (1946), W **Somerset Maugham**'s *Canaries Sometimes Sing* (1947) and *Affairs of State* (1952). She also played Gertrude in *Hamlet*, a role for which she went to Moscow with the Stratford Company. There she met **Guy Burgess**, a meeting which was dramatized by **Alan Bennett** in *An Englishman Abroad* (1983), and in which she appeared as her younger self, duly winning a BAFTA award for her performance. She married the actor Philip Pearman (d.1964) in 1950, and the US actor **Vincent Price** in 1974.

Browne, Hablot K(night), *pseudonym* Phiz 1815–82
English illustrator

Born in Kennington, London, he was apprenticed to a line-engraver, but soon started etching and watercolour painting, and in 1833 gained a medal from the Society of Arts for an etching of 'John Gilpin'. In 1836 he became illustrator of *The Pickwick Papers*, and he maintained his reputation by his designs for other works by **Dickens**. His son, Gordon F Browne (1858–1932), was a well-known book illustrator.

Browne, Robert c.1550–c.1633
English clergyman, and founder of the Brownists
Born in Tolethorpe, Rutland, he graduated from Cambridge in 1572, becoming a schoolmaster in London, and an open-air preacher. In 1580 he began to attack the established church, and soon after, with Robert Harrison, formed a distinct Church on Congregational principles at Norwich. In 1581, he and his followers were forced to flee to Holland. In 1584 he returned, and in 1586 became master of Stamford Grammar School, and in 1591 rector of Achurch, Northamptonshire. A man of violent temper, he was sent to Northampton jail at the age of 80 for an assault on a constable, and died there. The Brownists may be said to have given birth to the Independents or Congregationalists.

Browne, Sir Samuel James 1824–1901
British soldier
Born in India, the son of a doctor, he joined the Indian army in 1849 and fought in the battles of Chilianwalla and Goojerat in the Second Sikh War (1848–49). During the Indian Mutiny (1857–58) he saw much service, including action at Lucknow and at Seerporah, where he lost his left arm and won a VC. He was promoted to general in 1888; the 'Sam Browne' sword-belt is attributed to him.

Browne, Sir Thomas 1605–82
English writer and physician
He was born in London. Educated at Pembroke College, Oxford, he studied medicine, travelled in Ireland, France, and Italy, graduated as Doctor of Medicine at Leyden in the Netherlands and at Oxford, and settled in 1637 at Norwich, where he lived and practised the rest of his life. He was knighted by **Charles II** on his visit to Norwich in 1671. His greatest work is his earliest, the *Religio Medici* (c.1635, authorized edition 1643)—a sort of confession of faith, revealing a deep insight into the mysteries of the spiritual life. It was followed by *Pseudodoxia Epidemica, or Enquiries into…Vulgar and Common Errors* (1646), a discursive amalgam of humour, acuteness, learning, and credulity. In the 1650s he wrote *Hydriotaphia, or Urn Burial* (1658), considered to be the first archaeological treatise in English, and *The Garden of Cyrus* (1658), the most fantastic of Browne's writings, which aims to show that the number five pervaded not only all the horticulture of antiquity, but that it recurs throughout all plant life, as well as in the 'figurations' of animals. Posthumous publications include *Christian Morals* (1716), an incomplete work, intended to be a continuation of the *Religio Medici*. 🕮 F L Huntley, *Sir Thomas Browne* (1962)

Browne, Tom 1870–1910
English strip cartoonist, illustrator and painter
Born in Nottingham, he was first apprenticed to a lithographer and freelanced his first strip to *Scraps* (1880). Moving to London, he quickly became a popular cartoonist for magazines, posters and picture postcards. When *Comic Cuts* was launched (1890), his bold linear style proved suitable for cheap reproduction, and he was soon drawing front pages for several comics a week. His two tramps, *Weary Willie* and *Tired Tim*, inspired by Don Quixote and Sancho Panza, were instantly popular, and continued to appear in *Chips* 40 years after his death.

Browne, William 1591–1643
English pastoral poet
Born in Tavistock, Devon, he was educated at Exeter College, Oxford. He entered the Inner Temple, and was then tutor to Robert Dormer, the future Earl of Carnarvon. His best-known poetry is in *Britannia's Pastorals* (3 vols, 1613, 1616, 1852) and in the *Inner Temple Masque* (1615). 🕮 F W Moorman, *William Browne; his Britannia's Pastorals and the pastoral poetry of the Elizabethan age* (1897)

Browning, Elizabeth Barrett, *née* Barrett 1806–61
English poet
Born in Coxhoe Hall, Durham, she spent her childhood at Hope End, Herefordshire. At 10 she read **Homer** in the original, and at 14 wrote an epic on *The Battle of Marathon*. In her teens she damaged her spine, and was an invalid for a long time. Her *Essay on Mind, and Other Poems*, was published in 1826, and in 1833 she issued a translation of **Aeschylus'** *Prometheus Bound*, succeeded by *The Seraphim, and Other Poems* (1838), in which was republished the poem on **William Cowper's** grave. *Poems* (1844) contained 'The Cry of the Children', an outburst against the employment of young children in factories. In 1845 she met **Robert Browning**, and married him the following year. They settled in Pisa (1846) and then Florence (1847), where they became the centre of a literary circle. Her other works include *Casa Guidi Windows* (1851), *Aurora Leigh* (1856), *Poems before Congress* (1860), her best-known work *Sonnets from the Portuguese* (published in the *Poems* of 1850), and *Last Poems* (1851). 🕮 D Hewlett, *Elizabeth Barrett Browning* (1953)

Browning, John Moses 1855–1926
US gunsmith and inventor
Born in Ogden, Utah, the son of a Mormon gunsmith, he produced his first gun from scrap metal at the age of 13. He patented a breech-loading single-shot rifle in 1879, and the Browning automatic pistol in 1911. The Browning machine gun (1917) and the Browning automatic rifle (1918) were standard army weapons for many years.

Browning, Oscar 1837–1923
English schoolmaster, historian and educational reformer
Born in London, he was educated at Eton and King's College, Cambridge, where he was a Fellow from 1859 until his death. Assistant master and housemaster at Eton from 1860, he was dismissed in 1875 on unsubstantiated charges of intimacy with boys. He returned to King's where he became lecturer in history (1880) and university lecturer (1883). He helped to found the Cambridge University day training college and was principal from 1891 to 1909. He retired to Rome and wrote most of his historical works in his last years, including *A History of the Modern World, 1815–1910* (2 vols, 1912).

Browning, Robert 1812–89
English poet
Born in Camberwell, he attended lectures briefly at University College London and then travelled abroad. *Pauline*, a dramatic poem written at the age of 20, was published anonymously in 1833. He made a visit to St Petersburg, and on his return *Paracelsus* (1835) won him some recognition in literary circles. He wrote several dramas and collections of shorter dramatic poems and published them under the title *Bells and Pomegranates* (1841–46). It included *Dramatic Romances and Lyrics* (1845), which contained 'My Last Duchess' and 'The Pied Piper of Hamelin'. From 1846 he was married to **Elizabeth Barrett Browning**, settling first in Pisa (1846) and then in Florence (1847), where their son, Robert Wiedemann Barrett Browning (1849–1912), the sculptor, was born. In 1855 Browning published *Men and Women*, which contained such poems as 'Fra Lippo Lippi', 'Childe Roland to the Dark Tower Came' and 'Andrea del Sarto'. After the death of his wife (1861) he settled in London with his son, and wrote the famous *The Ring and the Book*, published in four volumes (1868–69). Browning's poetry is distinguished by its spiritual insight and psychological analysis; and he invented new kinds of narrative structure to

take the place of the epic and the pastoral. In his play *Pippa Passes* (1841), for example, a girl's song binds together a variety of scenes. His other chief works are *Dramatis Personae* (1864), *Fifine at the Fair* (1872), *The Inn Album* (1875), *Pacchiarotto* (1876) and *Asolando* (1889). □ T E F Blackburn, *Robert Browing: a study of his poetry* (1973); A Maurois, *Robert and Elizabeth Browning* (1955)

Brownlee, John 1900–69
Australian baritone
Born in Geelong, Victoria, he studied at Melbourne and Paris, where he made his debut in 1926. Later that year Nellie Melba engaged him to sing opposite her in *La Bohème* at Covent Garden, London. Thereafter, he was a regular soloist with the Paris Opera until 1936, a founding soloist with the Glyndebourne Festival Opera, and made many records. He made his first appearance with the Metropolitan Opera, New York, in 1937 as Rigoletto and appeared there regularly until 1958. As director of the Manhattan School of Music (1956–58) and president (from 1958), he spent the remaining years of his life in Manhattan.

Brownrigg, Sir Robert 1759–1833
English general
Governor of Ceylon from 1811 to 1820, he conquered the Kandyan kingdom in 1814–15 and was promoted to general in 1819.

Brown-Séquard, Édouard 1817–94
French physiologist
Born in Port Louis, Mauritius, he studied at Paris University, practised medicine in the USA, and was briefly professor at Virginia Medical College in Virginia. He was appointed Professor of Physiology at Harvard in 1864, at the School of Medicine in Paris (1869–73), and at the Collège de France from 1878. He proved an ingenious physiological researcher, experimenting in particular on blood, muscular irritability, animal heat, the spinal cord, and the nervous system. He also demonstrated the artificial production of epileptic states, and as a pioneer of endocrinology, he proved that removal of the adrenal glands would always produce death in animals.

Brownson, Orestes Augustus 1803–76
US clergyman and writer
Born in Stockbridge, Vermont, he was self-educated, and was successively a Presbyterian, a Universalist, a Unitarian pastor, and, from 1844, a Roman Catholic. He founded and edited *Brownson's Quarterly Review* (1844–65, and 1872 onwards), and wrote many books, including *The Convert* (1857) and *The American Republic* (1865).

Brubeck, Dave (David Warren) 1920–
US pianist, composer and bandleader
He was born in Concord, California. He was tutored by his mother, a classical pianist, and he went on to study music at the College of the Pacific, Stockton, California, leading a twelve-piece jazz band and at the same time studying composition under Darius Milhaud. Towards the end of World War II he was stationed in Europe, leading a service band, but in 1946 he resumed his studies and began to make his reputation as an experimental musician with his Jazz Workshop Ensemble. He reached a wider public with the Dave Brubeck Quartet formed in 1951, including alto saxophonist Paul Desmond. Desmond's composition 'Take Five' in 5/4 time, became one of the most popular recordings in jazz. From 1972, he involved his three sons in various combinations in his bands. He has composed larger-scale works such as ballets, a mass, and pieces for jazz group and orchestra, and continued to tour and record with small groups into the 1990s. He was made Officier, L'Ordre des Arts et des Lettres in 1990.

Bruce, C(harles) G(ranville) 1866–1939
English soldier and mountaineer
During his distinguished military career, he served in many parts of the world and attained the rank of general. While with the 5th Gurkha Rifles he explored the Himalayas and joined the 1892 expedition to the Karakoram led by Martin Conway. In 1907 he took part in the expedition on which T G Longstaff and three others climbed Trisul, the first peak over 7,000m (22,966ft) to be scaled. Despite having been wounded in World War I, he led two major British expeditions to Mt Everest (1922 and 1924), for which he became a national figure. It was his idea that Sherpas be employed as high-altitude porters, a suggestion which was to revolutionize Himalayan climbing.

Bruce, Christopher 1945–
English dancer and choreographer
Born in Leicester, he studied tap, acrobatics and ballet, and on graduating from the Ballet Rambert School immediately joined the company. In 1967 he established his reputation in Glen Tetley's *Pierrot lunaire* (1962). Within two years of this he had choreographed his first piece for Rambert, *George Frideric*, an abstract dance laced with drama. Later works include *Ancient Voices of Children* (1975), *Cruel Garden* (1977, with Lindsay Kemp), *Ghost Dances* (1981) and *Swansong* (1987). His work is a fusion of classical and modern dance idioms, with a strong undercurrent of social consciousness. He was associate choreographer of English National Ballet (formerly London Festival Ballet) from 1986 to 1991, has been a resident choreographer of Houston Ballet since 1989 and artistic director of the Ballet Rambert Dance Company since 1994.

Bruce, Sir David 1855–1931
Scottish microbiologist and physician
Born in Melbourne, Australia, whilst serving as an officer in the Royal Army Medical Corps (1883–1919), he identified in Malta the bacterium that causes undulant fever (brucellosis) in humans, named *Brucella* (1887). He was Assistant Professor of Pathology in the Army Medical School (1889–94), and worked to improve studies in pathology. In 1895 in South Africa he discovered that the tsetse fly was the carrier of the protozoal parasite (*Trypanosoma brucei*) responsible for the cattle disease nagana, and sleeping sickness in humans. Elected FRS in 1899 and knighted in 1908, he was Commandant of the Royal Army Medical College during World War I. □ J Mitchell, *David Bruce: The Early Naturalist Years* (1989)

Bruce, Frederick Fyvie 1910–90
Scottish classicist and biblical scholar
Born in Elgin, Morayshire, he was the son of a Plymouth Brethren preacher. He was educated at Aberdeen, Cambridge and Vienna, and taught at Edinburgh, Leeds and Sheffield before moving to the historic Rylands Chair of Biblical Criticism and Exegesis at Manchester (1959–78). A welcome speaker and lecturer in evangelical circles, he edited the *Evangelical Quarterly* (1949–80) and *Palestine Exploration Quarterly* (1957–71). An indefatigable writer, he produced commentaries on nearly every New Testament book. Among his many other works are *The Books and the Parchments* (1950), *Second Thoughts on the Dead Sea Scrolls* (1956), *Israel and the Nations* (1963), *New Testament History* (1969), *Paul and Jesus* (1974), *History of the Bible in English* (1979), the autobiographical *In Retrospect* (1980), and *The Real Jesus* (1985).

Bruce, James, *nicknamed* the Abyssinian 1730–94
Scottish explorer
Born in Kinnaird House, Stirlingshire, and educated at Harrow, he became consul-general in Algiers (1763–65), and in 1768 travelled to Abyssinia (Ethiopia) by the Nile,

Aswan, the Red Sea, and Massawa. In 1770 he reached the source of the Abbai, or headstream of the Blue Nile, then considered the main stream of the Nile. His *Travels to Discover the Sources of the Nile* was published in 1790, but contained such extraordinary accounts of Abyssinia that many considered them fictitious at the time. Their truth was later confirmed by **Richard Burton** and other travellers. ☐ J R Reid, *Traveller Extraordinary* (1968)

Bruce, James See Elgin, 8th Earl of

Bruce, Lenny, *originally* Leonard Alfred Schneider
1925–66
US satirical comedian
Born in New York, he had a variety of jobs after leaving the US navy in 1946, and first appeared as a night-club performer in Baltimore, Maryland. The satire and black humour of his largely improvised act often overstepped the limits of what was considered permissible. In 1961 he was imprisoned for obscenity, and in 1963, a year after his first appearance at the Establishment Club in London, he was refused permission to enter Great Britain to fulfil another engagement. In May 1963 he was found guilty of illegal possession of drugs; his death three years later was drugs-related. He was one of the first comedians who tried to disturb rather than amuse with his observation of the violence and brutalities of the mid-20th century. ☐ Albert Goldman and Lawrence Schiller, *Ladies and Gentlemen, Lenny Bruce!!!* (1974)

Bruce, Mary Grant 1878–1958
Australian novelist
Born in Sale, Victoria, she began writing as a child, and on moving to Melbourne in 1898, she ran the children's page of the *Leader* newspaper, in which some of her stories were serialized as *A Little Bush Maid* and later published in book form (1910). She published a book nearly every year until 1942, as well as much short fiction and numerous contributions to newspapers and periodicals. Although she is now considered mainly as a children's writer, her novels were at the time widely read and reviewed by adults. She is best known for her *Billabong* series of novels of Australian pastoral life and their heroine Norah Linton, perhaps the first Australian female character drawn in a realistic light, though she herself thought more highly of her book *The Stone Axe of Burkamukk* (1922), a collection of Aboriginal legends.

Bruce, Robert See panel p284

Bruce I, Robert de, *also spelt* Bruis or Breaux or Brus d.c.1094
Norman knight
He accompanied **William the Conqueror** to England in 1066. The name is traced to the domain of Bruis, near Cherbourg. He received extensive lands in Yorkshire.

Bruce II, Robert de c.1078–1141
Scottish nobleman
He was the son of **Robert de Bruce**, and a companion in arms of Prince David of Scotland, afterwards **David I**, from whom he got the lordship of Annandale. He renounced his allegiance to David in the war in England between **Stephen** and **Matilda**, niece of the King of Scots, so forfeiting Annandale (1138).

Bruce V, Robert de, 4th Lord of Annandale
d.1245
Scottish nobleman
He married Isabel, second daughter of David, Earl of Huntingdon and Chester, brother of King **William I**, the Lion, and thus founded the royal house of Bruce.

Bruce VI, Robert de, 5th Lord of Annandale
1210–95
Scottish nobleman
He did homage to **Henry III** (1251), and was made Sheriff of Cumberland and Constable of Carlisle. When the Scottish throne became vacant at the death (1290) of **Margaret**, Maid of Norway, granddaughter of **Alexander III**, **John de Balliol** and Bruce claimed the succession. **Edward I** of England decided in favour of Balliol (1292). To avoid swearing fealty to his successful rival, Bruce resigned Annandale to his eldest son, **Robert de Bruce** (1253–1304).

Bruce VII, Robert de 1253–1304
Scottish nobleman
The eldest son of **Robert de Bruce**, 5th Lord of Annandale, he is said to have accompanied **Edward I** of England on crusade to Palestine (1269). He married Marjory, Countess of Carrick (1271), and thus became Earl of Carrick, but resigned the earldom (1292) to his eldest son, **Robert Bruce**, the future King Robert I. On the death of his father (1295) he did homage to Edward for his English lands, was made constable of Carlisle, and fought for the English against **John de Balliol**. On Balliol's defeat he applied to Edward for the Crown of Scotland, but was refused it.

Bruce (of Melbourne), Stanley Melbourne Bruce, 1st Viscount 1883–1967
Australian statesman
Born in St Kilda, Victoria, he was educated at Cambridge, and spent much time in England because of business interests. After service in World War I with a British regiment, he entered Australian federal politics in 1918, and was Treasurer in **William Morris Hughes's** Nationalist government, but in 1923 joined with the Country Party in a coalition with himself as Prime Minister and Minister for External Affairs (1923–29). An ardent imperialist, he was active in the League of Nations. He became Australia's High Commissioner in London (1933–45), and played a leading part in **Churchill's** War Cabinet. He became Viscount Bruce in 1947 and was the first Chancellor of the Australian National University (1951–61).

Bruce (of Kinross), Sir William 1630–1710
Scottish architect
Born at Blairhall, Fife, he was appointed king's surveyor and master of works in 1671, and rebuilt the palace of Holyroodhouse in Edinburgh (1671–79). He also designed Kinross House (1685–93), and part of Hopetoun House in West Lothian (1699–1702). He is recognized as a founder of British Palladianism.

Bruch, Max 1838–1920
German composer
Born in Cologne, he became musical director at Coblenz in 1865, and conducted the Liverpool Philharmonic Orchestra (1880–83), introducing many of his choral works. He is best known, however, for his Violin Concerto in G minor (1868), the *Kol Nidrei* (1881) variations in which he employs the idioms of Hebrew and Celtic traditional melodies, and the *Konzertstück*.

Bruckner, Anton 1824–96
Austrian composer and organist
Born in Ansfelden, his early sacred choruses reflect a highly religious background. Following a rigorous, self-imposed training, and several posts as an organist, he wrote his Symphony No1 in 1865–66, becoming Professor of Composition at the Vienna Conservatory (1868–91). His fame rests chiefly on his nine symphonies (the last unfinished), but he also wrote four impressive masses, several smaller sacred works, and many choral

Bruce, Robert, *later* Robert I, *commonly known as* Robert the Bruce 1274–1329
King of Scotland from 1306, hero of the Scottish War of Independence

Robert the Bruce was born either at Turnberry in Ayrshire or in Essex. In 1296, as Earl of Carrick, he swore fealty to Edward I at Berwick, and in 1297 renewed his oath of homage at Carlisle. Shortly after, with his Carrick vassals, he joined the Scottish revolt under William Wallace. He was appointed one of the four guardians of Scotland in 1298, but did not fight against Edward again until the final rising in 1306. His stabbing of John Comyn ('the Red Comyn'), the nephew of John de Balliol and a rival with a better claim to the throne, in the church of the Minorite Friars in Dumfries (10 February 1306), allowed him to assert his own claim and two months later he was crowned king at Scone.

Between 1306 and 1314 he developed from a master of guerrilla warfare into a national leader, despite scepticism by some as to his legal status. Two defeats in 1306, one by an English army at Methven, near Perth, the other by the Lord of Argyll, a kinsman of the Comyns, at Dalry, near Tyndrum in Perthshire, forced him to flee, probably to Rathlin Island off the north coast of Ireland.

The turnabout in his fortunes between 1307 and 1309 began in his own south-west territory, with the defeat of an English force at Loudoun (May 1307). The death of Edward I the following July brought to the English throne a king, Edward II, who lacked his father's iron will and drive. By 1309 Robert was able to hold his first parliament (in St Andrews), which was, however, attended only by Bruce supporters.

Spectacular military success between 1310 and 1314, when he won control of northern Scotland, resolved the doubts of many. A series of strongholds were recaptured, leaving only Lothian outside his control. In early 1314 the castles of Edinburgh and Roxburgh also fell to him, leaving Stirling as the only English stronghold north of the Forth. The victory (24 June 1314) at Bannockburn, near Stirling, over a larger English army of nearly 20,000 men, did not end the Anglo-Scottish war, which went on until 1328 or later, but it did virtually settle the Scottish civil war, leaving Robert I unchallenged.

For 10 years the north of England was raided (Berwick was taken in 1318) and a second front was opened up by Robert's brother, Edward, in Ireland in 1315. The Declaration of Arbroath, a letter composed in 1320 by his chancellor, Bernard de Linton, and a mission to Avignon, finally persuaded Pope John XXII to recognize Robert as king in 1323. A truce with England brought a temporary suspension of hostilities, but Robert took advantage of the accession of the young Edward III in 1327 to force the Treaty of Northampton (1328), which secured English acknowledgement of Scottish independence and his own right to the throne. He was succeeded by David II, his son by his second wife.

📖 J Barbour, *The Brus* (c.1375); later editions by W W Skeat (ed), *The Bruce* (2 vols, 1894), and by M P McDiarmid and J A C Stevenson (eds), *Barbour's Bruce* (vols 2 and 3, 1980). See also G W S Barrow, *Robert Bruce and the Community of the Realm of Scotland* (1965).

The traditional tale about Robert Bruce and the spider is thought to originate from his time in exile on Rathlin Island (1306–07). Learning that Kildrummie Castle in Aberdeenshire, the last castle left to him, had been seized by the English, and his wife imprisoned and his brother slain, Bruce fell into despair. As he lay on his bed, wretchedly trying to decide whether to resign all attempts to restore freedom to Scotland, he noticed a spider hanging from the roof of the cabin (or, some say, cave) on a long thread. The spider was trying to swing itself from one roofbeam to another, to secure the thread for spinning its web. On its sixth unsuccessful attempt, Bruce spied an analogy with his own situation: he had fought six battles against the English without success. He decided that if the spider should secure its thread on its seventh attempt, he would try his luck in Scotland one more time. If it failed, he would go to the wars in Palestine and never return to his homeland.

The legend goes that the spider made an almighty effort and secured its thread, inspiring Bruce to his subsequent victories in Scotland. Walter Scott wrote: 'I have often met with people of the name of Bruce, so completely persuaded of the truth of this story, that they would not on any account kill a spider; because it was that insect which had shown the example of perseverance, and given a signal of good luck to their great namesake.' (See Walter Scott, *Tales of a Grandfather*, 1828, ch.8)

---

works. His music, which received a mixed reception during his lifetime, shows the influence of Wagner and Schubert.

Brudenell, James Thomas See Cardigan, 7th Earl of

Brueghel or Breughel, Jan, the Elder, *also called* 'Velvet' Brueghel 1568–1625
Flemish artist

He was born in Brussels, the younger son of Pieter Brueghel, the Elder. He painted still life, flowers, landscapes and religious subjects, generally on a small scale. His son, Jan, the Younger (1601–78), imitated him closely.

Brueghel Pieter, the Elder, *also spelt* Breughel or (after 1559) Bruegel, *also called* 'Peasant' Brueghel c.1520–1569
Flemish artist

He was born in the village of Bruegel, near Breda, and was the pupil of Pieter Coecke van Aelst (1502–50). An early influence on his work was Hieronymus Bosch. He was made a master of the Antwerp guild in 1551 and then went to Italy. His work was highly regarded, particularly by Rubens, and much of it was bought for royal collections, but his reputation went into decline until the beginning of the 20th century. His pictures, often highly sophisticated moral commentaries derived from everyday sayings and proverbs, mainly depict earthy peasants engaging in all sorts of activities against a backdrop of well-observed landscape, and the truthfulness of his rendering of peasant life and weather conditions marks his work out from the Italianate style of his Netherlandish contemporaries. This genre reached its highest expression in his later works, *The Blind Leading the Blind* (1568), *The Peasant Wedding* (1568) and *The Peasant Dance* (1568). His principal works are in Vienna but there are two examples, *The Adoration of the Kings* and *The Death of the Virgin*, in the National Gallery, London.

Brueghel or Breughel, Pieter, the Younger, *also called* 'Hell' Brueghel c.1564–1638
Flemish painter

Born in Brussels and educated by his grandmother, then in Antwerp, he was the son of Pieter Brueghel, the Elder. He was called 'Hell' Brueghel because he painted *diableries*, scenes with devils, hags or robbers.

Brugmann, Karl 1849–1919
German philologist

Born in Wiesbaden, he was Professor of Sanskrit at Freiburg (1884) and Leipzig (1887). He wrote a *Comparative Grammar of the Indo-Germanic Languages* (1886–83), supplemented by three volumes on syntax by Berthold

Delbrück (1842–1922). He was a leading exponent of the Neo-Grammarian school, and stressed the fixity of sound laws.

Brugsch, Heinrich Karl 1827–94
German Egyptologist
Born in Berlin, he first visited Egypt in 1853, and subsequently alternated between Egypt and Germany as professor, or as consul for Germany. He was director of the School of Egyptology in Cairo (1870–90), and published a hieroglyphic–demotic dictionary (1867–82). He wrote many books, including *Egypt under the Pharaohs* (1879).

Brühl, Heinrich, Count von 1700–63
Saxon politician
The Prime Minister of Augustus III, King of Poland and Elector of Saxony, he drained the treasury, and burdened the country with debt to allow the king a luxurious lifestyle. He maintained a costly establishment for himself as well.

Bruhn, Erik, *originally* Belton Evers 1928–86
Danish dancer and ballet director
Born in Copenhagen, he trained at the Royal Danish Ballet School, joining the company in 1947. An elegant classical dancer, and an impressive exponent of the buoyant Bournonville style, he toured the world as guest performer with many companies, appearing to critical acclaim in such ballets as *Sleeping Beauty* and *La Sylphide* (1976). He was equally sought after for dramatic roles from the modern repertory, such as Roland Petit's *Carmen* (1949), and Birgit Cullberg's *Miss Julie*. He later took on character roles, including Dr Coppelius in his own production of *Coppelia* (1975). He was the director of the Royal Swedish Ballet (1967–72) and artistic director of the National Ballet of Canada (1983–86).

Brumby, Colin James 1933–
Australian composer and teacher
Born in Melbourne, where he studied at the Conservatorium of Music, he subsequently studied in Europe with Philipp Jarnach and Alexander Goehr. On his return he became senior lecturer at the University of Queensland, Brisbane, where he was head of the music department (1975–80), and where he is now associate professor. His considerable output includes two operas, nine operettas for younger audiences, nine concertos, *Alice: Memories of Childhood* for the Queensland Ballet, choral works, film scores and chamber music, much of which has been recorded. Major works include a flute concerto and his *Festival Overture on Australian Themes* (1982), a symphony (1982), *Ballade for St Cecilia* (1971), and *The Phoenix and the Turtle* (1974).

Brummell, George Bryan, *known as* Beau Brummell 1778–1840
English dandy
He was born in London, the son of Frederick, Lord North's private secretary. At Eton, and during a brief period at Oxford, he was less distinguished for studiousness than for the exquisiteness of his dress and manners. After four years in the army, having come into a fortune, he entered on his true vocation as arbiter of taste and leader of early 19th-century fashionable society. A close friend and protégé of the Prince Regent (the future George IV), he quarrelled with him in 1813, and in 1816 gambling debts forced Brummell to flee to Calais. From 1830 to 1832 he held a sinecure consulate at Caen. He died there in the pauper lunatic asylum. 📖 Hubert Cole, *Beau Brummell* (1977)

Brun, Charles le See Le Brun, Charles

Bruna, Dick 1927–
Dutch artist and writer
The creator of a highly successful series of picture books for young children, he started in the book trade in Utrecht, London and Paris, but he gave this up to concentrate on graphic art. His first book was *The Apple*, published in England in 1966, 13 years after it appeared in Holland. His great success came from 1959 onwards when his books began to appear in their present format. Many of these featured Miffy, others the small dog Snuffy. Among his most popular books is *B is for Bear*, first published in Dutch in 1967.

Brundage, Avery 1887–1975
US international athletics administrator
Born in Detroit, he was a member of the US decathlon team in the 1912 Olympic Games at Stockholm, but was far more influential in his long spell as president of the US Olympic Association from 1929 to 1953, and in his 20 years as president of the International Olympic Committee (1952–72). He was criticized for his rigid adherence to the letter of the Olympian law and his insistence on the strictest tenets of amateurism, but fought hard to preserve the Games from some of the commercial excesses which have since afflicted them.

Brundtland, Gro Harlem 1939–
Norwegian Labour politician
Born in Oslo, the daughter of a doctor who became a Cabinet Minister, she studied medicine at Oslo and Harvard, qualifying as a physician. In 1960 she married a leader of the opposition Conservative Party, Arne Olav Brundtland. In 1969, after working in public medicine services in Oslo, she joined the Labour Party and entered politics. She was appointed Environment Minister (1974–79) and then, as leader of the Labour Party group, became Prime Minister for a short time in 1981, the first woman Prime Minister of Norway. She was re-elected Prime Minister in 1986, 1990 and 1993, but stepped down in 1996. In 1987 she chaired the World Commission on Environment and Development which produced the report *Our Common Future*. In 1988 she was awarded the Third World Foundation prize for leadership in environmental issues.

Brune, Guillaume Marie Anne 1762–1815
French soldier
Born in Brive-la-Gaillarde, he commanded the Revolutionary army in the Netherlands (1799) and defeated the Russo-British forces (the latter under the command of Frederick Augustus, Duke of York) at two battles of Bergen. He commanded under Napoleon I in Italy (1800). On the emperor's return from Elba in 1815 Brune joined him, and was murdered by a Royalist mob at Avignon.

Bruneau, Alfred 1857–1934
French composer and music critic
Born in Paris, he studied at the Paris Conservatory under Jules Massenet. Although he wrote a choral symphony, lieder and other distinguished works, he is best known for his operas based on Emile Zola's works, such as *Le Rêve* (1891, 'The Dream') and *Messidor* (1897). On its first production, *Messidor* was badly received because of the composer's and Zola's sympathies with Alfred Dreyfus. Three volumes of his criticism were published from 1900 to 1903.

Brunel, Isambard Kingdom 1806–59
English engineer and inventor
Born in Portsmouth, he was the son of Sir Marc Isambard Brunel, and in 1823, after two years spent at the Collège Henri Quatre in Paris, he entered his father's office. He helped to plan the Thames Tunnel, and in 1829–31 planned the Clifton Suspension Bridge, completed in 1864 with the chains from his own Hungerford Suspension Bridge (1841–45) over the Thames at Charing Cross. He designed the *Great Western* (1838), the first steamship built

to cross the Atlantic Ocean, and the *Great Britain* (1845), the first ocean screw-steamer. The *Great Eastern*, until 1899 the largest vessel ever built, was constructed to his design in collaboration with **John Scott Russell**, from whose yard in Millwall the 'Great Ship' was launched at the second attempt in January 1858. In 1833 he was appointed engineer to the Great Western Railway, and constructed all the tunnels, bridges, and viaducts on that line. Among docks constructed or improved by him were those of Bristol, Monkwearmouth, Cardiff, and Milford Haven. ⊞ Peter Hay, *Brunel: His Achievements in the Transport Revolution* (1973)

Brunel, Sir Marc Isambard 1769–1849
French engineer and inventor
He was born in Hacqueville, Rouen, but during the French Revolution fled from Paris to the USA (1793). In 1794 he was appointed to survey for the canal from Lake Champlain to the Hudson at Albany. He then worked as an architect in New York, and became chief engineer for the city. Returning to Europe in 1799, he married and settled in England. In 1806 he received £17,000 from the government as a reward for his plan for making block-pulleys by machinery. He constructed public works in Woolwich arsenal and Chatham dockyard, and made experiments in steam navigation on the Thames in 1812, but his scheme for steam-tugs was declined by the navy board. The destruction of his sawmills at Battersea by fire (1814) led to his bankruptcy in 1821, when he was imprisoned for debt. He was later released on receiving a £5,000 grant from the government. His most remarkable undertaking was the Thames Tunnel from Rotherhithe to Wapping (1825–43), for which he used the tunnelling shield he had patented in 1818. ⊞ Paul Clements, *Marc Isambard Brunel* (1970)

Brunelleschi, *properly* Filippo di Ser Brunellesco 1377–1446
Italian architect, goldsmith and sculptor
Born in Florence, he began as a goldsmith. He is said to have turned his talents to architecture after defeat by **Ghiberti** in the competition for the Florence Cathedral baptistery doors in 1402 (the competition panels entered by both men are in the Bargello Museum). He designed the dome of the cathedral in Florence: erected between 1420 and 1461, it is (measured diametrically) the largest in the world and served as the model for **Michelangelo's** design for Saint Peter's in Rome. Other well-known buildings by him in Florence include S Spirito, S Lorenzo, and the Spedale degli Innocenti (Foundling Hospital). The wooden crucifix in the church of S Maria Novella was designed by him in private competition with **Donatello**. He was one of the figures responsible for the development of the Renaissance style in Florence, and is also to be noted for his innovations in the use of perspective. ⊞ Antonio Manetti, *The Life of Brunelleschi* (1970)

Bruner, Jerome Seymour 1915–
US psychologist
Born in New York City, he was educated at Duke University and Harvard. He was Professor of Psychology at Harvard (1952–72), Oxford (1972–80), and the New School for Social Research, New York (1981–88) and Research Professor of Psychology at New York University (1987–). His book *The Process of Education* (1960) established his reputation as a curriculum innovator. He stressed the centrality of teaching for underlying cognitive structure and the usefulness of the 'spiral curriculum', and his humanities programme 'Man: A Course of Study', described in *Toward a Theory of Instruction* (1966), has been held to be a landmark in curriculum development. He also pioneered techniques for investigating infant perception. The leading advocate of the value of the phenomenological tradition in psychology, he has attacked the radical behaviourism of **B F Skinner** as having distracted the subject from a proper regard for the main problems of humanity. Recently, he published *Acts of Meaning* (1990).

Brunhilde c.534–613
Frankish queen
The daughter of the Visigothic King Athanagild, she married King Sigbert of Austrasia. After his assassination (575), as regent for her two grandsons, Theodebert II, King of Austrasia, and Theodoric II, King of Burgundy, she divided the government of the whole Frankish world with her rival **Fredegond**, who governed Neustria for **Clotaire II**. On Fredegond's death (598) she seized Neustria, and for a time united under her rule the whole Merovingian dominions, but was overthrown by the Austrasian nobles under Clotaire II, and put to death by being dragged at the heels of a wild horse.

Brunhoff, Jean de 1899–1937
French writer and illustrator of children's books
He was born in Paris. His creation Babar the Elephant is one of the most enduring characters of 20th-century children's literature. *L'Histoire de Babar, le petit éléphant* (1931, Eng trans *The Story of Babar the Little Elephant*, 1934), which de Brunhoff both wrote and illustrated, was visually outstanding, produced on large pages with coloured lithographic drawings and a hand-written text. Nothing like it had appeared previously, and **A A Milne** persuaded his publishers to bring out the first English edition. The stories proved popular, and de Brunhoff wrote seven *Babar* books in all, three of which were published posthumously. His son, Laurent de Brunhoff (1925–), continued to write and illustrate *Babar* stories after World War II.

Bruni, Leonardo, *styled* Aretino 1369–1444
Italian humanist
Born in Arezzo, he was Papal Secretary from 1405 to 1415. He then wrote *Historiarum Florentini populi libri XII* (1610, '12 Books of Histories of the Florentine People'), and was made Chancellor of Florence in 1427. Bruni aided the advance of the study of Greek literature mainly by his literal translations into Latin of **Aristotle, Demosthenes, Plato**, and others. He also wrote Lives of **Petrarch** and **Dante** in Italian.

Brüning, Heinrich 1885–1970
German politician
Born in Münster, he studied at Bonn and the London School of Economics. During the Weimar Republic he became in 1929 leader of the predominantly Catholic *Zentrum* (Centre Party) and then Chancellor (1930–32). Faced with the problems of economic depression, he attempted to rule by decree, but was eventually forced out of office by **Hindenburg**, to make way for the more conservative **Franz von Papen**. In 1934 he left Germany, spending most of the rest of his life in US universities.

Brunner, (Heinrich) Emil 1889–1966
Swiss Reformed theologian
He was born in Winterthur, near Zurich. Following service as a pastor (1916–24), he became Professor of Systematic and Practical Theology at Zurich (1924–55), and visiting professor at the International Christian University, Tokyo (1953–55). The author of nearly 400 books and articles, his reputation outside the Continent was established by translations of *The Mediator* (1927) and *The Divine Imperative* (1937). *The Divine-Human Encounter* (1944) reveals his debt to **Martin Buber's** 'I–Thou' understanding of the relationship between God and Man, but he parted company in 1934 with the dialectical theology of the early **Karl Barth** by holding that there *was* a limited universal revelation of God in creation.

Brunner, Heinrich 1840–1915
German legal historian
His work has been fundamental for the study and understanding of early German law and institutions. His main works were *Deutsche Rechtsgeschichte* (1887) and *Grundzüge der deutschen Rechtsgeschichte* (1901).

Brünnich, Morten Thrane 1737–1827
Danish naturalist and zoologist
Born in Copenhagen, he studied theology and oriental languages, but turned to the natural sciences under the influence of **Linnaeus**. He wrote *A History of the Eider Duck* (1763) and in 1764 published a book on northern birds, *Ornithologia Borealis*, followed by *Entomologia* in the same year. As lecturer in natural history and economy at Copenhagen, he established a natural history museum, and wrote *Zoologiae fundamenta* (1771). Regarded as the founder of Danish zoology, Brünnich's Guillemot is named after him.

Bruno, St, *known as* Bruno the Great 925–65
German prelate
Born in Cologne, he was Imperial Chancellor in 940. In 953 he crushed a rebellion against his brother, **Otto I**, the Great, became Archbishop of Cologne the same year, and Duke of Lorraine in 954. He was distinguished both for piety and learning. He was the son of **Henry the Fowler**. His feast day is 11 October.

Bruno, St, *also known as* Boniface 970–1009
German missionary
Born in Querfurt, he was educated at Magdeburg Cathedral School, and entered the monastery in Ravenna in 997. He worked as a missionary bishop in Poland, Hungary and the Ukraine. When he reached Prussia, he met fierce opposition, and was put to death with his companions. His feast day is 19 June.

Bruno of Cologne, St c.1030–1101
German churchman
Born in Cologne, he became rector of the cathedral school at Rheims, but withdrew in 1084 to the mountains of Chartreuse, near Grenoble. Here with six friends he founded the austere Carthusian order on the site of the present Grande Chartreuse. In 1091, at the invitation of Pope **Urban II**, he founded a second Carthusian monastery at Della Torre, Calabria. His feast day is 6 October.

Bruno, Frank (lin Roy) 1961–
English boxer
Born in London, he won the ABA Heavyweight championship when he was 18 years old. Early successes as a professional soon propelled him into the world top 10, and in October 1985 he took the European championship. In 1986 he challenged for the WBA world championship, but lost to the holder, **Tim Witherspoon**, and a second attempt at the world crown, against **Mike Tyson** in 1989, also failed. In 1993 he unsuccessfully challenged **Lennox Lewis** for the WBC world title which he eventually won in 1995. He retired in 1996 and has latterly become involved in pantomime and television, and has retained his great popularity.

Bruno, Giordano, *originally* Filippo Bruno, *nicknamed* Il Nolano 1548–1600
Italian hermetic thinker
Born in Nola, near Naples, he became a Dominican friar but was too unorthodox to stay in the order, and fled to Geneva (1578). He travelled widely, lecturing and teaching, in France, Germany, England and Italy. His pantheistic philosophy—whereby God animated the whole of creation as 'world-soul'—and his sympathy with **Copernicus**'s theory of the universe brought him into conflict with the Inquisition. He was arrested in 1592 in Venice and after an eight-year trial was burned at the stake in Rome. His most famous works are *De l'infinito universo et mondi* (1584, 'On the Infinite Universe and Worlds') and *Spaccio de la bestia trionfante* (1584, 'The Expulsion of the Triumphant Beast'). 📖 Giovanni Gentile, *Giordano Bruno e il pensiero del rinascimento* (1991)

Brunton, John Stirling 1903–77
Scottish reforming educationist
Born in Glasgow, he taught in Scottish schools then joined HM (Scottish) Inspectorate of Schools in 1932. He rose to occupy its top position as Senior Chief Inspector (1955–66), and during these years set about changing the role of school inspectors. He reduced their load of routine examining and visiting and channelled their energies into active leadership of 'Working Parties', whose membership included teachers and college lecturers. Such working parties produced influential reports on the Senior Secondary curriculum (1959) and on 'the vocational impulse' as motivation for non-academic learners (1963). Another working party produced the 'Primary Memorandum' (1965) which in due course transformed Scottish primary education.

Brunvand, Jan Harold 1933–
US folklorist and scholar
As a Fellow of the Folklore Society, editor of the *Journal of American Folklore* (1976–80), a regular newspaper columnist since 1987, and Professor of English at the University of Utah, he has carried out extensive research on urban legends that has contributed enormously to popular awareness of folklore in the modern world. His writings include *The Study of American Folklore: an introduction* (1980), *The Vanishing Hitchhiker: American Urban Legends and their Meanings* (1981), *The Choking Doberman and Other 'New' Urban Legends* (1984), *The Mexican Pet: More 'New' Urban Legends and Some Old Favorites* (1986) and *Curses! Broiled Again! The Hottest Urban Legends Going* (1989).

Brusilov, Aleksei 1856–1926
Russian soldier
He was born in Tiflis (now Tbilisi), Georgia. He served in the war against Turkey (1877) and in World War I led the invasion of Galicia (1914) and the Carpathians. From 1916 he distinguished himself on the Eastern Front, notably in command of the South Western Army Group in the only partly successful 'Brusilov Offensive' against the Austrians in 1916. He became Chief of Staff in 1917, but the second 'Brusilov Offensive' was frustrated, and many of his troops mutinied and added to the unrest that produced the Bolshevik Revolution. After the Revolution he commanded forces in the war against Poland (1920).

Brustein, Robert 1927–
US drama critic, teacher and director
He was born in New York City. As Dean of the School of Drama at Yale University, he founded the Yale Repertory Theater (1966). He is also director of the American Repertory Theater, which took up residence at Harvard University in 1980. He is the author of several books, including an erudite and entertaining book of collected essays entitled *Who Needs Theater* (1987), and *Re-imagining American Theater* (1991).

Bruton, John Gerard 1947–
Irish Fine Gael politician
Born in Dublin and educated at University College, Dublin, he was elected to the Dáil Éireann as a Fine Gael member in 1969. His farming background made him his party's spokesman for agriculture in 1981 and he was made Minister of Finance in 1981. He became leader of Fine Gael in 1990 and was elected Prime Minister in 1994. During the discussions over the future of Northern Ireland he proved to be conciliatory to Unionist feelings and has been a constant critic of republican terrorism.

Brutus, Lucius Junius fl.500BC
Roman hero

He established Republican government in Rome. The son of a rich Roman, on whose death Tarquinius Superbus seized the property and killed an elder brother, he himself escaped by feigning idiocy, from which he got his name (*Brutus* means 'stupid'). When popular indignation was roused at the outrage on Lucretia by Sextus, son of Tarquinius Superbus, Brutus drove the royal family from Rome. He was elected one of the first two consuls (509BC). He sentenced his own two sons to death for conspiring to restore the monarchy, and fell repelling an attack led by one of Tarquin's sons.

Brutus, Marcus Junius c.85–42BC
Roman politician

He sided with Pompey when the civil war broke out in 49BC, but, after the defeat at Pharsalia, submitted to Julius Caesar, and was appointed Governor of Cisalpine Gaul. He divorced his wife to marry Portia, the daughter of his master Cato. Cassius persuaded him to join the conspiracy to assassinate Caesar (44BC), and, defeated by Mark Antony and Octavian (Augustus) at Philippi, he killed himself.

Bruyère, Jean de la See La Bruyère, Jean de

Bry, Théodor de 1528–98
Flemish engraver and goldsmith

Born in Liège, he settled in Frankfurt am Main about 1570 and established a printing house there. His well-known print, *The Procession of the Knights of the Garter under Queen Elizabeth*, was produced after a visit to England.

Bryan, W(illiam) J(ennings) 1860–1925
US politician

Born in Salem, Illinois, he graduated from Illinois College in 1881 and studied law at Chicago. He served in the US House of Representatives as a Democrat from Nebraska (1891–95) and was a delegate to the 1896 Democratic national convention, where he delivered his famous 'Cross of Gold' speech in defence of free silver and so captured the presidential nomination. He lost to William McKinley in that year and in 1900; in 1908 he gained the nomination for the third time but lost to William Howard Taft. In the course of his campaigns he became known as a great populist stump-orator, styling himself as an advocate of the common people and denouncing expansionism and monopolies. He also promoted his views through a political weekly, *The Commoner*, which he founded and edited from 1901. He was appointed Secretary of State by Woodrow Wilson (1913), but as an ardent pacifist resigned in June 1915 over America's second *Lusitania* note to Germany. His last public act was assisting the anti-evolutionist prosecutor in the Scopes Monkey Trial in Dayton, Tennessee. He was the father of the feminist Ruth Rohde.

Bryant, William Cullen 1794–1878
US poet and journalist

Born in Cummington, Massachusetts, he graduated in law and practised in Great Barrington, Massachusetts, from 1816, but in 1817 published his majestic blank verse *Thanatopsis*. He practised law until 1825, but increasingly turned to newspaper contributions in prose and verse, becoming co-owner and editor of the New York *Evening Post* in 1829. The paper was Democratic, but, having anti-slavery views, assisted in 1856 in forming the Republican party. His public addresses and letters to his paper on his visits to Europe and the West Indies were published in book form as *Letters of a Traveller* (1850), and he also published volumes of his poetry. ☐ P Godwin, *A Biography of Willian Cullen Bryant* (1883)

Bryce, David 1803–76
Scottish architect

He was born and educated in Edinburgh and entered partnership with William Burn there. One of the pre-eminent architects of Victorian Scotland, he evolved and perfected the Scottish Baronial style for his country houses, drawing inspiration from 16th-century Scottish architecture. He also used Italianate and French styles, as in Fettes College (1864–70), which has been described as his Scottish Baronial–French Gothic masterpiece, and designed several classical banks in Edinburgh.

Bryden, Bill (William Campbell Rough) 1942–
Scottish stage director and dramatist

He was born in Greenock, Renfrewshire, and began his career as a documentary scriptwriter for Scottish Television (1963–64), before becoming assistant director at the Belgrade Theatre, Coventry (1965–67) and associate director of the Royal Lyceum Theatre, Edinburgh (1971–74). His productions at Edinburgh included two of his own plays, *Willie Rough* (1972) and *Benny Lynch* (1974), gritty dramas set in industrial urban Scotland. From 1975 to 1985 he was an associate of the National Theatre, where he was director of the small Cottesloe Theatre (1978–80) and where he became particularly associated with directing plays by US authors. From 1984 to 1993 he was head of drama for BBC Television Scotland. He has directed three films from his own screenplays: *Ill Fares the Land* (1982), *The Holy City* (1985) and *Aria* (1987), as well as *Parsifal* (1988) and *The Cunning Little Vixen* (1990) at Covent Garden. Also in 1990, he directed *The Ship*, a large-scale epic play about the Glasgow shipbuilding industry, set at a Clydeside shipyard, in the course of which a ship was built and launched. In 1991 he directed his own adaptation of Mark Baker's *Cops*, which was based on interviews with New York policemen. In 1994, he wrote and directed *The Big Picnic*, which was also performed at a Clydeside shipyard.

Bryussov, Valeri Yakovlevich 1873–1924
Russian poet, critic, editor and translator

Born in Moscow, he was one of the leaders of the Russian Symbolist movement which looked to France for its inspiration. Like Konstantin Balmont, his best work was done before 1910, but unlike him his technique remained unimpaired to the last. He translated major modernist writers in Europe, including Paul Verlaine, Stéphane Mallarmé, Maurice Maeterlinck and Gabriele D'Annunzio. He became an enthusiastic Bolshevist in 1917 and worked tirelessly for that cause until his death. His best-known prose works are the two novels *Ognennyy Angel* (1907–08), 'The Fiery Angel', which provided the basis of Prokofiev's opera *The Fiery Angel*, and *Altarpobedy* (1911–12), 'The Altar of Victory').

Brzezinski, Zbigniew 1928–
US academic and politician

Born in Warsaw, Poland, he settled in the USA and became a naturalized citizen in 1958. He taught at Harvard's Russian Research Center during the 1950s and then, as Professor of Public Law and Government, at Columbia University. A member of the State Department's policy planning council during the Johnson administration, he became national security adviser to President Jimmy Carter (1977–80) and was the chief architect of a tough human rights policy, directed against the USSR. From 1981 he resumed his position at Columbia and taught at Georgetown University, producing influential works on strategic relations with the USSR and Japan. His publications include *Out of Control* (1993).

Buber, Martin 1878–1965
Austrian Jewish theologian, philosopher and novelist

Born in Vienna, he studied philosophy at Vienna, Berlin and Zurich, then became interested in Hasidism. He was founding editor of the monthly journal *Der Jude* (1916–24, 'The Jew'), Professor of Comparative Religion at Frankfurt (1923–33), then director of the Central Office for Jewish Adult Education until 1938 when he fled to Palestine to escape the Nazis and became Professor of the Sociology of Religion at Jerusalem. He published profusely on social and ethical problems, but is best-known for his religious philosophy expounded most famously in *Ich und Du* (1922, Eng trans *I and Thou*, 1958), contrasting personal relationships of mutuality and reciprocity with utilitarian or objective relationships. Both his philosophy and his reworkings of Hasidic tales, collected in English translation in *The Legend of the Baal-Shem* (1955), *Tales of Rabbi Nachman* (1956), and elsewhere, have had a subtle influence on European and US literature. His only novel is *Gog and Magog* (1943, Eng trans *For the Sake of Heaven*), about the Hasidic world in Napoleonic times. ⌨ R Horwitz, *Buber's Way to 'I and Thou'* (1978); M Seymour-Smith, *Who's Who in Twentieth Century Literature* (1976)

Bubka, Sergei 1963–
Ukrainian field athlete
Born in Donetsk, he made his international debut as a pole-vaulter at the 1983 world championship in Helsinki, where he won the gold medal. He retained this title in 1987, 1991, 1993 and 1995, and also won gold at the 1988 Olympics. In his career he has broken 35 world records and in 1992, took the world pole vault record to 6.12m. Injury prevented him from defending his title in the 1996 Olympic Games in Atlanta, Georgia.

Bucer or Butzer, Martin 1491–1551
German Protestant reformer
Born in Schlettstadt, Alsace, he entered the Dominican Order, and studied theology at Heidelberg. In 1521 he left the order, married a former nun, and in 1523 settled in Strasbourg. In the disputes between **Martin Luther** and **Huldreich Zwingli** he adopted a middle course. At the Diet of Augsburg he refused to subscribe to the proposed Confession of Faith, and afterwards drew up the *Confessio Tetrapolitana* (1530). He advised **Henry VIII** on his divorce from **Catherine of Aragon** (1533). At Wittenberg in 1536 he made an agreement with the Lutherans, but when attacked for his refusal to sign the *Interim* in 1548, he came to England on **Thomas Cranmer**'s invitation (1549) as Regius Professor of Theology at Cambridge. In **Mary I**'s reign his remains were exhumed and burned. His chief work was a translation and exposition of the Psalms (1529).

Buch, (Christian) Leopold von 1774–1853
German geologist and traveller
Born in Stolpe, near Angermünde, Prussia, at the age of 15 he was sent to nearby Berlin to study mineralogy and chemistry and subsequently he went to Freiburg to study under **Abraham Werner**. He later contradicted Werner's teaching and accepted basalt as a product of volcanic activity. Fieldwork in the Canary Islands led to his proposal of a 'craters of elevation' hypothesis, now refuted. As a result of travels in Scandinavia (1806–08), he recognized the uplift of land relative to sea level. He published the first coloured geological map of Germany in 42 sheets (1826) and undertook important early studies of Alpine geology. He introduced the term gabbro and described other igneous rocks. In later years he turned his attention to palaeontology, and formulated a classification of cephalopods (1829–30).

Buchan, Alexander 1829–1907
Scottish meteorologist and oceanographer
Born in Kinnesswood, near Kinross, he was educated at the Free Church College for teachers at Edinburgh and later at Edinburgh University. He became secretary of the Scottish Meteorological Society in 1860 and held this position throughout his career. He was editor of the *Scottish Meteorological Society Journal* and from 1877 a member of the Meteorological Council which directed the operations of the Meteorological Office. It was largely through his efforts that observatories were established at the summit of Ben Nevis (1883) and near its base at Fort William. In 1868 he produced the first charts of storm tracks across the Atlantic. He prepared the meteorological report of the *Challenger* expedition of 1876 and contributed to the oceanographic section of that report. In his major work *Report on Atmospheric Circulation* (1889), he presented global charts of monthly mean temperature, pressure and wind direction for the whole year. His studies of weather charts led him to conclude that the British climate is subject to warm and cold spells falling approximately between certain dates each year, the so called Buchan spells. He was the first recipient of the Symons Gold Medal of the Royal Meteorological Society.

Buchan, Earl of See **Erskine, David Stewart**

Buchan, John, 1st Baron Tweedsmuir
1875–1940
Scottish writer and statesman
Born in Perth, the son of a Free Church minister, he was educated at Glasgow University and at Brasenose College, Oxford. In 1901 he was called to the Bar and became private secretary to Lord **Milner**, High Commissioner for South Africa. He returned in 1903 to become a director of Nelson's the publishers. During World War I he served on HQ staff until 1917, when he became Director of Information. He was MP for the Scottish Universities (1927–35), and was raised to the peerage in 1935, when he became Governor-General of Canada. In 1937 he was made a Privy Councillor, and Chancellor of Edinburgh University. His strength as a writer was for fast-moving adventure stories, which include *Prester John* (1910), *Huntingtower* (1922) and *Witch Wood* (1927). He became best known, however, for his spy thrillers featuring Richard Hannay: *The Thirty-Nine Steps* (1915), *Greenmantle* (1916), *The Three Hostages* (1924), and others. He also wrote biographies, including *Montrose* (1928) and *Sir Walter Scott* (1932). ⌨ J Adam Smith, *John Buchan* (1965)

Buchanan, Claudius 1766–1815
Scottish missionary
Born in Cambuslang, Glasgow, he became chaplain to the East India Company at Barrackpur in 1797, translated the Gospels into Persian and Hindustani, and made two tours through southern and western India. Returning in 1808 to England, he excited so much interest in Indian missions that before his death the first English bishop had been appointed to Calcutta.

Buchanan, George c.1506–1582
Scottish scholar and humanist
Born near Killearn in Stirlingshire, at the age of 14 he was sent by an uncle to study Latin at the University of Paris. He returned to Scotland in 1523 and studied at St Andrews University, then returned to Paris to teach. In 1537, King **James V** appointed him tutor to one of his illegitimate sons, the future Earl of **Moray**, but he was soon charged with heresy at St Andrews after writing a satirical poem about friars, *Franciscanus*, which offended Cardinal **Beaton**. He fled to France, where he taught at Bordeaux (1539–42) with **Montaigne** as one of his pupils, and wrote two tragedies in Latin, *Jeptha* and *Baptistes*. In 1547 he went to teach at Coimbra in Portugal, where he was arrested by the Inquisition as a suspected heretic. During his confinement (1547–53) he made a Latin paraphrase of the Psalms, which was published in 1566 with a dedication to **Mary, Queen of Scots**. He returned to Scotland in

1561 and was appointed Classical tutor to the 19-year-old queen, despite his acknowledged leanings towards Protestantism. He abandoned the queen's cause after the murder of Lord Darnley in 1567, and charged her with complicity in a scurrilous pamphlet, *Ane Detectioun of the Duings of Mary Quene* (1571). In 1567 he was elected Moderator of the newly-formed General Assembly of the Church of Scotland, and later was appointed Keeper of the Privy Seal of Scotland, and tutor to the four-year-old King James VI of Scotland (1570–78). His main works were *De juri regni apud Scotos* (1579, an attack on the divine right of monarchs and a justification for the deposition of Mary), and a monumental but unreliable history of Scotland, *Rerum scoticarum historia* (20 vols), which he completed shortly before his death. 🕮 I D McFarlane, *Buchanan* (1981)

Buchanan, James 1791–1868
15th President of the USA
Born in Stony Batter, near Mercersburg, Pennsylvania, the son of an immigrant Irish farmer, in 1812 he was admitted to the Bar, where he established a large practice. Initially a Federalist and later a conservative Democrat, he served in the US House of Representatives (1821–31) and was minister to Russia for two years before returning to the Senate (1834–45). As Secretary of State (1845–49) under President James K Polk, he dealt with the annexation of Texas and the Mexican War as well as the Oregon boundary negotiations. He helped draft the Ostend Manifesto while minister to Great Britain (1853–56), and on his return to the USA in 1856 gained the Democratic nomination and was elected President. His administration was plagued by rising sectional tensions, which his stand on slavery—he believed it wrong in principle but valid under the Constitution—did nothing to defuse. After his retirement in 1861, he took no part in public affairs, but in 1866 he published a defence of his administration. 🕮 Philip S Klein, *President James Buchanan: a Biography* (1962)

Buchanan, James McGill 1919–
US economist and Nobel Prize winner
Born in Tennessee, he was educated there and in Chicago. He was awarded the Nobel Prize for economics in 1986 for his work on the theories of public choice. He has held numerous professorships since 1950, and is currently at George Mason University (1983–). He was director of the Center for Public Choice (1969–88) then advisory general director (1988–).

Buchanan, John Young 1844–1925
Scottish chemical oceanographer
Born in Glasgow, he graduated from the university there, and continued his study of chemistry in mainland Europe. He devised a stop-cock water bottle to retain dissolved gases, used during the *Challenger* expedition (1872–76), for which he was in charge of shipboard chemistry. His observations and analyses of seawater resulted in the first reliable surface salinity and temperature map of the oceans. He demonstrated that vertical currents bring cold water to the surface, and from a study of temperate lakes established the concept of the thermocline—the base of the warm surface water (1886). He worked for a year in Edinburgh with John Murray, before continuing his research on his own yacht in the west of Scotland (1878–82), sailing aboard cable ships and frequently with Prince Albert of Monaco. He discovered a strong easterly flowing current below the westerly southern equatorial current which he proved to be an important factor in oceanic circulation.

Buchanan, Pat(rick Joseph) 1938–
US Republican politician
Born in Virginia, he was educated at Georgetown and Colombia universities before taking up a career in journalism. In 1969 he became a special assistant to the Republican leader Richard Nixon while continuing to write trenchant political columns for the *Chicago Tribune* and the *New York Times*. In 1996 he contested the presidential nomination of the Republican Party but lost to Senator Bob Dole.

Buchanan, Robert Williams 1841–1901
English poet, novelist and playwright
Born in Caverswall, Staffordshire, he was educated at Glasgow High School and Glasgow University, where his closest friend was David Gray, with whom he set out for London in 1860. They found life hard in London and success came too late for Gray. Buchanan is noted for his attacks in the *Spectator* on Algernon Charles Swinburne, and on the Pre-Raphaelites under the pseudonym of 'Thomas Maitland' in an article entitled 'The Fleshly School of Poetry' (1871). *London Poems* (1866) was his first real success. He also wrote novels and plays. 🕮 A Walker, *Robert Buchanan, the poet of modern revolt* (1901)

Buchman, Frank Nathan Daniel 1878–1961
US evangelist
He was born in Pennsburg, Pennsylvania, of devout Lutheran parents. Ordained in 1902, he became minister in charge of a hospice for underprivileged boys in Philadelphia (1902–07), travelled extensively, and in 1921, believing that there was an imminent danger of the collapse of civilization, founded at Oxford the 'First Century Christian Fellowship'. For its propagation it led parties of young men, including some Oxford undergraduates, to many parts of the world. The movement was misleadingly labelled the 'Oxford Group', until 1938, when it began to rally under the slogan 'Moral Rearmament' (MRA). The Buchmanites did not regard themselves as a new sect, but as a catalyst for existing religious institutions. They emphasized divine guidance, constant adherence to the four cardinal principles of honesty, purity, unselfishness, and love, fostered by compulsory, public 'sharing' of their shortcomings. After World War II the movement emerged in a more political guise as an alternative to capitalism and communism. He wrote *The Oxford Group and its Work of Moral Rearmament* (1954) and *America Needs an Ideology* (1957). 🕮 Garth Lean, *Frank Buchman: A Life* (1985)

Buchner, Eduard 1860–1917
German chemist and Nobel Prize winner
Born in Munich, he began his study of chemistry at the Technische Hochschule in Munich, finishing at the Bavarian Academy of Sciences. While working at the Institute of Plant Physiology, he became interested in alcoholic fermentation and showed that, contrary to Louis Pasteur's contention, the absence of oxygen is not necessary for fermentation. For these studies he received the Nobel Prize for chemistry in 1907. In 1893 he moved to the University of Kiel, and after appointments at the universities of Tübingen and Berlin, he became professor at the universities of Breslau in 1909, and of Würzburg in 1911. He was the brother of Hans Buchner.

Büchner, Georg 1813–37
German dramatist and pioneer of Expressionist theatre
He was born in Goddelau near Darmstadt, the brother of the physician and philosopher Ludwig Büchner (1824–99). After studying medicine and science, he became involved in revolutionary politics and fled to Zurich, where he died of typhoid at the age of 24. His best-known works are the poetical dramas *Dantons Tod* (1835, Eng trans *Danton's Death*, 1958) and *Woyzeck* (1837, Eng trans 1979), of which he left many unfinished manuscript versions. The true story of an uneducated and mentally-backward army

private who killed his girlfriend in a fit of jealousy, it was used by **Alban Berg** as the basis for his opera *Wozzeck*. 📖R Hauser, *Georg Büchner* (1974)

Buchner, Hans 1850–1902
German bacteriologist
Born in Munich, the brother of **Eduard Buchner**, he graduated in medicine from the University of Leipzig in 1874, became Professor at Munich (1880–1902), and was appointed Director of the Institute of Hygiene from 1894. His pioneering work on the proteins now known as gamma globulins showed that blood serum contains protective substances against infection. He is also known for developing methods for studying those bacteria only able to grow in the absence of oxygen.

Buck, Frank 1884–1950
US big-game hunter and collector
Born in Gainesville, Texas, from 1911 he led several expeditions all over the world to capture wild animals for zoos and circuses. Perhaps the most celebrated hunter in the world, he was enormously popular as a lecturer, and wrote many books, including *Bring 'Em Back Alive* (1930), *Wild Cargo* (1931) and *Fang and Claw* (1935), which were turned into movies starring Buck himself.

Buck, Pearl S (ydenstricker), *née* Sydenstricker, *pseudonym* John Hedges 1892–1973
US novelist and Nobel Prize winner
Born in Hillsboro, West Virginia, the daughter of Presbyterian missionaries, she lived in China from her childhood, but was educated in the USA. She returned to China as a missionary and teacher in 1921, after marrying another missionary, John Lossing Buck, in 1917 (they divorced in 1934). Her earliest novels are coloured by her experiences while living in China. *The Good Earth* (1931) was a runaway bestseller. In 1935 she returned to the USA, and most of her output after that date was concerned with contemporary US life. She was awarded the 1938 Nobel Prize for literature. Her other novels on China include *Sons* (1932), *A House Divided* (1935), *Dragon Seed* (1942) and *Imperial Woman* (1956), and amongst other works are *What America Means to Me* (1944) and *My Several Worlds* (1955). Five novels were written under her pseudonym. 📖 T F Hariss, *Pearl S Buck* (1969, 1971)

Buck, Sir Percy Carter 1871–1947
English musical educationist
Born in West Ham, London, he held successive posts at Wells and Bristol cathedrals, was director of music at Harrow, and then at Dublin University (1910) and London University (1923). The author of several sound textbooks, he was responsible for the inauguration of the teachers' course at the Royal College of Music.

Buck, Sir Peter Henry, *adopted Maori name* Te Rangi Hiroa 1879–1951
New Zealand anthropologist, surgeon, politician and athlete
Born in Urenui, Taranaki, he graduated from the University of Otago where he twice won the national long-jump title. Before serving in World War I in Egypt and Gallipoli, he represented the North Maori constituency in parliament (1908–14) and was Minister for Maori Affairs in the Executive Council (1912). He afterwards gained an international reputation in Polynesian anthropology and from 1927 was ethnologist at the Bernice P Bishop Museum in Honolulu, Hawaii. Director there from 1936 until his death, he was Visiting Professor of Anthropology at Yale (1932–34), and received many honorary degrees and fellowships.

Buckingham, George Villiers, 1st Duke of
1592–1628
English politician and court favourite

Born at his father's seat of Brooksby, Leicestershire, he was brought to the notice of **James VI and I** in 1614 and soon succeeded Robert Carr, Earl of Somerset as favourite. He was knighted, then raised to the peerage as Viscount Villiers in 1616, and also became Earl of Buckingham in 1617, and Marquis in 1618. He became, with a single exception, the wealthiest noble in England. In 1623 he failed to negotiate a Spanish match for Prince Charles (the future **Charles I**), but he later arranged the marriage of Charles I with **Henrietta Maria** of France. The abortive expedition against Cadiz exposed him to impeachment by the Commons, however, and only a dissolution rescued him. His expedition against France in 1627 failed, and while he was planning a second, he was assasinated by John Felton, a discontented subaltern. 📖 Roger Lockyer, *Buckingham: The Life and Political Career of George Villiers, First Duke of Buckingham* (1981)

Buckingham, George Villiers, 2nd Duke of
1627–87
English politician
He was born in London, son of the 1st Duke. After his father's assassination in 1628 he was brought up with **Charles I**'s children. At the outbreak of the Civil War he joined the Royalists. In 1648 he joined the rising by Lord Holland in Surrey and barely escaped with his life (his younger brother was killed). He went with **Charles II** to Scotland, and after the Battle of Worcester went into exile. Returning secretly to England, in 1657 he married the daughter of Lord **Fairfax**, the Parliamentary general to whom his forfeited estates had been assigned. At the Restoration he recovered his estates, became a Privy Councillor, and for the next 25 years excelled the other courtiers in debauchery and wit. In 1667 he killed in a duel the Earl of Shrewsbury, whose countess, his lover, watched disguised as a page. He was involved in **Clarendon**'s downfall and was a member of the infamous Cabal of Charles II. He lost influence to the Earl of **Arlington**, and in 1674 was dismissed from government for alleged Catholic sympathies. He was the author and part-author of several comedies, the wittiest of them being *The Rehearsal* (1671), a parody of **Dryden**'s tragedies, but he is better known as the 'Zimri' of Dryden's *Absalom and Achitophel*. 📖H W Chapman, *Great Villiers* (1949)

Buckland, Henry Seymour Berry, Baron
1877–1928
Welsh industrialist
He was born in Merthyr Tydfil. A protégé of Lord **Rhondda**, he directed his enterprises when Rhondda served in the Cabinet. He promoted mergers within the coal industry in South Wales with the aim of greater efficiency. He also held interests in newspapers with his brothers, lords **Camrose** and **Kemsley**.

Buckland, William 1784–1856
English geologist and clergyman
Born in Axminster, Devon, he was educated at Oxford, and became a Reader in Mineralogy there. He is known for his description of Kirkdale Cave, and his attempts to relate geology to the biblical description of the Creation. In 1845 he became dean of Westminster.

Buckle, George Earle 1854–1935
English journalist
Born in Twerton, Bath, he was editor of *The Times* from 1884 to 1912. He completed Monypenny's *Life of Disraeli* (1914–20) and edited six volumes of Queen **Victoria**'s Letters (1926–32).

Buckle, Henry Thomas 1821–62
English historian
Born in Lee, Kent, he was mostly self-educated. He mastered 18 foreign languages and amassed an enormous library to assist him in compiling the *History of Civilization*

in England (1857–61), only two volumes of which were written and in which he practised a scientific method of writing history, taking into account a country's climate, population, and other factors.

Buckley, William 1780–1856
Australian thief

Born near Macclesfield, England, he was a bricklayer, then joined the army, but was transported to Australia in 1802 for stealing. He escaped the following year from a new convict settlement at Port Phillip, near Melbourne, was adopted by an Aboriginal tribe, and lived with them for 32 years before being found by an expedition. He became a bodyguard to the colonel in command of the new colony, then moved to Van Diemen's Land (later renamed Tasmania).

Buckley, William F(rank), Jnr 1925–
US political writer and journalist

He was born in New York City. After serving in the military and the Central Intelligence Agency, he dedicated himself to combating creeping liberalism in US life. In 1955 he founded the conservative political journal *National Review*, which became the voice of the intellectual US right. He ran successfully in 1963 to become Mayor of New York City, a campaign detailed in *The Unmaking of a Mayor* (1966). He also taught at the New School for Social Research (1967–68). *Up From Liberalism* (1959) indicated his political position, but his best writing has been in a syndicated column called 'On the Right'. An author of fiction and non-fiction, he wrote many books including *God and Man at Yale* (1951), *Saving the Queen* (1976), *Stained Glass* (1978), *Who's On First?* (1980), *Marco Polo, If You Can* (1982), *The End of the Affair* (1992) and *A Very Private Plot* (1993). ⌨ *Overdrive: a Personal Documentary* (1983)

Buckner, Simon Bolivar, Jnr 1886–1945
US soldier

Born in Munfordville, Kentucky, he was the son of a Civil War general. Trained at West Point, he commanded the Alaska Defense Force (1940) and took part in operations for the recapture of the Aleutian Islands (1942–43). He commanded the 10th Army in the Central Pacific command, and led the invasion of the island of Okinawa in 1945. He was killed in action during the final stages of the capture of this key objective of US Pacific strategy.

Budaeus, *Latinized form of* Guillaume Budé
1467–1540
French scholar

He was born in Paris. Of his works on philology, philosophy, and jurisprudence, the best known are his *Annotationes in XXIV libros Pandectarum*, a work on ancient coins (1514), and the *Commentarii Linguae Graecae* (1519). Louis XII and Francis I also employed him in diplomacy. At his suggestion Francis founded the Collège de France. Though suspected of a leaning towards Lutheranism, he was royal librarian and founded the royal collection at Fontainebleau, which, moved to Paris, became the Bibliothèque Nationale. His collected works were published in 1557.

Budd, Zola, *married name* Pieterse 1966–
South African athlete

Born in Bloemfontein, she had a sports career that was dogged by controversy. She set a world record time of 15 minutes 1.83 seconds for the 5,000 metres while still a South African citizen. In 1984 she was accorded British citizenship on the strength of her parental background, and became eligible to participate in the 1984 Olympic Games. Her disappointing performance was best remembered for her accidental clash with the American Mary Decker. She set further world records for the 5,000 metres in 1984 and 1985, reducing the time to 14 minutes 48.07 seconds, but her refusal to condemn apartheid outright and her apparent lack of commitment to her British residency brought her career to a premature end.

Buddha See panel p293

Buddhaghosa 5th century AD
Indian Buddhist scholar

He was born near Buddh Gaya, or Ghosa, East India, the place of the **Buddha**'s enlightenment. He studied the Buddhist texts in Ceylon (now Sri Lanka) and is best known for the *Visuddhimagga* ('The Path of Purity'), a compendium of the Buddhist doctrines.

Budé, Guillaume See Budaeus

Budenny, Semyon Mikhailovich 1883–1973
Russian and Soviet soldier

He was the son of a Cossack farmer. He fought as a Cossack private in the Russo-Japanese War (1904–05) and as a non-commissioned officer in World War I. After the Russian Revolution (1917) he became a Bolshevik and defeated the Whites in the battles of Tsaritsyn (1918–19). He served in the war against Poland (1920), and was made a marshal in 1935. In 1941 he commanded the South West sector against the German invasion, but was relieved by General **Semyon Timoshenko** after a disaster at Kiev.

Budge, Don (John Donald) 1915–
US tennis player

Born in Oakland, California, the son of an immigrant Scot, he retains his reputation as one of the greatest tennis players ever. He was the first player to win all four Grand Slam events in the same year (1938). He won the Wimbledon singles, men's doubles (with Gene Mako) and, with US player Alice Marble, the mixed doubles (1937, 1938). He turned professional in 1939.

Budgell, Eustace 1686–1737
English writer

Born in Exeter, he contributed miscellaneous essays to the *Spectator* and was a cousin of **Joseph Addison**. He was the butt of **Pope's** mockery in *The Dunciad*. After losing a fortune in the South Sea Company collapse (1720) he worked as a literary hack. He drowned himself in the River Thames. ⌨ *A Vindication of Eustace Budgell Esq, by William Wilson* (1733)

Buecklelaer, Joachim See Beuckelaer, Joachim

Bueno, Maria Esther 1939–
Brazilian lawn tennis player

Born in São Paulo, she won Wimbledon in 1959 and 1960 and again in 1964, and was US champion on four occasions. Her graceful style disguised a classic backhand and powerful serve. With the US player Darlene Hard, she won the Wimbledon doubles title five times and the US doubles four times. Ill health brought her retirement from top-class tennis at the relatively early age of 29, although she attempted a comeback once, in 1976.

Buerk, Michael Duncan 1946–
English television reporter

Born in Solihull, West Midlands, he began working as a BBC television news correspondent from 1973, reporting on energy (1976–79), and Scotland (1979–81). He became a special correspondent (1981–82), and then went to Africa in 1983. He became a household name in 1984, when his reports on the famine in Ethiopia provided the impetus for vast fund-raising movements. After several more years as a foreign reporter he returned home to front the BBC's *Nine O'Clock News* (1988–). He was the Royal Television Society Journalist of the Year in 1984, and received the James Cameron Memorial award in 1987.

Buffalo Bill See Cody, William F(rederick)

Buddha ('the enlightened one') c.563–c.483BC
The title of Prince Gautama Siddhartha, the founder of Buddhism

Buddha was born the son of the rajah of the Sakya tribe ruling in Kapilavastu, 100 miles (160km) north of Benares, in Nepal. When about 30 years old, he left the luxuries of the court, his beautiful wife, and all earthly ambitions in exchange for the life of an ascetic; after six years of extreme self-mortification he saw in the contemplative life the perfect way to self-enlightenment. According to tradition, he achieved enlightenment when sitting beneath a banyan tree near Buddh Gaya in Bihar. For the next 40 years he taught, gaining many disciples and followers, and died at the age of about 80 in Kusinagara in Oudh.

His system was perhaps a revolutionary reformation of Brahmanism rather than a new faith, the keynote of it being that existence necessarily involves suffering, and that 'Nirvana', or nonexistence, the chief good, is to be attained by diligent devotion to Buddhistic rules. The death of the body does not bring Nirvana: the unholy are condemned to transmigration through many existences. Buddhism spread steadily over India, and during the 3rd century BC was dominant from the Himalayas to Cape Comorin. In the earlier centuries of our era it began to decline; it was relentlessly persecuted by triumphant Brahmanism in the 7th and 8th centuries, and stamped out of continental India (except Nepal) by invading Islam. Meanwhile it had spread to Tibet, Ceylon, Burma, Siam, China, and Japan, where it is still popular.

📖 Richard Gombrich, *Theravada Buddhism* (1988); M Carrithers, *The Buddha* (1983); H Oldenburg, *Buddha: His Life, His Doctrine, His Order* (Eng trans 1971); W T De Bary, *The Buddhist Tradition* (1969); Walpola Rahula, *What The Buddha taught* (1959).

'The Buddha, the Godhead, resides quite as comfortably in the circuits of a digital computer or the gears of a cycle transmission as he does at the top of a mountain or in the petals of a flower.' Robert M Pirsig, *Zen and the Art of Motorcycle Maintenance*, pt.1, ch.1 (1974).

Buffon, George-Louis Leclerc, Comte de
1707–88
French naturalist

He was born in Montbard, Burgundy, and after studying law at the Jesuit college in Dijon, he devoted himself to science. While on a visit to England (1733) he translated into French Isaac Newton's *Fluxions*. In 1739 he was appointed director of the Jardin du Roi and the Royal Museum, and formed the design of his monumental *Histoire naturelle* (44 vols, 1749–67), in which all the known facts of natural science were discussed. After receiving various high honours, he was made Comte de Buffon by Louis XV. His work was inclined to generalization, but he proposed several new theories (including a greater age to the Earth than proposed in Genesis). His writings were influential in arousing interest in natural history, and foreshadowed the theory of evolution, although he never entirely broke with the ideas of the Church. 📖 Otis E Fellows and Stephen F Milliken, *Buffon* (1972)

Bugatti, Ettore Arco Isidoro 1882–1947
Italian car manufacturer

Born in Milan, he began designing cars in 1899 and set up his works in Strasbourg in 1907. World War I caused him to move to Italy and later to France, where his racing cars won international fame in the 1930s.

Bugeaud, Thomas 1784–1849
French soldier

Born in Limoges, he served in the Napoleonic campaigns and in Algeria and Morocco (1836–44). In the February Revolution of 1848 he commanded the army in Paris.

Buhaina, Abdullah Ibn See Blakey, Art(hur)

Buhari, Muhammadu 1942–
Nigerian soldier and politician

Trained at military academies in Nigeria, England and India, he was Military Governor of North-Eastern State (1975–76), of Bornu State (1976), and then Federal Commissioner for Petroleum Resources (1976–78) and chairman of the Nigerian National Petroleum Corporation (1976–79). He returned to army duties (1976) but led the military coup which ousted Shehu Shagari (1983), when he became President. He was himself removed in a coup led by Ibrahim Babangida in 1985 and detained before being released in 1988.

Buhl or Boulle, Charles André 1642–1732
French cabinetmaker

Born in Paris, while in the service of Louis XIV he introduced *buhlwork*, a style of decorating furniture by inlaying metals, shells and pearls on ebony, which was carried on by his sons, Jean, Pierre, André and Charles.

Bühren, Ernst Johann See Biron, Ernst Johann

Buick, David Dunbar 1854–1929
US motor car manufacturer

Born in Arbroath, Tayside, Scotland, he was taken to the USA when he was two years old. In 1899 he sold his wholesale plumbing supply business and three years later established the Buick Manufacturing Company to make car engines. He built his first car in 1903 and formed the Buick Motor Company, but left the company after three years and in 1908 it was taken over by the General Motors Corporation. At the time of his death, he was a clerk in a Detroit trade school.

Bujones, Fernando 1955–
US dancer

Born in Miami, Florida, of Cuban extraction, he studied with Alicia Alonso in Havana and at the School of American Ballet in New York, and danced briefly with the Eglevsky Ballet. In 1972 he joined American Ballet Theater, becoming principal in 1974, when he became one of the first western dancers to win a gold medal at Varna International Competition in Bulgaria. Capable both of elegance and volatility, he has danced all the major classical roles for companies the world over and is equally at home in the modern repertoire.

Bukharin, Nikolai Ivanovich 1888–1938
Russian Marxist revolutionary and political theorist

Born in Moscow, he was active in the Bolshevik underground (1905–17), and after the February Revolution returned to Russia. He played a leading role in the organization of the October Revolution in Moscow and was dubbed by Lenin 'the darling of the party'. He was a considerable theorist, became editor of *Pravda* (1917–29), and was a member of the Central Committee of the Communist Party in Russia and a member of the politburo (1924–29), in which position he came round to supporting Lenin's New Economic Policy, but had an ambivalent attitude to Stalin's collectivization campaign. In 1937 he was arrested in Stalin's Great Purge, expelled from the party, tried on trumped-up charges, and shot. He was posthumously readmitted to the party in 1988.

Bukowski, Charles 1920–94
US poet and fiction writer

Born in Andernach, Germany, he was taken to the USA at the age of two, endured an unhappy childhood with an abusive father, and worked variously as a dishwasher and truck driver while learning to write. His first poetry collection was published in 1959, and he later published more than 40 other books of poetry, novels and short stories. A cult success as an underground writer, he evoked a world of low-lifers in a pared-down style influenced by Ernest Hemingway. He had a sardonic sense of humour and a liking for long titles, such as *Play the Piano Drunk Like a Percussion Instrument until the Fingers Begin to Bleed a Bit* (1979). He also wrote the screenplay for the 1987 film *Barfly*, dramatizing his own younger days as a hard-drinking writer. 🕮 H Fox, *Charles Bukowski: a biographical study* (1968)

Bulfinch, Charles 1763–1844
US architect

Born in Boston, he graduated from Harvard and from 1785 to 1787 he travelled in Europe, studying examples of Classical architecture suggested to him by Thomas Jefferson (whom he met in Paris). Ambitious to improve his native city, he returned to Boston and designed well-proportioned neoclassical buildings such as the Massachusetts State House (1798), New South Church (1814), and Massachusetts General Hospital (1820). Other works include the Connecticut State House (1796) and the Maine State Capitol (1831). Bulfinch succeeded Benjamin Latrobe as architect of the US Capitol in Washington DC.

Bulgakov, Mikhail Afanasevich 1891–1940
Russian novelist and dramatist

Born in Kiev, he studied at the Theological Academy and the university there, then practised as a country doctor for a short time. He settled in Moscow in 1921, and began a stormy association with the Moscow Art Theatre when he adapted part of his novel *Belaya gvardiya* (1925, Eng trans *The White Guard*, 1971) for the stage in 1926. His political attitudes in that play, and in others like *Beg* (1928, 'The Flight'), brought him much criticism, and only a personal appeal to Stalin restored him to some favour. However, he did gain success with a play (1930) about Molière, on whom he also wrote an imaginative biography. He described his tribulations with the theatre in *Tetralnyi roman* (1965, Eng trans *Black Snow, a Theatrical Novel*, 1967). His masterpiece is the novel *Master i Margarita* (1966, Eng trans *The Master and Margarita*, 1967), a remarkable fantasy. Although he died in obscurity with much of his work unpublished, his posthumous reputation has flourished.

Bulgakov, Sergei Nikolayevich 1871–1944
Russian philosopher, economist, and Orthodox theologian

Born in Livny, Central Russia, he was Professor of Political Economy at Kiev (1901–06) and then Moscow (1906–18), but became disillusioned with socialism after 1906 and became a priest in 1918. Expelled from Russia in 1923 like many other clergy, he was appointed Dean and Professor of the Orthodox Theological Academy in Paris (1925–44), where he expounded Sophiology, following Vladimir Soloviev and Florensky's interpretation of the Eastern fathers. Bulgakov's belief that Sophia (the Divine Wisdom) mediates between God and the world implied a fourth person of the Trinity and attracted accusations of heresy. English editions of his works include *The Orthodox Church* (1935) and *The Wisdom of God* (1937). Autobiographical notes and extracts from other French and Russian works appear in *A Bulgakov Anthology* (1976).

Bulganin, Nikolai Aleksandrovich 1895–1975
Soviet politician

Born in Nizhny Novgorod, he became an early member of the Communist Party, was Mayor of Moscow (1933–37) and a member of the Military Council during World War II. Created a marshal at the end of the war, he succeeded Stalin as Minister for Defence in 1946. After Stalin's death he became vice-premier in Giorgi Malenkov's government and was made premier after the latter's resignation in 1955, though Nikita Khrushchev held the real power as First Secretary. Unlike their predecessors, both men travelled extensively abroad in Yugoslavia, India, and Great Britain. Khrushchev ousted Bulganin from his nominal position in 1958 and, his authority totally eclipsed, he retained only the minor post of chairman of the Soviet State Bank.

Bulgya See Fadeyev, Aleksandr Aleksandrovich

Bull, John c.1563–1628
English organist and composer

Born in Somerset, he was appointed organist in the Queen's Chapel in 1586, first music lecturer at Gresham College in 1597 and organist to James VI an I in 1607. A Catholic, he fled to Belgium in 1613, and in 1615 became organist of Antwerp Cathedral. Considered one of the founders of contrapuntal keyboard music, he has been credited with composing 'God save the King'.

Bull, Olaf Jacob Martin Luther 1883–1933
Norwegian poet and bohemian

Born in Christiania (now Oslo), he rejected his family's altruistic Christianity for a life of wandering and self-examination. His poetry, from the early *Digte* (1909, 'Poems') onwards, combines a strongly Romantic and quasi-Symbolist treatment of themes like love and the natural world, with his interest in the creative act itself. He found his true voice early but continually experimented with styles. Among his more important later collections were *De hundrede år* (1928) and *Oinos og Eros* (1930). Still little-known outside Norway and France, he posthumously won the admiration of the US poet Robert Bly. 🕮 T Greiff, *Olaf Bull: Taper og seirer* (1952)

Bull, Ole Bornemann 1810–80
Norwegian violinist

Born in Bergen, he made his name in Paris, and made successful tours of Italy, England, Scotland, Ireland, Russia, Germany, and Norway. From 1843 he was often in the USA, and lost much of his considerable earnings through land speculations, especially an attempt to found a Scandinavian colony in Pennsylvania. He was a noted eccentric.

Bull, Phil, pseudonym William Temple 1910–89
English racing information service founder

He made racing accessible to everyone by starting the Timeform organization in Halifax, Yorkshire. Today it is the world's largest information service for racing form. Its annual publication in the *Racehorses* series contains ratings and comments for each horse that has run on the flat in Great Britain during that year and for the best horses in Ireland and France. As it is calculated in an unvarying scale, champions of different eras can be compared. Bull operated under his pseudonym and was considered to be one of the most influential racing personalities of the 20th century. His opinions and shrewd judgement on form were highly regarded.

Bullard, Sir Edward Crisp 1907–80
English geophysicist

Born in Norwich, Norfolk, he was educated at Clare College, Cambridge, gaining a PhD in geophysics (1935). He later accomplished the first British seismic experiment at sea under sail (1938). He initiated the measurement of heat flux from the interior of the Earth (1940) and made the first effective measurement of the heat flow through oceanic crust. During World War II he worked on degaussing ships to protect them from German magnetic mines. In Toronto as Professor of Physics (1946–49), he worked on the dynamo theory of the Earth's magnetic field (1949) then as director of the National Physical Laboratory in London (1950–55) he employed their early computer in the first numerical approach to dynamo theory. On returning to Cambridge as assistant director then as professor (1955–74), he brought the department of geodesy and geophysics into world recognition. His computer-fit of the continents (1965) was instrumental in bringing the theory of continental drift back into favour. The geophysical laboratories at Cambridge and a fracture zone joining the Mid-Atlantic Ridge to the Scotia Arc are named after him. He was elected FRS in 1941 and given a knighthood in 1953. 📖 D P McKenzie, *Sir Edward Bullard: A Biographical Memoir* (1987)

Bulleid, Oliver Vaughan Snell 1882–1970
British railway engineer
Born in Invercargill, New Zealand, he went to England in 1889. From 1901 he worked on the Great Northern Railway (GNR) at Doncaster under Ivatt, whose daughter he married. Later he worked with the Westinghouse Electrical Company in Paris, but in 1911 returned to the GNR under Sir Nigel Gresley and in 1923 went with him to the newly-formed London and North-Eastern Railway, where Bulleid introduced the first fully-articulated carriage set. In 1927 he moved to the Southern Railway, where he modernized the steam power of this predominantly electric system with his powerful Battle of Britain class of locomotive, and designed a prototype coalburner on two power bogies, on the Garratt pattern. In 1949 he joined the Irish state railway CIE (Coras Iompair Éireann) for which, to combat the high price of fuel, he re-engineered his Garratt design to burn the local peat.

Bullen, Arthur Henry 1857–1920
English editor
Born in London, he edited John Day, Thomas Campion, and other Elizabethans, and founded the Shakespeare Head Press at Stratford-upon-Avon (1904).

Bullen, Frank Thomas 1857–1915
English writer
He was a sailor until 1883, and made notable additions to the literature of the sea, including *Cruise of the Cachalot* (1898). He also wrote *Recollections* (1915). 📖 *With Christ at Sea: a religious autobiography* (1900)

Bullen, Keith Edward 1906–76
New Zealand mathematician and geophysicist
Born in Auckland, he studied mathematics, physics and chemistry at the university there, and received his PhD at Cambridge. He later became a lecturer at Auckland University College (1928–40) and Melbourne University (1940–45), and in 1946 was appointed Professor of Mathematics at the University of Sydney. As a research student under Harold Jeffreys, he studied the arrival times for primary and secondary waves and the locations for the epicentres of global earthquakes to revise the travel-time tables. This work resulted in the *Jeffreys–Bullen Tables* (1940) which are still in use, and revealed that the Earth has a layered structure with a dense core. Bullen divided the Earth into seven density layers consistent with the distribution of mass and seismic shadow zones. He was elected FRS in 1949.

Buller, Sir Redvers Henry 1839–1908
English general
He was born in Crediton, Devon. Educated at Eton, he joined the army in 1858 and fought in the war with China (1860), the Red River expedition (1870), the Ashanti War (1874), the Kaffir War (1878) and the Zulu War (1879),

where his rescue of fellow-soldiers in action at Inhlobane won him the Victoria Cross. He was Chief of Staff in the First Boer War (1881), and served in Egypt and the Sudan. As Commander-in-Chief in the Second Boer War (1899–1900), he raised the siege of Ladysmith (1900). He was succeeded by Lord Roberts and went on to command the 1st Army Corps (1901–06).

Bullinger, Heinrich 1504–75
Swiss reformer
Born in Bremgarten, he studied at the University of Cologne. In 1529 he married a former nun, and became a disciple of Huldreich Zwingli. He succeeded Zwingli in 1531 as leader of the reformed party in Switzerland in its struggle with the Catholics, as well as with the Zealots and the Lutherans. He drew up the Helvetic Confessions of 1536 and 1566.

Bullion, Old See Benton, Thomas Hart

Bullock, Alan Louis Charles Bullock, Baron 1914–
English historian
Educated at Bradford Grammar School and Wadham College, Oxford, he was appointed censor of St Catherine's Society, Oxford (1952–62), Vice-Chancellor of Oxford (1969–73), and Master of St Catherine's College, Oxford (1960–80). He was chairman of the Committee on Reading and Other Uses of English Language from 1972 to 1974, and the Bullock report (*A Language for Life*, 1975) was a response to suggestions that reading standards were declining and offered for the teacher beneficial, practical guidance on reading, writing, speech and language skills. He is also the author of numerous works on 20th-century Europe, including *Hitler: A Study in Tyranny* (1952) and *Hitler and Stalin: Parallel Lives* (1991).

Bülow, Prince Bernhard Heinrich Martin Karl von 1849–1929
German diplomat and politician
Born in Flottbeck, Holstein, he was Foreign Secretary (1897) and Chancellor (1900–09), and was made a count (1899) and a prince (1905). Identified with an aggressive foreign policy before World War I, he was guilty of a bad misjudgment in his threats to France in the 1905 Morocco crisis. He finally fell out of favour with the Emperor Wilhelm II after denying that he had approved an indiscreet interview given by Wilhelm to the *Daily Telegraph* that he had in fact seen, an incident which precipitated his dismissal.

Bülow, Hans Guido, Baron von 1830–94
German pianist and conductor
Born in Dresden, he studied law and joined radical social groups in Berlin, making the acquaintance of Richard Wagner in Zurich. He took piano lessons from Franz Liszt in Weimar, and married his daughter Cosima (1857). An impressive conductor, he was appointed court pianist and director of the music school in Munich in 1864. He resigned when Cosima left him for Wagner (1869), and undertook extensive conducting tours in England and the USA.

Bultmann, Rudolf Karl 1884–1976
German Protestant theologian
He was born in Wiefelstede, Oldenberg. As Professor of New Testament at Marburg (1921–51), he maintained that while Form Criticism of the Gospels showed it was next to impossible to know anything about the historical Jesus Christ, faith in Christ, rather than belief about him, was what mattered. The Gospels' existential challenge was, however, blunted for modern man by difficulties with miracles and other aspects of the New Testament worldview, which therefore needed to be 'demythologized'.

Such controversial views provoked sharp reaction: ultimately towards more confidence in the historicity of the Gospels or to a humanistic existentialism unconcerned with their subject. His books include *The History of the Synoptic Tradition* (1921), *Jesus and the Word* (1934), *Theology of the New Testament* (2 vols, 1952–55), Gifford Lectures on *History and Eschatology* (1957), *Jesus Christ and Mythology* (1960) and *Existence and Faith* (1964).

Bulwer, Sir (William) Henry Lytton Earle, Baron Dalling and Bulwer 1801–72
English diplomat and author

Born in London, he was educated at Harrow and Cambridge and entered the diplomatic service in 1827. He was attaché at Berlin, Brussels and The Hague. A Liberal MP, he became Secretary of Embassy (1837) at Constantinople (Istanbul), where he negotiated a very important commercial treaty. As minister plenipotentiary in Madrid, he negotiated the peace between Spain and Morocco (1849). His outspokenness resulted in his expulsion, and in 1849 he proceeded to Washington, where he concluded the Clayton–Bulwer Treaty. He was ambassador to the Ottoman Porte (1858–65), and ably carried out Lord Palmerston's policy on the eastern question. Among his works are *An Autumn in Greece* (1826), *Historical Characters* (1868–70) and an unfinished *Life of Palmerston* (1870–74). He was the elder brother of Bulwer Lytton.

Bulwer-Lytton, Edward George See Lytton, Bulwer

Bunau-Varilla, Philippe Jean 1859–1940
French engineer

He was born in Paris. The chief organizer of the Panama Canal project, he was instrumental in getting the waterway routed through Panama instead of Nicaragua, and worked to bring about the sale of the canal to the USA. After inciting the Panama revolution (1903) to further this end, he was made Panamanian minister to the USA and negotiated the Hay–Bunau-Varilla Treaty (1903) giving the USA control of the canal zone. He wrote *From Panama to Verdun* (1940).

Bunbury, Henry William 1750–1811
English caricaturist and sporting writer

Born in Mildenhall, Suffolk, he became a landowner in Norfolk, and found fame as an accomplished caricaturist with *Master of the Horse to the Doge of Venice*, which he illustrated with his own humorous designs. As a pioneer of the genre in Great Britain, he was the friend and peer of Thomas Rowlandson and James Gillray.

Bunche, Ralph Johnson 1904–71
US diplomat and Nobel Prize winner

Born in Detroit, the grandson of a slave, he studied at Harvard, Capetown, the London School of Economics, then became assistant Professor of Political Science at Howard University, Washington (1928). During World War II he advised the government on African strategic questions, and as an expert on trusteeship territories he drafted the appropriate sections of the UN Charter. As director (1947–54) of the UN Trusteeship Department, he followed Count Folke Bernadotte, after the latter's assassination (1948), as UN mediator in Palestine and arranged for a ceasefire. Awarded the Nobel Peace Prize (1950), he became a UN Under-Secretary for Special Political Affairs (1954–67) and played an important role in Suez, the Congo, and the Indo-Pakistan War of 1965. He was Under-Secretary-General of the UN from 1968. 📖 Peggy Mann, *Ralph Bunche: UN Peacemaker* (1975)

Buncho, Tani 1773–1840
Japanese painter

Born in Edo (now Tokyo), the son of a poet, he was familiar with the styles of various schools (Kano, Tosa, Nagasagik, Masumyama, Shijo) and with Chinese works, and attempted a synthesis of these with European techniques. An illustrator of books and a prolific painter, he excelled in landscapes. He also introduced the Nanga style of painting to Edo, which encouraged individualism and the expression of the artist's own feelings, a revolutionary concept for the period. He was regarded as the greatest Edo master of his time.

Bundy, McGeorge 1919–
US educator and government administrator

He was born in Boston, Massachusetts, and educated at Yale. He worked in public service, then taught at Harvard, where he became Dean of Arts and Sciences (1953–61). As National Security Adviser to Presidents Kennedy and Johnson he was one of the architects of the Vietnam War. He was Professor of History at New York University from 1979 to 1989, then emeritus. In 1988 he published *Danger and Survival*.

Bundy, Ted (Theodore Robert), assumed name Christopher Hagen 1946–89
US lawyer and serial killer

He was born in Vermont. An articulate and handsome man, he studied psychology and law. In 1974 he began a series of up to 40 murders in which he habitually raped and beat his victims. He stood trial in 1977 but escaped from custody, fleeing to Florida and assuming the name of Christopher Hagen. He finally murdered a 12-year-old girl. Three days afterwards the police checked the licence plates of his van, found it to have been stolen, and arrested Bundy. His trial took place in July 1979 in Miami, televised and watched by millions of people. He conducted his own defence with skill but was convicted and 10 years later executed in Florida.

Bung Karno See Sukarno, Ahmed

Bunin, Ivan Alekseyevich 1870–1953
Russian author and Nobel Prize winner

Born in Voronezh, he wrote lyrics and novels about the decay of the Russian nobility and of peasant life, and the disintegration of traditional rural patterns of life under the pressure of a changing world. They include *Derevnia* (1910, Eng trans *The Village*, 1923), *Gospodin iz San-Frantsisko* (1914, Eng trans *The Gentleman from San Francisco*, 1922), his best-known work, which has the vanity of all things earthly as its theme, and the autobiographical *The Well of Days* (1933, Eng trans 1946). He lived in Paris after the Russian Revolution (1917), and received the 1933 Nobel Prize for literature. His work belongs in the great Russian Realist tradition of Ivan Turgenev, Tolstoy and Chekhov. 📖 A Poggioli, *The Art of Ivan Bunin* (1953)

Bunny, Rupert Charles Wulsten 1864–1947
Australian artist

Born in St Kilda, Victoria, he studied in Melbourne, then in London at Calderons preparatory school for the Royal Academy. Moving to Paris, he exhibited there first at the Old Salon, receiving a 'Mention Honorable' (1890), and a Bronze Medal at the Paris Exhibition (1900). From 1901 he moved to the 'New' Salon and spent most of his working life in Paris. He held the first Loan Exhibition of an Australian artist at the National Gallery of Victoria in 1946. His work was influenced mainly by classical mythology, but he later turned to large decorative and exotic scenes.

Bunsen, Robert Wilhelm 1811–99
German chemist and physicist

Born in Göttingen, he studied at the university there and for his PhD produced a Latin dissertation on hygrometers. He became a professor at Kassel, went to Marburg in 1838 and, after a short period at Breslau (now Wrocław, Poland), he became a professor (1852) at Heidelberg, where he remained until his retirement. He was a talented experimentalist, although the eponymous burner, for which he is best known, is a modification of something developed in England by **Michael Faraday**. He did invent the grease-spot photometer, a galvanic battery, an ice calorimeter and, with Sir **Henry Roscoe**, an actinometer. He shared with **Gustav Robert Kirchhoff** the discovery, in 1859, of spectrum analysis, which facilitated the discovery of new elements, including caesium and rubidium. His most important work was his study of organoarsenic compounds such as cacodyl oxide. Following the partial loss of sight in one eye during an experiment, he forbade the study of organic chemistry in his laboratory.

Bunting, Basil 1900–85
English poet
Born in Northumberland, he was neglected for most of his career, and until the publication of *Loquitur* (1965) **Ezra Pound** seemed to be his sole aficionado. However, Bunting attracted more admirers with his long poem, *Briggflatts* (1966). He assisted **Ford Madox Ford** with the *Transatlantic Review* in Paris but he largely shunned literary society. His admirers have included **Herbert Read, Henry Tomlinson, Hugh MacDiarmid** and **Robert Creeley**, but he has a greater following in the USA than in Great Britain despite attempts to revive interest. His *Collected Poems* appeared in 1968.

Buntline, Ned See **Judson, Edward Zane Carroll**

Buñuel, Luis 1900–83
Spanish film director
He was born in Calanda, Spain, and educated at Madrid University. His first films, *Un Chien Andalou* (1928, *An Andalusian Dog*) and *L'Age d'or* (1930, *The Golden Age*), both made with **Salvador Dali**, were a sensation with their surrealistic, macabre, poetic approach. His first solo venture, *Las Hurdes* (1932, *Land Without Bread*), a documentary on Spanish poverty, was banned in Spain, and he eventually settled in Mexico (1947), his career in eclipse. *Los Olvidados* (1950, *The Young and the Damned*), a realistic study of juvenile delinquency, re-established him, and later films, such as *Nazarin* (1958), *Viridiana* (1961), *Belle de Jour* (1967), *La Voie Lactée* (1969, *The Milky Way*), *Le Charme discret de la Bourgeoisie* (1972, *The Discreet Charm of the Bourgeoisie*) and *Cet Obscur Objet de Désir* (1977, *That Obscure Object of Desire*), illustrate his poetic, often erotic, use of imagery, his black humour, and his hatred of Catholicism, often expressed in blasphemy. ▣ Francisco Aranda, *Luis Buñuel: A Critical Biography* (1976)

Bunyan, John 1628–88
English writer and preacher
Born in Elstow, Bedfordshire, he worked as a tinker. From 1644–45, he fought in the Parliamentary army, and in 1653 joined a Christian fellowship and became a preacher. In 1656 he was brought into discussions with the followers of **George Fox**, which led to his first book, *Some Gospel Truths Opened* (1656), a vigorous attack on Quakerism. To this Edward Burrough, the Quaker, responded, and Bunyan replied in *A Vindication of Gospel Truths Opened* (1657). In 1660 he was arrested while preaching in a farmhouse near Ampthill. During the 12 years' imprisonment in Bedford county gaol which followed, Bunyan wrote *Profitable Meditations* (1661), *I Will Pray with the Spirit* (1663), *Christian Behaviour* (1663), *The Holy City* (1665), *The Resurrection of the Dead* (1665), *Grace Abounding* (1666) and some other works. Briefly released

after the Declaration of Indulgence of 1672, Bunyan was then re-imprisoned for six months, during which period he wrote the first part of *The Pilgrim's Progress* (1678). There followed the *Life and Death of Mr Badman* (1680), the *Holy War* (1682), and *The Pilgrim's Progress, Second Part* (1684), containing the story of Christiana and her children. Bunyan became pastor at Bedford for 16 years until his death after a ride through the rain from Reading to London. ▣ R Sharrock, *John Bunyan* (1954)

Buononcini, Giovanni Maria See **Bononcini, Giovanni Maria**

Burbage, Richard c.1567–1619
English actor
He was the son of the actor James Burbage, who built the Shoreditch and Blackfriars theatres in London. Richard made his debut early, and had earned a considerable reputation as an actor, when the death of his father (1597) brought him a share in the Blackfriars Theatre. With his brother Cuthbert, he pulled down the Shoreditch house, and built the famous Globe Theatre as a summer playhouse (1599), taking as partners **Shakespeare**, Heminge, Condell, and others. He was widely admired by his contemporaries.

Burbank, Luther 1849–1926
US horticulturist
Born in Lancaster, Massachusetts, he received little formal education. He developed the Burbank potato, and in 1875 moved to Santa Rosa, California, where he spent over 50 years experimenting on the breeding of new fruits, flowers, grasses and vegetables. The city of Burbank is named after him. ▣ Peter Dreyer, *A Gardener Touched With Genius: The Life of Luther Burbank* (rev edn, 1987)

Burbidge, Geoffrey 1925–
English astrophysicist
Born in Chipping Norton, Oxfordshire, he graduated from Bristol University in 1946, and received his doctorate from University College London. He then went to the USA, working at the universities of Harvard (1951–52), Chicago (1952–53, 1957–64), Mount Wilson and Palomar (1955–57), and California at San Diego (1963–), where he is currently Professor of Physics. In the mid-1950s, in collaboration with Sir **Fred Hoyle**, he tried to assess some of the possible astrophysical consequences of antimatter. His most famous paper was published in 1957 and was written in conjunction with his wife **Margaret Burbidge**, Hoyle and **William Fowler**. This paper applied nuclear physics to an astrophysical situation, and in it they solved the problem of the creation of the higher elements in evolved stars. In 1967, again with his wife, Burbidge published an early and important book on quasars, objects which appear like faint stellar sources but which emit enormous amounts of radio energy. In 1970 he showed that light-emitting stars only account for 25 per cent of the total mass of their galaxies, highlighting the 'missing mass' mystery which continues to this day—most of the matter in the universe cannot be detected by its radiation.

Burbidge, (Eleanor) Margaret, *née* Peachey 1923–
English astronomer
She was born in Davenport, Cheshire, and educated at University College London (1941–47), and her lifelong interest in astronomical spectroscopy began in London, where she was assistant director of the university observatory (1948–51). In 1951 she moved to the USA, taking up appointments at Yerkes Observatory, the California Institute of Technology (Caltech) and the University of California at San Diego, where she was appointed Professor of Astronomy (1964–90), now emeritus, and

since 1990, Research Physicist. In 1972 she became director of the Royal Greenwich Observatory, but the following year she returned to her chair in California. She was director of the Center for Astrophysics and Space Science at San Diego from 1979 to 1988. In collaboration with her husband, **Geoffrey Burbidge**, Sir Fred Hoyle and **William Fowler**, she published the results of theoretical research on nucleosynthesis (the processes whereby heavy chemical elements are built up in the cores of massive stars), a discovery of fundamental importance to physics. On the observational side, Burbidge's main field of research is in the spectra of galaxies and quasars.

Burchfield, Robert William 1923–
English scholar and lexicographer

He was born in Wanganui, New Zealand, becoming lecturer in English language at Oxford (1952–63), Tutorial Fellow (1963–79), and Senior Research Fellow from 1979. From 1957 to 1986 he was editor of a new *Supplement to the Oxford English Dictionary* which appeared in four volumes between 1972 and 1986. Among his other works are *The Oxford Dictionary of English Etymology* (1966, with **Charles Onions** and G W S Friedrichsen) and *The English Language* (1985).

Burckhardt, Jacob Christopher 1818–97
Swiss historian

Born in Basle, he studied theology and art history in Berlin and Bonn. He became editor of the *Basler Zeitung* (1844–45), and from 1858 to 1893 was Professor of History at Basle University. He is known for his works on the Italian Renaissance and on Greek civilization.

Burdett, Sir Francis 1770–1844
English politician

Educated at Westminster and Oxford, he spent three years (1790–93) on the Continent, and witnessed the French Revolution. In 1793 he married the daughter of **Thomas Coutts**, of the great banking family. Entering the House of Commons in 1796, he opposed the war with France, and advocated parliamentary reform, Catholic emancipation, freedom of speech, prison reform and other liberal measures. His candidature for Middlesex in 1802 involved him in four years' costly and fruitless litigation. When, in 1810, he published, in **William Cobbett's** *Political Register*, a letter to his constituents declaring the conduct of the House of Commons illegal in imprisoning a radical orator, the Speaker's warrant was issued for his arrest. For two days he barricaded his house. The people supported him, but after two days an entry was forced, and Burdett was conveyed to the Tower of London. The prorogation restored him to liberty. In 1820 a letter on the 'Peterloo massacre' brought three months' imprisonment and a fine. In 1835 he joined the Conservatives.

Burdett-Coutts, Angela Georgina, Baroness 1814–1906
English philanthropist

Born in London, the daughter of Sir **Francis Burdett**, and granddaughter of **Thomas Coutts**, she inherited her grandfather's fortune in 1837 and used it to mitigate suffering. She established a shelter for fallen women, built model homes, and endowed churches and colonial bishoprics. In 1871 she received a peerage, and in 1872 she became the first woman to be given the freedom of the City of London. In 1881 she married William Ashmead-Bartlett (1851–1921), who assumed her name.

Buren, Abigail van See Van Buren, Abigail

Buren, Martin van See Van Buren, Martin

Bürger, Gottfried August 1747–94
German lyric poet and ballad writer

He was born in Molmerswende, near Halberstadt, and as a boy he showed an interest in verse. In 1764 he began to study theology, but in 1768 he went to Göttingen, where he began a course of jurisprudence and led a wild and extravagant life. He might have sunk into obscurity but for his friendship with **Johann Heinrich Voss**, and others. He studied the ancient and modern classics and translated **Thomas Percy's** *Reliques*. He revived the ballad tradition, and he wrote many, including *Lenore* (1774), which was translated (*William and Helen*, 1797) by Sir **Walter Scott**. ☐ W A Little, *Gottfried August Bürger* (1974)

Burger, Warren Earl 1907–95
US jurist

Born in St Paul, Minnesota, he was educated at the University of Minnesota. He taught and practised law in St Paul from 1931 before becoming assistant Attorney-General of the USA (1953), and in 1955 Judge of the US Court of Appeals for the District of Columbia. Appointed the 15th Chief Justice of the US Supreme Court by President **Richard Nixon** in 1969, he was inclined to judicial restraint, and was a conservative on criminal matters, but on social issues he proved to be more progressive that expected. He voted with the majority on Roe v. Wade (1973), which upheld the right to abortion, and wrote the majority opinion in the 1974 decision that forced Nixon to surrender the Watergate tapes to a special prosecutor. He retired in 1986, the longest-serving chief justice this century, and was awarded the Presidential Medal of Freedom in 1988. He wrote *It Is So Ordered* (1995).

Burges, William 1827–81
English architect and designer

Born in London, he trained with **Edward Blore**, and worked with the architect Matthew Digby Wyatt (1820–77). Much influenced by **August Pugin** and **Eugène Viollet-le-Duc**, he employed a strong medieval element in both his architecture and his furniture. Castell Coch (1876–81), near Cardiff, a reconstruction on 13th-century foundations, was designed as a hunting lodge for the 3rd Marquess of **Bute**. It combines archaeological seriousness with imaginative exuberance. His other project for the marquess, Cardiff Castle (1868–81), is a more eclectic mixture of medieval and exotic styles again applied to the remains of a fortress. His other major works include Cork Cathedral (1862–76), for which he also designed stained glass, a house in Park Place, Cardiff (1870s), and his own house in Melbury Road, London (1875–78). He also designed wallpapers, metalwork and jewellery.

Burgess, Anthony, *pseudonym of* John Anthony Burgess Wilson 1917–93
English novelist, critic and composer

He was born in Manchester, into a Catholic family of predominantly Irish background. His father ran a tobacconist's shop and his mother was a singer and dancer. He was educated at the Xaverian College, and at the University of Manchester where he studied language and literature. In World War II he served in the Royal Army Medical Corps and entertained the troops with his compositions. He married in 1942, and after the war taught in England before becoming an education officer (1954–59) in Malaya and Brunei, where his experiences inspired the three novels which became *The Long Day Wanes: Time for a Tiger* (1956), *The Enemy in the Blanket* (1958), and *Beds in the East* (1959). Invalided out of the Colonial Service with a suspected brain tumour, he was given a year to live and wrote five novels in a year to provide for his prospective widow, but it was she who died first. In 1968 he married the Contessa Pasi and went to live abroad, first in Italy, latterly in Monte Carlo and Switzerland. Among his many novels are his dark and violent vision of the future, *A Clockwork Orange* (1962), *Napoleon Symphony* (1974), *Earthly Powers* (1980), *The Kingdom of the Wicked* (1985), *Mozart and the*

Wolfgang (1991) and *A Dead Man in Deptford* (1993). He was fascinated by language, as his various works of exegesis demonstrate. He also wrote biographies, books for children, and libretti. 📖 *Little Wilson and Big God* (1987); *You've Had Your Time* (1990)

Burgess, Guy Francis de Moncy 1910–63
British double-agent
Born in Devonport, Devon, he was educated at Eton, at the Royal Naval College, Dartmouth, and at Trinity College, Cambridge, where he became a communist, and met Donald Maclean, Kim Philby and Anthony Blunt. Recruited as a Soviet agent in the 1930s, he worked with the BBC (1936–39), wrote war propaganda (1939–41), and again joined the BBC (1941–44) while working for MI5. After World War II he joined the Foreign Office and in 1950 became secretary of the British Embassy in Washington DC, where Philby was chief MI6 liaison officer. Recalled in 1951 for 'serious misconduct', he and Maclean disappeared, resurfacing in the USSR in 1956. 📖 John Fisher, *Burgess & Maclean: A New Look at the Foreign Office Spies* (1977)

Burgh, Hubert de, Earl of Kent d.1243
English statesman
He was the Chief Justice of England, under King John and Henry III (1215–32), and was virtual ruler for the last four years, but now is chiefly remembered as the jailer of Prince Arthur. He was created Earl of Kent in 1227. He was imprisoned (1232–34) after falling from favour, but later pardoned.

Burghley, 1st Baron See Cecil, William

Bürgi, Jost See Byrgius, Justus

Burgin, Victor 1941–
English photographer
Born in Sheffield, Yorkshire, he studied at the Royal College of Art, London, and at Yale in the USA. From 1973 to 1988 he lectured in the department of film and photographic arts at the School of Communication in the Polytechnic of Central London (now the University of Westminster). His work, which was influenced by the conceptual art of the 1960s, is always in black-and-white. Concerned with the social and cultural uses of photography, particularly in advertising, his pictures contain pieces of text superimposed on images of everyday urban life in a way that challenges and forces the viewer to participate.

Burgkmair, Hans 1473–1531
German painter and wood-engraver
Born in Augsburg, the father-in-law of the elder Hans Holbein, the Younger, and a friend of Albrecht Dürer, he is best known for his nearly 700 woodcuts.

Burgos Seguí, Carmen de, *pseudonym* Colombine c.1870–1932
Spanish feminist
Born in the remote province of Almería, the daughter of the consul of Portugal, she married young and then moved to Madrid after being abandoned by her husband. She became a teacher and was elected to the presidency of the International League of Iberian and Hispanoamerican Women. She was an outstanding advocate of women's rights and published a vast quantity of journalism both in Spain and Latin America (being the first Spanish female war correspondent in 1909) as well as many books on women's issues under the pseudonym 'Colombine'. Her novels include *Los inadaptados* (1909, 'The Misfits') and *El último contrabandista* (1920, 'The Last Smuggler').

Burgoyne, John 1722–92
English soldier and dramatist

Educated at Westminster School, he entered the army in 1740. In 1743 he eloped with a daughter of the Earl of Derby. In the Seven Years War (1756–63) he captured Valencia de Alcántara (1762), and sat in parliament. He was sent out to America where he fought at Bunker Hill (1775). In 1777 he led an expedition from Canada, and took Ticonderoga, but was later forced to surrender to General Horatio Gates at Saratoga. He was Commander-in-Chief in Ireland in 1782–83. He wrote plays including *The Maid of the Oaks* (1775) and *The Heiress* (1786).

Buridan, Jean c.1300–c.1358
French scholastic philosopher
Born probably in Béthune, Artois, he studied under William of Ockham and taught in Paris. He published works on mechanics, optics, and, in particular, logic. He gave his name to the famous problem of decision-making called 'Buridan's Ass', where an ass faced with two equidistant and equally desirable bales of hay starves to death because there are no grounds for preferring to go to one bale rather than the other.

Burke, Edmund See panel p300

Burke, John 1787–1848
Irish genealogist
Born in Tipperary, he was the compiler of *Burke's Peerage*—the first dictionary of baronets and peers of the UK in alphabetical order, published in 1826.

Burke, Sir John Bernard 1814–92
Irish genealogist
He was the son of John Burke and took over *Burke's Peerage* from his father, publishing it annually from 1847, as well as anecdotes of the aristocracy. An expert in heraldry, he was Ulster King of Arms (1853), and Keeper of the State Papers of Ireland (1855).

Burke, Kenneth Duva 1897–1992
US philosopher, critic and poet
Born in Pittsburgh, he was educated in Ohio and at Columbia University in New York City. He served as music critic for *The Dial* and *The Nation* during the 1920s, but gradually developed critical-theoretical constructs which put heavy emphasis on rhetoric as a means of revealing psychological, literary and cultural motives. His most important criticism is contained in *Counterstatement* (1931), *The Philosophy of Literary Form* (1941), *A Grammar of Motives* (1945) and *A Rhetoric of Motives* (1950). He also wrote short fiction, notably *The White Oxen* (1924), and a single, experimental novel, *Towards a Better Life* (1932), which he revised nearly 35 years after first publication. 📖 M E Brown, *Kenneth Burke* (1969)

Burke, Robert O'Hara 1820–61
Irish explorer
Born in St Clerans, County Galway, he was educated in Belgium, served in the Austrian army (1840), joined the Irish constabulary (1848), and emigrated to Australia in 1853. While an inspector of police in Victoria he accepted the leadership, with William Wills, of an expedition to cross the continent. They set off from Melbourne in 1860, and, after many hardships, Burke, John King and another man reached the tidal marshes of the Flinders River at the edge of the Gulf of Carpentaria. They were the first white men to cross the Australian continent from south to north but only King survived the return journey. Burke and the others died of starvation.

Burke, Thomas 1886–1945
English writer
Born in London, he is best known for his *Limehouse Nights* (1916), although he was the author of some 30 books in total, mostly on aspects of London or about inns. These include *Nights in Town* (1915), *The English Inn* (1930) and *The*

Burke, Edmund 1729–97
Irish statesman and philosopher

Edmund Burke was born in Dublin and educated at a Quaker boarding-school and at Trinity College, Dublin. In 1750 he entered the Middle Temple, London, but soon abandoned law for literary work. His early works include *Vindication of Natural Society* (1756) and *Philosophical Inquiry into the Origin of our Ideas of the Sublime and Beautiful* (1757). He was appointed Secretary for Ireland, and in 1765 entered parliament for the pocket borough of Wendover.

Burke's eloquence soon earned him a high position in the Whig Party. The best of his writings and speeches belong to the turbulent and corrupt period of Lord **North's** long administration (1770–82), and may be described as a defence of sound constitutional statesmanship against prevailing abuse and misgovernment. *Observations on the Present State of the Nation* (1769) was a reply to **George Grenville**; *On the Causes of the Present Discontents* (1770) deals with the **Wilkes** controversy. Perhaps the finest of his many efforts are the speech on *American Taxation* (1774), the speech *On Conciliation with America* (1775) and the *Letter to the Sheriffs of Bristol* (1777)—all advocating wise and liberal measures, which might have averted the troubles that ensued. Burke never systematized his political philosophy, which emerges with inconsistencies out of these writings and speeches. Opposed to the doctrine of 'natural rights', he takes over the concept of 'social contract', and attaches to it a divine sanction.

After the fall of the Whig ministry in 1783 Burke was never again in office and, misled by party feeling, he opposed **William Pitt's** measure for free trade with Ireland and the Commercial Treaty with France. In 1788 he opened the trial of **Warren Hastings** with the speech that will always rank among the masterpieces of English eloquence. His *Reflections on the Revolution in France* (1790) was read all over Europe.

Burke ranks as one of the foremost political thinkers of the British Isles. He had a vast knowledge of affairs, a glowing imagination, passionate sympathies, and an inexhaustible wealth of powerful and cultured expression; however, during his whole political life he had financial difficulties, despite two pensions granted him in 1794. He was buried in the little church at Beaconsfield, where in 1768 he had purchased the estate of Gregories.

S Ayling, *Edmund Burke: His Life and Opinions* (1988); G Fasel, *Edmund Burke* (1983); A P Miller, *Edmund Burke and His World* (1979).

'The age of chivalry is gone.—That of sophisters, economists, and calculators, has succeeded; and the glory of Europe is extinguished for ever.' From *Reflections of the Revolution in France* (1790).

Streets of London (1940). He also made a fine reconstruction of the Thurtell and Hunt case in *Murder at Elstree* (1936). He published an autobiography, *The Wind and the Rain*, in 1924. *Son of London* (1946)

Burke, Thomas Henry 1829–82
English politician

As permanent Irish Under-Secretary from 1868, he was brutally murdered with Lord Frederick Cavendish in Phoenix Park, Dublin (The 'Phoenix Park Murders').

Burke, William 1792–1829
Irish murderer

Born in County Cork, he moved to Scotland in 1818. With his partner William Hare (1790–1860) he committed a series of murders in Edinburgh, supplying dissection subjects to Dr Robert Knox, the anatomist. Hare turned king's evidence, and probably died some time in the 1860s, a blind beggar in London, while Burke was hanged, to great public satisfaction. James Bridie's play, *The Anatomist* (1931), was based on the case. Owen Dudley Edwards, *Burke & Hare* (1993)

Burkitt, Denis Parsons 1911–93
Northern Irish surgeon and nutritionist

Born in Enniskillen, County Fermanagh, and educated at Dublin University, he served with the Royal Army Medical Corps in Uganda, where he worked as a general surgeon after World War II, and began a series of clinical observations on a common childhood cancer found there (from 1957). It behaved as if it were infectious and subsequent research showed that the cancer—now known as Burkitt's lymphoma—was caused by a virus. Burkitt's other major contribution related the low African incidence of coronary heart disease, bowel cancer and other diseases to the high unrefined fibre in the native diet. He became one of the leading apostles of fibre in western diets, which earned him the nickname 'the bran man'. He was elected FRS in 1976, a rare honour for a surgeon.

Burks, Arthur Walter 1915–
US computer scientist and philosopher

Born in Duluth, Minnesota, he was educated at DePauw University and the University of Michigan, and by the end of World War II had joined **John Presper Eckert** and **John Mauchly** in the design and construction of the ENIAC (Electronic Numerical Integrator and Computer) and the EDVAC (Electronic Discrete Variable Computer) computing machines. In 1946 he worked at the Institute for Advanced Study in Princeton, and also wrote the influential paper *Preliminary Discussion of the Logical Design of an Electronic Computing Instrument*. He conducted pioneering work on cellular automata. Burks became Professor of Philosophy at the University of Michigan in 1954. He is co-author of *The First Electronic Computer: The Atanasoff Story* (1971), in which he examined the birth of the electronic digital computer.

Burlingame, Anson 1820–70
US diplomat

Born in New Berlin, New York, he was sent as US Minister to China by **Abraham Lincoln**, then was made Chinese envoy to the USA and Europe. He negotiated the Burlingame Treaty between China and the USA (1868), establishing reciprocal rights of citizenship.

Burlington, Richard Boyle, 3rd Earl of 1695–1753
Anglo-Irish politician and patron of the arts

A great admirer of **Andrea Palladio**, he was himself an enthusiastic architect. He redesigned the Burlington House in Piccadilly and by his influence over a group of young architects fostered the Palladian style which was to govern English building for half a century. He was Lord High Treasurer of Ireland in 1715.

Burn, William 1789–1870
Scottish architect

Born in Edinburgh, he trained under Sir **Robert Smirke** in London, and founded a successful business first in Edinburgh (with **David Bryce**), and then, after 1844, in London. He designed The Edinburgh Academy (1824), John Watson's School (now the Gallery of Modern Art) and the Music Hall in Edinburgh, and the Custom House in Greenock. He commissioned R W Billings (1813–74) to write the influential *Baronial and Ecclesiastical Architecture of Scotland* (1848–52).

Burnand, Sir Francis Cowley 1836–1917
English dramatist and journalist

He was called to the Bar in 1862, but the success of some early dramatic ventures altered his plans. He helped to start *Fun*, but in 1863 left that paper for *Punch*, of which he became editor (1880–1906). He wrote many burlesques, including *Black-Eyed Susan* (1866) and *Cox and Box*, which had music by **Arthur Sullivan** (1867). ⌑ *Records and Reminiscences* (1917)

Burne-Jones, Sir Edward Coley 1833–98
English painter

Born in Birmingham of Welsh ancestry, he studied at Exeter College, Oxford, where he became the close friend of **William Morris** and **Dante Gabriel Rossetti** and abandoned his studies for the Church. In 1861 he became a founder member of Morris, Marshall, Faulkner & Company (later Morris & Company), for which he designed tapestries and stained glass. His early works, mostly watercolours, such as *The Merciful Knight* (1864) and *The Wine of Circe* (1867), are brighter than his later oils which, inspired by the early art of the Italian Renaissance, are characterized by a romantic and contrived Mannerism. His subjects, drawn from the Arthurian romances and Greek myths, include *The Days of Creation, The Beguiling of Merlin, The Mirror of Vénus* (1877), and *Pan and Psyche* (1878). His *Love and the Pilgrim* is in the Tate Gallery, London. His son, Sir Philip Burne-Jones (1861–1926), also became a painter.

Burnell, Jocelyn Bell See Bell Burnell, (Susan) Jocelyn

Burnet, Sir Alastair, *originally* James William Alexander Burnet 1928–
English journalist and broadcaster

Born in Sheffield, South Yorkshire, he joined the *Glasgow Herald* as a sub-editor and leader-writer in 1951, then became leader-writer for *The Economist* (1958–62), before entering television as political editor of Independent Television News (ITN) (1963–65). He returned to *The Economist* as editor (1965) but continued to work for ITN as a newscaster, helping to launch *News at Ten* in 1967, before moving to the BBC as anchorman of *Panorama* in 1972. In 1974 he left television to become editor of the *Daily Express* but returned to ITN as a newscaster in 1976 and became associate editor on News at Ten in 1982. He was also anchorman for ITV's General Election and Budget programmes over many years and won the BAFTA Richard Dimbleby award a record three times. He was knighted in 1984 and retired in 1991.

Burnet, Gilbert 1643–1715
Scottish churchman and Anglican historian

Born in Edinburgh, he studied at Marischal College, Aberdeen, and in 1661 joined the Church of Scotland as a probationer. He became Professor of Divinity at Glasgow University in 1669, but in 1674 resigned his chair after a disagreement with his patron, the Duke of **Lauderdale**. Settling in London, where he associated with the Whig opposition, he was made chaplain to the Rolls Chapel, then lecturer at St Clements. He also published the first two volumes of his *History of the Reformation* (1679–81; vol 3, 1714). In 1680 he declined the bishopric of Chichester and in 1683 attended the execution of his friend William, Lord **Russell** for complicity in the Ryehouse Plot. **Charles II** deprived him of his lectureship and on James II's accession Burnet went to the Continent, eventually taking Dutch nationality. In 1684 he met the Prince of Orange (the future **William III**) and became his royal chaplain on the 'Glorious Revolution' of 1688. The following year he

was made Bishop of Salisbury. He published an *Exposition of the thirty-nine Articles* (1699) and a *History of My Own Time* (1724–34).

Burnet, Sir (Frank) Macfarlane 1899–1985
Australian immunologist and virologist and Nobel Prize winner

Born in Traralgon, eastern Victoria, he graduated in medicine from Melbourne University, and after postgraduate work there moved to London to work in bacteriological research at the Lister Institute. He returned to Melbourne in 1928 to the Walter and Eliza Hall Institute for Medical Research, where he later became assistant director (1934) and then director (1944). From 1931 to 1934, he began working on viruses at the National Institute for Medical Research in London, and for the next 20 years made important contributions to our understanding of many animal viruses, especially the influenza virus. From the end of the 1950s he turned his attention to immunological problems, particularly the phenomenon of graft rejection. His work transformed the understanding of how the entry of foreign substances (antigens) into the body results in the production of specific antibodies which bind and neutralize the invader. Burnet suggested that antibodies were present on specialized white blood cells, which would bind to an invading antigen and then reproduce, thus producing large quantities of its unique antibody. **Peter Medawar's** work provided the experimental evidence to support Burnet's theory, and in 1960 the two men shared the Nobel Prize for physiology or medicine. Burnet was elected FRS in 1942, knighted in 1951, and appointed to the Order of Merit in 1958.

Burnett, Carol 1933–
US comedienne and dramatic actress

Born in San Antonio, Texas, she studied at the University of California, Los Angeles, then moved to New York City, where she found work on children's television. Her Broadway debut was in *Once Upon a Mattress* (1960) and she became a television regular in *Stanley* (1956–57) and *The Garry Moore Show* (1959–62), for which she received her first Emmy award. A versatile comedy performer, she enjoyed enormous success with *The Carol Burnett Show* (1967–78, 1991) and *Carol and Company* (1990–91). She also appeared in the television films *Friendly Fire* (1979), *Life of the Party: The Story of Beatrice* (1982) and *Hostage* (1988). Her autobiography *One More Time* was published in 1986.

Burnett, Frances Hodgson, *née* Frances Eliza Hodgson 1849–1924
US novelist

Born in Manchester, England, the daughter of a manufacturer, she emigrated with her family to Knoxville, Tennessee, in 1865, and there turned to writing to help out the family finances. She married Dr Swan Moses Burnett in 1873 (divorced in 1898). There is speculation that a second marriage was made under the threat of blackmail. An unhappy alliance, it did much to cloud her later life. Her first literary success was *That Lass o' Lowrie's* (1877). Later works include plays, her most popular story *Little Lord Fauntleroy* (1886), *The One I Knew Best of All* (1893, autobiographical), *The Little Princess* (1905) and *The Secret Garden* (1909), still one of the best-loved classics of children's literature. In her lifetime she was rated one of the USA's foremost writers, and was a friend of **Henry James**. ⌑ A Thwaite, *Waiting for the Party: a life of Frances Hodgson Burnett* (1974)

Burnett, James See Monboddo, Lord

Burney, Charles 1726–1814
English musicologist

Born in Shrewsbury, Shropshire, he studied music there, at Chester, and under Dr Thomas Arne in London, later giving lessons himself. After composing three pieces, *Alfred*, *Robin Hood*, and *Queen Mab*, for Drury Lane (1745–50), he went as organist to King's Lynn, Norfolk (1751–60). He travelled (1770–72) in France, Italy, Germany, and Austria to collect material for his *Present State of Music in France and Italy* (1771), and his *General History of Music* (4 vols, 1776–89). His *General History* was long considered a standard work, superseding that of Sir John Hawkins, but its bias towards the then popular Italian style, to the neglect of Bach and his contemporaries, led to a fall in its influence. Burney also wrote a *Life of Metastasio* (3 vols, 1796), and nearly all the musical articles in *Rees's Cyclopaedia*. In 1783 he became organist to Chelsea Hospital. He was the father of Fanny Burney, and knew many of the eminent men of his day, including Edmund Burke, Dr Johnson and David Garrick.

Burney, Fanny (Frances), *later* Madame d'Arblay
1752–1840
English novelist and diarist
Born in King's Lynn, Norfolk, the daughter of Charles Burney, she educated herself by reading English and French literature and observing the distinguished people who visited her father. By the age of 10 she had begun scribbling stories, plays, and poems, but on her 15th birthday, in a fit of repentance for what she saw as a waste of time, she burned all her papers. However, she did not forget the plot of *Evelina*, her first and best novel, published anonymously in 1778, which describes the entry of a country girl into the gaieties of London life. Her father at once recognized his daughter's talent and confided the secret to Mrs Hester Piozzi, who, as well as Dr Johnson, championed the gifted young author. *Cecilia* (1782), though more complex, is less natural, and her style gradually declined in *Camilla* (1796) and *The Wanderer* (1814). She was appointed a second keeper of the robes to Queen Charlotte in 1786, but her health declined, and she retired on a pension and married a French émigré, General d' Arblay, in 1793. Her *Letters and Diaries* (1846) give a vivid and lively account of her life. As a portrayer of the domestic scene she was a forerunner of Jane Austen, whom she influenced. ▢ M E Adelstein, *Fanny Burney* (1968)

Burnham, Daniel Hudson 1846–1912
US architect and leader of the Chicago School
Born in Henderson, New York, he worked in partnership with John Wellborn Root (1850–91), and later with Charles B Atwood. His pioneering designs into urban planning in Chicago were widely influential. He continued the Romanesque revival and developed the Richardsonian style. With Root, in Chicago, he designed the Women's Temple and Masonic Building (1890–92), now demolished, the Reliance Building (1890–95), and the conservative skyscraper design, the Monadnock Building (1890–91). As chief of construction for the Chicago World's Fair (1893), he co-ordinated the creation of the White City, comprising formal monumental designs. The Rookery Building, New York (1901), the Selfridge Building, London (1908), and the Union Railroad Station, Washington DC (1909) are examples of his later commissions.

Burnham, Forbes 1923–85
Guyanese politician
British-educated, he represented the African element in the Guyanese population and was co-leader with Cheddi Jagan of the multiracial People's Progressive Party until 1955. In that year he split with Jagan over the latter's support for international communism and set up a rival African-based party, the People's National Congress (PNC). The PNC slowly gained adherents in Jagan's troubled years after 1961 and in 1964 Burnham became

Prime Minister. He negotiated an independence constitution in 1966, and in 1970 established Guyana as a 'co-operative socialist republic', remaining its President until his death.

Burnham, Sir Harry Lawson Webster Levy-Lawson, 2nd Baron and 1st Viscount
1862–1933
English politician
Born in London, he was educated at Eton and Oxford, was Liberal and later Unionist MP, succeeded his father as director of the *Daily Telegraph* in 1903 and helped to frame the Representation of the People Act of 1918. He was president of the International Labour Conference and the Empire Press Union for several years. He is chiefly known, however, as chairman of the committees which inquired into the salaries of teachers and which recommended the Burnham Scales.

Burningham, John 1936–
English illustrator and children's writer
Born in Farnham, Surrey, he was educated at A S Neill's Summerhill and the Central School for Arts and Crafts, London. Popular and amusing, he draws children with round, cherubic faces which belie their highly-aware resourcefulness, as in *The Shopping Basket* (1982). Distinctions include illustrating Ian Fleming's *Chitty Chitty Bang Bang* (1964) and receiving the Kate Greenaway award for *Borka* (1964) and *Mr Gumpy's Outing* (1970). More recent publications include *Harvey Slumfenburger's Christmas Present* (1993) and *Courtney* (1994).

Burns, Sir George 1795–1890
Scottish shipowner
He was born in Glasgow. With his brother James Burns (1789–1871) he pioneered steam navigation from Glasgow. In 1839, with Samuel Cunard and Robert Napier, he founded the future Cunard Line. He was succeeded by his son John Burns (1829–1911), later Lord Inverclyde.

Burns, George, *originally* Nathan Birnbaum
1896–1996
US comedian
Born in New York City, he first performed in a quartet of child singers and later broke into vaudeville as a comedian. He and his wife, Gracie Allen, performed as a comedy team (1923–58), in which he played the straight-man role of a sometimes patient, sometimes exasperated husband to her scatterbrained wife. They brought their vaudeville act to radio (1932–50), TV (1950–58), and films. Burns retired from show business after Allen's death in 1964, but he returned to acting in the late 1970s, winning an Academy Award for his performance as an old vaudevillian in *The Sunshine Boys* (1975), and appearing in numerous other films and TV specials.

Burns, John Elliot 1858–1943
British engineer and socialist politician
Born of Scottish parentage in London, he worked as an engineer, took to socialism, and, elected MP for Battersea in 1892, became president of the Local Government Board (1905), and of the Board of Trade (1914), but resigned when war began. He was the first working-class Cabinet Minister in Great Britain. Known as a brilliant orator, he advocated the cause of the working classes of South London.

Burns, Robert See panel p303

Burnside, Ambrose Everett 1824–81
US soldier and senator
Born in Liberty, Indiana, he commanded a brigade at Bull Run, and in 1862 captured Roanoke Island. His corps was repulsed with heavy losses in the Battle of Antietam later that year. Commanding the army of the Potomac he crossed the Rappahannock to attack Robert E Lee near

Burns, Robert 1759–96
Scottish poet and songwriter

Robert Burns was born in Alloway, near Ayr. The son of a poor farmer, he nonetheless received a literary education, and was also much influenced by the popular tales, ballads and songs of Betty Davidson, an old woman who lived with his family.

His father died bankrupt in 1784, leaving Burns to try to farm for himself. With his brother Gilbert, he took a small farm at Mossgiel, near Mauchline, but his husbandry was beset by problems. As his farm went to ruin in 1785, he produced a prolific output of poetry celebrating love, lust and country life. Poems written in this year include the 'Epistle to Davie', 'Death and Dr Hornbook', 'The Twa Herds', 'The Jolly Beggars', 'Halloween', 'The Cotter's Saturday Night', 'Holy Willie's Prayer', 'The Holy Fair' and 'The Address to a Mouse'.

Also in 1785, Elizabeth Paton, who had been a servant girl on his father's farm, gave birth to Burn's first illegitimate child, whom he welcomed in a poem. Around the same time, his entanglement with Jean Armour (1767–1834), the daughter of a stonemason, began. But when Jean's father refused to accept him as a son-in-law, despite the fact that Jean was pregnant by him, he took up (1786) with a Mary Campbell ('Highland Mary'), who died not long after their liaison had begun.

He decided to emigrate to Jamaica and, having produced a further output of verse, much of it satirical in nature, he published the famous Kilmarnock edition of his poetry, *Poems, Chiefly in the Scottish Dialect* (1786), to try to raise money for his journey. This edition includes the well-known poems 'The Twa Dogs', 'Address to the Deil' and 'To a Louse'; 'Address to the Unco Guid' and 'Address to a Haggis' were among the poems added to the 1787 Edinburgh edition.

The praise and admiration that his poetry received from country folk and the Edinburgh literati alike persuaded Burns to stay in Scotland, and he was greeted with acclaim on visiting Edinburgh in the winter of 1786. After a Highland tour, he returned to Edinburgh and began the epistolary flirtations with 'Clarinda' (**Agnes Maclehose**).

In 1788, he 'fell to his old love again' and married Jean Armour. He leased a farm at Ellisland, near Dumfries, and in 1789 was made an excise officer. From 1788 until 1792 he worked on **James Johnson**'s *Scots Musical Museum* (1787–1803), collecting, editing, writing and rewriting songs and music for the six-volume publication. The best-known songs accredited to him therein include 'John Anderson My Jo', 'Ae Fond Kiss', 'Ye Jacobites By Name', 'The Banks o' Doon', 'Afton Water', 'A Red Red Rose' and

'Auld Lang Syne'. Many of his songs also appeared in George Thomson's *Select Collection of Original Scottish Airs for the Voice* (5 vols, 1793–1818).

In 1790, by which time his farm was failing, he wrote his long narrative poem 'Tam o'Shanter'. He left his farm in 1791 and moved to Dumfries, flirted with the sentiments and fervour of the French Revolution, continued collecting and writing Scottish songs set to traditional airs, expressed radical opinions and made himself unpopular with the local lairds. He died of endocarditis induced by rheumatism, and is buried in Dumfries.

Commonly regarded as the national poet of Scotland, Burns also has an international reputation for both the lyrical quality of his poems and songs, especially those written in his native Scots, and for his championing of the common man. Known variously as a kind of rural **Don Juan**, a rebel against extreme Calvinism and religious orthodoxy, and as 'the ploughman poet', he is the object of celebratory Burns Suppers held annually worldwide on his birthday (25 January).

📖 James A Mackay, *Burns: A Biography of Robert Burns* (1992); James A Mackay (ed), *The Complete Letters of Robert Burns* (1987); C Carswell, *The Life of Robert Burns* (1930).

'Men and women quite suddenly realised that here lay one who was the Poet of his Country—perhaps of mankind—as none had been before, because none before had combined so many human weaknesses with so great an ardour of living and so generous a warmth of admission. Certainly none had ever possessed a racier gift of expression for his own people.'
Catherine Carswell, writing about the death of Burns, in *The Life of Robert Burns*, ch.30 (1930)

Is there, for honest poverty,
That hangs his head, and a' that?
The coward-slave, we pass him by—
We dare be poor for a' that!
For a' that, and a' that,
Our toils obscure, and a' that,
The rank is but the guinea's stamp—
The man's the gowd for a' that.
　…For a' that, and a' that,
It's comin' yet for a' that,
That man to man, the warld o'er,
Shall brothers be for a' that!
'For a' that and a' that', stanzas 1 & 5 (1795)

Fredericksburg, but was driven back with a loss of more than 10,000 men (1862). In 1863 he successfully held Knoxville, and in 1864 led a corps under **Ulysses S Grant** through the battles of the Wilderness and Cold Harbor. He was elected US senator in 1875. He gave his name to a style of side-whiskers called 'burnsides' (now 'sideburns'). 📖 Ben Perley Poore, *The Life and Public Services of Ambrose E Burnside* (1882)

Burnside, William 1852–1927
English mathematician

Born in London, he graduated from Cambridge, and eventually became Professor of Mathematics at the Royal Naval College, Greenwich (1885–1919). He worked in mathematical physics, complex function theory, differential geometry and probability theory, but his lasting work was in group theory. His *Theory of Groups* (1897) was the first English textbook on the subject and is still of value, containing much original research and posing the famous Burnside problem. This was not solved until 1962

by Walter Feit and John Griggs Thompson, opening the way to the complete classification of finite groups, accomplished in the late 1980s.

Burr, Aaron 1756–1836
US politician

Born in Newark, New Jersey, he was a graduate of Princeton, and was called to the Bar in 1782. After serving as a US senator from New York (1791–97), he tied with **Thomas Jefferson** in the presidential election of 1800, and by decision of the House of Representatives became Vice-President (1801–05) under Jefferson. For 20 years he carried on a personal and political rivalry with **Alexander Hamilton**, and his defeat in a contest for the governorship of New York prompted him to force a duel (1804) with Hamilton, whom he mortally wounded. Burr fled to South Carolina, and though indicted for murder, returned and completed his term as Vice-President. He then devised a secret plan to establish an independent nation in the south-west. When rumours of this scheme leaked out, his enemies claimed that his goal was to dismember the Union, and he was arrested and tried for treason (1807). Acquitted, he spent some years in Europe, and in 1812 resumed his law practice in New York but was shunned by society. ▢ Milton Lomask, *Aaron Burr* (2 vols, 1977–82)

Burra, Edward 1905–76
English artist

Born in London, he travelled widely in Europe and the USA. He is well known as a colourist, and his Surrealist paintings of figures against exotic (often Spanish) backgrounds are invariably in watercolour. His picture *Soldiers* (1942) is in the Tate Gallery, London. He also designed for the ballet.

Burrell, Sir William 1861–1958
Scottish shipowner and art collector

He was born in Glasgow, the son of a shipping agent. He entered his father's business at the age of 15, and during his lifetime he accumulated a magnificent collection of 8,000 works of art from all over the world, including modern French paintings, which he gave in 1944 to the city of Glasgow, with provision for an art gallery. In 1949 he gifted an art gallery and a number of pictures to Berwick-upon-Tweed. The Burrell Collection was finally opened to the public in 1983 in a new gallery built for it on the south side of Glasgow. ▢ Richard Marks, *Sir William Burrell, 1861–1958* (rev edn, 1985)

Burri, Alberto 1915–
Italian painter

Born at Città di Castello, Perugia, he was a doctor during World War II, and began to paint in a prison camp in Texas in 1944. He was one of the first to exploit the evocative potential of waste materials, and is best known for his use of sacking and old rags, as in *Sacking with Red* (1954, Tate, London), reminiscent of blood-soaked bandages. From 1956 he also used charred wood and melted down polyvinyl and metal, for example in *Combustione Plastica* (1964, Pompidou Centre, Paris).

Burritt, Elihu, *known as* the Learned Blacksmith 1810–79
US pacifist

Born in New Britain, Connecticut, he worked as a blacksmith in his native town and at Worcester, Massachusetts, but devoted all his leisure to mathematics and languages. Through his published works and his travels in the USA and Europe he was known as an apostle of peace. He founded the *Christian Citizen* in 1844. From 1865 to 1870 he was US consul in Birmingham, England.

Burroughs, Edgar Rice 1875–1950
US popular author, creator of Tarzan

Born in Chicago, he served in the US cavalry and fought against the Apache but was discharged when it was discovered he was under age. Thereafter he had several colourful occupations before he took to writing, his aim being to improve on the average 'dime' novel. *Tarzan of the Apes* (1914) was his first book to feature the eponymous hero, the son of a British aristocrat, abandoned in the African jungle and brought up by apes. It spawned many sequels, as well as films (in which Tarzan was played most memorably by **Johnny Weissmuller**), radio programmes and comic strips, making Burroughs a millionaire. ▢ R A Lopoff, *Edgar Rice Burroughs, master of adventure* (1965)

Burroughs, John 1837–1921
US naturalist and writer

Born in Roxbury, New York State, he became a teacher and later tax inspector, and settled down in 1874 on a farm near Aesopus, New York, where he built himself a secluded cabin for his studies. His books mostly deal with

country life, and include *Wake-Robin* (1871), *Winter Sunshine* (1875), *Birds and Poets* (1877), and *Locusts and Wild Honey* (1879).

Burroughs, William Seward 1855–98
US inventor

Born in Auburn, New York, he worked in his father's shop in St Louis, Missouri, from the age of 15, working on new inventions. He developed a mechanical calculating machine in 1885 with three other businessmen, and started up the American Arithmometer Company (1886), patenting an adding machine in 1892 which was a commercial success.

Burroughs, William S(eward) 1914–97
US writer

He was born into a wealthy family in St Louis, Missouri. After graduating from Harvard in 1936, he travelled throughout the USA and Europe. While in New York in 1944 he became a heroin addict and in 1953 he published *Junkie*, an account of this experience. His novels *The Naked Lunch* (1959) and *The Soft Machine* (1961) established him as a leading figure of the Beat movement, though one who stood somewhat apart. Intensely interested in the juxtaposition of apparently random ideas and observations, he was concerned in his later work with innovations in the novel form, such as the techniques of 'cut-up' and 'fold-in', by which words and phrases are either cut out and pasted together or formed by cross-column reading. Other works include *The Experimentor* (1960, with Brion Gysin), *The Ticket that Exploded* (1962), *The Yage Letters* (1963, with **Allen Ginsberg**), *Dead Fingers Talk* (1963), *Nova Express* (1964), *The Wild Boys* (1971), *Exterminator!* (1973), *Ah, Pook is Here* (1979), *Cities of the Red Night* (1981) and *My Education: A Book of Dreams* (1995). ▢ E Mottram, *The Algebra of Need* (1971)

Burrows, Eva 1929–
Australian Salvation Army leader

Born in Newcastle, New South Wales, and educated at the universities of Queensland, Sydney and London, she was the daughter of a Salvation Army officer, and committed herself to the Salvation Army while a student. She subsequently worked for the Salvation Army in Rhodesia (now Zimbabwe) from 1952 to 1969, and then in England (1970–77), Sri Lanka (1977–79), Scotland (1979–82) and Southern Australia (1982–86), organizing and developing work in such areas as education, battered women's refuges, and youth training schemes. From 1986 to 1993 she was general of the Salvation Army, only the second woman to hold this office.

Burstyn, Ellen, *née* Edna Rae Gillooly 1932–
US actress

Born in Detroit, she studied acting in California, and with **Stella Adler** and **Lee Strasberg** in New York City. She made her Broadway debut as Ellen McRae in *Fair Game* (1957). Her notable stage roles include *Same Time, Next Year* (1975, Tony award), *The Three Sisters* (1977), *84 Charing Cross Road* (1982) and *Shirley Valentine* (1989). She was artistic director of the Actors Studio (1982–88) and was also the first woman president of the Actors Equity Association (1982–85). She made her film debut in *Goodbye Charlie* (1964) and has received Academy Award nominations for *The Last Picture Show* (1971), *The Exorcist* (1973), *Same Time, Next Year* (1978) and *Resurrection* (1980). She won a Best Actress Academy Award for *Alice Doesn't Live Here Anymore* (1974). On television, she received Emmy nominations for *The People vs Jean Harris* (1981) and *Pack of Lies* (1987). Recent films include *The Cemetery Club* (1993) and *Spitfire Grill* (1995).

Burt, Sir Cyril Lodowic 1883–1971
English psychologist

Born in London, he was educated at Christ's Hospital and Jesus College, Oxford, and at Würzburg. He became Professor of Education at London (1924–31) and then Professor of Psychology (1931–50). He was also psychologist to the London County Council, was consulted by the War Office and the Civil Service Commission on personnel selection and was highly influential in the theory and practice of intelligence and aptitude tests, ranging from the psychology of education to the problems of juvenile delinquency. Since his death the authenticity of some of his research data has been questioned.

Burton, Beryl, *née* Charnock 1937–96
English cyclist
Born in Leeds, she is chiefly known for her time trial records, but in the early 1960s she was rarely beaten in any field of cycling. In 1967 her distance of 277.25 miles (446.12km) covered in an amateur 12 hours' time trial set a new British record. More importantly, it was 0.73 miles further than any man in the race could manage. In 1968 she rode 100 miles (161km) in 3 hours, 55.05 minutes—only 12 years after the previous Briton—a man—had broken four hours for that distance. In total Burton won seven world championships in her career.

Burton, Decimus 1800–81
English architect
Born in London, he was the son of a builder. At the age of 23 he planned the Regent's Park colosseum, an exhibition hall with a dome larger than that of St Paul's Cathedral, and in 1825 designed the new layout of Hyde Park and the triumphal arch at Hyde Park Corner. He designed the Palm House at Kew Gardens (1844–48) with engineer Richard Turner.

Burton, Richard, *originally* Richard Walter Jenkins 1925–84
Welsh stage and film actor
Born in Pontrhydfen, Wales, the son of a coal miner, he was adopted by his English teacher, Philip H Burton, and gained a scholarship to Exeter College, Oxford. He first appeared on stage in *Druid's Rest* at the Royal Court Theatre, Liverpool, and, after national service in the RAF, returned to the stage in 1948, the same year as his film debut in *The Last Days of Dolwyn*. He made his stage reputation in Christopher Fry's *The Lady's Not for Burning* (1949), which was enthusiastically received on Broadway. A triumphant season at Stratford (1951) was followed by his first Hollywood film, *My Cousin Rachel* (1952), for which he received one of his six Academy Award nominations, and *The Robe* (1953), for which he was also nominated. In 1954 he was the narrator in the famous radio production of Dylan Thomas's *Under Milk Wood*. Hailed as one of the most promising Shakespearean actors of his generation, a well-publicized romance with his co-star in *Cleopatra*, Elizabeth Taylor, whom he eventually married (twice), projected him into the 'superstar' category. His highly successful films include *Cleopatra* (1963), *Becket* (1964), *The Spy Who Came in from the Cold* (1965) and *Where Eagles Dare* (1969). Interest in his lifestyle was generally greater than in his performances, although his work in *Who's Afraid of Virginia Woolf* (1968), *Equus* (1977) and *1984* (released in 1984, after his death) was well received. 🕮 Melvyn Bragg, *Richard Burton: A Life* (1989)

Burton, Sir Richard Francis 1821–90
English explorer, linguist and diplomat
Born in Torquay, Devon, he was largely self-educated and won a place at Oxford, where he began to study Arabic. He is said to have mastered approximately 30 languages, many with various dialects. In 1842 he served in Sind, India (now Pakistan) under Sir Charles Napier, and having mastered Hindustani, Persian, and Arabic, made a pilgrimage to Mecca disguised as a Pathan (1853). He was then commissioned by the Foreign Office to search for the sources of the Nile, and in 1856 set out with John Hanning Speke on the journey which led to the discovery (1858) of Lake Tanganyika. In 1861 he became consul at Fernando Pó, and he was subsequently consul at Santos in Brazil, at Damascus, Syria and (1872) Trieste, Italy. He was knighted in 1886. His most important books include *First Footsteps in East Africa* (1851), *The Pilgrimage to Al-Medinah and Meccah* (1855), *The Lake Regions of Central Africa* (1860) and his translation of *The Arabian Nights* (16 vols, 1885–88). 🕮 Lady Burton, *Life of Sir Richard Burton* (1893)

Burton, Robert 1577–1640
English writer and clergyman
Born in Lindley, Leicestershire, he was educated at Brasenose College, Oxford, and in 1599 was elected a student of Christ Church. In 1616 he was presented to the Oxford vicarage of St Thomas, and about 1630 to the rectory of Segrave, Leicestershire. He kept both livings, but spent his life at Christ Church, where he died. The first edition of his great work, *Anatomy of Melancholy*, was written under the pseudonym 'Democritus Junior', and appeared in quarto in 1621 (final, sixth edition, 1651–52). This strange book is a vast and witty compendium of Jacobean knowledge about the 'disease' of melancholy, gathered from classical and medieval writers, as well as folklore and superstition. One of the most interesting parts is the long preface, 'Democritus to the Reader', in which Burton gives indirectly an account of himself and his studies. 🕮 B Evans, *The Psychiatry of Robert Burton* (1944)

Burton, Tim 1960–
US film director
Born in Burbank, California, he studied animation at the California Institute of the Arts and worked for Walt Disney Studios where he made the inventive short films *Vincent* (1982) and *Frankenweenie* (1984). In 1985 he made his feature-length directorial debut with *Pee Wee's Big Adventure* and subsequently showed his love of the macabre, and his offbeat sense of humour and strong visual sensibility in films like *Beetlejuice* (1988), *Batman* (1989), *Edward Scissorhands* (1990) and *Batman Returns* (1992). He has also produced the stop-motion animation films *The Nightmare Before Christmas* (1993) and *James and The Giant Peach* (1996). His most recent films as director are *Ed Wood* (1994) and the science-fiction comedy *Mars Attacks!* (1996).

Bury, Lady Charlotte Susan Maria 1775–1861
Scottish novelist
She was born in London, the youngest child of the 5th Duke of Argyll. In 1796 she married Colonel John Campbell, on whose death in 1809 she became lady-in-waiting to Caroline, Princess of Wales (see Caroline of Brunswick). In 1818 she married the Rev Edward John Bury (1790–1832). She published 16 novels, including *Flirtation* and *Separation*, and was reputedly the anonymous author of the spicy *Diary Illustrative of the Times of George IV* (2 vols, 1838).

Bury, John Bagnell 1861–1927
Irish historian and classical scholar
Born in County Monaghan, he was educated at Trinity College, Dublin. He became Professor of Modern History (1893–1902) and of Greek (1899–1902) at Dublin, and thereafter Regius Professor of Modern History at Cambridge. He wrote a monumental *History of the Later Roman Empire* (1889) at the age of 28, and other major histories of Greece and Rome, and edited Pindar and Edward Gibbon.

Bury, Richard de See Aungerville, Richard

Busby, Sir Matt 1909–94
Scottish footballer and football manager
Born in Bellshill, Lanarkshire, he became manager of Manchester United in 1945 after a comparatively un-distinguished playing career with Manchester City and Liverpool. Almost immediately the club won the FA Cup in 1948 and the League Cup shortly afterwards. Re-building the team, he seemed likely to win the Euro-pean Cup for Great Britain for the first time in 1958 but his young side (known as the 'Busby babes') was largely wiped out in an air crash at Munich airport. He him-self was severely injured, but patiently reconstructed the side until European Cup success eventually came in 1968. He retired as manager in 1969, but continued his in-volvement with the club, and served as its president from 1980.

Busby, Richard 1606–95
English schoolmaster
Born in Lutton-Bowine, Lincolnshire, and educated at Westminster School and Christ Church, Oxford, he was headmaster of Westminster from 1640 until his death. He was the prototype 17th-century headmaster, notable alike for learning, assiduity, and unsparing application of the birch. Among his pupils were Dryden, John Locke, Robert South, and Francis Atterbury.

Busch, Adolf 1891–1952
Swiss violinist
Born in Siegen, Westphalia, Germany, he formed the Busch Quartet and Busch Trio in 1919, with his younger brother Hermann (1897–1975) as cellist and his son-in-law Rudolf Serkin as pianist. He took Swiss nationality in 1935, and emigrated to the USA in 1939. He was the younger brother of Fritz Busch.

Busch, Fritz 1890–1951
German conductor
Born in Siegen, Westphalia, he became an eminent con-ductor and noted Mozartian, especially as music director of the Dresden Opera (1922–33), where he premiered operas by Richard Strauss. He was later music director at Glyndebourne (1934–39), then worked in South America (1940–45) and at the New York Metropolitan (1945–49). He was the elder brother of Adolf Busch.

Busch, Wilhelm 1832–1908
German cartoonist and writer
Born near Hanover, he worked as an illustrator for the *Fliegende Blätter* (1859–71), and wrote satirical verse-stories with his own illustrations, such as *Max und Moritz* (1865, the prototypes for Rudolph Dirks's *Katzenjammer Kids*) and *Herr und Frau Knopp* (1876).

Büsching, Anton Friedrich 1724–93
German geographer
Born in Schaumburg-Lippe, he was the founder of stat-istical geography. He became the director of a gymnas-ium in Berlin, and wrote *Neue Erdbeschreibung* (1754–92, Eng trans *A New System of Geography*, 6 vols, 1762). His son, Johann Gustav Büsching (1783–1829), published many works on German antiquities, literature, and art.

Bush, Alan Dudley 1900–95
English composer and pianist
Born in London, he studied at the Royal Academy of Music (1918–22), composition with John Ireland (1922–27), and piano with Benno Moiseiwitsch and Artur Schnabel. He was a respected composition teacher at the Royal Academy for most of the years from 1925 to 1978. He was founder of the Workers' Music Association (1936), of which he was president from 1941. His political and philosophical beliefs underlie much of his work which includes four operas (1953, *Wat Tyler*, 1956, *Men of Blackmoor*, 1966, *The Sugar Reapers*, and 1970, *Joe Hill—The*

Man Who Never Died), four symphonies, concertos for violin and piano, choral works including *The Winter Journey* (1946), folksong arrangements, songs including the cycle *Voices of the Prophets* (1952), many chamber works including *Dialectic* (1929) for string quartet, and a considerable quantity of piano music and organ works. In 1980 he published his collected essays, *In My Eighth Decade*.

Bush, George Herbert Walker 1924–
41st President of the USA
Born in Milton, Massachusetts, the son of a Connecticut senator, he served in the US navy (1942–45), becoming its youngest pilot, and after the war received a degree in economics from Yale and established an oil-drilling business in Texas. In 1966 he devoted himself to politics, and was elected to the House of Representatives. After his second unsuccessful bid for the senate in 1970 (his first was in 1964), he became US ambassador to the UN. During the Watergate scandal he was chairman of the Republican National Committee (1973–74) under President Nixon, and during the Ford administration he served as US envoy to China (1974–75), and then became director of the CIA (1976). In 1980 he sought the Republican presidential nomination, but lost to Ronald Reagan, later becoming his Vice-President. He became President in 1988, defeating the Democratic candidate, Michael Dukakis. His administration (1989–93) was marked by his aggressive foreign policy, which included ordering the invasion of Panama (1989) to oust Manuel Noriega and presiding over the US-led UN coalition to drive Iraqi forces from Kuwait in the Gulf War (1991). He signed nuclear arms limitation treaties with the USSR and Russia and the North American Free Trade Agreement (1992) with Canada and Mexico. His domestic record was considerably weaker, however, and in the 1992 pres-idential elections he lost the presidency to Democrat Bill Clinton. His autobiography, *Looking Forward*, was pub-lished in 1988. ▣ Mark Sufrin, *George Bush* (1989)

Bush, Vannevar 1890–1974
US electrical engineer and inventor
Born in Everett, Massachusetts, he graduated from Tufts College and the Massachusetts Institute of Technology. He devoted most of his considerable research effort from 1925 to the development of mechanical, electro-mechanical and latterly electronic calculating machines or analogue computers, which led directly to the digital computers universally used today. He also devised a cipher-breaking machine which was successful in breaking Japanese codes during World War II, and he was instru-mental in setting up the 'Manhattan Project' in 1942 which led to the creation of the US atomic bomb.

Busia, Kofi 1913–78
Ghanaian academic and politician
He was educated in Kumasi and at Achimota College, and at the universities of London and Oxford. He was one of the first Africans to be appointed an administrative of-ficer in the Gold Coast (now Ghana). He resigned his position to become a lecturer, and later Professor of Sociology, at the University College of Ghana. Elected to the Legco (1951), he became a leader of the National Liberation Movement (1954–59) in opposition to Kwame Nkrumah and went into exile (1959–66), taking up the chair of sociology at Leiden University. After the 1966 coup, he returned as adviser to the National Liberation Council and then founded, and led, the Progress Party which won the 1969 election. He was Prime Minister (1969–72) before being overthrown in another coup, going into exile again in 1972. He held various academic posts and died in Oxford.

Busoni, Ferruccio Benvenuto 1866–1924
Italian pianist and composer

Born in Empoli, Tuscany, he was an infant prodigy. In 1889 he became Professor of Pianoforte at Helsinki, and he subsequently taught and played the piano in Moscow, Boston, Berlin, Weimar and Zurich. The influence of **Franz Liszt** is apparent in his piano concerto. Of his four operas *Doktor Faust*, completed posthumously by a pupil in 1925, is his most impressive work. He was a noted editor of the keyboard music of **J S Bach** and Liszt, and his pupils included **Percy Grainger, Paul Hindemith** and **Kurt Weill**. He wrote *Entwurf einer neuen Ästhetik der Tonkunst* (1906, Eng trans *Outline of a New Aesthetic of Music*). 📖 E J Dent, *Ferruccio Busoni: A Biography* (1933)

Buss, Frances Mary 1827–94
English pioneer of higher education for women
Born in London, she was educated there and began teaching with her mother at the age of 14. At the age of 23 she founded the North London Collegiate School for Ladies (which became a model for the High School of the Girls' Public Day Schools Company) and was headmistress (1850–94)—the first woman to give herself the title. She also campaigned for women to be admitted to university. She appears in verse with **Dorothea Beale** of Cheltenham Ladies' College ('Miss Buss and Miss Beale, Cupid's darts do not feel'). 📖 J Kamm, *How Different From Us: A Biography of Miss Buss and Miss Beale* (1958)

Bustamante, Sir (William) Alexander, *originally William Alexander Clarke* 1884–1977
Jamaican politician
Born near Kingston, the son of an Irish planter, he was adopted at the age of 15 by a Spanish seaman called Bustamante and spent an adventurous youth abroad before returning in 1932 to become a trade union leader. In 1943 he founded the Jamaica Labour Party (JLP) as the political wing of his union, and in 1962, when Jamaica achieved independence, became its first Prime Minister.

Butcher, Rosemary 1947–
English choreographer
Born in Bristol, she was the first dance graduate of Dartington College in Devon, from where she went to New York and saw the experimental work of **Trisha Brown, Steve Paxton** and **Lucinda Childs**. She began choreographing her own work in 1976 and has made over 30 pieces, often performing them in unusual places—in art galleries and once on a Scottish mountainside. Her work is minimal and is often made in conjunction with other artists. The fast-moving *Flying Lines* (1985) incorporates music by **Michael Nyman** and an installation by Peter Noble. The meditative *Touch the Earth* (1986) also has a Nyman score, and sculpture by the artist Dieter Pietsch. *Spaces 4* (1997) requires the dancers to improvise within certain guidelines so that every performance is recognisably the same work, but new.

Bute, John Stuart, 3rd Earl of 1713–92
Scottish statesman
He succeeded his father in 1723, and about 1737 became a lord of the bedchamber of **Frederick Louis**, Prince of Wales. On the Prince's death (1751), Bute became Groom of the Stole to his son, afterwards **George III**, whom he strongly influenced. He was the main instrument in breaking the power of the Whigs and establishing the personal rule of the monarch through parliament. He was made Prime Minister in 1762, replacing the popular Earl of Chatham, thus making him the most disliked politician in the country. He resigned in 1763, after the Seven Years War. 📖 Alice Margaret Coats, *Lord Bute: An Illustrated Life of John Stuart, Third Earl of Bute, 1713–1792* (1975)

Butenandt, Adolf Friedrich Johann 1903–95
German biochemist and Nobel Prize winner

Born in Wesermuende, he studied medicine in Göttingen, and in 1929 he and **Edward Doisy** independently determined the structure of the female steroid hormone oestrone. In 1931 Butenandt isolated the male hormone androsterone. The work for which he became truly famous, however, was the isolation of a few milligrams of progesterone and the determination of its structure, employing microanalytical techniques pioneered by **Fritz Pregl**. Butenandt was awarded the 1939 Nobel Prize for chemistry jointly with **Leopold Ružička**, although he was forbidden to accept it by the Nazi regime. In 1936 he discovered the first insect hormone, ecdysone (1956), and soon afterwards, bombykol—the scent produced by female silkworms to attract the male. He was appointed director of the Max Planck Institute in 1960.

Buthelezi, Chief Gatsha 1928–
South African Zulu leader and politician
Born in Mahlabatini, he was expelled from Fore Hare University College in 1950 where he was a member of the ANC (African National Congress). Officially appointed as chief of the Buthelezi in 1953, he was assistant to the Zulu king Cyprian (1953–68) before being elected leader of the Zulu Territorial Authority in 1970. A political moderate, he became in 1976 chief minister of KwaZulu, the black South African homeland (which ceased to exist on 1 May 1994). He is founder-president of the Inkatha Freedom Party, a paramilitary organization for achieving a non-racist democratic political system. At first refusing to participate in the 1994 election, he lifted the boycott a week before polling day when agreement was reached that the Kingdom of Zululand would be recognized in the constitution. Since 1994 he has been Minister of Home Affairs in South Africa.

Butler, Alban 1710–73
English hagiographer
Born in Appletree, Northampton, he was educated at Douai in France, became a professor there and was for some time chaplain to the Duke of Norfolk. He later became head of the English College at St Omer. His great work, the *Lives of the Saints* (1756–59), primarily intended for edification, makes no distinction between fact and fiction. His nephew Charles Butler (1750–1832), a lawyer, wrote on legal and theological subjects.

Butler, Benjamin Franklin 1818–93
US lawyer, general and congressman
Born in Deerfield, New Hampshire, he was admitted to the Bar in 1840, and became noted as a criminal lawyer, champion of the working classes and an ardent Democrat, both in the legislature and in the state senate. In 1861 he was appointed major-general of volunteers, and in 1862 took possession of New Orleans, where prompt and severe measures crushed all opposition. In 1863 he received a command in Virginia, and the following year made an expedition against Fort Fisher, near Wilmington. Elected to Congress in 1866 he was prominent in Republican efforts for the reconstruction of the Southern states and the impeachment of President **Andrew Johnson**. In 1878 and 1879 he was nominated for Governor of Massachusetts by the National Party, and in 1882 was elected. His nomination (as candidate for the Greenback Party) for President in 1884 was not taken seriously. 📖 William D Driscoll, *Benjamin F Butler* (1987)

Butler, Lady Eleanor 1745–1829
Irish recluse
She was born in Dublin. In 1779 she and her friend Sarah Ponsonby (1755–1831) resolved to live in seclusion, and settled in a cottage at Plasnewydd in the vale of Llangollen in Wales, accompanied by a maidservant. They

became famous throughout Europe as the 'Maids of Llangollen' or 'Ladies of the Vale', and attracted visitors from far and wide.

Butler, Elizabeth Southerden *née* Thompson
1846–1933
English painter

She was born in Lausanne, the daughter of a scholar and concert pianist. She married the soldier Sir **William Butler** in 1877. She made her reputation with the *Roll Call* (1874) and *Inkermann* (1877) but is perhaps best known for *Scotland for Ever!* (1881), which depicts the charge of the Royal Scots Greys at the Battle of Waterloo. Her splendid pictures seem to glorify war, but her focus was on the heroism of the common soldier rather than on the officers, and her paintings became popular images of the Victorian era. She was the sister of **Alice Meynell**.

Butler, James See **Ormonde, 1st Duke of**

Butler, Joseph 1692–1752
English moral philosopher and theologian

Born in Wantage, Berkshire, he graduated from Oriel College, Oxford, in 1718. He took Anglican orders, and was appointed preacher at the Rolls Chapel where he preached the *Fifteen Sermons* (published, 1726), which set out his ethical system. He became, successively, Bishop of Bristol (1738), dean of St Paul's (1740) and Bishop of Durham (1750). His other great work was *The Analogy of Religion* (1736), a defence of revealed religion against the deists. Terence Penelhum, *Butler* (1985)

Butler, Josephine Elizabeth *née* Grey 1828–1906
English social reformer

Born in Millfield Hill, Northumberland, she promoted women's education and successfully crusaded against licensed brothels and the white-slave traffic, and against the Contagious Diseases Acts which made women in seaports and military towns liable for compulsory examination for venereal disease. She was married to George Butler (1819–90), canon of Winchester and author of educational works. She wrote *Personal Reminiscences of a Great Crusade* (1896).

Butler, Nicholas Murray 1862–1947
US educator and Nobel Prize winner

Born in Elizabeth, New Jersey, he studied philosophy at Columbia University and in Berlin and Paris. He was Professor of Education and Philosophy at Columbia from 1890, and as president of the university (1901–45) he founded the Teachers College. Working for peace throughout his life, he established the Carnegie Endowment for International Peace and served as its president from 1925 to 1945. He shared the Nobel Peace Prize with **Jane Addams** in 1931.

Butler, Reginald Cotterell 1913–81
English sculptor

He was born in Buntingford, Hertfordshire, and trained as an architect and engineer. He was a lecturer at the Architectural Association School of Architecture in London (1937–39), and later technical editor of the Architectural Press from 1946 to 1951, when he was appointed Gregory Fellow of Sculpture at Leeds University. In 1953 he won first prize in the international *Unknown Political Prisoner* sculpture competition with a steel and bronze working model (1955–56, Tate Gallery, London). He was recognized as one of the leading exponents of 'linear' sculpture, and produced many constructions in wrought iron, although he later turned to a more realistic style.

Butler, R(ichard) A(usten) Butler, Baron *also called* Rab 1902–82
English Conservative politician

Born in Attock Serai, India, the son of a distinguished administrator, he was educated at Marlborough and Cambridge, was president of the University Union in 1924, and Fellow of Corpus Christi College from 1925 to 1929, when he became MP for Saffron Walden, Essex. After a series of junior ministerial appointments from 1932, he was Minister of Education (1941–45). His name will always be associated with the Education Act of 1944 which reorganized the secondary school system and introduced the 11-plus examination for the selection of grammar school pupils. In the 1951 **Churchill** government he was Chancellor of the Exchequer, and in 1955 introduced the emergency 'credit squeeze' budget, which was to be his last. In the same year he became Lord Privy Seal (until 1959) and Leader of the House of Commons (until 1961). He was widely expected to succeed **Anthony Eden** as Prime Minister in 1957, but **Harold Macmillan** was chosen and Butler became Home Secretary (until 1962). First Secretary of State and deputy Prime Minister (1962–63), he again narrowly lost the premiership to **Alec Douglas-Home** in 1963, and became Foreign Secretary (1963–64). Once described as 'both irreproachable and unapproachable', he will go down as one of the most progressive, thoughtful, and dedicated of Tory leaders. In 1965 he was appointed Master of Trinity College, Cambridge, and was made a life peer.

Butler, Samuel 1612–80
English satirist

Born in Strensham, Worcestershire, the son of a small farmer, he was educated at Worcester Grammar School, and perhaps Oxford or Cambridge. He was in the service of Elizabeth, Countess of Kent, and became a friend of the antiquary, **John Selden**. After the Restoration, he became secretary to the Earl of Carbery, Lord President of Wales, by whom he was appointed steward of Ludlow Castle (1661). From 1670 to 1674 he was secretary to George Villiers, 2nd Duke of **Buckingham**. He is best known as the author of the poem *Hudibras* (published in three parts: 1663, 1664, 1678). A burlesque satire on Puritanism, it secured immediate popularity, and was a special favourite of **Charles II**. However, despite the king's generosity, Butler died in penury. George R Wasserman, *Samuel 'Hudibras' Butler* (1989)

Butler, Samuel 1835–1902
English author, painter and musician

He was born in Langar Rectory, near Bingham, Nottinghamshire, and educated at Shrewsbury and St John's College, Cambridge. Always quarrelling with his clergyman father, he abandoned the idea of taking orders and instead became a sheep farmer in New Zealand (1859–64). On returning to England he lived in London and wrote *Erewhon* (1872), a Utopian satire in which, for example, machines have been abolished for fear of their mastery over men's minds. The dominant theme of its supplement, *Erewhon Revisited* (1901), is the origin of religious belief. Butler was greatly influenced by Charles Darwin's *The Origin of Species* (1859), and in an earlier series of writings had tried to revive the 'vitalist' or 'creative' view of evolution, as in *Luck or Cunning* (1886), in opposition to Darwin's doctrine of natural selection. Butler also studied painting (his picture *Mr Heatherley's Holiday* is in the Tate Gallery, London), and loved music, composing two oratorios, gavottes, minuets, fugues, and a cantata. He later published translations of the *Iliad* (1898) and the *Odyssey* (1900), and his essay *The Humour of Homer* (1892) is a remarkable piece of literary criticism. He is best known, however, for his autobiographical novel *The Way of All Flesh*, published posthumously in 1903, a work of moral realism on the causes of strife between different generations which left its mark on **George Bernard Shaw** and much 20th-century literature. ▢ P N Furbank, *Samuel Butler* (1948); *The Life and Letters of Dr Samuel Butler* (1856)

Butler, Sir William Francis 1838–1910
Irish soldier and writer
Born in Suirville, Tipperary, he joined the British army in 1858, and served in Canada from 1867 to 1873, where his experiences provided the material for his popular book, *The Great Lone Land* (1872). He served on the Red River expedition (1870–71), on the Ashanti expedition (1873), and in the Sudan (1884–85) and South Africa (1888–99). He published biographies of Charles George Gordon and Sir Charles Napier, and several travel books. ▢ *Remember Butler* (1967)

Butlerov, Aleksandr Mikhailovich 1828–86
Russian chemist
Born in Chistopol (now in Tatarskaya), he became interested in chemistry at primary school and he eventually taught chemistry at the University of Kazan (1849–68) and was twice Rector. He was a gifted teacher, but most of his research was in entomology and his first thesis concerned the distribution of butterflies around the Volga River. After 1857 he carried out further chemical research and published a number of papers on the oxidation of organic compounds. In 1857 he made a long trip abroad, meeting many eminent German and French chemists, and was converted to a view of chemical structure essentially the same as we have today. From 1868 to 1885 he was professor at St Petersburg University, where he studied a number of polymerization reactions, and he continued lecturing there after his retirement. He fought tirelessly for the recognition of Russian science and was elected a full member of the St Petersburg Academy of Sciences in 1874. His many interests outside chemistry included bee-keeping, spiritualism and the higher education of women.

Butler-Sloss, Dame (Ann) Elizabeth Oldfield, née Havers 1933–
English judge
Born at Kew Gardens, Richmond, Surrey, the daughter of Sir Cecil Havers QC, a High Court judge, she wanted to study law from an early age, and was educated at Wycombe Abbey School. Called to the Bar in 1955, she practised there for 15 years. In 1958 she married Joseph Butler-Sloss and in 1959, during her first pregnancy, she contested the Conservative seat at Lambeth, but without success. She was a divorce registrar from 1970, until her appointment in 1979 to the Family Division of the High Court. Also that year she was appointed DBE. After chairing the Cleveland Sex Abuse Inquiry (1987–88), she became the first woman Lord Justice of Appeal. She is the sister of Michael Havers.

Butlin, Sir William Edmund, known as Billy Butlin 1899–1980
British holiday camp promoter
Born in South Africa, he moved with his parents to Canada. After serving in World War I, he worked his passage to England with only £5 capital. After a short period in a fun fair he went into business on his own. In 1936 he opened his first camp at Skegness, followed by others at Clacton and Filey. During World War II he served as director-general of hostels to the Ministry of Supply. After the war more camps and hotels were opened both at home and abroad.

Butor, Michel Marie François 1926–
French writer
Born in Mons-en-Baroeul, he was educated at the Lycée Louis-le-Grand, Paris, and studied at the Sorbonne. He taught in Egypt, England, Greece, Switzerland, the USA, and France, and is Professor Extraordinaire at the University of Geneva. He came to prominence during the 1950s, together with Alain Robbe-Grillet, Nathalie Sarraute, Claude Simon and others, who were known collectively as the 'New Novelists'. His novels include *L'Emploi du temps* (1956, Eng trans *Passing Time*, 1960), *Degrés* (1960, Eng trans *Degrees*, 1961 (US); 1962 (UK)) and *Le Génie du lieu* (1960, 'The Spirit of the Place'). He also wrote poetry, plays, and a series of critical volumes under the title *Répertoire 1–4* (1960–74), and has collaborated with the Belgian composer Henri Pousseur on an opera, *Votre Faust* (1968). Later fiction includes *Matière de rêves* (4 vols, 1975–77, 'The Stuff of Dreams'), *Vanité: Conversation dans les Alpes-Maritimes* (1980, 'Vanitas: A Conversation in the Alpes-Maritimes') and *Transit* (1992). ▢ M C Spencer, *Michel Butor* (1974)

Butt, Dame Clara Ellen 1873–1936
English concert and operatic contralto
She was born in Southwick, Sussex. In 1890 she won a scholarship to the Royal College of Music and in 1892 made her debut as Ursula in Arthur Sullivan 's cantata *The Golden Legend*, followed three days later by the role of Orpheus in Gluck 's *Orfeo ed Euridice*. Her career was principally one of the concert hall and especially of the English music festivals, which seemed incomplete without her imposing presence. Elgar wrote his *Sea Pictures* for her, which she premiered at the Norwich Festival of 1899. Her rendition of Elgar's *Land of Hope and Glory* was redolent of the Edwardian era and World War I. In 1900 she married the English baritone R(obert) Kennerley Rumford (1870–1957); they often performed together, toured the USA and Canada, and made four visits to Australia and New Zealand. In 1920 she made a brief return in her role of Orpheus for Thomas Beecham, at Covent Garden. ▢ Winifred Ponder, *Clara Butt: her life-story* (1928, foreword by Dame Clara Butt)

Butt, Isaac 1813–79
Irish politician
Born in Glenfin, County Donegal, and educated at Raphoe and Trinity College, Dublin, he was called to the Irish Bar in 1838 and soon became active in politics. He represented Youghal as a 'Liberal Conservative' and in 1871 was returned for Limerick to lead the Home Rule Party in the House of Commons; however he met with little success.

Butterfield, Sir Herbert 1900–79
English historian
Born in Yorkshire, he was educated at the Trade and Grammar School, Keighley, and he won a scholarship to Peterhouse College, Cambridge, where he became a Fellow (1923–55), Professor of Modern History (1944–63) and Regius Professor (1963–68). He won initial recognition as a diplomatic historian with *The Peace-Tactics of Napoleon 1806–08* (1929), but followed it with a widely influential attack on historians who assumed inevitable (Protestant, English constitutional) progress in *The Whig Interpretation of History* (1931). His other works include *The Englishman and his History* (1944), *The Origins of Modern Science* (1949), which inaugurated the development of the history of science, *Christianity and History* (1949), *George III and the Politicians* (1957) and *International Conflict in the Twentieth Century* (1960).

Butterfield, William 1814–1900
English architect
He was born in London. Associated with the Oxford Movement, he was a leading exponent of the Gothic revival, and was the architect of Keble College, Oxford, St Augustine's College, Canterbury, the chapel and quadrangle of Rugby, All Saints', Margaret Street, London, and St Albans, Holborn. He was also responsible for many controversial 'restorations'.

Butterick, Ebenezer 1826–1903
US tailor and inventor

Born in Sterling, Massachusetts, he invented in 1859 standardized paper patterns for garments. He founded *Metropolitan* fashion magazine in 1869 to promote his pattern sales.

Butterley, Nigel Henry 1935–
Australian composer and pianist

Born in Sydney, he studied at the New South Wales Conservatorium, and later in London. He worked as a producer and planner for the music department of the Australian Broadcasting Commission (ABC) from 1955, and in 1966 won the prestigious Italia prize with *In the Head the Fire*, a musical work for radio commissioned by the ABC. Other major works include *Fire in the Heavens*, which was performed at the opening of the Sydney Opera House in 1973, a violin concerto, *Meditations of Thomas Traherne*, *Letter from Hardy's Bay* and *Explorations for Piano and Orchestra*.

Butterworth, George 1885–1916
English composer, critic, and folk-song collector

Born in London, he is remembered for his songs from *A Shropshire Lad* (1913) and the orchestral *The Banks of Green Willows* (1914). He was killed in action at Pozières.

Buttrose, Ita Clare 1942–
Australian journalist, publisher and broadcaster

Born in Sydney, she began a journalistic career at the age of 21 and eventually edited several women's magazines during the 1970s. She was also a director of the Australian Consolidated Press (1974–81) and publisher of the women's publications by the Australian Consolidated Press (1977–81). Having been women's editor at the age of 28 for the *Daily Telegraph* and the *Sunday Telegraph*, she returned in 1981 as editor-in-chief, the first woman in Australia to be editor of either a daily or a Sunday newspaper. In 1983 she entered radio broadcasting and was given her own show by two stations, and in 1985 she became presenter of *Woman's Day* on television. Continuing her radio and television appearances, she also became a newspaper columnist and chairman of the National Advisory Committee on AIDS (1984–). In 1988 she became chief executive of Capricorn Publishing Pty Ltd and editor-in-chief of the *Sun Herald*, launching her own magazine, *Ita*, the following year and editing it until 1994.

Butzer, Martin See Bucer, Martin

Buxtehude, Diderik, *German* Dietrich c.1637–1707
Danish organist and composer

Born in Oldesloe or Helsingborg (now in Sweden), he was appointed to the coveted post of organist at the Marienkirche, Lübeck, in 1668. Here he began the famous *Abendmusiken*—evening concerts during Advent of his own sacred choral and orchestral music and organ works. In 1705 J S Bach walked 200 miles across Germany from Arnstadt and Handel travelled from Hamburg to attend the concerts and to meet Buxtehude, who was highly respected in his time as an organist and as a composer. His principles of 'free' organ and pure instrumental works were later to be developed by Bach.

Buxton, Sir Thomas Fowell, 1st Baronet
1786–1845
English social reformer

He was born in Earls Colne, Essex. As MP for Weymouth (1818–37) he worked for modification of the criminal law, abolition of the slave trade and prison reform, succeeding William Wilberforce as head of the antislavery party in 1824.

Buys Ballot, Christoph Hendrik Diederik
1817–90
Dutch meteorologist

Born in Kloetinge, Zeeland, he studied and taught at Utrecht University, where he became professor in 1867. In 1854 he founded the Royal Netherlands Meteorological Institute and later became its director. From 1852 onwards he compiled maps which were among the first weather charts, showing wind direction and speed and temperature anomalies in graded shadings. In 1857 he produced Buys Ballot's law. He organized the first service of weather forecasts and storm warnings (1860) and designed the aeroclinoscope, which indicates the position of the centre of a depression and the pressure gradient. He became president of a committee whose recommendations were confirmed at the Congress of Rome (1879), and he greatly improved and standardized the meteorological system internationally.

Byars, Betsy Cromer 1928–
US children's writer

Born in Charlotte, North Carolina, she was educated at Queen's College, New Jersey. She began to write in the 1960s but made no great impact until *The Summer of the Swans* (1970), the story of a girl and her retarded brother, which was awarded the Newbery Medal. Specializing in 'kitchen-sink drama'—contemporary realism—she produced a number of popular novels, at times perceptive and inventive, at others predictable and reminiscent of soap opera. Her titles include *The Eighteenth Emergency* (1973), *Goodbye, Chicken Little* (1979) and *The Animal, The Vegetable, and John D Jones* (1982).

Byatt, A(ntonia) S(usan), *née* Drabble 1936–
English novelist and critic

She was born in Sheffield and educated at the Mount School, York, and at Newnham College, Cambridge. After some years as a teacher and academic, she published *Degrees of Freedom* (1965), the first full-length study of Iris Murdoch's novels, whose philosophical style has influenced her own. Further highly respected critical works followed. She made her reputation as a novelist with her third novel, *The Virgin in the Garden* (1978). This was followed by *Still Life* (1985), *Possession* (1990), which won the Booker Prize, and *Babel Tower* (1996). She has also written on Ford Madox Ford and on 18th- and 19th-century poetry. Her interests extend to art and art history, literary and social history, and philosophy, all of which feature in her novels. She published a volume of short stories, *The Matisse Stories*, in 1994 and *The Djinn in the Nightingale's Eye*, a collection of fairy tales, in 1995. She is the elder sister of the novelist Margaret Drabble.

Byerley, Perry 1897–1978
US geophysicist

Born in Clarinda, Iowa, and educated at the University of California at Berkeley, he became an instructor at the University of Nevada (1924–25), and spent the rest of his career at the University of California, where he was appointed head of the seismograph stations (1925). He later became chairman of the department of geology and geophysics (1949–54) and emeritus professor from 1965. His 1961 paper on traveltimes of the seismic waves from a Montana earthquake prompted Harold Jeffreys to begin the *Jeffreys–Bullen Tables*. Byerley's work established seismology in the USA, his greatest contribution being the study of earthquake motions to determine the possible planes along which fault movement may have taken place. The seismological station at Berkeley is named after him.

Bygraves, Max, *originally* Walter William Bygraves
1922–
English singer and entertainer

Born in London, he gained his stage name doing impressions of the legendary **Max Miller** while in the RAF. He appeared at the Sheffield Empire and (with **Judy Garland**) at the London Palladium, before winning a part in BBC Radio's hugely popular *Educating Archie*. Seminovelty songs like 'The Cowpuncher's Cantata', 'Deck of Cards', and the Manning–Hoffman tongue-twister 'Gilly Gilly Oscenfeffer Katzenellen Bogen by the Sea' were inexplicably successful and he had straight hits, too, with 'You Need Hands' and 'Fings Ain't Wot They Used to Be'. He recorded a hugely successful sequence of standards albums, starting with *Singalongamax* in 1971. His television successes include *Max Bygraves*, *Singalongamax* and *Max Bygraves—Side by Side With*. He also hosted one series of the gameshow *Family Fortunes* and was in films such as *Skimpy in the Navy* (1949), *Tom Brown's Schooldays* (1951) and *Spare the Rod* (1961). 📖 *After Thoughts* (1988); *I Wanna Tell You a Story* (1976).

Byng, George, 1st Viscount Torrington
1663–1733
English naval commander
Born in Wrotham, Kent, he joined the navy at 15, and as a supporter of William of Orange (the future **William III**), gained rapid promotion. As rear admiral, he captured Gibraltar in 1704, and for his gallant conduct at Málaga was knighted by Queen **Anne**. In 1708 he commanded a squadron that frustrated a threatened landing in Scotland by the Old Pretender, **James Francis Edward Stuart**, and again in 1715. In 1718, as Admiral of the Fleet, he destroyed the Spanish fleet off Messina. In 1721 he was created Viscount Torrington.

Byng, John 1704–57
English sailor
He was the fourth son of **George Byng**, 1st Viscount Torrington. He joined the navy at the age of 14, and was rapidly promoted, becoming admiral in 1756. For his failure to relieve Minorca, blockaded by a French fleet, and for retreating to Gibraltar, he was found guilty of neglect of duty, and shot at Portsmouth. 📖 W B Tunstall, *Admiral Byng and the Loss of Minorca* (1928)

Byng (of Vimy), Julian Hedworth George Byng, 1st Viscount 1862–1935
English field marshal
Commissioned in the 10th Hussars in 1883, he served in the Sudan (1884) and South Africa (1899–1902). In World War I he commanded the 9th Army Corps in Gallipoli (1915), the Canadian Army Corps in France at the capture of Vimy Ridge (1916–17), and thereafter the 3rd Army (1917–18), executing the first large-scale tank attack at Cambrai (November 1917). He later became Governor-General of Canada (1921–26), and Commissioner of the Metropolitan Police (1928–31) and was appointed field marshal in 1932.

Bynkershoek, Cornelis van 1673–1743
Dutch judge and jurist
Born in Middelburg, Zeeland, he became a judge of the Supreme Court of Holland and Zeeland. He wrote on Roman law, notably *Observationum juris Romani* (1710–33), and on Roman-Dutch law, including *Quaestionum juris privati* (1744–47) and *Observationes tumultuariae* (1704–43), decisions of the Supreme Court. His international law publications, which included *De Dominio Maris* (1702), a classic of maritime law, *De Foro Legatorum* (1720), on diplomatic rights, and *Quaestiones juris publici* (1737), on war and neutrality, were works which emphasized the importance of treaties and the custom and usage of states as sources of international law. He is credited with proposing the three-mile rule, where a state can claim sovereignty over its territorial waters up to three miles from the coast.

Byrd, Harry Flood 1887–1966
US politician
Born in West Virginia, he was educated at Shenandoah Valley Academy, and started work at the age of 15 on the Winchester *Star*. He took up apple and peach farming from 1906, was president of the Valley Turnpike Company (1908–18), and played an important part in the development of Virginia state highways. Elected to the state senate, he served from 1915 to 1925, becoming Democratic State Committee chairman in 1922, and was successfully nominated for Governor (1926–30). He was unsuccessful in his attempt at presidential nomination in 1932. Appointed US senator for Virginia (1933–65), he became chairman of the Senate Finance Committee, and was distinguished for his extreme conservatism and support for segregation. He was the brother of **Richard Evelyn Byrd**.

Byrd, Richard Evelyn 1888–1957
US explorer and aviator
Born in Winchester, Virginia, he graduated from the US Naval Academy, Annapolis, in 1912 and joined the navy's aviation service. With **Floyd Bennett** he made the first aeroplane flight over the North Pole (1926), for which they received the Congressional Medal of Honour. In 1929 he established a base, 'Little America', in the Antarctic and was the first to fly over the South Pole. He made four more expeditions to the Antarctic (1933–35, 1939–41, 1946–47, 1955–56). 📖 Martin Gladych, *Admiral Byrd of Antarctica* (1960)

Byrd, William 1543–1623
English composer
He was born probably in Lincoln, and his early life is obscure, but it is likely that he was one of the children of the Chapel Royal, under **Thomas Tallis**. At the age of 20 he became organist of Lincoln Cathedral, where he remained until 1572, when he was made joint organist with Tallis of the Chapel Royal. Three years later, Queen **Elizabeth I** granted Byrd and Tallis an exclusive licence for the printing and sale of music, and their joint work of that year, *Piae Cantiones* (1575), was dedicated to her. Byrd was associated with **John Bull** and **Orlando Gibbons** in *Parthenia* (1611), the first printed music for virginals. A firm Catholic, Byrd was several times prosecuted as a recusant, but he wrote music of power and beauty for both the Catholic and the Anglican services, as well as madrigals, songs, and music for strings. 📖 Frank Howes, *William Bryd* (1928)

Byrd or Birde, William 1674–1744
American tobacco planter, colonial official and diarist
He was born in Virginia, the son of William Byrd (1652–1704), pioneer planter and early Virginian aristocrat. During two periods in London (1697–1705, 1715–26) as a student of law and a colonial agent, he proved himself an elegant socialite and a man of learning. In 1728 he took part in surveying the boundary line between Virginia and Carolina, in 1737 he founded the town of Richmond, and in 1743 he became president of the Council of State, of which he had been a member since 1709. At his mansion, 'Westover', he kept a magnificent library, and wrote a diary, published in 1958 as *The London Diary (1717–1721) and Other Writings*.

Byrds, The
US folk-rock and country-rock band
The Byrds made one of the most influential and enduring of all contributions to US rock music, despite a chaotic history and multiple changes of direction and personnel. The original band featured Jim (later Roger) McGuinn and David Crosby (who left in 1967 to co-lead Crosby, Stills and Nash) in a five-piece band, and had a major hit

Byron (of Rochdale), George Gordon, 6th Baron known as Lord Byron 1788–1824
English poet of Scottish antecedents

Byron was born in London, the grandson of naval officer John Byron, and the son of Captain 'Mad Jack' Byron (1756–91) and Catherine Gordon of Gight, Aberdeen, a Scottish heiress. He was lame from birth, and this together with his early years in the shabby surroundings and the violent temper of his deserted mother produced a repression in him which is thought to explain many of his later actions. In 1798 he succeeded to the title on the death of his great-uncle.

He was educated at Aberdeen grammar school, then privately at Dulwich and at Harrow School, and went on to Trinity College, Cambridge, in 1805, where he read much, swam and boxed, and led a dissipated life. An early collection of poems under the title Hours of Idleness was badly received, and Byron replied with his powerful Popian satire English Bards and Scotch Reviewers (1809). He then set out on a grand tour, visiting Spain, Malta, Albania, Greece, and the Aegean, returning after two years with 'a great many stanzas in Spenser's measure relative to the countries he had visited'; these appeared under the title of Childe Harold's Pilgrimage in 1812 and were widely popular. This was followed by a series of oriental pieces, including the Giaour (1813), Lara (1814) and the Siege of Corinth (1816).

During this time he dramatized himself as a man of mystery, a gloomy romantic figure, derived from the popular fiction of the day and not least from Childe Harold. He became the darling of London society, and lover of Lady Caroline Lamb, and gave to Europe the concept of the 'Byronic hero'. In 1815 he married an heiress, Anne Isabella Milbanke, who left him in 1816 after the birth of a daughter, Ada (later Countess of Lovelace). He was also suspected of a more than brotherly love for his half-sister, Augusta Leigh, and was ostracized. He left for the Continent, travelled through Belgium and the Rhine country to Switzerland, where he met Percy Bysshe Shelley, and on to Venice and Rome, where he wrote the last canto of

Childe Harold (1817). He spent two years in Venice and there met the Countess Teresa Guiccioli, who became his mistress.

Some of his best works belong to this period, including Beppo (1818), A Vision of Judgment (1822) and the satirical Don Juan (1819–24), written in a new metre (ottava rima) and in an informal conversational manner which enabled him to express the whole of his complex personality. He gave active help to the Italian revolutionaries and founded with Leigh Hunt a short-lived journal, The Liberal. In 1823 he joined the Greek insurgents who had risen against the Turks, and died of marsh fever at Missolonghi.

His body was brought back to England and buried at Hucknall Torkard in Nottingham. His reputation declined after his death despite the championship of Matthew Arnold. On the Continent he had a far-reaching influence both as the creator of the 'Byronic hero' and as the champion of political liberty, leaving his mark on such writers as Victor Hugo, Alfred de Musset, Giacomo Leopardi, Heinrich Heine, José de Espronceda, Alexander Pushkin and Mikhail Lermontov.

📖 Phyllis Grosskurth, Byron: The Flawed Angel (1997), which draws on the Lovelace Papers; P Quennell, Byron: A Portrait in his Own Words (1989) and Byron (1967); S Coote, Byron: The Making of a Myth (1988).

> There is a pleasure in the pathless woods,
> There is a rapture on the lonely shore,
> There is society, where none intrudes,
> By the deep Sea, and music in its roar:
> I love not Man the less, but Nature more,
> From these our interviews, in which I steal
> From all I may be, or have been before,
> To mingle with the Universe, and feel
> What I can ne'er express, yet cannot all conceal.
> Childe Harold's Pilgrimage, canto 4, stanza 178.

with Bob Dylan's 'MrTambourine Man' in 1965. Their folk-rock orientation grew more progressive in songs like 'Eight Miles High' (1966), then took another turn toward country music in the seminal Sweethearts of the Rodeo album in 1968, which featured Gram Parsons. The group continued to record until 1973, when McGuinn reformed the original quintet for an undistinguished album, before concentrating on a solo career. 📖 J Rogan, Timeless Flight (1990)

Byrgius, Justus, also known as Jost Bürgi
1552–1633
Swiss mathematician and inventor

He was born in the canton of St Gall, and as a court watchmaker assisted Johannes Kepler in his astronomical work, inventing celestial globes. He compiled logarithms, but did not publish them before John Napier.

Byrne, John 1940–
Scottish dramatist and stage designer

He was born in Paisley, trained at Glasgow Art School, and designed stage sets for the 7:84 Theatre Company before writing his first play, Writer's Cramp, produced at the Edinburgh Festival Fringe (1977). The Slab Boys (1978), concerning the lives of employees at a carpet factory, developed into a trilogy with the addition of Cuttin' A Rug (1980) and Still Life (1983). Other plays include Normal Service (1979) and Cara Coco (1982). He wrote the highly acclaimed Tutti Frutti (1987), a BBC Scotland television series about an ageing pop group, and followed it with the less universally-acclaimed Your Cheatin' Heart (1989).

He returned to writing for the stage in 1992 with Colquhoun and MacBryde, a play based on the lives of two Scottish artists.

Byrom, John 1692–1763
English poet and stenographer

Born in Broughton, near Manchester, he studied medicine at Montpellier, but returned to England in 1716 to teach a new system of shorthand he had invented. In 1740 he inherited the family estates. He patented his system in 1742, and it was published in 1767 as the Universal English Shorthand. He was the author of the hymn 'Christians awake! Salute the happy morn!', and his poetry was published in Miscellaneous Poems (1773).

Byron, Annabella (Anne Isabella), known as Lady Byron or Lady Noel Byron, née Milbanke
1792–1860
English philanthropist

Born at Elmore Hall, Durham, she married Byron in 1815, but the couple separated the following year after the birth of their daughter Ada (later the Countess of Lovelace). Lady Byron moved in radical circles and was a close friend of the art critic Anna Jameson (1794–1860) and Barbara Bodichon. She is noted particularly for her commitment to schemes for improving women's education, many of which she funded. In 1854 she purchased the Red Lodge in Bristol on behalf of the social reformer Mary Carpenter who opened it as a home for girl offenders. Lady Byron was also involved in agricultural and industrial reforms, co-operative movements, the anti-slavery movement (she was a friend of **Harriet Beecher Stowe**) and other radical causes.

Byron, Lord See panel p312

Byron, John, *known as* **Foulweather Jack** 1723–86
English naval officer
His account of his shipwreck on the coast of Chile in 1761 was used by Lord **Byron**, his grandson, in *Don Juan*. He commanded a voyage round the world (1764–66), and was Governor of Newfoundland (1769–72).

Byron, Robert 1905–41
English writer and Byzantinist

He was born in Wiltshire, and was educated at Merton College, Oxford, where he collected Victoriana. A visit to Mount Athos in Greece led him to write *The Station* (1928), which was followed by *The Byzantine Achievement* (1929) and *The Appreciation of Architecture* (1932). He is best remembered, however, for his vivacious and erudite travelogues, which include *First Russia, Then Tibet* (1933) and *The Road to Oxiana* (1937), a minor masterpiece conceived as a collection of diary jottings. Typically aggressive in its assertions, it is suffused with humour and sensibility, and won the *Sunday Times* Literary award. Other publications include *Europe in the Looking Glass* (1927), *The Birth of Western Painting* and *An Essay on India* (1931). He died during World War II when his ship was torpedoed.

Caballé, Montserrat 1933–
Spanish soprano

Born in Barcelona, she enjoys, in addition to her concert repertoire, great acclaim in a wide variety of stage roles from **Rossini** to **Puccini**, in contemporary opera, in zarzuela, and in the German tradition (notably **Wagner** and **Strauss**). She has sung at Covent Garden, Glyndebourne, the Metropolitan Opera, La Scala, Mexico City and at many other major houses, and has made numerous recordings. 📖 Robert Pullen, *Monserrat Caballé: Casta Diva* (1994)

Caballero, Fernán, *pseudonym of* Cecilia Francesca de Arrom 1797–1877
Spanish novelist

Born in Morges in Switzerland, the daughter of Nikolaus Böhl von Faber (1770–1836), a German merchant in Spain, she spent most of her childhood in Germany, but returned to Spain in 1813. She wrote on the history of Spanish literature and introduced in Spain the picturesque 'local-colour' novel. The first of her 50 romances was *La Gaviota* (1849, 'The Seagull'). Others include *Clemencia* (1852), *Un servilón y un liberalito* (1855, 'A Groveller and a Little Liberal') and *La Familia de Alvareda* (1856). She also collected Spanish folk-tales. 📖 L H Klibbe, *Fernán Caballero* (1973)

Cabanel, Alexandre 1823–89
French painter

Born in Montpellier, he was a strict classicist, who won great popularity as a portrait painter and as a teacher, and was, with **William Adolphe Bouguereau**, the most influential Academician of his day.

Cabell, James Branch 1879–1958
US novelist and critic

Born in Richmond, Virginia, he made his name with his romance *Jurgen* (1919), the best known of a sequence of 18 novels, collectively entitled *Biography of Michael*. Set in the imaginary medieval kingdom of Poictesme, and written in an elaborate, sophisticated style, they show Cabell's fondness for archaisms. He also published a book of criticism, *Preface to the Past* (1936). 📖 C van Doren, *James Branch Cabell* (1926)

Cabet, Étienne 1788–1856
French reformer

Born in Dijon, after the revolution of 1830 he was elected a deputy (1831), but was exiled in 1834 for his radical pamphleteering. He set out his social doctrine in a book, *Voyage en Icarie* (1840), a 'philosophical and social romance', describing a communistic utopia. In 1849 he led a group to Texas to found a utopian settlement called Icaria on the Red River, and later moved to Nauvoo in Illinois. He was president of the community from 1849, but withdrew in 1856 after internal disputes.

Cabezón, Antonio de 1500–66
Spanish composer

Born in Castrillo de Matajudíos, near Burgos, he was blind from birth. He was the first major Spanish keyboard composer, and was noted for his keyboard pieces and vocal works.

Cable, George Washington 1844–1925
US writer

He was born in New Orleans, and at the age of 19 volunteered as a Confederate soldier. After the Civil War he earned a precarious living in New Orleans, before taking up a literary career in 1879. In 1884 he went to New England. His Creole sketches in *Scribner's* made his reputation. Among his books are *Old Creole Days* (1879) *The Grandissimes* (1880, his finest work, a profound study of colour and caste in New Orleans at the time of the Louisiana Purchase), *The Silent South* (1885), *Bylow Hill* (1902), *Kincaid's Battery* (1908) and *Lovers of Louisiana* (1918). 📖 A Turner, *George Washington Cable: biography* (1956).

Cabot, John, *originally* Giovanni Caboto 1425–c.1500
Italian navigator and explorer, the discoverer of mainland North America

Born in Genoa, he moved to England and settled in Bristol around 1490. In 1497 under letters patent from King **Henry VII**, he sailed from Bristol with two ships in search of a route to Asia, accompanied by his three sons. On 24 June, after 52 days at sea, he sighted land (probably Cape Breton Island, Nova Scotia), and claimed North America for England. He is thought to have made further voyages in search of the Northwest Passage, and after setting out in 1498, died at sea. 📖 Henry Harisse, *John Cabot* (1896)

Cabot, Sebastian 1474–1557
Venetian navigator and cartographer

Born in Venice, Italy, or Bristol, England, he is thought to have sailed with his father, **John Cabot**, on expeditions in search of the Northwest Passage to Asia. In 1512 he made a map of Gascony and Guienne for King **Henry VIII**, then entered the service of King **Ferdinand the Catholic** of Aragon as a cartographer. As pilot-major for Emperor **Charles V** he explored the coast of Brazil and the River Plate in 1526, but after a failed attempt at colonization he was imprisoned and banished for two years to Africa. In 1533 he was once again appointed pilot-major in Spain, and in 1544 published an engraved map of the world (the only surviving copy is in the Bibliothèque Nationale in Paris). In 1548 he returned to England where he was made inspector of the navy by King **Edward VI**, and in 1551 founded the company of Merchant Adventurers of London. 📖 David Beers Quinn, *Sebastian Cabot and Bristol Exploration* (1968)

Cabral, Amilcar 1924–73
Guinean nationalist leader

Educated at Lisbon University, Portugal, he worked as an agronomist and agricultural engineer for the colonial authorities. He founded the PAIGC (Partido Africano da Independência da Guiné e Cabo Verde, 'Portuguese-African Party for an Independent Guinea and Cape Verde') in 1956 and, after abortive constitutional discussions with the Portuguese government, initiated a revolutionary war in 1963. Noted for his commitment to politicizing the peasantry and establishing alternative institutions in liberated territories, he presided over a successful war which forced the Portuguese to concede independence. He was murdered in 1973 just as his aim was being achieved. He was the brother of **Luiz Cabral**.

Cabral, Luiz 1931–
Guinean nationalist leader

He was educated in Portuguese Guinea (Guinea-Bissau) and became a clerk and a trade union organizer. As a member of the PAIGC (Partido Africano da Independência da Guiné e Cabo Verde, 'Portuguese-African Party for an Independent Guinea and Cape Verde'), he went into exile in 1960 and took part in the guerrilla struggle to win independence. Success made him President of the new republic (1974–80), but he was then overthrown in a coup. He was the brother of **Amilcar Cabral**.

Cabral or Cabrera, Pedro Álvarez c.1467–c.1520
Portuguese navigator

Born in Belmonte, he sailed from Lisbon in 1500 in command of a fleet of 13 vessels bound for the East Indies. Drifting into the South American current of the Atlantic Ocean, he was carried (in the same year as **Vincente Pinzón**) to the unknown coast of Brazil, which he claimed on behalf of Portugal. From there he made for India, but, after losing seven of his ships, landed at Mozambique; he was the first to provide a description of that country. From there he sailed to Calicut (Kozhikode, Kerala), where he made the first commercial treaty between Portugal and India. He returned to Lisbon in 1501.

Çabrera, Pedro Álvarez See **Cabral, Pedro Álvarez**

Cabrera Infante, Guillermo 1929–
Cuban novelist

Born in Gibara, and educated at Havana University, he emigrated to England in 1966 and became a British citizen. He is best known for *Tres Tristes Tigres* (1967, Eng trans *Three Trapped Tigers*, 1971), and *Vista del amanecer en el trópico* (1974, Eng trans *A View of Dawn in the Tropics*, 1978). *La Habana para un infante difunto* (1979, Eng trans *Infante's Inferno*, 1984) is set in Havana during the 1940s and 1950s, and skilfully blurs the distinction between autobiography and fiction, thereby demythologizing the Don Juan legend in Hispanic culture. He translated **James Joyce's** *Dubliners* into Spanish (1972), has also written journalism, and, writing as 'Guillermo Cain', film criticism (collected in *A Twentieth Century Job*, 1991) and screenplays.

Cabrini, St Francesca Xavier, *originally* Maria Francesca 1850–1917
US nun, the country's first saint

Born in Sant 'Angelo, Lodigliano, Italy, she founded the Missionary Sisters of the Sacred Heart (1880), emigrated to the USA in 1889 and became renowned as 'Mother Cabrini' for her social and charitable work. She founded 67 houses in the USA, Buenos Aires, Paris and Madrid. She was canonized in 1946. Her feast day is 13 November.

Caccini, Giulio c.1550–1618
Italian composer and singer

Born in Rome, he paved the way for opera with **Jacopo Peri**, by setting to music the drama *Eurydice* (1600). Particularly significant was his *Nuove Musiche* (1602, 'New Music'), a collection of canzonets and madrigals, whose preface became the manifesto for the new monodic style.

Cadalso Vasquez, José de 1741–82
Spanish writer

Born in Cadiz, he was an army officer, and wrote as a hobby. He is best known for his prose satire *Los eruditos a la violeta* (1772, 'The Scholars and the Violet'), which ridicules pedantry, and *Cartas marruecas* (1774, 'Moroccan Letters'), a work of social criticism in epistolary form. He was killed at the Siege of Gibraltar. 📖 R P Sebold, *Colonel Don José Cadalso* (1971)

Cadbury, George 1839–1922
English Quaker businessman and social reformer

Born in Birmingham, he was the son of **John Cadbury**. In partnership with his elder brother, Richard Cadbury (1835–99), he took over his father's Birmingham-based cocoa business in 1861 and built it into the highly successful firm Cadbury Brothers. They moved the factory in 1879 and in 1894, guided by his Quaker and liberal principles, established for the workers the model village of Bournville, near Birmingham. It was a prototype for modern methods of housing and town planning and included the unprecedented provision of decent housing for his workers. He also founded education and welfare trusts. In 1902 he became proprietor of the *Daily News* and campaigned actively for social reform through the newspaper. 📖 Walter Stranz, *George Cadbury* (1973)

Cadbury, Henry Joel 1883–1974
US Quaker scholar

Born in Philadelphia, he was educated at Haverford College and at Harvard. He taught biblical studies at Haverford, Bryn Mawr, and Harvard, where he was subsequently Professor of Divinity (1934–54). Active in the work of the American Friends Service Committee (he had two stints as chairman) and member of many learned societies, he wrote prolifically. Among his works were *Style and Literary Method of Luke* (1920), *The Peril of Modernizing Jesus* (1937), *George Fox's Book of Miracles* (1948), *The Book of Acts in History* (1955), and *Friendly Heritage* (1972).

Cadbury, John 1801–89
English Quaker businessman

He was born in Birmingham, the son of Richard Tapper Cadbury, who had settled in Birmingham in 1794. He founded the cocoa and chocolate manufacturing firm which his sons Richard and **George Cadbury** took over in 1861.

Cade, Jack d.1450
Irish rebel

After an unsettled early career, he lived in Sussex, England, possibly as a physician. He then settled in Kent. He assumed the name of Mortimer, and the title Captain of Kent, and led the insurrection of 1450 against King **Henry VI**. With a great many followers he marched on London, but after a promise of pardon, his forces began to disperse. Cade attempted to reach the coast but was killed on the way.

Cadell, Francis Campbell Boileau 1883–1937
Scottish painter

Born in Edinburgh, he studied in Paris, and visited Munich (1907–09). In 1912 he founded the Society of Eight, a group of artists that included **John Lavery** and **Samuel Peploe**. One of the 'Scottish Colourists', he painted landscapes, interiors and still life in broad patches of brilliant colour.

Cadillac, Antoine Laumet de La Mothe, Sieur de 1656–1730
French soldier and colonialist

Born in Gascony, he went to America with the French army in 1683, and founded in 1701 the settlement of Fort-Pontchartrain du Détroit which became the city of Detroit. In 1711 he was appointed Governor of Louisiana but returned to France in 1716 and died in his native Gascony.

Cadogan, Sir John Ivan George 1930–
Welsh chemist

Born in Pembrey, Dyfed, he graduated from King's College London and lectured there, working on a number of topics including reactions of free radicals in solution and the chemistry of phosphorus compounds. He was appointed professor at the University of St Andrews (1963) and in 1969 moved to the chair at the University of Edinburgh. He researched many areas of chemistry, but possibly the most important were studies of phosphorus compounds and synthesis of reactive intermediates. He also established many links with the British chemical industry, and in 1979 became chief scientist at the BP Research Centre, in 1987 being promoted to director of research there. Elected FRS in 1976 and knighted in 1991, he was president of the Royal Society of Chemistry from 1982 to 1984. He was appointed the first Director General of Research Councils in 1993.

Caesar, (Gaius) Julius 100 or 102–44BC
Roman general, statesman and dictator

Caesar was a member of the Julii, an ancient patrician family. His aunt was the wife of **Marius**, and in 83BC he married Cornelia, daughter of the radical **Cinna**; this alliance incurred the hostility of the conservative reformer **Sulla**. To avoid Sulla's revenge, Caesar took up a military command in Asia (81). On his way to Rhodes, to study under a Greek rhetorician, Caesar was captured by pirates for a ransom. After his release, he caught and crucified them as he had said he would. He was elected pontifex (73), supported the attack on Sulla's legislation (71–70), was quaestor in Spain (69), and supported **Pompey's** commands (67–66). In 65 as curule aedile (chief magistrate) he spent lavishly on games and public buildings; he was elected pontifex maximus in 63 and praetor for 62. He may have been implicated in or privy to the conspiracy of **Catiline**. He was elected consul for 59. He reconciled Pompey and **Crassus**, and with them established the informal alliance known as the 'First Triumvirate'. Caesar gave Pompey his daughter Julia in marriage, while he married Calpurnia (Cornelia had died in 67, and Caesar had divorced his second wife Pompeia because the wife of Caesar, according to **Plutarch**, 'must be above suspicion').

For a period of nine years (58–50), Caesar was occupied with military campaigns which extended Roman power to most of Gaul; these are vividly described in his *Commentaries*. He invaded Britain in 55 and 54; in the second year he crossed the Thames, and enforced at least the nominal submission of the south-east of the island. Pockets of unrest in Gaul were followed by a general rebellion headed by Vercingetorix. The struggle was severe; at Gergovia, the capital of the Arverni, Caesar was defeated. But by capturing Alesia (52) he crushed the united armies of the Gauls. In the meantime Crassus had been defeated and killed in Asia (53) and Pompey was moving away from Caesar.

The Senate called upon Caesar, now in Cisalpine Gaul, to resign his command and disband his army (50), and entrusted Pompey with large powers. Pompey's forces outnumbered Caesar's legions, but were scattered over the empire. Supported by his victorious troops, Caesar moved southwards (49) and famously crossed the Rubicon, the boundary between Cisalpine Gaul and Italy. Pompey withdrew to Brundisium, pursued by Caesar, and from there to Greece (49); in three months Caesar was master of all Italy. In contrast to others before and after him, Caesar showed mercy in dealing with his enemies, and earned a reputation for *clementia* ('clemency'). After defeating Pompey's legates in Spain, he was appointed dictator. Pompey had gathered a powerful army in the east, and his fleet controlled the sea. Caesar, crossing the Adriatic, was driven back with heavy losses from Dyrrhachium. But in a second battle at Pharsalia (48), the senatorial army was routed, and Pompey himself fled to Egypt, where he was murdered.

cont

Cadogan, William Cadogan, 1st Earl 1675–1726
English soldier

Born in Dublin, Ireland, he fought as a 'volunteer' at the Battle of the Boyne (1690), and was commissioned in the Inniskilling Dragoons. He served under **Marlborough** in 1703 and led the march into Bavaria which ended in the victory of Blenheim (1704). With Marlborough's fall from political favour he resigned all his appointments; but on the accession of **George I** was restored. In 1715 he succeeded the 2nd Duke of **Argyll** in Scotland in quelling the Jacobite rebellion. On Marlborough's death (1722) he was appointed Commander-in-Chief.

Cadoudal, Georges 1771–1804
French revolutionary

A miller's son, born in Auray, Lower Brittany, he led the royalist Chouans against the Republicans from 1793 to 1800, and was guillotined for conspiring, with **Charles Pichegru**, against **Napoleon I**.

Cadwallon d.634
Pagan Welsh King of Gwynedd

He ruled from c.625. Having been driven out of his kingdom by **Edwin** (St Edwin), King of Northumbria, with **Penda**, King of Mercia, he invaded Northumbria (633) and killed Edwin at the Battle of Heathfield (Hatfield Chase), near Doncaster. He ravaged the kingdom, according to the Venerable **Bede**, but was himself defeated and killed by King **Oswald** (St Oswald) of Bernicia at the Battle of Heavenfield, near Hexham (634).

Caecilius, Firmianus See **Lactantius, Lucius Caelius**

Caedmon 7th century
Anglo-Saxon poet

He is the earliest Christian English poet known by name. According to **Bede**, he was an uneducated herdsman who in his old age received a divine call in a dream to sing of the Creation. He then became a monk at Whitby under the rule of **St Hilda**, where he turned other biblical themes into vernacular poetry. But the original hymn of the Creation, only nine lines long, is the only extant poem that can be attributed to him with any certainty. 📖 E Dobbie, *The MSS of Caedmon's Hymn and Bede's Death Song* (1937)

Caesalpinus See **Cesalpino, Andrea**

Caesar, Julius See panel above

Caetano, Marcelo 1906–80
Portuguese politician

The son of a schoolteacher, he rose rapidly during the counter-revolution following the First Republic and played a key judicial role in the establishment of **António Salazar's** Estado Novo (New State). He was Minister of the Colonies (1944–47) and Deputy Prime Minister (1955–58). Extrovert, ambitious and less submissive than other ministers, he had tried in 1951 to replace Salazar as Prime Minister, but was nevertheless chosen as his successor as one of the most notable figures in Estado Novo politics. From 1969 to 1971 he liberalized the country in some respects but avoided establishing a liberal democracy. However, discontent within the army over the costly and militarily unsuccessful 13-year war waged in Portuguese Africa against independence movements led to a bloodless coup in April 1974 which, in its turn, resulted in the revolution of 1974–75. He died in exile in Brazil.

Cage, John 1912–92
US composer

Born in Los Angeles, he was a pupil of **Schoenberg** and of Henry Cecil. Developing as an avant-garde composer, he not only used such experimental resources as indeterminacy (where a dice might be thrown to determine the elements of a composition), chance, electronics and the 'prepared piano' (distorting the sound of the instrument with objects placed inside), but produced pieces, such as *4' 33"* (1952, silent throughout) and *Radio Music* (1956, for one to eight radios), that challenge received ideas about what music is. His books include *Silence* (1961),

Caesar, (Gaius) Julius *cont*

Caesar, again appointed dictator for a year, and consul for five years, instead of returning to Rome, went to Egypt where he engaged in the 'Alexandrine War' on behalf of Cleopatra, who was now his mistress (47). He overthrew a son of **Mithradates IV** in Pontus (Asia Minor), and after a short stay in Rome, routed the Pompeian generals, Scipio and **Marcus Porcius Cato**, the Younger, at Thapsus in Africa (46). After his victories in Gaul, Egypt, Pontus and Africa he had still to put down an insurrection by Pompey's sons in Spain (45). He received the title of 'Father of his Country', was made dictator for life, and consul for 10 years; his person was declared sacred, his statue placed in temples, his portrait struck on coins, and the month Quintilis renamed Julius in his honour.

Ambitious plans were ascribed to him. He proposed to codify the whole of Roman law, to found libraries, to drain the Pontine Marshes, to enlarge the harbour at Ostia, to dig a canal through the Isthmus, and to launch a war against the Dacians in central Europe and the Parthians in the east. In the midst of these vast designs he was assassinated on the Ides (15th) of March. The conspirators, mostly aristocrats led by **Marcus Junius Brutus** and **Cassius**, believed that they were striking a blow for the restoration of republican freedom, which Caesar's autocracy was negating. But they merely succeeded in plunging the Roman world into a fresh round of civil wars, in which the Republic was finally destroyed.

Caesar was of a noble presence, tall, thin-featured, bald, and close shaven. As general, if not as statesman, he ranks among the greatest in history. Highly talented, and with a wide range of interests, he was second only to **Cicero** as orator, and his historical writings (on the Gallic and Civil Wars) are simple and direct; yet for all his genius, he failed to find a solution to the political problems of the late Republic, and it was left to his adopted son Octavianus (the future emperor **Augustus**) to achieve this.

📖 Caesar is alone among the great generals of antiquity in having left a surviving account of his campaigns: the *Commentarii* (*Commentaries: notes on the Gallic and Civil Wars*). These are important historical evidence despite their undoubted propaganda value to Caesar (the *Civil War* is virtually a political pamphlet).

There is a biography by Plutarch. Other sources are those for the end of the Roman Republic generally, including the speeches and letters of Cicero.

There are many references to Casar in literature; notable ones are **Shakespeare**, *Julius Caesar* (c.1600) and George Bernard Shaw, *Caesar and Cleopatra* (1901).

Christian Meier, *Caesar* (Eng trans 1995); E Bradford, *Julius Caesar: The Pursuit of Power* (1984); J C Fuller, *Julius Caesar* (1965).

> *Veni, vidi, vici.*
> 'I came, I saw, I conquered.'
> Words written on a *titulus* (placard) carried along in triumph after the campaign in Pontus (46BC).

A Year from Monday (1967), *M* (1973) and *Themes and Variations* (1982). He carried on a lifelong collaboration with choreographer **Merce Cunningham**, composing music for his dances and often serving as his music director. He was an authority on mushrooms.

Cage, Nicolas, *originally* Nicholas Coppola
1964–
US actor

Born in Long Beach, California, he studied at the American Conservatory Theatre in San Francisco before making his television debut in the series *The Best of Times* (1982) and his film debut in *Fast Times at Ridgemont High* (1982). He was then seen in *Rumble Fish* (1983) directed by his uncle **Francis Ford Coppola**. An adventurous performer, he has brought an intensity and individuality to a range of films including *Birdy* (1984), *Peggy Sue Got Married* (1986), *Moonstruck* (1987) and *Wild at Heart* (1990). Recently, he received an Academy Award for his performance as a dying alcoholic in *Leaving Las Vegas* (1995) and starred in the blockbuster *The Rock* (1996). He is married to actress Patricia Arquette (1968–).

Cagliostro, Alessandro, Conte di, *originally* Giuseppe Balsamo 1743–95
Italian adventurer

He was born in Palermo, Sicily, to a poor family, but at the monastery of Caltagirone learned a little chemistry and medicine. He travelled around Europe selling an 'elixir of immortal youth' with the help of his beautiful wife. A gifted conman, he styled himself 'Count', and in London persuaded clients to invest in 'Egyptian freemasonry'. In 1785 he was involved with the Comtesse de La Motte (1756–91) and Cardinal **Rohan-Guéménée** in the 'Affair of the Diamond Necklace', which led to his imprisonment in the Bastille, Paris. He was arrested in Rome in 1789 for peddling freemasonry, and died in prison.

Cagney, James Francis 1899–1986
US film actor

Born on New York City's lower East Side, he spent 10 years as an actor and dancer in vaudeville, musicals and on Broadway. Seen there in *Penny Arcade* (1929), he was signed to a contract with Warner Brothers, making his film debut in *Sinner's Holiday* (1930). His film performance as the gangster in *The Public Enemy* (1931) brought him stardom. Popular films of the 1930s include *Lady Killer* (1933), *Angels with Dirty Faces* (1938), and *The Roaring Twenties* (1939). He also appeared as Bottom in *A Midsummer Night's Dream* (1935), and in *Yankee Doodle Dandy* (1942) for which he won an Academy Award. Later, he offered an incisive psychological portrait of a hoodlum in one of his best films *White Heat* (1949), and later displayed his comic skills in the frenetic *One, Two, Three* (1961). He retired in 1961, but returned for *Ragtime* (1981) and the television film *Terrible Joe Moran* (1984). A farmer, painter and poet, he wrote an autobiography, *Cagney on Cagney* (1976).

📖 Patrick McGillian, *Cagney* (rev edn, 1982)

Cagniard de la Tour, Charles 1777–1859
French physicist

Born in Paris, he studied at the École Polytechnique and the École du Génie Géographe. In 1819 he published his invention of a disc siren for measuring the frequency of sounds, and his investigations between 1820 and 1823 revealed the 'critical state' in liquids and their vapours. Subsequently, he worked on crystallization (1828–31) and fermentation (1836–38), concluding amidst great controversy that yeast was not inert but in fact contained microscopic living organisms.

Caiger-Smith, Alan 1930–
English potter

He studied at Camberwell School of Arts and Crafts and King's College, Cambridge, before training in pottery at the Central School of Art and Design in 1954. He established the Aldermaston Pottery in 1955, producing tin-glazed earthenware with free hand brushwork and, occasionally, rich lustres. His book, *Tin Glaze in Europe and the Islamic World*, was published in 1973.

Caillaux, Joseph Marie Auguste 1863–1944
French radical politician

Born in Le Mans, he trained as a lawyer. He was Finance Minister five times (1899–1902, 1906–09, 1911, 1913–14, 1925). As Prime Minister (1911–12), he negotiated the treaty with Germany, following the Agadir Incident, by which France was given a free hand to subjugate Morocco. He was attacked for being too conciliatory towards Germany, and was arrested in 1918 on a charge of contacting the enemy. Tried by the Senate, he was sentenced in 1920 to three years' imprisonment, and to loss of political rights. Amnestied in 1925, he resumed his political career in the influential post of President of the Finance Committee of the Senate, and as one of the leading elder statesmen of the Radical Party. In 1914 his second wife shot and killed Gaston Calmette, editor of *Le Figaro*, who had published letters written to her by Caillaux while he was married to his first wife. She was acquitted after a sensational trial.

Caillebotte, Gustave 1848–94
French painter and art collector

Born in Paris, a naval architect by profession, he began to paint from 1872. He enrolled at the École des Beaux-Arts in Paris, but probably attended only sporadically. In 1876 he exhibited at the Second Impressionist exhibition showing a work which was already technically accomplished and shrewdly observant, *Les Raboteurs de parquet* (1875, 'Floor Scrapers', Musée d'Orsay, Paris). By 1876 his paintings included *Déjeuner* and *Le Pont de l'Europe* (Geneva). He also became a leading philatelist, and his income from stamps helped to purchase work from other Impressionists, **Claude Monet** in particular. Caillebotte's other work includes *Man at his Bath* (1884, National Gallery, London), once considered shocking and kept in a special room in Brussels, but now regarded as a fine example of realism. On his death, he bequeathed his collection of Impressionist pictures to the state. Forty of them were accepted by the Luxembourg, and formed the nucleus of the Impressionist collection there.

Cailletet, Louis Paul 1832–1913
French physicist

Born in Châtillon-sur-Seine, he was educated at the École des Mines in Paris. In 1870 he began a series of measurements to determine whether real gases deviate from the behaviour predicted by the 'ideal' gas laws. From this an interest in the liquefaction of gases grew and during 1877–78 he managed to liquefy oxygen, nitrogen, carbon monoxide, hydrogen, nitrogen dioxide and acetylene. Similar success was achieved by **Raoul Pictet** around the same time. Cailletet's other achievements included the installation of a manometer on the Eiffel Tower and the study of a liquid oxygen respiratory apparatus designed for high-altitude ascents.

Cain
Biblical character

The eldest son of **Adam** and **Eve**, he was the brother of Abel and Seth. He is portrayed (in Genesis 4) as a farmer whose offering to God was rejected, in contrast to that of his herdsman brother Abel. He murdered Abel, and God's punishment was to make him a vagrant.

Cain, James M(allahan) 1892–1977
US thriller writer

He was born in Annapolis, Maryland, and his earliest ambition was to emulate his mother and become a professional singer. He subsequently tried various jobs, was a reporter for many years and also taught journalism, but hankered after 'the great American novel'. After moving to California he found the style which is his hallmark, publishing *The Postman Always Rings Twice* (1934), in which an adulterous couple murder the woman's husband but

betray each other, and *Serenade* (1937), *Mildred Pierce* (1941), *Double Indemnity* (1943) and *The Butterfly* (1947). Several of his stories were filmed with legendary success, but the script credits went to others. ⌑ R Hoopes, *Cain: the biography* (1982)

Caine, Sir (Thomas Henry) Hall 1853–1931
English novelist

Born in Runcorn, Merseyside, he trained as an architect, and became secretary to **Dante Gabriel Rossetti** (1881–82), and published *Recollections of Rossetti* (1882). He wrote a number of popular novels, many of them set in the Isle of Man, including *The Shadow of a Crime* (1885), *The Bondman* (1890), *The Manxman* (1894) and *The Prodigal Son* (1904). He also wrote a *Life of Christ* (1938), and published an early autobiography, *My Story* (1908). ⌑ C F Kenyon, *Hall Caine, the man and the novelist* (1901)

Caine, Michael, *originally* Maurice Micklewhite 1933–
English film actor

Born in the East End of London, he spent many years as a struggling small-part actor in a variety of media, before winning attention for his performance as an aristocratic officer in *Zulu* (1963). His belated stardom continued with roles as down-at-heel spy Harry Palmer in *The Ipcress File* (1965) and its two sequels, and as the Cockney romeo *Alfie* (1966). A prolific performer, his reputation for consummate professionalism has withstood several inferior films and enhanced superior material like *Sleuth* (1972), *California Suite* (1978) and *Educating Rita* (1983). Nominated four times, he won an Academy Award for *Hannah and Her Sisters* (1986, Best Supporting Actor). He is also a gourmet cook and restaurant owner. Awarded the CBE in 1992, he published his autobiography, *What's it all About?*, the same year. ⌑ William Hall, *Raising Caine: The Authorized Biography* (1981)

Cairns, Hugh John Forster 1922–
English molecular biologist

Educated at Oxford, he progressed through a series of medical appointments until 1950, when he became a virologist at the Hall Institute in Melbourne, Australia. He later worked at the Virus Research Institute, Entebbe, Uganda (1952–54), and the Australian National University, Canberra (1955–63), before moving to the USA to hold posts at the California Institute of Technology and Cold Spring Harbor. He then became Professor of Biology at the State University of New York at Stony Brook (1968–73) and Head of the Imperial Cancer Research Fund Laboratory at Mill Hill, London (1973–80). He was then Professor of Microbiology at Harvard School of Public Health (1980–91). Elected FRS in 1974, Cairns has worked extensively on the initiation and progression of cancer, contributing extensively to the understanding of cell and molecular biology. He demonstrated that cancer develops from a single abnormal cell probably initiated by mutation of the DNA sequence, but the further progression of a cancer depends on multiple factors such as smoking, diet and hormones, and does not require further alteration to the cell's DNA.

Cairns, Hugh MacCalmont Cairns, Earl 1819–85
British jurist and politician

Born in County Down, Northern Ireland, and educated at Belfast and Trinity College, Dublin, he was called to the Bar at the Middle Temple in 1844, entered parliament for Belfast in 1852 and quickly made his mark in the House as a debater. He became QC in 1856, in 1858 Solicitor-General, in 1866 Attorney-General under Lord **Derby** and then a Lord Justice of Appeal, and in 1867 Baron Cairns. Under **Disraeli** he was made Lord Chancellor (1868, 1874), and was created Viscount Garmoyle and Earl Cairns in 1878. For some years he led the Conservatives in the House of Lords.

Cairns, Sir Hugh William Bell 1896–1952
Australian surgeon
He was born in Port Pirie, South Australia. His medical studies at Adelaide University were interrupted by military service, but after World War I, a Rhodes Scholarship allowed him to continue his medical work, at Oxford, and after at the London Hospital. His interest gradually shifted to neurosurgery, especially after a year's work with Harvey Cushing, and he made the London Hospital an international centre. In 1937 he became Nuffield Professor of Surgery at Oxford. During World War II he became an adviser on head injuries to the Ministry of Health, and neurosurgeon to the army. He played a crucial role in organizing the evacuation and treatment of soldiers with neurological injuries and persuaded the army to make crash helmets compulsory for dispatch riders. Among his patients was T E Lawrence, whose injuries following a motorcycle accident ultimately proved fatal.

Cairoli, Charlie 1910–80
French circus clown
Born in France, the son of a juggler, he made his debut as a circus performer at the age of five. He moved to Great Britain in 1938 and was for 39 years a star attraction of the Blackpool Tower Circus, until he was forced to retire a year before his death due to ill health.

Caitanya c.1486–1533
Indian Hindu mystic
Born in Nadia, Bengal, he was a Sanskrit teacher before becoming an itinerant holy man. He was converted in 1510 to a life of devotion to Krishna. He spent the latter part of his life in Puri, inspiring disciples in both Bengal and Orissa with his emphasis on joy and love of Krishna, and the place of singing and dancing in worship. Though he wrote little, he is also remembered for influencing the development of Bengali literature, previously thought to be inferior to Sanskrit.

Caius, John 1510–73
English physician and scholar
Born in Norwich, Norfolk, he became a student at Gonville Hall, Cambridge in 1529, and a Fellow in 1533. He studied medicine at Padua under Andreas Vesalius, then was a lecturer on anatomy in London (1544–64). President of the College of Physicians nine times, he was physician to Edward VI, Mary I, and Elizabeth I. In 1557 he obtained a charter to refound and enlarge his old Cambridge college, Gonville Hall (founded by Edmund Gonville in 1348), and in 1559 became the first master of Gonville and Caius College. A loyal Catholic, he had trouble with his Protestant colleagues, who burned his Mass vestments while he sentenced them to the stocks. He was the author of various critical, antiquarian and scientific books, notably *A Boke of Counseill against the Disease commonly called the Sweate, or Sweating Sicknesse* (1552).

Cai Yuanpei (Ts'ai Yüan-p'ei) 1863–1940
Chinese educator, scholar and politician
One of the youngest candidates ever to obtain the highest degree in the classical Civil Service examination system, he taught in various schools and colleges in his home province of Zhejiang (Chekiang) and in Shanghai. He joined Sun Yat-sen's anti-Manchu republican movement and in 1911 became the first Minister of Education of the new Chinese Republic, presiding over the creation of a new school system. Although he resigned in 1912, Cai continued to be active in educational affairs, helping to promote a work-study programme for Chinese students in France. Appointed Chancellor of Beijing (Peking) University (1916), he encouraged free debate and scholarship at the university, transforming it into one of the country's foremost intellectual centres. He later became a member of the Guomindang (Kuomintang), but became increasingly critical of the party's suppression of free speech. He died in Hong Kong.

Cajander, Aimo Kaarlo 1879–1943
Finnish politician and forestry expert
He became Professor of Forestry at Helsinki, and was three times Prime Minister of Finland (1922, 1924, 1937–40).

Cajetan, *Italian* Gaetano, *properly* Thomas de Vio 1469–1534
Italian prelate and theologian
Born in Gaeta, he studied at Bologna and Padua, being made Professor of Metaphysics at Padua University in 1494. In 1508 he became General of the Dominicans, in 1517 a cardinal, in 1519 Bishop of Gaeta, and in 1523 a legate to Hungary. In 1518 he tried to force Martin Luther to recant at Augsburg.

Caks, Aleksandrs, *pseudonym of* Aleksandrs Cadarainis 1901–50
Latvian poet and short-story writer
He studied medicine in Moscow, served in the Latvian Red Guards in the Revolution, then settled in Riga as a teacher. His early collections, influenced by Vladimir Mayakovsky, broke with the pastoral traditions of Latvian poetry and caused scandal amongst both left and right elements by its frequent allusions to sexuality and drink. He later fell foul of the Soviet authorities, and his poetry suffered through his unconvincing attempts to become a socialist realist. His death was passed over in silence, but he was 'rediscovered' in 1966 and is now considered to be his country's leading modernist. Poetry in translation includes *Let's Get Acquainted* (1973) and *Selected Poems* (1979).

Calamity Jane, *originally* Martha Jane Burke c.1852–1903
US frontierswoman
Born possibly in Princeton, Missouri, she was celebrated for her bravery and her skill at riding and shooting, particularly during the gold rush days in the Black Hills of Dakota. She teamed up with the renowned US marshal, Wild Bill Hickok, at Deadwood, Dakota, before he was murdered. She is said to have threatened 'calamity' for any man who tried to court her.

Calas, Jean 1698–1762
French Huguenot tradesman
He was born in Lacabarède. In 1761 he was accused, on the flimsiest evidence, of murdering his eldest son (a suicide) in order to prevent him becoming a Catholic. He was found guilty, and executed by being broken on the wheel. A revision of the trial followed as a result of a campaign led by Voltaire, and in 1765 parliament declared Calas and all his family innocent.

Caldecott, Randolph 1846–86
English artist and illustrator
Starting as a bank clerk in Whitstable and Manchester, he moved to London to follow an artistic career. He illustrated Washington Irving's *Old Christmas* (1876), and several children's books such as *The House that Jack Built* (1878) and *Aesop's Fables* (1883). He also contributed to *Punch* and the *Graphic*. Since 1938 the Caldecott Medal has been awarded annually to the best US artist-illustrator of children's books.

Calder, Alexander 1898–1976
US artist, pioneer of kinetic art

Born in Lawnton, Philadelphia, he trained as an engineer (1915–19) before studying art at the Art Students' League in New York (1923–26). In 1926 he exhibited paintings in the Artists' Gallery, New York, and in 1929 he had a one-man show in Paris. A pioneer of kinetic art, from 1925 he increasingly specialized in abstract hanging wire constructions (**Marcel Duchamp** christened them 'mobiles' in 1932). Some of these were connected to motors and were inspired by his fascination with the motion of animals and acrobats at the Ringling Brothers – **Barnum** and Bailey Circus. His best-known works, however, were not powered, relying upon air currents to set them rotating and casting intricate, ever-changing shadows.

Calder, (Peter) Ritchie, Baron Ritchie-Calder 1906–82
Scottish journalist and educationist

Born in Forfar, Tayside, he specialized in the spread of scientific knowledge to lay readers and wrote numerous books including *Men Against the Desert* (1951), *Men Against the Jungle* (1954), *Living with the Atom* (1962) and *The Evolution of the Machine* (1968). Made a life peer in 1966 he took the title Baron Ritchie-Calder of Balmashannar.

Calderón de la Barca, Pedro 1600–81
Spanish dramatist

Born in Madrid, he was educated by Jesuits, studied law and philosophy at Salamanca (1613–19), and for 10 years served in Italy and Flanders. In 1635 he was summoned by **Philip IV** to Madrid, and appointed a sort of master of the revels. The Catalonian rebellion in 1640 made him return to the army, but in 1651 he entered the priesthood, and in 1653 withdrew to Toledo. Ten years later he was recalled to court and to the resumption of his dramatic activity, and he continued to write for the court, the Church, and the public theatres till his death. His *autos sacramentales*, outdoor plays for the festival of Corpus Christi, number 72, and have been divided into seven classes—biblical, classical, ethical, 'cloak and sword plays', dramas of passion, and so forth. The finest of them is *El divino Orfeo* ('Divine Orpheus'). Of his regular dramas 118 are extant, of which the most famous are *La vida es sueño* ('Life's a Dream') and *El alcalde de Zalamea* ('The Mayor of Zalamea'), both probably written in the 1630s. ▢ E W Hesse, *Calderón* (1967)

Caldwell, Erskine 1903–87
US writer

Born in White Oak, Georgia, he worked amongst the 'poor whites' in the southern states, where he absorbed the background for his best-known work *Tobacco Road* (1932), of which the dramatized version by Jack Kirkland (1933) had a record run in New York. Other books include *God's Little Acre* (1933), *Sure Hand of God* (1947), *A Lamp for Nightfall* (1952), *Love and Money* (1954) and *Close to Home* (1962). ▢ James E Devlin, *Erskine Caldwell* (1984)

Caldwell, Zoë Ada 1934–
Australian actress

Born in Melbourne, she made her professional debut there in 1953. She made her British debut at Stratford-upon-Avon in 1958, and joined the Royal Court Theatre in 1960. She acted in **Molière** and **Chekhov** productions in her first season on the US stage in Minneapolis in 1963, which was followed by her New York debut in **John Whiting**'s *The Devils* in 1965. Performing a wide range of roles, she was in the acclaimed *Medea* in 1982, and had outstanding success in the title role in *The Prime of Miss Jean Brodie* (1968). She has also directed a number of plays.

Calgacus, also called Galgacus 1st century AD
Caledonian chieftain in northern Britain

He was leader of the tribes defeated by **Agricola** at the Battle of Mons Graupius (AD83). Agricola's biographer, **Tacitus**, attributes to him a heroic speech on the eve of a battle, with a ringing denunciation of Roman imperialism ('They make a desolation, and call it peace').

Calhoun, John Caldwell 1782–1850
US politician

Born in Abbeville County, South Carolina, of Irish Presbyterian descent, he became a successful lawyer. In Congress he supported the measures which led to the war of 1812–15 with Great Britain, and promoted the protective tariff. In 1817 he joined **Monroe**'s Cabinet as Secretary of War, and reorganized the war department. He was Vice-President under **John Q Adams** (1825–29) and **Andrew Jackson**. His *Address to the People of South Carolina* (1831) set forth his theory of state rights. On the passing by South Carolina in 1832 of the nullification ordinance he resigned the vice-presidency, and entered the Senate, becoming a leader of the states-rights movement and a champion of the interests of the slave-holding states. In 1844, as Secretary of State, he signed a treaty annexing Texas, but once more in the Senate, he strenuously opposed the war of 1846–47 with Mexico. He, **Henry Clay**, and **Daniel Webster** were the 'great triumvirate' of US political orators.

Caligula, *properly* Gaius Julius Caesar Germanicus AD12–41
Roman emperor

The youngest son of **Germanicus Caesar** and **Agrippina**, the Elder he was born in Antium. He was nicknamed Caligula from his little soldier's boots (*caligae*). He ingratiated himself with **Tiberius**, and, on his death (AD37), was co-heir alongside the emperor's grandson Gemellus. The senate, however, conferred imperial power on Caligula alone. His rule then developed into an erratic despotism, though it is not easy to separate fact from fiction in a hostile tradition. He squandered the wealth left by Tiberius, banished or murdered his relatives, excepting his uncle **Claudius** and sister Drusilla (with whom he was suspected of committing incest), executed and confiscated the property of many citizens of Rome, and awarded himself extravagant honours, having aspirations towards deification. His brief but traumatic reign ended when he was assassinated. ▢ John P V D Balsdon, *The Emperor Gaius* (1934)

Calisher, Hortense 1911–
US novelist and short-story writer

She was born in New York City, and educated at Barnard College there (graduated 1932); her fictional characters are usually drawn from the city's upper middle-class. Her novels, *The New Yorkers* (1969), *Queenie* (1971) and *The Bobby-Soxer* (1986), though frequently of novella length are less successful than her powerfully and precisely written short stories, which include 'In Greenwich There Are Many Gravelled Walks'. Her memoirs were published in 1988 entitled *Kissing Cousins*. ▢ *Herself* (1972)

Calixtus or Callistus I d.222AD
Italian pope

According to **Hippolytus**, his bitter opponent who became antipope in AD217, he was originally a slave, who had twice undergone severe punishment for his crimes before he became a priest under Zephyrinus, whom he succeeded as pope (218). He was martyred.

Calixtus, *originally* Callisen Georg 1586–1656
German Lutheran theologian

Born in Medelbye, Schleswig, he studied at Helmstedt from 1603, where he was made Professor of Theology. Although acknowledged by Romanists to be one of their ablest opponents, he was declared guilty of heresy for some statements which appeared to favour Catholic dogmas, and others which approached too near to the Calvinistic standpoint. He was accused of apostasy at the Conference of Thom in 1645, but, with the support of his friends, was able to retain his chair.

Callaghan of Cardiff, (Leonard) James Callaghan, Baron, *also called* Jim Callaghan 1912–
English Labour politician and Prime Minister

Born in Portsmouth and educated at Portsmouth Northern Secondary School, he joined the staff of the Inland Revenue in 1929. In 1945 he was elected Labour MP for South Cardiff and from 1950 represented Southeast Cardiff. One of the chief contenders for the party leadership after the death of **Hugh Gaitskell**, he was made Chancellor of the Exchequer under **Harold Wilson** (1964–67). In this capacity he introduced some of the most controversial taxation measures in British fiscal history, including the corporation and selective employment taxes. He was Home Secretary (1967–70) and Foreign Secretary (1974–76), and was elected Prime Minister on Wilson's resignation (1976), remaining in office until the general election of 1979. A failure to anticipate or check the growing power of left-wing extremists within his party and in trade unionism is said to have contributed greatly to Labour's defeat by **Margaret Thatcher**'s brand of new-look Conservatism in 1979. He resigned as Leader of the Opposition in 1980 and was made a life peer in 1987. His autobiography *Time and Chance* was published in 1987. ▫ Peter Kellner and Christopher Hitchens, *The Road to Number Ten* (1976)

Callaghan, Morley Edward 1903–90
Canadian novelist, short-story writer and memoirist

Born in Toronto, of Irish descent, he was educated at Toronto University, and when a cub reporter on the Toronto *Daily Star* was befriended by **Ernest Hemingway**. They met up again in Paris, where Callaghan's boxing prowess earned him Hemingway's respect. Callaghan wrote about his time there in one of his most appealing books, *That Summer in Paris* (1963). He had been called to the Bar in 1928, but Hemingway encouraged him to renounce law for literature. His first novel was *Strange Fugitive* (1928) and his first collection of stories *A Native Argosy* (1930). Other novels include *More Joy in Heaven* (1937), *The Many Colored Coat* (1960), *A Fine and Private Place* (1975), and *Our Lady of Snows* (1985). ▫ A Conron, *Morley Callaghan* (1966)

Callas, Maria, *stage name of* Maria Meneghini, *née* Kalogeropoulos 1923–77
US soprano

Born in New York City of Greek parents, she studied at Athens Conservatory, and in 1947 appeared in Verona in *La Gioconda* ('The Joyful Girl'), where she won immediate recognition. Her 1956 debut at the Metropolitan Opera in New York City drew a record audience. She sang with great authority in all the most exacting soprano roles, and was particularly impressive in the intricate *bel canto* style of pre-Verdian Italian opera. The fierce but truthful drama of her performances, her tumultuous personal life (including a long relationship with **Aristotle Onassis**), and her transformation (after losing a great deal of weight) into an exceptional beauty all added to her fascination in the mind of the public. Driven perhaps too hard, her voice began to fail early, and she gave her last operatic performance at the Metropolitan in *Tosca* in 1965.

Callcott, Sir Augustus Wall 1779–1844
English landscape painter

Born in London, he was appointed Surveyor of Royal Pictures in 1834. He was considered the most fashionable English landscape painter of his time, and was knighted in 1837. His wife, Lady Maria Callcott (1785–42, *née* Graham), wrote *Little Arthur's History of England* (1835).

Callendar, Hugh Longbourne 1863–1930
English physicist

He was born in Hatherop, Gloucestershire, and went from Marlborough to Trinity College, Cambridge. He was Professor of Physics at the Royal Holloway College (1888), McGill University, Montreal (1893), University College London (1898), and the Royal College of Science (1902–30). In 1886 he described an accurate platinum resistance thermometer, which was later used to measure the thermal properties of water, and was eventually accepted as the international standard. In addition he devised a constant-pressure air thermometer (1891) and an electrical calorimeter designed to measure specific heats of liquids. *The Callendar Steam Tables* (1915) and his *Properties of Steam and Thermodynamic Theory of Turbines* (1920) were standard references for engineers and scientists.

Calles, Plutarco Elias 1877–1945
Mexican political leader

Born in Guaymas, Sonora, he became a schoolmaster and tradesman. He took part in the revolt against **Porfirio Diaz** (1910) and became Governor of Sonora (1917–19) and Secretary of the Interior (1920–24). From 1924 to 1928 he was President of Mexico. In 1928 he retired to become a landowner and financier, but founded the National Revolutionary Party (PRN) in 1929 through which he controlled succeeding presidents. Known for his fanatical anticlericalism and for his efforts to restrict foreign influence in the oil industry, he was defeated by **Lázaro Cárdenas** and was exiled to the USA in 1936, but allowed to return in 1941.

Callil, Carmen Thérèse 1938–
Australian publisher

Born and educated in Melbourne, of Irish–Lebanese descent, she went to London in 1960 and worked for Marks and Spencer before beginning a publishing career. She worked in various publicity departments before forming her own publicity company. In 1972, with Ursula Owen and Rosie Boycott, she founded the feminist publishing house, Virago Press, with the intention of securing a place for women in the publishing and writing of literature in English. The company earned renown for promoting successful female authors like **Maya Angelou**, **Edith Wharton** and **Margaret Atwood**. When Virago joined the publishing group of Chatto and Windus, Bodley Head and Cape in 1982, Callil remained chairman but also became managing director of Chatto and Windus and The Hogarth Press, where she remained for 11 years. In 1993 she was made Publisher-at-Large of Random House, the new owners of Chatto and Windus, but left in 1994. She resigned her chairmanship of Virago in 1995.

Callimachus c.305–c.240BC
Hellenistic poet, grammarian and critic

Born in Cyrene, Libya, he became head of the Alexandrian library, and prepared a catalogue of it, in 120 volumes. He wrote several prose works and plays which have not survived, a number of *Hymns* and *Epigrams* and a long elegiac poem, the *Aitia*. Some sixty-four of his epigrams remain, including one to his friend Heraclitus of Halicarnassus, made familiar in the translation by **William Cory** ('They told me, Heraclitus, they told me you were dead'). ▫ G Capovilla, *Callimaco* (1967)

Callinicus See **Seleucus II**

Callistratus 4th century BC
Athenian orator and statesman

His eloquence is said to have fired the imagination of the young **Demosthenes**. In 366BC he allowed the Thebans to occupy Oropus, and was prosecuted, but defended himself successfully in a brilliant speech. He was prosecuted again in 361BC for his Spartan sympathies and then was condemned to death, but fled before sentence was pronounced. He returned from exile in Macedonia, hoping to win public support, but was executed.

Callistus I See **Calixtus I**

Callot, Jacques c.1592–1635
French etcher and engraver
Born in Nancy, he joined a band of gypsies at the age of 12, and travelled with them to Florence, but was sent home. In 1612 he went to Rome to study and then moved to Florence where he earned a reputation for his spirited etchings. In 1621 he returned to Nancy. For Louis XIII, who invited him to Paris, he executed etchings of the Siege of La Rochelle, but he refused to commemorate the capture of his native town. His 1,600 engravings include *Miseries of War* and *Gypsies*, and provide a vivid insight into 17th-century life.

Callow, Simon Phillip Hugh 1949–
English actor, director and writer
He was born in London and made his London debut in *The Plumber's Progress* (1975). He joined the Joint Stock theatre company in 1977, touring in several plays including David Hare's *Fanshen* and Howard Brenton's *Epsom Downs*. In 1978 he played the title roles in *Titus Andronicus* at the Bristol Old Vic, and Brecht's *The Resistable Rise of Arturo Ui* at the Half Moon Theatre. At the National Theatre he played Orlando in *As You Like it* and Mozart in Peter Shaffer's *Amadeus* (1979), and later appeared in Alan Ayckbourn's *Sisterly Feelings* (1980). He returned to the National Theatre (1988) to play a shabby and ebullient Guy Burgess in *An Englishman Abroad*, part of Alan Bennett's double bill, *Single Spies*. In 1991 he directed the Rodgers and Hammerstein musical *Carmen Jones* at the Old Vic and made his debut as a film director with Carson McCullers's *Ballad of the Sad Café*. His film appearances include *Amadeus* (1983), *A Room with a View* (1986), *Four Weddings and a Funeral* (1994) and *Jefferson in Paris* (1995). He has directed several new plays in fringe theatres, two operas, and published the autobiographical books, *Being An Actor* (1984) and *Shooting the Actor* (1992), as well as biographies of Charles Laughton (1987) and Orson Welles (1995).

Calloway, Cab(ell) 1907–94
US jazz bandleader and singer
Born in Rochester, New York, he became a national figure when his band succeeded Duke Ellington's at Harlem's Cotton Club in 1931, and had hits that year with the songs 'Minnie The Moocher' (his signature tune) and 'Kicking The Gong Around', both containing streetwise drug references. His scat-style catchphrases (for example substituting nonsense syllables such as 'hi-de-ho' for words) and flamboyant presentation remained characteristic throughout a long career, in which he also acted in stage musicals and in films, including *Stormy Weather* (1943) and *The Blues Brothers* (1980). George Gershwin is said to have modelled the character of Sportin' Life in *Porgy and Bess* (1935) partly on Calloway, a role he eventually played in 1952. ▣ *Of Minnie The Moocher and Me* (1976)

Calmette, (Léon Charles) Albert 1863–1933
French bacteriologist
Born in Nice, he was a pupil of Louis Pasteur and founder of the Pasteur Institute in Saigon, where he discovered an anti-snakebite serum. In 1895 he founded the Pasteur Institute, Lille (director, 1895–1919). He is best known for the BCG vaccine (Bacille Calmette–Guérin), used in the inoculation against tuberculosis, which he discovered jointly with Camille Guérin (1908). They recognized that a virulent strain of tuberculosis could be weakened by using bile, but would still convey a certain amount of immunity to protect against infection. This attenuated strain was used to produce BCG which was introduced in continental Europe around 15 years after the discovery, and later in the UK and the USA.

Calonne, Charles Alexandre de 1734–1802
French politician
He was born in Douai, and held various legal and administrative positions before becoming Controller-General of Finance (1783). In 1786 he advised King Louis XVI to convoke the Assembly of Notables and distribute the burden of taxation more equally. In opening the Assembly (1787) he described the general prosperity of France, but confessed that the annual deficit of the treasury had risen to 115 million francs, and that from 1776 to 1786 the government had borrowed 1,250 million francs. The Notables demanded a statement of accounts; failing to satisfy them, he was banished to Lorraine. After this he lived chiefly in England, until in 1802 Napoleon I allowed him to return.

Calprenède, Gautier de Costes de La
c.1610–1663
French writer and soldier
Born in the château of Toulgon, near Sarlat, he was an officer of the guards and royal chamberlain of France. He wrote tragedies, tragi-comedies, and the internationally popular clever but tedious heroic romances, like *Cléopâtre* (12 vols, 1647–57), *Cassandre* (10 vols, 1642–45) and others.

Calpurnius Siculus, Titus fl.mid-1st century AD
Roman pastoral poet
He is best known for his seven surviving Eclogues.

Calvaert, Denys, *also called* Dionisio Fiammingo
c.1545–1619
Flemish painter
He was born in Antwerp, but in 1575 settled in Bologna, where he opened a school, painting in the Mannerist style. Among his students were Guido Reni, Domenichino, and Francesco Albani, who later became pupils of the Carracci family. His *Mystic Marriage of St Catherine* (c.1590, Stomhead, Wiltshire, and elsewhere) shows the influence of Raphael and Correggio on his work.

Calverley, Charles Stuart, *originally surnamed* Blayds 1831–84
English poet and parodist
Born in Martley, Worcestershire, he was educated at Marlborough, Harrow, Oxford and Cambridge. His father changed the family name back to Calverley in 1852. In 1858 he was elected a Fellow of Christ's College, Cambridge, and in 1865 he was called to the Bar, and settled in London. A skating accident in the winter of 1866–67 ended his career and his last years were spent as an invalid. He is remembered as a skilful parodist in his two small volumes, *Verses and Translations* (1862) and *Fly Leaves* (1872). His translation of Theocritus (1869) shows his scholarship and his mastery of English verse. ▣ R B Ince, *Calverley and the Cambridge Wits of the 19th Century* (1929)

Calvert, Edward 1799–1883
English engraver
Born in Appledore, Devon, he was given at his baptism not a Bible, but a copy of Virgil. The paganism of the Greek myths remained an inspiration when, after serving in the navy, he moved to London in 1824 and met Samuel Palmer and the Ancients—the disciples of William Blake. Impressed by Blake's illustrations to Virgil, Calvert produced an exquisite series of tiny erotic woodcuts, including *The Ploughman* (1827, Tate, London) and *The Chamber Idyll* (1831, Tate). He also engraved on copper, for example *The Bride* (1828, Tate), with its fertility theme. Regarding his work as a passion not a profession, he rarely exhibited and destroyed much of it, but there are further examples in the British Museum and in Luxembourg. He influenced Pierre Puvis de Chavannes.

Calvin, John 1509–64
French theologian, one of the most important reformers of the 16th century

Calvin was born in Noyon, in Picardy, where his father, Gérard Caulvin or Cauvin, was procureur-fiscal and secretary of the diocese. He studied Latin in Paris from 1523 and later, while studying law in Orleans, received from the Scriptures his first impulse to study theology. From Orleans he went to Bourges, where he learned Greek, published an edition of **Seneca**'s *De clementia* and began to preach the reformed doctrines. After a short stay (1533) in Paris, which had become a centre of the 'new learning' and of religious excitement, he visited Noyon. He went to Nerac, Saintonge, Angoulême, the residence of **Margaret of Angoulême**, Queen of Navarre, and then to Paris again. Calvin fled France to escape persecution; and at Basle in 1536 he issued his *Christianae Religionis Institutio* ('Institutes of the Christian Religion') with the famous preface addressed to **Francis I**.

In Geneva, **Guillaume Farel** persuaded Calvin to assist in the work of reformation. A Protestant Confession of Faith was proclaimed, and moral severity took the place of licence. The strain, however, was too sudden and too extreme. A spirit of rebellion broke forth under the 'Libertines', and Calvin and Farel were expelled from the city (1538). Calvin, withdrawing to Strasbourg, devoted himself to a critical study of the New Testament. In 1542 he was invited to return to Geneva, where, through his College of Pastors and Doctors, and his Consistorial Court of Discipline, he founded a theocracy, which was virtually to direct all the affairs of the city, and to control the social and individual life of the citizens. His struggle with the Libertines lasted 14 years, when the reformer's authority was confirmed into an absolute supremacy (1555).

Calvin rendered a double service to Protestantism: he systematized its doctrine, and organized its ecclesiastical discipline. His commentaries embrace the greater part of the Old Testament and the whole of the New except the Revelation. In 1559 he founded a theological academy at Geneva that later became the university.

📖 McGrath, Alister E, *A Life of John Calvin* (1990), W J Bouwsma, *Calvin* (1987); T H L Parker, *John Calvin: A Biography* (1975); Richard Stauffer, *The Humanness of John Calvin* (1971).

'That knuckle-end of England—that land of Calvin, oatcakes and sulphur.' **Sydney Smith**'s description of Scotland. Quoted in Lady Holland, *Memoir* (1855), vol 1, ch.2.

Calvert, Frederick Crace 1819–73
English chemist
Born in London, he was largely instrumental in the introduction of carbolic acid as a disinfectant.

Calvi, Robert, *originally* Gian Roberto Calvini 1920–82
Italian banker and financier
Born in Milan, he worked his way up through Banco Ambrosiano, becoming its chairman in 1975. He continued to build a vast financial empire. In 1978, a report by the Bank of Italy on Ambrosiano concluded that several billion lire had been illegally exported. In May 1981, Calvi was indicted and arrested along with ten others, and on 20 July he was found guilty and sentenced to four years' imprisonment and was fined 16 billion lire. Calvi was released pending his appeal. Throughout the 1970s, he had become increasingly involved in Propaganda 2 (P2), a secret masonic lodge. In 1981, he also became entangled in the P2 scandal when the extent of its influence became publicly known. Members of parliament, leading financiers, intelligence officers and media magnates were implicated. By 1982, the bank hovered on the verge of financial collapse, but it was temporarily saved by patronage letters from the Vatican's bank which, under the leadership of Paul Marcinckus, had jointly perpetrated with Ambrosiano several dubious business deals. On 10 June, Calvi flew to Rome and was reported missing the next day. On 18 June, his body was found hanging from scaffolding under Blackfriars Bridge in London, his pockets weighed down with bricks and concrete, and containing a large amount of cash. A verdict of suicide was recorded, which was overturned in 1983, when an inquest delivered an open verdict on the death. Calvi's family still maintain that he was murdered.

Calvin, John See panel above

Calvin, Melvin 1911–
US chemist and Nobel Prize winner
Born in Minnesota, USA, of Russian immigrant parents, he became Professor of Chemistry at the University of California (1947–71) and head of the Lawrence Radiation Laboratory there (1963–80). In 1948 he helped elucidate the Thunberg–Wieland cycle by which some bacteria, unlike animals, synthesize four-carbon sugars, and hence glucose, from acetate as shown by **Konrad Bloch**. The idea that the cycle, operating in reverse, might fix carbon dioxide gas led him to investigate this process in photosynthesis (1950). The outcome was the Calvin cycle for which he was awarded the Nobel Prize for chemistry in 1961. Since 1971 he has been University Professor of Chemistry at the University of California.

Calvino, Italo 1923–85
Italian novelist, essayist and journalist
Born in Santiago de las Vegas, Cuba, of Italian parents, he grew up in San Remo, Italy, and was educated at the University of Turin. A reluctant member of the Young Fascists, he participated in the Italian occupation of the French Riviera, but in 1943 he was able to join the Resistance, and until 1945 he fought with the Partisan forces in Liguria. Throughout the 1940s he wrote for the communist paper *L'unità* and later he succeeded **Cesare Pavese** at Einaudi, the Turin-based publishers. His first novel, *Il sentiero dei nidi di ragno* (1947, Eng trans *The Path to the Nest of Spiders*, 1956), was dubbed neo realist, but he became increasingly interested in fantasy, folk-tales and the nature of narrative. His early works include three fantastic 'historical' novels, collectively titled *I nostri antenati* (1960, Eng trans *Our Ancestors*, 1980), and *Fiabe Italiane* (1956, Eng trans *Italian Folktales*, 1980). Regarded as one of the most inventive of the European modernists, he combined fantasy and surrealism with a hard, satirical wit. His later books include *Le città invisibili* (1972, Eng trans *Invisible Cities*, 1974), *Si una notte d'inverno un viaggiatore* (1979, Eng trans *If on a Winter's Night a Traveller*, 1981) and *Palomar* (1983). In 1973 he won the prestigious Italian literary award, the Premio Feltrinelli. 📖 J Cannon, *Calvino: writer and society* (1981)

Calvo Sotelo, José 1893–1936
Spanish politician
Under the dictator **Miguel Primo de Rivera**, he was made the Director-General of Local Government, introducing the stillborn Municipal Statute in 1924. He was also a controversial Minister of Finance, attempting to overhaul the tax system (only to be thwarted by the banks) and creating state monopolies, in particular the petroleum company CAMPSA. His much-criticized monetary

policies contributed to the regime's fall (1930). He went into exile on the advent of the Second Republic in 1931, returning with the amnesty of 1934. Having founded the totalitarian National Bloc, he soon became the most powerful civilian figure on the extreme Right. His assassination (13 July 1936) triggered off the military rising that led to the Spanish Civil War.

Calwell, Arthur Augustus 1896–1973
Australian Labor politician

He was born in Melbourne. He entered federal politics in 1940, and as Minister for Immigration (1945–49) under Ben Chifley, he administered the influx of one million refugees from Europe after World War II. At the same time, in support of the Labor Party's 'White Australia' policy, he tried to expel Asian refugees. In 1960 he succeeded H V Evatt (1894–1965) as leader of the ALP opposition. He retired following a heavy defeat, and having survived an assassination attempt, in 1966.

Cam or Cão 15th century
Portuguese explorer

In 1482 he discovered the mouth of the Congo, near which an inscribed stone erected by him as a memorial was found in 1887. His voyages southwards along the west African coast later enabled Bartolomeu Diaz to find the sea route to the Indian Ocean around the Cape.

Camara, Helder Pessoa 1909–
Brazilian Roman Catholic theologian and prelate

He was born in Fortaleza, Ceará State. Archbishop of Olinda and Recife, north-east Brazil (1964–84), he has been a champion of the poor and of non-violent social change in his native Brazil and in the Catholic Church at large through his influence at Vatican Council II, and received international recognition with the award of the Martin Luther King Jnr Peace Prize (1970) and the People's Prize (1973). His theological and devotional writings have been translated into many languages. His works include *Race Against Time* (1971), *Revolution Through Peace* (1971) and *Hoping Against All Hope* (1984).

Camargo, Maria Anna de 1710–70
French dancer

Born in Brussels, Belgium, she became famous for her performances at the Paris Opera, where she made her debut in 1726 in Jean Balon's *Les Caractères de la danse*. She is said to have been responsible for the shortening of the traditional ballet skirt, allowing more complicated steps to be seen. She was also one of the first celebrities to lend her name to merchandizing, in her case, shoes and wigs.

Cambacérès, Jean Jacques Régis de, Duc de Parme 1753–1824
Italian politician

Born in Montpellier, France, he was Archchancellor of the Empire from 1804 and Duke of Parma from 1808. The *Projet de Code Civil*, published in his name, formed the basis of the *Code Napoléon*.

Cambio See Arnolfo di Cambio

Cambon, Joseph 1756–1820
French financier and revolutionary

Born in Montpellier, during the Revolution he was a member of the Legislative Assembly and the Convention (1792) and though a moderate, voted for the King's death. As head of the committee on finance (1793–95), he produced the 'Great Book of the Public Debt' in an attempt to stabilize the finances. He was exiled as a regicide in 1815.

Cambrensis, Giraldus See Giraldus Cambrensis

Cambridge, Ada 1844–1926
Australian novelist and poet

Born in Norfolk, England, she was educated privately, and by the time she met and married George Cross at the age of 26, she had already published short stories, poems and a book of hymns. They left almost immediately for Australia where her husband was to be a missionary priest, and settled eventually in Melbourne. In 1873 she began contributing to the *Australian* which, between 1875 and 1886, serialized nine novels, of which three were subsequently published: *In Two Years' Time* (1879), *A Mere Chance* (1882) and *The Three Miss Kings* (1891). A woman with a strong sense of class, she drew attention through her writing to women's social position and encouraged them to think for themselves. She wrote 18 novels in all, and attracted a wide English readership. Jane Austen is the most obvious influence. Her best work includes *A Marked Man* (1890), *Not All In Vain* (1892) and *Materfamilias* (1898). ⌑ *Thirty Years in Australia* (1903); *The Retrospect* (1912)

Cambyses II *Persian* Kambujiya d.522BC
Second King of the Medes and Persians

He succeeded his father, Cyrus the Great, in 529BC. He put his brother Smerdis to death and invaded and conquered Egypt (525BC), so establishing Persian rule there for two centuries. Further attempts at expansion failed, however. When news came in 522BC, that Gaumáta the Magian had usurped the Persian throne, Cambyses marched against him from Egypt, but died in Syria, either by accident or suicide.

Camden, William 1551–1623
English antiquary and historian

Born in London, he was educated at Christ's Hospital, St Paul's School and Oxford, and he became headmaster of Westminster School in 1593. He is best known for his pioneering topographical survey of the British Isles, *Britannia* (in Latin 1586, Eng trans 1610). He also published a list of the epitaphs in Westminster Abbey (1600), a collection of old English historians (1603), a narrative of the trial of Guy Fawkes and the Gunpowder Plotters (1607), and *Annals of the Reign of Elizabeth to 1588* (1615). He was buried in Westminster Abbey.

Camerarius or Camerer, Joachim, originally Joachim Liebhard 1500–74
German classical scholar and Lutheran theologian

He was born in Bamberg. He changed his original name of Liebhard to Camerarius because his forefathers had been *Kammerer* (chamberlains) to the bishops of Bamberg. A friend of Philip Melanchthon, he embraced the Reformation at Wittenberg in 1521, and helped to formulate the Augsburg Confession of 1530. Professor of Greek and Latin at Tübingen (1535) and Leipzig (from 1541), he produced several editions of the classical authors, wrote a biography of Melanchthon (1566) and edited his letters (1569), and wrote *Epistolae Familiares* (3 vols, 1583–95) on contemporary affairs.

Camerarius or Camerer, Joachim 1534–98
German botanist

The son of Joachim Camerarius, he wrote *Hortus Medicus et Philosophicus* (1588) and *Symbola et Emblem* (1590), and was one of the most learned physicians and botanists of his age. His most distinguished descendant was Rudolph Jacob Camerarius.

Camerarius or Camerer, Rudolph Jacob 1665–1721
German physician and botanist

Born in Tübingen, he was director of the botanic garden at Tübingen University and Professor of Botany, and was renowned for his experimental proof of sexuality in plants (*De Sexu Plantarum*, 1694).

Cameron, Sir David Young 1865–1945
Scottish artist

Born in Glasgow, he studied at the Glasgow School of Art (1881–85) and was introduced to the collector George Stevenson who discovered his pen and ink drawings in 1887. As a result of this he gave up a career in business and concentrated on art. A noted landscape painter, he was also one of the most romantic of British etchers, following the lead of James McNeill Whistler and Francis Haden. Turning to his native landscape for inspiration, he introduced dry-point to produce some of the most memorable images in 20th-century British printmaking.

Cameron (of Lochiel), Donald, known as Gentle Lochiel c.1695–1748
Scottish Highland chieftain

He was the grandson of Sir Ewen Cameron of Lochiel and succeeded to the clan chieftancy in 1719. His reluctant support of the Young Pretender (Charles Edward Stuart) in 1745 encouraged other chieftains. Seriously wounded at Culloden (1746), he died in exile in France. His brother Alexander was captured after Culloden and died in a prison hulk on the Thames, London, and his brother Archibald was executed in 1753, the last man to die for the Jacobite cause.

Cameron (of Lochiel), Sir Ewen 1629–1719
Scottish Jacobite and chief of clan Cameron

A huge figure, famous for his ferocity and prodigious feats of strength, he led his clan against the parliamentary forces of the English Commonwealth, then fought with Claverhouse (Viscount Dundee) at Killiecrankie (1689), and supported the Earl of Mar in the 1715 Rebellion. He is said to have killed the last wolf in Scotland.

Cameron, (Mark) James 1911–85
Scottish journalist

Born of Scottish parents in Battersea, London, his career began as an office boy for the *Weekly News* (1935) and progressed, via Dundee and Glasgow, to Fleet Street, London, in 1940. He worked as a sub-editor on the *Daily Express* (1940–45), then returned to reporting. Covering the atom bomb experiments at Bikini (1946) convinced him to become a member of CND. He resigned from the *Daily Express* in 1950 and later joined the *News Chronicle* (1952–60). An accomplished reporter, he covered some of the great events in world affairs, from the Vietnam War to ill treatment of the underprivileged in India. He was also a writer and presenter of television programmes, including *Men of Our Time* (1963), *Cameron Country* and the autobiographical *Once Upon a Time* (1984). His radio play *The Pump* (1973) won the Prix Italia and was dramatized for television in 1980. His books include *Witness in Vietnam* (1966) and the autobiography *Point of Departure* (1967).

Cameron, Julia Margaret, née Pattle 1815–79
British photographer

Born in Calcutta, India, she married an Indian jurist, Charles Hay Cameron (1795–1880) in 1838. At the age of 48 she was given a camera and she became a noted amateur photographer in the 1860s, making acclaimed close-up portraits of such Victorian public figures as Tennyson, Charles Darwin, Thomas Carlyle and Cardinal Newman. Her style was influenced by her friend G F Watts and the Pre-Raphaelites. 📖 Joanne Lukitsh, *Julia Margaret Cameron* (1986)

Cameron, Kate (Katharine) 1874–1965
Scottish artist and etcher

Born in Hillhead, Glasgow, she studied at the Glasgow School of Art and in Paris. Her early interior watercolours reflect the arts and crafts style of the 'Glasgow four' of Charles Rennie Mackintosh, Margaret Mackintosh, Frances MacDonald and Herbert MacNair (1868–1955). Although she illustrated many books, including children's fairy tales, she was much better known for her watercolour flower studies, in particular her delicate and stylized middle-to-later-period works, which often incorporated butterflies or bumble bees. She was the sister of the artist Sir David Young Cameron.

Cameron, Richard 1648–80
Scottish Covenanter

Born in Falkland, Fife, he studied at St Andrews (1662–65). He became a precentor and schoolmaster at Falkland under its Episcopal curate, but was subsequently converted by field preachers. In 1678 he went to Holland. On his return (1680), he published the *Sanquhar Declaration*, in which he and his followers (Cameronians) renounced their allegiance to the king and declared war on him and his agents. Cameron and some 60 armed friends hid in the hills between Nithsdale and Ayrshire, but after a month they were surprised by a troop of dragoons on Airds Moss, near Auchinleck, and, after a brave fight, he was killed. His hands and head were cut off and fixed on the Netherbow Port, Edinburgh.

Cameron, Simon 1799–1889
US politician

Born in Pennsylvania, he was a journeyman printer and newspaper editor. In 1845 he became a senator, was Abraham Lincoln's Secretary of War (1861–62), and minister plenipotentiary to Russia (1862–63).

Cameron, Verney Lovett 1844–94
English explorer

Born in Radipole, near Weymouth, Dorset, he joined the navy in 1857, taking part in the suppression of the slave trade. In 1872 he was appointed to lead an African east coast expedition to relieve David Livingstone. Starting from Bagamoyo in March 1873, in August, at Unyanyembe, he met Livingstone's followers carrying his remains to the coast. Cameron made a survey of Lake Tanganyika, and in the belief that the Lualaba was the upper Congo, he set out to follow its course to the west coast. Meeting some local hostility on his journey, he struck south-west, and reached Benguela on 7 November 1875, the first European to cross Africa from coast to coast. In 1878 he travelled overland to India, to satisfy himself of the feasibility of a Constantinople (Istanbul)–Baghdad railway, and in 1882, with Sir Richard Burton, he visited the Gold Coast. He died in a hunting accident.

Camillus, Marcus Furius 447–365BC
Roman general and statesman

He is best known for the capture and destruction in 396BC, of Rome's greatest rival of the day, the Etruscan city of Veii, and for driving the Gauls under Brennus out of Rome (387–386). For this he came to be regarded as the saviour and second founder of Rome. Many other military achievements were later attributed to him, as well as numerous civic offices, but most of these (including at least three of his five dictatorships) are no longer considered to be historical. There is a life of him by Plutarch.

Camm, Sir Sydney 1893–1966
English aircraft designer

Born in Windsor, Berkshire, he was secretary of the Windsor Model Aeroplane Club (1912) and designer to the Martinsyde Company (1914). He joined the Hawker Engineering Company (which later became Hawker Siddeley Aviation) in 1923, and became their chief designer (1925–66), a post he retained until his death. He had a unique design record of highly successful single-engined military aircraft, notably the Fury, Hart and Demon biplanes, and his first monoplane, the Hurricane. He also designed the Tornado, Typhoon, Tempest, and the jet-engined Sea Hawk, Hunter and the jump-jet Harrier, the only jet-lift type to enter long-term service with four air forces.

Camoëns or Camões, Luis de 1524–80
Portuguese poet

Born in Lisbon, he studied for the church at Coimbra, but declined to take orders. Returning to Lisbon, probably in 1542, he fell in love with Donna Caterina Ataide, but her father opposed the marriage. He was banished from Lisbon for a year, and joining a Portuguese force at Ceuta, served there for two years, losing an eye. In 1550 he returned to Lisbon, where he was thrown into prison for his share in a street brawl, and released only on his volunteering to go to India. While in Goa (1553–55) his denunciations of the Portuguese officials led to an honourable exile in Macao (1556). Returning to Goa (1558) he was shipwrecked and lost everything except his great epic poem, *Os Lusiadas* (the *Lusiads*). He was imprisoned in Goa, but after an exile of 16 years, he returned to Lisbon to spend the remainder of his life. He wrote plays, sonnets and lyrics but is best remembered for his *Os Lusiadas* which was published in 1572 and was an immediate success. It took as its subject the history of Portugal, and did for the Portuguese language what **Chaucer** did for English and **Dante** for Italian. The Portuguese came to regard it as their national epic. 💻 W Freitas, *Camoens and his Epic: a Historic, Geographic and Cultural Background* (1963)

Camp, Maxime See Du Camp, Maxime

Camp, Walter Chauncy 1859–1925
US footballer

He was born in New Britain, Connecticut. At Yale University (1888–92) he helped to shape American football rules, introducing the 11-man side (as against 15), the concept of 'downs' and 'yards gained', and the creation of a new points-scoring system. He also pioneered the notion of the All-American side, a somewhat bizarre concept since such a selection had no opposition abroad against which it could be measured. He is known as the 'father of American football'.

Campagnola, Domenico c.1490–c.1564
Italian painter

A pupil of **Giulio Campagnola** and assistant of **Titian**, he is known for his religious frescoes in Padua, and also for engravings and line drawings, such as *The Shepherd Musicians* (c. 1515, British Museum, London), in the manner of Titian.

Campagnola, Giulio 1482–c.1515
Italian engraver

Born in Padua, he designed type for **Aldus Manutius**, and produced engravings after **Andrea Mantegna**, **Giovanni Bellini** and **Giorgione**.

Campana, Dino 1885–1932
Italian poet

Originating from Marradi near Florence, he was for the last 12 years of his life a patient in a mental hospital, a victim of the manic depression which had dominated his life. He earned his living in many ways, and was often jailed as a vagrant. However, he was almost inordinately gifted as an incantatory and visionary poet, and his *Canti Orfici* (1914, Eng trans *Orphic Songs*, 1968), has been recognized as a work of genius.

Campanella, Tommaso 1568–1639
Italian philosopher

Born in Stilo, Calabria, he entered the Dominican order in 1583, and taught at Rome and Naples. He evolved an empirical, anti-Scholastic philosophy, presented in his work *Philosophia sensibus demonstrata* (1591, 'Philosophy Demonstrated by the Senses'), for which he was imprisoned and tortured by the Inquisition. He was arrested again in 1599 for heresy and conspiracy against Spanish rule, and was not finally released until 1626. From prison he wrote his famous utopian work, *La Città del Sole* (c.1602, *City of the Sun*), as well as other religious works and some poetry. He eventually fled to Paris in 1634, as a protégé of Cardinal **Richelieu**.

Campbell
Ancient Scottish family

Its members have held the titles of **Argyll**, Breadalbane and Cawdor. Sir Duncan Campbell of Lochow was created Lord Campbell (1445), and his successor was created Earl of Argyll (1457). From his younger son, Sir Colin Campbell of Glenorchy (c.1400–78), are descended the earls and marquises of Breadalbane and from the younger son of the second Earl of Argyll, who fell at Flodden (1513), the earls of Cawdor.

Campbell, Alexander 1788–1866
US pastor, leader of the Disciples of Christ, or Campbellites

Born near Ballymena, Antrim, Northern Ireland, he emigrated with his family to the USA in 1809, his father, **Thomas Campbell** (1763–1854), having emigrated earlier in 1807. In 1813 he succeeded his father as pastor of an independent church at Brush Run, Pennsylvania. He advocated a return to the simple church of New Testament times, and in 1826 published a translation of the New Testament, in which the word 'baptism' gave place to 'immersion'. In 1841 he founded Bethany College in West Virginia.

Campbell, Charles Arthur 1897–1974
Scottish philosopher

Born in Glasgow, he was educated at Glasgow Academy, Glasgow University, and Balliol College, Oxford. He was a teacher of moral philosophy in Glasgow before becoming Professor of Philosophy at the University College of North Wales, Bangor (1932). He returned to Glasgow as Professor of Logic and Rhetoric (1938–61). His unfashionable yet indefatigable pursuit of the traditional concerns of philosophy against the trend to reduce the subject to questions of linguistic analysis is demonstrated in *Scepticism and Construction* (1931), his 1953–55 Gifford Lectures expanded as *On Selfhood and Godhood* (1957), and selected essays written during the period 1935–62, were published as *In Defence of Free Will* (1967).

Campbell, Colen 1679–1726
Scottish architect

Born either in Nairn or in Argyll, he began work as a lawyer, moving to London c.1710. His earliest recorded design was Shawfield Mansion, Glasgow (1712, demolished 1795) and he was apparently associated with James Smith, a leading Scottish classicist architect, possibly as his pupil. A prime instigator of British neo-Palladianism, he produced the influential *Vitruvius Britannicus* (1712, 1718, 1725) named after the Roman architect **Marcus Vitruvius Pollio**. His designs set precedents from which British Palladianism evolved. In 1728 he published a revision of **Andrea Palladio's** *First Book of Architecture*. His best-known buildings include Rolls House (1717), Burlington House (1718–19) and Wanstead House, London (1714–20, demolished 1824), Mereworth Castle, Kent (1722–25), echoing a Palladian villa, Houghton Hall, Norfolk (1722–26), and Compton Place, Eastbourne (1726–27).

Campbell, Sir Colin, Baron Clyde 1792–1863
Scottish field marshal

Born in Glasgow, he assumed the name of Campbell from his mother's brother. He served on the Walcheren expedition (1809), and throughout the Peninsular War (1804–14) against **Napoleon I**, where he was twice badly wounded. He took part in the expedition to the USA (1814), then spent nearly 30 years in garrison duty at Gibraltar, Barbados, Demerara, and England, in 1837 becoming lieutenant-colonel of the 98th foot. He fought in the brief Chinese campaign of 1842, and in the second Sikh War (1848–49), afterwards commanding for three years at Peshawar against the frontier tribes. On the outbreak of the Crimean War (1854) he commanded the Highland Brigade, bringing about the victory of Alma and repulsing the Russians with the celebrated 'thin red line' at the Battle of Balaclava. On the outbreak of the Indian Mutiny (1857), Lord Palmerston offered him command of the forces in India: he effected the final relief of Lucknow (1857), was created Baron Clyde (1858), and brought the rebellion to an end (December 1858). He returned the next year to England and was made a field marshal.

Campbell, Donald Malcolm 1921–67
English car and speedboat racer

He was born in Horley, Surrey. An engineer by training, he sought to emulate the achievements of his father, Sir Malcolm Campbell (1885–1949), and set new world speed records several times on both land and water, culminating in 1964 with a water-speed record of 276.33 mph on Lake Dumbleyung in Australia, and a land-speed record of 403.1 mph at Lake Eyre salt flats in Australia. In an attempt to become the first man to break 300 mph on water, he was killed when his *Bluebird* turbo-jet hydroplane crashed on Lake Coniston in England. ▢ Phil Drackett, *Like Father Like Son: The Story of Malcolm and Donald Campbell* (1969)

Campbell, John Archibald 1859–1909
Scottish architect

He studied at the École des Beaux Arts, Paris, and is regarded as an early pioneer of the vertical articulation of tall buildings. From 1886 to 1897 he was in partnership with John J Burnet in Glasgow with whom he produced the Athenaeum Theatre (1891) in a wilfully asymmetrical free style. One of his major independent works was the Northern Insurance Building in Glasgow (1908–09) where he contrasted a vertically proportioned Scots Renaissance façade with a functional rear elevation, and pioneered a steel frame which gave maximum daylighting from the cramped rear court. He also designed numerous houses, especially around his own home at Bridge of Weir.

Campbell, John Campbell, 1st Baron
1779–1861
Scottish judge

Born in Cupar, Fife, he studied theology at St Andrews University, turned to law and journalism, and was called to the English Bar in 1806. A Whig MP (1830–49), he was knighted and made Solicitor General in 1832, becoming Attorney General in 1834, when he sponsored some important reforming Acts. Created a baron in 1841, he was appointed successively Lord Chancellor of Ireland (1841), Chancellor of the Duchy of Lancaster (1846), Chief Justice of the Queen's Bench (1850), and Lord Chancellor (1859). His *Lives of the Lord Chancellors* (1845–47) and *Lives of the Chief Justices* (1849–57) are marred by prejudiced comments and, in later volumes, by inaccuracy.

Campbell (of Islay), John Francis 1822–85
Scottish folklorist

Born on the island of Islay, Inner Hebrides, he was educated at Eton and Edinburgh University. He held offices at court, and was then secretary to the lighthouse and coal commissions. An enthusiastic Highlander and profound Gaelic scholar, he collected folk traditions which he translated and published in *Popular Tales of the West Highlands* (4 vols, 1860–62).

Campbell, Kim (Avril Phaedra) 1947–
Canadian politician

Born in British Columbia, she was a talented musician but decided to study political science at the University of British Columbia and then at the London School of Economics. After returning to Vancouver she trained in law and practised there, at the same time becoming involved in provincial politics. In the 1988 election, she switched to national politics when she was elected a parliamentary member of the Progressive Conservative Party under Brian Mulroney, whose controversial free trade agreement with the USA she openly supported. She soon became a Cabinet member as Justice Minister (1990–93) then Defence Minister (1993). She succeeded Mulroney in June 1993, becoming Canada's first woman Prime Minister, but in October that year she and all but two of her Party's candidates lost their parliamentary seats in the national election and the Liberal Party under Jean Chrétien took over.

Campbell, Mrs Patrick, *née* Beatrice Stella Tanner 1865–1940
English actress

She was born in Kensington, London, of mixed English and Italian parentage. She married in 1884, and went on the stage in 1888. Though her mercurial temperament made her the terror of managers, she possessed outstanding charm and talent, and leapt to fame in *The Second Mrs Tanqueray* (1893). Her first husband died in South Africa in 1900 and she married George Cornwallis-West in 1914. She played Eliza in George Bernard Shaw's *Pygmalion* (1914) and formed a long friendship with the author. ▢ Alan Dent, *Mrs Patrick Campbell* (1961)

Campbell, Reginald John 1867–1956
English clergyman

He was born in London. He entered the Congregational ministry in 1895 and was pastor of the City Temple, London (1903–15). In 1907 he startled the evangelical world by his exposition of an 'advanced' *New Theology*. He became an Anglican in 1916. He wrote a biography of David Livingstone in 1929. Other works included *The Call of Christ* (1933) and *The Peace of God* (1936).

Campbell, (Ignatius) Roy(ston) Dunnachie
1901–57
South African poet and journalist

Born in Durban, he moved to England in 1918. He subsequently returned to South Africa and lived in France. He became an ardent admirer of all things Spanish and claimed erroneously to have fought with General Franco's armies during the civil war. His great poems include 'Tristan de Cunha' and his books of poetry include *The Flaming Terrapin* (1924), *The Wayzgoose* (1928), *Adamastor* (1930), *The Georgiad* (1931), *Mithraic Emblems* (1936) and the pro-Fascist *Flowering Rifle* (1939). A collected edition of his poems appeared in 1949, and he published two autobiographical volumes: *Broken Record* (1934) and *Light on a Dark Horse* (1951). He was killed in a car crash in Portugal. ▢ P Alexander, *Roy Campbell* (1982); *Light on a Dark Horse* (1951, autobiography); *Collected Poems* (3 vols, 1949–60)

Campbell, Thomas 1763–1854
US clergyman and religious leader

Born in Ireland, he emigrated to Pennsylvania in 1807 and served a congregation of followers known as Campbellites. In 1809 he was joined by his son Alexander Campbell, also a clergyman. Nominally Baptists, they strove to practise a primitive Christianity based solely on the Scriptures, without church hierarchy or additional theology. In 1832 they joined with splinter groups from other sects to form the Disciples of Christ.

Campbell, Thomas 1777–1844
Scottish poet and journalist

Born and educated in Glasgow, he went to Edinburgh in 1797 to study law, but became increasingly interested in reading and writing poetry. *The Pleasures of Hope*, published in 1799, ran through four editions in a year. He travelled on the Continent from 1800 to 1801, but in 1803 he married and settled in London, having refused a professorship at Wilna. He contributed articles to *The Edinburgh Encyclopaedia*, compiled *The Annals of Great Britain from George II to the Peace of Amiens*, and in 1809 published *Gertrude of Wyoming*. In 1818 he visited Germany again, and on his return published his *Specimens of the British Poets* (1819). He lectured on poetry and edited *The New Monthly Magazine* (1820–30), contributing 'The Last Man' and other poems. He was buried in Westminster Abbey, London.'Hohenlinden','Ye Mariners of England'and 'The Battle of the Baltic' are among his best-known poems. 📖 W Beattie, *Life and Letters of Thomas Campbell* (1849)

Campbell, William Wallace 1862–1938
US astronomer

Born in Hancock County, Ohio, he joined the Lick Observatory in California in 1891, becoming director (1901–30) and was also president of the University of California (1923–30). He is best known for his work on the radial velocity of stars. He led seven expeditions to study solar eclipses and elucidated the Sun's motion within the galaxy.

Campbell, William Wilfred 1860–1919
Canadian poet

Born in Kitchener, Ontario, he became an Anglican clergyman, and joined the Canadian Civil Service in 1891. He was author of *Lake Lyrics* (1889) and other volumes of poetry, and was editor of the *Oxford Book of Canadian Verse* (1906). 📖 C Klinck, *William Campbell, a study in late provincial Victorianism* (1942)

Campbell-Bannerman, Sir Henry 1836–1908
Scottish Liberal statesman

Born in Glasgow, he was the second son of Sir James Campbell, Lord Provost of Glasgow from 1840 to 1843. Educated at Glasgow and Trinity College, Cambridge, he became Liberal MP for Stirling in 1868 and assumed the name Bannerman in 1872. He was Chief Secretary for Ireland (1884), Secretary for War (1886, 1892–95), Liberal leader (1899), and Prime Minister (1905–08). A 'pro-Boer', he granted the ex-republics responsible government out of which grew the Union of South Africa. He launched the campaign against the House of Lords to reduce its power, which culminated in the passing of the momentous Parliament Act of 1911 after the Lords had blocked David Lloyd George's 'Peoples Budget'. He resigned on 4 April 1908, and died 11 April. 📖 John Wilson, *CB: A Life of Sir Henry Campbell-Bannerman* (1974)

Campeggio, Lorenzo 1472–1539
Italian prelate

Born in Bologna, he studied law, married early, and after his wife's death took orders. He was made Bishop of Feltri (1512), a cardinal (1517), papal legate to England to incite Henry VIII against the Turks (1518), and Bishop of Salisbury and Archbishop of Bologna (1524). Joint judge with Cardinal Wolsey in the divorce suit against Catherine of Aragon, he ended by displeasing all parties.

Campen, Jacob van 1595–1657
Dutch architect and painter

Born in Haarlem, he was greatly influenced by Italian style and built the first completely classical building in Holland. His masterpiece was the Maurithuis, The Hague (1633) for Prince Johan Maurits von Nassau but the interior was destroyed in 1704. Other works include Amsterdam Theatre (1637), based on Andrea Palladio's Theatro Olympico, and Amsterdam Town Hall (1647–55, now the royal palace), a large classical building around

two courts with a huge sculptured pediment depicting the oceans paying homage to Amsterdam, which was both a monument to the Peace of Munster and to the city itself.

Campendonck, Heinrich 1889–1957
German Expressionist painter

Born in Krefeld, he was a member of the Blaue Reiter ('Blue Rider') group founded by Franz Marc and Wassily Kandinsky. He emigrated to Holland in 1933.

Campenhout, François von 1779–1849
Belgian composer and violinist

Born in Brussels, he wrote several works, but is best remembered for *La Brabançonne* (1830, the Belgian national anthem).

Camper, Pieter 1722–89
Dutch anatomist

He was born in Leyden. Professor at Franeker (1749–61), Amsterdam (1761–63), and Groningen (1763–73), he wrote a series of works on human and comparative anatomy, and discovered the large air content of the bones of birds.

Camphuysen, Dirck Rafaelsz 1586–1627
Dutch religious poet and painter

Born in Gorinchem, he studied painting, then became a priest, but was dismissed and persecuted because of his Arminianism, which denies the Calvinistic doctrine of predestination. Thereafter he lived in poverty, making a meagre living as a flax dealer. Translations of his poetry are in *Batavian Anthology* (1824). 📖 L A Rademaker, *Dirck Camphuysen* (1898, in Dutch)

Campi, Antonio c.1536–c.1591
Italian painter and architect

He was born in Cremona, and was the brother of Giulio and Vincenzo Campi. He was a successful imitator of Correggio.

Campi, Bernardino 1522–c.1592
Italian artist

He was born in Cremona, the son of a goldsmith. He imitated Titian with such success that it has been difficult to distinguish the copies from the originals. His works may be seen in Mantua and Cremona. He was possibly a kinsman of Antonio Campi.

Campi, Giulio 1502–72
Italian architect and painter

Born in Cremona, he was the elder brother of Antonio and Vincenzo Campi. He studied under Giulio Romano and has left a fine altarpiece in San Abbondio in Cremona.

Campi, Vincenzo 1536–91
Italian painter

Born in Cremona, he was the brother of Antonio and Giulio Campi. He was at his most impressive in small figures and painted portraits.

Campin, Robert, usually identified as the Master of Flémalle c.1375–1444
Netherlandish artist

He has been identified as probably the Master of Flémalle from three paintings in the Städelsches Kunstinstitut in Frankfurt that were erroneously held to have originated in Flémalle. About 1400 he settled in Tournai, where Rogier van der Weyden and Jaques Daret (1406–c.1468) were his pupils, and supposedly learned technical secrets from Hubet van Eyck, the brother of Jan van Eyck. His *Madonna* and the pair of portraits of a man and his wife in the National Gallery, London, show him to have been a painter of rude vigour who made innovative use of realism.

Campion, St Edmund 1540–81

English Jesuit

Born in London, he was educated at Christ's Hospital and St John's College, Oxford. He became a deacon in the Church of England (1569), but his Roman Catholic sympathies were noticed, so he escaped to Douai in France, and in 1573 joined the Society of Jesus in Bohemia. He became Professor of Rhetoric at Prague, but in 1580 was recalled for a Jesuit mission to England. He circulated his *Decem Rationes* ('Ten Reasons') against Anglicanism in 1581, was arrested, tortured, tried on a charge of conspiracy, and hanged in London. He was beatified in 1886 and canonized as one of the 40 Martyrs of England and Wales in 1970. His feast day is 25 October.

Campion, Jane 1954–

New Zealand film director

Born in Wellington, she was trained at the Australian Film, Television and Radio School in Sydney, Australia, and her debut short, *Peel* (1982), won the Cannes Palme D'Or for Best Short Film. Her first feature-length piece, *Two Friends* (1986) was for Australian television, and she made her feature film debut with *Sweetie* (1989), a character study of a schizophrenic. She then made the three-part television series *An Angel At My Table* (1990), a dramatization of the autobiographies of **Janet Frame**. She won seven awards at the Venice Film Festival of 1990, and shared the Cannes Palme D'Or for *The Piano* (1993), the first such award for an Australian production as well as for a woman director. The film also secured her an Academy Award for Best Original Screenplay. In 1996 she directed *Portrait of a Lady*, adapted from the novel by **Henry James**.

Campion, Thomas 1567–1620

English physician, poet and composer

Born in Witham, Essex, he studied at Cambridge and abroad, and set his own lyrics to music. As well as poetry in Latin and English he left several books of 'ayres' for voice and lute. He also wrote a treatise, *Observations in the Art of English Rhyme* (1602). ▢ M Kastendieck, *England's Musical Poet: Thomas Campion* (1938)

Campoamor, Clara 1888–1972

Spanish politician and feminist

Of working-class origins, she graduated in law in 1924, and from then onwards became one of the principal figures in the struggle for women's rights in Spain. In 1931 she was elected to the Constituent Cortes of the Second Republic as a deputy for the Radical Republican Party. She was largely responsible for the inclusion of women's suffrage in the Constitution of 1931. During the legislature of 1931–33 she was vice-president of the Labour Commission and participated in the reform of the Civil Code. She also represented Spain at the League of Nations and founded the Republican Feminine Union. She was Director-General of Charity (1933–34). During the 1930s she wrote extensively on women's rights and aspirations. In 1938 she chose exile in Buenos Aires, moving in 1955 to Lausanne, where she died.

Campoamor, Ramón de 1817–1901

Spanish poet

Born in Navia, he studied medicine, almost became a Jesuit, and ultimately chose a career in politics and literature. His short, epigrammatic poems, including those in *Doloras* (1858, 'Laments'), *Pequeños poemas* (1871, 'Little Poems') and *Humoradas* (1890), represent his most significant literary contribution, but he also wrote longer poems, including *El drama universal* (1869, 'The Universal Drama') and *El tren expreso* (1874, 'The Express Train'). ▢ V Gaos, *La Poética de Campoamor* (1955)

Campoli, Alfredo 1906–91

Italian violinist

Born in Rome, he went to London in 1911, and quickly won a reputation as a soloist. During the lean years of the 1930s he became better known for his salon orchestra. This was disbanded at the outbreak of World War II, after which he emerged as one of the most distinguished violinists of his time.

Campos Salles, Manuel Ferraz de 1841–1913

Brazilian politician

Regarded as the 'political architect of the Republic', he was a slave-owner, fazendeiro and lawyer in Campinas, then the centre of the coffee-growing region of Brazil. He became a Republican in the 1870s and was Minister of Justice in the Provisional Government of the Republic (1889–91), when he was responsible for the separation of Church and State and the introduction of civil marriage. He was Governor of São Paulo (1896–98), and then became President (1898–1902). Charged with radical financial reform, designed to protect the country from foreign intervention, and pledged to a privatization programme, he emasculated a nationalist Congress by agreeing a pact with incumbent governors: the President would protect them from federal intervention if they, in their turn, pledged their support for him in Congress. This system, known as the 'Politics of the Governors', led to one-party state administrations and provided the basis for political management until 1930; vestiges of it remain to this day.

Camrose, William Ewert Berry, 1st Viscount 1879–1954

Welsh newspaper proprietor

He was born in Merthyr Tydfil, South Wales. After working on local newspapers, he founded (in 1901), with his brother Gomer Berry, 1st Viscount Kemsley, *The Advertising World*. In 1915 the brothers acquired the *Sunday Times* and during the 1920s gained control of more than 100 national and provincial publications. In 1928 he became managing editor of the *Daily Telegraph*. He was made a peer in 1941, and in 1947, at the time of the Royal Commission on the Press, published *British Newspapers and their Controllers*.

Camus, Albert 1913–60

French writer and Nobel Prize winner

Born in Mondovi, Algeria, the son of a farm labourer, he studied philosophy at Algiers and, interrupted by long spells of ill health, became an actor, schoolmaster, playwright and journalist there and in Paris. Active in the French Resistance during World War II, he became co-editor with **Jean-Paul Sartre** of the left-wing newspaper *Combat* after the liberation until 1948, when he broke with Sartre and 'committed' political writing. Having earned an international reputation with his Existentialist novel, *L'Étranger* (1942, Eng trans *The Outsider*, 1946), 'the study of an absurd man in an absurd world', he set himself in his subsequent work the aim of elucidating some values for man confronted with cosmic meaninglessness. *Le Mythe de Sisyphe* (1942, Eng trans *The Myth of Sisyphus*, 1955), concerning suicide, *L'Homme révolté* (1951, Eng trans *The Rebel*, 1954), on the harm done by surrendering to ideologies, the magnanimous letters to a German friend (1945), and a second masterpiece *La Peste* (1947, Eng trans *The Plague*, 1948), were followed by a return to extreme ironical pessimism in *La Chute* (1956, Eng trans *The Fall*, 1957). *Le Malentendu* (1945, Eng trans *Cross Purpose*, 1947) and *Caligula* (1938, Eng trans 1947) are his best plays. His political writings are collected in *Actuelles I* (1950, 'Chronicles of Today I') and *II* (1953). He was awarded the 1957 Nobel Prize for literature. Three years later he died in a car accident and in his briefcase was found an unfinished autobiographical novel, *Le Premier Homme* (Eng trans *The First Man*, 1995), which was then edited and

published by his daughter Cathérine Camus in 1995. ⌨ P
Thody, *Albert Camus 1913–1960* (1962); H Lottman, *Camus: a biography* (1979)

Canaletto, *properly* Giovanni Antonio Canal
1697–1768
Italian painter

Born in Venice, the son of a theatrical scene-painter, he studied in Rome but returned to Venice in 1730. Between 1746 and 1756 he worked in England where his views of London and elsewhere proved popular, and on his return to Venice his dramatic and picturesque views of that city became immensely popular with foreign visitors, especially the English. He is essentially a topographical painter—even today the views of Venice he depicts are remarkably unchanged—but he often shows a poetic response to his subjects. Unlike his rival Francesco Guardi, he enjoyed extraordinary commercial success. His nephew and pupil Bernardo Bellotto, became known as Canaletto the Younger.

Canaris, Wilhelm 1887–1945
German naval commander

Born in Aplerbeck, he joined the Imperial German Navy in 1905, and served in the *Dresden* at the battles of Coronel and the Falklands in World War I. He escaped from internment in Chile and made his way back to Germany, and served in U-boats in the Mediterranean. He retired as rear admiral in 1934. Though disapproving of aspects of the Nazi regime, he rose under Hitler to become admiral in the German navy and chief of the *Abwehr*, the military intelligence service of the High Command of the armed forces. Involved in the anti-Nazi resistance and associated with the 1944 bomb plot against Hitler, he was arrested, imprisoned, and hanged in April 1945, just before the entry of the Russian army into Berlin.

Candela, (Outeriño) Felix 1910–
Mexican architect and engineer

Born in Spain, he studied at the University of Madrid and fled to Mexico in 1939 as a Republican refugee from the Spanish Civil War. He worked as construction foreman, builder, architect and structural engineer to become one of the world's foremost designers of slender reinforced-concrete hyperbolic paraboloid shell roofs. His creations have included the Sports Palace for the Olympic Games in Mexico City (1968). He emigrated to the USA in 1971.

Candlish, Robert Smith 1806–73
Scottish ecclesiastic

Born in Edinburgh, he was minister from 1834 of St George's, Edinburgh. After the Disruption (1843) he co-operated with Dr Thomas Chalmers in organizing the Free Church, and from Chalmers's death (1847) was, in effect, its leader. He was made Moderator of the Free Assembly in 1861, and Principal of the New College in 1862.

Candolle, Alphonse Louis Pierre Pyrame de
1806–93
Swiss botanist

He was born in Geneva, the son of Augustin Pyrame de Candolle, and succeeded his father as professor at Geneva University in 1842. He defined the methods for the study of plant geography, and published the great *Géographie botanique raisonnée* (2 vols, 1855) and *Origine des plantes cultivées* (1883). In these works he described extensively the role of temperature in geographic distribution, and established the optimum temperature range for plant growth, one of the major factors in determining the ranges of particular species. He also tackled the problem of the origins of existing species, concluding that their creation was successive and evolutionary.

Candolle, Augustin Pyrame de 1778–1841
Swiss botanist

Born in Geneva, he studied chemistry, physics and botany at the universities of Geneva and Paris, and became Professor of Botany at Montpellier (1808) and Geneva (1817). His earliest work, on lichens (1797), was followed by *Astragalogia* (1802) and *Propriétés médicales des plantes* (1804). He was the first to use the word 'taxonomy' for his classification of plants by their morphology, rather than physiology, as set out in his *Théorie élémentaire de la botanique* (1813), and he defined the natural method of plant classification, a system based on observation of the whole plant, rather than by concentrating on a single character. He continued his work in *Regni Vegetabilis Systema Naturale* (1818–21) and the multi-volume *Prodromus Systematis Naturalis Regni Vegetabilis* which began publication in 1824, and which greatly increased the number of recognized plant families.

Canetti, Elias 1905–94
Bulgarian writer and Nobel Prize winner

He was born in Rutschuk, Bulgaria, into a community of Spanish-speaking Jews. In his formative years he moved between England, Switzerland, Austria and Germany and was educated in Zurich and Frankfurt and at the University of Vienna. From 1938 Canetti lived in Great Britain. The works for which he is best known are his novel on the growth of totalitarianism, *Die Blendung* (1935–36, Eng trans *Auto-da-Fé*, 1946), and a speculative study of the psychology of mass behaviour, *Masse und Macht* (1960, Eng trans *Crowds and Power*, 1962). His autobiographies, *Die gerettete Zunge: Geschichte einer Jugenol* (1977, Eng trans *The Tongue Set Free*, 1979) and *Die Fackel im Ohr* (1980, Eng trans *The Torch in my Ear*, 1982), emphasized the origins of and inspiration for his life's work. He was awarded the Nobel Prize for literature in 1981. ⌨ D Barnouw, *Canetti* (1979)

Caniff, Milt(on Arthur) 1907–88
US strip cartoonist

Born in Hillsboro, Ohio, he joined Associated Press in 1922 to draw the daily jokes, *Mr Gilfeather* and *GayThirties*. In 1933 he created his first daily strip, *Dickie Dare*, the globe-trotting adventures of a young boy, then joined the *New York Daily News* to create a similar serial, *Terry and the Pirates* (1934), where the adventures grew increasingly adult as Terry grew older. In World War II, Caniff drew a sexy strip, *Male Call*, for servicemen. Suddenly abandoning *Terry*, he created a new series about an ex-pilot, *Steve Canyon* (1947), which continued until the artist's death.

Canmore, Malcolm See Malcolm III

Canning, Charles John, 1st Earl 1812–62
English politician

He entered Parliament in 1836 as Conservative MP for Warwick, but the next year was raised to the House of Lords as Viscount Canning by his mother's death, both his elder brothers having predeceased her. In 1841 he became Under-Secretary in the Foreign Office, and in 1856 succeeded Lord Dalhousie as Governor-General of India. The war with Persia (Iran) was brought to a successful close in 1857. In the same year, the Indian Uprising began with the outbreak at Meerut. Canning's conduct was described at the time as weak — he was nicknamed 'Clemency Canning' — but this opinion was later revised. In 1858 he became the first Viceroy of India, and in 1859 became an earl.

Canning, George 1770–1827
English statesman

Born in London, he was raised and educated by his uncle after the death of his father when Canning was only one year old. He attended Eton and Christ Church, Oxford, and was admitted to the Bar before entering Parliament in 1794 and becoming Under-Secretary of State under **William Pitt**, the Younger (1796). He was navy treasurer (1801), and as Foreign Affairs Minister from 1807 in Lord **Portland**'s Cabinet he planned the seizure of the Dutch fleet that prevented **Napoleon I**'s planned invasion. His dispute with Lord **Castlereagh** over the Walcheren expedition resulted in a duel between them in which Canning was slightly wounded. As MP for Liverpool from 1812, he was a strong advocate of Catholic emancipation, and continued to support Lord **Liverpool** until resigning in 1820 in protest at the Government's action against Queen **Caroline**. After Castlereagh's suicide in 1822, he became Foreign Minister again, and on the death of Liverpool in 1827 he became Prime Minister in a coalition with the Whigs, but died later the same year. A notable orator, he was buried in Westminster Abbey near Pitt. ◫ H W V Temperley, *Life of Canning* (1905)

Canning, Sir Stratford See **Stratford (de Redcliffe), 1st Viscount**

Cannizzaro, Stanislao 1826–1910
Italian organic chemist and legislator
Born in Palermo, he studied in Palermo, Pisa and Turin. Condemned to death for his part in the Sicilian Revolution in 1848, he fled to Paris, then taught in Alessandria, Piedmont, before becoming Professor of Chemistry at Genoa (1855). In 1860 he supported **Garibaldi**'s Sicilian revolt. He was appointed Professor of Chemistry at Palermo (1861) and Rome (1871). He did much to co-ordinate organic and inorganic chemistry, showing that the same laws apply to both. He realized the significance of the discovery by **Amedeo Avogadro** that equal volumes of different gases at the same temperatures and pressures contain equal numbers of molecules. His greatest achievement was to recognize the difference between atomic weight and molecular weight, a discovery fundamental to the future development of chemistry. He also discovered that benzaldehyde reacts with potassium hydroxide to form benzoic acid and benzyl alcohol (the Cannizzaro reaction) and gave the name 'hydroxyl' to the OH radical. An inspiring teacher, he devoted much energy to matters of public health and other civic duties and was made a senator in 1871.

Cannon, Annie Jump 1863–1941
US astronomer
Born in Dover, Delaware, the daughter of a wealthy shipbuilder, she was one of the first women from Delaware to attend university (Wellesley College), graduating in 1884. She then studied astronomy at Radcliffe College. In 1896 she joined the staff of Harvard College Observatory under its director **Edward Pickering** in a major programme of classification of stellar spectra. She classified the spectra of 225,300 stars brighter than magnitude 8.5, published in the nine volumes of the *Henry Draper Catalogue*. Pickering's successor **Harlow Shapley** decided to extend the catalogue to fainter stars, of which she classified 130,000. She received many honours, among them the Henry Draper Gold Medal of the US National Academy of Sciences and honorary doctorates from the universities of Groningen and Oxford. She was inducted into the National Women's Hall of Fame in 1994.

Cannon, Joseph Gurney, *also called* Uncle Joe 1836–1926
US politician
Born in Guilford County, North Carolina, he practised law in Illinois and was elected to the US House of Representatives as a Republican in 1872, serving a total of 46 years in Congress. While Speaker of the House (1903–11) he used his power autocratically to favour the 'Old Guard' Republicans, prompting his opponents to pass a bill reforming House rules and curtailing the speaker's power.

Cannon, Walter Bradford 1871–1945
US physiologist
Born in Prairie du Chien, Wisconsin, he was associated with Harvard University for most of his career. He investigated many physiological problems, including digestion (using X-rays to study the movement of barium in the alimentary tract), and argued that the sympathetic nerves prepared an animal for 'fight or flight', through increasing heart rate, blood pressure, etc, with the two branches of the autonomic system acting together to maintain a large number of physiological functions, which he named homeostasis. During World War I, he studied the mechanism of traumatic shock on the battlefield, and in 1939 discovered sympathin, a stimulant for certain organs. After the Spanish civil war he helped to find posts for scientists and physicians who opposed Franco, and also assisted many victims of Nazi Germany. His death at the age of 73 was the result of a neoplasm caused by exposure to X-rays during his research.

Cano, Alonso 1601–67
Spanish painter, sculptor and architect
Born in Granada, he studied in Seville, with **Velázquez**, under **Francisco Pacheco**. In 1639 he was appointed court painter and architect. He designed the façade of Coranada Cathedral (c.1664).

Cano or **Elcano, Juan Sebastian del** d.1526
Basque navigator
He was born in Guetaria, on the Bay of Biscay. In 1519 he sailed with **Ferdinand Magellan** in command of the *Concepción*, and, after Magellan's death in the Philippines, safely navigated the *Victoria* home to Spain, arriving in 1522. He was the first man to circumnavigate the globe.

Canova, Antonio 1757–1822
Italian sculptor
Born in Possagno, he studied in Venice and Rome, and after his *Theseus* (1782, Victoria and Albert Museum, London), came to be regarded as the founder of a new Neoclassical school. He created the tombs of popes Clement XIII (1787–92) and Clement XIV (1783–87), and in 1802 he was appointed curator of works of art by Pius VII, and was called to Paris to model a colossal statue of Napoleon I. Other works include a statue of Pauline Bonaparte (Princess Borghese) reclining as Venus Victrix (1805–07, Borghese Gallery, Rome), and the sculpture *The Three Graces* (begun 1814, National Gallery of Scotland, Edinburgh, and Victoria and Albert Museum, London). In 1815 the pope sent him again to Paris to recover the works of art removed from Rome, and he also visited England.

Cánovas del Castillo, Antonio 1828–97
Spanish politician and historian
A Conservative, he became a member of the Cortes in 1854, and was premier (1875–81, 1884–85, 1890–92, 1895–97). He was the architect of the oligarchical Restoration System, which survived until the dictatorship of General Primo de Rivera (1923–30). He was shot by an anarchist.

Cantacuzenus, John VI 1292–1383
Byzantine soldier and ruler
He was a powerful courtier in the reigns of **Andronicus II** and **III**, and at the death of Andronicus III (1341) he became guardian of his son, John V (1332–91), then nine years old. Cantacuzenus, however, proclaimed himself the child's colleague, and after a six-year civil war made himself emperor (1347) with John V as colleague. In a

second war, during which the Turks occupied Gallipoli, he was forced to abdicate (1354). He retired to a monastery, where he died.

Cantelupe, St Thomas de, *also called* St Thomas of Hereford c.1218–1282
English prelate

Born near Henley-on-Thames, Oxfordshire, he studied at Oxford, Paris and Orleans, and was made Chancellor of Oxford University (1262). He supported the barons against Henry III, and was appointed Chancellor of England by Simon de Montfort (1264–65). Made Bishop of Hereford (1275), he became well known for his sense of justice and his kindness. Excommunicated by his archbishop in 1282, he took his case to Rome, but died on the way in Orvieto, and was canonized by Pope John XXII in 1320. His relics were taken to Hereford.

Canth, Minna, *née* Ulrika Vilhelmina Johnsson 1844–97
Finnish playwright and feminist

Born in Tampere, she began writing at 40 after an intensive course of self-education in literary and social history. Her reading, and her experience as the single parent of seven children, turned her into a radical. A powerful exponent of the Realist school, her best-known plays are *Työmiehen vaimo* (1885, 'A Working-class Wife') and *Kovan onnen lapsia* (1888, 'The Hard Luck Kids'). Later she turned to psychological dramas about women, such as *Anna Liisa* (1895). 📖 G von Frenckell-Thesleff, *Minna Canth* (1943)

Canton, John 1718–72
English physicist

He was born in Stroud, Gloucestershire, and became a schoolmaster in London despite having little formal education. His keen interest in natural philosophy was noticed by a neighbour and Fellow of the Royal Society, Dr Henry Miles (1698–1763), who was instrumental in Canton's election to the Royal Society in 1749. He was especially interested in atmospheric electricity, and was the first in England (1752) to confirm Benjamin Franklin's conjecture about the electrical nature of lightning. He determined that clouds could be charged either positively or negatively, for which he designed experiments on electrostatic induction, invented a portable electroscope (1754) and was the first to make powerful artificial magnets. In 1762 he showed the compressibility of water. He received the Royal Society's Copley Medal in 1765.

Cantona, Eric 1966–
French footballer

He was born in Paris. Known for his outstanding flair and fiery temperament, he became the first player to win two successive Premier League Championship titles with two different clubs. After 45 caps for France, a dispute with the coach led to suspension from his national team. He played for the French clubs at Auxerre, Martigues, Marseilles, Bordeaux, Montpellier and Nîmes, then moved to England, and joined Leeds United (1991–92), then Manchester United (from November 1992), and became a national hero. In 1994 he was suspended from Manchester United for a year after he kicked a fan kung-fu style.

Cantor, Charles Robert 1942–
US molecular geneticist

Born in Brooklyn, New York City, he was educated at Columbia University and the University of California at Berkeley. He has taught at Columbia University since 1966, and since 1981 has been chairman of the department of genetics and development. In 1984 he developed a pulse field gel technique to separate very large DNA molecules. He was director of the Human Genome Project at the University of California at Berkeley (1989–

90) before becoming its principal scientist in 1990. This worldwide project is designed to completely map the human genome, which will make it possible to learn the amino acid sequence of genes as yet unknown (possibly important disease-causing entities) and to identify DNA sequences which will be important in controlling genetic processes.

Cantor, Georg Ferdinand Ludwig Philipp 1845–1918
German mathematician

Born in St Petersburg, Russia, he studied in Berlin and in 1877 became Professor of Mathematics at Halle University. Building on work by Lejeune Dirichlet and Bernhard Riemann, he worked out a highly original arithmetic of the infinite, extending the concept of cardinal and ordinal numbers to infinite sets. Other aspects of his ideas on the theory of sets of points have become fundamental in topology and modern analysis. He also did important work on classical analysis, particularly in trigonometric series. His friend Julius Dedekind simultaneously developed a naive theory of sets, and their work was fused together around 1900 to become the setting for much subsequent work on the foundations of mathematics. His work did not receive immediate acceptance, and this may have contributed to the mental illness which he suffered after 1884.

Cantú, Cesare 1804–95
Italian historian and novelist

He was born in Brivio. Imprisoned as a liberal in 1833, he described the sorrows of a prisoner in the historical romance, *Margherita Pusterla* (1838). As well as his major history of the world, *Storia universale* (35 vols, 1836–42, 'A History of the World'), he wrote many works on Italian history and literature, as well as lighter works, and *Manzoni: Reminiscinze* (2 vols, 1883, 'Manzoni: Reminiscences'). 📖 G Grabinski, *Cesare Cantú* (1896)

Canute See Knut Sveinsson

Cão See Cam

Cao Yu (Ts'ao Yü), *pseudonym of* Wan Jiabao (Wan Chia-pao) 1910–96
Chinese playwright

Born in Tianjin (Tientsin), he studied western literature at Qinghua University, where he was profoundly influenced by Ibsen and George Bernard Shaw to attack the corruption of traditional society. His best-known work, *Thunderstorm*, was staged in 1935. His other major plays are *Sunrise* (1935), *Wilderness* (1936), *Metamorphosis* (1940), *Peking Man* (1940) and *The Family* (1941), adapted from the novel by Ba Jin. He toured the USA in 1946, and after the foundation of the People's Republic in 1949 he was appointed to numerous official posts. In 1979 he wrote the play *The Consort of Peace*. He is considered by many to be the most significant 20th-century dramatist in China.

Capa, Robert, *originally* Andrei Friedmann 1913–54
US photojournalist

Born in Budapest, Hungary, he worked in Berlin before moving to Paris in 1933. He recorded the Spanish civil war (1935–37) and China under the Japanese attacks of 1938. In 1939 he emigrated to the USA and covered World War II in Europe from the invasion of Normandy. Subsequently he reported on the early days of the state of Israel. He was killed by a land mine in the Indo-China fighting, which preceded the war in Vietnam. His images of war were a compassionate portrayal of the suffering of both soldiers and civilians. His brother, Cornell Capa (1918–), was also a photographer.

Capablanca, José Raúl 1888–1942
Cuban chess player

He was born in Havana. At the age of four he learned chess by watching his father's games, and within nine years he had defeated the Cuban champion, Corzo, in a match. A local industrialist sponsored his education in the USA, where he took an engineering degree at the University of Columbia. His spare time was devoted to chess at the Manhattan Club, New York, where he achieved a sensational win in a 1909 match against US champion Marshall. On his first appearance in Europe he defeated most of the world's leading masters at the San Sebastian tournament, 1909, but he had to wait until 1921 for an opportunity to play for the world championship, defeating **Emanuel Lasker** without losing a game. He maintained a record of near invincibility from 1921 to 1927. His defeat by **Alexander Alekhine** in 1927 was a major surprise, and despite further tournament successes he never received the opportunity to regain his title.

Čapek, Josef 1887–1945
Czech writer and painter
He was born in Schwadonitz, the elder brother of **Karel Čapek**. His early literary works, written in collaboration with his brother, include the allegorical *Ze života hmyzu* (1921, Eng trans *The Insect Play*, 1923). From such anxious visions of the future he progressed to a philosophy of sceptical humanism which found expression in his novel, *Stín Kapradiny* (1930), and in his essays. He died in Belsen.
📖 J Peirha, *Josef Čapek* (1961)

Čapek, Karel 1890–1938
Czech novelist and playwright
He was born in Malé Svatoňovice, Bohemia, and educated in Prague, Paris and Berlin. He worked as a journalist and, in the early 1920s, as stage director at the Vinograd Theatre in Prague. Several early works, including the novel *Zářivé hlubiny* (1916, 'The Shining Depths'), were collaborations with his brother **Josef Čapek**, but he got international attention with the play *R.U.R.* (1920, Eng trans 1923), a satirical vision of a dehumanized post-industrial society. The title stands for 'Rossum's Universal Robots', and the play led the way for a new kind of science fiction, as well as introducing the word robot (Czech *robota*, 'drudgery') to the English language. The brothers later collaborated on *Ze života hmyzu* (1921, Eng trans *The Insect Play*, 1923), which has a similar theme, as does the late novel *Válka s mloky* (1936, Eng trans *The War with the Newts*, 1937), written when Czech independence was increasingly threatened by Nazi expansionism. Karel also wrote *Věc Makropulos* (1922), which formed the basis for his countryman **Leoš Janáček's** 1925 opera *The Makropulos Affair*. 📖 W E Harkins, *Karel Čapek* (1962)

Capell, Edward 1713–81
English scholar
Born near Bury St Edmunds, Suffolk, he published an edition of **Shakespeare** (10 vols, 1768) based on the Folio and Quarto texts, and a full commentary, *Notes and Various Readings to Shakespeare* (3 vols, 1783).

Capella, Martianus Mineus Felix fl.480AD
North African scholar and writer
His *Satiricon*, a kind of encyclopedia, highly esteemed during the Middle Ages, is a medley of prose and verse, full of curious learning.

Capet, Hugo or Hugh c.938–996
King of France
As Duke of Francia, he was elected King of France on the death of the last Carolingian **Louis V** (987). The Capetian dynasty he founded ruled France until 1328. 📖 Robert Fawtier, *Capetian Kings of France* (1960)

Capgrave, John 1393–1464
English chronicler and theologian
Born in Lynn, Norfolk, he studied, probably at Cambridge, and was ordained priest about 1418, having already entered the Augustine order in Lynn. His works include Bible commentaries, sermons, *Nova legenda Angliae*, *De illustribus Henricis*, the lives of 24 emperors of Germany, kings of England, etc, and *Vita Humfredi Ducis Glocestriae*. Among his English works are a life of St **Catherine** in verse and *A Chronicle of England from the Creation to 1417*. *Ye Solace of Pilgrimes*, a description of Rome, has been assigned to him.

Capistrano, Giovanni da See John of Capistrano

Capito or Köpfel, Wolfgang Fabricius 1478–1541
German reformer
Born in Hagenau, Alsace, he entered the Benedictine order, and in 1515 became Professor of Theology at Basle. He approved of **Martin Luther's** action, but did not declare for the Reformation until later, when he became a Protestant leader in Strasbourg.

Capo d'Istria, Giovanni Antonio, Count, *Greek* Ióannis Antónios Kapodístrias 1776–1831
Greek statesman
Born in Corfu, he entered the Russian diplomatic service in 1809. In 1828 he became President of Greece, but imbued as he was with Russian ideas, his autocratic measures proved unpopular, and he was assassinated in a church at Nauplia.

Capone, Al(phonse) 1899–1947
US gangster
Born in Brooklyn, New York City, the son of immigrants from Naples, Italy, he joined a street gang as a boy and while working as a bartender and bouncer received the razor slash across his cheek that led to his nickname 'Scarface'. He achieved worldwide notoriety as a racketeer during the Prohibition era in Chicago in the 1920s, amassing enormous profits from gambling, bootlegging and prostitution, buying off police with bribery and warring with rival gangs, most notoriously in the St Valentine's Day Massacre (1929). Federal investigators did not have sufficient evidence to charge him with his most serious crimes, but in 1931 he was indicted for income-tax evasion and on his conviction was sentenced to 11 years in prison. He was released on health grounds in 1939 and retired to his estate in Florida. 📖 Fred Pasley, *Al Capone* (1930)

Capote, Truman 1924–84
US writer
Born in New Orleans, of Spanish descent, he spent much of his childhood in Alabama. He won several literary prizes while at school in New York but showed little ability in other subjects. His short story 'Miriam', published in the magazine *Mademoiselle*, was selected for the O Henry Memorial Award volume in 1946. *Other Voices, Other Rooms* (1948), his first novel, revealed his talent for sympathetic description of small-town life in the deep South and centres on the homosexual awakenings of a young boy. *The Grass Harp* (1951) is a fantasy performed against a background of the Alabama of his childhood. Other works are *Breakfast at Tiffany's* (1958), which was highly successful, though cleaned up and sentimentalized, as a film (1961), and *In Cold Blood* (1966), a 'non-fiction novel' about a murder in Kansas. Latterly, he published a collection of short pieces, *Music for Chameleons* (1980) and the long-promised but unfinished novel *Answered Prayers*, extracts of which appeared in *Esquire* magazine in 1975. 📖 Gerald Clarke, *Capote: a biography* (1987); W L Nance, *The Worlds of Truman Capote* (1970)

Capp, Al, originally Alfred Gerald Caplin 1909–79
US strip cartoonist

Born in New Haven, Connecticut, he studied at a series of art schools in Pennsylvania and Massachusetts, then entered strips as assistant to **Bud Fisher** on *Mutt and Jeff* (1930). Joining Associated Press he took on a daily joke, *Mr Gilfeather* (1932), then became assistant to Ham Fisher on *Joe Palooka* (1933). In 1934 he began his own strip *L'il Abner*, set in the backwoods community of Dogpatch, USA, and featuring a cast of hill-billy characters as well as frequent caricatures of public officials. Capp's chunky artwork and gift for satire made the strip an enduring success, and he continued to draw it until his retirement in 1977. *L'il Abner* inspired two films, a stage musical, and an animated series.

Capra, Frank 1897–1991
US film director

He was born in Palermo, Italy, but his family emigrated to California when he was six. He took a degree in chemical engineering at the California Institute of Technology before moving into the film industry (1921), initially as a gag writer for silent comedies. His films include *It Happened One Night* (1934), *Mr Deeds goes to Town* (1936), *Lost Horizon* (1937), *You Can't Take it with You* (1938), which won Academy Awards, *Arsenic and Old Lace* (1942), *It's a Wonderful Life* (1946), *State of the Union* (1948), and his last *A Pocketful of Miracles* (1961). During World War II he also made a series of patriotic documentaries. His best known work as a director celebrates the decency and integrity of the common man as he combats corruption and wrongdoing in high places. After the commercial failure of *It's A Wonderful Life* (now a television perennial) his sure touch faltered. He retired in 1964. 📖 Joseph McBride, *American Madness: The Life of Frank Capra* (1989)

Capriati, Jennifer 1976–
US tennis player

Born in New York City, she was 24 days short of her 14th birthday when she became a professional tennis player and so is known as the player for whom the Tour changed its age limit. She advanced through five rounds in her first tournament before losing to **Gabriela Sabatini**; aged 14 she became the youngest Grand Slam semi-finalist. She reached the final in her third tournament, and won her eleventh, the Puerto Rican Open. By the age of 15, she had become one of the world's highest-paid athletes, but by the age of 18 she had never progressed beyond the semi-final of any Grand Slam, and had begun to have difficulty in raising her game. She retired from professional tennis in 1996.

Caprivi, Georg Leo, Graf von 1831–99
German soldier and statesman

Born in Berlin, he fought in the campaigns of 1864 and 1866, and in the Franco-Prussian war (1870–71) was Chief of Staff to the 10th Army Corps. As head of the Admiralty (1883–88) he reorganized the navy and then was made commander of his old army corps in Hanover. He became Imperial Chancellor (1890–94) on **Bismarck's** fall, and Prussian Prime Minister. His principal measures were the army bills of 1892–93 and the commercial treaty with Russia in 1894. He was dismissed in 1894.

Capus, (Vincent Marie) Alfred 1858–1922
French writer

Born in Aix-en-Provence, he left engineering for journalism, and became political editor of *Le Figaro*. He wrote *Qui perd gagne* (1890, 'The Loser Wins') and other novels, but is best remembered for his comedies of the Parisian bourgeoisie such as *La Veine* (1901, 'Luck'). 📖 E Quet, *Alfred Capus* (1904)

Caracalla, properly Marcus Aurelius Antoninus
AD188–217
Roman emperor

The son of the Emperor **Septimius Severus**, he was born in Lyons, France. Caracalla was a nickname given him from his long hooded Gaulish tunic. He succeeded his father (AD211) as joint emperor with his brother Publius Septimius Antoninius Geta, whom he murdered in 212. He next turned against all Geta's associates, killing many including the jurist **Aemilius Papinianus**. Cruel and obsessed with advancing his martial dreams, in imitation of his hero **Alexander the Great**, he campaigned extensively in Germany, on the Danube, and in the East, and was assassinated as he was preparing for war against the Parthians. He is remembered for his edict of 212 (the *Constitutio Antoniniana*) which granted Roman citizenship to all free members of the empire.

Caracciolo, Francesco, Duca (Duke) di Brienza 1752–99
Neapolitan naval commander

He was born in Naples and served with the British in the American Revolution, then entered the service of Ferdinand IV of Naples (later **Ferdinand I** of the Two Sicilies) and became supreme commander of the Neapolitan navy. In 1798 he fled with the king before the French from Naples to Palermo, but returned to Naples and entered the service of the short-lived Parthenopean Republic. For two months he ably directed the operations of the revolutionists, but was captured whilst trying to escape in peasant disguise, and was hanged.

Caractacus See Caratacus

Caradon, Baron See Foot, Hugh Mackintosh, Baron Caradon

Caramanlis, Konstantinos See Karamanlis, Konstantinos

Caran d'Ache, pseudonym of Emmanuel Poire
1858–1909
French caricaturist

Born in Moscow, he studied there and then moved to Paris. He contributed to many periodicals, and was a pioneer in the development of the *bande dessinée* (comic strip), and a major influence on **H M Bateman**. Several collections of his works were published. His pseudonym came from the Russian word for *pencil*.

Caratacus or Caractacus or Caradoc
fl.40–52AD
British chieftain

The son of **Cymbeline**, he fought against the Romans (AD43–50), but was eventually defeated by Publius Ostorius Scapula near Ludlow. His wife and daughters were captured, his brothers surrendered, and he himself was handed over by Cartimandua, Queen of the Brigantes. He was taken to Rome (51), and exhibited in triumph by the Emperor **Claudius**, but eventually pardoned. According to **Tacitus**, his forceful oratory saved his life.

Carathéodory, Constantin 1873–1950
Greek mathematician

He was born in Berlin, Germany. His father served as Turkish ambassador in Belgium from 1875, and Constantin attended the École Militaire there (1891–95). In 1900 he began to study mathematics at the University of Berlin, and he received his PhD from Göttingen University in 1904. He taught in Germany and then at the new University of Smyrna established by the Greeks. When this was destroyed in 1922, Carathéodory saved the library, transporting it to Athens where he remained until 1924 before accepting his final academic position at Munich University. His research covered differential equations, the calculus of variations, the theory of real and complex functions, conformal mappings and the theory of point-set measure. He also wrote on **Albert Einstein**'s special relativity and geometrical optics.

Carausius, Marcus Aurelius Mausaeus
d.293AD
Roman emperor in Britain

He was born in Menapia (Belgium). Originally a Batavian pilot, Carausius had been put in command of the Roman fleet (*Classis Britannica*) in the Channel to ward off pirates. A usurper, he ruled from AD287, and was murdered by one of his officers, Allectus, who later set himself up as emperor in Britain in his stead.

Caravaggio, *properly* Polidoro Caldara da Caravaggio c.1492–1543
Italian painter

Born in Caravaggio, he aided **Raphael** in his Vatican frescoes. His *Christ Bearing the Cross* is in Naples. He was murdered by his servant at Messina.

Caravaggio, *properly* Michelangelo Merisi da Caravaggio 1573–1610
Italian painter

Born in Caravaggio, near Bergamo, he trained in Milan, but moved to Rome in the 1590s, where Cardinal del Monte became his chief patron. His early work is strikingly homoerotic, characterized by voluptuously portrayed young man in various guises. With his first two commissions, however, his style changed. The *Life of Saint Matthew* cycle in the Contarelli Chapel of the church of San Luigi dei Francese and the *Conversion of Saint Paul* and the *Crucifixion of Saint Peter* in the Cerasi Chapel of S Maria del Popolo, both in Rome, incorporate highly original, strongly lit, intensely realistic figures emerging dramatically from dark shadow. His work was often controversial as he used models off the street for biblical characters. In 1606 he fled Rome after killing a man in a brawl, and spent the rest of his life wandering between Naples, Sicily and Malta. In the hope of a pardon, he tried to return to Rome, but on the journey he was wounded, lost all his baggage, and caught a fever and died. Unlike the Carracci family he had no pupils, but his influence throughout the rest of the century was immense. He is widely regarded as the greatest Italian painter of the 17th century.

Caraway, Hattie (Ophelia) Wyatt, *née* Wyatt 1878–1950
US Democratic politician

Born near Bakerville, Tennessee, she was married to Senator Thaddeus Horatius Caraway and, when he died in 1831 before his term had expired, she was appointed by the governor of Arkansas to fill his Senate seat. She ran successfully for the same seat in 1932, becoming the first woman ever elected to the US Senate. She served until 1945, the year she was appointed by President **Franklin D Roosevelt** to the Federal Employees Compensation Commission. An independent-minded Democrat, she sponsored an early version of the Equal Rights Amendment in 1943.

Carco, Francis, *pseudonym of* François Carcopino-Tusoli 1886–1958
French writer

Born in Nouméa, New Caledonia, he first gained recognition with his volume of poems *La Bohème et mon Cœur* (1912, 'Bohemia and My Heart'). His novels were chiefly set in Paris's Latin Quarter. He also wrote a colourful account of his early life in *De Montmartre au Quartier latin* (1934, 'From Montmartre to the Latin Quarter'). 📖 S Weiner, *Francis Carco, career of a literary Bohemian* (1952)

Cardano, Girolamo, *also called* Jerome Cardan or Hieronymus Cardanus 1501–76
Italian mathematician, naturalist, physician, philosopher, gambler and astrologer

Born in Pavia, he became famous as a physician and teacher of mathematics in Milan and became Professor of Medicine at Pavia (1543) and Bologna (1562). In 1551 he visited Scotland to treat the archbishop of St Andrews and in London cast the horoscope of **Edward VI**. In 1570 he was imprisoned by the Inquisition for heresy, recanted and went to Rome in 1571 where he was given a pension by Pope **Pius V**. He died a few weeks after finishing his candid autobiography *De propria vita* (Eng trans, *Book of My Life*, 1930). A strange mixture of polymath and charlatan, he wrote over 200 treatises on, among other things, physics, mathematics, astronomy, astrology, philosophy, music and medicine. His most famous work is his treatise on algebra, the *Ars Magna* ('The Great Skill'), in which the formulae for solving cubic and quartic equations were published for the first time. He was accused of plagiarism by **Niccolò Tartaglia** who claimed the solution of the cubic as his own, but the credit should perhaps go to Scipione da Ferro. Despite this the solution is still known as Cardano's formula. 📖 Oystein Ore, *The Gambling Scholar* (1953)

Carden, Joan Maralyn 1937–
Australian soprano

Born in Melbourne, Victoria, she has been a principal artist with the Australian Opera since 1971. She made her debut at Covent Garden, London, in 1974 as Gilda in *Rigoletto*, a role she has since made her own. Renowned for her performances of **Mozart**, she has appeared at the Glyndebourne Festival, as Donna Anna in **Peter Hall**'s production of *Don Giovanni*, and with the English National Opera and the Metropolitan, New York. Her repertoire extends from **Handel** to **Richard Strauss** and **Benjamin Britten**, and one of her most celebrated performances is of the four heroines in *Les Contes d'Hoffmann* ('The Tales of Hoffmann'). In 1987 she was awarded the Dame Joan Hammond Award for Outstanding Service to Opera in Australia. She had a heart bypass operation in 1995 but resumed her career.

Cardenal, Ernesto 1925–
Nicaraguan poet

Born in Granada, he was educated at the University of Mexico and Columbia University, New York. Later he became a Franciscan priest with very mixed beliefs, and ran a small religious commune. He was influenced by Jose Coronel Urtecho, an older Nicaraguan poet, and the poet-priest **Thomas Merton**. His poetry is modernist in form and rhetorical in tone, reflecting both his religious and radical political commitments. His published collections include *Epigramas: Poemas* (1961, 'Epigrams: Poems'), *Oracion por Marilyn Monroe* (1965, Eng trans *Marilyn Monroe*, 1975) and *Salmos* (1967, Eng trans *Psalms of Struggle and Liberation*, 1981) and he has also written a number of prose works, mainly on spiritual subjects.

Cárdenas, Garcia Lopez de mid-16th century
Spanish explorer

On **Francisco Coronado**'s expedition to the south-west of North America, he discovered the Grand Canyon of the Colorado in 1540.

Cárdenas, Lázaro, *properly* Lázaro Cárdenas del Rio 1895–1970
Mexican general and politician

Born in the Michoacán, the son of a peasant, he joined the revolutionary army in 1913, was a general by 1923 and became Governor of Michoacán (1928–32). He seized control of the government from his patron, President **Plutarco Calles**. His presidency (1934–40) shaped modern Mexico, and witnessed the creation of PEMEX

(*Petróleos Mexicanos*) from nationalized foreign (mainly British) companies, and the PRM (Partido de la Revolución Mexicana, Mexican Revolutionary Party), successor to the PRN, and precursor of the PRI. Left-wing in his sympathies, he introduced many social reforms and reorganized the ruling party.

Cardew, Michael 1901–82
English potter

After studying under **Bernard Leach** at St Ives, Cornwall (1923–26), he set up his own studio at Winchcombe in the Cotswolds. Influenced by early English pottery, he specialized in lead-glazed slipware for everyday use. In 1939 he moved to Wenford Bridge, Cornwall and experimented with stoneware and tin glazes. In 1942 he took over the Achimota College on the Gold Coast, and started his own pottery at Vumé on the Volta, where he produced stoneware and strove to bring to West Africa a new industry capable of developing a modern West African art form, alongside the existing traditional craft.

Cardigan, James Thomas Brudenell, 7th Earl of 1797–1868
English general

Born in Hambleden, Buckinghamshire, he was MP for Marlborough (1818–29) and North Northamptonshire (1832). In 1824 he joined the army, and in 1830 bought himself a command in the 15th Hussars as a lieutenant-colonel. His fiery temper brought him into conflict with fellow officers, and he was forced to resign in 1833. From 1836 to 1847 he commanded the 11th Hussars, on which he lavished his own money to make it a crack squadron; after a duel with one of his officers in 1841 he was acquitted on a legal technicality by the House of Lords. Appointed major-general in 1847, he commanded the Light Brigade ('the Six Hundred') in the Crimea, and led it to destruction in the charge against enemy guns at Balaclava (25 October 1854). Received home as a hero, he was appointed Inspector-General of the cavalry (1855–60). The knitted woollen jacket he wore against the cold of a Crimean winter is named after him. 📖 Piers Compton, *Cardigan of Balaclava* (1972)

Cardin, Pierre 1922–
French fashion designer

Born in Venice, Italy, after working during World War II for a tailor in Vichy, he went to Paris in 1944. He worked in fashion houses and on costume design, for example for **Jean Cocteau's** film *La Belle et La Bête* (1946, *Beauty and the Beast*). He opened his own house in 1953 and has since been prominent in fashion for both women and men, as well as in other fields of design and business. A retrospective of his work was shown at the Victoria and Albert Museum, London, in 1990.

Cardoso, Fernando Enrique 1931–
Brazilian politician

Born into a wealthy military family in Rio de Janeiro, he became a sociologist and an opponent of the military regime. After the restoration of Brazilian democracy in the mid-1980s, he entered politics, serving as a senator (1986–92) and as Foreign Minister (1992). He became Finance Minister in 1993 and won praise for his successful anti-inflation measures, and in 1994 he was elected President. His moderate free-market reforms won broad popular support by 1996, and he sought to curb the human rights abuses still rampant in Brazil by introducing a plan to extend federal authority in order to prosecute such offences.

Cardozo, Benjamin Nathan 1870–1938
US judge and jurist

Born in New York City, he was educated at Dartmouth College and Columbia University. On the bench of the New York Court of Appeals (1913–32), he was appointed to the US Supreme Court (1932–38), where he handed down important opinions on congressional power, control of inter-state commerce and the relationship of the Bill of Rights to states' rights. He was generally liberal and favoured greater involvement of courts in public policy. He also wrote some thoughtful books, now classics: *The Nature of the Judicial Process* (1921), *The Growth of the Law* (1924), and *The Paradoxes of Legal Science* (1928).

Carducci, Giosuè 1835–1907
Italian poet and Nobel Prize winner

Born in Valdicastello, he became Professor of Italian Literature at Bologna (1860), and set a new standard in scholarship. In 1876 he was returned to the Italian parliament as a Republican, and in 1890 became a senator. He published several volumes of verse, and was considered Italy's national poet. He was awarded the Nobel Prize for literature in 1906. 📖 J C Bailey, *Carducci* (1926)

Cardwell, Edward Cardwell, 1st Viscount 1813–86
English politician

The son of a Liverpool merchant, he was educated at Winchester and Balliol College, Oxford and called to the Bar in 1838, entering the Commons as MP for Clitheroe in 1842. First a Peelite, then a Liberal, he served as President of the Board of Trade (1852–55), Chief Secretary for Ireland (1859–61), Chancellor of the Duchy of Lancaster (1861–64), and Colonial Secretary (1864–66). As Secretary of State for War under **W E Gladstone** (1868–74), he carried out a major reorganization of the British army, including abolition of the purchase of commissions, the development of county regiments and the reserves system, and the significant change in the command structure whereby the Minister took supremacy over the commander-in-chief. He was made a peer in 1874.

Careless, William See Carlos, William

Carême, Marie Antoine 1784–1833
French chef and writer

Born in Paris, he was the author of *La Cuisine Française* (1828), and other works. As **Talleyrand's** cook, he had an important role at the Congress of Vienna.

Carew, Thomas 1595–1639
English Cavalier poet

Born in West Wickham, Kent, he studied at Merton College, and entered the Inner Temple to study law in 1612. He visited Holland as secretary to the ambassador (1613–16), but was dismissed for slandering his employers. After three years in London he went to France (1619–24) as secretary to the ambassador, and won the favour of **Charles I**. A friend of **Ben Jonson** and **John Donne**, he wrote witty songs and lyrics in the Cavalier tradition, as well as longer poems, notably the love poem 'A Rapture'.

Carey, George Leonard 1935–
English prelate

Born in London to working-class parents, he left school at the age of 15 without any qualifications. After National Service spent in Egypt and Iraq, he felt called to the priesthood. He graduated from the London School of Divinity, became curate of St Mary's, Islington (1962–66), then spent 10 years teaching in theological colleges. As vicar of St Nicholas's, Durham, he became interested in charismatic renewal, and introduced new forms of worship. Appointed Archbishop of Canterbury in 1991 after four years as Bishop of Bath and Wells, he frequently emphasizes his origins, and represents the liberal and modern aspects of the Church of England; he was a strong supporter of the ordination of women. He has published several books, including *I Believe in Man* (1975), *The Meeting of The Waters* (1985), *The Great God Robbery* (1989), *Sharing a Vision* (1993) and *Spiritual Journey* (1994).

Carey, Henry c.1687–1743
English poet and musician

Born in Yorkshire, possibly an illegitimate son of a member of the Savile family, he published his first volume of poems in 1713. He wrote innumerable songs, witty poems, burlesques, farces, and dramatic pieces, sometimes composing the accompanying music, as for his best-known poem 'Sally in our Alley'. He also invented the term 'Namby Pamby', as a nickname for the poet **Ambrose Philips**.

Carey, Henry Charles 1793–1879
US political economist

He was born in Philadelphia. His father, Mathew Carey (1760–1839), was a journalist who had been imprisoned for nationalist opinions and had emigrated to the USA from Ireland in 1784. In Philadelphia Henry Carey became a successful publisher and author, known especially for his *Vindiciae Hibernicae*, written to confute **William Godwin** and other English misrepresenters of Ireland. He became a partner in his father's book-selling business and when he retired in 1835, he was at the head of the largest publishing concern in the USA. Among his works were *Principles of Political Economy* (3 vols, 1837–40) and *Principles of Social Science* (3 vols, 1858–59). Originally a zealous free-trader, he came to regard free trade as an ideal, but impossible in the existing state of US industry: a period of protection was indispensable.

Carey, James 1845–83
Irish builder, Fenian and informer

Born in Dublin, he worked as a builder there and became a town councillor. He joined the Fenians about 1861 and helped to found the group called the Invincibles in 1881. He betrayed his associates in the murder of Lord Frederick Cavendish, 8th Duke of Devonshire, and **Thomas Henry Burke** (the Phoenix Park murders). Five of the murderers were hanged, but Carey was shot dead by a bricklayer, Patrick O'Donnell.

Carey, Peter 1943–
Australian novelist

Born in Bacchus Marsh, Victoria, he was educated at Geelong Grammar School, began a career as an advertising copywriter, then lived in London. His first book, *The Fat Man in History* (1974), was a collection of short stories, and he was quickly recognized as an innovative force in Australian writing. Other books include *Bliss* (1981), which explored the advertising world, and *Illywhacker* (1985) (Australian slang for a trickster or conman). He won the Booker Prize with *Oscar and Lucinda* (1988), in which a compulsive gambler and a Sydney heiress fascinated with the manufacture of glass are bizarrely united. It was filmed in 1996 by **Gillian Armstrong**. His other books include *The Tax Inspector* (1991), *The Unusual Life of Tristan Smith* (1994) and *Collected Stories* (1995). He has also written screenplays, and now lives in New York.

Carey, William 1761–1834
English missionary and orientalist

Born in Paulerspury, Northamptonshire, he was apprenticed to a shoemaker, before joining the Baptists in 1783, becoming a minister three years later. In 1793 he and John Thomas were chosen as first Baptist missionaries to India, where Carey founded the Serampur mission (1799). From 1801 to 1830 he was Oriental Professor at Fort William College, Calcutta.

Cargill, Donald c.1619–1681
Scottish Covenanter

Born near Blairgowrie, Tayside, he studied at Aberdeen and St Andrews, and in 1655 was ordained minister of the Barony parish in Glasgow. Ejected for denouncing the Restoration, he became a field preacher, fought and was wounded at Bothwell Brig (1679), and took part with **Richard Cameron** in the famous *Sanquhar Declaration* (1680). Having excommunicated the king, the Duke of York, and others at Torwood, Stirlingshire, he was seized, and executed at the Mercat Cross in Edinburgh.

Carissimi, Giacomo 1605–74
Italian composer

Born in Marini, Rome, he was organist in Tivoli, Assisi (1628–29), and from 1628 in Rome. He did much to develop the sacred cantata, and his works include the oratorio *Jephte* (1650, *Jephtha*).

Carl See also **Karl**

Carl XVI Gustaf 1946–
King of Sweden

Born in Stockholm, the grandson of King **Gustav VI**, he is the seventh sovereign of the House of **Bernadotte**. His father, Prince Gustav Adolf (1906–47), the heir apparent, was killed in an air crash, so Carl Gustaf became crown prince on his grandfather's accession (1950). Educated at boarding school, he did military service, mainly with the navy (1966–68), took a specially designed one-year course at Uppsala University, and studied economics at Stockholm University. On his accession (1973), in accordance with the new constitution being discussed by the Riksdag (parliament), he became a democratic monarch like his grandfather, although the constitution was not formally approved until 1975. He is head of state, but does not preside at cabinet meetings and is not supreme commander of the armed forces. In 1976 he married a commoner, Silvia Renate Sommerlath (1943–), daughter of a West German businessman. They have three children: Princess Victoria (1977–), hereditary Prince Carl Philip (1979–) and Princess Madeleine (1982–). Under a new Act of Succession (1980), Crown Princess Victoria is now heir to the Swedish throne.

Carle See **Vernet, Antoine Charles Horace**

Carle, Eric 1929–
US picture-book artist

He was born in Germany. He has written and illustrated several children's books, using a distinctive collage technique, but he is best known for *The Very Hungry Caterpillar* (1970), in which the voracious creature burrows through the pages of the book in search of delicacies.

Carleton, Sir Guy, 1st Baron Dorchester 1724–1808
British soldier and Governor of British North America

He was born in Strabane, Ireland. As General **James Wolfe**'s quartermaster at the capture of Quebec in 1759, he realized that the American colonies were close to rebellion and that British imperial authority would require a base, which he set out to establish in Quebec. He refused to consider the English-speaking settlers' demands for *habeas corpus* and other aspects of English law, yet it was they who took up arms against the US rebels when they invaded (1775–76). Criticized for the slowness with which he pursued the rebels, he resigned. Sent out as Governor of Quebec again in 1786, he became Governor-General after the Constitutional Act of 1791. His continued concern for the military defence of Canada was illustrated by his inflammatory speech made just before Jay's Treaty was signed in 1794, when he was sure that war with America was imminent. He resigned in 1794 and left the province in 1796.

Carleton, William 1794–1869
Irish novelist

He was born in Prillisk, County Tyrone, of peasant birth, the youngest of 14 children. He became a tutor and writer in Dublin, contributing sketches to the *Christian Examiner*, republished as *Traits and Stories of the Irish Peasantry* (1830). A second series (1833) was just as popular. In 1839 he published a long novel, *Fardorougha the Miser*, which was followed by *The Black Prophet* (1847), about the potato famine, *The Tithe Proctor* (1849), *The Squanders of Castle Squander* (1852), *The Evil Eye* (1860), and others.

Carlile, Richard 1790–1843
English journalist and radical reformer

Born in Ashburton, Devon, he became a chemist's boy and a tinman's apprentice. A disciple of **Thomas Paine**, he sold the prohibited radical weekly *Black Dwarf* throughout London in 1817. He then printed thousands of **Robert Southey's** *Wat Tyler* (1817), reprinted the *Parodies* of William Hone (1780–1848) and wrote a series of imitations of them, for which he spent 18 weeks in prison. He was also imprisoned for publishing his own *Political Litany* and Paine's works, and a journal *The Republican* (1819–26).

Carlile, Wilson 1847–1942
English Anglican clergyman

Born in Brixton, London, he founded the Church Army in 1882, and was made a prebendary of St Paul's in 1906.

Carling, Will(iam David Charles) 1965–
English rugby union player

Born in Bradford-on-Avon, he is England's most capped centre (60) and also holds the world record for the most international wins as captain (40 in 53 games). He made his senior debut for England in 1988 and at 22 was made England's captain. He played a vital role in England's three Grand Slam wins (1991, 1992, 1995) but was sacked in 1995 when he called Rugby Football Union administrators 'old farts', only to be reinstated two days later after support from the England World Cup squad. Press exposure over his friendship with Princess **Diana** coincided with the break-up of his marriage and he announced his retirement as captain of the England team later in 1995.

Carloman 751–71
Frankish prince

The younger son of **Pepin, the Short** and brother of **Charlemagne**, he ruled the eastern Franks from 768. At his death Charlemagne took over his lands.

Carlos, Don 1545–68
Spanish prince

Born in Valladolid, son of King **Philip II** of Spain by his first wife, Maria of Portugal, he was sent to study at Alcalá de Henares, where he showed so little improvement that the king invited a nephew, Archduke Rudolf, to Spain, intending to make him his heir. Weak, inascible, and cruel, and with a hatred of the king's advisers, on Christmas Eve 1567 Don Carlos confessed to a priest that he intended to assassinate a certain person. The priest believed that the king was the intended victim, and betrayed Don Carlos, who was tried and found guilty of conspiring against the life of his father. The sentence was left for the king to pronounce. Philip declared that he could make no exception in favour of such an unworthy son, but sentence of death was not formally recorded. When, shortly afterwards, Don Carlos died, it was suspected that he had been poisoned or strangled but no evidence was found to support this.

Carlos, Don 1788–1855
Spanish pretender

Born in Madrid, he was the second son of **Charles IV** of Spain. On the accession of his niece **Isabella II** (1833), he asserted his claim to the throne, and was supported by the Church, but he was defeated by the liberals in the first Carlist War (1834–39) and went into exile.

Carlos or Careless, William d.1689
English soldier

After the Battle of Worcester (1651), he hid with **Charles II** in the oak at Boscobel, and escaped with him to France.

Carlson, Carolyn 1943–
US dancer and choreographer

Born in California, she studied at San Francisco Ballet School and with **Alwin Nikolais**, in whose company she danced from 1966 to 1971. After freelancing in Europe, she was invited to create a piece for the Paris Opera Ballet in 1973. Her solo was so well-received that a special post, *danseuse étoile choreographique*, was invented for her. Her dream-like, ritualistic dance-spectacles and independent working methods had a great impact on French and European modern/experimental dance. From 1980 she directed her own troupe at Venice's Teatro Fenice, but later returned to Paris.

Carlson, Chester Floyd 1906–68
US inventor

Born in Seattle, Washington, he graduated in physics from the California Institute of Technology in 1930, then took a law degree and worked as a patent lawyer in an electronics firm. On his own he began to experiment with copying processes using photoconductivity and by 1938 had discovered the basic principles of the electrostatic 'xerography' process. Patented in 1940, it was subsequently developed and from 1959 marketed worldwide by the Xerox Corporation, making him a multimillionaire.

Carlsson, Ingvar Costa 1934–
Swedish statesman

Educated at Lund (Sweden) and North Western (USA) universities, he was secretary in the Prime Minister's office (1958–60) before entering active party politics. He became president of the youth league of the Social Democratic Labour Party (SAP) in 1961, and in 1964 was elected to the Riksdag (Parliament). After holding a number of junior posts (1967–76), he became Deputy Prime Minister to **Olof Palme** in 1982 and succeeded him as Prime Minister and SAP leader after Palme's assassination in 1986. He retired in 1996.

Carlstadt or Karlstadt, *properly* Andreas Rudolf Bodenstein d.1541
German reformer

He was born prior to 1483, at Carlstadt in Bavaria. In 1517 he joined **Martin Luther**, who in 1521 rebuked his iconoclastic zeal, and whom he afterwards opposed on the question of the Eucharist. Accused of participation in the Peasants' War, he fled to Switzerland, where he became Professor of Theology at Basle.

Carlucci, Frank Charles 1930–
US diplomat and politician

Born in Scranton, Pennsylvania, he was educated at Princeton and Harvard, and after fighting in the Korean War, he served as a career diplomat in Africa and South America. He returned to the USA in 1969 to work in the **Nixon** administration (1969–74) and then served, under Presidents **Gerald Ford** (1974–76) and **Jimmy Carter** (1977–81), as US ambassador to Portugal and, later, as Deputy Director of the CIA. A pragmatic and apolitical Atlanticist, he found himself out of step with the 'hawks' in the **Reagan** administration (1981–89) and left to work at Sears World Trade after barely a year as Deputy Secretary of Defence. In 1986 he replaced Rear-Admiral **Poindexter** as National Security Adviser, and served as Secretary of Defence (1987–89), supporting Soviet-US arms reduction initiatives.

Carlyle, Jane (Baillie) Welsh, *née* Welsh 1801–66
Scottish diarist, the wife of Thomas Carlyle

She was born in Haddington, East Lothian, and tutored by the revivalist minister **Edward Irving**, who introduced her in 1821 to his friend **Thomas Carlyle**, whom she married in 1826. They lived on her estate at Craigenputtock, Dumfriesshire, from 1828 to 1834, and then in Chelsea. She declined to become a writer despite Carlyle's promptings, and spent much of her life supporting her husband through his depressions and chronic ill health. She is, nevertheless, remembered for her vividly written letters and diaries, edited by Carlyle, which were eventually published after his death in 1883, and which show her to have been one of the best letter-writers in the English language.

Carlyle, Thomas 1795–1881
Scottish historian and essayist

Born in Ecclefechan, Dumfriesshire, the son of a stonemason, he was educated at Edinburgh University, studying arts and mathematics, and then became a teacher. Returning to Edinburgh in 1818 to study law, he wrote several articles for the *Edinburgh Encyclopaedia*, and immersed himself in the study of German literature, publishing a translation of **Goethe**'s *Wilhelm Meister*, in 1824 which brought him entry into literary London. He married Jane Baillie Welsh (**Jane Carlyle**) in 1826, and from 1828 they lived on her estate of Craigenputtock, near Dumfries. There Carlyle wrote his first major work on social philosophy, *Sartor Resartus*, which was published in instalments in *Fraser's Magazine* (1833–34) and as a book in the USA (1836), with an introduction by **Ralph Waldo Emerson**. It was partly a satirical discourse on the value of clothes, and partly a semi-autobiographical discussion of creeds and human values. In 1834 the couple moved to Chelsea, London, where Carlyle spent the rest of his life. Here he completed his romantic history of *The French Revolution* (3 vols, 1837), despite the accidental burning of the manuscript of most of the first volume by **John Stuart Mill**'s maidservant. He also wrote numerous essays and pamphlets which highlight his increasingly right-wing political attitudes, and his six-volume work *History of… Frederick the Great* (1858–65), a compelling portrait of the practical autocrat as a heroic idealist. His *Reminiscences* were published in 1881. 📖 J A Froude, *Thomas Carlyle: a history of his life* (1884)

Carmen Sylva 1843–1916
Pen name of Elizabeth, Queen of Romania

The daughter of Prince Hermann of Wied Neuwied, she married King (then Prince) **Carol I** of Romania in 1869. Her only child, a daughter, died in 1874, and in her grief she turned to writing. Two poems, printed privately at Leipzig (1880) under the name Carmen Sylva, were followed by *Stürme* (1881), *Leidens Erdengang* (1882, Eng trans *Pilgrim Sorrow* by H Zimmern, 1884), and other works. In the war of 1877–78 she endeared herself to her people by her devotion to the wounded.

Carmichael, Hoagy, *in full* Hoagland Howard Carmichael 1899–1981
US songwriter

Born in Bloomington, Indiana, a self-taught pianist and musician, he studied law at Indiana University and became friends with jazz bandleader **Bix Beiderbecke**, who recorded his composition 'Riverboat Shuffle' (1924). He went on to compose many popular songs, including 'Georgia on My Mind' (1930) and 'Lazy River' (1931), which were characterized by a melodic structure that allowed for solo improvisation against the rhythm. His song 'Stardust' (first version 1927) is reputed to be the most frequently recorded popular composition of all time.

Carmichael, Ian 1920–
English actor

Born in Hull, he trained at RADA and made his stage debut in Karel Čapek's *R.U.R* at the People's Palace, East London (1939). After wartime service as an army officer, he starred in the West End and on Broadway before making his name as a film star in *Simon and Laura* (1955) and becoming Britain's top box-office comedy actor in **Boulting Brothers** films such as *Private's Progress* (1956), *Brothers in Law* (1956), *Lucky Jim* (1957) and *I'm All Right, Jack* (1959). Later, he found television fame as Bertie Wooster in *The World of Wooster* (1966–68), single parent Peter Lamb in *Bachelor Father* (1970), the title role in *Lord Peter Wimsey* (1972–75) and Sir James Menzies in *Strathblair* (1992–93). 📖 *Will the Real Ian Carmichael…* (1979)

Carmichael, Stokely, *later known as* Kwam Touré 1941–98
US civil-rights activist

He was born in Port-of-Spain, Trinidad, and educated in the USA from 1952. He joined the Student Nonviolent Co-ordinating Committee in 1964, and became its president in 1966–67 after the murder of **Malcolm X**. He came to stand for 'black power' and was leader of the more militaristic Black Panthers from 1967 to 1969. In 1969 he moved for a time to Guinea, where he promoted pan-Africanism.

Carmona, Antonio 1869–1951
Portuguese general and politician

He entered the army in 1888 and became a general in 1922. After a military coup in 1926 he was made Prime Minister and Minister of War, with dictatorial powers. In 1928 he was elected President for life by plebiscite. In 1932 he appointed **António Salazar** as Prime Minister and virtual dictator.

Carnap, Rudolf 1891–1970
US philosopher and logician

Born in Wuppertal, Germany, he studied at the universities of Jena and Freiburg im Breisgau. He was a lecturer in Vienna (1926–31) and Professor of Philosophy at Prague (1931–35), before moving to Chicago (1936–52) and then California (1954–70). He was a leading member of the 'Vienna Circle' of logical positivists, who dismissed most traditional metaphysics as a source of meaningless answers to pseudo-problems. His important work on the foundations of knowledge, scientific method, logic and semantics is represented in *Der logische Aufbau der Welt* (1928, 'The Logical Construction of the World'), *Logische Syntax der Sprache* (1934, 'Logical Syntax of Language'), *Meaning and Necessity* (1947) and especially in *The Logical Foundations of Probability* (1950). 📖 Roger C Buck and Robert S Cohen, *PSA 1970: In Memory of Rudolf Carnap* (1971)

Carnarvon, George Edward Stanhope Molyneux Herbert, 5th Earl of 1866–1923
English amateur Egyptologist

Born at Highclere Castle, Berkshire, he was the son of the politician Henry Carnarvon (1831–90). From 1907 he sponsored **Howard Carter**'s excavations of the royal tombs at Thebes. He died shortly after the spectacular discovery of Tut'ankhamun's tomb in the Valley of the Kings in 1922.

Carné, Marcel 1909–96
French film director

Born in Paris, he worked in a bank, a grocery and an insurance company before securing the position of assistant to film director Jacques Feyder. He directed the documentary short *Nogent, Eldorado du Dimanche* (1929, 'Nogent Sunday's Eldorado') and made his fictional directorial debut with *Jenny* (1936), the beginning of a long and profitable collaboration with poet and screenwriter **Jacques Prévert**, that resulted in such admired fatalistic dramas as *Quai des brumes* (1938, *Port of Shadows*) and *Le Jour se lève* (1939, *Daybreak*). *Les Enfants du Paradis* (1944, 'Children of Paradise'), made during the German occupation, evokes a romantic theatrical past with wit and sensitivity and is considered his masterpiece. The quality of his work declined in the postwar years and he was swept aside by the contempt of the 'nouvelle vague' generation of film-makers. Later films include *Thérèse Raquin* (1953), *Les Tricheurs* (1958, 'Youthful Sinners') and his last, the television documentary, *La Bible* (1977). In 1992 he began work on *Mouche* but it was abandoned after several weeks of filming.

Carneades c.214–129BC
Greek philosopher
Born in Cyrene, North Africa, he became head of the Academy founded by **Plato** near Athens, which under his very different, sceptical direction became known as the New Academy. He had a reputation as a supremely skilled dialectician, who could argue equally persuasively for quite opposing points of view.

Carnegie, Andrew 1835–1919
US industrialist and philanthropist
He was born in Dunfermline, Scotland, the son of a weaver who emigrated to Pittsburgh in 1848. After several jobs, including factory hand, telegraphist, and railway clerk, Andrew resigned from the Pennsylvania Railroad in 1865 to found his first company, which grew into the largest iron and steel works in the USA. He retired in 1901, a multimillionaire, to Skibo Castle in Sutherland, Scotland, and died in Lenox, Massachusetts. His benefactions exceeded £70 million, including public libraries throughout the USA and Great Britain, Hero Funds, the Pittsburgh Carnegie Institute, the Washington Carnegie Institution, the Hague Peace Temple, the Pan-American Union Building, and substantial gifts to Scottish and US universities, Dunfermline, and numerous others. Besides an autobiography (1920), he wrote *Triumphant Democracy* (1886), *The Gospel of Wealth* (1889), and *Problems of Today* (1908). ▢ Joseph F Wall, *Andrew Carnegie* (1970)

Carnegie, Dale 1888–1955
US author and teacher of self-improvement techniques
He was born in Maryville, Missouri, and during his childhood his family lived meagrely on a small farm. He worked first as a salesman and later as a teacher of public speaking, and in 1936 he published *How to Win Friends and Influence People*, which offered anecdotes, advice, and optimistic maxims about success in business and private life. In the wake of the book's enormous popularity, he founded hundreds of branches of the Dale Carnegie Institute for Effective Speaking and Human Relations, which enrolled 50,000 people a year at the time of his death.

Carner, Josep 1884–1970
Catalan poet and essayist
He was born in Barcelona, and pursued a career as a diplomat until the advent of the **Franco** dictatorship, which he opposed. His masterpiece is the long narrative poem on the theme of Jonah and the Whale, *Nabí*. Carner is regarded as being responsible for the miraculous Catalan linguistic reintegration. His collected works were published in 1968. He died in exile in Brussels. ▢ A H Terry, *Catalan Literature* (1972)

Carnot, Lazare Nicolas Marguerite 1753–1823
French revolutionary and politician
Born in Nolay, Burgundy, he was known as the 'organizer of victory' during the French Revolutionary Wars. He entered the army as an engineer, in 1791 became a member of the Legislative Assembly, and in the Convention voted for the death of **Louis XVI**. Elected to the Committee of Public Safety, he raised 14 armies, and drew up a plan by which the forces of the European reaction were repelled from the frontier. Though he tried to restrict the power of **Robespierre** he was accused after the Reign of Terror, but

the charge was dismissed. In 1797, as a member of the Directory, he opposed the extreme measures of **Paul Barras**, and was sentenced to deportation as a suspected royalist. Escaping to Germany, he wrote a defence which led to the overthrow of his colleagues in 1799. The coup d'état of 18th Brumaire (1799) brought him back to Paris, where in 1800, as Minister of War, he helped to organize the successful Italian and Rhenish campaigns. He retired when he understood the ambitious plans of **Napoleon I**, but later commanded at Antwerp (1814). During the Hundred Days he was Minister of the Interior, but after the second restoration (1830) he was banished, retiring first to Warsaw and then to Magdeburg. He was the author of *De la défense des places fortes* (1810, 'On the Defence of Fortified Towns').

Carnot, Marie François Sadi 1837–94
French statesman
The grandson of **Lazare Carnot**, he studied at the École Polytechnique, and became a civil engineer. In 1887 he was elected President and proceeded to stand firm against the Boulangist movement. He was stabbed to death at Lyons by an Italian anarchist.

Carnot, (Nicholas Léonard) Sadi 1796–1832
French physicist
Born in Paris, he was the son of **Lazare Carnot**. After studying at the École Polytechnique and the École de l'Artillerie, he became a captain of engineers, but from 1819 concentrated on scientific research. In his sole published work, *Réflexions sur la puissance motrice du feu* (1824, Eng trans *Reflections on the Motive Power of Fire*, 1890), he applied for the first time scientific principles to an analysis of the working cycle and efficiency of the steam engine, arriving at an early form of the second law of thermodynamics and the concept of reversibility in the form of the ideal Carnot cycle. His work became known through the reinterpretation of **Bénoit Clapeyron**, and was taken up by **Rudolf Clausius** and Lord **Kelvin** from the late 1840s. ▢ Robert R Palmer, *Twelve Who Ruled* (1941)

Caro, Sir Anthony 1924–
English sculptor
Born in London, he studied engineering at Cambridge but turned to sculpture after World War II, attending the Regent Street Polytechnic (1946) and the Royal Academy Schools (1947–52) in London. From 1951 to 1953 he worked with Sir **Henry Moore**. He visited the USA in 1959, where he met avant-garde artists like **David Smith** and **Kenneth Noland**. In the early 1950s he made rugged bronze animal and human figures, but he soon developed his characteristic abstract style, typically large pieces of metal welded together and painted in primary colours, for example *Early One Morning* (1962, Tate Gallery, London). In 1966 he won the David E Bright Prize at the Venice Biennale, and he has had major solo exhibitions in London, Washington, New York, and Ottawa. From 1983 he worked at the Triangle Workshop, New York State, producing figurative bronzes. In his later work he has made reference to tradition of the West and of India. He was knighted in 1987. ▢ Terry Fenton, *Anthony Caro* (1986)

Carol I 1839–1914
King of Romania
Born Prince Karl of Hohenzollern-Sigmaringen, he was elected Prince of Romania (1866) after the deposition of Alexandru Cuza and became Romania's first king (1881). He promoted urban industrial development and military expansion, but failed to deal with rural problems, and brutally crushed a peasant rebellion (1907). He married (1869) Princess Elizabeth of Wied, a prolific writer under the pseudonym **Carmen Sylva**. At the outset of World War

I, King Carol declared Romanian neutrality, but his successor (his nephew King Ferdinand I) declared for the Allies (1916).

Carol II 1893–1953
King of Romania

He was born in Sinaia, the eldest son of King Ferdinand I (reigned 1914–27) and great-nephew of Carol I. His flamboyant private life created constant problems. In 1917 he made a morganatic marriage to Zizi Lambrini, whom he divorced to marry Princess Helen of Greece (1921) and by whom he had a son, King Michael. In 1925 he renounced his right of succession to the throne, deserted his wife, and went into exile with his mistress, Magda Lupescu. In 1930 he returned to Romania and became king in a coup that overthrew his son. His reign was made chaotic by pressures from both Russia and Germany. He admired the authoritarian methods of Mussolini and, in an attempt to counter the pro-Nazi Iron Guard movement, he banned all political parties (1938) and created a Front of National Rebirth. In 1940, after being forced to cede northern Transylvania to Hungary, he was deposed through German influence in favour of his son, and fled into exile in Spain, where he married Lupescu (1947).

Caroline of Ansbach 1683–1737
Queen of Great Britain and Ireland

Born in Ansbach, the daughter of the Margrave of Brandenburg-Ansbach, she married George, Electoral Prince of Hanover (1705), later George II, and went to England with him when his father became King George I (1714). As Princess of Wales she established a court of writers and politicians at Leicester House. Sensible, and avoiding abuse of the power she loved, she was a strong supporter of Sir Robert Walpole, and acted as regent during her husband's absences abroad. They had five children, including Frederick Louis (1707–51), Prince of Wales and father of George III, and William Augustus, Duke of Cumberland. 📖 Peter Quennel, *Caroline of England* (1939)

Caroline of Brunswick, Amelia Elizabeth
1768–1821
Queen of Great Britain and Ireland, and wife of George IV

Born in Brunswick, she was the daughter of George III's sister Augusta. She was married (1795) to the Prince of Wales (later George IV), her first cousin, and although she bore him a daughter, Princess Charlotte, he made her live by herself at Shooters Hill and Blackheath, and from 1814 she lived chiefly in Italy. When George came to the throne (1820), she refused an annuity of £50,000 to renounce the title of queen and live abroad. The government instituted proceedings against her for adultery, but they were dropped, largely due to public sympathy and the impressive defence of Lord Brougham. She was nevertheless turned away from Westminster Abbey at George IV's coronation a few days before she died. 📖 Thea Holme, *Caroline: A Biography of Caroline of Brunswick* (1979)

Carolus-Duran, *properly* Charles Auguste Émile Durand 1838–1917
French painter

Born in Lille, he was strongly influenced by Velázquez and the Spanish school. He was the teacher of John Singer Sargent.

Carossa, Hans 1878–1956
German writer and physician

He was born in Tölz, and worked as a doctor in Bavaria. He became prominent with *Eine Kindheit* (1922, 'A Childhood'), the first of an autobiographical sequence which also includes *Rumänisches Tagebuch* (1924, 'Romanian Journal'), a diary of World War I, and *Verwandlungen einer Jugend* (1928, 'Transformations of a Youth'), consciously echoing the life-affirming example of his literary master, Goethe. He wrote novels, including *Doktor Bürgers Ende* (1913, 'The End of Dr Bürger'), and *Ungleiche Welten* (1951, 'Different Worlds'), and some poems. 📖 A Haveis, *Hans Carossa* (1935)

Carothers, Wallace Hume 1896–1937
US industrial chemist and inventor

Born in Burlington, Iowa, he studied at the University of Illinois and at Harvard, and taught there and at various universities before concentrating on research. Working for the Du Pont Company at Wilmington, he produced the first successful synthetic rubber, neoprene, and followed this with nylon. He committed suicide, and the patent for nylon, awarded posthumously, was given to the Du Pont Company. 📖 E V Heyn, *Fire of Genius* (1972)

Carpaccio, Vittore c.1455–1522
Italian painter

Born in Venice, he was probably a pupil of Giovanni Bellini and became a painter of the Venetian school. His most characteristic work is seen in the cycle of painting on the life of St Ursula (1490–95), for the school of St Ursula, Venice (now in the Accademia de Belle Arti, Venice). Another cycle, *Scenes from the Lives of St George and St Jerome* (1502), painted for the Schola San Giorgio degli Schiavoni, is still preserved there. In 1510 he executed for San Giobbe his *Presentation in the Temple*, now in the Accademia.

Carpeaux, Jean Baptiste 1827–75
French sculptor

He was born in Valenciennes, and in 1854 won the Prix de Rome. His major work was the marble group, *The Dance*, for the façade of the Paris Opera House (1869, Musée d'Orsay, Paris). His style was exuberant, breaking with the neoclassical tradition.

Carpenter, Harry Leonard 1925–
English sports commentator

Born in London and educated at Selhurst Grammar School, Croydon, he worked on the *Greyhound Express* at the age of 16, and entered the Royal Navy at 18. After World War II he became a greyhound owner. He was with the BBC from 1949 to 1994 and has become known as the voice of boxing. He published his autobiography, *Where's Harry? My Story*, in 1992.

Carpenter, Mary 1807–77
English educationist and reformer

Born in Exeter, the daughter of a Unitarian minister, she was trained as a teacher. She opened a girls' school in Bristol in 1829 and took an active part in the movement for the reformation of neglected children. In 1846 she founded a ragged school in Bristol, and also several reformatories for girls. She visited India on four occasions, and published *Our Convicts* (1864), *The Last Days of Rammohun Roy* (1866), and *Six Months in India* (1868). She was sister of William Carpenter.

Carpenter, Mary Chapin 1959–
US singer and songwriter

Born in Princeton, New Jersey, the daughter of a *Life* magazine executive, she lived in Japan for a time before settling with her family in Washington DC. Naming her publishing company Getarealjob reflects her initial ambivalence about her chosen path, but her growing local reputation led to a recording contract with a major label based in Nashville. Her characteristic fusion of country with soft rock and folk on *Hometown Girl* (1987) was a success, and she has gone on to establish herself as a major commercial force. Her subsequent albums include *State of the Heart* (1989) and *Stones in the Road* (1994).

Carpenter, William Benjamin 1813–85
English biologist

Born in Exeter, he studied medicine at the universities of Bristol, London, and Edinburgh. His graduation thesis (1839) on the nervous system of the invertebrates led on to his *Principles of General and Comparative Physiology* (1839). In 1844 he was appointed Professor of Physiology at the Royal Institution, London, and Professor of Forensic Medicine at University College (1849). He took part in a deep sea exploration expedition (1868–71), and he did valuable research on marine zoology. His central work, however, lay in neurology, where he explored the interfaces between neurological organization and consciousness, developing the idea of 'unconscious cerebration'. His other works are *Principles of Human Physiology* (1846), *The Microscope and its Revelations* (1856), *Principles of Mental Physiology* (1874), and *Nature and Man* (1888). He was the brother of **Mary Carpenter**.

Carpentier, Alejo 1904–80
Cuban novelist

Born in Havana to a French mother and a Russian father, he lived in Europe from the age of 10, but returned to Cuba in the early 1920s. He studied architecture as a young man, and later became a musicologist. After founding the magazine *Revista de Avance* (1927), he was imprisoned as a communist, then lived in Paris (1928–39). After World War II he served in several official government posts, including cultural attaché in Paris to **Fidel Castro**. He also spent some years in the USA and Venezuela. A widely admired writer, his numerous books include *El reino de este mundo* (1949, Eng trans *The Kingdom of this World*, 1957), *Los pasos perdidos* (1953, Eng trans *The Lost Steps*, 1956) and *El siglo de las luces* (1962, Eng trans *Explosion in a Cathedral*, 1963). 📖 R Gonzalez Echevarria, *Carpentier: the pilgrim at home* (1977)

Carpini, John of Plano, *Italian* Giovanni da Pian del Carpini c.1182–c.1253
Italian Franciscan monk and traveller

Born in Umbria, a disciple of St **Francis of Assisi**, he was head of the mission sent by Pope **Innocent IV** to the Emperor of the Mongols, whose warlike attitude had alarmed Christendom. A big man, more than 60 years old, he started from Lyons in April 1245, and, crossing the Dnieper, Don, Volga, Ural, and Jaxartes, in the summer of 1246 reached the Karakoram mountains, beyond Lake Baikal, where he met the supreme emperor. He returned to Kiev in June 1247, and so back to Lyons to report to the pope. He was later appointed Archbishop of Autivari.

Carpocrates of Alexandria 2nd century AD
Greek religious leader

He founded the gnostic sect of Carpocratians. They sought through contemplation the union, or return, of the individual soul to God and claimed among their spiritual predecessors **Pythagoras**, **Plato**, **Aristotle** and **Jesus Christ**.

Carpzov, Benedict 1595–1666
German jurist

Regarded as the founder of legal science in Germany, he did much to systematize German law, and held high offices in Dresden and Leipzig.

Carr, John Dickson, *pseudonym* Carter Dickson 1905–77
US detective story writer

He was born in Uniontown, Pennsylvania. The author of over 70 novels, he pioneered the 'locked room' mystery, the principles of which are described in his first book, *It Walks By Night* (1929). The room in which the murder had taken place had 'no secret entrances; the murderer was not hiding anywhere in the room; he did not go out by the window; he did not go out by the … door … Yet a murderer *had* beheaded his victim there'. Carr's finest novel is perhaps *The Hollow Man* (1931), featuring his most enduring detective, Dr Gideon Fell, a portly, learned, rather dandyish Edwardian figure, partly modelled on **G K Chesterton**. Under the name Carter Dickson, he wrote over 20 novels in which the detective is the more buffoonish Sir Henry Merrivale.

Carrà, Carlo 1881–1966
Italian painter

Born in Quargnento, Alexandria, he studied at the Brera Academy, Milan, aligning himself first (1909–14) with the Futurists, with paintings like *Funeral of the Anarchist Galli* (1911). He was one of the signatories of the Futurist Manifesto at the Exhibition in Paris in 1911. In 1915 he met **Giorgio de Chirico** and was influenced by his metaphysical painting movement. Carrà's aim thereafter was to synthesize past and present, seeking a bridge between **Giotto** and **Cézanne**.

Carracci, Agostino 1557–1602
Italian engraver

Born in Bologna, he dabbled in poetry and literature, but made his reputation as a painter and engraver on copper. His brother **Annibale Carracci's** jealousy is said to have driven him from Rome (where they did the frescoes in the Farnese Palace) to Parma, where he died. He had an illegimate son, Antonio Marziale (1583–1618), also a painter. He was the cousin of **Ludovico Carracci**.

Carracci, Annibale 1540–1609
Italian artist

Born in Bologna, he was the brother of **Agostino Carracci** and cousin of **Ludovico Carraci**, and leading member of a Bolognese dynasty. He was responsible for the revival of Italian painting after the vapid excesses of the later Mannerist period. The chief influences on his style were **Raphael** and **Correggio**. He was a talented draughtsman, and many of the family's drawings are in the British Royal Collection at Windsor. Apart from being the inventor of caricature in the modern sense, he was also a lively genre painter. In his greatest work, the ceiling of the Palazzo Farnese in Rome (1597–1600), he combines the influence of the antique with those of the High Renaissance masters, **Michelangelo** and **Raphael**. He was also the father of the idealized landscape which reached perfection in the hands of **Claude** and **Nicola Poussin**. **Zampieri Domenichino** and **Guido Reni** were both students at the Carracci Academy.

Carracci, Ludovico 1555–1619
Italian painter

Born in Bologna, he studied art there and in Parma, Mantua and Venice, and became a distinguished teacher. With **Agostino Carracci** and **Annibale Carracci**, his cousins, he established an 'eclectic' school of painting in Bologna, the Accademia degli Incamminati. His own works include the *Madonna and Child Enthroned* and the *Transfiguration* (both still in Bologna).

Carranza, Venustiano 1859–1920
Mexican political leader

Born into a landowning family in Cuatro Ciénegas, he became governor of his native state, Cohuila, which he led (1910) in the revolution against Porfirio Díaz. In 1913 he became the leader of the forces that overthrew General Victoriano Huerta. After a power struggle with other revolutionary leaders, Carranza became President (1915); he was a moderate who favoured political reforms but opposed land redistribution and mistrusted the labour movement. After he failed to enforce the progressive constitution of 1917, he was overthrown (1920) by a reform coalition. He fled on horseback into the mountains but was overtaken and killed.

Carr-Boyd, Ann Kirsten 1938–
Australian composer, teacher and music historian
She was born in Sydney and educated at Sydney University. A leading authority on Aboriginal and early Australian music, her many orchestral, chamber and instrumental compositions include *Symphony in Three Movements* (1964), *Three Songs of Love* (1975), *Festival* (1980), *Australian Baroque* (1984) and *Suite Veronese* (1985). Commissions include *Fanfare for Aunty* (1974), for the opening of the ABC's FM transmissions, and *The Bells of Sydney Harbour* (1979) for the Sydney Organ Society.

Carré, John Le See Le Carré, John

Carrel, Alexis 1873–1944
US experimental surgeon, Nobel Prize winner
Born in Lyons, France, he studied medicine at Lyons University (from 1890) and was attached to hospitals in Lyons from 1893 to 1900, when he obtained his medical degree. He discovered a method of suturing blood vessels which made it possible to replace arteries. As an assistant in physiology at the University of Chicago (from 1904), he experimented with transplantation of organs, such as kidneys, in animals. Much of the later progress in this field relied upon his pioneering work. In 1906 he was appointed to the Rockefeller Institute for Medical Research in New York City, where he developed techniques for tissue culture. He was awarded the 1912 Nobel Prize for physiology or medicine for these experiments. During World War I, he helped Henry Dakin to develop 'Dakin's solution' for sterilizing deep wounds. After the outbreak of World War II he returned to France, and established the Institute for the Study of Human Problems, hoping to introduce a programme of eugenics, nutrition and hygiene. He died of heart failure during the German occupation.

Carreño de Miranda, Juan 1614–85
Spanish painter
He was born in Avilés. Velázquez's assistant and successor at the Spanish court, he painted religious pictures and frescoes, such as the altarpiece, *Founding of the Order of the Trinity* (Louvre, Paris), as well as portraits.

Carrera Andrade, Jorge 1903–78
Ecuadorean poet and diplomat
Born in Quito, he was a diplomat by profession. He helped to found the Ecuadorean Socialist Party in 1926. His first poetry was in the *modernista* vein of Rubén Darío, but he soon broke with this, and his first collection, *Estanque inefable* (1922, 'Ineffable Pond'), consisted of mostly rural poems. He also adapted the Japanese haiku into Spanish. Translations of his poems include *Selected Poems* (1972). His *Reflections on Spanish American Poetry* was published in the USA in 1972. 📖 A Flores, *The Literature of Spanish America* (1966–69)

Carreras, José Maria 1946–
Spanish tenor
Born in Barcelona, he made his debut at the Liceo there in 1970. He first appeared at Covent Garden, London and at the Metropolitan Opera in 1974, at La Scala in 1975 and at Salzburg in 1976. After severe illness in the mid-1980s, he returned to the stage. In 1990 he performed alongside Placido Domingo and Luciano Pavarotti in the acclaimed 'Three Tenors' concert at the open-air Caracalla Theatre in Rome. He also sang at the 1992 Barcelona Olympics.

Carrero Blanco, Luis 1903–73
Spanish politician and naval officer
Director of Naval Operations in 1939, he later rose to the rank of admiral (1966). He became an under-secretary to the presidency in 1941, and for the next 32 years he was effectively General Franco's right-hand man. He became a minister in 1951, vice-premier in 1967 and, in 1973, the first Prime Minister other than Franco since 1939. He was absolutely loyal to Franco and shared his ultra-reactionary outlook, hating 'communists', 'freemasons' and 'liberals', although his visceral anti-Semitism set him apart. After Franco, he was the key figure of the regime and the embodiment of continuity, and his assassination by the Basque nationalist organization ETA was a grave blow to the regime.

Carrier, Jean Baptiste 1756–94
French revolutionary
He was born in Yolai, near Aurillac. In the National Convention he helped to form the Revolutionary Tribunal, voted for the death of the Louis XVI, demanded the arrest of the Duke of Orléans, and assisted in the overthrow of the Girondins. At Nantes in 1793 he massacred in four months 16,000 Vendéens and other prisoners, chiefly by drowning them in the Loire (the *noyades*), but also by shooting them. After the fall of Robespierre he was tried and guillotined.

Carrier, Willis Haviland 1876–1950
US engineer and inventor
Born in Angola, New York State, he designed his first machine to control humidity for a New York printing plant in 1902. He formed the Carrier Engineering Corporation in 1915, and in 1939 invented a practical air-conditioning system for skyscrapers.

Carriera, Rosalba Giovanna 1675–1757
Italian painter
Born in Venice, she was famed for her flattering portraits and miniatures, some of them in pastel, especially on ivory, such as *Portrait of a Man* (National Gallery, London). She introduced the pastel technique to France, on a visit in 1720–21, and wrote an account of her visit, *Diario...* (1865).

Carrière, Eugène 1849–1906
French painter
Born in Gournay-sur-Marne, he lived and worked in Paris, specializing in domestic groups and portraits. His soft tonalities inspired Edmond de Goncourt to call him 'the modern Madonna painter'.

Carrière, Jean-Claude 1931–
French writer, actor and director
He was born in Colombières-sur-Orbes. An association with comedy director Pierre Étaix brought his first involvement with the cinema as co-director of the short films *Rupture* (1961) and *Heureux anniversaire* (1961, *Happy Anniversary*). *Le Journal d'une femme de chambre* (1964, *The Diary of a Chambermaid*) was the first of six films he wrote in collaboration with Luis Buñuel that revealed a dry, dark humour and ability to dissect the social and sexual hypocrisies of the middle-classes. Their subsequent collaborations include *Belle de jour* (1967), and *Le Charme discrèt de la bourgeoisie* (1972, *The Discreet Charm of the Bourgeoisie*). A prolific scenarist whose work is often laced with a sense of anti-authoritarianism and irony, his many screenplays include *The Tin Drum* (1979), *Danton* (1982), *The Unbearable Lightness Of Being* (1988) and *Cyrano de Bergerac* (1990). A novelist, he has also written for television and the theatre, most notably for Peter Brook's company.

Carrillo, Santiago 1915–
Spanish political leader
Secretary-General of the Socialist Youth at only 19, he was jailed for participation in the Asturian rising of 1934, and was a key figure in the merger of the Socialist Youth with the Communists before the Spanish Civil War. He has been widely held responsible for the massacre of Nationalist prisoners at Paracuellos de Jarama in 1936. Having become General-Secretary of the exiled Spanish Communist Party (PCE) in 1960, in the 1970s he led the

party from neo-Stalinism to Eurocommunism. He returned to Spain in 1976. Although the PCE won 23 seats in the 1979 general election, it won a mere four in 1982. Carrillo resigned to found his own communist party, finally entering the Partido Socialista Obrera Español (PSOE, Spanish Socialist Workers' Party) in 1991.

Carrington, Dora de Houghton, known as Carrington, married name Partridge 1893–1932
English painter

Born in Hereford, she went to the Slade School of Art in 1910 and became a member of the Bloomsbury Group. In around 1914 she worked for **Roger Fry's** Omega Workshops. She painted landscapes and portraits inspired by her many intense, relationships, notably her deep love for **Lytton Strachey**, with whom she set up home in 1916. Several weeks after his death she committed suicide.

Carrington, Leonora, married name Weisz 1917–
Mexican painter and writer

Born in Clayton Green, Lancashire, the daughter of a textiles tycoon, she trained at **Amédée Ozenfant's** Academy in London. In 1937 she became a close friend of **Max Ernst**. Fleeing to Spain in 1940, she suffered a nervous breakdown, and her book *Down Below* (1943) describes the horrors of her treatment in a Santander clinic. In Madrid and Lisbon she discovered the work of **Hieronymus Bosch** and her painting shows his influence, as in *The Temptation of St Anthony* (1947). She exhibited at the Venice Biennale in 1942 and the same year went to Mexico, becoming a Mexican citizen. In 1944 she met Edward James, the chief collector of her work, who introduced her to *The Tibetan Book of the Dead*, and she became a disciple of the **Dalai Lama**. After 1988 she divided her time between Mexico City and Chicago, continuing to paint vigorously. Among her best-known pictures are her *Self-Portrait* (1938), her *Portrait of Max Ernst* (1939) and *The Ancestor* (1968). There was a retrospective of her work at the Serpentine Gallery in London in 1992.

Carrington, Peter Alexander Rupert Carrington, 6th Baron (Ireland) 1919–
English Conservative politician

Born in London and educated at Eton and Sandhurst, after service in World War II, he held ministerial posts in the Conservative administrations of **Churchill** (1951–54), Anthony Eden (1954–56), Harold Macmillan (1957–63), Alec Douglas-Home (Baron Home) (1963–64), Edward Heath (1970–74) and Margaret Thatcher (1979–82). He also served as High Commissioner to Australia (1956–59). As Foreign Secretary (1979–82) he was instrumental in establishing independence for Zimbabwe (1980). He resigned in 1982, accepting responsibility for the Argentinian invasion of the Falkland Islands. He was Secretary-General of NATO (1984–88) and Chairman of the EC conference on Yugoslavia (1991–92). His autobiography *Reflect on Things Past* was published in 1988. 📖 Patrick Cosgrave, *Carrington: A Life and a Policy* (1985)

Carrington, Richard Christopher 1826–75
English astronomer

Born in Chelsea, London and educated at Trinity College, Cambridge, he became Observer at the University of Durham (1847–52) where he worked on comets and minor planets. He later set up his own private observatory at Redhill, near Reigate in Surrey, where he carried out a substantial programme of observations, resulting in a catalogue of 3,735 stars close to the celestial pole, for which he was awarded the Gold Medal of the Royal Astronomical Society (1859). He also worked on the Sun's rotation, noting the apparent motions of sunspots across

its disc. He was able to represent its rotation and its dependence on solar latitude by a formula which came to be universally adopted.

Carroll, Charles 1737–1832
American Revolutionary leader

Born in Annapolis, Maryland, into a powerful Irish Catholic family, he was the cousin of **John Carroll**, the first American Catholic bishop. After his education by the Jesuits in St Omer and at the Collège de Louis le Grand in Paris, he returned to the USA in 1765 and took possession of a large family estate. He was barred, as a Roman Catholic, from taking part in colonial politics, but he became involved in the pamphlet wars of the mid-1770s on behalf of the colonies. Joining the Patriots, he served on the Annapolis Committee of Correspondence, the Maryland Revolutionary Convention, and the Maryland Committee of Correspondence and Committee of Safety. He was a member of the Continental Congress (1776–78) and later became one of Maryland's first senators (1789–92). His politics were markedly conservative, as his Catholicism and his wealth might suggest, but his adherence to the Revolutionary cause represented an opportunity for full political participation and was inspirational to other American Catholics. He was later director of the Baltimore and Ohio Railroad, and at his death he was the last surviving signer of the Declaration of Independence.

Carroll, James 1854–1907
US physician

Born in Woolwich, England, he emigrated in childhood to Canada and then the USA. Serving as a surgeon in the US army, and in association with **Walter Reed**, he did valuable research on yellow fever, deliberately infecting himself with the disease in the process (1900). He and Reed were the first to implicate a virus in human disease. In 1902 Carroll became Professor of Bacteriology and Pathology at Columbian (now George Washington) University and the Army Medical School.

Carroll, John 1735–1815
American prelate

Born in Upper Marlbro, Maryland, he trained for the priesthood in France and then Belgium. He entered the Jesuit Order in 1753 and was ordained priest in 1769. The Maryland priests petitioned **Pius VI** for a bishop in America, and Carroll was appointed to the see of Baltimore in 1789, the first American Catholic bishop. In 1808 he was made archbishop and the diocese was divided into four sees.

Carroll, Lewis, pseudonym of Charles Lutwidge Dodgson 1832–98
English children's writer and mathematician

He was born in Daresbury, Cheshire, and educated at Christ Church, Oxford, where he lectured in mathematics after 1855 and took orders in 1861. His most famous book, *Alice's Adventures in Wonderland* (1865), had its origin in a boat trip which he made with Alice Liddell and her sisters, the daughters of the Dean of his college, Henry George Liddell. A sequel, *Through the Looking-Glass and What Alice Found There*, appeared in December 1871 (dated 1872). They were illustrated by Sir John Tenniel, and have since appeared in innumerable translations and editions. Their success among children was doubtless due to their cast of fantastic characters (Tweedledum and Tweedledee, the White Rabbit and the March Hare) and the fact that Carroll eschewed moralising. His other works include *Phantasmagoria and other poems* (1869), *The Hunting of the Snark* (1876), *Rhyme? and Reason?* (1883) and *Sylvie and Bruno* (2 vols, 1889 and 1893). Of his mathematical works *Euclid and his Modern Rivals* (1879) is still of interest. He was also a pioneer photographer, and took many portraits, particularly of young girls. His diaries appeared in 1953, and an edition of his letters in 1979.

Carson, Edward Henry Carson, Baron
1854–1935
Irish politician and judge
Born in Dublin, he was called to the Irish Bar, became QC of the Irish (1880) and English Bar (1894), Conservative MP for Dublin University (1892–1918) and the Duncairn division of Belfast (1918–21), Solicitor-General for Ireland (1892) and for England (1900–06), Attorney-General (1915), First Lord of the Admiralty (1917), and a member of the War Cabinet (1917–18). As leader of the Irish Unionists, he organized the Ulster Volunteers, and violently opposed Home Rule. He was a lord of appeal (1921–29).

Carson, Hampton Lawrence 1914–
US evolutionist
Born in Philadelphia, he was educated at the University of Pennsylvania and began his career at Washington University, where he was later appointed professor (1956–71). From 1971 to 1985 he was Professor of Genetics at the University of Hawaii, then emeritus. Carson is best known for his work on the evolution of new species in Hawaiian Drosophilidae (the fruit fly). He developed the idea of the 'founder effect' (originally proposed by Ernst Mayr), using chromosomal inversions to mark relationships, and devising probable evolutionary lineages. These ideas were summarized in *Genetics, Speciation and the Founder Principle* (1989).

Carson, Johnny (John William) 1925–
US television presenter
Born in Corning, Iowa, he studied journalism at Nebraska University and started his career as a radio comedy writer, before working as a television announcer in Omaha, Nebraska, and Los Angeles. He soon had his own television comedy show, *Carson's Cellar* (1951), then became a writer for *The Red Skelton Show*, later standing in for the star. That led to *The Johnny Carson Show* (1955–56). After hosting the game show *Who Do You Trust?* (1957–62), he took over from Jack Paar as presenter of *The Tonight Show* in 1962, soon becoming the highest-paid star on television. He wrote *Happiness is a Dry Martini* (1965) and formed his own company, Carson Productions, in 1980. He retired from *The Tonight Show* in 1992 and was awarded the Presidential Medal of Freedom the same year.

Carson, Kit (Christopher) 1809–68
US frontiersman
Born in Madison County, Kentucky, he became a trapper and hunter in New Mexico in 1825, ranging as far afield as California and Montana and marrying a woman of the Arapahoe people in 1836. His knowledge of Native American customs and languages led to his becoming guide in John C Frémont's explorations (1842–45), and Indian agent in New Mexico (1853). He took part in the conquest of California, and as a brigadier general of volunteers he fought Native American tribes that sided with the Confederacy in the Civil War. Several places are named after him, including Carson City, Nevada.

Carson, Rachel Louise 1907–64
US naturalist and science writer
Born in Springdale, Pennsylvania, she studied biology at Johns Hopkins University, taught at Maryland University (1931–36) and worked as a marine biologist for the US Fish and Wildlife Service (1936–49). She became well known with *The Sea Around Us* (1951), which warned of the increasing danger of large-scale marine pollution, and the hard-hitting *Silent Spring* (1962), which directed public concern to the problems caused by synthetic pesticides and their effect on food chains. The resulting controls on their use owe much to her work, which also contributed to the growing conservationist movement, from the 1960s onwards. 📖 Carol B Gartner, *Rachel Carson* (1983)

Carson, Willie (William Hunter Fisher) 1942–
Scottish jockey
Born in Stirling, he developed late, and was 19 before he rode his first winner, and was further held back by a car accident in 1967. In 1972, however, he became the first Scotsman to be champion jockey and recorded his first Classic success, on High Top in the 2000 Guineas. He recorded a notable royal double for Queen Elizabeth II in 1977 when winning the Oaks and the St Leger on Dunfermline. He had to wait until 1979 for his first Derby winner, Troy, but immediately won again on Henbit in 1980. In all, he has ridden 17 classic winners and is third in the all-time winners table. A serious accident in the summer of 1996 led to his retirement the following year.

Carstares, William 1649–1715
Scottish clergyman
Born in Cathcart, Glasgow, he studied at Edinburgh and Utrecht, Holland, and became friend and adviser to the Prince of Orange (William III). He was arrested as a spy in London (1675), and imprisoned in Edinburgh until 1679. In 1683 he was again arrested, and after an imprisonment of a year and a half, returned to Holland to be chaplain to the Prince of Orange. Afterwards, he secured good relations between the new king and the Church of Scotland. From 1693 to the death of the king in 1702 he had great influence in Scottish affairs, and was popularly called 'Cardinal Carstares' by the Jacobites. He was elected Principal of Edinburgh University in 1703, and between 1705 and 1714 was four times Moderator of the General Assembly. His influence helped to pass the Treaty of Union (1707).

Carstens, Asmus Jakob 1754–98
German painter
Born near Schleswig, he studied art at Copenhagen and from 1783 to 1788 barely supported himself by portrait painting in Lübeck and Berlin before his *Fall of the Angels* gained him a professorship in the Academy of Art in Berlin in 1790. He lived in Rome from 1792, working on classical themes. He was a precursor of Johann Friedrich Overbeck and Peter von Cornelius.

Carswell, Catherine Roxburgh, *née* Macfarlane
1879–1946
Scottish novelist and critic
Born in Glasgow, the daughter of a merchant, she was educated at the Park School there, and in Frankfurt-am-Main, Germany. She became a socialist after reading Robert Blatchford at the age of 17, and went on to study English at Glasgow University. Her first marriage having been annulled after her husband attempted to kill her, she married fellow journalist and critic Donald Carswell (1917). She made her reputation as a dramatic and literary critic for the *Glasgow Herald* (1907–15) but lost this position when she wrote a review of D H Lawrence's banned novel *The Rainbow*. Lawrence subsequently encouraged her in her work, including an autobiographical novel *Open the Door* (1920), and her *Life of Burns* (1930). She also wrote biographies of Lawrence, *The Savage Pilgrim: A Narrative of D.H. Lawrence* (1932), and Boccaccio, *The Tranquil Heart* (1937). 📖 *Lying Awake: an unfinished autobiography* (1952)

Cartan, Élie Joseph 1869–1951
French mathematician
Born in Dolomieu, his mathematical talent earned him a scholarship first to the Lycée and then to the École Normale Supérieure. He was professor in Paris from 1912 to 1940. One of the most original mathematicians of his time, he worked on Lie groups and differential geometry,

and founded the subject of analysis on differentiable manifolds, which is essential to modern fundamental physical theories. Among his discoveries are the theory of spinors, the method of moving frames and the exterior differential calculus. The novelty of his ideas and their somewhat obscure presentation meant that their importance was only fully appreciated during the later part of his life. He is now seen to be a seminal figure for much of the mathematics of this century. His son Henri(-Paul) Cartan (1904–) also became a mathematician.

Carte, Richard D'Oyly 1844–1901
English impresario and manager

He was born in London and after working in his father's musical instrument-making business, became a concert agent. From 1875 he produced the first operettas by Gilbert and Sullivan, with whom he formed a partnership. He built the Savoy Theatre in London (1881), the first public building to be lit by electricity. Another theatre building, the Royal English Opera House (1891), failed. After his death the D'Oyly Carte company continued to perform Gilbert and Sullivan in traditional style for many years. ⌑ Robert Wilson and Frederick Lloyd, *Gilbert and Sullivan: The Official D'Oyly Carte Picture History* (1984)

Carter, Angela Olive, *née* Stalker 1940–92
English novelist and short-story writer

Born in London and educated at Bristol University, she taught creative writing in England, the USA and Australia, and lived in Japan for two years, an experience recorded in *Nothing Sacred* (1982). Her fiction, characterized by imaginative use of fantasy, vibrant humour and psychological symbolism, includes the novels *The Magic Toyshop* (1967), *The Infernal Desire Machines of Dr Hoffman* (1972), *Nights at the Circus* (1984), and *Wise Children* (1991), and the short-story collections *Black Venus* (1985) and *American Ghosts and Old World Wonders* (1993). *The Sadeian Woman* (1979) is a feminist reinterpretation of the Marquis de Sade. She also wrote poetry, children's stories, and radio plays and, with Neil Jordan, wrote the screenplay for his film from her stories, *The Company of Wolves* (1984).

Carter, Benny (Bennet Lester) 1907–
US alto saxophonist, trumpeter and composer

Born in New York City, he was largely self-taught as a musician, and plays trumpet and clarinet in addition to his primary instrument, alto saxophone. His warm tone and elegant flowing lines were hugely influential in the style of the swing era, and he is among the most important writers of big band arrangements composing for the Benny Goodman orchestra, among others. He lived in London from 1936–38, where his influence was enormous, and settled in Los Angeles in 1942. He was one of the first black writers to work on film (and later television) soundtracks within the studio system in Hollywood. He played occasional concerts, but stepped up his activities in the 1970s, and continued into the 1990s, playing in a sophisticated mainstream style which registered his awareness of post-swing developments. ⌑ M and E Berger *A Life In American Music* (1982)

Carter, Betty, *professional name of* Lillie Mae Jones, *also called* Lorraine Carter 1929–98
US jazz singer

Born in Flint, Michigan, and raised in Detroit, she came of age in the bebop era, and sang with touring bebop musicians, including Charlie Parker and Dizzy Gillespie. Bandleader Lionel Hampton, who employed her from 1948, nicknamed her 'Betty Bebop', and although she resented the belittling echo of the famous cartoon character, she adopted the forename. A brilliant vocal improviser, and a genuine jazz singer, she always resisted commercial alternatives, even when times were hard. Popular in the 1950s, she toured with Ray Charles in

1961–63, then from 1969 toured with her own trio. In 1971 she set up her own Bet-Car record label. After being 'rediscovered' in 1975, she went on to re-establish herself as a major jazz name in the 1990s.

Carter, Elliott Cook, Jnr 1908–
US composer

Born in New York City, he was befriended by Charles Ives, who introduced him to contemporary music. He studied at Harvard with Walter Piston and in Paris with Nadia Boulanger, teaching Greek and mathematics at St John's College, Annapolis (1940–42), and later, music at Yale and Columbia universities. His first work to gain international recognition was a string quartet (1953), the first of four quartets, the second of which won a Pulitzer Prize in 1960. This and subsequent works display an intellectual yet emotionally charged style, with the serial element extended to great rhythmic and metrical complexity. His output includes symphonies, other orchestral music, several concertos, songs and chamber music. His collected writings were published in 1977.

Carter, Howard 1874–1939
English Egyptologist

Born in London, he joined Flinders Petrie's archaeological survey of Egypt as a draughtsman in 1891, drawing inscriptions and sculptures at Thebes and at the Dynasty XVIII temple of Hatshepsut at Dayr al-Bahri. He subsequently served as inspector-general of the Egyptian antiquities department, from 1907 conducting his own research under the patronage of George Herbert, 5th Earl of Carnarvon. His discoveries included the tombs of Hatshepsut (1907), Tuthmosis IV and, most notably, in 1922 the virtually intact burial of the Dynasty XVIII King Tut'ankhamun. The work of emptying the chambers, photographing, conserving and despatching the treasures to Cairo occupied him for the rest of his life, but he failed through ill health to produce a final, detailed report. ⌑ C W Ceram, *Gods, Graves and Scholars* (2nd edn, 1967)

Carter, Jimmy (James Earl) 1924–
39th President of the USA

Born in Plains, Georgia, he graduated from the US Naval Academy in 1946 and served in the US navy until 1953, when he took over the family peanut business and other business enterprises. As Governor of Georgia (1970–74) he expressed an enlightened policy towards the rights of blacks and women. In 1976 he won the Democratic presidential nomination over several much more prominent figures and went on to win a narrow victory over Gerald Ford for the presidency. Throughout his campaign he presented an air of informality, honesty, morality and religious fervour which appealed to an American electorate tired of the scandal and intrigue of the Nixon administration. On election, he promised to institute a populist form of government giving the people a greater say in the administration. He also promised to set up effective energy and health programmes, to concern himself with civil and human rights issues and to try to restrict the making of nuclear weapons. His presidency (1977–81) was notable for the Panama Canal Treaty, which provided for the eventual transfer of the canal to Panamanian control, and the Camp David Accords (1978), which he brokered between Israel and Egypt against considerable odds. As an outsider in Washington he had little success in dealing with Congress, which refused to ratify his arms limitation treaty with the Soviet Union. High inflation, recession and the energy crisis irritated the US public and eroded Carter's popularity, which plummeted in 1979–80 as a result of the seizure of US embassy hostages by Islamic fundamentalists in Iran. He was defeated by the Republican Ronald Reagan in the 1980 election. A prolific human rights campaigner, he has worked as a leader of international observer teams (1989–90), hosted peace negotiations (Ethiopia, 1989) and has been highly active in his role as UN ambassador, taking part in talks with Rwanda in 1996. He has received several awards including the 1993 Matsunaga Medal of Peace. He is the author of several books including *The Blood of Abraham: Insights into the Middle East* (1985) and he published his memoirs, *Keeping Faith*, in 1982. 📖 Peter Meyer, *James Earl Carter* (1978)

Carter, Rosalynn Smith, *née* Smith 1927–
US humanitarian and First Lady as wife of President Jimmy Carter

Born in Plains, Georgia, she married Jimmy Carter in 1946. When her husband was Governor of Georgia (1971–74), she began to devote herself to developing a national strategy for helping the mentally ill, a work which she continued as First Lady (1977–81). Since then she has served on numerous committees dedicated to helping the mentally ill, and promoting children's health and worldwide peace, including the board of Habitat for Humanity, being a sponsor of the National Alliance for Research on Schizophrenia and Depression, and chairing the Carter Center Mental Health Task Force. She received the Volunteer of the Decade Award from the National Mental Health Association (1980), the Notre Dame award for International Humanitarian Service (1992) and the Eleanor Roosevelt Living World award for peace links (1992). Her books include *First Lady from Plains* (1984) and *Helping Yourself Help Others: A Book for Caregivers* (1994).

Carter, Truda See Adams, Truda (Gertrude)

Carter Family
US country music artists

The Carter Family, along with Jimmie Rodgers, were the first stars of country music. The original group in 1927 featured A(lvin) P(leasant Delaney) Carter (1891–1960), his wife Sara Carter (1898–1979, *née* Dougherty) and her cousin, Maybelle Carter (1909–78, *née* Addington). Their seminal recordings of 1928–35 established a new style of harmony singing which has been hugely influential in the development of modern country music. The original trio broke up in 1943, but Maybelle continued to perform with her daughters as The Carter Sisters. A P and Sara made a comeback in 1952, while Maybelle and Sara later reunited as The Original Carter Family in 1967. Several of their children were involved in the group, the best known of whom is singer June Carter Cash (1929–), who was married for a time to Johnny Cash. 📖 J Atkins, *The Carter Family* (1973)

Carteret, John, 1st Earl Granville 1690–1763
English orator and politician

In 1719 he was ambassador extraordinary to Sweden and in 1721 he was appointed one of the two foreign secretaries under Sir Robert Walpole and, as such, attended in 1723 the Congress of Cambrai (1723). From 1730 to 1742 he led in the House of Lords the party opposed to Walpole and became the real head of the next administration, although nominally only Secretary of State. He was with George II at the Battle of Dettingen (1743).

Carteret, Philip d.1796
English navigator

He sailed as lieutenant in John Byron's voyage round the world (1764–66), and commanded the *Swallow* in Samuel Wallis's world expedition (1766). Separated from Wallis in the Strait of Magellan, he discovered Pitcairn and other small islands (one of the Solomon Islands is named after him) and returned round the Cape of Good Hope to England in 1769.

Cartier, Sir Georges Étienne 1814–73
Canadian politician

He was born in St Antoine, Quebec, and trained as a lawyer. In 1837 he took part in the rebellion led by Louis Papineau. He was attorney-general under John Macdonald in 1856 and then, as the leader of the *Bleu* bloc of Canada East, served with him as joint Conservative Prime Minister (1858–62). In 1858 the Macdonald–Cartier administration was defeated, but reformed as the Cartier–Macdonald ministry in a mutual exchange of posts. This lasted until 1862, and Cartier returned to government in the great coalition of 1864 which negotiated confederation. Because of his involvement with the Canadian Pacific Railway and Sir Hugh Allan, he was defeated in 1872.

Cartier, Jacques 1491–1557
French navigator

Born in St Malo, between 1534 and 1541 he made three voyages to North America searching for a westerly route to Asia. He discovered the St Lawrence River.

Cartier-Bresson, Henri 1908–
French photographer and artist

Born in Paris, he studied painting (with André Lhote in 1927–28) and literature, before taking up photography after a trip to West Africa in 1930. His first photographs were published in 1933. In the later 1930s he visited Mexico and the USA and worked as an assistant to film director Jean Renoir. After World War II, during which he escaped from imprisonment to join the Resistance, he co-founded the independent photographic agency, Magnum Photos. He worked only in black-and-white, concerned exclusively with the spontaneous capturing of moments illustrating contemporary life. His books include *Images à la sauvette* (1952, 'The Decisive Moment'), *The Europeans* (1955) and *The World of Henri Cartier-Bresson* (1968). In the mid-1970s he gave up photography, and returned to painting and drawing.

Cartland, Dame (Mary) Barbara Hamilton 1901–
English popular romantic novelist

She was born in Edgbaston, Birmingham, and is step-grandmother of Diana, Princess of Wales. She published her first novel, *Jigsaw*, in 1923, and has since produced well over 400 bestselling books, mostly novels of chaste romantic love designed for female readers, but also including biographies and books on food, health and beauty, and several volumes of autobiography. She earned a place in the *Guinness Book of Records* for writing 26 books in the year 1983. An ardent advocate of health foods and fitness for the elderly, she has championed causes like the St John's Ambulance Brigade and the provision of campsites for Romany gipsies. She was made DBE in 1991. Her most recent volume of autobiography is *I Reach for the Stars* (1994). 📖 *The Years of Opportunity, 1939–1945* (1948)

Cartwright, Edmund 1743–1823
English inventor and clergyman

He was born in Marnham, Nottinghamshire. Educated at Wakefield and University College, Oxford, he became rector of Goadby-Marwood, Leicestershire, in 1779, where he made various agricultural improvements. A visit in 1784 to Richard Arkwright's cotton-spinning mills resulted in his invention of the power loom (1785). He built a weaving mill at Doncaster (1787), but it met with opposition and did not come into practical use until the 19th century. He also took out patents for wool-combing machines (1790), and joined Robert Fulton in his efforts to develop steam navigation. His business went bankrupt in 1793, but in 1797 he patented an alcohol engine, and in 1809 the government awarded him £10,000 in recognition of the merit of his invention of the power loom. He was the brother of John Cartwright.

Cartwright, John, *known as* the Father of Reform
1740–1824
English reformer

Born in Marnham, Nottinghamshire, he served in the navy (1758–70), and in 1775 became major to the Nottinghamshire militia. He then began to write on politics, advocating annual parliaments, the ballot, and manhood suffrage, and afterwards taking up reform in farming, abolition of slavery, the national defences, and the liberties of Spain and Greece. In 1820 he was fined £100 for sedition. He was the brother of **Edmund Cartwright**.

Cartwright, Peter 1785–1872
US Methodist preacher

Born in Amherst County, Virginia, he received little education and lived a life of drinking and gambling on the frontier before becoming converted in 1801. He was ordained in Kentucky in 1806, and in 1846 was defeated by **Abraham Lincoln** in an election for congressman. He also published an autobiography (1856) and *The Backwoods Preacher* (1869).

Cartwright, William 1611–43
English playwright, poet and preacher

He was born in Northway, near Tewkesbury, Gloucester, and preached at Oxford. He wrote plays such as *The Royal Slave*, which was performed at Oxford before **Charles I** in 1636, and a play ridiculing Puritans, *The Ordinary* (c.1634). He was one of the group of young playwrights known as the 'sons' of **Ben Jonson**. A Chalmers, 'A Life', in *The Works of Early English Poets* (1810)

Caruso, Enrico 1873–1921
Italian tenor

He was born in Naples, the 18th of 20 children. He made his first professional appearance in *Faust* (1895), went to London (1902) and New York (1903). The great power and musical purity of his voice, combined with his acting ability, won him recognition as one of the finest tenors of all time. Dorothy Caruso, *Caruso, His Life and Death* (1945)

Carvalho e Mello, Marquês de Pombal See Pombal, Marquis de

Carver, George Washington c.1860–1943
US botanist and scientist

Born into slavery on a farm near Diamond Grove, Missouri, he worked his way through Iowa State College, obtaining an MA in agriculture in 1896. He was then invited by **Booker T Washington** to become director of agricultural research (1896–1943) at the Tuskegee Institute in Alabama. Hoping to improve the lives of disadvantaged black farmers and the economy of the South, he promoted peanuts and sweet potatoes as alternatives to soil-depleting cotton and developed numerous products that could be made from each of these crops. He lectured widely on his work and was influential in the crop diversification that occurred in the South in the early 20th century.

Carver, John c.1575–1621
English colonialist

Bor in the English Midlands, he emigrated to Holland in 1609. He joined the Pilgrim Fathers and became their agent for the expedition to the New World. He chartered the *Mayflower*, sailing in June 1620, and was elected first governor of the colony at New Plymouth, Massachusetts. He died within five months of their landing.

Carver, (Richard) Michael (Power) Carver, Baron 1915–
English field marshal

He was born in Surrey, educated at Winchester, and commissioned into the Royal Tank Corps in 1935. In World War II he served with distinction in North Africa

(1941–43), in Italy (1943) and Normandy (1944) before commanding the 4th Independent Armoured Brigade in North West Europe (1944–45). He became Chief of the General Staff (1971–73), field marshal (1973) and Chief of the Defence Staff (1973–76). He then became the designated British Resident Commissioner in Rhodesia (now Zimbabwe) from 1977 to 1978. He has written several historical, biographical and strategic studies, as well as *Out of Step: Memoirs of Field-Marshal Lord Carver* (1989). He was made a life peer in 1977.

Carver, Raymond 1939–88
US poet and short-story writer

Born in Clatskanie, Oregon, he married at 18 and struggled for many years to provide for a young family and further his career as a writer. He also fought against chronic alcoholism. Although he published a number of small-press books of poetry and one chapbook of fiction in the 1960s and early 1970s, it was not until the publication of the collection *Will You Please Be Quiet, Please?* (1976) that his work began to reach a wider audience. Both his fiction and his poetry are remarkable for their spare narratives, focusing on the lower and middle classes and dealing with states of transition: couples breaking up, people between jobs. He wrote no novels. He was a Guggenheim Fellow in 1979 and was twice awarded grants by the National Endowment for Arts. He taught at the University of Iowa, the University of Texas and the University of California. Other books include *Fire: Essays, Poems, Stories* (1984), *Elephant and Other Stories* (1988), and the poetry collections *Where Water Comes Together with Other Water* (1985) and *Ultramarine* (1985, published in Great Britain as *In A Marine Light: Selected Poems*).

Carver, Robert c.1484–c.1568
Scottish composer

He was canon of Scone, and attached to the Chapel Royal of Scotland. Five of his masses have survived, each showing an elaborate style with free use of counterpoint, and one of which is the only early 16th-century British example based on the *cantus firmus* 'L'Homme armé'. Of two surviving motets, *O bone Jesu* has 19 voice parts.

Cary, Henry Francis 1772–1844
English clergyman and translator

Born in Gibraltar and educated at Rugby, Sutton Coldfield, and Birmingham, he went to Christ Church, Oxford, and took holy orders in 1796. In 1805 he published a translation in blank verse of **Dante's** *Inferno*, and in 1814 of the whole *Divina Commedia*. He afterwards translated **Pindar's** *Odes* and **Aristophanes'** *Birds*, and wrote memoirs in continuation of **Samuel Johnson's** *Lives of the Poets*. He was buried in Westminster Abbey, London.

Cary, John c.1754–1835
English cartographer

He began as an engraver and became a land surveyor and publisher. His *New and Correct English Atlas* appeared in 1787 and county atlases followed, with a large *New Universal Atlas* in 1808. In 1794 he undertook a road survey of England and Wales, which was published as *Cary's New Itinerary* (1798). He was responsible for the *Improved Map of England and Wales etc* (1832) on the scale of half an inch to the mile. Sir Herbert George Fordham, *John Cary, Engraver, Map, Chart and Print-seller and Globemaker 1754 to 1835* (1925)

Cary, (Arthur) Joyce Lunel 1888–1957
English novelist

Born in Londonderry, Northern Ireland, of English parents, he was educated at Tunbridge Wells and Clifton College in England and later studied art in Edinburgh and Paris, graduating (1912) at Oxford. He served with the Red Cross in the Balkan War of 1912–13 and was decorated by the King of Montenegro. In 1913 he joined the

Nigerian Political Service and fought in a Nigerian regiment in World War I. Injuries and ill health forced his early retirement after the war to Oxford, where he took up writing. Drawing on his African experiences he wrote several novels, including *Mister Johnson* (1939). In 1941 he was awarded the James Tait Black Memorial Prize for *The House of Children*, and established himself with the trilogy, *Herself Surprised* (1940), *To be a Pilgrim* (1942) and *The Horse's Mouth* (1944). Other books include *Moonlight* (1946), *Prisoner of Grace* (1952), and *Not Honour More* (1955). He left an unfinished novel with a religious theme, *The Captive and the Free* (1959). 📖 W Allen, *Joyce Cary* (1953)

Cary, Tristram 1925–
Australian composer and teacher
Born in Oxford, England, the son of **Joyce Cary**, he went to Trinity College of Music (1948–50), and pioneered the development of electronic music, establishing his own studio in 1952. He became a director of the celebrated Electronic Music Studios in London and from 1967 to 1974 was Professor of Electronic Music at the Royal College of Music there. In 1979 he joined Adelaide University, South Australia, where he became Dean of Music, and is now honorary visiting Research Fellow. He has composed much music for films, theatre, radio and television.

Casals, Pablo, *also known as* Pau Casals 1876–1973
Spanish cellist, conductor and composer
Born in Vendrell, Tarragona, he studied at the Royal Conservatory, Madrid, and became Professor of Cello at the Conservatory in Barcelona (1896). After a period as lead cello for the Paris Opera (1895–98), he began to appear as a soloist. In 1905 he formed, with **Jacques Thibaud** and **Alfred Cortot**, a trio which became famous for its performance of classical works. He founded the Barcelona Orchestra (1919), which he conducted until he left Spain at the outbreak of the civil war (1936). In 1950 he founded an annual festival of classical chamber music in Prades, France. His own compositions consist of choral and chamber works. 📖 H L Kirk, *Pablo Casals* (1974)

Casanova (de Seingalt), Giacomo Girolamo 1725–98
Italian adventurer
Born in Venice, he was expelled from a seminary for scandalous conduct (1741), and by 1750 had been secretary to a cardinal, an ensign in the Venetian army, an abbé, a gambler, an alchemist and a violinist. In 1755 he was imprisoned in Venice for being a magician, but made a daring escape in 1756, and for the next 20 years wandered through Europe, meeting the great men and women of his time, and indulging in romantic escapades. He was the director of state lotteries in Paris, was knighted in the Netherlands, visited Russia but fled after a duel, and worked as a spy for **Louis XV** and as a police informer for the Venetian Inquisition. In 1785 he found a haven as librarian for Count von Waldstein in Bohemia. His reputation rests on his *Mémoires de J. Casanova de Seingalt*, which were first published in edited form in Leipzig (12 vols, 1828–38). The complete edition, *Histoire de ma vie* (Eng trans *History of my Life*) was first published in 1960. Primarily, and memorably, an account of his numerous sexual adventures, they also give an intriguing portrait of his age. 📖 J R Childs, *Casanova* (1987)

Casarès, Maria 1922–96
French actress
Born in Corunna, Spain, she was exiled during the Spanish civil war, and took up residence in Paris, where she had her intial success in **J M Synge's** *Deirdre of the Sorrows* in 1942. Her screen debut was made in **Marcel Carné's** *Les Enfants du Paradis* (1943, 'The Children of Paradise'). She became closely associated with the work of

the Existentialist playwrights **Albert Camus** and **Jean-Paul Sartre**, and had a success in **Racine's** *Phèdre* at the Comédie-Française before joining the Théâtre National Populaire (1955). She was France's leading tragic actress of her generation, and popularized a more tempestuous style than was traditional in classical French theatre.

Casella, Alfredo 1883–1947
Italian composer and musician
Born in Turin, he studied piano at the Paris Conservatory and first attracted attention as a composer in 1908. His work was varied but mainly neoclassical in character, and includes three operas, two symphonies, concertos for cello, violin and organ, as well as chamber music, piano pieces and songs. He produced editions of classical composers, and wrote books on **Igor Stravinsky**, **J S Bach** and **Beethoven**, and an autobiography (1941).

Casement, Sir Roger David 1864–1916
Irish patriot and British consular official
Born in Sandycove, County Dublin, he joined the British consular service and went to Africa where he condemned the treatment of native workers (1904). As consul-general at Rio de Janeiro he exposed the exploitation of rubber workers in the Congo and Peru, for which he was knighted in 1911. He joined the Irish Volunteers in 1913, and at the outbreak of World War I went to Berlin to try to obtain German help for Irish independence, attempting to form an Irish Brigade of prisoners of war with which he intended to invade Ireland and end British rule. In 1916 he was arrested on landing in Ireland from a German submarine to head the Sinn Féin rebellion. He was tried in England for high treason, and hanged. His controversial 'Black Diaries', revealing, among other things, homosexual practices, were long suppressed by the government, but ultimately published in 1959. In 1965, the British Government allowed his remains to be reinterred in Ireland. 📖 B L Reid, *The Lives of Roger Casement* (1976)

Casey, Richard (Gavin) Gardiner Casey, Baron 1890–1976
Australian statesman
He was born in Brisbane. He served in World War I, then in 1924 went to London as mediator for **Stanley Bruce**. Back home in 1931, he entered federal politics and became Treasurer in 1935. He became first Australian Minister to the USA in 1940, and Minister of State in the Middle East (a War Cabinet rank) in 1942. From 1944 to 1946 he was Governor of Bengal, and after his return to Australia, he was made Minister of National Development (1949–51) and was Minister for External Affairs from 1951 until 1960, when he became the first Australian life peer to sit in the House of Lords. He was Governor-General of Australia (1965–69) and was also made Australia's first Knight of the Garter.

Cash, Johnny (J R) 1932–
American country music singer, songwriter and guitarist
Born in Kingsland, Arkansas, into a cotton farming family. He was christened simply J R, and became Johnny by general usage. A complex and often deeply troubled personality, he became the best-known performer in country music in the 1960s, and helped spread it to a huge new audience. After discharge from the US air force, he signed to Sun records in 1955, where the success of 'I Walk The Line' established his style, and brought him a contract with Columbia. He turned out a string of hits in the 1960s, and had his own television show from 1969–71. Nicknamed 'The Man In Black' (he had a 1971 hit of that name), he has battled with many personal problems, but bounced back as a member of The Highwaymen with **Willie Nelson**, **Waylon Jennings** and Kris Kristofferson from 1985, while his 1994 album *American Recordings* sealed a remarkable renaissance. He was married to singer June

Carter Cash of the **Carter Family**. His brother, Tommy Cash (1940–), is also a country singer, while his daughter by an earlier marriage, Roseanne Cash (1932–), is an important contemporary country artist, although she has experienced — and chronicled in song — many of her father's personal problems in her own life. He published a religious novel in 1986 entitled *Man in White*. ▢ *The Man In Black* (1977)

Cash, Martin 1810–77
Australian thief and bushranger

Born in Enniscorthy, Ireland, in 1827 he was transported to Australia for seven years, for theft and attempted murder. In 1831 he received his ticket-of-leave, but was soon on the run again, accused of cattle-stealing. He fled to Hobart, Van Diemen's Land (Tasmania) in 1837 but three years later was sentenced to seven years for possession of stolen goods. With two others he escaped from the prison at Port Arthur, and became a bushranger. After shooting a constable in 1843 he was sentenced to death, which later commuted to life imprisonment on the penal settlement of Norfolk Island, where he became a model prisoner. He married a fellow-prisoner, received a pardon in 1853, returned to Hobart where he was appointed a constable and was for some years caretaker of the Botanic Gardens there.

Casimir, Hendrik Brugt Gerhard 1909–
Dutch physicist

Born in The Hague, he studied at the universities of Copenhagen and Leyden, and held various research appointments before joining the Philips company at Eindhoven (1942), where he became co-ordinator of the research laboratories (1946) and a member of the board of management (1957–72). He worked in numerous fields including quantum mechanics and paramagnetism. In 1934 he introduced an important theory of superconductivity called the 'two-fluid model', constructed on the assumption that in a superconductor electrons can exist either as a superfluid that moves through the crystal without hindrance by the lattice, or as a normal fluid that experiences resistance. He has also carried out research into the theory of hyperfine structure and irreversible thermodynamics. His books include *Magnetism and very Low Temperature* (1940) and *On the Interaction between Atomic Nuclei and Electrons* (1936). Later work by **John Bardeen** and others both includes and extends his ideas.

Čáslavská, Věra 1942–
Czech gymnast

Born in Prague, she switched from ice-skating to gymnastics as a 15-year-old, and went on to win 22 Olympic, World, and European titles (1959–68), and eight silver and three bronze medals. She won three Olympic gold medals in 1964, and four in 1968. She donated her medals (one each) to the four Czech leaders (**Alexander Dubček**, **Ludwik Svoboda**, **Oldřich Černík** and Smrkorsky) deposed following the Soviet invasion. Since 1990 she has been President of the Czech Olympic Committee.

Caslon, William 1692–1766
English type-founder

Born in Cradley, Worcestershire, he worked as an apprentice to a gunlock and barrel engraver before he set up his own business as a gun engraver and toolmaker in London in 1716. He soon began cutting type for printers, especially **William Bowyer**. His graceful 'old face' Caslon types were extensively used in Europe and the USA until the end of the 18th century, when they went out of fashion. Revived 50 years later, they have retained their popularity to the present day. His son William (1720–78) carried on the business.

Casona, Alejandro, *pseudonym of* Alejandro Rodriguez Alvarez 1903–65
Spanish dramatist

He was born in the Asturias. Starting out as a poet, he then became director of the Teatro del Pueblo (Theatre of the People) in 1931. His plays of the 1930s, grouped together as *teatro de evasión* (theatre of evasion), were influential—and, later, in the 1950s, were played all over eastern Europe. He fled to Buenos Aires (1939–62), having angered the Falangists with his *Nuestro Natacha* (1936,'Our Natacha'), about a reforming woman educator. One of his best-known plays is the sarcastic *Prohibido suicidarse en primavera* (1937,'It is forbidden to commit suicide in spring').

Casorati, Felice 1886–1963
Italian painter

Born in Novara, Piedmont, he was an exponent of Italian Neoclassicism and is noted for his series of portraits of women, such as *The Heiress* and *The Cousin*.

Cass, Lewis 1782–1866
US politician

Born in Exeter, New Hampshire, he was called to the Ohio Bar in 1803, but rose to be general in the war of 1812. He was then for 18 years civil Governor of Michigan, which under his administration became a settled state. He was Secretary of War (1831–36) and Minister in Paris (1836–42). He twice failed to win the presidency, sat in the Senate (1845–57), and was Secretary of State (1857–60). His position was generally one of compromise, but he was bitterly hostile to Great Britain. He published works on the Native Americans (1823) and France (1840).

Cassander c.358–297BC
King of Macedonia

He assumed power over Macedonia after the death of his father, **Antipater** (319BC), and became its king (305). An active figure in the power struggle after the death of **Alexander the Great** (323), he murdered Alexander's mother, widow and son, and contributed to the defeat of **Antigonus I Monophthalmos** at Ipsus (301). He married Thessalonica (Alexander's half-sister), for whom he built and named a city in Macedonia.

Cassatt, Mary 1844–1926
US Impressionist painter

Born of French descent into a wealthy family in Allegheny (now part of Pittsburgh), Pennsylvania, she studied in Spain, Italy and Holland. From 1874 she worked mainly in France, where she was a friend and follower of **Edgar Degas**, who persuaded her to exhibit with the Impressionists (1879–81, 1886). She often painted society women and domestic scenes, as in *Lady at the Tea Table* (1885, Metropolitan Museum, New York), and from 1889 she produced the oils and pastels of mothers and children for which she is best known, eg *Woman and Child Driving* (Philadelphia Museum). She also made a series of drypoint colour prints influenced by Japanese wood blocks and prints, as in *The Tramway* (1891, Museum of Modern Art, New York). Her eyesight began to fail early, and by 1914 she was obliged to stop working.

Cassavetes, John 1929–89
US filmmaker

Born in New York City, he studied at the American Academy of Dramatic Arts and acted in stock companies before making his film debut in *Fourteen Hours* (1951). Often cast as angry, alienated young men, he appeared in such films as *Crime in the Streets* (1956) and *Edge Of The City* (1957) before finding popularity in the television series *Johnny Staccato* (1959–60). He made his directorial debut with the experimental cinema-vérité drama *Shadows* (1960). His subsequent films as an actor include *The Dirty Dozen* (1967), *Rosemary's Baby* (1968) and *Whose Life Is It Anyway?* (1981). He earned great critical acclaim as a director of extemporized films of unflinching honesty which explore the darker side of human existence. Often starring his wife Gena Rowlands (1934–), these include *Faces* (1968), *A Woman Under the Influence* (1974), *Gloria* (1980) and *Love Streams* (1984).

Cassel, (Karl) Gustav 1866–1945
Swedish economist
Born in Stockholm, he was professor there from 1904. He became renowned as a world authority on monetary problems.

Cassell, John 1817–65
English publisher
He was born in Manchester, the son of an innkeeper. After an apprenticeship as a carpenter, he went to London in 1836 as a temperance advocate. In 1847 he became a tea and coffee merchant, and in 1850 turned to writing and publishing educational books and magazines for the working classes, including *Cassell's Magazine* (1852).

Cassian, St John c.360–c.435AD
Romanian monk and theologian
Born in Dobruja, Scythia, he spent some years as an ascetic in the Egyptian desert, before being ordained by St John Chrysostom at Constantinople (Istanbul) in AD403. He instituted several monasteries in the south of France, including the Abbey of St Victor at Massilia (Marseilles), which served as a model for many in Gaul and Spain. He was one of the first of the 'semi-Pelagians'. He was the author of *Collationes* (on the Desert Fathers), and a book on monasticism. His feast day is 23 July.

Cassin, René 1887–1976
French jurist and politician, and Nobel Prize winner
He was born in Bayonne and educated at Aix and Paris universities. He was Professor of International Law at Lille (1920–29) and at Paris (1929–60), combining this with membership of the French delegation to the League of Nations (1924–38). During World War II he joined General de Gaulle in London. He was principal legal adviser in negotiations with the British government and, in the later years of the war, held important posts in the French government in exile in London and Algiers, and subsequently in the Council of State (of which he was President, 1944–60) in liberated France. He was the principal author of the Universal Declaration of the Rights of Man (1948) and played a leading part in the establishment of UNESCO. He was also a member of the European Court of Human Rights from 1959, and its President (1965–68). In 1968 he was awarded the Nobel Peace Prize.

Cassini, César François 1714–84
French astronomer
He was the son of Jacques Cassini. In 1765 he succeeded his father as director of the Paris Observatory and in 1744 began a topographical map of France.

Cassini, Giovanni Domenico 1625–1712
French astronomer
Born in Perinaldo, near Nice, France (then in Italy), he was educated at a school in Genoa. He became Professor of Astronomy at the University of Bologna (1650), where his determinations of the rotation periods of the planets and his tables of the motions of Jupiter's satellites (1668) brought him fame. In 1669 he became the first director of the new Paris Observatory, where he made a host of observations of Mars, Jupiter and Saturn, and discovered the division of Saturn's rings which still bears his name (1675). He also discovered four satellites of Saturn. One of Cassini's great achievements was his determination of the distance of the planet Mars, and thereby of the distance of the Sun, from observations made simultaneously in Paris and in the French colony of Cayenne.

Cassini, Jacques 1677–1756
French astronomer
The son and successor of Giovanni Cassini, he wrote on astronomy and electricity, and measured an arc of the meridian from Dunkirk to Perpignan.

Cassini, Jacques Dominique, Comte de 1748–1845
French astronomer
The son and successor of César François Cassini as director of the Paris Observatory, he completed his father's topographical map. He was imprisoned for a time during the French Revolution, and created a count by Napoleon I.

Cassiodorus, Flavius Magnus Aurelius c.490–c.580
Roman historian and statesman
Born in Scylaceum (Squillace), Calabria, he was minister and counsellor to Theodoric the Great, King of the Ostrogoths in Italy, and after his death, chief minister to Queen Amalasontha. He retired c.540 to devote himself to study and writing. He founded monasteries, and promoted the transcription of classical manuscripts. He compiled an encyclopedia on learning and the liberal arts for his monks, *Institutiones divinarum et saecularium litterarum*, and a history of the Goths which, though no longer extant, was summarized by the 6th-century Gothic monk and historian Jordanes.

Cassirer, Ernst 1874–1945
German-Jewish neo-Kantian philosopher and historian of ideas
Born in Wrocław, Poland, and educated at various German universities, he was appointed Professor of Philosophy (1919), then Rector (1930), at Hamburg, but resigned when Hitler came to power. He then taught at Oxford (1933–35), Göteborg (1935–41), Yale (1941–44) and Columbia (1944–45). His published works include *Substanzbegriff und Funktionsbegriff* (1910, *Substance and Function*, 1923), *Die Philosophie der symbolischen Formen* (1923–29, 'The Philosophy of Symbolic Forms'), which analyses the symbolic functions underlying all human thought, language and culture, and *Sprache und Mythos* (1925, Eng trans *Language and Myths*, 1946).

Cassius, in full Gaius Cassius Longinus d.42BC
Roman conspirator
He was quaestor to Marcus Licinius Crassus in the Parthian War (54BC), and in 49 supported Pompey during the civil war. He was pardoned by Julius Caesar after their defeat at the Battle of Pharsalia (48). Despite gaining political advancement through Caesar, he played a leading part in the conspiracy to murder him (44), having persuaded Marcus Brutus to join him. However, popular feeling turned against them, and they were defeated at Philippi (42) by Mark Antony. Cassius subsequently committed suicide.

Cassius, Dio See Dio Cassius

Cassivellaunus 1st century BC
King of the Catuvellauni
As a chief of the British tribe living in the area of modern Hertfordshire, he led the Catuvellauni in resistance to Julius Caesar on his second invasion (54BC), and made peace after his principal base (probably situated at Wheathampstead) was stormed.

Casson, Sir Hugh 1910–
English architect
Educated at Cambridge, he was Professor of Interior Design at the Royal College of Art (1953–75), and was planning adviser to several authorities after World War II. Among his works are *Homes by the Million* (1947), *Permanence*

and Prefabrication (1947), *Victorian Architecture* (1948), *Japan Observed* (1991) and *The Tower of London* (1993). He was President of the Royal Academy from 1976 to 1984.

Casson, Sir Lewis 1875–1969
English actor-manager and producer

Born in Birkenhead, Merseyside, he is known especially for his productions of Shakespeare and George Bernard Shaw. He married Sybil Thorndike in 1908, and from 1942 to 1945 was director of drama to the Council for the Encouragement of Music and Arts (CEMA).

Castagno, Andrea del, *properly* Andrea di Bartolo de Simone c.1421–57
Italian painter

Born in Castagno, Tuscany, he studied in Florence and became a painter of the Florentine school. His style shows the influence of Masaccio and Donatello. In about 1440 he painted some effigies of rebels hanged by their heels, which established his reputation as a painter of violent scenes. After a period in Venice he returned to Florence, where he designed a stained-glass window for the cathedral. Soon afterwards he painted his celebrated *Last Supper* for Sta Apollonia (now in the Castagno Museum). His series *Famous Men and Women*, painted for a villa at Legnaia, are now also in the Castagno Museum. His last dated work is the famous equestrian portrait *Niccolò da Tolentino*—a companion piece to the fresco *Sir Nicholas Hawkswood* by Paolo Uccello—which is in Florence Cathedral. He died of the plague.

Castaños, Francisco Xavier de, Duke of Bailen 1756–1852
Spanish soldier

During the Peninsular War (1808–14) he compelled 18,000 French to surrender at the Battle of Bailén (1808), but was defeated by the French soldier Jean Lannes (1769–1809) at Tudela. Under the Duke of Wellington he took part in the battles of Albuera, Salamanca and Vitoria (1813). In 1843 he was appointed the guardian of Queen Isabella II of Spain.

Castelfranco, Giorgio Barbarelli See Giorgione

Castellanos, Rosario 1925–74
Mexican poet, writer and translator

Born in Mexico City, she received little attention for her poetry before publishing *Poemas 1953–5* (1957), which appeared at the height of her close involvement with the Native Americans of Chialas, where she had spent her childhood and adolescence. Her theme of suffering peoples who cling to hope in a world 'civilized' in the name of barbarism, reflects this involvement. Several of these works are translated in *The Selected Poems of Rosario Castellanos* (1988). Many of her novels and stories have been translated, including *Balún-canán* (1957, Eng trans *The Nine Guardians*, 1958). She was electrocuted on a visit to Israel while trying to change a light bulb. ☐ M Allgood, *A Rosario Castellanos Reader* (1988); D Meyer and M F Olmos (eds), *Contemporary Women Authors of Latin America: Introductory Essays* (1983)

Castelli, Ignaz Franz 1781–1862
Austrian poet

Born in Vienna, he wrote *Kriegslieder für die österreichische Armee* (1809, 'War Songs for the Austrian Army'), which was banned by Napoleon I.

Castello, De See Vergil, Polydore

Castelnau, Noël Marie Joseph Edouard, Vicomte de Curières de 1851–1944
French soldier

He was born in Aveyron of a military, royalist, Catholic family. Educated at St Cyr, he served on the Loire in the Franco-Prussian War (1870–71). He was a member of the Conseil de Guerre in 1913 and took command of the Army of Lorraine in 1914. As commander of all French armies in France, he directed the Champagne offensive (1915), and became General Joffre's Chief of Staff.

Castelnuovo-Tedesco, Mario 1895–1968
US composer

Born in Florence, Italy, he studied under Ildebrando Pizzetti, began composing as a boy, and composed his opera *La Mandragola* (1920–23, performed 1926), based on Machiavelli's book. In addition to two other operas he produced orchestral and instrumental works, but is probably best known for his songs, especially his complete series of the lyrics from Shakespeare's plays, *33 Shakespeare Songs*. He emigrated to the USA in 1939 and became a US citizen.

Castelo Branco, Camilo, Visconde de Correia Botelho 1825–90
Portuguese novelist

He was born in Lisbon, an illegitimate child whose love of literature and longing for adventure grew from his reading. He was brought up by relatives in austere conditions and studied medicine then for the priesthood irregularly before turning to writing. One of the most important of modern Portuguese novelists, with a deep understanding of the life of his people, his work ranges from romances like *Mysterios de Lisboa* (1958, 'The Mysteries of Lisbon'), to closely observed, imaginative interpretations of the everyday Portuguese scene, such as *The Crime of Father Amara*. His best known book is *Amor de Perdição* (1862, 'Fatal Love'). He was created viscount in 1885 for his services to literature. He committed suicide. ☐ A Pimentel, *O Torturado de Seide* (1921)

Castelo Branco, Humberto de Alencar 1900–67
Brazilian politician

He was educated at the Pôrto Alegre Military Academy in Rio Grande do Sul and at France's École Supérieure de Guerre, as well as the General Command course at Fort Leavenworth, USA. He went on to fight with the Brazilian army in Italy, and coordinated the anti-Goulart military conspiracy of 1964. Linked to other veteran officers in the Escola Superior da Guerra, founded in the 1940s in Rio de Janeiro, his foreign policy was anti-communist, and he believed that short-term arbitary technocratic measures should be taken to create the conditions for democracy. As President from 1964 to 1967, although the economy had been stabilized, the financial system reorganized and foreign debt renegotiated, his government failed to alter traditional patterns of authority and prevent the emergence of hard-line factions amongst the military, which established the 'tutelary regime' which survived until 1985.

Casti, Giambattista c.1721–1803
Italian poet

Born in Prato, Tuscany, he took holy orders, but in 1764 went to Vienna, where he became Poet Laureate. On Joseph II's death he returned to Florence, and in 1798 he went to Paris. He wrote the *48 Novelle galanti* (1793), and *Gli animali parlanti* (1802, 'The Talking Animals'), a political satire. ☐ H van den Bergh, *Giambattista Casti, l'homme et l'oeuvre* (1951)

Castigliano, (Carlo) Alberto 1847–84
Italian civil engineer

Born in Asti, he studied at the Polytechnic in Turin and worked as a railway engineer in northern Italy. He was noted for the introduction of strain energy methods of structural analysis in his two theorems of 1873 and 1875, the second of which also states the principle of least work. These theorems represented a great advance on the methods of classical theory of structures, especially in their application to statically indeterminate systems.

Castiglione, Baldassare, Count 1478–1529
Italian courtier and writer
He was born near Mantua. In 1505 he was sent by the Duke of Urbino as envoy to Henry VII of England, who made him a knight, and he was later Mantuan ambassador at the papal court in Rome (1513–24). Thereafter he was papal nuncio for Pope Clement VII in Spain, from 1524. His chief work, *Il libro del Cortegiano* (1528, 'The Courtier'), is a manual for courtiers, in dialogue form, and was translated into English by Sir Thomas Hoby (as *The Courtyer*) in 1561. His Italian and Latin poems are models of elegance. His *Letters* (1769–71) illustrate political and literary history. ⌨ J Cartwright, *Baldassare Castiglione, his life and letters* (1908)

Castle of Blackburn, Barbara Anne Castle, Baroness, *née* Betts 1910–
English Labour politician
Born in Bradford, and educated at Bradford Girls' Grammar School and St Hugh's College, Oxford, she worked in local government before World War II, married Edward Cyril Castle (1907–79), a journalist, in 1944, and entered parliament in 1945 as MP for Blackburn. During the 1950s she was a convinced 'Bevanite', outspoken in her defence of radical causes. Chairman of the Labour Party (1958–59), after Labour came into power in 1964 she attained Cabinet rank, becoming Minister of Overseas Development (1964–65). She was a controversial Minister of Transport (1965–68), introducing a 70mph speed limit and the 'breathalyzer' test for suspected drunken drivers, in an effort to cut down road accidents. She took over the newly-created post of Secretary of State for Employment and Productivity (1968–70) to deal with the government's difficult prices and incomes policy. In 1974 she became Secretary of State for Social Services. In 1976 when James Callaghan became Prime Minister she returned to the back benches. As an MEP (1979–89), she served as vice-chairman of the Socialist Group (1979–86). Two volumes of her diaries were published in 1980 and 1984 followed by her autobiography *Fighting All the Way* (1993). She was created a life peer in 1990. ⌨ Wilfred De'Ath, *Barbara Castle: A Portrait from Life* (1970)

Castle, Vernon, *originally* Vernon Blythe 1887–1918 and Irene Castle, *originally* Irene Foote 1893–1969
English champion ballroom dancers
Born in Norwich, Norfolk and New Rochelle, New York, respectively, they married in 1911 and became highly popular exhibition ballroom dancers and teachers. They performed throughout the USA and Europe, and he devised such famous dances as the One-step, the Maxixe, the Turkey-trot, the Castle Walk and the Hesitation Waltz. She retired from dancing after his death while serving as an airman in the Royal Flying Corps.

Castle, William Ernest 1867–1962
US biologist
Born in Ohio and educated at Harvard, he became Professor of Geology there (1897) and later of Genetics (1908–36), and carried out important research in the field of heredity and natural selection.

Castlereagh, Robert Stewart, Viscount 1769–1822
British politician
Born in Dublin, the son of an Ulster proprietor who in 1816 became Marquis of Londonderry, he was educated at Armagh and Cambridge (for one year) and entered the Irish Parliament in 1790 as Whig member for County Down. In 1795 he turned Tory, although he remained in favour of Catholic emancipation. As Irish Chief Secretary from 1797 he devoted himself to promoting William Pitt, the Younger's measure of union, but, with Pitt, retired from office when Pitt's Catholic pledges were defeated. As War Minister (1806–07, 1807–09), he was made scapegoat for the failed Walcheren expedition, the dispute ending in a duel with George Canning in which Canning was slightly wounded. In 1812 he achieved recognition as Foreign Secretary under Lord Liverpool, as well as the post of Leader of the House of Commons, but was responsible for introducing into the Commons the unpopular measures of the reactionary Home Secretary Lord Sidmouth. After working at the heart of the coalition against Napoleon I (1813–14), Castlereagh also represented England at Chaumont and Vienna (1814–15), Paris (1815), and Aix-la-Chapelle (1818). He advocated 'Congress diplomacy' among the great powers, to avoid further warfare. Believing that he was being blackmailed for homosexuality, he committed suicide. Great Britain and Europe were indebted to him for the 40 years of peace that succeeded Napoleon I's downfall, yet few politicians have been so disliked, and a shout of joy was given as his coffin was carried into Westminster Abbey.

Castner, Hamilton Young 1848–99
US chemist
Born in Brooklyn, New York City, he was educated at Brooklyn Polytechnical Institute and the Columbia School of Mines. After failing to find a US backer to develop a process he had invented to obtain sodium from caustic soda (sodium hydroxide), he moved to Great Britain in 1886 where a new company financed by Sir Henry Roscoe was formed to exploit his patent. Two years later the company pioneered a second method which Castner developed for the production of sodium, this time by the electrolysis of molten sodium hydroxide; he then devised a way of producing much purer sodium hydroxide by the electrolysis of brine. He overcame the difficulty of separating the sodium hydroxide solution from the original salt with his famous 'mercury rocking cell'. Carl Kellner in Germany developed a similar process, also using mercury, and sold his patent to Ernest Solvay's company. Rather than engage in expensive lawsuits over patents, the British and Belgian companies collaborated to found the Castner–Kellner Alkali Company in 1895. After the Castner–Kellner Alkali Company became very prosperous, it was taken over by Sir John Tomlinson Brunner and Ludwig Mond, becoming part of Imperial Chemical Industries in 1926.

Castro, Eugenio de 1869–1944
Portuguese poet
Born in Coimbra, he became Professor of Portuguese Literature there, and travelled widely in Europe. In Paris he became interested in Symbolism, and introduced it to Portuguese writing in his poetry, beginning with *Oaristos* (1890). Although derided at first, his work eventually became influential, and his later work reflected a return to more classical forms, and a growing fascination with folklore.

Castro (Ruz), Fidel 1927–
Cuban revolutionary
Born near Birán, he was the son of a successful sugar planter. He studied law and practised in Havana, fighting cases on behalf of the poor and against the official corruption and oppression which were rife under President Fulgencio Batista. In 1953, with his brother Raúl, also an ardent revolutionary, he led an unsuccessful rising and was sentenced to 15 years' imprisonment, but, released under an amnesty within a year, he fled to the USA and thence to Mexico, all the time organizing anti-Batista activities. In 1956 he landed in Cuba with a small band of insurgents, but he was betrayed and ambushed, barely

escaping into the Sierra Maestra mountains, from where he waged a relentless guerrilla campaign. The degeneration of Cuba into a police state brought many recruits to his cause, and in 1958 he mounted a full-scale attack and Batista was forced to flee. Castro, Prime Minister from February 1959, proclaimed a 'Marxist–Leninist programme' adapted to local requirements. He set about far-reaching reforms in agriculture, industry, and education, not all immediately successful, but sufficiently so to enable his regime to gather strength. His overthrow of US dominance in the economic sphere and routing of the US-connived émigré invasion at the Bay of Pigs (1961) was balanced by consequent dependence on communist (mainly Russian) aid and the near-disaster of the 1962 missile crisis. Despite problems in sugar and tobacco production and two mass exoduses, Castro's popularity remained high. In 1979 he became president of the non-aligned countries movement despite Cuba's continuing substantial economic and political involvement with the Kremlin, but by the late 1980s, Cuba's status as the world's largest supplier of sugar was beginning to suffer because of the industry's outdated and unrepaired equipment. The start of 1991 ominously heralded Cuba's worst economic crisis in its 32 years of Communist rule, caused mainly by flagging economic aid and a drastic fall in basic supplies from the economically-compromised USSR on which Cuba had come to rely for almost all the oil imports on which 90 per cent of the island's energy industry is based. In 1994 Castro suffered great embarrassment when his daughter fled Cuba and sought asylum in the USA, where she publicly criticised the way her homeland was being run. He published an autobiography, *Fidel*, in 1987 (with Frei Betto) amongst other books.

Castro, Inés or Inez de c.1323–55
Spanish noblewoman

She went to Portugal (1340) in the train of her cousin Costança, the bride of the Infante, Dom Pedro (the future King Pedro I). He was captivated by Inez's beauty, and after Costança's death (1345), he made her his mistress, and then his wife (1354), but on the orders of his father, Alfonso IV, she was stabbed to death. Her life forms the basis of plays by Antonio Ferreira, Antoine Hondar de La Motte, and others.

Castro, João de 1500–48
Portuguese naval commander

He was born in Lisbon. He volunteered against the Moors at Tangiers, accompanied Charles V to Tunis, and had already fought and travelled in the East when in 1545 he sailed to India at the head of a small expedition, where he relieved the city of Diu. He was appointed Portuguese viceroy, but died in the arms of St Francis Xavier.

Castro, Rosalía de 1837–85
Spanish poet and novelist

She was born in Santiago de Compostela, Spain. Her earliest works, such as the poetry collection *La Flor* (1857, 'The Flower'), were written in Spanish, but her fame rests on her later volumes in Galician, *Cantares Gallegos* (1863, 'Galician Songs') and *Follas Novas* (1880, 'New Leaves'). Her novels, written in Spanish, such as *La Hija del Mar* (1859, 'The Daughter of the Sea') and *Ruinas* (1867, 'Ruins') brought her to the attention of a wider public.

Castro y Bellvis, Guillén de 1569–1631
Spanish dramatist

Born in Valencia, he commanded a Neapolitan fortress, but later lived in Madrid. His early works were romantic comedies, after which he turned to epic subjects, notably in *La Mocedades del Cid* (c.1600), which formed the basis for Corneille's *Le Cid*. His other works include a realistic play about an unhappy marriage, *Los mal casados de Valencia*

('The Unhappy Marriages of Valencia'), and dramatizations of works by Cervantes. He died in poverty. 📖 W E Wilson, *Guillén de Castro* (1973)

Catalani, Alfredo 1854–93
Italian composer

Born in Lucca, he succeeded Amilcare Ponchielli as Professor of Music at Milan Conservatory in 1886. He aimed to reform the Italian opera as Richard Wagner had the German. His finest opera was his last, *La Wally* (1892).

Catchpole, Margaret 1762–1819
Australian pioneer

Born near Ipswich, Suffolk, England, she became a servant to the Cobbold family of brewers of that town. Twice sentenced to death (for stealing a horse and for escaping from Ipswich jail), she was transported to New South Wales in 1801, where she was assigned as a servant and nurse. She managed a farm, ran a store, acted as midwife and contributed much to the community, eventually dying of an illness brought about by helping a neighbour during the bad winter weather. Her letters home to her relations and to the Cobbold family, who remained interested in her welfare, formed the basis of the book *Margaret Catchpole* (1845) by Richard Cobbold (1797–1877), and give a valuable account of early 19th-century life in the new colony.

Catena, Vincenzo c.1480–1531
Venetian painter

His early work was heavily influenced by Giovanni Bellini and Giovannni Battista Cima da Conegliano. In 1506 he was mentioned as a 'colleague' of Giorgione and by c.1510 the influence of Giorgione was apparent. His mature style blends elements of Titian, Palma Vecchio and other masters of the time. Though never a great originator, he was a sensitive portraitist.

Catesby, Mark c.1679–1749
English naturalist

Born in London, he travelled widely in North America (1710–19, 1722–26), and published *The Natural History of Carolina, Florida and the Bahama Islands* (1731–48).

Catesby, Robert 1573–1605
English conspirator, leader of the Gunpowder Plot

He was born in Lapworth, Warwickshire, into a wealthy Roman Catholic family. As a recusant he suffered fines and imprisonment under Elizabeth I. He was named as an accomplice in the 1603 plot against James VI and I, and in 1605 he was the chief instigator of the Gunpowder Plot. He was shot dead while resisting arrest.

Cather, Willa Sibert 1873–1947
US fiction writer, poet and journalist

She was born on a farm near Winchester, Virginia, and her formative years were spent in Nebraska. After university there (1891–95), her career began with a well-written volume of poetry, *April Twilights* (1903). She moved to New York as editor of *McClure's* magazine (1906–12), and her first novel, *Alexander's Bridge* was published in 1912. She subsequently wrote three novels dealing with immigrants to the USA: *O Pioneers!* (1913), *The Song of the Lark* (1915), and *My Ántonia* (1918), which is generally regarded as her best book. A lesbian who wrote primarily about independent women, she was a prolific writer, and other novels include *Death Comes for the Archbishop* (1927) and *One of Ours* (1922, Pulitzer Prize). 📖 P C Robinson, *Willa: the life of Cather* (1983)

Catherine, St d.307AD
Egyptian royal virgin

Tradition maintains she was born in Alexandria. She is said to have publicly confessed the Gospel at a sacrificial feast appointed by Emperor Maximinus, and was

Catherine II, the Great 1729–96
Empress of Russia from 1762

Catherine was born in Stettin in the Prussian province of Pomerania (now Szczecin in Poland), the daughter of the Prince of Anhalt-Zerbst. In 1745 she married Peter, Grand Duke and heir to the Russian throne, but the marriage was stormy and unhappy, with many quarrels. Catherine became notorious for her love affairs with Count Gregory Orlov (1734–83) and also with **Stanislas II Augustus Poniatowski**. After Peter's accession in 1762 (as **Peter III**), Catherine was compelled to live separately; later Peter was dethroned by a conspiracy in which Catherine was probably implicated, and Catherine herself was made empress despite a weak claim to the throne. A few days afterwards Peter was murdered by Orlov and others. Around this time Catherine began to make a show of regard for the Greek Church, although her principles were those of the French philosophers.

The government was carried on with great energy, and the dominions and power of Russia rapidly increased. When discontent was voiced, the young Prince Ivan, the hope of the disaffected, was murdered in the castle of Schlüsselburg. In 1774 Catherine suppressed a popular rebellion led by **Yemelyan Pugachev**, defeating his Cossack troops at the battle of Tsaritsyn the following year. She sought the support of the nobility in Russia, and promoted their cause by establishing them as a separate estate by Charter in 1785. Under Catherine, internal politics consisted of court intrigues both for and against a

succession of favourites, **Grigori Potemkin** being the best known. Three partitions (with Austria) of Poland in 1772, 1793 and 1795, and two Turkish wars (1774 and 1792) vastly increased the empire, as did a war with Sweden (1790) and the incorporation of the Baltic territory of Courland.

Vincent Cronin, *Catherine, Empress of All the Russians* (1990); John T Alexander, *Catherine the Great: Life and Legend* (1989); Ian Grey, *Catherine the Great: Autocrat and Empress of All Russia* (1961).

Catherine was renowned for her intelligence and learning. She promoted French culture in Russia, and corresponded throughout her life with **Voltaire** and the Encyclopaedists. She appointed a Commission to draw up a new legal code, and was much influenced in this plan by **Montesquieu**. She is said also to have considered some over-ambitious schemes such as expelling the British from India.

Moi, je serai autocrate: c'est mon métier. Et le bon Dieu me pardonnera: c'est son métier.
'I shall be an autocrat: that's my trade. And the good Lord will forgive me: that's his.'
Attributed remark.

consequently beheaded, after being tortured on a spiked wheel (later known as a 'catherine' wheel). Her remains were miraculously transported to Mount Sinai, where her shrine is on display in St Catherine's monastery. Her feast day is 25 November.

Catherine of Siena, St, *properly* Caterina Benincasa 1347–80
Italian mystic

Born in Siena, she became a Dominican at the age of 16. She is their patron saint. Her enthusiasm converted many sinners, and she persuaded Pope **Gregory XI** to return from the papacy Avignon to Rome. Christ's stigmata were said to have been imprinted on her body in 1375. She wrote many devotional pieces, letters, and poems; her *Dialogue*, a work on mysticism, was translated in 1896. She was canonized in 1461. Her feast day is 29 April.

Catherine I, *originally* Martha 1684–1727
Empress of Russia and wife of Peter the Great

She was probably of Lithuanian peasant stock, and after her Swedish husband deserted her, she became mistress of **Peter I**'s Chief Minister, Prince **Aleksandr Menshikov**, and later of Peter himself, changing her name to Catherine and converting to Orthodoxy (1708). The tsar married her as his second wife (1712), and in 1722 he passed a law allowing the tsar to nominate his successor. Catherine was crowned empress in 1724, and after Peter's death (1725) Prince Menshikov ensured her succession to the throne. Illiterate and licentious, she allowed Menshikov to govern in her name. During her reign taxation was lowered and the power of local bureaucracies was reduced. She was succeeded by Peter's grandson, **Peter II**.

Catherine II, the Great See panel above

Catherine de Médicis, *Italian* Caterina de' Medici 1519–89
Queen and Regent of France

Born in Florence, the daughter of **Lorenzo de' Medici**, Duke of Urbino, she was to become the mother of three French kings. Married at 14 to Henri, Duke of Orléans

(the future King **Henri II** of France), as Henri's queen (1547–59) she was constantly humiliated by his influential mistress, **Diane de Poitiers**. When her husband died (1559), Catherine acted as queen regent (1559–60) during the brief reign of her eldest son, **Francis II**, the first husband of **Mary, Queen of Scots**, and again during the minority of her second son, **Charles IX**, whom she dominated throughout his reign (1560–74). She tried to pursue moderation, to give unity to a state increasingly torn by religious division and aristocratic faction, but she nursed dynastic ambitions and was drawn into political and religious intrigues. She was also implicated in the infamous St Bartholomew's Day Massacre (1572), together with Charles and her third son, Henri of Anjou, who succeeded to the throne (1574) as **Henri III**. Catherine's political influence waned during his troubled reign, but she survived long enough to ensure the succession of Henri IV, who married her daughter Margaret, and who restored royal authority. N M Sutherland, *Catherine de Medici and the Ancien Regime* (1966)

Catherine de Valois 1401–37
Queen of England, wife of Henry V

Born in Paris, she was the youngest daughter of King Charles VI (Charles, the Foolish) of France, and after a stormy courtship, when England and France went to war over England's dowry demands, she married **Henry V** of England at Troyes (1420). In 1421 she gave birth to a son, the future **Henry VI** of England. After her husband's death (1422), she secretly married (c.1431–32) Owen Tudor, a Welsh squire, despite parliamentary opposition. Their eldest son, Edmund, Earl of Richmond, was the father of Henry VII, the first of the Tudor kings of England.

Catherine Howard d.1542
English queen

She was the granddaughter of **Thomas Howard**, 2nd Duke of Norfolk, niece of **Thomas Howard**, 3rd Duke of Norfolk and cousin of **Anne Boleyn**. In 1540 she married **Henry VIII** as his fifth wife, immediately after his divorce from **Anne of Cleves**. In 1541 she was charged by **Thomas Cranmer** with sexual intercourse before her marriage with a musician (Henry Mannock), her secretary (Francis Dereham) and a kinsman (Thomas Culpepper), whom she had known before her marriage. The men were executed, and Catherine was attainted by parliament and beheaded. ⌨ Lacey Baldwin Smith, *A Tudor Tragedy: The Life and Times of Catherine Howard* (1961)

Catherine of Aragon 1485–1536
English queen, the first wife of Henry VIII
Born in Alcalá de Henares, Spain, the youngest daughter of **Ferdinand** and **Isabella** of Spain, she was first married (1501) to **Arthur**, Prince of Wales, the eldest son of **Henry VII**. Arthur died six months later, and in 1503 she was betrothed to his brother, the 11-year-old Prince Henry (later **Henry VIII**). They were married (1509), seven weeks after Henry's accession to the throne. Of their six children, only the Princess Mary (later **Mary I**) survived. In the years that followed, Henry's infidelities, and his anxiety for a son and heir, soured the marriage, and in 1527 he began proceedings for a divorce, in order to marry **Anne Boleyn**. Despite strong opposition from the pope, Henry and Anne were secretly married (1533), and the marriage to Catherine was annulled by Archbishop **Cranmer**. Catherine, who had offered a dignified, passive resistance throughout, was sent into retirement at Ampthill, Bedfordshire. In 1534 the pope pronounced her marriage valid, which provoked Henry's final break with Rome and began the Reformation in England. Catherine refused to accept the title of Princess Dowager, or to accept the Act of Succession (1534) which declared Princess Mary illegitimate, and retired to lead an austerely religious life at Kimbolton, Cambridgeshire. ⌨ Garrett Mattingly, *Catherine of Aragon* (1942)

Catherine of Braganza 1638–1705
English queen, the wife of Charles II
Born in Vila Viçosa, Portugal, the daughter of the Duke of Braganza (later King **John IV** of Portugal), she was a devout Roman Catholic. She married **Charles II** in 1662, bringing Tangier and Bombay as her dowry. She was forced to receive the king's mistress, **Barbara Villiers**, and their children, at court, and her own failure to bear children, and her parsimony, alienated her from the people. Charles resisted all pressure for a divorce, even defending her from malicious poisoning charges during the Popish Plot (1678–79), but forced her to live apart from him in retirement. In 1692 she went home to Portugal, where she became regent for her brother, Pedro II.

Catherine or Katherine Parr 1512–48
English queen
The daughter of Sir Thomas Parr of Kendal, she married first Edward Borough, and next Lord Latimer, before becoming Queen of England by marrying **Henry VIII** as his sixth wife (1543). A learned, spirited and tactful woman, she managed Henry better than his other wives, persuaded him to restore the succession to his daughters Mary (**Mary I**) and Elizabeth (**Elizabeth I**) and showed them much kindness. Shortly after Henry's death (1547) she married a former suitor, **Thomas Seymour** of Sudeley, and died in childbirth the following year. ⌨ Anthony Martienssen, *Queen Katherine Parr* (1973)

Catherine the Great See **Catherine II** (panel)

Catilina, Lucius Sergius, *also called* Catiline
c.108–62BC
Roman conspirator
An impoverished patrician, and adherent of **Lucius Sulla**, he was elected praetor in 68BC, and next year Governor of Africa, but was disqualified from the consulship in 66 on charges of maladministration. Disappointed and crippled by debt, he entered into a conspiracy with other Roman nobles. In 63 he planned a complete revolution, and the assassination of **Cicero** and the hostile senators.

Cicero discovered the plans and defeated the assassins; two days later, when Catilina appeared in the Senate, Cicero denounced him. Catilina's reply was drowned in jeers. He escaped from Rome, but some of the conspirators were arrested and executed. Insurrections in several parts of Italy were suppressed, and Catilina was defeated and killed by republican forces at Pistoria (now Pistoia).

Catiline See **Catilina, Lucius Sergius**

Catlin, George 1796–1872
US artist and author
Born in Wilkes-Barre, Pennsylvania, during 1832–40 he studied the Native Americans of the far west, painting 470 full-length portraits and other pictures illustrating their life and customs (now in the National Museum at Washington). He spent eight years in Europe with a Far West show, travelled in South and Central America (1852–57), and lived in Europe again until 1871. His works include *Manners of the North American Indians* (2 vols, 1841), *The North American Portfolio* (1844) and *Last Rambles in the Rocky Mountains* (1868). ⌨ R Plate, *Palette and Tomahawk: the story of George Catlin* (1962)

Cato, Dionysius ?4th century AD
Roman writer
He was the supposed author of a volume of 164 moral precepts in Latin hexameters, known as *Dionysii Catonis disticha de moribus ad filium* ('Couplets on Morals, to his Son'), which was a great favourite during the Middle Ages. An English version by Benedict Burgh was printed by **William Caxton** before 1479. ⌨ Plutarch, *Life of Cato* in *Works*, D Wyttenbach (ed) (1795–1830)

Cato, Marcus Porcius, the Elder, *also known as* 'the Censor' 234–149BC
Roman statesman and orator
He was born in Tusculum, of peasant stock. He distinguished himself in the Second Punic War (218–202BC) at the capture of Tarentum (209), and became successively quaestor, aedile, praetor, and consul (195). In Spain he crushed a formidable insurrection, and in 191, as legatus, he was instrumental in the defeat of **Antiochus III**. He advocated the simple, strict social life of ancient Roman tradition, and condemned Greek refinement and luxury. Elected censor (184), he introduced such rigorous legislative reforms that 'Censor' became his permanent surname. He repaired watercourses, paved reservoirs, cleansed drains, raised the rents paid by the tax-farmers and reduced the contract prices paid by the state. More questionable reforms related to the price of slaves, dress, furniture, equipages, and so on. He opposed good and bad innovations with equal intolerance. In 153 he was sent on a mission to Carthage, which so fuelled his fear of Carthaginian power that he subsequently ended every speech in the Senate with the words 'Carthage must be destroyed' (*Carthago delenda est*). He lived to see the start of the Third Punic War (149–146BC). He wrote several works, of which only the *De Re Rustica* and a few fragments of his *Origines*, a summary of the Roman annals, survive. ⌨ A E Astin, *Cato the Censor* (1978)

Cato, Marcus Porcius, the Younger, *also called* Uticensis 95–46BC
Roman politician
He served in the campaign against Spartacus (72BC). Military tribune in 67, he brought back with him from Greece the Stoic philosopher Athenodorus. As quaestor (65–64) he reformed the treasury offices. As tribune (63) he denounced **Julius Caesar** as an accomplice of **Catilina**, and his strenuous opposition to **Marcus Licinius Crassus**, **Pompey**, and Caesar, led to the formation of the first triumvirate. He later sided with Pompey, and after the Battle of Pharsalia (48) escaped into Africa, to defend Utica.

When he heard of Caesar's decisive victory at Thapsus (46), he committed suicide rather than surrender. His great-grandfather was Cato, 'the Elder'.

Catroux, Georges 1877–1969
French soldier

Born in Limoges, he served in World War I, was Governor-General of Indo-China (1939–40), commanded the Free French forces in Syria and the Near East in 1940–41, and became Governor-General of Algeria in 1943. In 1945–48 he was ambassador in Russia.

Cats, Jacob, nicknamed Father Cats 1577–1660
Dutch statesman and poet

Born in Brouwershaven, Zeeland, he studied law at Leyden and Orleans, then settled in Middelburg. He rose to a position of authority in the state, and was twice ambassador in England (1627, 1652). From then until his death, he lived near The Hague, writing the autobiography printed in the 1700 edition of his *Poems*.

Catt, Carrie Clinton Chapman, née Lane 1859–1947
US reformer and pacifist

Born in Ripon, Wisconsin and educated at Iowa State College, she joined the staff of the National American Woman Suffrage Association in 1890, and later became its president (1900-04, 1915–47), effecting dramatic changes in the organization and helping to bring about the 19th Amendment (1920), thus securing the vote for women. She organized the Women's Peace Party during World War I, helped establish the League of Women Voters (1919), and spent the later years of her life campaigning for world peace.

Cattell, Raymond B(ernard) 1905–
English psychologist

Born in Staffordshire, he was educated at London University, where he took a PhD in psychology following a first degree in chemistry. He taught at Harvard, Clarke and Duke universities before World War II, and after the War became Research Professor and director of the Laboratory of Personality Assessment at Illinois University. He later moved to the University of Hawaii. He applied the statistical techniques of factor analysis to the study of personality differences, with the aim of being able to establish psychological dimensions along which people could be measured and compared. He devised a lengthy questionnaire (the 16 PF scale) from which is derived a personality profile of 16 scores for the person tested. His contributions to psychology have been mainly methodological and theoretical, and he has written widely on various statistical techniques of multivariate analysis (ie, the analysis of empirical data in terms of many concurrent souces of variation), and is a recipient of the Wenner-Gren prize of the New York Academy of Science.

Cattermole, George 1800–68
English watercolour painter and book illustrator

Born in Dickleborough, Norfolk, he was known for his Romantic antiquarian and architectural paintings, and for his illustrations of Sir Walter Scott's *Waverley Novels*, and the works of Charles Dickens.

Catton, (Charles) Bruce 1899–1978
US historian

Born in Petoskey, Michigan, he spent most of his career as a journalist and government official, but maintained an interest in the Civil War, and in his 50s he began to publish classic histories on the subject. His history of the army of the Potomac comprised *Mr. Lincoln's Army* (1951), *Glory Road* (1952), and *A Stillness at Appomattox* (1953,

Pulitzer Prize). His other works include a three-volume history of the Civil War and a biography of Ulysses S Grant.

Catullus, Gaius Valerius c.84–c.54BC
Roman lyric poet

Born in Verona, he began to write verses at the age of 16. About 62BC he settled in Rome where he became friendly with Cicero, and met 'Lesbia', a married woman whom he addresses in some of his most beautiful, and some of his most bitter poems. A fiery, unscrupulous partisan, he assailed his enemies, including Julius Caesar, with equal scurrility and wit. His extant works comprise 116 pieces (though three are spurious), including love poems, satiric poems, mythological pieces (some of them adapted from the Greek), and 'Attis'. The text depends on a single manuscript discovered in the 14th century at Verona, inaccurately transcribed and subsequently lost. He exerted a wide influence on his succesors and on English poetry, notably Robert Herrick, Lord Byron, and Tennyson. 🕮 K Quinn, *Catullus, an interpretation* (1972); and other works by Quinn

Cauchy, Augustin Louis, Baron 1789–1857
French mathematician

Born in Paris, he taught mathematics at the École Polytechnique, and after the 1830 revolution lived in exile in Turin and Prague, returning to Paris in 1838. He did important work on ordinary and partial differential equations, advocated the wave theory of light following Augustin Fresnel's work, and gave a substantial impetus to the mathematical theory of elasticity. He is remembered as the founder of the theory of functions of a complex variable, which was to play a leading role in the development of mathematics during the rest of the 19th century. In algebra he gave a definitive account of the theory of determinants, and developed the ideas of permutation groups which had appeared in the work of Joseph Luis de Lagrange and Évariste Galois.

Cauer, Minna (WilhelmineTheodore Marie), née Schelle 1841–1922
German feminist and suffragist

She was born in Freyenstein (Ostprignitz) where her father was pastor. Widowed in 1866, she qualified as a teacher (1867) and taught for a year in Paris before moving with her second husband (Cauer) to Berlin. Widowed again in 1881, she held leading roles in the *Kaufmännischer Verband für Weibliche Angestellete* and in the *Verein Frauenwohl* during the 1880s. In 1900 she founded with Anita Augspurg the important *Verband fortschrittlicher Frauenvereine* ('Federation of Women's Associations) and in 1902 was a founder, with Augspurg and Lida Heymann, of the *Deutscher Verband für Frauenstimmrecht*, a women's suffrage organization. Later she was involved with Heymann and Augspurg in publishing the newspaper *Die Frau im Staat* (1919–33).

Caulfield, Patrick 1936–
English painter and printmaker

Born in London, he studied at Chelsea School of Art and the Royal College of Art. Influenced by Fernand Léger and Juan Gris, he has kept apart from the Pop movement, using cliché subjects ironically to criticize the debasing effect of mass culture. He uses deeply contrasting colour with hard lines and no modelling, giving a printed effect, as in his *Portrait of Juan Gris* (1963) and *Italian Girl* (1968, Cardiff). He is perhaps best known for his interiors, with their emphasis on design, as in *After Lunch* (1975, Tate, London), and for his series of disembodied household and office artefacts—pipes, lamps, desks etc—of the 1980s and 1990s, such as *Glass of Whisky* (1987, Saatchi Collection, London). Public commissions include the

London Life mural in Bristol (1983), and sets and costumes for the ballet *Party Games* (1984, Royal Opera House). He had a retrospective at the Serpentine Gallery in 1992.

Caulkins, Frances Manwaring 1795–1869
US educationist and historian

Born and brought up in Connecticut, she ran a girls' school in Norwichtown after her step-father impoverished the family. A convert to Congregationalism, she had become involved in evangelical works by 1831, and her religious tracts published between 1836 and 1842 by the American Tract Society sold millions of copies. Her two classics of local history, *A History of Norwich* (1845) and *A History of New London* (1852), remain unsurpassed in their field. In 1849 she was the first woman to be elected to the prestigious Massachusetts Historical Society.

Causley, Charles 1917–
English poet and children's writer

His close ties with his home town of Launceston in Cornwall provide him with a unique, rooted point of view on the world, and his naval war experiences inspired his early verse, as in *Farewell, Aggie Weston* (1951). His poetry has gradually become more conversational in style, yet his meditations on family memories, life, landscape and legend are far from simplistic. His *Collected Poems 1951–1975*, which combines verse intended for both adults and children, was published in 1975 and his *Collected Poems for Children* was published in 1995. ⊞ H Chambers (ed), *Causley at 70* (1987)

Cavaco Silva, Anibal 1939–
Portuguese politician

Born in Loule, after studying economics in Great Britain and the USA he became a university teacher and then a research director in the Bank of Portugal. With the gradual re-establishment of constitutional government after 1976, he was persuaded by colleagues to enter politics and was Minister of Finance (1980–81). He then became leader of the Social Democratic Party (PSD) and Prime Minister (1985–95). Under his cautious, conservative leadership, Portugal joined the European Community (EC) in 1985 and the Western European Union (WEU) in 1988.

Cavafy, Constantine, *pseudonym of* Konstantínos Pétron Kaváfis 1863–1933
Greek poet

He was born in Alexandria, Egypt, of a Greek merchant family. After his father's death in 1872 his mother took him to England for five years, and apart from three years in Istanbul (1882–85) he spent the rest of his life in Alexandria, where he worked as a civil servant. His work tends to diverge into the erotic, in which he was one of the first modern writers to deal explicitly with homosexuality, and the historical, in which he recreates the world of Greece and Alexandria in the Hellenistic period. His view of life is essentially tragic. His first book, containing 14 poems, was privately published when he was 41, and reissued five years later with an additional seven poems. He published no further work during his lifetime, but in recent years he has become regarded as one of the most influential modern Greek poets. His best-known poems are his earlier ones, such as *I Polis* ('The City') and *Perimenondas tous Várvarous* ('Waiting for the Barbarians'). His work has been translated into English as *Poems* (1951) and *Complete Poems* (1961). ⊞ R Liddell, *Cavafy: a critical biography* (1974)

Cavaignac, Louis Eugène 1802–57
French soldier and politician

Born in Paris, he was the son of General Jean Baptiste Cavaignac (1762–1829), a member of the National Convention. Exiled to Algeria as a republican (1832), he became governor-general there in 1848, but was soon recalled to Paris and became Minister of War. As military dictator he quelled the formidable insurrection of June 1848. In the coup d'état of December 1851 he was arrested but soon released.

Cavalcanti, Guido c.1240–1300
Italian poet

He was born in Florence. A friend of Dante, he married a Ghibelline, and was banished by the Guelfs. He returned to Florence only to die within the year. His works, which included ballads, sonnets and *canzoni*, were translated by Dante Gabriel Rossetti and Ezra Pound. He is said to have been studious and eccentric, and much of his poetry reflects his intellectualism, although he is also aware of the emotional depths of his usual subject, love. ⊞ Ezra Pound, 'Cavalcanti', in *Literary Essays* (1954); A Ribera, *Guido Cavalcanti* (1911)

Cavalieri, (Francesco) Bonaventura 1598–1647
Italian mathematician

Born in Milan, he was appointed Professor of Mathematics at Bologna University in 1629. His method of 'indivisibles', published in 1635, worked with the idea of figures being made up of lines in order to determine their areas. Although the complexity of the method made it rather inaccessible, it helped pave the way for the introduction of integral calculus. He also promoted the use of the logarithms for calculation in Italy following their introduction in the early 1600s.

Cavalieri, Emilio de' c.1550–1602
Italian composer

Born in Rome, he lived mainly at the Florentine court of the Medici, where he was Inspector General of Arts. His dramatic works were forerunners of opera and oratorio.

Cavalli, Francesco, *originally* Francesco Caletti-Bruni 1602–76
Italian composer

Born in Crema, he assumed the name of his patron. A pupil of Monteverdi, he was the organist and maestro di capella of St Mark's, Venice (1668). As an opera and church composer he prepared the way for Alessandro Scarlatti.

Cavallini, Pietro 1259–1344
Italian painter and artist in mosaic

He was born in Rome, a contemporary of Giotto. His mosaics in S Maria in Trastevere are notable, as is the fragmentary *Last Judgement* fresco in S Cecilia in Trastevere. Both date from the early 1290s.

Cave, Edward, *known as* Sylvanus Urban 1691–1754
English printer

Born in Newton, near Rugby, Warwickshire, he became a journalist and set up a small printing office in London. In 1731 he founded the *Gentleman's Magazine*, which he edited under the pseudonym 'Sylvanus Urban, Gent'. Samuel Johnson became its parliamentary reporter in 1740.

Cavell, Edith Louisa 1865–1915
English nurse

Born in Swardeston, Norfolk, she became a nurse in 1895, and in 1907 the first matron of the Berkendael Medical Institute in Brussels, which became a Red Cross hospital during World War I. In August 1915 she was arrested by the Germans and charged with having helped about 200 Allied soldiers to escape to the neutral Netherlands. Tried by court martial, she did not deny the charges and was executed. ⊞ Rowland Ryder, *Edith Cavell: A Biography* (1975)

Cavendish See Jones, Henry

Cavendish
English ducal House of Devonshire

The family is directly descended from the chief justice, Sir John Cavendish, who was beheaded (1381) at Bury St Edmunds by Jack Straw's followers, and from Sir William Cavendish of Cavendish, Suffolk (c.1505–1557), a brother of Cardinal Thomas Wolsey's biographer. His third wife Elizabeth, the celebrated Bess of Hardwick (1518–1608), afterwards Countess of Shrewsbury, brought Chatsworth into the family, and William, their second son, was made Earl of Devonshire (1618).

Cavendish, Henry 1731–1810
English natural philosopher and chemist

Born in Nice, France, into an aristocratic family, he was educated at Peterhouse College, Cambridge (1749–53), but left without a degree. Family wealth enabled him to devote an increasingly reclusive life entirely to scientific pursuits. He demonstrated chemical and physical methods for analysing the distinct 'factitious airs' of which normal atmospheric air was composed (1766). Among these were 'fixed air' (carbon dioxide), and 'inflammable air' (hydrogen), which Cavendish isolated. In 1784 he ascertained that hydrogen and oxygen, when caused to explode by an electric spark, combined to produce water which could not therefore be an element. Similarly, in 1795 he showed nitric acid to be a combination of atmospheric gases. The famous 'Cavendish experiment' (1798) employed a torsion balance apparatus devised by John Michell to estimate with great accuracy the mean density of the Earth and the universal gravitational constant. In 1771 a theoretical study of electricity had appeared and later Cavendish ingeniously confirmed the inverse square law of attraction, but it was not until 1879 that his electrical manuscripts (covering statics and dynamics) were edited and published by James Clerk Maxwell. The Cavendish Laboratory (established 1871) in Cambridge was named in his honour. 📖 A J Berry, *Henry Cavendish* (1960)

Cavendish, Spencer Compton, Marquis of Hartington and 8th Duke of Devonshire
1833–1908
English politician

He was born at Holker Hall, Lancashire, the eldest son of William Cavendish, afterwards 7th Duke of Devonshire. He was educated at Trinity College, Cambridge, and entered parliament in 1857. Between 1863 and 1874 he held office as Lord of the Admiralty, Under-Secretary for War, War Secretary, Postmaster-General and, from 1871, Chief Secretary for Ireland. In 1875, on W E Gladstone's temporary abdication, he was chosen leader of the Liberal Opposition, a post which he filled admirably and in 1880, on the fall of the Disraeli administration, was invited by Queen Victoria to form a ministry. He declined the offer, choosing to serve under Gladstone as Secretary of State for India (1880–82) and as War Secretary (1882–85). He disapproved of Irish Home Rule and became head of the Liberal Unionists from 1886, serving in the Unionist government as Lord President of the Council (1895–1903).

Cavendish, Thomas c.1555–c.1592
English circumnavigator of the globe

He was born in Trimley St Martin, near Ipswich, Suffolk, and after squandering his patrimony at court, shared in Sir Richard Grenville's expedition to Virginia (1585). In 1586, he sailed with three ships for the Pacific Ocean, where he burned three Spanish towns and 13 ships. With a rich booty, but only his largest vessel, the *Desire*, he returned by the Cape of Good Hope to England in 1588. Queen Elizabeth I knighted him. A second expedition, with John Davis (1591), ended in disaster, and Cavendish died off Ascension Island in the south Atlantic Ocean.

Cavendish, William, Duke of Newcastle
1592–1676
English soldier

The nephew of the first Earl of Devonshire, he was created Knight of the Bath by James VI and I in 1610 and Earl of Newcastle in 1628 by Charles I after munificent entertainment at the family seat at Welbeck. In 1638 he was appointed Governor to Charles's son, the future Charles II. His support for the King in the Civil War was generous. As general of all the forces north of the Trent, he had power to issue declarations, confer knighthoods, coin money and raise men; the last function he executed with great zeal. After Marston Moor (1644) he lived on the Continent, at times in great poverty, till the Restoration. In 1665 he was created Duke of Newcastle. He was the author of two works on horsemanship and of several plays. 📖 Geoffrey Tease, *Portrait of a Cavalier: William Cavendish, First Duke of Newcastle* (1979)

Cavendish, William, 1st Duke of Devonshire
1640–1707
English soldier and politician

A steadfast Whig under Charles II and James VII and II, he was leader of the anti-court and anti-Romanist party in the House of Commons, and was a strong supporter of the 'Glorious Revolution' of 1688 that brought William III to the throne. He was created Duke of Devonshire and Marquis of Hartington in 1694 in recognition of his services. He built Chatsworth House, Derbyshire.

Cavendish, William, 4th Duke of Devonshire,
also known (to 1755) as the Marquis of Hartington
1720–64
British statesman

His family connections enabled him to embark early upon a political career. He became a Whig MP in 1741 and Privy Councillor in 1751. He was appointed Lord Lieutenant and Governor-General of Ireland (1754), succeeding to the dukedom in 1755. He was appointed First Lord of the Treasury by George II in 1756 at the beginning of the Seven Years War, largely because William Pitt, 1st Earl of Chatham, whose inclusion in a war ministry was considered vital, refused to serve under Thomas Pelham-Holles, Duke of Newcastle. He was ineffectual in the post, resigning after six months. He was Lord Chamberlain of the Household from 1757 to 1762.

Caventou, Joseph Bienaimé 1795–1877
French chemist

Born in St Omer, Pas-de-Calais, he was educated in Paris and became professor at the École de Pharmacie there. In 1817, in collaboration with Pierre Joseph Pelletier, he isolated (and introduced the term) 'chlorophyll'. They also isolated strychnine and brucine from nux vomica (1819), and quinine and cinchonine from cinchona bark (1820). Cinchonine was particularly important for the treatment of fevers and the French physiologist François Megandie (1783–1855) introduced these new drugs into his 1821 pocket formulary. Caventou also isolated veratrine (1818) and was one of the first to extract caffeine from coffee beans (1822).

Cavour, Camillo Benso, Conte di 1810–61
Italian statesman

Abandoning his early military career, he spent most of the 1830s and 1840s concentrating on the scientific farming of his estates or travelling. His visits to England left him an admirer of the British liberal institutions, railways, industry and banking. In 1847 he founded a progressive journal, *Il Risorgimento*, but played no part in the events of 1848. He entered politics in 1849, and held various ministerial posts under Massimo D'Azeglio before replacing him as Prime Minister (1852); he was to remain premier until his death, except for a few months in 1859.

Cavour's early policy was based on the economic development and modernization of the Kingdom of Sardinia–Piedmont, fostering commerce, ending restrictions on banking and improving communications. From 1855, however, he concentrated increasingly on foreign affairs, perhaps achieving his greatest success with the Plombières Agreement which laid the basis for the Piedmontese acquisition of Lombardy. In 1860 the Expedition of the Thousand to Sicily and **Garibaldi's** subsequent victories in the Mezzogiorno made Cavour fear that the former Mazzinian might establish a republican government in the south or attempt to capture Rome, which would jeopardize good relations with France. He consequently tried to place the south under more moderate leadership. Having failed to achieve this, he sent Piedmontese troops through the Papal States (annexing Umbria and the Marche en route) to block Garibaldi's northward advance. Much to his relief, Garibaldi happily surrendered his conquests to **Victor Emmanuel II**. In the last months of his life, Cavour made an abortive attempt to secure Rome through purchase and diplomacy. 📖 Frank J Coppa, *Camillo di Cavour* (1973)

Cavour's Shadow See **Farini, Luigi Carlo**

Cawley, Evonne Fay, *née* Goolagong 1951–
Australian tennis player
Born in Barellan, New South Wales, she left for Sydney at the age of 10 to be coached in tennis. She married Roger Cawley, an English metal broker, in 1975. As a teenager she won 37 junior titles and in 1971 beat **Margaret Court** at Wimbledon, becoming the second-youngest woman to win, and the first Aboriginal to do so. During the 1970s, she won 92 major tennis tournaments, including the Australian Open four times, and was ranked second in the world. In 1980 she won her second Wimbledon title against **Chris Evert**, becoming the first mother to do so.

Caxton, William c.1422–c.1491
English printer
He was born in the Weald of Kent, possibly at Tenterden. In 1438 he was apprenticed to a London mercer, went to Bruges in 1446, and in 1471 attached himself to the household of Margaret, Duchess of Burgundy, **Edward IV's** sister. He probably learned the art of printing when he was in Cologne (1471–72). In Bruges he joined with the Flemish calligrapher Colard Mansion to set up a press, and in 1474–75 he printed the first book in English, the *Recuyell of the Historyes of Troye*, which he himself had translated. *The Game and Playe of the Chesse* was another of his earliest publications. Late in 1476 he set up his wooden press in Westminster. The *Dictes or Sayengis of the Philosophres* (1477), translated from the French by the 2nd Earl **Rivers**, is the first book proved to have been printed in England. He began to use woodcut illustrations around 1480. Of about 100 books printed by him, over a third survive in unique copies or fragments only. Among the important books to come from his press were two editions of **Chaucer's** *Canterbury Tales*, **John Gower's** *Confessio Amantis*, and Sir **Thomas Malory's** *Morte d'Arthur*.

Cayley, Arthur 1821–95
English mathematician
Born in Richmond, Surrey, he lived in Russia till the age of eight. He graduated from Trinity College, Cambridge, as Senior Wrangler in 1842. Called to the Bar in 1849, he wrote nearly 300 mathematical papers during 14 years' practice in conveyancing. In 1863 he was elected first Sadleirian Professor of Pure Mathematics at Cambridge. His main contributions to mathematics were his algebraic theory of invariants and covariants, his work on matrices, and his study of *n*-dimensional geometry. He did much to revive British mathematics. 📖 A R Forsyth, *The Collected Mathematical Papers of Arthur Cayley* (1895)

Cayley, Sir George 1773–1857
English amateur scientist and aviation pioneer
Born in Scarborough, Yorkshire, he became a pupil of George Walker, a scientist and skilled mechanic, and in 1808 constructed and flew a glider with a wing area of 300 square feet ($27.9m^2$), probably the first practical heavier-than-air flying machine. Over the next 45 years he conducted thousands of model tests. He foresaw that the power to fly must come from a sufficiently light engine and an efficient airscrew. Such an engine was still half a century away when in 1853 he constructed the first successful manned glider, which carried his coachman safely a few hundred yards across a valley. He was also interested in railway engineering, allotment agriculture, and land reclamation methods, and invented a new type of telescope, artificial limbs, the caterpillar tractor and the tension wheel. He helped to found (1839) the Regent Street Polytechnic in London, and was a sponsor of the first meeting of the British Association for the Advancement of Science in York (1832). 📖 Leonard Rivett, *Sir George Cayley: The Father of Aeronautics* (1991)

Ceadda, St See **Chad, St**

Ceauşescu, Nicolae 1918–89
Romanian politician
Born in Scorniceşti into a peasant family and educated at the Academy of Economic Studies, Bucharest, he joined the Communist Party in 1936 and was imprisoned for anti-government activities (1936–38). He became a member of the Central Committee of the Romanian Communist Party (RCP) in 1952 and of the politburo in 1955. In 1965 he succeeded **Gheorghe Gheorghiu-Dej** as de facto party leader, becoming General-Secretary of the RCP in 1965 and its first President in 1967. Under his leadership, Romania became increasingly independent of the USSR and pursued its own foreign policy, for which Ceauşescu was decorated by many Western governments. In internal affairs he extended the rigid programme of his Stalinist predecessor, instituting a strong personality cult and appointing family members to public office. He manipulated Romanian nationalism and ruthlessly forced national minorities to adopt Romanian culture. His policy of 'systematization' in the countryside, replacing traditional villages by collectives of concrete apartments, roused an international outcry in the late 1980s. Internal opposition to his repressive and increasingly bizarre policies also grew. In 1989 he was deposed when elements in the army joined a popular revolt. Following a trial by military tribunal, he and his wife, Elena, who had been second only to him in political influence, were shot. 📖 Mary E Fischer, *Nicolae Ceauşescu: A Political Biography* (1988)

Cecchetti, Enrico 1850–1928
Italian dancer, teacher and choreographer
Born in Milan, he is most closely associated with Russia, where he worked from 1887 to 1902. After performing in Italy, London and the USA he settled in Russia, first as dancer with the Imperial Ballet in St Petersburg and then as teacher, developing the talents of stars like **Anna Pavlova**. He was Ballet Master of **Diaghilev's** Ballets Russes for 15 years. Though he choreographed several works, he is remembered for the influential ballet technique he developed, which is still highly regarded today.

Cecchi, Emilio 1884–1966
Italian poet, critic, translator and essayist
He lived in Florence, Tuscany. His critical work, influenced by **Benedetto Croce** and in particular *Pesci rossi* (1920, 'Goldfish') had an enormous impact. He introduced the essay as a form into Italian literature, basing his style on that of **Charles Lamb** and **Thomas De Quincey**.

Cecchi D'Amico, Suso, originally Giovanna Cecchi 1914–
Italian screenwriter

Born in Rome, the daughter of Emilio Cecchi, she studied in Rome and Cambridge, then worked as a journalist and translator before writing the screenplay of the film *Mio Figlio Professore* (1946). An active post-war Italian neo-realist, she contributed to the screenplays of *Ladri Di Biciclette* (1948, 'Bicycle Thieves') and *Miracolo A Milano* (1950, 'Miracle in Milan'), but found some of her best opportunities working in collaboration with director Luchino Visconti, especially on a number of elegant literary adaptations, including *Il Gattopardo* (1963, 'The Leopard'), *Lo Straniero* (1967, 'The Stranger') and *L'Innocente* (1976, 'The Innocent'). Her other expertly crafted screenplays include *Salvatore Guiliano* (1961), *Jesus of Nazareth* (1977) and *Oci Ciornie* (1987, 'Dark Eyes').

Cech, Thomas 1947–
US biochemist and Nobel Prize winner

Born in Chicago, he trained at the universities of California and Chicago, and later moved to the University of Colorado, Boulder, where he has been professor since 1983. He was the first to discover the ability of ribonucleic acid (RNA) to act as a biological catalyst, and in 1977 he studied the repair mechanisms of damaged DNA and identified regions sensitive to splitting. He discovered that the protein-free precursor RNA performs its own cleavage and splicing, acting in the manner of an enzyme, but modifying the molecule in the process. Subsequently he identified other catalytic RNA species that act without self-modification, called 'ribozymes'. For these pioneer discoveries Cech shared with Sidney Altman the 1989 Nobel Prize for chemistry. He has since extended this work to examine enzymes which use inbuilt RNA to add short repeat sections of DNA to chromosomal DNA.

Cecil, Lord (Edward Christian) David Gascoyne 1902–86
English literary critic

Born in London, the younger son of James Edward Cecil 4th Marquis of Salisbury (1861–1947), he was educated at Oxford and was a Fellow of Wadham College (1924-30) and of New College (1936-69). He was Professor of English Literature at Oxford from 1948 to 1970. Known chiefly as a literary biographer—William Cowper (in *The Stricken Deer*, 1929), *Sir Walter Scott* (1933), *Jane Austen* (1935), *Thomas Hardy* (1943) and *Max Beerbohm* (*Max*, 1964)—he also wrote an effective political biography of Lord Melbourne in two volumes—*The Young Melbourne* (1939) and *Lord M* (1954). He also published a collection of essays, *The Fine Art of Reading* (1957).

Cecil, Henry Richard Amherst 1943–
Scottish racehorse trainer

He was born near Aberdeen, and his first job was as assistant (1964–68) to his stepfather, Captain Cecil Boyd-Rochfort, a trainer appointed by Queen Elizabeth II. He got his first licence in 1969 and took over Warren Place, which was in decline, on his father-in-law's retirement. His wins from 1969 increased—he trained 15 British Classic winners, and won the Derby three times. His best season was in 1987 with 180 winners and a stable of 170 horses. His serious and dedicated character has outlived his early playboy image.

Cecil, Robert, 1st Earl of Salisbury c.1563–1612
English statesman

Son of William Cecil, 1st Baron Burghley, he entered parliament in 1584. He became a Privy Councillor in 1591 and was appointed Elizabeth I's Secretary of State in 1596. His control in the last years of the reign helped to smooth the succession of James VI of Scotland to the English throne as James I, and he was rewarded with an earldom in 1605. His

James kept him in office and he negotiated peace terms ending the long war with Spain (1604). Lord Treasurer from 1608, he was an efficient administrator and financial manager who fought a losing battle against mounting royal debts.

Cecil, Robert Arthur James Gascoyne-, 5th Marquis of Salisbury 1893–1972
English Conservative statesman

He was born at Hatfield House, Hertfordshire, the son of James Edward Cecil (1861–1947) and educated at Eton and Oxford. He became MP for South Dorset in 1929, and in 1935 as Viscount Cranborne became Foreign Under-Secretary. He resigned with his chief, Anthony Eden, in 1938 over the 'appeasement' of Mussolini. In the Churchill government of 1940 he became Paymaster General and was Dominions Secretary until 1941 when he was called to the Lords. He was Colonial Secretary, and Lord Privy Seal, and represented Britain at the founding conference of UNO at San Francisco. As leader of the Opposition in the House of Lords (1945–51) he counselled acceptance by the Tory majority of most of the legislation in the political and economic revolution. In the Churchill government of 1951 he became Secretary of State for Commonwealth Relations and in 1952 Lord President of the Council (1952). From 1951 to 1957 he was leader of the House of Lords, which he wished (within limits) to see reformed. In 1957 he (and Churchill) advised Elizabeth II on the choice of Harold Macmillan (rather than R A Butler) to succeed Eden as Prime Minister. In 1957 he resigned the lord presidency in protest at the government's action in releasing Archbishop Makarios of Cyprus from his exile.

Cecil, Robert Arthur Talbot Gascoyne, 3rd Marquis of Salisbury 1830–1903
English Conservative statesman and Nobel Prize winner

Born at Hatfield House, Hertfordshire, and educated at Eton and Christ Church, Oxford, he was elected Conservative MP for Stamford (1853). In 1865 he became Viscount Cranborne and heir to the marquisate on the death of his elder brother. In the Derby ministry (1866), he became Secretary for India, but resigned, along with others, when Lord Derby and Disraeli introduced a reform bill. In 1868 he succeeded his father as 3rd Marquis of Salisbury. A strong opponent of the disestablishment of the Irish Church, in 1870 he supported the Peace Preservation Bill, but disapproved the Irish Land Act. In 1874 he again became Secretary for India, but before the end of the year he had again come into collision with his chief on the Public Worship Regulation Act. In 1878 he succeeded Lord Derby as Foreign Secretary and accompanied Disraeli to the Berlin Congress. On the death of Disraeli (1881), he succeeded to the leadership of the Conservative Opposition and became Prime Minister and Secretary of State for Foreign Affairs in 1885. The contentious Irish Home Rule Bill defeated the Liberals, and Lord Salisbury, backed by Liberal Unionists, was Prime Minister again in 1886 and in 1895, when a succession of foreign complications brought the country several times to the verge of war. He resigned as Foreign Secretary in 1900 and, having remained at the head of the government during the Boer War (1889–1902), retired from public life in July 1902.

Cecil (of Chelwood), Robert Cecil, 1st Viscount 1864–1958
English Conservative politician and Nobel Prize winner

Born in London, the son of Robert Cecil (3rd Marquis of Salisbury), he was educated at Eton and University College, Oxford. He was called to the Bar in 1887, and entered parliament (1903). He was Minister of Blockade (1916–18), and as Under-Secretary for Foreign Affairs (1918) helped to draft the League of Nations Covenant and was British representative at various disarmament conferences. He was President of the League of Nations Union (1923–45) and thereafter an honorary life president of UNA. He resigned from the Cabinet because of the cruiser question with the USA (1927) and was awarded the Nobel Peace Prize (1937). He published his autobiography, *All the Way*, in 1949.

Cecil, Thomas, 1st Earl of Exeter and 2nd Baron Burghley 1542–1623
English soldier
Son of **William Cecil**, 1st Baron Burghley by his first wife, he served in the Scottish War (1573) and against the Armada (1588), and crushed the Earl of **Essex's** rebellion (1601). Cecil was created Earl of Exeter in 1605.

Cecil, William, 1st Baron Burghley or Burchleigh 1520–98
English statesman
He was born in Bourn, Lincolnshire. In 1547 **Henry VIII** appointed him 'Custos Brevium' and in 1547, under the patronage of the Protector Somerset (**Edward Seymour**), he was made Master of Requests and his secretary in the following year. When Somerset fell from grace Cecil fell too, but in 1550 he returned to office as Secretary of State and in 1551 was knighted. During **Mary I's** reign he adopted Catholicism but had already begun correspondence with Princess Elizabeth (later **Elizabeth I**) who, on her accession to the throne in 1558, appointed him Chief Secretary of State. For the next 40 years he was the main architect of the successful policies of the Elizabethan era. He was created Baron Burghley in 1571 and Lord High Treasurer in 1572, an office he held until his death. He left lavish mansions which he had built or restored, including Burghley, Theobalds in Hertfordshire and Cecil House in the Strand. He was the father of **Thomas Cecil** and **Robert Cecil**, 1st Earl of Salisbury. ▢ *Lord Burghley and Queen Elizabeth* (1960); Conyers Read, *Mr Secretary Cecil and Queen Elizabeth* (1955)

Cecilia, St c.2nd century–c.3rd century AD
Roman Christian
Born possibly in Rome, she was, according to a dubious tradition, compelled to marry a young pagan, Valerian, despite a vow of celibacy. She succeeded in persuading him to respect her vow, and converted him to Christianity. They were both put to death for their faith. According to legend she was a singer, and so became the patron saint of music. Her feast day is 22 November.

Cedd, St d.664
Anglo-Saxon churchman
The brother of St **Chad**, he christianized the East Saxons and became their bishop in 654. He founded a monastery at Lastingham, Yorkshire, in 658.

Cela, Camilo José 1916–
Spanish novelist and Nobel Prize winner
He was born in Iria Flavia, La Coruña, and attended Madrid University. He served in **Franco's** forces, and his work is frequently interpreted as an eloquent, aggressive, response to that error of judgement. His first novel, *La familia de Pascual Duarte* (1942, Eng trans *The Family of Pascual Duarte*, 1946) was banned, having stunned readers with its seemingly gratuitous violence. The range of his work is vast but he is best known for *La Colmena* (1951, Eng trans *The Hive*, 1953), which recreates daily life in Madrid in the aftermath of the Spanish civil war with great sensitivity and feeling for the plight of ordinary people. Other notable titles are *Viaje a la Alcarría* (1948, Eng trans *Journey to the Alcarria*, 1948), *San Camilo 1936* (1970) and *Mazurca para dos muertos* (1984, 'Mazurka for Two Dead People') which won Spain's national literature prize. The dominant

novelist in Spain for over 40 years, he was awarded the Nobel Prize for literature in 1989. ▢ D W MacPheeters, *Camilo José Cela* (1963)

Celan, Paul, *pseudonym of* Paul Ancel or Antschel 1920–70
Romanian poet who wrote in German
Born into the Jewish community in Czernowitz, he studied in Romania and in France. He survived a Nazi labour camp, though both his parents died, and later became a lecturer in German literature in Paris, taking French nationality. His reputation was established by his second collection of poems, *Mohn und Gedächtnis* (1952, 'Poppy and Memory'), which includes his most famous poem, 'Todesfuge' ('Death Fugue'), about concentration camps. *Sprachgitter* (1959, Eng trans *Speech-Grille*, 1971) and *Die Niemandsrose* (1963, 'The No-One's Rose') reflect his ambiguous attitude to the Jewish God. The flowing style of his early work was influenced by the French Surrealists and Yvan Goll (1891–1950), but this became more concentrated in his later poems as a result of his wartime experiences. He committed suicide by drowning himself in the River Seine. ▢ J Glenn, *Paul Celan* (1973)

Celestine
Title assumed by five popes
Celestine I (422–32); II (1143–44); III (1191–98); IV (1241); and V, Pietro di Morrone (1215–96). The last mentioned was born in Naples and, after a long life of ascetic severities, was reluctantly elected pope in 1294. He resigned his office after five months—'the great refusal'—for which **Dante** places him at the entrance of Hell. He was imprisoned by his successor, **Boniface VIII**. He founded the Celestine Order, and was canonized in 1313.

Céline, Louis-Ferdinand, *pseudonym of* L F Destouches 1894–1961
French novelist
He was born in Paris, the son of a poor clerk and a lace seamstress. His education was rudimentary and he had various jobs until 1912 when he joined the cavalry. In the first year of World War I he was wounded in the head and shell-shocked in an action for which he was decorated. The suffering, both mental and physical, caused by his wounds dogged him to the end of his days. He was invalided out of the military, took a medical degree, worked as a staff surgeon at the Ford plant in Detroit and later ministered to the poor of Paris. His first novel, *Voyage au bout de la nuit* (1932, 'Journey to the End of Night'), brought international acclaim, which increased with his second novel, *Mort à crédit* (1936, 'Death on the Installment Plan'). His use of the demotic and his insights into working-class have influenced many writers, among them **Jean-Paul Sartre**, **William Burroughs** and **Henry Miller**. In the late 1930s he was a declared anti-Semite, and after the liberation of France (1944), fled to Denmark. He was tried and sentenced to death in absentia but this was later reversed and he spent his last years in France, with partial paralysis, tinnitus and close to insanity. His final novels, *D'un château à l'autre* (1957) and *Nord* (1960), are ranked with his best.

Cellini, Benvenuto 1500–71
Italian goldsmith, sculptor and engraver
He was born in Florence, from where he was banished after a duel. In Rome his skill as an artist in metalwork brought him to the notice of nobles and prelates, but he was imprisoned several times for murdering or maiming his rivals. For some years he lived alternately in Rome and Florence, Mantua and Naples. His best work includes the gold salt-cellar of *Neptune and Triton* made for **Francis I** of France (now in Vienna), and his bronze *Perseus with the Head of Medusa*, which was made in Florence while he worked

under the patronage of **Cosimo I de' Medici**. He is also remembered for his autobiography (1558–62, first translated into English by Thomas Nugent, 2 vols 1771).

Celsius, Anders 1701–44
Swedish astronomer
Born in Uppsala, he taught mathematics and became Professor of Astronomy at the University of Uppsala (1730). Between 1732 and 1736 he travelled widely in Europe and whilst in Nuremberg published an aurora borealis compendium (1733). He was responsible for the construction (1740) and subsequent direction of the Uppsala Observatory. The Celsius temperature scale originated with a mercury thermometer, described by him in 1742 before the Swedish Academy of Sciences. Two fixed points had been chosen: one (0 degrees) at the boiling point of water, the other (100 degrees) at the melting point of ice. A few years after his death, colleagues at Uppsala began to use the familiar inverted version of this centigrade scale.

Celsus 2nd century AD
Roman philosopher
He was a Platonist who published one of the first anti-Jewish and anti-Christian polemics in his *True discourse* (c.178AD), refuted by **Origen** in his *Contra Celsum* (c.248).

Celsus, Aulus Cornelius 1st century AD
Roman writer and physician
He compiled an encyclopedia on medicine, rhetoric, history, philosophy, war and agriculture. The only extant portion of the work is the *De Medicina*, rediscovered by Pope Nicholas V (1397–1455) and one of the first medical works to be printed (1478). In it Celsus gives accounts of symptoms and treatments of diseases, surgical methods and medical history. ⨂ N Scalinci, *La Oftalmiatria di Aulo Cornelio Celso* (1940)

Cenci, Beatrice 1577–99
Italian beauty
She was the youngest daughter of a wealthy Roman nobleman, Count Francesco Cenci, who conceived an incestuous passion for her. With her stepmother and her brother, Giacomo, she hired two assassins to murder him (1598). The Cenci family were arrested and tortured, and all three were beheaded, by order of Pope Clement VIII. She was the central figure of a tragedy by **Shelley** (1819).

Cendrars, Blaise, *originally* Frédéric Louis Sauser 1887–1961
Swiss novelist, poet and traveller
He was born in Chaux-de-Fonds, Switzerland, of a Scottish mother. When he was 15 he ran away from home to work for a jewel merchant, with whom he travelled through Russia, Persia and China; he later described the journey in a long poem, *Transsibérien* (1913). In 1910 he met **Guillaume Apollinaire**, who greatly influenced him. He wrote his first long poem in the USA, *Pâques à New York* (1912, 'Easter in New York'), which, with *Transsibérien* and his third and last long poem, *Le Panama ou Les Aventures de mes Sept Oncles* (written in 1918, published as *Panama; or the Adventures of my Seven Uncles* in 1931 in a translation by **John Dos Passos**), was important in shaping the spirit of modern poetry. His novels include *La Confession de Dan Yack* (1927–29; 1946; Eng trans *Antarctic Fugue*, 1948), and *L'Or* (1925, Eng trans *Sutter's Gold*, 1926). ⨂ M A Caws, *The Inner Theatre of Recent French Poetry* (1932)

Centlivre, Susannah, *also known as* Susannah Carroll, *née* Freeman c.1667– c.1723
English playwright and actress
She was born probably in Lincolnshire, in either Whaplode or Holbeach. According to some sources she was taught French by a tutor, and there is a story of her masquerading as a young man in order to gain entrance to Cambridge. There are also unsubstantiated stories of her being first married at 14, and twice widowed, all while a relatively young woman. In 1700 her first play, *The Perjured Husband*, a tragi-comedy, was produced at Drury Lane, and she subsequently appeared on the stage in Bath in her own comedy, *Love at a Venture* (1706). She dedicated another play, *The Platonick Lady*, written in the same year, to 'all the Generous Encouragers of Female Ingenuity'. Also in 1706, she married Joseph Centlivre, head cook to Queen **Anne** at Windsor. She wrote 19 plays, of which *The Busie Body* (1709), *A Bold Stroke for a Wife* (1717) and *The Wonder: A Woman Keeps a Secret* (1714) were enormously popular farcical comedies of intrigue. A great woman of the theatre, she knew many actors, dramatists and writers, including **George Farquhar** and **Nicholas Rowe**. ⨂ J H Bowyer, *The Celebrated Mrs Centlivre* (1952)

Centlivres, Albert van de Sandt 1887–1966
South African judge
Born in Cape Town and educated at the South African College there, he was a Rhodes Scholar at Oxford. He became a judge of the Cape Provincial Division of the Supreme Court of South Africa in 1935, a judge of appeal in 1939 and was Chief Justice from 1950 to 1957. Highly regarded in legal circles, he played a substantial part in restoring Roman-Dutch law in South Africa and in excising inappropriate importations from English law.

Cerdic d.534
Saxon leader
He invaded Britain, landing in Hampshire with his son Cynric in AD495. By c.500 he had created the kingdom of Wessex for himself and founded the West Saxon royal dynasty.

Cerezo Arevalo, Marco Vinicio 1942–
Guatemalan politician
Educated at San Carlos University, he joined the Christian Democratic Party (PDCG), founded in 1968. From 1974 there was widespread political violence and democratic government was virtually suspended. With the adoption of a new constitution in 1985 the PDCG won the congressional elections and Cerezo became the first civilian President for 20 years. He remained in office until 1991, struggling to deal with a still-maleficent military and an economy undermined by high foreign debt, and at its close his administration was widely perceived as corrupt and ineffective.

Cerinthus c.100AD
Jewish Gnostic heretic
Born in Alexandria, Egypt, he is said to have lived in Ephesus contemporaneously with the aged apostle **John**.

Černík, Oldřich 1921–94
Czechoslovak politician
A man of reasonable ability, he worked his way up through the official hierarchy to become chairman of the State Planning Commission in 1963. As such, he favoured moderate change to make the economy more efficient. However, when **Alexander Dubček** became General-Secretary (1968), Černík became Prime Minister and followed a more far-reaching reform policy. In July and August of the same year he tried to restrain the more radical supporters of the Prague Spring, and after the Soviet invasion he struggled to retain something of its achievements. But within two years, like Dubček, he was removed from the party and the government. His attempts to rekindle his career after the 1989 fall of the Communist regime were unsuccessful.

Cernuda, Luis 1902–63
Spanish poet and critic

He is often considered the greatest of all the famous 'Generation of '27', which included Federico García Lorca and Rafael Alberti. Cernuda is also highly prized as, with Constantine Cavafy and Sandro Penna (1906–77), one of the great homosexual poets of the 20th century. An anti-Francoist, he escaped from Madrid in 1938 and moved to Great Britain to be Professor of Spanish Literature at Glasgow University, then to the USA. His first teacher and mentor was Pedro Salinas (1891–1951) and his poetry is soaked in his Andalusian origins, and combines explicit homosexuality with all the sad and beautiful virtues of Mediterranean art. His militaristic father is present as a symbol of the unavoidable, unlovable hostility of reality in his work and his 11 collections were finally published as *La realidad y el deseo* (1964, 'Reality and Desire'). His work has been translated into English in *The Poetry of Luis Cernuda* (1971) and *Selected Poems of Luis Cernuda* (1977). 📖 D Harris, *Luis Cernuda: A Study of the Poetry* (1973)

Cervantes (Saavedra), Miguel de 1547–1616
Spanish writer, author of Don Quixote

He was born in Alcalá de Henares, near Madrid, the son of a poor medical practitioner. In 1569 he published his first known work, a collection of pieces on the death of the queen. He then travelled to Italy in the service of Cardinal Giulio Acquaviva, and enlisted as a soldier. After service against the Turks in Tunis, he was returning to Spain in 1575 when the galley he sailed in was captured by Algerian corsairs, and with his brother Rodrigo and others he was carried into Algiers, where he remained in captivity for five years, during which he made four daring attempts to escape. In 1580 he was ransomed by the efforts of Trinitarian monks, Algiers traders and his family. Finding no permanent occupation at home, he drifted to Madrid, and tried a literary career. In 1584 he married Catalina de Salazar y Palacios (1565–1626). The marriage was childless, but Cervantes had an illegitimate daughter, Isabel de Saavedra (c.1585–1652). His first important work was the pastoral romance *La Galatea* (1585, Eng trans 1867). For some years he strove to gain a livelihood by writing plays, *La Numancia* (1784, Eng trans 1870) and *El trato de Argel* (1798, Eng trans *The Commerce of Algiers*, 1870), have survived. In 1594 he was appointed collector of revenues for the kingdom of Granada, but in 1597, failing to make up the sum due to the treasury, he was sent to prison in Seville, released after three months, but not reinstated. Local tradition maintains that he wrote *Don Quixote*, the first part of which came out in Madrid in early 1605, in prison at Argamasilla in La Mancha. It was immediately popular, though Lope de Vega dismissed it, but instead of giving his readers the sequel they asked for, Cervantes busied himself with writing for the stage and composing short tales, published as *Novelas Ejemplares* (1613, Eng trans *Exemplary Novels*, 1972). His *Viage al Parnaso* (1614), a poem of over 3,000 lines in *terza rima*, reviews the poetry and poets of the day. In 1614 a pseudonymous writer brought out a spurious second part of *Don Quixote*, with an insulting preface, which spurred Cervantes to the completion of the genuine second part (1615). While it was in the press he revised his various plays and interludes, and a little before his death, he finished the romance of *Persiles y Sigismunda* (1617, Eng trans *The Travels of Persiles and Sigismunda*, 1619). Though it is the most carelessly written of all great books, *Don Quixote* is widely regarded as one of the best books in the world, and seen as the precursor of the modern novel, as well as a great comic epic in its own right. 📖 W Byron, *Cervantes, a biography* (1978); Manuel Duran, *Cervantes* (1974)

Cesaire, Aimé Fernand 1913–
West Indian poet and playwright

He was born in Basse-Point, Martinique, and his reputation is based largely on two plays, *La tragédie du roi Christophe* (1963, Eng trans *The Tragedy of King Christophe*) and an original adaptation of Shakespeare's *The Tempest*. He is also noted for the influential long poem, *Cahier d'un retour au pays natal* (1939, *Notebook of a Return to my Native Land*) which tells of his conscious adoption of an African identity, and for a biography of the revolutionary Pierre Toussaint L'Ouverture (1961). A militant Marxist and anti-colonialist, he played a large role in rallying decolonized Africans in the 1950s.

Cesalpino, Andrea, Latin Caesalpinus 1519–1603
Italian botanist, physician and physiologist

Born in Arezzo, he became the most original and philosophical botanist since Theophrastus, whose work he revived. He was Professor of Medicine and director of the botanic garden in Pisa from 1553 to 1592, when he became physician to Pope Clement VIII. After he had taught at the university for 30 years he published *De Plantis* (1583), in which he stated the basic principles of botany and made the first attempt at a scientific classification of plants. His dissection of plant tissues led to the identification of plant veins, and his experiments on plants laid the foundations for plant physiology. In medicine he was no less original, propounding a theory of blood circulation.

César, full name César Baldaccini 1921–
French sculptor

Born in Marseilles, he trained at the École des Beaux-Arts there, then at the Institute des Beaux-Arts in Paris. He became known in the 1950s with works such as *Petit déjeuner sur l'herbe* (1957, 'Breakfast Picnic'), consisting of a crushed metal tumbler and sardine can on a metal plate, and for his beaten metal *L'Homme de Saint-Denis* (1958, Tate, London). He then won fame in the 1960s with his 'compressions', or crushed cars, like *Yellow Buick* (1961, Museum of Modern Art, New York). In 1985 he was commissioned by Peugeot to produce *The Champions*, a permanent memorial to four damaged and burnt-out racing cars. Since around 1990 he has also compressed paper, glass and rags, and for the 1995 Venice Biennale he constructed a huge monument to scrap metal—a transfigured mountain of hundreds of crushed cars.

Cesari, Giuseppe, also called Il Cavaliere d'Arpino or Il Giuseppino c.1568–c.1640
Italian painter

He was born in Arpino. Honoured by five popes, he is best known for the frescoes in the Capitol at Rome (1590–1615).

Cesnola, Count Luigi Palma di 1832–1904
US army officer and archaeologist

Born near Turin, Italy, he fought in the Austrian, Crimean, and American civil wars, and, having taken US citizenship (1865), became US consul in Cyprus. He was director of the New York Metropolitan Museum from 1879 until his death, and to it he presented his collection of about 35,000 antiquities, taken from nearly 70,000 tombs in Cyprus.

Céspedes, Carlos Manuel de 1819–73
Cuban nationalist

He came from a wealthy plantation family and studied law in Spain before returning to Cuba. There he raised a revolt against the Spanish colonial government instigating the Ten Years War in Oriente. With 200 poorly-armed men, he took Santiago and freed the slaves and in 1869 devised a constitution and was elected provisional President of the incipient republic. However, in 1873 he was deposed by the revolutionary council; he went into hiding, but was captured by the Spanish and shot. He became known as 'The Father of the Country'.

Cézanne, Paul 1839–1906
French painter, a leading figure of Post-Impressionism and in the development of modern art

Cézanne was born in Aix-en-Provence, the son of a self-made businessman, and seemed destined to follow in his footsteps. From 1859 to 1861 he studied law at Aix, and there formed a friendship with **Émile Zola**, who persuaded him in 1862 to go to Paris to study art at the Académie Suisse, with a small allowance from his disgruntled father. His passion was for the Romantics, in particular **Delacroix**, whom he admired all his life. In Paris he met the circle of painters centred on **Manet**, but his main influence was **Camille Pissarro**, who brought him into the realm of Impressionism. He worked mainly at Aix and l'Estaque, with occasional visits to Paris, where he exhibited at the first and third Impressionist exhibitions in 1874 and 1877.

Cézanne turned to the study of nature, as in the famous *Maison du pendu* ('The Suicide's House') of this period (1873, now in the Louvre), and began to use his characteristic glowing colours. In his later period after 1886, when he became financially independent of his father, he emphasized the underlying forms of nature ('the cylinder, the sphere, the cone') by constructing his pictures from a rhythmic series of coloured planes, painting not light but plastic form, and thus becoming the forerunner of Cubism.

In 1886 he married Hortense Fiquet, with whom he had had a secret liaison since 1870. In the same year, his friendship with Zola was ended by the publication of Zola's novel *L'œuvre*, in which the central figure, an unsuccessful and unbalanced Impressionist painter, is in many respects identifiable as Cézanne.

Cézanne described his aim as being 'to make Impressionism something solid and durable like the art of the old masters'. He realized this especially in his many still lifes and landscapes. He achieved recognition only in the last years of his life, and two exhibitions of his work were held by Vollard, in 1895 and 1899.

Among his most famous paintings are *The Card Players* (1890–92) in the Musée d'Orsay, Paris; *L'Homme au chapeau de paille* (c.1871, 'Man in a Straw Hat'), in the Metropolitan Museum, New York; his self-portrait of 1869, *Aix: Paysage rocheux* (c.1887, 'Rocky Landscape in Aix') and *Le Jardinier* (c.1906, 'The Gardener'), all in the Tate Gallery, London; and *La Vieille au chapelet* (c.1897–98, 'The Old Woman with Beads'), in the National Gallery, London.

📖 M Schapiro *Cézanne* (1988); John Rewald *Paul Cézanne* (1986); Gersthe Mack *Paul Cézanne* (1935); R Verdi, *Cézanne*.

> 'May I repeat what I told you here: treat nature by the cylinder, the sphere, the cone, everything in perspective?' From a letter to Émile Bernard, 15 April 1904.

Céspedes, Pablo de 1538–1608
Spanish painter

Born in Córdoba, he studied under **Michelangelo** and **Raphael** in Rome. In 1577 he became a canon at Córdoba, where he established a school of art, and was also active as an architect and writer. He painted the *Last Supper* in Córdoba cathedral.

Cessna, Clyde Vernon 1879–1954
US aviator and aircraft manufacturer

He was born in Hawthorne, Louisiana. The flexible monoplane design of his aircraft, which incorporated his invention, the cantilever wing, made them suitable for bush flying and as forest and rescue planes. In the 1920s he teamed up with the businessman Victor Roos, and they produced Cessna–Roos aircraft until 1927, when Cessna took over his partner's share. The Cessna Aircraft Company eventually mass-produced about 8,000 planes each year.

Cetewayo or Cetshwayo c.1826–84
King of Zululand

Born near Eshowe, the nephew of **Shaka**, he was King of Zululand from 1873 to 1883. He destroyed the garrison at Isandhlwana when the British invaded Zululand (1879), but was later defeated at Ulundi and taken prisoner. After captivity in the Cape of Good Hope and England, where his proud and dignified bearing impressed, he was restored by the British to part of his kingdom (1883), but was soon driven out by his subjects. His grave in the Nkandla forest is a spot sacred to the Zulus. 📖 C T Binns, *The Last Zulu King* (1963)

Cetti, Francesco 1726–78
Italian Jesuit and naturalist

Born in Mannheim, Germany, he was educated in Lombardy and at the Jesuit College in Monza. In 1766, at the request of Charles Emmanuel III, King of Sardinia, he was appointed Professor of Mathematics at the University of Sassari. A distinguished naturalist as well as theologian and philosopher, his great work was a monumental *Storia naturale della Sardegna* (1774–77). The bird Cetti's Warbler (*Cettia cetti*) was named in his honour.

Ceulen or Keulen, Ludolph van 1540–1610
Dutch mathematician

Born in Hildesheim, Germany, he devoted himself to finding the value of *pi* and finally worked it out to 35 decimal places. Known as 'Ludolph's number', it was inscribed on his tombstone at Leyden.

Ceva, Giovanni c.1647–1734
Italian geometer

Born in Milan, he gave his name to a theorem on concurrent lines through the vertices of a triangle.

Cézanne, Paul See panel above

Chabaneau, François 1754–1842
French chemist

Born in Nontron, Dordogne, he began as a student of theology, but was expelled on account of his views on metaphysics. Professor of Mathematics at Passy when only 17, and with little knowledge of the subject, he turned to physics and chemistry. Subsequently he became lecturer in physics and chemistry at the Real Seminario Patriótico at Vergara, Spain, where he and **Don Fausto d'Elhuyar y de Suvisa** founded the Real Escuela Metalúrgica in the 1780s. They worked together on ways of separating platinum from its compounds and making it malleable, announcing their success in 1783.

Chabrier, (Alexis) Emmanuel 1841–94
French composer

Born in Ambert, he composed the operas *Gwendoline* (1886), *Le Roi malgré lui* (1887, 'The King in Spite of Himself'), and *Briséis* (unfinished), piano music and songs but the piece most performed today is his orchestral rhapsody *España* (1883, 'Spain'), inspired by the folk music of Spain.

Chabrol, Claude 1930–
French film director

He was born in Paris, and became a leading figure in the *Nouvelle Vague* movement with his early films *Beau Serge* (1958, *Bitter Reunion*) and *Les Cousins* (1959, *The Cousins*) and above all with *Les Biches* (1968, *The Girlfriends*). Other films include *La Femme Infidèle* (1969, *Unfaithful Wife*), *Le Boucher*

(1970, *The Butcher*), *Les Noces rouges* (1973, *Wedding in Blood*), *Masques* (1987) and *Une Affaire des Femmes* (1989, *Story of Women*). Many of his films are about murder and suspense, and were much influenced by **Alfred Hitchcock**.

Chad or Ceadda, St d.672
Anglo-Saxon churchman

Born in Northumbria, he was a pupil of St **Aidan** in Lindisfarne. He spent part of his youth in Ireland, and in 664 became abbot of Lastingham, and in 666 Bishop of York. Doubt was cast on the validity of his consecration, and he withdrew in 669, but was immediately made Bishop of Mercia, fixing the see at Lichfield.

Chadli Benjedid 1929–
Algerian politician and soldier

He was born in Sebaa. He joined the guerrillas who were fighting for independence as part of the National Liberation Front (FLN) in 1955. Under **Houari Boumédienne**, Defence Minister in the government of Ahmed Ben Bella, he was military commander of Algiers, and when Boumédienne overthrew Ben Bella in 1965 he joined the Revolutionary Council. He succeeded Boumédienne as Secretary-General of the FLN and President in 1979, a post he held until 1991.

Chadwick, Helen 1953–96
English photographer, installation and performance artist

Born in Croydon, London, she studied at Brighton Polytechnic and Chelsea School of Art, and lectured at the latter and at the Royal College, London. Her often autobiographical work covered a wide range of disciplines, including sculpture, photography, mixed media installation and performance art. It tended to question stereotypical attitudes in society, particularly her series of meat abstracts such as *Enfleshings1* (1989) and her portrayal of the body, which was open to many differing interpretations. Her suggestive *Cacao* (1994) was a fountain of molten chocolate. In 1987 she had a work shortlisted for the 1987 Turner Prize, and in 1995 had a solo show at the Museum of Modern Art in New York. Her work is represented in many major public collections both in the UK, including the Tate Gallery, the Victoria and Albert Museum and Birmingham Art Gallery, and around the world. She died unexpectedly of heart failure.

Chadwick, Sir James 1891–1974
English physicist and Nobel Prize winner

Born near Macclesfield, Cheshire, he studied at the universities of Manchester, Berlin and Cambridge, and worked on radioactivity with **Ernest Rutherford**. In 1932 he repeated the experiment previously performed by **Walther Bothe** and **Irène** and **Jean Frédéric Joliot-Curie** in which a neutral penetrating radiation was released from the bombardment of beryllium by alpha particles. He suggested that the radiation was due to a neutral particle whose mass was close to that of the proton. He named the particle the neutron and was awarded the 1935 Nobel Prize for physics for this discovery. He built Great Britain's first cyclotron in 1935 at Liverpool University and during World War II worked on the Manhattan Project to develop the atomic bomb in the USA. He was elected FRS in 1927 and knighted in 1945.

Chadwick, Lynn Russell 1914–
English sculptor

Born in London, he trained as an architect, but in 1945 turned to making constructions and mobiles. Like **Henry Moore**, he is an artist whose work, although abstract, nevertheless carries suggestions of the human figure, as in *Winged Figures* (1955, Tate Gallery, London). His first one-man show was at Gimpel Fils, London, in 1950. This was followed by others in New York, Venice and Zurich, and in 1956 he won the International Sculpture prize at the Venice Biennale. He owns a 150-acre sculpture park in

Gloucestershire, England, where he works, and his first retrospective exhibition was in 1991 in Yorkshire. In 1992 he was made Commandeur, L'Ordre des Arts et des Lettres.

Chadwick, Roy 1893–1947
English aeronautical engineer

Born in Farnworth, Greater Manchester, the son of a mechanical engineer, he was educated at the Manchester College of Technology. In 1911 he joined Alliott Verdon-Roe and Roy Dobson in the AVRO company, designing and manufacturing aeroplanes. During World War I he designed many famous types including the Avro 504 trainer. Other designs were the Baby (a truly light aircraft), Avian, Anson (used for RAF coastal reconnaissance) and in World War II the Manchester and the famous Lancaster heavy bombers. Following the war he designed the Tudor and Ashton, both jet-propelled. He was killed in a test flight of the Tudor II prototype.

Chagall, Marc 1887–1985
French painter

Born of Jewish parents in Vitebsk, Russia, in 1914 he held a one-man show in Berlin, and for a short time was commissar of fine arts at Vitebsk, but in 1922 he left Russia and settled near Paris. He spent the years 1941–47 in the USA. The books he illustrated include **Nikolai Gogol**'s *Dead Souls* and **Jean de la Fontaine**'s *Fables*, but he is most famous for fanciful pictures, in which a visual potpourri of animals, objects, and people from his past life and dreams, and from Russian folklore, is presented in an arbitrary colour scheme of blues, greens, yellows, and pinks, as in *Bouquet of Flying Lovers* (1947) in the Tate Gallery, London. The word 'Surrealist' is said to have been coined by **Guillaume Apollinaire** to describe his work. In 1945 he designed décors and costumes for **Igor Stravinsky**'s *Firebird*. He wrote his autobiography, *Ma Vie*, in 1931. 📖 Sidney Alexander, *Marc Chagall* (1978)

Chagas, Carlos Ribeiro Justiniano 1879–1934
Brazilian physician and microbiologist

Born in Oliveira, Minás Gerais, he studied at the Medical School of Rio de Janeiro. After a few years in private practice, he joined the staff of the Instituto Oswaldo Cruz, where its founder and leading light, Oswald Cruz, befriended him. Much of Chagas's early work was concerned with malaria prevention and control. During one of his field missions, in Lassance, a village in the interior of Brazil, he first described a disease (Chagas' disease) caused by a trypanosome (he named the organism *T. Cruzi* after Cruz). Chagas elucidated its mode of spread through an insect vector, established the trypanosome's virulence in laboratory animals and described its acute and chronic course in human beings.

Chaillu, Paul du See **du Chaillu, Paul**

Chain, Sir Ernst Boris 1906–79
British biochemist and Nobel Prize winner

Born in Berlin of Russian–Jewish extraction, he studied physiology and chemistry at Berlin, then taught in the biochemistry department at Cambridge (1933–35), where he identified an enzyme in snake venom which caused paralysis of the nervous system. He then joined Sir **Howard Florey** at the Dunn School of Pathology in Oxford (1935–48) to characterize lysozyme and determine its mode of action on bacteria. He encountered Sir **Alexander Fleming**'s paper on penicillin (1929), discovered that penicillin was not an enzyme but a new small molecule, and greatly improved its purification. Fleming, Chain and Florey shared the 1945 Nobel Prize for physiology or medicine. Chain became director of the International Research Centre for Chemical Microbiology in Rome in 1948–61, and then Professor of

Biochemistry at Imperial College, London (1961–73). He was elected FRS in 1949 and knighted in 1969. ⊞ R W Clark, *The Life of Ernst Chain: Penicillin and Beyond* (1985)

Chaitanya c.1486–1533
Indian Hindu mystic
Born in Nadia, Bengal, he was a Sanskrit teacher before becoming an itinerant holy man. In 1510 he converted to a life of devotion to Krishna, and spent the latter part of his life in Puri, inspiring disciples in both Bengal and Orissa with his emphasis on joy and love of Krishna, and the place of singing and dancing in worship. Though he wrote little, he is also remembered for influencing the development of Bengali literature, previously held as much inferior to Sanskrit.

Chaliapin, Feodor Ivanovich, *also spelt* Fyodor Ivanovich Shalyapin 1873–1938
Russian bass
Born in Kazan, he was a singer of great power. Also talented as an actor, he sang in opera at Tiflis, now Tbilisi (1892), Moscow (1896), and London (1913). He left Russia after the Revolution. ⊞ Victor Borovsky, *Chaliapin* (1988)

Chalker (of Wallasey), Lynda Chalker, Baroness, *née* Bates 1942–
English Conservative politician
Educated at the universities of Heidelberg and London, and at the Central London Polytechnic, she began a career in market research before entering parliament as MP for Wallasey in 1974, retaining her seat until 1992. During the Labour administration she was Opposition spokesperson on social services (1976–79), and when the Conservatives took power, she held two under-secretary positions (DHSS, 1979–82, and Transport, 1982–3) before becoming Minister of State in the Department of Transport in 1983. She moved to the Foreign and Commonwealth Office in 1986, and as Minister for Overseas Development (1989–97) controlled the world's fifth biggest aid budget. She earned much popularity in the developing world and in 1997 resigned from politics to undertake independent development work in Africa. She became a life peer in 1992.

Challoner, Richard 1691–1781
English prelate and writer
Born in Lewes, Sussex, he converted to Catholicism as a boy, and went to the English College at Douai in 1704. He was ordained there in 1716, and remained at the college as a professor until 1730. He then served as a missionary priest in London, until in 1741 he was consecrated titular Bishop of Debra and Coadjutor of Bishop Petre, whom he succeeded as Vicar Apostolic of the London district in 1758. During the 'No Popery' riots of 1780 he was hidden near Highgate. Among his 34 works are the *Catholic Christian Instructed* (1737, an answer to the controversialist clergyman Conyers Middleton's *Letters from Rome*), the *Garden of the Soul* (1740, still a most popular prayer book with English Catholics), his revision of the Douai version of the Bible (5 vols, 1750), *Memoirs of Missionary Priests 1577–1684* (2 vols, 1741), and *Britannia Sancta* (2 vols, 1745).

Chalmers, Alexander 1759–1834
Scottish journalist and biographer
Born in Aberdeen, he studied medicine there, but about 1777 became an active writer in London. He published editions of works by several major authors, and a glossary to Shakespeare (1797), but his reputation rests mainly on his vast *General Biographical Dictionary* (32 vols, 1812–17).

Chalmers, George Paul 1833–78
Scottish artist
Born in Montrose, he worked as errand boy to a surgeon and apprentice to a ship-chandler, but in 1853 came to Edinburgh and studied art under Robert Scott Lauder.

Primarily a portrait painter, he also did some memorable landscapes, although his output was relatively small. He was murdered by thieves in Charlotte Square, Edinburgh. He is represented in the National Gallery of Scotland by *The Legend* (c.1864–67).

Chalmers, James 1782–1853
Scottish bookseller and inventor
He was born in Arbroath, Tayside. A bookseller and newspaper publisher in Dundee, he advocated faster mail services in 1825, and in 1834 publicly exhibited his invention, adhesive postage stamps. He corresponded with Sir Rowland Hill, who introduced the penny postage system in 1840.

Chalmers, Thomas 1780–1847
Scottish theologian and reformer
Born in Anstruther, Fife, he was educated at St Andrews. Ordained in 1803, he became a minister in Glasgow (1815), where his impressive oratory was quickly noticed. He became Professor of Moral Philosophy at St Andrews (1823), and of Theology at Edinburgh (1827). In 1843 he led the Disruption, when 470 ministers seceded from the Established Church of Scotland to found the Free Church of Scotland. He was the first moderator of its assembly, and Principal of the Free Church College from 1843 to 1847, when he completed his *Institutes of Theology*. His works, in 34 volumes, deal especially with natural theology, apologetics and social economy.

Chalmers, William 1748–1811
Swedish merchant
Born in Gothenburg, Sweden, of British parents, he was a representative in China of the Swedish East India Company (1782–93) and returned to Gothenburg a rich man. He left half his fortune to the Sahlgrenska Hospital and half to the foundation of the Chalmers's Craft School (1829), which became the Chalmers's Technical University in 1937.

Chamberlain, Sir (Joseph) Austen 1863–1937
English politician and Nobel Prize winner
The eldest son of Joseph Chamberlain, he was Chancellor of the Exchequer (1903–06, 1919–21), Secretary for India (1915–17), a member of Lloyd-George's War Cabinet, Lord Privy Seal, Leader of the House and Unionist leader (1921–22). As Foreign Secretary (1924–29), he was made Knight of the Garter in 1925, and shared with Charles G Dawes the 1925 Nobel Peace Prize for negotiating the Locarno Pact. ⊞ C A Petrie, *The Life and Letters of Sir Austen Chamberlain* (2 vols, 1939-40)

Chamberlain, Houston Stewart 1855–1927
German writer and propagandist
Born in Southsea, Hampshire, England, the son of an admiral, he settled in Dresden in 1885, then in 1908 moved to Bayreuth and married, as his second wife, Eva, daughter of Richard Wagner. He wrote in German on music, Wagner, Immanuel Kant and philosophy. A committed supporter of the dogmas of Aryan supremacy, he was naturalized as a German in 1916. ⊞ W Vollrath, *Houston Stewart Chamberlain und sein britisches Erbgut* (1939)

Chamberlain, Joseph 1836–1914
English politician
Born in London, he was educated at University College School, entered Nettlefold's Birmingham screw factory, and retired in 1874 with a fortune. A Radical politician, in 1868 he became a Birmingham town councillor, and mayor (1873–75). Returned unopposed for Birmingham in 1876, in 1880 he was appointed President of the Board of Trade, with a seat in the Cabinet. He was responsible for the passing of the Bankruptcy Bill. Regarded as the leader of the extreme Radical Party, he produced an

'unauthorized' programme during the general election of 1886, which included the readjustment of taxation, free schools, and the creation of allotments by compulsory purchase. In 1886 he became president of the local government board, but resigned a month later because of his strong objections to Gladstone's Home Rule Bill, of which he became the most strenuous opponent. From 1889 he was leader of the Liberal Unionists, and in the coalition government of 1895 took office as Secretary for the Colonies. In 1903 he resigned office to be free to advocate his scheme of tariff reform, giving preferential treatment to colonial imports and protection for native manufactures. Subsequently, in 1919 and especially 1932, the scheme was carried out by his sons Neville and Austen Chamberlain. In 1906 he withdrew from public life after a stroke. ⌨ James L Garvin and Julian Amery, *The Life of Joseph Chamberlain* (6 vols, 1932–69)

Chamberlain, (Arthur) Neville 1869–1940
English statesman
He was born in Birmingham, the son of Joseph Chamberlain by his second marriage, and educated at Rugby and Birmingham University. He was Lord Mayor of Birmingham (1915–16) and a Conservative MP from 1918. He was Chancellor of the Exchequer (1923–24, 1931–37), Minister for Health (1924–29) and became Prime Minister in 1937. For the sake of peace, and with the country unprepared for war, he chose initially to follow a policy of appeasement of Italy and Germany and signed the 1938 Munich Agreement, claiming to have found 'peace in our time'. Having meantime pressed on with rearmament, he declared war in 1939. Criticism of his war leadership accompanied initial military reverses, and in 1940 he yielded the premiership to Churchill, dying six months later. Subsequent re-evaluations of his career have shown his policy of appeasement in a more favourable light.

Chamberlain, Owen 1920–
US physicist and Nobel Prize winner
Born in San Francisco, he was educated at Dartmouth College, England, and at the University of Chicago, where he received his doctorate in 1949. He became professor at the University of California (emeritus in 1989) after working on the Manhattan atomic bomb project (1942–46) and at the Argonne National Laboratory (1947–48). The first antiparticle (the anti-electron, or positron) had been discovered in 1932 by Carl Anderson, and in 1955, Chamberlain and Emilio Segrè set up an experiment to identify the anti-proton. They discovered a negatively charged particle with a mass very close to that of the proton, and later proved that these particles annihilated protons, confirming that they were indeed anti-protons. In 1959 Chamberlain and Segrè were awarded the Nobel Prize for physics for this discovery.

Chamberlain, Wilt (on Norman), *nicknamed* Wilt the Stilt 1936–
US basketball player
Born in Philadelphia, he was more than 7ft tall. He began his professional career with the Harlem Globetrotters, and in 1959 he signed for the Philadelphia (later San Francisco) Warriors of the National Basketball Association. At various times he played with the New York Knickerbockers as well as with the Philadelphia Seventy-Sixers and the Los Angeles Lakers, with whom he played in championship-winning teams. He was on four occasions the NBA's Most Valuable Player (MVP). ⌨ Bill Libby, *Goliath: The Wilt Chamberlain Story* (1977)

Chamberland, Charles Édouard 1851–1908
French bacteriologist
A collaborator with Louis Pasteur, he invented the unglazed porcelain filter.

Chamberlayne, William 1619–89
English poet
He practised as a physician at Shaftesbury, Dorset, and fought as a Royalist at Newbury, Berkshire. His works are *Love's Victory, a Tragi-Comedy* (1658), and *Pharonnida, An Heroick Poem* (1659) in five books of rhymed couplets, recounting the adventures of the knight Argolia in quest of his beloved, Pharonnida. ⌨ G Saintsbury, *Minor Poets of the Caroline Period* (1905)

Chamberlin, Thomas Chrowder 1843–1928
US geologist
Born in Mattoon, Illinois and educated at Beloit College, where he became Professor of Geology (1872–82), he was chief geologist of the Wisconsin Geological Survey and later Professor of Geology at Chicago (1892–1918). His best-known work was in connection with the fundamental geology of the solar system. His books include *The Origin of the Earth* (1916) and *The Two Solar Families, The Sun's Children* (1928).

Chambers, Sir E(dmund) K(erchever) 1866–1954
English scholar and critic
Born in Berkshire, he was educated at Marlborough and Corpus Christi, Oxford, and was a civil servant with the Board of Education (1892–1926). His major works are *The Medieval Stage* (1903), *The Elizabethan Stage* (1923), *Arthur of Britain* (1927) and *William Shakespeare* (1930).

Chambers, Ephraim c.1680–1740
English encyclopedist
He was born in Kendal, Cumbria, and while apprenticed to a globemaker in London he conceived the idea of a *Cyclopaedia, or Universal Dictionary of Arts and Sciences* (2 folio vols, 1728). A French translation inspired Denis Diderot's great French *Encyclopédie*.

Chambers, John Graham 1843–83
English sportsman
A champion walker and oarsman, he founded the Amateur Athletic Club in 1866 and drew up the rules for amateur athletic competitions. In 1867 he drew up the rules for boxing promulgated under the aegis of the 8th Marquis of Queensberry, which are still known as the Queensberry Rules.

Chambers, R(aymond) W(ilson) 1874–1942
English scholar
He was educated at University College London, where he became Professor of English Language and Literature (1922–41). His numerous learned works include studies of *Widsith* and *Beowulf*, an essay on *The Continuity of English Prose* (1932), editions of John Berners's translation of Jean Froissart (6 vols, 1901–03, with W P Ker), and other texts.

Chambers, Robert 1802–71
Scottish writer and publisher
Born in Peebles, he was the younger brother of William Chambers. He began as a bookseller with his brother in Edinburgh in 1819, and wrote in his spare time. In 1824 he produced *Traditions of Edinburgh*. The success of *Chambers's Edinburgh Journal*, started by his brother in 1832, was largely due to his essays and his literary insight. Later that year he and his brother formed the publishing house of W & R Chambers. In 1844 he published anonymously the pre-Darwinian *Vestiges of Creation*. A prolific writer of reference books, he edited the *Chambers Encyclopaedia* (1859–68) and *The Cyclopaedia of English Literature* (1842), and himself wrote *A Biographical Dictionary of Eminent Scotsmen* (1832–34), *Domestic Annals of Scotland* (3 vols, 1858–61), extracts from Scottish historical sources, and *The Book of Days* (2 vols, 1863, an almanac of historical data), which broke his health. His other works include *Popular Rhymes of Scotland* (1826), a *History of the Rebellions in Scotland, Life of*

James I, *Scottish Ballads and Songs* (1829), *Ancient Sea Margins* (1848), *The Life and Works of Robert Burns* (4 vols, 1851), and *Songs of Scotland prior to Burns* (1862). 📖 William Chambers, *Memoir of Robert Chambers* (1872)

Chambers, Sir William 1726–96
Scottish architect
Born of Scottish ancestry in Stockholm, and educated in Edinburgh and Ripon, Yorkshire, he studied in Italy and France and practised in England. He designed Somerset House (1776) and the pagoda in Kew Gardens, and also wrote a *Treatise of Civil Architecture* (1759). In Edinburgh he designed Dundas House (1771, now the Royal Bank of Scotland) and Duddingston House, and in Dublin, Charlemont House (1763).

Chambers, William 1800–83
Scottish publisher
Born in Peebles, he was the older brother of **Robert Chambers**. In 1814 he was apprenticed to a bookseller in Edinburgh, and in 1819 started in business for himself, first bookselling, then printing. Between 1825 and 1830 he wrote the *Book of Scotland* and, in conjunction with his brother Robert, a *Gazetteer of Scotland*. In 1832 he started *Chambers's Edinburgh Journal*, six weeks in advance of the *Penny Magazine*. He later joined Robert to found W & R Chambers. In 1859 he founded and endowed a museum, library and art gallery in Peebles. Lord Provost of Edinburgh from 1865 to 1869, he promoted a successful scheme for improving the older part of the city, and carried out at his own cost a restoration of St Giles' Cathedral. Besides many contributions to the *Journal*, he wrote a *Youth's Companion*, a *History of Peeblesshire* (1864), *Ailie Gilroy, Stories of Remarkable Persons, Stories of Old Families*, and a *Historical Sketch of St Giles' Cathedral* (1879).

Chambord, Henri Charles Dieudonné, Comte de 1820–83
French Bourbon pretender
He was born in Paris and after the assassination of his father, the Duc de **Berry**, he was taken into exile with the remaining **Bourbons** following the abdication in 1830 of King **Charles X**, whose grandson he claimed to be. On Charles' death in 1836, he was proclaimed King of France by the Legitimist Party. Another attempt was made after the fall of **Napoleon III** in 1870, since the National Assembly elected in 1871 had a royalist majority, but Chambord's refusal to accept the tricolour flag rendered this abortive; a motion to restore the monarchy was finally defeated in the National Assembly in 1874.

Chamfort, Sébastien-Roch Nicolas 1741–94
French writer
Born in Clermont, he entered the literary circles of Paris, and lived for years 'by his wit, if not by his wits'. He joined the Jacobins at the outbreak of the French Revolution (1789), but his remarks on the Terror brought him into disfavour. Threatened with arrest, he tried to commit suicide and died after several days' suffering. His works include tales, dramas, éloges, maxims and admirably observed anecdotes (published posthumously in 1795), which attack the corruption of the period. 📖 P J Richard, *Aspects de Chamfort* (1959)

Chamisso, Adalbert von, originally Louis Charles Adelaïde de Chamisso 1781–1838
German poet and biologist
Born in Champagne, France, his parents fled the French Revolution to Prussia, and he served in the Prussian army (1798–1807). In Geneva he joined the literary circle of Madame de Staël and later studied at Berlin University. In 1815–18 he accompanied a Russian exploring expedition round the world as naturalist, and on his return was appointed keeper of the Botanical Garden of Berlin. In 1819 he was the first to discover in certain animals what he

called 'alternation of generations' (the recurrence in the life cycle of two or more forms). He wrote several works on natural history, but his fame rests partly on his poems, still more on his quaint and humorous *Peter Schlemihl* (1813), the story of the man who lost his shadow.

Chamorro, Violetta 1919–
Nicaraguan politician
She is the widow of Pedro Joaquin Chamorro, whose murder in 1978 sparked off events leading to the Sandinista revolution and the overthrow of the Somozoa regime in 1979, and her political career began after her husband's death. She briefly joined the junta the Sandinistas set up but left in 1980. Owner of the influential *La Prensa* newspaper, her own family of four children were split idealogically: one son ran the Sandinista party newspaper *Barricada*, one daughter was a Sandinista diplomat, one daughter took over the editorship of *La Prensa* while another son joined the contras in exile. In 1990 Chamorro, representing the National Opposition Union (UNO) which consisted of 14 parties with widely differing ideologies, was elected President after a decisive win over **Daniel Ortega** in February 1990. She did not run in the 1996 election and was succeeded by Arnoldo Alemán.

Chamoun, Camille 1900–87
Lebanese politician
The curious constitutional provisions of Lebanon after its independence provided for a Muslim Prime Minister and a (Maronite) Christian President. Chamoun held the presidency from 1952 until 1958. A pro-USA Maronite, his reluctance to surrender the presidency to **Fuad Chehab**, a Maronite more acceptable to Lebanese Muslims, led to the outbreak of civil war. His policy aimed at peaceful coexistence between Christians and Muslims, but his support for France and Britain during the Suez Crisis seriously undermined the credibility of his regime. His position was only saved during the civil war by the intervention, in 1958, of US Marines (who caused a stir by coming ashore on the bathing beaches of the Lebanese coast). Although he did not seek re-election, he continued in politics and in 1980 his National Liberal Party split from the Phalangists. He survived an assassination attempt in 1987, but died later the same year.

Champaigne, Philippe de 1602–74
French painter
Born in Brussels, Belgium, he trained as a landscape painter there, but moved to Paris (1621). A lifelong friend of **Nicholas Poussin**, he assisted him in decorating the Luxembourg Palace, and in 1628 was appointed painter to Marie de' **Medici** and was patronized by **Louis XIII** and Cardinal **Richelieu**. The most prominent portrait painter of his day, his work resembles that of Sir **Anthony Van Dyck**, particularly his triple portrait of Richelieu which was painted for **Gian Lorenzo Bernini** to use as a model for a bust. He began to associate with the Jansenists after 1647. Thereafter, his work became more austere and all traces of the Baroque influence of **Rubens** disappeared.

Champfleury, assumed name of Jules Fleury-Husson 1821–89
French writer
Born in Laon, he was educated sporadically, and moved to Paris to live a bohemian lifestyle. He wrote several early pieces for the theatre, and a number of novels in Realist style, inspired by the example of **Gustave Courbet** in painting. He became head of the Porcelain Museum in Sèvres, and published important studies on the history of caricature, literature, art and pottery, and a manifesto, *Le réalisme* (1857). 📖 E de Mirecourt, *Champfleury* (1891)

Champlain, Samuel de 1567–1635
French explorer, 'founder of Canada'

Born in Brouage, Saintonge, he made his first voyage to Canada in 1603. From 1604 to 1607 he explored the coasts, and on his third voyage (1608) he founded Quebec. He was appointed Lieutenant of Canada in 1612. His explorations into the interior mapped many new areas. During the Anglo-French war, Quebec was seized by the English, and he successfully negotiated its return to French sovereignty. Lake Champlain is named after him.

Champmeslé, La, *stage name of* Marie Desmares
1642–98
French actress
Born probably in Rouen, she took her professional name from her second husband, the actor Charles Chevillet Champmeslé, and by 1668 was in Paris. Said to have had a particularly moving mode of delivery, she established herself as a leading actress of the day. She became the mistress of the playwright Racine, and gave the first performances of his most important works, including *Phèdre* in 1677. She became the leading lady of the newly-formed Comédie-Française in 1680, and retired through illness only shortly before her death.

Champollion, Jean François 1790–1832
French founder of Egyptology
Born in Figeac, he was educated at Grenoble and became Professor of History there (1809–16). He is remembered for his use of the Rosetta Stone to decipher Egyptian hieroglyphics (1822–24) and for promoting the study of early Egyptian history and culture. In 1828 he mounted a joint expedition with the Italian Ippolito Rosellini (1800–43) to record the monuments of the Nile as far south as Aswan; on his return a chair of egyptology was founded for him at the Collège de France. He died a few months later. His works include *Précis du système hiéroglyphique* (1824) and *Monuments de l'Égypte et de la Nubie* (2 vols, 1844, 1889).

Chance, Britton 1913–
US biochemist
Born in Wilkes-Barre, Pennsylvania, he was educated at Pennsylvania University, and at Cambridge, in physical chemistry and physiology. He then became assistant Professor (1941–49) and then Professor of Biophysics (1949–83) at the University of Pennsylvania, where he is now Emeritus Professor of Biophysics and Physical Biochemistry (1983–). His career embraced many problems in biochemical energetics and biophysics, his best-known work being his 1943 demonstration of the existence of a complex between an enzyme and its substrate. Such complexes had long been theoretically presumed to exist as an essential stage in enzyme action but had not been detected. He studied the reactive mechanisms of several types of enzymes, and did important work on the problems of energy generation in biological systems. In addition to his biochemical studies, he utilized his technical expertise in developing and improving many types of analytical equipment.

Chancellor, Richard d.1556
English seaman
Brought up in the household of Sir Philip Sidney's father, he was 'pilot-general' of Sir Hugh Willoughby's expedition (1553) in search of a Northeast Passage to India. The ships were parted in a storm off the Lofoten Islands, and Chancellor proceeded alone into the White Sea and travelled overland to Moscow, to conclude a treaty giving freedom of trade to English ships. When he returned to England in 1554, his optimistic reports led to the establishment of the Muscovy Company.

Chand, Dhyan 1905–79
Indian hockey player
Born in Allahabad, he captained India to three consecutive Olympic Golds (1928, 1932, 1936), revered as hockey's most prolific goal scorer. Roop Singh (his brother) and Dhyan scored 18 goals against the USA in the 1932 Olympics, to make the final score India-24, USA-1. He scored six goals against Germany in the 1936 Berlin Olympics final, when India won 8–1. After World War II, he became captain and coach for the Indian national hockey team, and when he retired he became head coach at India's National Sports Institute.

Chandler, Raymond 1888–1959
US novelist
Born in Chicago, he was brought up in England from the age of seven, and educated at Dulwich College and in France and Germany. He worked as a freelance writer in London before going to California in 1912, and then served in the Canadian army in France, and in the RAF during World War I. After a variety of jobs, during the Depression he began to write short stories and novelettes for the magazine *Black Mask*, or for the detective-story pulp magazines of the day. On such stories he based his subsequent full-length 'private eye' novels, *The Big Sleep* (1939), *Farewell, My Lovely* (1940), *The High Window* (1942) and *The Lady in the Lake* (1943), all of which were successfully filmed. Chandler himself went to Hollywood in 1943 and worked on film scripts. He did much to establish the conventions of his genre, particularly with his cynical but honest anti-hero, Philip Marlowe, who also appeared in such later works as *The Little Sister* (1949), *The Long Goodbye* (1953) and *Playback* (1958). □Tom Hiney, *Raymond Chandler* (1997)

Chandler, Seth Carlo 1846–1913
US astronomer
Born in Boston, he graduated from Harvard, where in 1881 he worked at the observatory and designed a science observer code—a system for transmitting astronomical information by telegraph. His most important contribution to science was the discovery of the periodic variations in latitude of points on the Earth's surface due to movement of the geographic poles, verifying a cyclic variation in latitude with a period of 14 months. Leonhard Euler had predicted a 10 month period. This became known as the 'Chandler wobble'.

Chandos, Oliver Lyttelton, 1st Viscount
1893–1972
English industrialist and politician
He belonged to a family with many political connections. Educated at Eton and Cambridge, he served in the Grenadier Guards in World War I, winning the DSO. By 1928 he was managing director of the British Metal Corporation, and during the years of depression played a big part in organizing international cartels in the metal world to mitigate the effects of the slump. On the outbreak of World War II he became controller of non-ferrous metals, and in 1940 was made President of the Board of Trade, and MP for Aldershot. He was subsequently Minister of State in Cairo, and Minister of Production. When the Conservatives were returned to office in 1951 he went to the Colonial Office, but resigned from politics to return to business in 1954, when he was raised to the peerage. His period of office was a difficult one, with outbreaks of violence in Kenya and Malaya, and a constitutional crisis in British Guiana. However, he played a leading part in drawing up plans of constitutional reform and advance for many of the African colonial territories.

Chandragupta or Sandracottus c.350–c.250BC
Hindu Emperor of Pâtaliputra or Palibothra
Megasthenes was sent to him by Seleucus I Nicator (c.300BC).

Chandrasekhar, Subrahmanyan 1910–95
US astrophysicist and Nobel Prize winner

Chanel, Coco (Gabrielle) 1883–1971
French couturier who designed the little black dress

Coco Chanel was orphaned at an early age. She worked with her sister as a milliner until 1912, when she opened a shop of her own, followed by a couture house in Deauville (1913). During World War I she served as a nurse. She opened her second couture house in the Rue Cambon in Paris (1924), and it was from here that she was to revolutionize women's fashions during the 1920s. For the first time in a century women were liberated from the restriction of corsets (an innovation with which Chanel's colleague Madeleine Vionnet is credited).

In 1920 she designed her first 'chemise' dress, and in 1925 the collarless cardigan jacket. The combination of simple elegance and comfort in her designs gave them immediate, widespread and lasting appeal, and many of the features she introduced, such as the vogue for costume jewellery, the evening scarf, and the 'little black dress', have retained their popularity.

At the height of her career she managed four businesses, including the manufacture of her world-famous perfume, Chanel No.5, and her great wealth and dazzling social life attracted great public interest. She retired in 1938, but made a surprisingly successful comeback in 1954, when, following her original style, she regained her prominence in the fashion world.

📖 Axel Madsen, *Chanel* (1990); Edmonde Charles-Roux, *Chanel and Her World* (1981); Claude Baillén, *Chanel Solitaire* (1974, trans by Barbara Bray).

> 'Fashion is made to become unfashionable.'
> Quoted in *Life*, 19 August 1957.

Born in Lahore, India (now in Pakistan), nephew of Sir **Chandrasekhara Venkata Raman**, he was educated at the Presidency College, Madras, before going to Cambridge, where he studied under **Paul Dirac**. In 1936 he moved to the USA to work at the University of Chicago and Yerkes Observatory. He studied the final stages of stellar evolution, showing that the fate of a star depends on its mass. He also concluded that stars with masses greater than about 1.4 solar masses will be unable to evolve into white dwarfs, and this limiting stellar mass, confirmed by observation, is known as the Chandrasekhar limit. He suggested that if the mass of a star is greater than this, it can become a white dwarf star only if it ejects its excess mass in a supernova explosion before collapse. He was awarded the 1983 Nobel Prize for physics, jointly with **William Fowler**. He was editor of the *Astrophysical Journal* (1952–71) and the author of ten books, the last being *Newton's "Principia" for the Common Reader* (1995). 📖 K C Wali, *Chandra: A Biography of S Chandrasekhar* (1991).

Chanel, Coco See panel above

Chaney, Lon, *originally* Alonso Chaney 1883–1930
US film and stage actor
He was born in Colorado Springs, Colorado, and became known as 'the man of a thousand faces' from his skill at make-up and miming. He made his film debut in 1913 and became famous for his portrayal of deformed villains and other spine-chilling parts, most notably in *The Miracle Man* (1919), *The Hunchback of Notre Dame* (1923) and *The Phantom of the Opera* (1925). His son, Lon Chaney, Jnr (1907–73), was also an actor in horror films, and starred in a film version of **John Steinbeck**'s *Of Mice and Men* (1939). 📖 Robert G Anderson, *Faces, Forms, Films: The Artistry of Lon Chaney* (1971)

Chang Heng 78–139 AD
Chinese scholar and inventor
Born in Wan (Nanyang), he was the astronomer royal at the court of the later **Han** emperors. Although none of his actual works has survived there are detailed accounts extant of several of his inventions. He introduced a complete armillary sphere at about the same time as **Ptolemy** did in the West, and went on to construct one that was water-powered and, it is thought, regulated by some primitive form of escapement. He is also credited with the construction of the world's first seismograph.

Channing, Carol Elaine 1921–
US singer and actress
Born in Seattle, Washington, she made her stage debut in the chorus of *No for an Answer* (1941). She also appeared in the revue *Lend an Ear* (1948) but achieved star status as Lorelei Lee in *Gentlemen Prefer Blondes* (1949, 1951–53).

Later stage work includes *Wonderful Town* (1954), *Show Girl* (1961), *Hello Dolly!* (1964–67, Tony award) and *Legends* (1986). She received a special Tony in 1968, returned to her earlier role in *Lorelei* (1973–75) and continues to tour in various stage versions of *Hello Dolly!*. Her rare film appearances include *The First Travelling Saleslady* (1956) and *Thoroughly Modern Millie* (1967), for which she received an Academy Award nomination.

Channing, William Ellery 1780–1842
US clergyman
Born in Newport, Rhode Island, he graduated from Harvard in 1798, and in 1803 was ordained to the Congregational Federal Street Church in Boston, where his sermons were famous for their 'fervour, solemnity, and beauty'. He was ultimately the leader of the Unitarians. In 1822 he visited Europe, and made the acquaintance of **Wordsworth** and **Coleridge**. Among his Works (6 vols, 1841–46) were his *Essay on National Literature*, *Remarks on Milton*, *Character and Writings of Fénelon*, *Negro Slavery*, and *Self-culture*. 📖 R Hudspeth, *Ellery Channing* (1973)

Chantrey, Sir Francis Legatt 1781–1841
English sculptor
Born in Norton, Derbyshire, he was a painter as a young man, but became enormously successful with his portrait statues and busts, and church monuments such as the Robinson children (1817) in Lichfield cathedral. He left the bulk of his fortune to the Royal Academy to purchase British works of art. The collection is now in the Tate Gallery, London.

Chao Tzu-yang See Zhao Ziyang

Chapelain, Jean 1595–1674
French poet and critic
An original member of the Académie Française (1634), he had a high reputation as a critic, as well as considerable political influence, firstly with Cardinal **Richelieu**, and later with **Jean Baptiste Colbert**. He also wrote *La Pucelle* (1656, 'The Maid of Orleans'), a poem in 24 long cantos on Joan of Arc, which received harsh criticism from **Nicolas Boileau**. 📖 G Colas, *Un poète protecteur des lettres au XVI siècle* (1912)

Chaplin, Charlie See panel p372

Chapman, George c.1559–1634
English dramatist
Born near Hitchin, Hertfordshire, he began to make a reputation in Elizabethan literary circles with his poems *The Shadow of the Night* (1594), and in 1595 saw the production of his earliest extant play, the popular comedy *The Blind Beggar of Alexandria*. His complete translation of *The*

Chaplin, Charlie (Sir Charles Spencer) 1889–1977
English film actor and director

Charlie Chaplin was born in Kennington, London, the son of music-hall performers. His father was an alcoholic and died when he was a child, leaving the family in a state of extreme hardship, and his mother was mentally unstable and unable to support him. His first regular education was in the school at the poorhouse, and he took work as a newsboy and glass-blower, indulging his performing ambitions by joining a team of clog dancers. By the age of eight he was a seasoned stage performer, and his skill in comedy developed when he joined the impresario Fred Karno. As a member of Karno's vaudeville company he went to Hollywood in 1914 and there entered the motion picture business, then in its infancy, making over 50 films between 1914 and 1916, including *The Pawn Shop* and *The Vagabond* (1916), and *Easy Street*, *The Immigrant* and *The Adventurer* (1917).

In these early comedies he adopted the bowler hat, out-turned feet, moustache and walking-cane which became the hallmarks of his consummate buffoonery in films such as *The Kid* (1920), *The Gold Rush* (1924), *The Champion* (1915) and *Shoulder Arms* (1918). He achieved greater control of his work by forming United Artists with **Douglas Fairbanks**, Snr and director **D W Griffith**. *The Circus* (1928) won him a special Oscar for 'versatility and genius in writing, acting, directing and producing'. His art was essentially suited to the silent film and, realizing this,

he experimented with new forms when sound arrived, as in *City Lights* (1931), with music only, and *Modern Times* (1936), a satire on the age of machines in part speech and part mime.

Eventually he entered the orthodox sound film field with the satirical caricature of **Adolf Hitler** in *The Great Dictator* (1940), for which he received his only Oscar nomination as best actor. After a long absence, he took on a very different role, that of mass murderer in the black comedy *Monsieur Verdoux* (1947), which was not popular. He returned to more traditional methods in *Limelight* (1952), in which he acted, as well as directing and composing the music and dances. His left-wing sympathies caused him to fall foul of the rabid anti-Communist factions of post-war America, and he emigrated to Switzerland. He made only two further films: *A King in New York* (1957), a biting satire mocking the US way of life, and a *Countess from Hong Kong* (1967). He was knighted in 1975.

📖 Chaplin published *My Autobiography* in 1964. In 1992 a film biography *Chaplin* was directed by Sir **Richard Attenborough**. See also D Robinson, *Chaplin: His Life and Art* (1984).

> 'All I need to make a comedy is a park, a policeman and a pretty girl.' Quoted in *My Autobiography*, ch.10.

Whole Works of Homer: Prince of Poets, appeared in 1611, after which he set to work on the *Odyssey* (completed 1616). His *Homer* is known to many through **Keats**'s poem 'On first looking into Chapman's *Homer*'. He joined **Ben Jonson** and **John Marston** in the composition of *Eastward Hoe* (1605), in which slighting references to the Scots earned the authors a jail sentence. Other plays include a graceful comedy, *The Gentleman Usher* (1606), the *Tragedie of Charles, Duke of Byron* (1608), full of fine poetry, *The Widow's Tears* (1612) and *Caesar and Pompey* (1631). Two posthumous tragedies (1654), *Alphonsus* and *Revenge for Honour*, bear his name, but it is doubtful that he wrote them. *The Ball*, a comedy, and *The Tragedie of Chabot* (1639) were the joint work of Chapman and **James Shirley**. Among his non-dramatic works are the epic philosophical poem *Euthymiae & Raptus* (1609), *Petrarch's Seven Penitentiall Psalmes* (1612), *The Divine Poem of Musaeus* (1616) and *The Georgicks of Hesiod* (1618). 📖 C K Spivack, *George Chapman* (1967)

Chapman, John, *also called* Johnny Appleseed 1774–1845
US pioneer

Born in Leominster, Massachusetts, he first appeared in the Ohio River Valley around 1800, planting apple seeds that he took from the pomace of cider presses and tending seedlings in the frontier region. He moved continually ahead of the coming line of settlement, and by 1828 he had carried his orchards as far west as Indiana. A religious mystic and Swedenborgian, he was raggedly dressed and eccentric, and his sudden appearances in the wilderness and acts of extraordinary kindness became legendary. In addition to apple seeds, he is said to have planted many healing herbs, including horehound and pennyroyal. Although John Chapman certainly existed, historians have debated the extent to which the selfless actions of Johnny Appleseed are verifiable or real.

Chapman, Mark David c.1955–
US murderer

A security guard in Hawaii, he shot and killed former Beatles member **John Lennon**, on 8 December 1980, outside Lennon's apartment in Manhattan. At the trial, his lawyer initially entered a plea of insanity which Chapman later overturned with a plea of guilty. Chapman had been a fan of the Beatles, and had idolized Lennon to the extent that he often imagined that he was Lennon. He was also obsessed with and inspired by **J D Salinger**'s novel *The Catcher in the Rye*, identifying with the central character who regarded the world as phoney. Chapman was found guilty of murder and was sentenced to life imprisonment. He was also ordered to receive psychiatric treatment.

Chapman, Sydney 1888–1979
English physicist and geophysicist

Born in Eccles, Lancashire, he was educated at the universities of Manchester and Cambridge. He worked at the Royal Greenwich Observatory supervising the installation of the new magnetic observatory. Noticing that few of the existing magnetic data had been interpreted, he began a lifelong study of these. In 1914 he returned to Cambridge as college lecturer, though during World War I, as a pacifist, he was sent back to Greenwich (1916–18). He was Professor of Mathematics at Manchester (1919–24), professor at Imperial College, London (1924–46) and Sedleian Professor of Natural Philosophy at Oxford (1946–53), seeking to improve the status of science at the latter. He solved problems of thermal conductivity and diffusion of gases, and identified thermal diffusion (1917). During 1922–28 he produced the first satisfactory theory of magnetic storms, later known as the Chapman–Ferraro theory. In 1918 he identified a lunar atmospheric tide. After 1953 he took research posts in Alaska and at the High Altitude Observatory in Boulder, Colorado. He was elected FRS in 1919.

Chapone, Hester, *née* Mulso 1727–1801
English essayist

She was born in Twywell, Northamptonshire. One of the 'blue-stocking' circle associated with **Elizabeth Montagu**, she published verse stories and wrote for the *Rambler* (No.

10), *Gentleman's Magazine* and other periodicals. She is chiefly remembered for her *Letters on the Improvement of the Mind* (1772). 📖 *An Account of Her Life and Character drawn up by her family* (1807)

Chappe, Claude 1763–1805
French engineer and inventor

Born in Brûlon, Sarthe, he was studying for a career in the church when the French Revolution began, and he decided instead to pursue his interest in telegraphy. Failing in his attempts to construct apparatus for electrical telegraphy, he turned in 1793 to a hand-operated semaphore system which with government backing was quite extensively used in France up to around 1850. Repeater stations at distances of 6 to 7 miles (10 to 12km) were required, and messages could be sent by day and by night with the aid of lamps on the semaphore arms. Later financial difficulties drove him to suicide.

Chappell, Greg (ory Stephen) 1948–
Australian cricketer

He was born in Unley, South Australia, the younger brother of **Ian Chappell**. One of the most graceful of modern batsmen, he played 87 times for his country and scored 24 Test centuries, and succeeded his brother as captain. At the Oval in 1972, he and his brother both made centuries in the same innings. He played in England for Somerset for two years.

Chappell, Ian Michael 1943–
Australian cricketer

He was born in Unley, South Australia, the elder brother of **Greg Chappell**. A more combative character than his brother, he played 75 times for Australia, scoring over 5,000 runs and 14 Test centuries. A grandson of Victor Richardson, himself an Australian Test cricketer, Chappell had a pugnacious, driving style of captaincy that gained the Australian side universal respect in the 1970s.

Chappell, William 1809–88
English antiquary

He was a member of a London music publishing house. His *Collection of National English Airs* (2 vols, 1838–40) grew into *Popular Music of the Olden Time* (2 vols, 1855–59). He took a principal part in the foundation in 1840 of the Musical Antiquarian Society, the Percy Society, and in 1868 of the Ballad Society. In 1874 he published the first volume of a *History of Music*.

Chaptal, Jean Antoine, Comte de Chanteloupe 1756–1832
French politician and chemist

Born in Nogaret, he became a member of the Senate, and took a leading part in the introduction of the metric system of weights and measures. He was equally successful as a chemical manufacturer and on industrial chemistry. He was ennobled by **Napoleon I** and served as a minister in his Hundred Days (1815).

Charcot, Jean Martin 1825–93
French pathologist and neurologist

Born and educated in Paris, he was appointed to a position at Salpêtrière Hospital, and eventually became the most eminent French physician of his day. He turned the Salpêtrière into an international centre for the investigation of neurological diseases, himself making important observations on multiple sclerosis, amyotrophic sclerosis and familial muscular atrophy. During the last twenty years of his life, he began using hypnosis in the diagnosis and treatment of functional disorders. His lectures stimulated the young **Sigmund Freud**, who also translated some of Charcot's work into German. 📖 A R Owen, *Hysteria, Hypnosis, and Healing: The Work of J M Charcot* (1970)

Chard, John Rouse Merriott 1847–97
English soldier

Born near Plymouth, as a lieutenant he was awarded one of the 11 VCs given in 1879 for the defence of Rorke's Drift against 3,000 Zulus with 80 men of the 24th Regiment.

Chardin, Jean Baptiste Siméon 1699–1779
French painter

Born in Paris, he was the son of **Louis XIV**'s billiard-table maker. He was selected to assist in the restoration of the royal paintings at Fontainebleau, and later attracted attention as a signpainter. In 1728 he exhibited, at the 'Exposition de la Jeunesse', a series of still-life paintings, and was elected to the Académie Française in the same year. Emerging as a genre painter, he produced many pictures of peasant life and domestic scenes. *Grace before Meal* (1740, Louvre), perhaps his masterpiece in this vein, earned the praise of **Denis Diderot**. In 1755 he was appointed treasurer of the Académie Française, with an apartment in the Louvre. As an exponent of still life and genre he is without equal in French painting, and his composition and colouring is comparable with that of the best Dutch and Flemish masters.

Chardonnet, (Louis-Marie-) Hilaire Bernigaud, Comte de 1839–1924
French industrial chemist

Born in Besançon, Franche-Comté, he studied in Paris at the École Polytechnique and the École des Ponts et Chaussées, where he was later appointed engineer. The manufacture of rayon (at first called 'artificial silk') is his best-known achievement. He patented the process in 1884 and, five years later, opened factories in his home town and in Satvar, Hungary. He also designed the actinograph, which measures solar radiation and is used in aviation, and studied the effects of ultraviolet light on different organisms.

Chargaff, Erwin 1905–
US biochemist

Born in Czernowitz, Czechoslovakia (now in the Ukraine), he studied in Vienna before spending two years at Yale (1928–30). He returned to Berlin (1930–33), where he extended his study of bacterial lipids, and briefly visited Paris before settling at Columbia University, New York, in 1935. He was appointed Professor of Biochemistry in 1952, then emeritus in 1974. After initial research on plant chromoproteins, he produced his best-known work on the base composition of DNA, which he found to be characteristic of a species and identical in different tissues of the same animal. His most significant finding, of general application to living systems for the understanding of the structure of DNA as proposed by **Francis Crick** and **James Watson** in 1953, was that the concentrations of the DNA bases were in pairs.

Charisse, Cyd, *originally* Tula Ellice Finklea, *also acting as* Lily Norwood 1921–
US dancer

Born in Amarillo, Texas, she trained as a ballet dancer from the age of eight, was signed to the Ballets Russes at 14, and toured in Europe and the USA. Moving to Los Angeles, she played small film roles under the name of Lily Norwood before signing a contract with MGM in 1946. Described by **Fred Astaire** as 'beautiful dynamite', she appeared in such classic musicals as *Singin' in the Rain* (1952), *The Band Wagon* (1953), *Brigadoon* (1954) and *Silk Stockings* (1957), partnering both Astaire and **Gene Kelly**. Her career faltered with the demise of the original screen musical, although she continued to appear on stage in dramatic roles, performing in *Charlie Girl* (1986) in London and *Grand Hotel* (1992) on Broadway. She has been married to singer Tony Martin (1912–) since 1948.

Charlemagne ('Charles the Great'), Latin Carolus Magnus 747–814
King of the Franks and Christian Emperor of the West

Charlemagne was the grandson of **Charles Martel** and the eldest son of **Pepin III, the Short**. On Pepin's death in 768 the Frankish kingdom was divided between Charlemagne and his younger brother **Carloman**; three years later, on Carloman's death, he became sole ruler.

The first years of his reign were spent in strenuous campaigns to subdue and Christianize neighbouring kingdoms, particularly the Saxons to the north-east (772–77) and the Lombards of northern Italy (773), where he was crowned King of Lombardy, and the Moors in Spain (778). In Spain, the celebrated rearguard action at Roncesvalles in which **Roland**, his chief paladin, is said to have been overwhelmed, inspired the heroic literature of the *Chanson de Roland*.

In 782 the Saxons rose again in rebellion and destroyed a Frankish army at Süntelberg, which Charlemagne avenged by beheading 4,500 Saxons, but it was not until 785 that the Saxon leader, Widukind, submitted and accepted baptism; he then became a loyal vassal.

Between 780 and 800, Charlemagne added Bohemia to his empire; subdued the Avars (Turko-Finnish nomads) in the middle Danube basin (795–96) to create an eastern 'March' to buttress his frontiers; created the 'Spanish March' on the southern side of the Pyrenees (795); and entered Italy (800) to support Pope **Leo III** against the rebellious Romans. There on Christmas Day in St Peter's Church, the pope crowned him Emperor of the Romans as 'Carolus Augustus'.

The remaining years of his reign were spent in consolidating his vast empire which reached from the Ebro in northern Spain to the Elbe. Bishoprics were founded in the Saxon country; many of the Slavs east of the Elbe were subjugated. The emperor established his capital and principal court at Aachen (Aix-la-Chapelle), where he built a magnificent palace and founded an academy to which many of the greatest scholars of the age, like **Alcuin** of York, were invited. He himself could speak Latin and read Greek, and letters and Latin poems ascribed to him are still extant.

In a reign which has become known as the Carolingian Renaissance, Charlemagne zealously promoted education, architecture, book-making and the arts, created stable administrations and good laws, and encouraged agriculture, industry and commerce. He fostered good relations with the east, and in 798 **Harun ar-Raschid**, the caliph of Baghdad, sent ambassadors and a gift of a white elephant. His reign was a noble attempt to consolidate order and Christian culture among the nations of the west, but his empire did not long survive his death, for his sons lacked both his vision and authority. He was buried at Aachen.

📖 Related epics: *La Chanson de Roland* (c.11th century); **Matteo Maria Boiardo**, *Orlando Innamorato* (1486, 'Orlando in Love'); **Ludovico Ariosto**, *Orlando Furioso* (1516, 'Orlando Enraged'). See also Friedrich Heer, *Charlemagne and His World* (1975); Donald A Bullough, *The Age of Charlemagne* (2nd edn, 1973); Einhard, *Vita Karoli Magni: The Life of Charlemagne*, translated from Latin by Evelyn Scherabon Firchow and Edwin H Zeydel (1972).

Charlemagne and his 12 followers or paladins are the central figures in most of the surviving *chansons de geste*. In Christian iconography, Charlemagne appears in his armour beside the Emperor **Constantine I**, crowned and holding either the orb and sceptre of kingship or a miniature model of the cathedral at Aachen, where his body is thought to lie.

Many legends are associated with Charlemagne. In the legend of St **Giles**, the holy man is Charlemagne's confessor. While celebrating mass one day, Giles saw before him a tablet let down from heaven bearing details of an unconfessed sin. The emperor broke down and confessed the sin (which has been speculatively identified as incest with his sister) and received absolution.

Like King **Arthur** and several others, a legend maintains that Charlemagne is only sleeping, awaiting the call of his country in its greatest need.

Charlemagne See panel above

Charles (Kings of Sweden) See **Karl**

Charles I 1887–1922
Emperor of Austria as Karl I and King of Hungary as Károly IV, the last of the Habsburg emperors

Born at Persenbeug Castle, the son of Archduke Otto and grand-nephew of Emperor **Franz Joseph**, he became heir presumptive (1914) on the assassination at Sarajevo of his uncle, Archduke **Franz Ferdinand**. On his great-uncle's death (1916) he proclaimed himself Emperor of Austria and King of Hungary. He made secret attempts (which failed) to withdraw Austria/Hungary from World War I. In 1918 he was deposed, and exiled to Switzerland (1919). In 1921 he made two unsuccessful attempts to regain the Crown of Hungary, and was deported to Madeira, where he died. In 1911 he had married Zita of Bourbon-Parma; their son Archduke Otto later renounced his right of succession.

Charles I See panel p375

Charles II See panel p376

Charles I, *called* **the Bald**, *also* **Charles II**
823–77
King of France and Holy Roman Emperor

The son of **Louis the Pious** and grandson of Charlemagne, he was king from 843 and emperor (as Charles II) of the West from 875. His reign was characterized by rivalries within the royal family, and aristocratic factionalism, but also saw the zenith of the Carolingian renaissance, mainly due to his patronage of art and letters.

Charles II, *called* **the Fat** 839–88
King of France and Holy Roman Emperor

He became emperor in Germany (as Charles III) in 881 and King of France in 884, but, listless and incompetent, he was deposed from the imperial throne after making a humiliating treaty with the Vikings in Paris (887).

Charles III, *called* **the Simple** 879–929
King of France

He ruled France from 893. He ceded Normandy to the Vikings under **Rollo**, and was deposed (922).

Charles IV, *called* **the Fair** 1294–1328
King of France and Navarre

King from 1322, he was the last of the Capetian dynasty.

Charles V, *called* **the Wise** 1338–80
King of France

He was born at Vincennes, and as Dauphin he acted as regent during the long captivity of his father **John II**, after the Battle of Poitiers (1356), and succeeded his father in

Charles I 1600–49
King of Great Britain and Ireland

Charles was born in Dunfermline, the son of **James VI** of Scotland (later James I of England) and **Anne of Denmark**. He suffered from childhood frailty, which meant he had to crawl on his hands and knees until the age of seven, but overcame this to become a skilled tilter and marksman, and he excelled as a student of theology. Having been baptized as the Duke of Albany, and made Duke of York at the age of five, he became Prince of Wales in 1616, four years after the death of his brother Prince Henry had left him heir to the throne. In 1623 he travelled incognito to Madrid with his closest adviser, the 1st Duke of **Buckingham**, to seek the hand of a Spanish princess, but in the absence of an undertaking to convert to the Catholic faith, he was rebuffed by Rome.

He was betrothed two years later to Princess **Henrietta Maria** of France, with the promise that she would be allowed to practise her religion freely and to have the responsibility for the upbringing of their children until they reached the age of 13. This arrangement received a hostile reception from the growing body of Puritans, but Charles was undeterred, and three months after succeeding his father James I to the throne, he welcomed his new bride at Dover, having married her by proxy six weeks earlier. But the retinue of a bishop, 29 priests and 410 attendants that arrived with her soon tried Charles's patience, and he had them returned to France within a year. In the 12 years following the murder of Buckingham in 1628, Henrietta Maria came to exercise growing influence over the affairs of state, and it was largely at her behest that Charles dissolved no fewer than three parliaments in the first four years of his reign, and then ruled without one for 12 years.

With England now at peace with France and Spain, Charles addressed the task of refreshing his dwindling treasury with unpopular taxation of the inland counties, and of pulling Presbyterian Scotland into line with the imposition of a common prayer book. The hostility that both measures engendered forced Charles to recall parliament in 1640, but it continued to frustrate almost his every action. Worse still, to divert hostility from the queen, he was compelled to approve the Act of Attainment, by which parliament could not be dissolved without its consent, and to allow in 1641 the impeachment and execution of his loyal Lord Deputy for Ireland, the Earl of **Strafford**, after his secret plan to suppress the king's opponents in Ireland and England was exposed. Resentful of the power that parliament now held, Charles went to Edinburgh in an unsuccessful bid to win over the Scottish lords.

The following year, his arrival in the Chamber of the House of Commons to supervise the arrest of **John Pym** and four other MPs, which had been prompted by his fear that the queen would soon be impeached, made civil war inevitable; on 22 August 1642 the royal standard was raised at Nottingham, marking the start of more than three years of bitter fighting. The war effectively came to an end with the defeat of the Royalist forces in June 1645 at the Battle of Naseby, but the king spent another year trying to rally support from his refuge in Oxford before finally surrendering to the Scots at Newark on 5 May 1646. In January 1647 he was handed over to parliament and held at Holmby House near Northampton, where he exploited his comparative freedom to negotiate a treaty with the Scots and to foment a brief resurgence of civil war.

In November 1647 he escaped to the Isle of Wight, but he and his family were soon recaptured and held at Carisbrooke Castle, until the king was returned to stand trial at Westminster. His three refusals to plead were interpreted as a silent confession, and on 30 January 1649 Charles was beheaded on a scaffold erected outside the Guildhall in Whitehall, within sight of the parliament whose authority he had never been able to accept. On 7 February his body was taken for internment in the vault of **Henry VIII** at Windsor. Two of Charles's three sons were eventually to take the throne, as **Charles II** and James II (see **James VII and II**), and he was also survived by three daughters, the last born 10 weeks after his death.

📖 Maurice Ashley, *Charles I and Cromwell* (1988); Christopher Hibbert, *Charles I* (1968); Veronica Wedgwood, *The King's Peace, 1637–1641* (1955), *The King's War, 1641–1647* (1958) and *Trial of Charles I* (1964).

'A rule that may serve for a statesman, a courtier, or a lover—never make a defence or an apology before you be accused.' Quoted in a letter to Thomas Wentworth, later 1st Earl of **Strafford**, 3 September 1636.

'I see all the birds are flown.' Charles's comment on his unsuccessful attempt to arrest the Five Members in the House of Commons, 4 January 1642.

1364. He reorganized the army, established a navy and regained most of the territory lost to the English. A patron of the arts, he redecorated the Louvre to house his splendid library. 📖 Joseph Calmette, *Charles V* (1979)

Charles VII, *called* the Victorious 1403–61
King of France

Born in Paris, the son of Charles VI (the Foolish), he came to the throne in 1422, when Paris and the north of the country were in the hands of the English, who proclaimed **Henry VI** of England King of France, and appointed the Duke of **Bedford** regent. Charles was compelled to evacuate Champagne and Maine, but at Montargis (1426) the Comte de **Dunois** gained the first victory over the English, who laid siege to Orleans (1426). **Joan of Arc** incited the nobles and the people, leading to the end of the siege (1429). The English gradually lost nearly all they had gained in France. After the Treaty of Arras (1435) between the French king and **Philip, the Good**, Duke of Burgundy, their cause was hopeless, and Charles entered Paris (1436). Bayonne fell (1451), and with the death of Sir **John Talbot**, 1st Earl of Shrewsbury, under the walls of Castillon (1453), the whole south finally passed to France, and the Hundred Years War came to an end. Charles devoted himself to the reorganization of the government, and during his reign France recovered in some measure from her terrible calamities. He increased his solvency by obtaining the permanent right to tax without the permission of the Estates General, and enhanced his control of the French Church by the Pragmatic Sanction of Bourges (1438). His last years were embittered by the conduct of his son, the Dauphin, (later **Louis XI**). His mistress and confidante from 1444 was **Agnès Sorel**. 📖 M G A Vale, *Charles VII* (1974)

Charles VIII, *called* the Affable 1470–98
King of France

Born in Amboise, he succeeded his father, **Louis XI**, in 1483. Until 1492 the government was run by his sister, Anne de Beaujeu, and her husband. In 1494 he invaded Italy, but he failed in an attempt to secure the Kingdom of Naples (1495–96) which inaugurated a series of French expeditions to Italy that lasted until 1559.

Charles II *called* the Merry Monarch 1630–85
King of Great Britain and Ireland

Charles was the son of **Charles I** and **Henrietta Maria** and the years of his reign are known in English history as the Restoration Period. As Prince of Wales during the 1642–46 Civil War, he was sent to govern the west of England and saw action at the Battle of Edgehill in 1642, but when the Royalist forces continued to suffer heavy defeats, he went into exile to Sicily, Jersey (where his mistresss, Lucy Walter, bore him a son, James, Duke of Monmouth) and France. When his father was executed in 1649, Charles was proclaimed monarch by Scotland; on arriving in Edinburgh he agreed to the Presbyterian Covenant and, despite the failure of his forces to defeat **Oliver Cromwell** at Dunbar, he was crowned at Scone on 1 January 1651. At the Battle of Worcester the following September, Cromwell's forces again triumphed and Charles fled to France and the Netherlands.

As a result of successful negotiations in 1659 to restore the monarchy, Charles returned to England. Promising a general amnesty and liberty of conscience in his Declaration of Breda, he entered London in triumph on 29 May 1660—his 30th birthday. Personally, Charles was inclined to favour Roman Catholicism, and in 1663 attempted to issue a Declaration of Indulgence (allowing religious toleration of the Roman Catholics and Nonconformists), but it was bitterly resented. Under the chancellorship of Edward Hyde, 1st Earl of **Clarendon**, the country enjoyed peace and sound government, until his promotion of an unsuccessful war with Holland (1665–67) brought Hyde's downfall, and the office of Lord Chancellor was replaced by a group of Ministers acting in concert, who effectively formed the country's first Cabinet.

By the late 1660s, anti-Catholic feeling was again growing in strength, partly because of the growing power of **Louis XIV** of France, and also because the Great Fire of London in 1666 was blamed by some on a Catholic conspiracy. Charles had already sold Dunkirk to France in 1662 and, having little wish to see a revival of the old enmity, or to jeopardize an important potential source of personal income, he concluded a secret treaty whereby he undertook to become a Catholic, together with his brother (the future **James II** of England), and to enter into an alliance against Holland in return for an annual payment from Louis of £200,000. Charles's second attempt to subdue the Dutch between 1672 and 1674 was barely more successful than the first, but meanwhile he took a Catholic wife, **Mary of Modena**, in 1673. His attempt to issue a second Declaration of Indulgence to annul the penal laws against the Catholics and dissenters was rejected by parliament, which instead passed the 1673 Test Act, which excluded Roman Catholics from sitting in parliament or holding government office. It was followed by repeated attempts to legislate against James's succession to the throne, or to drastically limit his powers if he did so.

Mary's failure to produce an heir after four years of marriage compelled Charles to consent to the marriage in 1677 of his Protestant niece Mary (the future **Mary II**) to William of Orange (the future **William III**), and anti-Catholicism returned in the light of the fabricated account by **Titus Oates** of a Popish plot to murder the king. The next three years saw the future of the Stuart dynasty hanging in the balance, and the emergence for the first time of party distinctions, with the Whigs favouring James's exclusion, and the Tories opposed to any tampering with the succession. The Tories and Charles won the day, and the king immediately legislated for changes to borough government that effectively excluded the Whigs from power. Despite the absence of parliamentary opposition after Charles seized total power in 1681, anti-Catholic sentiment grew, and reached a peak after the 1683 Rye House plot to murder Charles and James came to light. However, James's succession was now safe, and on his deathbed Charles finally publicly acknowledged his conversion to Roman Catholicism. He died without producing an heir, but through his affairs with **Barbara Villiers**, **Nell Gwyn**, Louise de Kéroualle, Duchess of **Portsmouth**, and many others, he fathered several children, most of whom were later ennobled.

📖 J R Jones, *Charles II* (1987); Richard Ollard, *The Image of the King: Charles I and Charles II* (1979); Antonia Fraser, *Royal Charles: Charles II and the Restoration* (1979).

> 'Whereas, women's parts in plays have hitherto been acted by men in the habits of women…we do permit and give leave for the time to come that all women's parts be acted by women.' Royal licence, sanctioning the appearance of actresses on the English stage (1662).

Charles IX 1550–74
King of France

Born in St Germain-en-Laye, the second son of **Henri II** and **Catherine de Médicis**, he succeeded his brother, **Francis II** (1560). His reign coincided with the Wars of Religion. He was dominated by his mother, whose counsels drove him to authorize the infamous slaughter of Huguenots known as the St Bartholomew's Day Massacre (1572). Although increasingly melancholy, he was an intelligent man, and patronized the Pléiade, a literary group that included **Pierre de Ronsard**.

Charles X 1757–1836
King of France

Born at Versailles, the grandson of **Louis XV**, he received the title of Count of Artois. After a dissolute youth, he lived abroad during the French Revolution, returning to France in 1814 as lieutenant-general of the kingdom. In 1824 he succeeded his brother **Louis XVIII** to become the last **Bourbon** king of France, but he failed to adapt divine right monarchy to the post-Revolution democratic spirit, and his repressive rule led to the July Revolution (1830), and his eventual abdication and exile. 📖 Vincent W Beach, *Charles X of France* (1971)

Charles I of Spain See Charles V

Charles II 1661–1700
Last Habsburg King of Spain

Born in Madrid, he was the younger son and successor in 1665 of **Philip IV**. During his minority (1665–75) his mother, Queen Mariana of Austria, acted as regent. In 1690 he joined the League of Augsburg and went to war against **Louis XIV** in the Grand Alliance (1688–97). The weak, indolent end-product of Habsburg inbreeding, he was childless despite two marriages, and bequeathed the Crown to Philip of Anjou (**Philip V**), grandson of Louis XIV. The prospect of a union of the Crowns of Spain and France under the House of **Bourbon** precipitated the War of the Spanish Succession (1701–13).

Charles III 1716–88
King of Spain, and King Charles IV of Naples and Sicily

Born in Madrid, he was the younger son of **Philip V,** and succeeded his half-brother **Ferdinand VI.** He became Duke of Parma (1732), and in the War of the Polish Succession (1734) he became King Charles IV of Naples and Sicily. When he succeeded to the throne of Spain (1759) he handed over Naples and Sicily to his third son, **Ferdinand I.** During the Seven Years War (1756–63) he sided with France against Great Britain and lost Florida, but then regained it (1783) by siding with the Americans during the Revolution (1775–83). He gave the Spanish Empire better administration, fewer commercial restrictions, and greater security against attack. Frugal, informal, and disliking court ostentation, he chose effective ministers. At home he reformed the nation's economy, creating the conditions for industry to flourish. He strengthened the Crown's authority over the Church, ending the Inquisition (1767), and he expelled the Jesuits (1767). He was succeeded by his son, **Charles IV.**

Charles IV 1784–1819
King of Spain

Born in Portici, Naples, the son and successor of **Charles III,** he was an ineffectual ruler (1788–1808), dominated by his wife Maria Louisa of Parma and her lover, **Manuel de Godoy,** whom he appointed Prime Minister (1792). During the Napoleonic wars the Spanish fleet was destroyed by Admiral **Nelson** off Cape Trafalgar (1805), France was invaded (1807) and Charles was forced to abdicate (1808) in favour of **Napoleon I**'s brother, **Joseph Bonaparte.** He died in exile in Rome.

Charles IV 1316–78
Holy Roman Emperor

He became Margrave of Moravia (1334) and gradually assumed the government of the Czech lands during the frequent absences of his father, King **John, the Blind.** After the latter's death (1346) he became King of Bohemia, he was elected King of Germany (1347) and crowned Holy Roman Emperor in Rome (1355), but unlike his predecessors tried to avoid being drawn into Italian affairs. Instead, through shrewd diplomacy, he built up a dynastic empire based round his hereditary domains of Bohemia and Moravia, with his capital at Prague, where he founded the first university within the Empire (1348). His *Golden Bull* of 1356 became the new constitutional framework for the empire; it laid down procedure for the election of the monarch, excluded papal pretensions, and defined the rights of the seven electors, whose domains were declared indivisible. He was the first emperor since **Frederick I, Barbarossa,** to be succeeded by his son as Wenceslas IV (1361–1419).

Charles V *also* Charles I of Spain 1500–58
Holy Roman Emperor

He was born in Ghent, Belgium, the son of Philip the Handsome (count of Flanders, son of the Holy Roman Emperor **Maximilian I** and briefly King of Spain as **Philip I**) and Joanna, the Infanta of Spain ('**Juana the Mad**', daughter of **Ferdinand the Catholic** of Aragon and **Isabella of Castile**). Charles's father died in 1506, and his mother, who was regarded as insane, was kept in confinement in Spain for the rest of her life by her father, who assumed control of Castile. Charles and his sisters were brought up in Flanders by their aunt, the Archduchess **Margaret of Austria,** who acted as Charles's regent in the Netherlands until 1515. In 1516 his maternal grandfather Ferdinand of Aragon died, and Charles inherited from him Spain, Naples and Spanish America. In 1519 his paternal grandfather, Maximilian, died, and from him Charles inherited the Crown of Germany. In 1519 he was crowned Holy Roman Emperor at Aachen, having defeated **Francis I** of France for the election, and thereby became the most powerful monarch in Europe at the age

of 19. The ensuing years were dominated by virtually continuous wars with France for possession of Italy, and by a series of fruitless attempts to achieve religious unity in Germany. The Treaty of Cambrai (1529) brought a temporary peace, and Charles made a triumphal procession through Italy and in 1530 was crowned by the pope in Bologna as emperor and King of Italy. In 1532 he defeated Sultan **Süleyman the Magnificent** at the Siege of Vienna. War broke out again in 1536, when Francis invaded Savoy, and again in 1542, until a final truce was arranged through the Treaty of Crépy (1544). During the Reformation, Charles tried to restore unity of faith to protect his empire. In 1521 he presided over the Imperial Diet of Worms, where **Martin Luther** was given a hearing but declared an outlaw. He also called the Diets of Augsburg (1530) and Regensburg (1541) which, however, failed to reconcile the differences between Catholics and Lutherans. In 1547 he defeated the Lutheran princes (the League of Schmalkalden) at Mühlberg, and imposed the Augsburg Interim (1548) which condemned Lutheranism, but the harsh treatment of the Protestant prisoners only provoked a rebellious uprising in Saxony where Charles was worsted and was forced to grant Protestantism legal recognition through the Treaty of Passau (1552) and the Peace of Augsburg (1555). Elsewhere, Charles extended Spanish dominions in the New World by the conquest of Mexico by **Hernán Cortés** (1519–21) and of Peru by Francisco Pizarro (1531–35). Towards the end of his long reign, his health broken by gout, Charles devoted himself to consolidating his vast dominions for the benefit of his heirs. In 1527 he had married Isabella of Portugal, by whom he had a son, Philip (the future **Philip II** of Spain). In 1553 he renounced his imperial crown in favour of his brother, **Ferdinand I** (although his abdication was not formally accepted until 1558), and in 1555–56 he resigned his kingdoms of Spain, the Netherlands, and the Spanish Americas to his son Philip. Having abdicated all his powers he retired to live in seclusion in the monastery of San Geronimo de Yuste, in Estremadura.

Charles (Karl Ludwig Johann) 1771–1847
Archduke of Austria

He was born in Florence, the son of Emperor **Leopold II** and brother of Emperor **Francis II.** He became Governor-General of the Austrian Netherlands (1793) and as commander of the Austrian army on the Rhine (1796), defeated **Jean Victor Moreau** and Comte **Jean-Baptiste Jourdan** in several battles, drove the French over the Rhine, and took Kehl. He defeated Jourdan again in 1799, only to be defeated by **André Masséna.** He was Governor-General of Bohemia but then returned to the chief command from 1800. He reformed the Austrian army, using French military organization and tactics, and founding military academies. After victory at Aspern, and defeat at Wagram, he retired (1809) and became Governor of Mainz (1815).

Charles, Prince of Wales, *in full* Charles Philip Arthur George 1948–
British prince

He is the eldest son of Queen **Elizabeth II** and Prince Philip, Duke of **Edinburgh,** and heir apparent to the British throne. He was given the title of Prince of Wales (1958), and invested at Caernarvon (1969). Educated at Cheam School, Berkshire and Gordonstoun School in Scotland, he spent a term at Geelong Grammar School, Australia (1966), and studied at Trinity College, Cambridge (1967–70). He served in the RAF and Royal Navy (1971–76), and in 1981 married Lady **Diana** Frances, younger daughter of the 8th Earl Spencer. They announced their separation in 1992 and were divorced in 1996. They have two children: Prince William (1982–), and Prince Harry (1984–). Since leaving the navy, he has taken a special interest in industry, the problems of the inner cities, and unemployed young people. He has expressed strong views on architecture, conservation, organic farming and education, and he is a skilled fisherman, skier and painter. ⌨ Graham and Heather Fisher, *Charles: The Man and the Prince* (2nd edn, 1981)

Charles d'Orléans See Orléans, Charles, Duc d'

Charles Martel c.688–741
Ruler of the Franks, founder of the Carolingian dynasty
He was the illegitimate son of **Pepin II, the Younger** and in 719 became 'Mayor of the Palace' of Austrasia and real ruler of all the Frankish kingdom. He earned his nickname by his defeat of the Moors in a desperate battle at Tours, near Poitiers, in 732, which turned back the tide of Arab conquest in Europe, then drove the Saracens out of Burgundy and Languedoc (737). After his death the Frankish kingdom was divided between his sons Carloman and **Pepin III, the Short**. His grandson was **Charlemagne**. ⌨ Jean Deviosse, *Charles Martel* (1978)

Charles of Anjou 1226–85
Angevin King of Naples and Sicily
The posthumous son of Louis VIII of France, he was crowned King of Naples and Sicily by Pope **Urban IV** (1265), and defeated his Hohenstaufen rivals **Manfred**, King of Sicily in 1266 and Conradin of Swabia (1252–68) in 1268. He conquered much of mainland Greece, but his rule was unpopular, partly because he used French officials. He aimed to re-establish the Latin Empire in Constantinople (Istanbul), but when Peter III of Aragon seized Sicily after the revolt known as the Sicilian Vespers (1282), his plans failed and he was expelled.

Charles of Jesus, Brother See Foucauld, Charles Eugène

Charles of Valois 1270–1325
French nobleman
The second son of **Philip III** of France and Isabelle of Aragon, he was put forward as French claimant to the Kingdom of Aragon which he was unable to conquer (1283–89), eventually receiving Anjou and Maine (1290) as compensation. He continued to figure in the diplomatic schemes of his brother **Philip IV** as unsuccessful candidate for the thrones of Constantinople (Istanbul) from 1301 to 1307 and the Holy Roman Empire in 1308, and achieved great influence during the short reigns of Philip's three sons **Louis X**, Philip V (1293–1322) and **Charles IV**, commanding French armies in Guyenne and Flanders. Three years after his death, his only son, **Philip VI**, became the first of the Valois Kings of France.

Charles Robert 1288–1342
First King of Hungary of the Angevin dynasty
Born in Naples, he claimed the throne (through his mother) on the death of the last male member of the House of Árpád, Andrew III (1301), and after the defeat of rival claimants was crowned in 1310. He restored the royal authority in a struggle against the rebellious great magnates, whose lands he redistributed to the minor nobility, thus creating a new aristocracy loyal to him. The reforms which followed included the reorganization of military service and the introduction of a royal monopoly on gold and silver production. He was pious and civilized, and his court was famous as a school of chivalry. He married Elizabeth, daughter of Casimir III, the Great, of Poland (1310–70), and in 1337 obtained recognition of his son Louis, the future **Louis I**, the Great, as heir also to the Polish throne.

Charles the Bold 1433–77
Duke of Burgundy

He was born in Dijon, and succeeded his father, **Philip, the Good**, as duke (1467). Hasty and obstinate, though nominally a French vassal, he was continually at war with **Louis XI** of France, aiming to restore the old Kingdom of Burgundy, by conquering Lorraine, Provence, Dauphiné, and Switzerland. He was successful until 1474, organizing his extended possessions, freed from French control. He gained power over Lorraine (1475) and invaded Switzerland, but was defeated at Granson and Morat (1476). He laid siege to Nancy, but was killed in the battle. Under him Burgundy reached the zenith of its power, but it was a fragile achievement which then fell apart in the minority of his daughter.

Charles, Dame (Mary) Eugenia 1919–
Dominican politician
Born in Pointe Michel, she qualified in London as a barrister, then returned to the West Indies to practise law in the Windward and Leeward Islands. She entered politics in 1968 and two years later became co-founder and first leader of the centrist Dominica Freedom Party (DFP). She became an MP in 1975. Two years after independence, the DFP won the 1980 general election and she became the Caribbean's first female Prime Minister, a position she maintained until 1995, being re-elected in 1985 and 1990. She became a DBE in 1993.

Charles, Jacques-Alexandre-César 1746–1823
French experimental physicist
Born in Beaugency, Loiret department, he made himself an expert in popular scientific display. From 1781 he gave ingenious public lectures using an extensive collection of apparatus. Collaborating with the Robert brothers he made the first hydrogen balloon ascent in Paris in December 1783. He became a member of the Academy of Sciences (1795), and Professor of Experimental Physics at the Conservatoire des Arts et Métiers. He invented a megascope, a hydrometer and a goniometer (for measuring angles of crystals). Unpublished experiments which he carried out between 1786 and 1787 showed that insoluble gas expansion followed the fundamental law which, in the UK, now bears his name. **Joseph Gay-Lussac** published the general law, extended to soluble gases, in 1802.

Charles, Ray, *originally* Ray Charles Robinson 1930–
US singer and pianist
Born in Albany, Georgia, he was blind from the age of five. Orphaned at the age of 15, he went to Seattle and, after writing arrangements for several pop groups, was contracted to Atlantic Records in 1952. With *I've got a Woman* (1955) he established an influential new style of rhythm and blues which introduced elements of gospel music. He was awarded the National Medal of Arts in 1993.

Charleson, Ian 1949–90
Scottish actor
Born in Edinburgh, he studied for two years at Frank Dunlop's Young Vic Company, London, and appeared as Hamlet with the Cambridge Theatre Company before joining the Royal Shakespeare Company and playing a variety of leading roles. He also performed many roles at the National Theatre, including Brick in Tennessee Williams's *Cat on a Hot Tin Roof* (1988). He had notable film success as the runner Eric Liddell in *Chariots of Fire* (1981). Terminally ill, he gave a moving stage performance of *Hamlet* at the National Theatre in 1989, directed by Richard Eyre, and his decision to request the announcement of his death from AIDS was a courageous final act. A leading player of charm and power, he was one of the finest British actors of his generation.

Charlevoix, Pierre François Xavier de 1682–1761
French Jesuit explorer

He was born in St Quentin, Picardy, and in 1720 was sent by the French regent to find a route to western Canada. For two and a half years he travelled by canoe up the St Lawrence River across the Great Lakes and down the Mississippi River to New Orleans, and was finally shipwrecked in the Gulf of Mexico. He became the only traveller of that time to describe the interior of North America, writing *Histoire et description de la Nouvelle France* (1774,'History and Description of New France').

Charlie, Bonnie Prince See **Stuart, Prince Charles Edward** (panel)

Charlier, Jean See **Gerson, Jean de**

Charlotte (Augusta), Princess 1796–1817
Princess of Great Britain and Ireland
Born at Carlton House, London, the only daughter of George IV and Caroline of Brunswick, who separated immediately after her birth, she was the heir to the British throne, and was brought up in strict seclusion. In 1816 she married Prince Leopold of Saxe-Coburg, the future Leopold I of Belgium and uncle of Victoria. She died in childbirth.

Charlotte Sophia 1744–1818
Queen of Great Britain and Ireland and wife of George III
She married George III (1761), shortly after his accession to the throne, and bore him 15 children during their long and successful marriage. Their eldest son was the future George IV.

Charlton, Bobby (Sir Robert) 1937–
English footballer
Born in Ashington, Northumberland, he made his full-team debut in 1956 and played with Manchester United throughout his career (1954–73). He survived the Munich air disaster (1958) which killed eight teammates, won three League championship medals (1956–57, 1964–65, 1966–67), an FA Cup winner's medal in 1963, and captained Manchester United to victory in the 1968 European Cup. He played 106 games for England, between 1957 and 1973, scoring a record 49 goals, and was a member of the England side that won the World Cup in 1966. In all he played 754 games, scoring 245 goals. After a brief spell of management with Preston North End, he turned to running highly successful coaching schools and also became a director of Manchester United. He was knighted in 1994. He is the younger brother of Jack Charlton.

Charlton, Jack (John) 1935–
English footballer
Born in Ashington, Northumberland, he was a vital part of the great Leeds United side of 1965–75 under the management of Don Revie (1927–89). He was almost 30 before he was capped for England, but then retained his place for five years. His playing days over, he became manager of Middlesbrough (1973), Sheffield Wednesday (1977) and Newcastle United (1984). In 1986 he was unexpectedly appointed manager of the Republic of Ireland, and inspired the team to the semi-finals of the European Nations Cup in 1988 and to their best finish in the World Cup when in 1990 they reached the second round. In 1994 the team were beaten in the quarter finals by Italy. He retired from international football, a national hero, in 1996 and published *Jack Charlton—the Autobiography* the same year. He is the elder brother of Bobby Charlton.

Charney, Jule Gregory 1917–81
US mathematician and meteorologist
Born in San Francisco, he graduated from the University of California at Los Angeles in 1938 and received a PhD in meteorology in 1946. He then worked at Chicago University (1946–47), Oslo University (1947–48) and the Institute for Advanced Study in Princeton (1948–56)

before being appointed professor at the Massachusetts Institute of Technology (1956–81). In his greatest work, Charney studied and solved the problem of how weather systems develop from a basic flow, and devised equations which could be used in a large computer to produce weather forecasts. He was one of the first to realize the important influence which different surfaces have on weather and climate. He made an important contribution to the planning of the Global Atmospheric Research Program (1979) and helped to establish the National Center for Atmospheric Research in Boulder, Colorado (1960). His many honours included the Symons gold medal of the Royal Meteorological Society (1961).

Charnley, Sir John 1911–82
English orthopaedic surgeon
Born in Bury, Lancashire, he was educated at Manchester University. He served as an orthopaedic specialist during World War II, then returned to the Manchester Royal Infirmary, soon devoting himself to the technical problems associated with replacing badly arthritic hip joints. In the 1960s he established polyethylene as a suitable material for making artificial joints, and with a good cementing material, and scrupulous attention to aseptic technique, he perfected the operation which has given enhanced mobility to many people. He also pioneered other joint operations, and his centre at Wrightington Hospital became world famous. Elected FRS in 1975, he was knighted in 1977. ⌑W Waugh, *John Charnley: The Man and the Hip* (1990)

Charnock, Job d.1693
English merchant
He joined the East India Company in 1656, and became chief agent at Húglí. In 1690, when Húglí was under siege, he moved its factories to the mouth of the Ganges, thus founding Calcutta.

Charpak, Georges 1924–
French physicist and Nobel Prize winner
Born in Dabrovica, Poland, he studied at the Collège de France, worked at the National Centre for Scientific Research, and moved in 1959 to CERN (the European nuclear research centre in Geneva), where he developed gaseous particle detectors. Previous particle detectors recorded information on photographic film, which limited their detection and made analysis time-consuming. In a crucial advance in detector technology, Charpak devised the multi-wire proportional chamber, allowing large-area detectors capable of operating at high rates to be built relatively cheaply, a development which has revolutionized high-energy physics experiments. The use of such detectors has not been limited to high-energy physics, as they have also been used in biology, medicine and astronomy. For this work he was awarded the 1992 Nobel Prize for physics.

Charpentier, Gustave 1860–1956
French composer
Born in Dieuze, Lorraine, he wrote and composed both music and libretti of the operas *Louise* (1900) and *Julien* (1913). He succeeded his teacher, Jules Massenet, in the Académie des Beaux-Arts, Paris.

Charteris, Archibald 1835–1908
Church of Scotland minister and innovator
Born in Dumfriesshire, he studied at Edinburgh University, then held ministries at St Qivox and Park Parish, Glasgow. He was subsequently given the chair of Biblical Criticism at Edinburgh University. Chaplain to Queen Victoria and to Edward VII, he was also appointed moderator of the General Assembly in 1892. In 1879 he founded *Life and Work*, the enduring magazine of the Church's life and, in 1887, the Women's Guild. He was also responsible for the revival of the order of Deaconesses,

the foundation of the Deaconess Hospital, and a wide-ranging commitment to social work. He was a man of inexhaustible energy, vision and dedication, and his writings include *The Church of Scotland and Spiritual Independence* (1874) and many volumes on biblical criticism.

Charteris, Leslie, *pseudonym of* Leslie Charles Bowyer Yin 1907–93
US crime-story writer

Born in Singapore, the son of an English mother and a Chinese father, he was educated at Cambridge. He was author of a series of books featuring a criminal hero, Simon Templar, 'the Saint', starting with *Meet the Tiger* (1928) and *Enter the Saint* (1930). He moved to the USA in 1932 and worked in Hollywood as a screenwriter. He was naturalized in 1941. 📖 W O G Lofts and D J Adley, *The Saint and Leslie Charteris* (1979)

Chartier, Alain c.1390–c.1440
French writer and courtier

Born in Bayeux, he became secretary to Charles VI and Charles VII and went on diplomatic missions to Germany, Venice and Scotland (1425–28). His much imitated poem, *La Belle dame sans merci* (1424, 'The Beautiful Woman with no Mercy'), is a piece of escapism in the midst of his preoccupation with the plight of France in the Hundred Years War. This forms the backdrop for his two best works, the *Livre des quatre dames* (1415–16, 'Book of Four Women'), in which four ladies on the day after Agincourt weep for their lost lovers, and the prose *Quadrilogue invectif* (1422, 'A Debate Between Four People, Containing Invective'), a debate apportioning the blame for France's ills between the people and the nobility, and an appeal for national unity. He also skilfully handled the *ballade* and other lyrical forms. 📖 D Delaunay, *Étude sur Alain Chartier* (1876)

Chase, James Hadley, *pseudonym of* René Raymond 1906–85
English novelist

Born in London, he served in the RAF during World War II. As a writer of mystery stories he adopted the manner of the US 'hard-boiled' school, and had an immediate success with his first novel, *No Orchids for Miss Blandish* (1939). He continued in a similar vein to write prolifically, creating for most of his books US settings derived from copious second-hand research since he rarely visited that country. He employed a number of different detectives in various series, but his hallmark is always an intricate plot, and a fast-moving, harshly realistic narrative.

Chase, Salmon Portland 1808–73
US jurist and politician

Born in Cornish, New Hampshire, he settled as a lawyer in Cincinnati in 1830, where he acted as counsel for the defence of fugitive slaves. In 1841 he helped to found the Liberty Party, which brought about Henry Clay's defeat in 1844. Chase was returned to the Senate in 1849 by the Ohio Democrats, but he separated from the party in 1852 when it committed itself to slavery. He was twice Governor of Ohio (1855–59), and from 1861 to 1864 was Secretary of the Treasury. In 1864 Abraham Lincoln appointed him Chief Justice of the USA; as such he presided at the trial of President Andrew Johnson (1868).

Chase, Samuel 1741–1811
American judge and jurist

He was born in Somerset County, Maryland, the son of an immigrant English Anglican clergyman. As an Annapolis advocate he was quickly identified with rising Revolutionary feeling against the Stamp Act (1765). He was a delegate to the Continental Congresses from 1774 and signed the Declaration of Independence, later leading opposition to British peace proposals in 1778. He opposed the new Constitution but unexpectedly became a supporter of the Washington administration in 1795, and

was elected to the US Supreme Court in 1796. He delivered many distinguished opinions, stressing the pre-eminence of national treaties over state laws, and limitations on legislative powers. He was impeached in 1804 at the instance of President Jefferson for his partisan hostility to political offenders, but was acquitted in 1805.

Chase, William Merritt 1849–1916
US painter

Born in Franklin, Indiana, from 1872 to 1878 he studied in Munich under Karl von Piloty (1836–86), and on returning to the USA gained a reputation as a teacher. He painted landscapes, portraits and still lifes.

Chasles, Michel 1793–1880
French geometer

Born in Épernon, he entered the École Polytechnique in 1812, where he later taught mathematics (1841–51), and became Professor of Geometry at the Sorbonne in 1846. He greatly developed projective geometry without the use of coordinates, by means of a systematic study of cross-ratio and homographies. His command of geometry led him to a lifelong interest in the history of the subject, on which he wrote valuable books, but in 1867 he became involved in controversy with the Academy after claiming to have come into possession of autographs which proved that Blaise Pascal had anticipated Sir Isaac Newton's discovery of the law of gravitation. Ultimately, however, he admitted that these were forgeries.

Chassériau, Théodore 1819–56
French Créole painter

Born in Samana, San Domingo, he studied under Paul Delaroche and Ingres, and executed murals and historical subject paintings. His *Tepidarium at Pompeii* and *Susanna* are in the Louvre.

Chateaubriand, (François) René, Vicomte de 1768–1848
French writer and statesman

Born of a noble Breton family in St Malo, he served for a short time as an ensign, and in 1791 sailed to North America. Returning to France, he married, but immediately joined the army of the émigrés. From 1793 to 1800 he lived in London, teaching and translating. *Atala* (1801, Eng trans 1802), an unfinished Romantic epic of Native American life (1801), established his literary reputation, and *Le Génie du Christianisme* (1802, Eng trans *The Beauties of Christianity*, 1813), a vindication of the Church of Rome, made him prominent among French men of letters. He was appointed secretary to the embassy in Rome (1803) and was sent as envoy to the little republic of Valais (1804), but after the murder of the Duc d'Enghien, he refused to hold office under Napoleon I. He visited Greece, Palestine and Egypt in 1806–07, and wrote *Itinéraire de Paris à Jerusalem* (1811, Eng trans *Travels in Greece, Palestine, Egypt and Barbary*, 1812). He supported the Restoration monarchy from 1814 and was made a peer and minister, and in 1822–24 was ambassador extraordinary at the British court. Disappointed in his hope of becoming Prime Minister, he figured as a Liberal from 1824 to 1830, but on the downfall of Charles X he went back to the Royalists. His celebrated *Mémoires d'outre-tombe* ('Memoirs from Beyond the Grave') was written during the reign of Louis Philippe. Parts of this eloquent autobiography were translated as *Memoirs* in three volumes in 1848, but the whole work, in six volumes, did not appear till 1902. 📖 G Painter, *Chateaubriand: a biography* (1977)

Châtelet-Lomont, Gabrielle Émilie, Marquise du 1706–49
French mathematician and physicist

She was born in Paris, and after her marriage in 1725 to the Comte du Châtelet-Lomont she studied mathematics and the physical sciences. In 1733 she met Voltaire, and became

Chatham, William Pitt, 1st Earl of, *known as* Pitt the Elder 1708–78
English statesman and orator

William Pitt was born in Westminster, the younger son of Robert Pitt of Boconnoc, in Cornwall. He was educated at Eton and Trinity College, Oxford. In 1735 he entered parliament for the family borough, Old Sarum. He sided with **Frederick Louis**, Prince of Wales, against the king, and as leader of the young 'Patriot' Whigs, offered a determined opposition to **Robert Walpole**. After Walpole's fall from power, the king admitted Pitt in 1746 to the new administration; he became Paymaster-General, but resigned in 1755.

In 1744 Pitt inherited an income from the Duchess of Marlborough, and the Somerset estate of Burton-Pynsent, which became the family seat of the Pitts. In 1756, on the outbreak of the Seven Years War with France, Pitt became Secretary of State in a coalition government with Sir **Thomas Pelham-Holles**, 1st Duke of Newcastle. He immediately put into effect his plan of carrying on the war with France, raised the militia, and strengthened naval power. **George III**'s hostility and German predilections led him to resign in April 1757, only to be recalled in June, in response to popular demands.

His vigorous war policy was widely successful against the French on land (in India, Africa, Canada, and on the Rhine) and at sea, but Pitt himself was compelled to resign (1761) when the majority of the cabinet refused to declare war with Spain. Pitt received a pension of £3,000 a year, and his wife, sister of **George Grenville**, was created Baroness Chatham.

His imposing appearance and his magnificent voice added greatly to the attractions of his oratory. His character was irreproachable, though his haughtiness irritated even his friends. He formed a new ministry from 1766 to 1768, with a seat in the House of Lords as Viscount Pitt and Earl of Chatham. However, ill health prevented him from taking any active part in this ministry, and after his resignation (1768) he held no further office. He spoke strongly against the arbitrary and harsh policy towards the American colonies, and warmly urged an amicable settlement. However when it was proposed to make peace on any terms, Chatham came down to the House of Lords (2 April 1778), and in his final speech secured a majority against the motion. But the effort exhausted him and he collapsed into the arms of his friends. A few weeks later, he was dead.

Chatham was honoured with a public funeral and a statue in Westminster Abbey; government voted £20,000 to pay his debts, and conferred a pension of £4,000 a year on his descendants. His second son was **William Pitt**, the Younger.

📖 Stanley Ayling, *The Elder Pitt: Earl of Chatham* (1976); Peter D Brown, *William Pitt, Earl of Chatham* (1938); Basil Williams, *Life of William Pitt, Earl of Chatham* (2 vols, 1913).

'Where laws end, tyranny begins.' From a speech to the House of Lords, 2 March 1770.

---

his mistress. Voltaire came to live with her at her husband's estate at Cirey, where they set up a laboratory and studied the nature of fire, heat and light. She connected the causes of heat and light, and believed that both represented types of motion. She wrote *Institutions de physique* (1740) and *Dissertation sur la nature et la propagation du feu* (1744. 'Dissertation on the Nature and Propagation of Fire'), but her chief work was her translation into French of Sir **Isaac Newton**'s *Principia Mathematica*, posthumously published in 1759.

Chatelier, Henri Louis le See **Le Chatelier, Henri Louis**

Chatham, William Pitt, 1st Earl of See panel above

Chatrian See **Erckmann-Chatrian**

Chatterjee, Bankim Chandra 1838–94
Indian writer and social critic

He was born in Katalpura, Bengal, and became a district magistrate there. A contemporary of **Rabindranath Tagore**, he founded (1872) *Bangadarshan*, a Bengali newspaper which soon became a vehicle for expounding Hindu philosophy and culture. His novels include *Durges Nandini* (1864), *Anandamath* (1882), a novel of the Sannyasi rebellion of 1772, from which the Nationalist song *Bande Mataram* ('Hail to thee, Mother') was adopted, and *Kamalakanter Daptar* (1885). One of the most influential figures in 19th-century Indian literature, he was also a social activist, and in his novels was able to forge a sense of Indian nationality while at the same time pointing out the inequities institutionalized in Hindu society. 📖 M Lala Dasa, *Bankim Chatterjee, prophet of the Indian Renaissance* (1938)

Chatterjee, Gadadhar See **Ramakrishna Paramahasa**

Chatterton, Thomas 1752–70
English poet

Born in Bristol, he was a scholar of Colston's Bluecoat Hospital (1760–65), and then was apprenticed to an attorney. He wrote and published pseudo-archaic poems purporting to be the work of a 15th-century Bristol monk, Thomas Rowley, and in 1769 he sent a history of painting in England, allegedly by Rowley, to **Horace Walpole**, who was only temporarily deceived. He was released from his apprenticeship in 1770 and went to London, where he worked on innumerable satires, essays and epistles, and a burlesque opera, *The Revenge*, but later that year he poisoned himself with arsenic. His 'Rowley' poems, although soon exposed as forgeries, are considered to have genuine talent, and he became a romantic hero to later poets. His story was dramatized by **Alfred de Vigny** in 1835, and is the subject of the celebrated painting by Henry Wallis, *The Death of Chatterton* (1856, Tate, London).

Chatwin, Bruce 1940–89
English writer and traveller

He was born in Sheffield, educated at Marlborough College, and worked at Sotheby's as an expert on modern art for eight years until he temporarily went blind. To recuperate, he went to Africa and the Sudan. He was converted to a life of nomadic asceticism and began writing beguiling books which defy classification, combining fiction, anthropology, philosophy and travel. They include *In Patagonia* (1977), which won the Hawthornden prize and the **E M Forster** award of the American Academy of Letters, *The Viceroy of Ouidah* (1980), *On The Black Hill* (1982, winner of the Whitbread award for the best first novel) *The Songlines* (1987), and *Utz* (1988), a novella which was shortlisted for the Booker Prize.

Chau, Phan Boi See **Phan Boi Chau**

Chaucer, Geoffrey See panel p382

Chauliac, Guy de c.1300–1368
French surgeon

Chaucer, Geoffrey c.1345–1400

English poet best known for The Canterbury Tales, the most influential English poetry of the Middle Ages

Chaucer was born in London, the son of John Chaucer, a vintner and probably deputy to the king's butler. In 1357 and 1358 Geoffrey was a page in the service of the wife of Lionel, Duke of Clarence; later he transferred to the household of Edward III. In 1359 he served in the war in France, was taken prisoner and was ransomed, the king contributing £16 towards the required amount. He returned home in 1360. About 1366 he married Philippa, a relative by marriage of John of Gaunt, who gave Chaucer his support throughout his life. In 1367 the king granted him a pension; he is described as 'our beloved yeoman', and as 'one of the yeomen of the king's chamber', and in 1368 he was one of the king's esquires.

His first work as a poet was the *Book of the Duchess* (1369), on the death by plague of John of Gaunt's first wife Blanche. In 1370 he went abroad on the king's service: in 1372–73 on a royal mission to Genoa, Pisa, Florence; in 1376, abroad again; in 1377, to Flanders and to France; and in 1378, to Italy again. Meanwhile in 1374 he was appointed Comptroller of the Customs and Subsidy of Wools, Skins, and Tanned Hides in the port of London; in 1382, Comptroller of the Petty Customs; and in 1385 he was allowed to nominate a permanent deputy. In 1374 the king granted him a pitcher of wine daily; and John of Gaunt conferred on him a pension of £10 for life. In 1375 he received from the Crown the custody of lands that brought him in £104. In 1386 he was elected a knight of the shire for Kent.

However about the end of 1386 Chaucer lost his offices, possibly owing to the absence abroad of John of Gaunt, and fell upon hard times. In 1389 he was appointed clerk of the King's Works, but this did not last and he fell into debt. In 1394 King Richard II granted him a pension of £20 for life; but the advances of payment he applied for, and the issue of letters of protection from arrest for debt, indicate his condition. On the accession in 1399 of Henry IV, he was granted a pension of 40 marks (£26 13s 4d), and his few remaining months were spent in comfort.

After his death he was laid in that part of Westminster Abbey which through his burial was thereafter called Poets' Corner. By common consent, his greatest achievement is the Prologue (1387) to *The Canterbury Tales*, which, as a piece of descriptive writing, is unique. Chaucer was the first great poet of the English race, and he established the southern English dialect as the literary language of England.

📖 Chaucer's greatest work, probably begun in the late 1380s and not completed, was *The Canterbury Tales*, some 17,000 lines of verse and prose recounting, with a prologue, the tales told by a group of pilgrims on their journey to Canterbury. The work shows a profound understanding of human nature, ranging from the urbane to the bawdy, and is written in a variety of metres, principally the rhyming couplet.

In the period 1369–87 he wrote *The Parliament of Fowls, The House of Fame, Troilus and Cressida* and *The Legend of Good Women*; and also what ultimately appeared as the Clerk's, Man of Law's, Prioress's, Second Nun's and Knight's Tales in *The Canterbury Tales*. Chaucer's earlier writings, including his translation of part of the *Roman de la Rose*, followed the current French trends, but the most important influence on him during this middle period of his literary life came from Italy. Much of his subject matter he derived from his great Italian contemporaries, especially from Boccaccio, but it was the spirit, not the letter of these masters which he imitated. The crowning work of the middle period of his life is *Troilus and Cressida*—a work in which his immense power of human observation, his sense of humour, and his dramatic skill are lavishly displayed. *The Legend of Good Women* has an admirable prologue, but was never finished.

Other works have been ascribed to Chaucer, and were long printed in popular editions, that are certainly not his, eg *The Court of Love, Chaucer's Dream, The Complaint of the Black Knight, The Cuckoo and Nightingale, The Flower and the Leaf*, and much of the extant *Romaunt of the Rose*.

📖 There is an enormous amount of literature on Chaucer. See especially D Pearsall, *The Life of Geoffrey Chaucer* (1992); B Rowland, *A Companion to Chaucer Studies* (1979); D S Brewer (ed), *Geoffrey Chaucer* (3rd edn, 1973).

> 'Whan that Aprill with his shoures soote
> The droghte of March hath perced to the roote,
> And bathed every veyne in swich licour
> Of which vertu engendered is the flour;
> Whan Zephirus eek with his sweete breeth
> Inspired hath in every holt and heeth
> The tendre croppes, and the yonge sonne
> Hath in the Ram his halve cours yronne,
> And smale foweles maken melodye,
> That slepen al the nyght with open ye
> (So priketh hem nature in hir corages);
> Thanne longen folk to goon on pilgrimages.'
> The opening of the Prologue to *The Canterbury Tales* (edited by F N Robinson).

Born in Chauliac, Auvergne, he became the most famous surgeon of the Middle Ages. His *Chirurgia Magna* (1363) was translated into French over a century later and used as a manual by generations of doctors.

Chaumette, Pierre Gaspard 1763–94

French revolutionary

Born in Nevers, he was a shoemaker's son. At the Revolution he joined with Camille Desmoulins, and soon gained such popularity by his extreme Sans-culottism that he was appointed Procurator of the Paris Commune. His extravagances disgusted Robespierre, and he was executed.

Chaussée, Pierre Claude Nivelle de la See La Chaussée, Pierre Claude Nivelle de

Chausson, Ernest 1855–99

French composer

Born in Paris, he studied under Jules Massenet and César Franck. Several of his orchestral works, including the *Poème* for violin and orchestra, and the Symphony in B Flat Major (1891), as well as a number of songs, are still popular.

Chauviré, Yvette 1917–

French dancer and teacher

Born in Paris, she studied at the Paris Opera Ballet School before creating her first role for the company in 1936. In 1941 her mentor, company director Serge Lifar, promoted her to the rank of *étoile*, a position she held almost continually until her retirement from the stage in 1972. Regarded as the leading French ballerina of her generation, she impressed in the classical repertoire and was a guest star with companies around the world. In 1970 she became director of the International Dance Academy in Paris and became a Commander of the French Legion of Honour in 1988.

Chekhov, Anton Pavlovich 1860–1904
Russian dramatist and short-story writer

Chekhov was born in Taganrog, the son of an unsuccessful shopkeeper and the grandson of a serf. He studied medicine at Moscow University, qualifying as a doctor in 1884. In 1892 he settled on a farm estate at Melikhovo, near Moscow; five years later, suffering from tuberculosis, he moved to the Crimea. He then moved to Yalta in 1900 and spent the rest of his life there. He was elected Fellow of the Moscow Academy of Science in the same year, but resigned when his fellow-member **Maxim Gorky** was dismissed by the order of the tsar. In 1901 he married Olga Knipper an actress of the Moscow Art Theatre, who for many years after his death performed the female roles in his plays.

As a student, he had written humorous stories, sketches and articles for various magazines, and his first book, *Pëstrye Rasskazy* (1886, 'Motley Stories'), was successful enough for him to think of writing as a profession. However, he continued to regard himself as a doctor rather than a writer, although he practised very little except during the cholera epidemic of 1892–93.

He developed an interest in the popular stage of vaudeville and French farce and, after the failure of his first full-length play, *Ivanov* (1887, Eng trans 1912), he wrote several one-act plays, such as *Medved* (1889, Eng trans *The Bear*, 1909) and *Predlozheniye* (1889, Eng trans *A Marriage Proposal*, 1914).

His next full-length plays, *Leshy* (1889, Eng trans *The Wood Demon*, 1926) and *Chayka* (1896, Eng trans *The Seagull*, 1912), were also failures and he had decided to concentrate on his stories (which had introduced him to **Tolstoy** and **Maxim Gorky**) when Nemirovich-Danchenko persuaded him to let the Moscow Art Theatre revive *Chayka* in 1898. The play was produced by **Stanislavsky**, who revealed its quality and originality, and its reception encouraged Chekhov to write his masterpieces for the same company: *Dyadya Vanya* (1896, Eng trans *Uncle Vanya*, 1912), *Tri Sestry* (1901, Eng trans *The Three Sisters*, 1916) and *Vishnyovy Sad* (1904, Eng trans *The Cherry Orchard*, 1908).

Meanwhile he continued to write short stories, the following being good examples of his skill in this genre: *Step*

('The Steppe'); *Khoristka* ('The Chorus Girl'); *Duel* ('The Duel'); *Palata No. 6* ('Ward No 6'); *Dushetska* ('The Darling'); *Dama s sobachkoï* ('The Lady with the Dog'); and *V ovrag'e* ('In the Ravine'). The bulk of his stories were translated in 13 volumes (*The Tales of Tchevov*, 1916–22) by Constance Garnett. He also wrote a research thesis, *Ostrov Sakhalin* (1891, 'The Island of Sakhalin'), after spending three months in 1890 on the remote island Sakhalin, observing the lives of the prisoners and workers on this notorious Russian penal colony. It had a considerable effect on subsequent criminal legislation.

Chekhov is perhaps the most popular Russian author outside his own country. His stories have influenced many writers (eg **Raymond Carver**), and his plays are firmly established in the classical repertoires of Europe. His technique is impressionistic—almost *pointilliste*. In all his work he equates worldly success with loss of soul. It is the sensitive, hopeful, struggling people, at the mercy of forces almost always too strong for them, who are his heroes. This is why his work, although also presenting a convincing picture of Russian middle-class life at the end of the 19th century, has a timeless quality; it reflects the universal predicament of the 'little man'.

📖 V S Pritchett, *Chekhov: A Spirit Set Free* (1988); R Hingley, *A New Life of Anton Chekhov* (1976, reprinted 1989); E J Simmons, *Chekhov: A Biography* (1962).

'No one understood so clearly as Anton Chekhov the tragic element in life's trivialities; before him no one was able to convey to people, with such ruthless truthfulness, the shamefulness and boredom of their life in all its monotony and dreariness.' Maxim Gorky, in his memoir of Chekhov.

'Medicine is my lawful wife and literature is my mistress. When I get tired of one I spend the night with the other.' From a letter to A S Suvorin, 11 September 1888. Quoted in L S Friedland (ed), *Anton Chekhov: Letters on the Short Story…* (1964).

Chavannes See **Puvis de Chavannes, Pierre**

Chávez, Carlos 1899–1978
Mexican composer

Born in Mexico City, he studied in New York and Europe, and, returning to Mexico, formed the Mexican Symphony Orchestra in 1928, becoming director of the National Conservatory. A founder and director of the National Institute of Fine Arts (1947–52), Chávez's influence on every aspect of Mexican music was considerable. His works are less known outside his own country, partly owing to their large scale, but are influenced by Mexican folk music and include ballets, symphonies, concertos and an unusual *Toccata for Percussion* (1942).

Chavez, Cesar Estrada 1927–93
US labour leader

Born near Yuma, Arizona, the son of a family of Mexican–American migrants, he worked in the fields from early childhood and received little formal schooling. In 1962 he founded the National Farm Workers Association, which sought to unionize migrant workers. He used strikes, pickets, and marches in the struggle to win contracts from growers and himself undertook long fasts to publicize the movement. In 1968 he promoted a nationwide boycott of California grapes, which led to the

table-grape growers recognizing of the union in 1970. In 1972 the United Farm Workers (UFW), with Chavez as its president, became a member union of the AFL-CIO.

Chayefsky, Paddy, originally Sidney Chayefsky 1923–81
US stage and television playwright and film screenplay writer

He was born in New York City, and studied at the City College of New York. His work includes *Marty* (1953, television), which won an Academy Award for Best Screenplay when filmed (1954), and *The Bachelor Party* (1954, screenplay), sensitive and affecting plays about ordinary people. Other screenplays include *Paint Your Wagon* (1969), *The Hospital* (1971, Academy Award for Best Screenplay), and *Network* (1976, Academy Award for Best Screenplay). 📖 J M Clun, *Chayevsky* (1976)

Chebyshev, Pafnutii Lvovich 1821–94
Russian mathematician

Born in Okatovo, he graduated from Moscow University. He became an assistant at St Petersburg University in 1847 and later professor (1860–82). In number theory he made important contributions to the theory of the distribution of prime numbers, and in probability theory he proved fundamental limit theorems. Later he studied the theory of mechanisms and developed a theory of approximation to functions by polynomials, which has become important in modern computing. The mathematical school that he founded at St Petersburg remained the dominant influence on Russian mathematics for the rest of the century.

Cheever, John William 1912–82
US short-story writer and novelist

Born in Quincy, Massachusetts, he began telling stories when he was eight or nine. He sold his first story, 'Expelled', to *The New Republic* after he was thrown out of Thayer Academy in South Braintree, Massachusetts, at the age of 17. By the time he was 22 the *New Yorker* was accepting his work and for years he contributed a dozen stories a year to it. His first collection of stories was published in 1943 when he was in the army. After the war he taught English and wrote scripts for television, but in 1951 a Guggenheim Fellowship allowed him to devote his attention to writing, and a second collection, *The Enormous Radio and Other Stories*, came out in 1953. His first novel, *The Wapshot Chronicle* (1957), won the National Book award and its sequel, *The Wapshot Scandal* (1964), was awarded the Howell's Medal for Fiction. A steady stream of novels and stories followed, many of them focusing on the isolation and discontent of contemporary US life. Invariably funny and ironic, sad and sophisticated, these include *Bullet Park* (1969), *The World of Apples* (1973), *Falconer* (1977) and *The Stories of John Cheever*, winner of the Pulitzer Prize and the National Book Critics award in 1979. 📖 *The Journals* (1990); S Cheever, *Home Before Dark* (1984)

Chehab, Fuad 1902–73
Lebanese politician and soldier

From a Maronite Christian family, he came to prominence when he was appointed to command the new Lebanese army in 1945. He rose to become Minister of Defence in Camille Chamoun's government, formed in the aftermath of the Suez affair (1956). During the disturbances following the declaration of the United Arab Republic of Egypt and Syria in 1958, Chehab refused to use the Lebanese army to crush the rebellion. Through this, and a call by the rebels for Chamoun's resignation, Chehab won the respect of the Muslim section of the community; and in July 1958 Chehab, who had by this time resigned command of the army, was elected President, to succeed Chamoun when the latter left office. Despite initial problems, he succeeded in restoring stability to Lebanon. His six-year term of office saw an attempt to improve conditions for the common people. That this was unsuccessful may be seen, to some extent, as a contributing factor to the disastrous currents which were to overwhelm Lebanon a decade later.

Cheke, Sir John 1514–57
English scholar

Born in Cambridge, he became Fellow of St John's College, Cambridge, in 1529. He adopted the doctrines of the Reformation, and in 1540 was appointed the first Regius Professor of Greek at Cambridge. With Sir Thomas Smith he introduced the Erasmian pronunciation of Greek despite opposition from Bishop Stephen Gardiner. In 1554 he was appointed tutor to the Prince of Wales (later Edward VI), whose accession secured him a seat in parliament (1547), the provostship of King's College, Cambridge (1548) and a knighthood (1552). After the accession of Mary I he was imprisoned (1553–54) for having served as Latin secretary to Lady Jane Grey, and thereafter went abroad to teach. In 1556 he was lured to Belgium and treacherously seized, and taken back to the Tower of London where he was forced to recant his Protestantism publicly.

Chekhov, Anton Pavlovich See panel p383

Chelčický, Petz c.1390–1460
Czech reformer and theologian

He was born in Chelčic, Bohemia. A radical follower of the Hussites, he shunned towns and commerce, and founded the sect which became the Moravian Brothers. The Christian doctrine of his *The Net of True Faith* (1450) was later promulgated by Leo Tolstoy.

Chelmsford, Frederick John Napier Thesiger, 1st Viscount 1868–1933
English colonial administrator

He was Governor of Queensland (1905–09), Governor of New South Wales (1909–13), Viceroy of India (1916–21), and First Lord of the Admiralty in 1924.

Chemnitz or Kemnitz, Martin 1522–86
German Lutheran theologian

Born in Treuenbrietzen, in Brandenburg, he studied at the University of Wittenberg (1545) under Philip Melanchthon. His skill in astrology led to his appointment as ducal librarian at Königsberg in 1549, where he devoted himself to theology. His opposition to Andreas Osiander (1498–1552) took him to Wittenberg (1553), and he was appointed a preacher at Brunswick in 1554, and superintendent in 1567. His works include *Examen Concilii Tridentini* (1565–73) and *De duabus Naturis in Christo* (1571).

Chen Boda (Ch'en Po-ta) 1905–89
Chinese political propagandist

Born in Huian, Fujian (Fu-chien) province, he joined the Chinese Communist Party (CCP) in 1927 and studied in Moscow until 1930. After teaching in Beijing (Peking), he went to the Communist base at Yan'an (Yen-an) in 1937. He became Mao Zedong's personal secretary and helped popularize Mao's concept of the 'Sinification of Marxism' (adapting Marxism to Chinese conditions). After 1949 he continued to be influential in the party's propaganda department, becoming the chief editor of the party organ, *Hongqi* (Red Flag), in 1958. During the Cultural Revolution (1966–69), he became associated with the radicals and in 1969 reached the apogee of his influence when he was appointed to the politburo. In the campaign against leftist excesses the following year, however, he was arrested and expelled from the CCP. In 1980–81 he was tried along with the Gang of Four and sentenced to 18 years in prison but was reportedly released later the same year. He spent his final years studying history in Beijing.

Chen Ning Yang See Yang, Chen Ning

Chen Yi (Ch'en I) 1901–72
Chinese Communist leader

He studied in France, and joined the Communist Party on his return. He supported Mao Zedong in the struggle with the Guomindang (Kuomintang), and the Japanese (1934). He formed the 4th Route Army in Jiangxi (Kiangsi) in 1940, and commanded the East China Liberation Army (1946), restyled the 3rd (East China) Army (1948). He prepared an amphibious operation against Taiwan, but failed to capture Quemoy island in 1949. Created Marshal of the People's Republic in 1955, he became Foreign Minister in 1958. He was dropped from the politburo during the Cultural Revolution in 1969.

Chenier, Clifton 1925–87
US Zydeco accordionist

Born in Opelousas, Louisiana, he was a key figure in the development of Zydeco, a distinctly black variant on the Cajun two-step tradition, spiced up with borrowings from rhythm and blues. He sang in French patois, Creole and English, and after a string of regional hits during the 1950s, he succeeded in bringing this vibrant musical form to a wider audience in the 1960s and 1970s. He recorded for many different labels, and was twice nominated for Grammy awards (1979, 1986). His brother Cleveland Chenier played *frottoir* (a corrugated steel breast-plate) in his band, while his son C J Chenier is also an accordionist.

Chénier, (Marie) André 1762–94
French poet

Born in Constantinople (Istanbul), he was the third son of the French consul-general and a Greek mother. At the age of three he was sent to France, and at 12 was placed at the Collège de Navarre, Paris, where Greek literature was his special subject. At 20 he joined the army, and served for six months in Strasbourg, but he returned to Paris to study, and wrote his famous idylls *Le Mendiant* ('The Beggar') and *L'Aveugle* ('The Blind Man'). He travelled in Switzerland, Italy and the Greek Islands, returned to Paris in 1786 and began several poems, most of which remained fragments. The most noteworthy are *Suzanne*, *L'Invention* and *Hermès*, the last being an imitation of **Lucretius**. In 1787 he went to England as secretary to the French ambassador, and in 1790 he returned again to Paris, at first supporting the Revolution but later offending **Robespierre** by political pamphlets promoting liberal monarchism. He was thrown into prison, and six months later was guillotined, three days before the end of the Reign of Terror. Almost nothing was published in his lifetime, but the appearance of his collected poems in 1819 made a notable impression on subsequent French poetry. ⬛V Loggins, *André Chénier, his life, death and glory* (1965)

Cheops 26th century BC
Hellenic form of Khufu, King of Memphis in Egypt

He was second of the fourth dynasty, and is famous as the builder of the Great Pyramid. An active ruler, he centralized the government and reduced priestly power. A son and successor, Chephren (Khafre) built the next largest pyramid.

Cher, *originally* Cheryl Sarkisian La Pier 1946–
US pop singer and film actress

Born in El Centro, California, of partly Cherokee parentage, she began her career as a backing vocalist, then teamed up with Salvatore 'Sonny' Bono. They married in 1964, and had their first major hit single, 'I Got You Babe', in 1965. They divorced in 1975, and she began to gain fame as a solo singer, but also pursued an acting career. She appeared in **Robert Altman**'s Broadway production of *Come Back to the Five and Dime, Jimmy Dean, Jimmy Dean* (1981, film version 1982), and went on to win an Academy Award nomination as the lesbian friend of union activist Karen Silkwood in *Silkwood* (1983), a Cannes Best Actress Award in *Mask* (1985), and a Best Actress Academy Award as an Italian widow in the romantic comedy *Moonstruck* (1987). Other films include *Mermaids* (1990), *Faithful* (1995) and *If These Walls Could Talk* (1996), which she also co-directed. Her private life and physical appearance have proved a fertile source of media speculation. ⬛ L Quirk, *Totally Uninhibited* (1991)

Cherbuliez, Charles Victor, *pseudonym* G Valbert 1829–99
French novelist and critic

Born in Geneva, Switzerland, he was educated at Paris, Bonn and Berlin, studying first mathematics, then philology and philosophy, after which he lived in Geneva as a teacher. In 1864 he went to Paris to join the staff of the *Revue des Deux Mondes*, writing many literary and political articles under the pseudonym of 'G Valbert'. He was elected to the Académie Française in 1881. His novels include *Le Roman d'une honnête femme* (1866, 'The Story of an Honest Woman'), *Samuel Brohl et Cie* (1877, 'Samuel Brohl & Co.'), *La Vocation du Comte Ghislain* (1888, 'Count Ghislain's Calling') and *Le Secret du précepteur* (1893, 'The Tutor's Secret').

Cherbuliez, Joel 1806–70
Swiss novelist and critic

Born in Geneva, the son of a prosperous bookseller, he succeeded to his father's business, and edited the *Revue critique* from 1833. His *Lendemain du dernier jour d'un condamné* (1829, 'The Day After a Condemned Man's Last Day') was a clever burlesque on **Victor Hugo**'s well-known tour de force, while his *Genève* (1867) was a solid contribution to the history of the city.

Cherenkov, Pavel Alekseyevich 1904–90
Soviet physicist and Nobel Prize winner

He was born in Voronezh in western Russia and educated at Voronezh University and the Soviet Academy of Sciences. In 1934 he observed blue light emission from water bombarded by gamma rays. This so-called 'Cherenkov effect' was explained by **Igor Tamm** and **Ilya Frank** as being produced by particles travelling through a medium at velocities greater than the speed of light in that medium. The three shared the Nobel Prize for physics in 1958. The principle was adapted in constructing a cosmic-ray counter mounted in the *Sputnik III* satellite, and has become important as an identification tool in high-energy particle experiments. Cherenkov also contributed to the development and construction of electron accelerators, and to the study of the interactions of photons with nuclei and mesons. He became a corresponding member of the Academy of Sciences in 1964 and a full member in 1970.

Cherkassky, Shura Alexander Isaakovich 1911–95
US pianist

Born in Odessa, Russia, he settled in the USA in 1922 and studied under **Josef Hofmann** at the Curtis Institute, Philadelphia. He excels in the Romantic repertoire and has toured and recorded widely.

Chermayeff, Serge, *originally* Serge Issakovitch 1900–96
US architect and designer

Born in the Caucasus Mountains, Russia, he was educated in England. After a period in journalism, he became a director of Waring & Gillow (1928) for which he established a 'Modern Art Studio'. His early design work was for interiors, including studios for Broadcasting House, London (1931). He also designed textiles, radio cabinets (for Ekco) and furniture, including a modular range called 'Plan' (1936). His architectural designs included the De La Warr Pavilion, Bexhill-on-Sea (1933–35), with **Erich Mendelsohn**, and some notable houses. In 1940 he emigrated to the USA where, in addition to his architectural work, he taught design and architecture. He gained US citizenship in 1945 and held professorships at Harvard (1952–62) and Yale (1962–69). His drawings were divided between Columbia University's Avery Library and the Royal Institute of British Architects Drawings Collection in London; unfortunately only a few pre-war examples survive.

Chernenko, Konstantin Ustinovich 1911–85
Soviet politician

Born of peasant stock in Bolshaya Tes in Central Siberia, he joined the Komsomol (Communist Youth League) in 1929 and the Communist Party (CPSU) in 1931. During the 1940s, he worked as a specialist in party propaganda in, first, Krasnoyarsk (Siberia) and then Moldavia, where he impressed **Leonid Brezhnev**, who adopted Chernenko as his personal assistant and took him to Moscow to work in the central apparatus in 1956. He was inducted into the CPSU Central Committee in 1971, the secretariat in 1976 and into the politburo, as a full member, in December 1978. During his final years in power, Brezhnev sought to promote Chernenko as his heir-apparent, but on Brezhnev's death in 1982 Chernenko was passed over in favour of **Yuri Andropov**. However, when Andropov died in 1984 Chernenko was selected as the CPSU's stop-gap leader by cautious party colleagues. In 1984 Chernenko was also elected State President. As Soviet leader he sought to promote a new era of détente, but from mid-1984, suffering from emphysema, he progressively retired from the public gaze. He was succeeded by **Mikhail Gorbachev**. 📖 Ilya Zemtsov, *Chernenko: Sovetskii Soiuz v kanum perestroiki* (1989)

Chernomyrdin, Viktor Stepanovich 1938–
Soviet politician

Born in Cherny-Otrog in the Orenburg district, he was educated at the Kuybyshev Polytechnic. He served in the army (1957–60) before entering the oil industry. Having entered politics in 1978, he became Minister for Gas (1985–89) and did much to exploit the USSR's natural gas and oil resources. Appointed Prime Minister of Russia in 1993, he assumed greater political authority when he deputised for **Boris Yeltsin** during the Russian President's lengthy spell of illness, and was able to replace the reform-minded Cabinet with members of the old guard in 1994.

Chernyshevsky, Nikolai Gavrilovich 1828–89
Russian writer and political activist

The son of a Saratov priest, he graduated in history from the University of St Petersburg, and became a journalist and the editor of the critical magazine *Sovremennik* ('Contemporary') (1855–62). He abandoned the liberalism of his predecessors and developed a primitive revolutionary socialist philosophy, based on his faith in the Russian peasantry. He was disappointed with **Alexander II**'s rather tentative reforms and, on somewhat doubtful evidence of political subversion, he was imprisoned in 1862 and sent to Siberia in 1864, where he was forced to remain until shortly before his death. His novel *Chto delat'?* (1864, 'A Vital Question', also known as 'What Is To Be Done?'), written during imprisonment, inspired a generation of merging revolutionaries, and is said to have in part provoked **Dostoevsky**'s *Zapiski iz podpol'ya* (1864, *Notes from Underground*). 📖 F B Randall, *Nikolai Gavrilovich Chernyshevsky* (1967)

Cherry, Don(ald Eugene) 1936–95
US jazz trumpet player

Born in Oklahoma City, he was one of the most individual voices in contemporary jazz and world music. In an age of technically fearsome trumpet players, he preferred to emphasize expression and musical communication over speed and technical prowess on his distinctive pocket trumpet. He first came to notice in the epochal **Ornette Coleman** Quartet in 1958, and was a crucial factor in that group. He recorded as a leader from the mid-1960s, and incorporated the ethnic musics and instruments of Africa, India and Asia into his work with groups like Codona in the early 1970s, and later his Multikulti band, and did so with greater integrity than many of his peers. His devotion to Coleman's 'harmolodic' teachings remained strong throughout his career, which also included collaborations with rock musicians.

Cherubini, Maria Luigi Carlo Zenobio Salvatore 1760–1842
Italian composer

Born in Florence, he studied in Bologna and Milan, and wrote a succession of operas, at first in Neapolitan style and, later (having moved to Paris) in French style. Few of these are now heard, apart from some of the overtures, such as that of *Les Deux journées* (1800, 'The Water-Carrier'), his most impressive opera. His later work was mainly ecclesiastical. In 1822 he became director of the Paris Conservatoire, whose reputation he advanced considerably. His work on counterpoint and fugue (1835) was a standard text.

Chervenkov, Vulko 1900–80
Bulgarian politician

He joined the Bulgarian Communist Party (BCP) in 1919 and went to the USSR where he studied at the Moscow Military Academy and Lenin International School and acted as secretary to **Georgi Dimitrov**. Returning to Bulgaria in 1944, he held a series of appointments within the BCP: Secretary for AgitProp (1949–50), deputy Prime Minister (1949–50), General-Secretary (1950–61), Prime Minister (1950–6) and deputy Prime Minister (1956–61). Known as Bulgaria's 'Little **Stalin**', he fell victim to **Nikita Khrushchev**'s anti-Stalinist campaign in the early 1960s. In 1962 he was expelled from the party and replaced by **Todor Zhivkov** who had denounced him at the 1961 and 1962 party conferences. Later he was rehabilitated (1969) and awarded a state pension.

Cherwell, Frederick Alexander Lindemann, 1st Viscount 1886–1957
English physicist

Born in Baden-Baden, Germany, he was educated at the University of Berlin and at the Sorbonne, Paris, where he worked on the problems of atomic heat. In 1914 he became director of the Royal Flying Corps Experimental Physics Station at Farnborough. He was the first to evolve and put into practice the mathematical theory of aircraft spin. He was Professor of Experimental Philosophy at Oxford (1919–56) and director of the Clarendon Laboratory, which he turned into one of the best on low-temperature research in Great Britain. A close friend of **Churchill**, he became his personal assistant in 1940. He was Paymaster-General from 1942 to 1945 and again in the 1951 government, advising on nuclear research and scientific matters generally. He resigned in 1953 to resume his professorship, and was made a viscount in 1956.

Cheshire, Geoffrey Chevalier 1886–78
English law teacher and jurist

Born in Hartford, Cheshire, he was educated at Denstone College and Merton College, Oxford. An impressive teacher, he was Vinerian Professor of Law at Oxford (1944–49), and wrote three classic, authoritative works, *The Modern Law of Real Property* (1925), *Private International Law* (1935) and, with C H S Fifoot, *The Law of Contract* (1945), all of which have appeared in many editions.

Cheshire, (Geoffrey) Leonard Cheshire, Baron 1917–92
English philanthropist

He was educated at Stowe School and Merton College, Oxford. A pilot in the RAF in World War II, he was promoted Group Captain and won the VC in 1944 on completing a hundred bombing missions, often at low altitude, on heavily defended German targets. With **William Penney** he was the official British observer of the destruction caused by the atomic bomb over Nagasaki (1945). This experience, together with his new-found faith in Roman Catholicism, made him decide to devote the rest of his life to the relief of suffering. He founded the 'Cheshire Foundation Homes' for the incurable sick in many countries. In 1959 he married Sue, Baroness **Ryder**, who founded the Sue Ryder Foundation for the sick and disabled of all age groups. He was created Baron Cheshire in 1991.

Chesler, Phyllis 1940–
US educator and writer

Her works on psychology in the 1970s were landmarks in that field, and influenced all future study of women's psychology. The first, *Women and Madness* (1972), analysed psychology and psychiatry as tools to oppress women. Later books include *Women, Money and Power*, written with Emily Jane Goodman in 1976, and *About Men* (1978).

Chesney, Charles Cornwallis 1826–76
English soldier
Nephew of Francis Rawdon Chesney, he was Professor of Military History at Sandhurst (1858–64) and the Imperial Staff College from 1864. He was author of the *Waterloo Lectures* (1861) delivered at Sandhurst, criticizing the Duke of Wellington and giving the credit to Marshal Blücher.

Chesney, Francis Rawdon 1789–1872
Irish soldier and explorer
He was born in Annalong, County Down. In 1829 he surveyed the route for a Suez Canal, and from 1831 made four explorations of a route to India by rail and sea via Syria and the Euphrates. He commanded the artillery in Hong Kong (1843–47).

Chesnius See Duchesne, André

Chesnut, Mary Boykin Miller, *née* Miller
1823–86
US diarist
Born in South Carolina and educated at private schools in Camden and Charleston, she married James Chesnut, a US senator from South Carolina (1859–60) in 1840. He resigned his position in order to assist in the formation of the Confederacy, and she accompanied him, keeping a diary of her experiences and observations on military and political leaders of the Confederacy from 1861 to 1865. The diary constitutes a highly regarded contribution to the literature and history of the period. Although her observations were intended to be published, *A Diary from Dixie* did not appear until 1905.

Chessman, Caryl Whittier 1921–60
US convict and writer
Born in St Joseph, Michigan, he was sentenced to death in 1948 on 17 charges of kidnapping, robbery and rape, but was granted eight stays of execution by the Governor of California amounting to a period of 12 years under sentence of death, without a reprieve. While in prison he conducted a brilliant legal battle, learned four languages and wrote the bestselling, autobiographical books against capital punishment *Cell 2455 Death Row* (1954), *Trial by Ordeal* (1955) and *The Face of Justice* (1958). His ultimate execution provoked worldwide criticism of US judicial methods.

Chesterfield, Philip Dormer Stanhope, 4th Earl of 1694–1773
English statesman and man of letters
Born in London, he was an MP from 1715 to c.1723. In 1730 he was made Lord Steward of the household. Until then, as a Whig, he had supported Sir Robert Walpole; but being ousted from office for voting against an excise bill, he became one of Walpole's bitterest antagonists. He joined the Pelham ministry in 1744, became Irish Lord Lieutenant in 1745, and was in 1746 one of the principal secretaries of state. Intimate with Jonathan Swift, Pope and Viscount Bolingbroke, he drew from Dr Johnson a famous indignant letter. Besides the *Letters to his Son* (a guide to manners and success), he also wrote *Letters to his Godson and Successor*. His *Letters to Lord Huntingdon* were published in 1923, his verse in 1927.

Chesterton, G(ilbert) K(eith) 1874–1936
English critic, novelist and poet
Born in London, he was educated at St Paul's School and studied art at the Slade School. However, he never practised professionally, although he contributed illustrations to Hilaire Belloc's novels. Much of his best work went into

essays and articles, some of which appeared in his own *G.K's Weekly*, founded in 1925. He became a Roman Catholic in 1922, a decision clearly foreshadowed in his writing, the best of which was published before that date. His early books include two collections of poetry, followed by *The Napoleon of Notting Hill* (1904), liberal and anti-Imperialist in outlook, brilliant literary studies of Robert Browning (1903), Dickens (1906) and Robert Louis Stevenson (1907), and the provocative *Heretics* (1908) and *Orthodoxy* (1908). The amiable detective-priest Father Brown, who brought Chesterton popularity with a wider public, first appeared in *The Innocence of Father Brown* (1911). He also wrote lives of St Francis of Assisi (1923), and St Thomas Aquinas (1933), *Collected Poems* (1933), and an *Autobiography* (published posthumously in 1936). An ebullient personality, quick-witted, with a robust humour, he was one of the most colourful and provocative writers of his day. He married Ada Elizabeth Jones, journalist and writer, who pioneered the Cecil Houses for London's homeless women. 📖 P Braybrooke, *Gilbert Keith Chesterton* (1922)

Chetham, Humphrey 1580–1653
English merchant and philanthropist
Born in Manchester, he became a cloth manufacturer there, and was the founder of Chetham Hospital and a public library in Manchester.

Chettle, Henry c.1560–c.1607
English dramatist and pamphleteer
Born in London, he was a printer by trade, and turned to writing when his printing-house failed. He edited Robert Greene's *Groat's-worth of Wit* (1592), and in 1593 published a pamphlet, *Kind Harts Dreame*, apologizing for Greene's attack on Shakespeare. He wrote a picaresque romance, *Piers Plainnes Seven Yeres Prentiship* (1595), and from 1598 turned to writing plays for Philip Henslowe's Rose Theatre in Bankside, especially *The Tragedy of Hoffman* (1602). He collaborated on many others, including *The Blind Beggar of Bednal-Green* (1600, with John Day), and also wrote an elegy for Queen Elizabeth I, *Englandes Mourning Garment* (1603). 📖 H Jenkins, *The Life and Work of Henry Chettle* (1934)

Chevalier, Albert 1861–1923
English entertainer
He acted at the Prince of Wales's Theatre, London, in 1877, and in 1891 became a music-hall singer. Writing, composing and singing barrow-boy ballads, he immortalized such songs as 'My Old Dutch', and 'Knocked 'em in the Old Kent Road'. In 1901 he published *Before I Forget*.

Chevalier, Maurice 1888–1972
French film and vaudeville actor, and entertainer
Born in Paris, he began his career as a child, singing and dancing in small cafés, and became dancing partner to Mistinguett at the Folies Bergères (1909–13). A prisoner during World War I, he won the Croix de Guerre, and became a member of the Legion of Honour. He first appeared in London in 1919 and made his first Hollywood film, *The Innocents of Paris*, in 1929. Other films included *The Love Parade* (1932). Almost 30 years later his individual, straw-hatted, *bon-vivant* personality, with his distinctive French accent, was still much admired, as in the musical *Gigi* (1958). He received a Special Academy Award in 1959. He wrote his autobiography, *Ma route et mes chansons* (Eng trans *The Man in the Straw Hat*, 1949), and *I Remember It Well* (1971). 📖 Gene Ringgold and DeWitt Bodeen, *Chevalier* (1973)

Chevallier, Gabriel 1895–1969
French novelist

Born in Lyons, after a series of less successful psychological novels he won wide acclaim with his *Clochemerle* (1934, Eng trans 1936), an earthy satire on petty bureaucracy in a small French town. Other books include *La Peur* (1930, 'Fear'), *Clarisse Vernon* (1933), *Sainte-Colline* (1937), *Les Héritiers Euffe* (1945, 'The Euffe Inheritance'), *Le Petit général* (1951, 'The Little General') and *Clochemerle Babylone* (1954).

Chevreul, Michel Eugène 1786–1889
French chemist and gerontologist

Born in Angers, Anjou province, he studied chemistry at the Collège de France in Paris and at Harvard. Most of his working life was spent at the Museum of Natural History in Paris. For some years he was director of the dyeworks at the Gobelins Tapestry factory. He investigated the physics and psychology of colour. *De la loi du contraste simultané* (1839, 'Of the Law of Simultaneous Contrast'), which influenced many of the Impressionists, argued that our perception of the intensity and hue of any colour is conditioned by the degree of contrast with neighbouring colours. Chevreul was also a pioneer of organic analysis. His studies of the saponification process demonstrated that soaps are combinations of a fatty acid with an inorganic base, a discovery which opened up vast industries. He noticed the phenomenon of isomerism, reported that diabetic urine contains glucose and studied the psychiatric effects of old age.

Chevrolet, Louis 1878–1941
US car designer and racing driver

Born in La Chaux-de-Fonds, Switzerland, he emigrated to the USA in 1900, became a racing car driver, and in his first motor race defeated **Barney Oldfield**. Thereafter he set records on every important racing circuit in the USA. In 1911 with William Crapo Durant he founded the Chevrolet Motor Company, but had little confidence in it and sold his interest to Durant in 1915, who incorporated it with General Motors in 1916. Other cars designed by Chevrolet won important races, including the Indianapolis in 1920 and 1921. He was also involved in motor boat racing, and an unsuccessful aircraft factory in Indianapolis. In 1936 he returned to work for General Motors in the Chevrolet Division, as a minor employee.

Chiabrera, Gabriello 1552–1637
Italian poet

Born in Savona and educated at Rome, he served Cardinal Cornaro, but was obliged to leave for revenging himself upon a Roman nobleman. An enthusiastic student of Greek, he skilfully imitated **Pindar** and **Anacreon**, while his *Lettere Famigliari* ('Family Letters') introduced the poetical epistle into Italian. ⌑ E N Girardi, *Esperienza e poesia di Gabriello Chiabrera* (1950)

Chiang Ch'ing See Jiang Qing

Chiang Ching-kuo 1910–88
Taiwanese politician

The son of **Chiang Kai-shek**, he studied in the USSR during the early 1930s, returning to China with a Russian wife in 1937 at the time of the Japanese invasion. After the defeat of Japan in 1945 he held a number of government posts before fleeing with his father and the defeated Guomindang (Kuomintang, or Nationalist Party) forces to Taiwan in 1949. He became Defence Minister (1965–72), and was Prime Minister from 1972 to 1978. He succeeded to the post of Guomindang leader on his father's death in 1975 and became State President in 1978. Under his stewardship, Taiwan's postwar 'economic miracle' continued, but in the political sphere there was repression. During the closing years of his life, with his health failing, he instituted a progressive programme of political liberalization and democratization, which was continued by his successor, **Lee Teng-hui**.

Chiang Kai-shek (Jiang Jieshi) 1887–1975
Chinese general and politician

Born in Fenghua, Zhejiang (Chekiang), he received his military training in Tokyo, Japan, where he met **Sun Yat-sen**, for whom he fought in the 1911 revolution. In 1926 he commanded the army which aimed to unify China, a task which he completed by 1928. Meanwhile he opposed communism and rid the Guomindang (Kuomintang, or Nationalist Party) of its influence. As President of the Republic (1928–31), he consolidated the nationalist regime, but dangerous left-wing splinter groups retained a foothold in several areas, which led to Chiang's ultimate downfall. Head of the executive from 1935 to 1945, he was also Commander-in-Chief of China united against Japanese aggression. He allowed corrupt right-wing elements to dominate the Guomindang, and the split with the Communists was intensified. In 1948 the Guomindang collapsed before the Communist advance and Chiang was forced to withdraw to Formosa (Taiwan). There the Chinese national government, 'White China', trained new forces, aided by the USA. He wrote *Summing up at Seventy* (1957). His second wife, Song Meiling (Mayling Soong, b.1897), was educated at American universities, and distinguished herself in social and educational work, and wrote a number of works on China.

Chiang Tse-min See Jiang Zemin

Chiarelli, Luigi 1884–1947
Italian playwright

Born in Trani, he was a journalist before he took to the stage. He had his first play, *Vita intima* ('Inner Life'), performed in 1909. His great success was *La Maschera e il volta* (1916, 'The Mask and the Face'), a farcical comedy, which was subsequently translated into nearly every European language. ⌑ M Lo Vecchio O Musti, *L'Opere di Luigi Chiarelli* (1942)

Chicago, Judy, originally Judy Gerowitz 1939–
US artist

She was born in Chicago, Illinois, and adopted the name of her home town. A great encourager of women artists, she co-founded the Feminist Art Program at the California Institute of the Arts to provide women artists with a hospitable place to practise their art. She herself works in a variety of media, including not only painting and sculpture but traditionally female-oriented crafts such as needlework. One of her best-known works is a massive multimedia work called *The Dinner Party* (1974–79), which uses place settings at a banquet table to represent important mythical and historic women and to explore their role in Western civilization. Her autobiography, *Through the Flower: My Struggle as a Woman Artist*, was published in 1975.

Chichele, Henry c.1362–c.1443
English prelate and diplomat

Envoy to the Vatican (1405, 1407), he became Bishop of St David's (1408), and Archbishop of Canterbury (1414). He was the founder of two colleges at Oxford (1437): St John's and All Souls.

Chichester, Sir Francis Charles 1901–72
English adventurer and yachtsman

Born in Barnstaple, Devon, and educated at Marlborough, he emigrated to New Zealand in 1919, and became a land agent. He took up flying, and made a solo flight to Australia in a Gipsy Moth plane. He was an air navigation instructor in Great Britain during World War II, then started a map-publishing business. In 1953 he took up yacht racing, and in 1960 won the first solo transatlantic yacht race, with his boat *Gipsy Moth III*, sailing from Plymouth to New York in 40 days. He made a successful solo cicumnavigation of the world (1966–67) in *Gipsy Moth IV*, sailing from Plymouth to Sydney in 107 days and from there back to Plymouth, via Cape Horn, in 119 days. He was knighted in 1967. He wrote *The Lonely Sea and the Sky* (1964) and *Gipsy Moth Circles the World* (1967). □ Anita Leslie, *Francis Chichester* (1975)

Chick, Dame Harriette 1875–1977
English nutritionist
Born in London, she was educated in west London and at University College London (1894–96). In 1905 she gained a position at the Lister Institute, despite calls by some staff to prevent the appointment of a woman. She remained at the Institute for the rest of her long working life, retiring aged 95. After World War I she was sent to Vienna by the British Medical Research Council (MRC) to study nutritional disorders and to investigate rickets, then thought to be infectious. With her colleagues Elsie Dalyell and Margaret Hume, she established that sunlight and dietary cod-liver oil, rich in vitamin D, could eliminate childhood rickets. On her return to London (1922) she made extensive studies into the role of vitamins. She served as secretary of the Accessory Food Factors Committee, established by the MRC and the Lister Institute, which co-ordinated, assessed and publicized research and information on nutritional matters. She became a DBE in 1949.

Chidzero, Bernard Thomas G 1927–
Zimbabwean politician
Educated in Southern Rhodesia (Zimbabwe) and Marianhill in South Africa, he attended Ottawa University and Oxford. He was successively assistant research officer Economic Commission for Africa in Addis Ababa (1961–63), representative of UN Technical Assistance Board in Kenya (1963–66), resident representative UNDP, Kenya (1966–68), director commodities division UNCTAD (1968–77) and deputy president general (1977–80). Elected to the Zimbabwe Senate (1980), he has been Minister of Economic Planning and Development since then. Although not a member of the politburo, he has been the chief architect of Zimbabwe's economic policy and the leading figure among reformists who prevailed over the radicals' wish for a more socialist state.

The Chieftains
Irish folk group
Possibly the best-known folk group in the world, the original band met while members of Seán Ó Riada's Ceoltóirí Cualann orchestra in the late 1950s. They took a low-key approach at first, but the reception their music received eventually saw them become full-time musicians in the early 1970s. They have worked with many artists from other musical areas over the years, including Mike Oldfield, **Van Morrison** and **James Galway**, contributed to a number of film soundtracks, and remain a major concert attraction. The members have varied over the years, but key players include Uillean piper Paddy Moloney, harpist Derek Bell, and flautist Matt Molloy. They influenced important Irish bands like Planxty, The Bothy Band and **De Danaan**.

Chifley, (Joseph) Ben(edict) 1885–1951
Australian politician
He was born in Bathurst, New South Wales. Briefly a federal Labor MP, he fought against 'Big Jack' Lang (1876–1975) in NSW Labor politics in the 1930s and returned to federal politics in 1940, becoming Treasurer under **John Curtin** a year later, and then Minister for Post-War Reconstruction. He became Prime Minister in 1945. His administration was marked by massive white immigration and the Snowy Mountains hydroelectric scheme, and unsuccessful attempts at a national health scheme and nationalization of the airlines and the banks. He was defeated by **Robert Menzies** in 1949.

Child, Francis James 1825–96
US scholar
He was born in Boston, Massachusetts, and graduated from Harvard in 1846. After a year or two spent in Europe, he was appointed Professor of Rhetoric in 1851, and of Anglo-Saxon and Early English literature in 1876. An authority on the ballad, his first work was *Four Old Plays* (1848), but more important were his annotated *Spenser* (5 vols, 1855) and *English and Scottish Ballads* (8 vols, 1857–59).

Child, Julia, *née* McWilliams 1912–
US author and chef
Born in Pasadena, California, she served in the Office of Strategic Services in Ceylon during World War II, and from 1948 to 1954 she and her diplomat husband lived in Paris, where she studied cooking at the Cordon Bleu. In 1951 she and two French partners, Simone Beck and Louisette Bertholle, founded a cooking school, and in 1961 the three women published the classic cookbook *Mastering the Art of French Cooking*. Child has written many other cookbooks and hosted a series of public television programmes, notably *The French Chef* (1963–76), for which she won an Emmy award in 1966. She co-founded the American Institute of Food and Wine in 1982.

Child, Lydia Maria 1802–80
US social campaigner, essayist and novelist
Born in Watertown, Massachusetts, she was a committed campaigner for social and political reform, becoming editor of the *National Anti-Slavery Standard* and publishing many essays on political and social issues. Her book *The History of the Condition of Women in Various Ages and Nations* (1835) suggested women's equal capacity in the workplace, and *An Appeal in Favor of that Class of Americans Called Africans* (1833) was particularly influential for the abolitionist cause. She also published several novels, including *Hobomok* (1824), describing the conflict between the Puritans and Native American tribes in the Massachusetts Bay Colony, *The Rebels* (1825), a romance, *Philothea* (1836), set in Ancient Greece and *A Romance of the Republic* (1867), a 19th-century anti-slavery story.

Childe, (Vere) Gordon 1892–1957
Australian archaeologist
He was born in Sydney. Educated at Sydney University and Oxford, he established a reputation with his first book, *The Dawn of European Civilisation* (1925), a brilliant and erudite work that charted the prehistoric development of Europe in terms of its various peoples and their archaeological cultures. With *The Most Ancient Near East* (1928) and *The Danube in Prehistory* (1929) it established him as the most influential archaeological theorist of his generation. A lifelong Marxist and prodigious traveller and linguist, he was Professor of Archaeology at Edinburgh University (1927–46) and director of the University of London Institute of Archaeology (1946–56). A companionable, eccentric but essentially lonely man, he returned to Australia on retirement, and soon after committed suicide by jumping to his death in the Blue Mountains near Sydney. □ Bruce G Trigger, *Gordon Childe: Revolutions in Archaeology* (1980)

Childers, (Robert) Erskine 1870–1922
Anglo-Irish writer and nationalist
Born in London and educated at Haileybury and Trinity College, Cambridge, he was a clerk in the House of Commons (1895–1910) and served as a volunteer in the Second Boer War (1899–1902). He wrote a popular spy novel about a German invasion of Britain, *The Riddle of the Sands* (1903) and several non-fiction works. In 1910 he devoted himself to working for Irish Home Rule, and used his yacht, the *Asgard*, to bring German arms to the Irish volunteers in 1914. Nonetheless he served in the

Royal Navy in World War I. In 1921 he became a Sinn Féin member of the Irish parliament for County Wicklow and Minister for Propaganda. He opposed the treaty that established the Irish Free State, joined the IRA, but was captured by the Free State authorities and executed in Dublin. One of his sons, Erskine Hamilton Childers (1905–74), became the 4th President of Ireland (1973–74). 📖 A F B Williams, *Erskine Childers: 1870–1922* (1926)

Childs, Lucinda 1940–
US dancer and choreographer
Born in New York City, she studied dance at Sarah Lawrence College, and then later trained with **Merce Cunningham**. A founder member of the experimental Judson Dance Theatre (1962–64), she was influenced by **Yvonne Rainer**, and developed a Minimalist style of choreography, often incorporating dialogue. After a five-year gap she made the first of her 'reductionist pattern pieces' in 1973 and in 1976 performed her own solo material in the **Robert Wilson** and **Philip Glass** opera *Einstein on the Beach*. Since the late 1970s she has worked with other artists in her choreography. *Dance 1–5* was set to a 90-minute score by Philip Glass and film by sculptor and painter Sol le Witt. Other works include *Relative Calm* (1981), *Available Light* (1983) and *Premier Orage* (1984), the year she put her choreography on *pointe* for the first time, as well as *Rhythm Plus* (1991) and *One and One* (1992).

Chinese Gordon See **Gordon, Charles George**

Ch'i Pai-shih See **Qi Baishi**

Chippendale, Thomas 1718–79
English furniture designer
Born in Otley, Yorkshire, he set up a workshop in St Martin's Lane, London, in 1753. He earned a reputation for graceful neoclassical furniture, especially chairs, which he made mostly from mahogany, then newly introduced from South America. His book *The Gentleman and Cabinet Maker's Director* (1754), the first comprehensive trade catalogue of its kind, had a widespread influence on later craftsmen like **George Hepplewhite** and **Thomas Sheraton**. His style became increasingly eclectic and elaborate, including Rococo, Chinese and neo-Gothic. His son Thomas (1749–1822) carried on his business until 1813. 📖 Oliver Brackett, *Thomas Chippendale: A Study of His Life, Work and Influence* (1924)

Chirac, Jacques René 1932–
French Conservative politician
Born in Paris, the son of a banker, he graduated from the École Nationale d'Administration and worked in the Court of Accounts, before joining the government secretariat of President **Georges Pompidou**. In 1967 he was elected to the National Assembly for the Corrèze constituency in central France and proceeded to build up a powerful base there as a department and regional councillor. During the Pompidou presidency (1969–74), Chirac served as a junior secretary in the finance ministry then as Minister for Agriculture and later Minister for Industry, gaining the nickname 'the bulldozer' for his drive and determination. Between 1974 and 1976 Chirac served as Prime Minister to President **Valéry Giscard d'Estaing**, but the relationship was uneasy. On resigning as Prime Minister in August 1976, Chirac went on to establish the new neo-Gaullist Rassemblement (Rally) pour la République (RPR). He was elected Mayor of Paris (1977) and, despite unsuccessfully contesting the first ballot of the 1981 presidential election, emerged as the National Assembly leader for the 'right coalition' during the Socialist administration of 1981–86. Following the 'right coalition's victory in the 1986 National Assembly elections, Chirac was appointed Prime Minister by President **François Mitterrand** in a unique 'co-habitation' experiment. However, he was subsequently defeated by

Mitterrand in the presidential election of 1988. His third attempt to win the presidency at last succeeded in May 1995. During his period of administration he has been harshly criticised for his decision to test nuclear weapons in the Pacific Ocean. 📖 Franz-Olivier Giesbert, *Jacques Chirac* (1987)

Chirico, Giorgio de 1888–1978
Italian artist
Born in Volo, Greece, of Sicilian parents, he worked in Paris, and with **Carlo Carrà** in Italy, where he helped to found the *Valori Plastici* review in 1918. About 1910 he began to produce a series of dreamlike pictures of deserted squares, such as *Nostalgia of the Infinite* (1911, in the Museum of Modern Art, New York). These had considerable influence on the Surrealists, with whom he exhibited in Paris in 1925. His style, with that of **Carlo Carrà**, is often called 'metaphysical painting', a term which he reserved for his work after 1915, which included semi-abstract geometric figures and stylized horses. In 1929 he wrote *Hebdomeros*, a dream novel, but in the 1930s he renounced all his previous work and reverted to an academic style and to a study of the techniques of the old masters. He published his autobiography, *Memorie della mia vita*, in 1945.

Chisholm, Caroline 1808–77
Australian social worker and philanthropist
Born near Northampton, England, she married an officer in the army of the East India Company, based in Madras. In 1838 they settled in Windsor, New South Wales, but two years later Captain Chisholm returned to duty. Concerned at the plight of abandoned and impoverished immigrant women in the colony, Caroline Chisholm, with the approval of Governor **George Gipps**, established an office to provide shelter for the new arrivals, and then set about finding them work. In the 1840s she cared for over 11,000 women and children, thereby helping to alleviate the overcrowding in Sydney. She persuaded the British government to grant free passage to families of convicts already transported, and established the Family Colonization Loan Society, to which in 1852 the New South Wales government voted £10,000 for her work. In 1854 she visited the gold-rush settlements of Victoria and publicized the appalling conditions there, but ill health caused her to return to Sydney, and in 1866 she left for England.

Chisholm, Erik 1904–65
Scottish composer
Born in Glasgow, he studied under **Donald Tovey** and from 1930, as conductor of the Glasgow Grand Opera Society, produced many rarely heard works, including the weighty *The Trojans* by **Hector Berlioz**. In 1945 he was appointed Professor of Music at Cape Town. His works include two symphonies, concertos for piano and violin, other orchestral music and operas.

Chisholm, Shirley Anita St Hill, *née* St Hill 1924–
US politician
Born in Brooklyn, New York City, she became an expert in the education of young children, working as consultant to the New York Bureau of Child Welfare (1959–64). She was elected to the New York State assembly (1964–68) and was elected as a Democrat in 1968, becoming the first black woman member of the House of Representatives. She remained in congress for seven terms, until 1983. She freely voiced her opposition to the Vietnam War, and the House seniority system, and voiced support for the urban poor. In the 1972 Democratic Convention she won a 10 per cent vote for the presidential nomination. She has published *Unbought and Unbossed* (1970) and *The Good Fight* (1973).

Chissano, Joaquim 1939–
Mozambique politician

Born in Chibuto, he joined the National Front for the Liberation of Mozambique (Frelimo) during the campaign for independence in the early 1960s and became secretary to its leader, **Samora Machel**. When internal self-government was granted in 1974 he was appointed Prime Minister. He then served under Machel as Foreign Minister, and on Machel's death in 1986 he succeeded him as President.

Chittenden, Russell Henry 1856–1943
US physiological chemist

Born in New Haven, Connecticut, he went to Sheffield Scientific School of Yale University in 1872. He then studied at the University of Heidelberg. He was appointed Professor of Physiological Chemistry (1882) and director at Sheffield Scientific School (1898). His later work was concerned with toxicology, alcohol and food additives, and he was involved in the provision of scientific evidence in a number of legal cases involving poisoning. His best-known work was about human protein requirements. He experimented on himself and a group of young men, and concluded that men could remain healthy on a diet of c.2,500 calories containing about 50g protein. He hypothesized that various health problems might be the result of diets which are over-rich in protein.

Ch'iu Chin See Qiu Jin

Chiyonofuji, *real name* Akimoto Mitsugu 1955–
Japanese sumo wrestler

Born in Hokkaido, weighing 70kg (154lb) at the age of 15, he was spotted by scout Chiyonoyama, a former Yokozuna and the then master of Kokonoe stable. He joined Kokonoe, worked frantically and made his debut at the Aki Basho in 1970 after gaining 32kg (70lb) in weight. He broke into the top division just five years later. Despite pressure on him to retire aged 30 and after 11 shoulder dislocations, he celebrated his 29th Basho victory aged 34. He is one of sumo wrestling's greatest champions and the second most successful Yokozuna in the sport's 2,000-year history.

Chladni, Ernst Florenz Friedrich 1756–1827
German physicist

Born in Wittenberg, Saxony-Anhalt, of Hungarian extraction, he graduated in law at the University of Leipzig in 1782. Combining music with physical science, he performed a series of acoustical experiments, measuring the variation of the velocity of sound in organ pipes and studying the vibration of strings, rods and plates. When his 'Chladni plates' (pieces of metal or glass clamped at the centre) were sprinkled with sand and forced to vibrate, a surprising diversity of patterns appeared (now known as 'Chladni figures'). He travelled widely throughout Europe performing on two variants of the glass harmonica he had designed: the clavicylinder and the euphonium, and in 1809 published a *Traité d'acoustique*. He was the founder of the science of acoustics.

Chlodwig See Clovis

Chocano, José Santos 1875–1934
Peruvian poet

He was born in Lima. Though not a *modernista* poet, he introduced—as an arch opportunist—*modernismo* to Peru, and at one point his reputation rivalled that of **Rubén Darío** himself. At his best, as in *Oro de indias* (1940,'Gold of the Indies'), Chocano is a genuinely indigenous poet, with full sympathy for the Native Americans, who helped turn Latin-American poetry away from European models and towards its mysterious interior. He was also a bigamist and a murderer. He was imprisoned (1925–27) for

murdering a young critic, Edwin Elmore, who had failed to agree with him—and then left Peru in disgrace. A supporter of **Pancho Villa**, he was then advisor to and apologist for the Guatemalan dictator Estrada Cabrera (the president of the *El presidente* of **Miguel Asturias**), almost executed on the latter's downfall, and finally assassinated on a Santiago tram by a madman. ⌨ L A Sanchéz, *Aladino* (1960)

Choibalsan d.1952
Mongolian revolutionary leader

Originally trained as a lamaist monk, he went to Siberia, where he made contact with Russian revolutionaries. He founded his first revolutionary organization in 1919 and joined up with Sukhe Bator in 1921 to establish the Mongolian People's Revolutionary Party. When Soviet Red Army units entered Urga, the capital of Outer Mongolia (which had broken free of Chinese control in 1912) in 1921 and sponsored the creation of a pro-Soviet government, Choibalsan became a deputy War Minister. In succeeding years he became the dominant leader of the Mongolian People's Republic (formally established in 1924) and had eliminated all his rivals by 1940. His policies were modelled on those of **Stalin**, including the cultivation of a personality cult and harsh treatment of landowners. He was also responsible for the execution of thousands of lamaist monks.

Choiseul, Étienne François, Duc de 1719–85
French politician

A minister of **Louis XV**, he served in the War of the Austrian Succession (1740–48), and, through Madame de **Pompadour**, became lieutenant-general in 1748, and Duc de Choiseul in 1758. He arranged the alliance between France and Austria against **Frederick the Great** of Prussia (1756), and obtained good terms for France at the end of the Seven Years War (1763). He improved the army and navy and developed industry and trade, particularly with India. He had spies in every court, and **Catherine the Great** nicknamed him *Le Cocher de l'Europe* ('Europe's Coachman'). However, Madame **du Barry** alienated Louis from him, and he retired in 1770. ⌨ Rohan Butler, *Choiseul* (1980)

Chomsky, (Avram) Noam 1928–
US linguist and political activist

Born in Philadelphia, Pennsylvania, the son of a distinguished Hebrew scholar and educated at Central High School, Philadelphia, he studied under Zellig S Harris at Pennsylvania, and then went to Harvard. In 1955 he began teaching modern languages and linguistics at the Massachusetts Institute of Technology (MIT), becoming a full professor in 1961, Ferrari P Ward Professor of Foreign Languages and Linguistics in 1966, and Institute Professor in 1976. He is one of the founders of transformational generative grammar, and his book *Syntactic Structures* (1957) began a revolution in the field of linguistics, although his grammatical theories developed first out of his interest in logic and mathematics and were only later applied to the description of natural languages. He views language and other facets of human cognitive behaviour as being the result of innate cognitive structures built into the mind, and is strongly critical of empiricism. Among his other major works on linguistic theory are *Aspects of the Theory of Syntax* (1965), *Cartesian Linguistics* (1966), *The Sound Pattern of English* (1968, with Morris Halle), *Language and Mind* (1968, enlarged edition 1972), *Reflections on Language* (1975), *The Logical Structure of Linguistic Theory* (1975), *Lectures on Government and Binding* (1981), and *Language and Problems of Knowledge* (1987). Politically radical, he was an outspoken opponent of American military involvement in Vietnam, and published *American Power and the New Mandarins* (1969) and *At War with Asia* (1970). He has continued his critiques of American policy with *Peace in the Middle East* (1974), *Human*

Rights and American Foreign Policy (1978), *The Political Economy of Human Rights* (1979, with Edward Herman), *Towards a New Cold War* (1982), *Turning the Tide* (1985), *Deterring Democracy* (1991), *Chronicles of Dissent* (1992) and *Powers and Prospects* (1996). ⊞ John Lyons, *Chomsky* (rev edn, 1977)

Chopin, Frédéric François 1810–49
Polish composer and pianist

Born in Zelazowa Wola, near Warsaw, where his father, a Frenchman, had settled, he first played in public at the age of eight, and published his first work, Rondo in C minor, at 15. From 1826 to 1829 he studied at the Warsaw Conservatory under Elsner, then visited Vienna and Paris (1831), where he became the idol of the salons. On a groundwork of Slavonic airs and rhythms, notably that of the mazurka, Chopin wrote clearly identifiable music, mainly for the piano. His compositions include 50 mazurkas, 27 studies, 25 preludes, 19 nocturnes, 13 waltzes, 12 polonaises, 4 ballades, 3 impromptus, 3 sonatas, 2 piano concertos, and a funeral march. In 1836 he was introduced to **George Sand** by **Franz Liszt**, and lived with her from 1838 to 1847, when they became estranged. He died from tuberculosis.

Chopin, Katherine, *née* O'Flaherty 1851–1904
US novelist, short-story writer and poet

Born in St Louis, Missouri, the daughter of an Irish immigrant and a French-Creole mother, she was well educated at the Sacred Heart convent, made her debut in society and married Oscar Chopin, a Creole cotton trader from Louisiana. It was a happy marriage, scarred only by business failure. After her husband died of swamp fever (1882) she returned with their six children to St Louis where she began to compose sketches of her life in 'Old Natachitoches', such as *Bayou Folk* (1894) and *A Night in Acadie* (1897). This work gives no indication of the furore she was later to arouse with the publication of a realistic novel of sexual passion, *The Awakening* (1899), which was harshly condemned by the public. Thereafter she wrote only a few poems and short stories. Interest in her work was revived by **Edmund Wilson**, and she has since been embraced by feminists as a fin de siècle iconoclast bravely articulating the plight of the 'lost' woman. ⊞ P Seyersted, *Kate Chopin, a critical biography* (1969)

Chorley, Richard John 1927–
English geomorphologist

Born in Minehead, Somerset, and educated at Exeter College, Oxford, he received a Fulbright scholarship to study geology at Columbia University. After various lecturing appointments in North America and the UK, he became a reader (1970–74) at Cambridge, where he was Professor of Geography (1974–94), then emeritus. He is a leader of the group which challenged traditional geography and led to the British phase of the so-called 'quantitative revolution'. He used general system theory in the study of landforms, advocated geography as human ecology and developed the use of models in explanation.

Chosroes or Khosrow I *called* Anushirvan ('Immortal Soul') d.579
Sassanid King of Persia

He ruled Persia (Iran) from 531 and waged war against the Roman Emperor **Justinian I** for 20 years. At home he promoted agriculture, commerce and science.

Chosroes or Khosrow II *called* Parviz ('the Victorious') d.628
Sassanid King of Persia

The grandson of **Chosroes I**, he became king in c.588 and conquered Syria, Palestine, Egypt and parts of Asia Minor (613–19), and almost defeated the Byzantine Empire. However, the Emperor **Heraclius** led a recovery and penetrated Persia (Iran), defeating Chosroes at Nineveh (627), after which he was deposed and executed by his son, Kavadh.

Chou En-lai See **Zhou Enlai**

Chow, Elizabeth Kuanghu See **Han Suyin**

Chowdhury, Eulie 1923–
Indian architect

Educated at the University of Sydney, Australia, she received her Bachelor of Architecture in 1947. She worked in the USA before returning to her native India (1951) to work on **Le Corbusier**'s new Punjab capital, Chandigarh. She worked as senior architect for two periods (1951–63, 1968–70) and then as chief architect, in charge of the second phase of planning (1971–76). She became principal of the Delhi School of Architecture (1963–65), then returned to private practice in 1966, becoming Chief Architect of Harayana State (1970) and of Punjab State (1976), a post she held until her retirement in 1981. The first Indian woman to qualify and be elected to the Royal Institute of British Architects and the Indian Institute of Architects, she had a remarkable career for a woman in post-independence India.

Chrétien, Jean Joseph Jacques 1934–
Canadian politician

A French Catholic, born in Shawinigan, Quebec, he studied law at Laval University, Quebec City, and was first elected to parliament in 1963, holding several ministerial positions in the next two decades. He opposed the Quebec separatist movement and was instrumental in securing the new Canadian constitution in 1982. In 1990 he won the leadership of the Liberal Party, and after his party's victory at the polls in 1993, he became Prime Minister. In 1995 he responded to renewed Quebec separatist sentiment by proposing to give the province greater autonomy within the Canadian federation.

Chrétien de Troyes d.c.1183
French poet and troubadour

Born in Troyes, he was author of the earliest romances dealing with the King **Arthur** legend. The greatest of the French medieval poets, he was a member of the court of the Countess Marie de Champagne, daughter of **Louis VII**, to whom he dedicated his metrical romance of courtly love, *Yvain et Lancelot*. His other romances were *Érec et Énide* (c.1160), *Cligès* (c.1164), and the unfinished *Perceval, ou le Conte du Graal* (c.1180, 'Percival, or the Story of the Holy Grail'). His works were popular throughout medieval Europe. ⊞ U T Holmes, *Chrétien de Troyes* (1970)

Christ, Jesus See **Jesus Christ** (panel)

Christaller, Walter 1893–1969
German geographer

Born in Berneck, he was educated at Erlangen and Freiburg. He was an advocate of the method of deductive reasoning and originator of the 'central place theory' (1933) which was inspired by economic theory and arose from a study of tertiary economic functions in southern Germany. Although his ideas were not available in English until the 1960s this approach has been used extensively in the analysis of the spacing and arrangement of central places, and it found practical application as a planning tool in North America and, after World War II, in the north-east polders of the Netherlands.

Christensen, Harold 1904–89 and Lew 1909–84 and Willam 1902–
US dancers

Born in Utah to a family of music and dance teachers of Danish-Mormon descent, all three toured as children in vaudeville, performing classical dance. In 1932 Willam opened a ballet school in Portland, Oregon, from which emerged the Portland Ballet. In 1938 he became ballet master and choreographer of the San Francisco Opera Ballet, which within a few years became an independent institution for which he choreographed the first full-length US productions of *Coppelia*, *Swan Lake* and *The Nutcracker*. In 1951 he established in Salt Lake City the first dance department at a US university and, in the following year, the Utah Ballet, which since 1968 has been called Ballet West. Harold, having studied at the School of American Ballet and danced for various companies on both sides of the USA, retired from the stage in 1946 and took charge of the San Francisco Ballet School until 1975. As a member of the American Ballet, Lew was cast as the first US Apollo in George Balanchine's ballet of the same name. In 1938 he choreographed *The Filling Station*, a piece of contemporary Americana, for Ballet Caravan, and in the mid-1940s was on the faculties of the School of American Ballet and New York City Ballet. In the 1950s he replaced Willam as director and choreographer of the San Francisco Opera Ballet, a position he held virtually until his death.

Christian (Kings of Denmark) See Kristian

Christian, Charlie (Charles) 1916–42
US jazz guitarist
Remembered for his melodic facility and harmonic boldness as the father of the modern jazz guitar, he was born in Dallas, Texas, and learned to play a home-made 'cigar box' guitar as a child. His skill developed to the point where he was hired by bandleader Benny Goodman in 1939, playing mainly with the Goodman sextet rather than the big band. Christian pioneered the use of the amplified guitar as a solo instrument, freeing the guitar from a purely rhythmic role. He was one of the musicians whose after-hours sessions at Minton's Playhouse in New York laid the basis of the bebop revolution.

Christian, Fletcher c.1764–c.1794
English seaman
Born in Cockermouth, Cumberland, he joined the navy at the age of 18. He was selected by Captain William Bligh as midshipman on the *Britannia* sailing to the West Indies in 1787, and as first mate on the *Bounty* on a voyage to Tahiti to collect bread-fruit plants for the West Indies. Christian was the ringleader of the mutiny against Bligh on the *Bounty* in 1789. After the mutiny Christian, along with eight other mutineers, including John Adams, took refuge on Pitcairn Island with some Tahitian men and women, where they founded a settlement. Christian was probably killed by the Tahitians, along with three other mutineers.

Christianissimus, Doctor See Gerson, Jean de

Christiansen, Jens Anton 1888–1969
Danish physical chemist
Born in Vejle, he graduated from the Polytechnic in Copenhagen in 1911 and became assistant to Søren Sørensen at the Carlsberg Laboratory. From 1915 he was at the University of Copenhagen, holding various positions including the chairs in inorganic chemistry (1931–48) and physical chemistry (1948–59). His many honours included honorary membership of the Chemical Society. Christiansen's doctoral thesis (1921) contained fundamental contributions to chemical kinetics, including a collision theory of unimolecular reactions and a rate theory essentially equivalent to the later transition state theory, both of which have provided the basis for later, more sophisticated treatments. Because the thesis was in Danish, the scientific world has been slow to appreciate Christiansen's role in these matters. His later researches

embraced work on a wide variety of solution processes, including the decomposition of hydrogen peroxide, periodic reactions and enzyme reactions.

Christie
Family of London auctioneers
The founder of the firm, in 1766, was James (1730–1803), two of whose sons were James (1773–1831), antiquary and auctioneer, and Samuel Hunter (1784–1865), student of magnetism and Professor of Mathematics at Woolwich (1806–50). Samuel's son, Sir William Henry Mahoney (1845–1922), was Astronomer Royal (1881–1910).

Christie, Dame Agatha Mary Clarissa, pen name also Mary Westmacott, née Miller 1890–1976
English writer
She was born in Torquay, Devon, and educated at home. Under the surname of her first husband (Colonel Christie, divorced 1928), she wrote more than 70 classic detective novels, including those featuring the popular characters Hercule Poirot, a Belgian detective, and Miss Jane Marple, a village spinster. Between December 1953 and January 1954, she achieved three concurrent West End productions, *The Spider's Web*, *Witness for the Prosecution* and *The Mousetrap*, which continued its record-breaking run into the 1990s. Her best-known novels are *The Mysterious Affair at Styles* (1920), first featuring Poirot, *The Murder of Roger Ackroyd* (1926), *Murder at the Vicarage* (1930), introducing Miss Marple, *Murder on the Orient Express* (1934), *Death on the Nile* (1937), *And Then There Were None* (1941) and *Curtain* (1975), in which Poirot met his end. She also wrote under the pen name Mary Westmacott. 📖 R Barnard, *A Talent to Deceive* (1975)

Christie, John Reginald Halliday 1898–1953
English murderer
Born in Yorkshire, he was hanged for the murder of his wife, and confessed to the murder by strangulation of five other women. He also confessed to the murder of Mrs Evans, wife of Timothy John Evans, who had lived in the same house. Evans had been convicted and hanged for the murder of his infant daughter in 1950. He had been charged at the same time with the murder of his wife, but the case never came to court. After a special inquiry by the Home Office, and several debates in the House of Commons, no definite conclusion was reached, but there was an increasing body of opinion that Evans was technically innocent and that Christie had killed both Mrs Evans and the child. In 1966 Evans was granted a free pardon. The trial of Christie played an important part in altering legislation affecting the death penalty.

Christie, Julie Frances 1940–
English actress
Born in Chukua, Assam, India, she studied at the Central School of Music and Drama and worked in repertory before a television serial, *A for Andromeda* (1962), led to a small film role in *Crooks Anonymous* (1962). Her portrayal of a free spirit in *Billy Liar* (1963) brought further offers and in 1965 she won an Academy Award for *Darling*. Judged to typify 'Swinging Sixties' London, she also enjoyed further success with *Dr Zhivago* (1965), *Far From the Madding Crowd* (1967) and *The Go-Between* (1971). Romantically linked with Warren Beatty, she co-starred with him in *McCabe And Mrs Miller* (1971, Academy Award nomination), *Shampoo* (1975) and *Heaven Can Wait* (1978). Other notable films include *Don't Look Now* (1973), *Heat and Dust* (1982) and *Power* (1985). Committed to a number of political causes, she has been an infrequent performer in recent years but returned to the stage in *Old Times* (1995) and to the cinema in *Dragonheart* (1996) and *Hamlet* (1996).

Christie, Linford 1960–
English athlete

He was born in St Andrews, Jamaica, and his family moved to the UK when he was a child. He was educated at Wandsworth Technical College. He made his international debut for Great Britain in 1980 and has since made over 50 appearances. He was, however, a relatively slow developer as a sprinter, only establishing himself as the fastest man outside the USA in 1986, the year of his 100 metres victory in the European championships. In 1988 he won the silver medal at the Seoul Olympics. He won silver again in 1990, and in the same year won a gold medal at the Commonwealth Games. The pinnacle of his career came at the Barcelona Olympics of 1992, when he captained the British men's team and won the 100 metres gold medal, displacing **Allan Wells** as the oldest man to take the title. In 1993 he won the 100 metres gold medal in the world championships in Stuttgart. He failed to retain his Olympic title at the 1996 Atlanta Olympics, after being disqualified after two false starts. He holds a number of records, including the world record for the 200 metres indoor event. His autobiography, *Linford Christie*, appeared in 1989.

Christine de Pisan c.1364–1431
French poet

Born in Venice, Italy, she was the daughter of an Italian who was court astrologer to **Charles V**. She was brought up in Paris, and by 1389 was widowed with three children and no money. Obliged to call upon her literary talents, she produced between 1399 and 1415 a number of impressive works in both prose and verse, including a biography of **Charles V** for Philippe, Duke of Burgundy; *Cité des dames* ('City of Women'), a translation from **Boccaccio**; and *Livres des trois vertus* ('Books of the Three Virtues'), an educational and social compendium for women. She also wrote love poems. She is noteworthy for her defence of the female sex, hitherto a target for satirists. Saddened by the misfortunes of the Hundred Years War she withdrew to a nunnery about 1418 but wrote in celebration of **Joan of Arc**'s early successes in 1429. 🕮 E M D Robineau, *Christine de Pisan. Sa vie, ses œuvres* (1883)

Christison, Sir (Alexander Francis) Philip 1893–1993
Scottish general and ornithologist

Born in Edinburgh, he was educated at the Edinburgh Academy and at Oxford. During World War I he won the MC and bar, and he later occupied several staff posts in India. An inspired corps commander in Burma during World War II, he inflicted the first heavy defeat on the Japanese forces at Arakan in 1944, and as Commander-in-Chief Allied Land Forces South-East Asia he completed the defeat of the Japanese a year later. For this achievement he was knighted in the field, a unique occurrence. In the aftermath of the war he commanded the allied forces in the Netherland East Indies, where he was instrumental in ending the fighting between the Dutch and the Indonesians. After his retirement in 1949 he led a busy public life and was particularly interested in the promotion of Gaelic culture. A noted ornithologist, he published *Birds of Northern Baluchistan* (1940) and *Birds of Arakan* (1946). He died in 1993 shortly after celebrating his one hundredth birthday.

Christo, originally Christo Javachef 1935–
US avant-garde artist

Born in Gabrova, Bulgaria, he studied art first in Sofia (1951–56), then briefly in Vienna (1957), before moving to Paris in 1958. In 1964 he moved permanently to New York. His work typically consists of wrapping objects, buildings, and landscapes in fabric, or of creating 'assemblages', for example of stacked oil drums. His homage to **Claude Monet**, *Surrounded Islands* (1980–83), transformed eleven small islands off Florida into water lilies using six million square feet of pink fabric. Between 1984 and 1991 he succeeded in linking Japan and the USA by means of *The Umbrellas*, an event involving the simultaneous opening of innumerable blue and yellow umbrellas and which survives only in its documentation. His *Wrapped Reichstag* in 1995 was the biggest piece of artwork of the year involving the covering of the German parliament building with 100,000 sq m of silver fabric and nearly 16km of blue rope.

Christoff, Boris 1914–93
Bulgarian bass-baritone

Born in Plovdiv, he studied law in Sofia, and singing in Rome and Salzburg. His debut recital was in Rome (1946). He also sang at La Scala, Milan (1947), and at Covent Garden, London (1949), and from 1956 in the USA. He was particularly impressive in the role of Boris Godunov.

Christophe, Henri, also known as Henri I 1767–1820
Haitian ruler

Born a slave on the island of Grenada, he joined the black insurgents in Haiti against the French in 1790, and with his gigantic stature and courage, proved an able lieutenant to their leader **Toussaint Louverture**. In 1802 he defended Cape Haiti against the French. In 1806 he assassinated the Emperor Jean Jacques I (**Jean Jacques Dessalines**) whose cruelty and debauchery had alienated all his supporters, and in 1807 was appointed President. After years of civil war, he was proclaimed King of Haiti as Henri I in 1811, and ruled with enthusiasm; but his own avarice and cruelty led to an insurrection, and he shot himself.

Christopher, St 3rd century AD
Syrian Christian

He was, according to tradition, a man some 3.5m tall. His name in Greek (*Christophoros*) means 'Christ-bearing', which gave rise to the legend that he had carried the Christ-child (and all the weight of the world's sin) across a river. He is said to have suffered martyrdom under the Emperor **Decius** (c.250AD). He is the patron saint of travellers, and his feast day is 25 July. 🕮 Peggy C Walwin, *St Christopher Today and Yesterday* (1968)

Christopher, Warren Minor 1925–
US diplomat

Born in Scranton, North Dakota, he began his career as a lawyer, then entered public service and was deputy Secretary of State in the **Carter** administration (1977–81), helping to negotiate the release of the hostages from Iran in 1981. As Secretary of State (1993–96) under President **Bill Clinton**, he furthered Middle East peace talks and struggled to find a diplomatic solution to the fighting in Bosnia.

Christophersen, Henning 1939–
Danish politician

Born in Copenhagen, he was a member of the Danish parliament (Folketinget) (1971–84), and led the Danish Liberal Party (Venstre) (1978–84). During 1978 and 1979 he was Minister of Foreign Affairs and from 1982 to 1984 was Minister of Finance and deputy Prime Minister. He became a member of the EC Commission in 1984 and was a vice-president until 1995, in charge of economic and monetary co-operation.

Christus, Petrus c.1420–1473
Netherlandish painter

Often said to have been the pupil or assistant of **Jan van Eyck**, in both style and composition he continued that painter's tradition, though in a simplified manner. Christus became the major Bruges master in 1444, on settling there three years after van Eyck's death. He may have visited Italy (he has been identified as the 'Piero di Burges' referred to in a Milanese document of 1457) and was perhaps an important source for the transmission of the Eyckian technique to Italian painters, in particular Antonello da Messina.

Christy, Edwin P(earce) 1815–62
US entertainer

He was born in Philadelphia, and began his Christy Minstrels show singing with two assistants at a public house in Buffalo (1842), but steadily increased the reputation of his troupe and the success of his 'black-face' ministrelsy in New York and London. Many of his songs were commissioned from Stephen Foster. Credited with establishing the minstrel show's format, he retired in 1855. He threw himself out of a window during the Civil War.

Christy, Henry 1810–65
English banker and archaeologist

With Édouard Lartet he explored the Palaeolithic caves of the Dordogne from 1862, excavating in the valley of the Vézère at Gorge d'Enfer, La Madeleine, Le Moustier and Les Eyzies.

Chrysander, Friedrich 1826–1901
German musical historian

A biographer and editor of Handel, he founded the Handel Society in 1856.

Chrysippus c.280–c.206BC
Stoic philosopher

Born in Soli, Cilicia, Asia Minor, he went to Athens as a youth and studied under Cleänthes to become the third and greatest head of the Stoa. Only fragments remain of over 700 works in which he developed the Stoic system into what became its definitive and orthodox form.

Chrysler, Walter Percy 1875–1940
US automobile manufacturer

Born in Wamego, Kansas, he started his working life as an apprentice in a Union Pacific Railroad machine shop. He worked his way up to become plant manager with the American Locomotive Company, but left in 1912 to become works manager of Buick Motor Company at half the salary. By 1916 he had become president, but resigned (1919) to become a director of Willys-Overland and Maxwell Motor Company (1921). This became the Chrysler Corporation in 1925. He introduced the Plymouth motor car and designed the first high compression engine. His autobiography, *The Life of an American Workman*, was published in 1937.

Chrysoloras, Manuel c.1355–1415
Greek scholar

Born in Constantinople (Istanbul), he was the first to transplant Greek literature into Italy. About 1391 he was sent by the Byzantine emperor, Manuel II Palaeologus, to England and Italy to seek assistance against the Turks, and in 1397 he settled at Florence and taught Greek literature. He was afterwards employed by Pope Gregory XII in an attempt to promote a union of the Greek with the Roman Church, and in 1413 went to the Council of Constance, where he died. His chief work was a Greek grammar, *Erotemata* ('Questions'). His nephew, John Chrysoloras, also taught Greek in Italy.

Chrysostom, St John c.347–407AD
Syrian churchman, and one of the Doctors of the Church

Born in Antioch, he was named from the Greek meaning 'golden-mouthed', due to his eloquence. He spent six years as a monk in the mountains, but illness forced his return in AD381 to Antioch, where he was ordained, and gained his reputation as a great religious orator. In 398 he was made Archbishop of Constantinople, where he carried out many reforms, but his reproof of vices caused the Empress Eudocia (wife of Arcadius) to have him deposed and banished (404), after which he moved from one place to another. His works are *Homilies*, *Commentaries* on the whole Bible, part of which have perished, *Epistles*, *Treatises* on Providence, the Priesthood, etc, and *Liturgies*. His feast day is 27 January.

Chubb, Charles 1772–1846
English locksmith

Born in London, he patented improvements in 'detector' locks, originally (1818) patented by his brother, Jeremiah, of Portsea. He was in the hardware business in Winchester and Portsea, before settling in London. Under his son, John Chubb (1816–72), further patents were taken out.

Chudleigh, Elizabeth, Countess of Bristol and Duchess of Kingston 1720–88
English courtesan and bigamist

Beautiful but illiterate, she had several liaisons at court before secretly marrying naval lieutenant, Augustus John Hervey, brother of the 2nd Earl of Bristol, in 1744. Having concealed the birth and death of a son, she obtained a separation from her husband, and later, when courted by the 2nd Duke of Kingston, she denied the first marriage on oath and married him in 1769. On being left heiress to the duke's estates in 1773, she was accused of bigamy by his nephew and found guilty in 1776. In the following year her marriage to Hervey, who had now succeeded his brother as 3rd Duke of Bristol, was declared valid. She was the prototype of Beatrix Esmond in William Makepeace Thackeray's *Henry Esmond* and *The Virginians*.

Chulalongkorn, Phra Paramindr Maha, also called Rama V 1853–1910
King of Siam (Thailand)

Born in Bangkok, he was the son of King Mongkut, and the model for the best-selling novel *Anna and the King of Siam*, which was subsequently adapted for stage and screen as *The King and I*. He was educated by English teachers, acquiring Western linguistic and cultural skills, after which he went, as traditionally prescribed, to a Buddhist monastery, where he remained until the age of 20, having ceremonially succeeded his father (1868). His ambitious structural reforms reduced arbitrary government and provincial autonomy, and he introduced conscription and compulsory primary education. He toured India and Indonesia, abolished slavery, freed his subjects from approaching him on hands and knees, proclaimed liberty of conscience, built schools, hospitals, roads and railways, and followed his father in extending the armed forces. He standardized the coinage, introduced posts and telegraphs, and established a police force and sanitary and electrical systems in Bangkok. He sent his crown prince to study in Great Britain, visited Queen Victoria, and ultimately paid for his westernization by being forced to accept treaties with France (weakening his power in Laos and Cambodia) and with Great Britain (removing his rule over four Malayan states). His reign was the longest in Thai history.

Chunder Sen, Keshub 1838–84
Indian Hindu reformer

Born in Calcutta, he received a traditional Brahmin education. He was the chief developer after 1858 of the Theistic society called the Brahma Samaj of India, which originated with Rammohun Roy. He visited Europe in 1870.

Chun Doo-Hwan 1931–
South Korean soldier and politician

Born in Taegu in Kyongsang province, he trained at the Korean military academy and at the US Army Infantry School. After President Park Chung-Hee's assassination in October 1979, he took charge of the Korean Central Intelligence Agency (KCIA) and led the investigation into Park's murder. He assumed control of the army and the government after a coup in 1979. In 1981 he was

Churchill, Sir Winston Leonard Spencer 1874–1965
English statesman

Winston Churchill was born at Blenheim Palace, Woodstock, the eldest son of Lord **Randolph Churchill** and a descendant of John Churchill, 1st Duke of **Marlborough**. Educated at Harrow and Sandhurst, he was commissioned in the 4th Queen's Own Hussars in 1895. He served in the 1897 Malakand and 1898 Nile campaigns and, as a London newspaper correspondent in the Boer War, was captured but escaped with a £25 reward offered for his recapture. In 1900 he entered parliament as a Conservative MP, but crossed the floor of the House to join the Liberal majority in 1906. He was appointed Colonial Under-Secretary, and as President of the Board of Trade (1908–10), he introduced labour exchanges. As Home Secretary (1910), he witnessed the famous Siege of Sidney Street, and as First Lord of the Admiralty from 1910 began strengthening Great Britain's army and navy in preparation for the war with Germany that he foresaw.

He succeeded in rebuilding his reputation after the disastrous Dardanelles expedition of 1915, and **David Lloyd George** appointed him Minister of Munitions in 1917. He was Secretary of State for War and Air from 1919 to 1921, but then found himself out of favour and was excluded from the Cabinet. His warnings of the rising Nazi threat in the mid-1930s and his criticisms of the National Government's lack of preparedness for war went unheeded, but in 1940, **Neville Chamberlain** at last stepped down and Churchill began his 'walk with destiny' as Prime Minister of the coalition that was to see the country through five of the most momentous years in its history.

The loyalty of the British people and the confidence of the allies was crucial in the first two years of the war; in winning both early on, Churchill gained two enormous advantages. In addition, he was the first premier since the Duke of **Wellington** to have first-hand experience of battle, and also, he was an accomplished orator, able to convince the people by a parliamentary statement or radio broadcast, that even in the blackest moments Great Britain would eventually be victorious. Churchill's compassion and loathing of the scale of allied casualties made him impatient for that victory, and in the course of four years he travelled thousands of miles, shaped the 1941 Atlantic Charter, drew an initially reluctant American people into the battle, masterminded the strategy adopted for the Battle of Britain, Alamein and the North African campaign, and, after the enemy had been defeated, contrived with **Franklin D Roosevelt** and **Joseph Stalin** the means of gutting Germany's historic status as an epicentre of territorial ambition.

In the general election of 1945 Churchill was rejected by the British electorate; but by 1951, at the age of 77, he was Prime Minister again. In 1951–52 he vigorously promoted the development of Great Britain's first nuclear weapons. Meanwhile, he set about reconstructing a country economically and physically ravaged by war, and when in 1955 he finally relinquished the premiership to **Anthony Eden** at the age of 81, its postwar recovery was nearly complete.

He was the only Prime Minister ever to be honoured by the attendance of the reigning monarch at No. 10 Downing Street, when **Elizabeth II** dined there with him and his wife Clementine on the occasion of his eightieth birthday. After his death, the public queued for hours to pay homage to their wartime and peacetime leader as he lay in state in Westminster Hall, and tens of thousands lined the route of his funeral procession in a display of affection and respect on a scale that had not been seen since the death of Queen **Victoria**.

Winston Churchill's son Randolph Churchill (1911–68) was a notable journalist and author and a Conservative MP from 1940 to 1945. His grandson, Winston Spencer Churchill (1940–), was elected a Conservative MP in 1970.

📖 Churchill's apparently limitless energy was directed also at writing some of the finest historical and biographical works of the century. They include *Lord Randolph Churchill* (1906), *My Early Life* (1930), *Life of the Duke of Marlborough* (1933–38), *Great Contemporaries* (1937), *History of the Second World War* (6 vols, 1948–54), and *A History of the English Speaking Peoples* (1956–58). In 1953 he was awarded the Nobel Prize for literature.

📖 See also the biography begun by his son Randolph S Churchill and continued by Martin Gilbert, *Winston S Churchill* (8 vols, 1966–88); W Manchester, *The Caged Lion* (1988) and *The Last Lion: Visions of Glory* (1983); and Lady Violet Bonham-Carter, *Winston Churchill: An Intimate Biography* (1965; UK title *Winston Churchill As I Knew Him*).

'I have nothing to offer but blood, toil, tears and sweat.' From a speech in the House of Commons on assuming the premiership, 13 May 1940.

'I have never accepted what many people have kindly said—that I inspired the nation. It was the nation and the race living around the globe that had the lion heart. I had the luck to be called upon to give the roar.' From a speech to both Houses of Parliament, on the occasion of his eightieth birthday (1954).

---

appointed President and retired from the army to head the newly formed Democratic Justice Party (DJP). Under his rule, the country's 'economic miracle' continued, but popular opposition to the authoritarian nature of the regime mounted, which eventually forced his retirement in 1988. Two years later he was allowed to return to live in Seoul.

Chung, Kyung-Wha 1948–
US violinist

Born in Seoul, South Korea, she moved to New York in 1960 and studied at the Juilliard School of Music until 1967, when she made her debut with the New York Philharmonic. Her London debut came three years later. Her sister Myung-Wha (1944–) is a distinguished cellist, and her brother Myung-Whung (1953–) a pianist and conductor who was appointed music director of the new Bastille Opera, Paris, in 1989.

Church, Frederick Edwin 1826–1900
US landscape painter

Born in Hartford, Connecticut, he studied with **Thomas Cole** and became a member of the Hudson River School, painting landscapes that emphasized dramatic effects of light and the grandeur of the natural world. His works include American subjects such as *Niagara Falls* (1857, Corcoran Gallery, Washington DC), but he was also fascinated by exotic places, and in the course of his extensive travels he painted scenes in South America, the Arctic regions and the East.

Church, Sir Richard, *known as* the Liberator of Greece 1785–1873
Irish general

Born in Cork, the son of a Quaker merchant, he ran away from school to join the British army, and was commissioned in the 13th Foot (later Somerset Light Infantry) in 1800. He served in the British and Neapolitan services in the Mediterranean (1808–09) and with Greek troops (1812–43). He took part in the Greek War of Independence (1821–32), and was appointed generalissimo of the Greek insurgent forces in 1827. He led the revolution in Greece in 1815, and was subsequently promoted to general.

Church, Richard Thomas 1893–1972
English novelist, poet and essayist

He was born in London, and until the age of 40 financed his writing by working as a civil servant. This and subsequent periods of his life form the subject of his two autobiographical volumes, *Over the Bridge* (1955) and *The Golden Sovereign* (1957). *The Porch* (1937) was among the best received of his novels, and won the Femina Vie-Heureuse Prize. He also wrote for children. His poetry, as represented in *Collected Poems* (1948), is well disciplined and restrained in both form and content.

Church, William c.1778–1863
US inventor

He devised the first typesetting machine, patented in England in 1822.

Churchill, Arabella 1648–1730
English aristocrat

She was the elder sister of John Churchill, 1st Duke of Marlborough. In 1665 she entered the service of the Duchess of York (**Mary of Modena**), wife of the future **James VII and II**, and soon became James's mistress. She was the mother by James of two daughters and two sons: James Fitzjames (Duke of **Berwick**), and Henry Fitzjames (Duke of Albemarle).

Churchill, Caryl 1938–
English dramatist

Born in London, she was educated in Montreal and at Queen Margaret College, Oxford, where she began writing plays. Her themes include history, the nature of the female spirit, and the effects upon the individual of living in a capitalist and sexist society. *Light Shining in Buckinghamshire* (1976), about the 17th-century Levellers during the English Civil War, brought her work to widespread attention. Other work includes *Cloud Nine* (1979), *Top Girls* (1982), *Fen* (1983), and *Softcops* (1984). In 1987 she had considerable commercial success with *Serious Money*, a rumbustious play in rhyming couplets satirizing the world of the young, get-rich-quick City financial brokers. However, her earlier writing is of greater dramatic quality. Later plays include the phantasmagoric *The Skriker* (1993).

Churchill, Charles 1731–64
English satirical poet

Born in Westminster, London, he was educated at Westminster School and St John's College, Cambridge, but ruined his academic career with a clandestine marriage at the age of 17. He was ordained priest in 1756, and in 1758 succeeded his father as curate of St John's, Westminster, but gave up the church in 1763. His *Rosciad* (1761) had already made him famous and *The Apology* (also 1761) was an onslaught on his critics, particularly **Tobias Smollett**. *The Ghost* (1762) ridiculed Dr **Johnson** and others. He went on to assist **John Wilkes** in *The North Briton*, and ridiculed the Scots in the satire, *The Prophecy of Famine* (1763). For *The Epistle to Hogarth* (1763) the artist retaliated with a savage caricature. Other works include *The Candidate* (1764), *Independence* (1794), *The Journey* (unfinished) and *Dedication*. He died suddenly on a visit to Wilkes in France. 📖 W C Brown, *Poet, rake and rebel* (1953)

Churchill, John See **Marlborough, 1st Duke of**

Churchill, Lord Randolph Henry Spencer
1849–95
English politician

Born in Blenheim Palace, he was the third son of the 7th Duke of Marlborough. He entered parliament in 1874 and became conspicuous in 1880 as the leader of a group of Conservatives known as the Fourth Party. He was Secretary for India (1885–86), and for a short while Chancellor of the Exchequer and Leader of the House of Commons. His powers rapidly diminished by syphilis, he resigned after his first budget proved unacceptable, and thereafter devoted little time to politics. He was the father of **Winston Churchill**. 📖 Winston Churchill, *Lord Randolph Churchill* (new edn, 1952)

Churchill, Randolph Frederick Edward Spencer 1911–68
English journalist

Born in London, the son of Sir **Winston Churchill**, he was educated at Eton and Christ Church, Oxford. He served in World War II in North Africa and Italy and in the Middle East as an intelligence officer on the general staff. He was Conservative MP for Preston (1940–45). He wrote *The Rise and Fall of Sir Anthony Eden* (1959), and published two volumes (1966, 1967) of a full-length biography of his father.

Churchill, Sarah, Duchess of Marlborough, *née* Jennings 1660–1744
English aristocrat

In 1673 she entered the service of the Duke of York (the future **James VII and II**), and became a close friend of his younger daughter, Princess (the future Queen) **Anne**. After the Glorious Revolution of 1688, when **William III** supplanted James II on the throne, she and her husband, John Churchill, 1st Duke of **Marlborough**, tried to draw Anne into Jacobite intrigues for the restoration of her father. After Anne became queen, Sarah, who was beautiful, but fiery and headstrong, dominated her household and the Whig ministry. Queen Anne broke with the Marlboroughs in 1711, and Sarah was replaced by her cousin, Mrs **Abigail Masham**. She had two daughters: Henrietta, who married (1698) Sidney, 1st Earl of **Godolphin**, and Anne, who married (1700) a son of the 2nd Earl of **Sunderland**. After her husband's death (1722) she devoted herself to the completion of Blenheim Palace, quarrelling with the architect, Sir **John Vanbrugh**.

Churchill, Winston 1871–1947
US historical novelist

He was born in St Louis, Missouri and trained at the US Naval Academy at Annapolis, Maryland before concentrating on writing. His works include *Richard Carvel* (1899) and *The Crisis* (1901), and show a significant insight into the workings of political life, which Churchill knew at first hand as New Hampshire delegate to the Republican National Convention (1904) and Progressive Party candidate for governorship (1912). 📖 R W Schneider, *The Life and Thought of Churchill* (1976)

Churchill, Sir Winston Leonard Spencer See panel p396

Churchward, George Jackson 1857–1933
English locomotive engineer

Born in Stoke Gabriel, Devon, he was chief mechanical engineer of the Great Western Railway from 1902 to 1921. Although not a great innovator he showed rare judgment in combining the best features of British and foreign locomotive practice in his designs, such as the 4-6-0 Star series introduced in 1906, which was the outstanding British express locomotive for the next 20 years. His use

Cicero, Marcus Tullius 106–43BC
Roman orator, statesman and man-of-letters

Cicero was born at Arpinum in Latium into a wealthy equestrian family that was distantly related to **Gaius Marius**. At Rome he studied law and oratory, Greek philosophy, and Greek literature. He saw military service in the Social War of 90–88BC under Pompeius Strabo, the father of **Pompey the Great**. His first important speech (*Pro Roscio Amerino*), in 80BC, was the successful defence of a client against a favourite of the dictator **Sulla**. After a visit to Athens (where he met his future friend and correspondent **Titus Pomponius Atticus**), and a tour in Asia Minor, he was elected quaestor (76), thereby qualifying for membership of the senate, and obtained an appointment in Sicily. At the request of the Sicilians he undertook his brilliant impeachment of the corrupt governor **Gaius Verres** in 70; Verres abandoned his defence after Cicero's first speech (*actio prima*), but Cicero completed and published the long *actio secunda*, which further enhanced his reputation.

In these speeches, Cicero made clear his support for Pompey and the supremacy of the senate. In 66 he became praetor, and supported in a great speech (*Pro Lege Manilia*) the appointment of Pompey to conduct the war with **Mithridates VI** of Pontus. In 63 he held the consulship, and foiled the plot of **Catilina** after the elections for 62, in which Catilina was unsuccessful a second time; the senate voted on the death penalty for the conspirators, and Cicero had the sentence carried out immediately. The 'father of his country' (*pater patriae*, as **Marcus Cato** called him) was for a brief time the great man of the day. His great political ambition, not achieved, was the 'harmony of the orders' (*concordia ordinum*, ie of the senatorial and equestrian classes).

Then the tide turned against him. In 59 Cicero had declined an invitation to join the triumvirate of Pompey, **Caesar** and **Crassus**. He was now without real support, and his enemies exploited the situation by accusing him of having violated the constitution, since a Roman citizen could not be put to death except by the sentence of the people in regular assembly. **Publius Clodius**, an old adversary of Cicero and tribune in 58, brought in a popular bill outlawing anyone who had put a Roman citizen to death without trial. Cicero took refuge at Thessalonica; he was condemned to exile, and his house at Rome and his country houses at Formiae and Tusculum were plundered.

But in 57 the people with Pompey's support almost unanimously voted his recall. In his subsequent speeches he tried to secure compensation for himself and his supporters, such as P Sestius, whom he defended against a charge of rioting brought by Clodius (d.52BC) (*Pro Sestio*, 56). However, he was no longer a power in politics; and, nervously sensitive to the fluctuations of public opinion, he could not decide between Pompey and the aristocracy and **Caesar** and the new democracy. He hoped for the breakdown of the triumvirate, but this hope was dashed when the arrangement was renewed at a conference at Luca. Although he ultimately inclined to Caesar, he lost the esteem of both parties, being regarded as a trimmer and time-server. In 52 he composed his speech (*Pro Milone*) in defence of Milo, who had killed Clodius in a riot; but the court was packed with the supporters of Clodius, and Cicero lost his nerve, to his subsequent great mortification; Milo was condemned and exiled. Next year Cicero was in Asia, as Governor of Cilicia. In 49–48 he was with Pompey's army in Greece, but after the defeat at Pharsalia (48) he threw himself on Caesar's mercy.

In 46 Cicero divorced his wife Terentia, to whom he had been married for 30 years, and married his ward Publilia. In 45 his daughter Tullia died, leaving Cicero overwhelmed with grief. Later he divorced Publilia. These personal catastrophes, combined with the realization that Caesar's supremacy meant the end of good republican government, forced him to withdraw from public life and take refuge in his writing. In 46–44 he wrote most of his chief works on rhetoric and philosophy, living in retirement and brooding over his disappointments.

In 43, after Caesar's death, his famous speeches against **Marcus Antonius**, the *Philippics*, were delivered, and cost him his life. As soon as Antony, Octavian and **Lepidus** had formed a second triumvirate, they proscribed their enemies, and Cicero's name was high on the list. Old and feeble, he fled to his villa at Formiae, pursued by the soldiers of Antony, and was overtaken as he was being carried in a litter. With calm courage he put his head out of the litter and bade the murderers strike. He was in his sixty-third year.

As orator and pleader Cicero stands in the first rank; of his speeches the most famous are those against Verres and Catiline; equally fine is his speech in defence of Milo. As a politician, though in the end defeated, he was one of the outstanding figures of the late Republic. He is also remembered as an essayist and letter-writer, especially for his essays *De Senectute* ('On Old Age'), *De Amicitia* ('On Friendship') and *De Oficiis* ('On Duty'). His extensive correspondence (notably with Atticus) is one of the principal sources of knowledge of the politics of his time (in some years we are told of events from day to day), and his prose style was a model for the orators of the next four centuries.

📖 E Rawson, *Cicero: A Portrait* (1983); D Stockton, *Cicero: a Political Biography* (1971) .

> *Salus populi suprema est lex.*
> 'The good of the people is the chief law.'
> From *De legibus*, bk 3, ch.3.
> *O fortunatam natam me consule Romam.*
> 'O lucky Rome, born when I was consul.'
> Cicero's only extant line of poetry, quoted by **Juvenal**, *Satires* 10, line 122.

---

of longer stroke, longer valve travel, tapered boiler and higher steam pressure showed the way to other designers in the first half of the 20th century.

Churchyard, Thomas 1520–1604
English soldier and writer

He was born in Shrewsbury, Shropshire, and served in Scotland, Ireland and the Low Countries under the Earl of Surrey. He published many verse and prose pieces, the best-known of which are *The Legend of Shore's Wife* (1563, in *A Mirror for Magistrates*), and *Worthiness of Wales* (1587).

Churriguera, Don José 1650–1725
Spanish architect

Born in Salamanca, he was royal architect to **Charles II** and developed the extravagant style which has come down to us as Churri-gueresque. He designed Salamanca Cathedral. His brothers Joaquin (1674–1720) and Alberto (1676–1750) were also architects.

Chu Ta See **Zhu Da**

Chu Teh See **Zhu De**

Chuter-Ede, Baron See **Ede (of Epson), Baron Chuter**

Ciano, Galeazzo, Conte di Cortellazzo
1903–44
Italian politician and diplomat
Born in Livorno, Tuscany, the son of an admiral, he took part in the March on Rome and had a successful diplomatic career from 1925 to 1930, when, after marrying Mussolini's daughter, he was rapidly promoted to Under-Secretary for Press and Propaganda and a seat on the Fascist Grand Council. In 1936 he became Foreign Minister. He negotiated the Axis Agreement with Germany and supported the Italian invasion of Albania (1939) and the Balkans (1940–41), but was unenthusiastic about the invasion of France, especially after Hitler's unilateral and early declaration of war. Dismissed as Foreign Minister (February 1943), Ciano was one of those who called for the Duce's resignation in July 1943. He fled to Germany after his father-in-law's arrest but was blamed by Hitler and Joachim von Ribbentrop for Mussolini's defeat and was executed.

Ciaran
The name of two Irish 6th-century saints
One was the founder of Clonmacnoise, and the other Bishop of Ossory.

Cibber, Mrs, *née* Susannah Maria Arne   1714–66
English actress and singer
She was born in London, the sister of the composer Thomas Arne. An accomplished contralto, she made her stage debut in her brother's *Rosamund* (1733), and the following year married Theophilus Cibber (1703–58), the son of Colley Cibber. Handel wrote parts for her in his *Messiah* and *Samson*. Thereafter she turned to drama and played opposite David Garrick at Drury Lane with enormous success.

Cibber, Colley   1671–1757
English actor and dramatist
He was born in London, the son of the Schleswig sculptor, Caius Gabriel Cibber (1630–1700), and educated at Grantham School, Lincolnshire. In 1690 he joined the Theatre Royal in Drury Lane, and there, except for short intervals, spent his whole career. His first comedy, *Love's Last Shift* (1696), established his fame both as dramatist and actor. From 1711 he was joint manager of Drury Lane. In 1730 he was appointed Poet Laureate. *An Apology for the Life of Mr Colley Cibber, Comedian* (1740), his autobiography, gives a vivid picture of the theatre of his time.

Cicero, Marcus Tullius   See panel p398

Cid, El, *properly* Rodrigo or Ruy Díaz de Vivar or Bivar, *also called* El Campeador   c.1043–1099
Spanish hero
He was born in Burgos and immortalized as 'El Cid' (The Lord) or 'El Campeador' (The Champion). Both soldier of fortune and patriot, he was constantly fighting. In 1081 he was banished and served both Spaniards and Moors. He besieged and captured Valencia from the Moors (1093–94) and became its ruler. The favourite hero of Spain, he has inspired many legends, poems, and ballads, as well as Corneille's *Le Cid* (1636).

Cidenas   4th century BC
Babylonian astronomer
The head of an astronomical school at Sippra, he discovered the precession of the equinoxes.

Cierva, Juan de la   1895–1936
Spanish aeronautical engineer
Born in Murcia, he originally trained as an engineer, but was interested in aviation from an early age. In 1923 he invented the autogiro, a predecessor of the helicopter.

Cilea, Francesco   1866–1950
Italian composer of operas
Born in Palmi, Calabria, he was director of the Naples Conservatorio (1916–36). He wrote several operas, of which the best-known is *Adriana Lecouvreur* (1902).

Cilento, Lady Phyllis Dorothy, *née* McGlew
1894–1987
Australian medical practitioner, author and broadcaster
Born in Sydney, she was educated at Adelaide University. After postgraduate work in Asia, Europe and the USA, she became lecturer in mothercraft and obstetric physiotherapy at the University of Queensland. Her life's work, for which she was awarded the Member of the Order of Australia, was devoted to family planning, childbirth education, and nutrition, on which subjects she broadcast and wrote many books and newspaper columns. She married Raphael West Cilento in 1920.

Cilento, Sir Raphael West   1893–1985
Australian medical administrator
Born in Jamestown, South Australia, and educated at Adelaide University, he later studied at the London School of Tropical Medicine. He was director of the Australian Institute of Tropical Medicine at Townsville, Queensland, from 1922, director of Public Health and Quarantine in New Guinea (1924–28), director-general of Health and Medical Services for Queensland (1934–45) and sometime Honorary Professor of Tropical and Social Medicine at the University of Queensland. Knighted in 1935, after World War II he served in Germany and New York, and worked with the United Nations from 1946 to 1951.

Cilian or Kilian, St   d.697
Irish apostle
Born in Franconia, he was martyred at Würzburg.

Çiller, Tansu   1946–
Turkish economist and politician
Born in Istanbul and educated in the USA, she married her husband Ozer as a teenager, becoming the first woman in Turkey's recent history to make her husband adopt her surname. She worked for a time as an academic economist and was the youngest professor in Turkey before becoming responsible for government finances when the conservative True Path Party took power (1991). In 1993 she was elected head of the Party and the first woman Prime Minister of Turkey. Despite the collapse of the Turkish lira, the stockmarket crash, and the rise of inflation, her premiership was approved to continue in the municipal elections of 1994. In 1995 the government resigned and the ensuing general election was won by the Welfare Party, though it failed to get enough seats to govern alone, and Çiller was acting Prime Minister in the coalition until 1996, when she became deputy Prime Minister and Foreign Minister. A formidably tough leader, she promised pro-European constitutional reforms concerning human rights, ethnic self-expression (though the Kurdish rebellion continued) and democratization.

Cimabué, Giovanni   c.1240–c.1302
Italian painter
Born in Florence, he is famous chiefly as the teacher of Giotto. He was the first artist to move away from the stylized and rigid conventions of Byzantine art. In doing so, he paved the way for his pupil's humanistic naturalism which in turn forms the basis of Italian art. He is mentioned by Dante as having his reputation eclipsed by Giotto. Early critics attribute the famous *Rucellai Madonna* to him, but this is now generally believed to be by Duccio. Cimabué is known to have been in Rome in 1272 and is documented as having worked on the mosaic figure of Saint John in the apse of Pisa Cathedral in 1302. He also executed several important works in the Lower Church of San Francesco at Assisi.

Cima da Conegliano, Giovanni Battista
c.1460–1508
Venetian religious painter

Born in Conegliano, he was strongly influenced by Giovanni Bellini. His *David and Jonathan* is in the National Gallery, London.

Cimarosa, Domenico 1749–1801
Italian composer of operas

Born in Aversa, he studied music at Naples, and produced his first opera there in 1772. In 1789 he was summoned to St Petersburg by Catherine the Great, in 1792 to Vienna; and in 1793 he returned to Naples, where his comic opera, *Il Matrimonio segreto* (1792, 'The Secret Marriage'), was repeated 70 times.

Cimon c.507–c.450BC
Athenian soldier and politician

His father was Miltiades the Younger, the conqueror at Marathon. He fought at the Battle of Salamis (480BC) and from 476 was in supreme command of the Delian League in the patriotic struggle against the Persians. He is most famous for his destruction of a Persian fleet and army at the River Eurymedon (c.476). He led an unsuccessful expedition to support the Spartans during the Helot uprising in 462, and was dismissed and ostracized in 461. He was recalled in 454, and may have been instrumental in obtaining a five-year armistice with Sparta. He died at the siege of a town in Cyprus.

Cincinnatus, Lucius Quinctius fl.460BC
Roman soldier

He was a favourite hero of the old Roman republic. In 460BC he was made consul, and two years later dictator. The story goes that when the messengers came to tell Cincinnatus of his new dignity they found him ploughing on his small farm. He rescued the consul Minucius, who had been defeated and surrounded by the Aequi, and 16 days later he laid down his dictatorship and returned to his farm.

Cineas d.270BC
Greek politician

He was born in Thessaly. The friend and minister of Pyrrhus, the King of Epyrus, he was said to be the most eloquent man of his time.

Cinna, Lucius Cornelius d.84BC
Roman politician

He supported Gaius Marius. Sulla, after driving Marius from Rome, and before setting out against Mithradates VI, allowed Cinna to be elected consul on his swearing not to disturb the existing constitution. No sooner, however, had he entered office (87BC) than he impeached Sulla, and agitated for Marius' recall. Cinna and Marius declared themselves consuls after a cruel massacre, but Marius died a few days later, and Cinna was killed by his own disaffected troops in 84. During his fourth consulate his daughter Cornelia had been married to Julius Caesar.

Cione, Andrea de See Orcagna

Cione, Andrea del See Verrocchio, Andrea del

Cipriani, Giambattista 1727–85
Italian historical painter

Born in Florence, in 1755 he accompanied Sir William Chambers to London, where his graceful drawings, engraved by Francesco Bartolozzi, gained great popularity. He was a member of the St Martin's Lane Academy and in 1768 was elected a foundation member of the Royal Academy.

Citrine of Wembley, Walter McLennan Citrine, 1st Baron 1887–1983
English trade union leader

Born in Wallasey, Cheshire, he became an electrician. He held office in the Electrical Trades Union (1914–23) and was General Secretary of the TUC (1926–46). From 1928 to 1945 he was president of the International Federation of Trades Unions, and was a member of the National Coal Board and chairman of the Miners' Welfare Commission (1946–47). Knighted in 1935 and created a peer in 1946, he became chairman of the Central Electricity Authority in 1947. A skilled trade-union diplomat, he was one of the more significant figures of the postwar social-democratic 'managerial revolution'.

Citroën, André Gustave 1878–1935
French engineer and motor manufacturer

Born in Paris, he was responsible for the mass production of armaments during World War I. After the war he applied these techniques to the manufacture of low-priced small cars. In 1934 he became bankrupt and lost control of the company which still bears his name.

Civilis, Claudius or Julius fl.69–70
Dutch folk-hero, from Roman times

He was one of the favoured Batavian tribe who took advantage of the imperial crisis after Nero's fall to lead his people into revolt in alliance with the Germans (especially the Frisians) and then also the Gauls. He seems to have been sufficiently Romanized to win over troops and captains, but Vespasian, once master of Rome, despatched Petillius Cerialis to end the revolt. He refused terms of surrender, but the Gauls and Roman mutineers were overawed and he was defeated by the Romans at Trier in 70, and after further fighting fell back on sea-protected Batavia.

Cixi (Tz'u Hsi), *known as* the Old Buddha
1835–1908
Dowager Empress of China

The daughter of a minor Manchu mandarin, she was presented as a concubine to the Manchu Emperor Xianfeng (Hsien-Feng) and on his death (1861) became regent, initially to her infant son, Tongzhi (T'ung-chih), and then, following his death (1874), to her nephew Guangxu (Kuang-hsü), despite a dynastic custom which forbade women to reign. A conservative force within the Chinese court and an inveterate intriguer, she worked to frustrate the country's late 19th-century modernization programme. She remained dominant even after Guangxu (1871–1908) formally assumed imperial power (1889) and from 1898, after the emperor had attempted to promote far-reaching reform, she confined him to the palace. In 1900 she helped foment the anti-foreigner Boxer agitation, and a day before her own death, she organized the murder of Guangxu. 📖 Marina Warner, *Dragon Empress: The Life and Times of Tz'u hsi, Empress Dowager of China: 1835–1908* (1972)

Cixous, Hélène 1937–
French academic and feminist

Born in Algiers, she was educated at the Lycée Bugeaud there, moving to France in 1955 where she began to teach while taking degrees in English. In 1965 she became an assistant lecturer at the Sorbonne and took an active part in the student uprisings of 1968. Later, as Professor of Literature at the University of Paris VIII-Vincennes, she established experimental literature courses. Her work is mostly concerned with the relationship between psychoanalysis and language, especially in its significance for women, and in exploring the links between the writer and reader. She encourages the expression in language of female sexuality and has become associated with a theory called 'écriture féminine' (feminine writing). Her work includes *Dedans* (winner of the 1969 Prix Médicis), *Neutre* (1972), *Angst* (1979), the essays *Le Rire de la Méduse* (1976,

'The Laugh of the Medusa') and *Le Sexe ou la Tête* (1976, 'Castration or Decapitation'), and the play *Portrait de Dora* (1976, Eng trans *Portrait of Dora*, 1991).

Claiborne, Craig 1920–
US food critic and cookery writer

Born in Sunflower, Missouri, he was food editor of the *New York Times* and has published cookery books such as *Craig Claiborne's Memorable Meals* (1985).

Claiborne, Liz 1929–
US fashion designer

Born in Brussels, Belgium, she studied fine art in Belgium and France before moving to the USA and winning a *Harper's Bazaar* design competition. Turning to fashion design, she worked with Omar Kiam in New York City and designed for the Youth Guild Inc, before founding her own company with her husband in 1976. Her medium-priced, ready-to-wear collections, targeted at working women, have made her company one of the largest and most successful womenswear firms in the world. Her trademark practical, wearable separates appeal to a mostly young, fashion-conscious public. The company went public in 1981 and Liz Claiborne retired in 1989, though the company continues.

Clair, René, *pseudonym of* René Lucien Chomette 1898–1981
French film director

Born in Paris, he established his reputation with avant-garde films like *Paris qui dort* (1923, *The Crazy Ray*) and *Entr'acte* (1924), and developed a gift for ironic, light comedy in a string of successful films made in France, and later in the USA, including *La Proie du vent, Un Chapeau de paille d'Italie* (1927, *The Italian Straw Hat*), *Paris* (1930), *Le Million* (1931), *Quatorze juillet* (1933, *July 14th*), *The Ghost Goes West* (1935) and *It Happened Tomorrow* (1944). He returned to France in 1946, and his final film was *Les Fêtes Galantes* (1965).

Clairaut, Alexis Claude 1713–65
French mathematician

Born in Paris, he was admitted to the French Academy of Sciences at the age of 18. He worked on celestial mechanics, including the figure of the Earth and the motion of the Moon. He took part in an expedition to Lapland to determine the shape of the Earth, which verified Isaac Newton's theory of gravity, and he successfully computed the date of the first return of Halley's comet in 1759. His analysis of the motion of the Moon won him a prize of the St Petersburg Academy, and helped establish Newton's theory of an inverse square law for gravity, both among experts and the public at large. He also wrote a popular elementary work on geometry which was only superseded at the end of the century.

Clairemont, Claire 1798–1879
English mistress of the poet Lord Byron

When she was three years old, her mother married William Godwin, widower of Mary Wollstonecraft. This union provided Claire with a step-sister, Mary Godwin (see Mary Shelley), whom she accompanied when Mary eloped with Shelley in 1814. On their return to London, Claire had a love affair with Byron, which resulted in the birth of their daughter, Allegra, in 1817. However Byron removed Allegra from her mother's care because he disapproved of her methods of raising children. Allegra died in a convent near Ravenna at the age of five and Claire lived abroad for the rest of her life.

Clairon, Mademoiselle, *stage name of* Claire Josèphe Hippolyte Léris de La Tude 1723–1803
French actress

Born into poverty in Condé-sur-l'Escaut, she first appeared on stage in 1736 with the Comédie-Italienne. She had a fine singing voice, and joined the Opéra in Paris in 1743, but quickly reverted to her original pursuit of acting, this time with the Comédie-Française. She became the leading tragic actress of her day, and is credited with developing both a new style of acting which moved beyond the stiff formal gestures and speech of established practice, and a greater concentration on costume which reflected something of the play, rather than simply ostentatious display. She quit the professional stage in 1765, acting only in private theatres thereafter, and died in poverty in Paris.

Claparède, Édouard 1873–1940
Swiss psychologist and educationist

He was born in Geneva, and after studying there and in Leipzig and Paris, he founded the journal *Archives de psychologie* (1901). As professor at Geneva from 1908, he was director of the experimental psychology laboratory and in 1912 founded the J J Rousseau Institute for the study of child psychology and educational science. An exponent of Functionalism, he pioneered studies in sleep and problem-solving.

Clapeyron, Bénoit Paul Émile 1799–1864
French civil engineer

Born in Paris, he was educated at the École Polytechnique and the École des Mines. After some time in Russia he returned to France and was principally engaged in the construction of railways and bridges, including the design of locomotives, where he was the first to make use of the expansive action of steam in the cylinder. For the analysis of beams resting on more than two supports he developed the 'Theorem of Three Moments', and in 1834 published an exposition of Sadi Carnot's classic but previously neglected paper on the power and efficiency of various types of heat engine, *Réflexions sur la puissance motrice du feu* (1824, Eng trans *Reflections on the Motive Powers of Fire*, 1890). Clapeyron was elected to the French Academy of Sciences in 1858.

Clapperton, Hugh 1788–1827
Scottish explorer

Born in Annan, Dumfriesshire, he went to sea at the age of 13, and in 1821 was sent with Dixon Denham and Walter Oudney to discover the source of the Niger. They travelled south across the Sahara to Lake Chad in 1823. From there Clapperton went on alone to Sokoto, returning to England in 1825. The journey had thrown light on Bornu and the Houssa country, but the source of the Niger remained unknown, and he set off again from the Bight of Benin in December 1825, travelling north with Richard Lander and others. Most of the party died early on the journey, and although Clapperton and Lander reached Sokoto, Clapperton was detained by the Sultan and died.

Clapton, Eric 1945–
English rock and blues guitarist

Born in London, he was once identified as 'God' by worshipful fans, but is rarely comfortable with the limelight. He publicly concurred with Enoch Powell's controversial views on immigration at a difficult point in his career, but he has been one of the most significant white exponents of black music, particularly the blues. He began his recording career with The Yardbirds and John Mayall's Bluesbreakers, before forming the enormously influential power trio, Cream, with Jack Bruce and Ginger Baker. He sought relative anonymity in the short-lived Blind Faith and Derek and the Dominoes, briefly retired, overcame heroin addiction, and returned with the laid-back *461 Ocean Boulevard* (1974), which established his subsequent middle of the road style. The tragic death of his four-year-old son is commemorated in one of his most successful songs, 'Tears In Heaven' (1992). In 1994, he returned to a straight blues idiom on his *From The Cradle* project. ☐ R Coleman, *Survivor* (1986)

Clare, St 1194–1253
Italian Christian saint

Born in Assisi, the daughter of Count Favorino Scifi, she became a follower of St **Francis of Assisi** at 18. With him and her younger sister she founded the order of Poor Ladies of San Damiano ('Poor Clares', formerly called 'Minoresses'), of which she became abbess. She was canonized in 1255, and in 1958 she was designated patron saint of television by Pope **Pius XII** on the grounds that at Christmas 1252, when she was in her cell at San Damiano, she 'saw and heard' Mass being held in the Church of St Francis at Assisi. She was the elder sister of **St Agnes**. Her feast day is 11 August. ☐ Nesta De Robeck, *St Clare of Assisi* (1951)

Clare, John 1793–1864
English peasant poet

Born in Helpston, Northamptonshire, he was almost without schooling, but studied **James Thomson's** *Seasons*, and then began to write verse. After serving in the Northamptonshire militia (1812–14), in 1817 he published *Proposals for Publishing a Collection of Trifles in Verse* at his own expense, but got no subscribers. It led, however, to the publication of his *Poems Descriptive of Rural Life* (1820), which were well received. His other published works were *Village Minstrel* (1821), *The Shepherd's Calendar* (1827) and *Rural Muse* (1835). He lived in poverty, became insane, and died in an asylum. ☐ J W Tibble and A Tibble, *John Clare: a life* (1972)

Clarence, George, Duke of 1449–78
English nobleman

Born in Dublin, Ireland, he was the third son of Richard, Duke of **York**, and brother of **Edward IV** and **Richard III**. He was created Duke of Clarence on Edward's accession (1461). He married Isabella, elder daughter of Richard Neville, Earl of **Warwick**, against Edward's wishes (1469), and supported Warwick against his brother in the brief restoration of **Henry VI** (1470), but deserted to his brother's side (1471). He quarrelled with his other brother, Richard, Duke of Gloucester, over Richard's marriage to his sister-in-law Anne Neville (1472), but was later reconciled. In 1478 he was impeached by his brothers for treason, and secretly executed. According to tradition, he was put to death in the Tower of London, drowned in a butt of malmsey wine. Despite his traditionally bad historical reputation, he had many of the good qualities of his time.

Clarendon, Edward Hyde, 1st Earl of 1609–74
English statesman

Born in Dinton, near Salisbury, he sat in the Short Parliament of 1640 and the Long Parliament, where he criticized **Charles I's** unconstitutional actions and supported the impeachment of the Earl of Strafford. In 1641 he broke with the revolutionaries and became a royal adviser, and when the Civil War broke out he followed the monarch to Oxford. On the King's defeat in 1646 he joined Prince Charles (later **Charles II**) in Jersey. In 1651 he became chief adviser to Charles II in exile and on the Restoration he was created Earl of Clarendon. He further increased his influence by marrying his daughter Anne to the Duke of York in 1660. He introduced the 'Clarendon Code' to ensure the supremacy of the Church of England but his moderate policies were opposed by the extremists. He lost the confidence of Charles II when he criticized his private life, and the disasters of 1667, when the Dutch sailed up the Medway, confirmed his downfall. He was

exiled to Rouen where he died, but was buried in Westminster Abbey, London. ☐ B H G Wormald, *Clarendon: Politics, History and Religion, 1640–1660* (1951)

Clarendon, George William Frederick Villiers, 4th Earl of 1800–70
English politician

Born in London, he studied at Cambridge and entered the diplomatic service when young. In 1833 he was appointed ambassador in Madrid, where he employed his great influence in helping Espartero to establish a constitutional government. In 1838 he succeeded his uncle as 4th Earl, and in 1840 was made Lord Privy Seal under Viscount **Melbourne**. When the Whigs fell (1841) he became an active member of the Opposition, but supported Sir **Robert Peel** and his own brother, Charles Pelham Villiers, in the abolition of the Corn Laws. He became president of the Board of Trade under Lord **John Russell** in 1846 and from 1847 to 1852 was Irish viceroy. His impartiality helped to reconcile party exasperations, though it did not avert the hatred of the Orangemen. Secretary of State for Foreign Affairs (1853), he incurred the responsibility for the Crimean War, and John Roebuck's resolution in 1855 cost him his office, which he resumed at Lord **Palmerston's** request. He was Foreign Secretary again in 1865 and 1868.

Claretie, Jules, *properly* Arsène Arnaud Claretie 1840–1913
French novelist

He was born in Limoges. While a schoolboy in Paris he published a novel, and he soon became a leading critic and political writer. His short story *Pierrille* (1863) was praised by **George Sand**. His novels also were generally popular. During the Franco-German War he sent a series of remarkable letters to the *Rappel* and *Opinion nationale*, and acquired the materials for a later series of bright and vigorous anti-German books. His first success on the stage was with his Revolution plays, *Les Muscadins* (1874, 'The Coxcombs'), *Le Régiment de Champagne* (1877) and *Les Mirabeau* (1878), and in 1885 he became director of the Comédie-Française. ☐ G G de Cherville, *Jules Claretie* (1883, in French)

Clarin See **Alas, Leopoldo**

Clark, Alan Kenneth McKenzie 1928–
English Conservative politician and historian

The son of the cultural historian Baron **Kenneth Clark**, he was educated at Eton and at Christ Church, Oxford. After leaving university he trained as a barrister and was elected Conservative MP for Plymouth Sutton in 1974. Between 1989 and 1992 he was Minister of State at the Ministry of Defence but failed to achieve Cabinet rank. He returned to politics in 1997 on being elected MP for Kensington and Chelsea, the seat of the deposed MP Sir Nicholas Scott. As a military historian he has written *The Donkeys* (1961), a study of British military leadership in World War I, and *Barbarossa* (1965), an examination of the Nazi invasion of Russia in 1941. His *Diaries* (1993) are a frequently indiscreet record of his political career.

Clark, (John) Grahame Douglas 1907–95
English archaeologist

He was born in Shortlands, Kent, and educated at Marlborough and Peterhouse, Cambridge. He taught at Cambridge from 1935, serving as Disney Professor of Archaeology (1952–74), and also became Master of Peterhouse (1973–80). His *Archaeology and Society* (1939) and *World Prehistory* (1961, 1977) pioneered the use of the archaeological record to document the economic and social life of prehistoric communities. Books such as *Prehistoric Europe: The Economic Basis* (1952) also played a major role in moving prehistory away from typology and encouraging the newly emergent discipline of environmental archaeology. Of his many excavations, the most famous is that of the Mesolithic hunting settlement of the mid-8th millennium BC at Star Carr near Scarborough, revealed 1949–51. His *Archaeology at Cambridge and Beyond* (1989) is partly autobiographical.

Clark, (Charles) Manning Hope 1915–91
Australian historian and writer
Born in Burwood, New South Wales, he was educated at Melbourne Grammar School, and Melbourne and Oxford universities. In 1949 he became the first Professor of Australian History at the Australian National University, Canberra. His *Select Documents in Australian History* (2 vols, 1950–55) and *Sources of Australian History* (1957) established his scholarly reputation. His strong republican views colour his *History of Australia* (6 vols, 1962–88) which was abridged into one volume in 1993. His partly autobiographical fiction *Disquiet and Other Stories* (1969) was republished with additional material as *Manning Clark: Collected Short Stories* in 1986, and he wrote a contentious biographical essay, *In Search of Henry Lawson* (1978). The first volume of a projected autobiography, *The Puzzles of Childhood*, was published in 1989, followed in 1990 by *The Quest for Grace*.

Clark, Jim (James) 1936–68
Scottish racing driver
Born in Berwickshire, and educated at Loretto School in Musselburgh, he won his first motor race in 1956, and became Scottish Speed Champion in 1958 and 1959. In 1960 he joined the Lotus team as a Formula One driver, and thereafter won the world championship in 1963 and 1965. Also in 1965 he became the first non-American since 1916 to win the Indianapolis 500. Of his 72 Grand Prix races, he won 25, breaking the record of 24 held by **Juan Fangio**, and took pole position 33 times. He was killed during a practice for a Formula Two race at Hockenheim, in Germany. 📖 Graham Gauld, *Jim Clark Remembered* (1975)

Clark, Joe (Charles Joseph) 1939–
Canadian politician
Born in High River, Alberta, and educated at Alberta and Dalhousie universities, where he was politically active, he worked for a short period as journalist and university lecturer. He was elected to the Federal Parliament in 1972 and four years later became leader of the Progressive Conservative Party (PCP). He defeated **Pierre Trudeau** in 1979 to become Canada's youngest Prime Minister, but was himself defeated a year later. In 1983 he was replaced as party leader by **Brian Mulroney** who, as Prime Minister in 1984, made Clark Secretary of State for External Affairs. In the last two years of the Mulroney administration he was Minister for Constitutional Affairs. From 1993 to 1996 he was the UN representative for Cyprus.

Clark, Josiah Latimer 1822–98
English electrical engineer
Born in Marlow, Buckinghamshire, he patented a pneumatic delivery tube in 1854, and made important inventions in connection with submarine cables. He also invented a single-lens stereo-camera.

Clark, Kenneth Bancroft 1914–
US psychologist
Born in the Panama Canal Zone and raised in Harlem, he became the first African-American to gain a permanent professorship at City College of New York and to serve on the New York State Board of Regents (1966–86). He is best known for his writings on the detrimental effects of school segregation, and his 1950 report on the subject was cited in the US Supreme Court decision, *Brown* v. *Board of Education*, in 1954. His books include *Dark Ghetto* (1965) and *A Possible Reality* (1972).

Clark, Kenneth MacKenzie Clark, Baron
1903–83
English art historian
Educated at Winchester and Trinity College, Oxford, he worked in Florence with **Bernard Berenson** and became an authority on Italian Renaissance art. He was keeper of the department of fine art at the Ashmolean Museum (1931–33), director of the National Gallery, London (1934–45), Slade Professor of Fine Art at Oxford (1946–50, 1961–62) and Professor of Art History at the Royal Academy (1977–83). He was a major cultural influence on British life, and was chairman of the Arts Council (1953–60), and chairman of the Independent Television Authority (1954–57) at the launch of commercial television in the UK. He wrote several books, including studies on **Leonardo da Vinci** (1935, 1939) and **Piero Della Francesca** (1951), and two surveys, *Landscape into Art* (1949) and *The Nude* (1955). He achieved fame with his pioneering television series, *Civilisation* (1969), which stimulated widespread popular interest in art.

Clark, Mark Wayne 1896–1984
US soldier
He was born in Maddison Barracks, New York, and graduated at West Point in 1917. He was designated as Commander II Corps under General **Eisenhower** for the invasion of North Africa, but subsequently became his deputy. Prior to the Allied landings in North Africa he was secretly landed in Algeria to make contact with friendly French officials, narrowly escaping capture by the Vichy Security Police. He commanded the 5th Army at the Salerno landing (1943) and Anzio, and the capture of Rome (1944) and was much criticized for choosing the latter instead of encircling the German forces. Commanding general of the US Forces in Austria after the war, he ceded nothing to Soviet hectoring. He commanded the US 6th Army in the Far East (1947–49), and relieved **Mathew B Ridgway** in command of UN forces in Korea (1952–53).

Clark, Michael 1962–
Scottish dancer and choreographer
Born near Aberdeen, where he took lessons in Scottish country dancing from the age of four, he went to the Royal Ballet School in London at 13, going on to dance with the Royal Ballet. A move to the Ballet Rambert led to roles in **Richard Alston**'s *Dutiful Ducks* and *Soda Lake*. After studying with **Merce Cunningham** in New York for a short time, he began to choreograph. While developing his own style he worked as a dancer with **Karole Armitage** in the USA, starting his own company there in 1984. His original style incorporates punk, 1960s fantasy, nudity, video, platform shoes and giant hamburgers, but it is his keen, sculptural choreography which makes him one of the most inventive artists today. Major full-length productions include *Our caca phony H. our caca phony H* (1985), *No Fire Escape in Hell* (1986), *Because We Must* (1987), *I Am Curious, Orange* (1988) and *Mmm...Modern Masterpiece* (1992), which combines punk music with **Stravinsky**'s *Rite of Spring*. Commissions include *Swamp* for the Ballet Rambert (1986), and he appeared as Caliban in **Peter Greenaway**'s film *Prospero's Books* (1991).

Clark, Petula, *originally* Sally Owen 1932–
English singer and actress
Born in Epsom, Surrey, she was a child singer, entertaining the troops during World War II, and had her own radio series, *Pet's Parlour* (1943). She made her film debut in *Medal for the General* (1944) and many subsequent film appearances include *Here Come the Huggetts* (1948) and *The Card* (1952). Sustaining an adult career, she became one of Britain's most successful pop singers, earning 10 gold discs, two Grammy awards and enjoying a string of international hits with such songs as 'Downtown' in 1964, and 'My Love' in 1966. Later, increasingly rare, film

appearances include the musicals *Finian's Rainbow* (1968) and *Goodbye Mr Chips* (1969) whilst stage work includes *The Sound of Music* (1981), *Someone Like You* (1987), which she co-wrote, and *Blood Brothers* (1993–94) on Broadway and *Sunset Boulevard* (1995) in London.

Clark, Sir Wilfred Edward le Gros 1895–1971
English anatomist

Born in Hemel Hempstead, Hertfordshire, he qualified in medicine in London in 1916 and served as medical officer in Borneo before returning to teach anatomy at London and from 1934 to 1962 in Oxford. Distinguished for his work on the anatomy of primates and especially the brain, he helped expose in the 1950s the 'Piltdown Man' hoax involving Charles Dawson.

Clark, William 1770–1838
US explorer

Born in Caroline County, Virginia, he joined the army in 1789, and was appointed joint leader with Meriwether Lewis of the successful transcontinental expedition to the Pacific coast and back (1804–06). He later became superintendent of Indian affairs in Louisiana Territory, and then Governor of Missouri Territory.

Clark, William Mansfield 1884–1964
US chemist

Born in Tivoli, New York, he was educated at Johns Hopkins University, where he later became Professor of Physiological Chemistry after some years working in government departments dealing with the dairy industry and public health. His studies of acidity in milk led him to develop, with Herbert Lubs, a reliable range of titration indicators. While working on dyes, he began the investigations of oxidation-reduction systems which continued for the rest of his working life and which contributed largely to our understanding of life processes.

Clarke, Adam 1762–1832
English Wesleyan divine

Born near Portrush, County Antrim, Northern Ireland, of English parents, he was the author of a *Bibliographical Dictionary* (8 vols, 1802–06) and a well-known edition of the Holy Scriptures (8 vols, 1810–26) with a commentary. He denied the eternal sonship of Jesus Christ, though maintaining his divinity, and held that Judas repented unto salvation, and that the tempter of Eve was a baboon.

Clarke, Alexander Ross 1828–1914
Scottish geodesist

He began as an army engineer and was later attached to the Ordnance Survey. He is remembered for his work on the principal triangulation of the British Isles, and for his book *Geodesy* (1880).

Clarke, Sir Arthur C(harles) 1917–
English science fiction writer

Born in Minehead, Somerset, he worked in scientific research before turning to fiction: he was a radar instructor in World War II, and originated the idea of satellite communication in a scientific article in 1945. A prolific writer, he focuses on themes of exploration—in both the near and distant future—and man's position in the hierarchy of the universe. His first book was *Prelude to Space* (1951), and he is credited with some of the genre's best examples—*Rendezvous with Rama* (1973) and *The Fountains of Paradise* (1979). However, his name will always be associated first with *2001: A Space Odyssey* (1968), which, under the direction of Stanley Kubrick, became a highly successful film. He emigrated to Sri Lanka in the 1950s and since 1979 has been Chancellor of the country's Moratuwa University. He was knighted in 1998.

Clarke, Austin 1896–1974
Irish poet and dramatist

Born in Dublin, he was educated at the Jesuit Belvedere College and University College. He spent 15 years in England as a book reviewer and journalist before returning to Dublin in 1937. *The Vengeance of Fionn*, the first of 18 books of verse, was published in 1917. His early verse is influenced by W B Yeats and his fascination with Irish mythology, but he became a technically accomplished poet, satirical and critical of Irish attitudes. *Collected Poems* was published in 1974. He was also a noted playwright and an adherent of verse drama, which he promoted through the Dublin Verse-Speaking Society, formed by him in 1941. His plays, drawing heavily on Irish legend, were collected in 1963. His first novel, *The Bright Temptation* (1932), was banned in Ireland until 1954. His *Twice Round the Black Church* (1962) and *A Penny in the Clouds* (1968) are autobiographical.

Clarke, Bryan Campbell 1932–
English geneticist and evolutionist

Born in Gatley, Cheshire, he was educated at Oxford and taught at Edinburgh University. He became Professor of Genetics at Nottingham University (1971–93) then Research Professor (1993–). Clarke is distinguished for studies of the ecological genetics of terrestrial snails and for his explanation of the evolution of new species on the Pacific Island of Moorea. His major contribution to the understanding of genetical processes in animal populations was in disproving the theory that most inherited variation is neutral to its possessors, thus re-establishing the neo-Darwinian interpretation of evolution in the 1970s. Clarke also developed the concept of frequency-dependent natural selection. He was elected FRS in 1981.

Clarke, Charles Baron 1832–1906
English botanist

Born in Andover, Hampshire, he was educated at Trinity College and Queen's College, Cambridge, where he developed on interest in political economy which was to continue throughout his life. Always a traveller, he was appointed to the Bengal Educational Department in 1865, so beginning his interest in the botany of the Indian subcontinent. From 1865 to 1874 he explored East Bengal and other regions, and in 1874 was transferred to Calcutta which allowed him to collect in the Punjab Himalayas. In 1875 he was stationed at Darjeeling, and in 1876 traversed Kashmir and the Karakoram. Arriving back in England in 1877, he worked at Kew on his collections, by now numbering 25,000. He also wrote some accounts for Sir Joseph Hooker's *Flora of British India*, and assisted Hooker in completing the rest of the Flora. He returned to India in 1883 and made further excursions in Sikkim, Assam and elsewhere. He was an energetic, tireless, careful and exact worker and an ideal collector.

Clarke, Charles Cowden 1787–1877
English Shakespearean scholar

Born in Enfield, Middlesex, where his father kept a school where Keats was a pupil, he formed friendships with Leigh Hunt, Shelley, William Hazlitt, and Charles Lamb. In 1820, he became a bookseller in London and soon a partner as music publisher with Alfred Novello, whose sister Mary Victoria (1809–98), he married in 1828—she compiled a *Concordance to Shakespeare's Plays* (1845). He gave public lectures on Shakespeare and other literary figures, some of which were published as *Shakespeare Characters* (1863), and *Molière Characters* (1865). With his wife he published *Shakespeare Key* (1879), an annotated edition of Shakespeare (1869), and *Recollections of Writers* (1878).

Clarke, David Leonard 1937–76
English archaeologist

Born in Kent, he studied at Dulwich College and at Peterhouse, Cambridge, of which he was a Fellow (1966–76). His spirited teaching and writing—particularly in *Analytical Archaeology* (1967)—transformed European archaeology in the 1970s. Matched in impact only by the work of **Lewis Binford** in the USA, it demonstrated the central importance of systems theory, quantification, and clearly stated scientific reasoning in archaeology, and drew ecology, geography, and comparative anthropology firmly within the ambit of the subject for the first time. *Analytical Archaeologist* (1979) is a collection of his writings, together with the reminiscences of colleagues.

Clarke, Frank Wigglesworth 1847–1931
US geochemist
Born in Boston and educated at Harvard, he became Professor of Chemistry and Physics, first at Howard University (1873–74) and then at the University of Cincinnati (1874–83). As chief chemist to the US Geological Survey (1883–1925), he undertook numerous analyses of rocks and minerals and compiled important lists of fundamental physical and chemical constants. He was simultaneously Honorary Keeper of Minerals at the US National Museum, Washington, where his active interest and painstaking efforts led to the excellence and comprehensiveness of the mineral collection. He completed much work on the recalculation of atomic weights and he was the first to present a consistent theory of the chemical evolution of geological systems. His books include *Data of Geochemistry* (1908) and *The Composition of the Earth's Crust* (1924, with Henry Stephens Washington, 1867–1934). The new uranium mineral clarkeite was named in his honour.

Clarke, Sir Fred 1880–1952
Radical English educationist
Born in Witney, Oxfordshire, then educated at elementary school and technical college, he studied Modern History at Oxford. He became Master of Method at the Diocesan Training College, York (1903), and successively Professor of Education at Hartley University College, Southampton (1906–11), South African College and University of Cape Town (1911–29) and McGill University, Montreal (1929). He was adviser (1935) and director (1936–45) of the Institute of Education, London. He wrote a number of books including *Foundations of History Teaching* (1929), but his really influential work was *Education and Social Change* (1940). Termed 'the **Beveridge** of education', he foresaw the significance of education in the postwar period. As early as 1922 he had regarded **R H Tawney**'s *Secondary Education for All* programme as inadequate. Influenced by the refugee sociologist **Karl Mannheim**, he argued that after World War II the old class-divided education offered in Great Britain would be intolerable, especially at secondary level. His work was a forerunner of the thinking behind the Education Act of 1944.

Clarke, Gillian 1937–
Welsh poet
She was born in Cardiff and educated at the city's University College. Her earliest collections of poems, *Snow on the Mountain* (1971) and *Sundial* (1978), were followed by the more widely-read *Letter from a Far Country* (1982). *Selected Poems* followed in 1985, then *Letting in the Rumour* (1989). She was editor of *The Anglo-Welsh Review* from 1976 to 1984, and since 1987 has been Chair of the Welsh Academy.

Clarke, James Freeman 1810–88
US theologian
Born in Hanover, New Hampshire, he studied at Harvard, became a Unitarian pastor, and in 1841 founded the Unitarian Church of the Disciples at Boston.

Professor of Natural Theology at Harvard from 1867 to 1871, he wrote many books, including *Ten Great Religions* (1871) and *Self-Culture* (1882).

Clarke, Jeremiah c.1674–1707
English composer
Born probably in London, he studied under **John Blow** at the Chapel Royal and became organist of Winchester College in 1692. Vicar-Choral of St Paul's Cathedral from 1695, he followed his master at the Chapel Royal in 1704. The real composer of the *Trumpet Voluntary* long attributed to **Henry Purcell**, Clarke wrote operas, theatre music, religious and secular choral works, and music for harpsichord. An unhappy love affair led to his suicide.

Clarke, Kenneth Harry 1940–
English Conservative politician
From Cambridge he was called to the Bar in 1963 and practised on the Midland Circuit (1963–79). An active member of the progressive Bow Group within the Conservative Party, he entered parliament, as MP for Rushcliffe, Nottinghamshire, in 1970. After junior posts in the **Heath** administration (1971–74) he joined **Margaret Thatcher**'s government in 1979. In 1988 he was appointed Secretary of State for Health, with the task of overseeing a major reform of the National Health Service, becoming Secretary of State for Education and Science (1990–92). Under **John Major** he was Home Secretary (1992–93), then succeeded **Norman Lamont** as Chancellor of the Exchequer (1993–97). After the Conservatives' defeat in the 1997 general election he entered the leadership contest but lost to **William Hague**. 📖 Malcolm Balen, *Kenneth Clarke* (1994)

Clarke, Marcus 1846–81
Australian novelist
He was born and educated in London. Following the collapse of the family fortunes he was sent to Australia, where relatives had held high office, and he contributed to the Melbourne press while working first as a bank clerk and then on sheep stations. As with many of his books, his first novel, *Long Odds* (1860), began life as a serial. He visited Tasmania to study its convict past, and the subsequent articles formed the basis for his best-known book, *His Natural Life* (1874, revised edition as *For the Term of His Natural Life*, 1882, under which title it was filmed and is now best known). His financial problems were temporarily abated by his writing for the stage and press, but he died destitute. Most of his ephemeral work was subsequently collected in *The Selected Works of Marcus Clarke* (1890), and three books of Australian tales published in 1896–97. 📖 B Elliott, *Marcus Clarke* (1958)

Clarke, Martha 1944–
US dancer and choreographer
Born in Baltimore, Maryland, she studied dance as a child and later trained with **José Limón, Alvin Ailey, Charles Weidman** and **Anna Sokolow** at the American Dance Festival in Connecticut and with **Martha Graham**'s associate Louis Horst at New York's Juilliard School of Music. She spent a few seasons in Anna Sokolow's company before moving to Europe. On her return to the USA she became (1972) one of the first female members of Pilobolus, a collectively-run dance-theatre ensemble. As the troupe achieved worldwide popularity, Clarke and dancers Robby Barnett and Felix Blaska formed the trio Crowsnest. Since the mid-1980s, she has concentrated on unclassifiable dance-theatre productions such as *Garden of Earthly Delights* (1984), *Vienna: Lusthaus* (1986), *The Hunger Artist* (1987), *Miracolo d'Amore* (1988, 'Miracle of Love') and *An Uncertain Hour* (1993).

Clarke, Oz Birthdate unavailable
British wine critic and writer

He was educated at Oxford and was an actor in London, working with the Royal Shakespeare Company among others, before turning to full-time writing in 1984. He became wine correspondent for the *Daily Telegraph*, contributes to several other magazines and newspapers, and has regular slots on television and radio. As co-presenter and resident wine expert, with Jilly Goolden, of BBC Television's *Food and Drink Programme*, he is known for the vivid and personal style of his language, and for encouraging more people to drink wine by debunking its élitist imagery. He has published widely on his subject, and his books include at least nine editions of *Oz Clarke's Wine Guide*, *Webster's Wine Guide*, the *Sainsbury's Regional Wine Guides* (1989) and the *Wine Atlas* (1995). He is also the author and presenter of Microsoft's *Wine Guide* (1995), the first CD-Rom on the subject.

Clarke, Ronald William 1937–
Australian athlete

He was born in Melbourne. A notable distance runner, as a youth he was selected to carry the Olympic torch at the Melbourne Games of 1956. At one time he held the world records for three miles, five miles, 10 miles, 3,000, 5,000 and 10,000 metres, but despite holding six world records simultaneously he only came sixth in the 10,000 metres in Mexico City in 1968, and was so badly affected by the altitude that he collapsed on completion of the race and was revived with some difficulty. Although he had the reputation of being a better runner against the clock than against rivals, he lost only 25 of 500 races. He retired in 1970 after the Commonwealth Games, and his performances were found to be all the more remarkable when he was diagnosed as suffering from a leaking heart valve.

Clarke, Samuel 1675–1729
English philosopher and theologian

Born in Norwich, Norfolk, he studied at Cambridge, where he became a friend and disciple of Sir Isaac Newton. He was chaplain to the Bishop of Norwich from 1698, to Queen Anne from 1706, and became rector of St James' Westminster in 1709. His Boyle Lectures of 1704–05 contained his 'Demonstration of the Being and Attributes of God' and expounded the famous 'mathematical' proof of God's existence. His extensive correspondence with Gottfried Leibniz (published in 1717) defended a Newtonian view of space, time and the universe.

Clarke, Thomas James 1858–1916
Irish nationalist and revolutionary

He was born in Hurst Castle, Isle of Wight, where his father was a British soldier. His family emigrated to South Africa when he was a child, and returned to Ireland when he was 10. At the age of 21 he emigrated to the USA, where he became involved in Clan-na-Gael, the clandestine US wing of the Irish Republican Brotherhood, promoting anti-British action. Sent to England in 1883, he was arrested for taking part in the dynamite campaign against London civilians and imprisoned for life. He served 15 years under the most severe conditions, during which time he translated the Bible into shorthand twice. After his release (1898) he wrote *Glimpses of an Irish Felon's Prison Life*, and, once again in the USA, became agent for the remilitarized John Devoy. He married Kathleen Daly, niece of a fellow-dynamiter and fellow-prisoner John Daly (1845–1916), Mayor of Limerick (1899–1901) after his release. Clarke returned to Ireland in 1907 as a US citizen and at his urging the Irish Republican Brotherhood set up a military council. Under Clarke's influence this brought about the Easter Rising of 1916, in which Clarke was a symbolic presence. After the surrender he was court-martialled and shot.

Clarke, William Branwhite 1798–1878
English geologist and clergyman

Born in East Bergholt, Suffolk, he was educated at Dedham and Cambridge, and took holy orders, becoming a practising cleric at Ramsholt (1821–24). He travelled widely in Europe and, after publishing important papers on the geology of Suffolk and Dorset, emigrated to New South Wales. From the time of his arrival until 1844 he was in clerical charge of the area north of what is now Sydney, before becoming Minister of Willoughby (1847–70). He was active in studying geology and mineral reserves and is widely credited as the first to discover gold in Australia in the alluvium of Macquarie (1841). He also was the first to report tin and diamonds. He studied coal deposits and the occurrence of gold in granites, examined the Palaeozoic rocks of the Great Dividing Range and worked on the geology of Tasmania. He was the first to identify Silurian rocks in Australia, and demonstrated the Carboniferous age of the coal-bearing strata of New South Wales. His labours in officially reporting on the geology and economic potential of 108,000 square miles of territory gained him the title 'Father of Australian Geology'.

Clarkson, Thomas 1760–1846
English antislavery campaigner

Born in Wisbech, Cambridgeshire, and educated at St Paul's School, and St John's College, Cambridge, he gained a prize for a Latin essay in 1785 on the question 'Is it right to make slaves of others against their will?', which in an English translation (1786) was widely read. In 1787, in association with William Wilberforce and Granville Sharp, he formed an antislavery society and after the passing of the British antislavery laws (1807) wrote *History of the Abolition of the African Slave trade* (2 vols, 1808). He campaigned for the abolition of slavery in the colonies and saw it attained in 1833. 📖 Ellen Gibson Wilson, *Thomas Clarkson: A Biography* (1989)

Claude, *in full* Claude Le Lorrain, *English* Claude Lorraine, *real name* Claude Gelée 1600–82
French landscape painter

Born near Nancy, by tradition he is believed to have trained as a pastry cook but by about 1613 he was in Italy, where he was apprenticed to Cavaliere d'Arpino and the landscapist Agostino Tassi. In 1625 he returned to Nancy, but in 1627 returned to Rome and soon achieved a distinguished reputation as a landscape painter. Around 1635 he began recording his compositions in a book of drawings, the *Liber Veritatis* (now in the British Museum, London), to guard against copyists. The sources of his landscape style are the romanticized landscapes of the later Mannerists, Adam Elsheimer and the Brils. He is somewhat restricted in his subjects and natural effects and tends to be rather repetitive, but his colour is always harmonious and mellow. He also produced about 30 etchings. Philip Hamerton pronounced *Le Bouvier* ('The Cattleman') 'the finest landscape etching in the world'. He was a major influence on virtually every landscape painter from the 17th to the 19th centuries, including Jean Antoine Watteau, Richard Wilson and J M W Turner. The latter painted his *Dido building Carthage* (London, National Gallery) in emulation of Claude.

Claude, Albert 1899–1983
Belgian biologist and Nobel Prize winner

Born in Longlier, he worked during World War I for British Intelligence, and later as a war veteran was permitted to enter the University of Liège to study medicine, although he had no high school diploma. He studied further at the Cancer Institute in Berlin, and in 1929 went to the Rockefeller Institute for Medical Research in New York to study the possibility that Rous sarcoma (a form of cancer) in chickens is of viral origin. Claude developed cell fractionalization using a high-powered centrifuge, isolating a tumour agent from cancerous cells, and applied the technique to the study of normal cells, separating various 'organelles'—the nucleus, mitochondria and microsomes (later known as ribosomes). In 1942 he began applying electron microscopy to biology, which led to important advances in understanding the structure of cells. In 1949 he became director of the Jules Bordet Institute in Brussels. He shared the 1974 Nobel Prize for physiology or medicine with George Palade and Christian de Duve.

Claude, Georges 1870–1960
French chemist and physicist
Born in Paris, he is noted for his work on gases, and is credited with the invention of neon lighting for signs.

Claudel, Camille 1864–1943
French sculptor
Born in La Fère-en-Tardenois, the daughter of a wealthy civil servant, and sister of the poet Paul Claudel, she decided to become a sculptor at an early age and in 1884 was introduced to Auguste Rodin. She became his student, model and mistress, and produced skilfully executed works which, while close to his, nonetheless show great individuality and vitality, such as *The Waltz* (1895, Musée Rodin, Paris, in bronze). After a fiery relationship, Claudel and Rodin parted company in 1898, but she continued to sculpt, and briefly achieved great renown (c.1900). However, the break with Rodin affected her mental stability and from 1913 until her death she was confined to various institutions.

Claudel, Paul 1868–1955
French poet, essayist and dramatist
He was born in Villeneuve-sur-Fère. He joined the diplomatic service and held posts in many parts of the world. This experience, with the early influence of the Symbolists, adds quality and richness to his work. His dramas, of which the most celebrated are *L'Annonce faite à Marie* (1892, 'The Annunciation'), *Partage de Midi* (1905, Eng trans *Break of Noon*, 1960), *L'Otage* (1909, Eng trans *The Hostage*, 1917) and *Le Soulier de satin* (1921, Eng trans *The Satin Slipper*, 1931), have a Wagnerian grandeur and, in many cases, an anti-Protestant violence that make them too strong for popular taste. His more memorable poetry—*Cinq grandes Odes* (1910, Eng trans *Five Great Odes*, 1967) and *Corona benignitatis anni dei* (1915, Eng trans *Coronal*, 1943)—and the libretti for two operas: *Jeanne d'Arc au bûcher* (1943, 'Joan of Arc at the Stake') by Arthur Honegger and *Christophe Colomb* (1930, Eng trans *Christopher Columbus*, 1930) by Darius Milhaud. His later writings were mainly devoted to biblical exegesis. ⊞ H A Waters, *Paul Claudel* (1970)

Claudian, *properly* Claudius Claudianus AD340–410
Roman poet
Born in Alexandria, Egypt, he was the last of the great Latin poets. He went to Rome in AD395, and obtained patrician dignity by favour of Flavius Stilicho. A pagan, he wrote first in Greek, though he was of Roman extraction. Several epic poems by him, including *The Rape of Proserpine*, panegyrics on Flavius Honorius, Stilicho and others, invectives against Rufinus (c.345–410) and Eutropius, occasional poems, and a Greek fragment, *Gigantomachia*, are still extant. ⊞ J H E Crews, *Claudian as Historical Authority* (1908)

Claudius I, *full name* Tiberius Claudius Drusus Nero Germanicus 10BC–AD54
Fourth Roman emperor
Born in Lyons, he was the younger son of the elder Drusus and nephew of the Emperor Tiberius. His supposed imbecility saved him from execution by Caligula, but he was a great scholar. After Caligula's assassination

(AD41), Claudius was the only surviving adult male of the imperial family, and was proclaimed emperor by the army, against the wishes of the senate. His reign was marked by expansion of the Roman Empire: he created new provinces (Mauretania and Thrace), and inaugurated the conquest of Britain, taking part in the opening campaign in person (43). He tried to integrate provincials in the empire through the extension of Roman citizenship, and, unsuccessfully, to secure the co-operation of the senate in government. A hostile tradition portrays him as a weak personality, too influenced by his freedmen and his wives. His third wife, Valeria Messalina, was notorious, and when she went through a form of public marriage with a young lover, Claudius had her executed (48). He next married his niece, Agrippina, the Younger, who persuaded him to adopt Nero, her son by an earlier husband, although Claudius had a son of his own, Britannicus. Agrippina is believed to have poisoned Claudius with a dish of mushrooms to secure the succession of Nero. ⊞ Vincent M Scramuzza, *The Emperor Claudius* (1940)

Claudius, Appius 5th century BC
Roman decemvir
Consul in 471BC, he was one of a 10-man commission (the decemviri) appointed in 451 in response to popular demand to publish Rome's first code of laws, the so-called Twelve Tables. The commission tried to hold on to power, but was forced to resign by a popular uprising in 449. In subsequent legend he was depicted as a figure of extreme wickedness.

Claudius, Appius (Caecus) fl.312BC
Roman statesman and law-giver
He was regarded by the Romans as being the father of Latin prose and oratory. He was censor in c.312–307BC, and held several other important posts. He promoted many reforms giving privileges to the plebeians, and built the Aqua Appia aqueduct and the Via Appia highway (the Appian Way).

Clausewitz, Karl Marie von 1780–1831
Prussian soldier
Born in Burg, he entered the Prussian army in 1792 and saw active service in the Revolutionary War (1793–94). He served as a Russian staff officer (1812), but returned to the Prussian service and in 1815 became Gneisenau's Chief of Staff, taking part in the Waterloo campaign. From 1818 to 1830 he was director of the General War School in Berlin. His great treatise *Vom Kriege* (1833, 'On War') has had a major impact on strategic studies. ⊞ Roger Parkinson, *Clausewitz* (1971)

Clausius, Rudolf Julius Emmanuel 1822–88
German physicist
Born in Köslin, Prussia, he studied at the University of Berlin (1840–44), where his predominant interest changed from history to science. After receiving a PhD (Halle, 1847), he taught physics at the Royal Artillery and Engineering School, Berlin (1850), the Zurich Polytechnicum (1855), Würzburg University (1867), and Bonn University (1869). In 1850 he postulated that heat cannot of itself pass from a colder body to a hotter one (the second law of thermodynamics) in order to validate Sadi Carnot's theorem of perfect engines whilst rejecting the caloric theory. After considering the dissipation of energy which Lord Kelvin had suggested in 1852, he introduced the term 'entropy' (1865) in such a way that dissipation was equivalent to entropy increase, thus enabling the two laws of thermodynamics to be stated succinctly. He studied electrolysis, calculated the mean speed of gas molecules, ignoring collisions (1857), and introduced the concepts of mean free path and effective radius (1858).

Claussen, Sophus Niels Christen 1865–1931
Danish poet

Born in Heletoft, he gave up law to concentrate on journalism and writing. He lived for many years in France, where he met the Symbolists, later translating Baudelaire, Heinrich Heine and Shelley. His best-known poem, 'Rejseminder' ('Recollections of a Journey'), establishes the characteristic tone of erotic reverie which runs through *Naturbørn* (1887, 'Children of Nature'), his first book. Later works were less realistic in detail and the poems in *Djaevlerier* (1904, 'Demonism') are overtly Symbolist and psychological. His complete works were published in seven volumes in 1910. ▭E Frandsen, *Sophus Claussen* (1950)

Clavell, James du Maresq 1924–94
US novelist, film producer and director

Born in Sydney, Australia, he served during World War II and was a prisoner-of-war in Changi Jail, Singapore. The clash of East and West runs through his 'Asian Saga' which covers three and a half centuries, beginning in the year 1600 with *Shogun* (1975), *Tai-Pan* (1966) and *Gai-Jin* (1983). *King Rat* (1962), *Noble House* (1980) and *Whirlwind* (1986) bring the story up to the year 1979. He has also published an edition of Sun Tzu's 4th-century BC classic, *The Art of War*. His work in film includes scripting the epic war movies *The Great Escape* (1960, from the book by Paul Brickhill) and *633 Squadron* (1963). He is now based in New York and became a naturalized US citizen in 1963.

Claverhouse, John Graham of See **Dundee, 1st Viscount**

Clavijero, Francisco Xavier 1721–87
Brazilian Jesuit priest and historian

Born in Veracruz, he wrote a valuable Italian *History of Mexico* (trans 1787).

Clay, Cassius Marcellus See **Ali, Muhammad**

Clay, Henry 1777–1852
US politician

Born in Hanover County, Virginia, the son of a Baptist preacher, at the age of 15 he became an assistant clerk in the chancery court of Virginia. In 1797 he was licensed to practise law, and went to Lexington, Kentucky. He entered the Lower House of Congress in 1811, and was chosen as Speaker, a post he filled for many years. As leader of the 'War Hawk' group he was active in bringing on the War of 1812 with Great Britain, and was one of the commissioners who arranged the Treaty of Ghent which ended it (1814). Because of his course regarding the Missouri Compromise of 1820 he was given the nickname of 'the great pacificator'. He was US Secretary of State (1825–29) and US senator (1831–42). In 1832 and 1844 he was an unsuccessful candidate for the presidency. The compromise of 1850 between the opposing free-soil and pro-slavery interests, by which he attempted to avoid civil war, was largely Clay's work. ▭ Glyndon G Van Deusen, *The Life of Henry Clay* (1937)

Clayton, John fl.1650
English scientist

Educated as a theologian, he first discovered that gas could be distilled from crude coal and stored, but did not realize the commercial importance of his discovery. He also carried out work on stained glass.

Clayton, John Middleton 1796–1856
US politician

Born in Sussex County, Delaware, he practised as a lawyer, then became a US senator in 1829. While Secretary of State from 1849 to 1850 he negotiated the Clayton–Bulwer Treaty with Great Britain.

Cleänthes c.331–232BC
Greek Stoic philosopher

Born in Assos, Troas, Asia Minor, he studied under **Zeno of Citium** in Athens for 19 years and succeeded him as head of the Stoa in 262BC. His own contributions to Stoicism were especially in the areas of theology and cosmology, and the best known of his surviving works is the *Hymn to Zeus*.

Cleary, Jon Stephen 1917–
Australian novelist

Born in Sydney, he served in the Middle East and New Guinea during World War II. His first book, *These Small Glories* (1946), was a collection of short stories, and was followed by *You Can't See Round Corners* (1947), which was set in wartime Sydney. He had his first big success with *The Sundowners* (1952, filmed 1960), and followed this with over 40 novels, including *The Climate of Courage* (1954, filmed as *Naked in the Night*, 1963), *The Commissioner* (1966, filmed as *Nobody Runs Forever*, 1968), *High Road to China* (1977, filmed 1982), *Dark Summer* (1992), *Autumn Maze* (1994), *Winter Chill* (1995) and *Endpeace* (1996).

Cleese, John Marwood 1939–
English comic actor and writer

Born in Weston-super-Mare, Avon, he studied at Cambridge, where he joined the Footlights Revue (1963), subsequently performing with them in London, New Zealand and New York. He appeared in the Broadway production of *Half a Sixpence* (1965) and returned to the UK to write and perform in such television series as *The Frost Report* (1966) and *At Last the 1948 Show* (1967). With Graham Chapman (1941–89) he wrote scripts for television (*Doctor in the House*, 1968) and film (*The Rise and Rise of Michael Rimmer*, 1970). He then joined *Monty Python's Flying Circus* (1969–74), an anarchic series that changed the face of British television humour with its surreal comedy and animated graphics. The Monty Python team subsequently collaborated on such films as *Monty Python's Life of Brian* (1979) and *Monty Python's Meaning of Life* (1983). He had further success as the writer and star of the series *Fawlty Towers* (1975, 1979) and the films *A Fish Called Wanda* (1988) and *Fierce Creatures* (1996). His other film appearances include *Privates on Parade* (1982), *Clockwise* (1985) and *Bullseye!* (1990). On television, he played a straight role in *The Taming of the Shrew* (1980) and guest-starred in *Cheers* (1987).

Clegg, Samuel 1781–1861
English inventor

Born in Manchester, he was taught some science by John Dalton, and then became an apprentice at Matthew Boulton and James Watt's engineering works, where he saw the early experiments of William Murdock with coal gas lighting. He left the firm in 1805 and continued to work on improved methods of producing coal gas, leading to his appointment in 1813 as chief engineer of the Chartered Gas Company, for whom in 1814 he successfully illuminated by gas an entire district of London. In the course of this work he patented several important innovations in gas production, including purification by lime, a gas meter, a self-acting gas pressure governor, and an advanced type of rotating retort that later came into general use in the gas industry.

Cleisthenes 6th century BC
Athenian politician

A member of the Alcmaeonid family, he was the founder of Athenian democracy. After the fall of the tyrant Hippias (see **Pisistratus**) in 510BC he completely reorganized the Athenian state. His constitutional reforms (c.507) undermined traditional local loyalties by dividing the citizen body of Athens into 10 tribes (phylai), each comprising citizens from all regions of Attica: the city, coast and inland areas. Each tribe contributed 50 members annually to the democratic council of 500, and in all respects the Cleisthenic tribes provided the organizational basis for the democracy as it developed in the 5th to 4th century BC.

Cleland, John 1709–89
English novelist

He was born in London, and was educated at Westminster School. After a spell in the consular service and in the East India Company, followed by travel in Europe, he published in 1750 a pornographic novel, *Fanny Hill, or the Memoirs of a Woman of Pleasure*, a bestseller in its time which achieved a second succès de scandale on its revival and subsequent prosecution under the Obscene Publications Act in 1963. He also wrote *Memoirs of a Coxcomb* (1751), and *The Surprises of Love* (1764). ⍌ W H Epstein, *John Cleland: images of a life* (1974)

Cleland, William c.1661–1689
Scottish Covenanter and poet

After studying in St Andrews and joining the Covenanters, he fought at Drumclog and Bothwell Brig (1679), and fled to Holland, where he studied at Leyden. He took part in the abortive rebellion by Archibald, 9th Earl of Argyll, in 1685, and fled back to Holland. After the Glorious Revolution of 1688 he returned to Scotland as colonel of the Cameronians, and fell in the defence of Dunkeld against the Jacobite rebels. His poetry was published posthumously (1697).

Clemenceau, Georges Eugène Benjamin
1841–1929
French statesman

Born in Mouillon-en-Pareds, he studied medicine and visited the USA (1865–69), where he married an American. Elected to the National Assembly (1871), he resigned his seat in protest at the actions of the government that provoked the uprising in Paris known as the Paris Commune. Re-elected in 1876, he became the leader of the radicals (on the extreme Left). Implication in the Panama Scandal led to his defeat in the 1893 elections. He was a leader of the campaign for the rehabilitation of Alfred Dreyfus, which allowed his return to parliament as a senator in 1903. As Prime Minister (1906–09, 1917–20), his determination spurred France to make the effort to pursue victory in World War I. He presided at the Paris Peace Conference (1919), where he sought unsuccessfully to obtain in the Treaty of Versailles a settlement that would preserve France from another German attack. Nicknamed 'the Tiger' for the ferocity of his oratorical attacks on his political opponents, he was equally renowned for his journalism, in *L'Aurore*, at the time of the Dreyfus Affair, and in his own newspaper, *L'Homme libre* (renamed *L'Homme enchaîné* after a quarrel with the censor) during the war. ⍌ David R Watson, *Georges Clemenceau: A political biography* (1974)

Clemens, Roger 1962–
US baseball player

Born in Dayton, Ohio, he became a pitcher for the Boston Red Sox in 1984 and won the Cy Young award in 1986, 1987, and 1991. He is known for his extraordinary pitching control, his 153kph (95mph) fastball, and his quick temper. In 1986 he set the major-league record for the most strikeouts (20) in a single game.

Clemens, Titus Flavius See Clement of Alexandria, St

Clément V c.1260–1314
French pope

Born in Bordelais region, and formerly Archbishop of Bordeaux, he was pope from 1305. He suppressed the Knights Templars, and removed the seat of the papacy to Avignon (1308), a move disastrous to Italy.

Clement VII *originally* Guilio de' Medici 1478–1534
Italian pope

Born in Florence, he became pope from 1523 and allied himself with Francis I of France against the Holy Roman Emperor Charles V, whose troops sacked Rome in 1527, and for a while became the prisoner of the Constable Bourbon. His indecisiveness, along with his refusal to sanction Henry VIII's divorce from Catherine of Aragon, hastened the Reformation. A patron of artists and scholars, he was a cousin of Pope Leo X.

Clement IX *originally* Giulio Rospiglioso 1600–69
Italian pope

He was papal ambassador to Spain (1644–53) and Secretary of State to Alexander VII. Becoming pope in 1667 he sought, through the so-called Clementine Peace (Jan 1669), to prevent Louis XIV of France from persecuting the Jansenists. The issue of Jansenism, however, took on a lesser significance than Louis's increasing insistence on Gallican rights to limit the authority of the papacy within France. Louis's refusal to respond to Clement's pleas that he assist the Venetians in their struggle against the Turks during the War of Candia further strained relations. The slight assistance the pope was able to offer was insufficient to avert Turkish victory and Clement died while mourning the Christians killed in the final stages of the conflict.

Clement X 1590–1676
Italian pope

Made a cardinal in 1669, he had previously held a number of important Church offices, including that of papal ambassador to Naples. As pope from 1670, he sought vainly to rouse Europe against the Turkish threat in the Mediterranean and in Eastern Europe. Absence of support from Louis XIV, coupled with a general lack of interest among other European princes, thwarted any chance of a general crusade. However, Clement did manage to strengthen papal finances sufficiently to provide subsidies for the Poles in their struggle against the Turks.

Clement XI *originally* Giovanni Francesco Albani
1649–1721
Italian pope

Born in Urbino, he was elected pope in 1700 at a difficult time for the papacy, with its political role in decline and its control of national Churches increasingly threatened. Although Clement hoped to avoid conflict with either of the great ruling houses of Europe, he succeeded in antagonizing first the Austrian Habsburgs, by supporting the recognition of Louis XIV's grandson, Philip of Anjou, as King of Spain (Philip V), and then the Bourbons, when he agreed to the demands of Joseph I of Austria to recognize his brother, Charles, as the rightful pretender to the Spanish throne. By the Treaties of Utrecht (1713) and Rastatt (1714), Clement was forced to concede suzerainty over Naples, Sicily, Parma and Piacenza, while papal influence in France was increasingly marginalized by the growth of Gallicanism and the rise of Jansenism. It was against this latter that, in September 1713, he issued the Bull *Unigenitus* which prompted widespread opposition among the many French clergy who supported the now outlawed heresy.

Clement XIII 1693–1769
Italian pope

He held several important ecclesiastical positions before becoming a cardinal in 1737. As pope from 1758, he faced considerable hostility from most of Europe's more powerful Catholic princes who, at the time, were seeking to

Cleopatra 69–30BC
Queen of Egypt, the last of the Macedonian dynasty of the Ptolemies

Cleopatra was the daughter of **Ptolemy XII Auletes**, who died in 51BC. By the terms of his will he appointed her joint successor, as Cleopatra VII, with her younger brother as Ptolemy XIII (who was also her husband in name, in the Egyptian manner), but she was ousted by Ptolemy's guardians, and was about to assert her rights when **Julius Caesar** arrived in Egypt in pursuit of Pompey (48). Caesar took her side, and after the Alexandrine war restored her to the throne (47). She was now Caesar's mistress, and she claimed that Caesarion, a son born to her the following year, was his. She followed Caesar to Rome in 46, but left after his assassination.

After the Battle of Philippi (42), **Mark Antony** (Marcus Antonius) summoned her to Tarsus in Cilicia; their meeting has been immortalized by **Plutarch**'s account. They spent the following winter in Alexandria, but Antony then married **Octavia** (40), sister of Octavian (the future **Augustus**), and did not see Cleopatra again until 37, by which time he had become estranged from his wife. He acknowledged the paternity of the twins (a son and a daughter) Cleopatra had borne him in 40, and a third child was born in 36.

From this time their personal and political careers were linked, although how far their aims coincided is not easy to determine. Cleopatra's ambition was most probably to achieve the restoration of Ptolemaic power. But Antony's position in the East and his relations with Cleopatra were ambiguous and susceptible to distortion for propaganda purposes, especially by Octavian, who was brilliantly successful in swaying Roman public opinion against his absent rival. War was declared against Cleopatra, who was presented as a threat to the power of Rome, and after the Battle of Actium (31), in which they were defeated, Antony and Cleopatra fled to Egypt. When Octavian appeared before Alexandria, Cleopatra opened negotiations with him to try to save her dynasty. Antony, misled by a false report of Cleopatra's death, committed suicide by falling on his sword. Finding that she could not move Octavian, and unwilling to bear the shame of being taken to Rome to be paraded in his triumph, she is said to have killed herself by causing an asp (the Egyptian symbol of royalty) to bite her breast.

📖 Lucy Hughes-Hallett, *Cleopatra* (1990); Jack Lindsay, *Cleopatra* (1971); Hans Volkmann, *Kleopatra* (1953, Eng trans *Cleopatra: A Study in Politics and Propaganda*, 1958).

> Plutarch's description of Cleopatra at Tarsus: 'Her beauty was not of that incomparable kind which instantly captivates the beholder. But the charm of her presence was irresistible, and there was an attraction in her person and her talk, together with a peculiar force of character which pervaded every word and action, and laid all who associated with her under its spell. It was a delight merely to hear the sound of her voice, with which, like an instrument of many strings, she could pass from one language to another, so that in her interviews with foreigners she seldom required an interpreter, but conversed with them quite unaided, whether they were Ethiopians, Troglodytes, Hebrews, Arabians, Syrians, Medes, or Parthians.' (Plutarch, *Mark Antony*, 27, translated by I Scott Kilvert, 1965).

---

exert greater control over their own national Churches. The Portuguese and the **Bourbon** rulers of Spain, Naples and France were all engaged in anti-Jesuit campaigns, and the **Habsburg** Empire was witnessing a surge of Febronianism, the German equivalent of Gallicanism. Despite Clement's attempts to defend the Jesuits, they were expelled from Portugal (1759), France and its dominions (1764), the Spanish Empire (1767) and the Kingdom of Naples and Sicily (1768). Finally in 1769 the ambassadors of the three Bourbon powers demanded that the Society of Jesus be suppressed totally. Clement refused, but within a month had a stroke and died.

Clement XIV *originally* Vincenzo Antonio Ganganelli 1705–74
Italian pope

Born near Rimini, he was educated by the Jesuits, and made a cardinal by **Clement XIII** (1759), who hoped he would prove a useful ally in his struggle against the rulers of Portugal, Naples, Spain and France. Naples had proved determined to destroy the Society of Jesus, not least because it was seen as a symbol of papal interference in their domestic affairs. However, when elected pope on Clement XIII's death in 1769, he feared that open schism might emerge unless he placated the great **Bourbon** powers. In July 1773, therefore, he issued the *Dominus ac Redemptor* ('Lord and Saviour') dissolving the society. The suppression lasted until 1814.

Clement of Alexandria, St, *also called* Titus Flavius Clemens c.150–c.215AD
Greek Church Father

Born probably in Athens, he lived chiefly in Alexandria, Egypt. He became head of the Catechetical school (c.180–201AD) and together with his pupil **Origen** made it a celebrated centre of learning, until forced to flee to Palestine during the persecutions of Emperor **Severus**. His chief surviving works are *Who is the Rich Man that is Saved* and the trilogy of *The Missionary*, *The Tutor* and *The Miscellanies*.

Clement, Clemens Romanus d.c.101AD
Roman pope

Born in Rome, he was pope (AD88–89 or AD92–101), and the first of the Apostolic Fathers. He is reckoned variously as the second or third successor of St **Peter** in the See of Rome. He may have been a freedman of Jewish parentage belonging to the imperial household. He was the author of an *Epistle to the Corinthian Church* (c.95), which discusses social dissensions and the Resurrection. A tradition suggests that he was martyred.

Clemente, Roberto Walker 1934–72
US baseball player

He was born in Carolina, Puerto Rico. An outstanding outfielder, he played for the Pittsburgh Pirates for 17 years (1955–72), led the National League in batting five times, and was in the World Series in 1971. In 1966 he was voted the Most Valuable Player (MVP). He was killed in an aircrash while flying on a relief mission to the victims of the earthquake at Managua in Nicaragua. In 1973 he was elected to the National Baseball Hall of Fame without the usual five-year wait.

Clementi, Muzio 1752–1832
Italian pianist and composer

Born in Rome, he was taken to England in 1766 by Peter Beckford, MP. He conducted the Italian Opera in London (1777–80), went on tour to Paris and Vienna, and later went into the piano-manufacturing business. In 1817 he wrote the *Gradus ad Parnassum* ('Steps to Parnassus'), on which subsequent piano methods have been based, and he left many charming and tuneful pieces.

Clementis, Vladimir 1902–52
Slovak politician
Born in Tesovec, Slovakia, he studied at Prague University, became a Czechoslovak Communist MP (1935) but criticized the Nazi–Soviet Pact (1939) and spent World War II in London. In 1945 he was made Vice-Minister of Foreign Affairs in the first postwar government. One of the organizers of the 1948 coup, he succeeded Jan Masaryk as Foreign Minister, but was forced to resign in 1950 as a 'deviationist'. During the Stalinist purges he was hanged.

Clements, Sir John Selby 1910–88
English actor and director
He was educated at St Paul's School, London, and St John's College, Cambridge, and first appeared on stage in London at the Lyric Hammersmith (1930). In 1946 his first marriage, to Inga Maria Ahlgren, was dissolved and he married the actress Kay Hammond (1909–1980). They became one of Great Britain's most famous theatrical partnerships, especially in *Marriage à la Mode* and *The Beaux' Stratagem* (500 performances at the Phoenix in 1949–50). From 1966 to 1973 he was director of Chichester Festival Theatre, enjoying seven very successful seasons.

Cleomenes I d.490BC
King of Sparta in the Agiad royal family
He reigned from c.520 to 490BC. He expelled the Pisistratid tyranny from Athens in 510BC (see Pisistratus) and continually tried and failed to bring Athens under Spartan influence. He inflicted a decisive defeat on Sparta's old rival Argos (c.494), but refused to aid Samos (c.517), and in 499 gave no support to the revolt of the Ionian Greeks from Persia. He secured the deposition of his fellow king, Demaratus (491), by bribing the Delphic oracle, but when detected fled from Sparta. According to Herodotus, he committed suicide, though he may have been murdered.

Cleomenes III c.260–219BC
King of Sparta in the Agiad royal family
He ruled from 235 to 222BC. Inspired by the example of Agis IV, whose widow he married, he conceived and eventually carried out (227) a revolutionary programme of reforms to augment Sparta's depleted citizen body and assert once more her ancient leadership in the Peloponnese. This involved producing 4,000 more citizen land holdings, and restoration of Spartan youth training. But his success alarmed Aratus of Sicyon, the leader of the Achaean League, who appealed to the Macedonian king, Antigonus Doson, to intervene. Defeated at Sellasia (222), Cleomenes fled to Alexandria where he committed suicide after an unsuccessful uprising. Plutarch's *Life of Cleomenes* is the principal source for his career.

Cleon d.422BC
Athenian soldier and politician
His origins were humble. He worked as a tanner, and became leader of the War Party during the Peloponnesian War (431–404BC). As a member of the Assembly he advocated (427) the slaughter of the Mytilenean prisoners, who were saved by a last minute reprieve. His first great success was the reduction of Sphacteria, in which a Lacedaemonian force had long held out (424). Success was largely due to his colleague Demosthenes, but in 422 he was sent to oppose the Spartan soldier Brasidas in Macedonia. He was killed at Amphipolis.

Cleopatra See panel p410

Clerk, Sir Dugald 1854–1932
Scottish mechanical engineer
Born in Glasgow, he studied at Anderson's College, Glasgow, and in Leeds, intending to become a chemical engineer. Having studied the properties of petroleum oils, from 1877 he devoted himself to research on the theory and design of gas engines. In 1881 he patented a gas engine working on the two-stroke principle which became known as the Clerk cycle, extensively used for large gas engines and later for small petrol engines. He was elected a Fellow of the Royal Society in 1908, and received its Royal Medal in 1924. He was knighted in 1917.

Clerk-Maxwell, James See Maxwell, James Clerk

Cleve, Cornelis 1520–67
Flemish painter
Born in Antwerp, he was the son of Joos van Cleve. He specialized in portraits of the rich Flemish bourgeoisie, and in 1554 he went to England, hoping for the patronage of Philip II of Spain, who was there for his marriage to Mary I (Tudor). However, his arrival coincided with that of a collection of pictures by Titian and others from Italy, which ousted the Flemish school from royal favour. The disappointment mentally deranged Cornelis, who never entirely recovered, being known thereafter as 'Sotte (ie mad) Cleve'. Some of his work is at Windsor Castle, England.

Cleve, Joos van c.1480–1540
Flemish painter
He was born in Antwerp, and most of his work was done there, although he also worked in Cologne and was invited to Paris to paint portraits of Francis I and his family. He is best known for his religious pictures and is sometimes called 'the Master of the Death of the Virgin' from two triptychs of that subject at Munich and Cologne.

Cleveland, (Stephen) Grover 1837–1908
US statesman and 22nd and 24th President
Born in Caldwell, New Jersey, the son of a Presbyterian minister, he was admitted to the Bar in 1859 and began to practise at Buffalo. From 1863 to 1866 he was assistant district attorney for Erie County, and in 1870 was chosen sheriff. As Mayor of Buffalo (from 1882), he became known as a reformer independent of political posses, and after a year in office was elected Governor in New York (1882). He was nominated by the Democrats for the presidency (1884), and took his seat as President in 1885 after a campaign marked by energetic mud-slinging on all sides. In his first term (1885–89) he advocated tariff reduction and Civil Service reform, and he invested much effort into making sure that government appointments and pensions were granted on the basis of merit. His stand on the tariff issue was unpopular, and he lost the 1888 election to the Republican candidate Benjamin Harrison, but four years later he defeated Harrison to win a second term as President (1893–97). The panic of 1893 prompted Cleveland to force the repeal of the Sherman Silver Purchase Act, thus angering free-silver advocates in the West, and his intervention on the side of the railroads in the Pullman strike of 1894 also aroused much protest. In foreign affairs he invoked the Monroe Doctrine to resolve Great Britain's boundary dispute with Venezuela, and he showed admirable integrity by refusing to recognize the Hawaiian government set up largely by US planters. By 1896 he had lost the support of his party, and the Democratic nomination went to William Jennings Bryan.

Cleveland, John 1613–58
English Cavalier poet
Born in Loughborough, Leicestershire, he entered Christ's College, Cambridge, in 1627, graduated BA and then moved to St John's College, where he was elected to a fellowship in 1634. He opposed Oliver Cromwell's election

to the Long Parliament for Cambridge, and for his loyalty was ejected from his fellowship in 1645. He joined the Royalist army, and was appointed judge advocate at Newark, but had to surrender with the garrison. In 1655 he was arrested at Norwich, but was released by Cromwell. In 1656 he published a volume of 36 poems—elegies on Charles I, the Earl of Strafford, Archbishop Laud and Edward King, and also some satires. His *Clievelandi Vindiciae* was published in 1677, with a short biography. 📖 B Morris, *John Cleveland, 1613–1658: a bibliography* (1967)

Cleves, Anne of See Anne of Cleves

Cliff, Clarice 1899–1972
English ceramic designer
Born in Tunstall, Staffordshire, she attended local art schools there and at Burslem, and set up a design studio at Wilkinson's Newport Showroom where she developed a unique style using bold designs stylized trees and abstract patterns in vivid colours. By 1929 the Newport Pottery was given over entirely to the decoration of her work, which was marketed under the name 'Bizarre', a range which also included work by contemporary artists such as Vanessa Bell and Laura Knight.

Clifford
English noble family
They were descended from Walter (fl.12th century), Richard FitzPonce's son, who by 1138 acquired Clifford Castle on the Wye, 17 miles west of Hereford. He was the father of Fair Rosamond, Henry II's mistress, who was possibly murdered by Queen Eleanor of Aquitaine. The family rose in achievement and honours. To a cadet branch belonged Thomas (1630–73), a Catholic member of the Cabal, who in 1672 was created Lord Clifford of Chudleigh.

Clifford, John 1836–1923
English clergyman
Born in Sawley, near Derby, he studied at the Baptist College in Nottingham and at University College London, and from 1858 to 1915 was pastor of Praed Street Baptist Church in Paddington. A leading passive resister to the Education Act of 1902 and a strong Nonconformist Liberal, he was created first president of the Baptist World Alliance (1905–11).

Clifford, William Kingdon 1845–79
English mathematician
Born in Exeter, he entered King's College London at the age of 15, and then Trinity College, Cambridge (1863), where he graduated as Second Wrangler in 1867. In 1871 he became Professor of Applied Mathematics at University College London. He was the first British mathematician to appreciate the work of Bernhard Riemann, which he translated in part and extended in some respects. He wrote on projective and non-Euclidean geometry, and on the philosophy of science, and his book *The Common Sense of the Exact Sciences* was completed by Karl Pearson in 1885. He had a reputation as an excellent lecturer on science to popular audiences.

Clift, Charmian 1923–69
Australian novelist and essayist
Born in Kiama, New South Wales, she married the novelist George Johnston in 1947. They travelled to London and then, with their three children, lived in Greece for 10 years, providing the setting for much of her writing. She wrote three novels in collaboration with Johnston, *High Valley* (1949), *The Big Chariot* (1953) and *The Sponge Divers* (1955). Her own work included two novels, *Walk to the Paradise Gardens* (1960) and *Honour's Mimic* (1964), and accounts of their life in Greece in *Mermaid Singing* (1956) and

Peel me a Lotus (1959). Johnston later edited two collections of Clift's essays, *Images in Aspic* (1965) and *The World of Charmian Clift* (1970).

Clift, (Edward) Montgomery 1920–66
US film and stage actor
Born in Omaha, Nebraska, he worked in summer stock as a teenager, moved to New York and for 10 years acted exclusively on stage. Finally accepting one of many film offers, he appeared in *Red River* (1946) and was briefly considered the most promising of postwar actors. His performances in *The Search* (1948), *A Place in The Sun* (1951) and *From Here to Eternity* (1953) earned him Academy Award nominations. A non-conformist, he turned down many prestigious films. Broodingly handsome, his slight, intense figure was particularly adept at conveying the introspective turmoil of society's drifters and outsiders, but a car accident in 1957 left him permanently scarred. Troubled by his homosexuality and by poor health, his later career never fulfilled its early promise, although his sincerity remained evident, particularly in his last major role *Freud* (1962).

Cline, Patsy, *stage name of* Virginia Petterson Hensley 1932–63
US country singer
Born in Winchester, Virginia, she was spotted on the television show *Talent Scout* (1957) and signed to Decca label. Her powerful voice allowed her to cross over from country to a wider pop audience, and songs like 'Crazy' (1961) and 'She's Got You' (1962) made her extremely popular worldwide. Like Buddy Holly, however, she has been more successful posthumously than in life, which ended suddenly in a plane crash in Tennessee.

Clinton, Bill (William) 1946–
US Democratic politician and 42nd President
Born in Hope, Arkansas, he was educated at Georgetown University and Yale Law School, and at Oxford (Rhodes Scholar). He taught law at the University of Arkansas (1973–76) before he was elected state Attorney-General (1976). Elected Governor of Arkansas in 1978, he was the youngest person ever to hold that office, and served for five terms (1979–81, 1983–92). In 1992, on a platform of hope and change in a climate of economic recession and voter disillusionment, he defeated George Bush and was elected President, thus ending a 12-year Republican hold on the office. Since his inauguration (20 January 1993) he has been faced with problems at home, such as the need to break his election promise and raise taxes to reduce budget deficit, and problems abroad involving decisions on the intervention of US troops in the Somalian and Yugoslav civil wars. In the 1996 elections he became the first Democrat President to gain re-election since Franklin D Roosevelt in 1936.

Clinton, DeWitt 1769–1828
US politician
Admitted to the New York Bar in 1788, he sat in the state legislature (1797) and the state senate (1798–1802), and in 1802 was elected to the US Senate, but resigned in the same year on being appointed Mayor of New York by his uncle. In this office he continued, except for two short intervals, until 1815; he was defeated by James Madison in the presidential contest of 1812. He pressed the Erie Canal scheme, was elected Governor of New York in 1817, and in 1825 opened the canal.

Clinton, George 1739–1812
American brigadier and politician
Born in Little Britain, New York, he fought with his father, Charles Clinton (1690–1773), and brother James Clinton in the French and Indian War (1755–63), including the expedition against Fort Frontenac (1758). He was a member of the New York Provincial assembly (1768–75),

and in 1775 attended the second Continental Congress. In the American Revolution (1775–83) he was a brigadier of militia, and in 1777 was chosen first Governor of New York, a post he held for six successive terms (1777–95). He conceived the idea of the Erie Canal. In 1804 and again in 1808 he was elected Vice-President of the USA.

Clinton, Sir Henry c.1738–1795
British soldier

He was born in Newfoundland, Canada, the son of George Clinton, Governor of Newfoundland, and afterwards of New York. He served in the Seven Years War (1756–63), and was sent to America in 1775, where he fought at Bunker Hill, and in 1776 was repulsed in an attack on Charleston. After John Burgoyne's surrender in 1778, Clinton succeeded Admiral Howe as Commander-in-Chief. In 1780 he captured Charleston and the entire Southern army, but after Lord Cornwallis's capitulation at Yorktown in 1781 he resigned and returned to England, where he published a *Narrative* of the campaign (1783). In 1794 he was appointed Governor of Gibraltar.

Clinton, Hillary Rodham, *née* Rodham 1947–
US politician and lawyer

Born in Chicago, Illinois, the daughter of a conservative Republican father, she was educated at Wellesley College and studied law at Yale. She then practised law privately, specializing in family issues and children's rights. She married Bill Clinton in 1975 and has campaigned vigorously for his political offices as Governor of Arkansas (1979–81, 1983–93) and as President of the USA (1993–). She serves as chief presidential adviser and was appointed head of his Health Care Task Force, which ran into problems in its plans for health-care reform. In 1996 she became the first wife of a president in office to appear before a grand jury in the so-called 'Whitewater affair', an inquiry concerning property deals in Arkansas in the 1980s involving Clinton's former law firm. She is the author of *Handbook on Legal Rights for Arkansas Women*.

Clinton, James 1736–1812
American soldier

Born in Little Britain, New York, he was the brother of George Clinton and son of Charles Clinton (1690–1773), who had emigrated from Ireland to New York State in 1729. He fought in the French and Indian War (1755–63) and as a brigadier-general during the American Revolution (1775–83).

Clitherow, St Margaret, *known as* the Pearl of York, *née* Middleton c.1556–1586
English religious martyr

She was born in York, married a butcher, and was converted to Catholicism in 1574. She harboured priests in her home during Elizabeth I's reign, for which she was tried, condemned and pressed to death. She was canonized in 1970, and her feast day is 25 March.

Clive, Kitty, *née* Catherine Raftor 1711–85
English comic actress

She was born in London, the daughter of a Jacobite lawyer from Kilkenny, Ireland. She made her debut at Drury Lane in about 1728, where she continued to play till 1769, when she left the stage. She had married George Clive, a barrister, in about 1731, but the marriage was brief. She was admired by David Garrick, Handel, Robert Walpole and Dr Johnson, who said to James Boswell that 'in the sprightliness of humour he never had seen her equalled'.

Clive (of Plassey), Robert Clive, Baron, *also called* Clive of India 1725–74
English general and colonial administrator

He was born near Market Drayton, Shropshire. In 1743 he joined the East India Company in Madras, where he tried to commit suicide. In 1751 he held Arcot with a small

force against a French-Indian army for 53 days before being relieved. In 1753 he married Margaret Maskelyne, sister of the astronomer Nevil Maskelyne, and returned to England in triumph. In 1755 Clive returned to India where he was called on to avenge the so-called Black Hole of Calcutta (1757). Calcutta was soon retaken, and Chandernagore, the French settlement, captured. At Plassey (1757) he defeated the Nawab of Bengal, Suraja Dowlah. For three years he was sole ruler in all but name of Bengal on behalf of the East India Company. In 1760 he returned to England, to be hailed by Lord Chatham (Pitt the Elder) as 'a heaven-born general'. In 1761 he entered parliament, and in 1762 was made Baron Clive of Plassey. Clive was sent to India again in 1764 as Governor and Commander-in-Chief of Bengal. He established British supremacy throughout India, but on his return to England in 1767 he was faced with a parliamentary storm about his handling of the East India Company's affairs, and although ultimately vindicated in 1773, committed suicide soon afterwards. 🕮 A M Davies, *Clive of Plassey* (1939)

Clodion See Michael, Claude

Cloots, Jean Baptiste du Val-de-Grâce, Baron de, *also called* Anacharsis Cloots 1755–94
French revolutionary

Born in Prussia, he established himself in France in 1776. There he became one of the Philosophes and lavished his money to promote the union of all nations in one family. In the French Revolution he saw the fulfilment of his dreams. He was both hated and feared by Robespierre, who involved him in Jacques René Hébert's downfall, and he was guillotined. He wrote *Certitude des preuves du Mohammédisme* (London 1780, 'Certitude of the Proofs of Mohammedism') and *La République du genre humain* (1793, 'The Republic of Mankind').

Clopinel, Jean See Meung, Jean de

Clopton, Sir Hugh d.1497
English silk merchant and philanthropist

Born in Stratford-upon-Avon, Warwickshire, he became a merchant in London, then a sheriff (1486) and finally mayor (1492). At Stratford he built New Place (c.1483), which was Shakespeare's home from 1597 to 1616. He also built a stone bridge over the river.

Close, Chuck (Charles Thomas) 1940–
US artist

Born in Monroe, Washington, he studied painting at Yale (1962–64), and has lived in New York since 1967. In 1967–68 he began copying portrait photographs, painstakingly reproducing every detail, and has since continued with this Photorealist method. His works are often large scale and many are monochromatic. In the 1980s, he adopted the techniques of finger painting and collage to achieve the same hyper-detailed results.

Close, Glenn 1947–
US film and stage actress

Born in Greenwich, Connecticut, she was a student of anthropology and acting and began her career in regional theatre before her Broadway debut in *Love for Love* (1974). Her theatre work includes *The Crucifer of Blood* (1978), *Barnum* (1980–81), *The Singular Life of Albert Nobbs* (1982), for which she received an Obie award, and *The Real Thing* (1984–85), for which she received a Tony award. She made her television debut in *Too Far to Go* (1979) and received an Emmy nomination for *Something About Amelia* (1984). Other television roles include *Sarah Plain And Tall* (1991) and *Serving in Silence* (1995). She made her film debut in *The World According to Garp* (1982, Academy Award nomination) and *Dangerous Liaisons* (1988, Academy Award nomination). Recent stage performances include *Death And*

The Maiden (1992, Tony award), and *Sunset Boulevard*, (1993–95, Tony award). In 1996 she starred as Cruella De Vil in the film *101 Dalmations*.

Clotaire or Chlotar I 6th century
King of all the Franks from 558
The son of the Frankish King **Clovis**, he inherited the kingdom jointly with his three brothers (511), but gradually added to his holdings until with the death of his brother Childebert I (558) he became ruler of all the Franks. Brutal and ruthless, he extended his rule into central Germany, but faced a serious rebellion by his son, Chram, whom he had burnt to death.

Clotaire II 584–629
King of the Franks
The grandson of **Clotaire I**, he assumed rule (613) after a period of regency, recovered lost territories and, by seizing Austrasia and Burgundy, extended rule over all the Franks.

Clotilda, St AD474–545
Queen of the Franks
The daughter of the Burgundian King Childeric, she married the Frankish King **Clovis** (AD493) and converted him to Christianity. After his death (511) she lived a life of austerity and good works at the abbey of St Martin at Tours, where she died.

Clouet, François c.1516–1572
French portrait painter
Born probably in Tours, the son of **Jean Clouet**, he succeeded his father as court painter to **Francis I** and continued in that office under **Henri II**, **Francis II** and **Charles IX**. His masterpiece, the Louvre portrait of Elizabeth of Austria (Louvre, Paris), is one of the finest examples of the period, and that of **Mary Queen of Scots** in the Wallace Collection, London, is attributed to him.

Clouet, Jean, *also known as* Jehan *or* Janet
c.1485–c.1540
French portrait painter
He was probably the son of Jehan Clouet (c.1420–c.1480), a Flemish painter who came to France as court painter to the Duke of Burgundy. He became court painter to **Francis I**, whose portrait in the Louvre, Paris, is supposed to be by him.

Clough, Anne Jemima 1820–92
English educationist
Born in Liverpool, she was a vigorous proponent of higher education for women. She secured the admission of women to Manchester and Newcastle colleges, and in 1871 she became the first principal of the first hall for women students at Cambridge, Newnham Hall, later called Newnham College. She was the sister of **Arthur Hugh Clough**.

Clough, Arthur Hugh 1819–61
English poet
Born in Liverpool, he was the son of a cotton merchant who emigrated to Charleston, West Virginia, USA, in 1823. The boy was sent back to England in 1828 and entered Rugby, where he became a pupil of **Dr Thomas Arnold** and a friend of **Matthew Arnold**. He was elected a Fellow of Oriel College and there lived through the crisis which resulted in **John Henry Newman's** conversion to Catholicism. His own difficulties with the Thirty-nine Articles led to his resignation in 1848. He became Principal of the new University Hall, attached to University College, Gower Street, which had a Unitarian bias little to Clough's liking. On his dismissal from University Hall he obtained an examinership in the education department, but before taking up that appointment he spent some months in Boston, Massachusetts,

where he met the Boston Brahmins. In England, he enjoyed the friendship of **John Ruskin**, Arnold, and **Thomas Carlyle**, and at Oriel as the leader of the Members of the Decade group, he took reading parties to the Lake District and to Scotland. The latter resulted in *The Bothie of Tober-na-Vuolich* (1848). His only other long poems were 'Amours de voyage', which was written in Rome in 1849, and 'Dipsychus' (1850), both published posthumously. Arnold wrote the poem 'Thyrsis' in Clough's memory in 1866. Clough's two-volume *Correspondence* was published in 1957. He followed the revolutionary doctrines of **George Sand**, called himself a republican, and disliked class distinction and the capitalist system. 📖 W V Harris, *Arthur Hugh Clough* (1970); Evelyn B Grenberger, *Arthur Hugh Clough* (1970)

Clough, Brian 1935–
English footballer and manager
Born in Middlesbrough, Cleveland, he became a manager when injury terminated his playing career. He took Derby County and Nottingham Forest to League championship wins and, in the case of Nottingham Forest, two European Cup successes. He was awarded the OBE in 1991 and the freedom of the city of Nottingham in 1993, the year he retired.

Clovio, Giulio, *also called* Jurni Glovichisch
1498–1578
Italian miniaturist
Born in Croatia, he was a monk for 50 years and is best known for a series of 12 miniatures on the victories of the Emperor **Charles V**.

Clovis, *Old German* Chlodwig AD465–511
Merovingian ruler of the Franks
The grandson of **Merovech**, he succeeded his father, Childeric I (AD481), as King of the Salian Franks. In 486 he overthrew the last Roman governor in Gaul, Syagrius, near Soissons, and took control of the whole country between the Somme and the Loire, making his capital at Soissons. He married **St Clotilda** of Burgundy (493), who converted him to Christianity, and he championed orthodox Christianity against the heretic Arians, defeating the Alemonni (496) and the Arian Visigoths under **Alaric II** (507). The Ostrogoth **Theodoric the Great** checked Clovis' progression through Gaul, and made his capital in Paris. A heroic figure, he was the traditional founder of the historic French monarchy, and when he died his Frankish kingdom was divided among his four sons, who further enlarged the empire by conquest. 📖 Jean Verseuil, *Clovis, ou, La naissance des rois* (1992)

Clowes, William 1780–1851
English nonconformist
Born in Burslem, Staffordshire, he became a potter, and in the course of a dissolute youth achieved a reputation as a champion dancer. In 1805 he was converted to Methodism, becoming in 1810 a co-founder with **Hugh Bourne** of the Primitive Methodists.

Clune, Frank (Francis Patrick) 1893–1971
Australian writer
He was born in Woolloomooloo, Sydney, of Irish extraction, and his early life was one of travel and adventure at sea, in Europe and the USA. He served with the Australian Imperial Forces in World War I and was wounded at Gallipoli. A vagabond life was followed by marriage, then a career in accountancy. At the age of 40 he published *Try Anything Once* (1933), the story of his early years, which includes a hilarious account of his brief career with a touring opera company. He went on to write over 60 books, often in collaboration with P R ('Inky') Stephensen, and became one of Australia's bestselling writers. His works including *Rolling down the Lachlan* (1935), *Wild Colonial Boys* (1948) and *Ben Hall the Bushranger*

(1947), were of popular appeal, and also aroused interest in Australian history. 📖 *Korean Diary* (1955); *Try Nothing Twice* (1946); B Adamson, *Francis Clune, author and ethnological anachronism* (1944)

Clunies Ross, Sir Ian 1899–1959
Australian veterinary scientist
Born in Bathurst, New South Wales, he joined the newly-formed Australian Council for Scientific and Industrial Research (CSIR) in 1926, but resigned in 1937 upon being appointed representative on the International Wool Secretariat. He served as chairman there until 1940, when he became Professor of Veterinary Science at Sydney University, returning to the CSIR in 1946 as a member of its executive committee. When the CSIR became the Australian Commonwealth Scientific and Industrial Research Organization in 1949, Clunies Ross became its first chairman. He played a leading role in research for the sheep and wool industries and established a sheep biology laboratory in Sydney. He was a member of the Australian delegation to the League of Nations in 1938, and president of the Australian Institute of International Affairs from 1941 to 1945.

Clurman, Harold Edgar 1901–80
US theatre director and critic
He was born in New York City, and was co-founder (1931) with **Lee Strasberg**, of the Group Theater, best remembered for the fervent dedication of its members and its staging of a sequence of plays by **Clifford Odets**. The Group disbanded in 1940, and Clurman went on to work extensively on Broadway. He directed, among others, **Carson McCullers**'s *The Member of the Wedding* (1950) and **Arthur Miller**'s *Incident at Vichy* (1964). He also directed productions in London (**Jean Giraudoux**'s *Tiger at the Gates* in 1955), Los Angeles, Israel and Japan. As a drama critic he wrote for the US magazine *The New Republic* (1949–53), and for the London *Observer* (1959–63). He published several books, including a history of the Group Theater, *The Fervent Years* (1945).

Cluverius or Clüver, Phillip 1580–1622
German geographer and antiquary
Born in Danzig, he is regarded as the founder of historical geography. He studied law at Leyden, and visited Norway, England, Scotland, France and Italy. He wrote *Introductio in universam geographium* (1624, 'Introduction to Universal Geography').

Clyde, Lord See **Campbell, Sir Colin**

Clynes, Joseph Robert 1869–1949
English Labour politician
Born in Oldham, Lancashire, he worked in a cotton mill from the age of 10 and educated himself. Organizer of the Lancashire Gasworkers' Union (1891), he was president (1892) and secretary (1894–1912) of Oldham's Trade Council. Entering parliament in 1910 he became Food Controller (1918), Vice-Chairman (1922) and Lord Privy Seal in Great Britain's first Labour Cabinet (1924). As Home Secretary (1929–31), he refused to allow **Trotsky** to settle in Britain, following his expulsion by **Stalin**. He became a Privy Councillor (1918).

Coanda, Henri 1885–1972
Romanian aeronautical engineer
He built the first jet-propelled aeroplane, which used a ducted fan, not a turbojet. Because of a phenomenon not then understood, the hot exhaust gases set fire to the structure. Coanda later investigated this effect, the entrainment of a free jet alongside a curved surface, which now bears his name. He subsequently became an aircraft designer with the British & Colonial Aeroplane Company (later the Bristol Aircraft Company).

Coates, Anne V 1925–
English film editor
Born in Reigate, Surrey, she began her working life as a nurse, but moved into film editing in the early 1950s. Her early films include *The Pickwick Papers* (1952). She went on to become a leading film editor, working both in Great Britain and in Hollywood, and has been responsible for cutting a number of very important films, including the epic *Lawrence of Arabia* (1962), for which she received an Academy Award. She was nominated again for *Becket* (1964), and also cut *Tunes of Glory* (1960), *The Eagle Has Landed* (1976) and *Greystoke* (1984).

Coates, Eric 1886–1957
English composer
Born in Hucknall, Nottinghamshire, he studied in Nottingham and at the Royal Academy of Music, working as violinist in chamber music groups. In 1912 he became leading violist in the Queen's Hall Orchestra under Sir **Henry Wood**, who produced several of his early works at Promenade Concerts. Success as a composer of attractive light music enabled him to devote himself to composition after 1918. Among his best-known compositions are the *London Suite* (1933), *The Three Bears* (1926), the suites *Four Centuries* (1941) and *The Three Elizabeths* (1944), and a number of popular waltzes and marches.

Coates, Wells Wintemute 1895–1958
English architect
Born in Tokyo, Japan, he was one of the principal figures of the modern movement in architecture, and practised as an architect from 1929. He studied in Canada and London, and in 1933 formed the MARS group of architects. He was responsible for the design of BBC studios, the EKCO laboratories, and many other buildings in Great Britain and in Canada, and he also played an important part in the development of industrial design. His work in this field included furniture and an innovative bakelite circular radio for EKCO.

Cobain, Kurt (Donald) 1967–94
US singer and guitarist
He was born in Aberdeen, Washington. He formed the band Nirvana, the chief catalyst in Seattle's grunge scene of the late 1980s. Their first album, *Bleach* (1989), established their characteristic sound, a dense compound of punk's ferocity with strong melodies. *Nevermind* (1991), and the single 'Smells Like Teen Spirit' from it, were an international success. Nirvana's sound largely defined the grunge ethos, while Cobain became its leading icon. He grew increasingly disaffected with the publicity which success brought, which reached a frenzy after he married guitarist and singer Courtney Love in 1992. His mental state was also affected by his heroin addiction, and after recording a third album, *In Utero* (1993), he committed suicide at his home in Seattle. 📖 C Sandford, *Kurt Cobain* (1995)

Cobb, Ty (rus Raymond), nicknamed the Georgia Peach 1886–1961
US baseball player
Born in Narrows, Georgia, he was considered the outstanding offensive player of all time. He played for the Detroit Tigers (1905–26) and the Philadelphia Athletics (1926–28), and until **Pete Rose** in 1985 was the only player with more than 4,000 hits in major league baseball. His career batting average was an astonishing .367, meaning that he had a hit more than once every three times at bat. He came first in the first ballot for the National Baseball Hall of Fame in 1936.

Cobbe, Frances Power 1822–1904
Irish social worker and feminist

Born in Newbridge House, Donabate, she travelled in Italy and the East, and wrote *Cities of the Past* (1864) and *Italics* (1864). A strong theist, a supporter of women's rights, and a prominent antivivisectionist, she was associated with **Mary Carpenter** in the founding of 'ragged' schools and published more than 30 works, mostly on social questions, including *The Duties of Women* (1881) and *The Scientific Spirit of the Age* (1888).

Cobbett, William 1763–1835
English writer and champion of the poor

Born in Farnham, Surrey, the son of a small farmer, he taught himself to read and write, and while serving as sergeant-major in New Brunswick (1785–91) studied rhetoric, geometry, logic and French. He bought his discharge in 1791, and the following year sailed for America. In Philadelphia he taught English to French refugees, opened a bookshop and published a paper, the *Porcupine's Gazette* (1797–99), in which he wrote fierce onslaughts on **Joseph Priestley**, **Tom Paine** and the native Democrats. On his return to England in 1800 the Tories welcomed him with open arms. In 1802 he started his weekly *Cobbett's Political Register*, which was Tory at first, but from 1804, he gradually became the most uncompromising champion of Radicalism. He initiated the publication of *Parliamentary Debate* (1806, later taken over by **Luke Hansard**) and *State Trials* (1809). He spent two years in Newgate Prison, London (1810–12), for his strictures on flogging in the army, and in 1817 financial problems and fear of further imprisonment drove him back to the USA, where he farmed on Long Island. Returning to England in 1819, he started a seed-farm at Kensington, defended himself against a charge of sedition (1831), and in 1832, after the First Reform Bill, became MP for Oldham. His celebrated *Rural Rides* (1830), a delightful picture of a vanishing world, were reprinted from the *Register*. His 40 or more other works include a savage *History of the Reformation* (1824–27), *The Woodlands* (1825) and *Advice to Young Men* (1830). 📖 G D H Cole, *The Life of Cobbett* (1924)

Cobden, Richard *known as* the Apostle of Free Trade 1804–65
English economist and politician

He was born in Heyshott, near Midhurst, Sussex. His father had to sell his farm in 1814 and Richard, the fourth of his eleven children, was sent for five years to a 'Dotheboys' school in Yorkshire, and afterwards went to work in an uncle's warehouse in London. Cobden set up an establishment for calico-printing with two friends in Lancashire (1831), and settled in Manchester (1832). He visited the USA (1835), and the Levant (1836–37), the result being two pamphlets, *England, Ireland, and America* (1835), and *Russia* (1836), the former preaching free trade and non-intervention, and the latter directed against 'Russophobia'. He failed to be elected to the parliament for Stockport on free-trade principles (1837). In 1838 seven Manchester merchants founded the Anti-Corn-Law League, its most prominent member being Cobden. His lectures all over the country and his speeches in parliament (to which Stockport had returned him in 1841) were characterized by clear, quiet persuasiveness. Sir **Robert Peel** acknowledged that Cobden had played a large part in abolition of the Corn Laws (1846). His public work had detracted from his business, but when he ended up a ruined man, a subscription of £80,000 was raised in recognition of his services. He was elected for both Stockport and the West Riding and he chose West Riding. He shared **John Bright's** unpopularity for opposing the Crimean War (1853–56) and on Lord **Palmerston's** appeal to the country to support him in his Chinese policy, of which Cobden was a firm opponent, he retired from the West Riding and contested Huddersfield, where, however, he was defeated (1857). In 1859 he revisited the USA,

and meanwhile was elected for Rochdale. Palmerston offered him the presidency of the Board of Trade but Cobden declined. Ill health prevented him from being active in parliamentary proceedings, but in 1859–60 he arranged the Treaty of Commerce with France. He spoke out strongly in favour of the North during the American Civil War (1861–65), and in 1864 strongly opposed intervention in favour of Denmark. His *Speeches on Questions of Public Policy* were edited by John Bright and Thorald Rogers (1870). 📖 Wendy Hinde, *Richard Cobden: A Victorian Outsider* (1987)

Cobden-Sanderson, Thomas James 1840–1922
English printer and bookbinder

He was born in Alnwick, Northumberland. A lawyer by training, he became a leader of the 19th century revival of artistic typography, working with **William Morris**, and in 1900 founded the Doves Press at Hammersmith from which was issued the beautiful *Doves Bible* (1903). In 1916 the press closed and he threw the type into the Thames.

Cobham, Lord See **Oldcastle, Sir John**

Coborn, Charles, *stage-name of* Colin Whitton McCallum 1852–1945
English comedian

He made his stage debut in 1875 and immortalized the songs 'Two Lovely Black Eyes' (1886) and 'The Man who Broke the Bank at Monte Carlo' (1890). In 1928 he published the autobiographical *The Man who Broke the Bank*.

Coburn, Alvin Langdon 1882–1966
British photographer

Born in Boston, Massachusetts, he studied photography from 1898 and was influenced by **Edward Steichen**, **James McNeill Whistler** and, later, the work of the Japanese painter **Sesshū**. In 1902–03 he worked in the studio of **Gertrude Kasebier**, with whom he later founded the Pictorial Photographers of America (1912). He joined **Alfred Stieglitz's** Photo-Secession Group in 1902, and its predecessor, the British Salon of the Linked Ring, in 1903. He first went to work in the UK in 1904 to photograph celebrities such as **George Bernard Shaw** (1906); this work was later published as *Men of Mark* (1913) and *More Men of Mark* (1922). Coburn later emigrated, becoming a British citizen in 1932. In 1917 he invented a kaleidoscopic mirror apparatus called a Vortograph which he used to make the earliest abstract, or nonobjective photographs, introducing vorticism into his pictorial work. He published *Alvin Langdon Coburn, Photographer: An Autobiography* in 1966. 📖 Mike Weaver, *Alvin Langdon Coburn: Symbolist Photographer* (1986)

Coburn, John 1925–
Australian artist and tapestry designer

He was born in Ingham, Queensland. During war service in the Far East he studied the arts of India, Burma and China, which influenced his subsequent work, in which he used formalized leaf designs to make two-dimensional patterns of shape and colour. This style lent itself to large-scale tapestry design, and most of his work in this medium has been woven on the famous looms at Aubusson, France. There he worked (1969–72) on his best-known commissions, the *Curtain of the Sun* and *Curtain of the Moon* for the prosceniums of Sydney Opera House. His tapestries also hang in the Australian Embassy in Paris and in the John F Kennedy Center for the Performing Arts in Washington DC.

Cochba, Simon Bar See **Bar Kokhba, Simon**

Cochise d.1874
Native American leader

Born in Arizona, he became a chief of the Chiricahua band of the Apache, and in 1861 a decade of co-existence with the US government was broken when Cochise was falsely accused of having abducted a white child. His imprisonment and escape from an army post led to the execution of hostages on both sides, and he began a campaign of fierce resistance to white settlement, terrorizing Arizona settlers in the 1860s. He led raids from his base in the Dragoon Mountains until 1871, when he was forced to surrender to General **George Crook**. He retired to an Arizona reservation the following year.

Cochran, Sir C(harles) B(lake) 1872–1951
English theatrical producer and manager
Born in Lindfield, Sussex, he began his career as an actor in the USA, then turned impresario, becoming agent for **Mistinguett**, **Houdini** and other famous figures. His spectacular presentation of *The Miracle* (1911) in London won him renown as a producer, but after a number of successes, the failure of his Wembley rodeo venture in 1924 made him bankrupt. He managed the Albert Hall from 1916 to 1938, and made a rapid comeback with the successful **Noël Coward** musicals *This Year of Grace* (1928), *Bitter Sweet* (1929) and *Cavalcade* (1931). His most successful production was *Bless the Bride* by Herbert and Ellis (1947), which ran for 886 performances.

Cochran, Jacqueline 1910–80
US aviator
Born in Pensacola, Florida, she received her pilot's licence in 1932, and became the first woman to fly in the Bendix transcontinental air race in 1935. In 1938 she secured the transcontinental record at 10 hours and 28 minutes. The International League of Aviators named her the world's outstanding woman pilot (1937–50, 1953). The first woman to pilot a bomber across the Atlantic Ocean in World War II, she became director of Women Auxiliary Service Pilots in the US air force in 1943. In 1953 she became the first woman to fly faster than sound (in an F-86 Sabre fighter), and in 1964 flew faster than twice the speed of sound.

Cochrane, Sir Ralph Alexander 1895–1977
Scottish Air Chief Marshal
Born in Springfield, Fife, he was educated at the Royal Naval College at Osborne and Dartmouth, then entered the Royal Navy in 1912. During World War I he transferred to the Royal Flying Corps and was commissioned in the RAF in April 1918. During the 1920s he was one of the officers responsible for the evolution of 'Air Power', the policy used by the RAF to police remote and recalcitrant areas of the empire, such as the north-west frontier and Kurdistan. After occupying various staff posts he became director of Flying Training and, on the outbreak of World War II, returned to Bomber Command. As the commander of 5 Group he was responsible for planning the British heavy bomber offensive against German industry, including the famous 'Dambuster' raid of October 1943. In the postwar years he commanded Flying Training Command and Transport Command before his retirement in 1952.

Cochrane, Thomas, 10th Earl of Dundonald
1775–1860
Scottish naval commander
Born in Annesfield, Lanarkshire, he joined the navy in 1793, and in 1800 received the command of a sloop, with which he defeated over 50 ships, including a 32-gun frigate. He was captured by the French, but was speedily exchanged, and returned to sea. By 1805 his share of prize money amounted to £75,000. By judicious bribery he was elected to parliament for Honiton (1806) and campaigned against naval abuses. In 1809 he was selected to burn the French fleet then blockaded in Aix Roads by Lord **Gambier**, but the operation was only partly successful. Discredited and on half-pay, Cochrane pursued his crusade against naval corruption, until he was arrested

on a charge of fraud (1814), accused, with two others, of spreading a rumour of **Napoleon I**'s overthrow that sent up the funds, and of then selling over a million sterling with a gross profit of £10,000. Cochrane was fined £1,000 and sentenced to a year's imprisonment and an hour in the pillory. Re-elected by Westminster, he broke out of jail in March 1815 and reappeared in the House, but was reimprisoned for the remaining three months of his sentence, and fined a further £100. In command of Chile's navy (1818–22) in the War for Freedom by Chile and Peru, he stormed Valdivia (1819), and made Chile mistress of her own waters. He also took command of the Brazilian navy (1823–25), and later the Greek navy (1827–28). In 1831 he succeeded to the earldom of Dundonald, and in 1832 was granted a free pardon for past misdeeds. He was restored to the navy as a rear admiral, and was later Commander-in-Chief on the North American station (1848–51), and rear admiral of the United Kingdom (1854). Considered one of Britain's greatest seamen, he was buried in Westminster Abbey, London.

Cockburn, Alison or Alicia, *née* Rutherford
1713–94
Scottish poet
Born in Selkirkshire, she married Patrick Cockburn in 1731, an advocate, and for over 60 years she was a leading figure in Edinburgh society. Of her lyrics, the best known is her version of 'The Flowers of the Forest' ('I've seen the smiling of Fortune beguiling'), which was first printed in 1765. She met **Walter Scott** in 1777, and thought him 'the most extraordinary genius of a boy', and in 1786 she made **Robert Burns**'s acquaintance. 📖 *Letters and Memoirs of Her Own Life* (1900)

Cockcroft, Sir John Douglas 1897–1967
English nuclear physicist and Nobel Prize winner
Born in Yorkshire and educated at the universities of Manchester and Cambridge, he became Jacksonian Professor of Natural Philosophy at Cambridge (1939–46). In 1932, with **Ernest Walton**, he induced the disintegration of a lithium nucleus by proton bombardment in the first successful use of a particle accelerator. The experiment verified **Albert Einstein**'s theory of mass–energy equivalence, and the particle accelerator was crucial for the understanding of nuclear substructures. Cockcroft and Walton were awarded the 1951 Nobel Prize for physics for this work. Cockcroft later assisted in the design of some special experimental equipment for the Cavendish Laboratory, including the cyclotron. During World War II, he was director of Air Defence Research (1941–44) and of the Atomic Energy Division of the Canadian National Research Council (1944–46). He became the first director of the UK's Atomic Energy Research Establishment at Harwell in 1946. He was appointed Master of Churchill College, Cambridge (1959), elected FRS in 1936 and knighted in 1948. 📖 Guy Hartcup and T E Allibone, *Cockcroft and the Atom* (1984)

Cocker, Edward 1631–75
English engraver
Based in London, he taught penmanship and arithmetic, and was reputedly the author of *Cocker's Arithmetic* (1678), which went through 112 editions. Its reputation for accuracy gave rise to the expression 'according to Cocker', but it was exposed as a poor and inaccurate forgery by its editor and publisher.

Cockerell, Charles Robert 1788–1863
English architect
The son of **Samuel Pepys Cockerell**, he travelled in the Levant and Italy (1810–17). He was Professor of Architecture in the Royal Academy (1840–57), and was the designer of the Taylorian Institute in Oxford and the Fitzwilliam Museum in Cambridge.

Cockerell, Sir Christopher Sydney 1910–

English radio-engineer and inventor of the hovercraft

Born in Cambridge and educated at Gresham's School and Peterhouse, Cambridge, he worked on radar in World War II, and later on hydrodynamics. In 1953 he pioneered the amphibious hovercraft, which rides on a cushion of jet-generated air. A prototype of it, the SRNI, made the Calais–Dover crossing of the English Channel in 1959.

Cockerell, Samuel Pepys 1754–1827

English architect

He laid out Brunswick and Mecklenburg Squares in London and designed the tower of St Anne's, Soho.

Cockerill, John 1790–1840

English industrialist

Born in Haslingden, Lancashire, he was the son of William Cockerill (1759–1832), an inventor who established a factory at Liège in Belgium for manufacturing spinning machines (1807). John and an elder brother, having taken over their father's business (1812), started a woollen factory in Berlin (1815), and the famous iron works at Seraing in Belgium (1817).

Cocteau, (Clement Eugène) Jean 1889–1963

French poet, playwright and film director

Born in Maisons-Lafitte, near Paris, success came early with *La Lampe d'Aladin* (1909, 'Aladdin's Lamp'), and he exploited it. He ran the gamut of experience, first enjoying a spectacular conversion to Roman Catholicism through Jacques Maritain. This was followed by a scornful repudiation of his mentor, the use of opium and a search for salvation through solitude. Nevertheless he had astonishing success with whatever he touched, and figured as sponsor of Picasso, Stravinsky, Giorgio de Chirico and the group of young French composers known as Les Six. As an actor, director, scenario writer, novelist, critic and artist, his work was marked by vivacity and a pyrotechnic brilliance. He was elected to the Académie Française in 1955. Significant works are his novels *Le Grand écart* (1923, Eng trans *The Grand Escort*, 1925), *Thomas l'imposteur* (1923, Eng trans *Thomas the Imposter*, 1925), *Les Enfants terribles* (1929, Eng trans *Children of the Game*, 1929), and plays: *Les Mariés de la Tour Eiffel* (1921, Eng trans *The Eiffel Tower Wedding Party*, 1963), *Orphée* (1926, Eng trans *Orpheus*, 1933) and *L'Aigle a deux têtes* (1946, Eng trans *The Eagle has Two Heads*, 1948). His films include *Le Sang d'un poète* (1930, *The Blood of a Poet*), *La Belle et la bête* (1945, *Beauty and the Beast*), *Orphée* (adapted from his play, 1949) and *Le Testament d'Orphée* (1960). 📖 F Brown, *An Impersonation of Angels: a biography of Cocteau* (1968)

Codrington, Sir Edward 1770–1851

English naval commander

Born in Dodington, Gloucestershire, he joined the navy in 1783 and in 1794 became lieutenant of Lord Howe's flagship in the action off Ushant. At Trafalgar (1805) he commanded the *Orion*. In 1826, as Commander-in-Chief of the Mediterranean squadron, he sought to advance Greek independence peacefully, in company with the French and Russian naval commanders. In this event the Turkish fleet was annihilated at the Battle of Navarino (1827). He was Admiral of the Red in 1837, and in 1839 Commander-in-Chief at Portsmouth.

Codrington, Sir Henry John 1808–77

English naval commander

The son of Sir Edward Codrington, he joined the navy in 1823, and was wounded at the Battle of Navarino under his father's command (1827). He was present at the bombardment of Acre in 1840, and served in the Baltic Sea during the Crimean War (1854–55). He was promoted Admiral of the Fleet in 1877.

Cody, Samuel Franklin 1862–1913

British aviator

Born in Texas, USA, he went to England in 1896 and acquired British nationality. He experimented with man-lifting kites, participated in the planning and construction of the first British dirigible, and built an early aeroplane in 1908. He was killed in a flying accident.

Cody, William F(rederick), *known as* Buffalo Bill 1846–1917

US showman

Born in Scott County, Iowa, he became an army scout and pony express rider. He earned his nickname after killing nearly 5,000 buffalo for a contract to supply meat to the workers on the Kansas Pacific Railway (1867–68). He served as a scout in the Sioux wars, but from 1883 toured with his own Wild West Show. The town of Cody in Wyoming is situated on part of his ranch.

Coe, Sebastian 1956–

English athlete and Conservative politician

Born in Chiswick, London, he won the 1,500 metres gold medal and the silver medal in the 800 metres at both the 1980 Moscow Olympics and at Los Angeles four years later. In 1981 he broke the world record for the 800 metres, 1,000 metres and the mile. Between September 1976 and June 1983 he did not lose the final of any race over 1,500 metres or a mile. He served as vice-chairman of the Sports Council (1986–89) and following the 1990 Commonwealth Games retired from athletics to pursue a career in politics. He was Conservative MP for Falmouth and Cambourne from 1992 to 1997.

Coello, Claudio 1621–93

Spanish religious painter

He is known for the sacristy altarpiece in the Escorial and many other church paintings in Toledo, Saragossa and Madrid.

Cœur de Lion See Richard I

Coesius, Willem Janszoon See Blaeu

Coetzee, J(ohn) M(ichael) 1940–

South African novelist

He was born in Cape Town. The political situation in his native country provided him with the base from which to launch his allegories and fables, attacking colonialism and demythologizing historical and contemporary myths of imperialism. His first work of fiction was *Dusklands* (1974), followed by *In the Heart of the Country* (1977), *Waiting for the Barbarians* (1980), *Life and Times of Michael K* (1983), for which he was awarded the Booker Prize, *Foe* (1986) and *The Master of Petersburg* (1994).

Coggan, (Frederick) Donald Coggan, Baron 1909–

English prelate, Archbishop of Canterbury

Born in London, he was educated at St John's College, Cambridge. He was a lecturer in Semitic languages at Manchester (1931–34), Professor of New Testament at Wycliffe College, Toronto (1937–44), Principal of London College of Divinity (1944–56), then Bishop of Bradford (1956–61). He was Archbishop of Canterbury from 1974 to 1980, when he was made a life peer. He is the author of several theological works, including *On Preaching* (1978), *Mission to the World* (1982), *God of Hope* (1991), *Voice from the Cross* (1993) and *The Servant Son* (1995). 📖 Margaret Pawley, *Donald Coggan, Servant of Christ* (1987)

Coggeshall, Ralph de d.c.1227

English chronicler

A native of Cambridgeshire, he was abbot from 1207 to 1218 of the Cistercian abbey of Coggeshall, Essex, and continued the Latin Chronicle (*Chronicon Anglicanum*) kept at the abbey, covering the period from 1187 to 1224.

Cogswell, Joseph Green 1786–1871
US bibliographer

He was born in Ipswich, Massachusetts, and was Professor of Geology at Harvard (1820–23). He established the Round Hill School at Northampton, Massachusetts, with **George Bancroft** in 1823, edited the *New York Review* (1836–42), and from 1848 was superintendent of the **Astor** Library.

Cohan, George M(ichael) 1878–1942
US showman and songwriter

Born in Providence, Rhode Island, he spent his childhood acting in vaudeville with a family theatrical group, The Four Cohans. He grew up to write, produce, and perform in musicals and dramas, which were usually centred on flag-waving patriots and the allure of show business, such as *Johnny Jones* (1904) and *The Song and Dance Man* (1923). He wrote many songs that have remained favourites, including 'Yankee Doodle Dandy' (1904), 'Give My Regards to Broadway' (1904), 'You're a Grand Old Flag' (1906), and 'Over There' (1917). In the film *Yankee Doodle Dandy* (1942), he was played with gusto by **James Cagney**. His autobiography *Twenty Years on Broadway* (1925) recalls the seething heap of New York's theatre world.

Cohan, Robert 1925–
British dancer, choreographer and director

Born in Brooklyn, New York City, he took British citizenship in 1989. After serving in World War II he dropped his career as a research naturalist to take up a training with the **Martha Graham** Company in New York. From 1946 to 1957 he was Martha Graham's partner, and created his first role in their *Diversion of Angels* (1948). Keen to develop his own choreography, he founded a company in 1957, but after five years returned to Graham's group, where he became co-director in 1966. From 1967 to 1983 he was the founding artistic director of London Contemporary Dance Theatre, which was to play a key role in the development of modern dance performance and education in Great Britain. His many works include *Cell* (1969), *Stages* (1971), *Class* (1975) and *Video-Life* (1987).

Cohen, Hermann 1842–1912
German Jewish philosopher

Born in Coswig, he studied at the Jewish Theological Seminary in Breslau, the University of Berlin, and the University of Halle. He was Professor of Philosophy at Marburg (1876–1912), where he founded the Marburg School of neo-Kantianism which applied Kantian methods to the presuppositions of science. He later taught at the Rabbinic seminary in Berlin, and proposed a synthesis of Judaism and idealism which had a deep influence on such early 20th-century Jewish thinkers as **Martin Buber** and **Franz Rosenzweig**.

Cohen, Leonard Norman 1934–
Canadian poet, novelist and singer

Though his background is Jewish, he was born and grew up in the predominantly Catholic city of Montreal, and the title of his first poetry collection, *Let Us Compare Mythologies* (1956), offers an indication of how he has moved between traditions. His novels include *The Favorite Game* (1963) and *Beautiful Losers* (1966). The first of his many albums as a singer-songwriter was *The Songs of Leonard Cohen*, which appeared in 1968, the same year as his *Selected Poems*. 📖 S Scobie, *Leonard Cohen* (1978)

Cohen, Nudie (Paul) 1908–84
US designer of country music stage costumes

Born in Brooklyn, New York City, he became famous as the creator of the Nudie suit, the bright, rhinestone-spangled stage costume which became a trademark of country music. He was a boxer for a time, but found his niche when he met country singer Tex Williams in Los Angeles in the early 1940s, and persuaded him to try his suit designs. The fashion for the Nudie suit quickly spread to cowboy stars like Gene Autry and Roy Rogers, and then into the mainstream of country music. He tried to tailor garments to individual personalities, and his designs are firmly part of country music lore.

Cohen, Seymour Stanley 1917–
US biochemist

Born and educated in New York City, he did valuable early work in the 1940s using radioactive labelling of bacteriophage which suggested, but did not prove, that DNA plays a key part in heredity.

Cohen, Stanley 1922–
US biochemist and Nobel Prize winner

Born in Brooklyn, New York City, he was educated at the University of Michigan and held posts at the universities of Colorado and Washington before moving to Vanderbilt University in 1959. From 1967 he was Professor of Biochemistry there, becoming Distinguished Professor in 1986. Following **Rita Levi-Montalcini**'s discovery of nerve growth factor, the substance that promotes the development of sympathetic nerves, Cohen helped to isolate the compound, and went on to isolate a further cell growth factor, named epidermal growth factor (EGF), which accelerated aspects of natural development in newborn mice. In further studies he demonstrated the effects of this compound on various developmental processes in the body, and described the mechanisms through which it is absorbed by, and interacts with, individual cells. In 1986 he was awarded the Nobel Prize for physiology or medicine jointly with Levi-Montalcini for their work on growth factors.

Cohl, Emile, *originally* Emile Courtet 1857–1938
French cartoonist, inventor of the animated cartoon film

Born in Paris, he began as a jeweller's apprentice, but later became a pupil of the caricaturist **André Gill**. His first cartoons were published in *Le Rire* (1880), and he was given a position as comedy film writer and director at the **Gaumont** Studio after accusing the company of basing scenarios on his comic strips. Using simple stick-figures he produced the first frame-by-frame animated cartoon film, *Fantasmagorie* (1908), projecting it in negative so that it looked like chalk drawings on a blackboard. Sent to New York by Eclair Films he adapted the George McManus strip, *The Newlyweds and Their Baby*, into the first animated series (1912).

Cohn, Ferdinand Julius 1828–98
German botanist and bacteriologist

Born in Breslau, Germany (now Wrocław, Poland), he was barred as a Jew from taking the degree examinations at Breslau University, and so went to Berlin, where he obtained his doctorate in botany at the age of 19. Professor of Botany at Breslau from 1859 and founder of the Institute of Plant Physiology, he is regarded as the father of bacteriology in that he was the first to account it a separate science, to define bacteria, and to designate the group as plants. He did important research in plant pathology, and worked with **Robert Koch** on anthrax. Through his experiments on the effects of heat on bacteria, he identified bacterial spores. His work was a major factor in the overthrow of the theory of spontaneous generation. 📖 Pauline Cohn, *Ferdinand Cohn* (1901)

Cohnheim, Julius Friedrich 1839–84
German pathologist

Born in Demmin, Pomerania (now in Poland), he graduated in Berlin, where he spent a year as **Rudolf Virchow**'s assistant, and then occupied chairs in Kiel, Breslau and Leipzig. A superb microscopist and experimentalist, he worked on many problems, including infectious diseases and cancer. He was also the first to elucidate completely the microscopical events of inflammation, provided the first proof that tuberculosis was an infectious disease, and made investigations into the obstruction of the coronary artery and the resulting lack of oxygen which leads to a heart attack. His *Lectures on General Pathology* (1877) summarized the field.

Coke, Sir Edward, *also called* Lord Coke or Lord Cooke 1552–1634
English judge and jurist

Born in Mileham, Norfolk, he studied at Norwich and Trinity College, Cambridge, and was called to the Bar in 1578. He became Speaker of the House of Commons (1593), Attorney-General (1594), Chief Justice of the Common Pleas (1606), Chief Justice of the King's Bench (1613), and Privy Councillor. He vigorously prosecuted the Earl of **Essex**, Sir **Walter Raleigh**, and the Gunpowder Plot conspirators, but after 1606 increasingly supported the idea of national liberties vested in parliament, against the royal prerogative. He was dismissed in 1617, and from 1620 led the popular party in parliament, serving nine months in prison. The Petition of Right (1628) was largely of his making. Most of his epoch-making Law Reports were published from 1600 to 1615. ⊞ Catherine Drinker, *The Lion and the Throne* (1957)

Coke, Thomas 1747–1814
Welsh Methodist churchman

Born in Brecon, Powys, he graduated in 1768 from Oxford, and became an Anglican curate in Somerset. In 1777, he joined the Methodists, and was attached to the London circuit, and in 1784 was appointed by **John Wesley** as the superintendent of the Methodist Church in the USA. He visited the USA nine times, and assumed the title of bishop in 1787. Besides religious works, he published extracts from his *Journals* (1790), a *History of the West Indies* (3 vols, 1808–11), and, with Henry Moore, a *Life of Wesley* (1792).

Coke, Thomas William See Leicester of Holkham

Colbert, Claudette, *originally* Lily Claudette Chauchoin 1903–96
US film and stage actress

Born in Paris and educated in New York, she wanted to be a fashion designer but a bit part on stage in *The Wild Westcotts* (1923) converted her to acting. Her first film, *For the Love of Mike* (1927), led to a long-term contract with Paramount. Petite, saucer-eyed and glamorous, with a deep-throated laugh, she played historical seductresses in *The Sign of the Cross* (1932) and *Cleopatra* (1934) but sparkled in spirited comedy roles in such films as *It Happened One Night* (1934, Academy Award), *Tovarich* (1937), *Midnight* (1939) and *The Palm Beach Story* (1942). She retired from the screen after *Parrish* (1961), but frequently emerged from her home in Barbados to appear in such plays as *The Kingfisher* (1978), *A Talent for Murder* (1981) and *Aren't We All?* (1984–87). She also appeared in the television miniseries *The Two Mrs Grenvilles* (1987).

Colbert, Edwin Harris 1905–
US palaeontologist

Born in Clarinda, Iowa, he was educated at the University of Nebraska and Columbia University. He carried out research into vertebrate palaeontology at the American Museum of Natural History, New York City (1930–66), the Academy of Natural Sciences of Philadelphia (1937–48) and the Northern Arizona Society of Science and Art (1949–69). Professor of Vertebrate Palaeontology at Columbia University (1945–69), he has been one of the foremost palaeontologists of this century and has carried out fieldwork in many countries. He was a strong supporter of the theory of continental drift proposed by **Alfred Wegener**, and his discovery of the fossil *Lystrosaurus*

provided conclusive palaeontological support for this theory; his *Wandering Lands and Animals* (1973) gives a popular account of the evidence. He was also involved in the discovery and excavation of fossil dinosaurs in the American Mid-West, and his *Evolution of the Vertebrates* (1955) is a standard text.

Colbert, Jean-Baptiste 1619–83
French statesman

Born in Rheims, he entered the service of Cardinal **Mazarin** (1651), and became the chief financial minister of **Louis XIV** (1661). His series of successful financial reforms doubled the revenue in 10 years, and he also reorganized the colonies in Canada, Martinique and St Domingo, provided a strong fleet, improved the civil code, and introduced a marine code. He founded the Academies of Inscriptions, Science, and Architecture, and became a patron of industry, commerce, art, science and literature. The wars and the extravagance of the court undid all that he had accomplished, however, and he died bitterly disappointed, hated by the people as the cause of their oppressive taxes.

Colburn, Zerah 1804–40
US child prodigy

Born in Vermont, he displayed such powers of calculation that in 1810 his father left Vermont to exhibit him. A few years later he could solve extremely complicated problems with great rapidity, and was shown in Great Britain and Paris. From 1816 to 1819 he studied at Westminster School at the expense of the Earl of Bristol. His father died in 1824, and he returned to the USA, where he was a Methodist preacher for nine years, and from 1835 Professor of Languages at the University of Norwich, Vermont. His remarkable faculty for mental calculation disappeared as he grew to adulthood.

Colchester, Charles Abbot, 1st Baron 1757–1829
English jurist and politician

Born in Abingdon, Berkshire, he was educated at Westminster and Christ Church, Oxford, and in 1779 entered the Middle Temple. Returned to parliament as a strong Tory in 1795, in his first session he improved the legislation regarding temporary and expiring laws, and it is because of him that municipal bodies receive a copy of all new acts as soon as they are printed. He was also mainly responsible for the Private Bill Office and the Royal Record Commission, whose proceedings he superintended for many years. But his greatest service was in the Act (1800) for taking the first national census of the British population (1801). He was Speaker from 1802 until 1817, when he retired with a peerage.

Colding, Ludvig August 1815–88
Danish engineer and physicist

Born in Holbaek, from a profoundly religious family, he trained as a carpenter, then entered the Copenhagen Polytechnic Institute. By 1845 he had become inspector of roads and bridges, eventually rising to occupy the specially created position of Engineer of Copenhagen (1857). Municipal duties continued after he became professor at the Polytechnique Institute in 1869. He is most famous for his independent measurement of the mechanical equivalent of heat, contemporaneous with **James Prescott Joule** and others. In 1843 Colding proposed to the Danish Society of Sciences that 'force' which disappeared with friction was converted directly into heat, and much more generally, that there was a universal 'imperishability' of all natural forces, which was a justification that explicitly allied experimental data with religion and metaphysics.

Coldstream, Sir William 1908–87
English painter and teacher

Born in Belford, Northumberland, he studied at the Slade School of Art, and subsequently joining the London Group in 1933, helped to found the Euston Road School (1837), which promoted a quiet, sober realism. During World War II he was an official war artist in Italy and the Middle East. From 1949 he was Slade Professor of Fine Art at University College London. He was a highly skilled administrator, who helped to reshape British art education, especially through his work on the National Advisory Committee (1958–71) which produced the two 'Coldstream Reports'.

Cole, George 1925–
English actor

Born in South London, and educated in Morden, he was 'discovered' as a teenager by **Alastair Sim** when they starred together in the West End stage play *Cottage to Let* (1941) and the subsequent film version (1941). He acted in **Laurence Olivier**'s film of *Henry V* (1944) and found fame in radio's *A Life of Bliss*. His best remembered films are the farcical *The Belles of St Trinian's* (1954), three *St Trinian's* sequels and *Too Many Crooks* (1959), in all of which he played flashy and incompetent minor crooks. His many television roles include Max Osborne in *A Man of Our Times* (1968), Arthur Daley in *Minder* (1979–94), Trevor in *The Bounder* (1982–83), Sir Giles Lynchwood in *Blott on the Landscape* (1985), Henry Root in *Root into Europe* (1992) and Peter Banks in *My Good Friend* (1995).

Cole, G(eorge) D(ouglas) H(oward)
1889–1958
English economist, historian and detective-story writer

Born in London, he was educated at St Paul's School and Balliol College, Oxford, where he became Reader in Economics (1925) and Chichele Professor of Social and Political Theory (1944). Historian, chairman (1939–46, 1948–50) and president of the Fabian Society from 1952, he wrote numerous books on socialism, including *Lives of* **William Cobbett** (1925) and **Robert Owen** (1925) and a history of the British working-class movements, 1789–1947 (1948), often in collaboration with his wife, **Margaret Isabel Cole** and her brother, Raymond Postgate. The Coles also collaborated in writing detective fiction.

Cole, Sir Henry, *pseudonym* Felix Summerly
1808–82
English designer, writer and civil servant

He was born in Bath, Somerset, and as assistant keeper at the Public Record Office from 1838, was responsible for saving many ill-preserved documents. He also was involved in setting up the penny postage system. Under the pseudonym 'Felix Summerly' he set up a firm for 'art manufacture', designed the 'Summerly tea service', produced by Minton, wrote a series of handbooks on famous buildings in London, produced illustrated children's books, and published the first English Christmas card (1856). He planned and largely organized the Great Exhibition of 1851 under the patronage of Prince **Albert**. He set up a national system of art education, and was director of the South Kensington Museum in London (1853–73), which later became the Victoria and Albert Museum. His autobiography was published posthumously in 1884.

Cole, Dame Margaret Isabel, *née* Postgate
1893–1980
English writer, historian and political analyst

Born in Cambridge, she was educated at Roedean School, Sussex, and studied classics at Girton College, Cambridge. A socialist and feminist, she taught for a time at St Paul's School, London, before becoming a researcher for the Fabian Society where she met her husband, **G D H Cole**. They married in 1918 and together they wrote *An Intelligent Man's Review of Europe Today* (1933), *A*

Guide to Modern Politics (1934) and 29 detective stories. In addition she wrote many distinguished works including *The Makers of the Labour Movement* (1948), and a highly acclaimed biography of **Beatrice Webb** (1945).

Cole, Nat 'King', *originally* Nathaniel Adams Coles 1919–65
US singer and pianist

Born in Montgomery, Alabama, the son of a Baptist minister, he was brought up in Chicago and played the organ in his father's church before embarking on a career as a jazz pianist in the 1930s. His King Cole Trio (1939–51) made its first hit record, 'Straighten Up and Fly Right', in 1943, and its continuing success was influential in the trend away from big band and toward the small jazz combo of piano, guitar, and bass. Remembered mainly as a vocalist, Cole's mellow, caressing voice and impeccable phrasing produced a series of hit ballads, including 'Mona Lisa' (1950) and 'Unforgettable' (1951). He began acting in films in 1943, and became the first black American to host his own television show in 1956, but was subject to racist harassment when he bought a house in Beverly Hills area. His daughter, Natalie Maria Cole (1949–), is also a singer. Her albums include *Everlasting* (1987), *Thankful*, *Good to Be Back* (1989) and *Unforgettable* (1991). 📖 L Gourse, *Unforgettable* (1992)

Cole, Thomas 1801–48
US painter

Born in Bolton, Greater Manchester, England, he went to the USA in 1819, settled in Catshill, New York, and became founder of the Hudson River school of landscape painters. In 1830 two of his pictures appeared in the Royal Academy, London, and he afterwards made sketching tours through England, France and Italy, but his best landscapes, for example the *Voyage of Life* series, were American.

Coleman, David 1926–
English sports commentator and broadcaster

Born in Alderley Edge, Cheshire, he began his sporting life as a middle-distance runner, winning the Manchester Mile in 1949. He entered journalism, working on the *Stockport Express* and other local newspapers, and, having begun freelance radio work in 1953, joined the BBC in 1959. Noted for his reporting at the 1972 Munich Olympics when Israeli athletes were taken hostage, he built up a reputation for high-quality coverage. He has covered every World Cup final since 1958 and every Olympic Games since 1960, and has hosted the long-running television quiz programme, *A Question of Sport*, since 1979.

Coleman, Ornette 1930–
American jazz musician and composer

He was born in Fort Worth, Texas, where he began playing alto saxophone in rhythm and blues and jazz bands, under the influence of **Charlie Parker**. He moved to Los Angeles, and began to experiment from the mid-1950s with free-form jazz and his own distinctive approach to melodic and harmonic organization, later dubbed Harmolodics. A series of important recordings in 1959–60 with sympathetic collaborators like **Don Cherry**, Charlie Haden and Ed Blackwell established him as a leading but controversial innovator, and he became the figurehead of the free jazz movement of the 1960s. His own music continued to develop, including the adoption of electric instrumentation in the 1970s, and he has also written for chamber groups and symphony orchestras. He recorded the soundtrack for the 1991 film *Naked Lunch* based on the 1959 **William Burroughs** novel of the same title, and his collected recordings were released in 1993 under the title *Beauty is a Rare Thing*. Although never fully accepted by some in the jazz community, he is among the handful of most important figures in the music. ⌨ John Litweiler *Ornette Coleman – The Harmolodic Life* (1992)

Colenso, John William 1814–83
English clergyman

Born in St Austell, Cornwall, he was a graduate of St John's College, Cambridge. In 1853 he was appointed first Bishop of Natal, where he learned the Zulu language, writing a grammar and dictionary, and translating the Prayer Book and part of the Bible. His *The Pentateuch and the Book of Joshua Critically Examined* (1862–79), which cast doubts upon biblical accuracy, was regarded as heretical and his Metropolitan, Bishop Gray of Capetown, attempted to have him deposed, even publicly excommunicating him (1864). He was also unpopular for supporting dispossessed Africans. He was eventually deposed in 1869. His publications include *Miscellaneous Examples in Algebra* (1848), *Plane Trigonometry* (1851) and *Village Sermons* (1853).

Colepeper or Culpeper, Lord John 1600–60
English politician

Born in Wigsell, Sussex, he served abroad, and in 1640 was elected to the Short Parliament for Rye, and for Kent to the Long Parliament. There he opposed the Grand Remonstrance, but supported episcopacy. In 1642 he was created Chancellor of the Exchequer, in and 1643 Master of the Rolls. He was an important adviser to **Charles I** and Prince Charles (the future **Charles II**), and spent many years in exile in France and Flanders. He died shortly after his return to England at the Restoration.

Coleridge, Hartley 1796–1849
English writer

The eldest son of **Samuel Taylor Coleridge**, he was born in Clevedon, Somerset. He was brought up by **Robert Southey** at Greta Hall, and educated at Ambleside school and Merton College, Oxford. He lost his Oriel College fellowship because of intemperance. His *Poems, Songs and Sonnets* were published in 1833. He also wrote biographies, published under the titles of *Biographia Borealis* (1833) and *Worthies of Yorkshire and Lancashire* (1836), contributed to Blackwood's Magazine and other literary journals, and edited **John Ford** and **Philip Massinger**. He was provided for by an annuity, and spent his later years in the Lake District, where he continued to write tender, sincere poetry. He was the subject of the poems 'Frost at Midnight' and 'The Nightingale' by his father. ⌨ Earl Griggs, *Hartley Coleridge, his life and work* (1929)

Coleridge, Samuel Taylor 1772–1834
English poet

He was born in Ottery St Mary, Devon. The son of a vicar, and the youngest of a very large family, he had an unhappy childhood. He was educated at Christ's Hospital and Jesus College, Cambridge, where he studied for the Church. His university career was interrupted in 1793 by a runaway enlistment in the 15th Dragoons from which he was rescued by his family. On a walking tour in 1794 he met **Robert Southey**, with whom he shared Romantic and revolutionary views. Together they planned, but never created, a 'Pantisocracy' or commune on the banks of the Susquehanna, in Pennsylvania. In 1795 he married Sarah Fricker, a friend of Southey's, who married her sister Edith. He had contributed some verses to the *Morning Chronicle* in 1793, and now he wrote, with Southey, a historical play, *The Fall of Robespierre*. He became immersed in lecturing and journalism in Bristol, interspersed with itinerant preaching at Unitarian chapels. The Bristol circle provided him with generous friends, including Joseph Cottle the bookseller, who published his first book of poems, *Poems on Various Subjects* (1796), which contained the 'Ode to France'. In 1797 the Coleridges moved to a cottage

at Nether Stowey, Somerset, and later that year met **William** and **Dorothy Wordsworth**. It was a significant meeting for English poetry—their discussions produced a new poetry which represented a revulsion from neoclassic artificiality and, consequently, the renovation of the language of poetry. *Lyrical Ballads* (1798), which opened with Coleridge's 'The Rime of the Ancient Mariner' and closed with Wordsworth's 'Tintern Abbey', was thus in the nature of a manifesto. A visit to Germany with the Wordsworths followed in 1798–99. German philosophy and criticism influenced Coleridge greatly and he published translations of **Schiller**'s *Piccolomini* and *Wallenstein*. In 1800 he settled at Keswick and for a time, with the Wordsworths at Grasmere and Southey already resident at Keswick, it looked as if a fruitful career was opening out for him, but he was deeply unhappy at this time, due partly to his addiction to opium, and partly to an increasingly unhappy marriage. His 'Ode to Dejection' (1802) is both a recantation of Wordsworth's animistic view of Nature and a confession of failure. From then on his association with Wordsworth was strained; his relations with Dorothy continued only through her devotion to him. In 1809 he began a weekly paper, *The Friend*, which ran for 28 issues and was published as a book in 1818. In 1810 he finally broke with Wordsworth and settled in London, where he engaged in miscellaneous writing and lecturing at the Royal Institution (his lectures on **Shakespeare** alone are extant). He also wrote a play, *Remorse* (1813), which had a mild success at Drury Lane. In 1816 he published *Christabel and other poems*, which included 'Christabel' and the fragment, 'Kubla Khan', both written in his earlier period of inspiration. He had relinquished the idea of renewing that inspiration but became the centre of a circle of young disciples and devoted himself to philosophical speculation. His critical writing in these middle years is important as the finest creative criticism in the language, collected in *Biographia Literaria* (1817), *Aids to Reflection* (1825), and *Anima Poetae* (edited from his *Notebooks*, 1895). He also wrote some moving late poems, including 'Youth and Age' and 'Constancy to an Ideal Object. ⌨ J L Lowes, *The Road to Xanadu* (1927); T D Campbell, *Samuel Taylor Coleridge: a narrative of the events of his life* (1894)

Coleridge, Sara 1802–52
English scholar

Born at Greta Hall, Keswick, the daughter of **Samuel Taylor Coleridge**, she was brought up in **Robert Southey**'s household. In 1822 she translated Dobrizhoffer's *Historia de Abiponibus*, and in 1825 the *Memoirs* of the Chevalier Pierre du Terrail de Bayard. In 1829 she married her cousin, Henry Nelson Coleridge, and helped to edit her father's writings. Her own works were *Pretty Lessons for Good Children* (1834) and *Phantasmion* (1837), a fairy tale. Her son, Herbert Coleridge (1830–61), educated at Eton and Oxford, was called to the Bar, but, devoting himself to comparative philology, worked for the Philological Society's dictionary, and wrote a *Thirteenth Century Glossarial Index* (1859) and an essay on King **Arthur**.

Coleridge-Taylor, Samuel 1875–1912
English composer

Born in London, the son of a West African doctor and an Englishwoman, he studied at the Royal College of Music. He composed *Hiawatha* (1898–1900), and other popular cantatas and orchestral works.

Colet, John c.1467–1519
English scholar and theologian

Born in London, the son of Sir Henry Colet, he studied at Oxford. In Italy (c.1493) he became acquainted with the views of **Savonarola**. Returning to England in 1496, he was ordained a priest, and became a lecturer at Oxford on the Epistles of St Paul (1496–1504), in which he opposed the interpretations of the scholastic theologians. He was a colleague of both Sir **Thomas More** and **Erasmus** while at Oxford. In 1505 he was made Dean of St Paul's, and continued to deliver controversial lectures on the interpretation of Scripture, and to preach against ecclesiastical abuses. Charges of heresy were brought against him, but Archbishop **William Warham** refused to support them. With the large fortune he inherited from his father he endowed St Paul's School in 1509–12. ⊞ J H Lupton, *Life of John Colet* (1887)

Colette, *properly* Sidonie-Gabrielle Colette, *also known as* Colette Willy 1873–1954
French novelist

She was born in Saint-Sauveur-en-Puisaye, Burgundy. Her early novels, the *Claudine* series, were published by her first husband, Henri Gauthier-Villars, under his pen name 'Willy'. From 1904 (the end of their collaboration) to 1916 she wrote under the name 'Colette Willy'. After their divorce in 1906 she appeared in music-halls in dance and mime, and out of this period came *L'Envers du music-hall* (1913, Eng trans *Music-Hall Sidelights*, 1957). Keenly perceptive, and writing in a musical, mellifluous prose, she writes with an intense, sensual responsiveness to the world of nature and to her childhood. Her novels include *Chéri* (1920, Eng trans 1929), *La Fin de Chéri* (1926, Eng trans *The Last of Chéri*, 1932), *La Chatte* (1933, Eng trans *The Cat*, 1936) and *Gigi* (1944, Eng trans 1953). She was the first woman to be made president of the Académie Goncourt. ⊞ J Richardson, *Colette* (1983)

Colfax, Schuyler 1823–85
US politician

He was born in New York City. Originally a newspaper editor, in 1868 he was elected Vice-President of the USA, in **Ulysses S Grant**'s first term. Unjustly implicated in the Crédit Mobilier charges of 1873, he spent the rest of his life in political retirement.

Coligny, Gaspard II de, Seigneur de Châtillon 1519–72
French Huguenot leader

Born in Châtillon-sur-Loing, he fought in the wars of **Francis I** and **Henri II** of France, and was made Admiral of France (1552). In 1557 he became a Protestant, and commanded the Huguenots during the second and third Wars of Religion. Disliking his influence over her son, **Charles IX**, **Catherine de' Médicis** made him one of the first victims in the St Bartholomew's Day Massacre in Paris (1572). ⊞ A W Whitehead, *Gaspard de Coligny, Admiral of France* (1904)

Colijn, Hendrikus 1869–1944
Dutch politician

His first career was in the Dutch colonial army (1892–1909). He became a member of the Dutch parliament for the Calvinist Anti-Revolutionary Party, of which he was the leader from 1920. He also had business interests (as director of the Batavian Oil Company) and was chief editor of the Calvinist daily newspaper the *Standard* from 1922. He first took cabinet office as Minister of War (1911–13) and then as Minister of Finance (1923–25). From 1925 to 1939 he was Prime Minister of no less than six cabinets, and was the figurehead of the tough deflationary Dutch government policies of the 1930s. When the Germans invaded his country in 1940 he toyed with accepting the New Order, but soon rejected this, and was interned in 1941. He died in Ilmenau in Germany.

Colleoni, Bartolommeo 1400–75
Italian soldier and condottiere

He was born near Bergamo. He fought on both sides in the conflict between Milan and Venice, where he finally settled in 1454, becoming generalissimo for life. He is the subject of the famous Venetian equestrian statue by **Andrea del Verrocchio**.

Collett, (Jacobine) Camilla, *née* Wergeland 1813–95
Norwegian novelist

Born in Kristiansand, she had a strict upbringing and in her adult life became a passionate champion of women's rights. Her novel *Amtmandens døttre* (1855, 'The Magistrate's Daughters') is notable for its sympathetic portrayal of young women trapped by stultifying convention. *I den lange naetter* (1862, 'Through the Long Nights') is an insomniac's pillow-book, reconstructing childhood scenes. Her occasional pieces were published in three volumes of *Sidtse blade* (1868, 1872, 1873). She was the sister of **Hendrik Arnold Wergeland**. ⊞ A Collett, *Camilla Colletts livshistorie* (1911)

Collier, Arthur 1680–1732
English philosopher

He was born in Steeple Langford rectory, Wiltshire, where he himself became rector in 1704. His *Clavis Universalis* (1713, 'Universal Key') independently argues for the idealist conclusions Bishop **Berkeley** reached on the impossibility of the existence of an external world.

Collier, Jeremy 1650–1726
Anglican Church historian and clergyman

Born in Stow, Cambridgeshire, and educated at Ipswich and Cambridge, he became rector of Ampton, and a lecturer at Gray's Inn, London. He opposed **William III** and **Mary**, refusing to take the Oath of Allegiance in 1689. Fierce in his polemics, he spent some time in prison and in temporary exile abroad as a political outlaw. He is best known, however, for *A Short View of the Immorality and Profaneness of the English Stage* (1698), a vehement attack on Restoration dramatists. Replies by **John Dryden**, **William Congreve**, Sir **John Vanbrugh** and others were generally considered to be ineffective. Collier's strictures did much ostensibly to reform, but actually to tame, comic drama in the 18th century. He also wrote the *Great Historical, Geographical, and Poetical Dictionary* (4 vols, folio, 1701–21) and the scholarly *An Ecclesiastical History of Great Britain* (2 vols, folio, 1708–14). He was consecrated a nonjuring bishop in 1713. ⊞ Sister Rose Anthony, *The Jeremy Collier Controversy* (1937)

Collier, John Payne 1789–1883
English journalist and critic

Born in London, he published editions of various authors, including **Shakespeare** and **Robert Dodsley**, and a *History of English Dramatic Poetry* and *Annals of the Stage to the Restoration* (both 1831). He is chiefly remembered for his forgeries and falsification of old manuscripts, especially for the so-called 'Perkins folio' (a Second Folio of Shakespeare's plays dated 1632, in which he falsified the marginal corrections). He was exposed in 1859.

Collings, Jesse 1831–1920
English politician

Born in Littleham-cum-Exmouth, Devon, he was elected Radical MP for Ipswich in 1880. He was MP for Bordesley as a Unionist (1886–1918), and was specially identified with the Agricultural Labourers' Union and measures for promoting allotments and smallholdings ('three acres and a cow'). He was also Under-Secretary for the Home Office (1895–1902).

Collingwood, Cuthbert, Lord 1748–1810
English naval commander

Born in Newcastle upon Tyne, he joined the navy at the age of 11, and from 1778 his career was closely connected with that of Lord Nelson. He played a prominent part in the naval victories of Lord Howe off Brest (1794), of Lord Jervis off Cape St Vincent (1797), and of Nelson off Cape Trafalgar (1805), where he held the second command. He died at sea, and was buried beside Nelson, in St Paul's Cathedral, London.

Collingwood, R(obin) G(eorge) 1889–1943
English philosopher, historian and archaeologist

Born in Coniston, Cumbria, the son of William Gershom Collingwood and educated at Rugby and Oxford, he taught at Oxford and was Professor of Philosophy there (1934–41). He was an authority on the archaeology of Roman Britain, and much of his philosophical work was concerned with the relations of history and philosophy. At first a follower of Hegel and Benedetto Croce, increasingly he saw philosophy as an irreducibly historical discipline, always influenced by its own time and culture. He was intellectually an unfashionable figure in his lifetime but was recognized as a writer of great style, originality and learning. His many books include: *Speculum Mentis* (1924), *Roman Britain and the English Settlements* (1936), *The Principles of Art* (1937), *Autobiography* (1939), *Essay on Metaphysics* (1940), *The New Leviathan* (1942), and two posthumous works *The Idea of Nature* (1945) and *The Idea of History* (1946).

Collingwood, William Gershom 1854–1932
English artist and archaeologist

Born in Liverpool, he studied philosophy and aesthetics at Oxford, then trained as an artist for four years in London under Alphonse Legros. He moved to Coniston in the Lake District to be private secretary and collaborator to John Ruskin, and was for a time a professor at Reading University. He is best known for his archaeological studies on Viking remains in the north of England, and for his *Pilgrimage to the Saga-Steads of Iceland* (1899), copiously illustrated with his own watercolours. He was the father of the philosopher R G Collingwood.

Collins, Albert 1932–93
US blues guitarist and singer

Born in Leona, Texas, he was a cousin of Lightnin' Hopkins, and inherited the Texas blues guitar tradition of Hopkins and T-Bone Walker. He had a regional hit in 1958 with 'The Freeze', and became known for an 'icy', spare guitar sound. He recorded in a crossover blues–funk style in the late 1960s, but did little more of note until he signed with Alligator Records in 1977. Both he and the label flourished in the blues revival of the 1980s, and his distinctive guitar style has influenced younger players like Robert Cray. He joined Cray and Johnny Copeland on the best-selling *Showdown* (1985), one of several records for which he received Grammy award nominations.

Collins, Charles Allston 1828–73
English painter

The second son of the artist William Collins and brother of Wilkie Collins, he began by painting pictures in the Pre-Raphaelite style and in 1860 married the younger daughter of Charles Dickens. Turning his attention to literature, he produced *The Eye-witness* essays (1860), two novels, and other works.

Collins, Joan Henrietta 1933–
English actress and writer

Born in London, she made her film debut in *Lady Godiva Rides Again* (1951) and used her sultriness and headline-catching private life to build a career as an international celebrity. By the 1970s she was appearing in low-budget horror films such as *Tales from the Crypt* (1972), but her fortunes were revitalized with a leading role in the popular television soap opera *Dynasty* (1981–89). Married four times, she has written a tell-all autobiography, *Past Imperfect* (1978); the novels *Prime Time* (1988) and *Too Damn Famous; My Secrets* (1994); and her memoirs, *Second Act* (1996). Her sister is the bestselling novelist Jackie Collins (1937–).

Collins, Michael 1890–1922
Irish politician and Sinn Féin leader

Born in County Cork, he became an active force in the Sinn Féin independence movement, and was imprisoned in England in 1916 for his part in the Easter Rebellion. On the declaration of independence, he raised funds for the movement and was subsequently responsible, with Arthur Griffith, for negotiating the 1921 treaty that created the Irish Free State (1922). But when Éamon de Valera and his supporters insisted on a fully-independent republic, civil war between the two factions broke out. Collins became head of the provisional Free State Government in 1922, but only 10 days after taking office he was killed in an IRA ambush. His life was the subject of a film, *Michael Collins*, in 1996. ▢ Edgar Holt, *Protest in Arms* (1960)

Collins, Michael 1930–
US astronaut

Born in Rome, Italy, he graduated from the US Military Academy, West Point. He joined the US air force in 1952 and became an experimental test pilot at the Air Force Flight Test Center, Edwards Air Force Base, California. He joined NASA as an astronaut in 1963 and was back-up pilot for Gemini 7 (a two-seater Earth satellite capsule) before orbiting as co-pilot in Gemini 10, which was launched on 18 July 1966. On the historic Apollo II Moon-landing mission in 1969 he was in the command module while Neil Armstrong and Buzz Aldrin set foot on the Moon. His publications include the autobiographical *Carrying the Fire* (1974) and *Mission to Mars* (1990).

Collins, Pauline 1940–
English actress

Born in Exmouth, Devon, but brought up in Liverpool, she played Dawn in the television series of *The Liver Birds* (1969) and followed her role of under-house parlourmaid Sarah in *Upstairs Downstairs* (1971–75) by starring with her husband, actor John Alderton, in the spin-off *Thomas and Sarah* (1979), as well as in *No Honestly* (1974) and *Forever Green* (1989–91). Following her success in the title role of *Shirley Valentine* in the West End and on Broadway (1988–89), winning her a Tony award, she was nominated for an Academy Award and won a BAFTA award when she starred in the film version (1989). She also played Sister Joan in the film *City of Joy* (1992).

Collins, Phil(ip) 1951–
English singer, drummer and songwriter

Born in Hounslow, West London, the son of a theatrical agent, he appeared on stage in *Oliver!* (1964), but decided to pursue a career in rock music. He began with the band Flaming Youth, joined Genesis as drummer in 1970, and took over as lead vocalist when singer Peter Gabriel left the group (1985). Under his leadership the band gained international success, which was maintained with *We Can't Dance* (1991), but as a solo artist his success was greater, with the albums *Face Value* (1981), *No Jacket Required* (1985), *But Seriously...* (1989) and *Both Sides* (1993). He has appeared on television, in *Miami Vice*, and starred in the films *Buster* (1987) and *Frauds* (1992).

Collins, Wilkie (William) 1824–89
English novelist

Born in London, the elder son of the artist William Collins, he was educated partly at Highbury, but from 1836 to 1839 was with his parents in Italy. After his return he spent four years in business, and then was called to the Bar, but gradually devoted himself to literature, beginning with a *Life* of his father (1848). His first work of fiction was a novel about the fall of Rome, *Antonina* (1850). With *Basil* (1852) he turned his attention to mystery, suspense and crime, writing the first full-length detective stories in English. His best work was written in the 1860s when he produced *The Woman in White* (1860), *No Name* (1862), *Armadale* (1866) and *The Moonstone* (1868). Perhaps because of his poor health and opium addiction, his later novels, often driven by pressing social issues, are more uneven in quality. ◫ K Robinson, *Wilkie Collins: a biography* (1951); William H Marshall, *Wilkie Collins* (1950)

Collins, William 1721–59
English poet
Born in Chichester, Sussex, and educated at Winchester and Magdalen College, Oxford, he went to London to make a living by literature. During this period, he wrote his *Odes*, upon which his fame rests, but which attracted no notice at the time of publication (1747). In 1749 he retired to Chichester and met **John Home**, the author of *Douglas*, and gave him his 'Ode on the Superstitions of the Highlands', a poem in which, says **James Lowell**, 'the whole Romantic School is foreshadowed'. ◫ P L Carver, *The Life of a Poet: a biographical sketch* (1967)

Collins, William 1788–1847
English landscape and figure painter
Born in London, he studied at the Royal Academy. He is remembered for his subject pictures of country scenes, such as *Blackberry Gatherers* and *The Bird-catchers* (1814). He was the father of **Wikie Collins** and **Charles Collins**.

Collins, William 1789–1853
Scottish publisher
He was born in Eastwood, Renfrewshire. A weaver by trade, he opened a private school for the poor in Glasgow in 1813. A friend of the evangelist **Thomas Chalmers**, in 1819 he set up business in Glasgow as a bookseller and publisher with Chalmers's brother. He specialized in church history and pioneered school textbooks. The company became the largest independent publishing house in Britain, and remained under family control until 1979.

Collinson, Peter 1694–1768
English botanist and naturalist
Born in London, he became a woollen draper, trading with the American colonies, and through his business and Quaker associations introduced American plant species into Great Britain, and vice versa, thereby assisting horticultural progress in both countries. He had a garden first at Peckham, and then at Mill Hill.

Collip, James Bertram 1892–1965
Canadian biochemist and Nobel Prize winner
Born in Belleville, Ontario, and educated at Toronto University, he became a lecturer in biochemistry at the University of Alberta at Edmonton (1915–17), and subsequently became assistant professor (1917–19) and associate professor (1919–28). In 1928 he became Professor of Biochemistry at McGill University, transferring in 1941 to a chair in endocrinology, and in 1947 he became Dean of Medicine at Western Ontario, where he also headed a department of medical research. His early research concerned the blood chemistry of vertebrates and invertebrates; he also examined the physiological effects of adrenaline and the mechanisms of brain stem function. Early in 1921 he went to the Toronto laboratory of **John Macleod**, where he worked with Sir **Frederick Banting** and **Charles Best** on the isolation and identification of insulin. Collip purified their pancreatic extract sufficiently for it to be tried in clinical trials; his experiments also alerted clinicians to the dangers of exceeding the calculated doses. This research earned the team the 1923 Nobel Prize, with Banting sharing his half with Best, and Macleod doing likewise with Collip. In 1922 Collip

returned to Edmonton to focus his career on biochemical aspects of endocrine function. In 1925 he discovered the active principal of the parathyroid gland, and in later years identified hormones from the placenta.

Collor de Mello, Fernando 1950–
Brazilian politician
Born into a family in the north-eastern state of Alagoas, he grew up in Rio de Janeiro where his family owned extensive media holdings. He managed to lever himself into the Prefecture of Maceió (1979–82) and then become Governor of Alagoas (1986). A political conservative, he leapt to prominence as a young and dynamic critic of 'corruption', leading his National Renovation Party in the race for the presidency in 1989. Once in office (1990), he embarked on a bold programme of economic reform, before he built up a significant base within Congress. Control over Congress lay in the hands of groups which had benefited from the 1988 Constitution, which protected special interests directly affected by the presidential programme. He resigned in 1992 as his impeachment, on charges of corruption, began in the Senate.

Collot d'Herbois, Jean Marie 1751–96
French revolutionary
Born in Paris, and originally an actor, he joined the Jacobin Club in 1791. His self-confidence, his loud voice and his *Almanach du Père Gérard* secured his election to the National Convention. In 1793 he became president of the Convention and a member of the murderous Committee of Public Safety. Sent by **Robespierre** to Lyons, he took revenge by guillotine and grapeshot on the inhabitants for having once hissed him off the stage. He joined in the successful plot against Robespierre (1794), but was himself expelled from the Convention, and banished to Cayenne (1795), where he died.

Collymore, Frank Appleton 1893–1980
Barbadian poet and story writer
He was educated at Combermere School, where he taught from 1910 to 1958. As founder and editor of the long-running literary magazine *Bim* (1942–1975), he was a major force in the rise of modern West Indian literature. His short stories were published in *Bim* between 1942 and 1971. He also published five books of poems, notable chiefly for their evocation of the sea and Caribbean landscape. His *Collected Poems* were published in 1959. ◫ E Baugh, in *Fifty Caribbean Writers*, ed D C Dance (1986)

Colman, St d.676
Irish monk
He was a monk on the island of Iona and became Bishop of Lindisfarne in 661, but in 664 withdrew to Iona on the defeat of the Celtic party at the Council of Whitby.

Colman, George, the Elder 1732–94
English playwright and manager
Born in Florence, the son of the English envoy, he was educated at Westminster School and Oxford, and called to the Bar in 1755. In 1760 his first piece, *Polly Honeycombe*, was produced at Drury Lane with great success. It was followed by *The Jealous Wife* (1761), and in 1766 *The Clandestine Marriage*, written in conjunction with **David Garrick**. In 1767 he purchased, with three others, Covent Garden Theatre, and held the office of manager for seven years, until he sold his share. In 1776 he purchased the Haymarket Theatre from the playwright Samuel Foote (1720–77). He was paralysed by a stroke in 1785. ◫ E R Page, *George Colman the Elder* (1935)

Colman, George, the Younger 1762–1836
English playwright

Born in London, the son of **George Colman**, the Elder, he was educated at Westminster School, Oxford and Aberdeen. During his father's illness he acted as manager of the Haymarket Theatre, London, and on his death the patent was transferred to him. As examiner of plays from 1824 he showed himself both arrogant and excessively precise. In industry he rivalled his father, and he made money from his *John Bull* (1803), *Iron Chest* (1796), *Heir at Law* (1797) and other comedies, and from songs like 'Mynheer Van Dunck'. He also wrote *Random Records of My Life* (1830). ⮺ J F B Collins, *George Colman the Younger* (1946)

Colman, Ronald 1891–1958
English film and stage actor

Born in Richmond, Surrey, he moved to Hollywood, where he made his screen debut in 1919 in *The Live Wire*. His dashing good looks, mellifluous voice and gentlemanly manner made him a popular romantic leading man for three decades, and he was one of the few major Hollywood stars to survive the transition to the sound era. His films include *The White Sister* (1923), *Raffles* (1930), *A Tale of Two Cities* (1935), *The Prisoner of Zenda* (1937) and *Random Harvest* (1942).

Colmcille See Columba, St

Colomb, Philip Howard 1831–99
Scottish naval officer and historian

Born in Scotland, he entered the navy in 1846 and served in the Burmese War (1852) and in China (1874–77). He devised the system of night signalling known as 'Colomb's Flashing Signals' (1858). The author of *Naval Warfare* (1891), on the importance of naval supremacy, he was promoted vice-admiral in 1892.

Colombine See Burgos Seguí, Carmen de

Colombo, Joe Cesare 1930–71
Italian designer

Born in Milan, he was interested in painting, sculpture and architecture, but became an industrial designer. One of the most versatile Italian designers of the 1960s, his interests included lighting, glass, furniture and, in particular, multifunction storage furniture. He designed compact 'core' units which required only connection to services to provide a fully functioning home, and included kitchen, bathroom, storage, radio, music centre and television. The best example was his 'Total Furnishing Unit' (1971) for the exhibition 'Italy: The New Domestic Landscape' at the Museum of Modern Art, New York. This, and many of his designs, made much use of plastics.

Colonna, Vittoria 1490–1547
Italian poet

Born into an important noble Roman family in Marino, she had an arranged marriage to the Marquis of Pescara but saw little of him. He died in battle at Pavi (1525), and she devoted herself to a religious life and good causes, later lamenting his death and that of her father in *Canzoniere* (1544). Her religious thinking was profound, as were her objections to corruption in the Church. An inspiration to her friend **Michelangelo**, she was admired by **Ariosto**, and became the intimate associate of the reforming party at the papal court. Her poems, which are Petrarchan in style, appeared at Parma in 1538. Other members of the ancient Colonna family, which took its name from a castle in the Alban Hills, include a pope (**Martin V**), several cardinals, generals, statesmen and noted scholars. ⮺ M F Jerrold, *Vittoria Colonna* (1906, reprinted 1969)

Colquhoun, Ithell, *originally* Margaret Ithell
1906–88
English artist and poet

Born in Assam, India, she studied at the Slade School of Art, London, before working in various studios in Paris and Athens. Associated with the English Surrealists, she met **André Breton** and **Salvador Dali** in 1933, and exhibited at the 1936 International Surrealist Exhibition. Prior to 1930, her work dealt with mythological and biblical subjects, but she turned to portraying dream-like states, and in the 1940s she painted fantastic plants using various media. From 1956 she lived in Cornwall, where she wrote about and painted themes from the occult and alchemy. She exhibited widely throughout Great Britain and abroad, and contributed articles and poems to the *London Bulletin*.

Colquhoun, Patrick 1745–1820
Scottish merchant and reformer

He was born in Dumbarton, Strathclyde. After visiting Virginia, America, he became a tobacco merchant in Glasgow and was Lord Provost in 1782. He founded the Glasgow Chamber of Commerce in 1783, the oldest of its kind in Great Britain. Moving to London in 1789 he became a police magistrate and wrote many reforming pamphlets, including *Police of the Metropolis* (1795).

Colquhoun, Robert 1914–62
Scottish artist

Born in Kilmarnock, Ayrshire, he studied at the Glasgow School of Art and in Italy, France, Holland and Belgium. His enigmatic, dreamlike figures, such as *Girl with a Circus Goat*, are usually presented in a characteristic colour scheme of reds and browns.

Colt, Samuel 1814–62
US inventor

Born in Hartford, Connecticut, he ran away to sea in 1827, and from about 1836 travelled throughout the USA, lecturing in chemistry. In 1836 he took out his first patent for a revolver, which after the Mexican War (1846–48) was adopted for the US army. He financed an immense armoury in Hartford, and also worked on submarine mines, and a submarine telegraph.

Coltrane, John William 1926–67
US jazz saxophonist and composer

Born in Hamlet, North Carolina, he emerged in the 1950s as one of the most influential jazz performers of the post-bebop era. His early engagements included working with **Dizzy Gillespie** and **Bud Powell**, but his distinctive style coalesced with the **Miles Davis** Quintet from 1955, and then with pianist **Thelonious Monk** in 1957. His so-called 'sheets of sound' style of harmonic exhaustiveness reached a logical culmination in *Giant Steps* (1959), by which time he was already immersed in the modal jazz experiments of Miles Davis. The freedom from conventional harmonic structures profoundly affected his improvising style. The intensity of his attack and dense flow of notes influenced a generation of future saxophone players, as did his adoption of the soprano saxophone as a second instrument to the tenor. His post-1960 quartet with pianist McCoy Tyner and drummer Elvin Jones helped redefine the process of interaction within the jazz group, and led to some of his most important recordings, notably *A Love Supreme* (1964). His music grew increasingly experimental toward the end of his life, when his collaborators (in both music and eastern philosophy) included his wife, Alice Coltrane (*née* McLeod, 1937–), who went on to have a significant musical career in her own right. Their sons, Ravi and Omar, are also musicians. ⮺ B Cole, *John Coltrane* (1976)

Coltrane, Robbie, *originally* Robin McMillan
1950–
Scottish actor

Born in Rutherglen, near Glasgow, he won the Scottish Council Film of the Year award for his 50-minute documentary *Young Mental Health* (1973). His career progressed via theatre work and especially an involvement with writer **John Byrne** on *The Slab Boys* (1978) and its sequel *Cuttin' A Rug* (1980). A talented mimic and wit, he displayed his comic skills on television in a succession of satirical sketch shows. His films include *Mona Lisa* (1986), *The Fruit Machine* (1987), *Henry V* (1989), in which he played Falstaff, and *Golden Eye* (1995). He played rock 'n' roller Danny McGlone in the television series *Tutti Frutti* (1987) and his reputation continued to grow through warmly received one-man stage shows such as *Yr Obedient Servant* (1987), in which he played Dr Johnson, and *Mistero Buffo* (1990), which was also televised, and as police psychologist Fitz in the television series *Cracker* (1993–96). Increasingly recognized internationally, he has starred in such comic films as *Nuns on the Run* (1990) and *The Pope Must Die* (1991). 📖 *Coltrane in a Cadillac* (1993)

Colum, Pádraic 1881–1972
Irish poet and playwright

Born in County Longford, he was educated at a school in Longford, and worked as a railway clerk in Dublin. He became a leader of the Irish literary revival, and wrote plays for the Abbey Theatre, including *Broken Soil* (1903, later called *The Fiddler's House*), *The Land* (1905) and *Thomas Muskerry* (1910). He published his first collection of poems, *Wild Earth*, in 1907. In 1916 he was co-founder of the *Irish Review*. From 1914 he lived in the USA, where he and his wife taught comparative literature at Columbia University. He published two studies on Hawaiian folklore (1924, 1926), the result of government-sponsored research. He wrote several further volumes of verse, including the lyric *She Moved Through the Fair*. His novel *The Flying Swans* (1957) was followed by the memoir *Our Friend James Joyce* (1958), written with his wife, Mary. 📖 Z R Brown, *Pádraic Colum* (1970)

Columba, St, *also known as* Colmcille ('Colm of the Churches') 521–97
Irish missionary in Scotland

He was born into the royal warrior aristocracy of Ireland at Gartan, County Donegal, and according to his 7th-century biographer, **Adomnan**, he studied under St **Finnian** at Clonard with St **Ciaran**. In 546 he founded the monastery of Derry. In 561 he was accused of having been involved in the bloody Battle of Cuildreimhne, for which he was excommunicated and sentenced to exile. In 563, accompanied by 12 disciples, he set sail to do penance as a missionary, and found haven on the Hebridean island of Iona, where he founded a monastery that became the mother church of Celtic Christianity in Scotland. He travelled to other parts of Scotland, especially to the north to evangelize amongst the Picts, and won the respect of the pagan King Brude (Bridei) at his stronghold near Inverness (possibly the hill-fort at Craig Phadrig). He and his missionaries founded numerous churches in the islands of the Hebrides (hence his Gaelic name of Colmcille). He organized his monastery on Iona as a school for missionaries, and played a vigorous role in the politics of the country. Although he spent the last 34 years of his life in Scotland, he visited Ireland on occasions, and towards the end of his life he founded the monastery of Durrow in Ireland. He was renowned as a man of letters, he wrote hymns, and is credited with having transcribed 300 books. He was also revered as a warrior saint, and his supernatural aid was frequently invoked for victory in battle. His feast day is 9 June. 📖 W D Simpson, *The Historical St Columba* (1927, rev edn 1963)

Columban or Columbanus, St, *known as* the younger Columba 543–615
Irish missionary

Born in Leinster, he studied under St **Comgall** at Bangor in County Down, and in c.585 went to Gaul with 12 companions, and founded the monasteries of Anegray, Luxeuil and Fontaine in the Vosges. His adherence to the Celtic Easter involved him in controversy, and his vigourous criticism of the vices of the Burgundian court led to his expulsion in 610. After a year or two in Bregenz, on Lake Constance, he went to Lombardy, and in 612 founded the monastery of Bobbio, in the Appenines, where he died. His writings, all in Latin, comprise a monastic rule, six poems on the vanity of life, 17 sermons and a commentary on the Psalms (Eng trans, ed G S M Walker, 1957). His feast day is 23 November. 📖 C W Dispham, *Columban, Saint, Monk and Missionary* (1903)

Columbus, Christopher See panel p428

Columella, Lucius Junius Moderatus
1st century AD
Roman writer on agriculture

Born in Gades (Cadiz), Spain, he wrote *De Re Rustica* (12 books), on arable and pasture lands, the culture of vines and olives, the care of domestic animals, and arboriculture. Book 10 (on gardening) is written in hexameters as an addendum to **Virgil's** *Georgics*. 📖 S Hedberg, *Contamination and Interpolation: a study of the 19th century manuscripts* (1968)

Colville, David 1813–98
Scottish industrialist

Born in Campbeltown, Argyll, he began making malleable plates and angles for Scottish shipbuilders in 1871, employing 200 men. In 1879 he built five of the largest Siemens furnaces for the production of steel, and in 1880 he obtained the contract to supply Siemens furnaces. In 1885 he took his three sons into partnership, but two of them died in 1916 and the third, John, became an MP. Thus the chairmanship passed to a former office boy, Sir John Craig (1874–1957), who made the firm the fourth largest steel concern in Great Britain.

Comaneci, Nadia 1961–
Romanian gymnast

Born in Onesti, Moldavia, at the 1976 Olympic Games at the age of 14, she won gold medals in the parallel bars and beam disciplines, and a bronze in the floor, becoming the first gymnast to obtain a perfect score of 10 for her performance on the bars and beam. She also won a gold medal in the beam at the 1978 world championships. She won both the beam and floor exercise gold medals in the 1980 Olympics. Later she became an international judge, and coach to the Romanian national team. In 1989 she defected to the USA via Hungary.

Combe, William 1741–1823
English writer and adventurer

Born in Bristol, the illegitimate son of a wealthy London alderman, he was educated at Oxford, inherited a fortune in 1762 and led the life of an adventurer, spending much time in debtors' jails. He wrote metrical satires like *The Diaboliad* (1776), but made his name with his three verse satires on popular travel-books: *The Tour of Dr Syntax in Search of the Picturesque* (1809), *The Second Tour of Dr Syntax in Search of Consolation* (1820) and *The Third Tour of Dr Syntax in Search of a Wife* (1821). Illustrated with cartoons by **Thomas Rowlandson**, they recounted the travels of 'Dr Syntax', a clergyman schoolmaster (based on **William Gilpin**). He also wrote the text for Rowlandson's *Dance of Death* (1815–16), *Dance of Life* (1816) and *Johnny Quae Genus* (1822), and for *The Microcosm of London* (1808). 📖 H Hamilton, *Doctor Syntax: a silhouette of William Combe Esq* (1969)

Columbus, Christopher 1451–1506
Genoese explorer, and discoverer of the New World

Christopher Columbus was born in Genoa, the son of a woolcomber. He went to sea at the age of 14, fought with Tunisian galleys, and in about 1470, shipwrecked in a fight off Cape St Vincent, reached the shores of Portugal on a plank. In Lisbon he married Filippa Moniz. As early as 1474 he had conceived the design of reaching India by sailing westward, a design in which he was encouraged by a Florentine astronomer Paolo Toscanelli; in 1477 he 'sailed 100 leagues beyond Thule', probably to or beyond Iceland; and, having also visited the Cape Verde Islands and Sierra Leone, he began to seek a patron for his intended expedition. Finally, after seven years of alternate encouragement and repulse, his plans were accepted by **Ferdinand** and **Isabella of Castile** in April 1492.

On Friday 3 August Columbus set sail in command of 50 men on the small *Santa Maria*; they were attended by two little caravels, the *Pinta* and the *Niña*, the whole squadron comprising only 120 adventurers. He first made the Canary Islands; and though he found it hard to keep up the courage of his crews, new land was descried on Friday 12 October, probably Watling's Island in the Bahamas. He then visited Cuba and Hispaniola (Haiti), planted a small colony, and set sail with his two caravels (for the flagship had been wrecked). After a difficult and stormy voyage, he re-entered the port of Palos on 15 March 1493, and was received with the highest honours by the court.

He set out on his second voyage on 25 September, with three carracks and 17 small caravels, and on 3 November sighted Dominica in the West Indies. After a succession of wretched quarrels with his associates, and a long illness in Hispaniola, he returned to Spain much dejected in 1496. His third voyage, begun in 1498, resulted in the discovery of the South American mainland. In 1500 Columbus and his brother were sent home in irons by a newly appointed royal governor, but the king and queen repudiated this action, and restored Columbus to favour. His last great voyage (1502–04), along the south side of the Gulf of Mexico, was accomplished in the midst of great hardships. He died at Valladolid in Spain, and was buried in a monastery near Seville. In 1536 his remains were taken to Santo Domingo in Hispaniola; they were brought back to Spain in 1899 and deposited in Seville Cathedral in 1902.

📖 James Axtell, *Beyond 1492* (1992); F Fernández-Armesto, *Columbus on Himself* (1992) and *Columbus* (1991).

> 'All Christendom ought to feel joyful and make great celebrations and give solemn thanks to the Holy Trinity with many solemn prayers for the great exaltation which it will have, in the turning of so many people to our holy faith, and afterwards for material benefits, since not only Spain but all Christians will hence have refreshment and profit.'
> From *Carta del descubrimiento* (1493, Eng trans *The Letter in Spanish of Christopher Columbus*, 1889).

Comenius or Komenský, John Amos 1592–1670
Czech educationist

Born in Eastern Moravia, to parents belonging to the Moravian Brethren, he became Rector of the Moravian school of Prerau (1614–16) and minister at Fulnek, but lost all his property and library in 1621 when the town was taken by the Imperialists. Settling at Lissa in Poland (1628), he worked out his new theory of education, wrote his *Didactica Magna*, and was appointed Bishop of the Moravian Brethren in 1632. He spoke four languages fluently and was a pioneer of new language teaching methods. In 1631 he published his *Janua Linguarum Reserata* and in 1639 his *Pansophiæ Prodromus*. In 1641 he was in England by invitation of parliament, planning a Baconian College of all the sciences, but the Civil War drove him to Sweden (1642). He returned to Lissa in 1648, and in 1650 went to Saros-Patak in Hungary, where he composed his *Orbis Sensualium Pictus* (1658), the first foreign language textbook to use pictures as a visual aid to learning. He finally settled in Amsterdam. 📖 Matthew Spinka, *John Amos Comenius: That Incomparable Moravian* (1943)

Comgall, St c.515–602
Irish abbot

Born in Ulster, he founded in c.558 the great Abbey of Bangor, in County Down. He is said to have lived on the Hebridean island of Tiree for a time, and accompanied St **Columba** on his journey to the north of Scotland.

Commines or Commynes Philippe de, *also called* M. d'Argenton 1445–1509
French statesman and historian

Born in the castle of Comines near Courtrai, he entered the court of Burgundy in 1463, but in 1472 began to serve **Louis XI** of France. He was rewarded with the rich estate of Talmont, married the heiress of Argenton and became one of Louis's most trusted advisers. Louis's death brought him the loss of much property and eight months' imprisonment in an iron cage, but in 1493 he regained favour. He accompanied **Charles VIII** on his expedition to Italy (1494), was present at the Battle of Fornovo, and met **Machiavelli**. His *Mémoires* (1524, first Eng trans by Thomas Danett, 1596) are the earliest French example of history as distinct from the chronicle and provide an important record of the times. 📖 Jean Liniger, *Philipe de Commynes* (1978)

Commodus, Lucius Aurelius AD161–92
Roman emperor

The son of **Marcus Aurelius**, he was carefully educated but proved unable to live up to the example of his virtuous father, and his reign (from AD186) degenerated into one of imperial despotism. After the discovery of his sister Lucilla's plot against his life (183), he gave uncontrolled vent to his savagery. He became increasingly unbalanced, imagining that he was the god Hercules and renamed Rome after himself. At length his mistress, Marcia, had him strangled by Narcissus, a famous athlete. His death brought to an end the dynasty of the Antonine emperors.

Commynes, Philippe de See Commines, Philippe de

Comnenus 1057–1461
Byzantine rulers

Originally Italian, many members of the family occupied the Byzantine throne (1057–85), and that of Trebizond (1204–1461). See **Alexius I Comnenus**, **Isaac I** and **Anna Comnena**. David Comnenus, the last in Trebizond, was executed at Adrianople with all his family (1462), by **Mohammed II**.

Compaoré, Blaise 1940–
Burkino Faso soldier and politician

Educated locally and in military academies in Senegal and France, including St Cyr, he joined the army in 1958, rising to command the Artillery Group (1975–76). In 1980 he was appointed Minister of Rural Development and was second in command to **Thomas Sankara** (1983–87). He overthrew Sankara and became Chairman of the Popular Front of Burkino Faso and Head of Government in 1987. Originally a very close friend and confrere, he came to reject the excessively egalitarian thrust of Sankara's policies. In 1991 military rule in Burkina Faso ended and Compaoré became President.

Compassion, Marie Augustine de la See Jamet, Marie

Compton, Arthur Holly 1892–1962
US physicist and Nobel Prize winner

Born in Wooster, Ohio, he studied at Princeton University and Cambridge, and held posts at Washington University in St Louis, and at Chicago University. He developed a theory to describe the interaction of X-rays with matter, based on Einstein's idea that light consists of particles, or photons. He confirmed the theory by measuring the wavelength of X-rays scattered by a target. For this important test of the particle nature of light, he shared the 1927 Nobel Prize for physics with Charles Wilson. A leading authority on nuclear energy, X-rays and nuclear chemistry, he was invited in 1941 to direct plutonium production for the atomic bomb. He was involved in the Manhattan Project and built the first reactor with Enrico Fermi in Chicago (1942). ▣ Marjorie Johnston (ed), *The Cosmos of Arthur Holly Compton* (1968)

Compton, Denis Charles Scott 1918–97
English cricketer and journalist

Born in Hendon, he first played for Middlesex in 1936, and was first capped for England the following year. He played in 78 Test matches, scoring 17 Test centuries. In his first-class career he scored over 38,000 runs, including 123 centuries; in 1947 he scored 3,816 runs and a record 18 centuries. He was also a talented footballer, a member of the Cup-winning Arsenal team in 1950, and was capped for England in 1943. He retired from professional cricket in 1957 to take up journalism and broadcasting.

Compton, Fay 1894–1978
English actress

She was born in London, the daughter of the actor Edward Compton (1854–1918) and sister of Compton Mackenzie. She first appeared on the stage in 1911. After a successful visit to the USA in 1914 she won acclaim in London as *Peter Pan* (1918), and subsequently played especially in plays by J M Barrie and in comedies like Dodie Smith's *Autumn Crocus* (1930) and *Call it a Day* (1935–37).

Compton, Henry 1632–1713
English prelate

Born in Compton Wynyates, Warwickshire, he was the youngest son of the 2nd Earl of Northampton. He studied at Oxford, and entered the Church in 1662. In 1674 he became Bishop of Oxford, and in 1675 of London. He was tutor to the daughters of James VII and II (Mary II and Anne), but was suspended for two years for his Protestantism. He welcomed William of Orange, and crowned him William III with his wife Mary.

Compton, John George Melvin 1926–
St Lucian politician

Born in Canouan in St Vincent and the Grenadines, he graduated at the London School of Economics and was called to the English Bar. In 1951 he established a law practice in St Lucia and three years later joined the St Lucia Labour Party (SLP), becoming deputy Leader. He left in 1961 to form the United Workers' Party (UWP). At independence in 1979 he was St Lucia's first Prime Minister. He was defeated that year by the Labour Party but returned in 1982 and was re-elected in 1987. He retired in 1996 and was replaced as UWP Leader and Prime Minister by Vaughan Lewis.

Compton-Burnett, Dame Ivy 1884/92–1969
English novelist

Born in London, she graduated in classics from the Royal Holloway College, London University, and published her first novel, *Dolores*, in 1911. She was a prolific writer, and her rather stylized novels have many features in common. They are often set in upper-class Victorian or Edwardian society, for example, and the characters usually belong to a large family, spanning several generations. She was noted for her skilful use of dialogue, which conveys the secret thoughts and understanding of the characters. Her works include *Pastors and Masters* (1925), *Brothers and Sisters* (1929), *Parents and Children* (1941), *Mother and Son* (1955, James Tait Black Memorial Prize), *A Father and his Fate* (1957), *The Mighty and their Fall* (1961) and *A God and His Gifts* (1963). ▣ H Spurling, *Ivy Compton-Burnett* (2 vols, 1984–85)

Comrie, Leslie John 1893–1950
New Zealand astronomer and pioneer in mechanical computation

Born in Pukekohe, Central Auckland, he was educated at Auckland University College and studied astronomy at Cambridge. He later accepted a teaching post in the USA and subsequently joined HM Nautical Almanac Office in 1926, becoming superintendent (1930–36). He completely revolutionized the computing methods used there by installing desk calculators and punched card machines and, more importantly, devising efficient numerical methods for use with these mechanical computing aids. He founded the Scientific Computing Service Ltd (1936), and was regarded as the foremost computer and tablemaker of his day. He was elected FRS in 1950.

Comstock, Anthony 1844–1915
US morals crusader

He was born in New Canaan, Connecticut. As founder and secretary (1873–1915) of the New York Society for the Suppression of Vice, he lobbied to keep obscene materials from being sent through the mail and worked to prosecute not only quack doctors and fraudulent advertisers but also many writers, poets, and painters. He brought legal proceedings against George Bernard Shaw's play *Mrs. Warren's Profession* in 1905; Shaw had already coined the term 'comstockery' to describe narrow-minded and puritanical crusading.

Comte, Auguste 1798–1857
French philosopher and social theorist

Born in Montpellier, he was educated at the École Polytechnique in Paris (1814–16). He taught mathematics, and from 1818 was influenced by the Comte de Saint-Simon. In 1826 he began teaching philosophy, but suffered a breakdown, and was largely supported by J S Mill, George Grote and other friends. His two major works were *Cours de Philosophie positive* (6 vols, 1830–42) and *Système de politique positive* (4 vols, 1851–54, 'System of Postive Philosophy'). His Positivism sought to expound the laws of social evolution, to describe the organization and hierarchy of all branches of human knowledge, and to establish a true science of society as a basis for social planning and regeneration; in this vision humanity itself becomes the object of religious reverence and love—'Catholicism minus Christianity', as T H Huxley dubbed it. He is generally regarded as the founder of sociology. ▣ Frederick J Gould, *Auguste Comte* (1920)

Comyn or Cumming or Cumyn
French noble family

It took its name from the town of Comines near Lille, on the Franco-Belgian frontier. While one branch remained there, and gave birth to Philippe de Commines, another followed William of Normandy (later known as William the Conqueror) to England. In 1069 William made Robert of Comines, or Comyn, Earl of Northumberland; his younger son, William, became Chancellor of Scotland

Confucius, *Latin for* Kongfuzi (K'ung-fu-tzu, 'the Master K'ung') 551–479BC
Chinese philosopher

Confucius was born of an aristocratic but impoverished family in the state of Lu, part of the present province of Shandong (Shantung), and his father died when he was two. He married at 19, and became a government official in Lu with a retinue of disciples, mostly young gentlemen whom he was preparing for government service. He was promoted to ministerial rank and enjoyed a successful and highly popular career, which eventually attracted jealousy and hostility and led to a breach with the ruler.

In 497 he left Lu and for a dozen years became an itinerant sage, wandering from court to court seeking a sympathetic patron and attended by a company of his disciples. In about 485 he returned to Lu and spent his final years teaching and possibly writing. After his death his pupils compiled a volume of memorabilia, the *Analects*, which record Confucius' sayings and doings; most of the other works attributed to him are later compilations which, like the philosophy of 'Confucianism' itself, are probably only loosely related to his own teachings.

Confucius emerges as a great moral teacher who tried to replace the old religious observances with moral values as the basis of social and political order. In his Way (*dao*) he emphasized the practical virtues of benevolence (*ren*), reciprocity (*shu*), respect and personal effort which were to be interpreted pragmatically with regard to individual circumstances and cases rather than any abstract system of imperatives. Succeeding generations revered him and Confucianism became the state religion of China, which, until recently, it remained.

📖 R Dawson, *Confucius* (1981); H Fingarette, *Confucius— The Secular as Sacred* (1972); H G Creel, *Confucius: The Man and the Myth* (1949).

'Man has three ways of acting wisely. First, on meditation; that is the noblest. Secondly, on imitation; that is the easiest. Thirdly, on experience; that is the bitterest.' From *The Analects* (c.479BC).

---

about 1133. By 1250 his descendants in Scotland included four Earls (Buchan, Monteith, Angus and Atholl) and 32 belted knights of the name of Comyn. Some 70 years afterwards this great house was overthrown.

Condamine, C M de La See **Lacondamine, Charles Marie de**

Condé, Louis I de Bourbon, Prince de 1530–69
French nobleman and Huguenot leader

Born in Vendôme, he was the younger brother of Antony of Bourbon, King of Navarre. Although a hunchback, he fought in the wars between Henri II of France and Spain (1551–57), and joined the Huguenots on the accession of Francis II (1559). He led the Huguenots during the French Wars of Religion and was defeated at Dreux during the first civil war (1562). In the second war (1567–69) he was defeated at Jarnac, taken prisoner, and shot. 📖 H Noel Williams, *The Love Affairs of the Condés, 1530–1740* (1912)

Condé, Louis II de Bourbon, 4th Prince de, *known as* the Great Condé 1621–86
French nobleman

The great-grandson of Louis I de Bourbon (Prince de Condé), he was born in Paris. Proud, hot-tempered, aggressively atheist, during the Thirty Years War he defeated Spain at Rocroi (1643) and Lens (1648). He was recalled (1649) to suppress the first French uprising (Fronde) against Cardinal Mazarin and the Regent Anne of Austria. In 1650 he rebelled and led the second Fronde, but fled to Spain, where he served for six years against France, until he was defeated by the Vicomte de Turenne and Cromwell's Ironsides at the Battle of the Dunes (1658). Pardoned in 1659, he became one of Louis XIV's greatest generals; he defeated the Spanish in Franche-Comté (1668), and with Turenne commanded the French armies in the Netherlands. After a last indecisive battle at Seneffe (1674) against William III of Orange, he retired, gout-ridden, to Chantilly, where he enjoyed the company of literary friends like Molière, Racine, Nicolas Boileau and Jean de La Bruyère. 📖 H Noel Williams, *The Love Affairs of the Condés, 1530–1740* (1912)

Conder, Charles Edward 1868–1909
Australian painter and lithogapher

Born in London, England, he arrived in Sydney in 1884, worked as a lithographer and contributed to the *Sydney Illustrated News*. In 1888 one of his oils was bought for the Art Gallery of New South Wales, and later that year he joined Tom Roberts, Arthur Streeton and Frederick McCubbin in their camp at Box Hill, Victoria. He also showed in the controversial '95 Impression' exhibition in the following year. In 1890 he went to Paris, where his portrait was painted by Toulouse-Lautrec, and later to London, where he was influenced by James McNeill Whistler and the 'Japonais' cult. From then until his death he worked in watercolours on silk, his delicate fan designs being especially notable.

Condillac, Étienne Bonnot de 1715–80
French philosopher and psychologist

Born in Grenoble, he was ordained a priest but became an associate of Denis Diderot, Jean Jacques Rousseau and others in the rationalizing and secularizing movements of the Enlightenment. He was also a great admirer of John Locke and in his *Essai sur l'origine des connaissances humaines* (1746, 'Essay on the Origin of Human Knowledge') and *Traité des sensations* (1754, 'Treatise on Sensations') he argued that all knowledge depends ultimately on the senses and on the association of ideas. He also wrote on logic, language and economics.

Condon, Edward Uhler 1902–74
US theoretical physicist

Born in Alamogordo, New Mexico, he was educated at the University of California and at Göttingen University in Germany, worked as a news reporter and held many posts including chairs in physics at the universities of Washington and Minnesota. Independently of George Gamow, Condon showed that alpha particle decay could be explained by the quantum-mechanical tunnelling of helium nuclei, and used this theory to derive the Geiger–Nuttall law that had been formulated empirically. During World War II Condon did notable work on the Manhattan Project to develop the atomic bomb, as associate director with Robert Oppenheimer, and was later director of a US Air Force study of unidentified flying objects from 1945 to 1951.

Condorcet, Marie Jean Antoine Nicolas de Caritat, Marquis de 1743–94
French mathematician, politician and philosopher

Born in Ribemont, he studied in Paris, where his work in mathematics brought the high approval of Alexis Clairaut and Jean le Rond D'Alembert. His *Essai sur le calcul intégral* (1765, 'Essay on Integral Calculus') won him a seat in the Academy of Sciences. He wrote five volumes of obituaries of famous scientists, amounting to intellectual biographies, and contributed to Denis Diderot's *Encyclopédie*. On the outbreak of the Revolution he was sent by Paris to the Legislative Assembly (1791), and in 1792 he became president of the Assembly, siding usually with the Girondins. Condemned by the extremist Jacobins, he hid for eight months, but, forced to move, was recognized and imprisoned; he was found dead the next morning. In his *Progrès de l'esprit humain* (1794, 'Progress of the Human Mind'), written in hiding, he insisted on the justice and necessity of establishing a perfect equality of civil and political rights between the sexes, and proclaimed the infinite perfectibility of the human race. ⊞ Keith M Baker, *Condorcet: From Natural Philosophy to Social Mathematics* (1975)

Cone, James Hal 1938–
US theologian

Born in Fordyce, Arkansas, he studied at Garrett Theological Seminary and received a PhD from Northwestern University. He became Charles A Briggs Professor of Systematic Theology at Union Theological Seminary, New York (1977–87, Distinguished Professor from 1987), and has written extensively. His angry criticisms of the presuppositions of White theology in *A Black Theology of Liberation* (1970) were followed by the more measured *God of the Oppressed* (1975), *For My People* (1984), *Speaking the Truth* (1986), the autobiographical *My Soul Looks Back* (1987) and *Martin and Malcolm and America* (1991).

Conegliano, Giovanni Battista Da See Cima Da Conegliano

Confucius See panel p430

Congreve, William 1670–1729
English dramatist and poet

Born in Bardsey near Leeds, he was educated in Ireland at Kilkenny School and Trinity College, Dublin, where he was a fellow student of Jonathan Swift. In London he entered the Middle Temple to study law, but never practised. In 1693 his first comedy, *The Old Bachelor*, produced under John Dryden's auspices, with the celebrated Mrs Bracegirdle as heroine, achieved brilliant success. His second comedy, *The Double Dealer* (also 1693), was in every way stronger, but the satire on the heartless sexual morals of the time was aimed too directly at the theatre's best customers, and it failed to please. His best-known play *Love for Love* (1695), generally regarded as his masterpiece, is more vital than its predecessors, and has a more coherent plot and truer characterization. In 1697 his only tragedy, *The Mourning Bride*, appeared, best remembered for the quotations 'music hath charms to soothe a savage breast' and 'nor hell a fury like a woman scorned' (often misquoted as 'hell hath no fury like a woman scorned'). He was next occupied busily in the famous Jeremy Collier controversy, defending the morality of the new stage (1698). His last play, *The Way of the World* (1700), was not a success and he wrote little more for the stage, apart from the words of a masque of *The Judgment of Paris*, set to music by the English composer John Eccles (1650–1735) in 1701. He died in a coach accident. ⊞ M E Novak, *William Congreve* (1971); E Goss, *The Life of William Congreve* (1888)

Congreve, Sir William 1772–1828
English scientist

Born in London, and educated at Woolwich Academy, he became comptroller of the Woolwich Laboratory in 1814, and in 1808 invented the 'Congreve rocket', first used in the Napoleonic Wars. The first friction matches, called 'Congreves' (alluding to the rockets) were not invented by him but by John Walker. He was MP for Gatton from 1818 to 1828.

Conkling, Roscoe 1829–88
US politician

Born in Albany, New York State, he was admitted to the Bar in 1850 and served as a Republican from New York in the House of Representatives (1859–63, 1865–67), and in the Senate (1867–81). A loyal machine politician and an advocate of punitive measures against the South during Reconstruction, he contended unsuccessfully for the Republican presidential nomination in 1876. In 1880, supporting Ulysses S Grant and opposing James G Blaine, he split the Republican Party.

Conley, Rosemary 1946–
British writer and dietician

She was a sickly child, and was told that she would not live past the age of 10. However she survived an operation, became a committed Christian and lived to devise her world-famous hip and thigh diet in response to the wide-ranging effects of eating a very low-fat diet. Starting with *Rosemary Conley's Complete Hip and Thigh Diet* (1989), many of her books on diet, cookery and exercise have been translated into five languages. She also owns a nationwide exercise franchise business and produces fitness videos such as *Rosemary Conley's Flat Stomach Plan* (1995). Between 1988 and 1995 the British Top Ten Paperback list always featured one of her books.

Connaught, Prince Arthur, Duke of 1850–1942
British prince and soldier

Born at Buckingham Palace, London, the third son of Queen Victoria, he trained at the Royal Military Academy, Woolwich, then served in Canada, Gibraltar, Egypt and India (1869–90). Thereafter he was Commander-in-Chief in Ireland (1900–04), Commander-in-Chief of the Mediterranean (1907–09) and Governor-General of Canada (1911–16). He was created Duke of Connaught and Strathearn (1874). In 1879 he married Princess Louise Margaret of Prussia (1860–1917). Of their children, Margaret (1882–1920) married the future King Gustav VI of Sweden (1905), and his son, Prince Arthur (1883–1938), was Governor-General of South Africa (1920–23).

Connelly, Marc(us) Cook 1890–1980
US dramatist

He was born in McKeesport, Pennsylvania, and worked as a journalist before turning to the theatre. He achieved several outstanding successes in collaboration with George S Kaufman, including *Dulcy* (1921), *To the Ladies* (1922), the 'Expressionist' comedy *Beggar on Horseback* (1924) and *Hunter's Moon* (1958). His greatest individual success was *Green Pastures* (1930, Pulitzer Prize). ⊞ P T Nolan, *Marc Connelly* (1969)

Conner, Denis Walter 1942–
US yachtsman

He was born in San Diego, California. He won the 1974 America's Cup, as co-skipper in *Courageous*. He was Star Class world champion twice and won an Olympic bronze in 1976. Before 1983 he was known as the most successful 12m US skipper. However, after 1983 he became the only US skipper to lose the America's Cup in 132 years, when *Liberty* was beaten by *Australia II* in a 4–3 victory. He regained the Cup from the Australians in *Stars and Stripes* in Perth (1987). He put up a successful defence against New Zealand in 1988, but lost to them (captained by Peter Blake) in 1995.

Connery, Sean Thomas 1930–
Scottish film actor

Born in Edinburgh, he had a succession of jobs, including milkman, lifeguard and coffin-polisher. His powerful physique won him a position in the chorus line of the London stage production of *South Pacific* (1951–52). Sporadic film work followed, as well as television drama, notably *Requiem for a Heavyweight* (1956) and *Anna Karenina* (1957). Cast as Ian Fleming's secret agent James Bond in *Dr. No* (1962) he became an international film star. He played the role on seven occasions until *Never Say Never Again* (1983). Other notable film roles include an army rebel in *The Hill* (1965), a 19th-century union leader in *The Molly Maguires* (1969), and a roistering adventurer in *The Man Who Would Be King* (1975). He won the BAFTA Best Actor Award for *The Name of The Rose* (1986) and an Academy Award for his portrayal of an ageing Irish cop with true grit in *The Untouchables* (1987). His many recent successes include *Indiana Jones and the Last Crusade* (1989), *The Hunt for Red October* (1990) and *The Rock* (1996). A highly competitive golfer and a stickler for fair play, he has also offered financial support to many causes. ⬤ John Parker, *Sean Connery* (1993)

Connolly, Billy 1942–
Scottish comedian

Born in Glasgow, he became a shipyard welder and entertained his workmates with caustic patter and tunes plucked out on a banjo. He performed as an amateur before turning professional in 1965 and for a time joined Gerry Rafferty and Tam Harvey in the folk group The Humblebums. Going solo, and affectionately known as the 'Big Yin', he gained a loyal following as a stand-up comic and singer. In 1975 he enjoyed a number-one hit with the single 'D.I.V.O.R.C.E.'. His stage act was captured in the documentary film *Big Banana Feet* (1975), and he has acted in such films as *Absolution* (1979), *Water* (1985) and *The Big Man* (1990). His other work includes a production of *Die Fledermaus* (1978) and such television dramas as *Just Another Saturday* (1975), *Androcles and the Lion* (1984) and *Dreaming* (1990). He starred in the US television sit-coms *Head of the Class* (1990–92) and *Billy* (1992), as well as British series such as *Billy Connolly's World Tour of Scotland* (1994) and the television play *Down Among the Big Boys* (1993).

Connolly, Cyril Vernon 1903–74
English author and journalist

He was born in Coventry, Warwickshire, and educated at Eton and Balliol College, Oxford. He contributed to the *New Statesman* and other periodicals and wrote regularly for the *Sunday Times*. He was founder-editor of *Horizon* (1939–50) with **Stephen Spender** and briefly literary editor of the *Observer*. Among his works are *The Rock Pool* (1936), his only novel, *Enemies of Promise* (1938), critical essays with 'A Georgian Boyhood' describing his own childhood, *The Unquiet Grave* (1944), under the pseudonym 'Palinurus', containing miscellaneous aphorisms and reflections, and various collections of essays. ⬤ Jeremy Lewis, *Cyril Connolly: A Life* (1997)

Connolly, James 1868–1916
Irish Labour leader and insurgent

Born in Edinburgh, Scotland, of Irish immigrant parents, he joined the British army at the age of 14 and was stationed in the Curragh and Dublin, but deserted to get married to an Irish girl in Scotland. Returning to Ireland in 1896 he organized the Irish Socialist Republican Party and founded *The Workers' Republic*, the first Irish socialist paper. He toured the USA as a lecturer (1902–10) and helped found the Industrial Workers of the World ('Wobblies'). Back in Ireland, in 1913 with the Irish Labour Leader James Larkin (1876–1947) he organized the great transport strike in Dublin. He organized socialist 'citizen armies', and took part in the Easter Rising (1916) in command of the GPO. Severely wounded, he was arrested and executed on 12 May, tied to a chair because he was unable to stand. He wrote *Labour in Irish History* (1912).

Connolly, Maureen Catherine, known as Little Mo 1934–69
US tennis player

Born in San Diego, California, she made tennis history by becoming the first woman to win the so-called Grand Slam of the four major titles (British, US, French and Australian) in the same year (1953). She won the US title in three consecutive years (1951–53) and the Wimbledon singles in three consecutive years (1952–54). Soon after her last Wimbledon triumph she broke her leg in a riding accident and retired from tournament play.

Connors, Jimmy (James Scott) 1952–
US tennis player

He was born in East St Louis, Illinois. He was Wimbledon men's singles champion in 1974 and 1982, won the Australian Open in 1974, and the US Open in 1974, 1976, 1978, 1982, and 1983. With Ilie Nastase, he won the Wimbledon men's doubles in 1973, and the US Open men's doubles in 1975. He was World Championship Tennis champion in 1977 and 1980, Masters champion in 1978, and was a member of the US Davis Cup team in 1976 and 1981. A left-handed player, he was one of the first to use the double-fisted backhand. His zest for the sport kept him at the top for many years.

Conon de Béthune, *also known as* Quesnes de Béthune d.1220
Northern French trouvère poet

Born into the royal house of Flanders, he became one of the leaders of the Fourth Crusade. He was hugely influential in the literary development of northern France, being one of the first poets writing in the dialect of the area to gain popular acceptance elsewhere.

Conrad I d.918
King of Germany

He was the son of the Count of Franconia, and nephew of the Emperor Arnulf. Elected king on the extinction of the direct Carolingian line (911), he gradually re-established imperial authority over most of the German princes, carried on an unsuccessful war with France, and at last fell mortally wounded at Quedlinburg in a battle with the Hungarians.

Conrad II c.990–1039
King of Germany and Holy Roman Emperor

The son of the Duke of Franconia and founder of the Salian dynasty (crowned king in Mainz, 1024), in 1026 he crossed the Alps, crushed a rebellion in Italy, was crowned in Milan and was anointed Holy Roman Emperor by the pope (1027). He was soon recalled to Germany to put down four revolts, which he achieved by 1033, when he was also crowned King of Burgundy. A fresh rebellion recalled him to Italy (1036); but this time he was forced to grant various privileges to his Italian subjects. Shortly after his return he died at Utrecht. He was succeeded by his son **Henry III**.

Conrad III 1093–1152
King of Germany

He was the first **Hohenstaufen** Holy Roman Emperor. His support for **Henry V** earned him the duchy of Franconia in 1115. On the death of Emperor Lothar III, the princes of Germany, fearing the growing power of the **Guelf** party, crowned Conrad at Aachen (1138). He quarrelled with the Guelf Henry the Proud, and then with Henry's son, **Henry the Lion**. When St **Bernard of Clairvaux** preached a new crusade, Conrad set out for Palestine with a large army (1147). He designated his nephew, **Frederick I Barbarossa**, as his successor.

Conrad, Joseph, *originally* Józef Teodor Konrad Nalecz Korzeniowski 1857–1924
British novelist

He was born of Polish parents in Berdichev, Poland (now Ukraine). His father was a revolutionary and writer (he translated **Victor Hugo's** *Les Travailleurs de la mer*) who was exiled to Vologda in 1862. In 1878 Joseph joined an English merchant ship, and he was naturalized in 1884 when he gained his certificate as a master. In the 10 years that followed, he sailed to Singapore, Borneo and the Belgian Congo, and his experiences at sea inspired much of his writing. In 1895 he married and soon afterwards settled in Kent, England, where he lived a sedentary life, devoted to writing. His first novel was *Almayer's Folly* (1894), followed by *An Outcast of the Islands* (1896), *The Nigger of the Narcissus* (1897), *Lord Jim* (1900), *Nostromo* (1904), *The Secret Agent* (1907) and *Under Western Eyes* (1911). He became famous with the publication of *Chance* in 1914, and it was only then that *Lord Jim* was recognized as a masterpiece. Perhaps the short story was his true medium—*Tales of Unrest* (1898), *Heart of Darkness* (1902), *Youth* (1902) and *Twixt Land and Sea* (1912). His semi-autobiographical *The Mirror of the Sea* (1906) and his *Personal Record* (1912) testify to his high artistic aims. He also wrote *Victory* (1919), but his later works, *The Arrow of Gold* (1919) and *The Rescue* (1920), owed their popularity largely to his earlier work. His unfinished novel *Suspense* was published in 1925. 📖 J Baines, *Joseph Conrad: a critical biography* (1960)

Conran, Jasper 1959–
English fashion designer

He was born in London, the son of **Terence** and **Shirley Conran**. He trained at the Parsons School of Art and Design in New York, leaving in 1977, when he joined Fiorucci briefly as a designer. He produced his first collection of easy-to-wear, quality clothes in London in 1978. He has designed clothes for several stage productions such as *My Fair Lady* (1992) and the Scottish Ballet's *Sleeping Beauty* (1994).

Conran, Shirley Ida, *née* Pearce 1932–
English designer, fashion editor and author

Born in London and educated at St Paul's Girls' School and Portsmouth College of Art, she was married to Terence Conran from 1955 to 1962, and she designed fabrics for and was director of Conran Fabrics. Their sons Jasper Conran and Sebastian both became designers. In 1964 she turned to journalism and became woman's editor for the *Observer* colour magazine, editor of the *Daily Mail*, then 'life and style' editor for *Over 21* (1972–74). After a debilitating illness she wrote the best-selling *Superwoman* (1975), a book telling working women and mothers how to cope, which was followed by four more superwoman books. In 1979 she moved to Monaco, and published her first fiction book, *Lace* (1982). Later novels include *Lace 2* (1985), *Crimson* (1991) and *Tiger Eyes* (1994).

Conran, Sir Terence Orby 1931–
English designer and businessman

Born in Esher, Surrey, and educated at Bryanston School, Dorset, he founded and ran the Habitat Company (1971), based on his own success as a furniture designer and the virtues of good design and marketing. He has since been involved in the management of several related businesses such as Richard Shops, Conran Stores and Habitat Mothercare, and several restaurants such as Le Pont de la Tour and Mezzo in London. He has published a variety of books about interior design, gardening and cookery including *The House Book* (1974), *Terence Conran's Kitchen Book* (1993) and *The Essential Home Book* (1994). He was married to **Shirley Conran** (1955–62) and is the father of **Jasper Conran**. He was knighted in 1983. 📖 Nicholas Ind, *Terence Conran: The Authorized Biography* (1995)

Conroy, Patrick See Oconaire, Pádraic

Conroy, Stephen 1964–
Scottish painter

Born in Helensburgh, Dunbartonshire, he studied at the Glasgow School of Art (1982–86), and whilst studying in his postgraduate year, he had some work included in The

Vigorous Imagination exhibition at the Scottish National Gallery of Modern Art, Edinburgh. He uses traditional qualities of figure drawing, light and shade, and very specific spatial organization, and his dark, crowded interiors and stiffly posed and dressed figures make his paintings seem Victorian or Edwardian in age. Such images received popular as well as critical attention, and he received a good deal of media coverage in 1989 when he was the subject of a legal dispute concerning the ownership of many of his paintings.

Consalvi, Ercole 1757–1824
Italian statesman and prelate

Born in Rome, he was made a cardinal and Secretary of State by Pius VII (1800). An able diplomat and administrator, he concluded the Papal Concordat with **Napoleon I** in 1801, and, at the Congress of Vienna (1814–15), managed to block Prince **Clemens Metternich's** schemes to establish an Italian Confederation under Austrian presidency along the same lines as that of Germany. In domestic affairs, he was a reformer, suppressing monopolies, feudal taxes and exclusive rights, but found his policies constantly opposed by reactionary cardinals (who were known as Zelanti). He was a liberal patron of science and art.

Conscience, Hendrik 1812–83
Flemish novelist

He was born in Antwerp, and worked as an assistant teacher before joining the army in 1831, then became director of the Wiertz Museum (1866). His *Phantazy* (1837), a fine collection of tales, and his most popular romance, *De Leeuw van Vlaenderen* (1838, 'The Lion of Flanders'), earned him the title 'the father of the Flemish novel'. His series of pictures of Flemish life, beginning with *Hoe man schilder wordt* (1843, 'How to become a Painter'), made his name throughout Europe. 📖 F Joster, *Hendrik Conscience* (1917)

Constable, Archibald 1774–1827
Scottish publisher

Born in Carnbee, Fife, he became a bookseller's apprentice in Edinburgh at the age of 14, and in 1795 started as a bookseller on his own account, quickly gathering round him the chief book-collectors of the time. He drifted into publishing, bought the *Scots Magazine* in 1801, and was chosen as publisher of the *Edinburgh Review* (1802). For his flair and respect for editorial independence he is regarded as the first modern publisher. He published for all the leading men of the time, and his quick appreciation of **Walter Scott** became the envy of the book trade. In 1812 he purchased the copyright of the *Encyclopaedia Britannica*, but in 1826 was financially ruined, heavily involving Scott in his bankruptcy. Incorrigibly innovative, in 1827 he launched *Constable's Miscellany*, a series of volumes on literature, art and science, moderately priced to encourage sales among the common man, but he died before he could capitalize on its success.

Constable, Henry 1562–1613
English poet

He was educated at St John's College, Cambridge. He became a Catholic, and went to Paris. He was pensioned by King Henri IV, and seems to have been employed in confidential missions to England and Scotland. In 1592 he published his *Diana*, a collection of 23 sonnets, and in 1594 a second edition appeared, containing 76, some by his friend, Sir **Philip Sidney**, and other poets. He was imprisoned in the Tower of London in 1604, but released the same year. His other poems included a set of *Spiritual Sonnets*, first published in 1815. 📖 G A Wickes, *Henry Constable: poet and courtier* (1954)

Constable, John 1776–1837
English landscape painter

Constantine I *known as* Constantine the Great,
properly Flavius Valerius Aurelius Constantinus c.274–337AD
Roman emperor

Constantine was born in Naissus, in Upper Moesia, the eldest son of **Constantius Chlorus** and **Helena**. He first distinguished himself as a soldier in **Diocletian's** Egyptian expedition (296), next under **Galerius** in the Persian war. In 305 the two emperors Diocletian and Maximian abdicated, and were succeeded by Constantius Chlorus and Galerius. Constantine joined his father, who ruled in the West, on the expedition against the Picts at Boulogne, and before Constantius died at York (306) he designated his son as his successor; the army proclaimed him Augustus. Galerius did not dare to quarrel with Constantine, yet he granted him the title of Caesar only, refusing that of Augustus. Political complications now increased, until in 308 there were actually no fewer than six emperors at once—Galerius, Licinius and Maximian in the East; and Maximian, Maxentius his son, and Constantine in the West. Maxentius drove his father from Rome, and after some intrigues, Maximian committed suicide (309). Maxentius threatened Gaul with a large army. Constantine, crossing the Alps by Mont Cénis, defeated Maxentius on three occasions; Maxentius was drowned after the last great victory at the Milvian Bridge near Rome (312).

Before the battle a flaming cross inscribed 'In this conquer' was said to have caused Constantine's conversion to Christianity; and the edict of Milan (313), issued conjointly with Licinius, gave civil rights and toleration to Christians throughout the empire. Constantine was now sole emperor of the West; and with the death of Galerius in 311 and of Maximian in 313, Licinius became sole emperor of the East. After a war (314) between the two rulers, Licinius was forced to cede Illyricum, Pannonia and Greece; and for the next nine years Constantine devoted himself vigorously to the correction of abuses and the strengthening of his frontiers. In 323 Constantine again defeated Licinius, and put him to death; he was now sole ruler of the Roman world. He chose Byzantium (modern day Istanbul) for his capital, and in 330 inaugurated it under the name of Constantinople ('City of Constantine').

Christianity became a state religion in 324, although paganism was not suppressed. In 325 the great Church Council of Nicaea was held, in which the court sided against the Arians and the Nicene Creed was adopted. Yet it was only shortly before his death that Constantine was baptised. The story of his baptism at Rome by Pope Sylvester I (pope 314–335) in 326, and of the so-called *Donation of Constantine*, long treated as an argument for the temporal power of the papacy, is unhistorical. His later years were vicious, seeing the execution of his eldest son Crispus (326) for treason and of his own second wife Fausta (327) on some similar charge. He proposed to divide the empire between his three sons by Fausta—**Constantius**, Constantine II and **Constans I**—but in 340 Constantine II lost his life in war with Constans.

📖 Joseph Burkhardt, *The Age of Constantine the Great* (1983, trans by Moses Hadas); Ramsay MacMullen, *Constantine* (1969); Norman H Baynes, *Constantine the Great and the Christian Church* (1929); **Eusebius of Caesarea**, *Constantine*.

> *In hoc signo vinces.*
> 'In this sign thou shalt conquer.'
> 'Constantine's Vision' (AD312), quoted in Eusebius, *Life of Constantine*.

Born in East Bergholt, Suffolk, he assisted his father for a year in the family mill (1794), but the landscape painter and art patron Sir George Beaumont (1753–1827) prevailed on his family to send him to London, where he studied at the Royal Academy schools. He exhibited his first picture at the Royal Academy in 1802. In 1828, on the death of his father-in-law, an inheritance of £20,000 enabled him to devote himself exclusively to his landscape work, which expressed its profound love of the country, and his interest in the effects of changing light and the movement of clouds across the sky. In 1824 he had a success with *The Haywain* (1821) in the Paris Salon, and in 1825 at Lille with his *White Horse*. Both gained gold medals and exercised a powerful influence upon **Eugène Delacroix** and other French Romantic artists. His later years were saddened by bereavements, ill health and depression, but he worked steadily, though his landscapes were frequently unsold. Some of his finest landscapes, including *The Valley Farm*, *Cornfield* and *The Haywain*, are in the National Gallery, London, and nearly as many are in the Tate Gallery. Other well-known works include *View on the Stour* (1819) and *Salisbury Cathedral* (1823, Victoria and Albert Museum, London).

Constans I, Flavius Julius c.320–350AD
Roman emperor

The youngest son of **Constantine I**, the Great, he received Illyricum, Italy and Africa as his share of the empire in AD337. After defeating his brother Constantine at Aquileia (340), he became sole ruler of the West until his death at the hands of Magnentius.

Constans II, Flavius Heraclius 630–68
Byzantine emperor

Born in Constantinople (Istanbul), he succeeded his father Constantine III in 641. His reign was marked by the loss of Egypt and much of the Middle East to the Arabs. His despotism and attempt at Church unity aroused antagonism, and he was murdered in his bath by a chamberlain five years after transferring his capital to Syracuse.

Constant, Benjamin, *pseudonym of* Henri Benjamin Constant de Rebecque 1767–1830
French writer and politician

Born in Lausanne, Switzerland, of French parents, he was educated at Oxford and Edinburgh, and at Erlangen in Germany. He settled in Paris as a publicist (1795) and entered the Tribunate in 1799, but was banished from France in 1803 for opposing **Napoleon I**. After travelling in Germany and Italy with Madame de Staël, he settled at Göttingen. On Napoleon's fall in 1814 he returned to Paris, and during the Hundred Days became one of his councillors, despite his previous stance. After the second restoration of the Bourbons he wrote and spoke in favour of constitutional freedom. He was returned to the Chamber of Deputies in 1819, and became leader of the Liberal Opposition. He is remembered not for his political career but for his remarkable psychological novel, *Adolphe* (1816), based on his relationship with Mme de Staël. His correspondence appeared in 1844, his *Œuvres politiques* ('Political Works') in 1875, and his *Journal intime* ('Personal Diary') in 1895. His *Cahier rouge* (1907, 'Red Notebook') contains a vivid account of his youth. The fictional fragment *Cécile* (published posthumously, 1951) is also based on his life. 📖 P L Leon, *Benjamin Constant* (1930)

Constantine I See panel above

Constantine I 1868–1923
King of Greece

Born in Athens, he was the son and successor (1913) of **George I**. As a military commander he was unsuccessful in the Turkish War (1897), but led the Greeks to victory in the Balkan War (1912–13). Brother-in-law to Kaiser **Wilhelm II** of Germany, he insisted on Greek neutrality in World War I, but was forced to retire in favour of his son Alexander by the rival government of **Eleutherios Venizelos** and the Allies (1917). In 1920 he was restored to the throne by plebiscite, but after a military revolt (1922), abdicated again in favour of his son **George II**.

Constantine II or XII 1940–
King of Greece
Born near Athens, he was the son and successor of **Paul I**. Soon after his accession (1964) he married Princess Anne-Marie, younger daughter of **Frederik IX** of Denmark and sister of Queen **Margrethe II** of Denmark. In 1967 the Colonels' Junta seized power in a military coup. The king made an abortive attempt to regain power, and fled into exile in Rome. He was formally deposed (1973), and the monarchy was abolished by national referendum (1974). He now lives in London. His heir is Crown Prince Paul (1967–).

Constantine IV d.685
Byzantine emperor
The son and successor (668) of **Constans II**, he gave up much territory to the Bulgarians, Serbs and Croats.

Constantine V Copronymus 718–75
Byzantine emperor
The son of **Leo III**, he was crowned co-emperor at the age of two. On the death of his father (741) he defeated a revolt by his brother-in-law, Artabasdus, and thereafter intensified Leo's iconoclastic policies. A well-managed Council of the Church (754) promulgated the destruction of icons, starting an era of persecution of the Orthodox party. A talented leader of soldiers, Constantine directed numerous expeditions against the Bulgarians, whom he defeated (763, 773), and died on campaign.

Constantine XI Palaeologus Dragases
1404–53
Last Byzantine emperor
Born in Constantinople (Istanbul), he was the fourth son of **Manuel II** and the Serbian princess, Helen Dragaš. During the reign of his elder brother, John VIII, he and his other brothers jointly ruled the despotate of Morea, a Byzantine appanage in the Peloponnese, and on John's death (1448) Constantine succeeded to an empire consisting of little more than Constantinople and its environs, threatened by the vast Ottoman Empire which surrounded it. His proclamation of the union of the Greek Church with Rome (1452) secured only limited military assistance from the West and was repudiated by his indignant subjects. Powerless to prevent the inevitable Ottoman siege, Constantine died fighting in the final Turkish assault.

Constantine Nikolayevich, *Russian* Konstantin Nikolayevich 1827–92
Russian grand-duke
The son of Tsar **Nicholas I**, he commanded the Russian fleet in the Crimean War (1854–56). He became president of the council in 1865 and 1878, but was dismissed in 1882 for revolutionary views.

Constantius AD317–61
Roman emperor
He was the third son of **Constantine I**, the Great. As Eastern Roman Emperor from AD337, he fought against the Persians, and after the death of his brother **Constans I** (350), he became sole emperor. He was a supporter of Arian Christianity and exiled catholic bishops.

Constantius Chlorus c.250–306AD
Roman emperor

The father of **Constantine I**, the Great, he took the title Caesar (AD292), and had Britain, Gaul and Spain as his government. After re-establishing Roman power in Britain and defeating the Alemanni, so strengthening the Rhine frontier, he took the title of Augustus (305). He died in York.

Conté, Lansana c.1945–
Guinean soldier and politician
Military commander of the Boke Region, he led a bloodless coup on the death of President **Ahmed Sékou Touré** (1984) and set up the Military Committee for National Recovery (CMRN) with himself as President. He relaxed the centralizing policies of Touré and successfully encouraged many exiles to return. An attempted coup was thwarted by loyal troops in 1985 and the process of reintegrating into the Western world was continued. In 1996 civil unrest forced him to take command of the army and to impose a military rule in Guinea.

Conti, Tom 1941–
Scottish actor
Born in Paisley, Strathclyde, of part-Italian extraction, he studied acting at the Royal Scottish Academy of Music and Drama. He made his stage debut in *The Roving Boy* (1959) then struggled for many years before finding theatrical success in *The Black and White Minstrels* (1972) and *Savages* (1973). His television work includes the series *The Glittering Prizes* (1976) and *The Norman Conquests* (1978). He was praised for his stage performance as the defiant paraplegic in *Whose Life Is It Anyway?* (1978), a role he later repeated on Broadway. His films include *Galileo* (1973), *Reuben, Reuben* (1983, Academy Award nomination). *Heavenly Pursuits* (1986) and *Shirley Valentine* (1989). His many stage performances include *Jeffrey Bernard Is Unwell* (1990) and the world première of **Arthur Miller's** *The Ride Down Mount Morgan* (1991).

Contucci, Andrea See **Sansovino**

Conway, Hugh, *pseudonym of* Frederick John Fargus 1847–85
English novelist
He was born in Bristol, where he was an auctioneer in succession to his father. He took his writing name from the school frigate *Conway*, where he was a student for a time, but he never fulfilled his ambition of joining the navy. He wrote clever newspaper verse and tales, but his greatest success was the melodramatic *Called Back* (1883), also popular as a play. Other works include *A Life's Idyll and other Poems* (1879), and the novels *Dark Days* (1884), *A Family Affair* (1885) and *Living or Dead* (1886). ⬜'A Sketch of the Author's Life', included in *Called Back* (1885)

Conway, Moncure Daniel 1832–1907
US abolitionist
He was born in Stafford County, Virginia. A Methodist turned Unitarian preacher, he lectured in England on the Civil War and became a pastor in London (1864–97). He published *Demonology and Devil-lore* (1879), *Thomas Carlyle* (1881), *The Wandering Jew* (1881) and *Life of Paine* (1892), and was co-editor of an anti-slavery newspaper, *Commonwealth*.

Conyngham, Barry Ernest 1944–
Australian composer, lecturer and performer
Born in Sydney, he studied under **Peter Sculthorpe** at Sydney University and **Raymond Hanson** at the New South Wales Conservatorium. Influenced by jazz in his early years, he has also used computer-generated sound, which he actively promotes, in his works. Japanese influences are also strong in his work. Much of his varied output is for film or theatre, including an opera *Edward John Eyre* based on the life of the explorer, *The Ballad of Bony Anderson*, and another opera *Ned* about **Ned Kelly**. His other works include a cello concerto, and *Southern Cross*, a

double concerto for piano and violin written for **Roger Woodward** and Wanda Wilkomirska. His opera *Fly* (1984) is based on the life of **Lawrence Hargrave**, and his ballet *Vast* (1989) was choreographed by **Graeme Murphy**. He was appointed Vice-Chancellor of the New Southern Cross University, NSW, in 1993.

Cook, Arthur James 1883–1931
Welsh miners' leader

Born in Wookey, Somerset, he became a coal miner in the Rhondda and a leading figure in the South Wales branch of the Union of Mineworkers. He became general secretary of the national union in 1924 and was one of the miners' leaders during the General Strike of 1926. A powerful orator, he fought successfully to hold the union together after the strike.

Cook, Beryl 1937–
English painter

Born in Plymouth, she started to paint in the early 1960s and was entirely self taught. Her humorous paintings of the inhabitants and views of her home town are often deemed 'naïve' and 'primitive' but her acute character observation is both penetrating and flamboyant. Refusing to admit to any significant artistic influences, she claims that television, in particular 'The Flintstones' cartoon characters, have influenced her work.

Cook, Eliza 1818–89
English poet

The daughter of a London tradesman, she contributed to magazines from an early age, and issued volumes of poetry in 1838, 1864 and 1865. She wrote *Eliza Cook's Journal* (1849–54), republished as *Jottings from my Journal* in 1860.

Cook, Frederick Albert 1865–1940
US explorer and physician

Born in Calicoon Depot, New York State, he studied medicine at the universities of Columbia and New York. He was the surgeon on an Arctic expedition to Greenland in 1891 led by **Robert Peary**. Two further expeditions to Greenland followed in 1893 and 1894, and a Belgian expedition to the Antarctic in 1897, led by Adrien de Gerlache, was recounted by Cook in *Through the First Antarctic Night* (1900). In 1906 he claimed to have made the first ascent of the highest mountain in North America, Mount McKinley, Alaska, reporting the expedition in *To the Top of the Continent* (1908). On 3 July 1907 he sailed from Gloucester, Massachusetts, and crossed Ellesmere Island, reaching Axel Heilberg Island on 17 March 1908. From there he apparently reached the North Pole on 21 April 1908. Although he was treated as a hero on his return, his claim to the Pole was questioned by Peary. An investigative committee set up by Copenhagen University discredited both Cook's claim to be the first man to the North Pole and his ascent of Mount McKinley. He denied this vehemently in public statements and in his book *My Attainment of the Pole* (1911). His subsequent imprisonment for fraud in 1923 brought his character into further question, and although he was pardoned shortly before his death the controversy continues.

Cook, James 1728–79
English navigator

He was born in Marton, Yorkshire, the son of an agricultural labourer. After a short time in a haberdasher's shop at Staithes, he was apprenticed to Whitby shipowners, and spent several years in the coasting and Baltic trade, then joined the navy (1755), becoming master in 1759. He was engaged in surveying around the St Lawrence and the shores of Newfoundland. He commanded the *Endeavour*, for the Royal Society expedition to the Pacific, to observe the transit of Venus across the Sun (1768–71). On the return, New Zealand was circumnavigated and charted, and the east coast of Australia was surveyed and claimed for Great Britain, the strait between Australia and New Guinea was sailed through, and the voyage completed by way of Java and the Cape of Good Hope. Made commander, he was given control of a second voyage of discovery in the *Resolution* and *Adventure* (1772–75), to discover how far the lands of the Antarctic stretched northwards, and sailed round the edge of the ice, reaching 71° 10' S. in longitude 110° 54' W. During the intervals between the Antarctic voyages, he visited Tahiti and the New Hebrides, and discovered New Caledonia and other groups. Owing to his precautions, there was only one death among his crews during all the three years. His next and last voyage (1776–79) was to discover a passage round the north coast of America from the Pacific, and was by way of the Cape, Tasmania, New Zealand, the Pacific Islands, the Sandwich Islands (now discovered), and the west coast of North America, which he surveyed from 45° N as far as Icy Cape in Bering Strait, where he was forced to turn back, reaching Kailua Bay in Hawaii, in January 1779. The inhabitants, at first friendly, changed their attitude, and on 14 February, when he landed on Kealakekua Beach to recover a stolen boat, he was killed. Cook did more than any other navigator to add to our knowledge of the Pacific and the Southern Ocean. ▢ J C Beaglehole, *The Life of Captain Cook* (1974)

Cook, Peter Edward 1937–95
English comedian and actor

Born in Torquay, Devon, he had his first success while reading languages at Cambridge as one of the writers and performers of the revue *Beyond the Fringe* (1960, sequel *Behind the Fridge*, 1971–72). He invented the stage character E L Wistey, a forlorn figure perplexed by the complexities of life. He collaborated with **Dudley Moore** in the irreverent television programme *Not Only... But Also* (1965–71) and made regular film appearances, notably as the devil in *The Wrong Box* (1966), and in *The Bed Sitting Room* (1969), *The Secret Policeman's Ball* (1979), *Yellowbeard* (1983), *Supergirl* (1984), *The Princess Bride* (1987) and *Without a Clue* (1988). He was co-founder of both The Establishment club in London and the satirical magazine *Private Eye*, and made many recordings with Moore under the names Derek and Clive.

Cook, Robin, *originally* Robert Finlayson Cook 1946–
Scottish Labour politician

Born in Bellshill, Lanarkshire, he was educated at Aberdeen Grammar School, the Royal High in Edinburgh and Edinburgh University. He was a teacher and an adult education organizer before embarking on a political career with the Labour Party. An Edinburgh town councillor (1971–74), MP for Edinburgh Central (1974–83) and then for Livingston (1983–), he became an Opposition spokesman on health and social security in 1987 and was promoted to chief Opposition health spokesman two years later. He became Trade and Industry spokesman in 1992, the same year that he organized the successful leadership campaign for **John Smith**, then Foreign and Commonwealth Affairs Spokesman in 1994. Widely recognized as one of the most intellectually formidable parliamentarians of recent years, he entered **Tony Blair**'s Cabinet as Foreign Secretary after Labour won the general election in 1997.

Cook, Stanley Arthur 1873–1949
English bible scholar

Born in King's Lynn, he was Professor of Hebrew at Cambridge from 1932 to 1938 and wrote on Old Testament history. His works include *The Place of the Old Testament in Modern Research* (1932) and *An Introduction to the Bible* (1945). He was joint editor of the *Cambridge Ancient History*.

Cook, Thomas 1808–92
English railway excursion and tourist pioneer
Born in Melbourne, Derbyshire, he left school at the age of 10 and worked at various jobs before becoming a Baptist missionary. He established a travel agency in London and his first railway trip (a temperance one) was made from Leicester to Loughborough in 1841, and was the first public excursion train journey in England. In 1844 the Midland Counties Railway Company agreed to make a permanent arrangement with him if he found passengers. In 1856 he introduced a railway tour of Europe, and in the early 1860s he began the travel firm, Thomas Cook and Sons, which included tours of the USA. His travel agency is now a worldwide organization. 🕮 G R Heath, *Thomas Cook of Melbourne, 1808–1892* (1981)

Cooke, (Alfred) Alistair 1908–
US journalist and broadcaster
Born in Salford, England, he was educated at Cambridge, and at Yale and Harvard. He joined the BBC in 1934 as a film critic but then became a foreign correspondent and specialized in US affairs. He returned to the USA in 1937 and became a US citizen in 1941. He has written numerous books, including *A Generation on Trial* (1950), *One Man's America* (1952), and *America Observed* (1988). He wrote and narrated the award-winning *America: a personal history of the United States* (1971–72), and has broadcast the weekly radio programme *Letter from America* since 1946. He was made an honorary KBE in 1973.

Cooke, Deryck Victor 1919–76
English writer and broadcaster on music
Born in Leicester, he became a distinguished **Mahler** scholar, and published a book on the composer (1960) and completed a realization of Mahler's Tenth Symphony (premiered 1964). He also wrote perceptively on **Bruckner** and **Richard Wagner**, notably a posthumously published study of *The Ring*, 'I Saw the World End' (1979).

Cooke, George Frederick 1756–1812
English actor
He was born in Westminster, London, and made his debut at Brentford in 1776. Between 1784 and 1800 he was one of the leading actors of his day, despite his heavy drinking. From 1801 to 1810 he played at Covent Garden both in comedy and in tragedy, and became as popular as **John Philip Kemble**. In 1810 he visited the USA, where he died. The monument in New York which marks his grave was erected in 1821 by **Edmund Kean**, who regarded Cooke as the greatest of actors.

Cooke, Sir Robin Brunskill 1926–
New Zealand lawyer
Born in Wellington, he graduated from Victoria University, Wellington, became a Research Fellow at Cambridge (1952–54) and was called to the Bar in London in 1954. He practised law in New Zealand from 1955 to 1992, becoming QC in 1964, a judge of the New Zealand Supreme Court (1972) and of the Court of Appeal in 1976 (president, 1986–96), serving also on the Courts of Appeal of Western Samoa and the Cook Islands. Cooke became a Privy Councillor in 1977 and a Fellow of All Souls, Oxford, in 1990, and was awarded a life peerage in January 1996.

Cooke, Sam, *originally* Sam Cook 1931–64
US soul, gospel, and rhythm and blues singer
Born in Clarksdale, Mississippi, he first sang in a gospel quartet with his siblings, and was a member of the innovative Soul Stirrers (1951–56). Record producer 'Bumps' Blackwell recognized his pop potential, but the label owner refused to issue the secular 'You Send Me', which was sold cheaply to a non-gospel label, and promptly sold 2 million copies. A string of pop, soul and rhythm and blues hits followed, but his career ended when he was shot by the manageress of a motel in Los Angeles over a dispute with a girl. The posthumously released classic 'A Change Is Gonna Come' was a poignant reminder of the loss of this highly influential artist. 🕮 D Woolf, *You Send Me* (1994)

Cooke, Sir William Fothergill 1806–79
English inventor
Born in Ealing, London, he studied medicine, then took up telegraphy, and in 1837 became the partner of Sir **Charles Wheatstone**. In 1845 they patented the single magnetic needle electric telegraph. The following year Cooke formed a company, which paid £120,000 for the partners' earlier patents. In 1867 he won the Albert Gold Medal.

Cookson, Dame Catherine Ann 1906–98
English popular novelist
She was born in East Jarrow, Tyneside, and her best-selling, mostly historical fiction is largely set in the north-east of England. The author of more than 70 books of tragedy and romance, including the Mallen trilogy and the Tilly Trotter series, a 1988 survey revealed that almost a third of all fiction borrowed from British public libraries was by Cookson. She was made a DBE in 1993 for her generous donations to hospitals and charities in the north-east. 🕮 *Our Kate* (1969)

Cookworthy, William 1705–80
English porcelain manufacturer
Born in Kingsbridge, Devon, a Quaker, he was an apprentice to an apothecary at the age of 14, who set him up in business as a pharmacist in Plymouth. He discovered kaolin near St Austell (1756), and established a china factory near Plymouth (1768).

Cooley, Denton Arthur 1920–
US cardiac surgeon
Born in Houston, Texas, he received his MD from the Johns Hopkins University Medical School. In 1954 he joined the staff of the Baylor University College of Medicine, where he was Professor of Surgery from 1962 to 1969, as well as the founder (1962) and chief of the surgical division of the Texas Heart Institute in Houston. With **Michael DeBakey** and others, he pioneered open-heart surgery as well as the surgical treatment of diseases of the arteries, especially the treatment of aortic aneurysms by graft replacement. His publications include *Essays of Denton A Cooley—Reflections and Observations* (1984).

Coolidge, (John) Calvin 1872–1933
30th President of the USA
Born in Plymouth, Vermont, the son of a farmer and storekeeper, he became a lawyer and then Governor of Massachusetts (1919–20), where he achieved renown in decisively using the state militia to break the Boston police strike in 1919. Vice-President from 1921 to 1923, he succeeded as President on **Warren G Harding**'s death (1923). A strong supporter of US business interests, he was triumphantly re-elected by the Republicans in 1924. Known for his reserved demeanour and cautious temperament, he adopted a laissez-faire attitude towards business, cutting taxes, reducing regulations and blocking the McNary–Haugen scheme to raise farm income by sending surplus crops abroad. He was not greatly interested in foreign policy, but his administration did see the signing of the **Dawes** Plan to reduce Germany reparations and the **Kellogg–Briand** Pact outlawing war. Although highly popular whilst in office, he declined to run for re-election in 1928. His policies were later thought to have contributed to the stock market crash, but by leaving his post when he did he escaped the

public acrimony that was visited on his successor, **Herbert Hoover.** ▢ C M Fuess, *Calvin Coolidge, The Man From Vermont* (1940)

Coolidge, Susan, *pseudonym of* Sarah Chauncy Woolsey 1835–1905
US children's writer and literary critic

Born in Cleveland, Ohio, she wrote the *Katy* books (*What Katy Did*, 1872, and its sequels) and other stories for girls, in an easy natural style, free from contemporary sentimentality. She also edited some correspondence by **Fanny Burney** and **Jane Austen.** ▢ Biographical sketch by 'EDWG' in *Last Verses* (1906)

Coolidge, William D(avid) 1873–1975
US physical chemist and inventor

Born in Hudson, Massachusetts, he studied at the Massachusetts Institute of Technology, and graduated with a PhD in physics from the University of Leipzig. He joined the General Electric Company at Schenectady, New York, in 1905, later becoming its director of research. He was consultant on X-rays (1945–61), and from 1961 to his death he was emeritus director of Research and Development. Among his many awards and honours was the Hughes Medal of the Royal Society (1927). The 'Coolidge tube' (1916), incorporating a hot tungsten cathode, was the prototype of modern X-ray apparatus. In association with **Irving Langmuir** he developed the first successful submarine detection system and during World War II his research interests extended to radar, the atomic bomb, rockets and anti-submarine devices.

Coombs, H(erbert) C(ole), *nicknamed* Nugget Coombs 1906–97
Australian economist and banker

Born in Kalamunda, near Perth, Western Australia, he studied at the London School of Economics, and then joined the Commonwealth Bank as an assistant economist, moving to the Treasury in 1939. He became a member of the board of the Commonwealth Bank in 1942, and its chairman in 1951. When the bank's regulatory and trading functions were separated in 1959, Coombs became the inaugural governor of the newly created Reserve Bank of Australia. He was personal adviser to seven Australian Prime Ministers, and his opinion was accepted accross the political spectrum. He also became Pro-Chancellor (1959) and Chancellor (1968) of the Australian National University. A keen environmentalist, he delivered the ABC's Boyer Lectures, 'The Fragile Pattern, Institutions and Man' in 1970. Committed to the advancement of the Aboriginal people, he became founding chairman of the Council for Aboriginal Affairs, and was one of the few whites to be adopted as a tribal member of the Yolgnu people of Arnhem Land. His publications include *The Fragile Pattern* (1970) and *Aboriginal Autonomy* (1993).

Coon, Carleton Stevens 1904–81
US anthropologist

Born in Wakefield, Massachusetts, and educated at Harvard, he was a professor there (1934–48), and at Pennsylvania (1948–63). His many archaeological expeditions led him to discover the remains of Aterian fossil man (North Africa, 1939), Hotu man (Iran, 1951) and Jebel Ighoud man No. 2 (Sierra Leone, 1965). His books include *A Reader in General Anthropology* (1948), *The Story of Man* (1954), *The Seven Caves* (1957) and the now discredited *The Origin of Races* (1962).

Cooney, Ray(mond George Alfred) 1932–
English dramatist, director and producer

Born in London, he made his debut as an actor in *Song of Norway* (1946), and appeared in several stage comedies and farces in the 1950s and 1960s, but is best known as an author and director. His first play, a farce, *One for the Pot*, appeared in 1961, and was followed by many others, including *Chase Me Comrade* (1964), *Move Over, Mrs Markham* (1969), *Two Into One* (1981), *Run for your Wife* (1983), which had a record-breaking nine-year run, *Wife Begins at Forty* (1986), *Out of Order* (1990), *Funny Money* (1994) and *One Good Turn* (1994). In 1983 he created the Theatre of Comedy, based at the Shaftesbury Theatre, London.

Cooper, Anthony Ashley See Shaftesbury, 3rd Earl of

Cooper, Sir Astley 1768–1841
English surgeon

Born at Brooke Hall, Norfolk, he studied in London and Edinburgh, then lectured on anatomy at St Thomas's Hospital (1789) and at the College of Surgeons (1793). In 1800 he became surgeon to Guy's Hospital, and in 1813 Professor of Comparative Anatomy in the College of Surgeons. In his work he raised surgery from its primitive state to a science, and was the first man to tie the abdominal aorta in treating an aneurysm. In 1820 he removed a tumour from the head of King **George IV**, and was made a baronet, and in 1828 he was appointed Sergeant-Surgeon to the King. His major work, *Anatomy and Surgical Treatment of Hernia* (1804–07) was followed by *Dislocations and Fractures* (1822), *Anatomy and Diseases of the Breast* (1829–40), and *Anatomy of the Thymus Gland* (1832).

Cooper, Sir (Alfred) Duff, 1st Viscount Norwich 1890–1954
English politician

Educated at Eton and Oxford, he served with the Grenadier Guards in World War I and was elected to parliament as a Conservative in 1924, becoming Secretary for War (1935–37). He resigned from the office of First Lord of the Admiralty in 1938 in protest against **Neville Chamberlain's** Munich Agreement, but became Minister of Information under **Churchill** (1940–42), and ambassador to France (1944–47). He wrote lives of **Talleyrand** (1932), Earl **Haig** (1935) and King **David** (1943), and other books.

Cooper, Eileen 1933–
English artist

Born in Glossop, Derbyshire, she studied at Goldsmiths' College and at the Royal College of Art, London, and became a visiting lecturer at Central St Martins College of Art, also in London. Her works, which explore a wide range of emotions, often from a feminist viewpoint, are executed in a bold linear fashion and are often haunting in their simplicity. She exhibits widely, and some of her work is in the collections of the Victoria and Albert Museum, London, the Contemporary Art Society and the Arts Council of Great Britain.

Cooper, Gary Frank James 1901–61
US film actor

Born in Helena, Montana, he was originally a cartoonist. He moved to Los Angeles and began working as an extra and stunt rider in Western films. A bit part in *The Winning of Barbara Worth* (1926) brought him a contract with Paramount and several years of minor roles before his work as the laconic cowboy in *The Virginian* (1929) made him a star. He then starred as the archetypal hero of many Westerns, and also made light comedy and high adventure. His many film credits include *A Farewell to Arms* (1932), *The Lives of a Bengal Lancer* (1935), *For Whom the Bell Tolls* (1943) and *Friendly Persuasion* (1956). He was nominated for an Academy Award for his performance in *Mr Deeds Goes to Town* (1936) and won Best Actor Academy Awards for performances as the World War I Quaker hero *Sergeant York* (1941) and as the sheriff who stood alone in *High Noon* (1952). He also received a Special Academy Award in 1960. ▢ Larry Swindell, *The Last Hero* (1980)

Cooper, Giles Stannus 1918–66
Irish playwright and actor

Born in Carrickmines, County Dublin, he wrote several stage plays, but his sensitivity to the voice and the use of sound resulted in his becoming an exceptional author for radio. His themes of the shortcomings of society, woven into largely naturalistic plays, such as *Mathry Beacon* (1956) and *Unman, Wittering and Zigo* (1958), were very popular at the time. He died after a fall from a moving train near Surbiton, Surrey. In 1978, the annual Giles Cooper awards for best radio scripts was inaugurated by the BBC and Methuen publishers.

Cooper, Dame Gladys Constance 1888–1971
English actress

Born in London, she became a child model and made her professional stage debut in *Bluebell in Fairyland* (1905). Her many performances include *The Importance of Being Earnest* (1911), *Milestones* (1912) and *The Second Mrs Tanqueray* (1922). One of the great beauties of her day, she made her film debut in 1913 but remained primarily a stage performer. Moving to Hollywood (1940), she appeared in over 30 films, and received three Academy Award nominations for her performances, but continued her stage work in London and New York. She starred in the television series *The Rogues* (1964–65) and made her final stage appearance in *The Chalk Garden* (1971).

Cooper, Henry 1934–
English boxer

Born in London, he was Amateur Boxing Association light-heavyweight champion in 1952 and 1953, then turned professional. In 1959 he beat Brian London to gain the British heavyweight title which he held, apart from a brief spell, until 1971. He floored **Muhammad Ali** (then known as Cassius Clay) in 1963, though he did not win the fight, and in 1966 he fought him for the World heavyweight title but was forced to retire in the sixth round on account of a bad cut. In 1971 he lost his British heavyweight title in a disputed contest against Joe Bugner, and announced his retirement. Since retiring from the ring he has appeared regularly as a guest on television. In 1993 he sold his Lonsdale Belts, following losses incurred after the Lloyds insurance company crash. He has published several books on boxing and an autobiography, *Henry Cooper* (1972).

Cooper, James Fenimore 1789–1851
US novelist

He was born in Burlington, New Jersey, the son of a wealthy Quaker and Federalist member of Congress. The family later moved to Cooperstown, New York, then in a wild frontier region of great natural beauty. He was educated at Yale, but was expelled during his third year, and joined the merchant marine (1806), and then the navy as midshipman (1808). He rose to the rank of lieutenant, but in 1811 resigned his commission and married Susan, a sister of Bishop De Lancey of New York, and settled down as a country gentleman. His first novel, *Precaution* (1819), was a failure, and the 32 which followed it are of uneven quality. The best are his stories of the sea and of Native American Indians—*The Spy* (1821), *The Pilot* (1823), *The Last of the Mohicans* (1826), *The Prairie* (1826), *The Red Rover* (1827), *The Bravo* (1831), *The Pathfinder* (1840), *The Deerslayer* (1841), *The Two Admirals* (1842), *Wing-and-Wing* (1842) and *Satanstoe* (1845). His other writings include a scholarly *Naval History of the United States* (1839), and *Lives of Distinguished American Naval Officers* (1846). After visiting England and France, he was US consul at Lyons (1826–29), and then travelled in Switzerland and Italy until 1831. His later years were much disturbed by literary and newspaper controversies and litigation. ▢ S Railton, *Cooper: a study of his life and imagination* (1978)

Cooper, Leon N(eil) 1930–
US physicist and Nobel Prize winner

Born in New York City and educated at Columbia University where he received his PhD in 1954, he moved to the University of Illinois to join **John Bardeen** and **John Schrieffer** in producing the BCS (Bardeen–Cooper–Schrieffer) theory of superconductivity. Cooper made a theoretical prediction that at low temperatures, electrons in a conductor could act in bound pairs (Cooper pairs). This work was extended to show that in a superconductor the Cooper pairs have a common momentum which is not affected by the random scattering of individual electrons, making the effective electrical resistance of the material zero. This theory won Bardeen, Cooper and Schrieffer the 1972 Nobel Prize for physics. Cooper became assistant professor at Ohio State University in 1957, and since 1958 he has held various appointments at Brown University, Providence, where he has been Thomas J Watson Snr Professor of Science since 1974.

Cooper, Paul 1869–1933
English architect and jeweller

Born in London, he entered the office of J D Seddings in 1889, where he undertook architectural work for the Duke of Portland. He took lessons in jewellery in 1890 and was appointed head of the metalwork department at Birmingham School of Art (1901). He abandoned his architectural career (1898) to devote his time to craft-work which dominated the rest of his working life. He produced a large amount of jewellery work throughout his career, all of which was detailed in his stock books.

Cooper, Peter 1791–1883
US manufacturer, inventor and philanthropist

He was born in New York and, although he had only one year's schooling, learned many trades when he was young. After starting a cloth-shearing business, a grocery store, and a glue factory, he erected the Canton Iron Works in Baltimore in 1828, and in 1830 built there *Tom Thumb*, the first locomotive engine ever made in the USA. He later built an iron-wire factory in New York and blast-furnaces in Pennsylvania, and helped Cyrus West in promoting the laying of the Atlantic cable. He also invented a washing machine, among other devices. He endowed the Cooper Union (1854–59) in New York, whose aim was to provide the working classes with educational advantages.

Cooper, Samuel 1609–72
English miniaturist

He was taught by his uncle, the miniaturist John Hoskins (c.1595–1665). His sitters included **Cromwell**, the wife of **Samuel Pepys**, **Milton**, **George Monk** and Cosimo III de' Medici. He also produced several portraits of monarchs and nobility in the royal collection. His work is in the true oil portrait style, as distinct from the tinted drawing of earlier schools.

Cooper, Susie (Susan Vera) 1902–95
English ceramic designer

She was born in Stoke-on-Trent, Staffordshire, and trained at Burslem School of Art under **Gordon Forsyth**. She joined Gray's Pottery in 1922 and set up her own firm in 1929, purchasing earthenware from local firms and decorating it with her individual designs of simple patterns: coloured bands and polka dots and animals and flowers. She also used lithographic transfers. She received her first major orders in 1935, became the first Royal Designer for Industry in 1940 and undertook many important commissions, which show the diversity and originality of her work. In the 1950s she added fine bone china to her range. In 1961 the Susie Cooper Pottery merged with R H & S L Plant which became part of the Wedgwood Group in 1966. Cooper was senior designer for Josiah Wedgwood & Sons until 1972, following which she continued to be active and produced new work for her ninetieth birthday.

Copernicus, Nicolaus, *Latin name of* Mikołaj Kopernik 1473–1543
Polish astronomer

Copernicus was born in Toruń in Prussia (now in Poland). He was brought up after his father's death (1483) by his uncle, later Bishop of Ermeland. After studying mathematics at the University of Cracow (1491–94) he went to Italy (1496) where he studied canon law and heard lectures on astronomy at the University of Bologna, while at Padua he studied medicine (1501–05). He was made a Doctor of Canon Law by the University of Ferrara (1503), and though nominated a canon at the cathedral of Frombork (1497), he never took holy orders.

On his return to Poland, he became his uncle's medical adviser and undertook administrative duties at Frombork, where he spent the rest of his life. He pondered deeply on what he considered the unsatisfactory description of the world by **Ptolemy**, which had the Earth as the stationary centre of the universe, and became converted to the idea of a Sun-centred universe. He set out to describe this mathematically in 1512. Copernicus hesitated to make his work public, having no wish to draw criticism from Aristotelian traditionalists or from theologians such as **Martin Luther** who had ridiculed him, but was eventually persuaded by his disciple **Rheticus** to publish his complete work, *De Revolutionibus Orbium Coelestium* (1543, 'The Revolutions of the Celestial Spheres'), which he dedicated to Pope **Paul III**.

In the new system, the Earth is merely one of the planets, revolving around the Sun and rotating on its axis.

The absence of any apparent movement of the stars caused by the Earth's annual motion was interpreted as due to the great size of the sphere of the stars. The transfer of the centre of the system from the Earth to the Sun in the new arrangement greatly simplified the geometry of the planetary system, though it did not dispense with all the epicycles of Ptolemy's model, a step which had to await **Johannes Kepler**.

Copernicus was already old and ill by the time his book was printed, and he was unaware that it carried an anonymous and unauthorized 'Preface to the Reader', presenting the work as a hypothesis rather than a true physical reality, written by Andreas Osiander (1498–1552), a Lutheran pastor of Nuremberg who supervised the last stages of the printing. Osiander's misguided intention was to forestall criticism of the heliocentric theory. The first printed copy of Copernicus's treatise, a work which fundamentally altered man's vision of the universe, reached its author on his death bed. It was later banned by the Catholic Church, and remained on the list of forbidden books until 1835.

📖 John Banville, *Doctor Copernicus* (1977); Jan Adamczewski and Edward J Piszek, *Nicolaus Copernicus and His Epoch* (1974); Thomas S Kuhn, *The Copernican Revolution* (1957); Angus Armitage, *Sun, Stand Thou Still* (1947, rev edn *The World of Copernicus*, 1956).

Cooper *or* Couper, Thomas c.1517–1594
English prelate and lexicographer

Born in Oxford, he studied at the university there. He subsequently became Master of Magdalen College School, Oxford (1549–68), Bishop of Lincoln (1570) and Bishop of Winchester (1584), and published a *Thesaurus Linguae Romanae et Britannicae* (1565), which became known as 'Cooper's Dictionary'.

Cooper, Thomas Joshua 1946–
US photographic artist and teacher

Born in San Francisco, he was educated at Humboldt State University (1965–69) and the University of New Mexico, Albuquerque (1970–72). After teaching at Trent Polytechnic, Nottingham, England, in 1982 he became the founding Head of the Department of Photography in the School of Fine Art of the Glasgow School of Art, Scotland. He was a committed practitioner and teacher, and his landscape works often deal with themes of myth, ritual and transformation; they are best represented in the books *Between Dark and Dark* (1985) and *Dreaming the Gokstadt* (1988).

Cooper (of Culross of Dunnet), Thomas Mackay Cooper, 1st Baron 1892–1955
Scottish judge and legal scholar

Born in Edinburgh, he was educated at George Watson's College and Edinburgh University. Successively Lord Advocate (1938), Lord Justice Clerk (1941) and Lord Justice General of Scotland and Lord President of the Court of Session (1947), he was a distinguished judge and leader of the court. In his judgements, many of permanent value, he stressed reliance on Scottish principles rather than indiscriminate following of English precedents. He was also keenly interested in legal history and published *Select Scottish Cases of the Thirteenth Century* (1944) and edited *The Register of Brieves* (1946) and Sir John Skene's *Regiam Majestatem* (1947).

Cooper, Tommy 1922–84
Welsh comic

Born in Caerphilly, Glamorgan, he first became interested in magic when given a present of tricks as a child. A member of the Horse Guards (1939–46), he began performing with the Combined Services Entertainment in the Middle East where he acquired his trademark headgear of a red fez. In 1947 he appeared at the Windmill Theatre and refined his act in clubs and music halls before achieving television renown in numerous variety shows and his own 1950s series *It's Magic*. His act thrived on his apparent ineptitude at performing elaborate tricks. He also made occasional appearances in films like *The Plank* (1967). He died during the transmission of the television show *Live From Her Majesty's*.

Coote, Sir Eyre 1726–83
Anglo-Irish soldier

He was born in Ash Hill, County Limerick. He entered the army early and saw service in Scotland, and from 1756 to 1762 served in India. It was he who induced **Robert Clive** to risk the Battle of Plassey (1757). In 1760 he defeated Thomas, Comte de Lally (1702–66), at Wandiwash and his capture of Pondicherry in 1761 completed the downfall of the French in India. In 1777 he became Commander-in-Chief in India, and in 1781, his rout of **Haidar Ali** at Porto Novo saved the presidency again.

Cope, Edward Drinker 1840–97
US palaeontologist

Born to a Quaker family in Philadelphia, he studied zoology and was a curator and professor at Haverford College, Pennsylvania, by the age of 24. From 1889 he was professor at the University of Pennsylvania. From 1868 he led a series of excavations in the American West which produced a wealth of dinosaur skeletons, especially from the Badlands of South Dakota and Como Bluff, Wyoming. A famous rivalry developed between him and **O C Marsh**, each descending to underhand tactics in the race for important fossils. Cope dynamited fossil localities to prevent Marsh from excavating there, while Marsh's employees re-addressed Cope's crates of fossils to his own laboratory. Cope wrote 1,400 books and articles on his fossil discoveries and also contributed to evolutionary theory, giving his name to two influential ideas: 'Cope's rule'—that animals have a tendency to ever increasing size during their evolution—and the Cope–Osborn theory for the origin of mammalian molars. He eventually sold most of his vast lifelong fossil collection to the American Museum of Natural History.

Cope, Sir John d.1760
English soldier

He was commissioned in the cavalry in 1707 and in the War of the Austrian Succession (1740–48), and in 1742 commanded the troops sent to assist the Empress Maria Theresa in 1742. On the landing of Prince Charles Edward Stuart in 1745, he was appointed Commander-in-Chief of the forces in Scotland. After a fruitless march to the Highlands, he returned by sea to Dunbar, and was routed at the Battle of Prestonpans (1745). He was ridiculed in the song 'Hey, Johnny Cope'.

Cope, Wendy 1945–
English poet

Born in Erith, Kent, and educated at Oxford, she worked as a primary-school teacher in London for 15 years before becoming a professional writer in 1986. Her talent for parody and for light-hearted demolitions of men targets male authors such as Ted Hughes or Philip Larkin. She is a little less cruel to T S Eliot in 'Limericks on The Wasteland'. The titles *Making Cocoa for Kingsley Amis* (1986) and *Men and their Boring Arguments* (1988) are fair indications of her approach. She has less tonal subtlety than Stevie Smith but more boisterous fun.

Copeau, Jacques 1879–1949
French theatrical manager, director, actor, teacher and critic

He was born in Paris, and as co-founder of the *Nouvelle Revue Française* (1908) and manager of the Théâtre du Vieux-Colombier (from 1913), he had a profound influence on French dramatic art, as well as drama training in Europe and the USA. In 1924 he formed an acting troupe, Les Copiaus (1924–29). 📖 John Rudlin, *Jacques Copeau* (1986)

Copeland, William Taylor 1797–1868
English china manufacturer

Born probably in Stoke-on-Trent, Staffordshire, he was the son of William Copeland, the partner of Josiah Spode, and managed the Spode concerns in Stoke and London, from 1827 to 1833, later gaining control. From 1846 onwards he produced Parian (imitation marble) groups and statuettes, and bone china. He also invented a filter press for working clay, and was one of the founders of the North Staffordshire Railway. He became Lord Mayor of London (1835), and MP for Stoke-on-Trent (1837–52, 1857–65).

Coper, Hans 1920–81
British studio potter

Born in Germany, he trained as an engineer before going to England in 1939. He worked with the Pioneer Corps, then joined the Studio of Lucie Rie as an assistant in 1947. He contributed works to her Berkeley Galleries Exhibitions in 1950 and 1951, and in 1958 established his own workshop in Hertfordshire. His work mainly consisted of thrown vases which are more sculptural and decorative than domestic. He worked as a consultant to a development group concerned with the use of clay products in building. Originally a painter and sculptor, he is widely remembered as one of the most influential of British studio potters.

Copernicus, Nicolaus See panel p440

Copland, Aaron 1900–90
US composer

Born in New York City, he studied under Rubin Goldmark, the teacher of George Gershwin, in New York, and in France, under Nadia Boulanger. After his return to the USA (1924), he was awarded a Guggenheim Fellowship (1925)—the first to be awarded to a composer. A series of early works influenced by Stravinsky, neo-classical in outlook and employing jazz idioms, was followed by compositions which drew on US tradition and folk music, of which the ballets *Billy the Kid* (1938) and *Appalachian Spring* (1944), and *A Lincoln Portrait* (1942), for orator and orchestra, are typical. As well as ballets and impressive film scores, he composed two operas and three symphonies. He published his autobiography, *Composer from Brooklyn*, in 1984. 📖 Julia F Smith, *Aaron Copland* (1955)

Copleston, Frederick Charles 1907–93
English Jesuit philosopher

Born near Taunton, Somerset, and educated at Marlborough, he joined the Society of Jesus in 1930 and was ordained in 1937. He became Professor of the History of Philosophy at Heythrop College (1939) and Professor of Metaphysics at the Gregorian University in Rome (1952). He wrote many critical studies of philosophers as well as the monumental eight-volume *A History of Philosophy* (1946–66). He took part in a famous broadcast debate with Bertrand Russell in 1948 on 'the existence of God'.

Copley, Sir Godfrey d.1709
English philanthropist

Born in Yorkshire, he left a fund in trust to the Royal Society which has been applied since 1736 to the provision of the annual Copley Medal, awarded for philosophical research.

Copley, John Michael Harold 1933–
English theatrical producer

He was born in Birmingham and after a brief career on the stage, became stage manager at Sadler's Wells, London, 1953, both for the ballet and the opera companies. He joined the Covent Garden Opera Company as deputy stage manager (1960), becoming resident producer in 1972. He has since produced most of the standard operatic repertoire, both at Covent Garden and at the London Coliseum, and also the Royal Silver Jubilee Gala at Covent Garden (1977). He has produced for many opera houses and festivals in Europe, the USA and Canada, and has had a long and successful connection with Australian Opera since his *Fidelio* in 1970, with productions including *Zauberflöte* (1973), and the Australian première of Leos Janácek's *Jenufa* (1984). He has also directed for the Victoria State Opera (1984–85).

Copley, John Singleton 1738–1815
American portrait and historical painter

Born in Boston, Massachusetts, of Anglo-Irish parents, he was executing portraits at the age of 16, and in 1755 George Washington sat for him. His vigorous and original portraits of colonial figures such as Paul Revere, Samuel Adams and John Hancock are now seen as his finest work, but he believed that by immersing himself in the European tradition he would become a better artist. In 1774 he left for England, where he was well received by Sir Joshua Reynolds, Benjamin West and Sir Robert Strange, and was commissioned to paint the king and queen for Governor Wentworth. He studied in Italy and returned to London at the end of 1776. *The Death of Chatham* (1779–80) and *The Death of Major Pierson* (1783) are both in the Tate Gallery, London. Other works include an enormous canvas of the Siege of Gibraltar painted for the City of London (1786–91) and a group of the royal princesses in Buckingham Palace.

Coppard, A(lfred) E(dgar) 1878–1957
English short-story writer and poet

Born in Folkestone, Kent, he left school when he was nine, and after being an office boy, then an accountant, he became a professional writer in 1919. In 1921 he published *Adam and Eve and Pinch Me*, and soon became celebrated for his tales of country life and character. His prose is remarkable for its detailed observations and poetic quality. Other volumes of stories include *The Black Dog* (1923), *The Field of Mustard* (1926) and *Lucy in Her Pink Jacket* (1954). His *Collected Poems* appeared in 1928. ▢ *It's Me, O Lord!* (1957); J Schwartz, *The Writings of A.E. Coppard* (1931)

Coppée, François 1842–1908
French poet

Born in Paris, he was a war-office clerk for three years. He soon turned to poetry, and with *Le Reliquaire* (1866, 'The Reliquary') and *Les Intimités* (1867, 'Intimacies') he became a leading Parnassian. Later volumes of poetry include *Les Humbles* (1872), *Olivier* (1876, his one long poem), and *Contes en vers* ('Stories in Verse'). His earliest dramatic poem, *Le Passant* (1869, 'The Wayfarer'), owed much to Sarah Bernhardt, and was followed by such works as *Le Luthier de Crémone* (1876, 'The Lute Maker from Cremona'), *Madame de Maintenon* (1881), and *Pour la couronne* (1895, 'For the Crown'). Other works include *Contes en prose* ('Prose Tales') and *Vingt Contes nouveaux* ('Twenty New Tales') and a novel about religious conversion, *La Bonne souffrance* (1898, 'The Healthy Pain'), written after he became a Catholic. He was a prominent associate of the anti-Semitic *Ligue de la patrie française* during the Dreyfus affair. ▢ L Le Meur, *La vie et l'œuvre de François Coppée* (1932)

Coppi, Fausto 1919–60
Italian racing cyclist

Although his career was interrupted by World War II he won the Tour of Italy five times and the Tour de France twice, the first man to win both in the same year (1949, 1952). His riding skill depended on strength, tenacity and a fast start rather than sheer pace, and his finishing sprint was always unremarkable, although his winning margins were often huge.

Coppin, Fanny Marion Jackson, *née* Jackson
1837–1913
US teacher

She was born a slave in the District of Columbia, and her aunt bought her freedom for her for $125 when she was young. From 1851 to 1857 she worked for the author George Henry Calvert who encouraged her education, and she went on to study at Oberlin College, Ohio (1860–65). She became principal of the girls' high school department of the Institute for Colored Youth, Philadelphia (1865), then became its head principal (1869–1902), the first black woman to hold such a position. During her 37 years at the Institute she extended its curriculum, raising academic qualifications and providing vocational training. Retiring in 1902, she went with her husband, the Reverend Levi Coppin, to Cape Town, where he was bishop from 1902 to 1912.

Coppola, Francis Ford 1939–
US film director and screenwriter

Born in Detroit, Michigan, he graduated from the University of California, Los Angeles, and worked on low-budget productions before directing the horror film, *Dementia 13* (1963), followed by the musical, *Finian's Rainbow* (1967). An accomplished screenwriter, he won an Academy Award for *Patton* (1970). Among his outstanding productions are *The Godfather* (1972; *Part II* 1974; *Part III*, 1990) and his controversial study of the Vietnam War, *Apocalypse Now* (1979). Commercial success allowed him to form his own company, American Zoetrope, which has supported directors like George Lucas and Wim

Wenders. Beset by financial difficulties throughout the 1980s, he has still created works as diverse as the romance *One from the Heart* (1982), the Existentialist *Rumble Fish* (1983), *The Cotton Club* (1984), *Peggy Sue Got Married* (1984) and *Tucker* (1988), a biography of the maverick automobile designer Preston Tucker. Later films include *Bram Stoker's Dracula* (1992).

Coram, Thomas c.1668–1751
English philanthropist

Born in Lyme Regis, Dorset, he became a shipwright, then went to America in 1693 and settled at Taunton, Massachusetts (1694–1704). There he strengthened the Anglican church, and promoted settlement schemes in Georgia and Nova Scotia. Back in London (c.1720) he projected and founded the Foundling Hospital (1741), of which William Hogarth was a patron.

Corbet or Corbett, Richard 1582–1635
English poet and prelate

Born in Ewell, Surrey, he was educated at Westminster School then went to Oxford, and in 1620 was made Dean of Christ Church. In 1624 he was consecrated Bishop of Oxford, and in 1632 transferred to Norwich. His *Certaine Elegant Poems* (1647), which reflects his jovial character, was published posthumously. His longest piece is *Iter Boreale*, a holiday tour of four students, and the best known is the *Faeries' Farewell*. His other volume of poems, *Poetica Stromata* (1648), was also published posthumously. ▢ J E V Crofts, *A life of Bishop Corbett* (1924)

Corbett, Harry H 1925–82
British actor

Born in Rangoon, Burma, the son of an army officer, he served with the Royal Marines during World War II. On demob, he joined Chorlton Rep, before gaining experience with Joan Littlewood's Theatre Workshop and acting in the West End. He played rag-and-bone man Harold Steptoe, alongside Wilfrid Brambell as his father Albert, first in *The Offer*, in the BBC's Comedy Playhouse series (1962), then in the long-running *Steptoe and Son* (1962–74). Fond of playing the classics on stage, he also starred in the television sitcoms *Mr Aitch* (1967) and *Grundy* (1980).

Corbett, 'Gentleman' Jim (James John)
1866–1933
US boxer

Born in San Francisco, California, he won the world heavyweight championship in 1892 by knocking out John L Sullivan (1858–1918) in the 21st round, and lost it in 1897 to Bob Fitzsimmons (1862–1917) in the 14th round. He failed to regain his title in two fights with his former sparring partner, James J Jeffries (1875–1953), in 1900 and 1903. Corbett, who is said to have introduced 'science' into the art of boxing, also made several appearances on stage and in films.

Corbett, Richard See Corbet, Richard

Corbett, Ronnie (Ronald Balfour) 1930–
Scottish comedian and actor

He was born in Edinburgh, and following national service in the RAF and 18 months as a civil servant in the Department of Agriculture, he entered showbusiness via amateur dramatics, seaside shows and stand-up comedy. Spotted in Danny La Rue's nightclub by David Frost, he appeared on television in *The Frost Report* (1966–67) and *Frost on Sunday* (1968–69). His small stature, impish sense of fun and inimitably discursive delivery of comic monologues soon gained him national popularity and his own television series have included *No—That's Me Over Here* (1967–70) and *Sorry!* (1981–88). A fruitful partnership with Ronnie Barker led to the long-running *The Two*

Ronnies (1971–87) and numerous cabaret appearances. His film appearances include *Casino Royale* (1967) and *No Sex Please, We're British* (1973).

Corbière, Tristan, *pseudonym of* Édouard Joachim Corbière 1845–75
French poet
He was born in Coat-Congar, Finistère. He was largely unknown until **Paul Verlaine** included him in his *Les Poètes maudits* (1884, 'The Accursed Poets'). Corbière's collection *Amours Jaunes* (1873, 'Yellow Loves') was an acknowledged influence upon **T S Eliot**. His bitter early work reflected the landscape of Brittany, and represented a powerful reaction against the excesses of Romanticism. His later, more ironic poetry reads as if it had been written at least 50 years after its time. ⬚ F C Burch, *Tristan Corbière* (1970)

Corbin, Margaret, *née* Cochran 1751–1800
American Revolutionary War heroine
Born in Franklin County, Pennsylvania, she was raised by her uncle from the age of five when her father had been killed fighting Native Americans and her mother had been taken prisoner. Her husband John Corbin enlisted in the Revolution and she accompanied him to assist in looking after the troops. When he was killed during the Battle of Harlem Heights (1776), she took over his artillery station and continued firing his cannon until she herself was shot. Her injuries resulted in the permanent loss of the use of one arm. In 1779 she became the first woman to receive a military pension from Congress, and a monument at West Point was erected in her honour in 1916.

Corday, Charlotte, *properly* Marie Charlotte Corday d'Armont 1768–93
French noblewoman
She was born in St Saturnin. Despite her aristocratic background she welcomed the Revolution at first, but was then so horrified by the behaviour of the Jacobins that she resolved to kill either **Robespierre** or **Jean Paul Marat**. After hearing of Marat's demand for 200,000 more victims, she entered his house in Paris by pretending to be a messenger. Marat was having a bath, and his heartless comment about the fugitive Girondins ('I will have them all guillotined at Paris') incited her to stab him to death. Unrepentant, she was brought before the Revolutionary Tribunal and guillotined four days later. ⬚ Jacqueline Dauxois, *Charlotte Corday* (1988)

Cordobes, El, *real name* Manuel Benitez Pérez 1937–
Spanish matador
He was born in Palma del Rio. He was the idol of the crowds in the 1960s. His athleticism and populist approach in the ring shocked purists who saw him as more of an acrobat than a torero, but his theatrical style and disregard of danger made him the highest paid matador in history. He retired in 1972.

Corea, Chick (Armando Anthony) 1941–
US jazz pianist, bandleader and composer
Born in Chelsea, Massachusetts, he was brought up in a musical family, and cut his professional teeth in Latin bands, an influence which has remained strong in his music. He first recorded as a leader in 1966, but came to prominence after joining **Miles Davis's** early jazz-rock fusion bands, then forming his own Return To Forever in that vein in 1971. He has written some works which are closer to a classical vein than jazz, but has continued to move between straight jazz and fusion settings with his clearly demarcated Akoustic and Elektric bands. He has been a significant influence on the style of many younger jazz musicians, as well as a major voice in the music.

Corelli, Arcangelo, *nicknamed* Il divino 1653–1713
Italian composer
He was born in Fusignano, near Bologna. His concerti grossi and his solo and trio sonatas for violin mark an epoch in chamber music, and had great influence on **J S Bach** and on contemporary string technique.

Corelli, Marie, *pseudonym of* Mary Mackay 1855–1924
English novelist
She was born in London, the illegitimate child of Charles Mackay, a journalist, and Ellen Mills, a widow whom he later married as his second wife. She was educated by governesses, and trained as a pianist but from 1885 devoted herself to writing. *A Romance of Two Worlds* (1886) was a bestseller, and marked the beginning of a prolific career. A sentimental, self-righteous moralist, she was the writer that critics loved to hate, but her admirers included **Gladstone** and **Oscar Wilde** and her readership was immense. Her novels include *Barabbas* (1893), *The Devil's Motor* (1910), *Eyes of the Sea* (1917) and *The Secret Power* (1921). ⬚ E Bigland, *Marie Corelli, the woman and the legend* (1953)

Corey, Elias James 1928–
US chemist and Nobel Prize winner
He was born in Methuen, Massachusetts, and, after studying at the Massachusetts Institute of Technology, he became an instructor at the University of Illinois (1951). In 1953 he became professor there, but in 1959 he moved to Harvard, where he was appointed Sheldon Emery Professor in 1965. He has made mechanistic and structural studies of many natural products, but is best known for computer-aided analyses of synthetic problems. Retrosynthetic analysis, the way a target molecule might be broken down into simpler, readily available compounds, is a valuable technique in designing organic syntheses, and he showed that the application of computers to retrosynthetic analysis can greatly assist the process. For this work he was awarded the Nobel Prize for chemistry in 1990. He has received many other awards and honours, including the National Medal of Science (1988).

Cori, Carl Ferdinand 1896–1984
US biochemist and Nobel Prize winner
Born in Prague, Czechoslovakia, he married and graduated in medicine there, and in 1922 emigrated with his wife **Gerty Cori**. Both became professors at Washington University in St Louis from 1931. In 1936 he studied an ester isolated from frog muscle and discovered that the enzyme involved in its formation existed in muscle, heart, brain and liver. He obtained it in crystalline form in 1942, and recognized that it had both inactive and active forms and required a prosthetic group, adenylic acid. He shared the 1947 Nobel Prize for physiology or medicine with his wife and **Bernado Houssay**. In 1951 he described the process which removes the side chains in glycogen breakdown, and used it to determine the length of the main chain and side branches of several polysaccharides. After Gerty's death, Carl Cori worked at the Massachusetts General Hospital from 1967.

Cori, Gerty Theresa Radnitz 1896–1957
US biochemist and Nobel Prize winner
Born in Prague, Czechoslovakia, she trained in medicine at the German University of Prague, and married her fellow student **Carl Cori** upon graduating. She emigrated with her husband to the USA, where she was employed at the State Institute for the Study of Malignant Disease, Buffalo, New York (1922–31) and then held a number of posts at the Medical School at the Washington University, St Louis, including Professor of Biochemistry (1947–57). With her husband she conducted research into carbohydrate metabolism, analyzing the process whereby glycogen, the stored form of carbohydrate, is

enzymatically broken down to glucose, liberating energy in the process. Their detailed analysis enabled them to reconstruct the pathways whereby glycogen was synthesized and stored in the body. They also studied the effects of many hormones including insulin, adrenaline and pituitary extracts, and examined glycogen and glucose metabolism in biochemically abnormal circumstances. The latter work led her to the first demonstration that glycogen storage disease could be caused by abnormalities or deficits in enzymes. Gerty and Carl shared the Nobel Prize for physiology or medicine with **Bernardo Houssay** in 1947; they were only the third husband-and-wife team to receive this award, following after the **Curies** in 1903 and the **Joliot-Curies** in 1935.

Corinth, Lovis 1858–1925
German painter
Born in Tapiau, East Prussia, he studied at Königsberg and Munich and under **William Bouguereau** in Paris. From conventional nudes, landscape painting and especially portraiture, his style became markedly Impressionistic, as in *Under the Chandelier* (1905), *After a Bathe* (1906) and his many *Waldensee* views, while later work, for example *Georg Brandes* (1924), verged on Expressionism. From 1900 he lived in Berlin and with **Max Liebermann** and **Max Slevogt** led the Secession movement, of which he became president (1915), against the Berlin academic school.

Coriolanus, Gaius, *also called* Gnaeus Marcius
5th century BC
Roman folk hero
Named after his capture of the Volscian town of Corioli, and the subject of **Shakespeare**'s play *Coriolanus*, he was banished by the Romans for tyrannical behaviour during a famine (491BC). He took refuge with the Volsci, and proceeded to lead them against Rome but after entreaties from his mother and wife, he spared Rome, and was executed by the Volsci.

Coriolis, Gustave Gaspard 1792–1843
French physicist
Born in Paris, he was educated at the École Polytechnique, where he became professor in 1816. Intrigued by the problem of motion above a spinning surface, he considered the problem from around 1835, and in this work identified the 'Coriolis force'. This apparent force acting on objects moving across the Earth's surface results from the Earth's rotation. In the northern hemisphere, the path of an object appears deflected to the right, in the southern hemisphere to the left. It is responsible for wind and ocean current patterns, and is applicable to rotating systems generally.

Corkery, Daniel 1878–1964
Irish writer and critic
Born in Cork, he was educated at University College, Cork, and was Professor of English there from 1931 to 1947. He published a collection of short stories, *A Munster Twilight* (1917), depicting ethnic and class division in Irish life, and a novel, *The Threshold of Quiet* (1917). He made a great attack on the literary historians who saw Ireland in terms of the 18th-century 'Big House', in his *The Hidden Ireland* (1925). He profoundly influenced new Irish writers such as **Frank O'Connor** and **Sean O'Faolain**. His love of the Irish language was the basis of his literary evangelism, as revealed in his *The Fortunes of the Irish Language* (1954). He also wrote *Synge and Anglo-Irish Literature* (1931) and several plays. He was elected to the Irish Senate in 1951.

Corliss, George Henry 1817–88
US engineer and inventor

He was born in Easton, New York State. Of his many improvements to the steam engine the most important were the 'Corliss valve', with separate inlet and exhaust ports, and his use of springs to speed up the opening and closing of valves. In 1856 he founded the Corliss Engine Co, which supplied the 1876 Philadelphia Centennial Exhibition with a huge 1,400hp engine, which worked continuously for six months, driving all the machines in the exhibition.

Cormack, Allan MacLeod 1924–98
US physicist and Nobel Prize winner
Born in Johannesburg, South Africa, he studied physics and engineering at Cape Town University and did postgraduate work at Cambridge. He worked as a medical physicist at Groote Shuur Hospital in Johannesburg before moving to the USA, where he held various appointments at Tufts University, Medford, Massachusetts, being appointed full professor in 1964, then emeritus in 1995. He pioneered the development of computerized axial tomography (CAT) scanning, which enables the production of detailed X-ray pictures of the human body. He shared the 1979 Nobel Prize for physiology or medicine with Sir **Godfrey Hounsfield**, who had independently developed a similar device. He was awarded the US National Medal of Science in 1990.

Corneille, Guillaume, *properly* Cornélis van Beverloo 1922–
Belgian painter
Born in Liège, he was a leading European exponent of 'action' painting. His works include *Drawing in Colour*, from the 'and the country loses itself in Infinity' series (1955), and *Summer Flowers* (1958).

Corneille, Pierre 1606–84
French dramatist
Born in Rouen, he was educated in a Jesuit school and studied law. He moved to Paris in 1629, where his comedy *Mélite* (1629, Eng trans *Melite*, 1776) proved highly successful. His other early pieces handle intricate and extravagant plots with ingenuity, but show little of his poetic genius. He became one of Cardinal **Richelieu**'s 'cinq auteurs' (five authors), engaged to compose plays on lines laid down by the cardinal, and produced such plays as *L'Aveugle de Smyrne* (1638, 'The Blind Man of Smyrna') and *La Grande pastorale* (1639, 'The Great Pastoral'), but he was too independent to retain Richelieu's favour. *Médée* (1635, 'Medea') showed a marked advance on his earlier works, and *Le Cid* (first produced in January 1637) took Paris by storm, and had a profound impact on French drama. Richelieu ordered his literary retainers to criticize it, but the general enthusiasm remained strong. Other major tragedies were *Horace* (1640, Eng trans *Horatius*, 1656), *Cinna* (1640, Eng trans *Cinna's Conspiracy*, 1713) and *Polyeucte* (1642, Eng trans *Polyeuctes*, 1655). *Le Menteur* (1643, Eng trans *The Mistaken Beau; or, The Liar*, 1685) entitles him to be called the father of French comedy as well as of French tragedy. From 1647, when he was made an academician, his plays show a decline in dramatic and poetic power. He made a verse translation of **Thomas à Kempis**'s *Imitatio Christi* (1651). He returned to the stage in 1659 with *Œdipe*, and in 1671 joined **Molière** and Quinault in writing the opera *Psyché*. His last works were *Pulchérie* (1672) and *Suréna* (1674, Eng trans *Surenas*, 1969). After his marriage in 1640 he lived in Rouen until 1662, when he settled in Paris. A master of the Alexandrine verse form, his plays deal with heroes; but he concerned himself with moral and mental conflict rather than physical action, exploring the tensions between duty and honour on one hand, and passion on the other, and exalting man's capacity for freedom, strength of will, and spiritual development.
📖 P J Yarrow, *Corneille* (1963)

Corneille, Thomas 1625–1709
French playwright

He was born in Rouen, the brother of **Pierre Corneille**. His tragedies, including *Camma* (1661), *Laodice* (1668), *Pyrrhus* (1690), *Bérénice* (1657), *Timocrate* (1656), *Ariane* (1672) and *Bradamante* (1696), are, in general, superior to his comedies. He also wrote a verse translation of **Ovid**'s *Metamorphoses*. ☐ D Collins, *Thomas Corneille, protean dramatist* (1968)

Cornelius Nepos See **Nepos, Cornelius**

Cornelius, Peter 1824–74
German composer

Born in Mainz, he went to Weimar in 1852, becoming a devotee of **Franz Liszt**, **Richard Wagner** and the New German school. He produced his famous comic opera, *der Barbier von Bagdad* ('The Barber of Baghdad') in 1858 (a failure at the time), and his grand opera, *Der Cid*, in 1865. He was the nephew of **Peter von Cornelius**.

Cornelius, Peter von 1783–1867
German painter

Born in Düsseldorf, he joined the group of **Philipp Veit**, **Friedrich Schadow** and **Johann Overbeck** in Rome in 1811, and assisted in the decoration of the Casa Bartoldi. From Rome he went to Düsseldorf, where he became director of the academy; in 1819 he was called to Munich by Crown Prince Ludwig of Bavaria (later **Ludwig I**). Here he remained until 1841, and executed the large frescoes of Greek mythological scenes in the Glyptothek and the New Testament frescoes in the Ludwigskirche, which was built to give scope for his art. In 1841 he was appointed director of the Berlin Academy. Among his productions in Berlin are the frescoes for the Campo Santo, or royal burial place, the finest being his *Four Riders of the Apocalypse*.

Cornell, Ezra 1807–74
US industrialist and philanthropist

Born in Westchester Landing, New York State, he became a carpenter and millwright, and in association with **Samuel Morse** devised insulation for telegraph wires on poles. He founded and organized telegraph companies, including the Western Union Telegraph in 1855. In 1865, in association with **Andrew Dickson White**, he founded and heavily endowed Cornell University, which opened in Ithaca, New York State , in 1868.

Cornell, Joseph 1903–72
US artist

He was born in Nyack, New York State. A self-taught artist, he was one of the first exponents of a form of sculpture called 'assemblage', in which unrelated objects are brought together to create new forms and sometimes suprising juxtapositions. His 'boxes' contain evocative and poetic collections of bric-à-brac, and show a Surrealist sense of fantasy, such as *Shadow Box: Interior white with yellow sand and 'sea-side' atmosphere*. His first one-man exhibition was in New York in 1932 and his work has been included in many subsequent exhibitions of Surrealist art. He is regarded as a pioneer of US Pop Art.

Cornell, Katharine 1893–1974
US actress, producer and manager

She was born in Berlin, Germany, of US parents and educated in New York City. She made her first stage appearance in 1916, and subsequently appeared in many stage productions such as *The Green Hat*, *The Letter* and *The Age of Innocence* before embarking on a career as producer. Her own productions include a number of Shakespearean and Shavian classics, as well as *The Constant Wife*, *The First-Born* and *Dear Liar*.

Cornforth, Sir John Warcup 1917–
Australian chemist and Nobel Prize winner

Born in Sydney, he studied at university there and at Oxford. From a young age he was increasingly deaf. He took part in the wartime effort to synthesize the new drug penicillin. He also studied the biosynthesis of cholesterol and other steroids. In 1962 he and George Popják were appointed co-directors of the Milstead Laboratory of Chemical Enzymology of Shell Research Ltd. Cornforth was also appointed professor at Warwick University. Cornforth and Popják studied in detail the stereochemistry of the interaction between an enzyme and its substrate and biological oxidation-reduction reactions. Cornforth has also collaborated extensively with Hermann Eggerer on the stereochemistry of enzyme action, developing the chiral methyl group. In 1975 he was awarded the Nobel Prize for chemistry, which he shared with **Vladimir Prelog**, for his work on the chemistry of enzyme action. From 1975 to 1982 he was Royal Society Fellow at the University of Sussex and was knighted in 1977.

Cornwall, Barry See **Proctor, Bryan Waller**

Cornwallis, Charles Cornwallis, 1st Marquis 1738–1805
English soldier

Born in London, he served as aide-de-camp to the Marquis of **Granby** during part of the Seven Years War. In the American Revolution (1775–83), although he opposed the taxation of the American colonists, he accepted a command in the war, and with an inferior force defeated **Horatio Gates** at Camden, South Carolina, in 1780 and more than held his own at Guildford (1781). Later that year he was besieged at Yorktown, Virginia, and forced to surrender—a disaster that proved the ruin of the British cause in America. From 1786 to 1793 he was Governor-General of India and Commander-in-Chief, defeating **Tippoo Sultán**. As Lord Lieutenant of Ireland (1798–1801) while Viscount **Castlereagh** was secretary, he crushed the 1798 rebellion. As plenipotentiary to France he negotiated the Peace of Amiens in 1802. He was reappointed Governor-General of India in 1804. ☐ Frank and Mary Wickwire, *Cornwallis: The American Adventure* (2 vols, 1970)

Cornyshe, William c.1465–1523
English composer

Born in Hylden, Kent, he was employed as musician, actor and producer of entertainments at the courts of **Henry VII** and **Henry VIII**. In 1509 he became Master of the Children of the Chapel Royal, and was in charge of the music at the Field of Cloth of Gold (1520). He composed religious and secular choral works.

Coronado, Francisco Vázquez de 1510–54
Spanish conquistador and explorer

He was born in Salamanca. In 1540 he commanded the expedition to New Mexico on which **Garcia Lopez de Cárdenas** discovered the Grand Canyon of the Colorado.

Corot, (Jean Baptiste) Camille 1796–1875
French landscape painter

Born in Paris, he became an assistant in a Paris drapery establishment, but in 1822 took up the study of art. He moved to Rome in 1825, but returned to Paris in 1872, and contributed his *Vue prise à Narni* and his *Campagne de Rome* to the Salon. His main sketching ground was at Barbizon, in the Forest of Fontainebleau, but he made two other visits to Italy in 1835 and 1843. It was not until about 1840 that he fully developed his style, characterized by breadth and delicacy, and sacrificing accuracy of detail to unity of impression and harmony of effect. The Universal Exhibition of 1855 established his fame. Among his masterpieces are *Danse de nymphes*, *Homère et les bergers*, *Orphée*, *Joueur de flûte* and *Le Bûcheron*. ☐ Ared Robaut, *L'Œuvre de Corot* (4 vols, 1905)

Correggio, Antonio Allegri da c.1494–1534
Italian painter

He was born in Correggio, near Parma. He painted for the Franciscan convent a *Virgin Enthroned* in 1514, now in the Dresden Gallery, and began his great series of mythological frescoes for the convent of San Paolo at Padua in 1518. *The Ascension* in the cupola of the Benedictine church of San Giovanni dates from 1521–24, and the decoration of the cathedral of Parma was commissioned in 1522. He also painted easel pictures, including *Ecce Homo* (National Gallery, London) and his celebrated nativity scene *The Night* commissioned in 1522, now in the Dresden Gallery. Five years later he painted *Il Giorno*, an exquisite picture of St Jerome (Parma Gallery). In 1530 he returned to Correggio and purchased an estate. *Jupiter and Antiope* (Louvre, Paris), *Education of Cupid* (National Gallery, London), *Danae* (Borghese Gallery, Rome) and *Leda* (Berlin Museum) have been assigned to his later years. *Reading Magdalene*, of which the picture in the Dresden Gallery is now regarded as merely a 17th century copy, was completed in 1528. His only son Pomponio (1521–c.1593) was also a painter, and an altarpiece by him is in the Academy in Parma.

Correns, Carl Franz Joseph Erich 1864–1933
German botanist and geneticist

Born in Munich, he was educated there and at Tübingen University, becoming professor at Münster University in 1909. From 1914 he was the first director of the Kaiser Wilhelm Institute for Biology in the Dahlem district of Berlin, and with Hugo de Vries and Erich von Tschermak-Seysenegg was a rediscoverer of Gregor Mendel's law of heredity. He proved that sex was inherited in a Mendelian fashion and cytoplasmic (non-nuclear) inheritance.

Corrigan(-Maguire), Mairead 1944–
Northern Irish peace activist and Nobel Prize winner

Born in Belfast, she was co-founder with Betty Williams of the Northern Ireland Peace Movement in 1976. A Roman Catholic secretary in Belfast, she started organizing peace petitions in the face of the sectarian violence in Northern Ireland. The initiative became a mass movement of Roman Catholic and Protestant women known as the Community of the Peace People. She shared with Betty Williams the 1976 Nobel Peace Prize. ☐ Richard Deutsch, *Mairead Corrigan, Betty Williams* (1977)

Cort, Henry 1740–1800
English ironmaster and navy agent

Born in Lancaster, Lancashire, he was a civilian in the Royal Navy then bought an ironworks near Plymouth (1775). He was the inventor of the 'puddling' process for purifying iron. Ruined by a prosecution for debt, he was ultimately pensioned.

Cortázar, Julio 1914–84
Argentine–French writer

Born in Brussels, Belgium, the son of Argentine parents, he grew up in Argentina, and was educated there. From 1935 to 1945 he taught in secondary schools in several small towns and in Mendoza, Argentina, and from 1945 to 1951 he was a translator for publishers. He then moved to Paris where he lived until his death, writing and freelancing for UNESCO, and he became naturalized in 1981. He is one of the most widely recognized Spanish–American writers outside the Spanish-speaking world, partly due to the filming in 1966 of his short-story 'Las babas del diablo' (1958, Eng trans 1963, in *Blow-Up and Other Stories*, 1968) as *Blow-Up* by the Italian director Michelangelo Antonioni. His other works of fiction include *Los premios* (1960, Eng trans *The Winners*, 1965), his

masterpiece *Rayuela* (1963, Eng trans *Hopscotch*, 1966), *62: modelo para armar* (1968, Eng trans *62: A Model Kit*, 1972), *Alguien que anda por ahí y otros relatos* (1977, Eng trans *A Change of Light and Other Stories*, 1980) and *Queremos tanto a Glenda* (1980, Eng trans *We Love Glenda So Much*, 1983). ☐ S Boldy, *The Novels of Cortázar* (1980)

Cortés, Hernán See panel p447

Cortona, Pietro Berrettini da 1596–1669
Italian painter and architect

Born in Cortona, he ranks, with Gian Lorenzo Bernini, as one of the great figures of the Roman Baroque. With Lanfranco and Guercino he was the founder of the Roman High Baroque style in painting. He specialized in highly illusionistic ceiling painting in which paint is combined with stucco and gilt to create arresting effects. The greatest of these is his *Allegory of Divine Providence* and *Barberini Power* (1633–39) in the Barberini Palace in Rome. There is similar work in the apse of the church of Santa Maria in Vallicella and the Pitti Palace in Florence. Although he once said that he regarded architecture as a pastime, his church of SS Martina e Luca in Rome is of high quality. His easel painting is usually less impressive.

Cortot, Alfred 1877–1962
French pianist and conductor

Born in Nyon, Switzerland, of French parents, he won the first prize for piano-playing at the Paris Conservatoire in 1896. Known in France as a distinguished player of Beethoven's concertos, he formed the Société de Festival Lyrique in 1902, and conducted the first Paris performance of Richard Wagner's *Götterdämmerung* ('The Twilight of the Gods') in 1902. In 1905, with Jacques Thibaud and Pablo Casals, he founded a trio whose chamber music performances became highly respected. Principally known in later years as an exponent of Chopin's music, he was Professor of Pianoforte at the Paris Conservatoire from 1917 to 1920 and the author of several books on musical appreciation, interpretation and piano technique.

Corvinus See Matthias I Hunyadi

Corvisart-Desmarets or Corvisart des Marets, Jean Nicolas, Baron de 1755–1821
French physician

He was born in Voliziers, Champagne, and became physician to Napoleon I in 1807. As professor at the Collège de France, he popularized the method of percussion in diagnosing heart diseases. He is regarded as the founder of pathological anatomy.

Corvo, Baron See Rolfe, Frederick William

Cory, Charles Barney 1857–1921
US naturalist and traveller

Born in Boston, he developed an early interest in ornithology and travelled widely in the eastern USA and the Caribbean. A founder-member of the American Ornithologists' Union, he published *The Birds of the Bahamas* (1878) and various other bird books. In 1906 he moved to Chicago, where he became curator of zoology at the Chicago Field Museum, and published his monumental *Birds of the Americas* (4 vols, 1918–19). Cory's Shearwater was named in his honour.

Cory, William Johnson, *originally* William Johnson 1823–92
English academic, translator and poet

Born in Torrington, Devon, he was educated at Eton and at King's College, Cambridge, where he became a Fellow. As assistant master at Eton (1845–72), he wrote the words of the 'Eton Boat Song'. He inherited an estate and in 1872 adopted the name Cory, went to Madeira, married, and

Cortés or Cortez, Hernán or Hernando 1485–1547
Spanish conquistador and conqueror of Mexico

Hernán Cortés was born into a family of low nobility in Medellin, Estremadura. He enrolled at the University of Salamanca at the age of 14, but left after only two years. In 1504 he sailed for San Domingo, and accompanied **Diego Velázquez de Cuellar** in his successful expedition to conquer Cuba in 1511. Inspired by the discoveries of **Pedro de Alvarado** and others, in 1518 Velázquez fitted out a small expedition of 550 men with 17 horses and 10 cannons and gave the command to Cortés. He landed first in the Yucatán, and subjugated Tabasco. At San Juan de Ulua, messengers from **Montezuma II**, the Aztec king, reached him, bringing presents. He founded Vera Cruz, and marched to Tlaxcala, whose warlike inhabitants, subdued after hard fighting, became his faithful allies. After some delay, he started on his march to Mexico, with his Tlaxcalan allies. He escaped a dangerous ambush at Cholula, and on 8 November 1519 he reached the capital, Tenochtitlán. There he was well received by Montezuma, who was abducted to the Spanish quarters, and forced to submit to a public act of vassalage to Spain.

In 1520 Cortés marched to the coast, leaving Alvarado in command to deal with a force sent by Velázquez to arrest him, and succeeded in winning them to his side. Meanwhile Alvarado's harshness had provoked the Mexicans to revolt, and Cortés was forced to evacuate Tenochtitlán with heavy losses (the 'Night of Sorrows'). In retreat, Cortés overcame a hugh Aztec army at Otumba, and eventually reached Tlaxcala. After rebuilding his forces he laid siege to Tenochtitlán in 1521, capturing it and razing it to the ground, building Mexico City in its place. In 1522 he was appointed Governor and Captain-General of New Spain. He sent Alvarado to subdue Guatemala (1524–25), and he himself made an expedition to Honduras (1524–26). In May 1528 he went back to Spain, was received with honour by **Charles V**, and was created a marquis. He returned in 1530 as Captain-General, but not as Civil Governor, of New Spain. Poor and broken in health, he returned to Spain in 1540, where he accompanied Charles in his unhappy expedition against Algiers, and died neglected near Seville. His remains were moved to Tezcuco in 1562, and to Mexico City in 1629.

📖 Salvador de Madriaga *Hernán Cortés, Conqueror of Mexico* (1942); William H Prescott, *History of the Conquest of Mexico* (1843).

His story has been used as the basis of an opera by **Gasparo Spontini**, with text by **Étienne Jouy**, *Fernand Cortez* (1809).

John Keats mentions Cortés in his poem 'On First Looking into Chapman's Homer' (1817):
'Then felt I like some watcher of the skies
When a new planet swims into his ken;
Or like stout Cortez when with eagle eyes
He stared at the Pacific—and all his men
Looked at each other with a wild surmise—
Silent, upon a peak in Darien.'

settled in Hampstead where he gave private lessons and spent his remaining years writing and translating. His 'Heraclitus' in *Ionica* (1858)—'They told me, Heraclitus, they told me you were dead. They brought me bitter news to hear and bitter tears to shed—', based on the epigram by Callimachus, ensured him a permanent place among English lyric poets. His *Letters and Journals* were published in 1897. 📖 Faith Compton Mackenzie, *William Cory* (1950)

Cosby, Bill (William Henry) 1937–
US comedian

Born in North Philadelphia, he served in the US navy (1956–60), and later studied at Temple University, Philadelphia, on a track and field scholarship. He began performing as a nightclub comic and gave up his studies to pursue this career full-time. An appearance on *The Tonight Show* (1965) led to him being cast in the television series *I Spy* (1965–68) where his role won him three of his eight Emmy awards and broke new ground in the portrayal of African-Americans on screen. Subsequent television series include *The Bill Cosby Show Kids* (1969–71), *The New Bill Cosby Show* (1972–73), *The Cosby Show* (1984–92), *The Cosby Mysteries* (1994) and *Cosby* (1996). He also voiced the children's animated series *Fat Albert and the Cosby Kids* (1972–79) and *The New Fat Albert Show* (1979–84), as well as hosting the quiz show *You Bet Your Life* (1992). A congenial figure, his wholesome humour is based on quirky observations of the world around him and offbeat anecdotes based on personal experience. He made his film debut in *Hickey and Boggs* (1971) and has appeared in *Uptown Saturday Night* (1974), *California Suite* (1978), *Leonard: Part VI* (1987), *Ghost Dad* (1990) and *Jack* (1996). He has recorded more than 20 albums and his book *Fatherhood* (1986) was a bestseller.

Cosgrave, Liam 1920–
Irish statesman

Born in Templeogue, County Dublin, the son of **William Thomas Cosgrave**, he was educated at St Vincent's College, Castleknock, Dublin. He was called to the Bar in 1943 and was a member of the Dáil (1943–81). He was Minister for External Affairs (1954–57), Leader of the Fine Gael Party (1965–77) and Prime Minister (1973–77).

Cosgrave, William Thomas 1880–1965
Irish statesman

Born in Dublin, he joined the Sinn Féin movement at an early age, and took part in the Easter Rising (1916). He became a Sinn Féin MP (1918–22), and after his years as first President of the Irish Free State (1922–32), was Leader of the Opposition (Fine Gael, 1932–44). He was the father of **Liam Cosgrave**.

Cosimo, Piero di See **Piero di Cosimo**

Cosmas, *called* Indicopleustes ('Indian Traveller')
fl.6th century
Merchant of Alexandria

He travelled much in Ethiopia and parts of Asia. He returned to Egypt about 550, and in monastic retirement wrote a Greek work on Christian topography to prove the authenticity of the biblical account of the world.

Cosmas and Damian or Damianus, Saints
d.303AD
Arabian brothers

Born traditionally in Cilicia region, Asia Minor, they were said to have been physicians at Ægæa in Cilicia, who were cast into the sea as Christians, but rescued by an angel. Thereafter, burning and stoning having proved ineffectual, they were beheaded.

Cossa, Francesco del c.1435–1477
Italian artist

He was born in Ferrara. His work is similar to that of **Cosima Tura**, and often equally austere, but his most famous work, the frescoes in the Palazzo Schifanoia at Ferrara, which were commissioned by Borso **d'Este**, consists of a number of mythological and court scenes. He also worked in Bologna.

Cossington-Smith, Grace 1892–1984
Australian painter
Born in Neutral Bay, New South Wales, she studied art at Dattilo Rubbo's Art School, Sydney, and in England and Germany in 1912–14. Credited with introducing Post-Impressionism to Australia, she was a pioneer of the Modernist movement and co-founded the Contemporary Group in 1926. Her paintings did not become popular until late in her career. They include *The Sock Knitter* (1915), a key work in the Australian Modernist movement, and *The Lacquer Room* (1935).

Costa, Afonso 1871–1937
Portuguese politician
He was born in Beira Baixa province. As Minister of Justice under the First Republic he led a vigorous anti-clerical campaign which culminated in the separation of Church and State in 1911. He headed the most popular Portuguese Republican Party (PRP) government of the Republican era (1913–14), being the only government to balance the budget. His PRP was the vehicle of the urban lower middle classes, disenfranchizing much of the working class by reducing the electorate by more than half to 400,000. Internal divisions within the PRP and the alienation of the army led to the fall of his government (1914). Premier again in 1916–17, he took Portugal into World War I on the side of the Allies, fearing for the future of its colonies in any postwar settlement. However, the economic impact of the war and military losses paved the way for a coup (1917), and Costa went into exile in Paris (1919).

Costa, Joaquín 1846–1911
Spanish historian and reformer
Born in Monzon, Huesca, he was a crusader for the political and economic regeneration of Spain and an investigator of Spain's oldest traditions. He co-founded the National League of Producers (1899), the National Union (1900), and in 1903 was elected as a deputy for the Republican Union. A unique publicist and reformer, Costa left a legacy of radical populism and corporatism, and all later regenerationists were to be in his debt. His work includes *Juridical and Political Studies* (1884) and *Agrarian Collectivism in Spain* (1898).

Costa, Lorenzo c.1460–1535
Italian painter
He was born in Ferrara. His *Madonna and Child Enthroned* is in the National Gallery, London. In 1506 he went to Mantua, where he succeeded **Andrea Mantegna** as court painter.

Costa, Lucio 1902–98
Brazilian architect
Born in Toulouse, France, of Franco-Brazilian parents, he studied in Rio de Janeiro. Influenced by **Walter Gropius**, **Mies van der Rohe** and **Le Corbusier**, from 1948 to 1954 he designed the award-winning Eduardo Gunile Apartments (1948–54). In 1957 his plan for the city of Brasilia was chosen by an international jury for its clarity and ability to integrate monumentality and daily life. He devoted much of his time to the Brazilian Society for Historical Preservation, and was an authority on the colonial architecture of Brazil. He is considered the father of modern Brazilian architecture.

Costa, Manuel Pinto da 1937–
São Tomé politician
Born in Agua Grande, he founded the Movement for the Liberation of São Tomé and Príncipe (MLSTP) in Gabon (1972) and in 1974, taking advantage of the new government in Portugal, returned and persuaded the new government in Lisbon to recognize the MLSTP as the sole representative of the people and to grant independence a year later. He became President in 1975 and set his country on a politically non-aligned course.

Costello, Elvis, *real name* Declan Patrick McManus 1955–
English singer-songwriter
The most important songwriter to emerge from the English new wave of the late 1970s and one of the finest pop chroniclers of Great Britain in the 1980s, he was born in Paddington, London, the son of big band singer Ross McManus. He started his own career with the unrecorded band Flip City and as a solo folk-club singer. Signed to Stiff Records in 1977, he established his reputation as an intense and vitriolic musician with his debut album *My Aim Is True*. For his second album, *This Year's Model* (1978), he was joined by the Attractions—a three-piece group consisting of Steve Nieve, Pete Thomas and Bruce Thomas who worked with Costello on most of his albums over the next eight years, although Costello also collaborated with many other musicians. His albums have included *Get Happy* (1980), *Almost Blue* (1981, a collection of country and western songs), *Imperial Bedroom* (1982), *Goodbye Cruel World* (1984) and *King of America* (1986).

Costello, John Aloysius 1891–1976
Irish politician
Born in Dublin and educated at University College, Dublin, he was called to the Bar in 1914 and became Attorney-General (1926–32). In 1948 he became Prime Minister of a government of several parties dominated by his own Fine Gael Party. As a foremost constitutional lawyer, one of his first acts was to repeal the External Relations Act, which paved the way that year for the formal change from the State of Eire to the Republic of Ireland. On the defeat of his government by **Eamon de Valera**'s Fianna Fáil Party in 1951, he became Leader of the Opposition in the Dáil, was Prime Minister from 1954 to 1957, and again Leader of the Opposition until 1959.

Costello, Lou See **Abbott, Bud**

Coster, Charles de 1827–79
Belgian storyteller
He was born in Munich, and studied at Brussels. His most famous work, the prose epic *La Légende et les aventures héroiques, joyeuses et glorieuses d'Ulenspiegel* (1866, Eng trans *The Legend of the Glorious Adventures of Tyl Ulenspiegel*, 1918), took 10 years to write. 💡 H Liebrecht, *La vie et le rêve de Charles de Coster* (1927)

Coster, Dirk 1889–1950
Dutch physicist
Born in Amsterdam, he studied at Leyden University, before taking a degree in electrical engineering at Delft Technological University. He returned to Leyden University for his doctoral thesis before moving on to Lund University (1922–23). He then joined **Niels Bohr** at his institute in Copenhagen. In 1923, Coster and **George Hevesy** discovered the naturally occurring element hafnium (atomic number 72) in zirconium compounds as suggested by Bohr. Coster then returned to the Netherlands where he was assistant to **Hendrik Lorentz** at the Teyler Laboratory in Haarlem, before accepting a chair in physics and meteorology at Groningen University, which he held until 1949.

Costner, Kevin 1955–
US film actor and director
He was born in Los Angeles, California, and graduated from California State University with a BA in marketing. He worked as a stage manager for Raleigh Studios before turning to acting and making his film debut in the low-budget *Sizzle Beach USA* (1981). A succession of small roles followed before he consolidated his leading-man status

with roles in *Silverado* (1985), *The Untouchables* (1987) and *No Way Out* (1987). His subsequent films include *Bull Durham* (1988), *Field of Dreams* (1989), *Robin Hood: Prince of Thieves* (1991) and *The Bodyguard* (1992). He won a Best Director Academy Award for the epic western *Dances With Wolves* (1990) in which he also starred. More recently, he weathered a hostile critical response to *Waterworld* (1995) and reasserted himself with *Tin Cup* (1996).

Coster, Laurens See Janszoon, Laurens

Cosway, Richard c.1742–1821
English miniaturist

Born in Tiverton, he painted in oils in the style of Antonio da Correggio, but it was in portraiture that he made his mark, and his miniatures became highly fashionable. The Prince of Wales appointed him painter-in-ordinary. In 1781 he married the Irish-Italian Maria Hadfield (1759–1838), herself a skilful artist, who established a conventual school at Lodi, and was made a baroness by Francis I.

Cotes, Roger 1682–1716
English mathematician

Born in Burbage, near Leicester, he was educated at St Paul's School, London, and Trinity College, Cambridge, where he became a Fellow in 1705, and Plumian Professor of Astronomy and Natural Philosophy in 1706. In 1713 he took holy orders. He collaborated with Isaac Newton in revising the second edition of Newton's *Principia* and contributed a preface defending Newton's methodology. His posthumously published *Harmonia mensurarum* (1722) contains work on logarithms and integration.

Cotman, John Sell 1782–1842
English landscape artist

Born in Norwich, he made journeys all over Great Britain sketching architecture and the countryside. In 1806 he returned to his birthplace and became a leading member of the 'Norwich School', but from 1811 to 1823 lived in Yarmouth, where he executed some fine oil paintings and etchings. In 1834 he became, thanks to J M W Turner, drawing master of King's College London. His work exhibits a variety of styles, the best being characterized by skilful arrangement of masses of light and shade, with a minimum of modelling, giving an effect reminiscent of a Japanese print or a modern poster, as in his famous *Chirk Aqueduct* and *Greta Bridge* (1805, in the British Museum, London).

Cottier, Daniel 1838–91
Scottish stained-glass artist, designer, interior decorator and art dealer

He was born in Glasgow, and little is known of his early education, except that in the 1850s he was apprenticed to a well-known stained-glass firm in Glasgow, and by 1862 he was working as chief designer for a firm in Leith, Edinburgh. In 1867 he established a studio in Glasgow, and began working with the famous Glasgow architect, Alexander 'Greek' Thomson. Cottier produced decorative schemes and stained-glass designs for at least two of Thomson's best-known commissions: painted panelling at the United Presbyterian Church, Queen's Park, Glasgow, and the interior decoration of the eastern section of Glasgow's Great Western Terrace. His early work reflects William Morris's influence, but he developed a distinctive personal style. In 1870, he went into partnership with Bruce Talbert, William Wallace and J M Brydon in London, and in 1873 branches were opened in the USA and Australia. While in the USA, Cottier collaborated with John La Farge to produce designs for a window in Holy Trinity Parish Church, Copley Square, Boston. He was a major exponent of the 'aesthetic movement', and

examples of his stained glass can be seen in Paisley Abbey, St Machar's Cathedral, Aberdeen, Dowanhill Church, Glasgow, and at Greenock West Kirk.

Cottin, Sophie, née Risteau 1770–1807
French writer

She was brought up in Bordeaux and at the age of 17 married a Parisian banker, but was left a childless widow at 20. For comfort she turned to writing, producing verses and a lengthy history, and romantic fiction. *Claire d'Albe* (1799) and *Mathilde* (1805) were followed in 1806 by her most successful work, *Élisabeth, ou les exilés de Sibérie*, ('Elisabeth, or the Siberian Exiles'). 📖 L C Sykes, *Madame Cottin* (1949)

Cotton, Charles 1630–87
English writer

He was born at his father's estate of Beresford in Staffordshire. His father was a friend of Ben Jonson, John Selden, John Donne and other illustrious men. Charles travelled on the Continent, and his early verses were circulated privately. Though a sincere loyalist, he seems to have lived securely under the Commonwealth. In 1664 he issued anonymously his burlesque poem, *Scarronides, or the First Book of Virgil Travestie*, and among his later works are his *Voyage to Ireland in Burlesque* (1670), *Burlesque upon Burlesque* (1675), *Planter's Manual* (1675), and a treatise on fly-fishing contributed in 1676 to the fifth edition of Izaak Walton's *Compleat Angler*. He also published a translation of Montaigne's *Essays* (1685). 📖 E R Miner, *The Cavalier Mode from Honson to Cotton* (1973)

Cotton, Frank Albert 1930–
US chemist

Born in Philadelphia, he studied at Temple University and at Harvard under Sir Geoffrey Wilkinson. He then went to Massachusetts Institute of Technology, and has been Robert A Welch Distinguished Professor of Chemistry at Texas Agricultural and Mechanical University since 1973. Cotton is famous as a transition metal chemist and has studied most aspects of the subject. His earlier work centred upon metal carbonyls, using nuclear magnetic resonance (NMR) to monitor the non-rigid behaviour of such molecules. He has also worked on the preparation and structural characterization of compounds with multiple metal–metal bonds, and discovered the first quadruple bond in 1963. He is author or co-author of several widely used university textbooks, including *Advanced Inorganic Chemistry* (1962, with Wilkinson) and *Chemical Applications of Group Theory* (3rd edn 1990). He was the first recipient of the American Chemical Society award in Inorganic Chemistry in 1962, won the Baekeland Medal in 1963 and was Royal Society of Chemistry Centenary Lecturer (1973–74).

Cotton, George Edward Lynch 1813–66
English teacher and clergyman

Educated at Westminster School and Trinity College, Cambridge, he was a master at Rugby School under Thomas Arnold and Archibald Campbell Tait from 1836 (in *Tom Brown's School Days* he appears as 'the young master'). In 1852 he became head of Marlborough College, whose academic position he boosted considerably, and in 1858 Bishop of Calcutta, where he founded schools for the children of the poorer Anglo-Indians and Eurasians. He was drowned in the Ganges.

Cotton, Sir (Thomas) Henry 1907–87
English golfer

Born at Holmes Chapel, Cheshire, and educated at Alleyn's School, he soon became a professional golfer. In the 1930s and 1940s he almost single-handedly defended the US challenge in the British Open championship, winning in 1934, 1937 and 1948. He won many other titles, and played in the Ryder Cup against the USA four times between 1929 and 1953. In his latter years he ran a golf complex in Portugal and was much in demand as a teacher and consultant.

Cotton, John, *known as* the Patriarch of New England 1585–1652
English Puritan clergyman

Born in Derby, Derbyshire, he was educated at Trinity College, Cambridge, became a tutor there, and from about 1612 held a charge at Boston, Lincolnshire. Cited for his Puritan views before Archbishop **Laud**, in 1633 he emigrated to Boston, Massachusetts, where he preached till his death. He became the head of Congregationalism in the USA. His many works include a catechism, forms of prayer, and his defence against **Roger Williams** of the civil authority in religious matters. He also wrote *The Keys of the Kingdom of Heaven* (1644) and *Spiritual Milk for Babes* (1646).

Cotton, Sir Robert Bruce 1571–1631
English antiquary

Born in Denton, Huntingdonshire, he was educated at Westminster School (where his master was the antiquary **William Camden**) and Jesus College, Cambridge. At Cotton House in Westminster, on the site of the present House of Lords, he accumulated books, manuscripts, coins, etc, dispersed by the dissolution of the monasteries. King **James VI and I** created him a baronet in 1611, and frequently consulted him, but imprisoned him for eight months in connection with the Overbury case (1615–16). Cotton, returned to parliament in 1604, identified himself from about 1620 with the constitutional opposition to the Crown. His protest against the proposed debasement of the coinage by King **Charles I** (1626), his frank criticisms in his *Raigne of Henry III* (1627), his *Dangers wherein the Kingdom now Standeth* (1628), and the frequent meeting in his house of Sir **John Pym**, **John Selden** and Sir **Edward Coke**, marked him out to the court as an enemy. He was imprisoned for his supposed connection with the publication of *A Proposition to Bridle the Impertinency of Parliaments*, but was released on the birth of an heir to the throne (May 29, 1630). His library, however, was not restored to him. His son, Sir Thomas (1594–1662), had the books restored to him and greatly increased the library; and his great-grandson, Sir John (1679–1731), bestowed them on the nation in 1700.

Coty, François 1874–1934
French industrialist and newspaper proprietor

Born in Ajaccio, Corsica, he built up the famous perfumery firm which bears his name, obtained control of the *Figaro* in 1924 and founded the *Ami du Peuple* in 1928. He was a member of the Corsican Senate.

Coty, René 1882–1962
French statesman

Born in Le Havre, he became a barrister, and was elected a Left Republican deputy in 1923. He entered the Senate in 1935 and was Minister of Reconstruction in 1947, and in 1953 became the last President of the French Fourth Republic (1953–59). After the constitutional crisis precipitated by the generals in Algeria in 1958, he assisted the return to power of General **de Gaulle** and the consequent birth of the new constitution and Fifth Republic in 1959, with de Gaulle as his successor.

Coué, Émile 1857–1926
French pharmacist and hypnotist

As a pharmacist in Troyes from 1882 he took up the study of psychotherapy, and in 1910 opened a free clinic in Nancy. His system became world-famous as 'Couéism', expressed in the famous formula: 'Every day, in every way, I am becoming better and better'.

Coughlin, Charles Edward 1891–1979
US Roman Catholic priest and political activist

Born in Hamilton, Ontario, he was ordained a priest in 1916. As pastor of the Shrine of the Little Flower in Royal Oak, Michigan, he gave radio addresses on political and economic issues during the Depression. He was hostile to big business and initially supportive of the New Deal, but he turned against **Franklin D Roosevelt** in 1935. By the late 1930s his programme, which at the height of his popularity reached as many as 40 million listeners, was becoming increasingly demagogic, anti-Semitic, and favourable to fascism. He was finally silenced by Church superiors in 1942.

Coulomb, Charles Augustin de 1736–1806
French physicist

Born in Angoulême, he completed his education in Paris at the École du Génie. At the outbreak of the Revolution, he was forced to leave Paris, but returned in 1795 when he was elected a member of the new Institut de France, and was appointed Inspector-General of Public Instruction (1802–06). His experiments on mechanical resistance resulted in 'Coulomb's law' concerning the relationship between friction and normal pressure (1779), and he became known for the torsion balance for measuring the force of magnetic and electrical attraction (1784–85).With 'Coulomb's law' he observed that the force between two small charged spheres is related to the charges and the distance between them. The unit of quantity of charge is named after him. ⌨ C W Gillmor, *Charles Augustin Coulomb* (1972)

Coulson, Charles Alfred 1910–74
English theoretical chemist

Born in Dudley, Worcestershire, he was educated at Cambridge, where he studied mathematics and natural sciences, and in 1938 became senior lecturer in mathematics at University College, Dundee. He worked at the Physical Chemistry Laboratory, Oxford (1945–47), was Professor of Theoretical Physics at King's College London (1947–52), and in 1952 was appointed Rouse Ball Professor of Mathematics at Oxford. He was chairman of Oxfam from 1965 to 1971, and in 1972 became Oxford's first Professor of Theoretical Chemistry; the chair of this subject at Oxford now bears his name. His many honours included the Davy Medal of the Royal Society (1970) and the Faraday Medal of the Chemical Society (1968). Coulson's research interests were almost entirely within theoretical chemistry, concerning the application of molecular orbital theory to chemical bonding and the electronic structures of molecules. Probably his most important contribution was his definition of fractional bond order and the relation of this to bond length. He extended quantum-mechanical methods to analyze giant molecules such as graphite and diamond, and his book *Valence* (1952) was highly influential. His ideas helped to establish the basis upon which today's more sophisticated calculations are performed.

Coulton, George Gordon 1858–1947
English historian

Born in King's Lynn, Norfolk, he became a lecturer at Cambridge, Oxford, Toronto and Edinburgh. His many works include *Five Centuries of Religion* (1923), *The Medieval Village* (1925), *Art and the Reformation* (1928), *Life in the Middle Ages* (1928–29) and *Medieval Thought* (1939). He also wrote an autobiography, *Fourscore Years* (1943).

Couper, Archibald Scott 1831–92
Scottish organic chemist

Born in Kirkintilloch, Strathclyde, he studied classics at Glasgow and philosophy at Edinburgh, then turned to chemistry and travelled in Germany and studied in Paris under **Charles Adolphe Wurtz**. In 1858 he asked Wurtz to present to the Académie Française his paper *On a New Chemical Theory*, the contents of which were fundamentally important in assigning structural formulae to organic compounds. Unfortunately Wurtz procrastinated in his presentation and August Kekule von Stradonitz published first. In many ways Couper's ideas were ahead of Kekule's, but Kekule forcefully pressed his superiority, Couper quarrelled with Wurtz, returned to Edinburgh ignored as a chemist, and suffered a permanent depressive illness. Kekule's successor at Bonn discovered Couper's early work in which he had used the graphic formulae, and his paper on chemical theory, and Couper's work was given belated recognition.

Couper, Thomas See Cooper, Thomas

Couperin, Charles 1638–79
French organist and composer
Born in Chaumes-en-Brie, one of the first generation of a celebrated family of musicians, he succeeded his brother Louis Couperin as organist of the church of Saint-Gervais, Paris. His son was François Couperin.

Couperin, François, *known as* le Grand 1668–1733
French organist and composer
Born in Paris, he was taught by his father, Charles Couperin, whom he eventually followed as organist of Saint-Gervais in 1685. In 1693 he became organist to Louis XIV, and taught harpsichord to the royal children. In 1717 he was appointed composer-in-ordinary of chamber music to the king. Internationally famous as a harpsichord composer whose principles are contained in his textbook *L'Art de toucher le clavecin* (1716, 'The Art of Playing the Harpsichord'), he had a great influence on J S Bach. His other compositions include many chamber concertos as well as motets and other church music.

Couperus, Louis Marie Anne 1863–1923
Dutch poet and novelist
Born in The Hague, he was largely brought up in Batavia, in the Dutch East Indies, and lived in Italy. His naturalistic first novel, *Eline Vère* (1889, Eng trans 1892), was a success, and he went on to write several more, including novels set in the Dutch East Indies, and a powerful, fatalistic tetralogy of life in The Hague, *Dr Adriaan* (1901–04, Eng trans *The Books of the Small Souls*, 1914). 📖 W J Simons, *Louis Couperus* (1963)

Courant, Richard 1888–1972
US mathematician
Born in Lublinitz, Germany, he studied in Breslau, Zurich and, as a pupil of David Hilbert, at Göttingen University, where he became professor in 1920, founding the Mathematics Institute in 1929. In 1933 he was forced by the Nazis to retire and after a year at Cambridge, he went to the USA where he became professor at New York University (1934), and director of the Institute of Mathematical Sciences (later the Courant Research Institute) from 1953 to 1958. His work in applied analysis, particularly in partial differential equations and the Dirichlet problem, was always motivated by its physical applications. His textbook *Methoden der mathematischen Physik* (1924–27), written jointly with Hilbert, became a classic immediately.

Courbet, Gustave 1819–77
French painter
Born in Ornans, he had little formal art training and scorned the rigid classical outlook, preferring Flemish and Spanish models, especially Velázquez. The founder of Realism, in 1844 he began exhibiting pictures in which everyday scenes were portrayed with complete sincerity and no idealism, as in *Peasants of Flagzey* (1850, Musée Beaux-Arts, Besançon) and *Burial at Ornans* (1850, Musée d'Orsay, Paris), both of which were condemned as 'socialistic' though not painted with any political intent. Perhaps his most famous canvas is the large *Studio of the*

Painter: an Allegory of Realism (1855), in the Louvre. Republican in sympathies, he joined the Commune in 1871, and on its suppression was imprisoned and fined for his part in the destruction of the Vendôme Column. On his release in 1873 he fled to Switzerland.

Courier, Paul Louis 1772–1825
French writer
He was born in Paris, and in 1816 issued the *Pétition aux deux chambres*, a scathing exposure of the wrongs of the peasantry. He was an accomplished translator from Greek, and a master of irony. His masterpiece, *Simple discours de Paul Louis, vigneron* (1821), derided the scheme to purchase Chambord for the Duc de Bordeaux by a 'national offering', and he was imprisoned. He was assassinated on his estate in Touraine.

Cournand, André Frédéric 1895–1988
US physician and Nobel Prize winner
Born in Paris, France, he was educated at the Sorbonne, and emigrated to the USA in 1930, where he became a citizen in 1941. A specialist in cardiovascular physiology, he was awarded the Nobel Prize for physiology or medicine in 1956 jointly with Werner Forssman and Dickinson Richards for developing cardiac catheterization. The technique made it possible to study heart functions in health and disease, and modifications of it are now important in treating heart disease. From 1934, he was on the academic staff of Columbia University, becoming Professor of Clinical Physiology in 1960, and Professor Emeritus of Medicine in 1964.

Courrèges, André 1923–
French fashion designer
Born in Pau, he studied civil engineering but later turned to fashion, in Paris. Trained by Cristóbal Balenciaga from 1952 to 1960, he opened his own house in 1961. Famous for his stark, futuristic, 'Space Age' designs, he introduced the miniskirt (1964), and has featured trouser suits for women, and white boots. Since 1966 he has produced ready-to-wear as well as couture clothes.

Court, Margaret Jean Smith, *née* Smith 1942–
Australian lawn tennis player
Born in Albury, New South Wales, she was the winner of more Grand Slam events (66) than any other player: 10 Wimbledon titles (including the singles—the first Australian to do so—in 1963, 1965, 1970), 22 US titles (singles in 1962, 1965, 1968–70, 1973), 13 French (singles 1962, 1964, 1969–70, 1973), and 21 Australian (singles 1960–66, 1969–71, 1973). In 1970 she became the second woman (after Maureen Connolly) to win all four major titles in one year. She retired in 1977.

Courtauld, Samuel 1876–1947
English industrialist
He was a descendant of Samuel Courtauld (1793–1881), the founder of the silk manufacturing company in 1816. As chairman of Courtaulds Limited he promoted the British rayon and nylon industry, and was a patron of art and music. He built the Courtauld Institute of Art in Portman Square, London, and donated it with his art collection to London University.

Courteline, Georges, *pseudonym of* Georges Moinaux 1860–1929
French dramatist
He was born in Tours. A humorous journalist who turned to the stage, he wrote satirical comedies, many of them one-acters, including *Boubouroche* (1893), *Un Client sérieux* (1897, 'A Serious Client') and *Le Commissaire est bon enfant* (1900, 'The Inspector is Good Natured'). He also published novels, such as *Le Train de 8h47* (1888, 'The 8:47

Train', dramatized 1909) and *Messieurs les Ronds-de-cuir* (1893, 'The Pen Pushers'). 💷 P Bournecque, *Le Théâtre de Georges Courteline* (1969)

Courtenay, Tom (Thomas Daniel) 1937–
English actor

Born in Hull, Humberside, he made his professional debut, as Konstantin in Chekhov's *The Seagull*, with the Old Vic company in Edinburgh in 1960. He has since appeared in a variety of roles including Hamlet at the 1968 Edinburgh Festival, and Norman in the Alan Ayckbourn comedy trilogy *The Norman Conquests* (1974). Other stage appearances include leading roles in *The Dresser* (1980), the title role in the musical *Andy Capp* (1982), Harpagon in a translation of Molière's *Le Misanthrope* (1991, 'The Miser') and *Art* (1996). A distinguished film actor, he made his first appearance in *The Loneliness of the Long-Distance Runner* (1962). Subsequent films include *Billy Liar* (1963), *King Rat* (1965), *Dr Zhivago* (1965), *One Day in the Life of Ivan Denisovitch* (1971) and *Boy From Mercury* (1996).

Courtneidge, Dame Cicely Esmerelda
1893–1980
English actress

She was born in Sydney, Australia, and was an actress from the age of eight. She made her London debut at 14 in a musical version of *Tom Jones* and later became widely known as an actress in musicals, pantomime and revue, having a great success in *By-the-Way* (1935), which also starred her husband, Jack Hulbert (1892–1978). They appeared together in many shows such as *Clowns in Clover* (1927), *Under Your Hat* (1938) and *Something in the Air* (1943). She also appeared in several straight comedies, including her final West End stage appearance in *Move Over, Mrs Markham*, by Ray Cooney (1971). She published an autobiography, *Cicely*, in 1953.

Courtney, Dame Kathleen D'Olier 1878–1974
English suffragette and world peace activist

Born in Gillingham, Kent, she read modern languages at Lady Margaret Hall, Oxford. A woman of independent means, she devoted her life to improving the position of women and to world peace. On the outbreak of World War I, like other constitutional suffragettes, she diverted her energies to international Quaker relief work. A founder of the Women's International League for Peace, she chaired the British section and was on the executive of the British League of Nations Union (1928–39). She took part in the drawing up of the UN Charter, and was vice-chairman, then chairman of the UN Association in Great Britain (1949–51). She was created DBE in 1952.

Courtois, Bernard 1777–1838
French chemist

Born in Dijon, he studied pharmacy in Auxerre and chemistry in Paris, later working in the laboratory at the École Polytechnique and at the Thénard Laboratory. While investigating opium with Baron Louis Guyton de Morveau he isolated morphine, the first alkaloid known. In 1804 he took over the management of his father's factory, which made saltpetre from seaweed ash. In 1811 he accidentally added too much sulphuric acid to the ash and produced a violet gas which condensed into dark crystals; his discovery of iodine was announced at the Institut de France in 1813. In the 1820s Courtois abandoned the ailing saltpetre industry and attempted unsuccessfully to make a living by preparing and selling compounds of iodine. He died in poverty.

Cousin, Jean 1501–c.1590
French sculptor, glass-stainer and painter

Born in Soucy, near Sens, he was responsible for the stained glass in the church of Saint-Gervais in Paris, in Sens Cathedral, and the Sainte Chapelle in Vincennes.

Cousin, Victor 1792–1867
French philosopher

Born in Paris, he studied under Pierre Royer-Collard and became a lecturer at the École Normale, Paris (1815). A charismatic lecturer and teacher who also had a lively, if uneven, public career, he visited Germany to study German philosophy (1817), and met Georg Hegel, Carl Jacobi and Friedrich Schelling. His liberalism resulted in various professional setbacks, but he prospered after the revolution of 1830 when his friend François Guizot became Prime Minister. He became a member of the Council of Public Instruction (1830), a peer of France and director of the École Normale (1832), and Minister of Public Instruction under Louis Thiers (1840). He was sympathetic to the Revolution of 1848 and assisted Louis Cavaignac, but retired from public life in 1849 and lived for many years in the Sorbonne, Paris. His eclectic learning resulted in many published works, including a translation of Plato and editions of Proclus, René Descartes, Peter Abelard and Blaise Pascal. His most original work was *Du vrai, du beau, et du bien* (1854, 'On the True, the Beautiful, and the Good').

Cousins, Frank 1904–86
English trade union leader

Born at Bulwell, Nottingham, a miner's son, he started work in the pits at the age of 14, became a lorry driver and by 1938 was a full-time union organizer. In 1955 he was appointed General Secretary of the Transport and General Worker's Union. He played a controversial part in the London transport strike (1958) and, defying the TUC and the leaders of the Labour Party, aligned his union behind a near unilateral nuclear disarmament policy in 1958. In 1965 he was elected MP for Nuneaton, having been appointed Minister of Technology (1964), a post he resigned in 1966 because of the government's prices and incomes policy. He gave up his parliamentary seat the same year and resumed his former union post. He was also chairman of the Community Relations Commission (1968–70).

Cousins, Samuel 1801–87
English engraver

Born in Exeter, he was apprenticed in 1814 to Samuel William Reynolds (1773–1835), a mezzotinter. In 1826 he set up on his own, and produced the *Master Lambton* after Sir Thomas Lawrence, which at once established his reputation. It was followed by a long series of plates after Sir Joshua Reynolds, Sir Edwin Landseer, Sir John Millais, and others.

Cousteau, Jacques Yves 1910–97
French naval officer and underwater explorer

Born in Saint André, Gironde, he was educated at Stanislas, Paris, and the Navy Academy, Brest. He served in the Resistance during World War II, for which he was made a Commander of the Legion of Honour and awarded the Croix de Guerre with Palm. As Lieutenant de Vaisseau (1939–43) he was partly responsible for the invention of the aqualung diving apparatus (1943). In 1946 he founded the French navy's undersea research group, and in 1950 became commander of the oceanographic research ship *Calypso* from which he made the first underwater film. Having retired from the navy in 1956, he was appointed director of the Musée Océanographique de Monaco (1957–88). His other achievements include developing an underwater television and the bathyscaphe, designing a diving saucer capable of descending to great depths, and promoting the Conshelf programme, which investigated the possibilities of undersea living (1962–65). He is best known for the popularization of marine biology with his many films, including *The Undersea World of Jacques Cousteau* (1968–76) and

Lilliput in Antarctica (1990). His books include *The Living Sea* (1963) and *Jacques Cousteau's Calypso* (1983). 📖 Axel Madsen, *Cousteau* (1987)

Coustou, Guillaume 1678–1746
French sculptor
Born in Lyons, he was the brother of **Nicolas Coustou**, and was trained by **Antoine Coysevox**. His many spectacular works include the *Chevaux de Marly* (1740–45) at the entrance of the Champs Elysées, Paris (originals in the Louvre). His style was vigorous in the manner of **Gian Bernini**, whose work he saw in Rome.

Coustou, Guillaume 1716–77
French sculptor
Born in Paris, he was the son of **Guillaume Coustou** (1678–1746). His works include the bronze bas-relief *Visitation* at Versailles, and the mausoleum of the Dauphin (father of **Louis XVI**) in the cathedral at Sens (c.1767).

Coustou, Nicolas 1658–1733
French sculptor
Born in Lyons, he was the brother of **Guillaume Coustou** (1678–1746), and sculpted the *Descente de la Croix* at Notre Dame, Paris.

Cousy, Bob (Robert Joseph) 1928–
US basketball player
Born in New York City, he is considered to be one of the greatest players ever. He played professionally with the Boston Celtics (1950–63), and then went on to coach with the Cincinatti Royals and the Kansas City-Omaha Kings. He became a sports commentator and was elected to basketball's Hall of Fame in 1971. He wrote *Basketball is my Life* (1956) and *The Killer Instinct* (1976).

Couthon, Georges 1756–94
French revolutionary
He was born in Orcet, in Auvergne. An advocate at the outbreak of the Revolution, he was sent by Puy de Dôme to the National Convention, and in July 1793 he became a member of the Committee of Public Safety. He crushed the Lyons insurrection with merciless severity (1793), and helped to usher in the Reign of Terror. **Robespierre's** fall brought down Couthon also; he was thrown into prison, freed by the mob with whom he was popular, recaptured by the soldiers of the Convention, and executed, with **Louis de Saint-Just** and Robespierre.

Coutts, Thomas 1735–1822
Scottish banker
He was born the son of the Edinburgh merchant and banker John Coutts (1699–1751) who was Lord Provost in 1742–44. He founded the London banking-house of Coutts & Co. with his brother James, on whose death in 1778 he became sole manager. In 1815 he married the actress **Harriot Mellon**. His granddaughter was **Angela Burdett-Coutts**. Keen and exact in matters of business, he left £900,000 when he died.

Coventry, Sir John d.1682
English politician
He sat in the Long Parliament (1640), and at the Restoration was knighted. Having become MP for Weymouth in 1667, he participated in a debate on playhouses (1670), and is remembered for asking a question about **Charles II's** love life, making the king furious. One night Coventry was pulled from his coach and his nose slit to the bone; the 'Coventry Act' made maiming a capital offence.

Coverdale, Miles 1488–1568
English Protestant reformer and biblical scholar
Born in Yorkshire, he studied at Cambridge, was ordained priest at Norwich in 1514, and joined the Augustinian Friars at Cambridge, where he was converted to Protestantism. He lived abroad from 1528 to 1534 to escape persecution and in 1535 published in Zurich the first translation of the whole Bible into English, with a dedication to **Henry VIII**. The Prayer Book retains the Psalms of this translation, and many of the finest phrases in the Authorized Version of 1611 are directly due to Coverdale. In 1538 he was sent by **Thomas Cromwell** to Paris to superintend another English edition of the Scriptures. **Francis I** had granted a licence, but during the printing an edict was issued prohibiting the work. Many of the sheets were burned, but the presses and types were hastily carried over to London. Grafton and Whitchurch, the noted printers of that day, were thus enabled to bring out in 1539, under Coverdale's superintendence, the 'Great Bible', which was presented to Henry VIII by Cromwell. The second 'Great Bible', known also as 'Cranmer's Bible' (1540), was also edited by Coverdale, who on Cromwell's fall found it expedient to leave England. In March 1548 he returned to England, was well received through **Thomas Cranmer's** influence, and in 1551 was made Bishop of Exeter. On **Mary I's** accession he was deprived of his see, but was allowed to leave the country, at the earnest intercession of the King of Denmark, whose chaplain, Dr Macchabaeus (MacAlpine), was Coverdale's brother-in-law. Returning to England in 1559, he did not resume his bishopric, but in 1564 he was collated by Edmund Grindal (1519–83) to the living of St Magnus, near London Bridge; this he resigned due to growing Puritan scruples about the liturgy in 1566.

Cowan, Clyde Lorrain, Jnr 1919–74
US physicist
Born in Detroit, he was educated at the universities of Missouri and Washington, and became a group leader at Los Alamos Scientific Laboratory (1949–57). He served as Professor of Physics at George Washington University (1947) and at the Catholic University of America (1948–74). Together with **Frederick Reines**, Cowan demonstrated the existence of nature's most elusive particle, the neutrino, the definitive experimental evidence being produced in 1956. In 1930 **Wolfgang Pauli** had proposed the existence of the neutrino, defining it to be a low-mass neutral particle that interacts only very weakly with matter. To overcome the detection problems caused by the neutrino's weak interaction with matter, Cowan and Reines required a source which produced large numbers of neutrinos. In an experiment to study the emissions from a nuclear reactor, they confirmed the existence of the neutrino, detecting three neutrino interactions per hour.

Coward, Sir Noël Peirce 1899–1973
English actor, playwright and composer
He was born in Teddington, Middlesex, and began acting at the age of 12. At 14 he appeared in *Peter Pan*, and his first play, written with Esme Wynne, was produced in 1917. He acted thereafter in other plays, including many of his own. His first play, *I'll Leave It to You* (1920), was followed by many successes, including *The Vortex* (1924), *Hay Fever* (1925), *Private Lives* (1930), *Blithe Spirit* (1941), *This Happy Breed* (1943) and *Nude With Violin* (1956), all showing his strong satiric humour and unique gift for witty dialogue. He was a gifted singer and wrote the music for most of his works, including his operetta *Bitter Sweet* (1929) and his play *Cavalcade* (1931), and for a series of revues, including *Words and Music* (1932) with its 'Mad Dogs and Englishmen', *This Year of Grace* (1928) and *Sigh No More* (1945). He produced several films based on his own scripts, including *In Which We Serve* (1942), *Blithe Spirit* (1945) and *Brief Encounter* (1945). He published two autobiographies, *Present Indicative* (1937) and *Future Indefinite* (1954). 📖 S Morley, *A Talent to Amuse* (1969)

Cowdrey, (Michael) Colin Cowdrey, Baron
1932–
English cricketer

Born in India, he was educated at Tonbridge School (where he played in his school XI at the age of 13) and Brasenose College, Oxford. He was captain of the Oxford XI in 1954 when he was already a Kent player. He played in a record 114 Tests for England (23 as captain), despite being dogged by injuries and illness, and made six tours of Australia, also a record. In his long first-class career (1951–75) he was captain of Kent from 1957 to 1971, and scored 107 centuries, of which 22 were in Test matches. He became International Cricket Council chairman between 1989 and 1993, overseeing the return of South Africa to international cricket and the agreement of the international code of conduct in 1991. Consequently the 1992 World Cup was the first in which every team could play every other team. His publications include *MCC: the Autobiography of a Cricketer* (1976). He was knighted in 1992.

Cowell, Henry Dixon 1897–1965
US composer

Born in Menlo Park, California, he was noted as a leader of the avant-garde in US music, developing many of the idosyncrasies of his style, before his more conventional studies at the universities of California and New York. His book, *New Musical Resources* (1919), and *The New Musical Quarterly*, of which he was founder (1927), reflect his interest in experimental composition perhaps more than his own works, where 'progressive' styles appear with more traditional types of material. He composed 20 symphonies and a large number of other orchestral works.

Cowen, Sir Zelman 1919–
Australian jurist, administrator and writer

Born in St Kilda, Victoria, he served in World War II with the Royal Australian Navy, then studied law at Oxford. He became a Fellow of Oriel College in 1947, and returned there as provost in 1982. From 1951 he was Professor of Public Law, and Dean of the Faculty of Law, at Melbourne University, and in 1967 was appointed emeritus professor. He was Vice-Chancellor of the University of New England, New South Wales (1966–70) and of the University of Queensland (1970–77). In 1977 he succeeded Sir John Kerr as Governor-General of the Commonwealth of Australia, beginning 'a touch of healing' after the controversy of the previous years. He served as chairman of the UK Press Council (1983–88) and was Pro-Vice-Chancellor of Oxford (1988–90).

Cowie, James 1886–1956
Scottish painter

Born in the parish of Monquhitter, Aberdeenshire, he attended the parish school there, and from 1901 to 1905 was a pupil teacher. He then studied English at Aberdeen University, but gave it up to study at the Glasgow School of Art (1912–14). From 1918 to 1935 he was art master at Bellshill Academy near Glasgow, and some of his best-known work dates from this period. He was appointed head of the painting department at Gray's School of Art, Aberdeen (1935), became an associate of the Royal Scottish Academy (1936), and in 1937 he became Warden of Hospitalfield near Arbroath, a summer school for the four Scottish Art Colleges. In 1948 he retired to Edinburgh, becoming secretary of the Royal Scottish Academy, and was awarded an honorary doctorate from Edinburgh University. His work ranged from landscape to still life, all solidly founded on drawing and linear design.

Cowley, Abraham 1618–67
English poet

Born in London, he was attracted to poetry by Edmund Spenser's *Faerie Queen*. He wrote verses at the age of 10, and at 15 published five poems. From Westminster School he went in 1637 to Trinity College, Cambridge, where he wrote a large portion of his epic the *Davideis*, which was published in 1656 with a reprint of his first book, *The Mistress*, and a number of other poems. During the Civil War he was ejected from Cambridge (1644) but studied at Oxford for another two years. In 1646 he accompanied or followed the queen (Henrietta Maria) to Paris, was sent on Royalist missions, and carried on her correspondence in cipher with King Charles I. He returned to England in 1654 and in 1655 was arrested and released on bail. On Cromwell's death he returned to Paris, but he went home to England at the Restoration. 📖 J G Taaffe, *Abraham Cowley* (1972)

Cowley, Hannah, *née* Parkhouse, *pseudonym* Anna Matilda 1743–1809
English playwright and poet

She was born in Tiverton, Devon, the daughter of a bookseller. Her first play, *The Runaway* (1776), was written in a fortnight and produced by David Garrick at Drury Lane Theatre, London. Before retiring to Devon in 1801, she rapidly produced 13 works for the stage, the most successful being *The Belle's Stratagem* (1780) which was frequently revived, notably by Henry Irving in 1881, with Ellen Terry as Letitia. She also wrote long narrative verses (1780–94) and, under her pseudonym carried on a sentimental, poetic correspondence in *The World*, satirized by William Gifford. The name Anna Matilda became a byword for sentimental fiction.

Cowley, Malcolm 1898–1989
US critic and editor

Born in Belsano, Pennsylvania, he was educated at Harvard. His struggle to make a living as a writer in New York and Paris proved a useful experience when he came to write *Exile's Return* (1934), about the illustrious group of US writers in Paris after World War I. He returned to the theme with *A Second Flowering: Works and Days of the Lost Generation* (1973) and *The Dream of the Golden Mountains: Remembering the 1930s* (1980). He also published a volume of poetry, *Blue Juniata* (1929), and several volumes of essays. Long associated with *The New Republic* as literary editor (1929–44) and responsible for recognizing the talent of John Cheever, he is credited with reviving the career of William Faulkner by editing *The Portable Faulkner* (1949). 📖 *Think Back on Us* (1967)

Cowper, William Cowper, 1st Earl c.1664–1723
English jurist

He was educated in St Albans, and became a barrister in 1688, MP for Hertford in 1695, Lord Keeper of the Great Seal in 1705, Baron Cowper in 1706, Lord Chancellor in 1707 and 1714, and Earl Cowper in 1718. He resigned in 1718, and from a Whig became a Leader of the Opposition. He played a large part in negotiating the Union with Scotland (1707), and made a substantial contribution to the development of modern equity.

Cowper, William 1666–1709
English surgeon and anatomist

Born in Petersfield, Sussex, he settled as a surgeon in London. He wrote *The Anatomy of Human Bodies* (1698), and discovered 'Cowper's glands'. Also called bulborethral glands, these are glands near the prostrate in mammals which produce mucus under sexual stimulation.

Cowper, William 1731–1800
English poet

Born in Berkhamstead, Hertfordshire, he was educated at Westminster School, where Warren Hastings and the poet Charles Churchill were contemporaries. He was called to the Bar in 1754, but made no attempt to practise. He showed signs of mental instability and in 1763 tried to commit suicide. With the clergyman **John Newton**, he wrote the *Olney Hymns* (1779), to which Cowper contributed some hymns which are still favourites. His other works include the ballad 'John Gilpin' (1783), 'Castaway', *The Task* (1785), a long poem on rural themes, and translations including **Milton**'s Latin poems. He is generally regarded as the poet of the evangelical revival and as the precursor of **Wordsworth** as a poet of nature. ⊞Lord David Cecil, *The Stricken Deer* (1933)

Cox, Allan 1927–87
US geophysicist

Born in Santa Ana, California, he served in the US Merchant Marine (1945–48), and after graduating in chemistry from the University of California at Berkeley (1951), joined the US army (1951–53). He returned to Berkeley to study geology and geophysics, studying under **Perry Byerley**, and then joined the US Geological Survey, setting up a successful palaeomagnetic laboratory. He later accepted a professorship at Stanford University (1967), where he became Green Professor of Geophysics in 1974 and Dean in 1979. His studies of palaeomagnetism and rock samples from around the world produced evidence for many reversals of the Earth's magnetic field at random intervals back in geological time, the implied geomagnetic reversal timescale being published in *Nature* (1963). He also worked on dating the age of the sea floors using magnetic anomalies, and his *Plate Tectonics and Geomagnetic Reversals* (1973) investigated the connection between plate tectonics and continental geology.

Cox, Brian Dennis 1946–
Scottish actor, teacher and director

Born in Dundee, he made his London debut as Orlando in *As You Like It* in 1967. His subsequent West End appearances include **Alan Bennett**'s *Getting On* (1971) and **Eugene O'Neill**'s *Strange Interlude* (1984). His Royal Shakespeare Company performances include Danton in **Pam Gems**'s *The Danton Affair* (1986), Petruchio in *The Taming of the Shrew* (1987), and the title role in *Titus Andronicus* (1987). His many television appearances include roles in *The Lost Language of Cranes* (1991), *The Cloning of Joanna May* (1992) and *Grushko* (1994). He has acted in films such as *Hidden Agenda* (1990) and *Braveheart* (1995).

Cox, David 1783–1859
English landscape painter

Born near Birmingham, he was a teacher in Hereford, having in 1813 joined the Society of Painters in Water-Colours, to whose exhibitions he was a regular contributor. He turned his attention seriously to oil painting in 1839, and in 1841 settled at Harborne, near Birmingham, where he produced his greatest works. They owe their inspiration mainly to the scenery of North Wales, and especially of Bettws-y-Coed, which he visited every autumn. Also that year Cox published *A Treatise on Landscape Painting and Effect in Water Colours*. The Birmingham Art Gallery has many examples of his work in both oil and watercolour, as has the Tate Gallery, London. His son, David Cox (1809–85), was also a noted watercolourist.

Cox, Richard 1500–81
English prelate and Protestant reformer

Born in Whaddon, Buckinghamshire, he was educated at Eton and King's College, Cambridge. He became headmaster of Eton and a favourite of Archbishop **Thomas Cranmer**. As Vice-Chancellor of Oxford (1547–52) he proscribed books, pictures and statues relating in any way to 'popery'. On the accession of Queen **Mary I** he was imprisoned; he went into exile in Frankfurt, where he was an opponent of **John Knox** and his Calvinist doctrines. He

returned to England when **Elizabeth I** came to the throne in 1558, and was appointed Bishop of Ely, serving from 1559 to 1580.

Cox, William 1764–1837
Australian road builder

Born in Wimbourne Minster, Dorset, England, he arrived in Australia in 1800 as a lieutenant in the New South Wales Corps, and purchased land to farm. In 1814 Governor **Lachlan Macquarie** made him superintendent of works for a new road over the Blue Mountains, which was to reach the rich farming land of the central plains and the town of Bathurst, the first European settlement west of the Great Dividing Range. With 30 strong convict labourers, in just six months, Cox constructed 101 miles (162km) of road through rugged hills with precipitous gradients, building more than a dozen bridges to cross the mountain streams. The workers started from Penrith, New South Wales, in July 1814 and reached Bathurst in January the following year, a road-building feat unequalled for many years. Cox received the first grant of land in the new district, returned to farming, and established a flock of sheep famous for the quality of its wool. He was appointed magistrate and later provisioned expeditions by John Oxley (c.1785–1828) into western New South Wales, the new territory which had been opened up by Cox's road.

Coxcie, Michiel See **Coxie, Michiel**

Coxey, Jacob Sechler 1854–1951
US social reformer

Born in Selinsgrove, Pennsylvania, he became a businessman in Ohio and gained fame after the panic of 1893 by leading a band of jobless men across the country to Washington DC to demonstrate for government spending to relieve unemployment. He promised that Coxey's Army would number 100,000 but managed to gather only 500 men and was arrested before he could finish his address on the Capitol steps (1894). He later became an advocate for public works as a remedy for unemployment and ran for President in 1932 and 1936 as the Farmer-Labor Party candidate.

Coxie or Coxcie or Coxius, Michiel 1499–1592
Flemish painter

Born in Mechelen, he introduced the Italian classical style into Flanders. He executed frescoes in S Maria dell' Anima in Rome and was court painter to **Philip II** of Spain.

Coxius, Michiel See **Coxie, Michiel**

Coysevox, Antoine 1640–1720
French sculptor

Born in Lyons, he became court sculptor to **Louis XIV** in 1666 and was responsible for much of the decoration at the Palace of Versailles, most notably the Galerie des Glaces and the Salon de la Guerre (containing an important relief equestrian sculpture of the king). His vigorous and decorative Baroque style—ultimately derived from **Gian Bernini**—was appropriate for the flamboyance of the French court, though he also sculpted very fine portrait busts of, and memorials to, many important figures of the time, including both a marble and a bronze bust of Louis XIV and a terracotta bust of **Charles Le Brun** (in the Wallace Collection, London), and also Cardinal **Mazarin** and Jean-Baptiste Colbert.

Cozens, Alexander 1717–86
English watercolour painter

Born in St Petersburg, Russia, he is believed to be one of the two illegitimate sons of **Peter the Great** by a woman from Deptford who accompanied the tsar to Russia. After studying in Italy, he settled in England in 1746. In

1785 he published a treatise describing his method of using accidental ink-blots as the basis for landscape compositions.

Cozens, John Robert 1752–c.1799
English watercolour landscape painter

Born in London, he was the son of **Alexander Cozens**. In 1776 he visited Switzerland, and in 1783 he returned from Italy. In 1794 he became insane, and in his later days was befriended by Sir **George Beaumont**. His drawings were copied by J M W **Turner** and Thomas **Girtin**, and John **Constable** pronounced that he was 'the greatest genius that ever touched landscape'.

Cozzens, James Gould 1903–78
US writer

Born in Chicago, he published his first novel, *Confusion* (1924), at the age of 19 while a student at Harvard. He fought with the US air force in World War II, and on his release from service wrote the Pulitzer Prize-winning *Guard of Honour* (1948). Among his other works are *S.S. San Pedro* (1931), *Ask Me Tomorrow* (1940), *The Just and the Unjust* (1942), *By Love Possessed* (1958) and *Children and Others* (1965). 📖 M Bruccoli, *James Gould Cozzens: a life apart* (1983)

Crabbe, George 1754–1832
English poet

Born in Aldeburgh, Suffolk, he had irregular schooling, but after a nine-month course in London, he set up as a surgeon in Aldeburgh. Having already published *Inebriety, a Poem* in 1775 and *The Candidate*, he ventured into the literary world in London in 1780, but lived in poverty, until, as the guest of **Edmund Burke** at Beaconsfield, he met the noted men of the day, published *The Library* (1781), and patronage followed. He was ordained in 1782 and the next year was established in the Duke of Rutland's seat at Belvoir. In 1783 *The Village*, a harshly realistic poem about village life sponsored by Burke and Dr **Johnson**, brought him fame, and he wrote nothing for 24 years. His narrative poems include *The Parish Register* (1807); *The Borough* (1810), a collection of 24 tales in letter form (which were later to form the basis of **Benjamin Britten's** opera *Peter Grimes*); *Tales* (1812); and *Tales of the Hall* (1819). 📖 T E Krebbel, *Life of George Crabbe* (1972)

Craddock, Charles Egbert, *pseudonym of* Mary Noailles Murfree 1850–1922
US writer

She was born in Murfreesboro, Tennessee. Her short stories were published in the *Atlantic Monthly* from 1878, and collected as *In the Tennessee Mountains* (1884). She went on to become a prolific novelist of mountain backwoods life. 📖 E Parks, *Charles Egbert Craddock* (1941)

Cragg, Tony 1949–
English sculptor

Born in Liverpool, he worked as a laboratory technician before attending art school in Cheltenham and London. He graduated from the Royal College of Art in 1977, and since then he has lived and worked in Wuppertal, Germany. He retrieves discarded materials such as plastic, glass, and masonry rubble, arranging them by colour into wall mosaics to express rejection of consumerism, as in *Britain Seen From the North* (1981, Tate, London). He has also produced freestanding forms suggestive of laboratory implements as a metaphor for procreation, eg *Mother's Milk* (1988) and *On the Savannah* (1988, Tate). He won the Turner Prize in 1988. He exhibited at the Venice Biennale in 1988 and 1993, and an exhibition of new work was held at the Whitechapel Gallery, London, in 1997.

Craig, Charles 1922–
English tenor

Born in London, he was 'discovered' by Sir **Thomas Beecham**. His fine, powerful tenor voice, coupled with a pleasing stage personality, made him naturally suited to opera and he joined the Carla Rosa Company in 1952. Three years later, he was playing principal roles for Sadler's Wells Opera and giving guest performances in many of the world's leading opera houses. He made his debut in **Puccini's** *Madama Butterfly*, an opera he was to sing often, but it was for his performances in roles like Otello and Sigmund that he was most celebrated. His versatility was such that he scored a great success in a revival of **Franz Léhar's** operetta *Land of Smiles*, at one time a vehicle for Richard **Tauber**.

Craig, Christopher c.1936–
English murderer

Born in south London, he was a young friend of **Derek Bentley**. On Sunday 2 November 1952, he and Bentley broke into a confectionery warehouse in Croydon. They were seen climbing over the fence, and the police were alerted. Bentley, who was carrying a knife and a knuckle-duster, and Craig, who was armed with a gun, were approached by the police. Bentley was quickly caught, but Craig fired several shots, initially wounding one policeman and then killing another. In a suicide attempt, he threw himself off the roof of the building, but succeeded only in fracturing his spine. Both were arrested and charged and a secret cache of arms was found in Craig's house. Craig's defence claimed that his actions were provoked by the violent comics and films he favoured. He and Bentley were both found guilty. Craig was sentenced to an indefinite period of detention, as he was too young to receive the death penalty, but Bentley was sentenced to be hanged. Despite vigorous attempts to gain a reprieve, Bentley was executed. Craig was released from prison in 1963.

Craig, (Edward Henry) Gordon 1872–1966
English actor, stage designer, director and theorist

He was born in Stevenage, Hertfordshire, the son of **Ellen Terry** and her lover, the architect **William Godwin**. He acted for eight years under **Henry Irving** at the Lyceum and retired from the stage in 1897, but his acting experience led him to approach theatrical design, with the aim of simplifying the scene and emphasizing the actors. His ideas were too advanced for England, where his three productions for his mother were failures, but he was acclaimed in Germany, Italy and Russia, where he produced *Hamlet* (1912) at the Moscow Arts Theatre. He settled in Italy (1906), published the journal *The Mask* (1908–29), and founded a theatrical art school in Florence (1913). He greatly influenced scenic design in the USA and Europe. His published works include *On the Art of the Theatre* (1911), *Towards a New Theatre* (1913), *The Theatre Advancing* (1921), *Ellen Terry and Her Secret Self* (1931) and the autobiographical *Index to the Story of My Days* (1957). 📖 Edward Craig, *Gordon Craig: The Story of His Life* (1968)

Craig, Sir James Henry 1748–1812
British soldier

Born in Gibraltar, he joined the army at the age of 15 and served in America, where he was wounded at Bunker Hill and helped capture Ticonderoga (1777). In 1795, as major-general, he took Cape Colony and served as its governor from 1795 to 1797. He was Governor-General of Canada from 1807 to 1811.

Craig, James, 1st Viscount Craigavon 1871–1940
Northern Ireland politician

Born in Belfast, he served with the British army in South Africa. He was a Unionist MP in the UK parliament (1906–21) where he vigorously campaigned to preserve the Act of Union against the Irish Nationalists. When the

Stormont parliament was established in 1921, he became the first Prime Minister of Northern Ireland (1921–40). His Unionist beliefs ensured that the interests of the Protestant majority in Northern Ireland would be paramount. He was created viscount in 1927 and died suddenly in office.

Craig, John 1512–1600
Scottish political reformer

He joined the Dominicans at St Andrews, but fell under suspicion of heresy, and after brief imprisonment (1536) went to Rome. Through Cardinal **Reginald Pole** he gained admission to the Dominican convent of Bologna, but **Calvin**'s *Institutes* converted him to Protestantism. On 18 August 1559 he was lying in the dungeon of the Inquisition condemned to suffer next morning at the stake, when Pope **Paul IV** died, and the mob set the prisoners free. A bandit befriended him and a dog brought him a purse of gold. He escaped to Vienna, and there preached in his friar's habit, one of his listeners being the Archduke Maximilian. Learning his whereabouts, the new pope demanded his surrender, but Maximilian protected him. He returned to Scotland and in 1563 was appointed coadjutor to **John Knox**. In 1567 he was criticized for proclaiming, although unwillingly, the banns between **Mary, Queen of Scots** and the 4th Earl of **Bothwell**, and in 1572 he was sent to 'illuminate the dark places' in Angus and Aberdeenshire. He went back to Edinburgh in 1579 as a royal chaplain, collaborated with **Andrew Melville** on the Second Book of Discipline, and drew up the 'Confession of Faith'.

Craig, John d.1731
Scottish mathematician

A pupil of the mathematician David Gregory (1659–1708) in Edinburgh, he later settled in Cambridge and joined the circle around Sir **Isaac Newton**. Between 1685 and 1718 he published a number of books and papers on the theory of fluxions, and in 1699 he published *Christianae Theologiae Principia Mathematica*, a curious attempt to apply mathematics to theology, in which he claimed that the world would end by the year 3144. He was ordained in 1708 and became FRS in 1711.

Craig, Roger 1960–
US footballer

Born in Preston, Mississippi, he became a running back with the San Francisco 49ers, and scored 18 points and three touchdowns, both records, in the 1985 Super Bowl. He also became the first player in National Football League history to rush for 1,000 yards and receive passes for 1,000 yards. He then became manager of the San Francisco Giants (1985–).

Craig (of Riccarton), Sir Thomas 1538–1608
Scottish legal writer

He was born either in Craigfintray (Aberdeenshire) or in Edinburgh. From St Andrews University he went in 1555 to Paris; in 1563 he was admitted a Scottish advocate; the following year he was appointed justice-depute of Scotland; and in 1573 he became sheriff-depute of Edinburgh. Besides a poem to celebrate the marriage of **Mary, Queen of Scots** to Lord **Darnley**, and some other Latin verses, he wrote the masterly *Jus Feudale* (1608), which is a Scottish legal classic relating the development of Scots law to that of European systems; *De Unione Regnorum* (Scottish History Society 1910); and Latin treatises on **James VI**'s right to the English throne and on the homage controversy between Scotland and England.

Craigie, Sir William Alexander 1867–1957
Scottish philologist and lexicographer

Born in Dundee, he was educated there and at St Andrews, and went to Balliol College, Oxford, for a year before going to Copenhagen to study Old Icelandic.

While he was assistant to the Professsor of Latin at St Andrews (1893–97), he produced *Scandinavian Folk-Lore* (1897). In 1897 he joined Sir **James Murray** in the compilation of the *Oxford English Dictionary* (joint editor, 1901–33). In 1916 he was appointed Professor of Anglo-Saxon at Oxford, and in 1925–36 was Professor of English at the University of Chicago, where he compiled the *Historical Dictionary of American English* (4 vols, 1936–44). From 1936 to 1955 he was editor of the *Dictionary of the Older Scottish Tongue*. A scholar of encyclopedic knowledge, he also wrote *The Icelandic Sagas* (1913), *The Pronunciation of English* (1917), *Easy Readings in Anglo-Saxon* (1923), *The Poetry of Iceland* (1925), and a monumental study of Iceland *rímur* ('rhymes'), *Sýnisbók íslenkra rímna* (3 vols, 1952). 🕮 J M Wyllie, *Sir William Craigie* (1953)

Craik, Dinah Maria, *née* Mulock 1826–87
English novelist

Born in Stoke-upon-Trent, Staffordshire, she settled in London at the age of 20, and went on to publish *The Ogilvies* (1849), *Olive* (1850), *The Head of the Family* (1851) and *Agatha's Husband* (1853). Her best-known novel is *John Halifax, Gentleman* (1857). Her short stories were collected as *Avillion* (1853), and *Collected Poems* appeared in 1881. She also wrote essays, children's stories, and fairytales. In 1865 she married George Lillie Craik, nephew of the Scottish scholar George Lillie Craik (1798–1866) and was assigned the benefits of a Civil List pension awarded in 1864 to less well-off authors.

Craik, Kenneth 1914–45
Scottish experimental psychologist

Educated at Edinburgh and Cambridge, he spent much of World War II on applied military research on topics which included servo-mechanisms and 'human factors' in design. In 1944 he was appointed director of the new Unit for Research in Applied Psychology at Cambridge set up by the Medical Research Council. He pioneered that major modern psychological school of thought in which the mind is considered as a complex example of an information-processing system. The development of this metaphor, with the help of digital computers, is known as 'cognitive science'. He died young following a cycling accident in Cambridge on the eve of VE Day.

Cram, Donald James 1919–
US chemist and Nobel Prize winner

Born in Chester, Vermont, he studied chemistry at Rollins College, Florida, and at the University of Nebraska, then took a doctorate at Harvard (1945–47) and became an instructor at the University of California at Los Angeles (UCLA). He was appointed assistant professor at UCLA in 1948, full professor in 1956 and S Winstein Professor in 1985. For his early work he received the American Chemical Society award for creative work in synthetic organic chemistry. His most highly praised work began in 1972, when he described the synthesis of chiral crown ethers. He also introduced the informative description host–guest chemistry, for which he shared the 1987 Nobel Prize for chemistry with **Jean-Marie Lehn** and **Charles Pedersen**. Since 1972 he has synthesized many novel three-dimensional host compounds.

Cram, Steve(n) 1960–
English middle distance runner

Born in Jarrow, Tyne and Wear, as a young athlete he was inspired by the feats of another runner from the north-east of England, Brendan Foster, and emerged from the shadows of **Sebastian Coe** and **Steve Ovett**, who had dominated 800 metre and 1,500 metre running. He won the 1,500 metre titles in the world championships (1983), European championships (1982) and Commonwealth Games (1982), as well as the silver medal in the 1984 Olympics. In 1985 he broke three world records in just 19 days—at 1,500 metres, one mile and 2,000 metres. Retaining only his mile record, not broken until 1993 by Noureddine Morceli of Algeria, he decided not to compete in the 1992 Olympics after his elimination at the semi-final from the 1991 world championships, and retired from all 1,500-metre and mile races.

Cramer, Johann Baptist 1771–1858
British pianist

Born in Mannheim, Germany, he was the son of Wilhelm Cramer (1745–99), a violinist who settled in London in 1772. From 1788, Johann undertook concert tours on the Continent, and gained a high reputation. He founded the London musical publishing firm of Cramer and Co in 1824, and, after some years in Paris, died in London. Most of his compositions are forgotten, except for his *Études*, an important work.

Crampton, Thomas Russell 1816–88
English engineer

Born in Broadstairs, Kent, he was a pioneer of locomotive construction and was responsible for the first successful cross-channel submarine cable, between Dover and Calais, in 1851. He built the Berlin waterworks (1855), and many railway systems.

Cranach, Lucas, the Elder 1472–1553
German painter

Born in Kronach, near Bamberg, he seems to have been instructed by his father, and became court painter at Wittenberg to the Elector Frederick the Wise of Saxony. In 1509 he accompanied an embassy to Emperor Maximilian I, and while in the Netherlands painted the future Charles V. In 1537, and again in 1540, he was elected Burgomaster of Wittenberg. His paintings include sacred and a few classical subjects, hunting scenes and portraits. He was closely associated with the German Reformers, including Martin Luther and Philip Melanchthon, who were painted by Cranach and his pupils. A *Crucifixion* in the Stadtkirche, Weimar, is his masterpiece. His wood engravings are numerous. Of three sons, all painters, the second, Lucas the Younger (1515–86), painted so like his father that their works are difficult to distinguish.

Crane, (Harold) Hart 1899–1932
US poet

Born in Garrettsville, Ohio, he had little formal education, but worked as an advertising copywriter in New York before he found a patron who enabled him to travel and devote himself to poetry. An alcoholic and homosexual, he placed a heavy burden on his friends' tolerance and wallets. He published two volumes—*White Buildings* (1926) and the long, symbolic *The Bridge* (1930)—variously hailed as masterpieces and unintelligible. Crane is now recognized as a major US poet, having much in common with Walt Whitman. Returning to the USA from Mexico, he drowned himself by leaping from a steamboat into the Caribbean. 📖 J Unterecker, *Voyager: a life of Crane* (1969)

Crane, Stephen 1871–1900
US writer and war correspondent

He was born in New Jersey, and worked as a journalist in New York before publishing his first novel, *Maggie: A Girl of the Streets* (1893). His reputation, however, rests on *The Red Badge of Courage* (1895), which relates vividly the experiences of a soldier in the American Civil War. (The surreal verse of *The Black Riders* dates from the same year.) He had no personal experience of the war but *The Red Badge of Courage* was received with acclaim, in particular for its psychological realism. He never repeated its success but was lionized by literary London (befriended by Joseph Conrad and meeting H G Wells) before succumbing to tuberculosis in Baden Baden. 📖 R W Stallman, *Crane: a biography* (1968)

Crane, Walter 1845–1915
English painter and illustrator

Born in Liverpool, he was the son of the portrait painter Thomas Crane (1808–59). As an apprentice to the wood-engraver, William James Linton (1812–98), he came under the influence of the Pre-Raphaelites, and became a leader with William Morris in the Arts and Crafts movement, and in early socialism. He was well known as an illustrator of children's books, but his main achievement was his illustrated edition of Edmund Spenser's *Faerie Queen* (1894–96). In his paintings he was much influenced by Botticelli. He was director of the Manchester School of Art (1893–96) and Reading College (1896–98), and Principal of the Royal College of Art (1898–99).

Cranko, John 1927–73
South African choreographer

Born in Rustenburg, he had an early interest in dance but from the age of 16, when he made a piece for the Cape Town Ballet Club, choreography was his overriding interest. In 1946 he moved to Great Britain to study, and joined Sadler's Wells Theatre Ballet (1946–61, becoming resident choreographer 1951–57). He made over 30 dances, including *Pineapple Poll* (1951) and his first full-length ballet, *Prince of the Pagodas*, with music by Benjamin Britten (1957). He also wrote the musical revue *Cranks* (1955). In 1961 he moved to Germany to become artistic director of the Stuttgart Ballet, which became, under his influence, an internationally famous company. A lover of drama and physical intensity, he choreographed ballets like *Romeo and Juliet* (1958), *Onegin* (1969) and *Carmen* (1971). One-act ballets include *Jeu de Cartes* (1965, 'Game Card') and *Initials R.B.M.E.* (1972).

Cranmer, Thomas See panel p459

Cranston, Kate (Catherine) 1850–1934
Scottish tea-room proprietress and patron of art

Born in Glasgow, she opened a chain of highly successful tea rooms there (1884–1904), known for their distinctive 'artistic' interiors. Charles Rennie Mackintosh redesigned the furniture and fittings in the Argyle Street tea rooms (1896), and later did the interior decoration for the Ingram Street branch (1900) and the Willow tea rooms in Sauchiehall Street (1911). She then commissioned George Walton to decorate the Buchanan Street tea rooms, opened in 1896, though Mackintosh also produced mural designs for these interiors. She also ran the tea rooms for the Glasgow International Exhibitions (1901–11). A highly respected business woman, who drew attention to the progressive nature of art and design in Glasgow, she retired in 1919.

Crashaw, Richard c.1613–1649
English religious poet

Born in London, he was educated at Charterhouse and Pembroke Hall, Cambridge, and became a Fellow of Peterhouse College (c.1636). In 1634 he published a volume of Latin poems, *Epigrammatum Sacrocorum Liber*. As his Catholic leanings prevented him from receiving Anglican orders, he lost his fellowship (1643) for refusing to take the Covenant. He went to Paris and became a Catholic, and in 1646 published his *Steps to the Temple*, which was republished in Paris in 1652 under the title *Carmen Deo Nostro*, with 12 vignette engravings designed by Crashaw. He was introduced by John Cowley to Queen Henrietta Maria, who recommended him at Rome, and in April 1649 he became a subcanon at Loretto. 📖 M Praz, *Richard Crashaw* (1945)

Crassus, Lucius Licinius 140–91BC
Roman orator

Cranmer, Thomas 1489–1556
English prelate and Archbishop of Canterbury

Thomas Cranmer was born in Aslacton or Aslockton, Nottinghamshire, and educated at Jesus College, Cambridge. He took holy orders in 1523. In 1529, during an epidemic of the plague, he and two of his pupils left Cambridge for Waltham, where he met **John Foxe** and **Stephen Gardiner** and with them discussed **Henry VIII**'s proposed divorce from **Catherine of Aragon**. Cranmer suggested an appeal to the universities of Christendom, which pleased Henry, and he subsequently became a counsel in the suit. Appointed a royal chaplain and archdeacon of Taunton, he was also attached to the household of **Ann Boleyn**'s father (Anne at the time being Henry's paramour), and was sent on two embassies, to Italy in 1530 and to **Charles V** in Germany in 1532.

Appointed Grand Penitentiary of England at Rome by Pope **Clement VII**, he was consecrated Archbishop of Canterbury in 1533, and took the oath of allegiance to the pope 'for form's sake'. In May, Cranmer pronounced Catherine's marriage null and void *ab initio* and the private marriage to Anne Boleyn, which had taken place four months earlier, valid; in September he was godfather to Anne's daughter **Elizabeth**. In 1536 he annulled Henry's marriage with Anne Boleyn, divorced him from **Anne of Cleves** (1540), informed him of **Catherine Howard**'s premarital affairs, then strove to coax her into confessing them (1541).

He did what he dared to oppose the Six Articles of 1539, which sought to impose uniformity of dogma. He promoted the translation of the Bible and a service book, and curtailed the number of holy days. In 1547 Henry died, and Cranmer sang mass of requiem for his soul. He had been slowly drifting into Protestantism, but now was quickly swept into great religious changes. In 1548 he compiled **Edward VI**'s First Prayer Book (which converted the Mass into Communion), composed the 42 articles of religion (1553), later called the 39 Articles, and in 1552 rephrased the Prayer Book.

During this, as during the preceding reign, he took little part in affairs of state, although he was one of the council of regency. However, he signed **Thomas Seymour**'s death warrant (1549); played a major part in the deposition and imprisonment of bishops **Edmund Bonner**, Gardiner and Day; and, won over by the dying boy-king's pleading, reluctantly subscribed the instrument diverting the succession from the princess Mary (later **Mary I**) to Lady **Jane Grey** (1553). By this he was guilty of conscious perjury, yet when the 12-day reign was over he made no attempt to escape. On 14 September he was sent to the Tower, on 13 November was arraigned for treason, and, pleading guilty, was condemned to die. In March 1554 he went to Oxford where he bravely faced his trial before the papal commissioner, whose jurisdiction he refused to recognize.

In October, from jail, he witnessed **Hugh Latimer**'s and **Nicholas Ridley**'s martyrdom, and on 14 February 1556, he was formally degraded. In rapid succession he signed seven increasingly submissive recantations. The last he transcribed on 21 March, and was immediately taken to St Mary's Church, where he heard that he was to be burnt. When the time came for him to read his recantation, he retracted all that he had written. Taken to the stake, he thrust his right hand into the flame and kept it there, crying: 'This hath offended! Oh this unworthy hand!'.

📖 Among Cranmer's 42 writings are his prefaces to the Bible (1540) and the first Prayer Book (1549); the *Reformatio Legum Ecclesiasticarum* (1571); and *A Defence of the Doctrine of the Sacrament* (1550). See also Diarmaid MacCulloch, *Thomas Cranmer: A Life* (1962); Jasper G Ridley, *Thomas Cranmer* (1962).

In 95BC he was elected consul, along with Quintus Scaevola, and during their consulship a rigorous law was enacted banishing from Rome all who had not the full rights of citizens. It was one of the chief causes of the Social War (90–88). Crassus is the chief speaker in Cicero's *De Oratore*, and represents the writer's own opinions.

Crassus, Marcus Licinius, *known as* Dives ('the Rich') c.115–53BC
Roman politician

He was a protégé and supporter of **Lucius Cornelius Sulla** in the civil war against **Gaius Marius** (88–82BC). As praetor he defeated **Spartacus** at the Battle of Lucania (71), and in 70 he was made consul with **Pompey**, whom he hated. The richest of Roman citizens (hence his byname), he became a friend of **Julius Caesar**, and formed the first triumvirate with him and Pompey (60). In 53, as Governor of Syria, he attacked the Parthians, but was routed and killed at the Battle of Carrhae. 📖 B A Marshall, *Crassus: A Political Biography* (1976)

Crates of Athens early 3rd century BC
Greek philosopher

He succeeded Potemo and preceded **Arcesilaus** as head of the Academy in Athens. He should not be confused with Crates of Tarsus, who was head of the Academy about 130BC, or Crates of Thebes, a disciple of **Diogenes of Sinope** in the 4th century BC. His main claims to fame were that he was teacher of **Zeno of Citium** and that he had sex in public to make a philosophical point about social conventions.

Crates of Chalkis fl.335–325BC
Greek engineer

He was one of several who carried out notable works for **Alexander the Great**, including the building of the new city and port of Alexandria in the Nile delta. Other projects with which he is thought to have been concerned include works of drainage, irrigation and water supply, as well as an attempt to drive two tunnels each more than a mile (1.6km) long which, however, was abandoned before completion.

Cratinus c.519–423BC
Greek comic poet

Next to Eupolis and **Aristophanes**, he best represents the Old Attic comedy. He limited the number of actors to three, and was the first to add biting personal attack to comedy—even **Pericles** did not escape his pen. Of his 21 comedies, nine of which obtained the first public prize and on one occasion beat Aristophanes' *Clouds*, only some fragments are extant; they are collected in Meineke's *Fragmenta Comicorum Graecorum* (1840, Berlin).

Cratippus 1st century BC
Greek Peripatetic philosopher

He was born in Mitylene, and was a contemporary of Cicero, whose son Marcus he taught at Athens in 44BC. Pompey visited him after the Battle of Pharsalus, and **Marcus Brutus** travelled to Athens to hear him, even while making preparations to meet **Augustus** and **Marcus Antonius**. Nothing that he wrote has survived.

Craven, William Craven, Earl of 1606–97
English soldier

The son of a Lord Mayor of London, he served in the Low Countries on behalf of **Elizabeth**, Queen of Bohemia, daughter of **James VI and I**, and was taken prisoner with her son, Prince **Rupert**, purchasing his liberty in 1639. Afterwards he attached himself to the exiled queen's court at The Hague. A man of great wealth, he assisted Charles I financially; his estates were sequestered in 1652 but returned at the Restoration. He was made an earl by Charles II in 1664, and Lord Lieutenant of Middlesex, but retained his attachment to Elizabeth of Bohemia.

Crawford, Cheryl 1902–86
US actress, theatre director and producer
Born in Akron, Ohio, she began as an actress with the Theatre Guild in New York in 1923, and became its casting manager in 1928. She was centrally involved in some of the most important US theatrical developments of her time, including the Group Theatre (1931, with Harold Clurman and Lee Strasberg), the American Repertory Theatre (1946, with Eva Le Gallienne and Margaret Webster (1905–72)) and the Actors Studio (1947). An important producer in her own right, she mounted productions ranging from the musical *Brigadoon* (1947) to Bertolt Brecht's *Mother Courage* (1963), and included four plays by Tennessee Williams.

Crawford, Cindy (Cynthia Ann) 1966–
US supermodel, actress and television presenter
Born in de Kalb, Illinois, she had plans to become a chemical engineer before being discovered by photographer Victor Skrebenski in Chicago. Moving to New York, she became established as a top model and has appeared on an unprecedented 300 magazine covers in her career. She has modelled for *Playboy* magazine, has produced exercise videos and calendars, and presented the fashion on MTV's *House of Style*. Her advertising contracts include Revlon and Pepsi. After cameo appearances in the films *The Secret of My Success* (1987) and *Unzipped* (1995), she starred in *Fair Game* (1995) and *Catwalk* (1995). In 1991–94 she was married to Richard Gere.

Crawford, F(rancis) Marion 1854–1909
US novelist
Born in Bagni di Lucca, Italy, he was educated in the USA and Europe before working as a journalist in India. He became a bestselling writer with the exotic *Mr Isaacs, A Tale of Modern India* (1882). Thereafter he spent most of his life in Italy, where many of his romantic and historical novels are set, including *Saracinesca* (1887), *Sant' Ilario* (1889), *Don Orsino* (1892) and *Corleone* (1897). His books were immensely popular at the time, but only his ghost stories such as 'The Upper Berth' (1885) and 'The Screaming Skull' (1908) remain widely read. ▢ J Pilkington Jnr, *Francis Marion Crawford* (1964)

Crawford, Joan, *originally* Lucille Le Sueur 1906–77
US film actress
Born in San Antonio, Texas, she arrived in Hollywood in 1924. Her early films include *Our Dancing Daughters* (1928) and *Our Blushing Brides* (1930). During the 1920s and 1930s she developed into the archetypal glamorous Hollywood Movie Queen. Declared 'box-office poison' in 1938, she returned as the wickedly witty husband-stealer in *The Women* (1939). Later, she continued to suffer in jewels and ermine as the older woman beset by emotional problems, such as in *Mildred Pierce* (1945, Academy Award) and *Whatever Happened to Baby Jane?* (1962), and she retired after *Trog* (1970). She published an autobiography, *Portrait of Joan* (1962), and her adopted daughter Christina wrote a scathing attack on her in *Mommie Dearest* (1978).

Crawford, Sir John Grenfell 1910–85
Australian economist and administrator
Born in Hurstville, Sydney, and educated at Sydney University, he held many senior positions in agricultural and rural economics including the directorship of the Commonwealth Bureau of Agricultural Economics

(1945–50). He was senior agricultural advisor to the World Bank, and a member of its economic mission to India (1964–65). He held the chair of economics at the Australian National University, Canberra (1960–67), and was Vice-Chancellor there (1968–73). He had a strong interest in developing countries, and was sometime chairman of the Papua New Guinea Development Bank, and Chancellor of the University of Papua New Guinea (1972–75). He was president of the Australian and New Zealand Association for the Advancement of Science (1967–68) and received many honours for his work, including the Japanese Order of the Sacred Treasure in 1972.

Crawford, Michael, *originally* Michael Patrick Smith 1942–
English actor and singer
Born in Salisbury, Wiltshire, as a boy he was in Benjamin Britten's *Let's Make an Opera* (1955) and *Noye's Fludde* (1958). His performance in *No Sex, Please—We're British* (1971–72) established him as a gifted comedy actor. He went on to star in such musicals as *Billy* (1974–76), *Flowers for Algernon* (1979) and *Barnum* (1981–83), and won awards for his role in *The Phantom of the Opera* (West End, Broadway and Los Angeles, 1986–90). The television series *Some Mothers Do 'Ave 'Em* (1974–78), in which he played the accident-prone Frank Spencer, made him a household name. His films include *The Knack...and how to get it* (1965), *A Funny Thing Happened on the Way to the Forum* (1966), *How I Won the War* (1967), *Hello Dolly!* (1969) and *Condorman* (1980). In 1995 he appeared in the Las Vegas special-effects spectacular *EFX*.

Crawford, Osbert Guy Stanhope 1886–1957
English archaeologist and aerial photographer
Born in Bombay, India, he was educated at Marlborough, England, and studied classics and then geography at Keble College, Oxford, developing an interest in field archaeology. Serving with the Royal Flying Corps on the Western Front in World War I, he identified the potential of aerial photography in archaeology, and produced the classic album *Wessex from the Air* (1928). He served as the first archaeology officer of the Ordnance Survey (1920–40) and did much to develop the cartographic recording of archaeology, especially in period maps such as the *Ordnance Survey Map of Roman Britain* (1924). In 1927 he founded the journal *Antiquity*, which he edited until his death. His idiosyncratic *Archaeology in the Field* was published in 1953 and an autobiography, *Said and Done*, in 1955.

Crawford, Thomas 1814–57
US sculptor
He was born in New York City, and studied in Rome with Bertel Thorvaldsen. His works, in a neoclassical style, include the fine Washington monument in Richmond, Virginia (1857) and the bronze *Indian Warrior, Armed Freedom* surmounting the dome of the Capitol at Washington DC (installed 1863).

Crawford, William Harris 1772–1834
US politician
Born in Virginia, he practised law at Lexington, Georgia, and was elected to the state senate in 1802 and to the US Senate in 1807 and 1811. Appointed Minister to France in 1813 and Secretary of the Treasury in 1816, he was a Democratic candidate for the presidency in 1824.

Craxi, Bettino 1934–
Italian politician
He was born in Milan. After being active in the Socialist Youth movement he became a member of the Central Committee of the Italian Socialist Party (PSI) in 1957 and a member of the National Executive in 1965. He was Deputy Secretary (1970–76) and then became General Secretary in 1976. After the general election of 1983 he became Italy's first Socialist Prime Minister, successfully

leading a broad-based coalition until 1987. In 1995 a warrant was issued for his arrest on charges of receiving bribes, but his self-imposed exile in Tunisia allowed his lawyers to argue that as a political refugee, he was protected under the extradition treaty between Tunisia and Italy.

Craxton, John 1922–
English painter

Born in London, he studied at Westminster Art School, the Central School of Art, and Goldsmiths College, before settling at Hania in Crete in 1948. His style is linear, and early work is pastoral, influenced by William Blake and Samuel Palmer, eg *Dreamers in a Landscape* (1942, Tate, London) and *Pastoral for P.W.* (1948, Tate). Later, however, he was impressed by the colour of Byzantine mosaics, as shown in *Sunlit Ravine* (1982–85, Christopher Hull Gallery, London). Voluntarily exiled from Greece under the 'Colonels', he worked on *Landscape with the Elements* (Cottrell Memorial Tapestry, 1971–74) for Stirling University, and returned to Crete in 1977. An exhibition of his work was organized in Hania in 1985 by the British Council in Athens.

Cray, Seymour R 1925–96
US computer designer

Born in Chippewa Falls, Wisconsin, he was educated at Minnesota University, and in 1950 he was awarded degrees in both electrical engineering and mathematics. He established himself at the forefront of large-scale computer design through his work at Engineering Research Associates (later Remington Rand, Sperry Rand UNIVAC Division) and Control Data Corporation (CDC). In 1972 he organized Cray Research Inc in Chippewa Falls to develop and market the most powerful computer systems available. These 'supercomputers' are used in military, weather-forecasting and advanced engineering design applications. The Cray 1, delivered in 1976, was the world's fastest computer, and by the 1980s this machine and its later derivatives dominated the supercomputer market. After serving first as president and then as chairman of Cray Research, he severed his connections with the company in 1989 to head the Cray Computer Corporation (a separate company) and to work on the Cray 3 supercomputer. This materialized in 1993, but the end of the Cold War and the cut in the government's spending brought about the folding of his company in 1995. Cray died as a result of injuries sustained in a motor accident.

Crazy Horse, *Sioux name* Ta-Sunko-Witko
c.1849–77
Oglala Sioux Chief

Born in South Dakota and regarded as the foremost Sioux military leader, he defeated General Custer at the Battle of Little Big Horn (1876) with a combined force of Sioux and Cheyennes. He and his followers surrendered the following year, and he died in custody in Fort Robinson, Nebraska.

Creasey, John 1908–73
English crime and espionage writer

Born in Southfields, Surrey, he was educated in London, and wrote full-time from 1935, two years after the first Department Z thriller was published. An astonishingly prolific writer, he used no less than 25 pseudonyms (male and female), of which J J Marric was perhaps the best known. His characters include Inspector Roger West and the former jewel thief John Mannering (known as 'The Baron'). He has more than 550 novels to his credit, and his total sale of books is around 70 million worldwide. Creasey stood for parliament as a Liberal candidate in 1950, and four times as a member of the All Party Alliance, which he had founded in 1967. ⊞ R E Briney and J Creasey, 'A John Creasey Bibliography', in *Armchair Detective* (October 1968)

Crébillon, Claude Prosper Jolyot de 1707–77
French novelist

He was born in Paris, the younger son of Prosper Jolyot de Crébillon. After writing a number of light plays, he acquired great popularity as an author of elegant but licentious stories satirizing the fashionable society in which he moved. When the indecency of his *Le Sopha, conte moral* (1742, 'The Sofa—A Moral Tale') offended Madame de Pompadour, he was banished from Paris for five years, but on his return in 1755 he was appointed official literary censor in succession to his father. ⊞ P P Brooks, *The Novel of Worldliness* (1969)

Crébillon, Prosper Jolyot de 1674–1762
French dramatist

He was born in Dijon, and studied law in Paris. His tragedy *Idoménée*, successfully produced in 1703, was followed by *Atrée et Thyeste* (1707), *Électre* (1709), and *Rhadamiste et Zénobie* (1711), his masterpiece. He wrote little over the next 20 years, but was then pushed forward as a dramatic rival to Voltaire by Madame de Pompadour, elected to the Academy, awarded a pension of 1,000 francs, and appointed royal censor and a royal librarian. His *Catilina* achieved great success in 1748. His son was the novelist Claude Prosper Jolyot de Crébillon. ⊞ P Le Clerc, *Voltaire and Crébillon Père* (1973)

Credi, Lorenzo di 1459–1537
Italian painter

Born in Florence, he was the fellow pupil, lifelong friend and executor of Leonardo da Vinci. He mainly painted Holy Families, examples of which may be seen in the National Gallery, London, and in the Louvre, Paris.

Creed, Frederick George 1871–1957
Scottish inventor of the 'Creed teleprinter'

Born in Nova Scotia, Canada, of Scottish parents, he left school at the age of 14 to qualify as a telegraph operator. After working in Canada, Chile and Peru he moved to Glasgow in 1897 where, after some initial setbacks, he successfully realized his idea of an automatic perforated tape teleprinter. In 1909 he opened a factory in Croydon, Surrey, to meet the demand for his invention from newspapers all over the world, but after being bought out by the International Telephone and Telegraph Corporation in 1927, he lost most of his fortune through a series of impractical inventions.

Creeley, Robert White 1926–
US poet

Born in Arlington, Massachusetts, he dropped out of Harvard and spent some years in Spain before being appointed by Charles Olson to the faculty at Black Mountain College in North Carolina in 1954. There he became linked with the Black Mountain school of poets and founded and edited the *Black Mountain Review*. In the mid-1950s he moved to California, where he mixed with prominent Beat writers like Jack Kerouac and Allen Ginsberg. His poems, characterized by dense syntax and abrupt endings, have appeared in numerous collections including *If You* (1956), *The Whip* (1957), *For Love: Poems 1950–60* (1962), *St Martin's* (1971), *The Collected Poems of Robert Creeley, 1945–75* (1982), *Memory Gardens* (1986) and *Places* (1990). He has written one novel, *The Island* (1963), and more prose in *The Collected Prose of Robert Creeley: A Story* (1984). He published his autobiography in 1990. ⊞ M Novik, *Robert Creeley, an inventory* (1973)

Creevey, Thomas 1768–1838
English politician and diarist

He was a Whig MP for Thetford in 1802, and later for Appleby, and became treasurer of ordnance (1830) and treasurer of Greenwich hospital. He is remembered for the journal *Creevey Papers*, an important source of Georgian social history.

Cremer, Sir William Randal 1838–1908
English pacifist and Nobel Prize winner

Born in Fareham, Hampshire, he was an active trade unionist and a strong advocate of British neutrality in the Franco-Prussian War. He founded the Workmen's Peace Association, the germ of the International Arbitration League. A radical MP from 1885, he edited the peace journal *Arbitor* from 1889. In 1903 he won the Nobel Peace Prize.

Crémieux, Benjamin 1888–1944
French writer and critic

Born in Narbonne, he is known for his works on modern European literature, including the *XX* siècle* (1924), and for his translation of the plays of Luigi Pirandello. He died in Buchenwald concentration camp.

Crerar, Henry Duncan Graham 1888–1965
Canadian soldier

He was born in Hamilton, Ontario, of Scottish parentage. He worked as a civil engineer while holding a commission in the militia. In World War I he served with the Canadian Artillery in France. In World War II he was Chief of Canadian Army Staff (1940–41), commanded the 2nd Canadian Division (1942) and the Canadian Corps in Italy (1942–44) and succeeded Andrew McNaughton in command of the Canadian Land Forces in Europe (1944).

Crerar, Thomas Alexander 1876–1975
Canadian politician

He was president of United Grain Growers Ltd (1907–29), making it one of the country's most successful co-operatives, and served as Minister of Agriculture (1917–19) in Sir Robert Borden's coalition Cabinet. He left the Liberals in protest against their high tariff budget of 1920 and founded the New Progressive Party, leading them second place in the 1921 elections. He resigned as leader in 1921 but re-entered politics on becoming Minister of Railways and Canals in Mackenzie King's administration in 1929. Although he lost his seat in 1930, he won again with the Liberals in 1933, and served in the government as Minister of Mines and Resources (1935–45). He then served in the Canadian Senate (1945–66).

Crespi, Giuseppe Maria, *called* Lo Spagnuolo 1665–1747
Italian painter of the Bolognese school

Born in Bologna, he painted religious and mythological subjects showing the influence of the Eclectic school of the Carracci.

Cresson, Edith 1934–
French politician

She was born in Boulogne-sur-Seine and educated at the Ecole des Hautes Études Commerciales. As an active member of the Socialist Party, she was its youth organizer in 1975, became Mayor of Thuré in 1977 and was elected a member of the European parliament in 1979. A close friend of President François Mitterrand for more than 25 years, and having a reputation as a fiery socialist equivalent of Margaret Thatcher, she held various portfolios during the 1980s and after a brief return to industry in 1990 became her country's first woman Prime Minister in 1991 after the resignation of moderate premier Michel Rocard, but she too resigned the following year.

Cretzschmar, Philipp Jakob 1786–1845
German naturalist and physician

He was born in Sulzbach, and studied medicine at the universities of Würzburg and Halle. After army service he settled in Frankfurt where he practised as a doctor and taught zoology. In 1817 he founded the Senckenberg Natural History Society in Frankfurt, and made the ornithological contributions to the works of Eduard Rüppell. The bird Cretzschmar's Bunting was named in his honour.

Crèvecoeur, Michel Guillaume Jean de, *pseudonym* J Hector St John Crèvecoeur 1735–1813
US essayist and farmer

Born in Caen, France, he served as a mapmaker in Canada during the French and Indian War, then settled in New York where he wrote a series of essay-letters (1770–81) collected under the title *Letters from an American Farmer*. The letters combined a realistic description of rural colonial life with a romantic vision of the nobility of a life close to nature and the freshness of the New World. Because of his Loyalist connections he was forced to flee to Europe in 1780. When he returned to New York in 1783 to serve as French consul he found his wife dead and his children missing, the result of a Native American raid. He recovered his children and became a popular figure in the new USA.

Crichton, James, *known as* the Admirable Crichton 1560–c.1585
Scottish prodigy of the Scottish Enlightenment

The son of the Scottish Lord Advocate, he was born in Cluny, Perthshire, and educated at St Andrews, where his tutor was George Buchanan. After graduating in 1575, he earned a reputation on the Continent as a scholar, poet, linguist and swordsman. He spent two years in France as a teenager, apparently in the French army, delivered a Latin oration before the senate in Genoa in 1579, and took part in a great scholastic disputation in Venice (1580), and in Padua (1581). Later he went to Mantua in the service of the duke, and was killed by the duke's son in a nocturnal brawl. His popular reputation rests on the fantastic account of his exploits written by Sir Thomas Urquhart in his panegyric on the Scots nation, *The Discoveryie of a Most Exquisite Jewel* (1652). 'Admirable Crichton' became synonymous with all-round talents, the ideal man; the phrase was used by J M Barrie for his play about a perfect butler, *The Admirable Crichton* (1902).

Crichton Smith, Iain See Smith, Iain Crichton

Crick, Francis Harry Compton 1916–
English molecular biologist and Nobel Prize winner

Born near Northampton, Northamptonshire, he studied physics at University College London. After World War II he joined the laboratory of Max Perutz to work on the structure of proteins. In the early 1950s, in Cambridge, he met James Watson and together they worked on the structure of DNA, publishing in 1953 their model of a double-helical molecule, consisting of two chains of nucleotide bases wound round a common axis in opposite directions. This structure suggested a mechanism for the reproduction of the genetic code, which Crick continued to study for the next decade. He worked at the Laboratory of Molecular Biology, Cambridge, from 1949 to 1977, when he became Kieckhefer Professor at the Salk Institute, California, carrying out research into the visual systems of mammals, and the connections between brain and mind. He has been JW Kieckhefer Distinguished Professor there since 1977 and President since 1994. With Watson and Maurice Wilkins he was awarded the Nobel Prize for physiology or medicine in 1962 and he received the Order of Merit in 1991. His publications include *The Astonishing Hypothesis: the scientific search for the soul* (1994). 📖 David E Newton, *James Watson and Francis Crick: Discovery of the Double Helix and Beyond* (1992)

Crile, George Washington 1864–1943
US surgeon and physiologist

Born in Chili, Ohio, he was educated at Northwestern Ohio Normal School and the University of Wooster. He became interested in surgical shock (abnormally low blood pressure) when a friend died following an emergency operation after an accident, and published his first monograph on the subject in 1899. In 1900 he became Clinical Professor and in 1911 Professor of Surgery at the Western Reserve School of Medicine in Cleveland, Ohio. He was founder and first director of the Cleveland Clinic Foundation (1921–40). Continuing his work on surgical shock, he devised a method (which he called 'anoci-association') of combining drugs and anaesthetics which relaxed the patient and made surgical complications easier to control. He was also an early advocate of blood-pressure monitoring during operations, and was one of the first to regularly use adrenaline and blood transfusions as a means of combating shock. He developed several operations for the endocrine glands, though some of his later physiological speculations were rather eccentric.

Crillon, Louis des Balbes de Berton de, *called* Le Brave 1541–1615
French soldier

Born in Murs, in Provence, as a young man he distinguished himself at the Siege of Calais (1558) and the capture of Guines. In the religious wars he fought against the Huguenots at Dreux (1562), Jarnac and Moncontour (1569). Though wounded at Lepanto (1571) while serving with the Knights of Malta, he was sent to carry the news of the victory to the pope and the French king (**Charles IX**). He abhorred the St Bartholomew's Day Massacre (1572), but took part in the Siege of La Rochelle (1573), and eventually died at Avignon.

Crippen, Hawley Harvey 1862–1910
US murderer

Born in Michigan, he studied medicine and dentistry there and in London. In 1896 he returned to London, settling there with his second wife, Cora Turner, an unsuccessful opera singer and music hall performer, with whom he was not happy. He fell in love with his secretary, Ethel le Neve, and poisoned his wife after a party at their home at Hilldrop Crescent, Holloway; he dissected the body, burned the bones, and buried the remains in the cellar. His wife's friends were told she had died on holiday in the USA. After the police had unsuccessfully investigated Cora's disappearance, Ethel took fright, and the pair fled to Antwerp, where they boarded an Atlantic liner as Mr and Master Robinson. The suspicious captain, who had read reports of the second and successful search at Hilldrop Crescent, contacted Scotland Yard by radio-telegraphy (the first use of radio for police purposes), and the couple were arrested and tried. Crippen was executed at Pentonville.

Cripps, Sir (Richard) Stafford 1889–1952
English Labour statesman, economist, chemist and patent-lawyer

Born in London, the son of the politician Charles Alfred Cripps (1852–1941), and of Theresa, sister of **Beatrice Webb**, he was educated at Winchester and won a scholarship to New College, Oxford. However, his chemistry papers attracted the attention of Sir **William Ramsay**, who persuaded him to work in his laboratory at University College London instead. At 22 he was part-author of a paper read before the Royal Society. He also pursued legal studies and was called to the Bar in 1913, became the youngest barrister in the country in 1926, and made a fortune in patent and compensation cases. In 1930 he was appointed Solicitor-General in the second Labour government, but refused to serve in **Ramsay MacDonald's** Coalition (1931–35). From then until the outbreak of

World War II, Cripps was associated with a succession of extreme left-wing movements, at first pacific in character, but later, as the Nazi threat increased, concerned with rallying everyone, and not only socialists, to active opposition to **Neville Chamberlain's** policy of appeasement. Cripps's 'popular front' brought about his expulsion from the Labour Party in 1939 and forced him to sit as an independent MP throughout the war. Appointed ambassador in Moscow (1940–42), under **Churchill's** leadership in 1942, he became Lord Privy Seal and Leader of the Commons. During the summer he was sent to India with the famous 'Cripps offer' of dominion status for a united India, rejected by both **Mahatma Gandhi** and **Muhammad Ali Jinnah**, and finally in November he succeeded **Max Beaverbrook** in the vital post of Minister of Aircraft Production; this he held for the remainder of the war. When Labour came to power in July 1945, Cripps was readmitted to the party and appointed President of the Board of Trade. In 1947 he became the first Minister of Economic Affairs and within a few weeks succeeded **Hugh Dalton** as Chancellor of the Exchequer. His at first unpopular policy of austerity caught the public conscience, and the trade unions took the unprecedented step of imposing a voluntary wage freeze. He only began to be challenged when he devalued the pound in 1949. Illness from overwork forced his resignation in 1950. Cripps firmly believed that politics was a proper sphere for the practice of Christianity, and he wrote *Towards a Christian Democracy* (1945). 📖 Colin Cooke, *The Life of Richard Stafford Cripps* (1957)

Crispi, Francesco 1819–1901
Italian statesman

Born at Ribera, Sicily, he was called to the Bar and became a member of the provisional government established in Palermo after the insurrection of 1848. He was exiled from the Kingdom of the Two Sicilies in 1849 and settled in Turin; he organized the successful movement of 1859–60, and re-entered Sicily with **Garibaldi**. In the restored kingdom of Italy he became Deputy, President of the Chamber, Interior Minister, and Premier (1887–90, 1894). A member of the Left, he was strongly anticlerical, and maintained the alliance with Germany at the cost even of alienating France. The Abyssinian disaster of the Battle of Adowa (1896) compelled his resignation.

Crispin, St d.287AD
Roman Christian

Born in Rome, according to legend, under the reign of **Diocletian**, he fled from there, with his brother St Crispinian, and worked as a shoemaker in Soissons, while striving to spread Christianity. He and his brother were martyred in AD287 by being thrown into molten lead. Their feast day is 25 October.

Crispus, Gaius Sallustius See **Sallust**

Cristofaloi, Bartolommeo See **Cristofori, Bartolommeo**

Cristofano, Francesco di See **Franciabigio**

Cristofori or Cristofaloi, Bartolommeo
1655–1731
Italian harpsichord-maker and inventor of the pianoforte

He was born in Padua and worked in Florence from about 1690. He is generally credited with inventing the pianoforte (c.1709), which was described in his time as *gravicembalo col piano e forte* ('harpsichord that plays soft and loud'). The name refers to the instrument's ability to be played either softly or loudly, according to the amount of pressure put on the keys. Three of his pianos survive, dated 1720, 1722 and 1726. 📖 Konstantin Restle, *Bartolomes Cristofori und die Anfänge des Hammerclaviers* (1991)

Critias c.460–403BC
Athenian orator and politician

He was a pupil of **Socrates**. Implicated with **Alcibiades** in the mutilation of the Hermae on the eve of the Sicilian expedition (415BC), he nonetheless escaped punishment. In 411 he took part in the oligarchical revolution that set up the government of Four Hundred. Exiled in 406, he returned in 404, and as a strong supporter of Sparta became one of the Thirty Tyrants set up by the Spartans after their defeat of Athens at the end of the Peloponnesian War (431–404). In the same year he was killed at Munychia, resisting **Thrasybulus** and the exiles. He had a high reputation as an orator, and wrote poetry and tragedies.

Crivelli, Carlo c.1430–1495
Italian painter of the Venetian school

Trained probably by the **Vivarini** family in Venice, he spent most of his time working elsewhere in the Marches. His style is a highly individual combination of old-fashioned International Gothic opulence with a contemporary Renaissance setting of figures in architectural frameworks and against landscapes. His style of draughtsmanship is similar to that of **Botticelli**, but the impression given by his works is more overpowering. His *Annunciation* is in the National Gallery, London.

Crnjanski, Milos 1893–
Serbian poet, novelist and dramatist

Born in Csongrád, Hungary, he was forced to fight for the Austro-Hungarian army in World War I, and his experiences turned him into a militantly right-wing pacifist. He remained abroad until 1965, when he was able to return to Belgrade as a revered national figure. His bold lyrical poetry much influenced the Serbs, and his long novel *Seobe* (1929–62, 'The Migrations'), a masterful account of the 18th-century Serbs in Vojvodina, is one of the most significant Yugoslav novels of the 20th century. He also wrote a renowned critical study of the sonnets of **Shakespeare**. ☐ T Eekman, *Thirty Years of Yugoslav Literature 1945–1975* (1978); A Kadic, *Contemporary Serbian Literature* (1964).

Croce, Benedetto 1866–1952
Italian philosopher, historian, literary critic and politician

Born in Pescasseroli, Aquila, he was buried and lost his parents and sister in an earthquake on the island of Ischia in 1883. He studied at Rome, and in Naples devoted himself at first to literature and antiquarian studies. He developed a phenomenology of the mind in which the four principal activities of the mind, art and philosophy (theoretical), political economy and ethics (practical), do not oppose, as they do for **Hegel**, but complement each other. His theory of aesthetics, with its denial of the physical reality of the work of art, considerably influenced **R G Collingwood**. He founded the review, *La Critica*, in 1903, and made major contributions to idealistic aesthetics in his *Estetica* (1902, 'Aesthetic') and *La Poesia* (1936, 'Poetry'). In 1910 he became senator, and was Minister of Education (1920–21) when, with the rise of **Mussolini**, he had to resign his professorship at Naples. He placed the highest value on liberty and was opposed to totalitarianism, and with the fall of Mussolini (1943) helped to resurrect liberal institutions in Italy. He became president of the Italian Liberal Party in 1947 and a member of the Constituent Assembly; he became a senator again in 1948. He had an enormous influence on European, particularly Italian, literature, and has been compared to **Montaigne** in his capacity as an educator. He also wrote literary studies of **Goethe, Dante, Ariosto** and **Corneille**. ☐ C Sprigge, *Benedetto Croce, Man and Thinker* (1952)

Crocker, Chester A(rthur) 1941–
US politician

Born in New York City, and educated at Ohio State and Johns Hopkins universities, he worked as a journalist on *African Report* during the mid-1960s and as a lecturer at the American University (1969–70). During the **Nixon** administration, he served briefly on the National Security Council as a staff officer (1970–72), before returning to academic life at Georgetown University, becoming its director of African Studies in 1976. An expert on southern African politics, he joined the **Reagan** administration (1981–89) as Assistant Secretary of State for African Affairs, being placed in effective charge of its new policy of 'constructive engagement' with Pretoria. This bore partial fruit with a peace settlement for Namibia. Since 1989 he has been Research Professor at Georgetown University and his publications include *High Noon in Southern Africa* (1992).

Crockett, Davy (David) 1786–1836
US frontiersman

Born near Greeneville, Tennessee, he grew up on the frontier, repeatedly moving westward with his family, and had little schooling. He distinguished himself against the Creek Indians in **Andrew Jackson**'s campaign of 1814, was elected to the Tennessee state legislature in 1821 and served in Congress (1827–31, 1833–35), where his colourful personality and humorous oratory drew much attention. Defeated in the 1835 election, he left his home state for Texas, and he died defending the Alamo during the Texas Revolution. ☐ J W Burke, *The Man Behind the Myth* (1984)

Crockett, Samuel Rutherford 1860–1914
Scottish novelist

Born in Little Duchrae, Kirkcudbright, he attended Edinburgh University and New College, Edinburgh, supporting himself by journalism and travelling tutorships. Becoming a Free Church minister in Penicuik, he wrote sardonic Congregational sketches, of which 24, collected as *The Stickit Minister* (1893), brought immediate fame. This was consolidated in 1894 with the publication of *The Raiders*, *The Lilac Sunbonnet* (a seemingly innocent love story which ridiculed narrow religious sects) and two novellas. Resigning the ministry in favour of full-time writing (1895), he wrote tales of Covenanting and medieval Scotland, European historical romances, and (often sensational) stories of mining, industrialism and Edinburgh slums. His posthumous works include one detective and one theological science-fiction novel. ☐ I M Donaldson, *Life and Work of Samuel Rutherford Crockett* (1989)

Croesus 6th century BC
Last King of Lydia

He succeeded his father, Alyattes, in c.560BC. He made the Greeks of Asia Minor his tributaries, and extended his kingdom eastward from the Aegean to the Halys. His conquests, his mines, and the golden sand of the Pactolus made his wealth proverbial. **Cyrus the Great** defeated and imprisoned him (546).

Crofts, Freeman Wills 1879–1957
Irish author of detective fiction

Born in Dublin, he abandoned a career as chief assistant engineer on the Belfast and Northern Counties Railway in 1929 in order to concentrate on his writing and, later, moved to England. He wrote 35 novels, of which 24 feature the character Inspector (later Superintendent) French of Scotland Yard, the first of these being *Inspector French's Greatest Case* (1925). Other novels include *The Starvel Tragedy* (1927) and *The Hog's Back Mystery* (1933).

Croke, Thomas William 1824–1902
Irish prelate

Born in Ballyclough, County Cork, he was educated in Paris and Rome, and is said to have fought at the barricades in Paris during the revolution of 1848. A close friend of Cardinal Henry Manning, he became Roman Catholic Bishop of Auckland, New Zealand, in 1870. In 1875 he was promoted Archbishop of Cashel and Emly. A strong nationalist, he backed the Gaelic League and the Land League, and supported the leadership of Charles Parnell. Croke Park in Dublin is named after him.

Croker, Boss See Croker, Richard

Croker, John Wilson 1780–1857
Irish politician and essayist
Born in Galway, the son of the surveyor-general of Irish customs, and educated at Trinity College, Dublin, he entered Lincoln's Inn in 1800, and in 1802 was called to the Irish Bar. His verse satire on the Irish stage (*On the Present State of the Irish Stage*, 1804) and his prose satire on Dublin society (*Intercepted Letters from Canton*, 1804) proved successful hits, as did his *Sketch of Ireland Past and Present* (1807), a pamphlet advocating Catholic emancipation. Elected MP for Downpatrick in 1807, he helped to found the *Quarterly Review* in 1809, and contributed 260 articles. He was rewarded with the lucrative secretaryship of the Admiralty (1809–30) for his defence of Frederick Augustus, Duke of York, in the case of Mary Anne Clarke (1776–1852; the Duke's mistress from 1803 to 1807 who trafficked in commissions). After 1832, he refused to re-enter parliament and would not even take office under Sir Robert Peel, his old friend (1834). He fell out with Peel over the repeal of the Corn Laws (1846). Among the 17 works that he wrote or edited were his *Stories for Children from English History* (1817), which suggested the *Tales of a Grandfather*; the *Suffolk Papers* (1823); his edition of James Boswell's *Life of Johnson* (1831); and *Essays on the Early French Revolution* (1857). He is better remembered for his attack on John Keats and for Thomas Macaulay's attack on him (Macaulay 'detested him more than cold boiled veal'), as the originator of the term Conservative, and as the 'Rigby' of Benjamin Disraeli's *Coningsby* (1844). 📖 M Brightfield, *John Wilson Croker* (1940)

Croker, Richard, *known as* Boss Croker 1841–1922
US politician
Born in County Cork, Ireland, he emigrated as a child with his family to New York. He entered New York City politics in 1862, joining the 'Young Democracy' faction opposed to Mayor 'Boss' Tweed (1823–78) in 1868. He secured control of the Tammany Hall machine in 1886 and, as 'Boss Croker', dominated Democratic Party politics for the next 16 years, surviving a major corruption scandal involving the police department in 1894. After the election as mayor in 1901 of the reforming idealist Seth Low (1850–1916), he left the USA (1903) and spent the rest of his life on a large estate in Ireland.

Croker, Thomas Crofton 1798–1854
Irish antiquary and folklorist
He was born in Cork and from 1818 to 1859 was a clerk at the Admiralty. At the age of 14 he began to collect songs and legends of the Irish peasantry and in 1818 he sent Thomas Moore about 40 old Irish melodies. In 1825 he published anonymously his *Fairy Legends and Traditions of the South of Ireland*, a work which charmed Sir Walter Scott and was translated into German by the brothers Grimm (1826). A second series followed in 1827. His other works include *Researches in the South of Ireland* (1824), *Legends of the Lakes* (1829), *The Adventures of Barney Mahoney* (1832) and *Popular Songs of Ireland* (1839).

Croll, James 1821–90
Scottish physicist and geologist

Born in Cargill, Perthshire, he received an elementary school education but his science was self-taught. Successively millwright, insurance agent and keeper of the museum of Anderson's College, Glasgow, he was appointed to the Scottish Geological Survey (1867–81) and came into contact with many of the best geologists of the time. He was broadly supportive of Lord Kelvin's calculations of the age of the Earth, and rejected the mathematically unconstrained vast length of time required by uniformitarianism. His main interests were in changes in climate over geological time and in glacial geology. He argued that the influence of ocean currents and the changing distribution of land and water have a great effect on climates.

Croly, George 1780–1860
Irish poet, romance-writer, biographer and Anglican preacher
Born in Dublin, he was educated at Trinity College. He took orders in 1804, and went to London in 1810, becoming rector of St Stephen's, Walbrook (1835). From 1817 he published some 40 works, the best-known of which is the weird romance of *Salathiel* (1829), based on the legend of the Wandering Jew. Other titles include the tragedy *Cataline* (1822), the satirical *May Fair* (1827), and a romance of the French Revolution, *Marston* (1846). 📖 R Herring, *A Few Personal Recollections* (1861)

Crome, John, *known as* Old Crome 1768–1821
English landscape painter
Born in Norwich, he was educated locally and taught himself to paint. He helped to found the Norwich Society of Artists in 1803, and became its president (1808). He occasionally visited London, where he exhibited in the Academy and the British Institution, and a tour through Belgium and France in 1814 resulted in *The Fishmarket on the Beach, Boulogne* and *The Boulevard des Italiens, Paris*. However, he nearly always painted the scenery of his native county, which, though influenced by the Dutch landscapists, he treated in a direct and individual fashion. He occasionally painted watercolours, and his etchings of *Norfolk Picturesque Scenery* were published in 1834. His son, John Berny Crome (1794–1842), known as Young Crome, was also a landscape painter.

Cromek, Robert Hartley 1770–1812
English engraver
Born in Hull, Humberside, he published Robert Blair's *The Grave*, with engravings after William Blake. He visited Scotland to collect and publish the *Reliques of Burns* (1808) and *Select Scottish Songs* (1810), and after meeting Allan Cunningham, published his literary fabrications in *Remains of Nithsdale and Galloway Song* (1810).

Cromer, Evelyn Baring, 1st Earl of 1841–1917
English colonial administrator
Born at Cromer Hall, Norfolk, he was private secretary to his cousin, Sir Francis Baring, Lord Northbrook (1796–1866), when Viceroy of India (1872–76). He later became British Controller-General of Egyptian Finance (1879–80), Finance Minister of India (1880–83), and Agent and Consul-General in Egypt (1883–1907). Effectively the ruler of Egypt, he reformed its administration and agricultural policies, and improved its finances. He also wrote *Political and Literary Essays (1908–16)*.

Crommelynck, Fernand 1888–1970
Belgian playwright and novelist
He was born in Paris of a French mother and a Belgian father. His first real success was *Le Cocu magnifique* (1920, 'The Magnificent Cuckold'), a study of obsessive jealousy, which was first produced in Paris by Aurélien-François Lugné-Poë (1869–1940), and was made into a film by Jean-Louis Barrault (1921). Later plays were less successful. After *Une Femme qui a le cœur trop petit* (1934, 'A Woman

Cromwell, Oliver 1599–1658
English soldier and statesman

Oliver Cromwell was born in Huntingdon and educated at Huntingdon Grammar School and Sydney Sussex College, Cambridge. He studied law in London, and developed a dislike for **Charles I** after first sitting in the House of Commons in 1628. When the king dissolved parliament the following year, he took up farming in Huntingdon and subsequently at St Ives and Ely. He was a member of the Short Parliament of 1640 which refused the king funds for the Bishops' War, and of the subsequent Long Parliament, in which he moved the Second Reading of a Bill to introduce annual sittings.

At the start of the English Civil War in 1642, he raised a troop of cavalry for the battles of Edgehill and Gainsborough, and in 1644 he brought the war nearer to an end with a cavalry charge against Royalist troops at Marston Moor. Back in parliament, he led the independent faction that rejected reconciliation with the king, and commanded the army that won a decisive victory over the king's forces at Naseby on 14 June 1645. Cromwell at first professed a willingness to negotiate terms by which the throne might be saved, but Charles' success in rallying the Scots from the Isle of Wight brought further fighting in 1648 and Cromwell resolved to rid himself of the king for ever. Charles was taken to Westminster for trial, and Cromwell's signature was among those on the death warrant that brought the king's execution on 30 January 1649. The monarchy was abolished and Cromwell declared the establishment of a Commonwealth with himself as chairman of its Council of State.

He brutally brought the last vestiges of Irish resistence to an end by massacring the Catholic garrisons at Drogheda and Wexford, and between 1650 and 1651 defeated at Dunbar and at Worcester the supporters of **Charles II** who had declared him King of Scotland.

Frustrated by the obstruction presented by the substantial body of Royalists remaining in the Commons, Cromwell dissolved the Long Parliament in 1653 and ruled briefly as head of the Puritan Convention and then, on the implementation of a new Constitution, as Lord Protector. He reorganized the Church of England and established Puritanism, brought prosperity to Scotland under his administration, and granted Irish representation in parliament.

He dissolved parliament again in 1655 with a view to imposing regional rule under 10 major-generals in England, but the experiment failed, and after recalling the Commons in 1656 he was offered the Crown. He declined it, but instead won the right to name his son, **Richard Cromwell**, as Lord Protector. However, his relations with parliament worsened to bring another dissolution in 1658, and Cromwell continued to rule absolutely until his death later that year. His son held the promised title of Lord Protector for just a year, but failed to emulate his father's iron grip and surrendered the office a year later. On the Restoration in 1660, Oliver Cromwell's body was disinterred from the tomb of kings in Westminster Abbey; it was later hung from Tyburn gallows and afterwards buried there.

📖 Barry Coward, *Oliver Cromwell* (1991); Antonia Fraser, *The Lord Protector, Cromwell* (1973); C V Wedgwood, *Oliver Cromwell* (1973).

'I had rather had a plain, russet-coated Captain, that knows what he fights for, and loves what he knows, than that which you call a Gentle-man and is nothing else.' From a letter (1643), quoted in **Thomas Carlyle**'s *Letters and Speeches of Oliver Cromwell* (1845).

---

whose Heart is too Small') he stopped writing for the theatre, and confined himself to a mystery novel and filmscripts. 📖 D Grossvogel, *20th Century French Drama* (1961)

Crompton, Richmal, *originally* Richmal Lamburn 1890–1969
English writer

Born in Bury, Lancashire, she was educated in Lancashire and Derby and at Royal Holloway College, London. An honours graduate in classics (1914), she taught for some years, but was struck down with poliomyelitis in 1923. She published 50 adult titles thereafter but she is best known for her *Just William* books, 38 short-story collections (and one novel, *Just William's Luck*) about a perpetual schoolboy, the 11-year-old William Brown. Children love the judicious deliberation with which his escapades are described and their reduction of ordered adult life to chaos. 📖 Kay Williams, *Just Richmal: The Life and Work of Richmal Crompton* (1986)

Crompton, Rookes Evelyn Bell 1845–1940
English engineer

Born near Thirsk, North Yorkshire, he designed and built first a model and then a full-size steam road locomotive while still a schoolboy, continuing with this work after army service in India. His road steamers were technically successful but could not compete with the rapid development of the railways in the second half of the 19th century. On his return to Great Britain he became involved in the generation and distribution of electricity for lighting, on which he became an international authority. He strongly supported standardization in industry and

was concerned in the establishment of the National Physical Laboratory and what is now the British Standards Institution. He was elected FRS in 1933.

Crompton, Samuel 1753–1827
English inventor of the spinning mule

Born in Firwood, Lancashire, the son of a farmer, he set out to invent a spinning-machine that would improve on that of **James Hargreaves**. In 1779, after five years' work, he produced his spinning mule, so called because it was a cross between Hargreaves' spinning-jenny and **Richard Arkwright**'s water frame. Too poor to apply for a patent, he sold the rights to a Bolton manufacturer for £67. In 1812 he was granted a reward of £5,000 by the House of Commons. He tried bleaching at Over Darwen, then failed as a partner in a cotton firm. Some friends purchased him an annuity of £63.

Cromwell, Oliver See panel above

Cromwell, Richard 1626–1712
English statesman

The third son of **Oliver Cromwell**, he served in the Parliamentary army, sat in parliament in 1654 and 1656, and was a member of the Council of State in 1657. In September 1658 he succeeded his father as Lord Protector, but he soon fell out with parliament, which dissolved in 1659. He recalled the Rump Parliament of 1653, but proved incapable of ruling, and was forced to abdicate in May 1659. After the Restoration (1660) he lived abroad, in France and Geneva, under the alias 'John Clarke', but returned to England in 1680, and spent the rest of his life at Cheshunt.

Cromwell, Thomas, Earl of Essex c.1485–1540
English statesman

Born in Putney, London, the son of a blacksmith and brewer, he lived from 1504 to 1512 on the Continent, where he may have served in the French army in Italy, and gained experience as a clerk and trader. He then became a wool-stapler and scrivener, practised some law, and entered the service of Cardinal **Wolsey** in 1514, and parliament in 1523. In 1525 he acted as Wolsey's chief agent in the dissolution of the smaller monasteries, and as his general factotum for the endowment of his colleges at Ipswich and Oxford. In 1529 he pleaded successfully in the House of Commons in favour of quashing the Bill of Attainder against Wolsey. In 1530 he entered the service of **Henry VIII** and quickly became his principal adviser, as Privy Councillor (1531), Chancellor of the Exchequer (1533) and Secretary of State and Master of the Rolls (1534). The guiding hand behind the Reformation acts of 1532–39 which made the king head of the English Church, as vicar-general from 1535, and as Lord Privy Seal and the king's deputy as the head of the Church (from 1536), he organized the dissolution of the monasteries (1536–39). He devoted himself single-mindedly to establishing the absolute authority of the Crown and Protestantizing the Church. Though appointed Lord Great Chamberlain in 1539 and ennobled as the Earl of Essex in 1540, he lost favour with the king after negotiating the disastrous marriage with **Anne of Cleves**. He was sent to the Tower, condemned by parliament under a Bill of Attainder, and executed. ⌑ A G Dickens, *Thomas Cromwell and the English Reformation* (1959)

Cronin, A(rchibald) J(oseph) 1896–1981
Scottish novelist

Born in Cardross, Dunbartonshire, he graduated in medicine at Glasgow in 1919, but in 1930 abandoned his practice as a result of a breakdown in his health, and turned to literature. He had an immediate success with his brooding and melodramatic autobiographical novel *Hatter's Castle* (1931). Subsequent works include *The Citadel* (1937), *The Keys of the Kingdom* (1941), *Beyond this Place* (1953), *Crusader's Tomb* (1956) and *A Song of Sixpence* (1964). The medical stories in his Scottish novels formed the basis of the popular radio and television series *Dr Finlay's Casebook* in the 1960s, and again in 1993. Towards the end of his life he lived largely in the USA and Switzerland. ⌑ *Adventures in Two Worlds* (1952)

Cronin, James Watson 1931–
US physicist and Nobel Prize winner

Born and educated in Chicago, he worked at the Brookhaven National Laboratory before moving to Princeton University, becoming Professor of Physics there in 1965, and at Chicago University from 1971. **Tsung-Dao Lee**, **Cheng Ning Yang** and others had shown to the surprise of physicists that neither charge conjugation nor parity was conserved in weak interactions between subatomic particles. In 1964, together with **Val Fitch**, J Christensen and R Turlay, Cronin made a study of neutral kaons and discovered that a combination of parity and charge conjugation was not conserved either, thus violating CP-conservation. Since it was known from the CPT theorem that a combination of parity, charge conjugation and time is conserved, this important result implied that the decay of kaons is not symmetrical with respect to time reversal. This is still not understood today, but the idea of CP violation has been used to explain the domination of matter over antimatter in the universe. Cronin and Fitch shared the 1980 Nobel Prize for physics for their work in particle physics.

Cronje, Piet Arnoldus 1835–1911
South African soldier

In the First Boer War (1880–81) he captured the British garrison at Potchefstroom (1881), and in 1886 he overpowered the **Jameson** Raiders. In the Second Boer War

(1899–1900) he defeated the British at Magersfontein (1899), but was forced to surrender to **Frederick Roberts** at Paardeberg (1900).

Cronkite, Walter Leland, Jnr 1916–
US journalist and broadcaster

Born in St Joseph, Missouri, he was a student of political science, economics and journalism at Texas University (1933–35). He dropped out in his junior year to work for the Houston *Post* and later at KCMO radio in Kansas City as a news and sports reporter. Employed by the United Press (1939–48), he provided vivid eyewitness accounts of World War II in Europe, and remained to cover the Nuremberg trials and work as the bureau chief in Moscow (1946–48). At CBS from 1950, he hosted a number of shows and narrated *You Are There* (1953–56) but became best known for his informative, straightforward reporting on the *CBS Evening News* (1962–81). He also hosted *Sabotage in South Africa* (1962), *D–Day Plus 20 Years* (1964) and *Vietnam: A War That Is Finished* (1975). In 1981 he was awarded the Presidential Medal of Freedom.

Cronquist, Arthur 1919–92
US botanist

Born in San José, California, and educated at Utah State University and the University of Minnesota, he was an authority on the family Compositae (Asteraceae) and wrote treatments of it for several US Floras. One of his major interests was the phylogeny of flowering plants, particularly at and above the level of family. In this field his major work was *An Integrated Classification of Flowering Plants* (1981), one of the most important 20th-century publications in plant taxonomy, which effectively supersedes the classification of **Adolf Engler**. The 'Cronquist system' of plant classification has been adopted in many later works. He also prepared several standard Floras, including *Vascular Plants of the Pacific North-West* (5 parts, 1955–69), *Manual of Vascular Plants of Northeastern United States and Adjacent Canada* (1963, 1991) and *Intermountain Flora* (6 vols, 1972), as well as several textbooks on botany.

Cronstedt, Axel Fredrik, Baron 1722–65
Swedish metallurgist and mineralogist

Born in Turinge, he studied mathematics at Uppsala and served in the army (1741–43) before embarking on a career in mining and metallurgy. He first isolated nickel (1751) and noted its magnetic properties. He is renowned for his *Essay towards a System of Mineralogy* (1758), in which minerals and stones were distinguished for the first time and chemical composition was advocated as the primary method of classification of minerals. He proposed a new classification based on the action of fire, water and oil on specimens, and introduced mineral analysis by the blowpipe.

Crook, George 1829–90
US soldier

Born in Ohio, he fought on the Federal side in the Civil War (1861–65), commanding the army of West Virginia in 1864. He then fought in the Indian wars (1866–77) in Idaho and Arizona (1873), capturing **Cochise**, pacifying the Apaches (1871), and fighting in the Sioux War (1876). He fought the Apaches again under **Geronimo** (1882–86).

Crookes, Sir William 1832–1919
English chemist and physicist

Born in London, he was a pupil and assistant of **August Hoffmann** at the Royal College of Chemistry there, then superintended the meteorological department of the Radcliffe Observatory, Oxford, and from 1855 lectured on chemistry at the Science College, Chester. He discovered the metal thallium (1861), and the sodium amalgamation process (1865). He also improved vacuum tubes and promoted electric lighting, invented the radiometer (1873–76) and the spinthariscope, and wrote *Select Methods of Chemical Analysis* (1871).

Crosbie, Annette 1934–
Scottish actress

Born in Edinburgh, she trained at Bristol Old Vic Theatre School and won two BAFTA Best Actress awards for her performances on television as Catherine of Aragon in *The Six Wives of Henry VIII* (1970) and Queen Victoria in *Edward the Seventh* (1975). She later played Dorothy Simcos in *Paradise Postponed* (1986), Margaret Meldrew in the sit-com *One Foot in the Grave* (1990–) and Janet MacPherson in *Doctor Finlay* (1993–). Her films include *The Slipper and the Rose* (1976) and *Leon the Pig Farmer* (1992).

Crosby, Bing, *originally* Harry Lillis Crosby 1904–77
US singer and film actor

Born in Tacoma, Washington, he began his career playing the drums while still at school and sang with Paul Whiteman's Rhythm Boys. He made his feature film debut in *King of Jazz* (1930). From the 1930s onwards his distinctive crooning style made him a top attraction on radio, and later on television. He is one of the greatest sellers of records this century, and his version of 'White Christmas' sold over 30 million copies. Consistently among the most popular pre-war film stars, his partnership with Bob Hope and Dorothy Lamour (1914–96) resulted in a series of 'Road to…' comedies and he won an Academy Award for *Going My Way* (1944). Later notable films include *The Bells of St Mary's* (1945), *Blue Skies* (1946), *White Christmas* (1954), *The Country Girl* (1954) and *High Society* (1956). A keen golfer, he continued to record and perform sell-out concerts until his death on a golf course in Spain.

Crosby, Caresse See Jacob, Mary Phelps

Crosby, Fanny (Frances Jane), *later* Mrs Van Alstyne 1820–1915
US hymnwriter

Born in Southeast, New York, she was blind from infancy, and was both pupil and teacher in New York City's Institute for the Blind. She composed about 6,000 popular hymns, including 'Safe in the arms of Jesus' (played at President Ulysses S Grant's funeral), 'Pass me not, O gentle Saviour' (reportedly a favourite of Queen Victoria) and 'Rescue the perishing' (prompted by her mission work on New York's Lower East Side). She would not allow blindness to interfere with her work, and Dwight L Moody and Ira Sankey (1840–1908) acknowledged a great debt to her.

Crosland, Tony (Charles Anthony Raven) 1918–77
English Labour politician

He was born at St Leonards-on-Sea, Sussex, and educated at Oxford (president of the Union, 1946), where he also taught after serving in World War II. He was elected MP for South Gloucester (1950–55) and for Grimsby from 1955. He held several government posts under Harold Wilson, becoming Secretary for Education and Science (1965–67), President of the Board of Trade (1967–69), Secretary for Local Government and Regional Planning (1969–70), and Environment Secretary (1974–76). He made an unsuccessful bid for the party leadership in 1976, but served James Callaghan as the Foreign and Commonwealth Secretary (1976–77) before dying suddenly at the age of 59. A strong supporter of Hugh Gaitskell, he was a key member of the revisionist wing of the Labour Party, aiming to modernize socialist ideology, and wrote one of its seminal texts, *The Future of Socialism* (1956).

Cross, Charles Frederick 1855–1935
English industrial chemist

Born in Brentford, Essex, he studied in London, Zurich and Manchester, and in 1885 joined Edward John Bevan (1856–1921) to form Cross and Bevan Research and Consulting Chemists, specializing in the chemistry of cellulose. They began to investigate the process invented by Hilaire de Chardonnet's process for making thread from nitrocellulose, and in 1892 patented the modern method for producing artificial silk from cellulose. Two years later they patented a similar process for making viscose film ('cellophane'). Cross joined C H Stearn in 1898 to form the Viscose Spinning Syndicate which amalgamated with Courtaulds, the silk manufacturers, in 1902 and began large-scale production in 1905. He was elected FRS in 1917.

Crossley, Ada Jemima 1871–1929
Australian contralto

Born in Tarraville, Victoria, she went to London in 1894 to study under Sir Charles Santley, and made her debut at the Queen's Hall, London, in 1895. After standing in at short notice for the indisposed Clara Butt, she was in demand for oratorios and festivals all over Great Britain, and within two years had given five 'command performances' for Queen Victoria. Her considerable repertoire included sacred songs and ballads. Able to sing in seven languages, she was admired both for her voice and for her interpretative skills, and toured the USA in 1902 and 1903, recording for the new Victor Company, and later became an established international recording artist. She returned to Australia for two tours in 1903 and 1907, with supporting artists including the young Percy Grainger. She later reduced her commitments but performed at many charity concerts during World War I.

Crossley, Sir Francis 1817–72
English carpet manufacturer and philanthropist

Born in Halifax, Yorkshire, he was Liberal MP for Halifax from 1852 to 1859 (then for the West Riding), and presented a public park (1857) to Halifax, as well as almshouses and an orphanage.

Crossman, Richard Howard Stafford 1907–74
English Labour politician

The son of a judge who was a strong Conservative but also a personal friend of Clement Attlee, he was educated at Winchester and New College, Oxford, where, after gaining a first-class degree, he stayed on as a Fellow, philosophy tutor and lay Dean. Having become leader of the Labour group on the Oxford City Council, he left the university in 1937 to lecture for the Workers' Educational Association and join the staff of the *New Statesman*. During World War II he worked in political and psychological warfare, and in 1945 became the Labour MP for Coventry East. A Bevanite activist, his brilliant intellect, and also perhaps his prosperous middle-class background, alienated him from some sections of the party, and neither Attlee nor Hugh Gaitskell appointed him to high government office. Harold Wilson, however, brought him into the Cabinet as Minister of Housing and Local Government (1964–66) and Leader of the House of Commons (1966–69). His last office was Secretary of State for Social Services and head of the Department of Health, and in 1970, on the defeat of the government, he returned to the *New Statesman* as editor until 1972. He began a political diary in 1952 during the internal struggles of the party, wishing to make a detailed record of the day-to-day workings of government as they occurred, rather than a reasoned and sifted account viewed with hindsight. Published posthumously in four volumes (1975, 1976, 1977, 1981), despite attempts to suppress them, the diaries provide an invaluable insight into the Wilson administration. 🕮 Tam Dalyell, *Dick Crossman: A Portrait* (1989)

Crowe, Mrs See Bateman, Kate Josephine

Crowley, Aleister, *originally* Edward Alexander Crowley 1875–1947
English writer and magician
He became interested in the occult while an undergraduate at Cambridge at the time of the 'magic revival' of the late 19th century, and was for a time a member of the Order of the Golden Dawn which **W B Yeats** also joined. Expelled for extreme practices, he founded his own order, the Silver Star, and travelled widely, settling for several years in Sicily with a group of disciples at the Abbey of Thelema near Cefalò. Rumours of drugs, orgies and magical ceremonies involving the sacrifice of babies culminated in his expulsion from Italy. In 1921 a series of newspaper articles brought him the notoriety he craved—he liked to be known as 'the great beast' and 'the wickedest man alive'—and certainly many who associated with him died tragically, including his wife and child. 🕮 Charles Richard Cammell, *Aleister Crowley* (1969)

Crowley, Bob (Robert) 1954–
English stage designer
He has worked at the Bristol Old Vic, the Royal Exchange, Manchester, and, in London, at the Greenwich Theatre and the National Theatre, where he designed **Bill Bryden**'s revival of *A Midsummer Night's Dream* (1982) and **Howard Davies**'s production of **Ibsen**'s *Hedda Gabler* (1989). Other stage work includes **Richard Eyre**'s productions of **David Hare**'s *Murmuring Judges* (1991) and **Tennessee Williams**'s *The Night of the Iguana* (1992), and **Edward Bond**'s *The Sea*. He has also worked extensively at the Royal Shakespeare Company. He is considered to be one of the finest of contemporary stage designers.

Crowther, Geoffrey Crowther, Baron 1907–72
English economist
Born in Claymont, Delaware, USA, he was educated at Leeds Grammar School, Oundle, and at Cambridge, Yale and Columbia universities. On the staff of *The Economist* from 1932, he was editor from 1938 to 1956. The *Crowther Report* (1959), produced during his period as chairman of the Central Advisory Council for Education (1956–60), held that 'the richest vein of untapped human resources' was those of middling ability; it recommended the raising of the school-leaving age to 16, the establishment of county colleges for those up to 17 not in full-time education, and more coherent, vocational education. It was the first British education report to seek systematic sociological answers and to consider the implications of economic and social change for the education of young people.

Crowther, Samuel Adjai 1809–91
African missionary
Born in Ochugu, West Africa, he was carried off as a slave in 1819, and sold more than once, but rescued by a British warship and put ashore at Sierra Leone in 1822. He was baptized in 1825, taking the name of a London vicar, ran a mission school at Regent's Town, and accompanied the Niger expeditions of 1841 and 1854. Ordained in London in 1842, he was consecrated Bishop of the Niger Territory in 1864. He translated the Bible into Yoruba.

Cruden, Alexander 1701–70
Scottish bookseller
He was born in Aberdeen and educated at the city's Marischal College. In 1732 he started as a bookseller in London. In 1737 he published his biblical *Concordance of the Holy Scriptures*. From then on he suffered frequent bouts of insanity. Working as a printer's proofreader he assumed

the title of 'Alexander the Corrector', and in 1755 began to travel the country denouncing Sabbath-breaking and profanity.

Cruft, Charles 1852–1939
English showman
He was for many years general manager of James Spratt, dog-biscuit manufacturers. He organized his first dog show in 1886, and the annual shows since then have become world-famous. Through his influence the popularity of dogs has increased and the standards of dog-breeding have been greatly improved.

Cruickshank, Andrew John Maxton 1907–88
Scottish actor
Born in Aberdeen, he made his London debut in the celebrated **Paul Robeson** production of *Othello* (1930). His many stage performances included *Dial M for Murder* (1952), *Inherit the Wind* (1960), *The Master Builder* (1962, 1972), *The Wild Duck* (1980) and his last in *Beyond Reasonable Doubt* (1987). His films included *The Cruel Sea* (1953) and *Richard III* (1955), but he gained his greatest renown on television as the gruff but kindly Dr Cameron in *Dr Finlay's Casebook* (1962–71). He also appeared on television in *Bleak House* (as John Jarndyce) and *The Old Men at the Zoo* (1983).

Cruikshank, George 1792–1878
English caricaturist and illustrator
Born in London, he illustrated some children's books and songs, and made his name as a political caricaturist with *The Scourge* (1811–16) and *The Meteor* (1813–14). He contributed coloured etchings to the *Humorist* (1819–21) and *Points of Humour* (1823–24), and his book illustrations included the etchings for *Peter Schlemihl* (1823) and **Grimm**'s *German Popular Stories* (1824–26). He also illustrated **Dickens**'s *Sketches by Boz* (1836) and *Oliver Twist* (1838), **Thackeray**'s *Legend of the Rhine*, and a series of books by **William Harrison Ainsworth**. From 1835 onwards he issued the *Comic Almanack*, one of the precursors of *Punch*. He devoted much of his later work to temperance, with a series of plates entitled *The Bottle* (1847), *The Drunkard's Children* (1848), and his cartoon *Worship of Bacchus* (1862). He is buried at St Paul's Cathedral. 🕮 Robert L Patten, *George Cruikshank's Life, Times and Art Volume 2: 1835–1878* (1996)

Cruise, Tom, *in full* Tom Cruise Mapother IV 1962–
US film actor
He was born in Syracuse, New Jersey, and after acting in high school plays moved to New York in 1980, making his film debut in *Endless Love* (1981). The success of the teen comedy *Risky Business* (1983) confirmed his stardom. A charismatic performer with a winning smile and great intensity, he has had many box-office successes including *Top Gun* (1986), *Rain Man* (1988), *A Few Good Men* (1992), *Mission Impossible* (1996) and *Jerry Maguire* (1996). He received a Best Actor Academy Award nomination for *Born on the 4th of July* (1989). He is married to actress Nicole Kidman (1967–), his co-star in *Days of Thunder* (1990), *Far and Away* (1992) and *Eyes Wide Shut* (1997).

Crum Brown, Alexander 1838–1922
Scottish chemist
Born in Edinburgh, he studied medicine at Edinburgh University, and in 1862 went to Germany to work with **Hermann Kolbe**. On his return he joined the chemistry department in Edinburgh, becoming professor in 1869, a position he held until 1908. His main interest was chemical structure, and he invented the 'ball and stick' graphical presentation of organic molecules, based on the earlier system of **Archibald Couper**. In addition, he devised 'Crum Brown's rule' to systematize the nomenclature of certain benzene compounds. He was also

interested in physiology, particularly the sensations of vertigo. Elected FRS in 1879, he served as president of the Chemical Society from 1891 to 1893.

Cruveilhier, Jean 1791–1874
French anatomist

Born in Limoges and educated at the University of Montpellier, he was a pioneer of the descriptive method, and the first to describe multiple sclerosis and progressive muscular atrophy ('Cruveilhier's paralyses'). He became Professor of Pathology at Montpellier in 1824 and of Anatomy at the University of Paris in 1825, then of Pathological Anatomy at Paris in 1836.

Cruyff, Johann 1947–
Dutch footballer

Born in Amsterdam, he became one of the great European forwards of his time. With Ajax Amsterdam he won three European Cup medals in succession and was European Footballer of the Year in 1973 and 1974. In 1974 he was captain of the Dutch side which lost to West Germany in the final of the World Cup. He afterwards moved to Barcelona, but he never quite recaptured the form of his earlier years in Holland. ⌨ Jacques Tilbert and Max Urbini, *Johan Cruyff, Superstar* (1975)

Cruz, Juan de la See John of the Cross, St

Cruz, Ramón de la, *properly* Ramón Francisco de la Cruz Cano y Olmedilla 1731–94
Spanish dramatist

He was born in Madrid. Although he began very much in the traditional neoclassicist mould, he subsequently turned to the popular portrayal of life in Madrid as encapsulated in the *sainete*, a short play or farce. He also wrote the libretti for many *zarzuelas* (light operas), again taking daily life in Madrid for his subject matter and transforming a genre whose subjects had previously been largely Classical gods and goddesses. He wrote over 400 sainetes (1786–91, 10 volumes), originating a strong tradition of which Carlos Arniches was to become the main inheritor.

Cruz, Sor Juana Inés de la 1648–95
Mexican feminist, poet and playwright

Born in San Miguel Nepantle, Amecameca, she was invited to live at the court after receiving attention for her scholarship. At the age of 19 she entered the Carmelite Order. However, the artificial rigour of this life revolted her, and she returned to court. A year later she joined the Hieronymite convent in Mexico City. When instructed by a bishop, an officer of the Inquisition, to give up learning as 'unbefitting to a woman' she issued the stately *Respuesta* (1691, 'Response'), a key document in the history of feminism. Her own parodic, mystical poetry, is individualistic, especially the 'Primero sueño' ('First Dream'). Her poems about male stupidity, in particular 'Rendonillas' ('Verses'), have hardly been forgiven, and have not been translated. Amongst the greatest and least understood of all writers, she sold all her books, scientific equipment and musical instruments, in order to care for the poor, and died of the plague while ministering to them. ⌨ E A Chávez, *Sor Juana dela Cruz* (1970); A Reyes, *The Position of America* (1950).

Čsiky, Gregor 1842–91
Hungarian dramatist

He was born in Pankota, Vilagos, and became Professor of Theology at Temesvar seminary. He published some tales from religious history ('Photographs from Life'), and in 1875 a comedy, *Jaslot* ('The Oracle'), which was a success. Other plays followed, including comedies like *Anna* (1883), and tragedies such as *Janus* (1877) and *A Mágusz* (1878, 'The Magician'). He also translated Sophocles, Plautus and Molière into Hungarian, as well as several English plays. *Az Ellenallhatatlan* ('The Irresistible'), which won a prize from the Hungarian Academy, typifies his talent for a direct, fresh approach to his subject. ⌨ G Hefedus, *Čsiky Gregor* (1953)

Čsokonai Vitéz, Mihály 1773–1805
Hungarian poet

Born in Debrecen, he was Professor of Poetry at the university there until his political sympathies lost him the post. His fame persists chiefly through his lyrics, which are based on old Hungarian folk-songs. Among his works are the drama *Tempefoi* (1793), the poems *Magyar-Musa* (1797) and *Dorottya* (1804), a mock-heroic poem. ⌨ V Julow, *Čsokonai Vitéz Mihály* (1975)

Ctesias 5th century BC
Greek historian and physician

He was physician to Artaxerxes II Mnemon of Persia, and accompanied him in the expedition against his rebellious brother Cyrus, the Younger (401BC). He wrote a history of Persia in 23 books, *Persika*, of which only some fragments remain.

Ctesibius 2nd century BC
Greek inventor

Born in Alexandria of Greek parents, he invented the force-pump and water organ, and improved the clepsydra or water-clock. He was the teacher of Hero of Alexandria.

Cubitt, Thomas 1788–1855
English builder

Born in Buxton, Norfolk, he revolutionized trade practices in the building industry, and was responsible for many large London projects, including Belgravia, and the east front of Buckingham Palace. ⌨ Hermione Hobhouse, *Thomas Cubitt: master builder* (1971)

Cubitt, Sir William 1785–1861
English civil engineer

Born in Dilham, Norfolk, he was a miller, a cabinet-maker and a millwright until 1812, and then chief engineer in Robert Ransome's Orwell Works at Ipswich, in which he was a partner (1821–26). He moved to London in 1823. The Bute Docks at Cardiff, the Southeastern Railway and the Berlin waterworks were constructed by him. He also invented the treadmill and was associated with the construction of the Great Exhibition buildings (1851). He was Lord Mayor of London in 1860–61, and Cubitt Town on the Isle of Dogs is named after him.

Cudworth, Ralph 1617–88
English philosopher and theologian

Born in Aller, Somerset, he was the leading member of the Cambridge Platonists. He became student, then Fellow, at Emmanuel College, Cambridge; Master of Clare Hall and Regius Professor of Hebrew (1645); rector of North Cadbury, Somerset (1650); and Master of Christ's College, Cambridge (1654), where he lived until his death. His monumental work, *The True Intellectual System of the Universe* (1678), was a systematic but unwieldy and uncompleted treatise which aimed to refute determinism and materialism and to establish the reality of a supreme divine Intelligence. An important work on ethics, directed against Thomas Hobbes, was published posthumously in 1731 as *Treatise Concerning Eternal and Immutable Morality*. ⌨ John Passmore, *Ralph Cudworth* (1951)

Cueva, Juan de la c.1550–1610
Spanish poet and dramatist

Born in Seville, he wrote a number of rather undistinguished poems, but is regarded as an important figure in the development of Spanish drama, writing such plays as *Tragedia de la muerte de Virginia* (1583, 'Tragedy of the Death of Virginia') and *La muerte del rey don Sancho* ('The Death of King Don Sancho'). He is particularly known for his use of new metrical forms, and for his introduction of historical material and overtly political themes into drama. ▭R F Glenn, *Juan de la Cueva* (1973)

Cugnot, Nicolas Joseph 1725–1804
French military engineer

Born in Void, he invented a three-wheeled steam-driven artillery carriage with a speed of 2–3mph (1.6–3.2kph) in c.1770. Lack of support prevented further development.

Cui, César Antonovich 1835–1918
Russian composer and engineer

Born in Vilna (now Vilnius, Lithuania), he was virtually self-taught as a musician and composed *William Ratcliff* (1861) and other operas. He was also an expert on fortification, and became lieutenant-general of engineers.

Cuijp, Albert See Cuyp, Albert

Cukor, George D(ewey) 1899–1983
US film director

He was born in New York City, and became involved with the theatre from an early age, making his Broadway debut with *Antonia* (1925). In Hollywood he worked as a dialogue director on *River of Romance* (1929) before making his directorial debut with *Grumpy* (1930). *A Bill of Divorcement* (1932) and *Little Women* (1938) began a 50-year association with Katharine Hepburn that resulted in a succession of polished entertainments including *The Philadelphia Story* (1940), *Adam's Rib* (1949) and *Love Among the Ruins* (1975). Drawn to sophisticated comedies and literary subjects, he enjoyed a reputation for his sensitive handling of many major stars in films like *Camille* (1936, with Greta Garbo), *The Women* (1939), *Gaslight* (1944, with Ingrid Bergman), *Born Yesterday* (1950, with Judy Holliday) and *A Star is Born* (1954, with Judy Garland). He won an Academy Award for *My Fair Lady* (1964).

Culkin, Macaulay 1980–
US film actor

Born in New York City, he made his film debut in *Rocket Gibraltar* (1988) and became a successful child star. Among his subsequent films are *Jacob's Ladder* (1990), *Home Alone* (1990), *Home Alone 2* (1992) and *The Good Son* (1993). Despite his youth, he is one of the most highly paid Hollywood stars.

Cullberg, Birgit Ragnhild 1908–
Swedish dancer, choreographer and ballet director

Born in Nyköping, she studied in England with Kurt Jooss, and later in New York with Martha Graham. In the mid-1940s she toured Europe with Svenska Dansteatern, a group she co-founded with Ivo Cramér. Her ballets are influenced by modern dance and characterized by their strong dramatic content, often of a psychological nature. Her best-known work, *Miss Julie*, dates from 1950. She was resident choreographer of the Royal Swedish Ballet (1952–57), after which she freelanced for companies including American Ballet Theatre and Royal Danish Ballet. She formed the Cullberg Ballet at the Swedish National Theatre in 1967, for which her sons Niklas and Mats Ek have danced and choreographed. She published *Ballet and Us* in 1954.

Cullen, Countee 1903–46
African-American poet

Born in New York City, the son of a Methodist Episcopal minister, he studied at New York University and Harvard. He began his literary career with *Color* (1925), a book of poems in which classical models such as the sonnet are used with considerable effect, and he became a leading figure in the Harlem Renaissance. He published several subsequent volumes of verse, and a novel, *One Way to Heaven* (1932), and collaborated with Arna Bontemps to write the play *St Louis Woman* (1946). ▭ M Perry, *A bio-bibliography* (1971)

Cullen, Paul 1803–78
Irish prelate

Born in Prospect, County Kildare, he studied at the College of Propaganda at Rome, and was ordained priest in 1829. He was successively Vice-Rector and Rector of the Irish College in Rome and Rector of the College of Propaganda. Consecrated Archbishop of Armagh and Primate of Ireland in 1850, he transferrred to Dublin in 1852, and helped to found the Catholic university in 1854 and Clonliffe College (the Dublin diocesan seminary) in 1859. His denunciations of Fenianism made him many enemies among activist Irishmen, but greatly increased the respect of English Protestants. He was the first Irishman to be created a cardinal priest (1866).

Cullen, William 1710–90
Scottish chemist and physician

Born in Hamilton, Lanarkshire, he obtained a post as ship's surgeon on a vessel bound for the West Indies, then returned to practise medicine in Hamilton, attending medical classes in both Edinburgh and Glasgow. In 1747 he began teaching chemistry in Glasgow with great success, being appointed to the chair in medicine in 1755. He also taught chemistry, materia medica and medicine in Edinburgh, and was the leading light of the Edinburgh Medical School during its golden age. He had hundreds of grateful and professionally successful pupils. He expounded his clinical ideas primarily through the nosologically arranged *First Lines of the Practice of Physic* (1778–79), which was frequently reprinted and translated during the next half-century. He emphasized the importance of the nervous system in the causation of disease, coining the word 'neurosis' to describe a group of nervous diseases, and bitterly opposed the Brunonian system (see John Brown, c.1735–1788).

Cullmann, Oscar 1902–
German biblical scholar and theologian

He was born in Strassburg (now Strasbourg, France). As professor at Basle (from 1938) and Paris (from 1948), he was the chief representative in New Testament studies of the 1950s and 1960s 'biblical theology' movement and an exponent of the concept of Salvation-history (*Heilsgeschichte*). In *Christ and Time* (1951), *Salvation in History* (1967) and *Immortality of the Soul or Resurrection of the Dead?* (1958), he maintains that biblical thinking is essentially historical—God reveals himself in historical events, not through the isolated personal challenges of Rudolf Bultmann's existential demythologizing approach. He has also written *The Christology of the New Testament* (1959), *Peter: Disciple, Apostle, Martyr* (1953), and several studies of early Church worship and practice.

Culmann, Karl 1821–81
German engineer

Born in Bergzabern, he graduated from the Polytechnikum in Karlsruhe, and from 1855 taught at the Polytechnic Institute in Zurich. His principal work was in graphical statics which he systematized and elevated into a major method of structural analysis, introducing the use of force and funicular polygons, and the method of sections.

Culpeper, Lord John See Colepeper, Lord John

Culpeper, Nicholas 1616–54
English physician

Born in London, he studied at Cambridge, and in 1640 started to practise astrology and medicine in Spitalfields, London. In 1649 he published an English translation of the College of Physicians' Pharmacopoeia, *A Physical Directory*, renamed in 1654 *Pharmacopoeia Londinensis, or the London Dispensatory*. This infringement of a close monopoly, together with his Puritanism, brought him many enemies. His *The English Physician Enlarged, or the Herbal* appeared in 1653. Both books had an enormous sale, the latter forming the basis of herbalism in the English-speaking world. ◻ Olav Thulesius, *Nicholas Culpeper, English Physician and Astrologer* (1992)

Cumberland, Richard 1631–1718
English philosopher and theologian
Born in London and educated at St Paul's School, London, and Magdalene College, Cambridge, he was successively rector of Brampton, Northamptonshire (1658), vicar of All Saints, Stamford (1667), and Bishop of Peterborough (1691). He is associated with the Cambridge Platonists. His *De legibus naturae* (1672, Eng trans *A Philosophical Enquiry into the Laws of Nature*, 1750) was written as a direct response to **Thomas Hobbes** and in some respects anticipated utilitarianism in recommending a principle of universal benevolence.

Cumberland, Richard 1732–1811
English playwright
Born in the lodge of Trinity College, Cambridge, the maternal grandson of **Richard Bentley**, he attended Westminster School, then returned to study at Trinity College, and was made a Fellow at the age of 20. Becoming private secretary to George Dunk, 2nd Earl of Halifax in 1761, he gave up his intention of taking orders, and was secretary to the Board of Trade from 1776 to 1782. Thereafter he retired to Tunbridge Wells, where he wrote farces, tragedies, comedies, pamphlets, essays and two novels, *Arundel* (1789) and *Henry* (1795). Of his sentimental comedies the best include *The Brothers* (1769), *The Fashionable Lover* (1772) and *The Wheel of Fortune* (1795). He was caricatured by **Richard Brinsley Sheridan** as Sir Fretful Plagiary in *The Critic*. ◻ S T Williams, *Richard Cumberland* (1917)

Cumberland, William Augustus, Duke of,
known as **the Butcher** 1721–65
English military commander
The third son of **George II** and Caroline of Ansbach, he was created duke in 1726. He was defeated at Fontenoy by Marshal **Saxe** in 1745, but nevertheless was sent to crush the 1745 Jacobite Rising in Scotland, which he achieved at Culloden (1746); his cruelties earned him the lasting title of 'Butcher'. In the latter stages of the War of the Austrian Succession he was defeated by Saxe at Langfeld (1747), and in the Seven Years War he had to surrender at Kloster-Zeven (1757), after which he retired. ◻ W A Speck, *The Butcher: The Duke of Cumberland and the Suppression of the 45* (1981)

Cumming See Comyn

cummings, e e, *properly* Edward Estlin Cummings 1894–1962
US writer and painter
Born in Cambridge, Massachusetts, he was educated at Harvard, and studied art in Paris. He is known for his verse, characterized by unusual typography and eccentric punctuations. His collections of poetry include *Tulips and Chimneys* (1923), and his best-known prose work, *The Enormous Room* (1922), describes his wartime internment—brought about by an error by the authorities—in France. He also wrote a travel diary, a morality play, *Santa Claus* (1946), and a collection of six 'non-lectures' delivered at Harvard entitled *i* (1953). A collection of his drawings and paintings was published in 1931. ◻ N Friedman, *The Growth of a Writer* (1964)

Cumyn See Comyn

Cunard, Sir Samuel 1787–1865
Canadian ship-owner
Born in Halifax, Nova Scotia, he succeeded early as a merchant and shipowner and emigrated to Great Britain in 1838. For the new steam rail service between Great Britain and the USA, he joined up with **George Burns** of Glasgow and David McIver of Liverpool to found (1839) the British and North American Royal Mail Steam Packet Company, later known as the Cunard Line. The first passage (1840) was that undertaken by the *Britannia*, in 14 days 8 hours.

Cunctator ('Delayer') See Fabius, Quintus Fabius Maximus Verrucosus

Cunegund, St See Kunigunde, St

Cunliffe, Barry (Barrington Windsor) 1939–
English archaeologist
Born in Portsmouth, he was educated at St John's College, Cambridge, then taught at Bristol and Southampton and in 1972 became Professor of European Archaeology at Oxford. Much influenced by **Mortimer Wheeler**, he has the same commitment to disciplined excavation and writing, and a flair for communication. An active field-worker even as a schoolboy, he established a reputation in his twenties with spectacular excavations at the Roman palace of Fishbourne near Chichester (1961–67). He has since worked at Roman Bath, and three sites in Wessex: the Roman fort of Portchester near Portsmouth, the Iron Age hillfort at Danebury near Stockbridge, and the late prehistoric trading settlement at Hengistbury Head near Christchurch. Among his general books are *The Celtic World* (1979), *Greeks, Romans and Barbarians* (1988), and *Wessex Before AD 1000* (1991).

Cunningham, Sir Alan Gordon 1887–1983
British general
Educated at Cheltenham College and the Royal Military Academy, Woolwich, he served with distinction in World War II. In 1941 he struck through Italian Somaliland from Kenya and freed Abyssinia and British Somaliland from the Italians. He was High Commissioner for Palestine (1945–48). His brother was Admiral Lord **Cunningham**.

Cunningham, Allan 1784–1842
Scottish poet and writer
He was born in the parish of Dalswinton, Dumfriesshire, and his father was a neighbour of **Robert Burns** at Ellisland. At the age of 10 he was apprenticed to a stonemason, but he became increasingly interested in songs and stories. His first publications were his old-ballad style poems and prose contributions to **Robert Cromek's** *Remains of Nithsdale and Galloway Song* (1810). Through James Hogg he met Sir **Walter Scott**, with whom 'Honest Allan' became a favourite. He moved to London, and became one of the best-known writers for the *London Magazine*, as well as manager of **Francis Chantrey's** sculpture studio (1815–41). Among his works are *Traditional Tales of the English and Scottish Peasantry* (1822), *Songs of Scotland, Ancient and Modern* (1825), *Lives of the most Eminent British Painters, Sculptors, and Architects* (6 vols, 1829–33) and a *Life of Wilkie* (3 vols, 1843). ◻ D Hogg, *The Life of Allan Cunningham* (1875)

Cunningham, Allan 1791–1839
English botanist and explorer
Born in Wimbledon, Surrey, he became clerk to the curator of Kew Gardens, and then plant collector for Sir **Joseph Banks**, first in Brazil and then, in 1816, in New South Wales, Australia. While searching for new specimens, Cunningham made many valuable explorations of the hinterland of New South Wales and Queensland, also visiting New Zealand and Norfolk Island before returning to Kew in 1831 to classify his specimens. Offered the

post of Colonial Botanist for New South Wales, he eventually accepted the invitation and returned to Sydney in 1837. He found that his duties included managing what he termed the 'Government Cabbage Garden' and growing vegetables for government officials, so he resigned and left for New Zealand, but returned to Sydney six months later. Many indigenous Australian trees now bear his name.

Cunningham (of Hyndhope), Andrew Browne Cunningham, 1st Viscount 1883–1963
British naval commander

The brother of Sir Alan Cunningham, he was educated at Stubbington and HMS *Britannia* at Dartmouth, and joined the navy in 1898. He commanded a destroyer in World War I, and in World War II he was Commander-in-Chief of British naval forces in the Mediterranean (1939–43). He defeated the Italian navy at Taranto (1940) and Cape Matapan (1941), and was in command of Allied naval forces for the invasion of North Africa (1942), and Sicily and Italy (1942). Promoted Admiral of the Fleet in 1943, he was First Sea Lord from 1943 to 1946.

Cunningham, E V See Fast, Howard Melvin

Cunningham, Imogen 1883–1976
US photographer

Born in Portland, Oregon, she worked with Edward Curtis before opening her own portrait studio in Seattle in 1910. Her personal style was pictorial romanticism, particularly in still-life flower studies. In 1915 she married a photographer, Roi Partridge, and moved to San Francisco, continuing the same photographic style until 1932, when she met Edward Weston and became part of his Group f/64, which insisted on sharply defined images and precise tonal gradation. After the break-up of the group she worked at her portrait gallery for almost 40 years more, and was still teaching at the Art Institute in San Francisco in her nineties.

Cunningham, John 1917–
English military and civil aircraft pilot

Born in Croydon, Surrey, he attended Whitgift School and was apprenticed to the De Havilland Aircraft Company at Hatfield (1935–38), joining the Auxiliary Air Force in 1935. He became a group captain in 1944, specializing in night defence against German bombers and earning the title 'Cat's Eyes Cunningham'. After World War II he became chief test pilot of the De Havilland Aircraft Company (1946–78), and was appointed chairman of the De Havilland Flying Foundation, founded in memory of Sir Geoffrey De Havilland, which gives grants to encourage young people to take part in flying.

Cunningham, Merce 1919–
US choreographer, dancer, teacher and director

Born in Centralia, Washington, he danced with the Martha Graham Dance Company (1939–45), began to choreograph in 1942, and gave his first solo concerts, with the composer John Cage, in 1944. His choreographic works include *Suite for Five* (1956), *Antic Meet* (1958), *Aeon* (1961), *Scramble* (1967), *Landrover* (1972), *Travelogue* (1977), *Duets* (1980) and *Loosestrife* (1991). In 1953 he founded the Merce Cunningham Dance Company. He is credited with redefining modern dance and developing a new vocabulary for it. He was awarded the US National Medal of Arts in 1990.

Cunninghame Graham, Robert Bontine
1852–1936
Scottish author and politician

Born in London, the grandson of the Scottish laird and songwriter Robert Cunninghame Graham (d.1797), he was educated at Harrow and from 1869 was chiefly engaged in ranching in Argentina, until he succeeded to the

family estates in 1883. In 1879 he had married a Chilean poetess, Gabriela de la Belmondiere. He was Liberal MP for North-West Lanarkshire (1886–92) and was imprisoned with the Socialist leader John Burns for 'illegal assembly' in Trafalgar Square during a mass unemployment demonstration in 1887. He was the first president of the Scottish Labour Party (1888). He travelled extensively in Spain and Morocco (1893–98), and wrote many travel books, but is best known for his highly individual, flamboyant essays and short stories, collections of which are entitled *Success* (1902), *Faith* (1909), *Hope* (1910), *Charity* (1912) and *Scottish Stories* (1914). He was elected the first president of the National Party of Scotland in 1928, and of the Scottish National Party in 1934. Joseph Conrad and W H Hudson were among his close literary friends. He died in Argentina, where he was known as 'Don Roberto'. 📖 A F Tschiffely, *Don Roberto: Tornado Cavalier* (1937)

Cunobelinus See Cymbeline

Cuomo, Mario Matthew 1932–
US politician

Born in the Queens borough of New York City, the son of Italian immigrants who ran a grocery store, he played minor-league baseball before deciding to study law. Admitted to the Bar in New York in 1956, he often served as an advocate for community groups on housing issues, and his energetic temperament and skills as a conciliator led him into state politics. During his three terms as Governor of New York (1983–95), he sought to strengthen the criminal justice system but opposed the death penalty, and despite his Catholic faith, he supported abortion rights. His powerful oratory, particularly his keynote address at the Democratic Convention in 1984, won him a national reputation; he was favoured to win the Democratic presidential nomination in 1988 and 1992, but declined to run.

Cupitt, Don 1934–
English theologian

Born in Oldham and educated at Cambridge, he was ordained to the Anglican priesthood in 1959. He followed an academic career and was appointed Vice-Principal of Westcott House, Cambridge, in 1962 and was Dean of Emmanuel College (1966–91). In addition to his teaching commitments at the university, he has been a prolific writer, often provoking controversial reaction to some of his more radical views. This was perhaps most notably illustrated by the response to *Sea of Faith* (1984), which was also a successful television series, demonstrating his ability to communicate theological concepts in terms accessible to a lay audience. Other works include *Christ and the Hiddenness of God* (1971), *Taking Leave of God* (1980), *The Long-Legged Fly* (1987), *The Time Being* (1992) and *The Last Philosophy* (1995).

Curie, Marie See panel p474

Curie, Pierre 1859–1906
French physicist and Nobel Prize winner

Born in Paris and educated at the Sorbonne, he was laboratory chief at the School of Industrial Physics and Chemistry until 1904, when he was appointed to a new chair in physics at the Sorbonne. With his brother Jacques, he discovered piezoelectricity in 1880 and used a piezo-electric crystal to construct an electrometer; this was later used by Pierre's wife Marie Curie in her investigations of radioactive minerals. In studies of magnetism, Pierre showed that a ferromagnetic material loses this property at a certain temperature—the 'Curie point'—and gained his doctorate for this work in 1895. Another of his important results in magnetism was 'Curie's law', which relates the magnetic susceptibility of a paramagnetic material to the absolute temperature. From 1898 he worked with his wife on radioactivity, and showed that the rays

---

Curie, Marie, *originally* Maria, *née* Skłodowska 1867–1934
Polish-born French physicist

Marie Curie was born in Warsaw and brought up in poor surroundings after her father, who had studied mathematics at the University of St Petersburg, was denied work for political reasons. After brilliant high school studies, she worked as a governess for eight years, during which time she saved enough money to send her sister to Paris to study. In 1891 she too went to Paris where she graduated in physics from the Sorbonne (1893) taking first place; she then received an Alexandrovitch Scholarship from Poland which allowed her to study mathematics.

She met **Pierre Curie** in 1894 and they married the following year. Together they worked on magnetism and radioactivity (a term she invented in 1898), and isolated radium, and polonium, which she named after her native Poland. They were jointly awarded the Nobel Prize for physics in 1903, with **Antoine Henri Becquerel**. After her husband's death in 1906 she succeeded him as Professor of Physics at the Sorbonne. She isolated pure radium in 1910, and received the 1911 Nobel Prize for chemistry.

During World War I she developed X-radiography and afterwards became director of the research department at the newly established Radium Institute in Paris (1918–34). She was also Honorary Professor of Radiology at Warsaw (1919–34). She died of leukaemia, probably caused by her long exposure to radioactivity. Her elder daughter was the nuclear physicist **Irène Joliot-Curie**; her second daughter Eve (1904–), became well known as a musician and writer, and in World War II worked in the USA on behalf of the French Resistance movement. She also wrote a biography of her mother.

📖 S Quinn, *Marie Curie: A Life* (1995); Eve Curie, *Madame Curie* (1937, Eng trans 1943) .

> 'In science, we must be interested in things, not in persons.'
> Quoted in Eve Curie, *Madame Curie* (1937, Eng trans 1943).

---

emitted by radium contained electrically positive, negative and neutral particles. With his wife and **Antoine Henri Becquerel** he was awarded the Nobel Prize for physics in 1903. 📖 Marie Curie, *Pierre Curie* (Eng trans 1923)

Curl, Robert Floyd, Jnr 1933–
US chemist and Nobel Prize winner

Born in Alice, Texas, he was educated at the William Marsh Rice University and the University of California at Berkeley. After working as a research fellow at Harvard (1957–58) he became assistant Professor of Chemistry at Rice University (1958–63), associate Professor (1963–67), then Professor (1967–). His research at the university with **Harold Kroto** and **Robert Smalley** led to the discovery of carbon C60 molecules named 'buckminsterfullerene' (known as 'buckyballs'), resulting in much further research. For this work Curl, with Kroto and Smalley, was awarded the 1996 Nobel Prize for chemistry.

Curlewis, Sir Adrian Herbert 1901–85
Australian judge, life-saver and administrator

Born in Sydney, the son of Judge Herbert Curlewis (1869–1942) and novelist **Ethel Turner**, he studied law at Sydney University, and was a judge of the New South Wales district court (1948–71). He was president of the Surf Life-Saving Association of Australia (1933–74, then life governor), and president of the International Council of Surf Life-Saving (1956–73). As chairman of the International Convention of Life-Saving Techniques in 1960, he was an outstanding advocate for the adoption of mouth-to-mouth resuscitation (the 'kiss of life' method) which has saved countless lives.

Curley, James Michael 1874–1958
US politician

Born into a working-class Irish Catholic family in Boston, Massachusetts, he joined the Democratic Party and cast himself as a champion of the immigrant poor. Between 1911 and 1950 he served as US congressman, Governor of Massachusetts, and Mayor of Boston. Elected four times to the mayor's seat, he served five months in prison for mail fraud during his final term, conducting city government from his cell.

Curran, John Philpot 1750–1817
Irish orator, lawyer and nationalist

Born in Newmarket, County Cork, he studied at Trinity College, Dublin, then spent two years at the Middle Temple, London, and in 1775 was called to the Irish Bar. There he earned a considerable reputation for his wit and powers of advocacy, but when he entered the Irish parliament in 1783 he met with less success. In the course of his turbulent career he fought five duels, all without serious injury. Although a staunch Protestant, he had much sympathy for his Catholic fellow countrymen, and strongly opposed the Union. He was master of the rolls in Ireland (1806–14), but towards the end of his life he suffered problems (relating to his daughter Sarah's secret engagement to **Robert Emmet**) and ill health. He moved to London in 1814.

Currie, Ken 1960–
Scottish painter

Born in North Shields, Tyne and Wear, he studied social sciences at Paisley College, then attended the Glasgow School of Art. He worked on two community-based films about Glasgow and the shipbuilding industry on the Clyde, which stimulated an interest in painting about Glasgow's social and industrial conditions. He is influenced by the social realist painters of the 19th century and by the 20th-century political realist art of Germany and Mexico. His most ambitious polemical work to date has been a series of murals for the People's Palace Museum in Glasgow, depicting the Socialist history of Glasgow.

Currier, Nathaniel 1813–88
US lithographer

Born in Roxbury, Massachusetts, he founded a lithography house in New York City in 1835, and in 1857 he entered into a partnership with James Merritt Ives (1824–95). Ives contributed drawings of his own, oversaw a staff of other artists, and chose subjects ranging from current events to country scenes. From 1840 to 1890 the firm produced more than 7,000 hand-coloured prints, now collectors' items, chronicling life in 19th-century America.

Curtin, John (Joseph Ambrose) 1885–1945
Australian Labor politician

Born in Creswick, Victoria, he was active in trade-union work, and edited a Perth newspaper. In 1928 he entered federal politics for Fremantle, Western Australia, and became leader of the Australian Labor Party in 1935. As Prime Minister (1941–45), he recognized Australia's vulnerable remoteness from Great Britain and placed it firmly under the control of the US forces during World War II, recalling Australian troops from the Middle East. He died in office and was succeeded first by his deputy **Frank Forde**, then by **Ben Chifley**.

Curtis, Charles 1860–1936
US politician

Born in Topeka, Kansas, he was one eighth Native American and lived briefly on the Kaw Reservation during his childhood. He served as a Republican congressman from Kansas (1892–1906), championing Native American rights and supporting farm and veterans' benefits. After several terms in the US Senate (1907–13, 1915–29), he served as the Vice-President (1929–33) under **Herbert Hoover**.

Curtis, Charles Gordon 1860–1953
US inventor

Born in Boston, he graduated at Columbia University as a civil engineer in 1881, then trained at the New York Law School before practising as a patent lawyer (1883–91). He is best known for his invention of the 'Curtis impulse steam turbine' in 1896, 12 years after the reaction turbine had been patented by Sir **Charles Parsons**. Present-day machines usually combine impulse and reaction stages for maximum efficiency.

Curtis, Edward Sheriff 1868–1952
US photographer and writer

Born in Madison, Wisconsin, he was brought up in Seattle, Washington. He devoted almost the whole of his career from 1896 to recording the North American peoples and their way of life, which was to vanish almost completely during the 35 years of his study. With financial assistance from **J Pierpoint Morgan**, he published the first of 20 volumes in 1907, combining evocative and detailed photographs with an equally informative text. In all, he took some 40,000 negatives, many hundreds of which were reproduced as large photogravure plates illustrating his volumes, the last of which appeared in 1930. In contrast to earlier US photographers who portrayed the Native Americans as warriors, Curtis stressed their peaceful arts and culture, perhaps in idealized terms.

Curtis, George William 1824–92
US writer

Born in Providence, Rhode Island, he spent four years in Europe (1846–50), then joined the staff of the New York *Tribune*, and became one of the editors of *Putnam's Monthly* (1852–69). He began the 'Editor's Easy Chair' papers in *Harper's Monthly* in 1853, and became principal leader-writer for *Harper's Weekly* on its establishment in 1857. A novel, *Trumps* (1862), and most of his other books first appeared in these journals. □W Payne, *Leading American Essayists* (1910)

Curtis, Heber Doust 1872–1942
US astronomer

Born in Muskegon, Michigan, he studied classics at Michigan University and then went on to teach classics, becoming Professor of Latin at Napa College, California. In 1897 he changed academic direction and became Professor of Mathematics and Astronomy at the University of the Pacific, subsequently moving to the Lick Observatory in California and then to Chile. In 1920 he became the director of the Allegheny Observatory and in 1930 director of Michigan University Observatory. From 1902 to 1909 he worked on **William Wallace Campbell**'s radial velocity programme, and thereafter concentrated on the photography and investigation of spiral nebulae. Curtis opposed **Harlow Shapley** in the 'great debate' of 1920 on the scale of the universe and was proved correct when, in 1924, **Edwin Hubble** demonstrated that the spiral Andromeda nebula lay well beyond our galaxy.

Curtis, Tony, *originally* Bernard Schwartz 1925–
US actor and painter

Born in New York, he served as a signalman during World War II and subsequently used the G I Bill Of Rights to study acting at the Dramatic Workshop in New York. He made his film debut in *Criss Cross* (1948) and quickly gained popularity as the athletic star of exotic adventure stories like *The Prince Who Was A Thief* (1950) and *Son of Ali Baba* (1952). A deft light comedian in films like *Some Like It Hot* (1959), he also proved himself a dramatic actor of merit in *Sweet Smell of Success* (1957), *The Boston Strangler* (1968) and *The Defiant Ones* (1958), for which he received an Academy Award nomination. Seen in increasingly unworthy roles, he found further popularity in such television ventures as *The Persuaders* (1971–72), *The Scarlett O'Hara War* (1980) and *Mafia Princess* (1986). He is also an accomplished painter. Actress Jamie Lee Curtis (1958–) is his daughter. □ With Barry Paris, *Tony Curtis—The Autobiography* (1994)

Curtis, Tony 1946–
Welsh poet

Born in Carmarthen, he was educated at University College, Swansea, and Goddard College, Vermont. He has published four collections of verse, a collection of prose-poems and short stories, two volumes of critical essays, and has edited several anthologies. A senior lecturer in English at the Polytechnic of Wales, he chaired The Welsh Academy from 1984 to 1987. In 1984 he won first prize in the National Poetry Competition.

Curtis, William 1747–99
English horticulturist and botanist

Born in Alton, Hampshire, he grew a collection of British plants on a plot of ground at Bermondsey, and established a botanic garden at Lambeth in 1777. He also established nurseries at Brompton and Chelsea, and became demonstrator and later director of the Chelsea Physic Garden (1772–77). His study of grasses led to the publication of *Enumeration of British Grasses* (1787) and *Hortus Siccus Gramineus* (1802). He began publication of the *Botanical Magazine*, the first periodical devoted exclusively to plants, in 1787. The work, consisting of a detailed description of a plant and a hand-coloured plate for each species, was extremely influential in the horticultural world and is still published today as *Kew Magazine*. His *Lectures in Botany* were published in 1802.

Curtiss, Glenn Hammond 1878–1930
US aviation pioneer and inventor

He was born in Hammondsport, New York. Originally a bicycle mechanic, he established a motorcycle factory in Hammondsport in 1902, and in 1905 set a world speed record of 137mph (220kph) on a motorcycle of his own design. He also designed motors for airships, and with **Alexander Graham Bell** formed the Aerial Experiment Association (1907). He gained the Scientific American award in 1908 for the first public flight of 0.62 miles (1km) in the USA with his third aeroplane, the *June Bug*, flying at 40mph (64.4kph). He won the James Gordon Bennett Cup in France in 1909 in his *Golden Arrow* at 46.65mph (75.1kph). In 1911 he invented the aileron, and also flew the first practical seaplane (Hydroplane) which he patented, as well as the flying boat. During World War I he produced military aircraft like the JN-4 (Jenny), the Navy-Curtiss flying boat, speedboats and Liberty engines. He was design adviser to his Curtiss Aeroplane and Motor Company at the time of his death.

Curtius, Ernst 1814–96
German archaeologist

He was born in Lübeck, the brother of **Georg Curtius**. He studied at Bonn, Göttingen and Berlin, visited Athens in 1837, and accompanied Karl Otfried Müller (1797–1840) in his travels through Greece. Tutor (1844–49) to Crown Prince Frederick of Prussia (the future **Frederick III**), he later became professor at Göttingen (from 1856) and then Berlin (from 1868). An energetic and careful excavator, he worked most notably at Olympia in Greece, under the auspices of the German Archaeological Institute

(1875–80), and later helped by young **Wilhelm Dörpfeld**. Over £30,000 was spent on the work, the expenses of the last season being borne personally by Emperor **Wilhelm I**.

Curtius, Georg 1820–85
German philologist

Born in Lübeck, he was the brother of **Ernst Curtius**. One of the greatest of Greek scholars, he was Professor of Classical Philology at Prague (1849), Kiel (1854) and Leipzig (1862–65). The most important of his many works were *Griechische Schulgrammatik* (1852, 'Textbook of Greek Grammar'), *Erläuterungen* (1863, 'To the Foregoing'), *Grundzüge der griechischen Etymologie* (1858, 'Fundamentals of Greek Etymology') and *Das griechisches Verbum* (1873–76).

Curtius, Mettus or Mettius 4th century BC
Roman hero

A noble youth, in 362BC he allegedly leapt on horseback into a chasm which had opened in the forum, and which the soothsayers declared could only be filled by throwing into it the most precious treasure of Rome.

Curtius, Theodor 1857–1928
German organic chemist

He was professor at Heidelberg from 1897, and became known especially for his discovery of hydrazine (1887) and other organic compounds.

Curwen, John 1816–80
English music theorist

Born in Heckmondwike, Yorkshire, the son of an Independent minister, he himself became an Independent minister at Plaistow in 1844. In 1841 he began to promote the sol-fa system, and in 1843 his *Grammar of Vocal Music* appeared. Resigning his ministry in 1864, he continued his work on the sol-fa system.

Curzon, Sir Clifford Michael 1907–82
English pianist

He was born in London and entered the Royal Academy of Music in 1919; he studied there with Charles Reddie, in Berlin with **Artur Schnabel**, and in Paris with **Wanda Landowska** and **Nadia Boulanger**. His repertory included the romantics, especially **Liszt**, but concentrated on Beethoven, Mozart and Schubert. He made a small number of famous recordings, including chamber music with Viennese groups. With **Solomon**, he is regarded as the finest British pianist of recent years. He was knighted in 1977.

Curzon (of Kedleston), George Nathaniel Curzon, Marquis 1859–1925
English statesman

Born in Kedleston Hall, Derbyshire, he was educated at Eton and Oxford. In 1886 he was elected MP for Southport, and the following year began extensive travels all over the East which provided material for three authoritative books, on Asiatic Russia (1889), on Persia (1892) and on problems of the Far East (1894). He became Under-Secretary for India in 1891, and for Foreign Affairs in 1895. In 1898, aged only 39, he became Viceroy of India and was given an Irish barony, having been unwilling to accept an English peerage with its accompanying bar from the House of Commons. A controversial and often turbulent viceroy, constantly at war with his officials, he introduced many reforms, both social and political, including the establishment of the NW Frontier Province and the partition of Bengal. After the arrival of Lord Kitchener as Commander-in-Chief in 1902, a difference of opinion arose which led to Curzon's resignation in 1905. He devoted himself to art and archaeology and to the question of university reform, returned to politics as Lord Privy Seal in the Coalition of 1915, and became a member of **David Lloyd George's** War Cabinet in 1916. In

1919 his long-standing ambition to become Foreign Secretary was fulfilled. On the resignation of **Bonar Law** in May 1923 he clearly hoped for and expected the premiership; the choice of **Stanley Baldwin** was a great blow, but he offered his support and continued as Foreign Secretary until 1924. He was created a marquis in 1921. 📖
Earl of Ronaldshay, *The Life of Lord Curzon* (3 vols, 1928)

Cusack, Cyril 1910–93
Irish actor, director and playwright

Born in Durban, South Africa, he was a child actor, appearing on stage from the age of seven and making his film debut in Knocknagow in 1918. A member of the Abbey Theatre (1932–45), he appeared in over 65 plays including the major works of **Sean O'Casey**, **J M Synge** and **George Bernard Shaw**. He subsequently formed his own company, touring Ireland and the world with a repertory of Irish and European plays. He received the International Critics award for his performance in **Samuel Beckett's** *Krapp's Last Tape* (1960) in Paris. London stage appearances include *The Physicists* (1963), *The Shaghraun* (1968) and *A Life* (1980). He was also known for telling cameo parts in films like *Odd Man Out* (1947), *Fahrenheit 451* (1966) and *Little Dorrit* (1988). Several members of his family have followed in his professional footsteps, including his daughter, actress Sinead Cusack (1948–).

Cusack, (Ellen) Dymphna 1902–81
Australian writer

Born in Wyalong, New South Wales, she was educated at Sydney University, and trained as a teacher. The first of her 12 novels, *Jungfrau*, was published in 1936 and dealt frankly (for its time) with sexual issues. This was followed in 1939 by *Pioneers on Parade*, written jointly with **Miles Franklin**. Illness forced her to retire from teaching in 1944. In 1948 she won the (Sydney) *Daily Telegraph* novel competition with *Come In Spinner*, the story of the lives of a group of women in wartime Sydney, written in collaboration with the New Zealand writer Florence James (1902–93). Its outspoken handling of adultery and abortion delayed its publication until 1951, and the full text was not published until 1988. Cusack wrote nine other novels and eight plays, which illustrate her preoccupation with social and political disadvantage. They have been translated into over 30 languages, and her plays have been broadcast on television. She also edited and introduced *Caddie, the Story of a Barmaid* (1953, filmed 1976).

Cushing, Caleb 1800–79
US politician

Born in Salisbury, Massachusetts, he was admitted to the Bar in 1821, sat in the state legislature and senate, and was elected to Congress (1835–43). He arranged the first treaty between China and the USA in 1844, and raised and commanded a regiment in the war with Mexico. He was US Attorney-General (1853–57), counsel for the USA at the Geneva Conference (1872), and Minister to Spain (1874–77).

Cushing, Harvey Williams 1869–1939
US neurosurgeon

Born in Cleveland, Ohio, he was educated at Yale and Harvard, became Professor of Surgery at Harvard (1912–32), served with the Army Medical Corps during World War I, and in 1933 became Sterling Professor of Neurology at Yale until his retirement in 1937. A talented and innovative neurosurgeon, he depended for much of his success on the important new techniques and procedures he developed to control blood pressure and bleeding during surgery. He discovered a new operative approach to the pituitary gland, and made a detailed study of its activity, characterizing the effects of underactivity, which caused dwarfism in a growing child, and of overactivity, which caused a form of gigantism in adults. He was also interested in the history of medicine and won a Pulitzer Prize in 1926 for his biography of the Canadian physician, Sir William Osler. 🕮 Elizabeth Harriet Thomson, *Harvey Cushing: Surgeon, Author, Artist* (1950)

Cushing, Peter 1913–94
English actor

Born in Kenley, Surrey, he studied at the Guildhall School of Music and Drama, and worked as an assistant stage manager at Worthing Repertory Company before making his stage debut in *The Middle Watch* (1935). A trip to the USA resulted in his Hollywood film debut in *The Man in the Iron Mask* (1939) and a New York stage appearance in *The Seventh Trumpet* (1941). After World War II he established himself as a classical actor with the Old Vic Company (1948–49) and was named Best Television Actor for his part in the television adaptation of George Orwell's *1984* (1955). However, lasting fame resulted from a long association with the gothic horror films produced by Hammer Films in which his cadaverous figure and gentlemanly manner brought conviction to a succession of misguided scientists and vampire hunters in films like *The Curse of Frankenstein* (1956), *Dracula* (1958) and *The Mummy* (1959). Other films include *Hamlet* (1948), *Dr Who and the Daleks* (1965), *Tales from the Crypt* (1972) and *Star Wars* (1977). He also enjoyed a long screen association with the character of Sherlock Holmes that included a 1968 television series and the film *The Hound of the Baskervilles* (1959). He published two volumes of autobiography: *An Autobiography* (1986) and *Past Forgetting* (1988).

Cushman, Charlotte Saunders 1816–76
US actress

Born in Boston, she appeared first in opera (1834), and as Lady Macbeth (1835). In 1844 she accompanied William Charles Macready on a tour through the northern states, and afterwards appeared in London, where she was well received in a range of characters that included Lady Macbeth, Rosalind, Meg Merrilies, and Romeo, with her sister Susan (1822–59) playing Juliet.

Custer, George Armstrong 1839–76
US soldier

Born in New Rumley, Ohio, he trained at West Point and served with distinction throughout the American Civil War (1861–65), becoming a brigadier general at the age of 23 (he returned to his permanent rank of captain at the war's end). From 1866 he commanded the 7th Cavalry against the Native American tribes of the Great Plains, and in 1874 he led an expedition that discovered gold in the Black Hills, which were sacred to the Cheyenne and the Sioux and protected by treaty. The gold rush that followed greatly escalated the conflict between Native Americans and whites and prompted the US government to adopt a more aggressive policy of removal. In 1876 Custer was ordered to lead the 7th Cavalry as part of a three-pronged campaign against an alliance of Cheyenne and Sioux organized by Sitting Bull, Crazy Horse and other chiefs. Discovering them in the valley of the Little Big Horn River (in present-day Montana), Custer attacked (25 June 1876) without waiting for reinforcements, pitting his regiment of 647 men against an army of thousands of warriors. He and his central unit of some 260 soldiers were surrounded and killed to the last man, an event that became known as 'Custer's Last Stand'. His death made him a legend, but many critics have called the attack vainglorious and suicidal. 🕮 Jay Monaghan, *Custer* (1959)

Cuthbert, St c.635–87
Anglo-Saxon bishop and missionary

Born probably in Lauderdale, in the Scottish Borders, he had a vision while working as a shepherd boy which made him resolve to become a monk. The same year (651) he entered the monastery of Old Melrose, and in 661 was elected prior. He travelled widely in the north of England as a missionary, and many miracles were reported. In 664 he left Melrose for the island monastery of Lindisfarne, of which he became prior, but in 676 left Lindisfarne for a hermit's cell built on Farne Island (Inner Farne). In 684 he reluctantly agreed to accept the bishopric of Hexham, but shortly after exchanged the see of Hexham for that of Lindisfarne. At the end of two years he returned to his cell, where he died. His body was elevated with a coffin-reliquary in 689, and the magnificent Lindisfarne Gospels book was made for the occasion. After many wanderings his body was finally buried in 999, in Durham, where, enclosed in an elaborate shrine, and believed to work many miracles daily, it remained until the Reformation. The grave was opened in 1826; inside the triple coffin his skeleton was found still apparently entire, wrapped in fives robes of embroidered silk. His feast day is 20 March. 🕮 Hilda Colgrave, *Saint Cuthbert of Durham* (1955)

Cuthbert, Betty, *known as* the Golden Girl 1938–
Australian sprinter

Born in the Merrylands district of Sydney, she won the Australian junior 100 metres title in 11.3 seconds at the age of 15. Shortly before the 1956 Olympic games, she broke the world record for the 200 metres, and went on to win Olympic gold medals for the 100 metres, 200 metres and 4 × 100 metres relay, setting three Olympic records and the world record for the relay. Over the next nine years she set 16 world records, 11 individual and 5 relay, culminating in a fourth gold medal (for the 400 metres) at the 1964 Olympics in Tokyo. The second woman to win four track gold medals (Fanny Blankers-Koen was the first), in 1981 she was diagnosed as having multiple sclerosis; she has since worked to raise public awareness of the disease.

Cuvier, Georges Léopold Chrétien Frédéric Dagobert, Baron 1769–1832
French anatomist

Born in Montbéliard, he studied for the ministry at Stuttgart but developed an interest in zoology while a tutor on the Normandy coast (1788–94). In 1795, through Étienne Geoffroy Saint-Hilaire, he was appointed Assistant Professor of Comparative Anatomy at the Jardin des Plantes at the Museum of Natural History in Paris, and in 1789 he became Professor of Natural History at the Collège de France. After the Restoration he was made Chancellor of the University of Paris, and admitted into the Cabinet by Louis XVIII. His opposition to the royal measures restricting the freedom of the press lost him the favour of Charles X, but under Louis Philippe he was made a peer of France in 1831, and Minister of the Interior in 1832. He worked hard for national education and the French Protestant Church. In his scientific work he originated the natural system of animal classification which anticipates the modern division of the animal kingdom into phyla. His studies of animal and fish fossils, through his reconstructions of the extinct giant vertebrates of the Paris basin, linked palaeontology to comparative anatomy. He was a militant anti-evolutionist, and accounted for the fossil record by positing 'catastrophism'—a series of extinctions due to periodic global floods after which new forms of life appeared. Cuvier's works include: *Leçons d'anatomie comparée* (1801–05, 'Lessons of Comparative Anatomy'), *L'Anatomie des mollusques* (1816, 'The Anatomy of Molluscs'), *Les Ossements fossiles des quadrupèdes* (1812, 'The Fossilized Bones of Quadrupeds'), *Histoire naturelle des poissons* (1828–49, 'The Natural History of Fish'), and *Le Règne animal distribué d'après son organisation* (1817, 'The Animal Kingdom

Distributes According to its Organization'). He is known as the father of comparative anatomy and palaeontology. 📖 William Coleman, *Georges Cuvier, Zoologist* (1964)

Cuvilliés, François de 1695–1768
Bavarian architect

Born in Belgium, he was taken as court dwarf and architect by **Maximilian II Emmanuel**, Elector of Bavaria, and trained in Paris under Jacques-François Blondel (1705–74). Becoming a leading exponent of the French Regency and Rococo styles in Bavaria, he employed natural motifs especially in the exquisitely refined Amalienburg Pavilion (1734–39) at Schloss Nymphenburg. He later adopted a heavier style, as seen in Residenztheater, Munich (1750–53), where a mass of rococo elements combine to produce a baroque heaviness. From 1738 he published a series of books of ornamental design which were influential throughout the Empire.

Cuyp or Cuijp, Albert 1620–91
Dutch painter

Born in Dordrecht, he travelled along his local rivers making sketches and studies from nature, but unlike many of his peers never went to Italy. Although he had little influence on the history of Dutch painting, he is widely regarded as one of the greatest Dutch landscapists. He excelled at depicting sunlight in scenes of munching cattle. He painted very little in the last decade of his life after marrying into a rich family. During the 18th and 19th centuries he was particularly appreciated in England, with the result that a great number of his works are still in English collections.

Cymbeline or Cunobelinus fl.c.5–41AD
British chief of the Catevellauni tribe

He is described by **Suetonius** as 'rex Britannorum' ('King of Britain'). Several of his coins are extant. **Shakespeare's** Cymbeline is loosely based on him, following his portrait in the chronicles of **Raphael Holinshed**.

Cynewulf c.700–c.800
Anglo-Saxon poet and scholar

He came from Mercia or Northumberland. The works attributed to him are now restricted to four poems which have his name worked into their runic inscriptions: *The Ascension of Christ* and *Elene* in the *Exeter Book*, and *St Juliana* and *The Fates of the Apostles* in the *Vercelli Book*.

Cyprian, St, properly Thascius Caecilius Cyprianus c.200–58AD
North African Christian and Father of the Church

Born probably in Carthage, Tunisia, he taught rhetoric there, and became a Christian in c.245AD. He was made Bishop of Carthage in 248, and became unpopular because of his efforts to restore strict discipline. In the persecution under **Decius** he had to leave home, but returned to Carthage in 251. Excommunicated by Pope Stephen I (d.257) for denying the validity of heretic baptism, at a synod in Carthage in 256 Cyprian maintained that the Roman bishop, in spite of **St Peter's** primacy, could not claim judicial authority over other bishops. He was martyred during the reign of **Valerian**. He wrote a treatise on church unity called *De unitate ecclesiae*. His feast day is 6 September. 📖 J A Faulkner, *Cyprian: The Churchman* (1977)

Cypselus fl.c.657–625BC
Tyrant of Corinth

He was one of the earliest self-made rulers who arose in many Greek cities in the 7th and 6th centuries. He seized power from the Bacchiads who had ruled Corinth since the 8th century, and founded the Cypselid dynasty. The earliest account of his rule in **Herodotus** is unfavourable, yet there are indications that Cypselus's rule enjoyed some popular support. He founded colonies in north-west

Greece, exported large amounts of local pottery, and cultivated good relations with the Oracle of Apollo at Delphi. He was succeeded by his son **Periander**.

Cyrankiewicz, Jozef 1911–89
Polish statesman

Born in Tarnow, he studied in Kraków, where he became Secretary of the Socialist Party in 1935. Taken prisoner by the Germans in 1939, he escaped and organized resistance in the Kraków Province, but was sent to Auschwitz in 1941. In 1945 he became Secretary-General of the Socialist Party and was Prime Minister from 1947 to 1952. He resumed the premiership from 1954 to 1970, then became chairman of the Council of State (1970–72) and, from 1973, of the All-Poland Peace Committee.

Cyrano de Bergerac, Savinien 1619–55
French writer and dramatist

He was born in Paris. As a soldier, in his youth he fought more than a thousand duels, mostly on account of his monstrously large nose. His works, often crude, but full of invention, vigour, and wit, include a comedy, *Le Pédant joué* (1654, 'The Pedant Outwitted') and the satirical science fantasies *Histoire comique des états et empires de la lune et du soleil* (1656 and 1662, Eng trans, 1 vol *Voyages to the Moon and the Sun*, 1754). He was the subject of **Edmond Rostand's** play, *Cyrano de Bergerac* (1897). 📖 E Harth, *Cyrano de Bergerac and the politics of modernity* (1970)

Cyril of Alexandria, St AD 376–444
Greek theologian and a Doctor of the Church

Born in Alexandria, he succeeded his uncle, Theophilus, as Patriarch of Alexandria (AD412), and vigorously implemented orthodox Christian teaching. He expelled the Jews from the city (415), and relentlessly persecuted the Patriarch of Constantinople, **Nestorius** (d.451), who was deposed at the Council of Ephesus (431). Pope **Leo XIII** declared him a Doctor of the Church in 1882. Among his extant works are a defence of Christianity, written against the Emperor **Julian** in 433, and a series of homilies and treatises on the Trinity, the Incarnation, and the worship of God in spirit and in truth. His feast day is 9 or 27 June.

Cyril of Jerusalem, St c.315–86AD
Middle Eastern Christian ecclesiastic and Doctor of the Church

Born in Jerusalem, he was ordained a presbyter in c.345AD, and in 351 Bishop of Jerusalem. He was twice expelled from his see, in 358 and by a synod at Constantinople (Istanbul) in 360, but on the accession of **Julian**, the Apostate, in 361 he resumed his duties till 367, when, by order of Valens, he was again expelled. He returned again on the death of Valens in 378, and took part, on the Orthodox side, in the second Council of Constantinople. He was the author of 23 *Katéchéseis* (instructions to catechumens). His feast day is 18 March.

Cyril 827–69 and Methodius 826–85, Saints, known as the Apostles of the Slavs
Greek Christian missionaries

They were born in Thessalonica. Cyril, traditionally the inventor of the Cyrillic alphabet, first worked among the Tartar Khazars (c.860), and Methodius among the Bulgarians of Thrace and Moesia (c.863). In Moravia they made Slav translations of the Scriptures and chief liturgical books, for which they were summoned to Rome to explain. After Cyril's death, Methodius continued as Bishop of Moravia to evangelize the Slavs, and he gained the approval of Pope John VIII when he was called to Rome (879) to justify his celebration of the Mass in the native tongue. Their feast day is 7 July.

Cyrrhestes See Andronicus

Cyrus the Great c.600–529BC
Founder of the Persian Empire

He was a cousin of **Darius** I. In c.550BC, he made Astyages, last King of Media, a prisoner, and took his capital, Ecbatana. By 548BC he was King of Persia (Iran), and with the support of the tribes on 'the Lower Sea', or Persian Gulf, he took Sippara (Sepharvaim) and Babylon itself (539BC). Cyrus, a polytheist, at once began a policy of religious conciliation, restoring enslaved nations, including the Jews, to their native countries, and granting them religious freedom. The empire of Lydia had fallen to Cyrus (c.546BC), and by 539BC he ruled Asia from the Mediterranean to the Hindu Kush. His friendliness towards the Phoenicians and Jews led to his being called, in the Old Testament, the 'Shepherd' and the 'Anointed of Jehovah'. He extended his empire from the Arabian desert and the Persian Gulf in the south, to the Black Sea, the Caucasus and the Caspian in the north. He became the epitome of the heroic conqueror: brave, magnanimous and tolerant. Cambyses II became King of Babylon. The *Cyropaedia* of **Xenophon** is a historical romance drawn from his life. ▢ Harold Lamb, *Cyrus the Great* (1976)

Cyrus, the Younger 424–401BC
Persian prince and satrap

He was the second son of the Achaemenid King **Darius II Ochus**. He was accused of conspiring against his brother, **Artaxerxes II Mnemon**, and was sentenced to death (404BC), but was afterwards pardoned and restored as Satrap of Asia Minor. In 401 he led an army of Greek mercenaries (which included Xenophon) against his brother, but was killed at Cunaxa.

Czartoryski, Adam Jerzy 1770–1861
Polish politician

Born in Warsaw, he was educated at Edinburgh and London. He fought against Russia in the Polish insurrection of 1794, and, sent to St Petersburg as a hostage, gained the friendship of the Imperial Grand Duke Alexander (later **Alexander** I) and the confidence of the Emperor **Paul**, who made him ambassador to Sardinia. When Alexander ascended the throne he appointed him assistant to the Minister of Foreign Affairs. As curator of the University of Wilno (1803) he exerted all his influence to keep alive a spirit of nationality, and when some of the students were sent to Siberia, he resigned his office. During the Revolution of 1830 he was elected president of a provisional government, and summoned a national diet which in January 1831 declared the Polish throne vacant and elected Czartoryski head of the national government. He immediately devoted half of his large estates to the public service, and, though in August he resigned his post, continued to fight as a common soldier. After the suppression of the rising, Czartoryski—excluded from the amnesty and with his Polish estates confiscated—escaped to Paris, where he afterwards lived, the liberal friend of his poor expatriate countrymen. In 1848 he freed all his serfs in Galicia, and during the Crimean War he tried to induce the allies to identify the cause of Poland with that of Turkey. He refused the amnesty offered to him by **Alexander II**.

Czerny, Karl 1791–1857
Austrian pianist and composer

Born in Vienna, he studied under **Beethoven** and **Muzio Clementi**, and himself taught **Franz Liszt**, Thelberg and Döhler. His piano exercises and studies were widely used.

Dacko, David 1930–
Central African Republic politician

Born in M'Baiki, he became the first President of the Central African Republic in 1960, after the accidental death of his uncle, the president-designate Barthelemy Boganda, who had been a leading campaigner for independence. Dacko was overthrown by **Jean Bédel Bokassa** in 1965. In 1976 he agreed to return as Bokassa's adviser, and ousted him in turn, with French help, in 1979. He was re-elected President for a six-year term in 1981, but within seven months was removed by the army Chief of Staff, **André Kolingba**.

Dacre, Winifred See **Nicholson, Winifred**

Dadd, Richard 1819–87
English painter

Born in Chatham, Kent, he travelled extensively in Europe and the Middle East. In 1843 he suffered a mental breakdown and murdered his father. He was sent first to the asylum of Bethlem, where he spent 20 years, and subsequently to Broadmoor. He is best known for the fantastically detailed fairy paintings which made up the bulk of his output after his incarceration; *The Fairy-Feller's Master Stroke* (1855–64) is a typical example.

Dafydd ap Gruffydd d.1283
Welsh prince

The brother of Llywelyn ap Gruffydd, he opposed his brother's accession, but eventually supported him in his battles with the English. He succeeded his brother as Prince of Gwynedd in North Wales (1282), but was betrayed and executed (1283), the last native prince of Wales.

Dafydd ap Gwilym c.1315–c.1370
Welsh poet and bard

Born near Aberystwyth, of noble birth, he introduced many elements of European writing into Welsh verse while managing to bring Welsh verse into the European mainstream. A poet in the wandering bard tradition, he wrote verse set in forests and peopled with birds and animals. Often hailed as the greatest of Welsh poets, he is sometimes credited with having invented the *cywydd* form of verse; he was certainly responsible for its becoming the dominant form in Welsh verse after his time. ▢ R Loomis (ed), *Dafydd ap Gwilym: The Poems, Translation and Commentary* (1982); T Parry, *History of Welsh Literature* (1955)

---

da Gama, Vasco See **Gama, Vasco da**

Dagover, Lil, *originally* Marie Antonia Sieglinde Marta Liletts 1897–1980
Dutch actress

Born in Java, where her Dutch father was a forest ranger, she was educated in Germany. She married the veteran actor Fritz Dagover (1872–1936) at the age of 20 and appeared in German films beginning with **Fritz Lang**'s *Harakiri* (1919), closely followed by Robert Weine's Expressionist classic *Das Kabinett des Dr Caligari* (1919, *The Cabinet of Dr Caligari*). Specializing in playing threatened heroines, she starred in many German films, as well as working in Sweden (1926–27) and France (1928–29). Her only US film was *The Woman from Monte Carlo* (1931). An important star in German Expressionist cinema, she continued acting until just before her death.

Daguerre, Louis Jacques Mandé 1789–1851
French photographic pioneer and painter

Born in Cormeilles, he became a scene painter for the opera in Paris. From 1826 onwards, and partly in conjunction with **Joseph Nicéphore Niepce**, he perfected his 'daguerrotype' process, in which a photographic image is obtained on a copper plate coated with a layer of metallic silver sensitized to light by iodine vapour. This reduced the exposure time required to produce an image from around eight hours for Niepce's original method to around 25 minutes. ▢ Helmut and Alison Gernsheim, *L J M Daguerre* (2nd rev edn, 1968).

Dahl, Anders 1751–87
Swedish botanist

He was a pupil of **Carolus Linnaeus**, and the genus *Dahlia* is named after him.

Dahl, Johann Christian Clausen 1788–1857
Norwegian landscape painter

He was the pioneer of a spirit of nationalism in Norwegian art, and his sketches, made in both Norway and in Italy, are also highly regarded. From 1821 until his death, he was Professor of Painting at the Academy in Dresden.

Dahl, Michael 1656–1743
Swedish portrait painter

Born in Stockholm, he settled in London in 1688, and painted royalty and other notables. His works can be seen in the National Portrait Gallery, London.

Dahl, Roald 1916–90
British children's author, short-story writer, playwright and versifier

He was born in Llandaff, Glamorgan, of Norwegian parents. His first stories were based on his wartime experiences in the RAF and were collected in *Over to You* (1946). He specialized in the macabre, and subsequent collections achieved enormous success: *Someone Like You* (1954), *Kiss, Kiss* (1960) and *Switch Bitch* (1974). Although he is among the most popular children's authors of all time, many parents, teachers and librarians disapprove of his anarchic rudeness and violence. *Charlie and the Chocolate Factory* (1964) is his best-known children's book and was successfully filmed. Others include *James and the Giant Peach* (1961, filmed 1996), *The Enormous Crocodile* (1978), *The BFG* (1982), *Matilda* (1988) and *EsioTrot* (1990). *The Minpins* and *The Vicar of Nibbleswick* were published posthumously in 1991. He also wrote the screenplays for *You Only Live Twice* (1967) and *Chitty Chitty Bang Bang* (1968), and a number of his stories were adapted for television as *Tales of the Unexpected*. ▢ *Boy* (1984); *Going Solo* (1986)

Dahlgren, John Adolphus Bernard 1809–70
US naval commander

Born in Philadelphia, he joined the navy in 1826 and founded an ordnance workshop in Washington DC. There he designed a new type of naval gun (1850), called the Dahlgren gun. Promoted rear-admiral, he commanded the South Atlantic blockade squadron in the Civil War (1863–65).

Dahmer, Jeffrey Lionel 1960–94
US serial killer

Born in Milwaukee, Wisconsin, he began drinking heavily at the age of 14 and murdered his first victim shortly after leaving high school. He joined the US army in January 1979 but by 1981 had been discharged for excessive drinking. He turned to killing again, murdering and dismembering young men and dissolving their bodies in acid. On capturing Dahmer in his flat at Oxford

Apartments in 1991, the police discovered the remains of at least 11 people in a barrel, the fridge, and the filing cabinet. He admitted to acts of dismemberment, necrophilia and cannibalism to 17 men and boys, and at his trial in 1992 he was sentenced to 15 life sentences. In 1994 he was beaten to death by a fellow prisoner.

Dahn, (Julius Sophus) Felix 1834–1912
German historian and poet

Born in Hamburg, he was educated at Munich and Berlin, and became Professor of German Jurisprudence at Königsberg and Breslau (now Wrocław, Poland). He wrote a number of novels, plays and books of poetry, and a notable history, *Die Könige der Germanen* (1861–1911, 'The Kings of the Germanic People').

Dahrendorf, Ralf Gustav Dahrendorf, Baron 1929–
British sociologist

Born in Hamburg, and educated at Hamburg University and the London School of Economics, he held posts at universities in Germany and the USA in the 1950s and 1960s. His works include *Class and Class Conflict in Industrial Society* (1957) and *Society and Democracy in Germany* (1965). In 1967 he joined the liberal Free Democrats (FDP) and briefly represented the party in the federal Bundestag and Baden-Württemberg Landtag. He was a member of the European Community Commission (1970–74) and then moved to the UK to become director of the London School of Economics (1974–84). He wrote *Life Chances* (1980), which stresses the need to broaden the range of opportunities available to each individual. In 1987 he was appointed warden of St Anthony's College, Oxford, and in 1996 announced that he would step down the following year. Included in his many publications is *LSE* (1995), a study of the London School of Economics from 1895 to 1995. He was knighted in 1982 and made a life peer in 1993. He adopted British nationality in 1988.

Dai, Ailian (Tai Ai-lien) 1916–
Chinese dancer and choreographer

Born in Trinidad, she studied during the 1930s in Great Britain with **Anton Dolin**, **Kurt Jooss** and **Rudolf von Laban**. She has been instrumental in bringing the principles and study of western ballet to China. Working in China from 1940, she performed in dance recitals with various groups before securing leading directorial positions in several companies and institutions, including the Central Song and Dance Ensemble (1949–54) and the Beijing (Peking) Dance Academy (1954–64). In 1959 she co-founded what is now known as the Central Ballet of China, originally an offshoot of the academy's Experimental Ballet Society. She is the company's artistic adviser, and a member of the All-China Dance Association and the International Council of Kinetography/Labanotation.

Daiches, David 1912–
Scottish critic

Born in Sunderland, the son of a rabbi, he was brought up in Edinburgh, and educated at Edinburgh University. He did research on English translations of the Hebrew Bible at Oxford before moving to Chicago University in 1937. He served in the British Embassy in Washington during World War II, then returned to academic life at Cornell University (1947–51), taught at Cambridge (1951–61), and was Professor of Literature at the University of Sussex (1961–77), before retiring to Edinburgh. He was then Director of the Institute for Advanced Studies in the Humanities at Edinburgh University (1980–86). He made many valuable contributions to literary criticism, especially in his insistence on the inclusion of modern literature within the academic syllabus. His works include a book on **Robert Burns** (1950, rev edn 1966), the first

serious study on the poet that incorporates the broader literary and intellectual movements of the period; a provocative study of the Scottish Enlightenment, *The Paradox of Scottish Culture* (1964); and an autobiographical account of his upbringing in Edinburgh, *Two Worlds* (1956). More recently he published *A Weekly Scotsman and other poems* (1994).

d'Ailly, Pierre See **Ailly, Pierre d'**

Daimler, Gottlieb Wilhelm 1834–1900
German engineer and inventor

He was born in Schorndorf, and studied engineering at the Stuttgart Polytechnic Institute. From 1872 he worked on improving the gas engine. In 1885 he built one of the earliest roadworthy motor cars, using a high-speed internal combustion engine, and in 1890 he founded the Daimler-Motoren-Gesellschaft in Cannstatt. 📖 Anthony Bird, *Gottlieb Daimler, Inventor of the Motor Engine* (1962)

Dainton (of Hallam Moors), Frederick Sydney Dainton, Baron 1914–97
English physical chemist and administrator

Born in Sheffield, he was educated at Oxford and then Cambridge, where he was appointed H O Jones Lecturer in Physical Chemistry (1946). From 1950 to 1973 he held professorships in chemistry at the universities of Leeds and Oxford, and was Vice-Chancellor of the University of Nottingham. He chaired the University Grants Committee (1973–78) and the British Library Board (1978–85), and was also chairman/president of the Faraday Society (1965–67), the British Association for the Advancement of Science (1980), and other bodies. His numerous honours include the Tilden (1950) and Faraday (1973) medals of the Chemical Society and the Davy medal of the Royal Society (1969). Knighted in 1971, he was created a life peer in 1986. His contributions to physical chemistry were in the areas of chemical kinetics, photochemistry and radiation chemistry.

Dakin, Henry Drysdale 1880–1952
English chemist

Born in London, he was trained in Marburg under **Albrecht Kossel** before returning to work at the Lister Institute where he independently synthesized adrenaline (1906). He carried out extensive research on the oxidation processes of the body (1908–12). After World War I, he emigrated to the USA and joined the staff of the Rockefeller Institute, New York, where he made early contributions to the understanding of protein structure. His most enduring contribution came from his study of antiseptics; 'Dakin's' or the 'Carrel–Dakin' solution (a 0.5 per cent solution of sodium hypochlorite) was widely used for treating wounds during the two world wars and is still used extensively as a safe, cheap sterilizing agent today. He was elected FRS in 1917.

Daladier, Édouard 1884–1970
French politician

He was born in Carpentras. He became leader of the radical socialists in 1927, and in 1933 Minister of War and Prime Minister of a short-lived government. Again Minister of War, he was asked to form a Cabinet in 1934, but his government immediately met the full force of the repercussions of the **Stavisky** crisis, and lasted only a few weeks. In 1936 he became War Minister in the Popular Front Cabinet, and in 1938 again took office as premier. Pacifist in outlook, he supported 'appeasement' and was a signatory of the Munich Pact. In 1940 he resigned, became successively War Minister and Foreign Minister, and on the fall of France was arrested and interned until 1945. 📖 André Geraud, *The Gravediggers of France* (1944)

Dalai Lama See panel p482

Dalai Lama, *originally* Tenzin Gyatso 1935–
Spiritual and temporal head of Tibet

Tenzin Gyatso was born into a peasant family in Taktser, Amdo province, and was designated the 14th incarnation of the Dalai Lama by the monks of Lhasa in 1937. He was enthroned in 1940, but his rights were exercised by a regency until 1950. He fled to Chumbi in southern Tibet after an abortive anti-Chinese uprising in 1950, but negotiated an autonomy agreement with the People's Republic the following year and for the next eight years served as nominal ruler of Tibet.

After China's suppression of the Tibetan national uprising in 1959 he was forced into permanent exile, and settled with other Tibetan refugees at Dharamsala in Punjab, India, where he established a democratically based alternative government and sought to preserve Tibetan culture. A revered figure in his homeland, the Dalai Lama has continually rejected Chinese overtures to return home as a figurehead, seeking instead full independence. In 1988 he modified this position, proposing the creation of a self-governing Tibet in association with China. The following year he was awarded the Congressional Human Rights award and the 1989 Nobel Prize for peace in recognition of his commitment to the non-violent liberation of his homeland.

📖 The Dalai Lama has written a number of books on Buddhist philosophy, as well as *My Land and People* (1961) and the autobiographical *Freedom in Exile* (1990). See also Claude B Levenson, *The Dalai Lama: A Biography* (1989) and M H Goodman, *The Last Dalai Lama* (1986).

> 'Frankly speaking, it is difficult to trust the Chinese. Once bitten by a snake, you feel suspicious even when you see a piece of rope.' Quoted in the *Observer Colour Magazine*, 5 April 1981.

Daldry, Stephen 1961–
English theatre director

He studied at Sheffield University, then ran away with a circus to Italy. On his return he was an associate director of the Metro Theatre (1984–86) and of the Sheffield Crucible Theatre (1986–88), then artistic director of the Gate Theatre in Notting Hill, London (1989–92). There he began to win awards for his work, which included *Damned for Despair* (1991). In 1992 he joined Max Stafford-Clark at the Royal Court Theatre, succeeding him officially as artistic director in 1993. His many successful productions include *An Inspector Calls* (1992), which won a Laurence Olivier award. It also won a Tony award for Best Revival when it was taken to Broadway in 1994. He left the Royal Court Theatre in 1997 to work for Working Title Films.

Dale, David 1739–1806
Scottish industrialist and philanthropist

Born in Stewarton, Ayrshire, he was apprenticed to a Paisley weaver and became a clerk to a Glasgow silk merchant. In 1763 he set up his own business in Glasgow, importing linen yarn from Holland and Flanders. He was a founder-member in 1768 of an independent dissenting sect, the 'Old Scotch Independents', who were firm believers in practical Christianity, and became their best-known lay preacher. In 1777 he married the daughter of an Edinburgh director of the Royal Bank of Scotland, and was appointed the first Glasgow agent of the bank (1783). In 1784 he met Richard Arkwright and set up a business partnership to build cotton mills at New Lanark; but the partnership was dissolved in 1785 when Arkwright lost his legal battle over patents for his 'water-frame' machines. Spinning began at New Lanark in 1786, followed by a mill at Blantyre in 1787. From 1791 he gave work and housing at New Lanark to destitute would-be emigrants from the Western Isles shipwrecked off the west coast, and started industrial ventures to provide more work, with spinning mills at Spinningdale in Sutherland and at Oban. He also employed hundreds of pauper children from Edinburgh and Glasgow at New Lanark, providing a school as well as accommodation for them. He became one of the first directors of the Glasgow Royal Infirmary in 1795, which was opened that year to help the sick and diseased poor. In 1799 he sold the New Lanark mills, with their tradition of benevolent management, to his son-in-law, Robert Owen.

Dale, Sir Henry Hallett 1875–1968
English physiologist and Nobel Prize winner

Born in London, he was educated at Cambridge and London, and became director of the National Institute for Medical Research, London, in 1928. He discovered acetylcholine, and in 1936 he shared with Otto Loewi the Nobel Prize for physiology or medicine for work on the chemical transmission of nerve impulses.

---

d'Alembert, Jean le Rond See Alembert, Jean le Rond d'

Dalén, Nils Gustav 1869–1937
Swedish physicist, engineer and Nobel Prize winner

Born in Stenstorp, he graduated as a mechanical engineer from the Chalmers Institute in Göteborg (1896), and after a year of further training in Zurich returned to Sweden to experiment on hot-air turbines, compressors and air-pumps. From 1900 to 1905 he was a member of Dalén and Alsing, the engineering firm founded to exploit inventions, then worked for the Swedish Carbide and Acetylene Company (later called the Swedish Gas Accumulator Company), becoming its managing director in 1909. He invented lighthouses, and buoys, and also invented a valve enabling the light to be flashed in such a way that the light source's location could be identified. To conserve acetylene, he produced a sun-valve that extinguished the flame during daylight hours. He was awarded the 1912 Nobel Prize for physics, but was unable to attend the award ceremony due to a serious accident, in which he lost his sight.

Daley, Richard Joseph 1902–76
US Democratic politician

Born in Chicago, he grew up in an Irish neighbourhood and worked in the Chicago stockyards before entering Illinois state politics in the 1930s. As Mayor of Chicago (1955–76) he sponsored extensive programmes of public works and made alliances with organized labour. He was an old-fashioned machine politician, and he wielded considerable power in the national Democratic Party, but became a controversial figure in 1968, when by his orders Chicago police officers brutally subdued a demonstration against the Vietnam War at the Democratic National Convention. His son, Richard M Daley (1942–), served as state's attorney for Cook County, Illinois, before he was elected Mayor of Chicago in 1989.

Dalgarno, George c.1626–1687
Scottish educationist

Born in Aberdeen, he studied there at Marischal College, and ran a school for 30 years in Oxford. He published a book on philosophy using letters of the alphabet for ideas,

Ars Signorum, *vulgo Character Universalis* (1661) and a sign language for those who could neither hear nor speak, *Didascalocophus, or the Deaf and Dumb Man's Tutor* (1680).

Dalglish, Kenny (Kenneth Mathieson) 1951–
Scottish footballer and manager
Born in Glasgow, he is considered one of Scotland's greatest internationals. He joined Glasgow Celtic in 1967 and in 10 years there won every honour in the Scottish game. Transferred to Liverpool in 1977 for a then record fee between two British clubs of £440,000, he won every major English honour in addition to three European Cups. Unexpectedly invited to manage Liverpool (1985) while he was still a player, he confounded the pundits by being an instant success. In his first season, Liverpool won both Cup and League. In 1991 he resigned from Liverpool and became manager of Blackburn Rovers, rising to director of football in 1995. Whilst there, he broke the transfer record twice by paying £3.3 million for Alan Shearer and £5 million for Chris Sutton, and led the team to win the 1994–95 Premiership, having been runners up the previous season. He left Blackburn in 1995 and succeeded **Kevin Keegan** as manager of Newcastle United in 1996. He is the only player to have scored 100 goals in both English and Scottish football. His records include playing 102 games for Scotland, and scoring 30 goals for them, a record he shares with **Denis Law**.

Dalhousie, James Andrew Broun-Ramsay, Marquis of 1812–60
Scottish politician and administrator in India
Born at Dalhousie Castle, Midlothian, and educated at Harrow and Christ Church, Oxford, he was the third son of the 9th Earl of Dalhousie. In 1837 he was elected MP for Haddingtonshire and in 1838, on the death of his father, entered the House of Lords as Earl of Dalhousie. In 1843 **Robert Peel** appointed him vice-president of the Board of Trade, and in 1845 he succeeded **Gladstone** as president. When Peel resigned office in 1846, Lord **John Russell** asked Dalhousie to remain at the Board of Trade in order to carry out the regulations he had framed for the railway system. In 1847 he was appointed Governor-General of India—the youngest viceroy ever sent there. He conquered Pegu and the Punjab and annexed Nagpur, Oudh, Sattara, Jhansi and Berar, and meanwhile encouraged the development of roads, railways, irrigation networks and telegraph. He also energetically opposed suttee, thuggee, female infanticide and the slave trade. He organized the Legislative Council, improved Civil Service training, and encouraged the development of trade, agriculture, forestry, mining and the postal service. Broken in health, he left India in 1856. The annexation of Oudh (1856) caused resentment which fuelled the 1857 Indian Uprising. ▥ William Lee-Warner, *The Life of the Marquis of Dalhousie* (2 vols, 1904)

Dalí, Salvador 1904–89
Spanish artist
He was born in Figueras, and after studying at the Academy of Fine Arts, Madrid, he moved to Paris. After joining the Surrealists in 1928, he became one of the principal figures of the movement. He made a deep study of abnormal psychology and dream symbolism, and represented 'paranoiac' objects in landscapes remembered from his Spanish boyhood with almost academic realism and highly finished craftsmanship. In 1940 he settled in the USA, and later became a Catholic and devoted his art to symbolic religious paintings. His publications include *The Secret Life of Salvador Dalí* (1942) and the Surrealist novel *Hidden Faces* (1944). He collaborated with **Luis Buñuel** in producing the Surrealist films *Le Chien Andalou* (1928) and *L'Age d'Or* (1930). His painting *The Persistence of Memory* (1931, also known as the *Limp Watches*) is in the Museum of Modern Art, New York, and his *Christ of*

St John of the Cross (1951) is in the St Mungo Museum of Religious Life and Art, Glasgow. ▥ James T Soby, *Salvador Dalí* (1946)

Dalin, Olof von 1708–63
Swedish poet, essayist and historian
Born in Vinberg, he became a tutor to the aristocracy, and also published a personal newspaper, *Then swänska Argus* (1732–34), in the tradition of **Joseph Addison's** and **Richard Steele's** *Tatler* and *Spectator*. Influenced by **Jonathan Swift**, it achieved considerable status and popularity and is regarded as the foundation stone of modern Swedish prose. Among his other works are a verse tragedy, *Brynilda* (1738), a brilliant prose allegory, *Sagan om hästan* (1740, 'The Story of the Horse'), which is his finest imaginative piece, and a monumental history of Sweden (1747–62). Between 1751 and 1756 he was tutor to the future King **Gustav III**. ▥ K J Warburg, *Olof Dalin* (1884)

Dallam, Thomas c.1570–c.1630
English organ-builder
He was born in Lancashire and in 1599–60 went to Constantinople (Istanbul) to deliver an organ to the sultan. He built organs for King's College, Cambridge, for Worcester Cathedral and for the Royal Chapel of Holyroodhouse, Edinburgh. His sons became organ-builders too: Robert (1602–65) was responsible for organs at New College, Oxford, York Minster, St Paul's Cathedral, Jesus College, Cambridge (1634), Canterbury Cathedral (1635) and St Mary Woolnoth (destroyed in the Fire of London); Ralph (d.1672) built organs for St George's Chapel, Windsor, and for Greenwich church.

Dallapiccola, Luigi 1904–75
Italian composer and teacher
He was born in Pisino d'Istria. His compositions, making wide use of twelve-note technique, include songs, a piano concerto, operas *Il prigioniero* (1944–48, 'The Prisoner') and *Ulisse* (1959–68, 'Ulysses'), the ballet, *Marsyas* (1942–43, 'Marsia'), and orchestral and choral works such as *Canti di Prigionia* (1938–41, 'Songs of Imprisonment'). His work was influential on composition in the USA.

Dallas, Alexander James 1759–1817
American lawyer
Born in Jamaica of Scottish parents, he went to the USA in 1783, settled in Philadelphia, and was later Secretary of the Treasury and War Secretary under President **Madison**. He is remembered for promoting a national banking institution and for restoring public credit.

Dallas, George Mifflin 1792–1864
US lawyer and politician
Born in Philadelphia, the son of **Alexander James Dallas**, he graduated at Princeton College in 1810, was admitted to the Bar and entered the diplomatic service. In 1831–33 he was sent to the US Senate by Pennsylvania. He was US Minister to Russia (1837–39), and in 1844 was elected Vice-President of the USA. In 1846 his casting vote as president of the Senate repealed the protective tariff of 1842, though he had been a Protectionist. Later he became Minister to Great Britain (1856–61). His writings include *Letters from London* (1869), a life of his father (1871), and his *Diary*. Dallas in Texas is named after him.

Dalou, (Aimé) Jules 1838–1902
French sculptor
He was born in Paris, and became the pupil of **Jean Baptiste Carpeaux**. After being the curator of the Louvre during the Commune, he fled to England in 1871, and taught at the Royal College of Art in London. His realistic modelling influenced many English sculptors of the time. The best-known of his works is the *Triumph of the Republic* monument in Paris (1879–99).

Dalrymple, Sir David See **Hailes, Sir David Dalrymple, Lord**

Dalton (of Forest and Frith), (Edward) Hugh John Neale Dalton, Baron 1887–1962
Welsh Labour politician

Born in Neath, Glamorgan, he was educated at Eton and King's College, Cambridge, and at the London School of Economics. He served in World War I and was a Labour MP (1924–31, 1935–59). He became Minister for Economic Warfare in 1940 and then President of the Board of Trade (1942) in Churchill's war-time coalition. In 1945 he became Labour Chancellor of the Exchequer, nationalized the Bank of England (1946) but resigned following 'budget leakages' to a journalist in 1947. He published his memoirs, *High Tide and After*, in 1962.

Dalton, John 1766–1844
English chemist and natural philosopher

Born in Eaglesfield, Cumbria, he received his early education at a Quaker school there and began teaching at the age of 12. In 1793 he moved to Manchester and taught mathematics at New College in Moseley Street (a predecessor of Manchester College, Oxford) but after about six years turned to private teaching and scientific research. In 1787 he began a lifelong meteorological journal, recording over 200,000 observations. In 1794 he described colour blindness (Daltonism), exemplified partly by his own case. In his chemical and physical research Dalton was a crude experimentalist, but his results led him to his atomic theory, on which his fame rests. Of particular importance were his studies showing that in a mixture of gases each gas exerts the same pressure as it would if it were the only gas present in the given volume (Dalton's law). This led to the interpretation of chemical analyses in terms of the relative weights of the atoms of the elements involved and to the laws of chemical combination. His atomic theory recognized that all matter is made up of combinations of atoms, the atoms of each element being identical. He concluded that atoms could be neither created nor destroyed, and that chemical reactions take place through the rearrangement of atoms. H E Roscoe, *John Dalton and the Rise of Modern Chemistry* (1895)

Dalton, Sir John Neale 1839–1931
English clergyman and philanthropist

Born in Kent and educated at Cambridge, he occupied various curacies and was chosen by Queen Victoria as tutor to her grandsons Albert Victor and George (the future George V), whom he taught from 1871 to 1884. He was canon and steward of St George's Chapel at Windsor from 1884, and proved himself a distinguished antiquary, inspired singing master and ruthless autocrat. His insistence on disinterring the corpse of Henry VI before a scholarly audience including Montague James seems to have inspired the sardonic portrait in James's ghost story *An Episode of Cathedral History*. Dalton published several notable works, including *Ordinale Exon* (3 vols, 1908, 1926), *The Collegiate Church of Ottery St Mary* (1917) and *The Book of Common Prayer, Proposals, and Suggestions* (1920). His protégés included the navvy poet Patrick MacGill whom he brought to the Windsor Cloisters as his secretary. His son was the politician Hugh Dalton, who had strong socialist ideas.

Dalton, Robert 1867–92
US outlaw

Born probably in Cass County, Missouri, he was originally a deputy US marshal in the Indian Territory (1888–89), but shifted to a career on the opposite side of the law after killing a rival in a love affair in 1889. He formed a gang that included his brothers Grattan and Emmet, and began stealing horses and robbing trains in Kansas,

Oklahoma and California. In 1892 they tried to rob a bank in Coffeyville, Oklahoma, but met heavy fire from the townspeople; Robert and Grattan were killed, and Emmet was wounded and captured.

Daly, (John) Augustin 1838–99
US dramatist and theatre manager

He was born in Plymouth, North Carolina. After a career as a drama critic, he went into management, opening the Fifth Avenue Theatre, New York City, in 1869, and his own theatre, Daly's, in 1879, with the company of which he visited London in 1884. In 1893 he opened the London Daly's with Ada Rehan in *The Taming of the Shrew*. He wrote and adapted nearly a hundred plays, of which the best was *Horizon* (1871), though the most popular were melodramas such as *Leah, the Forsaken* (1862) and *Under the Gaslight* (1867). He was chosen by Tennyson to adapt *The Foresters* for the stage in 1891. M Felheim, *The Theatre of Augustin Daly* (1956)

Daly, Mary 1928–
US feminist and theological writer

Born in Schenectady, New York, she studied theology at St Mary's College, Indiana, and Fribourg University, Switzerland, and taught at Fribourg (1959–66) and Boston College (from 1969). Having analysed the effects of male bias in *The Church and the Second Sex* (1968), she gave up her attempts to reform official Roman Catholic attitudes and became a post-Christian radical feminist (*Beyond God the Father*, 1973). Her emphasis on pre-Jewish/Christian religion and women's personal experience is developed in *Gyn/Ecology: The Metaethics of Radical Feminism* (1978) and *Pure Lust: Elemental Feminist Philosophy* (1984). Later publications include *Webster's First New Intergalactic Wickedary of the English Language*, written with Jane Caputi, and her autobiography *Outercourse: the Be-dazzling Voyage: Containing Recollections from my Logbook as a Feminist Philosopher (be-ing an account of my time/space travels and ideas—then, again, now, and how)* (1992).

Dalyell, Tam 1932–
Scottish Labour politician

Born into an ancient Scottish landed family, he was educated at Eton and Oxford, trained as a teacher at Moray House, Edinburgh, and taught at Bo'ness in West Lothian. A convert to the Labour Party, he was MP for West Lothian (1962–83), then for Linlithgow (1983–). During the Conservative administration he established a reputation as the quintessential backbencher—ready to champion unpopular causes and to question Ministers relentlessly. He opposed his own government's Scottish devolution legislation in the mid-1970s, and later campaigned tirelessly on such issues as the sinking of the *Belgrano* during the Falklands War (1982) and the environmental consequences of the Gulf War (1991).

Dalyell or **Dalzell, Thomas**, *known as* **the Muscovy General** c.1615–1685
Scottish soldier

Born at The Binns, West Lothian, the son of a laird, he served in the unsuccessful expedition against Rochelle led by the 1st Duke of Buckingham (1628), and fought for the Royalists in Ireland in the 1640s. In the attempted revolution he was taken prisoner at Worcester (1651), but escaped from the Tower of London in 1652 and joined Charles II in exile. In 1655 he entered the service of Russia and fought against the Tartars and Turks. In 1666, appointed Commander-in-Chief in Scotland, he defeated the Covenanters at Rullion Green in the Pentland Hills. Commander-in-Chief again from 1679 to 1685, he again brought about the bloody suppression of the Covenanters. He raised the Royal Scots Greys in 1681.

Dalziel, Edward 1817–1905
English engraver
Born in Wooler, he joined his brother George (1815–1902) in London in 1839 and gradually built (together with a third brother, Thomas, 1823–1906) the business of the Brothers Dalziel, wood-engravers.

Dam, (Carl Peter) Henrik 1895–1976
Danish biochemist and Nobel Prize winner
Born in Copenhagen, he taught there from 1923 until 1940, when he went to the USA. There he taught at the University of Rochester (1942–45) and became a member of the Rockefeller Institute for Medical Research in New York City in 1945. He was also on the staff of the Polytechnic Institute, Copenhagen (1941–65). For his discovery of the coagulant agent vitamin K (1934) he shared the Nobel Prize for physiology or medicine in 1943 with the US biochemist Edward Doisy.

Damaskinos, Demetrios Papandreou
1891–1949
Greek archbishop and regent
After serving in the army during the Balkan Wars, he was ordained priest (1917) and elected Bishop of Corinth (1922) and Archbishop of Athens (1938), but was exiled because of his opposition to Yanni Metaxas. Returning to Greece in 1941, he was able to give secret assistance to the British during the German occupation. After the withdrawal from Greece of German troops, Winston Churchill, eager to establish peace between the warring factions, agreed to Damaskinos's appointment as regent until a plebiscite could be held over the issue of the monarchy (December 1944). When the Greeks voted for the return of their king, Damaskinos resigned as regent (September 1946) and continued his work as archbishop.

Damasus I, St c.304–384AD
Roman deacon and pope
He was possibly of Spanish descent. His election in AD366 was violently contested, but confirmed by Valentinian I. He opposed Arianism, and condemned Apollinaris, the Younger at the Council of Constantinople in 381. In 382 he proclaimed the primacy of the see of Rome. He restored the catacombs and wrote epitaphs for the tombs of the martyrs. He commissioned St Jerome, his secretary, to revise the Bible, which resulted in the Vulgate version. His feast day is 11 December.

d'Amboise, Jacques 1934–
US dancer and choreographer
Born in Dedham, Massachusetts, he trained at George Balanchine's School of American Ballet and joined the New York City Ballet in 1949. A powerful and acrobatic dancer, he performed in new ballets such as *Stars and Stripes* (1958) as well as classical works such as *Swan Lake*. He also choreographed his own ballets, including *The Chase* (1963) and *Irish Fantasy* (1964). In 1976 he founded the National Dance Institute to bring dance instruction into the public schools, and in 1990 he was awarded a MacArthur fellowship.

Damian, St See Cosmas and Damian, Saints

Damian, St Peter See Damian, Pietro

Damiani, Pietro, *also called* St Peter Damian
1007–72
Italian ecclesiastic and Doctor of the Church
Born in Ravenna, he herded swine as a boy, and in 1035 joined the hermitage at Fonte Avellana; he rose to be Cardinal and Bishop of Ostia (1057). He supported the policy of Hildebrand (Gregory VII) without sharing his arrogance, and laboured strenuously to reform the clergy, which at the time was at a low ebb of immorality and indolence. His feast day is 23 February.

Damien, Father, *originally* Joseph de Veuster
1840–89
Belgian Roman Catholic missionary
Born in Tremelo, he is renowned for his work among the lepers of the Hawaiian island of Molokai, where he lived from 1873 until his death from the disease.

Damm, Sheila van See Van Damm, Sheila

Damocles 4th century BC
Greek courtier
He was a member of the court of Dionysius the Elder. Having praised the happiness of royalty, he was invited to a royal feast; but on looking upwards he saw a sword suspended over his head by a single hair—the 'Sword of Damocles'—symbolizing the precarious nature of happiness. The story is told by Cicero.

Damon and Pythias or Phintias 4th century BC
Pythagorean philosophers of Syracuse
Condemned to death by Dionysius the Elder, tyrant of Syracuse, Pythias begged to be allowed to go home to arrange his affairs, and Damon pledged his own life for his friend's. Pythias returned just in time to save Damon from death. Moved by so noble an example, Dionysius pardoned Pythias.

Dampier, William 1652–1715
English navigator, pirate and travel writer
He was born near Yeovil, Somerset, and as a young sailor gained a great knowledge of hydrography. However, in 1679 he joined a band of buccaneers who crossed the Isthmus of Darién (in central America) and ravaged the coast as far south as the Juan Fernández Islands. In another expedition (1683), after seizing a Danish ship at Sierra Leone, Africa, he sailed across the Pacific Ocean and reached the Philippines, China and Australia. He finally returned to England in 1691, where he published *A New Voyage round the World* (1697). After exploring the west coast of Australia (1699–1700), and the coasts of New Guinea and New Britain, he gave his name to the Dampier Archipelago and Strait, and published his findings in *A Voyage to New Holland* (1703–09). However, Dampier was apparently a better pilot than commander, and his cruelty to his lieutenant led to his being court-martialled. He was reappointed to the command of two privateers to the South Seas in 1703, but is again said to have been guilty of drunkenness and brutality. This is reputed to have been the voyage during which Alexander Selkirk (the model for Daniel Defoe's Robinson Crusoe) was sent—by his own request—into arid exile on one of the Juan Fernández Islands. Dampier returned home in 1707, poor and broken, but sailed again the following year as pilot on Woodes Rogers's ship, which rescued Selkirk.
📖 Christopher Lloyd, *William Dampier* (1966)

Dana, Charles Anderson 1819–97
US newspaper editor
Born in Hinsdale, New Hampshire, he spent two years at Harvard, and was a member of the Brook Farm community (1841–46) with George Ripley. From 1848 to 1862 he edited the New York *Tribune*, which opposed the extension of slavery to new territories. From 1863 until the end of the Civil War he was Assistant Secretary of War. In 1867 he purchased the New York *Sun*, and successfully managed it on democratic lines. He published translations and anthologies, collaborated in a life of Ulysses S Grant (1868), and with Ripley edited the *New American Cyclopaedia* (1857–63) and the *American Cyclopaedia* (1873–76).

Dana, James Dwight 1813–95
US mineralogist, crystallographer and geologist
Born in Utica, New York, he graduated from Yale then joined the US navy as a teacher of mathematics to midshipmen. This voyage resulted in his first scientific paper

in 1835, an observation *On the condition of Vesuvius*. In 1836 he became assistant in chemistry to his future father-in-law Benjamin Silliman, with whom he edited the *American Journal of Science* from 1846 until his death. He was appointed Professor of Natural History (1849–64) and Professor of Geology and Mineralogy (1864–90) at Yale. He was a scientific observer on a US exploring expedition visiting the Antarctic and Pacific (1838–42) during which his ship was wrecked. Following an overland trek to safety involving travelling down the Sacramento River to San Francisco, he reported the 'probable occurrence of gold in California' six years before its discovery. In 1837 he published the *System of Mineralogy*, the fifth edition (1868) of which is a monumental treatise which remains useful today. His 400 publications included *Manual of Mineralogy* (1848), two treatises on corals, *Manual of Geology* (1863), *Textbook of Geology* (1864), *Corals and Coral Islands* (1872) and *Hawaiian Volcanoes* (1890).

Dana, Richard Henry, Snr 1787–1879
US poet and critic

Born in Cambridge, Massachusetts, he was educated at Harvard, and admitted to the Bar at Boston in 1811. In 1818 he became associate editor of the *North American Review*, to which he contributed. His *Dying Raven* (1821), *The Buccaneer* (1827) and some of his other poems were praised by critics, but his best work was in criticism.

Dana, Richard Henry, Jnr 1815–82
US writer and lawyer

Born in Cambridge, Massachusetts, he was the son of **Richard Henry Dana, Snr**. He was obliged to suspend his studies at Harvard because of eyestrain, and he shipped out as a common sailor on a voyage round Cape Horn to California and back, which he described in *Two Years before the Mast* (1840). After graduating in 1837 he was admitted to the Massachusetts Bar in 1840, and was especially distinguished in maritime law. Among his works are *The Seaman's Friend* (1841) and *To Cuba and Back* (1859). He also edited **Henry Wheaton's** *International Law*, and was a prominent free-soiler and Republican. 📖 R Gale, *Dana* (1969)

Danby, Francis 1793–1861
Irish painter

Born near Wexford, Killinick County, he studied art at Dublin, moved to Bristol in 1813, but left England for Switzerland in 1829, returning to London in 1840. He painted landscapes, eg *Temple of Flora* (1840, Tate, London), and large biblical and historical pictures, such as *The Deluge* (1840, Tate). His later work was more tranquil, eg *The Evening Sun* (1857, private collection).

Dance, George 1700–68
English architect

Born in London, he designed the Mansion House (1739) and many other London buildings.

Dance, George 1741–1825
English architect and painter

Born in London, the son of **George Dance**, he rebuilt Newgate Prison (1770–83), and was one of the original Royal Academicians.

Dancourt, Florent Carton 1661–1725
French dramatist, actor and court favourite

Born in Fontainebleau, he studied law in Paris, and became popular in the court of **Louis XIV** by introducing comedy of manners to French theatre. He excelled in depicting the stupidity of the peasantry and the follies of the bourgeoisie. His best-known comedy is *Le Chevalier à la mode* (1687, 'The Fashionable Knight'). He became devout in his old age, which he spent in retirement in the country. 📖 J Le Maître, *Le Théâtre de Dancourt* (1882)

Dandolo, Enrico c.1110–1205
Doge of Venice

He became Doge of Venice in 1192 and sailed at the head of the Fourth Crusade in 1202. The Crusaders could not raise the sum which they had negotiated for the ships which the Venetians had supplied, so Dandolo proposed that the debt be paid in military service to Venice. This resulted in the subjugation of Trieste and Zara, the coasts of Albania and the Ionian Islands. Most notoriously, it led to the Sack of Constantinople (1204), from which much of the plunder was carried off to Venice. Three of his descendants were also Doge: Giovanni (1280–89), Francesco (1328–39), and Andrea (1342–54).

Dandridge, Dorothy 1920–65
US singer and actress

Born in Cleveland, Ohio, she was a child star in films, but broke through to adult roles in *A Day at the Races* (1937). The most beautiful African-American actress of her generation, and one of the first ever to be acclaimed a star, Dandridge had her greatest successes in *Carmen Jones* (1954) and *Porgy and Bess* (1959), though in neither case was her rather light voice used, being dubbed in by **Lena Horne** and others. She died young and an edited memoir, *Everything and Nothing: the Dorothy Dandridge Story*, appeared in 1970.

Dandy, Walter Edward 1886–1946
US neurosurgeon

Born in Sedalia, Missouri, he studied medicine at Johns Hopkins University, where **Harvey Cushing** encouraged his interests in neurosurgery. Dandy remained on the staff there until his death. He did important work on the pathophysiology and surgical treatment of hydrocephalus, and developed a number of fundamental diagnostic and neurosurgical techniques. He also demonstrated the significance of ruptured vertebra disks in cases of low back pain, and pioneered spinal surgery. Dandy and Cushing unfortunately later quarrelled and remained bitter rivals for the leadership of the US neurosurgical community.

Dane, Clemence, *pseudonym of* Winifred Ashton 1888–1965
English novelist and playwright

She was born in Blackheath, London, and educated in England and France. Her novels include *Regiment of Women* (1917), *Legend* (1919), *Broome Stages* (1931) and *The Flower Girls* (1954), the last two dealing with theatrical families. Many of her plays achieved long runs, including *A Bill of Divorcement* (1921); the ingenious reconstruction of the poet's life in *Will Shakespeare* (1921); the stark tragedy of *Granite* (1926); *Call Home the Heart* (1927); and *Wild Decembers* (1932), about the Brontës.

Dane, Nathan 1752–1835
US lawyer

He was born in Ipswich, Massachusetts. A delegate to the Continental Congress in 1785 and later a commissioner to revise the statutes of Massachusetts, he published a *General Abridgement and Digest of American Law*, the first comprehensive work on American law (9 vols, 1823–29). He arranged that the income from this work be used to establish a chair in the Harvard Law School provided that **Joseph Story** was the first holder. As Dane Professor, Story published his distinguished series of *Commentaries* and revitalized the School.

Dangerfield, Thomas 1650–85
English thief and conspirator

Born in Waltham, Essex, he was a thief, a soldier on the Continent, and a pseudo-convert to Catholicism. In 1679 he accused the Presbyterians of plotting to bring down the government. Imprisoned when this was shown to be a lie, he claimed he had been deceived by a Roman Catholic tale invented to screen a plot of their own against king Charles II. Papers proving this would, he alleged, be found in a meal-tub in the house of a Mrs Cellier (who was tried and acquitted). The case became known as the Meal-tub Plot. He was whipped and pilloried, and on returning from Tyburn was killed by a blow in the eye from a bystander.

d'Angers, David See David, Pierre Jean

Daniel, also called Belteshazzar 6th century BC
Judean exile and prophet

Born of noble descent, he was taken from Jerusalem after the capture of King Jehoiakim of Judah to serve in the court of Nebuchadnezzar. He quickly gained a reputation for wisdom, for faithfulness to his god and for the interpreting of dreams. Later he himself had visions prophesying the coming of the Messiah's kingdom. In translating the writing on the walls of the banqueting chamber, 'Mene mene tekel u-pharsin', he predicted the downfall of King Belshazzar. Because of his wisdom he was appointed third in rank in the kingdom and went on to serve Darius I, King of the Medes, and Cyrus, King of the Persians.

Daniel, Arnaut fl.late 12th century
Provençal poet

Born at the Castle of Rebeyrac, Périgord, he became a member of the court of Richard I and was esteemed one of the best of the troubadours, particularly for his treatment of the theme of love. He introduced the sestina, the pattern of which was later adapted by Dante and Petrarch. 📖 E Pound, in *Literary Essays* (1954)

Daniel, Glyn Edmund 1914–86
Welsh archaeologist

Born in Barry, South Glamorgan, he was educated at University College Cardiff, and St John's College, Cambridge. He lectured at Cambridge (1945–74) and was Professor of Archaeology there (1974–81). A companionable bon viveur, he devoted his career less to excavation and research than to stimulating popular interest in archaeology through writing, editing and broadcasting. He was a pioneer historian of archaeology and an energetic editor, both of the journal *Antiquity* (1958–86) and of the book series *Ancient Peoples and Places* published from 1955. On television he achieved popularity in the 1950s as chairman of the archaeological panel game *Animal, Vegetable, Mineral?* 📖 *Some Small Harvest* (1986)

Daniel, Samuel 1562–1619
English poet

Born near Taunton, Somerset, he entered Magdalen Hall, Oxford, in 1597, but left without a degree. He was a tutor to William Herbert, son of the 2nd Earl of Pembroke, and to Anne Clifford, daughter of the Earl of Cumberland, and in 1604 he was appointed to read new plays. In 1607 he became one of the queen's grooms of the privy chamber, and from 1615 to 1618 he had charge of a company of young players at Bristol. Although he was highly commended by his contemporaries, Ben Jonson described him as 'a good honest man...but no poet'. His works include sonnets, epistles, masques and dramas, but his chief production was a poem in eight books, *A History of the Civil Wars between York and Lancaster*. His *Defence of Ryme* (1602) is in admirable prose. 📖 C Seronsy, *Samuel Daniel* (1967)

Daniell, John Frederick 1790–1845
English chemist and meteorologist

He was born in London. He was employed in a sugar refinery run by a relative and he effected improvements in the processes. However, he soon left the business and held no definite appointment until he became Professor of Chemistry at the newly founded King's College

London in 1831. Around 1815 he began his publications on meteorology and in 1823 published his *Meteorological Essays*. In 1820 he invented a hygrometer and in 1830 a pyrometer, for which he was awarded the Royal Society's Rumford medal (1832). In 1835 he began the investigation of voltaic cells and in particular the reasons for their rapid loss of voltage. This led to a constant voltage (Daniell) cell, for which he was awarded the Royal Society's Copley medal (1837). He collapsed and died at a council meeting of the Royal Society, of which he was foreign secretary.

Daniels, Bebe (Phyliss) 1901–71
US actress

Born in Dallas, Texas, she was a member of her father's theatre company from the age of three and became known as 'The World's Youngest Shakespearean Actress'. A prolific stage performer, she is also reputed to have appeared in over 200 short silent comedies and westerns. She also proved an accomplished comedienne, often cast in mildly risqué roles as thrill-seeking playgirls. Her films include *Speed Girl* (1921), *Monsieur Beaucaire* (1924) and *She's a Sheik* (1928). She survived the transition to sound, appearing in musicals like *Rio Rita* (1929) and *42nd Street* (1933), but when her Hollywood career flagged she moved to London with her husband Ben Lyon (1901–79). They remained there throughout the war years, beginning the popular radio show *Hi Gang!* in 1939. Together they enjoyed long-running successes on radio and television, especially with the comedy series *Life With the Lyons* (1955–60). A dedicated entertainer of US servicemen, she is said to have been the first woman ashore following the D-Day landings in 1944 and was awarded the American Medal of Freedom in 1946 for her war work.

Danilova, Alexandra Dionysievna 1904–97
US dancer and teacher

Born in Petergof (Petrodvorets), she trained at the Imperial Ballet School, Petrograd (now St Petersburg), before joining the Maryinsky Theatre (now Kirov Ballet) in 1922. She defected on a tour to Europe in 1924 and that year became a member of Sergei Diaghilev's Ballets Russes, leaving in 1929. She danced for Colonel de Basil's Ballet Russe (1933–38) and its splinter group the Ballets Russes de Monte Carlo (until 1952), as well as making guest appearances with many companies. She formed her own group, Great Moments of Ballet (1954–56) before retiring in 1957. After this, she staged ballets for opera companies and in collaboration with George Balanchine, at whose School of American Ballet she earned an impressive reputation as a teacher. 📖 A E Twysden, *Alexandra Danilova* (1947)

Dankworth, John Philip William 1927–
English jazz musician and composer

Born in London, he studied at the Royal Academy of Music. He was a founder-member (on clarinet and alto saxophone) of the legendary Club 11 in 1948, before forming the first of his own influential groups in 1950. Cleo Laine sang with his big band from 1953, and went on to become a major artist in both jazz and musical theatre. After they married in 1958, he acted as her musical director, and concentrated on composition and arrangement. They have remained a significant musical partnership, and have run an annual workshop/festival for young musicians at Wavendon, Buckinghamshire, since 1970. Their son, Alec Dankworth, is a jazz bass player, and co-leads the Dankworth Generation Band with his father. 📖 G Collier, *Cleo and John* (1976)

d'Annunzio, Gabriele 1863–1938
Italian writer, adventurer and political leader

Born in Pescara, he began as a journalist on the *Tribuna* in Rome, then made his name as a poet in 1879 with the publication of *Primo vere* ('In Early Spring'). During the

---

Dante Alighieri 1265–1321
Italian poet, author of the Divina Commedia ('Divine Comedy')

Dante was born in Florence, the son of a lawyer of the noble **Guelf** family. He was baptized Durante, afterwards abbreviated to Dante. According to his own account, he first set eyes on his lifelong love, Beatrice Portinari (c.1265–1290), at the age of nine in 1274. There is no evidence that she returned his passion; she was married at an early age to one Simone de' Bardi, but neither this nor the poet's own subsequent marriage interfered with his pure and Platonic devotion to her, which intensified after her death. The story of his boyish but unquenchable passion is told with exquisite pathos in *La Vita Nuova* (c.1292).

Shortly after, Dante married Gemma Donati, daughter of a powerful Guelf family. They had seven children, six sons and one daughter, Beatrice, a nun at Ravenna. In 1289 he fought at Campaldino, where Florence defeated the Ghibellines, and was at the capitulation of Caprona. He was registered in the City Guild of the Apothecaries, being entered as 'Dante d'Alighieri, *Poeta*'. In 1300, after filling minor public offices, and possibly going on some embassies abroad, he became one of the six priors of Florence, but for only two months. It was towards the 'White Guelfs', or more moderate section, that his sympathies tended. As prior, he procured the banishment of the heads and leaders of the rival factions, showing characteristic sternness and impartiality to **Guelf** and Ghibelline, white and black, alike.

In 1301, in alarm at the threatened interference of Charles of Valois (1270–1325), second son of **Philip III** of France, he was sent on an embassy to Rome to Pope **Boniface VIII**. He never returned from that embassy, nor did he ever again set foot in his native city. Charles espoused the side of the *Neri* or Blacks, and their victory was complete. Dante was banished from Florence in 1309 and sentenced to death in his absence. From then on he led a wandering life, first in Verona, in Tuscany, in the Lunigiana, near Urbino, and then Verona again. He eventually settled in Ravenna (1318), where for the most part he remained until his death. He was buried with much pomp at Ravenna, where he still lies, having been restored in 1865 to the original sarcophagus there.

His most celebrated work is the *Divina Commedia*, begun around 1307, his spiritual testament, which narrates a journey through Hell and Purgatory, guided by **Virgil**, and finally to Paradise, guided by Beatrice. It gives an encyclopedic view of the highest culture and knowledge of the age, all expressed in the most exquisite poetry. The *Divina Commedia* (which Dante began in Latin) established Italian as a literary language. The next most important work is the fragment called *Il Convivio*, or 'The Banquet', which takes the form of a commentary on some of the author's *canzoni*, or short poems, of which there are only three, though the work, if completed, would have contained 14. The *De Monarchia* (in Latin) expounds Dante's theory of the divinely intended government of the world by a universal pope. Another unfinished work, *De Vulgari Eloquentia*, discusses the origin of language, the divisions of languages, and the dialects of Italian in particular. *Canzoniere* is a collection of short poems, *canzoni*, sonnets, etc; there are a dozen epistles addressed mainly to leading statesmen or rulers; and there are also some *Eclogues* and other minor works, as well as several of doubtful authenticity.

📖 W Anderson, *Dante the Maker* (1980); T C Chubb, *Dante and His World* (1966); E Auerbach, *Dante, Poet of the Secular World* (1961).

> *Lasciate ogni speranza voi ch'entrate.*
> Abandon all hope ye who enter here.
> Inscription above the gates of Hell in *Divina Commedia*, 'Inferno', canto 3, line 9.

> *Nel mezzo cammin di nostra vita*
> *mi ritrovai per una selva oscura*
> *che la diritta via era smarrita.*
> In the middle of the journey of our life
> I found myself in a dark wood
> where the straight path was lost.
> *Divina Commedia*, 'Inferno', canto 1, lines 1–3.

1890s he wrote 'Romances of the Rose'; a trilogy of novels with **Nietzsche** on heroes comprising *Il Piacere* (1889, 'The Child of Pleasure'), *L'Innocente* (1892, 'The Intruder') and *Il Trionfo della morte* (1894, 'The Triumph of Death'). He was elected a parliamentary Deputy in 1897, and became notorious for his passionate affair with the actress Eleanora Duse, for whom he wrote several plays, including the tragedites *La Gioconda* (1899) and *Francesca da Rimini* (1901). His greatest play is considered to be *La figlia di Jorio* (1904, 'The Daughter of Jorio'). An enthusiastic patriot, he urged Italian entry into World War I and served as a soldier, sailor and airman. In 1916 he lost an eye in aerial combat, and in 1918 carried out a sensational reconnaissance over Vienna. In 1919 he seized and held Fiume and ruled as dictator until he was removed by the Italian government (1920). He became a strong supporter of the Fascist Party under **Mussolini**. He is regarded as one of the most important Italian literary figures of the late 19th and early 20th centuries.

Dantas, Julio 1876–1962
Portuguese dramatist, poet and short-story writer

He was born in Lagos. In his light lyrical poems and stories he displayed considerable talent, but his other work, such as historical dramas, attempted under the influence of the Norwegian and French schools, was less successful. His *A ceia dos cardeais* (1902) was translated by H A Saintsbury as *The Cardinal's Collation* (1927). 📖 J Dias Cancho, *Julio Dantas* (1922)

Dante Alighieri See panel above

Danton, Georges Jacques 1759–94
French Revolutionary leader

He was born of peasant stock, in Arcis-sur-Aube. At the outbreak of the French Revolution he was practising as an advocate in Paris, where he had instituted the Revolutionists' Cordeliers' Club with **Jean Paul Marat** and **Camille Desmoulins**. He fled to England in 1791, but in 1792 he became Minister of Justice in the new republic following the fall of the monarchy. Elected to the National Convention, he voted for the death of the king in January 1793 and was one of the nine original members of the Committee of Public Safety, frequently undertaking missions to **Dumouriez** and other republican generals. He also contributed to the fall of the Girondins, or moderate party (October 1793), and to the subsequent supremacy of the extremist Jacobins. As president of the Jacobin Club he strove for domestic unity, government stability, and to abate the pitiless severity of the Revolutionary Tribunal (which he had himself set up) but he lost power to **Robespierre** in the Reign of Terror. Danton retired from active politics, but in March 1794 he and his followers were arrested for conspiracy to overthrow the goverment. His audacious, satirical defence moved the people so greatly that the Revolutionary Tribunal concocted a decree to shut the mouths of men who had 'insulted Justice', and on 5 April Danton was guillotined. ⬛ Norman Hampson, *Danton* (1978)

Dantzig, Rudi von 1933–
Dutch dancer, choreographer and ballet director
Born in Amsterdam, he studied with Sonia Gaskell. In 1952 he made his debut in her Ballet Recital Group, later known as the Netherlands Ballet and, eventually, the Dutch National Ballet. He became her choreographer, assistant, co-director and, in 1968, the company's sole director. He was one of the founding members of Netherlands DanceTheater, a group that broke away from the Netherlands Ballet in 1959. Dantzig's ballets are marked by their strong social themes, mix of academic and modern dance vocabularies, often abstract music scores and some technical experimentation. In 1993 he published *Rudolf Nureyev,The Trail of a Comet*.

Da Ponte, Lorenzo, *originally* Emanuele Conegliano 1749–1838
Italian poet
He was born in Ceneda, near Venice, of Jewish parents. After converting to Roman Catholicism, he became Professor of Rhetoric at Treviso until political and domestic troubles drove him to Vienna, where as a poet to the Court Opera he wrote the libretti for **Mozart's** operas *The Marriage of Figaro* (1786), *Don Giovanni* (1787) and *Così fan Tutte* (1790). In London he taught Italian and sold boots, before moving in 1805 to New York where he eventually became Professor of Italian Literature at Columbia College (1825).

Daquin or d'Aquin, Louis Claude 1694–1772
French composer, organist and harpsichordist
Born in Paris, he played before **Louis XIV** when six years old and displaced his master, Marin de la Guerre, as organist of Sainte Chapelle in 1706. He held many official posts, and became organist of the Chapel Royal in 1739. His works include religious music, and pieces for the organ and harpsichord, the most famous of which is *Le Coucou* (1735, 'The Cuckoo').

Darby, Abraham c.1678–1717
English iron-master
Born near Dudley, Worcestershire, he founded the Bristol Iron Company (1708), and is generally acknowledged to have been the first man to use coke successfully in the smelting of iron (1709). This was important because charcoal had become increasingly scarce and was too soft to allow larger furnaces to be used, and coal itself was almost always contaminated with sulphur and other undesirable impurities. Darby's works at Coalbrookdale produced the finest iron yet made. ⬛ Barrie Stuart Trinder, *The Darbys of Coalbrookdale* (1974)

Darby, Abraham 1711–63
English iron-master
The son of **Abraham Darby** (c.1678–1717), he is reputed to have discovered how to produce wrought iron from coke-smelted ore; if he did he kept the process such a close secret that no details of it are known. It is likely that the first man to achieve this on a commercial scale was **Henry Cort** in the 1780s with his puddling process. The Darby foundry at Coalbrookdale did, however, manufacture large numbers of cast-iron cylinders for **Thomas Newcomen's** atmospheric steam engines, and later the first high-pressure steam boiler for **Richard Trevithick**.

Darby, Abraham 1750–91
English iron-master and engineer

The son of **Abraham Darby** (1711–63), he raised the art of iron-founding to new heights in both decorative embellishment and structural prefabrication. His greatest achievement, the world's first cast-iron bridge of 100 feet (30m) span, was designed and built in the Darby foundry and erected over the River Severn in 1779. It is still in use as a footbridge.

Darby, Sir (Henry) Clifford 1909–92
Welsh geographer
Born in Glamorgan, he was educated at Neath County School and St Catharine's College, Cambridge. Following appointments at Cambridge, he was appointed Professor of Geography at Liverpool (1945–49). He was later professor at University College London (1949–66), and at Cambridge (1966–76). His particular interest was in medieval geography. He was a leader in promoting the relationships between geography and other subjects, especially history, thus transforming the study of historical geography and leading, for example, to the cross-sectional study of regions at certain times in the past. He was also an organizer of the study of the *Domesday Book* (general editor, *The Domesday Geography of England*, 7 vols, 1952–77) and the historical geography of the Fenlands.

Darby, John Nelson 1800–82
English churchman
Born in London, he was educated at Westminster School and Trinity College, Dublin. For a short time an Anglican clergyman, he became the principal founder in 1830 of the Plymouth Brethren, and in 1840 founded an exclusive sect of it known as the 'Darbyites'. He wrote 30 works.

Darbyshire, Jane Birthdate unavailable
British architect
After graduating from Newcastle University School of Architecture in the early 1970s, she set up her own practice in 1979 and was joined by her then husband, David Darbyshire, in 1980. In 1981 they won a competition to design St Oswald's Hospice, gaining positive publicity and several commissions for their practice. The building, which reflects the sensitive nature of Darbyshire's design ethos, was selected RIBA (Royal Institute of British Architects) Building of the Year (1987). In 1987 her marriage and business partnership broke up and she set up a new practice with David Kendall. She has been the recipient of RIBA and other awards for her work virtually every year since 1981.

Darcy, Patrick 1598–1668
Irish nationalist politician
Born in Galway, the seventh son of a Roman Catholic baronet of English descent, he sat for Navan, County Meath, in the Irish parliament of 1634, had risen to prominence by 1640, and supported his native Irish fellow Catholics in the Confederation of Kilkenny in 1641. He argued that no law of the English parliament could have force in Ireland unless enacted by the Irish parliament. A negotiator for the Catholic Confederates with **Charles I's** deputy **Ormonde** in 1649, he was then made a commissioner of the peace throughout Ireland, an appointment abrogated by the arrival of **Cromwell**.

Dare, Virginia b.1587
First child of English parents to be born in America
She was born on Roanoke Island during the second attempt to colonize Virginia, and disappeared along with the other members of Roanoke's 'Lost Colony' (c.1590).

Dargomizhsky, Aleksandr Sergeyevich 1813–69
Russian composer
Born in Tula, he was taught by **Mikhail Glinka** and influenced by other Russian nationalist composers. He set **Alexander Pushkin's** *Kamenny Gost* ('The Stone Guest') to

music (1866, completed by **Nikolai Rimsky-Korsakov** and performed in St Petersburg in 1872), which anticipated the work of **Mussorgsky** in dramatic power and naturalist treatment of words. He also wrote the operas *Esmeralda* (completed 1840) and *Rusalka* (1856), and almost 100 songs.

Darío, Rubén, *pseudonym of* **Felix Rubén García Sarmiento** 1867–1916
Nicaraguan poet
Born in Metapa, he wrote poetry from an early age and left Nicaragua in 1886 to work for newspapers in Chile and Argentina. He inaugurated the Spanish American Modernist movement with his major works *Azul* (1888, 'Blue') and *Prosas Profanas* (1896, Eng trans *Prosas Profanas and Other Poems*, 1922), which combined exotic imagery and simple, direct language and were influenced by the French Parnassian and Symbolist movements. A well-travelled man who held many diplomatic posts, he was plagued in later life by financial problems, heavy drinking and poor health. He wrote short stories, plays, travel books and literary criticism but is best known for his poetry, especially his collection *Cantos de Vida y Esperanza* (1905, 'Songs of Life and Hope'). His work greatly influenced Spanish-language writers both in Latin America and in Spain. ⏁ C D Watland, *Poet-Errant: a Biography of Darío* (1965)

Darius I 548–486BC
King of Persia
An **Achaemenid**, he ascended the Persian throne in 521BC, after putting to death the Magian Gaumáta, who pretended to be **Cambyses II**'s brother. There were revolts throughout his kingdom during his reign. He re-organized the administration and finances of the Persian Empire, making Susa the capital, while achieving conquests as far as the Caucasus and the Indus. His expedition against the Scythians (c.515) took him as far as the Volga, and enabled him to subdue Thrace and Macedonia. His expedition against the Athenians to punish them for supporting the Ionian revolt (499–994) was decisively defeated at Marathon (490). He died before the Egyptian revolt (487) had been quelled, and was succeeded by **Xerxes I**. Darius was a Persian by birth, and of the Zoroastrian faith, which under him became the state religion. He was also a great architect, and founded a new royal residence at Persepolis. ⏁ Albert ten Eyck Olmstead, *History of the Persian Empire* (1948)

Darius II *surnamed* **Ochus**, *surnamed in Greek* **Nothos ('Bastard')** d.404BC
King of Persia
The illegitimate son of **Artaxerxes I**, he seized power (c.424BC) in the dynastic struggle which followed his father's death, but was the tool of his cruel half-sister and spouse Parysatis. His reign was a long series of struggles and revolts ruthlessly suppressed. After the defeat of the Sicilian expedition of the Athenians (413), he resumed active Persian intervention in Greek affairs, and broke Athenian power (405). He died in Babylon, and was succeeded by his eldest son, **Artaxerxes II**.

Darius III *surnamed* **Codommanus** c.381–330BC
King of Persia
The grandson of **Artaxerxes II**, he was king from 336BC. He was defeated by **Alexander the Great** at the Granicus (334), at Issus (333) and at Gaugamela or Arbela (331), and was killed by a satrap, Bessus, on his retreat. He was the last king of the **Achaemenid** dynasty.

Dark, Eleanor, *née* O'Reilly 1901–
Australian novelist
Born in Sydney, the daughter of the writer Dowell O'Reilly (1865–1923), she was employed briefly as a stenographer, then in 1922 married a general practitioner,

and a year later moved to Katoomba in the Blue Mountains. Her earliest writings, short stories and verse, were contributed from 1921 to various magazines, mostly under the pseudonym 'Patricia O'Rane' or 'P. O'R'. *Slow Dawning*, her first novel, was completed in 1923, but not published until 1932. Her other novels include *Prelude to Christopher* (1934), *The Little Company* (1945), *Lantana Lane* (1959) and the trilogy comprising *The Timeless Land* (1941), *Storm of Time* (1948) and *No Barrier* (1953), which charts the early years of European settlement of New South Wales. A skilled writer, and a committed socialist and feminist, she was awarded the Australian Literature Society's gold medal in 1934 and 1936, and in 1978 received the Australian Society of Women Writers' Alice award. ⏁ H Anderson, *A Handlist of Books* (1954)

Darlan, Jean (Louis Xavier) François
1881–1942
French admiral and politician
He graduated from the École Navale in 1899, became captain in 1918, and navy Commander-in-Chief in 1939. He served in the Vichy government as Minister of the Navy and Mercantile Marine, Vice-President of the Council of Ministers, and Secretary of State for Foreign Affairs and the Navy. He then commanded French forces in North Africa (1942), where he concluded an armistice with the Allies. He was killed by an anti-Vichy assassin in Algiers.

Darley, Felix Octavius Carr 1822–88
US artist
He was born in Philadelphia. He illustrated the works of **Washington Irving, James Fenimore Cooper, Dickens**, and others.

Darling, Charles John Darling, 1st Baron
1849–1936
English judge
Born in Colchester, Essex, he was educated privately and articled to a Birmingham solicitor. He was called to the Bar (1874) and joined the Oxford circuit. A freelance journalist, he was a Conservative MP (1888–97) when his appointment as a judge of the King's Bench aroused widespread controversy. He presided over the Steinie Morrison (1911) and Armstrong (1922) murder trials, the Romney picture (1917) and Pemberton Billing (1918) cases, and heard the **Crippen** (1910) and **Casement** (1916) appeals. He deputized for the Lord Chief Justice, Lord **Reading**, when the latter was ambassador in Washington (1914–18), and was a member of several royal commissions. He never allowed his high office to dampen his sense of humour, and it enlivened his volumes of light verse which include *Scintillae Juris* (1877) and *On the Oxford Circuit* (1909). On his retirement, he was made a peer (1924).

Darling, Grace 1815–42
English heroine
She was born in Bamburgh, Northumberland, and with her father, William Darling (1786–1865), was a lighthouse keeper on one of the Farne Islands. On 7 September 1838, she rescued the survivors of the *Forfarshire*. ⏁ Jessica Mitford, *Grace Had an English Heart* (1988)

Darling, Sir James Ralph 1899–1995
Australian teacher
Born in Tonbridge, Kent, England, he attended Repton School and was taught in turn by **William Temple, Geoffrey Fisher** and **Victor Gollancz**. In 1924 he succeeded the Everest mountaineer Leigh-Mallory as history master at Charterhouse. He went to Australia in 1930 as headmaster of Geelong Grammar School, Victoria, and remained there until 1962, influencing several now-famous Australians including **Rupert Murdoch, Kerry Packer** and **Russell Drysdale**. In 1953 he inaugurated Timbertop, the school's campus in the foothills of the Australian Alps,

which the young Prince **Charles** attended in 1966. In retirement he was chairman of the Australian Broadcasting Commission (1961–67) and wrote two autobiographical books, *The Education of a Civilised Man* (1962) and *Richly Rewarding* (1978).

Darling, Jay Norwood, *known as* Ding 1876–1962
US cartoonist
He was born in Norwood, Michigan, and as a staff cartoonist on the Des Moines *Register* (1906–49) and the New York *Tribune* (later the *Herald Tribune*) from 1917 to 1949, he won the Pulitzer Prize in 1923 and 1943. An active wildlife conservationist, he was chief of the US Biological Survey (1934–35) and president of the National Wildlife Federation (1936).

Darlington, Cyril Dean 1903–81
English cytologist and geneticist
Born in Chorley, Lancashire, and educated at South Eastern Agricultural College, Wye, he began work at the John Innes Horticultural Institution, London (1923), was founding head of its cytology department in 1937, and director of the institute from 1939 to 1953. In 1953 he became Sherardian Professor of Botany at Oxford. In 1929–30 he travelled to Iran and Caucasia to investigate the origins of various plant species. He proposed 60 genetic terms and seven major theories, including the idea that chromosomes themselves were the objects of evolution and selection. In later life he studied the genetics of man and society, concluding that genius, or innovation, was the result of outbreeding and the environment. He was the author of *Chromosomes and Plant Breeding* (1932), *Darwin's Place in History* (1960) and *The Little Universe of Man* (1981). He exposed **Stalin**'s murder of Russian geneticists and was a strong critic of committees and the establishment.

Darlington, William 1782–1863
US botanist
He was born in Birmingham, Pennsylvania. The California pitcher plant (*Darlingtonia*) is named after him.

Darnley, Henry Stewart, Lord 1545–67
Scottish nobleman
Born in Temple Newsome, England, the eldest son and heir of Matthew, 4th Earl of Lennox, he was proposed as a husband for his cousin **Mary, Queen of Scots**, upon the death of her first husband, **Francis II** of France. In 1565 he married Mary at Holyroodhouse in Edinburgh in the presence of just seven witnesses, having been proclaimed Henry, King of Scots, the previous day. A son was born (the future **James VI and I**), but the marriage was disastrous. Darnley's participation in the plot to murder **David Rizzio**, the queen's Italian secretary, finally estranged him from her. He was himself murdered in Edinburgh when Kirk O'Field, the house in which he was sleeping, was blown up at the instigation of his wife's new suitor, the Earl of **Bothwell**, who subsequently married the queen.

Darrow, Clarence Seward 1857–1938
US civil liberties lawyer
Born in Kinsman, Ohio, he was admitted to the Bar in 1878. In 1907 he successfully defended 'Big Bill' **Haywood** and Charles Moyer of the Western Federation of Miners who had been implicated in the murder of Frank Steunenberg, ex-Governor of Idaho. In 1924, Darrow's defence of Richard Loeb and Nathan Leopold in a highly publicized murder trial saved them from the death penalty; and in the Scopes Monkey Trial of 1925, at Dayton, Tennessee, he defended the high school biology teacher John Scopes who was charged under the Tennessee state law forbidding the teaching of **Darwin**'s theory of evolution. Although Scopes was found guilty and fined, Darrow dismantled the arguments of the prosecution. In 1934 he was appointed to investigate Senator Gerald Nye's

charge that the codes introduced by the National Recovery Board were favouring monopolies. His report led eventually to the abolition of price control. Darrow was an advocate of progressive reforms and an opponent of the death penalty, and often used the courtroom as a platform for wry and eloquent arguments aimed at swaying the US public as well as the jury at hand. 📖 Miriam Gurko, *Clarence Darrow* (1965)

Dart, Raymond A(rthur) 1893–1988
South African anatomist
Born in Toowong, Australia, he graduated in medicine at Sydney University in 1917, and became Professor of Anatomy at Witwatersrand University, Johannesburg, in 1923. In 1925 he described an ape-like infant part-skull found in Botswana which he considered to be a human ancestor, *Australopithecus africanus*. Later work by Dart and others supports this view, and indicates that bipedalism preceded brain expansion, although whether the australopithecines were tool-users, and in the direct ancestral line to *homo sapiens*, remains uncertain.

Daru, Pierre Antoine Noël Bruno, Comte 1767–1829
French military administrator and historian
Born in Montpellier, he joined the army at the age of 16, and was imprisoned during the Terror, but was appointed Secretary of the war industry in 1800 and intendant-general in Austria and Prussia. He was Minister of War from 1811, and was later ennobled by **Louis XVIII**. He wrote histories of Venice and of Great Britain.

Darusmont, Frances See **Wright, Frances**

Darwin, Charles Robert See panel p492

Darwin, Erasmus 1731–1802
English physician and poet
Born near Newark, Nottinghamshire, he studied at the universities of Cambridge and Edinburgh. At Lichfield he became a popular physician and prominent figure on account of his ability, his radical and freethinking opinions, his poetry, his eight-acre botanical garden, and his imperious advocacy of temperance in drinking. After his second marriage in 1781, he settled in Derby, where he founded a Philosophical Society. He was grandfather of **Charles Darwin** by his first wife, and of **Francis Galton** by his second. He anticipated **Jean-Baptiste Lamarck**'s views on evolution, and also those of his own grandson. He edited translations of **Carolus Linnaeus**'s work, and wrote a long verse work, *The Botanic Garden* (1789). His chief prose works are *Zoonomia, or the Laws of Organic Life* (1794–96) and *Phytologia* (1799).

Das, Chitta Ranjan 1870–1925
Bengali patriot and politician
Called to the Bar in 1894, he soon acquired a reputation for skilfully representing nationalists, such as **Aurobindo** (1908), accused of terrorism by the British colonial government in India. He participated in the campaign against the partition of Bengal, chaired Bengal Provincial Congress (1917) and the Indian National Congress (1918), and renounced his legal practice and all his property to join **Mahatma Gandhi**'s Non-Cooperation Movement (1920). Imprisoned in 1921, he emerged in 1922 to help form the Swaraj Party to contest district and provincial council elections (then boycotted by the Indian National Congress). Opposed to Hindu communalism, he was popular with both Muslim and Hindu communities in Bengal. He was elected Mayor of Calcutta City Corporation in 1924. Soon after, he came to an agreement with Gandhi which allowed both Swarajists and Gandhians to campaign from the Congress platform. Although he himself rejected violence, many of his followers were either involved in terrorism or openly

Darwin, Charles Robert 1809–82

English naturalist, the originator (with Alfred Wallace) of the theory of evolution by natural selection

Charles Darwin was born in Shrewsbury, Shropshire, the grandson of **Erasmus Darwin** and of **Josiah Wedgwood**. He was educated at Shrewsbury grammar school, studied medicine at Edinburgh University (1825–27), and then, with a view to entering the church, entered Christ's College, Cambridge, in 1828. At Edinburgh he had joined the local Plinian Society; he took part in its natural history excursions, and read before it his first scientific paper—on Flustra or sea-mats. His biological studies began in earnest at Cambridge, where the botanist John Stevens Henslow encouraged his interest in zoology and geology. He was recommended by Henslow as naturalist to HMS *Beagle*, which was about to start for a scientific survey of South American waters (1831–36), captained by **Robert Fitzroy**.

Darwin visited Tenerife, the Cape Verde Islands, Brazil, Montevideo, Tierra del Fuego, Buenos Aires, Valparaiso, Chile, the Galapagos, Tahiti, New Zealand, Tasmania and the Keeling Islands; it was there that he started his seminal studies of coral reefs. During this long expedition he obtained an intimate knowledge of the fauna, flora and geology of many lands, which equipped him for his later many-sided investigations. By 1846 he had published several works on his geological and zoological discoveries on coral reefs and volcanic islands—works that placed him at once in the front rank of scientists. He formed a friendship with **Charles Lyell**, was Secretary of the Geological Society from 1838 to 1841, and in 1839 married his cousin, Emma Wedgwood (1808–96).

From 1842 he lived at Downe, Kent, enjoying his garden, conservatories, pigeons and fowls. The practical knowledge thus gained (especially as regards variation and interbreeding) proved invaluable; private means enabled him to devote himself unremittingly, in spite of continuous ill health, to science. At Downe he addressed himself to the great work of his life—the problem of the origin of species. After five years collecting the evidence, he 'allowed himself to speculate' on the subject, and drew up in 1842 some short notes, enlarged in 1844 into a sketch of conclusions for his own use. These embodied in embryo the principle of natural selection, the germ of the Darwinian theory; but Darwin delayed publication of his hypothesis, which was only precipitated by accident. In 1858 Wallace sent him a memoir on the Malay Archipelago, which, to Darwin's alarm, contained in essence the main idea of his own theory of natural selection. Lyell and **Joseph Dalton Hooker** persuaded him to submit a paper of his own, based on his 1844 sketch, which was read simultaneously with Wallace's before the Linnaean Society on 1 July 1858, although neither Darwin nor Wallace were present at that historic occasion.

Though not the sole originator of the theory of evolution, Darwin was the first thinker to gain for the concept a wide acceptance among biological experts. By adding his own specific idea of natural selection to the crude evolutionism of Erasmus Darwin, **Jean-Baptiste Lamarck** and others, Darwin supplied to the idea a sufficient cause, which raised it at once from a hypothesis to a verifiable theory.

He was buried in Westminster Abbey. His son, Sir Francis Darwin (1848–1925), who was also a botanist, became a Reader in Botany at Oxford (1888) and produced Darwin's *Life and Letters* (1887–1903). Another son, Sir George Howard Darwin (1845–1913) was Professor of Astronomy at Cambridge (1883–1912).

📖 At Downe, Darwin set about condensing a vast mass of notes, and assembled his great work, *The Origin of Species by Means of Natural Selection*, published in November 1859. This epoch-making work, received with great interest throughout Europe, was violently attacked and energetically defended; in the end it succeeded in obtaining recognition from almost all biologists of note. From the day of its publication, Darwin continued to work on a great series of supplemental treatises: *The Fertilisation of Orchids* (1862), *The Variation of Plants and Animals under Domestication* (1867) and *The Descent of Man and Selection in Relation to Sex* (1871), which derived the human race from a hairy quadrumanous animal belonging to the great anthropoid group, and related to the progenitors of the orang-utan, chimpanzee and gorilla. In it Darwin also developed his important supplementary theory of sexual selection. Later works were *The Expression of the Emotions in Man and Animals* (1873), *Insectivorous Plants* (1875), *Climbing Plants* (1875), *The Effects of Cross and Self Fertilisation in the Vegetable Kingdom* (1876), *Different Forms of Flowers in Plants of the same Species* (1877), *The Power of Movement in Plants* (1880) and *The Formation of Vegetable Mould through the action of Worms* (1881).

📖 John Bowlby, *Charles Darwin: A Biography* (1990); Peter Brent, *Charles Darwin: A Man of Enlarged Curiosity* (1981); Gavin de Beer, *Charles Darwin: A Scientific Biography* (1963).

'I have called this principle, by which each slight variation, if useful, is preserved, by the term of Natural Selection, in order to mark its relation to man's power of selection.' From *The Origin of Species by Means of Natural Selection*, ch.3.

---

advocated the use of violence in opposition to colonial rule. A strong supporter of the trade union movement, he campaigned on behalf of railway workers and labourers on the Assam tea plantations. He and his followers were thus a powerful force for radicalism within the Indian Nationalist movement, a radicalism that grew in the years following his death. Sadly, his achievements in forging unity between Hindus and Muslims in Bengal survived his death by only a few years: factionalism and violence led ultimately to the partition of the province on independence in 1947.

Dasent, Sir George Webbe 1817–96

English folklorist and scholar of Scandinavian studies

Born in St Vincent, Windward Islands, he was educated at Westminster School, King's College London and Magdalen Hall, Oxford, and was called to the Bar in 1852. He was an assistant editor on the London *Times* (1845–70).

In 1853 he became a professor at King's College London and from 1872 to 1892 he was a Civil Service commissioner. He is best known as a translator of classical Icelandic literature, including *The Prose or Younger Edda* (1842), *The Saga of Burnt Njal* (1861) and the *Story of Gisli the Outlaw* (1866). He also published *Popular Tales from the Norse* (1859) and *Tales from the Fjeld* (1874), both translated from Peter Asbjørnsen's Norwegian collections.

Dashkova, Yekaterina Romanovna 1743–1810

Russian princess and author

Born in St Petersburg, a member of the influential Vorontsov family, she married (1759) Prince Dashkov (d.1762). She was an intimate friend and leading supporter of Empress **Catherine II the Great** in the conspiracy that deposed her husband, **Peter III** (1762). Dashkova travelled widely in Europe, and was director of the Academy of

Arts and Sciences in St Petersburg (1783–96). She wrote several plays, and was the first president of the Russian Academy (1783).

Dashwood, Sir Francis 1708–81
English courtier and profligate
He was an MP (1741–63), Chancellor of the Exchequer (1761–63), joint Postmaster-General (1770–81) and succeeded his uncle as 15th Baron Le Depencer in 1763. He earned notoriety as the founder (c.1755) of a secret society, the Knights of St Francis of Wycombe, better known as the Hellfire Club, and later known as the Mad Monks of Medmenham because of their obscene cavortings in the ruins of Medmenham Abbey. The members included John Wilkes and the 4th Earl of Sandwich.

Dassault, Marcel, *originally* Marcel Bloch 1892–1986
French aviation pioneer, industrialist and politician
Born in Paris, he saw one of the Wright brothers in flight while a schoolboy, and was inspired to study aeronautical design and electrical engineering. After graduating from the École Nationale Supérieure de l'Aéronautique (1913), he joined Henri Potez in building aircraft during World War I. He spent several years in property speculation, then rejoined Potez to build twin-engined and tri-motor war planes. A Jew, he was imprisoned in Buchenwald concentration camp during World War II, but was later converted to Roman Catholicism. Following the war he adopted the name Dassault (which had been his brother's code name in the French Resistance) and founded his own company, Général Aéronautique Marcel Dassault. Building a series of highly successful craft in the 1950s, such as the Mystère and Mirage, guided weapons and specialized equipment, he became one of the wealthiest men in France. He was Deputy in the National Assembly (1951–55), Deputy for the Oise (1957–58), and was elected to the National Assembly in 1986.

Daswanth, *also spelt* Daswarth or Dasvanth 16th century
Indian Mughal painter
He was active at the court of the emperor Akbar the Great. Akbar was intent on developing an Indian school of painting, and established an academy in which about 100 Hindu artists worked under the guidance of Persian painters. Daswanth was one of its leading three artists. Most of the surviving paintings of the *Hamzanama*, the adventures of Amir Hamza, the uncle of the prophet leader, were painted there during Akbar's reign. The composition and architectural ornaments were Persian in origin, whereas the costumes, landscapes and figures began to show an Indian quality which was also evident in the toning down of the original brilliant colour scheme.

Daubié, Julie-Victoire 1824–74
French writer and feminist
Born in eastern France, she had little formal education, but was taught Latin and Greek by her brother and became a governess. In 1858 she won an essay competition organized by the Académie de Lyons. Encouraged by one of the competition judges, she sat the *baccalauréat* exam in 1861 despite government opposition, and became the first woman to obtain this qualification in 1862. She went on to pass the *licence,* a more advanced exam, in 1871. Her writings include *La femme pauvre au XIXe siècle* (1866, 'Poverty of Women in the 19th Century') and *L'émancipation de la femme* (1871, 'Women's Emancipation').

d'Aubigné See Merle, Jean Henri d'Aubigné

Daubigny, Charles François 1817–78
French artist
Born in Paris, he was a pupil of Paul Delaroche. A member of the Barbizon school, he painted landscapes, such as *The Banks of the Oise* (1872, Musée des Beaux-Arts). He painted moonlight and river scenes, a number of which are to be seen in the National Gallery in London.

Daubrée, Gabriel Auguste 1814–96
French economic geologist, mineralogist and mining engineer
Born in Metz, he studied at the École Polytechnique in Paris, and was admitted to the Corps des Mines in 1834. He was appointed Professor of Geology and Mineralogy (1838) and later Dean (1852) at the University of Strasbourg. He became Professor of Mineralogy and Geology (1862–72) and, subsequently, director at the École des Mines in Paris, being appointed Inspector-General of French Mines in 1867. He published more than 300 memoirs, chiefly on geological and mineralogical subjects with notable studies of meteorites, minerals and experimental petrology. He studied the permeability of rocks and was noted for the long-term and sometimes dangerous experiments which he conducted to ascertain to what extent it was possible to imitate the natural production of rocks.

Daudet, Alphonse 1840–97
French writer
Born in Nimes, he was educated at the Lyons Lycée, and at 17 went to Paris where he obtained an appointment in the office of the Duke of Morny. From 1862 he published a number of theatrical pieces, notably *L'Arlésienne* (1872, 'A Woman from Arles'), with incidental music by Bizet. His best-known work is his series of sketches and short stories of Provençal life, originally written for the newspaper *Le Figaro*, especially *Lettres de mon moulin* (collected 1869, 'Letters from my Mill') and the charming extravaganza of *Tartarin de Tarascon* (1872), continued in *Tartarin sur les Alpes* (1885) and *Port Tarascon* (1890). *Le Petit chose* (1868, 'Young What's His Name') is full of pathos and of reminiscences of Daudet's own early struggles. Other works include his long naturalistic novels on the social conditions of the day, such as *Fromont jeune et Risler aîné* (1874, 'Fromont Junior and Risler Senior') and *Le Nabab* (1877, 'The Nabob'), *Sapho* (1884), a tale of the infatuation of a young man for a courtesan, and *L'Immortel* (1888, 'The Immortal One'), in which Daudet's powers of ridicule are turned against the Académie Française. 📖 R H Sherard, *Alphonse Daudet* (1894)

Daudet, Léon 1867–1942
French writer and political activist
The son of Alphonse Daudet, he studied medicine but turned to journalism, and in 1899 helped to found the right-wing royalist newspaper *Action française*, of which he became editor in 1908. He sat in the Chamber of Deputies from 1919 to 1924. In 1925 his son was assassinated and subsequently he spent some time in Belgium as a political exile. He wrote several novels, but is best remembered for his numerous memoirs and critical works, especially *Le Stupide XIXe siècle* (1922, 'The Stupid Nineteenth Century'). 📖 J Marque, *Léon Daudet* (1971)

D'Aumale See Aumalle, Duc d'

Daumier, Honoré 1808–78
French caricaturist and painter
Born in Marseilles, he was taken to Paris as a child, and entered a lithographer's studio. He made his name as a satirical caricaturist, working for *La Caricature, Charivari* and other periodicals, and was imprisoned for six months for a caricature of Louis Philippe in 1832. He made more than 4,000 lithographs and 4,000 caricatures. Later he worked as a serious painter of realistic subject pictures, such as *Don Quixote* and *The Third Class Carriage*, and also as a sculptor. In his old age he became blind and was befriended by Camille Corot.

Daurat or Dorat, Jean c.1510–1588
French scholar and poet

As president of the Collège de Coqueret he supervised the studies of Pierre de Ronsard, Joachim du Bellay, Jean de Baïf and Rémy Belleau. These poets, with whom he was united in the famous Pléiade, he carefully trained for the task of reforming the vernacular and ennobling French literature by imitation of Greek and Latin models. He wrote copious verse in Greek and Latin, and was appointed court poet by Charles IX.

Dausset, Jean 1916–
French immunologist and Nobel Prize winner

Born in Toulouse, he studied medicine in Paris, and was Professor of Medicine there from 1958 to 1977, and Professor of Experimental Medicine at the Collège de France from 1977 to 1987. Service in a blood transfusion unit in World War II led to his special interest in transfusion responses and the way they can lead to antibody production. His results led to 'tissue typing' which greatly reduced rejection risks in organ transplant surgery. He shared the 1980 Nobel Prize for physiology or medicine with George Snell and Baruj Benacerraf.

Dauthendey, Max 1867–1918
German poet, philosopher, dramatist and novelist

Born in Würzburg, he lived a solitary life and his works run to nine volumes, including *Reliquien* (1899). His poetry is exotic, and his elaborate theories of life and art are forgotten, but he still has a few champions, who point to its 'orgiastic' qualities. ▢ H G Wendt, *Max Dauthendey: Poet-Philosopher* (1936)

D'Auvergne, Henri de la Tour See Turenne, Henri de la Tour d'Auvergne, Vicomte de

Davaine, Casimir Joseph 1812–82
French physician and microbiologist

He was born in St-Amand-les-Eaux, and after studying at Tournai and Lille, went to Paris in 1830 to embark on a medical course. He practised medicine in Paris, and although he never held an official university position, he contributed a steady stream of important experimental papers, mostly to do with the role of micro-organisms in the causation of human and animal diseases. He developed procedures to identify parasitical worms, and first identified the anthrax bacillus in the blood of animals dying from anthrax. He was an advocate of the germ theory of disease at the Academy of Medicine before it was taken up by Louis Pasteur, who always appreciated Davaine's work.

D'Avenant, Sir William 1606–68
English poet and playwright

He was born in Oxford. His father kept a tavern at which Shakespeare used to stay, thereby giving rise to the rumour that D'Avenant was Shakespeare's illegitimate son. He studied briefly at Lincoln College, Oxford, and later served in the household of the aged poet, Fulke Greville, Lord Brooke. From 1628 he produced many plays, including *The Cruel Brother* (1630) and *The Wits* (1636), and in 1638 he was appointed Poet Laureate in succession to Ben Jonson. About the same time he lost his nose through an illness, a calamity which exposed him to public ridicule. Although knighted by King Charles I in 1643, he was later imprisoned in the Tower of London (1650–52), where he completed his epic, *Gondibert* (1651). He is considered to have been the founder of English opera with his *Siege of Rhodes* (1656), and he opened a theatre, the Cockpit, in Drury Lane, London, in 1658. ▢ A Harbege, *Sir William D'Avenant, 1606–1668* (1935)

David, *Hebrew* 'beloved' 11th century BC
First king of the Judean dynasty of Israel

He was the youngest son of Jesse of Bethlehem, and is traditionally the author of several of the Psalms and the ancestor of Jesus Christ. His success as a warrior against the Philistines, especially in killing Goliath, aroused King Saul's jealousy, and he was forced to flee, but after Saul's death he became King over Judah in Hebron, and later was chosen King of all Israel. Jerusalem became the political and religious centre of his kingdom, and he built a palace for himself on its highest hill, Zion (the 'city of David'), and placed the Ark of the Covenant there under a tent. He united the many tribes of Israel, and extended his territory from Egypt to the Euphrates. The later part of his reign was troubled by attempted revolutions by his sons Absalom and Adonijah. He may have died as early as 1018BC, and was succeeded by his son Solomon, his son by Bathsheba.

David or Dewi, St c.520–601
Patron saint of Wales

Born near St Bride's Bay, Pembrokeshire, he presided over two Welsh synods, at Brefi and the 'Lucus Victoriae', or Synod of Victory. According to the *Annales Cambriae* (10th century) he died in 601 as Bishop of Moni Judeorum, or Menevia, afterwards St David's. His feast day is 1 March.

David I c.1080–1153
King of Scotland

He was the youngest of the six sons of Malcolm Canmore and St Margaret. In 1100 his sister Matilda married Henry I of England, and he accompanied her to the English court. When his brother Alexander I succeeded to the throne (1107), David became Prince of Cumbria, and, through marriage, became Earl of Huntingdon (1113). He was therefore loyal to England under Henry I's daughter, Matilda, Empress Maud, when he succeeded Alexander (1124), until Stephen took the English throne (1135). He invaded northern England in support of Matilda but made peace at the Treaty of Durham (1136), and when war broke out again (1138), he made a further treaty (1139). During his reign the authority of the monarch was consolidated, the first Scottish royal coinage issued, a common law of Scotland produced, and trade encouraged. The Scottish Church was reformed and reorganized, and three new dioceses established by 1154. Twenty monasteries were founded, including the Cistercians at Melrose and the Premonstratensians at Dryburgh. By 1154 the transformation of the Scottish Church that had begun with Malcolm Canmore and St Margaret was nearcomplete. ▢ Marjorie O Anderson, *Kings and Kingship in Early Scotland* (1973)

David II 1324–71
King of Scotland

He was born in Dunfermline, the only surviving son of Robert Bruce (King Robert I) and married the daughter of Edward II of England, Joanna (1328). In 1329 he succeeded his father, and he and his child queen were crowned at Scone (1331). The success of the victory by Edward de Balliol and Edward III at Halidon Hill (1333) forced David's guardians to send him and his consort to France (1334). He returned in 1341 and, five years later, invaded England, but at Neville's Cross, near Durham, was defeated and captured (1346), and was kept prisoner for 11 years. His release (1357), on promise of a heavy ransom, and the treaty of 1357 brought 27 years of truce with England, but strains over payment of the ransom brought increased customs duties and direct taxation, and caused resentment when the hostages of 1357 were abandoned (1363) as a result of defaulting on payments. Yet David maintained a firm grip of his kingdom, with little sign of the tensions between king and nobles which afflicted later reigns. Despite a second marriage to Margaret Drummond of Logie (1363), a year after Queen

Joanna died, he left no children, and was succeeded by his sister's son, **Robert II**. 📖 Marjorie O Anderson, *Kings and Kingship in Early Scotland* (1973)

David, (Père) Armand 1826–1900
French naturalist and Lazarist missionary
Born in Espelette in the Pyrenees, he was educated locally and at the Grand Séminaire de Bayonne. He entered the Lazarist Order of St Vincent de Paul (1848), hoping to go to China, but instead went to Savona, Italy (1851–61), where he taught science, continued his education and formed the foundation of the Savona Natural History Museum. After 10 years he was an expert in geography, geology and mineralogy, as well as a brilliant all-round naturalist. He was then ordained and sent to China as a missionary. Between 1866 and 1874 he explored the Peking plain, Mongolia, Tibet and central China, sending specimens to the Natural History Museum, Paris. He discovered the unique handkerchief tree named after him (*Davidia involucrata*), but he is best known for one of his zoological discoveries, Père David's deer (*Elaphurus davidianus*).

David, Elizabeth 1913–92
English cookery writer
Born in Sussex, she spent time in France, on a Greek island, and in Cairo, before returning to a Great Britain beset by food rationing (1946). Her early books, such as *Mediterranean Cooking* (1950) and *Italian Food* (1954), are a reminder of a culinary world unrestricted by the lack of butter, cream, and imported delicacies. Her best-known work is her influential *French Provincial Cooking* (1960), a work of reference as well as a collection of recipes. Other works include *English Bread and Yeast Cookery* (1977) and *An Omelette and a Glass of Wine* (1984).

David, Félicien 1810–76
French composer
Born in Cadenet, he was a chorister in Aix cathedral, then entered the Paris Conservatoire. He joined the Saint-Simonians in 1831 and composed for them, and on the break-up of the cult in 1833, travelled to the East. In 1835 he returned to Paris, but remained in obscurity till his *Le Désert* (1844, 'The Desert'), a grand 'ode-symphonie', had a sudden success. He failed to retain his popularity, but the oriental devices and motifs which he used influenced many other composers.

David, Gerhard c.1460–c.1523
Flemish painter
Born in Oudewater, the Netherlands, he entered the Painters' Guild of Bruges in 1484, becoming its dean in 1501. Among his best works are the two *Justice Scenes* (1498) in Bruges.

David, Jacques Louis 1748–1825
French painter
Born in Paris, he won the Prix de Rome in 1774, and in Rome devoted himself to drawing from classical models. It is in his works of the 1780s, such as the *Oath of the Horatii* (1784), *Death of Socrates* (1788) and *Brutus Condemning his Son* (1789), that the Neoclassical style is first clearly discernible and he became the leading artist of the Neoclassical movement. David entered with enthusiasm into the Revolution, and in 1792 became a representative for Paris in the Convention. He voted for the death of Louis XVI, was a member of the Committee of Public Safety, and was the artistic director of the great national fêtes founded on classical customs. After Robespierre's death he was twice imprisoned, and narrowly escaped with his life. Released in 1795, he produced his masterpiece, *The Rape of the Sabines* (1799), and in 1804 was appointed court painter by Napoleon I. After the Bourbon restoration he was banished in 1816 as a regicide.

David, Moses, *originally* David Brandt Berg 1919–
US cult leader
Born in California into a devoutly Christian home, he began a ministry with the Christian and Missionary Alliance Church, but involvement with the hippy lifestyle of 1960s California led to his adopting an increasingly independent style of ministry. In 1968 he founded the Children of God, which later became the Family of Love, and moved to London in 1971. This millenarian movement, based on the teaching of the Bible, and David's own *Mo Letters*, followed a radical anti-materialist philosophy, but the increasing use of controversial methods of attracting converts led to strong criticism of the sect, and to some decline in its influence. 📖 Shirley Harrison, *Cults—The Battle for God* (1990)

David d'Angers, Pierre Jean 1789–1856
French sculptor
He was born in Angers, the son of a wood carver, and studied under **Jacques Louis David** in Paris. In 1811 his relievo of the *Death of Epaminondas* won him the Prix de Rome, and he went to Rome, where he was influenced by **Jean Ingres** and **Antonio Canova**. From 1835 to 1837 he executed the pediment of the Panthéon, in Paris, his most prestigious commission, as well as the Gutenberg monument in Strasbourg. He was also a prolific sculptor of portrait busts and medallions. These reveal a talent for characterization, and include those of **Niccoló Paganini** (1834), **Jeremy Bentham** and **Goethe** (1828 and 1835, both in Saumur). In the Angers museum 200 of his works are preserved, as well as 400 of his medallions and many drawings.

David-Neel, Alexandra 1868–1969
French oriental scholar and traveller
Born in Paris, she studied Sanskrit in Ceylon (Sri Lanka) and India, and toured internationally as an opera singer. In 1911 she returned to India, visiting the Dalai Lama in exile at Darjeeling and studying Tibetan Buddhism. Invited to Sikkim, she overwintered in a high mountain cave with a religious hermit and her lifelong servant, Yongden. Having travelled illegally to Tashilhumpo in Tibet, she was expelled from India in 1916 and went to Burma, Japan and Korea with Yongden, arriving in Beijing (Peking) on 8 October 1917. Together they travelled 2,000 miles (3,220km) to the Kumbum monastery near the Koko Nor and on to Chengdu through northern Tibet, Mongolia and across the Gobi Desert; she then donned the disguise of a Tibetan pilgrim, as described in *My Journey to Lhasa* (1927). They returned to Tibet in 1934 to work at Kanting until forced to leave by the Japanese advance of 1944, and retired to Digne in France, where she died aged 100.

Davidson, Donald Herbert 1917–
US philosopher
Born in Springfield, Massachusetts, he received a PhD from Harvard in 1949 and taught at numerous US institutions, including the University of California, Berkeley (1981–), where he is professor. He has been one of the most influential analytical philosophers over the last two decades, with original and interrelated contributions to the philosophy of language, mind and action. His writings include *Essays on Action and Events* (1980), *Inquiries into Truth and Interpretation* (1983) and *Structure and Content of Truth* (1990).

Davidson, Eric Harris 1937–
US molecular biologist
Born in New York City, he studied at the University of Pennsylvania and Rockefeller University in New York, where he was a research associate (1963–65) and assistant professor (1965–71). He then moved to the California Institute of Technology as associate Professor of

Developmental Molecular Biology (1971–74) and Professor (1974–81), and since 1981 has been Norman Chandler Professor of Cell Biology there. He is a member of the US National Academy of Sciences, and has written many publications on DNA sequence organization, gene expression during embryonic development, and gene regulation. Together with **Roy Britten**, he elucidated genome organization in higher animals, and showed that the genome has enormous stretches of 'junk' DNA made up of longer sequences repeated a few times, and shorter sequences repeated many times. However its function remains unknown.

Davidson, John 1857–1909
Scottish poet, novelist and dramatist
Born in Barrhead, Renfrewshire, he was educated at the Highlander's Academy, Greenock, where he became a pupil-teacher (1872–76), and at Edinburgh University, before he became an itinerant teacher in Scotland. He had started to write in 1885 (four verse dramas and two novels), and in 1889 moved to London where, among other works, he wrote *Fleet Street Eclogues* (1893) and *Ballads and Songs* (1894). T S Eliot later acknowledged a debt to the urban imagery and colloquialism of his 'Thirty Bob a Week'. He wrote prolifically in the last years of his life, including a series of blank-verse *Testaments*, several other verse dramas, short stories and prose sketches. He committed suicide by drowning himself at Penzance. ⌑ J Townsend, *Davidson, poet of Armageddon* (1961)

Davidson, Jo(seph) 1883–1952
US sculptor
Born in New York City, he attended medical school at Yale before determining to become a sculptor and studying art in Paris from 1907. He was soon in demand as a maker of statues and portrait busts, and he sought to capture the intricacies of human character using a naturalistic style. He sculpted hundreds of famous political and cultural figures from life, including **Mahatma Gandhi**, **Albert Einstein** and **James Joyce**, and portrayed many of the leading statesmen and generals of both world wars.

Davidson (of Lambeth), Randall Thomas Davidson, Baron 1848–1930
Scottish Anglican prelate and Archbishop of Canterbury
Born in Edinburgh into a Presbyterian family, he studied at Harrow and Trinity College, Oxford, and became chaplain to Archbishop **Tait** (his father-in-law, whose biography he wrote in 1891) and to Queen **Victoria**. He was also dean of Windsor and Bishop of Rochester (1891) and of Winchester (1895). As Archbishop of Canterbury (1903–28) he worked hard to increase the role of the Church in society, and was not afraid to speak out on social and political issues.

Davie, Alan 1920–
Scottish painter and jazz musician
Born in Grangemouth, central Scotland, the son of a painter and etcher, he studied at Edinburgh College of Art (1937–40), later moving to Hertfordshire, Cornwall and the Carribean. During wartime service with the Royal Artillery he concentrated on his other major pursuit—jazz. He played the saxophone and in 1971 produced his first record, which was followed by concerts and broadcasts (1973–75). In 1948 he was introduced, through Peggy Guggenheim in Venice, to the work of **Jackson Pollock** and **Mark Rothko**, and his paintings of the 1950s had much in common with US Abstract Expressionism, eg *Birth of Venus* (1955, Tate, London). His bold and colourful images, suggestive of myth and magic, testify to his preoccupation with Zen and oriental mysticism, a continuing interest reflected in his solo exhibitions of the 1980s. ⌑ D Hall and M Tucker, *Alan Davie* (1992)

Davie, Elspeth, *née* Dryer 1919–95
Scottish novelist
Born in Kilmarnock, Ayrshire, she was educated at Edinburgh University and Edinburgh College of Art. She worked as an art teacher before settling in Edinburgh, where she married the philosopher George Elder Davie (1912–). Her first novel, *Providings*, was published in 1965. Edinburgh provides the backdrop for her fiction, which eschews high drama or lurid subject matter in favour of an exploration of the human vulnerability underlying ordinary, everyday behaviour. In 1978 she won the Katherine Mansfield award for her short stories, collections of which include *The Spark* (1968), *The Night of the Funny Hats* (1980) and *Death of a Doctor* (1992). Her novels include *Creating a Scene* (1971), *Climbers On A Stair* (1978) and *Coming to Light* (1989).

Davies, Arthur Bowen 1862–1928
US painter
Born in Utica, New York, he studied at the Art Institute of Chicago and at the Art Students League in New York City. Known for idyllic pastoral scenes and allegorical paintings, he belonged to the group of US artists known as the Eight or the Ashcan School, whose first exhibition he organized in New York in 1908. He was also the chief organizer of the Armory Show in 1913, which brought avant-garde European painters—Post-Impressionists, Cubists and Futurists—to New York for the first time, changing the direction of art in the USA.

Davies, Christian, *known as* Mother Ross 1667–1739
Irish woman soldier
Born in Dublin, she served for many years in the army, masquerading as a man. She went to Flanders in search of her husband, Richard Welsh, who had been pressed into the Duke of **Marlborough**'s army. There she enlisted under the name of Christopher Welsh, fought in the Battle of Blenheim (1704), and eventually was reunited with her husband in 1706. When he was killed at the Battle of Malplaquet (1709) she married a grenadier, Hugh Jones, who was killed the following year. In England she was presented to Queen **Anne**, and returned to Dublin where she married another soldier. She died in Chelsea Pensioners' Hospital for soldiers.

Davies, Clement Edward 1884–1962
Welsh politician
Born in Llanfyllin, Montgomeryshire, he was educated at Trinity Hall, Cambridge, and was called to the Bar in 1909. He became Liberal MP for Montgomeryshire in 1929, and in 1945 he was elected Leader of the decimated Liberal Party in the House of Commons, holding this office until September 1956, when he resigned. He declined a post as Education Secretary in **Churchill**'s 1951–55 government, did not enter into any political agreements with either of the two great parties and thus kept the Liberal Party a separate political entity. He conducted a brilliant parliamentary defence of **Seretse Khama** against the actions of successive Labour and Conservative Colonial Secretaries.

Davies, David 1818–90
Welsh industrialist and politician
Born in Llandinam, Montgomeryshire, he worked his way up through building and contracting work to railway construction in mid-Wales, and later became owner of the Ocean Colliery in the Rhondda Valley. A dispute about the Bute family interests in Cardiff docks led to his defiantly building his own docks at nearby Barry from which to ship his coal exports. He was elected Liberal MP for Cardigan in 1874, but in 1886 he resigned the Liberal whip.

Davies (of Llandinam), David Davies, 1st Baron 1880–1944
Welsh philanthropist and politician

He was born in Llandinam, Montgomeryshire, the grandson of the industrialist David Davies, whose great wealth he inherited. With his two sisters, Gwendoline and Margaret, he was a major benefactor of the University College of Wales, Aberystwyth, the National Library of Wales, and of a chain of tuberculosis sanatoriums established in memory of King Edward VII. A Liberal MP for Montgomeryshire (1906–29) and close associate of Lloyd George, after World War I he turned his attention to support for the League of Nations and to attempts to set up an International Police Force, which never materialized. In 1933 he founded the New Commonwealth Society. He erected the Temple of Peace and Health in the centre of Cathays Park in Cardiff.

Davies, Sir Henry Walford 1869–1941
Welsh composer, organist and broadcaster

Born in Oswestry, he became Professor of Music at Aberystwyth (1919–26), organist of St George's Chapel, Windsor (1927–32) and Master of the King's Musick (1934–41). He was a prolific composer of religious music, and an influential educationist through his radio talks on music.

Davies, Howard 1945–
English stage director

He was born in Reading, Berkshire, and after taking a director's course at Bristol University, became associate director of Bristol Old Vic. He joined the Royal Shakespeare Company (RSC) in 1975 and became an associate director to establish and run the Warehouse, the RSC's London studio theatre (1977–82). His other RSC work includes a cool, Brechtian *Macbeth* (1982), *Henry VIII* (1983) and *Troilus and Cressida* (1985), which he set during the Crimean War. He also directed William Saroyan's *The Time of Your Life* and Christopher Hampton's *Les Liaisons Dangereuses* at The Other Place. He became an associate director of the National Theatre in 1988. His first operatic production was *Idomeneo* (1991) for the Welsh National Opera.

Davies, Idris 1905–53
Welsh poet

Born in Rhymney, Gwent, he left school at 14 to become a miner in the pit where his father worked. He later took a correspondence course and went on to study at Loughborough College and Nottingham University, qualifying as a teacher. He published four volumes of verse, his work fired with anger and indignation at the social injustices that he had witnessed. From 1932 to 1951 he worked as a school teacher, in London and (after World War II) in the Rhymney Valley. 📖 I Jenkyns, *Idris Davies* (1972)

Davies, Sir John 1569–1626
English poet and statesman

Born in Tisbury, Wiltshire, he was educated at Winchester School, Queen's College, Oxford, and the Middle Temple, and was called to the Bar in 1595. He was returned to parliament for Corfe Castle and after the death of Elizabeth I found favour with James I (see James VI and I), who sent him to Ireland as Solicitor-General. Three years later he was made Irish Attorney-General and knighted. In Ireland he supported severe repressive measures and took part in the plantation of Ulster. He returned to the English parliament in 1614, representing Newcastle under Lyme, and practised as King's Sergeant in England. He had been nominated chief justice a month before his death of apoplexy. In 1622 he collected in one volume his three chief poems—*Orchestra, or a Poeme of Dancing* (1596), *Nosce Te Ipsum* (1599), a long didactic piece on the soul's

immortality, and *Hymns to Astraea* (1599), a collection of clever acrostics on the name Elizabeth Regina. 📖 M Seeman, *Sir John Davies, sein Leben und seine Werke* (1813)

Davies, Jonathan 1962–
Welsh rugby union and league player

Born in Carmarthenshire, he first played for Wales in 1985, won 27 caps and then left to join rugby league in 1988 after Wales won the Triple Crown, and he set a record of 13 drop goals. He made headlines with his transfer to Widnes in January 1989 and scored 1,000 points in 109 matches. In 1990 he toured Australia with Great Britian and set a club scoring record for one season with 342 points (30 tries and 112 goals). He moved to Warrington in 1993, and led Wales in league games. One high point was his memorable try for Great Britain against Australia at Wembley in the first Test in 1995, when it won the match. He returned to rugby union at the end of 1995.

Davies, Peter Maxwell See Maxwell Davies, Peter

Davies, (William) Robertson 1913–95
Canadian novelist, playwright and essayist

He was born in Thamesville, Ontario, and educated in Canada and at Balliol College, Oxford. A teacher, actor (he was Tyrone Guthrie's literary assistant) and journalist, he was editor of the *Examiner* (Peterborough, Ontario) from 1942 to 1963, a professor of English at the University of Toronto (1960–81) and a writer of international repute. His first novel was *Tempest-Tost* (1951), the first of the 'Salterton trilogy', but he is best known for the 'Deptford trilogy'—*Fifth Business* (1970), *The Manticore* (1972) and *World of Wonders* (1975). This work evolved from his earlier books set in Salterton, an imagined Ontario city, patently Kingston, which is dominated by its old families, Anglican Church, military school, university, and belief in the virtues of England and the English. Among his other novels are *What's Bred in the Bone* (1985), *The Lyre of Orpheus* (1988) and *The Cunning Man* (1995).

Davies, Sarah Emily 1830–1921
English feminist and educational reformer

She was born in Southampton, and was a vigorous campaigner for higher education for women. In 1869 she founded a small college for women students at Hitchin, which was transferred to Cambridge as Girton College in 1873. She was Mistress of Girton from 1873 to 1875, and honorary secretary (1882–1904). As a member of the London School Board (1870–73), she campaigned for London degrees for women, which were granted in 1874.

Davies, Siobhan, *originally* Susan Davies 1950–
English choreographer and dancer

Born in London, she was one of the first to study with London Contemporary Dance Theatre (LCDT) in the late 1960s. She began to choreograph early on in her career, becoming resident choreographer with LCDT in 1971, when she retired as a dancer. She created 17 pieces for the company including *New Galileo* (1984) and *Bridge the Distance* (1985). While still at LCDT, she also worked under commission for Ballet Rambert (1979, *Celebration*), ran Siobhan Davies and Dancers for a short period during 1981, and became a founding member of Second Stride (a development of Richard Alston's Strider) in 1982, for which she made six pieces. Working in a style which ranges from personal to abstract, she is also eclectic in her choice of music which includes scores by Benjamin Britten and Michael Nyman. In 1987 she left LCDT and travelled to the USA on a Fullbright Arts Fellowship. In 1988 she formed the Siobhan Davies Dance Company and in 1989 became associate choreographer for Ballet Rambert. Her work includes *Wyoming* (1988) and *Arctic Heart* (1991), both to music by John-Marc Gowans; *White Man Sleeps* (1988); *Different Trains* (1990) which combines live and taped music in the score by **Steve Reich**; and *Winnsboro Cotton Mill Blues* (1992). In 1993 she was awarded the **Laurence Olivier** Award for Outstanding Achievement in Dance.

Davies, Stephen Owen, *known as* S O 1886–1972
Welsh politician

Born in Abercwmboi, Glamorganshire, he was intended for the Non-Conformist ministry, but became active in Socialist politics and went into the coal mines. He was soon appointed a union official with a reputation for militancy. Deeply influenced by the Russian Revolution, he proved to be a rebellious member of the Labour Party after he was elected MP for MerthyrTydfil in 1934. A firm advocate of Welsh self-government, he supported Welsh cultural and educational institutions. He was critical of the National Coal Board and the government after the Aberfan Disaster (1966) and this, combined with his great age, led the constituency party to replace him as the official candidate in 1970. In the same year he stood as an Independent Socialist and won.

Davies, William Henry 1871–1940
Welsh poet

Born in Newport, Monmouthshire, he emigrated to the USA at the age of 22. He lived partly as a tramp and partly as a casual workman until the loss of a leg whilst 'jumping' a train caused him to return to England. There he began to write and worked as a pedlar to obtain money to have his poems printed. In 1907 **George Bernard Shaw** arranged a publication of his first work, *A Soul's Destroyer*. The success of this book was consolidated by *The Autobiography of a Super-tramp* (1908). He published volumes of poems and lyrics, gathered in the *Collected Poems* (1943), two novels, and the prose *Adventures of Johnny Walker,Tramp* (1926). He continued his autobiography with *Beggars* (1909), *The True Traveller* (1912), *A Poet's Pilgrimage* (1918) and *Later Days* (1925).

da Vinci, Leonardo See **Leonardo da Vinci**

Daviot, Gordon See **Mackintosh, Elizabeth**

Davis, Angela 1944–
African-American activist and writer

Born in Birmingham, Alabama, she was educated at the Sorbonne, Paris, and Brandeis University, and soon began to take part in radical protest and the civil rights movements. In the late 1960s she became involved with the Student Nonviolent Coordinating Committee and the Black Panthers, and in 1968 she joined the Communist Party. Her activist activities with the Black Panthers led her to support black political prisoners. She was arrested on charges of conspiracy, kidnapping and murder in 1970, but after a 10-month trial she was acquitted of all charges. She now teaches at the University of California, Santa Cruz. Among her many books are *Women, Race and Class* (1981) and *If They Came in the Morning: Voices of Resistance* (1971).

Davis, Benjamin Oliver 1877–1970
US general

Born in Washington DC, he began his career as a first lieutenant of volunteer troops in the Spanish–American War, and after being mustered out in 1899 he re-enlisted in the regular army with the rank of private. Promoted to major during World War I and colonel in 1930, he taught military science at Wilberforce University and the Tuskegee Institute. Davis became the first African-American general (1940–48) in the US army. His son, Benjamin Oliver Davis, Jnr (1912–), was the first African-American general (1954–70) in the US air force.

Davis, Bette (Ruth Elizabeth) 1908–89
US film actress

Born in Lowell, Massachusetts, she studied at the John Murray Anderson school, and worked with repertory and summer stock companies before her film debut in *Bad Sister* (1931), and her first Hollywood success in *The Man Who Played God* (1932). Her numerous leading roles included *Of Human Bondage* (1934) and *Dangerous* (1935, Academy Award), which established her as a major star for the next three decades. Highly dedicated, she brought an emotional honesty to the most unprepossessing of melodramas. She was nominated on 10 occasions for an Academy Award, winning her second for *Jezebel* (1938). She received great critical acclaim for her role in *Whatever Happened to Baby Jane?* (1962); later film appearances also included *Death on the Nile* (1979). Latterly more often on television, she won an Emmy award for *Strangers* (1979). Married four times, she wrote several volumes of autobiography:*The Lonely Life* (1962), *Mother Goddam* (1975, with Whitney Stine) and *This'n' That* (1987, with M Herskowitz).

Davis, Sir Colin Rex 1927–
English conductor

Born in Weybridge, Surrey, he was educated at Christ's Hospital and the Royal College of Music. He was assistant conductor of the BBC Scottish Orchestra (1957–59) from where he went to Sadler's Wells to be conductor (1959), principal conductor (1960) and musical director (1961–65). He was chief conductor of the BBC Symphony Orchestra (1967–71) and musical director at Covent Garden (1971–86). Principal guest conductor for the Boston Symphony Orchestra in 1972 and for the London Symphony Orchestra in 1974, he was then chief conductor of the Bavarian Radio Symphony Orchestra from 1983 to 1992. At Covent Garden he gained a reputation as a **Wagner** conductor of international standing with the *Ring* cycle, and conducted at the Bayreuth Festival in 1977. He is also a noted interpreter of **Berlioz**. Since 1995 he has been principal conductor of the London Symphony Orchestra and principal guest conductor of the New York Philharmonic Orchestra since 1996. He was knighted in 1980. ▢ Alan Blyth, *Colin Davis* (1972)

Davis, Dwight Filley 1879–1945
US public official

He was born in St Louis, Missouri. In 1900 he donated an international challenge cup for lawn tennis, competed for annually. The Davis Cup signifies the world team championship.

Davis, Fred 1913–98
English billiards and snooker champion

He was born in Whittingham Moor, Derbyshire, the younger brother of **Joe Davis**. In 1948 he succeeded his brother as world snooker champion — the first of 8 world championships wins — and in 1980 won the world billiards championship.

Davis, Jefferson 1808–89
US statesman, President of the Confederate States of the USA

Born in Christian County, Kentucky, he studied at West Point, and served in several frontier campaigns, but resigned his commission in 1835. He entered Congress in 1845 for Mississippi, and served in the Mexican War as colonel of volunteers (1846–47). He was a senator from 1847 to 1851, and from 1853 to 1857 he was Secretary of War, in which position he improved US military readiness. Returning to the Senate for a second term (1857–61), he, like **John Calhoun**, was a defender of states' rights; as leader of the Southern wing of the Democratic Party he carried in the Senate (1860) his seven resolutions asserting the inability of Congress or the legislatures of the territories to prohibit slavery. Disagreements in the Democratic Party were followed by the election of **Abraham Lincoln** to the presidency. In January 1861 Mississippi seceded from the Union; a few weeks later

Davis was chosen provisional President of the Confederate States, an appointment confirmed for six years in November. The history of his presidency is that of the Civil War (1861–65). He struggled to govern the Confederacy as a whole nation, despite calls for autonomy by political leaders in its constituent states, and astutely allowed General **Robert E Lee** to determine much of the strategy of the war. Lee's final surrender at Appomattox in April 1865 was made without his agreement, and intending to continue the struggle he fled south, only to be captured a month later by Union cavalry in Georgia. He was imprisoned for two years in Fort Monroe, Virginia, then released on bail. Though indicted for treason, he was never brought to trial and was included in the amnesty of 1868. He refused to take an oath of loyalty to the USA and so never regained his citizenship, and after 1879 he lived on an estate bequeathed to him in Mississippi. In 1881 he published *The Rise and Fall of the Confederate Government*. 📖 Hudson Strode, *Jefferson Davis* (4 vols, 1955–66)

Davis, Joe 1901–78
English billiards and snooker champion

Born in Whitwell, near Chesterfield, Derbyshire, he took up billiards at the age of 10 and two years later made his first break of 100. In 1927 he won the first world professional snooker championship and was never beaten until he retired from competitive snooker and billiards in 1946. In 1928 he won the billiards championship, which he held till 1933. A new event was introduced in 1934, and **Walter Lindrum** became the world champion, Davis continued to hold the UK championship. He continued to play both games, and in 1955 made the maximum snooker break of 147, later officially recognized as the world record. He was awarded the OBE in 1963. His younger brother **Fred Davis** followed the same career. The Davis brothers are the only players to have won both the world billiards and the world snooker championships.

Davis or Davys, John c.1550–1605
English navigator

He was born in Sandridge, near Dartmouth, Devon, and between 1585 and 1587 undertook three Arctic voyages in search of the Northwest Passage. In the last voyage he sailed as far north as 73°, and Davis Strait is named after him. He fought against the Spanish Armada in 1588, and took part in an unsuccessful venture with **Thomas Cavendish** (1591), sighting the Falkland Islands on the return journey. He also made two ill-fated voyages towards the South Seas and as pilot of a Dutch vessel to the East Indies. On his last voyage he was killed by Japanese pirates off Singapore. He wrote *World's Hydrographical Description* (1595) and *The Seaman's Secrets* (1594), and invented the navigational instrument Davis's Quadrant.

Davis, Judy 1955–
Australian actress

Born in Perth, Western Australia, she sang in jazz and pop groups, studied at the National Institute of Dramatic Arts in Sydney (1974–77) and made her film debut in *High Rolling* (1976). After graduating, she worked with the Adelaide State Theatre Company, appearing in such plays as *Visions* (1978). Her performance as the strong-willed, 19th-century heroine of the film *My Brilliant Career* (1979) earned her international attention. She has portrayed a range of forceful individuals in such films as *Winter of Our Dreams* (1981) and *Heatwave* (1981) whilst continuing a parallel stage career with *Piaf* (1980), *Lulu* (1981) and, in London, *Insignificance* (1982). She received Academy Award nominations for *A Passage to India* (1984) and *Husbands and Wives* (1992) and now divides her time between Australia and the USA. Recent films include the television production *Serving in Silence* (1995) and *Blood and Wine*.

Davis, Miles Dewey, III 1926–91
US jazz trumpeter and bandleader

Born into a wealthy middle-class black family in Alton, Illinois, and brought up in St Louis, he began playing the trumpet at the age of 13 and, while receiving private tuition and playing in his high school band, he was performing with a local rhythm-and-blues group. In 1944 he began studies at the Juilliard School of Music, New York, but left to perform in the 52nd Street clubs where the new bebop style was emerging. At 19 he became a member of the foremost of these groups, the **Charlie Parker** Quintet. Although not then the most technically accomplished of jazz trumpeters, Davis played in an understated style that became highly influential, and he continued to be at the forefront of new stylistic departures. In 1948, working with pianist-arranger **Gil Evans**, he led a nonet that inspired the 'cool jazz' school. In the late 1950s, his quartet featuring saxophonist **John Coltrane** introduced a 'modal' approach which broke away from the harmonic principles previously accepted in jazz. Ten years later, his bands were featuring electronic instruments and synthesizers as well as rock-style rhythms. He became known for his expressive lyricism (eg 'Round About Midnight', 1955), new modal structures (eg 'Milestones', 1958), solos in elegant orchestrations (eg 'Porgy and Bess', 1958), and fusion of jazz harmonies with rock instrumentation and rhythms (eg 'In a Silent Way', 1969). Davis retired from performing from 1975 to 1980, but he returned thereafter, further developing the use of electronics but using a commercial approach that did not find favour with all of his previous followers.

Davis, Peter Hadland 1918–92
English botanist

Born in Weston-super-Mare, Avon, and educated at Bradfield College and Maiden Erleigh, Reading, his first botanical publication appeared in *The Times* when he was 15. His apprenticeship at a plant nursery in East Grinstead in 1937 nurtured an all-consuming passion for plants. He began botanizing in the Middle East in 1938, eventually visiting almost every Mediterranean country, Brazil, and Malaysia, collecting some 70,000 specimens. He later studied botany at Edinburgh University, and began a distinguished career (1950–85) in its botany department. In 1961 he began preparing *The Flora of Turkey and the East Aegean Islands* (10 vols, 1965–88), widely regarded as a model Flora. He also published many papers on Mediterranean and south-west Asian botany and plant taxonomy, and was joint author with Vernon Heywood (1927–) of *Principles of Angiosperm Taxonomy* (1963), another landmark of 20th-century botanical literature.

Davis, Raymond, Jnr 1914–
US chemist and astrophysicist

Born in Washington, he was educated at the University of Maryland and at Yale, worked as a senior chemist at Brookhaven National Laboratory (1948–84), and since 1984 has been professor in the department of astronomy of the University of Pennsylvania. He devised the first experiment to detect neutrinos emitted from the Sun's core, placing a large tank of dry cleaning fluid in a deep mine, in which neutrinos interact with chlorine atoms to produce minute quantities of radioactive argon atoms. Running since 1969, all the results gathered so far have shown that there are only about a third of the neutrinos coming from the Sun that were predicted.

Davis, Richard Harding 1863–1916
US novelist, newspaper correspondent and dramatist

Born in Philadelphia, the son of the novelist Rebecca Harding Davis (1831–1910), he became known as 'the **Beau Brummell** of the Press'—a dashing dandy and an often unscrupulous correspondent. Although essentially superficial, he was a master storyteller, and his fiction can still be read with pleasure. It includes *Van Bibber and Others* (1892), sketches about a New York socialite, and the novel *Soldiers of Fortune* (1897), modelled on the formula established by **Anthony Hope** in *The Prisoner of Zenda*.

Davis, Steve 1957–
English snooker player
He was born in London. Between 1980 and 1985 he won three world titles, and of 96 major matches played he won all but 11. Calm and imperturbable, he was distinguished by the maturity of his play even while very young. In 1985 he lost on the final black of the world championship to Dennis Taylor in a 35-frame match regarded as the finest-ever televised snooker match. For most of the 1980s, when he won the world championships six times, he was ranked as the world's leading player, but was beaten by John Parrott in 1991 and **Stephen Hendry** in 1990 and 1992. He published *How to be Really Interesting* in 1988.

Davis, Stuart 1894–1964
US painter and graphic artist
Born in Philadelphia, he studied with **Robert Henri** in New York (1910–13), and worked as an illustrator for the left-wing journal *The Masses* (1913–16). The Armory Show in 1913 converted him to avant-garde French art, especially Cubism. He tried to develop a specifically American modernism; his imitation collages such as *Lucky Strike* (1921) anticipated Pop Art by 35 years.

Davis, William Morris 1850–1934
US geomorphologist
Born in Philadelphia and educated at Harvard, after a short spell as an astronomer in Córdoba, Argentina (1871–72), he became Professor of Physical Geography at Harvard (1875–1912). He participated in an expedition to Turkestan (1903) with Raphael Pumpelly (1837–1923) and undertook wide-ranging studies of the role of rain in erosion, the development of rivers, glacial erosion, the formation of coral reefs, arid landscapes, and the elevation and subsidence of land masses. He reinterpreted some geomorphological features in Europe and stimulated much debate with his ideas of the development of British, French and German rivers. He also introduced the concept of cycles of erosion and made significant contributions to meteorology.

Davison, Emily 1872–1913
English suffragette
Born in Blackheath, she was educated first at London University and then at Oxford, where she gained a first in English. In 1906 she became a militant member of the Women's Social and Political Union (WSPU). Her activities included stone-throwing, setting alight letterboxes and attacking a Baptist minister whom she mistook for **Lloyd George**. Frequently imprisoned, she often went on hunger-strike, and was repeatedly force-fed. Once, while in Holloway prison, she attempted suicide in protest against force-feeding. In the 1913 Derby, wearing a WSPU banner, she tried to catch the reins of the king's horse, but she was trampled underfoot and died several days later.

Davisson, Clinton Joseph 1881–1958
US physicist and Nobel Prize winner
Born in Bloomington, Illinois, he was educated at the universities of Chicago and Princeton, where he was instructor in physics before taking up industrial research at the Bell Telephone Laboratories. In 1927, with **Lester Germer**, Davisson was observing electron scattering from a block of nickel, when their vacuum system accidentally broke down. Upon continuing the experiment the results were completely different, as they found the familiar peaks and troughs of a diffraction pattern. They had observed the diffraction of electrons, confirming **Louis de Broglie**'s theory of the wave nature of particles.

This accidental discovery was crucial to the development of the quantum theory of matter. In 1937 he shared the Nobel Prize for physics with **George Paget Thomson**.

Davitt, Michael 1846–1906
Irish Nationalist politician and founder of the Irish Land League
Born a peasant's son, in Straid, County Mayo, he emigrated with his family to Haslingden in Lancashire, England (1851), where he lost his right arm through a machinery accident in a cotton factory in 1857. In 1866 he joined the Fenian movement, and was sentenced in 1870 to 15 years' penal servitude for sending guns to Ireland. He was released in 1877 and, supplied with funds from the USA, began an anti-landlord crusade which culminated in the Land League (1879). Davitt was thenceforward in frequent collision with the government, and was imprisoned in Portland for breaking his ticket-of-leave (1881–82). During this time he was elected an MP (1882) but disqualified from taking his seat. His *Leaves from a Prison Diary* were published in 1885. A strong Home Ruler, but socialistic on the question of land nationalization, he opposed **Charles Parnell** after the split in the party, and was returned to parliament in 1892 as an anti-Parnellite, but unseated on the ground of clerical intimidation (1893). In 1895 he was returned unopposed by South Mayo, but resigned in 1899. ▣ T W Moody, *Davitt and the Irish Revolution 1846-82* (1981)

Davout, Louis Nicolas 1770–1823
French general
Born in Annoux, Burgundy, he was educated with **Napoleon I** at the military school of Brienne. As general he accompanied Napoleon to the East, largely securing the victory at Aboukir (1799). A Marshal of the Empire (1804), he fought brilliantly at Austerlitz (1805) and Auerstädt (1806), and was made Duke of Auerstädt (1808). At Eckmühl and Wagram (1809) he checked the Austrian attack. As Governor of Poland he ruled despotically, and in the Russian campaign of 1812–13 he won victories at Mohilev and Vitebsk. After the retreat from Moscow he became Governor-General of the Hanse towns, and at Hamburg maintained a regime of repression until the first Restoration of the **Bourbons** (1814). On Napoleon's return from Elba in 1815 he was appointed Minister of War, and after Waterloo he received the command of the remnant of the French army under the walls of Paris. In 1819 he was made a peer of France.

Davy, Edward 1806–85
Australian physician and scientist
Born in Ottery St Mary, Devon, England, he studied medicine, then in 1829 established the firm of Davy & Co, supplying scientific apparatus, including some of his own inventions, such as 'Davy's blow-pipe' for chemical analysis, and 'Davy's diamond cement' for repairing broken china. He invented the electric relay and he deserves to stand alongside **Charles Wheatstone** and **William Cooke** as one of the inventors of wireless telegraphy. He lectured and wrote many papers on the subject, and demonstrated his system over a 1 mile (1.61km) wire in Regents Park, London. He later emigrated to Adelaide, South Australia (1838), where he continued his experiments, on subjects including starch production and the smelting of copper. In 1853 he moved to Victoria where he made an unsuccessful attempt at farming, before returning to medicine, which he practised for the rest of his life. In recognition of his earlier achievements he was made an honorary member of the Society of Telegraph Engineers in 1885.

Davy, Sir Humphry 1778–1829
English chemist and science propagandist

Born in Penzance, Cornwall, he was apprenticed to a surgeon and apothecary. **Thomas Lovell Beddoes** employed him as an assistant at the Pneumatic Institute in Bristol (1798), where Davy discovered the anaesthetic effect of laughing gas (nitrous oxide). He also showed that heat can be transmitted through a vacuum and suggested that it is a form of motion. His *Researches, Chemical and Physical* (1799) led to his appointment as assistant lecturer in chemistry at the Royal Institution (1801), where his research into electrochemistry was organized by **Jöns Jacob Berzelius** into a coherent system. He isolated the metals sodium and potassium, as well as barium, strontium, calcium and magnesium. Following up the work of **Bernard Courtois**, Davy showed that fluorine and chlorine are related to iodine, and his work also refuted **Antoine Lavoisier**'s theory that all acids contain oxygen. He also proved that diamond is a form of carbon. His *Elements of Agricultural Chemistry* (1813) was the first book to apply chemical principles systematically to farming. From 1813 to 1815 he travelled on the Continent, taking the young **Michael Faraday** as chemical assistant and valet. He invented the safety lamp (1815, the 'Davy lamp') which enabled greater coal production as deeper, more gaseous seams could be mined with less risk of explosion. Davy popularized science and interested industrialists in scientific research. He was one of the founders of the Athenaeum Club and of the Zoological Society, which in its turn founded London Zoo. He was made a baronet in 1812. 📖 Sir H Hartley, *Humphrey Davy* (1966)

Davys, John See Davis, John

Dawes, Charles G (ates) 1865–1951
US diplomat, politician and Nobel Prize winner
Born in Marietta, Ohio, he studied at Marietta College and Cincinnati Law School and was admitted to the Bar. He gained administrative experience as brigadier-general in charge of military procurement for US forces in France in World War I and was appointed director of the Budget in 1921. He was head of the commission that drew up the Dawes Plan (1924) for reducing and reorganizing German reparation payments. He shared the 1925 Nobel Peace Prize with Sir **Austen Chamberlain**, for negotiating the Locarno Pact. He served as Republican Vice-President (1925–29) under **Calvin Coolidge** and later became US ambassador to Great Britain. 📖 Bascom N Timmons, *Portrait of an American: Charles G Dawes* (1953)

Dawes, Sophia 1790–1840
English adventuress
She was born in St Helens on the Isle of Wight. She later became an inmate in a workhouse, an officer's mistress, and a servant in a brothel. She was mistress to the Duc de **Bourbon**, and married his aide-de-camp, the Baron de Feuchères, in 1818. She is thought to have murdered the Duc (1830).

Dawkins, (Clinton) Richard 1941–
British ethologist
Born in Nairobi, Kenya, he was educated at Oxford, and taught at the University of California at Berkeley before returning to Oxford (1970) where he is a Fellow of New College and has been a Reader in zoology since 1989. Working in the field of theoretical modelling of ethology, his major contribution has been his ability to explain complex evolutionary ideas, making them comprehensible to fellow biologists and laypersons alike. In *The Selfish Gene* (1976), he shows how natural selection acts on individual genes rather than at the individual or species level, and also describes how apparently altruistic behaviour in animals is designed to increase the probability of survival of genes. The ways in which small genetic changes or mutations form the basis for evolution are set out in *The Blind Watchmaker* (1986). *The Extended Phenotype*

(1982), a more advanced book, argues that genes can have effects outside the bodies that contain them. His later publications include *River Out of Eden* (1995).

Dawkins, Sir William Boyd 1837–1929
Welsh geologist
Born in Buttington, near Welshpool, Powys, he was educated at Rossall School and Jesus College, Oxford. He joined the Geological Survey in 1861, became curator of Manchester Museum in 1870, and the first Professor of Geology at Manchester in 1872. He wrote *Cave-hunting; or, Caves and the Early Inhabitants of Europe* (1874) and *Early Man in Britain* (1880).

Dawson (of Penn), Bertrand Edward Dawson, 1st Viscount 1864–1945
English physician
Born in Purley, he was physician-in-ordinary successively to **Edward VII**, **George V**, **Edward VIII**, **George VI** and Queen **Mary**. He was a major influence in the organization of medical services in interwar Great Britain.

Dawson, Charles 1864–1916
English solicitor and antiquary
Born in Sussex, he became an amateur geologist. He was the victim (or possibly the perpetrator) of the celebrated 'Piltdown skull' hoax, in which cranial fragments, found by him at Piltdown (1908–12), together with parts of a jawbone unearthed later, were accepted by anthropologists as the 'missing link' in **Charles Darwin**'s theory of evolution, and as such one of the greatest discoveries of the age, being named after him *Eoanthropus dawsoni* ('Dawson's Dawn Man'). Many experts had doubts, but it was not until 1953 that the skull was formally denounced as a fake, after scientific tests had established that the jawbone was that of a modern ape, coloured to simulate age, that the cranium had also been stained to match the gravel deposits in which it was found, and that the fragments had clearly been 'planted' on the site.

Dawson, George Mercer 1849–1901
Canadian geologist
He was born in Pictou, Nova Scotia, the son of Sir **John William Dawson**. Educated at McGill University, he did much pioneer geological work in British Columbia and the Yukon, where Dawson City was named after him.

Dawson, Henry 1811–78
English landscape painter
Born in Hull, Humberside, he was a Nottingham lace maker until 1835, then took to art. By the time of his death the price of his pictures had risen from £5 or less to £800 or more. He specialized in marine and river scenes, such as *The Wooden Walls of Old England*, perhaps his best-known work.

Dawson, James 1717–46
English Jacobite
Born in Manchester, he studied for the Church at St John's College, Cambridge, but having held a captaincy in Prince **Charles Edward Stuart**'s army, was hanged, drawn and quartered on Kensington Green, London. At exactly the same time his sweetheart, Jenny Dawson, died in her coach there. The incident gave rise to the ballad by **William Shenstone**, 'Jenny Dawson'.

Dawson, Sir John William 1820–99
Canadian geologist
Born in Pictou, Nova Scotia, he studied at Edinburgh, and subsequently studied the natural history and geology of New Brunswick and Nova Scotia, where he was superintendent of education (1850–55). From 1855 to 1893 he was Principal of McGill University, Montreal. He was an authority on fossil plants, the principal proponent of the organic nature of eozoon and systematically opposed

Charles Darwin's theories. In 1851 he discovered some of the earliest known terrestrial vertebrate fossils inside carboniferous fossil tree stumps at Joggins, Nova Scotia. His publications included *Acadian Geology* (1855), *The Story of Earth and Man* (1873), *Origin of the World* (1877), *Fossil Men* (1878) and *Relics of Primeval Life* (1897). He was knighted in 1884.

Dawson, Peter 1882–1961
Australian bass-baritone

Born in Adelaide, South Australia, he won a solo competition at Ballarat, Victoria, in 1901, and the following year went to London, where he studied for three years with Sir **Charles Santley** and toured with Madame Emma Albani (1852–1930). He made his debut in grand opera at Covent Garden, London, in 1909, and appeared regularly in oratorios, but he was best known for his ballad singing. From 1904, when he cut a cylinder record for the Edison-Bell company, until 1957, when he made a microgroove stereo recording for EMI, Dawson was a prolific recording artist, using a variety of pseudonyms, including Will Danby, Hector Grant and Will Strong. Many of the ballads he sang were written by Dawson himself, under the name J P McColl.

Day, Clarence Shepard, Jnr 1874–1935
US writer

Born in New York City, the son of a successful Wall Street stockbroker, he retired from his father's firm at 29 because of crippling arthritis and thereafter earned his living by publishing essays and drawings in magazines. He is best known for his light, witty sketches recalling his parents, included in collections such as *Life with Father* (1935) and *Life with Mother* (1937). Day wrote for the *New Yorker* for many years, and helped to set its famous tone.

Day, Doris, *originally* Doris Kappelhoff 1924–
US singer and film actress

Born in Cincinnati, Ohio, she was a vocalist with several big bands and a radio favourite before she made her film debut in *Romance on the High Seas* (1948). Her sunny personality, singing talent and girl-next-door image enlivened many standard Warner Brothers musicals of the 1950s. More satisfying material followed with *Calamity Jane* (1953), *Young at Heart* (1954) and *The Pajama Game* (1957). A top selling recording artist, she was also able to show her dramatic talent in *Storm Warning* (1950) and *Love Me or Leave Me* (1955). The popularity of the comedy *Pillow Talk* (1959) earned her an Academy Award nomination and a further career as the perennial virgin in a series of frothy farces where she was often partnered by Rock Hudson (1925–85). She retired from the screen after *With Six You Get Egg Roll* (1968), but appeared occasionally on television and also in *The Doris Day Show* (1968–73). Her autobiography, *Doris Day, Her Own Story* (1976), revealed much of the turmoil beneath her apparently carefree vivacity.

Day, Dorothy 1897–1980
US writer and radical social reformer

Born in Brooklyn, New York City, she became a life-long socialist, having worked in the New York slums as a probationary nurse. Converted to Catholicism in 1927, she co-founded the monthly *Catholic Worker* in 1933, drawing on her earlier experience as a reporter on Marxist publications like *Call* and *The Masses* in lower east side Manhattan. Under the influence of the French itinerant priest Peter Maurin (1877–1949), she founded the Catholic Worker Movement, which established 'houses of hospitality' and farm communities for people hit by the Depression as described in her *House of Hospitality* (1939). A pacifist and a fervent supporter of farm-worker unionization in the 1960s, she helped turn her church's attention to peace and justice issues. Her autobiography, *The*

Long Loneliness, was published in 1952. Other works include the autobiographical novel *The Eleventh Virgin* (1924) and *On Pilgrimage: the Sixties* (1972).

Day, John 1522–84
English printer

Born in Dunwich, Suffolk, he was one of the first English music printers. He produced the earliest church service book with musical notation (1560), and in the same year Archbishop **Matthew Parker**'s English version of the psalms, with music by **Thomas Tallis** and others. His most celebrated publication was **John Foxe**'s *Actes and Monuments* (1563), better known as the *Book of Martyrs*.

Day, John 1574–1640
English dramatist

He was born in Norfolk, and studied at Gonville and Caius College, Cambridge. He is mentioned in **Philip Henslowe**'s *Diary* in 1598 as an active playwright, and collaborated freely with **Henry Chettle**, **Thomas Dekker**, and others. His works, privately printed by **Arthur Henry Bullen** in 1881, include a graceful comedy, *Humour Out of Breath*, and *The Parliament of Bees*, an allegorical masque.

Day, Sir Judson Graham 1933–
British business executive

Born in Halifax, Nova Scotia, Canada, he was educated at Queen Elizabeth High School and Dalhousie University. He spent eight years in private practice as a lawyer before joining Canadian Pacific in 1964. In 1975 he went to British Shipbuilders as deputy chairman and chief executive designate, but left in 1977 to take a chair at Dalhousie University. Four years later he became a vice-president of Dome Petroleum for a short period. In 1983 he returned to British Shipbuilders as chairman and chief executive, moving to the Rover Group plc as chairman and chief executive from 1986 to 1991. He was then chairman of the electricity company PowerGen (1990–93). He was knighted in 1989.

Day, Sir Robin 1923–
English journalist and broadcaster

Born in London, he served in the Royal Artillery (1943–47), studied law at St Edmund Hall, Oxford, and was called to the Bar in 1952. He left for the British Council in Washington DC to become a freelance broadcaster in 1954, working at ITN from 1955 to 1959. He then joined the BBC's *Panorama*, which he presented from 1967 to 1972. He brought an acerbic freshness to interviewing techniques and has proved a formidable inquisitor of political figures. His radio work includes *It's Your Line* (1970–76) and *The World at One* (1979–88), while his television credits include *Question Time* (1979–89) and *The Parliament Programme* (1992). He received the Richard Dimbleby award for factual television in 1974. Among his books are *The Case for Televising Parliament* (1963), *Day by Day* (1975), *Grand Inquisitor–Memoirs* (1989) and *But With Respect–Memorable Interviews* (1993). He was knighted in 1981.

Day, Thomas 1748–89
English writer and barrister

He was born in London, and educated at Corpus Christi College, Oxford. He entered the Middle Temple, London, in 1765, and in 1775 was called to the Bar, but he never practised. A disciple of **Jean Jacques Rousseau**, he brought up an orphan and a foundling, one of whom, he presumed, would become his wife. That scheme miscarried, but in 1778 he married an heiress, Esther Milnes, and spent 11 happy years with her, until he was killed by a fall from a colt he was breaking in. He wrote two didactic, moral children's tales, *The History of Sandford and Merton* (3 vols, 1783–89), and *The History of Little Jack* (1788), and a long poem, *The Dying Negro* (1773). 📖 M Sadler, *Thomas Day, an English disciple of Rousseau* (1928)

Dayan, Moshe 1915–81
Israeli soldier and politician

Born in Palestine, he founded the Haganah underground militia. He was Chief of Staff of the Israeli army when Israel conquered Gaza and Sinai in the Suez War of 1956. In 1958 he left military service to study at the Hebrew University in Jerusalem. Dayan was elected to the Knesset as a Labour member in 1959 and made Minister of Agriculture by David Ben-Gurion (1959–64). He left the Labour Party in 1966 to set up the Rafi Party with Ben-Gurion. In 1967, as a member of the opposition, he was appointed Defence Minister, and masterminded the Israeli victory in the Six-Day War. Dayan then cleared Jerusalem of Arab/Jewish barriers and mines, and declared it a free city. He was Defence Minister again from 1969 to 1974, but his reputation was tarnished by Israel's disastrous start to the 1973 (Yom Kippur) War, and he was dropped from the Cabinet. In 1977, as Foreign Minister, he helped secure the historic peace treaty with Egypt. He resigned (1979) from the Begin government, and in 1981 he launched a new centre party, but died the same year. He wrote *Diary of the Sinai Campaign* (1966) and *Living with the Bible* (1978).

Daye, Stephen c.1610–1668
American printer

He was born in London, England. In 1639 he set up the first New England printing press at Harvard.

Day-Lewis, Cecil, *pen name* C Day Lewis, *pseudonym* Nicholas Blake 1904–72
Irish poet, critic and detective-story writer

Born in Ballintubbert, County Leix, he was educated at Sherborne School and Wadham College, Oxford. He published his first verse, *Beechen Vigil and Other Poems* in 1925. He made his name as a lyric poet with *Transitional Poems* (1929), and during the 1930s, with W H Auden and Steven Spender, became associated with left-wing causes, and also wrote literary criticism in *A Hope for Poetry* (1934). He became a member of the Communist Party, which he renounced in 1939. During World War II he worked in the Ministry of Information, and then published *Poetry for You* (1944) and his major critical work, *The Poetic Image* (1947). He became Professor of Poetry at Oxford (1951–56) and at Harvard (1964–65), and published his last critical work, *The Poetic Impulse*, in 1965. He made notable translations of Virgil and St Valery, and was appointed Poet Laureate in 1968. Under the pseudonym Nicholas Blake he wrote 20 sophisticated detective novels. His autobiography, *The Buried Day*, was published in 1960. He was the father of Daniel Day-Lewis.

Day-Lewis, Daniel 1958–
English actor

Born in London, the son of Poet Laureate Cecil Day-Lewis, he made an early film debut with a non-speaking role in *Sunday, Bloody Sunday* (1971) and acquired extensive stage experience before winning recognition for his West End appearance in *Another Country* (1982–83). His screen versatility was established with contrasting roles as the homosexual punk in *My Beautiful Laundrette*, the prissy Edwardian suitor in *A Room with a View* (both 1985), and a lover in *The Unbearable Lightness of Being* (1988). His stage work with the National Theatre includes *The Futurists* (1986) and *Hamlet* (1989). Highly selective in his choice of film roles, he won a Best Actor Academy Award as the handicapped writer Christy Brown in *My Left Foot* (1989). More recent films include *The Last of the Mohicans* (1992, Academy Award nomination), *The Age of Innocence* (1994), *In the Name of the Father* (1994) and *The Crucible* (1996).

d'Azeglio, Marchese See Azeglio, Marchese d'

Deacon, Sir George Edward Raven 1906–84
English physical oceanographer

Born in Leicester, he studied chemistry at King's College London and was appointed in 1927 as hydrologist to the Discovery Committee, a government agency studying the sustainability of whaling in the Falkland Island Dependencies. Further studies of the chemistry of the Southern Ocean between 1930 and 1937 revealed the Antarctic convergence, where cold water dips beneath warmer sub-Antarctic water, and that Antarctic bottom water extends northwards into all the major oceans. This report, *The Hydrology of the Southern Ocean* (1937), earned him fellowship of the Royal Society (1944). During World War II he led a group at the Admiralty Research Laboratory in Teddington which discovered a method of analysing ocean waves. This group became part of the new National Institute of Oceanography at Wormley, Surrey (1949), with Deacon as director. He was knighted in 1971. He had a major influence on the national and international development of marine science, and the Institute of Oceanographic Sciences (formerly the National Institute of Oceanography) Laboratory is named after him.

Deacon, Richard 1949–
British sculptor

Born in Bangor, Wales, he trained at Somerset College of Art in Taunton, and in London at St Martins School of Art, the Royal College of Art, and Chelsea School of Art. His work is abstract and varied, ranging from sinuous forms to bulky objects which expose the nuts and bolts of fabrication. He plays on associations between language and aspects of reality, as with *Listening to Reason* (1986), *Double Talk* (1987) and *The Back of my Hand* (1987). Since winning the Turner prize in 1987 he has exhibited widely abroad, continuing to explore meaning in sculpture, as in *Struck Dumb* (1988) and *Kiss and Tell* (1989). Public commissions include *Between the Eyes* (1990, Toronto), *Let's Not be Stupid* (1991, Warwick University) and *Never Mind* (1993, Antwerp).

Deák, Francis 1803–76
Hungarian politician

Born in Söjtör, Zala, he practised as an advocate, entered the National Diet in 1832 and played a moderate liberal role, dissociating himself from Lajos Kossuth's extreme Magyar nationalism and becoming in 1848 Minister of Justice. Hailed in 1861 as leader in the Diet, he restored Hungary's constitution by his efforts in 1867 and the dual monarchy of Austria–Hungary was established.

Deakin, Alfred 1856–1919
Australian statesman

Born in Collingwood, Victioria, he entered the Victorian Legislative Assembly in 1879 and held various offices, including that of Chief Secretary (1886–90). He was a member of the committees which drew up draft constitutions at both the National Australasian Convention in 1891 and the Federal Convention of 1897–98, and went to Great Britain with Edmund Barton's delegation to present the draft constitution to the British parliament in 1900. When Barton became the first Prime Minister of Australia's first federal government in 1901, Deakin was appointed Attorney-General and was largely responsible for the immigration legislation that created the White Australia Policy and the Judiciary Act which established the High Court. On Barton's retirement in 1903 he became Prime Minister until 1904 and was re-elected twice (1905–08, 1909–10). Failing health forced his political retirement in 1913.

Deakin, Arthur 1890–1955
English trade union leader

Born in Sutton Coldfield, Warwickshire, he and his family moved to Dowlais, South Wales, when he was 10 and at 13 he began work in a steelworks. A full-time trade union official from 1919, in 1935 he became assistant to

Ernest Bevin, General Secretary of the Transport and General Workers Union, following the Bevin tradition that a trade union leader should be a first-class organizer rather than an 'agitator'. In 1945 he became General Secretary of the 1.3 million-strong union and was president of the World Federation of Trade Unions from 1945 to 1949, when he led the British withdrawal from the organization because of its Communist domination. Subsequently he was one of the founders of the International Confederation of Free Trade Unions. He was chairman of the TUC in 1951 and continued to be one of the most influential members of its General Council until his death.

Dean (of Thornton-Le-Fylde), Brenda Dean, Baroness 1943–
English trade union leader

Born in Manchester, she left school in 1959 and became an employee of the printing trade union SOGAT. She was secretary of the Manchester branch (1976–83) before becoming president of the renamed and reconstituted SOGAT '82. From 1985 to 1991 she was general secretary and became a national figure during the printers' dispute with **Rupert Murdoch's** News International. She then became deputy chairman of the Graphical Paper and Media Union (1991–92), but resigned on being unsuccessful in the leadership contest. In 1993 she became chairman of the Independent Committee for Supervision of Standards of Telephone Information Services, and that same year was awarded a life peerage.

Dean, Christopher 1958–
English ice-skater

Born in Nottingham, he was a policeman before taking up skating full time. He formed a skating partnership with **Jayne Torvill** in 1975, and they set a new standard in the sport. They were six times British champions (1978–83) and won the Grand Slam of World, Olympic and European ice-dance titles in 1984, with a haunting interpretation of **Ravel's** 'Bolero'. After turning professional in 1985 he continued to tour the world with Torvill in their own ice show. They made a brief comeback to competitive ice-dancing at the Winter Olympics of 1994, in which they won bronze medals.

Dean, Dixie (William Ralph) 1907–80
English footballer

Born in Birkenhead, Merseyside, he voluntarily attended Borstal for part of his schooling because it had better football facilities. He turned professional with Tranmere Rovers at the age of 16, and scored 27 goals in 27 matches in the following season. He joined Everton in 1925, for whom he scored a record 349 goals in 399 games, despite a severe motor-cycle accident in 1926 which fractured his skull. In 1938 he played for Notts County for one season before injury ended his career. He still holds the remarkable scoring record of 60 League goals in one season.

Dean, Dizzy (Jay Hanna) 1911–74
US baseball player

Born in Lucas, Arkansas, he grew up in a family of migrant farm workers and left school early. In a short but brilliant tenure with the St Louis Cardinals (1932–37), he led the National League in strikeouts four times (1932–35) and proved himself one of the finest pitchers in the history of the game. His best year was 1934, when he was named the League's Most Valuable Player; with his brother Paul (1913–81), who joined the team as a pitcher a year after he did, he secured a victory for the Cardinals at the 1934 World Series. His career faltered after he injured his arm in 1937, though he played for three more seasons with the Chicago Cubs (1938–41). In the 1940s and 1950s

he was a radio broadcaster for the Cardinals and other teams, gaining millions of fans with his inspired malapropisms and buoyant personality.

Dean, James Byron 1931–55
US film actor

Born in Marion, Indiana, he started acting at California University and in 1952 he moved to New York City, where he joined the Actors Studio. After small parts in theatre, including *See the Jaguar* on Broadway, and in films and television, he gained overnight success in the film *East of Eden* (1955). He starred in only two more films, *Rebel Without a Cause* (1955) and *Giant* (released 1956), before he was killed in a car crash. In just over a year he had become a cult figure, the personification of contemporary US youth, restless and without direction. For many years after his death he remained a symbol of youthful rebellion and self-assertion. ⌨ John Howlett, *James Dean* (1984)

Dean, Laura 1945–
US dancer, choreographer and teacher

Born in Staten Island, New York City, she studied at Manhattan's High School of Performing Arts and School of American Ballet, danced in **Paul Taylor's** company (1965–66), and worked with **Meredith Monk**, Kenneth King and **Robert Wilson**. She began choreographing in 1967, developing a style based on her interest in simple, repetitive movement—spinning, stamping, jumping—aligned to rhythmic music. Formed in 1976, Laura Dean Dancers and Musicians mainly features her own scores and those of composer **Steve Reich**. She has made dances for other companies, including Joffrey Ballet and New York City Ballet.

Deane, Richard 1610–53
English general

He was born in Temple Guiting, Gloucestershire. During the Civil War he commanded the Parliamentary artillery in Cornwall and at the Battle of Naseby (1645), and led the right wing at Preston (1648). He was a commissioner at the trial of **Charles I**, and one of the signatories of the king's death warrant. Later he held commands on both land and sea. He was major-general at the Battle of Worcester (1651), Commander-in-Chief in Scotland (1652), general-at-sea with **Robert Blake** at the Battle of Portland (1653) and was killed in the Battle of Solebay.

Deane, Seamus 1940–
Irish writer

He was born in Derry, Northern Ireland, and educated in Belfast and at Cambridge. He became a Fulbright lecturer at the University of California at Berkeley (1966–8) before returning to Ireland to become Professor of Modern English and American Literature at University College Dublin. In 1971 he became co-director of the Field Day Theatre Company, a post he held until 1993. His three-volume *Field Day Anthology of Irish Writing* was published in 1991. Of his own work, *Gradual Wars* (1972) was one of the first poetry collections to address the political unrest in Ireland since the late 1960s. He has also published five subsequent collections and several volumes of essays, including *Heroic Styles: The Tradition of an Idea* (1985). His first novel, *Reading in the Dark*, was published in 1996.

Déat, Marcel 1894–1955
French politician

Born in Guerigny, he was the founder in 1933 of the Socialist Party of France, which was Fascist in outlook. His pro-Nazi sympathies procured him the post of Minister of Labour in the Vichy government, and having achieved notoriety by his ruthless deportations of French workers to Germany, he fled there himself in 1945. He was sentenced to death in absentia, but evaded arrest until his death in Turin.

DeBakey, Michael Ellis 1908–
US cardiovascular surgeon
He was born in Lake Charles, Louisiana, and received his
medical training at Tulane University. He subsequently
taught surgery there until 1948, when he moved to Baylor
University College of Medicine in Houston, Texas, where
he has been director of the De Bakey Heart Center since
1985. There, with **Denton Cooley** and others, he developed a centre of international reputation in the field of
cardiovascular surgery. DeBakey was particularly involved in the surgical treatment of aortic aneurysms and
arterial occlusion through replacement with grafts, but
also contributed to other aspects of surgery, including
gastric.

de Balliol, Edward See **Balliol, Edward de**

de Balliol, John See **Balliol, John de**

de Bary, Heinrich Anton See **Bary, Heinrich
Anton de**

de Basil, Colonel W(assili) See **Basil, Colonel
W(assili) de**

de Beauharnais, Eugène See **Beauharnais,
Eugène de**

de Beer, Esmond 1895–1990
English scholar, historian and philanthropist
He was born in Dunedin, New Zealand, and owing to his
grandfather Bendix Hallenstein (1835–1905), who had
established a chain of stores throughout New Zealand,
had sufficient wealth to devote his life to scholarship. In
1914 he went to Oxford, where he was influenced by the
eminent historian Sir Charles Firth (1857–1936) and
Firth's insistence on research from original documents.
After World War I Esmond studied at London University
and in 1931 started editing the first full text of John
Evelyn's diaries (6 vols, 1955), and then edited the
Correspondence of John Locke (8 vols, 1976–89). De Beer also
contributed the articles on Evelyn and **John Locke** to the
1969 edition of *Encyclopaedia Britannica*. **Enoch Powell**
described his work as 'a miniature example of the sort
of input which the antipodean members of the
Commonwealth have made into the mother country'. 📖
Michael Strachan, *Esmond de Beer (1895–1990) Scholar
and Benefactor: a personal memoir* (1995)

de Beer, Sir Gavin Rylands 1899–1972
English zoologist
Born in London, he graduated from Oxford and then
taught there (1923–38). After World War II he became
Professor of Embryology at London, and from 1950 to
1960, director of the British Museum (Natural History),
London. In *Introduction to Experimental Embryology* (1926)
and *Development of the Vertebrate Skull* (1935), he discussed
the processes whereby tissues are derived during the
course of development. In his *Embryos and Ancestors*
(1940), he proposed that the earlier sexual maturing of an
animal is a factor in evolution. De Beer also brought his
biological knowledge to bear on historical problems, reconstructing **Hannibal**'s route across the Alps via pollen
analysis and glaciology. He was awarded the Darwin
medal of the Royal Society and the Linnaean Society gold
medal, both in 1958, and knighted in 1954.

de Belloy, Dormont See **Belloy, Dormont de**

de Bergerac, Cyrano See **Cyrano de
Bergerac, Savinien**

de Bonivard, François See **Bonivard, François
de**

de Bono, Edward Francis Charles Publius
1933–
British psychologist and writer

Born in Malta, he took a degree in medicine at the Royal
University there, then went as a Rhodes Scholar to Christ
Church, Oxford, where he read psychology, physiology
and medicine. From 1976 to 1983 he was a lecturer in
medicine at Cambridge, and he is involved with a number
of organizations to promote the skills of thinking, including the Cognitive Research Trust, Cambridge
(director since 1971). His books include *The Use of Lateral
Thinking* (1967), *Handbook for a Positive Revolution* (1990),
Water Logic (1993) and *Textbook of Wisdom* (1996).

De Bono, Emilio 1866–1944
Italian Fascist politician and general
He was born in Cassano d'Adda. After an army career in
World War I, he took part in **Mussolini**'s March on Rome
(1922), became Governor of Tripolitania (1925), colonial
secretary (1939) and commanded the Italian forces in-
vading Abyssinia (1935) until he was replaced by **Pietro
Badoglio**. He voted against Mussolini in the Fascist
Supreme Council (1943) and was summarily tried and
executed as a traitor by Fascists in Verona.

Debray, Regis 1941–
French Marxist theorist
Educated at the École Normale Supérieure, he gained
international fame through his association with the
Marxist revolutionary **Che Guevara** in Latin America
during the 1960s and, in 1967, was sentenced to 30 years'
imprisonment in Bolivia. He was released from jail in
1970 and from 1981 to 1984 he was appointed a specialist
adviser to President **François Mitterrand** on Third World
affairs. His most influential writings have been *Strategy for
Revolution* (1970) and *The Power of the Intellectual in France*
(1979), the latter a broadside against the growing influence of 'mediacrats'.

Debré, Michel Jean Pierre 1912–96
French politician
He was born in Paris. After taking part in the Resistance,
he helped to set up the École Nationale d'Administration
in 1945. He was elected to parliament as a member of the
Gaullist Party (RPF) in 1948, and violently attacked the
constitution of the Fourth Republic. In 1958 he was appointed Minister of Justice and **Charles de Gaulle**
charged him with the task of producing the new constitution of the Fifth Republic (adopted later that year); he
was appointed its first Prime Minister in 1959, but displaced by **Georges Pompidou** in 1962. Between 1966 and
1973 he held the Finance, Foreign Affairs and Defence
portfolios, and in 1979 became an MEP.

Debrett, John c.1750–1822
English publisher and biographer
Presumed to have been born in London, he took over in
1781 the publishing business of John Almon (1737–1805),
editor of *The New Peerage* (first published 1769). This became *Debrett's Peerage of England, Scotland and Ireland* in 1802,
and was in its 14th edition by the time Debrett died. His
shop, opposite the Royal Academy in Piccadilly, became
the meeting place of the Whig intelligentsia, and Debrett
was the leading publisher of books on the new colony of
Australia, including Watkin Tench's *Narrative* (1789) and
Settlement at Port Jackson (1793), chief surgeon John White's
Journal (1790), and the official dispatches of Governor
Arthur Philip (1789). *Debrett's Peerage*, under various titles,
continued publication until the late 1980s.

Debreu, Gerard 1921–
US economist and Nobel Prize winner
Born in Calais, France, and educated at the University of
Paris, he went to the USA in 1950 as a researcher with the
Cowles Foundation at Chicago University, and became a
professor at Yale (1955–61) and then Professor of Math-
ematics and Economics at the University of Califor-
nia at Berkeley (1962–91). His work on the equilibrium

Debussy, (Achille-)Claude 1862–1918
French composer

Debussy was born in St Germain-en-Laye and educated at the Paris Conservatoire (1873–84), where he studied the piano under Marmontel. In 1884 he won the Prix de Rome with his cantata *L'Enfant prodigue*. His early work was influenced by **Robert Wagner**, for whom he had a great admiration, but he developed a more experimental and individual vein in his first mature work, the *Prélude à l'après-midi d'un faune*, evoked by **Stéphane Mallarmé**'s poem, which first won him fame. He further added to his reputation with his admired operatic setting of **Maurice Maeterlinck**'s *Pelléas et Mélisande*, begun in 1892 but not performed until 1902, and some outstanding piano pieces, *Images* and *Préludes*, in which he moved further from traditional formulae and experimented with novel techniques and effects, producing the pictures in sound which led to his work being described as 'musical Impressionism'.

He extended this new idiom to orchestral music in *La Mer* (1905), the orchestrated *Images*, and other pieces, and later elaborated his piano style still further, as in the scintillating *Feux d'artifice* and the atmospheric *La Cathédrale engloutie*. In his later period he composed much chamber music, including pieces for the flute and the harp, two instruments peculiarly suited to his type of music.

In his private life Debussy was shy and reserved, particularly in his last years, which were clouded by his suffering from cancer; he did not socialize much, except in literary circles. In 1899 he married Rosalie Texier, a dressmaker, whom he left in 1904 for Emma Bardac, his wife from 1905.

His intensely individual compositions explored new and original avenues of musical expression, and had a profound effect on French music in general and piano music in particular at the turn of the century.
R Nichols, *Debussy* (1973) and *Debussy Remembered* (1992).

'The colour of my soul is iron-grey and sad bats wheel about the steeple of my dreams.' From a letter, 1894.

---

between prices, production and consumer demand in a free-market economy was recognized by the award of the Nobel Prize for economics in 1983. He wrote *Theory of Value: An Axiomatic Analysis of Economic Equilibrium* (1959) and a collection of essays, *Mathematical Economics* (1983).

De Broglie, Louis-Victor Pierre Raymond
See **Broglie, Louis-Victor Pierre Raymond de**

Debs, Eugene V(ictor) 1855–1926
US politician and union leader

Born in Terre Haute, Indiana, the son of Alsatian immigrants, he became a railroad worker and served as the national secretary of the Brotherhood of Locomotive Firemen until 1893, when he resigned to organize an industrial union of railroad workers, the American Railway Union (ARU). He pledged the ARU's participation in the Pullman strike of 1894, which was broken by federal authorities and brought Debs a six-month prison sentence. He helped to found the Socialist Party of America, standing unsuccessfully as its candidate in all the presidential elections between 1900 and 1920, except that of 1916. His pacifism during World War I and his denunciation of the Espionage Act led to his imprisonment (1918–21); he conducted his final presidential campaign from an Atlanta penitentiary, receiving nearly a million votes.

Deburau, Jean Gaspard 1796–1846
French actor

Born in Bohemia, he moved to Paris in 1814. There he perfected the art of mime and romanticized the traditional harlequinade by his development of the Pierrot role, performing to great popular and critical acclaim.

Debussy, (Achille-)Claude See panel above

Debye, Peter Joseph Wilhelm, *originally* Petrus Josephus Wilhelmus Debije 1884–1966
US physicist, physical chemist and Nobel Prize winner

Born in Maastricht, the Netherlands, he initially studied electrotechnology but became Professor of Theoretical Physics at Zurich (1911–12) and Utrecht (1912–14) universities, and Professor of Theoretical and Experimental Physics at Göttingen (1914–20). He was director of the Physical Institutes at the Federal Institute of Technology (ETH) in Zurich (1920–27), at Leipzig University (1927–34) and of the Kaiser-Wilhelm-Gesellschaft, Berlin (1934–40), where increasing political interference led him to leave for the USA (1940). He was chairman of the Cornell chemistry department from 1940 until his retirement in 1950. Debye's work included development of the theory of the specific heats of crystalline solids (pioneered by **Einstein**) in 1911, followed by his work on dielectric constants and, in 1912, molecular dipole moments (now known as Debyes), which were used during the 1920s and 1930s to investigate the details of chemical bonding. In the Debye–Hückel theory of strong electrolytes (1923), their behaviour was related quantitatively to electrostatic forces between ions. The Debye–Scherrer X-ray diffraction powder method was developed in 1916–20 and the theory of X-ray scattering by gaseous molecules in 1925. Experimental studies of X-ray diffraction by gases and liquids were made from 1929 to 1933 and for this work Debye was awarded the 1936 Nobel Prize for chemistry. Later he made important studies by means of electron diffraction (1938). He also provided the theoretical treatments for the electro-optical Kerr effect (1925), adiabatic demagnetization (1926) and thermal diffusion (1939). After his move to the USA he worked on light scattering related to molecular and media structures (1944–66) and many aspects of polymer behaviour (1945–66). He was awarded the Rumford medal of the Royal Society (of which he became a Foreign Member in 1933), the Faraday medal of the Chemical Society (1933), and several medals of the American Chemical Society.

Decamps, Alexandre Gabriel 1803–60
French painter

Born in Paris, he was a pioneer of the Romantic school. He was a great colourist, specializing in oriental scenes and biblical subjects. One of his best pictures, *The Watering Place*, is in the Wallace collection in London.

Decatur, Stephen 1779–1820
US naval commander

Born in Sinepuxent, Maryland, of French descent, he served against the French, and in the war with Tripoli (1801–05) gained great distinction burning the captured *Philadelphia*, and escaping under the fire of 141 guns. Promoted captain in 1804 and commodore in 1810, in the War of 1812 with Great Britain he captured the British frigate *Macedonian*, but in 1814 surrendered. He was killed in a duel in Bladensburg, Maryland. C T Brady, *Stephen Decatur* (1900)

Decius, Caius Messius Quintus Trajanus c.200–251AD
Roman emperor

He was born in Lower Pannonia, and was sent (AD249) by the Emperor Philip I, the Arab, to reduce the rebellious army of Moesia. An able general and administrator, he was proclaimed emperor by the soldiers against his will, and he defeated and killed Philip near Verona. His brief reign was one of warring with the Goths and persecuting the Christians. He was killed near Abricium.

de Coster, Charles See Coster, Charles de

De Danaan
Irish traditional music group
The group formed in the early 1970s, at a time of great activity in traditional Irish music circles, and have gone on to establish themselves as the leading group to emerge from that era. While bands like The Bothy Band, Planxty and Moving Hearts later disbanded, De Danaan have remained loyal to their conception, combining superbly played traditional Irish music with US influences, as on *The Star Spangled Molly* (1981) and *½ Step In Harlem* (1991). Founder members Frankie Gavin (fiddle) and Alec Finn (bouzouki) remain at the heart of the group, which has featured many of the best-known Irish musicians, including singers Mary Black and Dolores Keane.

Dedekind, Julius Wilhelm Richard 1831–1916
German mathematician
Born in Brunswick, he wrote his doctoral thesis at the University of Göttingen under Carl Gauss in 1852, but the real influence on him was Lejeune Dirichlet, who led Dedekind into number theory. From 1854 to 1858 he taught at Göttingen, then in Zurich, and he returned to Brunswick in 1862 as professor at the Polytechnic. He gave one of the first precise definitions of the real number system, and his important work in number theory led him to introduce many concepts which have become fundamental in all modern algebra. With his friend Georg Cantor he did much to found mathematics on the naive concept of a set, and also made important contributions in the early history of lattice theory.

de Duve, Christian René 1917–
Belgian biochemist and Nobel Prize winner
Born in Thames Ditton, Surrey, England, he studied medicine at Leuven, Belgium, and returned there to teach in 1947. He was Professor of Biochemistry there from 1951, and from 1962 also held a chair of biochemistry at Rockefeller University, New York. He explored the new technique of differential centrifugation, separating a tissue into its separate constituents by centrifugation at different speeds, but he is best known as the discoverer of lysosomes, small organelles within cells which contain enzymes, whose malfunction causes some metabolic diseases, such as cystinosis. For this and other discoveries on the structure and biochemistry of cells he shared the 1974 Nobel Prize for physiology or medicine with Albert Claude and George Palade. His publications include *A Guided Tour for the Living Cell* (1985) and *Vital Dust* (1995).

Dee, John 1527–1608
English alchemist, geographer and mathematician
Born in London, he was educated in London, Chelmsford, and at St John's College, Cambridge, and became one of the original Fellows of Trinity College, Cambridge (1546). He earned the reputation of a sorcerer by using a mechanical beetle in a representation of Aristophanes's *Peace*. He claimed to have found in the ruins of Glastonbury a quantity of the Elixir, and his assistant, Edward Kelley, professed to confer with angels by means of Dee's magic crystal, and talked him into consenting to a community of wives. As astrologer to Queen Mary I, Tudor, he was imprisoned but acquitted on charges of plotting her death by magic (1555). For most of his life he was concerned with the search for the Northwest Passage to the Far East, aiding the exploration by his navigational and geographical knowledge. He wrote numerous works on logic, mathematics, astrology, alchemy, navigation, geography and the calendar (1583), but died in poverty. His eldest son, Arthur Dee (1579–1651), was also an alchemist, and a friend of Sir Thomas Browne. 📖 Thomas Smith, *The Life of John Dee* (1992)

Deeping, (George) Warwick 1877–1950
English novelist
Born in Southend-on-Sea, Essex, he qualified as a doctor, but turned to writing. It was not until after World War I, in which he served, that he gained recognition as an author with his bestseller, *Sorrell and Son* (1925), which was later filmed. Other novels include *Old Pybus* (1928) and *Roper's Row* (1929). In his sentimental stories, good breeding is represented as the cardinal virtue.

Deere, John 1804–86
US inventor and manufacturer
Born in Rutland, Vermont, he was apprenticed to a blacksmith at the age of 17, and after establishing himself in the trade, he moved to Grand Detour, Illinois, in 1837. He discovered that the dense prairie soil was too tough for cast-iron ploughs, which farmers often brought in for repairs, and in 1838 he designed a steel plough. His plough helped transform the prairie into a vast cropland, and the business which he founded to manufacture it (incorporated as Deere and Co in 1868) made his fortune.

de Fleury, André-Hercule See Fleury, André-Hercule de

Defoe, Daniel 1660–1731
English writer and adventurer
Born in Stoke Newington, London, the son of a butcher, he set up in the hosiery trade there in 1683, then joined William III's army in 1688 and up to 1704 strenuously supported the king's party. In Queen Anne's reign he ran into trouble with his famous satire *The Shortest Way with the Dissenters* (1702), which eventually cost him a ruinous fine, the pillory and imprisonment in Newgate Prison. After his release, he founded a newspaper, *The Review* (1704–13), which aimed at being an organ of commercial interests, but also expressed opinions on political and domestic topics, and included the feature the 'Scandal Club', anticipating such magazines as *Tatler* and the *Spectator*. From 1704 he undertook various secret commissions for the Tory minister Robert Harley, including dubious dealings with the Scottish commissioners for Union in 1706–07. He turned to writing fiction after 1714, and in 1719–20, at the age of nearly 60, published his best-known book, *Robinson Crusoe*. His other major fictions include *Journal of the Plague Year* (1722), *Moll Flanders* (1722), his most vivid and still one of the best tales of low life, and *Roxana* (1724). A writer of astonishing versatility, he published more than 250 works in all, among them a three-volume travel book (*Tour through the Whole Island of Great Britain*, 1724–27), *The Great Law of Subordination Considered* (1724) and *Augusta Triumphans, or the Way to make London the Most Flourishing City in the Universe* (1728). 📖 P Rogers, *Defoe: the critical heritage* (1972); B Fitzgerald, *Defoe, a History of Conflict* (1954)

De Forest, Lee 1873–1961
US physicist and inventor
Born in Council Bluffs, Iowa, he was educated at Yale and Chicago. He introduced the grid into the thermionic valve (1906), and invented the 'audion' and the four-electrode valve. He also did much early work on sound reproduction and on television, and received his last patent at the age of 84 for an automatic dialling device. A pioneer of radio and wireless telegraphy, he patented more than 300 inventions in all and is known as the 'father of radio' in the USA. He was a founder member of the Institute of Radio Engineers (1912), and was awarded its

de Gaulle, Charles André Joseph Marie 1890–1970
French general and first President of the Fifth Republic

Charles de Gaulle was born in Lille. He served as an army officer in World War I, and drew on this experience to develop a new theory of mechanized strategy, which was expounded in *The Army of the Future* published in 1932, and which, although largely ignored by the French military, clearly inspired the German *Blitzkrieg* of 1940. De Gaulle's prescience was rewarded with promotion to general and junior War Secretary the same year, but days before the signing of the French Armistice he sought refuge in England to found the Free French Army. Though largely ignored by both **Winston Churchill** and **Franklin D Roosevelt**, he served as a focus for the resistance movement, in which he played an active role during the rest of the war. He returned to Paris in 1944 with the first liberation forces.

He was the country's natural first choice as postwar leader. He failed to form an all-party coalition and resigned in 1946 to found a new party, Rally of the French People, which took 40 per cent of the votes in the 1947 election. He relinquished its leadership in 1953, and, in the wake of the failure by successive administrations to resolve the Algerian question, was free to accept office as first President of the Fifth Republic in 1958. In 1959–60 he granted self-government to all French African colonies (including Algeria, which finally achieved independence in 1962), and at home consolidated France's growing international importance by establishing its own nuclear deterrent, fostering better relations with West Germany,

blocking Great Britain's attempts in 1962 and 1967 to enter the Common Market, and recognizing the Peking (Beijing) government in 1964.

Despite his extensive use of the referendum, his autocratic presidential style and the growing popularity of the Left among the new young electorate created by the postwar baby boom, he won re-election in 1965 after a second vote, and recovered with an overwhelming victory in 1968 on seeking a mandate in the wake of violent student riots. However, in 1969 the electorate's rejection, in a referendum, of his proposals for Senate and regional reforms brought his resignation, and he died a year later.

To the British and Americans in particular, Charles de Gaulle epitomized Gallic obstinacy and self-interest, but while he could not match Churchill's brilliance in wartime, he may be regarded as a more influential and effective national leader in peacetime.

📖 His three-volume memoirs, *Mémoires de guerre*, were published between 1954 and 1959. See also Brian Crozier, *De Gaulle: The Warrior* (1973) and *De Gaulle: The Statesman* (1974); Aidan Crawley, *De Gaulle* (1969).

> 'The French will only be united under the threat of danger. How else can one govern a country that produces 246 different types of cheese?' From a speech (1951). Quoted in *Les Mots du Général* (1962).

Medal of Honour (1915). Among his other honours was the Cross of the Legion of Honour from France. 📖 Israel E Levine, *Electronic Pioneer: Lee De Forest* (1964)

Degas, (Hilaire Germain) Edgar 1834–1917
French artist

Born in Paris, he studied at the École des Beaux-Arts under Lamothe, a pupil of **Jean Ingres**, then went to Italy, where he was influenced by the art of the Renaissance painters. On his return to Paris he associated with the Impressionists and took part in most of their exhibitions from 1874 to 1886. He was also influenced by Japanese woodcuts and, in the seemingly casual composition of his paintings, by photography. He travelled in Spain and Italy and visited New Orleans, USA, in 1872–73, but most of his paintings and pastels of dancers and women at their toilet were produced in his Paris studio, often with the aid of wax and clay models. His interest lay in precision of line and the modelling of the human form in space. *Miss Lola at the Cirque Fernando* (1879) is in the Tate Gallery, London, *Rehearsal of the Ballet* (c.1874) is in the Louvre, Paris, *Dancer Lacing her Shoe* (c.1878) is in the Paris Museum of Impressionism, *Dancer at the Bar* is in the Metropolitan Museum, New York, and the well-known *Cotton-brokers Office* (1873) is in Pau Museum. In later life, because of failing sight, he concentrated on sculpture.

De Gasperi, Alcide 1881–1954
Italian statesman

He was born in Pieve Tesino in the Austrian province of Trentino and educated at Vienna University. He edited the journal *Il Nuovo Trentino* from 1906, and was elected to the Austrian parliament (1911–16, 1919). After Trentino was united with Italy, he became a member of the Italian Chamber of Deputies until 1925, when the Fascist regime of **Mussolini** banned political activity. A founder of the Italian Popular Party, he was arrested in 1926 but found refuge in the Vatican, as Vatican librarian, until Mussolini's overthrow in 1943. From 1945 he was a leading force in the creation of the Christian Democratic Party

(DC), of which he remained Secretary-General until his death, and, as Prime Minister (1945–53), was Italy's most notable postwar politician.

de Gaulle, Charles André Joseph Marie
See panel above

de Geer, Louis Gerhard See **Geer, Louis Gerhard de**

De Gennes, Pierre-Gilles 1932–
French theoretical physicist and Nobel Prize winner

Born in Paris, he was educated at the École Normale Supérieure and became professor at the University of Orsay (1961–71). Since 1971 he has been Professor of Solid State Physics at the Collège de France, and since 1976 director of the College of Industrial Physics and Chemistry in Paris. Amongst several honours, De Gennes was awarded the 1991 Nobel Prize for physics for outstanding work on molecules in substances undergoing phase transitions, and for increasing our understanding of polymers and liquid crystals. He explained how polymers flow, describing mathematically how the tangled long-chain molecules can move along their own lengths. This led to a totally new theory of polymer elasticity and viscosity. In studies of liquid crystals, he showed how their optical properties can be altered by applying a current.

Dehaene, Jean-Luc 1940–
Belgian politician

Born in Montpellier, France, and educated at the university of Namur, Belgium, he worked as an adviser to several government ministries before entering politics in 1981. He was appointed deputy Prime Minister in 1988 and became Prime Minister in 1992. A Flemish speaker and supporter of Flemish culture, he emerged as devolutionist in European politics and supports the concept of giving more to the regions. In 1994 he was a candidate for the presidency of the European Commission but lost to **Jacques Delors**.

De Havilland, Sir Geoffrey 1882–1965
English aircraft designer
Born near High Wycombe, Buckinghamshire, he was educated at Crystal Palace Engineering School. He built his first plane in 1908 and became director of the firm bearing his name, which produced many famous aircraft, including the Tiger Moth (1930), the Mosquito (1941, of revolutionary plywood construction) and the Comet jet airliner (1952). He established a height record for light aircraft in 1928, and won the King's Cup air race at the age of 51. ⌨ *Sky Fever* (1979)

de Havilland, Olivia Mary 1916–
US actress
She was born in Tokyo, Japan, of British parentage, and raised in California. Her early stage appearances brought her to the attention of **Max Reinhardt**, who cast her in both his stage and film versions of *A Midsummer Night's Dream* (1935). Subsequently under contract to **Warner** Brothers, she proved an excellent foil to such stars as **Errol Flynn** in boisterous tales such as *Captain Blood* (1935) and *The Adventures of Robin Hood* (1938). She received an Academy Award nomination for her portrayal of Melanie in *Gone With The Wind* (1939), secured a further nomination for *Hold Back The Dawn* (1941) and won the award for both *To Each His Own* (1946) and *The Heiress* (1949). In 1942, her case against Warner Brothers resulted in a landmark decision limiting all film contracts to seven years. Her later, less frequent, film appearances include *The Proud Rebel* (1958) and *Hush, Hush Sweet Charlotte* (1964). Her television work includes *Noon Wine* (1967), *The Screaming Women* (1972) and *The Mystery of Anna* (1986). She published her autobiography, *Every Frenchman Has One*, in 1963.

Dehmel, Richard 1863–1920
German poet
Born in Wendisch-Hermsdorf, Brandenburg, he worked for an insurance company, then served on the front line in World War I, where he was awarded the Iron Cross. He wrote intellectual verse, which showed the influence of **Nietzsche** and in which he practised rigorous self-discipline. His best-known collection is *Weib und Welt* (1896, 'Woman and World'). ⌨ E Ludwig, *Richard Dehmel* (1913)

Dehmelt, Hans Georg 1922–
US physicist and Nobel Prize winner
Born in Görlitz, Germany, he studied at Göttingen University, where he received his PhD in 1950, and moved to the USA in 1952, becoming professor at the University of Washington in 1961. He developed a device known as the 'Penning trap', which uses electromagnetic fields to isolate ions and electrons so that they may be studied over long periods of time. Using this trap, he measured the magnetic moment of an electron to an unprecedented accuracy. The device has also allowed very accurate measurement of the energy levels in atoms, which in turn will lead to increases in the accuracy of time measurement by atomic clocks. For this work Dehmelt shared the 1989 Nobel Prize for physics with **Wolfgang Paul** and **Norman Ramsey**. He became a US citizen in 1961.

de Honnecourt, Villard See Villard de Honnecourt

Deighton, Len (Leonard Cyril) 1929–
English thriller writer
Born in London, he has been an art student, a railway plate-layer and an air steward. His first novel, *The Ipcress File* (1962), was written when he was 33 and became a bestseller, as have almost all his books. Along with **John Le Carré**, **Graham Greene** and **Eric Ambler** he has been responsible for taking the spy novel out of the genre ghetto into mainstream literature. Notable titles are *Funeral in Berlin* (1965), *Only When I Larf* (1968) and the

Game, Set and Match trilogy: *Berlin Game* (1984), *Mexico Set* (1985) and *London Match* (1986). It was followed by another trilogy, *Spy Hook* (1988), *Spy Line* (1989) and *Spy Sinker* (1990). He also writes cookery books.

Deisenhofer, Johann 1943–
US molecular biologist and Nobel Prize winner
Born in Zusamaltheim, Bavaria, Germany, he graduated in physics at Munich University (1971) and then worked at the **Max Planck** Institute for Biochemistry in Martinsried until 1988, when he became Regental Professor and Professor of Biochemistry at the University of Texas Southwestern Medical Center in Dallas. Initially he worked with **Robert Huber** on the crystallographic X-ray analysis of the structure of biological macromolecules. From 1974 he studied pancreatic enzymes, and in 1976 he began a series of studies on immunoglobulin structure, identifying receptor and effector sites for other biomolecules and the nature of the interaction with other molecular components. He later collaborated with **Hartmut Michel** and Huber to determine the structure of the reaction centre of the bacterium *Rhodopseudomonas viridis*, work for which they shared the 1988 Nobel Prize for chemistry. Deisenhofer has studied another membrane-bound enzyme, cytochrome-c oxidase, indicating the presence in the molecule of alpha helical structures, and has also contributed to studies on protein–DNA interactions.

De Keersmaeker, Anne Teresa 1960–
Belgian dancer and post-modern choreographer
Born in Mechelen, she studied at the Mudra School in Brussels, founded by **Maurice Béjart**, and in New York, and created a style which blends the abstract qualities of new US dance with the expressionist energies of Europeans like **Pina Bausch**. Her own company, Rosas, opened in 1983 with *Rosas Danst Rosas*. She has set her pieces to both minimalist and classical music and has used film and speech in her work. Her recent interests in dance theatre led to a staging of *Verkommenes Ufer Medeamaterial Landschaft mit Argonauten*, by East German writer Heiner Müller. Other work includes *Elena's Aria* (1984) and *Bartók/Aantekeningen* (1986), a piece about the modern woman which transforms high-heeled restriction into school-girl freedom with precision choreography.

Dekker, Eduard Douwes, *pseudonym* Multatuli 1820–87
Dutch radical publicist and novelist
Born in Amsterdam, he served for many years in the Dutch Civil Service in Java. In his novel *Max Havelaar* (1860), and in many bitter satires, he protested against the abuses of the Dutch colonial system. ⌨ G Bron, *Multatuli* (1958)

Dekker, Thomas c.1570–1632
English dramatist and pamphleteer
He was born in London. Around 1598 he was employed by **Philip Henslowe** to write plays, and in 1600 published two comedies, *The Shoemaker's Holiday, or the Gentle Craft*, and *The Pleasant Comedy of Old Fortunatus*. His most powerful dramatic writing is seen in *The Honest Whore* (Part I, 1604, written with **Thomas Middleton**; Part II, written 1605, performed 1630). In 1607 he published three plays written in conjunction with **John Webster**, the *Famous History of Sir Thomas Wyat*, *Westward Ho!* and *Northward Ho!* These were followed by several other collaborative works: the excellent comedy, *The Roaring Girl* (1611, with Middleton), the *Virgin Martyr* (1622, with **Philip Massinger**), *The Sun's Darling* (licensed 1624, printed 1656, with **John Ford**), and a powerful tragedy, *The Witch of Edmonton* (1623, with Ford and **William Rowley**). From 1613 to 1616 he was mostly in prison for debt. His pamphlets include *The Wonderful Year* (1603), which gives a tragic

account of the plague, and *The Bellman of London* (1608), a lively account of London vagabonds. 📖 G R Price, *Thomas Dekker* (1969)

de Kéroualle, Louise See Portsmouth, Duchess of

de Klerk, F(rederik) W(illem) 1936–
South African politician and Nobel Prize winner

Born in Johannesburg into a political family, he graduated from Potchestroom University, established a legal practice in Vereeniging and became active in the National Party. He entered the South African parliament, representing Vereeniging, in 1972, and then served in the Cabinets of John Vorster and P W Botha (1978–89). De Klerk also became National Party leader for the Transvaal in 1982 and in 1989 replaced Botha as National Party leader and acting State President. He began gradual reform of the apartheid system and improved diplomatic relations and in 1989 he secured electoral victory for his party, but with a reduced majority. In February 1990 he ended the 30-year-old ban on the African National Congress (ANC) black opposition movement and sanctioned the release from imprisonment of its effective leader Nelson Mandela, with whom in 1993 he was jointly awarded the Nobel Peace Prize. By 1994 apartheid had been abolished and South Africa experienced its first democratic elections with de Klerk appointed Vice-President. He resigned his post as National Party leader in 1997.

de Kooning, Willem 1904–97
US painter

Born in Rotterdam, the Netherlands, he emigrated to the USA in 1926 and settled in New York City, where he was influenced by the work of Arshile Gorky. By the 1950s he had emerged as a leader of the Abstract Expressionist movement (New York school), though he retained some figurative elements in his work and was preoccupied by the human form, which he represented most famously in his controversial series *Woman I–V* (1952–53). He began in the late 1950s to spend much of his time in Long Island, chronicling this shift from city to country in works such as *Montauk Highway* (1958) and *Pastorale* (1963). From his studio near the ocean he continued to produce vibrant abstract paintings that echoed nudes and landscapes into the late 1980s, when he stopped painting due to illness.

De la Beche, Sir Henry Thomas 1796–1855
English stratigrapher and geologist

Born near London, he went to the Military School at Great Marlowe in 1810 and lived for a time in Switzerland and France, studying the natural phenomena of the Alps. From 1822 to 1826 he described in detail the secondary strata near Lyme Regis, Dorset. In 1832 he started mapping the geology of Dorset and Devon, and in 1835 was appointed to extend the survey into Cornwall, marking the beginning of the first national Geological Survey of which he became the first director. His work led to the establishment of the Mining Record Office (1839), the Museum of Practical Geology (1841) and the School of Mines and Science (1853). He became president of the Geological Society of London in 1847. He published many works, including *Manual of Geology* (1831), *Researches in Theoretical Geology* (1834), regional memoirs of parts of southern England and the first account of the geology of Jamaica (1834). He was knighted in 1842.

de la Bourdonnais, Bertrand François Mahé See La Bourdonnais, Bertrand François Mahé de

de La Calprenède, Gautier See Calprenède, Gautier de La

Delacroix, (Ferdinand Victor) Eugène
1798–1863
French painter

He was born in Charenton, the son of Charles Delacroix (1741–1805), who had been Foreign Minister under the Directory, and prefect of Marseilles. As a boy he developed a love of art and in 1861 he entered the studio of Pierre Guérin, where his fellow pupil was Theodore Géricault, whose famous *Raft of the Medusa* gave him early inspiration. In 1822 he exhibited *Dante and Virgil in Hell* at the Salon, and in 1824 *The Massacre at Chios* (Louvre, Paris). These pictures, particularly the latter with its loose drawing and vivid colouring, shocked the devotees of the austere Classical style and aroused a storm of criticism. John Constable's *Haywain*, which was hung in the same exhibition, profoundly impressed Delacroix, who moved even further away from traditional treatment with brilliant canvases of historical and dramatic scenes, often violent or macabre in subject, among them *The Execution of Faliero*, now in the Wallace collection, and the famous *Liberty Guiding the People* (1831, Louvre). A journey to Morocco and Spain with a diplomatic mission in 1832 led to several pictures with an oriental flavour, such as *Algerian Women* (1834), and he also turned to literary themes, notably from Shakespeare and Torquato Tasso. In 1838 he began work on a series of panels for the library of the Chamber of Deputies, choosing as his subject the history of ancient civilization, but despite this official recognition and despite the fact that the government had bought his *Massacre at Chios*, he was regarded as a rebel in the art world and was not elected to the Institut de France until 1857. Perhaps the greatest figure in 19th century French art, Delacroix was one of the most accomplished colourists of all time, and was responsible for a shift away from the meticulous but pallid techniques of Jean Ingres and Jacques Louis David. A man of immense energy, he interested himself in politics and literature (he was a friend of George Sand, whom he painted). The daily journal which he kept from the age of 23 until his death records fascinating details of his life and work. 📖 Lee Johnson, *Delacroix* (1963)

Delafield, E M, *pseudonym of* Edmée Elizabeth Monica Dashwood, *née* de la Pasture 1890–1943
English novelist

Born in Llandogo, Monmouth, Wales, she worked first as a nurse and then at the Ministry of National Service in Bristol during World War I, and then became a civil servant, and served as a magistrate. She was the prolific author of novels which took a mildly but affectionately satirical look at the mores of genteel provincial life. Her best-known works are the series which began with *Diary of a Provincial Lady* (1930). 📖 *A Note By the Way* (1933)

de la Hire, Philippe See La Hire, Philippe de

de la Huntly, Shirley Barbara, *née* Strickland
1925–
Australian athlete

Born in Guildford, Western Australia, she was the daughter of a professional male runner. She won seven Olympic medals over the course of the three Games from 1948 to 1956, specializing in the 80 metres hurdles, 200 metres and 100 metres sprint. A re-read of the photo finish at the 1948 Games suggests that she should have taken a bronze in the 200 metres, unofficially taking her medal total to eight. She also set world record times on successive days in the 80 metres hurdles at the Helsinki Olympics in 1952. Since retiring she has been involved in promoting junior competition.

De La Madrid Hurtado, Miguel 1934–
Mexican politician

Born in Colima, Mexico, he studied law in Mexico City and public administration at Harvard. He became an adviser to the Bank of Mexico, then entered government service in the Ministry of Finance. As Minister of Planning and Budget under **José López Portillo**, he formulated an economic development plan that sought to use Mexico's oil wealth to promote economic growth. A conservative who could be trusted to carry on the policies of his predecessor, he was chosen as the candidate of the ruling Institutional Revolutionary Party in 1981 and was President of Mexico from 1982 to 1988.

de la Mare, Walter John 1873–1956
English poet and novelist
Born in Charlton, Kent, of Huguenot descent, he was educated at St Paul's Choir School, London. He worked for the Standard Oil Company (1890–1908) then took up full-time writing. His first book of verse, *Songs of Childhood* (1902), was published under the pseudonym of Walter Ramal. A popular writer with adults and children, he has produced novels, poetry and short stories. His works include the prose romance *Henry Brocken* (1904), the children's story *The Three Mulla Mulgars* (1910), the novel of the occult *The Return* (1910), the collection of poetry *The Listeners* (1912), the fantasy novel *Memoirs of a Midget* (1921), and short stories in *On the Edge* (1930). He was buried in St Paul's Cathedral. A *Complete Poems* was issued in 1969. ⌨ L Clark, *Walter de la Mare* (1960)

de la Mettrie, Julien Offray See **La Mettrie, Julien Offray de**

de la Motte, Friedrich Heinrich Karl See **Fouqué, Friedrich Heinrich Karl de la Motte, Baron**

Delane, John Thaddeus 1817–79
English journalist
Born in London, he graduated from Magdalen Hall, Oxford. **John Walter**, his father's neighbour in Berkshire and proprietor of *The Times*, noticed him, and in 1841 he became joint editor of *The Times*. For 25 of the 36 years he held this post he was assisted by **George Dasent**. Under Delane *The Times* attained a circulation and an influence unparalleled in journalism. He did not write articles, but contributed reports and letters; his exposure of the railway mania, his attacks upon the management of the Crimean War, and his strong opposition to Great Britain's support of Denmark in 1864 were noteworthy.

Delaney, Shelagh 1939–
English playwright and screenwriter
Born in Salford, Lancashire, she left school at the age of 16 and completed her first and best-known play a year later. *A Taste of Honey*, produced in London in 1958, is the story of a young white girl's abrasive home life and her pregnancy following a casual affair with a black sailor. It was immediately seen as part of a young, 'angry' movement dealing realistically with working-class, provincial life, and which included the playwrights **John Osborne** and **Arnold Wesker**. None of Delaney's more recent writing has achieved equal critical acclaim. Among her later work is the screenplay for *Dance with a Stranger* (1985), a film depicting the fraught life of **Ruth Ellis**, the last woman to be hanged in England.

Delany, Mary, *née* Granville 1700–88
English writer
She was born in Coulston, Wiltshire, the niece of Lord Lansdowne, and after the death of her second husband, the Rev Patrick Delany (1685–1768), an Irish divine, and friend of **Jonathan Swift**, she lived chiefly in London. She is mainly remembered for her patronage of the writer **Fanny Burney** and for her *Autobiography and Correspondence* (6 vols, 1861–62).

de la Platière, Jeanne Manon Roland See **Roland de la Platière, Jeanne Manon**

de la Renta, Oscar 1932–
US fashion designer
He was born in Santo Domingo, in the Dominican Republic. After studying art there and in Madrid, he worked at **Cristóbal Balenciaga**'s couture house in Madrid. He joined the house of Lanvin-Castillo in Paris in 1961, but after two years went to **Elizabeth Arden** in New York. In 1965 he started his own company. He has a reputation for opulent, ornately trimmed clothes, particularly evening dresses, and he also designs daywear and accessories.

Delarivier Manley See **Manley, Delarivier**

de la Roche, Mazo 1885–1961
Canadian novelist
She was born in Newmarket, Ontario, and published *Jalna*, the first of a series of novels about the Whiteoak family, in 1927. *Whiteoaks* (1929) was dramatized with considerable success. She also wrote children's stories, history and travel books and an autobiography, *Ringing the Changes* (1957). ⌨ G Hendrik, *Mazo de la Roche* (1970)

Delaroche, (Hippolyte-) Paul, 1797–1856
French painter
Born in Paris, he studied under **Antoine Jean Gros**, and specialized in romantic historical subjects such as the *Death of Queen Elizabeth* (1827) and the *Execution of Lady Jane Grey* (1834). From this period until 1841 he was engaged on his largest work, the mural *Apotheosis of Art* in the École des Beaux-Arts, in which he was aided by **Edward Armitage** and other pupils.

de la Rochefoucault, François See **La Rochefoucault, François, 6th Duc de**

De la Rue, Warren 1815–89
British astronomer and physicist
Born in Guernsey, the Channel Islands, he was educated in Paris, and entered his father's paperware business, inventing an envelope-making machine, and becoming one of the first printers to adopt electrotyping. He also worked to improve the **Daniell** constant silver chloride cell, and did research on the discharge of electricity in gases. A pioneer of celestial photography, he invented the photoheliograph which permitted mapping the Sun's surface photographically, and showed that sunspots are depressions in the Sun's atmosphere. He was elected FRS (1850), and to the Royal Astronomical Society (president 1864–66), and was a member of the Royal Institution.

de la Tour, Frances 1944–
English actress
Born in Bovingdon, Hertfordshire, she made her stage debut with the Royal Shakespeare Company in *Timon of Athens* (1965) and stayed there until 1971, when she played Helena in *A Midsummer Night's Dream*. She is best known to television audiences as Miss Jones in the sitcom *Rising Damp* (1974–78), a role she recreated in the film version (1980), and as Carol Beasley in *A Kind of Living* (1988), Shirley Silver in *Every Silver Lining* (1993) and Rosemary in *Downwardly Mobile* (1994). On stage, her performances in *Duet for One* (1980) and *A Moon for the Misbegotten* (1983) won her Society of West End Theatres awards.

Delaunay, Robert 1885–1941
French painter
Born in Paris, he abandoned stage design for painting in 1905 and his first works are painted in a colourful Divisionist (Pointillist) technique. Under the influence of **Cézanne** he subdued his palette, but later returned to high-key colour in a series of pictures of Saint-Severin and the Eiffel Tower (c.1910) by which he is best known.

Later he started isolating areas of pure colour in his pictures, a method which he called Orphism and which he saw as a logical development of Impressionism and Neo-Impressionism. The breaking up of the surface of his pictures into planes of colour eventually led to almost pure abstraction. In 1912 he was visited by members of the Blaue Reiter group upon whom he was to exert considerable influence, and by 1914 he had become recognized as the most significant painter in Paris. ⊞ Michael Hoog, *Delaunay* (1977)

Delaunay, Sonia Terk, *née* Stern 1885–1979
French painter and textile designer

Born in the Ukraine, Russia, she was brought up in St Petersburg, and studied art at Karlsruhe and in Paris where, in 1905, she attended the Académie de la Palette. In 1910 she married the French painter **Robert Delaunay** and together they founded the movement known as Orphism. In 1918 they designed sets and costumes for **Sergei Diaghilev**. She was a textile designer of international importance, and her work was included in the Exposition des Arts Décoratifs in 1925.

de la Vega, Garcilaso See **Garcilaso de la Vega**

Delavigne, Jean François Casimir 1793–1843
French dramatist, satirist and lyricist

Born in Le Havre, he became popular through his *Messéniennes* (1818, 'Messenians'), satires upon the Restoration. *Les Vêpres siciliennes* (1819, 'Sicilian Vespers'), a tragic piece, was followed by *L'École des vieillards* (1820, 'The School of Old People'), *Les Comédiens* (1821, 'The Actors'), *Louis XI* (partly based on *Quentin Durward*, 1833) and *La Fille du Cid* (1839, 'The Daughter of El Cid'). ⊞ F Vaucheux, *Casimir Delavigne* (1893)

De la Warr, Thomas West, 3rd or 12th Baron 1577–1618
English soldier and colonist

After serving under Robert, 2nd Earl of **Essex**, he was appointed the first Governor of Virginia in 1610. Returning to England in 1611, he wrote the *Relation* on Virginia. He died on a return voyage to Virginia. The state of Delaware is named after him.

Delbrück, Max 1906–81
German biophysicist and Nobel Prize winner

Born in Berlin, he studied atomic physics at the University of Göttingen, where he received his PhD in 1930. He worked with **Niels Bohr** at Copenhagen University in 1932, moved to Berlin in 1935 to work with **Lise Meitner**, and in 1937 emigrated to the USA, where he held appointments at the California Institute of Technology (Caltech), and became Professor of Biology there in 1947. In the 1940s Delbrück began working on the genetics of the phage virus, a simple organism with a protein coat surrounding a coil of DNA. Independently of **A D Hershey**, he discovered in 1946 that viruses can exchange genetic material to create new types of virus, and together with **Salvador Luria** they set up the Phage Group, to encourage the use of phage as an experimental tool. The three were awarded the 1969 Nobel Prize for physiology or medicine for their work in viral genetics. ⊞ Ernst Peter Fischer, *Thinking About Science: Max Delbrück and the Origins of Molecular Biology* (1988)

Delcassé, Théophile 1852–1923
French politician

He was twice Foreign Minister (1898–1905, 1914–15), during which time he promoted the Entente Cordiale with Great Britain (1904), and worked towards the Triple Entente with Great Britain and Russia.

Deledda, Grazia 1875–1936
Italian writer and Nobel Prize winner

Born in Sardinia, she moved to Rome after her marriage in 1900, but her work in the next 20 years focused on peasant stories of her native island. The lyricism and intensity of novels like *Cenere* (1904, 'Ashes'), *L'edera* (1908, 'Ivy'), *Marianna Sirca* (1915) and *La madre* (1920, 'The Mother') won her a considerable reputation. Her later books left the Sardinian setting, but were similar in style. The posthumous *Cosima* (1937) is autobiographical. She won the 1926 Nobel Prize for literature. ⊞ N Zoja, *Grazia Deledda, saggio critica* (1939)

De Leon, Daniel 1852–1914
US radical

Born in Curaçao, in the Netherlands Antilles, the son of a Dutch Jewish surgeon on Dutch colonial military service, he studied in Hildesheim, Germany, and then in Amsterdam, emigrating to the USA in 1874. He worked on a Spanish newspaper for Cuban liberation and taught in Westchester County, New York, while studying law at Columbia, afterwards practising in Texas, and then lecturing in Latin American diplomacy at Columbia (1883–89). He supported the Socialist Labor Party from 1890, becoming its national lecturer and (unsuccessful) candidate for Governor of New York in 1891. He edited the party journal, *The People* (1890–1914). He founded the Socialist Trade and Labor Alliance in 1895, but a split developed in protest against his authoritarianism and the seceders of 1899 ultimately became the Socialist Party of America. He assisted in the formation of the Industrial Workers of the World (1905), merging it with his Alliance, but broke away from them and founded a rival body, the Workers' International Industrial Union. He wrote several Marxist treatises such as *The Socialist Reconstruction of Society*, translated **Karl Marx**'s *Eighteenth Brumaire of Louis Bonaparte* and profoundly influenced **Lenin**'s theoretical writings.

de León, Juan Ponce See **Ponce de León, Juan**

de León, Luis Ponce See **Ponce de León, Luis**

Delescluze, Louis Charles 1809–71
French politician and journalist

Born in Dreux, he was driven from France to journalism in Belgium (1835) following his Republican agitation at the 1830 Restoration, but the February Revolution (1848) brought him back to Paris. His writing made him popular with the masses but brought him imprisonment, and he was ultimately transported until 1859. His experiences are described in *De Paris à Cayenne; Journal d'un transporté* (1867, 'From Paris to Cayenne, Journal of a Convict'). In 1868 he started the *Réveil*, to promote the International. He played a prominent part in the Paris Commune (1871), and died on the last barricade.

Delfim Neto, Antônio 1929–
Brazilian economist and politician

The son of Italian immigrants, he is widely viewed as the typical technocrat, an econometrician who believed in rapid gross domestic product (GDP) growth and centralization as an antidote to the social problems of Brazil. He was Economic Secretary to São Paulo State (1966) and Planning Minister under Artur da Costa e Silva, becoming 'economic tsar' under his successor, **Emílio Médici**. He curbed the labour unions, became popular among the propertied class as the author of the 'Economic Miracle' (1968–73), and was recalled to office (1979–85). He attempted to sustain GDP and export growth as antidotes to soaring international oil prices, interest rates and a deteriorating balance of payments.

Delfont (of Stepney), Bernard Delfont, Baron, *originally* Boris Vinogradsky 1909–
British theatre producer

Born in Tokmak, Russia, the brother of Lew Grade, he moved with his family to Great Britain in 1912. He entered theatrical management in 1941, and during the next 20 years acquired many theatrical properties, notably the London Hippodrome which he converted into the Talk of the Town restaurant in 1958. He acquired control of more than 30 companies, embracing theatre, film, television, music and property interests. He also presented the annual Royal Variety Performance (1958–78) and has presented a record number of West End shows. He was made a life peer in 1976.

Delgado, Humberto 1906–65
Portuguese general and politician

Born into a modest military family, he keenly supported the counter-revolution as a junior officer in the 1920s. At the age of 46, he became the youngest general in the Portuguese armed forces. However, António Salazar never entirely trusted Delgado, considering him too independent, and his suspicions were confirmed when Delgado, having experienced democracy abroad, especially in the USA (1953–57), rejected the Salazar regime and stood against the official presidential candidate in 1958. His charismatic appeal led to huge demonstrations of support in Lisbon and Oporto, but a heavily-rigged vote ensured his defeat. The humiliated Salazar soon got rid of direct presidential elections, restrictive as they had been. Delgado tried to stage three coup attempts in 1958, but failed on each occasion for lack of support. He left Portugal in 1959 and attempted unsuccessfully to win over the armed forces from abroad. He was murdered in Spain, near the Portuguese border, by the PIDE (Portuguese secret police) in mysterious circumstances.

d'Elhuyar y de Suvisa, Don Fausto See Elhuyar y de Suvisa, Don Fausto d'

Delilah
Biblical character

At the instigation of the Philistines she enticed Samson to reveal the secret of his great strength, which was his uncut hair, according to his Nazirite vow. She contrived to cut his hair to weaken him (Judges 16).

Delille, Jacques 1738–1813
French poet

He was born near Aigueperse, Auvergne, and his popular verse translation of Virgil's *Georgics* (1769) was praised by Voltaire. After holding a canonry at Moissac, he was presented by the Comte d'Artois with the abbacy of Saint-Séverin. The didactic poem, *Les Jardins* (1782, 'The Gardens'), was generally accepted as his masterpiece. The Revolution compelled Delille to leave France, and he travelled in Switzerland and Germany, then to London, where he translated *Paradise Lost*. After his return to France in 1802 he produced a translation of Virgil's *Aeneid* (1804), and volumes of verse in *L'Imagination* (1806), *Les Trois Règnes de la nature* (1809, 'The Three Reigns of Nature') and *La Conversation* (1812). During his life he was regarded by his countrymen as the greatest French poet of the day.
📖 E Guitton, *Jacques Delille, 1738–1813* (1974)

de Lisle, Claude Joseph Rouget See Rouget de Lisle, Claude Joseph

Delisle, Joseph Nicholas 1688–1768
French astronomer

Born in Paris and educated at the University of Paris, he first attracted notice by an interesting though erroneous theory that the Sun's corona is produced by diffraction of light around the Moon (1715). In 1717, a meeting with Peter I of Russia in Paris led to an invitation from the Empress Catherine (later Catherine II) to St Petersburg (1745), where he founded an observatory and a school of navigation and cartography. He returned to Paris in 1747 to become astronomer to the navy. His main interest was in problems associated with the Sun, in particular with the apparent movements of Mercury and Venus when in transit across its disc. He worked out (1743) an alternative method of observing transits of Venus to that first used by Edmond Halley for finding the distance to the Sun.

De L'Isle, William Philip Sidney, 1st Viscount 1909–91
English soldier, businessman and politician

Educated at Eton and Magdalene College, Cambridge, he served in France and Italy during World War II and was awarded the VC at Anzio. He was elected to parliament in 1944, but on the death of his father in 1945 he entered the House of Lords as the 6th Baron De L'Isle and Dudley. He became a privy councillor in 1951 and until 1955 was Secretary for Air in Churchill's first postwar ministry. He was created 1st Viscount De L'Isle in 1956, and was the last Governor-General of Australia (1961–65). In his capacity as a chartered accountant he held many business directorships, trusteeships and charitable appointments.

Delius, Frederick 1862–1934
British composer

Born in Bradford, Yorkshire, of German–Scandinavian descent, he went to Florida in the USA as an orange planter at the age of 20, but studied music in his spare time. He entered the Leipzig Conservatory (1886) where he became a friend of Edvard Grieg. After 1890 he lived mainly in France. A prolific composer, he wrote six operas, including *A Village Romeo and Juliet* (1901), and a variety of choral and orchestral works, such as *Appalachia* (1902) and *On Hearing the First Cuckoo in Spring* (1912). By 1924 he was paralysed and blind from a syphilitic infection, but with the English musician Eric Fenby (1906–97) as his amanuensis from 1928, he produced a group of works, including the complex *A Song of Summer* (1930), *Songs of Farewell* (1930) and *Idyll* (1930–32).

Dell, Ethel Mary 1881–1939
English novelist

She was born in Streatham, London, and as a writer of light romantic novels enjoyed a tremendous vogue in the years between the wars. Her books include her enormously successful first novel, *The Way of an Eagle* (1912), *The Lamp in the Desert* (1919), *The Black Knight* (1926) and *Sown Among Thorns* (1939).

dell'Abbate, Niccolò See Abbate, Niccolò dell'

Della Casa, Lisa 1919–
Swiss soprano

Born in Burgdorf, near Bern, she studied in Zurich, and first appeared at Solothurn-Biel in 1943, subsequently joining the company at the Stadttheater, Zurich. Her appearance at the Salzburg Festival of 1947 led to her engagement with the Vienna State Opera Company. A specialist in the operas of Richard Strauss, she shares with Lotte Lehmann the distinction of having sung all three soprano roles in *Der Rosenkavalier* ('The Knight of the Rose').

della Gherardesca, Count Ugolino See Ugolino della Gherardesca, Count

Della Robbia or Robia, Luca c.1400–1482
Italian sculptor

He worked in Florence, and between 1431 and 1440 executed, in a warm natural style, 10 panels of angels and dancing boys (the Cantoria) for the cathedral there. He also made (1448–67) a bronze door for the sacristy, with 10 panels of figures in relief. From 1457 to 1458, he sculpted the marble tomb of the Bishop of Fiesole. He is equally famous for his figures in terracotta, including medallions and reliefs, and he established a business producing glazed terracottas.

Deller, Alfred George 1912–79
English counter-tenor

Born in Margate, Kent, he joined his first church choir at the age of 11. In 1943, while a member of Canterbury Cathedral Choir, he was heard by **Michael Tippett** who was looking for a counter-tenor to sing music by **Henry Purcell**, and arranged his first London concert. In 1946 he made his radio debut in the inaugural broadcast of the BBC's Third Programme, and in 1947 began a full-time musical career. He made many recordings of early English songs, notably those of **John Dowland** and Purcell, and in 1950 formed the Deller Consort, a small group of musicians devoted to the authentic performance of early music. In 1963 he founded the Stour Music Festival, at which he performed and conducted. Many composers wrote for his voice, including **Benjamin Britten**, who created the part of Oberon in *Midsummer Night's Dream* for him. It was largely due to him that the counter-tenor voice regained its popularity in performance and teaching. ⊞ Michael and Mollie Hardwick, *Alfred Deller: A Singularity of Voice* (1968)

De l'Obel, Matthias See L'Obel, Matthias de

Deloney, Thomas c.1550–1600
English writer

Nothing is known of his birthplace or education, although his works suggest familiarity with Latin and French. A London silk-weaver, he wrote a number of ballads, but is best known for his stories in pamphlet form, such as *Jack of Newbury* (1597) *Thomas of Reading* (c.1599) and *Gentle Craft* (1597–c.1598) which, with their lively dialogue and characterization, are seen as a forerunner of the novel. ⊞ R Howarth, *Two Elizabethan Writers of Fiction: Thomas Nashe and Thomas Deloney* (1956)

De Long, George Washington 1844–81
US explorer

He was born in New York City, and in 1879 commanded the *Jeanette* in an attempt to reach the North Pole via the Bering Strait. Having abandoned his ship in the pack ice in 1881, he travelled 300 miles (483km) by sledge and boat to the Siberian coast, but only two of his crew reached safety.

Deloria, Ella 1889–1971
US linguist, ethnologist and novelist

Born in White Swan in the Standing Rock Sioux reservation in South Dakota, she grew up in a family where traditional Dakota (Sioux) culture merged with Episcopal Protestantism. A graduate of Columbia University, she worked for several years in collaboration with the anthropologist, **Franz Boas**, gathering material on the Dakota language and culture that she was passionate to preserve. Her publications include *Dakota Texts* (1932), a bilingual collection of traditional stories, *Dakota Grammar* (1941), *Speaking of Indians* (1944), a description of Dakota culture written for the popular market, and a novel, *Waterlily*, which was written in the 1940s but unpublished until 1988. She also compiled a Dakota–English dictionary and translated several oral narratives and autobiographies.

Delorme, Marion 1613–50
French courtesan

She was born in Paris, where her beauty and wit gathered a group of high-born lovers round her—among them the 1st Duke of **Buckingham** and Charles, Seigneur de Saint-Évremond. Even Cardinal **Richelieu** was not insensible to her charms, and caused her to be separated from the

Marquis de Cinq-Mars, whose mistress she was until he was executed in 1642. During the early days of the Fronde uprising (1648–53) her house was the rallying-point of its chiefs. Cardinal **Mazarin** was about to imprison her when she suddenly died in poverty, having been expelled from the Place Royale by the government.

Delorme, Philibert c.1510–1570
French architect

Born in Lyons he was royal architect to **Henri II**. He built the Tuileries for **Catherine de Médicis**, and the châteaux of Anet, Meudon, and others.

Delors, Jacques 1925–
French Socialist politician

Born in Paris, the son of a bank employee, he served as social affairs adviser to Prime Minister Jacques Chaban-Delmas (1969–72). He joined the Socialist Party in 1973 and represented it in the European parliament from 1979, chairing the economic and monetary commission. He served as Minister of Economy and Finance in the Mitterrand administration (1981–84), overseeing a programme of austerity (*rigueur*). After being passed over for the post of Prime Minister in 1984, he left to become President of the European Commission in 1985 and was elected to a second two-year term as President in 1988, a position he held until 1995, when **Jacques Chirac** took over. As Commission President, he oversaw significant budgetary reforms and the move towards the removal of all internal barriers in the EC in 1992, with increased powers residing in Brussels.

de los Angeles, Victoria, *originally* Victoria López Cima 1923–
Spanish soprano

Born in Barcelona, where she gave her first public concert (1944), she made her operatic debut at the Liceo theatre, Barcelona, in 1945. She then performed at the Paris Opera and La Scala, Milan (1949), Covent Garden, London (1950), the New York Metropolitan (1951) and subsequently at all the great houses and festivals throughout the world. She notably portrayed Carmen, Dido, **Puccini**'s heroines, **Mozart** roles, and Elisabeth in *Tannhäuser* (1961, Bayreuth), and was an exponent of Spanish songs. After retiring from the stage in 1969 she carried on giving recitals.

del Piombo, Sebastiano See Sebastiano del Piombo

Del Rio, Andrés Manuel 1764–1849
Spanish geologist and mineralogist

Born in Madrid, he was educated at the San Isidoro College and Alcala de Henares University, where he studied experimental physics. After graduating, he continued his work at the Real Academia de Minas de Almaden. He then spent four years in Paris and attended **Abraham Werner**'s lectures on mineralogy at Freiburg, where he became a friend of Baron **Alexander von Humboldt**. He also studied mining at Schemnitz, and at mines in Saxony and England before returning to Paris to study chemistry with **Antoine Lavoisier**. In 1794 he travelled to Mexico to take up a post as Professor of Mineralogy at the newly founded Colegio de Mineria. He discovered a new metallic element, panchromium, subsequently known as vanadium (1801). Del Rio worked on the origin of mineral veins, the paragenesis of sulphide minerals and the effects of trace elements. He was author of the first textbook of mineralogy published in the Americas, *Elementos de Orictognosia* (1795).

del Sarto, Andrea See Sarto, Andrea del

Delvaux, Paul 1897–1994
Belgian Surrealist painter

Born in Antheit, he has lived mainly in Brussels, where he exhibited mainly Neo-Impressionist and Expressionist pictures until 1935. He was influenced by **Giorgio de Chirico** and **René Magritte**, and produced a series of paintings depicting nude and semi-nude girls in dream-like settings (eg *The Call of the Night*).

Delvig, Anton Antonovich, Baron von
1798–1831
Russian poet
Born in Moscow, he studied with **Alexander Pushkin** at the Tsarskoe Selo school and became keeper of the public library at St Petersburg. From 1825 to 1831 he published the miscellany *Severnye tsvety* ('Flowers from the North'). ⊞ L Koehler, *Anton Antonovich Delvig: a Classicist in the time of Romanticism* (1970)

Demades c.380–319BC
Athenian politician
A bitter enemy to **Demosthenes**, he supported **Philip II** of Macedon, and after the Battle of Chaeronea (338BC) secured an honourable peace. He also secured lenient treatment for Athens after the revolt of 335. In 332, after **Antipater** had crushed a revolt against Macedonian rule in the Lainian War, Demades arranged the death of Demosthenes and his followers, but was himself executed by Cascander, the son of Antipater.

Demarco, Richard 1930–
Scottish artist, broadcaster and teacher
Born in Edinburgh, he studied there at the College of Art (1949–53). He has been a leading promoter of modern art in Scotland, including the work of such international figures as **Joseph Beuys**, as well as contemporary Scottish artists, especially at the Edinburgh Festival since 1967, and has presented annual programmes of theatre, music and dance. He was co-founder of the Traverse Theatre Club, director (1966–92) of the Richard Demarco Gallery, and since 1993 has been Professor of European Cultural Studies at Kingston University. His publications include *A Life in Pictures* (1994).

Demetrius See Dmitri

Demetrius Phalereus c.350–c.283BC
Greek orator and statesman
He was named after the Attic seaport of Phalerum, where he was born. Educated with **Menander** in the school of **Theophrastus**, he began a public career in c.325BC, and in 317 **Cassander** made him Governor of Athens, which he ruled for 10 years. Towards the end of that time he became dissipated, and when Demetrius Poliorcetes captured Athens in 307 he had to flee—first to Thebes and next to the court of **Ptolemy I, Soter** at Alexandria, where he was involved with the establishment of the great Alexandrian library. On Ptolemy's death in 283 he retreated to Busiris in Upper Egypt, where he died of a snake-bite.

de Mille, Agnes George 1905–93
US dancer, choreographer and writer
Born in New York City, she went to London, after graduating from the University of California, and danced with **Marie Rambert's** company in the original production of **Antony Tudor's** *Dark Elegies* (1937). *Three Virgins and a Devil* (1941) marked her breakthrough into choreography and she went on to choreograph for such hit musicals as *Oklahoma!* (1943), *Carousel* (1945), *Brigadoon* (1947), *Gentlemen Prefer Blondes* (1949) and *Paint Your Wagon* (1951). She was also known for her wit and eloquent public speaking, and her contribution to television and film. Her books include *Dance to the Piper* (1952), *The Book of Dance* (1963) and *American Dances* (1980). She was the niece of the film director **Cecil B De Mille**.

De Mille, Cecil B (lount) 1881–1959
US film producer and director

Born in Ashfield, Massachusetts, he acted on the stage and wrote unsuccessful plays before discovering Hollywood with **Samuel Goldwyn** (with whom he founded Paramount Films) as a suitable place for shooting the first US feature film, *The Squaw Man* (1914). With the **Gloria Swanson** comedy, *Male and Female* (1919), he became the most 'advanced' of US film directors. His box-office spectacles included *The Ten Commandments* (1923, re-made in cinemascope, 1956), *The Sign of the Cross* (1932), *The Plainsman* (1936), *Reap the Wild Wind* (1942) and *The Greatest Show on Earth* (1952, Academy Award). A notable exception to the usual formula of a high moral theme, enlivened by physical violence and sex, was the filmed Passion Play, *King of Kings* (1927). He also organized the first commercial passenger airline service in the USA in 1917. In 1938 he declined nomination to the US Senate.

Demirel, Suleyman 1924–
Turkish politician
Born in Islam Köy, he qualified as an engineer at Istanbul Technical University and worked on hydro-electric schemes in the USA and Turkey before making the transition from public service to politics. In 1964 he became president of the centrist Justice Party (JP), now subsumed in the True Path Party (TPP). He served three terms as Prime Minister from 1965, until a military coup in 1980 resulted in a three-year ban on political activity. He was placed in detention and banned from participating in politics for 10 years, but was released in 1983. However, Demirel was not prevented from forming the True Path Party, and when **Turgut Özal's** party lost in the 1991 elections, Demirel became Prime Minister (1991–93) then President (1993–).

De Mita, Luigi Ciriaco 1928–
Italian politician
Born in Fusco, Avellino province, he joined the Christian Democratic Party (DC) and in 1963 was elected to the Chamber of Deputies. He held a number of ministerial posts in the 1970s and in 1982 became party Secretary-General. In 1988, following a series of unsuccessful attempts by others to form a stable coalition, he became Prime Minister, but his government lasted only one year.

Democritus c.460–c.370BC
Greek philosopher
Born in Abdera, Thrace, he was one of the most prolific of ancient authors, publishing many works on ethics, physics, mathematics, cosmology and music, but only fragments of his writings (on ethics) survive. He is best known for his physical speculations, and in particular for the atom theory he developed from **Leucippus**, whereby the world consists of an infinite number of everlasting atoms whose different characteristics and random combinations account for the different properties and qualities of everything in the world. Supposedly known as 'the laughing philosopher' in the ancient world because of his wry amusement at human foibles, he was an important influence on **Epicurus** and **Lucretius**, and he was the subject of **Karl Marx's** PhD thesis, 'The Atomic Theories of Democritus and Epicurus'. ⊞ David J Furley, *The Greek Cosmologists* (1987)

de Moivre, Abraham See Moivre, Abraham de

De Morgan, Augustus 1806–71
English mathematician
Born in Madurai, Madras, India, he was educated at several English private schools, went to Trinity College, Cambridge, and in 1828 became first Professor of Mathematics in University College London. In 1831 he resigned this office, but resumed it from 1836 to 1866. He was one of the founders of the London Mathematical Society and its first president in 1865. He wrote a number

Demosthenes 384–322BC
Athenian orator and statesman who opposed the Macedonians

Demosthenes was born in Athens, the son of a wealthy sword manufacturer, who died when Demosthenes was seven. Most of his inheritance was lost by the neglect or fraud of his guardians, and although he later prosecuted them, the money had gone. This litigation led him to take up law as a profession. Up to the age of 30 he confined himself to speechwriting for others, and gained a reputation as a constitutional lawyer.

He did not embark on his political career until 351BC, around which time the Greek cities were under threat from **Philip II** of Macedon; Demosthenes from the outset advocated a policy of total resistance. Philip's attack on the northern state of Olynthus gave occasion to the *Olynthiacs* (349), which, with the orations against Philip called the *Philippics* (351, 334 and 341), are Demosthenes' greatest speeches. Athens made war with Philip on behalf of Olynthus, but failed to save the city and settled for peace. From 346 to 340 Demosthenes was engaged in forming an anti-Macedonian Party and in indicting **Aeschines**, his political opponent, for betraying Athens.

War broke out again in 340, and ended in the fatal Battle of Chaeronea (338), in which Athens and her allies were totally defeated. The Macedonian Party in Athens seized on a proposal to present Demosthenes with a gold crown as a means of publicly discrediting him. The trial was held in 330, when in the famous speech *On the Crown* Demosthenes gloriously vindicated himself against Aeschines. Meanwhile, in 336 **Alexander the Great** had succeeded his father Philip to the Macedonian throne. In 324 Harpalus, Alexander's treasurer, absconded to Athens with an enormous sum of money. It was placed in the state treasury under the care of Demosthenes and others, and when Alexander demanded it, half was missing. Demosthenes was accused and condemned, but escaped from prison into exile.

In 323 Alexander died, and Demosthenes was recalled to head a fruitless attempt to throw off the Macedonian yoke. The Battle of Crannon ended the revolt; sentenced to death, Demosthenes fled to the island of Calauria, where he took poison.

📖 James J Murphy (ed), *Demosthenes' On the Crown: A Critical Case Study of a Masterpiece of Ancient Oratory* (1967); Werner Jaeger, *Demosthenes: The Origin and Growth of His Policy* (1938).

> 'There is one safeguard, which is an advantage and security for all, but especially to democracies against despots. What is it? Distrust.' From *Philippics II*, section 24.

---

of mathematical text books, but his most important work was in symbolic logic. He also had a deep knowledge of the history of mathematics and contributed 850 articles to the *Penny Cyclopaedia*. His son William Frend De Morgan (1839–1917) and daughter-in-law Evelyn (née Pickering, 1855–1919) were a Pre-Raphaelite ceramic artist and painter respectively.

Demosthenes d.413BC
Athenian soldier

During the Peloponnesian War (431–404BC) he captured Anacterium (425) and helped assist **Cleon** to reduce Sphacteria, but failed to conquer Boeotia in 424. In 413, having been sent to Sicily to the relief of **Nicias**, he was captured by the Syracusans during a brave rearguard action and was put to death.

Demosthenes See panel above

Dempsey, (William Harrison) Jack, *nicknamed* the Manassa Mauler 1895–1983
US boxer

Born in Manassa, Colorado, he worked in copper mines before taking to the ring as 'Kid Blackie' in 1914. In 1919 he defeated Jess Willard to win the world heavyweight title, which he lost to Gene Tunney in 1926. In a controversial re-match the following year, he knocked down Tunney but was himself too dazed to retire promptly to his corner, and so delayed the count; Tunney struggled to his feet during the 'long count' and went on to win the fight on points. Dempsey retired from the ring, but briefly made a comeback in the early 1930s, and became a successful restaurateur on Broadway in New York.

Demuth, Charles 1883–1935
US painter and book illustrator

Born in Lancaster, Pennsylvania, from 1912 to 1914 he was in Paris where he met **Gertrude Stein** and saw the work of the early Cubists, whose ideas he took back to the USA. From 1919 he was a major exponent of 'Precisionism', with its hard outlines and semi-abstract treatment of industrial or urban scenery, as seen in *My Egypt* (1927), a view of grain elevators. He was a significant influence on the poet **William Carlos Williams**.

Dench, Dame Judi (th Olivia) 1934–
English actress

She was born in York and studied at the Central School of Speech and Drama, London. She made her stage debut as Ophelia in *Hamlet* (1957) in Liverpool with the Old Vic Company, with whom she remained from 1957 to 1961. Her numerous stage appearances include *Macbeth* (1963), *Cabaret* (1968), *The Good Companions* (1974), *Mother Courage* (1984), *Antony and Cleopatra* (1987), *The Plough and the Stars* (1991), and **Peter Shaffer**'s *The Gift of the Gorgon* (1993). She is one of Great Britain's most distinguished classical actresses, and her distinctive voice and versatility have brought warmth and emotional veracity to a kaleidoscope of characters from the sensual to the homely. Her television credits include many individual plays and the popular sit-com *A Fine Romance* (1981–84) in which she co-starred with Michael Williams (1935–), her husband since 1971. She made her film debut in *The Third Secret* (1964) but has only recently become a regular film performer, with incisive character parts in *A Room With a View* (1985), *A Handful of Dust* (1987) and *Henry V* (1989). In 1995 she played 'M' in the James Bond film, *Goldeneye*. She was created DBE in 1988 and made her directorial debut in the same year with a production of *Much Ado About Nothing* for **Kenneth Branagh**'s Renaissance Theatre Company. She also directed *Look Back In Anger* for them (1989). In 1991, in Regent's Park, London, she directed *The Boys From Syracuse*, a **Rodgers** and **Hammerstein** musical based on *The Comedy of Errors*.

Denck, Hans c.1495–c.1527
German Anabaptist theologian

Born in Habach, Bavaria, he became Rector of the Sebaldusschule, Nuremberg, in 1523. From 1524 he preached a doctrine resembling Evangelical Quakerism in various parts of Germany, and in 1525 was expelled from the school, when he became a leader of the Anabaptists in Augsburg. He wrote a commentary on the book of Micah (1531,) and other learned works.

Deneuve, Catherine, *originally* Catherine Dorléac 1943–
French actress

Born in Paris, into a theatrical family, she made her film debut in *Les Collégiennes* (1956) and was occasionally cast as the sister of her real-life sister, actress Françoise Dorléac (1941–67). Her own career took off with the unexpected popularity of the musical *Les Parapluies de Cherbourg* (1964, *The Umbrellas of Cherbourg*). Her remoteness and image of exterior calm concealing passion or intrigue were seen to great effect as a psychopath in *Repulsion* (1965) and a bourgeois housewife turned prostitute in *Belle de Jour* (1967, 'Lady of the Day'). Her other successes include *Tristana* (1970), *La Sauvage* (1975, *The Savage*) and *Le Dernier métro* (1980, 'The Last Metro'). She has also made selective appearances in English language productions like *April Fools* (1969) and *Hustle* (1975). She received a Best Actress Academy Award nomination for *Indochine* (1992). Recent films include *Ma Saison Preferée* (1993) and *Les Voleurs* (1996). Married to the photographer **David Bailey** (1965–70), she has a child by director Roger Vadim (1928–), born in 1963, and a daughter by actor **Marcello Mastroianni** called Chiara (1972–) who is also an actress.

Deng Xiaoping (Teng Hsiao-p'ing), *originally* Deng Xixian 1904–97
Chinese Communist politician

Born in Sichuan (Szechwan) Province into a middle-class landlord family, he joined the Chinese Communist Party (CCP) in 1925 as a student in Paris, where he met a fellow-student, **Zhou Enlai**, and adopted the name Xiaoping, ('Little Peace'). He later studied in Moscow (1926) where he became associated with **Mao Zedong**. He took part in the Long March (1934–36) and served as a political commissar to the People's Liberation Army (PLA) during the civil war (1937–49). In 1954 he became Secretary-General of the CCP, but reacted strongly to the excesses of the Great Leap Forward (1958–59). During Mao's 1966–69 Cultural Revolution he was criticized and purged, along with **Liu Shaoqi**, and sent for 're-education' in a tractor factory in Nanchang, but was rehabilitated by Zhou Enlai in 1974, becoming vice-premier. When Zhou died in 1976 he was again forced into hiding, but following popular protests he was reinstated in 1977 and by 1978 had become the dominant figure in Chinese politics. Working with his protégés **Hu Yaobang** and **Zhao Ziyang** he proceeded to introduce a pragmatic new economic modernization programme. Despite retiring from the politburo in 1987, he remained influential. He attempted to create a 'socialism with Chinese characteristics', but his reputation was tarnished by his sanctioning of the army's massacre of around 3,000 unarmed pro-democracy demonstrators in Tiananmen Square, Beijing (Peking), in June 1989. ⌷U Franz, *Deng Xiaoping* (1988)

Denham, Dixon 1786–1828
English army officer and explorer

Born in London, he was educated at Merchant Taylor's School, then served with distinction in the Napoleonic Wars. He was sent as expedition leader to join **Hugh Clapperton** and Walter Oudney on their expedition to discover the source of the Niger (1821–25). In 1827 he was appointed Governor of Sierra Leone, where he died of fever. The bird Denham's Bustard was named in his honour.

Denham, Sir John 1615–69
Irish poet

Born in Dublin, the only son of an Irish judge of English birth, he was educated in London and at Trinity College, Oxford. He studied law at Lincoln's Inn, and was called to the Bar in 1639. At the outbreak of the Civil War he immediately joined the king, and on the capture of Farnham Castle, Sir **William Waller** sent him as a prisoner to London, but he was soon freed and went to Oxford. In 1641 he produced *The Sophy*, a historical tragedy of the Turkish court which was performed at Blackfriars, and in 1642 he published a long poem, *Cooper's Hill*, a description of the scenery around Egham, which **Pope** imitated in his *Windsor Forest*. Being discovered in secret services for **Charles I** in 1648, he fled to Holland and France. In 1650 he collected money for the young King **Charles II** from the Scots resident in Poland, and several times visited England on secret service. At the Restoration he was appointed Surveyor-General of works, with **Christopher Wren** as his deputy, and in 1661 he was created a Knight of the Bath. He was buried in Poet's Corner in Westminster Abbey, London. ⌷B O'Hehir, *Harmony from discords: a life of Sir John Denham* (1968)

Denikin, Anton Ivanovich 1872–1947
Russian soldier

He joined the army at the age of 15, and rose to lieutenant-general during World War I. After the Revolution of 1917 he led the White Army in the south against the Bolsheviks (1918–20). He won the Ukraine, but was defeated by the Red Army at Oryel (1919), and in 1920 resigned his command and escaped to Constantinople (Istanbul). Thereafter he lived in exile in France (1926–45) and the USA (1945–47), and wrote books on his military experiences.

De Niro, Robert 1943–
US film actor

Born in New York City, he studied acting with **Stella Adler** and **Lee Strasberg**, and worked off-Broadway before making his film debut as an extra in *Trois Chambres à Manhattan* (1965, 'Three Rooms in Manhattan'). He attracted critical attention as the baseball player in *Bang the Drum Slowly* (1973) and won an Academy Award for Best Supporting Actor for *The Godfather, Part II* (1974). He has become noted for his versatility and an obsessive quest for authenticity in his characterizations. His films made with **Martin Scorsese** include *Taxi Driver* (1976) and *Raging Bull* (1980), for which he won a Best Actor Academy Award. Others include *The Deer Hunter* (1978), *Awakenings* (1990), *Cape Fear* (1991), *Casino* (1995), *Heat* (1995) and *Sleepers* (1996). He made his directorial debut with *The Bronx Tale* (1994).

Denis or Denys, St, *properly* Dionysius
3rd century AD
Italian cleric and patron saint of France

Born probably in Rome, he was sent from Rome about 250 AD to preach the Gospel to the Gauls, and became the first Bishop of Paris. Under the persecutions of the Emperor **Valerian** (reigned 253–60) he was beheaded on Montmartre ('Martyrs' Hill'). Later his legend was confused with that of **Dionysius the Areopagite**, and he was supposed to have carried his own head to his burial place, the site of the abbey church of Saint-Denys. His feast day is 9 October. ⌷Ingeborg Bahr, *Saint Denis und seine Vita im Spiegel der Bilduberlieferung der französischen Kunst des Mittelalters* (1984)

Denis, Maurice 1870–1943
French artist and art theorist

Born in Grandville, he was one of the original group of Symbolist painters, and then of the Nabis ('prophets'), influenced by **Gauguin**. His comments on the aesthetics of the modern movement have obtained a wide currency. He wrote *Théories* (1913), *Nouvelles théories* (1921, 'New Theories'), *Histoire de l'art religieux* (1939, 'History of Religious Art') and a study of *Sérusier* (1942). He executed some large murals for the Théâtre des Champs Élysées and the Petit Palace. In 1919 he helped to found, with George-Olivier Desvallières (1861–1950), the Studios of Sacred Art, devoted to the revival of religious painting. His most famous picture is perhaps the *Hommage à Cézanne* (1900) in the Musée d'Art Moderne, Paris.

Denison, Edmund Beckett See Grimthorpe, 1st Baron

Denktaş, Rauf R 1924–
Cypriot politician

Born in Ktima, Paphos, and educated at the English School, Nicosia, he studied law in Lincoln's Inn, London, was called to the Bar, and after working in a Nicosia law practice (1947–49), became a Crown prosecutor, then acting Solicitor-General (1956–58). He was elected president of the Communal Chamber in 1960 and won re-election in 1970, and from 1975 served an eight-year term as President of the Turkish Federated State of Cyprus. In 1983 he was elected President and Prime Minister of the Turkish Republic of Northern Cyprus (recognized only by Turkey), and in 1991 called on UN Secretary-General Javier Pérez de Cuéllar to devise a solution to the island's split as Perez de Cuellar's last challenge before his retirement at the end of 1991.

Denman, Lady Gertrude Mary, née Pearson
1884–1954
English founder of the National Federation of Women's Institutes

Born in London and educated privately, she married Thomas, 3rd Baron Denman (1874–1954) in 1903, and accompanied him when he was appointed Governor-General of Australia in 1911. Following their return to Great Britain, she chaired a sub-committee of the Agricultural Organization Society (1915) which that year had founded the Women's Institutes. When the institutes were transferred to the Board of Agriculture in 1917, she insisted they should be self-governing, and the National Federation of Women's Institutes was formed, with herself as chairman until 1946. The institutes' aim was to improve the standard of women's lives through increased knowledge and training in 'citizenship'. She was also involved in the foundation of the National Birth Control (later Family Planning) Association, the Cowdray Club for Nurses and Professional Women, and the Women's Land Army, of which she was appointed director in 1939; she resigned in 1945 on the government's refusal to give the Land Army the grants being received by women in the civil defence and armed services. The Women's Institute residential college in Berkshire was named Denman College in her honour in 1948.

Dennery, Adolphe Philippe 1811–99
French playwright

Born in Paris, he was clerk to a notary, but from 1831 produced 133 dramas, vaudevilles and plays, the most successful being *Marie Jeanne* (1845). He also wrote the libretti for Charles Gounod's *Le Tribut de Zamora* (1881) and Jules Massenet's *Le Cid* (1885). He was the creator of the Norman watering-place, Cabourg.

Denning (of Whitchurch), Alfred Thompson Denning, Baron 1899–
English judge

He was educated at Andover Grammar School and Magdalen College, Oxford. Called to the Bar in 1923, he became a King's Counsel (1938), a judge of the High Court of Justice (1944), a Lord Justice of Appeal (1948), Lord-of-Appeal-in-Ordinary (1957) and Master of the Rolls (1962–82). In 1963 he held the inquiry into the circumstances of John Profumo's resignation as Secretary of State for War. As Master of the Rolls he showed a profound regard for justice but was responsible for many controversial decisions. Among his many legal publications are *The Road to Justice* (1955), *The Discipline of Law* (1979), *What Next in the Law* (1982), and several autobiographical books. 📖 Edmund Heward, *Lord Denning: A Biography* (1990)

Dennis, C(larence Michael) J(ames)
1876–1938
Australian poet and journalist

Born in Auburn, South Australia, he worked as a journalist in Adelaide then moved to Melbourne and contributed light verse to many periodicals, including the Sydney *Bulletin*. His poems were collected as *Backblock Ballads and Other Verses* (1915). Some of these poems, featuring the larrikin Bill, were republished as *The Songs of a Sentimental Bloke* (1915) and became immediately popular. Dennis's success was repeated in *The Moods of Ginger Mick* (1916), and the 'Trench' pocket editions of these books were popular among Australian troops during World War I. He published five more books in the next five years, all of which captured the vernacular working-class speech of the cities. However, the fashion passed, and in 1922 Dennis returned to journalism, contributing a daily column to the Melbourne *Age* for the next 16 years.

Dennis, John 1657–1734
English critic and playwright

He was born in London, and educated at Caius College, Cambridge. After a tour through France and Italy, he took his place among the wits and men of fashion, and produced biting criticism to support the Whigs. He wrote nine plays, including a satire, *A Plot and No Plot* (1697), and *Rinaldo and Armida* (1699), but had little success with them. Pope's *Essay on Criticism* (1711) contained a contemptuous allusion to another play, *Appius and Virginia* (1709), answered by Dennis a month later in *Reflections Critical and Satirical*, which triggered a long feud. Among his critical works are *The Grounds of Criticism in Poetry* (1704) and *An Essay on the Genius and Writings of Shakespeare* (1712). 📖 H G Paul, *John Dennis, his life and criticism* (1911)

Denny, Robyn 1930–
English painter

Born in Abinger, Surrey, he studied in Paris and in London at St Martin's School of Art and the Royal College of Art. In 1959 he helped to organize the exhibition *Place* in London's Institute of Contemporary Arts, at which canvases formed corridors—space seemingly generated by colour. The following year he was responsible for two more 'situation' exhibitions, aimed at bypassing dealers and promoting abstract art. Inspired by US abstract artists, his paintings are symmetrical and subtle in colour; they include *Baby is Three* (1960), *First Light* (1965–66) and *Garden* (1966–67), all in the Tate Gallery, London.

Denny-Brown, Derek Ernest 1901–81
US neurologist

Born in Christchurch, New Zealand, he received his early medical training at the University of New Zealand and then went on a Beit Fellowship to Oxford, where he worked with Charles Sherrington. After clinical work in London, and a brief spell as consultant neurologist at St Bartholomew's Hospital, he went to Harvard in 1941. He was equally at home in the laboratory or at the bedside, and was particularly interested in the diseases of the basal ganglia and of the muscles.

Dent, Joseph Malaby 1849–1926
English publisher

He worked as a bookbinder in London before opening his own bookbinding business in 1892. In 1888 he founded the publishing house of J M Dent & Sons, which brought out the pocket-sized *Temple Classics* from 1893, and also *Everyman's Library* from 1904.

Denton, Sir Eric James 1923–
English marine biologist

Born in Bridport, Dorset, he was educated at the universities of Cambridge and Aberdeen. He worked at the Biophysics Research Unit at University College London, before lecturing in physiology at Aberdeen University (1948–56). From 1955 he worked at the Plymouth Laboratory of the Marine Biological Association. He was also secretary of the Marine Biological Association of the United Kingdom, and director of the Plymouth Laboratory (1975–87). Elected a Fellow of the Royal Society (1964), he served as a member of the council (1984–85), receiving the society's Royal Medal in 1987. His notable research has focused on the physiology of marine animals, including the visual and acoustic physiology of fish, and luminescence and camouflage of oceanic species. In the 1950s and 1960s he undertook pioneering studies of buoyancy regulation amongst squids and other molluscs, finding this buoyancy to be attributable to the reduction of heavy substances through the replacement of heavy ions by lighter ions, increasing light substances (such as fats/oils), and the use of gas floats. His work on sound has concerned the schooling behaviour of clupeoid fish. He was knighted in 1987 and awarded the International Biology prize in 1989.

Denys, St See Denis, St

Depardieu, Gérard 1948–
French film actor

Born in Châteauroux, he was an unruly child, and was encouraged to act as therapy. He made his film debut in *Le Beatnik et le minet* (1965, 'The Beatnik and the Pussy Cat'), and continued in occasional film roles whilst appearing on stage and television, including the series *L'Inconnu* (1974, 'The Unknown'). In the cinema his imposing physique and peasant's looks were seen in an increasing variety of roles as he gained a reputation as one of the most versatile and skilled actors of his generation. Able to combine strength and gentleness, he has appeared in many films, including *Le Dernier métro* (1980, 'The Last Metro'), *Danton* (1982), *Le Retour de Martin Guerre* (1982, *The Return of Martin Guerre*), *Jean De Florette* (1986), *Sous le soleil de Satan* (1987, 'Under Satan's Sun'), *Cyrano de Bergerac* (1990) and *Germinal* (1993). His first English-speaking role was in *Green Card* (1990). He also directed *le Tartuffe* (1984). Recent films include *Les Anges Gardiens* (1995), *Unhook The Stars* (1996) and *Hamlet* (1996).

De Paul, St Vincent See Vincent de Paul, St

Depretis, Agostino 1813–87
Italian politician

A friend of both Garibaldi and Giuseppe Mazzini, he broke with the latter after the abortive Milanese insurrection of 1853. He played a key part in the Expedition of the Thousand to Sicily in 1860, serving for a while as the island's 'prodictator'. Although he began his parliamentary career on the political left, he abandoned his earlier radicalism and achieved ministerial office in 1862 and 1866. He was to be Prime Minister for all but two years from 1876 to 1887 and became the arch-exponent of 'trasformismo' (the practice of forming alliances in parliament, almost regardless of political ideology, in order to guarantee a government majority). He played a key part in steering Italy towards the Triple Alliance with Germany and Austria–Hungary (1882).

De Priest, Oscar Stanton 1871–1951
US politician

Born in Alabama, he ran away from home to Chicago where he was the first black to be elected to the city council (as a Republican in 1915). He became an alderman in 1927, and the first black congressman from the North in 1928. Holding office until 1934, when he was defeated by a black Democrat, he secured passage for a bill to reduce discrimination in the Civilian Conservation Corps.

De Quincey, Thomas 1785–1859
English critic and essayist

Born in Manchester, the son of a merchant, he was educated at Manchester Grammar School, but in 1802 ran away and wandered in Wales, and then to London, where he lived with a young prostitute called Ann. He later described this experience in his *Confessions of an English Opium-eater* (1822). He then spent a short time at Worcester College, Oxford, and it was here that he became addicted to opium. A visit to his mother in Bath brought him into contact with Coleridge, and through him with Robert Southey and Wordsworth. When these poets settled in the Lake District, De Quincey visited them there and, after a brief sojourn in London (where he met Charles Lamb, William Hazlitt and others of the 'Cockney' school), he went to stay in Grasmere in 1809. Except for *The Logic of Political Economy* (1841) and an unsuccessful novel, his whole literary output, including the *Confessions*, consisted of magazine articles. The *Confessions* appeared in 1821 as a serial in *The London Magazine*, and at once made him famous. In 1828 the lure of the Edinburgh literary scene drew him to the northern capital, where he lived and worked until his death. For 20 years he lent distinction to *Blackwood's Magazine*, *Tait's Magazine* and, occasionally, *The Quarterly*, with articles like *Murder Considered as One of the Fine Arts* (1827), *Lake Reminiscences* (1834–40), the fantasy *Levana and Our Ladies of Sorrows* (1845), and *Vision of Sudden Death* (1849). ◫ J S Lyon, *Thomas De Quincey* (1969); H S David, *Thomas De Quincey* (1964)

Derain, André 1880–1954
French artist

Born in Chatou, he is most famous for his Fauve pictures, executed from 1904 to 1908, when he was associated with Maurice de Vlaminck and Henri Matisse. Later landscape pictures show a romantic realism influenced by Cézanne. He also designed for the theatre (notably the Diaghilev ballet) and illustrated several books.

Derby, Earl of
English title

It was conferred in 1485 by Henry VII of England on Thomas, second Lord Stanley, two months after the Battle of Bosworth, where he had contributed to the victory of Richmond (later Henry VII) by withdrawing his promised support for Richard III. The Stanleys were descended from Adam de Aldithley, who came with William the Conqueror to England in 1066. His grandson married the heiress of Thomas Stanley, of Stafford, and exchanged the manor of Thalk, Staffordshire, his wife's marriage portion, for Stoneley, Derbyshire, and assumed the surname of Stanley. A descendant, Sir John Stanley, who had married the heiress of Lathom, got a grant of the Isle of Man (1405), which he and his descendants ruled until 1736.

Derby, Edward Geoffrey Smith Stanley, 14th Earl of 1799–1869
English statesman

Born at Knowsley Hall, Lancashire, he was educated at Eton and Christ Church, Oxford, and entered parliament for Stockbridge in 1820. In 1830 he became Chief Secretary for Ireland and in 1833 Colonial Secretary. In this capacity he carried the emancipation of West Indian slaves. In 1831 he seceded from the Whigs and, declining to join the administration under Sir Robert Peel, he and his supporters maintained an independent position. In 1844 he resigned his Commons seat and went to the Lords as Baron Stanley of Bickerstaffe. When Peel attempted to repeal the Corn Laws, Stanley headed the Protectionists in the Upper House, and was seen as Conservative leader. In 1851 he succeeded his father as Earl Derby and briefly became Prime Minister. He returned as premier in 1858, but resigned the following year on a vote of confidence. Returning to power in 1866, he passed the Reform Act of 1867 in conjunction with

Disraeli, to whom he passed the premiership in 1868. He was an accomplished scholar and an excellent parliamentary speaker. ⌑ Wilbur D Jones, *Lord Derby and Victorian Conservatism* (1956)

Derby, Edward Henry Smith Stanley, 15th Earl of 1826–93
English politician
He was born at Knowsley Hall, Lancashire, the eldest son of the 14th Earl of Derby. In 1848 he became MP for Lynn, and in 1852 was appointed Foreign Under-Secretary in his father's first ministry. After declining to join Henry, 3rd Viscount Palmerston's ministry in 1855, he became Secretary for India in his father's second administration (1858–59), and carried the measure transferring the government of India to the Crown. He was Foreign Secretary in the third Derby and first Disraeli ministries (1866–68). In 1874 he again became Foreign Secretary under Disraeli, but resigned in 1878 when the majority of the Cabinet determined to support Turkey by occupying Cyprus. In 1880 he joined the Liberal Party, and was Colonial Secretary (1882–85) prior to Home Rule.

Derby, James Stanley, 7th Earl of, *known as* the Great Earl of Derby 1606–51
English soldier
He fought on the Royalist side throughout the Civil War. After the Battle of Worcester in 1651, he helped Charles II to escape but was captured by the Parliamentary forces and beheaded at Bolton. His wife, Countess Charlotte de la Trémouille (d.1663), is famous for her heroic defence of Lathom House (1644) and of the Isle of Man (1651).

Derème, Tristan, *pseudonym of* Phillippe Huc 1889–1941
French poet of the Fantaisiste school
His works include *La Verdure dorée* (1922, incorporating eight previous collections of poems, 'The Gilded Foliage'), and *L'Enlèvement sans clair de lune* (1924, 'Kidnapping without Moonlight'). ⌑ H Martineau, *Tristan Derème* (1927)

Deren, Maya, *originally* Eleanora Derenkowsky 1917–61
US filmmaker
She was born in Kiev, but fled with her parents to New York, USA, in 1922. Educated at Syracuse University there, she was a left-wing activist in the 1930s and regional organizer of the Syracuse Young People's Socialist League. She was employed by choreographer Katherine Dunham (1941) and became fascinated with dance and movement. Her interest in the cinema was stimulated by Czech filmmaker Alexander Hammid (1907–), whom she married in 1942. They collaborated on *Meshes of the Afternoon* (1943) and *At the Land* (1944), both poetic, trance-like films that used devices such as slow motion to dispense with the conventional narrative requirements of time and space. Dance films like *A Study in Choreography for Camera* (1945), *Ritual in Transfigured Time* (1946), *Meditation on Violence* (1948) and *The Very Eye of Night* (1958) followed. A tireless worker in the 1940s on behalf of independent, experimental cinema, she wrote the pamphlet *An Anagram of Ideas on Art, Form and Film* (1946), and established the Creative Film Foundation (1954).

de Ribera, Jusepe See Ribera, Jusepe de

Deringer, Henry 1786–1868
US manufacturer of small arms
Born in Easton, Philadelphia, he supplied rifles to the US army, and in 1852 invented the pocket pistol known as a 'der(r)inger'.

Dernesch, Helga 1939–
Austrian soprano

Born in Vienna, where she studied at the Conservatory, she made her debut in Bern in 1961 and at Covent Garden, London, in 1970. She has sung throughout Europe and the USA, and is specially noted for her portrayals of Wagner, Strauss and the modern German repertory. Since 1979 she has sung mezzo-soprano roles.

DeRoburt, Hammer 1923–92
Nauruan statesman
Educated at Nauru Secondary School and Geelong Technical College in Victoria, Australia, he worked as a teacher in Nauru from 1940 but was deported to Japan in 1942 after the country's occupation. After his release (1946), he worked as an education liaison officer and teacher. He became head chief of Nauru in 1956 when his country achieved a measure of self-government, and, on full independence, was elected its first President (1968). Apart from brief breaks (1976–78, 1986), he remained President until August 1989, when he was ousted on a no-confidence motion and replaced by Kenas Aroi who is, allegedly, his 'unacknowledged natural son'.

Deroin, Jeanne-Françoise 1805–94
French journalist, teacher, feminist and socialist
Born in Paris and largely self-educated, she became a teacher and journalist. She was involved in the Saint-Simonian movement of the 1830s, editing the newspaper *La femme libre*. During the 1840s she was jailed for political activities. She was much involved with the revolutionary societies of 1848. Campaigning for women's emancipation, she wrote for the newspaper *La Voix des femmes* and founded the journal *L'Opinion des femmes* (1849). She insisted that the complementarity of the sexes necessitated women's participation in political affairs; a participation rejected by the National Assembly (1848). Her radical beliefs led to imprisonment, and eventually to exile in London, where she continued to publish such works as *Almanac des femmes* (1854). Her refusal to adopt her husband's surname (Desroches) after her marriage in 1832 was a source of continuing comment.

de Rossi, Giovanni Battista See Rossi, Giovanni Battista de

Derozio, Henry Louis Vivian 1809–31
Eurasian poet and patriot
He was born in Calcutta, and at the age of 19 he had published two books of poems and was lecturing on English history and literature at the city's Hindu College. In the next four years he translated Pierre de Maupertuis, lectured on philosophy, wrote a critique on Kant and edited four journals. He became involved in local politics, and instigated so much free thinking and social rebelliousness that he was dismissed from the college a few months before he died. Much of his verse is imitatively ornamental, but some of his sonnets put him among the lesser Romantics. ⌑ E W Madge, *Henry Derozio, the Eurasian poet and reformer* (1965)

D'Errico, Ezio 1892–1973
Italian writer, painter and dramatist
He was born in Agrigento, and his work now tends to be neglected. His avant-garde play *La foresta* (1959, 'The Forest') is a novel of terror, in which a technological nightmare is created by people who try to compensate for their lack of wisdom by creating over-sophisticated pseudo-scientific schemes.

Derrida, Jacques 1930–
French philosopher
Born in El Biar, Algeria, he studied in Paris, and taught at the Sorbonne (1960–64) and at the École Normale Supérieure (1965–84). His work is highly original, and has attracted great interest in the English-speaking world, spanning literary criticism, psychoanalysis and

linguistics as well as philosophy. He stresses the primacy of the written over the spoken text ('there is nothing outside the text') and his critique of the referentiality of language and the objectivity of structures founded the school of criticism known as 'deconstruction'. Among his works are the influential *La Voix et le phénomène* (1967, Eng trans *Speech and Phenomena*, 1967), *De la Grammatologie* (1967, 'Of Grammatology') and *L'Écriture et la différence* (1967, 'Writing and Difference'). His later publications include *Marges de la philosophie* (1972, Eng trans *Margins of Philosophy*), *La Dissémination* (1972, 'Dissemination'), *La Vérité en peinture* (1978, 'Truth in Painting'), *La Carte postale* (1980, 'The Postcard') and *Aporias* (1994). 📖 Christopher Norris, *Derrida* (1987)

de Ruyter, Michiel Adriaanszoon See **Ruyter, Michiel Adriaanszoon de**

Derwentwater, James Radcliffe or Radclyffe, 3rd Earl of 1689–1716
English Jacobite
Born in London and brought up in St Germain, France, he was a companion of Prince James Francis Edward Stuart, the 'Old Pretender'. His father had married Lady Mary Tudor, Charles II's natural daughter, and in 1715, at the time of the Jacobite Rising, a warrant was issued against him as a Catholic. He fled from Northumberland with a few retainers, and fought in the disastrous encounter at Preston. Derwentwater, with most of the rebel leaders, was taken prisoner, and conveyed to the Tower of London. At his trial for high treason at Westminster Hall he pleaded guilty, and threw himself on the king's mercy. Every effort for a pardon failed, and he was beheaded on Tower Hill.

der Weyden, Rogier van See **Weyden, Rogier van der**

Derzhavin, Gavril Romanovich 1743–1816
Russian poet
Born in Kazan, he joined the army as a private in 1762, but rose to officer rank, was transferred to the Civil Service, and later to governorships. In 1791 he became Secretary of State, in 1800 Imperial Treasurer, and in 1802 Minister of Justice. He published a variety of original and imaginative lyric poetry on many subjects, both personal and public, and is considered one of Russia's greatest poets. 📖 A V Zapadov, *Gavril Romanovich Derzhavin* (1958)

Desaguliers, John Theophilus 1683–1744
British scientist and inventor
Born in La Rochelle, France, his parents settled in England after 1685. He graduated from Oxford in 1709 and was appointed lecturer in experimental philosophy at Hart Hall. In 1713 he moved to London, where he assumed the duties of curator and demonstrator of experiments at the Royal Society. His experimental lectures popularizing the work of Isaac Newton earned him the Royal Society's prestigious Copley medal three times. A prolific author and translator, he brought out *A Course of Experimental Philosophy* in 1734, defining and illustrating the practical applications of the subject. He invented scientific instruments (eg a planetarium) and made improvements to machines, including Thomas Savery's steam engine and an air-pump used as a ventilator at the House of Commons.

Desai, Anita, *née* Mazumdar 1937–
Indian novelist
Born in Mussoorie, Uttar Pradesh, the daughter of a Bengali father and a German mother, she was educated at Delhi University. Her works include novels for adults and children, and short stories. *Clear Light of Day* (1980) and *In Custody* (1984) were both shortlisted for the Booker Prize and *The Village by the Sea* won the Guardian award for

children's fiction in 1982. In 1988 she published *Baumgartner's Bombay*, the grim story of a German expatriate adrift in India. More recently she published *Journey to Ithaca* (1995).

Desai, Morarji Ranchhodji 1896–1995
Indian politician
Born in Gujarat and educated at Bombay University, he was a civil servant for 12 years before embarking on a long and varied political career. He joined Congress in 1930, but was twice imprisoned as a supporter of Mahatma Gandhi's Civil Disobedience Campaign before becoming Revenue Minister in the Bombay government (1937–39). He was again imprisoned (1941–45) for his part in the 'Quit India' movement, before again serving as Bombay's Revenue Minister (1946) and later, Home Minister and Chief Minister (1952). Four years later, he entered central government, first as Minister for Commerce and Industry (1956–58) then as Finance Minister, resigning in 1963 to devote himself to party work. He was a candidate for the premiership in 1964 and again in 1966, when he was defeated by Indira Gandhi. Deputy premier and Minister of Finance in her administration, Desai resigned in 1968 over differences with the premier. In 1974 he supported political agitation in Gujarat, and the following year began a fast in support of elections in the state, being detained when a state of emergency was proclaimed. After his release in 1977 he was appointed leader of the Janata Party, a coalition opposed to Mrs Gandhi's rule, and he finally became Prime Minister after the elections that same year. The Janata government was, however, characterized by much internal strife, and Desai was forced to resign in 1979. 📖 *The Story of My Life* (1979)

de Saint-Pierre, Jacques Henri Bernardin See **Saint Pierre, Jacques Henri Bernardin de**

Desaix de Veygoux, Louis Charles Antoine 1768–1800
French soldier
Born in St Hilaire-d'Ayat, Auvergne, he won fame in 1796 in Jean Victor Moreau's famous retreat through the Black Forest. Behind the ruined fortress of Kehl he resisted the Austrians for two months. His greatest achievement was the conquest of Upper Egypt after an eight-month campaign (1799). He was killed in action in the Battle of Marengo.

Desalvo, Albert, *also known as* the Boston Strangler 1931–73
US sex offender
Born in Chelsea, Massachusetts, he was arrested in late 1964 for sex attacks on women in their homes. He then confessed to a psychiatrist that he was the Boston Strangler, who had murdered and sexually assaulted 13 women between 1962 and 1964 in Boston. He was never tried for the murders, because under Massachusetts law a doctor who receives information from a suspect cannot use it as evidence. His defence lawyer, Francis Lee Bailey, claimed that he made another confession in 1965 after an agreement that conversations with him would not be used in court. He was sentenced to life imprisonment for his other crimes. In 1973 he was found stabbed to death in his cell in Walpole Prison, Massachusetts.

Desani, Govindas Vishnoodas 1909–
US novelist
Born in Nairobi, Kenya, he went to Great Britain in 1926 and from 1928 was a correspondent for the *Times of India*, Reuters, and Associated Press. He was a broadcaster during World War II. From 1952 to 1966 he visited Buddhist and Hindu monasteries, studying yoga and meditation. Throughout the 1960s he filed a provocative column with the *Illustrated Weekly for India*. He has been a US citizen since 1979. His prose-poem *Hali* (1950) and some uncollected

Descartes, René 1596–1650
French philosopher and mathematician, usually regarded as the father of modern philosophy

Descartes was born near Tours in a small town now called La-Haye-Descartes, and was educated from 1604 to 1614 at the Jesuit College at La Flèche. He remained a Catholic all his life, and he was careful to modify or even suppress some of his later scientific views, for example his sympathy with **Nicolaus Copernicus**, no doubt aware of **Galilei's** condemnation by the Inquisition in 1634. He studied law at Poitiers, graduating in 1616; then from 1618 he enlisted at his own expense for private military service, mainly in order to travel and to have the leisure to think. He was in Germany with the army of the Duke of Bavaria one winter's day in 1619 when he had his famous intellectual vision in the 'stove-heated room': he conceived a reconstruction of the whole of philosophy, and indeed of knowledge, into a unified system of certain truth modelled on mathematics and supported by a rigorous rationalism.

From 1618 to 1628 he travelled widely in Holland, Germany, France and Italy; then in 1628 returned to Holland where he remained, living quietly and writing until 1649. Few details are known of his personal life, but he did have an illegitimate daughter called Francine, whose death in 1640 at the age of five was apparently a terrible blow for him.

In 1649 he left Holland for Stockholm on the invitation of Queen **Kristina** who wanted him to give her tuition in philosophy. These lessons took place three times a week at 5am and were especially taxing for Descartes whose habit of a lifetime was to stay in bed meditating and reading until about 11am. He contracted pneumonia and died. His last words were supposedly *a mon âme, il faut partir* ('So my soul a time for parting'). He was buried in Stockholm but his body was later removed to Paris and eventually transferred to Saint-Germain-des-Prés.

Descartes' more popular works were published in French, the more scholarly ones first in Latin. The *Discours de la méthode* (1637, 'Discourse on Method'), the *Meditationes de prima Philosophia* (1641, 'Mediations on First Philosophy') and the *Principia Philosophiae* (1644,

'Principles of Philosophy') set out the fundamental Cartesian doctrines: the method of systematic doubt; the first indubitably true proposition, *je pense, donc je suis* or *cogito ergo sum* ('I think, therefore I am'); the idea of God as the absolutely perfect Being; and the dualism of mind and matter.

Other philosophical works include *Regulae ad directionem ingenii* ('Rules for the Direction of the Mind', composed in the later 1620s, but unfinished and published posthumously in 1701) and *Les Passions de l'âme* (1649, 'Passions of the Soul'). He also made important contributions in astronomy, for example with his theory of vortices, and more especially in mathematics, where he reformed algebraic notation and helped to found co-ordinate geometry.

L J Beck, *The Method of Descartes* (1987); Leon Pearl, *Descartes* (1977); Elizabeth S Haldane, *Descartes: His Life and Times* (1905).

La lecture de tous les bons livres est comme une conversation avec les plus honnêtes gens des siècles passés, qui en ont été les auteurs, et même une conversation étudiée en laquelle ils ne nous découvrent que les meilleures de leurs pensées.
'The reading of good books is like a conversation with the best men of past centuries—in fact like a prepared conversation, in which they reveal their best thoughts.'
From *Discours de la méthode*, 1st discourse (trans by G E M Anscombe and Peter Geach).

Agnoscam fieri non posse ut existam talis naturae qualis sum, nempe ideam Dei in me habens, nisi revera Deus etiam existeret, Deus, inquam, ille idem cujus idea in me est.
'I could not possibly exist with the nature I actually have, that is, one endowed with the idea of God, unless there really is a God; the very God, I mean, of whom I have an idea.'
From *Meditationes*, 3rd meditation (trans by G E M Anscombe and Peter Geach).

stories notwithstanding, his claim to posterity is dependent on *All About H Hatterr* (1948). It reprinted the week after publication, then was neglected for several decades before being resurrected as a modern classic comparable to the work of **James Joyce** and **Flann O'Brien**.

Desargues, Gérard 1591–1661
French mathematician

Born in Lyons, he was in Paris by 1626, and he took part as an engineer in the Siege of La Rochelle in 1628. He founded the use of projective methods in geometry, inspired by the theory of perspective in art, and introduced the idea that parallel lines 'meet at a point at infinity'. His style of writing and a reluctance to publicize his ideas greatly hindered their reception and mostly they were independently rediscovered by others. From 1645 he began a new career as an architect in Paris and Lyons.

Desbarres, Joseph Frederick Wallet 1722–1824
English military engineer

Born of Huguenot parentage, he was aide-de-camp to **James Wolfe** at the siege of Quebec (1759). He surveyed the coast of Nova Scotia from 1763 to 1773. He was Lieutenant-Governor of Cape Breton (1784–1805) and Prince Edward Island (1805–13), and died at Halifax, Nova Scotia, at the age of 102.

Descartes, René See panel above

Deschamps, Eustache, *known as* Morel
c.1345–c.1406
French poet

Born in Vertus, Champagne, he was brought up by **Guillaume de Machaut**, who may have been his uncle and probably taught him to write. A soldier, a magistrate, a court favourite, and a traveller in Italy and Hungary, he held important posts in Champagne, but after his patron, **Charles V**, died, his possessions were ravaged by the English. He composed 1,175 lyrics, besides *Le Miroir de mariage* ('The Mirror of Marriage', a long poem satirizing women), two dramatic works, and several poems deploring the miseries of the Hundred Years War. He is known to have influenced **Chaucer**. A Sarradin, *Eustache Deschamps. Sa vie et ses œuvres* (1879)

De Sica, Vittorio 1902–74
Italian actor and film director

Born in Sera, he graduated from Rome University, and began in the film industry as an actor, making his debut in *Il Processo Clémenceau* (1918, *The Clemenceau Affair*). He established himself as a romantic star of stage and screen in the 1930s before turning to direction (1940). In the immediate postwar years he was at the forefront of the Neorealist movement, depicting the social problems of battle-ravaged Italy with compassion and sensitivity in films like *Sciuscia* (1946, *Shoeshine*), *Ladri di Biciclette* (1948, *Bicycle Thieves*) and *Umberto D* (1952). Later films tended to be more lighthearted although with *La Ciociara* (1960,

Two Women) and *Il Giardino dei Finzi Contini* (1970, *The Garden of the Finzi Continis*) he returned to the subject of earlier triumphs. An avuncular character actor, he also played minor roles in scores of international productions.

Desiderio da Settignano 1428–64
Italian sculptor
Born in Settignano, near Florence, he worked in the early Renaissance style, and was influenced by **Donatello** and **Luca della Robbia**. He is best known for his busts of women and children, for example *Virgin with Laughing Child* (Victoria and Albert Museum, London), the tomb of Gregorio Marsuppini in Santa Croce (after 1453), and the *Tabernacle of the Sacrament* in San Lorenzo, Florence (1461).

De Sitter, Willem See Sitter, Willem de

Deslandres, Henri Alexandre 1853–1948
French spectroscopist and astronomer
Born in Paris, he was educated there at the École Polytechnique, where he worked in laboratory spectroscopy with Marie-Alfred Cornu (1841–1902). He studied the band spectra of diatomic molecules, and found a formula for their frequencies, known as Deslandres' law (1885). In 1889 he took up astronomical spectroscopy on joining the Paris Observatory, but his greatest successes were in the field of solar spectroscopy, inventing the velocity spectrograph (1891), an instrument which allowed photographs of successive strips of the Sun to be taken in the light of a particular spectrum line. In 1897 Deslandres moved to the astrophysical observatory at Meudon, of which he became director in 1908. He was elected to the French Academy of Sciences in 1901 and was awarded the gold medal of the Royal Astronomical Society in 1913.

Desmares, Marie See Champeslé, la

Desmarets, Jean, Sieur de Saint-Sorlen
1596–1676
French writer
Born in Paris, he was a protégé of Cardinal **Richelieu**, and wrote many volumes of poetry and critical works, notably *Comparaison de la langue et la poésie française avec la grecque et la latine* (1670, 'Comparison of French Language and Poetry with Greek and Latin'). His play *Les Visionnaires* (1637, 'The Visionaries') was a great success, and he also wrote two verse epics and a novel on biblical and classical themes. He was the first chancellor and a co-founder of the Académie Française, and was a protagonist in the 'ancients' versus 'moderns' controversy.

Desmond, Earl of
Irish title
It was conferred (1329) on Maurice Fitzgerald along with County Kerry, and last borne by Gerald Fitzgerald, 15th Earl, who rebelled (1579–80) against Queen **Elizabeth I**, sacked Youghal by night and was proclaimed a traitor. He escaped the fate of the garrison at Smerwick, but was driven at last from his strongholds, wandered about for over two years, and was killed (1583) in a cabin in the Kerry Mountains.

Desmoulins, Camille 1760–94
French revolutionary and journalist
Born in Guise, he studied law as a fellow-student of **Robespierre** at the Collège Louis le Grand in Paris. He wrote on classical republicanism in his pamphlets, *La Philosophie du peuple français* (1788) and *La France libre* (1789), and took part in the destruction of the Bastille. His *Discours de la Lanterne aux Parisiens* (1789, 'The Streetlamp's Address to the Parisians') earned him the sinister title of 'Procureur-général de la Lanterne'. In November 1789 he began the witty, sarcastic *Révolutions de France et de Brabant* which appeared weekly until July 1792. Desmoulins had been a member of the Cordeliers' Club from its foundation, and was close to **Danton**. Elected by Paris to the National Convention, he voted for the death of the king. In the struggle between the Girondins and Danton he took an active part, but in late 1793 he brought out the *Vieux cordelier*, an eloquent expression of his and Danton's longing for clemency. Robespierre took fright at its reception, and soon became actively hostile. On 30 March 1794, Desmoulins was arrested with Danton; on 5 April he was guillotined. A fortnight later his wife, Lucile Duplessis (1771–1794), was also executed.

Desnos, Robert 1900–45
French poet, novelist and cinema critic
He was born in Paris. The author of profoundly ironic Surrealist poetry, much of which has a deceptively playful surface, he is particularly famous for his poems for children, and for his writings on the cinema, which were collected in *Cinéma* (1966). Deported by the Nazis to concentration camps for the part he had played in the Resistance, he died, weakened by starvation, of typhus at the notorious Terezin camp in Czechoslovakia. 📖 M A Caws, *The Poetry of Dada and Surrealism* (1970)

de Soto, Hernando See Soto, Hernando, de

Despard, Charlotte, *née* French 1844–1939
English social reformer
A sister of **John French** (1st Earl of Ypres), she was an advocate of women's rights, and Irish self-determination. Her politics seriously embarrassed her brother during his viceroyalty of Ireland.

Despard, Edward Marcus 1751–1803
Irish conspirator
Born in Queen's County, Ireland, he obtained an ensigncy at the age of 15, and from 1772 to 1790 served in the West Indies, but was then recalled on frivolous charges. His demands for compensation brought him two years' imprisonment (1798–1800). On his release he became involved in a conspiracy to assassinate the king, and to seize the Tower of London and Bank of England. For this, with six associates, he was drawn on a hurdle, hanged and beheaded.

Despenser, Hugh, Earl of Winchester
1262–1326
English baron
He became Chief Adviser to **Edward II** after the death of Piers de Gaveston (c.1284–1312), but was banished with his son, Hugh (1321). Recalled the next year by Edward II he was created Earl of Winchester. After Queen **Isabella** of France's landing in England (1326) he was captured by the queen's party and hanged at Bristol; his son was hanged at Hereford.

Despériers or Des Périers, Bonaventure
c.1500–1544
French writer
He was born in Autun, and became a member of the court of men of letters assembled by **Margaret of Angoulême**. In a dialogue, *Cymbalum mundi* (1537), under the pretence of attacking the superstitions of the ancients, he satirized the religious beliefs of his own day. The book raised a storm of indignation, against which Margaret was powerless to shield him, and rather than fall into the hands of his persecutors he is said to have killed himself. His *Nouvelles récréations et joyeux devis* (1558, 'Novel Recreations and Delightful Talks') consists of 129 short stories, both comic and romantic. Despériers has often been attributed with the chief authorship of Margaret's *Heptameron*. 📖 J Nodier, *Bonaventures Des Périers* (1867)

Despiau, Charles 1874–1946
French sculptor

He was born in Mont-de-Marsan, and discovered by **Auguste Rodin**, who took him as a pupil. He is noted for his sensitively Neoclassical portrait busts, such as *Head of Madame Derain* (1922, Washington DC). He exhibited at the Venice Biennale in 1930 and 1936.

Despréaux, Boileau See **Boileau, Nicolas**

Des Prez or Desprez, Josquin See **Josquin des Prez**

Dessalines, Jean Jacques c.1758–1806
Emperor of Haiti

Born in Guinea, he was imported into the French West Indian colony of Saint-Domingue (Haiti) as a slave and was bought by a French planter, whose name he assumed. In the slave revolt of 1791 he was second only to **Toussaint Louverture**. After the first compromise he became Governor of the southern part of the island, but after the arrest of Toussaint (1802) he renewed the war, and after infamous cruelties compelled the French to evacuate Saint-Domingue (1803). He was created governor in 1804, and in October of that year was crowned emperor of an independent Haiti as Jean Jacques I. However his cruelty, especially against whites and mulattos, and his debauchery soon alienated even his firmest adherents, and while trying to repress a revolt, led by the mulatto leader, Pétion, he was cut down by **Henri Christophe**, who succeeded him. ⌨ Dubroca, *La Vie de J J Dessalines, chef des noirs revoltes* (1804)

Dessau, Paul 1894–1979
German composer and conductor

Born in Hamburg, he studied in Berlin, after which he became an opera coach. He conducted opera at Cologne from 1919, Mainz from 1923 and the Berlin State Opera from 1925. During the Nazi era he moved to Paris (1933) and the USA (1939). From 1942 he collaborated with **Bertolt Brecht**, writing incidental music for *Mutter Courage* (1946, 'Mother Courage') and other plays. Like Brecht, he settled in 1948 in East Berlin, where he produced the operas *Die Verurteilung des Lukullus* (1949, 'The Trial of Lucullus', text by Brecht), *Puntila* (1957–59, text after Brecht), *Lanzelot* (1969) and *Einstein* (1971–73). Dramatic inventiveness and socialist commitment are also evident in his orchestral, choral and chamber works, and in his many songs.

Destivelle, Catherine 1960–
French rock-climber

Born in Oran, Algeria, she moved to France with her parents in her early teens, and before her seventeenth birthday had made significant climbs at Verdon, Freyr and in the Dolomites. She lost interest in rock-climbing after her early success until a television contract renewed her enthusiasm and she became a professional full-time climber in 1986. Since then, she has participated in competitions, advertising and filmmaking, and has popularized the sport while acquiring superstar status at home and abroad.

Destouches, Philippe, *originally* Philippe Néricault 1680–1754
French playwright

He was born in Tours, and wrote 17 comedies, initially in the manner, but without the talent, of Molière. They include *Le Philosophe marié* (1727, 'The Married Philosopher') and *Le Glorieux* (1732, 'The Boaster'), his masterpiece. He spent six years in England as a diplomat from 1717 to 1723, and adapted **Jospeh Addison**'s play *The Drummer* as *Le Tambour nocturne* (1733). ⌨ J Hankiss, *Destouches, l'homme et l'œuvre* (1918)

Detaille, (Jean Baptiste) Édouard 1848–1912
French battle painter

Born in Paris, he belonged to the school of **Ernest Meissonier** and painted battle scenes while serving in the Franco–Prussian War. He also painted portraits, including *Edward VII and the Duke of Connaught*, in the Royal Collection.

de Thierry, Baron Charles Philip Hippolytus 1793–1864
English settler in New Zealand

The English-born son of a French émigré, he claimed French or English nationality according to his needs. Through a friend he purchased 40,000 acres in the Hokianga area of New Zealand, styled himself the 'Sovereign Chief of New Zealand' and tried without success to obtain the backing of the French and English governments. Promising to establish a kingdom with no taxes, free trade and free medicine, de Thierry arrived in New Zealand in 1837 with a large family, big ideas and no money. Within a short time the colony was starving and being supported by the local Maoris. The historian Sir Keith Sinclair describes de Thierry's efforts to establish a feudal kingdom as 'the first and most exotic of a long line of utopias to be built in New Zealand's cloud-land'.

de Torres, Luis Vaez See **Torres, Luis Vaez de**

Deutsch See **Manuel, Nikolaus**

Deutsch, Babette 1895–1982
US poet, novelist and critic

Born in New York City, she published *Banners*, her first collection of poems, in 1919, the title piece celebrating the initial achievements of the Russian Revolution. Russia became a special interest for her. She translated **Alexander Blok**'s *The Twelve* with a Russian scholar she later married, and continued to translate from both Russian and German. Her *Epistle to Prometheus* (1931) is an ambitious, book-length poetic interpretation of human history. Her collected poems appeared in 1969. Her work is noted for its perceptive preoccupation with love, war and desolation, and the historical place and fate of women. Her novels include *A Brittle Heaven* (1926), while her criticism includes the highly regarded *Poetry in Our Time* (1952). ⌨ J Gould, *American Women Poets* (1980)

Deutscher, Isaac 1907–67
British Marxist historian of Russia

Born in Kraków, Poland, he became a journalist, joined the Communist Party in 1926, and edited Communist periodicals until his expulsion in 1932 for leading an anti-Stalinist opposition. He went to London in 1939, and worked on the editorial staff of *The Economist* (1942–49) and the *Observer* (1942–47), reporting extensively from Europe (1946–47). His *Stalin, a Political Biography* (1949) was a landmark in emancipating Marxists from Stalinophilia. His biography of **Trotsky** appeared in three volumes: *The Prophet Armed* (1954), *The Prophet Unarmed* (1959) and *The Prophet Outcast* (1963). He also wrote *Heretics and Renegades* (1955), *The Great Contest* (1960) and *The Unfinished Revolution: Russia 1917–1967* (1967). He was a visiting professor at many US universities in the 1960s, and was prominent in the 'Teach-In' movement against the USA's undeclared war in Vietnam.

de Valera, Éamon See panel p525

De Vere, Aubrey Thomas 1814–1902
Irish poet

Born in Curragh Chase, County Limerick, and educated at Trinity College, Dublin, he became a friend of **John Henry Newman**, Wordsworth and Tennyson. In addition to many volumes of poems he published poetical dramas on **Alexander the Great** (1874) and **Thomas à Becket** (1876), *Essays on Poetry* (2 vols, 1887), and works on Irish ecclesiastical politics and literary criticism.

de Valera, Éamon 1882–1975
Irish statesman

Éamon de Valera was born in Brooklyn, New York City, of Spanish-Irish parentage. He was brought up in Bruree, County Limerick, by a labourer uncle, and became a mathematics teacher. Taking up Irish, he joined the Gaelic League and married his teacher Sinéad Ni Flannagáin (who subsequently became the author of delicate and enjoyable Gaelic fairy stories). Under the influence of **Thomas MacDonagh** he rose in the Irish Volunteers, leading his men into action in the Easter Rising of 1916. The sentence of execution imposed on him after court-martial was commuted through the intervention by the US consul.

After his release from jail (1917), he was elected MP for East Clare, and became the focus of nationalist opposition to conscription (1918). He was again arrested, an act which helped his Sinn Féin Party to massive electoral victory (1918). After a sensational escape he toured the USA as President of the Irish Republic (actually of Dáil Éireann, the secret assembly of Irish MPs refusing participation at Westminster), 1919–20. He drew in massive funds and moral support.

Guerrilla warfare had exploded in Ireland without him and on his return he was believed a more moderate influence than **Michael Collins**, but ultimately Collins signed the Anglo-Irish Treaty of 1921 and incurred de Valera's anger. Narrow victory for the Treaty in the Dáil led de Valera to resign as President. He played only a symbolic part in the anti-Treaty forces during the civil war (1922–23), but was ultimately imprisoned (1923–24) and in 1926 formed a Republican Opposition party which entered the Irish Free State Dáil (1927), and which brought him to power there in 1932. He severed most of the remaining constitutional links with Great Britain, and introduced a new constitution (1937) under which his prime ministerial title was altered to *taoiseach* (to which he was re-elected until 1948, and then once more in 1951 and 1957). In international affairs he pursued neutrality, all the more because of anti-democratic threats from Right and Left. In 1959 he resigned his position as taoiseach and was elected as President, being re-elected in 1966 and remaining as head of state until he retired in 1973.

📖 O D Edwards, *Éamon de Valera* (1988); John Bowman, *De Valera and the Ulster Question, 1917–1973* (1982); T P Longford and Thomas P O'Neill, *Éamon de Valera* (1970).

> On being told that **David Lloyd George** had said talking to him was like trying to pick up mercury with a fork, de Valera replied, 'Why doesn't he use a spoon?' (1921).

---

de Victoria, Tomás Luis See Victoria, Tomás Luis de

Deville, Henri Étienne Sainte-Claire See Sainte-Claire Deville, Henri

Devine, George Alexander Cassidy 1910–65
English stage director, administrator, teacher and actor

Born in Hendon, Greater London, he began his career as an actor at Oxford during the 1930s, and taught at the London Theatre Studio (1936–39). After World War II he was director of the Old Vic School. He founded the English Stage Company (1956), which took up residence at the Royal Court Theatre, London. With plays such as John Osborne's *Look Back in Anger* (1956) and John Arden's *Serjeant Musgrave's Dance* (1959), he not only restored prestige to English theatre but set drama on a new course by encouraging the work of new writers. He made a return to acting in the year of his death, in Osborne's *A Patriot for Me* (1965). The George Devine award, inaugurated in 1966, gives encouragement to young theatre practitioners.

Devis, Arthur 1711–87
English painter

Born in Preston, Lancashire, he had settled in London by the 1740s and was painting small portraits and conversation pieces depicting, in fine detail, solidly middle-class patrons set within their own interiors or gardens. His brother Anthony (1729–1816) was a landscape painter, and his son, Arthur William (1762–1822), joined the East India Company and depicted the arts and industry of Bengal.

DeVito, Danny 1944–
US actor

Born in Asbury Park, New Jersey, he worked as a hairdresser in his sister's beauty parlour before enrolling at the American Academy of Dramatic Arts in New York City. Off-Broadway appearances preceded his film debut in *Lady Liberty* (1971). He played small roles in films like *One Flew Over the Cuckoo's Nest* (1975) before starring as a petty tyrant in the television show *Taxi* (1978–83). He made a return to film as a character actor in *Terms of Endearment* (1983) and *Romancing the Stone* (1984), and became a popular comic star in films like *Ruthless People* (1986),

Twins (1988) and *Batman Returns* (1992), in which he played the Penguin. He has also directed such films as *The War of the Roses* (1989) and *Hoffa* (1992). His company, Jersey Films, has been behind such films as *Pulp Fiction* (1994), *Get Shorty* (1995) and *Matilda* (1996), which he also directed, also co-starring with his wife, actress Rhea Perlman (1949–).

---

de Vlamingh, Willem Hesselsz See Vlamingh, Willem Hesselsz de

Devlin, Joseph 1872–1934
Irish nationalist

Born in Belfast, the son of poor Catholic parents, he was educated by the Christian Brothers. He built up Belfast Catholic nationalism on ghetto lines of mutual favour-sharing with close clerical links, learning from the prevailing Protestant use of Masonic-style organizations so that his command over the local section of the international Ancient Order of Hibernians functioned on joint use of rewards and comrades. The disarray of Irish nationalist politics caused by the **Parnell** divorce split meant that Belfast, up until then an area where Home Rule politics were directed from Dublin as far as parliamentary hopes were concerned, was now made very much self-dependent. He established good relations with the re-united Irish Party under **John Redmond** and **John Dillon** to the extent of being made Nationalist MP for Kilkenny North (1902–06), but then captured and retained West Belfast. In the general election of 1918 Irish repudiation of his party was not shared by Ulster Catholics who by a majority rejected Sinn Féin candidates. Devlin himself defeated **Éamon de Valera**. The Northern Ireland Settlement of 1920, confirmed in 1922 and 1925, abandoned the Ulster Catholics to Protestant Unionist overlordship. Devlin as leader oscillated between ostracism of the new sub-state and ineffectual opposition tactics, but he consolidated his own politico-economic machine over Catholics, as was shown by his representation in the Stormont parliament at various times of Armagh, Tyrone, Fermanagh and Catholic Belfast.

Devlin, Patrick Arthur Devlin, Baron 1905–92
English lawyer and judge

The son of an Ulster-born father and Scottish mother, he spent his early years in Aberdeen. He was educated at Stoneyhurst College, Lancashire, and Christ's College, Cambridge, and was called to the Bar in 1929, then appointed to the High Court in 1948. He presided over many famous trials, including that of **John Bodkin Adams**. In 1960 he became a Lord Justice of Appeal, and was raised to the peerage the following year. He resigned from the House of Lords in 1964. During the 1980s, he joined with Lord **Scarman** in the campaign for the review of the Guildford Four conviction.

Devonshire, 4th Duke of See **Cavendish, William**

Devoy, John 1842–1928
US journalist and nationalist

Born in Kill, County Kildare, Ireland, he became an agent for the Fenian secret society, oath-bound to seek an Irish Republic. He helped rescue the Fenian chief **James Stephens** from prison in 1865, and was sentenced (1866) to imprisonment for organizing cells, but amnestied on condition of exile from the UK. He settled in the USA as a journalist on the New York *Herald* and helped organize Clan-na-Gael, which offered terms of alliance ('the New Departure') in 1878 to **Charles Parnell**. The Parnell split drove Devoy from constitutionalism and his paper the *Gaelic American* returned to Anglophobian organization. Through **Thomas James Clarke** he helped tie the Easter Rising of 1916 to alliance with Germany in World War I, rousing US support for the victims of its repression. His hatred of **Woodrow Wilson** may have weakened the Irish cause. In any event, **Éamon de Valera**, President of Dáil Éireann, broke with Devoy and kept the Irish cause free from identification with any one US political faction, as Devoy now wished. He wrote *Recollections of an Irish Rebel* (1928).

Devoy, Susan 1964–
New Zealand squash player

Born in Rotorua, she went to England in 1982 and settled in Marlow, Buckinghamshire, but didn't cause a stir until she won the British championship in 1984. Improving steadily throughout her career, she won the world championship in 1985 and went on to take the world title another four times. She won the British Open another seven times, becoming the fourth-top winner of the title of all time, male or female, before she took a complete rest to start a family. A classically beautiful squash player, who was also noted for her dark good looks, she was the first New Zealand woman to win the world championships.

de Vries, Hugo Marie See **Vries, Hugo Marie de**

De Vries, Peter 1910–93
US novelist

Born in Chicago, of Dutch immigrant parents, he was the editor of a community newspaper in Chicago before working as a vending-machine operator, toffee-apple salesman, radio actor, furniture mover, lecturer to women's clubs, and associate editor of *Poetry*. In 1943 he lured **James Thurber** to Chicago to give a benefit lecture for *Poetry* and Thurber subsequently encouraged him to write for the *New Yorker*. This he did, later joining the editorial staff, and latterly restricting his contribution to captions for cartoons. A satirist in his mentor's mould, he favoured word play in the manner of **S J Perelman** and was an inveterate (and inventive) punster and epigrammatist. He wrote more than 20 novels such as *Reuben, Reuben* (1964), *The Glory of the Humming-bird* (1974) and *Parkham's Marbles* (1986), but none eclipsed the reception of his first, *The Tunnel of Love* (1954). 📖 Roderick Jellema, *Peter De Vries* (1966)

Dewar, Donald Campbell 1937–
Scottish Labour politician

Born in Glasgow, and educated at Glasgow University, he qualified as a solicitor. He won Aberdeen South for the Labour Party in 1966, but lost his seat in 1970, and spent eight years out of parliament before returning in the Glasgow Garscadden by-election of 1978. He retained the seat with ease in the general elections of 1979, 1983, 1987, 1992 and 1997. Chief Opposition Spokesman on Scottish Affairs from 1983, he moved to Social Security (1992–95) and was Opposition Chief Whip (1995–97). Following Labour's landslide win in 1997, he entered **Tony Blair's** Cabinet as Secretary of State for Scotland (1997–).

Dewar, Sir James 1842–1923
Scottish chemist and physicist

Born in Kincardine-on-Forth, Fife, and educated at Edinburgh University, he became a lecturer in chemistry at the Royal (Dick) Veterinary College in Edinburgh in 1869, and then Jacksonian Professor of Natural Philosophy at Cambridge (1875–1923). From 1877 onwards, however, he lived at the Royal Institution, London, where he was Fullerian Professor of Chemistry and the first director of the new Davy–Faraday Laboratory (from 1896). The rift with Cambridge was probably caused by his dissatisfaction with the research facilities. He devised the structure known as the 'Dewar formula', and, with Sir **Frederick Abel**, discovered cordite (1889). He also accomplished the liquefaction of hydrogen (1898) and invented the vacuum flask. He was elected FRS in 1877, and knighted in 1904. 📖 William Meiklejohn, *Tulliallan: Four Lads o' Pairts: Sir James Wylie, Sir James Dewar, Robert Maule, J P, Sir Robert Maule* (1990)

Dewar, Michael James Steuart 1918–
British chemist

Born in Ahmednagar, India, of Scottish parents, he specialized in chemistry at Oxford (1936–40), worked on explosives as part of the war effort, and during a fellowship with Sir **Robert Robinson** studied the chemistry of penicillin. After World War II he worked at Oxford on tropolone synthesis and benzidine rearrangement, and started on his celebrated book, *The Electronic Theory of Organic Chemistry* (1949). From 1945 to 1951 he worked in industry as a physical chemist, becoming increasingly interested in the application of molecular orbital theory to organic chemistry. In 1951 he became Professor of Chemistry at Queen Mary College, London, and began using these calculations to explain a number of phenomena in organic chemistry. In 1959 he moved to the University of Chicago, where he developed programmes for semi-empirical molecular orbital calculations which have provided powerful insights into mechanistic organic chemistry. This work was continued at the University of Texas at Austin (1963–90) and latterly at the University of Florida. Elected FRS in 1960, Dewar joined the US National Academy of Sciences in 1983.

de Wet, Christiaan Rudolf See **Wet, Christiaan Rudolf de**

De Wette, Wilhelm Martin Leberecht 1780–1849
German biblical critic

Born in Ulla, near Weimar, he studied from 1799 at Jena, and became a professor at Heidelberg in 1809, and in 1810 at Berlin. A letter sent in 1819 to his friend, the mother of Karl Ludwig Sand (the assassin of the playwright **August von Kotzebue**), cost him his chair. In 1822 he became Professor of Theology at Basle. He wrote introductions to the Old and New Testaments, and a manual of Hebrew archaeology.

Dewey, George 1837–1917
US admiral

Born in Montpelier, Vermont, he graduated from the US Naval Academy, Annapolis, and during the Civil War (1861–65) served with Admiral David Farragut. As Commodore in the Spanish–American War (1898) he defeated the Spanish fleet at Manila Bay without losing a man.

Dewey, John 1859–1952
US philosopher and educationist
Born in Burlington, Vermont, he was educated at the university there. He began his professional career as a high-school teacher, but went on to a series of university positions at Johns Hopkins, Michigan (1884), Chicago (1894) and Columbia, where he was Professor of Philosophy from 1904 until retirement in 1930. He was a leading exponent of pragmatism, in succession to Charles Peirce and William James, and his philosophy of education, which stressed development of the person, understanding of the environment, and learning through experience, was influential. He published widely on psychology and education as well as philosophy, and his many works include *The School and Society* (1899), *The Child and the Curriculum* (1902), *Reconstruction in Philosophy* (1920), *Experience and Nature* (1925), *The Quest for Certainty* (1929), and *Experience and Education* (1938). 🕮 George Dykhuizen, *The Life and Mind of John Dewey* (1973)

Dewey, Melvil 1851–1931
US librarian
Born in Adams Centre, New York, he was the founder of the 'Dewey System' of book classification by decimals. He designed the system for the Amherst College Library in 1876. He became chief librarian and Professor of Library Economy at Columbia (1883–88), and director of the New York State Library (1889–1906).

Dewey, Thomas Edmund 1902–71
US politician
He was born in Owosso, Michigan. After studying law at the universities of Michigan and Columbia, he became district attorney for New York County (1937) and Governor of New York State (elected 1942, 1946, 1950). He was Republican nominee for President in 1944 and 1948, when by virtue of the 'Dewey machine', his campaign organization, he appeared to be a much stronger candidate than President Harry S Truman.

Dewi, St See David, St

de Witt, Jan See Witt, Jan de

Dexter, Caroline, *née* Harper 1819–84
Australian writer and feminist
Born in Nottingham, England, she was educated there and in Paris, and having married the artist William Dexter in 1843, she emigrated to Sydney, Australia, in 1855. After their art school failed, the Dexters moved to Gippsland, Victoria, but the marriage ended and she moved to Melbourne. There, in 1861, she and Harriet Clisby (1830–1931) founded *The Interpreter*, the first Australian journal produced by women. She became a patron of many aspiring artists and writers, and is known to have been a friend of George Sand.

Dexter, John 1925–90
English stage director
He began as an actor in repertory and television before becoming a director in 1957. During the next 20 years, he directed 15 plays for the Royal Court Theatre, London, and became an associate of the National Theatre (1963–66). In New York his direction of *Equus* won him a Tony award in 1974. He was director of the Metropolitan Opera, New York (1974–81), and also directed opera in London, Paris and Hamburg. He co-founded the New Theatre Company in 1986.

Dharmapala, Anagarika, *originally* Don David Hewavitarne 1864–1933
Buddhist reformer
Born in Ceylon (Sri Lanka), he took the name Anagarika Dharmapala as a result of his activities with the Buddhist Theosophical Society. He wrote and spoke as the champion of Buddhist reformism and the interests of the Sinhala people, but never formed or led any significant political grouping. Instead he devoted his attention in his later years to campaigning for the return of Buddhist sacred sites in North India into Buddhist hands.

d'Hérelle, Felix See Hérelle, Felix d'

Dhu al-Nun Ayybub 1908–
Iraqi novelist
A professor of physics and chemistry, he wrote *Duktur Ibrahim* (1939, 'Doctor Ibrahim'), which analyses a Western intellectual to devastating effect. He was in exile in Vienna between 1954 and 1958 for political reasons, and wrote about this in a number of highly-regarded, short stories. *Wa ala al-dunya al-salam* (1972, 'Farewell to the World') depicts struggles in Iraq in the preceding decade.

Diaghilev, Sergei Pavlovich 1872–1929
Russian ballet impresario
Born in Novgorod, he obtained a law degree, but his real preoccupation was with the arts. In 1898 he became editor of *Mir Iskusstva* ('World of Art') and during the next few years arranged exhibitions and concerts of Russian art and music. He presented *Boris Godunov* in Paris (1908), and the next year brought a ballet company to the Châtelet. His permanent company, Ballets Russes de Diaghilev, was founded in 1911 (with headquarters in Monte Carlo, and Enrico Cecchetti as ballet master) and remained in existence for 20 years, successfully touring Europe, despite constant financial anxiety. Most of the great dancers, composers and painters of this period—among them the choreographers and dancers Vaslav Nijinsky, Léonide Massine and George Balanchine, artists Leon Bakst, Picasso and Natalia Goncharova, and composers Erik Satie and Stravinsky—contributed to the company's success, and many owed their subsequent fame to their association with it. A temperamental tyrant, who combined ruthlessness with charm, he seemed to activate the creation of works of art through his mere presence. 🕮 Arnold L Haskell and W Nouvel, *Diaghileff* (1955)

Diamond, I A L, *originally* Itek Dommnici 1920–88
US screenwriter
Born in Romania, he emigrated to the USA in 1929. After his graduation from Columbia University, New York, he displayed sufficient promise to secure a contract as a junior writer at Paramount Studios (1941–43). He first received screen credit as the writer of the minor musical thriller *Murder In The Blue Room* (1944). His subsequent work comprised a string of generally undistinguished broad comedies and musicals before he embarked on a 25-year collaboration with the writer-director Billy Wilder on *Love In The Afternoon* (1957). Together they created witty, incisive classics of contemporary US cinema, including the uproarious farce *Some Like It Hot* (1959) and bittersweet romantic comedies such as *The Apartment* (1960), for which he and Wilder won a joint Academy Award for best screenplay. He received the Writer's Guild Laurel award in 1979 and collaborated a final time with Wilder on *Buddy, Buddy* (1981).

Diamond, Jared Mason 1937–
US physiologist and ecologist
Born in Boston, he was educated at Harvard and Cambridge, and since 1968 has been professor at the University of California Medical Center. He has contributed significantly to the study of ecological diversity through his studies on islands, particularly on their bird

---

Dickens, Charles John Huffam 1812–70
English writer

Dickens was born in Landport, then a suburb of Portsmouth. His father was John Dickens, a clerk in the navy pay office at Portsmouth dockyard. In 1814 he was transferred to London, and in 1816 to Chatham where, already a great reader, he got some schooling. In 1821 the family fell into trouble; reforms in the Admiralty made his father's job redundant and they had to leave Chatham. They moved to London, where they took a small house in Camden Town, but John Dickens was arrested for debt in 1824 and sent to the Marshalsea prison with his whole family, apart from Charles, who was sent to work in a blacking factory at Hungerford Market. At night, Charles had four miles to walk to his lonely bedroom in lodgings in Camden Town; on Sundays he visited his parents in the prison.

On his father's release the family returned to Camden Town, and Charles was sent again to school, an academy in the Hampstead Road, for three or four years, after which he worked for a solicitor as an office boy (1827). Meanwhile his father had obtained a post as reporter for the *Morning Herald*, and Charles decided also to attempt the profession of journalist. He taught himself shorthand and visited the British Museum daily to supplement some of the shortcomings of his reading.

In 1828 he became a reporter of debates at the House of Commons for the *Morning Chronicle*, although at that time he was only interested in being an actor. It was not until 1835 that he obtained permanent employment on the staff of a London paper as a reporter, and in this capacity he was sent around the country. Meanwhile in December 1833, the *Monthly Magazine* published a sketch 'Dinner at Poplar Walk', under the pen-name 'Boz', which was the nickname of Charles's younger brother. Eventually he made an arrangement to contribute papers and sketches regularly to the *Evening Chronicle*, continuing to work as a reporter for the *Morning Chronicle*, and received an increased salary.

The *Sketches by Boz* were collected and published early in 1836. Dickens received £150 for the copyright; he later bought it back for 11 times that amount. In the last week of March 1836 the first number of the *Pickwick Papers* appeared; three days afterwards he married Catherine, the daughter of his friend George Hogarth, editor of the *Evening Chronicle*. She bore him seven sons and three daughters between 1837 and 1852, three of whom predeceased their father. They were separated in 1858.

Once he'd become established, Dickens for the rest of his life allowed himself little respite. In fulfilment of publishers' engagements he produced *Oliver Twist* (1837–39) which appeared in *Bentley's Miscellany*; *Nicholas Nickleby* (1838–39); and *Master Humphrey's Clock*, a serial miscellany which resolved itself into the two stories *The Old Curiosity Shop* (1840–41) and *Barnaby Rudge* (1841). From then on a great part of Dickens's life was spent abroad, especially notable being his visits to the USA in 1842 and 1867–68, his stay in Genoa in 1844–45 and in Lausanne in 1846, and his summers spent in Boulogne in 1853, 1854 and 1856. His reception in the USA was somewhat chilled by his criticism of US publishers for pirating English books, and by the unfavourable picture of the country given in *Martin Chuzzlewit*.

Dickens died suddenly at Gadshill, near Rochester (the place he had coveted as a boy, and purchased in 1856), and was buried in Westminster Abbey. His last work was *The Mystery of Edwin Drood*, a mystery story influenced by the work of his friend **Wilkie Collins**; it remained unfinished.

cont

---

faunas, following up the theory of island biogeography proposed by **Robert MacArthur** and **Edward Wilson**. He distinguished organisms which spread readily and easily ('super-tramps') from those which are less mobile, and calculated the turnover of species on a number of Pacific islands. His *Rise and Fall of the Third Chimpanzee* (1991) is an influential work of popular biology.

Diana, Princess of Wales, *née* Lady Diana Frances Spencer 1961–97
British princess

Born in Sandringham, Norfolk, she was educated at Riddlesworth Hall, West Heath, and at the Institut Alpen Videmanette in Switzerland. Following her work as a kindergarten teacher in London, she married **Charles, Prince of Wales**, in 1981. They had two children, William Arthur Philip Louis (1982–) and Henry Charles Albert David (1984–). She and Charles separated in 1992 (becoming divorced in 1996), but she continued to carry out her public engagements, taking a special interest in children and the sick (notably AIDS victims) until late 1993. In 1994 she announced that she would take an advisory role with the International Red Cross.

Diane de France 1538–1619
Duchess of Montmorency and Angoulême

An illegitimate daughter of **Henri II** of France and of a Piedmontese (according to some, of **Diane de Poitiers**), she was born in Paris. Formally legitimized, she was married to a son of the Duke of Parma, then to the eldest son of the 1st Duke of **Montmorency**. She enjoyed great influence at court under **Henri III** and **Henri IV**, and supervised the education of the future **Louis XIII**.

Diane de Poitiers 1499–1566
Mistress of Henri II of France

Married at 13, and left a widow at 32, she attracted the attention of the young Dauphin, Henri (later King **Henri II**), who was 20 years her junior and already married to **Catherine de Médicis**. On his accession in 1547 Diane, who was lively, cultivated, and the patron of poets, enjoyed great influence, and was created Duchess of Valentinois. After his death (1559) she retired to her château at Anet.

Diaz or Dias, Bartolomeu c.1450–1500
Portuguese navigator and explorer

At the royal court of Aragon he met many scientists, including the German cosmographer **Martin Behaim**. In 1486 King John II gave him the command of two vessels to follow up the discoveries already made on the west coast of Africa. Diaz soon reached the limit which had been attained in South Atlantic navigation, and first touched land in 26° S latitude. Driven by a violent storm, he sailed round the southern extremity of Africa, the Cape of Good Hope, without immediately realizing the fact, and discovered the southernmost point of Africa, so opening the route to India. He equipped **Vasco da Gama**'s expedition of 1497 and travelled with them as far as the Cape Verde Islands. He established a number of trading posts before joining the expedition of **Pedro Cabral** in 1500, the discoverer of Brazil, but was lost in a storm after leaving Brazil.

Díaz, Juan Martín See Empecinado, El

Díaz, (José de la Cruz) Porfirio 1830–1915
Mexican soldier and statesman

Dickens, Charles John Huffam *cont*

Dickens is the most widely known English writer after **Shakespeare**, and no other novelist has managed to find both popular success and critical respect on such a lavish scale. His novels are a vivid portrayal of social life in Victorian England, much of it derived from his own experiences. The breadth, perception and sympathy of his writing, his abiding concern with social deprivation and injustice, his ability to conjure up memorable characters in a few paragraphs, and the comic genius which permeates even his most serious works, have all ensured that he continues to find a receptive audience, both for the books themselves and in film and stage adaptations of his work.

📖 **Principal works**: *Sketches by Boz* (1833–36); *The Pickwick Papers* (1836); *Oliver Twist* (1837–39); *Nicholas Nickleby* (1838–39); *The Old Curiosity Shop* (1840–41); *Barnaby Rudge* (1841); *American Notes* (1842); *Martin Chuzzlewit* (1843); *The Christmas Tales: A Christmas Carol, The Chimes, The Cricket on the Hearth, The Battle of Life, The Haunted Man* and *The Ghost's Bargain* (1843, 1846, 1848); *Pictures from Italy* (1845); *Dombey and Son* (1846–48); *David Copperfield* (1849–50); *Bleak House* (1852–53); *A Child's History of England* (1854); *Hard Times* (1854); *Little Dorrit* (1855–57); *A Tale of Two Cities* (1859); *The Uncommercial Traveller* (1861); *Great Expectations* (1860–61); *Our Mutual Friend* (1864–65) and *The Mystery of Edwin Drood* (1870, unfinished). To these must be added public readings (1858–70), both in England and in the USA, private theatricals, speeches, innumerable letters, pamphlets, plays, and a popular magazine, first (1850) called *Household Words* and then (1859) *All the Year Round*.

📖 Peter Ackroyd, *Dickens* (1990); J Carey, *The Violent Effigy* (1973); P Hobsbaum, *A Reader's Guide to Charles Dickens* (1973); J Butt and K Tillotson, *Dickens at Work* (1957); G Orwell, 'Charles Dickens', *Inside the Whale* (1940), reprinted in *Collected Essays* (1968); J Forster, *The Life of Dickens* (1872–74).

A description of a place: 'Fog everywhere. Fog up the river, where it flows among green aits and meadows; fog down the river, where it rolls defiled among the tiers of shipping, and the waterside pollutions of a great (and dirty) city. Fog on the Essex marshes, fog on the Kentish heights. Fog creeping into the cabooses of collier-brigs; fog lying out on the yards; and hovering in the rigging of great ships; fog drooping on the gunwales of barges and small boats.'
From *Bleak House*, ch.1.

A description of a time: 'It was the best of times, it was the worst of times, it was the age of wisdom, it was the age of foolishness, it was the epoch of belief, it was the epoch of incredulity, it was the season of Light, it was the season of Darkness, it was the spring of hope, it was the winter of despair, we had everything before us, we had nothing before us, we were all going direct to Heaven, we were all going direct the other way.'
From *A Tale of Two Cities*, ch.1.

A description of marriage: 'As to marriage on the part of a man, my dear, Society requires that he should retrieve his fortunes by marriage. Society requires that he should gain by marriage. Society requires that he should found a handsome establishment by marriage. Society does not see, otherwise, what he has to do with marriage.'
Mrs Merdle in *Little Dorrit*, ch.33.

Born in Oaxaca City to a modest mestizo family, he studied for the priesthood and then for the law. As a student and follower of **Benito Juárez** he opposed the dictatorship of **Antonio de Santa Anna**, joined the Oaxaca National Guard and rose to the rank of general. Hero of the War of Reform (1857–60) and the French Intervention (1861–67), he was shunned by Juárez in peacetime and retired from public life during Juárez's third term (1867–71). In 1871 he rebelled against the unconstitutional fourth re-election of Juárez, rebelled again in 1876 in support of the principle of no re-election, and became President. When his term ended (1880) he relinquished office peacefully to Manuel González (1833–93), was elected again in 1884 and ruled without interruption until he was deposed in 1911. He and his positivist advisers pursued a programme of 'peace and progress', attracting foreign investment to modernize Mexico, which produced a remarkable growth in railroads and other material improvements. However, eventually the dictator's age and his neglect of political and social reforms led to the 1911 revolution of **Francisco Madero**. He died in poverty in Paris. 📖 José F Godoy, *Porfirio Diaz* (1976)

Díaz del Castillo, Bernal c.1492–1581
Spanish soldier and historian
He was one of the handful of conquistadors who accompanied **Hernán Cortés** in 1519. His *Historia de la conquista de la Nueva España* (1904, Eng trans 1908–16), written at the age of 84, is notable.

Díaz de le Peña, Narciso Virgilio 1807–76
French landscape painter
He was born in Bordeaux of Spanish parentage. Left an orphan, he was educated by a Protestant pastor at Bellevue, near Paris. At the age of 15 he was apprenticed to a porcelain painter and in 1831 he began to exhibit in the Salon. He especially painted nymphs, lovers and satyrs.

Dibdin, Charles 1745–1814
English songwriter
He was born in Southampton, and soon attracted notice for his singing. While still a boy, he composed an operetta, *The Shepherd's Artifice*, which was produced at Covent Garden in 1762. He subsequently lived an unsettled life as an actor and composer of stage music, and in 1788 began a series of musical entertainments which became popular. He wrote nearly 100 sea songs—among the best 'Poor Jack' and 'Tom Bowling'. He also wrote nearly 70 dramatic pieces. In 1803, he published his autobiography. Two of his sons, Charles (1768–1833) and Thomas John (1771–1841), wrote songs and dramas.

Dibelius, Karl Friedrich Otto 1880–1967
German Lutheran churchman and ecumenical leader
He was born in Berlin. Suspended from church duties as general superintendent of the Kurmark following a 1933 sermon to Nazi leaders stating that 'the dictatorship of a totalitarian state is irreconcilable with God's will', he continued to support the Confessing Church, despite being forbidden to speak or publish. As Bishop of Berlin (1945–61), chairman of the Council of the Evangelical Church in Germany (1949–61), and a president of the World Council of Churches (1954–61), he defended religious freedom in East Berlin and encouraged ecumenism. He wrote an autobiography, *In the Service of the Lord*, in 1965. His theologian cousin, Martin Dibelius (1883–1947), was the pioneer of the use of Form Criticism (*Formgeschichtliche Kritik*) in New Testament studies, as in *From Tradition to Gospel* (1934).

Dic, Penderyn See **Lewis, Richard**

Dick, Deadwood See **Love, Nat**

Dick, King See **Seddon, Richard John**

Dick, Philip K(indred) 1928–82
US science-fiction writer

Born in Chicago, Illinois, he worked as a record store manager and as a radio announcer. From 1952 to 1955 he published a profusion of short stories, but from 1962 he turned to writing novels. Despite a penchant for modish titles, such as *Do Androids Dream of Electric Sheep?* (1968) and *Galactic Pot-Healer* (1969), the story of a master-potter who has never thrown his own pots, he was not so much interested in technological gimmickry and space-age jargon as in his characters. A spare and humorous writer, he received the Hugo award in 1963.

Dicke, Robert Henry 1916–
US physicist

Born in St Louis, Missouri, he studied physics at the universities of Princeton and Rochester, and spent his career at Princeton as Professor of Physics from 1957 and Albert Einstein Professor of Physics from 1975. Independently of **Ralph Alpher** and **George Gamow**, he deduced in 1964 that a 'Big Bang' origin of the universe should have left an observable remnant of microwave radiation. This radiation was later detected by **Arno Penzias** and **Robert Wilson**. In the 1960s he carried out important work on gravitation, proposing that the gravitational constant G slowly decreases with time (the Brans–Dicke theory, 1961). After a critical review of **Roland von Eötvös's** work on showing that inertial mass is equal to gravitational mass (**Einstein's** equivalence principle), he verified this to one part in 10^{11}.

Dickens, Charles John Huffam See panel p528

Dickey, James Lafayette 1923–97
US poet and novelist

Born in Georgia, he writes with an intense concern for the fragile harmony of nature and human enterprise. This is the substance of much of his verse from the first collection *Into the Stone* (1960), *Drowning with Others* (1962, republished in part as *The Owl King*, 1977) and *Helmets* (1964). Dickey's wider fame depends on his one novel, *Deliverance* (1972), a Hemingwayesque rite of passage set against the damming and flooding of a wild valley. It was successfully filmed by **John Boorman**. Later poetry collections emphasized Dickey's deep narrative urge: *The Zodiac* (1976), *The Strength of Fields* (1977), whose title poem was written for President **Jimmy Carter's** inauguration, the remarkable *Head-Deep in Strange Sounds: Free Flight Improvisations from the UnEnglish* (1979) and *Falling, May Day Sermon and Other Poems* (1981). Dickey's poems have been collected in three volumes: *Poems, 1957–1967* (1967), *The Achievement of James Dickey* (1968) and *The Central Motion: Poems 1968–1979* (1983). Later publications include *Alnilam* (1987) and *To the White Sea* (1993). He also published *Self-Interviews* (1970). ▣ B Weigl and T R Hummer (eds), *The Imagination as Glory* (1984)

Dickinson, Emily Elizabeth 1830–86
US poet

Born in Amherst, Massachusetts, she was educated at Amherst Academy and Mount Holyoke Female Seminary in South Hadley. At the age of 23 she withdrew from most social contacts and lived a secluded life in Amherst, writing in secret over 1,700 poems, most in a period of creative ferment between 1858 and 1865. In later years she dressed in white and seldom consented to meet even family visitors, though she did correspond with a few friends and literary acquaintances such as **Thomas Wentworth Higginson**. Apart from several poems published anonymously, her work remained unknown and unpublished until after her death, when her sister Lavinia brought out three highly praised volumes (1890, 1891, 1896). Further collections appeared as *The Single Hound* (1914) and *Bolts of Melody* (1945). Her lyrics, which show great originality both in thought and in form, have had considerable influence on modern poetry. ▣ C G Wolf, *Emily Dickinson: a biography* (1986)

Dickinson, John 1732–1808
US writer and politician

He was born in Talbot County, Maryland, and studied law in Philadelphia and London. In the years that preceded the outbreak of the Revolution, he opposed British policies but maintained hope of a reconciliation. His *Letters from a Farmer in Pennsylvania* (1767–68) were an influential statement of protest against the Townshend Acts, and he came to be known as the 'penman of the Revolution'. Although he voted against the Declaration of Independence, he served in the militia during the war and in the Constitutional Convention in 1787.

Dick-Read, Grantly 1890–1959
English gynaecologist

He attended school in Hertfordshire before studying at St John's College, Cambridge, and the London Hospital. His unorthodox work, *Natural Childbirth* (1933), with its rejection of anaesthetics during childbirth and its advocacy of prenatal relaxation exercises, caused bitter controversy, but later found common acceptance. In 1948 he emigrated to South Africa, where he conducted a tour of African tribes in 1954 to investigate childbirth.

Dicksee, Sir Frank (Francis Bernard)
1853–1928
English painter

He is remembered for several much-reproduced historical subject paintings, such as *Romeo and Juliet* and *The Passing of Arthur*. His sister, Margaret Isabel (1858–1903), painted several equally well-remembered canvases, such as *The Children of Charles I* and *Swift and Stella*.

Dickson, Alec (Alexander Graeme) 1914–
Scottish educationist

Born in London, he was educated at Rugby and New College, Oxford. He trained as a journalist on the *Yorkshire Post*, but after war service in Africa he set up Community Service Volunteers (CSV) to enable young people to give voluntary service to the community in Great Britain. Since 1984 he has been consultant to International Baccalaureate schools worldwide. His publications include *A Community Service Handbook* (1967, with his wife Mora Dickson), *School in the Round* (1969), *A Chance to Serve* (1976) and *Volunteers* (1983).

Dickson, Carter See Carr, John Dickson

Dickson, Leonard Eugene 1874–1954
US mathematician

Born in Independence, Iowa, he studied at the University of Texas, and taught at Chicago University for most of his life, doing much to make that university a leading centre for research in mathematics in the USA. He did important work in group theory, finite fields and linear associative algebras, and discovered all the families of finite simple groups. His encyclopedic *History of the Theory of Numbers* (1919–23) is the definitive work on the subject.

Didelot, Charles-Louis 1767–1837
French dancer, choreographer and teacher

He was born in Stockholm, Sweden, where his father was principal dancer at the Royal Theatre. The king sent him to Paris for ballet training, and he made his debut there (1790). In London he choreographed the most famous of his 50 or so ballets, *Zephyr and Flora* (1796), in which his use of wired flying apparatus caused a sensation. From 1801 to 1811 he was master choreographer and teacher at the Imperial Ballet in St Petersburg, where he introduced a complete system of reforms influenced by his own French training. He returned to St Petersburg in 1816, having spent the interim in London and Paris. He was especially noted for his intense, innovative interests in stagecraft and costuming, his almost sculptural direction of group scenes, and the dramatic clarity that he brought to the ballet storyline.

Diderot, Denis 1713–84
French writer

Born in Langres, the son of a master cutler, he was trained by the Jesuits at home and in Paris. He refused to become either a lawyer or a physician, and worked instead as a tutor and bookseller's hack (1734–44). His *Pensées philosophiques* (1796, Eng trans *Philosophical Thoughts*, 1916) was burned by the parlement of Paris in 1746, and in 1749 he was imprisoned for his *Lettre sur les aveugles* (1749, Eng trans *An Essay on Blindness*, 1750). In 1748 he had published his first novel, *Les Bijoux indiscrets* (Eng trans *The Indiscreet Toys*, 1749), and he was then invited to edit an expanded translation of Ephraim Chambers's *Cyclopaedia* (1727) with Jean d'Alembert. In Diderot's hands the character of the work was transformed. He enlisted nearly all the important French writers of the time as contributors to his *Encyclopédie, ou Dictionnaire raisonné des sciences, des arts et des métiers* (35 vols, 1751–76, 'Encyclopedia, or Critical Dictionary of Sciences, Arts and Trades'), and produced a major work of the Enlightenment. However, it was seen as propaganda for the Philosophe Party, its sale was repeatedly prohibited, and Diderot ran a constant risk of imprisonment or exile. He was rescued from financial difficulties by Catherine II of Russia, to whom in 1773 he paid a five-month visit. His later works include the novel *La Religieuse* (1796, Eng trans *The Nun*, 1797), which exposed convent life, and *Le Neveu de Rameau* (1821, Eng trans *Rameau's Nephew*, 1897), an imaginary conversation between the author and a parasite, in which the follies of society are laid bare with sardonic humour and piercing insight. His plays are less successful, the best efforts being two short pieces: *Est-il bon? Est-il méchant?* (1784, 'Is He Good? Is He Bad?', not produced until 1913) and *La Pièce et le prologue* (1820, 'The Play and the Prologue'). His letters to Sophie Volland are the most interesting of his voluminous correspondence. As a critic he stood far in advance of his contemporaries, and anticipated the Romanticists. His *Salons* (4 vols, 1957–67) are the earliest example of modern aesthetic criticism. 📖 P France, *Diderot* (1974); L G Crocker, *The Embattled Philosopher: a Biography of Diderot* (1954, rev edn 1966)

Didi, *professional name of* Valdir Pereira 1928–
Brazilian footballer

Born in Campos, he was the master strategist of the Brazil side which won the 1958 World Cup in Sweden, despite a slightly crippled right leg. A spell with Real Madrid was unsuccessful because of a personality clash with Alfredo Di Stefano, but he later managed the Peruvian national side which reached the quarter-finals of the World Cup in Mexico in 1970.

Didion, Joan 1934–
US writer

She was born in Sacramento, California, and educated at the University of California at Berkeley (1952–56). From 1956 to 1963 she was associate feature editor of *Vogue* in New York and has worked and written for such magazines as the *Saturday Evening Post*, *Esquire* and the *National Review*. Her essays have been published as *Slouching Towards Bethlehem* (1968), *The White Album* (1979) and *After Henry* (1992). Her novels portray contemporary social tensions in a laconic style that has aroused much admiration. *Run River* (1963) was her first, but she is best known for *A Book of Common Prayer* (1977), set in a banana republic devoid of history. Her other works include the novels *Democracy* (1984) and *The Last Thing He Wanted* (1996), and non-fiction such as *Salvador* (1983) and *Miami* (1987). In 1964

she married the writer John Gregory Dunne (1932–). 📖 B Morton, *The Princess in the Consulate: the Novels of Joan Didion* (1980)

Didius Julianus, Marcus c.135–193AD
Roman soldier and emperor

A distinguished former Governor of Gaul, Dalmatia and Africa, he purchased power (193AD) by bribing the praetorian guard in a famous auction of the empire held after the death of Publius Helvius Pertinax. He did not hold power for long, as the Senate soon declared for his rival Lucius Septimius Severus and deposed him. He was murdered in his palace.

Didley, Bo See Bo Didley

Didot, Firmin 1764–1836
French printer

He was the grandson of François Didot and brother of Pierre Didot. As a printer, and especially as an engraver and founder, he raised the family name to the highest eminence. He revived and developed the stereotyping process, and produced fine editions of many classical, French and English works. He became a deputy, and obtained some reputation as an author by his tragedies, *La Reine de Portugal* ('The Queen of Portugal') and *La Mort d'Annibal* ('The Death of Hannibal'), and several volumes of metrical translations from the classics. His sons, Ambroise (1790–1876) and Hyacinthe (1794–1880), carried on and transmitted the business, as the firm of Firmin Didot Frères.

Didot, François 1689–1757
French printer and publisher

He was the founder of a great printing dynasty. His two sons were François Ambroise (1730–1804) and Pierre François (1732–95).

Didot, Pierre 1760–1853
French publisher

He was the grandson of François Didot. He brought out the magnificent Louvre editions of Virgil, Horace, Racine and Jean de La Fontaine, besides Nicolas Boileau's works and Voltaire's *Henriade*.

Didrickson, Babe See Zaharias, Babe

Diebenkorn, Richard 1922–93
US painter

Born in Portland, Oregon, he enrolled in 1946 at the California School of Fine Arts, San Francisco, where he taught from 1947 to 1950. During the 1950s he developed a style close to Abstract Expressionism while retaining suggestions of the Californian landscape and of city motifs; his two major series of paintings, developed over many years, focus on Berkeley and Ocean Park. The loose, gestural brushwork of the 1950s gave way to more geometrical compositions during the 1960s and 1970s. Diebenkorn evoked the dazzling Californian light by using bright, semi-translucent colours, particularly blues and yellows.

Diefenbaker, John G(eorge) 1895–1979
Canadian politician

Born at Normanby Township, Ontario, and educated at the University of Saskatchewan, he was called to the Bar in 1919. In 1940 he entered the Canadian Federal House of Commons, and was chosen as leader of the Progressive Conservatives in 1956. He became Prime Minister in 1957 when the Liberal Party was defeated after 22 years in office. His government extended the federal franchise to Canada's native peoples, but a recession eroded his party's support in 1962, and he lost office in 1963. Leader of the Opposition from 1963 to 1967, he remained an MP until his death.

Dieffenback, Johann Friedrich 1792–1847
German surgeon

He was born in Königsberg, Prussia (now Kaliningrad, Russia). Professor of Surgery at Berlin from 1840, he was a pioneer of transplant surgery and improved techniques relating to plastic surgery and blood transfusion.

Diels, Otto 1876–1954
German chemist and Nobel Prize winner

Born in Hamburg, he studied chemistry at Berlin (1895–99) under **Emil Fischer** and was on the staff there from 1899 to 1916. In 1916 he became professor at Kiel. He investigated a number of reactions, but is most famous for the discovery of the reaction of an activated olefin with a diene to give a cyclic structure with a predictable stereochemistry, a reaction of enormous synthetic value. It was discovered in collaboration with **Kurt Alder**, and they shared the 1950 Nobel Prize for chemistry for this work.

Diem, Ngo Dinh See Ngo Dinh Diem

Dieren, Bernard van 1884–1936
Dutch composer, critic and author

Born in Rotterdam, he lived in England from 1909. Although he trained as a scientist, he began to study music seriously in his twenties, and his earliest surviving works date from 1912. The complexity and intensity of his style, as well as his refusal to compromise for popular taste, leave his work little known. His compositions include an opera, *The Tailor* (1917), and a *Chinese Symphony* (1914) for soloists, choir and orchestra, as well as numerous songs and chamber compositions. He wrote a study of the sculptor **Jacob Epstein** (1920) and a volume of musical essays, *Down Among the Dead Men* (1935).

Diesel, Rudolf Christian Karl 1858–1913
German engineer

Born in Paris, France, of German parents, he studied at the Munich Polytechnic and trained as a refrigeration engineer, but in 1885 began work on internal-combustion engines. Subsidized by the Krupp Company, he set about constructing a 'rational heat motor', demonstrating the first practical compression–ignition engine in 1897. The diesel engine achieved an efficiency about twice that of comparable steam engines. He spent most of his life at his factory at Augsburg but in 1913 he vanished from the Antwerp–Harwich mail steamer, and was presumed drowned. ▢W Robert Nitske and Charles M Wilson, *Rudolf Diesel: Pioneer in the Age of Power* (1965)

Dietrich, Marlene, *originally* Maria Magdalena Von Losch 1901–92
US film actress and cabaret performer

Born in Berlin, Germany, she made her film debut as a maid in *Der Kleine Napoleon* (1922, 'The Little Napoleon'), but it was her performance as the temptress Lola in Germany's first sound film *Der blaue Engel* (1930, *The Blue Angel*) that brought her international attention and a Hollywood contract. With the director **Josef von Sternberg**, she developed a sensual film personality, used to effect in a succession of exotic films like *Morocco* (1930), *Blonde Venus* (1932), *The Scarlet Empress* (1934) and *The Devil Is a Woman* (1935). Labelled 'box-office poison' in 1937, she returned in triumph as the brawling saloon singer Frenchie in *Destry Rides Again* (1939). Later film work tended to exploit her legendary mystique, although she was effective in *A Foreign Affair* (1948), *Rancho Notorious* (1952) and *Judgment at Nuremberg* (1961). She made frequent tours to entertain US troops during World War II, and after the war pursued a career as an international chanteuse and cabaret star. Later she became increasingly reclusive, refusing to be photographed for the 1984 documentary *Marlene*, but she contributed a pugnacious vocal commentary. ▢S Morley, *Marlene Dietrich* (1977)

Dietrich von Bern See Theodoric the Great

Dietzenhofer
German family of architects

The family consisted of five brothers. They were active over the period 1643 to 1726, and their work was of great importance in the development of the Late Baroque in central Europe. They were the successors of **Francesco Borromini** and **Guarino Guarini**, and the precursors of **Balthasar Neumann**. A good example of their work is Christoph's St Nicholas in the Lesser Town Prague (1703–11), in which a system of ogival vaults supported on deep wall-pillars are arranged to create a spatial syncopation. The work of the brothers is brought to a logical conclusion by Christoph's son Killian Ignaz Dietzenhofer in St Nicholas in the Old Town (1732–37), where a greater spatial awareness is gained through complexity and lighting.

Dieudonné, Henri Charles See Chambord, Henri Charles Dieudonné, Comte de

Dieudonné, Jean Alexandre 1906–92
French mathematician

Born in Lille, he studied at the École Normale Supérieure in Paris, and held chairs in Rennes, Nancy, Chicago, the Institut des Hautes Études Scientifiques, and finally Nice (1964–70). He worked in many areas of abstract analysis, **Lie** groups, and algebraic geometry. His *Éléments d'analyse* (9 vols, 1960–82) carries on the French tradition of the definitive treatise on analysis. As a founder of the **Bourbaki** group, his ideas on the presentation of mathematics, emphasizing precise abstract formulation and elegance, have marked out a distinctively French school of mathematical writing whose influence has lasted for some 50 years. In later life he wrote the only histories of algebraic geometry and algebraic topology which come up to the present day. One of the leading French mathematicians of his generation, he was elected to the French Academy of Science in 1968.

Digby, Sir Kenelm 1603–65
English diplomat and writer

Born in Gayhurst, near Newport Pagnell, Buckinghamshire, he left Gloucester Hall, Oxford, without a degree and went abroad where, in Madrid, he met Prince Charles (later **Charles II**). He followed him back to England, was knighted and entered his service. After his wife's death he went into seclusion and made a Protestant, but soon announced his reconversion to Catholicism, and during the Civil War was imprisoned and had his estates confiscated. Despite this, he was successful in establishing close relations with **Cromwell**. At the Restoration he retained his office as chancellor to Queen **Henrietta Maria**. He was a founder member of the Royal Society (1663), but gained a reputation for duplicity, and was described by **William Stubbs** as 'the very **Pliny** of our age for lying'.

Digby, Kenelm Henry 1800–80
English writer

He was born in Ireland, the youngest son of the dean of Clonfert, and educated at Trinity College, Cambridge. He published a survey of medieval customs, *The Broad Stone of Honour* (1822, with additional volumes in 1828–29 and 1877), which was influential in the 19th-century cult of medievalism. After his conversion to Roman Catholicism he published *Mores Catholici* (1831–42) and other works, including poetry. ▢ K G Huston, *Sir Kenelm Digby: a checklist* (1969)

Digges, Leonard 1520–c.1559
English applied mathematician

He was probably self-educated, but his books on surveying and navigation went through many editions in the 16th century. His work in ballistics, based on his own experiments, appeared as *Stratioticos* (1579), published by his son, Thomas Digges (d.1595). He took part in Thomas Wyatt's rebellion in 1554, and was condemned to death, but later pardoned and fined.

Dijkstra, Sjoukje Rosalinde 1942–
Dutch figure skater
Born in Akkrum, she was given last place at the 1955 world championships when she was just 13 years old, and after that steadily progressed. She had her first major success in 1960, when she won the European title and finished second at both the Olympics and the world championships. Those victories proved the start of a string of wins which included another four European titles, three world titles (1962–64) and the Olympic title of 1964. She won the Grand Slam in 1964 by lifting the Olympic, European and World titles, as Sonja Henie had done twice in her time.

Dilas, Milovan See Djilas, Milovan

Dilke, Charles Wentworth 1789–1864
English critic and journalist
He graduated from Cambridge, served for 20 years in the navy pay office and edited *Old English Plays* (6 vols, 1814–16). In 1830 he became proprietor of the *Athenaeum* and he edited it until 1846, when he took over the *Daily News*, which he managed for three years.

Dilke, Sir Charles Wentworth 1843–1911
English radical politician
Born in Chelsea, London, the son of Charles Wentworth Dilke, he graduated from Trinity Hall, Cambridge, and was called to the Bar. His travels in Canada and the USA, Australia and New Zealand were described in his *Greater Britain* (1868). He was elected MP for Chelsea in 1868. Though a doctrinaire radical and republican, he sometime held office as Under-Secretary for Foreign Affairs and president of the Local Government Board under Gladstone. His connection with a Mrs Crawford, and a divorce case, led to defeat in 1886 and temporary retirement. But for this, he might have been Gladstone's successor. Author of *European Politics* (1887), *Problems of Greater Britain* (1890) and *The British Empire* (1899), he organized the Labour members into an influential party, and was an authority on defence and foreign relations. He returned to public life in 1892 as MP for the Forest of Dean.

Dill, Sir John Greer 1881–1944
Northern Irish field marshal
Educated at Cheltenham College and trained at Sandhurst, he served in the Second Boer War (1899–1902) and World War I, in which he was decorated and promoted brigadier-general. In World War II he commanded I Corps in France, and became Chief of the Imperial General Staff (1940–41) and field marshal (1941). His strategical insight and organizational ability made him head of the British Service Mission in Washington from 1941. He was posthumously decorated by the US President.

Dillenius, Johann Jacob 1687–1747
German botanist and botanical artist
Born in Darmstadt, he went to England in 1721, and from 1734 was first Sherardian Professor of Botany at Oxford. He was the author and artist of *Hortus Elthamensis* (1732) and *Historia Muscorum* (1741), of fundamental importance in the study of mosses.

Dillinger, John 1903–34
US gangster
Born in Indianapolis, Indianda, he was convicted of attempted robbery in 1923 and imprisoned for 10 years. On his parole in 1933 he and his gang began a series of violent bank robberies, terrorizing his native state of Indiana and neighbouring states. Designated 'public enemy number one' by the FBI, he was held responsible for 16 killings. After escaping from Crown Point county jail, where he was being held on a murder charge, he was betrayed by his girfriend's landlady and shot dead by FBI agents while leaving a theatre in Chicago.

Dillon, John 1851–1927
Irish nationalist politician
Born in Blackrock, County Dublin, the son of the nationalist John Blake Dillon (1816–66) and educated at the Catholic University medical school in Dublin, he qualified as a surgeon but turned to politics. He became a committed supporter of Charles Parnell in the Land League and in 1880 was returned MP for County Tipperary. In parliament he distinguished himself by the violence of his language, while speeches delivered by him in Ireland led to his imprisonment (1881, 1881–82, 1888). From 1885 to 1918 he was MP for East Mayo. After the divorce case involving Parnell in 1890 he became leader of the anti-Parnellite group (1896–99), but resigned in favour of John Redmond (1900). In 1918 he became leader of the remnant of the Irish Nationalist Party, but was defeated in the election of 1919 by Éamon de Valera and retired from politics.

Dilthey, Wilhelm 1833–1911
German philosopher and historian of ideas
Born in Biebrich, Hesse, he was a student of the great historian Leopold von Ranke. He taught at Basle, Kiel and Breslau (now Wrocław, Poland), and was Professor of Philosophy at Berlin (1882–1911). He was much influenced by Kant and is himself a key figure in the idealist tradition in modern social thought. One of his central themes is the radical distinction he made between the natural sciences (*Naturwissenschaften*) and the human sciences (*Geisteswissenschaften*), the former offering explanations of physical events through causal laws, the latter offering understanding (*Verstehen*) of events in terms of human intentions and meanings. He was an important influence on Martin Heidegger, R G Collingwood and José Ortega y Gasset, and he developed a typology of world-views (*Weltanschauungen*) which would set out the different ways of conceiving our relation to the world. He developed a theory of hermeneutics for the interpretation of historical texts, and favoured biography as the best historical method. His own biographies include studies of Friedrich Schleiermacher, the young Hegel, Gotthold Lessing and Goethe. 📖 Michael Ermath, *Wilhelm Dilthey: The Critique of Historical Reason* (1981)

DiMaggio, Joe (Joseph Paul), nicknamed Joltin' Joe and the Yankee Clipper 1914–
US baseball player
Born in Martinez, California, he was a powerful and elegant centre fielder and hitter, and played his entire career (1936–51) with the New York Yankees. His greatest achievement was hitting safely (recording a hit) at least once in 56 consecutive games in the 1941 season. He won the batting championship twice (1939, 1940), and was voted the American League's Most Valuable Player (MVP) three times. During his career he hit 361 home runs and compiled a lifetime average of .325. In 1954 he married (briefly) the film actress Marilyn Monroe. 📖 Jack G Moore, *Joe DiMaggio: Baseball's Yankee Clipper* (1987)

Dimbleby, David, Jonathan and Richard See panel p534

Dimitrov, Gemeto 1903–72
Bulgarian politician
After studying medicine in Belgrade and Sofia, he began to take an active part in left-wing politics as a member of the Pladne Group of the Agrarian Union. Like many

The Dimblebys
Family of English broadcasters

Dimbleby, Richard 1913–65

Richard Dimbleby was educated at Mill Hill School, and worked on the editorial staff of various newpapers before being appointed first news observer of the BBC in 1936. In 1939 he became the BBC's first war correspondent and went with the British Expeditionary Force to France. He was the first radio reporter in Berlin and at Belsen. In 1946 he became a freelance broadcaster and gave commentaries on many major events, particularly royal occasions, and reported royal tours abroad and state visits in Great Britain (notably that of **Charles de Gaulle** in 1960), as well as the funerals of US President **John F Kennedy** (1963) and **Winston Churchill** (1965).

He took part in the first Eurovision relay in 1951 and in the first live television broadcast from the USSR in 1961. He was presenter of a number of current affairs programmes, most famously of *Panorama* and *About Britain*, and was a member of *Twenty Questions* radio team for 18 years. He is commemorated by the annual BBC Dimbleby Lectures on topical subjects. His sons, David and Jonathan, followed their father into broadcasting.

Dimbleby, David 1938–

He was educated at Charterhouse and at Christ Church, Oxford, and has been with the BBC since 1960, when he was a reporter with BBC Bristol. He was a special correspondent with CBS News in 1966–68. After a period in children's programmes (including *Top of the Form*, 1961–63) he became a presenter of *Panorama* for several series and of BBC election results programmes from 1979 to 1992.

Dimbleby, Jonathan 1944–

He was educated at University College London, and joined the BBC in 1969, when, like his brother David, he became a reporter with BBC Bristol. Now a freelance broadcaster and author in current affairs, he has written an authorized biography of **Charles, Prince of Wales**, about whom he also made a television documentary (1994).

> 'The moment of the Queen's crowning is come.'
> Richard Dimbleby, in his commentary on the Coronation at Westminster Abbey, 2 June 1953.

---

others during the dictatorship of Boris III, he was arrested and tortured (1935). After the outbreak of World War II, he organized opposition to the Tripartite Pact and had to flee to Turkey. He returned to Bulgaria in 1944 and began to reorganize the Agrarian Party. Placed under house arrest, with US assistance he escaped to the USA, where he founded the Bulgarian National Committee and the newspaper *Free and Independent Bulgaria*.

Dimitrov, Georgi Mikhailovich 1882–1949
Bulgarian Communist politician

Born near Radomir, he was a printer by trade. A leading figure in the Bulgarian Socialist Party before World War I, he was imprisoned in 1917 for antimilitarist agitation. He helped to found the Bulgarian Communist Party in 1919, and after visiting Moscow, returned to Bulgaria and led an uprising which earned him a death sentence (1923). He fled to Yugoslavia, then lived under an assumed name in Vienna and Berlin. In 1933 he was one of those accused of setting fire to the Reichstag, but conducted a brilliant defence against the charges engineered by the Nazi prosecution and was acquitted. He then became a Russian citizen and served as Executive Secretary of the Comintern (1934–43). Returning to Bulgaria in 1945, he was elected president of the Central Committee of the Fatherland Front and became Prime Minister (1946–49) after the elections which established Communist rule. Despite overseeing the 'Sovietization' of the republic, he fell out of favour with **Stalin** because of his close relations with **Tito**. He died in Moscow while undergoing medical treatment. 📖 C A Moser, *Dimitrov of Bulgaria* (1979)

Dine, Jim (James) 1935–
US artist

Born in Cincinnati, Ohio, he studied at the Boston Museum of Fine Arts School. In 1959 he exhibited his first series of ready-made objects as images, alongside **Claes Oldenburg**, with whom he continued to collaborate, as in *The Ray Gun Show* of 1960 (New York), pioneering 'happenings'. His own happening, *The Car Crash* of 1960, was a classic of this type. One of the foremost US Pop artists, he had his first one-man show at the Reuben Gallery, New York, in 1960. He is essentially a collage painter, as in *Double Red Self-portrait (Green Lines)* (1964, New York), where clothing is fastened to canvas against a freely painted background. During the late 1960s he also collaborated with **Eduardo Paolozzi** on collages. He has since turned to more traditional painting, concentrating on colour and line under the influence of **Mark Rothko**, such as *Cardinal* (1976, Pace Gallery, New York). His publications include *Welcome Home, Lovebirds* (1969), which he also illustrated, and *Drawings from the Glyptothek* (1993), which he co-authored and illustrated.

Dines, William Henry 1855–1927
English meteorologist

Born in Oxshott, Surrey, he graduated from Cambridge in 1881, and after 1879 became a member of the Wind Force Committee of the Royal Meteorological Society. In 1901 he designed the pressure tube anemometer which bears his name, and also began upper-air investigations from his home. In 1905 he was appointed director of experiments of the upper air for the Meteorological Office, and in 1907 he started regular balloon ascents, the results of which he used to calculate correlations between pressure and temperature at the surface and at various heights. From these extensive analyses Dines concluded that a cyclonic circulation resulted from dynamical processes in the middle atmosphere. After World War I he studied solar and terrestrial radiation with **Lewis Fry Richardson** and designed numerous meteorological instruments, including the Dines radiometer (1920).

Ding See **Darling, Jay Norwood**

Dingaan d.1843
King of Zululand

He was the half-brother of **Shaka**, whose murder he instigated. King from 1828, he admitted the Boers (1837) and then treacherously massacred the colonists in Natal, but he was defeated by **Andries Pretorius** at Blood River in 1838 (Dingaan's Day). He fled to Swaziland, where he was overthrown and killed by one of his brothers.

Dingelstedt, Franz von 1814–81
German poet, novelist and theatre director

Born in Halsdorf, near Marburg, he began writing as a journalist and satirical novelist and poet with radical views, and published the novels *Die neuen Argonauten* (1839, 'The New Argonauts') and *Unter der Erde* (1840, 'Under the Earth'). He then adopted more establishment views, and became royal librarian at Württemberg (1843–1850), and director of the court theatres at Munich, Weimar and

Vienna. He wrote stories, novels and plays, but is best remembered for his work as director of these theatres. 📖 M Sauerlandt, *Franz von Dingelstedt* (1854)

Ding Ling (Ting Ling), *pseudonym of* Jiang Bingzhi (Chiang Ping-chih) 1902–86
Chinese feminist writer and Communist Party activist
Born in Linli County, Hunan Province, she went to Shanghai University (1923–24), where she started publishing stories of rebelliousness against traditional society, such as *The Diary of Miss Sophia* (1928), which dealt candidly with questions of female psychology and sexual desires, *Birth of an Individual* (1929) and *A Woman* (1930). She joined the League of Left-Wing Writers in 1930 and became editor of its official journal. Two years later she joined the Chinese Communist Party, and after a spell of imprisonment by the Guomindang (Kuomintang) authorities (1933–36), she succeeded in escaping to the Communist base at Yenan, where she became a star attraction for Western journalists. Her outspoken comments on male chauvinism and discrimination there led to her being disciplined by the Party leaders, until her novel *Taiyangzhaozai Sangganheshang* (1948,'The Sun Shines over the Sanggan River'), about land-reform, restored her to favour. In 1958, however, she was 'purged' and sent to raise chickens in the Heilongjiang reclamation area, known as the Great Northern Wilderness (Beidahuang). She was imprisoned (1970–75) during the Cultural Revolution, but was rehabilitated by the Party in 1979, and published a novel based on her labour camp experiences, *Comrade Du Wanxiang* (1979).

Diniz, Denis 1261–1325
King of Portugal
King from 1279, he strengthened the country by limiting the roles of the Church and the nobles. He founded the universities of Lisbon (1290) and Coimbra (1307), negotiated the first commercial treaty with England (1294), formed the Portuguese navy (1317), introduced improved methods of land cultivation, founded agricultural schools, and was both a patron of literature and music and a prolific poet.

Diniz or Dinis da Cruz e Silva, António 1731–99
Portuguese poet
Born in Lisbon, he took a law degree at the University of Coimbra in 1753, and became a founder member of the *Arcadia Lusitana*, a society dedicated to the revival of national poetry. He wrote the epic poem, *O Hyssope* (1774), and *Odes Pindaricas* (published posthumously in 1801), lyrics which earned him the title 'the Portuguese *Pindar*'. His later life was spent in Brazil.

Dinkins, David 1927–
US lawyer and politician
Born in Trenton, New Jersey, and educated at Howard and Brooklyn Law School, he practised as a lawyer and was elected to New York State Assembly in 1965. In 1990, following posts as New York City clerk (1975–85) and Manhattan borough president (1985), he became the first black Mayor of New York (1990–93). He stood for New York on a programme of crime and drug prevention following high-profile political scandals in the city. In 1993 he was appointed professor at Columbia University School of International and Public Affairs.

Dinwiddie, Robert 1693–1770
Scottish colonial administrator
Born near Glasgow, he was appointed Collector of Customs for Bermuda in 1727 and Surveyor-General for southern America in 1738. Appointed Lieutenant-Governor of Virginia in 1751, he tried to prevent French occupation of the Ohio district in 1753. He sent a young surveyor, George Washington, to demand a French withdrawal, followed by troops in 1754, but Washington was forced to surrender at Fort Necessity. In 1755 General Edward Braddock was defeated near Fort Duquesne in Ohio, thus precipitating the French and Indian War (1755–63). Dinwiddie was recalled in 1758.

Dio Cassius c.150–c.235AD
Roman historian
Born in Nicaea, Bithynia, he went to Rome (c.180AD), held high offices of state, and was twice consul. He became a close friend of Alexander Severus, who sent him as legate to Dalmatia and Pannonia. About 229 he retired to his native city. Of the 80 books of his *History of Rome*, from the landing of Aeneas in Italy until 229, only 19 (from the period 68BC–AD10) have survived complete.

Diocletian, *properly* Gaius Aurelius Valerius Diocletianus AD245–313
Roman emperor
He was born of humble parentage near Salona, Dalmatia. He served under Probus, Aurelian and Carus, and was proclaimed Emperor by the army (AD284). To aid him against barbarian attacks he made Maximian his co-Emperor over the Western Empire (286), and also pronounced Constantius Chlorus and Galerius Caesars (292). Diocletian ruled the East from Nicomedia, Maximian ruled Italy and Africa, Constantius Britain, Gaul and Spain, and Galerius Illyricum and the valley of the Danube. Britain, after maintaining independence under Marcus Aurelius Carausius and Allectus, was restored to the empire (296), the Persians were defeated (298), and the Marcomanni and other northern barbarians were driven beyond the Roman frontier. Diocletian's domestic reforms displayed his genius for administration. He strengthened the frontiers, increased the size of the army, revised legal codes, instituted new taxes and restored a sound coinage. A conservative, he attempted to preserve the ancient Roman virtues, but this led to severe persecution of the Christians (303). Diocletian and Maximian abdicated (305), and Diocletian retired to Salona (now Split) to philosophy and gardening. 📖 Stephen Williams, *Diocletian and the Roman Recovery* (1985)

Diodati, Jean 1576–1649
Swiss Calvinist theologian
Born in Geneva, he became Professor of Hebrew at the university there in 1597, pastor of the Reformed church in 1608, and in 1609, on Theodorus Beza's death, Professor of Theology. He was a preacher at Nimes (1614–17) and Genevese representative at the Synod of Dort (1618–19). He is remembered for his Italian translation of the Bible (1607) and his *Annotationes in Biblia* (1607).

Diodorus Siculus 1st century BC
Greek historian
Born in Agyrium, Sicily, he travelled in Asia and Europe, and lived in Rome. For 30 years he collected the material for his *Bibliotheke Historike*, a history of the world in 40 books, from the creation to the Gallic wars of Gaius Julius Caesar. Five of the books are extant entire, some are lost, and fragments of the rest remain.

Diogenes of Apollonia 5th century BC
Greek philosopher
He continued the pre-Socratic tradition of speculation about the primary constituent of the world, which he identified as air, operating as an active and intelligent life-force. He was caricatured along with Socrates in Aristophanes' comedy *The Clouds* (423BC).

Diogenes of Sinope c.412–c.323BC
Greek Cynic philosopher and moralist
Born in Sinope, Pontus, Asia Minor, he moved to Athens as a young man and became a student of Antisthenes, with whom he founded the Cynic sect, preaching an austere asceticism and self-sufficiency. Legendary for his

unconventional behaviour and ostentatious disregard for domestic comforts, he was said to have lived in a tub 'like a dog' (Greek *kyon*), the origin of the term 'Cynic'. When **Alexander the Great** visited him and asked what he could do for him he answered, 'you could move away out of the Sun and not cast a shadow on me'. According to another story he would wander around Athens by day with a lamp 'looking for an honest man'. Later he was captured by pirates while on a sea voyage and was sold as a slave to Xeniades of Corinth. He was soon freed, was appointed tutor to Xeniades' children and remained in Corinth for the rest of his life. ◻Ragner Höistad, *Cynic Hero and Cynic King* (1949)

Diogenes Läertius fl.2nd century AD
Greek writer
He was born in Läerte, Cilicia. His *Peri biōn domatōn kai apophthegmatōn tōn en philosophia endokimēsantōn* ('Lives of the Greek Philosophers'), in 10 books, gives a second-hand account of the principal Greek thinkers.

Dion 409–353BC
Syracusan magnate
He was both brother-in-law and son-in-law of **Dionysius the Elder**. This connection with the tyrant brought him great wealth, but he fell out with **Dionysius the Younger**, who banished him in 366BC. Thereupon he retired to Athens to study philosophy under **Plato**. A sudden attack upon Syracuse made him master of the city in 357, but his severity alienated the Syracusans, and he was murdered.

Dion or Dio Chrysostom, *literally* 'the golden-mouthed' c.40–c.112AD
Greek orator and philosopher
Born in Prusa, Bithynia, Asia Minor, he went to Rome under **Vespasian**, but was banished by **Domitian**. He next visited—disguised as a beggar, and on advice of the Delphic oracle—Thrace, Mysia and Scythia. On **Marcus Cocceius Nerva's** accession (96AD) he returned to Rome, and lived in great honour under him and **Trajan**. Fragments of his work survive, as well as around 80 orations or treatises on politics, morals and philosophy.

Dionysius See Denis, St

Dionysius Exiguus d.556
Scythian Christian scholar
Abbot of a monastery in Rome, he was one of the most learned men of his time. He fixed the dating of the Christian era in his *Cyclus Paschalis* (525).

Dionysius of Alexandria, St, *called* the Great
c.200–64AD
Greek theologian
Born in Alexandria, he was a pupil of **Origen**, and succeeded him as head of the Catechical school in Alexandria (AD231). He became Bishop of Alexandria in 247. In the persecutions under **Caius Decius** he escaped to a refuge in the Libyan desert, and was restored at the death of Decius in 251. He was banished again in 257, under **Valerian**, but returned in 261. Only fragments of his writings have survived. His feast day is 17 November.

Dionysius of Halicarnassus 1st century BC
Greek critic, historian and rhetorician
From 30BC he lived and worked in Rome. He wrote, in Greek, *Romaike Archaeologia*, a history of Rome down to 264BC, a mine of information about the constitution, religion, history, laws and private life of the Romans. Of its 20 books, only the first nine are complete. He also wrote a number of valuable critical treatises on literature and rhetoric, particularly *On the Arrangement of Words*. ◻S F Bonner, *The Literary Treatises of Dionysius* (1939)

Dionysius the Areopagite c.500AD
Greek or Syrian churchman

Born in Athens, he was one of the few Athenians converted by the Apostle **Paul** (Acts 17.34). Tradition makes him the first Bishop of Athens and a martyr. The Greek writings bearing his name were written, not by him, but probably by an unknown Alexandrian of the early 6th century. They include the treatises *On the Heavenly and Ecclesiastical Hierarchies*, *On Divine Names*, *On Mystical Theology*, and a series of 10 *Epistles*, and had a great influence on the development of theology.

Dionysius the Elder 431–367BC
Tyrant of Syracuse
He made himself absolute ruler of his native city in 405BC. After ferociously suppressing several insurrections and conquering some of the Greek towns of Sicily, he warred with the Carthaginians (397–392), when he concluded an advantageous peace. In 387 he captured Rhegium, gaining influence over the Greek cities of Lower Italy, while his fleets swept the Tyrrhenian and Adriatic seas. From 383 until his death he tried to drive the Carthaginians from Sicily. He was a poet, and patron of poets and philosophers, but a hostile tradition depicts him as the destroyer of Greek liberties.

Dionysius the Younger fl.367–343BC
Tyrant of Syracuse
The son of **Dionysius the Elder**, he succeeded him in 367BC. Reportedly indolent and dissolute, he fell out with **Dion** who had invited **Plato** to Syracuse. Dion was banished, but 10 years afterwards expelled Dionysius. He fled to Locri, and made himself master of the city, which he ruled despotically, until dissensions in Syracuse (346) enabled him to return there. However in 343 **Timoleon** went to free Sicily, and Dionysius was exiled to Corinth.

Dionysius Thrax fl.c.100BC
Greek grammarian
A native of Alexandria, he taught at Rhodes and at Rome. His *Techne Grammatike* is the basis of all European works on grammar.

Diop, Birago 1906–90
Senegalese writer, diplomat and veterinary surgeon
He was both a poet and a story writer, and in the last capacity became the greatest transcriber from the griots (oral storytellers) of his continent. His narrator was the Wolof, Amadou Koumba, a real griot. A selection of his incomparable and profound animal tales is translated in *Tales of Amadou Koumba* (1966).

Diophantus fl.3rd century AD
Greek mathematician
He lived in Alexandria, and his largest surviving work is the *Arithmetica*, which deals with the solution of algebraic equations. In contrast to earlier Greek works it uses a rudimentary algebraic notation instead of a purely geometric one. In many problems there is no uniquely determined solution, and these have become known as Diophantine problems. The study of Diophantus's work inspired **Pierre de Fermat** to take up number theory in the 17th century with remarkable results. ◻T L Heath, *Diophantus of Alexandria* (1910)

Dior, Christian 1905–57
French couturier
Born in Granville, Normandy, he first began to design clothes in 1935, and founded his own Paris house in 1947. He achieved worldwide fame with his long-skirted 'New Look' in that year, followed by the 'A-line', the 'Holine trapeze look', and 'the Sack'. ◻F Giroud, *Dior* (1987)

Diori, Hamani 1916–89
Niger politician

He was educated in Dahomey and then at the William Ponty School in Dakar. A teacher in the language school for colonial administrators (1938–46), he helped form the Rassemblement Démocratique Africain in 1946 and represented Niger in the French National Assembly (1946–51, 1956–57). In 1956 he became Prime Minister of Niger and in 1960, at independence, its first President. Building on close relations with France, he ran one of the most stable countries in West Africa, being re-elected in 1965 and 1970, but opposition within his party (the Niger Progressive Party) led to his overthrow in 1974 through a military coup led by army Chief of Staff, **Seyni Kountche**. He was placed under house arrest for 13 years, before he left for Morocco, where he died.

Dioscorides, Pedanius c.40–c.90AD
Greek physician

Born in Anazarb, Cilicia, he wrote *De materia medica*, the standard work on substances used in medicine and the science of their properties for many centuries.

Diouf, Abdou 1935–
Senegalese politician

Born in Louga, north-west Senegal, he studied at Dakar and Paris universities before graduating with a law degree and returning to Senegal to work as a civil servant. After holding a number of posts, including that of Secretary-General to President **Léopold Sédar Senghor**, he became Prime Minister in 1970 and succeeded Senghor on the latter's retirement (1981). He was re-elected President of Senegal in 1983, 1988 and 1993. He twice served as chairman of the Organisation of African Unity (OAU), in 1985–86 and 1992–93.

Dippel, Johann Konrad 1673–1734
German theologian and alchemist

Born in Burg Frankenstein, near Darmstadt, he invented a panacea known as 'Dippel's Animal Oil', a distillation of animal bone and offal, while living in Berlin. He also discovered Prussian blue.

Dirac, P(aul) A(drien) M(aurice) 1902–84
English mathematical physicist and Nobel Prize winner

He was born in Bristol, and educated at the universities of Bristol and Cambridge, completing his PhD in 1926. Using the matrix approach of **Max Born**, **Pascual Jordan** and **Werner Heisenberg**, he worked on his own interpretation of quantum mechanics, and in 1928 produced his relativistic wave equation, which explained the electron spin discovered by **George Uhlenbeck** and **Samuel Goudsmit** in 1925. This equation had negative energy solutions which he later interpreted as antimatter states (1930). He predicted that a photon could produce an electron–positron pair, which was confirmed experimentally by **Carl Anderson** in 1932. In 1930 Dirac published the classic work *The Principles of Quantum Mechanics* and in the same year he was elected FRS. Lucasian Professor of Mathematics at Cambridge (1932–69), he was awarded the Nobel Prize for physics in 1933 with **Erwin Schrödinger** for their work in quantum theory. His work on quantum electrodynamics (QED) predicted the existence of the magnetic monopole (not yet discovered), and in 1950 he proposed the idea of particles being not point-like, but string-like, an idea now gaining support following the work of **Michael Green**, John H Schwarz and Edward Witten. He became Professor of Physics at Florida State University in 1971. 📖 Helge Kragh, *Dirac: A Scientific Biography* (1990)

Dirceu See **Gonzaga, Tomás António**

Dirichlet, (Peter Gustav) Lejeune 1805–59
German mathematician

Born in Düren, he showed a precocious interest in mathematics and entered the Collège de France in Paris in 1822. After teaching privately, he became extraordinary professor at Berlin in 1828, and succeeded **Carl Friedrich Gauss** as professor at the University of Göttingen in 1855. His main work was in number theory, **Fourier** series, and boundary value problems in mathematical physics.

Dirks, Rudolph 1877–1968
US strip cartoonist

Born in Heinde, Germany, he went to Chicago at the age of seven. He started selling joke cartoons to *Life* magazine in 1894, then joined the *New York Journal* where he created the long-running strip, *The Katzenjammer Kids* (1897) based on **Wilhelm Busch**'s *Max und Moritz*. Dirks later retitled his characters as *The Captain and the Kids* (1914), while the original *Katzenjammer Kids* continued in parallel for decades. Dirks retired in 1958 and his strip was continued by his son, John.

Disney, Walt See panel p538

Disraeli, Benjamin See panel p539

D'Israeli, Isaac 1776–1848
English writer

He was born in Enfield, Middlesex, the son of a Jewish merchant of Italian descent, and became a British subject in 1801. Although he had wished to be a creative writer, and published one or two novels, his forte was in literary illustrations of people and history, as in his *Curiosities of Literature* (1791–1834), *Calamities of Authors* (1812) and a commentary on **Charles I** (1831). **Byron** was an admirer of his work. He was the father of **Benjamin Disraeli**. 📖 J Ogden, *Isaac D'Israeli* (1969)

Di Stefano, Alfredo 1926–
Argentine footballer and coach

Born in Buenos Aires of Italian descent, he first came to prominence in Colombia with the Bogota club, Millionarios. His lasting fame rests on his spell with Real Madrid, during which time he played in five European Cup successes. He did not like competition from clubmates and had **Didi** removed from the Real Madrid staff. With the Hungarian footballer Ferenc Puskas (1927–) he formed a partnership of equals, however, and between them they scored all the goals in Real Madrid's 7–3 win over Eintracht Frankfurt at Hampden Park, Glasgow, in the European Cup Final of 1960, Di Stefano scoring three. Later he became a coach and took Valencia to the Spanish League Championship in 1971.

Ditiatin, Aleksandr 1957–
Soviet gymnast

Born in Leningrad (now St Petersburg), he was educated at the Leningrad Lesgraft Institute of Physical Culture and was the first person to win eight medals in one Olympic Games—in Moscow, 1980. He won three golds for overall, team and rings, four silvers for parallel bars, horizontal bar, pommel horse and vault, and one bronze for floor. He was also the first male gymnast to receive a 10 in an Olympic event, with the longhorse vault. He was overall world champion in 1979 and overall champion in the Soviet Summer Games in 1975 and 1979.

Dittersdorf, Karl Ditters von 1739–99
Austrian composer and violinist

Born in Vienna, he wrote 13 Italian operas, and much orchestral and piano music. He was a friend of **Haydn**.

Dives See **Crassus, Marcus Licinius**

Divine, Father, *originally* **George Baker** 1877–1965
US religious leader

Disney, Walt(er Elias) 1901–66
US artist and film producer

Walt Disney was born in Chicago. He worked as a commercial artist before setting up a small studio in which he produced animated cartoons, his most famous character being Mickey Mouse, who first appeared in *Plane Crazy* and *Steamboat Willie* in 1928. Among his early successes were the *Silly Symphonies* (from 1929) and the first full-length coloured cartoon film, *Snow White and the Seven Dwarfs* (1937). This was followed by *Pinocchio* (1940), *Dumbo* (1941), and *Fantasia* (1940), the first successful attempt to realize music in images.

His other achievements include a series of coloured nature films (eg *The Living Desert*, 1953), and several swashbuckling colour films for young people, including *Treasure Island* (1959), *Robin Hood* (1952) and *The Swiss*

Family Robinson (1960), as well as family films such as *Mary Poppins* (1964). He opened the family theme park, called Disneyland, in California in 1955; others have since been built in Florida (1971), in Tokyo (1983) and on the outskirts of Paris (1992).

📖 Richard Schickel, *The Disney Version* (rev edn 1985); Christopher Finch, *The Art of Walt Disney: From Mickey Mouse to the Magic Kingdoms* (1973).

'Fancy being remembered around the world for the creation of a mouse!' Comment to his wife during his last illness (c.1966). Quoted in Leonard Mosley, *Disney's World* (1985).

An African-American born near Savannah, Georgia, he became an itinerant preacher, and spent several years travelling through the South under the name of 'the Messenger'. He moved to New York City (c.1915) and in 1919 founded the Peace Mission movement, which stressed communal living, celibacy, and complete racial equality. He also founded a series of settlements, at one time numbering more than 150, which were known as 'heavens', and achieved his greatest popularity during the Depression by offering nourishing 15-cent meals to the poor. He claimed to possess supernatural powers and once placed a curse on the New Jersey Turnpike after receiving a speeding ticket. Most of his followers believed that he was God, and after his death the movement faltered.

Dix, Dorothea Lynde 1802–87
US humanitarian and reformer

Born in Hampden, Maine, she established at the age of 19 her own school for girls in Boston (1821–35), and then lived in semi-retirement while she struggled to recover from tuberculosis. In 1841 she visited a Massachusetts prison and was shocked to find inmates confined because of insanity and subject to chaining, flogging and other forms of abuse. She began a lifelong crusade for specialized treatment of the mentally ill, and her efforts led to the founding of numerous state mental hospitals in the USA, Canada and Europe. She was also an advocate of prison reform, arguing for educational programs and the separation of prisoners according to the severity of their crimes. Throughout the Civil War she served as superintendent of women nurses in the army.

Dix, John Adams 1798–1879
US general and politician

He was born in Boscawen, New Hampshire. From 1833 he was successively Secretary of State of New York, US Senator, and US Secretary of the Treasury. In the Civil War (1861–65), as major-general, he effectively served the cause of the Union. He was Minister to France (1866–69) and Governor of New York (1873–75).

Dix, Otto 1891–1969
German Realist painter

Born in Gera-Unternhaus, he is best known for his etchings and paintings of World War I casualties, portrayed with biting realism, and of Berlin prostitutes in the decadent postwar period. He was a brilliant and savage portraitist and social commentator; his work was regarded as unwholesome by the Nazis who included it in the famous exhibition of Degenerate Art. After World War II he painted mostly religious subjects in isolation at Hemmenhofen. 📖 Brigid S Barton, *Otto Dix und Die neue Sachlichkeit, 1918–1925* (1981)

Dixon, Sir Owen 1886–1972
Australian judge

Justice of the Supreme Court of Victoria (1926), then Justice (1929–52) and Chief Justice (1952–64) of the High Court of Australia, he was a master of his subject. In constitutional cases he helped to make the Australian constitution a guarantee of freedom of trade and commerce between the states. He also served as Australian Minister to the USA (1942–44).

Dixon, Richard Watson 1833–1900
English poet

Born in Islington, London, he studied at King Edward's School, Birmingham and Pembroke College, Oxford. He became a canon of Carlisle in 1874 and vicar of Warkworth in 1883. A member of the Pre-Raphaelite circle with Edward Burne-Jones and William Morris, and a teacher and supporter of Gerard Manley Hopkins, he wrote seven volumes of poetry and a *History of the Church of England* (6 vols, 1877–1902). 📖 A Sambrook, *A Poet Hidden* (1962)

Dixon, William Hepworth 1821–79
English writer

He was born in Manchester. His two series of papers in the *Daily News* on 'The Literature of the Lower Orders' and 'London Prisons' attracted attention, and in 1850 he published *John Howard, and the Prison World of Europe*. *William Penn* (1851) is a defence against Thomas Macaulay's attack. From 1853 to 1869 he was editor of the *Athenaeum*. He also wrote a number of works on political history.

Djilas or Dilas, Milovan 1911–95
Yugoslav politician and writer

Born in Montenegro, he was active in the outlawed Yugoslav Communist Party in the 1930s and was subsequently imprisoned (1933–36). He was, with his friend Tito, a remarkable partisan leader during World War II. In the postwar government, he was Vice-President of Yugoslavia but concern for doctrine led him to criticize the Communist system practised in Yugoslavia. Expelled from the party in 1954 and imprisoned (1956–61, 1962–66), he was released under amnesty. He was formally rehabilitated by the Yugoslav authorities in 1989. He strongly opposed the break-up of Yugoslavia and the nationalist warfare which followed. His books include *The New Class* (1957) and *Conversations with Stalin* (1962), as well as novels, short stories and political memoirs. 📖 Dennis Reinhartz, *Milovan Djilas: A Revolutionary as Writer* (1981)

Dmitri or Demetrius 1583–91
Russian prince

The youngest son of Tsar Ivan IV he was murdered by the Regent Boris Godunov, but (c.1603) a runaway Moscow monk Grigorii Otrepiev (the 'false Demetrius') impersonated him and was crowned tsar by the army (1605)

Disraeli, Benjamin, 1st Earl of Beaconsfield 1804–81
English statesman and novelist

Benjamin Disraeli was born in London, the eldest son of Isaac D'Israeli, who, although a Jew, had him baptized in 1817. He was educated at a private school at Walthamstow by a Unitarian minister, was articled to a solicitor and kept nine terms at Lincoln's Inn. In 1826 he became the talk of the town with his first novel, *Vivian Grey*. After four unsuccessful attempts at election, he entered parliament for Maidstone in 1837. His over-ornate maiden speech was drowned in shouts of laughter, except for the closing words 'ay and though I sit down now, the time will come when you will hear me'. By 1842 he was head of the 'Young England' group of young Tories, and had married Mrs Wyndham Lewis, the widow of a fellow MP.

Robert Peel did not reward Disraeli's services with office and was fiercely attacked by him over the repeal of the Corn Laws (1846); this helped bring about Peel's political downfall. At the same time Disraeli wrote two political novels, *Coningsby* (1844) and *Sybil* (1845), in which his respect for tradition is blended with 'Young England' radicalism. As Chancellor of the Exchequer and leader of the Lower House in the brief Derby administration of 1852, he coolly discarded Protection, and came off on the whole with flying colours; but his budget was rejected, and Gladstone succeeded him in the Aberdeen coalition ministry.

In opposition (1858–66), Disraeli displayed talent as a debater, and a spirit and persistency under defeat that won for him the admiration of his adversaries. As Chancellor of the Exchequer in the third Derby administration (1866), he introduced and carried a Reform Bill (1867). In February 1868 he succeeded Lord Derby as premier; but, in the face of a hostile majority, he resigned in December. Disraeli returned to power in 1874 and from this time his curious relationship with Queen Victoria began. Disraeli's wife had meanwhile been raised to the peerage as Viscountess Beaconsfield; she died in 1872.

In 1875 Disraeli made Great Britain half-owner of the Suez Canal; and in 1876 he conferred on the queen the new title of Empress of India. The same year he was called to the Upper House as Earl of Beaconsfield. The Bulgarian insurrection which was brutally put down by the Turks did not move Disraeli as it did Gladstone. The Russians threatened Constantinople and at length a British fleet was dispatched to the Dardanelles, but war was averted by Disraeli's diplomacy at the Congress of Berlin (1878). Russia agreed to respect British interests, the Turkish empire was drastically reduced and Great Britain's share was 'Peace with honour' and Cyprus. Bismarck was full of admiration for Disraeli: 'Der alte Jude, das ist ein Mann' ('The crafty old Jew, now he's what I call a man'). But the increase of taxation and loss of trade brought about a catastrophic defeat for the Tories at the polls in 1880, and Disraeli retired to writing. He was buried at Hughenden, near High Wycombe.

📖 The most famous of his works are the trilogy *Coningsby* (1844), *Sybil* (1845) and *Tancred* (1847). He drew extensively on his travel experiences in his writing, notably in the trilogy *The Young Duke* (1831), *Contarini Fleming* (1832) and *Alroy* (1833), the last set in 12th century Azerbaijan. *Henrietta Temple* and *Venetia* were love stories, published in 1837. After a long gap, *Lothair* was published in 1870. His last finished novel was *Endymion* (1880). See also Sarah Bradford, *Disraeli* (1983); Daniel R Schwarz, *Disraeli's Fiction* (1979); William F Monypenny and G E Buckle, *The Life of Benjamin Disraeli, Earl of Beaconsfield* (6 vols, 1910–20, reissued in 4 vols, 1968).

> 'Read no history: nothing but biography, for that is life without theory.' From *Contarini Fleming*, part 1, ch.5 (1832).
>
> 'A Conservative government is an organized hypocrisy.' Speech, House of Commons, 17 March 1845.

but was killed in a rebellion (1606). A second and a third 'false Demetrius' appeared within the next few years, but their fate was no better.

Dobbie, Sir William George Sheddon
1879–1964
English soldier

Born in Madras, India, and educated at Charterhouse and the Royal Military Academy, Woolwich, he joined the Royal Engineers and served in South Africa in the Second Boer War (1899–1902). He was General Officer Commanding in Malaya from 1935 to 1939, and Governor of Malta from 1940 to 1942 during its resolute resistance to German and Italian air attack.

Dobell, Sydney Thompson 1824–74
English poet

Born in Cranbrook, Kent, he worked with his father as a wine merchant in London and Cheltenham, but lived for some time in the Scottish Highlands and abroad, and became a passionate advocate of oppressed nationalities. His dramatic poem, *The Roman* (1850), was written in sympathy with Italian aspirations for unity, and he also wrote sonnets on the Crimean War (1855) and *England in Time of War* (1856). His chief works were in the style of the so-called Spasmodic school, caricatured by William Aytoun, and appeared under the pseudonym Sydney Yendys. 📖 E Jolly (ed), *Life and Letters of Sydney Thompson Dobell* (1878)

Dobell, Sir William 1899–1970
Australian portrait painter

Born in Newcastle, New South Wales, he studied at the Julian Ashton Art School, Sydney, and the Slade School of Art in London, and exhibited at the Royal Academy. Returning to Sydney he worked during World War II in a camouflage unit with other artists including Joshua Smith. His portrait of Smith won the Archibald prize in 1944 and became the centre of a bitter artistic storm. Dobell won the ensuing legal battle but it resulted in permanent damage to his health. He was further vindicated in 1948 by not only winning the Archibald again, but also the Wynne prize for landscape painting. In 1959 he won the Archibald for a third time and the following year was commissioned by *Time* magazine to paint a portrait of the then Prime Minister of Australia, Robert Menzies. In 1964 his career was crowned by a retrospective exhibition at the Art Gallery of New South Wales. He left his estate to establish the art foundation which bears his name.

Döbereiner, Johann Wolfgang 1780–1849
German chemist

He was born in Bug bei Hof, Bavaria, and received little education but read extensively and attended science lectures. Professor at Jena from 1810, he is remembered as the inventor of 'Döbereiner's lamp', in which hydrogen, produced in the lamp by the action of sulphuric acid on zinc, burns on contact with a platinum sponge.

Dobi, Istvan 1898–1968
Hungarian politician

He spent the earlier part of his life as a day labourer on various large estates. He had a brief experience as a soldier in the Hungarian Red Army in 1919, but it was not until 1935 that he joined the Independent Smallholders Party. During and after World War II he rose within its ranks and, as leader of its left wing, became Prime Minister within the predominantly Communist government of 1949. He remained in office until 1952 during the worst of the Stalinist purges, and was president of the State Council until 1967, including during the Hungarian Uprising of 1956.

Döblin, Alfred 1878–1957
French novelist

Born in Stettin, Germany, he grew up in Berlin, studied medicine both there and in Freiburg, and practised as a doctor and psychiatrist from 1911. He published stories before writing epic novels like *Die drei Sprünge des Wang-Lun* (1915, 'The Three Leaps of Wan Lung'), the satirical fantasy *Wadzek's Kampf mit der Dampfturbine* (1918, 'Wadzek's Fight with the Steam Machine'), *Wallenstein* (1920), and the futuristic *Berge Meere und Giganten* (1924, Eng trans *Giganten*, 1932). *Berlin Alexanderplatz* (1929, Eng trans *Alexanderplatz Berlin*, 1931), the story of a reformed criminal in the dark underworld of Weimar Germany is considered to be his masterpiece. He left for France in 1933, and he became a French citizen in 1936. He continued to write ambitious works like *Pardon wird nicht gegeben* (1935, Eng trans *Men Without Mercy*, 1937) and the trilogies *Amazonas-Trilogie* (1937–47, 'The Amazon Trilogy') and *November 1918* (1948–50). His perilous 1940 flight to the USA is described in *Shicksalreise* (1949, 'Fateful Journey'). He then returned to Germany in 1945 and co-founded the Academy of Science and Literature (1949) before moving again to France (1951), prior to his death in Baden-Württemberg. His last novel was *Hamlet oder Die lange Nacht nimmt ein Ende* (1956, 'Hamlet, or the Long Night is Ended').

Dobrée, Bonamy 1891–1974
English literary scholar

He was Professor of English Literature at Leeds (1936–55), and wrote on Restoration Comedy (1924) and Tragedy (1929), Philip, 4th Earl of Chesterfield (1932), Charles Wesley (1933), Pope (1951), Rudyard Kipling (1951) and Dryden (1956).

Dobrynin, Anatoli Fyodorovich 1919–
Soviet diplomat and politician

Born in Krasnoya Gorka, near Moscow, he was educated at a technical college and worked as an engineer at an aircraft plant during World War II. He joined the diplomatic service in 1946, serving as counsellor at the Soviet Embassy in Washington (1952–55), assistant to the Minister for Foreign Affairs (1955–57), Under-Secretary at the UN (1957–59) and head of the USSR's American Department (1960–61), before being appointed the Soviet ambassador to Washington (1962–86). Dobrynin played an important part in resolving the Cuban Missile Crisis in 1962 and was influential in promoting Soviet–US entente. A member of the Communist Party (CPSU) from 1945, he became a full member of its Central Committee in 1971. In 1986, the new Soviet leader, Mikhail Gorbachev, appointed him Secretary for Foreign Affairs and head of the International Department. He retired in 1991.

Dobson, (Henry) Austin 1840–1921
English poet

Born in Plymouth, he was educated at Beaumaris, Coventry, and Strasbourg as a civil engineer, but from 1856 to 1901 was a Board of Trade clerk. His earliest poems, published in 1868 in *St Paul's Magazine*, were followed by *Vignettes in Rhyme* (1873), *Proverbs in Porcelain* (1877), *At the Sign of the Lyre* (1885), *The Story of Rosina* (1895) and *Collected Poems* (1897, rev edns 1902, 1909, 1913). His poems were often in rondeau, ballade or villanelle form. In prose he published monographs of Henry Fielding (1883), Richard Steele, Thomas Bewick (and his pupils), Horace Walpole, William Hogarth, Oliver Goldsmith, Fanny Burney and Samuel Richardson (1902). He also wrote *Eighteenth Century Vignettes* (1892–96), *Four Frenchwomen* and other collections of erudite essays.

Dobson, Frank 1888–1963
English sculptor

Born in London, he was associated with the London Group (including Eric Gill, Jacob Epstein and Roger Fry) for many years, and was Professor of Sculpture at the Royal College of Art until 1953. His sculptures show an extraordinary feeling for plastic form, and his very individual style (with simplified contours and heavy limbs) is shown at its best in his female nudes, such as *Cornucopia* (1925–27, University of Hull). Among his best known works are *The Man Child*, *Morning*, and a polished brass bust of Osbert Sitwell (1922, Tate, London) which was exhibited at the Venice Biennale in 1928.

Dobson, Rosemary de Brissac 1920–87
Australian poet

Born in Sydney, she was the granddaughter of the English poet and essayist Austin Dobson. She worked for some years with the Australian publishing firm Angus & Robertson and married Alec Bolton, then its London editor. Her poems reflect her love of antiquity, manuscripts and fine printing, as seen in 'The Missal'. She first published *In a Convex Mirror* (1944), then *The Ship of Ice*, which won an award in 1948. Later books were *Child with a Cockatoo* (1955) and *Cock Crow* (1965). She also edited the feminist anthology *Sister Poets* (1979), and in the same year received the Robert Frost prize. In 1984 she won the Patrick White Literary award.

Dobson, William 1610–46
English portrait painter

Born in London, he succeeded Van Dyck in 1641 as serjeant-painter to Charles I, and painted portraits of him and Prince Rupert, among others. He was imprisoned for debt and died in poverty shortly after his release.

Dobzhansky, Theodosius 1900–75
US geneticist

Born in Nemirov, the Ukraine, he studied zoology at Kiev University and taught genetics in Leningrad (St Petersburg), before going to the USA to join Thomas Hunt Morgan at Columbia University in 1927 to work on the genetics of the fruit fly *Drosophila*. He taught thereafter at the California Institute of Technology (Caltech, 1929–40), Columbia (1940–62) and Rockefeller University, New York (1962–71). He showed that the genetic variability in a population is large, including many potentially lethal genes which nevertheless confer versatility when the population is exposed to environmental change. His influential work is described in *Genetics and the Origin of Species* (1937) and in *Genetics and the Evolutionary Process* (1970). His work linked Darwinian evolutionary theory with Gregor Mendel's laws of heredity, and he applied his ideas to the concept of race in man, defining races as Mendelian populations differing in gene frequencies, as in his *Mankind Evolving* (1962). ⌨ Barbara Land, *Evolution of a Scientist: The Two Worlds of Theodosius Dobzhansky* (1973)

Dockwra or Dockwray, William d.1716
English merchant

Based in London, he devised a new penny postal system in London in 1683, and was alternately favoured and persecuted by the authorities.

Doctorow, E(dgar) L(awrence) 1931–
US novelist

Born in New York City, he was educated at Kenyon College and Columbia University. From 1960 to 1964 he was editor of the New American Library and he has held teaching posts in several colleges and universities. He is currently Gluckman Professor of American and English Letters at the University of New York (1987–). His first novel was *Welcome to Hard Times* (1961), followed by *Big as Life* (1966) and *The Book of Daniel* (1971), based on the story of the **Rosenberg**s, who were executed for spying. *Ragtime* (1975, filmed 1981) is generally regarded as his tour de force, in which he recreates the atmosphere of New York in the decades before World War II with wit, accuracy and appealing nostalgia. Later books include *Loon Lake* (1980), *Billy Bathgate* (1989) and *The Waterworks* (1994).

Dod, Charles Roger Phipps 1793–1855
Irish journalist

Born in Drumlease vicarage, Leitrim, he went to London in 1818, and for 23 years worked on *The Times*. He started the *Parliamentary Companion* (1832) and a *Peerage* (1841).

Dod, Lottie (Charlotte) 1871–1960
English sportswoman

She was born in Cheshire, and was tennis's first child protégé, winning her first Wimbledon title at the age of 15, becoming the youngest-ever champion. She then won another four singles titles, as well as defeating Wimbledon champion Ernest Renshaw in a handicapped exhibition match in 1885, and six-times winner **Willie Renshaw** later the same year. Turning her attention to hockey, she represented England in 1899, before taking up golf and going on to win the British Ladies Open Golf championships in 1904 at Troon. She then completed her career by winning a silver medal in archery at the 1908 Olympic Games in London. She is probably the greatest all-rounder that Great Britain has ever produced.

Dodd, C(harles) H(arold) 1884–1973
Welsh biblical scholar and Congregational pastor

Born in Clywd, he graduated from Oxford and served a Congregational church in Warwick. He returned to lecture at Oxford, held a theological chair at Manchester, then was elected to the Norris–Hulse chair of divinity at Cambridge (1936–49)—the first Nonconformist incumbent for nearly three centuries. In 1949 he became general director for the New English Bible translation. His own publications included *The Apostolic Preaching and Its Developments* (1936), *According to the Scriptures* (1952) and *Historical Tradition in the Fourth Gospel* (1963).

Dodd, Ken (Kenneth Arthur) 1927–
English stand-up comedian, singer and actor

Born in Liverpool, he made his debut at the Empire Theatre, Nottingham, in 1954, and played summer seasons all round Great Britain for the next 10 years. He created a record at his London debut in 1965 by starring in his own 42-week season of *Doddy's Here* at the Palladium. He has since appeared regularly on stage in variety and pantomime, on radio and, often supported by the famous Diddymen, in television programmes such as *The Ken Dodd Show* (1959–66), *Ken Dodd's World of Laughter* (1974–76), *The Ken Dodd Laughter Show* (1979), *Ken Dodd at the London Palladium* (1990) and *An Audience with Ken Dodd* (1994). He has also had hits with songs such as *Tears* and *Happiness*, and was in *The Guinness Book of Records* for telling 1,500 jokes non-stop in three-and-a-half hours.

Dodd, William 1729–77
English preacher and forger

Born in Bourn, Lincolnshire, he graduated from Clare Hall, Cambridge (1750), took orders and became a popular preacher. He was made a king's chaplain (1763) and was the tutor of Philip Stanhope, Lord **Chesterfield**'s nephew. Despite a large income, he fell into debt, and his attempt to buy the rich living of St George's, Hanover Square, led to his name being struck off the list of chaplains (1774). He went to Geneva, where he was welcomed by his pupil, now Lord **Chesterfield**, who granted him the living of Wing in Buckinghamshire. Still considerably in debt, however, he was forced to sell his chapel, and in 1777 offered a stockbroker a bond for £4,200 signed by Chesterfield. It proved to be a forgery, and Dodd, though he refunded a great part of the money, was tried and sentenced to death. Great efforts were made by Dr **Johnson** and others to secure a pardon, but the king refused to reprieve him, and Dodd was hanged.

Dodds, Johnny (John M) 1892–1940
US jazz clarinettist

Born in New Orleans, he was self-taught on the clarinet. His measured embroideries typified the role of his instrument in the early three-part ensemble style, and recordings in the 1920s with **King Oliver** and **Louis Armstrong** secured his reputation. Although he recorded little after 1929, Dodds's influence continues among clarinet players in the New Orleans style.

Dodge, Grenville Mellen 1831–1916
US soldier and engineer

Born in Danvers, Massachusetts, he fought in the Civil War, and was promoted to major-general in 1864. After the war, as chief engineer of the Union Pacific Railway from 1866, he was responsible for the construction of some of the most famous US railroads.

Dodge, Henry 1782–1867
US politician and pioneer

Born in Vincennes, Indiana, he served in the War of 1812 and the Black Hawk War of 1832, and became famous as a frontiersman. In 1836 he was appointed Governor of the Territory of Wisconsin and became a member of the House of Representatives in 1841. He was US Senator for Wisconsin from 1848 to 1857.

Dodge, Mary Elizabeth, *née* Mapes 1831–1905
US writer

Born in New York City, she married William Dodge, a lawyer, in 1851, and after his death in 1858 turned to writing books for children, notably *Hans Brinker; or, The Silver Skates* (1865), which became a children's classic. From 1873 she was the editor of *St Nicholas Magazine*.

Dodge, Theodore Ayrault 1842–1909
US soldier and military historian

Born in Pittsfield, Massachusetts, he fought in the Civil War, losing a leg at Gettysburg, and wrote such books as *A Bird's-eye View of our Civil War* (1885), *Alexander* (1890), *Hannibal* (1891) and *Caesar* (1892).

Dodgson, Charles Lutwidge See **Carroll, Lewis**

Dods, Meg See **Johnstone, (Christian) Isobel**

Dodsley, Robert 1704–64
English playwright

Born in Mansfield, Nottinghamshire, he was a stocking weaver's apprentice, then a footman. In 1735 his *Toy Shop*, a dramatic piece, was through **Pope**'s influence acted in Covent Garden, with great success. With his profits, and £100 from Pope, he set up as a bookseller, publishing **Edward Young**, **Mark Akenside**, **Oliver Goldsmith** and the as yet unknown Dr **Johnson**, among others. He founded the *Annual Register* with **Edmund Burke** in 1759. His other plays include the collection *Trifles* (1745) and the highly successful tragedy *Cleone* (1758). He is chiefly remembered for his *Select Collection of Old Plays* (12 vols, 1744–45) and his *Poems by Several Hands* (3 vols, 1748; 6 vols, 1758).

Doe, Samuel Kenyon 1951–90
Liberian politician and general

Born in Tuzon, Grand Gedeh county, he joined the army in 1969 and had attained the rank of sergeant by 1975. In 1980 he led a coup, in which President William Tolbert was killed, and Doe replaced him as head of state. The following year he made himself general and army Commander-in-Chief. In 1984 he established the National Democratic Party of Liberia, and in 1985 was narrowly elected President. Widespread dissatisfaction with his rule generated several opposition groups and a virtual civil war erupted in 1989, which the Economic Community of West African States (ECOWAS) attempted to mediate. Doe was killed in the ensuing internal struggle for power.

Doesburg, Theo van, *originally* Christian Emil Marie Kupper 1883–1931
Dutch painter, architect and writer

Born in Utrecht, he became a poet, but took up painting and exhibited at The Hague in 1908. With Piet Mondrian he founded the avant-garde magazine *De Stijl* (1917–31), and devoted himself to propagating the new aesthetic ideas of this movement, based on a severe form of geometrical abstraction known as Neo-Plasticism. By 1921 he was in touch with Le Corbusier, and with the leading figures of the Bauhaus design school at Dessau. He later became increasingly involved in architectural projects, and in 1930 published a 'Manifesto of Concrete Art'.

Doggett, Thomas c.1660–1721
Irish actor

Born in Dublin, he moved in 1691 to London, where he prospered as a comic actor, wrote a play called *The Country Wake* (1696), and became joint-manager of the Haymarket Theatre (1709–10). In 1716, to honour the accession of King George I, he founded a rowing prize, 'Doggett's Coat and Badge', still competed for by Thames watermen on 1 August.

Doherty, Peter Charles 1940–
Australian immunologist and Nobel Prize winner

Born in Brisbane, he studied at the University of Queensland and at Edinburgh University, and worked in Brisbane and Edinburgh before becoming a research Fellow in the department of microbiology at the John Curtin School of Medical Research, Canberra. There in 1973 he and Rolf M Zinkernagel made a breakthrough in the understanding of the human immune system that led to their joint Nobel Prize for physiology or medicine in 1996. In 1975 Doherty moved to the Wistar Institute in Philadelphia, returning to the Curtin School in 1982 as head of the department of experimental pathology. In 1988 he went to Tennessee, where he was appointed chairman of the department of immunology at St Jude's Children's Research Hospital in Memphis, and as adjunct Professor of Paediatrics and Pathology at the University of Tennessee. He received the Paul Ehrlich prize in 1983 and became FRS in 1987.

Dohnanyi, Ernst (Erno) von 1877–1960
Hungarian composer and pianist

Born in Pressburg, he achieved some success with his opera *The Tower of Voivod* (1922), but is perhaps best known for his piano compositions, especially *Variation on a Nursery Theme* (1913), for piano and orchestra.

Doi, Takako, *known in Japan as* the Iron Butterfly 1929–
Japanese politician

Born in Kobe, she studied law at Doshisha University, Kyoto. In the course of an academic career, she became Professor of Constitutional Law before being elected to the Diet, the House of Representatives, or Lower House, of the Japanese parliament in 1969. From 1983 to 1986 she was the vice-chairman of the *Shakaito*, or Japanese Social Party (now the Social Democrat Party of Japan), becoming chairman in 1986. In 1989 her party almost doubled its seats in the Upper House of parliament but she resigned in 1991 as a result of heavy losses in local elections. Despite this she is respected for her pragmatic approach to politics and was appointed Speaker in 1993.

Doig, Peter 1959–
British painter

Born in Edinburgh, he lived in Quebec and Ontario (1966–79) before moving to London and training at the Wimbledon, St Martin's, and Chelsea schools of art (1979–90). Since 1991 he has become known for his landscapes and snowscapes, which emerge out of layers, skeins and blots of paint. Just as landscape is manipulated for human needs such as leisure, so Doig manipulates his canvas, as in *Ski-Jacket* (1993, Tate, London), where the image is reflected across a split panel. Drawn to the woodland setting of Le Corbusier's Habitation, at Briey-en-Forêt, Doig became a resident, and exhibited six paintings of it in London in 1994. Works such as *Pond Life* (1993, McKinsey & Co Inc UK) and *Cabin Essence* (1994, Victoria Miro Gallery, London) also reveal a preoccupation with dwellings engulfed by nature as metaphors for human presence. The winner of the Whitechapel Gallery award, the John Moores Liverpool prize, and the inaugural Prix Eliette von Karajan, Salzburg, he was also nominated for the Turner prize in 1994.

Doisneau, Robert 1912–94
French photographer

Born in Gentilly, Seine, he began experimenting in photography while working in a graphics studio in the 1920s, then became assistant to the modernist photographer André Vigneau. After World War II Doisneau worked for several picture magazines, including the mass-circulation *US Life* magazine. A master of humour who could capture life's absurdities on film, he created images that radiated a mixture of satire and warmth and paid homage to the ordinary. *The Kiss* (1950) is perhaps his best-known picture.

Doisy, Edward Adelbert 1893–1986
US biochemist and Nobel Prize winner

Born in Hume, Illinois, he studied at Harvard, and was director of the department of biochemistry at St Mary's Hospital, St Louis (1924–65). In collaboration with US embryologist Edgar Allen (1892–1943) he conducted research on reproduction and hormones, and studied the female sex hormones estrone (1929), estriol (1930) and estradiol (1935). In his Porter Lectures at the University of Kansas (1936), he delineated the four stages of endocrinology as recognition of gland, detection of the hormone, its extraction and purification, and finally structure and synthesis. In 1939 he isolated two forms of the coagulant agent Vitamin K (discovered earlier by Henrik Dam), and they shared the 1943 Nobel Prize for physiology or medicine. He wrote *Sex Hormones* (1936) and *Sex and Internal Secretions* (1939).

Dolabella, Publius Cornelius c.70–43BC
Roman politician

Cicero's profligate son-in-law, he sought refuge from his creditors with Gaius Julius Caesar in 49BC. Two years later, as tribune, he brought forward a bill cancelling all debts, which led to bloody struggles in Rome. On Caesar's murder (44BC) he appropriated the consular insignia and gave his support to the conspirators; Marcus Antonius gave him the province of Syria. At Smyrna he murdered the proconsul, Trebonius, and so drained money from the towns of Asia that he was outlawed. He retreated to Laodicea, and when it fell to **Cassius**, Dolabella commanded one of his own soldiers to kill him.

Dolci, Carlo 1616–86
Italian painter

He was born in Florence. His works, which are scattered over all Europe, include many Madonnas, *St Cecilia* (Dresden), *Herodias with the Head of John the Baptist* (Dresden) and the *Magdalene* in the Uffizi, Florence.

Dolci, Danilo 1925–97
Italian social worker

Born in Trieste, he qualified as an architect, but decided to fight poverty in Sicily. He managed to extract municipal funds to launch his campaign in three of Sicily's poorest towns—Trappeto, Partinico and Montalepre—building schools and community centres to teach the people the methods by which they could raise themselves by their own efforts, helped by funds and social workers from many European countries, and becoming known as 'the **Gandhi** of Sicily'. Opposed by the government, his own Church and the Mafia, he was imprisoned in 1956 for four months for leading a gang of unemployed in repairing a road, unpaid and without permission, ie, an 'upside down strike', and again in 1957 for obscenity in publishing the pathetic life stories of little boys who sold themselves for vice in return for food. Although neither Communist nor fellow-traveller, he was awarded the Lenin Peace prize in 1956. His books include *To Feed the Hungry* (trans 1959), *Waste* (trans 1963), *The Man Who Plays Alone* (trans 1969) and *Sicilian Lives* (trans 1982), and some published poetry.

Dole, Bob (Robert) 1923–
US Republican politician

Born in Russell, Kansas, he served in the Kansas state legislature and the House of Representatives before he won a Senate seat in 1968. He has chaired the Republican national committee, and was an unsuccessful Republican nominee for the vice-presidency in 1976. Having sought the Republican nomination for the presidency in 1980 and 1988, without success, he became a presidential candidate in 1996, but lost the election to **Bill Clinton**.

Dole, Elizabeth Hanford, *née* Hanford 1936–
US politician and campaign organizer

Born in Salisbury, North Carolina, she trained as a lawyer and in 1975 married **Robert Dole**, who became US Senator for Kansas in 1969. She has held numerous posts in the US government, including that of a commissioner on the Federal Trade Commission and two Cabinet-level positions, Secretary of Transportation (1983–87) and Secretary of Labor (1989–90). In 1990 she became the president of the American Red Cross. She has also taken an active role in her husband's campaigns to be elected for the office of Vice-President of the USA in 1976, and supported his bid for the presidency in 1980, 1984, 1990 and 1996.

Dole, Sanford Ballard 1844–1926
Hawaiian politician

Born in Honolulu, the son of Protestant missionaries, he studied law at Williams College in Massachusetts and returned home to practice, eventually serving on the Hawaiian supreme court. In 1893 he helped organize the revolt that deposed Queen **Liliuokalani**, and in 1894, after President **Grover Cleveland** refused to annex Hawaii, he became the President of the Republic of Hawaii. When Cleveland left office and the USA agreed to take over Hawaii, Dole served as its first territorial governor (1900–03).

Dolet, Étienne, *known as* the Martyr of the Renaissance 1509–46
French printer and humanist

Born in Orleans, he studied at the University of Paris, and in Venice (1526–32) he learned about humanism. Living in Lyons from 1534, he wrote *Dialogus de imitatione ciceroniana* (1535) against **Erasmus**, and came under strong suspicion of heresy. He killed a man in self-defence and fled to Paris, where friends intervened with the king (1537). In Lyons he set up a printing press, on which he printed translations of the classics, as well as Erasmus and **Rabelais**. He was arrested more than once for publishing heretical books. In 1544 he was found guilty of heresy (on a charge mainly based on an alleged mistranslation of **Plato**, in which he was accused of denying the immortality of the soul) and was burned in Paris. His chief contribution to classical scholarship was his *Commentarii* (2 vols, 1536–38, 'Commentaries on the Latin Language').

Dolin, Anton, *originally* Patrick Healey-Kay 1904–83
English dancer and choreographer

Born in Slinfold, Sussex, he studied under Grace and Lilly Cone, Serafoma Astafoeva and **Bronislava Nijinska**, and was a principal with **Sergei Diaghilev's** Ballets Russes, from 1924, for which he danced in **Michel Fokine's** *Spectre de la Rose* and **George Balanchine's** *Le Bal* and *The Prodigal Son* (1929). He was a founder-member of the Camargo Society and a principal with the Vic-Wells Ballet during the 1930s, co-founding the **Markova**–Dolin Ballet in 1935. The partnership became known particularly for its interpretation of *Giselle*. From 1950 to 1961 he served as London Festival Ballet's first artistic director, choreographing for the company. His list of works includes *Rhapsody in Blue* (1928), *Variations for Four* (1957) and *Pas de deux for Four* (1967). He wrote *The Life and Art of Alicia Markova* (1953) and published his autobiography in 1960. 📖 *Last Words: A Final Autobiography* (1985)

Dollfuss, Engelbert 1892–1934
Austrian politician

Born in Texing, he studied at Vienna and Berlin. He became leader of the Christian Socialist Party, and as Chancellor (1932–34) he suspended parliamentary government, drove the Socialists into revolt and crushed them (February 1934). Purged of its Socialist majority, parliament then granted Dollfuss power to remodel the state but in July 1934 a Nazi putsch in Vienna culminated in his assassination. 📖 P R Sweet, *Mussolini and Dollfuss* (1948)

Döllinger, Johann Joseph Ignaz von 1799–1890
German Catholic theologian

Born in Bamberg, he was ordained in 1822, then became Professor of Ecclesiastical History and Law at Munich almost continuously from 1826 to 1871, when he was elected Rector. A staunch Ultramontane, he published *Die Reformation* (1846–48, 'The Reformation'), but a visit to Rome in 1857 caused a change in his opinions. In 1870 the Vatican Council promulgated the decree of papal infallibility, and in 1871 Döllinger issued a letter withholding his submission. Excommunicated, he took a leading part in the summoning of the congress in Munich out of which arose the Old Catholics. From this time Döllinger lectured in favour of the union of the various Christian churches and, in two conferences, agreement was reached on various points with the Anglican and Orthodox churches. He represented his university in the Bavarian Chamber from 1845 to 1847, and from 1849, sat in the Frankfurt Parliament of 1848–49. He published a history of moral controversies in the Catholic church since the 16th century (1888), *Akademische Vorträge* (1888–91) and other books.

Dollo, Louis Antoine Marie Joseph 1857–1931
Belgian palaeontologist
Born in Lille, he became an assistant (1882) and keeper of mammals (1891) at the Royal Museum of Natural History in Brussels. In 1893 he enunciated Dollo's law of irreversibility in evolution which states that complex structures, once lost, are not regained in their original form. While this is generally true, exceptions are found.

Dollond, John 1706–61
English optician
He was born in London, of Huguenot parentage. A silk weaver to trade, he became an optician in 1752, and devoted himself to the invention of an achromatic telescope (c.1747).

Dolmetsch, (Eugène) Arnold 1858–1940
British musical-instrument maker
Born in Le Mans, France, he went to England to study at the Royal College of Music (1883). Interested in early music and original instruments, he became involved in their restoration and manufacture around 1890. From 1892 he gave concerts at the Century Guild owned by Arthur Heygate Mackmurdo. He exhibited a harpsichord at the Arts and Crafts Exhibition in 1896, and his clavichord of 1897 was decorated by Edward Burne-Jones. In 1919 he made the first modern recorder and in 1928 the Dolmetsch Foundation was established to support his work. He was the author of *The Interpretation of the Music of the Seventeenth and Eighteenth Centuries* (1893). 📖 Margaret Campbell, *Dolmetsch: The Man and His Work* (1975)

Dolomieu, Déodat Guy Gratet de 1750–1801
French geologist, soldier and traveller
Born in Dolomieu, Dauphiné, he travelled extensively in Italy, Sicily, Portugal, the Alps and the Pyrenees, writing on earth tremors in Calabria and Italian volcanoes. He accompanied Napoleon I's expedition to Egypt (1799), but was imprisoned when returning to France. In 1800 he was freed from imprisonment in Sicily to become a professor at the Natural History Museum in Paris on the recommendation of René Just Haüy, but his health had been damaged by prison and he died shortly afterwards. The mineral dolomite is named after him and by extension the Dolomite mountain range of Italy.

Dolphy, Eric (Allan) 1928–64
US jazz saxophonist and clarinettist
Born in Los Angeles, he began to play clarinet at school, and developed into an important, iconoclastic jazz performer on several reed instruments, notably alto saxophone and bass clarinet. He came to notice with the Chico Hamilton Quintet in the 1950s, then moved to New York in 1959, where he worked with such seminal (and diverse) figures as Charles Mingus, John Coltrane, Ornette Coleman, Max Roach and Gunther Schuller, among many others. His own recordings, notably *Out To Lunch* (1964), are crucial works of the period. 📖 R Horricks, *The Importance of Being Eric Dolphy* (1990)

Domagk, Gerhard Johannes Paul 1895–1964
German biochemist and Nobel Prize winner
Born in Lagow (now in Poland), he graduated in medicine at Kiel University (1921), and taught at the universities of Greifswald and Münster before becoming director of the I G Farbenindustrie laboratory for experimental pathology and bacteriology in 1927. In a search for new dyes and new drugs, Domagk particularly sought a treatment against streptococci which caused widespread and generally lethal infections. One dye became of potent benefit when added to a substance called prontosil, which only worked in the living animal, being converted to sulfanilamide in the body. This discovery led to a new wonder drug and ushered in a new age in chemotherapy. In 1939 Domagk's original acceptance of the Nobel Prize for physiology or medicine was cancelled upon instruction from the German government, but he finally received the award in 1947.

Domenichino, *also called* Domenico Zampieri 1581–1641
Italian painter
He was born in Bologna and painted in the style of the Bolognese school. His masterpiece is the *Last Communion of St Jerome* (1614), in the Vatican.

Domenico Veneziano c.1400–1461
Italian painter
Known for his altarpiece in the Uffizi in Florence, he is represented in the National Gallery, London, by a *Madonna and Child*.

Domenico Zampieri See Domenichino

Domett, Alfred 1811–87
New Zealand statesman, journalist and poet
Born in London, England, of New Zealand origins, he was a friend of Robert Browning, who eulogized him in 'Waring'. Praised by Tennyson, he was among the first to use New Zealand scenery and Maori myths, evoked in typically Wordsworthian verse. An early settler in Nelson and its MP from 1855, he was involved in moves towards self-government and became premier of New Zealand briefly during the Land Wars (1862–63). 📖 *The Diary of Alfred Domett, 1872–1885* (1953)

Domingo, Placido 1941–
Spanish tenor
Born in Madrid, he moved to Mexico with his family and studied piano and conducting at the National Conservatory of Music, Mexico City. In 1959 he made his debut as a baritone, taking his first major tenor role, that of Alfredo in *La Traviata* ('The Strayed Woman'), in 1960. From 1962 to 1965 he was a member of the Israeli National Opera. He first sang in New York in 1965, at La Scala, Milan, in 1969 and Covent Garden, London, in 1971. His controlled, intelligent vocal technique and skilful acting have made him one of the world's leading lyric-dramatic tenors, and among his successes have been Puccini's *Tosca*, Giacomo Meyerbeer's *L'Africaine*, Verdi's *Otello*, Bizet's *Carmen*, and Jacques Offenbach's *Les Contes d'Hoffmann* ('The Tales of Hoffmann'). In 1990 he performed alongside José Carreras and Luciano Pavarotti in the acclaimed 'Three Tenors' concert held in the open-air Caracalla Theatre in Rome. He published his autobiography, *My First Forty Years*, in 1983. He made his Wagner debut in *Die Walküre* (1870, 'The Valkyrie') at Covent Garden in 1996 marking his 25th anniversary of performing there, and the same year he conducted Puccini's *Tosca* at the Royal Opera House. 📖 D Sussman, *The World of Placido Domingo* (1985)

Dominguín, *nickname of* Luis Miguel Gonzales Lucas 1926–96
Spanish matador
Born in Madrid, he became a first-rank matador at the age of 18, his style marked by an unflurried elegance and disdain. This sometimes angered the crowds but for purity of style and unruffled, detached courage no matador has ever bettered him. A friend of Hemingway and Picasso, he retired in 1961, but made a triumphant return to the bullring in 1971.

Dominic, St, *also called* Dominic de Guzman c.1170–1221
Spanish founder of the Order of Friars Preachers
Born in Calaruega, Old Castile, he studied at Palencia. His rigorously ascetic life was focused on missionary work, notably among Muslims, 'heretics', and the Albigenses of southern France, but his memory is stained

by his consent to the cruel crusade instigated by Innocent I against the Albigenses, who had murdered his legate, Peter of Castelnau. By the time Dominic died, the Dominican order, which he had founded in 1216, based on the Augustine rule, occupied 60 houses and had spread as far as England, where from their dress the monks were called 'Black Friars'. He was canonized in 1234 by Gregory IX and his feast day is 4 August.

Dominici, Gaston 1877–1965
French farmer and alleged murderer

Born in Digne, Provence, he was sentenced to death in 1954 after prolonged inquiries and a confession (afterwards retracted) for the murder near Lurs, Provence (1952), of Sir Jack Drummond, his wife and their 11-year-old daughter. The case was officially closed in 1956, with Dominici still in a Marseilles prison hospital. In 1957 his sentence was formally commuted to life imprisonment.

Domino, Fats (Antoine) 1928–
US rhythm and blues pianist and singer

Born in New Orleans, he learned to play the piano as a youngster, and performed in local clubs while working in a factory. He was discovered by producer Dave Bartholemew in 1949, and had the first of many collaborative hits with 'The Fat Man' in 1950. His light-toned singing and laid-back but infectious piano style, compounded from New Orleans's rich Creole, Cajun, Latin, blues and jazz heritage, made him one of the first stars of the rock and roll era with songs like 'Ain't That A Shame' and 'Blueberry Hill'. He has retained an affectionate following ever since, and continued to tour and record into the 1990s.

Domitian, *originally* Titus Flavius Domitianus
AD51–96
Roman emperor

The son of Vespasian, he succeeded his elder brother Titus as emperor in AD81. He ruled well at first, and was a zealous administrator and builder; he expanded Roman territory in Britain and tried to improve public morality. However his autocratic manner and severity alienated the Roman upper classes, and his reign declined into violence and terror. He eventually fell victim to one of many conspiracies, and the Flavian dynasty came to an end with him. 📖 J Janssen, *Domitian* (1919)

Donald, Ian 1910–87
Scottish obstetrician and inventor

The son of a Paisley doctor, he graduated in medicine at St Thomas's Hospital Medical School, London, where he was Reader in Obstetrics and Gynaecology. In 1954 he was appointed to the regius chair of midwifery in Glasgow, a post he held for 22 years. His *Practical Obstetric Problems* (2nd ed 1959) was a best-seller. With the help of the engineer Tom Brown and the Scottish electronics company Kelvin Hughes, he developed echo-sounding with radar techniques to create the first contact compound pregnancy scanner. His pioneering ultrasound diagnosis was reported in *The Lancet* in 1958. The first images were poor but he improved the apparatus and by the 1970s it was used routinely, Glasgow becoming a world centre in this field. He was a man of enthusiasm and strong opinions, and his anti-abortion stance gained him more media publicity than his contributions to obstetrics.

Donaldson, James 1751–1830
Scottish newspaper proprietor and philanthropist

Born in Edinburgh, he inherited the *Edinburgh Advertiser*, and left about £240,000 to found a 'hospital' (school) for 300 poor children. It was built (1842–51) from designs by William Playfair at a cost of about £120,000 and subsequently became Donaldson's School for the Deaf.

Donaldson (of Lymington), John Francis Donaldson, Baron 1920–
English judge

He was educated at Charterhouse and Trinity College, Cambridge. After practising at the Bar, mainly in commercial cases, he became a judge (1966), a Lord Justice of Appeal (1979) and Master of the Rolls (1982–92). As such he was known for his expeditious hearing of cases. He was made a life peer in 1988.

Donat, Aelius See Donatus Magnus

Donat, Robert 1905–58
English film and stage actor

He was born in Manchester, of Polish descent. Elocution lessons to cure a stammer led to his involvement with the theatre. His stage performances include parts in *Julius Caesar* (1921), *Knave and Queen* (1930), *Saint Joan* (1931) and *Precious Bane* (1932), which brought him a contract with Alexander Korda. One of the most popular stars of 1930s British cinema, he appeared in films like *The Private Life of Henry VIII* (1932), *The Thirty-Nine Steps* (1935) and *Goodbye Mr Chips* (1939), which earned him an Academy Award (Best Actor). His later career was blighted by ill health, although he continued to give much-admired performances. He died shortly after completing a poignant performance as the Chinese mandarin in *Inn of the Sixth Happiness* (1958).

Donatello See panel p546

Donati, Giambattista 1826–73
Italian astronomer

Born in Pisa, he was educated at the University of Pisa and became an assistant at the observatory in Florence in 1852. In 1864 he succeeded Giovanni Battista Amici as director there. He discovered the brilliant comet ('Donati's comet') of 1858. Noted for his research on stellar spectra, he was the first to observe the spectrum of a comet.

Donatus, Aelius fl.4th century AD
Roman grammarian

He taught grammar and rhetoric in Rome in about 360AD, amongst others to St Jerome. His treatises form a course of Latin grammar (*Ars grammatica*), and in the Middle Ages were the only textbooks used in schools, so that 'Donat' in western Europe came to mean a grammar book. He also wrote commentaries on Terence and Virgil.

Donatus Magnus, *also called* Aelius Donat
d.c.355AD
North African bishop

He was a leader of the Donatists, a 4th-century puritan Christian sect in North Africa who objected to Roman influences. As Bishop of Carthage (AD312–47), he was involved in the Donatist schism of the North African Church.

Don Carlos See Carlos, Don

Donders, Franciscus Cornelis 1818–89
Dutch oculist and ophthalmologist

Born in Tilburg, he studied at the military medical school at Utrecht and later at Utrecht University. In 1840 he graduated in medicine from the University of Leyden, returning to Utrecht where he pursued researches in physiological chemistry. Aided in part by Hermann von Helmholtz's invention of the ophthalmoscope, Donders established himself as a specialist in diseases of the eye, setting up a polyclinic for eye diseases at the university, improving the efficiency of spectacles by the introduction of prismatic and cylindrical lenses, and writing extensively on eye physiology. In 1862 he was appointed Professor of Physiology at Utrecht.

Donatello, *real name* Donato di Niccolo c.1386–1466
Florentine sculptor

Donatello was one of the most important artists of early Renaissance Italy. He trained in the Florence Cathedral workshop under **Ghiberti** and received his first commission in 1408. He was the first sculptor since classical times to produce works which were fully rounded and independent in themselves and not mere adjuncts of their architectural settings. The evolution of his highly-charged and emotional style can be traced in a series of figures of saints he executed for the exterior of Or San Michele and another series of prophets for the Campanile, in which his interest in classical antiquity is evident.

In the 1420s, in partnership with **Michelozzi**, he produced the monument to the antipope **John XXIII** in the Baptistery which influenced all subsequent tomb design.

In 1443 he migrated to Padua where he produced the bronze equestrian portrait of the military commander known as Gattemelata—the first lifesize equestrian statue since antiquity. The celebrated bronze statue of **David** is a key work of the Renaissance, as is the multiple-viewpoint *Judith and Holofernes* in the Piazza della Signoria in Florence. The anguished, expressive statue of **Mary Magdalene** has no counterpart elsewhere in the 15th century and not until **Michelangelo** was Donatello's expressive power equalled.

📖 C Avery, *Donatello: An Introduction* (1994); Bonnie A Bennett and David G Wilkins, *Donatello* (1984); H Janson, *The Sculpture of Donatello* (1957).

Dondi, Giovanni de' 1318–89 and Jacopo de'
1290–1359
Italian horologists and physicians
Son and father, they were born in Chioggia and Padua, and both studied medicine at the University of Padua, and returned there as teachers. First Jacopo designed and built an astronomical clock for the Prince of Padua which he completed in 1344, then Giovanni began in 1348 to construct an even more sophisticated one on which he was engaged for the next 18 years. In addition to the usual planetary motions it showed the feasts of the Church calculated in accordance with a perpetual calendar, and Giovanni described every detail of its construction in his *Planetarium*. The clock was so far ahead of its time, however, that only one replica is known to have been made until the 20th century.

Dönitz, Karl 1891–1980
German Nazi politician and naval commander
Born in Grünau, near Berlin, he joined the submarine service of the Imperial Germany Navy in 1916, and became a staunch advocate and supporter of U-boat warfare. He planned **Hitler's** U-boat fleet, was made its commander in 1936, and in 1943 succeeded **Erich Raeder** as Commander-in-Chief of the German navy. Becoming Führer on the death of Hitler, he was responsible for the final surrender to the Allies, and in 1946 was sentenced to 10 years' imprisonment for war crimes. 📖 Peter Padfield, *Dönitz the Last Fuhrer: Portrait of a Nazi War Leader* (1984)

Donizetti, (Domenico) Gaetano (Maria)
1797–1848
Italian composer
Born in Bergamo, he studied music there and in Bologna. His first opera, *Enrico di Borgogna*, was successfully produced at Venice (1818), but his first internationally famous work was *Anna Bolena*, produced at Milan in 1830. *L'Elisir d'amore* (1832, 'The Elixir of Love') and *Lucrezia Borgia* (1833) also achieved lasting popularity, as did *Lucia di Lammermoor* (1835). In Paris (1840), he staged *La Fille du régiment* ('The Daughter of the Regiment') and *La Favorita* ('The Favourite'), the last act of which was written in three to four hours. The comic opera *Don Pasquale* (1843) was his last success, soon after which he became paralysed and then insane. 📖 Herbert Weinstock, *Donizetti and the World of Opera in Italy, Paris and Vienna in the First Half of the Nineteenth Century* (1963)

Donkin, Bryan 1768–1855
English engineer and inventor
Born in Sandoe, Northumberland, he was first a land agent but then became apprenticed to a mechanic and within a few years had developed the first automatic paper-making machine (1804). He continued to improve the machine and by 1850 had built almost 200 of them,

effecting a radical change in the paper-making industry. In 1813 he patented one of the first rotary printing machines, but this was not successful. He also improved on the food-preserving invention of **Nicolas Appert** by using sealed tins instead of glass jars, and built a factory to supply the Royal Navy with canned meat and vegetables.

Donleavy, J(ames) P(atrick) 1926–
Irish author
He was born in Brooklyn, New York City, of Irish parents, and after serving in the US navy during World War II, studied microbiology at Trinity College, Dublin, where he became a friend of **Brendan Behan**. While living on a farm in Wicklow he began painting, then wrote his first novel, *The Ginger Man*, published in 1955. Picaresque, bawdy, presenting an apparently totally irrational hero, it was hailed as a comic masterpiece. The novels, plays and stories that followed are on the same theme, that of his own 'dreams and inner desires', and have been described as paler versions of *The Ginger Man*. He became an Irish citizen in 1967 and among his other works are *A Singular Man* (1963), *Meet My Maker,The Mad Molecule* (short stories, 1964), *The Beastly Beatitudes of Balthazar B* (1968), written as a play in 1981, *The Onion Eaters* (1971), *A Fairy Tale of New York* (1973, a novel written from the play of 1960), *The Destinies of Darcy Dancer, Gentleman* (1971), *Schultz* (1980), *Are you Listening, Rabbi Low?* (1987) and *That Darcy, That Dancer, That Gentleman* (1990). His paintings have been exhibited in Dublin (1950–51), New York (1955), London (1975–91) and Belfast (1987). Later works include the autobiographical *The History of the Ginger Man* (1994) and *The Lady Who Liked Clean Rest Rooms* (1995). 📖 Charles G Masinton, *J P Donleavy* (1975)

Donnay, Maurice 1859–1945
French dramatist
He was born in Paris, and originally studied to be a civil engineer. His brittle fin-de-siècle comedy *Amants* (1895, 'Lovers') achieved considerable popularity, as did *Lysistrata* (1893), an adaptation of **Aristophanes**. Later successes in that vein included *La douloureuse* (1897, 'The Sad Woman') and *L'autre danger* (1902, 'The Other Danger'). His more serious works concerned social problems, and were felt to be daring at the time in dealing with subjects such as the marriage between Jew and Gentile in *Le retour de Jérusalem* (1903, 'The Return from Jerusalem'). 📖 P Bathille, *Maurice Donnay. Son œuvre* (1931)

Donne, John c.1572–1631
English poet
He was born in London, the son of a prosperous ironmonger, and connected through his mother with Sir **Thomas More**. Although a Catholic, he was admitted to Hart Hall, Oxford, and later graduated at Cambridge,

where his friendship with Sir **Henry Wotton** began. He decided to take up law and entered Lincoln's Inn in 1592. After taking part in the 2nd Earl of **Essex**'s two expeditions to Cadiz in 1597 and the Azores in 1598 (reflected in his poems 'The Storm' and 'The Calm'), he became (1598) secretary to Sir **Thomas Egerton**, keeper of the Great Seal. His daring works and strong personality indicated a career as notable as that of his contemporary **Francis Bacon**, but he was dismissed and imprisoned after his secret marriage to Egerton's niece, Anne More. Having turned Protestant, he lived in Mitcham in Surrey, but still sought favour and employment at the court. Under the direction of Thomas (later Bishop) Morton he undertook a religious polemic against Catholics. He had already written his passionate and erotic poems, *Songs and Sonnets* and his six *Satires* and his *Elegies*, but published no verse until 1611 when his *Anniversarie* appeared, a commemorative poem for Elizabeth Drury, daughter of his benefactor, Sir Robert Drury, whose house in the Strand offered hospitality to the poet when in London. A second *Anniversarie* followed which displayed his metaphysical genius at its best. His religious temper is seen in more lyrical form in the *Divine Poems*, some of which certainly date from before 1607. These, like most of his verse, were published posthumously but his pieces circulated widely among learned and aristocratic friends. How difficult his journey to the Anglican faith was may be judged from the satirical 'Progresse of the Soule' (1601). This unfinished poem is antiheretical, but also sceptical in a disturbing way. Donne's ten-year hesitation to take orders is variously explained as due to an indecision, or to a sense of unworthiness because of his profligate youth, or to his still wanting civil employment. He courted the distinguished ladies of the time, in verse letters of laboured but ingenious compliment. More injurious to his name was a poem for the marriage (regarded as scandalous) of the king's favourite, Robert Carr, to the divorced Countess of Essex. In his funeral poems, of which the first and second *Anniversaries* are the best, he also paid court to the great. His prose works of this period include *Pseudo-Martyr* (1610), which is an acute polemic against the Jesuits. More interesting is his *Biothanatos*, which discussed the question of suicide, which he claimed to contemplate on occasion. He decides that suicide is permissible in certain cases, a conclusion at variance with that affirmed in his third *Satire*, but confirmed in a letter to his friend Sir Henry Wotton. King **James VI and I** encouraged him to go into the Church (1614), and promoted him to the deanship of St Paul's in 1621 when he relinquished his readership at Lincoln's Inn. Several of his sermons are still extant. In this middle period of his life he accompanied Sir Robert Drury to France and Spain. In 1619 and 1620 he was in Germany, where he preached one of his most noble sermons before the exiled Queen **Elizabeth** of Bohemia, King James's daughter. Donne's creative years fall into three periods: from 1590 to 1601, a time of action, passion and cynicism; from his marriage to his ordination in 1614, a period of anguished meditation and flattery of the great; and the period of his ministry, which includes two sonnet sequences, *La Corona* and *Holy Sonnets*, the latter containing (no. xvii) an anguished tribute to his wife, who died in 1617. Also of this period are the fine 'Hymne to God, the Father', 'To God My God, in my Sicknesse' and 'The Author's Last Going into Germany'. ⌑ J B Leishman, *The Monarch of Wit* (1951); R C Bald, *John Donne: a life* (1920)

Donnelly, Ignatius 1831–1901
US politician and writer

Born in Philadelphia, Pennsylvania, he qualified for the Bar in 1852, and moved to Minnesota in 1856, becoming Lieutenant-Governor and Governor (1859–63) and later Radical Republican congressman (1863–69). He became identified with reform, editing the *Anti-Monopolist* and later the *Representative*, and was for several years president of the State Farmers' Alliance in Minnesota, a forerunner of the Populist Party, which nominated him for Vice-President. As a prophet of reform his most enduring legacy is a horrific novel, *Caesar's Column* (1891), predicting tyranny and oppression. His *Atlantis, The Antediluvian World* (1882) was a highly popular development of the idea of a former continent drowned under the Atlantic Ocean. His *The Great Cryptogram* (1888) sought to prove **Francis Bacon** had written the plays usually attributed to **Shakespeare** and had hidden ciphered messages in the plays declaring his authorship. ⌑ M Ridge, *Ignatius Donnelly: portrait of a politician* (1962)

Donoso (Yanez), José 1928–96
Chilean novelist

Born in Santiago, he attended the University of Chile and spent two years at Princeton, USA, on a Doherty Foundation fellowship (1949–51). He worked as a longshoreman, teacher, editor and journalist. His first collection of short stories won Chile's Municipal prize in 1951, and in 1962 he received the William Faulkner Foundation prize for Chile for his novel *Coronación* (1957, Eng trans *Coronation*, 1965). His work reflects urban life with its madness, opulence and decay. Among his other novels are *El obsceno pájaro de la noche* (1970, Eng trans *The Obscene Bird of Night*, 1973), *Casa do Campo* (1978, Eng trans *A House in the Country*, 1984), *La Desesperanza* (1985, 'Desperation') and *Conjeturas sobre la memoria de mi tribu* (1996, 'Conjectures about the Memory of my Tribe'). ⌑ A C Polar, *Donoso: la destruccion de un mundo* (1975)

Donovan, Terence Daniel 1936–96
English photographer

Born in the East End of London, he left school at the age of 11 and attended a course in blockmaking at the London School of Engraving and Lithography. By the age of 15 he had become interested in photography and joined the studio of John French, a leading fashion photographer. He became famous for a style which juxtaposed the luxurious with the everyday, photographing models against harsh and bleak backgrounds. He published a collection of photographs, *Glances*, in 1983.

Doolittle, Hilda, *known as* H D 1886–1961
US Imagist poet

Born in Bethlehem, Pennsylvania, she was educated at Gordon School, the Friends' Central School in Philadelphia, and Bryn Mawr College (1904–06). She lived in London from 1911 and married **Richard Aldington** in 1913. After their divorce in 1937, she settled near Lake Geneva. Her many volumes of poetry include *Sea Garden* (1916), *The Walls do not Fall* (1944), *Flowering of the Rod* (1946) and *Helen in Egypt* (1961). She also wrote several novels, notably *Palimpsest* (1926), *Hedylus* (1928), *Bid Me to Live* (1960) and *Tribute to Freud* (1965). ⌑ *The Gift* (1982)

Doolittle, James Harold 1896–93
US air force officer

At the outbreak of war with Japan, he commanded 16 B-25 bombers which took off from Admiral **William Halsey**'s aircraft carriers to raid Tokyo in April 1942, with decisive effects on Japanese naval strategy. He and other survivors landed in China. He later commanded the 12th Army Air Force (AAF) in North Africa, the 15th AAF in Italy (1943) and 8th AAF in the UK for operations in north-west Europe (1944). After the war he was vice-president and director of Shell Oil (1945–59).

Doppler, Christian Johann 1803–53
Austrian physicist

Born in Salzburg, he showed early mathematical ability and after studying at the Polytechnic Institute in Vienna, he was appointed Professor of Mathematics and

Accounting at the State Secondary School in Prague. In 1851 he was appointed Professor of Physics at the Royal Imperial University of Vienna, the first such position to be created in Austria. 'Doppler's principle', which he enunciated in a paper in 1842 when he was Professor of Elementary Mathematics and Practical Geometry at the State Technical Academy in Prague, explains the frequency variation observed when a vibrating source of waves and the observer approach or recede from one another. The Doppler effect applies to all forms of electromagnetic radiation and is used in astronomy, where the changing wavelengths of approaching or receding celestial bodies provide important evidence for the concept of an expanding universe.

Dora, Sister See Pattison, Dorothy Wyndlow

Doran, John 1807–78
English journalist and theatre historian

Born in London of Irish parents, he was educated there. He wrote out a melodrama, *Justice, or the Venetian Jew* (1824), followed by many other works, including *A Lady of the Last Century* (1873, an account of **Elizabeth Montagu**), *Mann and Manners* (1876, the letters of Sir **Horace Mann** to **Horace Walpole**), and books on kings and queens and on stage history. He was frequently acting-editor of the *Athenaeum*, edited the *Church and State Gazette* (1841–52), and was editor of *Notes and Queries* (1870–78).

Dorat, Jean See Daurat, Jean

Dorati, Antal 1906–88
US conductor and composer

He was born in Budapest, Hungary, and studied at the Budapest Academy and University. After various opera and ballet posts in Europe, he went to the USA in 1945 and became a US citizen two years later. There he directed the Minneapolis Symphony Orchestra (1949–60) and made a number of acclaimed recordings with them. He recorded all the symphonies of **Haydn** with the Philharmonia Hungarica, an orchestra of expatriate Hungarians founded in 1957, who regularly performed with him. He also conducted 20th century music, notably that of **Stravinsky** and Les Six, and of his compatriot **Bartók**. He was principal conductor of the BBC Symphony Orchestra (1963–67), and had strong associations with other major orchestras, including the Royal Philharmonic Orchestra and the Detroit Symphony Orchestra (1977–81). He received an honorary knighthood in 1983.

Doré, Gustave 1832–83
French painter and book illustrator

Born in Strasbourg, he first became known for his illustrations to **Rabelais's** works (1854) and to *The Wandering Jew* and **Honoré de Balzac's** *Contes drolatiques* (1865). Other works include illustrated editions of **Dante's** *Inferno* (1861), the *Contes* of **Charles Perrault** and *Don Quixote* (1863), the *Purgatorio* and *Paradiso* of Dante (1868), the Bible (1865–66), *Paradise Lost* (1866), **Tennyson's** *Idylls of the King* (1867–68), **Jean de La Fontaine's** *Fables* (1867), and many other series of designs, which in the end deteriorated. He also executed much in colour.

Doren, Carl Clinton Van See Van Doren, Carl Clinton

Doren, Mark Albert Van See Van Doren, Mark Albert

Dorfman, Ariel Birthdate unavailable
Chilean playwright, novelist and short-story writer

Born in Argentina, he was brought up in Chile but was forced into exile in 1973, and did not return until 1990. He gained international acclaim with his play *Death and the Maiden* (1991, Laurence Olivier award for Best Play, 1992),

about a South American torture victim who takes revenge on her torturer. He also wrote the screenplay for the film of the same name by **Roman Polanski** (1995). Dorfman's other works include a book of essays, *Some Write to the Future* (1991), a collection of short stories, novels, such as *Konfidenz* (1995), and *The Reader* (1995), a play about a censor who discovers he is reading the story of his own life.

Doria, Andrea c.1466–1560
Genoese admiral and mercenary

Born in Oneglia, he served under various Italian princes then returned to Genoa in 1501. In 1513 he received command of the Genoese fleet, and in 1519 defeated the Turkish corsairs off Pianosa. When the imperial faction were restored to power in Genoa (1522), he transferred his allegiance to **Francis I** of France. In command of the French fleet, he defeated the Emperor **Charles V** in Italy and Provence, blockaded Genoa, and proclaimed the independence of the republic in 1527. After a period of papal service he rejoined the French, but in 1529, fearing Francis's power, he went over to Charles V, entered Genoa amid popular acclamation, and established an oligarchy which lasted to the end of the republic in 1797. The emperor gave him the Order of the Golden Fleece and the princeship of Malfi. He continued his war against the Turks and **Khair-Ed-Din Barbarossa**, but had as many setbacks (Algiers, 1541; Herba, 1560) as successes. His later years were disturbed by the conspiracy of the Fieschi in 1547 that forced him to flee Genoa. His family continued to rule after his death in Genoa until the end of the 18th century.

Dorn, Friedrich Ernst 1848–1916
German chemist

Born in Guttstadt, East Prussia, he was educated at Königsberg, taught physics at Darmstadt and Halle. In 1900 he noticed that radium apparently becomes radioactive if swept with a current of gas. This led him to the discovery of a radioactive gas which is emitted by radium as part of its decay processes. He called it 'niton' but it is now known as radon.

Dornberger, Walter Robert 1895–1980
US rocket engineer

Born in Giessen Hesse, Germany, he was an engineer and officer in the German army. He set up an experimental rocket station at Kummersdorf which successfully fired a 650lb-thrust motor (295kg) in 1932. By 1934 he had designed a 3,300lb-thrust rocket (1,497kg) which reached a height of 1.5 miles (2.4km). In World War II the work was transferred to Peenemünde where in 1942 a 46-foot (13.8m) 14-ton rocket was launched to the edge of the atmosphere. From 1944 to 1945, 1,500 of these V-2 rockets with explosive warheads were launched against Great Britain and 2,000 into Antwerp, Belgium. After spending three years as a prisoner of war in England (1945–47), he went to the USA as a consultant to the air force. In 1950 he joined the Bell Aircraft Corporation, and worked on the Rascal air-to-surface missile and the Dyna-Soar manned Space Glider programme. He wrote *V2* (1952), an account of his work in jet propulsion.

Dornier, Claudius 1884–1969
German aircraft designer

Born in Kempten, he was educated at technical college in Munich. He designed the first all-metal aircraft in 1911 after entering the service of Graf von Zeppelin, and in 1914 founded the Dornier works at Friedrichshafen on Lake Constance. He manufactured seaplanes and flyingboats, including the famous 12-engined Do X (1929), and the Dornier twin-engined bomber which was a standard Luftwaffe type in World War II.

Dörpfeld, Wilhelm 1853–1940
German archaeologist

Born in Barmen, he was **Heinrich Schliemann's** collaborator and successor at the site of Troy in Turkey, and became professor at Jena in 1923. The chronology of Troy set out in his *Troja und Ilion* (1902, 'Troy and Ilium') served to date European prehistory for the first 30 years of the 20th century.

Dorrell, Stephen James 1952–
English Conservative politician

Born in Worcester, he was educated at Uppingham and Oxford and gave up a career in his father's industrial overall business to become MP for Loughborough in 1979. During **John Major's** administration he rose from being a junior health minister (1990–92) to Financial Secretary to the Treasury (1992–94) and Secretary of State for National Heritage (1994–95). In 1995 he succeeded **Virginia Bottomley** as Secretary of State for Health. In 1996 problems arose relating to the safety of British beef following speculation that BSE ('mad cow disease') could be related to Creutzfeldt–Jakob disease in humans. In early 1997 he displayed his left-of-centre stance by voicing his party's commitment to fund the National Health Service out of taxes and by rejecting suggestions that it should become a safety-net for the poor. Following the Conservatives' election defeat that year, he lost the leadership contest to **William Hague**.

Dors, Diana, *originally* Diana Fluck 1931–84
English actress

Born in Swindon, Wiltshire, she was a student at RADA. She made her film debut in *The Shop at Sly Corner* (1946) and was signed to a long-term contract with Rank who groomed her for stardom in their 'Charm School'. Promoted as a sex symbol, she was cast in various low-budget comedies, and despite an effective dramatic performance in *Yield to the Night* (1956) and highly publicized visits to Hollywood she was soon typecast in blowsy supporting roles. Her accomplished stage work in *Three Months Gone* (1970) brought her a selection of good character parts in films like *Deep End* (1970) and *The Amazing Mr Blunden* (1972). Later roles were undistinguished but her personal popularity never dimmed as she performed in cabaret and as a television agony aunt. She returned to the screen in *Steaming* (1984) just before she died.

Dorsey, Thomas A(ndrew) 1899–1993
US gospel musician

Born in Villa Rica, Georgia, the son of a revivalist preacher, he began his career as a blues pianist, performing with blues greats such as **Ma Rainey** in the 1920s as well as with his own bands. He combined blues melodies and rhythms with Christian religious music in about 1,000 gospel songs, including 'Take My Hand, Precious Lord' (1931). He founded the first gospel choir at Ebenezer Baptist Church in Chicago (1931) and established the National Convention of Gospel Choirs and Choruses (1933) to promote gospel music. He is known as 'the father of gospel music'.

Dorsey, Tommy (Thomas) 1905–56
US trombonist and bandleader

Born in Shenandoah, Pennsylvania, the son of a bandleader, he formed big bands, sometimes co-led by his brother Jimmy (1904–57, alto saxophone, clarinet), that included many accomplished jazz soloists. They existed as the Dorsey Brothers Orchestra from 1932 to 1935, reforming again in 1953 until Tommy's death. Both brothers were in great demand as session musicians in the late 1920s, with the expansion of radio in the USA, and their fame was revived through a regular television show in the 1950s. Renowned for its sweet-toned instrumental style, his work hovered between jazz and dance music.

Dorson, Richard M 1916–
US historian and folklorist

Born in New York City, he studied American history at Harvard before teaching there (1943–44) and at Michigan State University (1944–56). He moved to Indiana University in 1957, becoming Distinguished Professor of History and Folklore in 1971. He organized the Folklore Institute and became its first director in 1963. He was general editor of the series *Folktales of the World* by Chicago University Press, and has produced numerous books, articles and essays, doing much to raise awareness of folklore both as a field of study and as a continuing feature of the modern world. His publications include *Buying the Wind: Regional Folklore in the US* (1964), *American Folklore and the Historian* (1971), *Folklore and Folklife: an introduction* (1972), *America in Legend* (1973), *Folktales Told Around the World* (1975), *Folklore and Fakelore: essays towards a discipline of folk studies* (1976) and *Folklore in the Modern World* (1978).

Doshi, Balkrishna Vithaldas 1927–
Indian architect

Born in Poona, he was educated there and in Bombay. He worked as senior designer with **Le Corbusier** at Chandigarh and Ahmedabad (1951–57). In 1956 he joined Stein and Bhalla in partnership. His architectural aesthetic derived from the vernacular, traditional and functional styles of India. The user of local materials and craftsmanship, he was influenced by the late works of Le Corbusier and **Louis Kahn**. His architectural works include the City Hall, Toronto (1958), several mills (1958–77), the Indian Institute of Management (1962–74, with Kahn), in Ahmedabad, and Vidyadhar Nagar New Town, Jaipur. He is founder and honorary director of Kanoria School of Arts, Ahmedabad (1984–) and was Architect of the Year in 1991.

Dos Passos, John Roderigo 1896–1970
US novelist, playwright and journalist

Born in Chicago, the grandson of a Portuguese immigrant, he was educated at Choate and Harvard. In 1916 he went to Spain to study architecture but was caught up in World War I and served in the US Medical Corps. Thereafter he lived in the USA but travelled widely on journalistic assignments. In middle age he led a simple life on Cape Cod and later he and his wife moved to his father's farm at Spence's Point, Virginia. He had a precocious start as an author, publishing *One Man's Initiation* in 1917 when he was 21. The fiercely anti-war *Three Soldiers* (1921) confirmed his talent and in *Manhattan Transfer* (1925) his confidence and ambition grew, its rapid narrative transitions and collectivist approach foreshadowing the monumental *U.S.A.* trilogy: *The 42nd Parallel* (1930), *1919* (1932) and *The Big Money* (1936). A digressive, dynamic epic, it consists of a medley of newsreel footage, snatches of popular songs, brief but vivid sketches of public figures and prose-poetry, disparate elements that together represent the character and course of US life in the early decades of the 20th century. He also wrote three plays. He was an anti-capitalist, but his second trilogy, *District of Columbia* (1939–49, 1952), was less radical in its criticism of the free-enterprise system, and his later work continued this trend towards conservatism. *The Best Times* (1966), his last book, was a reminiscence of his youth. ▢ V S Carr, *Dos Passos: a life* (1984)

Dos Santos, Jose Eduardo 1942–
Angolan politician and nationalist

Born in Luanda, he joined the People's Movement for the Liberation of Angola (MPLA) in 1961 and was forced into exile in what is now the Democratic Republic of Congo while the struggle for independence developed into a civil war between the MPLA and the National Union for the Total Independence of Angola (UNITA). In Congo he founded

Dostoevsky, Fyodor Mikhailovich, *also spelt* Dostoyevsky 1821–81
Russian novelist

Dostoevsky was born in Moscow, the second of a physician's seven children. His mother died in 1837 and his father was murdered by his serfs a little over two years later. After leaving a private boarding school in Moscow he studied from 1838 to 1843 at the Military Engineering College at St Petersburg, graduating with officer's rank. His first published short story was 'Poor Folk' which gained him immediate recognition. In 1849 he was arrested and sentenced to death for participating in the socialist 'Petrashevsky Circle', but during the preparations for his execution a commutation was announced and he was sent instead to Siberia, where he was confined in a convict prison at Omsk until 1854. There, among other works, he read Dickens's *Pickwick Papers* and *David Copperfield*; and he experienced a religious crisis in which he rejected socialism for Russian Orthodoxy. A result of his experience at Omsk was *The House of the Dead* (1860).

In 1861 he began the review *Vremya* ('Time') with his brother Mikhail, and he spent the next two years travelling abroad, which confirmed his anti-European outlook. At this time he met Mlle Suslova, the model for many of his heroines, and succumbed to the gaming tables. He fell heavily into debt but was rescued by Anna Grigoryevna Smitkina, whom he married in 1867. They lived abroad for several years but he returned to Russia in 1871 to edit *Grazhdanin*, to which he contributed his 'Author's Diary'.

Like **Dickens**, Dostoevsky was both horrified and fascinated by the Industrial Revolution, and his fiction is dark with the suffering caused by poverty and appalling living conditions, crime and the exploitation of children. Second only to those of **Leo Tolstoy**, his novels *Crime and Punishment* (1866), *The Idiot* (1868), *The Devils* (1872) and *The Brothers Karamazov* (1880) have been profoundly influential, and their impact on Robert Louis Stevenson's *Dr Jekyll and Mr Hyde* (1886), among many others, is conspicuous. Others have reacted with hostility to his work, including **Henry James**, **Joseph Conrad**, and above all **D H Lawrence** ('he is like the rat, slithering along in hate').

📖 J Frank, *Dostoevsky* (2 vols, 1976–83); R Hingley, *Dostoevsky: His Life and Work* (1978).

> 'All people seem to be divided into 'ordinary' and 'extraordinary'. The ordinary people must lead a life of strict obedience and have no right to transgress the law because... they are ordinary. Whereas the extraordinary people have the right to commit any crime they like and transgress the law in any way just because they happen to be extraordinary.' From *Crime and Punishment*, part 3, ch.5 (trans by David Magarshak).

the MPLA Youth and in 1963 was sent to Moscow to study petroleum engineering and telecommunications. He returned to Angola in 1970 and rejoined the war (which continued after independence in 1975) between the government (assisted by Cuba) and UNITA (supported by South Africa). He held key positions under President **Agostinho Neto** and when Neto died in 1979, succeeded him. By 1989, with US help, he had negotiated the withdrawal of South African and Cuban forces, and a ceasefire between MPLA and UNITA. A peace agreement was signed in 1991, and a general election was held in 1992. Dos Santos won 50 per cent of votes, not enough to avoid a second round of voting, and amidst accusations of rigging from UNITA, the civil war recommenced. To the relief of the UN negotiators who orchestrated it, an accord was signed by the Angolan government and UNITA representatives despite mutual accusations of default.

Dosso Dossi, *properly* Giovanni di Niccolò Lutero 1479–1542
Italian religious painter

Born near Mantua, he was a friend of **Ludovico Ariosto**, and painted some pictures jointly with his brother Battista (c.1497–1548).

Dostoevsky, Fyodor Mikhailovich See panel above

Doty, Paul Mead 1920–
US biochemist

He studied at Pennsylvania State College, Columbia University and at Cambridge, and became assistant professor (1948–50) and associate professor (1950–56) at Harvard, where he has been professor since 1956. He has been consultant to the Arms Control and Disarmament Agency of the National Security Council since 1973. In 1961 Doty discovered DNA renaturation, establishing the specificity and feasibility of the DNA bonding structure. A very special feature of DNA is that two of the constituent bases make chemical bonds to the other two bases, forming the double helix and allowing the transcription of DNA to its mirror image RNA. This structure also permits use of labelled specific nucleic acids to 'find' their counterpart DNA sequence *in vitro*, the basis for all experimental manipulation of nucleic acids.

Dou or Douw, Gerard 1612–75
Dutch painter

Born in Leyden, he studied under **Rembrandt** (1628–31). At first he mainly occupied himself with portraiture, but soon turned to genre painting characterized by precisely painted scenes of everyday life. He is known as the founder of the Leyden school of *fijnschilders* ('fine painters') and his 200 works include portraits of himself and his wife, *The Poulterer's Shop*, in the National Gallery, London, and his celebrated *Dropsical Woman* (1663), in the Louvre, Paris.

Doubleday, Abner 1819–93
US general and alleged inventor of baseball

He was born in Ballston Spa, New York. He served as a major-general of volunteer Union troops in the Civil War, fighting at Antietam, Fredericksburg and Gettysburg. He had been known for organizing team games during his boyhood, and in 1907 a commission reported that Doubleday had invented baseball at Cooperstown, New York, in 1839. This report has been discredited, and it is now known that a game similar to baseball was played in the USA and England long before Doubleday's time.

Doudart de Lagrée, Ernest-Marie-Louis de Gonzague 1823–68
French explorer

Born in Saint-Vincent-de-Mercuze, and educated at the École Polytechnique in Paris, he joined the navy and served in the Crimean War, then became French representative at the court of King Norodom of Cambodia in 1863. He was appointed to the Mekong River expedition (1866–68), which was charged with assessing the possibility of a navigable waterway to China. The expedition left Saigon in June 1866 and made the first survey of the ruined temples of Angkor before continuing northwards, crossing the Sambor rapids and going on to the forbidding Khone Falls on the Laos border, showing that the river was unsuitable for commercial traffic. Their scientific work continued but Doudart de Lagrée died in Huitse after persistent illness, and leadership of the expedition was taken over by Francis Garnier.

Douglas
Scottish noble family

It includes William the Hardy, a crusader, who harried the monks of Melrose, and was the first man of mark who joined William Wallace in the rising against the English (1297). His son, 'the Good' Sir James Douglas (c.1286–1330), called also 'the Black Douglas' from his swarthy complexion, was Robert Bruce's greatest captain in the War of Independence. The hero of 70 fights, he was slain fighting the Moors in Andalusia, bearing the heart of Bruce. Hugh, brother of Sir James, and a canon of Glasgow, made over the family's large propery (1342) to his nephew Sir William.

Douglas, Lord Alfred Bruce 1870–1945
English poet

The son of the 8th Marquis of Queensberry, he wrote a number of impressive sonnets, collected in *In Excelsis* (1924) and *Sonnets and Lyrics* (1935). He is remembered for his association with Oscar Wilde, to which his father objected, thereby provoking Wilde to bring the ill-advised libel action which led to his own arrest and imprisonment. He wrote two books on Oscar Wilde, and *The Autobiography of Douglas* (1929). 🕮 R C Cooke, *Bosie: the story of Lord Alfred Douglas* (1963)

Douglas, Bill 1934–91
Scottish film director

Born in Newcraighall, near Edinburgh, the illegitimate son of a miner, he was brought up amidst misery and penury, an experience which formed the basis of his famed autobiographical trilogy. After National Service he pursued a career as an actor and writer for the theatre, working as an assistant to Joan Littlewood and attending film school before making his directorial debut with *My Childhood* (1972). Together with *My Ain Folk* (1973) and *My Way Home* (1977), it formed an intense, dramatic interpretation of his childhood and adolescence. A painstaking, uncompromising artist, he made only one further feature film, *Comrades* (1986), an ambitious, epic account of the Tolpuddle Martyrs, partly conveyed as a pre-history of the cinema by an itinerant lanternist.

Douglas, David 1798–1834
Scottish botanist and plant collector

Born in Scone, Perthshire, he was apprenticed as a gardener at Scone Palace, and later went on many collecting trips with Sir William Hooker, becoming expert in preparing herbarium specimens. In 1823 he became a plant collector for the Horticultural Society of London, and left on an expedition to North America where he discovered many new species such as *Aster douglasii*, *Garrya elliptica* and *Paeonia brownii*. The most famous of the many plants Douglas introduced into cultivation was the Douglas fir (*Pseudotsuga taxifolia*), and the Douglas squirrel was also renamed after him. After some months in London, Douglas sailed again for western North America and explored southern California (1830–32), travelled up the Fraser and Simpson rivers in western Canada, and sailed to Hawaii, where he was gored to death by a bull.

Douglas, Donald Wills 1892–1981
US aircraft designer and manufacturer

Born in Brooklyn, New York City, he attended the US Naval Academy and the Massachusetts Institute of Technology (MIT). Chief engineer to the Glenn L Martin Aircraft Company in 1915, he set up his own company (Davis-Douglas Co) in California in 1920. His Douglas World Cruisers made a historic round-the-world flight in

1924, and the all-metal low wing Douglas DC-2 transport of 1934 was second in the England–Australia Air Race, with 14 passengers. The DC-3 (C-47, Dakota) followed in 1936, and the DC-4, -6 and -7 and the jet-engined transports DC-8, -9 and -10. During World War II he produced the B-19 bomber and other craft. He was chairman of his company, Douglas Aircraft, until it merged with McDonnell Aircraft as the McDonnell Douglas Corporation in 1967.

Douglas, Earls of Morton
Scottish nobility

The name was first recorded in 1248. Sir William Douglas, the Knight of Liddesdale (c.1300–1353), was assassinated by his kinsman, William, 1st Earl of Douglas. Sir James Douglas of Dalkeith married a daughter of James VI and I, and was created 1st Earl of Morton (1458). The earldom devolved the 3rd earl's youngest daughter's husband, the regent James Douglas Morton, and from him the present Earl of Morton is descended. James, 2nd Earl of Douglas and Mar, had an illegitimate son, Sir William Douglas of Drumlanrig, whose descendants were created viscounts of Drumlanrig (1628), earls of Queensberry (1633), marquises of Queensberry (1681), dukes of Queensberry (1683), earls of March (1697) and earls of Solway (1706). On the death of the 4th Duke of Queensberry (1810), the titles were split up among the Scottish nobility.

Douglas, Gawain or Gavin c.1474–1522
Scottish poet and prelate

Born in Tantallon Castle, East Lothian, he was educated at St Andrews, and possibly Paris, for the priesthood, and from 1501 to 1514 was dean or provost of the Collegiate Church of St Giles, Edinburgh. After the Battle of Flodden (1513), in which King James IV fell, Douglas's nephew, the 6th Earl of Angus, married the widowed Queen Margaret Tudor, and through her influence, Douglas became Bishop of Dunkeld (1515). On the fall of Angus in 1521, he fled to London to obtain the aid of Henry VIII, but died suddenly of the plague. His works include *The Palice of Honour* (c.1501) and a translation of Virgil's *Aeneid*, with prologues (finished c.1513), the first version of a Latin poet published in the vernacular. He was one of the first to point out the differences between Scots and the English language.

Douglas, George See Brown, George Douglas

Douglas, Keith Castellain 1920–44
English poet

Born in Kent, he began publishing verse in magazines during his teens. Edmund Blunden, his tutor at Merton College, Oxford, gave encouragement and later arranged for the publication of a slim *Selected Poems* (1943), using verses sent back from the Western Desert, where Douglas was serving with a tank regiment; it was the only book Douglas saw published in his lifetime. He was killed by a shell fragment. It was his faintly surreal and bluntly unoptimistic memoir of the fighting in the Western Desert, *Alamein to Zem Zem* (1946), that began to establish a posthumous reputation which only became secure two decades after his death when Ted Hughes, an admirer, introduced an important selection. The *Complete Poems* appeared in 1979, edited by Desmond Graham.

Douglas, Kirk, *originally* Issur Danielovich 1916–
US film actor

Born in Amsterdam, New York, the son of poor Russian immigrants, he acted on Broadway and served in the US navy before moving to Hollywood and making his film debut in *The Strange Love of Martha Ivers* (1946). An ambitious actor, noted for his intensity, he received Best Actor Academy Award nominations for *Champion* (1949), *The Bad and the Beautiful* (1952) and *Lust For Life* (1956), in which he played **Van Gogh**. His numerous films include *Paths of Glory* (1957), *Spartacus* (1960) and *Lonely Are the Brave* (1962). He directed the film *Scalawag* (1973) and *Posse* (1975). He has published an autobiography, *The Ragman's Son* (1988), and several novels. In 1996 he received a special Academy Award.

Douglas, Mary, *née* Tew 1921–
English social anthropologist

Born in Italy, she studied at Oxford, and carried out fieldwork among the Lele of the Belgian Congo in 1949–50 and 1953. From 1970 until 1978 she was Professor of Social Anthropology at University College London. In 1977 she moved to the USA, becoming Avalon Foundation Professor in the Humanities at Northwestern University (1980–85), professor emeritus in 1985, and visiting professor at Princeton (1986–88). She is especially known for her studies of systems of cultural classification and beliefs about purity and pollution, as in *Purity and Danger* (1966) and *Natural Symbols* (1973), themes to which she returned in her study of Old Testament practices, *In the Wilderness: The Doctrine of Defilement in the Book of Numbers* (1993). In addition, she has contributed significantly to economic anthropology in *The World of Goods* (1979, with Baron Isherwood), and to the sociology of risk in *Risk and Culture* (1982, with Aaron Wildavsky), *Risk Acceptability According to the Social Sciences* (1986) and *Risk and Blame* (1992). She was awarded the CBE in 1992.

Douglas, Michael (Kirk) 1944–
US film actor and producer

Born in New Brunswick, New Jersey, he gained experience of the film industry through his father, **Kirk Douglas**, and first appeared in *Hail Hero!* (1969). Working as a producer, he shared the Best Picture Academy Award won by *One Flew Over the Cuckoo's Nest* (1975). Among the films he has starred in are *Romancing the Stone* (1984), *Jewel of the Nile* (1985), *Fatal Attraction* (1987), *Wall Street* (1987), for which he won a Best Actor Academy Award, *Basic Instinct* (1992), *Disclosure* (1994) and *The Ghost in the Darkness* (1996).

Douglas, (George) Norman 1868–1952
Scottish novelist and essayist

He was born in Thüringen, Austria. His father was Scottish and his mother was part-German, and he was educated at Uppingham School and at Karlsruhe in Germany before joining the Foreign Office in 1894. He served in St Petersburg, then settled in Capri in 1896, where his circle embraced **Compton Mackenzie**, **Ouida** and **D H Lawrence**. His first book, *Unprofessional Tales* (1901), was co-authored with his wife and published under the pseudonym 'Normyx', but *Siren Land* (1911) first attracted critical attention. An account of his travels in southern Italy, it is an exotic collage of anecdote, philosophy and myth. *Old Calabria* (1915) garnished his reputation and is a minor classic. Other travel books are *Fountains in the Sun* (1912), *Alone* (1921) and *Together* (1923). Of his novels, the most famous is *South Wind* (1917). Set in Nepenthe (Capri) among a floating population of expatriates, it is an unapologetic celebration of hedonism to which its author was a happy convert. *Looking Back* (1933) is an unusual autobiography, in which he recalls his life and his friends by taking up their calling cards and describing them one by one, at length or tersely, depending on his mood. 📖 R D Lindeman, *Norman Douglas* (1965)

Douglas, Sir Roger Owen 1937–
New Zealand politician and economist

Born in Auckland, he was Labour MP for two Auckland electorates between 1969 and 1990, becoming Minister of Finance in the **Lange** ministry (1984–88). In 1985 *Euromoney* magazine named him Finance Minister of the Year; his stringent policies revived his country's economy

but ended New Zealand's years as a 'cradle-to-grave' welfare state. He resigned from parliament in 1990 and formed a new party, the Association for Consumers and Taxpayers (ACT), but left this to return to consultancy. His theories are propounded in two books, *There's Got to be a Better Way* (1981) and *Towards Prosperity* (1987).

Douglas, Stephen Arnold 1813–61
US judge and politician

Born in Brandon, Vermont, he studied law and moved to Illinois in 1833. He rose rapidly in state Democratic politics, then served in the US House of Representatives (1843–47) and the Senate (1847–61). Known as 'the Little Giant' because of his short stature, forceful presence and boundless energy, he argued for westward expansion and manifest destiny, supporting US claims to Oregon, the annexation of Texas and the Mexican War. On the question of slavery he maintained that each territory should decide whether to be a free or a slave state, and he helped win passage of the Compromise of 1850 and the Kansas–Nebraska Act. His 1858 campaign for re-election to the Senate against Republican candidate **Abraham Lincoln** became the occasion for a series of famous debates in which Lincoln returned again and again to the issue of slavery, and though Douglas won the election his effort to find a middle-ground on the subject only succeeded in alienating the South and eroding his popularity as a national political figure. He was the Democratic nominee for President in 1860 but was narrowly defeated by Lincoln.

Douglas, Sir William Fettes 1822–91
Scottish landscape and figure painter

Born in Edinburgh, he painted *Hudibras and Ralph visiting the Astrologer* and *David Laing in his Study*, and was appointed curator of the National Gallery of Scotland, Edinburgh, in 1771.

Douglas, William Orville 1898–1980
US judge

Born in Maine, Minnesota, he was educated at Whitman College and Columbia University. He was a law professor at Yale, then became a member (1934) and chairman (1937–39) of the Securities and Exchange Commission. He was a strong supporter of the New Deal, and was appointed to the Supreme Court in 1939. As a justice he supported civil rights and liberties, and guarantees of freedom of speech and of the press. He wrote *We the Judges* (1956), *A Living Bill of Rights* (1961), autobiographical works, and many books on his travels.

Douglas (of Kirtleside), William Sholto Douglas, 1st Baron 1893–1969
English air force officer

Educated at Tonbridge School and Lincoln College, Oxford, he served in World War I as a fighter pilot. After a brief career as a commercial test pilot, he rejoined the RAF, and at the outbreak of World War II was assistant Chief of Air Staff. He became Air Officer Commanding successively of Fighter Command (1940–42), Middle East Air Command (1943–44) and Coastal Command (1944–45), and directed the successful anti-submarine campaign which played a decisive part in the later stages of the war. After the war he commanded the British Air Force of Occupation in Germany (1945–46), and became military governor of the British zone of occupation (1946–48). He also chaired British European Airways (1949–64). He was knighted in 1941 and created a peer in 1948.

Douglas-Home, Alec See Home (of the Hirsel), Baron

Douglas-Home, William 1912–92
Scottish playwright

He was born in Edinburgh, and educated at Eton and Oxford. The author of a number of plays, principally light-hearted comedies, he is best known for *The Chiltern Hundreds* (1947), *The Thistle and the Rose* (1949) and *The Reluctant Debutante* (1955). ▫ *Mr. Home, pronounced Hume* (1979); *Half-Term Report: an autobiography* (1954)

Douglass, Andrew Ellicott 1867–1962
US astronomer
He was born in Windsor, Vermont. After research work at the Lowell Observatory at Flagstaff, Arizona, he became Professor of Physics and Astronomy at Arizona University (1906) and later director of the Stewart Observatory (1918–38). He investigated the relationship between sunspots and climate by examining and measuring the annual growth rings of long-lived Arizona pines and sequoias. He coined the term 'dendrochronology' ('tree-dating') in his *Climatic Cycles and Tree Growth* (3 vols, 1919–36).

Douglass, Frederick, originally Frederick Augustus Washington Bailey 1817–95
US abolitionist
Born a slave in Tuckahoe, Maryland, he learned to read and write in childhood as a household servant, then was returned to a plantation where he laboured as a field hand. He escaped from a Baltimore shipyard in 1838, and changed his name. He settled in New Bedford, Massachusetts, became an agent of the Massachusetts Anti-Slavery Society and wrote *Narrative of the Life of Frederick Douglas* (1845). He lectured on slavery (1845–47) in Great Britain, where £150 was collected to buy his freedom, and travelled in Ireland, but returned to the USA to buy his freedom, thus banishing his fear of recapture, and set up a campaigning antislavery newspaper, *North Star*. In 1847 he started *The North Star* in Rochester, New York, an abolitionist journal that he edited for 16 years. He held various public offices and was US Minister to Haiti (1889–91). He wrote two more autobiographical books, *My Bondage and My Freedom* (1855) and *Life and Times* (1881). ▫ Arna Bontemps, *Free at Last: The Life of Frederick Douglass* (1971)

Douhet, Giulio 1869–1930
Italian general
He was born in Caserta. From 1912 to 1915 he was commander of Italy's first military aviation unit, but in 1916 he was court-martialled and imprisoned for publicly deploring Italy's aerial weakness, until the truth of his claims was shown by the defeat of Italian arms by the Austrian air force at Caporetto. He became head of the Italian Army Aviation Service in 1918 and was promoted to general in 1921. A renowned military aviation strategist, he wrote books on strategic bombing and the future devastation of major cities by mass bomber raids, such as *Il domino dell'aria* (1921, 'The Command of the Air'), which influenced attitudes to civil defence prior to World War II.

Doulton, Sir Henry 1820–97
English pottery manufacturer
Born in Lambeth, London, he entered his father's pottery there, and in 1846 introduced stoneware drain pipes instead of flat-bottomed brick drains. In 1848 he started works, later the largest in the world, near Dudley. He furthered the revival in art pottery.

Doumer, Paul 1857–1932
French politician
Born in Aurillac, he worked as a jeweller, journalist and deputy (1888), before becoming Governor-General of French Indo-China (1897–1902), President of the Chamber (1905–06), President of the Senate (1927–31) and President of the Third Republic (1931–32). He was shot by a mad Russian émigré, Gorgalov.

Douw, Gerard or Gerrit See Dou, Gerard

Dove, Arthur Garfield 1880–1946
US painter
Born in Canandaigua, New York, he earned his living as a commercial illustrator from 1903. In 1910 he began a series of abstract paintings, such as *Nature Symbolized* (1914) and *Fog Horns* (1929), which bear comparison with contemporary works by **Wassily Kandinsky**. In the 1920s he experimented with collage incorporating mirrors, sand and metal. His later abstract work is suggestive of natural organic forms.

Dove, Heinrich Wilhelm 1803–79
German climatologist
Born in Liegnitz, Silesia (now in Poland), he was Professor of Natural Philosophy at Berlin University (1845–79), director of the Royal Prussian Meteorological Institute (1848–79), and was a great collector and organizer of meteorological observations. He established the first comprehensive network of meteorological observations over Europe, enabling specific weather situations to be studied in detail and providing an early climatology. From these and other observations, he produced monthly mean maps of isotherms over much of the globe, forming the basis of maps of temperature in many early atlases. He also investigated in detail some remarkable storms, notably that of 23–29 January 1850. His method of analysis using graphs of pressure and temperature along lines of latitude and longitude was later used by **Robert Fitzroy** to investigate the Royal Charter storm of 1859. He also applied the stereoscope to the detection of forged bank notes.

Dove, Rita Francis 1952–
US poet
Born in Akron, Ohio, she is Professor of English at the University of Virginia. Her first book was *Ten Poems* (1977). *The Yellow House On The Corner* (1980) contained a sequence of poems told from the point of view of Negro slaves, and historical figures have recurred throughout her work. She was awarded the Pulitzer Prize for poetry in 1987 for *Thomas and Beulah* (1986), in which she recreated the lives of her grandparents from courtship to death. Other collections include *Museum* (1983), *The Other Side of the House* (1988) and *Grace Notes* (1989). *Fifth Sunday* (1985) is a collection of short stories.

Dow, Neal 1804–97
US reformer
He was born in Portland, Maine, and as Mayor of Portland was the author of the Maine Liquor Law (1851), a stringent prohibition measure. In 1880 he was the Prohibition candidate for the presidency.

Dowden, Edward 1843–1913
Irish critic
Born in Cork, he was educated at Queen's College, Cork, and at Trinity College, Dublin, and in 1867 became Professor of English Literature there, only four years after graduating. He wrote several books on **Shakespeare** (1875–93), as well as *Studies in Literature* (1888–95), *Southey* (1879), *Life of Shelley* (1886), *History of French Literature* (1897), *A Woman's Reliquary* (poems, 1913), *Letters*, and *Poems* (1914).

Dowding, Hugh Caswall Tremenheere Dowding, 1st Baron 1882–1970
Scottish air force chief
Born in Moffat, Dumfriesshire, and educated at Winchester and at the Royal Military Academy, Woolwich, he joined the army in 1900 and the air force in 1914 and was decorated for service in World War I. As Commander-in-Chief of Fighter Command (1936–40), he organized the air defence of Great Britain, and in August to

September the German air force was defeated in the momentous Battle of Britain. He was relieved of his post in November 1940 and represented the Minister for Aircraft Production in the USA (1940–42) before retiring. Created a peer in 1943, he became interested in spiritualism, and his *Many Mansions* (1943) contained communications attributed to men killed in the war. 📖 Basil Collier, *Leader of the Few: The Authorized Biography of Air Chief Marshall, the Lord Dowding of Bentley Priory, GCB, GCVO, CMG* (1957)

Dowell, Sir Anthony 1943–
English dancer and director

Born in London, he trained at Sadler's Wells and the Royal Ballet School. A skilful and elegant technician, he first performed with the Royal Ballet in 1961 and was chosen to partner Antoinette Sibley in Sir Frederick Ashton's *The Dream* (1964), a partnership which was to be highly successful. He was promoted to principal dancer in 1966 since then has danced all the major roles in the classical repertoire as well as having many new roles created for him by major choreographers, some of the most notable being in *Monotones* (1965), *Enigma Variations* (1968) and *A Month in the Country* (1976), all by Ashton, *Shadowplay* (1967) by Antony Tudor, *Manon* (1974) by Kenneth Macmillan and *Four Schumann Pieces* (1975) by Hans van Manen. He was principal dancer of the American Ballet Theater (1978–80), but returned to the Royal Ballet as artistic director (1986–). He was knighted in 1995. 📖 Nicholas Dromgoole, *Sibley and Dowell* (1976)

Dowie, John Alexander 1847–1907
US religious leader

Born in Edinburgh, Scotland, he emigrated to Australia in 1860 and became a Congregational pastor in Sydney. In 1888 he emigrated to the USA, where he organized the Christian Catholic Church in Zion (1896). He became a faith healer, and proclaimed himself 'Elijah the Restorer', and in 1901 he founded near Chicago the prosperous industrial and banking community called 'Zion City'. He was deposed from his autocratic rule there in 1906 due to opposition to his fiscal irresponsibility (and to alleged polygamy).

Dowland, John 1563–1626
English lutenist and songwriter

Born possibly in Westminster, London, he gained a music degree at Oxford in 1588, later also graduating at Cambridge. Having failed, as a Catholic, to become a court musician to Queen Elizabeth I, he entered the service of the Duke of Brunswick in 1594, and subsequently went to Italy, where he met with some English Catholic refugees. Fearing for his own reputation he wrote to Sir Robert Cecil denouncing them, which restored him to favour in England, to where he returned in 1596. His *First Books of Songes or Ayres of Foure Partes with Tableture for the Lute* appeared in 1597 and ran to five editions by 1613. In 1598 he became lutenist to Kristian IV of Denmark. Back in London, he brought out his *Lachrymae* (1605), which contains some of the finest instrumental consort music of the period, and is dedicated to Anne of Denmark. He is now remembered chiefly for his songs, such as 'Weep you no more, sad fountains', and 'Awake, sweet love'. 📖 Diana Poulton, *John Dowland* (1972)

Dowling, Stephen 1904–86
English strip cartoonist

Born in Liverpool, he studied art and did advertising agency work before teaming with his brother, copywriter Frank Dowling. They created newspaper strips, starting with *Tich* (1931) in the *Daily Mirror*, followed by *Ruggles* (1935–60), a family soap opera, *Belinda Blue-Eyes* (1936–42), and the fantasy super-hero *Garth*.

Downing, Sir George, 1st Baronet c.1623–1684
English soldier and diplomat

Born in Ireland, he emigrated to New England with his parents in 1638 and attended the newly founded Harvard College. Returning to England, he fought for parliament and later undertook several diplomatic missions for Cromwell, including that of ambassador to The Hague, where he associated with the Royalist exiles so that at the Restoration he continued as ambassador and received other offices, as well as a baronetcy (1663). As a diplomat he was an expert in commercial matters, but achieved a reputation for contentiousness and duplicity which led Charles II to use him as an instrument in provoking the Dutch into war. Downing Street in London was named after him.

Downing, Sir George, 3rd Baronet 1684–1749
English landowner

Born in Cambridgeshire, he was the founder of Downing College, Cambridge. Being childless, he stipulated that his estates should pass to each of four cousins in turn, and if they died without issue the money should be used to found a college named after him. Even when the last cousin died childless in 1764, the widow refused to give up the estates, and Downing College did not receive its charter until 1800. He was the grandson of Sir George Downing.

Dowsing, William c.1576–1679
English Puritan

Born in Laxfield, Suffolk, he purged over 150 Suffolk churches of stained glass, brasses, paintings and other relics of 'popery' in 1644. He was also responsible for much iconoclasm in Cambridgeshire.

Dowson, Ernest Christopher 1867–1900
English poet

Born in London and brought up mainly in France, he studied at Oxford, then helped his father to manage the dry dock in Limehouse, but spent more time in literary activity. His friends included Lionel Johnson, Arthur Symons, Oscar Wilde and W B Yeats. From 1894 writing became his livelihood, and *Verses* appeared in 1896 and *Decorations* in 1899. He also published stories, a verse play and translations, and collaborated on two novels. From 1895 he lived mostly in France, but in 1899 he returned to London, where he died of tuberculosis. His poetry was influenced by Paul Verlaine and the Decadents. The two best-known poems, 'Vitae summa brevis' (1896) and 'Cynara' (1891), have contributed several stock phrases to English: 'days of wine and roses', 'gone with the wind' and 'I have been faithful to thee, Cynara! in my fashion'. 📖 *Letters* (1967, D Flower and H Maas eds); M Longaker, *Ernest Dowson* (1944, rev edn 1968)

Doyle, Sir Arthur Conan 1859–1930
Scottish writer of detective stories and historical romances, creator of Sherlock Holmes

Born of Irish parentage in Edinburgh, he was educated at Stonyhurst and in Germany, and studied medicine at Edinburgh. Initial poverty as a young practitioner in Southsea and as an oculist in London coaxed him into authorship. *A Study in Scarlet* introduced that prototype of the modern detective in fiction, Sherlock Holmes, and his good-natured friend Dr John Watson. *The Adventures of Sherlock Holmes* were serialized in the *Strand Magazine* (1891–93) and published as books under such titles as *The Sign of Four* (1890) and *The Hound of the Baskervilles* (1902). They became so popular that when Conan Doyle tried to kill off his hero, he was compelled in 1903 to revive him. However, his historical romances, *Micah Clarke* (1887), *The White Company* (1890), *Brigadier Gerard* (1896) and *Sir Nigel* (1906), have more literary merit and are underrated, and *Rodney Stone* (1896) is one of his best novels. He served as a physician in the Second Boer War (1899–1902), and his pamphlet, *The War in South Africa* (1902), justifying Great Britain's action, earned him a knighthood (1902). He used his detective powers to some effect outside fiction in attempting to show that the criminal cases of the Parsee Birmingham lawyer, Edaljee (1903), and alleged murderer Oscar Slater (1873–1948) in 1909 were instances of mistaken identity. He also wrote on spiritualism, to which he became a convert in later life. ⬚ O D Edwards, *The Quest for Sherlock Holmes* (1982); H Pearson, *Conan Doyle: His Life and Art* (1943)

Doyle, John, *pseudonym* H.B. 1797–1868
Irish political cartoonist
Born in Dublin, he settled in 1821 in England, where his loyalties were to liberal figures who brought about Catholic emancipation and reform. He revolutionized the art of caricature from the 18th-century grotesques. His subjects were striking likenesses, and included royalty and the Duke of Wellington (to whom Doyle bore a striking physical resemblance), handled critically as a politician but affectionately as a person. Doyle's 'Political Sketches' were issued as large single prints, collected in portfolios and signed 'H.B.' (from two IDs, his Latin initials, one on top of the other). Few knew H.B.'s identity. Doyle was widowed young and brought up an artistically talented family, including Richard Doyle and Charles, father of Arthur Conan Doyle.

Doyle, Richard 1824–83
English caricaturist, book illustrator and watercolour painter
Born in London, he was trained by his father, the noted caricaturist 'H.B.' (John Doyle). He became a contributor to *Punch* in 1843, designed the famous cover that was used from 1849 to 1956, produced the well-known 'Ye Manners and Customs of ye Englyshe' and the first of the famous 'Brown, Jones, and Robinson' travel and other adventures. In 1850 he left, resenting, as a Catholic, attacks on 'papal aggression'. He also illustrated John Ruskin (*King of the Golden River*), Thackeray (*Newcomes*), Dickens (*Battle of Life*) and Leigh Hunt.

Doyle, Roddy 1958–
Irish novelist
Born in Dublin, he worked for 14 years as a teacher in a community school in Kilbarrack (North Dublin), a deprived area which is the 'Barrytown' of his novels. *The Commitments* (1987), *The Snapper* (1990) and *The Van* (1991, filmed 1996) spoke for communities denied a media voice, their comic style acting as a vehicle for Doyle's statement on the plight of the urban dispossessed. The Booker Prize-winning *Paddy Clarke Ha Ha Ha* (1993), narrated through the sense and senses of a 10-year-old boy, similarly exhibits the tragedy that underlines all comedy, as does *The Woman who Walked into Doors* (1996), narrated by the vulnerable Paula, who finds the strength to escape from a violent and abusive marriage.

Drabble, Margaret 1939–
English novelist
Born in Sheffield, Yorkshire, she was educated at the Mount School, York (the Quaker boarding school where her mother taught), and Newnham College, Cambridge. She acted for a short time, then turned to writing. Divorced from her first husband, the actor Clive Swift, in 1972 (after having three children), she married Michael Holroyd in 1982. Frequently mirroring her own life, her novels concentrate on the concerns of intelligent, often frustrated middle-class women. *A Summer Bird-Cage* (1963), *The Garrick Year* (1964), *The Millstone* (1965), *Jersualem the Golden* (1967), *The Needle's Eye* (1972), *The Ice Age* (1977), *The Middle Ground* (1980), and the trilogy comprising *The Radiant Way* (1987), *A Natural Curiosity* (1989) and *The Gates of Ivory* (1991) are among her titles. She was the editor

of the fifth edition of the *Oxford Companion to English Literature*, and has written a biography of Arnold Bennett (1974) and Angus Wilson (1995). Her elder sister is the novelist A S Byatt. ⬚ V G Myer, *Margaret Drabble: Puritanism and Permissiveness* (1974)

Drachmann, Holger Henrik Herholdt
1846–1908
Danish writer and artist
He was born in Copenhagen, of a German family. A visit to London inspired him to revolutionary solidarity with the working class, particularly the exiled Communards, but his early poetry is mainly lyrical and subjective. Later volumes such as *Sange ved havet* (1877, 'Seaside Verses') and *Ranker og roser* (1879, 'Vines and Roses') are less conventional, and anticipate important elements of Danish Modernism. His novel *Derovre fra graensen* (1877, 'Over the Border') is nationalistic and anticipates Jonas Lie's stories of respectable middle-class families. Drachmann was also an accomplished sea painter. ⬚ J Ursin, *Holger Drachmann, Liv og vaerker* (1953)

Draco 7th century BC
Athenian legislator
His harsh codification of the law in 621BC produced the word 'draconian'. The code was largely abolished by Solon (594), and only his law on homicide remained.

Drago, Luis María 1859–1921
Argentine politician
He was born in Buenos Aires. As Minister of Foreign Affairs in Argentina, he objected to the blockade of Venezuelan ports (1902) conducted by Great Britain, Italy and Germany as a punitive measure for non-payment of debt. He formulated the Drago Doctrine, which stated that public debt could not be used as an excuse for armed intervention in or territorial occupation of a US state by a European power. Although never universally adopted, his doctrine was influential in international law.

Drake, Edwin Laurentine 1819–80
US oil pioneer
Born in Greenville, New York, he started as a railway conductor, later becoming a stockholder in the Pennsylvania Rock Oil Company, which sent him in 1857 to inspect its property at Oil Creek. He secured a lease himself and after three months of drilling struck oil in 1859 at a depth of 69 feet (21m), with an initial yield of 40 barrels a day. Having thus initiated the huge oil industry of today, he failed to patent his invention of a tube down to bedrock to protect the drill-hole, and by 1863 he had lost his savings in oil speculation.

Drake, Sir Francis c.1540–1596
English navigator
Born in Crowndale, near Tavistock, he worked in the coasting trade from the age of 13, but by 1565 was voyaging to Guinea and the Spanish Main. In 1567 he commanded the *Judith* in his kinsman Sir John Hawkins's ill-fated expedition to the Gulf of Mexico and in 1570 and 1571 sailed to the West Indies to make good the losses he had then sustained from the Spaniards, gaining great popularity in England in the process. In 1572, with two small ships, the *Pasha* and *Swan*, and a privateer's licence from Queen Elizabeth I, he plundered on the Isthmus of Panama and became the first Englishman to see the Pacific Ocean. On his return to Plymouth in 1573 he became a popular hero. In 1577 he set out with five ships to explore the Strait of Magellan, where he changed his ship's name to the *Golden Hind*. On entering the Pacific Ocean violent tempests were encountered for 52 days during which the *Marigold* foundered with all hands and the *Elizabeth* returned home. Drake sailed north alone, to Vancouver, but failing to find a Northwest Passage back into the Atlantic he turned south and moved across the

Pacific, and for 68 days did not sight land until he made the Pelew Islands. After refitting in Java, he headed for the Cape of Good Hope, and arrived in England in September 1580, the first Englishman to circumnavigate the world. The queen, in the face of Spanish protests, was at first uncertain how to receive him, but at length paid a visit to his ship at Deptford and knighted him. In the autumn of 1585 he sailed against the Spanish Indies, plundered Hispaniola, Cartagena and the coast of Florida, and brought home the 190 dispirited Virginian colonists, with tobacco and potatoes. Early in 1587 he pillaged Cadiz, and in 1588, as vice admiral under **Charles Howard**, took a leading part in harassing the Spanish Armada as it passed through the English Channel. Off Portland he captured the galleon *Rosario*. In 1589 he led a large expedition to aid the Portuguese against Spain, but the mission was unsuccessful. He died while on an expedition, with Sir **John Hawkins**, to the West Indies. 📖 J A Williamson, *Sir Francis Drake* (1951)

Drake, Samuel Gardner 1798–1875
US antiquary and historian

Born in Pittsfield, New Hampshire, he published many reprints and valuable works on the early history of New England, including *Indian Biography* (1832), enlarged as *Book of the Indians* (1841).

Drapeau, Jean 1916–
French–Canadian politician

He became Mayor of Montreal in 1954, backed both by those wanting improved municipal services and those who demanded the elimination of gambling and prostitution. He sought more autonomy for the city and became a strong critic of **Maurice Duplessis**. When the October Crisis occurred in 1970 Drapeau, along with the Montreal chief of police and **Robert Bourassa**, asked the federal government to implement the War Measures Act. He received 92 per cent of the votes in the following city elections. His administration backed Expo 67 (when General **De Gaulle** delivered his notorious 'Vive le Québec libre' speech), and Montreal's successful bid to hold the 1976 Olympic Games. He was mayor until 1986, then went on to become Ambassador to UNESCO in Paris (1987–91).

Draper, Henry 1837–82
US astronomer and pioneer of astronomical photography

Born in Prince Edward County, Virginia, he graduated in medicine at City University, New York, and taught natural science and later physiology there from 1860 to 1882. He retired in 1882 to devote himself to astronomical research. He applied the new technique of photography to astronomy and in 1872 obtained a photograph of the spectrum of the star Vega. In 1874 he directed the photographic section of the US commission that observed the transit of Venus. He was the first to notice that long photographic exposures at the focus of a large telescope revealed fainter stars than could be seen with the naked eye. After his death his widow established a fund to support spectroscopic work at Harvard, the result being the *Henry Draper Catalogue* of stellar spectra (9 vols, 1918–24).

Draper, John William 1811–82
US author and scientist

Born in St Helens, Lancashire, England, he began medical studies in London in 1829. In 1831 he emigrated to Virginia, qualified in medicine in 1836, and subsequently taught chemistry at the University of New York. Between 1850 and 1873 he was head of its medical department. He was an early pioneer of photography. In 1840 he made what is probably the oldest surviving photographic portrait, a picture of his sister, which required an exposure of 65 seconds. In the same year, he photographed the Moon and thereby initiated astronomical photography. In 1850

he made the first photomicrographs, which served as illustrations of a book called *Physiology*. He also made early ultraviolet and infrared photographs of the Sun, describing **Fraunhofer** lines in the solar spectrum. In 1841 he formulated Draper's law, the principle that only absorbed radiation can produce chemical change. He also established that all solids become incandescent at an identical temperature and, if heated enough, afford a continuous spectrum. Intellectually, he fell under the influence of **Auguste Comte** and his positivism, as is evident from his *A History of the Intellectual Development of Europe* (1863). A prolific author, he is best remembered today for his studies of the history of science, especially *History of the Conflict Between Religion and Science* (1874), which claimed to show how scientific progress had been impeded by religious, especially Roman Catholic, bigotry. 📖 Donald H Fleming, *John William Draper and the Religion of Science* (1950)

Draper, Ruth 1889–1956
US diseuse and monologuist

She was born in New York City, and made her stage debut in 1915. Following successful solo appearances for the US troops in France (1918), she toured extensively, appearing in 1926 before King **George V** at Windsor. Her repertoire comprised 36 monologues, which she wrote herself, and embraced 57 characters.

Drawbell, James Wedgwood 1899–1979
Scottish journalist

After a traumatic childhood with an alcoholic father, he left Scotland as a young man and worked as a newspaper reporter in Montreal and New York City. When he returned to Great Britain, his progress was meteoric and he became one of the youngest Fleet Street editors when he became editor of the *Sunday Chronicle* at the age of 24. Later, he pioneered the development of *Woman's Own* as a mass-circulation magazine, and achieved mild notoriety by publishing the memoirs of a royal governess, 'Crawfie'. His autobiography, *The Sun Within Us* (1963), includes a compelling account of his boyhood, spent in a Falkirk tenement.

Drayton, Michael 1563–1631
English poet

Born in Hartshill, near Atherstone, Warwickshire, he became a page in a wealthy household and spent the rest of his life in the households of patrons. His earliest work was *The Harmony of the Church* (1591), a metrical rendering of scriptural passages, which gave offence to the authorities. His first major poem, *Mortimeriados* (1596, recast in 1603 as *The Barons' Wars*) was followed by *England's Heroical Epistles* (1597). *Poems, Lyric and Pastoral* (c.1606) contains some of his most familiar poems, including the *Ballad of Agincourt* and *Fair Stood the Wind for France*. The first 18 'songs' or books of his greatest work, the panoramic *Polyolbion*, were published in 1613, with annotation by **John Selden**, and the complete poem appeared in 1622. In 1619 he collected in one volume all the poems (except *Polyolbion*) which he wished to preserve, and in 1627 he published a new volume of miscellaneous poems, among them the whimsical *Nymphidia, the Court of Fairy*. His last work, *The Muses' Elysium* (1630), contains some pastoral poems. His only surviving play is *The First Part of Sir John Oldcastle* (1600). He was buried in Westminster Abbey, London. 📖 J A Berthelot, *Michael Drayton* (1967)

Drebbel, Cornelis Jacobszoon c.1572–1633
British inventor

Born in Alkmaar, the Netherlands, he was apprenticed to a painter and engraver in Haarlem who was also an alchemist, and acquired an interest in chemistry and later in various branches of technology. He prepared a map of Alkmaar and designed a water-supply system for the town, then in 1604 moved to England where he spent most of the rest of his life. Among his inventions were a clock driven by changes in atmospheric pressure, a new method for the manufacture of sulphuric acid, a thermostat which could regulate the supply of air to a furnace, and a rudimentary submarine (1620) which was successfully tested in the River Thames.

Drechsler, Heiki, *née* Daute 1964–
German athlete

Born in Gera, she came to prominence when, competing for East Germany, she won the European youth long jump championship and heptathlon championship in 1981, setting a world junior record a year later for long jump. In 1983 she won the world championship, becoming the youngest-ever long jump world champion, and in 1985 added wins in the European and World Cup events. She consistently jumped over seven metres, winning 27 successive competitions at long jump before 1987, when she was injured, and setting three world records before 1988. She was also a strong sprinter, picking up a variety of Olympic and world medals at 100 and 200 metres and equalling Marita Koch's 200 metres world record. She is a former delegate of the *Volkskammer*, the East German parliament.

Drees, Willem 1886–1988
Dutch politician

Born in Amsterdam, he moved to The Hague as a government stenographer and then entered politics, joining the Socialist Democratic Workers' Party and becoming its chairman in 1911. He sat in the Second Chamber from 1933 until the German invasion of 1940, after which he played an important part in the Resistance movement. In 1947, as Minister of Social Affairs, he introduced the state pension and then became Prime Minister (1948–58). A modest, puritanical man, he became the most durable figure in Dutch politics, a special stamp being issued to commemorate his hundredth birthday.

Dreiser, Theodore Herman Albert 1871–1945
US novelist

Born in Terre Haute, Indiana, to a German immigrant father, he was brought up on the breadline and left home at the age of 15 for Chicago. He did odd jobs before becoming a successful journalist, and wrote *Sister Carrie* (1900), a powerful and frank treatment of a young working girl's climb towards worldly success. The publisher, fearful of accusations of obscenity, was diffident in its promotion and it flopped commercially. After suffering a nervous breakdown and abandoning serious literary work for a decade, he wrote *Jennie Gerhardt* (1911), on a similar theme, which established Dreiser as a novelist. He went on to write a trilogy about a power-hungry business tycoon: *The Financier* (1912), *The Titan* (1914) and *The Stoic* (published posthumously in 1947). *An American Tragedy* (1925), based on a real-life murder case, has survived as a classic, despite its leaden prose. A large, egocentric man with an excessive sexual appetite, he saw his literary powers decline in later years and he occupied himself increasingly with philosophical speculations and left-wing journalism. His best works have been admired by Saul Bellow. 📖 R Lingeman, *Dreiser: At the Gates of the City, 1871–1907* (1986), and subsequent volumes

Dresser, Christopher 1834–1904
English designer and writer

Born in Glasgow, he first studied botany, from which he developed the stylized plant motifs which became the basis for his interest in decorative design. He contributed to Owen Jones's *Grammar of Ornament* and later wrote *The Art of Decorative Design* (1862) and *The Principles of Decorative Design* (1873). As a pioneer consultant designer, he designed glass, ceramics and cast-iron furniture for a number of manufacturers, but his most impressive works were items of functional metalwork, such as teapots and soup tureens. These, in their unadorned, geometric forms, are some of the most striking 'modern' designs of the 19th century.

Dressler, Marie, *originally* Leila Marie Koerber 1869–1934
Canadian actress

Born in Coburg, Ontario, the daughter of a music teacher, she made her stage debut in *Under Two Flags* (1886) and toured with a light opera company before her first Broadway appearance in *Robber on the Rhine* (1892). A popular straight actress, vaudeville headliner and comedienne, she made her film debut in *Tillie's Punctured Romance* (1914) but her support for an actors' strike in 1917 adversely affected her career and she struggled for a decade before returning to the cinema in small supporting roles. Her effective dramatic performance opposite Greta Garbo in *Anna Christie* (1930) revived her fortunes and she was gainfully employed until her death. Her film appearances include *Min and Bill* (1930, Best Actress Academy Award), *Emma* (1932), *Dinner at Eight* (1933) and *Christopher Bean* (1933). She also published an autobiography, *The Life Story of an Ugly Duckling* (1924).

Drew, Charles Richard 1904–50
US physician

Born in Washington DC, he became a surgeon and professor at Howard University (1942–50). He developed a method of preserving blood plasma for transfusion, and as the leading expert in the field, he organized and directed blood-plasma programmes in Great Britain and the USA in the early years of World War II, becoming head of the first American Red Cross Blood Bank in 1941. Ironically, the Red Cross would not accept donations of his own blood because he was an African-American. He lobbied to change their policy, but when they responded only by establishing a separate supply of blood donated and used by African-Americans, he resigned in protest (1942).

Drew, Dame Jane Beverley 1911–96
English architect

Born in Thornton Heath, Surrey, she trained at the Architectural Association, London (1929–34). After establishing her own practice during World War II, she then worked (1945–78) with her husband Maxwell Fry. She spent many years in India, where she was a senior architect at Chandigarh, the new capital of Punjab, India (1951–54), supervising work for Le Corbusier and designing the Government College for Women and the High School. From 1947 to 1965 she often worked in western Africa, and her work there includes Wesley Girls School, Ghana (1946), and the Olympic Stadium and Swimming Pool in Kaduna, Nigeria (1965). Deeply influenced by the MARS group who were responsible for the introduction of the Modern Movement into Great Britain, she persuaded her political friends, including the Prime Minister, of the need for an Open University (Milton Keynes), a project on which she worked from 1969 to 1977. Her other works include the Hospital Building for the Kuwait Oil Company (1949–51) and the Festival of Britain Harbour Restaurant, London (1951). With her husband she wrote *Village Housing in the Tropics* (1945) and *Tropical Architecture in the Humid Zone* (1956). She was appointed DBE in 1996.

Dreyer, Carl Theodor 1889–1968
Danish filmmaker

Born in Copenhagen, he was raised in a strict Lutheran family. His early career as a journalist brought him into contact with the developing film industry and he began writing scripts in 1912. He made his debut as a director with *Praesidenten* (1919, *The President*). Works like *Blade af Satans Bog* (1920, *Leaves from Satan's Book*), *La Passion de Jeanne d'Arc* (1928, 'The Passion of Joan of Arc') and *Vampyr* (1932, *Castle of Doom*) combine technical experimentation with a desire to explore spiritual themes and the influence of evil through torment and martyrdom. An exacting perfectionist whose work rarely found commercial favour, he returned to journalism in the 1930s and subsequently concentrated on documentaries. Infrequent fictional works like *Vredens Dag* (1943, *Day of Wrath*) and *Ordet* (1955, *The Word*) continued his fascination with spirituality and deliverance through death. His last film was *Gertrud* (1964), about a woman seeking perfect love, although until his death he continued to work on a long-cherished project to film the life of Jesus Christ.

Dreyer, John Louis Emil 1852–1926
Danish astronomer

Born in Copenhagen, he was appointed in 1874 as an assistant at the observatory of William Parsons (3rd Earl of Rosse) at Birr Castle, Ireland. Four years later he moved to Dunsink, and in 1882 he became director of the Armagh Observatory. Dreyer is remembered for his catalogue of nebulae and star clusters. His *New General Catalogue*, published in 1888, was so influential that many nebulae are still referred to by their NGC number. Dreyer's two great literary contributions to astronomy were his biography of Tycho Brahe (1890) and his *History of Planetary Systems from Thales to Kepler* (1906). Dreyer was awarded the Gold Medal of the Royal Astronomical Society in 1916.

Dreyfus, Alfred c.1859–1935
French soldier

Born in Mülhausen, Alsace, he was the son of a rich Jewish manufacturer. He joined the army but in 1893–94 he was unjustly accused of delivering documents connected with the national defence to a foreign government. He was transported for life to Devil's Island, but the efforts of his supporters to prove his innocence provoked Émile Zola's *J'accuse* (1898), in which he denounced the government's militarism and anti-Semitism. In 1898 the then Chief of Military Intelligence, Major Hubert Joseph Henry (1846–98), confessed to forging the papers for the original trial with Major Marie Charles Esterhazy (1847–1923). Dreyfus was eventually found guilty but pardoned, but it was not until 1906 that the verdict was reversed by a civilian court. Dreyfus was restored to his rank of artillery captain, fought in World War I and was awarded the Legion of Honour. 📖 Douglas Johnson, *France and the Dreyfus Affair* (1966)

Dreyfuss, Henry 1903–72
US designer and writer on design

Born in New York City, he worked initially in stage design, and in 1928 he opened his own design office which continued in practice after his death (he and his wife committed suicide). He pioneered research into anthropometry, a study with clear implications for design, and he wrote *Designing for People* (1955) and *The Measure of Man* (1959). Functionalism took precedence over style in his design work. He was also concerned with the ethical standards of his profession, and restricted the number of his clients partly to prevent a conflict of commitment. Among the products which he designed were Bell telephones, Hoover vacuum cleaners, RCA televisions, John Deare agricultural machinery and Lockheed airliner interiors.

Drezen, Youenn 1899–
Breton poet, dramatist, translator and novelist

He began as a journalist. He has translated Greek tragedies and English and Spanish classics into Breton. *Chant à l'Ouest* is an epic poem about the Celts; however,

his acknowledged masterpiece, written before he devoted himself to the theatre, is the novel *Notre-Dame des Carmélites* (1941). His chief aim has been to elevate Breton literature and his books have become classics in their language.

Driesch, Hans Adolf Eduard 1867–1941
German physiologist and philosopher

Born in Bad Kreuznach, he was the son of a wealthy merchant. From 1886 to 1889 he studied zoology at the universities of Freiburg and Jena. During the following 10 years he conducted his most important experiments, mainly at the Zoological Station in Naples. In 1891 he separated the two cells produced by division of a fertilized sea-urchin egg, and showed that each cell could form a whole larva, thus providing evidence opposed to the theory of preformation—the idea that in the fertilized egg a whole individual already exists in miniature—and opening up new avenues in experimental embryology. He was later appointed Professor of Philosophy at the universities of Heidelberg (1911), Cologne (1920) and Leipzig (1921).

Drinkwater, John 1882–1937
English poet, dramatist and critic

Born in Leytonstone, London, he was an insurance clerk, and had published several volumes of poems when he achieved an immediate theatrical success with his play *Abraham Lincoln* (1918). He followed it with *Mary Stuart*, *Oliver Cromwell* (both 1921), *Robert E. Lee* (1923) and a comedy, *Bird in Hand* (1927). His first volume of poems appeared in 1903, and he also wrote critical studies of William Morris, Algernon Charles Swinburne and Byron, and of lyric poetry. He was one of the founders of the Pilgrim Players and became manager of the Birmingham Repertory Theatre. He published two volumes of an unfinished autobiography, *Inheritance* (1931) and *Discovery* (1932). 📖 G Matthews, *John Drinkwater: a lecture* (1925)

Driver, Sir Godfrey Rolles 1892–1975
English biblical scholar

The son of the Old Testament scholar Samuel Rolles Driver (1846–1914), he became Professor of Semitic Philology at Oxford (1938–62). From 1965 to 1970 he was joint director of the project to develop the new translation of the *New English Bible*.

Droeshout, Martin 17th century
Flemish engraver

Resident in London, he was widely known by his portrait of Shakespeare, prefixed to the folio edition of 1623.

Droste-Hülshoff, Annette Elisabeth, Baroness von 1797–1848
German poet

Born in Westphalia, she is regarded as Germany's greatest woman writer. She led a reclusive life and from 1818 to 1820 wrote religious verses, published posthumously as *Geistliche Jahre* (1851). Her long narrative poems, notably *Das Hospiz auf dem Grossen Sankt Bernard* (1838, 'The Hospice on the Great Saint Bernard') and *Die Schlacht im Loener Bruch* ('The Battle in the Loener Marsh'), were influenced by Byron. She also wrote a novella, *Die Judenbuche* (1841, 'The Jew's Beech Tree'). 📖 C Heselhaus, *Annette von Droste-Hülshoff. Werk und Lebel* (1971)

Drouet, Jean Baptiste, Comte d'Erlon 1765–1844
French soldier

Born in Reims, he served in the Napoleonic Wars in the campaigns of the Moselle, Meuse, Sambre and Peninsula. At the first Restoration the Bourbons gave him a command, but on Napoleon I's return he was put under arrest in Lille citadel. He seized and held it for the Emperor, and at Waterloo (1815) he commanded the first *corps d'armée*. After the capitulation of Paris he fled to Bavaria, returned for the July Revolution (1830), and became Governor-General of Algeria (1834–35) and Marshal of France (1843).

Droz, Antoine Gustave 1832–95
French novelist

Born in Paris, he devoted himself to art before achieving his first and greatest success with *Monsieur, Madame, et Bébé* (1866, Eng trans *Papa, Mamma and Baby*, 1887). Later came *Entre nous* (1867, 'Between Ourselves'), *Les Étangs* (1876, 'The Ponds'), *L'Enfant* (1885, 'The Child'), and others.

Druce, George Claridge 1850–1932
English botanist

Born in Potterspury, Northamptonshire, he was apprenticed to a Northampton chemist firm in 1866, and in 1879 he purchased a chemist's shop in Oxford. There, he helped to found the Ashmolean Museum and began his best work, a series of county Floras covering the Upper Thames Valley (*Flora of Oxfordshire*, 1886; *Flora of Berkshire*, 1897; *Flora of Buckinghamshire*, 1926; *Flora of Northamptonshire*, 1930). He wrote many papers on British botany, was extremely active in the Botanical Exchange Club, and also served on Oxford City Council.

Drucker, Peter Ferdinand 1909–
US management consultant

Born in Vienna, Austria, and educated in Austria and England, he became an economist with a London international bank before going to live in the USA in 1937. He was Professor of Philosophy and Politics at Bennington College (1942–50), Professor of Management at the Graduate School of Business, New York University (1950–72), and was appointed Professor of Social Sciences at the Claremont Graduate School in California in 1972. He is well known as a management consultant and has written numerous successful textbooks on management, including *The Effective Executive* (1967), *Management: Tasks, Practices, Responsibilities* (1974), *The New Realities* (1989) and *Managing at a Time of Great Change* (1995). He has also written two novels.

Drummond, Dugald 1840–1912
Scottish locomotive engineer

Born in Ardrossan, Ayrshire, he was the chief mechanical engineer of the London & South Western Railway from 1905. He made his reputation in Scotland (1876–78) with the 4-4-0 'Abbotsford' class, examples of which were still running in the 1960s. His younger brother, Peter Drummond (1850–1918), born in Polmont, Stirlingshire, was also a locomotive engineer with the Highland and Glasgow & South Western Railways.

Drummond, George 1687–1766
Scottish entrepreneur and philanthropist

Born in Perthshire, he is known as the founder of the New Town in Edinburgh. An anti-Jacobite Whig, he fought at the Battle of Sheriffmuir (1715) and commanded a company in the 1745 Rising. A skilled accountant, he worked on the accounts for the Union of Parliaments in 1707, and was appointed Accountant-General of Excise. He was Lord Provost of Edinburgh six times between 1725 and 1764. He was the driving force behind the building of the Royal Infirmary (1738) and the Royal Exchange (1760, now the City Chambers), the expansion of Edinburgh University, and the proposal to create a New Town to the north of Princes Street. He drained the Nor'Loch (1759), and in 1763 laid the foundation stone of the North Bridge.

Drummond, Henry 1786–1860
English banker, politician and religious leader

Born in Albury, Surrey, he studied at Oxford for two years, but did not finish his degree. He was MP for Plumpton Earls (1810–13) and West Surrey (1847–60). Living for a time near Geneva he continued a campaign begun by Robert Haldane (1764–1842) against the creed of Socinianism founded by **Faustus Socinus**. He founded a chair of economics at Oxford (1825), and became the founder and chief prophet of the Catholic Apostolic, or Irvingite, Church, based on the messianic creed of **Edward Irving**.

Drummond, Henry 1851–97
Scottish evangelical theologian and biologist

Born in Stirling, he studied at Edinburgh, and became lecturer (1877) and Professor of Natural Science (1884) at the Free Church College, Glasgow. He travelled in the Rocky Mountains, Central Africa, Japan and Australia. Attempting to reconcile Christianity and **Darwinism**, he wrote such works as *Natural Law of the Spiritual World* (1883), *The Ascent of Man* (1894) and *Tropical Africa* (1888).

Drummond, Thomas 1797–1840
Scottish engineer and politician

Born in Edinburgh and educated there and at Woolwich, he joined the Royal Engineers in 1815, and in 1820 joined the Ordnance Survey, whose work was immensely facilitated by his improved heliostat and limelight (the 'Drummond Light'); the latter was also developed at about the same time by Sir **Goldsworthy Gurney**. He became head of the boundary commission under the Reform Bill, and Under-Secretary for Ireland (practically its governor) in 1835.

Drummond (of Hawthornden), William 1585–1649
Scottish poet

Born in Hawthornden, near Edinburgh, he was educated at Edinburgh University, studied law at Bourges and Paris, then became Laird of Hawthornden (1610), and devoted his life to poetry and mechanical experiments. He enjoyed the friendship of **Ben Jonson** who paid him a memorable visit (1618–19), and Drummond wrote *Notes* of their talk. His chief works are the pastoral lament *Tears on the Death of Moeliades* (ie Prince Henry, 1613), *Poems, Amorous, Funereall, Divine, Pastorall in Sonnets, Songs, Sextains, Madrigals* (1614), *Forth Feasting* (1617), and *Flowers of Sion* (1623). In prose he wrote *A Cypress Grove* (1630) and a *History of the Five Jameses*, and his *History of Scotland 1423–1524*, was posthumously published in 1655. His death was hastened by grief for **Charles I**'s execution. ⌑ F R Fogle, *A Critical Study of William Drummond of Hawthornden* (1952)

Drury, Alfred 1857–1944
English sculptor

He was born in London, and trained there at the Royal Academy Schools. Among his works in London are *St Agnes* (1896, Chantrey Collection, Tate), Sir **Joshua Reynolds** (1931, Burlington House quadrangle) and the memorial to the London Troops of two world wars. He also sculpted the figures of **Victoria** and **Albert** over the entrance to the Victoria and Albert Museum (1903) and, between 1901 and 1924, worked on the Canada and Africa gates in the Mall, London.

Drusus, Nero Claudius, *also known as* Drusus Senior 39–9BC
Roman soldier

He was the son of Livia Drusilla, stepson of the Emperor **Augustus**, and younger brother of the Emperor **Tiberius**. His campaign against the Rhaeti and other Alpine tribes (15BC) was celebrated by **Horace** in his *Odes*. Until his death he was engaged chiefly in establishing Roman supremacy in Germany, and received the title Germanicus. **Germanicus Caesar** was his son.

Druten, John van 1901–57
US playwright

Born in London, England, he became famous with his play *Young Woodley* in 1928, which was first produced in the USA after falling foul of the British censor. After several years and considerable success, he was granted US citizenship in 1944. *The Voice of the Turtle*, one of his most successful plays, was produced in 1943 and his adaptation of sketches by **Christopher Isherwood**, *I Am A Camera*, in 1951. 📖 *The Way to the Present* (1938).

Dryden, John 1631–1700
English poet

He was born at the vicarage of Aldwinkle All Saints, Northamptonshire, and educated at Westminster School under **Richard Busby** and at Trinity College, Cambridge, where he stayed until 1657. Going up to London in that year he attached himself to his cousin Sir Gilbert Pickering, **Cromwell's** chamberlain, in the hope of employment, as both sides of his family were Parliamentarians. His *Heroic Stanzas*, in quatrains, on the death of Cromwell (1658), was soon followed by his *Astrea Redux* (1660), celebrating the Restoration in heroic couplets, which was to be his staple measure even in the myriad plays which he soon produced for the amusement of 'a venal court'. The first of these 'heroic' verse plays to win the public was *The Indian Emperor* (1665), dealing with the conquest of Mexico by **Hernán Cortés** and his love for the emperor's daughter, and the last was *Aurungzebe* (1676). In 1663 he married Lady Elizabeth Howard, eldest daughter of the Earl of Berkshire. In 1667 he published *Annus Mirabilis, The Year of Wonders, 1666*, which established his reputation, and he was appointed Poet Laureate in 1668 following Sir **William D'Avenant**, and historiographer royal in 1670. Meanwhile he was writing a series of comedies for the stage, including *The Rival Ladies* (1664, in rhymed verse), and culminating with *Marriage à la Mode* (1672). He used blank verse for *All for Love* (1677), his best play and comparable to **Shakespeare's** *Antony and Cleopatra*. His adaptation of another Shakespeare play, *Troilus and Cressida*, in 1678, was by comparison a failure. He had adapted *The Tempest* in 1670, **Milton's** *Paradise Lost* (as *The State of Innocence*, 1677), and **Corneille's** *The Mock Astrologer* (1668). He wrote a series of important critical essays as prefaces to his plays, including his charming *Essay of Dramatic Poesy* (1668) and the *Defence of the Epilogue* (to *The Conquest of Granada*, 1670). In 1680 he began a series of satirical and didactic poems, starting with the most famous, 'Absalom and Achitophel' (1681), and followed by 'The Medal' (1682) and 'MacFlecknoe' (1684), written some years before, which did much to turn the tide against the Whigs. To this era also belong the didactic poem *Religico Laici* (1682), which argues the case for Anglicanism, and *The Hind and the Panther*, marking his conversion to Catholicism in 1685. A place in the Customs (1683) was his reward for his political labours. At the Revolution of 1688 he lost the poet laureateship and took up translation to earn a living. Of these his fine translation of **Virgil** was most profitable, and that of **Juvenal** and **Persius** was prefaced by a *Discourse Concerning the Origin and Progress of Satire*. His final work, published in 1699, was *Fables, Ancient and Modern* which, with its paraphrases of **Chaucer**, **Ovid** and **Boccaccio**, has delighted generations of readers. These works are only the most outstanding of a lifetime's industry. Dryden is transitional between the Metaphysical poets of the school of **John Donne** and the neoclassic reaction which he did so much to create. 📖 G Wasermann, *John Dryden* (1964); C Ward, *A Life of John Dryden* (1961)

Drygalski, Erich Dagobert von 1865–1949
German geophysicist and explorer

Born in Königsberg, Prussia (now Kaliningrad, Russia) he headed expeditions to Greenland (1891–93), and in the *Gauss* to the Antarctic (1902–03), where he discovered and named the Gaussberg volcano.

Drysdale, Sir (George) Russell 1912–81
Australian painter

Born in Sussex, England, he settled in Melbourne in 1923 and, although he originally intended to work on the land, attended art school. In 1939 he took part in the first exhibition of the Contemporary Art Society of Australia. Eventually he settled in Sydney, and in 1942 had his first one-man exhibition. **Kenneth Clark** encouraged him to exhibit in London in 1950. In 1954 he represented Australia at the Venice Biennale. His paintings of the Australian outback often stress drought and erosion, and show the influence of abstract and Surrealist art.

dsh See **Houedard, Dom Sylvester**

Duarenus, *originally* François Douaren 1509–59
French humanist jurist

He was a professor at Bourges and wrote *Pro libertate ecclesiae Gallicae* (1551), *Commentarius in Consuetudines Feudorum* (1558) and a Commentary on **Justinian I's** *Digest*.

Duarte, José Napoleón 1925–90
El Salvadorean politician

Trained as a civil engineer in the USA at the University of Notre Dame in South Bend, Indiana, he founded the Christian Democratic Party (PDC) in 1960. After serving as Mayor of El Salvador (1964–70), he was elected President in 1972 but was soon impeached and exiled for seven years in Venezuela. He returned and in 1980 regained the presidency, with US backing. He lost the 1982 election and for two years witnessed a fierce struggle between the right- and left-wing elements. He returned as President in 1984 but in 1988, stricken by terminal cancer, was forced to resign.

Dubček, Alexander 1921–92
Czechoslovak statesman

Born in Uhrovek, Slovakia, he lived from 1925 to 1938 in the USSR, where his father was a member of a Czechoslovakian industrial co-operative. He returned home and joined the Communist Party in 1939, fought as a Slovak patriot against the Nazis (1944–45), and gradually rose in the party hierarchy until in 1968 he became First Secretary. He implemented a programme of far-reaching economic and political reforms, including abolition of censorship, increased freedom of speech, and suspension of ex-President **Antonín Novotný** and other former Stalinist party leaders. Despite his avowed declaration of democracy within a Communist framework, his policy of liberalization during the Prague Spring led in August 1968 to the occupation of Czechoslovakia by Warsaw Pact forces. In 1969 the Russians exerted strong pressure on the Czechoslovak government, and Dubček was replaced as First Secretary by **Gustav Husak**. He was elected president of the Federal Assembly for a few months in 1969, but expelled from the Presidium in September and deprived of party membership in 1970. He spent the next 18 years working as a clerk in a lumber yard in Slovakia, but having publicly pledged support for the reforms of **Mikhail Gorbachev**, he was given freedom to travel. Following the overthrow of the existing Communist regime in November 1989 in a bloodless 'Velvet Revolution', he dramatically re-emerged from retirement to be elected chairman of the Federal Assembly in December 1989 but lost his parliamentary seat in the elections of 1992. He was awarded the Sakharov Peace prize in 1989 and his book about the events of 1968, *The Soviet Invasion*, was published in 1990. He died as the result of a car accident.

Dubinsky, David 1892–1982
US labour leader
Born in Brest (now Brest Litovsk), Russian Poland, he was exiled to Siberia (1908) for union activity. In 1911 he escaped and reached the USA. He found a job as a cloak cutter and joined the International Ladies' Garment Workers Union, rising to become its president (1932–66). Dubinsky transformed the ILGWU into a model international union with 450,000 members, raising the workers' standard of living and pioneering initiatives in housing, pension plans, and health centres.

Dubois, Guillaume 1656–1723
French prelate
Born in Brive-la-Gaillarde, he studied for the priesthood, then was appointed first tutor and later secretary to the Duc de Chartres, and became very influential when his employer (now Duc d'Orléans) became regent in 1715. He was appointed Foreign Minister and Archbishop of Cambrai (1720), a cardinal (1721), and Prime Minister of France (1722).

Dubois, Marie Eugène François Thomas
1858–1940
Dutch palaeontologist
Born in Eijsden, Limburg, he studied medicine in Amsterdam and taught there from 1899. His interest in the 'missing link' between the apes and humans took him to Java in 1887, where in the 1890s he found the humanoid remains named as *Pithecanthropus erectus* (Java Man) and which he claimed to be the missing link. His view was contested and even ridiculed. When in the 1920s it eventually became widely accepted, Dubois began to insist that the fossil bones were those of a giant gibbon, and maintained this view until his death.

Du Bois, W(illiam) E(dward) B(urghardt)
1868–1963
African-American writer and editor
Born in Great Barrington, Massachusetts, he studied at Fisk University, Tennessee, and at Harvard, from where he was the first black person to be awarded a PhD (1895) and was later Professor of Economics and History at Atlanta University (1897–1910). He was co-founder of the National Association for the Advancement of Colored People (1908), and edited its magazine, *Crisis* (1910–34), but later disassociated himself from the Association, finding it too conservative. He wrote a number of important works on slavery and the 'colour problem', including *The Negro* (1915), *Black Reconstruction* (1935) and *Colour and Democracy* (1945). He also wrote novels, such as *The Dark Princess* (1928) and *Worlds of Color* (1961). A passionate advocate of radical black action and an early supporter of the suffragette movement—which he tried to link with the struggle for black rights—he joined the Communist Party in 1961, and moved to Ghana at the age of 91, renounced his US citizenship and became a naturalized Ghanian just before he died. 📖 *Autobiography* (1968)

Du Bois-Reymond, Emil Heinrich 1818–96
German physiologist
Born into a Swiss family which had settled in Berlin, he trained in medicine there, working under Johannes Müller, and graduating in 1843. He succeeded Müller as Professor of Physiology at Berlin in 1858, and was appointed head of the new Physiological Institute which opened in 1877. Du Bois-Reymond's importance lay in his investigations of the physiology of muscles and nerves, and in his demonstrations of electricity in animals. He improved the techniques for measuring such effects, first investigated by Luigi Galvani, and was able to detect an electric current in ordinary localized muscle tissues, tracing it to individual fibres. He demonstrated the

existence of electrical currents in nerves, and his experimental methods proved the basis for almost all future work in electrophysiology.

Du Bos, Charles 1882–1939
French writer
Born in Paris, of an English mother, he studied at Oxford (1900–01) and in Germany. He wrote critical works on Byron, François Mauriac, André Gide, and others, and published a collection of critical essays under the title *Approximations* (7 vols, 1922–27). His *Qu'est-ce que la littérature?* ('What is Literature?') was published posthumously in 1945, and contains a 'Hommage' by a number of writers including Charles Morgan.

Dubos, René Jules 1901–82
US bacteriologist
He was born in Saint-Brice, France, and studied at the Institut National Agronomique, Paris, and Rutgers University, New Jersey. He worked at Rockefeller University in New York City from 1927 and became a US citizen in 1938. In 1939 he discovered tyrothricin, the first commercially produced antibiotic.

Dubricius, St d.612
Welsh religious
He was the traditional founder of the Welsh bishopric of Llandaff.

Dubuffet, Jean 1901–85
French painter and printmaker
Born in Le Havre, he enrolled at the Académie Julian in Paris in 1918, but never studied seriously, enjoying life as the son of a rich wine-merchant whose business he took over in 1925. He began painting again during World War II, when he invented the concept of Art Brut and pioneered the use of rubbish such as discarded newspapers, broken glass, and rough plaster daubed and scratched like an old wall, to create 'pictures'. His artwork is regarded as presaging the Pop Art and Dada-like fashions of the 1960s, and his collected writings were published in 1967. 📖 Andreas Franzke, *Dubuffet* (1981)

Du Camp, Maxime 1822–94
French photographer and writer
Born in Paris, he was a close friend of Gustave Flaubert, with whom he travelled in the Middle and Near East in 1844–45 and 1849–51. His renown as a photographer dates from this time, and his pictures are testament to the fascination seen in the East by those involved in the Romantic movement. They are also early examples of topographical photography and were published in one of the first books illustrated by original photographs, *Égypte, Nubie, Palestine et Syrie* (1852). In 1848 Du Camp fought and was decorated as a counter-revolutionary; he also fought as a volunteer with the Italian revolutionary Garibaldi. He wrote books on Paris and was a founder of the *Revue de Paris* (1851), in which Flaubert's *Madame Bovary* was first published in serial form. His other writings include *Souvenirs littéraires* (2 vols, 1882–83, 'Literary Recollections') and several novels.

Duccio, Agostino di See Agostino di Duccio

Duccio di Buoninsegna c.1260–c.1320
Italian painter
He founded the Sienese school, and in his work the Byzantine tradition in Italian art is seen in its most highly developed state. His masterpiece is the *Maestà* for the altar of Siena Cathedral (1311), and the *Rucellai Madonna* in S Maria Novella at Florence, long attributed to Giovanni Cimabué, is now generally considered to be his work. He is represented in the National Gallery, London, by the *Annunciation*, *Christ Healing the Blind Man* and the *Transfiguration*.

Du Chaillu, Paul Belloni 1831–1903
US traveller

Born in Paris, France, he spent several years in Gabon and in 1852 went to the USA, where he was naturalized. From 1855 he spent four years exploring the interior of West Africa. He was received at first with much distrust, but his *Explorations in Equatorial Africa* (1861) made important contributions to geographical, ethnological and zoological science, especially as to the Ogowé River's source, the culture of Fang, and the natural history of the gorilla.

Duchamp, Marcel 1887–1968
US painter

Born in Blainville, France, he moved to Paris to join his two artistic brothers in 1904. Associated with several modern movements including Cubism and Futurism, he shocked his generation with such works as *Coffee-Mill* (1911) and *Nude Descending a Staircase* (1912, Philadelphia), and was one of the pioneers of Dadaism, the anti-art protest, which favoured the presentation of energy and change above classical aesthetic values and fulminated against mechanization. In 1914 he introduced the first 'ready-made' by inscribing a bottle-rack and declaring it to be art. In 1915 he left Paris for New York City, where he worked for eight years on a 10 feet (3m) high composition in glass and metal, *The Bride Stripped Bare by Her Bachelors Even*, known as *The Large Glass*, in which many of the shapes were obtained by chance effects, such as dust blown on to the drawings. He described this in his *Green Box* notes (1933). He edited the US art magazine, *VVV* (1942–44), and became a US citizen in 1955. He was the brother of **Jacques Villon** and half-brother of **Raymond Duchamp-Villon**. ▣ Calvin Thomkins, *The World of Marcel Duchamp* (1966)

Duchamp-Villon, Raymond 1876–1918
French sculptor

Born in Damville, Normandy, the brother of **Jacques Villon** and half-brother of **Marcel Duchamp**, he began as a medical student, turning to sculpture in 1898. By 1914 he was one of the leading Cubist sculptors in Paris. His most striking work is the bronze *Horse* (1914, Peggy Guggenheim Collection, Venice), in which realism is rejected in favour of an abstract swirl of forms that captures the energetic movement of the animal.

du Châtelet-Lomont, Gabrielle See Châtelet-Lomont, Gabrielle du

Duchenne, Guillaume Benjamin Amand
1806–75
French physician

Born in Boulogne-sur-Mer, he was educated at Douai and Paris. After 11 years as a general practitioner in Boulogne, he returned to Paris and devoted himself to the physiology and diseases of muscles. A pioneer of electrophysiology and electrotherapeutics, he did important work on poliomyelitis, locomotor ataxia and a common form of muscular ('Duchenne's') dystrophy. He also developed a method of taking small pieces of muscle (biopsy) from patients for microscopical examination. Although he never held a formal hospital appointment, he worked at the Salpêtrière Hospital, where **Jean Martin Charcot** was his patron.

Duchesne, André, *Latin* Chesnius *or* Quercetanus
1584–1640
French historian

He was royal historiographer, and is known as the 'Father of French history'. He wrote histories of England, Scotland and Ireland, of the popes up to **Paul V**, and of the House of Burgundy. He also made collections of the early Norman and French histories.

Duchesne, Père See Hébert, Jacques René

Duchesne, St Rose Philippine 1769–1852
French Roman Catholic nun and missionary

She was born in Grenoble and entered the women's community called the Society of the Sacred Heart in 1804, and in 1818 was sent as a missionary and teacher to the USA. That year she founded a branch of the society, a convent and school at St Charles, Missouri. Using this as her base, she went on to establish several convents, orphanages and schools, for example at St Louis, Missouri (1827), and at Grand Cocteau, Louisiana. In the early 1840s she worked to spread the gospel among the Potawatomi in Kansas. Beatified in 1940, she was canonized in 1988 and her feast day is 17 November.

Ducis, Jean François 1733–1816
French poet and playwright

He was born in Versailles. His own tragedies are regarded as mediocre and he is best known for his adaptations of **Shakespeare** for the French stage, which he completed from earlier French versions, since he knew no English. They did help popularize Shakespeare in France, despite wild inaccuracies, and such liberties as allowing Othello to discover his mistake and spare Desdemona.

Duckworth, Sir John Thomas 1748–1817
English naval commander

Born in Leatherhead, Surrey, he was educated at Eton, but left early to join the navy as a volunteer, and in 1759 saw action in the battles of Lagos Bay and Quiberon Bay, under **Edward Hawke**. He served at sea in the War of American Independence (1775–83) and in the French Revolutionary Wars (1792–1800), including the Battle of Ushant (1794). In 1801 he captured Swedish and Danish possessions in the West Indies, and was Commander-in-Chief at Jamaica from 1803 to 1813.

Ducos du Hauron, Louis 1837–1920
French scientist

Born in Langon, he became interested in photography from 1859, and his publication *Les Couleurs en photographie* (1869) outlined for the first time all the principles of additive and subtractive colour reproduction, although at that period suitably sensitive photographic materials were not available. In 1878 he published *Photographie en couleur*, describing practical methods which he patented, and in 1891 proposed the anaglyph method of viewing stereoscopic images.

Duddell, William du Bois 1872–1917
English engineer

He worked on radiotelegraphy and in 1897 invented an improved version of the oscillograph. He also designed a high-frequency generator. The Physical Society instituted the Duddell Medal in his honour.

Dudley, Edmund c.1462–1510
English lawyer and privy councillor

He was Sir **Richard Empson's** partner in collecting taxes and dues for **Henry VII**, whose son and successor **Henry VIII** had him executed.

Dudley, Lord Guildford d.1554
English nobleman

The fourth son of **John Dudley**, Earl of **Warwick** and Duke of Northumberland, he was persuaded by his father to marry the unwilling Lady **Jane Grey** (1553) as **Edward VI** lay dying, and then proclaimed her queen on 9 July. After the accession of **Mary I**, Tudor (Edward's sister), Dudley and his wife were imprisoned in the Tower of London and beheaded.

Dudley, Leon See Sorabji, Kaikhosru Shapurji

Dudley, William Stuart 1947–
English stage designer

He was born in London, and educated at St Martin's School of Art and the Slade School of Art, London. He designed his first stage set for *Hamlet* at the Nottingham Playhouse (1970). He subsequently designed many productions for the Royal Court, including **Alan Bennett's** *Kafka's Dick* (1986). He has worked extensively at the National Theatre, being associate designer there since 1981, and at the Royal Shakespeare Company. He has also worked extensively in opera in Great Britain and elsewhere, and designed **Peter Hall's** production of *The Ring* at Bayreuth (1983), and **Bill Bryden's** productions of *The Ship* (1990) and *The Big Picnic* (1994) in Glasgow.

Dudok, Willem Marinus 1884–1974
Dutch architect

Born in Amsterdam, he trained as an army engineer and became city architect of Hilversum in 1915. Mixing modern and traditional elements, his fully developed style is characterized by dramatic massing of asymmetrical plain brick blocks, deep-set windows and vertical elements. The Hilversum Town Hall (1928–30) was his master-work. His most important building outside Hilversum was the Bijenkorf Department Store in Rotterdam (now demolished) where large areas of glazing contrasted with plain brickwork. Dudok had no successors, but was widely imitated abroad.

Dufay, Charles François de Cisternay 1698–1739
French chemist

Born in Paris, he joined the army at the age of 14, leaving in 1721 and being appointed chemist at the Academy of Sciences (1723), rising to the position of director in 1733. His early research on mercurial phosphorus showed him to be a thorough and methodical investigator of natural phenomena. He reported his observations of natural magnetism and the effect of distance on the force between magnets, but his most important work concerned electrostatics, in which he defined the difference between positive and negative electricity and recognized that they exhibit repulsive as well as attractive forces. He worked in many areas including double refraction in crystals, the colouring of artificial gems, the heat of slaked lime and plane geometry.

Dufay, Guillaume c.1400–1474
French composer

Born probably in Cambrai, he was the most celebrated 15th-century composer. A choirboy at Cambrai, he returned there as canon in 1439 after extensive travel and residence in Italy. Almost 200 of his works are extant, including eight complete masses, many motets, and songs. His warmth of emotion, strong sense of melody and pioneering of the *cantus firmus* mass greatly influenced Renaissance composers. ▯ David Fallows, *Dufay* (1982)

Duff, Sir Lyman Poore 1865–1955
Canadian judge and jurist

Born in Ontario, he became a judge of the Supreme Court of British Columbia (1904–06) and of the Supreme Court of Canada (1906–33), and was later Chief Justice of that court (1933–44). He had an extensive knowledge of law, both common law and the modern civil law of France and Quebec, and wrote leading opinions on many important constitutional decisions. His influence was particularly significant on the question of the distribution of powers between the Federal Government and the provinces, and on that of upholding the Federal Government's power to abolish, without the consent of the provinces, appeals to the Privy Council. He also sat on the judicial committee of the Privy Council (1919–46).

Duffy, Carol Ann 1955–
Scottish poet

Born in Glasgow, she is considered one of the leading woman poets of her generation. Much influenced by the dramatic monologues of **Robert Browning**, and by **Laura Riding**, she is striking in her use of a kind of toughened and good-natured whimsicality in her verse. Her collections include *Standing Female Nude* (1985) and *The Other Country* (1990). In 1993 she won the Whitbread award for poetry for her collection *Mean Time*. ▯ *Bête Noir*, 6 (1989)

Duffy, Sir Charles Gavan 1816–1903
Irish nationalist and politician

Born in County Monaghan, he helped to start the *Nation* (1842), the Young Ireland organ, and for 12 years engaged in agitation, and was tried for sedition and treason. On the break-up of the Independent Irish Party, he emigrated in 1856 to Australia, where after the establishment of the Victorian constitution, he became Minister of Public Works (1857), Minister of Lands (1858, 1862), and Prime Minister (1871). In 1877 he was elected Speaker of the Legislative Assembly. His *Ballad Poetry of Ireland* became a household book in his native country. In 1880, when he returned to Europe, he published his *Young Ireland, 1840–50* (final edn 1896), followed in 1883 by *Four Years of Irish History, 1845–49*, and in 1898 by *My Life in Two Hemispheres*.

Dufour, Guillaume Henri 1787–1875
Swiss soldier and military writer

He served in the French army (1807–14), and founded the military academy at Thun, Switzerland, in 1818. Chief of Staff of the Swiss army from 1831, he commanded the new Swiss federal forces against the Sonderbund in 1847. He was also responsible for a topographical map of Switzerland (1864) and presided over the Geneva Convention in 1864 that led to the foundation of the Red Cross.

Du Fu (Tu Fu) 712–70
Chinese poet of the Tang dynasty

He was born in Xiangyang, and spent much of his youth travelling, during which time he soaked up impressions of his country's sharply juxtaposed cultural riches and social ills. One of the foremost lyricists in the language, his poems include 'The Ballad of Beautiful Women', 'The Newlyweds' Parting' and 'The Chariots' Song'. These last two reflect the violent uncertainties of life at the time, but they are also beautifully crafted and full of memorable imagery. In his later years, he was supported financially by an old friend, who enabled him to travel once more, in greater comfort than he had experienced in his youth. The best English-language source for Du Fu is still Florence Ayscough's two-volume *The Autobiography of a Chinese Poet* (1929); a definitive edition of the complete works appeared in Beijing (Peking) in 1979. ▯ W Hung, *Tu Fu, China's Greatest Poet* (1952)

Dufy, Raoul 1877–1953
French artist and designer

Born in Le Havre, he was much influenced by the brightness and colour of Fauvism, which he did much to popularize. Later he abandoned it, but retained his singing blues and reds. From 1907 he worked in woodcut and engraved many book illustrations, including **Guillaume Apollinaire's** *Bestiary* (1911), and produced woodcuts for making printed silk fabrics for dress designers. He also made pottery and tapestries, but in 1919 he returned to painting on the Riviera, where he produced a notable series of seascapes, bathers, sailing regattas and racecourse scenes.

Dugdale, Sir William 1605–86
English antiquary

Born in Shustoke, Warwickshire, he studied law and history under his father, and in 1625 purchased the neighbouring manor of Blythe. In 1638 he was created a pursuivant-at-arms extraordinary and in 1640 Rouge Croix pursuivant. During the Civil War he adhered to the

Royalist cause, and from 1642 to 1646 lived at the king's headquarters in Oxford, becoming a Chester herald, while pursuing his antiquarian researches. At the Restoration he received the office of Norroy, and in 1677 was made garter principal king of arms, and given a knighthood. His works include the *Monasticon Anglicanum* (1655, 1664, 1673), *Antiquaries of Warwickshire* (1656), *History of Imbanking and Drayning* (1662) and *Baronage of England* (3 vols, 1675–76).

Dughet, Gaspard, *also called* Gaspard Poussin
1615–75
Italian landscape painter

He was born in Rome of French descent. His sister married **Nicholas Poussin** and he called himself after his more famous brother-in-law. He specialized in landscapes which, while modelled on the Roman countryside, combine the classical manner of Poussin with the more lyrical style of **Claude Lorrain**. His works were avidly collected by 18th-century English travellers to Rome and were often taken as models for landscaped gardens and parks.

Duhamel, Georges 1884–1966
French novelist and poet

Born in Paris, he originally studied medicine and worked as an army surgeon in World War I. This provided the background for *La Vie des martyrs* (1917, 'Life of the Martyrs') and *Civilisation* (1918, awarded the Prix Goncourt). Many of his 50 volumes of vigorous, skilful writing have been translated. They include *Salavin* (1920–32), *Le Notaire du Havre* (1913, Eng trans *News from Le Havre*, 1934), the first of the 10 parts of *Chronique des Pasquier* (1933–44, Eng trans *The Pasquier Chronicles*, 1937–45) and *Positions françaises: Chronique de l'année 1939* (1940, Eng trans *Why France Fights*, 1940). He edited *Mercure de France*. 🕮 *Light on My Days*, translation of two volumes of autobiography (1948)

Duhamel du Monceau, Henri-Louis 1700–82
French technologist

Born in Paris, he proved the distinction between what we would now call potassium and sodium salts, showed that soda can be made from rock salt, and improved the making of starch, soap and brass. He reviewed agricultural practice and introduced **Jethro Tull's** methods into France.

Duhem, Pierre Maurice Marie 1861–1916
French philosopher and physicist

Born in Paris, he held teaching positions at Lille, Rennes and Bordeaux. A devout Catholic all his life, he began his scientific work in thermodynamics and many of his ideas were well in advance of their time. He made important contributions to the history of science, in particular reviving an interest in medieval science, his magnum opus being *Système du monde* (10 vols, 1913, 'The World System'). His philosophical views are developed in *La Théorie physique, son objet et sa structure* (1906, 'The Aim and Structure of Physical Theory') and present a formalistic account of science, whereby scientific theories and models should be regarded as useful predictive devices and psychological aids rather than direct descriptions or explanations of the world.

Duilius, Gaius fl.260BC
Roman general

As consul in 260BC he led 143 new Roman galleys to a decisive victory over the Carthaginians off Mylae, by the first use of new devices nicknamed *corvi* (ravens), combined grappling-hooks and boarding-bridges.

Dukakis, Michael 1933–
US politician

Born in Boston, Massachusetts, the son of Greek immigrants, he studied law at Harvard and served in Korea (1955–57) before concentrating on a political career in his home state. Elected as a Democrat to the Massachusetts legislature in 1962, he became Governor of that state in 1974. His first term was unsuccessful, marred by an unwillingness to compromise, and he was defeated in 1978. However he returned in 1982, committed to work in a more consensual manner, and was elected Governor again. His second term coincided with the state's emergence as a centre of US high technology and its new-found prosperity helped assure his re-election with an increased majority in 1986. He captured the Democratic Party's presidential nomination, defeating **Jesse Jackson** and presenting himself as a neo-liberal, but was defeated by the Republican **George Bush** in 1988. Governor until 1990, he now teaches at Florida Atlantic University (1991–).

Dukas, Paul Abraham 1865–1935
French composer

He was born in Paris. Some of his music was classical in approach, but he tended mainly towards musical Impressionism, and is noted for the symphonic poem *L'Apprenti sorcier* (1897, 'The Sorcerer's Apprentice') and the opera *Ariane et Barbe-Bleu* (1907, 'Ariadne and Bluebeard'). He also wrote several orchestral and piano pieces, and was Professor of Composition at the Paris Conservatoire from 1927. He wrote some musicological books, and edited works by **Jean Philippe Rameau** and **Alessandro Scarlatti**.

Dulac, Edmund 1882–1953
British artist and book illustrator

Born in France, he is best known for his illustrations of classics and fairy tales. He designed the coronation stamp for 1937 and 1953.

Dulbecco, Renato 1914–
Italian virologist and Nobel Prize winner

Born in Catanzaro, he studied medicine at the University of Turin, and in 1947 he emigrated to the USA, securing appointments at Indiana University and then at the California Institute of Technology (Caltech). From 1972 to 1977 he was assistant director of research at the Imperial Cancer Research Fund, London. He then returned to the USA as Professor of Pathology and Medicine at the University of California (1977–81), and since 1977 has been Research Professor at the Salk Institute, La Jolla, of which he is currently president emeritus (1993–). Dulbecco demonstrated how certain viruses can transform some cells into a cancerous state, such that those cells grow continuously, unlike normal cells. For this discovery he was awarded the 1975 Nobel Prize for physiology or medicine, jointly with his former students, **David Baltimore** and **Howard Temin**.

Dulles, Allen Welsh 1893–1969
US Intelligence officer

Born in Washington DC, into a clerical family with diplomatic links, he was educated at Princeton. After working in Allahabad, India, he entered the US diplomatic service when his uncle, **Robert Lansing**, was Secretary of State. He had served at Vienna, Berne, Paris, Berlin and Istanbul by 1920. He was chief of Division of Near Eastern Affairs, Department of State (1922–26), and worked for a law firm with powerful international links from 1926 to 1942. In World War II he served in Europe with the US Office of Strategic Services (1942–45), and played an important part in arranging the surrender of Italian forces without Russian knowledge, as described in his *The Secret Surrender* (1966). When the **Truman** administration decided on the formation of the Central Intelligence Agency (CIA), Dulles was made deputy director (1951), becoming director in 1953 coincident with his brother, **John Foster Dulles**, becoming Secretary of State. Under his direction the Agency had some success in clandestine operations, assisting in right-wing coups in Guatemala and Iran which were believed to be in the US interest, but the 1961 disaster at the Bay of Pigs in the attempt to overthrow **Fidel Castro** in Cuba was followed by his resignation. Two years later he served on the Warren Commission investigating **John F Kennedy**'s death. He also wrote *The Craft of Intelligence* (1963).

Dulles, John Foster 1888–1959
US Republican politician
Born in Washington DC, the brother of **Allen Welsh Dulles**, he was educated at Princeton and the Sorbonne. As a young lawyer from a family with a diplomatic tradition he attended the Hague Conference of 1907. At the Versailles Conference he was adviser to President **Woodrow Wilson** and was principal US spokesman on the Reparations Commission. During World War II he was a strong advocate of a world governmental organization. In 1945 he was adviser to Senator **Arthur Vandenberg** at the Charter Conference of the United Nations, and later served as US delegate to the General Assembly (1946–48, 1950). In 1953 he became US Secretary of State. By the end of 1954 he had travelled nearly 180,000 miles and had visited more than 40 countries, signing treaties and agreements and drawing the attention of the Western nations more strongly to the threat of Communism. In 1954 he launched the concept of SEATO (South-East Asia Treaty Organization) and backed the plan to bring Western Germany into NATO. In 1956, after the nationalization of the Suez Canal by Egypt, he proposed the Suez Canal Users' Association, and later opposed the Anglo-French military intervention. His advocacy of the policies of 'massive retaliation' and 'brinkmanship' raised tensions in the Cold War and seemed at odds with his belief that a moral purpose should inform international affairs. He resigned in 1959. Possibly the most powerful Secretary of State ever seen in the USA to that time, he was awarded the highest US civil decoration, the Medal of Freedom, shortly before his death from cancer. He published *War, Peace and Change* (1939) and *War or Peace* (1950). ⌨ *Richard Goold-Adams, John Foster Dulles: A Reappraisal* (1962)

Dulong, Pierre Louis 1785–1838
French chemist
Born in Rouen, he trained first as a doctor, and later became Professor of Chemistry and then of Physics in Paris. In 1813 he discovered the explosive nitrogen trichloride. With **Alexis Thérèse Petit** he carried out research on heat and enunciated the law of the constancy of atomic heats (1819).

Dumas, Alexandre See panel p566

Dumas, Alexandre, *known as* Dumas fils 1824–95
French writer
He was born in Paris, the illegitimate son of **Alexandre Dumas**, and at the age of 16, after a course of training at the Institution Goubaux and the Collège Bourbon, he joined the literary society to which his father belonged. 'Dumas fils' began by writing fiction, then turned, with equal success, to drama, and theoretical writings on art, morals, politics, and even religion. His novels include *La Dame aux camélias* (1848, Eng trans *The Lady with the Camelias*, 1856), and *L'Affaire Clémenceau* (1864, Eng trans *Wife Murder; or, The Clémenceau Tragedy*, 1866), which was a great success in dramatic form (1852). Of his 16 plays, *Le Demi-monde* (1855, Eng trans 1921), *Les Idées de Mme Aubray* (1867, Eng trans *Mme Aubray's Opinions*, 1965), *Monsieur Alphonse* (1873, Eng trans 1874) and *Denise* (1885, Eng trans 1885) are masterpieces. Other famous dramas in which he had a share include *Le Supplice d'une femme* (1865, 'The

Torture of a Woman'), whose chaotic original is due to **Émile de Girardin**. He may have assisted **George Sand** in preparing several of her works for the stage, and he completed and produced his father's *Joseph Balsamo* (1878). ⌨ *F H Gribble, Dumas, Father and Son* (1930)

Dumas, Jean Baptiste André 1800–84
French chemist
Born in Alais, he started his professional life as an apothecary there, but moved in 1816 to Geneva where he studied pharmacy, chemistry and botany. In 1823 he returned to France, where he taught chemistry at the École Polytechnique and at the Athenaeum to adults in the evening. He also lectured occasionally at the Collège de France and gave instruction in a private chemical laboratory. In 1840 he became the editor of *Annales de chimie et de physique*. His most important contribution to science was his attempts to classify organic compounds. He developed a simple method for the determination of vapour density, and thus relative molecular mass, but interpretation of the data was confused by the lack of distinction between an atom and a molecule. In 1834 he proposed that many organic compounds are formed by substitution of hydrogen by another element. This theory was developed further by **Auguste Laurent** and **Charles Frédéric Gerhardt**. After the French Revolution of 1848 he was elected to the legislative assembly. He was Minister of Agriculture (1850–51) and later became a senator. He was also vice-president and president of the Paris Municipal Council. ⌨ *Marcel Chaigneau, Jean-Baptiste Dumas, sa vie, son œuvre, 1800-1884* (1984)

du Maurier, Dame Daphne 1907–89
English novelist and short-story writer
Born in London, the daughter of the actor-manager Sir **Gerald du Maurier**, she wrote a number of highly successful period romances and adventure stories. Many of them were inspired by Cornwall, where she lived, including *Jamaica Inn* (1936), *Rebecca* (1938), *Frenchman's Creek* (1942) and *My Cousin Rachel* (1951). Several of these have been filmed, and her short story, 'The Birds' (published in *The Apple Tree*, 1952), became a classic **Hitchcock** movie. Later books include *The Flight of the Falcon* (1965), *The House on the Strand* (1969), *The Winding Stair*, a study of **Francis Bacon** (1976), *The Rendezvous and other Stories* (1980), and a volume of memoirs, *Vanishing Cornwall* (1967). ⌨ *Growing Pains: The Shaping of a Writer* (1977, published in the USA as *Myself When Young*); M Forster, *Daphne du Maurier* (1993)

du Maurier, George Louis Palmella Busson 1834–96
British artist, cartoonist and novelist
Born in Paris, he was the grandson of émigrés who had originally fled to England during the Revolution. In 1851 he went to London himself and studied chemistry, but returned to Paris to study art there, and in Antwerp and Düsseldorf. Back in England he made his name as an illustrator, with new editions of **Thackeray**'s *Esmond* and his ballads, **John Foxe**'s *Book of Martyrs*, and stories in periodicals like *Once A Week* and the *Cornhill Magazine*. He joined the staff of *Punch* (1864–96), and some of his illustrations were collected as *English Society at Home* (1880). He also wrote and illustrated three novels, *Peter Ibbetson* (1891), *The Martian* (1897), and the very successful *Trilby* (1894), the story of a young singer under the mesmeric influence of another musician, Svengali.

du Maurier, Sir Gerald Hubert Edward Busson 1873–1934
English actor-manager
He was born in London, and educated at Harrow. He left a business career for the stage. He played a small part in his father **George du Maurier**'s *Trilby* (1895), but became known for criminal roles, starting with a dramatization

Dumas, Alexandre, *in full* Alexandre Dumas Davy de la Pailleterie, *known as* Dumas père 1802–70
French novelist and playwright

Dumas was born in Villers-Cotterêts, the son of General Alexandre Davy-Dumas and Marie Labouret, the daughter of a tavern keeper and landowner. He moved to Paris in 1823, working as a clerk and taking up writing. At the age of 27, he became famous for his play *Henri III et sa cour* (1829, 'Henry III and his Court'), performed at the Théâtre Français, which revolutionized historical drama. In 1831 he did the same for domestic tragedy with *Antony*, and scored a tremendous success with *Richard Darlington*. In 1832 he carried the romantic 'history' to its culmination in *La Tour de Nesle* (in collaboration with Gaillardet). In that same year he fell ill with cholera, went to Switzerland to recuperate, and wrote for the *Revue des deux mondes* the first of his famous and delightful travelogues called *Impressions de voyage*.

Having returned to Paris, Dumas took a conspicuous part in the Days of July; in 1837 he received the red ribbon; in 1842 he married Mlle Ida Ferrier, from whom he promptly separated. In 1855 he went for two years into exile at Brussels; from 1860 to 1864 he was helping **Garibaldi** in Italy, and conducting and writing a journal, and in 1886 he produced the last but one of his plays. By this time he was ill and suffering from overwork. He had gone through a series of fortunes, and he left Paris for the last time with only a couple of napoleons in his pocket. He went to his son's villa in Dieppe, and stayed there until his death.

Dumas was a prodigious worker, and his output was enormous. Only a selection can be mentioned here. It was as a storyteller on historical themes that he gained enduring success. He decided to put the history of France into novels, and his earliest attempt was *Isabelle de Bavière* (1836). It was followed by *Pauline* (1838), *Acté* (1839), *Othon l'archer* (1840)—and others all on different lines. Then he turned again to the historical vein in *Le Chevalier d'Harmenthal* and *Ascanio* (1843).

In the 1840s, there appeared *Le Comte de Monte Cristo* (1844–45, *The Count of Monte Cristo*); the three works of *Les Trois mousquetaires* (1844, *The Three Musketeers*), *Vingt ans après* (1845, 'Twenty Years After') and *Dix Ans plus tard ou le Vicomte de Bragelonne*, (1848–50, 'Ten Years Later; or, The Vicomte de Bragelonne') which are set in the reign of **Louis XIII** and follow the adventures of d'Artagnan, who joins the king's musketeers and shares in the adventures of Athos, Porthos and Aramis; and *La Fille du régent* ('The Regent's Daughter'); *La Reine Margot* (1845, Eng trans *Queen Margot*, 1845), about the religious wars of 16th-century France; *La Guerre des femmes* ('The War of the Women'); *Le Chevalier de Maison Rouge* (1845), about the Chevalier de Rougeville's plot to rescue Marie Antoinette; *Le Bâtard de Mauléon* ('The Bastard of Mauléon'); *La Dame de Monsoreau* (1846, 'The Lady of Monsoreau'); *Les Mémoires d'un médecin, Joseph Balsamo* (1846–48, 'The Memoirs of Dr Joseph Balsamo'); and *Le Collier de la Reine* (1849–50, 'The Queen's Necklace'), about the 'Affair of the Diamond Necklace'.

There followed works as varied as *La Tulipe noire* (1850, 'The Black Tulip') and *Le Trou de l'enfer* (1850), and *La Femme au collier de velours* (1851, 'The Lady with the Velvet Collar'); the historical masterpiece *Olympe de Clèves* (1852); and from 1852 to 1854 the 10 delightful volumes of *Mes Mémoires*, with *Ange Pitou* (1851) and *La Comtesse de Charny* (1852–55). Other achievements in the romance of French history were *Ingénue* (1854), *Les Compagnons de Jéhu* (1857), *Les Louvres de Machecoul* (1859) and *Les Blancs et les bleus* (1867–68, 'The White and the Blue'), with which the sequence ended.

Claude Schopp, *Alexandre Dumas* (1988); F W Hemmings, *Alexandre Dumas* (1980); A Craig Bell, *Alexandre Dumas* (1950).

> *Tous pour un, un pour tous.*
> 'All for one, one for all.'
> From *Les Trois Mousquetaires*, ch.9 (1844).

---

of *Raffles* (1906). He became joint manager of Wyndham's Theatre (1910–25), and was knighted in 1922 for his services to the stage. He was manager of the St James's Theatre from 1926 until his death.

Dumont, Louis Charles Jean 1911–98
French social anthropologist

Born in Greece, he carried out fieldwork in southern India and became known for his studies of caste, as in *Homo hierarchicus* (1967), in which he distinguishes between the holistic, hierarchical ideology of traditional Indian society and the individualistic, egalitarian ideology of the modern West. The latter is explored in *Homo aequalis* (1977) and *Essais sur l'individualisme* (1983). His honours include the Académie Française prize (1984) and the Tocqueville prize (1987).

Dumont, Pierre Étienne Louis, *known as* the Apostle of Benthamism 1759–1829
Swiss churchman

Born in Geneva, he accepted the charge of the French Protestant church at St Petersburg in 1783. He became tutor in London to the sons of Lord Shelbourne (1785), his talents and liberalism recommending him to the Whigs. During the early years of the French Revolution he was in Paris, and became attached to Honoré, Comte de **Mirabeau**, about whom he wrote in his *Souvenirs sur Mirabeau* (1832, 'Memories of Mirabeau'). In 1791 he returned to England and met **Jeremy Bentham**. Convinced of the value of Bentham's views on legislation, he obtained permission to edit his unpublished writings. The results appeared in his *Traité de législation civile et pénale* (1802), *Théorie des peines et des récompenses* (1811), and others. Dumont returned to Geneva in 1814, and became a member of the Representative Council.

Dumont d'Urville, Jules Sébastien César 1790–1842
French naval explorer

Born in Condé, Calvados, he joined the navy in 1807. During hydrographic surveys of the eastern Mediterranean (1819–20) he secured the statue of the *Vénus de Milo*, which had been found on the Aegean island of Milos, for France. He first visited the Pacific as a member of the Louis-Isidore Duprey biological expedition (1822–15) and on his return proposed a second voyage. Sailing in the *Astrolabe*, he found the sunken remains of the Comte de La Pérouse's ship on the reefs of Vanikoro and also collected much important information on the ethnic groups, plants and geology of the Pacific Islands, revising the majority of existing maps (1826–29). From 1837 to 1840 he sailed to the Antarctic via the Magellan Strait but was stopped by ice at 63° S. The following year he returned south from Tasmania, and this time getting inside the ice barrier discovered Adelie and Joinsville Islands, so giving France its claim to Antarctica. He was promoted to rear admiral on his return. Forty-nine volumes of text and maps record his voyages.

Dumouriez, Charles François du Périer
1739–1823
French general
Born in Cambrai, he served during the Seven Years War from 1757. He was imprisoned for trying to help dissidents in Poland, but in 1778 Louis XVI made him commandant of Cherbourg. In 1790 he became one of the Jacobins, and was appointed commandant at Nantes. He now attached himself to the Girondins and was appointed Minister of Foreign Affairs in 1792, but resigned to command the northern army against Austria and Prussia. He prevented the allies from sweeping over Champagne, defeated the Prussians at Valmy (1792), and overthrew the Austrians at Jemappes. At Neerwinden (1793) he sustained a severe defeat from the Austrians. His leanings towards constitutional monarchy aroused the suspicion of the Revolutionists, and soon he was denounced as a traitor and summoned to Paris. To save his head he went over to the Austrian camp. After wandering through Europe he finally settled in England. Besides pamphlets, he wrote *Mémoires* (1794).

Dunant, Jean Henri 1828–1910
Swiss philanthropist and Nobel Prize winner
Born in Geneva, he inspired the foundation of the International Red Cross after seeing the plight of the wounded on the battlefield of Solferino (1859). His efforts brought about the conference at Geneva (1863) from which came the Geneva Convention (1864). In 1901, with Frédéric Passy, he was awarded the first Nobel Peace Prize. ⊞ H N Pandit, *The Red Cross and Henry Dunant* (1969)

Dunaway, (Dorothy) Faye 1941–
US actress
Born in Bascom, Florida, she trained at the Boston University School of Fine and Applied Arts and made her Broadway debut in *A Man for all Seasons* (1962). She was signed to a personal contract with producer-director Otto Preminger, and first appeared in *The Happening* in 1966. She quickly acquired popularity, winning a Best Actress Academy Award nomination for her performance in *Bonnie and Clyde* (1967). She also appeared in *The Three Musketeers* (1973), *The Towering Inferno* (1974), *Chinatown* (1974) and *Network* (1976, Academy Award). Her television work includes *The Disappearance of Aimee* (1976) and *Cold Sassy Tree* (1989). Later films include *Mommie Dearest* (1981), *Barfly* (1987) and *Don Juan De Marco* (1995). She published her autobiography, *Looking for Gatsby*, in 1995.

Dunbar, Paul Laurence 1872–1906
US poet
Born in Dayton, Ohio, he was the son of escaped black slaves. He gained a reputation with *Lyrics of Lowly Life* (1896), many of which were in dialect. He published several other volumes of verse, and four novels. His *Complete Poems* appeared in 1913. ⊞ A Gayle Jnr, *Oak and Ivy: a biography of Dunbar* (1971)

Dunbar, William c.1460–c.1520
Scottish poet
Born probably in East Lothian, he seems to have studied at St Andrews University (1475–79). He became a Franciscan novice, and travelled widely in England before leaving the order. He then became secretary to some of James IV's embassies to foreign courts. In 1500 the king gave him a pension. The following year he visited England, and as a courtier of James IV he wrote poems, including *The Thrissil and the Rois* and the *Lament for the Makaris*. In 1508 Walter Chepman (c.1473–1538) printed seven of his poems—the earliest specimen of Scottish typography. Dunbar also wrote satires, such as *The Twa Marriit Wemen and the Wedo* and *The Dance of the Sevin Deadly*

Synnis. His name disappears from the records altogether after the Battle of Flodden (1513). ⊞ J Baxter, *William Dunbar, a biographical study* (1952)

Duncan I c.1010–1040
King of Scots
He was the son of Bethoc and Crinan, Abbot of Dunkeld, and the grandson of Malcolm II. He succeeded to Strathclyde in 1034 and probably ruled over most of Scotland except the islands and the far north. He attempted southwards expansion, and a long and unsuccessful siege of Durham weakened his position. He was killed by Macbeth at Pitgaveney, near Elgin.

Duncan, Adam, Viscount 1731–1804
Scottish naval commander
Born in Dundee, he joined the navy in 1746, and commanded the *Valiant* in the sack of Havana (1762). He commanded the *Monarch* at Cape St Vincent (1780), and as admiral took command in 1795 of the North Sea Squadron to watch the Dutch fleet (Holland and France being at war with Great Britain). His blockade of the Texel was effective, and Dutch trade was almost ruined. In the spring of 1797 the mutiny of the Nore spread to Duncan's seamen, and his position was for some weeks critical, but in the autumn he gained an impressive victory over Jan de Winter at Camperdown.

Duncan, Isadora, *originally* Angela Duncan
1877–1927
US dancer and choreographer
Born in San Francisco, she travelled throughout Europe, performing her own choreography, and founded schools in Berlin, Salzburg and Vienna. A pioneer of modern dance, she based her work on Greek-derived notions of beauty and harmony, but also used running, skipping, and walking movements. In Moscow (1922) she married a young Russian poet, Sergei Yesenin, who later committed suicide. An influential and controversial figure, she held unconventional views for the time on marriage and women's liberation. She herself was accidentally strangled when her scarf caught in the wheel of her car. She published her autobiography, *My Life*, in 1926–27.

Duncan, Robert Edward, *originally* Edward Howard Duncan 1919–
US poet
Born in Oakland, California, he was adopted by Theosophists in 1920 and named Robert Edward Symmes. Educated at the University of California, he was editor of *Experimental Review* (1938–40) and *Phoenix and Berkeley Miscellany* (1948–49). Aligned with the Black Mountain school of poets, and influenced by George Barker and Ezra Pound, he wrote in a style that emphasized natural forms and processes. His collections include *Heavenly City, Earthly City* (1947), *The Opening of the Field* (1960), *Roots and Branches* (1964) and *The Years as Catches* (1966). His 1944 essay, 'The Homosexual in Society', is an important document in the development of homosexual cultural politics. ⊞ *The Truth and Life of Myth: an essential autobiography* (1968)

Duncan, Thomas 1807–45
Scottish painter
Born in Kinclaven, Perthshire, he is best known for historical and genre works, many with a Jacobite flavour, such as *Prince Charles's Entry into Edinburgh after Prestonpans* and *Charles Edward Asleep after Culloden*.

Duncan-Sandys, Duncan Edwin Sandys, Baron 1908–87
British Conservative politician
He was educated at Eton and Magdalen College, Oxford, worked for the diplomatic service (1930–33), and in 1935 entered politics as MP for Norwood, London (1935–45),

and later Streatham (1950–74). In 1951 he was made Minister of Supply in the **Churchill** government and in 1954 became Minister of Housing and Local Government. He introduced the Clean Air Act and the concept of Green Belts round cities, and was the founder of the Civic Trust (1956). As Minister of Defence (1957–59) he inaugurated a controversial programme of cutting costs and streamlining the forces. He was subsequently Minister of Aviation (1959–60), Secretary of State for Commonwealth Relations (1960–64) and Secretary of State for the Colonies (1962–64). In 1935 he married Diana, daughter of Sir Winston Churchill (divorced 1960). He published two books, *European Movement and the Council of Europe* (1949) and *The Modern Commonwealth* (1961).

Dundas, Henry, 1st Viscount Melville and Baron Dunira 1742–1811
Scottish jurist and politician

Admitted to the Scottish Bar in 1763, he was successively advocate-depute and Solicitor-General. In 1774 he became MP for Midlothian, in 1775 Lord Advocate, and in 1777 Keeper of the Signet for Scotland. Elected in opposition to the current administration, he soon became a strenuous supporter of Lord **North** and one of the most obstinate defenders of the war with America. When North resigned in 1781 Dundas continued as Lord Advocate under the Marquis of **Rockingham**. On the formation of the coalition he passed over to **William Pitt**, the Younger, and became his ablest coadjutor. When Pitt returned to power in 1784 Dundas was appointed president of the Board of Control, and introduced a bill for restoring the Scottish estates forfeited after the 1745 Jacobite rebellion. He resigned with Pitt in 1801, and in 1802, under the Addington (see **Sidmouth**) administration, was made Viscount Melville and Baron Dunira. For 30 years he was the effective ruler of Scotland. In 1805 he was impeached for 'gross malversation and breach of duty' as Treasurer of the Navy, but was acquitted by his peers on all charges involving his honour.

Dundas of Arniston
Scottish family distinguished for their legal and political talent

Sir James Dundas, the first of Arniston, was knighted by **James VI and I**, and was Governor of Berwick. His son, Sir James (d.1679), was a judge of the Court of Session under the title of Lord Arniston (1662), but was deprived of his office in 1663 for refusing to abjure the Covenant. His eldest son, Sir Robert (d.1726), was also a judge at the Court of Session, from 1689. The latter's son, Robert, was Solicitor-General for Scotland (1717), Lord Advocate (1720), and Lord President of the Court of Session (1748–53). His son, also Robert, was Solicitor-General for Scotland (1742), Lord Advocate (1754) and Lord President of the Court of Session (1760–87).

Dundee, John Graham of Claverhouse, 1st Viscount, *known as* Bonny Dundee or Bloody Claverse c.1649–1689
Scottish soldier

He served in both the French and Dutch armies as a professional soldier. In 1674 at the Battle of Seneff he is said to have saved the life of William of Orange (**William III**). In 1677 he returned to Scotland, and became lieutenant in a troop of horse commanded by his kinsman, the Marquis of **Montrose**, against the Covenanters. At Drumclog (1679) he was routed by Covenanters, but three weeks later he commanded the cavalry at Bothwell Brig, where the Covenanters were defeated. From 1682 to 1685 he was active in hunting down Covenanters in the southwest of Scotland. When William III landed in England in 1688 at the start of the 'Glorious Revolution', Dundee marched into England in support of **James VII and II**. In

Scotland, after leaving the Convention of 1689, he raised an army in the Highlands. He defeated the loyalist forces in a fierce encounter at Killiecrankie in July 1689, but in the process was mortally wounded. 📖 Andrew Murray Scott, *Bonnie Dundee* (1989)

Dundonald, Earl of See **Cochrane, Thomas**

Dunér, Nils Christofer 1839–1914
Swedish astronomer

Educated at Lund, he became Professor of Astronomy at Uppsala and director of the observatory there (1888–1909). He made a study of variable and double stars and was an expert on stellar spectroscopy.

Dunham, Katherine 1910–
US dancer, choreographer and teacher

Born in Chicago, she studied anthropology at the University of Chicago and researched dance in the West Indies before her appointment as dance director of the Federal Theatre Project (1938). Her first New York concert in 1940 launched her career as a leading choreographer of African-American dances. She subsequently worked on Broadway (most importantly for the musical *Cabin in the Sky*, 1940) and in Hollywood on *Stormy Weather* (1943) amongst other things, while developing a successful formula for live black performance revues. Her Dunham School of Dance (1945–55) exerted considerable influence on the direction of US black dance with its combination of elements of classical ballet, modern and Afro-Caribbean techniques. She choreographed for opera, toured extensively with her own company and wrote several books about her field. She published her autobiography, *A Touch of Innocence*, in 1959.

Dunhill, Thomas Frederick 1877–1946
English composer and teacher

Born in London, he studied under **Charles Stanford** at the Royal College of Music in London, and taught at Eton (1899–1908). In 1907 he organized concerts to publicize the works of younger British composers. He made his name with chamber works, songs, and the light opera *Tantivy Towers* (1931) to words by **A P Herbert**.

Dunlop, Frank 1927–
English stage director and administrator

He was born in Leeds and after founding and directing Piccolo Theatre, Manchester (1954), he became an associate director of the Bristol Old Vic (1956). From 1961 to 1964 he was director of Nottingham Playhouse, opening the first season in the new building. He directed *Saturday Night and Sunday Morning* in the West End (1965), and directed Pop Theatre, a company he founded himself, in *The Winter's Tale* and **Euripides**'s *The Trojan Women* at the Edinburgh Festival (1966). He became associate director at the National Theatre (1967–71), and also administrator (1968–71). He founded the Young Vic (1970), and was the company's director (until 1978, 1980–83). He was director of the Edinburgh Festival for eight years (1984–91).

Dunlop, Joey (William Joseph) 1952–
Northern Irish motorcyclist

Born in Ballymoney, Londonderry, he was an outstanding rider at Isle of Man Tourist Trophy (TT) races, winning 13 races between 1977 and 1988 (one short of the all-time record of **Mike Hailwood**), including the Senior Tourist Trophy in 1985 and 1987–88. He won the Formula One TT for the sixth successive season in 1988, and was Formula One World champion (1982–86). In 1988, he set the TT lap record at 118.54mph (190.73kmph).

Dunlop, John Boyd 1840–1921
Scottish inventor

Born in Dreghorn, Ayrshire, he became a veterinary surgeon in Edinburgh and then Belfast (from 1867). He is generally credited with inventing the pneumatic tyre, having in 1887 fitted his child's tricycle-wheels with inflated rubber hoses instead of solid rubber tyres. The principle had already been patented, in 1845, by Scottish engineer, **Robert William Thomson**, but in 1889 Dunlop formed the business that became the Dunlop Rubber Company Ltd, which produced commercially practical pneumatic tyres for bicycles and, later, motor cars.

Dunlop, Ronald Ossary 1894–1973
Irish painter
Born in Dublin, he was a member of the London Group, best known for his palette-knife painting with rich impasto and glowing colour. His work is represented in the Tate Gallery, London, and many provincial galleries, and his writings on art include *Landscape Painting* (1954) and the autobiographical *Struggling with Paint* (1956).

Dunn, Douglas 1942–
US post-modern dancer and choreographer
Born in Palo Alto, California, he studied dance while at Princeton, moving later to New York and the **Merce Cunningham** studio. While working there (1969–73) he met **Yvonne Rainer**. As well as performing in her works (including *Continuous Project Altered Daily*, 1969–70), he joined her as one of the founders of the experimental dance group Grand Union with which he was associated for six years until 1976. During that time, he made a solo piece, *101*, which required him to lie motionless for four hours a day, six days a week for two months. In 1977 he founded his own company and in 1980 created *Pulcinella* for Paris Opera Ballet. His fun, original and loose-limbed choreography has been seen in such recent works as *Landing* (1992), *Stucco Moon* (1994) and *Caracole* (1995).

Dunn, Douglas Eaglesham 1942–
Scottish poet
Born in Inchinnan, Renfrewshire, he was educated at Renfrew High and Camphill schools, Paisley, before attending the Scottish School of Librarianship and Hull University, where he was employed in the library simultaneously with **Philip Larkin**, who became a friend and mentor. His first collection of poems, *Terry Street* (1969), articulates contempt and warmth in almost equal measure for the working-class suburb of Hull where he was then living. The two subsequent collections—*The Happier Life* (1972) and *Love or Nothing* (1974)—rather disappointed readers who had been drawn to *Terry Street* by its bleak humour and tacky glamour. In *Barbarians* (1979), however, he echoed and extended that first collection. He returned to Scotland in 1984. *Elegies* (1985), written on the death of his first wife, is a moving valediction, emotionally raw but tightly controlled. It won the Whitbread prize. Other works include *Secret Villages* (1985), a collection of stories, *Selected Poems: 1964–1983* (1986), *Dante's Drum-kit* (1993) and another volume of stories, *Boyfriends and Girlfriends* (1994). He has been Professor of English at St Andrews University since 1991.

Dunne, Finley Peter 1867–1936
US humorist
Born in Chicago, he worked as a journalist there, and was editor of *Chicago Journal* (1897–1900). *Mr Dooley in Peace and War* (1898) established the character 'Mr Dooley', a Chicago Irish philosopher-bartender, and from 1900 Dunne was *the* exponent of US–Irish humorous satire on current personages and events. 📖 E J Bander, *Mr Dooley and Mr Dunne: The Literary Life of a Chicago Catholic* (1981)

Dunne, Irene, *originally* Irene Marie Dunn
1898–1990
US actress

Born in Louisville, Kentucky, she trained at the Chicago Musical College, establishing herself as a musical comedy star in her first Broadway appearance in *The Clinging Vine* (1922). Her Hollywood debut came with *Leathernecking* (1930) and she received the first of five Best Actress Academy Award nominations for the Western *Cimarron* (1931). An intelligent, versatile actress, she had many successes including *The Awful Truth* (1937), *Love Affair* (1939) and *I Remember Mama* (1948). She retired in 1952 and served as an alternate delegate to the United Nations 12th General Assembly in 1957. An active charity worker, she was honoured for her lifetime achievement at the Kennedy Arts Center in 1985.

Dunne, John William 1875–1949
English inventor and philosopher
He designed the first British military aeroplane (1906–07) and wrote the bestselling speculative works *An Experiment with Time* (1927), *The Serial Universe* (1934), *The New Immortality* (1938) and *Nothing Dies* (1940).

Dunnett, Sir Alastair MacTavish 1908–98
Scottish journalist
Born in Kilmacolm, Ayrshire, he was educated at Hillhead High School, Glasgow, and joined the head office of the Commercial Bank of Scotland at the age of 17. He gave up his job to publish a magazine for Scottish boys, and though short-lived, this venture launched him on his journalistic career. He was chief press officer to the Secretary of State for Scotland (1940–46) and editor of the *Daily Record* (1946–55) before becoming editor of *The Scotsman* from 1956 to 1972, thereafter serving as chairman of Thomson Scottish Petroleum (1979–87). Intensely committed to his native country, he served with distinction on the boards of several national bodies. He co-wrote the autobiographical *Among Friends* (1984) with his wife, the novelist **Dorothy Dunnett**. He became a Fellow of the Royal Society of Arts in 1987 and was knighted in 1995.

Dunnett, Dorothy, *née* Halliday 1923–
Scottish novelist
Born in Dunfermline, Fife, and educated at James Gillespie's High School for Girls, Edinburgh, she began her career with the Civil Service as a press secretary in Edinburgh. In 1946 she married the journalist **Alastair Dunnet**. A recognized portrait painter since 1950, she has exhibited at the Royal Academy and is a member of the Scottish Society of Women Artists. She has used her maiden name for a series of detective novels, starting with *Dolly and the Singing Bird* (1968), but her best-known works comprise a series of historical novels, including *Game of Kings* (1961) and *Checkmate* (1975), which continue the Scottish tradition of historical romance. In 1986 she embarked upon a second historical series, this time featuring the house of Charetty and Niccoló. She became a director of the Edinburgh Book Festival in 1990.

Dunning, John Ray 1907–75
US physicist
Born in Shelby, Nebraska, he studied at Wesleyan University, Nebraska, and at Columbia University, New York, where he worked from 1933, becoming professor in 1950. In 1940 he confirmed **Niels Bohr**'s hypothesis that the slow neutrons required to maintain nuclear chain reactions would only result in the fission of ^{235}U, which would have to be separated from the more abundant ^{238}U to obtain fissionable material for the Manhattan atomic bomb project. Dunning led the group which developed the gaseous diffusion technique, where the lighter ^{235}U passes through a diffusion filter faster than ^{238}U, leading

to an increase in the ^{235}U concentration. This process provided most of the ^{235}U used in the atomic bombs dropped on Japan.

Dunning, William Archibald 1857–1922
US historian and educator

Born in Plainfield, New Jersey, he studied and taught at Columbia University, New York. His major work was a three-volume *History of Political Theories* (1916), spanning two thousand years of European thought, but his chief significance lies in his direction of doctoral research on American history. In particular the 'Dunning School' (apart from his prize pupil, Ulrich Bonnell Phillips) produced detailed studies of individual states under Reconstruction.

Dunois, Jean d'Orléans, Count, *known as* the Bastard of Orléans 1403–68
French general

The illegitimate son of Louis, Duc d'Orléans, he was a general in the Hundred Years War. He defeated the English at Montargis (1427), defended Orleans with a small force until its relief by Joan of Arc (1429), then inflicted further defeats on the English, forcing the Duke of Bedford from Lagny and chasing them out of Paris. By 1453 he had also liberated Normandy and Guyenne. He joined the league of nobles against Louis XI, but remained loyal to Louis XII.

Dunoyer de Segonzac, André See Segonzac, André Dunoyer de

Dunsany, Edward John Moreton Drax Plunkett, 18th Baron 1878–1957
Irish novelist, poet and playwright

Born in London, and educated at Eton and Sandhurst, he served in the Second Boer War, and then settled in Ireland. In World War I he was an officer of the Inniskilling Fusiliers. By World War II, he was Byron Professor of English Literature at Athens, and was associated with the Irish revival led by W B Yeats and Lady Gregory. He became known for his poetic and imaginative literary works, such as *The King of Elfland's Daughter* (1924), and his 'Jorkens' stories, beginning with *The Travel Tales of Mr Joseph Jorkens* (1931). At Yeats's invitation he wrote many plays for the Abbey Theatre, Dublin, including *The Laughter of the Gods* (1919), which became popular both in Great Britain and the USA. His verse is contained in *Fifty Poems* (1930) and *Mirage Water* (1939). He also wrote an autobiographical series (1938–49). ⌨ M Amory, *Lord Dunsany* (1972)

Duns Scotus, John, *Latin* Joannes c.1265–1308
Scottish Franciscan philosopher and theologian

His brief life is scantily documented. Born probably in Duns, Berwickshire, he became a Franciscan and was ordained priest in St Andrews Church, Northampton, in 1291. He studied and taught at Oxford and Paris, probably also in Cambridge, and finally at Cologne where he died and was buried. His works, consisting mainly of commentaries on the Bible, Aristotle and the *Sentences* of Peter Lombard, many incomplete, were later collected and edited (not always very responsibly) by his associates. The main works are now taken to be the *Opus Parisiense* (the Parisian Lectures, as recorded by a student), the *Opus Oxoniense* (the Oxford lectures, also known as the *Ordinatio*, and probably revised by the author), the *Tractatus de Primo Principio* (Eng trans *A Treatise on God as First Principle*, 1966) and the *Quaestiones Quodlibetales*. His philosophy represents a strong reaction against both Aristotle and St Thomas Aquinas. He propounded the primacy of the individual (in the dispute about universals), and the freedom of the individual will. He saw faith as the necessary foundation of Christian theology, but faith was for him exercised through an act of will and

was practical, not speculative or theoretical. He also pioneered the doctrine of the Immaculate Conception. He rivalled Aquinas as the greatest theologian of the Middle Ages—the Franciscans followed Scotus as the Dominicans did Aquinas—and was known by contemporaries as 'Doctor Subtilis' for his dialectical skill. In the 16th century the Scotists were ridiculed by the English Reformers, and dubbed 'Dunses' (hence 'dunce') for their defence of the papacy against the divine right of kings. More recently he has been admired by figures as diverse as Charles Peirce, Martin Heidegger and Gerard Manley Hopkins, who found him 'of realty the rarest veinèd unraveller'. ⌨ Efrem Bettoni, *Duns Scotus* (1961)

Dunstan, St c.909–988
Anglo-Saxon prelate

Born near Glastonbury, Somerset, he was educated at the Abbey there, and took monastic vows. Appointed abbot of Glastonbury in 945, he transformed Glastonbury into a centre of religious teaching. An adviser of King Edmund I, he fled during Edwy's reign, but was recalled by King Edgar, who was now king of the country north of the Thames, and was created Bishop of Worcester (957) and of London (959). In that year, on Edwy's death, Edgar became King of all England, and immediately appointed Dunstan Archbishop of Canterbury. Dunstan strove to make the clergy real teachers of the people in secular as well as religious matters. He made the payment of tithes by landowners obligatory, and introduced the Benedictine rule into England. On Edgar's death he declared for Edward the Martyr, Edgar's elder son, and crowned him. On Edward's murder (978) Ethelred succeeded, whose hostility ended Dunstan's political career. His feast day is 19 May.

Dunwoody, Richard 1964–
Northern Irish National Hunt jockey

Born in Ulster, the son of a jockey, he rode his first winner in 1983 and thereafter shadowed the success of the champion jockey Peter Scudamore, until Scudamore retired in 1993. Dunwoody's highly impressive career includes victories at the Grand National (1986), Gold Cup (1988) and the Champion Hurdle (1990). Since 1993 he has been vice-president of the Jockey's Association. He is the co-author of two books, namely *Hell for Leather* (1993) and *Duel* (1994).

Duparc, Henri, *in full* Marie Eugène Henri Fouques-Duparc 1848–1933
French composer

Born in Paris, he studied under César Franck. Although he wrote a variety of works, he is remembered for his 15 songs, based on poems by Baudelaire and others which remain popular.

Dupleix, Joseph François 1697–1763
French colonial administrator

Born in Landrecies, he was appointed to a seat in the French East India Council in 1720. His skilful diplomacy among the native princes almost made the Carnatic a French province, and his power alarmed the English company. When war broke out in Europe between France and England, Bertrand de La Bourdonnais, who had taken Madras, was bribed with £40,000 to restore it to the English on payment of a ransom. This Dupleix refused to accede to, and violent disputes resulted in La Bourdonnais' recall. Dupleix skilfully defended Pondicherry, against Admiral Boscawen's five-week attack, but his ambitious project of founding a French empire in India was frustrated by Sir Robert Clive. The French Company refused to reimburse him for the vast sums he had spent out of his (alleged) private fortune, and he died in poverty and neglect in 1763.

Duplessis, Maurice le Noblet 1890–1959
French–Canadian politician

He led the Union Nationale to power in Quebec in 1936, gaining power through a methodical exploitation of nationalisme and fear of anglicization, yet he encouraged further encroachments by US corporations on Quebec's economic life. His campaign against radical reformers gained him the support of the Catholic Church, which he retained almost throughout his political career. His attitude towards labour was expressed in the notorious Padlock Act of 1937 which crippled the socialist Co-operative Commonwealth Federation (CCF), but it was his antagonistic attitude towards federal government (which he claimed was invading provincial rights through the War Measures Act) which contributed most to his defeat in 1939, when Ernest Lapointe and other French–Canadian ministers threatened to resign if he was returned to office. He did regain power in 1944, defeating both the incumbent Liberals under Adélard Godbout and the extremist Bloc Populaire, and maintained his pre-war policies. An alliance between labour, professionals, academics, and even some churchmen, eventually succeeded in demonstrating the scale of corruption in his government and although Duplessis himself died suddenly in 1959, the Union Nationale was defeated by the Liberals in 1960.

Dupond, Patrick 1959–
French dancer

Born in Paris, he was the youngest dancer ever accepted into the Paris Opera Ballet (at the age of 15), and at 17 won top honours at the Varna international competition. In 1980 he was made *étoile*, and he has since been a guest performer with various companies around the world. An unconventional and mercurial virtuoso, one of his most notable roles was that of **Vaslav Nijinsky** in **John Neumeier's** tribute to the dancer (1979). In 1988 he became artistic director of Ballet de Nancy.

du Pont (de Nemour), Éleuthère Irénée
1771–1834
US industrialist

Born in Paris, the younger son of **Pierre-Samuel du Pont de Nemours**, he worked in his father's printing plant until it was closed down in 1797. He emigrated to the USA (1800), and in 1802 established in Wilmington, Delaware, a gunpowder factory which developed into one of the world's largest chemical concerns. 📖 William H Carr, *The du Ponts of Delaware* (1964)

du Pont (de Nemours), Pierre-Samuel
1739–1817
US economist

Born in Paris, France, he was a disciple of **François Quesney** and expounded the theories of Quesnay's Physiocratic school in *Physiocratie* (1767). He was imprisoned in 1792 for his defence of **Louis XVI**, and he emigrated to the USA in 1799. He was approached by **Thomas Jefferson** to create a new American education system, but this was never implemented; however it was adopted as part of the French educational code. He returned to France in 1802, where he became Secretary to the provisional government, but finally settled in the USA in 1815. He also wrote *Origines et progrès d'une science nouvelle* (1768) and *Du pouvoir législatif et du pouvoir exécutif* (1795).

du Pont, Pierre Samuel 1870–1954
US businessman

Born in Wilmington, Delaware, he graduated from Massachusetts Institute of Technology (MIT) and joined the family gunpowder company. In 1902 he bought the company with his cousins, Thomas Coleman du Pont and Alfred Eugene du Pont, and decentralized many of its activities, although family control was maintained. As president (1915–20) he also introduced and developed many new industrial management techniques, including a systematic approach to strategic planning, control systems, and the pioneering of modern industrial accounting methods. He became president of General Motors (GM) in 1920 after the du Pont company had rescued it from near bankruptcy. He reorganized GM and appointed **Alfred Sloan, Jnr**, as its chief executive officer. 📖 William H Carr, *The du Ponts of Delaware* (1964)

du Pont, Samuel Francis 1803–65
US naval officer

Born in Bergen Point, New Jersey, he joined the navy in 1815, and commanded a sloop during the Mexican War in the Gulf of California and off San Diego. In the Civil War he organized the blockade of the South Atlantic area by Federal naval forces, and captured the ports of South Carolina and Georgia. Unjustly blamed for the failure of the Federal attack on Charleston in 1863, he was relieved of his command.

du Pré, Jacqueline Mary 1945–87
English cellist

Born in Oxford, she studied at the Guildhall School of Music with William Pleeth, with **Paul Tortelier** in Paris, **Pablo Casals** in Switzerland and **Mstislav Rostropovich** in Moscow. She made her concert debut at the Wigmore Hall aged 16, and subsequently toured internationally. In 1967 she married the pianist **Daniel Barenboim**. After developing multiple sclerosis in 1972 she pursued a teaching career, including master-classes on television. 📖 Carol Easton, *Jacqueline du Pré: A Biography* (1989)

Dupré, Marcel 1886–1971
French organist

Born in Rouen, he was chief organist at St Sulpice Church, Paris, and Notre Dame Cathedral. He won the Prix de Rome for composition in 1914, and became a professor at the Paris Conservatoire in 1926. A gifted improviser, he composed many chorales and an organ concerto, and was acclaimed throughout Europe for his organ recitals. 📖 Michael Murray, *Marcel Dupré, the Work of a Master Organist* (1985)

Dupuytren, Guillaume, Baron 1777–1835
French surgeon

Born in Pierre-Buffière, near Limoges, he was Professor of Clinical Surgery in Paris from 1812, and surgeon to **Louis XVIII** and **Charles X**. He invented many surgical instruments, and devised surgical techniques for many conditions, including 'Dupuytren's contracture', in which fibrosis in the palm causes the retraction of fingers.

Duquesne, Abraham, Marquis of 1610–88
French naval officer

Born in Dieppe, he distinguished himself from 1637 to 1643 in the war with Spain. Serving Sweden (1644–47) he became vice-admiral and won victories over a Danish-Dutch naval alliance. He returned to France and captured Bordeaux, which had declared for the Fronde (1650). He defeated **Michiel de Ruyter** and **Maarten Tromp** several times (1672–73), and the united fleets of Spain and Holland off Sicily in 1676. On the revocation of the Edict of Nantes, Duquesne was the only Protestant excepted.

Durack, Dame Mary 1913–94
Australian author

Born into a pioneering Western Australian family in Adelaide, she wrote historical novels such as *Kings in Grass Castles* (1959) and its sequel *Sons in the Saddle* (1983). Other works include *The Rock and the Sand* (1969) and the play *Swan River Saga* (1975). She has also written a number of books for children, some with illustrations by her younger sister, Elizabeth Durack (1916–). Her libretto for the opera *Dalgerie*, with music by Australian composer James Penberthy, was based on her own novel *Keep Him My Country* (1955) and was produced at the Sydney Opera House in 1973. Her husband was Horatio Clive ('Horrie') Miller (1893–1980), a pioneer of Australian aviation.

Duran See **Carolus-Duran**

Durand, Alice See **Gréville, Henry**

Durand, Asher Brown 1796–1886
US painter, engraver and illustrator

Born in New Jersey, as well as producing reproductions of the work of US artists, he made his own engravings of famous contemporary Americans. Between 1835 and 1840 he also painted portraits of eminent Americans. After a visit to Europe in 1840 he was associated with the Hudson River school and painted Romantic and dramatic landscapes. His graphic work strongly influenced the design of US paper currency.

Durand, Charles Auguste Émile See **Carolus-Duran**

Durand, Marguerite 1864–1936
French feminist writer

Born in Paris, she became an actress at the Comédie Française in 1881 but abandoned her acting career and married Georges Laguerre (1888), whom she later divorced. She became a feminist and was for a time vice-president of *La Ligue française pour le droit des femmes*. She established the first women's daily paper in the world, *La Fronde* ('The Insurrectionist'), and campaigned for better working conditions for women and for female suffrage. From 1908 until 1914 she was co-director of the Parisian newspaper *Les Nouvelles*. In 1922 she organized an exhibition of 19th-century women in Paris and five years before her death endowed a feminist archive, the Bibliothèque Marguerite Durand.

Durante, Jimmy 1893–1980
US comedian

Born in New York City, he played the piano and told jokes in saloons and nightclubs in the 1920s and performed on Broadway in the 1930s. A fixture in US show business for more than half a century, he appeared in many Hollywood films and had his own radio and television programmes. Known for his battered hat, gravelly voice, and oversized nose (he was nicknamed 'Da Schnozz'), he often mangled and invented words and repeated trademark lines such as his sign-off 'Goodnight, Mrs. Calabash, wherever you are'.

Duras, Marguerite, *pseudonym of* Marguerite Donnadieu 1914–96
French novelist

Born in Gia Dinh, Indo-China, she studied law and political science at the Sorbonne in Paris, and during World War II took part in the Resistance at great risk to herself as a Jewess. Her novels include *Un Barrage contre le Pacifique* (1950, Eng trans *The Sea Wall*, 1952 (US); 1953 (UK)), *Le Vice-Consul* (1966, Eng trans *The Vice Consul*, 1968) and *Détruire, dit-elle* (1969, Eng trans *Destroy, she said*, 1970). She also wrote film scripts such as *Hiroshima mon Amour* (1960, 'Hiroshima My Love'), and a number of plays, including *La Musica* (1965, Eng trans *The Music*, 1966). The semi-autobiographical *La Douleur* was published in 1985, (Eng trans 1986) and *L'Amant* (1984, Eng trans *The Lover*, 1985) won the Prix Goncourt. Remarkably, Duras, in her later life, survived a two-year period in a coma and continued to write. Her final novel *C'est tout* ('That's All') was published in 1995. She is considered one of the great European writers of the 20th century. 📖 A Cismaru, *Duras* (1971)

Durbin, Deanna, *originally* Edna Mae Durbin
1921–
Canadian entertainer

Born in Winnipeg, Manitoba, she and her family moved to California, where her singing voice attracted the attention of talent scouts. She first appeared in the short film *Every Sunday* (1936), and became an immediate star with *Three Smart Girls* (1936). Already popular on radio, she had box-office successes with *One Hundred Men and a Girl* (1937), *Mad About Music* (1938) and *Three Smart Girls Grow Up* (1939). Her flair for comedy was evident in *It Started With Eve* (1941) and she gave creditable dramatic performances in *Christmas Holiday* (1944) and *Lady on a Train* (1945). She made her last two films in 1948 and has enjoyed a long and contented retirement near Paris.

Durcan, Paul 1944–
Irish poet

Born in Dublin, he graduated in history and archaeology from University College, Cork, in 1973. His poems, which have won the Patrick Kavanagh award for poetry (1974) and the Whitbread Poetry prize (1990), are direct statements of commitment to a relentless humanist standpoint. His publications include *O Westport in the Light of Asia Minor* (1975), *Teresa's Bar* (1976), and *Jesus and Angela* (1988). A more meditative and reflective tone is present in the autobiographical *Daddy, Daddy* (1990) and the politically-informed *A Snail in my Prime* (1993). The loose long line structure he assimilated from the US Beat Poets and the Russian Modernists often conceals the craft and passion that is the emotional trademark of all his work.

Durcansky, Ferdinand 1906–74
Slovak Populist Party politician

Upset by the union of Czechs and Slovaks in a single state in 1918, he was active in the 1930s in trying to negotiate Slovak independence. After the Munich Agreement he visited **Hermann Goering** and others in Berlin and was encouraged to make trouble for the rump Czechoslovak government in Prague. Eventually **Hitler** virtually ordered him and his superior, **Jozef Tiso**, to declare independence. This was the signal for the Nazis to sweep into Prague in 1939 and establish the Bohemian Protectorate. He was immediately made Slovak Foreign Minister, although about a year later he was dismissed as insufficiently compliant. Condemned to death in absentia in 1947, he spent the remainder of his life abroad.

Dürer, Albrecht See panel p573

Durey, Louis 1888–1979
French composer

Born in Paris, he did not begin his musical education until he was 22. In 1916, under the influence of **Erik Satie**, he became one of the group of young French composers known as Les Six, but broke with them in 1921. He wrote large orchestral and choral works, but is chiefly known for his songs and chamber music.

D'Urfey, Tom (Thomas) 1653–1723
English dramatist and songwriter

He was born in Exeter, a nephew of **Honoré d'Urfé**. He was a prolific playwright, and his comedies, which include *The Fond Husband* (1676), *Madame Fickle* (1677) and *Sir Barnaby Whig* (1681), were especially popular. In 1683 he published his *New Collection of Songs and Poems*, which was followed by a long series of songs, collected as *Wit and Mirth, or Pills to Purge Melancholy* (6 vols, 1719–20). Several plays he had written in the meantime were criticized as being immoral by **Jeremy Collier**. 📖 R S Forsyte, *A Study of the Plays* (1916)

Durham, John George Lambton, 1st Earl of
1792–1840
English politician

Dürer, Albrecht 1471–1528
German painter and engraver

Albrecht Dürer was born in Nuremberg, the son of a goldsmith from Hungary. In 1486 he was apprenticed to **Michael Wolgemut**, the chief illustrator of the Nuremberg Chronicle, and in 1490 started on travels that lasted four years. In 1497 he set up on his own; he completed many paintings, among them the Dresden triptych, and the Baumgartner altarpiece in Munich.

In 1498 he published his first great series of designs on wood, the illustrations of the Apocalypse. The copperplates of this period include *The Prodigal Son* (1500) and *Adam and Eve* (1504). From 1505 to 1506 he visited Venice, and there produced the *Feast of the Rosaries*, now the property of Strahow monastery, Prague. On or before his return he painted *Adam and Eve* (1507), now in Madrid; and the triptych *Assumption of the Virgin*, the centre of which was destroyed by fire in Munich in 1674. It was followed in 1511 by the *Adoration of the Trinity*, now in Vienna.

Dürer did much work for **Maximilian I**, including several portraits, and 43 pen-and-ink drawings for his prayer book. In his honour Dürer drew the *Triumphal Car* and (with others) the *Triumphal Arch*, which were engraved on wood, the latter on 92 blocks, forming a surface of 100 square feet (9.3m²), the largest known woodcut.

From 1520 to 1521 Dürer visited the Netherlands. He met **Erasmus** in Antwerp, and was present at the coronation of **Charles V**, who appointed him his court painter. During his later years he met **Martin Luther** and showed great sympathy with the Reformation.

As an engraver on metal and a designer of woodcuts he ranks even higher than as a painter. His work is distinguished by an unerring perception of the capabilities of the material, his metalplates being executed with extreme finish and refinement, while his woodcuts are boldly drawn with a broad expressive line. His copperplates, over 100 in number, include the *Little Passion* (16 plates, 1508–13); the *Knight, Death, and the Devil* (1513); *St Jerome in his Study* and *Melancholia* (1514). He may also be regarded as the inventor of etching, as he produced several plates in which all the lines are bitten with acid. He completed about 200 woodcuts, including the *Greater Passion*, 12 subjects; *The Little Passion*, 37 subjects; and *The Apocalypse*, 16 subjects. He also wrote several treatises on measurement and human proportion.

📖 F Anzelewsky, *Dürer: His Life and Art* (1983).

'He that would be a painter must have a natural turn thereto. Love and delight are better teachers of the Art of Painting than compulsion is.' From *On Painting*. Quoted in William Martin Conway, *Literary Remains of Albrecht Dürer* (1889).

Born in London, he served in the dragoons, and in 1813 became a Whig MP. In 1828 he was created Baron Durham. He became Lord Privy Seal (1830) and helped to draw up the Reform Bill. He was made an earl in 1833, and became ambassador to St Petersburg (1835). As Governor-General of Canada (1838), he resigned when the House of Lords voted disapproval of his amnesty to several of the French–Canadian rebels. His report on Canada (1839) advocated the union of Upper and Lower Canada, which was accepted in 1841.

Durkheim, Émile 1858–1917
French sociologist

Born in Épinal, he was educated at the École Normale Supérieure, Paris, and he taught at the University of Bordeaux (1887–1902) and at the Sorbonne (1902–16). He was appointed to the first chair of sociology in France in 1913. He believed that sociology should be rigorously objective and scientific, and he developed a systematic sociological methodology based on the view that what he called 'social facts', that is, social phenomena, should be treated as 'things' to be explained solely by reference to other social facts, not in terms of any individual person's actions. This approach is presented in his methodological writings, such as *Les Règles de la méthode sociologique* (1894, 'The Rules of Sociological Method') and is applied particularly in his study of suicide (1897). Also central to his work is his concept of 'collective representations', which explains how the social power of ideas stems from their development through the interaction of many minds. He is generally regarded as one of the founders of sociology.

Durrell, Gerald Malcolm 1925–95
English writer and naturalist

He was born in Jamshedpur, India. His interest in zoology was sparked off when his family moved to Corfu in the 1930s, where he kept a menagerie of local animals. As he wrote in his bestselling memoir, *My Family and Other Animals* (1956), it was like living 'in one of the more flamboyant and slapstick comic operas'. He combined writing with zoology, published many popular books, including the autobiographical *Birds, Beasts and Relatives* (1969), and made many expeditions and wildlife films. He founded the Jersey Zoological Park in 1959, about which he wrote *The Stationary Ark* (1976), and the Jersey Wildlife Preservation Trust in 1963. In 1976 he established the International Training Centre next to the Jersey Zoo, an educational institute for scientists and fieldworkers from all over the world. His discovery in Madagascar of an aye-aye—a lemur which was thought to have been extinct—is described in his book *The Aye-Aye and I* (1992). He was the brother of **Lawrence Durrell**. 📖 David Hughes, *Himself and Other Animals* (1997)

Durrell, Lawrence George 1912–90
English novelist, poet, travel writer and playwright

He was born in Jullundur, India, and sent to England to be educated at St Edmund's School, Canterbury. He took numerous odd jobs—in nightclubs, as an estate agent and in the Jamaica police—and once said he had been driven to writing 'by sheer ineptitude'. He convinced his family, who had moved back to England following his father's early death, that life would be more congenial in a warmer climate and they moved to Corfu until the outbreak of World War II, during and after which he travelled widely as a journalist and in the service of the Foreign Office. His first novel was *Pied Piper of Lovers* (1935) and his second, *Panic Spring*, appeared two years later under the pseudonym Charles Norden, so woeful were the sales of its predecessor. He made his name with the 'Alexandria Quartet'—*Justine* (1957), *Balthazar* (1958), *Mountolive* (1958) and *Clea* (1960)—a complex, interlocking series set in Egypt, remarkable for its sensuous language. The *Avignon Quincunx—Monsieur* (1974), *Livia* (1978), *Constance* (1982), *Sebastian* (1983) and *Quinx* (1985)—is conceived on a similarly grand and elaborate scale. He also wrote travel books, *Prospero's Cell* (1945) and *Bitter Lemons* (1957), verse (*Collected Poems, 1931–1974*), comic sketches, criticism, plays and a children's novel, *White Eagles Over Serbia* (1957). His long friendship with **Henry Miller** is recorded in their correspondence published in 1988. 📖 J Unterecker, *Lawrence Durrell* (1964)

Dürrenmatt, Friedrich 1921–90
Swiss writer

Born in Konolfingen, Bern, he studied there and at Zurich. The theme which recurs in all his work is that life is a calamity which has to be accepted for what it is but without surrender. His novels include the detective story *Der Richter und sein Henker* (1952, Eng trans *The Judge and his Hangman*, 1954) and *Die Panne* (1956, Eng trans *A Dangerous Game*, 1960), and his plays *Romulus der Grosse* (1949, Eng trans *Romulus*, 1961) and *Die Ehe des Herrn Mississippi* (1952, Eng trans *The Marriage of Mississippi*, 1958), which established his international reputation. The play *Ein Engel kommt nach Babylon* (1953, Eng trans *An Angel Comes to Babylon*, 1962) is a parable in which an angel brings chaos instead of happiness, and *Der Besuch der alten Dame* (1956, Eng trans *The Visit*, 1958) is a play which portrays the return of an old lady to her native village to revenge herself on a seducer. Later works include the plays *Die Physiker* (1962, Eng trans *The Physicists*, 1963) and *Porträt eines Planeten* (1970, Eng trans *Portrait of a Planet*, 1973), and a novel, *Der Sturz* (1971, 'The Fall'). ⌨ M B Peppard, *Dürrenmatt* (1969)

Durruti, Buenaventura 1896–1936
Spanish revolutionary anarchist

He was the most prominent violent activist to emerge from the ferocious urban guerrilla warfare in Barcelona (1919–23) between the employers (backed by the state) and the Confederación Nacional de Trabajo (CNT, the National Confederation of Labour). While in exile in Europe and South America (1923–31), he was the principal leader of the revolutionary Iberian Anarchist Federation (FAI). During the Second Republic, he agitated for an immediate revolution from below, and was frequently jailed. He led the anarchist militia in the Spanish Civil War until he was shot dead in 1936 in mysterious circumstances, probably by a Nationalist sniper. His funeral procession in Barcelona was the last great demonstration of strength by the anarchist movement.

Duruflé, Maurice 1902–86
French organist, teacher and composer

He was born in Louviers and showed considerable talent as an organist from an early age. Moving to Paris, he became an organ student of Louis Vierne (1870–1937) at the Conservatoire, and took lessons in composition from Paul Dukas. In 1930 he became the organist at St Étienne-du-Mont in Paris. Twelve years later he returned to the Conservatoire and soon became Professor of Harmony (1943–69). Included in his comparatively small but valuable and interesting oeuvre is his *Requiem*; clearly modelled on Gabriel Fauré's, it is a thing of mystic beauty. Duruflé's *Three Dances for Orchestra* (1939) are arresting pieces and are sometimes programmed by adventurous orchestras.

Duse, Eleonora, *known as* the Duse 1859–1924
Italian actress

Born near Venice, she rose to fame in Italy, then triumphed (1892–93) throughout the European capitals, mainly acting in plays by Ibsen, contemporary French dramatists, and the works of her lover, Gabriele D'Annunzio. She returned to the stage in 1921 after years of retirement. She ranks among the greatest actresses of all time. ⌨ Jeanne Bordeux, *Eleonora Duse: The Story of her Life* (1925)

Dussek, Jan Ladislav 1760–1812
Czech composer and pianist

Born in Czaslau, Bohemia, he produced his earliest works for the piano in Amsterdam. After considerable success in London (1788–1800), he was instructor to Prince Louis Ferdinand of Prussia (1803–06), and in 1808 entered Talleyrand's service. He composed over 30 sonatas.

Dutrochet, (René Joachim) Henri 1776–1847
French physiologist

Born in Néon, he qualified in medicine at the University of Paris, becoming an army medical officer physician and serving as personal physician to Joseph Bonaparte of Spain. After the Peninsular War he conducted researches in animal and particularly plant physiology. Dutrochet believed that life processes were to be explained exclusively in physicochemical terms. He isolated stomata, identified the role of chlorophyll in photosynthesis, and made wide-ranging studies of osmosis.

Dutt, Michael Madhu Sudan 1824–73
Indian poet

Born in Sagandari, Bengal, he absorbed European culture and became a Christian. He wrote poetry and drama in English and Bengali, such as the plays *Sarmishtha* (1858), *Padmavati* (1859), and the blank-verse epics *Tillotama* (1860) and *Meghanad-Badha* (1861). ⌨ H M Das Gupta, *Studies in Western Influence on 19th Century Bengali Poetry* (1935)

Dutton, Geoffrey Piers Henry 1922–98
Australian poet, novelist, critic and editor

Born in Kapunda, South Australia, he began working in publishing after serving in World War II. His verse collections include *Night Flight and Sunrise* (1944), the prize-winning *Antipodes in Shoes* (1958) and *A Body of Words* (1977). Other works include the novels *The Mortal and the Marble* (1950), *Tamara* (1970) and *Queen Emma of the South Seas* (1976), and critical studies of Patrick White (1961) and Walt Whitman (1961). He also wrote three historical biographies of pioneering Australians, as well as art appreciation, short stories (*The Wedge-Tailed Eagle*, 1980), and books for children. His work as a scholarly and enthusiastic editor produced the acclaimed *The Literature of Australia* (1964, rev edn 1976) and representative anthologies of Australian verse. His history of the publishing house of Penguin Books in Australia, *Rare Birds*, was published in 1996.

Duun, Olav 1876–1939
Norwegian novelist

Born in Tosnes, he worked as a farmer and fisherman before training as a teacher, and the experience gave him a profound feeling for the lives of rural Norwegians. Between the wars he became an important exponent of the new 'national language', *Landsmål* (later known as *Nynorsk* or New Norwegian), for which he was twice shortlisted for the Nobel Prize, but which has thwarted international translation and recognition of his work. He is immensely prolific, and his major fictional achievement is the massive six-volume *Juvikfolke* (1918–23, 'The People of Juvik'), which asserts human indomitability in the face of large-scale natural forces. ⌨ A Overland, *Olav Duun* (1955)

Duval, Claude 1643–70
French highwayman

Born in Domfront, Normandy, he went to England at the Restoration (1660) in the train of the Duke of Richmond. Soon taking to the road, he pursued a successful career until, captured while drunk, he was hanged at Tyburn.

Duvalier, François, *known as* Papa Doc 1907–71
Haitian politician

Born in Port-au-Prince, he trained in medicine, and became director of the Public Health Service in 1946 and Minister of Health in 1949. After the military coup in 1950 he opposed the government, and in 1957 was overwhelmingly elected President of Haiti in army-supervised elections. His rule became increasingly autocratic and murderous, and saw the creation of the brutal civil militia of the so called Tontons Macoutes. A professed believer in voodoo, he fought off invasions and threatened uprisings with US economic help. He was

Dvořák, Antonín Leopold 1841–1904
Czech composer

Dvořák was born near Prague, the son of a butcher. He worked for a while in the business, but showed such musical talent that he was sent to the organ school in Prague in 1857. In 1859 he began to earn his living playing the viola in an orchestra and giving lessons, but all the while he was composing in secret. It was not until 1873 that he attracted attention with his *Hymnus*, a nationalistic cantata based on Halek's poem *The Heroes of the White Mountain*. In 1873 he married, and from 1874 to 1877 was organist at St Adalbert's church in Prague, during which time he made a name for himself with several compositions which were promising enough to bring him to the notice of the authorities and secure him a state grant.

In 1877 **Brahms** became a member of the committee which examined the compositions of grant holders. He recognized Dvořák's talent and introduced his music to Vienna by sponsoring the publication of the *Klänge aus Mähren*, which were followed by the *Slavonic Dances* (1878), a commissioned work. Brahms's friendship was a great influence and stimulus in the life of the young composer. His work, basically classical in structure, but characterized by colourful Slavonic motifs, won increasing recognition, culminating in European acclaim for his *Stabat Mater* (1877), first performed in London in 1883. He had now written six symphonies and much chamber and piano music, and enjoyed a worldwide reputation. In 1891 he was offered the directorship of the New York Conservatory.

It was in the USA in 1893 that he wrote his Ninth Symphony, the ever-popular 'From the New World', containing themes redolent of American folk music yet retaining a distinct Slavonic flavour. The beautiful solo for cor anglais in the slow movement is firmly established as a world favourite among classical melodies. At this time he also wrote some of his best chamber music. He returned to Prague in 1895. The last period of his life was spent composing chiefly orchestral music, but he also wrote three more operas, including *Rusalka* (1901) and *Armida* (1904) which, like their predecessors, were not highly successful.

📖 P Young, *Dvořák* (1970); J Clapham, *Antonín Dvořák* (1966); A Robertson, *Dvořák* (rev edn, 1964).

In a letter to **Sibelius**, Dvořák wrote: 'I have composed too much.'

made President for life in 1964 and was succeeded by his son, **Jean-Claude (Baby Doc) Duvalier**. 📖 E Abbott, *Haiti: The Duvaliers and their Legacy* (1988)

Duvalier, Jean-Claude, *known as* Baby Doc 1951–
Haitian politician

He was born in Port-au-Prince, son of **François (Papa Doc) Duvalier**. After studying law at the University of Haiti he followed his father into politics. At the age of 20 he became President-for-Life, ruling, as had his father, through a private army. In 1986 he was deposed in a military coup led by General Henri Namphrey and went into exile in Grasse, in the south of France.

Duve, Christian René de See de Duve, Christian René

Duveen (of Millbank), Joseph Duveen, 1st Baron 1869–1939
English art dealer

Born in Hull, Yorkshire, he began by working in his father's antique shop, then developed a business in the USA specializing in Old Masters and established significant collections in the USA and Europe. He was a benefactor of the National Gallery, London, and gifted a gallery in the British Museum to house the Elgin marbles.

Dvořák, Antonín See panel above

Dwight, John c.1637–1703
English potter

He was born in Oxfordshire, and at his pottery in Fulham (1671–98), he patented a 'transparent earthenware' resembling porcelain, thus pioneering the English pottery industry.

Dwight, Theodore 1764–1846
US journalist and politician

The brother of **Timothy Dwight**, he sat in the House of Representatives (1806–07), wrote in support of the Federalist Party, edited the Albany *Daily Advertiser* (1815–17), and founded its New York namesake, which he edited (1817–36). His son Theodore Dwight (1796–1866) edited *Dwight's American Magazine* (1845–52), and wrote travel books.

Dwight, Timothy 1752–1817
US clergyman and educationist

Born in Northampton, Massachusetts, he was taught by his mother before he went to Yale at the age of 13, graduating in 1769. Headmaster of Hopkins Grammar School in New Haven (1769–71) and a tutor at Yale from 1771, he was a chaplain with the Continental Army during the American Revolution (1775–83), and thereafter became minister of Greenfield Hill, Connecticut, where he also ran an academy. In 1795 he was elected president of Yale and Professor of Divinity. His principal works are an epic poem, *The Conquest of Canaan* (1785), *Theology Explained and Defended* (1818) and *Travels in New England and New York* (1821). His grandson, Timothy Dwight (1828–1916), was also president of Yale from 1886 to 1899, and a member of the US committee for revising the English Bible.

Dworkin, Andrea 1946–
US feminist and critic

Born in Camden, New Jersey, and educated at Bennington College, she worked as a waitress, a receptionist and a factory employee, before joining the contemporary women's movement. Her early publications include *Woman Hating* (1974), *Our Blood: Prophecies and Discourses on Sexual Politics* (1976) and *The New Women's Broken Heart* (1980). Her crusade against pornography is detailed in *Take Back the Night: Women on Pornography* (1980) and *Pornography: Men Possessing Women* (1981), where she identifies pornography as a cause rather than a symptom of a sexist culture. She portrays contemporary society as one that promotes the hatred of women via debased images of them, and sees this as creating an atmosphere conducive to rape and woman-battering. This view is shared by fellow polemicist **Catherine MacKinnon**, with whom Dworkin battled to have pornography legally condemned as an infringement of equal rights. Her later works include *Letters from a War-Zone 1976–1987* (1989) and *Mercy* (1990).

Dybwad, Johanne 1867–1950
Norwegian actress and director

Born in Bergen, she trained there at the National Scene and made her professional debut in 1887. She quickly established a reputation as Norway's leading actress with her natural, unaffected style, and became the leading actress of the new National Theatre when it opened in Oslo

Dylan, Bob, *originally* Robert Allen Zimmerman 1941–
US singer and songwriter

Bob Dylan was born in Duluth, Minnesota. He was instrumental in the popular revival of the folk tradition in the early 1960s, when his work, with its overt social and political concerns, was greatly influenced by the pioneering folk-singer and songwriter Woody Guthrie. His unconventional vocal style was immediately influential, and many of his songs, notably 'Blowing in the Wind' and 'The Times They are a-Changin'' were widely performed and imitated. Quickly tiring of his unsought role as spokesman for his generation, he turned in 1965 to rock and roll music with the group which later became The Band. The use of amplified instruments alienated many of his early admirers, initally at the Newport Folk Festival in 1965, and then on the infamous world tour of 1966, when he was accused of being Judas by a fan in England during a widely bootlegged concert.

Dylan soon reached a much wider rock audience, however, while songs like 'Mr Tambourine Man', 'Desolation Row', 'Subterranean Homesick Blues' and 'Like a Rolling Stone' had a profound influence. Self-consciously literary and often the product of his experiments with hallucinogenic drugs, they helped raise the latter form to new heights, and were treated by many critics as poetry, although his only novel, *Tarantula* (1971), was a reminder that *songs* were his forte. After a motorcycle accident in 1966 he briefly retired from public view, emerging to record more personal songs in a country-influenced style. The early 1970s saw a creative lull, but he returned to form in his records of the mid-1970s, which contain some of his most lasting work.

His subsequent conversion to evangelical Christianity (he was born into the Jewish faith) again alienated some of his audience, a controversy which obscured the quality of some of the music in his albums of the late 1970s and early 1980s, notably in songs like 'Precious Angel' and 'Every Grain of Sand'. He returned to Judaism in the 1980s, and while there was a slackening in his productivity, he remains one of the seminal influences on popular songwriting. He has issued records and toured at regular intervals into the mid-1990s, often reworking old songs in radical ways alongside new material on stage, although his records of the period have not achieved the kind of unanimity of approval bestowed on his indubitably classic works of the previous decades. His collaboration with four other big-name musicians (including George Harrison and Roy Orbison) as The Traveling Wilburys (1988–91) was largely disappointing, and certainly did not achieve the sum of its parts. Numerous live albums, both legitimate and bootlegged, have been issued, and he has appeared in or directed a number of films, including the celebrated documentary *Don't Look Back* (1967), the concert film *Hard Rain* (1976), and the sprawling *Renaldo and Clara* (1978).

♫ Major recordings include: *The Freewheelin' Bob Dylan* (1963), *Another Side of Bob Dylan* (1964), *Bringing It All Back Home* (1965), *Highway 61 Revisited* (1965), *Blonde On Blonde* (1966), *John Wesley Harding* (1968), *Nashville Skyline* (1969), *New Morning* (1970), *Planet Waves* (1973), *Blood On The Tracks* (1974), *Desire* (1975), *Street Legal* (1978), *Slow Train Coming* (1979).

📖 J Bauldie, *Wanted Man* (1992).

Speaking at an induction dinner in the Rock and Roll Hall of Fame in 1988, Bruce Springsteen said: 'Bob freed your mind the way Elvis freed your body. He showed us that just because music was innately physical did not mean that it was anti-intellectual. He had the vision and the talent to make a pop record that contained the whole world'.

---

in 1899, a position she retained for the next 40 years. She worked especially well with the great director Bjørn Bjørnson, and was particularly valued for her interpretations of Ibsen's plays. She also directed regularly from 1906, although she was sometimes criticised for a lack of fidelity to the works she undertook.

Dyce, William 1806–64
Scottish historical and religious painter
He was born in Aberdeen, and in 1825 went to Rome, where he developed sympathies with the German Nazarenes, which he transmitted to the Pre-Raphaelites. Professor of Fine Arts at King's College London from 1844, he executed frescoes in London in the new House of Lords, Osborne House, Buckingham Palace and All Saints', Margaret Street.

Dyck, Sir Anthony Van See Van Dyck, Anthony

Dyer, Anson, *originally* Ernest Anson-Dyer 1876–1962
English animator
Born in Brighton, Sussex, he studied at Brighton Art School, and designed stained-glass windows before trying animation with a series of *Dicky Dee's Cartoons* (1915). For the Cartoon Film Company he produced the bimonthly *John Bull's Animated Sketchbook* (1916), followed by 10 *Kine Komedy Kartoons* (1917). After World War I he made a series of *Shakespeare Burlesques* (1920). In 1935 he began a series of colour cartoons based on the Stanley Holloway character, *Old Sam*, his biggest popular success.

Dyer, Sir Edward c.1545–1607
English poet and diplomat
Born in Sharpham Park, Somerset, he studied at Balliol College or Broadgates Hall, Oxford, and became a courtier. He was a friend of Sir Fulke Greville and Sir Philip Sidney; the latter wrote a song in praise of their friendship, while Dyer commemorated Sidney's death in a moving elegy. Only six of his poems have survived, of which the best known is 'My Mind to Me a Kingdom is'.
📖 R M Sargent, *At the Court of Queen Elizabeth: the life and hymns of Sir Edward Dyer* (1935)

Dyer, George 1755–1841
English writer
He was born in London and educated at Christ's Hospital and at Cambridge. In 1792 he settled in Clifford's Inn, London, and, with 'poems' and a vast mass of hack work, produced the *History of the University of Cambridge* (1814) and *Privileges of the University of Cambridge* (1824). He contributed 'all that was original' to Valpy's classics (141 vols, 1809–31), and became totally blind soon after his life's work was done. 📖 *The Poet's Fate* (1797)

Dyer, John 1699–1757
Welsh poet and painter
Born in Llanfynydd parish, Dyfed, he was educated at Westminster School. He abandoned law for art, and in 1725 published his most successful work, *Grongar Hill*, inspired by the scenery of the valley of the River Towy in Carmarthenshire. In 1750 he published *The Ruins of Rome*, and was ordained the following year. His longest work, *The Fleece* (1757), a didactic poem, is praised by Wordsworth in a sonnet. 📖 'The Poems of John Dyer' and 'The Life of John Dyer' in Dr S Johnson, *The Lives of the English Poets* (1779–81)

Dyer, Reginald Edward Henry 1864–1927

British general

Born in Murree in the Punjab, India, of Irish parents, he was commissioned into the Queen's Royal Regiment before transferring to the Indian army. During World War I he commanded allied troops in south-east Persia, returning to India in 1917 to command a training brigade at Jullundur. There he gained a reputation as a strict disciplinarian and two years later was responsible for an incident which strained relations between the British and Indian nationalist politicians. Following an assault on a British lady missionary in Amritsar, Dyer banned all public meetings, but the order was disobeyed and troops fired into the crowd, killing around 400 people. An official enquiry blamed Dyer and he was forced to resign from the army. ⌨ Ian Colvin, *Life of General Dyer* (1951)

Dyke, Dick Van See Van Dyke, Dick

Dyke, Henry Van See Van Dyke, Henry

Dylan, Bob See panel p576

Dymoke, Sir John d.1381

English knight

By his marriage (c.1350) with the heiress of the Marmions he got the Lincolnshire manor of Scrivelsby, and became King's Champion at Richard II's coronation. The function (to challenge all comers to the king's title) was last exercised at George IV's coronation by Henry Dymoke (1801–65), but Dymokes bore the standard of England at the coronations of Edward VII, George V, George VI, and Queen Elizabeth II.

Dympna c.9th century

Irish princess

She is said to have been killed by her pagan father in Gheel, Belgium, for resistance to his incestuous passion. She is the patron of the mentally ill.

Dyskolos See Apollonius

Dyson, Sir Frank Watson 1868–1939

English astronomer

Born in Measham, Leicestershire, he was Astronomer Royal for Scotland (1905–10) and England (1910–33), and is known for his work on the distribution of stars and on solar eclipses.

Dzerzhinsky, Felix Edmundovich 1877–1926

Russian revolutionary

He was born in Dzerzhmovo, near Minsk, of Polish descent. In 1897 he was exiled to Siberia for political agitation, fought in the Russian Revolution of 1905, and in 1917, as one of the organizers of the coup d'état, became chairman of the secret police and a member of the Bolshevik Central Committee until his death. After 1921 he also reorganized the railway system, and was chairman of the Supreme Economic Council (1924–26), trying to combine industrialization with good relations with the peasantry.

Dzierzon, Jan 1811–1906

Polish apiculturist

Born in Lowkowitz, Upper Silesia, he discovered parthenogenesis in bees and introduced a new type of hive. He wrote *Rationelle Bienenzucht* (1861).

Eadgar See Edgar

Eadmer d.c.1124
English monk and historian
He was the devoted friend of Archbishop **Anselm**, to whom he had been
sent by Pope **Urban II**. In 1120 at
Alexander I's request he became
Bishop of St Andrews. He was the
author of *Historia Novorum in Anglia*
(c.1115) and a *Vita Anselmi* (c.1125,'Life
of Anselm').

Eads, James Buchanan
1820–87
US engineer and inventor
Born in Lawrenceburg, Indiana, he received little education due to frequent travelling, but read widely. He invented a diving bell and founded a salvage company that
made a fortune from sunken river steamboats. In 1861 he
built in 100 days eight iron-clad Mississippi steamers for
the government. He built the steel triple-arched Eads
Bridge (1867–74) across the Mississippi at St Louis, with
a central span of 520 feet (158.6m), and his works for
improving the Mississippi mouth were completed in
1875–79. ⊞ Florence Dorsey, *Road to the Sea and the
Mississippi River: The Story of James B Eads* (1947)

Eagleton, Terence Francis 1943–
British literary critic
He was a Fellow in English at Jesus College, Cambridge
(1964–69), Tutorial Fellow at Wadham College, Oxford
(1969–89), and lecturer in Critical Theory and Fellow of
Linacre College, Oxford (1989–92), before becoming
Thomas Warton Professor of English Literature and Fel-
low of St Catherine's College, Oxford in 1992. His works
include *Criticism and Ideology* and *Marxism and Literary
Criticism* (both 1976), *The Function of Criticism* (1984) and
The Crisis of Contemporary Culture (1993).

Eakins, Thomas 1844–1916
US painter and photographer
Born in Philadelphia, he was influenced by **Édouard
Manet** and went on to become the leading US Realist
painter. Fond of river scenes, he was a master of light effects. He introduced European educational techniques
into the USA. In the 1870s he allowed both sexes to draw
from the nude model at his class in the Pennsylvania
Academy, and as a result was forced to resign. His interest
in photography led him to extend the advances made by
Eadweard Muybridge in his studies of figures in motion,
and his composite plates inspired **Marcel Duchamp's** *Nude
Descending the Staircase* (1912). Having a private income, he
was never obliged to bow to the restrictive attitudes of the
US art establishment.

Ealdhelm, St See Aldhelm, St

Ealdred See Aldred

Eames, Charles 1907–78 and Ray, *née* Kaiser
c.1916–88
US designers and architects
Charles Eames was born in St Louis, Missouri. He started
a course in architecture which he did not complete, then
set up an office in 1930 as an architect and industrial designer. He taught at Cranbrook Academy of Art from
1936. He collaborated with colleagues **Eero Saarinen** and
Ray Kaiser on original furniture designs for a competition organized by **Eliot Noyes** at the Museum of Modern
Art, New York. The designs of this period used new materials such as moulded plywood, foam upholstery and
steel rod frames with great versatility. He and Kaiser were
married in 1941 and they set up an office in California.
They displayed a great ability to communicate in all

mediums, so much so that their Santa
Monica House (1949) is almost the
only building for which they are
known. Constructed entirely from
standard building components, it was
a prototype of worldwide interest and
a seminal building in postwar architecture, due to having industrial components in its construction and a
contrasting lighthearted feel to it as a
whole. They are best known for their
range of furniture designed in 1946,
and for such pieces as the 'Lounge
Chair' produced with the manufacturer Herman Miller (1956), ori-
ginally designed for **Billy Wilder**. In 1979 the couple were
awarded the RIBA (Royal Institute of British Architects)
Gold Medal for their record of innovation and excellence
in the fields of architecture, furniture design and, more
recently, film, graphics and exhibition design.

Eanes, António Ramalho Dos Santos 1935–
Portuguese general and politician
He was born in Alcains. For his role in quashing the Far
Left at the end of the Revolution of 1974–75, he was promoted from an unknown colonel to Chief of Staff. His
austerity associated him with the **Salazar** regime. In 1976
he was elected President as the principal non-Communist
candidate. During his 10-year presidency, Eanes upheld
the new democratic regime amidst the debilitating
squabbles of the political parties, and his honesty won
him wide popular support. From 1986 to 1987 he was
leader of the Portuguese Democratic Renewal Party.

Eardley, Joan 1921–63
English painter
Born in Warnham, Sussex, she began her studies at
Goldsmith's College of Art, London (1938) but moved to
study at the Glasgow School of Art in 1940. After World
War II she studied at Hospitalfield, Arbroath, and at
Glasgow School of Art, winning various prizes and travelling to France and Italy on a **Carnegie** bursary. Greatly
influenced by **Van Gogh**, both technically and in terms
of her choice of subjects, in 1949 she took a studio in
Cochrane Street, Glasgow, and began to paint poor children of the nearby tenements. In 1950 she first visited
Catterline, the tiny fishing village on the north-east
coast of Scotland which inspired her finest landscapes
and seascapes. She lived and worked there until her death.

Earhart, Amelia Mary 1897–1937
US aviator
Born in Atchison, Kansas, she was an army nurse and
social worker before becoming the first woman to fly the
Atlantic Ocean (from Newfoundland to Burry Point,
Wales) on 17 June 1928. Although merely a passenger on
that initial flight, she later became the first woman to fly
solo across the Atlantic (1932) and the first person to fly
alone from Hawaii to California (1935). Her records made
her a celebrity and a spokeswoman both for commercial
aviation and for feminism. In 1937 she attempted a round-
the-world flight, but her plane disappeared in the Pacific
somewhere between New Guinea and Howland Island.
Her autobiography, *Last Flight* (1938), was published
posthumously.

Early, Jubal Anderson 1816–94
US soldier
Born in Franklin County, Virginia, he commanded a
Confederate brigade at Bull Run (1861) and a division at
Fredericksburg and Gettysburg (1863). He was defeated
three times (1864) by **Philip Sheridan** and **George Custer**
on a raiding expedition down the Shenandoah Valley to-
wards Washington, and was relieved of his command

after a rout at Waynesboro. He fled to Canada, but returned in 1869 to his former profession as a lawyer in Virginia.

Earp, Wyatt (Berry Stapp) 1848–1929
US lawman and gunfighter

Born in Monmouth, Illinois, he served as assistant marshal in the Kansas cattle town of Dodge City, then moved (1878) to Tombstone, Arizona, where he worked as a Wells Fargo messenger, gambler, and saloon guard, while his brother Virgil served as marshal. His falling-out with the Clanton gang led to the famous shootout at the OK Corral (1881). Though they were represented later in the stories of the Old West as the champions of law and order, at the time Wyatt and his friends were seen by the townspeople of Tombstone as little more than criminals.

East, Sir Alfred 1849–1913
English painter and etcher

He was born in Kettering, Northamptonshire, where there is a gallery devoted to his work. He studied at the Glasgow School of Art, and is best known for his landscapes of Japan, which he visited in 1889. From 1902 he produced a large number of etchings, and in 1906 he wrote *The Art of Landscape Painting in Oil Colour*.

Eastaway, Edward See Thomas, (Philip) Edward

Eastham, George 1936–
English footballer

Born in Blackpool, he is more noted for the court case he pursued, *Eastham v Newcastle United and others*, than for his playing. Through this, he established the right of professional footballers to freedom of contract. This case, heard in 1961, led to a decision that the retain and transfer lists then operating were in restraint of trade and should be abolished. This outcome revolutionized the pay structure in association football.

Eastlake, Sir Charles Lock 1793–1865
English historical painter

Born in Plymouth, he studied under **Benjamin Haydon**. He made his name with two full-length portraits of **Napoleon I**, sketched while a prisoner on HMS *Bellerophon* in Portsmouth harbour (1815). He produced many Italianate genre paintings, and became a director of the National Gallery from 1855. He is also remembered for his *Materials for the History of Oil Painting* (1847).

Eastlake, Charles Lock 1836–1906
English architect, furniture designer and writer

He was born in Plymouth, and became the protégé of his uncle, the painter Sir **Charles Lock Eastlake**. He studied architecture at the Royal Academy, London, then studied art on the Continent, returning to England to write. Probably his most important book, *Hints on Household Taste in Furniture, Upholstery and Other Details* (1868), developed an aesthetic reasoning in reaction to 19th-century excesses. It was especially influential in the USA where it, and the robust furniture it illustrated, gave rise to the 'Eastlake' style. Another major book, *A History of the Gothic Revival*, was published in 1872. He was assistant secretary of the RIBA (Royal Institute of British Architects) from 1866, secretary from 1871 to 1877, and a keeper at the National Gallery in London (1878–98).

Eastman, Crystal 1881–1928
US suffragette

She graduated from New York University with a law degree (1907), then spent a year in Pittsburg researching *Work Accidents and the Law*, which illuminated the plight of working families debilitated by industrial accidents. In 1909 she drafted New York's first worker compensation law, which was later used as a model nationwide, and in 1913 she founded the forerunner of the National Women's Party, which campaigned for the Equal Rights Amendment of 1923. She was also a founder of the Feminist Congress which convened in New York in 1919. After her second marriage she moved to England where she became involved in the women's rights movement there.

Eastman, George 1854–1932
US inventor and philanthropist

Born in Waterville, New York, and educated in Rochester, he turned from banking to photography, producing a successful roll-film (1884), the 'Kodak' box camera (1888), and joining with **Thomas Edison** in experiments which made possible the moving-picture industry. He formed the Eastman Kodak Co in 1892 and produced the Brownie camera in 1900. He was the founder of the Eastman School of Music in Rochester, New York. 📖 Elizabeth Brayer, *George Eastman: A Biography* (1996)

Eastwick, Edward Backhouse 1814–83
English Orientalist

Born in Warfield, Berkshire, he worked for the East India Company then was appointed (1845) Professor of Hindustani at Haileybury College, and assistant political secretary in the India Office (1859). He was also secretary of legation in Persia in 1860–63 then later became MP for Penryn and Falmouth (1868–74). He produced many translations from the Persian, notably the *Gulistan* of **Sádi**. He also produced a *Hindustani Grammar* (1847) and *Journal of a Diplomate in Persia* (1864), and translated **Franz Bopp**.

Eastwood, Clint 1930–
US actor and director

Born in San Francisco, he was athletic and worked as a lumberjack and lifeguard before being signed to a standard Universal contract, making his film debut in *Revenge of the Creature* (1955). He found television fame in *Rawhide* (1958–65) and then became an international star with three Italian-made 'spaghetti' westerns as the laconic gunslinger, The Man with No Name, beginning with *Per un Pugno Di Dollari* (1964, *A Fistful of Dollars*). In the USA his box-office status was confirmed in adventure films and as tough detective *Dirty Harry* (1971). He was actor–director for the first time in the thriller *Play Misty for Me* (1971). Later films include *Bronco Billy* (1980), *Pale Rider* (1985), *Heartbreak Ridge* (1986), *Bird* (1988), *Unforgiven* (1992), for which he won a Best Director Academy Award, *In the Line of Fire* (1993) and *The Bridges of Madison County* (1995). From 1986 to 1988 he was Mayor of Carmel, where he now lives.

Eaton, Margaret, *known as* Peggy, *née* O'Neill 1799–1879
US socialite

She was born in Washington, DC, the daughter of an innkeeper. Her first husband died in 1828, and the following year she married John Henry Eaton, Secretary of State for War under President **Andrew Jackson**. The wives of the other cabinet ministers refused to mix with her because of her alleged premarital intimacy with Eaton and because of her background, forcing Eaton to resign (1831) despite the strenuous efforts of Jackson, who even transferred his support to a presidential candidate, **Martin Van Buren**, favourably disposed towards her. A great social success in Europe when Eaton became ambassador to Spain (1836), after his death she married a young dancing instructor.

Eban, Abba, *originally* Aubrey Solomon 1915–
Israeli diplomat and politician

Born in Cape Town, South Africa, and educated in England, he taught oriental languages at Cambridge before serving as a liaison officer at Allied HQ during World War II. In 1944 he worked in the Middle East Arab Centre in

Jerusalem and in 1948 was Israeli UN representative in New York and then ambassador in Washington (1950–59). He returned to Israel where he won a seat in the Knesset and joined **David Ben-Gurion**'s government. Between 1959 and 1974 he held several posts, under various prime ministers, and was Foreign Minister for eight years (1966–74). He remained a member of the Israel Labour Party in the Knesset until 1988. His publications include his 1978 autobiography and *Israel Through My Eyes* (1993).

Ebba, St, *also called* St Abb d.683
Northumbrian princess

The daughter of Æthelfrith, King of Northumbria, she founded the double monastery of Coldingham, and ruled it as abbess until her death.

Ebbinghaus, Hermann 1850–1909
German experimental psychologist

Born in Barmen, Prussia (Germany), he trained at the University of Bonn before becoming assistant professor at the Friedrich-Wilhelm University in Berlin and, from 1894, professor at the University of Breslau (Wrocław, Poland). He carried out pioneering experimental researches on memory to investigate higher mental processes, and discovered the so-called 'forgetting curve' that relates memory failure to time. He published his findings in *Über das Gedächtnis* (1885, 'Memory').

Eberhardt, Isabelle 1877–1904
Russian writer and traveller

She was born near Geneva, where her mother Nathalie de Moender, a Russian general's wife, had fled with her lover the anarchist Alexander Trophimovsky. She was reared as a boy, and spoke six languages, including Arabic. In 1897 she went to Bône (now Annaba) in Algeria with her mother where they both converted to Islam and Eberhardt began journeying in the Sahara disguised as an Arab. Though an enthusiast for all things Arab, she worked for the French government of North Africa. After an assassination attempt on her failed, she was expelled from Algeria, but returned after she married Slimène Ehnni, an Arab. In 1903 she was drowned while reporting for an Algerian newspaper on General **Louis Lyautey**'s campaign in Morocco.

Eberhart, Richard Ghormley 1904–
US poet

Born in Minnesota, he is the author of almost 30 collections, including *A Bravery of Earth* (1930), *Reading the Spirit* (1936), *The Quarry* (1960) and *Fields of Grace* (1972). With his *Selected Poems 1930–1965* he won a Pulitzer Prize in 1966, and with *Collected Poems 1930–1976* a National Book award in 1977. A traditional, lyrical, reflective writer, deliberating upon the natural world and the cycles of life and death, he writes in the romantic tradition of **William Blake**, **Wordsworth** and **Walt Whitman**. He is considered to be one of the most important of 20th-century US poets. Since 1972, he has been honorary president of the Poetry Society of America.

Ebers, Georg Moritz 1837–98
German Egyptologist and novelist

He was born in Berlin. Lecturer (1865) and professor (1868) at Jena, he visited the East in 1869, and from 1870 to 1889 was Professor of Egyptology at Leipzig. He discovered and published (1875) the celebrated hieratic medical *Papyrus Ebers* ('Ebers Papyrus'), and wrote on biblical sites in Goshen, Sinai and Egypt. He is best known as the author of numerous historical novels based on ancient Egypt.

Eberst, Jakob See Offenbach, Jacques

Ebert, Friedrich 1871–1925
German statesman

Born in Heidelberg, a tailor's son, he became a saddler there, then a Social Democrat journalist and Reichstag member (1912). Chairman of his party (1913), he was a leader in the Revolution of 1918–19. He was the first President of the German Republic (1919–25).

Ebert, Karl Egon 1801–82
Bohemian poet

He was born in Prague, and his poems include the national epic *Vlasta* (1829).

Eboussi-Boulaga, F Birthdate unavailable
Cameroonian theologian

He was born in Cameroon and is a former director of studies at the Nkol-Bisson Seminary, Yaounde. He is concerned with the search for a faith relevant to Africans, and speaks in his book, *Christianity without Fetishes* (1984), of the 'alienated belief' of African Christians, who need to understand Christ present in their own history and culture. This work offers an African critique of Christianity and seeks to reclaim an identity for the African Christian, a theme also addressed in *La Crise du Muntu: Authenticité africaine et philosophie* (1977).

Eça de Queiros, José Maria de 1845–1900
Portuguese novelist

He was born in Lisbon. Although essentially a 19th-century figure, Eça established realism in the Portuguese novel and was influenced by **Émile Zola** and **Gustave Flaubert** in his attempt to analyse what was wrong with his country's society. Though greatly admired in his own country, his work, in particular his self-study *Os Maias* (1888, Eng trans *The Maias*, 1965), has been neglected elsewhere. Other works include *O Crime do Padre Amero* (1876, Eng trans *The Sin of Father Amaro*, 1962), *O primo Basilio* (1878, Eng trans *Cousin Basilio*, 1958), a variation on the theme of Flaubert's *Madame Bovary*, and *Cartas de Inglaterra* (1903, Eng trans *Letters from England*, 1970). He died in a bitter Parisian exile. ⌂ M Seymour-Smith, *Introduction to Fifty European Novels* (1979)

Eccles, Sir John Carew 1903–97
Australian neurophysiologist and Nobel Prize winner

Born in Melbourne, he was educated at the universities of Melbourne and Oxford, where he collaborated with Sir **Charles Sherrington** in papers on neural inhibition. He was director of the Kanematsu Institute of Pathology at Sydney University (1937), then Professor of Physiology at Otago University (1944–51) and the Australian National University, Canberra. In 1968 he moved to the State University of New York at Buffalo, and was latterly Distinguished Professor Emeritus. His significant contributions to the neurosciences include the recording of the depolarization of a post-synaptic muscle fibre in response to a neural stimulus, the identification of inhibitory neurons, and the demonstration of how inhibitory synapses control the flow of information within the nervous system. He was awarded the 1963 Nobel Prize for physiology or medicine, with Sir **Alan Hodgkin** and Sir **Andrew Huxley**, for discoveries concerning the functioning of nervous impulses. He was elected FRS in 1941, knighted in 1958, and in 1990 was awarded the AC (Companion of the Order of Australia).

Ecevit, Bülent 1925–
Turkish writer and politician

Born in Istanbul, he worked as a government official and a journalist, before becoming an MP for the centre-left Republican People's Party in 1957. He was Minister of Labour for four years, and in 1966 became Secretary-General of his party and subsequently (1972) chairman. He became Prime Minister of a coalition government in 1974, during which he ordered the invasion of Cyprus. He resigned later that year over differences of opinion with the other coalition party. Again Prime Minister in 1978, he imposed martial law on Turkey but his government lasted for only 22 months. After the military coup of 1980, Ecevit was imprisoned twice for criticizing the military regime. A distinguished poet and writer, he was committed to maintaining Turkey's independence within NATO and to improving the country's traditionally poor relations with neighbouring Greece. In 1987 he announced his retirement from active politics. His political writings include *Bu düzen değismelidir* (1968, 'The System Must Change') and *Democratik Sol* (1974, 'Democratic Left').

Echegaray y Eizaguirre, José 1833–1916
Spanish dramatist and joint Nobel Prize winner

Born in Madrid, of Basque descent, he taught mathematics, held portfolios in various ministries (1868–74), then won literary fame through many plays in prose and verse. His plays are usually on simple themes, but with elaborate plot twists and rhetorical passages, and some incorporate social comment, as in his masterpiece, *El gran Galeoto* (1881, 'The Great Galeoto'). He was jointly awarded the Nobel Prize for literature (with **Frédéric Mistral**) in 1904. The following year he returned to politics as Minister of Finance, and to science as Professor of Physics at Madrid University. 📖 J Mathias, *Echegaray* (1970)

Echeverria, Estaban 1805–51
Argentine writer

Born in Buenos Aires, from 1826 until 1830 he lived in Paris, where he absorbed the essence of European Romanticism, which he later introduced to his country. His novella *El matadero* (1871, Eng trans *The Slaughter House*, 1959), written in about 1840, is one of the earliest of the great Latin-American anti-dictator documents; here the country is shown as an abattoir run by insane butchers. His famous poem is 'La cautiva' ('The Captive'). He died in exile because of his opposition to the dictator General Juan Manuel de Rosas.

Echeverría Alvarez, Luis 1922–
Mexican politician

He joined the Institutional Revolutionary Party and held many government posts, including Secretary of the Interior (1964–69). As President of Mexico from 1970 to 1976, he sponsored reforms such as land redistribution and the expansion of social security, but his administration was troubled by runaway inflation, high unemployment, and a declining balance of trade.

Eck, Johann Mayer von 1486–1543
German Catholic theologian

Born in Egg, Swabia, he studied at Heidelberg, Cologne, Tübingen and Freiburg im Breisgau universities. As Professor of Theology at Ingolstadt (1510–43), he was the ruling spirit of that university. He disputed with **Martin Luther** at Leipzig in 1519, wrote his *De Primatu Petri* and went to Rome in 1520, to return with the Bull which declared Luther a heretic. He also disputed with **Joannes Oecolampadius** at Baden and with **Philip Melanchthon** at Worms (1540).

Eckart, Johannes See Eckhart, Johannes

Eckener, Hugo 1868–1954
German aeronautical engineer

Born in Flensburg, he became a friend of **Ferdinand von Zeppelin** and in 1911 was made a director of his airship company. In 1924 he piloted the ZR3, later called the *Los Angeles*, from Friedrichshafen to Lakehurst, New Jersey, on the first flight by an airship directly from continental Europe across the Atlantic. He built the *Graf*

Zeppelin (1929) in which he circumnavigated the world, and made many other notable flights, including a polar expedition in 1931.

Eckermann, Johann Peter 1792–1854
German writer

He was born in Winsen, Hanover, and studied at Göttingen. After the publication of his *Beiträge zur Poesie* (1823, 'Contributions on Poetry') he moved to Weimar, where he assisted **Goethe** in preparing the final edition of his works. He achieved fame by his *Gespräche mit Goethe in den letzten Jahren seines Lebens, 1823–32* (1836–48, Eng trans as part of *Conversations with Goethe*, 1839). 📖 E Hitschman, *Johann Peter Eckermann, eine psychoanalytische-biographische Studie* (1933)

Eckert, J(ohn) Presper 1919–95
US engineer and inventor

Born in Philadelphia, he graduated in electronic engineering at the University of Pennsylvania where he remained for a further five years as a research associate. From 1942 to 1946, he worked on **John Mauchly** on the Electronic Numerical Integrator And Calculator (ENIAC), one of the first modern computers. It weighed several tons, used thousands of valves and resistors, and required 100kW of electric power. He and Mauchly continued to develop improved versions of their computer, including UNIVAC I which in 1951 became one of the first computers to be sold commercially. Eckert himself was granted more than 85 patents for his electronic inventions. He retired in 1989.

Eckhart or Eckart, Johannes, *also called* Meister Eckhart c.1260–1327
German theologian and mystic

Born in Hochheim, near Gotha, he entered the Dominican order, studied and taught in Paris. He acted as prior of Erfurt and as vicar of his order for Thuringia, was Dominican provincial in Saxony (1303–11), vicar-general of Bohemia (1307), and from 1312 preached at Strasbourg, Frankfurt and Cologne. Eckhart's teaching is a mystic pantheism, which influenced later religious mysticism and speculative philosophy. In 1325 he was accused of heresy by the Archbishop of Cologne, and two years after his death his writings were condemned by Pope **John XXII**. His extant works consist of Latin and German sermons and tractates. 📖 F E Copleston, *A History of Philosophy*, vol iii (1953); J M Clark (ed), *The Great German Mystics* (1949); *Meister Eckhart: An Introduction* (1957, with translations)

Eco, Umberto 1932–
Italian novelist and semiotician

Born in Alessandria, Piedmont, he was a student of philosophy at Turin University and was awarded a doctorate for his thesis on St **Thomas Aquinas**. He taught at Turin (1956–67), and was appointed Professor of Semiotics (the study of signs in all realms of culture) at the University of Bologna in 1971. Imbued with a 'taste and passion' for the Middle Ages, he undertook a prolonged study of the commentary of Beatus of Liébana, an 8th-century saint, on the Book of Revelation and of 11th-century illuminations, all of which bore fruit in *The Name of the Rose* (1980). A suspense story set in a medieval monastery, centring on the criminal investigation of Brother William of Baskerville, an English Franciscan, it is indebted to **Arthur Conan Doyle**'s Sherlock Holmes stories, despite having been described as 'a completely semiotic book'. It was an international bestseller and was successfully translated to celluloid in a film of the same name directed by Jean-Jaques Arnaud. He has published two other novels, *Foucault's Pendulum* (1989) and *L'isola del giorno prima* (1995, Eng trans *The Island of the Day Before*).

Edberg, Stefan 1966–
Swedish tennis player
He was born in Vasternik. He won the men's singles title at Wimbledon in 1988 and 1990. Other wins include the Australian Open (1985, 1987) and the US Open (1991–92). He retired in 1996.

Eddery, Pat (rick James John) 1952–
Irish jockey
Born in Newbridge, Kildare, he was champion jockey nine times between 1974 and 1993, and had several successes in the Classics, including Derby winners in 1975, 1982 and 1990, while he also won the Oaks twice, as well as the St Leger. He also had a particularly good record in France, winning the Prix de l'Arc de Triomphe in 1980, 1985, 1986 and 1987.

Eddington, Sir Arthur Stanley 1882–1944
English astronomer
Born in Kendal, Westmorland (Cumbria), he studied at Manchester and Cambridge. He was appointed chief assistant at the Royal Observatory Greenwich (1906) and Plumian Professor of Astronomy and Experimental Philosophy at Cambridge (1913), and in the following year also became director of the university observatory. His first book, *Stellar Movements and the Structure of the Universe* (1914), dealt with the kinematics and dynamics of stars in the Milky Way. In 1916 he deduced a theoretical relationship between the mass of a star and its total output of radiation, and suggested that extreme values of density may exist in stars such as white dwarfs. He published these investigations in *Internal Constitution of the Stars* (1926). Concurrently, he had become deeply interested in **Albert Einstein**'s theory of relativity, and published a non-mathematical account of the theory of relativity, *Space, Time and Gravitation* (1920), which he extended to his *Mathematical Theory of Relativity* (1923). He wrote a series of scientific books for the layman. In 1947 the Royal Astronomical Society instituted the Eddington Medal to be awarded for outstanding work on theoretical astronomy; the first recipient was the cosmologist **Georges Henri Lemaître** in 1953. Eddington was awarded the Gold Medal of the Royal Astronomical Society in 1924, was knighted in 1930 and received the Order of Merit in 1938. He was president of the Royal Astronomical Society (1921–23) and at the time of his death was president of the International Astronomical Union. 🕮 A Vibert Douglas, *The Life of Arthur Stanley Eddington* (1956)

Eddington, Paul Clark 1927–95
English actor
Born in London and trained at RADA, he joined Birmingham Rep in 1945. After making his West End debut in *The Tenth Man* (1961), he rose to become one of Great Britain's most authoritative actors. He joined the National Theatre to play George in *Who's Afraid of Virginia Woolf?* (1981) and acted the headmaster in *Forty Years On* (1984), George in *Jumpers* (1985), Orgon in *Tartuffe* (1991) and Spooner in *No Man's Land* (1992). On television, he played Jerry in *The Good Life* (1975–77) and Jim Hacker in *Yes Minister* and *Yes, Prime Minister* (1980–87), as well as straight roles in *The Prisoner* (1967), *The Camomile Lawn* (1992) and *King Henry IV* (1995). 🕮 *So Far So Good* (1995)

Eddy, Mary (Morse), née Baker 1821–1910
US founder of the Christian Science Church
She was born in Bow, New Hampshire, and brought up as a Congregationalist. After a brief first marriage (to George Glover, 1843–44), she was married a second time, in 1853, to Daniel Patterson (divorced in 1873). Frequently ill as a young woman, she later turned to faith healing and in 1862 came under the influence of Phineas P Quimby (1802–66). She developed the spiritual and metaphysical system she called Christian Science while recovering from a severe fall in 1866, and published her beliefs in *Science and Health with Key to the Scriptures* (1875), which proclaimed the illusory nature of disease. She married Asa G Eddy in 1877, and in 1879 founded at Boston the Church of Christ, Scientist, which attracted great numbers of followers. She founded various publications, including the *Christian Science Journal* (1883) and the *Christian Science Monitor* (1908). 🕮 Edwin F Dakin, *Mrs Eddy* (1929)

Ede (of Epsom), James Chuter Ede, Baron Chuter- 1882–1965
English politician
Born in Epsom, Surrey, he was educated at Epsom National School, Dorking High School, Battersea Pupil Teachers' centre, and Christ's College, Cambridge. Assistant master at Surrey elementary schools (1905–14), he was elected MP for Mitcham (1923) and for South Shields (1929–31, 1935–64). As Minister of Education (1940–45) he helped to bring about the Education Act of 1944. He was Home Secretary (1945–51) during which time he introduced the Criminal Justice Act of 1948 and was involved in controversy on capital punishment. He was leader of the House of Commons in 1951. A nonconformist with a passion for political liberty, he was greatly depended upon by **R A Butler** for his knowledge of the local authorities.

Edel, (Joseph) Leon 1907–97
US scholar and biographer
He was born in Pittsburgh, Pennsylvania. A professor at New York University from 1955, he edited the works of **Henry James** and won the Pulitzer Prize for parts of his five-volume biography (1953–72) of James. His other books include biographies of **James Joyce**, **Willa Cather**, and **Henry David Thoreau**, as well as literary histories such as *Bloomsbury: A House of Lions* (1979). He examined the art of biography in his book *Writing Lives: Principia Biographia* (1984), asserting that biography is a literary form in its own right, which must emulate the subtlety and structural inventiveness of fiction while remaining scrupulously faithful to the facts, a credo that is well borne out in his own works.

Edelfelt, Albert Gustav 1854–1905
Finnish artist
Born in Porvoeo, he worked in many different media in a naturalistic style. Among his best works are a portrait of **Louis Pasteur**, *Christ and the Magdalene* and *Women in the Churchyard*.

Edelinck, Gerard 1649–1707
Flemish copper engraver
He was born in Antwerp and in 1665 he went to Paris, where he produced more than 300 engravings and portraits. His portrait of **John Dryden**, after Sir **Godfrey Kneller**, is his best-known work.

Edelman, Gerald Maurice 1929–
US biochemist and Nobel Prize winner
Born in New York City, he was educated at the University of Pennsylvania and at Rockefeller University, where he has spent his entire research career. He became Professor of Biochemistry in 1966 and Vincent Astor Distinguished Professor in 1974. He purified the light chain from a human multiple myeloma, and reported the complete amino acid sequence (1969). He also analysed the antibody structure and the nature of the subunit interactions, subsequently investigating the number of antibody forms in different vertebrates. This work, together with **Rodney Porter**'s studies in England, enabled a picture of a typical Y-shaped human immunoglobulin (IgG) antibody molecule to be established. For these discoveries they shared the 1972 Nobel Prize for physiology or medicine.

Edelman's DNA interest continued in the 1970s with the development of a system for studying yeast plasmid DNA replication *in vitro*.

Eden, Sir (Robert) Anthony, 1st Earl of Avon 1897–1977
British statesman and Prime Minister

Born at Windlestone Hall, Bishop Auckland, County Durham, he was educated at Eton and Christ Church, Oxford. He won the MC in 1917, and became Tory MP for Warwick and Leamington (1923–57). In 1931 he became Foreign Under-Secretary, in 1934 Lord Privy Seal and in 1935 Foreign Secretary. He resigned in 1938 following differences with the Prime Minister, Neville Chamberlain, principally on the issue of the policy towards Fascist Italy. In 1940 he was Churchill's Secretary of State for War, issuing the historic appeal that brought the Home Guard into being. In 1940 he was Foreign Secretary again. Strenuous wartime work culminated in his leadership of the British delegation to the 1945 San Francisco Conference which established the United Nations. With Labour in power from 1945 to 1951, he was deputy Leader of the Opposition, returning to the Foreign Office once more in 1951 in Churchill's government. He succeeded Churchill as Prime Minister in 1955, a year marked by the summit conference at Geneva with the heads of government of the USA, France and the USSR. In 1956 he ordered British and French forces to occupy the Suez Canal Zone ahead of the invading Israeli army. His action was condemned by the UN and caused a bitter and prolonged controversy in Great Britain which did not subside when he ordered a withdrawal. In failing health, he abruptly resigned the premiership in 1957. He was created an earl in 1961. Regarded as one of the Western world's most experienced statesmen, he aimed principally for world peace based on respect for law. He wrote *Place in the Sun*, *Foreign Affairs* (1939), *Freedom and Order* and *Days for Decision* (1949), his memoirs (3 vols, 1960–65) and an account of his prepolitical life, *Another World* (1976). 📖 Sidney Aster, *Anthony Eden* (1976)

Eden, Dorothy 1912–82
New Zealand writer

She is best known for her suspense and historical novels, especially *Bride by Candlelight* (1954). Her early books, such as her first, *Singing Shadows* (1940), had a New Zealand setting. A move to London in the 1950s inspired contemporary themes such as Nazi Europe in *The Shadow Wife* (1968), and a spy plot in *Waiting for Willa* (1970). Her Gothic romances, mainly Victorian in period, ranged from England and Ireland to South Africa and to China during the Boxer Rebellion. She returned to her home province of Canterbury after her fortieth and last book, *An Important Family* (1982), was published.

Ederle, Gertrude Caroline 1906–
US swimmer

She won a gold medal at the 1924 Olympic Games, as a member of the US 400m relay team, and two bronze medals. On 6 August 1926 she swam the Channel from Cap Gris Nez to Kingsdown, the first woman to do so, in 14 hours 31 minutes, nearly two hours faster than the existing men's record. She later turned professional.

Edgar or Eadgar 944–75
English King

The younger son of King Edmund of Wessex, he was made King of Northumbria and Mercia (957) and succeeded to Wessex on his brother Eadwig's death (959), thus becoming ruler of a united England. He recalled St Dunstan from exile and made him his closest adviser and Archbishop of Canterbury. In 973 he was formally crowned and received the submission of all the kings in Britain. His reign was one of secure peace and prosperity,

with the acceptance of the Danelaw as a separate but integral part of England, under his nominal authority. He is renowned for his legal codes, his coinage reform and his revival of the English Church. His two sons became Edward, the Martyr, and Ethelred II (the Unready). 📖 Helen Panter, *King Edgar* (1971)

Edgar the Ætheling c.1050–c.1125
English prince

Born in Hungary, the son of Edward the Ætheling and grandson of Edmund II, Ironside, he was the legitimate heir to the English throne on the death of his great-uncle Edward, the Confessor (1066). He was passed over as king in favour of Harold Godwinsson, but after Harold's defeat and death at Hastings, some English nobles supported the Ætheling's claims against William the Conqueror, until he was compelled to submit to William (1067). In 1068 he fled to Scotland, where King Malcolm III (Canmore) welcomed him and married his sister, St Margaret. In 1074 the Ætheling made peace with William, and led the Norman expedition that conquered Apulia (1086) and an expedition to Scotland (1097) to depose the usurper Donald Bane and put Malcolm's son Edgar on the throne. He was captured by Henry I (1106) but was released and spent his last years in obscurity.

Edgar, David 1948–
English dramatist

Born in Birmingham, he studied drama at Manchester University, and was a journalist in Bradford before deciding to write for the stage full time. *Destiny* (1976), a large-scale play looking at the roots of fascism in British society, was produced by the Royal Shakespeare Company (RSC). His eight-hour adaptation of Dickens's *The Life and Adventures of Nicholas Nickleby* for the RSC (1980) brought his work to a massive audience. *Maydays* (1983), the first contemporary play to be presented by the RSC at the Barbican Theatre in London, was similarly ambitious. Other works include *Entertaining Strangers* (1985), *The Shape of the Table* (1990), which charts the negotiations between a Communist government and the forces acting against it in the autumn of 1989, a television documentary *Civil War* (1991), a radio play *A Movie Starring Me* (1991), several adaptations, including *The Strange Case of Dr Jekyll and Mr Hyde* (1991), and *Pentecost* (1994). He was appointed Honorary Professor by the University of Birmingham in 1992.

Edgerton, Harold Eugene 1903–90
US electrical engineer

Born in Fremont, Nebraska, he became Professor of Electrical Engineering at the Massachusetts Institute of Technology (MIT) in 1934. A specialist in stroboscopes and high-speed photography, he produced a krypton-xenon gas arc which was employed in photographing the capillaries in the white of the eye without hurting the patient.

Edgerton, Sidney 1818–1900
US politician

Born in New York City, he sat in Congress (1859–63), became first Chief Justice of Idaho Territory and as such was a founder of the new state (1864) of Montana, of which he was made the first Governor.

Edgeworth, Francis Ysidro 1845–1926
Irish economist

Born in Edgeworthstown, County Longford, he was educated at Trinity College, Dublin, and Baliol College, Oxford. Professor of Political Economy at Oxford (1891–1922), and first editor of the *Economic Journal* (1891–1926), he was perhaps the most outstanding mathematical economist of his time. He was best known for his *Mathematical Psychics* (1881), and he also carried out important work in the field of statistical theory.

Edison, Thomas Alva 1847–1931
US inventor and physicist

Born in Milan, Ohio, he lost much of his hearing as a boy and had little formal training. He worked as a railroad newsboy on the Grand Trunk Railway, and soon printed and published his own newspaper on the train, the *Grand Trunk Herald*. During the Civil War he worked as a telegraph operator in various cities, and invented an electric vote-recording machine. In 1871 he invented the paper ticker-tape automatic repeater for stock exchange prices, which he then sold in order to establish an industrial research laboratory at Newark, New Jersey. In 1876 he moved the laboratory to Menlo Park, New Jersey, where he was able to give full scope to the astonishing inventive genius that won him the name 'the Wizard of Menlo Park'.

He took out more than 1,000 patents in all, including the gramophone (1877), the incandescent light bulb (1879), and the carbon granule microphone as an improvement for **Alexander Graham Bell**'s telephone. To make possible the widespread use of electric light, he invented a system for generating and distributing electricity and designed the first power plant (1881–82). Amongst his other inventions were a megaphone, a storage battery, the electric valve (1883) and the kinetoscope (1891). He moved his laboratory to West Orange, New Jersey, in 1887, and in 1912 he produced the first talking motion pictures. He also discovered thermionic emission, formerly called the 'Edison Effect'. Tireless at experimentation but always practical and commercial in his goals, he was the most prolific inventor the world has ever seen.

📖 W Wachhorst, *Thomas Alva Edison: An American Myth* (1981); R Silverberg, *Light for The World* (1967); M Josephson, *Edison: A Biography* (1959).

Often called the 'Wizard' or 'Genius' of Menlo Park for the invention factory he created in New Jersey, Edison is cited as the originator of the proverb 'Genius is one per cent inspiration, ninety-nine per cent perspiration' (c.1903). Quoted in *Harper's Monthly Magazine*, September 1932.

Edgeworth, Maria 1767–1849
Irish novelist

Born in Blackbourton, Oxfordshire, the eldest daughter of the inventor and educationist Richard Lovell Edgeworth (1744–1817), she was educated in England, then returned to Edgeworthstown in County Longford, Ireland, in 1772 to act as her father's assistant and governess to his many other children. With her father, and to illustrate his educational ideas, she wrote *Letters to Literary Ladies* (1795), *The Parent's Assistant* (1796) and *Practical Education* (1798). In 1800 she published her first novel, *Castle Rackrent*, which was an immediate success, followed by *Belinda* in 1801. She was praised by Sir **Walter Scott** and was lionized on a visit to London and the Continent, where she turned down a proposal of marriage from the Swedish Count Edelcrantz for the sake of her father. The next of her 'social novels' of Irish life was *The Absentee* (1809), followed by *Ormond* (1817). All her works were written under the influence of her father, which may have inhibited her natural story-telling talent. After her father's death (1817) she did little more writing apart from a late novel, *Helen* (1834), but devoted herself to looking after the family property, and 'good works'. She is also remembered for her children's stories. 📖 P H Newby, *Maria Edgeworth* (1950)

Edinburgh, Prince Philip, Duke of 1921–
Consort of Queen Elizabeth II

The son of Prince Andrew of Greece and Princess Alice of Battenburg, grandson of **George I** of Greece and great-grandson of Queen **Victoria**, he was born in Corfu and educated at Cheam School, Gordonstoun and Dartmouth. He joined the Royal Navy (1939) as lieutenant Philip Mountbatten. In 1941 he joined HMS *Valiant*, on which he fought in the Battle of Cape Matapan, subsequently serving in the Pacific on HMS *Whelp*. In 1947 he became a naturalized British subject, and on 20 November 1947, as the Duke of Edinburgh, he married his third cousin, Princess Elizabeth, the future Queen **Elizabeth II**. As a prince of Great Britain and Northern Ireland since 1957, he has shown a keen and occasionally outspoken interest in science and technology, as well as in youth adventure training, through the Duke of Edinburgh's awards, and world wildlife. He is also interested in sports, especially carriage driving. His speeches and essays were published in *Men, Machines and Sacred Cows* (1984). 📖 Basil Boothroyd, *Philip: An Informal Biography* (1971)

Edison, Thomas Alva See panel above

Edmonds, Noel 1948–
English television presenter

Born in Ilford, Essex, he joined Radio Luxembourg as a disc-jockey in 1968 while still a student teacher, moved to BBC Radio 1 in 1969 and, later, to television. His first success was the children's show, *Multi-Coloured Swap Shop* (1976–81). Moving to peak-time, he became a regular fixture in the BBC's Saturday-evening ratings battle with ITV, presenting *The Late Late Breakfast Show* (1982–86) and *Noel's House Party* (1991–), as well as hosting the long-running quiz show *Telly Addicts* (1985–). His Unique Group company devises television shows and markets books, games and mineral water.

Edmonds, Sarah Emma 1841–98
Canadian soldier

Born in Nova Scotia, she was a habitual cross-dresser who claimed to be 'naturally fond of adventure, a little ambitious and a good deal romantic'. These qualities led her not only to pose as a door-to-door Bible salesman among other exploits, but also to enlist as a man in the Union Army's Michigan regiment during the Civil War, under the name of Frank Thompson. She became known as the 'Beardless Boy' by fellow soldiers, and her talent for subterfuge led her to be frequently assigned to serve as a spy, on one occasion infiltrating the Confederate camp as a young black male cook. She also took on the role of nursing the fatally wounded, still in her masculine disguise, and proved that she could shoot in cold blood when necessary, by firing a pistol at point-blank range into the face of a Confederate captain. Her autobiography, *Nurse and Spy in the Union Army* (1865), is a lively account of her contribution to the history of female impersonation of men as a means of access to masculine work.

Edmund, St c.841–870
King of East Anglia

According to tradition, he was the son of a Frankish king and succeeded **Offa** of Mercia as his adopted heir. When the great Danish invasion of 865 entered East Anglia (870), Edmund met them at Hoxne, Suffolk, and was defeated and killed. Tradition claims that he was taken captive, and when he refused to abjure his Christian faith he was tied to a tree and shot to death with arrows by the pagan Danes. A miracle cult quickly sprang up and in 903 his remains were moved from Hoxne to Bury St Edmunds, which became a popular pilgrimage centre.

Edmund, St, *originally* Edmund Rich 13th century
English ecclesiastic and scholar

Born in Abingdon, Oxfordshire, he studied and taught at Oxford and Paris and, acquiring fame as a preacher, was commissioned by Pope Gregory IX to preach the Sixth Crusade throughout England (c.1227). In 1234 he was made Archbishop of Canterbury, and became the spokesman of the national party against Henry III, even threatening him with excommunication if he did not dismiss foreign favourites. But his gentleness, generosity, austerity and purity led to his authority being diminished by the arrival of the papal legate, Cardinal Otho, in 1237, and in 1240 he retired to the Abbey of Pontigny in France. The last Archbishop of Canterbury to be canonized, his feast day is 16 November. St Edmund Hall, Oxford, was named in his honour. ▣ Lord Francis Hervey, *The History of King Eadmund the Martyr and of the Early Years of His Abbey* (1929)

Edmund I 921–46
King of the English

The son of Edward, the Elder, he succeeded his half-brother, Athelstan, in 939. He re-established English control of Mercia against the Norse Vikings of Northumbria, and re-conquered from them the Five Boroughs of the Danelaw whose Danish settlers now regarded themselves as English citizens. He subdued the Norsemen in Cumbria and Strathclyde, which he entrusted to Malcolm I of Scotland as an ally. He was killed at Pucklechurch, Gloucestershire, by an outlawed robber. His reign saw the beginning of the 10th century monastic revival.

Edmund II, Ironside c.990–1016
King of the English

The son of Ethelred II, the Unready, and half-brother of Edward the Confessor, he was lord of most of Mercia from 1015. When Knut Sveinsson (Canute) invaded England that summer, Edmund was elected king by the beleaguered defenders of London on his father's death (April 1016), while Knut was chosen king by the Witan (Council) in Southampton. Edmund raised an army, reconquered Wessex and relieved London, before being routed by Knut in a fierce battle at Ashingdon in Essex. He agreed to partition the country, but died a few weeks later, leaving Knut as sole ruler. Edmund's elder son, Edward the Ætheling, became the legitimate heir-apparent to the throne of his uncle, Edward the Confessor.

Edmunds, George Franklin 1828–1919
US politician

Born in Richmond, Vermont, he sat in the state legislature and senate, and in the US Senate (1866–91). He took an active part in the prosecution of President Andrew Johnson, and was author of the Edmunds Act for the suppression of polygamy in Utah.

Edrich, William John 1916–86
English cricketer

He was born in Norfolk. As a batsman he is always associated with his Middlesex partner, Denis Compton, but took longer to develop. He played 39 Tests and in 1938 became one of a handful of players to have scored 1,000 runs before the end of May. With Compton he shared a record third wicket Test partnership of 370 against South Africa at Lord's in 1947. After World War II he reverted to amateur status to make himself available for the England captaincy, but was never selected for the post.

Edrisi or Idrisi c.1100–1164
Arabic geographer

Born in Ceuta, he studied at Córdoba, and travelled in Spain, Barbary and Asia Minor. He then settled at the court of Roger II of Sicily, who invited him to write a description of the Earth. To this end travellers were sent on journeys of exploration, and were asked to send him an account of all they had seen or heard. This occupied many years, and Edrisi's 'Description of the World' (*Nuzhat-el-Mushtâk*) or 'Book of Roger', as it was also called, was not completed till 1154. It is one of the principal medieval geographies.

Edward, St *called* Edward the Martyr c.963–978
Anglo-Saxon King of England

The elder son of King Edgar, he succeeded to the throne at the age of 12 (975). His accession provoked rival claims on behalf of his younger half-brother, Ethelred II, the Unready, and in 978 he was treacherously murdered by Ethelred's household at Corfe Castle in Dorset. He was canonized in 1001. ▣ Christine Fell, *Edward, King and Martyr* (1971)

Edward the Confessor c.1003–1066
King of England and saint

Born at Islip, Oxfordshire, he was the elder son of Ethelred II, the Unready, by his wife Emma, and half-brother of Edmund II, Ironside. In 1016 the English throne passed to Knut Sveinsson (Canute), who married Ethelred's widow, and had a son by her, Hardaknut Knutsson. Edward meanwhile went to Normandy (1016–41) and became very religious, taking a vow of chastity. Hardaknut recalled him to England (1041) and Earl Godwin of Wessex helped him to the throne (1042). In 1045 he married Godwin's only daughter, Edith. His reign was marked by the conflict between the Norman party at court and the 'National' party led by Godwin and his son, Harold Godwinsson, later Harold II. Although his legitimate heir was Edgar the Ætheling (the grandson of Edmund Ironside), on his deathbed he allegedly nominated Harold Godwinsson as his successor. He was buried in Westminster Abbey, which he founded shortly before his death, and became the subject of a cult which saw him canonized in 1161. ▣ Frank Barlow, *Edward the Confessor* (1970)

Edward I *also known as* Edward Longshanks and the Hammer of the Scots 1239–1307
King of England

Born in Westminster, London, the elder son of Henry III and Eleanor of Provence, he married Eleanor of Castile (1254) and later Margaret of France, the sister of Philip IV (1299). He initially supported Simon de Montfort in the Barons' War (1264–67), but rejoined Henry III and defeated de Montfort at Evesham (1265). He became king on his father's death (1272) while away on the Eighth (and last) Crusade to the Holy Land (1270), but was not crowned until his return (1274). He annexed north and west Wales (campaigns in 1276–77, 1282–83) and tried to unite England and Scotland through the marriage of his infant son Prince Edward (later Edward II) to Margaret, Maid of Norway, Queen of Scotland. When Margaret died, he chose John de Balliol as king (1292) in preference to Robert de Bruce. However, Edward's insistence on full rights of suzerainty forced Balliol to refuse to recognize Edward and ally with France (1295), starting the Scottish Wars of Independence. Despite victories such as the defeat of William Wallace at Falkirk (1298), Edward could not subdue Scotland. Robert de Bruce (son of Robert de Bruce) had himself crowned King Robert I of Scotland at Scone (1306). Edward marched north, but died near Carlisle (1307). He was called the English Justinian for his improvement in the efficiency of royal justice, and several statutes (1275–90) reorganized the state both centrally and locally. He regularly summoned local representatives to central assemblies (such as the so-called 'Model' Parliament of 1295), which voted him useful revenues and gave him national approval for his actions. He expelled the Jews from England (they were not readmitted until 1655). ⌑T F Tour, *Edward the First* (1893)

Edward II *called* Edward of Caernarvon 1284–1327
King of England

Born in Caernarvon, Wales, the son of **Edward I** and **Eleanor of Castile**, he was created the first Prince of Wales in 1301. On his father's death (1307) he abandoned Edward I's plans to subdue the Scots and went to France (1308) to marry **Isabella**, daughter of **Philip IV**, leaving his foreign favourite, Piers Gaveston, Guardian of the Kingdom. Not an energetic ruler, Edward antagonized the barons, who wanted to regain their place in government and rid the country of such royal favourites. Edward invaded Scotland (1314), but was decisively defeated by **Robert de Bruce** at Bannockburn (1314). Bruce went on to capture Berwick (1318) and undid virtually every trace of the conquest of Edward I. Risings in Wales and Ireland followed, and two seasons of unprecedented famine and pestilence. Edward's authority was challenged by Thomas, Earl of Lancaster, but with the aid of his new favourites, **Hugh Despenser** and his son, Edward, he overthrew Lancaster (1321), and put him to death (1322). He made a truce with Scotland for 13 years in 1323, but then **Charles IV** of France, brother of his wife, Isabella, seized Edward's French territories. Edward sent Isabella to negotiate with Charles, but she despised her husband, hated the Despensers, and had fallen in love with Roger de Mortimer, one of the disaffected nobles. In 1326 she landed with a large body of malcontents on the coast of Suffolk. The Despensers were executed, and Edward was imprisoned in Kenilworth Castle and forced to abdicate (1327) in favour of his eldest son (**Edward III**). He was murdered at Berkeley Castle. ⌑Hilda Johnstone, *Edward of Caernarvon* (1946)

Edward III *called* Edward of Windsor 1312–77
King of England

Born in Windsor, he was the son of **Edward II**, who was forced to abdicate in his favour (1327). During his minority the country was governed by his mother, **Isabella**, sister of **Charles IV** of France, and her lover, Roger de Mortimer. Edward married **Philippa of Hainault** (1328), executed Mortimer, banished his mother and assumed full control of the government (1330). He successfully supported **Edward de Balliol** against **David II** of Scotland, and David sought refuge in France (1333–1341). Balliol failed to hold Scotland, and despite successive English invasions the Scots rallied each time. Edward then claimed the French Crown, declared war against **Philip VI** (1337), and started the Hundred Years War. He raised money for the war by tallages, forced loans, and by seizing wool, but was increasingly reduced to offering privileges in exchange for funds, which devalued royal authority and wrecked the country's public finances. He destroyed the French navy at Sluys (1340), and in 1346, with his son, **Edward, the Black Prince**, conquered a large part of Normandy and defeated the French at Crécy. There were further successes, and Calais fell after a year's siege. Meanwhile the Scots had been defeated at Neville's Cross (1346), and David II was captured and imprisoned. In England, a third of the population died from the Black Death (1349). War in France was renewed (1355) with a great victory at Poitiers (1356), where King **John II** of France was taken prisoner. Unable to raise his proposed ransom, he died in captivity in London (1364). A three-year truce was concluded in 1374, but Edward had failed to win the French crown, and his extravagance and constant betrayals of trust had alienated both parliament and public. His mistress, Alice Perrers, became increasingly influential, until his fourth (third surviving) son, **John of Gaunt**, took over the government. The Black Prince, opposed to his father's policy, died the year before the king. ⌑M Packe, *Edward III* (1983)

Edward IV 1442–83
King of England

Born in Rouen, France, he was the eldest son of **Richard**, Duke of York, and bore the title Earl of March. His father Richard claimed the throne as the lineal descendant of **Edward III**'s third and fifth sons (Lionel, Duke of Clarence, and Edmund, Duke of York), against the Lancastrian King **Henry VI** (the lineal descendant of Edward III's fourth son, **John of Gaunt**). Richard was killed at Wakefield (1460), but Edward entered London (1461) and was recognized as king when Henry VI was deposed (1461). With the support of his cousin, Richard Neville, Earl of **Warwick**, he defeated the Lancastrians at Towton (1461). He threw off his dependence on Warwick, and secretly married **Elizabeth Woodville** (1464), but Warwick forced him into exile in Holland (1470), and Henry VI regained the throne. Edward returned to England (March 1471), was restored to kingship (April), then defeated and killed Warwick at Barnet (April), and destroyed the remaining Lancastrian forces at Tewkesbury (May). Henry VI was murdered at the Tower of London soon afterwards, and Edward remained secure for the rest of his reign. Direct, straight forward and intelligent, he ensured his court rivalled the splendid court of Burgundy. He made his own decisions, periodically reviewed his grants of patronage, restored order, ended private war, subdued the nobility, and died solvent. In his financial reforms he foreshadowed the Tudors, but his advancement of his wife's family was to have serious repercussions in the royal minority that followed his death. ⌑Charles Ross, *Edward IV* (1974)

Edward V 1470–83
King of England

Born in Westminster, London, he was the son of **Edward IV** and **Elizabeth Woodville**. When his father died (1483), he and his younger brother, the Duke of York, were left to the guardianship of their paternal uncle, Richard, Duke of Gloucester (the future **Richard III**). The Woodvilles (headed by Edward V's uncle, Anthony Woodville, 2nd Earl **Rivers**) tried to gain influence over him, but Richard took Edward to London (May 1483), and the same month was appointed Protector. In June the Duke of York also reached London, and the two boys were placed in the Tower of London (then a royal residence as well as a prison). Parliament petitioned Richard to take over the throne the day after that originally set for Edward's coronation, and the 'Princes in the Tower' made no more public appearances. From about October 1483 there were rumours that Richard had had them murdered, and in 1674 some bones were discovered and re-interred as theirs in Westminster Abbey. In recent years it has been suggested that **Henry VII** may equally have been responsible for their deaths. ⌑ Alison Weir, *The Princes in the Tower* (1992)

Edward VI 1537–53
King of England and Ireland

Born in London, the son of **Henry VIII** and his third wife, **Jane Seymour**, he was 10 years old at his accession (1547). The government was at first in the hands of his uncle, **Edward Seymour**, Duke of Somerset, who, as Lord Protector, attempted to resolve the economic, social and religious problems of the realm. The publication of the conservative first *Book of Common Prayer* (1549) was an important step towards the establishment of uniform observance in the newly reformed English Church, but it caused the Western Rebellion in the south-west. **Robert Kett**'s rebellion in East Anglia in 1549 helped cause Somerset's fall; his moderate religious policy pleased neither adherents of the old faith nor the more zealous Protestants, while his cautious approach towards popular discontent worried those who advocated a harder line. He was executed (1552) and replaced by John Dudley, Earl of **Warwick**, who had achieved great influence over the young king. Edward was highly intelligent, with a mind of his own, but his religious views were intensely narrow. A revised prayer book was produced, confirmed by a second Act of Uniformity (1552) and the Forty-Two Articles (1553) were intended to give the English Church a definitive creed. As the English Reformation flourished, the king's health, never robust, deteriorated suddenly, and Warwick persuaded the dying boy to alter the succession in favour of his own daughter-in-law, Lady **Jane Grey**. Edward died of tuberculosis, and Lady Jane Grey was overthrown after only nine days on the throne by his Catholic half-sister, **Mary I**. 📖 W K Jordan, *Edward VI* (2 vols, 1968–70)

Edward VII 1841–1910
King of Great Britain and Ireland

The eldest son (Albert Edward) of Queen **Victoria** and Prince **Albert**, he was born at Buckingham Palace, London. He served a 60-year apprenticeship as Prince of Wales during his mother's long reign. He was educated privately, and also at Edinburgh University, Christ Church, Oxford, and Trinity College, Cambridge. In 1860 he made the first tour of Canada and the USA undertaken by a royal prince, and after his father's death (1861), took his seat in the House of Lords as Duke of Cornwall. In 1863 he married Princess **Alexandra**, eldest daughter of **Kristian IX** of Denmark. Considered too frivolous for responsibility by his mother, he was devoted to social and leisure activities such as horse-racing, theatre-going and yachting. He had several mistresses, and caused a scandal by being cited as a witness in a divorce suit (1870). He succeeded to the throne in 1901 and was crowned the following year. As king he restored vitality and flair to the monarchy, and endeavoured to promote international friendship by visits to Continental capitals, preparing the way for the Entente Cordiale with France (1904) and the Anglo-Russian agreement (1907). He and Queen Alexandra had six children: Albert Victor, Duke of Clarence (1864–92); George, later King **George V**; Louise, Princess Royal (1867–1931); Victoria (1868–1935); Maud (1869–1938), who married King **Haakon VII** of Norway; and Alexander (born and died in 1871). 📖 Sir Philip Magnus, *King Edward the Seventh* (1964)

Edward VIII 1894–1972
King of Great Britain and Northern Ireland

The eldest son of **George V**, he was born at White Lodge in Richmond, Surrey, and educated at Osborne, Dartmouth, and Magdalen College, Oxford. Invested as Prince of Wales (1911), he was in the navy and (in World War I) the army, travelled much, and achieved considerable popularity. He was forthright in his comments on poverty, especially in South Wales. He succeeded his father (20 January 1936), but abdicated (11 December) on account of general disapprobation of his proposed marriage to Mrs **Wallis Simpson**. He was thereupon given the title of Duke of Windsor, and the marriage took place in June 1937. From 1940 to 1945 he was Governor of the Bahamas, as described in his *A King's Story* (1951). After 1945 he lived in Paris and was not invited back to England with his wife to an official public ceremony until 1967. 📖 Frances Donaldson, *Edward VIII: A Biography of the Duke of Windsor* (1975)

Edward, *called* Edward the Elder c.870–c.924
King of Wessex

The son of **Alfred** the Great, he succeeded his father in 899. Tenacious and imaginative, he was the best Anglo-Saxon royal strategist. He brought back under English rule the whole of the Danelaw south of the Humber, building a series of fortresses to consolidate his rule. He took control of Mercia (918) after the death of his sister **Ethelflæd** (the 'Lady of the Mercians'), and subdued the Scots, the Norsemen in Northumbria, and the Welsh Britons of Strathclyde.

Edward, Prince, *in full* Edward Antony Richard Louis 1964–
British prince

The third son of Queen **Elizabeth II**, he was educated at Gordonstoun and then spent several months as a house tutor in New Zealand at Wanganui Collegiate School. After studying history at Jesus College, Cambridge, he joined the Royal Marines (1986) but left the following year and began a career in the theatre as a production assistant with **Andrew Lloyd Webber**'s Really Useful Theatre Company. In 1990 he set up his own production company, Ardent Productions.

Edward the Black Prince 1330–76
English heir to the throne

Born in Woodstock, Oxfordshire, the eldest son of **Edward III**, he was created Earl of Chester (1333), Duke of Cornwall (1337) and Prince of Wales (1343). While still a boy, he commanded the right wing at Crécy (1346), and is said to have won his popular title (first cited in the 16th century) from his black armour. He won several victories in the Hundred Years War, including the great victory of Poitiers (1356). In 1361 he married his cousin, Joan, the 'Fair Maid of Kent' (1328–85), who bore him two sons, Edward (1365–70) and the future **Richard II**. In 1362 his father created him Prince of Aquitaine, and he lived there until 1371, when a revolt forced him to return to England. In 1367 he espoused the cause of **Pedro**, the Cruel, of Castile and restored him to the throne, at Najera winning his third great victory and taking **Bertrand du Guesclin** prisoner. Worn out by sickness, he mercilessly sacked Limoges (1370), after which, mortally ill, he returned to England and took no further part in public life. A chivalric legend in his own lifetime, brave and inspirational, he tended to live beyond his means, and it is doubtful if he had the pragmatic realism necessary for medieval kingship. 📖 Richard Barber, *Edward, Prince of Wales and Aquitaine* (1978)

Edward the Ætheling, Prince d.1057
English nobleman

He was the son of **Edmund II, Ironside**, and nephew of the childless **Edward, the Confessor**. After Edmund's death (1016), he was taken for safe keeping to Hungary, where he had a son, **Edgar the Ætheling**. Edward the Ætheling was recognized as the proper heir to Edward the Confessor's throne, but he died shortly after landing in England (1057).

Edwardes, George 1852–1915
English theatrical manager

He was born, of Irish parents, in Clee, Lincolnshire. He became business manager at the Savoy Theatre, London (1881), leaving to enter into partnership with John Hollinshead at the Gaiety (1885), and taking over the sole management in the following year. In 1893 he built Daly's Theatre for **Augustin Daly**. He is known as the father of musical comedy, the form of which he standardized by his gift of foreseeing public taste and recognizing and developing talent. His many successes include *The Geisha*, *The Merry Widow*, *The Gaiety Girl* and *The Quaker Girl*.

Edwardes, Sir Michael Owen 1930–
British business executive

Born in South Africa and educated at Rhodes University, Grahamstown, he joined the Chloride Group of companies in Africa in 1951. In 1966 he first worked in Great

Britain, as commercial director and then as general manager of Chloride's smallest subsidiary, Alkaline Batteries. He proved his skills in reviving an ailing company, by defining sound business targets and building a team of competent and enthusiastic executives to achieve them. In 1974 he was appointed chairman of the Chloride Group and, in 1977, was asked to rescue British Leyland, Britain's major motor manufacturer, from commercial collapse, a task considered to be virtually impossible. In five years, however, Edwardes's strong leadership and expectations of excellence had turned the company round. He described this experience in his book *Back from the Brink* (1983). Since 1988 he has been chairman of Charter Consolidated Plc. He was knighted in 1979.

Edwards, Amelia Ann Blandford 1831–92
English novelist and Egyptologist

Born in London, she was the author of *My Brother's Wife* (1855), *Debenham's Vow* (1869) and *Lord Brackenbury* (1880). She founded the Egyptian Exploration Fund, and contributed papers on Egyptology to the principal European and US journals, and wrote *A Thousand Miles up the Nile* (1877) and *Pharaohs, Fellahs, and Explorers* (1891). ⬚ K S MacQuoid, *Amelia Blandford Edwards* (1897)

Edwards, Gareth Owen 1947–
Welsh rugby player

Born in Gwaun-cae-Gurwen, near Swansea, he was first capped for Wales in 1967 at the age of 19, and became their youngest-ever captain a year later. With Barry John and Phil Bennett he created the most famous Welsh half-back partnerships, and he also played full-back or centre. His 53 consecutive caps are a Welsh record. He played in 10 Lions Tests which included series victories against New Zealand and South Africa. ⬚ *Gareth* (1978)

Edwards, Sir George Robert 1908–
English aircraft designer

Born in Higham's Park, Essex, he studied engineering at London University, then joined the staff of Vickers-Armstrong at Weybridge, where he was experimental manager in World War II, becoming chief designer in 1945. Responsible for Viking, Valiant, Viscount and Vanguard aircraft, he was managing director and later chairman of the British Aircraft Corporation (1963–75). He received the US Guggenheim award and the Royal Aeronautical Society Gold Medal and was awarded the Order of Merit in 1971.

Edwards, Jimmy (James Keith O'Neill) 1920–88
English comedian

Born in London, he performed with Cambridge Footlights before serving during World War II in the RAF. His distinguishing feature was his huge handlebar moustache, worn to disguise the results of plastic surgery after his Dakota was shot down at Arnhem (1944). After the war he played Pa Glum in the hit radio series *Take It From Here* (1948–60), developing his bluff and blustering characterization, and headmaster 'Professor' James Edwards in the television series *Whack-O!* (1956–60, 1971). On television, he also played the title role in the series *John Jorrocks Esq.* His films included *Bottoms Up!* (1959), *The Plank* (1967), *The Bed Sitting Room* (1969) and *Rhubarb* (1970). ⬚ *Six of the Best* (1984)

Edwards, Jonathan 1703–58
American philosopher and theologian

Born in East Windsor, Connecticut, he was educated at Yale and succeeded his grandfather, Solomon Stoddard, as minister of the Congregationalist Church at Northampton, Massachusetts, in 1729. Renowned for his powerful preaching and hardline Calvinism, expressed in sermons such as 'Sinners in the Hands of an Angry God'

(1741), he helped inspire the revivalist movement known as the 'Great Awakening'. He was dismissed in 1750 for his zealous orthodoxy and became a missionary to the Housatonnuck people at Stockbridge, Massachusetts. In 1758, he became president of the College of New Jersey (now Princeton College). He is regarded as the greatest theologian of American Puritanism, his main doctrinal work being the *Careful and Strict Enquiry into the Modern Prevailing Notions of that Freedom of the Will* (1754). ⬚ Perry Miller, *Jonathan Edwards* (1949)

Edwards, Jonathan 1745–1801
US theologian

Born in Northampton, Massachusetts, he was the son of Jonathan Edwards. Graduating from New Jersey, he became a pastor at White Haven, Connecticut (1769), at Colebrook, Connecticut (1796), and president of the new college at Schenectady, New York in 1799. His works include *On the Necessity of the Atonement* (1785) and *A Dissertation Concerning Liberty and Necessity* (1797).

Edwards, Robert Geoffrey 1925–
British physiologist

He was educated at the universities of Wales and Edinburgh, and following a one-year research fellowship at the California Institute of Technology joined the National Institute of Medical Research, Mill Hill (1958–62). He moved to the University of Glasgow (1962–63) and to Cambridge (1963–89), where he became Ford Foundation Reader in Physiology (1969–85) and Professor of Human Reproduction (1985–89). His experimental researches focused on the mechanisms of human fertility and infertility, and the process of conception. In collaboration with Patrick Steptoe he contributed substantially to the successful development of the *in vitro* fertilization ('test-tube babies') programme. Edwards was able to analyse and then recreate the conditions necessary for the egg and sperm to survive outside the womb. He discovered the factors that would facilitate the ripening of immature eggs, and he provided the appropriate artificial conditions to ensure successful fertilization and subsequent maturation of the embryo. In July 1978 the first healthy baby was born as a result of their research. With Steptoe he established the Bourne Hallam Clinics, of which he became scientific director (1988–91).

Edwards, Robert Walter Dudley 1910–88
Irish historian

Born in Dublin, of an English father and Irish mother, he was one of the founders of modern Irish historiography. He studied at University College, Dublin, and then at the Institute of Historical Research, University of London. In 1938, with T W Moody, he founded the authoritative journal, *Irish Historical Studies*. He was Professor of Modern Irish History at University College, Dublin (1945–79). His most important published work was *Church and State in Tudor Ireland* (1936).

Edwards, Shaun 1966–
English rugby league player

Born in Wigan, he signed for Wigan at the age of 17 for £35,000—the world's biggest fee yet paid for a schoolboy. He went on to become the youngest player to appear in a Challenge Cup final and was the youngest international when he played against France at the age of 18. He played in 41 consecutive winning Challenge Cup games, as Wigan won the trophy for a record eight successive seasons. Whilst playing for Wigan (1983–95) he amassed a record 37 winners' or runners-up medals in major competitions.

Edwards, Tracy 1962–
English yachtswoman

Born in Reading, she learned to sail while serving as a stewardess and then as cook aboard motor and sailing yachts. In 1985 she competed in the Whitbread 33,000-mile round-the-world race aboard *Atlantic Privateer*, which won the leg to Auckland, making her the first woman ever to crew a winning yacht in the Whitbread. She formulated the idea of an all-female crew for the 1989–90 race and started the *Maiden* project, which she financed by selling her house. At the age of 27 she captained and navigated *Maiden* to win in her class on the second and third legs of the race, marking the first time a British yacht had won a leg for 12 years. She returned to racing in 1997 after buying the catamaran *Enza* sailed by **Robin Knox-Johnston** and **Peter Blake**, and planned to challenge their circumnavigation record in 1997–98.

Edwin, St c.585–633
King of Northumbria
The son of Ælla, King of Deira, he was kidnapped by Æthelfrith, King of Bernicia, when Ælla died (588). King Rædwald of East Anglia gave him sanctuary and with his support, Edwin killed Æthelfrith (616), creating a united Northumbrian kingdom. He extended this north to the Lothians in Scotland and west to Anglesey and the Isle of Man, and, when Rædwald died (c.625), into East Anglia, soon becoming master of all England except Kent. He accepted Christianity in order to marry the daughter of **Æthelbert**, King of Kent, who had been converted by St **Augustine** of Canterbury. His wife's chaplain, **Paulinus**, converted Edwin to Christianity (627). He was killed at Hatfield Chase, near Doncaster (633), defending Northumbria from invasion by **Cadwallon** of Wales and **Penda** of Mercia.

Egan, Sir John Leopold 1939–
English industrial executive
Born in Coventry and educated at Imperial College, London, as a petroleum engineer he spent five years in the oil industry before taking a degree at London Business School. In 1968 he entered the motor industry, first with General Motors, then with British Leyland and Massey Ferguson. In 1980 he became chairman and chief executive of the then ailing Jaguar company, and restored the company's high reputation in Great Britain and abroad. He moved to become chief executive of the British Airports Authority in 1990, implementing plans for a fifth terminal at Heathrow airport and a major programme to expand retailing space in airports.

Egan, Pierce 1772–1849
English sporting writer
He was born in London, and worked as a journalist there, and was the author of many works, including *Boxiana; or Sketches of Ancient and Modern Pugilism* (1812–13). He achieved fame with his description of the life of a 'man about town', *Life in London*, published in serial form in 1820 and as a book in 1821, with coloured illustrations by the **Cruikshank** brothers. In 1824 he launched a weekly sporting journal *Pierce Egan's Life in London*, incorporated into *Sporting Life* in 1859. 📖 J Reid, *Bucks and Bruisers: Pierce Egan and Regency England* (1971)

Egas Moniz, António Caetano de Abreu Freire 1874–1955
Portuguese neurosurgeon and Nobel Prize winner
He was born in Avanca. Professor of Neurology at Coimbra (from 1902) and Lisbon (1911–44), he did important work on the use of dyes in the X-ray localization of brain tumours and developed prefrontal lobotomy for the control of schizophrenia and other mental disorders. In 1949 he shared the Nobel Prize for physiology or medicine with **Walter Hess**. The early promise which lobotomy seemed to some to show was not substantiated and the operation, which frequently produces serious

long-term side-effects, has fallen into disrepute. Egas Moniz also had a successful political career, as a deputy in the Portuguese parliament (1903–17), Foreign Minister (1918), and the leader of the Portuguese delegation to the Paris Peace Conference.

Egbert d.839
West Saxon king, and first ruler of all the English
The son of Ealhmund of Kent, he was driven into exile by **Offa** of Mercia to **Charlemagne**'s court (789). In 802 he returned to England and was recognized as King of Wessex. He ended Mercian dominance at the Battle of Ellendun (Wroughton, Wiltshire), conquering Mercia itself (829), and the Northumbrians accepted his overlordship. He became *Bretwalda*, the (first) sole ruler of Britain, but by 830 he had lost Mercia again. His last years were dominated by Viking invasions, and in 839 he defeated an alliance of Cornish insurgents and Danish invaders at Hingston Down, near the River Tamar. His reign was important for consolidating West Saxon domination of the south-west and south-east of England.

Egede, Hans, *known as* the Apostle of Greenland 1686–1758
Norwegian missionary
A pastor at Vagen (1707–17), he learned to speak the language of the Inuit, and in 1721 set out with his family as the first missionary to Danish Greenland. He founded a permanent mission there (1721–36), and returned to Copenhagen where he founded a seminary for training missionaries to Greenland, and was appointed bishop (1740). He wrote *Det gamle Grönlands nye Perlustration* (1729), and published the first book written in Inuit (1742). His son, Paul (1708–89), succeeded him as bishop, and translated the New Testament (1766), as well as a catechism (1756) and prayer book (1783).

Egerton, Francis, 3rd Duke of Bridgewater 1736–1803
English engineer
From 1759 he constructed the earliest canal in England, the Bridgewater Canal. Designed by James **Brindley**, it was 42 miles (67km) long, and united Worsley with Manchester and Runcorn on the Mersey above Liverpool. He later built the Manchester–Liverpool canal (1772). He was known as the 'father of British inland navigation'.

Egerton, Francis Henry, 8th Earl of Bridgewater 1756–1829
English clergyman and antiquary
He was a prebendary of Durham, but lived in Paris for many years and kept his house and garden full of animals dressed up like manikins, because he was fond of shooting. He left £8,000 to be paid to the author of the best treatise on the subject of God manifested in Creation, which was eventually awarded to eight authors of the 'Bridgewater Treatises'.

Egerton, Sir Thomas, Baron Ellesmere and Viscount Brackley 1540–1617
English lawyer and statesman
Having been called to the Bar in 1572, he acquired a large practice in Chancery. He became Solicitor-General in 1581, a confidant of **Elizabeth I** and James VI and I, and a friend of **Francis Bacon** and Robert Devereux, Earl of **Essex**. He took part in the trial of **Mary, Queen of Scots** (1586) and of Essex (1600–01), and became Lord Chancellor in 1603. In the struggle with Sir **Edward Coke** and the courts of common law, he maintained the supremacy of his own court. He wrote *Privileges of Prerogative of the High Court of Chancery* (1641).

Eggan, Frederick Russell 1906–91
US cultural anthropologist

Born in Seattle and educated at the University of Chicago under both **Edward Sapir** and **Alfred Radcliffe-Brown**, he maintained links with his 'alma mater' throughout his academic life, lecturing there from 1935 to 1974. His main contribution to anthropological theory was his method of 'controlled comparison', a synthesis of the synchronic perspective of the British structural-functionalism school and the diachronic approach of American historical ethnology. His works include the edited volume *Social Anthropology of North American Tribes* (1937, enlarged edition 1955) and *Social Organization of the Western Pueblos* (1950).

Egge, Peter Andreas 1869–1959
Norwegian novelist

He was born in Trondheim. Too poor to pursue his education, he was discovered by **Knut Hamsun**, who arranged for the publication of his first novel, *Common People* (1891). His first real success was with *The Heart* (1917), which is a serious and penetrating study of marriage between two dissimilar personalities, and *Hansine Solstad* (1926), a delicate, sympathetic description of a woman wrongfully accused of theft. Egge also wrote plays, in which he followed **Ibsen** in creating drama from defects of character. 📖 C M Woel, *Peter Egge* (1929)

Eggleston, Edward 1837–1902
US writer and pastor

Born in Vevay, Indiana, he held a Methodist ministry in Minnesota, and was editor of journals like *Little Corporal*, *National Sunday School Teacher* and *Hearth and Home*. He also wrote several classic novels, among them *The Hoosier Schoolmaster* (1871), which was based on his brother's experience as a small-town teacher, *The Circuit Rider* (1874), on his own as an itinerant minister, and *The Graysons* (1888), in which **Abraham Lincoln** is a central character. 📖 W P Randel, *Eggleston, author of 'The Hoosier Schoolmaster'* (1946)

Egidius, St See Giles, St

Eginhard See Einhard

Egmont or Egmond, Lamoraal, Graf van
1522–68
Flemish soldier and Prince of Gavre

Born in the castle of La Hamaide, Hainault, he accompanied Emperor **Charles V** on many campaigns, notably against the French at St Quentin (1557) and Gravelines (1558), for which he was made Governor of Flanders and Artois. He opposed **Philip II** of Spain's Catholic policy, thus becoming a popular hero, but when he later broke with the Prince of Orange, he was executed as a traitor.

Ehrenberg, Christian Gottfried 1795–1876
German naturalist

Born in Delitzsch in Prussian Saxony, he became professor at Berlin University from 1839, and travelled in Egypt, Syria, Arabia and Central Asia. His works on microscopic organisms founded a new branch of science, and he discovered that phosphorescence in the sea is caused by living organisms.

Ehrenburg or Erenburg, Ilya Grigorevich
1891–1967
Soviet novelist and journalist

Born in Kiev, he was in exile in Paris before 1917 and returned to fight against the Communists. He went back to Paris as a correspondent, but was allowed to return to the USSR in 1923, and he subsequently wrote novels in praise of the Communist system. Among his best works are *The Extraordinary Adventures of Julio Jurenito* (1921), a satire on the aftermath of World War I, and *The Fall of Paris* (1941) and *The Storm* (1947), both novels about World War II. In the **Khrushchev** period he wrote in favour of an East–West thaw and managed to open the eyes of the Soviet

public to some genuine truths about the West. He published his memoirs *People, Years, Life* in six volumes from 1960 to 1966.

Ehrenfest, Paul 1880–1933
Austrian physicist

Born in Vienna, he studied at the universities of Göttingen and Vienna, where he completed his doctorate under **Ludwig Boltzmann** (1904). With his wife he recast the statistical mechanics of Boltzmann and **Josiah Gibbs**, their exposition of the foundations of this subject appearing in 1911. The following year Ehrenfest was appointed to the chair in theoretical physics at Leyden University. **Enrico Fermi** was one of his many students, and **Albert Einstein** and **Niels Bohr** were amongst his close friends. He demonstrated the comprehensibility of the early quantum-mechanical theory and its relation to classical physics, and his 'adiabatic principle' assumed a foundational status within quantum theory by linking it to statistical mechanics, a vital achievement during quantum theory's uncertain infancy.

Ehrlich, Paul 1854–1915
German bacteriologist and Nobel Prize winner

He was born of a Jewish family in Strehlen, Silesia (now Strzelin, Poland). He trained in medicine at Leipzig and developed his interests in chemistry and bacteriology there. A pioneer in haematology and chemotherapy, he synthesized salvarsan as a treatment for syphilis, and propounded the side-chain theory in immunology. He was joint winner, with **Elie Metchnikoff**, of the 1908 Nobel Prize for physiology or medicine. 📖 Ernst Bäumler, *Paul Ehrlich, Scientist for Life* (1984)

Eichendorff, Joseph, Freiherr von 1788–1857
German poet, novelist and critic

Born near Ratibor, he studied law and became a government official. His poems were set by a number of composers, including **Schumann** and **Felix Mendelssohn**, and reveal his profound veneration for the divine gifts of natural beauty. His novels include the idyllic *Aus dem Leben eines Taugenichts* (1826, Eng trans *Memoirs of a Good-for-Nothing*, 1955) and *Das Marmorbild* (1826, 'The Marble Statue'). He is regarded as one of the most important Romantic lyricists writing in German, known for *Gedichte* (1931) and the epic *Robert und Guiscard* (1955). 📖 L R Radner, *Eichendorff: the spiritual geometer* (1970)

Eichhorn, Johann Gottfried 1752–1827
German theologian and biblical scholar

Born in Dörrenzimmern, Franconia, he became Professor of Oriental Languages at Jena (1775), and at Göttingen (1788). His introductions to the Old and New Testaments (1780–1814) were the first attempt to apply the ordinary methods of literary criticism to Scripture. He derived each of the four gospels from one original Greek gospel.

Eichmann, (Karl) Adolf 1906–62
Austrian Nazi war criminal

Born in Solingen, and a fanatical anti-Semite, he became a member of the SS and organized anti-Jewish activities, particularly their deportation to concentration camps. Captured by US forces in 1945, he escaped from prison some months later, having kept his identity hidden, and in 1950 reached Argentina. He was traced by Israeli agents and in 1960 taken to Israel, condemned for crimes against humanity and executed. 📖 Hannah Arendt, *Eichmann in Jerusalem* (1963)

Eiffel, (Alexandre) Gustave 1832–1923
French engineer

Born in Dijon, he was the designer of many notable bridges and viaducts. The Eiffel Tower, 985ft (295.5m) high, was erected (1887–89) on the Champ-de-Mars in Paris at a cost of £260,000 for the World Exhibition of 1889, and was the highest building in the world until 1930. In 1893 he was condemned to two years' imprisonment and fined for breach of trust in connection with the abortive French Panama Canal scheme. ⌨ Bernard Marrey, *La vie et l'œuvre extraordinaires de Monsieur Gustave Eiffel* (1984)

Eigen, Manfred 1917–
German physical chemist and Nobel Prize winner
Born in Bochum and educated in Göttingen, he directed the Max Planck Institute for Physical Chemistry there from 1964. He developed methods for the study of very fast chemical reactions and for this work shared the Nobel Prize for chemistry in 1967 with **Ronald Norrish** and Sir **George Porter**.

Eijkman, Christiaan 1858–1930
Dutch physician, pathologist and Nobel Prize winner
He was born in Nijkerk and studied medicine at the University of Amsterdam. He investigated beriberi disease in the Dutch East Indies (Indonesia), and was the first to produce a dietary deficiency disease experimentally (in chickens) and to propose the concept of 'essential food factors', later called vitamins. He showed that the substance (now known as vitamin A) which protects against beriberi is contained in the husks of grains of rice, and carried out clinical studies on prisoners in Java to show that unpolished rice could cure the disease. After his return from the Dutch East Indies, he became Professor of Public Health and Forensic Medicine at the University of Utrecht in 1898. He shared the 1929 Nobel Prize for physiology or medicine with Sir **Frederick Gowland Hopkins**.

Einaudi, Luigi 1874–1961
Italian politician
Professor of Public Finance in Turin (1902–49), he was a senator (1915–45) and President of Italy (1948–55). His most important role was as Budget Minister (a post specially created for him in 1947 by **Alcide De Gasperi**). He devised a rigorous deflationary policy of tight monetary control and high interest rates which was not abandoned until 1950. While this arguably slowed Italy's postwar industrial recovery and certainly contributed to high unemployment, it also helped to revive confidence in the lira and to lay the foundation for growth in the post-1950 era.

Einem, Gottfried von 1918–96
Austrian composer
Born in Bern, Switzerland, his most successful works have been for the stage, including several ballets, and the operas *Dantons Tod* (1947, 'The Death of Danton') and *Der Besuch der alten Dame* (1970, 'The Visit of the Old Woman'). His *Jesu Hochzeit* (1980, 'Jesus's Wedding') offended the Catholic church and occasioned a national scandal. He also wrote orchestral, choral and chamber music, concertos and many songs.

Einhard or Eginhard c.770–840
Frankish historian
Born in East Franconia, he was sent to the court of **Charlemagne**, where he became a pupil of **Alcuin** and a favourite of the emperor, and of his successor **Louis I, the Pious**. For years lay abbot of various monasteries, he ultimately retired to Mühlheim. His *Life of Charlemagne* (c.820) is the great biographical work of the Middle Ages. He also wrote *Annales Francorum*, covering the period 741–829, and 62 *Epistolae*.

Einstein, Albert See panel p592

Einstein, Alfred 1880–1952
US musicologist
Born in Munich, Germany, he fled the Nazi regime in 1933, and lived in Florence and London (1933–39). He settled in the USA in 1939, becoming a US citizen in 1945. He collaborated in several well-known musical reference books, such as *Eaglefield's Dictionary of Modern Music*, but is perhaps best remembered for his work on **Mozart**, especially the revision of **Ludwig von Köchel**'s catalogue. His *Essays on Music* were published in 1958.

Einthoven, Willem 1860–1927
Dutch physiologist and Nobel Prize winner
Born in Semarang, Dutch East Indies (Indonesia), he trained in medicine at the University of Utrecht before becoming Professor of Physiology at Leyden in 1886. In 1903 he invented the string galvanometer, prompting great advances in electrocardiography. He was awarded the 1924 Nobel Prize for physiology or medicine.

Eiríksson, Leifur heppni See Leif the Lucky

Eisenhower, Dwight D See panel p593

Eisenstaedt, Alfred 1898–1995
US photojournalist
Born in Dirschau, Germany (now Tczew, Poland), he moved with his family to Berlin in 1906, and served in the German army in World War I. He started freelancing as a photojournalist in the 1920s, and emigrated to the USA in 1935, where he became one of the original photographers working on *Life* (1936–72). He was voted Photographer of the Year in 1951, and his worldwide assignments and telling photo essays made him one of the most impressive practitioners of the 20th century. His publications include *Witness to Our Time* (1966), *The Eye of Eisenstaedt* (1969), *Photojournalism* (1971) and *Eisenstaedt Remembrances* (1990). He was awarded the National Medal of Arts in 1990.

Eisenstein, Sergi Mikhailovich 1898–1948
Russian film director
Born in Riga, Russia (now Latvia), he served in the Red Army during the Russian Revolution (1916–18), and after training in theatrical scene painting was appointed to make propaganda films on the history of the Revolution with *The Battleship Potemkin* (1925, on the 1905 mutiny), and *Ten Days That Shook The World* (1928), on the October Revolution. His substitution of the group or crowd for the traditional hero, and his consummate skill in cutting and recutting to achieve mounting impressionistic effects, especially in the macabre Odessa steps sequence of *The Battleship Potemkin*, greatly influenced film art. Later he made the patriotic epic *Alexander Nevski* (1938), *The Magic Seed* (1941), the masterpiece *Ivan the Terrible* (1944), and its sequel, *The Boyars Plot*, which was banned in the USSR for many years. ⌨ Yon Barna, *Eisenstein* (1973)

Eisler, Hanns 1898–1962
German composer
Born in Leipzig, he studied under **Arnold Schoenberg** at the Vienna Conservatory (1919–23). A committed Marxist, he wrote political songs, choruses and theatre music, often in collaboration with **Bertolt Brecht**. From 1933 he worked in Paris, London and Copenhagen, and moved to Hollywood in 1938, teaching and writing film music. Denounced in the **McCarthy** anti-Communist trials, he returned to Europe in 1948. He settled in East Germany in 1952, composing popular songs and organizing workers' choirs. He wrote about 600 songs and choruses, music for over 40 films, and for nearly 40 plays. In his orchestral and chamber music he often adopted sophisticated techniques including the twelve-note technique.

Einstein, Albert 1879–1955
German–Swiss–US mathematical physicist

Albert Einstein, who ranks with **Galileo Galilei** and Sir **Isaac Newton** as one of the great contributors to the understanding of the universe, was born in Ulm, Bavaria, of Jewish parents, and educated in Munich, Aarau and Zurich. He took Swiss nationality in 1901, was appointed examiner at the Swiss Patent Office (1902–05), and began to publish original papers on the theoretical aspects of problems in physics. He achieved world fame by his special and general theories of relativity (1905 and 1916), and won the 1921 Nobel Prize for physics for his work. The special theory provided a new system of mechanics which accommodated **James Clerk Maxwell**'s electromagnetic field theory, as well as the hitherto inexplicable results of the **Michelson–Morley** experiments on the speed of light. He showed that in the case of rapid relative motion involving velocities approaching the speed of light, puzzling phenomena such as decreased size and mass are to be expected. His general theory accounted for the slow rotation of the elliptical path of the planet Mercury, which Newtonian gravitational theory had failed to do.

In 1909 a special professorship was created for Einstein at Zurich; and in 1911 he became professor at Prague. In 1912 he returned to Zurich and from 1914 to 1933 was director of the Kaiser Wilhelm Physical Institute in Berlin. By 1930 his best work was complete. After **Hitler**'s rise to power he left Germany and lectured at Princeton, USA, from 1934, becoming a US citizen and professor at Princeton in 1940. In September 1939 he wrote to President **Roosevelt** warning him of the possibility that Germany would try to make an atomic bomb, thus helping to initiate the Allied attempt to produce one (called the Manhattan Project).

After World War II Einstein urged international control of atomic weapons and protested against the proceedings of the un-American Activities Senate Subcommittee, which had arraigned many scientists. He spent the rest of his life trying, by means of his unified field theory (1950), to establish a merger between quantum theory and his general theory of relativity, thus bringing subatomic phenomena and large-scale physical phenomena under one set of determinate laws. His attempt was not successful.

His works include *About Zionism: Speeches and Letters* (1930), *Why War* (1933, with **Sigmund Freud**), *The Evolution of Physics* (1938) and *Out of My Later Years* (1950). See also Ronald W Clark, *Einstein: The Life and Times* (1971); Peter Michelmore, *Einstein: Profile of the Man* (1962).

> On his part in develping the atom bomb, he commented: 'If only I had known, I would have become a watchmaker'. Quoted in the *New Statesman*, 16 April 1955.

Eisner, Kurt 1867–1919
German journalist and politician

Born in Berlin, he was the leader of the successful Bavarian revolution of 1918–19. Appointed first President of the Bavarian republic in 1919, he was assassinated in Munich later the same year.

Eisner, Will (William Erwin) 1917–
US comic book artist and writer

Born in New York City, he studied at the Art Students League, then became staff artist on the *New York American*. In 1936 he submitted a strip, *The Flame*, to a new comic, *Wow*, and in 1937 he started mass-producing strips for *Wags*, in which he developed *The Flame* into the long-running weekly serial *Hawks of the Seas*. In 1940 he produced the first comic insert for Sunday newspapers, starring his own character, *The Spirit*.

Ekeberg, Anders Gustaf 1767–1813
Swedish chemist and mineralogist

Born in Stockholm, he was educated at Uppsala and became an assistant professor there in 1794 and full professor in 1799, the same year that he was elected a member of the Royal Swedish Academy of Sciences. In the 1790s he braved the hostility of his superiors to introduce the theories of **Antoine Lavoisier** into Sweden. Around 1795 he began investigating yttria, a newly discovered heavy metal from the quarry at Ytterby, Sweden, and in 1802 he found that it contained another unknown heavy metal. This he called 'tantalum', a reference to the tantalizing work of coaxing its oxide to react with an acid. One of his greatest distinctions was his role as the teacher of **Jöns Jacob Berzelius**.

Ekelöf, (Bengt) Gunnar 1907–68
Swedish poet

A leader of the postwar Modernists, he is considered one of the most significant Swedish poets of this century. Much influenced by the French Symbolists, he published his first book of poetry, *Sent på jorden* (1932, 'Late Arrival on Earth'), followed by *Dedikation* (1934, 'Dedication'), *Sorgen och stjärnan* (1936, 'Sorrow and the Star') and *Färjesång* (1941, 'Ferry Song'). *En Mölna-elegi* (1960), was translated into English (*A Mölna Elegy*, 1979), as were his *Selected Poems* (1966) and *Guide to the Underworld* (1967). S Karlsson and A Liffman, *En bok om Gunnar Ekelöf* (1956)

Ekelund, Vilhelm 1880–1949
Swedish poet and essayist

He was a Symbolist and early Modernist, and his works include poetry such as *Stella Maris* (1906), and volumes of essays inspired by **Nietzsche**, including *Classical Ideal* (1909). S Ahlstrom, *Vilhelm Ekelund* (1940)

Ekman, Vagn Walfrid 1874–1954
Swedish oceanographer

Born in Stockholm and educated at Uppsala University, he worked at the International Laboratory for Oceanographic Research in Oslo (1902–08) before returning to Sweden, where he was appointed Professor of Mathematical Physics at Lund University (1910–39). He explained the variation in direction of ocean currents with depth, basing his work on an observation made by the Norwegian explorer **Fridtjof Nansen**, who noted that the path of drifting arctic sea ice did not follow the prevailing wind direction, but deviated 45° to the right. Ekman explained this as an effect of the Earth's rotation (**Coriolis** force). He also showed that the general motion of near-surface water is the result of interaction between surface wind force, the Coriolis force, and frictional effects between different water layers. The resulting variation of water velocity with depth is known as the 'Ekman spiral'.

Ela, Jean Marc 1936–
Cameroonian theologian

He was born in Ebolowa and studied at the universities of Paris and Strasbourg, gaining doctorates in both theology and sociology. His major works, *My Faith as an African* (1985) and *African Cry* (1986), urge the rejection of colonial structures and of imposed Western symbols in the Church. He challenges African Christians to embrace the liberating God of Exodus and to re-read the Gospel through African eyes.

Elagabalus See **Heliogabalus**

Eisenhower, Dwight D(avid), *nicknamed* Ike 1890–1969
US general and 34th President of the USA

Dwight D Eisenhower was born in Denison, Texas, of immigrant stock originating in the Rhineland. He graduated from West Point Military Academy in 1915, took the war college course in 1928 and gained experience under the Secretary for War. By 1939 he had become chief military assistant to General **MacArthur** in the Philippines. On the outbreak of World War II he obtained leave to return to troop duty in the USA. Carefully groomed for the responsibility by General **George C Marshall**, in 1942 he assumed command of allied forces mustered for the amphibious descent on French North Africa. Without experience of high command, but perceptive and assimilative, he rapidly learned to translate strategic theory into terms of practical action. At the same time he exhibited a rare genius for smoothly co-ordinating the activities of an interallied staff, perhaps his most valuable contribution to the war effort.

His successful conduct of the North African operations, plus the preponderant American element in the forces earmarked for 'Operation Overlord', led to his selection as supreme commander for the 1944 cross-Channel invasion of the Continental mainland, which he resolutely launched despite unnervingly capricious weather conditions. With an acute appreciation of the psychology of his US forces, his strategic preference for the drive to cross the Rhine was for a shoulder-to-shoulder advance in line—a choice of method that found some justification in the failure of the 'left-hook' stroke at Arnhem. But his reluctance to push on beyond the Elbe and occupy Berlin, and his quiescence in the rather hasty dismantling of the Anglo-American armies, resulted in Russia's emergence as the leading military power in Europe.

Among many honours, he received an honorary Order of Merit in 1945, and in 1948 became for a while president of Columbia University. With the establishment of NATO in 1950 he was made Supreme Commander of the combined land forces, but in 1952 the popularity which he had gained in Europe swept him to nomination and ultimate victory in the presidential elections. Standing as a Republican, he won by a large majority despite the even balance of parties in the house, and he was re-elected in 1956. During his presidency the US government was preoccupied with foreign policy and the campaign against Communism, and undercurrents of extremism and excess of zeal often placed the President in an invidious position, but his political inexperience was balanced by sincerity, integrity and a flair for conciliation. More recently his presidency has been subject to a favourable reassessment, now seen as maintaining stablility during a difficult period.

📖 R A Melanson and D Mayers (eds), *Reevaluating Eisenhower* (1987); Stephen E Ambrose, *The Supreme Commander: The War Years of General Dwight D Eisenhower* (1970).

'The Eyes of the world are upon you. The hopes and prayers of liberty-loving people everywhere march with you.' From his speech despatching US forces on D-Day, 6 June 1944.

Elcano See **Cano, Juan Sebastian del**

Elder, Sir Thomas 1818–97
Australian businessman

Born in Kirkcaldy, Fife, Scotland, he emigrated to Adelaide, South Australia, in 1854 where he joined his brother, Alexander, in the firm of Elder and Company. They financed copper mines in South Australia. With the proceeds and in partnership with **Robert Barr Smith**, who was to marry his sister, Joanna, Elder founded the firm of Elder, Smith & Co in 1863. This grew into one of the world's largest woolbroking firms, which built up extensive pastoral holdings as a source for the supply of wool, stretching into Western Australia and Queensland. He brought in camels to provide efficient transport in the outback, and Afghans to manage them, and his stud of camels was invaluable, especially for some of the early expeditions into the 'centre' made by **Peter Warburton**, **James Ross** and **William Giles**, all of which were financed by Elder. He was appointed a knight of the Order of St Michael and St George in 1887.

Elders, M(innie) Joycelyn, *née* Jones 1933–
US paediatrician

Born in Skaal, Arkansas, she was educated at the Brock Army Medical School and the University of Arkansas. After post-graduate training and medical posts, she became Professor of Paediatrics at the University of Arkansas in 1974. Her research interests have focused on endocrine mechanisms in growth and development. In 1987 she was appointed director of the Arkansas Department of Health, and under the **Clinton** administration became the first female US surgeon-general (1993–94).

Eldh, Carl 1873–1954
Swedish sculptor

He studied in Paris (1896–1903) and his early work was much influenced by **Auguste Rodin**. His mature work after his return to Sweden is characterized by an idealized social realism. Among his public works are the August **Strindberg** and Karl **Branting** monuments in Stockholm, the young **Carolus Linnaeus** in Uppsala and **Engelbrekt** in Arboga. He also produced many portrait busts of the figures of his day.

Eldridge, Roy (David) 1911–89
US jazz trumpet player

Born in Pittsburgh, Pennsylvania, he was sometimes known as 'Little Jazz'. His originality and technical facility made him a jazz virtuoso to compare with **Louis Armstrong** and **Dizzy Gillespie** (on whom he was an early influence). He learned to play the drums as a child, before progressing to bugle and then trumpet. He worked with travelling shows and lesser-known jazz groups until 1930, when he moved to New York. A passionate improviser, able to play with ease in the ultra-high register, he was in demand as a featured soloist with top bands of the 1930s, such as McKinney's Cotton Pickers and the Teddy Hill and Fletcher **Henderson** Orchestras. He adapted to the changing demands of the modern jazz era after the late 1940s, and continued to perform until suffering a stroke in 1980.

Eleanor of Aquitaine c.1122–1204
Queen of France and of England

She was the daughter of William, Duke of Aquitaine, whom she succeeded as duchess (1137) when she married Prince Louis, who became King **Louis VII** of France a month later. Beautiful and volatile, she led her own troops on the Second Crusade (1147–49), dressed as an Amazonian warrior. In 1152 the marriage was annulled, and she married Henry Plantaganet, who became **Henry II** of England (1154). She took an active part in administration and the management of her own lands, making her court at Poitiers a model of courtly life. As a result of

Henry's infidelities she supported their sons, Richard and John, in a rebellion against him, and was imprisoned (1174–89). She acted as regent for her son **Richard I** during his crusading campaigns abroad (1189–94), and raised the ransom for his release. In 1200 she led the army that crushed a rebellion in Anjou against her second son, King **John**. 📖 Amy Kelly, *Eleanor of Aquitaine and the Four Kings* (1950)

Eleanor of Castile c.1245–1290
Queen of England

The daughter of **Ferdinand III** of Castile, she married the future **Edward I** of England in 1254. She accompanied him to the Crusades (1270–73), but the story that she saved his life by sucking the poison from a wound is probably apocryphal. She died in Harby, Nottinghamshire, and the Eleanor Crosses at Northampton, Geddington and Waltham Cross are survivors of the nine erected by Edward at the halting places of her cortège. The last stopping place was Charing Cross, where a replica now stands. 📖 John Carmi Parsons, *Eleanor of Castile: Queen and Society in Thirteenth-Century England* (1994)

Eleanor of Provence 1223–91
Daughter of Raymond Berengar IV, Count of Provence

In 1236 she married **Henry III** of England but alienated the barons by advancing her foreign uncles to high office. In the Barons' War (1264) she raised an army of mercenaries in France to support her husband, but her invasion fleet was wrecked. After the accession of her son, **Edward I**, she retired to a convent.

Eleonora of Arborea c.1350–1404
Sardinian ruler and national heroine

The daughter of a district chieftain (*giudice*), she defeated an incursion from Aragon (1383) and became Regent of Arborea for her infant son, Frederick. In 1395 she introduced a humanitarian code of laws (*Carta di Logu*), which was far ahead of its time. Her statue stands in the Piazza Eleonora in Oristano. She gave special protection to hawks and falcons, and Eleonora's Falcon is named after her.

Elgar, Sir Edward 1857–1934
English composer

Born in Broadheath, Worcestershire, he was the son of an organist and music dealer, but musically, was largely self-taught. In his youth, he worked as an orchestral violinist and became conductor of the Worcester Glee Club and the County Asylum Band, and organist of St George's Roman Catholic Church, Worcester, in succession to his father. Devoting himself to composition from 1891, he wrote the *Enigma Variations* (1899) and the oratorio *The Dream of Gerontius* (1900) which both consolidated his position as the leading figure in English music. Other works include the oratorios *The Apostles* (1903) and *The Kingdom* (1906), two symphonies and concertos for violin and cello as well as incidental music and, during World War I, topical occasional music. From 1924 he was Master of the King's Musick. His command of the orchestra and of late 19th-century musical styles within his own personal idiom were very influential in re-establishing English music internationally. He was knighted in 1904, after the Elgar Festival, held in London. 📖 Michael Hurd, *Elgar* (1969)

Elgin, James Bruce, 12th Earl of Kincardine and 8th Earl of 1811–63
English politician and colonial administrator

Born in London, the son of Thomas Bruce, 7th Earl of Elgin, he became Governor of Jamaica (1842–46) and Governor-General of Canada (1847–54). While on his way to China in 1857 as plenipotentiary, he heard at Singapore of the Indian Mutiny, and diverted the Chinese

expedition to India. His own mission, although delayed, resulted in the Treaty of Tientsin (1858). He also negotiated a treaty with Japan, and on his return home became Postmaster-General. In 1860 he was again in China to enforce the treaty, and in 1861 became Governor-General of India.

Elgin, Thomas Bruce, 11th Earl of Kincardine and 7th Earl of 1766–1841
British diplomat and art connoisseur

While ambassador to the Ottoman sultan (1799–1803) he became interested in the decorated sculptures on the ruined Parthenon at Athens, and, because they were in danger of damage and destruction, arranged for some of them to be transported to England. This action brought criticism and accusation of vandalism, but the earl was vindicated by a government committee and the Elgin Marbles were purchased for the nation in 1816 and ultimately placed in the British Museum, London.

El Greco See Greco, El

Elhuyar y de Suvisa, Don Fausto d' 1755–1833
Spanish chemist and metallurgist

Born in Logroño, Rioja, he studied medicine in Paris and mining in Freiberg, returning to Spain to teach mineralogy and geology at the Real Seminario Patriótico in Vergara. In the 1780s he and **François Chabaneau** founded the Real Esuela Metalúrgica and worked together to extract platinum and make it malleable. He collaborated with his brother Juan José in experiments to isolate tungsten (then known as wolfram) from wolframite. Subsequently the government sent him to be Director of Mines in Mexico, where he succeeded in revitalizing the mining industry until interrupted by the War of Independence in 1810. In 1821 he returned to Spain as Director-General of Mines and did much to reform mining law.

Eliade, Mircea 1907–86
Romanian historian and philosopher of comparative religion

He was born in Bucharest, and studied Indian philosophy and Sanskrit at Calcutta University (1928–31) before returning to Romania as a lecturer in the history of religion and metaphysics at Bucharest (1933–39). He served in the diplomatic service during World War II, and later taught at the Sorbonne, Paris (1946–48), and Chicago University (1957–85). A pioneer in the systematic study of world religions, he published numerous books and papers, including *The Myth of the Eternal Return* (1949), *Patterns in Comparative Religion* (1958), *Yoga: Immortality and Freedom* (1958), *The Sacred and the Profane* (1959), *A History of Religious Ideas, I–III* (1978–85), and two volumes of autobiography (1982, 1988). He was editor-in-chief of *The Encyclopaedia of Religion* (1987), and wrote a number of novels, including *The Forbidden Forest* (1955).

Eliezer, Israel ben See Baal-Schem-Tov

Eligius, St See Eloi, St

Elijah fl.c.900BC
Hebrew prophet

His story is told in 1 Kings 17–19, 21, and 2 Kings 1–2. His loyalty to God inspired him to oppose the worship of Baal in Israel under King **Ahab** and **Jezebel**, and was rewarded by his direct ascent into heaven in a whirlwind.

Elijah ben Solomon 1720–97
Jewish scholar

Born in Vilna (now Vilnius, Lithuania), he was a student of the Cabala and a commentator on the Halakah. He was revered for his exemplary life and was considered leader of the Jewish community of Vilna, the cultural centre of

Eliot, T(homas) S(tearns) 1888–1965

US-born British poet, critic and dramatist, one of the most important figures of 20th-century English literature

T S Eliot was born in St Louis, Missouri, the son of a successful businessman of New England origin. He attended the Smith Academy in St Louis and studied for four years at Harvard (1906–10), where the chief influence on his development was that of **Irving Babbitt** with his selective humanism and his resistance to modern trends. Eliot spent a year in Paris, attending lectures at the Sorbonne and improving his command of French, then returned to Harvard to study philosophy for three years. He had distinguished teachers, such as **Josiah Royce** and **George Santayana** and, for a time, **Bertrand Russell**. A travelling scholarship from Harvard took him to Merton College, Oxford, where he continued his work on a doctoral dissertation on **F H Bradley**, and read **Plato** and **Aristotle** under H H Joachim.

In 1914 he met **Ezra Pound**, to whom he had shown his poems; Pound persuaded him to remain in England, where he lived from then on, taking up naturalization in 1927. In 1915, he married Vivien Haigh-Wood. After a period of schoolteaching, he worked for eight years in Lloyds Bank before becoming a director of the publishing firm of Faber & Gwyer (later Faber & Faber). At Faber, he built up a list of new poets, including Auden and Spender, as well as Pound. Pound said of Eliot that 'he has actually ... modernized himself on his own', and his support led to the publication of Eliot's first volume of verse, *Prufrock and Other Observations* (1917). In the same year he became assistant editor of *The Egoist*, to which he contributed criticism, and he wrote reviews for the Times Literary Supplement and *Athenaeum*. He was introduced by Bertrand Russell into the Bloomsbury Circle, where the quality of his work was immediately recognized.

Ara vos prec (1920) included new poetry, notably the dramatically pessimistic 'Gerontion'. In 1921 both Eliot and his wife were affected by nervous disorders, and he was granted three months' leave to receive treatment in Lausanne. At this time he completed *The Waste Land* (1922), which was published by **Leonard** and **Virginia Woolf** at the Hogarth Press. It received wide attention and helped to reinforce his reputation. However *The Hollow Men,* which followed in 1925, gave more excuse for regarding Eliot at that point as a cynical defeatist. *The Waste Land* had appeared in the first number of *The Criterion*, a quarterly review which Eliot edited from 1923 to 1939. It aimed at impartiality in presenting opposed political philosophies and is indispensable for a study of ideas— political and religious—between the wars, as well as for the literary developments, in Great Britain and abroad, during that period. In 1933 Eliot divorced his wife Vivien; she was sent in controversial circumstances to a psychiatric hospital, where she died in 1947.

In 1939 Eliot published a collection of children's verse, *Old Possum's Book of Practical Cats*, which revealed another side of his character, influenced by **Edward Lear**. It has been one of his most popular works, and was adapted as a musical (*Cats*, 1981). *Four Quartets* (1944), the last of his major poems, is considered, despite its obscurity, to be one of the greatest philosophical poems in English. Each of its four sections depicts one of the

seasons against the background of historical events and of experiences of wartime London: 'Burnt Norton' is a Cotswold house Eliot often visited; 'East Coker' is a Somerset village; 'The Dry Salvages' is a rock formation off the coast of Massachusetts; and 'Little Gidding' is the Huntingdonshire home of **Nicholas Ferrar** and his 17th-century religious community.

Eliot's critical work consists of literary criticism, such as *The Sacred Wood* (1920, on Jacobean dramatists), the admirable *Homage to Dryden* (1924), *The Use of Poetry and the Use of Criticism* (1933), *Elizabethan Essays* (1934), *After Strange Gods* (1934), and *On Poetry and Poets* (1957); and social comment, such as *After Strange Gods* (1934), *Essays Ancient and Modern* (1936), *The Idea of a Christian Society* (1939) and *Notes towards the Definition of Culture* (1948). He was often highly provocative, as in his *Modern Education and the Classics* (1934), where he maintained that the Classics were to be studied not for their own sake but as a buttress for the Faith.

The new poetry, as announced by Ezra Pound, **T E Hulme** and Eliot, was to be related to modern life and expressed in modern idiom, preferably in free verse. Rhetoric and romantic clichés were to be avoided. In his late essay 'Milton II', in *On Poetry and Poets*, he confessed that he and his friends had insisted overmuch on these ideas and this was a sort of recantation for his abuse of **Milton**.

In 1927, the year in which he became a British subject, Eliot was baptized and confirmed in the Anglican Church, having been raised as a Unitarian. In the preface to a volume of essays *For Lancelot Andrewes* (1928), Eliot declared himself to be 'classicist in literature, royalist in politics, and anglo-catholic in religion'; the first fruit of this spiritual attitude was *Ash Wednesday* (1930). In the 1930s, Eliot developed his writing of poetic drama. The religious plays *The Rock* (1934) and *Murder in the Cathedral* (1935) further confirmed his reputation as the poet who had revived the verse play in the interests of Catholic devotion. *The Family Reunion* (1939) was a kind of comedy which dealt with social concerns; and his later dramas, *The Cocktail Party* (1950), *The Confidential Clerk* (1954) and *The Elder Statesman* (1958), were to be West End successes rather than sacred plays in church precincts. Catholic doctrine inspired all these plays, sometimes to the embarrassment of critics and audience alike.

Eliot's standing was greatly enhanced in 1948, when he received the Order of Merit and was awarded the Nobel Prize for literature. In 1957 he married Valerie Fletcher, his secretary at Faber. His poem 'A Dedication to My Wife' celebrates the evidently happy marriage that followed. Since his death, Valerie Eliot has edited his letters, the first volume of which appeared in 1988.

📖 There is a valuable biographical introduction by Valerie Eliot in the 1971 edition of *The Waste Land*. See also P Ackroyd, *T S Eliot* (1984); L Gordon, *Eliot's Early Years* (1977) and *Eliot's New Life* (1988); and for detailed criticism of Eliot's works, see H Gardner, *The Composition of Four Quartets* (1978).

East European Jewry. He was a vigorous opponent of Hasidism, denouncing its focus on miracles, visions, and collective joy as idolatrous.

Elin, Pelin, *pseudonym of* Dimitur Ivanov 1877–1949

Bulgarian writer and editor

He was born in Baylovo. In his many writings he depicted the peasantry (*shopi*) of the country around Sofia, where he lived, with a loving detachment and always with a

large dose of psychological realism. His rural tales are still read and loved; his collected work was published in Bulgaria (10 vols, 1958–59). He also wrote plays. He had the approval of the Communist government, but did not like socialist realism, and declared that the emotions of men, and not machines, should determine literature. He wrote little in the last 25 years of his life, but remained active in literary circles. 📖 C Manning and R Smal-Stocki, *The History of Modern Bulgarian Literature* (1960)

Elizabeth I 1533–1603
Queen of England and Ireland from 1558

Elizabeth was the daughter of **Henry VIII** and his second wife, **Anne Boleyn**. When her father married his third wife, Jane Seymour, in 1536, Elizabeth and her elder half-sister Mary Tudor (the future **Mary I**) were declared illegitimate by parliament in favour of Jane Seymour's son, the future **Edward VI**. Her childhood was precarious but well educated, and unlike her sister she was brought up in the Protestant faith. In 1549, during the reign of Edward VI, she rejected the advances of **Thomas Seymour**, Lord High Admiral of England, who was subsequently executed for treason. On Edward's death she sided with her half-sister Mary against Lady **Jane Grey** and the Earl of **Warwick** (Northumberland), but her identification with Protestantism aroused the suspicions of her Catholic sister, and she was imprisoned in the Tower.

Her accession to the throne in 1558 on Mary's death was greeted with general approval as an earnest advocate of religious tolerance after the persecutions of the preceding reigns. Under the able guidance of Sir **William Cecil** (later Lord Burghley) as Secretary of State, Mary's Catholic legislation was repealed, and the Church of England was fully established (1559–63). Cecil also gave support to the Reformation in Scotland, where **Mary, Queen of Scots** had returned in 1561 to face conflict with the Calvinist reformers led by **John Knox**. She was forced to abdicate in 1567, and in 1568 escaped to England, where she was placed in confinement and soon became a focus for Catholic resistance to Elizabeth. The Northern rebellion of 1569 was followed by the **Ridolfo** plot (1570); and also in 1570 the papal bull, *Regnans in Excelsis*, pronounced Elizabeth's excommunication and absolved her Catholic subjects from allegiance to her.

Government retribution against English Catholics, at first restrained, became more repressive in the 1580s. Several plots against the queen were exposed, and the connivance of Mary in yet another plot in 1586 (the **Babington** conspiracy) led to her execution at Fotheringay Castle in 1587. The harsher policy against Roman Catholics, England's support for the Dutch rebellion against Spain, and the licensed piracy of men like Sir **John Hawkins** and Sir **Francis Drake** against Spanish possessions in the New World, all combined to provoke an attempted Spanish invasion in 1588. The Great Armada launched by **Philip II** of Spain reached the English Channel, only to be dispersed by storms and English harassment, and limped back to Spain after suffering considerable losses.

For the remainder of her reign, Elizabeth continued her policy of strengthening Protestant allies and dividing her enemies. She allowed marriage negotiations with various foreign suitors but with no real intention of getting married, or of settling the line of succession; but with the death of Mary, Queen of Scots, she was content to know that the heir-apparent, **James VI** of Scotland, was a Protestant. She indulged in romances with court favourites such as Robert Dudley, Earl of **Leicester**, and later with Robert Devereux, Earl of **Essex**, until his rebelliousness led to his execution in 1601.

Her fiscal policies caused growing resentment, with escalating taxation to meet the costs of foreign military expeditions, and famine in the 1590s brought severe economic depression and social unrest, only partly alleviated by the Poor Law of 1597 which charged parishes with providing for the needy. England's vaunted seapower stimulated voyages of discovery, with Drake circumnavigating the known world in 1577 and Sir **Walter Raleigh** mounting a number of expeditions to the North American coast in the 1580s, but England's only real Elizabethan colony was Ireland, where opportunities for English settlers to enrich themselves at the expense of the native Irish were now exploited more ruthlessly than ever before and provoked a serious rebellion under **Hugh O'Neill**, Earl of Tyrone, in 1597.

At Elizabeth's death in March, 1603, the Tudor dynasty came to an end and the throne passed peacefully to the Stuart **James VI** of Scotland as James I of England. Her long reign had coincided with the emergence of England as a world power and the flowering of the English Renaissance; and the legend of the 'Virgin Queen', assiduously promoted by the queen herself and her court poets and playwrights, outlived her to play a crucial part in shaping the English national consciousness.

📖 S Bassnett, *Elizabeth the First* (1988); Roy Strong, *The Cult of Elizabeth: Elizabethan Portraiture and Pageantry* (1977); J B Black, *The Reign of Elizabeth, 1558–1603* (2nd edn 1959; J E Neale, *Queen Elizabeth* (1934, reissued as *Queen Elizabeth I*, 1971).

> 'I know that I have the body of a weak and feeble woman, but I have the heart and stomach of a king—and a King of England too; and think foul scorn that Parma or Spain, or any Prince of Europe, should dare to invade the borders of my realm.' From her address at Tilbury on the approach of the Spanish Armada (1588).

Elion, Gertrude Belle 1918–
US biochemist and Nobel Prize winner

Born in New York City, she studied at Hunter College and New York University, before joining Burroughs Wellcome in 1944 as a research associate of **George Hitchings**. She progressed through the company to become head of experimental therapy (1967–83), and since 1983 has been emeritus scientist. With Hitchings she worked extensively on drug development, synthesizing compounds that inhibited DNA synthesis, in the hope of preventing the rapid growth of cancer cells. From their work came drugs active against leukaemia and malaria, drugs used in the treatment of gout and kidney stones, and also drugs that suppressed the normal immune reactions of the body, proving vital in transplant surgery. In the 1970s they produced an anti-viral compound active against the herpes virus, which preceded the successful development of AZT, the anti-AIDS compound. In 1988 Elion and Hitchings, with Sir **James Black**, shared the Nobel Prize for physiology or medicine. She was appointed Research Professor of Pharmacology and Medicine at Duke University, North Carolina, in 1983.

Eliot, Charles William 1834–1926
US educationist

Born in Boston, he became a mathematician and chemist. As president of Harvard College (1869–1909) he carried out radical reforms of its faculties and teaching methods and turned it into a full university. During his tenure it doubled in strength, and the old undergraduate curriculum was abandoned for an optional system of studies. He also organized a graduate school of arts and sciences, and helped to establish Radcliffe College in Cambridge, Massachusetts. He published two manuals of chemistry and several books on education, and was editor of the *Harvard Classics*.

Eliot, George, *pseudonym of* **Mary Ann** or **Marian Evans** 1819–80
English writer

She was born on Arbury Farm in Astley, Warwickshire. Her father, Robert Evans, a Warwickshire land agent, was a man of strong character, and many of his traits were transferred by Eliot to her characters Adam Bede and Caleb Garth. She lost her mother, whom she loved devotedly, in 1836, and soon afterwards took entire charge of the household. She was taught German and Italian, and music, of which she was passionately fond throughout her life. She was also an immense reader. In 1841 her father moved to Coventry, and there she met Charles Bray, a writer on the philosophy of necessity from the phrenological standpoint, and his brother-in-law, Charles Hennell, who had published a rationalistic *Inquiry Concerning the Origin of Christianity* (1838). Under their influence she rejected her earlier evangelical Christianity. In 1844 she took on the laborious task of translating David Strauss's *Leben Jesu* (published 1846). After her father's death in 1849 she travelled on the Continent. Returning to England in 1850 she began to write for the *Westminster Review*, becoming assistant editor in 1851. She was also at the centre of a literary circle, two of whose members were Herbert Spencer and G H Lewes. She translated Ludwig Feuerbach's *Essence of Christianity* (1854), the only book that bore her real name. Her intimacy with Lewes grew, and in 1854 she formed a liaison with him which lasted until his death in 1878. In 1856 she attempted her first story, 'The Sad Fortunes of the Rev. Amos Barton', the beginning of *Scenes of Clerical Life*. It came out in *Blackwood's Magazine* in 1857, and at once showed that a new author of great power had risen. 'Mr Gilfil's Love Story' and 'Janet's Repentance' followed quickly. Her first novel, *Adam Bede* (1859), had enormous success. *The Mill on the Floss* (1860), *Silas Marner* (1861), *Romola* (1863) and *Felix Holt* (1866) appeared next. Her first poem, 'The Spanish Gypsy' (1868), was followed by 'Agatha' (1869), 'The Legend of Jubal' (1870) and 'Armgart' (1871), and in 1871–72 appeared *Middlemarch*, generally considered her greatest work. After that came *Daniel Deronda* (1876), her last great novel. After the death of Lewes, she was coaxed to write *Impressions of Theophrastus Such* (1879), a volume of miscellaneous essays. She fell in love with John Walter Cross (d.1924), a friend of long standing whom she married in 1880. As a novelist, George Eliot will probably always stand among the greatest of the English school. Her pictures of farmers, tradesmen, and the lower middle class, generally of the Midlands, are hardly surpassed in English literature. 🕮 G S Haight, *George Eliot* (1968); F R Leavis, *The Great Tradition* (1948)

Eliot, Sir John 1592–1632
English statesman
Born in Port Eliot, near St Germans in Cornwall, he entered parliament in 1614, was knighted in 1618 and in 1619 was appointed vice-admiral of Devon. Previously a follower of the 1st Duke of Buckingham, he broke with him in 1625 and was instrumental in securing his impeachment. In 1628 he denounced arbitrary taxation and helped to force the Petition of Right from Charles I. After further protests against the king he was sent to the Tower of London, where he was kept in confinement until his death.

Eliot, John, *known as* the Apostle to the Indians 1604–90
English missionary
Born in Widford, Hertfordshire, he graduated at Cambridge (1622), took orders, left England for America on religious grounds and settled in Roxbury, Massachusetts (1632), where he served as pastor. In 1646 he began to preach to the Native Americans at Nonantum, establishing his native converts, who numbered 3,600 in 1674, in 14 self-governing settlements nearby. However the numbers diminished after the war with the native King Philip (1675), and at the hands of the English. He was the author of *A Primer or Catechism, in the Massachusetts Indian Language* (1653). He also translated the Bible into the Native American language (1661–63), which was the first Bible printed in America. His book *The Christian Commonwealth* (1659) was suppressed for its Republican sentiments.

Eliot, Sir Thomas See Elyot, Sir Thomas

Eliot, T S See panel p595

Eliott, George Augustus See Heathfield, 1st Baron

Elisha 9th century BC
Hebrew prophet
He succeeded Elijah and his activities are portrayed in 1 Kings 19 and 2 Kings 2–9, 13. He was active in Israel under several kings from Ahab to Jehoash, was credited with miraculous signs, counselled kings, and attempted to guide the nation against her external enemies, especially the Syrians.

Elizabeth I See panel p596

Elizabeth II 1926–
Queen of Great Britain and Northern Ireland, and Head of the Commonwealth
Born in London, she was formerly known as Princess Elizabeth Alexandra Mary, being proclaimed Queen Elizabeth II on the death of her father, George VI (1952). She was crowned in 1953, which was the first major royal event to be televised. The queen is accepted as Head of the Commonwealth. She is Queen of Great Britain and Northern Ireland, Canada, Australia, New Zealand, and of several other more recently independent countries. Her husband was created Duke of Edinburgh on the eve of their wedding (1947), and styled Prince Philip (1957). They have three sons, Prince Charles, styled the Prince of Wales, Prince Andrew, and Prince Edward and a daughter, Princess Anne, styled the Princess Royal. The Queen has aimed to modernize the monarchy and make it more informal, instituting luncheon parties for distinguished individuals and pioneering royal walkabouts. She shows a strong personal commitment to the Commonwealth as a voluntary association of equal partners. 🕮 Ronald Flamini, *Sovereign: Elizabeth II and the Windsor Dynasty* (1992)

Elizabeth, *known as* the Winter Queen or the Queen of Hearts 1596–1662
Queen of Bohemia
The eldest daughter of James VI and I of Scotland and England and Anne of Denmark, she married Frederick V, Elector Palatine, in 1613. Intelligent and cultured, she enlivened the court at Heidelberg by her presence and, with Frederick's championship of the Protestant cause and his brief, unhappy winter as King of Bohemia, she became a potent symbol of the Protestant cause in Europe. Driven from Prague and deprived of the palatinate by Maximilian I of Bavaria, the couple lived in exile in The Hague with their numerous children, continually beset by financial difficulties. Frederick died in 1632, Elizabeth outliving him by 30 years. Her son, Charles Louis, was restored to the palatinate in 1648, but his mother remained in Holland. She died in London while on a visit to her nephew, the newly restored Charles II of England.

Elizabeth, *originally* Lady Elizabeth Bowes-Lyon 1900–
Queen Mother, and Queen Consort of Great Britain and Northern Ireland
Born in London, the daughter of the future 14th Earl of Strathmore, she spent much of her childhood at Glamis Castle in Scotland, where she helped the nursing staff in World War I. In 1920 she met the Duke of York, second son of George V and they were married in 1923. Princess

Elizabeth (later **Elizabeth II**) was born in 1926 and Princess **Margaret** in 1930. The Duke of York came to the throne as King **George VI** (1936). She was with the king when Buckingham Palace was bombed (1940), and travelled with him to visit heavily damaged towns throughout the war. After George VI's death (1952), the Queen Mother continued to perform public duties, becoming a widely-loved figure. She never retired and, from 1953 onwards, found a new interest in restoring the Castle of Mey, on the Pentland Firth, as her favourite Scottish home. In 1978 she became Lord Warden of the Cinque Ports, the first woman to hold the office. She is an expert fisherwoman, has great enthusiasm for horse-racing, and was Chancellor of London University (1955–80). ⮾ Grania Forbes, *My Darling Buffy: The Early Life of the Queen Mother* (1997)

Elizabeth 1st century BC – 1st century AD
Biblical character
Elizabeth was the wife of the priest Zechariah. Though the marriage was childless for many years, her husband received an angelic prophecy concerning the birth and mission of a son who would prepare people for the message of **Jesus Christ**. The apparent impossibility of this struck Zechariah dumb until their son John (later known as **John the Baptist**) was born, while Elizabeth believed and was thankful. When **Mary** was told by the angel Gabriel about the forthcoming birth of Jesus, she was also informed that her kinswoman Elizabeth was pregnant and went to visit her. When the two women met, Elizabeth prophesied, blessing Mary's faith, and stayed about three months.

Elizabeth of Hungary, St 1207–31
Hungarian princess
Born in Sáros, Patak, she was the daughter of Andreas II of Hungary. At the age of four she was betrothed to Louis IV, Landgrave of Thuringia, and educated at his father's court, the Wartburg, near Eisenach. At 14 she was married, and had two children. Louis, who admired her for her long prayers and generous charity, died as a crusader at Otranto in 1227, and Elizabeth was exiled by her husband's brother. At length, she was received into the monastery of Kitzingen by the abbess, her aunt. She was canonized by Pope **Gregory IX** in 1235. Her feast day is 17 November.

Elizabeth of Portugal, St, *known in Portugal as* Isabel 1271–1336
Portuguese saint and Queen of Portugal
The daughter of King Peter III of Aragon and great-niece of **Elizabeth of Hungary**, she married King Denis of Portugal and as queen became known for her piety, social concern and generosity, despite the corrupt life of court. The institutions she founded included a hospital, an orphanage and a women's hostel. She earned the sobriquet of 'peacemaker' because she brought about the reconciliation of Denis and their rebellious son Afonso, who had attempted an armed coup. In 1336 she rode on to the battlefield between the forces of her son (now Afonso IV) and Alfonso of Castile to avert a war between Portugal and Castile. Though her marriage was an unhappy one, she nursed her unfaithful husband through a long illness before his death. Afterwards she retired to live near a Poor Clare convent which she founded in Coimbra. She was canonized in 1625 and her feast day is 8 July.

Elizabeth of Romania See **Carmen Sylva**

Elizabeth Petrovna 1709–62
Empress of Russia
Born in Kolomenskaye, near Moscow, the daughter of **Peter I**, the Great, and **Catherine I**, she was passed over for the succession in 1727, 1730 and 1740, finally becoming empress on the deposition of Ivan VI in 1741. Attractive

and vivacious, she enjoyed food, clothes, parties and guards officers. A war with Sweden (1741–43) was brought to a successful conclusion, but her animosity towards Frederick II, the Great (1712–86) led her to take part in the War of the Austrian Succession (1740–48) and the Seven Years War (1756–63), which helped to establish Russia as a European power. At home, she contributed considerably to the extension and entrenchment of serfdom. She founded Russia's first university (in Moscow) and built the Winter Palace (now the Hermitage Art Gallery) in St Petersburg. She was succeeded by her nephew, **Peter III**. ⮾ R N Bain, *The Daughter of Peter the Great* (1899)

Elkin, Stanley Lawrence 1930–95
US writer and academic
He was born in Brooklyn, New York City, and educated at the University of Illinois, where he took a PhD. Some of his short stories in *Criers and Kibitzers, Kibitzers and Criers* (1966) are noteworthy, and *The Living End* (1979)—three stories about heaven and hell—is his most widely read book, but he is pre-eminently a novelist. *Boswell* (1964), about a professional wrestler obsessed with death and greatness, marked his debut and was followed by *A Bad Man* (1967), *The Dick Gibson Show* (1971) and *The Franchiser* (1976), all fixated with modern USA. His other novels include *George Mills* (1982), set in Sultanic Turkey, *The Magic Kingdom* (1985), *The Rabbi of Lud* (1987) and *Mac-Guffin* (1993). ⮾ P Bailey, *Reading Stanley Elkin* (1985)

Elkington, George Richards 1801–65
English inventor and manufacturer
Based in Birmingham, he introduced electroplating from 1832 in conjunction with his cousin, Henry Elkington (1810–52).

Ellery, William 1727–1820
US politician
Born in Newport, Rhode Island, he sat in the Congress of 1776, and was one of the signatories of the Declaration of Independence.

Ellesmere, Baron See **Egerton, Sir Thomas**

Ellet, Charles 1810–62
US civil engineer
Born in Bucks County, Pennsylvania, he was educated in France, and built the first wire suspension bridges in the USA, including one over the Schuylkill River at Fairmount (1842) and another over the Ohio River at Wheeling (1849). He also advocated and demonstrated the use of ram-boats, then build and commanded a fleet of them on the Mississippi, capturing Memphis (1862), but was killed in action. He was known as the 'Brunel of America'.

Ellington, Duke See panel p599

Elliotson, John 1791–1868
English physician
Born in London, he trained at Edinburgh, Cambridge and at hospitals in London. He became professor at London University (1831), and helped to establish University College Hospital. His conversion to **Mesmerism** (1837) cost him his professorship in 1838, but hardly injured his large practice. One of the first to use the stethoscope, he experimented on the action of drugs, encouraged clinical study, and founded the Phrenological Society.

Elliott, Denholm 1922–92
English actor
Born in London, he studied at RADA and served in the RAF during World War II, spending three years in a POW camp. He made his stage debut at Amersham in *The*

Ellington, Duke (Edward Kennedy) 1899–1974
US jazz pianist, composer and bandleader

Duke Ellington was born in Washington DC, into a middle-class black family. He received his only formal musical education as a child through elementary piano lessons, but he was influenced while young by church music and burlesque theatre. After forming bands to play at parties and dances he led his first regular group, the Washingtonians, when he succeeded Elmer Snowden as its leader in New York in 1925. In the next three years, his band increased in size from six to 10 or more players. In 1927 he began a four-year residence at the Cotton Club in Harlem, which not only offered him a high-profile live engagement (albeit to segregated white-only audiences), but regular access to radio airtime, then crucial in the dissemination of popular music, and recording contracts. His work at this time placed him in the forefront of orchestral jazz, a position he maintained throughout his career.

His music of this period was largely written and performed as the accompaniment for dance shows; but he began to emerge as the most important of jazz composers, and went on to produce around 2,000 works. He worked closely with his staff arranger, Billy Strayhorn (1915–67), who was an important composer in his own right, and wrote the tune which became the band's signature, 'Take The A Train'. He led some of the greatest big bands ever assembled by a jazz musician, and was highly skilled at drawing the optimum contributions from his outstanding soloists. He wrote much of his music with their specific qualities and sound characteristics in mind, a process that has led some critics to suggest the band rather than the piano was his real instrument, and he was not averse to borrowing themes and ideas from his sidemen, and incorporating them within his trademark sophisticated compositions.

He broke new ground in jazz by writing extended works and suites like *Black, Brown and Beige* (1943) and *The Perfume Suite* (1945). Such works remained a regular feature of his output until the end of his career. His use of instrumental colours and textures and innovative chord voicings make him a major figure in 20th-century music, irrespective of genre, although his real genius is arguably more accurately reflected in his shorter works, or in individual segments of extended suites, rather than genuine long-form works. Many of his song-length pieces, such as 'Mood Indigo' and 'Sophisticated Lady', became part of the standard jazz repertoire. He also wrote and performed music for films, the most important of which were *Anatomy of a Murder* (1959) and *Paris Blues* (1961). His son, Mercer Ellington (1919–96), continued to run the orchestra after his father's death, but an irreplaceable element was missing.

His vast discography is among the richest in jazz. He also wrote a highly selective memoir, *Music Is My Mistress* (1973), which stops short of being a proper autobiography. Mercer Ellington also wrote a memoir, *Duke Ellington In Person*, with critic Stanley Dance, whose own *The World of Duke Ellington* (1970) remains highly useful. See also J L Collier, *Duke Ellington* (1987).

> Ellington explained the genesis of a famous phrase inextricably associated with him in a 1965 interview: '[Trumpeter] Bubber [Miley] was the first man I heard use the expression, It don't mean a thing if it ain't got that swing. Everything, and I repeat, everything had to swing'.

Drunkard (1945) and his London debut the following year in *The Guinea Pig. Venus Observed* (1950) won him the Clarence Derwent award, whilst his New York debut in *Ring Round the Moon* (1950) received the Donaldson award. Following his first film appearance in *Dear Mr Prohack* (1949) he played breezy juveniles and heroic servicemen in films like *The Cruel Sea* (1953) and *They Who Dare* (1954). *Nothing But the Best* (1964) launched a second career as a distinguished character actor, playing largely rogues, bounders and life's losers, in films like *Alfie* (1966), *Saint Jack* (1979), *September* (1987), *Scorchers* (1992) and *Noises Off* (1992). A prolific performer in all media, and an inveterate scene-stealer, he won British Film awards for *Trading Places* (1983), *A Private Function* (1984) and *Defence of the Realm* (1985).

Elliott, Grace Dalrymple c.1758–1823
Scottish courtesan

She was the daughter of an Edinburgh advocate, and in 1771 married Sir John Elliott, MD (1736–86), who divorced her in 1774. She was the mistress successively or simultaneously of Lord Valentia, Lord Cholmondley, the Prince of Wales (the future George IV), Charles Windham, George Selwyn, Philippe Égalité (Duke of Orléans), and many others. She died at Ville d'Avray near Sèvres, leaving an interesting but untrustworthy *Journal of My Life during the Revolution*, which was published in 1859 by her granddaughter.

Elliott, Herbert James 1938–
Australian athlete

Born in Perth, Western Australia, he was winner of the gold medal in the 1,500 metres at the 1960 Olympics in Rome, and his time of 3 minutes 35.6 seconds for that event was unbeaten for 7 years. He was never beaten on

level terms over a mile or 1,500 metres, and he ran the sub-4-minute mile 17 times. He was noted for the rigour and severity of his training schedule.

Elliott, Ramblin' Jack, *professional name of* Elliott Charles Adnopoz 1931–
US folk-singer

Born in Brooklyn, New York, he rebelled against his middle-class upbringing by joining a rodeo as a teenager. He met Woody Guthrie in 1949, working with him until striking out on his own. He travelled and performed widely in Europe in the 1950s, and established an almost semi-legendary presence on the folk scene, even though he performed and recorded only intermittently, preferring to devote time to his love of boats and the sea. His music draws on both folk and country sources, peppered with more eclectic borrowings, and he uses his wit and engaging delivery to overcome his technical limitations as a singer.

Elliott, Sumner Locke 1917–1991
US novelist and playwright

Born in Sydney, Australia, the son of the writer Sumner Locke (1881–1917), he became an actor and wrote several plays, of which *Rusty Bugles* (1948) achieved great success and some notoriety when its realistic army language was heavily censored. By that time he had left for the USA, where he settled, becoming a US citizen in 1955. He was a scriptwriter for NBC and CBS television when his play, *Buy Me Blue Ribbons*, was produced on Broadway in 1951. His semi-autobiographical novel *Careful, He Might Hear You* (1963), dealing with the traumatic experiences of his own childhood and the battle for his custody, was translated into many languages and became a successful film in

1983. He also wrote *Water under the Bridge* (1977), which begins with the opening of Sydney Harbour Bridge in 1932, and ends in the early 1950s.

Ellis, Alexander John, *originally surnamed* Sharpe
1814–90
English philologist

Educated at Shrewsbury, Eton and Trinity College, Cambridge, he wrote much on mathematical, musical and philological questions, and did more than any other scholar to advance the scientific study of phonetics, of early English pronunciation, and of existing English dialects. His major work was *Early English Pronunciation* (1869–89).

Ellis, George 1753–1815
British satirist and poet

Born in Grenada, West Indies, the son of a planter, he won early popularity with his *Poetical Tales by Sir Gregory Gander* (1778). He contributed satires on William Pitt, the Younger, and others to the Whig *Rolliad*, though later he was co-founder with George Canning of the Tory *Anti-Jacobin*. A friend of Sir Walter Scott, he edited *Specimens of Early English Poets* (1790) and *Specimens of Early English Romances in Metre* (1805).

Ellis, (Henry) Havelock 1859–1939
English physician and writer

Born in Croydon, Surrey, the son of a sea captain, he travelled widely in Australia and South America before studying medicine at St Thomas's Hospital, London. In 1891 he married Edith Lees and throughout his life had a number of female followers, notably Olive Schreiner. His interest in human biology and his own personal experiences led him to compile his seven-volume *Studies in the Psychology of Sex* (1897–1928, rev edn 1936), which caused tremendous controversy, and was banned in Great Britain. He also founded the 'Mermaid' series on Elizabethan and Jacobean dramatists, and wrote *My Life* (1940).

Ellis, Ruth, *née* Neilson 1926–55
Welsh murderess

Born in Rhyl, Clwyd, she was a nightclub hostess. She shot dead her former lover, David Blakely, a racing-car driver, outside a Hampstead pub in April 1955. The case achieved notoriety as a 'crime passionnel'—Blakely was trying to extricate himself from their tempestuous, often violent, relationship at the time of his murder. Ellis was the last woman to receive the death penalty in Great Britain, and was hanged on 13 July 1955.

Ellis, William 1794–1872
English missionary

Born in London, he was sent as a missionary to the South Sea Islands, but his wife's illness obliged him to return home in 1825, after which he became secretary to the London Missionary Society. After 1853 he made four visits to Madagascar. His works included a history of Madagascar (1838), *Madagascar Revisited* (1867) and *The Martyr Church of Madagascar* (1870).

Ellis, William Webb 1805–72
English sportsman

According to a rather doubtful tradition, he was a pupil at Rugby School in 1823 when he broke the rules by picking up and running with the ball during a game of association football, thus inspiring the new game of rugby football.

Ellison, Ralph Waldo 1914–94
US novelist

Born in Oklahoma City, he studied music at Tuskegee Institute and served during World War II in the US Merchant Marine. He met Richard Wright in 1937, through whom he became aware of social and racial injustice, and

who encouraged him to write. His early work appeared in *New Challenge* magazine. *Invisible Man* (1952), his only completed novel, is the quest of a nameless black man, travelling from South to North, in search of a personal and racial identity. Allusive but highly original and ingenious, it had a seminal influence on other black writers and won the National Book award. He was Albert Schweitzer Professor in the Humanities at New York University (1970–79). He published two books of essays, *Shadow and the Act* (1964) and *Going to the Territory* (1986), but the long-awaited second novel never appeared. 📖 R Dietze, *Ellison: the genesis of an artist* (1982)

Ellmann, Richard 1918–87
US biographer and academic

Born in Detroit, Michigan, he graduated from Yale, and after World War II lived in Dublin for a year, where he wrote his first book, *Yeats: the Man and the Mask* (1948). Some 10 years later came his masterful biography of James Joyce, now accepted as one of the great 20th-century biographies, as much for its elegant composition as its astute judgement and erudition. A professor at Northwestern University, Illinois, until 1968, he moved to Oxford in 1970 as Goldsmiths' Professor of English Literature, remaining there until his death. His biography of Oscar Wilde (1987), a 20-year labour of love, was published posthumously to wide acclaim. Selected essays were published under the title, *a long the riverrun* in 1988. 📖 *Literary Biography: inaugural lecture* (pamphlet, 1971)

Ellsworth, Lincoln 1880–1951
US explorer

Born in Chicago, the son of a millionaire financier, he was the first person to fly over both the North Pole (in the airship *Norge* with Umberto Nobile and Roald Amundsen in 1926) and the South Pole (in 1935). In his Antarctic explorations (1935, 1939), he claimed thousands of square miles of territory for the USA (Ellsworth Land). He led an expedition to the Andes in 1924, helped survey the route for the Canadian transcontinental railway, and in 1931 financed Sir George Hubert Wilkins's transarctic submarine expedition in the *Nautilus*.

Ellsworth, Oliver 1745–1807
US politician and jurist

Born in Windsor, Connecticut, he studied at Yale (from which he was dismissed for mischievous behaviour) and the College of New Jersey, then practised law in Connecticut and became active in politics, representing the colony at the Continental Congress (1777–84). As a delegate to the Constitutional Convention (1787) he helped engineer the Connecticut Compromise, which gave all states equal representation in the US Senate and based representation on population in the House, thus resolving the conflict between large and small states that threatened to scuttle the convention. As a senator from Connecticut (1789–96), he was chiefly responsible for the Judiciary Act of 1789, which established the nation's federal judicial structure. He served as Chief Justice of the Supreme Court (1796–1800), and is noted for his defence of the tradition of English common law against the attacks of anti-Federalists.

Ellwood, Thomas 1639–1713
English Quaker

He was born in Crowell, Oxfordshire, and converted to Quakerism at the age of 20. In 1662 he befriended Milton, and in 1665 he hired a cottage in Chalfont St Giles so that the latter could escape the plague in London. Milton gave him the manuscript of *Paradise Lost* to read, and Ellwood's criticisms inspired Milton to write *Paradise Regained*.

El Malakh, Kamal 1918–
Egyptian archaeologist

In 1954 he recovered from a stone-slabbed pit in the shadow of the Great Pyramid a dismantled cedarwood rowing boat, probably one of the funeral vessels of King **Cheops** (d.2566BC). Reconstructed, it measures 43.6 metres (143ft) long with a beam of 5.9 metres (19.3ft).

Elman, Mischa 1891–1967
US violinist

Born in Talnoye, Ukraine, he was a child prodigy. His debuts were in Berlin (1904), London (1905) and New York (1908), and they confirmed him as an exceptional violinist. He settled in the USA in 1911 and became a US citizen in 1923.

Elms, Lauris Margaret 1931–
Australian singer

Born in Melbourne, Victoria, she studied in Paris and made her debut (1957) at Covent Garden, London, in Verdi's *Un Ballo in Maschera* ('A Masked Ball'), becoming principal resident artist there. She toured Australia with **Joan Sutherland** in 1965, and appeared at the royal opening of the Sydney Opera House in 1973. She has appeared with all the leading Australian companies, and is renowned for her Azucena in Verdi's *Il Trovatore* ('The Troubadour'). A frequent broadcaster, she gives regular lieder recitals with pianist Geoffrey Parsons. She has made a number of successful recordings including *Peter Grimes* under the composer **Benjamin Britten**.

Eloi or Eligius, St 588–658
Flemish Bishop of Noyon and Apostle of Flanders

He was originally a goldsmith, and so became patron of smiths. His feast day is 1 December.

Elphinstone, George Keith, Viscount Keith
1746–1823
Scottish naval officer

Born in Elphinstone Tower, Stirling, he joined the navy in 1761 and fought in the American War of Independence (1775–83). In the French Revolutionary wars (1792–1800) he helped capture Toulon. Promoted rear admiral, he commanded the expedition that captured Cape Town (1795) and Ceylon (1796). He helped to quell the Nore mutiny in 1797, and took Malta and Genoa (1800). He landed **Abercromby**'s army at Aboukir Bay (1801). As commander of the Channel fleet (1812–15), he arranged **Napoleon I**'s transfer to St Helena.

Elphinstone, William 1431–1514
Scottish churchman and statesman

Born in Glasgow, he was ordained priest, spent five years in France, and lectured on law at Paris and Orleans. He was appointed Bishop of Ross in 1481, and of Aberdeen in 1488. Under **James IV** he was ambassador to France (1491), and Keeper of the Privy Seal from 1492. It was chiefly through his influence that the first printing-press—that of Walter Chepman (c.1473–1538) and Andrew Myllar—was established in Scotland (1507). The University of Aberdeen (King's College) was founded by him in 1494. His *Breviarium Aberdonense* (1509–10) was printed by Chepman and Myllar.

Elsasser, Walter Maurice 1904–
US physicist

Born in Mannheim, Germany, he studied at Göttingen University before leaving Germany in 1933 for the Sorbonne, Paris. In 1936 he moved to the USA, working first at the California Institute of Technology (1936–41) and then for the US Signal Corps in radar research (1941–46). He subsequently held professorships at the universities of Pennsylvania, Utah, Princeton and Maryland. In 1939 he suggested a theory which provided an explanation of the Earth's permanent magnetic field. Considering the Earth as having a core of molten iron which would not retain any permanent magnetism, he suggested that eddy currents in the liquid core would cause the Earth to behave as an electromagnet. He was also interested in the relationship between the biological sciences and quantum mechanics.

Elsheimer, Adam 1578–1610
German painter

Born in Frankfurt, he worked in Venice after 1598 and in Rome after 1600. Basing his style on a close study of **Tintoretto** and other Italian masters, he excelled in the portrayal of atmosphere and effects of light, and exerted a profound influence on the development of German landscape painting.

Elssler, Thérèse 1808–78 and Fanny 1810–84
Austrian dancers

Born in Vienna, the younger of the two sisters, Fanny, was the more popular, with more than 25 years of successful world touring, first in Europe and then in the USA (1840–42), the only major Romantic ballerina to go there. As well as joining her sister on stage as a performer, Thérèse was one of the few female choreographers of the time. Fanny retired in 1851, and Thérèse married Prince Adalbert of Prussia, nephew of **Frederick William III**, in 1850.

Elster, Johann Phillipp Ludwig Julius
1854–1920
German physicist

Born in Bad Blankenburg, he studied with **Hans Geitel** in Heidelberg and then in Berlin, and both were appointed teachers of mathematics and physics at the Herzogliches Gymnasium in Wolfenbüttel, near Brunswick. They produced the first photoelectric cell and photometer and a Tesla transformer, but refused to take out patents, believing that such inventions should benefit all. Among other achievements, they determined in 1899 the charge on raindrops from thunderclouds, showed that lead in itself is not radioactive, and that radioactive substances producing ionization cause the conductivity of the atmosphere.

Elstracke, Renold c.1590–1630
Belgian engraver

Born probably in Hasselt, he was one of the earliest engravers in England. He worked chiefly for booksellers, and his engravings include portraits of the kings of England and **Mary, Queen of Scots**.

Elton, Ben (jamin Charles) 1959–
English comedian and writer

Born in Catford, South London, he made his first professional appearance as a stand-up comedian at the Comic Strip Club in 1981. At the forefront of the alternative comedy movement, he has co-written such popular television comedy as the anarchic *The Young Ones* (1982, 1984), *Happy Families* (1985), *Blackadder II* (1986), *Blackadder the Third* (1987), *Blackadder Goes Forth* (1989) and *The Thin Blue Line* (1995–). A regular fixture on the cabaret circuit and television, he has also written the stage plays *Gasping* (1990) and *Silly Cow* (1991), as well as the bestselling novels *Stark* (1989, filmed for television 1993), *Gridlock* (1991) and *Popcorn* (1996). His own television shows include *Ben Elton—The Man from Auntie* (1994). He also played Verges in the film *Much Ado About Nothing* (1993).

Elton, Charles Sutherland 1900–91
English ecologist

Born in Liverpool, he studied at Liverpool College and New College, Oxford, and spent most of his career there (1936–67). His four Arctic expeditions in the 1920s and his use of trappers' records for fur-bearing animals led to his classic books on animal ecology. His talents were turned to reduction of food loss in World War II through his studies of rodent ecology. His work on animal communities led to the recognition of the ability of many animals to counter environmental disadvantage by change of habitats, and to the use of the concepts of 'food chain' and 'niche'. His books include *Animal Ecology* (1927), *Animal Ecology and Evolution* (1930) and *The Pattern of Animal Communities* (1966). He exercised a formative influence on animal ecology through his founding and long editorship of the *Journal of Animal Ecology*, and was elected FRS in 1953.

Éluard, Paul, *pseudonym of* Eugène-Émile Paul Grindel 1895–1952
French poet

Born in Saint-Denis, he was founder with **André Breton** and **Louis Aragon** of the Surrealist movement, and was also involved with the Dada movement. He became France's leading 20th-century love poet. His early poetry showed Surrealist influence, as in *Le Devoir et l'inquiétude* (1917, 'Duty and Anxiety'), *Capitale de la douleur* (1926, 'The Capital of Pain') and *La Rose publique* (1934, 'The Public Rose'), but his chief Surrealist poetry is in *Les Dessous d'une vie ou la pyramide humaine* (1926, 'The Underbelly of Life or the Human Pyramid'). In 1938 he broke with the movement. During World War II he was active in the Resistance, joined the Communist Party in 1942, and circulated his poetry secretly (*Poésie et vérité*, 1942, and *Au rendez-vous allemand*, 1944). His postwar work was more lyrical and personal, especially his last volume, *Le Phénix*. English translations include *Thorns of Thunder* (1936), *Selected Writings* (1951) and *Last Love Poems* (1980). ⏛ P Nugent, *Paul Éluard* (1974)

Elvehjem, Conrad Arnold 1901–62
US biochemist

Born in McFarland, Wisconsin, he studied and spent most of his career at Wisconsin University, ultimately becoming president (1958–62). Studying pellagra, a human dietary disease, in 1935, Elvehjem showed that liver extracts cured pellagra-like symptoms caused by a steroid-limited diet. In 1937 he confirmed and extended his original finding by curing the related disease, black tongue in dogs. A year later, with collaborators, he showed that nicotinic acid too cured the canine disease, and they correctly anticipated its efficacy for curing pellagra in humans. Elvehjem also showed that certain elements are essential in animal nutrition in trace levels, including copper (necessary in the formation of haemoglobin), cobalt and zinc.

Elvström, Paul 1928–
Danish yachtsman

He is the only yachtsman to have won four individual Olympic gold medals: in the Firefly class in 1948 and the Finn class in 1952, 1956, and 1960. He was also the first to win the same event at four consecutive Olympics. He came fourth in the Tornado class at the 1984 Olympics, his seventh Games, with his daughter, Trine.

Elwyn-Jones, Frederick Elwyn-Jones, Baron 1909–89
Welsh jurist and Labour politician

Born in Llanelli, Dyfed, and educated there and at the universities of Aberystwyth and Cambridge, he was called to the Bar in 1935. He was a member of the British War Crimes Executive at Nuremberg in 1945, and was MP for the Plaistow division of West Ham (1945–50), West Ham South (1950–74), and for Newham South from 1974. He was involved in the founding of Amnesty International (1961). In 1964 he was appointed Attorney-General by **Harold Wilson** and while in this post, he led the team of

counsel to the investigating tribunal of the Aberfan pit disaster (1966). He was Lord High Chancellor (1974–79), and Lord of Appeal (1979–89).

Elyot or Eliot, Sir Thomas c.1490–1546
English scholar and diplomat

Born in Wiltshire, the son of a jurist, he was educated at Oxford and the Middle Temple, and in 1523 became clerk of the Privy Council. In 1531–32, as ambassador to Emperor **Charles V**, he visited the Low Countries and Germany, having orders to procure the arrest of **William Tyndale**. His chief work, *The Boke Named the Gouernour* (1531), is the earliest English treatise on moral philosophy. He also wrote a medical handbook, based on classical sources, *The Castel of Helth* (1538), and compiled the first English dictionary (1538).

Elytis, Odysseus, *pseudonym of* Odysseus Alepoudelis 1911–96
Greek poet and Nobel Prize winner

Born in Heraklion, Crete, he was educated at Athens University and at the Sorbonne, Paris, and has worked in broadcasting and as a critic of art and literature. His pseudonym is said to combine the three most prevalent themes in his work: Greece, hope and freedom. He was influenced by the Surrealists, both French and Greek, and his career as a poet dates from 1929. His early poems exude a love of Greece, sun and life, but after war experience in Albania a natural joie de vivre is set against violence and the imminence of death. His greatest achievement was *To axion esti* (1959, Eng trans *The Axion Esti*, 1974), a long, optimistic poem which took 14 years to write. His final poetic collection, ('West of Sorrow'), was published in Greek in 1995. In 1979 he was awarded the Nobel Prize for literature and in 1989 was made a Commander of the French Legion of Honour. ⏛ I Ivask, *Elytis: analogies of light* (1980)

Elzevir
Dutch family of printers

Based at Leyden, Amsterdam and elsewhere, between 1592 and 1681 they issued some 1,600 editions of Latin, French and Italian classics—many of them bibliographical prizes. The founder of the family, Louis (1540–1617), was born in Louvain, and settled in Leyden. Five of his sons carried on the business—Matthias, Louis, Aegidius (Giles), Jodocus (Joost) and Bonaventura; and Abraham and Isaac, sons of Matthias, were also notable. A Daniel, another Louis, another Abraham, and Peter, all maintained the traditions of the house.

Emanuel I See Manoel I

Emecheta, (Florence Onye) Buchi 1944–
British novelist

Born near Lagos, Nigeria, she was educated at the Methodist Girls' High School, Lagos, and the University of London, and has worked as a teacher, librarian and social worker. She moved to England with her student husband in 1962 and has since lived in London with her five children (she separated from her husband). She writes of marriage as a battle of the sexes, and her novels are powerful social documents, graphic in their depiction of man's inhumanity to woman. Her work includes *In the Ditch* (1972) and *Second-Class Citizen* (1974), which were published together as *Adah's Story* (1983), *The Slave Girl* (1977), *The Joys of Motherhood* (1979) and *The Rape of Shavi* (1983). *Gwendolen* (1989) focuses on the cultural isolation of a young Caribbean immigrant. She has also written children's stories and television plays. ⏛ *Head Above Water* (1986)

Emerson, Gladys Anderson 1903–
US biochemist

Born in Caldwell, Kansas, she was educated at Oklahoma College for Women, and later studied nutrition and biochemistry at the University of California, Berkeley. Following the identification of vitamin E, Emerson succeeded in isolating it in a pure form. At the Merck Pharmaceutical Company in New Jersey she studied the role of vitamin B deficiencies in diseases, and also investigated the possible dietary causes of cancer. In 1956 she became Professor of Nutrition at UCLA.

Emerson, Ralph Waldo 1803–82
US poet and essayist

Born in Boston, of a long line of ministers, he graduated from Harvard in 1821 and became pastor of the Second Church (Unitarian) in Boston (1829), but his controversial views resulted in his resignation. In 1833 he went to Europe and visited **Thomas Carlyle**, beginning their 38-year correspondence the next year. He moved to Concord, Massachusetts (1834), and in 1836 published a prose rhapsody entitled *Nature*, which was followed by 'The American Scholar', an oration delivered at Harvard. His 'address before the Divinity Class, Cambridge, 1838', produced a great sensation, especially among the Unitarians. In 1849 he revisited England to lecture on *Representative Men* (published in 1850). He also published *English Traits* (1856), *The Conduct of Life* (1860), *Society and Solitude* (1870) and *Letters and Social Aims* (1876). He was an idealist or transcendentalist in philosophy, a rationalist in religion, and a firm advocate of individualism and spiritual independence. 📖 G W Allen, *Emerson: a biography* (1981)

Emerson, Roy Stanley 1936–
Australian tennis player

Born in Queensland, he holds the record for the most Grand Slam titles—28 (12 singles and 16 doubles)—and won all four Grand Slam singles titles at least twice. These victories, however, were at a time when the majority of his rivals had turned professional and were ineligible for those championships. A classic all-court player, he is celebrated as the first man to play a serve-volley game for five sets. He won the French Open singles in 1963 and 1967, the Wimbledon singles in 1964 and 1965, the Australian Open singles six times, and the US Open singles in 1961 and 1964. He held the French doubles title for five consecutive years (1961–65) with different partners.

Emett, Rowland 1906–90
English cartoonist and designer of eccentric mechanical displays

Born in London, he studied art at Birmingham College and worked in a local commercial studio until 1939. A draughtsman during World War II, he helped develop the jet engine. After his earliest joke drawings for *Punch* (1939), he evolved a unique and fantastic style depicting a quaint, Victorian world of his own, culminating in Nellie the steam engine of the Far Tottering and Oyster Creek Railway. He built a replica of his railway for the Festival of Britain (1951). Many working models followed, including the famous Guinness Clock.

Eminescu, Mihail, *pseudonym of* Mihail Eminovici 1850–89
Romanian poet

Born in Ipoteşti, Moldavia, he studied at Czernowitz, Vienna and Berlin, and worked as a librarian, then editor. In 1883 he suffered a mental collapse, with recurring bouts of madness until his death. He wrote lyric verse which was widely read and translated posthumously. His works were collected in four volumes in 1939, and his masterpiece is generally considered to be the long poem *Luceafărul* (1883). He is remembered for creating an influential school of poetry. 📖 G Calinescu, *Mihail Eminescu* (1965)

Emin Pasha, *originally* Eduard Schnitzer 1840–92
German doctor, explorer and linguist

Born in Neisse, of Jewish parents, he studied medicine at Breslau and Berlin, and practised at Scutari (Albania), where he adopted the Muslim faith. After 1876, as Emin Effendi, he was in the Egyptian service, becoming bey and pasha. General **Charles Gordon** appointed him chief medical officer of the Equatorial Province, and in 1878 made him Governor of the province. A skilful linguist, Emin Pasha added enormously to the knowledge of African languages, made important surveys and wrote valuable geographical papers, and sent to Europe rich collections of plants and animals. He was 'rescued' by **Henry Morton Stanley**'s expedition in 1889, and, isolated by disaffection within his troops, he accompanied Stanley to Zanzibar, but immediately returned to extend the German sphere of influence around Lake Victoria. He never regained his old influence, and was marching for the west coast when he was murdered by Arabs in the Manyema country. 📖 A Symons, *Emin, the Governor of Equatoria* (1928)

Emlyn, Thomas 1663–1741
English Presbyterian clergyman

He was born in Stamford, Lincolnshire. The first person in England to describe himself as 'Unitarian', he was imprisoned and fined for blasphemy (1702–05).

Emma d.1052
Queen of England

The daughter of Richard II, Duke of Normandy, she was a forceful, ambitious and unscrupulous survivor, who played a leading part in English political life for 40 years. She married **Ethelred II, the Unready** (1002), and had a son, **Edward, the Confessor**. She fled to Normandy when **Svein Haraldsson, Fork-Beard** invaded England (1013), returning to England (1017) to marry Ethelred's successor, **Knut Sveinsson** (Canute). She tried to put their son, **Hardaknut Knutsson**, on the throne after Knut's death (1035), but was thwarted by **Harold I Knutsson**, Harefoot, her stepson, and fled to the Flemish court of Baldwin the Pious, father-in-law of **William the Conqueror**. When Hardaknut was elected king (1040), Emma returned to England, but on his death (1042) his successor, her other son, Edward, the Confessor, confiscated her property when she apparently favoured his rival, **Magnus I**, the Good, of Norway.

Emmerich, Anna Katharina, *known as* the Nun of Dülmen 1774–1824
German visionary

Born near Coesfeld, she entered the Augustinian Order in 1802, and from 1812 bore the stigmata of Christ's Passion. Her revelations were recorded by the poet **Clemens von Brentano**.

Emmet, Robert 1778–1803
Irish nationalist

Born in Dublin, he joined the United Irishmen in 1789, travelled on the Continent, interviewed **Napoleon I** and **Talleyrand** in 1802, and returned the next year to spend his fortune of £3,000 on muskets and pikes. He plotted to seize Dublin Castle and secure the viceroy, in conjunction with the expected French invasion of England, but was forced to begin his insurrection prematurely and it failed. He escaped to the Wicklow Mountains, but returning for a last meeting with his sweetheart, Sarah, daughter of the orator **John Curran**, was arrested, and hanged. 📖 Helen Landreth, *The Pursuit of Robert Emmet* (1948)

Empecinado, El, *real name* Juan Martín Díaz 1775–1825
Spanish general and patriot

He gained distinction as a guerrilla leader against the French in the Peninsular War (1808–14) and became a general (1814). However, he petitioned **Ferdinand III** to re-establish the Cortes and was banished to Valladolid (1818). On the outbreak of the insurrection in 1820 he joined the Constitutionalists. On the Absolutists' triumph in 1823 he was exhibited in an iron cage, and fatally stabbed by a soldier.

Empedocles fl.c.450BC
Greek philosopher and poet

He was born in Acragas (Agrigento), Sicily, and was by tradition a doctor, politician and soothsayer. He attracted various colourful but apocryphal anecdotes—such as the story that he jumped into Mount Etna's crater to support his own prediction that he would one day be taken up to heaven by the gods. His thought reflects both the Ionian and the Eleatic traditions, but we have only fragments of his writings from two long poems. *On Nature* describes a cosmic cycle in which basic elements, Earth, Air, Fire and Water, periodically combine and separate under the influence of dynamic forces akin to what we might call 'love' and 'strife'. This notion was adopted by **Aristotle** and the doctrine of four elements became central to Western thought for the following 2,000 years. *Purifications* has a Pythagorean strain and describes the Fall of Man, and the transmigration and redemption of souls. Empedocles was the first to demonstrate that air has weight. He was also aware of the possibility of an evolutionary process, and believed that some creatures less well-adapted to life on Earth had perished in the past. 📖 Jean Bollack, *Empédocle* (1965)

Empson, Sir Richard d.1510
English politician

In 1491 he became Speaker of the House of Commons, and in 1504, High Steward of Cambridge University and Chancellor of the Duchy of Lancaster. Throughout **Henry VII's** reign he was employed in exacting taxes and penalties due to the Crown. His conduct, which he defended as strictly legal, was regarded by the people as tyrannical, and in the second year of **Henry VIII's** reign he was convicted of tyrannizing and constructive treason, and beheaded on Tower Hill with his partner **Edmund Dudley**.

Empson, Sir William 1906–84
English poet and critic

Born in Howden, Yorkshire, he was educated at Winchester and Magdalene College, Cambridge, where he studied mathematics and literature. His first work of criticism was his university dissertation, published as *Seven Types of Ambiguity* (1930). From 1931 to 1934 he was Professor of English Literature in Tokyo, and at Peking (1937–39, 1947–53), having been in the meantime with the BBC's Far Eastern Service. In 1953 he became Professor of English Literature at Sheffield University. His other critical works include *The Structure of Complex Words* (1951) and *Milton's God* (1961). *Collected Poems*, noted for wit, concentration and complexity of thought, was published in 1955. 📖 R Gill, *William Empson, the man and his world* (1974)

Encina or Enzina, Juan del c.1469–c.1530
Spanish dramatist and poet

Born near Salamanca, he was secretary to the first Duke of Alva, then musical director in Pope **Leo X's** chapel at Rome, and later prior of León in Spain. He wrote *Cancionero* (1496, 'Songbook'), and in 1521 a poetical account of his pilgrimage to Jerusalem. His fame rests on 14 dramatic poems, seven of which were the first secular poems to be dramatized in Spain (1492). 📖 J R Andrews, *Juan del Encina* (1959)

Encke, Johann Franz 1791–1865
German astronomer

Born in Hamburg, he was educated at the University of Göttingen where he studied mathematics under **Carl Friedrich Gauss**. In 1816 he became assistant to Bernhard von Lindenau at the Seeberg Observatory, near Gotha, then succeeded him as director in 1822. Later he moved to Berlin (1825), where he superintended the building of a new observatory which had been promoted by Baron **Alexander von Humboldt**, and became Professor of Astronomy at the university there. His principal work was concerned with facilitating computations of the movements of comets and asteroids, and included a method of calculating the gravitational influences of the planets on the motion of comets. On investigating the orbit of a comet discovered by **Jean-Louis Pons** in Marseilles (1818), he demonstrated that the same comet had been observed on previous returns and deduced that it moved around the Sun in an elliptic orbit with a period of only 3.25 years. Encke's comet, as it is called, has the shortest known period of any comet. Encke was twice awarded the Gold Medal of the Royal Astronomical Society (1823, 1830).

Endecott, John c.1588–1665
English colonialist

Born in Dorchester, Dorset, he landed in America in 1628 to manage a plantation near Salem, where he also established an independent Puritan church. After **John Winthrop** arrived as governor with the main body of colonists in 1630, he served as an assistant. He headed a violent expedition against the Native Americans in 1636, was deputy governor (1641–44, 1650, 1654), and governor six times from 1644 to 1665.

Ender, Kornelia 1958–
German swimmer

Born in Bitterfeld, she won three Olympic silver medals in 1972, aged 13, and between 1973 and 1976 broke 23 world records (the most by a woman under modern conditions). At the 1973 and 1975 world championships she won 10 medals, including a record eight golds. In 1976 she became the first woman to win four gold medals at one Olympic Games, in the 100 metres and 200 metres freestyle, the 100 metres butterfly, and the 4×100 metres medley relay.

Enderby, Samuel fl.1830–39
English entrepreneur

The grandfather of General **Charles Gordon**, he was one of a firm of London merchants who fitted out three Antarctic expeditions (1830–39). The name Enderby Land was given in 1831 to a tract of Antarctica by its discoverer, John Biscoe, a whaler employed by the company.

Enders, John Franklin 1897–1985
US bacteriologist and Nobel Prize winner

Born in West Hartford, Connecticut, he studied literature at Harvard, but turned to science and received a PhD in bacteriology. He researched antibodies for the mumps virus, and in 1946 founded a laboratory for poliomyelitis research in Boston. He shared, with **Frederick Robbins** and **Thomas Weller**, the 1954 Nobel Prize for physiology or medicine for the cultivation of polio viruses in human tissue cells, thus greatly advancing virology and making possible the development of a polio vaccine by **Jonas Edward Salk**. In 1962 Enders developed an effective vaccine against measles.

Endlicher, Stephan Ladislaus 1804–49
Austrian botanist

Born in Pressburg (now Bratislava, Slovakia), he entered the archiepiscopal seminary in Vienna in 1823, became keeper of the botany department at the Naturaliencabinet in 1836, Professor of Botany at the University of Vienna, and director of the botanic garden in 1840. He formulated a system of plant classification, publishing *Genera Plantarum* (1836–41, 5 supplements 1840–50) along with other botanical works. He was also a noted sinologist, publishing a book on the elements of Chinese grammar.

Endo, Shusako Paul 1923–96
Japanese novelist and short-story writer

He was born in Tokyo. After his parents divorced, he and his mother converted to Roman Catholicism. He graduated in French literature from Keio University, then studied for several years in Lyons. He has gained wide recognition in the West and, although he is considered by some Japanese to be 'un-Japanese', has won many literary awards. In 1981 he was elected to the Nihon Geijutsuin, the Japanese Arts Academy. His books include *Chimmoku* (1966, Eng trans *Silence*), *Umi to dokuyaku* (1972, Eng trans *The Sea and the Poison*), *Obakasan* (1974. Eng trans *Wonderful Fool*), *Iesu no shogai* (1978, Eng trans *Life of Jesus*, Dag Hammarskjöld Prize) and *Samurai* (1982, Noma Literary Prize). He also published a play, *Ogon no kuni* (1966, Eng trans *The Golden Country*). Inveterately a moralist, he is often labelled 'the Japanese Graham Greene'.

Enesco, Georges, *originally* George Enescu
1881–1955
Romanian composer

Born in Dorohoiu, he studied in Vienna and under Jules Massenet and Gabriel Fauré in Paris (from 1895). Successful as a virtuoso and teacher of the violin (his pupils included Yehudi Menuhin), he was also active as a composer. His works include music in Romanian national style, an opera, *Oedipe* (1936), three symphonies, and orchestral and chamber music.

Engel, Johann Carl Ludwig 1778–1840
Finnish architect

Born in Berlin, Germany, he planned the layout of Helsinki as capital of Finland, and designed many churches and public buildings.

Engel, Johann Jakob 1741–1802
German writer

Born in Parchim, he intended to follow his father as a Lutheran pastor, but instead became a teacher. He wrote a number of plays, mainly in the comic manner of Gotthold Lessing, but is best known for the novel *Herr Lorenz Stark* (1795), and popular philosophical books, including the four-volume work *Der Philosoph für die Welt* (1775–1803, 'The World's Philosopher'). ▫C Schroeder, *Johann Jakob Engel* (1897)

Engelbrekt or Engelbrektsson c.1390–1436
Swedish rebel and military commander

He was born in Bergslagen of a German iron-mining family. When the war between King Erik VII of Pomerania and the Hanseatic League disrupted iron exports, he led a series of rebellions against the king, and in 1434 forced the Council of the Realm to retract its oath of loyalty to Erik. In 1435 at a meeting at Arboga ('the first Swedish Parliament'), he was appointed Commander-in-Chief of the Realm. The Council soon reversed its decision, but a year later Erik was again deposed, and Engelbrekt was reappointed. Shortly after this Engelbrekt was murdered in a personal quarrel. He is celebrated as a hero of national liberation in a play by Strindberg, among other works of literature.

Engels, Friedrich 1820–95
German philosopher and politician

Born in Barmen, he lived mostly in England after 1842. Having gained experience from working in his father's cotton factory in Manchester and established contacts with the Chartist movement, he wrote *Condition of the Working Classes in England in 1844* (1845). He first met Karl Marx at Brussels in 1844 and collaborated with him on the *Communist Manifesto* (1848), and returned to Germany with his mentor in 1848 to work on the *Neue Rheinische Zeitung* and fight on the barricades at Baden during the unsuccessful revolution of that year. After Marx's death in 1883, Engels devoted the remaining years of his life to editing and translating Marx's writings, including the second (1885) and third (1894) volumes of the influential *Das Kapital*, which established the materialist interpretation of history. ▫ Gustav Mayer, *Friedrich Engels: A Biography* (1936)

Enghien, Louis Antoine Henri de Bourbon, Duc d' 1772–1804
French soldier

He was the only son of Louis Henri Joseph, Prince de Condé. He commanded the emigré vanguard from 1796 to 1799. At the Peace of Lunéville (1801) he went to reside in Baden. Napoleon I, claiming that Enghien was involved in a conspiracy against him, violated the neutral territory of Baden, captured the duke and took him to Vincennes. In 1804 he was shot in the castle moat. Boulay de la Meurthe said of this act that it was worse than a crime, it was a blunder—a saying often wrongly attributed to Fouché or to Talleyrand.

Engler, (Heinrich Gustav) Adolf 1844–1930
German systematic botanist

Born in Sagan, Lower Silesia (now Zagan, Poland), he was educated at Breslau, and worked as keeper of the Royal Herbarium, Munich (1871–78), then became Professor of Botany and director of the botanic garden at Kiel University (1878–84). From 1884 to 1889 he was Professor of Botany at Breslau University and began *Die natürliche Pflanzenfamilien* (1887–1915). In 1889 he became Professor of Botany at Berlin University, where he developed the present botanic garden in the Dahlem district, and began *Das Pflanzenreich* (107 vols, 1900–53). In 1892 he published *Syllabus der Pflanzenfamilien*, his system of classification, which for many years was the most widely used.

Ennius, Quintus c.239–169BC
Roman poet

Born in Rudiae, Calabria, probably of Greek extraction, he is said to have served in the Punic Wars, and returned from Sardinia to Rome with Cato, the Elder. In Rome he taught Greek, gained the friendship of Scipio Africanus, the Elder, and attained the rank of Roman citizen. He introduced the Greek hexameter into Latin, using it in his *Annales*, which became the model for Latin epic poetry. In addition, he wrote satires, didactic verse, epigrams and numerous plays. Only fragments of his works survive. ▫O Skutsch, *The Annals of Quintus Ennius* (1953)

Enoch
Biblical character

The son of Jared and father of Methuselah, he was depicted as extraordinarily devout, and therefore was translated directly into heaven without dying (Genesis 5.24). In the Graeco-Roman era his name became attached to Jewish apocalyptic writings allegedly describing his visions and journeys through the heavens (1, 2, and 3 Enoch).

Enquist, Per Olov 1934–
Swedish playwright and novelist

Born in Hjoggböle, his best-known work for the theatre is a collection of three plays published in 1981 under the collective title *Triptych*, comprising *Lesbian Night* (about Strindberg and his wife), *To Phaedra* and *The Life of the Slow-Worms* (about Hans Christian Andersen). His major novel is *The Legionaries* (1968), a controversial documentary about the expulsion of Baltic refugees to Russia from Sweden after World War II. 🕮 A Landsmanis, *De misstolkade legionarerna* (1970)

Ensor, James Sidney Ensor, Baron 1860–1949
Belgian painter and engraver
He was born in Ostend, of Anglo-Belgian parentage, and trained at the Brussels Academy. He rarely left Ostend and was neglected as an artist for much of his life, but is now regarded as a pioneer of Expressionism. He is best known for his macabre carnival paintings of fighting skeletons and masked revellers, such as his *Entry of Christ into Brussels* (1888), which owe a great deal to Hieronymus Bosch, Pieter Brueghel, the Elder, and Goya. His later work is less fierce.

Ensor, Sir Robert Charles Kirkwood
1877–1958
English radical journalist and historian
Born in Somerset, he was educated at Winchester and Oxford. He joined the *Manchester Guardian* as a leaderwriter, and edited an anthology of speeches and writings, *Modern Socialism* (1904). He was active in the Labour movement and the Fabian Society (1907–19). He worked as leader-writer on the liberal *Daily News* (1909–11) and on the radical *Daily Chronicle* (1912–30), but left the *Daily Chronicle* when it merged with the *News*. He then became a lecturer at the London School of Economics (1931–32), and held various other academic posts. Chosen to write the late Victorian volume of the *Oxford History of England*, he produced *England 1870–1914* (1936), a masterpiece combining personal knowledge with massive research. His *Courts and Judges* (1933) compared the British, French and German legal systems.

Enver Pasha 1881–1922
Turkish soldier and politician
A leader in the 1908 revolution of Young Turks, as the pro-German Minister of War he steered the Turkish government into a secret alliance with Germany directed against Russia in August 1914. After the Turkish surrender in 1918 at the end of World War I, he fled to Russia and was killed in an insurrection in Turkestan. 🕮 E E Ramsaur, *The Young Turks* (1957)

Enzensberger, Hans Magnus 1929–
German poet
He was born in Kaufbeuren and educated at Nuremberg, Freiburg and Hamburg. He served with the militia towards the end of World War II then worked as an editor for the Süddeutsche Rundfunk broadcasting company at the end of the 1950s. His first significant poetry was published in *verteidigung der wölfe* (1957). He lived for a period in Norway (1961–66), but has since lived in Berlin and later in Munich. The first English translations of his work were made by Michael Hamburger (1966). His radical style is influenced by Georg Trakl, Gottfried Benn and Bertolt Brecht, and is most apparent in his long poem *Der Untergang der Titanic* (1978, Eng trans *The Sinking of the Titanic*, 1980). His other poetic works are *Die Gedichte* (1983, 'Poems'), published by Suhrkamp, Frankfurt, for whom he has acted as editor since 1960, and *Kiosk* (1995). Enzensberger has translated a wide range of literature, and like Günter Grass, has been a commentator on European unification. 🕮 R Grimm, *Über Enzensberger* (1984)

Enzina, Juan del See Encina, Juan del

Eoin See MacNeill, John

Eötvös, Roland von, Baron 1848–1919
Hungarian physicist
Born in Pest (Budapest), the son of the writer and statesman Josef von Eötvös (1813–71), he studied at the universities of Königsberg and Heidelberg, and was appointed to a professorship at Budapest University in 1872. His early research on liquids produced the 'Eötvös law', which described the relationship between surface tension, molar volume and temperature for liquids. His subsequent research into gravitation led him to devise the sensitive Eötvös torsion balance in 1888, to conclusively demonstrate Galileo's assertion that all bodies have the same acceleration in a gravitational field, and to provide a vital stepping-stone in Albert Einstein's later development of the general theory of relativity.

Epaminondas c.418–362BC
Theban general
His victory at the Battle of Leuctra (371BC) broke the military power of Sparta and made Thebes the most powerful state in Greece. Two years later, with Pelopidas, he marched into the Peloponnesus, and incited some of the allies to desert Sparta. In 368 war was renewed, and Epaminondas made a somewhat unsuccessful invasion into the Peloponnesus. To atone for this he advanced into Arcadia, and near Mantinea broke the Spartan phalanx, but was killed there.

Épée, Charles Michel, Abbé de l' 1712–89
French educationist
Born in Versailles, he became a preacher and canon at Troyes, but was deprived as a Jansenist. In 1765 he began to educate two sisters who could not hear or speak, and invented a language of signs. He also pioneered the use of 'spatial aids' to assist the memorizing of, for example, vocabulary by associating words with particular locations in space. His attempts succeeding, at his own expense he founded an institute for those who could neither hear nor speak, which was converted into a public institution two years after his death.

Ephialtes d.461BC
Athenian politician
Predecessor of Pericles in the leadership of the democratic party, he enacted the constitutional reforms (462–461BC) which broke the power of the Areopagus and ushered in radical democracy at Athens. He was assassinated in 457BC by his political opponents.

Ephraem Syrus, St c.306–378AD
Syrian churchman
Born in Nisibis, he went to a desert school near Edessa (now Urfa, Iraq) after the capture of Nisibis by the Persians in AD363. Devoting himself to prayer, fasting and the study of the Scriptures, Ephraem's orthodoxy, asceticism and learning were the admiration of his contemporaries, and his works, written in a fervid and popular style, maintain his reputation as an orator and poet. Part of them have come down to us in Syriac, part in Greek, Latin and Armenian translations. His feast day is 18 June.

Ephron, Nora 1941–
US screenwriter
Born in New York City, to parents who were both writers, she was educated at Wellesley College. Her debut screenplay collaboration *Silkwood* (1983) earned her an Academy Award nomination, and she went on to write two of the most successful romantic comedies of the period, *When Harry Met Sally* (1989) and *Sleepless in Seattle* (1993). She adapted *Heartburn*, her novel about her failed marriage to Carl Bernstein, one of the *Washington Post* journalists who uncovered the Watergate affair, for the screen in 1985, and added directing to her credits with *This Is My Life* (1992) and *Michael* (1997).

Epicharmus c.540–450BC
Greek poet

Born in Cos or Syracuse, he wrote 35 or more comedies performed in Syracuse. Only fragments of his works survive. 📖 L Berk, *Epicharmus* (1964)

Epictetus 1st century AD
Greek Stoic philosopher and moralist
Born in Hierapolis, Phrygia, he was a slave in Rome. After he was freed he taught philosophy there until banished by the Emperor **Domitian** along with other philosophers in AD90 when he settled at Nikopolis in Epirus. His pupil, the historian **Arrian**, collected his sayings into a manual entitled the *Enchiridion* and into eight volumes of *Discourses*, of which four survive. He taught a gospel of inner freedom through self-abnegation, submission to providence and the love of one's enemies.

Epicurus c.341–270BC
Greek philosopher and founder of the Epicurean school
Born on the island of Samos, he visited Athens at the age of 18, opened a school at Mitylene (310BC) and taught there and at Lampsacus. He returned to Athens and established a successful school of philosophy (305), known as the 'Gardens', where he led a life of temperance and simplicity. The Gardens became the model for other Epicurean communities, or communes, where members could live peacefully in friendship. Only three letters and a few fragments of his 300 or so works survive and most of our knowledge of his doctrines comes from **Cicero**, **Plutarch** and in particular, **Lucretius**. He believed that pleasure is the chief good and the only goal of morality, by which he meant freedom from pain and anxiety, not (as the term 'epicure' has since come to mean) one who indulges sensual pleasures without stint. These ethical views are supported by a materialistic psychology and an atomistic physics (largely derived from **Democritus**) which demonstrate that the world operates on mechanical principles and that neither death nor the gods are to be feared, that the gods do not intervene in the world or punish the guilty, and that the human soul and body are a combination of atoms that dissolve and perish together. Epicureanism and Stoicism were the two great philosophies of the Hellenic period, and both found many followers in Rome and endured for many centuries.

Epimenides fl.7th century BC
Semi-legendary Greek poet and priest
Born in Crete, he is said to have lived for 299 years, during 57 of which he received, while sleeping, the divine inspiration that determined his future career. **Goethe** wrote a poem on the subject, *Des Epimenides Erwachen*. Epimenides is said to have gone to Athens about 600BC, where he stayed, and with **Solon** reformed the Athenian constitution. He was the 'prophet' quoted by St **Paul** in 1 Titus, 12, but it is unlikely that he wrote the epic poems ascribed to him. 📖 H Demoulin, *Epimenides de Crète* (1901)

Épinay, Louise Florence, *née* Tardieu d'Esclavelles 1726–83
French writer
She was born in Valenciennes. After her marriage at the age of 19, to a 'worthless' cousin, she held a brilliant salon at La Chevrette and formed liaisons with **Jean Jacques Rousseau**, **Friedrich Melchior Grimm**, and others. Her *Conversations d'Émilie* (1774), a work on education, won her a gold medal from the Académie Française.

Epiphanes See Antiochus IV

Epiphanius, St c.315–403AD
Palestinian Christian Church Father
Born in Palestine, he founded a monastery near Eleutheropolis in AD335. He was Bishop of Constantia in Cyprus from 367 until his death. He showed intolerance

to St **John Chrysostom** and proclaimed **Origen** a heretic in 394. He wrote several works against Arianism and various other heresies.

Episcopius or Biscop, Simon 1583–1643
Dutch theologian
Born in Amsterdam, he studied at Leyden under **Jacobus Arminius** and **Francis Gomarus**, and succeeded to the latter's chair in 1612. He and 12 other Arminians were banished by the Synod of Dort (1618), and in the Spanish Netherlands he wrote his famous Arminian *Confessio* (1622). On the renewal of the war between Spain and Holland, he lived in France, and published a series of able controversial treatises. Permitted to return in 1626, he was a professor at the Arminian College at Amsterdam from 1634, where he produced his *Institutiones theologicae* and *Responsio*.

Epstein, Sir (Michael) Anthony 1921–
English microbiologist
Born in London, he was educated at Trinity College, Cambridge, worked at Middlesex Hospital Medical School and moved to the University of Bristol as professor and head of the pathology department (1968). In 1985 he moved to Oxford, taking up a fellowship at Wolfson College. In 1964 he discovered a new human herpes virus, known as the Epstein–Barr virus, which has been implicated in some forms of human cancer, notably **Burkitt**'s lymphoma. This was the first virus to be associated with cancer in man, and its discovery stimulated the current vast research on the viral origins of human tumours. He has received many national and international awards, was elected FRS in 1979, knighted in 1991, and from 1986 to 1991 served as foreign secretary and vice-president of the Royal Society, which awarded him with its Royal Medal in 1992.

Epstein, Sir Jacob 1880–1959
British sculptor
He was born in New York City, USA, a Russian-Polish Jew, and studied at the École des Beaux-Arts in Paris (1902). He became a British subject in 1907, and his early commissions included 18 nude figures for the façade of the British Medical Association building in the Strand, London (1907–08) and *Night and Day* (1929) for the London Transport Building. These and later primitivist sculptures, such as the marble *Genesis* (1930, Granada Television), the *Ecce Homo* (1934), and the alabaster *Adam* (1939), resulted in great controversy, and accusations of indecency and blasphemy. He modelled many impressive bronze portrait heads of famous people, such as **Joseph Conrad**, **Albert Einstein**, **T S Eliot** and **George Bernard Shaw**, and of children, such as *Ester* (1944), his youngest daughter. He also executed two bronze *Madonna and Child* works (1927, Riverside Church, New York; 1950, Holy Child Jesus Convent, London). In the 1950s, his last two large commissioned works, the aluminium *Christ in Majesty* (Llandaff Cathedral) and *St Michael and the Devil* (Coventry Cathedral), won more immediate critical acclaim. 📖 Richard Buckle, *Jacob Epstein, Sculptor* (1963)

Equiano, Olaudah c.1750–97
Nigerian autobiographer
Captured by slave traders at the age of 10, he was sold in the West Indies. After buying his freedom, he worked as a merchant seaman and was active in the English anti-slavery movement. He wrote *The Interesting Narrative of the Life of Olaudah Equiano, or Gustavus Vassa, the African* (1789).

Érard, Sébastien 1752–1831
French pianoforte maker
Born in Strasbourg, he set up a workshop in Paris, where he invented the harp with double pedals, the mechanical harpsichord, and the piano with double escapement.

Erasmus, Desiderius c.1466–1536
Dutch humanist and scholar, one of the most influential figures of the Renaissance

Erasmus was born in Rotterdam, and educated by the Brethren of the Common Life at Deventer. He joined an Augustinian monastery at Steyn near Gouda in 1487, and was ordained a priest in 1492; but he was already reacting against scholasticism and was drawn to the Humanists. He studied and taught in Paris, and later in most of the cultural centres in Europe, including Oxford (1499) and Cambridge (1509–14), where he was Professor of Divinity and of Greek. He travelled widely, writing, teaching and meeting Europe's foremost intellectuals (including, in England, **John Colet** and **Thomas More**).

He published many popular, sometimes didactic works, including *Adagia* (*Adages*, 1500, 1508), *Enchiridion Militis Christiani* (*Handbook of a Christian Soldier*, 1503), and the famous *Encomium Moriae* (*In Praise of Folly*, 1509). He also published scholarly editions of classical authors and the Church Fathers, and edited the Greek New Testament (1516). He became strongly critical of the pedantries and abuses of the Catholic Church, and his *Colloquia familiaria* of 1518 helped prepare the way for **Martin Luther** and the Reformation; but he also came to oppose the dogmatic theology of the Reformers and specifically attacked Luther in *De Libero Arbitrio* (1523). Despite these controversies he enjoyed great fame and respect in his last years, which he spent in Basle.

📖 J M Sowards, *Desiderius Erasmus* (1975); R H Bainton, *Erasmus* (1969).

In regione caecorum rex est luscus.
In the country of the blind, the one-eyed man is king.
Adages bk 3, century 4, no.96 (c.1500).

Erasistratus of Ceos fl.c.250BC
Greek physician

Born on the island of Ceos (Chios), he studied medicine in Athens, and later founded a school of anatomy at Alexandria. His writings are known largely through **Galen's** accounts. On the basis of vivisection and dissection of animals, accompanied by postmortems on humans, he built up an extensive grasp of human and comparative anatomy. He denied **Aristotle's** view that digestion was a process similar to cooking, and also rejected the theory likening it to fermentation, contending instead that food, once in the stomach, was torn to pieces and pulped by the peristaltic motion of the gastric muscles. He also traced arteries and veins to the heart, and like **Herophilus**, clearly recognized the difference between sensory and motor nerves. On the basis of such investigations, he is considered one of the founders of modern medicine.

Erasmus, Desiderius See panel above

Erastus, Thomas, *originally* Thomas Liebler or Lieber or Lüber 1524–83
Swiss theologian and physician

Born in Swiss Baden, he studied theology at Basle, philosophy and medicine in Italy, and was appointed physician to the counts of Henneberg. Professor of Medicine at Heidelberg and physician to the Elector Palatine (1558), he became Professor of Ethics at Basle in 1580. He was a skilful physician, and a vigorous writer against **Paracelsus** and witchcraft. In theology he followed Huldreich Zwingli, and represented his view of the Lord's Supper at Heidelberg (1560) and Maulbronn (1564). In England the name of Erastians was applied to the party that arose in the 17th century, denying the right of autonomy to the Church which was neither maintained nor denied by Erastus.

Eratosthenes c.276–194BC
Greek mathematician, astronomer and geographer

Born in Cyrene, he became the head of the great library at Alexandria and was the most versatile scholar of his time, known as 'pentathlos', or 'all-rounder'. He measured the obliquity of the ecliptic and the circumference of the Earth with considerable accuracy. In mathematics he invented a method, the 'sieve of Eratosthenes', for listing the prime numbers and a mechanical method of duplicating the cube. He also wrote on geography, chronology and literary criticism, but only fragments of this work remain. 📖 P M Fraser, *Eratosthenes of Cyrene* (1971)

Ercilla y Zúñiga, Alonso de 1553–c.1595
Spanish poet

Born in Bermeo on the Bay of Biscay, he entered the service of **Philip II**, and accompanied him in 1554 to England on the occasion of his marriage to Queen **Mary I, Tudor**. Shortly after, he joined the expedition against the Araucanians in Chile, whose amazing heroism inspired his monumental epic poem, *La Araucana* (1569–89, Eng trans 1945). When an unfounded suspicion of his complicity in an insurrection nearly led to his execution, he returned to Spain, but as Philip treated him with indifference he made a tour through Europe, and became chamberlain to the Emperor **Rudolf II**. In 1580 he returned to Madrid, where he lived in poverty until his death. 📖 J T Medina, *Vida de Ercilla* (1948)

Ercker, Lazarus c.1530–1593
German metallurgist

Born in Annaberg, Saxony, he held a variety of posts in mines and mints, and latterly served under Emperor **Rudolf II** as chief superintendent of the mines of the Holy Roman Empire and Bohemia. He was reputed to be both well informed and a careful observer, and his extensive influence was due to his book *Beschreibung allerfürnemisten mineralischen Ertzt und Berckwercksarten* (1574, 'Description of Leading Ore Processing and Mining Methods'). This was the first systematic account of analytical and metallurgical chemistry, describing how to test alloys and metallic compounds, and how to separate and refine the metals in them. It was translated into many languages and remained the leading manual until around the middle of the 18th century.

Erckmann-Chatrian
French writers

Émile Erckmann (1822–99) and Alexandre Chatrian (1826–90) were both from Lorraine: Erckmann was born in Phalsbourg and Chatrian in Abreschwiller. Their literary partnership dates from 1848, but they had little success until the publication of *L'Illustre Docteur Mathéus* (1859, Eng trans *The Illustrious Dr Mathéus*, 1872). *Le Fou Yégof* (1862, Eng trans *The Great Invasion of 1813–14; or, After Leipzig*, 1870) is one of a series of novels, to which also belong *Histoire d'un conscrit de 1813* (1864, Eng trans *The Conscript: A Tale of the French War of 1813*, 1865), *Waterloo* (1865, Eng trans 1865) and *Le Blocus* (1867, Eng trans *The Blockade*, 1869). Well-known plays by them include *Le Juif polonais* (1869, Eng trans *The Polish Jew*, 1871) and *Les Rantzau* (1882, Eng trans *The Rantzaus*, 1882). After the annexation of Alsace-Lorraine to Germany, they demonstrated a strong anti-German feeling in several of their books—the best of these is *L'Histoire du plebiscite* (1872, Eng trans *The Story of the Plebiscite*, 1872). They quarrelled over money just before Chatrian died.

Erdtman, Otto Gunnar Elias 1897–1973
Swedish palynologist

Born in Hjorted, Småland, he graduated from Stockholm University but could not then gain academic employment, and instead worked as a high school teacher. In 1933 he developed and published the acetolysis method to prepare pollen for microscopy, which is still used today. In 1944 he was allowed to set up a small palynological laboratory at a Stockholm school, and he became director of a palynological laboratory financed by the Swedish Research Council, which rapidly became the foremost of its kind. In 1952 he published the first of four volumes covering all spores (1952, 1957, 1965, 1971). In 1954 he founded the palynological journal *Grana Palynologica* and in 1970 initiated the *World Pollen and Spore Flora* project.

Erenburg, Ilya Grigorevich See **Ehrenburg, Ilya Grigorevich**

Erhard, Ludwig 1897–1977
German economist and politician

Born in Furth, North Bavaria, the son of a haberdasher, he studied economics at Nuremberg. His career was held back during the 1930s as a result of his refusal to join the Nazi Party. However, immediately after World War II, he became Professor of Economics at Munich University. In 1949 he was elected to the Bundestag (federal parliament) at Bonn and was appointed Finance Minister in the **Adenauer** Christian Democrat administration. He was the pioneer of the West German 'economic miracle' of recovery from wartime devastation, devising a successful policy of social free enterprise (Marktwirtschaft). He succeeded Adenauer as Chancellor (1963–66), but economic difficulties forced his resignation.

Eri, Vincent Serei 1936–
Papua New Guinean novelist

He was born in Moveave, and was educated by Catholic missionaries and at the University of Papua New Guinea, Port Moresby. He has held various government offices both at home and in Australia. His novel, *The Crocodile* (1970), the first significant novel from his country, describes the period of colonialism and concerns the opposition of traditional values with modernity. The crocodile itself is a symbol of power, magic, and both fertility and death, and the novel concludes ambiguously, its central character precariously balanced between worlds.

Erickson, Arthur Charles 1924–
Canadian architect

Born in Vancouver and educated at British Columbia and McGill universities, he established Arthur Erickson Architects after working in various other partnerships. Powerful articulation and theatricality mark his designs, and he had a strong preoccupation with technology and materials. The influences of Le Corbusier, Louis Kahn and Brutalism are evident in his works. He received international recognition with the Simon Fraser University buildings, British Columbia (1963), confirmed by his avant-garde design of Lethbridge University, Alberta (1971). Further major works include the Canadian Pavilion at Expo '70, Osaka, the Museum of Anthropology, British Columbia (1971–77), and Roy Thomson Hall, Toronto (1976–80).

Ericsson, John 1803–89
US inventor

Born in Långbanshyttan, Värmland, Sweden, he served as an officer of engineers in the Swedish army (1816–26), and in 1826 moved to England, where he set up as an engineering consultant. He built (1829) a formidable rival to George **Stephenson**'s *Rocket*, and in 1836 he patented, six weeks after Sir Francis Pettit **Smith**, one of the first

successful screw-propellers. In 1839 he went to the USA, where he designed the warship *Princeton*, the first steamer with engines and boilers entirely below the water-line. He became a naturalized US citizen in 1848. In 1861, during the Civil War, he designed the iron-clad *Monitor* (the first warship with an armoured revolving turret), and in 1878 *The Destroyer*, which could launch submarine torpedoes. His inventions largely revolutionized navigation and the construction of warships. He was the brother of the engineer Nils **Ericsson**. 📖 Ruth White, *Yankee from Sweden: Days of John Ericsson* (1960)

Ericsson, Nils 1802–70
Swedish engineer

After supervising the building of the new Trollhättan Canal and the Saima Canal in Finland, he became director of state railway building (1854–62) and was responsible for the main lines in southern and central Sweden. He was the brother of the inventor John **Ericsson**.

Erigena, John Scotus, *also called* Johannes Scotus Eriugena or John the Scot c.810–c.877
Irish philosopher and theologian

Born in 'Scotia' (Ireland), he taught at the court of Charles I, the Bald, in France, then supported Hincmar in the predestination controversy with his *De Praedestinatione* (851) which the Council of Valence condemned as *pultes Scotorum* ('Irishman's porridge') and 'an invention of the devil'. He also translated into Latin and provided commentaries on the Greek writings of the theologians of the Eastern Church. His major work *De Divisione Naturae* (c.865) tried to fuse Christian and neoplatonic doctrines and to reconcile faith and reason, but his work was later condemned for its pantheistic tendencies and eventually placed on the Index by Gregory **XIII** in 1685. An enigmatic and singular figure who stands outside the mainstream of medieval thought, tradition has it that, having become abbot of Malmesbury, he was stabbed to death by his scholars with their pens 'for trying to make them think'.

Erik VII, *also known as* Erik of Pomerania c.1381–1459
King of Denmark, Sweden (Erik XIII) and Norway (Erik III)

The son of Duke Wratislaw VII of Pomerania and Maria, niece of Queen **Margrethe** I, he was adopted as heir to the triple monarchy by his great-aunt (1389), and crowned at Kalmar, Sweden (1397) when the treaty of union between the three countries was formally sealed. He married Philippa, the daughter of King Henry **IV** of England (1405), but it was not until 1412, on Queen Margrethe's death, that he gained actual power. Aggressive commercial and military policies against Holstein and the Hanseatic League that ultimately failed led to economic disasters that provoked rebellion, and he was deposed by all three countries one by one: Sweden and Denmark (1438), and Norway (1442). He was succeeded by his nephew, Kristofer of Bavaria.

Erik IX Jedvardsson, *called* Erik the Saint d.1160
King and patron saint of Sweden

King of Sweden from c.1150, he is said to have led a Christian crusade for the conversion of Finland, and to have been murdered at Mass in Uppsala by a Danish pretender to his throne. He was married to Kristina, and was the father of King Knut Eriksson (d.c.1195).

Erik XIV 1533–77
King of Sweden

Born in Stockholm, the eldest son and successor of Gustav **I** Vasa, he ruled from 1560 to 1568. Tutored by a German Lutheran nobleman, he had the outlook of a Renaissance prince, although he was highly unstable. Suspicious of others to the point of paranoia, he imprisoned his half-brother, Johan, for treason (1563), and launched a war against Denmark for control of the Baltic ports, which ended inconclusively with the Peace of Stettin (1570). He had several of his courtiers butchered on suspicion of treason and, after various attempts to marry Queen Elizabeth I of England and Mary, Queen of Scots, he married a soldier's daughter, Karin Månsdotter, who alone seemed capable of controlling his paroxysms of fury. Her coronation (1568) provided a pretext for rebellion. He was dethroned (1568) in favour of his brother Johan III, and spent the rest of his life in captivity, listening to music and writing psalms, until he died, probably of arsenic poisoning.

Erik Haraldsson, called Erik Blódøx ('Bloodaxe')
d.954
King of Norway

The eldest son of **Harald I Halfdanarson**, he succeeded to the throne of Norway (c.942) when his father abdicated. His wife was Gunnlaug, sister of King **Harald Gormsson** of Denmark. His reign in Norway was violent, and Erik killed several of his half-brothers who had rebelled against him. He was deposed by his youngest brother, **Haakon I Haraldsson** (947) and sought refuge in England, where he was accepted as king in York of the Norse realm in Northumbria (948, 952–54). He was eventually expelled (954) and killed in battle at Stainmore, Yorkshire.

Erik of Pomerania See **Erik VII**

Erik the Red, *properly* Erik Thorvaldson 10th century
Norwegian sailor

He explored the Greenland coast and founded the Norse colonies there (985). His son **Leif the Lucky** landed in 'Vinland', often identified as America (1000). Both men are the subject of Icelandic sagas.

Eriksen, Gunn 1956–
Scottish chef and restaurateur

Born in Grimstad, Norway, an artist by training, she went to Ullapool in the Scottish Highlands to pursue her craft. There she met Fred Brown, owner of the Altnaharrie Inn across Loch Broom from Ullapool. She joined him there in 1980 and began to develop the distinctive cooking style which has brought her renown. With no formal culinary training, she continues to make memorable meals which reveal her Scandinavian origins. Given the hotel's somewhat isolated location (practical access only by boat), the willingness of visitors to seek out its cooking makes its own point.

Erikson, Erik Homburger 1902–94
US psychoanalyst

Born in Frankfurt am Main, Germany, to Danish parents, he trained in Vienna under **Sigmund Freud** and **Anna Freud**, specializing in child analysis. In 1933 he emigrated to the USA, where he engaged in clinical work and taught successively at Yale, Berkeley, and Harvard. Seeking to test the limits of Freudian theory and to determine the extent to which human psychology is modified by social and cultural forces, he carried on anthropological studies of children in various societies, including those of the Sioux and Yurok. His most important book, *Childhood and Society* (1950), divides human development into eight stages, each characterized by a crisis that the individual must resolve in order to continue his emotional progress. The originator of the concept of the adolescent 'identity crisis', Erikson expanded on his theory in books such as *Identity: Youth and Crisis* (1968) and traced the psychological development of historical figures in *Young Man Luther* (1958) and *Gandhi's Truth* (1969, Pulitzer Prize).

Erinna 4th century BC
Greek poet

Mistakenly believed in antiquity to have lived in the 7th century, she was born on the island of Telos, and though she died at the age of only 19, she won fame for her epic, *The Distaff*, which is on the joys of childhood and was apparently written in mourning for a friend. Only four lines of this and a handful of epigrams survive of her work. ☐C Latte, *Erinna* (1953)

Eriugena, Johannes Scotus See **Erigena, John Scotus**

Erixson, Sven, *known as* X-et 1899–1970
Swedish artist

Born in Tumba, he spent much time in the Mediterranean countries and took his motifs from there as well as from Sweden. His colourful paintings, with their mixture of folk-art and naivism, full of incident from everyday life, made him much in demand for large-scale public commissions, such as his tapestry *Melodies on the Square* (1937–39) in the Concert Hall in Gothenburg. He was also active as a scenic artist in the theatre.

Erlander, Tage Fritiof 1901–85
Swedish politician

He became active in the Social Democratic Party while he was studying at the University of Lund and was elected to parliament in 1933. He was Minister without Portfolio in the wartime coalition government from 1944, and was Minister for Ecclesiastical Affairs when chosen to succeed **Per Albin Hansson** as party leader and Prime Minister in 1946. He made way for the younger **Olof Palme** in 1969. He was a moderate, and his brand of consensual government was dubbed 'Harpsund democracy' after his country estate, where he consulted with leaders in all walks of society.

Erlanger, Joseph 1874–1965
US physiologist and Nobel Prize winner

Born in San Francisco, and educated at the Johns Hopkins Medical School, where he accepted an assistant professorship, he was subsequently appointed Professor of Physiology at Wisconsin University (1906–10) and then at Washington University, St Louis (1910–46). His early career was devoted to studying the heart and the circulation, but during World War I he studied different problems, including the treatment of wound shock. In 1921 he began collaborating with **Herbert Gasser** in analysing fundamental properties of the neural conduction of impulses, discovering that the velocity of the impulse was proportional to the diameter of the nerve fibre. For this research they shared the 1944 Nobel Prize for physiology or medicine. Their development of the necessary equipment, especially the cathode-ray tube, for the prosecution of their researches, heralded a new electronic age in neurophysiology.

Ermanaric, *Icelandic* Jörmunrekkr fl.c.375AD
King of the Ostrogoths

He is the oldest historical personage depicted in the heroic lays of Scandinavia. He built up a huge empire in the Ukraine, centred on the Dnieper, but was overthrown by the Huns, and may have committed suicide when wounded. In Germanic legend he is depicted as a cruel tyrant who had his wife trampled to death by wild horses, and was mortally wounded by her brothers in a suicidal revenge attack.

Ernest Augustus 1771–1851
King of Hanover

Born at Kew, the fifth son of **George III**, he was educated at the University of Göttingen. He then entered the Hanoverian army and was created Duke of Cumberland (1799). He married Princess Frederica of Mecklenburg-Strelitz in 1815, and in 1837 under Salic law succeeded his brother **William IV** of Great Britain as Ernest I of Hanover. His policy was reactionary, but in 1848 he saved his throne by the unwilling concession of liberal reforms. He was succeeded by his son, **George V**.

Ernst, Max 1891–1976
German painter and sculptor
He was born in Brühl, near Cologne. After studying philosophy and psychiatry at Bonn, he turned to painting, and in 1918 founded at Cologne the German Dada group. Later, in Paris, with **Paul Éluard** and **André Breton**, he participated in the Surrealist movement. He invented the technique of frottage (pencil rubbings on canvas), and settled in the USA in 1941, but returned to France in 1953. He won the Venice Biennale prize in 1954. ⊞W S Lieberman, *Max Ernst* (1961)

Ernst, Richard Robert 1933–
Swiss physical chemist and Nobel Prize winner
Born in Winterthur, he studied at the Swiss Federal Institute of Technology (ETH) in Zurich, worked as a research scientist with Varian Associates in Palo Alto, California (1962–68), and then joined the staff of the ETH, becoming full professor in 1976. Since 1978 he has been vice-president of the board of directors. He was awarded the Nobel Prize for chemistry in 1991, for innovations in nuclear magnetic resonance (NMR) spectroscopy, which has been an important tool for the determination of molecular structure in organic chemistry. During the first 20 years its applications were based on a restricted range of nuclei, which Ernst sought to extend after 1966 by increasing enormously the sensitivity of the instrumentation and developing his 'Fourier transform NMR'. His work is of particular value in probing very large molecules, such as are often involved in biology and medicine. His other awards include the 1986 Benoist prize and the 1990 Ampère prize.

Ernulf or Arnulf 1040–1124
French Benedictine monk
Appointed prior of Canterbury by **Anselm**, he was subsequently abbot of Peterborough (1097) and Bishop of Rochester (1114). He was remarkable for his skill in canon law and personal saintliness and compiled a great collection of documents about his own church, laws and papal decrees, which from the old name of the see (*Hrôlfe-ceaster*) was known as the *Textus Roffensis*. As 'Ernulphus' he was comprehensively cursed in Book III of **Laurence Sterne's** *Tristram Shandy* (1759–67).

Erpenius, *properly* Thomas van Erpen 1584–1624
Dutch Orientalist
Born in Gorkum, he studied at Leyden, and at Paris learned Arabic from an Egyptian. In 1613 he became Professor of Oriental Languages at Leyden, where he erected an Arabic press in his own house. His *Grammatica Arabica* (1613) enjoyed undisputed supremacy for two hundred years, like his *Rudimenta* (1620). His other works were *Proverborum Arabicorum Centuriae Duae* (1614), and an edition of El-Mekin (1625).

Ershad, Hossain Mohammad c.1929–
Bangladeshi soldier and chief martial law administrator
He was born in Rangpur in northern Bangladesh and joined the Pakistan army. He subsequently served in East Pakistan, rising to the rank of colonel during the 1971 civil war. He became Chief of Staff to the Bangladesh army and was appointed a lieutenant-general in 1979. Ershad assumed power in a military coup in 1982, became President in 1983 and proceeded to introduce a new rural-orientated economic programme. He was re-elected President in 1986 and lifted martial law, but he faced continuing political opposition and demands for a full return to civilian rule until he resigned in 1990. In 1991 he

was sentenced to 10 years' imprisonment for illegal arms possession, among other charges. In the 1996 general election he was elected to parliament as leader of the Jatiya Party.

Erskine, David Stewart, 11th Earl of Buchan 1742–1829
Scottish nobleman
He was a noble antiquary, though considered somewhat eccentric. He founded the Society of Antiquaries of Scotland (1780) and brought about a reform in the election of Scottish peers. He was the brother of **Thomas Erskine** and Henry Erskine (1746–1817).

Erskine, Ebenezer 1680–1754
Scottish clergyman
Born at Chirnside, in the Scottish Borders, he was minister of Portmoak in Kinross-shire from 1703 to 1711, and then in Stirling. He took the Evangelical side in the rise of the Marrow Controversy in 1718, and in the patronage dispute of 1733 advocated the right of the people to choose their own pastors, and with three other ministers was suspended and finally deposed (1740). Meanwhile, in 1733, he and his three colleagues formed an Associate Presbytery, setting up the Secession Church of Marrowkirk. In the divisions of 1747 (Seceders divided into Burghers and Antiburghers), Erskine led the Burghers. He was the brother of **Ralph Erskine**.

Erskine (of Carnock), John 1695–1768
Scottish jurist
He was called to the Bar in 1719, and became Professor of Scots Law at Edinburgh (1737). His two works, *Principles of the Law of Scotland* (1754) and the more important *Institutes of the Law of Scotland* (1773), have maintained their value, the latter being one of the classics of Scots law.

Erskine, Ralph 1685–1752
Scottish clergyman
Born in Chirnside, in the Scottish Borders, he was a minister in Dunfermline from 1711. He joined his brother **Ebenezer Erskine**, in the Secession (Associate Presbytery) in 1737, and also took part with the Burghers in the divisions of 1747. His sermons were highly thought of, and many of them were translated into Dutch. His *Gospel Sonnets* and *Scripture Songs* are well known, and his *Practical Works* were published in 1764.

Erskine, Thomas Erskine, 1st Baron 1750–1823
Scottish jurist
Born in Edinburgh, he was sent to sea (1764), and in 1768 bought a commission in the 1st Royals, studying English literature in Minorca (1770–72). He entered Lincoln's Inn (1775) and Trinity College, Cambridge (1776), and was called to the Bar in 1778. His acute legal mind led to immediate success and in 1783 he became a KC, and MP for Portsmouth. A sympathy with the French Revolution led him to join the 'Friends of the People', and to undertake the defence in many political prosecutions of 1793–94. His acceptance of a retainer from **Tom Paine** cost him the attorney-generalship to the Prince of Wales (held since 1786). Erskine's speeches for Paine, the Scottish radical Thomas Hardy (1794), and **John Tooke** (1794) are very fine examples of forensic skill, and his defence of Hadfield (1800), indicted for shooting at **George III**, dismantled the contemporary theory concerning the criminal responsibility of the mentally ill. In 1802 he was appointed Chancellor to the Prince of Wales, an ancient office revived for him, and in 1806 he was appointed Lord Chancellor, but resigned the following year. He published a pamphlet on army abuses (1772), a discussion of the war with France (1797), a political romance (*Armata*, 1817), a pamphlet in favour of the Greeks, and some poems. He was the brother of **David Erskine** and the jurist

Henry Erskine (1746–1817). 📖 Lloyd Paul Stryker, *For the Defense: Thomas Erskine, the Most Enlightened Liberal of His Times 1750–1823* (1947)

Ervin, Sam(uel James) 1896–1985
US senator

Born in Morgantown, North Carolina, he became a lawyer and served on the North Carolina supreme court. In 1954 he was elected to the US Senate, where he remained for the next 20 years. He was a conservative Democrat who led Southern filibusters against civil rights laws. As chairman of the Senate committee that investigated the Watergate scandal (1973–74), he fought President **Richard Nixon**'s efforts to withhold testimony on the ground of executive privilege.

Ervine, St John Greer 1883–1971
Irish playwright and writer

He was born in Belfast, and in 1900 emigrated to London, where he wrote novels and plays. From 1915 to 1916 he was manager of the Abbey Theatre, Dublin, where his first plays, *Mixed Marriage* (1911) and *Jane Clegg* (1914), were produced. After World War I, in which he served with the Dublin Fusiliers and lost a leg, he won a high reputation as a drama critic, working on the *Observer* and the *Morning Post*, and for the BBC (1932). His most successful plays are perhaps *Anthony and Anna* (1926), *The First Mrs Fraser* (1929) and *Robert's Wife* (1937). Other publications include seven novels and several biographies. 📖 *Some Impressions of My Elders* (1922)

Erving, Julius 1950–
US basketball player

Born in Hempstead, New York, he played for the American Basketball Association's Virginia Squires (1971–73) and New York Nets (1973–76) and the National Basketball Association's Philadelphia 76ers (1976–87). Nicknamed 'Dr J', he won fame for his dazzling moves and soaring slam dunks. He was named most valuable player four times (ABA, 1974–76; NBA, 1981) and placed third on the all-time scoring list with a career total of 30,026 points (in the ABA and NBA combined).

Erzberger, Matthias 1875–1921
German politician

He was born in Buttenhausen, Württemberg. He became controversial when, as a leading member of the Centre Party, he began to advocate peace without annexations as early as 1917 and again (1918–19) when, as a member of the armistice delegation, he advocated acceptance, despite fierce German opposition, of the terms of the Treaty of Versailles. Finance Minister and vice-premier in 1919, he drastically reformed the tax system and nationalized the German railways. Unsuccessful in a libel action against an unscrupulous political opponent, he resigned in 1921 and was assassinated in August of that year by members of an extremist group (Organisation Consul) in the Black Forest.

Esaki, Leo 1925–
Japanese physicist and Nobel Prize winner

Born in Osaka, he was educated at Tokyo University, working for his doctorate on semiconductors. In 1957, at the Sony Corporation in Tokyo, he investigated conduction by quantum mechanical 'tunnelling' of electrons through the potential energy barrier of a germanium p-n diode. He used the effect to construct a device with diode-like properties, the tunnel (or Esaki) diode. Their very fast speeds of operation, small size, low noise and power consumption, give these diodes widespread application in computers and microwave devices. He shared the Nobel Prize for physics in 1973 for work on tunnelling effects with **Brian Josephson** and **Ivar Giaever**. He worked at IBM in the USA from 1960 to 1992 where his research interests included man-made semiconductor superlattices. Since 1992 he has been President of the University of Tsukuba in Japan.

Esarhaddon d.669BC
King of Assyria

He was the younger son of **Sennacherib**, whom he succeeded in 680BC. He achieved the conquest of Egypt (675–671). A great builder, he established the city of Nineveh. He was succeeded by his son, **Ashurbanipal**.

Esau
Biblical character

The elder son of Isaac, he is depicted as his father's favourite son, but he was deprived of Isaac's blessing and his birthright by his cunning brother **Jacob** (Genesis 27). The story explains why Esau's descendants, the Edomites, were thereafter hostile to Jacob's descendants, the Israelites.

Eschenbach, Wolfram von See **Wolfram von Eschenbach**

Eschenmoser, Albert 1925–
Swiss chemist

Born in Erstfeld, Uri, he enrolled at the Swiss Federal Institute of Technology in Zurich in 1949, obtaining a doctorate in 1951 for work with **Leopold Ružička**. He first came to prominence when his group joined with that of **Robert Woodward** in uniting two halves of the vitamin B_{12} molecule (one made in Zurich and the other in Boston) to give a few micrograms of synthetic B_{12}. Since then he has worked on prebiotic chemistry (the type of chemistry which might have created the molecules now characteristic of living things), and has synthesized molecules analogous to DNA but containing non-naturally occurring sugars. He has received prizes and awards from all over the world, including the Davy Medal of the Royal Society (1978).

Escher, Maurits Cornelius 1898–1972
Dutch artist

Primarily a printmaker, he created whimsical visual fantasies in lithographs and woodcuts. He often used geometric distortions and tricks of perspective to deceive the eye.

Escoffier, Auguste c.1847–1935
French chef

Born in Villeneuve-Loubet, he served with a Russian Grand Duke, then became chef de cuisine to the general staff of the Rhine army in the Franco-Prussian War (1871) and of the Grand Hotel, Monte Carlo, before César Ritz persuaded him to go to the Savoy, London, and finally to the Carlton. He invented the '*bombe Nero*' of flaming ice and '*pêche Melba*', among other dishes, and wrote the *Guide culinaire* (1903, 'Culinary Guide') and *Ma cuisine* (1934). 📖 Timothy Shaw, *The World of Escoffier* (1994)

Eshkol, Levi 1895–1969
Israeli politician

Born in the Ukraine into a pious Jewish family, he settled in Palestine as an agricultural worker in 1914. After Israeli independence in 1948, he supervised the founding of several hundred new villages to absorb immigrants. A member of the Mapai Party, he served as Minister of Finance (1952–63) and as Prime Minister and Defence Minister (1963–69), transferring the latter post to **Moshe Dayan** during the Six-Day War of 1967. Eshkol established diplomatic relations with West Germany and was also the first Israeli leader to visit the USA. Despite internal political difficulties in 1964–65, he remained Prime Minister until his death.

Espert Romero, Nuria 1935–
Spanish actress and stage director
Born in Hospitalet, Barcelona, she began her professional career at the age of 12, at 16 played Juliet and at 19, Medea. At the age of 24 she co-founded the Nuria Espert Theatre Company, which she still leads. She has played the title role in *Hamlet*, and both Prospero and Ariel in the same production of *The Tempest*. Other productions include **Bertolt Brecht's** *The Good Person of Setzuan* and **Oscar Wilde's** *Salomé*. She has appeared as an actress in productions all over the world. In 1986 she directed a revival of **Federico García Lorca's** *The House of Bernarda Alba* in London, which won the *Evening Standard* Drama award, and also **Puccini's** *Madame Butterfly* for Scottish Opera.

Espinel, Vicente de 1551–1624
Spanish writer and musician
Born in Ronda, he served as a soldier in France and Italy, meeting with some of the adventures related in his *Relaciones de la vida del Escudero Márcos de Obregón* (1618, Eng trans *The History of the Life of the Squire Marcos de Obregon*, 1816). This book was much drawn upon by **Alain Lesage** for his *Gil Blas*. After his return to Spain he took holy orders. He also published a volume of poems (1591) and a translation of the *Ars Poetica* of **Horace**. He was, if not the inventor, the improver of the 10-line stanza, and is credited with adding the fifth string to the guitar. 📖 G Haley, *Vicente Espinel e Marcos de Obregon* (1959)

Espronceda, José de 1808–42
Spanish poet and revolutionary
Born in Almendralejo, Estremadura, he travelled widely in Europe, partly to escape persecution for his liberalism, and partly in pursuit of Teresa Marcha, who is commemorated in his unfinished poem, *El Diablo mundo* (1841, 'The Devil of the World'). He wrote romantic poems in the **Byronic** manner, and is considered by some the greatest lyricist of his time. 📖 J Casalduero, *Espronceda* (1961)

Espy, James Pollard 1785–1860
US meteorologist
Born in Westmoreland County, Pennsylvania, he obtained a degree at Transylvania University, Lexington, and later studied law. He taught in the Franklin Institute and became so impressed with the meteorological writings of **John Dalton** and **John Frederick Daniell** that he began to observe and study the weather. In 1840 he was appointed Chief of the Meteorological Bureau of the War Department (1842–57). He organized a service of daily synchronous weather observations and from these compiled charts for 1,100 days which he analysed to deduce the main characteristics of cyclones and tornadoes.

Esquivel, Manuel 1940–
Belizean politician
Born in Belize City, he was educated at the Loyola University in the USA and the University of Bristol in the UK. Following a career in teaching he joined the United Democratic Party and was elected to the Senate in 1979. He was Prime Minister between 1984 and 1989, and again in 1993. During those terms of office he was responsible for negotiating the reduction of British military forces in Belize.

Es-Sa'id, Nuri, *officially* **Nouri Said Pasha**
1888–1958
Iraqi politician
Born in Kirkuk and educated at the Istanbul Staff College for the Turkish Army, he fled to Egypt when his Pan-Arab activities became suspect. In World War I he fought against the Turks under King **Hussein Ibn Ali** of the Hejaz. In 1921 he became Iraq's first Chief of the General Staff and a year later Defence Minister. From 1930 he filled the office of Prime Minister many times until he was assassinated in 1958 after the coup d'état of Brigadier **Abdul Kassem**.

Essex, Robert Devereux, 2nd Earl of
1566/67–1601
Elizabethan soldier and courtier
Born in Netherwood, Herefordshire, the eldest son of **Walter Devereux**, he succeeded his father in 1676. Under Robert Dudley, Earl of **Leicester**, his stepfather from 1580, he served in the Netherlands (1585–86), distinguishing himself at Zutphen. At court he quickly rose in the favour of Queen **Elizabeth I**, despite his clandestine marriage (1590) with Frances Walsingham, the daughter of Sir **Francis Walsingham** and widow of Sir **Philip Sidney**. He became Master of the Horse (1587) and in 1591 he commanded the forces sent to help **Henri IV** of France against the Catholic League (1591). He took part in the capture of Cadiz (1596), but was largely responsible for the failure of an expedition to the Azores (1597). He became earl marshal (1597), and Chancellor of Cambridge University (1598), but because of his great quarrel with Elizabeth, when he turned his back on her, and she boxed his ears, they were never reconciled. When his six months' lord lieutenancy of Ireland proved a failure, he returned to England, and Elizabeth had him imprisoned. Unfortunately, although handsome and brave, and an ideal courtier, Essex aimed at the highest state office, despite being politically and administratively unskilled. He plotted to raise revolt in London and remove Elizabeth's councillors (1601), but was found guilty of high treason and beheaded. 📖 Robert Lacey, *Robert, Earl of Essex* (1970)

Essex, Robert Devereux, 3rd Earl of 1591–1646
English soldier
He was the eldest son of Robert Devereux, 2nd Earl of Essex. In 1604 the earldom was restored to him after his father's execution for treason in 1601. In 1606 he married Frances Howard (1592–1632). From 1626 Essex attached himself to the popular party, and in 1642 he received the command of the Parliamentary army. Though personally brave, he was a poor general, and the prolongation of the war was largely due to him. The drawn Battle of Edgehill, the capture of Reading, and the relief of Gloucester were followed by his blundering march into Cornwall, whence he fled by sea. In 1646 he resigned the command, and died soon afterwards.

Essex, Walter Devereux, 2nd Viscount Hereford and **1st Earl of** 1541–76
English colonialist
The scion of an old Herefordshire house, he earned notoriety as the merciless colonizer of Ulster from 1573. As Earl Marshal of Ireland he dealt severely with the rebellious Sorley Boy MacDonnell and his followers.

Estaing, Charles Hector Théodat, Comte d'
1729–94
French naval officer
He served in the East Indies, and was captured twice by the British. As a vice-admiral, he commanded French naval forces (1778) against the British in the American Revolution, and captured St Vincent and Grenada in 1779, but his operations on the mainland were unsuccessful. During the French Revolution he was guillotined for writing in support of **Marie Antoinette**.

Esterházy
Hungarian noble dynasty
A powerful Magyar family, originally founded by Ferenc Zerhazy (1563–94), it developed along the Frankó, Csesznek and Zólyom lines and produced diplomats, soldiers and art patrons into the 20th century. The

Franknó line was founded by Zerhazy's son Miklós Esterházy (1582–1645), whose goal was to free Hungary from Turkish dominance and whose son Pál Esterházy (1635–1713) was made a prince of the empire (1687) for his successes against the Turks, thus establishing the princely line. He also strongly supported the **Habsburg** monarchy, whose wealth the Esterházy dynasty exceeded, and helped to reduce the power held by the Magyar nobles. Prince Miklós Joseph (1714–90), a notable art patron, employed **Haydn** in his private orchestra for nearly 30 years. The fourth Prince Miklós (1765–1833) formed a splendid collection of pictures in Vienna, but his extravagance put his estates into sequestration. He raised an army to fight the French in the Napoleonic Wars and refused the honour of becoming king. Prince Pál Antal (1786–1866) represented Austria at London until 1842, and in 1848 was Hungarian Minister of Foreign Affairs. His extravagance caused the estates to be sequestrated again in 1860. Count Moritz (1807–1890) too was a diplomat; he served as Austrian Minister in Rome until 1856, and later as Minister without Portfolio (1861–66). 📖 Rebecca Gates-Coon, *The Landed Estates of the Esterházy Princes: Hungary during the reforms of Maria Theresa and Joseph II* (1994)

Estes, Richard 1932–
US painter

Born in Keewane, Illinois, he studied at the Art Institute of Chicago (1952–56) and moved to New York in 1959. For several years he worked in the illustration and advertising industry before becoming a full-time painter in 1966. In the late 1960s, he began painting precise copies of photographs, particularly of New York street-scenes, and for nearly three decades he has continued to produce meticulously detailed Photorealist works which can easily be confused with photographs. His works include *The Candy Store* (1969), *Downtown* (1978) and *The Plaza* (1991).

Esther 5th century BC
Biblical queen

She was the foster-daughter of the Jew **Mordecai**. According to the Book of Esther she was chosen by the Persian King Ahasuerus (**Xerxes I**) as his wife in place of the disgraced Queen Vashti, and brought about the deliverance of her people.

Estridsson See **Svein II Ulfsson**

Etchahounia, Pierre Topet d' 1786–1862
Basque poet

He was born in Etchahounia in the French Basque provinces. He is famous for having cursed his father for forbidding him to marry a poor girl; 'God curse Gaztelondo Topet and all those who fall in love with poor girls!' is now proverbial. He beat up the rich (and allegedly unfaithful) woman whom he did marry, killed her supposed lover, was refused permission to live at home, and spent much of his life as a beggar and travelling bard. His trenchant poetry, often questioning the existence of God, is considered the best there is in the Basque language. It survives only because it is easily memorable; his family burned it on a bonfire as soon as he died. It was collected in *Le Poète Pierre Topet, dit Etchahun, et ses œuvres* (1946). **Adelbert von Chamisso** told his story well.

Ethelbert or Æthelbert d.616/618
King of Kent

He was the first English king to adopt Christianity. During his reign, which historians now tend to date from c.590, Kent achieved hegemony over England south of the Humber. **Bede** describes him as powerful, but cautious and superstitious. He married Bertha, a Frankish Christian princess (c.580) and welcomed St **Augustine** in 596, allowing him to settle at Canterbury and set up

further bishoprics at Rochester and London. He himself was baptized with his court, and Canterbury became the capital of Roman Christianity in Britain. He was also responsible for the first written code of English laws.

Etheldreda or Æthelthryth or Audrey, St
c.630–79
Anglo-Saxon princess and abbess

She was the daughter of King Anna of East Anglia, and was widowed after three years of her first marriage, which was said never to have been consummated. In 660 she married Ecgfrith, future King of Northumbria, but refused to consummate the marriage. Instead she took the veil and withdrew to the double monastery at Coldingham founded by her aunt, **Ebba**, and in 672 founded a double monastery herself on the isle of Ely, of which she was appointed abbess.

Ethelflæd or Æthelflæd c.870–918
Anglo-Saxon ruler of Mercia

She was the daughter of **Alfred**, the Great, and sister of **Edward**, the Elder, of Wessex. She married Ethelred (Æthelred), the alderman of Mercia (c.886), and fought alongside him to repel the Danish invaders, their battle culminating in a decisive victory near Tettenhall in 910. She succeeded her husband (911) and built fortified strongholds throughout Mercia, including Tamworth and Stafford, and planned and led Mercian counter-attacks on the Danes. In 917, with her brother Edward, she captured Derby, and took Leicester in 918. She also kept up Mercian pressure on the Welsh. She died when poised to invade Danish-held Northumbria.

Ethelred or Æthelred I d.871
Anglo-Saxon King of Wessex

One of the five sons of King Ethelwulf (Æthelwulf) and elder brother of **Alfred**, the Great, he succeeded to the throne in 865. In that year a large Danish invasion army landed in East Anglia intent on permanent conquest, and captured York and Northumbria. Ethelred, with Alfred as his second-in-command, helped to defend Mercia against them. Early in 870 the Danes established a fortified camp at Reading in Wessex. Ethelred and Alfred defeated them at Ashdown in Berkshire but Ethelred died soon afterwards, to be succeeded by Alfred.

Ethelred or Æthelred II *wrongly referred to as* the Unready c.968–1016
King of England

The son of King **Edgar** and his second wife, Ælfryth (Elfryth), he was 10 when he succeeded to the throne (978) after the murder of his half-brother **Edward, the Martyr**. He married **Emma**, daughter of Duke Richard of Normandy. He at first attempted to buy off Viking invaders (hence his Anglo-Saxon nickname of *Unræd*, meaning 'lack of counsel'—mistranslated as 'Unready'—meant as a pun on his name Ethelred, which means 'good counsel'). However, in 1002, he ordered a savage massacre of all Danish settlers. In 1013, beleaguered by the invasion of **Svein I Haraldsson** of Denmark, he abandoned his throne and fled to Normandy but was recalled in 1014. Recent scholarship has seen his reign in more positive light than the hostile *Anglo-Saxon Chronicle*, and has emphasized the efficient financial and secretarial system and the flowering of vernacular literature. By a first marriage he left a son, **Edmund II, Ironside**, who succeeded him for a few months, and by Emma he was the father of **Edward, the Confessor**.

Etherege, Sir George c.1635–91
English dramatist

Born probably in Maidenhead, Berkshire, he was secretary to the ambassador at Constantinople (Istanbul) from 1668 to 1670 or 1671. He married a wealthy widow, and in

1685 was sent to be resident at the Imperial court at Ratisbon, where he drank, flirted with actresses, and engaged in correspondence with Thomas Middleton, Dryden and Thomas Betterton. In English literature he is founder of the comedy of intrigue. He sought his inspiration in Molière, and out of him grew the legitimate comedy of manners and the work of Richard Brinsley Sheridan and Oliver Goldsmith. His three plays are *The Comical Revenge or, Love in a Tub* (1664), *She Would if She Could* (1668) and *The Man of Modeor, Sir Fopling Flutter* (1676)—all highly popular in their day. 📖 D Underwood, *Etherege and the 17th-century Comedy of Manners* (1957)

Etheridge, Melissa 1962–
US singer and songwriter
Born in Leavenworth, Kansas, she gained her first Grammy nomination with her 1988 debut album, *Melissa Etheridge*, and her second album, *Brave and Crazy*, was released the following year. It was her more experimental album *Never Enough* (1992) that won her a Best Female Rock Perfomance Grammy for the single 'Ain't it Heavy'. After that, her albums and singles sold in millions and her concert tours (often for AIDS benefits) became sell-outs. In 1993 the album *Yes I Am* had two top-ten single hits. In 1995 she won her second Grammy for Best Female Rock Performance.

Etty, William 1787–1849
English painter
Born in York, the son of a baker, he went to London in 1806, and studied at the Royal Academy schools, for a year under Sir Thomas Lawrence. In 1822–23 he spent 18 months in Italy, half of them at Venice, where he was deeply influenced by the Venetian masters. Renowned for his nudes, he depicted historical and classical subjects, as in *The Combat* (1825, National Gallery of Scotland), but was at his best when working on a less ambitious scale.

Eucken, Rudolf Christoph 1846–1926
German philosopher and Nobel Prize winner
Born in Aurich, Ostfriesland, he was educated at the University of Göttingen. He became professor at Basle (1871) and at Jena (1874), and won the Nobel Prize for literature in 1908 in recognition of his 'earnest search for truth' and 'idealistic philosophy of life'. His distinctive philosophy of ethical activism was broadly in the idealist tradition of Immanuel Kant, and sought to identify and vindicate the spiritual significance of history and life. His works include *Philosophie der Geschichte* (1907), *Der Sinn und Wert des Lebens* (1908, Eng trans *The Meaning and Value of Life*, 1916) and *Mensch und Welt* (1918).

Eucleides of Megara fl.c.390BC
Greek philosopher
A disciple of Socrates, mentioned by Plato as one of those present during Socrates' last hours, he founded a school of Megarians, who were evidently influenced by Parmenides as well as by Socrates and are associated with various developments in logic like the 'liar paradox' (attributed to one of their number, Eubulides). Nothing of their writings survives.

Euclid fl.300BC
Greek mathematician
He taught in Alexandria, where he appears to have founded a mathematical school. His *Elements* of geometry, in 13 books, is the earliest substantial Greek mathematical treatise to have survived, and is probably better known than any other mathematical book, still being used as the basis of school textbooks in the earlier part of the 20th century. It was the first mathematical book to be printed and has stood as a model of rigorous mathematical exposition for centuries. It covers the geometry of lines in the plane, including Pythagoras's

theorem, and goes on to discuss circles, ratio, and the geometry of three dimensions. He wrote other works on geometry, including the theory of conics, and on astronomy, optics and music. 📖 Henry Albaugh, *Euclid* (1971)

Eudocia, *also called* Athenais AD401–65
Byzantine princess
She was the daughter of an Athenian professor of rhetoric. Pulcheria, sister of the Emperor Theodosius II (AD401–50), chose Eudocia to be his wife. Eudocia renounced paganism, changing her name from Athenais, and was married to Theodosius in 421. Pulcheria and Eudocia became fierce rivals, and despite defeating Eudocia's support of the controversial patriarch, Nestorius, Pulcheria was banished. Eudocia then backed Eutyches, head of an opposite heresy, until Pulcheria regained her influence shortly before Theodosius's death (450). Eudocia retired to Jerusalem, where she wrote a panegyric on Theodosius's victories over the Persians, paraphrases of Scripture, hymns and poetry.

Eudoxus of Cnidus 408–353BC
Greek mathematician, astronomer and geographer
Thought to have been a member of Plato's Academy, he spent over a year studying in Egypt with the priests at Heliopolis, and formed his own school in Cyzicus. He made many advances in geometry and it is possible that most of Euclid's Book XII is largely his work. He drew up a map of the stars and compiled a map of the known areas of the world. He correctly recalculated the length of the solar year and his philosophical theories are thought to have had a great influence on Aristotle.

Eugène of Savoy, Prince, *properly* François Eugène de Savoie Carignan 1663–1736
Austrian soldier
Born in Paris, he left France after his mother, a niece of Cardinal Mazarin, was banished from court by Louis XIV. He entered the service of the Emperor Leopold I against the Turks. He distinguished himself in the war against Louis XIV in Italy, and his defeat of the Turks at Zenta (1697) put an end to their power in Hungary. The War of the Spanish Succession (1701) recalled him to Italy, but Louis, Duc de Vendôme defeated him there (1702). In command of the imperial army he helped the Duke of Marlborough at Blenheim (1704). Eugène defeated the French in Italy, but his defeat by Claude, Duc de Villars at Denain (1712) was followed by other disasters, until the Peace of Rastadt (1714) ended the war. He continued to fight the Turks from 1716, and then the French in a war over the crown of Poland. After the peace he returned to Vienna.

Eugénie, Empress, *originally* Eugénie de Montijo 1826–1920
Spanish empress of France
Born in Granada, a Spanish noblewoman renowned for her beauty, she was consort of Napoleon III from 1853 until 1871. She used her political influence to oppose liberal and democratic ideas and to serve as an advocate of the church. She is also believed to have played a large role in the decision to create a French-sponsored kingdom in Mexico (1861). After Napoleon III's deposition during the Franco-Prussian War, she fled to England, where she was befriended by Queen Victoria.

Eugenius III *originally* Bernardo Paganelli
12th century
Italian pope
Born near Pisa, he was a disciple of Bernard of Clairvaux and became a Cistercian monk, being appointed pope in 1145. His predecessor (Lucius II) had died during a rebellion against the papacy in Rome, and so Eugenius was

obliged to flee to Viterbo immediately upon his election. Soon after his return he was again driven out by a revolt initiated by Arnold of Brescia and turned his attention to promoting a second crusade in France.

Eugenius IV, *originally* Gabriele Condulmer
1383–1447
Italian pope

Born in Venice, he was installed as pope in 1431, and quarrelled with the reforming Council of Basle convoked by his predecessor Martin V, which sought to limit papal power. Driven from Rome in 1434 by the Colonnas, he opened a new council, first at Ferrara, then at Florence, and excommunicated the bishops assembled at Basle. The Council of Basle deposed him (1439) and elected Amadeus VIII of Savoy, as Felix V. At the Council of Ferrara, John Palaeologus II, Emperor of Constantinople (Istanbul), appeared with 20 Greek bishops, and a union between the Greek and Latin Churches was effected for a short time in 1439. In 1444 Eugenius returned to Rome.

Euhemerus fl.c.300BC
Greek philosopher and mythographer

Born probably in Messene, Sicily, he wrote *Hiera anagraphe* or *Sacred History*, which 'Euhemerized' Greek mythology by explaining the gods as distorted representations of warriors and heroes from remote history.

Euler, Leonhard 1707–83
Swiss mathematician

Born in Basle, he studied mathematics there under Jean Bernoulli. In 1727 he went to St Petersburg to study at the Academy of Sciences newly founded by Catherine II, where he became Professor of Physics (1731) and then Professor of Mathematics (1733). In 1741 he moved to Berlin at the invitation of Frederick II, the Great, to be director of mathematics and physics in the Berlin Academy, but he returned to St Petersburg in 1766 after a disagreement with the king, and remained in Russia until his death. He published many books and papers on every aspect of pure and applied mathematics, physics and astronomy. He studied infinite series and differential equations, introduced or established many new functions, including the gamma function and elliptic integrals, and created the calculus of variations. His *Introductio in analysin infinitorum* (1748) and later treatises on differential and integral calculus and algebra became standard textbooks, and his notations such as e and i (the square root of -1) have been used ever since. In mechanics Euler studied the motion of rigid bodies in three dimensions, the construction and control of ships, and celestial mechanics. For the princess of Anhalt-Dessau he wrote *Lettres à une princesse d'Allemagne* (1768–72), a non-technical outline of the main physical theories of the time. His powerful memory enabled him to continue mathematical work though nearly blind. ▭ Otto Speiss, *Leonhard Euler* (1929)

Euler, Ulf Svante von 1905–83
Swedish pharmacologist

Born in Stockholm, the son of Nobel laureate Hans Euler-Chelpin, he qualified in medicine from the Karolinska Institute and joined the department of pharmacology there as Research Fellow (1926–30), before travelling on a Rockefeller Fellowship to work with, amongst others, Sir Henry Dale and Corneille Heymans (1930–31). He began studying neuroactive substances in the autonomic nervous system, and with John Gaddum he discovered a new active factor, a polypeptide. Returning to the Karolinska, he continued research on biologically active substances and in 1935 isolated a group of lipids he called prostaglandins. Later he reverted to the study of neurally active chemicals and isolated and characterized the principal transmitter of the sympathetic nervous system,

noradrenaline, in the early 1940s. For the next 30 years he continued to study noradrenaline and its chemical relatives in many situations. Appointed Professor of Physiology at the Karolinska (1939–71), he shared the 1970 Nobel Prize for physiology or medicine with Julius Axelrod and Bernard Katz.

Euler-Chelpin, Hans Karl August Simon von
1873–1964
Swedish biochemist and Nobel Prize winner

Born in Augsburg, Germany, after studying in Berlin, Göttingen and Paris, he became a lecturer in physical chemistry at Stockholm University (1900), then was appointed Professor of Chemistry and director of the Institute for the Biochemistry of Vitamins in 1929. Interested in a wide range of scientific areas, his many collaborations and publications were oriented towards elucidating the chemistry and kinetics of peptidases, zymase (yeast extract causing fermentation), and in particular, saccharase. He showed that zymase was markedly activated by vitamins A and B, and purified the system by alcohol fractionation and aluminium oxide adsorption. He also analysed the properties and reactions of the saccharases. With Sir Arthur Harden, Euler-Chelpin was awarded the Nobel Prize for chemistry in 1929 for his researches on enzymes and fermentation.

Eumenes II d.159BC
King of Pergamon

The son of Attalus I, he ruled from 197BC, and during his reign Pergamon reached the zenith of its importance. He was an ally of Rome against Antiochus III and Macedonia. He made Pergamon a centre of learning, founded a great library, and had the famous sculptured Altar of Pergamon built (now in Berlin museum).

Eumenes of Cardia c.360–316BC
Macedonian soldier

He was one of the ablest generals of Alexander the Great, after whose death he became governor of Cappadocia, Paphlagonia and part of Pontus. He was ultimately defeated in 317BC by Antigonus (Monophthalmos) and executed.

Eunomius d.c.399AD
Cappadocian prelate

Born in Cappadocia, Asia Minor, he was Bishop of Cyzicus (c.360AD) but was deposed for his Arian views. With Flavius Aëtius he became the leader of an extreme sect of Arians, known as the Anomoeans or Eunomians.

Euphranor 4th century BC
Greek painter and sculptor

Born in Corinth, he was famed for his decoration of the Stoa Basileios at Athens.

Euphronios fl.late 6th century–5th century BC
Greek potter and vase painter

His name is inscribed, as either painter or potter, on 15 vessels which constitute some of the finest surviving examples of vessels painted in the 'red figure' style.

Euripides 484 or 480–406BC
Greek tragic dramatist

Born probably in Salamis, he did not take much part in public life. In politics he was moderate, approving of a democracy, but not of demagogues. Of about 80 of his dramas whose titles are known, 18 survive complete. They include *Medea* (431BC, Eng trans 1959), *Andromache* (425BC, Eng trans 1957), *Supplices* (423BC, Eng trans 1957), *Troades* (415BC, Eng trans *The Women of Troy*, 1954), *Phoenissae* (410BC, Eng trans *The Phoenician Women*, 1959) and *Orestes* (408BC, Eng trans 1959). *The Bacchae* (405BC, Eng trans 1954) and *Iphigenia Aulidensis* (405BC, Eng trans *Iphigenia in Aulis*, 1959) were put on the Athenian stage only after the author's death. It is doubtful whether the *Rhesus* (Eng trans 1959) is genuine. He brought a new style to tragedy and the treatment of traditional mythology, and is notable for highlighting unusual opinions and portraying socially marginal characters. **Sophocles**, who deemed him 'the most tragic of poets', also commented that while he himself showed people as they ought to be, Euripides portrayed them as they are. ⌨ Gilbert Murray, *Euripides and His Age* (1913)

Eurytus of Croton late 5th century BC
Greek philosopher
A follower of **Pythagoras**, he is known only for the reported story that he used pebbles to represent the essential definitions of physical objects.

Eusebio, *in full* Eusebio Silva Ferreira da 1942–
Portuguese footballer
Born in Mozambique, he was one of the first great players to emerge from the African continent. He had a long and successful career with Benfica of Lisbon, with whom he won European Cup medals. He was nominated European Footballer of the Year in 1965 and in the Centenary Match to mark the foundation of the FA he played for the Rest of the World against England in 1963. In the World Cup of 1966 he was the top goal-scorer.

Eusebius of Caesarea, *known as* the Father of Church History c.264–340AD
Palestinian theologian and scholar
Born probably in Palestine, he became Bishop of Caesarea (c.313AD), and in the Council of Nicaea was the head of the semi-Arian or moderate party, which was averse to discussing the nature of the Trinity. His *Chronicon*, a history of the world to 325, contains extracts from lost works. His *Praeparatio Evangelica* is a collection of such statements in heathen authors as support the evidences of Christianity, and its complement is the *Demonstratio Evangelica* in 20 books, 10 of which are extant, intended to convince the Jews of the truth of Christianity from their own scriptures. His most important work, the *Ecclesiastical History*, is a record of the chief events in the Christian Church down to 324. Other works include the *Theophania* (discovered in 1839), and a life of **Constantine I, the Great**.

Eusebius of Nicomedia d.342AD
Syrian prelate
Born probably in Syria, he was Bishop first of Beryta (Beirut) in Syria, and then of Nicomedia. He defended **Arius** at the Council of Nicaea (AD325) and afterwards became the head of the Arian party. Exiled to Gaul for his views, he came back in 328 and influenced the Emperor **Constantine I, the Great**, to move towards Arianism, and baptized him in 337, just before Constantine died. He had also been responsible for the deposition of **Athanasius** in 335. In 339 he was appointed Patriach of Constantinople, and enjoyed the patronage of the Emperor **Constantius I**.

Eustachio, Bartolommeo 1520–74
Italian anatomist
Born in San Severino (now Ancona), he studied medicine in Rome, and after serving as a personal physican taught anatomy at the Collegia della Sapienza, Rome. He made considerable studies of the thoracic duct, larynx, adrenal glands, the teeth, and above all the kidneys. From 1552 he was involved in the production of a remarkable, but unpublished, series of anatomical illustrations. He is remembered for his precise account of the Eustachian canal (auditory tube) of the ear, and also of the Eustachian valve in the foetus. His most important work was the *Opuscula Anatomica* (1564).

Eustathius fl.mid 12th century
Greek scholar and commentator

Born in Constantinople (Istanbul), he was Archbishop of Thessalonica from 1160 and of Myra from 1174. He was the author of numerous chronicles and commentaries on classical writers. His commentary on **Homer** and other writings contain extracts from works which are no longer in evidence.

Euthymides fl.late 6th century–early 5th century BC
Greek vase painter of the so-called 'red figure' style
He was a contemporary of **Euphronios** and, seemingly, a rival since, among the six surviving signed vessels is one inscribed with the words 'Euphronios never did anything like it'. His painted figures are among the earliest to show foreshortened limbs.

Eutropius fl.4th century AD
Roman historian
He was secretary to Emperor **Constantine I** and fought against the Persians under **Julian**, the Apostate. He wrote a survey of Roman history, *Breviarium Historiae Romanae*, from the foundation of the city to AD364. Written in simple, concise style, it may have been intended for use in schools.

Eutyches c.384–c.456AD
Greek religious Archimandrite at Constantinople
He was the founder of 'Eutychianism', holding that after the incarnation, human nature became merged in the divine, and that **Jesus Christ** had therefore but one nature. He was condemned by a synod at Constantinople (Istanbul) in AD448, but the Council of Ephesus (449) decided in his favour and restored him, deposing his opponents. The Council of Chalcedon (451) annulled this decision, and Eutyches died in exile. His sect was put down by penal laws.

Euwe, Max (Machgielis) 1901–81
Dutch chess player
Born near Amsterdam, he was originally a professor of mathematics and mechanics. He was the only amateur to win the world championship in the history of chess, by defeating **Alexander Alekhine** (1935), but he lost the title in a return match two years later. After his academic retirement he served (1970–78) as president of FIDE (Fédération Internationale des Échecs), arbitrating over the turbulent **Fischer–Spassky** world championship match in Reykjavík, Iceland, in 1972. A prolific annotator, he contributed more to the literature of chess than any other Grand Master.

Evagrius, *known as* Scholasticus c.536–c.600
Byzantine church historian
He was born in Epiphanica, Syria, and was the patriarch of Antioch. His Greek *Ecclesiastical History, 431–594*, was a continuation of that of **Eusebius of Caesarea**.

Evans, Alice 1881–1975
US microbiologist
She received little formal education, but won a scholarship to study science at Cornell University. She worked for the Dairy Division of the US Department of Agriculture before moving to the US Public Health Service (later the National Institutes of Health) in 1918. Her investigations into the dangers of non-pasteurized cows' milk, and assertion that cattle brucellosis and human Malta fever had a common origin, were strongly resisted by veterinarians, dairymen and many physicians. Compelling confirmation during the late 1920s and 1930s led to the recognition of Evans's achievements and she received several honours, including that of being the first woman president of the Society of American Bacteriologists (1928).

Evans, Sir Arthur John 1851–1941
English archaeologist

He was born in Nash Mills, Hertfordshire. A curator at the Ashmolean Museum, Oxford (1884–1908), he developed an interest in the ancient coins and seals of Crete. Between 1899 and 1935 he excavated the Bronze Age city of Knossos (modern Kephala), discovering the remains of the civilization which in 1904 he named 'Minoan' after Minos, the Cretan king of Greek legend. He later rebuilt and repainted substantial parts of the Minoan palace in an effort to recreate its original appearance. 📖 Ann Brown, *Arthur Evans and the Palace of Minos* (1983)

Evans, Bill (William John) 1929–80
US jazz pianist and composer

Born in Plainfield, New Jersey, he played jazz while a student in Louisiana, but took up music seriously after leaving the army in 1954. He studied in New York, then began to play professionally with clarinettist Tony Scott in 1956, and was a member of the **Miles Davis** group which recorded the hugely influential *Kind of Blue* album in 1958. Although he recorded solo, in duos (with Jim Hall and Bob Brookmeyer), and even with orchestral accompaniment, his preferred format as leader was the piano trio. He is among the most important (and influential) pianists in jazz, and developed his essentially bop-based style in lyrical, highly sophisticated directions.

Evans, Caradoc, *pseudonym of* David Evans
1878–1945
Welsh short-story writer and novelist

Born in Llanfihangel-ar-Arth, Dyfed, he spent much of his childhood at Rhydlewis, but left home in 1893, to work as a shop assistant in Carmarthen, Barry, Cardiff and finally London. While in London, he attended evening classes and eventually found employment as a journalist (1906). His collections of short stories, *My People* (1915), *Capel Sion* (1916) and *My Neighbours* (1919), savagely exposed the hypocrisies, lust and greed of the chapel-going people of his native West Wales. His play *Taffy* (1923) was in similar vein and in his own time he was vilified by the Welsh as a traitor for his assaults on many cherished aspects of Welsh culture from Nonconformity and the Eisteddfod to the integrity and intelligence of the people themselves. 📖 T L Williams, *Caradoc Evans* (1970)

Evans, Dame Edith Mary 1888–1976
English stage and film actress

Born in London, she became known for her versatility, in many **Shakespeare** and **Shaw** plays, and in others, including *The Way of the World*, *The Late Christopher Bean* and *Daphne Laureola*, but her most famous role was as a memorable Lady Bracknell in *The Importance of Being Earnest* (also on film, 1952). During World War II she entertained the troops at home and abroad, and in 1946 was created DBE. She made her first film appearance in *The Queen of Spades* (1948) and continued to act until her eighties. 📖 Bryan Forbes, *Ned's Girl* (1978, also published as *Dame Edith Evans*)

Evans, Frederick Henry 1853–1943
English photographer

Retiring from his profession as a bookseller in 1898, he devoted himself to architectural photography, especially of the cathedrals of England, emphasizing their structural rhythms and repetitions. He found similar order and pattern in his studies of trees and in photomicrographs, as well as in his austerely formed landscapes. His best work was done in the early years of the 20th century, but he remained unsympathetic to the modern activism then emerging.

Evans, Sir Geraint Llewellyn 1922–92
Welsh baritone

He was born in Pontypridd, Mid Glamorgan. He studied singing in Hamburg and Geneva, and made his London debut with the newly formed Covent Garden Opera Company in 1948, singing the Nightwatchman in **Wagner**'s *Meistersinger*. He sang regularly at Covent Garden until 1984, establishing a reputation in many roles, notably Figaro and Leporello in **Mozart**, Beckmesser in Wagner, Don Pasquale in **Donizetti**, and Falstaff in **Verdi**. He also sang at Glyndebourne, San Francisco and elsewhere, created a number of roles, including Flint in **Benjamin Britten**'s *Billy Budd*, and produced works with Welsh Opera and in Chicago and San Francisco. He was knighted in 1971, and published his autobiography, *A Knight at the Opera*, in 1984, the year of his retirement.

Evans, Gil (Ian Ernest Gilmore Green) 1912–88
Canadian jazz pianist, composer and arranger

Born in Toronto of Australian parents, he spent his childhood in Washington State and California, and was self-taught as a musician. His first influential work was done in the mid-1940s when, apart from three years' military service, he was principal arranger for the Claude Thornhill Orchestra. Although basically a dance orchestra, its use of french horns and tuba to create dense textures attracted the interest of young jazz performers. The result was a series of collaborations between Evans and **Miles Davis**, starting in the late 1940s, which led to the emergence of the 'cool jazz' style. As an arranger and conductor, Evans continued to collaborate with Davis until 1960, covering a very influential period in the trumpeter's career. Evans went on to lead and write for a range of groups until his death, and was one of the first modern jazz arrangers to use electronics and rock influences successfully in combination with the swing and bebop idioms.

Evans, (Thomas) Godfrey 1920–
English cricketer

Born in Finchley, London, he was educated at Kent College, Canterbury, and joined the Kent county cricket staff at the age of 16. First capped for England in 1946, he played in 91 Test matches, and made many new records, including 218 Test dismissals (75 against Australia). He was the first wicket-keeper to have dismissed more than 200 batsmen and scored 2,000 runs in Test cricket. He scored two Test centuries and held records for both the fastest scoring and the slowest (his 10 not out in 133 minutes against Australia at Adelaide in 1946–47 saved the match). After his retirement he went into public relations.

Evans, Harold Matthew 1928–
English journalist

Born in Manchester, he started as a weekly reporter at the age of 16, then studied at Durham University and the University of Chicago. He worked on the *Manchester Evening News* and the *Northern Echo* before becoming editor of the *Sunday Times* (1967–81), and was a pioneer of investigative journalism during the thalidomide scandal. He was editor of *The Times* (1981–82) but resigned after its controversial takeover by **Rupert Murdoch**'s News International. He went to New York and became chief editor of *Traveler* magazine for Condé-Nast in 1986 and since 1990 has run Random House, the book publishing division belonging to the same company as Condé-Nast. He married **Tina Brown** in 1981. His books include five manuals on journalism, and *Good Times, Bad Times* (1983).

Evans, Janet 1971–
US swimmer

Born in Fullerton, California, she won three gold medals at the 1988 Olympics (400m freestyle, 800m freestyle and 400m medley) and one at the 1992 Olympics (800m freestyle). She holds the world record in the 400 metre freestyle, the 800 metre freestyle and the 1,500 metre freestyle, and was a Sullivan award winner in 1989.

Evans, Marian or Mary Ann See Eliot, George

Evans, Oliver 1755–1819
US inventor

Born in Newport, Delaware, he was apprenticed to a wagon-maker. By 1777 he had invented a high-speed machine for assembling the wire-toothed combs used in carding textile fibres. By 1785 he had established a continuous production line, with improved machinery, in a flour mill at Wilmington. Meanwhile he had engaged in a number of profitable business ventures, so that when he moved to Philadelphia he was able to devote his time to improving the very primitive steam engines then coming into use. Most engineers at that time followed the lead of **James Watt** in rejecting the use of high-pressure steam because of the practical difficulties and the danger of explosion, but by 1802 Evans had successfully built a high-pressure steam engine. For several years he tried to harness the power of steam for road vehicles without much success, although his amphibious steam dredging machine of 1804 is considered to have been the first US steam-powered road vehicle. He built 50 or so engines in total, and was largely responsible for the more rapid adoption of high-pressure steam in the USA than in Great Britain during the early years of the 19th century.

Evans, Walker 1903–75
US photographer

Born in St Louis, Missouri, he started as an architectural photographer in 1933. Moving to social studies, from 1935 he began to record the life of rural depression in the southern states for the US government Farm Security Administration (FSA), although he left this organization a few years later. The two themes were combined in his *American Photographs* (1938), the first section of which shows members of society and the second its buildings, all the images intended to be viewed in sequence. He worked with the writer **James Agee** for *Fortune* magazine to document the lives of the sharecroppers of the Deep South, and the material was eventually published as *Let Us Now Praise Famous Men* (1941). During his years as associate editor of *Fortune* (1945–65) he continued with architectural studies, but particularly impressive were his records of people in the New York City subways, published in 1966 as *Many Are Called*. He was Professor of Graphic Design at Yale from 1965 to 1974.

Evans-Pritchard, Sir Edward Evan 1902–73
English social anthropologist

Born in Crowbridge, Sussex, he studied history at Oxford, and succeeded his teacher **Alfred Radcliffe-Brown** in the chair of social anthropology (1946–70). He carried out fieldwork in East Africa in the 1920s and 1930s among the Azande and the Nuer, resulting in a number of classic monographs including *Witchcraft, Oracles and Magic among the Azande* (1937), *The Nuer* (1940) and *Nuer Religion* (1956). Though strongly influenced by the sociological theory of **Émile Durkheim**, he came to reject Radcliffe-Brown's view that social anthropology could be regarded as a natural science of society, choosing instead to emphasize its affinity with history, requiring interpretation and translation rather than scientific explanation. His later work on religion was strongly coloured by his own experience of conversion to Catholicism.

Evarts, William Maxwell 1818–1901
US lawyer and politician

He was born in Boston. He was Defense Counsel for President **Andrew Johnson** in the impeachment proceedings of 1868, US Attorney-General, US counsel before the *Alabama* Tribunal in Geneva (1872), Secretary of State (1877–81S), and sat in the Senate from 1885 to 1891.

Evatt, Elizabeth Andreas 1933–
Australian lawyer

Born in Sydney, the daughter of a barrister, she was the youngest student at Syndey University Law School, where she was the first woman to win the law medal, and at Harvard, before becoming a barrister in New South Wales at the age of 21. In 1958 she was called to the English Bar, and worked in England for several years, focusing on family law with the Law Commission. On returning to Australia, she became the deputy president of the Arbitration Commission (1973–89). She chaired the Royal Commission of Human Relationships (1974–77) and the Family Law Council (1976–79) and was chief judge in the Family Court of Australia (1976–88). A member of the UN Committee on the Elimination of Discrimination Against Women from 1984 until 1992, she joined the UN Human Rights Committee in 1993. Her other positions include being president of the Law Reform Commission (1988–93), a member of the Australian National Commission for UNESCO (1993–) and Chancellor of the University of Newcastle.

Eve
Biblical character

According to Genesis, Eve was made by God from one of Adam's ribs, as a companion for him. Adam, the first man, named the first woman 'Eve', meaning 'the mother of all living'. They tended the garden of Eden together, until they were expelled for eating the fruit of the tree of knowledge. Although both knew that God had forbidden this, Adam blamed Eve for tempting him. This view has coloured much later interpretation of Eve's character, starting with a brief mention in the New Testament of Eve as a weak seducer, and culminating in a negative assessment of women in general. A few commentators have considered Eve's fellowship with Adam more positively. If Christ can be seen as the Second Adam, reversing the effects of the Fall, then the Virgin Mary can be seen as the Second Eve, her 'Yes' to the birth of Jesus being an act of obedience to reverse Eve's disobedience. This interpretation, popular in medieval Catholicism, finds echoes in recent feminist and ecological spirituality that sees women far more in tune with creation than men.

Evelyn, John 1620–1706
English diarist and writer

Born in Wotton, near Dorking, Surrey, he was brought up in Lewes (1625–37), then entered Balliol College, Oxford, and in 1640 the Middle Temple. The Covenant being pressed on him, he travelled for four years on the Continent, and in Paris (1647) married the ambassador's daughter, Mary Browne (1635–1709). He settled at Sayes Court, Deptford, in 1652, but spent a lot of time at Court after the Restoration, and from 1685 to 1687 was one of the commissioners of the privy seal. From 1695 to 1703 he was treasurer of Greenwich Hospital and was a prominent FRS. He was always active in church affairs and was involved in the rebuilding of St Paul's Cathedral in London. Of his three dozen literary works the chief are *Fumifiguim, or the Inconvenience of the Air and Smoke of London dissipated* (1661), *Sculptura, or the Art of Engraving on Copper* (1662), *Sylva, or a Discourse of Forest-trees* (1664), and a *Diary* (discovered in an old clothes-basket at his brother's home at Wotton in 1817). It covers the years 1641–1706 and contains vivid portraits of his contemporaries. ⊞ B
Saunders, *Evelyn and His Times* (1970)

Everdingen, Allart van 1621–75
Dutch landscape painter and etcher

Born in Alkmaar, he visited Scandinavia in the 1640s and was inspired by mountain torrents there, as in *A Saw-Mill by a Torrent* (National Gallery, London). He thus inspired the waterfalls of **Jacob van Ruïsdael**. As an etcher, he is best known for *Reynard the Fox*. His brother, Caesar van Everdingen (1606–79), was a historical and portrait painter, whose *Portrait of a Dutch Commander* is in the National Gallery, London. He also helped to decorate the royal Huis ten Bosch at The Hague, for example *Four Muses with Pegasus* (c.1650).

Everest, Sir George 1790–1866
Welsh military engineer

Born in Gwernvale, Brecknockshire, he was Surveyor-General of India from 1830. He completed the trigonometrical survey of the Indian sub-continent in 1841. He was knighted in 1861 and Mount Everest was named after him in 1865.

Everett, Alexander Hill 1790–1847
US diplomat

Born in Boston, he was appointed Minister at The Hague (1818–24) and Madrid (1825–29). Proprietor and editor of the *North American Review* (1829–35), and elected to the Massachusetts legislature, in 1840 he was appointed US agent in Cuba, and in 1845 commissioner to China.

Everett, Edward 1794–1865
US politician and scholar

Born in Dorchester, Massachusetts, he studied at Harvard and in 1815 was elected Professor of Greek there. In 1820 he became editor of the *North American Review*, and in 1824 a member of the US Congress. From 1835 to 1838 he was four times Governor of Massachusetts, and from 1841 to 1845 Minister at the court of St James's. He was president of Harvard (1846–49), in 1852 succeeded **Daniel Webster** as Secretary of State, and in 1853 was returned to the US Senate. He wrote *Defence of Christianity* (1814), poems, and *Orations and Speeches* (1836–59). He was the brother of **Alexander Everett**.

Evers, Medgar (Wiley) 1925–63
US civil rights activist

Born in Decatur, Mississippi, he was an army veteran and an insurance salesman when he became (1954) first field secretary of the National Association for the Advancement of Colored People (NAACP) in Mississippi, working to recruit new members and organizing voter registration drives and economic boycotts. In 1963 he was shot and killed in an ambush in front of his home. The case attracted national attention, and Evers became a martyr to the cause of civil rights. His murderer was finally convicted in 1994, 30 years after the original trial. His brother Charles Evers (1923–) was appointed to the NAACP position, successfully continuing voter registration campaigns and promoting African-American candidates for local elective offices. His widow, Myrlie Evers-Williams, has chaired the NAACP since 1995, bringing with her the same drive and integrity her late husband exhibited.

Evert, Chris(tine) Marie 1954–
US tennis player

She was born in Fort Lauderdale, Florida. Renowned for her two-handed backhand, she was extremely cool on the courts and her success helped popularize women's tennis in the USA and Europe. She won 157 professional titles and was undefeated on clay from August 1973 until May 1979. She won 18 singles Grand Slam titles—the Australian Open twice (1982, 1984), the French Open seven times (1974–75, 1979–80, 1983, 1985–86), Wimbledon Championship three times (1974, 1976, 1981) and the US Open six times (1975–78, 1980, 1982). She was married for a time to the English tennis player, John Lloyd, and was co-author with him of *Lloyd on Lloyd* (1985). She retired in 1989 after reaching the quarter-finals of the US Open to become a mother and a television commentator. 📖 Betty L Phillips, *Chris Evert: First Lady of Tennis* (1977)

Everts, Jan See **Johannes Secundus**

Evita See **Perón, Eva Duarte de**

Evoe See **Knox, Edmund George Valpy**

Évremond, Seigneur de Saint See **Saint-Évremond, Charles Seigneur de**

Ewald, Johannes 1743–81
Danish Romantic poet and dramatist

Born in Copenhagen, he ran away from home at the age of 15 to fight in the Seven Years War (1756–63), then turned to writing. He was one of the first Danish poets to use national legends and myths as material, as in his biblical drama *Adam og Eva* (1769), the historical drama *Rolf Krage* (1770) and the lyrical drama *Balders Död* (1773). He also wrote an operetta, *Fiskerne* (1779, 'The Fishermen'), which contains the song 'King Kristian stood by the lofty mast', now the Danish national anthem. 📖 L Labe, *Johannes Ewald* (1943)

Ewart, James Cossar 1851–1933
Scottish zoologist

Born in Penicuik, Midlothian, he became Professor of Natural History at the universities of Aberdeen (1879–82) and Edinburgh (1882–1927), carried out notable experiments in animal breeding and hybridization, and disproved the theory of telegony (the transmitted influence of a previous mate on the offspring of a female by a later mate).

Ewart, William 1798–1869
English politician and reformer

Born in Liverpool, he was Liberal MP (1828–68) for Bletchingly, Liverpool, Wigan, and the Dumfries Burghs. He played a leading part in humanitarian reforms, including the abolition of capital punishment for minor offences and of hanging prisoners in chains. He carried a free libraries bill in 1850.

Ewell, Richard Stoddart 1817–72
US soldier

Born in Georgetown, Washington DC, he served in Mexico and against the Apaches. However in the Civil War (1861–65) he resigned from the army to join the Confederates (1861), and served under **Thomas Jackson** and **Robert E Lee**. He fought at Gettysburg and the Wilderness, and commanded the defences of Richmond. He was eventually captured with his entire force at Sailor's Creek in 1865.

Ewing, Sir (James) Alfred 1855–1935
Scottish engineer and physicist

Born in Dundee, he was educated at Edinburgh University. He became Professor of Engineering at Tokyo (1878–83), and Dundee (1883–90), Professor of Mechanism at Cambridge (1890–1903), director of Naval Education (1903–16), and Principal of Edinburgh University (1916–29). During World War I he was the head of the department of the Admiralty which worked on the deciphering of intercepted messages. His works include *Magnetic Induction in Iron and Other Metals* (1891) and *Thermodynamics for Engineers* (1920). He was knighted in 1911.

Ewing, Juliana Horatia, *née* Gatty 1841–85
English children's writer

Born in Ecclesfield, Yorkshire, she was the daughter of Margaret Gatty (1809–73), also a children's writer. She soon began to compose nursery plays, which are said to have prompted her mother to start *Aunt Judy's Magazine* (1866), which Juliana later edited, publishing in it many of her charming stories, such as *Jackanapes*. Her numerous books included *A Flat Iron for a Farthing* (1870), *Lob-lie-by-the-Fire* (1873) and *Daddy Darwin's Dovecot* (1881). Her *The Brownies and Other Tales* (1870) provided the name by which the junior section of the Girl Guide movement is known.
📖 G Avery, Mrs Ewing (1961)

Ewing, (William) Maurice 1906–74
US marine geologist

Born in Lockney, Texas, he became a research associate at the Woods Hole Oceanographic Institution, where he studied sound transmission in sea-water. In 1944 he joined the geology department at Columbia University and established the Lamont Geological Observatory, becoming director there in 1949. In 1972 he continued his work at the University of Texas. He pioneered marine seismic techniques which he used to show that the ocean crust is much thinner than the continental crust, and discovered the global extent of mid-ocean ridges. He also discovered the deep central rift in the Mid-Atlantic Ridge (1957). His discovery that the ocean sediment thickness increases with distance from the mid-ocean ridges lent support to the plate tectonic theory. He also published papers on seismology, the effects of nuclear explosions, heat flow, petrology and palaeontology.

Ewing, Winnie (Winifred Margaret) 1929–
Scottish Nationalist politician

Born in Glasgow, she was educated at Queen's Park School, Glasgow, and Glasgow University. She was a lawyer and president of the Glasgow Bar Association, and her victory at the Hamilton by-election (1967) established the Scottish National Party (SNP) as a major political force. Although ousted there in 1970, she won the Moray and Nairn seat in 1974. After losing this position in 1979 she was elected to the European Parliament in the same year, representing the Highlands and Islands, and re-elected in 1984, 1989 and 1994. One of the best-known figures in the SNP, she is known as 'Madame Écosse' because of her work in Europe. She became president of the party in 1988.

Ewins, Arthur James 1882–1957
English chemist

Born in Norwood, London, he was educated at Chelsea Polytechnic. In 1914, working with **Henry Dale**, he isolated the neurotransmitter acetylcholine. Moving to the pharmaceutical firm of May and Baker he conducted the research which resulted in the preparation of sulphapyridine, which opened a new era of sulphonamide drug treatment, effective against a series of previously intractable diseases. Related drugs were produced in the USA (sulfadiazine, sulfasoxazole). The finding that sulphonamides lower blood sugar levels led to the discovery of tolbutamide and carbutamide for the control of blood sugar levels in diabetes. Ewins was elected FRS in 1943.

Eworth, Hans c.1520–after 1573
Flemish painter

He was recorded in the Antwerp Guild in 1540, but was active chiefly in England, being based in London from c.1545 for about 20 years. His surviving paintings are mainly portraits, but he is known also to have undertaken work for masques and pageants. In their careful technique and delicate rendering of detail his portraits owe much to **Hans Holbein**, the Younger, but in style and imagery they are more closely related to the sophisticated Mannerism fashionable in contemporary European court circles. Among his most elaborate allegorical portraits is *Sir John Lutterell* (1550).

Ewry, Ray(mond Clarence) 1873–1937
US athlete

After suffering poliomyelitis as a child, he used calisthenic exercises to strengthen his legs, which helped him to a record 10 track and field Olympic gold medals between 1900 and 1908. The three gold medals he won in one day at the Paris Olympics at the age of 26 are still a record for track and field athletics, although the events in which he competed are now disbanded—standing high jump, standing long jump and standing triple jump.

Exekias or Execias fl.late 6th century BC
Greek potter and vase painter

He worked in the 'black figure' style. The most famous of his vessels—on which is inscribed 'Exekias made and decorated me'—is in the Vatican Museum, Rome, and depicts Achilles and Ajax playing dice.

Exmouth, Edward Pellew, 1st Viscount 1757–1833
English naval commander

Born in Dover, he joined the navy at the age of 13 and took part in the battle on Lake Champlain (1776). He was captured at Saratoga in 1777. In 1798 he was sent to the French coast, where he had many successes. He was appointed Commander-in-Chief in India (1804), and then in the North Sea and in the Mediterranean. Promoted admiral in 1814, he was sent to Algiers (1816) to enforce the treaty abolishing Christian slavery. With English and Dutch vessels he inflicted such immense damage on the city that the Dey consented to every demand, and Pellew was honoured with the title of Viscount Exmouth.

Eyadéma, (Etienne) Gnassingbe 1937–
Togolese politician and general

Born in Pya, Lama Kara district, he joined the French army in 1953 and served in Africa for several years. In 1965 he became army Chief of Staff in Togo. In 1967 he led a bloodless coup to oust President Nicolas Grunitzky, and as President of Togo he banned all political activity until 1969, when he founded the Assembly of the Togolese People (RPT), as the only legal party. Although there have been several attempts to overthrow him, he has begun to introduce a degree of democracy into the political system. In 1980–81 he chaired the West African customs union ECOWAS.

Eyck, Jan van c.1389–1441
Flemish painter

He was born near Maastricht, and nothing is known of his training. He was successively in the service of John of Bavaria, Count of Holland, and **Philip, the Good**, of Burgundy, for whom he undertook diplomatic missions in Spain and Portugal. From 1431 he lived in Bruges. All the works which can be definitely attributed to him date from the last 10 years of his life. During this period there is evidence of his increasing wealth and importance as court painter, diplomat and city official. His style is created from a meticulous attention to detail, accuracy in rendering textures and realistic light effects, and his oil-technique attained near-perfection. There are three works by him in the National Gallery, London, including the *Man in a Red Turban* (1433), which some have thought to be a self-portrait, and the mysterious Arnolfini marriage portrait. By far his most famous work is the altarpiece *The Adoration of the Holy Lamb* (1432) in the church of Saint Bavon, Ghent, which consists of 24 panels. He is regarded as the greatest Flemish artist of the 15th century.

Eyde, Samuel 1866–1940
Norwegian engineer

Born in Arendal, he was educated in Germany, where he worked as a structural engineer for some time. He became increasingly interested in the potential in his native land for electro-chemical industries, and with **Kristian Birkeland** developed an economic electric arc process for the fixation of nitrogen, using Norway's abundant hydro-electric power.

Eyre, Edward John 1815–1901
English explorer and colonist

Born in Hornsea, Yorkshire, the son of a clergyman, he emigrated to Australia at the age of 17, settled on the Lower Murray as a sheep farmer, and was appointed a magistrate. In 1840–41 he explored the region between South and Western Australia, and discovered Lake Eyre. In 1847 he became Governor of New Zealand, in 1854 of St Vincent, and in 1862 of Jamaica. In 1865 he suppressed a native rebellion at Morant Bay with the utmost severity, and the alleged ringleader (a wealthy Baptist mulatto who was also a member of the Jamaica House of Assembly) was court-martialled and hanged. Eyre was recalled to England and prosecuted amidst great public controversy, but was cleared. 📖 Geoffrey Dutton, *The Hero as Murderer: The Life of Edward John Eyre* (1967)

Eyre, Sir Richard Charles Hastings 1943–
English stage director

He was born in Barnstaple, Devon, and was educated at Cambridge, beginning his career in 1965 at the Phoenix, Leicester. He became associate director of the Lyceum Theatre, Edinburgh (1967) and director of productions (1970–72). He was artistic director of the Nottingham Playhouse (1973–78), and afterwards producer of the BBC Television *Play for Today* series (1978–81). Other television plays include *Tumbledown* (1988), a Falklands War saga. He has made three films, including *The Ploughman's Lunch* (1983). He became associate director of the National Theatre, London (1981), and in 1988 was appointed director, taking over from Sir **Peter Hall**. His aims have included opening up the National Theatre to young directors such as **Deborah Warner** (*The Good Person of Setzuan*, 1989; *King Lear*, 1990) and increasing the performance of multicultural work and children's drama. In 1996 he directed productions of **Ibsen**'s *John Gabriel Borkman* and *The Prince's Play*, translated by **Tony Harrison** from the **Victor Hugo** play *Le Roi s'amuse* (1832). The same year, he announced that he planned to leave in 1997, when he will be replaced by **Trevor Nunn**. He was knighted in 1997.

Eyring, Henry 1901–81
US physical chemist

Born in Chihuahua, Mexico, he studied chemistry at the University of California, Berkeley, from 1927 to 1929 was an instructor at the University of Wisconsin, and in 1929–30 held a research fellowship at the Kaiser Wilhelm Institute for Physical Chemistry in Berlin. From 1931 to 1946 he was on the chemistry faculty at Princeton, and in 1946 moved to the University of Utah as Professor of Chemistry and Graduate Dean. His many honours and awards included the Debye award of the American Chemical Society (1964), and he was president of the society in 1965. Eyring's interest in chemical kinetics was further stimulated in Berlin by **Michael Polanyi**, with whom he pioneered the quantum-mechanical technique used to calculate the rate of chemical reactions from the forces between the atomic nuclei and electrons of reactants and products. He continued to make major contributions to such transition state theories for many years. He also worked extensively on isotope effects, bioluminescence, and liquid structures, and wrote some influential books.

Eysenck, Hans Jürgen 1916–97
British psychologist

Born in Berlin, he left Germany in 1934 and studied psychology at London University under Sir **Cyril Burt**. He began his career in the field of clinical psychology, which led to psychometric research into the normal variations of human personality and intelligence. He was a prolific and gifted writer, and a merciless critic of psychoanalysis in its various forms. He frequently championed the view that genetic factors play a large part in determining the psychological differences between people, and often held controversial views, particularly with his study of racial differences in intelligence in *Race, Intelligence and Education* (1971). From 1955 to 1983 he was Professor of Psychology at the Institute of Psychiatry, London University, then emeritus. He received the American Psychological Association's Distinguished Scientific award in 1988. His other publications include *Uses and Abuses of Psychology* (1953), *Know Your Own IQ* (1962) and the autobiographical *Rebel with a Cause* (1990). 📖 H B Gibson, *Hans Eysenck* (1981)

Eyskens, Gaston 1905–88
Belgian economist and politician

After studying in Leuven and the USA, he became Professor of Economics at Leuven (1934–75). In 1939 he was elected MP for the Christian People's Party (Belgium), and in 1965 became a senator in the Upper House. He was Minister of Finance (1945, 1947–49), and from 1949 to 1950 was Prime Minister for the first time. In the mid-1950s he was Minister for Economic Affairs, and led the government again in 1958–61. Appointed Minister for Finance (1965–66), he became Prime Minister twice more (1968–72, 1972–73). He led coalitions with both left and right, and was one of the pivotal figures of postwar Belgian politics, playing a key role in the negotiations which led to the abdication of **Leopold III**, the debate on education funding, and the decolonization of the Congo.

Eyvindur, *known as* Skáldaspillir ('the Plagiarist'), *properly* Eyvindur Jónsson d.c.990
Norwegian court poet of the Viking Age

Born of a noble family, he was a devoted follower of King Haakon I, the Good, of Norway, whom he eulogized in his *Hákonarmál*. He later wrote a eulogy in praise of Earl Haakon of Norway (*Haleygjatal*), and an *íslendingadrápa* about Icelanders.

Ezekiel c.6th century BC
Old Testament prophet

He was the successor to **Isaiah** and **Jeremiah**. According to the Book of Ezekiel, he was carried captive to Mesopotamia by **Nebuchadnezzar** in 597BC. The prophecies were composed during the Babylonian captivity, and looked forward to a new Jerusalem after the destruction of the old.

Ezra, the Scribe 4th century–5th century BC
Old Testament reformer

He was living in Babylon either during the reign of **Artaxerxes I**, Longimanus (465–425BC), or during that of **Artaxerxes II** (404–359). He was commissioned to lead a band of his fellow countrymen from Babylon to Jerusalem (458 or 397) to reorganize the returned Jews there. He is believed to have arranged the books of the Mosaic law (the Pentateuch) as they are now. The Book of Ezra records the return of the Jews after the Babylonian captivity in c.537BC, and the rebuilding of the Temple.

Faber, Frederick William
1814–63
English hymn writer

Born in Calverley, Yorkshire, he graduated from Oxford, where he won the Newdigate prize for poetry (1836). He took Anglican orders, but under the influence of Cardinal John Newman he turned Roman Catholic and founded in 1845 a lay community of converts (the 'Wilfridians'). He wrote many theological works, and is remembered for his *Hymns* (1861), such as 'My God, how wonderful Thou art' and 'Hark, hark my soul'.

Fabergé, Peter Carl, *properly* Karl Gustavovich Fabergé 1846–1920
Russian goldsmith and jeweller

He was born in St Petersburg, of Huguenot descent, and educated in Germany, Italy, France and England. He inherited his father's establishment in 1870, and moved from the design and manufacture of conventional jewellery to the creation of more elaborate objects, such as the celebrated imperial Easter eggs, first commissioned by Alexander III for his tsarina in 1884. Fabergé's skilled artists and craftsmen produced exceptionally delicate and imaginative flowers, animals, groups of figures, etc, much prized by Russian, European and Asian royalty. He died in exile in Lausanne after his business had been destroyed during the Russian Revolution. 🕮 G Hill et al (eds), *Fabergé and the Russian Master Goldsmiths* (1989)

Fabius, Caius Fabius, *also called* Pictor ('Painter')
fl.304BC
Roman general

He earned his surname by decorating the temple of Salus in Rome with the earliest known Roman paintings (304BC).

Fabius, Laurent 1946–
French socialist statesman

The son of a wealthy Jewish art dealer in Paris, he had a brilliant academic career there at the École Normale Supérieure and the École Nationale d'Administration. He joined the Council of State as an auditor in 1973 and became economic adviser to the Socialist Party (PS) leader, François Mitterrand, in 1976. Elected to the National Assembly in 1978, representing the Seine-Maritime constituency, he was appointed Budget Minister when the PS gained power in 1981, and Minister for Research and Industry in 1983. In 1984 he was appointed Prime Minister at the age of 37, in an effort to revive the PS's sagging fortunes. He introduced a more free-market economic programme, which had some success, but resigned following his party's electoral defeat in 1986. He was President from 1988 to 1992, thereafter being appointed First Secretary of the PS from 1992 to 1993, and was also re-elected to the National Assembly the same year.

Fabius, Quintus Fabius Maximus Verrucosus, *also called* Cunctator ('Delayer')
d.203BC
Roman soldier

He was five times consul and twice censor. In the Second Punic War (218–202BC) he was elected dictator (217) after the Roman defeat at Lake Trasimene, and became known by his defensive tactics as Cunctator ('Delayer'). Avoiding direct encounters, he carried on guerrilla warfare and allowed Rome to muster her forces. The derisive nickname took on an honourable connotation after the disastrous Roman defeat at Cannae (216), and the 'Fabian' tactics were resumed. He recovered Tarentum in 209 and was made consul for the fifth time. He died just before the successful conclusion of the war.

Fabius Quintus Fabius Rullianus 4th century BC
Roman general

He fought in the Second Samnite War. He was dictator (315BC), censor (304), and six times consul.

Fabre, Jean Henri 1823–1915
French entomologist

Born in St Léon, Aveyron, he taught in schools at Carpentras, Ajaccio and Avignon before retiring to Sérignan in Valcluse. He is remembered for his detailed and carefully observed accounts of insect behaviour and natural history, which resulted in the *Souvenirs entomologiques* (10 vols, 1879–1907). These dealt with the activities of insects such as scarab beetles, ant lions and parasitic wasps, from which observations he deduced that much of the wasp's behaviour is inherited and not learned. 🕮 G V Legros, *Fabre* (1971)

Fabre d'Églantine, Philippe François Nazaire 1750–94
French dramatist, poet and revolutionist

Born in Carcassonne, he wrote *Le Philinte de Molière* (1790), a sequel to Molière's *Le Misanthrope*. A member of the National Convention, he devised some of the new names of months for the Revolutionary Calendar, but, having fallen out of favour with Robespierre, was guillotined. 🕮 L Jacob, *Fabre d'Églantine, chef des Fripons* (1946)

Fabriano, Gentile da, *properly* Niccolò di Giovanni di Massio c.1370–1427
Italian painter

Born in Fabriano in the Marches, along with Lorenzo Ghiberti he was the major exponent in Italy of the International Gothic Style. He first achieved fame with his decorations for the Doge's Palace in Venice (all now lost) and then went on to work throughout Italy's main centres before reaching Rome, where he executed frescoes in the church of S Giovanni in Laterano (also lost). His greatest surviving work is the *Adoration of the Magi*, now in the Uffizi Gallery, Florence, showing all the facets of his opulent style: complex lighting effects, rich use of colour and gilding, and careful attention to detail. The overall impression is intensely decorative. Gentile's style is often considered old-fashioned for the period, but in comparison with that of his contemporary Masaccio, Gentile's work was thought advanced in his own day.

Fabrici, Girolamo See Fabricius ab Aquapendente, Hieronymous

Fabricius, David 1564–1617
German astronomer and clergyman

Born in Esens, he was a skilled observer and his observations (1602–04) of the positions of Mars (together with those made by Tycho Brahe) were used by his friend Johannes Kepler in his analysis of planetary orbits. Fabricius discovered the first known variable star (Mira, in the constellation Cetus) in 1596. He was pastor at Resterhaave and Osteel in East Friesland, where he was murdered by one of his parishioners.

Fabricius, Johann Christian 1745–1808
Danish entomologist

Born in Tondern in Schleswig, he became Professor of Natural History at Kiel University in 1775. His classification of insects was based on the structure of the mouth. He was one of the founders of entomological taxonomy.

Fabricius, Johannes 1587–c.1615
Dutch astronomer and physician

He was born in Resterhaave, the son of David Fabricius. He made pioneering observations of sunspots, whose discovery was announced publicly in 1611.

Fabricius ab Aquapendente, Hieronymus,
Italian name Girolamo Fabrici 1537–1619
Italian anatomist

Born in Acquapendente, he studied at Padua under Gabriele Falloppius and succeeded him as Professor of Anatomy there (1562). One of his pupils was William Harvey. A remarkable anatomist of his time, and a pioneer of modern embryology, he studied foetal development, the function of the larynx as a vocal organ and the changing size of the pupil in the eye.

Fabritius, Carel 1622–54
Dutch painter

Born in Beemster, he worked under Rembrandt around 1641 and lived mainly at Delft, where he was killed in an explosion. He is important for the influence of his sensitive experiments in composition and the painting of light (as in the tiny *View of Delft*, 1652, in the National Gallery, London) upon his pupil Jan Vermeer. Some of his paintings have been attributed to his brother Barent Fabritius (1624–73), also a pupil of Rembrandt.

Fabry, (Marie Paul Auguste) Charles 1867–1945
French physicist

Born in Paris, he graduated from the École Polytechnique, Paris, became professor at Marseilles (1904) and the Sorbonne, Paris (1920), and was appointed first director of the latter's Institute of Optics. Inventor of the 'Fabry–Perot interferometer', he is also known for his researches into light in connection with astronomical phenomena, and he confirmed experimentally the Doppler effect for light in the laboratory. Previously, such measurements had been made using stellar sources. He was also interested in ways of increasing the public's scientific understanding.

Fadeyev, Aleksandr Aleksandrovich,
pseudonym Bulgya 1901–56
Russian novelist

Born in Kimry, near Tver, he was educated in Vladivostock. He was deeply influenced by Leo Tolstoy, and wrote *Razgrom* (1926, Eng trans *The Rout*, 1926), set in the Russian Civil War, and *Molodaya gvardiya* (1945, Eng trans *The Young Guard*, 1962), portraying Russian resistance against the Germans in World War II. A Socialist Realist and general-secretary of the Soviet Writers' Union (1946–55), he mercilessly exposed any literary 'deviationism' from the party line. However, he later became a target himself and, compelled to revise *Molodaya gvardiya*, took to drink and finally shot himself. 🕮 V M Ozerov, *Aleksandr Aleksandrovich Fadeyev* (1960)

Faed, John 1819–1902
Scottish painter

Born in Burley Mill, Kirkcudbrightshire, he studied at the Edinburgh School of Design from 1841. He became a noted painter of miniatures in London, and also painted figure subjects like *The Cottar's Saturday Night* (1854). He was the brother of Thomas Faed.

Faed, Thomas 1826–1900
Scottish painter

Born in Burley Mill, Kirkcudbrightshire, he studied at the Edinburgh School of Design. He was elected an associate of the Royal Scottish Academy in 1849 when he produced *Scott and his Friends at Abbotsford*, engraved by his brother, John Faed. He went to London in 1852 and made his name with paintings of humble incidents in Scottish life. Elected to the Royal Academy in 1864, he resigned in 1893.

Fagan, Garth 1940–
West Indian dancer, choreographer and artistic director

Born in Kingston, Jamaica, he toured Latin America as a teenager with Ivy Baxter and Rex Nettleford's Jamaican National Dance Company. He later attended college in the USA and danced with, and choreographed for, several Detroit-based companies. Soon after joining the faculty of the State University of New York, Brockport (1970), he began teaching untrained urban youths at nearby Rochester. The fruit of these classes was The Bottom of the Bucket But... Dance Theatre, shortened to Bucket Dance Theatre a decade later. He fashions his pupils into a disciplined professional ensemble who expertly convey the Fagan style, a fusion of modern and jazz dance with the influences of both Afro-Caribbean and classical ballet movement. He occasionally choreographs dances for other companies and directs stage shows.

Fahd (ibn Abd al-Aziz al-Saud) 1923–
King of Saudi Arabia

Born in Riyadh, a son of Ibn Saud, he served as Minister of Education (1953) and Minister of the Interior (1962–75), before becoming first deputy Prime Minister and effective ruler in 1975 on the assassination of his half-brother Faisal. He officially became king in 1982 on the death of his other half-brother Khalid. Promoting the modernization of his country, he helped to shape Saudi Arabia's foreign policy in the 1970s and 1980s, and countered Soviet influence through financial assistance to moderate Arab states such as Egypt. During the 1990–91 Gulf War he permitted the deployment of US, British and other forces on his territory in order to contain Iraqi expansionism.

Fahrenheit, (Gabriel) Daniel 1686–1736
German instrument-maker and physicist

Born in Danzig (now Gdansk, Poland), he was sent (1701) to Amsterdam, where he learned the trade of instrument-maker. He produced high-quality meteorological instruments, devising an accurate alcohol thermometer (1709) and a commercially successful mercury thermometer (1714). Adopting what he believed to be Olaus Roemer's practice of taking thermometric fixed points as the temperatures of melting ice and of the human body, Fahrenheit eventually devised a temperature scale with these points calibrated at 32 and 96 degrees, and zero fixed at the freezing point of ice and salt. He was the first to show that the boiling point of liquids varies at different atmospheric pressures, and suggested this as a principle for the construction of barometers.

Fa Hsien See Fa Xian

Faidherbe, Louis Léon César 1818–89
French general and colonial administrator

He was born in Lille. As Governor of Senegal (1854–61, 1863–65) he greatly extended the frontiers of his province, laying the foundation of France's empire in Africa. In the Franco-Prussian War (1870–71) he commanded the army of the North, but was defeated near St Quentin (1871). He was twice elected as a Deputy (1871, 1879). He wrote on Numidian and Phoenician inscriptions (1870–74), the anthropology of Algiers and the French Sudan (1874–84), a work on Senegal (1889), and treatises on the Fula (or Poul) and Berber languages (1875–77), besides *Campagne de l'armée du nord* (1871, 'Campaign of the Army of the North').

Fairbairn, Sir William 1789–1874
Scottish engineer

Born in Kelso, in the Scottish Borders, he was apprenticed in 1804 to an engine-wright at North Shields, where he also studied mathematics and met **George Stephenson**. Moving to London in 1811 he invented a steam excavator and a sausage-making machine, neither of them much of a commercial success. By 1817, however, he had established an engineering works in Manchester making machinery for water wheels and cotton-mills, and within a few years he had gained a reputation as one of the most capable engineers in the country. From about 1840 until his death the Manchester works also built over 400 locomotives. In 1830 he took a lead in the building of iron boats, and his works at Millwall, London (1835–49) turned out hundreds of vessels. He developed the rectangular wrought-iron tubes for Stephenson's railway bridge over the Menai Strait (1850), the two main spans of which measured almost 460 feet (140m), and were not surpassed for the next 25 years. He also aided **James Joule** and William Thomson, 1st Baron **Kelvin** in geological investigations from 1851, and guided the experiments of a government committee (1861–65) on the use of iron for defensive purposes. He was elected FRS in 1850 and made a baronet in 1869.

Fairbanks, Douglas Elton, Snr, *originally* Douglas Elton Ullman 1883–1939
US film actor

Born in Denver, Colorado, he first appeared in stage plays (from 1901), but in 1915 went into films and specialized in swashbuckling hero parts, as in *The Three Musketeers* (1921), *Robin Hood* (1922) and *The Thief of Baghdad* (1924) in which he did all his own stunts. He was a founder of United Pictures. In 1920 he married **Mary Pickford** (divorced 1935). His son **Douglas Fairbanks, Jnr**, followed in his footsteps.

Fairbanks, Douglas Elton, Jnr 1909–
US film actor

He was born in New York City, the son of **Douglas Fairbanks, Senior**. In his youth he made Hollywood movies in his father's style, including *Catherine the Great* (1934), *The Prisoner of Zenda* (1937) and *Sinbad the Sailor* (1947), and also gained a reputation as a producer. He later became interested in international affairs, and made a name for himself as a diplomat. He distinguished himself in World War II and was created an honorary KBE in 1949. He has published two volumes of autobiography, *The Salad Days* (1988) and *A Hell of a War* (1993).

Fairclough, Sir John Whitaker 1930–
English computer scientist

He graduated in technology from Manchester University, then joined Ferranti and moved to the USA to develop and sell computer components. In 1958 he returned to England to join IBM's Hursley laboratory, where his work led to the development of the control store, an important technological feature in IBM's highly successful System/360 machines. Fairclough later managed the development of IBM Model 40, which was the first System/360 model. He became chairman of IBM's UK laboratories in 1983, and was Chief Scientific Adviser to the Cabinet from 1986 to 1990. He was knighted in 1990.

Fairey, Sir (Charles) Richard 1887–1956
English aeronautical inventor and industrialist

He was born in Hendon, London, and studied electrical engineering at Finsbury Technical College. He was also a skilled model aircraft builder, and became chief engineer to aircraft manufacturers Short Brothers in 1913. He formed Fairey Aviation Company in 1915, starting by building Short designs, and by 1925 half the aircraft in the RAF were of Fairey origin. Famous types from his factory include Hendon, Fantome, Swordfish, Barracuda and Firefly. Following World War II the company worked on guided weapons and helicopters, and in 1956 the Fairey 'Delta' became the first aircraft to fly at over 1,000mph (1,609kph). In 1927 he took up yachting, designing advanced hulls and winning many races.

Fairfax, John 1804–77
Australian newspaper proprietor

He was born in Warwick, Warwickshire, England, and was apprenticed to a printer at the age of 12. In 1828 he founded a newspaper in Leamington, and in 1835 became part-owner of another. After twice successfully defending a libel action he was unable to meet his costs, was declared insolvent and with his family went to Sydney in 1838. Three years later he and a partner bought, on credit, the established daily newspaper *The Sydney Herald* which in 1842 became *The Sydney Morning Herald*. For the first few years the two partners performed every function, writing, editing and printing, and their success was such that in 1851 Fairfax returned to Leamington and repaid all his creditors in full. He also purchased a steam printing-press which on its arrival in Sydney (1853) became the first of its kind to print a newspaper in Australia.

Fairfax (of Cameron), Thomas Fairfax, 3rd Baron 1612–71
English general

Born in Denton, Yorkshire, he was the son of Ferdinando, Lord Fairfax. From 1629 he served in the Netherlands, under Sir Horace, 1st Baron Vere, whose daughter Anne he married (1637). In the Civil War (from 1642) he was general of Parliamentary horse and after distinguished action at Marston Moor (1644) was appointed to succeed the 3rd Earl of **Essex** in the supreme command in 1645, and defeated **Charles I** at the decisive Battle of Naseby (1645). In 1650, on Fairfax's refusal to march against the Scots, who had proclaimed **Charles II** king, **Cromwell** was appointed Commander-in-Chief, and Fairfax withdrew into private life. After Cromwell's death he assisted **George Monk**, 1st Duke of Albermarle against **John Lambert** and was head of the commission dispatched to The Hague in 1660 to arrange for the return of Charles II.

Fairweather, Ian 1891–1974
Australian painter

Born in Bridge of Allan, Stirlingshire, Scotland, he served in the army in World War I then studied forestry in London and Edinburgh. He later attended the Slade School of Art, London, from 1920, where he developed an interest in Oriental art. He eventually became a student of Chinese and his abstract painting was very much influenced by the art of non-European cultures. From 1924 he travelled extensively, living and working in Germany, Canada, China, Japan, India and Australia. His *Bathing Scene, Bali* was acquired by the Tate Gallery, London, in 1934. In 1940 he served in the British army in India until, invalided out in 1943, he returned to settle in Australia. In 1952 he attempted to sail from Darwin to Indonesia in a home-made raft. Although he eventually landed, he had been presumed lost at sea and an obituary had already appeared in the Australian press. After several more adventures, he returned to Australia in 1953 and lived and worked in a hut he built on Bribie Island off the Queensland coast. He exercised considerable influence over the younger generation of artists in Sydney during the 1960s as his work became more abstract, as in *Monastery* (1961, Rudy Komon Gallery, Sydney).

Faisal, *in full* Faisal ibn Abd al-Aziz 1905–75
King of Saudi Arabia

He was born in Riyadh, and was declared crown prince and foreign minister on the accession of his brother **Saud** in 1953. He was given full executive powers during the economic crisis of 1958, which he retained until 1960, and was made viceroy in 1964, succeeding to the throne when

Saud abdicated later in the year. He showed himself to be an able and energetic ruler, especially in financial affairs. His foreign policy was cautious, although he joined the Arab states in the Arab–Israeli War of 1967. He was shot dead in the royal palace by his nephew.

Faisal I 1885–1933
King of the Hejaz

Born in Ta'if, he was the son of **Hussein ibn Ali**. He played a prominent role in the Arab revolt against Turkey (1916–18) and became King of Iraq (1921). He negotiated with Great Britain a treaty (1930) that gave Iraq independence and League of Nations membership (1932). 📖 Vincent Sheean, *Faisal, the King and his Kingdom* (1975)

Faisal II *in full* Faisal ibn Ghazi ibn Faisal el Hashim
1935–58
King of Iraq

Born in Baghdad, the great-grandson of **Hussein ibn Ali** and cousin of King **Hussein** of Jordan, he succeeded his father, King Ghazi, who was killed in an accident in 1939. After an education at Harrow he was installed (1953) as the third King of modern Iraq, thus ending the regency of his uncle, Emir Abdul Illah. He paid a state visit to Great Britain in 1956. Although, in the aftermath of the Suez intervention (1956), he formally declared that Iraq would continue to stand by Egypt, rivalry later grew between the two incipient Arab blocs. In 1958 he therefore concluded (with King Hussein of Jordan) a federation of the two countries in opposition to the United Arab Republic of Egypt and Syria. In July that year, he and his entire household were assassinated during a military coup d'état and Iraq became a republic.

Faithfull, Emily 1835–95
English publisher and feminist

Born at Headley Rectory, Surrey, she founded in London a printing house with women compositors in 1860, and was appointed printer and publisher-in-ordinary to Queen **Victoria**. In 1863 she started *Victoria Magazine*, which she edited until 1880, advocating the claims of women to renumerative employment. In 1865 she founded a penny weekly, *Women and Work*, and she published *Change upon Change*, a novel, in 1868.

Faithfull, Marianne 1946–
English singer, songwriter and film actress

Born in Hampstead, London, she was 'discovered' by the **Rolling Stones'** manager and at the age of 18 had a hit with 'As Tears Go By', followed by 'Summer Nights' (1965) and others. As **Mick Jagger's** girlfriend, she received headline attention when the Stones were arrested on drugs charges. Her acting career began with *I'll Never Forget Whatshisname* (1967) and *Girl on a Motorcycle* (1968). Faithfull's singing career seemed to be over in the 1970s, but the extraordinary *Broken English* (1979) revived her fortunes. Subsequent records include *Dangerous Acquaintances* (1981) and *Strange Weather* (1987). Her autobiography, *Faithfull*, was published in 1994.

Faithorne, William 1616–91
English engraver

Born in London, he fought as a Royalist, and having been banished for refusing allegiance to **Cromwell**, he spent several years in Paris, where he made engravings of prints from the vast collection of the Abbé de Villeloin. Allowed home in 1650, he achieved fame as a portraitist and also engraved Newcourt's maps of London and Westminster, and of Virginia and Maryland. He published *The Art of Graving and Etching* in 1662.

Fajans, Kasimir 1887–1975
US physical chemist

Born in Warsaw, Poland, he was educated at the universities of Leipzig and Heidelberg, obtaining his doctorate in 1909. He later carried out research at Zurich and with **Ernest Rutherford** at Manchester (1910–11). From 1911 to 1917 he was on the staff of the Technische Hochschule, Karlsruhe, and from 1917 to 1935 he worked at the University of Munich as director of the Institute for Physical Chemistry (1932–35). From 1936 until his retirement in 1957 he was Professor of Chemistry at the University of Michigan, Ann Arbor. Among his numerous awards and honours was honorary membership of the Royal Institution. In 1912 he discovered the radioactive displacement law at around the same time as **Frederick Soddy** and Alexander Smith Russell. Later he pioneered the use of adsorption indicators in precipitation titrations. He also formulated the factors that govern whether an element tends to form ionic or covalent compounds in terms of ideas which became known as Fajans's rules (1924). He also contributed extensively to thermochemistry and photochemistry.

Falco, Louis 1942–93
US modern dancer and choreographer

Born in New York City, he studied with **José Limón**, **Martha Graham**, and **Charles Weidman**, joining the Limón company in 1960. In his ten years with them he performed in Limón's *The Demon*, *Missa Brevis*, *The Winged*, and *The Exiles and Psalms*. In 1967 he formed his own company and began to choreograph. His works, popular with audiences, have since been included in the repertoires of many of the world's major contemporary dance companies including Boston Ballet, Rambert Dance Company and Netherlands Dance Theater. His film work includes the dance element of the successful theatre school story, *Fame* (1980).

Falcone, Aniello 1600–56
Italian artist

He founded a school of battle painters in Naples, and was the teacher of **Salvator Rosa**.

Falconer, Hugh 1808–65
Scottish botanist and palaeontologist

Born in Forres, Grampian, he studied medicine at Aberdeen and Edinburgh, then went to India as assistant surgeon at the Bengal Medical Establishment (1830). He then became superintendent at the botanic gardens at Saharanpur in 1832 and discovered many extinct Lower Pliocene fossil vertebrates in the Siwalik Hills. He also conducted the first experiments on growing tea in India. He later returned to Great Britain (1842) and wrote on Indian botany and palaeontology, arranged Indian fossils in the British Museum and East India House, and prepared his great work *Fauna Antiqua Sivalensis* (1846–49). He returned to India in 1848 as superintendent of the botanic garden and Professor of Botany at the medical college in Calcutta. He retired from the Indian Service in 1855, returning once again to England where he undertook studies of the Pleistocene faunas of Great Britain, Sicily, France and Gibraltar.

Falconer, Ion Keith or Ion Keith-Falconer
1856–87
Irish orientalist, missionary and athlete

He was the third son of the Earl of Kintore. While studying at Cambridge he began evangelistic work, which he continued at Mile End in London. A keen cyclist, he defeated the then fastest cyclist in the world (1878), and cycled from Land's End to John o' Groats. Professor of Arabic at Cambridge, he settled at Shaikh Othman near Aden as a Free Church missionary, shortly before he died of fever. In 1885 he translated the Fables of Bidpai.

Falconet, Étienne Maurice 1716–91
French sculptor

He was born in Paris, became a pupil of François Le Moyne, and was director of sculpture at the Sèvres Porcelain Factory from 1757 to 1766. His figures of *Venus*, bathers and similar subjects (in the Louvre) epitomize the Rococo style of the period of Louis XV and were very popular with patrons such as Madame de Pompadour. It was through the influence of Denis Diderot that Catherine II, the Great, invited him to Russia in 1766 to execute what is his most impressive work, a bronze equestrian monument to Peter I, the Great, in St Petersburg (1767–78). After suffering a stroke in 1783, he turned to writing art theory, nine volumes of which had been published by 1787.

Faldo, Nick (Nicholas Alexander) 1957–
English golfer

He was born in Welwyn Garden City, Hertfordshire. Within seven years of turning professional he was the European top player. His early successes included winning the Professional Golfers' Association (PGA) championships in 1978, 1980 and 1981. However he was unhappy with his performance and spent two years reworking his swing with golf instructor David Leadbetter. This resulted in six major victories: the Open championship (1987, 1990, 1996) and the Masters (1989, 1990, 1996). He has been a member of the Ryder Cup team since 1977. His greatest victory was perhaps the 1996 Masters when he overcame a six-stroke deficit to win the competition by five shots.

Falguière, Jean Alexandre Joseph 1831–1900
French sculptor and painter

Born in Toulouse, he was celebrated more for his portrait statues than his larger compositions. Several sculptures and paintings are now in the Luxembourg Palace in Paris, and his statue of the Marquis de Lafayette stands in Washington DC.

Falk, Johann Daniel 1768–1826
German writer and philanthropist

Born in Danzig, he founded the 'company of friends in need' for helping destitute children, and established the Falk Institute at Weimar. Of his writings the best known are his satirical works like *Der Mensch* (1795) and a study of Goethe.

Falkeberget, Johann Petter, *originally* Johann Petter Lillebakken 1879–1967
Norwegian novelist

Born in Nordre-Rugel, he was a miner from the age of eight, and wrote realistic novels of working-class life in his area. His first novel was *Svarte Fjelde* (1907, 'Black Mountains'). He also wrote *Den fjerde nattevakt* (1923, 'The Fourth Night-Watch'), and two trilogies, *Christianus Sextus* (1927–35) and *Nattens brød* (1940–59, 'Night's Bread').

Falkender, Marcia Matilda Falkender, Baroness, *originally* Marcia Williams 1932–
English political worker

She took a history degree at Queen Mary College, London, then worked at Labour Party headquarters before becoming Private and Political Secretary to Prime Minister Harold Wilson (1956–83). Her background influence during the 1964–70 Labour government is chronicled in her book *Inside No.10* (1972). She was given a life peerage in 1974.

Falkenhayn, Erich von 1861–1922
German soldier

Following a varied military career, he succeeded Helmut von Moltke as Chief of the German General Staff in 1914. He decided against a German retreat in the West, despite the French success at the first Battle of the Marne (1914) and in 1916 he launched the offensive at the Battle of Verdun. His failure led to his replacement by Paul von Hindenburg and Erich von Ludendorff in 1917. He brilliantly commanded the German forces in the occupation of Romania when it entered the war, and continued to serve successfully as a field commander in Palestine and Lithuania.

Falla, Manuel de 1876–1946
Spanish composer

Born in Cadiz, he played the piano as a child, and after two years studying under the composer Felipe Pedrell (1841–1922), won prizes both for his piano-playing and for his opera *La Vida Breve* ('Short Life') in 1905. During his seven years in Paris, up to the outbreak of World War I, he composed in a less exclusively national style, but after his return to Spain in 1914 his music returned to his original colourful Spanish idiom, of which the most famous piece was the ballet *El Sombrero de Tres Picos* (1919, 'The Three-Cornered Hat'). His other works include the opera *El Retablo de Maese Pedro* (1919–22, 'Master Peter's Puppet Show'), the ballet *La Vida Breve* (1904–05, 'Love, the Magician'), and the piano and orchestra suite *Noches en los Jardines de España* (1909–16, 'Nights in the Gardens of Spain'). With the outbreak of the Spanish Civil War, he settled in Argentina. 📖 G Chase and A Budwig, *Manuel de Falla* (1986)

Fallada, Hans, *pseudonym of* Rudolf Ditzen 1893–1947
German writer

Born in Greifswald, he achieved international fame with his novel of German social problems, *Kleiner Mann, Was Nun?* (1932, Eng trans *Little Man, What Now?*, 1969) in which a devoted young couple struggle against the hardship of rampant inflation and unemployment. *Wolf unter Wölfen* (1937, Eng trans *Wolf Among Wolves*, 1938) is a tragic novel of post-World War I Germany. Several important works appeared posthumously, including *Der Trinker* (1950, Eng trans *The Drinker*, 1952). 📖 H Schulder, *Hans Fallada, humanist and social critic* (1970)

Faliero, Marino c.1274–1355
Doge of Venice

He defeated the Hungarians at Zara (1346), captured Capo d'Istria, was ambassador to Rome and Genoa, and became Doge in 1354. After conspiring unsuccessfully to overthrow the oligarchs, he was arrested and beheaded. His fate is the theme of tragedies by Byron and Algernon Swinburne, and of a painting by Eugène Delacroix.

Fallersleben, Hoffmann von See Hoffmann von Fallersleben

Fallopio, Gabriello See Falloppius, Gabriele

Falloppius, Gabriele, *Italian* Gabriello Fallopio or Falloppia 1523–62
Italian anatomist

He was born in Modena, and became Professor of Anatomy at Pisa (1548) and Padua (1551). He particularly studied bones and the reproductive organs, and the Fallopian tube connecting the ovaries with the uterus is named after him.

Falls, Cyril Bentham 1888–1971
English military historian

Educated at Bradfield College, Portora Royal School, Enniskillen, and London University, he served as a staff officer in World War I and won the Croix de Guerre. He was military correspondent of *The Times* (1939–53) and Chichele Professor of the History of War at Oxford (1946–53). He wrote the official history of the British campaigns in Egypt, Palestine, Macedonia and France, studies of Rudyard Kipling and Ferdinand Foch, *A Short History of the Second World War* (1948), *The First World War* (1960), and other works.

Faludi, Susan 1960–
US journalist and writer

Born at Yorktown Heights, New York, and educated at Harvard University, she has been a staff member of the *New York Times* and is attached to the San Francisco bureau of the *Wall Street Journal*. In 1991 she was awarded the Pulitzer Prize for her investigative journalism as well as the 1991 National Book Critics Award for non-fiction for *Backlash* (1991), which argues that despite appearances, women are still controlled and repressed in contemporary society. She is also a contributor to *Ms* and *Mother Jones* magazines.

Falwell, Jerry 1933–
US evangelist

Born in Lynchburg, Virginia, he studied engineering there, but after a religious conversion graduated from Baptist Bible College, Springfield, Missouri. In 1956 he became pastor of Thomas Road Baptist Church, Lynchburg, which he founded. There he inaugurated the television 'Old-Time Gospel Hour', and founded Liberty Baptist College. In 1979 he established Moral Majority Inc., which formed a rallying point for conservative opinion in the 1980 and 1984 presidential election campaigns, and in 1982 an influential publication listed him among the 20 most prominent people in the USA. He wrote *Listen, America!* (1980), *The Fundamentalist Phenomenon* (1981), *Wisdom for Living* (1984) and the autobiographical *Strength for the Journey* (1987).

Faneuil, Peter 1700–43
US merchant and philanthropist

Born in New Rochelle, New York, he made a fortune in Boston and built the Faneuil Hall in Boston, known as 'the cradle of American liberty' (1742), and presented it to the town.

Fanfani, Amintore 1908–
Italian politician

He was born in Pieve Santo Stefano. A former Professor of Political Economics, he was Prime Minister six times (1954, 1958–59, 1960–63 (twice), 1982–83, 1987). Nominated a life senator in 1972, he was president of the Italian Senate (1968–73, 1976–82). He is a member (and former secretary and chairman) of the Christian Democratic Party and was both Minister of the Interior (1953, 1987–88) and Budget Minister (1988–1989).

Fangio, Juan Manuel 1911–95
Argentine racing driver

Born in Balcarce, of Italian descent, he served his racing apprenticeship first as a mechanic and then by driving a car he had built himself in South American events. He first took part in European Grand Prix racing in 1949, and in 1951 won the first of his five world championships; he was world champion again for four consecutive years from 1954 to 1957. His record of 24 Grand Prix wins was only bettered 10 years later by Jim Clark. Fangio retired in 1958 and became an executive for Mercedes-Benz. 📖 Denis Jenkinson, *Fangio* (1973)

Fan Kuan (Fan K'uan) fl.c.990–1030
Chinese landscape painter

Born in Huayuan, Shaanxi (Shensi) Province, he was a representative of the Monumental style of Chinese painting which began between the fall of the Tang (T'ang) dynasty and the foundation of the Song (Sung) dynasty in 960. The painted silk hanging scroll *Travelling in Streams and Mountains* (Palace Museum, Taiwan), one of the few surviving paintings of the period and possibly the greatest single example of the style, is attributed to him. His work was based on Taoism and the contemplation of nature— in his case the austere grandeur of the Shaanxi mountains, to which he retired.

Fanon, Frantz 1925–61
French West Indian doctor and revolutionary writer

He was born in Martinique. Educated as a psychiatrist in France and sent to Algeria, he changed sides and joined the rebels. His study of the Algerian revolution, *Les Damnés de la terre* (1961, 'The Wretched of the Earth'), became the inspiration and manifesto for liberation struggles throughout the Third World. He died of leukaemia before seeing the achievement of independence for Algeria.

Fanshawe, Richard 1608–66
English poet, translator and diplomat

Born at Ware Park, Hertfordshire, he attended Jesus College, Cambridge, and went abroad to study languages. In the Civil War he fought for the Royalists, and became an MP on the accession of Charles II. In 1648 he became treasurer to the navy under Prince Rupert, in 1651 he was taken prisoner at Worcester, and on Cromwell's death he withdrew to the Continent. After the Restoration he was appointed ambassador at the courts of Portugal and Spain. He translated Horace, Giovanni Guarini's *Il Pastor Fido*, and the *Lusiads* (1655) of Camoëns. His wife Ann's *Memoirs* were published in 1829.

Fanthorpe, U(rsula) A(skham) 1929–
English poet

She was educated at Oxford and the University of London Institute of Education, where she obtained a teacher's diploma. Since the mid-1970s, however, she has worked as an admissions clerk in a Bristol hospital. Her style, evident in her first collection, *Side Effects* (1978), is discreetly gossipy, and her ironically polite evasions echo Philip Larkin and John Betjeman. In writing of the natural or the wider human scene, she is quizzical, but capable of genuine wonder. Later volumes are *Four Dogs* (1980), *Standing To* (1982) and *Voices Off* (1984). A major selection appeared in 1986.

Fantin-Latour, (Ignace) Henri Joseph Théodore 1836–1904
French painter and printmaker

Born in Grenoble, he studied at the École des Beaux Arts under Gustave Courbet and was a regular exhibitor at the French Salon from 1861 to 1899. Despite his academic background he also showed work at the controversial Salon des Refusés of 1863, and became friendly with some of the most advanced painters of his day, such as Édouard Manet, James Whistler and Courbet. He made several visits to London and exhibited at the Royal Academy. His subject matter was varied: in France he was particularly admired for his portrait groups, in England for his still lifes, especially of flowers. He was a devotee of Romantic composers such as Hector Berlioz and (especially) Richard Wagner, and made a series of lithographs illustrating their music. 📖 Edward Lucie-Smith, *Henri Fantin-Latour* (1977)

Fanu, Sheridan Le See Le Fanu, (Joseph) Sheridan

Farabi, Abu Nasr al-, Latin Alfarabius 878–c.950
Islamic philosopher

Born in Farab, he studied at Baghdad and published commentaries on Aristotle and Porphyry. He was much influenced by Plato's *Republic* and can be regarded as the first Islamic Neoplatonist. He also published a utopian political philosophy of his own, known under the title *The Perfect City*.

Faraday, Michael 1791–1867
English chemist and physicist, creator of classical field theory

Born in Newington Butts near London, the son of a blacksmith, he was apprenticed to a bookbinder whose books sparked his interest in science. In 1813, after applying to **Humphry Davy** for a job, he was taken on as his temporary assistant, accompanying him on a European tour during which he met many top scientists and gained an unconventional but invaluable scientific education. In 1827 he succeeded to Davy's chair of chemistry at the Royal Institution, in that year publishing his *Chemical Manipulation*. His early publications on physical science include papers on the condensation of gases, limits of vaporization and optical deceptions. He was the first to isolate benzene, and he synthesized the first chlorocarbons. His great life work, however, was the series of *Experimental Researches on Electricity* published over 40 years in *Philosophical Transactions*, in which he described his many discoveries, including electromagnetic induction (1831), the laws of electrolysis (1833) and the rotation of polarized light by magnetism (1845). He received a pension in 1835 and in 1858 was given a house in Hampton Court. As adviser to the Trinity House in 1862 he advocated the use of electric lights in lighthouses. Greatly influential on later physics, he nevertheless had no pupils and worked with only one assistant. He is generally considered the greatest of all experimental physicists. ⌨ L Pearce, *Michael Faraday* (1987)

Farborough, Lord See **May, Sir Thomas Erskine**

Farel, Guillaume 1489–1565
French reformer
Born in Gap in Dauphiné, he became a convert to Protestantism in 1521. He fled to Basle, and in 1524 supported 39 Protestant theses. He moved to Geneva in 1532 and, after being twice compelled to leave, settled there in 1534. In 1535 the town council proclaimed the Reformation, but people reacted against the sudden severity of the ecclesiastical discipline imposed by **John Calvin**, and in 1538 the two reformers were expelled from the city. He became a pastor in Neuchâtel in 1538, and worked there for the rest of his life.

Farge, John La See **La Farge, John**

Farhi, Nicole Birthdate unavailable
British fashion designer
Born in Nice, France, she worked there as a freelance designer before moving to London to work with Stephen Marks on French Connection and the Stephen Marks label. Launching her own company in 1983, she has become known for her comfortable, uncomplicated clothes which feature soft structure, subtle colouring and fine quality fabrics. She has been a nominee in the British Fashion awards four times, and won the British Classis award in 1989. She recently launched a swimwear collection and has shops in London, Glasgow, Manchester, New York, Oslo and Tokyo, and her collections wholesale to top stores in Europe, the USA and the Far East.

Faria y Sousa, Manuel de 1590–1649
Portuguese poet
Born near Pombeiro, he went to Madrid in c.1613, and from 1631 to 1634 was secretary to the Spanish embassy in Rome. He wrote on Portuguese history and on **Camoëns**, and left around 200 Portuguese sonnets, 12 eclogues, and 3 treatises on poetry.

Farina, Battista, nicknamed **Pinin** 1893–1966
Italian car designer
Born in Turin, he worked at the Fiat factory early in his career in the 1920s, and visited the USA, where he studied Ford's production methods, before setting up his own bodywork establishment in Turin (1930). Although always associated with classic designs for the prestigious Italian makers like Ferrari, Lancia and Alfa-Romeo, he also designed for mass production. Among his firm's successful popular cars were Austin's innovative A40 'hatchback' of 1958, and the 1100 model (actually designed by his son Sergio) which appeared under a number of BMC names after 1963. His nickname, Pinin, was adopted in the company name—Pininfarina—in 1961.

Farina, Guiseppe La See **La Farina, Guiseppe**

Farina, Johann Maria 1685–1766
Italian perfumier
Born in Novara, he settled in Cologne in 1709, and was the inventor of eau-de-Cologne.

Farinacci, Roberto 1892–1945
Italian politician
Born in Isernia, he became Fascist Party Secretary (1924–26), a member of the Fascist grand council (1935) and Minister of State (1938). An ardent racist and anti-Semite, notorious for his extremism and pro-Nazi tendencies, he edited the *Regime Fascista*, the party organ. He was ultimately captured and shot, on the same day and by the same band of partisans as **Mussolini**, while attempting to flee to Switzerland.

Farinelli See **Broschi, Carlo**

Farini, Luigi Carlo, nicknamed **Cavour's Shadow** 1812–66
Italian statesman and revolutionary
Born near Ravenna, he was involved in the Bologna uprising against papal rule in 1831 and expelled from the Papal States in 1843, then summoned back to Rome by **Pius IX**, who appointed him Under-Secretary of State. When Pius fled to Gaeta after the murder of Count Pellegrino Rossi (1787–1848), Farini followed, but he was subsequently dismissed and exiled because of his liberal sympathies. He settled in Turin and collaborated with the Conte di **Cavour** on *Il Risorgimento*. He became a minister in the D'Azeglio government and supported Cavour during the 1850s. In 1859 he was appointed as Commissioner Extraordinary in Modena and the following year was recognized as 'dictator' in Parma and the Papal Legations. In 1860 he orchestrated their transfer by plebiscite to the new united Italy. After the annexation of the Kingdom of the Two Sicilies, he was made lieutenant-general of Naples. He became Prime Minister on the resignation of **Urbano Rattazzi** (1862), but resigned himself due to ill health in 1863. His admiration and close co-operation with Cavour earned him his nickname.

Farjeon, Eleanor 1881–1965
English writer
Born in Hampstead, London, she wrote fantasies and children's stories, beginning with her successful first novel, *Martin Pippin in the Apple Orchard* (1921). She collaborated with her brother Herbert in *Kings and Queens* (1932) and the play *The Glass Slipper* (1944). Her childhood is described in her autobiographical *A Nursery in the Nineties* (1935). There is an annual Eleanor Farjeon award for outstanding service to children's literature. ⌨ D Blakelock, *Eleanor, a portrait* (1966)

Farman, Henri 1874–1958
French pioneer aviator and aircraft manufacturer
With his brother Maurice (1878–1964) he made the first flight in a Voisin biplane (1908) which they had built. In 1912 they established a factory at Boulogne-sur-Seine to manufacture the Farman biplane, and built the first long-distance passenger plane, the *Goliath*, in 1917.

Farmer, Fannie Merritt 1857–1915
US cookery expert

Born in Boston, she suffered a stroke at the age of 16 and was unable to attend college, so she turned to cooking at home and then attended the Boston Cooking School. After graduation (1889), she became a director there (1891–1902), during which time she edited the *Boston Cooking School Cook Book* (1896). In 1902 she opened Miss Farmer's School of Cookery in Boston, the first to offer courses designed for housewives and nurses rather than servants or teachers, and her insistence on precise measurements in her recipes was innovatory. She also wrote for the *Woman's Home Companion* for 10 years.

Farnaby, Giles c.1563–1640
English composer
Born probably in Truro, Cornwall, he spent most of his active life in London. His works include madrigals and settings of the psalms in verse paraphrases for East Psalter, but he is best remembered for his keyboard music.

Farnese, Alessandro 1546–92
Spanish soldier
Born in Rome, he was the son of the 2nd Duke of Parma and the illegitimate daughter of the emperor Charles V, and nephew of Philip II of Spain. He distinguished himself under his uncle, John of Austria, at the sea battle of Lepanto (1571), and became one of the great land-force commanders of his era as well as a gifted diplomat. He joined his uncle in the Spanish Netherlands in 1577, then in 1578 defeated the rebellious Dutch at Gembloux and captured Maastricht. As Governor-General himself he captured Antwerp in 1585. He prepared forces for the invasion of England in concert with the Great Armada in 1588. In 1590 he compelled Henri IV of France to raise the Siege of Paris.

Farouk I 1920–65
King of Egypt
Born in Cairo, he was educated privately in England. On ascending the throne, he dismissed the premier, Nahas Pasha, and for a while devoted himself to schemes of economic development and land reform. In 1942, with Axis troops threatening Egypt, Great Britain insisted on the re-appointment of Nahas Pasha. After the war, his lifestyle became increasingly flamboyant, and he alienated the armed forces, especially after defeat by Israel (1948). In 1948 he dissolved his first marriage with Princess Farida, and he married Narriman Sadek (1951). General Neguib's coup d'état (1952) forced Farouk to abdicate. He was exiled to Italy and in 1959 he became a citizen of Monaco. ▣ Barrie St Clair McBride, *Farouk of Egypt: A Biography* (1968)

Farquhar, George c.1677–1707
Irish playwright
He was born in Londonderry, possibly in 1677 (but he is said to have fought at the Boyne). Educated at Trinity College, Dublin, he became an actor in a Dublin theatre, but the accidental wounding of a fellow actor so shocked him that he quitted the boards, and shortly after received a commission in a regiment stationed in Ireland. His first comedy, *Love and a Bottle* (1698), proved a success, and the *Constant Couple* (1700) met with an enthusiastic reception. In 1703 he produced *The Inconstant*, founded on John Fletcher's *Wild Goose Chase*, and in 1706 *The Recruiting Officer*. He wrote the best of his plays, *The Beaux Stratagem* (1707), during an illness but died before he could enjoy its success. He is one of the best of the comic dramatists, and had on the whole more variety and character than any of his contemporaries. ▣ E Rothenstein, *George Farquhar* (1967)

Farragut, David Glasgow 1801–70
US naval commander

He was born near Knoxville, Tennessee, of Spanish origin, and after being adopted by Captain David Porter and made a midshipman in the navy at the age of nine, he joined the navy in 1810 and served against the British (1812), and against pirates (1820). In the American Civil War he served with the Federal forces and commanded the ships fitted out for the capture of New Orleans (1862). He took part in the siege and capture of Vicksburg (1863) and helped establish Union control of the Mississippi River. His most famous victory occurred at Mobile Bay (1864), into which he sailed his fleet despite floating mines (he cried 'Damn the torpedoes!'), defeating the Confederate flotilla and bringing about the town's surrender. He was made vice-admiral, the rank being created for him by special Act of Congress, as was also that of admiral (1866).

Farrakhan, Louis, *originally* Louis Eugene Wolcott, *formerly known as* Louis X 1933–
US leader of the Nation of Islam
He was born in New York City and his tough upbringing led him to join Malcolm X's Black Muslim movement. The sect was plagued by factionalism and in 1978 Farrakhan was excommunicated by the World Community of Islam and revived the Nation of Islam, which promotes self-reliance, healthy eating and abstinence from drugs. More radical than the leaders of the Civil Rights movement, he has been widely criticised for his anti-Jewish rhetoric, but the growing influence among African-Americans of his message of self-respect was demonstrated in the 1995 Million Man March in Washington DC. In 1996 *Time* magazine included him in its list of the 25 most influential people in the USA.

Farrar, Frederic William 1831–1903
English clergyman and writer
Born in Bombay, he was ordained in 1854, taught at Harrow, became headmaster of Marlborough (1871–76), honorary chaplain to Queen Victoria (1869–73), and later became a chaplain-in-ordinary. He was made a canon of Westminster and rector of St Margaret's in 1876, archdeacon of Westminster in 1883, chaplain to the House of Commons in 1890, and dean of Canterbury in 1895. His theological writings were many, but he is chiefly remembered for the bestseller *Eric, or Little by Little* (1858), one of several school stories that he wrote. ▣ *My Object in Life* (1883)

Farrar, Geraldine 1882–1967
US soprano
Born in Melrose, Maine, she studied in Boston, Paris and Berlin, making her professional debut in Charles Gounod's *Faust* in Germany. Her first role in the USA came five years later, again in Gounod's work, as Juliet. She retired from the opera stage in 1922, but continued giving recitals until the early 1930s. Many of her finest roles, including Cio-Cio San and Carmen, were recorded. She wrote her autobiography, *The Story of an American Singer*, in 1916, later revised as *Such Sweet Compulsion*.

Farrell, James T(homas) 1904–79
US novelist, short-story writer, critic and essayist
Born in Chicago, he paid for his own education at the University of Chicago (1925–29) and lived in Paris in the early 1930s. His first novel was *Young Lonigan* (1932), which began the *Studs Lonigan* trilogy of life on Chicago's South side, realistically and graphically portrayed. A lapsed Catholic and a naturalist in the mould of Émile Zola, he owes much to the style of Sherwood Anderson. The other volumes were *The Young Manhood of Studs Lonigan* (1934) and *Judgement Day* (1935). An accomplished study of defeat (the hero dies aged 29), it was a landmark in US fiction. This was followed by a five-novel sequence centred on Danny

O'Neill (1936–53), and another trilogy, on Bernard Clare (1946–52). He published more than 50 novels in all. ▣ A M
Wald, *Farrell: the revolutionary socialist years* (1978)

Farrell, Suzanne 1945–
US ballerina

Born in Cincinnati, Ohio, she graduated from the School of American Ballet at the age of 16. From there, she went to the New York City Ballet (NYCB), where she became an inspiration to the choreographer-artistic director George Balanchine. She and her husband, dancer Paul Majia, left the company to join Maurice Béjart's Ballet of the 20th Century (1971–75). Upon her return to NYCB in 1975, she formed a fruitful onstage partnership with dancer Peter Martins. Tall, strong and supple, with great musical sensitivity, she is the ideal Balanchine dancer. She retired as a dancer in 1989 but has continued to teach and to stage Balanchine ballets, notably at the John F Kennedy Center for the Performing Arts in Washington DC in 1995. That year she helped initiate a yearlong celebration of its 25th anniversary by staging a weeklong season of seven Balanchine works, entitled 'Suzanne Farrell Stages Balanchine'.

Farren-Price, Ronald William 1930–
Australian pianist

Born in Brisbane, Queensland, he was educated at Melbourne University, then studied in Germany and, under Claudio Arrau, in London. From 1967 he toured extensively in the USA, England and Europe, and was the first Australian pianist to tour the USSR. A regular broadcaster and recitalist, he performed as a soloist with many major orchestras, and has recorded widely. In 1955 he joined the Melbourne Conservatorium of Music (now the faculty of music at Melbourne University) where he became Reader in Music.

Farrer, Reginald John 1880–1920
English botanist, plant-collector and writer

Born in Clapham, Yorkshire, he was educated at home before going to Balliol College, Oxford. He travelled extensively in Europe, Japan, China (1914–16) and Upper Burma (1919–20) in search of plants. Farrer introduced many species into cultivation, and his herbarium collection is distinguished by the expressiveness and detail of his field notes. A prolific author, he wrote five horticultural works, among them *Alpines and Bog-Plants* (1908) and *The Rock-Garden* (1912), and six travel books. From his student days he had an interest in politics, in 1911 standing unsuccessfully as Liberal candidate for Ashford, Kent.

Farrer, William James 1845–1906
English agriculturist

Born in Docker, Westmorland (Cumbria), he studied medicine at Cambridge, but tuberculosis forced him to give up and emigrate to Australia in 1870. He found work as a surveyor, but in 1886 he settled on his own property near Tharwa, New South Wales, where an early interest in grasses led him to several experiments with various varieties of wheat. He crossbred over 200 strains each year in an endeavour to find one which would be resistant to diseases such as rust yet would give good baking qualities, and be suitable for Australian climatic conditions and farming methods. A pioneer of scientific wheat-breeding, he introduced many valuable varieties for stock and for commercial use, culminating in his 'Federation' strain of 1901. Farrer's work was almost solely responsible for the growth and success of the Australian wheat industry.

Farrow, Mia (Maria de Lourdes Villiers) 1945–
US actress

She was born in Los Angeles, the daughter of the film director John Farrow and the actress Maureen O'Sullivan. She made her Broadway debut in 1963 and first came to notice in *Peyton Place* on television in the 1960s. Her films include *Rosemary's Baby* (1968), *The Great Gatsby* (1974), and a number of Woody Allen films, notably *Hannah and Her Sisters* (1986). She has developed into an authoritative actress, and her high-profile marriages to Frank Sinatra (1966–68) and André Previn (1970–79), and her subsequent relationship with Woody Allen, which ended in court in 1992, have attracted significant media attention.

Farson, James Negley 1890–1960
US writer

Born in Plainfield, New Jersey, he trained as a civil engineer but moved to England and went from there to Russia, where he had an export business and where he witnessed the 1917 Revolution. From then on he led an adventurous life as airman, sailor and journalist, which is reflected in his varied works. These include *Sailing Across Europe* (1926), *Seeing Red* (1930), *Bomber's Moon* (1941) and *A Mirror for Narcissus* (1957). ▣ *The Way of a Transgressor* (1935)

Fasch, Johann Friedrich 1688–1758
German composer

Born in Buttelstedt, Weimar, he was educated at the Thomasschule, Leipzig, and founded the *Collegium Musicum* there, the forerunner of the *Gewandhaus* concerts. In 1722 he was appointed kapellmeister at Zerbst. He wrote overtures in the style of Georg Telemann, orchestral suites admired by J S Bach, three operas (since lost), and also several masses, a requiem, trios and sonatas. His son, Carl Friedrich Christian (1736–1800) was a harpsichordist and composer, and was appointed accompanist (1756) to Frederick II, the Great, who played the flute. He was twice visited by Beethoven (1796).

Fassbinder, Rainer Werner 1946–82
German film director

Born in Bad Wörishofen, he began his career as an actor in fringe theatre in Munich, founding his own 'anti-theatre' company, for whom he wrote original works and adapted classical pieces. Moving into films (1969), he was much influenced by Jean-Luc Godard, believing that films should have a social purpose. His first film to gain international recognition was *Warum läuft Herr R. Amok?* (1970, *Why Does Herr R. Run Amok?*). He made over 40 films, usually politically committed criticisms of contemporary Germany, contrasting personal failure and frustration with the country's superficial economic success, and illustrating the misuse of power and social oppression. Notable among these were *Die bitteren Tränen der Petra von Kant* (1972, *The Bitter Tears of Petra von Kant*), *Effi Briest* (1974, based on a classic novel of the 1890s by Theodor Fontane), and *Die Ehe der Maria Braun* (1979, *The Marriage of Maria Braun*), an allegory of postwar Germany, which won the first prize at the 1979 Berlin Film Festival. Before his death he had completed *Lili Marleen* and *Lola*, two of a planned series of films dealing with recent German history as seen through the eyes of women. ▣ R Katz, *Love is Colder than Death* (1987)

Fassett, Kaffe 1937–
US designer

Born in San Francisco, he was brought up in Big Sur, California, and the community there remains the biggest influence on his work, although his career has been made in the UK. Originally a painter, he learned to knit after moving to the UK in 1964. His colourful, highly individual designs and the sources of many of his ideas are seen in such books as *Glorious Knitting* (1985), *Glorious Needlepoint* (1987), *Glorious Inspirations* (1991) and *Glorious Interiors* (1995).

Fast, Howard Melvin, *pseudonym* E V Cunningham 1914–92
US novelist, playwright and political commentator

Born in New York City, he came of age during the radical 1930s and wrote on this time in a sequence of historical novels, *The Unvanquished* (1942), *Citizen Tom Paine* (1943) and *Freedom Road* (1944), whose contemporary relevance was transparently obvious. His allegiance to Popular Front Communism eventually led to his being imprisoned for 'contempt of Congress' in 1947, and to his blacklisting by Hollywood, but he later recanted in a much-quoted account of writers' dealings with the Party, called *The Naked God* (1957). A prolific writer, he wrote *Spartacus* (1951) which owed its success to the absence of ideological speeches, and to a powerful Hollywood adaptation. With slightly ironic timing, he was awarded the Stalin Peace Prize in 1953.

Fastolf, Sir John 1378–1459
English soldier
Born in Caister, Norfolk, he distinguished himself at Agincourt (1415), and still more at the 'Battle of the Herrings' (1429). He was less successful against Joan of Arc, and at Patay, according to the chronicler Monstrelet (c.1390–1453), displayed such cowardice that the Duke of Bedford stripped him of his Garter. This, however, is doubtful, since on his return to Norfolk in 1440, he was granted a pension of £20 'for notable and praiseworthy service and good counsel'. His Norfolk life is recorded in the *Paston Letters*. His identification with 'Sir John Falstaff' is unlikely, for Sir John Oldcastle was certainly the prototype used by Shakespeare.

Fateh Singh, Sant 1911–72
Sikh religious leader
Born in the Punjab, India, he was a campaigner for Sikh rights and was involved in religious and educational activity in Rajasthan, founding many schools and colleges there. In 1942 he joined the Quit India Movement, and was imprisoned for his political activities. During the 1950s he agitated for a Punjabi-speaking state, which was achieved once Haryana was created as a separate state in 1966.

Fatima c.605–33
Arab religious figure
Born in Mecca, Arabia, she was the youngest daughter of Muhammad, and wife of the fourth Muslim Caliph, 'Ali. Their descendants were the Fatimids, a radical Shiite movement, who ruled over Egypt and North Africa (909–1171), and later over Syria and Palestine.

Faulkner, William 1897–1962
US novelist and Nobel Prize winner
Born near Oxford, Mississippi, he became a pilot in the Canadian Flying Corps in World War I, and later attended Mississippi University. He took various jobs, and while working in New Orleans met Sherwood Anderson, who offered to recommend his first novel, *Soldier's Pay* (1926), to a publisher on condition that he did not have to read it! In 1929 Faulkner took a job as a coal-heaver and while on night-work at a local power station apparently wrote *As I Lay Dying* (1930) in just six weeks, working between midnight and 4am. *Sanctuary* (1931) was intended as a potboiler and was more successful commercially, but had a profound impact on Jean-Paul Sartre and Albert Camus. However, it is the lyrical style of novels like *The Sound and the Fury* (1929), *Light in August* (1932), *Absalom, Absalom!* (1936), *The Hamlet* (1940) and *Intruder in the Dust* (1948) that account for his reputation as one of the modern masters of the novel. Other titles include *Sartoris* (1929), *The Town* (1957) and *The Mansion* (1959), set, like most of the earlier books, in the imaginary Yoknapatawpha County, and *A Fable* (1954), an ambitious but unsuccessful reworking of Christ's Passion, set on the Western Front. He received the 1949 Nobel Prize for literature. ⌨ J Blotner, *Faulkner: a biography* (2 vols, 1974)

Faure, Edgar Jean 1908–88
French politician
Born in Béziers, he trained as a lawyer in Paris, entered politics as a Radical-socialist, and was Minister of Finance and Economic Affairs (1950, 1951, 1954, 1958). He served as Prime Minister (1952, 1955–56), was Professor of Law at Dijon University (1962–66), and became Minister of Agriculture (1966), Minister of Education (1968), Minister of State for Social Affairs (1969), and president of the National Assembly (1973–78). He was a member of the European Parliament from 1979. He also published several detective novels under the pseudonym Edgar Sanday.

Fauré, Gabriel Urbain 1845–1924
French composer
Born in Pamiers, he became organist (1896) at La Madeleine, Paris, and director of the Conservatoire (1905–20). Though he is chiefly remembered for his songs, including 'Après un rêve' (c.1865), he also wrote operas and orchestral pieces, such as *Masques et bergamasques* (1919, 'Masks and Bergamasks'), and a requiem (1887–90).

Faust, Frederick Schiller See Brand, Max

Fautrier, Jean 1898–1964
French painter and printmaker
Born in Paris, he went to England in 1909 and studied at the Royal Academy and Slade schools, London, returning to Paris in 1917. He depicted animal and human flesh in thick impasto so undefined that he was considered the forerunner of postwar abstraction. Early examples are *The Flayed Wild Boar* (1927, Pompidou Centre, Paris) and his lithographs to Dante's *Inferno* (1928). In 1943 he exhibited his series *Otages* ('Hostages'), based on the mass deportations of World War II. In 1946 he exhibited at the Salon des Réalités Nouvelles. His *Femme Douce* (1946, 'Gentle Woman', Pompidou Centre, Paris) belongs to this period. From 1950 he became a pioneer of printmaking (examples in the Tate Gallery, London). He won the Grand Prix at the 1960 Venice Biennale.

Favart, Charles Simon 1710–92
French dramatist
He was born in Paris, and had his first success with the comic opera *Deux jumelles* (1734, 'The Twin Girls'). He went on to direct the Opéra-Comique, and in 1745 married the actress Marie Justine Benoîte Duronceray (1727–72), with whom he pioneered a new realism in costume. At the end of 1745 the Favarts went to Flanders with a company of actors attached to Marshal de Saxe. The Marshal attempted to make Madame Favart his mistress, and when she fled from him took out a lettre de cachet against her husband. Favart had to remain in hiding until the Marshal's death in 1750, when he was finally able to return to Paris. Among his best comic operas are *Les amours de Bastien et Bastienne* (co-written with his wife, 1753, 'The Loves of Bastien and Bastienne') and *Les Trois sultanes* (1776, 'The Three Sultans' Wives'). ⌨ E Maddelen, *Goldoni e Favart* (1889)

Fawcett, Henry 1833–84
English political economist and reformer
Born in Salisbury, he was blinded in a shooting accident in 1858. He became Professor of Political Economy at Cambridge in 1863 and was elected Liberal MP in 1865. He advocated women's suffrage and helped pass the Reform Act of 1867. As Postmaster-General from 1880 he introduced the parcel post, postal orders and sixpenny telegrams. He was the husband of Millicent Garrett Fawcett.

Fawcett, Dame Millicent, née Garrett 1847–1929
English suffragette and educational reformer

Born in Aldeburgh, Suffolk, the wife of **Henry Fawcett** (m.1867) and younger sister of **Elizabeth Garrett Anderson**, she opposed the militancy of the Pankhursts, but campaigned for women's suffrage and higher education for women. She was a founder of Newnham College, Cambridge (1871), and was president of the National Union of Women's Suffrage Societies (1897–1919). She wrote *Political Economy for Beginners* (1870) and *The Women's Victory—and After* (1920). 📖 David Rubinstein, *A Different World for Women: The Life of Millicent Garrett Fawcett* (1991)

Fawcett, Percy Harrison 1867–1925
English explorer

Born in Torquay, Devon, he joined the army at the age of 19, rose to become lieutenant-colonel, and after service in Ceylon (Sri Lanka), Hong Kong and elsewhere was in 1906 given a border delimitation assignment on behalf of the Bolivian government. This led to several hazardous expeditions in the Mato Grosso area in search of traces of ancient civilizations. In 1925 he disappeared near the Xingú River.

Fawkes, Guy 1570–1606
English conspirator

Born in York of Protestant parentage, he developed his fervent Catholicism while still a schoolboy, having been taught about **Henry VIII's** ruthless subjugation of the Catholics 40 years earlier, and appalled by the persecution of his Catholic friends. In 1592, he fought with the Spanish in the Netherlands, and in 1603 rode to Spain in a fruitless attempt to persuade the king to raise an army against his Protestant homeland. The following year, Fawkes secretly returned to London to join the small group of conspirators, led by **Robert Catesby**, who devised a plan to blow up the House of Lords during the State Opening. The plot was supposedly discovered with only hours to spare, and Fawkes and seven other conspirators were beheaded. There is strong evidence, however, to suggest that they were merely pawns in an elaborate hoax, engineered by the state to discredit Rome. 📖 Henry Garnett, *Portrait of Guy Fawkes* (1962)

Fawkner, John Pascoe 1792–1869
Australian pioneer

Born in Cripplegate, London, he moved with his family to the colony of Port Phillip in 1803, after his father was sentenced to transportation. When the colony was abandoned, the convicts and settlers were shipped across to Van Diemen's Land (Tasmania), where the Fawkner family secured a land grant. He chartered a ship (1835) to explore Western Port and Port Phillip Bay on the mainland of Australia, and made camp at the mouth of the Yarra River, the future site of the city of Melbourne. Fawkner's camp was found by another party of settlers, led by **John Batman**, who had previously 'purchased' land from the local Aboriginals. The new town prospered and Fawkner became a member of its council. Later, when the new colony was separated from New South Wales, he became a member of the first legislative council for Victoria.

Fa Xian (Fa Hsien) fl.400AD
Chinese Buddhist monk and traveller

Born at Shanxi (Shansi), at the beginning of the 5th century AD, he made a pilgrimage to India across the Takla Makan Desert and Pamirs, following the Upper Indus River south to Sri Lanka in search of holy texts. He returned by sea through south-east Asia.

Fay, András 1786–1864
Hungarian poet, playwright and novelist

He lived in Budapest, and was a pioneer of the social novel. He also wrote a set of fables in the manner of **Aesop** which achieved great success.

Fay, Sir (Humphrey) Michael Gerard 1949–
New Zealand businessman

Born in Auckland and educated at Victoria University, Wellington, he was the co-founder (with David Richwhite) of the merchant bank Fay, Richwhite. He was chairman of the Australia/New Zealand Bicentennial Committee in 1988, and chairman of three New Zealand challenges for the America's Cup in 1987, 1988 and 1992.

Fayette, Comtesse de la See La Fayette, Marie Madeleine Pioche de Lavergne, Comtesse de

Fazy, Jean James 1794–1878
Swiss journalist and politician

Born in Geneva, he founded the *Revue de Genève*, became the leading spirit in the Radical movement (1846), and until 1862 was the real ruler of Geneva, which he modernized. He wrote *History of Geneva* (1838–40) and also wrote on constitutional law. He was deposed in 1862 and fled to Paris, where he edited *La France Nouvelle*. He later returned to Geneva and became Professor of International Law there (1871).

Feather, Vic(tor Grayson Hardie Feather), Baron 1908–76
British trade union leader

Educated at Hanson Grammar School, Bradford, he began work at the age of 14, and joined the Shopworkers' Union. Shop steward at 15 and chairman of his branch committee at 21, he was a stirring speaker and in 1937 joined the staff of the TUC. He travelled widely as assistant secretary (1947–60), reorganizing trade unions in Europe after World War II, and in India and Pakistan in 1957. In 1969 he succeeded **George Woodcock** as General Secretary, and achieved success in restoring industrial peace following the economic crisis despite opposition from the TUC's left wing. He fought the Conservative government's anti-union Industrial Relations Bill and when this became law in 1972 he joined representatives of British industry to establish an independent advisory organization to settle labour disputes. He retired in 1973, becoming president of the European Trade Union until 1974, when he became a life peer. 📖 Eric Silver, *Victor Feather, TUC* (1973)

Fechner, Gustav Theodor 1801–87
German physicist, psychologist and philosopher

Born in Gross-Särchen, near Halle, he studied medicine at the University of Leipzig but took up physics as a career and became Professor of Physics at Leipzig in 1834. He worked mainly on galvanism (the original term for current electricity), electromagnetism and colour. He then became interested in the connections between physiology and psychology, which he explored in his *Elemente der Psychophysik* (1860), and helped to formulate the **Weber**–Fechner law relating stimuli to sensations. He also published *Das Büchlein vom Leben nach dem Tode* (1836) and *Vorschule der Aesthetik* (1876). His psychophysics later evolved into experimental psychology through **Wilhelm Max Wundt** and others.

Fedden, Sir (Albert Hubert) Roy 1885–1973
English aero-engine designer

Born in Bristol, he trained as an engineer at Bristol Merchant Venturers Technical College. He joined Brazil Straker and Co in Bristol (1906) and produced Rolls-Royce aero-engines during World War I. Taking his aero-engine design 'Jupiter' to form the engine department of the Bristol Aeroplane Company in 1920, he was chief engineer there until 1942. Initiating a famous range of piston engines—Mercury, Pegasus, Perseus, Taurus, Hercules and Centaurus—he was also notable for his unique development of the sleeve-valve engine. He held a variety of governmental and international posts until 1960, and was president of the Royal Aeronautical Society in 1938, 1939 and 1945.

Feigan, Li See Ba Jin

Feininger, Lyonel Charles Adrian 1871–1956
US artist and cartoonist

Born in New York City of German immigrant parents, he studied music there and then in Germany, where he turned to art, and studied in Berlin and Hamburg, and then worked as a newspaper strip cartoonist. From 1907 he devoted himself to painting, working in a style reminiscent of Cubism. After World War II he taught at the Bauhaus at Weimar (1919–24) and Dessau (1925–33). When the Nazis came to power he returned to the USA where, with **Walter Gropius** and **Ludwig Mies van der Rohe**, he founded the Chicago Bauhaus.

Feinstein, Dianne, *née* Goldman 1933–
US politician

Born in San Francisco, California, and educated at Stanford University, she was on the San Francisco Board of Supervisors (1969–78), served as board president (1970–72, 1974–76, 1978), then became Mayor of San Francisco in 1978 following the assassination of George Mascone. She was elected Mayor in 1979 and re-elected in 1983, remaining in the position until 1988. She was elected to the US House of Representatives in 1984 and was senator for California in 1986 and 1992. In 1994 she won a second term in the US Senate.

Feith, Rhijnvis 1753–1824
Dutch poet

Born in Zwolle, he became mayor there in 1780. He wrote some sentimental love novels, and the lyrical *Oden en Gedichten* (1796–1810, 'Odes and Poems'). Of his tragedies, the best known are *Thirza* (1784), *Johanna Gray* (1791) and *Ines de Castro* (1793). He also published a collection of criticism, *Brieven* (1784–94, 'Letters').

Feld, Eliot 1942–
US dancer and choreographer

Born in Brooklyn, New York, he trained in both the classical and modern idioms at the School of American Ballet. He appeared in the 1957 Broadway and 1961 Hollywood versions of *West Side Story* before joining American Ballet Theater (ABT) in 1963, where he quickly rose to the status of soloist, especially in character roles. Thanks to the support of **Jerome Robbins**, he made his choreographic debut in 1967 with *Harbinger* and *At Midnight*, for which he was hailed as Robbins' natural successor. He left ABT to found the short-lived American Ballet Company (1969–71), rejoined ABT for a few seasons and formed Eliot Feld Ballet in 1974. In 1978 he started the New Ballet School, an organization to offer inner-city children the chance to become dance professionals. He is a prolific choreographer with a gift for setting neo-classical, folk-influenced and even gymnastic movement to a wide range of music. His works include *Papillon* (1979), *The Jig is Up* (1984), *Charmed Life* (1990) and *Paper Tiger* (1996).

Felix See Sulla, Lucius Cornelius

Felix II d.365AD
The first antipope

He was consecrated when Liberius was banished (AD355) for refusing to condemn **Athanasius**. When Liberius was restored in 357, Felix retired, but he was ultimately regarded as a saint and martyr.

Felix V See Amadeus VIII

Fell, Dame Honor Bridget 1900–86
British cell biologist

Educated at the University of Edinburgh, she became the director of Strangeways Research Laboratory in Cambridge (1929–70), was Foulerton Research Fellow of the Royal Society from 1941 to 1967, and Royal Society Research Professor from 1963 to 1967. She greatly advanced biochemical study through her investigations using the organ culture method, which demonstrated that excess vitamin A could destroy intercellular material, and which led to the use of such organ cultures in studies of the physiological effects of vitamins and hormones. In later life she investigated the pathogenesis of arthritis. Elected FRS in 1952, she was made a DBE in 1963.

Fell, John 1625–86
Anglican divine

He was born in Longworth, Berkshire. With three others he contrived to maintain the Church of England services during the Commonwealth, and after the Restoration he was made dean of Christ Church, Oxford, royal chaplain and doctor of divinity. He governed the college strictly, restored its buildings, was liberal to poor scholars, and did much to promote learning. In 1676 he became Bishop of Oxford. He rebuilt the episcopal palace at Cuddesdon. 'I do not love thee, Dr Fell' is ascribed to **Thomas Brown**.

Feller, William 1906–70
US mathematician

Born in Zagreb, Croatia, he studied at the universities of Zurich and Göttingen, and after teaching at Kiel University, left Germany in 1933 for Stockholm. In 1939 he emigrated to the USA, holding chairs at the universities of Brown (1939–45), Cornell (1945–50) and Princeton (1950–70). His work in probability theory introduced new rigour without losing sight of practical applicability, and his textbook *Introduction to probability theory and its applications* (1950) is an enormously influential classic, unique as a textbook starting from first principles, yet containing original research often leading to surprising results, and packed with practical examples.

Fellini, Federico 1920–93
Italian film director

Born in Rimini, and educated at Bologna University, he started as a cartoonist, journalist and scriptwriter, before becoming an assistant film director (1942). His highly individual films, always from his own scripts, include *I Vitelloni* (1953, *The Young and the Passionate*), *La Strada* (1954, 'The Road'), which won an Academy Award for Best Foreign Film (1957), *Le Notte di Cabiria* (1957, *The Nights of Cabiria*, Academy Award, 1958), *Giulietta degli Spiriti* (1964, *Juliet of the Spirits*), *Satyricon* (1969), *Fellini's Roma* (1972), *Amarcord* (1974, 'I Remember'), *Casanova* (1976), *Orchestra Rehearsal* (1979), *Città delle Donne* (1980, 'City of Women'), *The Ship Sails On* (1983), and *Ginger and Fred* (1986). His most famous and controversial work, *La Dolce Vita* (1960, 'The Sweet Life', Cannes Festival prize winner), was a cynical evocation of modern Roman high life. *Otto e Mezzo* (1963, 8½) is his most obviously autobiographical work, juxtaposing the dreams and fantasies of its film director hero against the Baroque settings of the film world. In 1943 he married the actress **Giulietta Masina**, star of several of his films.

Fellowes, Edmund Horace 1870–1951
English musicologist

Born in London, he was a minor canon at St George's, Windsor, from 1900. He edited *The English Madrigal School* (36 vols, 1912–24) and *The English School of Lutenist Songwriters* (31 vols, 1920–28).

Fellows, Sir Charles 1799–1860
English archaeologist

In 1838 he discovered in Turkey the ruins of Xanthus, ancient capital of Lycia, and those of Tlos, and in 1839 the ruins of 13 cities. From these he selected marbles, casts, and other artefacts for the British Museum, London.

Felltham, Owen c.1602–68
English writer
Born in Suffolk, he lived in Great Billing, Northamptonshire, and was the author of a series of moral essays, *Resolves, Divine, Morall, Politicall* (1620–28).

Felsenfeld, Gary 1929–
US molecular biologist
Born in New York City, he studied at Harvard and the California Institute of Technology, then was a postgraduate National Science Foundation Fellow at Oxford. Since 1961 he has been chief of the physical chemistry section of the molecular biology laboratory at the National Institute for Digestive and Kidney Diseases in Washington DC. Felsenfeld's best-known work has been on the association of regulatory protein molecules with chromatin, using DNA footprinting to investigate the precise binding location and the interaction between protein molecules which regulate the activity of the globin genes.

Fénelon, François de Salignac de la Mothe 1651–1715
French Catholic prelate and writer
Born in Fénelon, Périgord, he studied at the Saint-Sulpice Seminary in Paris. He was ordained in 1675, and became director of an institution for women converts to the Catholic faith in 1678. Here he wrote *Traité de l'éducation des filles* (1678, Eng trans *The Education of Young Gentlewomen*, 1699), urging a more liberal education for women, and criticizing the coercion of Huguenot converts. From 1689 to 1699 he was tutor to **Louis XIV**'s grandson, the young Duke of Burgundy, and wrote *Fables* (1690), *Les Dialogues des morts* (1690, 'Dialogues of the Dead'), *History of the Ancient Philosophers* and *Les Aventures de Télémaque* (1699, 'The Adventures of Telemachus'), which displeased the king because of its alleged political satire on the court. As Archbishop of Cambrai from 1695, he wrote a defence (*Explication des maximse des saints sur la vie intérieure*, 'Explanation of the Maxims of the Saints on the Interior Life') of the doctrines of the celebrated quietist mystic Madame **Guyon** (1697, 'Explanation of the Sayings of the Saints on the Interior Life'). After a fierce controversy the pope condemned the book. ⌺ P Janet, *Fénelon, une biographie* (1892)

Feng Guozhang (Feng Kuo-chang) 1859–1919
Chinese militarist
He trained at the Beiyang Military Academy, one of the military schools established during the last decades of the Qing (Ch'ing) Dynasty. On graduating, he entered the service of **Yuan Shikai**, commander of the Beiyang Army, China's first modern army. After the creation of a republic in 1912 he became one of a number of influential militarists known as the 'Beiyang Clique', and served as a provincial military governor before becoming acting President of the Chinese Republic (1917–18). During his one year in office China declared war on Germany.

Feng Youlan (Fung or Feng Yu-lan) 1895–1990
Chinese philosopher
Born in Tanghe County, Henan (Honan) Province, he is best known for his *History of Chinese Philosophy* (2 vols, 1931–33, with a supplement in 1936). He held academic posts in many universities, including Pennsylvania (1946–47). Denounced in 1968 during the Cultural Revolution as a counter-revolutionary, he did not reappear until 1973. He was also a leader in the movement to revive neo-Confucianism.

Feng Yuxiang (Fung or Feng Yü-hsiang), *known as* the Christian General 1882–1948
Chinese warlord
Born in Hsing-chi-chen, Hopeh Province, he rose through the ranks to command an independent force. In 1924 he took Beijing (Peking), and set up a government which included members of the Nationalist Party. He supported the Nationalist government in 1927, but became apprehensive of the growing personal power of **Chiang Kai-shek**, and joined in two successive revolts, both of which failed. He left China in 1947 to visit the USA, and died in a ship fire on his return journey.

Fenley, Molissa 1954–
US dancer and choreographer
Born in Las Vegas, she studied dance at Mills College, California, before moving to New York, where she made her choreographic debut in 1978. Although she created ensemble pieces for her own now-defunct group and other companies, her reputation rests on physically demanding, high-energy solos like *Eureka* (1982), *State of Darkness* (1988) and *Regions* (1995).

Fenning, Frederick William 1919–88
British nuclear physicist
He was educated at Clacton County High School before graduating from Cambridge in 1940, when he joined the team at the Cavendish Laboratory which investigated neutron diffusion problems associated with the possibilities for an atomic bomb. Later in World War II he played a major role in starting up the ZEEP reactor at Chalk River, Canada, and after the war returned to the new research establishment at Harwell where he was closely concerned with the design of early nuclear reactors in Great Britain. As chief physicist and then director of reactor technology at Risley he worked on the Advanced Gas-Cooled Reactor (AGR) which led to the operation of the Windscale (Sellafield) AGR. He returned to Harwell as deputy director in 1966 and from 1979 to 1984 was the deputy director of the Atomic Energy Research Establishment.

Fenton, James 1949–
English poet
He was born in Lincoln. A highly thought of, intellectual poet, who has deliberately set himself apart from the mainstream, Fenton publishes little. He is mainly a political and satirical rather than a 'personal' poet, who makes a virtue out of reticence. He wrote some sharply satirical poems in collaboration with John Fuller in *Partingtime Hall* (1987). His own main collections are *Terminal Moraine* (1972), *The Memory of War* (1982), *Children in Exile* (1984), *Poems 1968–83* (1985) and *Out of Danger* (1993). He has written for *The Independent* since 1993 and has been Professor of Poetry at Oxford since 1994.

Fenton, Roger 1819–69
English photographer
Born in Lancashire, he studied painting in Paris and exhibited at the Royal Academy, London (1849–51). He photographed in Russia in 1852 and was a founder and the first honorary secretary of the Photographic (later Royal) Society in 1853. Queen **Victoria** became its patron, and Fenton photographed the royal family at Balmoral and Windsor. In 1855 he went to the Crimea as the world's first accredited war photographer, using the large cameras and wet plates of the period to record both the men and the campaign conditions. It is for this work that he is best known. He subsequently travelled widely throughout Great Britain, producing fine architectural and landscape studies, but gave up photography in 1862 to become a lawyer.

Ferard, Elizabeth Catherine fl.1858–73
English deaconess

She went to stay at the Lutheran Kaiserwerth community in Germany in 1858. Here, the deaconess order or diaconate, comprising an order of nurses, had been revived by Theodor Fliedner (1800–64) in 1836, the same time as the first Protestant hospital was established. Inspired by the work of the order, she offered to promote it in London, but under the auspices of the Church of England. Ferard and two companions undertook a common rule of life in 1861 in a house near Kings Cross, and she was 'set apart' as a deaconess the following year, by Archibald Campbell Tait, Bishop of London. She resigned as leader in 1873, due to ill health, but by that time the idea had spread to other dioceses and the bishops had drawn up guidelines for deaconesses in the Church at large.

Ferber, Edna 1885–1968
US writer

Born in Kalamazoo, Michigan, she became a journalist in Wisconsin at the age of 17. She was the author of numerous novels and short stories, including *Dawn O'Hara* (1911), *Gigolo* (1922), *So Big* (1924, Pulitzer Prize), *Cimarron* (1929) and *Saratoga Trunk* (1941). Her work gives a lively, though sometimes sentimental, account of 1920s and 1930s US life, and she is probably best remembered as the writer of *Show Boat* (1926), which inspired the musical play of that name. She also wrote plays with George Kaufman, such as *Dinner at Eight* (1932) and *Stage Door* (1936). ⊞ J G Gilbert, *Edna Ferber: a biography* (1978)

Ferdinand, the Catholic, *also known as* Ferdinand V of Castile (from 1474), Ferdinand II of Aragon and Sicily (from 1479), and Ferdinand III of Naples (from 1503) 1452–1516
The first monarch of all Spain

Born at Sos, Aragon, he was the son of John II of Navarre and Aragon, and married (1469) Isabella of Castile, sister of Henry IV of Castile, ruling Castile jointly with her after Henry's death (1474). When his own father died (1479), the crowns of Aragon and Castile were united to form the basis of modern Spain. During their reign Ferdinand and Isabella suppressed local bandits by forming a *santa hermandad* ('holy brotherhood') of militia police, and also introduced the Inquisition (1478). They completed the reconquest of Granada (1482–92) and expelled the Jews from Spain (1492). He and Isabella sponsored the voyage of Columbus to the New World (1492), giving Spain the resources for foreign expansionism. In 1495 he formed a Holy League to help the pope drive the French from Naples, for which he gained the title of 'the Catholic', and Naples became a Spanish possession (1503). When Isabella died (1504), Ferdinand became regent in Castile for their insane daughter, the Infanta Juana. In 1505 he married Germaine de Foix, a niece of Louis XIII of France. He conquered Oran, North Africa (1509), and also Navarre (1512), thus becoming monarch of all Spain from the Pyrenees to Gibraltar. He was succeeded by his grandson, the Holy Roman Emperor Charles V.

Ferdinand I 1503–64
Holy Roman Emperor

Born in Alcalá de Henares, Spain, he was the second son of Philip I, the Handsome (briefly King of Castile), and younger brother (and successor) of Emperor Charles V. In 1521 Charles recognized Ferdinand as ruler of the family's hereditary possessions in Austria and in the same year Ferdinand married Anna, daughter of Ladislas II of Bohemia. He was elected King of Bohemia (1526), but failed to secure Hungary, where John Zapolya (1487–1540) was made king (1527), although an eventual compromise maintained the integrity of the Habsburg possessions in both nations. Left to rule the empire during Charles's frequent absences, Ferdinand was elected King of the Romans (1531) and recognized as the heir to the imperial throne (1551). The main threats to the empire were twofold: the external threat posed by the expansionist policy of the Ottoman Sultan Süleyman, the Magnificent, and the internal threat from the religious divisions between Catholics and Lutherans. Unable to prevent Süleyman's attacks on Hungary, the Imperial forces under Charles V successfully relieved Vienna (1529), but the Austrian lands were again threatened by the Turks (1532, 1541). Philip of Hesse, the political leader of the Lutheran princes, seized Württemberg from Habsburg control (1534), and Ferdinand supported the emperor (1546–47) in his campaign to crush the Protestant Schmalkaldic League. His appraisal of the religious situation was more realistic than his brother's and it was Ferdinand who was principally responsible for the religious compromise at Augsburg (1555) that brought the religious wars to an end. The abdication (1556) of Charles V became effective on his death in 1558, when Ferdinand succeeded as Holy Roman Emperor. An admirer of Erasmus (who dedicated the second edition of *Handbook of the Christian Prince* to Ferdinand), he strove to emulate the Erasmian virtues of compromise and reconciliation.

Ferdinand I 1751–1825
King of the Two Sicilies

He was born in Naples, the third son of Charles III of Spain. When Charles ascended the Spanish throne (1759) he succeeded him as Ferdinand IV of Naples (1759–99, 1799–1806, 1815–16) and as Ferdinand III of Sicily (1759–1816). After his marriage (1768) to Maria Carolina, daughter of Maria Theresa, he fell completely under her influence, and lost his popularity. He joined England and Austria against France (1793), but was forced to make a treaty with Napoleon I (1801). A violation of this treaty compelled him to take refuge in Sicily (1806). The French took possession of Naples, but Ferdinand was reinstated by the Congress of Vienna (1815), and in 1816 united his two states into the Kingdom of the Two Sicilies. Despite the demands for a constitutional government, he maintained a harsh absolutism. He was succeeded by his son, Francis I.

Ferdinand I 1861–1948
Prince and first King of modern Bulgaria

Born in Vienna, Austria, the youngest son of Prince Augustus I of Saxe-Coburg and Princess Clementine of Orléans, he served in the Austrian army. On the abdication of Prince Alexander of Battenberg, he accepted the Crown, as prince (1887). Dominated at first by the premier, Stephan Stambolov, he later took increasing control of the government. After proclaiming Bulgaria independent of the Ottoman Empire (1908), he took the title of king. Territorially ambitious, he joined the Balkan League against Turkey (1912), and, allying himself with the Central Powers, invaded Serbia (1915). His armies routed, he abdicated in 1918, to be succeeded by his son, Boris III (1894–1943). He retired to live in Coburg.

Ferdinand II 1578–1637
King of Bohemia and of Hungary, and Holy Roman Emperor

The grandson of Ferdinand I, he was born in Graz, Austria, and educated at the Jesuit University of Ingolstadt (1590–95). Privately genial and kind-hearted, he was ruthless in enforcing abolutism and religious orthodoxy as King of Bohemia (1617–27) and of Hungary (1618–26), and Holy Roman Emperor from 1619. He instigated the Thirty Years War (1618–48) by compelling his Protestant subjects on his Austrian lands to choose between conversion and exile. Threatened by the election of the Protestant Elector Palatine, Frederick V, as King of Bohemia, and of the Protestant Prince of Transylvania, Bethlen Gabor, as King of Hungary, he assembled a formidable pan-Catholic force. Troops from Spain and

Bavaria overran the Palatinate, while the forces of the Catholic League routed the Bohemian Protestants at the White Mountain, near Prague (1620), and Polish forces under **Sigismund III** forced Gabor to renounce his throne. An alliance of Protestant nations was defeated by the Catholic League and the Imperial army under **Albrecht von Wallenstein**, resulting in the peace of Lübeck (1629). The Protestants found **Gustav II Adolf** of Sweden a more effective leader, while Cardinal **Richelieu** of France provided financial support for the German Protestants. Although the Battle of Lützen (1632) was a Protestant victory, Gustav Adolf was killed and the Swedish army was defeated at Nördlingen (1634). The Edict of Restitution (1629) ordered the restoration within the empire of all Church lands, secularized by the Protestants since 1552, but Ferdinand failed to extirpate Protestantism. The compromise Peace of Prague (1635) was primarily effected by his son, the future **Ferdinand III**.

Ferdinand II 1810–59
King of the Two Sicilies
Born in Palermo, he was the son of Francis I, whom he succeeded in 1830. In 1836, the year his first wife died, he gave himself up to Austrian counsels and his state became one of the most reactionary in Europe. He granted a constitution in 1848, but the Sicilians mistrusted him and declared that he had forfeited the Sicilian Crown. He subdued the revolt in Sicily by bombarding its chief cities, thus earning himself the epithet Bomba. He then set aside the constitution, while all who had taken part in reforms were subjected to those persecutions which were brought to international light by **William Gladstone**. On his death he was succeeded by his son Francis II (1836–94), just before his kingdom was incorporated into the new kingdom of Italy (1860).

Ferdinand III c.1200–52
King of Castile and of Leon
The son of Alfonso IX of Leon, he attacked from 1224 the weakened Almohad caliphate in Andalusia. After capturing Córdoba (1236), he went on to take Jaen (1246), Seville (1248), Cadiz (1249) and the surrounding territories, settling his conquests with Christian inhabitants. By his death he had annexed more Muslim territory than any other Spanish king, and reduced the remaining Muslim states, now confined to Granada, to vassal kingdoms of Castile. He was canonized in 1671, and his feast day is 30 May.

Ferdinand III 1608–57
King of Hungary and of Bohemia, and Holy Roman Emperor
The son of Emperor **Ferdinand II**, he was born in Graz, Austria. Although scholarly, shy and artistic, he ruled with vigour and skill as ruler of Hungary from 1626, of Bohemia from 1627, and Holy Roman Emperor from 1637. He conspired in the overthrow of **Albrecht von Wallenstein** and succeeded him as commander of the Imperial armies. As emperor he continued the struggle against the Protestants but opened negotiations at Münster (1644), and signed the Peace of Westphalia (1648) which ended the Thirty Years War.

Ferdinand III 1769–1824
Grand Duke of Tuscany and Archduke of Austria
Born in Florence, he succeeded his father **Leopold II** (1790). He was the first to recognize the French Republic (1792). Russia and Great Britain constrained him to become a passive member of the coalition against France, but on the French occupation of Piedmont (1795) he resumed friendly relations with France. In 1797 he concluded an unfavourable treaty with **Napoleon I** but was driven into an Austrian alliance. In 1799 he retired to Vienna, and at the Peace of Lunéville (1801) renounced all claim on Tuscany. However, he was reinstated by the

Peace of Paris (1814). At home he continued his father's liberal economic and social reforms, and stood out among Italian princes for his enlightened moderation.

Ferdinand VI 1713–59
King of Spain
He was born in Madrid, the son of **Philip V**, whom he succeeded in 1746. Gloomy and mediocre, he did appoint very capable ministers, and was a patron of art and scholarship. He did his best to keep Spain neutral in European conflicts following the disadvantageous Treaty of Aix-la-Chapelle (1748). He became acutely depressed during the last years of his life.

Ferdinand VII 1784–1833
King of Spain
He was born in Escorial, near Madrid, the eldest son of **Charles IV** and Marie Luisa of Parma, who banished him from Madrid (1807). When **Napoleon I** invaded Spain (1808), Charles abdicated in favour of Ferdinand, but he was replaced by Napoleon's brother **Joseph Bonaparte**. For six years he lived in exile on the estate of the French Foreign Minister, **Talleyrand**, at Valençay, where the treaty was signed with Napoleon (1813) that restored him to the throne. In 1820 a revolution obliged him to recognize Napoleon's liberal Constitution of Cadiz (1812) but repressive absolutism was reinstated three years later and lasted until his death (1833), which signalled the outbreak of the first Carlist war (1833–39). By 1826 all the Spanish possessions in the USA had gained their independence.

Ferdusi See **Firdausi**

Ferguson, Adam 1723–1816
Scottish philosopher and historian
Born in Logierait, Perthshire, he studied at St Andrews University, and served as a Black Watch chaplain before settling in Edinburgh, where he became Professor of Natural Philosophy (1759) and then of Moral Philosophy (1764). He travelled to Philadelphia, America, as secretary to the 1778–79 commission sent by Lord **North** to negotiate with the American colonists. A member of the Scottish 'Common Sense' school of philosophy, together with **Thomas Reid** and **Dugald Stewart**, his works include *The History of the Progress and Termination of the Roman Republic* (1783) and *Principles of Moral and Political Science* (1792). His *Essay on the History of Civil Society* (1767) was a major contribution to political thought. Underlining the necessity and fact of conflict in society, it influenced **Hegel**, **Schiller** and **Karl Marx**. It has been credited with an influence on the Greek revival, with planting the seed of sociology, and with articulating decisively the problem called 'alienation'.

Ferguson, Alex(ander) 1941–
Scottish football manager
Born in Govan, Glasgow, he was a schoolboy international who became one of football's most successful managers. He began his managerial career at East Stirling in 1974, but after three months he left to manage St Mirren, whom he took to the Second Division in his first season with them. As manager of Aberdeen (1978–86), he won the Scottish League Championship three times, the Scottish Cup four times, and the Scottish League Cup once with the European Cup Winners Cup and Super Cup in 1983. With Manchester United he won the FA Cup (1990), the Cup Winners Cup (1991), the League Cup (1992), the League Championship (1993), and the double (the League Championship and the FA Cup) in 1994 and 1996, when they became the first team to have won the double twice.

Ferguson, Harry George 1884–1960
Irish engineer and inventor

Born in Hillsborough, County Down, he started a garage business in Belfast at the age of 16, and while working with his brother on the repair of cars and cycles built his own aeroplane, which made the first flight from Irish soil in 1909. Over many years he developed the famous 'Ferguson farm tractor' with a hydraulic linkage which controlled the depth of ploughing, and made the tractor itself more stable and efficient. These machines played a large part in the mechanization of British agriculture during and after World War II.

Ferguson, James 1710–76
Scottish astronomer

He was born in Keith, Banffshire. The starry sky which he observed on clear winter's nights as a shepherd inspired him to study the movements of the Moon and planets, and to demonstrate these movements by mechanical models. He was eventually able to make a living from writing and lecturing. His books and his 'machines', many of which survive, aroused in the general public a widespread interest in astronomy. According to **Caroline Herschel**, Ferguson's books were among those which influenced **William Herschel** to take up the study of astronomy.

Ferguson, Patrick 1744–80
Scottish soldier and inventor

He was born in Pitfour, Aberdeenshire. He served in the army in Germany and Tobago. In 1776 he invented a breech-loading rifle, firing seven shots a minute, and sighted for ranges of from 100 to 500 yards. With it he armed a corps of loyalists, who helped win the Battle of Brandywine in Pennsylvania, America (1777). He was killed at the Battle of King's Mountain, South Carolina.

Ferguson, Robert, *also called* the Plotter
c.1637–1714
Scottish conspirator

He was born near Alford, Aberdeenshire. In 1662 he was ousted as a Presbyterian from the vicarage of Godmersham in Kent. For 10 years he played a leading part in every treasonable scheme against the last two Stuart kings, and twice had to leave the country. However after the Revolution of 1688 (of which he published a history in 1706), he conspired as busily for the Jacobite cause. He was arrested for treason in 1704, but not tried.

Ferguson, Sir Samuel 1810–86
Irish poet and Celtic scholar

Born in Belfast, he was called to the Irish Bar in 1838, and in 1867 he was appointed the first deputy keeper of Irish Records. As president of the Royal Irish Academy he gave a powerful impetus to the study of early Irish art. His spirited poems were published as *Lays of the Western Gael* (1865), *Congal* (1872), *Poems* (1880) and *The Forging of the Anchor* (1883). His edition of the *Leabhar Breac* appeared in 1876, and his *Ogham Inscriptions* in 1887. ⌨ A Dearing, *Sir Samuel Ferguson, Poet and Antiquarian* (1931)

Ferguson, Sarah See **York, Duchess of**

Fergusson, Bernard Edward, Baron Ballantrae 1911–80
Scottish soldier and military historian

Born in London, of Scottish parentage, he was commissioned into the Black Watch in 1931, an experience which caused him to write *The Black Watch and the King's Enemies* (1950). During World War II he served with the Chindit forces in Burma, whose successes were a great boost to British morale in the war against Japan. After the war Fergusson became assistant Inspector-General of the Palestine Police and took part in anti-terrorist operations during the last days of the British mandate and the civil war between Arabs and Zionists. He was promoted to brigadier in 1956 and became Governor-General of New

Zealand (1962–67) and chairman of the British Council (1972–76). He wrote about his wartime experiences in *Beyond the Chindwin* (1945) and *The Trumpet in the Hall* (1970). He was granted a life peerage in 1972.

Fergusson, John Duncan 1874–1961
Scottish painter

Born in Perthshire, he took up painting after a medical training. Along with **Samuel John Peploe** and **Francis Cadell**, he emphasized colour rather than line. Trips to North Africa, Spain (1897) and Paris (which he made his home before and after World War I) brought him into contact with Mediterranean light and landscape, and with the painting of the Post-Impressionists and Fauves. He is best known for his series of World War I paintings of naval dockyards and his portraits of the female nude.

Fergusson, Robert 1750–74
Scottish poet

Born in Edinburgh, he was educated at the high schools of Edinburgh and of Dundee, and at St Andrews University. He was employed in the commissary office in Edinburgh, contributing poems to *Weekly Magazine* from 1771, which gained him local fame. A religious interest, inspired by the minister John Brown (1722–81), was followed by deep depression, and he became insane after a fall downstairs, and died in a public asylum. He was a major influence on **Robert Burns**, who placed a headstone on his grave in 1789. He left 33 poems in Scots, and 50 poems in English. Essentially an Edinburgh poet, he is most famous for *Auld Reekie* (1773), tracing a day in the life of the city. Other well-known poems are *Elegy on the Death of Scots Music*, *The Daft Days* (his first published poem), *Hallow Fair*, *To the Tron Kirk Bell*, *Leith Races* and the satirical *The Rising of the Session*. ⌨ A Law, *Robert Fergusson and the Edinburgh of his Time* (1974)

Ferishtah or Firishtah c.1550–c.1615
Persian historian

Born in Astrabad, he went as a child to India, became captain in the bodyguard of the prince of Ahmednagar, and on his deposition went to Bijapur (1589). He wrote a great history of the Muhammadan power in India (1609, Eng trans 1831–32).

Ferlinghetti, Lawrence 1919–
US poet and publisher

Born in Yonkers, New York, he studied at the University of North Carolina, Columbia University, and the Sorbonne, and served in the US Naval Reserve (1941–45). After working for *Time* magazine in New York, he moved to San Francisco in 1951, where he contributed to the so-called 'San Francisco Renaissance'. He was co-founder of the City Lights Bookstore, which acted as a cultural forum and publishing house for radical poets. His work made a major contribution to Beat poetry and beyond, beginning with *Pictures of the Gone World* (1955) and *A Coney Island of the Mind* (1958). He has published over 40 books of poetry, including *Endless Life: The Selected Poems* (1981) and *When I Look at Pictures* (1990), two novels, and a number of plays. ⌨ N Cherkassky, *Ferlinghetti: A Biography* (1979)

Fermat, Pierre de 1601–65
French mathematician

Born in Beaumont, he studied law at Toulouse University, where he became a councillor of parliament. His passion was mathematics, most of his work being communicated in letters to friends containing results without proof. His correspondence with **Blaise Pascal** marks the foundation of probability theory. He studied maximum and minimum values of functions in advance of the differential calculus, but is best known for his work in number theory, the proofs of many of his discoveries being first published by **Leonhard Euler** a hundred years later. His 'last theorem' is the most famous unsolved problem in mathematics, stating that there are no integers positive x, y, and z with $x^n + y^n = z^n$ if n is greater than 2. In optics Fermat's principle was the first statement of a variational principle in physics, saying that the path taken by a ray of light between two given points is the one in which the light takes the least time. 📖 Michael S Mahoney, *The Mathematical Career of Pierre de Fermat 1601–1665* (1973)

Fermi, Enrico 1901–54
US nuclear physicist and Nobel Prize winner

Born in Rome, Italy, he studied at Pisa University, at Göttingen University under **Max Born**, and at the University of Leyden. He became Professor of Theoretical Physics at Rome University in 1927. Between 1927 and 1933 he expanded upon the work of **Wolfgang Pauli**, published his semiquantitative method of calculating atomic particles, and in 1934 he and his colleagues split the nuclei of uranium atoms by bombarding them with neutrons, thus producing artificial radioactive substances. This led to the discovery that slow neutrons are much more efficient than high-energy neutrons in initiating nuclear reactions, which proved an important step in the development of nuclear power and weapons. He was awarded the 1938 Nobel Prize for physics. Fearing for the safety of his Jewish wife in the light of Italy's anti-Semitic legislation, he went straight from the prize presentation in Stockholm to the USA, where he became professor at Columbia University (1939). He played a prominent part in interesting the US Government in atomic energy, constructed the first US nuclear reactor at Chicago (1942), and produced the first controlled chain reaction. The element fermium is named after him. 📖 Emilio Segrè, *Enrico Fermi: Physicist* (1970)

Fermor, Patrick Michael Leigh 1915–
English travel writer

He was of English and Irish descent. Expelled from King's School, Canterbury, he set out in 1933 on a leisurely walk from Rotterdam to Constantinople (Istanbul). *A Time of Gifts* (1977) recounted the journey as far as Hungary, and *Between the Woods and the Water* (1986) the remainder. Both have been praised for their incisive grasp of the mood of pre-war Europe, and few doubted the veracity of his account despite its being more than 40 years in gestation. He spent World War II in Albania, Greece and Crete where, disguised as a shepherd, he lived for two years organizing the Resistance and the capture and evacuation of the German commander, General Kreipe. Among his other books are *The Traveller's Tree*, about the West Indies, which won the Heinemann Foundation prize in 1950, *Mani* (1958, Duff Cooper Memorial prize) and *Three Letters from the Andes* (1991), vivid accounts of a journey in the early 1970s. 📖 *A Time to Keep Silent* (1953)

Fernandel, *pseudonym of* Fernand Joseph Désiré Contandin 1903–71
French film comedian

Born in Marseilles, he worked in a bank and soap factory before his stage debut in 1922. From 1930 he appeared in over 100 films, interrupted only by military service and Nazi occupation. He established himself internationally with his moving portrayal of the naive country priest in *The Little World of Don Camillo* (1953), and with his versatile handling of six separate roles in *The Sheep has Five Legs* (1953), which gave full rein to his memorable facial mobility.

Fernández, Juan c.1536–c.1604
Spanish navigator

In 1563 he discovered the Pacific islands named after him. He also discovered San Felix and San Ambrosio Islands.

Fernández de Lizardi, José Joaquín 1776–1827
Mexican writer

Born in Mexico City, he became a radical journalist and a leading figure in the national liberation movement. He was known as 'El Pensador Mexicano' ('the Mexican Thinker') after a journal he founded and edited, and when his anticlerical and anti-absolutist articles and poems were censored by the government, he turned to fiction. His picaresque satire *El periquillo sarniento* (1816, 'The Itching Parrot'), considered the first Latin American novel, is a tale of adventure in the Spanish tradition mined with Lizardi's explosive assessments of colonial society in Mexico. 📖 J R Spell, *The Life and Works of José Fernández de Lizardi* (1931)

Fernandez de Quiros, Pedro See Quiros, Pedro Fernandez de

Fernel, Jean François 1497–1558
French physician

Born in Montdidier, he turned to medicine only after several years studying philosophy, mathematics and astrology. He soon became a popular medical teacher and his reputation as a physician soared when he saved the life of the Dauphin's (later **Henri II**) mistress. Despite his essential adherence to **Galenism**, he was an astute observer whose many writings synthesized 16th-century medical orthodoxy and rejected magic and astrology. He coined the Latin words which became 'physiology' and 'pathology'. His magnum opus, the *Universa medicina* (1567), was edited by a disciple after his death.

Ferrabosco, Alfonso 1543–88
Italian composer

Born in Bologna, the son of **Domenico Maria Ferrabosco**, he went to England before 1562, and was for some time in the service of **Elizabeth I**. Leaving England in 1578, he entered the service of the Duke of Savoy. His musical works include madrigals, motets, and compositions for viols.

Ferrabosco, Alfonso c.1575–1628
English composer

Born in Greenwich, London, the son of **Alfonso Ferrabosco**, he was in the service of **James VI and I** and **Charles I**. He wrote music for masques, songs and, most notably, for viol consorts, showing his impressive grasp of counterpoint and invention. His sons Alfonso (c.1610–c.1660), Henry (c.1615–c.1658) and John (1626–82) all held court appointments.

Ferrabosco, Domenico Maria 1513–74
Italian composer

Born in Bologna, he composed madrigals and motets. He was also a singer and became maestro di cappella of San Petronio in Bologna. He was the father of **Alfonso Ferrabosco**.

Ferranti, Sebastian Ziani de 1864–1930
English electrical engineer and inventor

Born in Liverpool, of Italian extraction, he was educated in a Roman Catholic college at Ramsgate and at evening classes at University College London. From his early experiments with dynamos and alternators he conceived the idea of the large-scale generation and distribution of electricity at high voltages, and in 1887 he was appointed chief electrician to the London Electric Supply Corporation which planned to provide power to the whole of London north of the Thames from a power station at Deptford. This scheme was temporarily frustrated by the Electricity Lighting Act of 1888, but it nevertheless contained all the elements of the national electricity grid system which came into being some 40 years later. From 1882 to 1927 he took out 176 patents, and founded the firm of Ferranti Ltd in 1905. 🕮 J F Wilson, *Ferranti and the British Electrical Industry, 1864–1930* (1988)

Ferrar, Nicholas 1592–1637
English theologian and mystic
He was born in London. An Anglican deacon, he founded a Utopian religious community (1625) at Little Gidding in Huntingdonshire (Cambridgeshire). The 30 adherents held constant services and occupied themselves with fine bookbinding. They printed and published the first edition of **George Herbert's** *The Temple* (1633). The community was not broken up by the Puritans until 1647.

Ferrara, Andrea fl.16th century
Italian broadsword maker
Born probably in Ferrara, he was famous, with his brother, as an armourer in Belluno in 1585. It is said that he tempered sword blades by the method employed by the smiths of Damascus.

Ferrari, Paolo 1822–89
Italian dramatist
Born in Modena, he wrote many excellent comedies, including *Goldoni* (1852) and *Parini e la satira* (1857, 'Parini and the Lampoon'). He became Professor of History at Modena (1860), and afterwards at Milan. 🕮 N de Belli, *Il Teatro di Paolo Ferrari* (1922)

Ferraro, Geraldine Anne 1935–
US Democrat politician
Born in Newburgh, New York, the daughter of Italian immigrants, she was educated at Marymount College, Fordham University and New York Law School and, after marrying wealthy businessman John Zaccaro in 1960, established a successful law practice (1961–74). She served as assistant district attorney for the Queens district of New York between 1974 and 1978 and worked at the Supreme Court from 1978, heading a special bureau for victims of violent crime, before being elected to the House of Representatives in 1981. In Congress, she gained a reputation as an effective, liberal-minded politician and was selected in 1984 by **Walter F Mondale** to be the first female vice-presidential candidate of a major party, in an effort to add sparkle to the Democrat 'ticket'. After the Democrats' convincing defeat she returned to law practice and in 1992 unsuccessfully sought the New York Democratic nomination for US senator. In 1994 and 1995 she served as US representative on the UN Human Rights Commission. Her publications include *My Story* (1985) and *Changing History: Women, Power and Politics* (1993).

Ferreira, Antonio, *known as* The Portuguese Horace 1528–69
Portuguese poet
Born in Lisbon, he studied law at Coimbra, and became a judge in Lisbon, where he spent his life. Having little time for the popular Iberian subjects of commerce and war, he turned to classical models for his inspiration, and introduced a classical style into Portuguese verse and drama, earning the title 'The Portuguese **Horace**'. His best-known work is the two-act historical tragedy on classical lines, *Inês de Castro* (1587). 🕮 A Roig, *Antonio Ferreira, études sur sa vie et son œuvre* (1970)

Ferrel, William 1817–91
US mathematician
Born in Bedford County, Pennsylvania, he attended Marshall College, Pennsylvania, and Bethany College, West Virginia. He taught in Missouri and Kentucky before obtaining a scientific post at the American Nautical Almanac in 1858. In 1867 he joined the US Coast Survey and in 1882 became professor in the US army's signal service. He was elected a member of the US National

Academy of Sciences in 1868. He gave the first mathematical formulation of atmospheric motions on a rotating Earth and applied his theory to the general circulation of both the atmosphere and the oceans (1859–60). He produced models of three-dimensional motion in a cyclone and also indicated that the general circulation in each hemisphere could be considered on similar lines. He derived the concept of the thermal wind which gives the relationship between horizontal temperature gradient and the change of wind with height. He also dealt with tidal theory, and in 1880 he derived a mechanical tide predictor.

Ferrier, James Frederick 1808–64
Scottish philosopher
Born in Edinburgh, he became Professor of History at Edinburgh (1842) and Professor of Moral Philosophy at St Andrews (1845). His book *The Institutes of Metaphysic* (1854) was the first important work of the British Idealist (neo-**Hegelian**) movement. He introduced the term 'epistemology' into English and propounded also an 'agnoiology', or theory of ignorance.

Ferrier, Kathleen 1912–53
English contralto
Born in Higher Walton, Lancashire, she was an accomplished amateur pianist. After winning a prize for singing at a local music festival, she was encouraged to study seriously (1940). The range and richness of her voice, together with her technical control, rapidly won her great respect. In 1946 she sang Lucrezia in **Benjamin Britten's** *The Rape of Lucrezia*, and Orpheus in **Gluck's** *Orfeo* at Glyndebourne, and thereafter was in great demand throughout Europe and the USA. Her greatest success, perhaps, was in **Mahler's** *Das Lied von der Erde* ('The Song of the Earth'), at the first Edinburgh Festival (1947) and at Salzburg (1949). 🕮 Winifred Ferrier, *Kathleen Ferrier* (1955)

Ferrier, Susan Edmonstone 1782–1854
Scottish novelist
She was born in Edinburgh, the tenth child of a lawyer who became principal clerk to the Court of Session with Sir **Walter Scott**. On the death of her mother in 1797 she took over the running of the house, and she looked after her father until his death in 1829. Her first work, *Marriage* (1818), a novel of provincial social manners, was followed by *The Inheritance* (1824) and *Destiny* (1831), a Highland romance. She enjoyed a close friendship with Scott, who was for a time credited by some with the authorship of her books. Following the publication of these works she was converted to evangelical Christianity, and became a member of the Free Church, concentrating on charitable works rather than on writing. Towards the end of her life she lived in relative seclusion, her eyesight failing badly. 🕮 A Grant, *Susan Ferrier of Edinburgh* (1957)

Ferry, Jules François Camille 1832–93
French statesman
Born at Saint Dié in the Vosges, he studied law and was admitted to the Paris Bar (1854), but became well known as a critic, supporting the opponents of the empire. He was elected (1869) to the Corps Législatif, where he voted against the war with Prussia, and during the Siege of Paris (1870–71) he was Mayor of the city. As Minister of Public Instruction (1879) he brought forward a bill excluding Jesuits from the schools. It was rejected, but the expulsion of the Jesuits was effected by decrees founded on obsolete laws, which brought about the dissolution of the Ministry in 1880. Ferry then formed a cabinet, which lasted until later the following year. His last ministry (1883–85) fell through his policy of 'colonial expansion', involving war in Madagascar and Indo-China.

Fersen, Frederik Axel, Count von 1719–94
Swedish field marshal and politician

He was born in Stockholm. A descendant of the Scottish Macphersons, he served successively in the French and Swedish armies, and was made a field marshal in 1770. He became leader of the anti-Royalist opposition and was ultimately assassinated in Stockholm.

Fersen, Hans Axel von 1755–1810
Swedish soldier and politician

The son of Count **Frederik Axel von Fersen**, he fought as a volunteer with the French army in America during the Revolution (1775–83). On his return, he served at the French court, where he became closely attached to Queen **Marie Antoinette**. In 1791, disguised as a coachman, he drove the royal family on their flight to Varennes. He returned to Sweden (1799) and in 1801 was appointed Earl Marshal. He rode in the funeral procession of Christian August of Augustenburg, the recently-elected heir to the Swedish throne, and was murdered by a mob who suspected him of having poisoned the prince.

Fessenden, Reginald Aubrey 1866–1932
US radio engineer and inventor

Born in East Bolton, Quebec, and educated in Canada, he moved first to Bermuda, where he developed an interest in science while acting as Principal of the Whitney Institute, and then to New York (1886) where he met **Thomas Edison** and became the chief chemist in his research laboratories in New Jersey. By 1892 he had returned to academic life, first at Purdue University and then as Professor of Electrical Engineering at the University of Pittsburgh (1893–1900). Of his many patents (over 500), the one of most fundamental importance was his invention of amplitude modulation. On Christmas Eve, 1906, he used this to broadcast what was probably the first US radio programme from the transmitter he had built at Brant Rock, Massachusetts. Another of his discoveries was the heterodyne effect, which soon developed into the superheterodyne circuit that rapidly became an integral part of the design of radio receivers. Among his other patents were the sonic depth finder, the loop-antenna radio compass and submarine signalling devices.

Fessenden, William Pitt 1806–69
US politician

Born in Boscawen, New Hampshire, he was admitted to the Maine Bar in 1827, and rose in the Whig Party. His antislavery sympathies won him his election to the US Senate as a Republican in 1854, his maiden speech being an attack on the Kansas-Nebraska bill which sought to make slavery optional for those territories. **Abraham Lincoln** made him Secretary of the Treasury in 1864 and he returned to the Senate in 1865. Lincoln's successor, **Andrew Johnson**, a Democrat, convinced Fessenden that the Republican Party was being endangered by a judicious presidential amnesty to former Confederates who would then swamp the House of Representatives and perhaps imperil the Union war debt or legalize the Confederate debt. Thus Fessenden, as Chairman of the Joint House and Senate Committee of Fifteen, framed in the Fourteenth Amendment to the US Constitution (adopted 1868) a measure which would specifically avert either, and protect the rights of emancipated slaves. Historians now realize that it was largely Fessenden, and not more radical figures, who set the tone.

Festinger, Leon 1919–89
US psychologist

Born in New York City, he was educated at the State University of Iowa. Between 1943 and 1955 he taught successively at Rochester University, the Massachusetts Institute of Technology (MIT), and Michigan and Minnesota universities. He then moved to Stanford University (1955–68) and later to the New School for Social Research in New York (from 1968). His contribution to postwar social psychology has centred on the introduction and development of the deceptively simple concept of 'cognitive dissonance'. According to the theory, people are unable to tolerate conflicting cognitions (beliefs, thoughts, perceptions) for any length of time, and have to resolve such internal conflicts by rejecting or devaluing one or more of the cognitions. The theory has proved useful in the understanding of a variety of psychological phenomena, and led to certain counter-intuitive predictions that were successfully borne out experimentally. He received the Distinguished Scientist award of the American Psychological Association in 1959.

Fétis, François Joseph 1784–1871
Belgian writer on music

He was born in Mons in the Austrian Netherlands (now Belgium). He was professor at the Paris Conservatoire (1821) and director of the Brussels Conservatory (1833). He produced a *Universal Biography of Musicians* (1835–44) and *General History of Music* (1868–76).

Fettes, Sir William 1750–1836
Scottish merchant and philanthropist

He made a fortune from tea and wine, was twice Lord Provost of Edinburgh and left £166,000 to found Fettes College there (1870), designed by **David Bryce**.

Feuchtwanger, Lion 1884–1958
German writer

Born in Munich, he studied literature and philology there and at Berlin universities. He won a reputation in Europe with the 18th-century historical novel *Jud Süss* (1925, Eng trans *Jew Süss*, 1926), presenting an elaborately detailed picture of the lives, sufferings and weaknesses of central European Jewry. The 14th-century tale *Die hässliche Herzogin* (1923), translated as *The Ugly Duchess* (1927) was a great success in Great Britain. During World War I he was interned in Tunis. His thinly disguised satire on Hitler's Munich putsch, *Erfolg* (1930, 'Success'), earned him the hatred of the Nazis. In 1933 he fled to France, where in 1940 he was interned by the German army, but escaped to the USA. He also wrote numerous dramas, and collaborated with **Brecht** in a translation of **Christopher Marlowe**'s *Edward II*. His later works included detailed part-biographies of **Goya** (1952) and **Jean Jacques Rousseau** (1954). 📖 L Boettche and P G Krohn, *Lion Feuchtwanger* (1960)

Feuerbach, Ludwig Andreas 1804–72
German philosopher

Born in Landshut, Bavaria, the son of the jurist Paul Feuerbach (1775–1833), he was a pupil of **Hegel** at Berlin but reacted against his Idealism. His best-known work, *Das Wesen des Christentums* (1841), which was translated by Mary Ann Evans (**George Eliot**) as *The Essence of Christianity* (1854), claims that religion rises from one's alienation from oneself, and is 'the dream of the human mind', projecting ideal qualities onto a fictitious supreme 'other'. His ideas strongly influenced **Karl Marx** and **Friedrich Engels**. 📖 C A Wilson, *Feuerbach and the Search for Otherness* (1989)

Féval, Paul Henri Corentin 1817–87
French novelist

He was born in Rennes. His many novels include *Les Mystères de Londres* (1844, 'The Mysteries of London') and *Le Bossu* (1858, 'The Hunchback'). A number of them were dramatized with great success. 📖 A Delaigue, *Un homme de lettres* (1898)

Feydeau, Ernest Aimé 1821–73
French novelist

He was a stockbroker and an archaeologist, and achieved notorious success with his novel *Fanny* (1858). His writing depicts the worst features of society in the time of the Empire. *Sylvie* (1861) is particularly powerful.

Feydeau, Georges Léon Jules Marie 1862–1921
French dramatist

Born in Paris, the son of **Ernest Aimé Feydeau** and a prostitute, he wrote his first play, *Le Tailleur pour dames* (1886, Eng trans *A Gown for his Mistress*, 1969), when he was 24 and subsequently maintained a prolific output. His name is synonymous with French bedroom farce. His characters are Parisian bourgeois couples seeking diversion from each other, and his farces rely on the twin themes of adultery and the chase. Among his plays are such enduring classics as *Le Dindon* (1896, Eng trans *Paying the Piper*, 1972), *L'Hôtel du libre échange* (1899, Eng trans *Hotel Paradiso*, 1957) and *Une Puce à l'oreille* (1907), produced as *A Flea in Her Ear* (trans by **John Mortimer**) at the National Theatre, London, in 1965. A Shenkan, *Georges Feydeau* (1972)

Feynman, Richard Phillips 1918–88
US physicist and Nobel Prize winner

Born in New York City, he studied at the Massachusetts Institute of Technology (MIT) and Princeton, where he received his PhD. Overcoming moral doubts, he worked on the Manhattan atomic bomb project at Los Alamos and after World War II he was appointed professor at Cornell University. There he worked with **Hans Bethe** on quantum electrodynamics, the application of quantum theory to interactions between electromagnetic radiation and particles. He devised his own pictorial way of describing quantum processes, the 'path integral approach', which has proved to be a very powerful theoretical tool. Using this he further developed quantum electrodynamics and introduced 'Feynman diagrams', which provide a pictorial representation of particle interactions. For his work on quantum electrodynamics he was awarded the Nobel Prize for physics in 1965 together with **Julian Schwinger** and **Sin-Itiro Tomonaga**. The most successful and accurate physical theory ever developed, quantum electrodynamics is the model on which other quantum field theories are based. Working with **Murray Gell-Mann**, he at the California Institute of Technology (Caltech), he created the V–A model of weak interactions which can describe parity conservation violation. He also studied how deep inelastic scattering can reveal the structure of protons and investigated the properties of liquid helium. A James Gleick, *Genius: The Life and Science of Richard Feynman* (1992)

Fiacre or Fiachrach, St d.670
Irish hermit

He founded a monastery in France, on the site of the village of Saint-Fiacre-en-Brie, near Paris. In 1640 Nicholas Sauvage, a hirer of hackney carriages, lived at the Hôtel St Fiacre in the Rue St Martin, Paris; hence the name 'fiacre'. He is the patron saint of cab drivers and gardeners, and his feast day is 30 August.

Fiammingo, Dionisio See Calvaert, Denys

Fibich, Zdeněk (Antonin Václav) 1850–1900
Czech composer

Born in Seboric, he wrote operas, symphonies, and works for solo piano and was kapellmeister in Prague from 1878. One of his melodies, *Poème*, from the symphonic poem *V podvečer* (1893, 'At Twilight'), has remained popular.

Fibiger, Johannes Andreas Grib 1867–1928
Danish pathologist and Nobel Prize winner

Born in Silkeborg, he studied in Berlin under **Robert Koch** and **Emil von Behring**, and became professor and head of the Institute of Pathological Anatomy at Copenhagen in 1900. The first to induce cancer experimentally, feeding rats with cockroaches carrying the parasite *spiroptera neoplastica*, he won the Nobel Prize for physiology or medicine in 1926.

Fibonacci, Leonardo, *also called* Leonardo of Pisa c.1170–c.1250
Italian mathematician

He popularized the modern Arabic system of numerals, which originated in India. His main work *Liber abaci* (1202, 'The Book of Calculation') illustrated the virtues of the new numeric system, showing how it can be used to simplify highly complex calculations. The book also includes work on geometry, the theory of proportion and techniques for determining the roots of equations. His greatest work, the *Liber quadratorum* (1225, 'The Book of Square Numbers') contains remarkably advanced contributions to number theory and is dedicated to his patron, Holy Roman Emperor **Frederick II**, of Germany. He discovered the 'Fibonacci sequence' of integers in which each number is equal to the sum of the preceding two (1,1,2,3,5,8,...). He was the first outstanding mathematician of the Middle Ages. A Joseph and Frances Gies, *Leonardo of Pisa and the New Mathematics of the Middle Ages* (1969)

Fichte, Johann Gottlieb 1762–1814
German philosopher

Born in Rammenau, Saxony, he studied at the University of Jena, made a precarious living for some years as an itinerant tutor in philosophy, in the course of which he met **Kant** at Königsberg and became a devoted disciple. He was appointed Professor of Philosophy at Jena in 1794. His *Wissenschaftslehre* (1785, 'The Science of Knowledge') modified Kant's doctrine of the 'thing-in-itself' as the absolute reality, substituting the 'Ego', a more subjective reality, affirming itself in the act of consciousness and constructing the external world (the 'non-Ego') as its field of action. *Grundlage des Naturrechts* (1796, Eng trans *The Science of Rights*, 1869, 1889) and *System der Sittenlehre* (1798, Eng trans *The Science of Ethics*, 1897) elaborate his system of thought. He went on to teach at Berlin (1799), after an accusation of atheism, and became Professor of Philosophy at Erlangen (1805), where he published *Grundzüge des gegenwärtigen Zeitalters* (1806, Eng trans *The Characteristics of the Present Age*, 1844) and *Anweisung zum seligen Leben und Religionslehre* (1806, Eng trans *The Way Towards the Blessed Life*, 1844). He delivered a famous series of patriotic lectures, *Reden an die Deutsche Nation* (1807–08, 'Addresses to the German Nation'), in which he tried to foster German nationalism in resistance to **Napoleon I**. In this context Fichte's metaphysical 'Ego' became the German nation, an idea that was later perverted into the Nazi concept of the *Herrenvolk*. In 1810 he became the first Rector of the new University of Berlin, whose constitution he had drawn up. His son Immanuel Hermann von Fichte (1797–1879) also became a Professor of Philosophy (at Bonn, then Tübingen) and was ennobled in 1867. A Robert Adamson, *Fichte* (1881)

Ficino, Marsilio 1433–99
Italian philosopher

He was born in Figline, Florence. **Cosimo de' Medici** appointed him head of the Platonic Academy in Florence, and commissioned from him translations (into Latin) from and commentaries on **Plato**, **Plotinus** and the *Corpus Hermeticum*. He was ordained a priest in 1473, and became rector of two churches and canon of the cathedral in Florence. He retired to the country when the Medici were expelled from Florence in 1494. He was a major influence in the Renaissance revival of Platonism and his own rather eclectic system was largely an attempt to reconcile Platonism with Christianity.

Fick, Adolph Eugen 1829–1901
German physiologist

Professor at the universities of Zurich and Würzburg, a law of diffusion in liquids was named after him when he discovered that the mass of solute diffusing through unit area per second is proportional to the concentration gradient.

Fick, August 1833–1916
German philologist

Born in Petershagen, he was a professor at Göttingen (1876) and Breslau (1887), and pioneered the comparative study of Indo-European vocabulary with his Indo-Germanic dictionary (1870). He also wrote works on Greek personal names, and the original language of the *Iliad*.

Fiedler, Arthur 1894–1979
US conductor

Born in Boston, he studied music in Berlin and joined the Boston Symphony Orchestra as a violinist. In 1930 he founded the Boston Pops Orchestra, which gave free outdoor concerts that blended both classical and popular music. He served as its director for nearly 50 years until his death.

Field, Cyrus West 1819–92
US merchant

Born in Stockbridge, Massachusetts, the younger brother of **David Dudley Field** and **Stephen Johnson Field**, he made a small fortune in the paper business, then conceived the idea of a transatlantic telegraph cable. He organized companies in England and the USA, and after repeated attempts, he had a brief success (1858). During the three weeks before the cable failed, Queen **Victoria** used it to send a message to President **James Buchanan**. Field laid a new transatlantic cable in 1866, and later promoted other oceanic cables.

Field, David Dudley 1805–94
US jurist

Born in Haddam, Connecticut, he was educated at Williams College, Williamstown, Massachusetts. He was admitted to the New York Bar in 1828, and worked to reform the judiciary system. An advocate of codification, he was appointed by the state in 1857 to prepare penal, political and civil codes, of which the first was adopted by New York, and all by other states. He made great contributions to international law and to law reform, and his *Outlines of an International Code* (1872) was translated into several languages. He was the brother of **Cyrus West Field** and **Stephen Johnson Field**.

Field, Eugene 1850–95
US writer

Born in St Louis, Missouri, he became a journalist at the age of 23, and from 1883 was a columnist with the *Chicago Morning News*, achieving a reputation as humorist and poet with his column 'Sharps and Flats'. He wrote the well-known nursery lullaby 'Wynken, Blynken, and Nod' and the sentimental 'Little Boy Blue', and published several books of children's verse. 📖 S Thompson, *The Life of Eugene Field* (1927)

Field, John 1782–1837
Irish pianist and composer

Born in Dublin, he was an infant prodigy, and was the apprentice of **Muzio Clementi**, who used him to demonstrate the capabilities of his pianos. He accompanied Clementi in 1802 to Paris, Vienna and St Petersburg, where he settled in 1804 as a music teacher, returning to London in 1832. His 19 nocturnes and other keyboard music influenced **Chopin**.

Field, Marshall 1834–1906
US merchant

Born in Conway, Massachusetts, he worked as a clerk before moving to Chicago (1856), where he became founder of the Chicago department store known from 1881 as Marshall Field and Company, one of the world's largest and most progressive emporiums.

Field, Nathan 1587–c.1620
English actor and dramatist

He was born in London and educated there at St Paul's School. In 1600 he became one of the children of the Queen's Chapel, and subsequently one of the comedians of the Queen's Revels (1604–13) and various other troupes. As a playwright he collaborated with **Francis Beaumont** and **John Fletcher**, and with **Philip Massinger** in the latter's *The Fatal Dowry* (1632). He also wrote two comedies, *A Woman is a Weathercocke* (1612) and *Amends for Ladies* (1618). 📖 R F Brinkley, *Nathaniel Field, actor-playwright* (1928)

Field, Sally 1946–
US film actress

Born in Pasadena, California, she studied at the Actors Studio in California and gained popularity as the star of lightweight television series like *Gidget* (1965) and *The Flying Nun* (1966–70). She later proved her credentials as a dramatic actress, winning an Emmy for the mini-series *Sybill* (1976) and Academy Awards for *Norma Rae* (1979) and *Places in the Heart* (1984). Her notable films include *Absence of Malice* (1981), *Steel Magnolias* (1989), *Mrs Doubtfire* (1993) and *Forrest Gump* (1994).

Field, Stephen Johnson 1816–99
US judge

Born in Haddam, Connecticut, he practised law in New York City before moving to California in 1849. He helped to draw up the California state codes and became Chief Justice there in 1859, serving as a judge of the US Supreme Court from 1863 to 1897. He was the brother of **Cyrus West Field** and **David Dudley Field**.

Fielding, Henry 1707–54
English novelist

Born at Sharpham Park, near Glastonbury, Somerset, he was educated at Eton. He went to London and in 1728 published a satirical poem, *The Masquerade*, and a comedy, *Love in Several Masques*. Thereafter he studied at the University of Leyden (1728–29), before returning to London, and in the space of eight years he wrote 25 dramatic pieces: light comedies, adaptations of **Molière**, farces, ballad operas, burlesques (including *Tom Thumb*), and a series of satires attacking Sir **Robert Walpole** and his government. This last prompted the introduction of the Theatrical Licensing Act of 1737 and effectively ended his career as a playwright and theatre manager (he had formed his own company, and was running the Little Theatre, Haymarket). He turned to the law, was admitted as a student at the Middle Temple, and was called to the Bar in 1740, but was hampered by his disabling gout. As a student he turned to journalism and edited *The Champion* (1739–41). Incensed by the publication of **Samuel Richardson**'s prudish *Pamela*, he ridiculed it in a pseudonymous parody, *An Apology for the Life of Mrs Shamela Andrews* (1741). In 1742 came *The Adventures of Joseph Andrews and his Friend, Mr Abraham Adams*. The three volumes of *Miscellanies* (including *The Life of Jonathan Wild the Great*) followed in 1743. In the interim he caused a scandal by marrying Mary Daniel, the maid of his first wife, Mary Craddock (d.1744). He was made a justice of the peace for Westminster and Middlesex in 1748, and campaigned vigorously against legal corruption, helping his half-brother, Sir John Fielding (1721–80) to found the Bow Street Runners as an embryo detective force. In 1749 *The*

History of Tom Jones, a Foundling was published to public acclaim, though its reception by some literary luminaries was unenthusiastic. Dr Johnson called it vicious and there were those who held it responsible for two earth tremors that shook London shortly after its publication. However, it has endured as one of the great comic and picaresque novels in the English language, and Coleridge thought the plot one of the three most perfect ever planned. He followed it with *Amelia* in 1751. In 1752 he was heavily involved with *The Covent Garden Journal*, which contains some of his most acerbic satire. During his last years, however, illness overtook him. He was still ardent in his fight against corruption but at the age of 45 he could not move without the help of crutches. 📖 I P Watt, *The Rise of the Novel* (1957); F H Dudden, *Henry Fielding* (2 vols, 1952)

Fields, Dorothy 1904–74
US lyricist

Born in Allenhurst, New Jersey, the daughter of the comedian Lew Fields (1867–1941), she is best known for her successful partnership with Jimmy McHugh (1894–1969), with whom she wrote 'I Can't Give You Anything But Love, Baby' for the Cotton Club revue *Blackbirds of 1928*. Their *International Revue* (1930) included 'On the Sunny Side of the Street'. Fields also wrote numbers for *Annie Get Your Gun* (1946), *A Tree Grows in Brooklyn* (1951) and *Sweet Charity* (1966); her best song in the last of these was 'Big Spender'.

Fields, Dame Gracie, *originally* Grace Stansfield 1898–1979
English variety artist and singer

Born in Rochdale, Lancashire, she first appeared on stage at the age of 10, making her London debut in 1915. She became one of the country's top music-hall attractions. Affectionately known as 'Our Gracie', she had a chirpy, natural talent and was adept at both comic songs and sentimental ballads. Her long career spanned radio, recordings, television and films like *Sally in Our Alley* (1931), *Sing As We Go* (1934) and *Holy Matrimony* (1943). In semi-retirement from the 1950s, she won a Silvania TV award for her performance in *The Old Lady Shows Her Medals* (1956) and, in 1960, published her autobiography *Sing As We Go*. A royal favourite, she appeared in 10 Command Performances between 1928 and 1978, the year she was created a DBE. 📖 David Bret, *Gracie Fields: The Authorized Biography* (1995)

Fields, W C, *originally* William Claude Dukenfield 1880–1946
US comedian

Born in Philadelphia, he was a carnival juggler as a teenager. He moved on to vaudeville, appearing all over the USA and Europe before settling as the star attraction at the *Ziegfeld Follies* (1915–21). He made his film debut in *Pool Sharks* (1915) and appeared in many short comedies during the silent era. A bulbous nose and gravelly voice enhanced his creation of a tippling, child-hating misanthrope, continually at odds with the world. The writer and performer of several classic comedies like *It's a Gift* (1934), *The Bank Dick* (1940), *My Little Chickadee* (1940) and *Never Give a Sucker an Even Break* (1941), he also played Micawber in *David Copperfield* (1935). Illness and a reputation for being difficult restricted later creative opportunities, and his final appearance was as a guest artist in *Sensations of 1945*. 📖 Carlotta Monti and Cy Rice, *W C Fields and Me* (1973)

Fiennes, Celia 1662–1741
English writer

Born at Newton Toney, near Salisbury, into a Puritan, anti-monarchist family, she travelled extensively throughout England and Scotland, on horseback and by coach, staying at inns or with relatives, and recorded vivid descriptions of her journeys. These journeys, supposedly for her health, were mostly undertaken between 1685 and 1703; during her 'Great Journey' of 1698 she travelled over 1,000 miles. Her travel diaries were first published in 1888 under the title *Through England on a Side Saddle in the time of William and Mary*, and in them she comments on towns, roads, inns, religious practices and particularly on local trade and industry. She admitted that her journeys were inspired by curiosity.

Fiennes, Sir Ranulph Twisleton-Wykeham 1945–
English explorer

Born in Windsor, Berkshire, he was educated at Eton, served with the Royal Scots Greys and the SAS, and fought with the Sultan of Oman's armed forces. He was the leader of six major expeditions between 1969 and 1986, including a journey up the White Nile by hovercraft, parachuting onto the Jostedal glacier in Norway (1970), travelling 4,000 miles (6,440km) up rivers in northern Canada and Alaska (1971), and over land towards the North Pole (1976–78). Between 1979 and 1982 he organized the Transglobe expedition which traced the Greenwich Meridian crossing both Poles. Since then he has made several attempts to reach the North Pole unsupported, reaching the record 88° 58' N in 1990. In 1993 he and Dr Michael Stroud successfully completed the first-ever unsupported crossing of the Antarctic on foot. This involved walking 1,350 miles (2,172km) in 88 days, dragging sleds of supplies behind them. In 1996 he set off on an unsupported and solo crossing of the Antarctic but had to give up after two days due to illness. Fiennes's published works include the autobiography *Living Dangerously* (1987), *The Feather Men* (1991) and *The Sett* (1995).

Fierlinger, Zdenek 1891–1976
Czechoslovak diplomat and politician

He was appointed ambassador in Moscow in 1937 and therefore played an important role in maintaining a liaison between Eduard Beneš and Stalin before, during and after the Munich Agreement and again following the Soviet entry into World War II. A social democrat by persuasion, he inclined increasingly to the Communist point of view, was Prime Minister in the interim postwar government (1945–46), and then Minister of Industry in Klement Gottwald's coalition government (1946–48). In 1948 he played a crucial role in persuading most of the social democrats to join the Communists in taking over power and putting an end to traditional Czechoslovak democracy for more than 40 years. His influence declined particularly after Gottwald's death in 1953, but he remained useful for propaganda purposes.

Fierstein, Harvey Forbes 1954–
US playwright and actor

Born in Brooklyn, New York, he studied art at the Pratt Institute, and then entered show business as a female impersonator in gay nightclubs. A gravelly-voiced, overweight figure at this time, he made his dramatic debut as an asthmatic lesbian cleaning-woman in the Andy Warhol play *Pork* (1971). His own plays include *In Search Of The Cobra Jewels* (1973) and *Flatbush Tosca* (1975), a transvestite version of the opera. In 1976 he wrote and acted in *The International Stud*, the first of three bittersweet, semi-autobiographical plays covering the life of sardonic, incurably romantic New York drag queen Arnold Beckoff. Premiered on Broadway as *Torch Song Trilogy* (1982), it won Tony awards for Best Play and Best Actor; Fierstein also wrote and starred in the film adaptation (1988). He won a further Tony for the book of the long-running Broadway musical *La Cage Aux Folles* (1983). Later plays include *Spookhouse* (1984) and *Legs Diamond* (1989).

Fieschi, Count Giovanni Luigi de' c.1523–1547
Italian nobleman

He was born into an illustrious Genoese family, hereditarily at feud with the family of Admiral **Andrea Doria**, who had restored Republican government in Genoa. Fieschi, with his three brothers and others, organized a plot to overthrow Doria and establish an oligarchy. The gates of the city were forced in 1547, the fleet captured, and Doria put to flight. But Fieschi, stepping from one galley to another at night, fell overboard, and was drowned in the harbour. The scheme ended there, and Doria returned to take his revenge on the other plotters. The conspiracy is dealt with in a drama by **Schiller**.

Fieschi, Joseph 1790–1836
Corsican conspirator

Dismissed from a minor government post for fraud, with several accomplices he constructed and fired a mechanism of 25 guns at King **Louis Philippe** in 1835. Eighteen people were killed, but the king escaped almost unhurt, and Fieschi was executed after trial.

Figes, Eva, *née* Unger 1932–
British feminist writer

Born in Berlin, she escaped from Nazi Germany and went to England in 1939, taking British nationality. She was educated at Kingsbury Grammar School, London, and Queen Mary College, London University. Her first novel, *Equinox*, was published in 1966, and in 1967 she became a full-time writer. Her other works include *Patriarchal Attitudes: Women in Society* (1970), a radio play *The True Tale of Margery Kempe* (1985), a highly acclaimed work written in 17th-century prose entitled *The Tree of Knowledge* (1990), and *The Tenancy* (1993).

Figueres Ferrer, José Don Pepe 1906–
Costa Rican politician

In 1948 he led a civilian rising against an attempt to annul the legal election of Otilio Ulate. Figueres headed a junta for 18 months, during which he carried through fundamental reforms of a social democratic nature, including the abolition of the armed forces, nationalizing the banking system, creating an electoral law and another law promoting rural co-operatives, and the modernization of the educational and social security systems. The constitution of 1949 embodied these reforms. He was President twice (1953–58, 1970–74), and is commonly known as the person who created a regime which was strong enough to survive the buffeting of civil war in neighbouring Nicaragua and El Salvador. His son, José Maria Figueres Olsen, became President of Costa Rica in 1994.

Figuero, Ana 1908–70
Chilean feminist and political activist

Born in Santiago, she studied at the University of Chile and became a teacher. During World War II she studied at Columbia University and Colorado State College. On returning to Chile, she campaigned for women's suffrage, directed the National School System, and headed the Woman's Bureau in the Ministry of Foreign Affairs. Having become Chile's special envoy to the United Nations in 1951, she went on to become the first woman head of a UN Committee of the General Assembly, the first woman member of the Security Committee, and the first woman assistant director-general of the International Labor Organization.

Figueroa, Leonardo de c.1650–1730
Spanish architect

Born in Seville, he was an innovative exponent of Hispanic Baroque. He was interested in surface complexity and was the first to use exposed brickwork in Seville at the Hospital de los Venerables Sacerdote (1687–97). In the Magdalena Church in Seville (1691–1709) he used the undulant cornice for the first time in Spain in this rebuilding of a mudéjar building. His most influential and important work, which presents a glittering assembly of Figueroa's most distinctive forms, is the San Tolemo doorway, Seville (1724–34), where balcony walls part in many layers to reveal a Borrominesque window (see **Francesco Borromini**) beneath an oval medallion.

Filaret See **Philaret**

Filarete, Antonio, *originally* Antonio di Pietro Averlino c.1400–c.1469
Florentine sculptor, architect and theorist

Born possibly in Florence, he may have trained with **Lorenzo Ghiberti**, though the bronze doors of Old St Peter's, Rome (c.1433–1445), his earliest surviving work, are more archaic in style than those of the Florentine Baptistry. Banished from Rome for the alleged theft of a relic, he travelled north and in 1450 settled in Milan, where he worked for **Francesco Sforza** (1451–65). His major project there was the Ospedale Maggiore (begun 1457), a vast enterprise never completed to his design, which introduced the concept of the centrally planned building and other Renaissance ideas to Lombardy. His remarkable *Trattato d'Architettura* (1460–64) includes a scheme for an ideal city built to a symmetrical plan, called Sforzinda.

Filchner, Wilhelm 1877–1957
German geographer and explorer

Born in Munich, he studied cartography and geography at Munich University and later worked with the Berlin Earth-Magnetic Institute and the Potsdam Astrophysics Institute. In 1910 he led the second German Antarctic expedition, and during a preparatory trip crossed and mapped Vestspitsbergen. In the ship *Deutschland* (1910–12), the expedition travelled to Vahsel Bay, the furthest south yet reached in that sector of the Antarctic. There they became stuck in the ice of the Weddell Sea, drifting for 700 miles (1,127km) northwards before escaping nine months later, having carried out useful observations of ice drift and disproving the theory of a second Antarctic continent. Filchner had travelled to Tibet (1903–05), and returned there twice more (1926–28, 1934–38), traversing the length of the region and exploring the upper Hwang Ho. He also undertook a magnetic survey of Nepal (1939–40) and established magnetic stations in China and Tibet. He lived in India during World War II as his anti-Nazi feelings were well known, and then returned to Zurich to write.

Fildes, Sir (Samuel) Luke 1844–1927
English painter

Born in Liverpool, he became known as a woodcut designer for magazines, such as *The Graphic*, the first issue of which (1869) included Fildes' illustration of homeless people. He also illustrated **Dickens**'s *Edwin Drood* (1870), and painted many subject pictures, such as *The Doctor* (c.1891, Tate, London), which showed the reality of Victorian England. He also painted romantic scenes, for example *An al Fresco Toilette* (1889, Leven Gallery, Port Sunlight).

Filicaia, Vincenzo da 1642–1707
Italian lyric poet

Born in Florence, he studied there and at Pisa, and held a post under the Grand Duke of Tuscany. He is remembered for his patriotic sonnets, and his ode on the liberation of Vienna from the Turks (1684). 📖 G Caponi, *Filicaia e son opere* (1901)

Fillan, St d.777
Irish churchman

He was the son of a Munster prince. He became abbot of the monastery on the Holy Loch in Argyll, Scotland, but withdrew to Upper Glendochart (Strathfillan). In 1318 **Robert Bruce** re-established an Augustinian priory there. His square-shaped bronze bell, and the quigrich, or bronze head of his pastoral staff, are in the Museum of Antiquities in Edinburgh. St Fillans, on Loch Earn, is associated with an earlier saint called 'the leper'.

Fillmore, Millard 1800–74
13th President of the USA

Born in Summer Hill, New York, the son of a farmer, he grew up in poverty but educated himself and became a lawyer. He entered New York state politics, then served in the US House of Representatives (1833–35, 1837–43), first as a member of the Anti-Masonic Party and then as a Whig. He was elected Vice-President under **Zachary Taylor** in 1848 and became President (1850) on Taylor's death. A moderate on the slavery issue, he signed the Compromise of 1850 and tried to enforce the Fugitive Slave Act. His efforts to purge the Whig Party of radicalism alienated many in the party and led to his being passed over for the presidential nomination in 1852. Four years later he ran unsuccessfully for the presidency as the candidate of the nativist Know-Nothing (American) Party.

Filmer, Sir Robert c.1590–1653
English writer

Born in East Sutton, Kent, he was an extreme advocate of the divine right of kings in his *Patriarcha* (1680). He also strenuously opposed witch hunting.

Finch, Alfred William 1854–1930
Finnish painter and ceramic artist

Born in Brussels, of Belgian and British parentage, he worked with **Georges Seurat**, and was an exponent of Pointillism. He abandoned painting for ceramics and moved to Finland in 1897, where he was head of the Iris pottery at Porvoo, and served to link Finnish and European arts and crafts. He later resumed painting, in an Impressionist style.

Finch, (Frederick George) Peter Ingle 1916–77
British actor

Born in London, of Australian parents, he moved to Australia permanently during the Depression when he worked in vaudeville and the newly-established Australian film industry. A popular radio actor who formed his own theatre group, he was encouraged to move back to Great Britain by **Laurence Olivier**. Rugged and authoritative, with an off-screen reputation as a hellraiser, he gained international fame in a wide variety of film roles, including *The Nun's Story* (1959), *Far From the Madding Crowd* (1967), *Sunday, Bloody Sunday* (1971) and *Network* (1976), for which he received the first ever posthumous Academy Award.

Findlater, Andrew 1810–85
Scottish editor

Born near New Aberdour, Aberdeenshire, he graduated from Aberdeen University, and from 1842 to 1849 was headmaster of Gordon's Hospital there. He went to Edinburgh (1853) to supervise for Messrs **William** and **Robert Chambers** a new edition of the *Information for the People* (1857). He also edited the first edition of *Chambers' Encyclopaedia* (1860–68), and wrote manuals on astronomy, philology, and physical geography.

Findlater, Jane 1866–1946
Scottish novelist

She was born in Lochearnhead, Perthshire, the daughter of a Free Church minister, and sister of **Mary Findlater**. She had a great success with her first novel, *The Green Graves of Balgowrie* (1896), an 18th-century story based on

family papers. It was followed by *A Daughter of Strife* (1897), *Rachel* (1899), *The Story of a Mother* (1902) and *The Ladder to the Stars* (1906). In collaboration with her sister she wrote the novel *Crossriggs* (1908) and other works. 🕮 E MacKenzie, *The Findlater Sisters* (1964)

Findlater, Mary 1865–1963
Scottish novelist

She was born in Lochearnhead, Perthshire, the sister of **Jane Findlater**. She wrote several novels of her own, including *Betty Musgrave* (1899) and *The Rose of Joy* (1903), a volume of *Songs and Sonnets* (1895), and collaborated with her sister on the novel *Crossriggs* (1908) and other works. 🕮 E Mackenzie, *The Findlater Sisters* (1964)

Fine, Anne 1947–
English novelist

She was born in Leicester and educated at Warwick University. Primarily a writer for children and teenagers, she started with such titles as *The Summer-House Loon* (1978), but made her reputation with *Goggle Eyes* (1989, published in the USA as *My War with Goggle Eyes*), a moving but witty account of a young girl coming to terms with her divorced mother's new boyfriend. This won the Carnegie Medal, as did *Flour Babies* (1993), while *Madame Doubtfire* (1987, published in the USA as *Alias Madame Doubtfire*, 1988) was turned into a successful Hollywood movie (1994, *Mrs Doubtfire*). A two-edged writer, whose characters often combine wisdom with a faint degree of malice, Fine has also written adult novels, including *The Killjoy* (1986), a disturbing and powerful novel about obsessive love, the blackly comic *Taking the Devil's Advice* (1990) and *In Cold Domain* (1994).

Finger, Godfrey, *originally* Gottfried Finger
fl.1685–1717
Czech composer

Born in Olomuc, he went (c.1685) to England where he became a musician at the court of **James VII and II**. He wrote a number of instrumental works for flute and violin, and composed incidental music for the plays of **William Congreve** and others. He left England in 1701 because of xenophobic prejudice against his work, and became a chamber musician to Queen Sophia Charlotte of Prussia (1668–1705).

Fini, Thommaso di Cristoforo See Masolino da Panicale

Fink, Albert 1827–97
US structural engineer

Born in Lauterbach, Germany, and educated in engineering and architecture at Darmstadt, he emigrated to the USA in 1849. He invented the Fink truss bridge (1852) which became widely used on US and other railways. Fink also carried out pioneering studies of transportation costs which inaugurated the science of railway economics.

Finlay, Ian Hamilton 1925–
Scottish artist, poet and writer

Born in the Bahamas to Scottish parents who returned to Scotland when he was a child, he spent a brief period at Glasgow School of Art before World War II. In the 1950s he began his career as a writer, and his writings of the early 1960s played a leading part in the foundation of the 'concrete poetry' movement. Since then the major theme of his art has been the relationship between words and images. In 1966 he moved with his wife to a farmhouse near Dunsyre in the Pentland Hills, later named Little Sparta, and transformed the grounds into an original modern conception of a classical garden, with sculptures and stone inscriptions carefully placed within the landscape. Like his prints, posters and other works, these are produced in collaboration with a number of skilled craftsmen. He also designed the garden at Stockwood Park, Luton, another monument to classical culture.

Finlayson, James 1772–1852
Scottish industrialist and philanthropist

He was born probably in Penicuik, and little is known of his early life. He is credited with having effectively founded the city of Tampere in Finland, and with setting in motion that country's industrial revolution. His travels took him from Scotland to Imperial Russia, where he became a master machinist in St Petersburg. In 1820 Tsar **Alexander I** helped him set up a textile factory in Tammerfors (now Tampere) in the Grand Duchy of Finland. The company, now called Oy Finlayson Ab, remains Scandinavia's largest textile manufacturer. Finlayson was led by his Quaker principles to undertake philanthropic works too, for which he is remembered. Forced by ill health to sell out, he returned to Scotland in 1838. ⌨ Brian Denoon, monograph in *Aberdeen University Review*, Vol LIV, 2; No.186 (Autumn 1991)

Finley, James 1762–1828
US civil engineer

Born in Pennsylvania, he was a judge and justice of the peace when he conceived the idea of building a bridge on the suspension principle, with masonry towers and wrought-iron chains. His first bridge of 70ft (21m) span was completed in 1801, one of the earliest of its type anywhere in the world, and in 1810 a similar bridge of 244ft (73m) span was built at Newburyport on the Merrimack River. His bridges had particularly substantial decks and unlike those of some other builders, there is no record of a Finley bridge having been blown down by strong winds.

Finnbogadóttir, Vígdis 1930–
Icelandic stateswoman

She was born in Reykjavík, and studied French language and literature at the University of Grenoble and the Sorbonne, Paris (1949–53). She returned to Iceland to work for the National Theatre, and for ten years (1962–72) she taught French in senior school in Reykjavík and French drama and theatre history at the university there. In 1980 she was persuaded to stand for the non-political office of President of Iceland, winning a narrow victory against three male candidates, becoming the first woman in world history to be elected head of any state. She was returned unopposed in 1984, was re-elected in 1988 and was to retire in 1996.

Finney, Albert 1936–
English actor

Born in Salford, Lancashire, he was a student at RADA, before making his stage debut at Birmingham in *Julius Caesar* (1956) and his London debut in *The Party* (1958). At Stratford in 1959 he appeared in *King Lear*, *Othello* and *A Midsummer Night's Dream*. He made his film debut in *The Entertainer* (1960) but it was his definitive portrayal of the working-class rebel in *Saturday Night and Sunday Morning* (1960) that established him as a star. On stage he appeared in *Billy Liar* (1960) and *Luther* (1961), joining the National Theatre in 1965 and serving as associate artistic director of the Royal Court Theatre (1972–75). Recent stage work includes *The Biko Inquest* (1984) and *Orphans* (1986). On film he directed *Charlie Bubbles* (1967) and received Academy Award nominations for his appearances in *Tom Jones* (1963), *Murder on the Orient Express* (1974), *The Dresser* (1983) and *Under the Volcano* (1984). His television work includes the series *The Green Man* (1990) and the **Dennis Potter** plays *Karaoke* (1996) and *Cold Lazarus* (1996). Recent films include *Miller's Crossing* (1990), *The Browning Version* (1994) and *Washington Square* (1997).

Finney, Sir Tom (Thomas) 1921–
English footballer

Born in Preston, Lancashire, he was regarded as one of the greatest wingers ever to play football. More direct than his contemporary, Sir **Stanley Matthews**, he gained 76 England caps. He played for Preston North End all his footballing life and so did not gain any major domestic honours in English football. He was knighted in 1998.

Finnian, St d.549
Irish churchman

He was born probably at Idrone, County Carlow. He is said to have taught 3,000 pupils at the monastery of Clonard, in County Meath, which he had founded.

Finniston, Monty, *properly* Sir Harold Montague Finniston 1912–91
Scottish engineer and industrialist

Born in Glasgow, he studied at Allan Glen's School in Glasgow, and went on to Glasgow University and the Royal College of Science and Technology (now Strathclyde University), where he lectured in metallurgy (1933–35). He entered the steel industry, then served in the Royal Navy Scientific Service from 1940 to 1946, and in Canada until 1947. He was chief metallurgist at the UK Atomic Energy Authority in Harwell (1948–58), then returned to industry, serving on many advisory committees. He was on the planning committee which set up the British Steel Corporation, of which he was made chief executive (1971) and later chairman (1973–76). He served on a wide range of public, educational and industry bodies, including the Policy Studies Institute (1968–84) and the Prison Reform Trust (1981–88).

Finsch, Friedrich Hermann Otto 1839–1917
German naturalist and traveller

Born in Silesia, he became assistant curator at the Dutch National Museum in Leyden, before becoming curator of the Bremen Museum (1864–78). He travelled all over the world and published accounts of the birds in every quarter of the globe, particularly East Africa and Polynesia, but is best remembered as an expert on the parrots of the world (*Die Papageien*, 1867). In 1884 he was appointed **Bismarck**'s imperial commissioner to New Guinea, which led to the formation of German protectorates in the area (Kaiser Wilhelm's Land and the Bismarck Archipelago). From 1905 he was head of the ethnographical department of the Municipal Museum in Brunswick. Finsch's Wheatear was named in his honour. He was one of the greatest ornithological explorers of his age.

Finsen, Niels Ryberg 1860–1904
Danish physician, scientist and Nobel Prize winner

Born in the Faroe Islands, he studied medicine at the University of Copenhagen and was appointed demonstrator in anatomy, but soon abandoned academic medicine to pursue an interest in the therapeutic uses of light. Founding the science of phototherapy, he showed that the light-induced inflammation of the skin occurring in patients with smallpox was caused by the blue and ultraviolet parts of the spectrum, but that red and infrared rays promoted healing. An institute for the study of phototherapy was formed in Copenhagen in 1896 and placed under his direction. For many years he suffered restrictive pericarditis and he died aged 44, shortly after he was awarded the 1903 Nobel Prize for physiology or medicine.

Finzi, Gerald Raphael 1901–56
English composer

Born in London, he was introspective by nature, and was attracted to the countryside and the folk idiom, and from 1922 to 1925 he lived and worked in isolation in Gloucestershire. He then took a course in counterpoint in London, meeting **Gustav Holst** and **Ralph Vaughan**

Williams, and from 1930 to 1933 taught composition at the Royal Academy of Music. A lover of literature, he is best known for his songs, setting to music many poems by **Thomas Hardy** and the metaphysical poets, sonnets by **Milton**, and **Wordsworth**'s ode on the *Intimations of Immortality*, which was first performed at the 1950 Three Choirs Festival. Among his orchestral compositions are the *Grand Fantasia and Toccata* (1953), and his church music includes *Lo, the full final sacrifice* (1946). He did considerable research into 18th-century English music, and his fine collection of music of this period is housed at St Andrews University.

Fiorelli, Giuseppe 1823–96
Italian archaeologist

Born in Naples, he became Professor of Archaeology at Naples University and director of excavations from 1860 to 1875. His work at Pompeii helped preserve the ancient city. He made the first layer by layer excavation, working on a large scale to reveal complete buildings and blocks of the city, and devised a method for making plaster casts of the humans and animals who had been buried by the volcanic ash which covered Pompeii in AD79. He founded a training school to teach archaeological technique, and made a particular study of the materials and building methods used in the city. Director of the National Museum at Naples from 1863, he was director-general of Italian antiquities and fine arts (1875–96).

Firbank, (Arthur Annesley) Ronald 1886–1926
English novelist

Born in London, he was educated at Cambridge, where he converted to Roman Catholicism, but left university without taking a degree and travelled extensively in Spain, Italy, the Middle East and North Africa. Sunstroke as a child left him delicate, and he was by nature solitary. He cultivated various eccentricities, such as growing a palm tree in his apartment and employing a gardener to water it twice a day. In 1905 he published a volume containing two short stories in a volume entitled *Odette d'Antrevernes*, and several novels followed, among them *Vainglory* (1915), *Valmouth* (1919) and *Prancing Nigger* (1924), inspired by a visit to Haiti. His novels (written on piles of blue postcards) are slight, but witty and innovative, anticipating **Evelyn Waugh**, **Anthony Powell**, **Ivy Compton-Burnett**, and he was championed by **Edith, Osbert** and **Sacheverell Sitwell**. His last complete work before his premature death from a lung disease was *Concerning the Eccentricities of Cardinal Pirelli* (1926), in which the hero meets his end while in ardent pursuit of a choir boy. 📖 M Berkowitz, *Ronald Firbank* (1970)

Firdausi or Ferd(a)usi, *pseudonym of* Abú Al-Qásim Mansúr c.935–c.1020
Persian poet

Born near Tús, Khorasan, he spent some years when he was about 60 at the court of **Mahmud of Ghazni**, where he wrote his masterpiece the *Shah Náma* (1010, 'Book of Kings'), based on actual events from the annals of Persia. He also wrote a number of shorter pieces, kasidas and ghazals. His *Yusuf u Zulaykha* is based on the story of **Joseph** and Potiphar's wife. 📖 H T Anklescriz, *Firdausi* (1934)

Firenzuola, Agnolo 1493–1548
Italian writer

Born in Florence, he became abbot of Prato, where he wrote the rather worldly tales in *Ragionamenti* (1525), and paraphrased the *Metamorphoses* of **Lucius Apuleius**. He was absolved of his vows in 1526 and spent 11 years in silence, but returned to writing in the last decade of his life, including religious works.

Firestone, Harvey Samuel 1868–1938
US industrialist

Born in Columbiana, Ohio, he started by selling solid rubber carriage tyres in Chicago and in 1900 he founded the Firestone Tire and Rubber Company in Akron, Ohio, with a \$10,000 investment which gave him half interest. The company grew to be one of the biggest industrial corporations in the USA. He pioneered the pneumatic tyre for the Ford Model T, non-skid treads, and tyres for farm tractors and motor trucks. To break the monopolistic power of rubber growers in Southeast Asia he started rubber plantations in Liberia in 1924. 📖 Alfred Lief, *Harvey Firestone* (1951)

Firth, John Rupert 1890–1960
English linguist

Born in Keighley, Yorkshire, he was Professor of English at the University of the Punjab, Lahore, in India from 1919 to 1928. He was senior lecturer in phonetics at University College London, (1928–38), becoming a senior lecturer in the School of Oriental and African Studies (1938), and head of the department of phonetics and linguistics there in 1941. In 1944 he was appointed Professor of General Linguistics at London University, the first such chair in Great Britain. In contrast to, for example, **Leonard Bloomfield**, he insisted that meaning was central to the study of language. He is particularly remembered for his development of prosodic phonology and the contextual theory of meaning. He wrote many articles but only two books, *Speech* (1930) and *The Tongues of Men* (1937), both deliberately written as popular works.

Firth, Mark 1819–80
English industrialist and philanthropist

He was born in Sheffield, and in 1849 with his father and brother he established there the great Norfolk steelworks. He was a munificent benefactor to Sheffield, his gifts including almshouses, a park and the Firth College (1879), now part of the university.

Firth, Sir Raymond William 1901–
English social anthropologist

Born and educated in Auckland, New Zealand, he studied under **Bronisław Malinowski** at the London School of Economics (LSE) and carried out fieldwork (1928–29) on the island of Tikopia in the Solomon Islands. He spent two years at Sydney University before returning to England in 1932 to take up a lectureship at the LSE, becoming reader in 1935 and professor from 1944 to 1968. His major contributions have been in the fields of economic anthropology, social change, and anthropological theory (especially social organization). Among his monographs are *We, the Tikopia* (1936), *Primitive Polynesian Economy* (1939) and *Social Change in Tikopia* (1959). Other significant contributions include studies of Malay peasant fishermen, kinship in London, and a major work on symbolism entitled *Symbols: Public and Private* (1973). The more recent *Religion: a Humanist Interpretation* (1996) is a cross-cultural survey of religion as 'art', which looks at a variety of religious features (eg prayer, spirit possession and sacrifice) and examines the use of religion as a tool for economic and political manipulation.

Fischart, Johann c.1545–90
German satirist

He was born in Strasbourg. His **Rabelais**ian works attack with inexhaustible humour the corruptions of the clergy, the astrological fancies and other follies of the time. *Flöhhatz, Weibertratz* (1573) is outrageously comic and original. Essentially different are *Das glückhafft Schiff von Zürich* (in verse, 1576, 'The Lucky Ship of Zurich'), a narrative poem, and his spiritual songs. 📖 A Hauffer, *Fischart* (1921)

Fischer, Bobby (Robert James) 1943–
US chess player

Born in Chicago, he became the first Western player to make a living solely by playing chess and was world champion from 1972 to 1975. Early in his career, he won both the US junior and senior chess titles (aged 14), and dictated terms of finance and playing conditions to tournament organizers. He had many phobias, including hidden cameras, shiny chess pieces, glaring lights, restless opponents and bugged seating, but his brilliance over the board led to his achieving the highest results rating (Elo 2,785) in the history of chess. In 1972 he won the world championship title in an acrimonious battle with **Boris Spassky** in Reykjavík, Iceland, and thereafter withdrew from competitive chess. Failure to agree terms and conditions in 1975 for a defence of his title against **Anatoli Karpov** resulted in FIDE (Fédération Internationale des Échecs) stripping him of it by default. For the next two decades Fischer lived in virtual seclusion, but in 1992 he beat Spassky in an exhibition match in Yugoslavia, violating US economic sanctions against that nation and prompting US officials to issue a warrant for his arrest. He was unable to return home, and has remained in Eastern Europe. 📖 Max Euwe, *Bobby Fischer—The Greatest?* (1979)

Fischer, Edmond Henri 1920–
US biochemist and Nobel Prize winner

Born in Shanghai, China, he was educated at the universities of Geneva, Montpellier and Basle, and moved to the USA in 1953. In 1961 he became professor at the University of Washington, Seattle, where he has been Professor Emeritus since 1990. He studied the enzyme phosphorylase and, with **Edwin Krebs**, he showed in 1955 that conversions to and from compounds of phosphorus are involved in activating glycogen phosphorylase. This fundamental mechanism controls a wide variety of processes from muscle contraction to the expression of genes, and for this work they were jointly awarded the 1992 Nobel Prize for physiology or medicine.

Fischer, Emil Hermann 1852–1919
German chemist and Nobel Prize winner

Born in Euskirchen, Prussia, he studied chemistry in Bonn. He worked with **Johann von Baeyer** in Strassburg and Munich. In 1882 he became professor in Erlangen, then in Würzburg (1882) and finally he succeeded **August von Hofmann** in Berlin (1892). He made important studies of the chemistry of sugars. After his discovery of phenylhydrazine in 1875, he found that it reacted with aldehydes to give phenylhydrazones. By a series of related reactions, phenylhydrazine reacts with a simple sugar to give an osazone and this permits the interconversion of simple sugars. This, together with studies of optical activity, led to the elucidation of the structures of the 16 possible aldohexoses (which include glucose). Textbook diagrams of the 16 isomers are known as Fischer projections. The frequent use of phenylhydrazine impaired his health and probably shortened his life, but it was for this work that he was awarded the Nobel Prize for chemistry in 1902. With his cousin Otto Fischer he elucidated the structure of rosaniline dyes. He also made significant discoveries concerning the structures of caffeine and related compounds. From 1899 he turned his attention to proteins and later to tanins. 📖 Edward Farber (ed), *Great Chemists* (1961)

Fischer, Ernst Otto 1918–
German organic chemist and Nobel Prize winner

Born in Munich, he was educated at the Munich Institute of Technology. In 1951, independently of Sir **Geoffrey Wilkinson** with whom he shared the Nobel Prize for chemistry in 1973, he deduced the structure of the synthetic compound ferrocene. Concluding that its molecule consists of a sandwich of two carbon rings with an iron atom centrally placed between them, he confirmed his theory by X-ray crystal analysis. This novel and peculiar class of organometallic sandwich compounds now numbers thousands. Fischer himself synthesized compounds from arenes, olefins, carbenes and carbonyls.

Fischer, Hans 1881–1945
German chemist and Nobel Prize winner

Born in Frankfurt am Main, he gained a PhD in chemistry from Marburg University and qualified in medicine from Munich University. Medical work in Munich was followed by chemical research in Berlin at **Emil Fischer's** institute. From Berlin he moved to Innsbruck (1916) to become Professor of Medical Chemistry and then back to Munich as Professor of Organic Chemistry in 1921. His most important research concerned the structure of the naturally occurring pigments haemin and chlorophyll. He was awarded the Nobel Prize for chemistry in 1930 for the synthesis of haemin.

Fischer-Dieskau, Dietrich 1925–
German baritone

Born in Berlin, he made his professional debut at Freiburg in 1947 then joined the Berlin Municipal Opera as a principal baritone, but he soon became one of the foremost interpreters of German lieder, particularly the song-cycles of **Schubert**. In 1990 he was made a Chevalier of the French Legion of Honour. 📖 Kenneth S Whitton, *Dietrich Fischer-Dieskau* (1981)

Fischer von Erlach, Johann Bernard 1656–1723
Austrian architect

Born in Graz, he was the founder and a principal exponent of the Austrian Baroque style. He trained in Rome under **Gian Bernini** and moved to Vienna as architect to the Habsburg court in 1687. His major works there are the Kariskirche (1716) and Hofbibliotek (1723). He also designed the Kollegienkirche in Salzburg (1707), and several palaces like the Schönbrunn Palace in Vienna (1711). He wrote a history of architecture in 1721. 📖 H Sedlmayr, *Johann Bernhard Fischer von Erlach* (1956)

Fish, Hamilton 1808–93
US politician

Born in New York City, he graduated from Columbia College and was admitted to the Bar in 1830. After serving as a senator from New York (1851–57), he negotiated treatment and exchanges of prisoners in the Civil War. As Secretary of State (1869–77) under **Ulysses S Grant** he proved himself an exceptionally skilful and far-sighted diplomat, partially redeeming an otherwise lacklustre administration. He improved relations between the USA and Great Britain, negotiating the Treaty of Washington (1871), and resolving the *Alabama* claims. He also sought to limit US expansionism and to ensure neutrality towards Cuba, and when Spanish authorities executed US sailors aboard a Cuban-owned ship, he prevented the incident from escalating into war.

Fishbein, Morris 1889–1976
US physician, writer and editor

He was born in St Louis, Missouri. Soon after receiving his medical degree from Rush Medical College, Chicago, he joined the staff of the *Journal of the American Medical Association* where as assistant editor (1913–24) and editor (1924–49) he gradually acquired enormous influence in US medical politics. For decades he was known as the 'voice of the AMA', where he campaigned against government involvement in medical practice and in favour of the traditional contractual fee-for-service structure. He castigated unorthodox medical practitioners and sought to increase health consciousness among lay people through his syndicated newspaper column and his *Modern Home Medical Adviser* (1935) and many other popular books.

Fisher, Allison 1968–
English snooker player

Born in Peacehaven, Sussex, she began playing snooker at the age of eight. She played on her first full-size table aged 12, and joined the ladies professional circuit shortly after her 15th birthday. With over 80 titles to her credit, she has won a record seven ladies world titles, five UK titles, four British Opens, three world mixed doubles (with partner Steve Davis) and a world Masters ladies doubles with her chief rival, Stacey Hillyard. The greatest-ever female competitor in the sport, she boasts a top break of 144 and a competition best break of 133, and was also the first woman to make a televised century.

Fisher, Andrew 1862–1928
Australian politician

He was born in Crosshouse, Ayrshire, Scotland, where he was a coal-miner from the age of 12, and emigrated to Queensland in 1885. From mining, he gradually moved into trade union activity and politics, entering the Queensland state assembly in 1893 and the first federal parliament in 1901. He became leader of the Australian Labor Party (ALP) in 1907 and then Prime Minister (1908–09, 1910–13, 1914–15). At the start of World War I he made the dramatic promise to support the war effort 'to the last man and the last shilling'. He was Australian High Commissioner in London (1916–21).

Fisher, Bud, *originally* Harry Conway 1885–1954
US strip cartoonist

Born in Chicago, he left university early to become staff cartoonist of the *San Francisco Chronicle* (1905). He introduced a regular strip, *A.Mutt*, illustrating the racing tips of a gambler named Mr A Mutt, and involving Mutt's family and cat (1907). Fisher moved to the *San Francisco Examiner*, where Jeff, Mutt's partner, was introduced in 1908, but the title did not change to *Mutt and Jeff* until 1915. In the 1920s he was the highest paid cartoonist in the world, and he later set up an animation studio and produced a weekly *Mutt and Jeff* cartoon.

Fisher, Doris Birthdate unavailable
US businesswoman

She founded The Gap Inc with her husband Donald, a San Francisco real estate developer, in 1969, because they had had enough of jeans stores that did not cater for them. The name 'Gap' refers to the generation gap of the time. Originally selling records and jeans from a small shop on the USA's west coast, Gap now has around 1,370 shops worldwide comprising Gap, Gapkids, babyGap (sic), Banana Republic Brands and Old Navy Clothing Co. Jeans, t-shirts, khaki trousers and checked shirts are the staple stock, continuing the original idea of selling the world the affordable US lifestyle. Fisher is currently a Gap director as well as being the company's merchandizing consultant.

Fisher (of Lambeth), Geoffrey Francis Fisher, Baron 1887–1972
English prelate and Archbishop of Canterbury

Born in Higham-on-the-Hill, near Nuneaton, Warwick, and educated at Marlborough and Oxford, he was ordained in 1912 and was from 1914 to 1932 headmaster of Repton School. He was 45 when he took up his first ecclesiastical appointment as Bishop of Chester (1932). In 1939 he became Bishop of London. As Archbishop of Canterbury (1945–61) he crowned Queen Elizabeth II in Westminster Abbey in 1953. He was created a life peer in 1961.

Fisher, Irving 1867–1947
US economist

Born in Saugerties, New York, the son of a Congregational minister, he earned a PhD in mathematics from Yale in 1891 and joined the faculty, soon switching from mathematics to political economics and remaining at the university until his retirement in 1935. He helped to make economics a more rigorously statistical science, but his interest was always in its practical applications, and much of his work was on the problem of monetary stability. He examined the relation of money supply to prices and clarified the forces of inflation. He proposed the 'compensated dollar', suggesting that by reducing or increasing the amount of gold behind the dollar in proportion to fluctuating prices, the purchasing power of the dollar could be kept virtually constant. He also devised the 'index number', an important tool for measurement in the study of price trends. His publications include *Stabilizing the Dollar* (1920) and *The Making of Index Numbers* (1922).

Fisher, St John 1469–1535
English prelate and humanist

Born in Beverley, Yorkshire, he was educated at Michaelhouse, Cambridge, of which he became Master (1497). He was made chaplain to Margaret, Countess of Richmond, Henry VII's mother, in 1502. In 1503 he was appointed first Lady Margaret Professor of Divinity, and in 1504 Chancellor of Cambridge University and Bishop of Rochester. He zealously promoted the New Learning, and advocated reformation from within. He resisted the Lutheran schism, and in 1527 he firmly pronounced against Henry VIII's divorce from Catherine of Aragon. In 1534 he was accused of treason and, for refusing the Oath of Succession, was sent with Sir Thomas More to the Tower. In May 1535 Pope Paul III made him a cardinal, and on 17 June he was tried for refusing to recognize Henry as head of the Church of England. On 22 June he was beheaded on Tower Hill, London. He was canonized in 1935, and his feast day is 9 July.

Fisher (of Kilverstone), John Arbuthnot Fisher, 1st Baron 1841–1920
English naval commander

Born in Ceylon (Sri Lanka), he joined the navy in 1854, and served in the China Wars (1859–60) and the Egyptian War (1882). A Lord of the Admiralty from 1892 to 1897, he became Commander-in-Chief on the North American and West Indies station (1897–99). He was appointed First Sea Lord in 1904. He effected great improvements in naval training, and introduced Dreadnought battleships and 'Invincible' battle cruisers in preparation for war against Germany. He resigned in 1915 in protest against the Dardanelles expedition.

Fisher, M(ary) F(rances) K(ennedy), *née* Kennedy 1908–92
US cookery writer

Born in Albion, Michigan, and educated in California and Illinois, she moved with her first husband to California in 1935, where she took a part-time job and spent some time in a library containing old cookery books, some dating from Elizabethan times, writing about what she had read. Her first published book, *Serve It Forth*, appeared in 1937, published under her initials to conceal the fact she was a woman (at the time only men wrote about food). She also translated *The Physiology of Taste* by Anthelme Brillat-Savarin, whose philosophy she admired. Compared sometimes to that of Elizabeth David, her writing is not so much about cookery itself, but a collection of culinary essays celebrating US regional food and offering anecdotes and reflections. Her books include the wartime *How to Cook a Wolf* (1942), *The Art of Eating* (1976) and *With Bold Knife and Fork* (1979). She later became a Hollywood screenwriter and joined the American civil rights movement.

Fisher, Sir Ronald Aylmer 1890–1962
English statistician and geneticist

Born in East Finchley, London, he was educated at Harrow and Cambridge. In 1919 he became statistician at the Rothamsted Agricultural Research Institute, where he developed techniques for the design and analysis of experiments. These were expounded in his classic work *Statistical methods for research workers* (1925), and have become standard in medical and biological research. The leading figure in biological and agricultural statistics in the first half of the 20th century, he also worked on genetics and evolution, and studied the genetics of human blood groups, elucidating the rhesus factor. He became Professor of Eugenics at University College, London (1933–43), and of Genetics at Cambridge (1943–57). He moved to Australia after his retirement.

Fisk, Sir Ernest Thomas 1886–1965
English pioneer of radio
Born in Sunbury-on-Thames, Middlesex, he was trained by the Marconi company as a ship's radio operator. He arrived in Australia in 1910 to demonstrate the company's equipment and became resident engineer the following year. In 1918 he successfully received a morse signal in Sydney from Guglielmo Marconi's transmitter at Caernarvon, North Wales, the first direct radio signal between the two countries. He made the first human voice contact between Australia and England in 1924 when he spoke to Marconi in England. He had already established the Amalgamated Wireless (Australasia) Company, becoming its managing director in 1916 and chairman in 1932. He was knighted in 1937, and in 1944 resigned from AWA to return to England as managing director of EMI. He returned to Sydney on his retirement in 1951.

Fisk, James 1834–72
US financial speculator
He was born in Bennington, Vermont, and led an uncertain existence as a peddler, waiter, and circus hand before discovering the trick of success as a stockbroker in the 1860s. With Daniel Drew (1797–1879) and Jay Gould he took part in the struggle for control of the Erie Railroad in 1868, making millions by manipulating Erie stock. A year later he and Gould attempted to corner the gold market, a scheme that was foiled by the government but which caused a disastrous drop in the market on 'Black Friday' (24 September 1869). These speculations made Fisk one of the most notorious of the robber barons, and his life of dishonourable luxury ended abruptly when he was shot by a rival in a quarrel over his mistress.

Fitch, Val Logsdon 1923–
US physicist and Nobel Prize winner
Born in Merriman, Nebraska, he was originally interested in chemistry, but after working on the Manhattan atomic bomb project at Los Alamos his interests switched to physics. He was educated at McGill and Columbia universities, and in 1954 moved to Princeton University where he became professor in 1960 and James S McDonnell Distinguished University Professor of Physics in 1984. Using the Nevis cyclotron, Fitch and James Rainwater studied muonic atoms. These are atoms where an orbital electron is replaced by its heavier relative, the muon. From observations of one of the spectral lines (the K-line) they deduced that the nuclear radii was smaller than had previously been believed, which was later verified in the experiments of Robert Hofstadter. In 1964 together with James Cronin and others, Fitch observed the non-conservation of the combined symmetry of parity and charge conjugation in the weak decays of neutral kaons. For this work Fitch and Cronin shared the 1980 Nobel Prize for physics.

Fitt, Gerry (Gerard) Fitt, Baron 1926–
Northern Ireland politician

Born in Belfast, he was a merchant seaman (1941–53) before he entered local politics (1958). He represented (1966–72) the Dock Division of Belfast as a Republican Labour MP in the Northern Ireland parliament, then founded and led the Social Democratic and Labour Party (SDLP). He was an SDLP MP for nine years, resigning the leadership in 1979 to sit as an Independent Socialist. He had earlier been a member of the Northern Ireland Executive (1973–75), and was its Deputy Chief Executive in 1974. Fitt, an opponent of violence who has had to endure the animosity of both Republican and Loyalist extremists, lost his Belfast seat in the 1983 general election and the same year was made a life peer.

Fittig, Rudolf 1835–1910
German scientist
Professor of Organic Chemistry at Tübingen (1869) and at Strassburg (1876), he was famous for his work on organic compounds. His name is associated with the 'Wurtz–Fittig reaction' with Charles Adolphe Wurtz.

Fitton, Mary c.1578–1647
English courtier
She became maid of honour to Queen Elizabeth I. She was the mistress of William Herbert, Earl of Pembroke in 1600, and has been identified by some as the 'dark lady' of Shakespeare's Sonnets cxxvii–cliv.

Fitzball, Edward, *originally* Edward Ball 1792–1873
English popular dramatist
He won outstanding popularity in the 1820s for his countless fantastically staged and highly intricate melodramas. He looted his material where he chose and took wild liberties with originals, such as *The Flying Dutchman* (1827), derived from John Howison's *The Pilot*, from James Fenimore Cooper's *The Red Rover* (1829) and from Edward Bulwer Lytton's *Paul Clifford* (1835). His *Jonathan Bradford* (1833), based on a famous murder case, ran for 260 nights at the Surrey Theatre. He wrote a vivid autobiography, *Thirty-Five Years of a Dramatic Author's Life* (1859), which is an invaluable source for 19th-century English theatre history.

Fitzgerald, Barry, *stage name of* William Joseph Shields 1888–1961
Irish actor
Born in Dublin and educated at Merchant Taylor's School there, he joined the Irish Civil Service (1911) and, after a period of amateur acting, played in the Abbey Theatre out of office hours (1916–29) under a stage name, in conformity with Civil Service Requirements. He became a full-time actor, toured the USA and was acclaimed as Fluther Good and Captain Boyle in Sean O'Casey's *The Plough and the Stars* and *Juno and the Paycock* respectively, both on stage and screen. He moved to Hollywood (1937) and made over 40 films, notably *The Long Voyage Home* (1940), and *And Then There Were None* (1945), as well as the phenomenally successful *Going My Way* (1944) and the police thriller *Naked City* (1948). He returned to Ireland to film *The Quiet Man* (1952) and *Happy Ever After* (1954), and moved back permanently in 1959.

Fitzgerald, Lord Edward 1763–98
Irish nationalist politician
Born in Carton House, County Kildare, he was a younger son of the Duke of Leinster. He served in the American Revolution (1775–83), was MP for Athy in the Irish parliament and was drawn to Paris in 1792 by the Revolution. There he renounced his title, and married. He returned to Ireland in 1793 to plunge into political conspiracy. He joined the United Irishmen in 1796, and went to France to arrange for a French invasion of Ireland. The plot was betrayed and Fitzgerald, with a price of £1,000 on his head, was seized and fatally wounded in Dublin.

Fitzgerald, Ella (Jane) 1917–96
US jazz and popular singer

Ella Fitzgerald was born in Newport News, Virginia, and raised in New York City by her mother and stepfather. She was briefly in an orphanage after her mother's death in 1932, and even lived on the streets for a short time. She participated in talent contests in Harlem, then began her professional career with the Tiny Bradshaw Band, before moving to the Chick Webb Orchestra, where she recorded her first substantial body of songs. She made her first record in 1935 (and her last in 1992, giving her one of the longest recording histories of any artist), and had her first hit with the novelty song 'A Tisket, A Tasket' in 1938. She became the nominal leader of the band after Webb's death in 1939, and continued in that capacity until 1942.

She embarked on her solo career in earnest at that point, and worked with both swing-based musicians and the emerging bebop generation in the 1940s. In 1948, her first husband, the bass player Ray Brown, persuaded her to come onstage at one of Norman Granz's famous Jazz At The Philharmonic concerts, and by 1950 she was a regular feature on the JATP bills. Granz, initially sceptical, became the major influence on her career, and added a more commercial facet to her mastery of jazz phrasing, rhythm and scat singing, notably in the series of *Songbook* recordings of great US songwriters, which began in 1956, and brought her to a new mass audience. It is one mark of her greatness that she was able to encompass both aspects of her work throughout her long career, moving comfortably between an overtly jazz approach and a more mainstream pop vein as the occasion demanded, and often transcending throwaway material in the process.

She sang with orchestras in the later part of her career, initially at the invitation of Arthur Fielder of the famous Boston Pops, but remained equally at home with a jazz trio, and worked with some of the finest piano accompanists in jazz, including Tommy Flanagan, Jimmy Rowles, and Hank Jones. The only idiom to elude her light vocal timbre and expressive singing was the blues, and she rarely ventured into that area. She appeared in cameo roles in a handful of films, including a memorable singing part in *Pete Kelly's Blues* (1955). Only Louis Armstrong has succeeded in emerging from jazz to achieve a similar level of global recognition and popularity, and she remained a major influence on jazz and popular singing throughout her lengthy performing career, which was halted by declining health in 1992.

♫ Her copious discography includes a number of landmark records. Her early work with Chick Webb and as a soloist for the Decca label (1935–56) is now available in collected editions. From 1956, she recorded for Norman Granz's Verve label, beginning with the *Cole Porter Songbook*, the first of an important series. She recorded with Duke Ellington, Count Basie, Louis Armstrong, Nelson Riddle, and her Verve co-stars Oscar Peterson and Joe Pass, among many others.

📖 S Nicholson, *Ella Fitzgerald* (1994).

> In his book *Jazz Singing*, Will Friedwald pays tribute to Fitzgerald's exceptional musical and improvisational abilites: 'There are enough sultry saloon singers and balladeers in this world; we don't need to cry all the time. We need singers like Fitzgerald to remind us that our great songwriters wrote music as well as words.'

Fitzgerald, Edward 1809–83
English scholar and poet

Born near Woodbridge, Suffolk, he was educated at Trinity College, Cambridge, where he developed close literary friendships with Thackeray, Thomas Carlyle and Tennyson. He wrote poetry, and in 1851 published *Euphranor: A Dialogue on Youth* (a comment on English education), followed by a book of aphorisms, *Polonius: A Collection of Wise Saws and Modern Instances* (1852). After studying Spanish, he published blank-verse translations in 1853 of six plays by Pedro Calderón de la Barca, but is best known for publishing (1859, anonymously at first) his free poetic translation of quatrains or *Rubáiyát of Omar Khayyám* (4th revision, 1879). He also translated Aeschylus and Sophocles, and two more plays by Cald-erón, and left letters, which were edited and published after his death. 📖 J Richardson, *Edward FitzGerald* (1960)

Fitzgerald, Ella See panel above

Fitzgerald, F(rancis) Scott (Key) 1896–1940
US novelist

Born in St Paul, Minnesota, he was educated at Newman School, New Jersey, and Princeton, where one of his contemporaries was Edmund Wilson. He enlisted in the US army in World War I but never left the USA. He married Zelda Fitzgerald (*née* Sayre, 1900–47), and in 1920 published his first novel, *This Side of Paradise*, based on his experience at Princeton. He captured the spirit of the 1920s ('The Jazz Age'), especially in *The Great Gatsby* (1925), his best-known book. Other novels include *The Beautiful and Damned* (1922) and *Tender is the Night* (1934). His short stories were equally notable, published in *Flappers and Philosophers* (1920), *Tales of the Jazz Age* (1922), *All the Sad Young Men* (1926) and *Taps at Reveille* (1936). In keeping with his fiction, which revealed both a fascination with the rich and a moral dismay at the aridity of their lives, he led the strenuous life of a playboy in Europe and the USA, exhausting both his financial and emotional resources and exacerbating his wife's mental illness. He described his own problems—and those of his generation—in an influential essay, 'The Crack Up' (1935). Driven by debts and alcoholism himself, he wrote short stories for popular journals, notably the *Saturday Evening Post*, and in the same spirit went to Hollywood in 1937 as a scriptwriter, where he wrote a final, unfinished novel, *The Last Tycoon* (1941). He was largely dismissed at his death as the darling of a fatuous decade, but the durable grace and purity of his best prose have since won him a place in the canon of major American writers. 📖 M Bruccoli, *Some Sort of Epic Grandeur: a biography of Fitzgerald* (1981); A Mizener, *The Far Side of Paradise* (1951, rev edn 1965)

Fitzgerald, Dr Garrett Michael 1926–
Irish politician

He was born in London, the son of Desmond Fitzgerald, who was Minister for External Affairs in the Irish Free State (1922–27) and for Defence (1927–32). He was educated at Belvedere College, University College and King's Inns, Dublin, became a barrister, lectured in political economy at University College, Dublin (1959–73), and was elected Fine Gael member of the Irish parliament for Dublin South-East in 1969. Minister for Foreign Affairs (1973–77), he then became leader of the Fine Gael Party (1977–87), and Prime Minister (1981–82, 1983–87). In 1985 he took part in the formulation and signing of the Anglo-Irish Agreement and since 1989 he has been European Deputy Chairman of the Trilateral Commission. In 1995 he became a Commander of the French Legion of Honour. His autobiography, *All in a Life*, was published in 1991. 📖 Raymond Smith, *Garret: The Enigma of Dr Garret Fitzgerald* (1985)

Fitzgerald, George Francis 1851–1901
Irish physicist

He was born in Dublin and educated at home by the sister of the mathematician **George Boole**, before going to Trinity College, Dublin, to study mathematics and experimental science. In 1881 he became Professor of Natural and Experimental Philosophy, a post which he held until his death. One of the first physicists to take **James Maxwell**'s electromagnetic theory seriously, he made important discoveries in this field and also in electrolysis and cathode rays, but his name is associated with the 'Fitzgerald–Lorentz contraction' suggested to account for the negative result of the **Michelson–Morley** experiment. It was one of the steps that eventually led to **Einstein**'s theory of relativity, which provided a new physical description of the contraction of bodies when moving at high speed relative to an observer. Elected Fellow of the Royal Society in 1883, he was awarded the Royal Society's Royal Medal in 1889.

Fitzgerald, Gerald, 8th Earl of Kildare, *known as the* Great Earl d.1513
Irish political leader

He succeeded to the title in 1477, and was appointed Lord Deputy by **Edward IV** in 1481 and retained by **Richard III** and, for a time, by **Henry VII**. He was suspected of plotting against the Crown and was ousted from his command, convicted of treason before a parliament in Drogheda (1494), and sent to the Tower while Sir **Edward Poynings** was Deputy. He was pardoned two years later and made Deputy again, and presided over the first Irish parliament held under Poynings's Act in 1498. He defeated Southern chieftains at Knockdoe, County Galway, in 1505, but died of wounds during a campaign against Gaelic rebels.

Fitzgerald, Gerald, 9th Earl of Kildare, *known as* the Young 1487–1534
Irish political leader

The son of **Gerald Fitzgerald**, 8th Earl, he was educated in England as a hostage for his father, whose return to full trust was symbolized by his own return to Ireland in 1504 and appointment as Lord High Treasurer. He succeeded his father as earl and Lord Deputy in 1513. He fell foul of **Thomas Wolsey**, but survived this and other attempts at his overthrow in 1519 and 1526. He was wounded in battle and became vulnerable to a second group of enemies, the Butlers of Ormond, relatives of the new Queen **Anne Boleyn**. On their instigation he was summoned to London, where he died in the Tower.

Fitzgerald, Thomas, 10th Earl of Kildare, *known as* Silken Thomas 1513–37
Irish political leader

Son of **Gerald Fitzgerald**, 9th Earl, he was made acting Deputy by his father on the latter's final summons to England in 1534. On hearing rumours that his father had been executed in London, he renounced his allegiance to **Henry VIII**, attacked Dublin Castle unsuccessfully, lost his base at Maynooth and surrendered on a guarantee of personal safety from the English commander. He was imprisoned in the Tower and hanged, drawn and quartered with his five uncles at Tyburn.

Fitzgibbon, John, 1st Earl of Clare 1749–1802
Irish Unionist politician

Born near Donnybrook, Dublin, he studied at Trinity College, Dublin, and Christ Church, Oxford, and was called to the Irish Bar in 1772. He entered the Irish House of Commons in 1778 and became Irish Attorney-General in 1783. In 1789 he was appointed the first native to be Lord Chancellor of Ireland for almost a century, raised to the peerage as Baron Fitzgibbon and later promoted, receiving his earldom in 1795 and a British peerage as Lord Fitzgibbon of Sidbury (Devonshire) in 1799. He resisted concessions to Irish Catholic sentiment, played a part in the ousting of Lord Lieutenant Fitzwilliam in 1795, and was a prominent supporter of the Act of Union of the British and Irish Parliaments (1800). At his funeral in Dublin his coffin was pelted with dead cats.

Fitzherbert, Mrs Maria Anne, *née* Smythe 1756–1837
English wife of George IV

Born into a Roman Catholic family in Hampshire, she was widowed for the second time in 1781 and secretly married the Prince of Wales, later **George IV** (1785). This marriage, contracted without King **George III**'s consent, was invalid under the Royal Marriage Act (1772) and the prince afterwards denied that there had been a marriage at all. On his marriage to Princess **Caroline of Brunswick** (1795) the connection was interrupted, but it was later resumed with the pope's consent, and finally broken off in 1803.

Fitzjames, James See Berwick, 1st Duke of

Fitz-John See Winthrop, John

Fitzpatrick, Sean (Brian Thomas) 1963–
New Zealand rugby union player

Born in Auckland, he is New Zealand's most capped player. From 1986 he was a mainstay of the All Black front row, becoming the world's most capped hooker, and his ability to avoid injury enabled him to set a world record of 63 consecutive caps (1986–95). He first captained New Zealand in 1992 and went on to play a total of 33 caps as captain (1992–95). At one time he was considered to be the world's best lineout thrower and he was the first hooker to play over 100 times for his home team, Auckland, since his debut in 1984.

Fitzroy, Sir Charles Augustus 1796–1858
English administrator

Born in Shipley Hall, Derbyshire, the second son of the 3rd Duke of Grafton, he married a daughter of the 4th Duke of Richmond. He secured rapid preferment via his many ducal connections, first in 1837 as Lieutenant-Governor of Prince Edward Island and then from 1841 to 1845 as Lieutenant-Governor of the Leeward Islands in the Caribbean. He was appointed Governor-in-Chief of New South Wales in 1846. He was soon faced with disputes between the various Australian colonies and he recommended to the British parliament that some superior post should be established in Australia to which such matters could be referred. In 1851 he received the commission of 'Governor-General of All Her Majesty's Australian Possessions', thus paving the way for the federation of Australian colonies 50 years later. His period of office was marked by a number of key constitutional innovations: the separation from New South Wales of the new colony of Victoria, the establishment of legislative councils there, in Tasmania, and in South and Western Australia, and a constitution conferring responsible government upon New South Wales.

Fitzroy, Robert 1805–65
English naval officer and meteorologist

Born at Ampton Hall, Suffolk, he was educated at Royal Naval College (1819–28) and as commander of the *Beagle*, he surveyed the coasts of South America (1828–30). In 1831 he circumnavigated the globe in the *Beagle* accompanied by **Charles Darwin**, with whom he collaborated in publishing *Narrative of the Surveying Voyages of HMS Adventure and Beagle* (1839). He was made Governor of New Zealand (1843–45) and was elected FRS in 1851. In 1854 he was attached to the meteorological department of the Board of Trade and became the first director of the Meteorological Office (1855). He set up a network of telegraph stations for the rapid collection of meteorological observations and was a pioneer in making weather charts. For these he introduced a set of symbols for wind speed and direction, pressure and temperature, and he invented the term 'synoptic chart'. Using these charts he began a system of gale warnings for shipping. He went on to produce weather forecasts for the press, but these attracted considerable opposition. He wrote *The Weather Book* (1863), which contains pictures of storms remarkably like present-day satellite pictures. He analysed the famous Royal Charter storm of 1859. He also invented the 'Fitzroy barometer' and was awarded the Gold Medal of the Royal Geographical Society.

Fitzwilliam (of Meryon), Richard, 7th Viscount 1745–1816
Irish peer
He was founder by bequest of the Fitzwilliam Museum in Cambridge.

Five, Kaci Kullmann 1950–
Norwegian politician
She was born in Oslo. She was deputy chairman of the Conservative Party from 1977 to 1981, when she first entered the Storting, and vice-chair of the parliamentary party until her appointment as Minister of Trade and Shipping (1989), in the right-wing coalition that collapsed in 1990. In 1991 she was elected leader, in the expectation that she would breathe new life into the main opposition party after five years of decline under three elderly male leaders. Her election made her Norway's third female political leader, with Gro Harlem Brundtland, Labour Prime Minister, and Centre Party chief Anne Enger Laghnstein.

Fizeau, Armand Hippolyte Louis 1819–96
French physicist
Born in Paris, he cut short his medical studies because of poor health and moved into the physical sciences, being greatly influenced by the lectures of François Arago. He collaborated with Jean Foucault to obtain the first detailed photographic image of the Sun (1845). In 1849 Fizeau was the first to measure the velocity of light by a laboratory experiment in which a ray of light was cut by a toothed wheel, producing intermittent flashes. His estimate was not as accurate as that produced by astronomical calculations, but he showed the practicability of this approach. He also demonstrated the use of the shift in light frequency (the 'red-shift') in determining a star's velocity, although unknown to him, Christian Doppler had already published this effect.

Flaccus, Aulus Persius See Persius

Flagstad, Kirsten 1895–1962
Norwegian soprano
Born in Hamar, she studied in Stockholm and Oslo, where she made her operatic debut in 1913. She distinguished herself in Wagnerian roles such as Sieglinde at Bayreuth (1934) and Isolde in New York (1935), and was acclaimed in most of the world's major opera houses. In 1958 she was made director of the Norwegian State Opera. 📖 Edwin McArthur, *Flagstad: A Personal Memoir* (1965)

Flahaut de la Billarderie, Auguste Charles Joseph, Comte de 1785–1870
French soldier and diplomat
Believed to be the illegitimate son of Talleyrand, he fought under Napoleon I. He was the lover of Napoleon's sister, Caroline Murat, and of Napoleon's stepdaughter, Hortense de Beauharnais, whose son by him became the Duc de Morny. In exile after Waterloo, he married the Baroness Keith and Nairne (1788–1867). After 1830 he

returned to France, was ambassador at Vienna (1842–48) and London (1860–62), and was Grand Chancellor of the Legion of Honour.

Flaherty, Robert Joseph 1884–1951
US pioneer documentary film-maker and explorer
Born in Iron Mountain, Michigan, and brought up in Canada, he trained as a mining prospector. He took a movie camera on his expeditions to Hudson Bay in 1913, and made the silent *Nanook of the North* (1922, the story of an Inuit family), followed by documentaries about the South Seas, *Moana* (1926), and *Tabu* (1930). His last great success was *Louisiana Story* (1948). He also produced *Man of Aran* in Ireland (1932–34) and *Elephant Boy* (1937). 📖 Francis H Flaherty, *The Odyssey of a Film-maker: Robert Flaherty's Story* (1953)

Flambard, Rannulf or Ralph d.1128
Norman ecclesiastic and Justiciar of England under William II
He was Bishop of Durham in 1099. He raised money to fund King William II's vices and extravagances by oppressive extortion of the people.

Flaminius, Gaius d.217BC
Roman general
Consul in 223BC, he distributed the Ager Gallicus tribal lands left uninhabited since 283. He was the first Roman commander to cross the Po when he defeated the Insubres at the Addua (223). He extended his road, the Via Flamina, from Rome to Ariminum (Rimini) in 220, and built the Circus Flaminius (the biggest arena for chariot-racing in Republican times). Consul again in 217, he tried to stem Hannibal's invasion of Etruria but was defeated and killed at Lake Trasimene.

Flammarion, Nicolas Camille 1842–1925
French astronomer
Born in Montigny-le-Roi, Haute-Marne, he became an apprentice astronomer at the age of 16 at the Paris Observatoire. He left in 1882 to establish *L'Astronomie*, a monthly magazine. He founded the observatory of Juvisy-sur-Orge in 1883 and the French Astronomical Society in 1887. He is also remembered as a popularizer of astronomy. Among his many books, *L'Astronomie populaire* (1879, Eng trans *Popular Astronomy*, 1907) is the best known and was translated into many languages. He was convinced that there were many life forms in the universe, a proposition that he developed in his first book *La Pluralité des mondes habités* (1862).

Flamsteed, John 1646–1719
English astronomer
Born in Denby, near Derby, he was the only son of a maltster. Following early astronomical studies pursued privately and a spell at Cambridge (1871–74), he was appointed to a commission concerned with finding longitude at sea. The commission's report induced King Charles II to found a national observatory at Greenwich, which was built in 1675–76 with Flamsteed as director and first Astronomer Royal. With a salary of only £100, no assistant and imperfect instruments assembled at his own expense, he was in a difficult position until his private financial circumstances improved in the 1680s. He then acquired from an instrument-maker, Abraham Sharp, a mural arc with which he started an immense programme of stellar positional observations. Aiming at the highest possible accuracy, he was slow with the reductions of his observations, much to the annoyance of Isaac Newton who claimed that he needed them for the perfection of his lunar theory. After much commotion, the *Historia Coelestis*, embodying the first Greenwich star catalogue was printed in 1712 under the editorship of Edmond Halley. Flamsteed, denouncing the production as surreptitious, burnt 300 copies of it. He pressed for an

adequate publication of his work, but died before its 1725 completion as the *Historia Coelestis Britannica*. Its three volumes were supplemented by the *Atlas Coelestis*, published by Abraham Sharp and Flamsteed's assistant Joseph Crosthwait in 1729. 📖 Francis Baily, *An Account of the Rev John Flamsteed and Supplement to the Account* (1935)

Flanagan, Barry 1941–
British sculptor

Born in Prestatyn, North Wales, he worked gilding picture frames in London before training at St Martin's School of Art. He at first reacted against the current vogue for steel, experimenting instead with stuffed hessian, as in *aaing j gni aa* (1965, Tate, London), and sand poured into tubes of cloth, such as *Four Casb* (1967, Tate). After 1975, however, he returned to stone and gilded bronze carving. He was a prize-winner at the Venice Biennale in 1982. He demonstrated an impish humour and an affinity with animals in works like *A Nose in Repose* (Tate), his *Leaping Hare* series of the 1980s, the *Unicorn and Oak Tree* (1991, Royal Academy), and his *Field Day* horses of 1996. He became a member of the Royal Academy in 1991.

Flanders, Michael 1922–75
English entertainer and writer

Born in London, he was confined to a wheelchair by polio from 1943. He contributed words and lyrics to a number of London revues during the 1950s, including *Penny Plain* (1951), and *Airs on a Shoestring* (1953), and co-translated Stravinsky's *The Soldier's Tale* for the Edinburgh Festival (1954). In 1956 he wrote the words and lyrics, and Donald Swann the music, for *At the Drop of a Hat* in which they both made their names. It was followed by *At the Drop of Another Hat* (1963).

Flandrin, Jean Hippolyte 1809–64
French painter

Born in Lyons, he won the Prix de Rome in 1830, and in 1842 began frescoes in the church of St Germain-des-Prés, Paris. He also executed many fine portraits.

Flanner, Janet, *pseudonym* Genêt 1892–1978
US journalist and novelist

Born in Indianapolis, Indiana, she settled in Paris in 1922, and for half a century (1925–75) she served as the Paris correspondent for the *New Yorker*, reporting on French life and culture in her bi-weekly 'Letter from Paris'. She was a leading member of the influential coterie of (mostly) homosexual women, which included Natalie Barney, and Djuna Barnes. She wrote pieces from elsewhere in Europe as well as profiles of famous people, and her journalism is of lasting historical value, providing a social and political anatomy of her era enlivened by her insight into human character and her novelistic eye for detail. Her writings are collected in books such as *An American in Paris* (1940), *Paris Journal, 1944–1965* (1965) and *Janet Flanner's World* (1979). 📖 S Weinstock, *Women of the Left Bank* (1986); I Drutman (ed), *Janet Flanner's World: Uncollected Writings, 1932–1975* (1979)

Flather (of Windsor), Shreela Flather, Baroness 1938–
British politician

Born in Lahore, India (now in Pakistan) she attended University College London, and was called to the Bar in 1962. After working as a teacher, she entered politics in 1976 as the first female member of an ethnic minority in Great Britain to be elected a councillor, and has since served on numerous advisory committees concerned with prison reform, housing, social services, and ethnic rights. She was a member of the Commission for Racial Equality from 1980 to 1986, in which year she was elected Mayor of Windsor and Maidenhead. In 1987, she was chosen as UK delegate to the European Community's economic and social committee. She became Britain's first Asian woman life peer in 1990.

Flatt and Scruggs, *in full* Lester Flatt (1914–79) and Earl (Eugene) Scruggs (1924–)
US bluegrass and country music artists

Guitarist Flatt was born in Overton County, Tennessee, and banjo virtuoso Scruggs was born in Cleveland County, North Carolina. They met as members of Bill Monroe's Bluegrass Boys in 1945, and went on to be a hugely influential partnership in both bluegrass and country music from 1948. They evolved a more commercial approach to bluegrass music in the 1950s, and found a substantial new audience on the folk and college circuits in the 1960s. They parted company in 1969, with Flatt continuing in bluegrass, and Scruggs forming his more rock-oriented Earl Scruggs Revue.

Flaubert, Gustave 1821–80
French novelist

Born in Rouen, the son of a doctor, he reluctantly studied law at Paris, where his friendship with Victor Hugo, the writer Maxime du Camp (1822–94), and the poet Louise Colet (1810–76), his lover from 1846 to 1854, stimulated his already apparent talent for writing. As a young man he was afflicted by a nervous disease, which may to some extent account for the morbidity and pessimism which characterize much of his work. This, together with a violent contempt for bourgeois society, is revealed in his best-known novel, *Madame Bovary* (1857, Eng trans 1881). The book achieved a succès de scandale after it had been condemned as immoral and its author prosecuted (unsuccessfully), but it has held its place among the classics. His second work, *Salammbô* (1862, Eng trans 1886), was followed by *L'Éducation sentimentale* (1869, Eng trans *Sentimental Education*, 1896) and *La Tentation de St Antoine* (1874, Eng trans *The Temptation of St Anthony*, 1895), a masterpiece of its kind. *Trois contes: Un Cœur simple, La Légende de Saint Julien l'Hospitalier, Hérodias* (1877, Eng trans *Stories*, 1903) reveals his mastery of the short story and foreshadows the work of Guy de Maupassant. *Bouvard et Pécuchet* (1881, Eng trans *Bouvard and Pecuchet*, 1896) and his correspondence with George Sand (1884) were published posthumously. He brought to the novel a new awareness of form, structure and aesthetic detachment. 📖 E Starkie, *Flaubert: the making of the novelist* (1967)

Flavell, Richard Anthony 1945–
British molecular biologist

Educated at the University of Hull, he was appointed Royal Society European Fellow at the University of Amsterdam, and Postdoctoral Fellow at the University of Zurich. During 1973–79 he worked at the University of Amsterdam, and he subsequently became head of the Laboratory of Gene Structure and Expression at the National Institutes of Medical Research, Mill Hill, London (1979–82). He was the president of Biogen Corporation (1982–88), and since 1988 has been professor at Yale University School of Medicine. He was elected FRS in 1984. Flavell is best known for his examinations of the structure of the human globin genes. An especially important facet of this work has been the demonstration that for a group of inherited anaemias, the genetic defects involve the total deletion of a specific globin gene, while in other types of this group of diseases, the defect resides at large distances from the affected gene. Work of this kind on naturally occurring mutations has been invaluable in identifying DNA sequences which regulate globin gene control, and has been used to prove the role of precise DNA elements and thus allow the introduction of gene therapy as a treatment for these anaemias. He was awarded the Colworth Medal in 1990 by the American Association of Immunologists.

Flavin, Dan 1933–96
US artist

Born in New York City, he attended the US Air Force Meteorological Technician Training School, Maryland University and the New York School of Social Research, but had no art education. In 1961 he began to make his 'electric light icons', fluorescent tubes hung on walls or set up as free-standing 'proposals' (he preferred this term to 'sculptures'). His work has been described by some critics as 'Luminism', and has obvious links with Minimalism, for example his *Monument for V Tatlin* (1966–69, Tate, London, and Stedelijk Museum, Amsterdam). In 1969 he exhibited in Ottawa, Canada. He continued to create his mystical and serene light sculptures for three decades. In 1983 he established the Dan Flavin Art Institute in New York.

Flaxman, John 1755–1826
English sculptor and draughtsman

Born in York, he displayed an early talent for drawing and modelling, and in 1769 became a student at the Royal Academy of Art, London. His style was Neoclassical, and he worked for 12 years, from 1775, as a designer for Josiah Wedgwood. He then directed the Wedgwood studio in Rome (1787–94), where he also executed several classical groups and began his drawings for the *Iliad* and *Odyssey* (published in 1793), the tragedies of Aeschylus (1795) and Dante's *Divine Comedy* (1787). In 1810 he was appointed the first Professor of Sculpture at the Royal Academy. His sculptures include monuments to the Earl of Mansfield (1795–1801, Westminster Abbey, London), to the poet William Collins (1795, Chichester Cathedral), to the poet Thomas Chatterton (St Mary Redcliffe, Bristol), and to Lord Nelson (1808–18, St Paul's Cathedral, London). He also created statues of Robert Burns (1822, National Portrait Gallery, Edinburgh) and John Kemble (1823, Westminster Abbey).

Fleck, Alexander Fleck, Baron 1889–1968
Scottish physical and industrial chemist

Born in Glasgow, he attended Glasgow University and lectured there for two years before working on radium with Frederick Soddy. In 1917 he was appointed chief chemist to the Castner–Kellner Co. at Wallsend-on-Tyne. In 1937 he became chairman of the Billingham division of Imperial Chemical Industries and in 1953 chairman of the whole company; he retired from ICI in 1960. He was also chairman of Scottish Agricultural Industries (1947–51) and deputy chairman of African Explosives and Chemical Industries Ltd (1953–60). He was a prominent member of many government committees and chaired the committee which investigated the nationalized coal industry from 1953 to 1955. Elected FRS and knighted in 1955, he was created a baron in 1961.

Flecker, James Elroy 1884–1915
English poet

Born in Lewisham, London, he was educated at Uppingham, and studied Oriental languages at Trinity College, Cambridge, then entered the consular service. He was posted first to Constantinople (Istanbul) and then to Beirut. He wrote two posthumously published verse dramas, *Hassan* (staged 1923) and *Don Juan* (1925), and published several volumes of verse, *The Bridge of Fire* (1907), *The Golden Journey to Samarkand* (1913) and *Old Ships* (1915). His *Collected Poems* appeared in 1947. 📖 G E Hodgson, *James Elroy Flecker* (1925)

Flecknoe, Richard c.1600–c.1678
Irish poet

After travelling (1640–50) in Europe, Asia, Africa and Brazil, he went to London, where he wrote five plays, and published his *Short Discourse on the English Stage* (1664). This provoked Dryden to caricature him as 'MacFlecknoe' in his satire on Thomas Shadwell, and inspired a good-humoured lampoon by Andrew Marvell.

Fleetwood, Charles c.1618–1692
English soldier

He was born in Northamptonshire. After commanding a cavalry regiment at the Battle of Naseby (1645), he was elected MP for Marlborough (1646). He commanded the Parliamentary forces in England before the Battle of Worcester (1651) and became Commander-in-Chief in Ireland (1652–55). He married Cromwell's daughter, the widow of Henry Ireton, in 1652. He was Commander-in-Chief in 1659, but had to give way to George Monk, Duke of Albermarle, and was deprived of office at the Restoration.

Fleetwood Mac
British–US pop group

Originally an English cult blues group, Fleetwood Mac gradually transformed itself into a British–US rock band. Early line-ups reflected the blues purism of English founder-members drummer Mick Fleetwood (1942–) and the guitarist Peter Green (1946–). Green's haunting lines made the instrumental 'Albatross' (1968) a hit at a time when the group seemed to be drifting toward a middle-of-the-road pop approach. After 'Man of the World' (1969), 'Oh Well' (1969) and the proto-heavy-metal surrealism of 'Green Manalishi (With the Two-Pronged Crown)' (1970), Green left and was replaced by former Chicken Shack vocalist Christine McVie (1945– , born Christine Perfect, wife of the group's bass player). Various personnel changes took place and during the early 1970s the group became Americanized, hiring Lindsay Buckingham (1947–) and singer Stevie Nicks (1948–) who helped create the smooth, high-finish rock of *Fleetwood Mac* (1975) and then *Rumours* (1976), which topped the charts in the UK and USA. Legal, contractual and 'relationship' problems abounded (there were at one point two Fleetwood Macs, moving obscurely amid a blizzard of writs) and the music became progressively tamer. Their early material is still highly rated. Mick Fleetwood published *Fleetwood* in 1990.

Fleischer, Max 1883–1972
US cartoonist, inventor and animated film producer

Born in Vienna, Austria, he was taken to New York City at the age of four. Joining the staff of *Brooklyn Eagle* (1900) as errand boy, he soon moved to the art department. As art editor of *Popular Science* (1914) he developed an inventive talent, and his invention, the rotoscope (patented 1917), is still used for transferring live action film into animated cartoon via tracing. With his brother Dave (1894–1979) he produced many *Out Of The Inkwell* films, which combined live action with animation. The brothers also created the 'bouncing-ball' singalong cartoons, silent but synchronized to the cinema orchestras. Having made the first experimental sound-on-film cartoons in the mid-1920s, Max went on to produce the *Betty Boop Talkartoons* (1930) and his best-remembered series, *Popeye the Sailor* (1933) from the strips by Ezie Crisler Segar, followed by the feature-length cartoons, *Gulliver's Travels* (1939) and *Mr Bug Goes to Town* (1941).

Flémalle, Master of See Campin, Robert

Fleming, Sir Alexander See panel p657

Fleming, Amalia, *née* Coutsouris 1909–86
Greek-British bacteriologist and politician

Fleming, Sir Alexander 1881–1955
Scottish bacteriologist, and the discoverer in 1928 of penicillin

Alexander Fleming was born in Loudoun, Ayrshire, and educated in Kilmarnock. He worked as a shipping clerk in London for five years before embarking on a brilliant medical studentship, qualifying as a specialist surgeon at St Mary's Hospital, Paddington (1909), where he spent the rest of his career. It was only by his expert marksmanship in the college rifle team, however, that he managed to find a place in Sir **Almroth Wright**'s bacteriological laboratory there.

In his research he became the first to use anti-typhoid vaccines on human beings, and pioneered the use of salvarsan against syphilis (see **Paul Ehrlich**). During World War I he served as a medical officer in France and continued researching antibiotics, and in 1922, while trying unsuccessfully to isolate the organism responsible for the common cold, he discovered lysozyme, an enzyme present in tears and mucus that kills some bacteria without harming normal tissues. While this was not an important antibiotic in itself, as most of the bacteria killed were non-pathogenic, it inspired Fleming's search for other antibacterial substances.

In 1928 by chance exposure of a culture of *staphylococci* he noticed a curious mould, penicillin, which he found to have unsurpassed antibiotic powers. Unheeded by colleagues and without sufficient chemical knowledge, he had to wait 11 years before two brilliant experimentalists at the William Dunn School of Pathology at Oxford, **Howard Florey** and **Ernst Chain**, with whom he shared the 1945 Nobel prize for physiology or medicine, perfected a method of producing the volatile drug. Fleming was appointed Professor of Bacteriology at London in 1938, elected FRS in 1943 and knighted in 1944.
📖 John Malkin, *Sir Alexander Fleming* (1985); Gwyn MacFarlane, *Alexander Fleming* (1985); André Maurois, *The Life of Sir Alexander Fleming* (trans 1959); John Rowland, *The Penicillin Man* (1957).

Born in Constantinople (now Istanbul) to Greek parents, she studied medicine at Athens University. During World War II she joined the Resistance, was captured, sentenced to death, and rescued by the Allied Advance. After the War she went to London, where she worked at the Wright–Fleming Institute with Sir **Alexander Fleming**, whom she married in 1953. After his death, she continued her research as a bacteriologist. Returning to Greece in 1967, she protested against the military regime which had seized power. Arrested in 1971, she was deported to London. She returned to Greece in 1973, becoming an MP, a European member of parliament, leader of the Greek committee of Amnesty International, and a member of the European Human Rights Commission.

Fleming, Ian Lancaster 1908–64
English novelist

Born in London, he was educated at Eton and Sandhurst, studied languages at Munich and Geneva universities, then worked as a foreign correspondent with Reuters in Moscow (1929–33), and as a banker and stockbroker (1933–39). He was a senior naval intelligence officer during World War II, and then became the foreign manager of *The Sunday Times* (1945–59). His varied career gave him the background for a series of 12 novels and seven short stories featuring Commander James Bond, the archetypal, suave British Secret Service agent 007, starting with *Casino Royale* (1953) and including *From Russia with Love* (1957), *Dr No* (1958), *Goldfinger* (1959), *Thunderball* (1961) and *The Man with the Golden Gun* (1965). They sold millions of copies worldwide, and have been turned into highly successful films. He was the brother of **Peter Fleming**.
📖 J Pearson, *The Life of Ian Fleming* (1966)

Fleming, Sir John Ambrose 1849–1945
English physicist and electrical engineer

Born in Lancaster, he won an entrance exhibition to St John's College, Cambridge, where he studied under **James Clerk Maxwell**. After three years at University College, Nottingham, he was appointed as a consultant to the Edison Electric Light Company, and he also served for 26 years as consultant to the Marconi Wireless Telegraph Company. During his tenure of the chair of electrical engineering at University College London (1885–1926), he invented in 1904 the thermionic rectifier or 'Fleming valve', which for half a century was a vital part of radio, television and early computer circuitry, until superseded by the transistor diode in the early 1950s. He was also a pioneer in the application of electricity to lighting and heating on a large scale. He was elected FRS in 1892, and knighted in 1929. 📖 J T MacGregor-Morris, *The Inventor of the Valve* (1954)

Fleming, Paul 1609–40
German lyric poet

Born in Hartenstein, he was the first German to use the sonnet form, and is best known for his lyrical and religious poetry in *Geistliche und weltliche Poemata* (1642, 'Spiritual and Worldly Poems'). His love poems, inspired by Elsabe Niehus, are for their time unusually sincere and direct in feeling and expression.

Fleming, Peggy 1948–
US figure skater, winner of the only gold medal won by the USA in the 1968 Olympics

Born in San José, California, she became the youngest woman ever to win the women's national senior championships in 1963, a victory that was to be the first of five consecutive wins. Three years later she won the world figure-skating championship, the first American woman to win the competition in more than a decade, and successfully defended her title for the next two years. After retiring from amateur competition in 1968, she launched a successful commercial career.

Fleming, (Robert) Peter 1907–71
English travel writer and journalist

He was born in London. Educated at Eton and Christ Church, Oxford, he took a stop-gap job in the Economic Advisory Council before being appointed assistant literary editor of *The Spectator*. In 1932 he read an advert in *The Times* for members to make up an expedition to explore rivers in Central Brazil and ascertain the fate of **Percy Fawcett** who had disappeared without trace in 1925. It provided the colourful copy which surfaced in *Brazilian Adventure* (1933), a landmark in travel literature and an immediate bestseller. In a similar vein are *One's Company* (1934) and *News From Tartary* (1936), an account of 'an undeservedly successful attempt' to travel overland from Peking to Kashmir. He was the brother of **Ian Fleming**. 📖 D Hart-Davis, *Peter Fleming, a biography* (1986)

Fleming, Sir Sandford 1827–1915
Canadian railway engineer

Born in Kirkcaldy, Scotland, he went to Canada in 1845, and became chief engineer of the Inter-colonial Railway (1867–76) and of the Canadian Pacific Railway (1872–80). He surveyed such famous routes as Yellowhead and Kicking Horse passes, and in 1884 devised the internationally adopted system of standard time or 'times zone'.

Fleming, Tom 1927–

Scottish actor, director and poet

Born in Edinburgh, he made his first speaking appearance as Bruce McRae in **Emlyn Williams**'s *The Late Christopher Bean* during a tour of India in 1945. He co-founded the Gateway Theatre, Edinburgh (1953), and until 1962 appeared in and directed many productions there. He joined the Royal Shakespeare Company (1962), appearing in the title role in *Cymbeline*, and the following year returned to Stratford-upon-Avon to play Prospero in *The Tempest*. In 1965 he was appointed the first director of the Edinburgh Civic Theatre Trust, and founded a new company at the Royal Lyceum Theatre in the city. He revived **David Lyndsay**'s *Ane Satyre of the Thrie Estaitis* for the Edinburgh Festival (1984, 1991). He has subsequently appeared as an actor and director in many Scottish theatres. His books of poetry include *So That Was Spring* (1954) and *Sax Roses for a Luve Frae Hame* (1961). He has also been a radio and television commentator since 1952, specializing in state and royal events.

Fleming, Williamina Paton, *née* Stevens

1857–1911

US astronomer

Born in Dundee, Scotland, she emigrated to Boston and after her marriage failed took up domestic work for the director of the Harvard College Observatory, **Edward Pickering**. She joined the research team at the Observatory in 1881 and frequently collaborated with Pickering; some feel the discovery of the duplicity of Beta Lyrae has been wrongly accredited to Pickering rather than to Fleming. Her technique, known as the Pickering–Fleming technique, involved the study of many thousands of celestial photographs. She also discovered new stars and variables, investigated stellar spectra, including 10 of the 24 novae recorded up until 1911, and categorized 10,351 stars in the Draper Catalogue of Stellar Spectra (1890). In 1906 she became the first US woman to be elected to the Royal Astronomical Society.

Flemming, Walther 1843–1905

German biologist

Born in Sachsenberg, he studied medicine in five German universities, going on to become Professor of Anatomy at Kiel University. Flemming is renowned for his investigations of cell division (mitosis), in which chromosomes divide lengthwise, the indistinguishable halves move to opposite sides of the cell, and the cell then divides, giving two daughter cells. Flemming provided a superb account of the process in 1882. He also made significant advances in microscope techniques.

Fletcher (of Saltoun), Andrew 1655–1716

Scottish patriot

He sat in the Scots parliament in 1681, and opposed Stuart policy so consistently that twice he had to flee to Holland. Joining William of Orange (**William III**), he returned to Scotland at the Glorious Revolution of 1688. He was the first patron of **William Paterson**, the projector of the Darien expedition, and the bitterness caused in Scotland by the treatment of the Darien colonists empowered Fletcher and the nationalist party in the struggle against the inevitable union with England. His famous 'limitations' aimed at constructing a federative instead of an incorporating union. After the Union, Fletcher retired in disgust from public life, to promote agriculture; he introduced fanners and the mill for pot-barley. His writings were reprinted in London in 1732.

Fletcher, John 1579–1625

English dramatist

He was born in Rye, Sussex. All that we know of him, apart from his work for the theatre, is that he entered Benet (now Corpus) College, Cambridge, and that he died of the plague in 1625. Much of his writing was achieved in collaboration with **Francis Beaumont, Philip Massinger, William Rowley** and Shakespeare. The best of his own plays are *The Faithful Shepherdess*, which ranks as a pastoral with **Ben Jonson**'s *Sad Shepherd* and **Milton**'s *Comus*, *The Humorous Lieutenant*, acted in 1619, and *Rule a Wife and Have a Wife* (1624), on the favourite theme of conjugal mastery. The 10 or so plays on which he collaborated with Beaumont include the romantic comedy *Philaster* (1610), *A King and No King* (1611) and *The Maid's Tragedy* (1611), generally considered their best work. Collaboration with Shakespeare probably resulted in *Two Noble Kinsmen* (c.1613), a melodramatic version of **Chaucer**'s *Knight's Tale*, and *Henry VIII* (or insertions therein). A vein of tender poetry in Fletcher and his relaxed type of versification are useful evidence in disentangling his various collaborations. He was the nephew of Giles Fletcher, the Elder (1546–1611) and cousin of the **Spenser**ian poets Giles Fletcher (c.1588–1623) and Phineas Fletcher (1582–1650).

Fletcher, John Gould 1886–1950

US poet and essayist

Born in Little Rock, Arkansas, he followed the Imagists while living in London and Paris (1908–33). He later turned to American subjects and became a leading spirit of the Southern Agrarian movement, contributing to *I'll Take My Stand* (1930). He won the Pulitzer Prize in 1939 for his *Selected Poems*. *South Star* (1941) contains a verse history of his native state. He published his autobiographical *Life is my Song* in 1937. ▢ E B Stephens, *John Gould Fletcher* (1967)

Fleury or Flory, André-Hercule de 1653–1743

French prelate and politician

He was born in Lodève. As a young priest, he entered court service (1679), became almoner to **Louis XIV** (1683), and Bishop of Fréjus (1698). Tutor to the future **Louis XV** from 1715, he replaced the Duc de **Bourbon** as Chief Minister (1726) and was made a cardinal, effectively controlling the government of Louis XV until 1743. Through skilful diplomacy he limited the involvement of the French in the War of the Polish Succession (1733–38), restoring the country's prestige as a mediator. His moderation gave France the stability her finances needed, and he carried out legal and economic reforms that stimulated trade.

Fleury-Husson, Jules See **Champfleury**

Flexner, Simon 1863–1946

US microbiologist and medical administrator

He was born in Louisville, Kentucky. His passion for medical research was awakened by the pathologist William Henry Welch (1850–1943) at Johns Hopkins University, and after another year's study in Europe he joined Welch's department of pathology before moving to Pennsylvania University (1899–1903), and then to the newly established Rockefeller Institute for Medical Research, New York City, as director of laboratories (1903–35). Among important contributions to bacteriology, virology and immunology he isolated the dysentery bacillus (1900), developed a serum for cerebrospinal meningitis (1907), and led the team that determined the cause of poliomyelitis. Equally importantly, he shaped the Rockefeller Institute into a powerful and productive centre of medical research. He encouraged both John Davison Rockefeller and his son, John Davison II, to establish research fellowships in the natural sciences, and edited (1905–46) the outstanding US periodical of medical research, *Journal of Experimental Medicine*.

Flieg, Helmut See **Heym, Stefan**

Flinders, Matthew 1774–1814

English explorer

Born in Donington, Lincolnshire, he became a naval officer and hydrographer. From 1795 to 1800 he surveyed the coast of New South Wales and the strait between Australia and Tasmania with **George Bass**, and from 1801 to 1803 was commissioned to circumnavigate Australia. On the return voyage he was wrecked, and detained by the French Governor of Mauritius until 1810. The Flinders River in Queensland, and the Flinders Ranges in South Australia are named after him. ▢ J D Mack, *Matthew Flinders* (1966)

Flint, Frank Stewart 1885–1960
English poet and translator
Born in London, he became a civil servant in the Ministry of Labour, and made important contributions to the Imagist movement in *Cadences* (1915). His poetry in *In the Net of Stars* (1909) and *Otherworld* (1920) is more lyrical and romantic. A talented linguist, he also produced many translations.

Flint, Sir William Russell 1880–1969
Scottish artist and illustrator
Born in Edinburgh, he settled in London in 1900, where he painted many watercolours to illustrate books (such as Chaucer, Matthew Arnold), and paintings of Scottish and foreign subjects. He wrote *Models of Propriety* (1951).

Flitcroft, Henry 1679–1769
English architect
He was born in Hampton Court, London, where his father was the king's gardener. The Earl of **Burlington** became his patron, and he held various official appointments, becoming comptroller of the works in 1758. He designed the London churches of St Giles in the Fields and St John at Hampstead, and he rebuilt parts of Wentworth House in Yorkshire and Woburn Abbey.

Flodoard of Rheims c.893–966
French annalist and divine
He was canon of Rheims, which had become a major centre of learning during the Carolingian Empire, and taught there in the library. Flodoard's annals, which cover the years 919–66, are an important historical source for information on western Europe in the period, and are particularly vivid in their account of the Norse invasions of the Northern French coasts.

Flo-Jo See Griffith-Joyner, Florence

Flood, Henry 1723–91
Irish politician
He became a leader in the popular party in the Irish parliament after his election in 1759. He became Vice-Treasurer of Ireland in 1775, but he was removed in 1781 as a strong Nationalist. Considering **Henry Grattan's** reform bills inadequate, Flood strove without success to carry a more sweeping measure, and became involved in a bitter quarrel with his former friend. In 1783 he was returned as MP for Winchester, and in 1785 for Seaford, but he failed to make a great mark at Westminster.

Florence of Worcester fl.1100
English chronicler
He was a monk at the abbey of Worcester and was the first in a series of English monastic historians in the 12th and 13th centuries. His Latin *Chronicle* is an important historical source for late Saxon and early Norman England, and drew heavily on the *Anglo-Saxon Chronicle*, a version of which was kept at Worcester.

Flores, Juan José 1801–64
Ecuadorean statesman
Born in Puerto Cabello, Venezuela, he became one of Simón Bolívar's principal aides, fought in the Spanish-American Wars of Independence and became the first President of Ecuador (1830–35, 1839–43) following the collapse of Gran Colombia. Illiterate and capricious, he imposed an autocratic constitution in 1830. As the representative for conservative Quito, he alternated in government with his Liberal opponent, Vicente Rocafuerte (1835–39), returning in 1839 and retaining power until 1845. He eventually sided with Gabriel García Moreno (1821–75) against the Liberals of Guayaquil under Guillermo Franco to create a conservative state in 1860.

Florey, Howard Walter See panel p660

Florio, John c.1533–1625
English lexicographer
Born in London, of Italian Protestant parentage, he became a tutor in foreign languages at Oxford (c.1576), and in 1578 published his *First Fruits*, accompanied by *A Perfect Induction to the Italian and English Tongues*. *Second Fruits* (1591) included some 6,000 Italian proverbs. His Italian and English dictionary, entitled *A World of Words*, was published in 1598. In 1603 Florio was appointed Reader in Italian to Queen **Anne** and in 1604 groom of the privy-chamber. His famous translation of **Montaigne** (1603) has appeared in several modern editions.

Floris, Cornelis, *originally* de Vriendt c.1514 or 1520–1575
Dutch sculptor, ornamentalist and architect
He was born in Antwerp and studied sculpture under Giambologna (1529–1608), visiting Rome in c.1538. He brought Italian and French Renaissance details to Flanders and diffused his style through a book of engravings, *Veeldlerleijniuwe inventien van Antychsche* (1556–57). His works were published later in Hans Vredeman de Vries's *Architectura*. Most remarkable among his works were the Town Hall, Antwerp (1561–66) and the marble reredos at Tournai Cathedral (1572).

Flory, André-Hercule de See Fleury, André-Hercule de

Flory, Paul John 1910–85
US physical chemist and Nobel Prize winner
Born in Sterling, Illinois, he was educated at Ohio State University and in 1934 obtained a research post under **Wallace Hume Carothers** at Du Pont, Wilmington. In 1938 he moved to a basic science research laboratory at the University of Cincinnati, but in 1940 returned to industry at the Linden laboratory of standard oil. In 1943 he became leader of the Goodyear fundamental research group, professor at Cornell University (after giving the Baker Lectures there) in 1948 and executive director of the Mellon Institute in 1957. From 1961 until his retirement in 1976 he held chairs at Stanford University. He was awarded the Nobel Prize for chemistry in 1974. His many other honours and awards included the Debye award (1969) and Priestley Medal (1974) of the American Chemical Society. His main research area was the physical chemistry of polymers. From the 1950s he also worked on liquid crystal behaviour.

Flotow, Friedrich, Freiherr von 1812–83
German composer
Born in Teutendorf, he made his reputation with *Le Naufrage de la Méduse* (1839), *Alessandro Stradella* (1844) and *Martha* (1847). From 1856 to 1863 he was director of the theatre at Schwerin.

Flourens, Pierre Jean Marie 1794–1867
French physiologist
He became secretary of the Academy of Sciences (1833) and professor at the Collège de France (1835). Elected to the Chamber of Deputies in 1838, he was made a peer of France in 1846. He wrote on neurophysiology and on animal instinct, and was the first to demonstrate the functions of the different parts of the brain. He was the

Florey, Howard Walter, Baron Florey of Adelaide and of Marston in the City of Oxford 1898–1968
Australian pathologist, developer of the antibiotic penicillin

Howard Florey was born in Adelaide, the son of an immigrant footwear manufacturer. He went to Oxford in 1922 as a Rhodes Scholar to study physiology, later doing post-graduate research in pathology at Cambridge and in the USA, where he made contacts that in due course were to prove invaluable.

Returning to Oxford as Professor of Pathology in 1935, he worked with **Ernst Chain** in purifying the antibiotic penicillin, which had been discovered in 1928 by **Alexander Fleming**. Florey supervised clinical testing of the drug in the USA where it was put into mass production; by 1943 it was readily available, and by the end of World War II had already saved many lives. Florey was knighted in 1944 and he, Chain and Fleming were jointly awarded the Nobel Prize for physiology or medicine in 1945. Florey became the first Australian President of the Royal Society

in 1960, and was awarded a life peerage in 1965. He retired from his Chair in 1962 to become Provost of Queen's College, Oxford, and was Chancellor of the Australian National University, Canberra (1965–67).

☐ Florey jointly authored *Antibiotics* (1949), edited and contributed to *General Pathology* (3rd edn 1962), and wrote for scientific journals on physiological and pathological subjects. See also Gwyn MacFarlane, *Howard Florey: the making of a great scientist* (1980).

> 'Science has made the world too healthy. There are too many people, and the quality of human life is going to suffer ... in the future.' From his Installation Speech as Chancellor of the Australian National University, Canberra, 1966.

father of Gustave Flourens (1838–71), who as an ardent republican took part in the Cretan insurrection against the Turks (1866), wrote such books as *La Science de l'homme* (1865), and fell fighting for the Paris Commune.

Flower, Sir William Henry 1831–99
English anatomist and zoologist

Born in Stratford-upon-Avon, Warwickshire, he studied medicine at University College London and the Middlesex Hospital. After serving as a surgeon in the Crimean War, he was appointed as a demonstrator in anatomy, and later curator of the museum, at the Middlesex Hospital. In 1861 he became conservator of the Hunterian Museum in London, and in 1870, was appointed Hunterian Professor of Comparative Anatomy and Physiology. He was the first director of natural history at the British Museum (1884–98) where he revolutionized museum displays, making them accessible to both scholars and the public alike. He was knighted in 1892.

Floyd, Keith 1943–
English chef and cookery writer

Born in Somerset and educated at Wellington, he began his career as a journalist and broadcaster. As a chef he is best known for the flamboyant style of his television programmes, demystifying cooking from around the world, including Australia, Spain, Italy and Africa. He has produced 14 books, including *The Best of Floyd* (1995), and nine major television series. Also the owner of several restaurants, he now divides his time between Great Britain and Ireland.

Fludd, Robert 1574–1637
English physician, mystic and pantheistic theosophist

Born in Bearsted, Kent, he studied at St John's College, Oxford. Influenced by **Paracelsus**, he recognized the three cosmic elements of God (archetypus), world (macrocosmos) and man (microcosmos). He wrote a treatise in defence of Rosicrucians, *Apologia Compendiaria Fraternitatem de Rosea Croce* (1616, 'Brief Apology for the Fraternity of the Rosy Cross').

Flynn, Errol, *originally* Leslie Thomson Flynn 1909–59
US film actor

Born in Hobart, Tasmania, Australia, he attended various Australian and English schools and worked briefly as a shipping-clerk, and other more adventurous occupations such as searching for gold in New Guinea. After his first film role as **Fletcher Christian** in the Australian film, *In the Wake of the Bounty* (1933), he moved to England to gain

acting experience with the Northampton Repertory Company. A part in a film led to a Hollywood contract. His first US film, *Captain Blood* (1935), established him as a hero of historical adventure films, and his good looks and athleticism confirmed him as the greatest Hollywood swashbuckler, in such films as *The Charge of the Light Brigade* (1936), *The Adventures of Robin Hood* (1938) and *The Sea Hawk* (1940). His legendary reputation for drinking, drug-taking and womanizing eventually affected his career, which was briefly revived by his acclaimed performance as a drunken wastrel in *The Sun Also Rises* (1957). His last, unsuccessful film, was *The Cuban Rebel Girls* (1959), a semi-documentary which he wrote, co-produced and narrated, in tribute to **Fidel Castro**. ☐ P Valenti, *Errol Flynn* (1984)

Fo, Dario 1926–
Italian dramatist and actor

Born in San Giano, Lombardy, he began his career as a stage designer and author of comic monologues, and from 1959 to 1968 ran a small theatre company in Milan with his wife, the actress Franca Rame. His reputation as a comic author was established before the abolition of stage censorship in 1962 allowed him to align himself openly with the political left in plays attacking government corruption and bureaucracy. His international fame rests primarily upon *Morte accidentale di un anarchico* (1970, Eng trans *Accidental Death of an Anarchist*, 1979), in which a political prisoner falls from a window while in police custody, and the frenetic *Non si paya, no si paya* (1974, Eng trans *Can't Pay, Won't Pay*, 1981), a protest against taxation which achieved popularity in Great Britain during the heated debate over the Poll Tax. Both use traditional techniques of farce in order to propound a socialist point of view. ☐ P Puppa, *Il Teatro di Fo* (1978); Tony Mitchell, *Dario Fo* (1984)

Foch, Ferdinand 1851–1929
French marshal

He was born in Tarbes. He taught at the École de Guerre, proved himself a great strategist at the Battle of the Marne, Ypres (both 1914), and other World War I battles, and became Allied Commander-in-Chief in 1918. He quarrelled with the French Prime Minister, **Georges Clemenceau**, about the peace settlement, regarding it as not providing adequately for French security. He wrote *Principles of War* (Eng trans 1919) and his *Memoirs* (1931). ☐ Basil H Liddell-Hart, *Foch: The Man of Orleans* (1931)

Fock, Vladimir Aleksandrovich 1898–1974
Soviet theoretical physicist

Born in St Petersburg, he graduated from the State Optical Institute of the university there in 1922, and became professor there in 1932. His most important work was in quantum mechanics. In the 1920s he generalized Erwin Schrödinger's wave equation to the relativistic case to produce the Klein–Fock equation, and he later developed Douglas Hartree's approach to the quantum mechanics of multi-particle systems (1930) to solve the wave equation for multi-electron atoms (the Hartree–Fock technique). Fock also studied general relativity and demonstrated that Isaac Newton's equations and the law of universal gravity follow directly from the general theory of gravity for finite masses. He received many awards, including the Lenin prize (1960).

Fokine, Michel, *originally* Mikhail Mikhailovich Fokine 1880–1942
US dancer and choreographer
Born in St Petersburg, he trained at the Imperial Ballet there. After teaching at his old school, he joined Sergei Diaghilev's Ballets Russes in 1909 as a choreographer. On leaving the company he worked in Europe, teaching and choreographing for both theatre and ballet. He is credited with the creation of a more expressive approach to the ballet than the artificial, stylized mode prevalent at the turn of the century. He settled in New York City from 1923. ⚏ Cyril W Beaumont, *Michel Fokine and his Ballets* (1935)

Fokker, Anthony (Anton Herman Gerard) 1890–1939
US aircraft engineer
Born in Kediri, Java, of Dutch parentage, he taught himself to fly and built his first plane in 1911. In 1913 he founded the Fokker aircraft factory at Schwerin in Germany, which made warplanes for the German air force in World War I. He also developed the apparatus allowing machine guns to shoot through revolving propeller blades. After the war he set up a factory in the Netherlands. He emigrated to the USA in 1922, where he became president of the Fokker Aircraft Corporation of America. He published his autobiography, *The Flying Dutchman*, in 1931. ⚏ Henri Hegener, *Fokker, the Man and the Aircraft* (1961)

Foley, John Henry 1818–74
Irish sculptor
Born and trained in Dublin, he went to London in 1834, and executed many statues of public figures in a lively and natural style, notably the gilded bronze seated figure of Albert, Prince Consort, for the Albert Memorial, London (1874). Other major commissions were statues of Edmund Burke (1868) and Oliver Goldsmith (1864) at Trinity College, Dublin, Henry Grattan on College Green, Dublin, and in London, Sidney Herbert on the Crimean War Memorial, London (1867), and John Hampden (1850) and John Selden in the House of Commons. He also made the design for the Daniel O'Connell Monument in Dublin (1866–83), and the group *Asia* on the Albert Memorial in London.

Folkers, Karl August 1906–
US biochemist
Born in Decatur, Illinois, he studied at the universities of Illinois, Wisconsin and Yale, and later directed research at Merck and Co, at the Stanford Research Institute, and at Texas University. Folkers worked on the synthesis and structure of a range of antibiotics, but is remembered for leading the Merck teams which isolated the anti-pernicious anaemia factor, cyanocobalamin (vitamin B_{12}) in 1948, isolated mevalonic acid in 1956 from a commercial yeast by-product, and discovered in 1970 the structure of porcine thyrotrophin-releasing hormone. In 1990 he was awarded the Presidential National Medal of Science.

Follete, Robert Marion la See La Follette, Robert Marion

Fonda, Henry Jaynes 1905–82
US actor
Born in Grand Island, Nebraska, he became involved with the Omaha Community Playhouse and enjoyed some success on Broadway, before moving to Hollywood (1935). His Hollywood debut in *A Farmer Takes A Wife* (1935) was followed by over 100 films, notably *Young Mr. Lincoln* (1939), *The Grapes of Wrath* (1940), *The Lady Eve* (1941) and *The Oxbow Incident* (1943), which established him in the role of the honest US folk hero. Later films include *Twelve Angry Men* (1957) and *On Golden Pond* (1981), for which he won an Academy Award. A frequent stage performer, he enjoyed long runs with *Mister Roberts* (1948–51), *Two for the Seesaw* (1958) and *Clarence Darrow* (1974–75). He was married five times, and his children include actors Jane Fonda and Peter (1939–).

Fonda, Jane Seymour 1937–
US actress
Born in New York City, she made her stage debut, with her father Henry Fonda, in *The Country Girl* (1955). A student at the Actor's Studio and part-time model, she made her film debut in *Tall Story* (1960). She worked in Europe and married director Roger Vadim (1928–), with whom she made *La Ronde* (1964) and *Barbarella* (1968). Later her 'sex kitten' image receded and she became established as a versatile dramatic actress of considerable emotional depth and sensitivity in such films as *Klute* (1971, Academy Award), *Coming Home* (1978, Academy Award), *The China Syndrome* (1978), *On Golden Pond* (1981), *The Dollmaker* (1983, Emmy Award), *The Old Gringo* (1989) and *Stanley and Iris* (1990). Noted for her anti-nuclear and feminist activities, as well as the anti-war stance which earned her the name of 'Hanoi Jane' during the Vietnam War, in the 1980s she also became involved with women's health and fitness, through bestselling videos and books.

Fonseca, Manoel Deodoro da 1827–92
Brazilian politician
He was born in Alagoas, and was the first President of Brazil (1889–91).

Fonsesca, Juan See Marsé, Juan

Fontaine, Jean de la See La Fontaine, Jean de

Fontana, Carlo 1634 or 1638–1714
Italian architect
Born in Switzerland, he was a pupil of Gian Bernini. He worked as papal architect in Rome, where he designed many major works including the fountain in the Piazza di San Pietro, and the tombs of popes Clement XI and Innocent XII, and Queen Kristina of Sweden, in St Peter's. He designed Loyola College in Spain and the Palazzo Durazzo at Genoa.

Fontana, Domenico 1543–1607
Italian architect
He was born in Melide, near Lugano, Switzerland. He was papal architect in Rome, and worked on the Lateran Palace and the Vatican Library. He was afterwards royal architect in Naples.

Fontana, Lucio 1899–1968
Italian artist
Born in Rosario, Argentina, he signed the first Manifesto of Italian Abstract Artists in 1935. After World War II, he made his name as the inventor of *Spazialismo* (Spatialism) and as a pioneer of 'environmental art'. He is best known for his bare or monochrome canvases, holed or slashed to create what he called *Attese*. These in turn looked forward to the 'gesture' or 'performance' art of the 1960s.

Fontane, Theodor 1819–98

German poet and novelist

Born in Neuruppin, he worked in the family chemist's business until in 1849 he turned to literature in Berlin. Periods of residence in Great Britain as a newspaper correspondent (1855–59) led to ballads such as 'Archibald Douglas' and 'Die Brücke am Tay' ('The Tay Bridge'). He was a war correspondent in 1866 and 1870–71, and became the secretary of the Prussian Royal Academy of Arts. He wrote his first novel, *Vor dem Sturm* (1878, 'Before the Storm'), at the age of 56. It is set against the events of the Franco-Prussian War in 1812–13, and is considered by many to be his best. *L'Adultera* (1882, Eng trans *The Woman Taken in Adultery*, 1979) and *Effi Briest* (1895, Eng trans 1967) focused on the position of women in German society, and he extended his appraisal of social mores into the realms of politics and power in *Die Poggenpuhls* (1896, Eng trans *The Poggenpuhl Family*, 1979) and *Der Stechlin* (1898). His novels influenced **Thomas Mann**. 📖 A R Robinson, *Fontane: an introduction to the man and his work* (1976)

Fontenelle, Bernard le Bovier de 1657–1757

French writer

Born in Rouen, he was a nephew of **Pierre Corneille**, and began his literary career in Paris. In the great quarrel of Moderns versus Ancients, he sided with the Moderns, assailing the Greeks and their French imitators, and receiving in return the satiric attacks of **Nicolas Boileau, Racine, Jean Jacques Rousseau** and **Jean de La Bruyère**. After the failure on the stage of his *Aspar*, he produced an imitation of **Lucian**, *Nouveaux dialogues des morts* (1682, Eng trans *New Dialogues of the Dead*, 1683), and the 'precious' *Lettres diverses de Monsieur le Chevalier d'Her…* (1687, Eng trans *Letters of Gallantry from Monsieur le Chevalier d'Her…*, 1687). In 1697 he was made secretary to the French Academy of Sciences, of which he was later president. He attempted almost every form of literature—idylls, satires, dialogues, tragedies, histories and critical essays—but his *Entretiens sur la pluralité des mondes* (1686, Eng trans *A Discourse on the Plurality of Worlds*, 1687) and *Histoire des oracles* (1686, Eng trans *The History of the Oracles*, 1688) are considered his best works.

Fonteyn, Dame Margot, *in full* Margot Fonteyn de Arias, *née* Margaret Hookham 1919–91

English ballerina

Born in Reigate, Surrey, she studied dance in Hong Kong and in London under **Nikolai Legat** and **Ninette de Valois** among others, then joined the Vic-Wells Ballet, which later became Sadler's Wells Ballet and finally the Royal Ballet, with which she spent her entire career. She created many roles under the choreography of Ninette de Valois and Sir **Frederick Ashton**, among them her first solo appearance, *The Haunted Ballroom* (1939), *Symphonic Variations* (1946) and *The Fairy Queen* (1946). She rose in the Royal Ballet to become one of the most impressive technicians of the 20th century. Her career was extended and enhanced in the 1960s by her acclaimed partnership with **Rudolph Nureyev**. She performed work by **Roland Petit** and **Kenneth MacMillan**, and also wrote and introduced a six-part television series, *The Magic of Dance* (1979). Her publications include an autobiography (1975) and a study of **Anna Pavlova**. She married Roberto Emilio Arias (1918–90), then Panamanian ambassador to the Court of St James in London, in 1955. 📖 Keith Money, *Fonteyn: The Making of a Legend* (1973)

Foot, Sir Dingle Mackintosh 1905–78

English lawyer and politician

He was educated at Oxford, where he was president of the Liberal Club (1927) and of the Union (1928). He was Liberal MP for Dundee (1931–45), joined the Labour Party in 1956 and was Labour MP for Ipswich (1957–70),

and Solicitor-General (1964–67). He was made QC in 1954, and was knighted in 1964. He published *British Political Crises* in 1976.

Foot, Hugh Mackintosh, Baron Caradon 1907–90

English administrator

The son of **Isaac Foot**, he was educated at Cambridge and was president of the Union in 1929. He held several government administrative posts abroad, in Palestine, Transjordan, Cyprus, Jamaica and Nigeria and from 1961 his work was mainly in connection with the United Nations (permanent representative 1964–70) and as a consultant to the UN development programme. He was awarded a life peerage in 1964.

Foot, Isaac 1880–1960

English politician

He was a solicitor in Plymouth and Liberal MP for Bodmin (1922–24, 1929–35), and was the father of **Dingle, Hugh** and **Michael Foot**.

Foot, Michael Mackintosh 1913–

English Labour politician and journalist

Born in Plymouth, Devon, the son of **Isaac Foot**, he was educated at Oxford, where he was president of the Union (1933). He was assistant editor of *Tribune* (1937–38), joint editor (1948–52) and editor (1955–60). He was also acting editor of the *Evening Standard* (1942–44) and a political columnist on the *Daily Herald* (1944–64), and Labour MP for Ebbw Vale (1960–83) and Blaenau Gwent (1983–92). He was Secretary of State for Employment (1974–76), and was deputy Leader of the Labour Party (1976–80) and Leader of the House of Commons (1976–79). In 1980 he became Leader of the Labour Party, replacing **James Callaghan**. A man of undoubted political integrity, he was known as a master of rhetoric in parliamentary debates, but proved no match for **Margaret Thatcher** in the media-dominated election of 1983, in which his party was heavily defeated. He was replaced that year by **Neil Kinnock**. A prominent figure on the left of the Labour Party and a pacifist, he has long been a supporter of the Campaign for Nuclear Disarmament (CND). His books include the influential *Guilty Men*, written with colleagues and published in 1940, a two-volume biography of **Aneurin Bevan** (1962, 1973) and a biography of **H G Wells** (whom he had known), entitled *HG: The History of Mr Wells* (1995). 📖 Mervyn Jones, *Michael Foot* (1994)

Foote, Albert Horton 1916–

US dramatist

Born in Wharton, Texas, he studied acting at the Pasadena Playhouse in California and in New York City, then began to write plays. His work is characterized by a fascination with family relationships and with the act of storytelling, and he is best known for a series of plays about rural Texas called the Orphans' Home Cycle, including *The Widow Claire*, *Valentine's Day*, and *1918*. His screenplays for *To Kill a Mockingbird* (1962) and *Tender Mercies* (1983) won Academy Awards, and his play *Young Man from Atlanta* (1995) won the Pulitzer Prize.

Foote, Andrew Hull 1806–63

US naval officer

Born in New Haven, Connecticut, he joined the navy in 1822, and was promoted captain in 1849. He helped to abolish the liquor ration in the US navy (1862). In 1856 at Canton he stormed four Chinese forts, which had fired on him. In the Civil War he organized the western flotilla, and in 1862 attacked Fort Henry. Shortly afterwards he was wounded and resigned as rear admiral.

Foote, Shelby 1916–

US novelist and historian

Born in Greenville, Mississippi, he established his name with his second novel, *Follow Me Down* (1950), which gives a multiple view of a violent murder. *Shiloh* (1952) is a historical novel, dealing with the Civil War. Foote is now even better known for his detailed history, *The Civil War: A Narrative* (1958–74), than for his novels. ⌨ *Mississippi Quarterly* (October, 1971)

Foppa, Vincenzo c.1427–c.1515
Italian painter
He was the leader of the Lombard school of painting which lasted until the time of Leonardo da Vinci.

Forbes, Bryan, *originally* John Theobald Clarke 1926–
English actor and director
He was born in London and studied at the Royal Academy of Dramatic Arts. After a number of years in acting, he founded Beaver Films with Sir Richard Attenborough in 1959. His film productions include *The Angry Silence* (1960), *The Slipper and the Rose* (1976) and *International Velvet* (1978). In the theatre he has directed *Macbeth* (1980) and *The Living Room* (1987). He has also produced drama for television. He married the actress Nanette Newman (1939–) in 1958, and published his autobiography, *Notes for A Life*, in 1974.

Forbes, Edward 1815–54
British naturalist
Born in Douglas, Isle of Man, he studied medicine at the University of Edinburgh, but in 1836 he gave up medicine altogether to devote himself completely to the natural sciences. In 1841 he joined the crew of the *Beacon* as naturalist during the survey around parts of Asia Minor. He later became Professor of Botany at King's College London (1843), and shortly afterwards was appointed curator of the Museum of the Geological Society of London. In 1844 he became the first palaeontologist to HM Geological Survey, was made Professor of Natural History at the Royal School of Mines (1851), and in 1854 was appointed Regius Professor of Natural History at Edinburgh University. A versatile natural historian, he undertook important studies of quaternary changes in molluscan faunas and relict floras, and made formative observations in oceanography, and effectively laid the foundations for the sciences of biogeography and palaeoecology.

Forbes, George 1849–1936
Scottish physicist and engineer
He was born in Edinburgh, where his father, James David Forbes, was Professor of Natural Philosophy. He was educated at St Andrews and Cambridge universities, and had a varied life as an astronomer, inventor, traveller and war correspondent. He was for some years Professor of Experimental Philosophy at Anderson's College, Glasgow, and while there took charge of one of the British Transit of Venus expeditions of 1874, to Hawaii. In his later life he worked on dynamos and invented the carbon brush. He made improvements in the method of measuring the velocity of light (with James Young), and in the field of range-finding. He forecast the existence of Pluto in 1880.

Forbes, James David 1809–68
Scottish physicist and glaciologist
Born in Edinburgh, he was privately educated until the age of 16 when he went to Edinburgh University. Here, despite an early interest in science, he pursued legal studies at the request of his father, George Forbes. On his father's death (1828) he received a modest inheritance, and abandoned law and returned to science. He became professor at Edinburgh University (1833–60) and Principal of St Andrews College (1860–68). In 1834, using instruments employed by Macedonio Melloni

(1798–1854), he carried out work which contributed to the concept of a continuous radiation spectrum. After 1840 his interests turned to geology and to glaciers. He visited the Alps with Jean Agassiz in 1841, later causing a lifelong controversy with him by claiming priority in noting that the surface of a glacier moves faster than the ice beneath it, and that glacier velocity is directly related to the steepness of the slope. Forbes fought successfully for reforms in Scottish higher education, including the instigation of degree-level examinations.

Forbes, Malcolm Stevenson 1919–90
US publisher
He was born in Brooklyn, New York City, where his father, a Scot, founded *Forbes* (1917), then the only business magazine in the USA. For the first dozen years the magazine prospered but in the 1930s its circumstances—and the family's—changed when rivals like *Fortune* and *Business Week* appeared on the scene. It was nevertheless kept alive and he became its editor-in-chief and publisher in 1957, since when circulation and profits have escalated, making its owner the talk of gossip columns and a multi-millionaire. Notorious for his extravagance, he had a passionate interest in ballooning as well as Fabergé eggs, of which he had one of the world's foremost collections.

Forbes, (Joan) Rosita 1893–1967
English writer and traveller
She was born in Swinderby, Lincolnshire. Having visited almost every country in the world and particularly Arabia and North Africa, she used her experiences as the raw material for exciting travel books, including *The Secret of the Sahara-Kufara* (1922), *From Red Sea to Blue Nile* (1928), *The Prodigious Caribbean* (1940), *Appointment in the Sun* (1949) and *Islands in the Sun* (1950). ⌨ *Gypsy in the Sun* (1967)

Forbes Mackenzie, William See Mackenzie, William Forbes

Forbes-Robertson, Sir Johnston 1853–1937
English actor
Born in London, he made his debut in 1874 and soon established himself as a West End favourite. In 1895 he became actor-manager of the London Lyceum and crowned his productions there with *Hamlet* (1897). In later years he had great success in *The Passing of the Third Floor Back* (1913). He married Gertrude Elliot (1900), a US actress who often partnered him. A daughter, Jean (1905–62), carried on the tradition and became actress-manager in *The Lady of the Camellias* (1934).

Ford, Betty (Elizabeth), *née* Bloomer 1918–
US health administrator and First Lady as the wife of President Gerald Ford
Born in Chicago, Illinois, she was originally a dancer, and toured with the Martha Graham Concert Group. In 1948 she married Gerald Ford, who later became President of the USA (1974–77). As First Lady, Betty Ford's public battle with breast cancer created awareness of health problems for women. Her struggle with substance abuse led her to found the Betty Ford Center, of which she is president of the board of directors. She has written two autobiographies, *The Times of My Life* (1979) and *Betty: A Glad Awakening* (1987).

Ford, Edmund Brisco 1901–88
English geneticist
Born in Papcastle, Cumberland, he studied and then taught at Oxford throughout his career, becoming Professor of Ecological Genetics and director of the Genetics Laboratory. He was stimulated by Julian Huxley, his tutor at Oxford, and with whom he carried out pioneering work on gene action rates. He wrote *Mendelism and Evolution* (1931), the first major published work leading to the neo-Darwinian synthesis. With Sir Ronald Fisher he

studied microevolution in Lepidoptera, and was responsible for the first experimental evidence of modifying dominance of an interested trait, confirming Fisher's theory of the evolution of dominance. He showed that the appearance of a specific trait in successive generations was under genetic control, and that selection could change its inheritance in the direction of either dominance or recessivity. He also demonstrated that the maintenance of different inherited forms of a character in the same population often resulted from natural selection. Ford's New Naturalist books on *Butterflies* (1945) and *Moths* (1955) were influential, and he was elected FRS in 1946.

Ford, Ford Madox, *originally* Ford Hermann Hueffer 1873–1939
English novelist, editor and poet

He was born in Merton, Surrey, the son of Francis Hueffer, the music critic of *The Times*, and grandson of the Pre-Raphaelite painter Ford Madox Brown. Brought up in Pre-Raphaelite circles, he published his first book when he was only 18, a fairy story entitled *The Brown Owl* (1891), and a novel, *The Shifting of the Fire*, appeared the following year. In 1894 he eloped with and married Elsie Martindale, presaging a life of emotional upheaval. He met Joseph Conrad in 1898 and they co-authored various works including *The Inheritors* (1901) and *Romance* (1903). In 1908 he founded the *English Review*, which he edited for 15 months and in which he published Thomas Hardy, H G Wells, D H Lawrence and Wyndham Lewis among others. In 1924, while living in Paris, he was founder-editor of the *Transatlantic Review*, which gave space to James Joyce, Ezra Pound, Gertrude Stein and the young Ernest Hemingway. He wrote almost 80 books in a hectic career but is best remembered for three novels: *The Fifth Queen* (1906), *The Good Soldier* (1915) and *Parade's End*, the title he gave to what is often known as the 'Tietjens war' tetralogy: *Some Do Not* (1924), *No More Parades* (1925), *A Man Could Stand Up* (1926) and *Last Post* (1928). 📖 A Mizener, *The Saddest Story* (1972)

Ford, Gerald R(udolph) 1913–
38th President of the USA

Born in Omaha, Nebraska, he attended the University of Michigan on a football scholarship, studied law at Yale and served in the US navy during World War II. From 1949 to 1973 he was a Republican member of the House of Representatives, becoming minority leader in 1965. On the resignation of Spiro Agnew in 1973 he was appointed Vice-President, becoming President in 1974 when President Richard Nixon resigned as a result of the Watergate scandal. Ford assumed the presidency during a time of economic difficulties and was faced with a resurgent, Democrat-dominated Congress which firmly resisted his domestic and external policy initiatives. His relations with congress were made worse by his controversial decision to grant a full pardon to former president Nixon in September 1974. In the 1976 presidential election he was defeated by Jimmy Carter. His publications include *Humor and the Presidency* (1987). 📖 Charles Mercer, *Gerald Ford* (1975)

Ford, Harrison 1942–
US film actor

Born in Chicago, he appeared in summer stock theatre before making his film debut in *Dead Heat on a Merry-Go-Round* (1966). He made small appearances in films and television and pursued a secondary career as a carpenter, before achieving fame in *Star Wars* (1977) and its two sequels. Cast as resourceful, swashbuckling heroes, he found great popularity as an archaeological adventurer in *Raiders of the Lost Ark* (1981) and its sequels *Indiana Jones and the Temple of Doom* (1984) and *Indiana Jones and the Last Crusade* (1989). Other successes include *Witness* (1985,

Academy Award nomination), *The Mosquito Coast* (1986), *Presumed Innocent* (1990), and *The Fugitive* (1993). His second wife is the screenwriter Melissa Matheson.

Ford, Henry 1863–1947
US car engineer and manufacturer

Born near Dearborn, Michigan, and apprenticed to a machinist in Detroit at the age of 15, he produced his first petrol-driven motor car in 1893. In 1899 he became chief engineer of the Detroit Automobile Company and in 1903 founded the Ford Motor Company. He pioneered the modern 'assembly line' mass-production techniques for his famous Model T (1908–09), 15 million of which were produced up to 1928. He also branched out into aircraft and tractor manufacture. An eccentric who once declared that 'history is bunk', he espoused pacifism during World War I and tried to negotiate a European peace in 1915 by chartering a 'Peace Ship' to Europe. He paid his employees far more than the standard rate, advancing the influential argument that decently paid industrial workers themselves provided a market for the product they were manufacturing, and his refusal to abandon this policy led to violent disagreements with the code laid down in the Franklin D Roosevelt recovery programme in 1931. Autocratic and paternalistic in his administration of the company, he tenaciously opposed the establishment of labour unions. In 1919 Ford was succeeded by his son Edsel Bryant Ford (1893–1943), and in 1945 by his grandson Henry Ford, II, despite his stubborn attempts, at 82, to regain absolute control of the ailing company. His philanthropies include the establishment of the Ford Foundation. 📖 Roger Burlingame, *Henry Ford: A Great Life in Brief* (1955)

Ford, Henry, II 1917–87
US car manufacturer

Born in Detroit, he was educated at Hotchkiss School, Connecticut and Yale. After the death of his father, Edsel Bryant Ford (1893–1943), he seized control of the Ford Motor Company from his grandfather, Henry Ford, in 1945. The company was in difficulties, but he reorganized it and rebuilt the management teams. He stepped down as chief executive officer in 1979 and as chairman in 1980, but stayed as a member of the board of directors.

Ford, John c.1586–c.1640
English dramatist

Born in Ilsington, Devon, he studied for a year at Oxford and entered the Middle Temple in 1602. He was expelled for debt but readmitted. He was greatly influenced by Robert Burton, whose *Anatomy of Melancholy* (1621) turned Ford's dramatic gifts towards stage presentation of the melancholy, the unnatural and the horrible in *The Lover's Melancholy* (1629), '*Tis Pity She's a Whore* (1633), *The Lady's Trial* (1639), and others. He also wrote a masterful chronicle play, *Perkin Warbeck* (1634). Ford often collaborated with Thomas Dekker, William Rowley and John Webster. 📖 D Anderson, *John Ford* (1972)

Ford, John, *originally* Sean Aloysius O'Fearna 1895–1973
US film director

Born in Cape Elizabeth, Maine, of Irish immigrant parents, he went to Hollywood in 1913, where he worked as a stunt man, actor and assistant director, before directing his first western, *The Tornado* (1917). An affectionate chronicler of American history in films like *The Iron Horse* (1924), *Young Mr. Lincoln* (1939) and *My Darling Clementine* (1946), he enjoyed a long association with actor John Wayne which resulted in such classics as *Stagecoach* (1939), *The Searchers* (1956) and *The Man Who Shot Liberty Valance* (1962). He frequently explored his Irish roots, as in *The Informer* (1935, Academy Award), but became identified with the Western genre, chronicling its rugged heroes, pioneering families and sense of male camaraderie. His other Academy Awards were for *The Grapes of Wrath* (1940), *How Green Was My Valley* (1941) and *The Quiet Man* (1952). He also received the first American Film Institute Life Achievement award in 1973, and co-directed the first film in Cinerama, *How the West Was Won* (1962). 📖 Andrew Sinclair, *John Ford* (1979)

Ford, Richard 1796–1858
English travel-writer
Born in Winchester, he studied at Trinity College, Oxford, and was called to the Bar, but never practised. He spent the years 1830–34 on riding tours in Spain, and wrote the popular and characterful *Handbook for Travellers in Spain* (1845), followed by *Gatherings from Spain* (1846). He introduced the British public to the works of **Velazquez**. 📖 B Ford, *Richard Ford en Sevilla* (1963)

Forde, Daryll 1902–73
English anthropologist
Born in Tottenham, Middlesex, he studied geography at University College London, and taught there (1923–28) and later at the University of Wales (1930–45), before returning to University College as Professor of Anthropology (1945–69). He carried out fieldwork in Arizona and New Mexico (1928–29), Nigeria (1935, 1939) and the Gambia (1945). He made extensive contributions to the anthropology of Africa, and was director of the African Institute, London, from the end of World War II until his death. In his major works, which include *Habitat, Economy and Society* (1934), *Marriage and the Family among the Yakö* (1941) and *The Context of Belief* (1958), he explored patterns of kinship and marriage, relations between environment, economy and social organization, and the role of anthropology as practised by indigenous scholars.

Forel, Auguste Henri 1848–1931
Swiss psychologist and entomologist
He was born in La-Gracieuse, near Morges, and studied at the University of Zurich before moving to specialize in neuroanatomy at Vienna. An authority on the psychology of ants, he was Professor of Psychiatry at Zurich (1879–98) and made notable contributions in the fields of the anatomy of the brain and nerves, hypnotism, and forensic psychiatry. He was also a pioneer in sex hygiene and other social reforms relating to the prevention of mental illness caused by syphilis and alcoholism.

Foreman, George 1949–
US boxer
Born in Marshall, Texas, he grew up in troubled circumstances in Houston and won a gold medal at the 1968 Olympics in Mexico City after only 18 amateur fights. He turned professional in 1969, and defeated Joe Frazier to win the world heavyweight championship in 1973. In 1977 he lost the title to **Muhammad Ali**, in one of the most famous fights of all time—the Rumble in the Jungle— and following a religious conversion that year, he was ordained and gave up boxing for 10 years. In 1987, short of funds for the youth and community centre he founded in Houston, he decided to return to boxing. His age and excessive weight led to much scepticism about his comeback, but in 1994, aged 45, he knocked out reigning heavyweight champion Michael Moorer to regain the title, becoming the oldest boxing champion ever in any weight division.

Forest, Lee De See De Forest, Lee

Forester, C(ecil) S(cott) 1899–1966
British writer
Born in Cairo, of British parents, he studied medicine at Guy's Hospital, London, but turned to writing full-time after the success of his first novel, *Payment Deferred* (1926). He also wrote *The African Queen* (1935, filmed 1951), *The General* (1936) and *The Ship* (1943). He is best known for his creation of Horatio Hornblower, a British naval officer in the Napoleonic era whose career he chronicled in a series of popular novels, starting with *The Happy Return* (1937) and *Ship of the Line* (1938, James Tait Black Memorial Prize). He also wrote biographical and travel books and collaborated with C E Bechhofer Roberts on a play about **Edith Cavell**. 📖 C Parkinson, *The Life and Times of Hornblower* (1970)

Forgan, Liz (Elizabeth Anne Lucy) 1944–
British journalist and broadcaster
She was born in Calcutta, where her Scottish father was posted in the army, and attended Benenden School in England, then Oxford. She began her career with the *Hampstead and Highgate Express* (1969–74) in London, and as chief leader-writer on the *Evening Standard* (1974–78). In 1978 she was appointed women's editor of *The Guardian*, where she developed a strong feminist commitment. In 1981 she was asked to join Channel Four Television as commissioning editor of factual output. She introduced programmes such as *Right to Reply* and by 1988 had become director of programmes and the most powerful woman in British television. In 1993 she left to become managing director of BBC Network Radio.

Forman, Miloš 1932–
US film director
Born in Caslav, Czechoslovakia, he received internation recognition for two feature films, *Lásky jedné plavovlásky* (1965, 'A Blonde in Love') and *Hoří, má panenko!* (1967, 'The Fireman's Ball'), made in Prague. He moved to the USA in 1970 and made his English-language debut with *Taking Off* (1971). He received Best Director Academy Awards for *One Flew Over the Cuckoo's Nest* (1975) and *Amadeus* (1984). His other films include *Ragtime* (1981), *Valmont* (1989) and *The People Vs Larry Flynt* (1996). He has published an autobiography: *Turnaround* (1994).

Forman, Simon 1552–1611
English astrologer and quack-doctor
Born in Quidhampton, Wiltshire, he studied at Magdalen College, Oxford. He set up a lucrative practice in 1583 in London, particularly in love potions for ladies of the court, and was constantly prosecuted by the Church and the College of Physicians. He left in manuscript form a *Booke of Plaies* containing the earliest accounts of the performances of some of **Shakespeare**'s plays.

Formby, George 1904–61
English entertainer
Born in Wigan, Greater Manchester, the son of a North Country comedian, he briefly pursued a career as a jockey before following in his father's footsteps. He developed an act in music halls throughout England that was subsequently transferred to film. In a series of low-budget, slapstick comedies he portrayed a shy young man with an irrepressible grin and ever-ready ukelele to accompany his risqué songs. From *Boots Boots* (1934) to *George in Civvy Street* (1946) he was one of Great Britain's most popular film stars. Falling out of favour with postwar cinema audiences, he returned to the stage. Latterly dogged by ill health he was long dominated by his formidable wife Beryl, who died in 1960.

Forrest, Edwin 1806–72
US actor
He was born in Philadelphia, where he made his debut (1820). At the age of 20 he appeared as Othello in New York with great success. He had favourable seasons in London (1836–37), but in 1845 his Macbeth was hissed by the audience. A resentment which prompted him to hiss **William Macready**'s performance in Edinburgh destroyed his reputation in Great Britain. The hissing of Macready's Macbeth by Forrest's sympathizers in New York in 1849

led to a riot which cost 22 lives. He retired temporarily in 1853, but returned to the stage (1860) and made his last appearance as Cardinal Richelieu in Boston (1871). ▭ Richard Moody, *Edwin Forrest, First Star of the American Stage* (1960)

Forrest, George 1873–1932
Scottish plant collector and botanist

Born in Falkirk, Lothian, he was employed in the Royal Botanic Garden of Edinburgh by Sir Isaac Bayley Balfour. His first expedition was to Yunnan and Tibet (1904–06) and he returned to the area several times between 1910 and 1930. He sent home several hundred pounds (weight) of seed from each trip. His explorations in Upper Burma and China resulted in the discovery and introduction of many plants, two of his most significant introductions being *Pieris formosa* variety *forrestii* and the widely grown *Gentiana sino-ornata*. Plants named after him include *Rhododendron forrestii* and *Gentiana forrestii*.

Forrest (of Bunbury), John Forrest, 1st Baron 1847–1918
Australian explorer and politician

He was born in Bunbury, Western Australia, and from 1864 was a colonial surveyor. In 1869 he penetrated inland from Perth as far east as 123°, and the next year reached South Australia from the west along the south coast. With his brother Alexander (1849–1901) he made an eastward journey in 1874. Surveyor-General for the colony from 1883, he was the first premier of Western Australia (1890–1901), and later Minister for Defence, Minister for Home Affairs, and Treasurer. He died at sea (off Sierra Leone) on his way to London, where he was due to receive a peerage, the first to an Australian.

Forrestal, James 1892–1949
US politician

Born in Beacon, New York, he entered US government service in 1940 after a business career. From 1944 to 1947 he was secretary of the navy and, until his resignation shortly before he committed suicide, Defense Secretary.

Forrester, Jay Wright 1918–
US computer engineer

Born in Anselmo, Nebraska, and educated at Nebraska University, he became a pioneer in the development of computer storage devices. He supervised the building in 1944–51 of the Whirlwind computer at the Massachusetts Institute of Technology (MIT), during the course of which (1949) he devised the first magnetic core store (memory) for an electronic digital computer. From 1951 to 1956 he was a founder and director of the Digital Computer Laboratory. He has published several books, including *Industrial Dynamics* (1961), *Principles of Systems* (1968) and *World Dynamics* (1971).

Forschammer, Johann Georg 1794–1865
Danish chemical oceanographer

Born in Husum, he entered Kiel University in 1815 to study physics and chemistry, and moved (1818) to Copenhagen, where he attended lectures by Hans Oersted and became director of the Polytechnic Institute. In 1831 he was appointed Professor of Mineralogy and Geology at the University of Copenhagen. He determined the major components of sea-water and found their relative concentrations to be almost constant, allowing the salinity of any sample to be determined by measurement of any single major component. In his *On the Components of Sea-water* (1859) he postulated the idea of a geochemical balance related to a sedimentary cycle of material washed into the sea by rivers, the balance being inversely proportional to the time the organo/chemical particles spend in the soluble state. His *Danmarks*

Geognostiske Forhold (1835) was the first work on the structural geology of Denmark, for which he was termed 'the father of Danish geology'.

Forssman, Werner 1904–79
German physician, surgeon and Nobel Prize winner

Born in Berlin, he studied at university there, served as an army doctor until 1945, then practised urological surgery at various places including Bad Kreuznach and Düsseldorf. He became known for his pioneering work in the late 1920s on cardiac catheterization, in which he carried out dangerous experiments on himself. He abandoned them in the face of criticism, but was awarded the 1956 Nobel Prize for physiology or medicine jointly with André Cournand and Dickinson Richards, who had extended Forssman's original techniques and demonstrated their clinical and experimental usefulness. By then, however, it was too late for Forssman to catch up with subsequent advances in cardiology and to contribute further to the procedure he had pioneered. His autobiography was published in 1974.

Forster, E(dward) M(organ) 1879–1970
English novelist and critic

Born in London, he was educated at Tonbridge School and King's College, Cambridge, where he revelled in the 'Bloomsbury circle' of G E Moore, G M Trevelyan and Lowes Dickinson (1862–1932), with whom he founded the *Independent Review* in 1903. In his novels he examined with subtle insight the pre-1914 English middle-class ethos and its custodians the Civil Service, the Church and the public schools. Early titles include *Where Angels Fear to Tread* (1905), *The Longest Journey* (1907), *A Room with a View* (1908) and *Howards End* (1910). He became secretary to the Maharajah of Dewas Senior in India in 1921, and in 1924 published his masterpiece, *A Passage to India*, in which he puts English values and Indian susceptibilities under his finest scrutiny. It was awarded the James Tait Black Memorial and Femina Vie Heureuse prizes in 1925. He also wrote short stories, essays, the Cambridge Clark lectures *Aspects of the Novel* (1927), biographies of Lowes Dickinson (1934) and Marianne Thornton (1958), and in 1951 he collaborated with Eric Crozier on the libretto of Benjamin Britten's opera, *Billy Budd*. He was elected a Fellow of King's College, Cambridge, in 1946. His novel *Maurice* (written 1913–14), on the theme of homosexuality, was published posthumously in 1971. ▭ N Beauman, *Morgan: a biography of E M Forster* (1993); J Beer, *The Achievement of E M Forster* (1962)

Förster, Johann Reinhold 1729–98
German naturalist and clergyman

Born in Dirschau (now Tczew) of parents of Scottish extraction (Forrester), he studied theology at Halle and became a country minister near Danzig. He left the church in 1765 and began a survey of new German colonies on the Volga, in south-west Russia. A teacher at the Dissenter's Academy in Warrington, Lancashire (1766–69), he (and his son, Johann Georg Adam Förster, 1754–94) accompanied James Cook as naturalist on his second world voyage on the *Resolution* (1772–75). A pioneer ornithologist of Antarctica, New Zealand and the Pacific, he was appointed Professor of Natural History at Halle in 1780. He wrote a *Catalogue of the Animals of North America* (1771), although he never went there, and *Observations made during a Voyage round the World* (1778) of his expedition with Cook. Förster's tern is named after him.

Forster, John 1812–76
English biographer, historian and journalist

Born in Newcastle upon Tyne, he was educated for the Bar, but in 1833 began to write political articles in the *Examiner*. He went on to edit the *Foreign Quarterly Review*, the *Daily News* and the *Examiner* (1847–56). He was the author of many biographical and historical essays and an admirable series dealing with the Commonwealth,— *Lives of the Statesmen of the Commonwealth* (1836–39), *Debates on the Grand Remonstrance* (1860), *Arrest of the Five Members* (1860), and *Sir John Eliot, a Biography* (1864). He is, however, best remembered for his *Life and Times of Goldsmith* (1848), *Landor* (1868), *Life of Dickens* (1871–74), and volume one of a *Life of Swift* (1875).

Forster, William Edward 1819–86
English politician

Born of Quaker parentage in Bradpole, Dorset, he abandoned the Bar for the wool industry. During the Irish famine of 1845 he visited the distressed districts as almoner of a Quaker relief fund. In 1850 he married Jane, the daughter of Dr Thomas Arnold. In 1861 he became Liberal MP for Bradford, rose to Cabinet rank and in 1870 carried the Elementary Education Act. Under the Gladstone administration of 1880 he was Chief Secretary for Ireland. He was attacked unceasingly in parliament by the Irish members, and his life was threatened by the 'Invincibles' for his measures of coercion. A strong opponent of Home Rule, he was a severe critic of Charles Stewart Parnell and, determined to re-establish law and order, had him and other Irish leaders arrested. When in 1882 a majority of the Cabinet determined to release the 'suspects', Forster and Lord Cowper (the Lord Lieutenant) resigned.

Forsyth, Alexander John 1769–1843
Scottish inventor and clergyman

Born in Belhelvie, Aberdeenshire, he succeeded his father as Presbyterian minister there (1791). In 1807 he patented his improved detonating mechanism for firearms, which resulted in the adoption of the percussion-cap by the British forces. Napoleon I offered him £20,000 for the secret of his invention, but he patriotically refused. The first instalment of the pension belatedly awarded to him by the British government arrived on the day of his death.

Forsyth, Bill (William David) 1946–
Scottish filmmaker

Born in Glasgow, he entered the film industry in 1963 and started making his own documentaries after the death of his employer. He dropped out of the National Film School after a year (1971), but his *That Sinking Feeling* ('a fairytale for the workless'), a comedy using actors from the Glasgow Youth Theatre, was warmly received at the 1979 Edinburgh Film Festival. His other feature films include the adolescent romance *Gregory's Girl* (1980) and *Local Hero* (1983), which focused on the impact of the oil business on a remote Scottish community. Particularly interested in exploring the lives of characters on the edge of society, he has also explored the more fragile melancholy of dislocated individuals: a love-struck radio DJ in *Comfort and Joy* (1984), and an eccentric hobo in *Housekeeping* (1987), his first US film since moving to Hollywood in the mid-1980s. His other films include *Breaking In* (1989) and *Being Human* (1994).

Forsyth, Bruce, originally Bruce Joseph Forsyth-Johnson 1928–
English entertainer

Born in Edmonton, London, he trained as a dancer, making his debut as 'Boy Bruce—The Mighty Atom' at the Theatre Royal, Bilston (1942). His vast showbusiness experience includes a spell as the resident comedian at the Windmill Theatre (1949–51) as well as innumerable appearances in cabaret and music hall. He made his television debut in *Music Hall* in 1954 but gained national popularity as the compere of *Sunday Night at the London Palladium* (1958–60). An all-round song'n'dance man and comic with a jaunty manner, catchphrases and deftness at audience participation, he has won affection as the host of game shows like *The Generation Game* (1971–78, 1990–95), *Play Your Cards Right* (1980–87) and the chat show *Bruce's Guest Night*. His musical talents have been seen in television specials and on stage in one-man shows and productions like *Little Me* (1964), *Birds on the Wing* (1969), *The Travelling Music Show* (1978) and *Bruce Forsyth on Broadway* (1979). A perennial Royal Command performer and charity golfer, he has appeared in a few films including *Star!* (1968) and *Bedknobs and Broomsticks* (1971).

Forsyth, Frederick 1938–
English writer

Born in Ashford, Kent, he was educated at Tonbridge School, Kent. He served in the RAF and later became a journalist. His reputation rests on three taut suspense thrillers, *The Day of the Jackal* (1971), *The Odessa File* (1972) and *The Dogs of War* (1974), meticulously researched and precisely plotted. Others include *The Fourth Protocol* (1984, filmed 1987), *The Deceiver* (1991) and *The Fist of God* (1993).

Forsyth, Gordon Mitchell 1879–1953
Scottish ceramic designer and teacher

Born in Fraserburgh, Aberdeenshire, he trained in Aberdeen and at the Royal College of Art, London, winning a travelling scholarship to Italy in 1902. From 1902 to 1905 he was art director of Minton, Hollins & Co before moving in 1906 to Pilkington Tile & Pottery Co, where he specialized in lustre ware. He frequently made use of lettering and mottoes as titles to his work. He encouraged throwers to produce individual decorative designs and to sign and date their own work. He served as a designer to the RAF (1916–19), before his appointment as superintendent of art instruction at the Stoke-on-Trent School of Art. Among his many pupils there were Clarice Cliff and Susie Cooper. He was art adviser to the British Pottery Manufacturers Federation and was noted for his knowledge of art education and aspects of design, and his awareness of the demands of industry. His publications include *The Art and Craft of the Potter* (1934) and *20th Century Ceramics* (1936).

Forsyth, Sir Michael Bruce 1954–
Scottish Conservative politician

Born in Montrose and educated at the University of St Andrews, he entered politics as a student and was a prominent member of the Federation of Conservative Students. As Conservative MP for Stirling (1983–97), he held several posts in the Scottish Office, including a difficult year as chairman of the Scottish Conservative Party (1989–90). His closeness to Margaret Thatcher helped his early political career but it made him many enemies in Scotland where her free market policies were unpopular. Nevertheless, under John Major he proved to be an effective Secretary of State for Scotland (1995–97). He lost his seat in the 1997 general election when Labour came to power and was knighted in 1998.

Forsyth, Peter Taylor 1848–1921
Scottish Congregational theologian and preacher

He was born in Aberdeen. Influenced in his student days by Albrecht Ritschl at Göttingen, he rejected theological liberalism in the early 1880s, and came to a deep belief in God's holiness and the realities of sin and grace. As Principal of Hackney Theological College, Hampstead, London (1901–21), he championed a high doctrine of church, ministry, sacrament, and preaching in the Congregational Church. His *The Cruciality of the Cross* (1909), *The Person and the Place of Jesus Christ* (1909), and *The Work of Christ* (1910), in some ways anticipating the neo-orthodoxy of Karl Barth and Emil Brunner, have enjoyed renewed popularity since World War II.

Forsythe, William 1949–
US dancer, choreographer and artistic director

Born in New York City, he trained at the Joffrey Ballet School before dancing with the company (1971–73). **John Cranko** invited him to the Stuttgart Ballet in 1973. His first ballet, *Urlicht* (1976), led to an appointment as resident choreographer there. He became artistic director of Frankfurt Ballet in 1984, establishing himself as a leading figure of European contemporary dance theatre by extending the classical ballet vocabulary into his own distinctive language. His controversial works, including *Say Bye Bye* (1980), *Artifact* (1984), *Impressing the Czar* (1988) and *Eidos: Telos* (1995), frequently use spoken text and stage mechanics to enhance the steps.

Fort, Paul 1872–1960
French poet

Born in Reims, he settled in Paris, where in 1890 he founded the Théâtre des Arts to present a wide range of European drama and recitals of Symbolist poetry. He is best known for his popular *Ballades françaises* (1st vol 1897, 'French Ballads'), which eventually numbered 17 volumes, and in which he brought poetry closer to the rhythms of everyday speech. He also wrote several plays, founded and edited the literary magazine *Vers et Prose* (1905–14), and wrote *Histoire de la poésie française depuis 1850* (1927, 'History of French Poetry since 1850'). 🕮 A Lowell, *Six French Poets* (1915)

Forte, Charles Forte, Baron 1908–
Scottish catering and hotel magnate

Born in Italy, he was educated there and at Alloa Academy and Dumfries College. He entered the catering trade via the family ice-cream business, and then became proprietor of the first milk bar in London (1933). He built up a successful catering network, and diversified into hotels and other business interests. A merger created Trusthouse Forte in 1970, and he won a boardroom battle to be chief executive of the new company from 1971 to 1978. He was executive chairman until 1981, and became chairman in 1982. Ten years later the chairmanship passed to his son Rocco Forte (1945–) and Forte became life president. He was made a life peer in 1986, and the same year published an autobiography, *Forte*.

Fortes, Meyer 1906–83
British social anthropologist

Born in Britstown, Cape Province, South Africa, he was educated in Cape Town, and trained in psychology before studying anthropology at the London School of Economics under **Charles Seligman**, **Bronisław Malinowski** and **Raymond Firth**. In 1946 he became Reader at Oxford, and from 1950 to 1973 he was Professor of Social Anthropology at Cambridge. During the 1930s he carried out fieldwork in West Africa among the Tallensi and the Ashanti, which resulted in several classic monographs including *The Web of Kinship among the Tallensi* (1949) and *Time and Social Structure* (1970). These studies laid the foundations for the theory of descent, a cornerstone of the 'structural-functionalism' dominating the social anthropology of the 1950s and 1960s. His most complete theoretical statement is in *Kinship and the Social Order* (1969), where he argues that kinship relations have an irreducible moral content. His early and enduring interest in psychology is particularly apparent in his studies of ancestor worship, as in *Oedipus and Job in West African Religion* (1959). His last work, *Rules and the Emergence of Society* (1983), a critique of sociobiological theories of human kinship and social organization, remained incomplete at his death.

Fortescue, Sir John c.1385–c.1479
English judge and jurist

Born in Somerset, and educated at Exeter College, Oxford, he was called to the Bar, then became Lord Chief Justice of the King's Bench in 1442. He sided with the Lancastrians, fled with **Margaret of Anjou** and her son to Scotland, and in 1463 embarked with them for Holland. During his exile he wrote his *De Laudibus Legum Angliae* (published 1537,'In Praise of the Laws of England') for the instruction of Prince Edward, a work which came to be of great value to later jurists. After the defeat of the Lancastrians at the Battle of Tewkesbury (1471), he surrendered to **Edward IV**. He also wrote *The Governance of England*, which was not published until 1714.

Fortescue, Sir John William 1859–1933
English military historian

Born in Madeira, he was brought up near Barnstaple, Devon. He became private secretary to the Governor of the Windward Islands and from 1886 to 1890 was private secretary to the Governor of New Zealand. He was also librarian of Windsor Castle (1905–26). As well as his monumental *History of the British Army* (13 vols, 1899–1930), his writings include *Statesmen of the Great War 1793–1814* (1911), *County Lieutenancies and the Army, 1803–1814* (1925), *Wellington* (1925) and, in a different vein, *The Story of a Red Deer* (1897).

Fortesque-Brickdale, Mary Eleanor 1872–1945
English painter and illustrator

Born in Surrey, she trained at the Crystal Palace School of Art and then at the Royal Academy schools, London. She began exhibiting at the Royal Academy in 1896 and in 1897 won a prize for the RA dining room design. She illustrated many books of poetry and prose, and taught at the Byam Shaw School of Art, London, before travelling extensively through Italy and the south of France. She designed posters for the government during World War I, after which her stained glass window designs were in great demand. She continued to work into the 1940s, and was the first woman to be elected a member of the Royal Institute of Oil Painters and to be an associated member of the Royal Society of Painters in Water Colour.

Fortin, Jean Nicolas 1750–1831
French scientific instrument-maker

Born in Mouchy-la-Ville, he worked for many eminent scientists including **Antoine Lavoisier**, **Joseph Gay-Lussac**, **François Arago**, and **Pierre Dulong**. He was notable for precision-balances, dividing engines and comparators, but especially for an improved barometer to which his name is given. Although he did not invent the leather bag, the ivory point or the glass tube in the cistern, he appears to have been the first to use all three together in 1797 in a sensitive portable barometer.

Fortune, Robert 1813–80
Scottish horticulturist and plant collector

Born in Kelloe, Berwickshire, he gained horticultural training in Berwickshire, at Moredun, near Edinburgh, and at Edinburgh's Royal Botanic Garden. In 1840 he was employed by the Horticultural Society at Chiswick, which sent him to China in 1842 to collect plants. In 1848 the East India Company asked him to help in expanding tea production in India's north-west provinces. This entailed a second three-year expedition to China, collecting tea seeds and plants, quickly followed by a third in search of black tea, and a fourth (1858–59) for the US Patent Office. His last journey (1861–62) was to Japan and northern China. From his many expeditions, Fortune introduced several well-known plants to British gardens, including the Japanese anemone, the Chinese fan palm (*Trachycarpus fortunei*), the winter jasmine, the Japanese golden-rayed lily (*Lilium auratum*) and the Chusan daisy, progenitor of today's pompom chrysanthemums. His travel notes were published as *Three Years Wanderings in the Northern Provinces of China* (1847), *Two Visits to the Tea Mountains of China* (2 vols, 1853), *A Residence Among the Chinese* (1857) and *Yedo and Peking* (1863).

Fortuny y Carbo, Mariano 1839–74
Spanish painter

Born in Reus, Tarragona, he followed the Spanish army in the war against Morocco and filled his portfolios with studies of Eastern life. The best of his Rococo pictures are *The Spanish Marriage, Book-Lover in the Library of Richelieu* and *Academicians Choosing a Model*.

Fosbury, Dick (Richard) 1947–
US athlete

He was born in Portland, Oregon. He pioneered a new technique in high jumping which revolutionized this event after he won the Olympic gold medal at Mexico City in 1968 with a jump of 2.24m (7ft 4in), using what came to be known as the 'Fosbury Flop'. This cut across conventional athletics coaching in that the bar was jumped head first and backwards.

Foscari, Francesco 1373–1457
Doge of Venice

He was doge from 1423, and his warlike policies on the Italian mainland, especially against Milan, were vital to the creation of a territorial state under Venetian rule. However, the losses of territory to the Turks, his princely style of government and his promotion of the interests of his family resulted in his deposition, and to his death from rage and grief soon afterwards. His career is the subject of a play by **Byron**.

Foscolo, Ugo 1778–1827
Italian writer

Born in Zante, he was educated at Spalato (now Split) and Venice. After Venice was ceded to Austria he wrote the *Lettere di Jacopo Ortis* (1802, Eng trans *Letters of Ortis*, 1818), and published his best poem, *I Sepolcri* (1807, Eng trans *The Sepulchres*, 1820). He translated Laurence **Sterne's** *Sentimental Journey*, and wrote two tragedies, *Ajace* and *Ricciarda*. In 1809 he was for a few months Professor of Eloquence in Pavia. After 1814, when the Austrians entered Milan, he sought refuge in London, where he published his *Saggi sul Petrarca* (1847, 'Essays on Petrarch'), his commentaries on **Boccaccio's** *Decameron*, **Dante** and **Petrarch**, and various papers in the *Quarterly Review* and *Edinburgh Review*. He left a long poem, *Le Grazie* (1848, 'The Graces'), incomplete on his death. 📖 L Fabiani, *Ugo Foscolo* (1972)

Fosdick, Harry Emerson 1878–1969
US Baptist minister

Born in Buffalo, New York, and ordained in 1903, he was a professor at Union Theological Seminary, New York, from 1915, and pastor of the interdenominational Riverside Church in New York from 1926 to 1946. An outstanding preacher, he was a leading 'modernist' in the controversy over Fundamentalism in the 1920s. His publications include *The Manhood of the Master* (1913), *The Secret of Victorious Living* (1934), *On Being a Real Person* (1943), *A Faith for Tough Times* (1952) and *The Living of These Days*, an autobiography (1956).

Foss, Lukas, *originally* Lukas Fuchs 1922–
US composer

Born in Berlin, Germany, he settled in the USA in 1937. He studied under Paul **Hindemith** and first attracted attention with his cantata, *The Prairie* (1941). His numerous works include *A Parable of Death* (1953), for soloist, narrator, choir and orchestra, and the operas *The Jumping Frog of Calaveras County* (1950) and *Griffelkin* (1955), as well as symphonies, concertos and chamber music. His later music is in aleatory style and also includes radical reworkings of Renaissance Baroque music, for example in his *Renaissance Concerto* (1986). Professor of Music Composition at Boston University since 1992, he has been a guest conductor with many US and European orchestras.

Fosse, Bob (Robert Louis) 1927–87
US theatre and film choreographer and director

Born in Chicago, the son of a vaudeville entertainer, he started performing on stage at the age of 13. He made his Broadway debut in the revue *Dance Me a Song* (1950), but it was his contribution to the musical *The Pajama Game*, a witty number called 'Steam Heat', which established him as a choreographer. During his long career he choreographed 11 Broadway shows, including *Damn Yankees* (1955), *Red Head* (1959), *Little Me* (1963), *Sweet Charity* (1966), *Pippin* (1973) and *Dancin'* (1978), and won six Tony awards. Moving into film, he was both director and choreographer of *Cabaret* (1972, Best Director Academy Award), and continued his success with *All That Jazz* (1979), which he directed and choreographed, and for which he supplied the screenplay.

Fossey, Dian 1932–85
US zoologist

She was born in San Francisco, and in 1963 went to Africa where she met the anthropologists Louis and Mary **Leakey**, and first encountered gorillas in the Virunga mountain range of central Africa. In 1966, encouraged by the Leakeys, she returned to Tanzania and set up the Karisoke Research Centre in Rwanda in order to study the gorilla population. Her 18-year study is documented in her 1983 book *Gorillas in the Mist* (filmed 1988). Fossey advocated 'active conservation', rallying international opposition to the threats posed to the gorillas by poaching and local farming methods. In 1985 she was murdered at the Centre.

Foster, (Myles) Birket 1825–99
English artist

Born in North Shields, Tyne and Wear, he produced (1841–46) several designs for wood-engravings, many of them for the *Illustrated London News*. After 1859 he devoted himself primarily to watercolours, mainly of rustic scenes.

Foster, Jodie, *originally* Alicia Christian Foster 1962–
US film actress

She was born in Los Angeles, and started her career as a toddler in commercials. She made her film debut in *Napoleon and Samantha* (1972, Academy Award), and progressed to playing streetwise adolescent characters in films such as *Alice Doesn't Live Here Anymore* (1974) and *Taxi Driver* (1976, Academy Award). Her adult roles include *Hotel New Hampshire* (1984), *The Accused* (1988), for which she won an Academy Award, *The Silence of the Lambs* (1991), *Sommersby* (1992), *Nell* (1995) and *Contact* (1997). She made her directorial debut in 1991 with *Little Man Tate* followed by *Home for the Holidays* in 1996.

Foster, Sir Michael 1689–1763
English judge and writer

Born in Marlborough, Wiltshire, he was educated at Exeter College, Oxford. He became justice of the King's Bench (1745), and was a widely respected judge who held a deep concern for personal liberty. He published *Examination of the Scheme of Church Power* (1735), setting out the superiority of parliament and the common law over the claims asserted by the High Church faction of the Church of England. His major work was *Crown Cases and Discourses upon a Few Branches of the Crown Law* (1762), a collection of reports, largely of his own criminal cases, and of commentaries on major problems of legal principle such as treason and homicide. It had a great influence on the development of modern criminal law.

Foster, Sir Michael 1836–1907
English physiologist

Born in Huntingdon, Huntingdonshire, he was educated there and at University College London, where he taught physiology until 1870. He then moved to Cambridge, where he became professor in 1883. He was MP for London University (1900–06). His *Textbook of Physiology* (1877) became a standard work.

Foster, Sir Norman 1935–
English architect

Born in Manchester, he trained there and was a founder member with **Richard Rogers** and their wives of Team 4, producing in 1966 Reliant Controls Factory, Swindon. In the 1970s he experimented with simplicity and with pushing technology to the limits, as seen in Willis Faber Dumas Building, Ipswich (1975) and Sainsbury Centre at the University of East Anglia (1978), which won international acclaim as a highly serviced single pure space. His Hong Kong and Shanghai Bank, Hong Kong (1979–85), with boldly expressive structure and immaculate detailing, was highly praised. His first commission in Japan, the Century Tower in Tokyo, was completed in 1991, and has led to other work there. Other 1991 commissions included a new terminal at Stansted Airport, a communications tower for the 1992 Barcelona Olympics, the ITN headquarters in London and a remodelling of the Royal Academy. His technological innovation can be seen in the cultural centre at Nîmes in France (1984–92). In 1996 he unveiled his plan for the Millennium Tower, due to be completed by the year 2001 and built on the site of the 1992 IRA bomb in London's City area. He was knighted in 1990 and made Officier, L'Ordre des Arts et des Lettres in 1994. He is recognized as a leading exponent of the technological approach to architecture.

Foster, Stephen Collins 1826–64
US songwriter

Born in Pittsburgh, he was a largely self-taught musician who began his career as a bookkeeper in Cincinnati and spent his spare time writing songs inspired by African-American life and the South. Himself a white Northerner, he published *Foster's Ethiopian Melodies* in 1849, the same year his song 'O Susannah' became the popular favourite of the migrants to the California Gold Rush. Of his 125 compositions the best known are 'The Old Folks at Home', 'Nelly Bly', 'Camptown Races', 'Beautiful Dreamer', 'Jeannie with the Light Brown Hair' and 'Old Kentucky Home'. He wrote both words and music for his songs, which vary in tone from the compelling simplicity of folk music to the sentimentality of 19th-century popular music. The **Edwin P Christy** minstrel troup helped make his work widely known, but by the time of his death in New York City he was in debt and living in poverty.

Foucauld, Charles Eugène, Vicomte de,
known as **Brother Charles of Jesus** 1858–1916
French soldier, explorer, monk and mystic

Born in Strasbourg, he achieved fame through his exploration of Morocco (1883–84), then in 1886 turned his attention to Catholicism, embarking on a life-long spiritual journey. He felt called to imitate **Jesus Christ** in a life of personal poverty in small contemplative communities financed solely by their own manual labour. He spent time as a Trappist monk in France and Syria, a hermit in Nazareth, a garrison priest at Beni-Abbès, Algeria, and a nomadic hermit among the Tuareg around Tamanrasset. He was murdered, but his ideals survived in the foundation of the Little Brothers (1933) and Little Sisters (1939) of Jesus, now active worldwide.

Foucault, Jean Bernard Léon 1819–68
French physicist

Born in Paris, he began a career as a physician but gave up as he detested the sight of blood. Turning to experimental physics, he determined the velocity of light by the revolving mirror method originally proposed by **François Arago**, and proved that light travels more slowly in water than in air (1850), showing the inverse relation between the speeds in the two media and their refractive indices. This was convincing evidence of the wave nature of light and earned Foucault his doctorate. In 1851, by means of a freely suspended pendulum, he convincingly demonstrated the rotation of the Earth. In 1852 he constructed the first gyroscope, in 1857 the Foucault prism and in 1858 he improved the mirrors of reflecting telescopes.

Foucault, Michel 1926–84
French philosopher and historian of ideas

Born in Poitiers, he was a student of the Marxist philosopher **Louis Althusser** and became Professor of History of Systems of Thought at the Collège de France, Paris (1970). He wrote a series of very influential and provocative books including *Histoire de la folie* (1961, Eng trans *Madness and Civilization*, 1971), *Les Mots et les choses* (1966, Eng trans *The Order of Things*, 1970), *L'Archéologie du savoir* (1969, Eng trans *The Archaeology of Knowledge*, 1972) and *Histoire de la sexualité* (1976, Eng trans *The History of Sexuality*, 1984). His basic thesis in tracing the changing historical assumptions about what counts as 'knowledge' at any one time was both relativistic and cynical. Prevailing social attitudes are manipulated by those in power, both to define such categories as insanity, illness, sexuality and criminality, and to use these in turn to identify and oppress the 'deviants'.

Fouché, Joseph, Duc d'Otrante 1763–1829
French revolutionary politician

Born in Nantes, he was a member of a Catholic teaching order before 1789, then was elected to the National Convention (1792), then becoming an extreme revolutionary. He was noted for his zealous support of attacks on the Christian religion, and for his part in the bloody suppression of opposition at Lyons. He then turned against **Robespierre**, being one of the main organizers of the Thermidor coup. Appointed chief of police in 1799, he helped to bring **Napoleon I** to power, and retained the post until 1815, surviving all the rapid changes of 1814–15. The First Empire gave him his titles of nobility and great wealth. He was banished in 1816. 💻 Hubert Cole, *Fouché, the Unprincipled Patriot* (1971)

Foucquet, Nicolas See **Fouquet, Nicolas**

Foulds, John 1880–1939
English composer

Born in Manchester and largely self-taught, he played cello in the Hallé Orchestra under **Hans Richter**, who premiered his cello concerto (1911). A tone poem, *Epithalamium*, was conducted by Sir **Henry Wood** in London (1906). Known mainly for light music during his lifetime, Foulds had an innovative style, the value of which was long overlooked. From 1915 he became fascinated with oriental (especially Indian) music, and fused these in his works. His major works include *A World Requiem* (1921), a tone poem, *April-England* (1926–32), *Mantras* for orchestra (1930), *Quartetto Intimo* (1932, his ninth string quartet) and other chamber, orchestral, vocal and piano pieces. He emigrated to India in 1935.

Fouqué, Friedrich Heinrich Karl de la Motte, Baron 1777–1843
German writer

Born in Brandenburg, he served as a Prussian cavalry officer in 1794 and 1813. Between campaigns he devoted himself to literary pursuits, and the rest of his life was spent in Paris, on his estate at Nennhausen and, after

1830, in Halle. He published a long series of romances based on Norse legend and Old French poetry, the best-known of which is the fairy romance *Undine* (1811).

Fouquet, Jean c.1420–c.1480
French painter
Born in Tours, he visited Rome between 1445 and 1448 when Pope **Eugenius IV** commissioned a portrait from him. Returning to Tours, he opened a prosperous workshop. In 1475 he received the official title of King's Painter. A copy of **Flavius Josephus**'s *Antiquities of the Jews* contains paintings which have been attributed to him. To him also are attributed the *Hours of Étienne Chevalier* at Chantilly, and several panel portraits, including that of **Charles VII**, and **Agnés Sorel** as the Virgin. In his miniatures he combined Italian influences like architectural perspectives and ornamental detail, with the more northern traits of realistic and unidealized portrayal.

Fouquet or Foucquet, Nicolas, Vicomte de Melun et de Vaux and Marquis de Belle-Isle
1615–80
French statesman
Born in Paris, he was made Procureur-Général to the parliament of Paris by Cardinal **Mazarin** (1650) and superintendent of finance (1653). He became very rich, and was ambitious to succeed Mazarin as Chief Minister, but **Louis XIV** himself took over the position on Mazarin's death, and Fouquet was arrested for embezzlement (1661) and sentenced to life imprisonment in the fortress of Pignerol, where he died.

Fouquier-Tinville, Antoine Quentin 1747–95
French Revolutionary politician
Born in Herouël, he was public prosecutor to the Revolutionary tribunal from 1793. He superintended all the political executions during the Reign of Terror until July 1794, when he sent his friends, among them **Robespierre**, **Danton** and **Hébert**, to execution. He himself was guillotined.

Fourcroy, Antoine François, Comte de
1755–1809
French chemist
Born in Paris, he studied medicine, qualifying in 1780. He became professor at the Jardins des Plantes in 1784, and from 1786 onwards promulgated the revolutionary chemical theories of **Antoine Lavoisier**, both in the classroom and in print. He improved methods of analysing mineral waters, discovered the double salts of ammonia and magnesia, and studied the physiology of muscles. With **Nicolas-Louis Vauquelin** he discovered iridium and made extensive chemical investigations of animal organs and fluids, isolating urea in 1808. Before the Revolution he was one of the leaders of the scientific community and one of the founders of the influential journal *Annales de chimie*. He also helped Antoine Lavoisier, **Marcellin Berthelot** and Baron **Louis Bernard Guyton de Morveau** to develop a new system of chemical nomenclature. During the Revolution he was a member of the Committee of Public Instruction and the Committee of Public Safety, working to reorganize higher education and munitions manufacture, and helping to establish the Institute National des Sciences et des Arts. In 1802 **Napoleon I** appointed him director-general of public instruction and in 1808 made him a Count of the Empire.

Fourdrinier, Henry 1766–1854 and Sealy d.1847
English paper-makers and inventors
With the assistance of **Bryan Donkin**, in 1806 the brothers patented an improved design of a paper-making machine capable of producing a continuous sheet of paper. The liquid pulp was fed on to a wire-mesh belt through which the water drains away, and the resulting damp web of paper was first heated and then passed between heavy rollers which gave it the required smooth finish. The same basic type of machine, with further improvements, is still in use today.

Fourier, (François Marie) Charles 1772–1837
French social theorist
Born in Besançon, he worked for some years as a commercial traveller but became repelled and obsessed by the abuses of civilization. After the Revolution (in which he was imprisoned, and only just escaped the guillotine) he published a number of Utopian socialist works, *Théorie des quatre mouvements et des destinées générales* (1808, Eng trans *The Social Destiny of Man*, 1857), *Traité d'association domestique agricole* (1822, 'A Treatise on Domestic Agricultural Association') and *Le Nouveau monde industriel et sociétaire* (1829, 'The Industrial New World'). In these he advocated a reorganization of society into self-sufficient units (*phalanstères*, 'phalanxes') which would be scientifically planned to offer a maximum of both co-operation and self-fulfilment to their members. Conventional living arrangements, property ownership and marriage would all be radically redesigned. Several experimental 'phalanxes' were founded in France and the USA, and although these failed, his ideas attracted great popular interest and many adherents.

Fourier, (Jean Baptiste) Joseph, Baron de
1768–1830
French mathematician
Born in Auxerre, he joined the staff (1795) of the École Normale in Paris, where his success led to the offer of the chair of analysis at the École Polytechnique. He accompanied **Napoleon I** to Egypt in 1798, and on his return in 1802 was made Prefect of Isère in Grenoble, and later baron (1808). He was later made a member of the Academy of Sciences of Paris (1817). Fourier introduced the expansion of functions in trigonometric series, now known as Fourier series, which proposed that almost any function of a real variable can be expressed as a sum of the sines and cosines of integral multiples of the variable. This method has become an essential tool in mathematical physics and a major theme of analysis. His *Théorie analytique de la chaleur* (1822, 'Analytical Theory of Heat') applied the technique to the solution of partial differential equations to describe heat conduction in a solid body. He also discovered an important theorem on the roots of algebraic equations. 📖 Grattan-Guiness, *Joseph Fourier, 1768–1830* (1972)

Fourneyron, Benoît 1802–67
French engineer and inventor
Born in St-Étienne, Loire, he was educated at the École des Mines. In the early 19th century traditional water wheels were still an important source of power in many industries, and Fourneyron determined to improve on their very low efficiency by 20 per cent. He developed a prototype outward-flow radial turbine in 1827, and by 1833 he had built a larger 50 horse-power turbine with an efficiency of about 75 per cent. In 1895 Fourneyron turbines were installed in the Niagara Falls hydroelectric generating station, but their inherent drawback of a poor part-load performance led to their being replaced after a few years by **Francis** type machines.

Fournier, Alain- See Alain-Fournier

Fournier, Henri-Alban See Alain-Fournier

Fou Ts'ong 1934–
Chinese pianist
Born in Shanghai, he studied under the Italian pianist and founder of the Shanghai Symphony Orchestra, Mario Paci. He won third prize in the International Chopin Competition in Warsaw (1955). He is distinguished

interpreter of **Mozart** and **Chopin**, and basing himself in London since 1958, has performed extensively on the international circuit.

Fowke, Francis 1823–65
British engineer and architect

Born in Belfast, he obtained a commission in the Royal Engineers on the strength of his drawing and in 1856 he was appointed architect and engineer to the government Department of Science and Art. The designer of the original plans for several major museums in Great Britain, he planned the Albert Hall in London, produced the original designs for the Victoria and Albert Museum in London (completed by Sir **Aston Webb**), and planned the Royal Scottish Museum in Edinburgh.

Fowler, Henry Watson 1858–1933
English lexicographer

Born in Tonbridge, Kent, he was educated at Rugby and Balliol College, Oxford, became a schoolmaster at Sedbergh (1882–99), then went to London to try journalism. After the failure of his *Collected Essays*, published in 1903 at his own expense, he went to Guernsey where his brother Frank George Fowler (1871–1918) was a tomato-grower. Together they produced *The King's English* (1906) and the *Concise Oxford Dictionary* (1911). After the death of his brother, Fowler produced the *Pocket Oxford Dictionary* (1924) and his immensely successful, if mannered, *Dictionary of Modern English Usage* (1926). The US counterpart is Margaret Nicholson's *A Dictionary of American English Usage, Based on Fowler.* ◫ Ernest Gowers, H W Fowler (1957)

Fowler, Sir John 1817–98
English civil engineer

Born in Wadsley Hall, Sheffield, he constructed railways from an early age. These included the London Metropolitan Railway, the original London Underground, and Victoria Station, London. River improvement and dock construction also occupied his attention. He was consulting engineer to **Ismail Pasha**, the Khedive of Egypt (1871–79). He designed the Pimlico Railway Bridge (1860), and, with Sir **Benjamin Baker**, the Forth Railway Bridge (1882–90).

Fowler, Sir (Edward) Michael Coulson 1929–
New Zealand architect, writer and politician

Born in Marton, near Wanganui, he was educated at Christ's College, Christchurch, and Auckland University. After working in architectural practices in New Zealand, and in the London offices of **Ove Arup** (1955–56), he became a partner (1959) in a Wellington practice which has designed several major Wellington buildings. He was elected to Wellington City Council (1968–74), and was mayor from 1974 to 1983. Widely travelled, he has written a number of popular architectural books including *The Architecture and Planning of Moscow* (1980), *Wellington Wellington—a History* (1981) and *University of Auckland* (1993). These books are illustrated with his own sketches which themselves have been the subject of several one-man exhibitions.

Fowler, William Alfred 1911–95
US physicist and Nobel Prize winner

Born in Pittsburgh, Pennsylvania, he studied at Ohio State University, obtained his PhD from the California Institute of Technology (Caltech, 1936) for work on radioactive nuclides, and became professor there in 1946. He made detailed measurements of nuclear reactions at low energies and extrapolated to obtain a better idea of what occurs at higher stellar energies. Fowler established the existence of the excited helium state predicted by Sir **Fred Hoyle**, which proved a crucial link in the stellar evolution theory which he developed with Hoyle, and **Geoffrey** and **Margaret Burbidge**, to explain the synthesis of heavy elements in stellar cores. Fowler continued to work on the details of stellar nucleosynthesis, including solar neutrino flux calculations. In 1974 he won the US National Medal of Science and for his work on stellar evolution and nucleosynthesis he shared the 1983 Nobel Prize for physics with **Subrahmanyan Chandrasekhar**.

Fowles, John Robert 1926–
English novelist

Born in Leigh-on-Sea, Essex, he was educated at Bedford School, Edinburgh University and New College, Oxford, where he studied French. He served in the Royal Marines (1945–46), and thereafter taught in schools in France, Greece (1951–52) and London. An allusive and richly descriptive writer, he wrote his first novel, and still perhaps his most sensational, *The Collector* in 1963. However, *The Magus* (1965, rev edn 1977) is the book which made his name. Drawing on his own experience, it is set in the 1960s on a remote Greek island. It is a disturbing and much-imitated tale about an English schoolteacher, his bizarre experiences, and his involvement with a master trickster. *The French Lieutenant's Woman* (1969), however, exceeded it in popularity, in large part due to the film version with **Meryl Streep** in the title role. Later books—*Daniel Martin* (1977), *Mantissa* (1982) and *A Maggot* (1985)—suffered a critical backlash but underlined his willingness to experiment, as well as the fecundity of his imagination. He also published a collection of short stories, *The Ebony Tower* (1974). An essay on the significance of nature in his work, originally written in 1979, was re-issued as *The Tree* (1992), and was followed by *Tessera* (1993), which Fowles describes as 'a piece of juvenilia'. ◫ Robert Huffaker, *John Fowles* (1980)

Fox, Sir Charles 1810–74
English civil engineer

Born in Derby, he built the Crystal Palace in London for the Great Exhibition (1851). He also did much railway construction with his two sons, Sir Charles Douglas Fox (1840–1921) and Sir Francis Fox (1844–1927), themselves both eminent engineers.

Fox, Charles James 1749–1806
English politician

Born in London, he was the third son of the 1st Lord Holland. Educated at Eton and Hertford College, Oxford, he became the MP for Midhurst at the age of 19. He later became a supporter of Lord **North**, and a Lord of the Admiralty. In 1772 he resigned, but the next year was named a commissioner of the Treasury. North dismissed him in 1775 after a quarrel. During the American War Fox was the most formidable opponent of the coercive measures of government. After the downfall of North (1782), he was a Secretary of State. In 1783 the North and Fox coalition was formed, and Fox resumed his former office, but the rejection of his India Bill by the Lords led to the resignation of his government. When **William Pitt**, the Younger, came to power, the long contest between him and Fox began. The regency, the trial of **Warren Hastings** and the French Revolution afforded scope to his talents, and he employed his influence to modify and counteract the policy of his rival. He was a strenuous opponent of the war with France, and an advocate of non-intervention. After Pitt's death in 1806, Fox, recalled to office, set into motion negotiations for a peace with France. He was on the point of introducing a bill for the abolition of the slave trade when he died. Although Fox was addicted to gambling and drinking, **Edmund Burke** called him 'the greatest debater the world ever saw'. He was buried, near Pitt, in Westminster Abbey, London. ◫ John W Derry, *Charles James Fox* (1972)

Fox, George 1624–91
English religious leader, and founder of the Society of Friends, or 'Quakers'

Born in Fenny Drayton, Leicestershire, he seems to have received little formal education and was apprenticed to a cobbler. A Puritan by upbringing, at the age of 19 he rebelled against the formalism of the established Church, and the state's control of it. He travelled around the country, attracting many followers and often interrupting services to expound his own teaching. He inveighed against sacerdotalism and formalism, and was equally vehement against social convention. In 1646 he had a divine revelation that inspired him to preach a gospel of brotherly love, and call his society the 'Friends of Truth'. His life is a record of insults, persecutions and imprisonments. In 1656, the year after he and his followers refused to take the Oath of Abjuration, nearly 1,000 of them were in prison. He went to Barbados, Jamaica, America, Holland and Germany, latterly accompanied by **William Penn**, **Robert Barclay**, and other Quaker leaders. His preaching and writings were often turgid, incoherent and mystical, but as a writer he will be remembered for his *Journal* (1874). ▢ Vernon Noble, *The Man in Leather Breeches* (1953)

Fox, Henry Richard See Holland, 3rd Baron

Fox, Richard See Foxe, Richard

Fox, Richard 1960–
English canoeist
The first man to be five times world champion in singles kayak, he was also a member of the British team who won the title five times during the 1980s. Kayaking was not an Olympic event between 1972 and 1992, denying this talented paddler an Olympic title, and in the kayak slalom singles in the 1992 Barcelona Olympics he finished a disappointing fourth. However the following year he won the world championship title for the fifth time.

Foxe, John 1516–87
English martyrologist
Born in Boston, Lincolnshire, he entered Brasenose College, Oxford, at the age of 16, and became a Fellow of Magdalen College (1538–45). During the reign of **Mary I, Tudor** he lived on the Continent, where he met **John Knox**, Edmund Grindal (1519–83) and Whittingham. On **Elizabeth I**'s accession he received a pension and a prebend of Salisbury (1563), but lived chiefly in London. He published numerous controversial treatises and sermons, besides an apocalyptic Latin mystery play called *Christus Triumphans* (1556). His best known work is *History of the Acts and Monuments of the Church*, popularly known as *Foxe's Book of Martyrs*, the first part of which was published in Latin at Strasbourg in 1554 (trans 1563).

Foxe or Fox, Richard c.1448–1528
English prelate
Born near Grantham, Lincolnshire, he studied at Oxford, Cambridge and Paris, and latterly became Bishop successively of Exeter, Bath and Wells, Durham and Winchester. He founded Corpus Christi College, Oxford, in 1517.

Foyt, A(nthony) J(oseph), Jnr 1935–
US racing driver
He was born in Houston, Texas, and became arguably America's most successful driver. He was the first to win the prestigious Indianapolis 500 (the 500-mile, 200-lap race in the USA, started in 1911) four times (1961, 1964, 1967, 1977). He also won the equally famous Le Mans 24-hour race in 1967. The only racing driver to have won seven national championships, he retired in 1993. He also breeds and trains racehorses. ▢ *A.J.: The Life of America's Race Car Driver* (1983)

Fra Angelico See Angelico, Fra

Fra Bartolommeo See Bartolommeo, Fra

Fracastoro, Girolamo 1483–1553
Italian scholar and physician
He was born in Verona. In 1502 he became Professor of Philosophy at Padua, but he also practised successfully as a physician at Verona, and excelled as an astronomer, geographer and mathematician. He wrote on the theory of music and left a Latin poem on the 'new' venereal disease, *Syphilis sive morbus Gallicus* (1530), from which the word 'syphilis' is derived. His works on contagion developed the older notions of the 'seeds of disease' and pointed to the importance of *fomites* (clothes, beddings, etc) in the spread of certain diseases.

Fra Diavolo, *properly* Michele Pezza 1760–1806
Italian brigand and renegade monk
Born in Itri, he headed a band of desperados in the Calabrian mountains for years and evaded capture by skilful guerrilla warfare. In 1806 he attempted to excite Calabria against France, but was taken prisoner and executed at Naples.

Fraenkel-Conrat, Heinz 1910–
US biochemist
Born in Breslau, Germany (now Wrocław, Poland), he studied medicine there and biochemistry in Edinburgh before moving to the USA in 1936. He returned to work in Europe before joining the staff of the University of California at Berkeley in 1952, becoming Professor of Virology in 1958 and later Professor of Molecular Biology. Working with viruses, he showed that an active virus could be reconstituted from its inactive protein and nucleic acid components, and that it was a 'living chemical' and a basic unit in the new science of molecular biology (1955). Later he studied methods for the sequence analysis of RNA and chemical modification in relation to protein–RNA interactions.

Fraga Iribarne, Manuel 1922–
Spanish politician and academic
As Minister of Information and Tourism under General Franco (1962–69), he liberalized the regime, above all through the Press Law of 1966. By contrast, he was a hardline Minister of the Interior (1975–76). In 1976 he founded Alianza Popular (AP, Popular Alliance), which became the main opposition party to the Spanish Socialist Workers Party (PSOE) in 1982 and was renamed the PP in 1988. A conservative of authoritarian temperament, he was a dynamic, if abrasive, leader of the AP (1979–86) and was elected again in 1989. In 1990 he was elected president of the regional government of Galicia, his home region.

Fragonard, Jean Honoré 1732–1806
French painter and engraver
Born in Grasse, he studied under **François Boucher** and **Jean Chardin** in Paris, and gained the Prix de Rome in 1752. He painted, with luscious colouring and a loose touch, genre pictures of contemporary life, the amours of the French court (notably *The Progress of Love*, 1770, for Madame **du Barry**), and landscapes foreshadowing Impressionism. His *Bacchante endormie* ('The Sleeping Baccante'), *La Chemise enlevée* and other works are in the Louvre, Paris, and he is also represented in the Wallace Collection, London. The French Revolution ruined his career. ▢ Jean-Pierre Cuzin, *Fragonard* (1988)

Frame, Janet Paterson 1924–
New Zealand novelist and short-story writer
She was born in Dunedin, and educated at Otago University Teachers Training College. Her first book was a collection of short stories, *The Lagoon: Stories* (1952), which she followed five years later with a novel, *Owls Do Cry*. She spent much time in psychiatric hospitals after severe mental breakdowns, and her novels describe an existence in which the looming threat of disorder both

attracts and frightens. She was applauded in her homeland, but only belatedly received international recognition with her key books *Scented Gardens for the Blind* (1963), *A State of Siege* (1966), *Intensive Care* (1970) and *Living in the Maniototo* (1979). Her short stories have been collected in *The Reservoir and Other Stories* (1966) and *You Are Now Entering the Human Heart* (1983), and some early verse was published as *The Pocket Mirror* (1967). The background to her work is implicit in three volumes of autobiography, *To the Island* (1982), *An Angel at my Table* (1984, filmed, 1990) and *The Envoy from Mirror City* (1985). *The Carpathians* was published in 1988 and *An Autobiography* in 1990.

Frampton, Sir George James 1860–1928
English sculptor

He was born in London, and studied at Lambeth School of Art under William Frith. With Sir Alfred Gilbert and Hamo Thornycroft he produced work in a naturalistic and sensitive style, notably a bronze *Peter Pan* in Kensington Gardens, London (1912), the group of Quintin Hogg and boys at the London polytechnic at Langham Place (1906), and the tinted marble and bronze *Dame Alice Owen* (1897, Potters Bar, London). He also produced the Edith Cavell memorial in London (1920) and the Lions at the British Museum.

Franca, Celia 1921–
English dancer

Born in London, she trained under Marie Rambert, Antony Tudor and Vera Volkova, performing with Ballet Rambert (1937–40), and moving to Sadler's Wells Royal Ballet in 1941 where she created roles in Robert Helpmann's *Hamlet* (1942) and *Miracle in the Gorbals* (1944). Soon after returning to Ballet Rambert in 1950 she was invited by a group of dance patrons in Toronto to set up a new ballet company for Canada. In 1951 the National Ballet of Canada was founded under her directorship, and until her retirement in 1974 she built up a repertoire strong on Russian classics and work from British choreographers like Frederick Ashton and Antony Tudor.

France, Anatole, *pseudonym of* Anatole François Thibault 1844–1924
French writer and Nobel Prize winner

Born in Paris, he began his literary career as a publisher's reader, 'blurb' writer and critic, and published his first volume of stories, *Jocaste et le chat maigre* ('Jocasta and the Thin Cat'), in 1879, followed by his first novel, *Le Crime de Sylvestre Bonnard* (1881). Under the literary patronage of Madame de Caillavet, whose love affair with him brought about his divorce (1893), he poured out a number of graceful, lively novels, critical studies and the like, such as the Parnassian *Le Livre de mon ami* (1885, 'My Friend's Book'), a picture of childhood happiness, which stands in strong contrast to later satirical, solipsistic and sceptical works such as *Les Opinions de Jérôme Coignard* (1893). The Dreyfus case (1896) stirred him into politics as an opponent of Church and State and champion of internationalism. His *Île des pingouins* (1908, 'Isle of Penguins'), in which the evolution of mankind is satirically treated, was followed by *Les Dieux ont soif* (1912, 'The Gods are Thirsty'), a fable about the Terror, and *La Révolte des anges* (1914, 'The Angels' Revolt'), a satire on Christianity and theology. He was awarded the Nobel Prize for literature in 1921. 📖 R Virtanen, *Anatole France* (1968); J Roujon, *La vie et les opinions d'Anatole France* (1925)

Francesca da Rimini d.c.1285
Italian noblewoman

She was the daughter of Guido da Polenta, Lord of Ravenna. She was married to Giovanni, Lord of Rimini, but she already loved Paolo, Giovanni's brother, and

Giovanni, catching the lovers together, murdered them both. Her story was immortalized in Dante's *Inferno*, and was the subject of an opera by Rachmaninov.

Francesco di Giorgio 1439–1501/2
Italian painter, sculptor and architect

He was born in Siena. Most of his paintings were executed in his early career, and now he is best known as an architect and architectural theorist. By 1477 he was working in Urbino where, as a military engineer, he designed the city's fortifications and, it is generally accepted, exploded the first land-mine (1495) at a siege of Naples. He wrote a treatise on architecture and town planning, and Leonardo da Vinci, who knew him, owned one of his architectural manuscripts. He was appointed chief architect of Siena Cathedral in 1498.

Francesco di Paula, San See Francis of Paola, St

Francesca, Maria See Cabrini, St Francesca Xavier

Francesca, Piero Della See Piero Della Francesca

Franchet d'Espérey, Louis Félix Marie François 1856–1942
French marshal

Born in Algeria, he had a varied military career and was made Commanding General of the French 5th Army in 1914, gaining success at the Battle of the Marne. In 1918 Georges Clemenceau appointed him Commander-in-Chief of Allied armies in Macedonia, where from Salonika he overthrew Bulgaria and advanced as far as Budapest. Only the end of the war prevented his dash for Berlin. He was made Marshal of France in 1922. He had some links to the French extreme right but refused to support Philippe Pétain and the Vichy State in 1940.

Francheville or Franqueville, Pierre 1548–1616
French sculptor, painter and architect

Born in Cambrai, he was long domiciled in Italy, where he studied under Giovanni Bologna. He executed the two colossal statues of Jupiter and Janus in the courtyard of the Grimaldi palace, Genoa, and five statues in the Nicolini Chapel in Florence. Recalled to France by Henri IV in 1604, he made the marble statue of David in the Louvre, Paris, and *Saturn carrying off Cybele* in the Tuileries Gardens.

Francia, *properly* Francesco di Marco di Giacomo Raibolini 1450–1517
Italian goldsmith and painter

Born in Bologna, he achieved fame as a craftsman in metal and niello, and he designed the first italic type for Aldus Manutius. As a painter in oils or in fresco he is noted for his madonnas. His sons, Giacomo (c.1486–1557) and Giulio (1487–1543), were also painters.

Francia, José Gaspar Rodriguez de 1756–1840
Dictator of Paraguay

Born near Asunción, he studied theology, was a professor of divinity, and practised law for 30 years with a high reputation. He assumed a prominent role in Paraguay's movement for independence and held absolute power from 1814 until his death, adopting a policy of isolating Paraguay from the outside world. Frugal and honest, but intensely cruel, he banned foreign trade, attempted national self-sufficiency through agricultural and industrial reform, and abolished noble privileges, together with the Inquisition. 📖 José Antonio Vazquez, *El doctor Francia, visto y oido por sus contemporaneos* (1975)

Franciabigio, *also known as* Francesco di Cristofano 1482–1525
Florentine painter

Born possibly in Florence, he worked in collaboration with **Andrea del Sarto** on the church of the Annunziata and the Chiostro dello Scalzo, and was much influenced by him and **Raphael**. His *Madonna del Pozzo* (c.1508) was long thought to be by Raphael. His *Portrait of a Knight of Rhodes* is in the National Gallery, London.

Francis I 1494–1547
King of France

Born in Cognac, he was the son of Charles, Count of Angoulême, and nephew and son-in-law of **Louis XII**, whom he succeeded (1515) when France's rivalry with the Austrian Habsburg dynasty was at its most intense. His military reputation was established when he gained control of Milan at Marignano (1515). On the death of Emperor **Maximilian I** (1519) he became a candidate for Holy Roman Emperor, but lost the election to Charles I of Spain (Emperor **Charles V**). In 1520 he met **Henry VIII** of England at the Field of the Cloth of Gold, near Calais, a costly and portentous occasion intended to woo England away from its alliance with Charles, and subsequently waged intermittent war against the emperor. A number of reverses followed, including Francis' capture at Pavia (1525) the price of his release (1526) being Flanders, Artois, Burgundy, and all his Italian possessions. He joined the Holy League with the pope, England and Venice to check Charles's growing power, but once again lost Italy in the ensuing Treaty of Cambrai (1529). In a final peace at Crépy (1544) he abandoned all his Italian claims. In religious affairs he won control over the French Church through the Concordat of Bologna (1516) and in general he tried to act the part of a peacemaker. However, in the later years of his reign he became increasingly hostile to Protestants allowing the persecution of heretics (1534), becoming involved in the massacre of the Vaudois (Provençal peasants) in 1554. A notable patron of the Renaissance, he extended protection to humanist scholars like **Erasmus** and the French humanists of the Cercle de Meaux. Brilliant, flamboyant and cultured, he fostered learning and the arts, and created the Palace of Fontainebleau.

Francis II 1544–60
King of France

He was the eldest son of **Henri II** and **Catherine de Médicis**. As the Dauphin of France, in 1558 he married **Mary, Queen of Scots**. He was a sickly boy, and his short reign (1559–60) was dominated by the Guise family in their struggle against the Protestants. ⬚ Marie-Thérèse de Martel, *Catalogue des actes de François II* (1991)

Francis I 1708–65
Holy Roman Emperor

Born in Nancy, Lorraine, the eldest son of Leopold, Duke of Lorraine and Grand Duke of Tuscany, he married **Maria Theresa** of Austria in 1736 and became emperor in 1745. Capable but easy-going, he was overshadowed by his wife, and had little influence on government, except in economic matters.

Francis II of the Holy Roman Empire and I of Austria 1768–1835
Holy Roman Emperor, King of Hungary and of Bohemia

Born in Florence, he succeeded his father, **Leopold II** as Holy Roman Emperor (1792). In Austria's wars against France, she lost the Netherlands and Lombardy in return for Venice, Dalmatia and Istria (1797), and after defeats at Ulm and Austerlitz and the capture of Vienna (1805), Francis renounced the title of Holy Roman Emperor, and retained that of Emperor of Austria (Francis I), which he had assumed in 1804. In 1809 Austria lost Salzburg, Carinthia, Trieste, part of Croatia, Dalmatia and Galicia. After a short alliance with France he allied with the Russians and Prussians, assailed **Napoleon I** and won the

Battle of Leipzig (1813). Through the Treaty of Vienna (1815) he recovered, thanks to Prince **Clemens Metternich**, Lombardy, Venetia and Galicia. He was the King of Hungary until 1830, and of Bohemia until his death. His policy was conservative and anti-liberal, but personally he was an urbane and popular ruler, introducing railways and steamships on the Danube. ⬚ Victor Bibl, *Kaiser Franz* (1938)

Francis II Rákóczi See **Rákóczi, Francis II**

Francis of Assisi, St, *baptized* **Giovanni** *originally* **Francesco di Pietro di Bernardone** c.1181–1226
Italian founder of the Franciscan Order

Born in Assisi, the son of a wealthy merchant, he was highly sociable and fond of good living. In c.1205, however, he joined a military expedition, then halted by a dream, returned to live as a hermit and devoted himself to the care of the poor and the sick. By 1210 he had a brotherhood of 11 for which he drew up a rule repudiating all property, which was originally approved by Pope **Innocent III**. In 1212 he also founded the 'Poor Clares', a Franciscan order for women. At the first General Assembly in 1219, 5,000 members were present, and 500 more were claimants for admission. Francis went to Egypt (1223) and preached in the presence of the sultan, who promised better treatment for his Christian prisoners, and for the Franciscan order gave the privilege they have since enjoyed as guardians of the Holy Sepulchre. On his return to Italy he is said to have received, while praying, the stigmata of the wounds of **Jesus Christ** (1224). His works consist of letters, sermons, ascetic treatises, proverbs and hymns, including the well-known *Canticle of the Sun*. He was canonized by Pope **Gregory IX** in 1228, and in 1980 was designated patron saint of ecology. His feast day is 4 October. ⬚ Thomas of Celano, *First and Second Life of St Francis with Selections from Treatises on the Miracles of Blessed Francis* (1963)

Francis of Paola, St, *Italian* **San Francesco di Paula** 1416–1507
Italian Franciscan monk

He was born in Paola, Calabria. He went to live in a cave at the age of 14 and was soon joined by others. He founded his order of Minim friars in 1436. Communities were established throughout Europe, but not in the British Isles. **Louis XI** of France summoned Francesco to his death-bed, and **Charles VIII** and **Louis XII** built him convents at Plessis-les-Tours and Amboise. He died at Plessis on Good Friday, and was canonized in 1519. His feast day is 2 April.

Francis of Sales, St 1567–1622
French Roman Catholic prelate and writer

Born in Sales, Savoy, he was educated by the Jesuits in Paris. He studied civil law at Padua, took orders and became a distinguished preacher. He successfully converted the Calvinistic population of Chablais, and in 1599 was appointed Bishop of Nicopolis. In 1602 in Paris he was invited to preach at the Louvre and his lectures had so much influence in converting several Huguenot nobles that the king offered him a French bishopric, which he declined. The same year, he became Bishop of Geneva. He established a congregation of nuns of the Order of the Visitation under the direction of Madame de Chantal. His *Introduction to a Devout Life* (1608), was the first manual of piety addressed to those living in society. In 1665 he was canonized by **Alexander VII**. He is the patron saint of writers and his feast day is 24 January. ⬚ A J M Hamon, *Life of St Francis de Sales* (2 vols, 1925–29)

Francis, Clare Mary, *née* **Norman** 1946–
English yachtswoman and writer

Born in Surbiton, she was educated at the Royal Ballet School and London University. The first woman to make a singlehanded crossing of the Atlantic (1973), she was the first woman home in the *Observer* Singlehanded Transatlantic Race, and holds the women's record for 1976. She was also the first woman to captain a boat in the Whitbread Round the World Race (1977–78). She now writes both fiction and non-fiction.

Francis, Connie, *originally* Concetta Rosa Maria Franconero 1938–
US pop singer and film actress

Born in Newark, New Jersey, she was discovered on a television talent show aged 11, and had her first hit with 'Who's Sorry Now' (1957). In the late 1950s, she rivalled fellow-Newarkian Frank Sinatra for records sold, and capitalized on the new pop boom with songs like 'Lipstick on Your Collar'. Her first film appearance was in *Where the Boys Are* (1951), and she became known for appearances on military bases and for charity work. Her later career was interrupted by a violent sexual assault in 1974, but her records continue to sell in large numbers.

Francis, Dick (Richard Stanley) 1920–
English jockey and writer

Born in Surrey, he turned professional jockey at the age of 28, and was on the point of winning the 1956 Grand National when his horse Devon Loch collapsed. He retired the following year and became a racing correspondent with the *Daily Express*. He also began writing popular thrillers with a racing background, and in 1980 he won the Golden Dagger Award of the American Crime Writers' Association. He has written an autobiography of Lester Piggott (1986) and over 30 novels in total, latterly *Wild Horses* (1994) and *Come to Grief* (1995). 🕮 *The Sport of Queens* (1957)

Francis, James Bicheno 1815–92
US engineer and inventor

Born in South Leigh, Oxfordshire, England, in 1833 he emigrated to the USA, working first on railroad construction. By 1837 he had been appointed chief engineer to the 'Proprietors of the Locks and Canals on the Merrimack River', and when they decided to develop the river's power potential in 1845 he began to work on the design of an inward-flow turbine that now bears his name. He is also remembered for the 'Francis formula' describing the flow of water over weirs.

Francis, Sir Philip 1740–1818
British civil servant

Born in Dublin and educated at St Paul's School, London, he became a member of the Council of Bengal in 1773. In 1780 he fought a duel with Warren Hastings, with whom he was always arguing, and was seriously wounded. In 1781 he returned home with a fortune gained at whist. He entered parliament in 1784. He was energetic in the proceedings against Hastings, wrote many pamphlets, and was made a KCB in 1806. He was devoted to the prince regent, supported William Wilberforce against the slave trade and founded the Friends of the People. In 1814 he married a second wife who believed that he was the author of the Letters of Junius, printed in the *Public Advertiser* (1769–72).

Francis, Sam 1923–
US abstract painter

Born in San Mateo, California, he began as a medical student but in 1945 turned to painting, studying at the California School of Fine Arts, San Francisco. He visited Paris in 1950 and had his first one-man show there in 1952. He also visited Japan, and his technique, applying thinned paint in small irregular blots which he allowed to trickle down the surface to create an all-over pattern, reflects both US Action Painting of the late 1940s and

early 1950s, and traditional oriental calligraphy, for example *The Over Yellow* (1957–58, Stuttgart), and *In Lovely Blueness* (1957, Pompidou Centre). His later work created a sense of space by the use of white canvas with blots of colour, as in *Untitled L.A.* (1982).

Francis Xavier, St, *known as* the Apostle of the Indies 1506–52
Spanish missionary

Born at Xavier near Sanguesa, in the Basque country, he was the youngest son of Juan de Jasso, Privy Councillor to the King of Navarre. He studied, then lectured, at Paris, becoming acquainted with Ignatius Loyola with whom he founded the Jesuit Society (1534). Ordained priest in 1537, he lived in Rome, and was sent in 1542 by John III of Portugal as a missionary to Goa, where he worked among both the native population and the Europeans. He visited Malacca, the Banda Islands, Amboyna, the Moluccas and Ceylon, where he converted the King of Kandy and many of his people. In 1548 he founded a mission in Japan which flourished for 100 years. He returned to Goa (1552) to organize a mission to China, but died in the effort. He was canonized in 1622, and his only literary remains are *Letters* (1631) and a catechism, with some short ascetic treatises. His feast day is 3 December.

Franck, César Auguste 1822–90
French composer

Born in Liège, Belgium, of German parents, he studied at the Liège Conservatory, and later in Paris, where he acquired French nationality. His early compositions were considered rather bizarre in France, but were given a better reception in Germany, where they were sponsored by Franz Liszt. In 1848 he settled in Paris as a teacher and organist, composing in his spare time, and in 1872 he was made organ professor at the Conservatory. Much of his considerable output was undistinguished, and his reputation rests on a few great works all written after the age of 50, the best known being his String Quartet (composed in the year of his death), his Symphony in D minor (1886–88), his Violin Sonata (1886), his *Variations symphoniques* for piano and orchestra (1885), and his tone poem *Le Chasseur maudit* (1881–82, 'The Accursed Hunter'). Some of his organ music is also performed. 🕮 Vincent d'Indy, *César Franck* (1906)

Franck, James 1882–1964
US physicist and Nobel Prize winner

Born in Hamburg, Germany, he was educated in Heidelberg and Berlin, and became Professor of Physics at Göttingen University (1920). He left Germany in 1933 in protest against Nazi policies and eventually settled in the USA where he became Professor of Physical Chemistry at the University of Chicago (1938–49). He worked with Gustav Hertz in researching the laws governing energy transfer between molecules, for which they were jointly awarded the Nobel Prize for physics in 1925. They showed that atoms would only absorb a fixed amount of energy, thus demonstrating the quantized nature of the atom's electron energy levels. Franck was also one of the formulators of the Franck–Condon principle of vibrational transitions, and later worked on the development of the nuclear bomb in World War II at Los Alamos, although he headed the Franck Committee of scientists who urged that the bomb should not be used.

Franco, Francisco See panel p677

François II See Francis II

François, Mary Joseph See Garnier, Francis

Francome, John 1952–
English horse-racing jockey, television commentator and author

---

Franco, Francisco, *in full* Francisco Paulino Hermenegildo Teódulo Franco Bahamonde 1892–1975
Spanish general and dictator

Franco was born in El Ferrol, Galicia, and graduated from Toledo military academy in 1910. He rose rapidly through the ranks in Spanish Morocco to become Europe's youngest general (1926). He oversaw the repression of the Asturias miners' revolt (1934), and during 1935 served as Chief of Staff. In 1936, at the last moment, he joined the conspiracy against the newly elected Popular Front government, which was launched on 17–18 July; the rebellion led to the Spanish Civil War.

Franco's leadership of the vital Army of Africa, and his close relations with the rebels' Italian and German allies, led to his becoming (September 1936) *generalissimo* of the rebel forces and chief of the Nationalist state. Between October 1936 and April 1939 he led the Nationalists to victory, and presided over the construction of an authoritarian regime that endured until his death. During World War II, he wanted to join Germany and Italy, but **Hitler** was not prepared to pay his price of France's north African territories. Franco therefore kept Spain out of the war, but

sent the Blue Division to fight in the USSR, and provided Germany with logistical and intelligence support.

In 1947, Franco was declared head of state for life by the reconstituted parliament (Cortes). During the 1950s, his anti-communist stand made possible a rapprochement with the Western powers, the 1953 Bases Agreement with the USA providing Franco with his breakthrough. The greatest paradox of Franco was that he oversaw the modernization of the Spanish economy in the 1950s and 1960s which undermined the political foundations of his police state and prepared it for the transition to democracy. In 1969 he announced that on his death the monarchy would return in the person of **Juan Carlos I**, grandson of Spain's last ruling king. Franco died in Madrid, and within two years almost every vestige of his dictatorship had disappeared.

📖 Paul Preston, *Franco: A Biography* (1993); J W D Tryhall, *El Caudillo: A Political Biography of Franco* (1970); Brian Crozier, *Franco: A Biographical History* (1967).

Born in Swindon, he first rode a winning horse in 1969. Between then and his retirement in 1985, he established a National Hunt record of 1,138 wins, his best season being 1983–84, with 131 wins. He was champion jockey seven times. Resourceful and adaptable, he has since continued his involvement with the sport as a trainer, a commentator for Channel 4 television, and as a writer. *Born Lucky*, his autobiography, was published in 1985, and he has since written several novels set in the racing world.

Franjiyeh, Suleyman 1910–92
Lebanese politician

President of Lebanon (and thus a Maronite) from 1970 to 1976, he began his presidency at a particularly tense period, when Palestinian guerrillas ejected from Jordan (1970–71) began conducting their operations from Palestinian refugee camps in Lebanon. He was President when civil war broke out in 1975 and left office in 1976, the year of the Syrian invasion. He was, however, still active in Maronite politics in 1978 when, as a result of his pro-Syrian stance (which lasted until 1984), a split occurred in Maronite ranks and Phalangist militia murdered his son, Tony Franjieh, and other members of his family.

Frank, Anne See panel p678

Frank, Bruno 1887–1945
German writer

Born in Stuttgart, he wrote historical novels, such as *Die Fürstin* (1915, 'The Princess'), *Aus vielen Jahren* (1937, 'From Many Years') and *Die Tochter* (1943, 'The Daughter'), in a style reminiscent of **Thomas Mann**. His lyric poetry is also noteworthy. Of Jewish descent, he fled the Nazi regime and went to Beverly Hills, California, USA. His *Der Reisepass* (1937, 'The Travel Pass') was directed against National Socialism.

Frank, Hans 1900–46
German Nazi politician

He was born in Karlsruhe and studied at the universities of Munich, Vienna and Kiel. He was Minister of Justice in Bavaria (1933), president of the German Law Academy (1934) and in 1939 became Governor-General of Poland, where he established concentration camps and conducted a policy of persecution and extermination. He was condemned as a war criminal and hanged.

Frank, Ilya Mikhailovich 1908–90
Soviet physicist and Nobel Prize winner

Born in Leningrad (now St Petersburg), he was educated at Moscow State University, and in 1944 was appointed Professor of Physics there, after working for four years at the State Optical Institute. By 1937, working with **Pavel Cherenkov** and **Igor Tamm**, he and his colleagues were able to explain the 'Cherenkov effect', which arises when a charged particle traverses a medium when moving at a speed greater than the speed of light in that medium. The effect is dramatically visible in the blue glow in a uranium reactor core containing heavy water. Cherenkov, Frank and Tamm shared the Nobel Prize for physics in 1958.

Frank, Johann Peter 1745–1821
German physician, medical reformer and author

Born in Rotalben in the Palatinate, he studied medicine at several German and French universities. He held various university, hospital, court and administrative positions in Italy, Austria, Germany and Russia. One of his patrons was **Joseph II** of Austria. He wrote many medical works, most notably the multi-volume *System of a Complete Medical Police*, published between 1779 and 1825, in which he described a comprehensive system of medical care which, in combining preventative and curative medical services, was an early vision of the welfare state.

Frank, Leonhard 1882–1961
German novelist

Born in Würzburg, he published (1914) the novel *Die Räuberbande* ('The Gang of Robbers'), which describes the adventures of a gang of roguish boys. After fighting in World War I he conceived a horror of war which led to his strongly pacifist *Der Mensch ist gut* (1917, 'Man is Good'). *Die Ursache* (1915, 'The Cause') attacked the repressive educational system in Germany, and *Der Bürger* (1924, 'The Citizen') is about the deadening effect of bourgeois society on the spirit. His *Karl und Anna* (1926, 'Carl and Anna'), also a war story, was successfully turned into a play. He left Germany and went to the USA to live in Hollywood, where he wrote several books, including *Von drei Millionen drei* (1932, 'From Three Million and Three'), and the autobiographical novel *Links wo das Herz ist* (1952, 'On the Left, Where the Heart Is'). 📖 C French and H Jobs, *Leonhard Frank: 1882–1961* (1962)

Frank, Robert 1924–
Swiss–US photographer and filmmaker

He was born in Zurich and was an industrial photographer during his early twenties before joining *Harper's Bazaar* magazine in Paris. He worked in fashion photography until 1948 and then travelled in the USA, South

Frank, Anne 1929–45
German Jewish diarist

Anne Frank was born in Frankfurt am Main, the second daughter of Otto Frank, a member of a banking family who took his family to Holland in 1933 to establish a pharmaceutical company in Amsterdam. After the Nazi occupation of Holland, Anne hid with her family and four others in a specially prepared hiding place in the two upper floors of an office building used by Frank's firm. There, supported with essential supplies by their friends (especially Miep Gies, who later wrote a memoir of her), they lived from July 1942 to August 1944, when they were betrayed. Anne was sent to Auschwitz and later Bergen–Belsen concentration camps, and died along with the other members of her family except for her father, who devoted the rest of his life to promoting the message of his daughter's diary.

The lively, moving diary she kept from 14 June 1942 and during her concealment was published in 1947 as *Het Achterhuis*, and was translated into English as *The Diary of Anne Frank* in 1952. It has since been published in over 50 languages, and has been dramatized and filmed. Anne Frank's name was given to villages and schools for refugee children throughout western Europe. In 1989 further entries from the diary, previously suppressed, were also published; these afford moving insights into Anne's repressed sexual feelings. A recent edition is *The Diary of a Young Girl: Ann Frank. The Definitive Edition* (1997).

📖 M Gies, *Anne Frank Remembered* (1987); E Schnabel, *The Footsteps of Anne Frank* (1959).

'I want to go on living after my death. And therefore I am grateful to God for giving me this gift…of expressing all that is in me.'

America and Europe. During the mid-1950s in the USA he created a series of photographs which were to establish him as one of the most influential photographers of his time. Bold images of US culture capturing often shocking pictures of everyday trivia, they were published, with text by **Jack Kerouac**, as *The Americans* (1959) and exemplified Frank's eye for bold composition and his often ironical point of view. He subsequently made films, including *Pull My Daisy* (1959, screenplay by Kerouac) about the authors of the Beat generation.

Frank, Waldo David 1889–1967
US novelist and journalist
Born in Long Branch, New Jersey, he co-edited *The Seven Arts* (1916–17), and later wrote novels and other works coloured by mysticism and Expressionism. Titles include *The Unwelcome Man* (1917), *City Block* (1922), *The Rediscovery of America* (1929) and *New Year's Eve* (1939, a play). 📖 P J Carter, *Waldo Frank* (1867)

Frankau, Gilbert 1884–1953
English novelist
He was born in London, the son of Julia Frankau (who wrote under the name of 'Frank Danby'). His early works were great successes and he continued as a professional writer, with a flair for anticipating popular taste. Of his many bestsellers, the most notable are *One of Us* (1912), *Peter Jackson, Cigar Merchant* (1919), *Men, Maids and Mustard-Pots* (1923) and *World without End* (1943). He was the father of **Pamela Frankau**. 📖 *Gilbert Frankau's Self-Portrait: a novel of his own life* (1940)

Frankau, Pamela 1908–67
English novelist
She was the daughter of **Gilbert Frankau**. In her first novel, *The Marriage of Harlequin* (1927), and her other early novels, she epitomized the era of the 'bright young things'. Her later novels were more serious in intent, and include *The Willow Cabin* (1949) and *A Wreath for The Enemy* (1954). *The Offshore Light* (1952) was written under the pseudonym 'Eliot Naylor'. 📖 *I Find Four People* (1935)

Frankenthaler, Helen 1928–
US abstract painter
Born in New York City, she studied under the Mexican painter **Rufino Tamayo** and at Bennington College, Vermont. Influenced by **Hans Hofmann**, with whom she studied briefly at the Art Students' League in New York (1950), and **Jackson Pollock**, she developed a technique of applying very thin paint to unprimed canvas, allowing it to soak in and create atmospheric stains and blots on the surface. Her best-known picture is *Mountains and Sea* (1952). She married the artist **Robert Motherwell** in 1958.

Frankfurter, Felix 1882–1965
US law teacher and judge
Born in Vienna, he emigrated to the USA as a child, and was educated at the College of the City of New York and at Harvard. He taught at Harvard Law School (1914–39) and served as an associate justice of the US Supreme Court (1939–62). He was a noted supporter of civil liberties and founded the American Civil Liberties Union, though in court he advised judicial restraint in opposing legislative and executive policy. In constitutional cases he claimed that judges should consider whether legislators could reasonably have enacted such a law. His major works are *The Business of the Supreme Court* (1927, with J M Landis) and *The Public and its Government* (1930).

Frankl, Ludwig, Ritter von Hochwart 1810–93
Austrian poet
Of Jewish origin, he became Professor of Aesthetics at the Vienna Conservatory (1851), and established the first Jewish school in Jerusalem (1856). He wrote epics, ballads and satirical poems, many of which have been translated. 📖 Biographical note in *Moderne Klassiker* (1852)

Frankland, Sir Edward 1825–99
English chemist
Born in Churchtown, Lancashire, he was attracted to chemistry while apprenticed to a pharmacist, and later studied under **Lyon Playfair** in London, **Robert Wilhelm Bunsen** in Marburg and **Justus von Liebig** in Giessen. From 1847 to 1851 he was science master at Queenwood School, Hampshire, and he then became the first Professor of Chemistry at the newly founded Owen's College, Manchester. He returned to London in 1857 to lecture at St Bartholomew's Hospital, and from 1863 to 1865 was Professor of Chemistry at the Royal Institution in succession to **Michael Faraday**. In 1865 he followed **August Wilhelm von Hofmann** at the Royal School of Mines, where he remained for 20 years. His pioneering work in organometallic chemistry around 1850 led to his development of the theory of valency, which underlies all structural chemistry. With Sir **Norman Lockyer** he studied the solar spectrum and in 1868 they jointly discovered helium in the Sun's atmosphere. In applied chemistry Frankland did important work on water supply and sanitation. He was elected a Fellow of the Royal Society in 1853, received its Copley Medal in 1894 and was knighted in 1897. 📖 Colin Archibald Russell, *Lancastrian Chemist: The Early Years of Sir Edward Frankland* (1986)

Franklin, Aretha 1942–
US soul singer and pianist

Franklin, Benjamin, *pseudonym* Richard Saunders 1706–90
US statesman, diplomat, printer, publisher, inventor and scientist

Benjamin Franklin was born in Boston, the youngest son of a chandler and the fifteenth of 17 children. He was apprenticed at the age of 12 to his brother James, a printer, who started a newspaper, the *New England Courant*, in 1721. The two brothers later fell out and Benjamin drifted to Philadelphia, where he secured work as a printer. During 1724–26 he worked for 18 months in London, before returning to Philadelphia to establish his own successful printing house, and in 1729 he purchased the *Pennsylvania Gazette*. A year later, he married Deborah Read, by whom he had two children, a son who died young, and a daughter, Sally. He also had an illegitimate son, William (later a Loyalist and the last royal governor of New Jersey).

In 1732 Franklin commenced the publication of *Poor Richard's Almanac*, which became popular for its witty aphorisms and attained an unprecedented circulation. He was an energetic citizen of Philadelphia, taking the lead in founding its first subscription library, paid police force and hospital, volunteer fire department, as well as its academy (later the University of Pennsylvania). He was appointed Clerk of the Assembly (1736), Postmaster of Philadelphia (1737), then deputy Postmaster-General for the colonies (1753), being elected and re-elected a member of the Assembly almost uninterruptedly until his first mission to England.

His invention of the Franklin stove and its commercial success encouraged him to turn from printing to the natural sciences in the 1740s, and in 1746 he commenced his famous researches in electricity. He brought out fully the distinction between positive and negative electricity, proved that lightning and electricity are identical, and suggested that buildings could be protected by lightning-conductors. Furthermore, he discovered the course of storms over the North American continent, the course of the Gulf Stream, its high temperature, and the use of the thermometer in navigating it; and the various powers of different colours to absorb solar heat.

A staunch advocate of colonial rights, he proposed to the Albany Congress a Plan of Union for the colonies in 1754, and in 1757 he was sent to England where he successfully insisted upon the right of the province to tax the proprietors of land held under the **Penn** charter for the cost of defending it from the French and the Native Americans. In 1764 he was again sent to England to contest the pretensions of parliament to tax the American colonies without representation. The differences, however, between the British government and the colonies became too grave to be reconciled by negotiation, and in 1775 Franklin returned to the USA, where he helped draft the Declaration of Independence.

To secure foreign assistance in the war Franklin was sent to Paris in 1776. His skill as a negotiator and his personal popularity, reinforced by the antipathy of French and English, favoured his mission, and in February 1778 a treaty of alliance was signed, while munitions of war and money were sent from France that made possible the American victory in the Revolutionary War. He helped negotiate the Treaty of Paris (1783), ending the war with Great Britain, and remained US Minister in Paris till 1785, when he returned to Philadelphia.

In 1787, frail and elderly, he was a delegate to the convention which framed the Constitution of the USA. He retired from public life in 1788, but his mind remained active, and at the age of 83 he invented bifocal eyeglasses. His classic *Autobiography*, not published in its entirety until 1868, reflects the wide-ranging interests and passion for self-improvement that generated his achievements, although it reveals little of the irreverant temperament that makes Franklin one of the most appealing of the US founding fathers.

📖 E Wright, *Benjamin Franklin: His Life As He Wrote It* (1990); T Fleming, *The Man Who Dared The Lightning* (1964); Benjamin Franklin, *Autobiography of Benjamin Franklin*, ed L Larabee et al (1964).

> As an important negotiator and mediator in getting individuals to work together to establish an independent USA Franklin warned his colleagues, on signing the Declaration of Independence: 'We must indeed all hang together or, most assuredly, we shall surely all hang separately.' (4 July 1776).

She was born in Memphis, Tennessee, the daughter of a well-known Detroit preacher and gospel singer, she had established her name on the gospel circuit touring with the choir of his New Bethel Baptist Church before she signed a recording contract with Columbia Records (1960). Although she spent six years with that label and recorded several successful albums, it was only after moving to Atlantic Records in 1967 that her full potential was realized. Producer Jerry Wexler capitalized on both her piano-playing skills and her gospel roots, most notably on *I Never Loved A Man The Way I Love You* (1967) and *Lady Soul* (1968). In 1972 she returned to the church with her album *Amazing Grace*, a two-record set of gospel songs recorded live in Los Angeles. Subsequent recordings have included *With Everything I Feel in Me* (1974), *Almighty Fire* (1978), *Love All The Hurt Away* (1981), *Aretha* (1980), *Get It Right* (1983) and *Jazz to Soul* (1992). In 1987 she recorded *One Lord, One Faith, One Baptism* in her father's Detroit church. Variously known as 'Lady Soul' and the 'Queen of Soul', she has had more million-selling singles than any other female recording artist.

Franklin, Benjamin See panel above

Franklin, Frederic 1914–
English dancer, ballet director and teacher

He was born in Liverpool, and worked in cabarets and casinos in London and Paris, until **Anton Dolin** invited him to join the **Markova**-Dolin Ballet (1935–37). He consolidated his international status as a member of Ballets Russes de Monte Carlo (1938–49, 1954–56), originating roles in such ballets as **Léonide Massine**'s *Gaîté Parisienne* (1938, 'Parisian Gaiety') and **Agnes De Mille**'s *Rodeo* (1942, as the Champion Roper). He became company ballet master in 1944. Later he worked with various companies including his own Slavenska-Franklin Ballet (founded 1951), National Ballet of Washington (artistic director, 1962–74), Pittsburgh Ballet Theatre (co-director) and Chicago Ballet.

Franklin, Lady Jane, *née* Griffin 1792–1875
English traveller and expedition benefactor

Born in England, she travelled widely with her father before marrying the explorer Sir **John Franklin** in 1828. She accompanied him on his tours through Syria, Turkey and Egypt, and whilst he was Governor of Van Diemen's Land (Tasmania) she campaigned vociferously for the rights of women prisoners. When her husband disappeared on a voyage in search of the Northwest Passage, she financed a series of search expeditions, some of them in co-operation with the navy. After 10 years her husband's diaries were recovered, showing he had proved the existence of the Northwest Passage. She was awarded the

Royal Geographical Society's Founder's Medal for her contribution to the exploration of the Canadian Arctic, becoming the first woman to be thus honoured.

Franklin, Sir John 1786–1847
English explorer

Born in Spilsby, Lincolnshire, he joined the navy at the age of 14 and was present at the battles of Copenhagen (1801) and Trafalgar (1805). From 1818 he made extensive land journeys along the Coppermine River and the Canadian Arctic coast, including the Mackenzie River (1819–22, 1825–27). He was Governor of Van Diemen's Land (Tasmania) from 1834 to 1845. In 1845 he commanded the *Erebus* and *Terror* in an attempt to discover the Northwest Passage. Leaving Baffin Bay via Lancaster Sound, they wintered at Beechey Island, then worked along the coast of the North American mainland, but were beleaguered by thick ice in the Victoria Strait (1846). Franklin died during the following year. The 105 survivors under Captain Crozier attempted to walk to Back's River, but died of starvation and scurvy. One of the numerous relief expeditions sent out found a record of the expedition to April 1848 with definite proof that Franklin had discovered the Northwest Passage. Franklin's Gull is named after him. ▢ Paul Nanton, *Arctic Breakthrough: Franklin's Expeditions, 1819–1847* (1970)

Franklin, John Hope 1915–
US historian

Born in Rentiesville, Oklahoma, the son of a black attorney, he was educated at Fisk University and Harvard. He taught at several black institutions, joining Howard University in 1947 when he published his survey of the African-American historical experience, *From Slavery to Freedom: A History of American Negroes* (1947). In 1956 he became chairman of the department of history at Brooklyn College, and published *The Militant South*. His *Reconstruction after the Civil War* (1961) laid a judicious foundation for a reappraisal of the post-Civil War era from the African-American standpoint, and his generosity to whites and understanding of blacks was apparent in *The Emancipation Proclamation* (1963). He was Professor of American History at Chicago University (1964–82), James B Duke Professor of History at Duke University (1982–85), then emeritus, and was the first black president of the American Historical Association (1978–79). He also wrote *Racial Equality in America* (1976) and *The Color Line: Legacy for the 21st Century* (1993).

Franklin, (Stella Marian Sarah) Miles,
pseudonym **Brent of Bin** 1879–1954
Australian novelist

Born in Talbingo, near Tumut, New South Wales, she spent her first 10 years at a farm in the bush country, described in *Childhood at Brindabella* (1963). Later the family moved 'downmarket' to the district fictionalized in *My Brilliant Career* (1901) as Possum Gully, and eventually settled in a Sydney suburb. She briefly took up nursing, then turned to journalism, became involved in the feminist movement, and in 1906 emigrated to the USA, where she worked as secretary to the Women's Trade Union League. Moving to England in 1915, she helped with the war effort, serving with the Scottish Women's Hospital at Ostrovo, Macedonia. In 1932 she returned permanently to Australia, and began the 'Brent of Bin' series, starting with *Up the Country* (1928). Her best work appeared under her own name, including the early autobiographical novels *All That Swagger* (1936) and *My Career Goes Bung* (1946), and a collection of essays on Australian literature, *Laughter, Not for a Cage* (1956). The Miles Franklin awards are among Australia's most prestigious literary prizes. The popularity of her novels has tended to obscure the considerable contribution which she made to the social and professional development of Australian women. ▢ M F Barnard, *Miles Franklin* (1967)

Franklin, Rosalind Elsie 1920–58
English X-ray crystallographer and posthumous Nobel Prize winner

Born in London, she studied physical chemistry at Cambridge and held a research post at the British Coal Utilization Research Association (1942–46), where her work was important in establishing carbon fibre technology. At the Central Government Laboratory for Chemistry in Paris (1947–50) she became experienced in X-ray diffraction techniques. She returned to London in 1951 to work on DNA at King's College. She produced X-ray diffraction pictures of DNA which were published in the same issue of *Nature* (1953) in which **James Watson** and **Francis Crick** proposed their double-helical model of DNA. Finding it difficult to co-operate with **Maurice Wilkins**, who was also working on DNA at King's College, Franklin left to join **John Bernal**'s laboratory at Birkbeck College, London, to work on tobacco mosaic virus. She died four years before she could be awarded the 1962 Nobel Prize for physiology or medicine jointly with Watson, Crick and Wilkins for the determination of the structure of DNA. ▢ Anne Sayre, *Rosalind Franklin and DNA* (1975)

Franqueville, Pierre See **Francheville, Pierre**

Franz Ferdinand 1863–1914
Archduke of Austria

Born in Graz, he was the nephew and heir apparent (from 1896) of Emperor **Franz Joseph**. On a visit to Sarajevo (now in Bosnia) in 1914 he and his wife Sophie were assassinated by a group of young Serbian nationalists led by **Gavrilo Princip**. Austria used the incident as a pretext for attacking Serbia, which precipitated World War I.

Franz Joseph, *properly* Franz Joseph I 1830–1916
Emperor of Austria, and King of Hungary

Born at the Schönbrunn Palace, Vienna, he was the son of the Archduke Francis (Emperor **Francis I**'s son), and the nephew of Ferdinand I (1793–1875), whom he succeeded (1848). He reigned longer than any other European monarch. His first task was to subdue the Hungarian revolt and pacify Lombardy. Having accomplished this, the aspirations of the various nationalities of the empire were rigorously suppressed, and a determined effort made to fuse them into one state. The emperor reasserted his claim to rule as an absolute sovereign, he reverted to a policy of bureaucratic centralization, and a close alliance was entered into with the Church to combat liberal progress. In 1859 Lombardy was wrested from Austria by Sardinia. Through the war with Prussia (1866) Austria was ostracized by Germany, and compelled to surrender Venetia to Sardinia, Prussia's ally. Hungary was granted autonomy in the Compromise of 1867, and Franz Joseph took the additional title of King of Hungary. The emperor then adopted a more conciliatory policy towards the various national groups within the empire. His annexation of Bosnia-Herzegovina (1908) agitated Europe and his attack on Serbia (1914) precipitated World War I. By the suicide at Mayerling of his son Rudolf (1858–89), and the murder at Sarajevo of his heir apparent, **Franz Ferdinand**, eldest son of the emperor's brother Charles Louis (1833–96), the crown passed to **Charles**. Elizabeth of Bavaria (1837–98), Franz Joseph's wife, was fatally stabbed in Geneva by an anarchist.

Franzos, Karl Emil 1848–1904
Austrian novelist

He was born in Podolia on the Austro-Russian border, of Jewish parentage, and his novels take their themes and settings from Galicia, the Bukovina, south Russia and

Romania. They present vivid pictures of life among the Jews and peasants, and include *Aus Halbasien* (1876, 'From Asia Minor'), *Die Juden von Barnow* (1877, 'The Jews of Barnow'), *Ein Kampf ums Recht* (1882, 'A Struggle over the Law') and *Der Pojaz* (1905, 'The Pojaz').

Frasch, Hermann 1851–1914
US industrial chemist
Born in Gailsdorf, Württemberg, Germany, he emigrated to the USA in 1868 and worked in Philadelphia, Cleveland and London, Ontario, as a chemist and oil worker. In the 1880s he developed a process for removing sulphur from petroleum, afterwards known as the Frasch process. In 1891 he patented a method (also known as the Frasch process) for extracting sulphur from deep deposits using superheated steam. He founded the Union Sulphur Company, which became the largest sulphur mining company in the world, and was subsequently also director of the International Sulphur Refineries of Marseilles.

Fraser, Lady Antonia, *née* Pakenham 1932–
British writer
She is the daughter of the 7th Earl of Longford. She was educated at St Mary's Convent, Ascot, and Lady Margaret Hall, Oxford, and has written a series of historical biographies, including *Mary Queen of Scots* (1969, James Tait Black Memorial Prize), *Cromwell Our Chief of Men* (1973), *King James VI and I* (1974), *King Charles II* (1979) and *Kings and Queens of England* (1975, reissued 1988). She has also written mystery stories, including *Quiet As A Nun* (1977) and *Have A Nice Death* (1983). She was married to Hugh Fraser (1956–77), and married Harold Pinter in 1980.

Fraser (of North Cape), Bruce Austin Fraser, 1st Baron 1888–1981
English naval officer
Educated at Bradfield College, he joined the navy in 1902 and became a gunnery specialist. He served at sea in World War I and was Chief of Staff Mediterranean fleet (1938–39). In World War II he was Controller of the Navy (1939–42) and Commander-in-Chief Home fleet (1943–44), Eastern fleet (1944) and British Pacific fleet (1945–46). He was a British signatory at the Tokyo Bay Peace Ceremony (1945). He was First Sea Lord from 1948 to 1951.

Fraser, Dawn 1937–
Australian swimmer
She was born in Balmain, Sydney, and her talent was discovered as a schoolgirl. In her swimming career she broke 27 world records and won 29 Australian championships. Her outstanding achievement was in winning gold medals at three successive Olympic Games— Melbourne (1956), Rome (1960) and Tokyo (1964), in each case setting a new Olympic record. At the Rome Olympic Games she broke three world records within one hour. In 1964 she became the first woman to break the 'magic minute' for the 100 metres with a time of 58.9 seconds, a record which was to stand for 20 years. She was often in conflict with the swimming authorities, but was awarded the MBE in 1967.

Fraser, George MacDonald 1925–
English historical novelist
He grew up in Carlisle and Glasgow. Trained as a journalist, he was deputy editor of the *Glasgow Herald* (1968–69), but following the success of his first novel *Flashman* (1969) he left to become a full-time writer. He is best known for this and subsequent novels, starting with *Royal Flash* (1970), in which he turned the bully of Thomas Hughes's *Tom Brown's Schooldays* into a representative figure of the English caste system and of imperial values. Other books include a parallel sequence of novels with the more down-to-earth hero, McCauslan, as in *Mr America* (1980) and *The Pyrates* (1983). He also wrote the screenplays for

the James Bond film *Octopussy* (1983) and a 1987 adaptation of the life of Casanova. His war experiences fuelled the surprisingly lyrical and elegiac *Quartered Safe Out Here* (1992). More recently he published *Flashman and the Angel of the Lord* (1994).

Fraser, (John) Malcolm 1930–
Australian politician
Born in Melbourne, he was educated at Melbourne Grammar School and at Oxford. In 1955 he became the youngest MP in the House of Representatives and was Minister for the Army (1966–68), Minister for Defence (1969–71), and Minister for Education and Science (1968–69, 1971–72). He succeeded Billy Snedden as leader of the Liberal Party in 1975. After the constitutional crisis of November 1975 he was asked to lead a caretaker government until the elections in December, in which the Liberal-National Country coalition he was leading was returned to power. He remained Prime Minister until his party's defeat in the elections of 1983 by the Labor Party (for which it was only the second victory in 33 years). Soon after, he resigned his parliamentary seat. Since then he has worked as a member of the Commonwealth Group of Eminent Persons which advised on global troublespots, and was briefly special envoy to Africa for the Howard Goverment. (1996).

Fraser, Marjory Kennedy 1857–1930
Scottish singer and folk-song collector
Born into a large musical family in Perth, she trained in Paris as a concert singer. In 1882 she started studying Gaelic music, took lessons in Gaelic, and began collecting Hebridean folk-songs, to which she gave modern harmonic settings. In 1909 she published *Songs of the Hebrides*. She also wrote the libretto of Granville Bantock's opera *The Seal Woman* (1924).

Fraser, Peter 1884–1950
New Zealand politician
He was born in Fearn, Ross and Cromarty, Scotland, and emigrated to New Zealand (1910), and became involved in trade union organization. A founder member of the New Zealand Labour Party (1916), he was imprisoned during World War I for opposing conscription. He entered parliament in 1918, became deputy Party Leader in 1933, and Leader and Prime Minister in 1940, holding office until 1949, when his government was defeated.

Fraser, Simon See Lovat, Lord

Fraser, Simon 1776–1862
Canadian fur-trader and explorer
Born in Bennington, New York (now in Vermont), USA, he settled in Cornwall, Ontario, after the death of his Scottish father, who was killed fighting in the American Revolution. Working as a clerk in the North West Company he was promoted to partner in 1801, and was sent in 1805 to establish the first trading posts in the Rocky Mountains. Following Alexander Mackenzie's route, he opened up a vast area which he called New Caledonia between the plains and the Pacific Ocean, and in 1808 followed the Fraser River, named after him, to its mouth. He headed the Red River department of the North West Company during conflict with settlers of the rival Hudson's Bay Company, before his retirement in 1818.

Fraser, Sir William 1816–98
Scottish archivist
A deputy keeper of records of Scotland (1880–92), he issued a series of sumptuous family histories with original charters, which were valuable as sources for Scottish history. By his will he endowed the Edinburgh chair of Scottish history, financed the *Scottish Peerage*, and founded the Fraser Homes.

Fraser Darling, Sir Frank 1903–79
English ecologist and conservationist

Born in Chesterfield, Derbyshire, he attended agricultural college at Sutton Bonnington and obtained a doctorate from the department of animal genetics at the University of Edinburgh. From 1930 to 1934 he studied the ecology of the red deer, publishing *A Herd of Red Deer* (1937), and subsequently carried out research on sea birds, showing how to improve the breeding of colonial birds by stimulating other members of the species, a phenomenon now known as the 'Fraser Darling effect'. He became convinced of the importance of living in ecological balance with the environment, and was one of the early champions of conservation. He was director of the West Highland Survey (1944–50), a senior lecturer in ecology and conservation at Edinburgh (1953–58) and vice-president of the Conservation Foundation, Washington DC (1959–72). He wrote many books, carried out official ecological surveys and advised several government bodies. He also served as a member on the Royal Commission on Environmental Pollution (1970–72). He was knighted in 1970.

Fraunhofer, Joseph von 1787–1826
German physicist

Born in Straubing, Bavaria, he went in 1806 to the optical workshop of the Munich Philosophical Instrument Company, where his skill in glass-making and scientific knowledge enabled him to transform the firm's fortunes, becoming a director of the company by 1811. In 1823 he was appointed director of the Physics Museum of the Bavarian Academy of Sciences. Fraunhofer advanced the design of achromatic doublet lenses, showing how to minimize their spherical aberration, and using these improved designs he developed the prism spectrometer to discover the dark lines in the Sun's spectrum which now bear his name (1814–17). He invented the transmission diffraction grating in 1821, and subsequently the reflection grating. Diffraction phenomena observed at very large distances from the diffracting aperture are known as Fraunhofer diffraction. His work laid the foundation for Germany's subsequent supremacy in the design and manufacture of optical instruments.

Frayn, Michael 1933–
English dramatist, journalist and humorist

He was born in London. A journalist by training, he has published a number of comic novels, among them *The Tin Men* (1965), and *Towards the End of the Morning* (1967), about the newspaper business. Other novels are *The Trick of It* (1989), *A Landing on the Sun* (1990) and *Now You Know* (1992). His stage plays include *Alphabetical Order* (1975), set in the library of a provincial newspaper, *Clouds* (1976), about two rival journalists in Cuba, *Noises Off* (1982), a frenetic farce about putting on a frenetic farce, *Benefactors* (1984), a piece about middle class mores, and *Look Look* (1990). His finest play is *Make and Break* (1980), a satirical look at the lives of salesmen at a foreign trade fair. He also wrote the script for the film *Clockwise* (1986), and is a translator of **Chekhov**.

Frazer, Sir James George 1854–1941
Scottish social anthropologist, classicist and folklorist

Born in Glasgow, he was educated at Larchfield Academy in Helensburgh, Glasgow University and Trinity College, Cambridge, where he became a Classics Fellow. His interest in anthropology, in combination with his classical studies, produced his major work, *The Golden Bough: A Study in Comparative Religion* (1890, rewritten in 12 vols, 1911–15). In addition to other anthropological works he published an edition of **Sallust** (1884), and a translation of **Pausanias**'s *Description of Greece* (1898). He was Professor of Social Anthropology at Liverpool (1907–08) and at Cambridge (from 1908). ▢ Robert Ackerman, *J G Frazer: His Life and Work* (1987)

Frears, Stephen Arthur 1941–
English film director

He was born in Leicester. After making his directorial debut with the 30-minute drama *Burning* in 1967, he directed the feature-length *Gumshoe* (1971) and worked extensively for television over the next decade with such feature-length plays as *A Day Out* (1972) and *Walter* (1982). He returned to the big screen with *The Hit* (1984) and went on to direct the feature films *My Beautiful Laundrette* (1985), *Prick Up Your Ears* (1987), *Sammy and Rosie Get Laid* (1987), *Dangerous Liaisons* (1988) and *The Grifters* (1990), before returning to television with *The Snapper* (1993).

Frece, Lady de See **Tilley, Vesta**

Fréchette, Louis Honoré 1839–1908
Canadian poet

Born in Lévis, Quebec, he was called to the Bar, and elected to the Dominion parliament in 1874. He published prose works and plays, and his poems *Mes loisirs* (1863), *La voix d'un exil* (1867, 'The Voice of an Exile'), which attacked Canadian politics, and others such as *Les Oiseaux de Neige* (1879, 'The Snow Birds'), were highly acclaimed by the Académie Française. ▢ M Dugas, *Un romantique canadien* (1934)

Fredegond, *also spelt* Fredegund *or* Frédégonde d.598
Frankish queen

She was first mistress, then wife, of Chilperic, King of Neustria. Monstrously cruel, she waged a relentless feud with **Brunhilde**, wife of Sigebert, King of Austrasia, and sister of Chilperic of Neustria's first wife, a feud which was intensified by the rivalry between the two kingdoms.

Frederic, Harold 1856–98
US novelist

He was born in Utica, New York. After a poverty-stricken youth, he became a journalist and was in 1884 appointed European correspondent of the *New York Times*. He wrote *Seth's Brother's Wife* (1887), *The Return of the O'Mahony* (1892) and other novels depicting his own background, but his best work is *The Damnation of Theron Ware* (1896), about the intellectual awakening of a young minister. ▢ A Briggs, *The Novels of Harold Frederic* (1969)

Frédérick See **Lemaître, Antoine Louis Prosper**

Frederick I 1657–1713
King of Prussia and Elector of Brandenberg

Born in Königsberg, Prussia (now Kaliningrad, Russia), the second son of **Frederick William**, the Great Elector, he married (1684) Sophia Charlotte (1668–1705), sister of **George I** of Great Britain, and succeeded his father as Frederick III, Elector of Brandenberg (1688). In return for military aid to Emperor **Leopold I** in the War of the Spanish Succession (1701–14), he was made the first King of Prussia (1701). He reclaimed land, doubled Prussian revenues, and encouraged the influx of Huguenots to create new industries. He maintained a large court, and was a great patron of the arts and of learning, especially of **Gottfried Leibniz**. During his reign the Academy of Sciences at Berlin and the University of Halle were founded. ▢ Linda and Marsha Frey, *Frederick I, the Man and His Times* (1984)

Frederick II, the Great See panel p683

Frederick III 1831–88
King of Prussia and German emperor

Frederick II *known as* Frederick the Great 1712–86
King of Prussia

Frederick was born in Berlin, the son of **Frederick William I**, and of Sophia-Dorothea, daughter of **George I** of Great Britain. His early years were devoted to military training and a rigid system of education, against which he initially rebelled to no avail. In 1733 he dutifully accepted as his bride the Princess Elizabeth of Brunswick-Wolfenbüttel (1715–97), and he was restored to favour.

From 1734 Frederick resided at Rheinsberg, where he avidly studied music and French literature. He achieved a high level of proficiency on the flute, and some of his music is still played. He corresponded with **Voltaire**, who in 1750 visited Berlin, and studied his work. On 31 May 1740 Frederick became king; and in October the accession of **Maria Theresa** separated the Crown of Austria from the imperial diadem. Frederick, in possession of a fine army and a well-filled treasury, seized the opportunity. He entered Silesia (December 1740), defeated the Austrians at Mollwitz (1741) and Chotusitz (1742), and, after concluding an alliance for 15 years with France, forced Maria Theresa to yield him Upper and Lower Silesia by the Treaty of Breslau (1742).

The second Silesian War (1744–45) left Frederick with increased territories and a reputation as one of the first military commanders of the day. The next 11 years were years of peace; but Frederick's energetic internal reforms were coloured by the expectation of renewed war. In 1756 the third Silesian War, the 'Seven Years War', began. Frederick anticipated attack by himself taking the offensive, and during all this momentous struggle displayed great courage and military genius.

In 1772 he shared in the first partition of Poland, by which he acquired Polish Prussia and a portion of Great Poland. In 1778 he completed the acquisition of the Franconian duchies. One of his last political actions was the formation of the 'Fürstenbund', which marked the emergence of Prussia as a rival to Austria for the lead in Germany.

Frederick was an able administrator, and contrived to carry on his wars without incurring any debt. He regarded himself as the first servant of the state, and he governed Prussia as one huge camp. With a view to providing treasure for future wars he fostered woollen and other manufactures by a high protective tariff, but he made himself unpopular by the introduction of the French excise system.

During Frederick's reign the country rapidly recovered from the ravages of war, while the army was raised to a strength of 200,000 men. By the end of his reign the area of Prussia had doubled, and, despite a temporary eclipse under **Napoleon I**, the foundation of Prussia's greatness was laid. Frederick was essentially a just, if somewhat austere man, and the administration of justice under his rule was pure; the press enjoyed comparative freedom; and freedom of conscience was promoted.

📖 Frederick was a prolific writer on political, historical and military subjects. He wrote wholly in French, and his works were published by the Berlin Academy (31 vols, 1846–57), as was his *Political Correspondence* (1879 onward). See also R B Asprey, *Frederick the Great* (1988); E Simon, *The Making of Frederick the Great* (1974); **Thomas Carlyle**, *The History of Friedrich II of Prussia, Called Frederick the Great* (6 vols, 1858–65, reprinted 8 vols, 1974).

'Troops always ready to act, my well-filled treasury, and the liveliness of my disposition—these were my reasons for making war on Maria Theresa.' From a letter to Voltaire (1741).

The only son of **Wilhelm I**, he was born in Potsdam. In 1858 he married **Victoria**, Princess Royal of England. As crown prince of Prussia (from 1861) he protested against **Bismarck**'s reactionary policy in relation to constitutional questions and the press. In the Franco-Prussian War he commanded the third army and was made field marshal (1870). He became crown prince of the German Empire (1871) and in 1878, when Emperor Wilhelm I was wounded by an assassin, he was appointed provisional regent. He became Emperor Frederick III on Wilhelm's death (1888), but he died at Potsdam three months later, of cancer of the throat. He had a great horror of war and of autocratic ideas, and he sought to liberalize German institutions.

Frederick I, Barbarossa c.1123–1190
Holy Roman Emperor and King of Germany and Italy

Of the **Hohenstaufen** family, he was the son of Frederick, Duke of Swabia. He succeeded his uncle **Conrad III** as Emperor in 1152. Earnest and distinguished, he channelled his intelligence and enthusiasm into establishing German predominance in western Europe. In 1162 his conquest of Milan subdued the rebellious Italian states, but his failure to defeat the pope led to revolt in Lombardy. After his defeat at Legnano (1176) he won Lombard support by more lenient rule, and in 1177 he acknowledged **Alexander III** as pope, and finally achieved peace (1183). In Germany, Frederick increased the authority of his strongest rebels and checked the weaker by supporting their municipal communities. Duke Ladislas of Bohemia became a king, Austria became a duchy, and Brunswick and Lüneburg went to the **Guelf** princes. He subdued **Henry the Lion** of Bavaria, and gained authority over Poland, Hungary, Denmark and Burgundy. In 1189 he led the Third Crusade against **Saladin**, defeating the Muslims at Philomelium and Iconium, but drowned at Cilicia. His son, **Henry VI**, succeeded him.

Frederick II 1194–1250
Holy Roman Emperor and King of Germany

The last great ruler of the **Hohenstaufens**, he was born in Jesi, near Ancona, the grandson of **Frederick I, Barbarossa** and son of Emperor **Henry VI**. He inherited Sicily from his mother (1198). In 1212 he took the imperial crown from **Otto IV**, gaining Pope **Innocent III**'s sanction (1215) for his coronation in 1220. Frederick consolidated his power in Italy by reducing the pope's, organizing his Italian territories, supporting the arts and education, and creating a legal code for Germany and Italy. During his crusade (1228–29) he captured Bethlehem and Nazareth, and crowned himself King of Jerusalem, but when he returned to Italy he experienced difficulties with the papacy, and was temporarily deposed. In 1235 he married the daughter of King **John** of England and sister of **Henry III**. Frederick tolerated Jews and Muslims, encouraged free trade, recognized popular representation by parliaments, and anticipated the humanistic movement, but persecuted heretics, and upheld absolute sovereignty. He wrote poetry and a book on falconry. A complex figure of sharp contradictions, he was named *stupor mundi* ('the amazement of the world'). However his claim of imperial pre-eminence coincided with the development of separate nation states. 📖 Thomas Curtis Van Cleve, *The Emperor Frederick II of Hohenstaufen, immutator mundi* (1972)

Frederick III 1415–93
Holy Roman Emperor and King of Germany

Born in Innsbruck, Austria, the son of Duke Ernest of Austria, he was elected King of Germany as Frederick IV (1440) and crowned emperor (1452). His reign was one of anarchy, wars raging on the frontiers of the empire, and disorders within. During its course Frederick lost his hold upon Switzerland, purchased peace from his brother Albert in Upper Austria, allowed Francesco Sforza to take Milan, George of Podiebrad (1420–71) to take the throne of Bohemia, and Matthias I Hunyadi that of Hungary, and failed to oppose two Turkish invasions (1469, 1475). Nevertheless, by the marriage (1477) of his son, Maximilian I, to Mary, daughter of Charles, the Bold, of Burgundy, he laid the foundation of the subsequent greatness of the Habsburg dynasty. Although he neglected government for alchemy, astrology and botany, he lost no opportunity to aggrandize his own family, and from his time the Holy Roman Empire was almost exclusively ruled by the House of Austria.

Frederick V, known as the Winter King 1596–1632
Elector Palatine and King of Bohemia

The son of Elector Frederick IV, he was born in Amberg, Upper Palatinate, and educated at the Huguenot academy at Sedan. He became Elector Palatine (1610–23) and in 1613 married Elizabeth, daughter of James VI and I of Scotland and England. Their daughter Sophia became the mother of George I of Great Britain. Under the refined young couple, Heidelberg, the capital of the Palatinate, became known for its artistic and cultural life. During his father's reign, the Protestant Union had been formed under Palatine leadership (1608), and when in 1619 the crown of Bohemia was offered to Frederick his Calvinist ministers urged him to accept. His regal power lasted only one winter (1619–20), hence his nickname, and the Bohemian Protestants were routed by imperial forces at the White Mountain, near Prague (1620). He also lost his hereditary lands, which passed to his Catholic cousin, Maximilian I of Bavaria. Frederick died while in exile in The Hague with his wife and young family, dependent on English and Dutch aid. His son, Charles Louis, recovered his electorate at the Peace of Westphalia (1648).

Frederick Augustus, Duke of York and Albany 1763–1827
English nobleman

Born at St James's Palace, London, the second son of George III of Great Britain, he was a soldier by profession, but was unsuccessful both in the field in the Netherlands (1793–99) and as British Commander-in-Chief (1798–1809), and earned the nickname of the 'grand old Duke of York' in the nursery rhyme. However, his painstaking reform of the army proved of lasting benefit, especially to the Duke of Wellington. He founded the Duke of York's School in London, and is commemorated by the Duke of York's column in Waterloo Place, London.

Frederick Charles, Prince, called the Iron Prince or the Red Prince 1828–85
Prussian field marshal

Born in Berlin, he was the nephew of the emperor Wilhelm I. He served in the Schleswig-Holstein War (1848), commanded the right wing in the Danish War (1864), and in the Seven Weeks War of 1866 against Austria helped to win the victory of Königgrätz. In the Franco-German War (1870–71) he commanded the second army, drove Marshal Achille Bazaine into Metz, which capitulated, and, promoted to field marshal, captured Orléans, broke up the army of the Loire, and scattered Antoine Chanzy (1823–83) and his troops at Le Mans.

Frederick Louis 1707–51
Prince of Wales

Born in Hanover, he was the eldest son of George II and Caroline of Ansbach, and father of George III. He quarrelled with his father over his allowance. He married Princess Augusta of Saxe-Gotha (1736). In 1737 he joined the parliamentary opposition, which was centred on his new home, Leicester House, and was banished from court.

Frederick William I 1688–1740
King of Prussia

Born in Berlin, he succeeded his father, Frederick I, in 1713. Boorishly contemptuous of art and learning, but thrifty and practical, he had a passion for soldiering which brought him Swedish Pomerania, with Stettin. He laid the foundation of the future power of Prussia by establishing a centralized hierarchy of administrative offices and an efficient army which he increased to 80,000 men. He encouraged native industries, particularly wool (to clothe the army), did away with vestiges of the old feudal system, introduced compulsory primary education, resettled his eastern provinces, and pursued a policy of religious toleration. He was succeeded by his son Frederick II, the Great.

Frederick William II 1744–97
King of Prussia

Born in Berlin, he was the nephew and successor in 1786 of Frederick II, the Great. The abolition of some of his predecessor's oppressive measures, including the coffee and tobacco duties, made him very popular, but he replaced them by increasing the excise duty on beer and sugar. He soon lost the regard of his subjects by his predilection for unworthy favourites, and his abrogation of the freedom of the press and religion (1788). He dissipated the fortune his uncle left in the treasury in a useless war with Holland. He acquired large areas of Polish Prussia and Silesia by the partitions of Poland (1793, 1795), and also Ansbach, Bayreuth and Danzig. He presided over a flourishing Berlin culture; he played the cello, and Mozart and Beethoven dedicated chamber music to him.

Frederick William III 1770–1840
King of Prussia

Born in Potsdam, he succeeded his father, Frederick William II in 1797. At first he was neutral towards Napoleon I but eventually declared war against him in 1806. After defeat at Jena and Auerstädt, he fled into East Prussia, and by the Treaty of Tilsit (1807) lost all his territories west of the Elbe. Although defeated at Lützen and Bautzen, Prussia was finally victorious at Leipzig (1813). The territories west of the Elbe were returned at the Treaty of Vienna (1815) and Prussia also gained Pomerania and parts of Saxony and Westphalia, but gave up most of her Polish acquisitions. The latter part of his reign was one of reaction. The democratic movements of 1819 and 1830 were rigorously suppressed, and the freedom of the press curtailed. Nevertheless, provincial diets were established (1823), the finances were situated on a better footing, education was encouraged, and the *Zollverein*, or customs union, was established. 📖 Thomas Stamm, *Konig in Preussens grosser Zeit: Friedrich Wilhelm III* (1992)

Frederick William IV 1795–1861
King of Prussia

Born in Cölln, near Berlin, he succeeded his father, Frederick William III, in 1840, and began his reign by granting minor reforms and promising, but never fulfilling, radical changes. He was possessed by vague ideas of the divine right of kings, and by a mystic pietism. He refused the Imperial Crown offered to him by the liberal Frankfurt Diet (1849), and opposed the popular movement of 1848, but was forced to grant a representative parliament (1850). In 1857, having become insane, he re-signed the administration to his brother, who from 1858 acted as regent until his accession as Wilhelm I.

Frederick William, *known as* the Great Elector
1620–88
Elector of Brandenburg
He was born near Berlin, and his childhood was greatly affected by the Thirty Years War (1618–48). He lived in Holland (1634–38), where he studied briefly at the University of Leiden, and gained an appreciation of Dutch art, architecture and technology. After his accession in 1640 he was responsible for rebuilding the war-ravaged and sparsely populated electorate, adding to the Hohenzollern territories, trebling his revenues, establishing an effective standing army, crushing the Estates, and reorganizing the privy council and Civil Service. He supported Sweden, then Poland in the First Northern War (1655–60), switched from the anti-French alliance of 1674 to support for Louis XIV in 1679, and returned to his anti-French stance in the 1680s. Tolerant over religion, he granted asylum by the Edict of Potsdam (1685) to Huguenots expelled from France following Louis's revocation of the Edict of Nantes, recognizing their economic potential. A discriminating patron of the arts and education, he established the Royal Library and Art Gallery in Berlin, and founded the University of Duisberg. ⬚ Ferdinand Schevill, *The Great Elector* (1947)

Frederik I 1471–1533
King of Denmark and Norway
The son of Kristian I and uncle of Kristian II, he was Duke of Holstein before being chosen king (1523) when Kristian II, who had just lost Sweden to Gustav I Vasa, was dethroned by a rebellion in Denmark. An invasion of Norway (1531–32) by the ex-king failed. Frederik died soon afterwards, on the verge of accepting Lutheranism, and was succeeded by his son Kristian III.

Frederik II 1534–88
King of Denmark and Norway
Born in Hadenslev, he succeeded his father, Kristian III (1559) and soon became involved in a seven-year war against Sweden and its deranged king, Erik XIV, which ended with the inconclusive Treaty of Stettin (1570). The remainder of his reign was a period of peace and prosperity, in which he rebuilt Denmark's economy and defences, imposing a toll on all ships passing through the Sound. He built the magnificent Renaissance castle of Kronborg at Elsinore, to which he brought English musicians to provide entertainment, and was a patron of the astronomer Tycho Brahe and other scientists. He was succeeded by his young son, Kristian IV. His daughter, Anne of Denmark, married King James VI and I of Scotland and England.

Frederik III 1609–70
King of Denmark and Norway
The son and successor of Kristian IV, he was born at Haderslev. The first half of his reign (1648–70) was taken up with costly wars against Sweden, but after the peace settlement of 1660 he established absolute hereditary monarchy over Denmark, Norway and Iceland, embodied in the Royal Law (*Kongelov*) of 1665. He was an enlightened patron of scientific and antiquarian studies, and founded the Royal Library in Copenhagen. Under him the bourgeoisie were able to increase its hold over the government and former crown lands.

Frederik VI 1768–1839
King of Denmark and Norway
Born at Kristiansborg Castle, the son of Kristian VII, he was appointed regent (1784) when his father was declared insane, and became king of both Denmark and Norway in 1808. He abolished serfdom, amended the criminal code, prohibited the slave trade in Danish colonies, and promoted free trade and industrial development. During the Napoleonic Wars, the Danish fleet was destroyed off Copenhagen by Nelson (1801), and in 1807, despite Danish neutrality, Copenhagen was bombarded for three days. This forced Denmark into the arms of Napoleon I, and with the overthrow of Napoleon's empire (1814), she lost Norway to Sweden. Under his rule the Danish economy recovered from bankruptcy. He granted a new constitution with four consultative provincial assemblies (1834), which was the start of parliamentary democracy in Denmark. He was succeeded by his son, Kristian VIII.

Frederik VII 1808–63
King of Denmark
Born at Amalienborg Castle, the son and successor (1848) of Kristian VIII, he was the last of the Oldenburg line. In 1849 he promulgated a new and liberal constitution abolishing monarchical absolutism. He died childless, and was succeeded by Kristian IX.

Frederik VIII 1843–1912
King of Denmark
Born in Copenhagen, he was the son and successor (1906) of Kristian IX, and brother of Queen Alexandra of Great Britain. In 1907 he made a state visit to Iceland to celebrate the granting of home rule there (1904). He married Princess Louise of Sweden, and was well-liked for his simple lifestyle. His second son, Prince Carl, became King Haakon VII of Norway. He was succeeded by his eldest son, Kristian X.

Frederik IX 1899–1972
King of Denmark
Born at Sorgenfri Castle, near Copenhagen, he was the son and successor (1947) of Kristian X. A naval officer (rising to rear admiral in 1946), he was crown prince of Denmark from 1912. In 1935 he married Ingrid, daughter of King Gustav VI of Sweden. During World War II he assisted his father in resistance to the German occupation, and was held under house arrest (1943–45). He was crowned in 1947 and was a popular monarch. He granted home rule to the Faroe Islands (1948), and in 1953 a new constitution provided for female succession to the throne. His eldest daughter became Crown Princess and succeeded him as Queen Margrethe II (1972). His youngest daughter, Anne-Marie, married ex-King Constantine II of Greece (1964).

Fredrik I 1676–1751
King of Sweden
Born in Kassel, Germany, he fought for England in the War of the Spanish Succession (1701–13). As Prince Frederick of Hesse-Kassel, he married (1715) Ulrika Eleonora, the younger sister of King Karl XII and future Queen of Sweden. In 1720 his wife abdicated the throne in his favour, under a new constitution which deprived the Crown of most of its authority. He spent most of his time on hunting and love affairs, leaving the government to his chancellor, Arvid Horn. He died childless, and was succeeded by Adolf Fredrik.

Fredriksson, Gert 1919–
Swedish canoeist
He won eight Olympic medals (1948–60), including six golds, and 13 world titles, all in either kayak singles or pairs. His winning margin of 6.7 seconds in the 1948 Olympic singles final was the biggest for any kayak race other than the 10,000 metres. When he won his last Olympic gold in 1960, he was 40 years 292 days old, the oldest canoeing gold medallist.

Freedman, Barnet 1901–58
English painter and lithographer

He was born in Stepney, London, the son of Russian Jewish immigrants, and was a pioneer in the revival of colour lithography. His first one-man show (1929) was held at the Literary Bookshop. He designed posters, book illustrations and book covers. He was visiting instructor at the Royal College of Art from 1928, and at the Ruskin School in Oxford. He worked for London Transport, Shell-Mex, BP Ltd, the BBC and the General Post Office. In 1935 his design was selected for the George V jubilee stamp. In 1940 he was appointed official war artist to the Admiralty and painted coastal defences, naval portraits and studies on battleships and submarines.

Freeman, John 1880–1929
English poet

Born in London, he rose from clerk to become secretary and director of an insurance company (1927). His *Stone Trees* (1916) and other volumes of poetry established his reputation. He won the Hawthornden prize with *Poems New and Old* in 1920 and wrote studies of George Moore (1922) and Herman Melville (1926). 📖 G Freeman and Sir John Squires (eds), *John Freeman's Letters* (1936)

Freeman, Morgan 1937–
US actor

He was born in Memphis, Tennessee. After serving in the US air force, he worked at various jobs whilst pursuing an active career. He performed as a dancer at the 1964 World's Fair, appeared as an extra in *The Pawnbroker* (1965), made his Broadway debut in *Hello, Dolly!* (1967) and starred as Easy Rider in the children's television series *The Electric Company* (1971–76). As a theatre actor, he won the Clarence Derwent award for *The Mighty Gents* (1978) and Obie awards for *Coriolanus* (1980), *Mother Courage* (1980) and *The Gospel at Colonus* (1984). After small and infrequent film roles, he received an Academy Award nomination for his performance as a vicious pimp in *Street Smart* (1987). He was nominated again, recreating his stage performance as the patient, compassionate chauffeur in *Driving Miss Daisy* (1989). He has subsequently established himself as a versatile character actor, bringing distinction to such popular films as *Glory* (1989), *Robin Hood: Prince of Thieves* (1991), *Unforgiven* (1992) and *Seven* (1995). He has directed the film *Bopha!* (1993) and received a further Academy Award nomination for *The Shawshank Redemption* (1994).

Freeman, Sir Ralph 1880–1950
English civil engineer

Born in London, he was educated at the City and Guilds of London Institute. In 1901 he joined the firm of consulting engineers which in 1938 became Freeman, Fox & Partners, specializing in the design of steel bridges. His first notable design was for Sydney Harbour Bridge, a construction of 1,670ft (501m) span (1932). He was later involved with his partner Sir Gilbert Roberts in the design of the long-span suspension bridges over the estuaries of the Forth, Severn and Humber rivers, though he did not live to see any of them built. He was knighted in 1947.

Freeman, Walter 1895–1972
US neurologist

He was born in Philadelphia, and was a leading expert on neurosurgery, developing the operation of prefrontal lobotomy, used in some specific mental illnesses but now largely discredited.

Frege, (Friedrich Ludwig) Gottlob 1848–1925
German logician, mathematician and philosopher

Born in Wismar, he was educated at the University of Jena, where he spent his whole professional career, becoming professor in 1879. His particular contribution to logic was the theory of quantification. His main works are *Begriffschrift* (1879), *Die Grundlagen der Arithmetik* (1884, Eng trans *The Foundations of Arithmetic*, 1950), and *Die Grundgesetze der Arithmetik* (2 vols, 1893, 1903). These have

all been translated into English, as has a collection of his still influential philosophical essays analysing such basic logical concepts as meaning, sense and reference. He also attempted to derive the whole of arithmetic from logic. He is now regarded as the founding father of modern mathematical logic and the philosophy of language. 📖 Michael Dummet, *Frege: Philosophy of Language* (1974)

Frei (Montalva), Eduardo 1911–82
Chilean politician

He became one of the leaders of the Social-Christian Falange Party in the late 1930s, and of the new Christian Democratic Party after 1957. His presidency (1964–70) saw an ambitious programme of social reform, which brought Chile substantial international support. His initial scepticism about the Pinochet regime turned into outright opposition. By the time of his death, he was widely seen as the father of opposition to the dictatorship.

Freiligrath, Ferdinand 1810–76
German poet and politician

Born in Detmold, he abandoned commerce for literature, but became an upholder of German democracy, when his writings became increasingly political. He was forced to seek refuge in Belgium and Great Britain for his *Glaubensbekenntnis* (1844, 'Confession of Beliefs'). He returned to Germany in 1848 and became leader of the Democratic Party. He was again expelled for his poem *Die Toten an die Lebenden* (1848, 'The Dead and the Living'), and returned to London in 1851. He translated many English classics into German. He lived in Stuttgart from 1868, and published his *Neue Gedichte* ('New Poems') in 1870. 📖 H Eulenberg, *Ferdinand Freiligrath* (1948)

Frelinghuysen, Frederick 1753–1804
US politician

He raised a corps of artillery, fought in the American Revolution (1775–83), and was a member of the Continental Congress (1778, 1782–83) and a US senator from 1793 to 1796.

Frémont, John Charles 1813–90
US explorer and politician

Born in Savannah, Georgia, he became a teacher of mathematics in the navy and in 1838 started surveying. In 1842 he crossed the Rocky Mountains (where a peak is named after him), and demonstrated the feasibility of an overland route across the continent. In 1843 he explored the Great Salt Lake, advancing to the mouth of the Columbia River, and in 1845 examined the continental watershed. After participating in the annexation of Upper California in 1847, he started (1848) upon a fourth expedition along the upper Rio Grande. In 1849 he crossed over to California, where he settled, and the next year became senator of the new state. In 1853 he conducted a fifth expedition. He was the Republican and antislavery candidate for the presidency in 1856 but was defeated by James Buchanan. Nominated again in 1864, he withdrew in favour of Abraham Lincoln. He served in the regular army as major-general (1861–62), but resigned rather than serve under General John Pope. In 1873 the French authorities sentenced him in absence to imprisonment for fraud in connection with the Southern Pacific railway scheme. He was Governor of Arizona from 1878 to 1882.

Frémy, Edmond 1814–94
French chemist

Born in Versailles, he became Professor of Chemistry at the École Polytechnique and later at the Museum of Natural History. He is chiefly remembered for his work on fluorine, which he attempted to isolate, also preparing anhydrous hydrogen fluoride and many of its salts. He wrote on the synthesis of rubies and worked on the ferrates, the colouring of flowers and the saponification of fats.

French, Annie 1872–1965
Scottish artist and illustrator

Born in Glasgow, she studied at the Glasgow School of Art, where she was a contemporary of **Jessie Marion King**, and exhibited first at the Brussels Salon (1903). She married the artist George Woolliscroft Rhead (1854–1920) in 1914. Her watercolours have a Pre-Raphaelite feel and are Romantic in subject matter, drawing parallels with the work of Sir **Edward Burne-Jones** and, although less sinister, **Aubrey Beardsley**. She illustrated a number of fairy tales and poems and designed a highly decorative series of postcards and posters. She exhibited regularly at the Royal Academy, Royal Glasgow Institute of Artists and Royal Scottish Academy and settled in Jersey in the late 1950s.

French, Daniel Chester 1850–1931
US sculptor

Born in Exeter, New Hampshire, he studied sculpture in New York and in 1873–74 produced *The Minuteman* monument to the American Revolution for the town of Concord, Massachusetts. Its good notices brought him numerous commissions for public monuments, such as the bronze figure of **John Harvard** (1884) at Harvard University. Following a period in Florence, he studied at the École des Beaux-Arts in Paris from 1886 to 1888. He produced a 60-foot (18.3m) high *Statue of Republic* for the 1893 Chicago World's Fair and the seated figure of **Abraham Lincoln** for the Lincoln Memorial in Washington DC (1918–22).

French, Dawn 1957–
English comedienne and actress

Born in Holyhead, she trained at the Central School of Speech and Drama, where she met **Jennifer Saunders**. Starting at the Comedy Store in London, they created a double act that took them to the forefront of the 'alternative' comedy of the time, and in 1980 they joined the new Comic Strip club. After appearing in *The Comic Strip Presents...* films on television (1982–93), the duo were given their own successful BBC series, *French and Saunders* (1987–). They also wrote and starred in *Girls on Top* (1985–86). Outside the partnership, she has appeared on television in *Murder Most Horrid* (1991–) and *The Vicar of Dibley* (1994). She has also starred on stage in Sharman MacDonald's *When I was a Girl I Used to Scream and Shout* and Ben Elton's *Silly Cow*, and was in the films *The Supergrass* (1985) and *The Strike* (1988). She married comedian **Lenny Henry** in 1984.

French, Sir John Denton Pinkstone, 1st Earl of Ypres 1852–1925
English field marshal

He was born in Ripple, Kent. He joined the navy in 1866, but transferred to the army in 1874. He was with the 19th Hussars in Sudan (1884–85), and was cavalry commander in South Africa in the Second Boer War (1899–1901). Chief of the Imperial General Staff from 1911–14, he was promoted field marshal in 1913 and took command of the British Expeditionary Force in France in 1914. He was superseded by General **Haig** and became Commander-in-Chief of the home forces in 1915. He was Lord Lieutenant of Ireland (1918–21) during the Anglo-Irish War.

Freneau, Philip Morin 1752–1832
US sailor and poet

Born in New York City, he wrote satirical verse in the pre-Revolutionary period, commanded a privateer in the American Revolution and was captured by the British. He wrote *The British Prison Ship* (1781) and a number of shorter poems, including 'The Indian Burying Ground' and 'The Wild Honeysuckle'. ▣ P M Marsh, *Freneau: Poet and Journalist* (1967)

Freni, Mirella 1936–
Italian soprano

She was born in Modena where her mother worked in the same cigarette factory as the mother of **Luciano Pavarotti** —later to be her operatic partner in many productions. Freni trained locally and made her first public appearance aged 11. By the age of 20 she had appeared with the Modena Opera as Micaela in *Carmen*. International success followed quickly with, among others, Netherlands Opera (1959), Glyndebourne (1960), Covent Garden (1961) and La Scala (1962). In 1963 she played Mimi in Herbert von Karajan's film of *La Bohème*. She frequently gives concerts with her husband, the Bulgarian bass Nicolai Ghiaurov (1929–).

Frenssen, Gustav 1863–1945
German novelist

Born in Barlt, Holstein, he studied for the Church but turned to writing and attracted attention by his *Jörn Uhl* (1901), a novel of peasant life. *Hilligenlei* (1906, 'Holy Land'), a life of **Jesus Christ** set in a Germanic background, aroused much controversy. ▣ W Johnson, *Gustav Frenssen. Art und Ahnen* (1934)

Frere, Sir Henry Bartle Edward 1815–84
Welsh colonial administrator

Born in Clybach, Brecknock, as chief commissioner of Sind, India (now in Pakistan) he kept order during the Mutiny. He was Governor of Bombay from 1862 to 1867. In 1872 he signed a treaty with the Sultan of Zanzibar abolishing the slave trade. In 1877 he was appointed Governor of the Cape and High Commissioner in South Africa, where his actions led to the onset of the Zulu War (1879). He was recalled in 1880.

Frescobaldi, Girolamo 1583–1643
Italian composer

Born in Rome, he studied the organ at Ferrara Cathedral, and became organist at Santa Maria in Trastevere, Rome. From 1608 until his death he was organist at St Peter's in Rome. He composed chiefly organ works and madrigals.

Fresenius, Karl Remigius 1818–97
German chemist

He was a professor at the Agricultural Institute from 1845. His revised tables for qualitative and quantitative analysis are still in use.

Fresnaye, Roger de la 1885–1925
French artist

Born in Le Mans, he studied in Paris and was influenced by **Cézanne**, **Robert Delaunay**, and the Cubists from 1912, as in *L'Homme assis* (1913–14, 'The Seated Man', Pompidou Centre) and *The Conquest of the Air* (1913, Museum of Modern Art, New York). Whilst serving in World War I, he developed chronic tuberculosis, and his output was curtailed. Later work was linear and decorative, and no longer abstract.

Fresnel, Augustin Jean 1788–1827
French physicist

Born in Broglie, he was head of the department of Public Works in Paris. His intensive study of the problem of projecting well-defined beams of light led to the celebrated multi-faceted lighthouse lens (the 'Fresnel lens'). His experimental and theoretical investigations into the interference, diffraction and polarization of light, coupled with his facility with new mathematical ideas, contributed greatly to the establishment of the undulatory theory of light. He also invented a special prism ('Fresnel's rhomb') to produce circularly polarized light. His most

Freud, Sigmund 1856–1939
Austrian neurologist, the founder of psychoanalysis

Freud was born in Freiburg, Moravia. He studied medicine at Vienna and joined the staff of the Vienna General Hospital in 1882, specializing in neurology. He collaborated with the Austrian neurologist Joseph Breuer in the treatment of hysteria by the recall of painful experiences under hypnosis, then moved to Paris in 1885 to study under **Jean Martin Charcot**; it was there that he changed from neurology to psychopathology. Returning to Vienna, he developed the technique of conversational 'free association' in place of hypnosis and refined psychoanalysis as a method of treatment.

In 1895 he published, with Joseph Breuer, *Studien über Hysterie* ('Studies in Hysteria'), but two years later their friendship ended as a result of Freud's theories of infantile sexuality. He developed his revolutionary thinking despite opposition from friends, patients and medical colleagues, and in 1900 he published his seminal work, *Die Traumdeutung* ('The Interpretation of Dreams'), arguing that dreams, like neuroses, are disguised manifestations of repressed sexual desires. He was appointed Extraordinary Professor of Neuropathology at the University of Vienna in 1902; there he began to hold weekly seminars in his home with kindred minds like **Alfred Adler**, and produced the further crucial works, *The Psychopathology of Everyday Life* (1904), and *Three Essays on the Theory of Sexuality* (1905), which met with intense and uncomprehending opposition. In 1908 these weekly meetings became those of the Vienna Psychoanalytical Society, and, in 1910, the International Psychoanalytical Association, with **Carl Jung** as its first president.

Both Adler (1911) and Jung (1913) broke with Freud to develop their own theories. Undeterred, Freud produced *Totem and Tabu* (1913), *Beyond the Pleasure Principle* (1919–20) and *Ego and Id* (1923), elaborating his theories of the division of the unconscious mind into the 'Id', the 'Ego', and the 'Super-Ego'. In 1927 he published a controversial view of religion, *The Future of an Illusion*. He was awarded the prestigious Goethe prize in 1930, and in 1933 published *Why War?*, written in collaboration with **Albert Einstein**. Under the Nazi regime psychoanalysis was banned, and in 1938, after the annexation of Austria, Freud was extricated from Vienna and brought to London with his family. He made his home in Hampstead, but died of cancer the following year.

📖 H S Decker, *Freud, Dora and Vienna 1900* (1990); E M Thornton, *Freud and Cocaine: The Freudian Fallacy* (1983); Lionel Trilling and Stephen Marcus, *The Life and Works of Sigmund Freud* (1961).

> 'The more the fruits of knowledge become accessible to men, the more widespread is the decline of religious belief.'
> From *The Future of an Illusion* (1927).

brilliant papers were a series published in 1818–21 relating polarization phenomena to **Thomas Young**'s hypothesis of transverse waves, and his *uvres Complètes* ('Complete Works') published in three volumes in the 1860s, contain practically everything that was known in optics up to the time of his death.

Freud, Anna 1895–1982
British psychoanalyst

Born in Vienna, Austria, the youngest daughter of **Sigmund Freud**, she taught at the Cottage Lyceum there, and emigrated (1938) with her father to London, where she organized (1940–45) a residential war nursery for homeless children. A pioneer of child psychoanalysis, she founded the Hampstead Child Therapy Clinic. Her works include *The Ego and the Mechanism of Defence* (1937) and *Beyond the Best Interests of the Child* (1973). 📖 U H Peters, *Anna Freud* (1985)

Freud, Lucian 1922–
British painter

Born in Berlin, Germany, he was the grandson of **Sigmund Freud**. After moving to Great Britain in 1931, he studied at the Central School of Arts and Crafts in London (1938–39) and the East Anglian School of Painting and Drawing, Dedham (1939–42). His first sketch (a self-portrait) was published when he was 17. In his early years he was one of the Neo-Romantic group of English painters along with **Graham Sutherland** and **John Piper**, but since the mid-1940s he has developed a linear, realistic style. This is seen best in his acutely observed portraits and nude studies, such as *Girl with a White Dog* (1951–52, Tate, London). From c.1958, he developed a freer style, painting his figures from disconcerting angles, shown in *Standing by the Rags* (1988–89, Tate). Exhibitions of his work in 1974 (London) and 1987 (Washington DC) contributed to international interest in his traditional, representational style, which continued into the 1990s, with a major exhibition in 1996 in Kendal, Cumbria, attracting over 25,000 visitors. He became a British citizen in 1939, and was appointed to the Order of Merit in 1993.

Freud, Sigmund See panel above

Freund, Wilhelm 1806–94
German philologist and lexicographer

Born in Kempen in Posen, he compiled the *Wörterbuch der lateinischen Sprache* (1834–45), on which most English–Latin dictionaries are based.

Freyberg, Bernard, 1st Baron Freyberg 1889–1963
New Zealand soldier

Born in London, he was educated at Wellington College, New Zealand. At the outbreak of World War I he enlisted in England and served in Gallipoli and France, winning the VC at Beaumont Hamel. In World War II he was given command of the New Zealand forces in the Middle East. He commanded Commonwealth forces in ill-fated operations in Greece and Crete (1941) and in the Sahara. He commanded the New Zealand Corps in Italy (1944–45), and was Governor-General of New Zealand (1946–52) and Lieutenant Governor of Windsor Castle (1956–63).

Freyre, Gilberto de Mello 1900–87
Brazilian writer and intellectual

Born in Recife, he was educated in Rio de Janeiro and in Texas and New York City. After working as a journalist in his native city (1927–30), he moved to an academic career. A prolific author, he came to prominence with a large-scale historical work, *Casa-grande & Senzala* (1933, Eng trans *The Masters and the Slaves*, 1946), which altered previous thinking about colonial Brazil and its relations with Europe. The book won him the Felippe d'Oliveira award (1934), the first of many prestigious prizes and honorary doctorates. He represented Brazil in the UN General Assembly in 1949. 📖 D de Melo Menezes, *Gilberto Freyre* (1944, in Spanish)

Freyssinet, Marie Eugène Léon 1879–1962
French civil engineer

Born in Objat, Corrèze, he graduated from both the École Polytechnique and the École des Ponts et Chaussées in Paris. His intuitive rather than analytical approach to reinforced concrete design reached its height in his airship hangars at Orly (1916–24, destroyed 1944) where he used corrugated parabolic arches over 200ft (61m) high yet only 3in (9cm) thick. Realizing that concrete's great weakness is its lack of strength in tension, he sought ways of putting concrete structures into a state of permanent compression even under load, and succeeded in developing practical techniques for pre-stressing concrete by the use of stretched steel tendons. From 1930 he was one of the leading exponents of this virtually new structural material, employing it to full advantage in bridges, foundations, a dam in Algeria, the airport runway at Orly and a water tower at Orleans.

Freytag, Gustav 1816–95
German novelist and playwright

He was born in Kreuzburg, Silesia, and from 1839 to 1847 he was *Privatdozent* (lecturer) of German at Breslau University. A deputy to the North German Diet, he attended the Prussian crown prince in the Franco-German campaign (1870). His comedies and other plays, such as *Die Valentine* (1846) and *Die Journalisten* (1853, Eng trans *The Journalists*), proved brilliant successes, but his greatest achievement is *Soll und Haben* (1855, Eng trans *Debit and Credit*, 1857), a realistic novel of German commercial life. It was followed by *Die Verlorene Handschrift* (1864, Eng trans *The Lost Manuscript*, 1865), and the series called *Die Ahnen*, (1872–81, 'The Ancestors'). He set down his dramatic theories in *Technik des Dramas* (1863, 'Technique of Drama'). 📖 H Lindau, *Gustav Freytag* (1907)

Frey-Wyssling, Albert Friedrich 1900–
Swiss botanist

Born in Küsnacht, he studied in Zurich, Jena and Paris and became Professor of Botany in Zurich in 1938. He did much to establish ultrastructural studies on plant cells by the use of polarization microscopy, in the period before about 1940. Later, X-ray diffraction and electron microscopy techniques became available to confirm and extend his results by these more direct methods.

Frick, Henry Clay 1849–1919
US industrialist and philantropist

Born in West Overton, Pennsylvania, he received little education, but capitalized on post-Civil War expansion by forming a company to supply the Pittsburgh steel mills with coke, and was a millionaire at 30. **Andrew Carnegie** was associated with Frick from 1884, and invited him to become chairman of the Carnegie steel company in 1889. He reorganized the company and made a highly profitable investment for the firm in iron ore at Lake Superior. He was a hard and ruthless employer, unsuccessfully using 200 hired Pinkerton guards in pitched battle to dislodge strikers at the Carnegie Steel Plant at Homestead, Pennsylvania (1892), and on their failure, called in the Pennsylvania National Guard. The strike was broken, but Frick was shot and stabbed by Alexander Berkman, an associate of the anarchist **Emma Goldman**, although was ultimately recovered. He broke with Carnegie in 1900, and became director of **John Pierpont Morgan**'s United States Steel (1901). He built up the distinguished Frick Collection of fine art, now a museum in New York City. He also endowed hospitals, schools and a large park in Pittsburgh. 📖 G B M Harvey, *Henry Clay Frick, the Man* (1928)

Frick, Wilhelm 1877–1946
German Nazi politician

Born in Alsenz, he participated in **Hitler**'s Munich putsch (1923), led the Nazi faction in the Reichstag from 1924, and as Minister of the Interior from 1933 banned trade unionism and freedom of the press, and encouraged anti-Semitism. Ousted by **Heinrich Himmler** in 1943, he became 'Protector' of Bohemia and Moravia. He was found guilty of war crimes at Nuremberg and executed.

Fricker, Peter Racine 1920–90
English composer

Born in London, he studied at the Royal College of Music, was musical director of Morley College, London (1952–64), and then moved to the University of California, Santa Barbara (1964). The influence of **Béla Bartók** and **Arnold Schoenberg** is apparent in such works as the String Quartet in One Movement (1948), the First Symphony (1948–49) and the Sonata for Violin and Piano (1950). Later works include symphonies, a cello sonata (1956), an oratorio, *The Vision of Judgement* (1957–58), and other chamber, choral and keyboard works.

Friday, Nancy 1937–
US feminist author

She was born in Pittsburgh, Pennsylvania, the daughter of a financier, and was educated at Wellesley College. She worked as a reporter on a newspaper in San Juan, Puerto Rico (1960–61) and as editor of *Islands in the Sun* magazine (1961–63), before turning to freelance writing. Her best known work, *My Secret Garden* (1976), which exploded the myth surrounding women's sexual fantasies, sold over 1.5 million copies worldwide. In 1980 she published *Men In Love*, an exploration of men and their sexuality fantasies. *Women on Top* (1991) re-examines modern women in the context of feminism and renewed sexual freedom, and documents the manner in which women appear to have incorporated male pornography into their own sexual fantasies. These issues are dealt with again in *Forbidden Flowers* (1994).

Frideswide, St d.c.735
Anglo-Saxon abbess and patron saint of Oxford

The daughter of Didanus, an ealdorman, she founded a nunnery at Oxford on the site of what is now Christ Church. She was canonized in 1481. Her feast day is 19 October.

Fried, Alfred Hermann 1864–1921
Austrian pacifist and Nobel Prize winner

He was born in Vienna, and founded the *Deutsche Friedensgesellschaft* (German Society for Peace) in Berlin in 1892. In World War I he lived in Switzerland, and on its conclusion he protested against the terms of the Treaty of Versailles, while maintaining his pacifist stance. He shared the Nobel Prize for peace with **Tobias Asser** in 1911.

Friedan, Betty (Elizabeth Naomi), *née* Goldstein 1921–
US feminist and writer

Born in Peoria, Illinois, she was educated at Smith College. She wrote a best-selling book, *The Feminine Mystique* (1963), which analyzed the role of women in US society and articulated their frustrations. She was founder and first president of the National Association for Women (1966), and headed the National Women's Strike for Equality (1970). In *The Second Stage* (1981), she emphasized the importance of both the new and the traditional female roles. She also wrote *It Changed My Life* (1977) and *The Fountain of Age* (1993), which explores the virtues and possibilities of old age.

Friedel, Charles 1832–99
French chemist

Latterly Professor of Organic Chemistry at the Sorbonne, Paris, he worked on the production of artificial minerals (diamonds). He and the US chemist James Mason Crafts (1839–1917) gave their names to the Friedel–Crafts reaction for the synthesis of benzene homologues.

Friedman, Herbert 1916–
US astrophysicist

Born in New York City and educated at Brooklyn College and Johns Hopkins University, he spent his career at the US Naval Research Laboratory in Washington. He carried out pioneering work on the use of rockets in astronomy and in the study of astronomical X-ray sources. From the 1940s he initiated the use of rockets carrying detectors to study X-rays from space. In 1949 he began investigations of the X-ray activity of the Sun, producing the first X-ray and ultraviolet photographs of the Sun in 1960. Following Bruno Rossi's discovery in 1962 of the first non-solar X-ray source, Friedman showed that one such source in the constellation Taurus coincided with the remnant of a luminous supernova in the Crab nebula (1964). After this early work, X-ray astronomy developed as an important area of astrophysics, as has the use of rockets to transport astronomical instruments above the absorbing layer of the Earth's atmosphere.

Friedman, Jerome Isaac 1928–
US physicist and Nobel Prize winner

Born in Chicago, he was educated and worked at the university there, then moved to Stanford University and the Massachusetts Institute of Technology (MIT), where he became professor in 1967. He became director of the Laboratory of Nuclear Science (1980–83) then head of the physics department. In the 1960s, with **Henry Kendall** and **Richard Taylor**, he led a group at the Stanford linear accelerator investigating electron scattering from nucleons (protons and neutrons). They studied the properties of quarks, establishing that quarks have spin and fractional charges of $+\frac{2}{3}$ and $-\frac{1}{3}$ times electronic charge, as had been postulated by **Murray Gell-Mann** and others. The supreme achievement of the group was in providing the first incontrovertible evidence for quarks as real entities rather than abstract mathematical concepts. For this work they won the 1990 Nobel Prize for physics.

Friedman, Milton 1912–
US economist and Nobel Prize winer

He was born in New York City and educated there and in Chicago. After eight years at the National Bureau of Economic Research (1937–45), he became Professor of Economics at Chicago University (1946–83), now emeritus, where he became the foremost exponent of monetarism. In such works as *A Monetary History of the United States, 1867–1960* (1963) and *Inflation: Causes and Consequences* (1963) he argued that a country's economy can be controlled through its money supply. He was awarded the 1976 Nobel Prize for economics, and was a policy adviser to the **Reagan** administration (1981–88). His ideas were applied in Great Britain, with almost messianic zeal by the Conservative government of **Margaret Thatcher** after the 1979 general election. A later publication is *Money Mischief* (1992). ▢ E Butler, *Milton Friedman* (1985)

Friedrich, Caspar David 1774–1840
German painter

Born in Pomerania, he studied at the Academy of Copenhagen from 1794 to 1798 then spent the rest of his life in Dresden. His work won the approval of **Goethe**, and in 1805 he won a Weimar Art Society prize. His paintings from c.1808 were highly controversial in their treatment of landscape as vast and desolate expanses in which man—often a solitary figure—is depicted as a melancholy spectator of Nature's awesome power. Such works helped to establish the notion of the sublime as a central concern of the Romantic movement. He taught at the Dresden Academy from 1816 and became a professor in 1824.

Friel, Brian 1929–
Northern Irish playwright and short-story writer

He was born in Omagh, County Tyrone, and studied for the priesthood in Maynooth, Ireland, choosing not to enter it upon graduation in 1948. He returned to Northern Ireland and taught for 10 years in Londonderry, during which time he started to write, his first short stories appearing in the *New Yorker*. His first play, *This Doubtful Paradise* (1959), was produced in Belfast. His first major success was *Philadelphia, Here I Come!* (1964), a play about emigration and the relationship between a man and his son. Friel's writing is poetic, sometimes ironic, always compassionate and poignant. He often concentrates upon the relation between people, language, custom and the land, these forming the principal theme of the plays *Translations* (1980) and *Dancing at Lughnasa* (1990), both of which are set in County Donegal. With actor Stephen Rea, Friel was a co-founder of the Field Day Theatre Company (1980). His short-story collections include *A Saucer of Larks* (1962) and *The Diviner: Brian Friel's Best Short Stories* (1983). In 1995 a critically acclaimed revival of *Translations* was staged at the Plymouth Theater in New York. ▢ U Dantanus, *Brian Friel* (1988)

Friel, George 1910–75
Scottish novelist

Born in Glasgow, he was educated at St Mungo's Academy and Glasgow University, then trained as a teacher at Jordanhill College, Glasgow. He served in the Royal Army Ordnance Corps during World War II, then went back to teaching, a profession he grew to loathe and distrust, although he always retained his concern for children. His teaching experiences are at the heart of his popular novel *Mr Alfred M.A.* (1972), which describes the disillusionment and downfall of a teacher betrayed by one of his female pupils. Other novels include *The Bank of Time* (1959), *The Boy Who Wanted Peace* (1964), *Grace and Miss Partridge* (1969) and *An Empty House* (1975).

Friend, Charlotte 1921–87
US oncologist and medical microbiologist

Born in New York City, she attended Hunter College before serving in the US Navy during World War II. The GI Bill of Rights enabled her to enrol at Yale, from which she gained a PhD (1950). She joined the Sloan-Kettering Institute for Cancer Research, and was associate Professor of Microbiology there until 1966, when she was appointed professor at the Mount Sinai School of Medicine, where she remained until her death. Her discovery that a fatal leukaemia could be induced in experimental animals by a virus, now known as the Friend Leukaemia Virus (FLV), was initially received with hostility, but colleagues soon recognized that some viruses were able to produce cancers. She received numerous honours worldwide and was elected to the National Academy of Sciences in 1976.

Fries, Elias Magnus 1794–1878
Swedish botanist

He was professor at Uppsala University, and keeper of the botanic garden there. He wrote on fungi, lichens and the flora of Scandinavia, and introduced a new classificatory system. The genus *Freesia* is named after him.

Friese-Greene, William, originally William Edward Green 1855–1921
English photographer and inventor

Born in Bristol, Avon, he designed a camera in the 1880s to expose a sequence of photographs for projection as a moving image by lantern slides. He is thus claimed by some as the English inventor of cinematography. However, he did not in fact propose perforated strips of film for either photography or projection. ▢ Ray Allister, *Friese-Greene: Close-up of an Inventor* (1948)

Friesz, (Émile) Othon 1879–1949
French painter

Born in Le Havre, where he attended the École des Beaux Arts, he went to Paris in 1898 and painted in the Fauve style, until 1908, when his work became more traditional. In 1935 he designed a Gobelius tapestry, *Peace*.

Friml, (Charles) Rudolf 1879–1972
US pianist and composer

Born in Prague, he studied at the Prague Conservatory under Antonin Dvořák, and settled in the USA in 1906. He wrote a piano concerto, film music for Hollywood, piano pieces and many operettas, including the popular *Rose Marie* (1924) and *The Vagabond King* (1925). His songs include 'The Donkey Serenade' (1937).

Frink, Dame Elisabeth 1930–93
English sculptor

Born in Thurlow, Suffolk, she entered Guildford Art School in 1947, then trained at Chelsea School of Art under Bernard Meadows, himself influenced by Henry Moore. She taught there for 10 years and at Central St Martins College of Art, London, and was visiting lecturer at the Royal College. She was appointed a trustee of the British Museum in 1977. Her work displays a combination of sensuality, strength and vulnerability, seen particularly in her series of horse and rider sculptures. She has exhibited in many places including the Tate Gallery, London, and the Museum of Modern Art, New York. She undertook many major public commissions and worked in France (1967-73) before returning to live and work in Dorset. She was appointed DBE in 1982.

Frisch, Karl von 1886–1982
Austrian ethologist, zoologist and Nobel Prize winner

Born in Vienna, he studied medicine there before abandoning it for zoology, which he studied at the universities of Munich and Trieste. After teaching at several universities he settled at Munich, where he established the Zoological Institute in 1932. He was a key figure in developing ethology using field observation of animals combined with ingenious experiments. His early work showed that fish perceive colours and that their visual acuity is superior to that of humans, but he is mainly remembered for his later work on honey bees. He demonstrated that bees are able to distinguish odours, tastes and colours, and that the honey bee's visual spectrum allows it to see ultraviolet light, and described how hive bees communicate the location of a source of food by means of coded dances. In 1949 he further showed that bees can navigate even on cloudy days by making use of the pattern of polarized light in the sky. In 1973 he shared the Nobel Prize for physiology or medicine with other pioneers of ethology, Konrad Lorenz and Nikolaas Tinbergen. His books include *The Dancing Bees* (1927, Eng trans 1954) and *Animal Architecture* (1974).

Frisch, Max Rudolph 1911–91
Swiss novelist and playwright

Born in Zurich, he was forced by economic circumstances to abandon the study of German literature at Zurich University (1933), and became a journalist, then trained as an architect. *Blätter aus dem Brotsack* (1940, Eng trans *Leaves from a Knapsack*, 1942), was published while he was serving with the Swiss frontier guard. In 1958 he became the first foreigner to be awarded the Büchner prize of the German Academy for language and poetry. As a novelist he is chiefly known outside German-speaking Europe for the novels *Stiller* (1954, Eng trans *I'm Not Stiller*, 1958), *Homo Faber* (1957, Eng trans 1959) and *Der Mensch erscheint im Holozän* (1979, Eng trans *Man in the Holocene*, 1980). As a playwright, he was a disciple of Bertolt Brecht in the 1940s, and his *Biedermann und die Brandstifter* (1953, Eng

trans *The Fire Raisers*, 1962) and *Andorra* (1961, Eng trans 1962) have become modern stage classics. ⌨ U Weisstein, *Frisch* (1967)

Frisch, Otto Robert 1904–79
British physicist

Born in Vienna, Austria, and educated at Vienna University, he became assistant to Otto Stern in 1930 and worked with him and Emilio Segrè on diffraction experiments. In 1933, under the Nazi racial laws, Frisch left Germany to work with Patrick Blackett at Imperial College, London, before moving to Niels Bohr's institute in Copenhagen. In 1939, with Lise Meitner (his aunt), he correctly interpreted and later confirmed that Otto Hahn's observation of uranium splitting was due to nuclear fission. During World War II he worked at Birmingham University, where he and Sir Rudolf Peierls studied the possibility of nuclear chain reactions. This work led to his involvement in the British and US atom bomb projects, and he worked for a time at Los Alamos on the Manhattan Project. After the war he returned to England to become head of the nuclear physics division of the Atomic Energy Research Establishment at Harwell, and later accepted a chair at Cambridge. He received an OBE in 1948 and was elected FRS in the same year. ⌨ *What Little I Remember (1979)*

Frisch, Ragnar Anton Kittil 1895–1973
Norwegian economist and Nobel Prize winner

Born in Oslo, he studied there, and was Professor of Economics at Olso University from 1931 to 1965, and editor of *Econometrica* (1933–55). He was a pioneer of econometrics, the application of statistics to economic planning. He shared the first Nobel Prize for economics in 1969 with Jan Tinbergen.

Frith, Francis 1822–98
English topographical photographer

Born in Chesterfield, Derbyshire, he became interested in photography while working with a printing firm. Between 1856 and 1859 he travelled extensively in Egypt and the Near East, using the large 40 × 50cm cameras and complicated wet-plate process of the period to produce the first photographic traveller's records to be seen in Great Britain. From 1864 he toured throughout Britain and established a nationwide service of photographs of local scenes as prints and postcards, a business which by the end of his life had extended into Europe and survived commercially until 1971.

Frith, John 1503–33
English Protestant religious

Born in Westerham, Kent, he was educated at Eton and King's College, Cambridge. From there Thomas Wolsey summoned him to his new foundation at Oxford in 1525. A year later suspicion of heresy drove him to Marburg, where he befriended William Tyndale and Patrick Hamilton, and wrote several Protestant treatises. Returning in 1532, he was burned at Smithfield.

Frith, Mary, known as Moll Cutpurse 1584–1659
English highwaywoman, pickpocket and receiver of stolen goods

Born in London, she proved inept and uninterested in all the traditional feminine virtues and joined the groups of pickpockets who frequented the crowded markets and fairs of the city, adopting masculine clothing to consolidate her equality among them. A long period of highway robbery followed this apprenticeship, when she gained her nickname from her use of a sharp knife to cut the belts on which travellers carried their purses. She became notorious and rich. A declared Royalist, she asserted that she would only rob the king's enemies. By the end of her life she was running a brothel. She left instructions that she was to be buried face down, so that she would remain as preposterous in death as in life.

Frith, William Powell 1819–1909
English painter

Born in Aldfield, he made himself the wealthiest artist of his time by selling both paintings and their copyright. The Pre-Raphaelites criticized the vulgarity of his historical and genre works, but he took a new direction with his huge canvases of Victorian scenes, *Ramsgate Sands* (1854, bought by Queen Victoria for Buckingham Palace), *Derby Day* (1858, Tate, London) and *The Railway Station* (1862, Holloway College), which achieved huge popular success and were hailed by John Ruskin as the art of the future.

Fritsch, Elizabeth 1940–
English potter

Born in Shropshire, she studied harp and piano at the Royal Academy of Music before attending the Royal College of Art, London. One of the most talented contemporary potters of her generation, she is sometimes inspired by music, and she uses coiling spires and geometric patterns in coloured slips with a matt texture akin to ivory frescoes. She was influenced by Hans Coper and Lucie Rie.

Frobenius, Ferdinand Georg 1849–1917
German mathematician

Born in Berlin, he studied at the universities of Göttingen and Berlin, where he gained a PhD, and from 1875 to 1892 taught at the university of Zurich, before returning to Berlin as professor. After early work on the theory of differential equations, he founded the theory of group representations, using it both to clarify the notion of an abstract group and also to derive the properties of groups inaccessible by more direct methods. Representation theory later became essential in quantum mechanics, and a major theme in the mathematics of the 20th century.

Froberger, Johann Jakob 1616–67
German composer

Born in Stuttgart, he was a pupil of Girolamo Frescobaldi. Court organist at Vienna (1637–57), he made concert tours to Italy, Paris, London and Brussels. Of his many compositions, the best remembered are his suites for harpsichord.

Frobisher, Sir Martin c.1535–1594
English sailor

Born in Altofts, near Wakefield, Yorkshire, he was sent to sea as a boy. In 1576, with the *Gabriel* and the *Michael*, he set off in search of a Northwest Passage to Cathay. The *Michael* was abandoned, but Frobisher reached Labrador and discovered Frobisher Bay. From two expeditions (1577, 1578) he brought back 'black earth' which was supposed to be gold from Frobisher Bay. He commanded a vessel in 1585 in Francis Drake's expedition to the West Indies, and was knighted for his services against the Armada in command of the *Triumph*. He was mortally wounded at the siege of Crozon, near Brest, France.

Fröding, Gustav 1860–1911
Swedish poet

Born in Alstern, near Karlstad, he studied at Uppsala, and became a schoolmaster and journalist, but suffered from mental illness. He is considered the greatest Swedish lyric poet, often compared to Robert Burns, combining dialect and folksong rhythm in his portrayal of local characters, as in *Guitarr och dragharmonika* (1891, 'Guitar and Concertina'), *Nya dikter* (1894, 'New Poems') and *Rägglerå paschaser* (1896, 'Drops and Fragments'). 📖 J Landquist, *Gustav Fröding, en biografi* (1956)

Froebel, Friedrich Wilhelm August 1782–1852
German educationist and founder of the kindergarten system

Born in Oberweissbach, he studied at Jena, Göttingen and Berlin, and in 1805 began teaching at Frankfurt-am-Main. In 1816 he put into practice his educational system at a school which he founded at Griesheim. He expounded its aim (to help the child's mind to grow naturally and spontaneously) in *Die Menschenerziehung* (1826). Catholic opposition foiled his attempts to establish a school near Lucerne (1831). After starting an orphanage at Burgdorf in Bern, where he began to train teachers for educational work, he opened his first kindergarten school at Blankenburg (1836). 📖 Irene M Lilley, *Friedrich Froebel: A Selection from his Writings* (1967)

Frohschammer, Jakob 1821–93
German Catholic theologian and philosopher

Born near Ratisbon (now Regensburg), he became widely known for his history of dogma (1850) which was banned by the pope. In another work he championed freedom of science from the church. He founded the first Liberal Catholic paper, *Athenä*, in which he gave an account of Darwin's theory. He was excommunicated in 1871.

Froissart, Jean c.1333–c.1404
French chronicler and poet

Born in Valenciennes, Hainault, he was educated for the Church, but at the age of 19 began to write the history of the wars of his time. He served Philippa of Hainault, wife of Edward III of England (1361–69), and travelled in Scotland, France and Italy. Returning to Hainault, he resumed work on his *Chroniques* (Eng trans *Chronicles*, 1523–25), which cover European history from 1325 to 1400. Mainly occupied with France, England, Scotland and Flanders during the Hundred Years War (1337–1453), he also supplies valuable information about Germany, Italy and Spain. He wrote poems for noble patrons and became private chaplain to Guy of Châtillon.

Froment, Nicolas fl.1450–90
French painter

His work exemplifies the late Gothic style, containing features surprisingly Flemish in appearance. He was court painter to King René, whose portrait is incorporated in his masterpiece, a triptych in the cathedral of Aix-en-Provence, having as its centrepiece Moses and the burning bush.

Fromentin, Eugène 1820–76
French novelist and painter

He was born in La Rochelle, and visits to Algeria and the Near East provided him with abundant material for his paintings, which betray the influence of Eugène Delacroix. His three travel books also provide vivid pictures of Algeria. However, he is best known as the author of *Dominique* (1862, Eng trans 1932), a nostalgic autobiographical novel, and *Les Maîtres d'autrefois* (1876, Eng trans *Masters of Past Time*, 1948), which was written during a tour of Belgian and Dutch art galleries and contains some impressive art criticism. 📖 A R Evans, *The Literary Art of Eugène Fromentin* (1964)

Fromm, Erich 1900–80
US psychoanalyst and social philosopher

Born in Frankfurt, Germany, he was educated at the universities of Frankfurt, Heidelberg and Munich, and at the Berlin Institute of Psychoanalysis. He emigrated to the USA in 1934, and after holding various university appointments became professor at New York (1962). He emphasized social and economic and cultural factors on human behaviour. His works include *Man for Himself* (1947), *Psychoanalysis and Religion* (1951), *Sigmund Freud's Mission* (1959) and *The Heart of Man* (1964).

Frost, Robert Lee 1874–1963
US lyric poet

Robert Frost was born in San Francisco, the son of a New England father and Scottish mother. He studied at Dartmouth and Harvard but did not graduate and as a teacher, cobbler and New Hampshire farmer he wrote poetry that he was unable to get published. From 1912 to 1915 he lived in Great Britain, where, encouraged by **Rupert Brooke** and others, he published *A Boy's Will* (1913) and *North of Boston* (1914), which brought him an international reputation.

Returning in glory to the USA, he became Professor of English at Amherst (1916), and continued to write lyric and narrative poetry which draws its characters, background and imagery from New England. His choice of rural subjects and use of traditional verse forms has contributed perhaps to the misperception of Frost as a homely and comfortable poet, but the dark and ambiguous vision that underlies his work is in no way conventional.

His volumes of poetry include *West-Running Brook* (1928), *A Witness Tree* (1942), *Steeple Bush* (1947) and *In the Clearing* (1962). He was awarded the Pulitzer Prize in 1924, 1931, 1937 and 1943, and he was Professor of Poetry at Harvard from 1939 to 1943 before returning to Amherst

(1949–63). Recognized as a major US poet, he read his poem 'The Gift Outright' at President **John F Kennedy's** inauguration in 1961. His *Complete Poems* appeared in 1967.

📖 S Burnshaw, *Robert Frost Himself* (1986); E C Latham, editor, *Robert Frost's Poetry and Prose* (1984); L Thompson and R H Winnick *Robert Frost: A Biography*, edited by E C Latham (1981); R Brower, *The Poetry of Robert Frost* (1963).

> 'I shall be telling this with a sigh
> Somewhere ages and ages hence:
> Two roads diverged in a wood, and I—
> I took the one less travelled by,
> And that has made all the difference.'
> From 'The Road Not Taken' (1916).

> 'He is a poet of the minor theme, the casual approach, and the discreetly eccentric attitude.' Yvor Winters in *Robert Frost: A Collection of Critical Essays*, edited by J Cox (1982).

Frontenac, Louis de Buade, Comte de
1622–98
French–Canadian politician

He served in the army, and in 1672 was appointed Governor of the French possessions in North America. He was recalled for misgovernment in 1682, but had gained the confidence of the settlers and the respect of the Native Indians, and in 1689 was sent out again. He extended the boundaries of New France down the Mississippi, launched attacks on New England villages, repulsed the British siege of Quebec (1690), and defeated the Iroquois.

Frontinus, Sextus Julius c.40–103AD
Roman soldier and writer

He was appointed Roman Governor of Britain in AD75, and established the legionary fortress at Isca (Caerleon on the Usk). In 97 he was made superintendent of the waterworks at Rome. He wrote the *Strategematica*, a treatise on war in four volumes, and the *De Aquis Urbis Romae*, a detailed account of the Roman water system which also contains important information on the history of architecture.

Fronto, Marcus Cornelius c.100–c.176AD
Roman orator

Born in Cirta, Numidia (North Africa), he was entrusted by **Antoninus Pius** with the education of **Marcus Aurelius** and Lucius Verus. In AD143 he was consul with **Herodes Atticus**. Two series of his letters to Marcus Aurelius were discovered in Milan in 1815. He was a champion of the early Latin stylists.

Frost, Sir David Paradine 1939–
English broadcaster and businessman

Born in Tenterden, Kent, and educated at Cambridge, he entered television in 1961. He hosted *That Was The Week That Was* (1962–63), a late-night revue show with topical satire and an irreverent attitude to authority. Shows in Great Britain and the USA include *The Frost Report* (1966–67), *Frost on Friday* (1968–70), *The David Frost Show* (1969–72) and *Breakfast with Frost* (1993–). His shows on US television include *The Guinness Book of World Records* (1981–) and *The Spitting Image Movie Awards* (1987), and he has been a diligent interviewer of world leaders in *The Nixon Interviews* (1976–77) and *The Shah Speaks* (1980). A producer of films like *The Slipper and the Rose* (1976), he was also a co-founder

and presenter of Britain's *TV–am* (1983–92). His many international honours include the Golden Rose of Montreux (1967) and the Emmy (1970, 1971). His publications include *How to Live Under Labour* (1964), *I Gave Them A Sword* (1978) and *The World's Shortest Books* (1987). His first volume of autobiography, *From Congregations to America*, was published in 1993, the same year he was knighted.

Frost, John d.1877
Welsh political leader

Born in Newport, he was a prosperous tailor and draper, and became Mayor of Newport (1836–37). In 1839 he led a Chartist insurrection designed to seize control of Newport, which was repulsed by troops with heavy loss of Chartist lives. He was sentenced to be hanged, drawn and quartered, but the sentence was commuted to transportation for life to Tasmania. Given an unconditional pardon in 1856, he returned to a triumphant welcome in Newport.

Frost, Robert Lee See panel above

Frost, Sir Terry (Terence Ernest Manitou)
1915–
English painter

Born in Leamington Spa, Warwickshire, he was taken prisoner in Crete in 1941 and spent World War II in prisoner-of-war camps. After the war, he attended evening classes at Birmingham Art College, and also at Camberwell School of Art, where he studied under **Victor Pasmore** (1947–50). He then moved to St Ives, Cornwall, and has constantly returned there. His first abstract paintings date from 1949 and typically consist of segments of colour, as in *Green, Blue and White Movement* (1951, Tate, London). Since 1952 he has had over 30 one-man shows in Great Britain, Europe and the USA, and has held teaching posts in both Britain and California, including being Professor of Painting at the University of Reading (1977–81), then emeritus. He co-authored *Terry Frost* in 1994.

Froude, James Anthony 1818–94
English writer and historian

He was born in Dartington, Devon, and was educated at Westminster and Oriel College, Oxford. In 1842 he was elected a Fellow of Exeter College, Oxford. His early controversial novels, *Shadows of the Clouds* (1847) and *The Nemesis of Faith* (1848), cost him both his fellowship and an educational post in Tasmania. For the next few years he wrote for *Fraser's Magazine* (which he edited for a while) and the *Westminster Review*, and produced his *History of England from the Fall of Wolsey to the Spanish Armada* (12 vols, 1856–69). His essays include *English in Ireland in the Eighteenth Century* (1871–74) and *Caesar* (1879). As literary executor of Thomas Carlyle he edited his *Reminiscences* (1881) and Jane Welsh Carlyle's *Letters* (1882), and wrote Carlyle's biography (1882–84). Other works are *Two Lectures on South Africa* (1880), *Oceana* (1886), *The English in the West Indies* (1888), *The Earl of Beaconsfield* (1890), *The Spanish Story of the Armada* (1892) and *Lectures on the Council of Trent* (1896). He later became Rector of St Andrews (1869) and Professor of Modern History at Oxford (1892). He was the brother of Richard Hurrell Froude and William Froude.

Froude, Richard Hurrell 1803–36
English tractarian

Born in Dartington, Devon, he became Fellow and tutor of Oriel College, Oxford, in 1827. With John Henry Newman and John Keble he helped to initiate the 'Oxford Movement', which favoured the early and medieval church, and wrote Tracts 9 and 63. His diaries, posthumously published as *Remains* (1838–39), betrayed hostility to the leaders of the Reformation and encouraged the development of Anglo-Catholicism. He was the brother of James Anthony Froude and William Froude.

Froude, William 1810–79
English engineer and applied mathematician

Born in Dartington, Devon, he became an assistant to Isambard Kingdom Brunel in 1827. Retiring in 1846 from professional work, he devoted himself to investigating the conditions of naval construction. He was the brother of James Anthony Froude and Richard Hurrell Froude.

Frumentius, St 4th century AD
North African bishop

Born in Phoenicia (now Tunisia), he was captured by Ethiopians whilst on a voyage, and was made the king's secretary. He gradually secured the introduction of Christianity and became known as 'the Apostle of Ethiopia'. In AD326 he was consecrated Bishop of Axum by Athanasius in Alexandria.

Frundsberg, Georg von 1473–1528
German soldier

Founder and leader of German *Landsknechte* during the Italian wars of Maximilian I and Charles V, he was largely responsible for winning the Battle of Pavia (1525).

Frunze, Mikhail Vasilevich 1885–1925
Russian revolutionary and professional soldier

A Bolshevik from 1904, active in both the 1905 and 1917 revolutions, he rose to prominence during the Russian Civil War with successful commands on the eastern and southern fronts. He exercised profound influence upon Soviet military doctrine but was soon engaged in debate with Leon Trotsky, Commissar for War, about creating a Red Army fit for the future. In 1925 he displaced Trotsky but died during an operation, often claimed to have been a medical murder.

Fry, Christopher Harris 1907–
English dramatist

Born in Bristol, and educated at Bedford Modern School, he was a schoolmaster before being appointed director of Tunbridge Wells Repertory Players (1932–36). In 1940 he became director of the Playhouse at Oxford, having in the meantime written two pageant plays, *Thursday's Child* and *The Tower* (1939), and also *The Boy with a Cart* (1937), a rustic play on the subject of the Sussex saint, Cuthman. After service in the Non-Combatant Corps during World War II he began a series of outstanding plays in free verse, often with religious and mystic undertones, including *A Phoenix too Frequent* (1946), *The Lady's Not for Burning* (1949),

Venus Observed (1950), *A Sleep of Prisoners* (1951), *The Dark is Light Enough* (1954), *Curtmantle* (1962) and *A Yard of Sun* (1970). Other publications include *One More Thing, or Caedman Construed* (1987). He has also produced highly successful translations of Jean Anouilh and Jean Giraudoux. 📖 D Stanford, *Christopher Fry* (1954)

Fry, Elizabeth, *née* Gurney 1780–1845
English Quaker prison reformer

Born in Norwich, Norfolk, she became a preacher for the Society of Friends in 1810. Visiting Newgate Prison for women in 1813 she found 300 women, with their children, in terrible conditions, and thereafter devoted her life to prison and asylum reform at home and abroad. She also founded hostels for the homeless, as well as charitable societies, despite her husband's bankruptcy in 1828. She was the sister of Joseph John Gurney. 📖 June Rose, *Elizabeth Fry* (1980)

Fry, Joseph 1728–87
English Quaker businessman and type-founder

Born in Sutton Benger, Wiltshire, he settled in Bristol as a doctor but later went into a pottery enterprise. He founded the chocolate business that bears his name. From 1764 onwards he became eminent as a type-founder, founding types that were similar to those of William Caslon. He also brought out a five-volume version of the Bible (1774–76).

Fry, Laura Ann 1857–1943
US wood carver, ceramicist, designer and sculptor

The daughter the wood carver William Henry Fry, she studied at the Cincinnati School of Design, in Trenton, New Jersey, and in France and England. A founder-member of the Cincinnati Art Pottery Club in 1879, she became the first employee of the Rookwood Pottery in 1881. In 1884 she introduced the use of the atomizer for applying slips to moist pots, and due to her work with underglazing techniques, 'Standard' Rookwood ware became the best-known feature of the firm's Arts and Crafts pottery. After leaving Rookwood in 1887, she was a Professor of Industrial Art (1891) and worked at the Lonhuda Pottery in Steubenville, Ohio (1891–94).

Fry, Roger Eliot 1866–1934
English artist and art critic

He was born in London and was educated at Cambridge. A landscape painter himself, he became a champion of modern artists, particularly Cézanne, and organized the first London exhibition of Post-Impressionists in 1910. He wrote extensively on art and aesthetics, propounding a theory of 'significant form' and colour, rather than content, as the only criteria for great art. He founded the Omega Workshops in London (1913–21), in association with Vanessa Bell and Duncan Grant and others of the Bloomsbury Group, to design textiles, pottery and furniture. His writings include *Vision and Design* (1920), *Transformations* (1926), *Cézanne* (1927), *Henri Matisse* (1930), *French Art* (1932) and *Reflections on British Painting* (1934).

Fry, Stephen John 1957–
English actor and writer

Born in London, he studied at Queen's College, Cambridge, during which time he appeared in more than 30 plays. He wrote his first play *Latin* (1980), which won a Fringe First at the Edinburgh Festival of that year, and appeared with the Cambridge Footlights revue. He also wrote the book for the long-running West End musical *Me and My Girl* (1984–). Frequently partnered by his Cambridge Footlights compatriot Hugh Laurie, he has appeared with him in *A Bit of Fry & Laurie* (1989–), *Jeeves and Wooster* (1990–93) and the film *Peter's Friends* (1992). He was also on television in *Stalag Luft* (1993) and *Cold Comfort Farm* (1995). His stage appearances include *Forty Years On* (1984), *The Common Pursuit* (1988) and *Look Look* (1990). He was in the films *A Handful of Dust* (1988),

A Fish Called Wanda (1988), and the **Oscar Wilde** biopic *Wilde* (1996). His novels include *The Liar* (1991) and *Making History* (1996). He caused a media sensation in 1995 when he walked out of the **Simon Gray** play *Cell Mates* (1995), shortly before its opening in London's West End, and disappeared for a time.

Frye, (Herman) Northrop 1912–91
Canadian literary critic
Born in Sherbrooke, Quebec, he graduated from the University of Toronto and later earned a master's degree in English from Oxford. He joined the faculty at Toronto in 1940 and remained at the university for half a century. Two early works established him as one of the most eminent literary critics of his generation: *Fearful Symmetry* (1947), a study of the writings of **William Blake**; and *Anatomy of Criticism* (1957), an examination of literary archetypes and of the social needs satisfied by myths and symbols. Subsequent writings include *The Educated Imagination* (1964), *Secular Scripture* (1976) and *The Great Code* (1982).

Fuad I 1868–1936
Egyptian ruler
Born in Cairo, the son of Khedive **Ismail Pasha** and father of **Farouk I**, he was Sultan of Egypt from 1917 and king from 1922, when the British protectorate was terminated. His reign was a period of uneasy relations with Egyptian nationalists, represented by the Wafd Party.

Fuchs, Klaus (Emil Julius) 1912–88
British spy and physicist
Born in Rüsselsheim, Germany, he escaped from Nazi persecution to the UK in 1933, was interned during World War II, then naturalized in 1942. From 1943 he worked in the USA on the atom bomb, and in 1946 became head of the theoretical physics division at Harwell, UK. He was sentenced in 1950 to 14 years' imprisonment for disclosing nuclear secrets to the Russians, but was released (1959) and worked in the nuclear research centre of East Germany until 1979. 📖 *Robert Chadwell Williams, Klaus Fuchs, Atom Spy (1987)*

Fuchs, Leonhard 1501–66
German botanist
He was professor at Tübingen University, a pioneer of German botany, and wrote *Historia stirpium* (1542). The genus Fuchsia was named after him.

Fuchs, Sir Vivian Ernest 1908–
English explorer and scientist
Born in Kent, the son of a farmer of German origin, he was educated at Brighton College and St John's, Cambridge. After four geological expeditions in East Africa (1929–38), he served in West Africa and Germany during World War II. As director of the Falkland Islands Dependencies Survey (1947) he set up scientific bases on Graham Land peninsula, and while marooned there for a year, conceived the plan for an overland crossing of Antarctica, which materialized in 1955 when he was appointed leader of the Commonwealth expedition. With a party of 10 he set out by snow tractor from Shackleton Base, Weddell Sea, on 24 November 1957, reached the South Pole on 19 January 1958, and continuing via Depot 700 with the assistance of Sir **Edmund Hillary** and his New Zealand party, reached Scott Base, Victoria Land, on 2 March. He was awarded the gold medal of the Royal Geographical Society (1951), and its Polar medal (1953) and clasp (1958). His publications include his autobiography *A Time to Speak* (1990).

Fucini, Renato, *pseudonym* Neri Tanfucio
1843–1921
Italian writer
Born in Monterotondo, near Pisa, he studied agriculture and engineering in Pisa, and became city engineer in Florence. He had a bright wit which found an outlet in dialect verse, published as *Cento Sonetti* (1872, 'A Hundred Sonnets'). When Florence ceased to be a capital city he lost his post and retired to the country. *Le veglie di Neri* (1884, 'The Vigils of Neri'), a collection of tales, is his best-known work. *All'aria aperta* (1897, 'In the Open') is considered the best modern collection of Italian humorous novellas. He also wrote books for children, and personal anecdotes. 📖 *Renato Fucini (1943)*

Fuentes, Carlos 1928–
Mexican novelist and playwright
Born in Panama City, the son of a diplomat, he was educated at the Colegio Frances Morelos, then at the National University of Mexico and the Institut des Hautes Études Internationales in Geneva, which led to a career in international affairs. A secretary of the Mexican delegation to the International Labor Organization, he eventually became cultural attaché to the Mexican Embassy in Geneva (1950–52) and press secretary to the United Nations Information Centre, Mexico City. He served as the Mexican ambassador to France (1975–77), and has held a variety of teaching posts. An energetic cultural promoter, writer of articles and reviewer, he has published prolifically since his first collection of fantastic, myth-inspired short stories, *Los dias enmascarados* ('The Masked Days') in 1954. Many of his novels have been published in English, among them *Terra nostra* (1975, Eng trans 1976 (US); 1977 (UK)), regarded as his masterpiece, the culmination and synthesis of his novel-writing technique and his ideas on the identity and destiny of Spain and Latin America. His novel *El Gringo viejo* (1985, 'The Old Gringo'), concerning the final days of US writer **Ambrose Bierce**, was filmed in 1989. His novel *Diana, the Goddess who Hunts Alone* was published in 1995. 📖 *D de Guzman, Carlos Fuentes (1972)*

Fugard, Athol 1932–
South African dramatist and theatre director
He was born in Middelburg, Cape Province, and educated at Port Elizabeth Technical College and Cape Town University. He worked as a seaman and journalist before settling firmly into a theatrical career in 1959 as actor, director and playwright. Since 1965 he has been director of the Serpent Players in Port Elizabeth, and in 1972 he co-founded the Space Experimental Theatre, Cape Town. His plays are mostly set in contemporary South Africa, but his presentation of the bleakness and frustration of life for those especially on the fringes of society raises them to the level of universal human tragedy. His work has met with official opposition: *Blood Knot* (1960), about two coloured brothers, one light- and one dark-skinned, was censored, and some of his work has only been published and produced abroad. His plays include *Statements After an Arrest under the Immorality Act* (1972), *A Lesson from Aloes* (1979), *Master Harold and the Boys* (1982), *The Road to Mecca* (1984) and *A Place with the Pigs* (1987), which was inspired by a newspaper story about a Red Army deserter who hid in a pigsty for over 40 years. He has also written film scripts and a novel, *Tsotsi* (1980). *The Road to Mecca* opened in the Promenade Theater in New York in 1988, gaining much praise for Fugard's direction, writing ability and acting in his role as a Dutch Reformed pastor.

Fugger
South German family of bankers and merchants
In the early 16th century the family founded lines of counts and princes. Johannes (1348–1409), was a master-weaver, who settled in Augsburg (1368). His second son, Jakob (d.1469), was extremely successful in his business, and three of his sons were even more successful, married into noble families, and were themselves ennobled by Emperor **Maximilian I**, who mortgaged to them for 10,000

gold gülden the county of Kirchberg and the lordship of Weissenhorn. The family attained the height of its prosperity and influence under **Charles V**, its chief members being the sons of George (d.1506), founders of the two chief lines of the House of Fugger. The brothers were zealous Catholics, opponents of **Martin Luther**. Charles V then made them counts, invested them with the still-mortgaged properties of Kirchberg and Weissenhorn, and gave them the rights of princes. The Fuggers continued in business, increased their immense wealth, and were appointed to the highest posts in the empire. They owned great libraries and art collections, maintained painters and musicians, and encouraged art and science.

Fujii, Shozo 1950–
Japanese judo fighter

World middleweight champion four times (1971–79), he did not make selection to the Japanese Olympic team in 1972 and 1976, and Japan boycotted the Moscow Olympics in 1980. However, despite the lack of an Olympic title, he gained international appreciation due to his style of attack. His first three title wins came after he beat Japanese finalists, but the fourth was against Bernard Tchoullouyan of France (1979). Fujii mastered a special double-handed shoulder throw; he curled below his opponent, ran two steps, and then threw his opponent onto the mat. He would then land on top of his opponent, victorious.

Fujimori, Alberto Kenyo 1939–
Peruvian politician

He was born in Lima. He founded and led the conservative Cambio '90 (Change 90) Party, and, promising reform, succeeded **Perez Alan García** to become President (1990–). Within two years he had dismantled the existing order in Peru by dismissing Congress (1992), sacking senior judges, imposing order through an 'Emergency National Reconstruction Government', and changing the constitution. His administration has been dogged throughout by violence from the Maoist Sendero Luminoso ('Shining Path') guerilla group.

Fukui, Kenichi 1918–98
Japanese chemist and Nobel Prize winner

Born in Nara prefecture, he graduated in industrial chemistry at Kyoto University in 1941, and worked (1941–45) in the Army Fuel Laboratory. In 1943 he joined the staff of Kyoto University and obtained a PhD in engineering. He was made Professor of Hydrocarbon Physical Chemistry in 1951. Initially he studied a diverse set of topics, but gradually his interest in the way atomic structure affects the course of a chemical reaction eclipsed all his other interests. He published his conclusions in highly mathematical terms and it was not until **Robert Woodward** and **Roald Hoffmann** produced their rules for the conservation of orbital symmetry that the value of Fukui's approach was appreciated. His frontier orbital theory has been widely used in rationalizing organic reactivity and preceded sophisticated computer calculations. Fukui shared the Nobel Prize for chemistry with Hoffmann in 1981. The recipient of many honours, he was president of the Kyoto Institute of Technology (1982–88), president of the Japanese Chemical Society (1983–84) and became director of the Institute for Fundamental Chemistry in Kyoto in 1988.

Fulbright, J(ames) William 1905–95
US politician

Born in Sumner, Missouri, and educated at the University of Arkansas, and George Washington University Law School, he was a Rhodes scholar at Oxford, and taught law in Washington and Arkansas. He was elected to the US House of Representatives as a Democrat in 1942 where, in 1943, he introduced a resolution advocating the creation of the United Nations, and was elected to the Senate in 1944. He sponsored the Fulbright Act (1946), which established an exchange scholarship system for students and teachers between the USA and other countries. He distinguished himself in 1954 by his opposition to **Joseph McCarthy**. As chairman of the Senate Foreign Relations Committee, he became a major critic of the escalation of the Vietnam War. He lost his Senate seat in 1974. He wrote *Old Myths and New Realities* (1965) and *The Arrogance of Power* (1967). He was made an honorary KBE in 1975. 📖 E J Brown, *William Fulbright* (1985)

Fuller, (Richard) Buckminster 1895–1983
US engineer

Born in Milton, Massachusetts, he studied at Harvard and the US Naval Academy, Annapolis, Maryland. In 1917 he discovered energetic/synergetic geometry, and he later devised a structural system known as Tensegrity Structures. Following the machine aesthetic, he experimented with structural designs, aimed at economical, efficient, trouble-free living (developed from systems of aircraft and chassis construction), intended for mass-production. Dymaxion House (1927) embodied these practical ideas. After 1945 he designed geodesic domes, great space-frame enclosures, based on polyhedra. The largest design was realized at the Union Tank Car Repair Shop, Louisiana (1958), and the best known at the US Pavilion, Montreal Exhibition (1967). 📖 Hugh Kenner, *Bucky* (1973)

Fuller, Charles H, Jnr 1939–
US playwright

Born in Philadelphia, he is noted for his unbiased, sensitive exploration of relationships, especially those between blacks and whites, and between blacks and a white-dominated bureaucracy. His successful plays include *The Brownsville Raid* (1976), based upon a true incident in 1906, in which an entire US Army regiment was honourably discharged after none of the 167 black soldiers admitted inciting a riot in Brownsville, Texas. His Pulitzer Prize-winning *A Soldier's Play* (1981), also set in the army, is on the murder of an unpopular sergeant. He is co-founder and co-director of the Philadelphia Arts Theater.

Fuller, John Frederick Charles 1878–1966
English soldier

He was born in Chichester, West Sussex. He served in the Second Boer War (1899–1902), and during World War I he advocated the armour-cum-fighter-plane war of movement as subsequently exploited by **Hitler's** *Reichswehr* (army). He retired in 1933 and became renowned for his writings on theory of war, particularly relating to mobile and armoured forces, including *Reformation of War* (1923), *Foundations of the Science of War* (1926), *Memoirs of an Unconventional Soldier* (1936) and *Decisive Battles* (3 vols, 1956).

Fuller, Loie, originally Marie Louise Fuller 1862–1928
US dancer, choreographer and producer

Born in Fullersburg, Illinois, she began her career in vaudeville and as a circus artist (1865–91). She was a pioneer in the field of performance art, and her exotic solo skirt-dance, using multi-directional coloured lights on the yards of swirling silk she wore, created a sensation in 1891, especially in Europe. Her Paris debut in 1892 was met with great acclaim and in 1900 she appeared at the Paris World Fair. Group pieces also figured among her (more than 100) dances. She founded a dance school in 1908, and was a model for **Toulouse-Lautrec**, **Auguste Rodin** and many other prominent artists.

Fuller, (Sarah) Margaret, Marchioness Ossoli 1810–50

US feminist, writer and revolutionary

Born in Cambridgeport, Massachusetts, she was educated by her father before attending the local school at the age of 14. She went on to teach in Boston (1836–37) and Providence (1837–39). There she assumed an important role in the transcendentalist circle that centred around Ralph Waldo Emerson. From 1840 to 1842 she was editor of *The Dial*, the transcendentalist journal, and in 1844 went to New York where she became literary critic for the *New York Tribune*. Moving to Italy in 1847, she worked as a foreign correspondent and there met and married Marquis Giovanni Ossoli, an Italian nobleman and re-publican. After becoming involved in the unsuccessful Revolution of 1848, she sailed for New York with her husband and infant son, but the ship was wrecked off Fire Island and all aboard were drowned. Her publications include *Summer on the Lakes* (1844) and *Woman in the 19th Century* (1855), the earliest major piece of US feminist writing. ⪚ Paula Blanchard, *Margaret Fuller* (1978)

Fuller, Melville Weston 1833–1910

US jurist

Born in Augusta, Maine, he graduated from Bowdoin College in 1853 and briefly attended Harvard Law School. He practised law in Chicago from 1856 and became active in the Democratic Party, befriending Grover Cleveland, who in 1888 appointed Fuller Chief Justice of the Supreme Court. Although he lacked a national reputation at the time of his appointment, he soon won praise for his skilful leadership on the court and his ability to engineer compromises. He sought to protect traditional civil liberties and tended toward a strict construction of the Constitution, and in 1895 he wrote two important decisions weakening the Sherman Antitrust Act and striking down the first personal income tax passed by Congress. He remained Chief Justice until his death, and from 1900 he also served as a member of the Permanent Court of Arbitration at The Hague.

Fuller, Roy Broadbent 1912–91

English poet and novelist

Born in Oldham, Lancashire, he went to school in Blackpool, trained as a solicitor, and worked as a solicitor with building societies. His first collection of poetry, *Poems*, which appeared in 1939, was strongly influenced by W H Auden. His experience of war in the Royal Navy (1941–45) prompted *The Middle of a War* (1942) and *A Lost Season* (1944). His traditionalist attitude kept him apart from the neo-Romantic revival initiated by Dylan Thomas after the war, but his *Brutus's Orchard* (1957) and *Collected Poems* (1962) established him as a major poet. His later poetic works include *Buff* (1965), *Song Cycle from a Record Sleeve* (1972), *Retreads* (1979) and *Available for Dreams* (1989), and his novels include *Second Curtain* (1953), *The Ruined Boys* (1959), *The Carnal Island* (1970) and *Stares* (1990). He was Professor of Poetry at Oxford (1968–73), and collected his lectures in *Owl and Artificers* (1971). He also published the autobiographical *Souvenirs* (1980), *Vamp Till Ready* (1982), *The Strange and the Good* (1989) and *Spanner and Pen* (1991). ⪚ A E Austin, *Roy Fuller* (1979)

Fuller, Thomas 1608–61

English clergyman and writer

Born in Aldwinkle St Peter's, Northamptonshire, he studied at Sidney Sussex College, Cambridge, and be-came prebendary of Salisbury in 1631 and rector of Broadwindsor, Dorset, in 1634. His first ambitious work, *The History of the Holy War* (1639), was about the Crusades. Just before the outbreak of the Civil War he was appointed preacher to the Chapel Royal at the Savoy in London, and during the war he was chaplain to the Royalist comman-der, Ralph Hopton (1598–1652). He compiled a collection

of miscellanies in *The Holy State and The Profane State* (1642), and wrote tracts for the troops, *Good Thoughts in Bad Times* (1645), *Good Thoughts in Worse Times* (1647), and *The Cause and Cure of a Troubled Conscience* (1647), and a satire directed at Oliver Cromwell called *Andronicus, or the Unfortunate Politician* (1646). In 1649 he was given the curacy of Waltham Abbey, and in 1655 he brought out his long-projected *Church History of Britain*, to which was appended his *History of Cambridge University*. With the Restoration he published *Mixt Contemplations in Better Times* (1660) and was appointed chaplain-extraordinary to Charles II. He did not live to complete his most famous work, *History of the Worthies of Britain*, an encyclopaedic miscellany about the counties of Great Britain and their notable men. It was published the year after his death.

Fulton, Rikki 1924–

Scottish actor and comedian

Born in Glasgow, he began his broadcasting career there in drama, features, children's and religious programmes for the BBC. He also appeared at several Scottish re-pertory theatres and from 1951 to 1955 presented various weekly programmes. He starred in the *Five past Eight* variety shows in Edinburgh and Glasgow, and since the 1950s has regularly appeared in pantomime in both cities, recognized as one of the great pantomime dames. He also has a stage double-act with Jack Milroy in which they appear as the teddy boys Francie and Josie. On television, he appeared in his own comedy sketch series, *Scotch and Wry*, *Rab C Nesbitt's Seasonal Greet* (1988) and played Macphail in *The Tales of Para Handy* (1994–95). He also acted in the film *The Girl in the Picture* (1985). In 1985 he adapted and starred in *A Wee Touch of Class*, a successful transposi-tion of Molière's *Le Bourgeois Gentilhomme* from 17th-century France to 19th-century Edinburgh.

Fulton, Robert 1765–1815

US engineer

Born in Lancaster County, Pennsylvania, of Irish parents, he painted miniature portraits and landscapes in Philadelphia from 1782, and in 1786 went to London to study under the painter Benjamin West. However he began to apply his energies wholly to mechanical engineering, and in 1794 patented a double-inclined plane to supersede locks, and invented a mill for sawing and polishing marble. In 1797 he went to Paris, where he developed a submarine torpedo boat, and made two experiments on the Seine with small steamboats (1803). He returned to the USA, to New York, in 1806, and the next year launched on the Hudson River a steam vessel, the *Clermont*, which accomplished a voyage of nearly 150 miles (241.4km) to Albany in 32 hours. Although he was not the first person to apply steam to inland navigation, he was the first to do so successfully. He was employed by the US government on canals and other works, and in constructing (1814) the world's first steam warship, *Fulton the First*. ⪚ H W Dickinson, *Robert Fulton, Engineer and Artist* (1913)

Fung Kuo-chang See Feng Youlan

Funk, Casimir 1884–1967

US biochemist

Born in Warsaw, Poland, he studied in Berlin and Bern, and worked as a research assistant at the Lister Institute, London (1910–13), where he attempted to isolate vitamin B_1, a cure for the dietary disease beri-beri. He suggested the general name 'vitamine', later altered to 'vitamin'. Funk became head of the biochemical department at the Cancer Hospital Research Institute (1913–15), emigrated to the USA in 1915, and later headed research institutes in Warsaw (1923–27) and Paris (1928–39). He achieved a crude extract of the male sex hormone androsterone from human urine in 1929.

Funk, Walther 1890–1960
German Nazi politician
One of Hitler's chief advisers, he succeeded Hjalmar Schacht as Minister of Economics and president of the Reichsbank, and played a leading part in planning the economic aspects of the attack on Russia, and in the exploitation of occupied territories. Captured in 1945, he was sentenced to life imprisonment as a war criminal, but was released in 1957 on account of illness.

Furetière, Antoine 1619–88
French scholar and lexicographer
The Abbé of Chalivoy and a writer of comic verse and fables, he compiled a massive *Dictionnaire universel*, only to be expelled from the Académie, which claimed a monopoly on its collections (1674). It was eventually published in Rotterdam in 1690.

Furness, Christopher Furness, 1st Baron
1852–1912
English shipowner
Born in West Hartlepool, Teeside, he became a shipbroker in 1876 and soon afterwards established the Furness Line. He went into partnership with Edward Withy in 1885, which marked the beginning of a huge shipbuilding and engineering business. A Liberal MP, he was one of the first to initiate a co-partnership scheme among his employees. He was knighted in 1895 and created baron in 1910. He was succeeded by his son, Marmaduke (1883–1940), who was created a viscount in 1918.

Furness, Horace Howard 1833–1912
US Shakespearean scholar
Born in Philadelphia, he became a lawyer by profession. He devoted his life to his *Variorum* edition of Shakespeare, starting with *Romeo and Juliet* in 1871. The work was later continued by his son Horace Howard II (1865–1930).

Furniss, Harry 1854–1925
Irish caricaturist
Born in Wexford, of an English father, he went to London in 1873, and worked as a caricaturist on the *Illustrated London News* (1876–84) and *Punch* (1884–94). He made the illustrations for Lewis Carroll's *Sylvie and Bruno*, and editions of Dickens and Thackeray. He edited and published his own cartoon magazine, *Like Joka* (1894), and wrote *Confessions of a Caricaturist*. He also worked in the film industry with Thomas Alva Edison (1912–13), acted in films, and was a pioneer of the animated cartoon film (1914).

Furnivall, Frederick James 1825–1910
English philologist
The son of a doctor at Egham, he studied at London and Cambridge universities, won fame as an oarsman and racing-boat designer, and was called to the Bar. Influenced by Frederick Denison Maurice and Christian socialism, he helped to found the Working Men's College in London. It was, however, as a philologist and editor of English texts that he became famous, giving a great impulse to Early English scholarship. He founded the Early English Text Society, the Chaucer, Ballad, New Shakespeare, John Wycliffe and Shelley Societies, and edited many texts, including Chaucer and the Thomas Percy *Ballads*, Robert Mannyng's *Handlying Synne*, William Harrison's *Description of England*, John Stubbes's *Anatomy of Abuses*, and Hoccleve (c.1368–1426), besides writing the introduction to the 'Leopold' Shakespeare. He also edited the Philological Society's dictionary (from 1861) that later became the *Oxford English Dictionary*.

Furphy, Joseph 1843–1912
Australian writer
Born in Yering, Yarra Valley, Victoria, of Irish immigrant parents, he described himself as 'half bushman and half bookworm'. From 1883 he worked at an iron foundry in Shepparton, Victoria, and contributed, under the name 'Tom Collins', a series of articles to the *Bulletin* magazine. He also wrote a 1,220-page manuscript, *Such is Life: Being Certain Extracts from the Diary of Tom Collins*, which was eventually published, after much revision and abridgment, in 1903. Some excised sections were published after his death as *Rigby's Romance* (1921, rev edn 1946) and *The Buln-Buln and the Brolga* (1948). His major work, it was in 'temper, democratic; bias, offensively Australian', and marked a move away from the common romantic concept of Australia's pioneering days. *The Poems of Joseph Furphy* was published posthumously in 1916. ▢ M Franklin, *Joseph Furphy* (1944)

Furtseva, Yekaterina Alekseyevna 1910–74
Soviet politician
She had a technical education, then became a party worker and rose to be district secretary in Moscow (1942) and a member of the Central Committee (1956). A supporter of Nikita Khrushchev, she was brought into the politburo in 1957 in the aftermath of the Anti-Party Plot (the name given by Khrushchev to the attempt made by senior opponents to oust him from his position as First Secretary of the Communist Party). She was not considered a major political figure, however, and was pushed out in 1961. Nevertheless from 1960 until her death she was Minister of Culture and apparently had no difficulty in insisting on ever greater conformity.

Furtwängler, (Gustav Heinrich Ernst Martin) Wilhelm 1886–1954
German conductor
Born in Berlin, he was the son of Adolf Furtwängler (1853–1907), the celebrated classical archaeologist. He succeeded Arthur Nikisch in 1922 as conductor of the Gewandhaus concerts in Leipzig and of the Berlin Philharmonic. His reputation was established by international tours, though his highly subjective interpretations of the standard German repertoire aroused controversy. His apparently ambivalent attitude to the Hitler regime caused him some unpopularity outside Germany, but after World War II he quickly re-established himself.

Fuseli, Henry *originally* Johann Heinrich Füssli
1741–1825
British painter and art critic
Born in Zurich, Switzerland, he studied theology at the Collegium Carolinum there. He settled in England in 1764, and was encouraged by Sir Joshua Reynolds to go to Italy (1770–78). He became Professor of Painting at the Royal Academy, and Keeper in 1804. His 200 paintings include *The Nightmare* (1781) and two series to illustrate Shakespeare's and Milton's works, for which he is chiefly known. An edition of his literary works, with a biography, was published by Knowles (1831).

Fust, Johann c.1400–1466
German printer and goldsmith
He was born in Mainz. In 1450 and 1452 he made loans to the printer Johannes Gutenberg, to help complete the printing of his Bible. When the loans were not repaid he sued for the debt, receiving, in lieu of payment, Gutenberg's printing plant, with which he started his own business, taking Peter Schöffer, his son-in-law, as partner. They published the Gutenberg Bible in 1465.

Futabatei Shimei 1864–1909
Japanese novelist
Born in Edo (Tokyo), he was the first writer of Japanese fiction to attempt to make the written word as intelligible as the spoken, in contrast to his predecessors, who wrote in a form of literary Japanese far removed from everyday

speech. *Ukigumo* (1887, 'Drifting Clouds') broke new ground in being written in the vernacular. He was also the first translator into Japanese of the works of **Nikolai Gogol** and **Ivan Turgenev**, again employing vernacular language.
📖 M G Ryan, *Japan's First Modern Novel* (1967)

Fyfe, Sir David Patrick Maxwell See **Kilmuir, 1st Earl of**

Fyffe, Will(iam) 1885–1947
Scottish comedian, singer and actor
Born in Dundee, he made his stage debut as a child, playing 'Little Willie' in his father's repertory version of *East Lynne*, and by the age of 15 was playing Polonius in *Hamlet*. He wrote several character sketches for **Harry Lauder**, but when they were rejected decided to perform them himself. Making his London debut at the Middlesex Theatre in 1916, by 1921 he was topping the bill at the Palladium. He appeared in the Royal Variety Performance (1922), the first of four, and made his film debut in *Elstree Calling* (1930), in which he sang his popular serenade to Scotch, 'Twelve and a Tanner a Bottle'. His character studies included a ship's engineer 'Sailing Up the Clyde', and his most popular song was 'I Belong to Glasgow'. He was King Rat of the Water Rats for six years, and acted engagingly in over 20 films, both British and American, such as *Annie Laurie* (1936), *Owd Bob* (1937), *Rulers of the Sea* (1939) and *They Came By Night* (1940).

Fysh, Sir (Wilmot) Hudson 1895–1974
Australian civil aviation pioneer
Born in Launceston, Tasmania, he was educated at Launceston Grammar and Geelong Grammar schools. He served with the Australian Imperial Forces at Gallipoli in World War I and later, having transferred to the Australian Flying Corps, was awarded the Distinguished Flying Cross. He surveyed a route between Darwin and Longreach, Queensland, for the 1919 Britain–Australia air race, and in the following year, with the backing of local pastoralists, he established the Queensland and Northern Territory Aerial Services Limited, now known as QANTAS. In 1931 he was involved in the pioneering Australia–England airmail flights, which led to the formation of Qantas Empire Airways as a joint venture with Imperial Airways of the UK. In 1947 Qantas was acquired by the Australian government. Fysh became managing director, was knighted in 1953, and retired as chairman in 1966. He was a notable aviation historian, and wrote books on the subject.

Gabain, Ethel Leontine
1883–1950
English artist and printmaker

Born in Le Havre, France, she studied at the Slade School of Art and the Central School of Arts and Crafts in London, and in Paris. She became known for her many female portraits, such as **Flora Robson** in the role of Lady Audley, purchased by Manchester City Art Gallery, which won the De Laszlo Silver Medal in 1933. In 1940 she was appointed an official war artist, painting the departing evacuees before turning to the depiction of women in traditionally male occupations. A remarkable draughtsperson, she was elected to the membership of both the Royal Society of British Artists and the Royal Institute of Oil Painters.

Gabelsberger, Franz Xaver 1789–1848
German bureaucrat
Born in Munich, in 1809 he entered the Bavarian Civil Service. He was the inventor of the chief German system of shorthand.

Gabin, Jean, *originally* Jean Alexis Moncorgé
1904–76
French actor
Born in Paris into a showbusiness family, he worked in the Folies Bergères and the Moulin Rouge, before making his film debut in *Chacun sa chance* (1930). In subsequent films, such as *La Grande illusion* (1937, *Grand Illusion*) and *Le Jour se Lève* (1939, *Daybreak*), his world-weary anti-heroes seemed to embody the pessimistic spirit of pre-war France. He escaped to the USA during World War II, later joining the Free French navy. Returning to France, he continued to dominate the French film scene until his death. Later films include *Touchez pas au Grisbi* (1954, *Grisbi*) and *Le Chat* (1971, *The Cat*).

Gable, Christopher 1940–98
English dancer
Born in London, he studied at the Royal Ballet School there, and was soon dancing solo roles as a principal and partner to **Lynn Seymour**. He retired as a dancer in 1967, having created roles in **Kenneth Macmillan**'s *Images of Love* (1964) and **Frederick Ashton**'s *The Two Pigeons* (1961). He was chosen to play the lead in Macmillan's new *Romeo and Juliet* with Seymour, but they were replaced in the première at the last minute by **Rudolf Nureyev** and **Margot Fonteyn**. He was the founder and artistic director (1982–98) of the Central School of Ballet, and in 1987 became director of the Northern Ballet Theatre. His innovative approach was evident in his staging of *Swan Lake* in 1992, which was set during a coup in 1870s Russia and ended in massacre. As an actor he had roles in films such as **Ken Russell**'s *The Boy Friend* (1972). In 1987 he danced again, in *A Simple Man*, based on the life of the artist **L S Lowry**.

Gable, (William) Clark 1901–60
US film actor
He was born in Cadiz, Ohio, and his early stage experience was intermingled with casual labour and work as an extra in silent films. A concentrated assault on Hollywood stardom resulted in a role in *The Painted Desert* and 11 other film appearances in 1931. He won an Academy Award for *It Happened One Night* (1934), and was voted 'King of Hollywood' in 1937. His sympathetic, ruggedly masculine and humorous persona made him the perfect Rhett Butler in *Gone With the Wind* (1939). He returned to the cinema after World War II army service and remained in demand as a sparring partner in films like *Mogambo* (1953) and *Teacher's Pet* (1958), and as an ageing cowboy in his last film, *The Misfits* (1961). Married five times, his third wife was the actress **Carole Lombard**. 📖 Lyn Tornabene, *Long Live the King* (1977)

Gabo, Naum, *originally* Naum Neemia Pevsner 1890–1977
US constructivist sculptor
Born in Bryansk, Russia, he first studied medicine and engineering, then art in Munich (1911–12). With his brother, **Antoine Pevsner**, and **Vladimir Tatlin** and **Kasimir Malevich**, he was associated with the Moscow Suprematist Group (1913), and in 1920 he broke away with his brother and Tatlin to form the group of Russian Constructivists, who have had considerable influence on 20th-century architecture and design. In 1920 they published their *Realistic Manifesto*. As their theories did not coincide with those of Russian official art circles, he was forced into exile, and lived in Berlin (1923–33), Paris (1933–35) and England (1936–45), before going to the USA in 1946. He was naturalized in 1952. There are several examples of his completely non-figurative geometrical 'constructions in space', mainly made in transparent plastics, in the Museum of Modern Art, New York.

Gabor, Dennis 1900–79
British physicist and Nobel Prize winner
Born in Budapest, he received a doctorate in engineering in Berlin (1927), and worked there as a research engineer, but left Germany in 1933. After spending some years with the British Thompson Houston Company in Rugby—during which time he wrote the first book on the electron microscope—he was appointed to a readership at Imperial College, London (1948), and later became Professor of Applied Electron Physics (1958–67). He is best remembered for conceiving in 1947 the technique of (and the name) holography, a method of photographically recording and reproducing three-dimensional images, for which he was awarded the 1971 Nobel Prize for physics. In the late 1960s he developed an acute interest in the socio-political and environmental questions raised by the Club of Rome, and visited many countries to lecture on economic expansionism and the limitations imposed by the Earth's finite resources.

Gaboriau, Émile 1835–73
French writer
Born in Saujon in Charente-Inférieure, he had already contributed to some of the smaller Parisian papers when he leapt to fame with his crime novel *L'Affaire Lerouge* (1866, 'The Lerouge Affair'), featuring his detective Lecoq. It was followed by *Le Dossier 113* (1867), *Monsieur Lecoq* (1869), *Les Esclaves de Paris* (1869, 'Slaves of Paris'), *La Corde au cou* (1873, 'Rope Around the Neck'), and several others.

Gabriel, Jacques Ange 1698–1782
French architect
Born in Paris, he was a court architect to **Louis XV**. He planned a number of additions to Versailles and other palaces, and designed the Petit Trianon (1768). He also laid out the Place de la Concorde (1753).

Gabrieli, Andrea c.1533–1586
Italian composer
Born in Venice, he studied under **Adrian Willaert**, and was later appointed organist of St Mark's Church. He wrote masses and other choral works, and his organ pieces include toccatas and ricercare, the latter foreshadowing the fugue.

Gabrieli, Giovanni c.1555–1612
Italian composer

Born in Venice, he composed choral and instrumental works in which he exploited the acoustics of St Mark's in Venice with unusual antiphonal and echo effects, using double choirs, double ensembles of wind instruments and other devices. He published much of his uncle, Andrea Gabrieli's music, and became a renowned teacher.

Gadamer, Hans-Georg 1900–
German philosopher
He was born in Marburg, Hesse, and was a pupil of Martin Heidegger, before becoming Rector at Leipzig and professor at Frankfurt am Main (1947) and Heidelberg (1949–68). His major work is *Wahrheit und Methode* (1960, Eng trans *Truth and Method*, 1975), and he is known particularly for his theory of hermeneutics, which has been useful both in philosophy and in related subjects in explaining the nature of understanding and interpretation.

Gaddafi or Qaddafi, Muammar (Muhammad al-) 1942–
Libyan soldier and political leader
Born into a nomadic family, he abandoned university studies to attend military academy in 1963. He formed the Free Officers Movement which overthrew the régime of King Idris in 1969. Gaddafi became chairman of the Revolutionary Command Council, promoted himself to colonel (the highest rank in the revolutionary army) and became Commander-in-Chief of the Libyan armed forces. As effective head of state, he set about eradicating colonialism by expelling foreigners and closing down British and US bases. He also encouraged a religious revival and return to the fundamental principles of Islam. He has been President of Libya since 1977. A somewhat unpredictable figure, Gaddafi has openly supported violent revolutionaries in other parts of the world while following a unique blend of democratic and autocratic government at home, ruthlessly pursuing Libyan dissidents both at home and abroad. He has waged a war in Chad, and in 1988 saw his territory bombed by the USA. He declared his unqualified support of Iraq's invasion of Kuwait in 1990, and found himself increasingly isolated after the UN's announcement at the end of the Gulf War that it would not entertain his formal participation in any future negotiations on the issue. 📖 David Blundy, *Qaddafi: A Biography* (1987)

Gaddi, Agnolo c.1333–1396
Florentine painter and architect
The son of Taddeo Gaddi, he painted the frescoes of the *Discovery of the Cross* in S Croce, Florence and of the *Legends of the Holy Girdle* in the cathedral at Prato. His work shows the influence of Giotto.

Gaddi, Gaddo c.1260–1332
Italian painter
The founder of the Gaddi family, he worked in mosaic in Rome and Florence.

Gaddi, Taddeo c.1300–1366
Italian painter
The son of Gaddo Gaddi, he was Giotto's best pupil and also his godson. His finest work is seen in the frescoes of the *Life of the Virgin* in the Baroncelli chapel of S Croce, Florence. Though he was the best-known of Giotto's followers, he deviated from the style of his master, whom he did not match in figure painting, but excelled in architectural perspective.

Gaddis, William 1922–
US novelist
Born in New York City, and educated at Harvard, he worked for the *New Yorker* (1946–47), and lived and travelled abroad. He then freelanced as a speech and filmscript writer from 1956 until the 1970s. He has written four novels: *The Recognitions* (1955), a densely allusive post-Christian epic about art, forgery, money and magic, followed by *JR* (1976), about an 11-year-old 'ragged capitalist' operating from pay phones, *Carpenter's Gothic* (1985), in which a Vietnam War veteran works as a media consultant for a fundamentalist preacher, and *A Frolic of His Own* (1994), a story of litigiousness and greed in US society. An ambitious satirist, he is one of the USA's most prominent contemporary novelists. He won the National Book award in 1976 and 1994. 📖 S Moore, *A Reader's Guide to William Gaddis's The Recognitions* (1982)

Gade, Niels Wilhelm 1817–90
Danish composer
Born in Copenhagen, he studied at Leipzig and became a friend of Schumann and Mendelssohn, from whom he took over the Gewandhaus orchestra in 1847. He composed eight symphonies, a violin concerto, several choral works and smaller pieces. The Scandinavian element in his music distinguishes him from the Leipzig school.

Gades, Antonio 1936–
Spanish dancer, choreographer and teacher
Born in Alicante, he made his debut in cabaret as a teenager, then joined Pilar Lopez's company for nine years. In the early 1960s he worked mainly in Italy, collaborating with Anton Dolin and staging dances at La Scala, Milan. The company he formed for the New York World's Fair of 1964 has since toured the world. He has appeared in various films, the most acclaimed being the flamenco trilogy directed by Carlos Saura: *Blood Wedding* (1981), *Carmen* (1983) and *El Amor Brujo* (1986).

Gadolin, Johan 1760–1852
Finnish chemist
Born in Turku, he studied in Uppsala, Sweden, becoming Professor of Chemistry there from 1797 to 1822. Travels on the Continent put him in touch with some of the leading scientists of the day, and he soon accepted Antoine Lavoisier's discoveries about combustion and his system of chemical nomenclature. He is remembered for his investigations of the rare earth elements, analysing a new black mineral from Ytterby, Sweden, and isolating from it a rare earth mineral, yttria, in 1794. This was an important step towards identifying the remaining undiscovered elements. Over the next century yttria was found to contain the oxides of nine new rare earth elements, leading eventually to the establishment of the whole series. Around 30 years after Gadolin's death, one of these was discovered by Jean Charles Galissard de Marignac and Paul Emile Lecoq de Boisbaudran, who named it gadolinium in his honour.

Gadsden, Christopher 1724–1805
American Revolutionary leader
Born in Charleston, South Carolina, he was a member of the first Continental Congress (1774), became a brigadier-general in the Continental army during the Revolution, and was Lieutenant-Governor of South Carolina.

Gadsden, James 1788–1858
US soldier and diplomat
Born in Charleston, South Carolina, he served in the War of 1812 and against the Seminoles. He spent a decade as a railroad company executive and was a continuing advocate of a transcontinental railroad along a southern route. In 1853 he was appointed Minister to Mexico, and negotiated the purchase (the 'Gadsden Purchase') of part of Arizona and New Mexico for railway construction.

Gaetano See Cajetan

Gaffky, Georg Theodor August 1850–1918
German bacteriologist

Born in Hanover, he was educated at the University of Berlin, where he graduated in medicine. He served as Ludwig Koch's assistant from 1880 to 1885, and after holding the chair of hygiene at the University of Giessen (1888–1904), he became director of the institute which was renamed the Koch Institute in 1912. He isolated and obtained a pure culture of the typhoid bacillus for the first time (1884), and during trips to Egypt and India (1883–84), he and Koch discovered the *Vibrio* responsible for cholera. He made a further visit to Egypt in 1897 to work on the bubonic plague.

Gagarin, Yuri Alekseyevich 1934–68
Soviet cosmonaut

Born near Gzhatsk, he joined the Soviet air force in 1957, and in 1961 became the first man to travel in space, completing a circuit of the Earth in the *Vostok* spaceship satellite. Nominated a Hero of the Soviet Union, he shared the Galabert Astronautical prize with John Glenn in 1963. He was killed in a plane accident while training. 📖 Mitchell Sharpe, *Yuri Gagarin: First Man in Space* (1969)

Gage, Matilda Joslyn, *née* Joslyn 1826–98
US feminist and women's rights activist

Born in Cicero, New York, she developed a radical feminist perspective and incisive analysis of the nature of patriarchal society, working with the more conservative reformers Susan B Anthony and Elizabeth Cady Stanton to launch the first wave of the American suffrage movement. With them, she later compiled the four-volume *History of Woman Suffrage* (1881–1906). She joined the National Woman Suffrage Association (NWSA) in 1869 and became president of both the national and New York State organizations. However, she withdrew in protest at the union between NWSA and the conservative Women's Christian Temperance Union. Believing that Church and State colluded to oppress women, she founded the Women's National Liberal Union (1890), whose aim was to separate Church and State. She expressed her ideas in her *Woman, Church and State: the Original Exposé of Male Collaboration Against the Female Sex* (1893).

Gage, Thomas 1721–87
English soldier

He was born in Firle, Sussex. He became military Governor of Montreal in 1760, Commander-in-Chief of the British forces in America (1763–72), and Governor of Massachusetts (1774). In April 1775 he sent a force to seize arms from the colonists at Concord, and the next day the skirmish at Lexington took place which began the American Revolution. After the Battle of Bunker Hill (June 1775) he was relieved by William Howe.

Gahn, Johan Gottlieb 1745–1818
Swedish chemist and mineralogist

Born in Voxna, Gävleborg, he studied at Uppsala, and after some years as a laboratory assistant there he was sent by the College of Mining to the famous copper mine at Falun. Here he so improved smelting methods and the use of by-products that industrialists and scholars flocked to learn from him. He isolated metallic manganese, developing a way to prepare it on a larger scale. He also discovered selenium, and in conjunction with Carl Wilhelm Scheele, found phosphoric acid in bones. The mineral gahnite (zinc aluminium oxide) is named after him.

Gainsborough, Thomas 1727–88
English landscape and portrait painter

Born in Sudbury, Suffolk, he copied Dutch landscapes in his youth and at the age of 14 was sent to London where he learned the art of Rococo decoration under Hubert Gravelot and Francis Hayman. *The Charterhouse* (1748) marks the end of his apprenticeship. He settled as a portrait painter at Ipswich in 1745. *Mr and Mrs Andrews* (1748)

and several 'chimney-piece' paintings belong to this, his Suffolk period. In 1760 he moved to Bath, where he established himself with his portrait of *Earl Nugent* (1760). His portraits combine the elegance of Van Dyck with his own characteristic informality, although in his later work he increasingly tends towards fashionable artificialities. Among his early masterpieces are *Lord and Lady Howe*, *Mrs Portman* (Tate, London) and *Blue Boy* (Huntington Collection, Pasadena), and the great landscapes *The Harvest Wagon* (1767, Barber Institute, Birmingham) and *The Watering Place* (1777, Tate) in which Rubens's influence is discernible. He became a foundation member of the Royal Academy in 1768, and exhibited there annually, until somewhat discontented with the place assigned to *The King's Daughters* in 1784, he retired. He moved to London in 1774. To this last period belong the character study *Mr Truman*, the luxuriant *Mrs Graham* (1777, Edinburgh), *George III* and *Queen Charlotte* (1781, Windsor Castle), and *Mrs Siddons* (1785). Landscapes include *Cottage Door* (1780, Pasadena), *The Morning Walk* (1780), which is closer to his 'fancy pieces' based on Bartolomé Murillo's paintings than to nature, and *Cattle Crossing a Bridge* (1781), the most rococo of all his work. 📖 Isabelle Worman, *Thomas Gainsborough: A Biography* (1987)

Gairy, Sir Eric Matthew 1922–97
Grenadian politician

In 1950 he founded the country's first political party, the left-of-centre Grenada United Labour Party (GULP) and was soon a dominant figure in Caribbean politics. He held the posts of Chief Minister in the Federation of the West Indies (1957–62), Premier of Grenada (1967–74) and, at independence, in 1974, Prime Minister. He was ousted by the left-wing leader Maurice Bishop in 1979.

Gaiseric or Genseric c.390–477AD
King of the Vandals and Alans

The son of the Vandal leader Godigisel, he succeeded his half-brother Gunderic in AD427. Invited by Bonifacius, the Roman governor of Africa, Gaiseric entered Numidia (429), captured and sacked Hippo (430), and seized Carthage (439). He established a formidable maritime power, ranging as far as the Peloponnese. An Arian, he ferociously persecuted Catholics. Eudoxia, the widow of Valentinian III, invited Gaiseric to Rome to destroy her husband's murderer Maximus. Gaiseric's fleet took and sacked the city (455), and one of Eudoxia's daughters married his son and successor, Huneric. Fleets sent against the Vandals (457, 468) were defeated.

Gaisford, Thomas 1780–1855
English Greek scholar

He became Regius Professor of Greek at Oxford in 1812 and in 1831 was made Dean of Christ Church. He produced editions of Herodotus, Hephaestion, Johannes Stobaeus and Suidas. The Gaisford prizes were founded in his memory.

Gaitskell, Hugh Todd Naylor 1906–63
English Labour politician

Born in London, he was educated at Winchester and at New College, Oxford, becoming a socialist during the 1926 general strike. On leaving Oxford he became a Workers' Educational Association lecturer in economics in the Nottinghamshire coalfield. In 1938 he became Reader in Political Economy at the University of London. Elected MP for Leeds South in 1945, he became Parliamentary Secretary to the Ministry of Fuel and Power in 1946 and Minister in 1947. Appointed Minister of State for Economic Affairs in 1950, he became (1950–51) the youngest Chancellor of the Exchequer since Arthur Balfour. His introduction of National Health Service charges led to the resignation of Aneurin Bevan as Minister of Health and to a long feud with Bevan and the hostile left wing of the Labour Party. However his ascendancy in the party grew steadily and in 1955 he was elected Leader of the Opposition by a large majority over Bevan, succeeding **Clement Attlee**. He bitterly opposed **Anthony Eden**'s Suez action (1956), attempted to modify Labour policy from total nationalization to the development of a shareholder state, and refused to accept a narrow conference vote for unilateral disarmament (1960). This caused a crisis of leadership in which he retained the loyalty of most Labour MPs. Gaitskell was also a keen European, and in his final years in office strongly supported Great Britain's entry into the EEC. He wrote *Money and Everyday Life* (1939). ⊞ Geoffrey McDermott, *Leader Lost: A Biography of Hugh Gaitskell* (1971)

Gaius fl.AD130–180
Roman jurist

His *Institutes* formed the basis for those of **Justinian** and are the only substantial texts of classical Roman law that have survived. His other works were largely used in the compilation of the *Digest*. The *Institutes*, lost until Barthold Niebuhr (1776–1861) discovered a manuscript at Verona in 1816, have been repeatedly edited, and a fragment of an older manuscript was printed in *Oxyrhynchus Papyri* (vol 17, 1928).

Gaj, Ljudevit 1809–72
Croatian nationalist

Inspired in his youth by the romantic nationalism of writers such as **Jan Kollár** and Pavel Šafařík (1795–1861), he believed in the common nationality of the South Slavs (whom he referred to as Illyrians) which led him to formulate a standard South Slav literary language and found a Croatian newspaper. He became increasingly involved in opposition to Hungarian and German political and cultural influence in Croatia, founding the Illyrian National Party (1841), which espoused the ideas of the Illyrian Movement and championed Croatian state-right. Ever-hopeful for the support of Vienna against the Hungarian nationalists, he concluded a pact with the Hungarian conservatives in a move designed to gain the confidence of Prince **Clemens Metternich** (1845). Under the government of Count Josip Jelačić (1801–59) Gaj led a delegation to Vienna in 1848 and presented the emperor with the Croats' requests for the reorganization of the **Habsburg** monarchy as a federation. Later that year, he was elected to the Croatian sabor (parliament) but shortly afterwards he was forced to leave political life, after his apparent involvement in a financial scandal with the Serbian prince, Miloš Obrenović.

Gajdusek, Daniel Carleton 1923–
US virologist, paediatrician and Nobel Prize winner

Born in Yonkers, New York, he studied physics at Rochester and medicine at Harvard. He spent much time in Papua New Guinea, studying the origin and dissemination of infectious diseases amongst the Fore people, especially a slowly developing lethal viral disease called kuru. He identified the causative agent as a 'slow virus', now implicated in many other diseases, which may take years to induce symptoms. He shared the 1976 Nobel Prize for physiology or medicine with **Baruch Blumberg** for his work on slow virus infections, which cause such diseases as Creutzfeld–Jakob disease.

Gál, Hans 1890–1987
Austrian composer and writer on music

Born in Brunn, near Vienna, he studied at Vienna University, and subsequently taught there (1919–29) and in Mainz (1933). He returned as a conductor to Vienna, but the Anschluss drove him out and, at **Donald Tovey**'s suggestion, he settled in Edinburgh where he became a university lecturer (1945), remaining in Scotland for the rest of his life. A writer and lecturer of perception and wit, he was a composer of exquisite craftsmanship, whose musical style remained that of late Romanticism. He wrote five operas, four symphonies, other orchestral music, part-songs, four string quartets, and many other chamber and piano works.

Galawdewos d.1559
Emperor of Ethiopia

Emperor from 1540, with Portuguese aid he defeated the Muslims who, under **Ahmad ibn Ibrahim Al-Ghazi**, had dominated Ethiopia in the early years of the century. He strengthened the monarchy and reformed the cultural and religious institutions of the empire. Towards the end of his reign he was preoccupied with the migration of Galla tribesmen but, despite having various successes in battle (1554–55), was unable permanently to check their advance.

Galba, Servius Sulpicius 3BC–AD69
Roman emperor

He became consul (AD33), and administered Aquitania, Germany, Africa and Hispania Tarraconensis with competence and integrity. In 68 the Gallic legions rose against **Nero**, and proclaimed Galba emperor. However he soon made himself unpopular by favouritism, ill-timed severity and avarice, and was assassinated by the praetorians in Rome.

Galbraith, John Kenneth 1908–
US economist

Born in Ontario, Canada, and educated at the universities of Toronto, California and Cambridge, he emigrated to the USA in 1931. In 1939 he became assistant Professor of Economics at Princeton University and held various administrative posts before becoming Paul M Warburg Professor of Economics at Harvard from 1949 to 1975. He was US ambassador to India (1961–63). A Keynesian economist, he advocated government spending to stimulate the economy, and he criticized the US mania for consumer goods, arguing that a greater portion of wealth should be spent on infrastructure, education and other improvements shared by the public. His written works include *American Capitalism: The Concept of Countervailing Power* (1952), *The Great Crash* (1955), *The Affluent Society* (1958), *The Liberal Hour* (1960), *The New Industrial State* (1967), *The Age of Uncertainty* (1977), which was made into a BBC television series, *The Anatomy of Power* (1983), *The Culture of Contentment* (1992) and *The Good Society* (1996). He also wrote his autobiography, *A Life In OurTimes* (1981). ⊞ Peggy Lamson, *Speaking of Galbraith: A Personal Portrait* (1991)

Galdós See Pérez Galdós

Gale, Zona 1874–1938
US novelist, story writer and dramatist

Born in Portage, Wisconsin, she began writing sentimental romances, as in her first novel, *Romance Island* (1906). She was scorned and disliked for her increasing pacifism and feminism, but gained some recognition for her novel *Birth* (1918), which was dramatized in 1924 as *Mr Pitt*. However, she found fame with her novel *Miss Lulu Bett* (1920), and her dramatization of it won her a Pulitzer Prize (1921). She later turned to the mysticism of **Georgei Gurdjieff** which strengthened her work, such as the autobiographical *Portage, Wisconsin* (1928), the story collection *Yellow Gentians and Blue* (1927) and the novel *Papa le Fleur* (1933). She became an avid supporter of **Robert La Follette**'s Progressive Party. The title of the biography of her by her fellow-Wisconsin author August Derleth (1909–71) is singularly appropriate: *Still, Small Voice* (1940). ⊞ Derleth, August, *Still, Small Voice* (1940)

Galen, properly Claudius Galenus c.130–c.201AD
Greek physician

Galileo, *properly* Galileo Galilei 1564–1642
Italian astronomer, mathematician and natural philosopher

Galileo was born in Pisa, the son of a musician. He matriculated at Pisa University (1581) where he accepted the chair of mathematics in 1589. From watching the movement of a lamp in the cathedral of Pisa, he discovered (1582) the principle of the isochronism of the pendulum (equality in time whatever the range of its swing), which indicated the value of the pendulum as a timekeeper. In his study of falling bodies, Galileo showed that, contrary to the Aristotelian belief that the rate at which a body falls is proportional to its weight, all bodies would fall at the same rate if air resistance were not present. He also showed that a body moving along an inclined plane has a constant acceleration, and demonstrated the parabolic trajectories of projectiles.

In 1592 he moved to the University of Padua, where his lectures attracted pupils from all over Europe. He made his first contribution to astronomy in 1604 when he demonstrated that a bright new star which had appeared in the constellation Ophiuchus was more distant than the planets, confirming **Tycho Brahe**'s conclusion that changes take place in the celestial regions beyond the planets. In 1610 he perfected a refracting telescope, which he used in the course of many astounding astronomical revelations published in his *Sidereus Nuncius* (1610, 'Sidereal Messenger'). These included the mountains of the Moon, the multitude of stars in the Milky Way, and the existence of Jupiter's four satellites. Galileo was appointed Chief Mathematician and Philosopher by the Grand Duke of Tuscany.

On a visit to Rome in 1611 he was elected a member of the Accademia dei Lincei and fêted by the Jesuit mathematicians of the Roman College. Further discoveries included the phases of Venus, spots on the Sun's disc, the Sun's rotation, and Saturn's appendages (though not then recognized as a ring system). These brilliant researches led Galileo to affirm the truth of the **Copernican** system with the sun at its centre, which he defended in his *Dialogue on the Two Principal Systems of the World* (1632). Its sale was prohibited by the ecclesiastical authorities; Galileo was brought before the Inquisition and under threat of torture recanted. He was finally allowed to live under house arrest in his own home at Arcetri, near Florence; there he continued his researches and completed his *Discourses on the Two New Sciences* (1638), in many respects his most valuable work, in which he discussed at length the principles of mechanics.

In 1637 he became blind, but he continued working until his death on 8 January 1642. The sentence passed on him by the Inquisition was formally retracted by Pope **John Paul II** on 31 October 1992.

📖 Pietro Redondi, *Galileo: Heretic* (1988); Stillman Drake, *Galileo at Work—His Scientific Biography* (1978) and *Discoveries and Opinions of Galileo* (1957); M Allan-Olney, *The Private Life of Galileo* (1970); Georgio de Santillana, *The Crime of Galileo* (1955).

Legend relates that following his recantation Galileo remarked under his breath: 'Eppur si muove' ('But it [the earth] does move'), but the story is probably apocryphal.

Born in Pergamum in Mysia, Asia Minor, he studied medicine there and at Smyrna, Corinth and Alexandria. He was chief physician to the gladiators in Pergamum from AD157, then moved to Rome and became friend and physician to the emperor **Marcus Aurelius**. He was also physician to emperors **Lucius Aurelius Commodus** and **Lucius Septimius Severus**. He was a voluminous writer on medical and philosophical subjects, and collated all the medical knowledge of his time, especially promoting the work of **Hippocrates**. An active experimentalist, and dissector of animals, he elaborated a physiological system whereby the body's three principal organs—heart, liver and brain—were central to living processes, and he was the first to use the pulse as a diagnostic aid. Although not a Christian, he was a monotheist and thus his work was easily assimilated into Christian orthodoxy in the centuries after his death. His *De usu partium* ('The Uses of the Parts') was in essence a hymn to the creator, whereby the organs of the body were seen as perfectly adapted to the functions which they served. He was long venerated as the standard authority on medical matters. 📖 G Sarton, *Galen of Pergamon* (1954).

Galerius, *properly* Gaius Galerius Valerius Maximianus d.311AD
Roman emperor

Born near Serdica, Dacia, he rose to a high rank in the army. He was made Caesar by **Diocletian** (AD293), and on Diocletian's abdication (305) became, with **Constantius Chlorus**, joint ruler of the Roman Empire, Galerius taking the eastern half. When Constantius died in York (306) the troops in Britain and Gaul transferred their allegiance to his son, **Constantine I, the Great**, but Galerius retained the east until his death. Christian tradition presented him as a persecutor of their faith, though in his last year he granted full toleration throughout the empire.

Galgacus See **Calgacus**

Galileo (Galileo Galilei) See panel above

Galindo, Beatriz, *also known as* La Latina 1465/75–1535
Spanish humanist and scholar

She was born probably in Salamanca, and may have been educated in Italy. A famous classical scholar, she became tutor to Queen **Isabella of Castile** and her daughters, and the wife of Francisco Ramirez, secretary to Isabella's husband **Ferdinand, the Catholic**. Her position of teacher at the University of Salamanca was rare for a woman of her time. She also founded schools and hospitals throughout Spain, notably the hospital in Madrid where she was buried. A commentary on **Aristotle** and some Latin poems have been attributed to her.

Galitzin, Dimitri Augustine See **Gallitzin, Dimitri Augustine**

Gall, St c.550–645
Irish monk

He was one of the 12 who followed St **Columban** to the Continent in c.585. In 614 he fixed his cell at a point on the Steinach river in Switzerland, around which grew up a great Benedictine abbey and the town of St Gall. His feast day is 16 October.

Gall, Franz Joseph 1758–1828
German physician, founder of phrenology

Born in Tiefenbrunn, Baden, he settled in Vienna as a physician in 1785. He gradually evolved theories by which he traced talents and other qualities to the functions of particular areas of the brain, and the shape of the skull. His lectures on phrenology were a popular success, but were suppressed in 1802 as being subversive of religion.

Gallacher, Bernard 1949–
Scottish golfer

Born in Bathgate, Midlothian, he turned professional in 1967, and the following year was voted Rookie of the Year. He has been Scottish professional champion on four occasions, and his significant tournament wins include the Spanish Open (1977) and the French Open (1979). First selected for the Ryder Cup team in 1969, when he was regarded as something of a child prodigy, he was a regular member of the team until 1983. In 1991 he was the non-playing captain of the side which came close to retaining the cup at Kiawah Island, South Carolina, co-authoring *Captain at Kiawah* the same year.

Gallacher, Willie (William) 1881–1966
Scottish Communist politician
Born in Paisley, Strathclyde, he attended Camphill School then worked as a brassfounder. Involved with the revolutionary Socialist Labour Party before 1914, he was a leader of the militant shop-stewards' movement during the wartime unrest on Clydeside. Arrested and deported in 1916, he met **Lenin** in Moscow after the Russian Revolution, and helped found the Communist Party of Great Britain. He was MP for Fife West from 1935 to 1951, making him the longest-serving Communist MP in British history. He steadfastly advocated the Communist line, although in private he disapproved of the Nazi–Soviet pact. After losing his seat he wrote several volumes of autobiography.

Galland, Antoine 1646–1715
French Orientalist
Born in Rollot, Picardy, he travelled in Syria and the Levant, and became Professor of Arabic at the Collège de France. His translation of the *Arabian Nights* (1704–08) was the first in any western language.

Gallant, Mavis 1922–
Canadian short-story writer and novelist
She was born in Montreal, to an English father and a German–Russian–Breton mother, and attended 17 different schools as a child, which made education 'virtually impossible'. In 1941 she began working at the *Montreal Standard* and for the National Film Board, before travelling abroad after 1950. She settled in Paris in 1950 and has earned her living entirely by writing, contributing numerous stories to the *New Yorker*. Her fiction often focuses on the lives of exiles and chronicles their alienation with a narrative intelligence that mingles satire, sympathy and cool observation. She has written two novels, *Green Water, Green Sky* (1959) and *A Fairly Good Time* (1970), several collections of short stories, and a diary of the 1968 street troubles in Paris. Her *Collected Stories* appeared in 1996.

Gallatin, Albert 1761–1849
US financier and politician
Born in Geneva, Switzerland, he studied at the university there then went to the USA in 1780. He taught French at Harvard, and bought land in Virginia and Pennsylvania. In 1793 he was elected a senator, in 1795 a member of the House of Representatives, and from 1801 to 1813 was US Secretary of the Treasury. He played an important part in the peace negotiations with Great Britain in 1814, and signed the Treaty of Ghent. He was Minister at Paris (1815–23) and at London (1826). He wrote on finance, politics and the Indian peoples. He was a cousin of Madame de **Staël**.

Gallaudet, Thomas Hopkins 1787–1851
US educator
Born in Philadelphia, he studied European methods for the instruction of those unable to hear or speak and in 1817 opened the first free US school for the deaf in Hartford, Connecticut. He enlarged the school with state aid and trained teachers who started schools elsewhere in the country. His son Edward Miner Gallaudet (1837–1917) founded a school for the deaf (now Gallaudet University) in Washington DC.

Gallé, Émile 1846–1904
French designer and glass maker
Born in Nancy, he studied botany, and this influenced much of his work, including the decoration of his father's ceramics. His own interests turned towards glass. By 1874 he was settled in Nancy running a glass workshop, which grew to employ 300 workers, as well as managing what had been his father's pottery. His distinctive designs for glass, reflecting his experiments with materials and techniques, were generally Art Nouveau in style, as was his furniture. He exhibited work at several major exhibitions, including those in Paris in 1889 and 1900. With Victor Prouvé (1858–1943) and Louis Majorelle (1859–1926) he formed the École de Nancy in 1901.

Galle, Johann Gottfried 1812–1910
German astronomer
Born in Pabsthaus, near Wittenberg, and educated at Berlin University, he graduated in mathematics and physics in 1833. He taught for two years in a school before being invited by **Johann Encke** to become his assistant at the newly-established Berlin Observatory. After 16 years in this post he became director of the observatory at Breslau (now Wroław, Poland, 1851–91). He took a special interest in comets, discovered three new ones and for many years computed ephemerides of comets and minor planets for the *Astronomisches Jahrbuch*. His most dramatic discovery, made in Berlin, was of the planet Neptune, whose existence had been theoretically predicted and whose expected position had been calculated by **Urbain Leverrier**. In 1872 he proposed the use of asteroids rather than regular planets for determinations of the solar parallax, a suggestion which bore fruit in a successful international campaign (1888–89). The method was last used during the closest approach of the minor planet Eros in 1930–31.

Gallegos, Rómulo 1884–1969
Venezuelan politician and novelist
He was born in Caracas. In his country's first democratic elections (1948) Gallegos became President, but his liberalism displeased the military and certain powerful elements in the United States, and he was deposed within a few months. He lived in exile until 1958, when he was welcomed back as an honoured hero. He published a collection of stories in 1913, and in 1920 his first novel, *El último Solar* ('The Last of the Solars'), a lively and pessimistic account of corrupt politicians, failed idealism, and decadent artists. His best-known novel is *Doña Bárbara* (1929, Eng trans 1931), about a barbaric cattle rancher and her encroachments on the land of her neighbour. In 1931 he fled Venezuela for a voluntary exile of four years, until the death of the dictator Juan Vicente Gómez (1857–1935). 📖 L Dunham, *Rómulo Gallegos: vida y obra* (1957)

Gallén-Kallela, Akseli Valdemar 1865–1931
Finnish painter
Born in Pori, he studied in Helsinki and worked in Paris from 1884 to 1890, developing a naturalistic style. He was a pioneer of the Finnish national Romantic style and chose his themes mainly from Finnish mythology, particularly his illustrations in the 1920s for the folk epic, *Kalevala*.

Galliano, John, *originally* Juan Carlos Galliano 1961–
British fashion designer
Born in Gibraltar of a Gibraltan father and Spanish mother, he moved with his family to England when he was six years old. Trained at the Central St Martin's School of Art and Design, he graduated in 1984 and gained the

five-year financial support of Peder Bertelson, a wealthy Danish oil-trader. Noted for the unusual way the fabric is cut—on the bias so that it clings to the body—his designs are inspired by a range of historical and cultural references. He was Designer of the Year in 1987, and showed in Paris in 1990, the first British designer to show in the Louvre tent. In 1992 he found new backing and set up a new workshop in Paris and in 1995, he replaced Hubert de Givenchy as designer-in-chief at his eponymous Paris fashion house. After only one year there, however, Galliano left to become designer-in-chief at the House of Dior in 1996.

Galli-Curci, Amelita 1882–1963
Italian soprano
Born in Milan, she was a prize-winning piano student at Milan Conservatorio, but was self-taught as a singer, and first appeared in opera in 1909. Her style was attractive enough to compensate for deficiencies of technique, and in 1916 she joined Chicago Opera Company. From 1919 onwards, she worked principally at the Metropolitan Opera, New York, and was first heard in Great Britain in 1924. She was forced to retire early, following a throat injury.

Galliéni, Joseph Simon 1849–1916
French soldier
He was born in St Béat, Haute Garonne. He served in the Franco-Prussian War of 1870–71, also in West Africa and Tonkin, was Governor of Upper Senegal from 1886, and Governor-General of Madagascar from 1897 to 1905. As Minister for War, and Military Governor of Paris from 1914, he saw to its fortifications and contributed to the victory of the Marne (1914) by his foresight and planning. He was posthumously created Marshal of France in 1921.

Galliene, Richard Le See Le Gallienne
Gallienne, Eva Le See Le Gallienne, Eva

Gallienus, Publius Licinius c.218–268AD
Roman emperor
He ruled jointly with his father, Publius Licinius Valerian, from AD253 until 260. His authority was constantly challenged (for example, by Postumus in Gaul and Gothic raids into Greece), while the legions frequently proclaimed their commanders Caesars. He abandoned Valerian's persecution of Christians, and developed a formidable force of cavalry. In 268, while besieging one of his rivals in Milan, he was murdered by his own officers.

Gallio, Junius Annaeus fl.AD52
Roman politician
He was proconsul of Achaia under Claudius I and brother of Seneca, the Younger. He dismissed the charge brought by the Jews against St Paul at Corinth in AD52.

Gallitzin or Galitzin or Golitsyn, Dimitri Augustine 1770–1841
US priest
Born in The Hague, the Netherlands, he was the son of a Russian ambassador and a Prussian-born Catholic mother. He entered the Roman Catholic church in 1787, and emigrated to the USA in 1792. Ordained a priest in 1795, he was sent as a missionary to Cambria County, Pennsylvania, where he founded the town of Loretto (1799) and became known as 'Father Smith' and 'the Apostle of the Alleghenies'. He was vicar-general for western Pennsylvania, and wrote several tracts, including *Defence of Catholic Principles* (1816), *Letter to a Protestant Friend* (1820) and *Appeal to the Protestant Public* (1834).

Gallup, George Horace 1901–84
US public opinion pollster
Born in Jefferson, Iowa, he became Professor of Journalism at Drake University (1929–31) and also at Northwestern University (1931–32). He was then director of research for the Young & Rubicam advertising agency in New York (1932–47). In 1935 he founded the American Institute of Public Opinion, and evolved the Gallup Polls for testing the state of public opinion, which made its name by correctly predicting the outcome of the 1936 US presidential elections. He wrote *Public Opinion in a Democracy* (1939) and *Guide to Public Opinion Polls* (1944, 1948).

Gallus, Gaius Cornelius c.70–26BC
Roman poet
Born in Forum Julii (now Fréjus) in Gaul, he lived in Rome and was a friend of Virgil. Appointed prefect of Egypt by Augustus, he was recalled and banished, and committed suicide. He was considered the founder of the Roman love elegy, from his four books of elegies upon his mistress 'Lycoris' (in reality the actress Cytheris). Only part of one line of his verse survives. ◻ J P Boucler, *Gaius Cornelius Gallus* (1966)

Galois, Évariste 1811–32
French mathematician
Born in Bourg-la-Reine, he entered the École Normale Supérieure in 1829, but was expelled in 1830 due to his extreme Republican sympathies. He was politically active and was imprisoned twice. His mathematical reputation rests on fewer than 100 pages of work of original genius, which include a memoir on the solubility of equations by radicals, and a mathematical testament giving the essentials of his discoveries on the theory of algebraic equations and Abelian integrals. Some of his results had been independently obtained by Niels Henrik Abel, but Galois put them in a theoretical setting for them which proved to be very useful to later mathematicians. The brevity and obscurity of his writing delayed the understanding of his work, but it gradually came to be seen as a cornerstone of modern algebra, in which the concept of a group first became of central importance.

Galsworthy, John 1867–1933
English novelist and playwright, and Nobel Prize winner
Born in Coombe, Surrey, he was educated at Harrow and New College, Oxford, and was called to the Bar in 1890, but chose to travel and set up as a writer. He met Joseph Conrad and they became lifelong friends. He published his first book, a collection of short stories, *From the Four Winds*, in 1897, under the pseudonym John Sinjohn. In 1906 he had a success with his first play, *The Silver Box*, and in the same year published *The Man of Property*, the first in his celebrated *Forsyte Saga* series—the others being *In Chancery* (1920) and *To Let* (1921). In these novels he describes both nostalgically and critically the life of the affluent middle class which ruled England before World War I. The second cycle of the saga, *A Modern Comedy* (1929), includes *The White Monkey* (1924), *The Silver Spoon* (1926) and *Swan Song* (1928), and examines the plight of the postwar generation, whose world has collapsed. Among his other novels are *The Island Pharisees* (1904), *The Country House* (1907), *Fraternity* (1909) and *The Patrician* (1911). A prolific playwright, he produced more than 30 plays for the London stage, including *Strife* (1909), *Justice* (1910), *The Skin Game* (1920), *A Bit o' Love* (1915) and *Loyalties* (1922). They best illustrate his reforming zeal, and also his sentimentality, for while technically first-rate theatre, they are marred, especially in the later ones, by the parsimony of his dialogue. He won the Nobel Prize for literature in 1932. ◻ D Holloway, *John Galsworthy* (1968)

Galt, Sir Alexander Tilloch 1817–93
Canadian politician

He was born in London, England. From 1844 to 1855 he was High Commissioner of the British American Land Company, which made huge profits from lands obtained through its influence with the Château Clique and in London. As Finance Minister in the Macdonald–Cartier administration he introduced the high tariffs of 1859 and served in the 'great coalition' of 1864 that negotiated the terms of confederation. In 1880 he became the first Canadian High Commissioner in London.

Galt, John 1779–1839
Scottish novelist and pioneer in Canada

Born in Irvine, Ayrshire, the son of a sea captain, he was educated at Greenock Grammar School, then became a junior clerk in a local merchant's firm (1796). He moved to London in 1804 and set up in business as a merchant, but the venture was not a success, and from 1809 to 1811 he travelled for his health's sake in the Levant, where he met Byron. On his return he published *Letters from the Levant* and other accounts of his travels. He later started to write novels for *Blackwood's Magazine*. The *Ayrshire Legatees* appeared in 1820, followed by *The Steam-Boat* in 1821. Its successor, *The Annals of the Parish* (1821), is his masterpiece, and its description of events in the life of a parish minister throws interesting light on contemporary social history. He produced in quick succession *Sir Andrew Wylie* (1822), *The Provost* (1822) and *The Entail* (1823), then in 1826 went to Canada, where he founded the town of Guelph, and played a prominent part in organizing immigration. He returned ruined in 1829, but wrote a new novel, *Lawrie Todd* (1830), followed by *The Member* (1832), on corruption in politics. He also wrote a *Life of Byron* (1830) and an autobiography (1834). In his depiction of life in small towns and villages Galt has few rivals. He possesses rich humour, genuine pathos and a rare mastery of Scottish dialect. ⌐I Gordon, *John Galt: a life of a writer* (1972)

Galtieri, Leopoldo Fortunato 1926–
Argentine soldier and statesman

He was born in Caseras, in the province of Buenos Aires. After training at the National Military College he was commissioned in 1945 and progressed steadily to the rank of lieutenant-general in 1979, when he joined the junta which had been in power since the military coup which ousted Isabelita Perón in 1976. In 1981 the leader of the junta, General Viola, died of a heart attack and Galtieri succeeded him as President. The state of the Argentine economy worsened and, to counter mounting domestic criticism, in 1982 Galtieri ordered the invasion of the long-disputed Malvinas (Falkland) Islands. Their recovery by Great Britain, after a brief and humiliating war, brought about his downfall. He was court-martialled in 1983 and sentenced to twelve years' imprisonment for negligence in starting and losing the Falklands War. He was released in 1989.

Galton, Sir Francis 1822–1911
English scientist

Born in Birmingham, he studied medicine at the Birmingham Hospital and King's College London and graduated from Trinity College, Cambridge. In 1846 he travelled in North Africa, and in 1850 explored unknown territory in South Africa, publishing *Narrative of an Explorer in Tropical South Africa* and *Art of Travel* (1853). His investigations in meteorology in *Meteorographica* (1863) were the basis for modern weather maps. He supported the evolutionary thinking of his cousin Charles Darwin, and devoted himself to heredity, founding and endowing the study of eugenics (the science of creating superior offspring), and publishing *Hereditary Genius* (1869), *English Men of Science: their Nature and Nurture* (1874) and *Natural Inheritance* (1889). He also devised the system of fingerprint identification with *Finger Prints* (1892). His researches into colour blindness and mental imagery were

also of great value. He was elected FRS in 1856, and knighted in 1909. ⌐ Karl Pearson, *The Life, Letters, and Labours of Francis Galton* (3 vols in 4, 1914–30)

Galuppi, Baldassaro 1706–85
Italian composer of light operas

Born near Venice, he lived in London from 1741 to 1744 and wrote the popular *I filosofo di campagna* (1754, 'The Country Philosopher'), as well as sacred music and sonatas.

Galvani, Luigi 1737–98
Italian physiologist

Born in Bologna, he became a lecturer in anatomy in 1768, and from 1782 was Professor of Obstetrics. He is famous for the discovery of animal electricity, inspired by his observation that dead frogs suffered convulsions when fixed to an iron fence to dry. He then showed that paroxysms followed if a frog was part of a circuit involving metals, wrongly believing the current source to be in the material of muscle and nerve. Galvani's name lives on in the word 'galvanized', meaning stimulated as if by electricity, and in the galvanometer, used from 1820 to detect electric current. ⌐ Percy Dunsheath, *Giants of Electricity* (1967)

Galway, James 1939–
Northern Irish flautist and conductor

Born in Belfast, he gained experience playing in flute bands in Northern Ireland, before training at the Royal College and the Guildhall in London. He was an orchestral player, notably as part of the woodwind section of the Berlin Philharmonic Orchestra, before establishing himself as an internationally renowned soloist in his own right from 1975. His repertoire includes not only classical and contemporary music, but a great deal of popular music, which, along with frequent television exposure, helped him to win a mass audience. He plays a 14-carat gold flute, and even in slight pop-derived material, his sound and technique are impeccable.

Gama, Vasco da c.1469–1525
Portuguese navigator

Born in Sines, Alemtejo, he distinguished himself at an early age as a mariner, and was selected by King Manoel I to discover a route to India round the Cape of Good Hope. The expedition left Lisbon in 1497, and after rounding the Cape, despite hurricanes and mutinies, made Malindi (in East Africa) early in the following year. Here da Gama found a skilful Indian pilot, crossed the Indian Ocean, and arrived at Calicut in 1498, the first westerner to sail round the Cape to Asia. The ruler of Calicut soon became actively hostile, and da Gama had to fight his way out of the harbour, but he arrived safely back in Lisbon in 1499, and was ennobled. However, 40 other Portuguese left behind were murdered, and to avenge them the king sent out a squadron of 20 ships under da Gama (1502), which founded the colonies of Mozambique and Sofala, bombarded Calicut, and returned to the Tagus with 13 richly-laden vessels in 1503. In 1524 da Gama became Viceroy of India. ⌐ K G Jayne, *Vasco de Gama and his Successors 1460–1580* (1910)

Gamage, Albert Walter 1855–1930
English merchant

Born in Hereford, he became a draper's apprentice in London, and in 1878 founded the famous store in Holborn which bore his name.

Gamaliel d.c.50AD
Palestinian rabbi

He was the teacher of St Paul. A prominent Pharisee, he taught 'the law' early in the 1st century. Tolerant and peaceful, he seems to have placed Christianity on a par with other sects.

Gambetta, Léon Michel 1838–82
French statesman

Born in Cahors, of Genoese–Jewish extraction, he became a member of the Paris Bar in 1859, attracted attention by his advanced liberal views, and in 1869 was elected deputy. After the surrender of Napoleon III he was one of the proclaimers of the Republic (September 1870). As Minister of the Interior in the Government of National Defence, he escaped from Paris under siege by balloon to Tours, and for five months was dictator of France. Despite the surrender of Metz he demanded that the war with Germany should be carried on to the end. After the fall of the Commune he became the chief of the advanced Republicans. When Albert, 4th Duc de Broglie (1821–1901), took office (1877) in the hope of restoring the monarchy, a civil war seemed imminent, but he averted it. He was imprisoned and fined for having declared regarding President MacMahon 'Il faudra ou se soumettre, ou se démettre' ('Give in or give up'), but two months later he was re-elected for Belleville, and in 1879 Mac-Mahon resigned. In 1880, on the resignation of the Ferry ministry, Gambetta succeeded in forming a Cabinet, but when in 1882 the chamber rejected his reform proposal he immediately resigned. He died from appendicitis while recovering from the effects of 'an accidental wound in the hand from a revolver'. 📖 Harold Stannard, *Gambetta and the Foundation of the Third Republic* (1921)

Gambier, James Gambier, 1st Baron 1756–1833
English naval commander

Born in the Bahamas, he fought with distinction in Richard Howe's action off Ushant (1794), was promoted rear admiral (1795) and served as lord commissioner of the Admiralty (1795–1801, 1804–06). He was Governor of Newfoundland (1802–04). As admiral he commanded the British fleet at the bombardment of Copenhagen in 1807. At the Battle of Aix Roads in 1809 he disregarded signals from Thomas Cochrane, but was acquitted by a court martial. He was made Admiral of the Fleet in 1830.

Gamble, Josias Christopher 1776–1848
Irish industrialist

Born in Enniskillen, Northern Ireland, he spent a period as a cleric before manufacturing chemicals in Dublin and then in Glasgow, and most profitably in partnership with James Muspratt in St Helens, making bleaching powder, soda ash, and sulphuric acid.

Gambon, Sir Michael John 1940–
Irish actor

Born in Dublin, he moved to England where he joined the National Theatre, London (1963). Subsequent performances include Alan Ayckbourn's *The Norman Conquests* (1974) and *Just Between Ourselves* (1977), as well as the title role in John Dexter's production of Bertolt Brecht's *The Life of Galileo* (1980). The leading actor in the National Theatre company (1986–87), he has also made several television appearances, notably as Dennis Potter's *The Singing Detective* (1986), and as Georges Simenon's *Maigret* (1992). His films include *Paris by Night* and *The Cook, The Thief, His Wife and Her Lover* (both 1989).

Gamelin, Maurice Gustave 1872–1958
French soldier

He was appointed aide-de-camp to Joseph Joffre in 1906, and became his chef de cabinet in 1911. In 1935 he became Chief of Staff of the army and a member of the Conseil Supérieur de la Guerre, but his theory that 'To attack is to lose' exposed his poor grasp of strategy. In 1940 his defensive 'solid fronts' crumbled under the German Blitzkrieg. He was replaced by General Maxime Weygand, tried and imprisoned (1943–45).

Gamow, George 1904–68
US physicist

Born in Odessa, Ukraine, he was educated at Leningrad (now St Petersburg) University, where later he was Professor of Physics (1931–34). After research at the universities of Göttingen, Copenhagen and Cambridge he moved to the USA as Professor of Physics at George Washington University (1934–55) and at Colorado University (1956–68). In 1948, with Ralph Alpher and Hans Bethe, he suggested an explanation for the universal abundance of chemical elements based on thermonuclear processes in the early universe, and he was a major expounder of the 'Big Bang' theory, still the accepted model for the creation of the universe. In molecular biology he made a major contribution to the problem of how the order of nucleic acid bases in DNA chains governs the synthesis of proteins from amino acids. He realized that short sequences of the bases could form a 'code' capable of carrying information directing the synthesis of proteins, a proposal shown by the mid-1950s to be correct.

Gandhi, Indira Priyad Arshini 1917–84
Indian politician

Born in Allahabad, the daughter of Jawaharlal Nehru, she was educated at Visva-Bharati University (Bengal) and Somerville College, Oxford. She was deeply involved in the independence issue, and spent a year in prison. She married Feroze Gandhi (d.1960) in 1942 and had two sons, Rajiv Gandhi and Sanjay (1946–80), who died in an aircrash. She became a member of the central committee of Indian Congress (1950), president of the Indian Congress Party (1959–60), and Minister of Information (1964). She took over as Prime Minister in 1966 after the death of Lal Bahadour Shastri. In 1975, after her conviction for election malpractices, she declared a state of emergency in India. Civil liberties were curtailed and strict censorship imposed. These restrictions were lifted in 1977 during the campaign for a general election, in which the Congress Party was defeated and Mrs Gandhi lost her seat. Acquitted after her arrest on charges of corruption, she resigned in 1978 from the Congress Parliamentary Party, and became leader of the new Indian National Congress (I), returning to power as Prime Minister following the 1980 general election. She was recognized for her work as a leader of the developing nations, but failed to suppress sectarian violence at home. She was assassinated in 1984 by members of her Sikh bodyguard, resentful of her employment of troops to storm the Golden Temple at Amritsar. This murder provoked a Hindu backlash in Delhi, involving the massacre of 3,000 Sikhs. She was succeeded by her elder son, Rajiv. 📖 Mary C Carras, *Indira Gandhi* (1979)

Gandhi, Mahatma See panel p709

Gandhi, Rajiv 1944–91
Indian politician

The eldest son of Indira Gandhi and the grandson of Jawaharlal Nehru, he was born in Bombay, into a Kashmiri–Brahmin family which had governed India for all but four years since 1947. He was educated at Doon School and Cambridge, where he failed his engineering degree. He married an Italian, Sonia Maino, in 1968. In contrast to his younger brother Sanjay (1946–80), he showed little interest in politics and worked as a pilot for Air India (1972–81). Following Sanjay's death in an air crash he inherited his brother's Amethi parliamentary seat in 1981 and was appointed a General-Secretary of the Congress (I) Party in 1983. After the assassination of Indira Gandhi in 1984 he became Prime Minister and secured a record majority in the parliamentary elections later that year. He attempted to cleanse and rejuvenate the Congress (I), inducting new technocrats and introducing a freer market economic programme. Congress (I) suffered heavy losses in the 1989 general election, and he

Gandhi, Mahatma ('Great Soul'), *properly* Mohandâs Karamchand Gandhi 1869–1948
Indian leader

Gandhi was born in Porbandar, Kathiawar, the son of a politician. His mother was a devout Hindu, and Gandhi derived much of his pacifist belief from her. He studied law in London, and in 1893 gave up working in a Bombay legal practice to live on £1 a week in South Africa, where he spent over 20 years opposing discriminatory legislation against Indians. He supported the British in the Boer War (1899–1902).

In 1914 he returned to India. While supporting the British in World War I, he took an increasing interest in the Home Rule movement (*Swaraj*), acquiring control of the Congress Movement, which he reformed. His civil disobedience campaigns of 1919–20 led to violence, notably the massacre at Amritsar in which several hundred people were killed by British soldiers. From 1922 to 1924 he was imprisoned for conspiracy and in 1930 he led a 200-mile (320km) march to the sea to collect salt in symbolic defiance of the government monopoly. He was rearrested and on his release in 1931 negotiated a truce between congress and the government and attended the London Round Table Conference on Indian constitutional reform.

Back in India, he renewed the civil disobedience campaign and was arrested again; this formed the pattern, along with his 'fasts unto death', of his political activity for the next six years. He assisted in the adoption of the constitutional compromise of 1937 under which Congress Ministers accepted office in the new provincial legislatures. When war broke out, Gandhi, convinced that only a free India could give Britain effective moral support, urged complete independence more and more strongly. He described the **Cripps** proposal in 1942 for a constituent assembly with the promise of a new Constitution after the war as 'a post-dated cheque on a crashing bank'. In August 1942 he was arrested for concurring in civil disobedience to obstruct the war effort, and was released in May 1944.

In 1946 Gandhi negotiated with the British Cabinet Mission which recommended the new constitutional structure eventually realized in the formation of India and Pakistan. In May 1947 he hailed Britain's decision to grant India independence as 'the noblest act of the British nation'. His last months were darkened by communal strife between Hindu and Muslim; but his fasts to shame the instigators helped to avert deeper tragedy. He was assassinated in Delhi by a Hindu fanatic on 30 January 1948.

In his lifetime Mahatma ('a great soul') Gandhi was venerated as a moral teacher, a reformer who sought an India as free from caste as from materialism, a dedicated patriot who gave the Swaraj movement a new quality. Critics, however, thought him the victim of a power of self-delusion which blinded him to the disaster and bloodshed his supposedly non-violent campaigns invoked. In Asia above all he has been regarded as a great influence for peace whose teaching had a message not only for India but for the world.

⌨ His publications include the autobiographical *The Story of My Experiment with Truth* (2 vols, 1927–29; reissued as 1 vol, 1983), his autobiography (1948), and *The Collected Works of Mahatma Gandhi* (90 vols, 1958–84). See also Yogesha Chadha, *Rediscovering Gandhi: The Definitive Biography* (1997); J M Brown, *Gandhi, Prisoner of Hope* (1990); Robert Payne, *The Life and Death of Mahatma Gandhi* (1969); Pyarelal, *Mahatma Gandhi* (2nd edn, 2 vols, 1965–66); Dinanath G Tendulkar, *Mahatma: Life of Mohandas Kamarchand Gandhi* (8 vols, 1960–63).

> 'Non-violence is not a garment to be put on and off at will. Its seat is in the heart, and it must be an inseparable part of our very being.' From 'War and Peace' in *Young India* (1926).

---

resigned as premier after his party's defeat. He was killed by a bomb hidden in the clothing of a woman who handed him flowers during an election campaign.

Gangeśa c.1200
Indian philosopher

He founded the *Navya-nyaya* or new *Nyaya* school of Hindu philosophy, in Mithila, Bihar. His approach, emphasizing philosophical logic rather than knowledge of the external world claimed in *Nyaya* philosophy stemming from **Gautama**, was continued by his son Vardhamana. Later eminent exponents included Pakshadhara (1400–95) and Raghunatha (1477–1547).

Ganivet, Angel 1865–98
Spanish essayist, novelist and thinker

His works include the profoundly argued *Idearium español* (1897, Eng trans *Spain: An Interpretation*, 1946), in which he analyses Spain as sick with *aboulia*—lack of will, chronic apathy, fixed ideology. (The term was coined by **Miguel de Unamuno** from whom Ganivet gained much of his inspiration, and with whom Ganivet had an important and eventually published correspondence.) His two semi-autobiographical novels are *La conquista del reino de maya por el último conquistador español Pío Cid* (1897, 'The Conquest of Maya's Kingdom by the Last Spanish Conquistador Pío Cid'), and *Los trabajos del infatigable creador Pío Cid* (1898, 'The Labours of the Indefatigable Creator Pío Cid'). Knowing that he had syphilitic paralysis, he drowned himself in the Dvina in Riga, where he was Spanish consul. ⌨ H Ramsden, *Angel Ganivet's 'Idearium español': A Critical Study* (1967)

Gao Gang (Kao Kang) c.1902–1955
Chinese political leader

In the mid-1930s he was in charge of a small independent Communist area at Baoan, Shaanxi (Shensi), where the Long March led by **Mao Zedong** ended (1935). Mao and Gao Gang became close political allies, and Gao Gang later became Chief Party Secretary of Manchuria (1949). He set the national pace in economic development, but in 1955 was accused of attempting to set up a 'separate kingdom'. He apparently committed suicide.

Gapon, Georgi Apollonovich 1870–1906
Ukrainian priest and reformer

In 1902 he became leader of the so-called Union of Russian Factory Workers. Without his knowledge, this seems to have been financed by the Tsarist police as a means of penetrating and controlling the working-class movement. However, with deteriorating economic conditions, its numbers grew and in 1905 Gapon led them in a procession to the Winter Palace in the sincere belief that Tsar **Nicholas II** would accede to their demands. The result was Bloody Sunday. Thereafter, idealists like Gapon could exercise less and less influence on Russian developments.

Garbarek, Jan 1947–
Norwegian saxophonist and composer

Born in Mysen, he became interested in jazz through the recordings of **John Coltrane** and Albert Ayler, although his own style developed in a contrary direction. Self-taught at first, he was playing at European jazz festivals by 1966 and one year later joined the Scandinavian orchestra led by US avant-garde composer George Russell. He

Garbo, Greta, *professional name of* Greta Lovisa Gustafsson 1905–90
Swedish-born US film actress, a glamorous star of 1930s films

Greta Garbo was born in Stockholm. She became a shop assistant and model, and won a bathing beauty competition at 16, then won a scholarship to the Royal Theatre Dramatic School in Stockholm. She was given a starring role in *Gösta Berling's Saga* (1924) by the Swedish director **Mauritz Stiller**; he also gave his star the name Garbo (chosen before he met her), trained her in acting technique, and insisted that she be given a contract at MGM in Hollywood when he moved there in 1925. He co-directed her in *The Temptress* (1926).

She was an actress of remarkable talent and legendary beauty, as her appearances in *Flesh and the Devil* (1927), *Love* (1927) and *A Woman of Affairs* (1928) showed. Her first talking role was in *Anna Christie* (1930), and this was followed by her greatest successes, *Queen Christina* (1933), *Anna Karenina* (1935), *Camille* (1936), *Conquest* (1937), in which she played **Napoleon I**'s mistress, and *Ninotchka* (1939), a romantic comedy in which she

caricatured her own aloof image and famously laughed. She retired from films in 1941, distressed by the scathing reviews of *Two-Faced Woman*.

She became a US citizen in 1951 but lived in New York as a total recluse for the rest of her life. In 1955 she was awarded an honorary Academy Award for her 'unforgettable screen performances'; the award was accepted for her by Nancy Kelly. Later attempts to persuade her to return to the screen were all unsuccessful.

📖 A Walker, *Garbo* (1980); John Bainbridge, *Garbo* (1971); M Conway, *The Films of Greta Garbo* (1968).

> 'I want to be alone.' The media have frequently attributed these words to Garbo, although she always denied she said them. In the film *Grand Hotel* (1932) Grusinskaya (played by Garbo) says 'I want to be left alone'.

---

worked with experimental US musicians like Keith Jarrett and Don Cherry in the early 1970s, but his own projects have moved increasingly away from jazz in favour of an exploration of influences from Norwegian folk music, and also the ethnic music of India, Pakistan and South America, sometimes with musicians from those traditions. His haunting saxophone sonority has grown more starkly and dramatically etched the further he has moved from the harmonic complexities of jazz.

Garbett, Cyril Foster 1875–1955
English prelate

Born in Tongham, near Aldershot, and educated at Keble College and Cuddesdon College, Oxford, he was Bishop of Southwark from 1919 to 1932 and of Winchester from 1932, until he was appointed Archbishop of York in 1942. He was one of the most outspoken leaders of the Church, a prelate of great pastoral gifts and a humanitarian remembered for his warmth of personality and strength of character. His publications include *The Church and Social Problems* (1939) and a trilogy on Church and State (1947–52).

Garbo, Greta See panel above

Garborg, Arne Evenson 1851–1924
Norwegian writer

Born in Jaeren, he rejected his agricultural upbringing and became a rural schoolmaster, working subsequently as a journalist and junior civil servant. The conflict precipitated his father's suicide. Garborg later lost his government post when he published *Mannfolk* (1886, 'Men'), in which he passionately argued that economic and social pressures drove respectable young Norwegians into the arms of prostitutes. He also wrote a series of realistic novels, such as *Bondestudenter* (1883, 'Peasant Students'), *Fred* (1890, 'Peace') and *Traette Maend* (1891, 'Tired Men'), and a cycle of lyric poems, *Haugtussa* (1895, 'The Hill Innocent'). He was a leader in the movement to establish a new Norwegian literary language (*Landsmål*, 'country language') based on western country dialects (later called *Nynorsk*, 'New Norwegian'), and from 1877 edited the periodical *Fedraheimen*, which provided him with a mouthpiece for his lifelong attack on **Luther**an theology.
📖 R Thesen, *Arne Garborg og det norske folket* (1944)

Garcia, Jerry (Jerome John) 1942–95
US rock and country guitarist and singer

Born in San Francisco, he began playing in folk and bluegrass bands, before drifting into San Francisco's Haight-Ashbury hippie scene of the mid-1960s, which led to the formation of The Grateful Dead in 1967. The

band became an institution in US music, with Garcia, Bob Weir and Phil Lesh as its key members. They moved from psychedelia into a more blues and country oriented sound in the early 1970s, but remained famous for their long, improvised live performances, and retained a huge worldwide following—the 'Deadheads'—through every change of pop and rock fashion. He performed in various other contexts, notably with an acoustic bluegrass band. His health, exacerbated by drug addiction, grew fragile, and his death ended an era in US rock music.
📖 W Ruhlmann, *History of The Grateful Dead* (1990)

García, Manuel 1775–1832
Spanish tenor and composer

Born in Seville, he made his reputation as a tenor in Cadiz and Madrid, and from 1808 travelled to Paris, Italy and London. In 1825 he visited New York and Mexico, where he was robbed of all his money, which compelled him to teach singing on his return to Paris. Several of his compositions, such as *Il Califo di Bagdad* ('The Thief of Baghdad'), became popular. His daughter was **Pauline Viardot**.

García, Paulina See Viardot, Pauline

Garcia, Perez Alan 1949–
Peruvian politician

He was born in Lima and studied law at the Catholic University there. He continued his studies in Guatemala, Spain and France before returning to his country and winning election to the National Congress as a moderate left-winger (1978). Four years later he was appointed Secretary-General, and in 1985 succeeded **Fernando Belaúnde Terry** in the first democratic election of a civilian president. He inherited an ailing economy which forced him to trim his socialist programme. By 1991 the economy was in tatters, and he became locked into the deepening struggle between the Sendero Luminoso and the armed forces in the Andes, and a conservative congress in Lima. He was succeeded as President by the conservative **Alberto Fujimori** and sought political asylum in Colombia in 1992.

García Gutiérrez, Antonio 1813–84
Spanish dramatist

Born in Chiclana, he abandoned his medical studies to become a soldier. His first success, *El trovador* (1836, 'The Troubadour'), provided **Verdi** with his opera *Il Trovatore* (1853), and he went on to write some 50 plays. His Romantic theatre includes some deliberately sensational writing but at its best, as in *Juan Lorenzo* (1865), is exceedingly skilful, written in a clever combination of prose and verse, and presenting unusually acute portrayals of women. 📖 N B Adams, *The Romantic Drama of García Gutiérrez* (1922)

García Lorca, Federico 1898–1936
Spanish poet and playwright

Born in Fuente Vaqueros, he is best known for his powerful dramatic tragedies, which deal with elemental themes in a striking fashion. The best of these plays are *Bodas de Sangre* (1933, Eng trans *Blood Wedding*, 1947), *Yerma* (1934, Eng trans 1947) and *La Casa de Bernarda Alba* (first performed in 1945, Eng trans *The House of Bernarda Alba*, 1947). His gypsy songs, which include *Canciones* (1927, Eng trans 1976) and *Romancero Gitano* (1928, 1935, Eng trans *Gypsy Ballads*, 1963), reveal a classical control of imagery, rhythm and emotion. The elegiac poems in *Llanto por la meurta de Ignacio Sánchez Mejías* (1935, Eng trans *Lament for the Death of a Bullfighter and Other Poems*, 1937) have been seen as a foreshadowing of his own death. He was assassinated on the orders of the Nationalist Civil Governor early in the Spanish Civil War at Granada. 📖 I Gibson, *The Death of Lorca* (1973)

García Márquez, Gabriel See **Márquez, Gabriel García**

García Robles, Alfonso 1911–
Mexican diplomat and Nobel Prize winner

After studying law at universities in Mexico and Paris and at the Academy of International Law in the Netherlands, he became a member of the Mexican Foreign Service. From 1964 to 1971 he was Under-Secretary for Foreign Affairs. In this capacity he furthered his interest in international nuclear disarmament, and was instrumental in forming the Treaty of Tlateloco (1967), which aimed to abolish nuclear weapons in Latin America. Since 1977 he has been Mexican delegate on the UN Disarmament Committee. His publications include *338 Days of Tlateloco* (1977). He was awarded the 1982 Nobel Peace Prize, jointly with **Alva Myrdal**.

Garcilaso de la Vega 1503–36
Spanish poet and soldier

Born in Toledo, he fought bravely in the wars of **Charles V**, and died in battle of a wound. He introduced the **Petrarchan** sonnet into Spain, and wrote odes in imitation of **Virgil**. 📖 D Castanian, *El Inca Garcilaso de la Vega* (1969)

Garcilaso de la Vega, *called* El Inca c.1540–c.1616
Spanish writer

He was born in Cuzco, Peru, the son of one of the conquerors of Peru and an Inca princess, and at the age of 20 he went to Spain, where he spent the rest of his life. His account of the conquest of Florida by **Hernando de Soto** (1605) was followed in 1609–17 by his great *Comentarios*, in which he movingly describes the legends and beliefs of his mother's people (Eng trans by Markham, 1869).

Garden, Mary 1874–1967
Scottish soprano

Born in Aberdeen, she was taken to the USA as a child. She studied singing in Chicago and then in Paris, and her career began sensationally when in 1900 she took over in mid-performance the title role in **Gustave Charpentier's** new opera *Louise* at the Opéra-Comique, when the singer was taken ill. In 1902 she created the role of Mélisande in **Debussy's** *Pelléas et Mélisande* at the composer's request, and in 1903 she recorded songs with Debussy. **Jules Massenet** and Frédéric d'Erlanger also wrote leading roles for her. She sang at Covent Garden (1902–03), starring in roles such as Thaïs, Salomé, Carmen and Juliet (**Charles Gounod**). She made her US debut as Thaïs (1907), and in 1910 she began a 20-year association with Chicago Grand

Opera, which she also briefly directed (1921–22). She returned to Scotland in 1939. 📖 Michael T R B Turnbull, *Mary Garden* (1996)

Gardiner, Gerald Austin Gardiner, Baron 1900–90
English jurist and legal reformer

Educated at Harrow and Magdalen College, Oxford, he was called to the Bar in 1925, and his cases included the *Lady Chatterley's Lover* trial, in which he acted as counsel for the defence. His support for law reform was expressed in *Capital Punishment as a Deterrent* (1956), and he was joint chairman (with Sir **Victor Gollancz**) of the National Campaign for the Abolition of Capital Punishment. In 1964 he was appointed Lord Chancellor during the government of **Harold Wilson**. During his six years in office, capital punishment was abolished, laws regarding abortion and homosexuality were reformed, and the Law Commission was set up. He appointed the first woman judge to the High Court, and introduced a compulsory training programme for Justices of the Peace. He retired in 1970 when Labour went into Opposition, and became Chancellor of the Open University in 1973.

Gardiner, Samuel Rawson 1829–1902
English historian

Born in Ropley, Hampshire, he was educated at Winchester and Christ Church, Oxford. For some years he was Professor of Modern History at King's College London but resigned in 1885 to continue his *History of England from the Accession of James I to the Restoration* at Oxford on an All Souls' Fellowship. The first instalment appeared in 1863, and at his death he had completed the work to 1656. He also published *The Thirty Years' War* (1874), *Introduction to the Study of English History* (1881), written in conjunction with J Bass Mullinger, and *The Student's History of England* (1890–92).

Gardiner, Stephen c.1483–1555
English prelate

Born in Bury St Edmunds, Suffolk, he received a PhD in civil and canon law at Cambridge (1520–21), and was made Master of Trinity Hall, Cambridge (1525–49, 1553–55). He became **Thomas Wolsey's** secretary (1525), then Bishop of Winchester (1531), and was sent to Rome to further **Henry VIII's** divorce from **Catherine of Aragon** (1527–33). He supported the royal supremacy, but opposed doctrinal reformation, and for this was imprisoned and deprived of his bishopric on **Edward VI's** accession. Released and restored by **Mary I, Tudor** (1553), he became a vigorous persecutor of Protestants.

Gardner, Alexander 1821–82
US photographer and journalist

He was born in Paisley, Scotland, and emigrated to the USA in 1856. Employed by **Mathew B Brady**, he became manager of Brady's Washington studio in 1858, but left, following a dispute over copyright, to open his own gallery in Washington (1863). He specialized in documentary projects, the best-known of which are his work on the American Civil War (some of it produced while he and his son James were employed in making maps at the headquarters of the army of the Potomac); on the Lincoln Conspiracy (he had earlier made several portraits of **Abraham Lincoln**); on the building of the Union Pacific Railroad; and on several Indian Peace Conferences. His most significant published work is his *Photographic Sketchbook of the War* (1865), which contains fully-attributed photographs by other photographers, including **Timothy H O'Sullivan**, in addition to his own original prints.

Gardner, Ava, *originally* Lucy Johnson 1922–90
US film actress

Born in North Carolina, she was signed by MGM as a teenager, emerging from the ranks of decorative starlets with her portrayal of a femme fatale in *The Killers* (1946). A green-eyed brunette, once voted the world's most beautiful woman, she remained a leading lady for two decades, portraying an earthy combination of sensuality and cynicism in films like *Mogambo* (1953), *The Barefoot Contessa* (1954) and *Night of the Iguana* (1964). She continued to work as a character actress in films and on television. She was married to **Mickey Rooney, Artie Shaw** and **Frank Sinatra**. She published an autobiography, *Ava*, in 1990.

Gardner, Erle Stanley 1889–1970
US crime novelist
Born in Malden, Massachusetts, he was educated at Palo Alto High School, California, studied in law offices and was admitted to the Californian Bar, where he became an ingenious lawyer for the defence (1922–38). A hugely prolific writer, he dictated up to six or seven novels simultaneously to a team of secretaries and used a number of pseudonyms. His best-known creation is the lawyer-sleuth Perry Mason, hero of 82 courtroom dramas, who first appeared in *The Case of the Velvet Claws* (1933). With a little help from Della Street, his faithful secretary, and private eye Paul Drake, Mason frequently defied the rulebook in his quest to clear his client's name. With Raymond Burr (1917–93) playing Perry Mason, the books enjoyed enhanced popularity when they were made into a long-running television series. He also wrote a series of detective novels featuring the District Attorney Doug Selby ('the DA'). 🕮 A Johnston, *The Case of Erle Stanley Gardner* (1947)

Gardner, George 1812–49
Scottish botanist and explorer
Born in Glasgow, he studied medicine before becoming a botanist under the guidance of Sir **William Hooker**. His plant-collecting expeditions in the drier provinces of north-eastern Brazil (1836–41) took him northwards from Rio de Janeiro to Ceara and Maranhao, and resulted in substantial collections for the Royal Botanic Gardens at Kew, London. He published a major work on this subject, *Travels in the Interior of Brazil*, in 1846. He went on to become director of the botanical garden at Peradeniya in Ceylon (now Sri Lanka).

Gardner, Isabella 1915–81
US poet
Born in Newton, Massachusetts, she worked in the theatre and was unpublished until after her third marriage in 1947. Her first collection, *Birthdays from the Ocean*, appeared in 1955. Other volumes include *The Looking Glass* (1961), *West of Childhood: Poems 1950–65* (1965) and *That Was Then: New and Selected Poems* (1980). Admired by many, including the poet **Sylvia Plath**, she received the first **Walt Whitman** Citation of Merit in 1981.

Gardner, Isabella Stewart 1840–1924
US art collector
Born in New York City, she married a wealthy Bostonian and led a cultural salon in Boston. She collected art with the advice of connoisseur **Bernard Berenson** and built a gallery on the plan of an Italian villa with an interior garden, living on the fourth floor and opening the remainder to the public as the Isabella Stewart Gardner Museum in 1903. At her death she willed it to the city of Boston with the proviso that nothing should be altered, added, or removed, and its idiosyncratic Victorian arrangement has remained unchanged excepting the blank spaces left after 1990, when thieves posing as policemen stole a number of priceless works from the museum, including paintings by **Rembrandt** and **Vermeer**.

Gardner, Peter 1836–1902
Scottish potter

At the age of 30 he took over the family business of Dunmore Pottery. Animals feature a great deal in his work and his pioneering style in applied design and glaze techniques ranged from tiles and teapots to garden seats and umbrella stands. He was encouraged by the Earl and Countess of Dunmore and received royal recognition in 1871 when he was visited by the Prince of Wales (later **Edward VII**). He is generally regarded as one of the principal makers of Art Pottery in the second half of the 19th century.

Garfield, James Abram 1831–81
20th President of the USA
Born near Orange, Ohio, he already added to his widowed mother's income by doing farm work at the age of 10, and despite their poverty managed to graduate from Williams College in 1856. After teaching in a school and serving as a lay preacher, he became a lawyer and was elected to the state senate in 1859. On the outbreak of the Civil War he commanded a regiment of volunteers, seeing action at Shiloh and winning promotion to major-general for gallantry at Chickamauga in 1863. That year he resigned his command to enter Congress as a representative from Ohio, and he kept his seat for 17 years, becoming leader of the Republicans. In 1880 he was elected to the Senate, but he never occupied the seat because a deadlock at the Republican national convention led to his being chosen as the compromise presidential candidate. Elected President by a slim margin, he took office in 1881 and at once alienated **Roscoe Conkling** and the stalwart faction of the Republican Party by asserting the right of the President to make political appointments without regard to party patronage. On the morning of 2 July he was shot by a deranged admirer of the stalwarts, Charles Guiteau (tagged historically as a 'disappointed office seeker'). He died on 19 September and was succeeded by Vice President **Chester Arthur**. His speeches were published in 1882. 🕮 Allan Peskin, *Garfield* (1978)

Garfinkel, Harold 1917–
US sociologist
Born in Newark, New Jersey, he was educated at Harvard, where he was a student of **Talcott Parsons**. He taught briefly at Ohio State University and then in the department of sociology at the University of California, Los Angeles (1954–88). He is the founder of the sociological tradition of ethnomethodology, an approach to social science which focuses on the practical reasoning processes that ordinary people use in order to understand and act within the social world.

Garibaldi, Giuseppe 1807–82
Italian Revolutionary, soldier and politician
He was born in Nice, French Empire (now in France), the son of a sailor. The greatest figure of the Risorgimento, he was a member of Young Italy and took part in an abortive **Mazzinian** insurrection in Genoa in 1834. He subsequently fled to South America, where he fought in defence of the Rio Grande do Sul Republic against the Brazilian Empire and in Uruguay against the Argentine dictator **Juan Manuel de Rosas**. He returned to Italy (1848) and offered his services to King Charles Albert (1798–1849) against the Austrians. Rejected, he instead took part in the government and defence of the Roman Republic, before attempting to relieve the Venetian republic of **Daniele Manin**. After the Revolutions of 1848–49 he visited the USA before settling on the island of Caprera. In 1856 he backed the Italian National Society and played a minor but brilliant part in the 1859 campaign against the Austrians. In 1860 he set sail from Genoa with 1,000 volunteers ('Red Shirts') to assist the anti-**Bourbon** rebellion which had broken out in Sicily. Having seized control of the island, he crossed to the mainland of the Kingdom of the Two Sicilies and overran much of the

Mezzogiorno before handing it over to **Victor Emmanuel II**. In 1862 he attempted to march on Rome but was stopped by Piedmontese troops at Aspromonte. A similar attempt to seize the papal capital was blocked by French forces at Mentana in 1867. He fought with limited success against the Austrians in 1866 and in 1870 he offered his services to the French after the Battle of Sedan. In 1870 he was elected a Deputy at the Bordeaux Assembly. He spent his last years as a farmer on Caprera. ▣ Jasper Ridley, *Garibaldi* (1974)

Garioch, Robert, *pseudonym of* Robert Garioch Sutherland 1909–81
Scottish poet

Born in Edinburgh and educated at the Royal High School and University there, he spent most of his professional career as a teacher in Scotland and England. He made his literary debut in 1933 with the surrealistic verse play *The Masque of Edinburgh* (published in expanded form in 1954). His first publications, *Seventeen Poems for Sixpence* (1940), in which he collaborated with **Sorley Maclean**, and *Chuckies on the Cairn* (1949), were hand-printed. His later work included *Selected Poems* (1966), *The Big Music* (1971), *Dr Faust in Rose Street* (1973) and *Collected Poems* (1977). He wrote in the Scots language in various styles and moods, from the colloquial to the literary. He also translated into Scots works as diverse as **Pindar**, **Hesiod**, **George Buchanan**'s Latin plays *Jeptha* and *Baptistes*, Anglo-Saxon elegies, and 19th-century Italian poems. His prose works include *Two Men and a Blanket* (1975), an account of his experience in POW camps during World War II. **Robert Fergusson** in particular influenced his poetry, as is most clearly seen in his sonnet on Fergusson's grave 'To Robert Fergusson', and 'The Muir'.

Garland, (Hannibal) Hamlin 1860–1940
US writer

Born in West Salem, Wisconsin, he often interrupted his schooling to help his father farm in Iowa, but in 1884 he went to Boston to teach and finally to write. In short stories such as the collections *Main Travelled Roads* (1887) and *Prairie Folks* (1892), in verse and in novels, he vividly, often grimly, described the farming life of the Midwest. *Rose of Dutcher's Coolly* (1895) was an important forerunner of the 1920s 'revolt from the village'. *A Daughter of the Middle Border* (1921), the sequel to his autobiographical novel *A Son of the Middle Border* (1917), won the Pulitzer Prize. *Crumbling Idols* (1894) was a collection of essays, setting out Garland's theories of 'veritism'. ▣ J Holloway, *Hamlin Garland: a biography* (1960)

Garland, Judy, *originally* Frances Ethel Gumm 1922–69
US actress and singer

Born in Grand Rapids, Minnesota, she made stage appearances in vaudeville with her parents and partnered two sisters in an act that led to a film contract. She became a juvenile film star in *Broadway Melody of 1938* and appeared in several fine film musicals, among them *The Wizard of Oz* (1939), *Meet Me in St Louis* (1944) and *Easter Parade* (1948). Personal appearances confirmed the emotional power of her voice, and in *A Star is Born* (1954) she gave an impressive dramatic performance. Despite emotional and medical difficulties and a reputation for unreliability, she achieved the status of a legendary performer and actress. She was married five times, once to director Vincente Minnelli, and her daughters **Liza Minnelli** and Lorna Luft have followed in her footsteps. ▣ E R Coleman, *The Complete Judy Garland* (1990)

Garner, Errol (Louis) 1921–77
US jazz pianist

Born in Pittsburgh, Pennsylvania, he was performing on radio at the age of 10, and playing professionally as a teenager. He moved to New York City in 1944, where he worked in both the jazz clubs of 52nd Street and the cabaret and cocktail lounge circuit. He never learned to read music, but evolved a distinctive, fearsomely virtuosic piano style which is readily identifiable in almost any setting. His growing popularity, bolstered by successful records like *Concert By The Sea* (1955), saw him lean increasingly toward the lucrative cabaret circuit, although jazz remained the cornerstone of his style. His compositions include the ballad 'Misty', now a jazz standard. ▣ J Doran, *The Most Happy Piano* (1985)

Garner, Helen 1942–
Australian writer

Born in Geelong, Victoria, she taught in Melbourne schools until being dismissed for answering pupils' questions on sex. Her adult fiction appeals strongly to adolescents because it examines contemporary problems in a clear-sighted and non-judgemental manner. *Monkey Grip* (1977), dealing with the subculture of drug addiction, won the National Book Council award that year and was filmed in 1981, gaining her instant popularity. Other works include two novellas, *Honour* and *Other People's Children* (both 1980), *The Children's Bach* (1984), and the collections of short stories *Postcards from Surfers* (1985) and *Cosmo Cosmolino* (1993). *First Stone* (1995) drew upon a Melbourne academic *cause célèbre* and attracted strong criticism from parts of the feminist movement. She has also written screenplays, such as *The Last Days of Chez Nous* (1993) for **Gillian Armstrong**.

Garner, John Nance 1868–1967
US politician

Born in Red River County, Texas, he served as a Democratic congressman from Texas (1903–33) and became Speaker of the House in 1931. As Vice President (1933–41) under **Franklin D Roosevelt**, Garner steered much New Deal legislation through Congress during his first two terms.

Garnerin, André Jacques 1769–1823
French aeronaut

A former balloon inspector in the French army, he gave the first public demonstration of a descent by parachute from a free-flying balloon in Paris in 1797, and thereafter made exhibition jumps in many countries, including one of 8,000 feet in England (1802). He was assisted in making improvements to the design of his parachutes by his brother, Jean Baptiste Olivier Garnerin (1766–1849).

Garnett, David, *nicknamed* Bunny 1892–1981
English novelist

He was born in Brighton, the son of **Edward Garnett**, and studied botany at the Royal College of Science, London. His first novel, *Lady into Fox* (1922), won both the Hawthornden and the James Tait Black Memorial prizes. *A Man in the Zoo* (1924) and *The Sailor's Return* (1925) were also successful, as were several other novels. Associated with the Bloomsbury Group of artists and writers, he was literary adviser to the Nonesuch Press (1923–32) and literary editor of the *New Statesman* (1932–34). He joined the RAF in 1939, and used this experience for *War in the Air* (1941). ▣ *The Golden Echo: memoirs 1892–1914* (1915)

Garnett, Edward 1868–1937
English writer and critic

Born in London, the son of **Richard Garnett**, as a publisher's reader he fostered the careers of many literary figures, including **Joseph Conrad**, **John Galsworthy** and **D H Lawrence**. He was the author of the set of critical essays *Friday Nights* (1922). He also wrote plays, including

The Breaking Point (1907) and *The Trial of Jeanne d'Arc* (1912). His wife Constance (*née* Black, 1862–1946) was a distinguished translator of Russian literature.

Garnett, Eve 20th century
English children's author and illustrator
Born in Worcestershire, she studied at the Royal Academy of Art and has combined life as an author with her work as a professional artist. Her artistry has included a commission for murals at Children's House, Bow, London, and an exhibition at the Tate Gallery, London, in 1939. Her name as an author rests upon *The Family from One End Street* (1937, Carnegie Medal), one of the first attempts to present working-class family life sympathetically in children's fiction. This book and its sequel, *Further Adventures of the Family from One End Street* (1956), remain popular. 📖 *First Affections* (1982)

Garnett, Richard 1835–1906
English writer and bibliographer
Born in Lichfield, Staffordshire, he worked as a clerk then became keeper of printed books at the British Museum, London (1890–99). He was the author of verse, critical works and biographies, including *Shelley* (1862), *Carlyle* (1883) and *The Age of Dryden* (1895). His best-known original work is his collection of tales on pagan themes, *Twilight of the Gods* (1888). His son was Edward Garnett. 📖 H Cordier, *Le Docteur Richard Garnett* (1906)

Garnett, Tony 1936–
English television and film producer
Born in Birmingham, Midlands, he studied psychology at London University before becoming an actor, appearing in television plays and the film *The Boys* (1962). He joined the BBC drama department (1964) as a script editor working on the Wednesday Play series. As a producer, he enjoyed a long association with director Ken Loach on such influential television work as *Cathy Come Home* (1966), *Days of Hope* (1975) and *The Price of Coal* (1977). His films, also in collaboration with Loach, include *Kes* (1969), *Family Life* (1971) and *Black Jack* (1979). He made his directorial debut with *Prostitute* (1980). Now resident in Los Angeles, he has directed *Handgun* (retitled *Deep in the Heart*, 1983), and returned to production on *Fat Man and Little Boy* (1989), *Earth Girls Are Easy* (1989) and *Beautiful Thing* (1996).

Garnier, Francis, *properly* Marie Joseph François 1839–73
French explorer
He was born in St Étienne, and as a naval officer fought in the Chinese War (1860–62). Appointed to a post in Cochin-China (now in Vietnam), he was second-in-command to Doudart de Lagrée on the Mekong River Expedition (1866–68) during which he mapped 3,100 miles (4,991km) of unknown territory in Cambodia and Yunnan. He aided in the defence of Paris (1870–71), and in the Tonkin War (1873) took Hanoi.

Garnier, Robert 1534–90
French poet and playwright
Born in Maine, USA, he was the most distinguished of the predecessors of Pierre Corneille. His *Œuvres complètes* (2 vols, 1923, 1949, 'Complete Works') include the tragedies *Antigone* (1580) and *Les Juives* (1583, 'The Jewesses'). 📖 M Mouflard, *Robert Garnier: 1545–1590* (1961)

Garnier, Tony (Antoine) 1869–1948
French architect
Born in Lyons, he studied at the École des Beaux-Arts, Paris. As architect of Lyons he made a major contribution to the forming of 20th-century architectural and urban planning through his Utopian ideal *Une Cité industrielle*, exhibited in 1904 and published in 1917. It combined functionalism with political and social reform, using the latest technology and materials. Through it he produced sophisticated reinforced concrete buildings at Lyons, including the Grange Blanche hospital (1911–27) and the Stadium (1913–18), and the Hôtel de Ville at Boulogne-Billancourt (1931–33). His early designs were published in *Les grands travaux de la ville de Lyons* (1920).

Garofalo, *originally* Benvenuto Tisi 1481–1559
Italian painter
Born in Ferrara, he was the last and foremost artist of the Ferrarese school. He worked chiefly in the churches and palaces of his native city, in Bologna and in Rome. The church of S Lorenzo, Ferrara, contains his *Adoration of the Magi*, and his *Sacrifice to Ceres* is in the National Gallery, London.

Garrick, David 1717–79
English actor, theatre manager and playwright
He was born in Hereford and educated at Lichfield Grammar School. In 1736 he was sent to study Latin and Greek under Dr Johnson at Edial, and in 1737 he set off for London to study law, but became a wine merchant with his eldest brother (1738–40). He then turned to the stage. His first play was performed at Drury Lane in 1740 and in 1741 he made his successful debut as an actor at Ipswich, as Aboan in Thomas Southerne's *Oroonoko*. The same year he appeared in London at Goodman's Fields, where his success as Richard III was so great that within a few weeks the two patent theatres were deserted, and crowds flocked to the unfashionable East End playhouse. When Goodman's Fields closed, he played at both Drury Lane and Covent Garden, but ultimately settled at Drury Lane, of which he became joint-manager (1747), and from where he dominated the English stage for 30 years. He played continually, his only long rest being a trip to Europe (1763–65), when he thought his popularity was in danger of diminishing. He married Eva Marie Violetti (1724–1822), a Viennese dancer (1749). He was buried in Westminster Abbey, London. 📖 George W Stone, Jnr and George M Kahrl, *David Garrick* (1979)

Garrison, William Lloyd 1805–79
US journalist and antislavery campaigner
He was born in Newburyport, Massachusetts. A printer to trade, he became editor of the *Newburyport Herald* (1824) and the *National Philanthropist* (1828). Encouraged by Benjamin Lundy, he denounced slavery so vigorously that he was imprisoned. He was founder-editor of *The Liberator* (1831–65) which argued the case for immediate abolition, visited Great Britain on lecture tours, and in 1833 founded the American Anti-Slavery Society. After the abolition of slavery, he turned his crusading attention to women's suffrage and the plight of the Native American peoples.

Garrod, Sir Archibald Edward 1857–1936
English physician
Born in London, he was educated at Oxford and St Bartholomew's Hospital, London, where he later did important work on arthritis, on an inherited metabolic disorder called alkaptonuria, and on several other rare hereditary conditions including albinism, cystinuria and pentosuria. His work was an early application of the new Mendelian genetics in the study of human disease, and in *The Inborn Factors in Disease* (1931) he developed his ideas of biochemical individuality. During World War I, he served in Malta as a colonel in the Royal Army Medical Corps, where he developed an interest in classical archaeology. A pioneer of clinical investigation, he succeeded Sir William Osler as Regius Professor of Medicine at Oxford in 1920. 📖 Alexander G Bearn, *Archibald Garrod and the Individuality of Man* (1993)

Garrod, Dorothy Annie Elizabeth 1892–1968
English archaeologist

Born in London, the daughter of Sir **Archibald Garrod**, she studied at Newnham College, Cambridge, directed expeditions to Kurdistan (1928) and Palestine (1929–34), and took part in the excavations in the Lebanon (1958–64). An expert on the Palaeolithic or Old Stone Age, in 1939 she became the first woman to hold a professorial chair at Cambridge.

Garscadden, Kathleen 1897–1991
Scottish broadcaster
Born in Glasgow, she was educated there at Hutchesons' Girls' Grammar School. Her career in broadcasting began when she acted as an all-round announcer, pianist and singer on her father's private broadcasting station. When this was bought by Lord **Reith** she joined the British Broadcasting Company (later Corporation) as a programme assistant (1923), working mainly on vocal concerts and the *Woman's Hour* series. Involved in the world's earliest experiments in broadcasting to schools, she started to run the early *Children's Hour*. She worked as a presenter, broadcaster, programme organizer and producer throughout the 42-year life of *Children's Hour*, and during World War II was responsible for organizing the broadcasting link between Scottish families and their evacuated children.

Garshin, Vsevolod Mikhailovich 1855–88
Russian writer
Born in Bachmut, he served in the Turkish War, and was wounded and invalided home in 1878. His story about a wounded soldier, *Chetyre Dnya* (1877, Eng trans *Four Days*, 1912), was a huge success. His work, which is narrow but emotionally intense, was greatly influenced by **Leo Tolstoy**, but without his breadth. His other stories include *Krasnyi Tsvetok* (1883, 'The Red Flower'), which is set in a lunatic asylum, and *Signal* (Eng Trans 1912, 'The Signal'). He suffered from depression, and eventually committed suicide. ☐ N Byelyaev, *Garshin* (1938)

Garson, Greer 1903–96
British actress
Born in County Down, Northern Ireland, and educated at the University of London, she worked in an advertising agency and participated in amateur dramatics before making her professional stage debut in 1932 with the Birmingham Repertory Company. In 1934 she moved to London's West End and was seen by Hollywood mogul **Louis B Mayer** in *Old Music* (1938). He signed her to a contract at MGM, and she made her film debut as Mrs Chipping in *Goodbye Mr Chips* (1939). She won a Best Actress Academy Award for her role as the English matriarch in *Mrs Miniver* (1942) and generally portrayed wholesome, independent women in romantic dramas like *Random Harvest* (1942), *Mrs Parkinton* (1944) and *That Forsyte Woman* (1949). She played **Eleanor Roosevelt** in *Sunrise at Campobello* (1960) and made her last film appearance in *The Happiest Millionaire* (1967). Her later stage work included *Auntie Mame* (1958) on Broadway, and she appeared on television as Aunt March in *Little Women* (1978).

Garstin, Sir William Edmund 1849–1925
English engineer
Born in India, he was educated at Cheltenham and King's College London, then became an official in the Indian Public Works Department (1872). Transferred to Egypt in 1885, he was responsible for the plans and building of the Aswan Dam and the barrages of Asyut and Esna, compiled two valuable reports on the hydrography of the Upper Nile, initiated the geological survey of Egypt (1896) and erected the new buildings of the National Museum of Egyptian Antiquities (1902).

Garvey, Marcus Moziah Aurelius 1887–1940
African-American leader and advocate of black nationalism
Born in St Ann's Bay, Jamaica, he founded the Universal Negro Improvement Association (UNIA) in 1914 to foster worldwide black unity and pride and moved its headquarters from Jamaica to New York City two years later. Rejecting integration, he called for a 'back to Africa' movement, in which people of African descent from the USA and elsewhere would settle in Liberia and build a modern black state. Through his stirring oratory and his newspaper *Negro World* he became the most influential African-American leader of the early 1920s, but in 1924 the Liberian government rejected his plans for resettlement, fearing that he intended to rule the country. After the collapse of his Black Star Steamship Line, which had been financed by the sale of stock to UNIA members, he was convicted of mail fraud (1925) and deported to Jamaica (1927). He eventually died in obscurity in London.

Garvin, James Louis 1868–1947
English journalist
He was born in Birmingham, and after a spell as leader-writer for the *Daily Telegraph*, he became editor of the *Observer* (1908–42). He also edited the 14th edition of the *Encyclopaedia Britannica*, and wrote a biography of **Joseph Chamberlain** (1932–34).

Gascoigne, George c.1525–1577
English poet and dramatist
Born in Cardington, Bedfordshire, he studied at Trinity College, Cambridge, entered Gray's Inn, wrote poems, and sat in parliament for Bedford (1557–59), but was disinherited for his extravagance. He married **Nicholas Breton's** widowed mother (to improve his finances), but, still persecuted by creditors, served in Holland under the Prince of Orange (**William I, the Silent**) from 1573 to 1575. He collected and published his poems, and translated in prose and verse, from Greek, Latin and Italian. *The Complaynt of Phylomene*, a verse narrative in the style of **Ovid**, was begun in 1563. *The Supposes* is from *I Suppositi* of **Ludovico Ariosto**, *Jocasta* (1566, with Francis Kinwelmersh) is practically a translation from Dolce's *Giocasta*, and *The Glasse of Government* (1575) is an original comedy. He also wrote *The Steele Glas*, the earliest blank verse satire, and *Certayne Notes of Instruction on Making of Verse* (1575), the first significant English essay on the subject. ☐ L T Prouty, *George Gascoigne, Elizabethan Courtier, Soldier and Poet* (1942)

Gascoigne, Paul John, *known as* Gazza 1967–
English footballer
Born in Gateshead, Tyne and Wear, an unpredictable, at times explosive, midfielder, he was voted England's Young Player of the Year in 1988 while still with his first club, Newcastle. Transferred to Tottenham that same year for a then record sum of £2 million, he soon established himself as the creative heart of the English international team. His performances during the 1990 World Cup in Italy brought him to the attention of the Roman club Lazio, for whom he eventually signed for £5.5 million in June 1992, after an injury sustained in the 1991 FA Cup Final had delayed the move. In 1995 he moved again from Lazio to Glasgow Rangers.

Gaskell, Mrs Elizabeth Cleghorn, *née* Stevenson 1810–65
English novelist
She was born in Cheyne Row, Chelsea, London. Her father was successively a teacher, preacher, farmer, boarding-house keeper, writer and keeper of the records to the Treasury, and she was brought up by an aunt in Knutsford—the Cranford of her stories. In 1832 she married William Gaskell (1805–84), a Unitarian minister in Manchester. There she studied working men and women, and made important contributions to what came to

be known as the 'Condition of England' novel. *Mary Barton* was published anonymously in 1848, followed by *The Moorland Cottage* (1850), *Cranford* (1853), *Ruth* (1853), *North and South* (1855), *Round the Sofa* (1859), *Right at Last* (1860), *Sylvia's Lovers* (1863), *Cousin Phillis* (1865) and *Wives and Daughters* (1865). She also wrote *The Life of Charlotte Brontë* (1857). ▣ M Allott, *Elizabeth Gaskell* (1960)

Gaskell, Walter Holbrook 1847–1914
English physiologist

He was born in Naples, Italy, and studied physiology at Cambridge, where he came under the influence of Sir Michael Foster. He studied with Karl Ludwig at Leipzig University and returned to Cambridge in 1875. His initial research topic identified by physiological experimentation the nerves which control dilation of the blood vessels, and in the 1880s he turned his attention to the question of the heartbeat. His work provided convincing evidence that the muscles of the heart exhibited inherent rhythmicity, independent of external influences, which supported the 'myogenic' theory of the heart's action. He extensively examined the autonomic nervous system, which his detailed physiological work revealed to consist of two major complementary branches, the sympathetic and the parasympathetic systems. As a result of these studies, Gaskell devoted himself almost completely to the problem of vertebrate evolution for the rest of his life.

Gasperi, Alcide de See De Gasperi, Alcide

Gass, William H(oward) 1924–
US novelist

He was born in Fargo, North Dakota, and educated at Ohio Wesleyan University, Delaware, and Cornell University. His novels are *Omensetter's Luck* (1966) and *Willie Masters' Lonesome Wife* (1971), an essay-novella, and his stories are collected as *In the Heart of the Heart of the Country* (1968). A philosopher and literary critic as well as novelist, he is linked with the Symbolists, New Critics and the Structuralists. His aesthetic theories are set out in *Fictions and the Figures of Life* (1970) and in subsequent years he engaged in public debate with fellow novelist John Champlin Gardner, Jnr (1933–82), a defender of 'moral fiction'. His massive autobiographical novel, *The Tunnel* (1995), was in progress for more than 20 years. ▣ A Saltzman, *The Fiction of William Gass: The Consolations of Language* (1986)

Gassendi or Gassend, Pierre 1592–1655
French philosopher and scientist

Born in Champtercier, Provence, he was ordained a priest in 1616, and became Professor of Philosophy at Aix University in 1617 and Professor of Mathematics at the Collège Royal in Paris in 1645. He was a strong advocate of the experimental approach to science and tried to reconcile an atomic theory of matter with Christian doctrine. He may be best known as an early critic of Descartes, but he also wrote on Epicurus, Tycho Brahe and Copernicus. His other works include *Exercitationes Paradoxicae adversus Aristoteleos* (1624), *Institutio Astronomica* (1647) and the *Syntagma Philosophicum* ('Philosophical Treatise', published posthumously in 1658).

Gasser, Herbert Spencer 1888–1963
US physiologist and Nobel Prize winner

Born in Plattville, Wisconsin, he graduated in medicine from Johns Hopkins University in 1915, and moved in 1916 to the department of physiology at Washington University in St Louis, to rejoin Joseph Erlanger, an instructor from his student years, thus beginning a fruitful collaboration in neurophysiology. Gasser and Erlanger used powerful new electrical equipment to dissect and analyse the nature and function of the nerve fibres, sharing the Nobel Prize for physiology or medicine in 1944. In 1931 Gasser moved to Cornell University as Professor of

Pharmacology, and in 1935 he was appointed director of the Rockefeller Institute for Medical Research in New York. His personal research continued into nerve trunks and nerve fibres, having an important bearing on understanding the physiology of sensation.

Gasset, José Ortega y See Ortega y Gasset, José

Gates, Bill (William Henry) 1955–
US computer scientist and businessman

He was born in Seattle, Washington, and attended Harvard but left without graduating. In 1975, at the age of 19, he founded Microsoft Corporation with Paul Allen, and in 1980 they licensed a computer operating system to International Business Machines (IBM) for use in the fledgling personal computer industry. This system (MS-DOS) and their applications software have been phenomenally successful, updated versions of which (such as Windows 95) have allowed Gates to maintain its PC hegemony. He has made aggressive attempts to expand into new markets, such as his 1995 purchase of the Bettmann Archives to enable the transformation of historical photographs into digital images for use on-line and his effort in 1996 to win a large stake in the Internet market. Gates became a billionaire by 1986 and Microsoft grew into one of the world's largest producers of microcomputer software. ▣ James Wallace and Jim Erikson, *Overdrive* (1997)

Gates, Henry Louis, Jnr 1950–
US historian

Born in Keyser, West Virginia, he studied history at Yale and received a PhD from Cambridge. He won a Macarthur 'genius' award in 1981 and has held professorships at several US universities, including Harvard (1991–). Perhaps the most eminent African-American scholar since W E B Du Bois, he has written critical works on race and identity and brought to light neglected black fiction and poetry as well as autobiographical texts such as early slave narratives. His works include *The Signifying Monkey* (1988), *Loose Cannons* (1992), and *Colored People: A Memoir* (1994). His essays on black life and culture are published regularly in the *New Yorker*.

Gates, Horatio 1728–1806
American Revolutionary general

Born in Maldon, England, he entered the English army, served in America under Edward Braddock, escaped from the disaster of the Duquesne expedition (1755) and, on the peace of 1763, purchased an estate in Virginia. In the American Revolution (1775–83) he sided with his adoptive country, and in 1775 was made adjutant-general, and in 1776 commander of the army which had just retreated from Canada. In August 1777 he commanded the northern department, and compelled the surrender of the British army under John Burgoyne at Saratoga in October. This success gained him a great reputation, and he sought to supplant George Washington, the Commander-in-Chief. In 1780 he commanded the army of the South, but was routed by Charles Cornwallis near Camden, South Carolina. He retired to Virginia until 1790, emancipated his slaves and settled in New York, where he died. ▣ Paul D Nelson, *Horatio Gates* (1976)

Gatling, Richard Jordan 1818–1903
US inventor

He was born in Money's Neck, North Carolina. He studied medicine but never practised, and is known for his invention (1861–62) of the rapid-fire 'Gatling gun', a revolving battery gun with 10 parallel barrels, firing 1,200 shots a minute.

Gatting, Mike (Michael William) 1957–
English cricketer

Born in Kingsbury, Middlesex, he made his mark as a forceful batsman with Middlesex; at the beginning of the 1988 season he had played 58 Tests and made nine Test hundreds, including 241 against India at Madras in the tour of 1984–85. As captain, he was involved in a dispute with a Pakistan umpire during the 1987–88 tour of that country and lost the captaincy after the first Test against the West Indies in England in 1988. He was banned from Test competitions for five years in 1990 after leading a rebel tour to South Africa, but the ban was lifted in 1992 and he joined the tour to India that year, which was captained by Graham Gooch.

Gaudí (i Cornet), Antoni 1852–1926
Spanish architect
Born in Riudoms, Catalonia, he was apprenticed to a blacksmith, then studied architecture at the Escuela Superior de Arquitectura in Barcelona. He became the leading exponent of Catalan Modernism (a branch of the Art Nouveau movement in architecture) inspired by a nationalistic search for a romantic medieval past. Strikingly original and ingenious, he designed a number of highly individualistic and unconventional buildings, such as the Palacio Güell (1886–89) and Parque Güell (1900–14) for his chief patron, Don Basilio Güell; the Casa Batlló (1904–17) and the Casa Milá (1905–09). His most celebrated work, the ornate church of the Sagrada Familia in Barcelona, occupied him from 1884 until his death. It is still under construction. ◻ César Martinell, *Gaudi: His Life, His Theories, His Work* (1975)

Gaudier-Brzeska, Henri, *originally* Henri Gaudier 1891–1915
French sculptor
He was born in St Jean de Braye, near Orleans. In Paris (1910) he met the Polish artist Sophie Brzeska and from 1911 they both used the hyphenated name. In 1911 they settled in London and met leading members of the British avant-garde. He became a founder member of the London Group (incorporating groups of younger artists) in 1913, and the following year signed the Vorticist Manifesto. He drew inspiration from African tribal art, but rapidly developed a personal abstract style exemplified in both carvings and drawings, for example *Red Stone Figure* (1913, Tate, London), *Crouching Figure* (1913–14, Minneapolis), and *Two Men With a Bowl* (1914, bronze, National Museum of Wales, Cardiff). He was killed in action at Neuville-Saint-Vaast.

Gaudron, Mary Genevieve 1943–
Australian lawyer
She was born in Moree, New South Wales, and trained at Sydney University, where she won the law medal. She was the youngest person ever to be appointed a federal judge when she became deputy president of the Arbitration Commission (1975–80), as well as the youngest ever Solicitor-General for New South Wales (1981–87). In 1987 she became a judge in the High Court of Australia in Canberra, the first woman to reach that position, and was appointed justice in 1991.

Gauguin, Paul See panel p718

Gaulle, Charles de See de Gaulle, Charles
(panel)

Gaultier, Jean-Paul 1952–
French fashion designer
He was born in Paris. Since launching his first collection in 1978 with a Japanese colleague, he has earned international renown for his fashions for both women and men. He also designs for ballet and for film (for example *The Cook, The Thief, His Wife and Her Lover*, 1989), has co-released a record, *How to Do That* (1989), and launched his own perfume in 1993.

Gaumont, Léon Ernest 1864–1946
French cinema inventor
He synchronized a projected film with a phonograph in 1901 and was responsible for the first talking pictures, demonstrated at the Académie des Sciences in Paris in 1910, and at the Royal Institute, London, in 1912. Also in 1912, he introduced an early form of coloured cinema-film, using a three-colour separation method with special lenses and projectors.

Gaunt, John of See John of Gaunt

Gauss, (Johann) Carl Friedrich 1777–1855
German mathematician, astronomer and physicist
Born in Brunswick to poor parents, he came to the notice of the Duke of Brunswick who paid for his education at the Collegium Carolinum, Brunswick, and the University of Göttingen. A notebook kept in Latin by him as a youth and discovered in 1898 showed that, from the age of 15, he had conjectured and often proved many remarkable results, including the prime number theorem. In 1796 he announced that he had found a ruler and compass construction for the 17-sided polygon, and in 1801 published his *Disquisitiones arithmeticae*, containing wholly new advances in number theory. The same year he was the first to rediscover the asteroid Ceres found by Giuseppe Piazzi in 1800 and since lost behind the Sun. In 1807 he became director of Göttingen Observatory, while studying celestial mechanics (on which he published a treatise in 1809), and statistics, where he was the first to use the method of least squares. From 1818 to 1825 he directed the geodetic survey of Hanover, and this and his astronomical work involved him in much heavy routine calculation, leading to his study of the theory of errors of observation. He also worked on pure mathematics, including differential equations, the hypergeometric function, the curvature of surfaces, four different proofs of the fundamental theorem of algebra, six of quadratic reciprocity and much else in number theory. In physics he studied the Earth's magnetism and developed the magnetometer in conjunction with Wilhelm Eduard Weber, and gave a mathematical theory of the optical systems of lenses. Manuscripts unpublished until long after his death show that he had made many other discoveries, including the theory of elliptic functions that had been published independently by Niels Henrik Abel and Carl Gustav Jacobi, and had come to accept the possibility of a non-Euclidean geometry of space, first published by János Bolyai and Nikolai Lobachevski in the 1820s. ◻ G Waldo Duddington, *Carl Friedrich Gauss: Titan of Science* (1955)

Gautama, *also known as* Gotama 1st century AD
Indian philosopher
Born in Bihar, he founded *Nyaya*, one of the six classical systems of Hindu philosophy. His *Nyaya Sutras* are principally concerned with ways of knowing and of reaching valid logical conclusions. They are thought to have been written in the 1st century AD, though tradition maintains Gautama lived in the 3rd century BC. Their claim that one can obtain real knowledge of the external world was disputed by Śriharsha and the *Navya-nyaya* school founded by Gangeśa.

Gautier, Hubert 1660–1737
French civil engineer
Born in Nimes, he was one of the first to recognize the importance of applying scientific principles to the design and execution of engineering works. After nearly 30 years as chief government engineer of the province of Languedoc, he was appointed inspector of the newly-created Corps des Ponts et Chaussées in 1716, responsible for virtually all public works throughout France. At the time he had just published the two classic textbooks, the *Traité des chemins* (1715, Eng trans *Treatise on the Constructions of*

Gauguin, (Eugène Henri) Paul 1848–1903
French Post-Impressionist painter

Gauguin was born in Paris, the son of a journalist and a half-Peruvian Creole mother. He went to sea at the age of 17, but settled down in Paris in 1871 and became a successful stockbroker with a fondness for painting and for collecting Impressionist paintings. By 1883 he had already exhibited his own work with the help of **Camille Pissarro** and determined to devote himself entirely to art. He left his Danish wife and five children, and went to Pont Aven, Brittany, where he became the leader of a group of painters and met the painter and theorist **Émile Bernard**.

He travelled to Martinique (1887–88), and gradually evolved his own style, *synthesism*, in accordance with his hatred of civilization and identification with the emotional directness of primitive peoples. He moved more permanently to Tahiti in 1891–1901, and from there to the Marquesas Islands. His output developed markedly from the earlier Brittany seascapes—the *Still Life with Three Puppies* (1888, Museum of Modern Art, New York), the stained-glass effects of *The Vision after the Sermon* (1888, National Gallery, Edinburgh) with its echoes of Romanesque, Japanese and Breton folk art, to the tapestry-like canvases, painted in purples, greens, dark-reds and browns, of native subjects on Tahiti and at Dominiha on the Marquesas Islands, such as *No Te Aha*

De Riri, Why are you angry? (1896, Chicago), and *Faa Iheihe, decorated with ornaments* (1898, Tate, London), which echoes his great allegorical painting dashed off prior to an unsuccessful suicide attempt, *D'où venons-nous? Que sommes-nous? Où allons-nous?* ('Whence do we come? What are we? Where are we going?' 1898, Boston).

Gauguin also excelled in wood carvings of pagan idols and wrote an autobiographical novel, *Noa-Noa* (1894–1900). He is remembered not only because of the tragic choices he made, and as the subject of many popular novels (particularly **Somerset Maugham**'s *The Moon and Sixpence*, 1919), but because he directed attention to primitive art as a valid field of aesthetic exploration and consequently influenced almost every school of 20th-century art.

📖 B Thomson, *Gauguin* (1987).

'Some advice: do not paint too much after nature. Art is an abstraction; derive this abstraction from nature while dreaming before it, and think more of the creation which will result than of nature.' From a letter to Emile Schuffenecker (1888).

Roads in France) and the *Traité des Ponts* (1716, Eng trans *Treatise on Bridges*), in which he summarized ancient and contemporary engineering practice, emphasizing the importance of strict supervision, careful testing of materials, and observance of the principles of structural mechanics. One of the most important of his recommendations was to reduce the width of bridge piers, in order to avoid excessive obstruction of waterways and the creation of dangerously high water levels in times of flood.

Gautier, Théophile 1811–72
French poet and novelist

Born in Tarbes, Gascony, he turned from painting to literature, and became at first an extreme Romantic. In 1830 he published his first long poem, *Albertus*, and in 1832 the *Comédie de la mort* ('The Comedy of Death'). His best remembered collection, *Émaux et camées* (1856, 'Enamels and Cameos'), marked a turning away from Romanticism towards the Parnassian school of poetry. His celebrated novel, *Mademoiselle de Maupin*, with its defiant preface, appeared in 1835. He wrote many other novels, short stories, theatrical criticisms, articles on the Salon, and *Ménagerie intime* (1869), a kind of informal autobiography. His daughter Judith Gautier (1845–1917) wrote novels, plays, poems and translations. 📖 R Grant, *Théophile Gautier* (1975)

Gavaskar, Sunil Manohar, *nicknamed* the Little Master 1949–
Indian cricketer

Born in Bombay and educated at St Xavier's College and Bombay University, he has become the most prolific run-scorer in Test cricket history. The perfection of his style as well as his short stature earned him his nickname. He has played in 125 Test matches for India since 1971, and scored 10,122 runs, including 34 test centuries. He holds the world record for scoring two separate hundreds in a Test, three times (against the West Indies, 1970–71; Pakistan 1978–79; West Indies 1978–79), as well as the highest score by an Indian batsman in Test cricket: 236 not out against the West Indies at Madras (1983–84).

Gawain Poet, The fl.c.1370
Anonymous English poet

He is the presumed author of *Cleanness*, *Patience*, *Pearl* and *Sir Gawain and the Green Knight*, the Arthurian masterpiece after which he is named. All four poems, written in the same north-of-England dialect, are found together in a single surviving manuscript. Each of the shorter poems has an explicitly religious theme: *Cleanness* discusses spiritual purity with reference to several biblical episodes, *Patience* is the retold tale of **Jonah** and the whale, and *Pearl* is a dream-poem of the afterlife. *Gawain* itself is a richer, longer, less overtly didactic work: the story of one of King **Arthur**'s knights and a threatening stranger who comes to Camelot, it can be read as a straightforward adventure or as a quest for spiritual knowledge. Either way it is one of the most remarkable works in the history of English poetry.

Gay, John 1685–1732
English poet

Born in Barnstaple, Devon, he was educated at Barnstaple Grammar School, and apprenticed to a silk mercer in London, but soon returned home to write. In 1708 he published his first poem, *Wine*, and in 1711 a pamphlet on the *Present State of Wit*. Appointed secretary to the Duchess of Monmouth (1712), in 1713 he dedicated to **Pope** the georgic *Rural Sports*. In 1714 he published *The Fan* and *The Shepherd's Week*, and accompanied Lord Clarendon, envoy to Hanover, as secretary. With Pope and **John Arbuthnot**, he wrote the play *Three Hours after Marriage* (1717), and in 1727 he produced the first series of his popular *Fables*. His greatest success was *The Beggar's Opera* (1728), set to music by **Johann Pepusch**, the outcome of a suggestion made by **Jonathan Swift** in 1716. Running for 62 performances, it attained unprecedented popularity. He wrote another opera, *Achilles* (produced posthumously in 1733). He was buried in Westminster Abbey, London. 📖 P M Sparks, *John Gay* (1965)

Gaye, Marvin 1939–84
US soul singer

Born in Washington DC, the son of a clergyman, he started singing and playing the organ in church and at 15 joined the 'doo-wop' group, The Rainbows. Moving to Detroit, he signed a recording contract with the Tamla/Motown company in 1961 after the company's founder **Berry Gordy, Jnr**, had heard him singing at an informal party. Most of his early recordings were in the 'beat ballad' idiom although there were notable exceptions including the dance-oriented 'Hitch Hike', and the 12-bar blues of 'Can I Get A Witness'.'I Heard It Through The Grapevine' (1968) was his last standard Motown recording and from 1970, despite arguments with the company management, he adopted a more independent attitude towards recording. *What's Going On* (1971) was a concept album that showed a fluidity and intelligence far removed from his previous teen ballad hits. Subsequent albums included *Here My Dear* (1979), *In Our Lifetime* (1981) and *Midnight Love* (1982). He was killed by a gunshot during a quarrel with his father.

Gay-Lussac, Joseph Louis 1778–1850
French chemist and physicist
Born in Saint-Léonard, Haute Vienne, he was educated at the École Polytechnique and the École des Ponts et Chaussées. He became assistant to Claude Louis Berthollet in 1800 and subsequently held various posts, including Professor of Chemistry at the École Polytechnique (from 1810), Professor of Physics at the Sorbonne (1808–32), Professor of Chemistry at the National Museum of Natural History (from 1832), superintendent of the government gunpowder factory (from 1818) and chief assayer to the Mint (from 1829). He became an Academician (1806), member of the Chamber of Deputies (1831) and member of the Upper House (1839). He was elected an honorary Fellow of the Chemical Society in 1849. His earliest research work was on the expansion of gases with temperature increases, and he discovered independently the law which in Great Britain is commonly known as Charles's law. In 1804 he made balloon ascents in association with Jean Baptiste Biot to make magnetic and atmospheric observations, and he travelled with Baron Alexander von Humboldt (1805–06), making measurements of terrestrial magnetism. In 1808 he published his important law of gas volumes. This was based on work which he had begun with Humboldt in 1805. From around 1808 Gay-Lussac's work became more purely chemical, and much of it was done in collaboration with Louis Jacques Thénard. Their work included the isolation and investigation of sodium, potassium, boron and silicon, extensive studies of the halogens (involving controversy with Sir Humphry Davy), and the improvement of methods of organic analysis. His last great pure research was on prussic acid and cyanogen and their derivatives. During the later part of his career, he did much work as a technical adviser to industry. ☐ Maurice Crosland, *Gay-Lussac, Scientist and Bourgeois* (1978)

Gaynor, Janet, *originally* Laura Gainor 1906–84
US actress
Born in Philadelphia, Pennsylvania, she was educated in San Fransisco then moved to Los Angeles, hoping to break into the film industry, and working as a bookkeeper and usherette before securing work as an extra. After various small comedy roles, she made her first notable appearance in *The Johnstown Flood* (1926). She then went on to win the first ever Best Actress Academy Award for a trio of performances in *Sunrise* (1927), *Seventh Heaven* (1927) and *Street Angel* (1928). She became a major star in the 1930s, and her many movies include *State Fair* (1933) and *A Star Is Born* (1937). She retired in 1938, making a one-off return to the screen in *Bernadine* (1957). She occasionally performed on television and the stage, and her later theatre work included *Harold and Maude* (1980) on Broadway.

Gayoom, Maumoon Abdul 1937–
Maldivian politician
Educated at the Al-Azhar ur Cairo, he lectured in Islamic studies at the American University, Cairo (1967–69) and Nigeria University (1969–71). He returned to the Maldives to head the government shipping (1972–73)

and telephone (1974) departments, before being appointed special Under-Secretary to Prime Minister Ahmed Zaki in 1974. Between 1975 and 1978 he held a variety of diplomatic and ministerial posts, before succeeding Ibrahim Nasir as Executive President and Minister of Defence in 1978. He was re-elected President in 1983 and 1988. Soon after the 1988 re-election a coup led by the exiled businessman Abdullah Luthufi was foiled by Indian paratroops. Gayoom then continued his programme of rural development and non-alignment.

Gazza See Gascoigne, Paul John

Gdlyan, Telman Khorenovich 1940–
Soviet lawyer
Born of Armenian extraction, with Nikolai Ivanov he helped to expose misdemeanours in Uzbekistan involving the late Leonid Brezhnev's son-in-law. He then proceeded to attack other figures such as Yegor Ligachev but encountered hostility even among Mikhail Gorbachev's supporters. He and Ivanov were very popular with the public, and they certainly undermined Communist credibility.

Geber 14th century
Spanish alchemist
Nothing is known about him except his name as the author of books on chemical and alchemical theory and practice. He took the name 'Geber' (Latin for 'Jabir') from Abu Musa Jabir ibn Hayyan, a famous Islamic alchemist and physician of the 8th century. It was through Geber's works that the discoveries of the early Arab chemists, along with many basic laboratory techniques, were relayed to Europe. His works, written in Latin, were translated into several languages and continued to be influential until the 16th century. Because of their clarity, and in many respects their accuracy, they helped to make alchemy more respectable.

Geddes, Jenny c.1600–c.1660
Scottish vegetable-seller
She is traditionally reputed to have started the riots in St Giles' Cathedral, Edinburgh, when Archbishop Laud's prayer book was introduced on Sunday, 23 July 1637. According to the popular legend she threw her folding stool at Bishop Lindsay, shouting: 'Thou false thief, dost thou say mass at my lug?' There is no historical evidence of this. Sydserf in 1661 mentions 'the immortal Jenet Geddes' as having burned 'her leather chair of state' in a Restoration bonfire, and the story appears in full detail in Edward Phillips's continuation of Sir Richard Baker's *Chronicle* (1660).

Geddes, Norman Bel 1893–1958
US designer and architect
Born in Adrian, Michigan, he first won acclaim for his theatrical designs in New York City, discarding ornamentation in favour of simple, functional sets. He was known for popularizing the concept of 'streamlining', and in the 1930s his sleek, rounded designs for radios and refrigerators as well as for skyscrapers were highly influential.

Geddes, Sir Patrick 1854–1932
Scottish biologist, sociologist and pioneer of town planning
Born in Ballater, Aberdeenshire, he was educated at Perth Academy and University College London (under T H Huxley), and became Professor of Botany at Dundee (1889–1914). Taking the theory of evolution as a basis for ethics, history and sociology, he wrote *The Evolution of Sex* (1889). In 1892 he established the 'world's first sociological laboratory' in the Outlook Tower on Castlehill, Edinburgh, to demonstrate regional differentiation. He also wrote *City Development* (1904) and *Cities in Evolution*

(1915), in which he coined the terms 'megalopolis' and 'kakatopia'. After World War I he was Professor of Civics and Sociology at Bombay University (1920–23), and in 1924 moved to France and established an unofficial 'Scots College' at Montpellier.

Geer, Gerhard Jacob de, Baron 1858–1943
Swedish Quaternary geologist

Born in Stockholm, the son of Louis Gerhard de Geer, he was educated at Uppsala. He later worked as Professor of Geology there (1897–1924), before founding the Geochronological Institute of the University of Stockholm, serving as its first director from 1924. He was an MP from 1900 to 1905. He devised a novel and valuable method for dating deposits by comparing sequences of varves (the annual deposits of sediment under glacial meltwater). He was able to decipher an annual chronology reaching back 15,000 years from the present day. He successfully correlated the Swedish varve sequence with others from elsewhere, demonstrating global climatic events and greatly advancing knowledge of the last Ice Age. The method was eventually enhanced by the use of increasingly sophisticated radioisotope methods.

Geer, Louis Gerhard de 1818–96
Swedish politician

In 1858 he was appointed Minister of Justice, a post which made him in effect Prime Minister, and which he held until 1870. He was largely responsible for the replacement in 1866 of the Diet of four estates (nobles, clergy, burghers and peasants) with a parliament of two houses, one indirectly elected through county councils and one directly elected on a narrow franchise. He was appointed Prime Minister (the title being then accepted) in 1876, but resigned four years later after defeat in parliament.

Geertgen Tot Sint Jans c.1460–c.1490
Dutch painter

He was born in Leyden. Little is known about his life. His name means 'little Gerard of the Brethren of St John' and he worked for this religious order in Haarlem. Only about 15 paintings are now attributed to him. These works, mostly fragments of larger altarpieces, and all religious in subject, are characterized by strong colours, convincing landscape and highly individual figures.

Geertz, Clifford James 1926–
US cultural anthropologist

Born in San Francisco, he studied at Antioch College and Harvard, and was Professor of Anthropology at the University of California (1958–60) and at Chicago (1960–70), before becoming Professor of Social Science at Princeton's Institute of Advanced Study (1970). He carried out fieldwork in Java (1952–54) and Bali (1957–58), which resulted in a series of works on environment and economy, social change and religion. These include *The Religion of Java* (1960), *Agricultural Involution* (1963), and *Person, Time and Conflict in Bali* (1966). In the 1960s and 1970s he made several field trips to Morocco, from which he developed a comparative approach to religion, as in *Islam Observed* (1968), and to processes of social change. His eloquent theoretical essays on topics ranging from art and ideology to politics and nationalism, collected in *The Interpretation of Cultures* (1973) and *Local Knowledge* (1983) were particularly influential. In these he advocates an interpretative stance, in which cultures are compared to literary texts. Other publications include *Works and Lives: The Anthropologist as Author* (1988), for which he won the National Book Critics Circle award for criticism, and *After the Fact* (1995).

Gegenbaur, Karl 1826–1903
German comparative anatomist

Born in Würzburg, he studied medicine at the university there. He became professor at Jena University in 1856 and at Heidelberg University in 1873. He won a towering contemporary reputation for his knowledge of vertebrate musculature and expertise in comparative anatomy and morphology. On this basis he became one of the leading German advocates of evolutionary theory. His chief work, *Comparative Anatomy* (Eng trans 1878), threw much light on the evolution of the skull from his study of cartilaginous fishes.

Gehlen, Arnold 1904–76
German philosopher and sociologist

He was born in Leipzig. He is particularly associated with 'philosophical anthropology', which tried to connect coherently biological, cultural and philosophical aspects of human nature. His most important works are *Der Mensch: seine Natur und seine Stellung in der Welt* (1940, 'The Nature of Man and His Place in the World'), *Urmensch und Spätkultur* (1956, 'Primeval Man and Modern Culture'), *Die Seele in technischen Zeitalter* (1960, 'The Soul in the Age of Technology') and *Moral und Hypermoral* (1965, 'Morals and Hypermorals').

Ge Hong (Ko Hung) c.280–340AD
Chinese alchemist

Born near Nanjing (Nanking), he was educated in the literary and philosophical traditions of his country, and became a successful and stern military commander. His most famous book, *Bao-pu zi* ('He Who Holds to Simplicity'), is the result of his travels and study with several teachers. It contains accounts of methods of producing solutions of minerals (including cinnabar and gold) in order to make immortality elixirs. He also describes the apparent production of gold from other metals. Some of his claims can be understood in terms of modern chemistry.

Gehrig, Lou (Henry Louis), *nicknamed* the Iron Horse 1903–41
US baseball player

Born in New York City, he earned his nickname through his endurance. He played a record number of 2,130 consecutive major league games for the New York Yankees (1925–39), and was voted Most Valuable Player (MVP) four times (1927, 1931, 1934, 1936). His career was cut short by motor neurone disease. In 1939 he was elected to the National Baseball Hall of Fame. The story of his life was told in the film *Pride of the Yankees* (1942). 📖 R Robinson, *Iron Horse* (1990)

Gehring, Walter Jacob 1939–
Swiss geneticist

Born in Zurich, he was educated at the universities of Zurich and Yale, where he was associate Professor of Anatomy and Molecular Biophysics from 1969 to 1972. Since 1972 he has been Professor of Genetics and Developmental Biology at the University of Basle. His career has mainly been concerned with the genetics of the fruit fly, in the mid-1980s discovering the short DNA sequence, called the homeobox, which controls genetic mutation and development in the insect. It was later found that similar control sequences occur in mammals, thus encouraging new lines of research to understand the molecular biology of such major developmental pathways.

Gehry, Frank 1929–
US–Canadian architect

Born in Toronto, Canada, he settled in Los Angeles with his family in 1947, and after studying architecture at the University of Southern California (1954), he studied city planning at the Harvard Graduate School of Design. He established his own firm, Frank O Gehry and Associates, in Los Angeles in 1962, and he soon became known for his playful, almost surreal designs using inexpensive materials such as chain-link fencing, plywood and raw concrete. Despite his irreverent temperament and his penchant for treating buildings as sculpture, he favours the abstraction of modernist architecture over the eclectic borrowings of post-modernism, and incorporates historical references into his work only when they are directly appropriate to their surroundings. Thus his recent ING Office Building (1996) in Prague is topped with twisting stainless-steel globes in homage to the onion-topped domes of that city. Other important works include the Los Angeles Children's Museum (1980), the California Aerospace Museum (1984) in Los Angeles, and the American Center (1994) in Paris.

Geibel, Emmanuel von 1815–84
German poet
Born in Lübeck, he studied at Bonn, and was tutor (1838–39) in Athens to the family of the Russian ambassador. He made many translations from Greek, Spanish and Italian authors, and with **Paul von Heyse** founded the Munich school of poetry, which emphasized harmony and form. He also wrote plays in classical form. ▣ C L Leimbach, *Emmanuel von Geibel. Des Dichters Leben und Werke* (1877)

Geiger, Hans Wilhelm 1882–1945
German physicist
Born in Neustadt-an-der-Haardt, he was educated at the University of Erlangen where he received his PhD in 1906. He then worked under **Ernest Rutherford** at Manchester (1906–12). With Rutherford, he devised a means of detecting alpha particles (1908), and subsequently showed that two α-particles are emitted in the radioactive decay of uranium. With J M Nuttall he demonstrated the linear relationship between the logarithm of the range of α-particles and the radioactive time constant of the emitting nucleus, now called the Geiger–Nuttall rule. In 1912 he became head of the Physikalisch Technische Reichsanstalt in Berlin, and in 1925 professor at Kiel University. There, he and Walther Müller made improvements to the particle counter, resulting in the modern form of the Geiger–Müller counter, which also detects electrons and ionizing radiation.

Geijer, Erik Gustav 1783–1877
Swedish poet and historian
Born in Ransäter, Värmland, he studied at Uppsala, and was appointed Professor of History there in 1817. A founder in 1811 of the Gothic Society and its journal, *Iduna*, in which he published much of his best poetry, he had a profound influence on both literature and historiography in Sweden, promoting a Romantic aesthetic. Among his works are *Impressions of England* (1809–10, Eng trans 1932) and a *History of the Swedish People* (1832–36), both of which are included in *Samlade Skrifter* (13 vols, 1849–82). He was also the first person to make a full Swedish translation of a **Shakespeare** play, *Macbeth* (1815). ▣ S Stolpe, *Geijer. En essay* (1947)

Geikie, Sir Archibald 1835–1924
Scottish geologist
Born in Edinburgh and educated at the university there, he was appointed to the Geological Survey in Scotland in 1855 and in 1867 he became its director. From 1871 to 1881 he was Professor of Geology at Edinburgh University. He subsequently became director-general of HM Geological Survey (from 1882) and also head of the Geological Museum of London. He undertook notable work on the Old Red Sandstone, volcanic geology and the scenery of Scotland, and did much to encourage microscopic petrography. He was elected FRS at the young age of 29 and knighted in 1907. His brother James Geikie (1839–1915)

was also an accomplished geologist and prehistorian who became Professor of Geology at Edinburgh University (1882–1914).

Geikie, Walter 1795–1837
Scottish printmaker and painter
Born in Edinburgh, he could neither hear nor speak and was taught to read and write by **Thomas Braidwood**. Best known for his scenes of everyday life, he was influenced by his contemporary **David Wilkie**, but unlike Wilkie, he remained in Edinburgh, and his topographical drawings of the city provide the most vivid image of life there at that time. Although he was a painter, his most notable work is a collection of etchings published posthumously under the title *Sketches of Scottish Life and Character*.

Geisel, Ernesto 1908–96
Brazilian general and dictator
He was born in Rio Grande do Sul. He became prominent in the administrations of both **Jânio da Silva Quadros** and **Humberto de Alencar Castelo Branco** during the 1960s, took part in the coup that overthrew **João Goulart** in 1964, and from 1969 to 1974 was director of Petroleo Brasileiro (Petrobras), helping the expansion of the country's oil industry. His ascendancy in 1973–74 was largely due to his brother Orlando's control of the military and saw the re-emergence of Golberi de Couto e Silva, nemesis of the hardliners who believed in an uncompromising dictatorship. While Geisel was President (1974–79), he and Golberi successfully masterminded a return to a regime in which the military acted in their traditional role as a moderating power. His support for the presidential nominee Tancredo Neves (1910–85) in early 1985 was decisive in persuading the army to acquiesce in a return to democratic civilian rule.

Geissler, Heinrich 1814–79
German inventor
Born in Saxony, he became a glass-blower and settled in Bonn in 1854. The 'Geissler tube', by which the passage of electricity through rarefied gases can be seen, and the 'Geissler mercury pump', are among his inventions.

Geitel, Hans Friedrich 1855–1923
German physicist
He was born in Brunswick, and published almost all his work with **Julius Elster**. They invented the first practical photoelectric cell, a photometer and a Tesla transformer. Geitel received honorary doctorates from the universities of Göttingen and Brunswick, and after his retirement he was made an honorary professor at Brunswick.

Gelasius I, St 5th century–6th century
African pope
Born in Africa, he was pope from AD492 to 496, and was one of the earliest bishops of Rome to assert the supremacy of the papal chair. He repressed Pelagianism, renewed the ban against the oriental patriarch, drove out the Manichaeans from Rome, and wrote against the Eutychians and Nestorians.

Gelasius II originally John of Gaeta
11th century–12th century
Italian pope
Born in Gaeta, Kingdom of Naples, he was a cardinal and chancellor under **Urban II** and Paschal II. On the death of the latter in 1118, he was chosen pope by the party hostile to the Emperor **Henry V**. Gelasius fled to Gaeta to escape the advancing imperialists, and excommunicated Henry and Gregory VIII, the antipope Henry had set up. Shortly afterwards he was able to return to Rome, but in the same autumn had to flee to France.

Geldof, Bob 1954–
Irish rock musician and philanthropist

Born in Dublin and educated at Black Rock College, he worked in Canada as a pop journalist then returned home in 1975 to form the successful rock group, the Boomtown Rats (1975–86). Moved by television pictures of famine-stricken Ethiopia, he established the pop charity 'Bandaid' trust in 1984. This raised £8 million for African famine-relief through the release of the record 'Do they know it's Christmas?'. In 1985, simultaneous 'Live Aid' charity concerts were held in London and Philadelphia, which, transmitted by satellite throughout the world, raised a further £48 million. Further charitable events followed and Geldof was awarded an honorary KBE in 1986, as well as a variety of international honours. In 1996 he was thrust into the eye of the media when he and his wife, Paula Yates, divorced.

Gelfand, Izrail Moiseyevich 1913–
Soviet mathematician

Born in Krasnye Okny, he studied in Moscow, and became professor at Moscow State University (1940–91). The leader of an important school of Soviet mathematicians, he has worked mainly in Banach algebras, the representation theory of Lie groups (important in quantum mechanics), and in generalized functions, used in solving the differential equations that arise in mathematical physics. In particular, his work has been used in symmetry theories for fundamental particles. Gelfand has also contributed to the life sciences through his mathematical studies of neurophysiology and cell biology.

Gellert, Christian Fürchtegott 1715–69
German poet and moralist

Born in Hainichen, Saxony, he was educated at Leipzig, and in 1751 became a professor there. He was a prolific writer of stories and fables, and two of his comedies, *Das Los in der Lotterie* (1746, 'The Lottery Ticket') and *Die kranke Frau* (1747, Eng trans *The Sick Wife*, 1928), were popular favourites. His moralistic novel *Leben der schwedischen Gräfin von G* (1747–48, Eng trans *The History of the Swedish Countess of G*, 1757) shows the influence of Samuel Richardson. 📖 L Spriegel, *Der Leipziger Goethe und Gellert* (1934)

Gellhorn, Martha Ellis 1908–98
US journalist and writer

Born in St Louis, Missouri, and educated at Bryn Mawr College, she became a foreign correspondent for *Collier's Weekly*, covering, among other things, the Spanish Civil War. She almost certainly saw more violent action than her first husband, Ernest Hemingway. Her interest in human conflict remained undimmed and she continued to report on wars in Java (1946), Vietnam (1966), the Middle East (1967) and Central America (1983–85). Her earlier reportage was collected in *The Face of War* (1959). Her novels include *What Mad Pursuit* (1934), *A Stricken Field* (1939), *Liana* (1943) and *The Wine of Astonishment* (1948). The short stories in *The Trouble I've Seen* (1936), *The Honeyed Peace* (1953), *Two by Two* (1958) and *The Weather in Africa* (1978) are marked by acute observation, and contain sympathy for the weak or oppressed and moral straightforwardness. 📖 *Travels with Myself and Another* (1978)

Gellius, Aulus c.123–c.165AD
Roman writer

Born probably in Rome, where he practised law, he studied philosophy in Athens, and there began to collect the material for *Noctes Atticae* ('Attic Nights'), a collection of dinner-table conversations on literature, history, law, antiquities and miscellaneous subjects. The value of *Noctes Atticae* is chiefly in the numerous quotations it gives from Greek and Roman books which would otherwise be completely unknown.

Gell-Mann, Murray 1929–
US theoretical physicist and Nobel Prize winner

Born in New York City, he went to Yale when he was only 15 years old, and graduated in 1948. He gained his PhD from the Massachusetts Institute of Technology (MIT), spent a year at the Institute of Advanced Studies in Princeton, then joined the Institute for Nuclear Studies at Chicago University, where he worked with Enrico Fermi. He became Professor of Theoretical Physics at the California Institute of Technology (Caltech) in 1956 then Robert Andrews Professor of Theoretical Physics (1967–93), now emeritus. When he was 24 he made a major contribution to the theory of elementary particles by introducing the concept of 'strangeness', a new quantum number which must be conserved in any so-called 'strong' nuclear interaction event. Gell-Mann and Yuval Ne'eman (independently) used 'strangeness' to group mesons, nucleons (neutrons and protons) and hyperons, and thus they were able to form predictions in the same way that Dmitri Mendeleyev had about chemical elements. The omega-minus particle was predicted by this theory and observed in 1964. Gell-Mann and George Zweig introduced the concept of quarks which have one-third integral charge and baryon number. (The name 'quark' is an invented word, associated with a line in James Joyce's *Finnegans Wake*.) Six quarks have been predicted, and five have so far been indirectly detected: the six are named as Up, Down, Strange, Charm, Bottom and Top. For this work he was awarded the Nobel Prize for physics in 1969. In 1994 he published *The Quark and the Jaguar*.

Gemayel, Amin 1942–
Lebanese politician

Son of Pierre Gemayel and brother of Bachir Gemayel, he trained as a lawyer. He supported Bachir in the 1975–76 civil war, and was his successor to the presidency in 1982. Politically more moderate, he initially proved no more successful in determining a peaceful settlement of the problems of Lebanese government. In 1988 his presidency came to an end and no obvious Christian successor, as required by the constitution, was apparent until the appointment of Rene Muawad and then Elias Hrawi in 1989. 📖 Matthew S Gordon, *The Gemayels* (1988)

Gemayel, Bashir 1947–82
Lebanese army officer and politician

He was the brother of Amin Gemayel and son of Pierre Gemayel. He joined the militia of his father's Phalangist Party at the age of 11, and was later appointed the party's political director in the Ashrefieh sector of East Beirut. He was an active leader of the Christian militia in the 1975–76 civil war, and led the military forces of East Beirut. His evident distancing of his party from Israeli support, and wish to expel all foreign influence from Lebanese affairs, effected his election as President in 1982. Having twice escaped assassination, he was killed in a bomb explosion while still President-Elect. 📖 Matthew S Gordon, *The Gemayels* (1988)

Gemayel, Sheikh Pierre 1905–
Lebanese politician

The father of Amin Gemayel and Bachir Gemayel, he was a member of the Maronite Christian community of Lebanon, and was educated at the University of St Joseph, Beirut, and Cochin Hospital, Paris, where he trained as a pharmacist. In 1936 he founded the Kataeb or Phalangist Party, modelled on the Spanish and German Fascist organizations, and in 1937 became its leader. He was twice imprisoned, in 1937 and in 1943, the year in which he organized a general strike. He held various ministerial posts (1960–67), and led the Phalangist Militia in the 1975–76 civil war. 📖 Matthew S Gordon, *The Gemayels* (1988)

Gems, Pam (Iris Pamela), *née* Price 1925–
English dramatist

She was born in Bransgore, Hampshire. Among her best-known plays are *Piaf* (1978) and *Camille* (1984), portraying women as victims in worlds ruled by men. She had written several radio and television scripts and stage plays before the mid-1970s, but it was *Dusa, Stas, Fish and Vi*, staged in London in 1975, which brought her widespread recognition. A study of the lives of four contemporary women, it was a courageous piece of feminist drama. Other plays include *The Danton Affair* (1986), dealing with the conflict between Danton and Robespierre; a musical stage adaptation of the 1930 film *The Blue Angel* (1991); *Deborah's Daughter* (1994); translations including Chekhov's *The Seagull* (1994); and *Stanley* (1997), for which she won an Olivier award.

Geneen, Harold Sydney 1910–
US accountant and industrialist

Born in Bournemouth, England, he worked as a clerk for a firm of Wall Street stockbrokers (1926–32) while studying at night to obtain a degree from New York University. He became a director of International Telephone and Telegraph (ITT) in 1959, taking on the role of chairman in 1964. He stepped down as chief executive in 1977, having seen the annual sales of the company rise from $766m to $22,000m in a 17-year period. He published his views on management in his book *Managing* (1984).

Genet, Edmond Charles, *known as* Citizen Genet 1763–1834
French diplomat

Born in Versailles, the son of a diplomat, he entered the foreign service at a young age. As French Revolutionary Minister to the USA (1793–94), he sought to draw the USA into France's war against Great Britain and Spain. After he outfitted privateers to attack British ships and attempted to raise troops against Spanish Florida, President George Washington demanded his recall. Realizing that he faced arrest in the Reign of Terror if he returned to France, Genet chose to stay in the USA as a citizen and farmer.

Genet, Jean 1910–86
French author

Born in Paris, he spent many years in reformatories and prisons, in France and abroad, for theft, male prostitution, and other crimes, and began to write in 1942 in Fresnes prison where he was serving a life sentence. His first novel, *Notre-Dame des fleurs* (1944, Eng trans *Our Lady of the Flowers*, 1949), portraying his world of homosexuals and criminals in a characteristically ceremonial and religious language, created a sensation. Later novels include *Miracle de la rose* (1946, Eng trans *Miracle of the Rose*, 1965) and *Pompes funèbres* (1947, Eng trans *Funeral Rites*, 1969). In 1948 he was granted a pardon by the President after a petition by French intellectuals, and Jean-Paul Sartre's book *Saint Genet* (1952, Eng trans 1963) later spread his fame among the intelligentsia. On release from prison he was associated with revolutionary movements in many countries. Several plays, including *Les Bonnes* (1946, Eng trans *The Maids*, 1954), *Les Nègres* (1958, Eng trans *The Blacks*, 1960) and *Les Paravents* (1961, Eng trans *The Screens*, 1962), and poems such as 'Les Condamnés à mort' (1942, 'Those Condemned to Death') and 'Chants Secrets' (1947, 'Secret Songs'), share the criminal underworld setting and profoundly pessimistic outlook of the novels. His autobiography, *Le Journal du voleur*, was published in 1949 (Eng trans *Thief's Journal*, 1954). 📖 Jean-Paul Sartre, *Saint Genet: actor and martyr* (1963)

Genêt See Flanner, Janet

Geneviève, St c.422–512AD
French patron saint of Paris

Born at Nanterre, near Paris, she took the veil from St Germanus. She acquired a reputation for sanctity, increased by her assurance that Attila and his Huns would not touch Paris in AD451, and by her expedition for the relief of the starving city during Childeric's Frankish invasion. In 460 she built a church over the tomb of St Denis, where she herself was buried. Her feast day is 3 January.

Genghis Khan See panel p724

Genlis, Stéphanie Felicité Ducrest de St Aubin, Comtesse de 1746–1830
French writer

She was born in Champcéri, near Autun, and at the age of 16 married the Comte de Genlis. In 1770 she was made lady-in-waiting to the Duchess of Chartres, to whose husband, Louis Philippe d'Orléans 'Égalité', she became mistress. She wrote four volumes of short plays entitled *Théâtre d'éducation* (1779) for her charges, the royal children, including the future King Louis Philippe, and nearly a hundred volumes of historical romances and 'improving' works. Her *Mémoires* (1825) contain interesting social comments on the period. 📖 J Hammond, *Keeper of Royal Secrets* (1913)

Gennaro, San See Januarius, St

Gennep, Charles-Arnold Kurr van 1873–1957
French ethnographer and folklorist

Born in Württemberg, Germany, of a Dutch father and French mother, he grew up in France. He worked for the French government in various cultural organizations (1903–10, 1919–1921), and also held brief academic appointments at Neuchâtel, Oxford and Cambridge. He became a collector and publisher of folklore materials, including the *Manuel de folklore français contemporaine* (1937–58), but he is best known for his earlier work, *Les Rites de passage* (1909), a comparative study of rituals marking transitions of social status. His other publications include *Religions, mœurs et légendes* (1908–14).

Gennes, Pierre-Gilles de See De Gennes, Pierre-Gilles

Genscher, Hans-Dietrich 1927–
German politician

Born in Reideburg, he was briefly a member of the Hitler Youth like many other children of the period, and fought in the army during World War II. After the war he remained in East Germany, or the German Democratic Republic (GDR), studying law at Leipzig and joining the Liberal-Democratic Party, before fleeing to West Germany (the Federal Republic of Germany) in 1952 as a result of the increasing repression of the GDR's Communist regime. He became Secretary-General of the Free Democratic Party (FDP) in 1959 and served as Interior Minister (1969–74), before being appointed FDP Chairman, Vice-Chancellor and Foreign Minister in 1974 when the party's leader, Walter Scheel, was elected federal President. Genscher, who served as Foreign Minister until 1992, emerged as a committed supporter of Ostpolitik and advocate of European co-operation. As FDP Leader, he masterminded the party's switch of allegiance from the Social Democratic Party to the Christian Democratic Union which resulted in the downfall of the Schmidt government in 1982. He resigned as FDP Chairman in 1985, but, as Foreign Minister, remained an influential force, seeking to pursue a new 'second phase' of détente. 📖 *Erinnerungen* (1995)

Genseric See Gaiseric

Genghis Khan, *also spelt* Jingis, Chingis, Chinghiz or Chingiz, *originally* Temujin c.1162–1227
Mongol warrior and ruler

Genghis Khan was born in Deligun Bulduk on the River Onon, the son of a Mongol chief. He was called at 13 to succeed his father, and faced a long and hard struggle against hostile tribes to establish his authority. Continued success stimulated his ambition, and he spent six years in subjugating the Naimans between Lake Balkhash and the Irtysh, and in conquering Tangut, south of the Gobi Desert. The Turkish Uigurs voluntarily submitted, and from them the Mongols derived their civilization, their alphabet and their laws.

In 1206 he was able to change his name from Temujin to Genghis Khan, 'Universal Ruler'. In 1211 he overran the empire of North China, and in 1217 he conquered and annexed the Kara-Khitai Khanate empire from Lake Balkhash to Tibet. In 1218 he attacked the powerful empire of Khwarezm, bounded by the Jaxartes, Indus, Persian Gulf and Caspian, took Bokhara, Samarkand, Khwarezm and other chief cities, and returned home in 1225. Two of Genghis's lieutenants penetrated northwards from the southern shore of the Caspian through Georgia into southern Russia and the Crimea, everywhere routing and slaying, and returned by way of the Volga.

Meanwhile in the far east another of his generals had completed the conquest of all northern China (1217–23) except Honan. After a few months' rest Genghis set out to punish the King of Tangut. He brought the country under control, but died on 18 August 1227.

Genghis was not just a warrior and conqueror, but a skilful administrator and ruler. He conquered empires stretching from the Black Sea to the Pacific, and organized them into states of some permanence, on which his successors were able to build.

📖 P Brent, *Genghis Khan* (1976).

'Happiness lies in conquering one's enemies, in driving them in front of oneself, in taking their property, in savouring their despair, in outraging their wives and daughters' (c.1210). Quoted in Witold Rodzinski, *The Walled Kindgom: A History of China* (1979).

Genth, Frederick Augustus 1820–93
US mineralogist, chemist and collector

Born in Wächtersbach, near Hanau, Germany, he was educated at Heidelberg, Giessen and the University of Marburg, where he received his PhD. He spent three years as a chemical assistant to **Robert Wilhelm Bunsen** before emigrating to the USA, where he established an analytical laboratory in Philadelphia. He was superintendent of the Washington Mine, North Carolina, from 1849 to 1850 but returned thereafter to his laboratory. He was appointed Professor of Chemistry at the University of Pennsylvania (1872–88) and was chief chemist and mineralogist to the Second Pennsylvania Geological Survey. He worked in mining geology for much of his life, although he also undertook important research on meteorites, chemistry and rare minerals. He produced an important monograph on the ammonium–cobalt compounds (1856) and discovered 23 new mineral species. The mineral genthite is named in his honour.

Gentile da Fabriano See Fabriano, Gentile da

Gentile, Giovanni 1875–1944
Italian philosopher, educationist and politician

He was born in Castelvetrano, Sicily. He was Professor of Philosophy successively at Naples (1898–1906), Palermo (1906–14), Pisa (1914–17) and Rome (1917–44). He collaborated with **Benedetto Croce** in editing the periodical *La Critica* (1903–22) and in developing a distinctive strain of Italian idealism, but they came to disagree both philosophically and politically. Gentile proposed a theory of 'actualism', in which nothing is real except the pure act of thought, the distinctions between theory and practice, subject and object, and past and present being mere mental constructs. He also became an apologist for Fascism and an ideological mouthpiece for **Mussolini**. He was the Fascist Minister of Public Instruction (1922–24), and presided over two commissions on constitutional reform and over the Supreme Council for Public Education (1926–28). Possibly his most important achievement was to plan the new *Enciclopedia Italiana* (35 vols, 1929–36), which became the main cultural monument of the regime. He was assassinated by anti-Fascist partisans in Florence after Mussolini's overthrow. His main philosophical work was the *Theory of Mind as Pure Act* (1916), and he also wrote a number of works on education.

Gentileschi, Artemisia, *properly* Artemisia Lomi
c.1597–c.1652
Italian painter

Born in Rome, she was the daughter of **Orazio Gentileschi**. She moved to Naples in 1630, and visited her father in England (1638–39), leaving a fine self-portrait at Hampton Court. She often depicted the decapitation of a man by a woman, and her chief work is a *Judith and Holophernes* in the Uffizi, Florence.

Gentileschi, Orazio, *properly* Orazio Lomi
1563–1647
Italian painter

Born in Pisa, he settled in England in 1626, the first Italian painter called to England by **Charles I**, having been patronized by the Vatican and the **Medicis** in Genoa. He was responsible for the decoration of the Queen's House at Greenwich (partly transferred to Marlborough House), and painted *Discovery of Moses* (Prado, Madrid), *Flight into Egypt* (Louvre, Paris) and *Joseph and Potiphar's Wife* (Hampton Court, London). His attempt to introduce the Italian style of decoration into England was unsuccessful.

Gentili, Alberico 1552–1608
Italian jurist and writer

Born in Sangenesio in the March of Ancona, he was educated at the University of Perugia. Exiled as a Protestant, he settled in England in 1580 and lectured at Oxford. He was the first true scholar in international law and his works, especially *De Jure Belli* (1598, 'Law of War'), are fundamental.

Gentz, Friedrich von 1764–1832
German publicist and diplomat

Born in Breslau, he entered public service in Prussia in 1786, and in 1802 in Austria. He wrote bitterly against **Napoleon I**. An adherent from 1810 of Prince **Clemens Metternich**, he was First Secretary at the Congress of Vienna in 1814.

Gény, François 1861–1959
French legal theorist

He was Professor of Law at Nancy, and his major work is *Méthodes d'interprétation et sources en droit privé positif* (1899, 'Codes in Private Law and Methods of Interpretation Thereof'), in which he contended that lawyers must supplement the norms derived from the codes, case-law and doctrine by objective factors such as social data, history and reason, so as to arrive at a decision which takes account of surrounding circumstances. His approach influenced legal thinking in many countries.

Geoffrey of Monmouth, *Latin name* Gaufridus Monemutensis c.1100–c.1154
Welsh chronicler and ecclesiastic

Thought to be the son of Breton parents, he studied at Oxford, was archdeacon of Llandaff or Monmouth (c.1140) and was appointed Bishop of St Asaph (1152). He compiled a fictitious history of Great Britain, *Historia Regum Britanniae* (c.1136), which traced the descent of British kings back to the Trojans, and he claimed to have based it on old Welsh chronicles that he alone had seen. Composed before 1147, it brought enduring romance by introducing the legends of King Arthur to European literature.

Geoffrin, Marie-Thérèse, *née* Rodet 1699–1777
French patron of literature

Born in Paris, she married a rich man at the age of 15 and when he died soon after, he left her an immense fortune. She had a genuine love of learning and art, and her salon became a rendezvous of the men of letters and artists of Paris, especially the *philosophes*.

Geoffroy Saint-Hilaire, Étienne 1772–1844
French zoologist

Born in Étampes, he became Professor of Zoology at the Museum of Natural History, Paris, in 1793 and began its great zoological collection. In 1798 he was a member of the scientific commission which accompanied Napoleon I to Egypt, and in 1809 he was appointed Professor of Zoology at the Faculty of Sciences in Paris. Comparing embryonic forms, he proposed that organs do not arise or disappear suddenly during evolution but appear gradually, that one organ grows at the expense of another, and that the equivalent organs and structures are to be found in all animals. In *Philosophie anatomique* (2 vols, 1818–20) he greatly enhanced the status of one of his major interests, teratology, the study of animal malformations. He also wrote *L'Histoire naturelle des mammifères* (1820–42, 'Natural History of Mammals'), *Philosophie zoologique* (1830, 'Zoological Philosophy') and *Études progressives d'un naturaliste* (1835, 'Progressive Studies of a Naturalist').

Geoffroy Saint-Hilaire, Isidore 1805–61
French zoologist

He was born in Paris, the son of Étienne Geoffroy Saint-Hilaire. In 1824 he became assistant naturalist at the National Museum of Natural History, Paris, and later was appointed Professor of Comparative Anatomy (1837) and Professor of Zoology (1850) at the Faculty of Sciences of Paris. He studied teratology, the analysis of anatomical abnormalities, and published *Histoire générale et particulière des anomalies de l'organisation chez l'homme et les animaux* (4 vols, 1832–37, 'General and Specific History of the Anomalies of the Organization in Man and in Animals'). He was interested in the domestication of animals and the way in which domestic animals adapt to different climates, and his study of alien animals in France appeared in *Domestication et naturalisation des animaux utiles* (1854, 'Domestication and Naturalization of Useful Animals'). In 1852 he published the first volume of his *Histoire naturelle générale des règnes organiques* ('General Natural History of Organic Kingdoms').

Georg, Callisen See **Calixtus**

George, St early 4th century AD
English patron of chivalry and guardian saint of England and Portugal

He may have been put to death by **Diocletian** at Nicomedia in AD 303, or died at Lydda in Palestine (c.250), where his alleged tomb is exhibited. By many writers, for example **Edward Gibbon**, he has been confused with the Arian George of Cappadocia (d.361). St George of the Eastern Church was no doubt a real personage of an earlier date than George of Cappadocia, but beyond this nothing is known of him, and his name was early obscured by fable. The famous story of his fight with the dragon cannot be traced much earlier than **Jacobus de Voragine**'s *Legenda Aurea*. The crusades gave a great impetus to his cult, many chivalrous orders assumed him as their patron, and he was adopted as guardian saint by England, Aragon and Portugal. In 1348 **Edward III** founded St George's Chapel, Windsor, and in 1344 the Order of the Garter was instituted. His feast day is 23 April.

George I 1660–1727
King of Great Britain and Ireland and Elector of Hanover

He was born in Osnabrück, Hanover, the eldest son of Ernest August, Elector of Hanover, and **Sophia**, daughter of **Elizabeth** of Bohemia. Elector of Hanover himself from 1698, he was a great-grandson of **James VI and I** of Scotland and England, and succeeded to the British throne in 1714 on the death of Queen **Anne** in accordance with the Act of Settlement (1701). He was the first Hanoverian King of Great Britain and Ireland. As a young man he held a military command in the War of Succession against **Louis XIV** of France. He married his cousin, Sophia Dorothea of Zell (1666–1726), in 1682, but divorced her in 1694 for adultery and, although he lived openly with his own mistresses, kept her imprisoned in the castle of Ahlden until her death. The Hanoverian succession was unpopular in England, with widespread demonstrations against the new king on his accession, but Whig support for him was strengthened by the unsuccessful Jacobite rising in 1715 to restore the exiled **Stuarts**, who were debarred from the throne on account of their Roman Catholicism. The '15 was exploited by the Whigs to discredit the Tories in the light of their lukewarm support for the Hanoverian king, while George's own preference for the Whigs served to give them a monopoly of power which was to last for another 50 years. The Septennial Act of 1716 extended the period between parliamentary elections to seven years and further reduced the level of popular participation in the political affairs of the nation. George never learned English, but although he preferred whenever possible to spend time in Hanover, he was no mere figurehead in the government of Great Britain. His reign saw an unprecedented dominance of the court party over parliament, intensified during the premiership of Sir **Robert Walpole**, from 1721 onwards. His relatively low political profile is attributed to the power and cohesion of the alliance between monarch and ruling oligarchy, rather than any evidence of weakness or indifference on the part of the king. 📖 R Hatton, *George I* (1978)

George II 1683–1760
King of Great Britain and Ireland and Elector of Hanover

He was born in Herrenhausen, Hanover, the son of **George I**, whom he succeeded in 1727. In 1705 he married **Caroline of Ansbach**. Despite the personal antipathy that had existed between father and son during most of George's adult life and his opposition to his father's government, he maintained his father's principal minister, Sir **Robert Walpole**, in power. Walpole dominated British politics until his fall in 1742, and thereafter the system that he had established continued to operate, little altered, under his successors. Walpole's peace policy was breached by war with Spain in 1737 and British participation in the War of Austrian Succession (1742–48). The king, the last British monarch to take part in a battle, took the field as commander of the British army at the Battle of Dettingen (1743), which he won. In 1745 a Jacobite rising in Scotland under the Young Pretender, **Charles Edward Stuart**, was at first alarmingly successful, but without the hoped-for aid from France the Scots had little real chance against the British army and were savagely cut down at Culloden by George's second son, William Augustus, the Duke of **Cumberland**. British involvement (1756–57) in the Seven

Years War (1756–63) was largely undertaken in defence of Hanover, but, while Great Britain suffered reverses in Europe, this was more than offset by successes further afield. **Robert Clive's** victory at Plassey in 1757 helped to lay the foundations of British India and the capture of Quebec by **James Wolfe** in 1759 established British supremacy in North America. ⊞ Charles Trench, *George II* (1973)

George III See panel p727

George IV 1762–1830
King of Great Britain and Ireland and of Hanover
Born in London, he was the eldest son of **George III**, and owing to his father's insanity he became prince regent (1811), succeeding in 1820. Until the age of 19 he was kept under strict discipline, against which he sometimes rebelled. Secretly, in 1785, he went through the ceremony of marriage (1785) with Mrs **Maria Fitzherbert**, a Roman Catholic, which was canonically valid, but not acceptable in English law. In 1795 he married Princess **Caroline of Brunswick**, but later tried to divorce her, causing a scandal in which the people sympathized with the queen. Though a professed Whig when Prince of Wales (out of antagonism to his father), as George IV he governed, as his father had done, with the aid of the Tories. He was a man of culture and wit, leaving to the nation a valuable collection of books and paintings, and also a patron of the arts, recognizing the genius of **John Nash** as an architect and town planner, and supporting Wyatville's restoration of Windsor Castle. ⊞ Joanna Richardson, *George the Magnificent* (1966)

George V 1865–1936
King of Great Britain and Northern Ireland
Born at Marlborough House, London, he served in the navy, travelled in many parts of the empire, and was created Prince of Wales in 1901. He succeeded his father, **Edward VII**, in 1910. His reign was marked by various important events, such as the Union of South Africa (1910), his visit to India for the Coronation Durbar (1911), World War I (1914–18), the adoption of the surname Windsor (1917), the Sinn Féin Rebellion (1916), the Irish Free State settlement (1922), the first Labour governments (1924, 1929–31), a General Strike (1926), Scottish Church union (1929), economic crisis and a National government (1931), the Statute of Westminster, defining Dominion status (1931), and the Government of India Act (1935). He originated the famous Christmas Day broadcasts to the nation in 1932. In 1893 he married **Mary of Teck**. Although he was without intellectual curiosity and suspicious of new ideas, he was responsible for the development of the monarchy as a symbol of national unity, and his Silver Jubilee (1935) was celebrated with genuine popular enthusiasm. He had five sons: Edward VIII, George VI, Prince Henry, Duke of Gloucester, Prince George, Duke of Kent, and Prince John (1905–19), and one daughter, Mary, Princess Royal (1897–1965), who married the 6th Earl of Harewood. ⊞ Kenneth Rose, *King George V* (1983)

George VI 1895–1952
King of Great Britain and Northern Ireland
The second son of **George V**, and father of **Elizabeth II** and Princess **Margaret**, he was born at Sandringham House, Norfolk, and educated at Dartmouth and at Trinity College, Cambridge. He served in the Grand Fleet at the Battle of Jutland (1916), and later in the Royal Naval Air Service and the RAF (1917–19). Keenly interested in the human problems of industry, he became president of the Boys' Welfare Association and originated the summer camps for public school and working-class boys. In 1920 he was created Duke of York and he married **Elizabeth** (Lady Elizabeth Bowes-Lyon) in 1923. An outstanding tennis player, he played at Wimbledon in the All-England championships (1926). The following year, he and the

duchess toured Australia. On the abdication of his elder brother, **Edward VIII**, he ascended the throne in 1936. During World War II he set a personal example over wartime restrictions, continued to reside in bomb-damaged Buckingham Palace, visited all the theatres of the war and delivered many broadcasts, for which he overcame a speech impediment. In 1947 he toured South Africa and substituted the title of Head of the Commonwealth for that of Emperor of India, when that subcontinent was granted independence by the Labour government. By then his health was rapidly declining, although he persevered with his duties. His last great public occasion was the opening of the Festival of Britain (1951). He died in his sleep on 6 February 1952 and was succeeded by his daughter **Elizabeth II**. ⊞ Denis Judd, *King George VI 1895–1952* (1982)

George I 1845–1913
King of Greece
The second son of King **Kristian IX** of Denmark, he was born in Copenhagen. He served in the Danish navy and on the deposition of King Otto of Greece (1832–62) he was elected king (1863) by the Greek national assembly. He married (1867) Grand Duchess Olga, niece of Tsar **Alexander II** of Russia. His reign was a formative period in Greece's emergence as a modern European state. It saw the consolidation of Greek territory in Thessaly and Epirus, and the suppression of a Cretan insurrection (1896–97). Involved in the Balkan War of 1912–13, he was assassinated at Salonika, and succeeded by his son **Constantine I**.

George II 1890–1947
King of Greece
The son of **Constantine I** and grandson of **George I**, he was born in Tatoë, near Athens, and succeeded to the throne on his father's second abdication (1922), but was deposed (1923) by a military junta. Restored to the throne by plebiscite (1935), he worked closely and controversially with his dictatorial Prime Minister, **Yanni Metaxas**. When Greece was overrun by the Germans (1941) after successfully resisting the Italian invasion of 1940–41, he withdrew to Crete and then to England. In 1946 he was restored to the throne, again by plebiscite. He was succeeded by his brother **Paul I**.

George V 1819–78
Last King of Hanover
Born in Berlin, he became blind through an accident (1833). He ruled from 1851 to 1866. A complete absolutist, by siding with Austria he lost Hanover to Prussia and died an exile in Paris. His son was **Ernest Augustus**, Duke of Cumberland.

George, David Lloyd See **Lloyd-George (of Dwyfor), 1st Earl**

George, Henry 1839–97
US economist
Born in Philadelphia, Pennsylvania, he left school at the age of 13, went to sea, and in 1858 arrived in California where he became a printer. He wrote for several newspapers, and became the owner of the *San Francisco Daily Evening Post* (1871–75). He took an active part in public questions and published *Our Land and Land Policy* in 1870 and *Progress and Poverty* (1877–79). His fundamental remedy for poverty was a 'single tax' levied on the value of land exclusive of improvements, and the abolition of all taxes which fall upon industry and thrift.

George, Mlle, *originally* **Marguerite Joséphine Weimar** 1787–1867
French tragic actress

George III *in full* George William Frederick 1738–1820
King of Great Britain and Ireland and of Hanover

George was born in London, the eldest son of **Frederick Louis**, Prince of Wales. In 1760 he succeeded his grandfather, **George II**, as King of Great Britain and Ireland and Elector of Hanover (King of Hanover from 1815). He was the first of the House of Hanover to command general respect on becoming sovereign, and at the outset he conciliated all classes of his subjects. In 1761, he married **Charlotte Sophia**, Princess of Mecklenburg-Strelitz, although various affairs and an illegitimate child were rumoured.

George was eager to govern as well as reign, and friction soon arose between him and his people. William Pitt, Earl of **Chatham**, was the popular idol; but the king disliked Pitt and his policy, and for much of his reign appointed others as Prime Minister. During the two years' administration of **George Grenville**, the first attempt to tax the American colonies was made. In Lord **North** George III found a Minister after his own heart, and North remained at the head of the government from 1770 to 1782. During his administration the American colonies, exasperated at renewed attempts at taxation, declared their independence (4 July 1776) and eventually achieved it by the treaty of peace with Great Britain signed in 1783.

The determination of the king not to grant any concessions to those whom he deemed rebels caused the struggle to be much protracted. Lord North was succeeded by the Marquess of **Rockingham**, who died after four months in office. Among his colleagues were **Charles James Fox**, **Edmund Burke** and **Richard Brinsley Sheridan**, whom George detested, and who, when Lord **Shelburne** took Lord Rockingham's place, refused to serve with him; but he secured **William Pitt**, the Younger, as Chancellor of the Exchequer. The friends of Fox and the followers of Lord North overthrew Shelburne in 10 months; and the coalition ministry of **William Cavendish Bentinck**, 3rd Duke of Portland, lasted only eight months (1783). In the interval the king compelled his Ministers to resign, called Pitt to office in December 1783, then dissolved parliament. Pitt remained in office for 18 years. The complete victory of his party at the general election in 1784 was a triumph for the king as much as for Pitt; there was now an end to the supremacy of the old Whig families.

When the union between Ireland and Great Britain was proposed, George III wrote to Pitt characterizing it as one of the most useful measures of his reign; but when the union was effected (1 January 1801), and Pitt proposed carrying out his pledges as to Catholic emancipation, the king refused his assent. Pitt resigned; he later resumed office, but died in 1806.

In 1810 the Princess Amelia, George's favourite child, fell dangerously ill; this preyed on the king's mind, and hastened an attack of mental derangement, not the first he had had. He also lost his sight, and his ailment is now believed to have been caused by porphyria. In 1811 the Prince of Wales was appointed regent, and although the king lived on until January 1820 he did not recover.

📖 John Brooke, *George III* (1972); J Clarke, *The Life and Times of George III* (1972); J Steven Watson, *The Reign of George III* (1960).

> The reign of George III was marked by decisive battles in America, India and Europe, and by many great conquests. Great statesmen, such as the Earl of Chatham, Pitt and Fox, adorned it; as did great captains, such as **Nelson** and **Wellington**; and many great names in modern English literature: **Johnson**, **Gibbon**, **Burns**, **Cowper**, **Crabbe**, **Scott**, **Byron**, **Coleridge**, **Wordsworth**, **Southey**, **Shelley** and **Keats**.
>
> When George III ascended the throne the national debt stood at £138 million sterling; before his death it was more than £800 million. On the other hand, trade and commerce made gigantic strides: during his reign both imports and exports had increased more than fourfold in monetary value.

Born in Bayeux, she was acclaimed at the Comédie Française, playing in both classical tragedy and the early romantic dramas. In her *Mémoires* she left an account of her liaison with **Napoleon I**.

George, Stefan 1868–1933
German poet

Born in Büdesheim, near Bingen, he edited (1892–1919) *Blätter für die Kunst*, a journal devoted to the work of a group of advanced poets and writers to which he belonged. He wrote lyric verse in *Hymnen* (1890, 'Hymns'), *Der siebente Ring* (1907, 'The Seventh Ring') and *Der Stern des Bundes* (1914, 'The Federal Star'), which shows the influence of the French Symbolists and the English Pre-Raphaelites. He also translated the works of **Baudelaire**, **Shakespeare** and **Dante**. In his poems he dispensed with punctuation and capitals. In *Das neue Reich* (1928, 'The New Reich') he advocated a new German culture, not in accord with that of the Nazis. 📖 E K Bennett, *A Critical Study* (1954)

George-Brown, George Alfred Brown, Baron 1914–85
English Labour politician

Born in Southwark, London, he left school at the age of 15, attended further education classes, and was an official of the Transport and General Workers Union before entering parliament as MP for Belper division in 1945. After holding minor posts in the Labour Government of 1945–51, he became Opposition spokesman on defence (1958–61), when he supported **Hugh Gaitskell** in opposing unilateral disarmament. He unsuccessfully contested **Harold Wilson** for party leadership in 1963. Vice-Chairman and deputy Leader of the Labour Party from 1960, he was first Secretary of State and Secretary of State for Economic Affairs (1964–66), when he instigated a prices and incomes policy which fell victim to the later freeze on wages and prices. He resigned in July 1966, but resumed his post and became Foreign Secretary in August. A flamboyant, impetuous and controversial figure, Brown finally resigned and returned to the back benches in 1968 during the gold crisis. He lost his seat in the 1970 general election and was created a life peer. 📖 *In My Way: The Political Memoirs of Lord George-Brown* (1972)

Gerald of Wales See **Giraldus Cambrensis**

Gérard, François Pascal Simon, Baron 1770–1837
French painter

Born in Rome, but brought up in Paris, he became a pupil of **Jaques Louis David** and a member of the Revolutionary Tribunal in 1793. His full-length portrait of the miniaturist **Jean Baptiste Isabey** (1796) and his *Cupid and Psyche* (1798), both in the Louvre, Paris, established his reputation, and leading men and women of the Empire and the Restoration sat for him. He also painted mythological, historical and battle scenes. After the fall of **Napoleon I** in 1815 he became court painter to **Louis XVIII**.

Gerard, John 1545–1612
English herbalist

He was born in Nantwich, Cheshire, and his London garden became famous for its rare plants. For 20 years (1577–98) he was superintendent of William Cecil's gardens. He wrote *The Herball, or general histoire of plantes* (1597).

Gérard, Marguerite 1761–1837
French artist

Born in Grasse, she was the sister-in-law and informal apprentice of the celebrated Rococo painter Jean Honoré Fragonard, and moved to Paris to live with the Fragonard family in the 1780s. She achieved success painting genre scenes of Enlightenment women in domestic surroundings, and when the Salon opened to women artists in the 1790s, she exhibited regularly until 1824, when she retired from professional painting. She was one of the first French women painters to achieve professional success, and some of her works were bought by Napoleon I and Louis XVIII.

Gere, Richard 1949–
US film actor

Born in Philadelphia, Pennsylvania, he studied at the University of Massachusetts before gaining extensive experience in the theatre. His stage appearances include *Grease* (1972) in London, *Killer's Head* (1975) off-Broadway and *Bent* (1979–80) on Broadway. He made his film debut in *Report to the Commissioner* (1975) and rose to stardom playing narcissistic loners and rebels in films like *Looking For Mr Goodbar* (1977), *American Gigolo* (1980) and *An Officer and a Gentleman* (1982). His popularity dimmed in the late 1980s, but he re-asserted himself with a chilling performance as a corrupt policeman in *Internal Affairs* (1989) and showed a deft comic touch in the box-office hit *Pretty Woman* (1990). Subsequent films include *Sommersby* (1993), *First Knight* (1995), *Primal Fear* (1996) and *The Day Of The Jackal* (1997). A committed Buddhist and spokesman for various Tibetan causes, he was briefly married (1991–94) to Cindy Crawford.

Gerhard, Roberto 1896–1970
British composer

Born in Valls, near Tarragona, Spain, of Swiss parentage, he studied piano with Enrique Granados y Campiña (1915–16), and composition with Arnold Schoenberg (1923–28) and Felipe Pedrell (1841–1922) from 1916 and 1922. After the Republican collapse in the Civil War he left Barcelona to settle in England (1939), becoming a British subject in 1960. Most of his music was written in England and was characterized by orchestral, rhythmic and melodic inventiveness. He composed ballets, an opera, *The Duenna* (1945–47), five symphonies, concertos for violin and piano, chamber music, incidental music and some electronic music.

Gerhardie or Gerhardi, William Alexander 1895–1977
English novelist

He was born in St Petersburg, Russia, of English parents, and educated there. He then served in the British Embassy at Petrograd (again St Petersburg) from 1917 to 1918, and later with the military mission in Siberia, before going to Worcester College, Oxford, where he wrote *Futility: A Novel on Russian Themes* (1922), and a lively study of Chekhov (1923). In 1925 he published *The Polyglots*, his most celebrated novel, described by Anthony Powell as 'outstanding…particularly in the rare gift of making child characters come alive'. Among his later novels, only *Of Mortal Love* (1936) stands comparison with his early fiction. Other works include *Memoirs of a Polyglot*, his autobiography, published in 1931, a biographical history of

The Romanoffs (1940), and *God's Fifth Column* (posthumous, 1981) an idiosyncratic account of the years 1890 to 1940. 📖
D Davies, *William Gerhardie: a life* (1990)

Gerhardsen, Einar 1897–1987
Norwegian politician

Of working-class origin, he rose to prominence in the Norwegian Labour Party between the wars but was not a member of the Labour government which was in power when the German invasion of Norway took place (1940). This, together with his active participation in the Resistance, made him well qualified to lead the first postwar government in Norway. As Prime Minister (1945–51, 1955–65), he led Norway into membership of NATO in 1949 and presided over a long period of economic growth and social welfare legislation.

Gerhardt, Charles Frédéric 1816–56
French chemist

Born in Strasbourg, he studied chemistry at the Polytechnicum in Karlsruhe and later attended a commercial college in Leipzig. He refused to join his father in running the family factory and after a violent quarrel joined a regiment of lancers, leaving shortly afterwards to study chemistry with Justus von Liebig (1836–37). After a final but unsuccessful attempt at reconciliation with his father he left for Paris to study with Jean-Baptiste André Dumas. He then secured a staff appointment (1841) in Montpellier, but resigned in 1851 and returned to the capital. In 1854 he was offered two chairs in Strasbourg, but died two years later. His contribution to chemistry was the 'theory of types' in which he proposed that all organic molecules belong to one of a small number of families or types.

Géricault, (Jean Louis André) Théodore 1791–1824
French painter

Born in Rouen, he became a pupil (1810) of Pierre Guérin, in whose studio he met and befriended Eugène Delacroix. A great admirer of the 17th-century Dutch and Flemish schools, Géricault revolted against the current classicism, and his unorthodox approach and bold use of colour incurred the disapproval of his teacher, who advised him to give up painting. His first important exhibition piece was *Officer of Light Horse* at the Salon of 1812, which was followed by other canvases noteworthy for their realism. In his quest for authenticity he spent much time studying the raw material of his pictures, thus achieving the great effectiveness of his masterpiece *The Raft of the Medusa* (1818–19, Louvre, Paris), based on a shipwreck which had shortly before caused a sensation in France. It impressed Delacroix but was harshly criticized and Géricault withdrew to England, where he did a number of paintings of racing scenes and landscapes and came to admire Constable and Richard Bonington, whose work he brought to the notice of the French. Towards the end of his life he made five portraits of the insane (1822–23). 📖
Eitner and S A Nash, *Theodore Géricault* (1989)

Germain, Sophie 1776–1831
French mathematician

Born in Paris, she was not admitted, as a woman, to the newly established École Polytechnique, but in the guise of a male student she submitted a paper which so impressed Joseph de Lagrange that he became her personal tutor. She gave a more generalized proof of Pierre de Fermat's 'last theorem' than had previously been available, developed a mathematical explanation of the figures of Ernst Chladni and went on to derive a general mathematical description of the vibrations of curved as well as plane elastic surfaces. Her *Recherches sur la théorie des surfaces élastiques* ('Research on the Theory of Elastic Surfaces') was published in 1821.

German, Sir Edward, *originally* Edward German Jones 1862–1936
English composer

Born in Whitchurch, Shropshire, he studied at the Royal Academy of Music, London. In 1888 he was made musical director of the Globe Theatre, London, and became known for his incidental music to Shakespeare. In 1901 he emerged as a light opera composer, when he completed Sir Arthur Sullivan's *Emerald Isle* after the composer's death. His own works include *Merrie England* (1902), *Tom Jones* (1907), *Fallen Fairies* (1909), several symphonies, suites, chamber music and songs and the *Welsh Rhapsody* (1904). 📖 Brian Rees, *A Musical Peacemaker: The Life and Work of Sir Edward German* (1986)

Germanicus Caesar 15BC–AD19
Roman soldier

Son of Nero Claudius Drusus, and of Antonia, daughter of Mark Antony and niece of Augustus, he was adopted by the emperor Tiberius. In AD13 he was appointed to command the eight legions on the Rhine, and two years later he marched to meet Arminius, whom he overthrew in two desperate battles. Tiberius, jealous of his popularity, sent him to the East in AD17, appointing Calpurnius Piso as viceroy of Syria, in order secretly to counteract him. Germanicus died at Ephidaphnae, near Antioch, probably of poison. His wife, Agrippina, the Elder, and two of her sons were eventually put to death, but the third son, Caligula, survived to become emperor. The notorious Agrippina, the Younger, was his daughter.

Germanus, St c.378–448AD
French religious

Born near Augustodunum, Gaul (now Autun, France), he was made Bishop of Auxerre. He was invited to Britain to combat Pelagianism in AD429, and under him the Christian Britons won the bloodless 'Alleluia Victory' over the Picts and Saxons at Maes Garmon ('Germanus's field') in Flintshire. His feast day is 31 July.

Germer, Lester Halbert 1896–1971
US physicist

He was born in Chicago, and while on the research staff of the Western Electric Co (1917–53), he worked with Clinton Davisson on experiments that demonstrated the diffraction of electrons by crystals (1927), which confirmed the theories of Louis-Victor de Broglie.

Gérôme, Jean Léon 1824–1904
French historical genre painter

He was born in Vesoul and began to exhibit in 1847. In 1863 he became Professor of Painting in the École des Beaux-Arts, Paris, where he taught Odilon Redon and Thomas Eakins. His *Polytechnic Student* is in the Tate, London. A first-rate draughtsman, he achieved distinction as a sculptor and a decorative painter of anecdotal and erotic subjects.

Geronimo, *Apache name* Goyathlay ('One Who Yawns') 1829–1909
Apache leader

Born in Arizona, he became a chief of the Chiricahua Apaches and warred against the Mexicans (who killed his mother, wife and children) as well as the US soldiers and settlers who arrived in the region after Mexico ceded it to the USA in 1848. Confined to a series of reservations outside their ancestral lands, he and his followers escaped repeatedly and led raids against the settlers for more than a decade. On their final surrender in 1886, they were placed under military confinement. Geronimo later became a farmer in Oklahoma with his people and adopted Christianity. He dictated his autobiography, *Geronimo: His Own Story* (1906). 📖 Alexander B Adams, *Geronimo* (1971)

Gerry, Elbridge 1744–1814
US politician

Born in Marblehead, Massachusetts, he graduated from Harvard in 1762, served in the Continental Congress (1776–81, 1783–85), and was a signer of the Declaration of Independence. He was a delegate to the Constitutional Convention (1787), where he opposed a strong central government. Elected Governor of Massachusetts in 1810, he signed a bill (1812) creating an oddly shaped electoral district favouring his own Republican Party. The district was caricatured as a salamander in the press and as dubbed a 'gerrymander'. Gerry later became Vice-President of the USA (1813–14) under James Madison.

Gershwin, George, *originally* Jacob Gershvin 1898–1937
US composer

Born in Brooklyn, New York City, the son of Russian Jewish immigrants, he studied piano as a boy, published his first popular song at the age of 14 and left high school to work for Jerome H Remick and Co., a Tin Pan Alley music-publishing company. In 1920 he had his first hit with 'Swanee', recorded by Al Jolson, and he began to compose songs for Broadway reviews. In 1924 he wrote his first successful musical comedy, *Lady Be Good*, collaborating with his brother Ira Gershwin, a brilliant lyricist who was to be his partner in songwriting until his death. In the 1920s and early 1930s he scored a series of hit musicals, including *Of Thee I Sing* (1931), and in the process produced numerous classics of US popular song, such as 'Someone to Watch Over Me', 'Embraceable You' and 'I Got Rhythm'. He also wrote songs and scores for motion pictures, notably several screen musicals with Fred Astaire and Ginger Rogers. In 1924 a commission from the conductor Paul Whiteman led to his composition of *Rhapsody in Blue*, a concert work combining Romantic emotionalism and the jazz idiom with unusual success, and this was followed with the *Concerto in F* (1925) and *An American in Paris* (1928), exploiting the same forces. His and Ira's black opera, *Porgy and Bess* (1935), was commercially unsuccessful when it was first staged but has won worldwide popularity. At the age of 38, at the height of his powers, he died of a brain tumour. Gershwin, who described jazz as 'a very powerful American folk-music', showed genius in his innovation of 'symphonic jazz' in his blithe dexterity with modern popular song and musical comedy, and he was influential in winning recognition of the legitimacy of US popular music. 📖 David Ewen, *George Gershwin* (1970)

Gershwin, Ira, *originally* Israel Gershvin 1896–1983
US lyricist

Born in Brooklyn, New York City, he was the brother of George Gershwin, with whom he collaborated to produce more than 20 successful Broadway musicals. Ira first wrote under the pseudonym of Arthur Francis, and wrote the lyrics for Vincent Youmans's *Two Little Girls in Blue* (1921), which includes 'Oh Me, Oh My'. Later, under his own name, he wrote lyrics for the *Ziegfeld Follies* (1936), and, most importantly, *Lady in the Dark* (1941, composed by Kurt Weill), which contains 'Jenny' and 'This is New'.

Gerson, Jean de, *originally* Jean Charlier, *known as* Doctor Christianissimus 1363–1429
French theologian and mystic

Born in Gerson, near Rheims, he was educated in Paris. He was a nominalist, opposed to scholasticism, but a Christian mystic. As Chancellor of the University of Paris from 1395 he supported the proposal for putting an end to the Great Schism between Rome and Avignon by the resignation of both the contending pontiffs, especially at the councils of Pisa and Constance (1414). Having provoked the animosity of the Duke of Burgundy for denouncing the murder of the Duc d'Orléans, Gerson prudently retired to Rattenburg in Tirol, where he composed his *De Consolatione Theologiae*. It was only after several years that he was able to return to France and settle in a monastery in Lyons.

Gerstäcker or Gerstaecker, Friedrich 1816–72
German writer and traveller

Born in Hamburg, he worked his way through the USA, South America, Polynesia and Australia, and wrote colourful adventure stories, collected in *Mississippi-Bilder* (1847, Eng trans *Western Waters*, 1864). 📖 *Gerstaecker's Travels* (1854)

Gertler, Mark 1891–1939
British painter

Born in London to Jewish Austrian émigrés, he studied at the Regent Street Polytechnic and was apprenticed at Bell's Stained Glass Works before going to the Slade School of Art, London. His friends included Sir **Stanley Spencer**, **Edward Wadsworth**, **Paul Nash** and **Dora Carrington**, with whom he had a traumatic affair. He developed a linear primitive style in his best work, such as *The Rabbi and his Grandchild* (1913, Southampton) and *The Merry-Go-Round* (1916, Tate, London). After 1917 his style became more lyrical and he was invited by **Roger Fry** to work for the Omega Workshops in 1918. From 1920 he was treated for tuberculosis and during this period he painted sensuous nudes and female portraits which brought him success without satisfaction. Paintings of the 1930s such as *The Spanish Fan* and *The Red Shawl* (1938) show a return to his flatter, more monumental style. He suffered from depression all his life and committed suicide in his London studio. 📖 Royal Academy Exhibition Catalogue, *British Art in the 20th Century* (1987)

Gertrude, St 626–59
Frankish religious

She was the daughter of Pepin the Elder (d.c.640), founder of the Carolingian dynasty. She became abbess of the monastery at Nivelles, Brabant, on the death of her mother, after refusing to marry the Frankish king Dagobert I (605–39). Her feast day is 17 March.

Gertrude of Helfta, St, *sometimes called* Gertruda the Great 1256–c.1302
German mystic

She entered the convent of Helfta near Eisleben at the age of five, and when she was 15 began to have visions which she described in Latin treatises. She was never formally canonized.

Gervase of Canterbury c.1141–c.1210
English monk and chronicler

He chronicled the reigns of **Stephen**, **Henry II** and **Richard I**, and was author of a history of the archbishops of Canterbury.

Gervase of Tilbury c.1150–c.1220
English historical writer

Born probably in Tilbury, Essex, he lectured on canon law at Bologna, and was Marshal of the kingdom of Arles, and perhaps provost of the nunnery at Ebsdorf. Of his *Otia Imperialia*, composed about 1212 for the entertainment of the emperor **Otto IV**, the first two books consist of an abstract of geography and history, the third contains a collection of curious beliefs about British sirens, the magnet, etc. He also prepared a *Liber Facetiarum* or book of anecdotes for **Henry II**'s son Henry, which is no longer in existence.

Gesell, Arnold Lucius 1880–1961
US psychologist

He was born in Alma, Wisconsin, and educated at Clark University and at Yale. He was Professor of Child Hygiene at Yale School of Medicine (1915–48) and established the Yale Psychological Clinic (now the Clinic of Child Development of the Yale School of Medicine), of which he was director (1911–48). He was research consultant to the Gesell Institute of Child Development (1950–58). A pioneer in the study of child psychology, he was particularly concerned with early infant development and devised standard scales for measuring its progress. His writings were supplemented by an original and extensive use of film as a medium for scientific and educational communication. His books include *Infant and Child in the Culture of Today* (1943), *The Child from Five to Ten* (1946) and *Child Development* (1949).

Gesner, Conrad, *Latin* Conradus Gesnerus 1516–65
Swiss naturalist and physician

Born in Zurich, he became Professor of Greek at Lausanne University in 1537, and in 1541 he was appointed Professor of Philosophy and Natural History at Zurich University. He published 72 works, and left 18 others in progress. His *Bibliotheca Universalis* (1545–49) contained the titles of all the books then known in Hebrew, Greek and Latin, with criticisms and summaries of each. His *Historia Animalium* (1551–58) attempted to describe all animals then known. He collected over 500 plants not recorded by the ancients, and his third major work contains beautiful and accurate engraved illustrations which were reprinted most recently in eight volumes between 1973 and 1980. He also wrote on medicine, mineralogy and philology. He was the first to allude to the concepts of genus and species, and stressed the significance of flowers, fruit and seed in identification and discrimination. He was one of the most versatile and industrious scholars of the 16th century.

Gessner, Salomon 1730–88
Swiss pastoral poet, and landscape painter and engraver

He was born in Zurich, where he became a bookseller. *Daphnis* (1754), a sentimental bucolic collection of poetry, was followed two years later by a volume of *Idyllen* ('Idylls') and by *Inkel und Yariko* ('Inkel and Yariko'). His *Tod Abels* (1758, 'Abel's Death'), a type of idyllic heroic prose poem, had the greatest success. His landscape paintings are all in the conventional classic style, but his engravings are more impressive. In 1772 he published a second volume of *Idyllen* and a series of letters on landscape painting. 📖 R Zuerchner, *Salomon Gessner, 1730–1788* (1968)

Gesualdo, Prince Carlo of Venosa c.1561–1613
Italian lutenist and composer

Born in Naples, he wrote many sacred vocal works and published six books of madrigals, remarkable for bold homophonic progressions and telling use of dissonance. He achieved notoriety for ordering the murder of his unfaithful wife and her lover in 1590.

Getty, Jean Paul 1892–1976
US oil executive, billionaire and art collector

Born in Minneapolis, he studied at the University of California, Berkeley, and Oxford, and then entered the oil business in his early twenties, making $250,000 in his first two years. His father (also a successful oil man) died in 1930, leaving him about $500,000. He merged his father's interests with his own and went on to acquire and control more than 100 companies, making most of the major policy decisions himself. He became one of the richest men in the world and his personal wealth was estimated in 1968 at over $1billion. Over the years he acquired a huge and extremely valuable art collection. He was married and divorced five times, and developed a legendary reputation for miserliness, installing a pay-telephone for guests in his English mansion. He wrote several books, including a history of the family oil busi-ness and two autobiographies, *My Life and Fortunes* (1963) and *As I see It* (1976). 📖 R Lenzner, *The Great Getty* (1986)

Getz, Stan(ley) 1927–91
US jazz saxophonist

He was born in Philadelphia, Pennsylvania, and educated in New York, where he started playing professionally at the age of 15. While still a teenager he was working under such important bandleaders as **Stan Kenton** and **Benny Goodman**. With the **Woody Herman** Orchestra from 1947 to 1949, he was a member of the 'Four Brothers' saxophone section which gave the band a unique ensemble sound. He later led his own small groups, and during the 1960s he helped to popularize the bossa nova jazz style. With his light tone and articulate phrasing, he was one of the most copied of tenor saxophone stylists.

Geulincx, Arnold, *also known as* Philaretus 1624–69
Belgian philosopher

Born in Antwerp, he taught at the Catholic University of Louvain but was expelled for his anti-scholasticism (1658). He later converted to Calvinism and became Professor of Philosophy at Leyden (1665). He was a lead-ing exponent of **Descartes**'s philosophy and is best known for his doctrine of 'Occasionalism': God himself 'occasions' every mental or physical process, while body and mind operate separately, without causal interaction, like two clocks which are perfectly synchronized. His principal works are *Quaestiones Quedlibeticae* (1653, 'Miscellaneous Questions'), re-edited by him as *Saturnalia* (1665), *Logica Restituta* (1662, 'Logic Restated') and *De Virtute* (1665, 'On Virtue'). After his death further works were published under his pseudonym, Philaretus, in-cluding six treatises on ethics under the title *Gnothi Seauton* (1675, 'Know Thyself') and *Metaphysica Vera* (1691, 'True Metaphysics').

Geyl, Pieter 1887–1966
Dutch historian and patriot

Born in Dordrecht, he was educated in The Hague, Leyden and Italy. After serving as London correspondent of the *Nieuwe Rotterdamsche Courant* (1913–19), he was ap-pointed the first Professor of Dutch Studies at London University (1919–36) and Professor of Modern History at Utrecht (1936–58). During World War II he was im-prisoned in Nazi concentration camps. He was a believer in a 'greater Netherlands', and mourned the loss of Dutch-speaking Flanders and Brabant during the Eighty Years War in the late 16th century. He was a climatologist and environmentalist as a historian, arguing that the outcome of the Dutch revolt against **Habsburg** Spain was dictated by movements of rivers and water currents rather than religion or economics. His multi-volume history of the Eighty Years War and its sequels were published in the 1930s, translated into English as *The Revolt of the Netherlands* and *The Netherlands Divided*, while his struggle against **Hitler**'s domination of Europe is reflected in his *Napoleon, For and Against* (1944). He was also a poet and essayist, debating with numerous living and dead historians, and was the leading interpreter of the Dutch past to his country and the world.

Gezelle, Guido 1830–99
Flemish poet

Born in Bruges, he was ordained in 1854, and for 28 years was a priest in Courtrai. He published many volumes of lyrical verse, wrote on philology and folklore, founded literary magazines, and is regarded as the founder of the West Flemish school. He inaugurated a revival in the use of Flemish as a literary language. 📖 K de Busschere, *Guido Gezelle* (1959)

Ghazali, al- 1058–1111
Islamic philosopher, theologian and jurist

He was born in Tus, Persia (near the modern Meshed). In 1091 he was appointed to the prestigious position of Professor of Philosophy at Nizamiyah College, Baghdad, where he exercised great academic and political influ-ence. However, in 1095 he suffered a spiritual crisis which led to a nervous breakdown and a speech impediment that prevented him from lecturing. He abandoned his position for the ascetic life of a mendicant Sufi (mystic), spending his time in meditation and spiritual exercises. Although he taught again briefly, he eventually retired to Tus to found a monastic community. His doctrines re-present a reaction against Aristotelianism and an attempt to reconcile philosophy and Islamic dogma. He was a prolific author, and his main works include *The Intentions of the Philosophers*, *The Incoherence of the Philosophers*, *The Deliverance from Error* and the monumental *The Revival of the Religious Sciences*.

Gheeraerts, Marcus, the Younger 1562–1636
British artist

He was born in Flanders, the son of Marcus Gheeraerts, the Elder (c.1510–c.1590). They moved to England in 1568 and Marcus, the Younger became court painter to **James VI and I**, specializing in portraits. Many pictures attrib-uted to him are of doubtful authenticity, but among the best of those that are certainly his are *Lady Russell* (1625, Woburn Abbey), and *William Camden* and *Sir Henry Savile* (both 1621, Bodleian, Oxford).

Gheorgiu-Dej, Gheorghe 1901–65
Romanian Communist politician

Born in Bîrlad, he became a railway worker, then joined the Romanian Communist Party (RCP) in 1930 and was imprisoned in 1933 for his role in the Grivita railway strike. On his release in 1944, he became Secretary-General of the RCP and Minister of Communications (1944–46). In 1945 he was instrumental in the ousting of the coalition government of Nicolae Radescu (1874–1953) and the establishment of a Communist regime. He then served in a variety of economic posts (1946–52) and as Prime Minister (1952–55), before becoming state President in 1961. A Stalinist, he nonetheless retained the support of **Nikita Khrushchev**'s Moscow, while develop-ing increasingly independent policies during the 1950s and 1960s.

Ghiberti, Lorenzo 1378–1455
Italian goldsmith, bronze-caster and sculptor

Born in Florence, he executed frescoes in the palace of Pandolfo Malatesta at Rimini in 1400, and in 1402 won the competition to make a pair of bronze doors for the Florence Baptistery. His chief competitor was **Filippo Brunelleschi** and both the panels they entered for this prestigious competition can be seen today in the Bargello Museum, Florence. Much of Ghiberti's life was spent completing this set of doors, and as soon as they were finished in 1424 he was entrusted with the execution of another set (1425–52), made to emulate the first pair, and dubbed by **Michelangelo** the 'Gates of Paradise'. Ghiberti was also responsible for the three bronze figures of the saints **Matthew**, **Stephen** and **John** the Baptist which adorn the exterior of Or San Michele. His large and flourishing workshop was a training ground for a dis-tinguished generation of Florentine artists, including **Donatello**, **Michelozzo Michelozzi** and **Paolo Uccello**. In true Renaissance fashion, he was also a humanist and scholar and wrote *I commentarii*, a wide ranging history of art. 📖 Richard Krautheimer and Trude Krautheimer-Hess, *Lorenzo Ghiberti* (1956)

Ghirlandaio, Domenico, *properly* Domenico di Tommaso Bigordi 1449–94
Italian painter

Born in Florence, he was apprenticed to a goldsmith, most probably his father. A metal garland-maker or 'ghirlandaio', he became a painter when he was 31, painting principally frescoes in his native city. Among these are six subjects from the life of St Francis (1485) and an altarpiece, the *Adoration of the Shepherds* (Florentine Academy), for the church of S Trinità, and, in the choir of S Maria Novella, a series illustrating the lives of the Virgin and the Baptist (1490). Between 1482 and 1484 he painted for Pope Sixtus IV, in the Sistine Chapel, the fresco *Christ Calling Peter and Andrew*. His easel pictures include the *Adoration of the Magi* (1488), in the church of the Innocenti at Florence, and the *Visitation of the Virgin* (1491), in the Louvre, Paris. His mosaics include the *Annunciation* in the cathedral of Florence. The many figures in his religious scenes are beautifully characterized with faces full of expression, but his composition tends to be unimaginative and the grouping formal and repetitive. His work is of great historical value for its detailed portrayal of costume and of domestic features. He was assisted by his brothers David (1452–1525) and Benedetto (1458–97).

Giacometti, Alberto 1901–66
Swiss sculptor and painter
Born in Stampa, he was the son of an artist. He studied at Geneva and worked mainly in Paris, at first under Émile Bourdelle. He joined the Surrealists in 1930, producing many abstract constructions of a symbolic kind, arriving finally at the characteristic 'thin man' bronzes, long spidery statuettes, rigid in posture yet trembling on the verge of movement, suggesting transience, change and decay, such as *Pointing Man* (1947, Tate, London). A major retrospective of his work was held in 1996 in the Scottish National Galley of Modern Art in Edinburgh and the Royal Academy in London. ▢ James Lord, *Giacometti* (1985)

Giaconni, Ricardo 1931–
US astrophysicist
Born in Genoa, Italy, he studied at the University of Milan before becoming a research associate at the University of Bloomington, Indiana, in 1956. In 1958 he moved to Princeton. His career was concerned principally with space X-rays, proposing a new type of space X-ray telescope mirror in 1960, and in 1962 leading a project which discovered the first extrasolar source of X-rays (the star Scorpious X-1), and which also revealed the extragalactic background radiation. Giacconi's group also built the first orbiting X-ray detector, which led to the discovery of a host of X-ray stars. In 1966 Giaconni showed that absorption of X-rays by interstellar gas and dust limited studies at long X-ray wavelengths. He has recently taken up the post of director of the European Southern Observatory (1992–).

Giacosa, Giuseppe 1847–1906
Italian dramatist
He was born in Colleretto-Parella, Piedmont, and wrote many different types of play. His historical dramas and comedies in verse include *Il Conte Rosso* (1880, 'Count Rosso') and *La Contessa di Challant* (1891, 'The Countess of Challant'). *Diritti dell'anima* (1894, 'Rights of the Soul'), *Come le foglie* (1900, 'Like the Leaves') and *Il piu forte* (1904, 'The Strongest') address contemporary social problems, emphasizing the importance of established institutions and bourgeois ideals of decency. With Luigi Illica he collaborated on the libretti for *La Bohème*, *Madame Butterfly* and *Tosca*.

Giaever, Ivar 1929–
US physicist and Nobel Prize winner
Born in Bergen, Norway, he studied electrical engineering in Trondheim, served in the Norwegian army (1952–53), then emigrated to Canada in 1954 to work for the General Electric Company. After moving in 1956 to the General Electric Research and Development Center in Schenectady, New York, he examined tunnelling effects in superconductors. Using structures consisting of a sandwich of various different materials, he created a simple technique of measuring superconductor energy gaps, and his subsequent research on current–voltage characteristics led to a significant advance in the understanding of the nature of superconductors. His field of work, of great value in microelectronics, had previously been the subject of related work by Leo Esaki and was later further developed by Brian Josephson, and all three men shared the Nobel Prize for physics in 1973 for their contributions. Giaever's research interests later shifted to immunology. Since 1988 he has been Institute Professor of the physics department at the Rensselaer Polytechnic Institute, Troy, New York.

Giannini, Amadeo Peter 1870–1949
US banker
Born in San Jose, California, the son of Italian immigrants, he made a small fortune in the wholesale produce business, then founded the Bank of Italy in San Francisco in 1904. The bank grew rapidly through his innovative policies, which included making loans to small farmers and businessmen on modest collateral and acquiring branch banks elsewhere in California. Renamed the Bank of America in 1930, it was the largest private bank in the world at the time of Giannini's death.

Giap, Vo Nguyen See Vo Nguyen Giap

Giauque, William Francis 1895–1982
US physical chemist and Nobel Prize winner
Born in Niagara Falls, Ontario, Canada, he received his chemical education at the University of California, Berkeley, where he became professor (1922–62) and emeritus professor from 1962. He was awarded the Nobel Prize for chemistry in 1949. A member of the US National Academy of Sciences, he received the Gibbs Medal of the American Chemical Society in 1951. He developed low-temperature calorimetry and cryogenic apparatus, was the first to use the magnetic method for attaining temperatures to within one degree of absolute zero, and he invented the carbon thermometer for measurements at temperatures in the liquid helium range. He also developed spectroscopic methods for determining entropy values. In 1929 Giauque and Herrick Johnston discovered the isotopes oxygen-17 and -18.

Gibb, Sir Alexander 1872–1958
Scottish civil engineer
Born near Dundee, he was the fifth generation in a line of civil engineers, begun by his great-great-grandfather William (1736–91). His great-grandfather John (1776–1850) became Thomas Telford's deputy on bridges and harbour works in Scotland, then turned to contracting. His grandfather Alexander (1804–67) was apprenticed to Telford, worked with Robert Stevenson, and built railways in Scotland and England. His father Easton (1841–1916) built reservoirs, railways, and the bridge over the Thames at Kew. Alexander joined the firm of Easton Gibb & Son in 1900, and from 1909 to 1916 worked on the construction of Rosyth naval dockyard, then, after five years in government posts, set up in practice as a consulting engineer. His firm became one of the world's largest, its work at home and abroad including hydroelectric schemes, bridges, docks and harbours, and many other kinds of civil engineering project.

Gibbings, Robert John 1889–1958
Irish illustrator and writer

Born in Cork, he is famous for the engravings and woodcuts with which he illustrated most of his own river-exploration books, such as *Sweet Thames Run Softly* (1940), *Lovely is The Lee* (1945) and *Sweet Cork of Thee* (1951). He was director of the Golden Cockerel Press from 1924 to 1933, and through it was instrumental in reviving the art of wood-engraving. He travelled widely and was perhaps the first artist to use diving equipment to make under-water drawings.

Gibbon, Edward 1737–94
English historian

Born in Putney, Surrey, he was educated at Westminster and Magdalen College, Oxford. His *Autobiography* contains a scathing attack on the Oxford of his time and also tells of his return to Protestantism and of his forbidden love for Suzanne Curchod who afterwards became Madame Necker and the mother of Madame de Staël. On a visit to Rome in 1764 he decided to write *The Decline and Fall of the Roman Empire* (6 vols, 1776–88), the work for which he remains best known. Acclaimed as literature as well as history, and markedly pessimistic in tone, the work has as its chief concept the continuity of the Roman Empire down to the fall of Constantinople (Istanbul). Gibbon entered parliament in 1774, and as a devoted follower of Lord North was made Commissioner of Trade and Plantations. After 1788, he spent much of the remainder of his life with Lord Sheffield, who published his *Miscellaneous Works* (1796). 📖 Sir Gavin de Beer, *Gibbon and his World* (1968)

Gibbon, Lewis Grassic, *pseudonym of* James Leslie Mitchell 1901–35
Scottish novelist

Born near Auchterless, Aberdeenshire, he was educated at the local school before attending Mackie Academy, Stonehaven, which he left after a year to become a newspaper reporter. Stirred by the promise of the Russian Revolution he became a member of the Communist Party. In 1919 he moved to Glasgow where he was employed on the *Scottish Farmer*, but he was dismissed for fiddling expenses. He attempted suicide, returned home and decided to enlist. He spent three and a half years with the Royal Army Service Corps in Persia, India and Egypt, and then served in the RAF as a clerk until 1929. His first published book was *Hanno, or the Future of Exploration* (1928), followed by *Stained Radiance* (1930), *The Thirteenth Disciple* (1931), *Three Go Back* (1932) and *The Lost Trumpet* (1932). *Sunset Song*, his greatest achievement, was published in 1932, the first of his books to appear under his pseudonym. Written in less than two months it was published under his mother's name as the first in a projected trilogy of novels, *A Scots Quair*, on the life of a young girl called Chris Guthrie. The second volume, *Cloud Howe*, appeared in 1933 and the third part, *Grey Granite*, in 1934. An unfinished novel, *The Speak of the Mearns*, was published in 1982. He also wrote a biography of the Scottish explorer, Mungo Park (1934), and published *The Conquest of the Maya* (1934). He died following an operation on a perforated ulcer. 📖 D Young, *Beyond the Sunset* (1973)

Gibbons, Grinling 1648–1721
English sculptor and woodcarver

He was born in Rotterdam, the Netherlands, and had for some time practised his art in England when he was discovered by John Evelyn carving a copy of Tintoretto's *Crucifixion*. He was appointed by Charles II to a place on the Board of Works, and was employed to decorate the king's rooms at Windsor and the choir at St Paul's Cathedral, London. At Chatsworth, Burghley, Hampton Court, Blenheim, and other mansions, he carved, often in lime-wood, and with controlled exuberance, the festoons of fruit and flowers and the cherubs's heads for which he is famous. A ceiling at Petworth, Sussex, is a

tour de force. He also produced several fine pieces in marble and bronze, including the statues of Charles II at the Chelsea Hospital, London, and James VII and II in Trafalgar Square.

Gibbons, James 1834–1921
US prelate

Born in Baltimore, Maryland, he became archbishop of that city in 1877, and a cardinal in 1886. He was largely responsible for the growth of the Roman Catholic Church in the USA. He wrote *The Faith of Our Fathers* (1876), *Our Christian Heritage* (1889), and many other books.

Gibbons, Orlando 1583–1625
English composer

Born in Oxford, he was appointed organist of the Chapel Royal, London, in c.1615. He studied at Cambridge and Oxford, and in 1623 became organist of Westminster Abbey, London. His compositions include the anthems, 'O Clap your Hands','God is Gone Up', and 'Almighty and Everlasting God'; and the madrigals, 'The Silver Swan','O that the Learned Poets' and 'Dainty, Fine Sweet Bird'. Besides these he left hymns, fantasies for viols, and pieces for the virginals. 📖 Edmund H Fellowes, *Orlando Gibbons and his Family* (2nd edn, 1951)

Gibbons, Stella Dorothea 1902–89
English writer

Born in London, she was educated at North London Collegiate School for Girls and University College London, where she studied journalism. She worked as a journalist and later began a series of successful novels. She also wrote poetry and short stories, but her reputation rests on *Cold Comfort Farm* (1933), a light-hearted satire on the melodramatic rural novels such as those written by Mary Webb, which won the Femina Vie Heureuse prize, and established itself as a classic of parody.

Gibbs, James 1682–1754
Scottish architect

Born in Aberdeen, he studied in Holland as a protégé of the exiled Earl of Mar, and then in Italy under Carlo Fontana. A friend and disciple of Christopher Wren, he became (1713) one of the commissioners for building new churches in London, but was dismissed in 1715 for his Roman Catholicism. He designed St Mary-le-Strand (1717), the steeple of St Clement Danes (1719), St Peter's, Vere Street (1724), and St Martin-in-the-Fields (1726), the latter being perhaps his most influential and attractive work. He was also responsible for St Bartholomew's Hospital (1730), the circular Radcliffe Camera at Oxford (1737–47) and the Senate House at Cambridge (1730). His *Book of Architecture* (1728) helped to spread the Palladian style and influenced the design of many churches of the colonial period in America.

Gibbs, Josiah Willard 1839–1903
US theoretical physicist

Born in New Haven, Connecticut, he graduated from Yale. A thesis treating the design of gears exhibited his geometrical expertise and earned him the first Yale engineering doctorate (1863). His academic career continued with an (initially) unsalaried appointment to the Yale chair of mathematical physics (1871) which he retained until his death, in spite of more lucrative offers from the new Johns Hopkins University. Thermodynamics was his main topic of scientific inquiry, and his most famous work appeared in the vast memoir *On the Equilibrium of Heterogeneous Substances* (1876–78). This paper introduced a concept of 'chemical potential' which has been a foundation for physical chemistry. Studies of the electromagnetic theory of light, advocacy of the use of vectors and the publication of a book of *Elementary*

Principles in Statistical Mechanics (1902) show the diversity of Gibbs's activities. ⌨ Lynde Phelps Wheeler, *Josiah Willard Gibbs* (1970)

Gibbs, William Francis 1886–1967
US naval architect

Born in Philadelphia, Pennsylvania, he was educated at Harvard and Columbia where he studied law, but became interested in the design of ships, especially from the point of view of safety in the event of a collision. In partnership with his brother Frederick, he designed yachts, luxury liners, and, from 1933, US naval vessels and the 'Liberty Ships' of World War II. His most famous design was the 53,330 ton *United States* which regained the Blue Riband of the North Atlantic for the USA in 1952, making the crossing at an average speed of 35.6 knots, still unbeaten by a passenger liner.

Gibbs-Smith, Charles Harvard 1909–81
English aeronautical historian

Born in Teddington, London, he was educated at Westminster School and Harvard, and in 1932 he joined the Victoria and Albert Museum as an assistant keeper, later becoming director of the photographic collection (1945), and keeper of the public relations and education department (1947–71). He became instructor in aircraft recognition at the Ministry of Information during World War II and developed a keen interest in the history of aeronautics. He wrote the definitive *Aviation—an Historical Survey From its Origins to the End of World War II* (1960) for the Science Museum, London, *Sir George Cayley's Aeronautics, 1796–1855* (1962) and *The Rebirth of European Aviation* (1974). He took up a research fellowship at the Science Museum in 1976 and in 1978 he became the Smithsonian Institution's first Lindbergh Professor of Aerospace History at the Aerospace Museum in Washington DC.

Gibran or Jibran, Kahlil 1883–1931
Syrian mystical writer, poet and artist

He was born in Bisharri in the Lebanese mountains, but became a permanent resident of New York City from 1912. Early on he discovered a spiritual affinity with William Blake, especially as expressed in his drawings, and later with the work of Nietzsche. Among his earliest works is *al-Ajnihah al-mutakassirah* (1911, Eng trans *Broken Wings*, 1922), in which he liberated Arabic from its archaic, classical roots and replaced it with the language of nature, allegory, metaphor and symbolism. He is best known for *The Prophet* (1923), which was written in English. His books have sold more than 20 million copies worldwide, and his poetry has been translated into more than 20 languages. Later works include *Jesus the Son of Man* (1928) and *The Garden of the Prophets* (1934) ⌨ M Naimy, *Kahlil Gibran: His Life and His Work* (1965)

Gibson, Sir Alexander Drummond 1926–95
Scottish conductor

Born in Motherwell, near Glasgow, he studied the piano at the Royal Scottish Academy of Music, Glasgow, and read music at Glasgow University. In 1948 he won a scholarship to the Royal College of Music, London, and after studying in Salzburg and Siena joined Sadler's Wells Opera as a répétiteur. From 1952 to 1954 he was associate conductor of the BBC Scottish Symphony Orchestra, then returned to Sadler's Wells in 1957 as the company's youngest musical director. In 1959 he moved to Scotland as the first native-born principal conductor and artistic director of the Scottish National Orchestra, bringing many new works to Scotland, often in advance of their London performances. In 1962 he helped to form Scottish Opera and as its artistic director until 1985 he was responsible for many notable successes, such as the first complete performance of Hector Berlioz's *Les Troyens* ('The

Trojans') in 1969 and, in 1971, the first production in Scotland of Richard Wagner's *Ring* cycle in German. He retired from the Scottish National Orchestra in 1984. ⌨ Conrad Wilson, *Alex: The Authorised Biography of Sir Alexander Gibson* (1993)

Gibson, Charles Dana 1867–1944
US illustrator and cartoonist

Born in Roxbury, Massachusetts, he was an accomplished black-and-white artist who drew society cartoons for various periodicals such as *Life*, *Scribner's*, *Century* and *Harper's*. In his celebrated 'Gibson Girl' drawings, he created the idealized prototype of the beautiful, well-bred US woman.

Gibson, Edmund 1669–1748
English Church jurist

He was born in Westmorland, and became Bishop of Lincoln (1716), then of London (1720). He edited the *Anglo-Saxon Chronicle* and translated William Camden's *Britannia*, but he is best known for his great *Codex iuris ecclesiastici Anglicani* (1713, 'The Code of English Ecclesiastical Law'). One of his life's ambitions was to reconcile the clergy and universities to the Hanoverian dynasty.

Gibson, Guy 1918–44
English airman

As a wing-commander in the RAF he led the famous 'dambusters' raid on the Möhne and Eder dams in 1943, for which he received the VC. He was killed on a later operation. His experiences are described in *Enemy Coast Ahead* (1946). ⌨ Richard Morris, *Guy Gibson* (1994)

Gibson, James Jerome 1904–79
US psychologist

Born in McConnelsville, Ohio, he was educated at Princeton and Edinburgh universities, and taught psychology at Smith College, Massachusetts (1928–49), and at Cornell University (1949–72). During World War II he served as director of the Research Unit in Aviation Psychology for the US air force, and his later research was partly a result of his wartime studies of such visual skills as those needed to land an aeroplane. He rejected the traditional reductionist approach of the psychological laboratory as inappropriate, and developed the concept of 'direct perception' of 'invariant' attributes of the visual world. His emphasis on the role of vision as the handmaiden for bodily action rather than as a means of achieving awareness of our surroundings has proved increasingly influential in the psychology of perception. He gained the Distinguished Scientist award of the American Psychological Association in 1961, and was elected to the National Academy of Sciences in 1967.

Gibson, John 1790–1866
British sculptor

Born in Gyffin, Gwynedd, Wales, the son of a market-gardener, he found a patron in the historian William Roscoe (1753–1831), and from 1817 lived mainly in Rome, where he studied under Antonio Canova and Bertel Thorvaldsen. His best works, in a neoclassical style, are *Psyche borne by Zephyrs*, *Hylas surprised by Nymphs* and *Venus with the Turtle*. He defended the innovation of tinting his figures, as in his *Venus* (1851–56, Walker Art Gallery, Liverpool), by reference to Greek precedents. Upon his death, all models of his marble works were left to the Royal Academy for the instruction of young sculptors. His public statuary includes those of William Huskisson (1936, Pimlico, London), Sir Robert Peel (1852, Westminster Abbey), and Queen Victoria (1856, House of Lords).

Gibson, Josh 1911–47
US baseball player

He was born in Buena Vista, Georgia. He was barred from major league baseball because he was black, and could play only in the black league. Playing for the Pittsburgh Homestead Grays and the Pittsburgh Crawfords, he became a legendary hitter. It is estimated that he hit more than 950 home runs in his career. In 1972 he was elected to the National Baseball Hall of Fame.

Gibson, Mel 1956–
US – Australian film actor

Born in Peekskill, New York, he emigrated to Australia in 1968 and studied at the National Institute of Dramatic Arts before making his film debut in *Summer City* (1977). He showed promise as the mentally retarded young man in *Tim* (1978) and gained international recognition in *Mad Max* (1979) and its two sequels. His many films include *Lethal Weapon* (1987) and its two sequels, *Hamlet* (1990), and *Maverick* (1994). He provided the voice of Captain John Smith in *Pocahontas* (1995). He has also acted and directed *The Man Without a Face* (1993) and *Braveheart* (1995), which won him Academy Awards for Best Director and Best Film. He subsequently made *Ransom* (1996) and *The Conspiracy Theory* (1997).

Gibson, Mike (Cameron Michael Henderson) 1947–
Irish rugby player

He was born in Belfast, Northern Ireland. A brilliant centre-threequarter, he established a worldwide reputation while still at Cambridge. He became Ireland's most capped player with a total of 69 caps, 25 of which came at fly-half, four on the wing, and the rest as centre. He and fellow Irishman Willie John McBride are the only players to have gone on five British Lions tours.

Gibson, Richard 1615–90
English painter of miniatures and court dwarf

He was a page to Charles I and Henrietta Maria, and the king gave away the bride when he married Anne Shepherd (1620–1709), like himself only 3ft 10in high. He later made several portraits of Cromwell and was himself painted by Sir Peter Lely.

Gibson, Robert 1935–
US baseball player

Born in Omaha, Nebraska, he was a noted pitcher with the St Louis Cardinals from 1959. He was twice named best pitcher in the National League and in 1968 became Most Valuable Player (MVP) in the league on the strength of his exceptionally low earned-run average of 1.12. He set a World Series record of strike-outs against the Detroit Tigers in 1968.

Gibson, Wilfrid Wilson 1878–1962
English poet and playwright

Born in Hexham, Northumberland, he was educated privately. From 1902 he wrote numerous volumes of verse, starting with *Urlyn the Harper and Other Songs*, on the plight of ordinary people faced with industrial change. Later volumes include *The Island Stag* (1947). He also wrote plays, such as *Daily Bread* (1910), and a collection of verse plays, *Within Four Walls* (1950). A realist, he was concerned with everyday matters, particularly industrial poverty. 📖 J Gawsworth, *Ten Contemporaries* (1932)

Giddings, Joshua Reed 1795–1864
US politician and antislavery campaigner

Born in Athens, Pennsylvania, he sat in Congress (1838–59) and in 1861 was appointed Consul-General in Canada.

Gide, André Paul Guillaume 1869–1951
French novelist, writer, diarist, and Nobel Prize winner

Born in Paris, the only child of a law professor, he was educated in a Protestant secondary school in Paris, and privately. He embarked on his career by writing essays, then poetry, biography, fiction, drama, criticism, memoirs and translation, and eventually completed more than 50 books. By 1917 he had emerged as the prophet of French youth and his unorthodox views were the subject of much debate. Although he married his cousin in 1892, he was bisexual and strongly attracted to men. His international reputation rests largely on his stylish novels in which there is a sharp conflict between the spiritual and the physical. They include *L'Immoraliste* (1902, Eng trans *The Immoralist*, 1930), *La Porte étroite* (1909, Eng trans *Strait is the Gate*, 1924), *Les Caves du Vatican* (1914, Eng trans *The Vatican Swindle*, 1925), *La Symphonie pastorale* (1919, Eng trans *Two Symphonies*, 1931) and *Les Faux-monnayeurs* (1926, Eng trans *The Counterfeiters*, 1927, rev edn 1950, *The Coiners*). He was a founder of the magazine *La Nouvelle Revue Française*, and was a critic of French bureaucracy at home and in the African colonies. His *Journals*, covering the years from 1889 to 1949, are an essential supplement to his autobiography, *Si le grain ne meurt* (1920–21, Eng trans *If It Die…*, 1935). He was awarded the Nobel Prize for literature in 1947. 📖 G D Painter, *Gide: a critical biography* (1968); R H S Crossman, in *The God That Failed* (1950)

Gideon
Biblical Israelite judge

Most eminent of the judges of Israel, he was the son of Joash. He suppressed Baal-worship, and put an end to the seven years' domination of the Midianites by routing them near Mount Gilboa.

Gielgud, Sir (Arthur) John 1904–
English actor and producer

He was born in London and made his debut there in 1921. He established his reputation in *The Constant Nymph* (1926), *Hamlet* (1929) and *The Good Companions* (1931), becoming a leading Shakespearean actor of the British theatre and directing many of the Shakespeare Memorial Theatre productions, as well as *The Cherry Orchard* (1954) and *The Chalk Garden* (1956) in London. He has also appeared in many films, notably as Disraeli in *The Prime Minister* (1940) and as Cassius in *Julius Caesar* (1952). He played Othello at Stratford (1961) and Prospero at the National Theatre (1974). Like Laurence Olivier, he adapted to changing dramatic styles and to the new wave of plays popularized by the Royal Court Theatre, appearing during the 1960s and 1970s in plays by David Storey, Edward Bond and Harold Pinter. He now appears increasingly in cameo roles in films, although he won an Academy Award for Best Supporting Actor for *Arthur* (1981), and played the lead role and voiced all the others in Peter Greenaway's *Prospero's Books* (1991). More recent film appearances include *Shine* (1996) and *Portrait of a Lady* (1996). He also returned to the stage (1988), playing in Hugh Whitemore's *Sir Sydney Cockerell: The Best of Friends*. He published an autobiography, *An Actor in his Time* (1979), and was awarded the BAFTA fellowship award for his lifetime contribution to showbusiness (1992). His other published works include *Shakespeare—Hit or Miss* (1991) and *Notes from the Gods* (1994). He was knighted in 1953 and was appointed to the Order of Merit in 1996. 📖 Ronald Hayman, *John Gielgud* (1971)

Gielgud, Maina 1945–
English dancer, artistic director and teacher

Born in London, she studied with many distinguished teachers prior to her 1961 debut with Roland Petit's company. She performed with such companies as Ballet of the 20th Century (1967–71), London Festival Ballet (1972–75) and the Royal Ballet (1977–78), before working freelance from 1978. In 1983 she was appointed artistic director of the Australian Ballet, for which her productions include *Giselle* (1992). She is the niece of the actor Sir John Gielgud.

Gierek, Edward 1913–
Polish politician

Born in Porabka (Bedzin district), the son of a miner, he lived in France (1923–34) during the Piłsudski dictatorship, and joined the French Communist Party in 1931. He was deported to Poland in 1934, and lived in Belgium (1937–48), becoming a member of the Belgian Resistance. On his return to Poland in 1948, he joined the ruling Polish United Workers' Party (PUWP), being inducted into its politburo in 1956, and was appointed party boss of Silesia. He became PUWP leader in 1970 when Władysław Gomułka resigned after strikes and riots in Gdansk, Gdynia and Szczecin. Head of the party's 'technocrat faction', he embarked on an ambitious industrialization programme. This plunged the country heavily into debt and, following a wave of strikes in Warsaw and Gdansk, spearheaded by the 'Solidarity' free trade union movement, he was forced to resign in 1980.

Gieseking, Walter 1895–1956
German pianist

Born in Lyons, France, of German parents, he studied in Hanover and made his first public appearance in 1915. After World War I he established an international reputation, especially in the works of Debussy and Ravel. At his death he was recording the complete piano works of Mozart, and Beethoven's piano sonatas.

Giffard, Henri 1825–82
French engineer and inventor

Born in Paris, he studied there at the Collège Bourbon and the École Centrale. In 1852 he built a light 3 horse-power steam engine, fitted it with a propeller and succeeded in piloting a balloon, steered by a rudder, over a distance of 17 miles (27.4km). This can be considered as the first powered and controlled flight ever achieved, in a craft which was a primitive example of the dirigible or semi-rigid airship. In 1858 he patented a steam injector which became widely used in locomotives and other types of steam engine, and made him a fortune. He continued with his aeronautical experiments, and bequeathed his money to the state for humanitarian and scientific purposes.

Giffen, Sir Robert 1837–1910
Scottish economist and statistician

He was born in Strathaven, Strathclyde. At first a journalist, he eventually became comptroller-general of the commercial, labour and statistical department of the Board of Trade. His works include Essays in Finance (1879–86), The Growth of Capital (1890) and Case against Bimetallism (1892).

Gifford, Adam 1820–87
Scottish judge

Born in Edinburgh, he was called to the Bar in 1849, and was raised to the bench as Lord Gifford in 1870. In his will he left endowments to Edinburgh, Glasgow, Aberdeen and St Andrews universities for a regular series of lectures on natural theology, which have enabled many leading thinkers to expound their views on society and morals.

Gifford, William 1756–1826
English editor and critic

Born in Ashburton, Devon, the son of a glazier, he went to Exeter College, Oxford, and after graduating, travelled on the Continent. His first poem, the Baviad (1794), was a satire on the Della Cruscan school of poetry, the Maeviad (1796), against corrupt drama. His translation of Juvenal, with his autobiography, appeared in 1802. He edited Philip Massinger, John Ford, James Shirley and Ben Jonson, and was the first editor of Walter Scott's Quarterly Review (1809–24). He possessed much satirical acerbity, but little merit as a poet, and as a critic was unduly biased.

Gigli, Beniamino 1890–1957
Italian tenor

Born in Recanati, he won a scholarship to the Liceo Musicale in Rome. He made his operatic debut in Amilcare Ponchielli's La Gioconda ('The Joyful Girl') in 1914, and by 1929 had a worldwide reputation. A lyric-dramatic tenor of great natural gifts, he compensated for technical deficiencies and weakness as an actor by the vitality of his singing, and was at his best in the works of Verdi and Puccini.

Gijsen, Marnix, pseudonym of Jan-Albert Goris 1899–
Flemish writer and diplomat

He was born in Antwerp. For long regarded as the most important living author in the Flemish–Dutch language, he has also written in English and French. He pursued a dual career as a writer and diplomat, retiring in 1968. He first emerged as a poet, much influenced by the third phase of German Expressionism. His ironic, elegant fiction began to appear after World War II, for example Het boek van Joachim van Babylon (1947, Eng trans The Book of Joachim of Babylon, 1951) and Klaaglied om Agnes (1951, Eng trans Lament for Agnes, 1957). In the first he presents the biblical Susanna as a modern wife, and the second is an autobiographical story about the woman whom he loved in his youth. He was a Catholic who turned agnostic, and his revulsion at the intolerance of his church is portrayed in De leejaren van Jan-Albert Goris (1975, 'Jan-Albert Goris's Years of Apprenticeship'). 📖 R P Meijer, Literature of the Low Countries (1978); M Gijsen, Belgian Letters (1946)

Gilbert of Sempringham, St c.1083–1189
English priest

Born in Sempringham, Lincolnshire, he was educated in Paris. In 1148 he founded, at his birthplace, the Gilbertine Order for both monks and nuns, and lay sisters and brothers. It was dissolved at the Reformation. His feast day is 4 February.

Gilbert, Sir Alfred 1854–1934
English sculptor

Born in London, he studied in France and Italy, where he was influenced by the work of Donatello, and executed work of remarkable simplicity and grace, including his aluminium statue of Eros (1886–93, Piccadilly Circus, London), his bronze Icarus (1884, National Museum of Wales, Cardiff) and Comedy and Tragedy (1892, Leeds). He was also a considerable goldsmith. In Windsor he executed the tomb of the Duke of Clarence in the Albert Memorial Chapel (1892–1926, polychrome metal with marble), considered to be his masterpiece. His final work was the Alexandra Memorial (1928–32, London). He was professor at the Royal Academy, London, from 1900 to 1909.

Gilbert, Cass 1859–1934
US architect

Born in Zanesville, Ohio, he was educated at the Massachusetts Institute of Technology (MIT). He is remembered as the designer of the first tower skyscraper, the flamboyant 66-storey Woolworth Building in New York (1912), then the tallest building in the world (not counting the Eiffel Tower). He designed many equally outstanding public buildings, including the US Customs House in New York City (1907) and the Supreme Court Building in Washington DC (1935), and the campuses of the universities of Minnesota (Minneapolis) and Texas (Austin).

Gilbert, Grove Karl 1843–1918
US geomorphologist, stratigrapher, structural geologist and cartographer

Born and educated in Rochester, New York, he joined the Ohio Geological Survey (1869–71), working on the 'Wheeler' survey of territories west of the 100th meridian (1874–76). In subsequent survey work in the Henry Mountains (1875–76) he recognized the nature of the intrusions named laccoliths. On joining the US Geological Survey he worked in Utah and studied the ancient lakes of the Great Basin. His *Monograph on Lake Bonneville* (1890) describes the history of the Pleistocene climate and hydrography of the Great Basin, and discusses the subsequent deformation of the old shore levels as throwing light on the problem of isostatic readjustments of the Earth's crust. He also made notable studies in glacial geology, the history of the Niagara River and recession of the falls.

Gilbert, Sir (Joseph) Henry 1817–1901
English agricultural chemist
Born in Hull, he was educated at Glasgow and London. From 1843 he was associated with Sir **John Bennet Lawes** in the Rothamsted Agricultural Laboratory and in 1884 became Professor of Rural Economy at Oxford. He is particularly noted for his work on nitrogen fertilizers.

Gilbert, Sir Humphrey 1537–83
English navigator
Born in Buxham, he served under Sir **Henry Sidney** in Ireland (1566–70), was made Governor of Munster, then campaigned in the Netherlands (1570–75). In 1578 he led an unsuccessful colonizing expedition to the New World. In a second attempt in 1583 he landed in Newfoundland, claiming it for the Crown, and established a colony at St John's. He was drowned on the homeward journey. He was the half-brother of Sir **Walter Raleigh**.

Gilbert, Walter 1932–
US molecular biologist and Nobel Prize winner
Born in Boston, he studied physics and mathematics at Harvard and Cambridge. From 1959 he taught physics at Harvard, where he was Professor of Biochemistry (1968–72), Professor of Molecular Biology (1972–81) and Carl M Loeb University Professor since 1987. In 1978 he founded the genetic engineering company Biogen NV and served as its chairman for three years. During the 1960s he isolated the repressor molecule, which **Jacques Monod** and **François Jacob** had suggested to be centrally involved in controlling gene action. Using methods developed by **Frederick Sanger**, he described the nucleotide sequence of DNA to which the repressor molecule binds. For this work he shared the 1980 Nobel Prize for chemistry with Sanger and **Paul Berg**. Since the late 1980s he has been a vigorous supporter of the Human Genome Initiative, a project to map and sequence all genes in the human body.

Gilbert, William 1544–1603
English physician
Born in Colchester, Essex, he was elected Fellow of St John's College, Cambridge, in 1561 and in 1573 settled in London, where he was appointed physician to Queen **Elizabeth I** (1601), and King **James VI and I** (1603). In his *De Magnete* (1600) he established the magnetic nature of the Earth and he conjectured that terrestrial magnetism and electricity were two allied emanations of a single force. He was the first to use the terms 'electricity', 'electric force' and 'electric attraction', and to point out that amber is not the only substance which when rubbed attracts light objects. The gilbert unit of magnetomotive power is named after him.

Gilbert, William 1804–89
English novelist
Born in Bishopstoke, Hampshire, he abandoned the East India Company's service for the study of surgery, and that in turn for literature. His 30 works, published from 1858 onwards, include the delightful *King George's Middy* (1869),

a biography of **Lucrezia Borgia**, and several novels in the style of **Daniel Defoe**. 🕮 *The Doctor of Beauweir: an autobiography* (2 vols, 1869)

Gilbert, Sir W(illiam) S(chwenck) 1836–1911
English parodist and librettist
Born in London, he studied at King's College London and became a clerk in the Privy Council Office (1857–62). Called to the Bar in 1864, he failed to attract lucrative briefs and made his living from magazine contributions to *Punch* and *Fun*, for which he wrote much humorous verse under his boyhood nickname 'Bab'. This verse was collected in 1869 as the *Bab Ballads*. He also wrote a Christmas burlesque, *Dulcemara, or The Little Duck and The Great Quack* (1866) and *The Palace of Truth* (1870), which both made a hit on the stage, followed by *Pygmalion and Galatea* (1871). But it is as the librettist of Sir **Arthur Sullivan's** light operas that he is best remembered. Their famous partnership, which began in 1871, scored its first success with *Trial by Jury* under **Richard D'Oyly Carte's** able management at the Royalty Theatre, London, in 1875. Jibing, topsy-turvy wit, accentuated by Sullivan's scores, was characteristic of the light operas that followed, from *The Sorcerer* (1877), *HMS Pinafore* (1878) and *The Pirates of Penzance* (1879) to *The Gondoliers* (1889) and *The Grand Duke* (1896). Their works were performed initially at the Opéra Comique and from 1881 in the new Savoy Theatre which had been specifically built for them by D'Oyly Carte. It was a carpet in the Savoy, considered too costly by the ever-argumentative Gilbert, that touched off a quarrel between him and Sullivan. They created only three more pieces before Sullivan's death and **Edward German's** efforts to fill the gap in *Fallen Fairies* (1909) proved unsuccessful. 🕮 H Pearson, *Gilbert: his life and strife* (1957)

Gilbert and George, *properly* Gilbert Proesch 1943– and George Passmore 1944–
English avant-garde artists
Born in Italy, Gilbert studied at the Academy of Art in Munich and then at St Martin's School of Art, London, where he met Plymouth-born George, who had studied at Dartington Hall and at the Oxford School of Art. They made their name in the late 1960s as performance artists (the 'singing sculptures'), with faces and hands painted gold, holding their poses for hours at a time. Continuing to pose as 'living sculptures', they have also more recently concentrated on photopieces, assembled from a number of separately framed photographs which key together to make a single whole, such as *Death Hope Life Fear* (1984, Tate, London). Their work now internationally exhibited, they talk and seem to think as one, seldom dropping their act. They won the Turner Prize in 1986 and have exhibited at the Venice Biennale in 1978, 1979 and 1993 (in the 'Art against AIDS' exhibition).

Gilbey, Sir Walter 1831–1914
English wine merchant
Born in Bishop's Stortford, Hertfordshire, he was founder of the well-known wine company, and was also a horse-breeder and agriculturist.

Gilbreth, Frank Bunker 1868–1924
US engineer and efficiency expert
Born in Fairfield, Maine, he began work as an apprentice bricklayer in 1885, and from that time devoted himself to developing time-and-motion studies of industrial processes as a means of increasing efficiency. Later he and his wife Lillian Evelyn (1879–1972) made detailed laboratory studies of the basic elements involved in manual work which they called 'therbligs', such as search, find, select, grasp, assemble, and so on. With **Frederick Winslow Taylor** they were the founders of scientific management

as it is universally practised today. The Gilbreths had 12 children, two of whom collaborated in writing the popular book and film *Cheaper by the Dozen* (1949–50).

Gilchrist, Percy Carlyle 1851–1935
English metallurgist

Born in Lyme Regis, Dorset, he studied at the Royal School of Mines, London, where he became a Murchison Medallist. He took a post as chemist first at Cwm Avon ironworks in south Wales, and then at Blaenavon ironworks. There he reluctantly agreed to the requests of his cousin, Sidney Gilchrist Thomas, that he should assist in carrying out the experimental work necessary to test and develop Thomas's ideas on dephosphorization to remove the phosphate impurities in iron ore. The Gilchrist–Thomas process greatly increased the potential steel production of the world by making possible the use of the large European phosphoric iron ore fields. After Thomas's early death, Gilchrist became active in the steel industry, working hard to promote basic steelmaking both by Bessemer converter and open-hearth furnace.

Gildas, St c.493–570
Roman-British historian and monk

Born in Strathclyde, he fled the strife that raged in his neighbourhood and went to Wales. After his wife died he became a monk. His famous treatise, *De Excidio et Conquestu Britanniae*, probably written between 516 and 547, is the only extant history of the Celts, and the only contemporary British version of events from the invasion of the Romans to his own time. His feast day is 29 January.

Giles or Aegidius or Egidius, St d.c.700
Greek hermit

Born in Athens, traditionally of royal descent, he renounced his patrimony, and lived two years with St Caesarius at Arles. He then retired to a hermitage, where he lived on herbs and the milk of a hind. A Frankish king, hunting the hind, discovered him and was so impressed with his holiness that he built a monastery on the spot and made him its abbot. He is the patron of lepers, beggars and cripples, and his feast day is 1 September.

Giles, *properly* Carl Ronald Giles 1916–95
British cartoonist and animator

Born in London, he was a self-taught artist, and worked his way up from film company office boy (1930) to animator on advertising films, then worked on the *Come On Steve* cartoons (1935). He joined *Reynolds News* in 1938 to draw weekly topical cartoons and a strip, *Young Ernie*, before transferring to the *Daily Express* and *Sunday Express* (1943) where he developed his 'Giles Family' cartoons, dominated by Grandma.

Giles, (William) Ernest (Powell) 1835–97
Australian explorer

Born in Bristol, England, he was educated at Christ's Hospital, London, then emigrated to Adelaide in 1850, where he worked in the Victoria goldfields. From 1861 to 1865 he searched for pastures inland from the Darling River. Under the sponsorship of Sir Ferdinand Mueller, he was sent to explore areas to the west of the Central Overland telegraph between Adelaide and Darwin, first in 1872 when he discovered Lake Amadeus and again in 1874 when he penetrated the Gibson Desert, named after a companion of his who died there. He tried again (1875–76), and managed to cross from Port Augusta to Perth, a distance of 2,500 miles (4,025km) in five months, and back along a line just south of the Tropic of Capricorn. This extraordinary feat of endurance is described in his *Australia Twice Traversed* (1889).

Giles, Herbert Allen 1845–1935
English scholar and linguist

Born in Oxford, he had a career in the diplomatic service in China between 1867 and 1892. He returned to Great Britain and from 1897 to 1932 was Professor of Chinese at Cambridge. Although interest in the Chinese language was initially small and he had few pupils, he published a great number of books on Chinese language and civilization which did much to arouse a serious interest in Chinese culture in Great Britain. He modified the romanization system of Sir Thomas Wade, his predecessor at Cambridge, and his use of this Wade–Giles system (as it came to be known) in his *Chinese–English Dictionary* (1892, 1912) established it as the preferred transliteration system in English-speaking countries for most of this century. Among his other works are a *Chinese Biographical Dictionary* (1898), *A History of Chinese Literature* (1901, 1923) and *An Introduction to the History of Chinese Pictorial Art* (1905, 1918).

Gill, (Louis) André, *pseudonym of* Louise André Gosset de Guines 1840–85
French caricaturist

He lampooned the famous of the day by drawing them with outsized heads and dwarfish bodies.

Gill, Sir David 1843–1914
Scottish astronomer

Born in Aberdeen and educated at Marischal College, Aberdeen (1858–60), he was inspired by the teaching of James Clerk Maxwell. He became a watch-maker and his serious scientific career did not begin until 1872, when he was put in charge of Lord Lindsay's private observatory at Dunecht, Aberdeenshire. He achieved recognition for his high-precision determinations of the solar distance made on expeditions to Mauritius (1874) and Ascension Island (1877). Soon afterwards he was appointed HM Astronomer at the Royal Observatory, Cape of Good Hope (1879–1907). He initiated a photographic survey of the southern sky and became responsible for the immense projects of the *Carte du Ciel* and the *Astrographic Catalogue*; some 22,000 photographs were taken in the Cape's allotted part in this undertaking. Among his other contributions was the geodetic survey of South Africa. He was twice awarded the Gold Medal of the Royal Astronomical Society (1882, 1908), of which he became president after his retirement (1909–11). He was knighted in 1900.

Gill, (Arthur) Eric (Rowton) 1882–1940
English sculptor, engraver, writer and typographer

Born in Brighton, Sussex, he trained as an architect, but then took up letter-cutting and masonry and later engraving. In 1907 he settled in Ditchling, East Sussex, where he founded an ideal community. His *Mother and Child* (1910–11) is in the National Museum of Wales, Cardiff. Through the influence of Augustus John he exhibited at the Chenil Galleries, Chelsea, in 1911 (the year he carved *Ecstasy*, in the Tate, London), and from then on he maintained a steady output of stone and wood carvings, as well as engravings (for his own press, St Dominic, and also for the Golden Cockerel Press). He also created type designs, such as Perpetua, Bunyan and Gill Sans-serif, subsequently adopted by Monotype and used all over the world. He also wrote a stream of books dealing with his various crafts, his thoughts and religious beliefs, including *Art* (1934) and *Autobiography* (1940). His sculptures include the *Stations of the Cross* in Westminster Cathedral, London (1913), war memorials up and down Great Britain after World War I, the gigantic figure *Mankind* (1928, Tate) and *Prospero and Ariel* (1931, Broadcasting House, London). He joined the Fabian movement, but later found the socialist ethic limited and joined the Catholic Church. In 1928 he founded the Order of St Dominic at High Wycombe, Buckinghamshire, in

1930 he executed the League of Nations panels in Geneva, and in 1933 he became a founder member of Artists International, set up to oppose Fascism.

Gillespie, Dizzy (John Birks) 1917–93
US jazz trumpeter, composer and bandleader
He was born in Cheraw, South Carolina, and studied musical theory and harmony at Laurinburg Institute, North Carolina. He began his career in swing bands led by Teddy Hill, Cab Calloway, Benny Carter and Charlie Barnet. Along with Charlie Parker, Thelonious Monk and others, he was involved in informal jam session experiments in New York that produced the bebop style in the 1940s. In 1945 Gillespie formed the first of his several big bands working in the new idiom, and in 1956 he led an orchestra on two international tours as cultural missions for the US State Department. Although Gillespie worked intermittently with large orchestras, he is best known as a leader of small combos and as a virtuoso who extended the working range of the trumpet. 📖 Tony Gentry, *Dizzy Gillespie: Musician* (1991)

Gillespie, James 1726–97
Scottish snuff and tobacco merchant
Based in Edinburgh, he bought the estate of Spylaw, and left money to found a hospital (designed by William Bush) in 1801–03 which became a school run by the Merchant Taylors' Company, known as James Gillespie's.

Gillette, King Camp 1855–1932
US inventor and businessman
He was born in Fond du Lac, Wisconsin, and educated in Chicago. After working for years as a travelling salesman, he invented a safety razor and disposable blade, which he started marketing in 1901. A Utopian socialist, he set up a 'World Corporation' in Arizona in 1910 to advocate a world planned economy. He wrote on social theories in various publications like *Gillette's Industrial Solution* (1900) and *The People's Corporation* (1924).

Gilliatt, Penelope Ann Douglas 1932–
English film and theatre critic, novelist and screenwriter
She was born in London. She has written a handful of novels, including *The Cutting Edge* (1978), which describes the relationship between two brothers, and six collections of short stories, including *Splendid Lives* (1977), a sympathetic study of a fleet of eccentrics. She was nominated for an Academy Award for her screenplay for *Sunday Bloody Sunday* (1971), based upon her novel *One By One* (1965). Her profiles of filmmakers, such as Jean Renoir and Jacques Tati, several of which appeared in the *New Yorker*, are considered among the best of their kind.

Gilliéron, Jules 1854–1926
Swiss linguist
Born in Neuveville, he studied under the philologist Gaston Paris (1839–1903) at the École des Hautes Études in Paris, where he himself was Professor of Romance Dialectology (1883–1926). His *Atlas linguistiques de la France*, produced in collaboration with Edmond Edmont and published between 1902 and 1912, was a stimulus to, and provided a basic model for, further studies in linguistic geography. Among Gilliéron's other works are *La Généalogie des mots qui désignent l'abeille* (1918, 'The Etymology of Words Relating to the Bee') and *Pathologie et thérapeutique verbales* (1915–21, 'The Pathology and Treatment of Words ').

Gillies, Sir Harold Delf 1882–1960
New Zealand plastic surgeon
Born in Dunedin, he was educated at Wanganui College and Cambridge. In 1920 he published his *Plastic Surgery of the Face*, which established this art as a recognized branch of medicine. During World War II he was responsible for setting up plastic surgery units throughout Great Britain and was personally in charge of the largest one at Park Prewett Hospital, Basingstoke. In 1957 he published *The Principles and Art of Plastic Surgery*, which became a standard work on the subject.

Gillies, Sir William George 1898–1973
Scottish artist
Born in Haddington, East Lothian, he studied at the Edinburgh College of Art, in Italy, and under André Lhote in France. His finely organized interpretations of Scottish landscape, many in watercolour, are well known, and his work is represented in the Tate Gallery, London. He was Principal of Edinburgh College of Art (1961–66).

Gilligan, Carol 1936–
US psychologist
She was born in New York City. Her studies in gender differences in moral development, published in *A Different Voice* (1982), point out the biases in studies that establish male behaviour as normal and female behaviour as different or abnormal. In 1984 she was recognized by *MS Magazine* (founded by Gloria Steinem) as Woman of the Year, and in 1987 she founded the Harvard Project on Women's Psychology and the Development of Girls. Her other books include *Mapping the Moral Domain: A Contribution of Women's Thinking to Psychological Theory and Education* (1988) and *Meeting at the Crossroads: Women's Psychology and Girls' Development* (with Lynn Mikel Brown, 1992).

Gillray, James 1757–1815
English caricaturist
Born in Chelsea, London, the son of a Lanark trooper, he first became known as a successful engraver about 1784, and between 1779 and 1811 issued 1,500 caricatures. They are full of humour and satire aimed against the French, Napoleon I, George III, the leading politicians and the social follies of his day. For the last four years of his life he was insane.

Gilly, Friedrich 1772–1800
German architect
Born in Berlin, he was the son of an architect. His work displayed considerable geometric control, evidently inspired by that of the French visionary architects in Paris. After a travelling scholarship in 1797, he became Professor of Optics and Perspective at the Academy of Architecture in Berlin (1798). His designs include the Funerary Precinct and Temple to Frederick II, the Great of Prussia (1796), and the Prussian National Theatre, Berlin (1798), both severe, classical designs.

Gilman, Charlotte (Anna) Perkins, *née* Perkins, first married name Stetson 1860–1935
US feminist and writer
Born in Hartford, Connecticut, she was educated at Rhode Island School of Design. Moving to California, she published her first stories, most memorably 'The Yellow Wall-Paper' (1892), and a collection of poetry, *In This Our World* (1893). She was married to Charles Stetson from 1884 to 1894, and married George Gilman in 1900. She lectured on women's issues, as well as wider social concerns, and in 1898 wrote *Women and Economics*, now recognized as a feminist landmark. She also founded, edited and wrote for the journal *The Forerunner* (1909–16). Her later works include *The Man-made World* (1911) and *His Religion and Hers* (1923). She committed suicide on being told that she was suffering from incurable cancer. 📖 *The Living of Charlotte Perkins Gilman: An Autobiography* (1935)

Gilman, Harold 1878–1919
English artist

Born in Rode, Somerset, he studied at the Slade School, London, and in Spain. He was associated with the Camden Town Group (1910), and was later the first president of the London Group. Influenced by Camille Pissarro and Van Gogh, he used Fauve colouring to paint interiors and portraits, as seen in his *Mrs Mounter* (Tate, London).

Gilmore, Dame Mary Jean 1865–1962
Australian poet and author

She was born in Cotta Walla, near Goulburn, New South Wales. Her early teaching career in the mining town of Broken Hill gave her a lasting interest in the labour movement and she became the first woman member of the Australian Workers' Union. In 1896 she joined William Lane's Utopian 'New Australia' settlement in Paraguay, South America. There she married a shearer, William Gilmore, and they returned to Australia (1902) and settled in Sydney (1912). She campaigned for the betterment of the sick and the helpless through the women's column, which she edited for over 20 years, in the Sydney *Worker* newspaper, but also in her poetry. *Marri'd and Other Verses* (1910) was followed by *The Passionate Heart* (1918), *The Wild Swans* (1930) and *Battlefields* (1939), and in her 89th year she published her last collection, *Fourteen Men* (1954). Her memoirs *Old Days: Old Ways* (1934) and *More Recollections* (1935) illustrate her lifelong efforts to preserve early Australian traditions and folklore. She was created DBE in 1937, and William Dobell's controversial portrait of her was unveiled on her 92nd birthday (1957). A collection of tributes to her was published in 1965, and an edition of her letters in 1980. 📖 W H Wilde, *Three Radicals* (1969)

Gilmour, John Scott Lennox 1906–86
English botanist

Born in London and educated at Uppingham and Clare College, Cambridge, he was curator of the herbarium at Cambridge (1930–31) but then went to Kew (1931–46), becoming assistant director in 1946. From 1946 to 1951 he was director of the Royal Horticultural Society's gardens at Wisley. He then returned to Cambridge, where he was director of the botanic gardens from 1951 to 1973. One of the original proponents of the 'deme' terminology, a flexible classification system, he was one of the founder-members of the Classification Society (later Systematics Association) in 1937. Gilmour was a philosopher, poet, musician, bibliophile, athlete and humanist, as well as a botanist. He published many papers on the theory and philosophy of systematics, chaired many committees on horticultural nomenclature, and was influential in the establishment of the International Code of Nomenclature of Cultivated Plants.

Gilpin, Bernard, *known as* the Apostle of the North
1517–83
English Anglican clergyman

Born in Kentmere Hall, Westmorland, he studied at Queen's College, Oxford, and at Louvain and Paris, and became archdeacon of Durham in 1556. His honesty against pluralites brought accusations of heresy which, however, were unsuccessful, and on Queen Elizabeth I's accession in 1558 he was appointed rector of Houghton le Spring. He turned down many lucrative offers, preferring to minister to his parish and to make preaching excursions into the remotest parts of northern England, which earned him his nickname.

Gilpin, John 1930–
English dancer

Born in Southsea, Hampshire, he was a child actor. He studied at the Rambert School, joining Ballet Rambert in 1945. In 1949 he was a principal with Roland Petit's Ballets de Paris, returning to Great Britain in 1950 to join London Festival Ballet, where he became artistic director

(1962–65). Known for his exacting technique, he created roles in Robin Howard's *The Sailor's Return* (1947), Frederick Ashton's *Le Rêve de Leonor* (1949) and Anton Dolin's *Variations for Four* (1957). He returned to dancing in the late 1960s and now combines teaching and acting.

Gilpin, Laura 1891–1979
US photographer

Born in Colorado, she was given a Kodak 'Brownie' camera in 1903, and made autochromes (the first true colour photographic process to be widely available) in Colorado Springs from 1908. In 1916 she photographed in the Grand Canyon. Also that year, she studied at the Clarence H White School of Photography in New York. She opened a portrait studio in 1918, worked on commercial commissions from the 1920s, and held solo exhibitions from 1924. She undertook public relations photography for the Boeing Aircraft Company in Wichita, Kansas (1942–45), and in 1945 photographed the Rio Grande from source to mouth, documenting the lifestyle of the Navaho people. She had an important solo exhibition at the Witkin Gallery in New York (1973–74), and a retrospective at the Museum of New Mexico, Santa Fe (1974–75). Her publications include *The Rio Grande: River of Destiny* (1949) and *The Enduring Navaho* (1968).

Gilpin, William 1724–1804
English clergyman, writer and artist

Born in Scaleby, Cumbria, he was educated at Oxford, and in 1777 became vicar of Boldre in Hampshire. A leader of the 18th-century cult of the picturesque, he was the author of works on the scenery of Great Britain, illustrated by his own aquatint engravings. He is satirized by William Combe in *Dr Syntax* (1809). His brother Sawrey Gilpin (1733–1807) was a successful animal painter, especially of horses.

Gil Polo, Gaspar c.1535–1591
Spanish poet

Born in Valencia, he continued Jorge de Montemayor's *Diana* in his *Diana enamorada* (1564, 'Diana in Love'), which was very popular throughout Europe, and was used by both Cervantes and Shakespeare as a basis for a plot. It marks a stage in the history of the novel.

Gil Robles, José María 1898–1980
Spanish politician and academic

As a young and pugnacious leader of the Spanish Confederation of Autonomous Rightist Groups (CEDA), he was the principal figure of the Right during the Second Republic. Effectively dominating the governments of 1933 to 1935, as Minister of War he prepared the army for the 1936 uprising which began the Civil War. Exiled as a member of the monarchist opposition to the Franco regime (1936–53, 1962–65), he was the founder and first president of the Popular Democratic Federation, and also created the Christian Social Democratic Party. However, in the 1977 general election his party was annihilated.

Gilruth, Robert Rowe 1913–
US engineer

Born in Nashwauk, Minnesota, he graduated from the University of Minnesota in aeronautical engineering, and has been associated ever since with the design and operation of high speed and supersonic aircraft, guided missiles, and space vehicles. In 1958 he was appointed head of the NASA man-in-space programme which put the first American, John Glenn, into earth orbit in 1962. The next objective, known as the Apollo lunar landing project, was achieved under his direction on 20 July 1969 when Neil Armstrong, on the Apollo 11 mission, became the first man to set foot on the Moon.

Gilson, Étienne 1884–1978
French historian and philosopher

Professor at the Sorbonne (1921–32) and the Collège de France (1932–51), he was founder of the Pontifical Institute of Medieval Studies at Toronto University (1929). He is known especially for his works on medieval Christian philosophy.

Gil Vicente See Vicente, Gil

Gimson, Ernest William 1864–1919
English architect and furniture designer

Born in Leicester, he was recommended by William Morris to take up articles with J D Sedding in London, where he met Ernest Barnsley (1863–1926) and his brother Sidney (1865–1926). Gimson designed, within the idiom of the Art and Crafts movement, a number of houses around Leicester, and other buildings. However, he is mainly associated with the design of furniture. After a short-lived furniture-making enterprise, Kenton & Co (1890–92), he and the Barnsley brothers moved in 1895 to the Cotswolds where they all designed or made furniture. Gimson's own designs included ladder-back chairs and cabinets, mostly in untreated native timbers, as well as metalwork such as sconces and firedogs.

Ginckell or Ginkel, Godert de, 1st Earl of Athlone 1630–1703
British soldier

Born in Utrecht, the Netherlands, he accompanied William III to England in 1688. He fought in the Battle of the Boyne (1690), and on the king's return to England was left as Commander-in-Chief in Ireland. He reduced Ballymore and Athlone, defeated St Ruth at Aughrim, and finally captured Limerick (1691). In 1692 he was created Earl of Athlone. He afterwards commanded the Dutch troops under the Duke of Marlborough (1702).

Giner de los Ríos, Francisco 1839–1915
Spanish educationist

Born in Ronda, Malaga, he became Spain's leading 20th-century educational philosopher and reformer. After his career as Professor of Philosophy had twice been interrupted, the second time by imprisonment because of his refusal to grovel to reactionary authority, he founded, with a group of intellectuals, the *Instituto Libre de Enseñanza* in Madrid (1876). This was a kind of free university through which three generations of distinguished writers and artists passed, such as Federico García Lorca, whose generation enjoyed a brief flowering in the Republic (1931–36). Pedagogically ahead of his time, Giner saw education as primarily 'making man' (*formar hombres*). His Instituto rejected textbooks and examinations, and students were encouraged to go to primary sources. Essential activities included visits to factories, farms, and the mountains, and workshop discussions. His educational ideas, which owe much to the philosophers Krause and John Locke, are set out in *Ensayos sobre educación* (1902).

Gingrich, Newt (Newton Leroy) 1943–
US politician

Born in Harrisburg, Pennsylvania, he was elected to Congress as a US representative from Georgia in 1978. He became a leader of conservative Republicans and launched scathing attacks on House Democrats, successfully using ethics charges to force the resignation of Speaker Jim Wright. He became House minority whip in 1989 and Speaker of the House in 1995, but his popularity dropped sharply in 1996 as the public tired of his stridency. He was fined $300,000 in 1997 for violating House rules and then misleading the Congressional committee investigating his case.

Ginkel, Godert de See Ginckell, Godert de

Ginsberg, Allen 1926–97
US poet

Born in Newark, New Jersey, he was brought up in a Jewish community and educated at Columbia University. A homosexual and drug experimentalist, he was associated with the Beat movement, coined the phrase 'flower power' and was a friend of Jack Kerouac, William S Burroughs and others. *Howl and Other Poems* (1956), his first book, was a succès de scandale. Numerous other poetry collections were published, including *Kaddish and Other Poems* (1961), *White Shroud, Poems 1980–85* (1986), *Snapshot Poetics* (1993) and *Cosmopolitan Greetings: Poems 1986–92* (1994). Despite his initial anti-establishment stance, he gained many honours and awards. His prose *Journals* were published in 1977. 📖 E Mottram, *Ginsberg in the 60s* (1972)

Ginsburg, Ruth Bader, *née* Bader 1933–
US federal judge

Born in Brooklyn, New York City, she was educated at Cornell University, and at Harvard and Columbia law schools. She taught law at Rutgers in the 1960s before becoming professor at the Columbia University School of Law (1972–80). She was US circuit court judge with the US Court of Appeals (1980–93), then was nominated by President Bill Clinton to the Supreme Court of the USA, the highest court in the country. As well as being the second woman Supreme Court justice (Sandra Day O'Connor was the first), she was also the second Jewish justice.

Ginzburg, Vitali Lazerevich 1916–
Soviet astrophysicist

Born in Moscow, he studied at the university there, before joining the Physics Institute of the Academy of Sciences, where he has been head of the sub-department of theoretical physics since 1940. There he applied quantum theory to the study of Cherenkov radiation, subsequently suggesting that the non-thermal radio emission produced in our galaxy is due to radiation produced by electrons gyrating in the galactic magnetic field. He also proposed in 1964 (in a classic book entitled *The Origin of Cosmic Rays*) that all cosmic rays come from within our own galaxy, originating from regions near the galactic nucleus. Professor at Gorky University from 1945 to 1968, he is now a professor at the Moscow Technical Institute of Physics (1968–). He was awarded the Royal Society Astronomical Society Gold Medal in 1991.

Gioberti, Vincenzo 1801–52
Italian (Piedmontese) writer and politician

Born in Turin, he was ordained in 1825 and expelled from Piedmont in 1833 because of his outspoken defence of the Polish cause. He wrote extensively on Italian history and politics. His most important work, *Del primato morale e civile degli italiani* ('On the Moral and Civil Primacy of the Italians'), written in exile in Brussels and published in 1843, called for an Italian confederation under papal presidency. His dreams seemed to have been realized with the election of the apparently liberal Pius IX in 1846 and the outbreak of revolution in 1848. Briefly Prime Minister of Piedmont (1848–49), he became disillusioned with, and retired from, politics and was condemned by an increasingly reactionary Pius.

Giolitti, Giovanni 1842–1928
Italian politician

Born in Mondovì, he was an astute and unprincipled parliamentary manager. He entered parliament in 1882 as a Liberal and became Francesco Crispi's Minister of Finance in 1889. Prime Minister from 1892 to 1893, he was brought down by a banking scandal. He returned to politics as Interior Minister under Roman Zanardelli in 1901, becoming Prime Minister again from 1903 to 1909, except for a brief spell out of office in 1905–06. As Prime Minister, he sought to combat leftist strikes and disorders through economic policy rather than confrontation, and in foreign policy he strengthened Italy's ties with Austria and Germany. During his fourth spell as Prime Minister (1911–14), he brought Italy into the Tripolitanian War, gaining Libya, Rhodes and the Dodecanese. However, the war resulted in unpopular tax increases and a general strike forced him from office in 1914. In opposition, he tried unsuccessfully (1915) to keep Italy neutral during World War I. His fifth ministry (1920–21) failed to cope with postwar disorder or the violence of the squadristi, and he was unable to block **Mussolini's** ascent to power.

Giordano, Luca 1632–1705
Italian painter

Born in Naples, he was able to work with great speed (hence his nickname 'Luca Fa Presto', 'Luca works quickly') and to imitate the great masters. In Florence he painted the ceiling frescoes in the ballroom of the Palazzo Medici-Riccardi. From 1692 to 1702 he was in Madrid as court painter to **Charles II** of Spain, and embellished the Escorial. His oils and frescoes are in most European collections.

Giordano, Umberto 1867–1948
Italian composer of operas

Born in Foggia, he is remembered especially for *Andrea Chenier* (1896) and *Fedora* (1898). There followed *Siberia* (1903) and other operas, the last being *Il Re* (1929).

Giorgione, *also called* Giorgio Barbarelli *or* Giorgio del Castelfranco c.1478–1511
Italian painter

Born near Castelfranco, he probably studied at Venice under **Giovanni Bellini**, and soon developed a freer and larger manner, characterized by intense poetic feeling and richness of colouring. Several early portraits by him have disappeared, but an *Enthroned Madonna* is an altarpiece at Castelfranco. In Venice he was extensively employed in fresco painting, but fragments in the Fondaco de''Tedeschi are all that now remain of this work. *The Tempest* at Venice is attributed to him, while *The Family of Giorgione* in Venice, *The Three Philosophers* in Vienna and the *Sleeping Venus* in the Dresden Gallery are genuine. Many of his pictures, such as the *Sleeping Venus* and *The Three Philosophers*, were completed by other painters, including **Titian**. Giorgione was a great innovator; he created the small intimate easel picture with a new treatment of figures in landscape, aimed at private rather than public collections, and his work marks a turning point in Venetian painting. He was the first great Romantic artist.

Giotto (di Bondone) c.1267–1337
Italian painter and architect

Born near Florence, he was the most innovative artist of his time, and is generally regarded as the founder of the Florentine school. At the age of 10, he was supposedly found by **Giovanni Cimabué** tending sheep and drawing a lamb on flat stone and was taken by him to study art in Florence. His earliest work may have been connected with the making of mosaics for the Florence Baptistery. As a painter he worked in all the major artistic centres of Italy, but his most important works are the frescoes in the Arena Chapel, Padua, the Navicella mosaic in Saint Peter's, Rome, the cycle of frescoes depicting scenes from the life of Saint **Francis of Assisi**, frescoes in the Peruzzi Chapel in the church of S Croce, Florence, and the Ognissanti Madonna, now in the Uffizi, Florence. Stylistically he broke with the rigid conventions of Byzantine art typified by the work of Cimabué, and composed simplified and moving dramatic narratives peopled by realistically observed and believable figures. Irrelevant detail is absent and the figures are left to tell the

stories for themselves. The repercussions of these innovations can be seen in the work of **Masaccio** a century later and ultimately in the work of **Michelangelo** himself, who studied and made copies of Giotto's compositions. In 1334 Giotto was appointed Master of Works for the cathedral and city of Florence. Aided by **Andrea Pisano** he decorated the façade of the cathedral with statues and designed the campanile himself. It still bears his name, though much altered.

Giovanni di Paolo, *also known as* Giovanni dal Poggio c.1403–1482/83
Italian painter

Born in Siena, he may have trained with **Taddeo di Bartoli**, and was certainly influenced by **Gentile da Fabriano**, who was in Siena from 1424 to 1426. Though little is known of his life many works by him have survived. Like his contemporary **Sassetta** he worked in a style that continued the tradition of Sienese Trecento masters. Nevertheless, his narrative abilities and highly personal vision give his paintings considerable charm and appeal.

Gippius *or* Hippius, Zinaida Nikolayevna 1869–1945
Russian poet, novelist and critic

She was born in Belev, Tula. After she went into exile (1919) she spelled her name 'Hippius'. She was married to the poet **Dmitri Merezhkovsky**. In her capacity as a critic (under the names of 'Anton the Extreme' and 'Comrade Herman') she poured deserved scorn on many now-forgotten writers. She and her husband, weary of the Orthodox Church and its hypocrisy, founded a new mystical faith, a compound of the ideas of **Dostoevsky**, **Vladimir Soloviev**, and others, with which she combined an extreme wit and a mordant sensibility. She had welcomed the February Revolution of 1917, but rejected the Bolsheviks on account of their godlessness. Her memoirs, *Zhivye litsa* (1925, 'Living Faces'), deserve to be read as sober prophecies of the fall of Stalinism. Selections from her diaries have been translated into English as *Between Paris and St Petersburg* (1975). Her best work is, however, her pellucid love lyrics and her religious poetry. *Moy lunny drug* (1925, 'My Moonlight Friend') is the most evocative of all portraits of **Aleksandr Blok**. There are English translations of her work in *Selected Works of Zinaida Gippius* (1972) and *Intellect and Ideas in Action: Selected Correspondence* (1972). 📖 V Zlobin, *A Difficult Soul: Zinaida Gippius* (1980); O Maslenikov, *The Frenzied Poets: Andrey Biely and the Russian Symbolists* (1952)

Gipps, Sir George 1791–1847
English colonial administrator

Born in Ringwould, near Deal, Kent, he served in the Royal Engineers and was Governor of New South Wales (1838–46). His policy of land selling by auction instead of the colonial office policy of a fixed price showed him to be an unpopular but farsighted opponent of land monopoly. Gippsland in Victoria is named after him.

Giraldi, Giambattista, *surnamed* Cynthius, Cinthio, Centeo *or* Cinzio 1504–73
Italian writer

Born in Ferrara, he was Professor of Natural Philosophy, then of Belles Lettres, at Florence. Later, he held the chair of rhetoric at Pavia. He is the author of nine plays in imitation of **Seneca**, the Younger, of which *Orbecche* (1541) is regarded as the first modern tragedy on classical lines to be performed in Italy. His *Ecatommiti* (1565) is a collection of tales that was translated into French and Spanish and gave **Shakespeare** his plots for *Measure for Measure* and *Othello*. 📖 P R Horne, *The Tragedies of Giambattista Giraldi* (1962)

Giraldus Cambrensis, *also called* **Girald de Barri or Gerald of Wales** c.1146–c.1223
Norman-Welsh chronicler and ecclesiastic

Born in Manorbier Castle, Pembrokeshire, he was educated at the abbey of St Peter, Gloucester, and later studied in Paris. He became archdeacon of St David's, but his nomination for Bishop of St David's (1176) was rejected by King **Henry II** of England because he was a Welshman. He was appointed royal chaplain (1184–89), and in 1185 accompanied Prince (later King) **John** on a military expedition to Ireland. He wrote *Topographia Hibernica* (c.1188), a record of the natural history, inhabitants and folk-tales of Ireland, and collected material for his *Expugnatio Hibernica* (c.1189), an account of the conquest of Ireland by Henry II. In 1188 he accompanied Archbishop **Baldwin** of Canterbury on a preaching tour of Wales to recruit support for the Third Crusade, and recorded his impressions in *Itinierarium Cambriae* (1191). He wrote an autobiography, *De Rebus a se Gestis: Gemma Ecclesiastica*, a handbook for the instruction of the clergy, and *De Principis Instructione*, a manual on the upbringing of a prince. ⮘ Robert Bartlett, *Gerald of Wales 1145-1223* (1982)

Girard, Stephen 1750–1831
US businessman and philanthropist

Born near Bordeaux, France, he was successively cabinboy, mate, captain and part-owner of a US coasting vessel. In 1776 he settled as a trader in Philadelphia, where he established a bank which became the mainstay of the US government during the War of 1812. He was a sceptic, a miser and an exacting master, yet in the yellow fever epidemic in 1793 he nursed many of the sick in the hospitals, and in public matters his generosity was remarkable. In 1816 he underwrote almost all of the $3 million stock issue to capitalize the Second Bank of the United States. Among other bequests he left $2 million for founding Girard College in Philadelphia for male white orphans, with the stipulation that no minister of any sect was to be allowed on its board or to visit it.

Girardelli, Marc 1963–
Luxembourg skier

Born in Lustenau, Austria, he has won the overall World Cup title more times than any other skier. Regarded as a true competitor and a classic all-rounder, he skis all the disciplines—downhill, slalom, giant slalom and super G—and has won 11 world championship medals (four gold, four silver, three bronze) and two Olympic silver medals. He won the 44th victory of his long career at Kitzbühl where he won the combined event of downhill and slalom. After a disagreement with his Austrian coaches, he adopted Luxembourgeois nationality to make a one-man team.

Girardin, Delphine de, *née* **Gay** 1804–55
French writer

Born in Aix-la-Chapelle, she married **Émile de Girardin**, and contributed feuilletons to her husband's paper under the pseudonym 'Vicomte Charles de Launay'. She also wrote elegant sketches of society life and some poetry, plays and novels, of which *Le Lorgnon* (1831, 'The Eyeglasses') is probably the best. ⮘ L Séché, *Muses romantiques* (1910)

Girardin, Émile de 1806–81
French journalist

Born in Paris, he was the illegitimate son of General Alexandre de Girardin. In 1827 he published an autobiographical novel, *Émile*, and the following year he founded the periodical *Le Voleur*. After the July Revolution (1830) he started the *Journal des Connaissances Utiles*, and in 1831 married **Delphine de Girardin**. In 1836 a charge that the halfpenny Orleanist *La Presse* was subsidized

by the government led to a fatal duel with Armand Carrel, the editor of the *National* (1800–36). From then Girardin gradually became a republican. He promoted **Louis Napoleon**'s election to the presidency, but was exiled for disapproving of the coup d'état and became a socialist, proposing the splitting of France into 15 federal states. In 1874, however, he founded *La France*, in which he again supported the republic.

Girardon, François 1630–1715
French sculptor

Born in Troyes, he studied in Rome, and after 1650 settled in Paris and joined the Le Brun Group of artists painting in the flamboyant, illusionistic style of **Charles Le Brun** at Versailles. He worked on decorative sculpture in **Louis XIV**'s galleries, gardens and palaces, mostly at Versailles (1666–73), where he is noted for the fountain figures, and designed the tomb of Cardinal **Richelieu** (1694) in the chapel of the Sorbonne, Paris.

Giraud, Henri Honoré 1879–1949
French soldier

In World War I he became Chief of Staff of the Moroccan Division. In early 1940 he commanded the French 7th and 9th Armies, suffering capture and internment by the Germans. On his escape in 1942 he was picked up by a British submarine and persuaded to support the Allied cause as a subordinate of General **Eisenhower**, and to collaborate as joint chairman of the French Committee of National Liberation with General **De Gaulle**. On the abolition of his post of Commander-in-Chief of the French forces, he refused the appointment of Inspector-General of the forces to become a highly critical right-wing deputy in the Second Provisional Assembly of 1946.

Giraudoux, (Hippolyte) Jean 1882–1944
French writer

He was born in Bellac, Limousin. After a brilliant academic career at the École Normale Supérieure, Paris, and extensive travel, he joined the diplomatic service and became head of the French Ministry of Information during World War II, until his affiliations became suspect. As a poet and novelist he was much affected by psychoanalytic theories, and pioneered an Impressionistic technique in literature, exemplified particularly in *Provinciales* (1909), *Simon le Pathétique* (1918), and his reflection on his war experiences, *Retour d'Alsace, août 1914* (1916, 'Return from Alsace in August 1914'). His plays are mainly fantasies based on Greek myths and biblical lore, satirically treated as commentary on modern life. They include *La Folle de Chaillot* (1945, Eng trans *The Madwoman of Chaillot*, 1949), *La Guerre de Troie n'aura pas lieu* (1935) and *Pour Lucrèce* (1953). The last two were translated as *Tiger at the Gates* (1955) and *Duel of Angels* (1958) by **Christopher Fry**. He also wrote literary criticism, some short stories, and two film scripts. ⮘ L LeSage, *Giraudoux: his life and works* (1959)

Giroud, Françoise, *originally* **Françoise Gourdji** 1916–
French journalist, feminist, broadcaster and politician

Born in Geneva and educated at the Lycée Molière, Paris, and the Collège de Groslay, she began her career as a typist but was soon writing screenplays. In 1953 she co-founded the news magazine *l'Express* which she also edited. She has been prominent in postwar feminism and from 1974–76 was the Minister for the Status of Women in **Valéry Giscard d'Estaing**'s government. Much of her writing has been translated into English, including *Ce que je crois* (1975, 'What I Believe'), *La Comédie du pouvoir* (1977, 'The Comedy of Power') and the bestseller *Les hommes et les femmes* (1993, 'Men and Women').

Girtin, Thomas 1775–1802
English painter

He was a close friend and a contemporary of **J M W Turner**, with whom he worked in the studio of John Raphael Smith (1750–1812), colouring prints. He painted some of his best landscapes in the north of England and in France, which he visited in 1801–02 for his health. His paintings were among the first in which watercolour was exploited as a true medium as distinct from a tint for colouring drawings, as in *The White House at Chelsea* (1800, Tate, London). His breadth of vision was in sharp contrast to the detailed fussiness of the majority of early watercolourists, and he was one of the greatest of the earlier landscape painters in watercolours. He influenced **John Constable** considerably.

Giscard d'Estaing, Valéry 1926–
French Conservative statesman

Born in Koblenz, Germany, the son of a wealthy Auvergne-based inspector of finance with distant connections to **Louis XV**, he was educated in Paris. He was awarded the Croix de Guerre for his activities for the Resistance during World War II. After the war he graduated from the École Nationale d'Administration and worked in the Ministry of Finance, before being inducted into the private 'Cabinet' of Prime Minister **Edgar Faure** in 1953. He entered the National Assembly, representing Puy-de-Dome, in 1956 as an Independent Republican and became Finance Minister to President **De Gaulle** in 1962. Giscard fell out with De Gaulle in 1966, but returned as Finance Minister during the **Pompidou** presidency (1969–74). Following Pompidou's death he was narrowly elected President in May 1974 and proceeded to introduce a series of liberalizing reforms. However, faced with deteriorating external economic conditions, he was defeated in 1981 by his 1974 opponent **François Mitterrand**. Giscard was re-elected to the National Assembly in 1984 and was the influential leader of the Union pour la Démocratie Française (Union for French Democracy), a centre-right grouping which he formed in 1978, until 1996. In 1989 he resigned from the French National Assembly to play, instead, a leading role in the European parliament. His publications include a volume of memoirs (1988) and a novel (1994). ⚏ Charles Hargrove, *L'autre Giscard: Valéry Giscard d'Estaing vu par un Anglais* (1981)

Gish, Lillian Diana, *originally* Lillian de Guiche 1893–1993
US actress

Born in Springfield, Ohio, she made her stage debut at the age of five, and acted in touring theatre companies with her sister, with whom she made a joint film debut in *An Unseen Enemy* (1912). A long association with **D W Griffith** brought her leading roles in *Birth of a Nation* (1915), *Intolerance* (1916) and *Broken Blossoms* (1919) and she created a gallery of waif-like heroines with indomitable spirits. Unsuited to talking pictures, she returned to the stage in 1930 where her many credits include *The Trip to Bountiful* (1953), *Romeo and Juliet* (1965) and *Uncle Vanya* (1973). She continued to play supporting roles in television and on film, including *Duel in the Sun* (1946) and *The Night of the Hunter* (1955), and returned to a major screen role in *The Whales of August* (1987). She directed one film, *Remodelling Her Husband* (1920), and wrote several volumes of autobiography. She received an honorary Academy Award in 1971.

Gissing, George Robert 1857–1903
English novelist

Born in Wakefield, Yorkshire, he earned a scholarship to Owens College (now the University of Manchester), and from there won another scholarship to the University of London. However, before he could take it up he fell in love with Marianne ('Nell') Harrison, thought to have been a prostitute, from whom he contracted venereal disease. Intent on setting her up as a seamstress, he stole money from his fellow students, for which he was sentenced to a month's hard labour and expelled from college. He was packed off to the USA in disgrace, and while in Chicago wrote a melodramatic tale of English life which was bought by the *Chicago Tribune*. He returned to England in 1877, started his first novel, *Workers in the Dawn* (1880), and married Nell in 1879. He was doggedly productive, feeding the circulating libraries with novels such as *The Nether World* (1889), one of the most graphic accounts of Victorian poverty ever written, but the couple struggled financially until Nell died in 1888. Now better off, Gissing travelled on the Continent, and went on to produce some of his finest fiction: *New Grub Street* (1891), a grim rebuke to all aspiring authors, *Born in Exile* (1892) and *The Odd Women* (1893). He moved to the south of France for the sake of his lungs, and wrote several books in the last five years of his life, including a notable critical biography of **Dickens** (1898), a travel book, *By the Ionian Sea* (1900), and *The Private Papers of Henry Ryecroft* (1902), a spoof autobiography that was instantly successful. His *Commonplace Book* was published in 1962 and *The Diary of George Gissing, Novelist* appeared in 1982. ⚏ G Tindall, *The Born in Exile* (1974)

Giugiaro, Giorgio 1938–
Italian motor car and industrial designer

Born in Garessio, near Cuneo, he worked in the 1960s for the bodywork designers Bertone and Ghia, before establishing his own firm, Ital Design, in 1969. While he has designed for such makers as Alfa-Romeo and Lancia, the models have mostly been those aimed at a popular market. He is especially associated with impressive small cars such as the first Volkswagen 'Golf' (1974), and the Fiat 'Panda' (1980) and 'Uno' (1983). Since the late 1970s Ital has extended its scope to product design, including cameras for Nikon, sewing machines for Necchi and watches for Seiko.

Giulini, Carlo Maria 1914–
Italian conductor

He was born in Barletta and quickly showed musical gifts. After studying at the Santa Cecilia Academy in Rome, he joined the city's Augusteo Orchestra as a viola player. By 1946 he had become director of music for Italian Radio. Five years later he was conducting at La Scala, Milan, where in 1954 he conducted **Maria Callas** in some memorable performances. Between 1969 and 1984 he worked as principal conductor of the Chicago Symphony, Vienna Symphony, and Los Angeles Philharmonic orchestras and gave guest performances all over the world. Giulini is a 'romantic' conductor with a small but perfectly formed repertoire, who achieves his results quietly and without histrionics. Outside the opera house, where he excels in **Mozart** and **Verdi**, he is most often to be heard in **Mahler**, **Tchaikovsky**, **Debussy** and **Ravel**. With the exception of **Benjamin Britten**, contemporary music has little appeal for him.

Giulio Romano, *properly* Giulio Pippi de' Giannuzzi c.1492–1546
Italian painter and architect

Born in Rome, he assisted **Raphael** in the execution of several of his finest works, and at his death in 1520 completed the *Transfiguration* in the Vatican. In 1524 he went to Mantua on the invitation of the duke. The drainage of the marshes and the protection of the city from the floods of the Po and Mincio rivers attest his skill as an engineer. His genius as an architect found scope in the restoration and adornment of the Palazzo del Tè, the cathedral, and a ducal palace. In Bologna he designed the façade of the church of S Petronio. Among his oil paintings are the *Martyrdom of St Stephen* (Genoa), a *Holy Family* (Dresden) and the *Madonna della Gatta* (Naples).

Gladstone, William Ewart 1809–98
English Liberal statesman

Gladstone was born in Liverpool, the son of a merchant and MP. He was educated at Eton and Christ Church, Oxford. In 1832 he was returned by Newark as a Conservative to the reformed parliament, serving under **Robert Peel**. After several junior appointments, he was appointed President of the Board of Trade in 1843. In December 1845 he was made Colonial Secretary. He later gave up his seat, and did not re-enter parliament until the corn-law struggle was over; then, at the general election of 1847 he was elected by the University of Oxford, still as a Tory.

When Peel died in July 1850 Gladstone was brought more directly to the front; and he compelled the House of Commons and the country to recognize in him a supreme master of parliamentary debate. His first really great speech in parliament was made in the debate on **Disraeli**'s budget in 1852. On the fall of the short-lived Tory administration, Lord **Aberdeen** formed the famous Coalition Ministry, with Lord **Palmerston** for Home Secretary, Lord **John Russell** for Foreign Secretary and Gladstone for Chancellor of the Exchequer. His speech on the introduction of his first budget was again masterly.

Gladstone was again Chancellor in 1859 when Palmerston was Prime Minister. In 1865, on Lord Palmerston's death and Lord Russell's accession to the premiership, Gladstone became Leader of the House of Commons. A minor reform bill was introduced enlarging the franchise in boroughs and counties. The Conservative Party opposed it, and were supported by a considerable section of the Liberals. The bill was defeated: the Liberals went out of office (1866).

The serious condition of Ireland, however, and the Fenian insurrection brought the Liberals to power with Gladstone as Prime Minister in 1868. He was frequently in office until 1894, when he resigned. He disestablished and disendowed the Irish Church. For the first time in English history a system of national education was established. He also introduced a measure to improve university education in Ireland, but Catholic members voted against it, and it was rejected (1873). Gladstone offered his resignation, but Disraeli declined to undertake any responsibility, and Gladstone had to remain at the head of affairs. But the by-elections began to tell against the Liberals; Gladstone suddenly dissolved parliament and Disraeli came back to power (1874). For some time Gladstone took the opportunity to concentrate on his literary studies.

Parliament was dissolved in 1880, the Liberals came in with an overwhelming majority, and Gladstone (now member for Midlothian) became Prime Minister once more. He succeeded in carrying out a scheme of parliamentary reform, which went a long way towards universal male suffrage. After a further period out of office, he attempted to introduce a Home Rule bill for Ireland, but a split was caused in his party, the bill was rejected and after an appeal to the country he was defeated at the polls. In 1893, after his final return to office, the Home Rule Bill was carried in the Commons, but was thrown out by the Lords. His advanced age made him resign in March 1894. He died at Hawarden, and was buried in Westminster Abbey.

📖 Roy Jenkins, *Gladstone* (1995); H C G Matthew, *Gladstone 1875–1898* (1995) and *Gladstone 1809–1874* (1986); E J Feuchtwanger, *Gladstone* (1975); P Magnus, *Gladstone* (1954).

'Remember the rights of the savage, as we call him. Remember that the happiness of his humble home, remember that the sanctity of his life in the hill villages of Afghanistan, among the winter snows, is as inviolable in the eye of Almighty God as can be your own.' From a speech at Edinburgh Foresters' Hall, during the Midlothian Campaign (26 November 1879).

Giuseppino, Il Cavaliere d'Arpin See **Cesari, Giuseppe**

Giusti, Giuseppe 1809–50
Italian poet and political satirist

Born near Pistoia, he mercilessly denounced the enemies of Italy and the vices of the age in a series of elegantly crafted satirical poems. He was elected to the Tuscan Chamber of Deputies in 1848. 📖 S Horner, *The Tuscan Poet* (1928)

Givenchy, Hubert James Marcel Taffin de 1927–
French fashion designer

Born in Beauvais, he was two years old when his father died, and his grandfather, who had at one time studied painting, was an early influence. He attended the École des Beaux-Arts and the Faculté de Droit in Paris. He obtained a job with Jacques Fath in 1944, then worked with Piguet, Lelong and **Schiaparelli**. He opened his own house in 1952 and his Bettina blouse in white cotton became internationally famous. In the early 1950s he met **Cristóbal Balenciaga**, who influenced and encouraged him. His clothes are noted for their elegance and quality. He produces ready-to-wear clothes under his Nouvelle Boutique label. He retired in 1995 after 43 years as designer-in-chief at his eponymous Paris fashion house, and was replaced by John Galliano.

Gladstone, Herbert John Gladstone, 1st Viscount 1854–1930
English politician

He was born in London, at No12 Downing Street, which his father **William Ewart Gladstone** then occupied as Chancellor of the Exchequer. He was Liberal MP for Leeds (1880–1910) but during this time he was criticized when a journalist made use of a private conversation with him about his father's intention to support Irish Home Rule (1885). He became Liberal Chief Whip in 1899, and was Home Secretary from 1905 to 1910, when he was appointed first Governor-General of the Union of South Africa and raised to the peerage. He was head of the War Refugees Association from 1914 to 1919.

Gladstone, William Ewart See panel above

Glaisher, James 1809–1903
English meteorologist

Born in Rotherhithe, London, he was self-educated. After taking part in the trigonometrical survey of Ireland, he became assistant to the director of Cambridge University Observatory. In 1835 he went to Greenwich Observatory and in 1840 became superintendent of the magnetic and meteorological department. In 1845 he produced tables for the calculation of dewpoints of the air which became standard. He was later invited to produce reports on the meteorology of England for the registrar-general's quarterly returns (1849), which he did for 54 years. He was a founder-member in 1850 of the British Meteorological Society (which later became the Royal Meteorological Society). He is best known for 29 balloon ascents between 1862 and 1866, which were carried out in every month of the year and with different weather conditions. The main aim was to measure temperature, dewpoint and wind at different heights, and the highest ascent is believed to have reached 30,000 feet. He was a member of many learned societies and was elected FRS in 1849.

Glanvill, Joseph 1636–80
English philosopher and clergyman

Born in Plymouth, Devon, he studied at Oxford. He served as vicar of Frome (1662), rector of the Abbey Church in Bath (1666) and prebendary of Worcester (1678). A sympathizer with the Cambridge Platonists against the rigid Aristotelianism current in Oxford, he attacked scholastic philosophy in his famous work *The Vanity of Dogmatising* (2nd edn, 1665), supported experimental science and appealed for freedom of thought. He dedicated the work to the newly-established Royal Society, of which he had become a Fellow in 1664. After his death Henry More edited and published his *Sadducismus Triumphatus* (1681) which, surprisingly perhaps, attacked the rationalizing scepticism of those who denied the existence of ghosts, witches and other apparitions of the spirit.

Glanvill, Ranulf de d.1190
English jurist

Born in Stratford St Andrew, near Saxmundham, Suffolk, he was Chief Justiciary of England (1180–89). An adviser to Henry II, he reputedly wrote the earliest treatise on the laws of England, the *Tractatus de Legibus et Consuetudinibus Angliae* (c.1187), which briefly but lucidly describes the procedure of the king's courts and is based on the writs which initiated actions. In 1174 he raised a body of knights and captured King William I of Scotland at Alnwick. He joined the Third Crusade and died at the Siege of Acre (1190).

Glanville-Hicks, Peggy 1912–90
Australian composer

Born in Melbourne, Victoria, she studied at the Conservatorium of Music there, at the Royal College of Music, London, and with Ralph Vaughan Williams, Nadia Boulanger, Arthur Benjamin and Egon Wellesz. Between 1948 and 1958 she was music critic of the *New York Herald Tribune* and in 1959 she went to Greece where her opera *Nausicaa* (to a text by Robert Graves) was produced for the 1961 Athens Festival. Much of her output was for theatre and ballet. Other major works include the operas *The Transposed Heads* (story by Thomas Mann) and *Sappho* (by Lawrence Durrell), *Etruscan Concerto, Letters from Morocco* and *Concerto Romantico*. From 1975 she was director of Asian studies at Australian Music Centre, Sydney.

Glas, John 1695–1773
Scottish sectarian

Born in Auchtermuchty, Fife, he was minister of Tealing near Dundee from 1719, and when he was deposed in 1728, formed a congregation of Glassites or Sandemanians based on simple apostolic practice. They held that church establishments were unscriptural and that congregations should be self-governing. The name Sandemanians was from his son-in-law Robert Sandeman (1718–71).

Glaser, Donald Arthur 1926–
US physicist and Nobel Prize winner

Born in Cleveland, Ohio, he was educated at the Case Institute of Technology, Cleveland, and at the California Institute of Technology (Caltech), then became a professor at the University of Michigan (1949–59), and at the University of California at Berkeley (1960–). He was awarded the 1960 Nobel Prize for physics for inventing the 'bubble chamber' for observing the paths of elementary particles. Bubble chambers were used to discover many subatomic particles and reached their pinnacle in 1971 with the construction of 'Gargamelle', a thousand-tonne detector, but have now largely been superseded by

electronic or gas detectors capable of providing data immediately. From 1964 Glaser's research interests have been in the application of physics to molecular biology.

Glasgow, Ellen Anderson Gholson 1874–1945
US novelist

Born in Richmond, Virginia, she spent most of her life there apart from various trips to Europe from 1896. She was best known for her stories of the South, including *The Descendant* (1897), *The Voice of the People* (1900), *Virginia* (1913), and *In This Our Life* (1941, Pulitzer Prize). *Barren Ground* (1925) is a more optimistic and progressivist narrative. ▢ L W Wagner, *Ellen Glasgow: beyond convention* (1982)

Glashow, Sheldon Lee 1932–
US physicist and Nobel Prize winner

Born in New York City, he studied at the universities of Cornell, Harvard, Copenhagen and Geneva, before becoming Professor of Physics at Harvard in 1967 and Higgins Professor of Physics in 1979. Glashow developed one of the first models to describe simultaneously two of the four forces of nature, the electromagnetic and weak forces, and subsequently developed the 'electroweak' theory of Steven Weinberg and Abdus Salam by introducing a new particle property known as 'charm'. He was a major contributor to the theory of quantum chromodynamics, which assumes that strongly interacting particles such as the protons and neutrons which form the nucleus are made of quarks and that 'gluons' bind the quarks together. He shared the 1979 Nobel Prize for physics with Salam and Weinberg for their contributions to 'the standard model' of all particle interactions.

Glaspell, Susan 1882–1948
US writer

She was born in Davenport, Iowa, and studied at Drake University in Des Moines, Iowa. She began by writing short stories, collected in *Lifted Masks* (1912). Her novels include *Fidelity* (1915), *Brook Evans* (1928) and *The Fugitive's Return* (1929). She also wrote plays, among them *Trifles* (1917) and *Alison's House* (1930), based on the life of Emily Dickinson, which won a Pulitzer Prize. ▢ A Waterman, *Susan Glaspell* (1966)

Glass, Philip 1937–
US composer

Born in Baltimore, Maryland, he studied with Nadia Boulanger (1964–66) and Ravi Shankar. He was much influenced by Far Eastern music with its static harmonies, by the melodic repetition found in North African music, and by rock music. The resulting 'minimalist' style, often cast over long periods with unremitting rhythmic patterns and simple diatonic chords, gained him a considerable following, especially in such stage works as *Einstein on the Beach* (1976), *Satyagraha* (1980), *Akhnaton* (1984), *The Making of the Representative for Planet 8* (1988) and *The Voyage* (1992). His other compositions include the film score for *Hamburger Hill* (1989), and the opera *Orphee* (1993).

Glatstein, Jacob 1896–1971
US Yiddish poet and critic

Born in Lublin, Poland, he emigrated to the USA just before World War I. After he arrived in New York at the age of 18, he started to write poetry in English. This short period turned out to be a useful one, for he came under the influence of Rabindranath Tagore, whose mysticism stayed with him. He then met a number of Yiddish poets, and, together with Nokhem Minkoff (1893–1958) and Aaron Glanz-Leyeles (1889–1966), he established the In Zikh movement—it derived its name from the Yiddish magazine, and meant 'within the self'. However, Glatstein was never dogmatic, and he helped to introduce a carefully cadenced free verse into Yiddish poetry. His own poetry, which is vital, sharply ironic, and true to his inner self, is paramount in the Yiddish (and Jewish) poetry of the 20th century. His published work includes *Poems* (1970) and *The Selected Poems of Jacob Glatstein* (1972). He also wrote two outstanding autobiographical volumes about his return to Poland in the mid-1930s to see his dying mother: *Ven yash iz geforn* (1938, Eng trans *Homeward Bound*, 1969) and *Ven yash iz gekumen* (1940, Eng trans *Homecoming at Twilight*, 1962). 💭 Commentary (January 1972); J R Hadda, *Yankev Glatstein* (1980)

Glauber, Johann Rudolph 1604–70
German physician

He was born in Karlstadt, Bavaria, but settled in the Netherlands. In 1648 he discovered hydrochloric acid, and he was probably the first to produce nitric acid. He also discovered 'Glauber's salt' (sodium sulphate), the therapeutic virtues of which he greatly exaggerated, and acetone, benzine and alkaloids. He was likened to Robert Boyle in achievement, and became known as the 'father of chemistry'.

Glauber, Roy Jay 1925–
US theoretical physicist

Born in New York City, he was a member of the theoretical physics division at Los Alamos (1944–46), and then studied at Harvard. He was appointed as a lecturer at the California Institute of Technology (Caltech) from 1951 to 1952, and in 1962 became Professor of Physics at Harvard. He established the theoretical foundations of quantum optics in two epic papers in 1963, and also made pioneering contributions to nuclear physics and to statistical mechanics (showing how a bulk magnetic moment in matter can be generated by the alignment of the atomic magnetic moments). He has been a member of the Advisory Board of the Program for Science and Technology for International Security at the Massachusetts Institute of Technology (MIT).

Glazebrook, Sir Richard Tetley 1854–1935
English physicist

He was born in Liverpool and educated at Dulwich College, Liverpool College and Trinity College, Cambridge. He was appointed assistant director of the Cavendish Laboratory (1891), Principal of University College, Liverpool (1895), and director of the National Physical Laboratory (1900–19). During his career he also held the presidencies of the Physical Society (1903–05), the Optical Society (1904–05, 1911–12), the Institution of Electrical Engineers (1906), the Faraday Society (1911–13) and the Institute of Physics (1919–21). He wrote several physics textbooks and is known for his work on electrical standards. He was elected FRS in 1882, and knighted in 1917.

Glazunov, Aleksandr Konstantinovich 1865–1936
Russian composer

Born in St Petersburg, he studied under Rimsky-Korsakov, and was director of the St Petersburg Conservatory from 1906 until the Revolution of 1917, when the Soviet government gave him the title of People's Artist of the Republic. Among his compositions are eight symphonies and works in every branch except opera. In 1927 he emigrated to Paris.

Gleim, Johann Wilhelm Ludwig 1719–1803
German poet

Born in Ermsleben, near Halberstadt, he held religious and political offices. He was the leader of the Anacreontic school of lyric poets, celebrating the joys of wine, love and friendship, as in *Lieder* (1745, 'Songs') and *Lieder nach dem Anakreon* (1766, 'Anacreontic Songs'). His patriotic *Lieder eines Preussischen Grenadiers* (1758–78, 'Songs of a Prussian Grenadier') contributed to the war poetry of the age of Frederick II, the Great.

Glemp, Jozef 1929–
Polish ecclesiastic

He studied at the Primatial Spiritual Seminary in Gniezno, was ordained in 1956 and became Bishop of Warmia in 1979. In 1968 he was appointed secretary to Cardinal Stefan Wyszynski, whom he succeeded as Archbishop of Gniezno and Warsaw and primate of Poland after Wyszynski's death in 1981. A specialist in civil and canonical law, Glemp was a prominent figure during Poland's internal political unrest. He was made a cardinal early in 1983 and was sent to Russia in 1989 by Pope John Paul II, where he became the first cardinal to be interviewed by *Pravda*. Later that year he was criticized for his handling of the furor over the siting of a Carmelite convent at the Auschwitz concentration camp.

Glen, Esther 1881–1940
New Zealand journalist and children's writer

Aware of the lack of children's reading material in newspapers, she started writing a children's supplement for the family newspaper, the Christchurch *Sun*, and later for the *Press*. Her first novel for younger readers was *Six Little New Zealanders* (1917), followed by its sequel *Uncles Three at Kamahi* (1926). Although she only wrote four books—the others were *Twinkles on the Mountain* (1920) and *Robin of Maoriland* (1929)—her influence on New Zealand children's writing was considerable, and in 1945 the New Zealand Library Association established the annual Esther Glen award for distinguished contributions to the genre.

Glencorse, Lord See Inglis, John

Glendower, Owen, *properly* Owain Glyndwr c.1350–c.1416
Welsh rebel

Born in Montgomeryshire, he claimed descent from Llywelyn ap Gruffydd. He quarrelled with Lord Grey (1401) over some lands and, unable to obtain redress from Henry IV, carried on a guerrilla warfare against the English lords of the Marches which became a national war of independence. He proclaimed himself Prince of Wales, and in 1402 captured Lord Grey and Sir Edmund Mortimer, both of whom married Glendower's daughters and joined him in coalition with Henry Percy (Hotspur). That coalition ended in the Battle of Shrewsbury (1403), won by Henry IV. In 1404 Glendower entered into a treaty with Charles VI of France, who in 1405 sent a force to Wales. Glendower, though often defeated, kept fighting until his death.

Glenn, John Herschel 1921–
US astronaut and politician

Born in Cambridge, Ohio, he was educated at Maryland University. He joined the US Marine Corps in 1943, and served in the Pacific during World War II, and later in Korea. In 1957 he completed a record-breaking supersonic flight from Los Angeles to New York. He became an astronaut in 1959, and in 1962 became the first American to orbit the Earth in a three-orbit flight in the Friendship 7 space capsule. He resigned from the Marine Corps in 1965, and from 1975 served as Democratic senator for Ohio. He sought the Democratic nomination for the presidency unsuccessfully in 1984 and 1988. He announced his retirement in 1997. 💭 Frank Van Riper, *Glenn: The Astronaut Who Would Be President* (1983)

Glennie, Evelyn 1965–
Scottish percussion player

Born in Aberdeen, she studied timpani and percussion from the age of 12, and trained at the Royal Academy of Music, London. Judged to be a percussionist of outstanding abilities, she is additionally remarkable in her achievements as she experienced a gradual but total loss of hearing in her early teens. The only full-time professional percussionist in the world, she has received innumerable prizes and awards and is a Fellow of the Royal College of Music. Many leading composers have written specially for her, and she has recorded and appeared widely throughout Europe, the USA, Australia and the Far East. Her autobiography, *Good Vibrations*, was published in 1990.

Gleyre, Charles 1806–74
Swiss painter

Born in Chevilly in the Swiss canton Vaud, he studied in Italy, travelled in Greece and Egypt and took over Paul Delaroche's teaching school in Paris. Monet, Renoir and Alfred Sisley numbered among his pupils. Much of his work is at Lausanne.

Glinka, Mikhail Ivanovich 1804–57
Russian composer

Born in Novopasskoi, Smolensk, he became a civil servant, but after a visit to Italy began to study music in Berlin. Returning to Russia, he produced his opera *A Life for the Tsar* (1836, known earlier as *Ivan Susanin*). His *Russlan and Ludmilla* (1842), based on a poem by Alexander Pushkin, pioneered the style of the Russian national school of composers.

Glock, Sir William Frederick 1908–
English music critic and impresario

He was born in London and won an organ scholarship to Cambridge. After studying piano with Artur Schnabel in Berlin, he became music critic of the *Daily Telegraph* (1934), the *Observer* (1934–45) and the *New Statesman* (1958–59). He was also director of the Dartington Hall summer school of music (1953–79) and as controller of music at the BBC (1959–72) greatly extended the range of its repertory, notably in the Henry Wood Promenade Concerts. He was knighted in 1970.

Glória, Maria Da See Maria II

Gloucester, Prince Henry, Duke of 1900–74
British prince

The third son of George V, he was educated privately and at Eton. He became a captain in the 10th Hussars and was created Duke of Gloucester (1928). In 1935 he married Lady Alice Montagu-Douglas-Scott, and they had two children: Prince William (1941–72) and Prince Richard, who succeeded him. He was Governor-General of Australia (1945–47).

Gloucester, Prince Humphrey, Earl of Pembroke and Duke of, nicknamed Good Duke Humphrey 1391–1447
English prince and literary patron

The youngest son of King Henry IV, as Regent of England (1420–21) and Protector (1422–29) during the minority of Henry VI, he was overshadowed by his elder brother, the Duke of Bedford, and greatly increased Bedford's difficulties by his greed, irresponsibility, and factious quarrels with their uncle, Cardinal Henry Beaufort. In 1447 he was arrested for high treason by Suffolk, Beaufort's successor as First Minister, at Bury St Edmunds and five days later was found dead in bed (apparently from natural causes). The first great figure in the English Renaissance, he cultivated friendships with literary figures like John Lydgate and the Italian humanists who supplied him with manuscript books. He later presented these to Oxford to form

the nucleus of the Bodleian library. He learnt his nickname from his patronage of literature. 📖 K H Vickers, *Humphrey, Duke of Gloucester* (1907)

Gloucester, Prince Richard, Duke of 1944–
British prince

The younger son of Prince Henry, Duke of Gloucester and grandson of George V, he trained as an architect. In 1972 he married Brigitte Eva van Deurs, the daughter of a Danish lawyer, and they have one son, Alexander, Earl of Ulster (1974–), and two daughters, Lady Davina Windsor (1977–) and Lady Rose Windsor (1980–).

Gloucester, Prince Robert, Earl of d.1147
English prince

An illegitimate son of Henry I, he was the principal supporter of his half-sister Matilda, the Empress Maud, in her civil war against Stephen.

Gloucester, Gilbert de Clare, 8th Earl of, known as the Red Earl 1243–95
English nobleman

He was born in Christchurch, Hampshire, the son of Richard de Clare, 7th Earl of Gloucester. He sided with Simon de Montfort and helped him win the Battle of Lewes (1264) against the king's forces, but after quarrelling with de Montfort, he joined Prince Edward (later Edward I), and won the Battle of Evesham (1265). He married Joan, daughter of Edward I, and built Caerphilly Castle in south Wales.

Gloucester, Gilbert de Clare, 9th Earl of 1291–1314
English nobleman

Also 10th Earl of Clare and 8th Earl of Hertford, he was the son of Gilbert de Clare, 8th Earl of Gloucester. His younger sister Margaret was married to Piers Gaveston, the favourite of Edward II, and after Gaveston's execution Gloucester acted as mediator for the barons with the king. He was killed in the English defeat by the Scots at Bannockburn (1314). Another sister, Lady Elizabeth de Clare (c.1291–1360), endowed Clare College, Cambridge (1336).

Gloux, Olivier See Aimard, Gustave

Glover, Jane Alison 1949–
English conductor and musicologist

Born in Helmsley, Yorkshire, she was educated at St Hugh's College, Oxford, where she became a lecturer in music (1976) and carried out research on the Italian composer Francesco Cavalli. She joined the Open University faculty of music in 1979, and also became a television presenter of such BBC programmes as *Orchestra* (1983) and *Mozart* (1985). She made her conducting debut at the Wexford Festival (1975), and went on to conduct nearly all the top orchestras in the world. After joining the Glyndebourne Opera in 1979, she worked as chorus director (1980–84) and as musical director of the touring opera (1982–85). She made her first appearance at the Royal Opera House, Covent Garden, in 1988, and was artistic director of the London Mozart Players (1984–91).

Glovichisch, Jurni See Clovio, Giulio

Glowacki, Aleksander See Prus, Boleslaw

Glubb, Sir John Bagot, known as Glubb Pasha 1897–1986
English soldier

He was born in Preston, Lancashire. After service in the Royal Engineers in World War I, he was the first organizer of the police force in the new state of Iraq in 1920. In 1926 he became an administrative inspector in the Iraqi government. Between 1930 and 1956 he organized and commanded British-mandated Transjordan's Arab Legion's

Desert Patrol, which became the most efficient Arab army (the Jordanian army) in the Middle East. He was abruptly dismissed from his post following Arab criticism, despite his prestige among the Bedouin and great influence in Arabia. His publications include *The Story of the Arab Legion* (1948), *A Soldier with the Arabs* (1957), *Britain and the Arabs* (1959), *The Course of Empire* (1963), *The Middle East Crisis: A Personal Interpretation* (1967). He also wrote *Into Battle: A soldier's diary of the Great War* (1977). 📖 James Lunt, *Glubb Pasha* (1984)

Gluck, Christoph Willibald 1714–87
German composer
Born in Erasbach, Bavaria, he studied in Milan, and began to write operas in 1741. In collaboration with the librettist Ranieri Calzabigi, he produced such works as *Orfeo ed Euridice* (1762, 'Orpheus and Eurydice') and *Alceste* (1767). In the late 1770s, Paris was divided into two—the Gluckists who supported Gluck's French opera style and the Piccinnists who supported the traditional Italian style of Niccola Piccinni, but Gluck won great accolades with his *Iphigénie en Tauride* (1778), and retired honourably from Paris.

Gluckman, Max Herman 1911–75
British social anthropologist
Born in Johannesburg, South Africa, he studied at Witwatersrand and Oxford, then carried out field research in southern and central Africa among the Zulu (1936–38), Barotse (1939–47) and Tonga (1944). He was director of the Rhodes–Livingstone Institute, Northern Rhodesia (1941–47), then was a lecturer at Oxford (1947–49) and in 1949 was appointed to the chair of social anthropology at Manchester, becoming research professor in 1971. During this period he built up a distinctive school of social anthropological research with a strong regional focus on central African societies, stressing the role of conflict in the maintenance of social cohesion. His major works were in the anthropology of law, politics and ritual, and include *Custom and Conflict in Africa* (1955) and *Politics, Law and Ritual in Tribal Society* (1965).

Glyn, Elinor, *née* Sutherland 1864–1943
British novelist
Born in Jersey, Channel Islands, she began writing with *The Visits of Elizabeth* (1900), but found fame with *Three Weeks* (1907), a book which gained a reputation for being risqué. She kept her public enthralled with such books as *Man and Maid* (1922), *Did She?* (1934) and *The Third Eye* (1940). Her novels were nonsensical, faulty in construction and ungrammatical, but were nevertheless avidly read. From 1922 to 1927 she lived in Hollywood, where 'it' (her version of sex appeal) was glamorized on the screen. 📖 *Romance Adventure* (1936)

Gmelin, Johann Georg 1709–55
German botanist, natural historian and geographer
Born in Tübingen, he graduated in medicine aged 18, and only four years later had become Professor of Chemistry and Natural History at St Petersburg University. In 1733 he took part in a lengthy scientific expedition to eastern Siberia, continued along the Yenisei River, and then turned south, returning to St Petersburg nearly nine and a half years after setting out. He became the first person to determine that the Caspian Sea lay at a lower level than the Black and Mediterranean seas, and he published the expedition's botanical results as *Flora Sibirica* (4 vols, 1747–69). In 1747 he returned to Tübingen, where from 1749 he was Professor of Botany, Chemistry and Medicine.

Gmelin, Leopold 1788–1853
German chemist and physiologist
Born in Göttingen, he studied in Germany and Italy and taught at the University of Heidelberg, where he became professor and director of the Chemical Institute in 1817,

posts that he held until 1851. His interests ranged from physiology to chemistry and mineralogy. He worked towards a definition of organic chemistry and introduced the terms 'ester' and 'ketone'. One of the pioneers of physiological chemistry, he prepared uric acid, formic acid and potassium ferricyanide (Gmelin's salt). He also developed a test which shows the presence of bile pigments (Gmelin's test).

Gmelin, Samuel Theophilus, *originally* Samuel Gottlieb Gmelin 1745–74
German botanist
He was born in Tübingen. He became Professor of Botany at St Petersburg University (1767) and explored the Don, the Volga and the Caspian Sea. His two most important works were *Historia Fucorum* (1768), dealing with the brown alga *Fucus* and its allies, and the account of his travels, *Reise durch Russland*, published in four volumes in the 1770s and 1780s. He was the nephew of Johann Georg Gmelin.

Gneisenau, August Wilhelm Anton, Graf Neithardt von 1760–1831
Prussian soldier
Born in Schildau in Prussian Saxony, he accompanied the German auxiliaries of England to America in 1782, joined the Prussian army in 1786, and in 1806 fought against Napoleon I at Saalfeld and Jena. His defence of Colberg (1807) led to his appointment on the commission with Gerhard von Scharnhorst for the reorganization of the Prussian army. In the War of Liberation (1813–14) he served at Leipzig (1813). In the 1815 Waterloo campaign, as Chief of Staff under Gebbard von Blücher he directed the strategy of the Prussian army.

Göbbels, (Paul) Joseph See Goebbels, (Paul) Joseph

Gobbi, Tito 1913–84
Italian baritone and opera producer
Born in Bassano del Grappa, he studied law, but took up singing in Rome, and made his operatic debut in Gubbio (1935). A regular performer with the Rome Opera from 1938, he was an acclaimed actor and soon made an international reputation, especially in Verdian roles such as Falstaff and Don Carlos. He also produced operas and appeared in films.

Gobelin
French family of dyers
Probably from Rheims, they founded a factory in about 1450 on the outskirts of Paris which later became famous for its tapestries.

Gobind Singh 1666–1708
Last of the 10 Sikh Gurus
He completed the process by which the Sikhs developed from the quietist faith propagated by Guru Nanak to a militant creed. Gaining the leadership on the execution by the Mughals of his father, Guru Tegh Bahadur (1664–75), he was implacably hostile to them, and in the final years of the 17th century established a small Sikh state in the Punjab foothills by military means. At the Baisakhi festival in 1699 he instituted the Khalsa, the new Sikh brotherhood marked by a new code of discipline, the 'Five Ks' (visible symbols, including the uncut hair and beard), and common adoption of the name Singh for males and Kaur for females. Following Aurangzeb's death in 1707, moves towards an accommodation between Sikhs and Mughals ended by Gobind Singh's death at the hands of Pathan assassins the next year. Traditionally, Gobind Singh declared on his deathbed that guruship would henceforth reside in the Sikh scripture (*Guru Granth*) and the Sikh community (*Guru Panth*), his sons having already died in battle or been executed by the Mughals.

Gobineau, Joseph Arthur, Comte de 1816–82
French Orientalist and diplomat

Born in Bordeaux, he was a member of the French diplomatic service and secretary to **Alexis de Tocqueville** (1849–77). He wrote several romances and a history of Persia, but is best known for his essay *The Inequality of Human Races*. He has been called the 'intellectual parent' of **Nietzsche** and the real inventor of the 'superman' and super-morality.

Godard, Benjamin Louis Paul 1849–95
French composer and violinist

Born in Paris, he studied under **Henri Vieuxtemps**, and is now remembered chiefly for the 'Berceuse' from his opera *Jocelyn* (1888).

Godard, Jean-Luc 1930–
French film director

Born and educated in Paris, he began his career as a cinema critic (1950), and contributed to *Cahiers du Cinéma* (1952–65). He started making short films in 1954 and his first feature film *A Bout de souffle* (1960, *Breathless*), established him as a leader of the *Nouvelle vague* ('New Wave') cinema. His elliptical narrative style and original use of jump cuts, freeze frames and so on, gained him much critical attention, both enthusiastic and otherwise. He wrote his own filmscripts on contemporary themes, such as *Vivre sa vie* (1962, *My Life to Live*). Other work from the 1960s includes *Pierrot le fou* (1965), *Alphaville* (1965) and *Week-end* (1967). After an unsuccessful trip to the USA, he submerged himself in 'revolutionary anti-capitalist' films, although he returned to more mainstream concerns in the 1980s. Later feature films include *Sauve Qui Peut* (1980, 'Slow Motion'), *Détective* (1984), *Je vous salue, Marie* (1985, 'Hail Mary'), a highly idiosyncratic *King Lear* (1987) and *Hélas pour moi* (1993, 'Woe is Me').

Goddard, Rayner Goddard, Baron 1877–1971
English judge

Born in London, he was educated at Marlborough and Trinity College, Oxford. Called to the Bar in 1899, he was appointed a High Court judge in the King's Bench Division in 1932, and became a Lord Justice of Appeal and a Privy Councillor in 1938. In 1944 he was made a life peer and became a Lord-of-Appeal-in-Ordinary, serving as Lord Chief Justice from 1946–58. A strong traditionalist and a believer in both capital and corporal punishment, he stressed that 'punishment must punish'.

Goddard, Robert Hutchings 1882–1945
US physicist, rocket engineer and inventor

Born in Worcester, Massachusetts, he received a PhD in physics from Clark University, Worcester, in 1911, and subsequently taught physics there for almost 30 years. Fascinated by the idea of space travel, he published *A Method of Reaching Extreme Altitudes* (1919) and in 1926 his first liquid-fuel rocket was launched. By 1929 he had developed the first instrument-carrying rocket able to make observations in flight. The following year he launched rockets at 500mph (804.5kph) to 2,000 feet (610 metres) and in 1935 they exceeded the speed of sound. He developed jet vanes and gyroscopic control 10 years before the Germans, and described the prospects for electric propulsion, a solar-powered generator and electrostatically accelerated jets of ionized gas. In all, he was granted 214 patents. In 1937 one of his rockets attained an altitude of 1.8 miles (3km), but even during World War II the US government showed little interest in his achievements. Only after his death was he given due recognition for his pioneering work, which led directly to NASA and the US space exploration programme. ▢ Milton Lehman, *This High Man: The Life of Robert H Goddard* (1963)

Godden, (Margaret) Rumer 1907–98
English novelist, poet and children's author

Born in Eastbourne, Sussex, she lived for many years in India, a country and culture which provide the backdrop to much of her fiction. Her third novel and first major success, *Black Narcissus* (1939), describes the struggles of nuns attempting to found a mission in the Himalaya region. Her first book for children was *The Dolls' House* (1947). She often wrote from the point of view of a young person, most notably in *The Greengage Summer* (1958). Her later books include *Coromandel Sea Change* (1991), a love story set in southern India, *Pippa Passes* (1994) and *Cromartie vs The God Shiva* (1998). ▢ *A House with Four Rooms* (1989); *A Time to Dance, No Time to Weep* (1987)

Gödel or Goedel, Kurt 1906–78
US logician and mathematician

Born in Brünn, Moravia (now Brno, Czech Republic), he studied and taught in Vienna, then emigrated to the USA in 1940 and joined the Institute for Advanced Study at Princeton University. He stimulated a great deal of significant work in mathematical logic and propounded one of the most important proofs in modern mathematics, namely Gödel's theorem, published in 1931, which demonstrated the existence of formally undecidable elements within any formal system of arithmetic. This result put an end to hopes of giving a truly rigorous foundation to all mathematics on essentially finite terms. His contact with **Einstein** led him to discover novel solutions to Einstein's field equations which seem to infer the physical possibility of time travel.

Goderich, Frederick John Robinson, Viscount, *afterwards* 1st Earl of Ripon 1782–1859
English politician

He was born in London and educated at Harrow and Cambridge. He entered parliament as a Tory MP in 1806, becoming president of the Board of Trade (1918–23, 1841–43) and Chancellor of the Exchequer (1823–27). He was associated with financial reforms to reduce government debt and promote greater freedom of trade. His success led **William Cobbett** to name him 'Prosperity Robinson'. He was Secretary of State for War and the Colonies (1827) under **George Canning**, whom he succeeded as Prime Minister. His weak leadership was soon exposed and he resigned willingly before meeting parliament as Prime Minister (1827–28), the only premier to do so. Briefly changing parties, he served in Lord **Grey's** Whig governments as Secretary for War and the Colonies (1830–33) and Lord Privy Seal (1834–35). His last government office was under Sir **Robert Peel** as president of the Board of Control (1843–46) and he introduced the bill to repeal the Corn Laws (1846).

Godfree, Kitty (Kathleen), *née* McKane 1896–1992
English tennis player

Born in London, she lost to **Suzanne Lenglen** in the 1923 Wimbledon final as Kitty McKane, and defeated the young US player, Helen Wills, the next year. In 1926, as Kitty Godfree, she defeated Lili de Alvarez to win the title again. In 1986 she presented a silver salver to **Martina Navratilova**, when the latter won her seventh title.

Godfrey of Bouillon c.1060–1100
French crusader

The eldest son of Count Eustace II of Boulogne and Ida of Bouillon, he became Count of Verdun and Lord of Bouillon in the Ardennes in 1076 as heir to his maternal uncle Godfrey (the Hunchback). He had to fight to maintain this inheritance against rival claimants and other local enemies, even after his appointment as Duke of Lower Lotharingia by the Emperor **Henry IV** (1089), and in 1096 he sold or mortgaged all of his lands and joined the First Crusade. In 1099 he was elected ruler of Jerusalem, taking the title of 'Advocate' or Defender of the Holy Sepulchre, and the next month defeated an Egyptian invasion at Ascalon. He had begun to extend the territory held by the Christians when he died after a reign of only a year.

Godfrey, Bob (Robert) 1921–
British animated cartoon producer and director

He was born in New South Wales, Australia, and brought to England as a baby. After training in animation as a background artist, he went on to make his own animated cartoons: *Watch the Birdie* (1954), which brought a new bawdy humour to British cartoons, *Polygamous Polonius* (1960), *Henry 9 till 5* (1965), *Kama Sutra Rides Again* (1971), and others. His musical cartoon, *Great*, on the life of Isambard Kingdom Brunel, won an Academy Award in 1975.

Godfrey, Sir Dan(iel Eyers) 1868–1939
English conductor

Born in London, he conducted opera and symphony concerts throughout Great Britain and from 1893 to 1934 was director of music to the Corporation of Bournemouth and its symphony orchestra. His father, Daniel (1831–1903), was bandmaster of the Grenadier Guards (1856–96). His uncle, Charles (1839–1904), was bandmaster of the Scots Fusiliers and the Royal Horse Guards and Professor of Military Music at the Royal College of Music, London. Another uncle, Adolphus Frederick (1837–82), was bandmaster of the Coldstream Guards, as was Charles (1790–1863), Sir Dan's grandfather, who founded *Jullien's Journal*, was devoted to military music, and was appointed musician-in-ordinary to King William IV (1831).

Godfrey, Sir Edmund Berry 1622–78
English politician

A London wood merchant and justice of the peace, he was knighted in 1666. His unsolved murder, one of the most celebrated of historical mysteries, was used by Titus Oates to advance his 'Popish Plot'.

Godiva, Lady d.c.1080
English noblewoman and religious benefactor

She was the wife of Leofric, Earl of Chester (d.1057). According to the 13th-century chronicler Roger of Wendover, she rode naked through the market-place of Coventry in order to persuade her husband to reduce the taxes he had imposed. A later embellishment of the legend suggests that she requested the townspeople to remain indoors, which they all did except for 'Peeping Tom', who was struck blind. Godiva built and endowed monasteries at Coventry and Stow, Lincolnshire. 📖 Ronald Aquilla Clarke and Patrick A E Day, *Lady Godiva: Images of a Legend in Art and Society* (1982)

Godolphin, Sidney, 1st Earl of 1645–1712
English statesman

Born in Helston, Cornwall, he became a royal page in 1662, entered parliament in 1668, and in 1684 was made head of the Treasury and Baron Godolphin. On William III's landing in 1688 Godolphin remained loyal to James VII and II, and started negotiations with William on his behalf. When James fled, he voted for a regency. However in 1689 William reinstated him as first commissioner of the Treasury where he remained until 1696, when he was replaced by a Whig. Queen Anne on her accession made him her sole Lord High Treasurer (1702) and in 1706 he was created earl. In 1698 he married Henrietta, daughter of the Duke of Marlborough. His able management of the Treasury financed Marlborough's campaigns without increasing the public debt by more than one million annually. To prevent his own overthrow, he forced Anne to dismiss Robert Harley (1708). However, the influence of Harley's friend and relative, Abigail Masham, helped Harley to power, and in 1710 Godolphin was himself dismissed. 📖 Sir Tresham Lever, *Godolphin, His Life and Times* (1952)

Godowsky, Leopold 1870–1938
US pianist and composer

Born near Vilna, Lithuania, he toured in Russia as a boy, studied briefly in Berlin, and then went to the USA where he spent much of his subsequent life. He worked at the Chicago Conservatory of Music (1895–1900) and was a professor at Vienna (1909–14). A skilful exponent of the keyboard, he developed the possibilities of the instrument (and left-hand technique in particular) to the utmost. However complex his compositions and many transcriptions may appear to be, they remain innately pianistic. He became a US citizen in 1891.

Godoy, Manuel de, Duke of Alcudia 1767–1851
Spanish politician

Born in Badajoz, he was a member of Charles IV's bodyguard and became the royal favourite. Having deposed the Count of Aranda, he achieved dictatorial power at the age of 25 through the favour of the queen, Maria Luisa, whose lover he was. In 1795 he assumed the title Prince of the Peace, following Spain's defeat by Revolutionary France. In 1796 he allied with France against England—a disastrous move which turned Spain into a virtual French satellite, and greatly contributed to her losing her American Empire. On the French invasion of 1808, the king was obliged to imprison Godoy as a protection from popular fury. He subsequently intrigued with Napoleon I and spent the rest of his life in exile in Rome and Paris. 📖 Jacques Chastenet, *Godoy: Master of Spain* (1953)

Godric, St c.1065–1170
English hermit

Born in Norfolk, he worked as a pedlar, mariner (possibly pirate), pilgrim and seer. From 1110, and for the rest of his long life, he lived as a hermit in a hut at Finchale, on the River Wear near Durham. His feast day is 21 May.

Godwin d.1053
Anglo-Saxon nobleman and warrior

The father of King Harold II, he was probably the son of the South Saxon Wulfnoth, but later stories indicate that his father was a peasant. He was made Earl of Wessex by King Knut (Canute) (1018), and in 1042 helped raise Edward, the Confessor, to the throne, marrying him to his daughter Edith (1045). He was ambitious for his five sons, all of whom received earldoms (1043–57) and collectively their wealth almost equalled that of the royal family. His struggle against the king's Norman favourites caused Edward to confine Edith to a monastery, and banish Godwin (1051). However, in 1052 Godwin won the support of Edward's forces and subjects, so that Edward was forced to reinstate him. His son Harold was for a few months Edward's successor.

Godwin, Edward William 1833–86
English architect and designer

Born in Bristol, he trained there and from 1854 practised as an architect. Northampton Town Hall (1861) dates from his early Gothic period. In 1865 he moved his practice to London. His mainly domestic architecture included the White House (1877), a studio house in Chelsea for his friend James McNeill Whistler. He was a central figure in the Aesthetic movement, and his furniture designs after 1875 were much influenced by the Japanese style which that movement made fashionable. Much of it, in ebonized pine, was remarkably advanced in its simple unornamented structure. He was also a theatrical designer, dress reformer and journalist. He was the lover of Ellen Terry, and their son was Edward Gordon Craig.

Godwin, Fay Simmonds 1931–
English photographer

Born in Berlin, Germany, she was educated in numerous schools worldwide. She began by taking photographs of her two young sons but has become best known for her landscapes, including Welsh and Scottish scenes. They now often make a sociological or ecological statement by incorporating pollution, in order to alert people to the potential for environmental disaster. Since 1970 she has worked as a freelance photographer, based in London. Her many publications include *The Oldest Road: The Ridgeway* (1975, co-authored with J R L Anderson) and *Our Forbidden Land* (1990).

Godwin, Francis 1562–1633
English prelate and author

Born in Hannington, Northamptonshire, the son of Bishop Thomas Godwin (1517–90), he was educated at Oxford. He became rector of Sampford, then Bishop of Llandaff (1601) and of Hereford (1617). His eight works include *A Catalogue of the Bishops of England* (1601), but he is best known for his science-fiction romance, *Man in the Moon or a Voyage Thither, by Domingo Gonsales* (1638), used as a source by Bishop John Wilkins, Cyrano de Bergerac and Jonathan Swift.

Godwin, Sir Harry 1901–85
English botanist

Born in Holmes, Rotherham, Yorkshire, he was educated at University College, Nottingham, and Clare College, Cambridge. From 1923 to 1968 he was on the staff of Cambridge, as Professor of Botany from 1960 to 1968. He was also the first director of the sub-department of quaternary research at the Cambridge Botany School (1948–66). He pioneered British pollen analysis, and is also known for his contributions to the science of radiocarbon dating, and studying changes in land/sea levels in recent geological time. In 1930 he wrote *Plant Biology*, whose emphasis on physiology secured a deeper understanding of the basic role of the green plant, but his major published work was *The History of the British Flora* (1956). Elected FRS in 1945, he was knighted in 1970.

Godwin, Mary See Wollstonecraft, Mary

Godwin, William 1756–1836
English political writer and novelist

Born in Wisbech, Cambridgeshire, he spent his childhood in Guestwick, Norfolk, and then attended Hoxton Presbyterian College (1773–78). During a five years' ministry at Ware, Stowmarket and Beaconsfield, he turned Socinian and republican, and by 1787 was a 'complete unbeliever'. His *Enquiry Concerning Political Justice* brought him fame, and captivated Coleridge, Wordsworth, Robert Southey, and later and above all Shelley, who became his disciple, son-in-law and subsidizer. It was calmly subversive of everything (law and 'marriage, the worst of all laws'), but it deprecated violence, and its author escaped prosecution. His masterpiece, *The Adventures of Caleb Williams* (1794), was designed to give 'a general review of the modes of domestic and unrecorded despotism'. In 1797 he married Mary Wollstonecraft, who was pregnant by him, but she died soon after their daughter, Mary Wollstonecraft Shelley was born. Four years later he married Mrs Clairemont. A bookselling business long involved Godwin in difficulties, and in 1833 he was glad to accept the sinecure post of yeoman-usher of the Exchequer. His tragedy, *Antonio* (1800), was widely criticized. The best of his later prose works are *The Enquirer* (1797) and *St Leon* (1799). 🕮 F K Brown, *The Life of William Godwin* (1926)

Godwin-Austen, Henry Haversham 1834–1923
English soldier and surveyor

A lieutenant-colonel, he was attached to the trigonometrical survey of India (1856–77). The second highest mountain in the world, in the Karakoram Range, Pakistan, was named Mt Godwin-Austen after him in 1888, although it is more commonly known as K2.

Goebbels or Göbbels, (Paul) Joseph 1897–1945
German Nazi politician

Born in Rheydt, the son of a Rhenish factory foreman, he was educated at a Catholic school and Heidelberg University. A club foot absolving him from military service in World War I, he won a number of scholarships and attended eight universities. He became Hitler's enthusiastic supporter, and was appointed editor of the Nazi sheet *Voelkische Freiheit* and led the Nazi Party in Berlin in 1923. With the Führer's accession to power 'Jupp' was made head of the Ministry of Public Enlightenment and Propaganda. A bitter anti-Semite, he had a gift for mob oratory which made him a powerful exponent of the more radical aspects of the Nazi philosophy. Wartime conditions greatly expanded his responsibilities and power, and by 1943, while Hitler was running the war, Goebbels was virtually running the country. He retained Hitler's confidence to the last, and in the Berlin bunker he and his wife committed suicide after they had taken the lives of their six children. His diaries now represent a major historical source. 🕮 Helmut Heiber, *Goebbels* (1972)

Goedel, Kurt see Gödel, Kurt

Goehr, (Peter) Alexander 1932–
British composer

Born in Berlin, the son of a conductor, he was taken to England in 1933, and studied at the Royal Manchester College (1952–55) and in Paris. He was made Professor of Music at Leeds University in 1971 and at Cambridge in 1976. Sometimes referred to as one of the Manchester School with Peter Maxwell Davies and Harrison Birtwistle, and typically exploratory in style, he wrote (1992) the piano cycle … *In Real Time*, a series of studies in the tensions between 'real' and 'experimental' time. That year his choral work *The Death of Moses* had its first performance at the Seville Expo. His other compositions include the operas *Arden Must Die* (1967) and *Behold the Sun* (1985), concertos, choral, orchestral and chamber music.

Goeppert-Mayer, Maria, *née* Goeppert 1906–72
US physicist and Nobel Prize winner

Born in Kattowitz, Germany (now Katowice, Poland), she graduated at Göttingen University in 1930, emigrated to the USA and taught at Johns Hopkins University, where her husband, Joseph Mayer, was Professor of Chemical Physics. From 1960 she held a chair at the University of California. Based on the fact that certain nuclei are very stable, having 'magic numbers' of protons and neutrons, she drew an analogy with atomic physics in which stable atoms have a closed shell of electrons and developed the shell model of the nucleus, resolving some initial problems by discussions with Enrico Fermi. A similar model was developed in Germany by Hans Jensen. Goeppert-Mayer shared the 1963 Nobel Prize for physics with Eugene Wigner and Jensen.

Goerdeler, Carl 1884–1945
German politician

Born in Schneidemühl, he served under Hitler as Commissar for Price Control (1934), but resigned from his post as Mayor of Leipzig in 1937 and became one of the leaders of opposition to Hitler. He was executed together with a number of generals following Count Claus von Stauffenberg's unsuccessful bomb plot of 20 July 1944.

Goering or Göring, Hermann Wilhelm
1893–1946
German Nazi politician
He was born in Rosenheim, Bavaria. One of the first in-fantry officers to fight on the Western Front in World War I, he transferred to the air force in 1915, became an ace pilot and later commanded the famous 'Death Squadron'. An anti-Semite, he joined the Nazi party in 1922 and next year commanded the **Hitler** storm troopers, the Brownshirts (SA), but went into exile for five years after the failure of the November Munich putsch. In 1928 he became one of the 12 Nazi deputies to the Reichstag. In the troubled economic crisis years his influence increased and in 1932 he became President of the Reichstag. When Hitler assumed power (1933) Goering entered the Nazi government, his several posts including that of Reich Air Minister and, in 1938, War Minister. As Hitler's Chief Lieutenant he instigated the Reichstag fire, his pretext for outlawing his Communist opponents. He founded the Gestapo, set up the concentration camps for political, racial and religious suspects, and, in the great purge of 30 June 1934 ('night of the long knives'), had his comrades murdered. Two years later the international phase of his career opened when he mobilized Germany for total war under the slogan 'Guns Before Butter'. He was director of the Four Year Plan, renewed in 1940, to prepare the economy for war, and played a major part in the Anschluss with Austria, (1938) and in the annexation of the Sudetenland (1938). When the Munich Agreement was made in 1938, he announced a five-fold extension of the Luftwaffe. Early in 1940 he became economic dictator of Germany and in June reached the pinnacle of his power when Hitler made him Marshal of the Reich, the first and only holder of the rank. However, the Battle of Britain, the failure of the 1941 Nazi bombing attacks to disrupt the British ports and cities, and the mounting Allied air attacks on Germany in 1942 and 1943 led to a decline in his prestige. By the time of the Allied liberation of Normandy in 1944 he was in disgrace. As the war drew to a close, he attempted a revolution. Hitler condemned him to death, but he escaped and was captured by US troops. In 1946 he was the principal defendant at the Nuremberg War Crimes Trial when his record of un-scrupulous intrigue and merciless oppression was laid bare. He was condemned for guilt 'unique in its en-ormity', but committed suicide by poison a few hours prior to his intended execution. ▣ Leonard Mosley, *The Reich Marshall* (1974)

Goes, Hugo van der c.1440–1482
Flemish painter
Born probably in Ghent, and dean of the painters' guild at Ghent (1473–75), he painted the magnificent Portineri Altarpiece containing *The Adoration of the Shepherds* (now in the Uffizi, Florence) for the S Maria Nuova Hospital in Florence, and many other notable works. He spent the last years of his life in the monastery of Soignies, near Brussels.

Goethals, George Washington 1858–1928
US engineer
Born in Brooklyn, New York City, he graduated from West Point in 1880 and served as an officer in the army's engineer corps. As chief engineer of the Panama Canal (1907–14), he supervised a corps of 30,000 workers and directed the excavation and construction, completing the project six months ahead of schedule. He later served as Civil Governor of the Canal Zone (1914–16).

Goethe, Johann Wolfgang von See panel p754

Goetz von Berlichingen See Götz von Berlichingen

Goffe, William c.1605–1679
English Parliamentarian
Born in Stanmer, Sussex, he became major-general in the Parliamentary army, sat in the House of Commons, and signed **Charles I**'s death-warrant. In 1660 he fled to America, where he lived for many years in seclusion at Hadley, Massachusetts.

Goffman, Erving 1922–82
Canadian sociologist
Born in Alberta, Canada, he was educated at the universities of Toronto and Chicago, and from 1949 to 1951 he carried out research at Edinburgh University. He then returned to Chicago, before serving as a visiting scientist at the National Institute for Mental Health (1954–57). In 1958 he joined the department of sociology at the University of California, Berkeley, remaining there until 1968, when he moved to Pennsylvania University. Renowned for his work on patterns of human communication, he was particularly interested in the way in which people present themselves to each other, and what happens when they deviate from accepted norms. His later work was concerned with language. His books include *Asylums* (1961), *Stigma* (1963), *Behavior in Public Places* (1963), *Relations in Public* (1972) and *Forms of Talk* (1981).

Gogarty, Oliver St John 1878–1957
Irish poet and memoir-writer
He was born in Dublin. Also a playwright, politician and surgeon, he knew **James Joyce** and was the model for 'stately, plump Buck Mulligan' in *Ulysses*. He was a senator of the Irish Free State from its foundation in 1922 until 1939, when he moved to the USA. His garrulous, witty prose is at its best in *As I Was Going Down Sackville Street* (1937) and *Tumbling In The Hay* (1939). It is on these volumes, rather than the *Collected Poems* (1952), that his lessened reputation now rests.

Gogh, Vincent Van See Van Gogh, Vincent Willem (panel)

Gogol, Nikolai Vasilevich 1809–52
Russian novelist and dramatist
Born in Sorochinstsi, Poltava, he settled in St Petersburg in 1829, and in 1831–32 published his first major work, *Vechera na khutore bliz Dikanki* ('Evenings on a Farm near Dikanka'). This was followed by two short-story collections, *Mirgorod* (1835, Eng trans 1928) and *Arabesques* (1835, Eng trans 1982) which contained some of his finest stories, like 'Shinel' ('The Overcoat'), 'Nevsky Prospect', and 'Zapiski symashedshevo' ('The Diary of a Madman'), introducing a nightmarish world of his fantastic imagi-nation, detailing his fears, frustrations and obsessions. In 1836 he brought out his play, *Revizor* (Eng trans *The Inspector-General*, 1892), the best of Russian comedies, a wild and boisterous satire exposing the corruption, ig-norance and vanity of provincial officials. He left Russia for Italy in 1836, and in Rome wrote the first part of *Myortvye dushi* (1842, Eng trans *Dead Souls*, 1854), one of the great novels in world literature. It deals with an attempt by small landowners to swindle the government by the purchase of dead serfs whose names should have been struck off the register. His later work shows increasing obsession with his own 'sinfulness' and he burnt many of his remaining manuscripts, including the second part of *Myortvye dushi*. He returned to Russia in 1846. ▣ H Troyat, *Nikolai Gogol* (1971)

Goh Chok Tong 1941–
Singapore politician
Born in Singapore, he was educated at the Raffles Institute and at Williams College in the USA. He worked as a civil servant before joining the Neptune Orient Lines as a businessman in 1969. Elected to parliament in 1976, he specialized in trades union legislation and became the

Goethe, Johann Wolfgang von 1749–1832

German poet, dramatist, scientist and court official, one of the greatest figures in European literature

Goethe was born in Frankfurt-am-Main, the son of a lawyer. He was educated privately and reluctantly studied law at Leipzig (1765–68); however, a love affair inspired him to write his first two plays, *Die Laune des Verliebten* (1767, 'The Beloved's Whim') and *Die Mitschuldigen* (staged 1787,'The Accomplices'). After a protracted illness he continued his law studies at Strasbourg from 1770 where he came under the influence of **Johann Herder**, the pioneer of German Romanticism.

In 1771 he qualified and returned to Frankfurt, where he became a newspaper critic and captured the spirit of German nationalism in an early masterpiece of drama, *Götz von Berlichingen* (1773), which epitomized the man of genius at odds with society. *Faust* was begun, and Goethe followed up his first triumph with his self-revelatory cautionary novel, *Leiden des jungen Werthers* (1774,'The Sorrows of Young Werther'), which mirrored his own doomed affair with Charlotte Buff, the fiancée of a friend. *Clavigo*, a Hamlet-like drama, followed in the same vein, based on **Beaumarchais'** *Mémoires*. A romance with Lili Schönemann inspired the love lyrics of 1775.

In the autumn Goethe (perhaps surprisingly) accepted the post of court-official and privy councillor (1776) to the young Duke of Weimar. He conscientiously carried out all his state duties, interested himself in a geological survey, and exerted a steadying influence on the inexperienced duke. His 10-year relationship with the young widow, **Charlotte von Stein**, served as a psychological support, but did little to help his development as a creative writer.

Goethe also took an interest in the life sciences; in 1782 he extended his researches to comparative anatomy, discovered the intermaxillary bone in man (1784), and formulated a vertebral theory of the skull. In botany he developed a theory that the leaf represented the characteristic form of which all the other parts of a plant are variations, and made unsuccessful attempts to refute **Isaac Newton's** theory of light. He wrote a novel on theatrical life, *Wilhelm Meisters Theatralische Sendung* ('Wilhelm Meister's Theatrical Mission', not discovered until 1910), which contains the enigmatic poetry of Mignon's songs, epitomizing the best in German romantic poetry, including the famous 'Nur wer die Sehnsucht kennt' ('Only He Who Knows Longing'). His visits to Italy (1786–88, 1790) cured him of his emotional dependence on Charlotte von Stein and contributed to a greater preoccupation with poetical form, as in the severely classical verse version of his drama, *Iphigenie* (1789), and the more modern *Egmont* (1788) and *Torquato Tasso* (1790).

His love for classical Italy, coupled with his passion for Christiane Vulpius, whom he married in 1806, found full expression in *Römische Elegien* (1795, 'Roman Elegies'). From 1794 he formed a friendship with **Schiller**, with whom he conducted an interesting correspondence on aesthetics (1794–1805) and carried on a friendly contest in the writing of ballads which resulted in Schiller's part in *Die Glocke* and Goethe's in the epic idyll *Hermann und Dorothea* (1798). They wrote against philistinism in the literary magazine *Horen*.

Goethe's last great period saw the prototype of the favourite German literary composition, the *Bildungsroman* in *Wilhelm Meisters Lehrjahre* (1796, 'Wilhelm Meister's Apprenticeship') continued as *Wilhelm Meisters Wanderjahre* (1821–29,'Wilhelm Meister's Travels'). *Wilhelm Meister* was to become the idol of the German Romantics, of whom Goethe increasingly disapproved. He disliked their enthusiasm for the French Revolution, which he satirized in a number of works, including the epic poem *Reineke Fuchs* (1794), based on a medieval theme, and the drama *Die natürliche Tochter* (1803, 'The Natural Daughter'), and their disregard for style, which he attempted to correct by example in his novel *Die Wahlverwandtschaften* (1809,'Elected Affinities') and the collection of lyrics, inspired by Marianne von Willemer, *West-östlicher Divan* (1819), an attempt to marry East with West.

Goethe's masterpiece, however, is his version of **Christopher Marlowe's** drama of *Faust*, on which he worked for most of his life. Begun in 1775, the first part was published after much revision and Schiller's advice in 1808, and the second part in 1832. Faust, the disillusioned scholar, deserts his 'ivory tower' to seek happiness in real life, and makes a pact with Satan, who brings about the love-affair, seduction and death of Gretchen, an ordinary village girl, and subtly brings Faust by other such escapades to the brink of moral degradation.

Goethe took little part in the political upheavals of his time, although he saw in **Napoleon I** the saviour of European civilization; Napoleon made a point of meeting Goethe at the congress of Erfurt (1803). When he died, Goethe was buried near Schiller in the ducal vault at Weimar.

📖 Goethe's autobiography is *Poetry and Truth* (1811–14). See also Benjamin C Sax, *Images of Identity* (1987); T Reed, *Goethe* (1984); Victor Lange (ed), *A Collection of Critical Essays* (1967); George H Lewes, *The Life of Goethe* (1965).

♪ Many of Goethe's songs have been set to music. Famous examples are *Das Veilchen* (*The Violet*, **Mozart**), *Erlkönig* (*The Erl King*, **Schubert** and **Loewe**), *Ganymed* (*Ganymede*, **Schubert** and **Hugo Wolf**), *Klärchens Lied* (*The Song of Klärchen*, **Beethoven**), *Gretchen am Spinnrade* (*Gretchen at her Spinning-Wheel*, **Schubert**), *Heidenröslein* (*Wild Rose*, **Schubert**).

> *Wer nie sein Brot mit Tränen aß,*
> *Wer nie die kummervollen Nächte,*
> *Auf seinem Bette weinen saß,*
> *Der kennt euch nicht, ihr himmlischen Mächte.*
>
> 'Who never ate his bread in sorrow,
> Who never spent the darksome hours
> Weeping and watching for the morrow
> He knows ye not, ye heavenly powers.'
> From *Wilhem Meisters Lehrjahre* (1796).

---

first secretary of the Peoples' Active Party. In parliament he held a number of ministerial posts including Trade and Industry (1979–81) and Defence (1982–85) before becoming Deputy Prime Minister in 1985. He was appointed Prime Minister in 1990 and remains a member of the National Trades Union Congress.

Gokhale, Gopal Krishna 1866–1915

Indian politician and social reformer

Born in Kotluk, Bombay, he became Professor of History at Fergusson College, Poona, resigning in 1904, when he was selected representative of the Bombay legislative council at the supreme council. He founded the Servants of India Society in 1905 to work for the relief of the underprivileged, and in the same year was elected president of the Indian National Congress. He was a leading protagonist of Indian self-government and influenced **Mahatma Gandhi**, advocating moderate and constitutional methods of agitation and gradual reform. 📖 B R Nanda, *Gokhale: The Indian Moderates and the British Raj* (1977)

Gold, Jimmy See **Naughton and Gold**

Gold, Thomas 1920–
US astronomer
Born in Vienna, Austria, he studied at Cambridge and
worked in the UK before moving to the USA in 1956.
While in England he worked with **Hermann Bondi** and
Fred Hoyle on the steady-state theory of the origin of the
universe. The theory was later displaced through new
evidence, but it was a valuable contribution to cosmology.
From 1959 to 1981 Gold was director of the Center for
Radiophysics and Space Research at Cornell University,
and in 1968 he suggested the currently accepted theory
that pulsars (discovered by **Jocelyn Bell Burnell** and
Antony Hewish in that year) are rapidly rotating neutron
stars, dense collapsed stars which produce beams of radio
waves from their poles which appear as radio pulses on
Earth. His unorthodox theory of the origin of petroleum
and natural gas proposed that some deposits arise from
gas trapped in the Earth's interior from the time of the
planet's formation. He was Professor of Astronomy at
Cornell University from 1971 to 1986, then emeritus, and
became an honorary Fellow of Trinity College, Cambridge, in 1986.

Goldberg, Arthur Joseph 1908–90
US jurist and diplomat
He was born in Chicago. As a lawyer in private practice he
was an advocate of organized labour, and in 1955 he
helped to found AFL–CIO, a national federation of labour unions formed by the merger of the American
Federation of Labor, an organization composed primarily of craft unions founded in 1886, and the Congress
of Industrial Organizations, a federation of industrial
unions founded in 1938. He served as an associate justice
of the Supreme Court (1962–65), resigning to become a
US representative to the United Nations (1965–68), but
never realized his goal of negotiating an end to the
Vietnam War (1975).

Goldberg, Reuben Lucius, *known as* Rube
1883–1970
US cartoonist
Born in San Francisco, he studied engineering at the
University of California, but soon after graduating (1904)
he embarked on a career as a newspaper cartoonist, first
in San Francisco and then (from 1907) in New York City,
where he worked for the New York *Evening Mail* and other
journals. Syndicated from 1915, his popular cartoons often mocked the pointless complications of modern life,
and he was famous for his drawings of ridiculously elaborate machines designed to accomplish simple tasks. He
turned to editorial cartooning after 1938 and won the
Pulitzer Prize in 1948.

Goldberg, Whoopi, *originally* Caryn Johnson
1949–
US actress
Born in New York City, she appeared on stage from the
age of eight, and gradually developed her talent as a
mimic and stand-up comedienne, which culminated in
her Broadway triumph *Whoopi Goldberg* (1984–85). She
made her major film debut in *The Color Purple* (1985), for
which she won a Best Actress Academy Award nomination. Determined not to be restricted by her colour, sex
or perceived image as a comic, she made the best of the
choices offered to her but was rarely faced with first-rate
material. Unsurprisingly, she turned to television, finding a recurring role as Guinan in the series *Star Trek: The
Next Generation* and in the short-lived sit-com *Bagdad Café*.
She acquired further recognition for her performance in
Ghost (1990) which brought her a Best Supporting Actress
Academy Award, and for the commercially successful
Sister Act (1992) and *Sister Act 2* (1993). Along with the

comedians Billy Crystal and **Robin Williams**, she has organized a cable-television show *Comic Relief* for several
years in order to raise money for the homeless in the USA.
Later films include *Boys on the Side* (1995) and *Ghosts of
Mississippi* (1996).

Goldberger, Joseph 1874–1929
US physician and epidemiologist
Born in Girált, Hungary, he went to the USA as a child
and studied medicine at the Bellevue Hospital Medical
College in New York City. After private medical practice
he joined (1899) the US Public Health Service, where he
investigated the mechanisms of the spread of a number of
infectious diseases, including measles, typhus and yellow
fever. His brilliant epidemiological studies of pellagra
within institutions in the southern USA demonstrated
that pellagra is a nutritional disorder caused by an unbalanced diet and cured by the addition of fresh milk,
meat or yeast. He used himself in a series of well-
designed experiments which demonstrated that, contrary
to contemporary opinion, pellagra was not an infectious disease. The deficiency was later shown to be niacin,
one of the vitamins of the B complex.

Goldie, Charles Frederick 1870–1947
New Zealand painter
He was born in Auckland and in his day was one of New
Zealand's most successful artists. Now considered more
of historical than artistic interest, he began working in
Paris in 1892, winning the Prix Julian in 1896, and returned to Auckland in 1898. Apart from a 10-year break
through ill health, up to 1916 and in the 1930s he worked
strenuously on portraiture, especially on *moko*, the traditional and elaborate Maori facial tattoos. His detailed and
meticulous life studies and portraits provide a valuable
insight into a disappearing society.

Goldie, Sir George Taubman 1846–1925
British soldier and trader
After service as an army officer, he became a trader in
West Africa. He foresaw the developing partition of
Africa and believed that British interests must be secured
against the French in the Oil Rivers region and along the
Niger as a great commercial highway to the interior. By
1884 he had amalgamated all the British companies as the
National Africa Company and set out to secure treaties
from chiefs throughout the Niger Delta and in northern
Nigeria. In 1886 he secured a charter for his renamed
Royal Niger Company and effectively ruled the Niger regions until 1898. He employed **Frederick Lugard**, who
conquered the emirates of Northern Nigeria.

Golding, Sir William Gerald 1911–93
English novelist and Nobel Prize winner
Born in St Columb Minor, Cornwall, he was educated at
Marlborough Grammar School and Brasenose College,
Oxford, where he took examinations in sciences but then
transferred to English literature. After five years at
Oxford he published his first book, *Poems* (1934), a rarity
which he later disowned. He spent the next five years
working in small theatre companies, as an actor, director
and writer, and in 1958 he adapted the short story 'Envoy
Extraordinary' for the stage as *The Brass Butterfly*. He married in 1939, spent World War II in the Royal Navy, and
from 1945 to 1961 was a teacher. He gained international
celebrity with *The Lord of the Flies* (1954). A chronicle of the
increasingly malevolent actions of a group of schoolboys
shipwrecked on a desert island in the wake of a nuclear
war, Golding said that it arose from his five years' war
service, and 10 years of teaching small boys. *The Inheritors*
(1955) was his second novel and is similar in theme and
tone. Next came *Pincher Martin* (1956), *Free Fall* (1959), *The
Spire* (1964) and *The Pyramid* (1967). There was a gap of 12
years before *Darkness Visible* (1979), during which he wrote

short stories, a film script and aborted novels. *Rites of Passage* (1980), the first of a trilogy about a 19th-century voyage from England to Australia, won the Booker Prize. *Close Quarter* (1987) was its sequel and the trilogy closed with *Fire Down Below* (1989). His only other novel was *The Paper Men* (1984). He was awarded the Nobel Prize for literature in 1983. 📖 M K Weeks and I Gregor, *William Golding: a critical study* (1967)

Goldman, Emma, *known as* Red Emma 1869–1940
US anarchist, feminist and birth-control advocate

She was born in Kaunas, Lithuania, and her Jewish family moved to Russia but were forced to go to Germany to avoid persecution. In 1885 she emigrated to the USA, where she began active anarchist agitation against tyrannical employers and was jailed in 1893 for incitement to riot in New York City. She founded and edited the anarchist monthly *Mother Earth* (1906–17) and became internationally known for her stirring speeches and her visits to anarchist congresses in Paris (1899) and Amsterdam (1907). She also worked extensively in US urban slums. In 1917 she was imprisoned for opposing government policy on registration of military recruits; she was deported to the USSR but returned to the USA in 1924, supporting the anarchists in the Spanish Civil War. Her publications include an autobiography, *Living My Life* (1931), and such other works as *Anarchism and Other Essays* (1910) and *My Disillusionment in Russia* (1923). She eventually settled in France. 📖 Richard Drinnan, *Rebel in Paradise: A Biography of Emma Goldman* (1961)

Goldmark, Carl 1830–1915
Hungarian composer

Born in Keszthely, he studied in Vienna and composed *Die Königin von Saba* (1875, 'The Queen of Sheba'), *Merlin* (1886) and other lavishly colourful operas, two symphonies, two violin concertos and other works. His nephew was Rubin Goldmark (1872–1936), the US composer who taught Aaron Copland and George Gershwin.

Goldmark, Peter Carl 1906–77
US engineer and inventor

Born in Budapest, Hungary, he studied at Vienna and Berlin. He emigrated to the USA in 1933 and found employment in the laboratories of the Columbia Broadcasting System, where he developed the first practical colour television system, used for experimental transmissions in New York City in 1940. He led the team that invented the long-playing microgroove record in 1948, and later built a special type of camera for the lunar orbiting space vehicle, which transmitted very high definition pictures of the moon's surface back to Earth.

Goldoni, Carlo 1707–93
Italian dramatist

Born in Venice, he studied law, but turned to writing for the stage. After several years in north Italy, he settled in Venice in 1740, and over the next 20 years wrote no fewer than 250 plays, in Italian, French and the Venetian dialect. He was greatly influenced by Molière and the 'commedia dell'arte', although many of his subjects are derived from direct observation of daily life. His best-known plays are *La locandiera* (1753, Eng trans *La Locandiera (The Mistress of the Inn)*, 1912), *I rusteghi* (1760, Eng trans *The Boors*, 1961) and *Le baruffe chiozzote* (1762, Eng trans *The Squabbles of Chioggia*, 1914). In 1762 he began to write for the Italian theatre in Paris, and he was attached to the French court until the Revolution. He published his *Mémoires* in 1787 (Eng trans 1814). 📖 H Taylor, *Goldoni: a biography* (1914)

Goldschmidt, Berthold 1903–96
British composer

Born in Hamburg, Germany, he was a younger contemporary of many avant-garde composers. He had a promising career in Germany, and became artistic adviser

to Karl Ebert at the Berlin City Opera (1931–33). In 1932 his first opera, *Der gewaltige Hahnrei* ('The Magnificent Cuckold'), was premiered at Mannheim. He fled to London in 1935, and shortly after composed his 2nd String Quartet (1936), expressing the sorrow of his race. In 1951 he was one of four winners in a competition for a new opera sponsored by the Arts Council for the Festival of Britain, but neither his opera (*Beatrice Cenci*) nor any of the others was performed. An expert on the music of Gustav Mahler, he helped to complete Mahler's unfinished 10th Symphony in 1960, and conducted its first performance in London in 1988. He continued to compose until his death.

Goldschmidt, Hans 1861–1923
German chemist

Born in Berlin, he studied under Robert Bunsen at Heidelberg. In 1905 he invented the highly inflammable mixture of finely divided aluminium powder and magnesium ribbon known as thermite. The high temperatures obtained from this mixture make it useful for welding and for reducing metals such as chromium, manganese and cobalt from their oxide ores. It has also been used in incendiary bombs. Around 1910, he developed a commercial process for extracting beryllium, a rare metal which is used in the manufacture of hard alloys and some scientific instruments.

Goldschmidt, Meïr Aron 1819–87
Danish journalist and novelist

He was born in Vordingborg, of Jewish parentage, and was educated in Copenhagen before turning to a career in journalism. He founded a satirical periodical, *Corsaren*, in 1840. His best-known novels are *En Jøde* (1845, Eng trans *Bendixen the Jew*, 1852, and as *The Jew of Denmark*, 1952), and *Hjemløs* (1853, Eng trans *Homeless*, 1857). They are acutely psychological and relate characters to social pressures in a distinctively 'modern' way. He also wrote an autobiography (1877). 📖 M Brøndstadt, *Meïr Goldschmidt* (1965)

Goldschmidt, Richard Benedikt 1878–1958
German biologist

Born in Frankfurt am Main, he was appointed biological director of the Kaiser Wilhelm Institute, Berlin (1921), and in 1935 went to the USA where he became Professor of Zoology at the University of California (1936–58). He experimented on the role of the X chromosomes using butterflies, and proposed the idea that the chromosomes themselves, and not the individual genes, are the units of heredity. One of his more important contributions was to show that much geographical variation is genetic and not environmental in origin. He also demonstrated that environmental effects could mimic some of the effects of genetic mutations. His books include *Physiological Genetics* (1938), *The Material Basis of Evolution* (1940) and *Theoretical Genetics* (1955).

Goldschmidt, Victor Moritz 1888–1947
Norwegian geologist and crystallographer

Born in Zurich, Switzerland, he moved to Christiania (renamed Oslo in 1925) with his family in 1905. After studying chemistry, geology and mineralogy at Christiania, he became a professor and director of the Mineralogical Institute there in 1914. From 1916 to 1922 he was chairman of the materials supply committee of the Norwegian Government. In 1927 he took up the chair of mineralogy at Göttingen, initially commuting by air from Oslo, but he resigned the Norwegian position and settled in Göttingen in 1929. In 1935 he was forced to leave Germany by the Nazis and returned to Oslo, where he was immediately granted a chair. When Germany invaded Norway in 1940, he worked secretly for the Allies for some time. In the end he fled to Sweden and then to

Great Britain, where he worked at the Macaulay Institute and at Rothamsted. In 1946 he returned to Norway. His earliest work was on the petrology of southern Norway. Following the development of X-ray crystallography by **William** and **Lawrence Bragg**, he undertook an extensive X-ray study of the binary compounds of the elements. This led to his rationalization of crystal structures in terms of ionic radii and polarizabilities. His interests in crystallography and petrology came together in research on the distribution of the elements in the Earth. His massive book *Geochemistry* was published posthumously in 1954.

Goldsmith, Oliver 1730–1774
Irish playwright, novelist and poet
Born in Pallasmore, County Longford, he was educated at local schools and Trinity College, Dublin. In 1752 he went to Edinburgh to study medicine, but was more noted for his social gifts than his professional skills and drifted to Leyden, set out to make the 'grand tour' on foot, but returned penniless in 1756. He practised as a poor physician in Southwark, and was proofreader to **Samuel Richardson**, before publishing a translation of the Memoirs of Jean Marteilhe, a persecuted French Protestant, in 1758. An *Enquiry into the Present State of Polite Learning in Europe* (1759) attracted some notice. Goldsmith started and edited a weekly, *The Bee* (1759), and wrote essays for **Tobias Smollett's** *British Magazine*. For **John Newbery's** *Public Ledger* he wrote the *Chinese Letters* (1760–71, republished as *The Citizen of the World*). *The Vicar of Wakefield* (1766) secured his reputation as a novelist, *The Deserted Village* (1770) as a poet, and three years later he also achieved high regard as a playwright with *She Stoops to Conquer*. 🕮 G S Rousseau, *Oliver Goldsmith: The Critical Heritage* (1974); S Gwinn, *Oliver Goldsmith* (1935)

Goldstein, Eugen 1850–1930
German physicist
Born in Gleiwitz, Upper Silesia (now Gliwice, Poland), he was educated at Ratobor Gymnasium and the University of Breslau before going to the University of Berlin (1878) where he worked with **Hermann von Helmholtz**. He then spent his career as a physicist at the Potsdam observatory. In 1876 he showed that cathode rays could cast sharp shadows and were emitted perpendicular to the cathode surface. This led to the production of concave cathodes which were useful in many experiments. In 1886 he published his discovery of 'Kanalstrahlen', literally canal rays, known as positive rays in English, which emerged from channels or holes in anodes, and were eventually shown to be positively charged particles of atomic mass. This apparatus was developed into the mass spectrograph by **J J Thomson**, **Francis Aston** and others.

Goldstein, Joseph Leonard 1940–
US molecular geneticist and Nobel Prize winner
Born in Sumter, South Carolina, he graduated with a medical degree from the University of Texas, Dallas, in 1966, where he later became head of the Division of Medical Genetics (1972), Professor of Internal Medicine (from 1976), and Professor of Medical Genetics (from 1977). With **Michael Brown**, he has worked on cholesterol metabolism in the human body, particularly studying the low-density lipoproteins (LDLs) which carry cholesterol in the blood. In some diseases the liver cells cannot remove cholesterol from the bloodstream because they are missing a receptor site for the LDLs, but in 1984 Goldstein and Brown described several mutations in the LDL receptor gene, opening up possibilities for new drugs to combat these diseases. For this work, they were jointly awarded the 1985 Nobel Prize for physiology or medicine. Goldstein was also awarded the 1988 US National Medal of Science.

Goldstein, Vida 1869–1949
Australian feminist
Born in Portland, Victoria, and educated in Melbourne at the Presbyterian Ladies' College and at Melbourne University, she ran a school with her sister and became involved with the campaign for women's suffrage. She was a member of the first Australian suffrage group, the Woman's Suffrage Society, and later formed the Woman's Federal Political Association. She also founded the feminist publication *Australian Woman's Sphere* and stood as an independent candidate in Victoria five times (1903–17). Full suffrage and eligibility to stand in national elections was granted to women in Australia in 1902, just after federation, and she became the first woman in the British Empire to stand in national parliamentary elections.

Goldwater, Barry M(orris) 1909–98
US Republican politician and author
Born in Phoenix, Arizona, the son of a Jewish father of Polish descent, he was educated at Arizona University and served as a ferry pilot during World War II. He worked at his family's department store, becoming president (1937–53), marketing a popular brand of men's undergarments, before representing his home state in the US Senate (1952–64). He was a conservative Republican, supporting **Joseph McCarthy** and opposing President **Dwight D Eisenhower** and state intervention in economic affairs. He contested the 1964 presidential election for the Republicans, but was heavily defeated by **Lyndon B Johnson**. Returning to the Senate in 1969, he chaired the Armed Services Commission, before retiring in 1987. He was one of the architects of the conservative revival within the Republican Party and many of his ideas were later adopted by the Republican 'New Right' and implemented by the **Reagan** administration. He wrote *The Conscience of a Conservative* (1960) and published his autobiography, *Goldwater*, in 1988.

Goldwyn, Samuel, *originally* Samuel Goldfish 1882–1974
US film producer
Born of Jewish parents in Warsaw, Poland, he was orphaned and, at the age of 11, ran away to relatives in England, and again, at 13, to the USA. After working as a glove-salesman, he founded a film company with a depressed playwright, **Cecil B de Mille**, as director and produced *The Squaw Man* (1913). In 1917 he founded the Goldwyn Pictures Corporation, in 1919 the Eminent Authors Pictures, and finally in 1925 the Metro-Goldwyn-Mayer Company, allying himself with United Artists from 1926. His 'film-of-the-book' policy included such films as *Bulldog Drummond* (1929), *All Quiet on the Western Front* (1930), *Stella Dallas* (1937) and *Wuthering Heights* (1939). He also produced *Little Foxes* (1941), *The Best Years of Our Lives* (1946, Academy Award), *The Secret Life of Walter Mitty* (1947), *Guys and Dolls* (1955) and *Porgy and Bess* (1959). Well known 'Goldwynisms' include 'include me out', and 'a verbal contract isn't worth the paper it's written on'. 🕮 A S Berg, *Goldwyn: A Biography* (1989)

Golgi, Camillo 1843–1926
Italian cytologist and Nobel Prize winner
He was born in Corteno, Lombardy. He began his career as a physician in Abbiategrasso, where he made the invaluable discovery of how to stain nerve tissue using silver nitrate (1873). As Professor of Pathology at Pavia (1876–1918), he discovered the 'Golgi bodies' in animal cells which, through their affinity for metallic salts, are readily visible under the microscope, and opened up a new field of research into the central nervous system, sense organs, muscles and glands. He shared with **Santiago Ramón y Cajal** the 1906 Nobel Prize for physiology or medicine.

Goliath 11th century BC
Biblical character
Described (in 1 Samuel 17) as a giant from Gath in the Philistine army, he entered into single combat with the young David and was slain by a stone from David's sling, resulting in Israel's victory. Some confusion exists over a similar name in 2 Samuel 21.19 (also 1 Chronicles 20.5).

Golitsyn, Dimitri Augustine See **Gallitzin, Dimitri Augustine**

Gollancz, Sir Hermann 1852–1930
British rabbi and scholar
He was born in Bremen, Germany, and was educated at University College London, before preaching at synagogues around England from 1876. An authority on Hebrew language and literature, he became professor at University College London (1902–24), and later a preacher at the Bayswater synagogue (1892–1923). He was the first British rabbi to be knighted (1923), sat on several government commissions and did much philanthropic work. He was the brother of Sir Israel Gollancz.

Gollancz, Sir Israel 1864–1930
English scholar
Born in London, he was appointed Professor of English Literature at University College London, in 1906. An authority on early English texts, he was a founder and first secretary of the British Academy. He was the brother of Sir Hermann Gollancz.

Gollancz, Sir Victor 1893–1967
English publisher, author and philanthropist
He was born in London into a family of Jewish businessmen and was educated at St Paul's School and New College, Oxford. As a young man he was in revolt against orthodox Judaism, which he eventually rejected. He became a teacher, went into publishing in 1920, and founded his own firm in 1928, becoming known for his innumerable campaigns and pressure group activities. In 1919 he was secretary of the Radical Research Group, in 1936 he founded the Left Book Club which influenced the growth of the Labour party, and during World War II he helped to get Jewish refugees out of Germany. After the war he worked hard to relieve starvation in Germany and tried to oppose the belief in German collective guilt for Nazi crimes. He founded the Jewish Society for Human Service. He also launched national campaigns for the abolition of capital punishment and for nuclear disarmament. 📖 Ruth Dudley Edwards, *Victor Gollancz: A Biography* (1987)

Golssenau, Arnold Friedrich von See **Renn, Ludwig**

Gomarus or **Gommer, Francis** 1563–1641
Dutch Calvinist theologian
He was born in Bruges, Belgium, and as Professor of Divinity at Leyden (1594) he became known for his hostility to his colleague, Jacobus Arminius. At the Synod of Dort (1618) he secured the Arminians' expulsion from the Reformed Church. From then until his death he was a professor at Groningen.

Gomberg, Moses 1866–1947
US chemist
Born in Kirovograd, Russia, he fled with his family to Chicago in 1884. He went to the University of Michigan in 1886. He received his PhD there and joined the faculty in 1893, remaining there for the rest of his professional life. He studied in Munich and Heidelberg, where he was successful in preparing molecules which had proved difficult to assemble because they contain bulky groups. When he returned to Michigan Gomberg attempted the synthesis of the compound hexaphenylethane. His work alerted chemists to the possibility of long-lived radicals in solution and this is now accepted as an important type of reactive intermediate. He was elected to the US National Academy of Sciences and served as president of the American Chemical Society in 1931.

Gombrich, Sir Ernst Hans Josef 1909–
British art historian
Born in Vienna, he studied at the university there. He then emigrated to England, where he joined the staff of the Warburg Institute, London (1936), becoming its director and Professor of History of the Classical Tradition (1959–76). During World War II he worked for the BBC Monitoring Service. His books include *The Story of Art* (1950), *Art and Illusion* (1960)—an influential study of the psychology of pictorial representation—and *The Sense of Order* (1979). He was knighted in 1972 and awarded the Order of Merit in 1988.

Gombrowicz, Witold 1904–69
Polish novelist
He was born in Maloszyce, studied law and economics in Warsaw and Paris, and spent most of his working life as a bank employee in Argentina, where he had gone on a visit on the eve of World War II. Beginning with the short stories in *Pamietnik z okresu dojrzewania* (1933, 'A Recollection of Adolescence'), Gombrowicz's work is much concerned with patterns of sexual and psychological dependency, and it is clear from his journal, published as *Dziennik, 1953–1966* (3 vols, 1957–66), that many of the complexes and inhibitions portrayed are his own. The slightly pathological tone of the early stories largely disappears in his best books, *Ferdydurke* (1937, Eng trans 1961) and *Pornografia* (1960, Eng trans *Pornography* 1966), which sustain a certain ironic distance from their vulnerable characters and claustrophobic situations. His collected works, *Dziela zebrane* (11 vols, 1969–77) began to appear in the year of his death. The strange *Opetani* (1973, Eng trans *Possessed, or The Secret of Myslotch*, 1980) was published posthumously. 📖 E Thompson, *Gombrowicz* (1979)

Gomme, George Laurence 1853–1916
British folklorist
He was a founder-member and subsequently president of the Folklore Society (1890–94). His first publication, *Primitive Folk Moots; or Open-Air Assemblies in Britain* (1880), revealed his approach to folklore, not as a relic of myth but as the vehicle of preserved 'remnants of archaic social existence'. Thus for him the proper field of folklore was untutored classes in a civilized society, not primitive societies themselves. A member of the same group as Andrew Lang and Alfred Nutt, he was the most crusading in his desire to see folklore recognized as a scientific discipline. He expanded these issues in *Ethnology in Folklore* (1892) and *Folklore as an Historical Science* (1908). In 1890 he produced a *Handbook of Folklore*, the first fieldwork guide for amateur collectors.

Gommer, Francis See **Gomarus, Francis**

Gompers, Samuel 1850–1924
US labour leader
Born in London, England, he emigrated to the USA in 1863, where he followed his father's trade as a cigar maker, joining a union the following year. Self-educated, he studied and rejected Marxism and socialism, developing instead the US practice of nonpolitical trade unionism. He helped found (1886), and was long-time president of, the American Federation of Labor (AFL), and with the AFL's triumph as the main force in organized labour he became a major public figure. 📖 Harold Livesay, *Samuel Gompers and Organized Labor in America* (1978)

Gomułka, Władysław 1905–
Polish Communist leader

Born in Krosno, South East Poland, he became a local trade union leader. He organized underground resistance to the Germans during World War II and took an active part in the defence of Warsaw. In 1943 he became secretary of the outlawed underground Communist Party. He became vice-president of the first postwar Polish government, but from 1948 was gradually relieved of all his posts for 'non-appreciation of the decisive role of the Soviet Union' and was arrested in 1951. But for Stalin's death in 1953, he would have been executed. Later in 1954 he was released from solitary confinement. He was rehabilitated in August 1956 and returned to power as party First Secretary in October—thus preparing the way for a new course for Polish society. He was re-elected to this post in 1959. Braving the risk of a 'Stalinist' military putsch, Gomułka sought to put Poland on the road to a measure of freedom and independence, allowing freer discussion within a Marxist framework. He resigned office in 1971, following a political crisis. ⩗Nicholas Bethell, *Gomułka: His Poland and His Communism* (1969)

Gonçalves, Nuno fl.1450–72
Portuguese painter

He is recorded, in 1463, as court painter to **Alfonso V.** He was virtually forgotten until the discovery of his only extant work, an altarpiece for the convent of St Vincent (the patron saint of Portugal) in 1882. This work was exhibited in Paris in 1931 and established him as the most important Portuguese painter of the 15th century. The altarpiece, comprising six panels, shows the influence of contemporary Flemish painting, notably that of **Dierick Bouts.**

Gonçalves Dias, António 1823–64
Brazilian poet, dramatist and translator

Born in Maranhão, he went to Coimbra to study law, but became enamoured of poetry, in which he showed great technical skill. He was himself of Native American, African and European extraction, and his fervent patriotism and ability to identify with all three races made him the Brazilian national poet. He was one of the first poets whose so-called 'Indianism' was genuine rather than merely exotic and decorative. He drowned within sight of his native town.

Goncharov, Ivan Aleksandrovich 1812–91
Russian novelist

Born in Simbirsk, he graduated from Moscow University (1834), and led an uneventful life in the Civil Service, punctuated by a trip to Japan, which he described in *Freget Pallada* (1858, Eng trans *The Frigate Pallas: Notes on a Journey*, 1965). He wrote three novels, the most important being *Oblomov* (1857, Eng trans 1915), one of the greatest and most typical works in the Russian Realist style. Neither *Obyknovennaya istoriya* (1847, Eng trans *A Common Story*, 1894) nor *Obryv* (1870, Eng trans *The Precipice*, 1916) attained the same heights. ⩗V Sechkarov, *Ivan Goncharov: his life and works* (1974)

Goncharova, Natalia Sergeyevna 1881–1962
French painter and designer

Born in Ladyzhino, Tula province, Russia, she began as a science student but turned (c.1898) to sculpture, studying at the Moscow Academy of Art. She began painting in 1904 and, like **Mikhail Larionov** (with whom she lived and whom she eventually married on her 74th birthday) and **Kasimir Malevich,** chose the flat colours and primitive forms of Russian folk art, combining these with the new influences of Cubism and Fauvism with an original flair. She moved to Geneva in 1915 with Larionov to design for **Sergei Diaghilev's** ballets, and went to Paris in 1921. She took French nationality in 1938.

Goncourt, Edmond de 1822–96 and Jules de, *known as* the Goncourt Brothers 1830–70
French novelists

Born in Nancy and Paris respectively, they were primarily artists, but after collaborating in studies of history and art they turned to writing novels. Their subject was the manners of the 19th century, and the enormous influence of environment and habit upon people. The first of their novels, *Les Hommes de lettres* (1860, 'The Men of Letters', new edn as *Charles Demailly*, 1868), was followed by *Sœur Philomène* (1861, Eng trans *Sister Philomène*, 1890), *Renée Mauperin* (1864, Eng trans 1864 (US); 1887 (UK)), *Germinie Lacerteux* (1865, Eng trans 1887), *Manette Salomon* (1867), and *Madame Gervaisais* (1869), their greatest novel. After Jules's death, Edmond published the extraordinarily popular *La Fille Élisa* (1878, Eng trans *Elisa*, 1959), *La Faustin* (1882, Eng trans 1902) and *Chérie* (1885, 'Darling'). The interesting *Idées et Sensations* (1866, 'Ideas and Sensations') had already revealed their morbid acuteness of sensation, and *La Maison d'un artiste* (1881, 'An Artist's House') had shown their love for bric-à-brac. In the *Lettres de Jules de Goncourt* (1885) and in the *Journal des Goncourt* (9 vols, 1888–96) they revealed their methods and their conception of fiction. Various translations of these have been made, including *The Journal of the De Goncourts* (1908), *Paris under Siege, 1870–1871* (1969), and *Edmond and Jules de Goncourt, with letters and leaves from their journals* (1894). Edmond, in his will, founded the Académie Goncourt to foster fiction with the annual Prix Goncourt. ⩗ R B Grant, *The Goncourt Brothers* (1972); A Billy, *La vie des Frères Goncourt* (1956)

Gondi, Jean François Paul de See Retz, Jean François Paul de Gondi, Cardinal de

Góngora (y Argote), (Don) Luis de 1561–1627
Spanish lyric poet

Born in Córdoba, he studied law, but in 1606 took orders and became a prebendary of Córdoba, and eventually chaplain to **Philip III.** His earlier writings were sonnets, romances and satirical verses, but he is best known for his longer poems, such as *Soledades* (1613, Eng trans *The Solitudes*, 1931), *Polifemo* (1613, Eng trans *Polyphemus and Galatea*, 1977) and *Piramo y Tisbe* ('Pyramus and Thisbe'), written in an affected style which came to be called 'gongorism', which his followers designated the *estilo culto*. ⩗ D W and V R Foster, *Góngora* (1973)

Gonne, Maud, *married name* MacBride 1865–1953
Irish nationalist and actress

The daughter of an English colonel, she was an agitator for the cause of Irish independence and edited a nationalist newspaper, *L'Irlande libre*, in Paris. She met **W B Yeats** in the early 1890s and, though Yeats wished to marry her, she ultimately rejected him and married Major John MacBride, who fought against the British in the Boer War and was executed as a rebel in 1916. She was one of the founders of Sinn Féin. Her son **Seán MacBride** was Foreign Minister of the Irish Republic from 1948 to 1951.

Gonzaga, Luigi, *known as* St Aloysius 1568–91
Italian Jesuit

Born near Brescia, the eldest son of the Marquis of Castiglione, he renounced his title to become a missionary and entered the Society of Jesus in 1585. When Rome had an epidemic of the plague in 1591 he devoted himself to the care of the sick, but was himself infected and died. He was canonized in 1726, and in 1926 was declared the patron saint of Christian youth by Pope **Pius XI.** His feast day is 21 June.

Gonzaga, Tomás António, *pseudonym* Dirceu 1744–1809
Portuguese poet

Born in Oporto, of an English mother and Brazilian father, he studied law, and was sent to Vila Rica in Brazil in 1782 where he met the 'Marilia' of his verses. He was exiled to Mozambique for his revolutionary activities, and there he married a rich mulatta and became a leading citizen. His *Marilia de Dirceu* (1792) contains impressive verses in the Arcadian tradition, considered second only to those of **Manoel Bocage**, and deemed masterpieces of the Mineiro school.

Gonzalès, Eva 1849–83
French painter

Born in Paris, she was noted for her great beauty at an early age. She studied with Charles Chaplin, an academic who was also the teacher of **Mary Cassatt**. When she was 20, **Manet** requested her family's permission to paint her portrait, and she became both his model and his pupil. She was the only artist permitted by him to sign 'pupil of Manet' on Salon entries, and her first entry to the Salon in 1870, *L'Enfant de troupe* ('The Boy Soldier'), was purchased by the government. She married the engraver Henri Guérard in 1876 and bore her first child in 1883, dying of an embolism five days later, one day after Manet.

González (Márquez), Felipe 1942–
Spanish politician

Born in Seville, he studied law and practised as a lawyer, and in 1962 joined the Spanish Socialist Workers' Party (PSOE), at that time an illegal organization. The party regained legal status in 1977, three years after he became Secretary-General. He persuaded the PSOE to adopt a more moderate, less overtly Marxist line, and in the general elections of 1982 they won a substantial overall majority to become the first left-wing administration since the Socialist-led coalition of 1936, and González was made Prime Minister, remaining in power until 1996, when the conservative Popular Party, led by José María Aznar, won the election.

González, Julio 1876–1942
Spanish sculptor

He was born in Barcelona, and studied there, then in 1900 went to Paris, where he joined the avant-garde circle around **Picasso**. He began as a painter, but in 1927 turned to sculpture, mainly in wrought and welded iron. Like Picasso he was inspired initially by African masks, and worked in a Cubist style, but his work also had Surrealist features. His works include *Angel* (1933, Pompidou Centre, Paris) and *Maternity* (1934, Tate, London), and he made a life-size figure of a peasant mother (1936–37), a symbol of popular resistance in the Spanish Civil War, for the Paris Exposition Universelle.

Gonzalvo de Córdoba, Hernández, *known as* the Great Captain 1453–1515
Spanish soldier

Born in Montilla, near Córdoba, he served with distinction against the Moors of Granada and afterwards in Portugal. Sent to assist **Ferdinand, the Catholic** (Ferdinand III of Naples) in his Holy League against the French (1495), he conquered most of the kingdom of Naples and expelled the French. After the partition of Naples in 1500, he again set out for Italy, but first took Zante and Cephalonia from the Turks and restored them to the Venetians. He then landed in Sicily, occupied Naples and Calabria, and demanded that the French keep the treaty. When they refused he waged war against them. Ultimately Gonzalvo won a great battle (1503) at the Garigliano river, which he crossed five miles above Minturno at a spot where in 1943 the 56th British Division found a crossing. His victory secured Naples for Spain. Recalled in 1506, and neglected by the king, he withdrew to his estates in Granada.

Gooch, Sir Daniel 1816–89
English engineer

Born in Bedlington, Northumberland, he was early associated with **George** and **Robert Stephenson** in railway construction, became locomotive superintendent of the Great Western Railway (1837–64), and then distinguished himself in submarine telegraphy by laying the first Atlantic cable (1865–66). His three brothers, Thomas Longridge (1808–82), John Veret (1812–1900) and William Frederick (b.1825), were also civil or locomotive engineers.

Gooch, Graham 1953–
English cricketer

Born in Leytonstone, London, he made his debut for Essex in 1973, and was captain of the club (apart from 1988) from 1986. First capped for England in 1975, he has since played in over 100 Test matches, and he recorded his highest score of 333 runs against India at Lord's in 1990. In July 1993 he resigned as captain of England after their eighth defeat in nine Test matches. He became England's highest-scoring Test player in August 1993 when he reached a career total of 8,293 runs. He has published two volumes of autobiography, *Testing Times* (1991) and *Gooch: My Autobiography* (1995, co-written with Frank Keating).

Goodall, Jane 1934–
English primatologist and conservationist

Born in London, she worked in Kenya with the anthropologist **Louis Leakey**, obtained her PhD from Cambridge in 1965, and subsequently set up the Gombe Stream Research Centre in Tanzania. She has been a visiting professor at the Department of Psychiatry and Program of Human Biology at Stanford University (1971–75) and visiting Professor of Zoology at Dar es Salaam (1973–). Since 1967 she has been scientific director of the Gombe Wildlife Research Institute. She has carried out a study of the behaviour and ecology of chimpanzees which has transformed the understanding of primate behaviour by demonstrating its complexity. She discovered that chimpanzees modify a variety of natural objects to use as tools and weapons, and showed that they hunt animals for meat. She is active in chimpanzee conservation in Africa, and her books include *In the Shadow of Man* (1971), *The Chimpanzees of Gombe: Patterns of Behavior* (1986) and *The Chimpanzee: The Living Link between "Man" and "Beast"* (1992). She has received many awards including the Albert Schweitzer award (1987), the Encyclopaedia Britannica award (1989) and the Kyoto prize for science (1990).

Goode, George Brown 1851–96
US ichthyologist

Born in New Albany, Indiana, he was on the staff of the Smithsonian Institute in Washington from 1827, was US fish commissioner (1887–1888) and author of *American Fishes* (1888) and *Oceanic Ichthyology* (1895).

Goodhart, Arthur Lehman 1891–1978
US jurist

Born in New York City, he was educated at the Hotchkiss School and Yale. He lived most of his life in England, becoming Professor of Jurisprudence at Oxford and Master of University College there (1951–63). His major scholarly work was his editorship of the *Law Quarterly Review* (1926–75) to which he contributed many valuable articles and a series of case notes examining recent decisions analytically and critically, but constructively. He also published a few small books on legal theory.

Goodman, Benny (Benjamin David) 1909–86
US clarinettist and bandleader

Born in Chicago to a poor immigrant family, he was a musical prodigy who was working in dance bands by the age of 13, and joined the Ben Pollack Orchestra at 15. He formed his own orchestra in New York in 1934 and, thanks to media exposure, became one of the best known leaders of the era with the sobriquet 'King of Swing'. Hiring top black musicians such as pianist **Teddy Wilson** and vibraphone-player **Lionel Hampton**, Goodman successfully defied racial taboos of the time. He led a succession of large and small bands for three decades, occasionally performing as a classical player, and was noted for his technical facility and clean tone. ▣ James L Collier, *Benny Goodman and the Swing Era* (1989)

Goodman, Isador 1909–82
Australian pianist and composer

Born in Cape Town, South Africa, he studied at the Royal College of Music, London, and appeared in concerts in England and Europe before emigrating in 1930 to Australia where he taught at the New South Wales Conservatorium. For the next 50 years he performed in recital and as a soloist with leading orchestras, in concert and for television and radio. In 1944 he wrote his *New Guinean Fantasy* on that island at the height of the battle there. He was a renowned exponent of the Romantic repertoire, and especially of **Rachmaninov** and **Liszt**. He played Liszt's 1st piano concerto in London at the age of 14 with Sir **Malcolm Sargent** and made his Australian debut with the same work in 1930.

Goodrich, Samuel Griswold, *pseudonym of* Peter Parley 1793–1860
US publisher

Born in Ridgefield, Connecticut, he was self-educated. He edited in Boston *The Token* (1828–42) to which he contributed moralistic poems, tales and essays for children and in which the best of **Nathaniel Hawthorne's** 'Twice-told Tales' appeared. He published some 200 volumes, mostly for the young as 'Peter Parley' books, starting with *The Tales of Peter Parley about America* (1827).

Goodricke, John 1764–86
English astronomer

Born in Groningen, the Netherlands, he was unable to hear or speak from an early age. He was the first, in 1782, to recognize that the star Algol (Beta Persei) is an eclipsing binary and that its periodic diminutions in brightness are due to one of the binary stars passing in front of the other. Two years later he discovered the regular variability of the stars Delta Cephei and Beta Lyrae. He was awarded the Copley Medal of the Royal Society in 1783.

Goodsir, John 1814–67
Scottish anatomist

Born in Anstruther, Fife, he attended the University of St Andrews and then Edinburgh University. Specializing in surgery, he joined his father's practice and published early in dentistry. He developed a passionate interest in marine biology, and was appointed in 1840 Conservator in Comparative Anatomy at the Edinburgh University Museum, in 1846 becoming Professor of Anatomy at the university. His researches attempted to apply the mathematics of form to problems of living structures, in particular to cell biology. He also cultivated the theory of the triangle as the basic natural living form.

Goodyear, Charles 1800–60
US inventor

He was born in New Haven, Connecticut. Having failed as an iron manufacturer, he began research into the properties of rubber in 1834. Amid poverty and ridicule he pursued the experiments which culminated, in 1844, in the invention of vulcanized rubber, which led to the development of the rubber-manufacturing industry and the production of the well-known tyres named after him.

Googe, Barnabe 1540–94
English poet

Born in Alvingham, Lincolnshire, he studied both at Cambridge and Oxford, travelled on the Continent, and became one of the gentlemen-pensioners of **Elizabeth I**. His best works are a series of eight *Eclogues, Epytaphes and Sonnets* (1563), which are one of the earliest examples of the pastoral form in English, and his *Cupido Conquered*.

Goolden, Jilly Birthdate unavailable
British wine critic and writer

She entered journalism after school, first working on the *Field* magazine. She later became co-presenter, with **Oz Clarke**, of BBC Television's *Food and Drink Programme* (which she joined for its first programme in 1982) and is renowned for her imaginative descriptions of the flavours of wine, such as 'a wheelbarrow full of Ugli fruit'. She is a strong advocate of the value of wine produced for drinking rather than keeping. Her publications include *The Taste of Wine* (1990).

Goossens, Eugène 1845–1906
Belgian conductor

Born in Bruges, he studied at the Brussels Conservatory, and became the conductor of several opera companies in Belgium, France and Italy. He made his name, however, in Great Britain, in comic opera with the Carl Rosa Company (from 1873). He founded the Goossens Male Voice Choir in Liverpool in 1894.

Goossens, Eugène 1867–1958
Belgian violinist and conductor

Born in Bordeaux, France, he studied at the Brussels Conservatory and at the Royal Academy of Music, London. From 1884 to 1886 he played with the Carl Rosa Company under his father, the Belgian conductor **Eugène Goossens**, and with the orchestra at Covent Garden, London (1893–94). He was principal conductor of the Carl Rosa Company from 1899 to 1915.

Goossens, Sir Eugène 1893–1962
English composer and conductor

Born in London, the son of the Belgian violinist and conductor **Eugène Goossens**, he studied in Bruges and London, and became associate conductor to Sir **Thomas Beecham** (1916–20) in his opera seasons. In 1921 he gave a successful series of orchestral concerts, in which he brought out some of his own music. From 1923 to 1945 he worked in the USA, as conductor of the Rochester (New York) Philharmonic Orchestra and of the Cincinnati Symphony Orchestra. Conductor of the Sydney Symphony Orchestra and director of the New South Wales Conservatorium from 1947 to 1956, he became a major influence on Australian music. His own music includes the operas *Judith* (1929) and *Don Juan de Mañara* (1937), a large-scale oratorio *The Apocalypse* (1950–54), and two symphonies.

Goossens, Léon 1897–1988
English oboist

Born in Liverpool, he studied at the Royal College of Music, London. After 1913, he held leading posts in most of the major London orchestras. He then retired from orchestral work to devote himself to solo playing and teaching. He was the brother of the composer and conductor Sir **Eugene Goossens**. ▣ Carole Rosen, *The Goossens: A Musical Century* (1993)

Göransson, Göran Fredrik 1819–1900
Swedish industrialist and engineer

He made the Bessemer process of producing steel a practical possibility in 1858. He was one of the founders of the Sandviken Iron Works company in 1868 and under

Gorbachev, Mikhail Sergeyevich 1931–
Soviet statesman and Nobel Prize winner

Mikhail Gorbachev was born in Privolnoye in the North Caucasus, the son of an agricultural mechanic. He went to Moscow University to study law in 1950, where he met and married a philosophy student, Raisa Titorenko, who was to play an important part in his later career (see **Raisa Gorbachev**). Having joined the Communist Party (CPSU) in 1952, he worked actively for it in Stavropol, introducing reforms and becoming local party leader in 1970. Having impressed his influential fellow countryman, **Yuri Andropov**, he was admitted to the CPSU secretariat as Agriculture Secretary in 1978. He was promoted to full membership of the politburo in 1980, and in 1983, following Andropov's election as party general-secretary, took broader charge of the Soviet economy.

During the **Chernenko** administration (1984–85) he established himself as the second-ranking figure in what was a 'dual key' administration and was swiftly appointed party general-secretary after Chernenko's death. He soon made his presence felt as party leader, forcing the retirement of obstructive colleagues and bringing into the politburo and secretariat a new group of younger technocrats, who were more supportive of his vision of reform. He also introduced a major campaign against alcoholism and corruption during 1985–86 and, after strongly criticizing the **Brezhnev** era, unveiled, under the slogans *glasnost* ('openness') and *perestroika* ('restructuring'), a series of liberalizing economic, political and cultural reforms which had the aim of making the Soviet economy and society more efficient and open. A major setback occurred in April 1986 with the disaster at Chernobyl in Ukraine, where an explosion in a nuclear reactor led to the immediate death of over 30 people, the hospitalization of at least 500, and radioactive fallout from the atmosphere caused disease and contamination in many parts of eastern and northern Europe. However, the effectiveness of Gorbachev's reforms was evidenced by the apparent availability of information about the disaster.

In foreign policy, Gorbachev launched a new 'detente offensive', meeting US President **Ronald Reagan** in several summits (1985–88) and signing an Intermediate Nuclear Forces (INF) abolition treaty in 1987. He sanctioned the USSR's military withdrawal from Afghanistan (1989), and its progressive disengagement from eastern Europe. He was elected head of state in 1988, and became an executive President with increased powers in 1990. Through seeking to transform the USSR into a new 'socialist pluralist' democracy, he encountered internal opposition on all sides from party conservatives, radicals, and nationalists, particularly in the Baltic republics, which sought and eventually achieved their independence. In particular, he faced a continuing challenge in **Boris Yeltsin**, who urged more radical reform and supported the breakaway republics. It was an embarrassment to Gorbachev when Yeltsin was elected to the Russian presidency in 1990, although he endeavoured to establish a working relationship with him.

In 1990 Gorbachev was awarded the Nobel Peace Prize, in acknowledgement of his contribution to the improvement in relations between the USSR and the West. The following year in August, he survived a coup staged by conservative elements, and Yeltsin again emerged as the principal focus of opposition to him. Later in the year Gorbachev had no choice but to resign, when the Communist Party was abolished and the Soviet Union disintegrated.

His works include *Perestroika: New Thinking for our Country and the World* (1987), *The August Coup: The Truth and the Lessons* (1992) and *Memoirs* (1996). See also Robert G Kaiser, *Why Gorbachev Happened* (1991); Richard Sakwa, *Gorbachev and His Reforms* (1991); Zhores Medvedev, *Gorbachev* (1986).

Commenting on her first meeting with Gorbachev in 1984, **Margaret Thatcher** said: 'I like Mr Gorbachev. We can do business together'.

And in his speech proposing Gorbachev to the Supreme Soviet as party leader in 1985, **Andrei Gromyko** said: 'This man, Comrades, has a nice smile, but he has iron teeth'.

---

his leadership it achieved international repute. His son Henrik and grandson Fredrik succeeded him in turn as directors of the company.

Gorbachev, Mikhail Sergeyevich See panel above

Gorbachev, Raisa Maksimova, *née* Titorenko
1934–
Soviet educationist

Born in the Altai region, she graduated from Moscow University and pursued a career in sociological research and lecturing. She worked as a sociologist at Stavropol Teacher Training Institute (1957–61) and was a lecturer at Moscow University (1977–85). She had gained standing in her own right before 1985 when, as the wife of **Mikhail Gorbachev**, the then General Secretary of the Communist Party of the USSR, she accompanied him on special occasions and overseas tours. Since the end of his presidency she has continued as a member of the board of the Cultural Heritage Commission (1987–). *I Hope: Reflections and Reminiscences* (1991)

Gorbunovs, Anatolijs 1942–
Latvian politician

He was born in the Ludza District and educated at the Riga Polytechnic Institute and Moscow Academy of Social Sciences. He worked as a mechanic before serving in the Red Army (1962–65) and rising through the Latvian Communist Party to become chair of the Supreme Council of Latvia (1988–93). He followed Lithuania and Estonia in declaring (1990) his intention for Latvia to become independent of the USSR; this independence was recognized in 1991. Gorbunovs served as President from 1990 to 1993.

Gorchakov, Prince Aleksandr Mikhailovich
1798–1883
Russian politician

Born in St Petersburg, he was ambassador at Vienna (1854–56) and succeeded Count **Karl Nesselrode** as Foreign Minister. As Chancellor of the Empire (1863) he was, until **Bismarck's** rise, the most powerful minister in Europe. He secured Austrian neutrality in the Franco-German War of 1870, and in 1871 absolved Russia from the Treaty of Paris (1856). After the conclusion of the Russo-Turkish war, the repudiation of the Treaty of San Stefano and the signing of the Treaty of Berlin, his influence began to wane. He was the cousin of Prince **Mikhail Gorchakov**.

Gorchakov, Prince Mikhail Dmitriyevich
1795–1861
Russian soldier

He served against the French in the Napoleonic campaign of 1812–14 and in the Russo-Turkish war of 1828–29. He helped to suppress the Polish revolution of 1831 and the Hungarian insurrection in 1849. On the outbreak of the

Crimean War (1853–56) he commanded in the Danubian Principalities and, now Commander-in-Chief in the Crimea (1855), was defeated on the Tchernaya, but defended Sebastopol. The cousin of Prince **Aleksandr Gorchakov**, he was military Governor of Poland from 1856 to 1861.

Gordimer, Nadine 1923–
South African novelist and Nobel Prize winner

Born in Springs, Transvaal, she was educated at a convent school, and at the University of the Witwatersrand, Johannesburg. Her first book was a collection of short stories, *Face to Face* (1949), followed by another collection, *The Soft Voice of the Serpent* (1952). In 1953 she had published her first novel, *The Lying Days*, in which a white girl triumphs over the provincial narrowness and racial bigotry of her parents, though she too has to come to terms with the limitations of her social background. This recurrent theme dominates Gordimer's early books, such as *Occasion for Loving* (1963) and *The Late Bourgeois World* (1966). Apartheid, and her characters' reaction to it, is ever present in her fiction, most powerfully in *The Conservationist* (1974), joint winner of the Booker Prize. Other important titles are *A Guest of Honour* (1970), *Burger's Daughter* (1979), *July's People* (1981) and *A Sport of Nature* (1987). Much fêted, she has received many awards, including the Malaparte prize from Italy, the Nelly Sachs prize from Germany, the Scottish Arts Council's Neil Gunn Fellowship and the French international award, the Grand Aigle d'Or. She was awarded the Nobel Prize for literature in 1991. Later publications include *None to Accompany Me* (1994) and *Writing and Being* (1995). 📖 R H Haugh, *Nadine Gordimer* (1974)

Gordon, Adam Lindsay 1833–70
Australian poet

Born in Fayal in the Azores, where his mother's father had a plantation, he completed his education in England but vanished to Australia after a series of reckless adventures. He had a brief career in the South Australian Mounted Police, and established a livery stable in Victoria. His ballads such as 'The Sick Stockrider', 'How We Beat the Favourite' and 'The Ride From the Wreck' reflect his interest in horses. Much of his best work is collected in *Sea Spray and Smoke Drift* (1867, reissued 1876 with a preface by **Marcus Clarke**) and in *Bush Ballads and Galloping Rhymes* (1870). His poem 'The Swimmer', with its undertones of suicide, was set as the last song in **Elgar's** *Sea Pictures*. A succession of unfortunate incidents precipitated a mental breakdown and his suicide. He is the only Australian poet honoured in the Poets' Corner of Westminster Abbey, London.

Gordon, Charles George, *known as* Chinese Gordon 1833–85
English general

Born in Woolwich, London, he joined the Royal Engineers in 1852, and in 1855–56 fought in the Crimean War. In 1860 he went to China, where he crushed the Taiping Rebellion. In 1877 he was appointed Governor of the Sudan. He resigned in poor health in 1880, but returned in 1884 to relieve Egyptian garrisons which lay in rebel territory. He was besieged at Khartoum for 10 months by the troops of the Mahdi (**Muhammad Ahmed**) and killed there two days before a relief force arrived. 📖 Anthony Nutting, *Gordon of Khartoum: Martyr and Misfit* (1966)

Gordon, Cyrus Herzl 1908–
US Hebrew scholar

Born in Philadelphia, Pennsylvania, he graduated at the University of Pennsylvania and taught Hebrew there before becoming field archaeologist in Bible lands with the American Schools of Oriental Research (1931–35).

Thereafter he taught at Johns Hopkins University, Princeton, Dropsie College and Brandeis University before retirement in 1973. His books include *The Living Past* (1941), *Adventures in the Near East* (1957), and various technical handbooks on Ugaritic. Since 1982 he has been director of the Center of Ebla Research at New York University.

Gordon, David 1936–
US dancer and choreographer

Born in Brooklyn, New York City, he studied painting before he began dancing with James Waring's company in New York (1958–62). He was a founding member (1962) of the seminal Judson Dance Theater and, in the following decade, the improvisational dance-theatre collective Grand Union. In 1974 he formed his own Pick-Up Company. He became known for his often humorous experimentation, and several of his works are in the repertories of major US and British classical and modern dance companies. He is married to the English-born ex-**Cunningham** dancer, Valda Setterfield.

Gordon, George, 2nd Earl of Huntly d.c.1502
Scottish nobleman

He married Princess Annabella, daughter of **James VI** of Scotland, in 1459. Their second son married the Countess of Sutherland and was progenitor of the earls of Sutherland. Their third son was progenitor of the turbulent Gordons of Gight, from whom **Byron's** maternal ancestors were descended. He served as Lord High Chancellor of Scotland from 1498 to 1501.

Gordon, George, 1st Marquis of Huntly and 6th Earl 1562–1636
Scottish nobleman

He was the head of the Roman Catholics in Scotland. He defeated a royal force under the 7th Earl of **Argyll** in 1594 at Glenlivet but, after submitting to the king, was pardoned and made marquis and joint Lieutenant of the North (1599).

Gordon, Lord George 1751–93
English anti-Catholic agitator

Born in London, he became an MP in 1774. With the aim of repealing the Catholic Relief Act of 1778, Lord George, as president of a Protestant association, led a mob of 50,000 to the House of Commons to present a petition for its repeal (1780). For five days, serious rioting took place during which many Catholic chapels and private houses, Newgate, and the house of the Chief Justice, Lord Mansfield, were destroyed. Five days later the troops were called out, and almost 300 of the rioters were killed, 21 being executed. Lord George was tried for high treason, but **Thomas Erskine's** defence earned his acquittal. He subsequently converted to Judaism, and was known as Israel Abraham George Gordon. In 1787 he was convicted for a libel on **Marie Antoinette**, and taken to Newgate Prison, where he died.

Gordon, Hannah Campbell Grant 1941–
Scottish actress

Born in Edinburgh, she won the James Bridie Gold Medal at the College of Music and Dramatic Art, Glasgow (1962), and made her television debut in *Johnson Over Jordan* (1965), following it with the situation comedies *My Wife Next Door* (1972) and *Joint Account* (1988–90), as well as such popular drama series as *Upstairs, Downstairs* (1976) and *Telford's Change* (1979). Rare film appearances include *Spring and Port Wine* (1969), *Alfie Darling* (1974) and *The Elephant Man* (1980). Her stage performances include *Can You Hear Me at the Back?* (1979), *The Jeweller's Shop* (1982), *The Country Girl* (1983) and *Shirley Valentine* (1989).

Gordon, John Rutherford 1890–1974
Scottish journalist

Born and educated in Dundee, he left school at the age of 14 to join a local newspaper, and worked as a sub-editor in London. Appointed editor of the *Sunday Express* in 1928, he turned a failing title into one of the most profitable newspapers in the world, increasing its circulation from 450,000 to 3,200,000 by the end of his reign. He introduced the first crossword puzzle and the first astrology column in a British newspaper. When he retired as editor (1952), he began an acerbic weekly column for the paper, called 'Current Events', which he continued until his death.

Gordon, Noele 1922–85
English actress
Born in East Ham, London, she made her first stage appearance at the age of two in a concert staged by the Maud Wells Dancing Academy. After studying at RADA she worked in repertory and pantomime before such London successes as *Diamond Lil* (1948) and *Brigadoon* (1949–51). She assisted John Logie Baird with his early experiments in colour television and first appeared on that medium in *Ah, Wilderness* (1938). She later studied television techniques in the USA, and returned to Great Britain as an adviser to ATV (Associated Television) and host of such series as *Lunch Box* (1955) and *Fancy That* (1956). She became a household name as the owner of the motel in the television soap-opera *Crossroads* (1964–81). Unceremoniously dismissed from the series, she returned to the stage in barnstorming musicals like *Gypsy* (1981), *Call Me Madam* (1982–83) and *No, No Nanette* (1983).

Gordy, Berry, Jnr 1929–
US record executive, producer and songwriter
He was born in Detroit, Michigan. He opened a jazz record shop in 1955, but its failure left him working in a car plant until Jackie Wilson had a hit with his song 'Reet Petite' in 1957. He became an independent producer in 1958, and launched Tamla Records the following year, the company which he built into Tamla Motown, one of the most famous labels in the history of US popular music. He oversaw the whole operation in the 1960s, when his artists like Diana Ross and The Supremes, Stevie Wonder, The Four Tops, Marvin Gaye and Smokey Robinson ruled the charts. He became increasingly involved in the business side of the company, including a move to California in the early 1970s and a venture into films, by which time its creative peak was already past. He sold the company to MCA (Music Corporation of America) in 1988. ▭ *To Be Loved* (1994)

Gore, Catherine Grace Frances, *née* Moody
1799–1861
English novelist
Born in East Retford, Nottinghamshire, she was a prolific and immensely popular writer of novels, mainly of fashionable life in the manner of the 'silver fork' school. They include *Mothers and Daughters* (1831), *Mrs Armytage* (1836) and *The Banker's Wife* (1843). She also wrote three plays, and short stories.

Gore, Charles 1853–1932
English Anglican prelate and theologian
The nephew of the 4th Earl of Arran, he was educated at Harrow and Oxford. He became a Fellow of Trinity College, Oxford, in 1875 and first Principal of Pusey House in 1884. His contribution to *Lux Mundi* (1889) abandoned the strict tractarian view of biblical inspiration, and his Bampton Lectures (1891) were equally controversial. He founded the Community of the Resurrection at Pusey House in 1892, and became successively Bishop of Worcester (1901), Birmingham (1904) and Oxford (1911–19).

Gore, Spencer Frederick 1878–1914
English painter

Born in Epsom, Surrey, he joined the New English Art Club in 1909. He was a founder member and first president of the Camden Town Group (1911), and became a member of the London Group in 1913. He met Walter Sickert in Dieppe, France, in 1904 and was inspired to paint theatre and music hall subjects, using a quasi-Pointilliste technique learned from Lucien Pissarro. In 1912 he contributed to Roger Fry's second Post-Impressionist exhibition.

Goren, Charles Henry 1901–
US contract bridge expert and author
Born in Philadelphia, Pennsylvania, he practised law there until 1936, when he abandoned it to concentrate on bridge. He wrote numerous books, including *Winning Bridge Made Easy* (1936) and *Contract Bridge in a Nutshell* (1946). He also wrote on backgammon (*Goren's Modern Backgammon Complete*, 1974), and contributed a daily newspaper column, syndicated in the USA.

Gorenko, Anna Andreeyevna See Akhmatova, Anna

Gorgas, William Crawford 1854–1920
US military doctor
Born near Mobile, Alabama, he trained in medicine at Bellevue Hospital Medical College in New York City, and joined the US Army Medical Corps in 1880. Following the discovery of the role of the mosquito in the transmission of yellow fever, Gorgas directed the mosquito eradication programme in Havana and the Panama Canal Zone, the latter permitting the successful construction of the canal (1904–14). He was surgeon-general to the US army during World War I and established the systematic medical examination of recruits, which greatly improved the quality of medical care among troops.

Gorges, Sir Ferdinando c.1566–1647
English colonialist
Born in Ashton, Somerset, he founded two Plymouth companies (1606–19, 1620–35) for settling lands in New England. In 1639 he received a charter making him proprietor of Maine. His grandson sold his rights to Massachusetts in 1677.

Görgey, Artúr 1818–1916
Hungarian rebel soldier
He was born in Toporcz, North Hungary. During the revolt of 1848 he compelled Josip Jelačič (1801–59) and his 10,000 Croats to capitulate at Ozora. As Hungarian Commander-in-Chief, despite conflict with Lajos Kossuth, he relieved Komorn by inflicting a series of severe defeats on the Austrians, practically driving them out of the country. In 1849 he was repeatedly defeated and in August surrendered to the Russians with his army of 24,000 men at Világos, near Arad. Görgey was imprisoned at Klagenfurt, but was eventually released and returned to Hungary in 1868.

Gorgias c.490–c.385BC
Greek philosopher and rhetorician
Born in Leontini, Sicily, he was one of the sophists who were professional itinerant teachers of oratory and political skills. He went to Athens as ambassador in 427BC and quickly became a celebrity for his public performances. His philosophy was an extreme form of scepticism or nihilism: that nothing exists, that if it did it would be unknowable, that if it were knowable it would be incommunicable to others, and that we live in a world of opinion, manipulated by persuasion. He is memorably portrayed in Plato's dialogue, the *Gorgias*, where he and Socrates debate the morality implicit in his teachings and activities.

Goria, Giovanni 1943–94
Italian politician

He was born in Asti, Piemonte Region, where he became provincial secretary of the Christian Democratic Party (DC). Elected to the Chamber of Deputies in 1976, he held a number of ministerial posts in DC-led coalition governments before being made Treasury Minister in 1982. In 1987, after a near constitutional crisis had been averted when the Socialists withdrew their support for the Christian Democrats, Goria managed to form another coalition which he led until it collapsed in 1988. He resigned in 1993, caught up in a government corruption investigation, and was brought to trial in 1994. He was acquitted of one charge with another pending at the time of his death.

Göring, Hermann Wilhelm See Goering, Hermann Wilhelm

Goring, Marius 1912–98
English actor
Born in Newport, Isle of Wight, he was educated at universities in Frankfurt, Munich, Vienna and Paris, made his West End debut in *The Voysey Ineritance* (1934) and took the title role in *Hamlet* at the Old Vic (1935). After serving in intelligence during World War II, he continued his film career with pictures such as *The Magic Box* (1951), *The Adventures of Quentin Durward* (1955), *The Barefoot Contessa* (1955) and *I Was Monty's Double* (1958). On television, he played the title role in *The Adventures of the Scarlet Pimpernel* (1955–56) and police pathologist Dr John Hardy in *The Expert* (1968–76).

Goris, Jan-Albert See Gijsen, Marnix

Gorky, Arshile, *originally* Vosdanig Manoog Adoian 1905–48
US painter
Born in Khorkom Vari, in Turkish Armenia, he emigrated to the USA in 1920 and studied at the Rhode Island School of Design and in Boston before moving to New York City in 1925. His art combined ideas from the European Surrealists who had fled to New York in the early 1940s with the biomorphic abstraction of such artists as Joán Miró, and he played a key role in the emergence of the New York school of Action Painters in the 1940s.

Gorky, Maxim, *pseudonym of* Aleksei Maksimovich Peshkov 1868–1936
Russian novelist
Born in Nizhny Novgorod, he was a pedlar, scullery boy, gardener, dock hand, tramp and writer, leading a restless, nomadic life which he described brilliantly in his autobiographical trilogy, *Detstvo* (1913–14, Eng trans *My Childhood*, 1915), *V lyudakh* (1915–16, Eng trans *In the World*, 1918) and *Moi universitety* (1922, Eng trans *My University Days*, 1923). He first achieved fame with his story *Chelkash* (1895), followed by others in a romantic vein, with vividly drawn characters, mostly tramps and down-and-outs. *Foma Gordeyev* (1899, Eng trans 1902) marks his transition from Romanticism to Realism. In 1902 he produced his best-known play, *Na dne* (Eng trans *A Night's Lodging*, 1905, better known as *The Lower Depths*, 1912). Involved in strikes and imprisoned in 1905, he lived abroad until 1914 and then engaged in revolutionary propaganda. From 1922 to 1928 he lived abroad again on account of his health, but then returned, a whole-hearted supporter of the Soviet regime. He sponsored 'Social Realism' as the official school in Soviet literature and art. 📖 Dan Levin, *The Stormy Petrel: The Life and Work of Maxim Gorky* (1965); R Hare, *Maxim Gorky, Romantic Realist and Conservative Revolutionary* (1962)

Gormley, Antony Mark David 1950–
English sculptor
Born in London, as a child he acquired a love of the natural world from his German grandparents. He read archaeology, anthropology and art history at Cambridge, before training at the Central School of Art and Design, Goldsmiths College, and the Slade School of Art, London. In 1981 he began to make moulds from his own body in various poses, to express the space, or spirit, within and the body's receptiveness to life, for example *Untitled (for Francis)* (1985, Tate, London). In 1982 and 1986 he exhibited at the Venice Biennale. After 1990 his bodies expanded into bulbous forms, such as *Still Running* (1990–93, Galerie Nordenhake). In 1993 his exhibition *Testing a World View*, which toured Malmö, Liverpool and Dublin, featured five identical figures, their bodies bent at right angles, 'testing' themselves against walls, floor and ceiling. More recently, his *Field for the British Isles* (1993) toured Liverpool, Edinburgh and the Hayward Gallery, London (1996–97), and his *Angel of the North* (1997–98), a figure some 20 metres high with a wingspan of 54 metres, was erected in Gateshead, north-east England.

Görres, Johann Joseph von 1776–1848
German writer
He was born in Coblenz, which in 1812 became the literary centre of the National movement. Denouncing political and religious absolutism with great vigour, he angered the Prussian government, and had to flee the country (1820). In 1827 he was made Professor of Literature at Munich, where he devoted himself to literature and controversial theology. His chief work was his *Christliche Mystik* (1842, 'Christian Mysticism'). 📖 J N Sepp, *Görres* (1873)

Gorshkov, Sergei Georgiyevich 1910–88
Soviet admiral
He joined the navy in 1927, graduated from the Frunze Naval Academy in 1931, and served in the Black Sea and in the Far East. From 1940 to 1955 he served mostly in the Black Sea fleet, commanding the fleet by 1951. He was appointed Commander-in-Chief of the Soviet navy by Nikita Khrushchev in 1956, with the brief to cut back expenditure. However, after the Cuban Missile Crisis (1962) and Khrushchev's ousting (1964), the new Soviet leader, Leonid Brezhnev, pressed for naval expansion. Supporting this view, Gorshkov oversaw a massive naval build-up, creating a force capable of challenging the West by the 1970s. Although he was in command of the navy until his death, his influence declined rapidly after Mikhail Gorbachev came to power (1985).

Gort, John Standish Surtees Prendergast Vereker, 6th Viscount 1886–1946
English field marshal
Educated at Harrow and the Royal Military College, Woolwich, he served with the Grenadier Guards in World War I and won the VC in 1918. He was appointed Chief of the Imperial General Staff in 1938. In World War II he was Commander-in-Chief of the British forces overwhelmed in the initial German victories of 1940. Afterwards he was Governor of Gibraltar (1941–42) and of Malta (1942–44), and was promoted field marshal in 1943. He was High Commissioner for Palestine and Transjordan from 1944 to 1945.

Gorton, Sir John Grey 1911–
Australian politician
Educated at Geelong Grammar School and Brasenose College, Oxford, he joined the Royal Australian Air Force in 1940, serving in Europe, Malaya and Australia. Seriously wounded, he was discharged in 1944. He was a Liberal senator for Victoria (1949–68) and a member of the House of Representatives (1968–75). He served in the governments of Sir Robert Menzies and Harold Holt and,

when Holt died in 1967, succeeded him as Prime Minister. In 1971 he was defeated on a vote of confidence and resigned in favour of **William McMahon**, becoming Deputy Leader of his party.

Gorton, Samuel 1592–1677
American colonist and religious leader
Born in Gorton, Lancashire, England, he emigrated in 1637 to Massachusetts Colony in New England, where he founded the sect of 'Gortonites'. Denying the doctrine of the Trinity and the existence of heaven and hell, he was tried for heresy (1637–38) and banished. Returning to London in 1644, he was given a letter of safe conduct by John Rich, the 2nd Earl of **Warwick**, to settle in Rhode Island (1648). He renamed the township of Shawomet, Warwick, and lived there peacefully with a few faithful Gortonite adherents.

Gossaert, Jan See **Mabuse, Jan**

Gosse, Sir Edmund William 1849–1928
English poet and critic
Born in London, the son of **Philip Henry Gosse**, he was educated privately. He became assistant librarian in the British Museum (1867–75), then translator to the Board of Trade (1875–1904) and finally librarian to the House of Lords (1904–14). His reputation as a critic was damaged after attacks on his accuracy and scholarship by Churton Collins in 1885, an incident which troubled him throughout his life. He initially regarded himself as a poet, and published several works, including the volumes *On Viol and Flute* (1873) and *Collected Poems* (1911). His *Studies in the Literature of Northern Europe* (1879), and other critical works, first introduced Ibsen to English-speaking readers. He also wrote on **William Congreve** (1888), John Donne (1899), Jeremy Taylor (1904), Sir Thomas Browne (1905), Algernon Charles Swinburne (1917) and François de Malherbe (1920), although his special field was *Seventeenth-Century Studies* (1897). His finest work is considered to be the autobiographical *Father and Son* (1907), in which he describes his puritanical father's domineering character and beliefs and his own escape into the literary world. 📖 A Thwaite, *Edmund Gosse, a literary landscape* (1984)

Gosse, Philip Henry 1810–88
English naturalist
Born in Worcester, he went to North America in 1827 and became a professional naturalist in Jamaica, with a particular interest in coastal marine biology. His *Manual of Marine Zoology* (1855–56) and *History of British Sea-anemones and Corals* (1860), written on his return to England, greatly expanded interest in marine organisms. He published *Omphalos* (1857) in opposition to evolutionary theory. His best-known work was the *Romance of Natural History* (1860–62).

Gosse, (Laura) Sylvia 1881–1968
English artist and printmaker
Born in London, she was a daughter of the writer Sir Edmund Gosse. She studied at St John's Wood School of Art, then the Royal Academy Schools, London. In 1908 she met **Walter Sickert**, who encouraged her, and she became co-principal at his school of painting and etching at Rowland House. In 1913 she had the first of many solo shows and the following year became a founder-member of the London Group. She was influenced by Sickert and Spencer Gore, encompassing genre subjects and everyday interiors, often with a single figure, as well as urban, town and Continental scenes. Her work includes accomplished etchings and features in many public collections throughout the UK.

Gosse, William Christie 1842–81
Australian explorer

He was born in Hoddesden, Hertfordshire, England, but his family emigrated to Adelaide, South Australia (1850), where he was educated privately and then joined the South Australian Surveyor-General's department. In 1873 Gosse led an expedition from Alice Springs in the Northern Territory (at that time administered by South Australia), in search of an overland route to Perth on the west coast of the continent. Gosse reached the massive sandstone monolith which had been sighted by **Ernest Giles** the previous year, and named it Ayers Rock after Sir Henry Ayers. Although his group was forced to turn back, his maps proved invaluable to Sir **John Forrest's** successful 1874 expedition from Perth.

Gotama See **Gautama**

Gottfried von Strassburg fl.1200
German poet
He wrote the masterly German version of the legend of *Tristan and Isolde*, based on the Anglo-Norman poem by Thomas. He is also noteworthy as an early exponent of literary criticism, having left appraisals of the work of poets of the period. 📖 M S Bates, *Gottfried von Strassburg* (1971)

Gottlieb, Adolph 1903–74
US painter
Born in New York City, he attended the Art Students' League in New York, and from 1921 to 1923 studied in Paris. In 1935 he joined the New York avant-garde group The Ten, whose members included **Mark Rothko**. From 1941 he painted an unusual series of pictographs in which a grid system is drawn on to the canvas and a primitive symbol inserted in each space. A strong interest in African and Native American art informed these works. After 1950 his paintings became radically simplified, consisting of gestural marks of bright colour which evoke imaginary landscapes. He stands as one of the most original of the Abstract Expressionist school of painters.

Gottlieb, Robert Adams 1931–
US publisher and editor
Born in New York City, he was educated at Columbia University and at Cambridge. After serving as editor-in-chief at Simon & Schuster (1955–68) and at Alfred Knopf (1968–87), he became editor of the *New Yorker* (1987–92).

Gottschalk, Laura Riding See **Riding, Laura**

Gottschalk, Louis Moreau 1829–69
US pianist and composer
Born in New Orleans, he studied in Paris (1842–46), and impressed **Chopin** and **Berlioz**. After touring in France, Switzerland and Spain, he returned to the USA (1853) and enjoyed success with his piano and piano-orchestral compositions, many of which explore Creole, African and Spanish idioms.

Gottwald, Klement 1896–1953
Czechoslovak politician
Born in Dedice, Moravia, he fought with the Austro-Hungarian army in World War I. He then joined the Communist Party, whose Secretary-General he became in 1927. He opposed the Munich Agreement of 1938 and later went to Moscow, where he was trained for eventual office. In 1945 he became vice-premier in the Czechoslovak provisional government. Prime minister in 1946, he carried out the Communist coup d'état which averted a defeat for his party at the polls in February 1948. In June he became President. Strong in the support of **Stalin**, whose line he followed closely, he established a complete dictatorship in Czechoslovakia. He died of an illness contracted while he was attending Stalin's funeral.

Götz or Goetz von Berlichingen 1480–1562
German soldier

He was born in Jaxthausen in Württemberg, and gained the nickname 'Götz mit der eisernen hand' ('Götz with the iron hand') because of a steel replacement for his right hand lost in the Siege of Landshut (1505). From 1497 he was involved in continual feuds, in which he displayed both lawless daring and chivalrous magnanimity. Twice he was placed under the ban of the empire. He fought for Duke Ulrich of Württemberg (1519) against the Swabian league, and after his heroic defence of Möckmühl was taken prisoner. In the Peasants' War of 1525 he led a section of the insurgents, was captured by the Swabian league, kept prisoner at Augsburg for two years, and sentenced to life imprisonment. He was only freed on the dissolution of the league in 1540. In 1542 he fought in Hungary against the Turks, and in 1544 in France. He wrote an autobiography, published in 1731, on which **Goethe** based his drama *Götz von Berlichingen*.

Goudimel, Claude c.1514–1572
French composer

Born in Besançon, he composed masses, motets, songs and psalm tunes. He taught music in Rome, and died in Lyons as a Huguenot just after the St Bartholomew's Day Massacre.

Goudsmit, Samuel Abraham 1902–78
US physicist

Born in The Hague, the Netherlands, he studied in Amsterdam and Leyden and emigrated in 1927 to the USA, where he was professor at Michigan University (1932–46) and later worked at the Brookhaven National Laboratory, Long Island (1948–70). Aged 23, he and his fellow student **George Uhlenbeck** proposed the idea that electrons in atoms can have intrinsic spin angular momentum. Initially physicists found it difficult to accept this rotational property of electrons, but **P A M Dirac's** 1928 theory of relativistic quantum mechanics showed that spin is an intrinsic property of the electron. During World War II, Goudsmit headed the secret Alsos mission charged with following German progress in atomic bomb research (1944), which led to the award of the US Medal of Freedom, and to his book *Alsos* (1947).

Goudy, Frederic William 1865–1947
US printer and type designer

Born in Bloomington, Illinois, he worked in printing shops before founding his own small press in 1895. While operating this and two subsequent presses, he designed more than 90 typefaces still admired for their simplicity and beauty, including Goudy Old Style, Hadriano, and Garamond.

Gough, Sir Hubert de la Poer 1870–1963
Irish general and mutineer

He was born in Gurteen, County Waterford. Educated at Eton and Sandhurst, he served in the Boer War, and relieved Ladysmith against orders. He returned to Ireland where, in 1914, he and 57 other officers threatened to resign rather than take arms in Ulster to impose Home Rule against Sir **Edward Carson's** Ulster Volunteers, and won the day. The episode convinced extreme Irish nationalist elements that reliance on government Home Rule promises was hopeless and only force would be respected. Gough was rapidly promoted in World War I, but his command of the 5th Army at the third Ypres campaign impaired his reputation. He was made a scapegoat for British military failure during the German advance of March 1918 and retired in 1922. He wrote a self-vindication in his *Fifth Army* (1931). His memoirs, *Soldiering On*, appeared in 1954.

Gough, Hugh Gough, 1st Viscount 1779–1869
Anglo-Irish soldier

Born in Woodstown, County Limerick, he served in the West Indies (1797–1800), through the Peninsular War, and in India, and in 1838 was made Commander-in-Chief of the forces sent against China during the first Opium War. After storming Canton, he compelled the Chinese to sign the Treaty of Nanking (1842), and in 1843 defeated the Marathas in India. In the Sikh War in 1845 he defeated the enemy in the battles of Mudki, Ferozeshah and Sobraon. In 1848 the Sikhs renewed the war, but Gough again defeated them at Ramnagar, Chillianwalla and Gujerat, victories which resulted in the annexation of the Punjab.

Goujon, Jean c.1510–c.1568
French sculptor

He was a Huguenot, but seems to have died before the St Bartholomew Massacre (1572). From 1555 to 1562 he worked in the Louvre, Paris, where some of his finest works can be seen there, such as *Diana reclining by a Stag*, and the reliefs for the *Fountain of the Innocents* (1549). He also created the monument to the Duke of Brézé in Rouen Cathedral (1541–44).

Goulart, João (Belquior Marques) 1918–76
Brazilian politician

Born in Rio Grande do Sul, he became the wealthy landowning neighbour of **Getulio Vargas**. He was linked with the Brazilian Labour Party (PTB) in the late 1940s and, as Vargas's protégé, became Minister of Labour in 1954. He became Leader of the PTB in 1960 and, having been accused by the army of nurturing pro-Communist sympathies, was elected Vice-President against military hostility. The army reluctantly agreed to allow him to become President of a parliamentary regime in 1961. A weak and vacillating leader (1963–64), he alienated moderate opinion by flirting with nationalist and left-wing groups. He was ejected by a coup (1964) engineered by the army and supported by powerful conservative politicians in the Brazilian Democratic Union (UDN).

Gould, Benjamin Apthorp 1824–96
US astronomer

Born in Boston and educated at Harvard and Göttingen, he founded the *Astronomical Journal* (1849–61), was director of the Dudley Observatory at Albany (1856–59) and in 1866 determined, by aid of the submarine cable, the difference in longitude between Europe and the USA. He helped to found and was director of the National Observatory at Córdoba, Argentina, from 1868. He published *Uranometria Argentina*, which complemented **Friedrich Argelander's** *Atlas* of the northern heavens.

Gould, Bryan Charles 1939–
British politician

Born in New Zealand, the son of a bank official, he won a university scholarship at the age of 15, entering Auckland University two years later. A Rhodes Scholarship took him to Balliol College, Oxford, and in 1964, instead of returning to New Zealand, he joined the British diplomatic service. He was, however, more interested in a political career and in 1968 left the Civil Service to teach at Worcester College, Oxford (1968–74). His own background and distaste for the British class system made the Labour Party his natural choice and, after experience in local politics, he entered the House of Commons as MP for Southampton Test (1974–79). He lost his seat in the 1979 general election but returned in 1983 to represent Dagenham, having spent the intervening four years as a television journalist. His rise in the Labour Party was rapid and he was elected to the Shadow Cabinet (1986), but resigned in 1992 over the party's policy on Europe. He stood unsuccessfully for both the leadership and deputy leadership of the Labour Party in 1992, and then resigned from British politics to return to New Zealand, where he has been Vice-Chancellor of Waikato University since 1994. He published his memoirs, *Goodbye to All That*, in 1995.

Gould, Chester 1900–85
US strip cartoonist

Born in Pawnee, Oklahoma, he won a cartoon contest in *American Boy* magazine (1916), and drew sports cartoons for *Daily Oklahoma* whilst at college. After a year at the Zuckerman Art Studio in Chicago (1921), he joined the art staff of the *Chicago American*, creating his first strip, *Fillum Fables* (1924), then moving to the *Chicago Tribune* to draw *Girl Friends* (1929). He submitted a new idea in continuity strips, *Plainclothes Tracy*, the first 'tough detective' in comics, to the *New York Daily News*, who rechristened it *Dick Tracy*. It kept Gould busy until his retirement in 1977, when his former assistant took it over.

Gould, Glenn 1932–82
Canadian pianist and composer

Born in Toronto, he started to play the piano at the age of three, and studied at the Royal Conservatory of Music there before making his debut, at 14, as a soloist with the Toronto Symphony Orchestra. He toured extensively in the USA and Europe and made many recordings, particularly of works by Bach and Beethoven. His own work, *A String Quartet*, was premiered in 1956. In 1964 he retired from the concert platform, believing concerts were obsolescent, and devoted himself to recording and broadcasting. His writings were collected together as *The Glenn Gould Reader* (1987).

Gould, Jay (Jason) 1836–92
US financier

Born in Roxbury, New York, he made a survey of parts of the state, engaged in lumbering, and in 1857 became the principal shareholder in a Pennsylvania bank. He began to buy up railroad bonds, started as a broker in New York (1859), and manipulated shares to seize the presidency of the Erie railway company (1868–72). He tried to corner the gold market, causing the 'Black Friday' stock market crash of September 1869. He bought up huge areas of railroad companies.

Gould, John 1804–81
English ornithologist and publisher

Born in Lyme Regis, he became curator and preserver (taxidermist) to the new Zoological Society's museum in London in 1827. An accomplished artist, he travelled widely, drawing birds whose skins he collected for the museum. Working with the newly developed technique of lithography, he produced 18 monumental books of sumptuous bird illustrations, including *Birds of Europe* (5 vols, 1832–37), *Birds of Australia* (7 vols, 1840–48), *Birds of Asia* (1849–83) and *Birds of Great Britain* (5 vols, 1862–73). One of his assistant draughtsmen at the Zoological Society was Edward Lear.

Gould, Morton 1913–96
US composer

He was born in New York City. His music is national in style and exploits the various aspects of popular music from both North and South America. He composed symphonies and a variety of works in more popular style, including a *Tap-dance Concerto* (1952). He won a Pulitzer Prize for *Stringmusic* in 1995, written for and premiered by the National Symphony of Washington DC.

Gould, Nat(haniel) 1857–1919
English writer

He was born in Manchester, and began as a journalist on provincial and London newspapers. He went to Australia in 1884 and became racing editor of the Sydney *Referee*, for which he was a successful tipster under the name 'Verax', and also published two serials, the second of which, 'With

the Tide', was later published as *The Double Event* (1891). Two years later it was made into a highly successful melodrama, staged in Melbourne with 20 horses in the 'cast', and his subsequent books became popular both in Australia and Great Britain. He returned to England in 1895 and from that time wrote over 130 novels, mainly thrillers of racing or other sporting plots. He wrote three volumes of autobiography, *On and Off the Turf in Australia* (1895), *Town and Bush* (1896) and *The Magic of Sport; Mainly Autobiographical* (1909).

Gould, Shane Elizabeth 1956–
Australian swimmer

She was born in Brisbane, Queensland, and between 1971 and 1972 set world records at every freestyle distance from 100 metres to 1,500 metres. Her time of 58.5 seconds for the 100 metres freestyle broke the record set by Dawn Fraser in 1964. Gould also became the first woman to win three individual swimming golds in world record times at the 1972 Olympics—in the 200 metres individual medley and 200 metres and 400 metres freestyle—and also won a silver and a bronze. As well as breaking or equalling 11 world records throughout her short career, she won numerous Australian individual championships, all before retiring at the age of 17 to marry and become a social welfare worker.

Gould, Stephen Jay 1941–
US palaeontologist

Born in New York City and educated at Antioch College, and the universities of Ohio and Columbia, he has been Professor of Geology since 1973 and Alexander Agassiz Professor of Zoology since 1982 at Harvard. In an influential paper published in 1972 he, together with the palaeontologist Niles Eldgredge, posited the theory of 'punctuated equilibrium' and he has also championed the idea of 'hierarchical evolution'. He has been critical of the 'adaptationist program', emphasizing that many characters of organisms are not 'adaptive' in the strict sense. He has popularized his ideas in a monthly column in *Natural History* magazine and a series of collected essays, including *Ever Since Darwin* (1977), *The Panda's Thumb* (1980), *Hens' Teeth and Horses' Toes* (1983), *The Flamingo's Smile* (1985), *Bully for Brontosaurus* (1991) and *Eight Little Piggies* (1993). His books have won many awards, including the 1990 Science Book prize for *Wonderful Life* (1989), a reinterpretation of the Cambrian Burgess Shale fauna. Gould has admitted to Marxist influence in his scientific work and has been a forceful speaker against pseudoscientific racism and biological determinism; *The Mismeasure of Man* (1981) is a critique of intelligence testing. He was also a witness in a courtroom trial about the teaching of evolution in US public schools.

Gouled Aptidon, Hassan 1916–
Djiboutian politician

Born in the city of Djibouti, he was a representative of French Somaliland in France while becoming increasingly active in the independence movement. He joined the African People's League for Independence (LPAI) in 1967 and when independence was achieved, in 1977, became the country's first President. Later the LPAI was amalgamated with other parties to become the People's Progress Party (RPP) and Djibouti's sole political party. He pursued a largely successful policy of amicable neutralism in a war-torn region and was re-elected in 1987 for a final six-year term.

Gounod, Charles François 1818–93
French composer

Born in Paris, he studied at the Paris Conservatoire and in Rome. He became organist of the Church of the Missions Etrangères, Paris, where his earliest compositions, chiefly polyphonic in style, were performed. His major works include the comic opera *Le Médecin malgré lui* (1858, 'The Mock Doctor') and *Faust* (1859). He also published hymns, masses, and anthems, and was popular as a songwriter. He fled to England during the Franco-Prussian War (1870). He was a member of the Institute (1866) and a commander of the French Legion of Honour (1877).

Gourd, Emilie 1879–1946
Swiss feminist and writer
She founded and edited the newspaper *Le mouvement féministe*. She campaigned on behalf of women's rights, and continually lobbied the Swiss authorities at both regional and national level on behalf of the cause of women's suffrage. She was president of the Swiss Women's Association (1914–28), and was also secretary of the International Alliance of Women. Her writings include a biography of the US suffragist Susan B Anthony.

Gourmont, Rémy de 1858–1915
French poet, novelist and critic
Born in Bazoches-en-Houlme, Normandy, he studied law at Caen University. He was dismissed from his post at the Bibliothèque Nationale, Paris, because of an allegedly pro-German article in *Mercure de France*, of which he was a co-founder. After that he lived the life of a recluse. His creative work—poetry and novels in the Symbolist vogue—is cerebral and stylistic, betraying a 'fin de siècle' obsession with words as sound more than as sense. However his evaluative work, which includes *Le Livre des masques* (1896–98) and *Promenades philosophiques* (1905–09), is clear-sighted and individualistic, exhibiting scholarship and intellectual curiosity. His novels include *Sixtine* (1890, Eng trans *Very Woman*) and *Un Cœur virginal* (1907, Eng trans by Aldous Huxley, *A Virgin Heart*, 1921).

Gow, Ian 1937–90
English Conservative politician
Educated at Winchester School, he later studied law, and after army service as a commander of the 15th/17th Hussars (1956–62), he practised as a solicitor. He entered parliament for the Conservatives in 1966, and served as parliamentary Private Secretary to Margaret Thatcher after his party's 1979 election victory, then as Minister of Housing (1983–85) and Treasury Minister, until resigning in 1986 in protest at the Anglo-Irish Agreement. His continuing fierce condemnation of IRA activities and of any relaxation of Great Britain's obligation to the Province, together with his continuing closeness to Thatcher, who frequently sought his informal counsel, singled him out as a prime IRA target, and he was killed by a car bomb.

Gow, Niel 1727–1807
Scottish violinist and songwriter
Born in Inver, near Dunkeld, Perthshire, he was the son of a plaid weaver, and started playing the fiddle at the age of five. He was largely self-taught, but went on to become Scotland's most famous fiddler and songwriter, known as 'the father of Strathspey and Reel players'. Patronized by the dukes of Atholl, he was much in demand as a player at important balls and parties. His compositions include Strathspeys, jigs, reels, and laments. His open, honest character, unique style of playing, long career and fine compositions combined to make him a household name during his lifetime and a legend after it. His influence on Scottish music continued through the work of his sons Andrew, John and Nathaniel, all of whom were practising musicians.

Gower, David Ivon 1957–
English cricketer
Born in Tunbridge Wells, Kent, he came to the fore quickly chiefly because of the elegance of his left-handed stroke play. A consistent rather than heavy scorer, he had by 1988 accumulated 7,000 runs in Test cricket, including 14 centuries. He was captain of England in the mid-1980s, though without particular success. He was recalled as captain in 1989, only to lose the captaincy and his place in the team after a crushing defeat in the Test series against Australia. He has become a cricket commentator on both radio and television and also regularly appears on *They Think It's All Over*. He published his autobiography in 1992.

Gower, John c.1325–1408
English medieval poet
Born in Kent, he spent most of his life in London and had contacts with the court in the service of Richard II and Henry IV. A friend of Chaucer, he wrote *Speculum Meditantis*, in French verse, which was discovered at Cambridge only in 1898, and 50 French ballads. Other works include the *Vox Clamantis*, elegiacs in Latin (1382–84), describing the rising under Wat Tyler, and the long English poem *Confessio Amantis* (c.1383), consisting of over 100 stories taken from Ovid's *Metamorphoses*, the *Gesta Romanorum*, and medieval histories of Troy. Gower was blind from about 1400. 📖 J A Burrows, *Ricardian Poetry: Chaucer, Gower, Langland and the Gawain Poet* (1971)

Gowers, Sir Ernest Arthur 1880–1966
English civil servant
The son of the neurologist Sir William Richard Gowers (1845–1915), he was educated at Rugby and Clare College, Cambridge, and called to the Bar in 1906. After a distinguished career in the Civil Service he emerged as the champion of *Plain Words* (1948) and *ABC of Plain Words* (1951), designed to maintain standards of clear English, especially in official prose.

Gowing, Sir Lawrence Burnett 1918–91
English painter and writer on art
Born in Stoke Newington, London, he studied at the Euston Road School under William Coldstream, and his Impressionist style is often applied to portraits, such as *Mrs Roberts* in the Tate Gallery, London. One of his best-known pre-war paintings is *Mare Street, Hackney* (1937). He was Professor of Fine Art at the University of Durham (1948–58), Principal of the King Edward VII School of Art, Newcastle upon Tyne (1948–58), principal of Chelsea School of Art (1958–65), Professor of Fine Art at Leeds (1967–75) and Slade Professor of Fine Art at University College London (1975–85). His studies of *Renoir* (1947) and *Vermeer* (1952) initiated his reputation as an art historian. Among his other publications are works on John Constable (1961), Goya (1965) and Matisse (1979).

Gowon, Yakubu 1934–
Nigerian soldier and politician
Born in Garam, Plateau state, he was a Christian in a Muslim area and was educated at a missionary school. After military training in Ghana and Great Britain (Sandhurst), he joined the Nigerian army (1956), serving with the UN force in the Congo (Zaire) from 1960 to 1961. He became adjutant-general in 1963 and Chief of Staff in 1966. The ethnic conflicts in the country precipitated a coup in January 1966, led by Ibo officers, and Gowon headed a counter-coup (July 1966). He then became head of the Federal Military Government and Commander-in-Chief. Unable to prevent a civil war, with US and Soviet aid he successfully retained Biafra (the eastern region) within a single Nigeria, while acceding to ethnic concerns by increasing the number of states. However, his delayed return to democracy encouraged another military coup. He was deposed in 1975 and went into exile. Although he returned to Nigeria in 1983 he was forced to leave and now lives in Togo.

Goya y Lucientes, Francisco (José) de
1746–1828
Spanish artist

Born in Fuendetodos, near Saragossa, he returned to Spain in 1775 after travelling in Italy, to design for the Royal Tapestry Works. He worked quite conventionally at first, painting scenes of court pastorals strongly influenced by Giovanni Tiepolo and the Neapolitans, but he soon began introducing scenes from everyday Spanish life, such as *Stilt Walkers*, *Blind Guitarist*, which show his passion for reality. At the same time he studied Velázquez in the Royal Collections, and this prompted him to begin painting the portraits for which he became famous. In 1786 he was appointed court painter to Charles IV (chief painter in 1799). The portraits, particularly those done of the Spanish royal family (eg *The Family of Charles IV*, 1800, Prado, Madrid) are painted in an uncompromising and unflattering style which makes one wonder how acceptable they were to their subjects. Other works include *Maja nude* and *Maja clothed* (c.1797–1800, Prado, Madrid). In a series of 82 satirical etchings called *Los Caprichos* issued in 1799, Goya castigated the follies of the court. After the Napoleonic occupation he produced an equally sardonic series entitled *The Disasters of War*. His religious paintings, particularly the frescoes (1798) for the church of San Antonio de la Florida, Madrid, are extremely freely painted. After 1792 he became increasingly deaf and in later life retired to the outskirts of Madrid, where he painted some extraordinary decorations for his own house (*House of the Deaf Man*, now in the Prado, Madrid). In 1824, on the accession of Ferdinand VII, he went into voluntary exile in France where he continued to work. His work has influenced virtually every major painter from Eugène Delacroix to Picasso.

Goyen, Jan Josephszoon van 1596–1656
Dutch painter

Born in Leyden, he produced many sea and river pieces in soft browns and greys, and, unusually for his time, omitted small details and developed a broad atmospheric effect. Jan Steen, who became his son-in-law, was one of his pupils. His *River Scene* (c.1645) is in the National Gallery, London.

Goytisolo, Juan 1931–
Spanish novelist and critic

Born in Barcelona, he was associated with progressive, anti-Franco writers in his early career, when he co-founded the group 'Turia' with Ana María Matute (1926–) and others. Then in 1957, unlike his brother Luis Goytisolo (1937–), he left Spain for Paris, where he worked for the publisher Gallimard. His early novels, such as *Juegos de manos* (1954, Eng trans *The Young Assassins*, 1959) show the influence of both his bisexuality and the Arabic elements in Spanish literature. He became a determined and influential Modernist and Postmodernist, and his best-known novels are *Reivindicación del conde Don Julian* (1970, Eng trans *Count Julian*, 1974) and *Juan sin tierra* (1976, Eng trans *John the Landless*, 1977), which are essentially a 'deconstruction' of Spain's official history (1939–64). ▣ J Ortega, *Juan Goytisolo* (1972, in Spanish)

Gozzi, Count Carlo 1720–1806
Italian dramatist

He was born in Venice. His *Tartana* (1757), a satirical poem against Carlo Goldoni, was followed by a very popular comedy, *Fiaba dell'amore delle tre Melarance* (1761, Eng trans *The Love of Three Oranges*, 1949). He also wrote several similar 'dramatic fairy-tales', of which the best-known, from Schiller's translation of it, is *Turandot* (Eng trans *Turandot, Princess of China*, 1913). ▣ E Borghesani, *Carlo Gozzi e l'opera sua* (1904)

Gozzoli, Benozzo, *properly* Benozzo di Lese
c.1420–97
Italian painter

Born in Florence, he was a pupil of Fra Angelico. In Florence (1456–64) he adorned the Palazzo Medici-Riccardi with scriptural subjects, including his famous *Journey of the Magi* in which Florentine councillors appear accompanied by members of the Medici family. He painted similar frescoes at San Gimignano (1464–67) and in the Campo Santo at Pisa (1468–84).

Graaf, Regnier de 1641–73
Dutch physician and anatomist

Born in Schoonhoven, he studied medicine at Utrecht and Leyden, where he was a student of Franciscus Sylvius and a contemporary of Jan Swammerdam (with whom he was later involved in violent priority disputes), and then practised at Delft. In 1672, on the basis of human and animal dissection, he discovered the 'Graafian vesicles' of the female gonad, coining the term 'ovary' for the organ. Not noticing the rupture of the ovarian follicles, Graaf was not able to develop a satisfactory theory for explaining the role of the ovary, and the mammalian egg was not discovered until the work of Karl Ernst von Baer in 1827. Graaf is rightly credited with having been one of the founders of experimental physiology.

Graaff, Robert J (emison) Van de See Van de Graaff, Robert J (emison)

Grabbe, Christian Dietrich 1801–36
German playwright

He was born in Detmold, and died at the age of 35 from tuberculosis and alcoholism. Together with his contemporary, Georg Büchner, he was associated with the 'Young Germany' movement. The first of his plays to be staged was *Don Juan und Faust* (1822), in which he attempted to emulate Goethe. *Kaiser Friedrich Barbarossa* (1829) is a similarly ambitious tragedy. *Napoleon* (1831) is less cohesive, but notable as the first German play in which the crowd is the main character. His recklessly satirical *Scherz, Satire, Ironie und tiefere Bedeutung* ('Joke, Satire, Irony and Deeper Significance'), written in 1822, but not performed for 70 years, is now considered to anticipate the Theatre of the Absurd. ▣ A Bergmann, *Christian Dietrich Grabbe* (1954, in German)

Grable, Betty (Elizabeth Ruth) 1916–73
US actress

Born in St Louis, Missouri, she lived in Los Angeles from 1928 and studied dancing, subsequently making her film debut as a chorus girl in *Let's Go Places* (1930). She appeared in numerous small roles throughout the next decade but began to build a following after Twentieth Century-Fox appearing in such popular films as *Down Argentine Way* (1940) and *Moon Over Miami* (1941). Her girl-next-door good looks and shapely legs made her a favourite pin-up girl of wartime troops. Her most successful films, usually musicals, include *The Dolly Sisters* (1945), *Mother More Tights* (1947) and *How To Marry A Millionaire* (1953). Her last film appearance was in *How To Be Very Very Popular* (1955) but she continued to work in cabaret and on stage in such productions as *Hello, Dolly!* (1965–67) and *Belle Starr* (1969).

Gracchus, Gaius Sempronius c.159–121BC
Roman politician

After the murder of his brother Tiberius Sempronius Gracchus he continued trying to solve major social and economic problems—the growing landlessness of the Roman peasantry and the consequent decline in army recruitment—by enacting reforms. He was Tribune of the Plebs in 123 and 122BC, and when he failed to achieve a third term he led a demonstration that turned into a riot. Many of his followers were killed and he committed suicide. The legislation and reforms enacted by Gauis and his brother were influential in the last century of the Republic.

Gracchus, Tiberius Sempronius 168–133BC
Roman statesman
In 137BC he was quaestor in Spain, where his family's popularity enabled him to gain better terms from the Numantines for 20,000 conquered Roman soldiers. He was concerned by the poverty of thousands of the Roman citizens, and agitated for reform. Elected Tribune in 133, he reimposed the agrarian law of Licinius Stolo, requisitioned all land held in excess and distributed it in allotments to the poor. The authority of the Senate was threatened when he deposed Tribune Marcus Octavius, who had vetoed his proposal. When Attalus, King of Pergamus, bequeathed his wealth to the Roman people, Gracchus proposed that it should be divided among the poor. But he was accused of having violated the character of the tribuneship by the deposition of his colleague Caecina. The common people deserted him, and during the next election for the tribuneship he was murdered, along with 300 of his friends. He was the brother of **Gaius Sempronius Gracchus**. ☐ A H Bernstein, *Tiberius Sempronius Gracchus: A Tradition and Apostasy* (1978)

Grace, W(illiam) G(ilbert) 1848–1915
English cricketer and doctor
Born in Downend, near Bristol, he is considered the first genuinely great cricketer of modern times. He started playing first-class cricket for Gloucestershire in 1864, and was immediately picked for the Gentlemen Players match. He scored 2,739 runs in a season in 1871, and in 1876 he scored 344 runs in an innings for MCC. He took his medical degree in 1879 and had a practice in Bristol, but devoted most of his time to cricket. He toured Canada and the USA, and twice captained the Test team against Australia, in 1880 and 1882. By 1895 he had scored 100 first-class centuries. In his long career in first-class cricket, from 1864 to 1908, he made 126 centuries, scored 54,896 runs and took 2,864 wickets, becoming a national hero. ☐ Eric Midwinter, *W G Grace: His Life and Times* (1981)

Gracian, (y Morales) Baltasar 1601–58
Spanish philosopher and writer
Born in Belmonte, Aragon, he entered the Jesuit order in 1619 and later became head of the college at Tarragona. His early works such as *El Héroe* (1637, Eng trans *The Hero*, 1652), *El Político* (1640, 'The Politician'), *El Discreto* (1646, Eng trans *The Compleat Gentleman*, 1729) and *Oráculo manual y arte de prudencia* (1647, Eng trans *The Courtier's Manual Oracle and the Art of Prudence*, 1685) are all heavily didactic guides to life. He set out his literary ideas on *conceptismo*, the art of conceited writing, in *Agudeza y arte de ingenio* (1642, 'Subtlety and the Art of Genius'). He is best known, however, for his three-part allegorical novel, *El Criticón* (1651, 1653, 1657, 'The Critic'), in which civilization and society are portrayed through the eyes of a savage. ☐ A Coster, *Baltasar Gracian* (1958)

Grade (of Elstree), Lew Grade, Baron, *originally* Louis Winogradsky 1906–98
British theatrical impresario
Born near Odessa, Russia, he was the eldest of three brothers who were to dominate British showbusiness for over 40 years. He moved to Great Britain in 1912, with his parents and brothers Boris (later Bernard, Baron **Delfont** of Stepney) and Leslie. Lew and Boris became dancers (semi-professional at first), winning competitions during the 'Charleston' craze of the 1920s but gave up dancing to become theatrical agents, booking variety acts into theatres. Lew joined forces with his youngest brother Leslie and was joint managing director of their theatrical agency until 1955. He also became an impresario, helping to establish such stars as **Norman Wisdom** and **Morecambe and Wise**. He launched the ITV company ATV in 1956, and headed several large film entertainment and communications companies, producing films such as *The Cassandra Crossing* (1976) and the television film *The Lady and the Highwayman* (1989). He was made a life peer in 1976.

Grade, Michael Ian 1943–
English television administrator
Born in London, he began in print journalism as a *Daily Mirror* trainee in 1960, and was a sports columnist (1964–66) on the same paper. He then became a theatrical agent for his family's Grade Organization. In 1973 he was appointed deputy controller of London Weekend Television, where he remained until 1977. He was the controller of BBC1 (1984–86), then became the BBC's director of programmes (1986–88). In 1988 he sought a new challenge by becoming chief executive officer of Channel 4, but unexpectedly resigned in 1997. He was made a Fellow of BAFTA in 1994, and CBE in 1998.

Graebe, Karl 1841–1927
German organic chemist
Born in Frankfurt-am-Main, he was professor at Königsberg (1870) and Geneva (1878–1906). With Carl Theodore Liebermann (1842–1914), he first synthesized alizarin from anthraquinone (1869), a process of great importance to the German dyestuffs industry.

Graebner, (Robert) Fritz 1877–1934
German ethnologist
Born in Berlin, he studied history there, and joined the staff of the Royal Museum of Ethnology in 1899, but moved to the Rautenstrauch-Joest Museum in Cologne in 1906 (director in 1925), and became honorary professor at Cologne University (1926). He is best known for developing the theory of *Kulturkreise*, clusters of diffusing cultural traits, which he used to explain cultural similarities and differences. His main work, *Methode der Ethnologie* (1911, 'Method of Ethnology'), became the cornerstone for the German culture-history school of ethnology.

Graells, Mariano de la Paz 1809–98
Spanish naturalist
Born in Tricio, Lograno, he studied at Barcelona University and became curator of the Natural History Museum at the Academy of Science and Arts there. He was Professor of Zoology at Madrid University (from 1837) and later Professor of Comparative Anatomy, and director of the National Museum of Natural Sciences and of the botanical gardens there. An outstanding entomologist, he discovered the Spanish Moon Moth. He also published a *Flora of Catalonia* (1831). He is known as the 'father of Spanish natural history'.

Graf, Steffi 1969–
German tennis player
Born in Bruehl, she first came to prominence in 1984 when she won the Olympic demonstration event and reached the last 16 at Wimbledon. In 1988 she won the Grand Slam of singles titles—the US, French, Australian and Wimbledon—as well as the gold medal at the Seoul Olympics. She was surprisingly defeated by Arantxa Sanchez in the 1989 French final, but the retention the same year of her Wimbledon title confirmed her position as world number one. Other singles wins include the French Open (1987, 1993), the Australian Open (1989–90), the US Open (1989, 1993, 1996), and the Wimbledon championship (1991–93). She has also won various doubles titles. She is only the third woman to win all four major titles in the same year, but her 1988 Grand Slam was unique—she won an Olympic gold at Seoul, making hers a Golden Grand Slam.

Grafton, Richard c.1513–c.1572
English printer and historian

A grocer by trade, he went to Antwerp in 1537 and there printed the Matthews Bible, the revised Coverdale New Testament and the 'Great' (folio) Bible. He became printer to Edward VI and produced the Book of Common Prayer (1549), but fell into disfavour for printing Lady Jane Grey's proclamation. He also wrote three histories of England, and sat in parliament.

Graham, Billy (William Franklin) 1918–
US evangelist

He was born in Charlotte, North Carolina. After studying at Florida Bible Institute (now Trinity College) from 1938 to 1940, he was ordained a minister of the Southern Baptist Church (1940). In 1943 he graduated in anthropology from Wheaton College, Illinois, and in the same year married Ruth Bell. He made his first high-profile preaching crusade in Los Angeles in 1949 and has since conducted his crusades on all continents, preaching in the former USSR during the Cold War and in other East European countries. Through his crusades and the subsidiary ministries of broadcasting, films and the printed word it is claimed that millions have been won to Christianity. A charismatic figure who has been the friend and counsellor of many in high office, including Richard Nixon, Graham has consistently emerged from investigative reporting as a person of high integrity, and his Billy Graham Evangelistic Association as a model of financial accountability. His books include *Peace with God* (1952), *World Aflame* (1965), *Angels* (1975), *Storm Warning* (1992) and his autobiography, *Just as I Am* (1997). 📖 Marshall Frady, *Billy Graham: A Parable of American Righteousness* (1979)

Graham, George 1944–
Scottish football player and manager

He was born in Bargeddie, North Lanarkshire. His career as a player started at Aston Villa in 1961, and he played for Chelsea, Arsenal, Manchester United, Portsmouth and Crystal Palace, as well as for California (1978). He gained winner's medals in the FA Cup and League in 1971, and was capped 12 times for Scotland. He was manager of Millwall from 1982 to 1986, when he became manager of Arsenal for nine years (1986–95). In that time the team won the League title in 1988–89 and 1990–91, the Football League Cup and FA Cup in 1993, and the European Cup Winner's Cup in 1994. Dismissed in February 1995 following proceedings relating to the receipt of a 'bung', or cash gift, from a players' agent, he nevertheless returned to football as manager of Leeds in September 1996.

Graham, Sir James Robert George, 2nd Baronet 1792–1861
British politician

He was born in Netherby, Cumberland (now Cumbria), and educated at Westminster and Christ Church, Oxford. In 1813 he became private secretary to the British minister in Sicily. He entered parliament as a Whig in 1826, and supported Catholic emancipation and the Reform Bill. Earl Grey made him (1830) First Lord of the Admiralty, but in 1834 he resigned over the Irish church question and in 1841 became Home Secretary under Robert Peel. In 1844 he issued a warrant for opening the letters of Giuseppe Mazzini, and the information thus obtained was communicated to the Austrian minister. His dealing with the Scottish Church increased the troubles which ended in the Disruption of 1843. He supported Peel over the Corn-Law Repeal Bill, and resigned (1846) as soon as it was carried. On Peel's death in 1850 he became leader of the Peelites, and from 1852 to 1855 was First Lord of the Admiralty in the Coalition ministry.

Graham, Katherine Meyer, *née* Meyer 1917–
US newspaper proprieter

Born in New York City, the daughter of the publisher Eugene Meyer (1875–1959), she was educated at Vassar College and the University of Chicago. In 1939 she joined her father's newspaper, the *Washington Post*, as an editor. In 1940 she married Philip Graham, who also joined the *Post* as associate publisher in 1946. When Meyer sold the paper to his daughter and her husband in 1948, they formed the Washington Post Company, bought *Newsweek* magazine (1961), and began to enlarge their circulation. When Philip committed suicide in 1963 after suffering from a mental illness, Katherine Graham took over the presidency (1963–73) and emerged as a tough media tycoon, also taking charge of several television and radio stations. In 1972 the *Post* editors investigated the Watergate scandal, which led to the resignation of President Richard Nixon in 1974. She was succeeded by her son Donald Graham in 1979, who became the company's president and chief executive in 1991.

Graham, Martha See panel p773

Graham, Otto Everett, Jnr 1921–
US football player

Born in Waukegan, Illinois, he was a quarter-back with the Cleveland Browns, the most successful team in the American Football Conference (formed in 1946 in opposition to the already established National Football League). In 1950, the Browns went into the NFL and he led them to championship victories in 1950, 1954 and 1955. He was head coach of the Washington Redskins from 1966 to 1968.

Graham, Robert Bontine Cunninghame See Cunninghame Graham, Robert

Graham, Thomas 1805–69
Scottish chemist

Born in Glasgow, he was educated at Glasgow and Edinburgh universities. He began to teach chemistry in Glasgow, at first privately and then at the Mechanics Institute. In 1830 he became Professor of Chemistry at Anderson's College and in 1837 moved to London as Professor of Chemistry at University College. He held this chair until 1854, when he was appointed Master of the Mint, a post he held until his death. His earliest work (1825) was on the solubility of gases in liquids, but his most famous research was on the diffusion of gases and related phenomena; Graham's law states that the velocity of effusion of a gas is inversely proportional to the square root of its density. He discovered the properties of colloids and their separation by dialysis. He was elected Fellow of the Royal Society in 1836 and received its Copley Medal in 1862. He was a founder-member and first president of the Chemical Society (1841). 📖 Robert Angus Smith, *The Life and Works of Thomas Graham, DCL, FRS* (1884)

Graham-Smith, Sir Francis 1923–
English radio astronomer

He spent most of his early research life at Cambridge, moved to Jodrell Bank in 1964, and in 1976 became director of the Royal Greenwich Observatory, where he supervised the establishment of the Northern Hemisphere Observatory at Las Palmas on the Canary Islands. He moved back to Jodrell Bank in 1981 as director, and was the Astronomer Royal of England between 1982 and 1990. In 1950 he showed that fluctuations in radio source signals were caused by diffraction in the ionosphere, in 1951 he proposed a method of measuring electron densities in a star's outer layer by astronomical observations, and during the 1950s participated in a systematic survey of radio sources. He also made the first investigation of radio noise from above the atmosphere.

Graham, Martha 1894–1991
US dancer, teacher, choreographer and pioneer of modern dance

Martha Graham was born in Pittsburgh. She trained in Los Angeles with the Denishawn School and appeared on stage first in vaudeville and revue. In 1926 she made her independent debut in New York, and set up her School of Contemporary Dance the following year. She was much influenced by the composer Louis Horst, and her early work constitutes a major contribution to the American Expressionist movement and to the development of modern dance. *Lamentation* (1930) and *Frontier* (1935) are among her better-known early works.

In 1930 she founded the Dance Repertory Theatre, and trained the company in her own method, which was to use every aspect of the body and mind to dramatic purpose, including movement, breathing and muscular control. Her ballets are based on the same idea of unity, in décor, choreography and music and, frequently, spoken dialogue. One of her best-known ballets, *Appalachian Spring* (1958, music by **Aaron Copland**), was a product of her great interest in Native American life and mythology and the early American pioneer spirit, and much of her work was based on the reinterpretation of ancient myths and historical characters. Her method of dance training has been widely adopted in schools and colleges around the world.

📖 Martha Graham published *The Notebooks of Martha Graham* in 1973. See also Agnes de Mille, *Martha: The Life and the Works of Martha Graham* (1991); Don McDonach, *Martha Graham* (1973); LeRoy Leatherman, *Martha Graham* (1966).

> 'We look at the dance to impart the sensation of living in an affirmation of life, to energize the spectator into keener awareness of the vigor, the mystery, the humor, the variety, and the wonder of life. This is the function of the American dance.' From 'The American Dance' in Virginia Stewart (ed), *Modern Dance* (1935).

From 1964 to 1974 he concentrated on pulsars, in 1968 discovering that they emitted polarized radiation. He was Langworthy Professor of Physics at Manchester University (1987–90), then emeritus. He was elected FRS in 1970, and knighted in 1986.

Grahame, James 1765–1811
Scottish poet

Born in Glasgow, he studied law at Glasgow University and was called to the Bar, but was forced to give up his career because of ill health. He took Anglican orders in 1809 and became a curate in Shipton, Gloucestershire, and later in Sedgefield, Durham. He wrote a dramatic poem, *Mary, Queen of Scots* (1801), but most of his poetry was evocative of the quiet Scottish countryside, in particular *The Sabbath* (1804) and *The Birds of Scotland* (1806), with an introduction that popularised ornithology. 📖 Memoir in *The Sabbath* (1839, 9th edition)

Grahame, Kenneth 1859–1932
Scottish children's writer

Born in Edinburgh, the son of an advocate, he was educated at St Edward's School, Oxford, and in 1876 entered the Bank of England as a clerk. He became its secretary in 1898 and retired for health reasons in 1908. His early work consisted of collected essays and country tales, such as *Pagan Papers* (1893), *The Golden Age* (1895) and *Dream Days* (1898), which revealed a remarkably subtle, delicate and humorous sympathy with the child mind. In 1908 he published his best-known work, *The Wind in the Willows*, originally written in the form of letters to his son Alastair, and featuring the quaint and unforgettable riverside characters, Rat, Mole, Badger and Toad. It did not at first win acclaim, but within a few years of Grahame's death had become a children's classic. 📖 P Green, *Kenneth Grahame* (1959)

Grahame-White, Claude 1879–1959
English aviator and engineer

He was born in Burseldon, Hampshire, and was the first Englishman to be granted a British certificate of proficiency in aviation (1910). In 1909 he founded the first British flying school at Paris, and in 1910 founded his own company to build aircraft. He helped to establish London Aerodrome at Hendon (1911) and published books on the aeroplane and flying.

Grahn, Lucile 1819–1907
Danish ballerina

Born in Copenhagen, she made her official debut at the age of only seven. She subsequently studied and worked in the Royal Danish Ballet with **Auguste Bournonville**, creating Astrid in his *Valdemar* (1835) and then becoming his first *La Sylphide* in 1836. In 1838 she moved from Copenhagen to base herself in Paris, also dancing in Hamburg, St Petersburg and London. Retiring from dancing in 1856, she was ballet mistress at the Leipzig State Theatre (1858–61) and then with the Munich Court Opera (1869–75), where she assisted **Richard Wagner** in the production of *Die Meistersinger von Nürnberg* (1868, 'The Mastersingers of Nuremberg') and *Das Rheingold* (1869, 'The Rhine Gold'). A street in Munich is named after her.

Grainger, (George) Percy Aldridge
1882–1961
Australian–US composer and pianist

Born in Brighton, Victoria, as a child he toured as a concert pianist under the management of his mother, whose maiden name Aldridge he adopted. He studied under Pabst and **Ferruccio Busoni**, then in 1914 settled in the USA, after collecting folk tunes in the UK and Europe. He took US nationality and served in the US army as a bandsman. A friend and admirer of **Edvard Grieg**, he followed his example in championing the revival of English and Scandinavian folk music in such works as *Molly on the Shore* (1914) and *Shepherd's Hey* (1911), which make skilful use of traditional dance themes. He also experimented with 'free form' music and mechanical music machines, and wrote *The Warriors: Music to an Imaginary Ballet*. He often returned to Australia, and in 1935 founded the Grainger Museum in Melbourne.

Gram, Hans Christian Joachim 1853–1938
Danish bacteriologist

Born in Copenhagen, he developed in 1884 the most important staining technique in microbiology, which is still in use today. The stain divides bacteria into two groups, *Gram-positive* or *Gram-negative*, depending on the structure of their cell walls. Gram took up a clinical career, and was appointed Professor of Medicine at Copenhagen University in 1900.

Grammaticus ('the Grammarian') See Ælfric

Gramme, Zénobe Théophile 1826–1901
Belgian electrical engineer

He was born in Jehay-Bodegnée. In 1869 he built the first successful direct-current dynamo, incorporating a ring-wound armature (the 'Gramme ring'), which after various improvements he manufactured from 1871. It was the first electric generator to be used commercially, for electroplating as well as electric lighting. In 1873 he showed that a dynamo could function in reverse as an electric motor.

Gramont or Grammont, Philibert, Comte de
1621–1707
French courtier
He served under Louis, 4th Prince de Condé and Henri, Vicomte de Turenne, and became a favourite at the court of Louis XIV, but was exiled from France in 1662. He found congenial society at the court of Charles II of Great Britain, and married Elizabeth Hamilton, with whom he afterwards returned to France. At the age of 80 he inspired his *Mémoires* of the amorous intrigues at Charles's court, or revised them when written by his brother-in-law, Count Anthony Hamilton. It was first printed anonymously in 1713.

Gramsci, Antonio 1891–1937
Italian journalist, politician and political thinker
Born in Ales, Sardinia, into a poor family, he was educated at Turin University, where he was drawn into political activity in the Socialist Party. A founder member of the PCI (Italian Communist Party) in 1921, he was Italian delegate at the Third International in Moscow (1922). In 1924 he became leader of the Communists in parliament. He was one of a number of outspoken Communist critics of the Fascist regime to be arrested in 1928 and was sentenced to 20 years' imprisonment; he spent the rest of his life in prison. His reputation rests primarily on his *Lettere del carcere* (1947, *Prison Notebooks*), which were a collection of thoughts and reflections written while in confinement and published posthumously. They are regarded as one of the most important political texts of the 20th century.

Gran, Ahmad See Ahmad ibn Ibrahim al-Ghazi

Granados y Campiña, Enrique 1868–1916
Spanish composer and pianist
Born in Lerida, he studied in Barcelona and Paris, and made his concert debut at the age of 16. He was a composer of Spanish dances, and his *Goyescas* (1911, 'Goya-like works') for piano are his most accomplished works. He was drowned when the *Sussex* was torpedoed by the Germans in the English Channel.

Granby, John Manners, Marquis of 1721–70
English soldier
He was born in Scarborough, Yorkshire. MP for Grantham in 1742, he served on the Duke of Cumberland's staff. As colonel of 'The Blues' and second-in-command of the British horse at Minden (1759), he witnessed the failure of Lord George Sackville (1716–85) to lead the cavalry into action, which earned his commander the contemptuous title of 'The Great Incompetent'. In 1760 Granby redeemed the cavalry's reputation with the spectacular victory of Warburg. He became 'the mob's hero', in Horace Walpole's sneering phrase, and in 1763 was appointed Master-General of the Ordnance, succeeding the aged John, 1st Earl of Ligonier (1680–1770) as Commander-in-Chief in 1766.

Grand, Sarah, *pseudonym of* Frances Elizabeth Bellenden McFall, *née* Clarke 1854–1943
British novelist
She was born in Donaghadee, Ireland, of English parentage, and at the age of 16 married an army doctor, D C McFall (d.1898). In 1923 and from 1925 to 1929 she was Mayoress of Bath. Her reputation rests on *The Heavenly Twins* (1893) and *The Beth Book* (1898), in which she skilfully attacks immorality and marital hypocrisy. Her later works, including *The Winged Victory* (1916), are advocacies of feminine emancipation.

Grandi, Dino, Count of Mordano 1895–1988
Italian politician and diplomat
Born in Mordano, near Bologna, he studied law and joined the Fascist quadrumvirate during the 1922 March on Rome. He became Mussolini's Foreign Minister (1929–32), then Italian ambassador in London (1932–39), during which time he unsuccessfully warned Mussolini of British opposition to the Abyssinian invasion (1935). He was created count in 1937. He was recalled in 1939 after the formation of the Berlin-Rome Axis, and appointed Minister of Justice. He became extremely concerned about Mussolini's regard for Hitler's policies and in 1943 he moved the motion in the Fascist grand council that full constitutional powers be restored to Victor Emmanuel III. This brought about Mussolini's resignation. Grandi then fled to Portugal before being sentenced to death in absentia by a Fascist Republican court at Verona. For many years he lived in exile in Brazil, then returned to Italy in 1973 and wrote two acclaimed books, *The Foreign Policy of Italy, 1929–32* and *My Country.*

Grange, Kenneth Henry 1929–
English industrial designer
Born in London, he studied at Willesden School of Arts and Crafts before working as a technical illustrator. After some years in architectural and design practices, he ran his own design consultancy from 1958 to 1971. In 1971 he co-founded the multidisciplinary practice Pentagram. His product designs include food mixers for Kenwood, cameras for Kodak, a sewing machine for Frister-Rossmann, pens for Parker, locomotives for British Rail and parking meters for Venner. He became a Royal Designer for Industry in 1969 and was made an honorary professor at Heriot-Watt University, Edinburgh, in 1987.

Grange, Red (Howard Edward) 1903–91
US football player and coach
He was born in Forksville, Pennsylvania. He played from 1923 to 1925 for Illinois University, where he gained 4,280 yards and was described as the 'greatest broken-field runner in the history of the game'. When he signed for the Chicago Bears in 1925 it caused a great controversy over the registration of student players. He was the first man to earn $100,000 in a season. He went on to play in New York before returning to the Bears (1929–34), retiring in 1935.

Granger, James 1723–76
English biographer
Born in Shaftesbury, he published a *Biographical History of England…adapted to a Methodical Catalogue of Engraved British Heads* (1769) and insisted 'on the utility of a collection of engraved portraits', by publishing later editions with blank interleaved paper for inserting extra illustrations. This led to extraordinary zeal in the collection of portraits, and 'grangerized copies' were embellished with engravings clipped from every conceivable source, even the most valuable early books. He himself is said to have cut some 14,000 engraved portraits from other books. At his death he was vicar of Shiplake, Oxfordshire.

Granger, Stewart, *originally* James Stewart 1913–93
English actor
Born in London, he trained at the Webber–Douglas School of Dramatic Art, then entered the acting profession as a film extra and lowly supporting figure at the Old Vic. He then progressed via repertory companies in Hull and Birmingham to the West End and a leading role in the film *So This is London* (1939). After wartime service in the Black Watch, his handsome looks and virile manner made him a popular leading man in costume melodramas like *The Man in Grey* (1943), *Caravan* (1946) and *Blanche Fury* (1948). He made a successful Hollywood debut in *King*

Solomon's Mines (1950) and proved an adept swashbuckler and man of adventure in the likes of *Scaramouche* (1952) and *Moonfleet* (1955). He later starred in a succession of 'continental westerns' and the television series *The Men from Shiloh* (1970) before curtailing his acting career to concentrate on business interests. An abrasive figure, he has published an autobiography, *Sparks Fly Upward* (1981), and made his Broadway debut in *The Circle* (1989–90).

Granit, Ragnar Arthur 1900–
Swedish physiologist and Nobel Prize winner

Born in Helsinki, Finland, he studied psychology and medicine at Helsinki University, specializing in neurophysiology. After graduating he was appointed instructor in physiology in 1927, and the following year visited England to work for a short period in Sir **Charles Sherrington**'s laboratory at Oxford. He won a fellowship in 1929 in medical physics to work at the Johnson Foundation at the University of Pennsylvania, where he met both **George Wald** and **Haldan Hartline**, with whom he was to share the 1967 Nobel Prize for physiology or medicine. After two years he returned to Helsinki and became Professor of Physiology in 1937. After the Soviet invasion of Finland he escaped to Sweden, where he became Professor of Neurophysiology at the Karolinska Institute in Stockholm (1940–67). His analyses of retinal processing revealed that visual mechanisms were complex responses to light and dark, and he pioneered the recording of the mass response of the retina, the electroretinogram (ERG). From these studies he was able to explain the mechanisms of colour discrimination. He has also contributed to research on the spinal cord, on pain mechanisms and on the philosophy of science.

Grant, Alexander Marshall 1925–
New Zealand dancer and director

Born in Wellington, he won a scholarship to London and the Royal Ballet, Covent Garden, where he was to spend his entire dancing career. A soloist by 1949, he became best known for character roles like Bottom in **Frederick Ashton**'s *The Dream* (1964). He was director of the Royal Ballet's off-shoot, Ballet For All (1971–75), and from 1976 to 1983 he was director of the National Ballet of Canada. Guest artist at the Royal Ballet (1985–89) and Joffrey Ballet (1987–89), he was also senior principal at the London Festival Ballet (now English National Ballet) from 1989 to 1991.

Grant, Anne, *née* MacVicar 1755–1838
Scottish poet and essayist

Born in Glasgow, she lived in North America as a child (1758–68). In 1779 she married the Rev James Grant, minister of Laggan. Left a widow in 1801, she turned to writing and published *Poems* (1803), *Letters from the Mountains* (1806), *Memoirs of an American Lady* (1808) and *Superstitions of the Highlanders* (1811). In 1810 she moved to Edinburgh, where she mixed in literary circles, and in 1825 she received a pension of £50 through the influence of Sir **Walter Scott**.

Grant, Bernie (Bernard Alexander Montgomery) 1944–
British Labour politician

Born in Georgetown, Guyana, he was educated at St Stanislaus College, Georgetown, Tottenham Technical College, London, and at Heriot-Watt University in Edinburgh. He worked as an analyst in Guyana before moving to Great Britain in the early 1960s, where he found employment as a railway clerk and, from 1969 to 1978, as a telephonist. An area officer with the National Union of Public Employees (1978–83), he worked as a development officer for the Black Trade Unionists Solidarity Movement (1983–84), before entering local government service in London (1985–87). He was elected

MP for Tottenham in 1987. He is founder and chairman of the Parliamentary Black Caucus, which promotes greater parliamentary representation of ethnic minorities in Britain.

Grant, Cary, *originally* Archibald Leach 1904–86
US film actor

Born in Bristol, England, he worked as an acrobat and juggler, before moving (1920) to the USA, where he stayed to pursue a stage career. He went to Hollywood in 1928 and made his film debut in *This is the Night* (1932). A suave, debonair performer opposite **Marlene Dietrich** and **Mae West**, he played leads in sophisticated light comedy, displaying metronomic timing and a sense of the ridiculous in films like *Bringing Up Baby* (1938), *His Girl Friday* (1940) and *Arsenic and Old Lace* (1944). He was also notable in **Alfred Hitchcock**'s thrillers, including *Suspicion* (1941), *Notorious* (1946), *To Catch a Thief* (1955) and *North By Northwest* (1959). Married five times, he retired from the screen in 1966 and received a special Academy Award (1970) for his 'unique mastery of the art of screen acting'. 📖 Albert Govoni, *Cary Grant* (1971)

Grant, Duncan James Corrowr 1885–1978
Scottish painter

Born in Rothiemurchus, Inverness, he studied at the Westminster and Slade School of Art, London, and in Italy and Paris. He was associated with **Roger Fry**'s Omega Workshops, and later with the London Group. His works were mainly landscapes, portraits and still-life, but he also designed textiles and pottery. His *Girl at the Piano* is in the Tate Gallery, London. Through his cousin, **Lytton Strachey**, he became friends with many of the Bloomsbury Group. He collaborated on many projects with **Vanessa Bell**, with whom he lived for many years.

Grant, Sir Francis 1803–78
Scottish painter

Born in Edinburgh, he painted sporting scenes, and his portrait groups were in great demand, such as the *Meet of HM Staghounds* and the *Melton Hunt* executed for the Duke of **Wellington**. He was president of the Royal Academy in 1866.

Grant, Hugh 1960–
English actor

Born in London, he studied English literature at Oxford where he appeared on stage as part of the Dramatic Society and made his film debut in *Privileged* (1982). He worked at the Nottingham Playhouse and performed comedy revues with the Jockeys of Norfolk. A prolific actor in often forgettable films and television mini-series, his screen appearances include *Maurice* (1987), *The Lair of the White Worm* (1988), *Impromptu* (1991) and *Bitter Moon* (1992). The phenomenally popular *Four Weddings and a Funeral* (1994) revealed him as a polished light comedian with charm and wit, whilst the character of a bumbling, emotionally repressed Englishman endeared him to audiences worldwide. Subsequent films include *Nine Months* (1995), *Sense and Sensibility* (1995) and *Extreme Measures* (1996).

Grant, James Augustus 1827–92
Scottish soldier and explorer

Born in Nairn, in the Scottish Highlands, he was educated at Marischal College, Aberdeen. He joined the Indian army, eventually reaching the rank of colonel, and fought in the Battle of Gujerat, the Indian Mutiny, and in the Abyssinian campaign of 1868. With **John Hanning Speke** he explored the sources of the Nile (1860–63) and made important botanical collections. On Speke's death he took over as the main spokesman for the expedition, becoming a leading African specialist. He wrote *A Walk Across Africa* (1864).

Grant, Ulysses S (impson), *originally* Hiram Ulysses Grant 1822–85
18th President of the USA

Born in Point Pleasant, Ohio, he graduated from West Point in 1843 and fought in the Mexican War (1846–48), gaining promotion to the rank of captain in 1853. He resigned from the army (1854) and settled on a farm near St Louis, Missouri. However, on the outbreak of the Civil War in 1861 he returned to the army, swiftly becoming a brigadier-general, and in 1862 he captured Fort Henry and Fort Donelson in Tennessee, securing for the Union its first major victory. He was criticized for high Union casualties at Shiloh, but in 1863 he besieged Vicksburg, Mississippi, and forced its surrender, thus capturing the last major Confederate stronghold on the Mississippi River and cutting the Confederacy in half. Having driven the enemy out of Tennessee, he was made a lieutenant-general and given command of the Union forces in 1864. His strategy was to concentrate all the national forces into several distinct armies, which should operate simultaneously against the enemy, with General **Sherman** moving toward Atlanta, while Grant accompanied the army of the Potomac against Richmond. He encountered General **Robert E Lee** in the wilderness, and fought a desperate battle, driving the enemy within the lines of Richmond and culminating in Lee surrendering his entire army in April 1865. The fall of Richmond substantially ended the war. In July 1866 Grant was appointed a full general but relinquished the rank when in 1868 and 1872 he was elected President as the candidate of the Republicans. Despite his military skill, he was politically naïve, and his administration (1869–77) was marked by corruption and incompetence. Most of the achievements of his presidency were traceable to his brilliant Secretary of State, **Hamilton Fish**, who negotiated the Treaty of Washington (1871) with Great Britain and resolved the *Alabama* claims. The proposal of a third term of presidency not having been approved, Grant returned to private life and became a sleeping partner in a banking-house but was robbed of all he possessed by two of the partners. In the hope of providing for his family, he had begun his autobiography, when in 1884 a sore throat proved to be cancer at the root of the tongue. The sympathies of the nation were aroused, and in March 1885 Congress restored him to his rank of general which he had lost on accepting the presidency, thus qualifying his dependants for an army pension. His *Personal Memoirs* (2 vols, 1885–86) are a classic of US military history. 📖 Bruce Catton, *U S Grant and the American Military Tradition* (1954)

Grant, William 1839–1923
Scottish distiller

Born in Dufftown, Banffshire, he began his career in quarrying and lime-burning. He then worked as book-keeper and manager at the Mortlach distillery in Banffshire for almost two decades. Having bought second-hand equipment from a neighbouring distiller he proceeded, with his six sons, to build the Glenfiddich distillery, where most of the whisky would be sold for blending. This accomplished, production began in 1887, and it was so successful that a second distillery was opened at Balvenie in 1893. Grant then sent both his son and his son-in-law to Glasgow to set up the family's own blending business. From this time Glenfiddich became established as a popular five-year old, and William's eldest son, John, took over to run the company.

Grant, William 1863–1946
Scottish lexicographer

Born in Elgin, Grampian, he studied in France, Belgium and Germany, and became a lecturer in English, modern languages and phonetics at Aberdeen University. He was until his death editor of the *Scottish National Dictionary*, and published various works on Scottish dialects.

Granville, 1st Earl See **Carteret, John**

Granville-Barker, Harley 1877–1946
English actor, playwright and producer

He was born in London. His career as an actor was noted for his appearances in plays by **George Bernard Shaw**, who chose him to play Marchbanks in *Candida* (1900). In 1904 he became co-manager of the Court Theatre with John Vedrenne, and there followed a four-year season that was a landmark in the history of the British theatre. First performances in England of plays by Count **Maurice Maeterlinck**, **Arthur Schnitzler**, **Gerhart Hauptmann**, **W B Yeats**, **John Galsworthy**, **John Masefield** and Shaw were performed in circumstances that set new standards of acting and design. He left the Court (1907) and continued his success with a series of **Shakespeare** plays at the Savoy. He retired from the stage in the early 1920s. His plays include *The Marrying of Ann Leete* (1902), *The Voysey Inheritance* (1905), *Waste* (performed privately in 1907, publicly in 1936) and *The Madras House* (1910). With William Archer he devised a scheme for a national theatre. He was married first to Lillah McCarthy and then to Helen Huntington Gates, with whom he made the standard translations of plays by **Gregorio Martínez Sierra** and the **Álvarez Quintero** brothers. His prefaces to Shakespeare's plays (4 vols, 1927–45) are valuable for their original criticism and ideas on production. 📖 Dennis Kennedy, *Granville-Barker and the Dream of Theatre* (1985)

Grapelli, Stephane 1908–97
French jazz violinist

He was born in Paris and had a classical training on violin and other instruments. With the Belgian gipsy guitarist **Django Reinhardt** as co-leader, he was a founder-member of the Quintette du Hot Club de France which brought a European influence into jazz from the mid-1930s. Grapelli worked as a solo artist in London during World War II, returning later to France. He went on to perform prolifically throughout the world, usually leading a quartet and adhering to the bright swing-based style of which he was a recognized master. 📖 Geoffrey Smith, *Stephane Grapelli: A Biography* (1987)

Grass, Günter Wilhelm 1927–
German novelist

Born in Danzig (now Gdansk, Poland), he was educated at Danzig Volksschule and Gymnasium. Having trained as a stonemason and sculptor, he attended the Academy of Art, Düsseldorf, and the State Academy of Fine Arts, Berlin. He served in World War II and was a prisoner-of-war. He worked as a farm labourer, apprentice stone-cutter, miner and jazz musician, and then was a speech-writer for **Willy Brandt** when he was Mayor of West Berlin. *Die Blechtrommel* (1959, Eng trans *The Tin Drum*, 1962) was the first of the novels that have made him Germany's greatest living novelist. Ostensibly the autobiography of Oskar Matzerath, detained in a mental hospital for a murder he did not commit, it caused a furore in Germany because of its depiction of the Nazis. Intellectual and experimental in form, theme and language, his books consistently challenge the status quo and question our reading of the past. A prolific playwright, poet and essayist, he excels in fiction. Important books are *Katz und Maus* (1961, Eng trans *Cat and Mouse*, 1963), *Hundejahre* (1963, Eng trans *Dog Years*, 1965), *Örtlich betäubt* (1969, Eng trans *Local Anaesthetic*, 1970), *Der Butt* (1977, Eng trans *The Flounder*, 1978), *Das Treffen in Telgte* (1979, Eng trans *The Meeting at Telgte*, 1981), *Die Ratten* (1987, Eng trans *The Rats*, 1987) and *Unkenrufe* (1992, Eng trans *The Call of the Toad*,

1992). He has illustrated many of his own book jackets. In 1995 he published *Ein weites Feld* ('A Broad Field'), one of the first major novels to tackle the issue of German re-unification. 📖 K Miles, *Günter Grass* (1975)

Grasse, François Joseph Paul, Comte de
1722–88
French admiral
Born into nobility at Château du Bar, near Grasse, he entered the navy in 1738 and served in the War of the Austrian Succession and the Seven Years War. As commander of the French fleet in Chesapeake Bay during the American Revolution, he blockaded the York and James rivers and trapped **Charles Cornwallis** at Yorktown, which made possible the American victory that ended the war.

Grassic Gibbon, Lewis See **Gibbon, Lewis Grassic**

Grassmann, Hermann Günther 1809–77
German mathematician and philologist
Born in Stettin, he studied theology and classics at Berlin University (1827–30), then became a schoolmaster in Berlin and Stettin. His book *Ausdehnungslehre* (1844) set out a new theory of n-dimensional geometry expressed in a novel language and notation. Despite its almost complete neglect by mathematicians of the time, its importance has gradually been recognized, as it anticipated much later studies in quaternions, vectors, tensors, matrices and differential forms. From 1849 he studied Sanskrit and other ancient Indo-European languages, work which met with immediate acceptance.

Gratian, *properly* Flavius Augustus Gratianus
AD359–83
Roman emperor
The son of the Emperor **Valentinian I**, he was born in Sirinium, Pannonia, and in AD367 his father made him Augustus in Gaul. He and his half-brother **Valentinian II** succeeded their father on his death (375). Gaul, Spain and Britain fell to Gratian's share, but as his brother was only four years old he virtually ruled the whole Western Empire, and in 378, on the death of his uncle Valens, he suddenly became sovereign also of the Eastern Empire. Thereupon he recalled **Theodosius I**, the Great from Spain, and appointed him his colleague (379). He was much influenced by St **Ambrose**, and persecuted pagans and heretics. He was eventually overthrown by the usurper **Magnus Maximus**, and was murdered at Lyons.

Gratian, *Latin* Franciscus Gratianus 12th century
Italian jurist and Carmaldulensian monk of Bologna
Between 1139 and 1150 he compiled the collection of canon law known as the *Decretum Gratiani*, which was to become the basic text for all studies of canon law.

Grattan, Henry 1746–1820
Irish politician
Born in Dublin and educated at Trinity College, Dublin, and at the Middle Temple, he became such a fervent supporter of **Henry Flood** that his father disinherited him. He deserted law for politics in 1775 when he entered the Irish parliament for Charlemont. When Flood, who had been leading the fight for Irish independence, accepted a government post Grattan immediately took his place, attempting to secure the removal of the restrictions imposed on Irish trade. When the concessions he won were revoked in 1779, he began the struggle for legislative independence. He secured the abolition of all claims by the British parliament to legislate for Ireland in 1782, but was unable to prevent the Act of Union and sat in the parliament at Westminster until his death.

Gravelet, Jean François See **Blondin, Charles**

Graves, Alfred Perceval 1846–1931
Irish writer and educationist
He was born in Dublin, and worked as an inspector of schools in England. He wrote much Irish folk-verse and songs, including 'Father O'Flynn', and an autobiography, *To Return to All That* (1930). A leader of the Celtic revival, he helped to found the Irish Literary Society in London.

Graves, Michael 1934–
US architect
Born in Indianapolis, Indiana, he studied architecture in Cincinnati and at Harvard, and after spending two years as a Fellow at the American Academy in Rome, he began to teach at Princeton University in 1962. His designs in the 1960s, influenced by **Le Corbusier**, were in the sleek, functional style of orthodox Modernism, but in the late 1970s he began to incorporate into his work 'quotations' from earlier architectural styles, including pyramids, columns, pilasters, and vaults. His colourful, irreverently ornamented works in the 1980s included the Portland Building (Portland, Oregon), the Walt Disney Co Corporate Headquarters (Burbank, California), and the Humana Building (Louisville, Kentucky). He has also designed furniture and housewares. Denounced by some as a maker of empty and arbitrary historical allusions and praised by others for the energy and inventiveness of his designs, Graves is one of the leading proponents of Postmodernism in architecture.

Graves, Richard 1715–1804
English writer
Born in Mickleton, Gloucestershire, and educated at Pembroke College, Oxford, he became a Fellow of All Souls, Oxford, in 1736, and also rector of Claverton, near Bath. Of his great output, only his novel *The Spiritual Quixote* (1772), a comic tilt at changing Methodist views which satirizes the evangelical preacher **George Whitefield**, is remembered. His other novels, though little read, contain well-observed portraits of the social conditions of his age. 📖 F Kilvert, *Richard Graves of Claverton* (1858)

Graves, Robert James 1796–1853
Irish physician
Born in Dublin, he studied medicine in Edinburgh but qualified in 1818 from Dublin. After three years' travel in Europe (several months of it with the painter **J M W Turner**), he returned to Dublin when he was appointed physician to the Meath Hospital. There he reorganized medical teaching along the lines advocated in France, with emphasis on physical examination and systematic note-taking and autopsies. He was an excellent diagnostician, best remembered today for his description of a form of hyperthyroidism ('Graves' disease'), and his *Clinical Lectures on the Practice of Medicine* (1843) won an international reputation.

Graves, Robert Ranke 1895–1985
English poet, novelist, essayist and critic
Born in London and educated at Charterhouse, he was Professor of English at Cairo and Professor of Poetry at Oxford (1961–66). His first poetry, such as *Over the Brazier* (1916) and *Fairies and Fusiliers* (1917) was published during World War I, and his poems also appeared in the popular anthology *Georgian Poetry*. In 1925 he met **Laura Riding** with whom he went into exile to Majorca on the proceeds of his autobiography, *Goodbye to All That* (1929). He returned to England in 1939 for World War II, but settled permanently in Majorca in 1946. His best known novels are *I, Claudius* (1934) and *Claudius the God* (1934), which were adapted for television in 1976. *The White Goddess* (1948) is his most significant non-fiction title, and his interest in myth prompted *Greek Myths* (1955) and *Hebrew*

Myths (1963). He is generally regarded as the best love poet of his generation. ☐ M Seymour-Smith, *Robert Graves' Life and Work* (1983)

Gray, Alasdair James 1934–
Scottish novelist, painter and playwright

Born in Glasgow, he was educated at Whitehill Secondary School and Glasgow School of Art. Painting was his first vocation and he came late to novel writing; *Lanark*, his first novel, was published in 1981. His novel *1982, Janine* (1984), is typically erotically charged and very funny. His other novels include *The Fall of Kelvin Walker* (1985), *Something Leather* (1990), *McGrotty and Ludmilla* (1990), 'the Aladdin story set in modern Whitehall', and *A History Maker* (1994). He has also published volumes of short stories, including *Unlikely Stories, Mostly* (1983) and *Mavis Belfrage* (1996), a volume of poetry, *Old Negatives* (1989) and the autobiographical *Saltire Self-Portrait no 4* (1989).

Gray, Asa 1810–88
US botanist

Born in Sauquoit, New York, he was educated there and in Clinton, Iowa, before going to Fairfield Academy, to whose medical school he transferred after a year. He practised medicine briefly at Bridgewater, New York (1831–32), and began collecting plants. In 1836 he became Professor of Natural History at the University of Michigan, Ann Arbor (1838–42). Following a tour of European botanical institutes, he became Professor of Natural History at Harvard (1842–73) on the understanding that he specialised in botany. He eventually became the USA's leading 19th-century plant taxonomist, was also a strong Darwinian, and using Charles Darwin's theory to explain the distribution of plants occurring in both eastern Asia and eastern North America. His works include *Manual of Botany of the Northern United States* (1848, known as 'Gray's Manual'), *Genera Florae Americae Boreali-Orientalis Illustrata* (1845–50) and *A Free Examination of Darwin's Treatise* (1861). ☐ A Hunter Dupree, *Asa Gray* (1988)

Gray, David 1838–61
Scottish poet

Born in Merkland, near Kirkintilloch, Dunbartonshire, he studied divinity at Glasgow University, but took an interest in poetry and in 1860 moved to London with Robert Buchanan. His only collection of poetry was *The Luggie and Other Poems*, published posthumously in 1874. Its title piece is a long lyrical poem in praise of the stream near his birthplace, written in the manner of James Thomson's *The Seasons* (1730). It also contained 'In the Shadows'. ☐ A V Stuart, *David Gray, Poet of the Luggie* (1961)

Gray, Edward Whitaker 1748–1806
English botanist and physician

Born probably in London, he was appointed librarian to the Royal College of Physicians in 1773, and from 1787 to 1806 was keeper of the department of natural history at the British Museum, arranging the collections according to the Linnaean system. In 1788 he was made one of the first associates of the newly formed Linnaean Society of London. Elected FRS in 1779, he became its secretary in 1797. He sent a collection of plants from Oporto, Portugal, to Sir Joseph Banks in 1777, and was the author of *On the Class of Animals Called by Linnaeus Amphibia* (1789). He was the uncle of Samuel Frederick Gray.

Gray, Eileen 1878–1976
Irish architect and designer

Born in Enniscorthy, County Wexford, she studied at the Slade School of Art, London (1898), then moved to Paris in 1902, studying at the Académie Colarossi and Académie Julian. She also worked with Japanese craftsman Sugawara. Specialising in lacquering, she began to design furniture and started making carpets, lamps and wall hangings. In 1922 she opened her Galerie Jean Désert in the Rue du Faubourg Saint-Honoré, where she showed her famous lacquer screens. Among her patrons were Jacques Doucet and Suzanne Talbot. Self-taught as an architect, she worked in the modern movement with Jean Badovici. She later exhibited at the Paris 1937 Exhibition with Le Corbusier. In the 1960s her work was 're-discovered' and she witnessed the revival of her art while in her nineties. Her furniture designs were reproduced in Italy, France and the UK.

Gray, Elisha 1835–1901
US inventor

Born in Barnesville, Ohio, he was a manufacturer of telegraphic apparatus. His firm became the Western Electric Co, and his 60 patents included a multiplex telegraph. He also claimed the invention of the telephone, but lost the patent rights to Alexander Graham Bell after a long legal battle in the US Supreme Court.

Gray, George Robert 1808–72
English ornithologist and entomologist

Born in London, he was the son of Samuel Frederick Gray and brother of John Edward Gray. Educated at Merchant Taylor's School, he became zoological assistant at the British Museum in 1831. His first task was cataloguing insects, and he published *Entomology of Australia* (1833). From 1831 to 1872 he ran the ornithological section of the museum, where he produced his most important work, the *Genera of Birds* (3 vols, 1844–49). Gray's Grasshopper Warbler is named after him.

Gray, Gordon Joseph 1910–93
Roman Catholic archbishop and cardinal

Born in Leith, near Edinburgh, he was educated at Holy Cross Academy, Edinburgh, St Joseph's Seminary, Sussex, and St John's, Surrey, and was ordained a priest in 1935. Following various appointments, he was appointed Archbishop of St Andrews and Edinburgh in 1951. In 1969 he was named cardinal by Pope Paul VI, the first such appointment in Scottish history (apart from exiled clerics in Rome). In 1982 he played a major part in bringing Pope John Paul II to Scotland. A traditionalist in manner, he was a valuable force in furthering ecumenical advances, and made possible the great improvement in the acceptability of Catholics in Scottish life.

Gray, Gustave Le 1820–82
French photographer and inventor

His early training was as a painter, but he is remembered as a pioneering photographer who in 1851 invented the waxed-paper process to replace the calotype process. His photographs were mainly of the landscape and architecture of France.

Gray, Hanna Holborn, *née* Holborn 1930–
US historian

She was born in Heidelberg, Germany, the daughter of the historian Hajo Holborn who fled the Nazis with his family in 1934 and settled in the USA. As a Renaissance and Reformation scholar, she worked in various universities during the 1950s and 1960s. She was appointed Professor of History and provost of Yale in 1974, and became acting president (1977–78). Her appointment as president of the University of Chicago (1978–93) made her the first woman to head a major US university.

Gray, Sir James 1891–1975
English zoologist

Born in London, he studied at Cambridge, where he was made a demonstrator in the zoology department in 1924, a Reader in Experimental Zoology in 1931, and later Professor of Zoology (1937–61). His investigations into the cellular mechanisms underlying fertilization, cell division and growth resulted in his 1931 *Text-book of*

Experimental Cytology. His subsequent research interests were in the mechanics of locomotion, much of his research dealing with swimming and the problems of size and scale. He was one of the first workers to make use of cinematography to analyse movement and used this technique in his examination of ciliary movement. He was a member of the Advisory Committee on Fisheries Research (1932–65, chairman from 1949), president of the Marine Biological Association (1945–55) and a trustee of the British Museum (1948–60). He was knighted in 1954.

Gray, John Edward 1800–75
English zoologist and botanist
Born in Walsall, Staffordshire, he was the son of **Samuel Frederick Gray** and brother of **George Robert Gray**. He studied medicine in London, but was much more interested in botany, and was co-author with his father of *The Natural Arrangement of British Plants* (1821). In 1824 he joined the British Museum as assistant keeper of zoology (keeper, 1840–74) and enormously increased its collections. He published 1,162 books, memoirs and notes, mostly zoological, but including a *Handbook of British Waterweeds* (1864).

Gray, Milner Connorton 1899–
English graphic designer
Born in London, he studied at Goldsmith's College there. He has always been associated with multidisciplinary design practices, forming in 1922 one of the first in Great Britain, with Charles Bassett (Bassett-Gray), and later co-founding with **Misha Black** the Industrial Design Partnership (1935) and the Design Research Unit (1945). He was also, in 1930, one of the founders of the designers' professional body, The Society of Industrial Artists (Chartered Society of Designers). He worked for the Ministry of Information during World War II and was involved in two major exhibitions, 'Britain Can Make It' (1946) and the 'Festival of Britain' (1951). Although he designed ceramics and furniture, he is best known for his co-ordinated corporate identity schemes for organizations such as Ilford, Austin Reed, ICI, Gilbey and British Rail. He became a Royal Designer for Industry in 1937.

Gray, Robert 1755–1806
US explorer
He was born in Tiverton, Rhode Island. He became the first US captain to sail around the world (1787–90), carrying sea otter skins from the north-west to China and then returning to Boston with a Chinese cargo, and in doing so he established the three-cornered China trade. His explorations of the north-west coast, especially his discovery of the Columbia River (1792), became the basis for the successful US claim to the Oregon country.

Gray, Samuel Frederick 1766–1828
English botanist and pharmacologist
Born in London, he moved to Walsall, Staffordshire, in 1797, and practised as a pharmaceutical chemist until 1800. In that year he returned to London and lectured on botany and materia medica. He published *Supplement to the Pharmacopoeia* (1818) and with his son **John Edward Gray** wrote *Natural Arrangement of British Plants*. Gray was the first person to establish fungal genera such as *Amanita*, *Lepiota* and *Corticium*.

Gray, Simon James Holliday 1936–
English dramatist, director and novelist
Born on Hayling Island, Hampshire, he studied at Cambridge. He has written novels and several television plays, but is best known as a stage dramatist. His first play, *Wise Child*, was produced in 1967. Subsequent plays include *Butley* (1971), *Otherwise Engaged* (1975), *The Rear Column* (1978), *Quartermaine's Terms* (1981), *The Common Pursuit* (1984, televised 1992), *Melon* (1987) and *Cell Mates* (1995), whose staging was the focus of much media attention following the walk-out and disappearance of **Stephen Fry**. This episode is central to Gray's autobiographical *Fat Chance* published later in 1995. He was a lecturer in English literature at Queen Mary College, London (1965–85), and many of his plays are set in the world of academics, publishers, or academics who publish. His best television play is *After Pilkington* (1987), a wry thriller set in Oxford. *They Never Slept* (1991), also for television, is a comedy about ghosts in World War II, with characteristically serious comment on war and the position of women. He has also published books about the process of staging a play, *An Unnatural Pursuit* (1985) and *How's That for Telling 'Em, Fat Lady?* (1988).

Gray, Stephen 1666–1736
English physicist
He was born in Canterbury, and his first scientific paper (1696) described a microscope made of a water droplet, similar to the simple glass bead microscopes made so famous by **Antoni van Leeuwenhoek** in the following decade. He was one of the first experimenters in static electricity, using frictional methods to prove conduction; this work had a great influence on the electrical theory of **Charles Dufay**.

Gray, Thomas 1716–71
English poet
Born in London, he was educated at Eton and Peterhouse, Cambridge. At Eton he met **Horace Walpole**, whom he accompanied (1739) on a two-and-a-half-year tour of France and Italy, but they quarrelled at Reggio and parted. Gray returned to England and in 1742 he wrote his 'Ode on a Distant Prospect of Eton College' (1747), and began the 'Elegy Written in a Country Churchyard' (1751), in Stoke Poges, Buckinghamshire. He then went back to Cambridge, where he wrote his *Pindaric Odes* (1757). He declined the laureateship in 1757. In 1768 he collected his poems in the first general edition, and became Professor of History and Modern Languages at Cambridge.
📖 R Cremer, *Thomas Gray, a biography* (1955)

Graziani, Rodolfo, Marchese di Neghelli 1882–1955
Italian soldier
He was born near Frosinone. He served in Libya in 1913 and on the Italian front during World War I. In 1930 he became Vice-Governor of Cyrenaica and in 1936 led the Italian forces on the Somalian front during the conquest of Abyssinia. He succeeded **Pietro Badoglio** as Viceroy of Ethiopia. He was placed in charge of the Italian forces in North Africa (1940–41) but was replaced after a series of defeats by the British under Lord **Wavell**. He accepted **Mussolini's** invitation to become Defence Minister of the Republic of Salò in 1943, but was captured in 1945 and tried for war crimes. In 1950 he was sentenced to 25 years in prison, but was released the same year. He was active in the Italian Social Movement until his death.

Greathead, James Henry 1844–96
British inventor
Born in Grahamstown, Cape Colony, South Africa, he went to England (1859) and after studying civil engineering as an apprentice, he undertook to build a subway under the Thames in London (1869). To penetrate the difficult water-bearing strata he devised the 'Greathead shield', a cylindrical wrought-iron tube pushed forward by powerful screws as material was excavated in front of it. In 1884 he patented further improvements to his shield, incorporating the use of compressed air and forward propulsion by hydraulic jacks instead of screws. The improved shield was used in the building of the City and South London railway tunnels (1886).

Greatrakes or Greatorex, Valentine 1629–83
Irish physician, the 'touch doctor'

He was born in Affane, County Waterford, and from 1649 to 1656 was an officer in the Parliamentary army in Ireland. From 1662 he became famous for curing 'king's evil' and all manner of diseases by 'touching' or 'stroking'. He failed at Whitehall before the king in 1666, but his gratuitous cures were attested by **Robert Boyle**, **Ralph Cudworth**, **Henry More**, and others. He replied to scepticism in his *Brief Account* (1666).

Grechko, Andrei Antonovich 1903–76
Soviet marshal and politician

He fought in the cavalry during the civil war which followed the Revolution of October 1917, and held several cavalry commands in the first half of World War II. As Commander-in-Chief in East Germany he helped put down the Berlin rising (1953), and he was Commander-in-Chief of the Warsaw Pact when the Berlin Wall was erected (1961). He became Minister of Defence in 1967 and a politburo member in 1973. In the debate about East–West détente he was regarded as a hardliner.

Greco, El, *properly* Domenico Theotocopoulos
1541–1614
Spanish painter

Born in Candia, Heraklion, Crete, of Greek descent, he studied in Italy, possibly as a pupil of **Titian**. Around 1570 he painted a *View of Mount Sinai and the Monastery of St Catherine* (Historical Museum of Crete, Heraklion, the sole example of his painting to be found in his native Crete). He is known to have settled in Toledo about 1577, when he was commissioned to execute the decorations for the new church of S Domingo el Antiguo, the centrepiece being the *Assumption of the Virgin* (1577, now at Chicago). He became a portrait painter whose reputation fluctuated because of the suspicion which greeted his characteristic distortions. His painting is a curious blend of Italian Mannerism and Baroque rhythm, with elongated flame-like figures, arbitrary lighting and colour, and, in his later pictures, almost Impressionist brushwork. The most famous of his paintings is probably the *Burial of Count Orgaz* (1586) in the Church of S Tomé, Toledo. Many of his works are to be seen in Toledo (Museo del Greco). His *Crucifixion* and *Resurrection* (1604) are held in the Prado, Madrid, his *Self-portrait* and *View of Toledo* (c.1600–1610) are in New York, and the National Gallery, London, has a version of the *Purification of the Temple* (c.1600). ☐ Harold E Wethey, *El Greco and His School* (2 vols, 1962)

Gréco, Juliette 1927–
French singer and actress

Born in Montpellier, she began her career in Left Bank clubs at the end of World War II. In 1949, at the height of Existentialism, she made her first cabaret appearance at Le Boeuf sur le Toit, establishing herself as the archetypal interpreter of world-weary lyrics, delivered in a half-sung, half-spoken style. She recorded many songs by **Jacques Prévert** and Josef Kosma (notably 'Les feuilles mortes', 'Dead Leaves'), Charles Aznavour ('Je hais les dimanches', 'I Hate Sundays') and above all Jacques Brel ('Je suis bien'). She had a much-publicized relationship with **Miles Davis**. Her film appearances include *Au Royaume des cieux* (1949, 'In the Kingdom of Heaven'), *The Sun Also Rises* (1957) and *Crack in the Mirror* (1957).

Greeley, Horace 1811–72
US editor and politician

Born in Amherst, New Hampshire, he worked as a printer. He went to New York in 1831, started the weekly *New Yorker* in 1834 and in 1841 the daily New York *Tribune*, of which he was the leading editor until his death, exerting a supreme influence on US opinion. The *Tribune* was at first Whig, then antislavery Whig, and finally extreme Republican; it advocated, to a certain extent, the social

theories of **Charles Fourier**. He published in the *Tribune* his 'Prayer of Twenty Millions', and within a month the emancipation proclamation was issued. After **Robert E Lee**'s surrender he advocated a universal amnesty, and his going to Richmond and signing the bail-bond of **Jefferson Davis** awakened a storm of public indignation. In religious faith he was a Universalist. He was an unsuccessful Liberal Republican candidate in 1872 for the presidency. ☐ G G Van Deusen, *Horace Greeley, Nineteenth Century Crusader* (1953)

Greely, Adolphus Washington 1844–1935
US explorer

Born in Newburyport, Massachusetts, he was a volunteer in the Civil War, and later joined the regular army as lieutenant. In 1881 he conducted a US expedition to Smith Sound to set up a meteorological station during which one of the team travelled to within 396 miles (638km) of the North Pole, the farthest point reached until then. The relief boat failed to turn up in 1883, and when rescue came in 1884, only six of the party of 25 were still alive. In 1887 Greely became chief of the signal service. Becoming major-general in 1906, he retired in 1908 and was awarded the Congressional Medal of Honour in 1931.

Green, George 1793–1841
English mathematician and physicist

Born in Sneinton, near Nottingham, he was largely self-taught and in 1828 published a pamphlet entitled *An essay on the application of mathematical analysis to the theories of electricity and magnetism*, containing Green's theorem and Green's functions. Green's theorem relates integrals taken over a volume with those taken over the surface enclosing that volume, and has valuable implications for potential theory. His functions are a valuable technical tool for solving partial differential equations. He went to Caius College, Cambridge, in 1833, published several papers on wave motion and optics, and was elected a Fellow of the college in 1839. Green's theorem was made known to European mathematicians through **Joseph Liouville** and his *Mathematical Works* (1850–54) were edited by William Thomson (later Lord **Kelvin**). ☐ D M Cannell, *George Green: Mathematician and Physicist 1793–1841* (1993)

Green, Henry, *pseudonym of* Henry Vincent Yorke
1905–73
English novelist

Born in Tewkesbury, Gloucestershire, and educated at Oxford, he became managing director in his father's engineering company in Birmingham, but pursued a parallel career as a novelist. His first novel, *Blindness* (1926), was published while he was still an undergraduate. *Living* (1929) gave a unique insight into life on the factory floor in Birmingham. An elliptical and highly stylized writer, he was partial to terse and sophisticated titles, such as *Party Going* (1939), *Caught* (1943), *Loving* (1945), *Back* (1946), *Concluding* (1948), *Nothing* (1950) and *Doting* (1952). He was a contemporary of **Anthony Powell** and **Evelyn Waugh**, and like **Ivy Compton-Burnett** he relies heavily on dialogue, plot being conspicuous only by its absence. His influence and reputation extended beyond the literary cognoscenti, and his writing was much admired in Europe. *Pack My Bag: A Self Portrait* (1940) is autobiographical.

Green, John Richard 1837–83
English historian

Born in Oxford, he was educated at Magdalen School and Jesus College there. He took orders and became curate and vicar of two East End London parishes, and also contributed historical articles to the *Saturday Review*. In 1868 he became librarian at Lambeth, but the next year developed tuberculosis, which made all active work impossible. Thus he began his *Short History of the English People* (1874), the first complete history of England from the social side related to geography and the antiquities. Its instant success encouraged a larger edition, *A History of the English People* (1877–80). His *Making of England* (1881) and the *Conquest of England* (1883) are fragments of an intended history of early England.

Green, Julien 1900–98
French novelist

Born in Paris, of US parents, and educated partly in the USA, he was bilingual, and became a convert to Catholicism. He began a successful series of psychological studies in a melancholy vein, written in French but later translated, with *Mont-Cinère* (1926, Eng trans *Avarice House*, 1927 (US); 1928 (UK)). His other works include *Adrienne Mesurat* (1927, Eng trans *The Closed Garden*, 1928), *Léviathan* (1929, Eng trans *The Dark Journey*, 1929), which won the Harper Prize Novel contest, and *Moïra* (1950, Eng trans 1951). He also published a series of *Journals*, the first eight of which were translated in two volumes as *Journal 1928–66* in 1969. *Memories of Happy Days* (1942) and *Memories of Evil Days* (1976) both written in English also describe his life. A more recent publication is the novel *Dixie* (1995). 📖 G S Burne, *Julien Green* (1972)

Green, Lucinda, *née* Prior-Palmer 1953–
British three-day eventer

Born in London, she won the Badminton Horse Trials a record six times (1973, 1976–77, 1979, 1983–84), and the Burghley Horse Trials in 1977 and 1981. At the European championships she won an individual gold medal in 1975 and 1977, a team gold in 1977, 1985, and 1987, and an individual and team silver in 1983. She was the 1982 world champion on Regal Realm, when she also won a team gold medal.

Green, Michael Boris 1946–
English theoretical physicist

Born in London, he was educated at Cambridge, studied at the Institute for Advanced Study at Princeton University (1970–72), and from 1972 to 1977 worked at Cambridge. He was then a Science and Engineering Council Advanced Fellow at Oxford from 1977 to 1979, became professor at Queen Mary and Westfield College, London, in 1985, and returned to Cambridge in 1993 as John Humphrey Plummer Professor of Theoretical Physics. With John H Schwarz and Edward Witten, he was the founder of superstring theory. This is based on the idea that the ultimate constituents of nature, when inspected at very small scales, do not exist as point-like particles but as 'strings' in more than three dimensions. String theories are now considered very good candidates for the actual laws of physics at the ultimate small scale. For this work he was awarded the Maxwell Medal by the Institute of Physics (1987), the William Hopkins prize by the Cambridge Philosophical Society (1987) and the Dirac Medal of the International Centre for Theoretical Physics (1989). He was elected FRS in 1989.

Green, William 1873–1952
US labour leader

Born in Coshocton, Ohio, the son of a coal miner, he became a miner himself at the age of 16, and he rose through the ranks of the United Mine Workers of America (UMW), to become president of the American Federation of Labor (AFL) in 1924. He held the post for the rest of his life and is remembered for his effort to eliminate radicalism from the labour movement. He led the AFL's struggle with the more militant Congress of Industrial Organizations (CIO), expelling the CIO unions in 1936 and breaking with his former mentor, UMW president John L Lewis.

Greenaway, Kate (Catherine) 1846–1901
English artist and book illustrator

Born in London, she started publishing her popular portrayals of child life in 1879 with *Under the Window*, followed by *The Birthday Book* (1880) and *Mother Goose* (1881). The Greenaway Medal is awarded annually for the best British children's book artist. 📖 Rodney K Engen, *Kate Greenaway* (1976)

Greenaway, Peter 1942–
English filmmaker and painter

Born in London, he trained as a painter, and first exhibited at the Lord's Gallery in 1964. Employed at the Central Office of Information (1965–76), he worked as an editor and began making his own short films. He later gained a reputation for originality and invention on the international festival circuit with such works as *A Walk Through H* (1978) and *The Falls* (1980) before *The Draughtsman's Contract* (1982) won him critical acclaim and a wider audience. He has subsequently pursued a prolific career utilizing ravishing visual composition, a painterly sense of colour and the distinctive music of **Michael Nyman** to explore such preoccupations as sex, death, decay and gamesmanship in films like *The Belly of An Architect* (1987), *Drowning By Numbers* (1988) and *The Cook, The Thief, His Wife and Her Lover* (1989). His *Prospero's Books* (1991) was based on *The Tempest* and starred **John Gielgud** playing the leading role and voicing all the others. Later films include *The Baby of Mâcon* (1993) and *The Pillow Book* (1996).

Greene, (Henry) Graham 1904–91
English writer

Born in Berkhamsted, Hertfordshire, he was educated at Berkhamsted School where his father was headmaster. In *A Sort of Life* (1971), the first of two autobiographies (*Ways of Escape*, the second volume, appeared in 1980), he recounts how he played Russian roulette and of how, aged 13, he tried to cut open his leg with a penknife. He went to Balliol College, Oxford, and while there published *Bubbling April* (1925), a collection of verse. He became a Roman Catholic in 1926 and became a journalist with *The Times*. He married in 1927 and was later separated but not divorced. His first novels, *The Man Within* (1925), *The Name of Action* (1930) and *Rumour at Nightfall* (1932), made little impression and he subsequently disowned them though he later allowed the first to be included in the Collected Edition. *Stamboul Train* (1932) was his first fully successful novel, although he termed it an 'entertainment'. Like many of his subsequent novels it is sombrely romantic, fusing tragedy and comedy in a peculiar no-man's land that critics christened 'Greeneland'. *It's a Battlefield* (1934) and *England Made Me* (1935) are likewise 'entertainments'. A prolific writer, he wrote a great number of novels, stories, plays and biographies as well as film criticism. He was the film critic for *Night and Day*, and was partly responsible for its demise when the magazine was successfully sued after he had accused Twentieth Century Fox of 'procuring' **Shirley Temple** 'for immoral purposes'. His career as a so-called Catholic novelist began with *Brighton Rock* (1938), a thriller which asserts that human justice is inadequate and irrelevant to the real struggle against evil. A recurring theme in his work, this is explored in other of the Catholic novels—*The Power and the Glory* (1940), *The Heart of the Matter* (1948) and *The Quiet American* (1955)—whose unorthodoxy often led him into controversy with the Church's hierarchy. Other notable novels include *The Third Man* (1950, filmed by **Carol Reed**), *The End of the Affair* (1951), *Our Man in Havana* (1958), *A Burnt-Out Case* (1961), *The Comedians* (1965), *Travels With My Aunt* (1969), *The Honorary Consul* (1973), *The Human Factor* (1978), *Doctor Fischer of Geneva* (1980), *Monsignor Quixote* (1982) and *The Captain and the Enemy* (1988). The multifarious settings reflect his wanderlust and his fascination with uncomfortable countries—Argentina, the Congo, Mexico,

Vietnam—as well as his seeming disregard for his personal safety. He settled in Antibes in 1966, where he lived for the rest of his life. In 1982 he broke his relative seclusion by publishing an incendiary pamphlet, *J'Accuse*, which brought him into conflict with the local authorities in Nice. He published travel books: *Journey Without Maps* (1936), *The Lawless Roads* (1939) and *In Search of a Character: Two African Journals* (1961). The *Collected Essays* appeared in 1969, the *Collected Stories* in 1972. His plays include *The Living Room* (1953), *The Potting Shed* (1957) and *The Complaisant Lover* (1959). *A World of My Own—A Dream Diary* was published in 1992. Few modern writers have his range and power, critical acclaim and popular success. He is often cited by his peers as the greatest novelist of his time, although there are dissenting voices from that judgement, including that of **Anthony Burgess**. 📖 J A Atkins, *Graham Greene* (1957, rev edn 1966)

Greene, Sir Hugh Carleton 1910–87
English journalist and television executive

He was born in Berkhamsted, Hertfordshire, and after studying at Merton College, Oxford, he moved to Germany, working as a foreign correspondent for the *Daily Herald* and later the *Daily Telegraph* (1934–39). He joined the BBC (1940) to work on propaganda broadcasts to Germany, and in 1946 he became controller of broadcasting in the British zone of Germany and rebuilt the country's peacetime radio service. He worked with the BBC's Overseas Service (1952–56) and was the BBC's first director of news and current affairs (1958–60) before becoming director-general (1960–69). He encouraged the BBC to compete with Independent Television and he created a liberal climate in which programme makers flourished. He was the brother of **Graham Greene**. 📖 Michael Tracey, *A Variety of Lives: A Biography of Sir Hugh Greene* (1983)

Greene, Nathanael 1742–86
American soldier

Born in Warwick, Rhode Island, he was a Quaker's son. At the Brandywine (September 1777) he commanded a division and saved the American army from complete destruction. In 1780 he succeeded **Horatio Gates** in command of the army of the South, which had just been defeated by **Charles Cornwallis**, and improved its condition. Although defeated by Cornwallis at Guilford Courthouse (March 1781) he conducted a masterly retreat into South Carolina which, with Georgia, was rapidly retaken, until at Eutaw Springs (September 1781) the war in the South was ended in what was virtually an American victory. A general second perhaps only to **George Washington**, he died at Mulberry Grove, Georgia. 📖 George Greene, *Life of Nathanael Greene* (3 vols, 1867–71)

Greene, Robert 1558–92
English dramatist

Born in Norwich, Norfolk, and educated at Cambridge, he wrote plays and romances. The latter are often tedious and insipid, but they abound in beautiful poetry. One of them, *Pandosto* (1588), supplied **Shakespeare** with hints for the plot of *The Winter's Tale*. The most popular of his plays was *Friar Bacon and Friar Bungay* (c.1591). As Greene helped to lay the foundations of the English drama, even his worst plays are valuable historically. After his death appeared the pamphlet entitled *The Repentance of Robert Greene, Master of Arts*, in which he lays bare the wickedness of his former life. His *Groatsworth of Wit bought with a Million of Repentance* (1592) contains one of the few authentic contemporary allusions to Shakespeare. 📖 W H Chapman, *William Shakespeare and Robert Greene: The Evidence* (1912)

Greenhow, Rose O'Neal 1817–64
US Confederate spy

Born in Port Tobacco, Maryland, she married the doctor and historian Robert Greenhow, and lived in Washington DC during the Civil War. As a society hostess she overheard information regarding Union troop movements which she is reputed to have passed to the Confederate government. She was placed under house arrest in 1861 and later exiled to the Confederacy (1862). She ran the blockade and travelled to England and France representing the Confederate states, but her ship foundered on her return and she drowned off the North Carolina coast. She published *My Imprisonment and the First Year of Abolition Rule at Washington* (1863).

Greenough, Horatio 1805–52
US sculptor and writer

Born in Boston, Massachusetts, he spent two years at Harvard, then moved to Italy (1825), becoming a leading member of the US artistic colony there. His principal work is a colossal statue in classical style of **George Washington** as Zeus, commissioned for the Capitol Rotunda but now in the Smithsonian Institution, Washington. His advanced views on functionalism and freedom from ornament in design, as expressed in his *Travels, Observations and Experience of a Yankee Stonecutter* (1852), probably influenced the architectural ideas of **Louis Sullivan** and **Frank Lloyd Wright**.

Greenspan, Alan 1926–
US businessman and financier

Born in New York City, he became president and chief executive officer of Townsend-Greenspan and Co Inc, New York City (1954–74, 1977–). He was consultant to the US Treasury and to the Federal Reserve Board (1971–74). He has been a consultant to the congressional budget office since 1977, and was a member of the president's economic policy advisory board from 1981 to 1989. A free-market economist, he has served as chairman of the board of governors of the Federal Reserve Bank since 1987 and has favoured tight monetary policies to keep inflation in check.

Greenway, Francis Howard 1777–1837
Australian architect

Born in Mangotsfield, Gloucestershire, England, of a West Country family of builders and stonemasons, he was a student of **John Nash**. He set up his own architecture firm but went bankrupt and in 1812 he was transported for forgery, arriving in Sydney two years later. He was soon given parole and established himself in practice as an architect in the town. Governor **Lachlan Macquarie** appointed him civil architect, and Greenway designed most of the early colony's public buildings. He made effective use of local material and the best remaining examples of his work, including St James's Church, Sydney, and St Matthew's Church, Windsor, New South Wales, are elegant examples of the Georgian style. Later, his abrasive manner caused him to lose his influential supporters, but he is depicted today on the Australian $10 note.

Greenwood, Arthur 1880–1954
English politician

Born in Leeds and educated at the university there, he became a wartime member of **Lloyd George**'s secretariat. He became an MP in 1922 and deputy leader of the parliamentary Labour Party in 1935, showing himself an outspoken critic of 'appeasement'. In the 1940 government he was Minister without Portfolio, in 1945 he became Lord Privy Seal, resigning from the government in 1947. He remained treasurer of the Labour Party, of whose national executive he became chairman in 1953. He did much to shape Labour's social policies. His son, Anthony Greenwood (1911–82), was also a Labour MP, entering parliament in 1946.

Greenwood, Joan 1921–87
English actress

Born in Chelsea, London, she studied at RADA before making her stage debut in Molière's *Le Malade Imaginaire* (1938, 'The Hypochondriac'). Her film debut came in *John Smith Wakes Up* (1940) and her early theatre work included *The Women* (1939) and *Peter Pan* (1941–42). She toured with the Entertainment National Service Association (ENSA) during World War II and afterwards joined Donald Wolfit's company. She was a woman of distinctive style, and her husky tones, wit and sensuality were evident in both classical roles and contemporary femmes fatales. Her film credits include the influential and enduring Ealing comedies *Whisky Galore* (1948), *Kind Hearts and Coronets* (1949) and *The Man in the White Suit* (1951). Later stage successes include *Lysistrata* (1957), *Hedda Gabler* (1960) and *Oblomov* (1964). Later films were *Tom Jones* (1963) and *Little Dorrit* (1987). She married actor André Morell in 1960.

Greenwood, Walter 1903–74
English writer

He was born in Salford, Lancashire, of working-class parents, and educated at the local grammar school. His novel *Love on the Dole* (1933), inspired by his experiences of unemployment and depression in the early 1930s, made a considerable impact as a document of the times and was subsequently dramatised. He also wrote other novels with a social slant, and several plays. 🕮 *There Was a Time* (1967)

Greer, Germaine 1939–
Australian feminist and author

Born in Melbourne, she attended the universities of Melbourne, Sydney and Cambridge, becoming a lecturer in English at Warwick University (1968–73). Since 1989 she has been special lecturer and unofficial Fellow at Newnham College, Cambridge. Her controversial and successful book *The Female Eunuch* (1970) portrayed marriage as a legalized form of slavery for women, and attacked the denial and misrepresentation of female sexuality by male-dominated society. A regular contributor to newspapers and periodicals, and a frequent television panellist, she became (1979) director of the Tulsa Centre for the Study of Women's Literature. Her later works include *Sex and Destiny: the Politics of Human Fertility* (1984) and *The Change* (1991), which documents her discoveries and conclusions concerning the menopause in women. 🕮 David Plante, *Difficult Women: A Memoir of Three* (1983)

Greg, William Rathbone 1809–81
English essayist

Born in Manchester, he became the manager of mills at Bury, then a commissioner of customs (1856), and comptroller of HM Stationery Office (1864–77). His numerous essays on political and social history were collected in *Essays on Political and Social Science* (1854), *Literary and Social Judgments* (1869) and *Miscellaneous Essays* (1884). His *Rocks Ahead* (1874) took a highly pessimistic view of the future of Great Britain, anticipating with foreboding the political supremacy of the lower classes, industrial decline and the divorce of intelligence from religion.

Gregg, John Robert 1867–1948
US publisher, inventor of the 'Gregg shorthand system'

He was born in Shantonagh, County Monaghan, Ireland. While working in Liverpool he invented a new shorthand system, published in *Light Line Phonography* and the *Gregg Shorthand Manual* (1888). Emigrating to the USA in 1893, he established the Gregg Publishing Company. He published *Gregg Speed Studies* (1917), and also founded the *American Shorthand Teacher* in 1920 (later renamed *American Business World*).

Gregg, Sir Norman McAlister 1892–1966
Australian ophthalmologist

Born in Burwood, Sydney, he was educated at Sydney University, and served with the Royal Australian Medical Corps in World War I, winning the MC in France. He later studied ophthalmology in London before returning to Sydney. After an epidemic of German measles there in 1939, his research proved the link between the incidence of that illness in pregnancy and cataracts or blindness in children.

Grégoire, Henri 1750–1831
French prelate and revolutionary

Born in Vého, Lorraine, he took orders and was sent to the Estates General of 1789 as a deputy of the clergy. The first of his order to take the oaths of loyalty to the new constitution, he was elected 'Constitutional Bishop' of Loir-et-Cher (1790). After the 18th Brumaire, he became a member of the Corps Législatif, and the Concordat (1801) forced him to resign his bishopric. He died unreconciled with the Church. Among his works are *Essai sur la régénération des juifs* (1789, 'Essay on the Regeneration of the Jews'), which became widely popular, *Histoire des sectes religieuses* (1814, 'History of the Religious Sects') and *L'Eglise gallicane* (1818, 'The Gallic Church').

Gregor, William 1761–1817
English chemist and clergyman

Born in Trewarthenick, Cornwall, he analysed local minerals, particularly the sand known as ilmenite, in which he discovered titanium.

Gregory, St, *known as* the Illuminator c.240–332AD
Armenian Christian

Born in Cappadocia, of Armenian parents, he is said to have been of the royal Persian race of the Arsacids. Known as 'the Apostle of Armenia', he was kept a prisoner for 14 years by Tiridates III for refusing to condone idolatry but, after converting the king (AD301), he was made patriarch of his country.

Gregory I, the Great See panel p784

Gregory II, St 669–731
Italian pope

Born in Rome, he was elevated in 715. The authority of the Eastern emperors had shrunk in the West into little more than a name, and the draconian measures of the Emperor Leo the Isaurian against image-worship weakened the tie even more. Gregory protested strongly against the imperial policy, the result being a notable increase of the political authority and influence of the popes in Italy. Under Gregory's auspices, St Boniface began to carry out his missionary work in Germany. His feast day is 11 or 13 February.

Gregory III d.741
Syrian pope

Born in Syria, he became pope in 731, succeeding Gregory II, and excommunicated the Iconoclasts. The threat of the Lombards became so formidable that, the Eastern emperors being powerless to help, the Romans compelled Gregory to send a deputation to Charles Martel, asking for his help, and offering to make him a consul of Rome. This offer is of historical significance, in that it failed to enlist the aid of Charles, but it was a step towards the independence of the West.

Gregory VII, St, *originally* Hildebrand c.1020–85
Italian pope

Born near Soana, Tuscany, he was educated at the monastery of St Maria, Rome. He became a cardinal in 1049. As pope (1073–85), he worked to change the secularized condition of the Church, which led to conflict with the Holy Roman Emperor Henry IV, who declared Gregory

Gregory I *known as* Gregory the Great c.540–604
Pope (from 590) and saint, a Doctor of the Church

Gregory was born in Rome and though appointed by Justin II as praetor of Rome, he relinquished this office, distributed his wealth among the poor and withdrew into a monastery at Rome. It was while he was here that he is said to have seen some Anglo-Saxon youths in the slave-market, and to have been seized with a longing to convert their country to Christianity. He embarked on this but was called back, and Pelagius II sent Gregory as nuncio to Constantinople for aid against the Lombards.

Gregory reluctantly agreed to become pope on the death of Pelagius. He proved to be a great administrator, and during his period of office the Roman Church underwent a complete overhaul of its public services and ritual and the systematization of its sacred chants, from which arose the Gregorian chant. He entrusted the mission to convert the English to Augustine, and the Gothic kingdom of Spain, long Arian, was reconciled with Rome.

Gregory was tolerant towards heathens and Jews, and he used all his efforts to repress slave-dealing and to mitigate slavery. He is buried in St Peter's basilica, Rome, and his feast day is 12 March.

📖 In his writings the whole dogmatical system of the modern church is fully developed. He left homilies on Ezekiel, Job and on the Gospels, the *Regulae Pastoralis liber* ('Book of Rules for Pastors'), and the *Sacramentarium* and *Antiphonarium*. See also Carole Straw, *Gregory the Great* (1988); F H Dudden, *Gregory the Great: His Place in History and Thought* (2 vols, 1905).

> *Scriptura sacre mentis oculis quasi quoddam speculum opponitur, ut interna nostra facies in ipsa videatur.*
> 'Holy scripture is placed before the eyes of our mind like a mirror, so that we may view our inner face therein.'
> From *Moralia* in *Job*, bk 2, ch.1, section 1.

deposed in a diet at Worms (1076), but then yielded to him after excommunication. In 1080 Henry resumed hostilities, appointing an antipope (Clement III), and after a siege took possession of Rome (1084). Gregory was freed by Norman troops, but was forced to withdraw to Salerno. He was canonized in 1606, and his feast day is 25 May. 📖 Allan J MacDonald, *Hildebrand: A Life of Gregory the Seventh* (1932)

Gregory IX, *originally* Ugo or Ugolino de Segni
1148/55–1241
Italian pope

He was the nephew of Pope Innocent III, by whom he was created cardinal-deacon in 1198. A strong supporter of the Franciscans and the Dominicans, he became pope in 1227 and constantly feuded with Emperor Frederick II, of Germany, asserting the supremacy of papal power. After a phase of uneasy collaboration with the emperor, in which the pope supported him in his relations with the Lombard cities, while he supported the pope against opposition in Rome, a ferocious conflict broke out over Frederick's Constitutions of Melfi which subjected Sicily to his will. Rome itself was under siege when the pope died. He was responsible for ordering the first authoritative collection of papal decretals (1234), which were to remain the basic source of canon law in the Catholic Church until 1917.

Gregory XI, *originally* Pierre Roger de Beaufort
1329–78
French pope

He became pope in 1370, and despite the opposition of France and his own family, he ended the Babylonian Captivity of the papacy, moving its seat from Avignon to its original place in Rome (1377). He was the last French pope, and the elections held after his death began the Great Schism.

Gregory XIII, *originally* Ugo Buoncompagni 1502–85
Italian pope

Born in Bologna, he studied at the university there and became Professor of Law (1531–39). He became one of the theologians at the Council of Trent, then in 1565 a cardinal and legate to Spain. As pope (1572–85), he did much to promote education, and endowed many of the colleges in Rome. His pontificate is notable for the correction of the calendar and the introduction of the Gregorian Computation in 1582, but his reputation was damaged by his ordering a *Te Deum* for the slaughter of

French Protestants in the St Bartholomew's Day Massacre in 1572. Gregory published a valuable edition of the *Decretum Gratiani*.

Gregory XV, *originally* Alessandro Ludovisi
1554–1623
Italian pope

Born in Bologna, he became pope in 1621. He established the still-used procedure for papal elections, set up the congregation of the Propagation of the Faith, regained Moravia and Bohemia to the Roman faith, and canonized Francis Xavier, Ignatius Loyola and Teresa of Ávila, among others.

Gregory XVI, *originally* Bartolomeo Alberto Mauro Cappellari 1765–1846
Austrian pope

Born in Belluno, Venetia, he went to the monastery of San Michele de Murano, near Venice, and became a member of the Camaldolese order. He was pope from 1831 and represented reaction and Ultramontanism in a revolutionary period. He favoured the Jesuits, and increased the papal debt by spending on buildings and museums.

Gregory of Nazianzus or Nazianzen, St
c.330–c.389AD
Greek prelate and theologian

Born of Greek parents in Cappadocia, he was educated at Caesarea, Alexandria and Athens. He became a close friend of Basil the Great, and was made Bishop of Sasima, but withdrew to a life of religious study at Nazianzus. The Emperor Theodosius I, the Great made him patriarch of Constantinople (Istanbul) in AD380, but he also resigned this in the following year. His theological works were largely concerned with upholding Nicene orthodoxy and include discourses, letters and hymns. His feast day in the West is 2 January.

Gregory of Nyssa AD331–95
Greek Christian theologian

Born in Caesarea, Cappadocia, he was consecrated Bishop of Nyssa in Cappadocia (c.371AD) by his brother Basil the Great. During the persecution of the adherents of the Nicene Creed in the reign of Valens, Gregory was deposed, but on the death of Valens was welcomed back (378). He was present at the Council of Constantinople in 381, and was appointed to share in the overseeing of the diocese of Pontus. He travelled to Arabia and Jerusalem to set in order the churches there, and was again at a synod in Constantinople (Istanbul) in 394. His chief works are his

Twelve Books against Eunomius, a treatise on the Trinity, several ascetic treatises, many sermons, 23 epistles, and his great *Cathechetical Oration* (1903).

Gregory of Tours c.538–94
Frankish prelate and historian
Born in Arverna (now Clermont), to a distinguished Roman family of Gaul, he made a recovery from sickness through a pilgrimage to the grave of St Martin of Tours. This led Gregory to devote himself to the Church, and he was elected Bishop of Tours in 573. As a supporter of Sigbert of Austrasia and his wife Brunhilde against Chilperic and his wife Fredegond, he was relentlessly persecuted. His *Historia Francorum* ('History of the Franks') is the chief authority for the history of Gaul in the 6th century. His *Miraculorum libri vii* is a hagiographical compilation.

Gregory, Augustus Charles 1819–1905
Australian surveyor and explorer
Born in Farnsfield, Nottingham, England, he went to Australia in 1829, joining the Western Australian Survey Department in 1841. He set out to explore a large area north of Perth in 1846 and discovered coal on the Irwin River. In 1848 he travelled inland from Shark Bay and found lead in the Murchison River. He then headed the Northern Australian expedition (1855–56), instigated by the Royal Geographical Society and financed by the British government, which discovered new pastures along the reverse of the route of Ludwig Leichhardt. In 1858 his explorations showed that many rivers drained into Lake Eyre and so solved the mystery of the South Australian Lakes. He was Surveyor-General of the new state of Queensland (1859).

Gregory, Isabella Augusta, Lady, née Persse
1852–1932
Irish playwright
She was born at Roxborough House near Coole, County Galway, the daughter of a wealthy family. The Gregory family were nearby landowners, and in 1880 Augusta Persse married Sir William Henry Gregory (1817–92) who was Governor of Ceylon (1872–77). After her husband's death, Lady Augusta furthered her study of Irish mythology and folklore, an interest which led in 1896 to her meeting W B Yeats. She shared his vision of a resurgent Irish drama and, with Yeats and the writer Edward Martyn (1859–1923), co-founded the Abbey Theatre, Dublin, which opened in 1904. Lady Gregory wrote or translated about 40 short plays about the Irish rural peasantry, including the comedy, *Spreading the News* (1904), the patriotic *Cathleen ni Houlihan* (1902, with Yeats) and *The Rising of the Moon* (1907). *The Gaol Gate* (1906) is a tragedy, while *The White Cockade* (1905) and *The Deliverer* (1911) are history plays. She also translated Molière and wrote versions of the Irish legends in dialect. She was a leading figure in the Irish literary revival, and her home at Coole Park became a focus for the movement.
📖 A Saddlemayer, *In Defence of Lady Gregory* (1966)

Gregory, James 1638–75
Scottish mathematician
Born in Drumoak, Aberdeenshire, he graduated from Aberdeen University and went to London in 1662, and the following year published *Optica promota*, containing a description of the Gregorian reflecting telescope that he had invented in 1661. From 1664 to 1667 he was in Padua, where he published a book on the quadrature of the circle and hyperbola, giving convergent infinite sequences for the areas of these curves. In 1668 he became Professor of Mathematics at St Andrews University, before taking the chair at Edinburgh in 1674. Much of his later work was concerned with infinite series, a term which he introduced into the language.

Gregory, John Walter 1864–1932
English geologist and explorer
Born in London, he started his career (1887–1900) at the British Museum, London, before becoming the first Professor of Geology at the University of Melbourne (1900–04) and at the University of Glasgow (1904–29). He accompanied the first British East African Expedition, describing the Great Rift Valley of Kenya and Tanzania (1893), and subsequently visited the Middle East, Tibet and the Americas. Gregory wrote more than 300 geological papers on diverse topics such as corals, tectonics, glacial phenomena, and the origin of oceans. His publications included *The Dead Heart of Australia* (1906), *The Rift Valleys and Geology of East Africa* (1921), *To the Alps of Chinese Tibet* (1923) and *Elements of Economic Geology* (1927). He was killed in the gorge of the River Urubamba in the Peruvian Andes.

Gregory Thaumaturgus c.213–c.270 AD
Roman Christian
Born in Neocaesarea in Pontus, he became a disciple of Origen, and was consecrated Bishop of Neocaesarea. His *Ekthesis* ('Confession of Faith') is a summary of Origen's theology. The genuineness of two other treatises is doubtful. His *Panegyricus* (which contains an auto-biography) is printed among the works of Origen. His name means 'wonder-worker' in Greek.

Greif, Andreas See Gryphius, Andreas

Greig, John 1942–
Scottish footballer and manager
Born in Edinburgh, he spent his entire senior career, from 1960 to 1978, with Rangers, much of it as club captain. He won five league championships and six Scottish Cups while with the club, as well as the European Winners' Cup in 1972. Winning 44 caps for Scotland, he was voted Scottish player of the year in 1966 and 1976. Retiring as a player in May 1978, he immediately became Rangers' manager, holding the post until 1983. He then became a radio football commentator, before returning to take up a position in Rangers' publicity department in 1990. He is remembered as a player for his inspirational captaincy, his fierce shot, and commanding defensive qualities.

Greig, Maysie Coucher, properly Jennifer Greig Smith 1901–71
Australian journalist and writer
Born in Sydney, she moved to England in 1920, writing short stories and serials for London newspapers. Her first romantic novel, *Peggy of Beacon Hill* (1920), was later filmed, and was followed by nearly 200 other novels. She was hugely popular in the circulating libraries until the 1950s, both under her own name and as Jennifer Ames.

Greig, Sir Samuel 1735–88
Scottish naval commander in the Russian navy
Born in Inverkeithing, Fife, he transferred to the Russian navy in 1763, just after the assumption of power by Empress Catherine II, and fought in the war with the Turks (1768–72) and the victory at Çesme (1770). Promoted rear admiral (1770) and vice-admiral (1773), he reformed the fleet and led it in the Baltic war against Sweden (1788–90).

Grenfell, Joyce 1910–79
English entertainer
Born in London, she made her debut in *The Little Revue* in 1939. After touring hospitals with concert parties during World War II, she appeared in revue until the early 1950s, performing comic monologues. She later appeared in her own one-woman shows, such as *Joyce Grenfell Requests the Pleasure*. Her monologues gently mocked the habits and manners of middle-class, English schoolmistresses and

ageing spinster daughters. She wrote her autobiography, *Joyce Grenfell Requests the Pleasure* (1976), and *George, Don't Do That* (1977).

Grenfell, Julian Henry Francis 1888–1915
English poet

Educated at Eton and Balliol College, Oxford, he was killed in World War I. He is remembered for his war poem 'Into Battle' which was published in *The Times* in 1915 and is often selected by anthologists. V Meynell, *Julian Grenfell* (1917)

Grenfell, Sir Wilfred Thomason 1865–1940
English physician and missionary

He was born in Parkgate, Cheshire. An Oxford rugby blue and house surgeon to the London Hospital, he took a master mariner's certificate and became a medical missionary in the North Sea fisheries. In 1892 he went to Labrador and founded hospitals, orphanages and other social services as well as fitting out hospital ships for the fishing grounds. He was knighted in 1927.

Grenville, Sir Bevil 1596–1643
English soldier

Born in Brinn, Cornwall, he was the hero of Robert Hawker's ballad, *Song of the Western Men*. He entered parliament in 1621, and sided for some years with the popular party. From 1639 he espoused the king's cause, and helped defeat the Parliamentarians at Bradock Down (1643), but fell at the head of the Cornish Infantry in the Royalist victory of Landsdowne.

Grenville, George 1712–70
English politician

He practised as a lawyer and became an MP in 1741, rising to Lord of the Admiralty (1744–47), Lord of the Treasury (1747–54) and Treasurer of the Navy (1754–55, 1756–62). He was briefly Secretary of State for the Northern Department (1762–63) and then became Prime Minister (1763–65). During his period in office, John Wilkes was arrested for seditious libel for his attack on the king's speech (1763). The closer supervision of revenue collection (1764–65) and Stamp Act (1765) began to alienate the American colonies from British rule. His tactlessness and clumsy handling of arrangements to cover a possible regency during George III's first serious illness (1765) led to his dismissal by the king, and he remained in opposition for the rest of his life.

Grenville, Sir Richard c.1541–1591
English naval commander

Born in Buckland Abbey, Devon, he fought in Ireland (1566–69) and Hungary. He was knighted (c.1577) and was an MP for Cornwall (1571–84). In 1585 he commanded the seven ships carrying his cousin Walter Raleigh's first colony to Virginia. He contributed three ships to the English fleet against the Spanish Armada (1588). In 1591, as commander of the *Revenge*, he fought alone against a large Spanish fleet off the Azores, dying of wounds on board a Spanish ship. A L Rowse, *Sir Richard Grenville of the Revenge* (1937)

Grenville, William Wyndham Grenville, 1st Baron 1759–1834
English politician

The son of George Grenville, he studied at Eton and Oxford, and became an MP in 1782. In 1783 he was Paymaster-General, in 1789 Speaker, and while Home Secretary (1790) was created baron. He became Foreign Secretary in 1791, and resigned, along with his cousin William Pitt, the Younger, in 1801 on the refusal of George III to assent to Catholic emancipation. In 1806 he formed the government of 'All the Talents' which, before its dissolution in 1807, abolished the slave trade. From 1809 to

1815 he acted along with Charles, 2nd Earl Grey, and generally supported George Canning. Peter Jupp, *Lord Grenville 1759-1834* (1985)

Gresham, Sir Thomas 1519–79
English financier and philanthropist

Born probably in London, the son of Sir Richard Gresham (c.1485–1549), he founded the Royal Exchange, and became Lord Mayor of London (1537). From Cambridge in 1543 he passed into the Mercers' Company, and in 1551 was employed as 'king's merchant' at Antwerp. In two years he paid off a heavy loan and restored the king's credit. As a Protestant he was dismissed by Queen Mary I, Tudor, but soon reinstated by Queen Elizabeth I, who made him ambassador to the Netherlands (1559–61). In 1569, on his advice, the state borrowed money from London merchants instead of from foreigners. He made the observation, known as 'Gresham's Law', that of two coins of equal legal exchange value, that of the lower intrinsic value would tend to drive the other out of use. Having lost his only son, Richard, in 1564, from 1566 to 1568 he devoted a portion of his great wealth to building an Exchange, in imitation of that of Antwerp. He made provision for founding Gresham College, London, and he left money for eight alms-houses.

Gresley, Sir (Herbert) Nigel 1876–1941
English locomotive engineer

Born in Edinburgh, he was the foremost British locomotive designer for 30 years from 1911, of such classic trains as the streamlined 'Silver Jubilee' and 'Coronation' in the mid-1930s. His A4 class Pacific 4-6-2 'Mallard' achieved a world record speed for a steam locomotive of 126mph (201.5kph) in July 1938 which has never been exceeded.

Grétry, André Ernest Modeste 1741–1813
French composer

Born in Liège, Belgium, he settled in Paris in 1767. He was the composer of over 40 comic operas, of which *Le Huron* (1768) and *Lucile* (1769) were the earliest, and among the bestknown are *Raoul* and *Richard Cœur-de-Lion* (1784, 'Richard the Lionheart'). He became inspector of the Paris Conservatoire and a member of the Institute. He published his memoires in 1796.

Gretzky, Wayne 1961–
Canadian ice-hockey player

Born in Brantford, Ontario, he played for the Edmonton Oilers (1978–88), then joined the Los Angeles Kings (1988–96) and signed with the New York Rangers in 1996 after a brief stint with the St Louis Blues. He set numerous records, including most goals scored in a season (92 in 1981–82) and most career points (he scored his 2,500th point in 1995 and continues to add to his total). Nine times named the National Hockey League's Most Valuable Player (1980–87, 1989), he is nicknamed the Great One and considered the greatest player in the history of the game. Ted Ferguson, *Superkid Wayne Gretzky 99* (1983)

Greuze, Jean Baptiste 1725–1805
French genre and portrait painter

Born in Tournus, near Mâcon, he painted Italian subjects after a visit to Italy (1755), but he is seen at his best in such studies of girls as *The Broken Pitcher* in the Louvre, Paris, and *Girl with Doves* in the Wallace Collection, London. He died in poverty.

Greville, Charles Cavendish Fulke 1794–1865
English diarist

He was educated at Christ Church, Oxford, and became private secretary to Earl Bathurst, and was clerk of the privy council (1821–59). His position gave him particular access for studying court and public life, which is reflected in his noted *The Greville Memoirs* (1875–87), and also in his *Letters* (1924) and *The Greville Diary* (1927).

Greville, Sir Fulke, 1st Baron Brooke 1554–1628
English poet and courtier

Born in Beauchamp Court, Warwickshire, he was educated at Shrewsbury and Jesus College, Cambridge. A friend of Sir **Philip Sidney** and a favourite of **Elizabeth I**, he held many important offices, including Secretary for Wales (1583–1628) and Chancellor of the Exchequer (1614–21). He was created baron in 1620. He wrote several didactic poems, over a hundred sonnets and two tragedies, including *The Tragedy of Mustapha* (1609), printed in 1633. His best-remembered work is his *Life of the Renowned Sir Philip Sidney* (published 1652) with its vivid pictures of contemporary figures. He was murdered by an old retainer who thought himself cut out of his master's will.
R A Rebholz, *The Life of Fulke Greville* (1971)

Gréville, Henry, *pseudonym of* Alice Durand, *née* Fleury 1842–1902
French novelist

Born in Paris, she accompanied her father in 1857 to St Petersburg, and wrote Russian society novels.

Grévy, François Paul Jules 1807–91
French politician

The vice-president of the Constituent Assembly of 1848, he opposed **Napoleon III**, and after the coup d'état retired from politics. In 1871 he was elected president of the National Assembly and in 1879 he became President of the Republic. Re-elected in 1885, he resigned in 1887 after a financial scandal involving his son-in-law.

Grew, Nehemiah 1641–1712
English botanist and physician

Born in Atherstone, Warwickshire, and educated at the universities of Cambridge and Leyden, he practised at the universities of Coventry and London, and was author of *Comparative Anatomy of the Stomach and Guts* (1681) and of the pioneering *Anatomy of Plants* (1682). In this work he used the microscope to elucidate plant structure and gave the first complete account of plant anatomy, and it remained the most significant and authoritative work in this field for more than 150 years. He discovered some of the crucial differences between plant root and stem tissue, described in detail the complex folding of unexpanded leaves in buds, and accepted the idea that the stamen is the male organ of the plant. As well as making enormous contributions to anatomy and physiology, his analytical studies presaged the development of phytochemistry.

Grey, Dame Beryl, *stage name of* Mrs Beryl Svenson 1927–
English ballerina

Born in London, she won a scholarship to Sadler's Wells Ballet School at the age of nine. Her first solo appearance at Sadler's Wells Theatre was in the part of Sabrina, in *Comus* (1941). The youngest Giselle ever at the age of 16, she was prima ballerina of the Sadler's Wells Ballet (1942–57), and also appeared with the Bolshoi Ballet in Russia (1957–58)—the first English ballerina to do so—and the Chinese Ballet in Peking (1964). She was artistic director (1968–79) of the London Festival Ballet, which became the English National Ballet in 1988, and became a DBE in 1988. Her publications include *My Favourite Ballet Stories* (1981). David Gillard, *Beryl Grey, an autobiography* (1977)

Grey, Charles, 2nd Earl 1764–1845
English statesman

He was born in Fallodon, Northumberland, and educated at Eton and King's College, Cambridge. He joined the Whig Opposition in parliament in 1786, and wasted little time in attacking the Government of **William Pitt**, the Younger, for its domestic and foreign policies and its union with Ireland in particular. On the Whigs' return to power in 1806, he became First Lord of the Admiralty, and as Foreign Secretary on the death of **Charles Fox**, piloted the abolition of the African slave trade. After succeeding his father to the earldom in 1807, he withdrew from doing battle in the Commons, but after the 1830 general election returned as Prime Minister of the new Whig Administration. He introduced his first Reform Bill a year later, and after its defeat and the dissolution of parliament, he returned even more resolved to secure its provisions. When the second bill was carried by the Commons but rejected by the Lords, there were violent demonstrations, and Grey piloted a third attempt that reached its second reading in the Lords but collapsed when Ministers resigned over its disenfranchisement clauses. After the Duke of **Wellington** failed to form a Government, Grey returned as premier and persuaded **William IV** to create a sufficient number of new peers to guarantee the legislation's adoption in the Upper House. His bill finally received royal assent in 1832, and Grey continued to lead the reformed parliament, extending his earlier antislavery measures to the colonies. However, a Cabinet split over reform of the Church of Ireland made Grey's position untenable, and he resigned in 1834.
G M Trevelyan, *Lord Grey of the Reform Bill* (1920)

Grey, Sir George 1799–1882
English politician

Born in Gibraltar, the nephew of Charles, 2nd Earl **Grey**, he graduated from Oriel College, Oxford, and relinquished the law after succeeding his father in 1828 in the baronetcy in 1828. MP for Devonport (1832–47) and Under-Secretary for the colonies (1834–35), he ably defended Lord **John Russell's** bill for the temporary suspension of the Lower Canadian constitution. In 1839 he became judge-advocate, in 1841 Chancellor of the Duchy of Lancaster, and in 1846 Home Secretary. During the Chartist disturbances he discharged his duties with much vigour and discrimination. He carried the Crown and Government Security Bill, the Alien Bill, and a measure for the further suspension in Ireland of the Habeas Corpus Act (1849). In 1854 he became Colonial Secretary, and in 1855, under Viscount **Palmerston**, took his old post of Home Secretary. From 1859 he was Chancellor of the Duchy of Lancaster, and Home Secretary again from 1861 to 1866.

Grey, Sir George 1812–98
British explorer and administrator

He was born in Lisbon, Portugal. He made two expeditions (1837, 1839) to the north-west of Western Australia, and was later appointed magistrate at King George Sound, where he produced a vocabulary of local Aboriginal dialects. In 1840 he was appointed Governor of South Australia. His stringent reform of the colony's finances resulted in economic success, but led to his transfer to New Zealand as Lieutenant-Governor in 1845. In 1854 he became Governor of Cape Colony and High Commissioner of South Africa, and in 1861 was sent back to New Zealand for a second term (1861–68) when he brought the Maori Wars to a close. He was a member of the New Zealand House of Representatives (1874–94) and premier (1877–79), before retiring to England in 1894.

Grey, Henry, 3rd Earl 1802–94
English politician

The son of Charles, 2nd Earl **Grey**, he entered parliament in 1826 as Lord Howick, became Under-Secretary for the colonies in his father's ministry, retired in 1833, but was subsequently Under-Secretary in the home department, and in 1835 Secretary for War. In 1841 he opposed Sir **Robert Peel's** policy, in 1845 succeeded to the peerage, in 1846 became Colonial Secretary, and in 1852 published his *Defence of Lord John Russell's Colonial Policy*. He was an opposer of the Crimean War, and condemned Disraeli's Eastern policy. In 1858 he issued his *Essay on Parliamentary Government as to Reform*, and then in 1867 his father's *Correspondence with William IV*.

Grey, Lady Jane 1537–54
Queen of England for nine days

Born in Bradgate, Leicestershire, she was the great-granddaughter of Henry VII and the eldest daughter of Henry Grey, Marquess of Dorset. Educated under the tutorship of John Aylmer (later Bishop of London), she proved an able pupil, especially proficient at languages. During the final illness of Edward VI, she was married against her will to Lord Guildford Dudley, fourth son of John Dudley, Duke of Northumberland, as part of the latter's scheme to make sure of a Protestant succession. Declared queen three days after Edward's death (9 July 1553), she was forced to abdicate nine days later in favour of Edward's sister, Mary I, Tudor, and imprisoned in the Tower of London. Following a rebellion in her favour under Sir Thomas Wyatt, the Younger, in which her father (by then Duke of Suffolk) also participated, she was beheaded with her husband. 📖 H W Chapman, *Lady Jane Grey* (1962)

Grey, Maria Georgina, *née* Shirreff 1816–1906
English pioneer of women's education

The sister of Emily Shirreff, she married her cousin William Thomas Grey in 1841. She helped to found the National Union for Promoting the Higher Education of Women (1871), which created the Girls' Public Day School Company, later Trust, in 1872 to establish 'good and cheap Day Schools for Girls of all classes above those attending the Public Elementary Schools', and eventually had some 38 schools which set new academic standards for girls' education. One of the first schools, Croydon, had a kindergarten and with her sister she revived interest in the work of the German educationist Friedrich Froebel and promoted the Froebel Society. The Women's Educational Union opened what was later called Maria Grey College in 1878 as a training college for teachers in higher grade girls' schools. She also published a novel and works on women's enfranchisement and education.

Grey, Zane 1875–1939
US novelist

Born in Zanesville, Ohio, he began his working life as a dentist, but after a trip out west in 1904 turned out 'westerns' with machine-like regularity, totalling 54 novels and an overall sale estimated at around 12 million copies. His best known, *Riders of the Purple Sage*, sold nearly two million copies. His hobby of big-game fishing off the coasts of Australia and New Zealand was utilized in such books as *Tales of Fishing* (1919). His success was due to the 'escapist' lure of his simple adventure plots and attractive, authentic settings. 📖 C Jackson, *Zane Grey* (1973); J Kerr, *Man of the West* (1957)

Griboyedov, Aleksandr Sergeyevich 1795–1829
Russian writer and diplomat

Born in Moscow, he wrote *Gore ot Uma* (1824, Eng trans *Wit Works Woe*, 1933), a comedy in rhymed iambics, which satirized the contemporary Moscow society so aptly that it provided household phrases for the Russian people. Involved in the Decembrist Revolt, he was nevertheless cleared and in 1828 became Russian ambassador to Persia (Iran). He was killed in an anti-Russian demonstration at the embassy in Teheran. 📖 V N Orlov, *Griboyedev* (1954); and other works by V N Orlov

Grieg, Edvard Hagerup 1843–1907
Norwegian composer

Born in Bergen of Scots descent, he studied at the Leipzig Conservatory, where he was influenced by Schumann's music. He made Copenhagen his main base between 1863 and 1867, and there was in close contact with Niels Gade, Hans Christian Andersen and the young Norwegian poet-composer Nordraak. With their encouragement, he evolved into a strongly national Norwegian composer with an intense awareness of his folk heritage. After some years teaching and conducting in Christiania (Oslo), the success of his incidental music for Ibsen's *Peer Gynt* (1876) on top of the award of a state pension in 1874 enabled him to settle near Bergen. Apart from his Piano Concerto in A minor, some orchestral suites, three violin sonatas and one quartet, his large-scale output was small, although he wrote many songs. In 1867 he married his cousin, Nina Hagerup, a well-known singer. 📖 Henry T Finck, *Grieg and his Music* (1929)

Grieg, (Johan) Nordahl Brun 1902–43
Norwegian poet and dramatist

Born in Bergen, he studied at Oslo and Oxford, and spent much of his youth travelling, as reflected in his early poetry volumes, such as *Rundt Kap det Gode Haab* (1922, 'Round the Cape of Good Hope') and *Norge i våre hjerter* (1925, 'Norway in our Hearts'). His novel, *Skibet gaar videre* (1924, 'The Ship Sails On'), about his experiences on a voyage to Australia as an ordinary seaman, was the model for Malcolm Lowry's *Ultramarine*. A committed anti-fascist, he wrote dramas about national freedom, as in *Vår ære og vår makt* (1935, 'Our Honour and Our Might') and *Nederlaget* (1937, 'Defeat') about the Paris Commune of 1871. During World War II he joined the Resistance, escaped to London, and broadcast his patriotic verses to Norway. His plane was shot down over Berlin in 1943. 📖 F J Hallund, *Nordahl Grieg. En dikter og hans tid* (1962)

Grien, Hans See Baldung, Hans

Grierson, John 1898–1972
Scottish documentary film producer

Born in Kilmadock, Stirlingshire, he studied communications in the USA and then joined (1928) the Empire Marketing Board, with whom he made his reputation with *Drifters* (1929), a film about herring fishermen. He headed the British General Post Office from 1933, inspiring hundreds of short films (including *Night Mail*, with a verse commentary by W H Auden). During World War II he set up the National Film Board of Canada, and was then appointed director of mass communications for UNESCO (1946–48) and film controller at the Central Office of Information in London (1948–50). Known as the 'father of British documentary', he was also the presenter of an anthology of international documentary films on television (1957–65).

Griesbach, Johann Jakob 1745–1812
German New Testament scholar

Born in Butzbach, he studied theology at Tübingen, Halle and Leipzig. He lectured at Halle, and in 1775 became a professor at Jena and devoted himself to critical revision of the New Testament text, reclassifying the MSS into three recensions, Alexandrian, Western and Byzantine. See his *Commentarius Criticus* (1811, 'Critical Commentary'), in which he coined the term 'synoptic' for the first three Gospels.

Griffin, Bernard 1899–1956
English prelate

Born in Birmingham, he was educated at the English and Beda colleges, Rome, then became Archbishop of Westminster in 1943, and cardinal in 1946. He toured postwar Europe and the USA and in 1950 was papal legate for the centenary celebrations of the reconstitution of the English hierarchy.

Griffin, Donald Redfield 1915–
US zoologist
Born in Southampton, New York, and educated at Harvard, he demonstrated for the first time that the ultrasound produced by bats is used in echolocation, and later showed that it is also used in hunting. During World War II he studied the effects of background noise on radio communication, and investigated night vision using infrared light. Continuing his pre-war studies on birds' homing abilities, he showed in 1968, by the use of radar, that migrating birds are able to maintain their orientation while flying blind in clouds. He launched the study of 'cognitive ethology' in 1981, an investigation of the way in which non-humans think and feel. His published works include *Animal Minds* (1992).

Griffin, Gerald 1803–40
Irish novelist
Born in Limerick, County Limerick, he wrote for local journals and went to London in 1823 to make a career in literature. He failed as a dramatist, but was more successful with collections of short stories of southern Irish life such as Holland Tide (1826) and *Tales of the Munster Festivals* (1827). His novel, *The Collegians*, on which Dion Boucicault's drama *Colleen Bawn* is founded, was published anonymously in 1829. In 1838 he burned his manuscripts and entered a monastery. ▢ *The Dead March Past* (1940)

Griffin, Marion See Mahony, Marion Lucy

Griffin, Walter Burley 1876–1937
US architect and town planner
Born in Maywood, Illinois, he graduated from Illinois State University and was for some years an associate of Frank Lloyd Wright before establishing his own practice in 1905. In 1910 he married a colleague, Marion Mahony. In 1912 he won an international competition for the design of the new federal capital of Australia, Canberra, which was to be built on a virgin site in the south of New South Wales. His original design was set aside but Griffin was invited to Melbourne in 1913 and became director of design and construction for the new city. He remained as director until late 1920 but refused to serve on the committee which superseded him, although his last grandiose and geometric plan was adopted officially in 1925. He then went into private practice in Australia, designing a number of notable buildings and the eccentric Castlecrag estate in north Sydney. He developed something of a speciality in municipal incinerators, designing 12 such buildings, one of which is now preserved. In 1935 he went to India following an invitation to design a library for Lucknow University

Griffith, Arthur 1872–1922
Irish nationalist politician
Born in Dublin, he was a compositor for a time, and joined the Gaelic League. He lived for a time in South Africa where he worked as a gold-miner and as a journalist. Back in Ireland he edited a new weekly paper, *The United Irishman*. In 1905 he founded a new political party, Sinn Féin ('We Ourselves'), and a paper of that name in 1906. A supporter of the Irish Volunteers, he took no part in the Easter Rising of 1916, but was imprisoned as a nationalist. He became vice-president in Éamon De Valera's provisional government (1919). During the Anglo-Irish War (1919–21) he was imprisoned again (1920–21), but signed the Anglo-Irish Treaty of 1921 that brought about the Irish Free State. He was a moderate president of Dáil Éireann (1922), but died suddenly, as further fighting broke out between those who opposed and those who supported the 1921 Treaty. ▢ Padraic Colum, *Arthur Griffith* (1959, US *Ourselves Alone!*)

Griffith, D(avid Lewelyn) W(ark) 1875–1948
US pioneer film director
Born in Floydsfork, Kentucky, he began as an actor and short-story writer, before turning to the film industry, learning his trade in hundreds of silent films. Using technical innovations such as close-ups, fade-outs, flashbacks and moving cameras, he did much to create the conventions of modern cinematic art. His first great film, *The Birth of a Nation* (1915), was both hailed as a masterpiece for its subtlety and dramatic force and bitterly criticized by African-American groups appalled by its racism. Subsequent films include his epic *Intolerance* (1916) and his war film *Hearts of the World* (1918), which incorporated battle scenes actually filmed at the front. He discovered many stars, including Lillian Gish, who appeared in his films *Broken Blossoms* (1919) and *Orphans of the Storm* (1922). ▢ Robert M Henderson, *D W Griffith: His Life and Work* (1972)

Griffith, Nanci 1954–
US folk and country music singer and songwriter
She was born near Austin, Texas, into a musical family, and began to perform while still at school. She recorded her first album in 1978, and began to attract attention both for her winsome vocal style, which encompasses both folk and country, and her sophisticated, acutely observed songs. A string of increasingly successful records followed, and she formed her backing band, The Blue Moon Orchestra, in 1986. She has built a large audience for her work in both the USA and Europe, and is now one of the major stars of the genre, as well as making inroads into the rock and pop audience. She recorded an album of songs by her favourite songwriters, *Other Voices, Other Rooms*, in 1993, followed by the more introspective and personal material on *Flyer* (1994).

Griffith, Sir Richard John 1784–1878
Irish soldier, geologist and engineer
Born in Dublin, he joined the Royal Irish Regiment in 1800, but he resigned shortly afterwards and studied chemistry, mining and geology in London and Edinburgh. He returned to Ireland in 1808, surveyed the coalfields of Leinster and examined the Irish bogs for a government commission. As commissioner of valuations after the Irish Valuation Act of 1827, he created 'Griffith's valuations' for country rate assessments. He published the first complete geological map of Ireland in 1838, with a major revision in 1855, and made major contributions to the knowledge of its strata. He was knighted in 1858.

Griffith, Samuel Walker 1845–1920
Australian judge
Born in Merthyr Tydfil, Glamorgan, Wales, he emigrated to Australia in 1854, and studied at Sydney University. From 1867 he practised law in Queensland, and became Prime Minister of that state three times. He was an active proponent of federation, and as chairman of the Constitutional Committee of the National Australian Convention in 1891, had a major role in drafting what became in 1900 the Australian Commonwealth Constitution. Chief Justice of Queensland from 1893, he was first Chief Justice of the High Court of Australia (1900–19). In this position he had considerable responsibility for the Court's assumption of authority to rule on the legislative validity of Commonwealth and state legislation. His judgements in non-constitutional cases were also highly regarded.

Griffith-Joyner, Florence, *known as* Flo-Jo 1959–98
US track and field sprinter
Born in Los Angeles, California, she excelled at athletics in high school and college, and won the National Collegiate Athletic Association 200-metre title in 1982. Two years later she won an Olympic silver medal in the 200 metres. At the 1988 Olympics, she won three gold

medals: for the 100 metres and 200 metres—setting world records of 10.54 seconds for the former and 21.34 seconds for the latter—and for the 4 × 400 metre relay. That year her awards included the 1988 Sullivan award for the top amateur athlete in the USA and the 1988 Associated Press Female Athlete of the Year award. She died of an apparent heart attack aged 38.

Griffiths, James 1890–1975
Welsh miners' leader and politician
Born in Bettws, Ammanford, Carmarthenshire, he became a leading official in the miners' union in South Wales, and was elected Labour MP for Llanelli (1936–70). In the Labour governments of 1945 to 1951, he was Minister of National Insurance and Secretary of State for the Colonies. A strong believer in a measure of devolution for Wales, he argued for a separate Welsh Office, and became the first Secretary of State for Wales (1964–66). He was a moderating influence in Labour Party politics during the tensions of the Gaitskell–Bevan disputes in the 1950s.

Griffiths, Trevor 1935–
English dramatist
He was born in Manchester, and his first plays, *The Wages of Thin* (1969) and *Occupations* (1970), were staged there. These were followed in 1973 by *The Party*, at the National Theatre, London. Set in May 1968, the play revolves around a discussion of left-wing politics, with Laurence Olivier, in his last stage role, playing an eloquent Glaswegian Trotskyist. *Comedians* (1975) is the story of a group of young apprentice comedians learning their craft under the guidance of an ageing comic. Other plays include *Real Dreams* (1986), a typically angry political piece, *The Gulf Between Us* (1992), which tackles the issues of the Gulf War in the style of a dream play, *Hope in the Year Two* (1994) and *Thatcher's Children* (1994).

Grignard, (François Auguste) Victor 1871–1935
French chemist and Nobel Prize winner
Born in Cherbourg, he joined the chemistry department in Lyons, where he became 'Chef de travaux pratiques' (1898) and began his work on the use of organomagnesium compounds in organic synthesis. Since then such compounds (Grignard reagents) have proved to be among the most useful and versatile reagents available for the synthesis of complex molecules, giving many different types of molecules under mild conditions. He received the Nobel Prize for chemistry in 1912 for this work. During World War I he worked on war gases and in 1919 he was appointed to the chair in Lyons, where he remained until his retirement.

Grigorovich, Yuri Nikolayevich 1927–
Soviet dancer, artistic director, teacher and choreographer
Born in Leningrad (now St Petersburg), he trained at the Leningrad Choreographic School before joining the Kirov Ballet as a soloist in 1946. His first major ballet, *The Stone Flower* (1957), marked a new stage for Soviet choreography, which he followed with *Legend of Love* (1961). In 1964 he switched allegiance from the Kirov, where he was ballet master, to become chief choreographer and artistic director of the Bolshoi Ballet. His idea of a 'total theatre' for ballet means the dancing springs more from the music and is freer from mime than was previously the case in Russia. Acting as his own librettist, he has brought an elegance to the Bolshoi's celebrated athletic style in ballets like *Spartacus* (1968), for which he was awarded the Lenin prize in 1970, and *Ivan the Terrible* (1975). He has also staged new versions of the classics, such as *Swan Lake* (1969) and *Romeo and Juliet* (1978). Made a People's Artist of the USSR in 1973, he is married to Bolshoi dancer Natalia Bessmertnova. His resignation from the Bolshoi in 1995 prompted a strike by the dancers, led by Bessmertnova,

which caused a performance to be cancelled for the first time in the company's 219-year history. The ringleaders were subsequently fined and sacked.

Grigson, Geoffrey Edward Harvey 1905–85
English poet, critic and editor
He was born in Pelynt, Cornwall, and was the founder of the influential magazine *New Verse* (1933–39). He published several volumes of precisely observed and tersely expressed verse, gathered in *Collected Poems, 1924–62* (1963). A later *Collected Poems* included his subsequent work of 1963 to 1982, and was followed by *Montaigne's Tree* (1984). As a literary critic he was often outspoken. He was married to the cookery writer Jane Grigson. 📖 *The Crest on the Silver* (1950)

Grigson, (Heather Mabel) Jane 1928–90
English cookery writer
After graduating from Newnham College, Cambridge, she worked as an editorial assistant (1953–55) and as a translator from Italian (1956–67) before writing her first book, *Charcuterie and French Pork Cookery* (1967), which acknowledged Elizabeth David's influence on her work. She became cookery correspondent for the *Observer* magazine and continued to write books, much influenced by her country lifestyle, including the three now regarded as cookery classics: *English Food* (1974), *Jane Grigson's Vegetable Book* (1978) and *Jane Grigson's Fruit Book* (1982). Her husband was the poet Geoffrey Grigson.

Grillo, Adelaide del See Ristori, Adelaide

Grillparzer, Franz 1791–1872
Austrian dramatic poet
Born in Vienna, he was in the imperial Civil Service from 1813 to 1856. He first attracted notice in 1817 with a tragedy, *Die Ahnfrau* ('The Ancestress'), followed by *Sappho* (1818, Eng trans 1820), *Das goldene Vlies* (1820, Eng trans *Medea*, 1879), *Des Meeres und der Liebe Wellen* (1831, Eng trans *Hero and Leander*, 1938), *Der Traum ein Leben* (1834, Eng trans *A Dream is Life*, 1946), and others. He wrote lyric poetry and one notable prose novel entitled *Der arme Spielmann* (1848, 'The Poor Musician'), the only one of his works set in the Vienna of his day. 📖 J Nadler, *Franz Grillparzer* (1952)

Grimald, Nicholas 1519–62
English poet and playwright
Born of Genoese ancestry in Huntingdonshire, he went to Christ's College, Cambridge, and became Nicholas Ridley's chaplain, but recanted under Mary I, Tudor. He contributed 40 poems to Richard Tottel's *Songes and Sonettes* (1557), known as *Tottel's Miscellany*, and translated Virgil and Cicero. He also wrote two Latin verse tragedies on religious subjects. 📖 L R Merrill, *The Life and Poems of Nicholas Grimald* (1925)

Grimaldi, Francesco Maria 1618–63
Italian physicist
Born in Bologna, he joined the Society of Jesus (Jesuits) at the age of 14, and was educated at his Order's houses at Parma, Ferrar and Bologna, where he became Professor of Mathematics (1648). At this time the Jesuits were notable teachers of the new science. Among many other contributions, he verified Galileo's laws of falling bodies, produced a detailed lunar map, and more notably, discovered diffraction of light, and researched into interference and prismatic dispersion. He was one of the first to postulate a wave theory of light.

Grimaldi, Joseph 1779–1837
English comic actor, singer and acrobat
Born in London, he first appeared at Sadler's Wells, London, in 1781 as an infant dancer. He appeared as the pantomime clown ('Joey') there and at Drury Lane, and

from 1806 to 1823 was engaged at Covent Garden. Many of his innovations became the character's distinctive characteristics. His memoirs were edited by Dickens. ⌧ Richard Findlater, *Grimaldi, King of Clowns* (1955)

Grimbald, St c.820–903
Flemish monk
He was prior of a Flemish monastery near St Omer. Alfred the Great invited him to England in c.893. He became abbot of the New Minster in Winchester. His feast day is 8 July.

Grimké, Angelina Emily 1805–79
US feminist and social reformer
Born in Charleston, South Carolina, she joined her sister Sarah Grimké in 1829 in Philadelphia, where she vigorously appealed to the women of the USA to support their fight against slavery in *Appeal to the Christian Women of the South* (1836) and *Appeal to Women of the Nominally Free States* (1837). In the wake of Angelina having a letter published in the anti-slavery newspaper *The Liberator* (1835), they became public figures, and Angelina went on a speaking tour. In 1838 she married the abolitionist Theodore Weld and gave up public life. With Sarah she continued, however, to be committed to reform. Their most significant work was *American Slavery as it is: Testimony of a Thousand Witnesses* (1838). ⌧ Gerda Lerner, *The Grimké Sisters from South Carolina* (1967)

Grimké, Sarah Moore 1792–1873
US feminist and social reformer
Born in Charleston, South Carolina, the daughter of a slave-owning judge, she deplored slavery. Moving to Philadelphia in 1821, she became a Quaker, and was joined by her sister Angelina Grimké in 1829. Together they campaigned for the abolition of slavery, moving to New York City, where they lectured for the American Anti-Slavery Society (the first women to do so), and broadened their concern to include women's emancipation. Sarah's works include *Epistle to the Clergy of the Southern States* (1836), aimed at changing their views on slavery, and *The Condition of Women* (1838). ⌧ Gerda Lerner, *The Grimké Sisters from South Carolina* (1967)

Grimm, Friedrich Melchior Grimm, Baron von 1723–1807
German critic and journalist
Born in Ratisbon, and educated at Leipzig, he accompanied a nobleman to Paris, and became reader to the crown prince of Saxe-Gotha. He became acquainted with Jean Jacques Rousseau in 1749, and through him with Denis Diderot and Louise Florence d'Épinay. Through the Encyclopédistes he became secretary to the Duke of Orléans, and began to write for several German princes a series of fortnightly private newsletters on Parisian life (1757–73), collected as *Correspondance Littéraire* (1812). In 1776 he was made a baron by the Duke of Gotha, and appointed minister plenipotentiary at the French court. At the Revolution he withdrew to Gotha, and afterwards to the court of Catherine II, the Great, from where he was sent in 1795 as Russian minister to Hamburg.

Grimm, Jacob Ludwig Carl 1785–1863 and Wilhelm Carl 1786–1859
German folklorists and philologists
Born in Hanau, Hesse-Kassel, they were brothers who both studied at Marburg. In 1808 Jacob became librarian to Jérôme Bonaparte, King of Westphalia, and published a work on the Meistersingers (1811). In 1812 the brothers published the first volume of the famous *Kinder und Hausmärchen* (*Grimm's FairyTales*, first translated as *German Popular Stories*, 1823). This work formed a foundation for the science of comparative folklore. The second volume followed in 1815, the third in 1822. In 1829 the two moved to Göttingen, where Jacob became a professor and

librarian, and Wilhelm under-librarian (professor 1835). They were among the seven professors dismissed in 1837 for protesting against taking the oath of allegiance to the King of Hanover. In 1841 the brothers received professorships in Berlin, where they began to compile the monumental *Deutsches Wörterbuch* (1854–1961, 'German Dictionary'). As a philologist, Jacob Grimm published *Deutsche Grammatik* (1819, 'German Grammar'), perhaps the greatest philological work of the age, and formulated 'Grimm's Law' of consonant sound changes, an elaboration of earlier findings by Johan Ihre and Rasmus Rask, but an important contribution to the subject. Wilhelm's chief independent work was *Die deutsche Heldensage* (1829, 'The German Heroic Myth'). ⌧ H Gerstner, *Die Brüder Grimm* (1974)

Grimmelshausen, Hans Jacob Christoffel von c.1622–1676
German novelist
Born in Gelnhausen, Hesse-Kassel, he served on the Imperial side in the Thirty Years War (1618–48), then led a wandering life, but ultimately settled down in Renchen near Kehl, where he became a senior civil servant of the town. In later life he produced a series of remarkable novels, the best of which are on the model of the Spanish picaresque romances. The sufferings of the German peasantry at the hands of lawless troopers who overran the country have seldom been more powerfully pictured than in his *Der Abenteuerliche Simplicissimus Teutsch und Continuatio* (1669, Eng trans *Simplicissimus the Vagabond*, 1924). It was followed by *Trutz Simplex* (1669, Eng trans *Mother Courage*, 1965), *Der seltzame Springinsfeld* (1670, Eng trans *The Singular Life Story of the Heedless Hopalong*, 1981), *Das wunderbarliche Vögelnest* (1672, 'The Amazing Bird's Nest'), and others. ⌧ K Negus, *Grimmelshausen* (1974)

Grimond, Jo(seph) Grimond, Baron 1913–93
Scottish Liberal politician
Born in St Andrews and educated at Eton and Balliol College, Oxford, he was called to the Bar in 1937, and served during World War II with the Fife and Forfar Yeomanry. In 1945 he contested the Orkney and Shetland seat, which he ultimately won in 1950. From 1956 to 1967 he was leader of the Liberal Party, during which time Liberal representation in parliament was doubled. His aim of making the Liberal Party the real radical alternative to Conservatism was only partially realized in the creation of the Social Democratic Party, and later the (Social and) Liberal Democrats. He served again as party leader for a short period following the resignation of Jeremy Thorpe (1976). He retired from parliament in 1983, when he was made a life peer. He published his *A Personal Manifesto* the same year.

Grimthorpe, Edmund Beckett Denison, 1st Baron 1816–1905
English lawyer, and authority on architecture and horology
Born in Carlton Hall, near Newark, Nottinghamshire, he was educated at Doncaster, Eton, and Trinity College, Cambridge. He made a fortune at the Bar, then turned his attention to church architecture and clock-making. He designed a new casement for Big Ben in the Palace of Westminster, London, and restored St Albans Abbey.

Gringoire or Gringore, Pierre c.1475–1538
French poet and dramatist
Born in Caen, he was active in the production of pantomime farces, and is one of the creators of the French political comedy. He attacked the enemies of Louis XII and thus found cover for his comments on the vices of the nobility, the clergy and even the pope himself. In later life he was a herald to the Duke of Lorraine, and wrote religious poetry. His works include the famous *Mystère de*

Monseigneur Saint Loys (c.1524). Gringoire figures in **Victor Hugo**'s *Notre Dame*, and in a play by **Théodore de Banville**.
📖 E Bardel, *Gringoire* (1925)

Grinnell, Henry 1799–1874
US shipping merchant
Born in New Bedford, Massachusetts, he financed an Arctic expedition to search for Sir **John Franklin** in 1850, and another in (1853–55) under **Elisha Kent Kane**. Grinnell Land was named after him.

Gris, Juan, *pseudonym of* José Victoriano González 1887–1927
Spanish painter
Born in Madrid, he went in 1906 to Paris, where he associated with **Picasso** and **Matisse** and became an exponent of synthetic Cubism. He exhibited with the Cubists in the Section d'Or exhibition in Paris (1912), and in 1920 at the Salon des Indépendants. He settled at Boulogne and in 1923 designed the décor for three productions by **Sergei Diaghilev**. He also worked as a book illustrator. In most of his paintings the composition of the picture dictates the deliberate distortion and rhythmic rearrangement of the subjects, as in *Still Life with Dice* (1922) in the Musée d'Art Moderne, Paris.

Grisebach, August Heinrich Rudolph 1814–79
German botanist and plant geographer
Born in Hanover and educated there and at Ifeld University, he went to Göttingen University in 1832, but completed his studies at Berlin University. In 1838 he published his vast work, *Genera et Species Gentianearum*. In 1839 he set off on an important expedition to the Balkan Peninsula and Bithynia, then largely unexplored botanically. This journey laid the foundation for his phytogeographical work which culminated in *Vegetation der Erde* (1872). Later he studied Caribbean and South American botany and published another of his most important works, *Flora of the British West Indian Islands* (7 parts, 1859–64).

Grishin, Viktor Vasilevich 1914–
Soviet politician
He was a supporter of **Leonid Brezhnev**, whom he expected to succeed. A genuine railwayman, he only took up party work during World War II. From 1956 to 1967 he was head of the Soviet trade unions and managed to keep them firmly in line. In 1967 he became First Secretary of the Moscow party and succeeded in making it toe the line for 18 years. In 1985 **Mikhail Gorbachev** replaced him almost immediately and put **Boris Yeltsin** in his place.

Grisi, Carlotta 1819–99
Italian ballerina
Born in Visinada in the Austrian Empire (now in Croatia), she studied under **Jules Perrot**, who became her husband. She was the original Giselle (1841) in Paris, and was a cousin of the Italian sopranos **Giuditta** and **Giulia Grisi**.

Grisi, Giuditta 1805–40
Italian mezzo-soprano
Born in Milan, she was the sister of **Giulia Grisi** whom she taught. She was the original Romeo in **Vincenzo Bellini**'s *I Capuleti ed i Montecchi* (1830), but retired on marrying Count Barni in 1833.

Grisi, Giulia 1811–69
Italian soprano
Born in Milan, she was renowned for her roles in **Vincenzo Bellini**'s operas, especially *I Puritani* ('The Puritans'), which was written for her, and *Norma*. She was the sister of **Giuditta Grisi**, who taught her.

Grivas, Georgeios Theodoros 1898–1974
Greek-Cypriot nationalist leader
Born in Trikomo, Cyprus, he commanded a Greek Army division in the Albanian campaign of 1940–41 and was leader of a secret organization called 'X' (Khi) during the German occupation of Greece. In 1945 he headed an extreme nationalist movement against the Communists. Some nine years later he became head of the underground campaign against British rule in Cyprus. As founder and leader of EOKA (Ethnikí Orgánosis Kipriakoú Agónos, or the National Organization of Cypriot Struggle), he began to call himself 'Digenes Akritas' after a legendary Greek hero. His secret diaries were found in 1956 when he had a price of £10,000 on his head. After the Cyprus settlement (February 1959), Grivas left Cyprus and, acclaimed a national hero by the Greeks, was promoted general in the Greek army. In 1964 he returned to Cyprus until 1967, when he was recalled to Athens. He returned secretly to Cyprus in 1971 and directed a terrorist campaign for *enosis* (union with Greece) until his death. He was given a hero's funeral.

Grobbelaar, Bruce 1957–
Zimbabwean footballer
Born in Bulawayo of a South African father, he still holds the Rhodesian under-16 baseball record for pitching strikeouts. After two years in the Rhodesian army, he played for the Vancouver Whitecaps and then made 24 appearances for Crewe Alexander. Between 1981 and 1994 he made 500 appearances for Liverpool FC, whose many honours include being six times League champions, three times FA Cup winners, and once European Cup winners. In 1994 he was given a free transfer on a two-year contract to Southampton and in 1996 he began playing for Plymouth Argyle.

Grock, *stage name of* Adrien Wettach 1880–1959
Swiss clown
Born in Reconvilier, he became world-famous for his virtuosity in both circus and theatre. He wrote several books, including *Ich lebe gern* (1930) and *Grock, King of Clowns* (1956, trans Creighton).

Grocyn, William c.1446–1519
English scholar and humanist
Born in Colerne, Wiltshire, he was educated at Winchester, and went to New College, Oxford, in 1465. He studied in Italy (1488–91), acquiring his knowledge of Greek from the Greek exile and scholar Demetrios Chalkondylas (1424–1511), and then settled again in Oxford, where he was the first to teach Greek publicly and where Sir **Thomas More** was his pupil. **Erasmus** lived at Oxford in Grocyn's house, and spoke of him as his 'patronus et praeceptor'. In 1506 he became Master of All Hallows' College near Maidstone.

Groen van Prinsterer, Guilaumme 1801–76
Dutch historian and politician
Born in Voorburg, he became secretary to the king's Cabinet and archivist to the Dutch royal family, and edited the massive *Archives de la maison d'Orange-Nassau* (1835–61). In 1847 he published a seminal critique of the French Revolution, *Ongeloof en Revolutie* ('Unbelief and Revolution'); it became the classic statement of a renascent Calvinist political movement in the Netherlands. He served as a member of the Second Chamber of Government (1849–57, 1862–66). His spiritual and intellectual political heir was **Abraham Kuyper**.

Grofé, Ferde 1892–1972
US composer
Born in New York City, he is known for a number of orchestral suites—all named after places in the USA—which are descriptive of the US scene, such as the *Grand Canyon Suite* (1931). He worked as an arranger for **Paul Whiteman**'s 'symphonic jazz' band, and orchestrated

Rhapsody in Blue for **George Gershwin** (1924). The modern-style orchestra based upon saxophones rather than strings is attributed to Grofé.

Grolier, Jean Vicomte d'Aguisy 1479–1565
French bibliophile
He was born in Lyons. He was attached to the court of **Francis I**, went to Italy as intendant-general of the army, was long employed in diplomacy at Milan and Rome, and then became Treasurer General of France (1547). He built up a magnificent library of 3,000 volumes, dispersed in 1675. He acquired choice copies of the best works, and had them magnificently bound, with the inscription *Io. Grolierii et Amicorum* ('for Grolier and his friends'). About 350 of his books have come to light.

Gromyko, Andrei Andreyevich 1909–89
Soviet politician and diplomat
Born near Minsk into a peasant family, he studied agriculture and economics and became a research scientist at the Soviet Academy of Sciences. In 1939 he joined the staff of the Soviet embassy in Washington DC, becoming ambassador in 1943 and attending the famous 'big three' conferences at Teheran, Yalta and Potsdam. In 1946 he was elected a Deputy of the Supreme Soviet, and in the same year became Deputy Foreign Minister and was made permanent delegate to the UN Security Council, achieving an unenviable reputation through his use of the power of veto no fewer than 25 times. For a few months (1952–53) he was ambassador to the United Kingdom. He succeeded Dmitri Shepilov (1905–) as Foreign Minister in 1957, holding this post until 1985, and being responsible for conducting Soviet relations with the West during the Cold War, showing no relaxation of the austere and humourless demeanour for which he had become notorious in diplomatic circles. During the 1970s, however, he adapted to the new policy of détente. **Mikhail Gorbachev** promoted him to the largely ceremonial and mainly domestic post of President in 1985, but he retired from office in 1988, when he was replaced in a much stronger presidency by Gorbachev himself. 📖 *Memories* (1989)

Groot, Huig de See Grotius, Hugo

Gropius, Walter Adolph 1883–1969
US architect
Born in Berlin, Germany, he studied in Munich and worked in the office of **Peter Behrens** in Berlin. After World War I he was appointed director of the Grand Ducal group of schools in art in Weimar, which was amalgamated and reorganized to form the Bauhaus, which aimed at a new functional interpretation of the applied arts, utilizing glass, metals and textiles. His revolutionary methods and bold use of unusual building materials were condemned as 'architectural socialism' in Weimar, and the Bauhaus was transferred (in 1925) to Dessau, housed in a building which Gropius had designed for it. When the Nazis came to power the Bauhaus became a Nazi training school and Gropius went (1934–37) to London, where he worked on factory designs and housing estates for the Home Counties, including a revolutionary adjunct to Christ Church, Oxford, which was never built. In 1937 he emigrated to the USA, where he became Professor of Architecture at Harvard (1938–52), and designed the Harvard Graduate Center (1949) and the American Embassy in Athens (1960). His other major constructions include the Fagus shoe factory at Alfeld (1911), a model factory and office for the Cologne Exhibition (1914), and large housing estates in Germany. He also designed Adler car bodies (1929–33). 📖 James Marston Fitch, *Walter Gropius* (1960)

Gros, Antoine Jean, Baron 1771–1835
French historical painter
Born in Paris, he studied under **Jaques Louis David**, and later travelled with **Napoleon I**'s armies and acquired celebrity by his depictions of battles (1797–1811). His *Charles V and Francis I* (1812), *Departure of Louis XVIII for Ghent* (1815) and *Embarkation of the Duchess of Angoulême* (1815) combine Classicism and Romanticism. He subsequently attempted a return to Classicism, but found his work ignored and drowned himself in the Seine.

Gross, Hans 1847–1915
Austrian criminologist and lawyer
He was born in Graz, and became a pioneer in the field of scientific detection of crime. From 1905 he was Professor of Criminal Law at Graz, where he established the first criminal museum. His *Handbuch für Untersuchungsrichter* (1893, Eng trans 1907) is a standard work.

Gross, Michael, *also called* the Albatross 1964–
German swimmer
Born in Frankfurt, a butterfly and freestyle swimmer, he won a record 13 gold medals between 1981 and 1987 for West Germany at the European championships. He was the world 200 metres freestyle and 200 metres butterfly champion in 1982 and 1986, and has won three Olympic gold medals: the 100 metres butterfly and 200 metres freestyle in 1984, and the 200 metres butterfly in 1988.

Grosseteste, Robert c.1175–1253
English prelate
Born in Stradbroke, Suffolk, he was educated at Lincoln, Oxford and Paris. After teaching for a number of years in Oxford, he became Bishop of Lincoln in 1235. He undertook the reformation of abuses, including the granting, by Pope **Innocent IV**, of English benefices to priests who used the income of their offices, but seldom appeared in their parishes. Grosseteste's opposition to this earned him a temporary suspension from his bishopric and a continual threat of excommunication. In the last year of his life he refused the pope's request to promote his nephew, an Italian, to a canonry. The pope is said to have excommunicated him, but his clergy continued to work with him regardless. His catalogue of works included 'treatises on sound, motion, heat, colour, form, angles, atmospheric pressure, poison, the rainbow, comets, light, the astrolabe, necromancy and witchcraft'.

Grossi, Tommaso 1791–1853
Italian poet
Born in Bellano on Lake Como, he studied law at Padua and practised in Milan. His first poem, *La Prineide* (1814, 'The Prineide'), was a battle poem in the Milanese dialect. There followed several historical romances, the most notable of which is *Marco Visconti* (1834, Eng trans 1836), and the epic poem for which he is best known, *I Lombardi alla prima crociata* (1826, 'The Lombards on their First Crusade'), which **Verdi** used for his opera *I Lombardi*. 📖 E Flori, *Scorci e figure del romanticismo* (1938)

Grossmith, George 1847–1912
English humorist, actor and writer
He was born in London and for several years was a police court reporter for The Times. In 1870 he became a singer and entertainer, creating several leading roles in the premières of operettas by **Gilbert** and **Sullivan**. He published his *Reminiscences of a Clown* in 1888, and *Piano and I* in 1910. He is best remembered, though, for his collaboration with his brother **Weedon Grossmith** on *The Diary of a Nobody*, serialized first in *Punch* and published in book form in 1892. An imaginary journal of domestic life in Holloway, London, it records the doings of the amiable, pompous city clerk Mr Pooter, striving to better himself culturally and socially but who, unwittingly, becomes the butt of numerous jokes he fails to understand. 📖 T Joseph, *George Grossmith* (1982)

Grosz, George 1893–1959
US artist

Born in Berlin, Germany, he was associated with the Berlin Dadaists in 1917 and 1918. While in Germany he produced a series of bitter, ironic drawings attacking German militarism and the middle classes. He fled to the USA in 1932 (becoming naturalized in 1938) and went on to produce many oil paintings of a symbolic nature. He returned to Berlin in 1959, where he died. 📖 Beth Lewis, *George Grosz: Art and Politics in the Weimar Republic* (1971)

Grósz, Károly 1930–96
Hungarian politician

Born in Miskolc, the son of a steel worker, he began his career as a printer and then a newspaper editor. He joined the ruling Hungarian Socialist Workers' Party (HSWP) in 1945 and moved to Budapest in 1961 to work in the agit-prop department, becoming its deputy head in 1968 and its head in 1974. Grosz served as Budapest party chief (1984–87) and was inducted into the HSWP politburo in 1985. He became Prime Minister in 1987 and succeeded János Kádár as HSWP leader in 1988, giving up his position as Prime Minister six months later. Following the lead given by Mikhail Gorbachev in Moscow, he became a committed and frank-speaking reformer in both the economic and political spheres, seeking to establish in Hungary a new system of 'socialist pluralism'. However when, in 1989, the HSWP reconstituted itself as the new Hungarian Socialist Party (HSP), he was replaced as party leader by Rezso Nyers, a radical social democrat.

Grote, George 1794–1871
English historian and politician

He was born in Clay Hill, Beckenham, Kent, and educated at Charterhouse. In 1810 he became a clerk in the bank (which was founded in 1766 by his grandfather) in Threadneedle Street, of which he became governor (1830–43). From 1832 to 1841 he was MP for the City of London. During his first session he brought forward a motion for the adoption of the ballot; it was lost, but Grote continued to advocate the measure until he retired from parliamentary life and banking to devote himself to literature, mainly his *History of Greece* (1846–1856). In 1865 he finished *Plato and the other Companions of Socrates*, but his *Aristotle* was unfinished. He also wrote *Fragments on Ethical Subjects* (1876). He was buried in Westminster Abbey, London.

Grotell, Maija 1899–1973
Finnish potter

Born in Helsinki, Finland, she studied under Alfred William Finch and in 1927 she moved to the USA, where she worked for a ceramics studio in New York and then taught at Rutgers University in New Jersey (1936–38). She won prizes in Barcelona and Paris for her early Art Deco work. She became head of the ceramics department of the Cranbrook Academy of Art, Michigan, in 1938, continuing to teach there until 1966, and became noted for rough-textured glazes, including a cratered glaze achieved by using a stoneware glaze over Albany Slip. She came to be regarded as the 'mother of American ceramics', and her work is in many private and public collections in the USA.

Groth, Klaus 1819–99
German poet

Born in Heide, Holstein, he became a schoolteacher, and in 1866 Professor of German Language and Literature at Kiel. His masterpiece, *Quickborn* (1852), is a series of poems in Low German (*Plattdeutsch*) dealing with life in Dithmarshen. Some of his work is in High German, and he published children's tales and short stories. 📖 H Siercks, *Klaus Groth* (1899)

Grothendieck, Alexandre 1928–
French mathematician

Born in Berlin, Germany, he became a French citizen after fleeing Germany in 1941. After early important work on infinite-dimensional vector spaces, he switched to algebraic geometry, where he revolutionized the subject. His work led to a unification of geometry, number theory, topology and complex analysis, and helped to resolve the important conjectures of André Weil. His work has also had profound implications for the theory of logic. His remarkably powerful introduction of the ideas at the very basis of algebraic geometry have extended the language of geometry from fields to rings, and has opened up many problems concerning the integers by allowing the use of geometrical techniques hitherto available only when dealing with rational or real numbers. He was awarded the Fields Medal (the mathematical equivalent of the Nobel Prize) in 1966.

Grotius, Hugo, *also called* Huig de Groot 1583–1645
Dutch jurist, politician, diplomat, poet and theologian

Born in Delft, he studied at Leyden, practised in The Hague, and in 1613 was appointed Pensionary of Rotterdam. He was a political champion of the Remonstrants, and in 1618 religious and political conflicts led to his imprisonment. In 1621 he escaped in a trunk from Loevestein Castle to Paris, where Louis XIII for a time gave him a pension. Recognized as one of the founders of international law, he published his great work on the subject, *De Jura Belli et Pacis* ('On the Law of War and Peace') in 1625. He led diplomatic missions for Sweden from 1634 until his death. He also wrote Latin and Dutch verse. His tragedy, *Adamus Exsul*, was one of Milton's sources, and he wrote the famous *De Veritate Religionis Christianae* (1627) and annotated the Bible (1641–46). His most impressive historical work is *Annales de Rebus Belgicis* (1657).

Grotowski, Jerzy 1933–99
Polish theatre director, teacher and drama theorist

Born in Rzeszów, he trained at the Kraków Theatre School. He founded the Theatre of 13 Rows in Opole (1959–64), which moved to Wrocław as the Theatre Laboratory (1965–84). In 1968 the company visited the Edinburgh Festival, and went on to London and New York City. Also in 1968, he published *Towards a Poor Theatre*, detailing many of his ideas about theatre and performance. In 1976 he disbanded his Laboratory Theatre and began working with actors and students on shows of his own devising to which no audiences were admitted. His work had a major impact on experimental theatre and actor training in the West in the 1960s and 1970s. A later publication is *Teksty and Performer* (1990).

Grouchy, Emmanuel, Marquis de 1766–1847
French soldier

Born in Paris, he was second to Lazare Hoche (1768–97) in the abortive expedition to Ireland (1796), and fought also in Italy (1798). Later he fought at Hohenlinden, Eylau, Friedland and Wagram, and in the 1812 Russian campaign, and after Leipzig covered the retreat of the French. On Napoleon I's escape from Elba he destroyed the Bourbon opposition in the south of France, and helped to rout Gebbard von Blücher at Ligny. After Waterloo (1815), where he failed to play an effective part due to misleading orders, he was Commander-in-Chief of the broken armies of France and led them skilfully back towards the capital before retiring to the USA. He returned in 1819, and was reinstated as marshal in 1831.

Grouès, Henri Antoine See Pierre, Abbé

Groulx, Abbé Lionel 1878–1967
French–Canadian nationalist, historian and novelist

In reaction to the more moderate interpretations of the early 20th century, he depicted French–Canadian history as an unremitting struggle against English domination. In such works as *Notre maître le passé* (1944) he celebrated the clerical and agrarian elements of that past, although he never explicitly advocated separatism.

Grove, Sir George 1820–1900
English musicologist, biblical scholar and civil engineer

Born in London, he trained as a civil engineer, and erected the first two cast-iron lighthouses in the West Indies, and worked on the Britannia tubular bridge. He was secretary to the Society of Arts (1849–52), and became secretary and director of the Crystal Palace Company in 1852. Editor of *Macmillan's Magazine* (1868–83), he was a major contributor to Sir William Smith's *Dictionary of the Bible*. His major work was as editor of the *Dictionary of Music and Musicians* (4 vols, 1878–89; 6th ed 1980). On a journey with Sir Arthur Sullivan to Vienna in 1867 he participated in the discovery of compositions by Schubert. His *Beethoven and his Nine Symphonies* (1896; new ed 1956) remained a standard work for years. Knighted in 1883 on the opening of the Royal College of Music, he was its director until 1895. ▢ Percy M Young, *George Grove: A Biography, 1820-1900* (1980)

Grove, Sir William Robert 1811–96
Welsh physicist and jurist

Born in Swansea, he was educated at Oxford, but had to abandon his law career because of poor health. Concentrating instead on electrochemistry, he invented a new type of voltaic cell named after him (1839), and also a 'gas battery', the first fuel cell. He also invented the earliest form of filament lamp intended for use in mines. As Professor of Physics at the London Institution (1841–64), he studied electrolytic decomposition and demonstrated the dissociation of water. Thereafter he returned to law, was raised to the bench (1871), and became a judge in the High Court of Justice (1875–87). He was one of the original members of the Chemical Society, and one of the leaders of the Royal Society's reform movement (elected FRS in 1840). He was knighted in 1872.

Groves, Sir Charles Barnard 1915–92
English conductor

He was born in London and studied at the Royal College of Music. He was appointed chorus master of the BBC Chorus (1938–42), and conductor of the BBC Northern Symphony Orchestra (1944–51), the Bournemouth Symphony Orchestra (1951–61), the Royal Liverpool Philharmonic Orchestra (1963–77), and the Leeds Philharmonic Society (1988–92). He also conducted with Welsh National Opera (1961–63) and English National Opera (1978–79). He was knighted in 1973, and established a wide reputation especially for his work in the early Romantics and in English music.

Groza, Petru 1884–1958
Romanian politician

During the 1930s he led the Ploughmen's Front which drew its support from the Transylvanian peasantry. When Romania entered World War II in 1944, he joined the Communist front organization, the National Democratic Front (FND). In 1944, together with his fellow 'home Communist' Gheorghe Gheorghiu-Dej, he represented the FND in the government of Sănătescu. In 1945 Stalin approved his appointment as presiding minister in the FND government, a post he held until 1952 when he became president of the presidium of the Romanian Communist Party (RCP).

Grubb, Sir Howard 1844–1931
Irish engineer and builder of astronomical instruments

Born in Dublin, he studied civil engineering at Trinity College, Dublin, then worked with his father, Thomas Grubb (FRS), engineer to the Bank of Ireland and also a maker of optical instruments. In 1865 his father was commissioned to build a 48 inch reflecting telescope for Melbourne, Australia, and Grubb was given charge of the work under his father's supervision. This instrument, one of the largest in the world at the time, established his reputation on an even higher level than his father's. On his father's retirement in 1868, the firm moved to larger premises in Dublin, and (c.1880) he completed a 27 inch refracting telescope for Vienna, for some years the most notable telescope of its kind in the world. In 1900 he patented a new type of optical gun sight, and developed and perfected the submarine periscope. In 1925, at the age of 81, he retired from active participation in the business, and it was acquired by Sir Charles Algernon Parsons (1854–1931) and moved to Newcastle upon Tyne as the Sir Howard Grubb Parsons Company. Grubb was elected FRS in 1883 and knighted in 1887.

Grubb, Sir Kenneth George 1900–80
English missionary, ecumenist, and Anglican lay churchman

He was born in Oxton, Nottinghamshire. Following extensive research on religious and social conditions in South America in the 1930s and wartime service with the Ministry of Information, he became president of the Church Missionary Society (1944–69), chairman of the Churches Committee on International Affairs (1946–68), and chairman of the House of Laity in the Church Assembly (1959–70). Author of several studies on South America and successive editions of the *World Christian Handbook* (1949–68), he revealed his waspish assessments of himself and others in *A Layman Looks at the Church* (1964) and his autobiography *Crypts of Power* (1971).

Gruenberg, Louis 1884–1964
US composer

Born near Brest-Litovsk, Russia, he was taken to the USA at the age of two. A pupil of Ferrucio Busoni, he worked as a concert pianist until 1919, and then retired to devote himself to composition. He wrote extensively for orchestra, chamber music combinations and voices, but is best known for his opera *The Emperor Jones* (1933), based on Eugene O'Neill's play.

Grumman, Leroy Randle 1895–1982
US engineer and aircraft pioneer

Born in Huntington, New York, he studied engineering at Cornell University, and served as a navy pilot in World War I. From 1921 to 1929 he was general manager of the Loening Aeronautical Corporation, thereafter forming the Grumman Aircraft Engineering Corporation at Bethpage, Long Island. He produced a series of successful navy aircraft—Wildcat, Hellcat, Bearcat and Tiger Cat—which played vital roles in the naval wars in the Pacific and the Atlantic in World War II. These were followed by jet fighters Panther, Cougar and Tiger, and several attack and search aircraft. Grumman built the Lunar Excursion Module (LEM) for the Apollo flights to the Moon.

Grün, Anastasius See Auersperg, Anton Alexander, Graf von

Grün, Hans See Baldung, Hans

Grundtvig, Nikolai Frederik Severin 1783–1872
Danish theologian, historian, poet and educator

Born in Udby, Zealand, he studied theology in Copenhagen. He wrote *Northern Mythology* (1801) and *The Decline of the Heroic Age in the North* (1809), and some volumes of patriotic poetry. He became a curate in 1815 in his father's church, but because of his criticisms of the rationalist tendency in the Danish Church, he was suspended from preaching (1825). His antiquarian interests continued with translations of Snorri Sturluson's *Heimskringla* and of Saxo Grammaticus, followed by a translation of *Beowulf* (1820). As a result of visits to England, he was the inspiration behind the Folk High School movement, begun in 1844, which provided adults with education in practical subjects and the humanities, and which contributed to the transformation of rural life in Denmark after the German–Danish War of 1864.

Gruner, Elioth 1882–1939
Australian painter

Born in Gisborne, New Zealand, of Norwegian and Irish parentage, he arrived in Sydney as an infant, and in 1894 trained at Julian Ashton's Art school. He won the Wynne prize for landscape painting in 1916, and was to win it six more times. Regarded as one of Australia's leading landscape artists, he captures, in his best work, the special quality of the Australian light, for example in *On the Murrumbidgee* (1929, Sydney). He organized the exhibition of Australian art shown at the Royal Academy, London, in 1923, and his work was exhibited at the Royal Academy and the Paris Salon.

Grünewald, Isaak 1889–1946
Swedish painter

Born in Stockholm, he was a leader of Scandinavian Expressionism. His wife, Sigrid Grünewald-Hjerten (1885–1946), was also a painter.

Grünewald, Matthias, *originally perhaps* Mathis Nithardt, *otherwise* Gothardt c.1475–1528
German artist, architect and engineer

Born probably in Würzburg, Bavaria, very little is known of his life, but he was trained in Alsace in the style of Martin Schongauer, and became court painter to the Archbishop of Mainz (1508–14) and to Cardinal Albrecht of Brandenburg (1515–25), and he designed waterworks for Magdeburg (c.1526). In 1516 he completed the great Isenheim altarpiece (Colmar Museum, Alsace), the nine paintings of which exhibit his rare livid colours and his use of distortion to portray passion and suffering. Towards 1524 he painted an even more dramatic *Crucifixion* (Karlsruhe, Kunsthalle) with its greenish, blood-spattered body of Christ. Grünewald is the *Mathis der Maler* of Paul Hindemith's opera. ⌨ Arthur Burkhart, *Matthias Grünewald: Personality and Accomplishment* (1936)

Gryphius or Greif, Andreas 1616–64
German lyric poet and dramatist

Born in Glogau, Silesia, he travelled in Holland, France and Italy, studying medicine and astronomy, then returned to his native town. His early misfortunes led him to the 'all is vanity' theme of his lyrics, expressed in deep gloom, collected under the title *Sonn-und-Feiertagssonette* (1639, 'Sonnets for Sundays and Holidays'). His dramas, mainly concerned with martyrdom, include *Leo Armenius* (1650), *Catharina von Georgien* (1657) and *Papinianus* (1659). He also wrote the pastoral *Die geliebte Dornrose* (1660, Eng trans *The Beloved Hedgerose*, and 1928), the comedies, *Herr Peter Squentz* (1663, Eng trans *Absurda Comica, or Master Peter Squentz*, 1964), which resembles the scenes with Bottom in Shakespeare's *A Midsummer Night's Dream*, and *Horribilicribrifax* (1663), satirizing the Thirty Years War. He was indirectly influenced by Shakespeare and Joost van den Vondel. ⌨ H Becker, *Andreas Greif, poet between epochs* (1973)

Gryphius, Sebastian 1493–1556
German printer

He was born in Reutlingen, Swabia. In 1528 he went to Lyons and there between 1528 and 1547 printed more than 300 works, notable for their accuracy and clear type. Among the more noted are the fine Latin Bible of 1550 and Étienne Dolet's *Commentaria Linguae Latinae* (1536, 'Commentaries on the Latin Language').

Guardi, Francesco 1712–93
Italian painter

Born in Pinzolo, he was a pupil of Canaletto, and was noted for his views of Venice, full of sparkling colour, with an Impressionist's eye for light effects. His *View of the Church and Piazza of S Marco* is in the National Gallery, London. His brothers, Giovanni Antonio (1669–1760) and Nicolò (1715–86), often collaborated with him.

Guardia, Fiorello H(enry) la See La Guardia, Fiorello H(enry)

Guare, John 1938–
US dramatist

Born in New York City, he studied at the Yale School of Drama and began to write tragicomic plays influenced by the Theatre of the Absurd. He won an Obie award for *The House of Blue Leaves* (1971), which investigated the grotesquely inappropriate ambitions and necessary self-deceptions of a family in the borough of Queens. In recent plays such as *Six Degrees of Separation* (1990) and *Four Baboons Adoring the Sun* (1992), he has written in a style more naturalistic but still highly inventive and has reached a level of accomplishment seldom matched in US theatre. His screenplays for *Atlantic City* (1981) and for the film version of *Six Degrees of Separation* (1991) were nominated for Academy Awards.

Guareschi, Giovanni 1908–68
Italian journalist and writer

He was born in Parma, and became editor of the Milan magazine *Bertoldo*. After World War II, in which he was a prisoner, he returned to Milan and journalism, but it was *Mondo piccolo 'Don Camillo'* (1950, Eng trans *The Little World of Don Camillo*, 1951) which brought him fame. These stories of a village priest and a Communist mayor, with their broad humour and rich humanity, have been translated into many languages. They were followed by *Mondo piccolo 'Don Camillo e il figliol prodigo'* (Eng trans *Don Camillo and the Prodigal Son*, 1952) and others. He illustrated his books with his own drawings. ⌨ *Diario clandestino, 1943–1945* (1949)

Guarini, Giovanni Battista 1538–1612
Italian poet

Born in Ferrara, he was entrusted by Duke Alfonso II with diplomatic missions to the pope and the emperor, and was sent to Venice and Poland. His chief work was the famous pastoral play, *Il Pastor Fido* (1585, 'Fido the Shepherd'), an imitation of Torquato Tasso's *Aminta*. ⌨ V Russi, *Battista Guarini ed il Pastor Fido* (1885)

Guarini, Guarino, *originally* Camillo 1624–83
Italian Baroque architect, philosopher and mathematician

Born in Modena, he became a Theatine monk at the age of 15. In Rome he studied the work of Francesco Borromini, from which he developed his own style. A love of complexity and movement in all dimensions is the keynote of his work. He designed several churches in Turin, of which the only two survivors are San Lorenzo (1668–80) and Capella della SS Sindone (1668), and the Palazzo Carignano (1679), as well as palaces for Bavaria and Baden. He also published books on mathematics, astronomy and architecture. His influential *Architectura Civile* (published posthumously in 1737), concerning the relationship of geometry and architecture, also included a defence of Gothic architecture.

Guarnieri or Guarneri
Italian family of violin makers

From Cremona, the most important were Andrea (fl.1650–95), his sons Giuseppe (fl.1690–1730) and Pietro (fl.1690–1725), and Giuseppe's son Giuseppe (fl.1725–45), the last commonly known as Giuseppe del Gesò (of Jesus) because he signed his violins with IHS (Iesu hominum salvator) after his name.

Gubaydulina, Sofiya Asgatovna 1931–
Russian composer

Born in Chistopol in the Tatar SSR, she has been resident in Germany since 1991. Educated at Kazan (1949–54) and Moscow (1954–63) conservatories, she worked for the next decade in the Soviet theatre and film industry, as accompanist and composer, with a special interest in electronic music. In 1975, her choral/orchestral *Steps* won an International Composers' Competition in Rome, and in the same year she co-founded the improvising ensemble Astreja, of which she remains a member. Her major works include the violin concerto *Offertorium* (1980–86), *Seven Words* (1982), which was initially suppressed, and the symphony *Stimmen…Verstummen* (1986).

Guderian, Heinz (Wilhelm) 1888–1953
German general

After serving in World War I, he stayed in the small army allowed to Germany by the Treaty of Versailles, and pioneered mechanized warfare. Created general of panzer (armoured) troops in 1938, he advocated fast-moving *Blitzkrieg* warfare which he later put into brilliant effect, commanding forces in France and the USSR under Fedor von Bock. He had a stormy relationship with Hitler and was dismissed and reinstated several times. He wrote *Panzer Leader* (1952).

Guedalla, Philip 1889–1944
English writer

Born in London, he was educated at Rugby and Oxford, and became a barrister (1913–1923). He was a highly popular historian and wrote *Second Empire* (1922), *Palmerston* (1926), *The Hundred Days* (1934), *The Hundredth Year* (1940), *Two Marshals* (about Jean René Bazaine and Philippe Pétain, 1943) and *Middle East* (1944).

Guelf, *properly* Welf c.825–1866
German dynasty

The first known Welf was a Frankish noble with lands in Bavaria and Swabia (c.825). The family was most powerful under Henry the Lion, Duke of Saxony and Bavaria, but Frederick I, Barbarossa took both duchies, only allowing him the area of Braunschweig-Lüneburg, which became a duchy in 1235 for Henry's grandson Otto. They became electors (1692) and later kings (1814) of Hanover, and in 1714 the Elector George Ludwig became George I of England. The death of William IV (1837) separated the British and Hanoverian crowns, when Salic Law prevented Victoria from ruling Hanover. Her cousin, George V of Hanover, lost his throne to Prussia in 1866. In medieval Italy, the term Guelfs represented political factions supporting the papacy and the Angevin rulers of Naples. Their opponents were the imperialist Ghibellines, who were originally supporters of the Hohenstaufen dynasty.

Guillaume, 9th Duke of Aquitaine
See Guilhem, 9th Duke of Aquitaine

Guercino, *literally* 'the Squint-Eyed', *properly* Gian-Francesco Barbieri 1590–1666
Italian painter of the Bolognese school

Born in Cento, he painted the famous *Aurora* at the Villa Ludovisi in Rome for Pope Gregory XV. In 1642, after the death of Guido Reni, he became the dominant painter of Bologna, combining in his work the liveliness and movement of the Carracci with a warmer, more Venetian colouring.

Guericke, Otto von 1602–86
German engineer and physicist

Born in Magdeburg, he worked in Leipzig, Helmstadt, Jena and Leyden, studying law and mathematics, mechanics and the art of fortification. An engineer in the Swedish army, he became one of the four burgomasters of Magdeburg from 1646 to 1681, elected for his service to the town as an engineer and diplomat during its siege in the Thirty Years War. He developed a primitive vacuum pump which enabled the natural philosophers of the day to study new areas of physics. He arranged a dramatic demonstration of the effect of atmospheric pressure on a near vacuum in 1654 at Regensburg before the Emperor Ferdinand III. Two large metal hemispheres were placed together and the air within pumped out. They could not then be separated by two teams of eight horses, but fell apart when the air was allowed to re-enter. He showed that in a vacuum candles cannot remain alight and small animals die, and he devised several experiments that demonstrated the elasticity of air. He also carried out some experiments in electricity and magnetism.

Guérin, Charles 1873–1907
French Symbolist poet

Born in Lunéville, he travelled in Germany and Italy, and periodically stayed in Paris. His work is confined to a few collections, including *Le Cœur solitaire* (1898, 'The Lonely Heart') and *L'Éros funèbre* (1900, 'Eros in Mourning'). A later series, *L'Homme intérieur* (1906, 'The Inner Man'), echoed his late conversion to the Catholic faith.
📖 Joseph B Hanson, *Le Poète Charles Guérin* (1935)

Guérin, Pierre Narcisse, Baron 1774–1833
French historical painter

Born in Paris, a skilful painter of classical subjects but inclined to melodrama, he was appointed Professor at the École des Beaux-Arts (1814), where he counted among his pupils Theodore Géricault and Eugène Delacroix. From 1822 to 1829 he was director of the French Academy of Painting in Rome.

Guerra, Tonino (Antonio) 1920–
Italian screenwriter

Born in Sant'Arcangelo, Emilia Romagna, he was a poet and novelist before writing for the cinema collaborating on the script for *Uomini E Lupi* (1956, 'Men and Wolves'). *L'Avventura* (1960, 'The Adventure') began a lengthy partnership with director Michelangelo Antonioni, and their most notable films include *La Notte* (1961, 'The Night') and *Il Deserto Rosso* (1964, 'The Red Desert'). He received Academy Award nominations for his contribution to the screenplays for *Casanova '70* (1965), *Blow-Up* (1966) and *Amarcord* (1973). He has worked extensively with some of the most distinguished filmmakers in contemporary European cinema, and his finest scripts include *Cadaveri Eccellenti* (1976, 'Illustrious Corpses') for Francesco Rosi, *La Notte Di San Lorenzo* (1981, 'The Night of San Lorenzo') for the Taviani brothers, *Landscape In The Mist* (1988) for Theo Angelopoulos, and *Stanno Tutti Bene* (1990, 'Everybody's Doing Fine') for Guiseppe Tornatore.

Guerra González, Alfonso 1940–
Spanish politician

He was born in Seville. A close friend of Felipe González from the early 1960s, Guerra was largely responsible for the transformation of the Spanish Socialist Workers' Party (PSOE) into a major political organization during the 1970s. An able administrator, he complemented the charismatic appeal of González, though his control of the party machine has been heavily personalized and intolerant of dissent. A deputy in every election since 1977, he was Deputy Prime Minister from 1982 until his major split with González in 1991.

Guerrero, José Gustavo 1876–1958
El Salvadorian lawyer and judge
He practised in San Salvador and was the author of many books on international law. A judge of the Permanent Court of International Justice from 1930, he became its president (1937–39). He was a judge (1946–55) and was president of the International Court of Justice (1946–49).

Guesclin, Bertrand du c.1320–1380
French soldier, Constable of France
Born near Dinan, he took part in the contests for the dukedom of Brittany. After King John II's capture at Poitiers in 1356, du Guesclin displayed military skill against the English particularly at Rennes (1356) and Dinan (1357), until he was taken prisoner at Auray, and ransomed. He next supported Henry of Trastamare against Pedro, the Cruel, King of Castile, but was defeated and taken prisoner by Edward, the Black Prince (1367). Again ransomed, he defeated Pedro in 1309, and crowned Henry of Trastamare, but was recalled by Charles V of France to be made Constable of France. In 1370 he opened his campaigns against the English, and soon nearly all their possessions were in the hands of the French. He died during the Siege of Châteauneuf de Randon.

Guest, Sir Josiah John 1785–1852
Welsh industrialist
Born in Dowlais, Glamorgan, he inherited the Dowlais Iron Company founded by his grandfather, John Guest, and made it the leading iron producer in South Wales. Guest was interested in the welfare of his workers and in Welsh culture. In 1833 he married Lady Charlotte Bertie, later Charlotte Schrieber, and she participated fully in his industrial and cultural concerns.

Guettard, Jean Étienne 1715–86
French botanist, invertebrate palaeontologist, stratigrapher and geomorphologist
Born in Étampes, Ile-de-France, he studied medicine in Paris. He subsequently became a physician and accompanied the Duke of Orléans on his travels as keeper of his natural history collections. In 1746 he published a geological map of part of northern France with stratal boundaries and later produced another in which he attempted to link the geology of France with that of England; these were amongst some of the earliest geological maps to be prepared. Guettard demonstrated that the distribution of plants could be used as a means of mapping outcrops. He independently recognized that fossils are the remains of once-living organisms and named some invertebrate genera. He also perceived the erosion and depositional roles of running water, and was the first to conclusively demonstrate the volcanic character of the Auvergne (1752). His mineralogical map of western Europe was published in 1780.

Guevara, Che, *properly* Ernesto Guevara de la Serna 1928–67
Argentine Communist revolutionary leader
Born in Rosario, he graduated in medicine at the University of Buenos Aires (1953), then joined Fidel Castro's revolutionary movement in Mexico (1955), played an important part in the Cuban revolution (1956–59) and afterwards held government posts under Castro. An activist of revolution elsewhere, he left Cuba in 1965 to become a guerrilla leader in South America, and was captured and executed by goverment troops in Bolivia while trying to foment a revolt. He became an icon for left-wing youth in the 1960s. He wrote *Guerrilla Warfare* (1961) and *Reminiscences of the Cuban Revolutionary War* (1968). ⌑ John Lee Anderson, *Che Guevara: A Revolutionary Life* (1997)

Guevara, Luis Vélez de 1570–1644
Spanish dramatist
Born in Ecija, he wrote many plays in the style of Lope de Vega. His novel *El Diablo cojuelo* (1641, 'The Limping Devil') was used as the model for Alain Lesage's *Diable boiteux*. ⌑ F E Spencer and R Schevil, *The Dramatic Works of Luiz Vélez de Guevara* (1937)

Guggenheim, Meyer 1828–1905
US industrialist
Born in Langnau, Switzerland, he emigrated to the USA in 1847 and made a fortune in the copper industry. He had seven sons, who included the famous philanthropists Simon Guggenheim (1867–1941), who established the Guggenheim Foundation (1925) to provide scholars, writers, and artists with grants for studying or working abroad, and Solomon Robert Guggenheim (1861–1949), who endowed the Solomon R Guggenheim Museum (1937) in New York City. His granddaughter, Peggy Guggenheim, was also an art patron.

Guggenheim, Peggy (Marguerite) 1898–1979
US art collector
Born in New York City, she married in 1922 but divorced after eight years and went to live in Paris (1930–1941), socializing with all the prominent artists of the time, and purchasing many paintings by new (now famous) artists. During World War II she returned to the USA with the artist Max Ernst, to whom she was married (1941–45), and opened a gallery called 'Art of This Century' in New York. There the works of the European artists, including Jackson Pollock, Mark Rothko and Hans Hofmann, were exhibited, changing the course of US art. After the war, Guggenheim moved to Venice, where she lived on the Grand Canal in the Palazzo Venier dei Leoni, which now houses the famous Guggenheim Collection.

Guicciardini, Francesco 1483–1540
Italian historian, lawyer and diplomat
Born in Florence, he became Professor of Law there, and also practised as an advocate. He served as Florentine ambassador in Spain (1512–14), and became papal Governor of Modena (1516), Reggio (1517), Parma (1521), the Romagna (1523) and Bologna (1531). Retiring from the papal service in 1534, he secured the election of Cosimo de' Medici as Duke of Florence, but, disappointed by the post of mayor of the palace, withdrew to Arcetri, where he wrote his *Storia d'Italia*, an analytical history of Italy from 1494 to 1532. ⌑ Roberto Ridolfi, *The Life of Francesco Guicciardini* (1960, Eng trans 1968)

Guiccioli, Teresa Gamba Ghiselli, Countess 1801–73
Italian noblewoman and mistress
The daughter of a Ravenna noblewoman, she was married in 1817 to the 60-year-old Count Alessandro Guiccioli. In 1851 she married the French Marquis de Boissy (1798–1866). She was the mistress of Lord Byron and later wrote *Lord Byron jugé par les témoins de sa vie* (1868).

Guido d'Arezzo, *English* Guy of Arezzo, *also called* Guido Aretino c.990–1050
Italian Benedictine monk and musical theorist
Born probably in Arezzo, he was a monk at Pomposa, and is said to have been prior of the Camaldolite monastery of Avellana. He contributed much to musical science and ascribed to him are the invention of the staff and the introduction of the system of using syllables to name the notes of a scale.

Guilbert, Yvette c.1869–1944
French comedienne

Born in Paris, she was a seamstress before she went on the stage. She became famous for her songs and sketches of all facets of Parisian life and, after 1890, for her revivals of old French ballads. Later, she founded a school of acting in New York City. She wrote two novels, and *La Chanson de ma vie* (1919, 'Song of My Life').

Guilhem or Guillaume, 9th Duke of Aquitaine, 7th Count of Poitou 1071–1126
The earliest known troubadour

The establishment in his territory (richer than those of the King of France) of the proto-Catharist mystical order of Fontrvrault, offers the key to the understanding of a man who, on the one hand, sacrificed an army of 60,000 men in a pointless crusade (1101), and on the other possibly 'invented' *amour courtois* ('courtly love') and who was, according to a contemporary, 'one of the most courtly men in the world'. He left 11 poems whose high quality no one has doubted: five are capably and amusingly obscene, one is an exercise, and the rest are exquisitely cryptic. ⊞ *Romanische Forschungen*, LXXIII (1961); R R Bezzola, *Les Origines de la littérature courtoise en occident* (1944–62)

Guillaume, Charles Édouard 1861–1938
Swiss physicist and Nobel Prize winner

Born in Fleurier, he was educated at Neuchâtel University and at the Zurich Polytechnic, and in 1883 joined the staff and eventually became director of the Bureau of International Weights and Measures at Sèvres. In the course of the Bureau's efforts to improve the precision of its standards, he redetermined the volume of the litre, and investigated the effect of thermal movement on standards of length. His search for a material with little or no thermal expansion or contraction led to the discovery of a nickel–steel alloy, christened 'Invar', the use of which significantly improved the accuracy and stability of timekeeping devices, precision instruments and standards of measurement. For this discovery Guillaume was awarded the Nobel Prize for physics in 1920.

Guillaume de Machaut c.1300–1377
French poet and musician

Born possibly in Rheims, he worked successively under the patronage of John of Luxemburg and John II of France. *Le Livre du voir-dit*, written in the form of letters from the elderly poet to a girl, influenced Chaucer. He was one of the creators of the harmonic art, and wrote a mass, motets, songs, ballads and organ music.

Guillemin, Roger (Charles Louis) 1924–
US physiologist and Nobel Prize winner

Born in Dijon, France, he graduated from Dijon University in 1942 and began a medical course. In 1949 he graduated in medicine from Lyons University and went to Montreal to study the role of the hypothalamus (a structure at the base of the brain) in regulating the activity of the pituitary gland. In 1953 he accepted an appointment at Baylor University School of Medicine in Houston. He was promoted to the chair of physiology at Baylor in 1963, and in 1970 moved to the Salk Institute, San Diego, where he remained until 1989. Guillemin and his colleagues were responsible for isolating and identifying the chemical structures of hypothalamic hormones, principally the hormone which stimulates the thyroid gland, and the hormones which release and inhibit the growth hormone. These discoveries have important applications, and potential applications for the treatment of various endocrinological diseases. Guillemin and Andrew Schally shared half of the 1977 Nobel Prize for physiology or medicine, with the other half awarded to Rosalyn Yalow. He was appointed Distinguished Scientist at the Whittier Institute for Diabetes and Endocrinology, La Jolla, California, in 1989 and director in 1993.

Guillén, Nicolás 1902–89
Cuban poet

He was born in Camagüey. His poetry is famous for its relating of Negro to Latin-American themes. He was the first to recognize that the black presence on his island was not merely exotic. He became Cuba's best-known poet, celebrated even by the illiterate. Much of his poetry is political, as was natural from a man who for many years was a leading member of the Communist Party of Cuba. He received a state funeral. There are two volumes of his poetry in translation: *Man-Making Words* (1972) and *The Great Zoo* (1972). ⊞ L V Williams, *Self and Society in the Poetry of Nicolás Guillén* (1982)

Guillotin, Joseph Ignace 1738–1814
French doctor and revolutionary

He was born in Saintes. As a deputy in the Estates General in 1789, he proposed to the Constituent Assembly the use of a decapitating instrument, which was adopted in 1791 and was named after him, although similar apparatus had been used earlier in Scotland, Germany and Italy.

Guimarães Rosa, João 1908–69
Brazilian novelist and short-story writer

Born in Cordisburgo, Minas Gerais, he practised as a doctor before becoming a diplomat in 1932. The chief area of his concern was that of Euclydes da Cunha, the backlands of Brazil. He shared a mutual admiration with Peruvian José María Arguedas (1911–69), who also tried to write in a 'native' form of their own European language. *Sagarana* (1946, rev edn 1958, Eng trans 1966) collects nine 'parables of the sertão', some of them about animals. One of the most important Latin-American writers of the 20th century, he is best known for *Grande Sertáo: veredas* (1956, rev edn 1958), for which its translators chose the title *The Devil to Pay in the Backlands* (1968). Of all the Brazilian novelists of such high calibre only the more accessible Graciliano Ramos has had similar power.

Guimard, Hector Germain 1867–1942
French architect

Born in Lyons, he was the most important Art Nouveau architect active in Paris between 1890 and World War I. For his impressive architectural scheme, the *Castel Béranger* apartment block (1894–98), he designed every aspect of the building and its interiors. He is best known for the famous Paris Métro entrances of the early 1900s, many of which are still in place.

Guimerá, Ángel 1849–1924
Catalan poet and dramatist

He was born in Santa Cruz, Tenerife. His work falls into three periods, of which the first and third—for the most part, historical plays—show the influence of the French Romantics. His middle period owes its preoccupation with contemporary life to Ibsen. He is regarded as the greatest Catalan dramatist. His best-known play is *Terra Baixa* (1896, 'Lowlands'), on which Eugen d'Albert based his opera *Tiefland*. ⊞ J Minack, *Guimerá* (1959)

Guin, Ursula K le See Le Guin, Ursula K(roeber)

Guinness, Sir Alec 1914–
English actor

Born in London, he worked briefly as a junior copywriter for an advertising firm before training to become an actor at the Fay Compton Studio of Dramatic Art. He made his stage debut in *Libel* (1934). He appeared as Osric in John Gielgud's production of *Hamlet* (1934–35) and joined the Old Vic in 1936 where he played *Hamlet* (1938). He rejoined the company in 1946 after serving in the Royal Navy throughout World War II. He made his film debut as an extra in *Evensong* (1934) but began his cinema career in earnest with the Dickens adaptations *Great Expectations* (1946) and *Oliver Twist* (1948). Long associated with Ealing Studios, his many comic triumphs include *Kind Hearts and Coronets* (1949), *The Lavender Hill Mob* (1951) and *The Ladykillers* (1955). He received a Best Actor Oscar for *The Bridge on the River Kwai* (1957). Other films include *Tunes of Glory* (1960), *Lawrence of Arabia* (1962), *Star Wars* (1977) and *Little Dorrit* (1988). Although increasingly infrequent, his many distinguished stage performances include *The Cocktail Party* (1949–50), *Ross* (1960), *Dylan* (1964), *Macbeth* (1966), *A Voyage Round My Father* (1971), *The Old Country* (1977) and *A Walk in the Woods* (1989). His television work includes two appearances as inscrutable spycatcher George Smiley in *Tinker, Tailor, Soldier, Spy* (1979) and *Smiley's People* (1982) as well as *Foreign Field* (1993). He was knighted in 1959 and has published the autobiographies *Blessings in Disguise* (1985) and *My Name Escapes Me* (1996). 📖 R Tanitch, *Guinness* (1989)

Guinness, Sir Benjamin Lee 1798–1868
Irish brewer

Born in Dublin, the grandson of Arthur Guinness (1725–1803), founder of Guinness's Brewery (1759), he joined the firm at an early age, and became sole owner at his father's death (1855). Under him the brand of stout became famous and the business grew into the largest of its kind in the world. He was the first Lord Mayor of Dublin in 1851 and an MP from 1865 to 1868. He restored St Patrick's Cathedral (1860–65) at his own expense.

Guinness, Edward Cecil, 1st Earl of Iveagh
1847–1927
Irish brewer

The third son of Sir Benjamin Lee Guinness, he spent much of his huge fortune on philanthropic projects including housing in Dublin and London, and gave the mansion of Kenwood at Highgate, London, with its collection of paintings, to the nation.

Güiraldes, Ricardo 1886–1927
Argentine novelist, poet and editor

Born in Buenos Aires, he founded the leading periodicals *Martin Fierro* and *Proa* with the young Jorge Luis Borges, and others. He lived between Buenos Aires and Paris, and was thus in touch with European influences. His best novel is *Don Segundo Sombra* (1926, Eng trans 1935), the story of a childhood on a gaucho ranch. Its style is an elegant blend of literary Argentinian and the vernacular. He was an adherent of Vedanta, and his record of his search, *El sendero* ('The Way'), was published in 1932. 📖 G Previtali, *Ricardo Güiraldes and Don Segundo Sombra* (1963)

Guiscard, Robert c.1015–1085
Norman adventurer

He was born near Coutances, and as the champion of Pope Nicholas II, he campaigned with his brother Roger I of Sicily against the Byzantine Greeks in southern Italy and Sicily (1060–76). In 1059 the papacy recognized him as Duke of Apulia, Calabria, and Sicily. He defeated the Byzantine emperor, Alexius I Comnenus, in 1081 at Durazzo. He interrupted his march on Constantinople (Istanbul) to liberate Pope Gregory VII from the Emperor Henri IV in Italy (1084), and died during his second attempt on Constantinople. 📖 Finch Allibone, *In Pursuit of the Robber Baron: Recreating the Journeys of Robert Guiscard, Duke of Apulia, and 'The terror of the World'* (1988)

Guise
French ducal family of Lorraine

The name was taken from the town of Guise. The direct line became extinct on the death (1675) of François Joseph, the 7th Duke. 📖 H D Sedgwick, *The House of Guise* (1938)

Guise, Charles of 1525–74
French prelate

He was the son of Claude of Lorraine, 1st Duke of Guise and brother of Mary of Guise and Francis, 2nd Duke of Guise, with whom he became all-powerful in the reign of Francis II. Archbishop of Rheims, he was created Cardinal of Guise in 1547. He introduced the Inquisition into France and exerted a great influence at the Council of Trent (1562–64).

Guise, Claude of Lorraine, 1st Duke of
1496–1550
French nobleman and soldier

Born at the Château of Condé, Lorraine, the fifth son of René II, Duke of Lorraine, he fought under Francis I at Marignano, Italy, in 1515, but subsequently remained at home to defend France against the English and Germans, and defeated the army of the Holy Roman Emperor, Charles V, at Neufchâteau. He was regent during the captivity of Francis (1525–26). For suppressing a peasant revolt in Lorraine (1527) he was created Duke of Guise. His daughter, Mary of Guise, married James V of Scotland and became mother of Mary, Queen of Scots.

Guise, Francis, 2nd Duke of, *called* Le Balafré ('the Scarred') 1519–63
French soldier and politician

The son of Claude of Lorraine, 1st Duke of Guise, he commanded the expedition against Naples in 1556, and took Calais (1558), bringing about the Treaty of Château Cambrésis (1559). He and his brother, Cardinal Charles of Guise, shared the main power in the state during the reign of Francis II (of France). They headed the Roman Catholic Party, sternly repressing Protestantism. With the Duc de Montmorency, he defeated the Huguenots at Dreux (1562), and was besieging Orleans when he was assassinated by a Huguenot.

Guise, Henri, 3rd Duc de 1550–88
French soldier and politician

The son of Francis, 2nd Duke of Guise, he was one of the contrivers of the St Bartholomew's Day Massacre (1572) and was the head of the Holy League against the Bourbons (1576).

Guise, Mary of See Mary of Guise

Guitry, Sacha 1885–1957
French actor and dramatist

Born in St Petersburg, Russia, the son of French actor-manager Lucien Guitry (1860–1925), he first appeared on the stage in Russia with his father's company. His first appearance in Paris was in 1902, still under his father's management. He went to London in 1920 with *Nono*, a play written when he was 16. It starred the second of his five wives, Yvonne Printemps. He wrote nearly a hundred plays, mostly light comedies, many of which have been successfully performed in English. He also wrote and directed several delightful films, including *Le Roman d'un tricheur* (1936, *The Tale of a Cheat*) and *Les Perles de la couronne* (1937, *The Pearls of the Crown*). 📖 J Harding, *Sacha Guitry, the last boulevardier* (1968)

Guizot, François Pierre Guillaume 1787–1874
French historian and politician

Born in Nîmes, of Huguenot stock, he went to Paris in 1805 to study law, but soon drifted into literature, and in 1812 became Professor of Modern History at the Sorbonne. As a Liberal, he was deprived of his appointments in 1821, and in 1825 was prohibited from lecturing. With some friends he then published *Mémoires relatifs à l'histoire de France jusqu'au 13 siècle* (31 vols, 'Memoirs Concerning the History of France up to the 13th Century) and *Mémoires relatifs à la Révolution d'Angleterre* (25 vols, 'Memoirs Concerning the English Revolution'), and edited translations of **Shakespeare** and Henry Hallam (1777–1859). Restored to his chair in 1828, he began his famous lectures, later published, on the history of civilization. Elected to the Chamber (1830), he became Minister of the Interior (1830), then Minister of Public Instruction (1832), establishing a system of primary education. In 1840 he went to London as ambassador, but was recalled to replace **Louis Thiers** as the king's chief adviser. He relapsed into reactionary methods of government which were partly responsible for the Revolution of 1848 and the fall of **Louis Philippe**, with whom he escaped to London. After the coup d'état of 1851 he devoted himself entirely to historical scholarship.

Gulbenkian, Calouste Sarkis 1869–1955
British financier, industrialist and diplomat
Born in Scutari, Turkey, of Amernian descent, he entered his father's oil business in Baku in 1888. After becoming a naturalized British subject in 1902 he brought the Russians into the new Royal Dutch-Shell merger and in 1907 he arranged for the latter to break into the US market, thus laying the foundations of an important British dollar asset. In 1916 he organized French entry into the Turkish Petroleum Company, instead of the Germans, and between 1921 and 1928 he did the same for the Americans. In 1940 in Vichy France, the five per cent Iraq Petroleum Company interest was confiscated by Great Britain, and he was declared an 'Enemy under the Act', whereupon he assumed Persian citizenship. From 1948 to 1954 he negotiated oil concessions between the USA and Saudi Arabia. He left $70 million and vast art collections to finance an international Gulbenkian Foundation. His son Nubar Sarkis Gulbenkian (1896–1972), philanthropist and bon vivant, was commercial attaché to the Iranian embassy (1926–51, 1956–65) and until his father's death worked with him. 📖 Ralph Hewins, *Mr Five Per Cent: The Biography of Calouste Gulbenkian* (1957)

Guldberg, Cato Maximilian 1836–1902
Norwegian mathematician and chemist
Born in Christiania (Oslo), he went to the University of Christiania in 1854 to study mathematics and science. He became a teacher at the Royal Military Academy (1860), Professor of Applied Mathematics in the Royal Military College (1862), a lecturer at the University of Christiania (1867) and finally Professor of Applied Mathematics there (1869). He is best known for his work in collaboration with his brother-in-law **Peter Waage**, which established the law of mass action, stating that the rate of a homogeneous chemical reaction is proportional to the concentrations of the reacting substances (1864).

Gullstrand, Allvar 1862–1930
Swedish ophthalmologist and Nobel Prize winner
Born in Landskrona, he studied medicine at the universities of Uppsala and Vienna, before becoming chief physician, and in 1892, director, at the Stockholm Eye Clinic. Two years later he became Professor of Ophthalmology at Uppsala University. In his investigations into physiological optics, Gullstrand developed mathematical formulae which facilitated the treatment of conditions such as astigmatism and coma. He also developed new techniques for the examination of the eye including the Gullstrand ophthalascope, used to examine the eye for arteriosclerosis and diabetes mellitus. He was awarded the 1911 Nobel Prize for physiology or medicine.

Gully, John 1783–1863
English sportsman
He was born in Wick, near Bristol. A butcher to trade, he was imprisoned for debt, which he paid from the proceeds of an informal boxing match. He later became the British heavyweight boxing champion (1806–08). After he retired from the ring he took up horse-racing and his

horses won the Derby three times (1832, 1846, 1854) as well as the St Leger in 1832 and the Two Thousand Guineas in 1844 and 1854. He was MP for Pontefract (1832–37), and bought coalmines in County Durham. He was also the father of 24 children (by two wives).

Gumilev, Nikolai Stepanovich 1886–1921
Russian poet
He was a leader of the Acmeist school which revolted against Symbolism. His exotic and vivid poems include *Kolchan* (1915, 'The Quiver'), about war and adventure, and *Kostyor* (1918, 'The Pyre') and *Ognennyi stolp* (1921, 'The Pillar of Fire'), which contain his best pieces. He also wrote criticism and translated French and English poetry. He was shot as a counter-Revolutionary. He was married to the poet **Anna Akhmatova**. 📖 I Strekhobsky, *Craftsman of the Word* (1949)

Gummer, John Selwyn 1939–
English Conservative politician
Born in Stockport, he was educated at King's School, Rochester, and Selwyn College, Cambridge. After graduating from university he became a successful business publisher. In 1970 he was elected Conservative MP for Lewisham West. Although he was defeated in the 1974 general election he returned to parliament in 1979 as Conservative MP for Eye (Suffolk Coastal from 1983). He was Secretary of State for Agriculture (1989–93) and Secretary of State for the Environment (1993–97). He retained his seat in the 1997 general election when Labour came to power. A high churchman, he resigned from the Church of England in 1993 over the question of the ordination of female priests.

Gundelach, Finn Olav 1925–81
Danish diplomat
Born in Vejle, he attended the University of Aarhus, gaining a degree in economics. He had a distinguished career in the Danish diplomatic service, culminating in his appointment as ambassador to the European Economic Community in 1967. He directed the negotiations for Denmark's entry into the Community on 1 January, 1973 and became his country's first European Commissioner. He was promoted to vice-president of the new European Commission under **Roy Jenkins** in 1977 and was given charge of the EEC's common agricultural policy, in which he attempted to maintain a better balance between farmers and consumers than had previously been the case.

Gundicarius, *also known as* Gunther *or* Gunnar
c.385–437 AD
First recorded King of the Burgundians
He was an ally of the Romans, but was killed when his army was annihilated by the Huns. In later Germanic and Norse heroic legend he was cast as the brother-in-law of **Attila** the Hun, who had not, in fact, taken part in the war against the Burgundians, but who was said to covet their gold, for which he put Gunnar/Gundicarius to death in a snake pit.

Gundulf 1024–1108
Norman prelate
A monk at Bec and Caen, he followed **Lanfranc** to England in 1070. Bishop of Rochester from 1077, he built the Tower of London, rebuilt Rochester Cathedral and founded St Bartholomew's Hospital in Chatham. The keep of Rochester Castle is also attributed to him.

Gunn, Neil M(iller) 1891–1973
Scottish novelist
He was born in Dunbeath, Caithness, the son of a fisherman. Educated at the village school, and privately in Galloway, he passed the Civil Service examination in 1907, and moved to London. He was in the Civil Service

until 1937, from 1911 as an officer of customs and excise in Inverness and elsewhere in Scotland. After writing a number of short stories, he published his first novel, *Grey Coast* (1926), which was immediately acclaimed, then *The Lost Glen* (serialized in 1928) and the even more successful *MorningTide* (1931). Other works include a historical novel on the Viking age, *Sun Circle* (1933), *Butcher's Broom* (1934), *Highland River* (1937, James Tait Black Memorial Prize), *Wild Geese Overhead* (1939), *The Silver Darlings* (1941), and the contrasting war-time novels *Young Art and Old Hector* (1942) and *The Green Isle of the Great Deep* (1944). Gunn was at his best when describing the ordinary life and background of a Highland fishing or crofting community, and when interpreting in simple prose the complex character of the Celt. His last novels are *The Well at the World's End* (1951), *Bloodhunt* (1952) and *The Other Landscape* (1954). *The Atom of Delight* (1956) is a philosophical autobiography. 📖 F R Hart and J B Pick, *Neil M Gunn: a Highland life* (1981)

Gunn, Thom(son) William 1929–
English poet

Born in Gravesend, Kent, he attended Trinity College, Cambridge, and moved to the USA in 1954. Since 1990 he has been a senior lecturer in English at the University of California, Berkeley. His first collection, *Fighting Terms* (1954), labelled him a 'Movement' poet. Other volumes include the existentialist *The Sense of Movement* (1957), the contemplative *My Sad Captains* (1961), *The Passages of Joy* (1982), about his homosexuality, and *The Man with Night Sweats* (1992), which includes a series of elegies on men who died as a result of AIDS. *Collected Poems* and *Shelf Life* were published in 1993. 📖 A Bold, *Thom Gunn and Ted Hughes* (1976)

Gunnar See Gundicarius

Gunnarsson, Gunnar 1889–1975
Icelandic novelist

Born in Fljótsdalur, East Iceland, he went to Denmark at the age of 18 to seek fame and fortune, and he wrote all his major works in Danish before rewriting them in Icelandic. His first novel, *Af Borgslægtens Historie* (1920, Eng trans *Guest the One-Eyed*, 1920), was the first Icelandic work to be turned into a feature film. He was a prolific writer, but his acknowledged masterpiece is the autobiographical novel, *Kirken paa Bjerget* (5 vols, 1923–28, Eng trans *Ships in the Sky* and *The Night and the Dream*, 1938). 📖 E O Gelsted, *Gunnar Gunnarsson* (1926)

Gunnell, Sally (Jane Janet) 1966–
English track and field athlete

Born in Chigwell, Essex, she is the only female British athlete to have won world, Olympic, European and Commonwealth titles. Her first national title was the long jump at the Women's Amateur Athletic Association junior championships in 1980. She later won a gold medal in the 100 metre hurdles at the Commonwealth Games in 1986, and silver in 1990. She made her debut in the 400 metre hurdles in 1987, came fifth at the Olympics in 1988, and won gold medals at the Commonwealth Games in 1990, and at the Olympic Games in 1992. She became world champion in 1993 in a record time of 52.74 seconds and set a new world record in the 400 metre hurdles in Stuttgart, also winning that event in the European Cup. She won the European and Commonwealth titles in 1994, but she was put out of action for most of 1995 due to injury, and her 400 metre record was broken by Kim Batten.

Gunning, Elizabeth 1734–90
Irish socialite

Born near St Ives, Cambridgeshire, England, she was the sister of Maria Gunning. She married the 6th Duke of Hamilton (1752) and, on his death (1759), the future Duke of Argyll. She was created Baroness Hamilton in 1770.

Gunning, Maria 1733–60
Irish socialite

Born near St Ives, Cambridgeshire, England, she was the sister of Elizabeth Gunning. She went to London with her sister (1751) and married the 6th Earl of Coventry (1752).

Gunter, Edmund 1581–1626
English mathematician and astronomer

Born in Hertfordshire and educated at Christ Church, Oxford, he received a Southwark living in 1615, but in 1619 became Professor of Astronomy at Gresham College, London. He invented many measuring instruments that bear his name: 'Gunter's chain', the 22 yard (20.1m) long 100-link chain used by surveyors, 'Gunter's line', the forerunner of the modern slide-rule, 'Gunter's scale', a 2 foot (60cm) rule with scales of chords, tangents and logarithmic lines for solving navigational problems, and the portable Gunter's quadrant. He made the first observation of the variation of the magnetic compass, and introduced the words 'cosine' and 'cotangent' into the language of trigonometry. On some accounts it was his reliability that gave rise to the familiar US expression 'according to Gunter', but others connect the expression to the chain.

Gunther See Gundicarius

Günther, Johann Christian 1695–1723
German lyric poet

Born in Strugan, Silesia, he studied medicine but went on to live a somewhat dissolute life, and died in poverty, rejected by his family. His poems, such as the *Leonorenlieder*, have a surprising range, and are for that period unusually direct in language and emotional expression. He wrote love lyrics notable for their sensitivity and their lack of affectation, as well as satires, political poems, religious poems, student songs and drinking songs.

Gunther, John 1901–70
US author and journalist

Born in Chicago, he was a foreign correspondent for the *Chicago Daily News* and for NBC. He established his reputation with the bestselling *Inside Europe* (1939), followed by a series of similar works, in which first-hand material is blended with documentary information to present penetrating social and political studies. Other books include *Death Be Not Proud* (1949) and *A Fragment of Autobiography* (1962).

Guðjónsson, Halldór See Laxness, Halldór Kiljan

Guo Morno (Kuo Mo-jo) 1892–1978
Chinese poet, academic and revolutionary

Born into a bourgeois Sichuan (Szechwan) family, he studied medicine in Japan, starting his writing career whilst there by translating foreign classics into Chinese from Japanese sources. He returned to China to fight in the civil war of 1925, and his work was banned by the nationalist Guomindang (Kuomintang). His early work, including his first collection of verse, *Nü shen* (1921, Eng trans *The Goddesses*, 1958), is liberal-democratic in tone, but it became increasingly didactic and polemical as he embraced communism. His play *Zhu yuan* (1942) is a reworking of a traditional piece about a hero-poet, now with a pro-communist message grafted on to it. In 1949, immediately after the revolution, his status as grand old man of revolutionary literature was confirmed by his being appointed president of the First All-China Federation of Literature and Art Circles. He was attacked during the Cultural Revolution but returned to power in the early 1970s.

Gurdjieff, Georgei Ivanovich c.1865–1949
Armenian thinker

He was born in or near Kars. He practised as a healer in St Petersburg (1910–17) and in 1914 met **Peter Ouspensky**, who became his disciple. He left Russia during the Revolution and in 1922 moved to Fontainebleau, France, where he set up the Institute for the Harmonious Development of Man. It was here that **Katherine Mansfield** died in 1923. His *Beelzebub's Tales to His Grandson* (1949) circulated in manuscript during his lifetime, but was not published until after his death. A charismatic modern Christian gnostic, Gurdjieff synthesized an extraordinary and profound system—to which his novel is a non-literary and deliberately shocking guide—which influenced many writers, including **Rudyard Kipling, Aldous Huxley, J B Priestley, Christopher Isherwood** and many others. 📖 J Moore, *Gurdjieff* (1992)

Gurdon, Sir John Bertrand 1933–
English geneticist

Born in Dippenhall, Hampshire, he was educated at Oxford, became a lecturer in the zoology department there (1965–72), and was a staff member at the Medical Research Council Laboratory of Molecular Biology, Cambridge (1972–83). Since 1983 he has been John Humphrey Plummer Professor of Cell Biology at Cambridge, and since 1991, chairman of the Wellcome Cancer Research Campaign Institute. He was elected FRS in 1971, and became a foreign member of the US National Academy of Sciences in 1980. Gurdon solved one of the central questions in biology this century, investigating the mechanism by which one cell type (the fertilized egg) gives rise to all the different cell types in the adult animal. In 1968 he transplanted a nucleus derived from frog gut into a fertilized egg, and produced a normal tadpole. This demonstrated that fully differentiated animal cells retain the genetic information to become any cell type under the correct environmental stimuli. He has been Master of Magdalene College, Cambridge, since 1995 and was knighted the same year.

Gurevich, Mikhail Iosifovich 1893–1976
Soviet aircraft designer

Born in Rubanshchina, near Kursk, he graduated in 1925 from the aviation faculty of Kharkov Technological Institute. He was best known for the fighter aircraft produced by the design bureau he headed with **Artem Mikoyan**, the MiG (Mikoyan and Gurevich) series.

Gurney, Sir Goldsworthy 1793–1875
English inventor

He was born in Treator, near Padstow, Cornwall. He studied medicine and practised in Wadebridge, Cornwall, and in London, but gave up to work on scientific problems. He devised an improved limelight known as the 'Drummond light', and built a series of steam carriages, one of which in 1829 travelled from London to Bath and back at the rate of 15mph (24.1kph).

Gurney, Ivor 1890–1937
English composer and poet

Born in Gloucester, he studied composition at the Royal College of Music, London, under **Charles Stanford**. Gassed and shell-shocked in 1917, he published two volumes of poems from hospital: *Severn and Somme* (1917) and *War's Embers* (1919). He returned to the Royal College to study with **Ralph Vaughan Williams**, and published his first songs, *5 Elizabethan Songs* (1920), which are considered his best work. From 1922 he was confined in an asylum. Some 300 of his songs survive, and there are also around 900 poems.

Gurney, Joseph John 1788–1847
English Quaker banker and reformer

Born at Earlham Hall, he became a minister for the Society of Friends in 1818, visited North America and the West Indies (1837–40), and campaigned actively for Negro emancipation, prison reform and the abolition of capital punishment. He was the brother of **Elizabeth Fry**.

Gustav I Vasa 1496–1560
King of Sweden and founder of the Vasa dynasty

He was born in Lindholmen, Uppland, into an aristocratic Swedish family. He was taken to Denmark (1518) as a hostage, on the orders of King **Kristian II**, but managed to escape. After the death of his father in the infamous Stockholm Bloodbath (1520), he led an uprising against Kristian, captured Stockholm (1523) and was elected king by the Diet, effectively ending the Kalmar Union. An orator of impressive presence and a hard worker, Gustav imposed order and peace on the demoralized kingdom. He introduced the Lutheran Reformation, made himself head of the Swedish Church, and confiscated Catholic Church properties, using the revenues to build up a well-organized standing army and navy. He fostered schools, promoted trade, and built roads, bridges and canals. In 1544 he persuaded the Riksdag (parliament) to declare the monarchy hereditary, and was succeeded by his son by his first wife, **Erik XIV**. Ruthless in dealing with opponents, he crushed a series of revolts, and left the country united and stable.

Gustav II Adolf, *originally* Gustavus Adolphus, *known as* the Lion of the North 1594–1632
King of Sweden, a champion of Protestantism

Born in Stockholm, he was the son and successor of **Karl IX** and grandson of **Gustav I Vasa**. When he came to the throne in 1611 he found the country immersed in wars and disorder, but he quickly conciliated the nobility, reorganized the government, and revitalized the army. He made a favourable peace at Knäred (1613) with Denmark which, under **Kristian IV**, invaded Sweden in 1611. He defeated Russia (1613–17) and received a large part of Finland and Livonia from Poland through the Treaty of Stolbova (1617). He fought King **Sigismund III Vasa** of Poland (1621–29) for the Swedish throne, took Livonia and forced a favourable six-year truce with the Treaty of Altmark (1629). This left him free to intervene directly in the Thirty Years War (1618–48), on behalf of the Protestants against the Catholic League of the Habsburg Holy Roman Emperor, **Ferdinand II**, and his victorious general **Albrecht von Wallenstein**. Leaving the government in the care of the chancellor, **Axel Oxenstjerna**, he crossed to Pomerania in 1630 with 15,000 men and took Stettino. In 1631 he failed to prevent the massacre of Magdeburg by Count von Tilly, who had supplanted Wallenstein, but in September of that year he decisively defeated Tilly at Breitenfeld, near Leipzig, and took the Palatinate and Mainz. In the spring of 1632 he advanced into Bavaria, defeated and killed Tilly and captured Augsburg and Munich. The Emperor Ferdinand recalled Wallenstein, and in November 1632 the two armies met in a furious battle at Lützen, near Leipzig. The Swedes won, but Gustav Adolf was killed. A compelling leader of impressive abilities and military achievement, he left Sweden the strongest power in Europe and reformed the country's central and local administration, establishing Stockholm as the administrative capital.

Gustav III 1746–92
King of Sweden

Born in Stockholm, he was the son of King **Adolf Fredrik** and Louisa Ulrika, sister of King **Frederick II, the Great** of Prussia. A brilliant and captivating figure, when he ascended the throne in 1771 he was determined to break the power of the oligarchy of nobles. He arrested the council, declared a new form of government (1772), purged the bureaucracy, and encouraged agriculture, commerce and science. He granted religious toleration, but also created a secret police system and introduced censorship. He was a patron of the arts, and wrote plays. His court became a northern Versailles, with the foundation of the Royal Opera House (1782), the Swedish Academy (1786) after the French pattern, and the Royal Dramatic Theatre (1788). With poor harvests and a failing economy creating discontent, as a diversion he launched into a war against Russia (1788–90) that proved unpopular and inconclusive, and in 1789 he assumed new royal prerogatives as absolute monarch. At the beginning of the French Revolution he encouraged Count **Hans Axel von Fersen** to rescue the French royal family in the abortive Flight to Varennes (1791), and planned to use his army to help **Louis XVI**, but in 1792 he was shot by a former army officer, **Johan Jakob Anckarström**, and later died. Married to Sofia Magdalena of Denmark, he was succeeded by his young son, **Gustav IV Adolf.**

Gustav IV Adolf 1778–1837
King of Sweden

Born in Stockholm, he was the son and successor (1792) of **Gustav III.** During his minority, the regent was his uncle Karl (Charles), Duke of Södermanland. In the first years of his reign as an absolute monarch he did much to improve Swedish agriculture with a General Enclosure Act (1803). He abandoned Swedish neutrality to declare war on France (1805) and when Russia became an ally of **Napoleon I**, the Swedes lost their last German possessions. In 1808 Sweden was attacked by Denmark and Finland was simultaneously invaded by Russia. Tactless and autocratic, he spurned an offer of help by a British force under Sir **John Moore**, and Finland was annexed by Russia (1809). He was arrested in a military coup and forced to abdicate (1809). He was exiled with his family, and after divorcing his wife (1812) wandered alone in Europe for 25 years as Colonel Gustafsson until he died in Switzerland.

Gustav V 1858–1950
King of Sweden

Born in Stockholm, the son and successor (1907) of **Oskar II**, he was shy and reserved by nature. He disliked pomp and spectacle and refused a coronation ceremony, thus becoming the first uncrowned king on the Swedish throne. Nevertheless, he sought to assert the personal power of the monarchy, and in 1914 he challenged the government with a call for greater spending on defence. Demands for his abdication were stilled by the outbreak of World War I, when Sweden mobilized but remained neutral. Thereafter he reigned as a popular constitutional monarch, and in World War II came to symbolize the unity of the nation. He was the longest-reigning king in Swedish history. In 1881 he married Princess Viktoria, daughter of the Grand Duke of Baden and granddaughter of Sofia of Sweden (**Gustav IV Adolf**'s daughter), thus uniting the reigning Bernadotte dynasty with the former royal House of Vasa. His nephew was Count Folke **Bernadotte**. He was succeeded by his son, **Gustav VI.**

Gustav VI 1882–1973
King of Sweden

He was born in Stockholm, the son and successor of **Gustav V**, and became a respected scholar and archaeologist and an authority on Chinese art. He married (1905) Princess Margaret (1882–1920), daughter of Prince Arthur, Duke of Connaught, and granddaughter of Queen **Victoria**, by whom he had four sons and a daughter, Ingrid, who married King **Frederik IX** of Denmark. In 1923 he married Lady Louise Mountbatten (1889–1965), sister of Earl **Mountbatten** of Burma. On Gustav's accession (1950) Lady Louise became the first British-born queen in Swedish history. A new constitution was under preparation during his reign, and the king worked

to transform the Crown into a democratic monarchy, which helped to preserve it against political demands for a republic. As his eldest son, Gustav Adolf (1906–47), was killed in an air crash, he was succeeded by his grandson, **Carl XVI Gustav.**

Guston, Philip 1913–80
US painter

Born in Montreal, Canada, he settled in New York City in 1936 where he was involved with the Federal Works of Art Project (1935–40). His work of the 1950s was in the Abstract Expressionist style, but from the late 1960s he introduced brightly coloured and crudely drawn comic-strip characters into his painting. A major series depicted the Ku Klux Klan.

Gutenberg, Beno 1889–1960
US geophysicist

Born in Darmstadt, Germany, he studied geophysics and mathematics at Darmstadt Technische Hochschule, and gained a PhD from Göttingen University. From 1913 to 1916 he was an assistant at the International Seismological Association in Strassburg (now Strasbourg, France) where he made two important contributions; he deduced from earthquake shock waves the existence of a zone in the mantle where seismic waves travel with low velocities (1913) and in 1914 he made the first correct determination of the depth to the Earth's core, which he concluded is liquid. At the University of Frankfurt (1924–30) he taught seismology and worked on the structure of the atmosphere. In 1929 he moved to the USA where he accepted the chair in geophysics at the California Institute of Technology (Caltech, 1930) and became director of the Seismological Laboratory when it moved from the Carnegie Institution to Caltech in 1937.

Gutenberg, Johannes Gensfleisch See panel p805

Gütersloh, Albert Paris von, *pseudonym of* Albert Conrad Kiehtreiber 1887–1973
Austrian painter and novelist

He was born in Vienna. A practitioner of Expressionism, he worked as a stage designer for **Max Reinhardt**, but was also a Professor of Fine Arts, until the Nazis forced him to work in a factory. The most extraordinary of his Baroque novels is *Sonne und Mond* (1962, 'Sun and Moon'), which is, simultaneously, a massive allegory of Austria as it tottered from grand empire to shabby and always menaced republic, and a 'huge gloss on the perennially puzzling parable of the Unjust Steward'. He started this major work as early as 1935.

Guthlac, St c.673–714
English monk

He was a monk at Repton in 697, and a hermit at Crowland Abbey in 699, where he lived a life of severe asceticism. His feast day is 11 April.

Guthorm or Guthrum d.890
Danish King of East Anglia

An opponent of King **Alfred** the Great, he led a major Viking invasion of Anglo-Saxon England in 871 (the 'Great Summer Army'), seized East Anglia, and conquered Northumbria and Mercia. He attacked Wessex (878) and drove Alfred into hiding in Somerset. Alfred recovered sufficiently to defeat the Danes at the crucial Battle of Edington, Wiltshire (878). In the ensuing treaty, Guthorm agreed to leave Wessex and accept baptism as a Christian, and he and his army settled down peacefully in East Anglia. He issued coinage modelled on Alfred's and there were substantial links between the English and Danes.

Guthrie, Sir James 1859–1930
Scottish painter

Gutenberg, Johannes Gensfleisch 1400–68
German printer, regarded as the inventor of printing

Gutenberg was born in Mainz, the son of a patrician called Friele Gensfleisch or Gutenberg. Between 1430 and 1444 Gutenberg was in Strasbourg, probably working as a goldsmith, and it is there (by 1439) that he may have begun printing. Living in Mainz again by 1448, he entered into partnership (c.1450) with **Johann Fust** who financed a printing press. This partnership ended in 1455; Fust sued him for the debt when the loan was not repaid, and received the printing plant in lieu of payment. He carried on the concern with the assistance of his son-in-law **Peter Schöffer** and completed the famous Bible which Gutenberg had begun, while Gutenberg, aided by Konrad Humery, set up another printing press.

Although Gutenberg is credited with the invention of printing, it is probable that rudimentary printing was practised before Gutenberg's development of the art. Apart from his 42-line bible, Gutenberg is credited with the *Fragment of the Last Judgment* (c.1445), and editions of **Aelius Donatus'** Latin school grammar.

📖 M E Gekker, *Gutenberg* (1991); Janet Ing, *Johann Gutenberg and His Bible: A Historical Study* (1988); Victor Scholderer, *Johann Gutenberg* (1963).

The Gutenberg Bible, also known as the Mazarin Bible because the first copy went into the library of Cardinal **Mazarin**, was a three-volume Latin work printed in columns of 42 lines, hence its other name, the Forty-Two-Line Bible.

Born in Greenock, Renfrewshire, the son of a minister, he began to study law at Glasgow, but abandoned this in 1877 to become an artist. Almost entirely self-taught, he was a follower of the Glasgow school, and attracted some attention in Paris with his early works. He later turned from genre to portraiture, of which he became a notable exponent. As president of the Royal Scottish Academy he was instrumental in improving the conditions and facilities of the National Galleries of Scotland.

Guthrie, Janet 1938–
US motor-racing driver, the first woman to complete the Indianapolis 500

Born in Iowa City, Iowa, she began building and racing cars in 1962. In 1976 she became the first woman to race in a NASCAR Winston Cup event, and also that year qualified for the Indianapolis 500, but was unable to compete because of equipment failure. The following year she became the first woman to compete in the Indianapolis 500, though she did not finish, and in 1978 she competed and finished ninth, establishing herself as the first woman to complete the race. Her 1978 Indianapolis 500 driver's suit and helmet are in the Smithsonian Institution in Washington DC, and she is in the International Women's Sports Hall of Fame.

Guthrie, Samuel 1782–1848
US chemist and physician

Born in Brimfield, Massachusetts, he studied at the College of Physicians and Surgeons, New York City, and at the University of Pennsylvania. During the 1812 War with Britain, he served in the Army Medical Corps and later practised medicine in Sacketts Harbor, New York. He is reputed to have invented percussion priming powder, and in 1830 he devised a process which rapidly converted potato starch into molasses. The following year he made chloroform by distilling chloride of lime with alcohol in a copper vessel.

Guthrie, Sir (William) Tyrone 1900–71
English theatrical producer

He was born in Tunbridge Wells, Kent, and educated at Wellington College and Oxford. After being director of the Scottish National Players and the Cambridge Festival Theatre, he produced many successful **Shakespeare** plays at the Old Vic during the 1930s, becoming administrator of the Old Vic and Sadler's Wells (1939–45), and director of the Old Vic (1950–51). He directed many plays at the Edinburgh Festival and abroad, and founded the Tyrone Guthrie Theatre in Minneapolis, USA, in 1963. He wrote *A Life in the Theatre* (1960). He was knighted in 1961. 📖 James Forsyth, *Tyrone Guthrie* (1976)

Guthrie, Woody (Woodrow Wilson) 1912–67
US folk-singer, songwriter and author

He was born in Okemah, Oklahoma. A folk-poet in the true sense, he travelled the length and breadth of the USA and wrote hundreds of songs about his experiences, using mostly traditional country-music and blues themes. His deep concern about the plight of the poor people of the USA turned into active campaigning for trade unions and racial equality in the 1930s and 1940s, and, along with **Pete Seeger**, he formed the influential radical group, the Almanac Singers. At the same time he wrote many much-loved songs for children, but it is for classic folk-song statements like 'This Land is Your Land', 'So Long It's Been Good to Know You', and 'Pastures of Plenty' that he is best remembered. His colourful autobiography, *Bound for Glory*, was published in 1943. In the 1950s his career was prematurely ended by Huntington's chorea, an inherited wasting disease; a young **Bob Dylan** was among the supplicants who visited his sick-bed. His son, Arlo Guthrie (1947–), became a popular figure on both the folk and rock scenes from the late 1960s. 📖 Joe Klein *Woody Guthrie: A Life* (1986)

Gutiérrez, Gustavo 1928–
Peruvian theologian

He was born in Lima. Abandoning medical studies for the Roman Catholic priesthood, he studied philosophy and psychology at Louvain (1951–55) and theology at Lyons (1955–59) before ordination in Lima, becoming Professor of Theology at the Catholic university there in 1960. His seminal work *A Theology of Liberation* (1971, Eng trans 1973) is dedicated to 'doing' theology. This is defined as 'critical reflection on historical praxis' and is based on responding to the needs of the poor and the oppressed rather than on imposing solutions from the outside. His arguments have challenged supporters of the status quo in Latin America and practitioners of academic theology elsewhere. He explores the biblical and spiritual roots of liberation theology more deeply in *The Power of the Poor in History* (1984), *We Drink from Our Own Wells* (1984) and *On Job* (1987).

Guttuso, Renato 1912–87
Italian painter

Born at Bagheria, near Palermo, he worked for some time in Milan and settled in Rome in 1937. He joined the outlawed Communist party in 1940, and much of his work is an allegory of life under Fascism such as *Flight from Etna* (1938–39) and his *Crucifixion* (1941). He also opposed the Mafia, as in his *Assassination* (1948). After the war, he began to paint dramatic Realist pictures of the lives of working people, such as *The Discussion* (1959–60, Tate, London), and in 1972 he was awarded the **Lenin** Peace Prize. In 1984 he completed a cycle of paintings on the theme of female gymnasts and football players (exhibited by the Olympic Committee in Rome and then in Los

Angeles). He left major works to the Galleria d'Arte Moderna in Rome, and a collection of his paintings to the town of Bagheria (Museo Guttuso, Bagheria).

Gutzkow, Karl Ferdinand 1811–78
German writer
He was born in Berlin. He was influenced by the French Revolution of 1830, and for his *Wally die Zweiflerin* (1835, 'Doubting Wally') got three months' imprisonment as a champion of the 'Young Germany' movement. He next became a journalist, and in 1847 director of the Court Theatre at Dresden, having meanwhile written many dramas, the most successful being *Richard Savage* (1839) and *Zopf und Schwert* (1844, 'Pigtail and Sword'). Among his romances is *Die Ritter vom Geiste* (1850–52, 'The Knights of the Spirit'). ▢ E W Dubert, *Karl Gutzkow und seine Zeit* (1968)

Gu Yanwu (Ku Yen-wu) 1613–82
Chinese scholar and official
He is celebrated for his loyalty to the Ming Dynasty and his refusal to serve the succeeding Manchu Qing (Ch'ing) Dynasty. He participated in the Ming resistance movement against the Manchus in the late 1640s and later led the life of an independent scholar, rejecting all offers by the Qing authorities to enter officialdom. Gu was to serve as an inspiration for early 20th century anti-Manchu revolutionaries.

Guy of Arezzo See Guido D'Arezzo

Guy of Lusignan d.1194
French crusader
He became King of Jerusalem in 1186 as consort of Sibylla, daughter of Amalric I, but was defeated and captured at Hattin (1187) by Saladin, who overran most of the kingdom. On the death of his wife in 1190 the throne passed to Conrad of Montferrat (d.1192), but Guy received Cyprus as compensation, where his family ruled until 1474.

Guy, Buddy (George) 1936–
US blues guitarist and singer
Born in Lettsworth, Louisiana, he began playing in his native Louisiana, but his mature style was not formed until he moved to Chicago in 1957, where he inherited the electric urban blues style of Muddy Waters, B B King and Guitar Slim. His frenetic style won him fans in the rock audience in the 1960s, helped by admiring endorsements from Jimi Hendrix and Eric Clapton. He opened his own blues club in Chicago in 1989, and remains a major figure in the music, and one of its most exciting live performers. ▢ With D Wilcock, *Damn Right I Got The Blues* (1994)

Guy, Thomas c.1644–1724
English bookseller and philanthropist
Born in Horselydown, Southwark, he began business in 1668 importing English bibles from Holland and later he contracted with Oxford for the privilege of printing bibles. By this means and by selling out South Sea shares, he amassed a fortune. He was MP from 1695 to 1707. In 1707 he built and furnished three wards of St Thomas's Hospital, London, and in 1722 he founded the hospital in Southwark, Guy's Hospital, which bears his name. He also built and endowed almshouses.

Guy, William 1859–1950
English dentist
Born in Kent, he studied medicine at Edinburgh, was a general physician in Cumberland, then returned to Edinburgh to learn dentistry and became partner to the Dental School's founder, John Smith, whose daughter, Helen, he married. He was Dean of the school from 1899 to 1933. He put Scotland in the forefront of the drive for professionalization in dentistry, lobbying for the 1921 Act

to outlaw amateur and untrained dentists from practice, and pressurizing other scientific bodies to accept dentistry as a respectable science. In 1948 he published *Mostly Memories—Some Digressions*.

Guyon, Jeanne Marie de la Mothe, *née* Bouvier 1648–1717
French mystic
Born in Montargis, she had planned to become a nun, but was married at the age of 16 to the wealthy and elderly Jacques de la Motte Guyon. A widow at only 28, she determined to devote her life to the poor and needy, and to the cultivation of spiritual perfection. To this end, she went to Geneva (1681), but three years later was forced to leave on the grounds that her Quietist doctrines were heretical. In Turin, Grenoble, Nice, Genoa, Vercelli and Paris, where she finally settled in 1686, she became the centre of a movement for the promotion of 'holy living'. In 1688 she was arrested for heretical opinions, and for having been in correspondence with Miguel de Molinos (1640–97), the leader of Quietism in Spain. Released by the intervention of Madame de Maintenon, she was again imprisoned in 1695, and not released from the Bastille until 1702. Her works include *Les Torrents spirituels, Moyen court de faire oraison* (1685, 'The Short and Very Easy Method of Prayer'), a mystical interpretation of the Song of Solomon, an autobiography, letters, and some spiritual poetry.

Guyot, Arnold 1807–84
US geographer
Born in Boudevilliers, Switzerland, he became Professor of Geology at Neuchâtel (1839), and studied glaciers in Switzerland with Louis Agassiz. In 1848 he followed Agassiz to the USA, where he lectured at the Lowell Institute on *Earth and Man* (1853), and in 1854 became Professor of Physical Geography and Geology at Princeton. In charge of the meteorological department of the Smithsonian Institution, he published *Meteorological and Physical Tables*. He wrote *Earth and Man* (1849), and was joint editor of *Johnson's Cyclopaedia* (1874–77).

Guyton de Morveau, Louis Bernard, Baron 1737–1816
French lawyer and chemist
Born in Dijon, Burgundy, he practised law during much of his life, notably as a provincial prosecutor, but devoted his leisure to studying and teaching chemistry. In 1791 he was elected a member of the legislative assembly. From 1795 to 1805 he was director of the École Polytechnique and was Master of the Mint from 1800 to 1814. He was made a baron of the French Empire in 1810. He adopted the views of Antoine Lavoisier on combustion, and in the 1780s he was involved with Lavoisier, Claude Louis Bertholet and Antoine François Fourcroy in revising chemical nomenclature and publishing *Méthode d'une nomenclature chimique* (1787, 'Method of Chemical Nomenclature'). He wrote many scientific articles and several books, and his interests spanned mineralogy, applied chemistry, metallurgy and balloon flight.

Guzman, Martín Luis 1887–1976
Mexican novelist, editor and journalist
He was born in Chihuahua. Originally a lawyer, he became a supporter of Francisco Madero, and then, after the latter's assassination, private secretary to Pancho Villa. Later a revolutionary who could not abide revolutionaries, he abandoned Mexico for New York and Madrid, but finally returned in 1936. With Mariano Azuela, Guzmán was the most important novelist of the revolution, all the events of which he recorded in his fiction. *El águila y la serpiente* (1928, Eng trans 'The Eagle and the Serpent', 1930), which is partly autobiographical, became the most famous of all Mexican novels of the

Revolution. *La sombra del caudillo* (1929, 'In the Shadow of the Leader'), his best novel, deals with the dominance of Obregón. His *Memorias de Pancho Villa* (1938–51, Eng trans *Memoirs of Pancho Villa*, 1965) is certainly a novel, but is told in the authentic voice of the illiterate caudillo. 📖 W M Langford, *The Mexican Novel Comes of Age* (1971); J S Brushwood, *Mexico in its Novel* (1970)

Guzmán Blanco, Antonio 1829–99
Venezuelan politician
Born in Caracas and educated in Europe, he was violently anticlerical and a bitter opponent of José Antonio Páez. He was Vice-President from 1863 to 1868, when he was driven from office. He then headed a revolution which restored him to power in 1870, and became dictator, holding the presidency on three occasions (1873–77, 1879–84, 1886–88). He was prevented from returning from a visit to Paris by a rising in Caracas, and died in exile. 📖 George S Wise, *Caudillo: A Portrait of Guzman Blanco* (1951)

Gwathmey, Charles 1938–
US architect
Born in Charlotte, North Carolina, he studied at the University of Pennsylvania and at Yale. As a member of the 'New York Five' in the 1960s he was encouraged by the patronage of Philip Johnson. He has won the American Institute of Architects (AIA) House award 10 times (1968–82), and became a Fellow of the AIA in 1981. Having become a partner in Gwathmey Seigel and Associates (1971), he is now known particularly for business architecture, including buildings such as the Library and Science Building, Westover School, Connecticut (1979), and the Fogg Art Museum extension, Harvard (1991). 📖 Peter Arnell and Ted Bickford (eds), *Charles Gwathmey and Robert Seigel: Buildings and Projects, 1964–1984* (1984)

Gwyn, Nell (Eleanor), *also spelt* Gwynn or Gwynne c.1650–1687
English actress, and mistress of Charles II
Born of humble parents, she lived precariously selling oranges before establishing herself as a comedienne at Drury Lane, London, especially in breeches parts. 'Pretty, witty Nell's' first protector was Lord Buckhurst, but the transfer of her affections to Charles II was genuine. She had at least one son by the king—Charles Beauclerk, Duke of St Albans—and James Beauclerk is allegedly a second. She is said to have urged Charles to found Chelsea Hospital. 📖 Bryan Bevan, *Nell Gwyn* (1969)

Gwynn, Stephen Lucius 1864–1950
Irish biographer and literary historian
Born in Dublin, the grandson of William Smith O'Brien, and educated at Brasenose College, Oxford, he became a schoolmaster and then a journalist in London (1896–1904). He moved into Irish nationalist politics as MP for Galway (1906–18), and later wrote a fine memoir of his leader, *John Redmond's Last Years* (1919). His wife became a Roman Catholic and their sons prominent Roman Catholic intellectuals. His literary output was prodigious, his *Masters of English Literature* (1904) proving a great bestseller. Perhaps his most remarkable work is *Experiences of a Literary Man* (1926), on the meaning of life in the midst of literature.

Gwynne, Nell See Gwyn, Nell

Gwynne-Vaughan, Dame Helen Charlotte Isabella, *née* Fraser 1879–1967
English botanist and servicewoman
Educated at Cheltenham Ladies' College and King's College London she became head and later Professor of Botany at Birkbeck College, London (1909). She became an authority on fungi. In World War I she was organizer (1917) and later controller of the Women's Army Auxiliary Air Force in France, and commandant of the Women's Royal Auxiliary Air Force (1918–19). In World War II she was chief controller of the Women's Auxiliary Territorial Service (1939–41). She retired from Birkbeck in 1944.

Gyatso, Geshe Kelsang 1931–
Tibetan Buddhist teacher and monk
He was born in western Tibet and spent 15 years at Sera Je monastery and a further 20 years in meditation in the Himalayas before moving to Great Britain in 1977. He is resident teacher at the Manjushri Buddhist Centre in Ulverston, Cumbria, and has founded several centres in the UK, North America and Mexico. He is the founder of the New Kadampa Tradition of Buddhism, which seeks to preserve and promote the essence of Buddhist teaching in a form suited to the modern world and way of life. His books include *Clear light of Bliss* (1982), *The Joyful Path of Good Fortune* (1990) and *Introduction to Buddhism* (1992).

Gyges d.c.648BC
King of Lydia
He came to power in c.685BC, when he murdered his predecessor Candaules, married his wife, and became King of Lydia. He also founded the Marmnad dynasty. Under him, Lydian power and wealth began to grow, and close relations developed with the Greeks. He initiated an aggressive policy towards the Greek cities of Asia Minor which his successors continued down to Croesus, also cultivating good relations with the Oracle of Apollo at Delphi, and with Ashurbanipal of Assyria. He died fighting an invasion of the Cimmerians.

Gylberde, William See Gilbert, William

Gyllenhammar, Pehr Gustaf 1935–
Swedish industrialist
Born in Gothenburg, he was educated at Lund University and studied international law in England, the USA and Switzerland. He joined the Volvo motor company in 1970, was managing director (1971–83), became chairman in 1983, and executive chairman of the board of directors from 1990 to 1993. He has written numerous articles and a number of books, including *Jag tror på Sverige* (1973, 'I Believe in Sweden') and *En industripolitik för människan* (1979, 'Industrial Policy for Human Beings').

Gyp, *pseudonym of* Comtesse de Mirabeau de Martel 1849–1932
French novelist
She was born in the château of Koëtsal in Brittany, and wrote a series of humorous novels describing fashionable society. The best known are *Petit Bob* (1868, 'Little Bob') and *Mariage de Chiffon* (1894, 'Chiffon Marriage'). 📖 *Sac à papier, correspondence with Trois Étoiles* (1886)

Haakon I Haraldsson, the Good c.914–961
King of Norway

The youngest son of Harald I Halfdanarson, he was brought up in England at the Christian court of King Athelstan. Co-ruler of Norway from c.940, he returned to Norway on his father's death (c.945) and seized the Crown with his half-brother, Erik Haraldsson, Blood-Axe. Haakon proved to be an able legislator and administrator. He brought missionaries from England and built some churches, but his attempts to convert Norway to Christianity met stubborn resistance. He had to fight off several attempts on the throne by the sons of Erik Blood-Axe, led by Harald II Eriksson, Grey-Cloak, and eventually died in battle against them.

Haakon or Hakon IV Haakonsson, the Old 1204–63
King of Norway

He was the illegitimate grandson of the usurper Sverrir Sigurdsson. His uncle, Duke Skúli, put him on the throne at 13 and acted as regent, but was defeated by his nephew and killed (1240). Haakon strengthened relationships with the Church, and was ceremoniously crowned (1247). He annexed Iceland and Greenland to the Norwegian Crown (1262), but on an expedition to the Western Isles of Scotland to reassert Norwegian power there (1263), he suffered a setback at the Battle of Largs against Alexander III of Scotland and died at Kirkwall in Orkney on his way back to Norway.

Haakon VII 1872–1957
King of Norway

Born in Charlottenlund, Denmark, he was Prince Carl of Denmark, being the second son of King Frederick VIII, and was elected King of Norway (1905) when the country voted for independence from Sweden. In 1896 he married Princess Maud, youngest daughter of King Edward VII of Great Britain. Known as the 'people's king', he dispensed with much of the pomp of royalty. When Germany invaded Norway (1940) he refused to abdicate, and when further armed resistance was impossible, carried on the resistance from Great Britain, returning in triumph in 1945. He was succeeded by his son, Olav V.
📖 Tim Greve, *Haakon VII of Norway, Founder of a New Monarchy* (1983)

Haba, Alois 1893–1972
Czech composer

Born in Vyzovice, he studied in Prague, Vienna and Berlin and was made a professor at the Prague Conservatory in 1924. He composed prolifically, and was interested in the division of the scale into quarter-tones. His works include an opera, *Matka* (1931, 'The Mother'), and orchestral, chamber and piano music. His brother Karel (1898–1972) was a violinist, teacher and composer.

Haber, Fritz 1868–1934
German physical chemist and Nobel Prize winner

Born in Breslau (Wrocław, Poland), he was the son of a dyestuffs merchant and took up chemistry initially with a view to entering the family business. After study at the universities of Berlin and Heidelberg, he obtained his doctorate at the Technische Hochschule, Charlottenberg. In 1894, he became an assistant at the Technische Hochschule in Karlsruhe, and began the study of physical chemistry and its technical applications. He became *Privatdozent* in 1896, professor extraordinary in 1898, and in 1906 became Professor of Physical Chemistry and Electrochemistry. In 1904 he began to study the direct synthesis of ammonia from nitrogen and hydrogen gases, work which continued after his move to Berlin and which, in association with Carl Bosch, led to the large-scale production of ammonia. This was important in maintaining an explosives supply for the German war effort from 1914 to 1918. It also led to Haber receiving the Nobel Prize for chemistry in 1918. This occasioned some criticism because he had been involved in the organization of gas warfare. In 1911 he moved to Berlin to direct the Kaiser Wilhelm Institute for Physical Chemistry and Electrochemistry; however he resigned in 1933 in protest at the anti-Jewish policies of the Nazi regime. He accepted an invitation to work in Cambridge, but decided to spend the winter first in Italy, and he died while travelling south. 📖 M Goran, *The Story of Fritz Haber* (1967)

Haberl, Franz Xaver 1840–1910
German musicologist

Born in Ober Ellenbach, he was kapellmeister at Passau Cathedral (1862–67). He is known for his researches on 16th-century music, especially that of Palestrina, whose 33-volume edition of works he completed from volume X onwards.

Habermas, Jürgen 1929–
German philosopher and sociologist

Born in Düsseldorf, he was educated at Göttingen, Zurich and Bonn. He became Professor of Philosophy at Heidelberg (1961) then Professor of Philosophy and Sociology at Frankfurt (1964) and was director of the Max Planck Institute, Starnberg (1971–80). The central theme of his work is the possibility of a rational political commitment to socialism in societies in which science and technology are dominant. His books include *Erkenntnis und Interesse* (1968, Eng trans *Knowledge and Human Interests*, 1971) and *Theorie des kommunikatives Handelns* (1981, Eng trans *The Theory of Communicative Action*, 1984). Since 1983 he has been Professor of Philosophy at Frankfurt University.

Habington, William 1605–54
English poet

He was born in Hindlip, Worcestershire. His father was imprisoned, and his uncle Edward executed, for complicity in Babington's plot. William was educated at St Omer and Paris, and married Lucy Herbert, daughter of the first Lord Powis. He immortalized her in his *Castara* (1634), a collection of metaphysical lyrics, and was the author of *The Historie of Edward the Fourth* (1640), and a play, *The Queen of Aragon* (1640). 📖 K Allott, introduction and commentary to *The Poems of William Habington* (1948)

Habré, Hissène c.1930–
Chadian nationalist and politician

The son of a desert shepherd, he worked as a clerk for the French army before becoming an administrator. He joined the FAN (Forces Armées du Nord) guerrillas in the early 1970s but, having made his peace with President Malloum in 1978, he was appointed Prime Minister. When Goukouni seized power in 1979, Habré first became Defence Minister, then, supported by the CIA, took power himself in 1982. With French military assistance and support from African heads of state, he forced Libya to withdraw from northern Chad and, although uneasily, retained power until he was ousted in a coup led by his military commander Idriss Deby (1990). He went to live in Cameroon.

Habsburg or Hapsburg
Royal dynasty of Austria-Hungary

The name comes from the castle of Habichtsburg (Hawk's Castle) on the River Aare in the Upper Rhine region (now in Switzerland), first built in the 11th century. The first Count of Habsburg was Werner I (d.1096). His descendant, Count Rudolf IV, was elected King of Germany (1273) as **Rudolf I**, *de facto* the first Habsburg emperor although he was never anointed by the pope. The first recognized emperor was **Frederick III** of Germany, crowned in 1452. From that time, with one interruption from 1742 to 1745, the imperial Crown was a family possession until the empire was dissolved in 1806. The zenith of Habsburg power was reached under the Emperor **Charles V** (Charles I of Spain) who presided over an empire stretching from the Danube to the Caribbean. After his death the House of Habsburg divided into two lines; the Spanish line died with **Charles II** of Spain (1700), but the Austrian line continued until the abdication of **Charles** (1887–1922), the last Habsburg-Lorraine emperor of Austria and Hungary, in 1918.

Habyarimana, Juvenal 1937–94
Rwandan soldier and politician

He was born in Gasiza, in Gisenji prefecture. He joined the National Guard and by 1973 had risen to the rank of major-general and head of the Guard. In the same year, as fighting between the Tutsi and Hutu tribes recommenced, he led a bloodless coup against President Gregoire Kayibanda and established a military regime. He founded the National Revolutionary Development Movement (MRND) as the only legal party and promised an eventual return to constitutional government.

Hácha, Emil 1872–1945
Czechoslovak lawyer and politician

Born in Trhové Sviny, Bohemia, he became President of Czechoslovakia in 1938 on **Eduard Beneš's** resignation following the German annexation of Sudetenland; under duress, he made over the state to **Hitler** in 1939. He was puppet President of the subsequent German protectorate of Bohemia and Moravia. Arrested after liberation in 1945, he died in prison.

Häckel, Ernst Heinrich Philipp August See
Haeckel, Ernst Heinrich Philipp August

Hackett, Deborah Vernon 1887–1965
Australian businesswoman

She was born in Guildford, Western Australia, the daughter of Frederick Drake-Brockman, a member of a pioneering family, and Grace Vernon Bussell, the heroine of a shipwreck from which she saved some 50 lives in 1875. Deborah's first husband, Sir John Hackett, died in 1916; in 1918 she married Frank Moulden, who became Mayor of Adelaide (1920–22) and was knighted in 1922. Inheriting a passion for geology from her father, she formed a syndicate in 1923 to mine tantalite at Port Hedland, in the north of Western Australia, and was later involved in mining tungsten in the Northern Territory; these rare metals both became invaluable in World War II. Also a lover of flying, she would sometimes travel over 20,000 miles in single-engined airplanes over Australia, and was a passenger on the first commercial flight from Australia to England in 1934. Her son by her first husband was General Sir **John Hackett**.

Hackett, Sir John Winthrop 1910–97
British soldier and academic

Born in Perth, Australia, and educated at Geelong Grammar School, Australia, and New College, Oxford, he was commissioned in the 8th Hussars in 1931. In World War II he served with distinction in the Middle East, Sicily, Italy and notably with the 4th Parachute Brigade at Arnhem in 1944. After the war he commanded the 7th Armoured Division as major general (1956), and was Commandant of the Royal Military College of Science (1958). He was Commander-in-Chief, Northern Ireland, in 1961 and of the British Army of the Rhine and of the Northern Army Group in 1966. He was Principal of King's College, University of London (1968–75), where he was Professor of Classics from 1977. His publications include *I was a Stranger* (1977), *The Untold Story* (1982) and *The Profession of Arms* (1983).

Hackman, Gene (Eugene Alden) 1930–
US actor

Born in San Bernardino, California, he was a marine and had studied journalism before pursuing acting at the Pasadena Playhouse. Working in television from 1959, he made his film debut in *Mad Dog Coll* (1961). He received Academy Award nominations for *Bonnie And Clyde* (1967) and *I Never Sang For My Father* (1970) before winning the award for his performance as the obsessive cop 'Popeye' Doyle in *The French Connection* (1971). His star roles include *The Poseidon Adventure* (1972), *The Conversation* (1974), *Night Moves* (1975) and *Eureka* (1982). One of American cinema's most respected and prolific character actors, he received a further Academy Award nomination for *Mississippi Burning* (1988) and won the Best Supporting Actor award for *Unforgiven* (1992). Recent films include *Get Shorty* (1995), *The Birdcage* (1996) and *The Chamber* (1996). In 1992 he made a rare stage appearance on Broadway in *Death and the Maiden*.

Hackworth, Green Haywood 1883–1973
US lawyer and judge

He was a legal adviser to the State Department (1925–46) and the author of an authoritative *Digest of International Law* (1940–43). He became a judge of the International Court of Justice (1946–61) and was its president from 1955 to 1958.

Hackworth, Timothy 1786–1850
English locomotive engineer

Born in Wylam, Northumberland, he was manager of the Stockton to Darlington railway (1825–40), and builder of a number of famous engines, including the *Royal George* and the *Sans Pareil*, rival of **George Stephenson's** *Rocket*.

Hadamard, Jacques Salomon 1865–1963
French mathematician

Born in Versailles and educated in Paris, he became lecturer in Bordeaux (1893–97), the Sorbonne (1897–1909), Paris, and then professor at the Collège de France and the École Polytechnique until his retirement in 1937. He was a leading figure in French mathematics throughout his career, working in complex function theory, differential geometry and partial differential equations. In 1896 he and the Belgian mathematician Charles de la Vallée Poussin independently proved the definitive form of the prime number theorem, previously conjectured in cruder forms by both **Adrien-Marie Legendre** and **Carl Friedrich Gauss**, and proved in a weaker form by **Pafnutii Chebyshev**. He lived to an exceptional age, and was still publishing mathematical work in his eighties.

Haden, Sir Francis Seymour 1818–1910
English etcher

Born in London, he founded the Royal Hospital for Incurables, and pursued his career as a surgeon alongside that of etching. His work, which was largely concentrated in the period 1859 to 1863, revived the art of creative printing, and in 1880 he founded the Royal Society of Painter-Etchers and Engravers.

Hadfield, Sir Robert Abbott 1858–1940
English metallurgist and steel manufacturer

Born in Sheffield, he was educated locally and trained as a chemist before joining his father's steelmaking firm in 1879, becoming chairman of Hadfields in 1888 until his death. His discovery of manganese steel in 1882, when he was only 24, established his reputation. The alloy proved ideal for tramway and railway trackwork, excavating equipment and mining machinery. He followed this with research on silicon steel and on armour-piercing projectile steels. Hadfield was vain, autocratic and very hard working, and his entrepreneurial ability placed Hadfields among the world's leading steel firms by World War I. A prolific technical writer and publicist, he wrote several important books on metallurgy and the development of special steels, such as *Metallurgy and its Influence on Modern Progress* (1925). He was knighted in 1908, elected FRS in 1909 and made a baronet in 1917.

Hadid, Zaha 1950–
Iraqi architect

Born in Baghdad and educated at the Architectural Association, London (1972–77), she left college to start her own architectural practice. Her work, which is characterized by zig-zag lines and geometric shapes, showing the influence of the Russian Constructivists earlier in the 20th century, includes the 'What a Wonderful World' Project (a centre for music, video and architecture) and one of the Pavilions at the Groningen Museum. Her design for the Vitra Fire Station was nominated for the 1994 BBC design awards. She won the competition to design the Cardiff Bay Opera House in 1994, sparking off a lively debate among the local population over the value of modernist architecture.

Hadlee, Sir Richard John 1948–
New Zealand cricketer

He was born in Christchurch. He and his father Walter and brother Dayle represented New Zealand at Test level. He started his first-class career with Canterbury (1971–72), and has also played for Nottinghamshire and Tasmania. In England in 1984, he made 1,000 runs and took 100 wickets. He made his Test debut for New Zealand in 1973. In 1988 he became the first bowler to take more than 400 Test wickets, several times taking 10 or more wickets in a match. He set a new world record of 431 wickets in 1990, the year he retired, and the record was surpassed in 1994 by Kapil Dev. However he still holds the New Zealand record for most wickets in a series. He was cricket's first player to be knighted during his Test career. ⌨ Gerry Cotter, *The Test Match Career of Sir Richard Hadlee* (1991)

Hadley, John 1682–1744
English mathematician

Born in Hertfordshire, he invented a reflecting telescope (1720) and the reflecting ('Hadley's') quadrant (1730). A prominent member of the Royal Society (FRS 1717), he became its vice-president in 1728.

Hadow, Sir William Henry 1859–1937
English scholar, educationist and musicologist

Born in Ebrington, Gloucestershire, a minister's son, he was educated at Malvern and Worcester College, Oxford, where he was successively scholar, lecturer (1884), Fellow, tutor and dean (1889) and honorary Fellow (1909). A noted lecturer in classics and music, his *Studies in Modern Music* (1892, 1895) are widely held to have marked a milestone in musical criticism. Other publications include *Sonata Form* (1896) and his highly-regarded *The Viennese Period* in the *Oxford History of Music*. He was Principal of Armstrong College, Newcastle upon Tyne (1909–19), and then the Vice-Chancellor of Sheffield University (1919–30). He was also chairman of the Consultative Committee set up by the Education Act of 1918, and of the Board of Education (1920–34). The most influential of the reports of the board was *The Education of the Adolescent* (1926) which called for the reorganization of elementary education, the abandonment of all-age schools and the creation of secondary modern schools. Other reports include those of 1931 (Primary School) and

1933 (Infant and Nursery Schools). He was a leading influence in English education at all levels in the 1920s and 1930s.

Hadrian, *in full* Publius Aelius Hadrianus AD 76–138
Roman emperor

Born probably in Rome, of Spanish origin, he was the ward and protégé of the Emperor Trajan. He became prefect of Syria (AD114), and after Trajan's death was proclaimed emperor by the army (117). He concluded a peace with the Parthians, having resolved to limit the boundaries of the empire in the East, and after appeasing the invaders of Moesia, he established his authority at Rome, and suppressed a conspiracy against his life (118). He spent little of his reign in Rome, and from c.120 he visited Gaul, Germany, Britain (where he built the wall named after him from the Solway Firth to the Tyne), Spain, Mauretania, Egypt, Asia Minor and Greece, returning to Rome at the end of 126. After crushing a major revolt in Judea (132–34), he returned to Italy, where he died. Although at times ruthless and tyrannical, he was an able administrator, and probably the most intellectual and cultivated of all the Roman emperors. He reorganized the army and the imperial bureaucracy. A patron of the arts and architecture, he founded the Athenaeum at Rome, and among his buildings were the Pantheon, his mausoleum (now part of the Castle of St Angelo) and the magnificent villa at Tibur. He also founded Adrianopolis. ⌨ Bernard W Henderson, *The Life and Principate of the Emperor Hadrian, AD 76–138* (1923)

Hadrian IV See Adrian IV

Haeckel or Häckel, Ernst Heinrich Philipp August 1834–1919
German naturalist

Born in Potsdam, he studied medicine at the universities of Würzburg, Berlin and Vienna, but later quit medicine to study anatomy at the University of Jena, where he became Professor of Zoology (1862–1909). He made expeditions to the Mediterranean, Madeira, Canaries, Arabia, India and elsewhere. He wrote on the radiolarians (1862), calcareous sponges (1872) and jellyfishes (1879), and contributed *Challenger* reports on deep-sea medusae (1882), Radiolaria (1887) and Siphonophora (1888). The first to attempt a genealogical tree of all animals, he postulated the idea that in its embryological development, each species illustrates its evolutionary history. Known as the 'German Darwin', he was a charismatic and enthusiastic ambassador for evolution, and many of his books, including *Generelle Morphologie* (1866), *The Natural History of Creation* (1868), *The Evolution of Man* (1874) and *Welträtsel* (1899, 'The Riddle of the Universe'), became bestsellers. ⌨ Wilhelm Bölsche, *Haekel: His Life and Work* (1906)

Haffkine, Waldemar Mordecai Wolff 1860–1930
British bacteriologist

Born in Odessa, Russia, he worked as an assistant to Louis Pasteur (1889–93), and as bacteriologist to the government of India (1893–1915) he introduced his method of protective inoculation against the bacteria which cause cholera, using a heat-killed culture prepared from a highly virulent strain. He became a British subject in 1899.

Hafiz or Hafez, *pseudonym of* Mohammad Shams od-Din Hafez c.1326–90
Persian lyric poet

Born in Shiraz, he was named by his contemporaries Chagarlab (Sugar-lip) because of the sweetness of his poetry. His *ghazals* (short poems) are all on sensuous subjects—wine, flowers, beautiful damsels—but they also possess an esoteric significance. Like nearly all the great poets of Persia, he was of the sect of Sufi philosophers, the mystics of Islam. His name is a household word throughout Iran, and his tomb, two miles northeast of Shiraz, has been magnificently adorned by princes, and is visited by pilgrims from all parts of the country. 📖 G M Wickens, 'Hafez', in *Encyclopaedia of Islam* (1971)

Hagar 19th century BC
Biblical character
She was the maid of **Abraham's** wife, **Sarah**. Due to Sarah's barrenness, Abraham had a son, **Ishmael**, by Hagar (Genesis 16), but Hagar and her son were later reluctantly expelled into the wilderness by Abraham on the request of Sarah, who was granted a child, Isaac (Genesis 21). A divine messenger came to Hagar's aid, when they had run out of water, and assured her that Ishmael would become a great nation.

Hagen, Uta Thyra 1919–
US actress
Born in Göttingen, Germany, the daughter of an art historian, she emigrated to the USA with her family in 1924 and grew up in Wisconsin. After studying briefly at the Royal Academy of Dramatic Art in London, she made her Broadway debut in 1938 as Nina in *The Seagull*. It was the first of a series of famous performances, others being her Desdemona opposite **Paul Robeson** in *Othello* in 1943 (her friendship with Robeson led to her being blacklisted in Hollywood) and the title role in *Saint Joan* in 1951. She also originated the role of Martha in *Who's Afraid of Virginia Woolf?* (1962). A dedicated teacher of acting, she devoted much time from 1947 to the Herbert Berghof Studio, a drama school that she founded with Herbert Berghof (1909–90), her second husband. She returned to the stage in *Mrs Klein* (1995) at an off-Broadway theatre.

Hagen, Walter Charles, *nicknamed* the Haig 1892–1969
US golfer
Born in Rochester, New York State, he was the first US-born winner of the British Open championship, which he won four times (1922, 1924, 1928–29). He won the US Open twice (1914, 1919), the US Professional Golfers' Association championship a record five times (1921, 1924–27), and captained the first six US Ryder Cup teams (1927–37). He published an autobiography, *The Walter Hagen Story*, in 1956.

Hägerstrand, Torsten 1916–
Swedish geographer
Born in Moheda, he was educated at Lund University, and was professor there (1957–71). An instigator of the quantitative revolution in Europe, he made Lund a major centre of innovation in geographical studies and established a new economic theory in which time and space are regarded as scarce resources.

Haggard, Sir H(enry) Rider 1856–1925
English novelist
He was born in Bradenham Hall, Norfolk, the son of a lawyer. Educated at Ipswich Grammar School, he went to Natal in 1875 as secretary to Sir Henry Bulwer, and next year accompanied Sir Theophilus Shepstone to the Transvaal. He returned to England in 1881, married, and settled down to a literary life. He wrote a number of books on South Africa, including *Cetewayo and his White Neighbours* (1882), which pleased the Cape politicians, but attracted no attention elsewhere. He is remembered for his 34 vivid and pacy adventure novels, especially *King Solomon's Mines* (1885). This was followed by *She* (1887), *Allan Quatermain* (1887), *Eric Bright-eyes* (1891), *The Pearl Maiden* (1903), *Ayesha: The Return of She* (1905) and many other stories. Other publications include *Rural England* (1902) and an autobiography, *The Days of My Life* (1926). 📖 M Cohen, *Rider Haggard* (1960)

Haggard, Merle (Ronald) 1937–
US country music singer and songwriter
Born in Bakersfield, California, he is one of the most influential artists in the history of country music, as well as one of its greatest practitioners. His early experiences included serving prison sentences for various crimes, material which later surfaced in his music, as did his parents' experiences as migrants from the Oklahoma dust bowl in the 1930s. He made his first record in 1963, and went on to achieve stardom with a string of hits later in the decade. His tribute albums helped restore interest in pioneering figures **Jimmie Rodgers**, **Bob Wills** and Lefty Frizzell. Admired by both traditional country audiences and the emerging country rock (who forgave his occasional polemical right-wing views) and later new country factions, he has proved an enduring artist, and continues to record and perform into the mid-1990s.

Haggett, Peter 1933–
English geographer
Born in Pawlett, Somerset, he studied at Cambridge. After various university appointments at home and abroad, he became Professor of Urban and Regional Geography at Bristol University (1966–). He was a leading exponent in the advance towards a unifying philosophical and methodological basis for human geography, as exemplified in his book, *Locational Analysis in Human Geography* (1965). Focusing on the 'region' as an open system, this work presented a new framework for human geography and emphasized the critical association of the earth sciences, social sciences and geometrical sciences. Later publications include *The Geographer's Art* (1990) and *Measles: an historical geography* (1993).

Hague, William Jefferson 1961–
English Conservative politician
Born in Wentworth, Yorkshire, he addressed the 1977 Tory conference and received a standing ovation. He was educated at Oxford, became a political adviser to the Treasury (1983) and entered parliament as MP for Richmond, Yorkshire, in 1989. He rose quickly to be Secretary of State for Wales (1995–97) and entered the leadership contest on the resignation of **John Major** following Labour's landslide win in the 1997 general election.

Hahn, Kurt Matthias Robert Martin 1886–1974
German educationist
Born in Berlin, he was educated at Wilhelm Gymnasium, Berlin, and Christ Church, Oxford, and the universities of Berlin, Heidelberg, Freiburg and Göttingen. He founded a school at Castle Salem in Germany, based on his ideas of what an English public school was supposed to be. In 1933 he fled from Nazi Germany to Great Britain, and in 1934 founded Gordonstoun School in Morayshire, Scotland. On similar lines to his school in Germany, Gordonstoun emphasized physical rather than intellectual activities in education, giving boys opportunities for self-discovery through practical tasks and allowing them to move up academically at their own pace. His ideas attracted the attention of the Admiralty and the War Office, and greatly affected the development of such establishments as the Outward Bound Schools (1941) and the Atlantic Colleges (1957).

Hahn, Otto 1879–1968
German radiochemist and Nobel Prize winner
Born in Frankfurt am Main, he studied at the universities of Marburg and Munich. He was appointed as an assistant at Marburg, but soon a growing interest in radiochemistry took him to the laboratories of Sir **William Ramsay** in London (1904–05) and Lord **Rutherford** in Montreal (1905–06). From 1906 to 1912 he was at the University of Berlin under **Emil Fischer** and from 1912 to 1944 (with an interruption for service in World War I) he

worked at the Kaiser Wilhelm Institute for Chemistry, of which he was director from 1928. When the Kaiser Wilhelm institutes were reorganized after World War II, Hahn became president of the Max Planck Gesellschaft in Göttingen. His research from 1904 onwards was devoted entirely to the chemistry of the radioactive elements and their decay products. From 1907 to 1938 much of his work was done in collaboration with the Austrian physicist Lise Meitner. Hahn was involved in the discovery of several new radioelements, among them radiothorium, radioactinium and mesothorium, but his best-known research was on the irradiation of uranium and thorium with neutrons. This work, initially in association with Meitner and later with Fritz Strassmann, led to the discovery of nuclear fission (1938). For this Hahn received the Nobel Prize for chemistry in 1944. Greatly upset that his discovery led to the horror of Hiroshima and Nagasaki, he became a staunch opponent of nuclear weapons.

Hahn, Reynaldo 1874–1947
French composer, singer, conductor and writer on music

Born in Caracas, Venezuela, he was taken to Paris at the age of three. He studied composition with Jules Massenet, and soon showed precocious musical gifts, especially in his early songs. He became a salon favourite and the intimate friend of Marcel Proust. He was for many years director of music at the Casino of Monte Carlo. His compositions included ballets, musical comedies (1923, *Ciboulette*, 1925, *Mozart*) and instrumental works, but he is best remembered for his songs, especially the *Chansons grises*, settings of lyrics by Paul Verlaine. He also wrote musical settings for Proust's *Les plaisirs et les jours* (1896).

Hahnemann, (Christian Friedrich) Samuel
1755–1843
German physician and founder of homeopathy

Born in Meissen, he studied at Leipzig, and for 10 years practised medicine. After six years of experiments on the curative power of bark (the source of quinine), he came to the conclusion that drugs produce a very similar condition in healthy persons to that which they relieve in the sick. This was the origin of his famous principle, *similia similibus curantur* (like cures like), which he contrasted to the belief of allopathic (ie ordinary) practitioners. His own infinitesimal doses of medicine provoked the apothecaries, who refused to dispense them. Accordingly, he illegally gave his medicines to his patients, free of charge, and was prosecuted in every town in which he tried to settle from 1798 until 1810. He then returned to Leipzig, where he taught his system until 1821, when he was again driven out. He retired first to Köthen, and then in 1835 to Paris. He spent much time undertaking 'proving' of a number of drugs, which then entered the homeopathic pharmacopoeia. Many of these were herbal in origin, and subsequent homeopathists have continued to emphasize natural remedies. By the time of his death, his system had been taken up by practitioners throughout Europe and North America, although their relations with ordinary doctors were often bitter. ⌨ T M Cook, *Samuel Hahnemann: The Founder of Homeopathic Medicine* (1981)

Hahn-Hahn, Ida Marie Luise Gustave, Gräfin,
née Hahn 1805–80
German novelist

She was born in Tressow, Mecklenburg-Schwerin, and wrote society novels influenced by the 'Young Germany' movement. She later became converted to Catholicism and founded a convent in Mainz (1854). ⌨ E I Schmid Juergens, *Ida, Gräfin Hahn-Hahn* (1933)

Haidar or Hyder Ali 1728–82
Indian soldier and Muslim ruler of Mysore

He was born in Budikote, and by his bravery he attracted the notice of the Maharaja of Mysore's Prime Minister, and soon rose to power, ousting both Prime Minister and raja (c.1761). He conquered Calicut, Bednor and Cannanore, and by 1766 his dominions included more than 84,000 square miles (218 000 sq km). He waged war against the Marathas and the British. Defeated by the Marathas (1772), he claimed British support, but when this was refused he became their enemy. Taking advantage of the war between Great Britain and the French (1778), he and his son Tippoo Sahib routed the British in the Carnatic, but were defeated in three battles by Sir Eyre Coote. ⌨ N K Sinha, *Haidar Ali* (1941)

Haig, Alexander Meigs 1924–
US soldier and public official

Born in Philadelphia, Pennsylvania, and educated at West Point, the Naval War College and Georgetown University, he joined the US army in 1947. He served in Korea (1950–51) and Vietnam (1966–67) and was made a general in 1973. During the Nixon presidency he was deputy to Henry Kissinger in the National Security Council, and became White House Chief of Staff (1973–74) at the height of the Watergate scandal. Returning to military duty in 1974 he became NATO's Supreme Allied Commander, Europe (1974–79) but went back to civilian life as president of United Technologies Corporation. He was President Reagan's Secretary of State (1981–82), but resigned as a result of policy differences. He unsuccessfully sought the Republican Party's presidential nomination in 1988. In 1992 he published his autobiography, *How America Changed the World*. ⌨ Roger Morris, *Haig: The General's Progress* (1982)

Haig (of Bemersyde), Douglas Haig, 1st Earl
1861–1928
Scottish field marshal

Born in Edinburgh, he was educated at Oxford and Sandhurst. Active service in Egypt and South Africa, followed by assignments in India, led to his appointment in 1911 as General Officer Commanding Aldershot. In August 1914 he took the 1st Corps of the British Expeditionary Force to France, and succeeded Sir John French as Commander-in-Chief in December 1915. Haig was forced to forgo a war of movement and wage a costly and exhausting war of attrition, for which he was much criticized; it was a task hampered by the progressive deterioration of the French after the failure of the Nivelle offensive of 1917, and by Lloyd George's distrust and attempts to control strategy. However, under the overall command of Marshal Foch, Haig led the final successful offensive of August 1918. In the post-war years he devoted himself to the care of ex-servicemen, organizing the Royal British Legion. His earldom was awarded in 1919. ⌨ John Charteris, *Field Marshal Earl Haig* (1929)

Haigh, John George 1909–49
English murderer

Born in Stamford, he was a company director. He shot a widow (1949) and subsequently disposed of her body by reducing it in sulphuric acid. A vital clue leading to his conviction and execution was a plastic denture which had resisted the acid. He probably murdered five others in the same way, and although the motive was money, it is possible that he drank his victims' blood.

Hailes, Sir David Dalrymple, Lord 1726–92
Scottish jurist and historian

Born in Edinburgh, he became a judge of the Court of Session and a judge of the High Court of Justiciary in 1776. He is best known for his historical work, the chronological *Annals of Scotland* (1776–79), which is still a valuable work.

Haile Selassie I *previously* **Prince Ras Tafari Makonnen** 1891–1975
Emperor of Ethiopia
He was born near Harer. Son of Ras Makonnen, he led the revolution (1916) against Lij Yasu, and became regent and heir to the throne. In 1930 he became Emperor of Ethiopia. A Coptic Christian, he westernized the institutions of his country and took it into the League of Nations. He settled in England after the Italian conquest of Abyssinia (1935–36), but in 1941 was restored after the liberation by British forces. In the early 1960s he played a crucial part in the establishment of the Organization of African Unity (OAU). Opposition to his reign had existed since 1960, and the disastrous famine of 1973 led to economic chaos, industrial strikes and mutiny among the armed forces. In 1974 he was deposed in favour of the Crown Prince, though he was allowed to return to his palace at Addis Ababa. Suspicion persists about the cause of his death. Accusations of corruption levelled against him and his family have not destroyed the unique prestige and reverence in which he is held by certain groups, notably the Rastafarians. 🕮 Peter Shwab, *Haile Selassie I* (1979)

Hailey, Arthur 1920–
Canadian novelist
He was born in Luton, Bedfordshire, England, and became a naturalized Canadian in 1947. He has written many bestselling blockbusters about disasters, several of which enjoyed a new lease of life when filmed. Titles include *Hotel* (1965), *Airport* (1968), *Wheels* (1971), *Strong Medicine* (1984, filmed 1986) and *The Evening News* (1990).

Hailsham, Quintin McGarel Hogg, 2nd Viscount 1907–
English jurist and politician
He was born in London, the son of Douglas Hailsham. Educated at Eton College and Christ Church, Oxford (president of the Union, 1929), he became a Fellow of All Souls in 1931. In 1932 he was called to the Bar and from 1938 to 1950 he was MP for Oxford City. He succeeded to the title in 1950, and, among several political posts, was First Lord of the Admiralty (1956–57), Minister of Education (1957), Lord President of the Council (1957–59, 1960–64), and chairman of the Conservative Party (1957–59). He was Minister for Science and Technology (1959–64), and Secretary of State for Education and Science (1964). In the Conservative leadership crisis of 1963, he renounced his peerage for life, and was re-elected to the House of Commons in the St Marylebone by-election. He was Opposition Minister for the Home Office from 1966. In 1970 he was created a life peer (Baron Hailsham of Saint Marylebone) and became Lord Chancellor (1970–74, 1979–87). His publications include *The Case for Conservatism* (1947), his autobiography, *A Sparrow's Flight* (1990), *On the Constitution* (1992) and *Values: Collapse and Cure* (1994). 🕮 *The Door Wherein I Went* (1975)

Hailwood, Mike, *properly* **Stanley Michael Bailey Hailwood** 1940–81
English motorcyclist
He was born in Oxford. He took nine world titles: the 250cc in 1961 and 1966–67, the 350cc in 1966–67, and the 500cc in 1962–65, all using Honda or MV Augusta machines. In addition, he won a record 14 Isle of Man Tourist Trophy (TT) races between 1961 and 1979, and during the 1960s he also had a career in motor racing. He was killed in a car accident.

Haitink, Bernard 1929–
Dutch conductor
Born in Amsterdam, his first appearance with the Amsterdam Concertgebouw Orchestra was in 1956. In 1961 he became its principal conductor and in 1964 its chief conductor. He was appointed principal conductor of the London Philharmonic Orchestra in 1967, and was its artistic director from 1969 to 1978. He was appointed music director of the Glyndebourne Festival (1977), and of the Royal Opera House, Covent Garden (1987). He has toured internationally and, in addition to opera, is an acclaimed interpreter of **Bruckner** and **Mahler**. He has been musical director of the European Union Youth Orchestra since 1994 and principal guest conductor of the Boston Symphony Orchestra since 1995. He was created an honorary KBE in 1977.

Hajek, Jiri 1913–93
Czechoslovak academic, diplomat, politician and dissident
A political scientist and social democrat, he was imprisoned in a concentration camp for much of World War II. On the left wing of his party, he joined with the Communists in 1948 and soon began to rise. He became ambassador in London (1955–58), deputy Foreign Minister (1958–62), ambassador to the UN (1962–65), and Minister of Education (1965–68). In 1968 **Alexander Dubček** appointed him Foreign Minister, in which post he tried to act as broker between the USSR and the West and, after the Soviet invasion (August 1968), tried to condemn the Soviet action by flying to the UN in New York. But he was summoned home and soon deprived of all his positions and privileges. In 1977 he was one of the founders of Charter 77 and was frequently harassed thereafter. Thoroughly disillusioned by the Communist subversion of Socialism, he had the satisfaction of witnessing the so-called Velvet Revolution (November 1989). He became a member of the French Legion of Honour in 1993 and his writings include *Munich* (1958) and *Dix Ans après* (1978, 'Ten Years After').

Hakim, al- 985–1021
Sixth Fatimid caliph of Egypt
He succeeded his father in 996. The early part of his reign, one of the most turbulent of the Fatimid dynasty, was characterized by persecution of the Christian and Jewish minorities and the destruction of thousands of churches, including the Holy Sepulchre in Jerusalem (1003–13). His extreme Shiite policies antagonized the predominantly Sunni population. From 1017 he became convinced of his own divinity, which was publicly preached by his followers Hamza and al-Darazi, and in the midst of a growing crisis the caliph disappeared in mysterious circumstances. His cult became the basis of the Druze religion which took root in Lebanon, Syria and Galilee.

Hakluyt, Richard c.1552–1616
English geographer, cleric and historian
Born in Hertfordshire, he was educated at Westminster School and Christ Church, Oxford, where he became the first ordained lecturer on geography. He introduced the use of globes into English schools. The publication of *Divers Voyages touching the Discovery of America* (1582), commissioned by Sir **Walter Raleigh**, advocating colonization of North America as a base for exploration via the Northwest Passage to the Orient, seems to have procured for him in 1584 the chaplaincy of the English embassy in Paris. While in Paris he wrote *Discourse concerning Western Discoveries* (1584), and decided to devote himself to publishing accounts of English navigations. On his return to England in 1588 he began to collect materials for his *Principal Navigations, Voyages, and Discoveries of the English Nation* (1589, and enlarged in 3 vols, 1598–1600), which contained accounts of the voyages of the **Cabots**, Sir **Francis Drake**, Sir **Humphrey Gilbert**, Sir **Martin Frobisher** and many others. The *Hakluyt Society* was instituted in 1846 to promote an interest in geography and the maintaining of records of expeditions and geographical writings. 🕮 G B Parks, *Richard Hakluyt and the English Voyages* (2nd edn, 1961)

Hakon IV Haakonsson See **Haakon IV Haakonsson**

Halas, Frantisek 1901–49
Czech poet

Born in Brünn, Moravia (now Brno, Czech Republic), he began as a proletarian poet, but soon, after a brief period during which he was a part of the Czech inter-war 'poetist' movement—an optimistic, playful affair, in defiance of the realities which threatened Czechoslovakia—adopted an extreme 'subjectivism'. His most characteristic collection, *Staré ženy* (1935, Eng trans *Two Women*, 1947), expresses his anxiety and his view of the human predicament as something essentially tragic, which yet might be overcome by true hope. 'Halasism' was a term of opprobrium amongst the clerks in charge of Czech Communist culture. He had at first welcomed the Stalinist takeover, but died feeling betrayed. ▣ A French, *The Poets of Prague* (1969)

Halas, George Stanley 1895–1983
US football coach and team owner

Born in Chicago, he was the coach of the Chicago Bears, and owner of the team. A co-founder of the National Football League (1920), he helped shape the modern professional game, bringing large crowds in to watch the sport for the first time. In 1968 he retired as head coach to the Bears for the fourth and last time. After more than 40 years of coaching his record showed 320 wins, 147 defeats and 30 draws.

Halas, John, *originally* John Halasz 1912–
British animated cartoon producer

Born in Budapest, Hungary, he started as a magazine joke cartoonist in 1930, then turned to animation and moved to London, where he met and married **Joy Batchelor** and formed the Halas–Batchelor animation unit. The producers of more than 2,000 films between 1940 and 1980, they also made the world's first fully digitized film, *Dilemma*, in 1982.

Haldane, Elizabeth Sanderson 1862–1937
Scottish writer

Born in Edinburgh, she was the sister of **John Scott Haldane** and **Richard Burdon Haldane**. She studied nursing, for a while managed the Royal Infirmary, Edinburgh, and became the first woman justice of the peace in Scotland (1920). She wrote a Life of **Descartes** (1905) and edited his philosophical works, translated **Hegel** and wrote commentaries on **George Eliot** (1927) and Mrs **Gaskell** (1930).

Haldane, James Alexander 1768–1851
Scottish minister

Born in Dundee, he was educated there and at Edinburgh, and then served with the East India Company (1785–94). With **Charles Simeon** of Cambridge he made a holiday-preaching tour of Scotland in 1796, but it was for his 119-day evangelistic tour that he became known and from which Congregational Churches developed. He became Scotland's first Congregational minister in 1799. He opened a tabernacle in Edinburgh with his brother Robert Haldane (1801), where he preached for 50 years, and which became Baptist in 1808. His pamphlets were widely read.

Haldane, J(ohn) B(urdon) S(anderson) 1892–1964
Indian biologist

Born in Oxford, England, he was the son of physiologist **John Scott Haldane**, and the brother of **Naomi Mitchison**. Educated at Eton, he graduated at Oxford in classics and philosophy, later moving to genetics. He became Reader in Biochemistry at Cambridge (1922–32), conducting research on enzymes, then switched to population genetics and the mathematics of natural selection. He became Professor of Genetics at London University (1933–37), but again switched to the chair of biometry at University College London (1937–57), and studied underwater conditions and submarine safety. He was chairman of the editorial board of the Communist *Daily Worker* (1940–49), but left the Communist Party in 1956 over the Lysenko controversy and 'Soviet interference in science'. In 1957 he emigrated to India, adopted Indian nationality, and became professor at the Indian Statistical Institute in Calcutta, but resigned in 1961. He became head of the Orissa State Genetics and Biometry Laboratory in 1962. His numerous popular works included *Animal Biology* (with **Julian Huxley**, 1927), *Possible Worlds* (1927), *Science and Ethics* (1928), *The Inequality of Man* (1932), *Fact and Faith* (1934), *Heredity and Politics* (1938), and *Science in Everyday Life* (1939). ▣ Ronald W Clark, *JBS* (1968)

Haldane, John Scott 1860–1936
Scottish physiologist

Born in Edinburgh, he was the younger brother of Richard Burdon, 1st Viscount **Haldane**, and father of **J B S Haldane** and **Naomi Mitchison**. He graduated in medicine at Edinburgh University in 1884, became a demonstrator and Reader in Medicine at Oxford (1887–1913), and was elected a Fellow of New College, Oxford. He developed the famous Haldane gas analysis apparatus in 1898, but his best-known research was concerned with the chemical control of ventilation, in which he emphasized the importance of the partial pressure of carbon dioxide. He became an authority on the effects of industrial occupations upon respiration and served as a director of a mining research laboratory at Birmingham from 1912. He produced an important report upon causes of death in mining accidents, focusing particularly on the role of carbon monoxide. He also conducted research into breathing in deep-sea diving and at high altitudes.

Haldane, Richard Burdon Haldane, 1st Viscount 1856–1928
Scottish jurist, philosopher and Liberal politician

Born in Edinburgh, the grandson of **James Alexander Haldane**, he was educated at Edinburgh and Göttingen, and was called to the Bar in 1879. He entered parliament in 1879 as a Liberal. He is remembered for his period as Secretary of State for War (1905–12), when he remodelled the army, founded the Territorial Army and made the plans by which British mobilization took place in 1914. He was Lord Chancellor (1912–15 and again in 1924 following his move to the Labour Party) and ranked high as a judge. He also wrote on the philosophical aspects of relativity, and helped to found the London School of Economics (1895). ▣ Dudley Sommer, *Haldane of Cloan* (1960)

Hale, Edward Everett 1822–1909
US Unitarian clergyman and writer

He was born in Boston, Massachusetts, and became pastor of the South Congregational Church there in 1856. He did much philanthropic work and his book *Ten Times One is Ten* (1870) inspired numerous 'Lend a Hand' clubs. He edited religious and other journals, and documents on the founding of Virginia, and wrote short stories. He was the grand-nephew of **Nathan Hale**.

Hale, George Ellery 1868–1938
US astronomer

Born in Chicago, he studied at the Massachusetts Institute of Technology and he established in 1891 the Kenwood Observatory in Chicago, a private institution which became well known through its work in solar spectroscopy. In that year, simultaneously with **Henri Deslandres** in France but independently of him, he invented the spectroheliograph. In 1892 he was appointed

Professor of Astrophysics at the University of Chicago and in 1897 became the first director of the newly founded Yerkes Observatory near Chicago. When in 1905, following his initiative, the Carnegie Institution established the Mount Wilson Observatory in California, he was appointed its director and in 1906 he set up the first tower telescope for solar research there. Hale's scientific work at Mount Wilson included his discovery and measurement of magnetic fields in sunspots. ⌑ David Oakes Woodbury, *The Glass Giant of Palomar* (1970)

Hale, Sir Matthew 1609–76
English judge

Born in Alderley, Gloucestershire, he studied at Oxford. He entered Lincoln's Inn in 1628, and in 1637 was called to the Bar. He was a Justice of the Common Pleas from 1654 until Cromwell's death in 1658 and, after the Restoration in 1660 (which he zealously promoted), he was made Chief Baron of the Exchequer, and Chief Justice of the King's Bench (1671). Much of his writing was left in manuscript form, and published after his death. Devout, acute, learned and sensible, although a believer in witchcraft, he wrote a *History of the Common Law* (1713), a *History of the Pleas of the Crown* (1736), both still important, and the *Prerogatives of the King* (printed 1776), as well as religious works.

Hale, Nathan 1755–76
American Revolutionary war hero

He was born in Coventry, Connecticut. He joined the Continental Army in 1775 and a year later volunteered to procure intelligence for George Washington from behind British lines on Long Island. He was captured and before being hanged as a spy reportedly stated, 'I regret that I have but one life to lose for my country.' Revered as a national hero, he is also the 'patron saint' of US espionage agencies, and his statue stands at the headquarters of the CIA in Langley, Virginia.

Hale, Sarah Josepha, *née* Buell 1788–1879
US writer

Born in Newport, New Hampshire, she embarked on a literary career on the death of her husband in 1822, in order to support herself and her five young children. In 1828 she became the first female editor of the *Ladies' Magazine* in Boston. She wrote a novel, *Northwood* (1827), and a book of *Poems for Our Children* (1830), which contained 'Mary had a Little Lamb'. From 1837 to 1877 she was editor of the popular and influential women's magazine the *Lady's Book* (later called *Godey's Magazine and Lady's Book*). She advocated the education of women and wrote *Woman's Record: Or, Sketches of All Distinguished Women from 'the Beginning' till A.D. 1850* (1853, 1869, 1876), a series of profiles of women notable for their contributions to society and literature. Also partly due to her work is the establishment of the national Thanksgiving day celebration. ⌑ R Finley, *The Lady of Godey's* (1931)

Hales, Stephen 1677–1761
English botanist and chemist

Born in Bekesbourne, Kent, he entered Corpus Christi College, Cambridge in 1696. Well-grounded in all branches of contemporary science and inspired by Isaac Newton's experimental philosophy, he was elected a Fellow of Corpus Christi College in 1702 and became in 1709 perpetual curate of Teddington. He was elected FRS in 1718, receiving the Royal Society's Copley Medal in 1739, and became a Foreign Member of the Académie Française in 1753. He was one of the founder-members of the Society for the Encouragement of the Arts and Manufactures and Commerce, now the Society of Arts. He was also chaplain to Prince George, later George III. Hales's *Vegetable Staticks* (1727) was the foundation of plant physiology, setting standards in the methodology of biological experimentation. His most important work was on the water balance of plants, and he was the first to measure root and leaf suction and root pressure. In *Haemastaticks* (1733) he discussed the circulation of blood and blood pressure. Besides a work on dissolving stones in the bladder, he wrote on a variety of subjects including ventilation, electricity and the analysis of air. He also invented machines for ventilating, distilling sea water, preserving meat and other practical applications of science. ⌑ D G C Allan, *Stephen Hales: Scientist and Philanthropist* (1986)

Halevi, Jehuda 1075–1141
Spanish Jewish poet, philosopher and physician

He was born in Toledo. His experience of anti-Semitism in Córdoba led him to expound and celebrate the superiority of Judaism over Aristotle's philosophy, and over Christianity and Islam, in various highly-wrought prose and poetic works. He encouraged a vision of the Jewish people and the land of Israel which has endeared him to modern Zionists. His main philosophical work (in Arabic) is the *Book of the Khazars* (in full, the 'Book of Argument and Proof in Defence of the Despised Faith'), and there is a collection of his poems entitled *Diwan*, including *Zionide* ('Ode to Zion'), the most widely translated Hebrew poem of the Middle Ages.

Halévy, (Jacques François) Fromental (Élie), originally Elias Lévy 1799–1862
French composer

Born in Paris, he had early success with the opera *Clari* (1828), followed by the comic opera *Le Dilettante d'Avignon* (1829). His masterpiece, *La Juive* (1835, 'The Jewess'), made him famous across Europe. The same year, he produced the comic opera, *L'Éclair* ('The Lightning Flash'), and followed it with about a dozen other operatic works. He continued the school of French opera, midway between Maria Cherubini and Giacomo Meyerbeer. Admitted to the Academy of Fine Arts in 1846, he became perpetual secretary in 1854. His *éloges* were collected as *Souvenirs et portraits* (1861–63, 'Souvenirs and Portraits'). Among his pupils were Bizet and Charles Gounod, and his brother was the writer Léon Halévy (1802–83).

Halévy, Ludovic 1834–1908
French playwright and novelist

He was born in Paris, the son of the writer Léon Halévy (1802–83), and in 1861 became secretary to the Corps Législatif. With Henri Meilhac he wrote libretti for the best-known operettas of Offenbach, and for Bizet's *Carmen*, and produced vaudevilles and comedies. His *Madame et Monsieur Cardinal* (1873) and *Les petites Cardinal* (1880) are delightful sketches of Parisian theatrical life. Other works include *L'Invasion* (1872), *Criquette* (1883, Eng trans 1891), *Deux mariages* (*Un mariage d'amour*, 1880, Eng trans *Marriage for Love*, 1890), *Un grand mariage* (1883, 'A Grand Marriage'), *Princesse* (1884) and *Mariette* (1893). ⌑ *Carnets* (1935)

Haley, Alex Palmer 1921–92
US novelist and biographer

Born in Ithaca, New York State, and brought up in North Carolina, he worked as a coastguard for 20 years from 1939. He turned to writing with the publication of *The Autobiography of Malcolm X* (1965), which he co-wrote after the assassination of the black activist. *Roots* (1976) was a phenomenal success, being adapted for television and winning a Pulitzer Prize the following year. Beginning with the life of Kunta Kinte, an African who was enslaved and taken to the USA, this novel documented the history of black Americans, and its essentially optimistic approach rendered it accessible to a large white audience.

Haley, Bill, originally John Clifton Haley 1925–81
US pioneer of rock and roll music

Born in Highland Park, Michigan, he began his career as a country music singer. With his band The Comets he had an international hit with 'Rock Around the Clock' (1955), which featured in the US film *The Blackboard Jungle* (1955), directed by Richard Brooks (1912–92). Since then Haley has become synonymous with the beginnings of rock and roll. Other songs include 'Shake, Rattle and Roll' and 'See You Later Alligator'.

Haliburton, Thomas Chandler 1796–1865
Canadian writer and jurist
Born in Windsor, Nova Scotia, he was called to the Bar in 1820, and became a member of the House of Assembly, Chief Justice of the Common Pleas (1828), and judge of the Supreme Court (1842). In 1856 he retired to England, and from 1859 to 1863 he was Conservative MP for Launceston. He is best known as the creator of 'Sam Slick', a sort of US version of Dickens's 'Sam Weller', in sketches printed in the Halifax newspaper *Nova Scotian*, and collected between 1837 and 1840 as *The Clockmaker, or Sayings and Doings of Samuel Slick of Slickville*, continued as *The Attaché, or Sam Slick in England* (1843–44). Other works include *Traits of American Humour* (1843) and *Rule and Misrule of the English in America* (1850). ☐ V Chittick, *Thomas Chandler Haliburton* (1924)

Halifax, Charles Montagu, 1st Earl of
1661–1715
English statesman and poet
He was born in Horton, Northamptonshire, and educated at Westminster and Trinity College, Cambridge. As a poet his most notable achievement was the parody of Dryden's *The Hind and the Panther*, entitled *The Story of the Country Mouse and the City Mouse* (1687), jointly written with Matthew Prior. As a lord of the Treasury in 1692 he established the National Debt with a loan of £1 million sterling. In 1694 he originated the Bank of England, as proposed by William Paterson three years earlier, and was appointed Chancellor of the Exchequer. His friend Isaac Newton became Warden of the Mint, and Halifax raised a tax on windows to pay for the recoinage in 1695; he first introduced Exchequer bills. In 1697 he became Prime Minister, but he was unpopular, and when the Tories came into power in 1699 he retired from the Commons to the Exchequer. He was unsuccessfully impeached in 1701, and again in 1703. He strongly supported the union with Scotland and the Hanoverian succession. On Queen Anne's death he was appointed a member of the Council of Regency, and on George I's arrival he became an earl and First Lord of the Treasury. His uncle was the Parliamentary general, the Earl of Manchester.

Halifax, Edward Frederick Lindley Wood, 1st Earl of (2nd creation) 1881–1959
English Conservative politician
Born at Powderham Castle, Devon, he was the grandson of Sir Charles Wood, 1st Viscount Halifax (1800–85) and a descendant of Charles Montagu, 1st Earl of Halifax (1st creation). He became (as Baron Irwin 1925) Viceroy of India (1926–31), Foreign Secretary (1938–40) under Neville Chamberlain, whose appeasement policy he implemented, and ambassador to the USA (1941–46). He was created earl in 1944.

Halifax, George Savile, 1st Marquis of 1633–95
English statesman
Born in Thornhill, Yorkshire, he was created viscount (1668) for his part in the Restoration, and in 1672 was made marquis and Lord Privy Seal. In 1675 he opposed Lord Danby's (see Duke of Leeds) Test Bill, and in 1679 by a display of extraordinary oratory he procured the rejection of the Exclusion Bill. On the accession of James II in 1685 he became President of the Council, but was dismissed soon after for opposing the repeal of the Test and

Habeas Corpus Acts. One of the three commissioners appointed by James II to negotiate with William of Orange (later William III) after he landed in England, on James's flight he gave allegiance to William and resumed the office of Lord Privy Seal, but joined the Opposition and resigned his post in 1689. His defence is to be read in his *Character of a Trimmer* (1688).

Halimi, Gisèle Zeïza Elise, *née* Taïeb 1927–
French lawyer, writer and feminist
Born in La Goulette, Tunisia, she was educated in Tunis and at the Institute of Political Studies in Paris. She became an advocate in 1948 and practised as a lawyer in Tunisia (1949–56) before being called to the Bar in Paris, becoming known there for her high-profile cases and clients, such as Jean-Paul Sartre and Simone de Beauvoir. She also acted as defence lawyer for the Algerian National Liberation Front (FLN) during the Franco-Algerian war, and for the defendants in the notorious Bobigny test-case abortion trial (1972). In 1966 she chaired the Commission of Inquiry into War Crimes in Vietnam. Her publications include two co-authored works, *La Cause des femmes* (1973, 'Women's Brief') and *Le Programme commun des femmes* (1978, 'Women's Common Programme'), as well as *Le Lait de l'oranger* (1988, 'The Milk of the Orange Tree'). She was elected to the French National Assembly in 1981.

Halkett, Samuel 1814–71
Scottish scholar
He was librarian to the Advocates' Library in Edinburgh (from 1848), and compiled the *Dictionary of Anonymous Literature* (4 vols, 1882–88) completed by the Rev John Laing (1809–80). From 1850 he was librarian of New College, Edinburgh.

Hall, Asaph 1829–1907
US astronomer
Born in Goshen, Connecticut, he was self-educated and was employed as an assistant at Harvard in 1857. From 1862 to 1891 he was on the staff of the Naval Observatory at Washington, and he later returned to Harvard as Professor of Astronomy. In 1877 he discovered the two satellites of Mars which he named Deimos and Phobos. In 1876 he discovered a white spot on Saturn and used this as a marker in order to obtain the rotation period of the planet.

Hall, Ben (jamin) 1837–65
Australian bushranger
Born in New South Wales, son of an English convict, at 16 he married the daughter of a wealthy cattleman and settled down to farming. In 1862 he was arrested for armed robbery but was acquitted and freed. On returning home he found that his wife had left him, taking their young son. In anger Hall joined a gang led by Frank Gardiner, and was soon re-arrested, on suspicion of involvement with the Eugowra gold robbery. Again released, Hall returned to his farm to find it burned down by the police and all his cattle killed. He was now committed to a life of outlawry and a series of audacious raids followed, most notably on the Bathurst and the Sydney–Melbourne roads. After the shooting of two policemen by one of the gang, he went into hiding, but was betrayed by a companion and shot dead by the police at the age of 28.

Hall, Charles Francis 1821–71
US explorer
Born in Rochester, New Hampshire, he was a blacksmith, journalist, stationer and engraver, then became interested in the fate of the explorer Sir John Franklin whose expedition to the Northwest Passage had been lost in 1847. He made two search expeditions (1860–62, 1864–69), bringing back relics and the bones of one of Franklin's men. In 1871 he sailed in command of the *Polaris* on an expedition to the North Pole, and on 29 August reached,

via Smith's Sound, 82° 16' N, then the highest latitude reached. Heading southwards, he went into winter quarters at Thank God Harbour, Greenland, where he became ill, and died.

Hall, Charles Martin 1863–1914
US chemist

Born in Thompson, Ohio, and educated at Oberlin College, in 1886 he discovered (independently of **Paul Héroult**) the first economic method of obtaining aluminium. Hall eventually secured the financial support of **Andrew W Mellon** and others and began aluminium production in 1888 in Washington, Pennsylvania. Two years later Hall became vice-president of the Aluminum Company of America.

Hall or Halle, Edward c.1499–1547
English historian

Born in London, he was educated at Eton and King's College, Cambridge, where he was elected Fellow, and at Gray's Inn. He became a Common Serjeant in 1532. His *Union of the Noble Families of Lancastre and Yorke* (1542, commonly called *Hall's Chronicle*) was completed only to 1532; the rest, to 1546, was completed by the editor, **Richard Grafton**. Hall's work was used as a source by **Shakespeare**, and is valuable to the student of **Henry VIII**'s reign.

Hall, Sir Edward Marshall 1858–1927
English lawyer

Born in Brighton, he was educated at Rugby and Cambridge. He was called to the Bar in 1883, and, although the victim of hostility in the **Harmsworth** press, built up his reputation through a series of impressive victories in murder cases such as Robert Wood (1907), Edward Lawrence (1909), Ronald Light (1920) and Harold Greenwood (1920), where his powers of classical advocacy offset his legal ignorance. His notable failures included Frederick Henry Seddon and the murderer George Joseph Smith (1872–1915), who drowned his three 'brides in the bath'. His greatest civil triumph was *Russell* v *Russell* (1923). Despite his oratorical powers he made little mark as Conservative MP for Southport (1900–06) and East Toxteth (1910–16), while his legendary reputation owed much to his biographer Edward Marjoribanks.

Hall, G(ranville) Stanley 1844–1924
US psychologist and educationist

He was born in Ashfield, Massachusetts. He studied at Leipzig under **Wilhelm Wundt**, then became successively professor at Antioch College, Ohio, lecturer at Harvard (1876–81) and professor at Johns Hopkins University, where in 1882 he introduced experimental psychology on a laboratory scale. In 1887 he founded the *American Journal of Psychology*. He exercised a profound influence on the development of educational psychology and child psychology in the USA, and became the first president of Clark University (1889–1920). His works include *The Contents of Children's Minds* (1883), *Educational Problems* (1911) and *Life and Confessions of a Psychologist* (1923).

Hall, James 1811–98
US palaeontologist and stratigrapher

Born in Hingham, Massachusetts, he was educated at Rensselaer Polytechnic Institute in Troy, New York. After a short spell as a librarian, he worked as an assistant to Amos Eaton (1776–1842) and then in 1836 was appointed to the Geological Survey of New York State at the start of a long association. From 1855 to 1858 he was State Geologist of Iowa. He was author of 13 volumes on the palaeontology of New York State (1847–94) and many other works on its Palaeozoic fossils and stratigraphy. He undertook important studies of crinoids and other echinoderms and named many new fossil genera and species.

He was also the director of the New York Museum of Natural History (1871–98), and the first president of the Geological Society of America.

Hall, Sir James 1761–1832
Scottish geologist

Born in Dunglass, East Lothian, he studied at the universities of Cambridge and Edinburgh. He initially disagreed strongly with the views of his friend **James Hutton**, but subsequently became a strong supporter, publishing *Illustrations of the Huttonian Theory* (1802, with **John Playfair**). In pioneering studies in experimental petrology, he melted and recrystallized local basalts and dolerites to demonstrate their igneous origin. He conducted more than 500 melting experiments and was able to demonstrate that molten magma could metamorphose existing limestones. He also produced a machine to demonstrate the folding of geological strata.

Hall, Sir John 1933–
English property developer and football club chairman

The multi-millionaire owner of Newcastle United FC, he made his fortune from developing Europe's biggest shopping centre—the MetroCentre on Tyneside. He spent more than £30 million rebuilding Newcastle's stadium, St James Park. On the field he has invested huge amounts attempting to make Newcastle successful and has used a similar philosophy with his Newcastle Sporting Club, by buying the best players for each sport. Newcastle Sporting Club comprises Newcastle Comets (basketball); Newcastle (rugby union: formerly Newcastle Gosforth); and Newcastle Cobras (ice hockey, formerly Durham Wasps).

Hall, Joseph 1574–1656
English prelate and writer

Born in Ashby-de-la-Zouch, Leicestershire, he studied at Cambridge from 1589. A Fellow of Emmanuel College, Cambridge (1595), he became dean of Worcester (1617). In the same year he accompanied **James VI and I** to Scotland to help establish episcopacy. As Bishop of Exeter (1627–41) he was suspected by Archbishop **Laud** of Puritanism. As Bishop of Norwich (1641–47) he protested with other prelates against the validity of laws passed during their enforced absence from parliament, and was imprisoned for seven months in the Tower of London. Soon afterwards he was deprived of his living, and in 1647 retired to a small farm in Higham. Among his works are *Contemplations, Christian Meditations, Episcopacy*, and *Mundus Alter et Idem* (c.1605, 'The World Different and the Same'). His poetical satires *Virgidemiarum* (1597–98) were admired by **Alexander Pope**.

Hall, Marshall 1790–1857
English physician and physiologist

Born in Basford, Nottinghamshire, he studied medicine at Edinburgh University. After further study in Paris, Göttingen and Berlin, he returned to Nottingham in 1817, where he practised medicine, being elected honorary physician to the General Hospital in 1825. The following year he moved to London, where he was elected a Fellow of the Royal College of Physicians. He wrote copiously on many aspects of medicine, including the circulation of the blood and respiration, developed a successful technique for resuscitating the drowned, and also canvassed changes in clinical practice, notably opposing the immoderate blood-lettings then considered an essential part of treatment. His researches on the physiology of reflex function built on the work of **François Magendie** and **Charles Bell**, and provided the foundation for the influential concept of the neural arc.

Hall, Sir Peter Reginald Frederick 1930–
English theatre, opera and film director

Born in Bury St Edmunds, Suffolk, he was educated at the Perse School and St Catherine's College, Cambridge. While at university he produced and acted in more than 20 plays. After working in repertory and for the Arts Council, he was artistic director of the Elizabethan Theatre Company (1953), assistant director of the London Arts Theatre (1954) and director in 1955–56, and he formed his own production company, The International Playwrights' Theatre, in 1957. After several productions at the Stratford Memorial Theatre, including *Love's Labour's Lost* (1956), he became director of the Royal Shakespeare Company (RSC), and remained as managing director of the company's theatres in Stratford and London until 1968, making his name by giving many of the classics a social context. Among his many productions during this period were the *Wars of the Roses* trilogy (*Henry VI parts 1, 2* and *3*, and *Richard III*, 1963), **Harold Pinter's** *The Homecoming* (1965) and **Nikolai Gogol's** *The Government Inspector* (1966). Continuing to direct for the RSC, he was also from 1969 to 1971 director of the Covent Garden Opera. His operatic productions there and at Glyndebourne include *The Magic Flute* (1966), *The Knot Garden* (1970), *Tristan and Isolde* (1971), *The Marriage of Figaro* (1973), *Fidelio* (1979) and *A Midsummer Night's Dream* (1981). In 1973 he succeeded **Laurence Olivier** as director of the National Theatre; his notable productions there include *No Man's Land* (1975), *Tamburlaine the Great* (1976), *Amadeus* (1979), *Othello* (1980), and *The Oresteia* (1981). In 1983 he became artistic director of the Glyndebourne Festival. Among his films are *Work is a Four Letter Word* (1968), *Perfect Friday* (1971) and *Akenfield* (1974). Hall left the National Theatre in 1988, ending his directorship with a sequence of three late Shakespearian plays: *The Winter's Tale*, *Cymbeline*, and *The Tempest*. He still directs opera, but in 1988 set up the Peter Hall Company, the inaugural project being his own production of **Tennessee Williams's** *Orpheus Descending*. That was followed in 1989 by Hall's production of *The Merchant of Venice*, with **Dustin Hoffman** as Shylock. Other productions include Williams's *The Rose Tattoo* (1991), starring **Julie Walters**, and **Stephen Poliakoff's** *Sienna Red* (1992). His autobiography, *Making an Exhibition of Myself*, was published in 1993 and in 1996 he became artistic director of London's Old Vic theatre. Hall was knighted in 1977. 📖 Stephen Fay and R E Schofield, *Power Play: The Life and Times of Sir Peter Hall* (1995)

Hall, (Marguerite) Radclyffe 1880–1943
English writer

She was born in Bournemouth, Dorset, and educated at King's College London, and then in Germany. She began as a lyric poet with several volumes of verse, some of which have become songs, but turned to novels beginning with *The Forge* and *The Unlit Lamp* (both 1924). Her *Adam's Breed* (1926) won the Femina Vie Heureuse and the Tait Black Memorial prizes, but *The Well of Loneliness* (1928), which deals openly with female homosexuality, was prosecuted for obscenity, and was banned in Great Britain for many years, despite the support of **Virginia Woolf**, **E M Forster** and others. It was republished in 1949.

Hall, Willis 1929–
English dramatist

Born in Leeds, he first wrote for radio. His first stage success was *The Long and the Short and the Tall* (1958), dealing with the members of a British military patrol lost in the Malayan jungle in 1942. He followed this with the short plays *Last Day in Dreamland* and *A Glimpse of the Sea* (both 1959). He has since collaborated extensively with **Keith Waterhouse**, notably on *Billy Liar* (1960), derived from the latter's novel, and on the farce, *Say Who You Are* (1965). *Saturday, Sunday, Monday* (1973) and *Filumena* (1973), based on plays by the Italian dramatist Eduardo de Filippo, were both enormous successes.

Halle, Edward See Hall, Edward

Hallé, Sir Charles 1819–95
British pianist and conductor

Born in Hagen, Westphalia, he studied first at Darmstadt, and from 1840 in Paris, where his reputation was established by his concerts of classical music. Driven to England by the Revolution of 1848, Hallé settled in Manchester, where in 1858 he founded his famous orchestra. This did much to raise the standard of musical taste by familiarizing the British public with the great classical masters, and he was knighted in 1888. In the same year he married the violinist Wilhelmine Neruda (1839–1911). 📖 Charles Rigby, *Sir Charles Hallé: A Portrait for Today* (1952)

Halleck, Fitz-Greene 1790–1867
US poet

Born in Guilford, Connecticut, he became a clerk in New York, and in 1832 private secretary to **John Jacob Astor**. In 1849 he retired to Guilford on an annuity left him by Astor. He published numerous poems, including the long mock-**Byron**ic poem, *Fanny* (1819), a satire on the literature, fashions and politics of the time. 📖 N F Adkins, *Fitz-Greene Halleck* (1930)

Halleck, Henry Wager 1815–72
US soldier

Born in Westernville, New York, he served in the Mexican War (1846–48) and, having taken a leading part in organizing the State of California, in the Civil War was appointed commander of the Missouri (1861). In 1862 he captured Corinth and was made general-in-chief, but in 1864 he was superseded by General **Ulysses S Grant**. Chief of Staff until 1865, Halleck commanded the military division of the Pacific until 1869, and that of the South until his death. He published *Elements of Military Science* (1846), and books on mining laws.

Haller, (Viktor) Albrecht von 1708–77
Swiss anatomist, botanist, physiologist and poet

Born in Bern, he studied anatomy and botany in Tübingen and Leyden, and started practice in 1729. In 1736 he became Professor of Anatomy, Surgery and Medicine in the new University of Göttingen. Here he organized a botanical garden, an anatomical museum and theatre, and an obstetrical school, helped to found the Academy of Sciences, wrote anatomical and physiological works, and took an active part in the literary movement. He experimented with injection techniques to investigate human blood vessels, and recognized the mechanical automatism of heart muscle function. In 1753 he resigned and returned to Bern, where he became magistrate and director of a saltworks. After this he wrote three political romances, and prepared bibliographies of botany, anatomy, surgery and medicine. His *Elementa physiologiae corporis humani* (8 vols, 1757, 'Physiological Elements of the Human Body') was a major contribution to the understanding of the functioning of the body. 📖 Adolf Haller, *Albrecht von Hallers Leben* (1954)

Hallesby, Ole Kristian 1879–1961
Norwegian theologian and preacher

Professor of the Free Faculty of Theology, Oslo (1909–52), he wrote several theological textbooks, but is best known outside Norway for translations of his devotional and apologetic writings: *Prayer* (1948), *Why I am a Christian* (1950) and *Under His Wings* (1978). Imprisoned like other religious leaders during World War II for opposing Nazi control of the Church, he influenced lay Christians through his chairmanship of the Norwegian Lutheran Home Mission, and students as first president of the International Federation of Evangelical Students (1947).

Halley, Edmond 1656–1742

English astronomer and mathematician

Born in London, he was educated at St Paul's School and Queen's College, Oxford. He left for St Helena in 1676 to make the first catalogue of the stars in the southern hemisphere (*Catalogus Stellarum Australium*, 1679). In 1680 he was in Paris with **Giovanni Cassini**, observing comets, and his calculation of the orbital parameters of 24 comets enabled him to predict correctly the return (in 1758, 1835 and 1910) of a comet that had been observed in 1583 (Halley's comet). He was the first to make a complete observation of the transit of Mercury and the first to recommend the observation of the transits of Venus in order to determine the Sun's parallax. He established the mathematical law connecting barometric pressure with heights above sea level (on the basis of **Boyle**'s law). He published studies on magnetic variations (1683), trade winds and monsoons (1686), investigated diving and underwater activities, and voyaged in the Atlantic Ocean to test his theory of the magnetic variation of the compass, which he embodied in a magnetic sea chart (1701). Halley predicted with considerable accuracy the path of totality of the solar eclipse that was observed over England in 1715, and was the first to realize that the Moon's mean motion had a secular acceleration. He also noticed that stars such as Aldebaran, Acturus and Sirius had a proper motion and that they had gradually changed their positions over the previous two millennia. In mapmaking he was the first to use an isometrical representation. He was also the first to predict the extraterrestrial nature of the progenitors of meteors. He encouraged **Isaac Newton** to write his celebrated *Principia Mathematica* (1687) and paid for its publication himself. With his *Breslau Table of Mortality* (1693) he laid the actuarial foundations for life insurance and annuities. In 1703 he was appointed Savilian Professor of Geometry at Oxford, where he built an observatory on the roof of his house which survives today, and in 1720 he succeeded **John Flamsteed** as Astronomer Royal of England. 📖 C A Ronan, *Edmond Halley: Genius in Eclipse* (1969)

Hallgrímsson, Jónas 1807–45

Icelandic lyric poet

Born in Hraun, northern Iceland, he attended the Latin School at Bessastaðir, where he read classical and Old Icelandic literature, and then studied law at Copenhagen University before turning to natural history and literature. As a student he and his friends founded the periodical *Fjölnir* (1835–47), which added inspiration to the independence movement led by **Jón Sigurðsson**. His poetry combined fervent nationalism—as in 'Island' (1835), with which *Fjölnir* was launched—and lyrical romanticism. His collected poems were first published in 1847; an English edition appeared in 1930. 📖 T V Gíslason, *Jónas Hallgrímsson* (1903)

Halliday, Michael Alexander Kirkwood 1925–

English linguist

He was born in Leeds, and studied Chinese language and literature at London University, and linguistics in China and at Cambridge. In 1963 he was appointed director of the Communication Research Centre at University College London, and two years later Professor of General Linguistics. There he undertook a research project on linguistics and English teaching, which resulted in two reports, *Breakthrough to Literacy* for primary schools and *Language in Use* for secondary schools. In the 1970s he worked in Chicago and Sydney, and held visiting professorships at Yale, Brown and Nairobi. He has worked extensively on the semantics and grammar of modern English, and developed the systemic and functional principles established by **J R Firth** and his school, as described in *A Short Introduction to Functional Grammar* (1984).

Halliwell, James Orchard, *later surname* Halliwell-Phillipps 1820–89

English Shakespearean scholar and antiquary

Born in Chelsea, London, he studied at Jesus College, Cambridge, and contributed much to Shakespearean studies by his *The Life of William Shakespeare* (1848) and *Outlines of the Life of Shakespeare* (1881–87) and a Folio edition of Shakespeare (1853–65). He also published *Nursery Rhymes and Tales of England* (1845), *Dictionary of Archaic and Provincial Words* (1847) and *Popular Rhymes and Nursery Tales* (1849).

Hallstrom, Sir Edward John Lees 1886–1970

Australian refrigerator manufacturer and philanthropist

Born in Coonamble, New South Wales, he left school at 13 and worked in a furniture factory, later opening his own works to make first ice-chests and then wooden cabinets for refrigerators. Eventually he started making the units themselves, to his own design, and marketed the first popular domestic Australian refrigerator. With the expansion of demand after World War II he was able to channel his wealth into philanthropic acts, particularly towards medical research and children's hospitals. He had a keen practical interest in zoology and was an active collector, preserver and breeder of wild animals. He made many gifts to the Taronga Zoo in Sydney.

Hals, Frans, *sometimes known as* Frans Hals the Elder c.1580–1666

Dutch portrait and genre painter

Born probably in Antwerp, he studied under **Karel van Mander** and settled permanently in Haarlem (c.1603). He was twice married, led a ramshackle domestic life with many children and, despite many commissions, was constantly overshadowed by poverty. Among his early conventional portraits are those of *Paulus von Berestyn* and his wife *Catherine* (1620), *Jacob Pietersz Olycan* and *Aletta Hanemans* (1625), and the dignified, sumptuously costumed *Portrait of a Man* (1622). But it is his studies of every nuance of smile, from the vague, arrogant amusement of *The Laughing Cavalier* (Wallace Collection, London) to the broad grins and outright vulgar leers of the low life sketches *Gypsy Girl* (c.1628–30, Louvre, Paris), *Malle Babbe* (c.1630–33, Berlin) and *Jolly Toper* (Amsterdam), which belong to the period 1625–35, that have won him his perennial popularity. Another formal masterpiece is *Pieter van den Broecke* (1633, Kenwood, London). But from 1640 onwards the virile, swaggering colours give way to more contemplative sombre blacks and greys, as in *Man in a Slouch Hat* (c.1660–66, Kassel). His own struggles and disappointments no doubt contributed to the bitter psychological study of old age *The Seated Man* (Kassell), as well as the last of the eight portrait groups in the Frans Halsmuseum at Haarlem, *The Women Guardians of the Haarlem Almshouse* (1664). They are a world apart from an earlier group, the *Banquet of the Company of St Adrian* (1627), in which the mood of robust merrymaking is symbolized by the upturned glass in the hand of one of the officers, the whole assembly a feast of many-splendoured colour. Two of his brothers were also artists, as well as five of his sons, including Frans Hals the Younger (1637–69).

Halsey, William F(rederick), Jnr, *known as* Bull Halsey 1884–1959

US naval officer

Born in Elizabeth, New Jersey, he was educated at the US Naval Academy, Annapolis (1904). He served in the White fleet (1908–09), and held destroyer commands in World War I and until 1925. He commanded the USS *Saratoga* and Naval Air Station Pensacola, and the Carrier

Division as rear admiral (1938) and vice-admiral (1940). He distinguished himself throughout the Pacific War (1941–45), latterly as commander of the Third fleet in the battles for the Caroline and Philippine islands, and for carrier attacks on the Japanese mainland. In October 1944 he defeated the Japanese navy at the Battle of Leyte Gulf. He retired as fleet admiral in 1949, and became president of International Telecommunications Laboratories (1951–57).

Halsted, William Stewart 1852–1922
US surgeon

He was born in New York, and trained at the College of Physicians and Surgeons there and in Vienna under Theodor Billroth. In 1881 he administered what is thought to be the first blood transfusion in the USA. Professor at Johns Hopkins University from 1886, where he established the first US school of surgery, he first used cocaine injections for local anaesthesia, and devised successful operative techniques for cancer of the breast and inguinal hernias. He pioneered the use of antiseptics and rubber gloves in surgery.

Ham
Biblical character

One of Noah's three sons, he was the brother of Shem and Japheth, and father of Canaan. He is described as helping Noah to build the ark, but after the Flood his son Canaan was cursed by God for Ham's apparent sin of having seen 'the nakedness of his father' (Genesis 9.22). This curse may be an attempt to explain the later subjugation of the Canaanites to Israel due to Canaanite sexual perversion.

Hamada, Shoji 1894–1978
Japanese potter

He studied and held a professorship at the Institute of Pottery in Kyoto. He worked primarily in stoneware using ash or iron glazes producing utilitarian wares in strong, simple shapes brushed with abstract design. He visited England in 1920 with Bernard Leach and experimented with lead-glazed slipware. On his return to Japan in 1923, he joined a pottery community in Okinawa, and later lived and worked in Mashiko alongside country potters, epitomizing his belief in the simple beauty of the handmade as opposed to the influences of industrialization. Widely recognized as one of the great modern potters, he became director of the Folk Art Museum in 1962.

Hamadhani, al- 969–1007
Arabic poet

He was the creator of the *maqamah*, the short story written out in rhymed prose. Two characters feature in his inventions, the *rawi* or narrator, and the unscrupulous wanderer or vagabond—one of the earliest representations of the trickster in post-classical literature. Al-Hamadhani's creations in the *Maqamat* (Eng trans 1913–17) played their part in the genesis of the picaresque novel.

Hamaguchi Osachi 1870–1931
Japanese politician

He began his career as a Finance Minister bureaucrat and was elected to the lower house of the Diet in 1915. In 1927 he assumed the presidency of the Minseito, one of the two main political parties of the time, and became Prime Minister of a Minseito government in 1929. Renowned for his incorruptibility and dogged determination, he adopted a policy of domestic financial austerity and better relations with the USA and Great Britain. He aroused the bitter hostility of the navy when, in 1930, he pushed through the Diet ratification of the London Naval Treaty, which placed restrictions on Japan's naval development. In assuming sole responsibility for the ratification of the treaty and ignoring the opinions of the navy, Hamaguchi was accused by both the military and ultra-nationalists

of infringing the Emperor's prerogative of supreme command. In November of that year he was shot by a right-wing fanatic and died the following year.

Hamann, Johann Georg 1730–88
German philosopher and theologian

Born in Königsberg, Prussia (now Kaliningrad, Russia), he became a friend of Immanuel Kant, and seems to have been largely self-educated and to have had a desultory early career as private tutor, merchant, commercial traveller and secretary, and eventually (1767–84) as a government employee in the excise office and custom house. After 1784 private patronage brought him a more comfortable income. His writings attempt to reconcile Christianity and philosophy, and his impatient distrust of rationalism and abstraction led him to emphasize the role of faith and develop an original form of fideism. His style is notoriously cryptic and opaque, but he was an important influence on Johann Herder, Goethe, Hegel and Kierkegaard, and interest in his work has returned.

Hambling, Maggi (Margaret) 1945–
English artist

Born in Sudbury, Suffolk, she attended Ipswich and Camberwell schools of art and the Slade, London, where she won a travelling scholarship to New York. She became artist in residence at the National Gallery in London, where she met Max Wall, and became best known for her powerful and expressive portraits of him. She paints in a wide range of other styles and has exhibited regularly since 1967.

Hamburger, Michael Peter Leopold 1924–
British poet and translator

Born in Berlin, Germany, into a German family which emigrated to England in 1933, he served in the Royal Army Education Corps during World War II, and after it became a university teacher. He established an international reputation for his distinguished translations of poets, including Friedrich Hölderlin, Günter Grass and Nelly Sachs. Among his own collections of poetry are *Flowering Cactus* (1950) and *Ownerless Earth* (1973). A *Collected Poems 1941–1983* was published in 1984, following an important essay collection on German literature, *A Proliferation of Prophets* (1983), and then *Collected Poems 1941–1994* was published in 1995. 📖 *A Mug's Game: Intermittent Memoirs 1924–1954* (1973, revised and reprinted as *String of Beginnings*, 1991)

Hamer, Fannie Lou, née Townsend 1918–77
US civil rights leader

Born in Montgomery County, Mississippi, the granddaughter of a slave, she worked as a plantation worker until 1962 when she began work for the Student Non-Violent Co-ordinating Committee. Her growing commitment to the civil rights movement was affected by her own experiences: in 1961 she was sterilized without her consent, and dismissed for attempting to register as a voter. Throughout the 1960s and 1970s she campaigned for voter registration and the desegregation of schooling in Mississippi and other states. In 1964, with her co-workers, she founded the Mississippi Freedom Democratic Party. She was elected to the Central Committee of the National Women's Political Caucus when it was founded in 1971.

Hamerton, Philip Gilbert 1834–94
English writer on art

Born in Laneside, Oldham, he began as an art critic by contributing to the *Saturday Review*, and later was founder-editor of the art periodical, *The Portfolio*. He wrote several books, including *The Intellectual Life* (1873, letters of advice addressed to literary aspirants and others), *Human Intercourse*, *The Graphic Arts* (1882), and *Landscape* (1885).

Hamilcar, *also called* **Barca**, *Hebrew* **Barak**
('Lightning') c.270–228BC
Carthaginian soldier
He and his son **Hannibal** were the greatest of the
Carthaginians. From 247BC he fought in the First Punic
War, seizing the Sicilian stronghold of Ercte with a small
band of mercenaries, from which he waged war for three
years against Rome. He occupied Mount Eryx (244–242)
and defended it against a Roman army. At the end of the
First Punic War (241) Sicily was surrendered to Rome and
the Carthaginian mercenaries revolted; Hamilcar crushed
the rebellion after a terrible struggle in 238. He aimed to
compensate for the loss of Sicily by creating in Spain an
infantry capable of coping with Roman legionaries. He
entered Spain in 237, and conquered most of the south
and east of the peninsula before his death.

Hamill, Dorothy 1956–
US ice-skater
She was born in Riverside, Connecticut, and began competing early. During the course of her amateur figure-
skating career, she gained one world title and three
national titles, culminating in a gold medal in the 1976
Olympics. She is the inventor of the figure-skating move
named the Hamill Camel, a spiral spin to a sit spin. After
retiring from amateur competition in 1976, she began a
successful commercial and media career. She became a
member of the US Olympic Hall of Fame in 1991.

Hamilton, Alexander 1757–1804
US politician
Born on the island of Nevis in the West Indies, he studied
at King's College (now Columbia) in New York City and
wrote a series of pamphlets in defence of the rights of the
colonies against Great Britain. On the outbreak of the
American Revolution, as captain of artillery, he served in
New York and New Jersey, and in 1777 became **George
Washington**'s aide-de-camp. In 1781, after a quarrel, he
resigned his appointment, but fought at Yorktown. After
the war he studied law, and became one of the most
eminent lawyers in New York. In 1782 he was elected to
the Continental Congress. In 1786 he played the leading
role in the convention at Annapolis, which prepared the
way for the great Constitutional Convention that met at
Philadelphia in 1787. In the same year he conceived the
series of essays arguing in favour of ratification afterwards collected as *The Federalist*, and himself wrote 51 out
of the 85. On the establishment of the new government in
1789, he was appointed Secretary of the Treasury and restored the country's finances to a firm footing. He devised
a system of taxation, insisted on payment of the national
debt and proposed the creation of the Bank of the United
States. He and his supporters favoured a strong central
government and were mistrustful of an unbridled democracy; they clashed politically with **Thomas Jefferson**'s
followers, who favoured limited government and envisaged an agrarian republic unsullied by commercial
interests. In 1795 Hamilton resigned his office, but he
remained the actual leader of the Federalist Party until his
death. His successful effort to thwart the ambition of his
rival, **Aaron Burr**, prompted Burr to challenge him to a
duel in Weekauken, New Jersey, in which Hamilton was
mortally wounded after firing into the air. 📖 Nathan
Schachner, *Alexander Hamilton* (1946)

Hamilton, Alice 1869–1970
US physician and social reformer
Born in New York City, she graduated in medicine from
the University of Michigan. After further training in
pathology and bacteriology in Europe, she was made
Professor of Pathology at the Woman's Medical College of
North Western University (1897). She combined medical
practice with social concerns, particularly the links between environment and disease, and served on state and

national advisory committees on occupational disease. In
1919 she became the first woman professor at Harvard,
almost 30 years before Harvard accepted women medical
students, and retired in 1935. Considered the leading authority on lead poisoning in particular and industrial
diseases in general, she published extensively, including a
classic textbook, *Industrial Toxicology* (1934).

Hamilton, Edith 1867–1963
US classical scholar and educationist
Born in Dresden, Germany, and raised in Fort Wayne,
Indiana, she was educated at home and at Miss Porter's
School, Farmington, Connecticut. She became Bryn
Mawr Fellow in Latin (1894–95), and held the Bryn Mawr
European Fellowship in 1895 when she attended Munich
and Leipzig universities. She was headmistress of Bryn
Mawr preparatory school in Baltimore from 1896 to 1922.
Showing her devotion to classical studies, her publica-
tions include *The Greek Way* (1930), *The Roman Way* (1932),
The Great Age of Greek Literature (1943), and her translation
of ancient myths, *Mythology* (1942). She was made an
honorary citizen of Athens at the age of 90.

Hamilton, Edmond 1904–77
US writer of science fiction
Born in Ohio, he started writing in the 1920s, contribut-
ing to the pulp magazines under a range of pseudonyms.
It was largely through his work for *Weird Tales and Amazing
Stories* that certain basic sci-fi concepts (galactic civiliza-
tions, cosmic radiation) took hold. His most enduring
fictional creation was the tritely-named Captain Future.
Hamilton's wife, Leigh Brackett, also wrote science
fiction.

Hamilton, Emma, Lady, *née* **Amy Lyon**
c.1761–1815
English woman, mistress of Lord Nelson
Born in Great Neston, Cheshire, into a poor family, her
girlhood was passed at Hawarden. Known for her great
beauty, she had had two children by a navy captain and a
baronet when in 1782 she became the mistress of the Hon
Charles Greville (1749–1809), and subsequently of his
uncle, Sir **William Hamilton** (1786). After five years in
Naples, she married Hamilton (1791). Lord **Nelson** first
met her in 1793; they became lovers, and she gave birth to
a daughter, Horatia (1801–81), later acknowledged by
Nelson as his child. After Nelson's death she squandered
her inheritance from her husband, was arrested for debt
(1813) and died exiled and impoverished.

Hamilton, Gavin 1723–98
Scottish painter and picture-dealer
Born in Lanarkshire, he studied at Glasgow University
before going to Italy in the mid-1740s. On his return
(1751) he worked, as a portrait painter but returned to
Rome in 1756 where he remained for the rest of his life.
There, he became a leading member of a circle of artists
and scholars concerned with Roman archaeology, and he
made many archaeological excavations which resulted in
important additions to antique art collections. He was
best-known in Britain as an art dealer, but his paintings,
mostly of Homeric subjects, became widely known
throughout Europe through engravings, and influenced
the development of the Neoclassical movement.

Hamilton, Hamish 1900–88
Scottish publisher
Born in Indianapolis, USA, of a Scottish father and a
US mother of Dutch stock, he spent his childhood in
Scotland and was educated at Rugby School and Caius
College, Cambridge, studying medicine (briefly) and
then modern languages, and becoming an accomplished
Olympic oarsman. He joined Harper & Brothers, the
New York publishers, as London manager in 1926. In 1931
he founded his own firm, Hamish Hamilton Ltd, with

the support of Harpers, who helped him build up a particularly strong list of US writers. In 1965 he sold his company to Thomson Publications Ltd, who later sold it to Viking-Penguin. He retired as chairman in 1981.

Hamilton, Iain Ellis 1922–
Scottish composer

Born in Glasgow, he originally trained as an engineer, entering the Royal College of Music in 1947. He first attracted attention when his Clarinet Quintet was played at a concert of the Society for the Promotion of New Music. In 1951 he won the Royal Philharmonic Society's prize for his Clarinet Concerto, and an award from the Koussevitsky Foundation for his Second Symphony, which was followed by the Symphonic Variations (1953). He moved to the USA in 1962. He has produced many orchestral and chamber works as well as operas, including *The Royal Hunt of the Sun* (1967–69) and *The Cataline Conspiracy* (1972–73). Since moving back to London in 1981, he has completed several large-scale choral works, the operas *Lancelot* (1982–83) and *Raleigh's Dream* (1983), and a wind octet, *Antigone* (1992).

Hamilton, Sir Ian Standish Monteith
1853–1947
English general

He was born in Corfu, Greece. He entered the army in 1873, and served with distinction in Afghanistan (1878) and the Boer wars (1881, 1899–1901). In World War I, as a general, he led the disastrous Gallipoli expedition (1915). Relieved of his command, he later became Lieutenant of the Tower (1918–20).

Hamilton, James, 2nd Earl of Arran and Duke of Châtelherault c.1515–1575
Scottish nobleman and Regent of Scotland

The grandson of James, 1st Baron Hamilton (d.1479) by the niece of Cardinal Beaton, he was a young man when the death of James V (1542) left only an infant, the future Mary, Queen of Scots, between him and the throne. He was chosen regent and tutor to the young queen, and held these offices until 1554, when Mary of Guise became regent. His regency was characterized by indecision and attention to family interest. He was granted the duchy of Châtelherault (1548) by Henri II of France.

Hamilton, James, 3rd Earl of Arran 1530–1609
Scottish nobleman

The eldest son of James Hamilton, the 2nd Earl, he was proposed as the husband both of Mary, Queen of Scots and of Queen Elizabeth I of England, but he became insane in 1562, and remained locked away until his death.

Hamilton, James, 3rd Marquis and 1st Duke of 1606–49
Scottish nobleman

He led an unsuccessful army of 6,000 men to support King Gustav II Adolf of Sweden (1631–32), and later played a conspicuous part in the contest between Charles I and the Covenanters. Created duke in 1643, he led a Scottish army into England (1648) but was defeated by Cromwell at Preston, and beheaded.

Hamilton, Sir James Arnot 1923–
Scottish aeronautical engineer

He was born in Edinburgh. Graduating in civil engineering from Edinburgh University, he joined the Marine Aircraft Experimental Establishment at Helensburgh in 1943. He worked initially on the design and development of airborne anti-submarine weapons and later undertook full-scale flight research associated with the design of seaplanes and flying boats. In 1948 he was appointed head of Flight Research. He joined the Royal Aircraft Establishment at Farnborough in 1951 to work on the aerodynamics of supersonic flight, and became head of

the Project Assessment Group (1963). Becoming director of Anglo-French Military Aircraft (1964), he was project director of Jaguar and Tornado aircraft, and became the first director-general of the Concorde project (1966), taking the aircraft from early concepts to the first flights of the two prototypes. In 1976 he became Permanent Under-Secretary of State at the Department of Education and Science, the first engineer to become permanent head of a Government department. He retired from the Civil Service in 1983.

Hamilton, James Douglas, 4th Duke of
1658–1712
Scottish nobleman

He fought against the Duke of Monmouth, led Scottish opposition to the Union, but discouraged bloodshed. He was created 1st Duke of Brandon (1711), a title challenged by the House of Lords. He helped to negotiate the Treaty of Utrecht (1713). As described in Thackeray's *Henry Esmond*, he fought a duel with Lord Mohun in which both men were killed.

Hamilton, John, 1st Marquis of 1532–1604
Scottish nobleman

The brother of James Hamilton, 3rd Earl of Arran, he was a devoted adherent of Mary, Queen of Scots, and he helped end her captivity on Loch Leven and reinstate her on the throne (1568). He fled to France and England (1579), but was reconciled with King James VI of Scotland (later James I of England) in 1585. In 1588 he was sent to negotiate the king's marriage to Anne of Denmark, and was created marquis in 1599.

Hamilton, Patrick 1503–28
Scottish Lutheran theologian and martyr

Born in Glasgow, the son of Catherine Stewart, the illegitimate daughter of the Duke of Albany, second son of James II, he was educated in Paris, then went to Louvain. He returned to Scotland and was in St Andrews in 1523, but was forced to leave in 1527 on account of his Lutheranism. After a brief stay in Wittenberg, where he met Martin Luther and Philip Melanchthon, he settled for some months in Marburg, where he wrote (in Latin) a series of theological propositions known as 'Patrick's Places', propounding the doctrines of the Lutherans. In 1528 he was summoned to St Andrews by Archbishop James Beaton, and on a renewed charge of heresy was burned before St Salvator's College. His death did more to extend the Reformation in Scotland than ever his life could have done.

Hamilton, Patrick 1904–62
English novelist

Born in Hassock, Sussex, he portrayed in his writing a particular brand of English middle-class existence, marked by reticence, fear and sublimated desire. *Craven House* (1926) was his first novel, but it was with *Rope* (1929) and *Gaslight* (both filmed by Alfred Hitchcock) that he became well known. Apart from *Hangover Square* (1940), his most substantial achievement was the 'Gorse' trilogy: *The West Pier* (1951), *Mr Stimpson and Mr Gorse* (1953) and *Unknown Assailant* (1955). 📖 S French, *Patrick Hamilton* (1994)

Hamilton, Richard 1922–
English painter

Born in London, he studied painting at the Royal Academy schools. During World War II, he was trained as an engineering draughtsman. In 1948 he entered a further period of study, at the Slade School of Art, and subsequently taught at the Central School of Art and Crafts, London, and at Durham University. During the 1950s, he devised and participated in several influential exhibitions, notably 'This is Tomorrow' (1956, Whitechapel Art Gallery, London), with its entrance display, the collage picture *Just What is it that Makes Today's Homes so Different, so Appealing?* This introduced the concept of Pop Art, of which Hamilton became a leading pioneer. His work in this vein fuses painting with printed imagery derived from such things as advertisements and pin-up photographs to comment ironically on contemporary life, politics and popular culture. Among his best-known works are *Hommage à Chrysler Corp* (1952), *Study of Hugh Gaitskell as a Famous Monster of Film Land* (1964) and his replica of **Marcel Duchamp**'s *The Bride Stripped Bare by her Bachelors, Even (The Large Glass)* (1965, Tate, London). He is an articulate exponent of his art and ideas, and his publications include *Collected Words* (1953–82). At the 1993 Venice Biennale he shared the Leone d'Oro prize for best artist with **Antoni Tàpies**, exhibiting *The Citizen* (1981–83, Tate), derived from the 1980 BBC TV film about IRA prisoners in the Maze.

Hamilton, Thomas 1784–1858
Scottish architect

Born in Glasgow, he studied as a mason with his father, beginning independent practice in Edinburgh before 1817. He was a leading figure in the international Greek Revival, together with his contemporary in Edinburgh, **William Henry Playfair**. In 1826 he was among the founders of the Royal Scottish Academy. His Grecian designs include the Burns Monument, Alloway (1820), the Royal High School, Edinburgh (1825–29), and the Royal College of Physicians, Edinburgh (1844–45). Cumston (Compstone) House, Kirkcudbright (1828), in a Tudor style, and a handful of gothic church designs, demonstrate his versatility. As a prime mover of the Edinburgh Improvement Act (1827) to create the New Town, he designed the George IV bridge which followed, among other projects.

Hamilton, William 1704–54
Scottish poet

Born in Bangour, West Lothian, he was educated at the High School of Edinburgh, and Edinburgh University, and contributed romantic songs and ballads to **Allan Ramsay**'s *Tea-table Miscellany* (1724). He joined the Jacobite Rising of 1745, and on its collapse escaped to Rouen, but he was permitted to return in 1749 and to succeed to the family estate, Bangour. The first collection of his poems was edited by **Adam Smith** in 1748. He is best known for his ballad, 'The Braes of Yarrow'.

Hamilton, Sir William 1730–1803
Scottish diplomat and antiquary

He was British ambassador at Naples from 1764 to 1800, and he married **Emma Hamilton** there in 1791. He took an active part in the excavation of Herculaneum and Pompeii, and formed rare collections of antiquities, one of them purchased in 1772 for the British Museum. He wrote several works on Greek and Roman antiquities.

Hamilton, Sir William 1788–1856
Scottish philosopher and scholar

Born in Glasgow and educated at Glasgow, and Balliol College, Oxford, he first made his name with papers in the *Edinburgh Review* where, among other subjects, he deplored the decayed state of Oxford and the high degree of illiteracy that was tolerated in England. These papers had a great influence on subsequent educational reform. He also wrote on philosophy, religion, psychology and logic, a subject that he did much to revive. As Professor of Civil History at Edinburgh (1821–38) and of Logic and Metaphysics (1838–56), he also revived philosophical scholarship. His main work was published posthumously as *Lectures on Metaphysics and Logic* (1859–60), presenting views on perception and knowledge that were later (unjustly) criticized in **John Stuart Mill**'s *An Examination of Sir William Hamilton's Philosophy* (1865). Many of his articles were collected in 1852 under the title *Discussions on Philosophy and Literature, Education and University Reform*, and he edited a major edition of the works of **Thomas Reid** (1846), in itself a considerable achievement. He was in his day a figure of great importance in the revival of philosophy in Great Britain.

Hamilton, William Donald 1936–
English zoologist

Born in Cairo, Egypt, he studied at the universities of Cambridge and London, and taught in London (1964–77), in Brazil and at the University of Michigan (1977–84) before becoming Royal Society Research Professor at Oxford in 1984. His main interests have been in evolutionary biology and his researches paved the way for the development of sociobiology. In 1964 he proposed his theory of 'kin selection' which accounted for the altruistic behaviour observed in animal societies by demonstrating that an individual may influence the survival and successful breeding of a relative, thus increasing the probability of survival of shared genes, even though the individual may be sterile. He subsequently developed the concept of 'reciprocal altruism', arguing that natural selection favours such behaviour in social animals. More recent research has demonstrated that choice of a sexual partner is affected by parasite load. His major contribution has been to provide a theoretical framework for some of the problems in modern evolutionary biology. He was elected a Fellow of the Royal Society in 1980, and received its Darwin Medal (1988) and the Scientific Medal of the Linnaean Society (1989).

Hamilton, Sir William Rowan 1805–65
Irish mathematician

He was born in Dublin. At the age of nine he had a knowledge of 13 languages, and at 15 he read **Isaac Newton**'s *Principia* and began original investigations. In 1827, while still an undergraduate, he was appointed Professor of Astronomy at Trinity College, Dublin, and Irish Astronomer Royal. His first published work was on optics, and he then adopted a new approach to dynamics, later and independently proposed by **Carl Jacobi**, which became of considerable importance in the 20th-century development of quantum mechanics. In 1843 he introduced quaternions after realizing that a consistent algebra of four dimensions was possible. The discovery led to work on other abstract algebras and so proved to be the seed of much modern algebra. Because quaternions split naturally into a one- and a three-dimensional part, their discovery allowed the successful introduction of vectors into physical problems. He was knighted in 1835. ⚏ Reginald Percival Graves, *Life of Sir William Rowan Hamilton* (3 vols, 1882–89)

Hamilton and Brandon, Douglas Douglas-Hamilton, 14th Duke of 1903–73
Scottish aviator

Educated at Eton and Balliol College, Oxford, he held many distinguished royal positions, such as hereditary keeper of Holyroodhouse and Lord Steward of HM Household (1940–64). He developed an interest in aviation during the 1920s and 1930s, first as pilot, then as commander of the 602 Squadron of the Auxiliary Air Force (1927–36). In 1932 he was the chief pilot in the Houston Mount Everest Expedition, about which he wrote in *The Pilot's Book of Everest* (1936). He played a large part in the formation of Scottish Aviation Ltd at Prestwick Airport (now part of British Aerospace). During World War II he held various senior positions in the RAF, and commanded the Air Training Corps in Scotland. In 1941 **Rudolf Hess** flew to Scotland seeking the duke's help as an intermediary in possible peace negotiations. The duke flew in his Hurricane to report to

Churchill, who was unimpressed, and Hess remained a prisoner for the rest of his life. In 1964 the duke received the Royal Victorian Chain from the queen.

Hamlin, Hannibal 1809–91
US politician

Born in Paris Hill, Maine, he practised law (1833–48), was Speaker of the Maine House of Representatives, and was returned to Congress in 1842 and 1844. He sat in the US Senate as a Democrat from 1848 to 1857, when he was elected governor by the Republicans, having separated from his party over his antislavery opinions. In the same year, he resigned to return to the Senate, and in 1861 became Vice-President under Abraham Lincoln. After a further period in the Senate (1869–81), he was appointed Minister to Spain (1881–82).

Hammarskjöld, Dag Hjalmar Agne Carl 1905–61
Swedish statesman and Nobel Prize winner

He was born in Jönköping. In 1933 he became an assistant professor at Stockholm University, and subsequently secretary (1935) and then chairman (1941–48) of the Bank of Sweden. He was Swedish Foreign Minister (1951–53), and a delegate to the Organization for European Economic Cooperation, the British–Scandinavian Economic Community (UNISCAN), the Council of Europe and the UN General Assembly. He became Secretary-General of the UN in 1953. Hammarskjöld, who once described himself as 'the curator of the secrets of 82 nations,' played a leading part in the setting up of the UN Emergency Force in Sinai and Gaza in 1956, and worked for conciliation in the Middle East (1957–58). He was awarded the 1961 Nobel Peace Prize after his death in an air crash near Ndola in Zambia, while he was engaged in negotiations over the Congo crisis. ⚏ Brian Urquhart, *Hammarskjöld* (1972)

Hammer, Armand 1899–1990
US business executive

Born in New York City, he trained as a physician at Columbia, and served with the US army medical corps (1918–19). In 1921, soon after taking his medical degree, he went to the USSR to help with an influenza epidemic, but turned to business, and exported grain to the USSR in exchange for furs, dealing face to face with Lenin and subsequent Soviet leaders. He founded the A Hammer Pencil Company in 1925, operating in New York, London and Moscow, and maintained strong trading and political connections with the USSR, acting as intermediary between it and the US government on a number of occasions, including the Soviet troop withdrawal from Afghanistan in 1987. In 1961 he bought the small Occidental Petroleum Corporation of California, and turned it into a giant. He founded Hammer Galleries Inc (New York) in 1930. Convicted of making illegal contributions to President Nixon's re-election fund, he was put on a year's probation and fined $3,000. President Bush pardoned him in 1989. ⚏ Carl Blumay with Henry Edwards, *The Dark Side of Power: The Real Armand Hammer* (1992)

Hammerstein, Oscar c.1847–1919
US theatre manager

Born in Stettin, Germany, he emigrated to the USA in 1863, made a fortune by inventing a machine for spreading tobacco leaves, and founded and edited the *United States Tobacco Journal*. He leased, built or opened numerous theatres in New York, Philadelphia and London.

Hammerstein, Oscar, II 1895–1960
US lyricist and librettist

Born in New York City, the grandson of Oscar Hammerstein, he graduated from Columbia College in 1916 and by the early 1920s was writing books and lyrics for Broadway musicals. Among his several collaborators were composers Jerome Kern, with whom he wrote *Showboat* (1927), and Richard Rodgers, with whom he formed a famous partnership in 1943. Together he and Rodgers produced such classic musicals as *Oklahoma!* (1943), *Carousel* (1945), *South Pacific* (1949, Pulitzer Prize), *The King and I* (1951) and *The Sound of Music* (1959). Hammerstein's sharp dialogue and ability to create dramatic movement through song helped to transform US musical theatre. In his hands musical comedies were no longer flimsy melodramas with songs tacked on, but seamless and powerful dramatic works. ⚏ Hugh Fordin, *Getting to Know: A Biography of Oscar Hammerstein II* (1986)

Hammett, (Samuel) Dashiell 1894–1961
US crime writer

Born in St Mary's County, Maryland, he grew up in Philadelphia and Baltimore and left school at 14. He was a messenger boy, newsboy, clerk, time keeper, yardman, machine operator, and stevedore before joining the Pinkerton Detective Agency in New York as an operator. Having served his literary apprenticeship writing stories for magazines like *Black Mask*, he became the first US author of authentic 'private eye' crime novels. Original, unsentimental and an acute social observer, his four best novels are *Red Harvest* (1929), *The Dain Curse* (1929), *The Maltese Falcon* (1930) and *The Glass Key* (1931). In New York he met Lillian Hellman, with whom he lived for the rest of his life. Already a chronic alcoholic, his subsequent work never equalled his first literary successes. *The Thin Man* (1934), written in a brief period of sobriety, was made into a popular film, as were all his novels, notably *The Maltese Falcon*. He made a living scriptwriting, and enlisted during World War II, but was discharged with emphysema, and continued to drink immoderately until 1948 when an attack of delirium tremens turned him to temperance. Politically a radical, he was anti-McCarthy and served a six-month jail sentence for his sympathies. A collection of short stories, *The Big Knockover and Other Stories* (1966), appeared posthumously. ⚏ D Johnson, *Dashiell Hammett: a life* (1983)

Hammett, Louis Plack 1894–1987
US physical chemist

Born in Wilmington, Delaware, he graduated from Harvard in 1916, worked for a year with Hermann Staudinger at the Swiss Federal Institute of Technology, Zurich, and after wartime research he joined the chemistry faculty of Columbia University, New York, in 1920, becoming full professor in 1935. He is regarded as a founder of physical organic chemistry, a field greatly influenced by his book *Physical Organic Chemistry* (1940). In structure–reactivity relationships he devised the 'Hammett equation' to summarize the reactivities of certain benzene derivatives, and he was also a pioneer in using the acidity function to study the effects of acidic solutions on organic reactions. His honours included the Priestley Medal (1961) and other awards of the American Chemical Society, and honorary fellowship of the Royal Society of Chemistry.

Hammond, Eric Albert Barratt 1929–
English trade union leader

He became active in trade union affairs in his early twenties and rose from shop steward in 1953 to general secretary of the Electrical, Electronics, Telecommunications and Plumbing Union (EETPU) in 1984. He was a long-time outspoken critic of what he considered as old-fashioned unionism and concluded single-union, 'no strike' agreements with employers, in defiance of Trades Union Congress (TUC) policy. Criticism of him and his union came to a head in 1988 when the EETPU was dismissed from the TUC. He retired from the EETPU in 1992, the same year that the union merged with the

TUC-affiliated Amalgamated Engineering Union to form the Amalgamated Engineering and Electrical Union, and the publication year of his autobiography, *Maverick: The Life of a Union Rebel*.

Hammond, Henry 1605–60
English clergyman

Born in Chertsey, Surrey, he was educated at Eton and Magdalen College, Oxford. In 1633 he became rector of Penshurst, and in 1643 archdeacon of Chichester. His loyalty to **Charles I** cost him his living but he officiated as chaplain to the king until 1647, when he returned to Oxford, and was chosen sub-dean of Christ Church. Imprisoned by the Parliamentary Commissioners in 1648, he retired to Westwood in Worcestershire. He published *Paraphrase and Annotations on the New Testament* in 1653.

Hammond, Dame Joan Hood 1912–96
Australian soprano

Born in Christchurch, New Zealand, she studied at the Sydney Conservatorium of Music, originally as a violinist. An active sportswoman, she won a number of golf and swimming championships up to 1935. When an arm injury forced her to give up the violin, she turned to singing, performing in **Handel**'s *Messiah* in London in 1938 and making her operatic debut the following year in Vienna. From 1945 she sang leading roles in some 30 operas, and made many recordings; her 'O mio babbino caro' was the first classical record to win a gold disc for sales of over one million. She retired from singing in 1971 to become the artistic director of the Victoria Opera Company, and was head of vocal studies at the Victorian College of the Arts (1975–92), then consultant in vocal studies at the University of Melbourne. In 1970 she received the Sir **Charles Santley** award (for Musician of the Year) from the Worshipful Company of Musicians in London and was made a DBE in 1974. She wrote an autobiography entitled *A Voice, A Life* (1970).

Hammond, John Lawrence le Breton 1872–1949
English reforming journalist and social historian

Born in Yorkshire, he was educated at Bradford Grammar School and Oxford. His politics were Liberal-Labour, shown in his early editorship of the *Speaker* (1899–1906), but he went to the Civil Service Commission and then (after armed service) to the Ministry of Reconstruction until 1918. He later became a major figure on the *Manchester Guardian*. Married from 1901 to Lucy Barbara Bradby (1873–1961), together they revealed the harshness of English social conditions from 1760 to 1832, in *The Village Labourer* (1911), *The Town Labourer* (1917) and *The Skilled Labourer* (1919). *The Age of the Chartists* (1930), reworked as *The Bleak Age* (1934), addressed later stages of social injustice. Hammond also wrote biographies of **Charles James Fox** (1903) and the *Guardian*'s editor **C P Scott** (1934), but his major work was *Gladstone and the Irish Nation* (1938), based on the **Gladstone** manuscripts.

Hammond Innes, Ralph 1913–98
English author and traveller

Born in Horsham, Sussex, he worked as a journalist on the *Financial Times* (1934–40), then served with the Royal Artillery for the next six years, during which time he began writing adventure novels. The first, *Wreckers Must Breathe* (1940), was followed by over 30 books, many with exotic locations and a maritime theme. Each is intensively researched and several have been made into successful films. Among the most popular are *The Lonely Skier* (1947), *Maddon's Rock* (1948), *The Mary Deare* (1956) and *The Strode Adventurer* (1965). Other publications include *Target Antarctica* (1993) and *Delta Connection* (1996).

Hammurabi d.c.1750BC
Amorite King of Babylon

He ruled from c.1792 to 1750BC, and is best known for his Code of Laws (a tablet inscribed with it is in the Louvre, Paris). He is also famous for his military conquests that made Babylon the greatest power in Mesopotamia. 📖 F M T Bohl, *King Hammurabi of Babylon in the Setting of His Time* (1946)

Hamnett, Katharine 1952–
English fashion designer

She was born in Gravesend, Kent, the daughter of a diplomat. Educated at Cheltenham Ladies College, she studied fashion at St Martin's School of Art in London, then worked as a freelance designer, setting up a short-lived company (1969–74) and then her own business in 1979. She draws inspiration for designs from workwear, and from movements such as the peace movement which she supports. In 1991 she produced her first theatrical designs for a production of Japanese writer **Yukio Mishima**'s *Madame de Sade*.

Hamp, Pierre, *pseudonym of* Pierre Bourillon 1876–1962
French writer

Born in Nice, he was a self-made and self-educated man, and his novels display a realism bred of firsthand experience. Among his works are *Marée fraîche* (1908, 'Fresh-Caught Fish'), *Le Rail* (1912), *Les Métiers blessés* (1919, 'The Injured Trades'), *Le Lin* (1924, 'Flax') and *La Laine* (1931, 'Wool'), novels of industrial life forming a cycle he called *La Peine des hommes* ('The Suffering of Men').

Hampden, John 1594–1643
English Parliamentarian

He became an MP in 1621 and in 1626 he helped to prepare the charges against the Duke of **Buckingham**. The next year, having refused to pay his proportion of the general loan which **Charles I** attempted to raise on his own authority, he was imprisoned, and in 1634, when Charles levied a tax for outfitting the navy ('ship-money'), he again refused to pay his share, and was prosecuted before the Court of Exchequer (1637). Seven of the 12 judges found against him, but the prosecution made Hampden the most popular man in England. He was MP for Buckinghamshire, both in the Short and the Long Parliaments. He was one of the five members whose attempted seizure by Charles in 1642 precipitated the Civil War. When hostilities broke out he raised a regiment of infantry for the Parliamentary army, and demonstrated bravery and generalship at the battles of Edgehill and Reading, but was killed at Thame. He was the most moderate, tactical, urbane and single-minded of the leaders of the Long Parliament. 📖 John Adair, *John Hampden* (1976)

Hampson, Frank 1918–85
English strip cartoonist

Born in Audenshaw, Manchester, he became a Post Office telegraph boy. After studying art at Southport, he contributed his first strip to the Post Office staff magazine in 1937. In 1950 he designed a Christian comic for boys which eventually became *Eagle*, made popular by his two-page weekly serial, *Dan Dare, Pilot of the Future*, a painted strip which introduced a unique authenticity through Hampson's use of human models and carefully modelled spaceships.

Hampton, Christopher 1946–
English dramatist

He was born in the Azores, and educated at Oxford. His first play, *When Did You Last See My Mother?* (1964), led to his appointment as the first resident dramatist at the Royal Court Theatre, London. The Court produced all his earlier plays, including *Total Eclipse* (1968), *The Philanthropist* (1970), *Savages* (1973), set in Brazil, and *Treats* (1976). His finest play is considered to be *Tales From Hollywood* (1982), but the most commercially successful has been *Les Liaisons Dangereuses* (1985, filmed 1988), a penetrating study of sexual manners, morality and responsibility, adapted from the novel by **Pierre Choderlos de Laclos**. *White Chameleon* was staged at the National Theatre, London, in 1991. He has made many adaptations and translations, including the serialization of Oswald Wynd's *The Ginger Tree* for television in 1989. Later he wrote and directed the film *Carrington* in 1995, based on the life of **Dora Carrington**.

Hampton, Lionel 1909–
US jazz musician and bandleader

Born in Louisville, Kentucky, he began as a drummer but was given xylophone tuition while a young man in Chicago. He later introduced the vibraphone into jazz, recording with **Louis Armstrong** in 1930. Hampton was a member of **Benny Goodman's** small groups in the late 1930s. He first formed a permanent big band in 1940, continuing as a leader until the 1980s and taking his entertaining brand of musicianship and showmanship on many overseas tours.

Hampton, Wade c.1751–1835
American general

Born in Halifax County, Virginia, he served in the American Revolution (1775–83), and became a member of the US House of Representatives. He rejoined the army in 1808, rose to the rank of major-general by 1813, and made an unsuccessful attempt to invade Canada.

Hampton, Wade 1818–1902
US soldier

He was born in Columbia, South Carolina, the grandson of **Wade Hampton**. In the Civil War (1861–65) he raised 'Hampton's Legion'. As brigadier-general he commanded a cavalry force (1862–63), was wounded at Gettysburg, received the command of **Robert E Lee's** cavalry (1864), and served in South Carolina against **William Sherman** (1865). He later became State Governor in 1876, when he was instrumental in restoring white rule to South Carolina, and was a US senator (1878–91).

Hamsun, Knut, *pseudonym of* Knut Pedersen 1859–1952
Norwegian novelist and Nobel Prize winner

Born in Lom, Gudbrandsdal, he had no formal education, and spent his boyhood with his uncle, a fisherman on the Lofoten Islands. He worked at various odd jobs, including shoemaking, coal-mining and teaching, and twice visited the USA (1882–84, 1886–88), where he worked as a streetcar attendant in Chicago and a farmhand in North Dakota. He sprang to fame with his novel *Sult* (1890, Eng trans *Hunger*, 1899), followed by *Mysterier* (1892, Eng trans *Mysteries*, 1927) and the lyrical *Pan* (1894). His masterpiece is considered *Markens grøde* (1917, Eng trans *Growth of the Soil*, 1920), which was instrumental in his award of the 1920 Nobel Prize for literature. His last novel was the unfinished *Ringen sluttet* (1936, Eng trans *The Circle is Closed*, 1937). A recluse during the inter-war years, he lost popularity during World War II for his Nazi sympathies and support of the **Quisling** regime, for which he was imprisoned in 1948, but his reputation has been largely re-established. 📖 R Ferguson, *The Life of Knut Hamsun* (1987)

Hanbury-Brown, Robert 1916–
British radio astronomer

Born in Aruvankadu, India, he studied engineering at Brighton Polytechnic before joining a radar research programme during World War II. In 1949 he moved to Jodrell Bank (University of Manchester). He was elected Fellow of the Royal Society in 1960, and in 1962 took up the chair of astronomy at the University of Sydney, Australia. In 1951, with Cyril Hazard, he obtained the first radio map of an external galaxy, but the map's poor resolution led him to construct a radio interferometer which had much greater resolution. In 1956 he demonstrated the 'intensity interference' phenomenon at optical wavelengths, which proved to be one of the key discoveries in the development of quantum optics in the early 1960s. In 1962, at the Narrabri Observatory, Australia, he used as interferometers two visual telescopes with large mirrors, the telescopes being mounted on a circular track. This equipment allowed the measurement of the diameters of around 30 previously inaccessible giant stars.

Hanbury-Tenison, (Airling) Robin 1936–
English explorer and author

Brought up in Ireland, and educated at Eton and Oxford, in 1958 he achieved the first land crossing of South America at its widest point. In 1964, with Sebastian Snow, he travelled from the Caribbean to the South Atlantic through South America, in three months. His concern for Indian tribes led to his being one of the founding members of the charity Survival International, of which he is now president. He took part in both British Hovercraft expeditions in Amazonas (1968) and Trans-Africa (1969). In 1971 he undertook a three-month expedition for the Brazilian government, visiting 33 tribes, and publishing a report on their plight. He took part in the British Trans-Americas expedition of 1972, crossing the Darién gap and writing a report on the impact of the road on the Cuna Indians, and led the Royal Geographical Society's Gunung Mulu (Sarawak) Expedition (1977–78), a multidisciplinary survey of a tropical forest ecosystem. In more recent years he has ridden on horseback from Cornwall to the Camargue, along the Great Wall of China (1986), and south to north through New Zealand (1986). His publications include the autobiographical *Worlds Apart* (1984) and *Spanish Pilgrimage* (1990).

Hancock, Herbie (Herbert Jeffrey) 1940–
US jazz pianist, bandleader and composer

Born in Chicago, he studied classical music as a child, but began performing jazz as a student. He went to New York with trumpeter Donald Byrd, made his first record as a leader in 1962, and joined the seminal **Miles Davis** Quintet in 1963, where he confirmed his escalating reputation while continuing to make important records under his own name. He followed Davis's example in turning to electric jazz–funk with his Headhunters sextet, and has worked back and forth in both genres ever since, including signing to two different record companies in the 1990s, one for each form. He has exerted a wide-ranging influence in each field, and is also a successful composer of film music. He won an Academy Award for his music for the jazz film *Round Midnight* (1987), in which he also appeared.

Hancock, John 1737–93
American revolutionary and political leader

Born in Quincy, Massachusetts, he graduated from Harvard and became a merchant in Boston. He opposed the Stamp Act (1765), and in 1768 his sloop *Liberty* was seized by the British for smuggling. As president (1775–77) of the Continental Congress, he was the first to sign the Declaration of Independence, writing his name in a bold hand. He remained in the Congress until 1780, when he was elected Governor of Massachusetts.

Hancock, Lang(ley) George 1909–92
Australian mining industrialist

Born in Perth, Western Australia, he leased claims for the mining of 'blue' asbestos at Wittenoom, Western Australia in 1934, and developed a processing plant in partnership with Peter Wright. Hancock pioneered the use of light aircraft for prospecting, after having discovered substantial iron ore deposits in the Pilbara region. Having established his claim, he concluded mining agreements with a number of companies, thus initiating the growth of Australian extractive industries. He went on to discover further deposits (1963–69), including Rhodes Ridge, the largest deposit in the world, of an estimated 10 million tonnes. He held controversial views on politics and Aboriginal affairs and in 1974 formed a secessionist movement in Western Australia with the aim of better political representation.

Hancock, Sheila 1933–
English actress

Born in Blackgang, Isle of Wight, she trained at RADA and made her name on television as shop treasurer Carole in the sitcom *The Rag Trade* (1961–62). She followed it with the roles of Thelma Teesdale in *Mr Digby, Darling* (1969), Mag Plant in *Gone to Seed* (1992), Frances in *Brighton Belles* (1993–94), Dowager Duchess in *The Buccaneers* (1995) and Sarah Ryan in *Dangerous Lady* (1995). Her films include *Doctor in Love* (1960), *Carry On Cleo* (1964), *The Anniversary* (1968), *Buster* (1988) and *3 Men and a Little Lady* (1990). On stage, she appeared in the West End in *The Anniversary* (1966) and on Broadway in *Entertaining Mr Sloane*. She is married to the actor John Thaw (1942–). ▢ *Ramblings of An Actress* (1987)

Hancock, Thomas 1786–1865
English inventor and manufacturer

Born in Marlborough, Wiltshire, he obtained in 1820 a patent for the 'application of a certain material (rubber) to render various parts of dress and other articles more elastic'. In experimenting with the preparation of rubber for waterproofing and other purposes, he built what was intended to be a shredding machine but found that it produced a solid homogeneous block of rubber, in a form that was much more suitable for manufacturing purposes. He took out patents for his 'masticator' and a number of other devices and processes, including (1843) the first English patent for vulcanization of rubber. For a time he was in partnership with Charles Macintosh.

Hancock, Tony (Anthony John) 1924–68
English comedian

Born in Birmingham, he tried his hand as a stand-up comic in RAF concert parties and touring gang shows before making his professional stage debut in *Wings* (1946). Pantomimes, cabaret and radio appearances in *Educating Archie* (1951) contributed to his growing popularity and he made his film debut in *Orders is Orders* (1954). The radio series *Hancock's Half Hour* (1954), written by Alan Simpson and Ray Galton, allowed him to refine his lugubrious comic persona as a pompous misfit whose changeable social ambitions and blinkered patriotism are frequently thwarted or belittled. The series transferred to television (1956–61), gaining large viewing figures and rare public affection. Dispensing with his regular co-stars and writers, he made ill-advised attempts at solo projects and serious 'artistic' endeavours in films like *The Rebel* (1960) and *The Punch and Judy Man* (1963). A chronic alcoholic beset by self-doubt, he spent his final years in a self-destructive round of aborted projects and unsatisfactory performances, and committed suicide while attempting a further comeback on Australian television.

Hancock, Sir William Keith 1898–1988
Australian historian and writer

Born in Fitzroy, Victoria, and educated at Melbourne University, he became a Rhodes scholar in 1922 and was the first Australian to be elected a Fellow of All Souls, Oxford. From 1924 he held professorships at Adelaide, Birmingham and Oxford universities, before becoming director of the Institute of Commonwealth Studies in London (1939–57). He returned to Australia in 1957 as foundation director of research studies and was later Professor of History at the Australian National University, Canberra. Author of many important works including *Australia* (1930) and a biography of Jan Smuts (1962–68), he gave the ABC's Boyer Lectures entitled 'Today, Yesterday and Tomorrow' in 1973.

Hancock, Winfield Scott 1824–86
US soldier

Born in Montgomery County, Pennsylvania, he organized the Army of the Potomac in 1861, was prominent at South Mountain, Antietam and Fredericksburg, and in 1863 took command of the 2nd Corps. At Gettysburg he was in command until George G Meade's arrival, and was severely wounded. In 1864 he was conspicuous in the battles of the Wilderness, Spottsylvania and Cold Harbor. Democratic candidate for the presidency in 1880, he was defeated by James A Garfield.

Hand, (Billings) Learned 1872–1961
US judge and jurist

Born in Albany, New York State, into a dynasty of New York judges, he graduated from Harvard University and its Law School. He practised law in New York City and at the state capital Albany, until he was appointed US judge for the Southern District of New York (1908–24), when he became a judge of the US 2nd Circuit Federal Court of Appeals (1924–51). His judgements extended into all branches of law, and exerted so much influence on the US Supreme Court that although never appointed to it, he was known as the Supreme Court's 'tenth man'. He was hostile to judicial 'legislation' and held that judges should not go beyond the immediate case in hand, but also opposed Congressional attempts to limit judicial discretion. From 1951 to 1961 he continued to hear special cases. He published *The Bill of Rights* (1958) and *The Spirit of Liberty* (1952, 1960).

Handel, George Frideric   See panel p828

Handke, Peter 1942–
Austrian dramatist and novelist

Born in Griffen, he trained as a lawyer, and his first play, *Publikumsbeschimpfung*, was published in 1966 (Eng trans *Offending the Audience*, 1970). It presents four characters who speak randomly and insult the audience, and, like much of his work, has been the subject of some controversy. Other plays are *Das Mündel will Vormund sein* (1966, Eng trans *My Foot My Tutor*, 1971) and *Wünschloses Unglück* (1972, Eng trans *A Sorrow Beyond Dreams*, 1975 (US); 1976 (UK)). His novels include *Die Angst des Tormanns beim Elfmeter* (1970, Eng trans *The Goalie's Anxiety at the Penalty Kick*, 1972 (US); 1977 (UK)). ▢ J Schlueter, *The Plays and Novels of Peter Handke* (1981)

Handley, Tommy (Thomas Reginald) 1892–1949
English comedian

Born in Liverpool, he worked in variety and concert parties during World War I, and in the early days of radio he became a regular broadcaster. In 1939 he achieved nationwide fame through his weekly programme *ITMA* (*It's That Man Again*), which, with its endearing mixture of satire, parody, slapstick and wit provided a major boost to wartime morale. The programme remained a favourite until his sudden death. ▢ Bill Grundy, *That Man: A Memory of Tommy Handley* (1976)

Handlin, Oscar 1915–
US historian

Born in Brooklyn, New York City, he was the son of Russian–Jewish immigrants. After graduating from Brooklyn College and teaching there (1936–38), he taught at Harvard, where he took his doctorate in 1940, and remained on its staff in chairs of increasing honour,

Handel, George Frideric, *German (until 1715)* Georg Friedrich Händel 1685–1759
German–English composer

Handel was born in Halle, Saxony, the son of a barber-surgeon. He became organist of Halle Cathedral at the age of 17 while studying law at the university. After some experience playing in the Hamburg opera orchestra, and four years in Italy, he was appointed in 1710 to the court of the Elector of Hanover. He took frequent leaves of absence to try his fortune in London, introducing himself with the opera *Rinaldo* (1711). These frequent absences displeased the Elector, whose succession to the English throne as **George I** led at first to some awkwardness; the *Water Music*, composed for a river procession, is said to have been a peace offering.

Between 1713 and 1720 Handel was attached to the households of the Earl of **Burlington** and the Duke of Chandos. Later he devoted himself to the promotion of opera at the King's Theatre, Haymarket, under the auspices of the newly founded Royal Academy of Music. Attempting to satisfy the fickle taste of the fashionable London world with Italian opera was difficult, and his success varied. The Royal Academy of Music came to an end in 1728, was resuscitated temporarily, but collapsed again, after which Handel went into partnership with John Rich at his theatre in Covent Garden. Eventually he turned to a new form, the English oratorio, which proved to be enormously popular.

In 1735 Handel conducted 15 oratorio concerts in London. Despite a stroke in 1737, in the next five years he produced the oratorios *Saul* (1739), *Israel in Egypt* (1739), and the *Messiah* (1742), which had been first performed in Dublin. *Samson* followed in 1743, succeeded by *Joseph and His Brethren* (1744), *Semele* (1744), *Judas Maccabeus* (1747), *Solomon* (1749), and others; his last, *Jephtha*, appeared in 1751. His *Music for the Royal Fireworks* had appeared in 1749, only serving to enhance his reputation in the eyes of the British people.

A sociable, cultivated, cosmopolitan figure, and a very prolific composer like his exact contemporary **J S Bach**, he wrote for the most part in the current Italianate style, though in his settings of English words there are reflections of **Henry Purcell**. His output included 46 operas, 32 oratorios, large numbers of cantatas, sacred music, concerti grossi and other orchestral, instrumental and vocal music. Regarded as the greatest composer of his day, Handel was buried in Westminster Abbey.

📖 D Burrows, *Handel* (1994); Christopher Hogwood, *Handel* (1985); Jonathan Keates, *Handel: The Man and His Music* (1985).

> 'Whether I was in my body or out of my body as I wrote it I know not. God knows.' Of the 'Hallelujah Chorus' in his *Messiah*. Quoted in Romain Rolland, 'Essays on Music' (1948).

latterly Carl M Loeb University Professor (1984–). His doctoral thesis and first book, *Boston's Immigrants 1790–1865* (1941) is his main work, and it was updated as *The Uprooted* (1951, Pulitzer Prize 1952), a comprehensive survey of all US immigration. With his sociologist wife, Mary Flug Handlin, he published *Commonwealth* (1947), a history of Massachusetts, and some of her work and influence are also present in his essays, *Race and Nationality in American Life* (1957). His later works include *The Americans* (1963), *Truth in History* (1979), *The Distortion of America* (1981) and *Liberty in Peril* (1991).

Hands, Terry (Terence David) 1941–
English stage director

Born in Aldershot, Hampshire, he was educated at Birmingham University, and co-founded the Everyman Theatre, Liverpool, in 1964. He joined the Royal Shakespeare Company (RSC) in 1966, became an associate director (1967), joint artistic director with **Trevor Nunn** (1978), and sole artistic director and chief executive (1986–91), now director emeritus. He was consultant director at the Comédie Française (1975–77), and has directed **Shakespeare** at the Burgtheater in Vienna. Among his more recent RSC productions are *Othello* (1985), with **Ben Kingsley** in the title role, *Romeo and Juliet* (1989) and Chekhov's *The Seagull* (1990), his last production before he handed over his directorship in 1991. In 1992, he returned to the RSC to direct an award-winning production of **Christopher Marlowe**'s *Tamburlaine the Great*, with **Antony Sher** in the lead role. Hands attracted much criticism in 1988 by producing at Stratford a pop opera, *Carrie*, based on a horror novel. It received profoundly hostile reviews and subsequently crashed on Broadway. More recent productions include *The Merry Wives of Windsor* (1995) with the Royal National Theatre and *The Importance of Being Earnest* (1995) with the Birmingham Repertory Theatre.

Handy, Charles Brian 1932–
Irish teacher and writer on management

Born in Dublin and educated at Oxford, he was a manager in Shell Petroleum and an economist in the City of London. In 1972 he became Professor of Management Development at the London Graduate School of Business and, in 1977, was appointed Warden of St George's House, Windsor (the Church of England's staff college). His comparative study of managers in Great Britain, the USA, Europe and Japan, *The Making of Managers* published in 1988, has helped to shape current management education. Later publications include *The Empty Raincoat* (1994) and *Beyond Certainty* (1995).

Handy, W(illiam) C(hristopher) 1873–1958
US musician and composer

He was born in Florence, Alabama, and despite the opposition of his Methodist preacher father to his choice of a musical career, he joined a minstrel show as a cornet player. In 1903 he formed his own band in Memphis, Tennessee, and drew on various genres of African-American music, including spirituals, folk ballads, work songs and early jazz, to develop the form of music known as the blues. His earliest known composition 'The Memphis Blues' (1911), was followed by 'St Louis Blues' (1914), 'Beale Street Blues', 'Yellow Dog Blues', 'Careless Love' and many others. He was the first to introduce the blues style to printed music, founding a music publishing company with a partner in Memphis in 1913 and continuing to run the firm independently in New York City in the 1920s and afterwards. Long known as the 'father of the blues', he used that epithet as the title of his autobiography, published in 1958.

Hani, Motoko, *originally* Matsuoka Moto 1873–1957
Japanese journalist and educationist

Born in Hachinohe, Aomori Prefecture, and educated at the Meiji Girls' School, Tokyo, she taught briefly in Aomori before returning to Tokyo where she joined the newspaper *Hochi Shimbun*. In 1897 she became its first full-time woman reporter. After her marriage to fellow reporter Yoshikazu Hani (1901), she and her husband joined the magazine *Katei no tomo* in 1903, which, under their ownership, became the highly influential woman's magazine *Fujin no Tomo*. In 1921 the Hanis founded the progressive school Jiyu Gakuen, which combines Christian and Confucian ethics.

Hanif, Mohammed 1934–
Pakistan cricketer

Born in Junagadh, and a member of the great cricketing family which produced two other Test players (his brothers Mushtaq and Sadiq), he made the first of his 55 appearances when only 17. In his Test career he scored twelve centuries, including two in the match against England at Dacca in 1961–62. A natural stroke-maker, he holds the world's second-highest score, with 499 runs for Karachi against Bahawalpur in 1958–59 (**Brian Lara** broke his record in 1994 with 501).

Hanks, Tom (Thomas J) 1956–
US actor

Born in Concord, California, he made his film debut in the thriller *He Knows You're Alone* (1980) and was praised for his performance in the television sitcom *Bosom Buddies* (1980–82) before the unexpected popularity of the film *Splash* (1984) boosted his career. His relaxed manner and mischievous grin made him one of the USA's most popular young performers in comedies like *Bachelor Party* (1984) and *The Money Pit* (1985). Nominated for an Academy Award for his role as a young boy trapped in an adult world in *Big* (1988), he later won the award for his performance as a defiant AIDS sufferer in *Philadelphia* (1993) and as the retarded but triumphant *Forrest Gump* (1994). His many popular successes include *A League of Their Own* (1992), *Sleepless in Seattle* (1993) and *Apollo 13* (1995). He made his feature-length directorial debut with *That Thing You Do* (1995).

Hanley, Ellery 1961–
English rugby league player

Born in Leeds, he played for a Leeds amateur club and signed for Bradford Northern in 1978. He waited three years for a Division 1 match, then scored 55 tries in 1984–85. He transferred to Wigan in 1985 for the record fee of £150,000 and transferred to Leeds in 1991 for £250,000. He was contemplating retirement when he was offered a job by the Australian Rugby League and signed as coach for a reputed £433,000 in May 1995. In March 1995 he had 422 tries to his credit.

Hanna, Mark (Marcus Alonzo) 1837–1904
US businessman and politician

Born in New Lisbon, Ohio, he and his family moved to Cleveland, where he worked in his father's wholesale grocery. He served in the Union army (1864) and, starting in partnership with his father in coal and iron, made the most of the great post-war expansion. He helped organize the Union National Bank, bought the Cleveland Opera House, invested in Cleveland street-railways, and moved into politics to protect business interests, backing Ohio candidates for the presidency successfully (**James A Garfield**, 1880), unsuccessfully (**John Sherman**, 1888), and very successfully (**William McKinley**, 1896). He transformed local and state Republican boss systems into a massively-organized national fighting force for the 1896 election, carrying campaign finance to unprecedented lengths. He refused Cabinet office, but accepted a seat in the Senate in 1897.

Hanna, William Denby 1910–
US animated cartoonist

Born in New Mexico, he became a structural engineer, then turned to cartooning and was one of the first directors at the new MGM animation studio in 1937, making **Rudolph Dirks**'s *Captain and the Kids*. With **Joseph Barbera**, he created the immortal cat-and-mouse duo, *Tom and Jerry*.

Hannibal See panel p830

Hannington, James 1847–85
English missionary

Born in Hurstpierpoint, Sussex, he studied at Oxford. In 1882, after a seven-year curacy in his native parish, he went out to Uganda for the Church Missionary Society. Fever and dysentery forced him to return to England, but in 1884 he was consecrated first Bishop of Eastern Equatorial Africa. In 1885 he travelled to Uganda, where he was murdered by King Mwanga.

Hanno 5th century BC
Carthaginian navigator

He undertook a voyage of exploration along the west coast of Africa. He founded colonies, and reached Cape Nun or the Bight of Benin. An account of his voyages, known as *Periplus of Hanno*, survives in a Greek translation.

Hanratty, James c.1936–1962
English murderer

He was found guilty of the murder of Michael Gregsten, who was shot while in his car with his lover, Valerie Storie, on 22 August 1961. Storie, who had been raped, and paralysed by several bullets, picked out Hanratty from an identity parade. Hanratty, who was reportedly a petty criminal of low intelligence, was charged. He denied the charge but refused to name his alibis, saying that to do so would be to betray his friends' trust. He then changed the location of his alibi from Liverpool to Rhyl. The jury found him guilty. After he was hanged on 4 April 1962, several witnesses came forward who believed they had seen him in Rhyl. Following over 30 years of campaigning by his family, a police inquiry in 1997 concluded that Hanratty was wrongly convicted, and the alleged miscarriage of justice was passed to the Criminal Cases Review Commission.

Hansard, Luke 1752–1828
English printer

He was born in Norwich, Norfolk. After joining the office of Hughes, printer to the House of Commons, he became acting manager in 1774, and in 1798 succeeded as sole proprietor. He and his descendants printed the parliamentary reports from 1774 to 1889 and the official reports of proceedings in Parliament are still called 'Hansard' in his honour. **William Cobbett**'s *Parliamentary Debates* was continued from 1806 by Hansard's son, Thomas, and successors.

Hansberry, Lorraine 1930–65
US playwright

She was born in Chicago, where her father was a successful real-estate broker, and his efforts to move the family into a segregated neighbourhood in the late 1930s (their victory came only after he carried a lawsuit all the way to the Supreme Court) provided an early lesson in the explosive drama of race relations in the USA. Her play *A Raisin in the Sun* (1959), about a black family seeking to escape a Chicago ghetto, became the first work by an African-American woman to be produced on Broadway and won the New York Drama Critics Circle Award. She also wrote *The Sign in Sidney Brustein's Window* (1964), staged shortly before her death from cancer at the age of 34. Selections from her writings and letters were assembled posthumously as a dramatic self-portrait in *To Be Young, Gifted and Black* (1969).

Hansen, Christian Frederik 1746–1845
Danish neoclassical architect

Born in Copenhagen, he studied in Rome and was influenced by **Andrea Palladio**, **Claude Ledoux** and geometry. The most important architect of his day, he was responsible for the rebuilding of Copenhagen after the 1807 British bombardment. Roman models inspired the strong simple masses of the Court House (1803–16),

Hannibal, 'the grace of Baal' 247–182BC
Carthaginian soldier

Hannibal was the son of **Hamilcar** and at the age of nine his father made him swear eternal enmity to Rome. He served in Spain under Hamilcar and his brother **Hasdrubal**, and was elected general after Hasdrubal's death. He won control of southern Spain up to the Ebro (221–219), and the fall of Saguntum in 218 sparked off the Second Punic War with Rome. In 218 he surprised the Romans by marching from Spain through southern Gaul, and crossing the Alps into Italy with an army including elephants. His troops, used to the African and Spanish climate, perished by the thousand amid ice and snow; but he defeated the Taurini, forced Ligurian and Celtic tribes to serve in his army, and at the River Ticinus drove back the Romans under **Publius Cornelius Scipio**, the Elder (218).

The first great battle was fought in the plain of the River Trebia, when the soldiers of the Roman consular army were either cut to pieces or scattered in flight. Hannibal wintered in the valley of the Po, and in spring crossed the Apennines, devastating Etruria and marching towards Rome. He awaited the consul **Gaius Flaminius** by Lake Trasimene, where he inflicted on him a crushing defeat; the Roman army was annihilated. Passing through Apulia and Campania, he wintered at Gerunium, and in the spring at Cannae (216) on the Aufidus utterly destroyed another Roman army under **Quintus Fabius** ('Cunctator').

After Cannae the tide turned. Rome's allies remained loyal, and Hannibal received inadequate support from Carthage. Although he was not defeated, as his veterans were lost to him he had no means of filling their places, while the Romans could put army after army into the field. He spent the winter of 216–215 at Capua. The Romans wisely avoided a further pitched battle, and allowed the Carthaginians to overrun Italy, taking towns and gaining minor victories. However, Capua fell in 210; and in 207 Hasdrubal, marching from Spain to his aid, was defeated and killed at the River Metaurus.

For four years Hannibal stood at bay in the hill-country of Bruttium, until in 203 he was recalled to Africa to meet a Roman invasion by Scipio. In the next year he met Scipio at Zama, his decisive defeat there ending the war. On the conclusion of peace, Hannibal devoted himself to political reform, but he aroused such strong opposition that he fled to the court of **Antiochus III** at Ephesus, and then to Bithynia. When the Romans demanded his surrender, he took poison.

📖 Bernard Levin, *Hannibal's Footsteps* (1986); D S Bradford, *Hannibal* (1981); Dennis Proctor, *Hannibal's March in History* (1971); Gavin De Beer, *Hannibal* (1969).

---

linked by bridges to its forbidding detention block. Only the chapel remains of his rebuilding of the Christenborg Palace, a porticoed rectangle surmounted by a saucer-dome. In the cathedral (1811–29) he re-used the old walls, but introduced a bold geometrical interplay.

Hansen, Gerhard Henrik Armauer 1841–1912
Norwegian physician and bacteriologist
He was born in Bergen, and in 1869 discovered the ba-cillus that causes leprosy, also known as Hansen's disease.

Hansen, Marcus Lee 1892–1938
US historian
Born in Neenah, Wisconsin, he was educated in Michigan, Minnesota and Iowa, and then studied at Harvard under **Frederick Turner**. He studied the European background, and toured Europe inspecting archives and newspapers (1925–27), and made a special study of the ethnic composition of the USA in 1790 for the American Council of Learned Societies. He taught at Illinois University from 1892 to 1938. All his books were pub-lished posthumously in 1940: *The Mingling of the Canadian and American Peoples*, *The Immigrant in American History* and *The Atlantic Migration 1607–1860*.

Hansen, Martin Alfred, *pseudonym of* Jens Alfred Martin Hansen 1909–55
Danish novelist
Born in Stroby, he came from a farming family, and worked on the land and as a teacher, but after 1945 devoted himself to writing. His early novels, *Nu opgiver han* (1935,'Surrender') and *Kolonien* (1937, 'The Colony'), deal with social problems of the 1930s. *Jonathans Rejse* (1941, 'Jonathan's Journey') and *Lykkelige Kristoffer* (1945, 'Lucky Christopher'), are outwardly picaresque novels, but in reality are closely related to his work for the Danish un-derground press during the Occupation. With *Løgneren* (1950, 'The Liar'), a psychological novel intended first for broadcasting as a serial, he reached a wider public. His most original work is the metaphysical *Orm og Tyr* (1952, 'The Serpent and the Bull'). Other writings include the short stories collected as *Torne-busken* (1946, 'The Thorn Bush'). 📖 C M Woel, *Martin Alfred Hansen. Liv og digtning* (1959)

Hansford Johnson, Pamela 1912–81
English novelist, playwright and critic
Born in London, into a theatrical family, she left school at 18, working in a bank and as a book reviewer. For a short time in the early 1930s she was engaged to be married to **Dylan Thomas**. Her background provided what **Margaret Drabble** has called 'a peculiar vantage point for an un-prejudiced insight into a wide range of behaviour'. Her first novel, *This Bed Thy Centre* (1935), was set in working-class south London, and her many subsequent novels, such as the tragi-comical *The Unspeakable Skipton* (1958), are observant of both the world of her youth, and of society in the sixties and seventies, and range from the comic to the morally insightful. Her critical works include writings on **Thomas Wolfe** and **Marcel Proust**. In 1950 she married the novelist **C P Snow** and they col-laborated on many literary projects. 📖 I Lindblad, *Pamela Hansford Johnson* (1982)

Hanslick, Eduard 1825–1904
Austrian music critic and writer on aesthetics
Born in Prague, he studied law at Prague University and gained a PhD from the University of Vienna. He was professor at Vienna University from 1861. He supported **Schumann** and **Brahms** against **Richard Wagner** in his critical writings. He propounded a form theory of aes-thetics in his *Vom Musikalisch-Schönen* (1854, Eng trans *The Beautiful in Music*, 1891), which did for music what the Bell–Fry theories later did for painting.

Hansom, Joseph Aloysius 1803–82
English inventor and architect
Born in York, he invented the 'Patent Safety (Hansom) Cab' in 1834, and designed Birmingham Town Hall and the Roman Catholic cathedral at Plymouth.

Hanson, Duane 1925–96
US sculptor
He was born in Alexandria, Minnesota, and studied at the Cranbrook Academy of Art in Bloomfield, Michigan, before going to Germany, where he lived from 1953 to 1961. He specialized in life-size figures made from polyester resin stiffened with fibreglass, then painted realistically and clothed. His earlier work was violent (for

example *Abortion*, 1966), but he later shifted to mildly satirical pieces like *Woman with Shopping Trolley* (1969) and *Tourists* (1970, Scottish National Gallery of Modern Art, Edinburgh). He lived in south Florida from 1973 until his death, modelling with relish, and perhaps condescension, the ordinary people he saw around him.

Hanson, Howard 1896–1981
US composer

Born in Wahoo, Nebraska, of Swedish descent, he was awarded the US Prix de Rome in 1921. After three years' study in Italy, he was appointed director of the Eastman School of Music in Rochester, New York State, a post he held until 1964. Under his leadership, the School became a highly important centre of US musical life. His compositions, firmly in the tradition of 19th-century Romanticism, include an opera, *The Merry Mount* (1933), and seven symphonies.

Hanson, James Edward Hanson, Baron
1922–
English business executive

Born in Huddersfield, West Yorkshire, he was for a time engaged as a young man to the then unknown actress **Audrey Hepburn**. Following army service (1939–46), he inherited the family transport business, and turned his entrepreneurial skills to a successful greetings-card business with his partner, Gordon White. He became chairman of Hanson Trust in 1965, building up a huge and diversified conglomerate of businesses under that umbrella. He was chairman of Trident Television in 1974, has been a director of Lloyds Bank since 1984, and was made a member of the Royal College of Surgeons in 1991. He was created a Life Peer in 1983.

Hanson, Raymond 1913–76
Australian composer and teacher

Born in Sydney, he studied at the New South Wales Conservatorium of Music, to which he returned to lecture from 1948 until his death. He had a considerable formative influence on the new generation of Australian composers and also, through his teaching, on the future of music education in Australia. Of his own work, his Trumpet Concerto is well known and was one of the first Australian recordings to be released internationally. Other works include operas, a ballet, a symphony, four concertos, chamber music and film scores, and music for piano including a bitter piano sonata, written between 1938 and 1940, which was his protest against war.

Hanson-Dyer, Louise Berta Mosson
1884–1962
Australian music publisher and patron

Born in Melbourne, she was an accomplished pianist, studying in Edinburgh and at the Royal College of Music, London. After marrying James Dyer she became the centre of Melbourne's musical life and helped establish the British Music Society there in 1921. In 1927 she went to London, then Paris, where she established Éditions du Oiseau-Lyre, a music publisher. In 1933 she brought out a complete edition of the works of **Couperin**, followed by works of **Purcell** and **John Blow** and became a leader in the revival of early music. In the 1950s the press was among the first to issue on LP some of the works of **Monteverdi**, Purcell and **Handel**. She became Mrs Hanson-Dyer in 1939, on her remarriage after the death of her first husband. She was permanently resident in France and, after World War II, in Monaco, but maintained her links with Australia, and published the works of such leading Australian composers as **Peggy Glanville-Hicks** and **Margaret Sutherland**. Her considerable Australian estate was left to Melbourne University for music research.

Hansson, Ola 1860–1925
Swedish poet and novelist

Born in Hönsinge, he became known for his naturalistic lyric poetry. He left Sweden for Germany in 1890 in the face of negative criticism and public apathy on the publication of his erotic volume, *Sensitiva amorosa* (1887). Thereafter he wrote mostly in German, much influenced by **Nietzsche**, concentrating on the kind of moral anarchism he sketched out in *Parias* (1890, 'Pariahs'). The verses in *Ung Ofegs visor* (1892, Eng trans *Young Ofeg's Ditties*, 1893) are notable. ◻ O Friesen, *Kylfverstenen, Af von Friesen och Hansson* (1909)

Hansson, Per Albin 1885–1946
Swedish politician

He rose to prominence in the Social Democratic youth movement and was elected to parliament in 1918. He served as Minister of Defence in Social Democrat administrations (1918–25) under **Karl Hjalmar Branting**, whom he succeeded as Leader of the party (1925). He became Prime Minister of a minority Social Democrat government in 1932, but secured the support of the Agrarians in the so-called 'cow deal' the following year and, apart from a brief period in 1936, was in office from then until his death. He presided over the foundation of the modern welfare state in Sweden and guided his country's successful policy of neutrality during World War II.

Han Suyin, *originally* Elizabeth Kuanghu Chow
1917–
British novelist

Born in Peking (Beijing), China, the daughter of a Belgian mother and a Chinese railway engineer, she studied medicine at Peking, Brussels and London, where after the death in the civil war of her husband, General Tang, she completed her studies. She then practised in Hong Kong, which provided the background for her first partly-autobiographical novel, *A Many Splendoured Thing* (1952, filmed 1955). It describes the love affair of an emancipated Chinese girl and an English journalist, symbolizing the political and ideological conflicts of the British colony. From 1952 she practised in an anti-tuberculosis clinic in Singapore. Her other novels include *And the Rain my Drink* (1954) and *Four Faces* (1963). She also wrote *China*, a semi-autobiographic and historical work in six volumes, comprising *The Crippled Tree* (1965), *A Mortal Flower* (1966), *Birdless Summer* (1968), *My House has Two Doors* (1980), *Phoenix Harvest* (1980) and *Wind in My Sleeve* (1992), and two volumes of contemporary Chinese history (1972).

Hantzsch, Arthur 1857–1935
German organic chemist

Born in Dresden, Saxony, he became professor at Zurich, Würzburg and Leipzig, and investigated the arrangement of atoms in the molecules of nitrogen compounds and the electrical conductivity of organic compounds.

Hapsburg See Habsburg

Hara Kei 1856–1921
Japanese politician

From a samurai family, he worked as a newspaper editor before joining the Ministry of Foreign Affairs (1882). He resigned from government service to join the Seiyukai, a political party formed in 1900, and shortly afterwards gained a seat in the lower Diet. As Home Minister in various non-party cabinets (1906–08, 1911–12, 1913–14) and Leader of the Seiyukai, he was able to advance the party's interests by appointing pro-Seiyukai provincial governors and promoting regional economic development. As the head of the majority party in the Diet, he became Prime Minister in 1918 and presided over the first party cabinet since the establishment of the Meiji Constitution. He proved to be a conservative premier, moving cautiously on political and social reform. Although he expanded the electorate by lowering tax qualifications, he did not endorse the principle of universal manhood suffrage. He was assassinated by an ultra-nationalist fanatic.

Harald I Halfdanarson, Finehair or Fairhair
c.860–c.945
King of Norway

He was the first ruler to claim sovereignty over all Norway. The son of Halfdan the Black (King of Vestfold), he achieved power and became king after the naval Battle of Hafursfjord, off Stavanger (c.890). His authoritarian rule caused many of the old aristocratic families to emigrate west to Orkney, Hebrides and Ireland, and to newly-settled Iceland. He made several punitive expeditions across the North Sea to subdue his former subjects and impose Norwegian rule over the Northern and Western Isles of Scotland. In 942 he abdicated in favour of his eldest son, **Erik Haraldsson, Blood-Axe**.

Harald II Eriksson, Greycloak d.c.970
King of Norway

The eldest son of **Erik Haraldsson, Blood-Axe**, he retreated to Denmark with his mother, Gunnhild, the sister of King **Harald Gormsson** (Blue-Tooth) after his father's death in England (954). With Danish support he and his four brothers made several assaults on Norway from 960 against their uncle, King **Haakon I Haraldsson, the Good**, and eventually killed him in battle off Hardangerfjord (c.961) and Harald became king. His reign was unpopular, especially when he tried to impose Christianity on his subjects. When he tried to break free of his alliance with Denmark one of his enemies, Earl Haakon of Lade, enlisted Harald Blue-Tooth's help for another invasion, and Greycloak was caught and killed at Limfjord.

Harald III Sigurdsson, also called Harald Hardraade (the Ruthless) 1015–66
King of Norway

The half-brother of **Olaf II Haraldsson** (St Olaf), he retreated to Kiev with his nephew, **Magnus I Olafsson** after St Olaf had been killed. He served as a Viking mercenary with the Varangian Guard in Constantinople (Istanbul), and returned to Norway (1045) to demand, and receive, a half-share in the kingdom from his nephew. He became sole king on his nephew's death (1047). He expanded Norway's possessions in Orkney, Shetland and the Hebrides, and after long wars against King **Svein II Ulfsson** of Denmark, he invaded England (1066) to claim the throne after the death of **Edward, the Confessor**, but although he captured York, he was defeated and killed by **Harold II** at Stamford Bridge.

Harald V 1937–
King of Norway

Born in Oslo, like his father **Olav V** he was educated at Oslo University, at a military academy, and at Oxford. He served briefly in each of the country's three armed services, and in 1968 took the then unprecedented step of marrying a commoner, Sonja—a shopkeeper's daughter—after strenuous efforts by his father to obtain Cabinet approval. As prince regent, he effectively served as monarch after the king suffered a stroke in 1990, and he formally succeeded to the throne (the coronation ceremony having been discarded in 1957, in a pledge to the Constitution) on Olav's death in January 1991. A lover of nature, he has been president of the Norwegian branch of the World Wildlife Fund since its foundation in 1970.

Harald Gormsson, Blue-Tooth c.910–985
King of Denmark

The son of Gorm the Old and father of **Svein I Haraldsson, Fork-Beard**, he became king in c.940 and was the first king to unite all the provinces of Denmark. He was converted to Christianity by a German missionary, Poppo (c.960), and made Christianity the state religion of Denmark. He is thought to have built the fortified military barracks at Trelleborg and elsewhere in Denmark as well as the Jelling Stone, proclaiming his conversion. He strengthened the unity and central administration of the country, and repelled attacks from Norway and Germany. He was deposed by his son Svein (985), and died in exile soon afterwards.

Harcourt, Dame Catherine Winifred, known as Kate Harcourt 1927–
New Zealand actress

Born in Amberley, North Canterbury, she studied music at Melbourne Conservatorium and in 1954 joined the Joan Cross Opera Studio at Sadler's Wells in London. Since returning to New Zealand in 1956, she has spent over 35 years in theatre, being active in radio, film and television drama. In 1996 she was appointed the first Dame Commander of the New Zealand Order of Merit.

Harcourt, Sir William Venables Vernon
1789–1871
English chemist and clergyman

Born in Sudbury, Derbyshire, the son of the Archbishop of York, he was educated at home then spent five years in the Royal Navy before going to Christ Church, Oxford, in 1807, intending to become a clergyman. At Christ Church he met John Kidd, who interested him in the sciences. After graduation he undertook clerical duties at Bishopsthorpe and set up his own chemical laboratory there, taking advice from **William Wollaston** and **Humphry Davy**. He was an amateur scientist whose importance lay in his influence and the stimulation he gave to others. He became the first president of the Yorkshire Philosophical Society and played an essential part in the establishment of the British Association for the Advancement of Science, which was to be open to all interested in science, at a time when the Royal Society was becoming more restrictive and professional in its membership.

Harcourt, Sir William Vernon 1827–1904
English Liberal politician

He was born in York, graduated from Trinity College, Cambridge, and was called to the Bar in 1854, becoming a QC in 1866. He was a noted contributor to the *Saturday Review*, and to *The Times* by his letters signed 'Historicus' (collected 1863). He entered parliament as Liberal MP for the city of Oxford (1868). From 1869 he was Professor of International Law at Cambridge. He was Solicitor-General (1873–74), Home Secretary (1980–85), and was Chancellor of the Exchequer under **Gladstone** (1886, 1892–94). On Gladstone's retirement in 1893 Sir William became Leader of the House of Commons. He is best remembered for his revision of death duties and his 1894 budget. He resigned the Liberal leadership in 1898, but remained a private member of the party.

Hardaknut Knutsson or Hardacanute or Hardicanute 1018–42
King of Denmark and of England

He was the son of **Knut Sveinsson** (Canute the Great) and **Emma** (the widow of King **Ethelred II, the Unready**), and was Knut's only legitimate heir. He inherited Denmark on his father's death (1035), but the English elected his illegitimate half-brother, **Harold I Knutsson** (Harefoot), as regent, confirming Harold as king in 1037. Hardaknut prepared to invade England to claim the Crown, but Harold died before he arrived. Hardaknut was made king (1040), and promptly punished the English by imposing a savage fleet-tax to pay for his expedition. His reign was universally disliked, and he died of convulsions at a wedding party.

Harden, Sir Arthur 1865–1940
English chemist and Nobel Prize winner

Born in Manchester, he worked in the Jenner (later Lister) Institute from 1897, becoming head of the biochemistry section from 1907 until his retirement in 1930. He was appointed emeritus professor by London University in 1912. Investigating the fermentation of sugars by bacteria, he made the crucial discovery that the first step in fermentation was the phosphorylation of the sugar to form an ester (1905), and isolated fructose 1,6-bisphosphate. Later he isolated two other intermediates. Harden also showed that dialysis destroyed activity, thereby implicating a dialysable co-factor in fermentation, and he recognized the presence of more than one enzyme. For this work he shared the 1929 Nobel Prize for chemistry with **Hans Euler-Chelpin**. He studied vitamins and the nutritional problems of the army during World War I. He was elected Fellow of the Royal Society in 1909, awarded its Davy Medal in 1935 and knighted in 1936.

Hardenberg, Karl August, Fürst von 1750–1822
Prussian politician
Born in Essenrode, Hanover, he held appointments in Hanover, Brunswick, Ansbach and Bayreuth, and became a Prussian Minister on Bayreuth's union with Prussia in 1791. In 1803 he was the Prussian Foreign Minister. His policy was to preserve neutrality in the war between France and Great Britain, but in 1806, under **Napoleon**'s influence, he was dismissed. In 1810 he was appointed Chancellor and completed the reforms begun by Baron von **Stein**. He played a prominent part in the war of liberation, and after the Treaty of Paris (June 1814) was made a prince. He took part in the Congress of Vienna, and in the Treaties of Paris (1815). He reorganized the Council of State (1817), of which he was appointed president, and drew up the new Prussian system of imposts. He was responsible (with Stein) for improvements in the Prussian army, the abolition of serfdom and the privileges of the nobles, and the reform of education.

Hardicanute See Hardaknut Knutsson

Hardie, Gwen 1962–
Scottish painter
Born in Newport-on-Tay, Fife, she studied at Edinburgh College of Art, then moved to West Berlin where she studied under **Georg Baselitz**. She first received critical notice in her postgraduate diploma show at Edinburgh, in which she exhibited a number of large-scale paintings of close-ups of female heads and torsos. She has continued to explore the theme of the female form from a feminist viewpoint, sometimes opening the figure up to reveal internal organs. The importance of these works lies particularly in the intention to re-invent the female form in pictorial art.

Hardie, (James) Keir 1856–1915
Scottish Labour leader and politician
Born near Holytown, Lanarkshire, he worked from the age of seven and was employed in a coalmine from the age of 10. Victimized as champion of the miners (whom he organized) he moved to Cumnock and became a journalist. The first of all Labour candidates, he stood as candidate for the Scottish Labour Party in Mid-Lanark (1888), but sat for West Ham, South (1892–95), and Merthyr Tydfil (1900–15), and in and out of parliament worked strenuously for socialism and the unemployed. In 1893 he founded the Independent Labour Party, then edited the *Labour Leader*, which became the party's official voice in 1903. He was chairman of the party until 1900 and again in 1913–14 (the party having been renamed the Labour Party). He strenuously opposed Liberal influence on the trade unions and strongly advocated the formation of a separate political party, as distinct from the existing Labour Representation League. A strong pacifist, he

opposed the Boer War, and lost his seat in 1915 after opposing Britain's involvement in World War I. 📖 Ian McLean, *Keir Hardie* (1975)

Hardie Boys, Sir Michael 1931–
New Zealand Governor-General
Born in Wellington and educated at Victoria University, Wellington, he joined his father's legal practice and was a member of the Legal Aid Board, becoming chairman (1978) until his appointment as a judge of the New Zealand High Court (1980–89). He became a Privy Councillor on his move to the Bench of the Court of Appeal in 1989, serving until 1996. In that year he was nominated to succeed Dame **Catherine Tizard** as Governor-General of New Zealand.

Harding (of Petherton), John Harding, 1st Baron 1896–1989
English field marshal
He was born in South Petherton, Somerset. A subaltern in World War I, he rose to Chief of Staff of the Allied Army in Italy in 1944. From 1955 to 1957, as Governor-General of Cyprus during the political and terrorist campaign against Great Britain, he reorganized the security forces to combat terrorism, re-established order through the imposition of martial law and press control, banished Archbishop **Makarios**, and, although he failed to bring about a political settlement, was widely respected for his straightforward approach. He was knighted in 1944 and created a peer in 1958.

Harding, John See Hardyng, John

Harding, St Stephen d.1134
English churchman
Born in Sherborne, Dorset, he was educated at Sherborne Abbey. He was the co-founder and, from 1109 to 1133, third abbot of the monastery of Cîteaux, south of Dijon. He endeavoured to restore the Cistercian rule to its original simplicity. His feast day is 16 July.

Harding, Tonya 1971–
US skater
She won the 1994 US Figure Skating Championships when Nancy Kerrigan, the then favourite, was unable to compete, having been clubbed on the right knee by a hitman while training. When Harding and Kerrigan took to the ice at the 1994 Lillehammer Olympics, Harding came eighth, Kerrigan won the silver. On their return to the USA, Harding was stripped of her title and had to resign from the US Figure Skating Association when found guilty of withholding information concerning the injury to Kerrigan. Her ex-husband and her bodyguard were given prison sentences for their role in the attack, and she was fined $100,000. She began a new career as a wrestling manager and singer.

Harding, Warren G(amaliel) 1865–1923
29th President of the USA
Born in Blooming Grove (now Corsica), Ohio, a doctor's son, he was a journalist and newspaper owner (the *Marion Star*), then entered politics as a Republican and served as a state senator (1899–1903) and Lieutenant-Governor (1902–06) of Ohio. During his term in the US Senate (1915–20), he proved himself an unremarkable party loyalist, and perhaps because he was offensive to nobody, in 1920 he was the compromise choice as the Republican presidential candidate. He promised a 'return to normalcy' after World War I, and his presidency (1921–23) saw the conclusion of peace treaties with Germany, Austria and Hungary, and the negotiation (1921) of a naval arms-limitation treaty at the Washington Naval Conference. Politically naive, he had little notion of the real activities of his appointees and advisers until 1923, when during a transcontinental tour he received word that the corrupt

schemes of several of his Cabinet members were on the verge of being exposed. This shock probably contributed to his sudden death in San Francisco soon afterwards. The investigations that followed brought to light the Teapot Dome scandal and revealed a level of corruption seldom matched in US presidential history. 📖 Andrew Sinclair, *The Available Man: The Life Behind the Masks of Warren Gamaliel Harding* (1965)

Hardinge (of Lahore), Henry Hardinge, 1st Viscount 1785–1856
English soldier and administrator

He was born in Wrotham, Kent. From 1809 to 1813 he was deputy quartermaster-general of the Portuguese army. After Napoleon's escape from Elba he was appointed commissioner at the Prussian headquarters. He lost an arm at Ligny. From 1820 to 1844 he was an MP, Secretary of War under the Duke of Wellington (1828–30, 1841–44) and Chief Secretary for Ireland (1830, 1834–35). In 1844 he was appointed Governor-General of India. During the First Sikh War he was present at the battles of Mudki, Firozshah and Sobraon as second in command to Lord Gough and negotiated the peace of Lahore (1845). Returning to England in 1848 he succeeded Wellington as Commander-in-Chief (1852), but was demoted to field marshal in 1855 following the disasters early in the Crimean War (1854–56).

Hardwick, Philip 1792–1870
English architect

Born in London, he was the son of the architect Thomas Hardwick (1752–1829). He designed Euston railway station, the hall and library of Lincoln's Inn, Goldsmiths' Hall in London, and Limerick Cathedral, Ireland.

Hardwicke, Sir Cedric Webster 1893–1964
English actor

He was born in Lye, Worcestershire, and served in World War I. He made his name in the Birmingham Repertory Company's productions of George Bernard Shaw's plays and in *The Barretts of Wimpole Street* (1934), before establishing himself as a leading character actor in Hollywood. He played the leading roles in a number of films, including *Dreyfus* (1931), *Things to Come* (1936), *The Winslow Boy* (1948) and others. He was knighted in 1934 and was Cambridge Rede Lecturer in 1936.

Hardwicke, Philip Yorke, 1st Earl of 1690–1764
English judge

He was born in Dover. He became successively Attorney General (1725), Chief Justice of the King's Bench (1733) and Lord Chancellor (1737). A supporter of Sir Robert Walpole, he held office under Thomas Pelham, Duke of Newcastle, presided at the trial of the Jacobite lords in 1745, and promoted the laws that proscribed tartan and abolished heritable jurisdiction in Scotland. His Marriage Act of 1754 abolished Fleet marriages, and he did much to establish the doctrine of equity in its modern form and systematize its principles. His son, Philip, 2nd Earl (1720–90) held public offices, wrote *Athenian Letters* and edited *Walpoliana*, and his second son, Charles (1722–70) became Lord Chancellor, but died three days later.

Hardy, Alexandre c.1570–c.1631
French dramatist

He was born in Paris, and wrote over 500 melodramatic pieces, largely taken from Spanish authors. He is notable for reducing the role of the chorus in French drama. 📖 K Garsche, *Hardy als Barockdramatiker* (1971)

Hardy, Sir Alister Clavering 1896–1985
English marine biologist

Born in Nottingham, and educated at Oxford, in 1921 he was appointed assistant naturalist at the Fisheries Laboratory in Lowestoft, where he initiated his classic studies on feeding of all life stages of herring, and their dependence on zooplankton. He was appointed chief zoologist (1924–27) on the *Discovery* expedition to study the plankton communities in the Antarctic, and his results provided an unparalleled illustration of the relationships between the whales and their zooplankton prey. He became Professor of Zoology and Oceanography at University College, Hull (1928–42), where he directed research on his plankton indicator and continuous plankton recorder, devices which allowed the detailed study of ocean life. In 1942 he was appointed to the regius chair of natural history at Aberdeen University, and he subsequently became Linacre Professor of Zoology at Oxford (1945–61). He was elected FRS in 1940 and knighted in 1957.

Hardy, Bert 1913–95
English photojournalist

Born in London, he started work as a messenger and laboratory assistant in a photographic agency and although self-taught was, in 1938, one of the first to use a Leica 35mm camera. He was on the staff of *Picture Post* until 1957, except for service as an army photographer from 1942 to 1945, during which period he recorded scenes in concentration camps. Later assignments took him to the Korean and Vietnam wars. After the closure of *Picture Post* he was much in demand for advertising until his retirement in 1967. In both war and peace his portrayal of ordinary people was of very high quality, and his records of London during the Blitz rank among the most impressive of the period. 📖 *Bert Hardy: My Life* (1985)

Hardy, Godfrey Harold 1877–1947
English mathematician

Born in Cranleigh, Surrey, he was educated at Cambridge, and became a Fellow of Trinity College in 1900. In 1920 he became Savilian Professor at Oxford, but returned to Cambridge as Sadleirian Professor (1931–42). An internationally important figure in mathematical analysis, he was chiefly responsible for introducing English mathematicians to the great advances in function theory that had been made abroad. In much of his work in analytic number theory, the Riemann zeta-function, Fourier series and divergent series, Hardy collaborated with John Littlewood. He brought the self-taught Indian genius Srinivasa Ramanujan to Cambridge and introduced his work to the mathematical world. With Ramanujan, he found an exact formula for the partition function, which expresses the number of ways a number can be written as a sum of smaller numbers. His mathematical philosophy was described for the layman in his book *A Mathematician's Apology* (1940), in which he claimed that one of the attractions of pure mathematics was its lack of practical use. In his one venture into applied mathematics, he developed (concurrently with, but independent of William Weinberg) the Hardy–Weinberg law, fundamental to population genetics.

Hardy, Oliver, *originally* Norvell Hardy Junior 1892–1957
US comic actor

Born near Atlanta, Georgia, he ran away from home at the age of eight to become a boy singer in a travelling minstrel show, but later returned home to enter films in 1913 with an appearance in the silent short *Outwitting Dad*. He played the straight man to many comedians and the Tin Man in the 1925 version of *The Wizard of Oz*. By then, he had already teamed up with Stan Laurel, as Laurel and Hardy; they made their screen debut together in *A Lucky Dog* (1917). The partnership produced more than 100 films, including silent shorts such as *Leave 'Em Laughing* (1928), *The Finishing Touch* (1928), *Liberty* (1929) and *Big Business* (1929), the sound shorts *Men o' War* (1929), *Perfect*

Day (1929) and *The Music Box* (1932), and the feature *Way Out West* (1937). Hardy also made more than 200 films outside the partnership.

Hardy, Robert 1925–
English actor
Born in Cheltenham, Gloucestershire, he began his career with the Royal Shakespeare Company and appeared on television as Coriolanus in *The Spread of the Eagle* (1963), as Robert Dudley, Earl of Leicester, in *Elizabeth R* (1971) and as Prince Albert in *Edward the Seventh* (1975). He also played Winston Churchill in *Winston Churchill—The Wilderness Years* (1981), *The Woman He Loved* (1988), *War and Remembrance* (1989) and *Bomber Harris* (1989), Siegfried Farnon in the television series *All Creatures Great and Small* (1978–90) and Arthur Brooke in *Middlemarch* (1994). His films include *The Spy Who Came in From the Cold* (1965), *10 Rillington Place* (1970) and *Sense and Sensibility* (1995).

Hardy, Thomas   See panel p836

Hardyng or Harding, John 1378–c.1465
English chronicler
In 1390 he entered the household of Henry Percy ('Hotspur'), whom he saw fall in battle on Shrewsbury Field in 1403. Pardoned for his treason, he became Constable of Warkworth Castle, and fought at Agincourt (1415). He served the Crown in confidential missions to Scotland. His chronicle, composed in stanzas, deals with the history of England from the earliest times to Henry VI's flight into Scotland. He extended it and presented it to Edward IV just after his accession. Its interest lies more in its eye-witness account of the Agincourt campaign than as a historical record or work of poetry. Richard Grafton continued it to Henry VIII.

Hare, Sir David 1947–
English dramatist, director and filmmaker
Born in Bexhill, Sussex, he graduated from Cambridge and was active in fringe theatre for many years, co-founding Portable Theatre in 1968 and Joint Stock in 1974. He succeeded Christopher Hampton as resident dramatist and literary manager of the Royal Court Theatre in London (1969–71), and at Nottingham Playhouse in 1973, before becoming associate director of the National Theatre, London (1984). *Slag* was staged in 1970, *The Great Exhibition* in 1972, and *Knuckle* in 1974, but the best of his early works is *Teeth 'n' Smiles* (1975), a commentary on the state of modern Britain. *Racing Demon* (1990) and *Murmuring Judges* (1991) were the first two parts of a trilogy about British institutions. His plays often have linked films, such as *The Secret Rapture* (1988) and the complementary political film *Paris by Night* (1988). His television films include *Dreams of Leaving* (1980), *Saigon… Year of the Cat* (1983) and the play *Heading Home* (1991). He wrote and directed his first feature film, *Wetherby*, in 1985. Later plays include *The Absence of War* (1993), *Skylight* (1995) and *The Judas Kiss* (1998). 📖 Joan Fitzpatrick Dean, *David Hare* (1990)

Hare, (John) Robertson 1891–1979
English actor
He was born in London, where he built up his reputation as a consummate comedian in the famous Aldwych farces, such as *A Cuckoo in the Nest* (1925), *Rookery Nook* (1926), *Thark* (1927) and *Plunder* (1928), cast invariably as the 'little man' whose ultimate 'debagging' became proverbial. He also featured in many other stage comedies and films.

Hare, William   See Burke, William

Harewood, Sir George Henry Hubert Lascelles, 7th Earl of 1923–
English nobleman and arts patron
The elder son of Mary, Princess Royal, and cousin of Queen Elizabeth II, he was born in Harewood, near Leeds. Educated at Eton and King's College, Cambridge, he was a captain in the Grenadier Guards in World War II, and was a prisoner of war. Keenly interested in music and drama, he was artistic director of the Leeds Festival (1958–74) and of the Edinburgh International Festival (1960–65), and managing director of English Opera North (1978–81). From 1985 to 1996 he was president of the British Board of Film Classification. 📖 *The Tongs and the Bones: The Memoirs of Lord Harewood* (1981)

Hargrave, Lawrence 1850–1915
Australian aeronautical pioneer
Born in Greenwich, England, he arrived in Sydney in 1865, and spent five years exploring in New Guinea before being appointed to a post at the Sydney Observatory (1878). He resigned in 1883 to devote his time to aeronautical experiments. In 1893 he developed the box-kite to produce a wing form used in early aircraft. In 1894, four tethered kites successfully lifted Hargrave five metres from the ground. His later work on curved wing surfaces presaged the wing shape of the Wright brothers' aeroplane of 1903. He also designed a radial rotary engine in 1899, the predecessor of the engine which drove most aircraft in the early days of aviation. His other projects included wave-driven ships and a one-wheel gyroscopic car.

Hargraves, Edward Hammond 1815–91
English colonialist
Born in Gosport, Hampshire, he travelled as a youth to Australia, then to the Californian gold diggings in 1849. From similarities in geological formation he suspected that gold would be found in Australia also. Finding it in the Blue Hills, New South Wales in 1851, he was appointed commissioner of Crown lands, and a government reward of £10,000. In 1855, a year after his return to England, he published *Australia and its Goldfields*.

Hargreaves, Alison, *married name* Ballard 1962–95
English mountaineer
Born in Belper, Derbyshire, she learned to climb whilst at the high school there. She then joined her boyfriend Jim Ballard (whom she later married) in his outdoor climbing business. In 1988, six months pregnant with her first child, she became the first British woman to climb the north face of the Eiger. She scaled the six main Alpine north faces unaccompanied—the Eiger, Matterhorn, Grandes Jorasses, Dru, Badille and Cima Grandesolo—in a single season during 1993. She then turned her attention to Mount Everest, which she climbed on her second attempt, alone and without supplementary oxygen (May 1995). Having moved to the Scottish Highlands with her family, Hargreaves went on to climb the world's second biggest mountain, K2, but died in a blizzard on the descent on 13 August 1995.

Hargreaves, James c.1720–1778
English inventor
Born probably in Blackburn, Lancashire, he worked as a weaver and carpenter in Standhill. About 1764 he invented the spinning-jenny, an early type of spinning-machine, with several spindles, but his fellow workers (fearing its effect on employment) broke into his house and destroyed his frame (1768). He then moved to Nottingham, where he erected a spinning mill, but his patent proved invalid, as he had disclosed his invention.

Häring, Georg Wilhelm Heinrich, *pseudonym* Willibald Alexis 1798–1871
German writer
He was born in Breslau (now Wrocław, Poland), and wrote the historical romance *Walladmor* (1823–24), claiming its author to be Sir Walter Scott, a fraud that led to its translation into several languages (into English, very

Hardy, Thomas 1840–1928
English novelist, poet and dramatist

Thomas Hardy was born in Upper Bockhampton, near Dorchester in Dorset, the son of a stonemason. As a boy he read a lot, learned to play the fiddle and developed a love of nature. He was educated in Dorchester and at the age of 16 was apprenticed to a local architect. In 1862 he went to London, where he spent five years working as an assistant architect, returning home in 1867 to pursue his chosen profession. However, he had already begun his first novel, The Poor Man and the Lady, which was never published.

There is speculation that around this time he met and fell in love with Tryphena Sparks, to whom he was related. The nature of their relationship is unclear but in 1870 he was sent to St Juliot, Cornwall, where he met Emma Gifford, whom he married in 1874, after the success of his novel Far From the Madding Crowd (1874). This was his fourth published novel in as many years: Desperate Remedies (1871), Under the Greenwood Tree (1872) and A Pair of Blue Eyes (1873) had been less successful. His marriage to Emma was not without difficulties but, ironically, when she died in 1912, Hardy was inspired to write some of the most moving love poems in the language ('Poems of 1912–13', in Satires of Circumstance, 1914).

A flood of novels continued to appear until 1895, with vibrant, brooding descriptive passages providing the backdrop to potent tragi-comedies. Among the most durable are The Return of the Native (1878), The Mayor of Casterbridge (1886) and Tess of the D'Urbervilles (1891).

Alhough Hardy was held in high esteem, critics carped at his seemingly inbred pessimism, and both Tess and Jude the Obscure (1895) were attacked virulently.

Thereafter, Hardy turned his attention to poetry, which he had always regarded as superior to fiction, and produced several volumes of lyrics, many of which express his love of rural life. His first collection, Wessex Poems, appeared in 1898; his last, Winter Words, posthumously in 1928, the year of his death. The Dynasts, a gargantuan drama in blank verse, occupied him for many years and was published in three instalments (1904, 1906, 1908). After Emma's death he married Florence Dugdale (1879–1937) and lived in Dorset, and was much visited there by aficionados and the literati. A biography published initially in two parts in 1928 and 1930 is thought to have been largely dictated by Hardy to Florence although it appeared under her name.

📖 M Seymour-Smith, Hardy (1994); R Little Purdy and M Millgate (eds), The Collected Letters of Thomas Hardy (7 vols, 1978–88); E Hardy, Thomas Hardy, a critical biography (1954).

'When the Present has latched its postern behind my tremulous stay,
And the May month flaps its glad green leaves like wings,
Delicate-filmed as new-spun silk, will the neighbours say,
He was a man who used to notice things.'
('Afterwards', 1917, stanza 1)

freely, by **Thomas De Quincey**, in 1824). It was followed by Die Gächteten (1825, 'The Outlaws'), Schloss Avalon (1827, 'Castle Avalon'), as well as books of travel, sketches and dramas. 📖 P K Richter, Willibald Alexis, als Literatur und Theaterkritiken (1931)

Haring, Keith 1958–1990
US artist

Born in Kutztown, Pennsylvania, he was involved in the New York graffiti movement in the 1980s, and came to public attention with his drawings of dancing children and animals and AIDS-inspired images, such as Ignorance = Fear (1989). He also designed stage sets, murals, record sleeves and book covers, including Painted Velum (1986, Stedelijk Museum, Amsterdam).

Harington, Sir Charles Robert 1897–1972
British chemist

Born in North Wales, he studied at Cambridge and then Edinburgh (1919–20), inspired by George Barger (1878–1939) with whom he later reported the constitution and synthesis of thyroxine (1927). Moving to the Royal Infirmary in Edinburgh, he studied protein metabolism and then spent a year in the USA with D D Van Slyke and Henry Dakin before becoming a lecturer (1922–31) and Professor of Pathological Chemistry (1931–42) at University College London. From 1942 to 1946 he was director of the National Institute for Medical Research in London. His numerous publications included The Thyroid Gland; its Chemistry and Physiology (1933). He was elected FRS in 1931, and knighted in 1948.

Harington, Sir John 1561–1612
English courtier and writer

He was born in Kelston, near Bath, and educated at Eton and King's College, Cambridge. From Cambridge he went to the court of his godmother, Queen **Elizabeth I**. His wit made him popular, but the freedom of his satires, as well as his The Metamorphosis of Ajax (1596), containing the earliest design for a water closet, brought a period of exile from the court. In 1599 he served under the Earl of **Essex** in Ireland, and was knighted by him on the field, much to the Queen's displeasure. To strengthen his amazing application to King **James VI and I** for the office of Chancellor and Archbishop of Ireland he composed in 1605 A Short View of the State of Ireland, an interesting and singularly modern essay. He is remembered as the metrical translator of **Ariosto**'s Orlando Furioso (1591), and his other writings include Rabelaisian pamphlets, epigrams, and a Tract on the Succession to the Crown. 📖 T Rich, Harington and Ariosto (1940)

Hariot, Thomas See Harriot, Thomas

Hariri, al-, in full Abu Mohammed al-Qasim ibn 'Ali al-Hariri, known as the silk merchant 1054–1122
Arabic writer

He was born in Basra, Iraq. As well as works on Arabic grammar and syntax, he wrote Maqamat ('Literary Gatherings'), a collection of witty rhymed tales of adventure in the maqamah ('assembly') style.

Harker, Alfred 1859–1939
English petrologist and structural geologist

Born in Kingston-upon-Hull, Humberside, he was educated at Cambridge, where he was appointed university demonstrator in geology at the Sedgwick Museum (1884) and university lecturer in 1904. Whilst undertaking fieldwork in Scotland for the Geological Survey (1895–1905) he did his most important work, publishing the authoritative memoirs The Tertiary Igneous Rocks of Skye (1904) and The Geology of the Small Isles of Invernessshire (1908). With these works he established the general succession of rocks in the igneous complexes and identified the hybrid rocks produced by the mixing of magmas. He also made great advances in the field of petrology, particularly with his idea that areas which contain similar rock types should be grouped together, and his studies of metamorphism and the physics of glacial erosion.

Harlan, John Marshall 1833–1911
US judge and jurist

Born in Boyle County, Kentucky, he graduated from Central College, Kentucky, and was admitted to the Bar in 1853 after reading law at Transylvania University. He was an unsuccessful candidate for the House of Representatives in 1858, and a presidential elector on the Bell–Everett (Constitutional Union) ticket in 1860. He supported the Union in the Civil War (1861–65), Kentucky having declared its neutrality, and commanded a volunteer Union regiment, resigning in 1863 to be elected as the Kentucky Attorney-General. By 1867, he was a radical Republican, and was appointed to a commission to decide between rival state governments in Louisiana, and then to the Supreme Court. He served from 1877 to 1911, invariably and often solely defending Black civil rights, denouncing the Court's acceptance of 'separate but equal' schools and stating that the Constitution was 'colour-blind'. His grandson, John Marshall Harlan (1899–1971), was also a distinguished jurist, and a Supreme Court judge from 1955 to 1971.

Harland, Sir Edward James 1831–96
Northern Irish shipbuilder

In Belfast in 1858 he founded the firm that later became Harland and Wolff, builders of many famous Atlantic liners and warships. Gustav William Wolff (1834–1913), his partner from 1860, was born in Hamburg, Germany, but learned engineering in Liverpool and Manchester.

Harland, Henry, *also known as* Sidney Luska 1861–1905
US novelist and short-story writer

Born in New York, not, as he claimed, in St Petersburg, after briefly attending Harvard Divinity School and a period working as a clerk, he turned to writing sentimental melodramatic novels about Jewish immigrants to the USA, such as *My Uncle Florimund* (1888), which he wrote under the pseudonym Sidney Luska. In 1889 he moved to Paris, and in the following year to London. He is best known as the founder and editor of the infamous quarterly *The Yellow Book* (1894–97) which became one of the leading influences on turn-of-the-century tastes and aesthetics. He also wrote popular fiction, including *The Cardinal's Snuff Box* (1900). ⌑ K Beckson, *Henry Harland* (1978)

Harlech, William David Ormsby Gore, 5th Baron 1918–85
English Conservative politician

He was educated at Eton and New College, Oxford. After service in World War II he managed the family estate. In 1950 he became Conservative MP for Oswestry, and became Minister of State at the Foreign Office (1956). During the Kennedy administration in the USA he served as British ambassador in Washington (1961–65), and was very close to the US President. He had succeeded his father in 1964, and on his return to Great Britain he obtained the franchise for Harlech Television (1967). As president of the British Board of Film Censors at a time of increasing permissiveness, Harlech made the controversial decision to license Sam Peckinpah's *Straw Dogs* (1972), with its graphic depiction of violence. He was active on many committees and for many causes. He supported Britain's entry into the European Community and was chairman of the National Committee for Electoral Reform.

Harley, Robert, 1st Earl of Oxford and Mortimer 1661–1724
English statesman

He was born in London. A Whig MP from 1689, he became Secretary of State in 1704. He soon joined the Tories, however, and was Chief Minister to Queen Anne from 1711 to 1714. His administration included the Treaty of Utrecht (1713) but he was dismissed for alleged treasonable acts and imprisoned in the Tower of London for two years. He then retired. His large collection of books and manuscripts is now in the British Library.

Harlow, Harry Frederick 1905–81
US psychologist

He was born in Fairfield, Iowa, and educated at Stanford University. He taught at Wisconsin University (1930–50, 1952–74), was director of the Regional Primate Center there from 1961 to 1971, and became research professor at Arizona University in 1974. His two major contributions to psychology both derived from his research on the behaviour of captive monkeys and were a departure from the traditional methods of laboratory investigations of animal behaviour. Firstly, he argued that 'learning to learn' a particular type of problem was a much more appropriate index of animal intelligence than any individual test, and secondly, he studied the effects of a number of early manipulations upon an infant monkey's social development. He also contributed to the growing field of neuropsychology, particularly to the vexed question of the putatively differential effects of brain damage sustained in infancy and in adulthood. He received the National Medal of Science in 1967.

Harlow, Jean, *originally* Harlean Carpentier 1911–37
US actress

Born in Kansas City, Missouri, she eloped with a business tycoon at the age of 16 and moved to Los Angeles, where she made her film debut in *Moran of the Marines* (1928) and worked as an extra before being signed to a contract by Howard Hughes and featuring in *Hell's Angels* (1930). Roles in *Platinum Blonde* (1931) and *Red Dust* (1932) established her screen image as a fast-talking, wisecracking blonde. With MGM (from 1932) she made the notorious *Red-Headed Woman* (1932), and developed into a deft comedienne in films like *Dinner at Eight* (1933), *Bombshell* (1933) and *Libelled Lady* (1936). She died at the age of 26 from cerebral oedema.

Harman, Harriet 1950–
English Labour politician

Born in London, she trained as a lawyer and became an outstanding legal officer for the National Council of Civil Liberties (1978–82), before entering parliament as MP for Peckham (1982). She was Opposition Chief Secretary to the Treasury (1992–94), a member of the Labour Party's National Executive Committee (1993–), and Opposition front bench spokesperson on employment (1994–95), on health (1995–96) and on social security (1996–97) before entering Tony Blair's Cabinet as Secretary of State for Social Security in 1997. In 1996 she received criticism for her decision to send her son to St Olave's grammar school in Kent rather than to a non-selective school. Her publications include *The Century Gap* (1993).

Harmodius d.514BC
Athenian murderer

With Aristogeiton in 514BC, he murdered Hipparchus, son of Pisistratus and younger brother of the tyrant Hippias, and intended to kill Hippias also. Harmodius was killed, while Aristogeiton, who fled, was later captured and executed. Subsequently they were regarded as patriotic martyrs, and were revered in Athens as champions of liberty.

Harmsworth, Alfred Charles William, 1st Viscount Northcliffe 1865–1922
Irish journalist and newspaper magnate

Born in Chapelizod, County Dublin, he was brought up in London and became one of the pioneers of mass circulation journalism. He was editor of *Youth* and, with his brother **Harold Sydney Harmsworth**, started *Answers to Correspondents* (1888). He founded *Comic Cuts* (1890) and an imitation, *Chips*, to discourage competitors. In 1894 he took over the *London Evening News* and sponsored the Jackson Arctic expedition. He also published some Sunday magazine papers and in 1896 revolutionized Fleet Street with his US-style *Daily Mail*. With Harold he bought the *Sunday Dispatch* and many provincial papers, pioneered the first newspaper for women, the *Daily Mirror* (1903), founded the Amalgamated Press for periodical and popular educational literature and acquired vast forests in Newfoundland for newsprint. In 1908 he became proprietor of *The Times* and in 1914 lowered its price to one penny to restore its falling circulation. An aspiring politician, he debated **Lloyd George**'s policies during World War I, and his attack on Lord **Kitchener** in the *Daily Mail* reduced its circulation by nearly 300,000. 📖 Henry Hamilton Fyfe, *Northcliffe: An Intimate Biography* (1930)

Harmsworth, Harold Sydney, 1st Viscount Rothermere 1868–1940
Irish newspaper magnate

Born and educated in London, he was closely associated with his brother **Alfred Harmsworth**, and founded the *Glasgow Daily Record*. In 1910 he established the King Edward chair of English literature at Cambridge and received a baronetcy. He dissociated himself from his brother in 1914 and concentrated on the *Daily Mirror*, which reached a circulation of three million by 1922. He also founded the *Sunday Pictorial* (1915), was Air Minister (1917–18), and after his brother's death acquired control of the *Daily Mail* and *Sunday Dispatch*.

Harnack, Adolf Karl Gustav von 1851–1930
German theologian

Born in Dorpat, the son of the Lutheran dogmatic theologian Theodosius Harnack (1817–89), he became a professor at Leipzig (1876), Giessen (1879), Marburg (1886) and Berlin (1889). His major writings include works on Gnosticism, St **Ignatius of Antioch**, Monasticism, the history of dogma, and on early Christian literature. He also wrote a history of the Berlin Academy. From 1893 his criticism of the Apostles' Creed caused him to be suspected of heresy. From 1905 to 1921 he was Keeper of the Royal (later State) Library, Berlin. His brother Otto (1857–1914) was Professor of Literature and History at Darmstadt, then at Stuttgart, and wrote on **Goethe** and **Schiller**.

Harnett, William Michael 1848–92
US painter

Born in County Cork, Ireland, he emigrated to Philadelphia with his parents and was trained as a silver engraver. He later became a painter of *trompe l'oeil* still lifes, in which he rendered common objects such as guns, pipes, books, musical instruments, and sheet music in meticulous detail and with photographic realism. His works include *After the Hunt*, *The Old Violin*, and *Artist's Card Pack*.

Harold I Knutsson, Harefoot d.1040
King of England

He was the younger son of **Knut Sveinsson** (Canute the Great) and his English mistress Ælfgifu of Northampton. On Knut's death the English elected Harold Harefoot regent for his half-brother **Hardaknut**, King of Denmark, the legitimate heir to the throne, who could not leave Denmark to claim the Crown. In 1037 Harold was elected king, but died just as Hardaknut was poised to invade England.

Harold II c.1022–1066
Anglo-Saxon King of England

He was the second son of Earl **Godwin**. By 1045 he was Earl of East Anglia. In 1053 he succeeded to his father's earldom of Essex and became the right hand of King **Edward the Confessor**. His brother Tostig became Earl of the Northumbrians in 1055, and two years later two other brothers were raised to earldoms. Meantime Harold drove back the Welsh, and added Herefordshire to his earldom. In 1063, provoked by the fresh incursions of the Welsh King Gruffyd, he marched against him, defeated the enemy at every point, and gave the government to the dead king's brothers. In c.1064 he made a celebrated visit to the court of **William**, Duke of Normandy, to whom he seems to have made some kind of oath and whom he helped in a war with the Bretons. On his return he married Ealdgyth, Gruffyd's widow, though Ealdgyth Swanneck, who had borne him his five children, was still alive. In 1065 the Northumbrians rebelled against Tostig, and Harold acquiesced in his replacement by Morcar and Tostig's banishment. In January 1066 King Edward died, and Harold, his nominee, was chosen king, and crowned in Westminster Abbey. He defeated Tostig and **Harald III** Sigurdsson, King of Norway, at Stamford Bridge in September 1066, but four days later Duke William landed in the south of England at Pevensey. Harold marched southwards and the two armies met at Senlac, about nine miles from Hastings. On 14 October 1066, the English fought stubbornly all day but were defeated. Harold, the last Anglo-Saxon King of England, was killed; he was supposedly pierced through the eye with an arrow. 📖 Hope Muntz, *Golden Warrior* (1970)

Harold Godwinsson See Harold II

Harper, Edward James 1941–
English composer

Born in Taunton, Somerset, he studied at Oxford and at the Royal College of Music, and in Milan. He became a lecturer in music at Edinburgh University, and directs the New Music Group of Scotland. Early works owed much to serial and aleatoric (where chance influences the choice of notes) styles, but with the orchestral *Bartók Games* (1972) and a one-act opera *Fanny Robin* (1975) he evolved a more tonally-based style. Other works include the operas *Hedda Gabler* (1985), *The Mellstock Quire* (1988), a symphony, concertos, choral works, two string quartets and other chamber and vocal pieces. Later pieces include *The Lamb* (1990) and *And Winds, Austere and Pure* (1993).

Harper and Brothers
New York publishers

The firm consisted originally of James (1795–1869), John (1797–1875), Joseph Wesley (1801–70) and Fletcher (1806–77). James and John began publishing in 1818. The firm of Harper and Brothers, established in 1833, is carried on by descendants, and issues *Harper's Magazine* (monthly since 1850), and other publications.

Harpignies, Henri 1819–1916
French landscape painter and engraver

Born in Valenciennes, he went to Italy and later became associated with the Barbizon school. His work includes *Ilex Trees at Villefranche* (Tate Gallery, London).

Harriman, E(dward) H(enry) 1848–1909
US financier and railroad executive

Born in Hempstead, New York, he became a Wall Street stockbroker, then applied his business acumen to the railroad business, directing the financial success of the Illinois Central and Union Pacific Railroads and controlling the Southern Pacific and Central Pacific (1901). He battled with **James J Hill** to gain control of the Chicago, Burlington & Quincy (1901–04), and they settled the dispute by forming, with **J P Morgan**, the Northern Securities Co, a railroad trust that was dissolved by the Supreme Court (1904).

Harriman, W(illiam) Averell 1891–1986
US politician and diplomat

He was born in New York City and educated at Yale. A close friend of President **Franklin D Roosevelt**, he was prominent in the National Recovery Administration in 1934. In 1941 he was Roosevelt's special war-aid representative in Britain. In 1943 he was appointed ambassador to the USSR and in 1946 to Britain. He was Secretary of Commerce (1946–48) and special assistant to President **Harry S Truman** (1950–51), helping to organize NATO. From 1951 to 1953 he was Director of Foreign Aid under the Mutual Security Act and was Governor of New York (1955–58). He was ambassador-at-large (1961, 1965–69), and US representative at the Vietnam peace talks in Paris (1968). Chief negotiator for the partial nuclear test-ban treaty between the USA and USSR in 1963, he continued to visit the USSR on behalf of the government until the age of 91. ⬚ Ruby Abramson, *Spanning the Century: The Life of W Averell Harriman 1891–1986* (1992)

Harriot or Hariot, Thomas c.1560–1621
English mathematician and scientist

Born in Oxford, he was mathematical tutor to Sir **Walter Raleigh** (1584–85) and was sent to survey Virginia, on which he published *A Briefe and True Report of the New Found Land of Virginia* (1588). He corresponded with **Johannes Kepler** on astronomical matters, observed **Halley's** comet in 1607 and made observations with the newly discovered telescope from 1609, as early as **Galileo**. His map of the Moon and drawings of sunspots and the satellites of Jupiter survive. He studied optics, refraction by prisms, and the formation of rainbows. Most of his work was never published and remains in manuscript, although his *Artis analyticae praxis*, a treatise on algebra, was published posthumously in 1631, showing that he had developed an effective algebraic notation for the solution of equations.

Harris, Sir Arthur Travers, *nicknamed* Bomber Harris 1892–1984
English air force officer

Born in Cheltenham, Gloucestershire, he was educated at Allhallows School and emigrated to Rhodesia in 1910. He served with the 1st Rhodesian Regiment in South West Africa (1914–15) and with the Royal Flying Corps in France and in defence of London. On the formation of the Royal Air Force (April 1918) he received a permanent commission. He commanded No. 4 Group Bomber Command (1937–38), and RAF Palestine and Transjordan (1938–39). He was deputy chief of Air Staff (1940–41), and head of the RAF Delegation in the USA (1941). As Commander-in-Chief Bomber Command RAF (1942–45) he organized bombing raids on industrial targets in Germany, earning his nickname. ⬚ Dudley Saward, 'Bomber Harris' (1984)

Harris, Barbara Clementine 1930–
US cleric in the US Episcopal Church

Born in Philadelphia, she worked as a public relations executive, a social activist in the 1960s, and a supporter of the ordination of women and of homosexuals in the 1970s. She attended Villanova University in the late 1970s, gaining some of her theological training through correspondence courses. Ordained in 1980, after parish and prison chaplaincy work she was appointed director of the Episcopal Church Publishing Co in 1984. She was consecrated suffragan (assistant) bishop of Massachusetts in 1989. Though not a diocesan bishop, she was the first female bishop in the Anglican Communion. Her consecration was ratified in 1990 when Penelope Jamieson (1942–) was consecrated the first female Anglican diocesan bishop, in Dunedin, New Zealand.

Harris, Bomber See Harris, Sir Arthur Travers

Harris, Emmylou 1947–
US country singer

Born in Birmingham, Alabama, she began her career as a folk singer, but moved into country rock through her association with Gram Parsons (1946–73). She continued her explorations after his death in records like *Pieces of the Sky* (1975) and *Elite Hotel* (1976). Her Hot Band was one of the best units in Nashville, and she experimented with more traditional country and bluegrass in *Roses in the Snow* (1980) and *Angel Band* (1987). She led a fine acoustic group, The Nash Ramblers, in the early 1990s, before making a surprise change of direction into the evocative, ambient country of *Wrecking Ball* (1995), a collaboration with guitarist/producer Daniel Lanois. She remains among the few important contemporary country artists.

Harris, Frank, *properly* James Thomas Harris 1856–1931
Irish writer and journalist

He was born, according to his autobiography, in Galway, but according to his own later statement, in Tenby, Dyfed. He ran away to New York at the age of 15 and, after various jobs, began studying law in 1874 at the University of Kansas. Returning to England about 1876, he entered the newspaper world. He had a considerable impact on Fleet Street as editor of the *Fortnightly Review*, *Saturday Review*, *Vanity Fair* and of the *Evening News*, with its provocative headlines and sensationalism. His best known work is his boastful and unreliable autobiography *My Life and Loves* (4 vols, 1923–27), which was banned for pornography. He is also remembered for his *Contemporary Portraits* (1915–30), as well as biographies of **Oscar Wilde** (1920) and **George Bernard Shaw** (1931), some novels, short stories and plays, and two works on **Shakespeare**.

Harris, Sir Henry 1925–
Australian–British geneticist

Educated at the universities of Sydney and Oxford, he became head of the department of cell biology at the John Innes Institute (1960–63), and returned to Oxford as head of the Sir William Dunn School of Pathology (1963–92), Professor of Pathology (1963–79), and Regius Professor of Medicine (1979–92). He was elected Fellow of the Royal Society in 1968. In 1965 he successfully fused somatic mammalian cells in culture to produce the first cells in which the cytoplasm fuses but the nuclei do not, and later true cell hybrids in which the nuclei of the parent cells coalesce. By the use of this technique, hybrid cells from different animal species could be produced. These permitted for the first time the genetic analysis of somatic cells. Such activator molecules have now been identified and purified. Perhaps the most important consequence of this technique was the demonstration that normal cells contained genes that suppressed the malignant character of tumour cells. These genes are now known as tumour suppressor genes. He was knighted in 1993.

Harris, Howel 1714–73
Welsh clergyman

Born in Trefecca, Brecon, he was the founder of Welsh Calvinistic Methodism. He became a Methodist preacher in 1735, and in 1752 went back to Trefecca and founded a kind of Protestant monastery, whose members he referred to as the 'family'. His autobiography was published in 1791.

Harris, James Rendel 1852–1941
English Quaker scholar

Born in Plymouth, after graduating from Cambridge, where he became Fellow of Clare College, he taught New Testament Greek at Johns Hopkins University (1882–85) and at Haverford College (1886–92), and palaeography at Cambridge (1892–1903). He was director of studies at the Friends' Settlement at Woodbrooke (1904–18), and then Curator of Manuscripts at the John Rylands Library, Manchester (1918–25), whence he travelled extensively in the Near and Middle East. His numerous books include *New Testament Autographs* (1882), *Biblical Fragments from Mount Sinai* (1890), *The Guiding Hand of God* (1905), *Leyden Documents Relating to the Pilgrim Fathers* (1920), and *The Migration of Culture* (1936).

Harris, Joel Chandler 1848–1908
US writer
Born in Eatonton, Georgia, he was in turn printer, lawyer, and journalist on the staff of the Atlanta *Constitution* (1876–1900). Having absorbed much Georgia Negro folklore and many sayings and stories, he began to publish his 'Uncle Remus' tales in the *Constitution*. His *Uncle Remus: His Songs and Sayings* (1880) made him internationally famous, both to children and to students of folklore. A gifted storyteller, he also wrote *Nights with Uncle Remus* (1883), *Minervy Ann* (1899), and several other children's books, as well as a history of Georgia (1899). ⏀ P M Cousins, *Joel Chandler Harris: A Biography* (1968)

Harris, Julie (Julia Ann) 1925–
US actress
Born in Grosse Point, Michigan, she made her New York debut in 1945 as a student at Yale School of Drama, and in 1946 won critical acclaim as a member of the Old Vic New York company for her roles in *Henry IV Part Two* and Sophocles' *Oedipus*. She established her reputation as a leading actress with her performance as Frankie Adams in Carson McCullers's *The Member of the Wedding* (1950), following this with an appearance as Sally Bowles in *I am a Camera* (1951). She played Juliet at Stratford Ontario (1960) and Ophelia in Joseph Papp's production of *Hamlet* in New York (1964). She has appeared since in numerous notable US plays, and is renowned for her solo performance as Emily Dickinson in *The Belle of Amherst* (1976). Her books include *Juliet Harris Talks to Young Actors* (1972). Later film appearances include *Gorillas in the Mist* (1988) and *Housesitter* (1992).

Harris, Patricia, *née* Roberts 1924–85
US lawyer and politician
Born in Mattoon, Illinois, she studied at Howard University in Washington DC (1945) and at the University of Chicago (1947). She later studied at the American University (1950) and at George Washington University (1960), both in Washington DC, and was appointed Dean of Howard University Law School in 1969. She became a director of IBM in 1971, and was appointed ambassador to Luxembourg under President Lyndon B Johnson. She became the first African-American woman to hold a US Cabinet post on being appointed Secretary of Housing and Urban Development (1977–79) by President Jimmy Carter. She then served as Secretary of Health, Education and Welfare (in 1980 redesignated Health and Human Services) from 1979 to 1981.

Harris, Paul 1868–1947
US lawyer
Born in Racine, Wisconsin, he was the founder in 1905 of the Rotary movement in Chicago. It began as a young businessmen's luncheon club and expanded in 1912 into Rotary International, now a worldwide organization dedicated to the maintenance of high standards of service and integrity in commercial and professional life.

Harris, Reg(inald Hargreaves) 1920–92
English track cyclist
Born in Bury, Lancashire, he came to prominence in 1947 when he won the world amateur sprint championship, and followed this with silver medals in sprint and tandem in the 1948 Olympic Games in London. That same year he turned professional and was world sprint champion from 1949 to 1951 and again in 1954, setting records in the process which stood for 20 years.

Harris, Renatus or René, the Elder c.1640–c.1715
British organ-builder
Born in France, he moved to England around 1660 with his father, whom he assisted in building organs for Salisbury, Gloucester and Worcester cathedrals. In 1684 he engaged in a contest with his great rival, Bernard Smith, over a commission for the Temple Church, London. Both constructed organs, challenging the other to make improvements. In this way the vox humana, cromorna and double bassoon stops were heard for the first time. Henry Purcell and John Blow performed on Smith's organ, and Giovanni Draghi (fl.1670s) on Harris's. Harris lost the contest. He built 39 organs in all, many for London churches as well as for James VII and II's private chapels, and for several cathedrals including Chichester (1678), Winchester (1681), Bristol (1685) and Hereford (1686), as well as King's College, Cambridge (1686). His two sons were both organ-builders: John (fl.1737) and Renatus 'the Younger' (d.1727).

Harris, Rolf 1930–
Australian entertainer and artist
Born in Bassendean, Perth, Western Australia, he won a radio 'Amateur Hour' competition at the age of 18, and after graduating from the University of Western Australia, went to London in 1952 where he studied art. While there he performed at the 'Down Under Club' and in 1954 he started working for the BBC children's department. He returned to Perth in 1960 to present a children's television programme and then had commercial success with records such as *Tie Me Kangaroo Down Sport* (1960), *Sun Arise* (1962) and the No 1 single 'Two Little Boys' (1969). His many television shows have included *The Rolf Harris Show* (1967–72), *Rolf's Cartoon Club*, *Animal Hospital Live* (1994), *Cat Crazy* (1995), *Zoo Watch Live* (1995) and *Animal Hospital* (1995–). He also played Jake the Peg in the film *The Little Convict* (1979).

Harris, Rosemary Jeanne 1930–
English actress
She made her debut in New York City in 1952, and in London a year later, in *The Seven Year Itch*. She appeared with the Bristol Old Vic and the Old Vic in London, before visiting New York again (1956), this time with the Old Vic Company, as Cressida in Tyrone Guthrie's modern-dress version of *Troilus and Cressida*. She appeared in many plays in the USA before returning to Great Britain, joining the Chichester Festival Theatre for its inaugural 1962 season. She won huge acclaim in London in 1969, playing three characters in Neil Simon's *Plaza Suite*. In 1991 she appeared as the old aunt in *Arsenic and Old Lace* and in Arthur Wing Pinero's *Preserving Mr Panmure*. A leading character actor, she has continued to alternate between Great Britain and the USA, playing the British and US classics.

Harris, Roy Ellsworth 1898–1979
US composer
Born in Lincoln County, Oklahoma and brought up on a farm in California, he had no specialized musical training until the age of 24, but studies in Los Angeles led to a Guggenheim Fellowship, which enabled him to study in Paris under Nadia Boulanger. Ruggedly American in character, his compositions are strongly rhythmic and

melodic and draw on influences ranging from folk music to the poetry of **Walt Whitman**. He wrote some 15 symphonies, of which the best known are his *Third Symphony* (1938) and his *Folksong Sympathy* (No.4, 1940). Other works include the orchestral pieces *When Johnny Comes Marching Home* (1935) and *Kentucky Spring* (1949) and choral pieces such as the *Walt Whitman Suite* (1944).

Harris, Thomas Lake 1823–1906
US spiritualist

Born in Fenny Stratford, Buckinghamshire, England, he was taken to the USA at the age of three, and in 1843 became a Universalist pastor. In 1850 he set up as a spiritualistic medium, and about 1855 he founded the Church of the Good Shepherd, based on doctrines compounded from **Swedenborg** and **Charles Fourier**. His followers included **Laurence Oliphant**.

Harris, (Theodore) Wilson 1921–
British novelist

Born in New Amsterdam, British Guiana (now Guyana), he was educated at Queen's College, Georgetown and worked as a surveyor. In 1959 he moved to London. His masterpiece is *The Guyana Quartet* (1960–63), which begins with a poetic exploration, and evolves into a composite picture of the various landscapes and racial communities of Guyana. Later works include *The Waiting Room* (1967), *The Tree of Life* (1978), *Carnival* (1985), *The Four Banks of the River of Space* (1990) and *Resurrection at Sorrow Hill* (1993).

Harrison, Benjamin 1833–1901
23rd President of the USA

Born in North Bend, Ohio, the grandson of **William Henry Harrison**, he studied at Miami University in Ohio, and in 1854 settled as a lawyer in Indianapolis. During the Civil War (1861–65) he joined the Union army in 1862, and was first lieutenant and then colonel of the 70th Regiment Indiana Volunteers. He served in General **Sherman**'s Atlanta campaign, and fought in the battles of Resaca, Peach Tree Creek and Nashville, and in 1865 he became brevet-brigadier-general. Returning to Indiana after the war, he took an active part in **Ulysses S Grant**'s presidential campaigns of 1868 and 1872, and was nominated by the Republicans for the state governorship in 1876, but was defeated. In 1880 he was chairman of his state delegation to the Republican national convention. As a US senator for Indiana (1881–87) he supported Civil Service reform and the Interstate Commerce Act of 1887. In 1888 he was nominated for President against the Democrat **Grover Cleveland**. The contest turned on the issue of free trade, and Harrison's election was a triumph for protectionism. His administration (1889–93) saw the adoption in 1890 of the **McKinley** Tariff, which set the highest tariff rates in US history, as well as the passage of the **Sherman** Silver Purchase Act. He took an active interest in foreign affairs, pressing for the establishment of US military bases overseas and sponsoring the first Pan-American Conference (1889). In 1892 he failed to gain re-election against Cleveland, and returned to legal practice. He later served as chief counsel for Venezuela in its boundary dispute with Great Britain.

Harrison, Frederic 1831–1923
English jurist and philosopher

Born in London, he was educated at King's College School there, and Wadham College, Oxford. He became Fellow and tutor of his college, but was called to the Bar in 1858. He sat on the Royal Commission upon Trade Unions (1867–69), was Secretary to the Commission for the Digest of the Law (1869–70), Professor of Jurisprudence and International Law at Lincoln's Inn Hall (1877–89), and an alderman of London County

Council (1889–93). A Positivist and an advanced Liberal, he wrote *The Meaning of History* (1862), *The Philosophy of Common Sense* (1908), *On Society* (1918) and other works.

Harrison, George See Beatles, The (panel)

Harrison, John 1693–1776
English inventor and horologist

He was born in Foulby, Yorkshire, and by 1726 had constructed a timekeeper with compensating apparatus for correcting errors due to variations of climate. In 1713 the British government had offered three prizes for the discovery of a method to determine longitude accurately. After long perseverance he developed a marine chronometer which, in a voyage to Jamaica (1761–62) determined the longitude within 18 geographical miles (or 29 km). After further trials, he was awarded the first prize (1765–73). He also invented the gridiron pendulum (1726), the going fusee, and the remontoir escapement.

Harrison, Sir Rex, originally Reginald Carey Harrison 1908–90
English actor

Born in Houghton, Lancashire, he joined the Liverpool Playhouse on leaving school and later toured before making his West End debut in *Getting Gertie Married* (1930) and his film debut in *The Great Game* (1930). Film and stage roles followed, including his Broadway debut in *Sweet Aloes* (1936) and the long-running *French Without Tears* (1936–38). His films include *Storm in a Teacup* (1937), *Major Barbara* (1940), *Blithe Spirit* (1945), *Anna and the King of Siam* (1946), *Cleopatra* (1962) and *Dr Dolittle* (1967). His urbane and somewhat blasé style led to many leading comedy roles, including that of Professor Higgins in *My Fair Lady* (1956–58), which he was the first to play and which he repeated on film (1964, Academy Award). Later stage work included *The Kingfisher* (1978), *Heartbreak House* (1983) and *The Admirable Crichton* (1988). He married six times and published his autobiography, *Rex* (1974). He was knighted in 1989. ⌨ Alexander Walker, *Fatal Charm: The Life of Rex Harrison* (1992)

Harrison, Ross Granville 1870–1959
US biologist

Born in Germantown, Pennsylvania, he entered Johns Hopkins University in 1889, received his PhD in zoology, and joined the staff at Johns Hopkins, first as an instructor in anatomy in 1896, and then as Professor of Biology (1899–1907). In 1907 he moved to Yale University where he was successively appointed Professor of Comparative Anatomy (1907), Professor of Biology (1927) and Emeritus Professor (1938). He introduced the hanging-drop method of tissue culture (1907), which has proved of great value not only in embryology, but also in oncology, genetics, virology and other fields.

Harrison, Thomas 1606–60
English soldier

Born in Newcastle-under-Lyme, Staffordshire, he joined the Parliamentary army and fought at Edgehill (1642), Marston Moor (1644) and the decisive Battle of Naseby (1645). He commanded the guard which took **Charles I** from Hurst Castle to London, and signed his death warrant (1649). He fought at Worcester (1651), but was too uncompromising in both religion and politics to favour **Cromwell**'s tolerant ideas. Deprived of his commission, he was later imprisoned for taking part in plots. He refused to go into exile at the Restoration and was executed.

Harrison, Tony 1937–
English poet

He was born in Leeds, and educated at Leeds Grammar School and Leeds University. His working-class background and subsequent education in the classics create a social tension which has proved his most fruitful theme.

The desire to give a poetic voice to those who have historically lacked one informs much of his work, and he skilfully combines vernacular speech and traditional poetic forms. He has gained international recognition for his verse translations and adaptations for the theatre, notably of the York Mystery Plays and the Greek tragedies. He has also explored the possibilities of poetry on television with an effective broadcast of his poem *V* (1985), a denunciatory journey through modern British life. His publications include *Earthworks* (1964), *Bow Down* (1977), *Selected Poems* (1984), *The Gaze of the Gorgon* (1992, Whitbread Poetry Award) and more recently, *Permanently Bard* (1995). He was elected a Fellow of the Royal Society of Literature in 1985.

Harrison, William Henry 1773–1841
9th President of the USA

Born in Charles City County, Virginia, he joined the troops **Anthony Wayne** led against the Native Americans, and distinguished himself at the Battle of Fallen Timbers in 1794. Resigning his captaincy in 1798, he became Secretary and then US representative of the Northwest Territory. When Indiana Territory was formed in 1800 he was appointed Governor. He attempted to avoid war with the Indians, but was compelled to quell the Shawnee Chief **Tecumseh's** outbreak, ending in the Battle of Tippecanoe (1811). In the War of 1812 he received the command in the north-west, reoccupied Detroit, and following the victory of **Oliver Perry** on Lake Erie was able to pursue the British and Native Americans into Canada, where, in 1813, he routed them at the Battle of the Thames. He represented Ohio in Congress (1816–19) and in the US Senate (1825–28). Gaining the Whig presidential nomination in 1840, he joined with vice-presidential nominee **John Tyler** in waging an energetic and image-conscious campaign, emphasizing his log-cabin frontier days and employing the slogan 'Tippecanoe and Tyler too!'. Elected by an overwhelming majority, he caught pneumonia at his inauguration and died a month later (April 1841). He was the grandfather of **Benjamin Harrison**. 📖 James A Green, *William Henry Harrison: His Life and Times* (1941)

Harrisson, Tom 1911–76
English ethnologist and sociologist

Educated at Harrow and Pembroke College, Cambridge, he became curator of Sarawak Museum in 1947. He was known for his exploration and research in Borneo, where he organized guerilla activities against the Japanese in World War II, and for his application of the techniques of social anthropology to the study of British urban communities by 'mass observation'. His books include *Borneo Jungle* (1938), *Mass Observation* (1937), *Living among Cannibals* (1942), and *World Within* (1959).

Harrod, Sir Henry Roy Forbes 1900–78
English economist

Born in London, he was educated at Oxford, where he became a don in 1922. He was Nuffield Professor of International Economics at Oxford from 1952 to 1967. He wrote widely, as a biographer and on philosophy and logic, as well as on economics. His major contributions to economic theory are dynamic concepts of conditions of economic growth, particularly the Harrod–Domar model of economic growth. The Polish-born US economist Evsey Domar (1914–) developed a similar insight independently at about the same time.

Harry, Blind fl.1470–92
Scottish poet

Blind from birth, he lived by telling tales, and from 1490 to 1492 was at the court of **James IV**, receiving occasional small gratuities. His major known work is *Wallace*, on the life of the Scottish patriot **William Wallace**, written in rhyming couplets. The language is frequently obscure, but the work is written with vigour, sometimes breaking into poetry. The poem transfers to its hero some of the achievements of **Robert the Bruce**, and contains many mistakes or misrepresentations, but much of the narrative can bear the test of historical criticism.

Harry, Deborah, *also known as* Debbie Harry
1945–
US singer and actress

Born in Miami, Florida, she worked as a beautician, waitress and Playboy Bunny before recording with the short-lived Wind in the Willows. In 1973, with her partner Chris Stein, she formed the Stilettoes, which later became Blondie. People tended to believe that the name referred to her alone, and after a string of new wave hits such as 'Heart of Glass', 'Presence Dear' and 'Denise', and the albums *Parallel Lines* and *Eat to the Beat*, she went solo under her own name, a decision compounded by Stein's long illness. Her first solo record was *Koo-Koo*, followed by *Rockbird*. She also turned to acting, with parts in *Atlantic City* (1980) and *Videodrome* (1982), geared to her almost Monroe-like appearance.

Hart, Gary, *originally* Gary Hartpence 1936–
US Democrat politician

He was born in Ottawa, Kansas, educated at Yale University, and where he became immersed in Democratic Party politics, working as a volunteer during John F Kennedy's 1960 presidential campaign. He moved to Denver, Colorado, where he established a law practice and, after managing **George McGovern's** presidential campaign between 1970 and 1972, entered the US Senate in 1974. He acquired a reputation for his advocacy of realistic liberal reforms, seeking to combine social and environmental improvement with enhanced economic efficiency. He contested the Democrats' presidential nomination in 1980 and almost defeated the 'party insider', **Walter Mondale**. He retired from the Senate in 1986 to concentrate on a bid for the presidency, but in 1987 he withdrew from the race when his wholesome, family image was put in issue by newspaper reporting of his private life. He re-entered the race in 1988 but withdrew shortly afterwards.

Hart, Herbert Lionel Adolphus 1907–
English jurist

He was educated at Cheltenham College and at New College, Oxford. He practised at the Chancery Bar and taught philosophy at Oxford, becoming Professor of Jurisprudence (1952–68), and later Principal of Brasenose College (1973–78). He wrote extensively, his most significant works including *Causation in the Law* (1959, with A M Honore), *Law, Liberty and Morality* (1963), and *Essays on Bentham* (1982). He also edited some of **Jeremy Bentham's** works, notably *Of Laws in General* (1970). Particularly important is Hart's *The Concept of Law* (1961) in which he contends that a defining characteristic of a legal system is that it should include a fundamental rule for the identification of the other rules of the system. This has been an influential book, widely studied and discussed in English-speaking countries.

Hart (of South Lanark), Dame Judith Constance Mary Hart, Baroness 1924–91
English Labour politician

Born in Burnley, Lancashire, she was educated at the London School of Economics. A life-time Labour Party member, she entered the House of Commons, representing Lanark, in 1959, and joined **Harold Wilson's** government in 1964, reaching Cabinet rank as Paymaster-General in 1968. She then had three successful terms as Minister of Overseas Development (1969–70, 1974–75, 1977–79). She was a popular and influential left-winger, with a strong concern for the needs of Third World countries. She was created a DBE in 1979 and awarded a life peerage in 1988. She retired from parliament in 1987.

Hart, Lorenz Milton 1895–1943
US lyricist

Born in New York City, he studied at Columbia University and was rejected for service in World War I because of his height (he was less than five feet tall). He met the young composer **Richard Rodgers** in 1918, and over the next two decades they collaborated on 28 Broadway musicals, including *A Connecticut Yankee* (1927), *The Boys from Syracuse* (1938) and *Pal Joey* (1940). Hart contributed lyrics marked by wit and metrical complexity, and his classic songs with Rodgers included 'The Lady Is a Tramp', 'Blue Moon', 'My Funny Valentine', and 'This Can't Be Love'. Hart's alcoholism eventually forced Rodgers to seek another collaborator in **Oscar Hammerstein II**, and Hart died of pneumonia while still in middle age.

Hart, Moss 1904–61
US dramatist and director

Born in the Bronx, New York City, he began his career as office boy to the impresario Augustus Pitou, to whom he sold his first play, *The Beloved Bandit*, when still a teenager. His second, *Once in a Lifetime* (1930), was successfully produced after extensive rewriting by **George S Kaufman**. Although he continued to write on his own, his most successful work was collaborative. With Kaufman he wrote several plays, the most popular being the wry comedies *Merrily We Roll Along* (1934), *You Can't Take It With You* (1936) and *The Man Who Came to Dinner* (1939), described by one reviewer as 'a merciless cartoon' of the critic **Alexander Woollcott**'s 'bad manners, shameless egoism, boundless mischief, and widely assorted friendships'. Hart is also remembered for writing the sketches for the **Irving Berlin** revue, *As Thousands Cheer* (1933), and the book for the **Kurt Weill/Ira Gershwin** musical, *Lady in the Dark* (1941). 📖 *Act One: An Autobiography* (1959)

Hart, Nancy, *née* Morgan 1735–1830
US heroine of the American Revolution

She was born into a frontier family who moved to Georgia (c.1771) and who during the 'War of Extermination' chose to stay and fight the Tories (Loyalists). None of her exploits have been formally documented, though they are well known in folklore. When five Tories appeared at the family cabin demanding food, she is said to have plied them with whiskey, seized one of their rifles, killed a soldier, and held the rest hostage until her daughter succeeded in signalling for help.

Hart, William S(urrey) 1865–1946
US actor and filmmaker

Born in Newburgh, New York State, he worked for the New York City post office, studied acting and toured the country before Broadway successes in *Ben Hur* (1899), *The Squaw Man* (1905) and *The Virginian* (1907–08). After his first film, *The Fugitive* (1913) he went on to enjoy great popularity in a series of westerns as a defender of truth, justice and the honour of good women. He often devised the original story and directed his own films, including *Wild Bill Hickok* (1923) and *Tumbleweeds* (1925). He published several volumes of fiction and an autobiography, *My Life East and West* (1929).

Harte, (Francis) Bret(t) 1836–1902
US author

Born in Albany, New York State, he went to California in 1854, and became a compositor and secretary of the US Mint in San Francisco (1864–70). He was US consul in Krefeld (1878–80) and in Glasgow (1880–85), and then lived in London. His most famous poems, written in San Francisco, include 'John Burns of Gettysburg' and 'The Society upon the Stanislaus'. His humorous verse includes 'Plain Language from Truthful James' (1870), commonly referred to as 'The Heathen Chinee'. In 1868 he founded and edited the *Overland Monthly*, to which he contributed short stories, later collected in *The Luck of Roaring Camp and Other Sketches* (1870). 📖 R O'Connor, *Bret Harte, a biography* (1966)

Hartington, Marquis of See **Cavendish, Spencer Compton**

Hartley, David 1705–57
English philosopher, physician and psychologist

Born in Luddenden, Halifax, Yorkshire, and educated at Cambridge, he first studied for the Church but changed direction and became a successful medical practitioner. His *Observations on Man, His Frame, His Duty and His Expectations* (1749) relates psychology closely to physiology, and develops a theory of the association of sensations with sets of ideas which forms part of an associationist tradition running from **David Hume** through to **John Stuart Mill** and **Herbert Spencer**.

Hartley, David 1732–1813
English inventor

Born in Bath, Somerset, the son of the philosopher **David Hartley**, he was a Fellow of Merton College, Oxford, and MP from 1774 to 1784. With **Benjamin Franklin**, he drafted the Treaty of Paris between Great Britain and the USA in 1783 that ended the American Revolution. However, his main claim to fame is that he invented a system of fireproofing houses which he demonstrated to crowds by using his own house.

Hartley, L(eslie) P(oles) 1895–1972
English writer

He was born near Peterborough, Cambridgeshire, and educated at Harrow and at Balliol College, Oxford. His early short stories, *Night Fears* (1924) and *The Killing Bottle* (1932), established his reputation as a master of the macabre. Later he transferred his Jamesian power of 'turning the screw' to psychological relationships and made a new success with such novels as his Eustace and Hilda trilogy *The Shrimp and the Anemone* (1944), *The Sixth Heaven* (1946) and *Eustace and Hilda* (1947). Among his finest work is *The Boat* (1950), and his best-known novel *The Go-Between* (1953). Later novels include *A Perfect Woman* (1955), *The Hireling* (1957) and *My Sister's Keeper* (1970). 📖 A Mulkeen, *Wild Thyme, Winter Lightning: the symbolic novels of L P Hartley* (1974)

Hartley, Marsden 1877–1943
US painter and writer

Born in Lewiston, Maine, he visited France and Germany in 1912–15, experimenting with the latest styles. Inspired by **Wassily Kandinsky** and **Franz Marc** his work became abstract, and he exhibited with the Blaue Reiter group, but landscapes—especially mountains—always attracted him. He travelled widely in the 1920s and did not settle finally in Maine until 1934. He was one of the pioneers of US modern art.

Hartline, Haldan Keffer 1903–83
US physiologist and Nobel Prize winner

Born in Bloomsburg, Pennsylvania, he graduated in medicine from Johns Hopkins Medical School, and in 1931 he joined the US neurophysiologist **Detlev Bronk** at the Johnson Foundation of the University of Pennsylvania, where he remained until 1949, apart from a brief intermission at Cornell (1940–41). In 1949 he moved with Bronk to Johns Hopkins, where he was appointed Professor of Biophysics, and in 1954 he again moved with Bronk, to the Rockefeller Institute for Medical Research, New York City, as head of the biophysics laboratory, later becoming Professor of Biophysics, and in 1972 Detlev Bronk Professor. Inspired by the work of Bronk and **Edgar Adrian** in recording the electrical activity of single nerve fibres, Hartline carried out experiments in the optic nerve of the horseshoe crab and the visual system of the frog, analysing the several physiological stages by which an eye distinguishes shapes. His work led directly to that of **David Hubel** and **Torsten Wiesel**, and he shared the 1967 Nobel Prize for physiology or medicine with **George Wald** and **Ragnar Granit**.

Hartmann von Aue c.1170–1215
German poet

He took part in the Crusade of 1197. His poetry is of the Middle High German period and the most popular of his narrative poems is *Der arme Heinrich* (c.1195, 'Poor Heinrich'), which, based on a Swabian tradition, is utilized in **Henry Wadsworth Longfellow**'s *Golden Legend*. *Erec* (c.1180–85) and *Iwein* (c.1200) are both drawn from the Arthurian cycle, and closely follow **Chrétien de Troyes**. In *Gregorius* (c.1188), he relates how worldly passion is expiated by religious faith. His songs are mainly on love.

Hartnell, Sir Norman 1901–78
English couturier and court dressmaker

Born in London, he was educated at Magdalene College, Cambridge. He started his own business in 1923, receiving the Royal Warrant in 1940. Costumes for leading actresses, wartime 'utility' dresses, the Women's Royal Army Corps uniform and Princess **Elizabeth**'s wedding and coronation gowns all formed part of his work. He published his autobiography, *Silver and Gold* in 1955.

Hartnett, Sir Laurence John 1898–1986
Australian automotive engineer

Born in Woking, Surrey, England, he was head of General Motors' English subsidiary, Vauxhall, and went to Australia in 1934 to take over GM–Holden. His enthusiasm for a locally-built mass production car, despite the opposition of his New York bosses, won over the Australian government. War production intervened and the first 'Holden' car appeared in 1946, by which time Hartnett had resigned from the company to produce his own small car. This project, and a later joint venture with a Japanese motor company, foundered due to government opposition.

Hartree, Douglas Rayner 1897–1958
English mathematician and physicist

He was born in Cambridge, where he graduated after working on the science of anti-aircraft gunnery during World War I. From 1929 to 1945 he was Professor of Applied Mathematics and Theoretical Physics at Manchester University, returning to Cambridge as Professor of Mathematical Physics in 1946. He worked mainly on computational methods applied to a wide variety of problems ranging from atomic physics, where he invented the method of the self-consistent field in quantum mechanics, to the automated control of chemical plants. At Manchester University he developed the differential analyser, an analogue computer, and was deeply involved in the early days of the electronic digital computer.

Hartshorne, Richard 1899–
US geographer

Born in Kittanning, Pennsylvania, and educated at Chicago University, he taught at Minnesota University (1924–40), and then at Wisconsin University as Professor of Geography (1940–70). Following distinguished research in North America in the 1920s and 1930s, and in Europe (1938–39), he published what has become a major milestone in the history of geographical ideas, *The Nature of Geography: a critical survey of current thought in the light of the past*

(1939). In this he argued for regional geography as the core of a non-theoretical discipline. A retrospective view, *Perspective on the Nature of Geography*, appeared in 1959.

Hartung, Hans 1904–89
French artist

Born in Leipzig, Germany, he studied in Basle, Leipzig, Dresden and Munich. Although in his earlier years he was influenced by the German Impressionists and Expressionists, from 1928 onwards he produced mainly abstract work. During World War II he served in the French Foreign Legion and gained French citizenship in 1945. His later paintings, which have made him one of the most famous French abstract painters, show a free calligraphy resembling that of Chinese brushwork. An exhibition of his work, *Hans Hartung: Works on Paper 1922–56*, was held at the Tate Gallery, London, in 1996.

Harty, Sir (Herbert) Hamilton 1880–1941
Northern Irish composer, conductor and pianist

Born in Hillsborough, County Down, he conducted the Hallé (1920–33) and other orchestras. His compositions include an 'Irish' Symphony (1887), and many songs. He also made well-known arrangements of **Handel**'s 'Fireworks' and 'Water Music' suites.

Harun al-Rashid, *in full* Harun al-Rashid ibn Muhammad al-Mahdi ibn al Mansur al-'Abbasi 766–809
Fifth Abbasid caliph

His reign, and that of his son al-Mamun (786–833) marked the apogee of the Abbasid caliphate, which ruled an empire stretching from North Africa to Central Asia. Harun came to the throne on the death of his brother al-Hadi (786) with the help of the influential Barmakid family which he permitted to dominate his early reign, but gradually removed from power. A great patron of the arts, enthusiastic in waging war against the Byzantines, but less interested in the detail of central government, he weakened the empire through his attempts to divide it among his three sons. He is the caliph who figures in many of the tales of the *Arabian Nights*.

Harvard, John 1607–38
American colonial clergyman

Born in Southwark, London, he studied at Emmanuel College, Cambridge, and in 1637 went out to Charlestown, Massachusetts, where he preached. He bequeathed £779 and over 300 volumes to the newly-founded college at Cambridge that was later named in his honour.

Harvey, David 1935–
English geographer

Born in Gillingham, Kent, he was educated at St John's College, Cambridge. Following various research and teaching posts, including posts at Lund (with **Torsten Hägerstrand**, 1960–61), Pennsylvania State (1965–66) and Johns Hopkins (1966–69) universities, he was appointed Halford Mackinder Professor of Geography at Oxford in 1987. He was a founder member of the so-called 'positivist' school, and his book, *Explanation in Geography* (1969), was regarded by the positivists as the fundamental reference. He has subsequently become one of its major critics, and his advocacy of 'radical' geography (in which the subject is viewed as a tool of social revolution) was crystallized in *Social Justice and the City* (1973). His other works include *The Limits to Capital* (1982), *The Urbanisation of Capital* (1985), *Consciousness and the Urban Experience* (1985) and *The Condition of Postmodernity* (1989). He has been Professor of Geography and Environmental Engineering at Johns Hopkins University since 1993.

Harvey, Ethel, *née* Browne 1885–1965
US embryologist

Born in Baltimore, Maryland, she was educated at Bryn Mawr School, the Women's College of Baltimore, and Columbia University. In 1916 she married Edmund Harvey, a Professor of Biology at Princeton, and worked there as an independent research worker for most of her career. Her work in cytology (the study of cells), using sea urchin eggs as her experimental model, was internationally recognized and she was awarded many honours, including fellowships of the American Association for the Advancement of Science and the New York Academy of Sciences.

Harvey, Gabriel c.1550–1630
English poet

Born in Saffron Walden, and educated at Christ Church, Cambridge, he became a Fellow of Pembroke Hall. He was a friend of **Edmund Spenser**, and published some satirical verses in 1579, attacking both **Robert Greene** and **Thomas Nashe**. He claimed to be 'the father of the English hexameter'. 📖 W Schrickx, *Shakespeare's Early Contemporaries* (1956)

Harvey, Sir John Martin 1863–1944
English actor-manager

Born in Wivenhoe, Essex, he intended to follow in his father's footsteps as a naval architect, but soon decided that he preferred the stage. From 1882 to 1896 he was with **Henry Irving** at the Lyceum. He also toured the provinces in **Shakespeare**, and in 1899 under his own management produced at the Lyceum *The Only Way*, adapted from *A Tale of Two Cities*, in which he played Sydney Carton, his most successful role. He became world-famous as a romantic actor and manager. He married Angelita da Silva, who was his leading lady for many years.

Harvey, William 1578–1657
English physician, discoverer of the circulation of the blood

Born in Folkestone, Kent, he studied medicine at Caius College, Cambridge, and after graduating in 1597, went to Padua to work under **Hieronymus Fabricius**. In 1602 he set up as a physician in London. Elected a Fellow of the Royal College of Physicians in 1607, two years later he was appointed physician to St Bartholomew's Hospital, and in 1615 he was Lumleian Lecturer at the College of Physicians. His celebrated treatise, *Exercitatio Anatomica de Motu Cordis et Sanguinis* ('An Anatomical Exercise on the Motion of the Heart and the Blood in Animals'), in which the circulation of the blood was first described, was published in 1628. He was successively physician to **James VI and I** (from 1618) and **Charles I** (from 1640), attending Charles at the Battle of Edgehill (1642) then accompanying him to Oxford, as Warden of Merton College. Harvey returned to London in 1646, and devoted himself entirely to his researches. His *Exercitationes de Generatione Animalium* ('Essays on Generation in Animals'), in which he confirmed the doctrine that every living being has its origin in an egg, appeared in 1651. The key claim of his earlier, distinguished work on the cardiovascular system was that the heart was a muscle functioning as a pump, and that it effected the movement of the blood through the body via the lungs by means of the arteries, the blood then returning through the veins to the heart. His views contradicted ideas central to medicine since **Galen**, and he was widely ridiculed by traditionalists, notably in France. He was not able to show how blood passed from the arterial to the venous system, there being no connections visible to the naked eye. However, he rightly supposed that the links existed but must be too minute to see, and **Marcello Malpighi** observed them with a microscope, shortly after Harvey's death. 📖 Gweneth Whitteridge, *William Harvey and the Circulation of the Blood* (1971)

Harvey, William Henry 1811–66
Irish botanist

Born in Summerville, Limerick, in 1831 at Killarney he discovered the moss *Hookeria laetevirens*, previously not known to exist in Ireland, which led to his becoming acquainted with **William Hooker**. He sailed in 1835 for Cape Town, where he was Colonial Treasurer (1836–42) and worked hard on South African botany. He returned to England in 1842, and quickly became the foremost authority of his day on algae. In 1844 he became curator of the Herbarium at Trinity College, Dublin, where he was appointed Professor of Botany in 1856. Between 1853 and 1856 he travelled extensively to Ceylon, India, Australia, Fiji and elsewhere to collect seaweeds, and published many important works on algae, including *Manual of British Algae* (1841) and *Phycologia Britannica* (4 vols, 1846–51) and was co-author of volumes 1–3 of *Flora Capensis* (1859–65).

Harvey-Jones, Sir John Henry 1924–
English industrial executive

Born in Kent, he was educated at Dartmouth Naval College and served in the navy until 1956, when he joined ICI. As chairman (1982–87) he was largely responsible for reshaping the company, and since 1987 he has been chairman of Parallax Enterprises. His publications include his autobiography, *Getting it Together* (1991), *Managing to Survive* (1993) and *All Together Now* (1994). He was knighted in 1985.

Harvie Anderson, Betty 1914–79
Scottish Conservative politician

Born into a political family, she was elected MP for Renfrewshire (East) in 1959, gaining a reputation as a good, hardworking constituency MP and becoming a member of the 1922 Committee of Backbench MPs. In 1970 she became the first woman to take the Speaker's Chair, keeping order during turbulent times, especially through the passing of the Industrial Relations Act (1970–71) and the Common Market debates. She was appointed a Privy Councillor in 1974.

Harwood, Gwen (doline Nessie), *née* Foster 1920–95
Australian poet and librettist

Born in Taringa, Brisbane, she first studied, then taught music, and did not publish her first book of verse, *Poems*, until 1963. *Poems, Volume Two* followed in 1968, and then *Selected Poems* (1975), *The Lion's Bride* (1981), *Bone Scan* (1988) and her final collection, *The Present Tense* (1995). During that period she wrote libretti for leading Australian composers, including **Larry Sitsky**, with the operas *The Fall of the House of Usher* (1965), *Lenz* (1972) and *The Golem* (1979), James Penberthy, with *Choral Symphony*, and Ian Cugley, with *Sea Changes*. She received the **Robert Frost** award in 1977, and the **Patrick White** Literary award in 1978, and won the Melbourne *Age* Book of the Year award for 1990 with *Blessed City*, a collection of letters from her Brisbane home of the 1940s to a friend in the navy.

Harwood, Harold Marsh 1874–1959
English dramatist

Born in Eccles, Lancashire, he served as an army physician during World War I, and married in 1918 F **Tennyson Jesse**, the author with whom he collaborated on many light plays. He was best known for his political play, *The Grain of Mustard Seed* (1920). He managed the Ambassadors Theatre, London (1920–32).

Harwood, Sir Henry 1888–1959
English naval commander

As commander of the South American division, he commanded the British ships at the Battle of the River Plate, in which the German battleship *Graf Spee* was trapped in Montevideo, and later scuttled (December 1939). He was made Commander-in-Chief of the Mediterranean fleet in 1942.

Hasdrubal, *also called* Hasdrubal Barca ('Lightning')
d.207BC
Carthaginian general
The son of Hamilcar, and the brother of Hannibal, he was left in command of the Carthaginian army in 218BC when Hannibal invaded Italy at the start of the Second Punic War (218–201). From 218 to 208 he fought successfully against the great Roman general Scipio Africanus Major and his son Gnaeus Scipio Africanus. In 207 Hasdrubal marched across the Alps to Italy to support his brother, but was intercepted at the river Metaurus and killed.

Hašek, Jaroslav 1883–1923
Czechoslovakian novelist and short-story writer
Born in Bohemia, he was a compulsive practical joker who despised pomposity and authority. He is best known for the novel *The Good Soldier Schweik* (1920–23), a brilliantly incisive satire on military life. The character of Schweik, an irresponsible and undisciplined drunkard, liar, scrounger and philistine, is widely thought to be at least partly autobiographical in inspiration. In 1915 he deserted the Austrian army (Austria ruled Czechoslovakia at the time) and crossed over to the Russian side. Characteristically, however, he managed to make satirical attacks on both regimes. 📖 Emanuel Frynta, *Hasek, the Creator of Schweik* (1965)

Haselrig or Heselrige, Sir Arthur d.1661
English Parliamentarian
He was one of the five members whose attempted seizure by Charles I in 1642 precipitated the Civil War. He sat in the Long and Short Parliaments for his native county of Leicestershire, commanded a Parliamentary regiment of cuirassiers, and in 1647 became Governor of Newcastle. After the Restoration, he died imprisoned in the Tower of London.

Hasenclever, Walter 1890–1940
German dramatist and poet
Born in Aachen, he attended Oxford, Lausanne and Leipzig universities, studying history, literature and philosophy. He wrote the lyrical poems *Der Jüngling* (1913, 'The Youngster') and *Tod und Auferstehung* (1916, 'Death and Resurrection'), and pioneered German Expressionism with his father-son drama *Der Sohn* (1914, 'The Son'). He later wrote a series of comedies, including *Ein besserer Herr* (1927, 'A Better Gentleman'), and film scripts. A pacifist, he committed suicide in a French internment camp. 📖 P J Cremers, *Walter Hasenclever* (1922)

Haslam, Robert Haslam, Baron 1923–
English industrialist
Educated at Birmingham University, where he studied coal mining, he joined Manchester Collieries in 1944, and the National Coal Board in 1947, before moving to ICI as a mining engineer during the same year. Remaining with the company for 36 years, he became deputy chairman in 1966, and was finally chairman of ICI plc from 1980 to 1983. He joined the British Steel Corporation as chairman (1983–86), and then became deputy chairman of British Coal (1986–90). He has held many directorships in business and industry, including that of the Bank of England (1985–93). He was made a life peer in 1990.

Hasluck, Dame Alexandra Margaret Martin
1908–93
Australian writer and historian
She was born in Perth, Western Australia. Her contributions to the literature of colonial women include a study of Australian botanist Georgiana Molloy (1955), and editions of the letters of the writer and early New Zealand

colonist Lady Broome (1963) and of Lady Audrey Tennyson (1978). Other books include a life of her mother Evelyn Hill (1963), the biographies of *Thomas Peel of Swan River* (1965) and the prison reformer *Sir Edmund du Cane* (1973), a history of early Western Australia entitled *Unwilling Emigrants* (1959), and a collection of short stories (1970). She was the wife of Sir Paul Hasluck; their son Nicholas Hasluck (1942–) is also a writer. 📖 *Portrait in a Mirror* (1981)

Hasluck, Sir Paul Meernaa Caedwalla
1905–93
Australian statesman and historian
Born in Fremantle, Western Australia, he was educated at the University of Western Australia. A journalist on the *West Australian* (1922–38), he was afterwards a lecturer in history at the University of Western Australia (1939–40). Seconded during World War II to the Australian Department of External Affairs, he became head of the Australian mission to the United Nations, returning to the university in 1948. He entered federal politics in 1949, and was successively Minister for Territories (1951–63), for Defence (1963–4), and for External Affairs (1964–9). He was Governor-General of Australia from 1969 to 1974.

Hassal, Joan 1906–88
English artist and illustrator
Born in Notting Hill, London, she studied at the Royal Academy schools in London prior to moving to the London Central College School of Photo Engraving and Lithography, where she studied wood engraving under Ralph Beedham. She was a prolific artist and her subject matter ranges from natural history to illustrations for editions of English literary classics. Her perfectionist, sensitive approach, similar in style to Thomas Bewick, found many admirers, and she became the first woman master member of the Art Workers Guild.

Hassall, John 1868–1948
English artist and cartoonist
Born in Walmer, Kent, he studied art at Antwerp and Paris, and in 1895 entered the advertising field, becoming the acknowledged pioneer of modern poster design. Among railway posters, his 'Skegness is so bracing' holds the record for longevity and ubiquity. He also illustrated children's books, and drew cartoons for many magazines.

Hassam, (Frederick) Childe 1859–1935
US painter
Born in Boston, he studied in Paris in the 1880s and was influenced by the French Impressionists. He became one of the group of American Impressionists known as The Ten and a member of the American Academy of Arts and Letters. His work was characterized by broad brush strokes and bright, clear colours and often featured atmospheric scenes of New England and New York City. Works include *Isles of Shoals* and *July 14th Rue Daunou* (Metropolitan Museum, New York City).

Hassan II 1929–
King of Morocco
He was born in Rabat, the eldest son of Sultan Mulay Mohammed Bin Yusuf, who was proclaimed king as Mohammed V in 1957. Educated in France at Bordeaux University, Crown Prince Hassan served his father as head of the army (1955) and, on his accession to the throne (1961), also became Prime Minister. After initially introducing a new constitution, with a popularly elected legislature, he suspended parliament and established a royal dictatorship in 1965, after riots in Casablanca. Despite constitutional and socio-economic reforms (1970, 1972), he retained supreme religious and political authority. His forces occupied Spanish (Western) Sahara (1975), and he mobilized a large army to check the incursion of Polisario guerrillas across his western Saharan

frontier (1976–88). Unrest in the larger towns led Hassan to appoint a coalition government of national unity under a civilian Prime Minister in 1984.

Hassel, Odd 1897–1981
Norwegian physical chemist and Nobel Prize winner

Born in Oslo, he was educated at the universities of Oslo, Munich (in the laboratory of **Kasimir Fajans**), and Berlin. From 1925 until his retirement in 1964 he was on the staff of the department of physical chemistry of the University of Oslo, as professor and director from 1934. He received the Nobel Prize for chemistry jointly with Sir **Derek Barton** in 1969, and was an Honorary Fellow of the Royal Society of Chemistry. Hassel's most distinguished research was carried out in the 1930s and involved the application of X-ray and electron diffraction, and the measurement of dipole moments. He elucidated the details of the molecular structure of cyclohexane and related compounds, and thereby helped to establish the concepts and procedures of 'conformational analysis'. His later work was on charge-transfer complexes.

Hastings, Francis Rawdon-Hastings, 1st Marquis of 1754–1826
English soldier and administrator

He was born in Dublin and educated at Harrow. He fought with distinction (1775–81) in the American War of Independence and in 1794 he led reinforcements to **Frederick Augustus**, Duke of York, at Malines. He became active in politics, and in 1813 was made Governor-General of India. Here he fought successfully against the Gurkhas (1814–16) and the Pindaris and Marathas (1817–18), encouraged Indian education and the freedom of the press, reformed the law system, and elevated the Civil Service. In 1821, however, he resigned after apparently unfounded charges of corruption had been made against him, and from 1824 until his death was Governor of Malta.

Hastings, (Andrew) Gavin 1962–
Scottish rugby player

Born in Edinburgh and educated at George Watson's College, Edinburgh, and Cambridge, he made his debut for Scotland in 1986, in the same match as his younger brother Scott. A powerful attacking full-back, he played in the 1987, 1991 and 1995 World Cups, and was an indispensable member of the Scotland team which won the Grand Slam in 1990. He has also played three times for the British Lions and captained them in the 1993 tour of New Zealand. He plays club rugby for his old school team, Watsonians, and became captain of the Scotland side for the first time in the 1992–93 season. Having broken **Andy Irvine**'s record number of points scored for Scotland in international matches, he stood down after the 1995 World Cup in South Africa, making way for Rob Wainwright.

Hastings, Warren 1732–1818
English colonial administrator

Born in Churchill, Oxfordshire, he was educated at Westminster School. In 1750 he went to Calcutta as a writer in the service of the East India Company, was British Resident at Murshidabad (1758–61), and then a member of council at Calcutta. He returned to England in 1764, and in 1769 went back to India as second in council at Madras. In 1772 he became Governor of Bengal and President of the Council. A year later he was created Governor-General. Hastings extended the power of the East India Company in India, improving the administration of justice, organizing the opium revenue, and waging vigorous war with the Marathas. He experienced continual conflict with his council, appointed from England and led by Sir **Philip Francis**, whom he later wounded in a duel (1780). In 1777 an attempt was made to depose Hastings, which was only frustrated by the action of the Supreme Court. He resigned office in 1784 and sailed for England, where he was charged with cruelty and corruption, and impeached at the Bar of the House of Lords. The trial began on 13 February 1788, at Westminster Hall, among the managers for the Commons being **Edmund Burke**, **Charles James Fox**, **Richard Brinsley Sheridan** and **Charles Grey**. The trial occupied more than seven years and 145 sittings. Finally, in April 1795, Hastings was acquitted on all the charges, but he left the court a ruined man, since most of the £80,000 that he had brought from India went in expenses. The East India Company made generous provision for his declining years, which he spent as a country gentleman at Daylesford, Worcestershire. 📖 Keith Feiling, *Warren Hastings* (1954)

Hatoum, Mona 1952–
British sculptor and performance artist

Born in Beirut of Palestinian origin, she settled in London in 1975. She trained at the Byam Shaw School of Art and at the Slade School. She became known in 1982 for her installation *Under Siege* (London Film Makers' Co-op), when she was trapped for seven hours in a glass tank at a low temperature, forced to keep moving while constantly slipping because of the wet clay covering her naked body. Subsequent installations, such as *Light Sentence* (1992, Cardiff), also induced curiosity and even fear in the spectator. In 1995 she was shortlisted for the Turner Prize on the strength of her *Foreign Body* video exhibition (1994, Pompidou Centre, Paris), in which she subjected herself to endoscopic and coloscopic examination, accompanied by the sound of her heartbeat.

Hatoyama Ichiro 1883–1959
Japanese politician

He was first elected to the Diet in 1915 and became a prominent leader of the Seiyukai in the 1930s. As Education Minister (1931–34), he clamped down hard on liberal university teachers who questioned the nature of the Japanese state. In 1946 he organized the conservative Japan Liberal Party (Nihon Jiyuto), which gained a victory in the elections of that year. On the verge of becoming Prime Minister, he was purged from official life by the US occupation authorities for his role in supporting the military cabinets of the 1930s. Although he was rehabilitated in 1951, he found that leadership of the Liberal Party was now firmly in the hands of **Yoshida Shigeru**. He formed a new conservative party, the Japan Democratic Party (Nihon Minshuto), which successfully ousted Yoshida from power (1954), and became premier. During his premiership (1954–56), relations with the USSR were normalized, thus paving the way for Japan's entry into the UN in 1956, and the two conservative parties were merged in 1955 to form the Liberal Democratic Party (Jiyu Minshuto).

Hatry, Clarence Charles 1888–1965
English forger

Born in Hampstead, London, he became an insurance broker in 1911 and went on to register several companies, including his Commercial Bank of London (1920). A gambler, he often lost large amounts of money. In 1929 one of his companies, Corporation and General Securities, failed in its attempt to take over United Steel. This led to substantial losses for his investors, and he was prosecuted. He confessed to forgery and was sentenced in 1930 to 14 years in prison. He was released in 1939, and, despite his past record, successfully resumed his work as a financier.

Hatshepsut c.1540–c.1481BC
Queen of Egypt of the 18th dynasty

She was the daughter of Tuthmosis I, and married Tuthmosis II, his son by another wife. Tuthmosis II succeeded in 1516BC, and was himself succeeded in 1503 by Tuthmosis III, his son by a minor wife, for whom Hatshepsut ruled as regent. She had herself crowned Pharaoh with full powers and titles. She was represented in male attire, including an artificial beard. During her 20-year reign, she built her mortuary temple at Deir el Bahri, erected obelisks at Karnak and despatched a trading expedition to Punt (now Eritrea/Somalia). 📖 Joyce Tyldesey, *Hatshepsut, the Female Pharaoh* (1996)

Hattersley, Roy Sydney George Hattersley, Baron 1932–
English Labour politician
Born in Sheffield, Yorkshire, and educated at Hull University, he was a journalist and Health Service executive as well as a member of Sheffield City Council before becoming a Labour MP (1964–97). A supporter of Britain's membership of the EEC, he was Minister of State at the Foreign Office for two years, then Secretary of State for Prices and Consumer Protection in the Callaghan government (1976–79). He later served as Opposition spokesman on the Environment, on the Treasury, and on Home Affairs. Regarded as being on the right wing of the party, he was elected deputy Leader of the Labour Party (1983–92), with Neil Kinnock as Leader. Though re-elected in 1988, following the defeat of Labour in the 1992 general election they were replaced, Kinnock by John Smith and Hattersley by Margaret Beckett. He is a regular contributor to newspapers and periodicals and has written novels and his autobiography *Who Goes Home?: Scenes From a Political Life* (1995). He was made a life peer in 1997.

Hauff, Wilhelm 1802–27
German novelist
Born in Stuttgart, he studied at Tübingen, and became a tutor, then editor of a paper. His fairy tales and short stories are admirable for their simplicity and playful fancy, particularly *Die Bettlerin vom Pont des Arts* (1826, Eng trans *The Beggar-Girl of the Pont-des-Arts*, 1844) and *Phantasien im Bremer Ratskeller* (1827, Eng trans *The Wine-Ghosts of Bremen*, 1889). *Lichtenstein* (1826, Eng trans 1846) is an imitation of Sir Walter Scott.

Haughey, Charles James 1925–
Irish politician
Born in Castlebar, County Mayo, and educated at University College, Dublin, he was called to the Bar in 1949. A former chartered accountant, Haughey became a Fianna Fáil MP in 1957, and from 1961 held posts in justice, agriculture and finance, until his dismissal after a political disagreement with the Prime Minister Jack Lynch (1970). He was subsequently tried and acquitted on a charge of conspiracy illegally to import arms. He succeeded Lynch as Prime Minister in 1979, and governed for two years. Premier again in 1982 and from 1987 to 1992, he was succeeded by Albert Reynolds.

Hauksbee or Hawksbee, Francis, the Elder d.1713
English physicist
Little is known about his origins. His nephew of the same name (1688–1763), who had similar scientific interests and assisted his uncle until his death, was called 'the Younger'. Francis, the elder, is chiefly noted for his experiments on electroluminescence, static electricity and capillarity. He carried further the observations by the physician William Gilbert on electricity and Robert Boyle on air, inventing the first glass friction electrical machine, and improved the air-pump. He was elected Fellow of the Royal Society in 1705 and was appointed as the Royal Society's Curator of Experiments.

Hauptman, Herbert Aaron 1917–
US mathematical physicist and Nobel Prize winner
Born in New York City, he was educated at the City College of New York, Columbia University and at the University of Maryland. While working at the US Naval Research Laboratories in Washington with Jerome Karle during the 1950s and 1960s, he helped develop a statistical technique that increased the speed of methods by which X-ray crystallography mapped structures of molecules. Using this 'direct method' the time taken to establish a molecular structure was reduced from years to days. In 1985, 22 years after publishing the work, Hauptman and Karle were jointly awarded the Nobel Prize for chemistry. Hauptman became professor at the University of Buffalo in 1970 and since 1972 has continued his research on X-ray crystallography at the Medical Foundation of Buffalo, of which he has been president since 1986 under its present name, the Woodward Medical Research Institute.

Hauptmann, Gerhart Johann Robert 1862–1946
German dramatist and novelist, and Nobel Prize winner
Born in Obersalzbrunn, Silesia, he studied sculpture in Breslau and Rome before settling in Berlin (1885). His first play, *Vor Sonnenaufgang* (1889, Eng trans *Before Dawn*, 1909), introduced the new social drama of Ibsen, Émile Zola and August Strindberg to Germany, but Hauptmann's Naturalism was alleviated by a note of compassion. *Die Weber* (1892, Eng trans *The Weavers*, 1899) introduces a new theatrical phenomenon, the collective hero. *Florian Geyer* (1896, Eng trans 1894), marks a transition to a mixture of fantasy and naturalism, maintained in other such outstanding works as *Die Versunkene Glocke* (1896, Eng trans *The Sunken Bell*, 1898) and *Rose Bernd* (1903, Eng trans 1913). His later plays, in a variety of styles, include the comedies *Der Biberpelz* (1893, Eng trans *The Beaver Coat*, 1912) and *Der rote Hahn* (1901, Eng trans *The Conflagration*, 1913); they were later adapted and revised by Bertolt Brecht to suit the East German Communist censorship. His novels include *Der Narr in Christo: Emanuel Quint* (1910, Eng trans *The Fool in Christ: Emanuel Quint*, 1911) and *Atlantis* (1912, Eng trans 1912). He was awarded the Nobel Prize for literature in 1912. 📖 C F W Behl, *Hauptmann: his life and work* (1958)

Hausdorff, Felix 1868–1942
German mathematician
Born in Breslau (now Wrocław, Poland), he studied at the universities of Leipzig and Berlin, and taught at Leipzig (1896–1910). In 1910 he moved to Bonn, where he remained until, as a Jew, he was forced by the Nazis to resign his chair in 1935. He is regarded as the founder of point set topology, introducing the basic concepts of topological spaces and metric spaces, and the fractal dimension of a set is often called the 'Hausdorff dimension'.

Hauser, Gayelord (Helmut Eugene Benjamin Gellert) 1895–1984
US popular nutritionist
Born in Germany, he emigrated to the USA after World War I and set up business in California in 1927, advocating special vegetable diets featuring 'wonder foods' like brewer's yeast, skimmed milk, wheat germ and blackstrap molasses. He made a fortune with bestselling books such as *Look Younger, Live Longer* (1950) and *Be Happier, Be Healthier* (1952).

Hauser, Kaspar c.1812–33
German foundling, a 'wild boy'
He was found in the marketplace of Nuremberg in May 1828. Though apparently 16 years old, his mind was a blank, and his behaviour that of a little child. He later gave an account of himself as having lived in a hole, looked after by a man who had brought him to the place

where he was found. He died in December 1833 from a wound in the side, dealt he said, by 'the man'. Many have considered him an impostor who committed suicide, but others regarded him as a person of noble birth, who was the victim of a crime.

Hausschein See Oecolampadius, Joannes

Haussmann, Georges Eugène, Baron 1809–91
French financier and town-planner
Born in Paris, he entered the public service, and under Napoleon III became prefect of the Seine (1853). He then began his task of improving Paris by widening streets, laying out boulevards and parks, building bridges, etc. For these services he was made baron and senator, but the heavy tax burden laid upon the citizens led to his dismissal in 1870. In 1871 he was appointed director of the *Crédit mobilier*, and in 1881 was elected to the Chamber of Deputies. 📖 Howard Saalman, *Haussmann: Paris Transformed* (1971)

Hauteclocque, Vicomte de See Leclerc, Jacques Philippe

Haüy, René Just 1743–1822
French crystallographer and mineralogist
Born in St Just, Picardy, he initially studied botany and embryology before developing his interests in mineralogy and crystallography. Following the French Revolution, He became Professor of Physics at the École Normale (1794) and curator of the École des Mines, Paris (1795). It was there that he wrote his *Traité de minéralogie* ('Treatise of Mineralogy'), published in 1801, the same year that he succeeded Déodat de Dolomieu as Professor of Mineralogy at the Museum of Natural History in Paris. He is widely regarded as the father of crystallography. Recognizing the importance of higher education in building the nation's prosperity, Napoleon I commissioned Haüy to write a treatise on physics to be used in the lycées of France.

Havel, Václav 1936–
Czech dramatist and statesman
Born in Prague, where he was educated at the Academy of Dramatic Art, he began work as a stagehand at the Prague *Theater Na zábradlí* (Theatre on the Balustrade), becoming resident writer there (1960–69). His work includes *Zahradní slavnost* (1963, Eng trans *The Garden Party*, 1969), *Spiklenci* (1970, 'The Conspirators') and *Audience* (1976, Eng trans *Temptation*, 1976). He was one of the founders of Charter 77 in 1977. Deemed subversive, he was frequently arrested, and in 1979 was imprisoned for four and a half years. He was again imprisoned in February 1989, but was released three months later. In December 1989, after the overthrow of the Czechoslovak Communist Party during the so-called Velvet Revolution, he was elected President by direct popular vote. He oversaw the peaceful division of Czechoslovakia into separate Czech and Slovak states in 1992, and was elected President of the Czech Republic in 1993. His later publications in English translation include *Selected Plays* (1991) and *Towards a Civil Society* (1994). 📖 M Goetz-Stankiewicz, *The Silenced Theatre: Czech dramatists without a stage* (1979)

Havelock, Sir Henry 1795–1857
English soldier
He was born in Bishop-Wearmouth, Sunderland. A lawyer by training, he entered the army after the Battle of Waterloo (1815), and went to India in 1823. He distinguished himself in the Afghan and Sikh Wars, and in 1856 commanded a division in Persia (Iran). On the outbreak of the Indian Mutiny (1857–58), he organized a column of 1,000 Higlanders and others at Allahabad with which to relieve Cawnpore and Lucknow, then defeated the rebels at Fatehpur, and entered Cawnpore, having

marched 125 miles and fought four actions in nine days, in the heat of July. Crossing the Ganges, he fought eight victorious battles, but, through cholera and dysentery in his army, had to retire to Cawnpore. In September General James Outram arrived with reinforcements, and Havelock again advanced, Outram waiving his superior rank and serving under Havelock as a volunteer. The relieving force fought their way to the Lucknow Residency, where they in turn were besieged by the determined rebel forces until November, when Sir Colin Campbell forced his way to their rescue. Four days later Havelock died of dysentery.

Havergal, William Henry 1793–1870
English hymnwriter
He was born in High Wycombe, Buckinghamshire, and took holy orders at Oxford. He composed hymn tunes, chants and songs, wrote *History of the Old 100th Tune*, and also published sermons and pamphlets.

Havers (of St Edmundsbury), (Robert) Michael (Oldfield) Havers, Baron 1923–92
English lawyer and politician
Educated at Westminster School and Cambridge, he saw wartime service in the Royal Navy, was called to the Bar in 1948 and made a QC in 1964. He was a successful advocate and judge before entering the House of Commons, as Conservative MP for Wimbledon, in 1970. He was Solicitor-General under Edward Heath (1972–74), leading the prosecution council that wrongly convicted the Maguire family for possession of nitroglycerine, and Attorney-General under Margaret Thatcher (1979–87), being responsible for the prosecution of the murderer Peter Sutcliffe. Knighted in 1972, he was made a life peer in 1987 and after a brief period as Lord Chancellor, retired in 1988. His sister is Elizabeth Butler-Sloss.

Havilland, Sir Geoffrey De See De Havilland, Sir Geoffrey

Havilland, Olivia Mary de See de Havilland, Olivia Mary

Hawes, Stephen c.1475–1525
English allegorical poet
Born probably in Aldeburgh, Suffolk, he was attached to the court from 1502 as groom of the chamber to Henry VII. His chief work is the allegory, *The Passetyme of Pleasure* (1509), printed by Wynkn de Worde, dedicated to the king. He also wrote *The Example of Virtue* (1504), *The Conversion of Swearers* (1509), an attack on blasphemy, and *A Joyful Meditation* (1509), a celebration of the coronation of Henry VIII. 📖 W Murison, *Stephen Hawes* (1908)

Haw-Haw, Lord See Joyce, William

Hawke, Bob (Robert James Lee) 1929–
Australian trade union executive and politician
Born in Bordertown, South Australia, he was educated at the University of Western Australia and University College, Oxford (Rhodes Scholar 1953). He worked for the Australian Council of Trade Unions for over 20 years (president, 1970–80) before becoming an MP in 1980. His Labor Party defeated the ruling Liberals in the 1983 general election only one month after adopting him as leader and he became Prime Minister (1983–91). In the 1987 general election the Labor Party narrowly increased its majority in the House of Representatives although it failed to control the senate. Frequently described as colourful, he is a skilled orator who won praise for his handling and settling of industrial disputes. In 1990, he became the first Labor prime minister to win a fourth term in office, but in 1991 he was challenged and replaced as Prime Minister by Paul Keating. Since 1992 he has been

Adjunct Professor at the Research School of Pacific Studies and Social Sciences at the Australian National University. *The Hawke Memoirs* were published in 1994.

Hawke (of Towton), Edward Hawke, 1st Baron 1705–81
English admiral

Born in London, he joined the navy in 1720. As a young commander he fought against the French and Spanish. In the Seven Years War (1756–63) he destroyed the French fleet in Quiberon Bay in November 1759, thus preventing an invasion of Great Britain. He became an MP (1747), First Lord of the Admiralty (1766–71), Admiral of the Fleet (1768) and a baron (1776). 🕮 Ruddock F Mackay, *Admiral Hawke* (1965)

Hawker, R(obert) S(tephen) 1803–75
English poet

Born in Stoke Demerel, Devonshire, he was educated at Pembroke College, Oxford, and won the Newdigate Prize for poetry in 1827. In 1834 he became vicar of Morwenstow, on the Cornish coast, and was noted for his eccentricity. His poetry includes *Tendrils* (1821), the Cornish ballads in *Records of the Western Shore* (1832–36), *Reeds Shaken with the Wind* (1843) and *The Quest of the Sangraal* (1864), the first part of a projected Arthurian epic. His best-known ballad is 'The Song of the Western Men', with its refrain 'And shall Trelawny die?', based on an old Cornish ballad which was printed anonymously in a local newspaper in 1826. Twelve hours before his death he was admitted to the Roman Catholic Communion. 🕮 M F Burrows, *Robert Stephen Hawker* (1926)

Hawkes, Jacquetta, *née* Hopkins 1910–96
English archaeologist and writer

Born in Cambridge and educated at the Perse School and Newnham College, Cambridge, she was the first woman to study archaeology and anthropology to degree level. Her first excavation was directed by Christopher Hawkes, whom she married in 1933, and with whom she published *Prehistoric Britain* (1944). Her earlier publications include *The Archaeology of Jersey* (1939), *Early Britain* (1945) and *A Land* (1951). She also wrote on Egyptian topics, produced a biography of *Sir Mortimer Wheeler*, and wrote a book of poetry, *Symbols and Speculations* (1948). With her second husband, J B Priestley, she wrote *Journey Down the Rainbow* (1955), a jovial indictment of US life in letter form, as well as fictional works. Her later publications include *The World of the Past* (1963) and the *Shell Guide to British Archaeology* (1986). She also served on the Central Committee of UNESCO (1966–79), and was a co-founder of the Campaign for Nuclear Disarmament in 1957.

Hawkesworth, John c.1715–73
English writer

He was born in London, and in 1744 succeeded Dr Johnson on the *Gentleman's Magazine*. In 1752 he started, with Johnson and others, *The Adventurer*, half of whose 140 numbers were written by Hawkesworth. He published a volume of fairytales, *Almoran and Hamet* (1761), wrote a play, *Edgar and Emmeline* (1761), edited Jonathan Swift, and compiled an account of Captain Cook's first voyage, which formed volumes two and three of Hawkesworth's *Voyages* (3 vols, 1773).

Hawking, Stephen William 1942–
English theoretical physicist

Born in Oxford, he graduated from the University of Oxford and received his PhD from Cambridge. He was elected FRS in 1974, and became Lucasian Professor of Mathematics at Cambridge in 1980. His early research on relativity led him to study gravitational singularities such as the 'Big Bang' when the universe originated, and 'black holes' where space–time is curved due to enormous gravitational fields. The theory of black holes,

which result when stars collapse at the end of their lives, owes much to his mathematical work. Since 1974 he has shown that a black hole could actually evaporate through loss of thermal radiation, and predicted that mass can escape entirely from its gravitational pull. This loss of mass is known as the Hawking process. His book *A Brief History of Time* (1988) is a bestselling popular account of modern cosmology. His achievements are even more remarkable because from the 1960s he has suffered from a highly disabling and progressive neuromotor disease. A later publication is *Black Holes and Baby Universes* (1993). 🕮 John Gribbin and Michael White, *Stephen Hawking: A Life in Science* (1992)

Hawkins, Coleman 1904–69
US tenor saxophonist

Born in St Joseph, Missouri, he received piano lessons as a child and studied music at Washburn College, Topeka. In 1923 he joined the Fletcher Henderson Orchestra, where he laid the foundations of the tenor saxophone's future pre-eminence as a jazz solo instrument. During the 1930s he worked in Europe for five years, becoming the most influential jazz 'exile' of that period. Following his return to the USA in 1939, his recording of the ballad 'Body and Soul' became a benchmark for jazz saxophonists in the swing style. Renowned for his full tone and well-constructed improvisations, Hawkins later embraced the bebop movement and was also a member of the touring Jazz at the Philharmonic groups.

Hawkins, Erick 1909–
US dancer, choreographer and teacher

Born in Trinidad, Colorado, he read Greek at Harvard and studied at the School of American Ballet and with Harald Kreutzberg, a pupil of Mary Wigman. He joined American Ballet (1935–37), and Ballet Caravan (1936–39) where he created his first choreography. In 1938 he became the first man to dance with the Martha Graham company, creating roles in many of her most famous dances until 1951. He formed his own company in the mid-1950s, in association with the composer Lucia Dlugoszewski and sculptor Ralph Dorazio. Influenced by Greek and Asian philosophy, his mainly abstract dances reflect his unforced, natural approach to movement. He was married to Martha Graham from 1948 to 1954.

Hawkins, Jack (John Edward) 1910–73
English actor

Born in Wood Green, London, he trained for the theatre at the Italia Conti School of Acting, before making his debut in *Where the Rainbow Ends* (1923), then subsequently performing in the original production of *Saint Joan* (1924). His adult debut was in *Young Woodley* (1929), and his first New York appearance was in *Journey's End* (1930). His first film *Birds of Prey* (1930) began a prolific cinema career that ran parallel with a series of admired Shakespearean roles opposite John Gielgud. A colonel in the Royal Welsh Fusiliers (1940–46) during World War II, after the war he gave an acclaimed performance in *Othello* (1946). He became one of Great Britain's most popular film stars, playing heroes with stiff upper-lips and authoritarian figures in such films as *The Cruel Sea* (1953), *The Bridge on the River Kwai* (1957) and *Lawrence of Arabia* (1962). Stricken with throat cancer in 1966, he courageously continued to act with fellow actors dubbing his voice. He published an autobiography, *Anything for a Quiet Life* (1973), and made his final appearance in the television mini-series *QB VII* (transmitted 1974).

Hawkins or Hawkyns, Sir John 1532–95
English navigator and naval commander

Born in Plymouth, he became the first Englishman to traffic in slaves (1562), taking slaves from West Africa to the Spanish West Indies. During his third voyage (1567), he and **Francis Drake** were intercepted and their fleet destroyed by the Spanish. He was knighted for his services against the Armada (1588), and in 1595, with his kinsman Drake, he commanded an expedition to the Spanish Main, but died in Puerto Rico. His only son, Sir Richard (c.1562–1622), was also a naval commander and fought against the Armada. He went on a round-the-world plundering expedition (1593) but was captured in Peru and held prisoner in Spain until 1602. He wrote *Observations on His Voyage into the South Seas* (1622).

Hawks, Howard Winchester 1896–1977
US film director

Born in Goshen, Indiana, he graduated in mechanical engineering, then worked as a prop man, served in the US army air corps and wrote scripts for silent films before making his directorial debut with *The Road to Glory* (1926). He survived the transition to sound, establishing himself as one of the great American filmmakers, noted for his versatility, storytelling skills, love of dialogue, interest in male camaraderie and focus on women who could be just as tough and sassy as their male counterparts. His many successful films include *Bringing Up Baby* (1938), *His Girl Friday* (1940), *To Have and Have Not* (1944), *The Big Sleep* (1946), *Red River* (1948) and *Rio Bravo* (1959). He received an honorary Oscar in 1975.

Hawksbee, Francis, the Elder See Hauksbee, Francis, the Elder

Hawkshaw, Sir John 1811–91
English engineer

Born in Leeds, he was a mining engineer in Venezuela (1831–34), chief engineer of the Manchester and Leeds railway (1845–50), and consulting engineer in the construction of Charing Cross and Cannon Street stations and bridges, and the Inner Circle underground railway in London. He designed the Narmada bridge in India, was engineer for the Amsterdam Ship Canal (1862), and wrote a report on the route chosen for the Suez Canal (1863). From 1872 to 1886 he was one of the engineers of the original Channel Tunnel project, and he also constructed the Severn Tunnel (1887).

Hawksmoor, Nicholas 1661–1736
English architect

Born in Nottinghamshire, he became a clerk to Sir **Christopher Wren** and also assisted Sir **John Vanbrugh** at Blenheim Palace and Castle Howard. His most individual contributions are the London churches St Mary Woolnoth, St George's, Bloomsbury, St Anne's, Limehouse and Christ Church, Spitalfields, as well as parts of Queen's College and All Souls, Oxford.

Hawley, Christine 1949–
English architect

Born in Shrewsbury and trained at the Architectural Association, London (1969–75), she registered as an architect in 1978. With her business partner, Peter Cook, she was a member of Archigram, an influential group of teachers at the Architectural Association in the 1960s and 1970s, motivated by the possibilities of 'high technology' and 'dense urban design'. Their work, which reflects this ethos, includes the unbuilt Stained Glass Museum, Hesse (1989), exhibition pavilions in Nagoya, Japan (1989) and Osaka, Japan (1990), and apartments and shops for the Internationale Bau Ausstellung, Berlin (1984–90). In 1988 Hawley was appointed head of the Department of Architecture at the Polytechnic of East London.

Hawn, Goldie Jeanne 1945–
US film actress

Born in Washington DC, the daughter of a professional musician, she trained in ballet and tap and dropped out of college to form her own dancing school. Turning to tele-vision, she soon became popular as one of the ensemble troupe in *Rowan and Martin's Laugh-In* (1968–70). She won a Best Supporting Actress Academy Award in *Cactus Flower* (1969) and starred in many comedy roles throughout the 1970s. She was the executive producer and star of the popular film *Private Benjamin* (1980) and since then has taken considerable control over her career. Her notable successes include *Bird on a Wire* (1990), *Housesitter* (1992), *The First Wives Club* (1996) and *Everyone Says I Love You* (1996).

Haworth, Adrian Harvey 1766–1833
English botanist and entomologist

Born in Hull, Humberside, he at first studied to be a solicitor, but left the legal profession to study botany, entomology and ornithology. Shortly after moving to Chelsea, London, he joined the Linnaean Society, and also founded the Aurelian Society in 1802. He then helped to found the Entomological Society of London. In 1812 he helped to form the Hull botanical garden. Haworth was an authority on succulent plants, his chief botanical work being *Synopsis Plantarum Succulentarum* (1812). His entomological publications include *Prodromus Lepidopterorum Britannicorum* (1802) and *Lepidoptera Britannica* (3 parts, 1803–12).

Haworth, Sir (Walter) Norman 1883–1950
English chemist and Nobel Prize winner

Born in Chorley, Lancashire, he learned most of his early chemistry from working in his father's linoleum factory and it was 1903 when he enrolled at the University of Manchester. A scholarship enabled him to study at Göttingen, and he then returned to Manchester. In 1911 he moved to Imperial College, London, but was there for only one year before moving to a post at the University of St Andrews. In 1920 he moved to King's College, Newcastle and in 1925 took up the chair of organic chemistry at the University of Birmingham, where he was joined by **Edward Hirst** for his most productive period. He shared the Nobel Prize for chemistry with **Paul Karrer** in 1937, for determining the structure of vitamin C. He was elected FRS in 1928, and knighted in 1947.

Hawthorne, Nathaniel 1804–64
US novelist and short-story writer

He was born in Salem, Massachusetts. At the age of four he lost his father, and he and his mother lived in straitened circumstances. At the age of 14 he went with her to a lonely farm in the woods of Raymond, Maine, and there he and his reclusive mother lived a solitary life. He attended Bowdoin College, Brunswick, where **Henry Wadsworth Longfellow** was a fellow pupil, and where he began his first novel in 1825. After his return to Salem he shut himself away for 12 years, writing tales and verses. His first novel, *Fanshawe* (1828), which was published anonymously, was unsuccessful. Continuing to contribute to annuals and magazines, such as *The Token*, he edited in 1836 a short-lived periodical. Meanwhile some of his short stories were favourably reviewed in the London *Athenaeum*, and were collected as *Twice-told Tales* (1837), but his talent was not yet appreciated in his own country. In 1839 the historian **George Bancroft** appointed him weigher and gauger in the customs-house, a post he held until 1841. In that year he spent several months at the Brook Farm, an idyllic, semi-socialistic community near Boston. Meanwhile he wrote and published a series of simple stories for children from New England history: *Grandfather's Chair*, *Famous Old People* and *Liberty Tree* (1841). Moving to Concord, Massachusetts, in 1842 he issued *Biographical Stories* for children, and brought out an enlarged edition of the *Twice-told Tales* (1842). His sketches and studies written for the *Democratic Review* were collected as *Mosses from an Old Manse* (1846). The *Review* failed and, having lost all his savings at Brook Farm, he was forced to accept a place in the customs-house again—this time as surveyor in Salem. In 1850 he published *The Scarlet Letter*, still the best-known of his works. At Lenox, Massachusetts, he then entered upon a phase of remarkable productiveness, writing *The House of the Seven Gables* (1851), *Wonder Book* (1851), *The Snow Image* (1852) and *The Blithedale Romance* (1852), which drew upon his Brook Farm experience. He settled in Concord in 1852, and wrote a campaign biography of his old schoolfriend, President **Franklin Pierce**, and on Pierce's inauguration became consul at Liverpool (1853–57). He completed *Tanglewood Tales* in 1853, as a continuation of *Wonder Book*. A year and half spent in Rome and Florence, from 1858 to 1860, supplied him with the materials for *The Marble Faun* (1860), published in Great Britain as *Transformation*. Returning to Concord, he wrote for the *Atlantic Monthly* the brilliant papers on England collected as *Our Old Home* (1863). He began a new romance, based on the idea of an elixir of immortality, which remained unfinished at his death. Only belatedly recognized in his own country, his reputation has continued to grow in the 20th century. ⬛F Crews, *The Sins of the Fathers* (1966); H James, *Hawthorne* (1879)

Hawthorne, Sir Nigel Barnard 1929–
English actor

Born in Coventry, he moved to South Africa with his parents as a child and made his stage debut there in *The Shop at Sly Corner* (1950). Returning to Great Britain in 1951, he quickly conquered the London stage and his long list of distinguished productions includes *Rosencrantz and Guildenstern Are Dead* (1971), *Julius Caesar* (1972), *Privates on Parade* (with the Royal Shakespeare Company, 1977), *The Magistrate* (1986) and *Hapgood* (1988). He made his Broadway debut in *As You Like It* (1974) and performed *Shadowlands* in the West End (1989) and on Broadway (1990–92). He is best known on television as Sir Humphrey Appleby in *Yes Minister* (1980–92) and *Yes, Prime Minister* (1986–88). The film version of *The Madness of King George* (1994) earned him a Best Actor Academy Award nomination and he has subsequently starred in such films as *Richard III* (1995) and *Twelfth Night* (1996). Other television work includes *The Fragile Heart* (1996). He was knighted in 1998.

Hay, Ian, *pseudonym of* John Hay Beith 1876–1952
Scottish novelist and dramatist

Born in Manchester, he was educated at Fettes College, Edinburgh and St John's College, Cambridge, and became a language master at his old school. He served in World War I, and was awarded the Military Cross. His light popular novels, *Pip* (1907), *A Safety Match* (1911) and *A Knight on Wheels* (1914), were followed by the war books *The First Hundred Thousand* (1915), *Carrying On* (1917) and *The Last Million* (1918). Many novels and comedies followed, the best known of the latter being *Tilly of Bloomsbury* (1919) and *Housemaster* (1936). He also dramatized some of his novels for the stage, and wrote other plays and dramatizations, many of them in collaboration with other writers, such as *Leave it to Psmith* (1930) with **P G Wodehouse**, and *Off the Record* (1947) with Stephen King-Hall. He was director of public relations at the War Office (1938–41).

Hay, John Milton 1838–1905
US politician

Born in Salem, Indiana, he was admitted to the Illinois Bar in 1861. He became private secretary to President **Lincoln**, and served for some months during the Civil War. He was secretary of legation at Paris (1865–67) and Madrid (1868–70), and chargé d'affaires at Vienna (1867–68). He returned to the USA and joined the staff of the *New York Tribune* (1870–75), and went on to write poetry, fiction, and a multi-volume biography of Lincoln (1891). He became first Assistant-Secretary of State (1878–81),

ambassador to Great Britain (1897) and in 1898 Secretary of State to President **William McKinley**. ⬛ Tyler Dennett, *John Hay: From Poetry to Politics* (1933)

Hay, Will 1888–1949
Scottish comic actor

Born in Aberdeen, he was an apprentice engineer and entertained at charity shows before turning professional. He worked in music halls and radio prior to his film debut in *Know Your Apples* (1933). Appearing as seedy, disreputable figures of authority with delusions of grandeur in comedies like *Boys Will Be Boys* (1935) and *Oh, Mr Porter!* (1937), he was one of the country's top film attractions between 1937 and 1942. Ill health caused him to retire from the screen after *My Learned Friend* (1943), but he remained a popular radio panellist until his death. Also a respected amateur astronomer, he published *Through My Telescope* (1935).

Hay, William Gosse 1875–1945
Australian writer

Born in Burnside, South Australia, he was related to Sir **Edmund Gosse** and to the explorer **William Gosse**. Hay's first novels, set in a fictionalized Australia, were *Stifled Laughter* (1901), *Herridge of Reality Swamp* (1907) and *Captain Quadring* (1912). His mother and sister were lost on a ship returning to England and Hay retreated to Tasmania, the setting for his last books, which were published between 1919 and 1937. His only other completed work was *An Australian Rip Van Winkle* (1921). His novels had a Gothic element, introduced, according to Hay, to 'raise Australian literature ... to her tragic and ballad-like history'.

Haya de la Torre, Víctor Raúl 1895–1979
Peruvian politician and political thinker

Educated in Lima, he was the founder (1924) of the Alianza Popular Revolucionaria Americana, known as the Aprista Party, the voice of radical dissent in Peru. Imprisoned in 1931, after standing against Colonel Luis Sánchez Cerro, he was released on the latter's assassination (1933), and went into hiding (1934–45). The Aprista Party changed its name to the Partido del Pueblo (People's Party) in 1945, and supported the successful candidate, José Luis Bustamante; control of the government, however, lay in Haya's hands. On Bustamante's overthrow (1948), Haya sought refuge in the Colombian embassy in Lima and later left for Mexico (1954). He returned to Peru when constitutional government was restored in 1957 and fought the bitter 1962 election campaign which, after army intervention, he lost to **Fernando Belaúnde Terry**. Haya was instrumental in drafting the constitution of 1979 restoring parliamentary democracy, but died before the People's Party finally gained power in 1985 under **Perez Alan García**.

Hayashi, Chusiro 1920–
Japanese astrophysicist

Born in Kyoto, he graduated from the university there, becoming Professor of Physics in 1957. In 1950 he showed that in the first two seconds after the Big Bang, temperatures would exceed 10^{10} kelvin, and that after that time the neutron to proton ratio in the universe would result in a fixed hydrogen-to-helium ratio and negligible amounts of heavier elements. In 1961 his work on stellar surface temperature demonstrated that certain pre-main-sequence stars must be in convective equilibrium, and so must have large luminosities. There is thus a zone on the Hertzsprung–Russell diagram, a graph which plots stellar luminosity against surface temperature, through which these stars cannot pass. This is known as the Hayashi forbidden zone.

Hayashi Razan 1583–1657
Japanese Confucian scholar and ideologist

He served as adviser to the **Tokugawa** shogunate. As the promoter of Neo-Confucianism, with its emphasis on loyalty and its assumption that a hierarchical and harmonious polity reflected the natural order, Hayashi provided ideological support for the shogunate and the political ascendancy of the warrior class.

Haydee, Marcia 1939–
Brazilian dancer and director

Born in Niteroi, she studied with Vaslav Veltchek, making an early debut with the Rio de Janeiro Teatro Municipal. Further study with the Sadler's Wells Ballet School led to her joining the Grand Ballet du Marquis de Cuevas in 1957 and then Stuttgart Ballet in 1961. She was directed at Stuttgart by **John Cranko**, for whom she created roles in *Romeo and Juliet* (1962), *Onegin* (1965), *Carmen* (1971) and *Initials R.B.M.E.* (1972). A highly successful dramatic ballerina, she worked all over the world, and for major choreographers such as **Kenneth Macmillan** and **Glen Tetley**. In 1976 she was appointed artistic director of Stuttgart Ballet.

Hayden, Bill (William George) 1933–
Australian politician

He was born in Brisbane, the son of a working-class Californian who had settled in Australia during World War I and an Irish mother. He served in the state civil and police services, joining the Australian Labor Party and entering the federal parliament in 1961. He served under **Gough Whitlam** and replaced him as party leader in 1977. In 1983 he surrendered the leadership to the more charismatic **Bob Hawke** and was Foreign Minister in his government (1983–88). From 1989 to 1996 he was Governor-General of Australia.

Hayden, Ferdinand Vandeveer 1829–87
US geologist

Born in Westfield, Massachusetts, he went to Oberlin College and worked to pay his own expenses. After graduating in 1850 he went on to Albany Medical College and was awarded an MD. Following work on geological surveys in Dakota, the Badlands, Missouri and Yellowstone (1853–62), he was appointed as a surgeon in the Union army (1862–65), and subsequently became Professor of Geology at Pennsylvania University (1865–72). He resigned from this post because of the increasingly onerous duties of his simultaneous position as head of the US Geological Survey (1867–79). One of the great geological pioneers of western North America, he was given the name 'the man who picks up rocks running' by the Sioux. He was influential in securing the establishment of Yellowstone National Park.

Hayden, Robert E(arl) 1913–80
US poet

He was born in Detroit, and brought up by foster parents. He worked as a researcher for the Federal Writers' Project from 1936 to 1940, in which year he published his first collection *Heart-Shape in the Dust* (1940). His *Selected Poems* (1966) reveals a profound and compassionate insight into the African-American experience. He became the first black poet to be invited to take up the prestigious office of Consultant in Poetry to the Library of Congress. His *Collected Poems* appeared posthumously in 1985.

Haydn, Franz Joseph See panel p854

Haydn, Michael 1737–1806
Austrian composer

Born in Rohrau, he was a cathedral chorister with his brother **Franz Joseph Haydn** in Vienna and ultimately became musical director and concert master to the archbishop in Salzburg, where he remained until his death.

Some of his compositions are of considerable merit and charm, and several of his church pieces and instrumental works are still performed. **Carl Weber** was his pupil.

Haydon, Benjamin Robert 1786–1846
English historical painter

Born in Plymouth, he studied at the Royal Academy but later became a severe critic of it. While he was painting *The Raising of Lazarus* (1823, Tate Gallery, London), he was arrested for debt. His *Mock Election* was purchased by **George IV** and he had some success with other large paintings like *The Reform Banquet* (1832) and *Cassandra* (1834). But poverty continued to dog him, and he shot himself in his studio. He is best remembered for the selections from his journals posthumously published as *Autobiography and Journals* in 1853 (complete text in 5 vols, 1960, 1963).

Hayek, Friedrich August von 1899–1992
British political economist and Nobel Prize winner

He was born in Vienna and became director of the Austrian Institute for Economic Research (1927–31). He lectured at Vienna (1929–31) and was appointed Tooke Professor of Economic Science at London (1931–50). His *Prices and Production* (1931), *Monetary Theory and the Trade Cycle* (1933) and *The Pure Theory of Capital* (1941) dealt with important problems arising out of industrial fluctuations. He was appointed to a professorship at Chicago in 1950 and was at the University of Freiburg from 1962 to 1969. Strongly opposed to **Keynes**ianism, his later works, *The Road to Serfdom* (1944), *Individualism and Economic Order* (1948) and *The Constitution of Liberty* (1960) show an increasing concern for the problems posed for individual values by increased economic controls. Works published during the same period on theoretical psychology and the history of ideas indicate a further broadening of interests, manifested by his *Studies in Philosophy, Politics and Economics* (1967) and *The Political Order of a Free People* (1979). He was awarded the Nobel Prize in economic science in 1974, jointly with **Gunnar Myrdal**.

Hayem, Georges 1841–1920
French physician

Born in Paris, he studied medicine there, receiving his MD in 1868. He became Professor of Therapy and Materia Medica in 1879, working for much of his long career at the Hôpital Tenon. He first described the platelets in the blood, and did classic work on the formation and diseases of the red and white blood cells. He also published important accounts of diseases of such organs as the stomach, liver, heart and brain. His work was notable for its attempt to apply the results of experimental physiology or pathology to the clinical setting.

Hayes, Helen 1900–93
US actress

Born in Washington DC, the daughter of an actress and a travelling salesman, she made her Broadway debut in 1909 and went on to become one of the premier stage actresses of her generation. She appeared in a wide variety of stage productions, including *Dear Brutus* (1919), *Victoria Regina* (1935–39), *The Wisteria Trees* (1951) and *A Touch of the Poet* (1958). She appeared in such films as *The Sin of Madelon Claudet* (1931, Academy Award, British title *The Lullaby*), *A Farewell to Arms* (1932), *Airport* (1970, Academy Award) and *Candleshoe* (1977).

Hayes, Isaac Israel 1832–81
US explorer

Born in Chester County, Pennsylvania, he sailed as surgeon in the **Elisha Kane** Arctic expedition (1853–55) and wrote *An Arctic Boat-journey* (1860). He led a second Arctic expedition in 1860–61, and in 1869 a third which he described in *The Land of Desolation* (1871).

Haydn, (Franz) Joseph 1732–1809
Austrian composer

Haydn was born in Rohrau, Lower Austria, the son of a farmer and wheelwright. He was educated at the Cathedral Choir School of St Stephen's, Vienna, earning his living to begin with by playing in street orchestras and teaching. When his voice broke, he gained valuable experience from acting as accompanist and part-time valet to the famous Italian opera composer and singing teacher, **Niccola Porpora**, and as musical director (1759–60) for Count von Morzin, who kept a small company of court musicians for whom he wrote his earliest symphonies.

His marriage in 1760 to the sharp-tempered Maria Anna Keller was unhappy. He entered the service of Prince Pál Antal **Esterházy** (d.1762) in 1761, and remained in his service and that of his successor, Prince Miklós Joseph, until 1790. As musical director of a princely establishment, his duties included the performance and composition of chamber and orchestral music, sacred music and opera for domestic consumption.

These favourable conditions led to a vast output, notable, technically, for his near-standardization and development of the four-movement string quartet and the 'classical' symphony, with sonata or 'first movement' form as a basic structural ingredient. This was to influence the whole course of European music. Although he rarely travelled during his Esterházy period, his compositions gained an international reputation and were in demand in France, Germany, England, Spain and Italy. Retiring in fact though not in name from Esterháza in 1790, he later paid

two visits to London, sponsored by the violinist and impresario J P Salomon (1745–1815), during which he directed performances of the specially commissioned 'Salomon' or 'London' Symphonies (Nos 93–104). He was made a Doctor of Music of Oxford in 1791.

During the closing years of his life in Vienna, his main works were *The Creation* (1798), *The Seasons* (1801) and his final string quartets. He was the most famous composer of his day, but was quick to recognize the genius of the young **Mozart**, although slower to appreciate the turbulent, questing spirit of **Beethoven**, who was his pupil in 1792. His spontaneity, melodiousness, faultless craftsmanship and a gift for the expression of both high spirits and gravity were strongly tinged in the 1770s by the prevailing *Sturm und Drang* ('storm and stress') atmosphere as well as by personal problems. His output includes 104 symphonies, about 50 concertos, 84 string quartets, 24 stage works, 12 masses, orchestral divertimenti, keyboard sonatas, and various chamber, choral, instrumental, and vocal pieces.

📖 H C Robbins Landon, *Haydn: Chronicle and Works* (5 vols, 1976–81); Neil Butterworth, *Haydn* (1978); Rosemary Hughes, *Haydn* (1950, rev edn 1978).

> When Mozart advised Haydn against visiting England because he could not speak the language, he replied, 'But all the world understands my language.' (1790).

Hayes, Rutherford B(irchard) 1822–93
19th President of the USA

Born in Delaware, Ohio, he graduated from Kenyon College, Ohio, and practised law in Cincinnati (1849–61). He served in the Civil War with distinction, retiring as major-general. He represented Ohio in Congress (1865–67) and was elected Governor of Ohio three times (1867, 1869, 1875). In 1876 he was Republican candidate for the presidency, the Democratic candidate being **Samuel J Tilden**. When the returns from four states were disputed, a Republican-dominated electoral commission awarded all the questionable votes to Hayes, securing him a majority of one in the electoral college. As President (1877–81) he withdrew the last remaining federal troops from the South, ending Reconstruction, and he pressed for Civil Service reform, making government appointments based on merit rather than party loyalty. He pursued a hard-money policy, bringing about the resumption of specie payments and opposing the Bland–Allison Silver Act (1878), which passed over his veto. He chose not to run for re-election in 1880. 📖 Harry Barnard, *Rutherford B Hayes and His America* (1954)

Hayley, William 1745–1820
English poet and writer

He was born in Chichester, Sussex. He became a popular writer, although his most ambitious works, *The Triumphs of Temper* (1781) and *The Triumphs of Music* (1804), were ridiculed by **Byron**. **William Blake** illustrated his *Ballads founded on Anecdotes of Animals* (1805). A prolific author, he also wrote essays, plays, and biographies of **John Milton**, **George Romney** and his friend **William Cowper**. 📖 W T Le Viness, *The Life and Work of William Hayley* (1945)

Hayman, Francis 1708–76
English painter and illustrator

He was born in Exeter. His most ambitious work was the decoration of the boxes and pavilions at Vauxhall Gardens, London. He also painted portrait groups which influenced **Thomas Gainsborough** who, for a time, worked under him. As a designer and illustrator he

worked in the London studio of Hubert Gravelot, the most important link between French and English art of the time and, amongst other work, illustrated the books of **Samuel Richardson**. From 1760 he was president of the Society of Artists and, in 1768, a founder-member and the first librarian of the Royal Academy.

Haynau, Julius Jakob, Baron von 1786–1853
Austrian soldier

Born in Cassel, he gained notoriety during the Italian campaigns (1848–49) for his ruthless severity, especially at the capture of Brescia, where his flogging of women gained him the nickname the 'Hyena of Brescia'. From the Siege of Venice he was summoned to the supreme military command in Hungary in 1849, and his successes at Raab, Komorn and Szegedin did much to secure Austrian supremacy. Appointed Dictator of Hungary in 1849 after its pacification, he was dismissed in 1850 for excessive violence, and that same year in London was assaulted by a mob.

Hayne, Robert Young 1791–1839
US politician

Born in South Carolina, he was admitted to the Bar in 1812, and served in the war with Great Britain. He became Speaker of the state legislature and Attorney-General of the state, and sat in the US Senate (1823–32). He opposed protection, and in 1832 supported the doctrine of nullification (the power of a state to render federal laws void within its borders). South Carolina in 1832 adopted an ordinance of nullification, Hayne was elected Governor, and the state prepared to resist the federal power by force of arms. A compromise, however, was agreed to, and the ordinance was repealed. His nephew, Paul Hamilton (1830–86), the 'Laureate of the South', wrote war songs, sonnets, etc, which were collected in 1882.

Haynes, Elwood 1857–1925
US inventor

He was born in Portland, Indiana, and was trained as an engineer and a chemist. In 1893 he constructed a one-horse power, one-cylinder vehicle, the oldest US automobile in existence, now preserved in the Smithsonian Institution. He also patented a number of alloys, including a type of stainless steel (1919), and ran his own company, Haynes Automobile Company, from 1905 to 1925.

Hays, Will (iam Harrison) 1879–1954
US politician and film censor

Born in Sullivan, Indiana, he was a lawyer by training. He was Republican national chairman (1918–20), engineered **Warren G Harding**'s presidential campaign, and became US Postmaster General (1921–22). As the first president of the Motion Picture Producers and Distributors of America (1922–45), he formulated the Production Code (1930), known as the Hays Code, which imposed a rigorous code of morality on US films, and which remained in force until 1966.

Hayter, Stanley William 1901–88
English artist and engraver

Born in Hackney, London, he studied chemistry and geology at King's College London for a career in the oil industry. He worked for the Anglo-Iranian Oil Company in Abadan (1922–25), then returned to London in 1926 to exhibit the portraits and landscapes he had painted in the Middle East. He then moved to Paris to study art at the Académie Julian, where he learned printmaking and line-engraving. In 1927 he founded a studio in which artists of all nationalities could work together. Later known as Atelier 17, it was based in New York during World War II but returned to Paris in 1950. As a painter, Hayter became one of the earliest members of the Surrealist movement, under the influence of **André Breton**, but he is best known as an innovator in printmaking. His publications include *New Ways of Gravure* (1949) and *About Prints* (1962).

Hayward, Abraham 1802–84
English essayist

Born in Wishford, Wiltshire, he was called to the Bar in 1832, founded and edited the *Law Magazine*, and was made a QC in 1845. Many of his best articles, including 'The Art of Dining', were reprinted in his *Biographical and Critical Essays* (1858–73) and *Eminent Statesmen and Writers* (1880).

Hayward, Susan, originally Edythe Marrenner 1917–75
US film actress

Born in Brooklyn, New York, she left her job as a cloth designer in a Manhattan handkerchief factory in 1936, and used her modest savings to enrol at the Feagin School of Dramatic Arts. She then pursued a modelling career and was offered a screen test for the part of Scarlet O'Hara in *Gone With The Wind*. Though unsuccessful, she remained in Hollywood, changed her name and took elocution lessons to deepen her voice and remove her Brooklyn accent. Her abrasive personality combined successfully with her roles as crisis-ridden women and she received the first of five Best Actress Academy Award nominations for her performance as an alcoholic in *Smash-Up: The Story of a Woman* (1947, UK: *A Woman Destroyed*). She went on to win this award for her role in *I Want to Live!* (1958) as the first woman in California to be sent to the gas chamber. She continued to act until the early 1970s and spent her last years battling with brain tumours, making a final, typically defiant, public appearance as a presenter at the 1974 Academy Award ceremony.

Haywood, Eliza, née Fowler c.1693–1756
English novelist

She was born in London. After being deserted by her husband, she became an actress and wrote plays, as well as a number of scandalous society novels, in which the characters resembled living persons so closely (their names being thinly concealed by the use of asterisks) as to be libellous. **Pope** denounced her in *The Dunciad*. She issued the periodicals *The Female Spectator* (1744–46) and *The Parrot* (1747). Her works include *Memoirs of a Certain Island adjacent to Utopia* (1725), *The History of Miss Betsy Thoughtless* (1751) and *The History of Jemmy and Jenny Jessamy* (1753).

Haywood, William D (udley), known as Big Bill 1869–1928
US labour leader

Born in Salt Lake City, Utah, he worked as a miner, homesteader, and cowboy, then joined the Western Federation of Miners (1896) and quickly became prominent. In 1905 he helped to found the Industrial Workers of the World, which was committed to revolutionary labour politics and to the organization of all workers in one big union. An active socialist, he was convicted of sedition in 1917 for his opposition to World War I, then fled from the USA (1921) and took refuge in the Soviet Union.

Hayworth, Rita, originally Margarita Carmen Cansino 1918–87
US film actress and dancer

She was born into a showbusiness family in New York City, a cousin of **Ginger Rogers**. Nightclub appearances led to a succession of small roles in B-pictures. Blossoming into an international beauty, she appeared in many films, sometimes cast as an enigmatic temptress, as in *Blood and Sand* (1941) and *Gilda* (1946). She appeared in a number of musicals, and although her singing voice was dubbed, she was a skilled dancer, notably partnering **Gene Kelly** in *Cover Girl* (1944), and **Fred Astaire** in *You'll Never Get Rich* (1941) and *You Were Never Lovelier* (1942). Later roles were largely lacklustre, although she was effective as the faded beauty in *Separate Tables* (1958). Her five husbands included **Orson Welles** and Prince Aly Khan. She suffered from Alzheimer's disease for many years prior to her death.

Hazelius, Artur Immanuel 1833–1901
Swedish ethnologist and museum curator

His collection of artefacts illustrative of the old folk and peasant culture of Sweden led him to found, in 1873, the ethnographic museum in Stockholm that became the Nordic Museum. His greatest achievement, however, was the foundation in 1891 of Skansen in Stockholm, the world's first major open-air museum and a monument to his belief in popular education.

Hazlitt, William 1778–1830
English essayist

He was born in Maidstone, Kent, the son of a Unitarian minister and spent much of his childhood in Wem, Shropshire. At the age of 15 he was sent to Hackney College, London, to study for the ministry, but he had abandoned the notion by 1796 when he met **Coleridge**, who encouraged him to write *Principles of Human Action* (1805). He turned briefly to portrait painting, then published *Free Thoughts on Public Affairs* (1806), *Reply to Malthus* (1807), and in 1812 found employment in London on the *Morning Chronicle* and *Examiner*. From 1814 to 1830 he wrote essays on literary criticism and other subjects for the *Edinburgh Review* and the *London Magazine*. He also lectured at the Surrey Institute on *The English Poets, English Comic Writers*, and *Dramatic Literature of the Age of Elizabeth* (1818–21). A passion for Sarah Walker, the daughter of a tailor with whom he lodged, found expression in the frantic *Liber Amoris* (1823). His *Spirit of the Age, or Contemporary Portraits* appeared in 1825, and his *Life of Napoleon Bonaparte* between 1828 and 1830. He was a deadly controversialist, and a master of epigram, invective and withering irony. Other essay collections include *Table Talk* (1821) and *Plain Speaker* (1826). His last years darkened by ill health and money difficulties, he died with the words 'Well, I've had a happy life'. S Jones, *William Hazlitt* (1982); P Howe, *The Life of William Hazlitt* (1922)

Hazzard, Shirley 1931–
US novelist
Born and educated in Sydney, Australia, she moved to the USA in 1951 and spent a decade working for the United Nations. She resigned to take up writing full time. Her first book, *The Evening of the Holiday*, was published in 1966. Her second novel, *People in Glass Houses* (1967), satirized the UN, and she later published a factual exposé of that organization in *Defeat of an Ideal* (1973), followed by *Countenance of Truth* (1990). Other novels include *The Bay of Noon* (1970), and *The Transit of Venus* (1980), which explored the tension btween romantic love and moral courage and established her as a major contemporary writer. Many of her short stories have appeared in the *New Yorker* magazine, and some are collected in *Cliffs of Fall* (1963).

H B See Doyle, John
H D See Doolittle, Hilda

Head, Edith 1907–81
US costume designer
Educated at UCLA and Stanford, California, she taught art and languages for a time before joining Paramount in the late 1930s. She became one of the leading Hollywood costume designers, later moving to Universal in 1967. She designed opulent dresses for many of the major stars of the era, including Barbara Stanwyck, Elizabeth Taylor, Audrey Hepburn and Bette Davis, as well as the stylish suits worn by Robert Redford and Paul Newman in *The Sting* (1973), one of eight films for which she received an Academy Award for costume design.

Head, Sir Henry 1861–1940
English neurologist
Born in Stamford Hill, London, he studied natural sciences at Trinity College, Cambridge, and clinical medicine at University College Hospital, London. His interest in the functions and diseases of the nervous system dated from his student days, when he was taught by Sir Michael Foster and John Langley among others. He became a consulting physician at the London Hospital, and is best known for his neurological research. His famous observations on the sensory changes in his own arm, after cutting some nerve fibres, provided important information about the physiology of sensation, and reinforced his reputation as a leading scientifically-inclined neurologist. He wrote widely on aphasia (disorders of speech), summarizing many of his ideas in *Aphasia and Kindred Disorders of Speech* (1926) which reported on the clinical disturbances of speech that he observed in a large number of men suffering from gunshot wounds. He edited the influential neurological journal *Brain* (1905–21) and also published poetry. He was knighted in 1927.

Heal, Sir Ambrose 1872–1959
English furniture designer
Born in London, he was educated at Marlborough and at the Slade School of Art, London. He served an apprenticeship as a cabinetmaker before joining the family firm in 1893, and began designing furniture influenced by the Arts and Crafts movement. From the 1930s, the firm adopted a fashionable modern style, providing homes with an inexpensive alternative to reproduction furniture and costly Arts and Crafts pieces.

Healey, Denis Winston Healey, Baron 1917–
English politician
Born in Keighley, Yorkshire, and educated at Oxford, he served with the Royal Engineers in North Africa and Italy (1940–45), attaining the rank of major. For seven years after World War II he was secretary of the Labour Party's international department before becoming MP for Leeds in 1952. He was a member of the Shadow Cabinet for five years before becoming Secretary of State for Defence in the Wilson government of 1964, a post which he held for six years. His five years (1974–79) as Chancellor of the Exchequer were a rather stormy period marked by a sterling crisis and subsequent intervention by the International Monetary Fund. Healey unsuccessfully contested the Labour Party leadership in 1976 and again in 1980 when he was somewhat unexpectedly defeated by Michael Foot. He was, however, elected Deputy Leader ahead of his left-wing opponent Tony Benn. In 1987 he resigned from the Shadow Cabinet and became a life peer in 1992. His publications include the autobiography *The Time of My Life* (1989), and *My Secret Planet* (1992). Bruce Reed and Geoffrey Williams, *Denis Healey and the Politics of Power* (1971)

Healy, Timothy Michael 1855–1931
Irish Nationalist leader
He was born in Bantry, County Cork. He sat in parliament (1880–1918), headed the 1890 revolt against Charles Stewart Parnell, and became an Independent Nationalist. He was the first Governor-General of the Irish Free State (1922–28).

Heaney, Seamus Justin See panel p857

Hearn, (Patricio) Lafcadio Tessima Carlos 1850–1904
Greek novelist, journalist and travel writer
Born in Levkás, one of the Ionian Islands, he grew up in Dublin, Ireland, was educated in France and England, and emigrated to the USA in 1869, where he set about a writing career. He was hampered by his partial blindness and a morbid sense of inferiority, and caused a scandal through his relationship with a mulatto woman. His writings of the period include the novel *Chita* (1889), set on the Gulf Coast of Louisiana, a volume of stories translated from Théophile Gautier (1882), the Negro-French proverbs collected in *Gombo Zhèbes* (1885), and many newspaper sketches of Creole life. After two years spent in Martinique, in 1890 he travelled to Japan, where he settled, became a Japanese citizen, and took the name Koizumi Yakumo from his wife's family name from 1895. He wrote a series of books sympathetically portraying Japanese life and manners, including *Out of the East* (1895), and *Japan: an attempt at interpretation* (1904). P Murray, *A Fantastic Journey* (1993)

Hearne, Samuel 1745–92
English explorer
Born in London, he served in the Royal Navy and then joined the Hudson's Bay Company, who sent him to Canada in 1769. During a journey in search of copper in 1770 he became the first European to travel overland by canoe and sled to the Arctic Ocean by following the Coppermine River north of the Great Slave Lake. He gave detailed reports of the frozen wastes and the Inuit conflicts he observed. In 1774 he set up the first interior trading post for the Company at Cumberland House, and then he became Governor of Fort Prince of Wales (Churchill), where he was captured and taken to France in 1782. There his release was negotiated on condition he publish an account of his travels. He returned to reestablish Churchill as a trading post in 1783, but ill health forced him back to England in 1787. *A Journey from Prince of Wales' Fort … to the Northern Ocean* was published in 1795.

Hearns, Tommy (Thomas), nicknamed Hit Man and Motor City Cobra 1958–
US boxer

Heaney, Seamus Justin 1939–
Northern Irish poet and critic and Nobel Prize winner

Seamus Heaney was born in Castledawson, County Derry. He was educated at St Columba's College, Londonderry, and at Queen's College, Belfast, where he later lectured (1966–72), while also a member of the Belfast writers' group. An Ulster Catholic, he was so disturbed by the violence in the North that he moved to the Republic in 1972, and taught at Caryfort College, Dublin (1975–81). He has been Boylston Professor of Rhetoric and Oratory at Harvard since 1985, and has been Professor of Poetry at Oxford since 1989.

He made his debut as a poet with *Eleven Poems* (1965). Redolent of the rural Ireland in which he grew up, his work seems nurtured by the landscape—lush, peaty and, to an extent, menacing. One of the greatest modern poets writing in English, he is regarded as a worthy successor to **W B Yeats**. He was awarded the Nobel Prize for literature in 1995 and won the Whitbread prize in 1997 for his latest collection, *Spirit Level*.

📖 Significant collections are *Death of a Naturalist* (1966), *Wintering Out* (1972, much influenced by the outbreak of sectarian violence in Northern Ireland), *North* (1975), *Bog Poems* (1975), *Stations* (1975, prose poems as recollections of childhood), *Field Work* (1979), *Station Island*

(1984, which has dialogues with the dead, including the ghost of **Henry James**), *The Haw Lantern* (1987) and *Seeing Things* (1991). *Selected Poems 1965–75* appeared in 1980, and *New Selected Poems 1966–87* in 1990. His first play, *The Cure at Troy* (1991), is a translation of **Sophocles**'s *Philoctetes* and was written for the Field Day Theatre Company in Dublin, and *Sweeney's Flight* (1992) is Heaney's version of the Irish odyssey of Mad Sweeney. A collection of essays, *Preoccupations*, was published in 1980. See also Michael Parker, *Seamus Heaney: The Making of the Poet* (1994); Blake Morrison, *Seamus Heaney* (1982); Tony Curtis (ed), *The Art of Seamus Heaney* (1982).

By Heaney:
'Between my finger and my thumb
The squat pen rests.
I'll dig with it.'
Death of a Naturalist, 'Digging'.

On Heaney:
'He's very popular among his mates.
I think I'm Auden, he thinks he's Yeats.'
Gavin Ewart, 'Seamus Heaney' (1986).

Born in Memphis, Tennessee, he became the first man to win world titles at four different weights in 1987, and in 1988 was the first to win titles at five different weights. His WBA (World Boxing Association) championship title wins include welterweight (1980) as well as super-welterweight (1982), and WBC (World Boxing Council) title wins include junior-middleweight (1984), light-heavyweight and middleweight (1987), and super-middleweight (1988).

Hearst, Phoebe, *née* Apperson 1842–1919
US philanthropist

Born in Missouri, she married the mining magnate George Hearst (1820–91) in 1862. He became US senator of California in 1886, and he allowed his wife to use money to endow schools, kindergartens, libraries and hospitals and to sponsor archaeological expeditions. Their son, **William Randolph Hearst**, took over the *San Francisco Examiner* from his father in 1887. Phoebe Hearst gave him $7.5 million and with it he built up the largest newspaper chain in the USA. One of Phoebe Hearst's most enduring philanthropies was the endowment of some of the buildings of the main campus of the University of California at Berkeley in 1873, for which she was honoured with the position of first woman Regent of the university.

Hearst, William Randolph 1863–1951
US newspaper publisher

He was born in San Francisco, the son of a newspaper proprietor. After studying at Harvard he took over the *San Francisco Examiner* in 1887 from his father. Invading the territory of **Joseph Pulitzer**, he acquired the *New York Morning Journal* (1895), launching the *Evening Journal* a year later. He revolutionized journalism by the introduction of banner headlines, lavish illustrations and other sensational methods, nicknamed by critics 'the yellow press' and designed to win readers away from Pulitzer's *New York World*. In 1897–98 he published exaggerated and fabricated reports on the Cuban struggle for independence, which boosted circulation enormously and incidentally helped bring about the Spanish–American War. He made himself the head of a national chain of newspapers and periodicals, which included the *Chicago Examiner*, *Boston American*, *Cosmopolitan* and *Harper's*

Bazaar. He was a member of the US House of Representatives (1903–07), but failed to become mayor and governor of New York. He built an impressive residence at San Simeon, California, furnished with some of the huge collection of antiquities and paintings that he compulsively acquired, on which he spent much of his vast wealth. It is now a museum. His career inspired the **Orson Welles** film *Citizen Kane* (1941). 📖 W A Swanberg, *Citizen Hearst* (1961).

Heartfield, John, *originally* Helmut Herzfelde 1891–1968
German photomonteur and painter

He was the son of the poet Franz Held. Together with **George Grosz**, he was a leading member of the Berlin Dada group after World War I, producing satirical collages from pasted, superimposed photographs cut from magazines. A lifelong pacifist and staunch Communist, he moved to East Berlin in 1950, and anglicized his name as a gesture of sympathy with the USA.

Heath, Sir Edward Richard George, *also called* Ted Heath 1916–
English Conservative politician

Born in Broadstairs, Kent, he was a scholar of Balliol College, Oxford. After service in World War II he entered parliament in 1950, one of R A Butler's 'One Nation' new Tory intellectuals. He became Chief Whip (1955–59), then Minister of Labour (1959–60). He was the chief negotiator for Great Britain's entry into the European Common Market, and although the French attitude prevented the UK from joining, he was awarded the German Charlemagne prize (1963). In the **Douglas-Home** administration (1963) he became Secretary of State for Industry and President of the Board of Trade (1963). Elected Leader of the Conservative Party in July 1965, he was Opposition leader until, on the Conservative victory in the 1970 general election, he became Prime Minister. After a long confrontation with the miners' union in 1973 the Conservatives narrowly lost the general election of February 1974, the loss being confirmed by another election in October 1974. In 1975 he was replaced as leader by **Margaret Thatcher**. From 1975 he became an increasingly outspoken critic of what he regarded as the extreme policies of 'Thatcherism'. He has resisted attempts to move him to the Lords, and retained his seat (Old Bexley and Sidcup) in the 1997 general election. His international credibility was evident from his meetings with **Saddam Hussein** before and after the 1991 Gulf War, which were instrumental in securing the release of British hostages and prisoners. He is an expert yachtsman, and, after winning the 1969 Hobart Ocean race, captained the British crew for the Admiral's Cup races of 1971 and 1979. He is also an accomplished musician. 📖 Margaret Laing, *Edward Heath: Prime Minister* (1973)

Heathcoat, John 1783–1861
English inventor

He was born near Derby, and in 1808 designed a machine for making lace. He set up a factory in Nottingham, but it was destroyed in 1816 by the Luddites, and he subsequently moved his business to Tiverton in Devon. He also invented ribbon and net-making machinery, and devised methods of winding raw silk from cocoons. He was MP for Tiverton from 1832 to 1859.

Heathcoat Amory, Derek See Amory, Derek Heathcoat Amory, 1st Viscount

Heathfield, George Augustus Eliott, 1st Baron 1717–90
Scottish soldier

He was born in Stobs in Roxburghshire. Educated at Leyden, the French military college of La Fère, and Woolwich, he served in the War of the Austrian Succession (1740–48), the Seven Years War (1756–63) and in Cuba (1762), returning as lieutenant-general. When Great Britain became involved in hostilities with Spain in 1775, he was sent out to Gibraltar. His heroic defence, from June 1779 to February 1783, ranks as one of the most memorable achievements of British military forces.

Heaviside, Oliver 1850–1925
English physicist

Born in London, a telegrapher by training, he spent much of his life living reclusively in Devon. There he made various important advances in the study of electrical communications, and in 1902, independently of **Arthur Kennelly**, he predicted the existence of an ionized gaseous layer capable of reflecting radio waves, the 'Heaviside layer' (now known as the ionosphere), which was verified 20 years later. He was elected FRS in 1891, and became an honorary member of the Institution of Electrical Engineers in 1908.

Hebb, Donald Olding 1904–85
Canadian psychologist

Born in Chester, Nova Scotia, he was educated at Dalhousie and McGill universities, and subsequently studied at Harvard with **Karl Lashley**, with whom he later worked at the Yerkes Laboratories of Primate Biology in Florida (1942–47). In 1947 he rejoined McGill University where he remained until his retirement, becoming chairman of the psychology department (1948–58) and later university Chancellor (1970–74). He was the first non-American to become president of the American Psychological Association. His best-remembered theoretical contributions to psychology were embodied in his book *The Organization of Behaviour* (1949), in which he argued that long-term memories could be encoded in the brain by means of changes occurring at the synapse (the point at which one nerve cell can communicate chemically with another), and that repeated use would itself strengthen such a synapse. There is now good physiological evidence for such 'Hebb synapses'. He also introduced and developed the concept of the 'cell assembly', a diffuse network of nerve cells which could be activated for relatively short periods and which would be the

physical embodiment of transient thoughts and perceptions. His ideas have had a renaissance in the field of 'computational neuroscience'.

Hebbel, Friedrich 1813–63
German dramatist

Born in Wesselburen, Dithmarshen, he studied in Hamburg from 1835 and later settled in Vienna (1846). He wrote *Maria Magdalena* (1842, Eng trans 1914) and several historical or biblical plays, such as *Herodes und Mariamne* (1849, Eng trans *Herod and Mariamne*, 1914) and his masterpiece, the *Nibelungen* trilogy (1855–60, Eng trans *The Nibelungs*, 1921). 📖 T Campbell, *The Life and Works of Friedrich Hebbel* (1919)

Heber, Reginald 1783–1826
English prelate and hymnwriter

Born in Malpas, Cheshire, he studied at Oxford, where he wrote his prize poem *Palestine* (1803). Inducted into the family living of Hodnet in Shropshire (1807), he was appointed Bampton lecturer (1815), a prebendary of St Asaph (1817), and a preacher of Lincoln's Inn (1822). In 1823 he was appointed Bishop of Calcutta. He carried out his duties for three years, but died very suddenly at Trichinopoly. He was a frequent contributor to the *Quarterly Review*, and published sermons, *A Journey through India*, and other works, and edited **Jeremy Taylor's** *Works* (1822). As a poet, his fame rests upon *Palestine* and his *Hymns* (1812), which include 'From Greenland's Icy Mountains' and 'Holy, Holy, Holy'. His half-brother, **Richard** (1774–1833), was a famous bibliomaniac with a collection estimated at 146,827 volumes.

Heberden, William 1710–1801
English physician

Born in London, he studied and practised in Cambridge, then in 1748 set up in London. He distinguished chickenpox from smallpox and described angina pectoris (a disease of the heart) and prescribed treatment for it. He attended Dr **Johnson**, and was the last to write medical papers in Latin.

Hébert, Jacques René, *also called* Père Duchesne 1755–94
French revolutionary

He was born in Alençon. A servant in Paris, he was dismissed more than once for embezzlement, but soon after the outbreak of the Revolution became a prominent Jacobin and editor of the satirical newspaper *Le Père Duchesne* (1790). As a member of the Revolutionary Council, he was active in the September Massacres. He was on the commission appointed to examine **Marie Antoinette** and raised the trumped-up charge of incestuous practices with the Dauphin. He was instrumental in converting Notre Dame into a Temple of Reason. After denouncing the Committee of Public Safety for its failure to help the poor, he tried to incite a popular uprising, but he incurred the suspicion of **Danton** and **Robespierre** and was guillotined with 17 of his followers (Hébertists).

Hecataeus of Miletus c.550–476BC
Pioneer Greek historian and geographer

He attempted to demythologize Greek history in his prose *Genealogies* (or *Histories*) by giving the poetic fables about the divine or heroic ancestries of leading Milesian families a pseudo-chronological framework. He travelled widely, visiting Greece, Thrace, Persia, and parts of Italy, Spain and Africa, and wrote a *Tour of the World* (of which only fragments remain) describing local customs and curiosities, and which he published with an improved version of the map made by **Anaximander** of Miletus.

Hecht, Ben 1894–1964
US writer

Born in New York City, he worked as a journalist in Chicago from 1910 and wrote a series of novels. His initial efforts to write for the stage were unsuccessful, but in 1928 he teamed up with his fellow newspaperman Charles MacArthur to write *The Front Page*, a fast-paced comedy about the moral ambiguities of the newspaper business. He scored a hit with this play and its subsequent film adaptation, and later wrote numerous screenplays, including *Wuthering Heights* (1939), *Spellbound* (1945) and *Notorious* (1946). His 1946 play, *A Flag is Born*, reflected his dedication to Zionism. ⌨ *A Child of the Century* (1955)

Heck, Barbara Ruckle, *née* Ruckle 1734–1804
Irish–American immigrant

Born in Ballingrane, Ireland, of a German Palatinate refugee family, she converted to Methodism at the age of 18 and, after marrying, migrated with a group of people to New York in 1760. Upset by a lack of spiritual zeal in her companions, she encouraged her cousin Philip Embury (1728–73), a carpenter, to hold the first Methodist meeting in the USA in his own home (1766), and prompted him to build the first chapel (1768). Her family was forced to move to Canada by the Revolutionary War.

Heckel, Erich 1883–1970
German painter

A founder of the Expressionist school Die Brücke ('The Bridge') about 1905, he studied architecture at Dresden before turning to painting. He excelled in lithography and the woodcut (for example his *Self-portrait*, 1917, Munich). Vilified by the Nazis, he stayed in Berlin and was professor at Karlsruhe (1949–56).

Heckel, Johann Adam c.1812–1877
German woodwind instrument-maker

In 1831 he established his own workshop in Biebrich, near Wiesbaden, and with the guidance of a bassoon player, Carl Almenraeder, introduced improvements in the structure and key-system of bassoons, which, when standardized, distinguished the German from the French type. His son, Wilhelm (1856–1909), and grandsons, Wilhelm Hermann (1879–1952) and August (1880–1914), carried on the business, which introduced several instrumental novelties such as the Heckel-phone (1904).

Hecker, Isaac Thomas 1819–88
US clergyman

Born in New York City, he was educated in Europe. He passed from Brook Farm socialism to Behmenite mysticism, became a Catholic in 1844 and, after studies in England, a Redemptorist Father. Forced to leave that order, he founded the Missionary Priests of St Paul (Paulists), and greatly extended Catholicism in the USA. His tendency to democratize Catholicism caused much controversy. His works include *Questions of the Soul* (1850) and *The Church and the Age* (1888).

Hedin, Sven Anders 1865–1952
Swedish explorer and geographer

Born in Stockholm, he first went to Persia (Iran) in 1885 as a tutor, and was attached to a Swedish–Norwegian embassy to the Shah in 1890. From then until 1908 he travelled constantly, particularly in the Himalayas, the Gobi Desert, and Tibet, of which he made the first detailed map (1908). After World War I he organized and led the Sino–Swedish scientific expedition to the northwest provinces of China (1927–33). The Sven Hedin Foundation in Stockholm contains some 8,000 geological specimens and artefacts collected by him.

Hedley, William 1779–1843
English inventor

He was born in Newburn, near Newcastle upon Tyne. A colliery 'viewer' and lessee, in 1813 he improved on Richard Trevithick's locomotive, proving that loads could be moved by the traction of smooth wheels on smooth rails. His locomotive, known as *Puffing Billy*, was the first commercial steam locomotive.

Hedwig, Johannes 1730–99
German botanist and physician

Born in Kronstadt (now Brasov, Romania), he studied medicine at the University of Leipzig, and after practising as a physician became Professor of Botany there (1789). He gave special attention to cryptogams, with his posthumous *Species Muscorum Frondosorum* (1801), based on natural groupings, being internationally accepted as the starting point for the scientific naming of mosses. He defined for the first time the characters which separate mosses and liverworts, and he described, essentially accurately, the life cycles of bryophytes in *Theoria Generationis et Fructificationis Plantarum Cryptogamicarum* (1784).

Heem, Jan Davidsz de c.1606–1684
Dutch still-life painter

Born in Utrecht, he settled in Antwerp in 1636. His paintings of flowers and exquisitely laid tables are in most galleries in Europe and the USA. He is arguably the greatest Dutch still-life painter. His son Cornelis (1631–95) was also a painter and a close follower of his father.

Heemskerck, Maerten van 1498–1574
Dutch portrait and religious painter

Born in Heemskerck, by c.1528 he was working in Haarlem with the Italianate painter Jan van Scorel. Following his lead, van Heemskerck also travelled to Italy and spent the period 1532 to 1535 in Rome, where he was attracted to the work of Michelangelo and Raphael. While in Rome he also studied antiquities, and his surviving sketchbooks (now in Berlin) are valuable historical documents, giving vivid impressions of the ancient monuments of the city as they appeared in the 16th century. He spent the remainder of his life in Haarlem.

Heenan, John Carmel 1905–75
English Roman Catholic archbishop

Born in Ilford, Essex, and educated at Ushaw and the English College, Rome, he was ordained in 1930. He became a parish priest in east London, and during World War II worked with the BBC, becoming well-known as 'the Radio Priest'. He became Bishop of Leeds in 1951, Archbishop of Liverpool in 1957, and Archbishop of Westminster in 1963. A convinced ecumenical, he supported the causes of religious liberty and reconciliation with the Jews at the Second Vatican Council, and was created cardinal in 1965. He wrote several doctrinal and autobiographical works. ⌨ Alan Lloyd, *The Great Prize Fight* (1977)

Heeren, Arnold Hermann Ludwig 1760–1842
German historian

Born near Bremen, he became Professor of Philosophy (1787) and of History (1801), at Göttingen. His first great work was an economic history of the ancient world (1793–96). He also wrote on the study of the classics since the Renaissance (1797–1802), a history of the states of the ancient world (1799) and *Political System of Europe and its Colonies* (1800). His economic interpretation of history foreshadowed Karl Marx and Friedrich Engels.

Heezen, Bruce Charles 1924–77
US oceanographer

Born in Vinton, Iowa, he graduated in palaeontology from the University of Iowa in 1948, worked with William Ewing at Columbia University (1948–77), and later moved to the university's department of geology as assistant professor (1960–64) and associate professor from 1964. In 1952 he was able to deduce the existence of a rapid sediment slump, or turbidity current, which had moved massive quantities of undersea sediment. Using the new continuously recording echo-sounder to map sea-floor topography, he demonstrated how the Atlantic Ocean fracture zones offset the mid-ocean ridge. He also discovered the undersea location of earthquake epicentres, which led him to realize that ridges were tensional features and propose that new sea-floor formed there (1960).

Heffer, Eric Samuel 1922–91
English Labour politician
Apprenticed as a carpenter-joiner at the age of 14, he worked in the trade, apart from war service in the RAF, until he entered the House of Commons, representing Liverpool, Walton, in 1964. He had joined the Labour Party as a youth, and was Liverpool president (1959–60) and a Liverpool city councillor (1960–66). A traditional socialist, favouring public ownership and strongly unilateralist, he distrusted centrist tendencies and had a brief, uncomfortable period as a junior minister (1974–75). He unsuccessfully challenged **Roy Hattersley** for the deputy leadership in 1988. His autobiography, *Never a Yes Man*, was published posthumously in 1991.

Hefner, Hugh Marston 1926–
US editor and publisher
He was born in Chicago into a family of Methodists and his upbringing was strict. He attended Illinois University, did postgraduate work in psychology, and worked as a personnel manager, advertising copywriter and in the subscriptions department of *Esquire* magazine until 1952, when he resigned to start a new magazine. Investing $10,000, he published the first issue of *Playboy* in December 1953, with **Marilyn Monroe** posing nude. 'Girly' photographs, practical advice on sexual problems, men's talk and articles of high literary standard combined to make him conspicuously wealthy and the magazine a notorious success. The *Playboy* empire extended into real estate, clubs (with 'bunny-girl' hostesses) and sundry products.

Hegel, Georg Wilhelm Friedrich See panel p861

Heiberg, Gunnar Edvard Rode 1857–1929
Norwegian dramatist and director
He was born in Christiania (now Oslo). As artistic director of the Bergen Theatre he staged the first performances of **Ibsen**'s *Vildanden* (*The Wild Duck*) and *Rosmersholm*. His own first play, *Tante Ulrikke* (1884), was in the same 'socially aware' vein. He wrote Expressionist plays in the radical and rational tradition of Norwegian literature, such as *Balkonen* (1894, 'The Balcony') and *Kjaerlighetens Tragedie* (1904, 'The Tragedy of Love'). 📖 E Skavlan, *Gunnar Heiberg* (1950)

Heiberg, Johan Ludvig 1791–1860
Danish playwright
The son of the writer Peter Andreas Heiberg (1758–1841), he wrote a series of enormously popular musical comedies, of which his masterpiece was *Nej!* (1836, 'No!'). He is seen as the creator of Danish vaudeville. His romantic play *Elverhøj* (1828, 'Hills of the Elves'), is considered a classic. He later became director of the Theatre Royal in Copenhagen (1849–56). He also wrote on philosophy and was significant as an interpreter of **Hegel**. 📖 M Borup, *Johan Ludvig Heiberg* (1947)

Heidegger, Martin 1889–1976
German philosopher
Born in Messkirch, Baden, the son of a Catholic sexton, he joined the Jesuits as a novice and went on to teach philosophy at Freiburg, where he wrote a dissertation on **Duns Scotus**. He was Professor of Philosophy at Marburg (1923–28) and then succeeded **Edmund Husserl** as Professor of Philosophy at Freiburg (1929–45), where he was appointed Rector in 1933. In a notorious inaugural address he declared his support for **Hitler**. He was officially retired in 1945 but continued to be an influential teacher and lecturer. He succeeded Husserl as a leading figure in the phenomenological movement, but was also much influenced by **Sören Kierkegaard**, and though he disclaimed the label of 'existentialist' he was a key influence on **Jean-Paul Sartre** through his writings on the nature and predicament of human existence, the search for 'authenticity' and the distractions of *Angst* (dread). His major work is the original but almost unreadable *Sein und Zeit* (1927, 'Being and Time'), which presents an exhaustive ontological classification of 'Being' and an examination of the distinctively human mode of existence (*Dasein*) characterized by participation and involvement in the world of objects. His deliberate obscurity and riddling style partly account for his poor reception in the Anglo-Saxon world, but he is a continuing influence in other parts of Europe. 📖 George Steiner, *Heidegger* (1978, US Martin Heidegger, 1979)

Heiden, Eric Arthur 1958–
US speed skater
Born in Madison, Wisconsin, he won all there was to win in speed skating between 1977 and 1980. In 1976, his first winter Olympic Games, he was seventh in the 1,000 metres race and nineteenth in the 5,000 metres. He became US world speed skating champion in 1977 and senior world all-round champion in 1977, 1978 and 1979. At the 1980 Winter Olympics at Lake Placid he won all five gold speed skating medals (500m, 1,000m, 1,500m, 5,000m and 10,000m). A medical student, he trained in short, intensive bursts, and after becoming a professional cycle racer in 1981, won the US professional cycling championships in 1985.

Heidenstam, (Karl Gustav) Verner von 1859–1940
Swedish writer and Nobel Prize winner
Born in Olshammar, he lived in southern Europe and the Middle East (1876–87). He published his impressions in a volume of poetry, *Vallfart och Vandringsår* (1888, 'Pilgrimage and Years of Wandering') which, together with his programmatic work, *Renässans*, inspired a literary renaissance in Sweden and established him as the leader of the new Romantic movement of the 1890s. His other volumes of poetry included *Endymion* (1889), the epic *Hans Alienus* (1892), *Dikter* (1895, 'Poems') and *Ett folk* (1897–98, 'One People'). Later he turned to historical fiction, as in *Karolinerna* (1897–98, 'The Carlists') and *Folkungaträdet* (1905–07, 'The Tree of the Folkungs'). He was once a friend of **Strindberg**, but they later became bitter rivals. He was awarded the 1916 Nobel Prize for literature. 📖 H Kamras, *Den unge Heidenstam* (1942)

Heifetz, Jascha 1901–87
US violinist
Born in Vilna, Lithuania, he began studying at the St Petersburg Conservatory in 1910, and toured Russia, Germany, and Scandinavia at the age of 12. After the Russian Revolution he settled in the USA and took US citizenship (1925). **William Walton**'s Violin Concerto is among other works commissioned by him from leading composers.

Heijn or Heyn, Piet 1578–1629
Dutch naval commander
Born in Delfshaven, he was a galley-slave of the Spanish and a merchant captain. In 1623 he became vice-admiral under the Dutch East India Company, and in 1624 he defeated the Spaniards near San Salvador, Brazil, and again in 1626 off Bahia, returning with an immense booty. In 1626 he captured the Spanish silver flotilla,

Hegel, Georg Wilhelm Friedrich 1770–1831
German philosopher

Hegel was born in Stuttgart, the last and perhaps the most important of the great German idealist philosophers in the line from **Kant**, **Fichte** and **Schelling**. He studied theology at Tübingen, and taught at Berne (1793), Frankfurt am Main (1796) and Jena (1801), but his academic career was interrupted in 1806 by the closure of the university after **Napoleon I**'s victory at Jena. When headmaster of the gymnasium at Nuremberg (1808–16), he published in 1807 his first great work *Phänomenologie des Geistes* ('The Phenomenology of Mind'), which describes how the human mind has progressed from mere consciousness through self-consciousness, reason, spirit and religion to absolute knowledge.

This work was followed by *Wissenschaft der Logik* (2 vols, 1812 and 1816, 'Science of Logic'), in which he set out his famous dialectic, a triadic process whereby thesis generates antithesis and both are superseded by a higher synthesis which incorporates what is rational in them and rejects the irrational. His work gained him the chair at Heidelberg in 1816, and he now resumed his university career and produced in 1817 a compendium of his entire system entitled *Encyclopädie der philosophischen Wissenschaften in Grundrisse* ('Encyclopedia of the Philosophical Sciences, Comprising Logic, Philosophy of Nature and of Mind').

In 1818 he succeeded **Fichte** as professor in Berlin and remained there until his death from cholera in 1831. His later works include the *Grundlinien der Philosophie des Rechts* (1821, 'The Philosophy of Right'), which contains his political philosophy, and his important lectures on the history of philosophy, art and the philosophy of history. Hegel was a system-builder of the most ambitious and thorough kind, and though his philosophy is difficult and obscure it has been a great influence on later philosophies, including Marxism, Positivism, and Existentialism.

📖 R C Solomon, *From Hegel to Existentialism* (1987); Peter Singer, *Hegel* (1983); Raymond Plant, *Hegel* (1973); Walter A Kaufmann, *Hegel: Reinterpretation, Texts and Commentary* (1965).

'In England, even the poorest of people believe that they have rights; that is very different from what satisfies the poor in other lands.' From *The Philosophy of Right* (1821).

---

valued at 12 million guilders, and was made Admiral of Holland in 1629. He died in a sea-fight against the privateers of Dunkirk.

Heilbron, Dame Rose 1914–
English judge

Educated at Liverpool University, she won a scholarship to Gray's Inn in 1936. Called to the Bar in 1939, she progressed quickly to become a QC in 1949, and Recorder of Burnley, the UK's first woman Recorder, from 1956 until 1974, when she was appointed a judge of the High Court in the Family Division. She also chaired the Home Secretary's Advisory Group on Rape in 1975, and was presiding judge of the Northern Circuit (1979–82). She retired from the High Court in 1988. Her daughter Hilary (1949–) is also a barrister.

Hein, Piet, pseudonym Kumbel 1905–96
Danish poet, designer and inventor

He was born in Delfshaven. His poems include several collections of aphoristic *Gruk* (10 vols, 1940–49, 'Grooks'). He defined the 'super-ellipse' (a special curve) and used it for architectural and design purposes, and also devised the 3D Soma Cube. From 1969 to 1976 he lived in Great Britain. His pseudonym is an Old Norse word for a gravestone. 📖 *Kumbelslyre* (1950)

Heine, (Christian Johann) Heinrich 1797–1856
German poet and essayist

Born of Jewish parents in Düsseldorf, he studied banking in Frankfurt and law in Bonn, Berlin and Göttingen. In Berlin in 1821 he published *Gedichte* ('Poems'), which was an immediate success, followed by *Lyrisches Intermezzo* (1823, 'Lyrical Intermezzo'), the first and second volumes of the prose *Reisebilder* (1826–27, 'Pictures of Travel') and the well-known *Das Buch der Lieder* (1827, revised 1844, Eng trans *Book of Songs*, 1856). In 1825 he became a Christian to secure the rights of German citizenship, but because of his revolutionary opinions, he could not be employed in Germany. He went into voluntary exile in Paris after the 1830 revolution. Having written two more volumes of *Reisebilder* (1830–31, all four vols Eng trans *Pictures of Travel*, 1855), he turned to politics, becoming leader of the cosmopolitan democratic movement. He wanted to make the French and the Germans acquainted with one another's intellectual and artistic achievements, and produced many works about both cultures, such as *Französische Zustände* (1833, Eng trans *French Affairs*, 1889), first printed in the *Allgemeine Zeitung*; *De l'Allemagne* (1835), and the French version of *Die Romantische Schule* (1836, Eng trans *The Romantic School*, 1882). His attack on **Ludwig Börne**, *Ludwig Börne: Eine Denkschrift* (1840, Eng trans *Ludwig Börne: Portrait of a Revolutionist*, 1881) resulted in a duel. From 1848, while confined to bed by spinal paralysis, his publications included *Neue Gedichte* (1844, revised 1851, Eng trans *New Poems*, 1910) and three volumes of *Vermischte Schriften* (1854, 'Various Writings'). Many of his poems were set to music, most notably by **Franz Schubert** and **Robert Schumann**. 📖 H Spencer, *Heinrich Heine* (1982)

Heinemann, Gustav 1899–1976
German statesman

Born in Schwelm, in the Ruhr district, and educated at Marburg and Münster, he practised as an advocate from 1926 and lectured on law at Cologne (1933–39). After World War II he was a founder of the Christian Democratic Union (CDU), and was Minister of the Interior in **Adenauer**'s government (1949–50), resigning over a fundamental difference over defence policy. A pacifist, he opposed Germany's rearmament. He formed his own neutralist party, but later joined the Social Democratic Party (SPD), was elected to the Bundestag (1957) and was Minister of Justice in **Kiesinger**'s 'Grand Coalition' government from 1966. In 1969 he was elected President but resigned in 1974.

Heinemann, William 1863–1920
English publisher

Born in Surbiton, London, he studied music in England and Germany, but turned to publishing instead. He founded his publishing house in London in 1890 and established its reputation with the works of **Robert Louis Stevenson**, **Rudyard Kipling**, **H G Wells**, **John Galsworthy**, **Somerset Maugham**, **J B Priestley**, and others.

Heinkel, Ernst Heinrich 1888–1958
German aircraft engineer

Born in Grunbach, he was chief designer of the Albatros Aircraft Company in Berlin before World War I. He founded the Heinkel Flugzeugwerke at Warnemünde in 1922, making at first seaplanes, and later bombers and fighters which achieved fame in World War II. He built the first jet plane, the HE-178, in 1939, and also the first rocket powered aircraft, the HE-176.

Heinse, (Johann) Wilhelm 1746–1803
German writer and poet

He was born in Thuringia, and studied law at Erfurt University. His romantic verse was admired by **Goethe**, although its overt sensuality and lasciviousness shocked him. He wrote several novels in a similarly unrestrained vein, including *Ardinghello und die glückseligin Inseln* (1787, 'Ardinghell and the Blessed Islands') and the partly autobiographical *Hildegard von Hohenthal* (1795–96, 'Hildegard of Hohenthal'). ▢ R Terras, *Wilhelm Heinses Ästetik* (1972)

Heinz, H(enry) J(ohn) 1844–1919
US food manufacturer and packer

He was born of German parents in Pittsburgh, Pennsylvania. In 1876 he became co-founder, with his brother and cousin, of F & J Heinz, a firm producing pickles and other prepared foods. The business was reorganized as the H J Heinz Company in 1888, and he was its president from 1905 to 1919. He invented the advertising slogan '57 Varieties' in 1896, which was used until 1969, promoted the pure food movement in the USA, and was a pioneer in staff welfare work. ▢ Robert C Alberts, *The Good Provider: H J Heinz and His 57 Varieties* (1973)

Heinze, Sir Bernard Thomas 1894–1982
Australian conductor and teacher

Born in Shepparton, Victoria, he was educated at Melbourne University, the Royal College of Music, London, and, after World War I, in Paris and Berlin. He was appointed Ormond Professor of Music at Melbourne University in 1925, a post which he held until 1956 when he became director of the New South Wales Conservatorium of Music. From 1933 to 1956 he was conductor of the Victorian Symphony Orchestra, and recorded with the Melbourne and Sydney orchestras. He pioneered the introduction of good music to schools from 1924 with his 'Young People's Concerts', which he continued with the Australian Broadcasting Corporation (ABC) as its music adviser from 1932. With the ABC, he was instrumental in founding symphony orchestras in each Australian state.

Heisenberg, Werner Karl 1901–76
German theoretical physicist and Nobel Prize winner

Born in Würzburg, Bavaria, he was educated at the universities of Munich and Göttingen, before becoming Professor of Physics at Leipzig University (1927–41). He then became professor at Berlin University and director of the Kaiser Wilhelm Institute (1941–45). From 1945 to 1958 he was director of the **Max Planck** Institute in Göttingen, which later moved to Munich. In 1925 he reinterpreted classical mechanics with a matrix-based quantum mechanics where phenomena must be describable both in terms of wave theory and quanta. For this theory and its applications he was awarded the Nobel Prize for physics in 1932. In his revolutionary principle of indeterminacy or uncertainty principle (1927), he showed that there is a fundamental limit to the accuracy to which certain pairs of variables (such as position and momentum) can be determined. A consequence of the wave description of matter, the principle may be interpreted as a result of disturbance to a system due to the act of measuring it. In 1958, he and **Wolfgang Pauli** announced the formulation of a unified field theory, which if established would remove the indeterminacy principle and reinstate **Albert Einstein**. ▢ David C Cassidy, *Uncertainty: The Life and Science of Werner Heisenberg* (1992)

Heiss, Carol, *married name* Carol Heiss-Jenkins 1940–
US ice-skater

Born in New York City, she took up figure-skating and in 1956 became the youngest woman to skate for the USA, winning a silver medal at the Olympics. She won her first world title at the 1957 world championships. Between then and 1960 she won four straight US national ladies singles titles, two North American crowns and four consecutive world titles. She won a gold medal at the 1960 Olympics and retired from amateur competition that year, turning to sports teaching, coaching and media work.

Hekmatyar, Gulbuddin 1949–
Afghan guerrilla leader

Formerly an engineer, in the 1970s he opposed the Republican government of General Mohammad Daud Khan, and rose to prominence during the 1980s in the fight to oust the Soviet-installed Communist regime in Afghanistan. As leader of one of the two factions of the Hizb-i Islami (Islamic Party), he was seen as the most intransigently fundamentalist, refusing to join an interim 'national unity' government with Afghan Communists as the USSR began to wind down its military commitment. He was injured in a car bomb attack on his group's headquarters in Peshawar in 1987, and in 1988 briefly served as President of the seven-party Mujahadeen alliance. He became Prime Minister of Afghanistan in 1993.

Held, Al 1928–
US painter

Born in Brooklyn, New York City, he studied at the Art Students League in New York City (1948–49) and then in Paris (1950–52). He returned to New York and during the 1950s painted in the Abstract Expressionist manner. From 1960 he adopted a more geometric style, using acrylic paints to render brightly-coloured, 'hard-edge' forms thrusting outwards from deep perspectival space, as in *Echo* (1966, New York). From 1967 he painted complex cube-like structures with heavy impasto worked up into low relief. In the mid-1970s he became interested in space travel, which is reflected in work such as *Mercury Zone II* (1975). By the 1980s he was exploring optical illusions in art (Op Art).

Helena, St c.255–330AD
Roman empress

She was the wife of the Emperor **Constantius Chlorus** and mother of **Constantine I**, the Great. Traditionally she came from Bithynia, the daughter of an innkeeper. For political reasons Constantius divorced her (292), but when Constantine was declared emperor by his army in York in 306, he made her dowager empress. In 312, when toleration was extended to Christianity, she was baptized. According to tradition, she visited Jerusalem (326), discovered Christ's cross, and founded the basilicas on the Mount of Olives and at Bethlehem. Her feast day is 18 August (21 May in the East).

Heliodorus fl.3rd and 4th century
Greek writer and Sophist

He was born in Emesa, Syria. One of the earliest Greek novelists, he was the author of *Aethiopica*, which narrates in poetic prose, at times with almost epic beauty and simplicity, the loves of Theagenes and Chariclea.

Heliogabalus or Elagabalus, *divine name of* Caesar Marcus Aurelius Antonius Augustus, *originally* Varius Avitus Bassianus AD204–22
Roman emperor

Born in Emesa, Syria, he was appointed High Priest of the Syro-Phoenician sun god Elagabal, and assumed the name of that deity. In AD218 he was proclaimed emperor by the army and defeated his rival Macrinus on the borders of Syria and Phoenicia. His brief reign was marked by extravagant homosexual orgies and intolerant promotion of the god Elagabal (Baal). He was murdered by the praetorians in a palace revolution.

Heller, Joseph 1923–
US novelist

Born in Brooklyn, New York City, he served in the US army air force in World War II and drew on the experience for his black comedy, *Catch 22* (1961), which is based on the simple premise that men on dangerous missions must be considered insane, and may therefore ask to be excused from duty, but by making the request they prove that they are sane and fit to fly. After selling slowly for some years it became an international bestseller and a byword for war's absurdity. Heller returned to the theme with a play, *We Bombed in New Haven* (1968). Later books—*Something Happened* (1974), *Good as Gold* (1979), *God Knows* (1984), a fictional monologue by the biblical King David, and *Picture This* (1988)—tended to receive churlish notices but are no less satiric, and the first is an Existentialist masterpiece. During the later period his output was hampered by a neurological ailment, described in his autobiographical account *No Laughing Matter* (with Speed Vogel, 1986). He published a sequel to *Catch 22*, entitled *Closing Time*, in 1994.

Hellman, Lillian Florence 1907–84
US playwright

Born into a Jewish family in New Orleans, she was educated at New York and Columbia universities, then worked for the New York *Herald Tribune* as a reviewer (1925–28) and for MGM in Hollywood as reader of plays (1927–32). She lived for many years with the detective writer **Dashiell Hammett**, who encouraged her writing. Her first stage success, *The Children's Hour* (1934), ran on Broadway for 86 weeks. It was followed by *Days to Come* (1936), and *The Little Foxes* (1939). During World War II she wrote the anti-fascist plays *Watch on the Rhine* (1941, winner of the Critics Circle award) and *The Searching Wind* (1944). When she came before the House Un-American Activities Committee in 1952 during the **Joseph McCarthy** era, she coined the famous phrase 'I can't cut my conscience to fit this year's fashions'. This period was described in her controversial memoir *Scoundrel Time* (1976). Her other plays include *The Autumn Garden* (1951) and *Toys in the Attic* (1960). Among her autobiographical works are *An Unfinished Woman* (1969) and *Pentimento* (1973). A left-wing activist, and sensitive to social injustice and personal suffering, she was one of the most persuasive playwrights in the modern US theatre. ⊞ *An Unfinished Woman* (1969); *Pentimento* (1973); *Scoundrel Time* (1976)

Hellyer, Arthur George Lee 1902–93
English horticulturalist, writer and journalist

Born in London, he suffered from tuberculosis. His horticultural career began after he was sent for a period of convalescence to a tomato farm in Jersey. He became assistant editor of *Amateur Gardening* in 1927, becoming editor 19 years later and holding that post for 21 years. During that time he wrote 10 books, including *Amateur Gardening Pocket Guide* (1941) and *Popular Encyclopedia of Flowering Plants* (1957). He was awarded the Dean Hole Medal for his contributions to horticulture and given the Victoria Medal of Honour in Horticulture by the Royal Horticultural Society.

Helmholtz, Hermann von 1821–94
German physiologist and physicist

Born in Potsdam, Brandenburg, he was successively Professor of Physiology at the universities of Königsberg (1849), Bonn (1855), and Heidelberg (1858). In 1871 he became Professor of Physics in Berlin. He was equally distinguished in physiology, mathematics, and experimental and mathematical physics. His physiological works are principally connected with the eye, the ear, and the nervous system, with his work on vision regarded as fundamental to modern visual science. In 1850 he invented an ophthalmoscope independently of **Charles Babbage**. He is also important for his analysis of the spectrum, his explanation of vowel sounds, his papers on the conservation of energy with reference to muscular action, his paper on *Conservation of Energy* (1847), his two memoirs in Crelle's *Journal*, on vortex motion in fluids, and on the vibrations of air in open pipes, and for researches into the development of electric current within a galvanic battery. He was elected a Foreign Member of the Royal Society and in 1873 was awarded the Society's Copley Medal. ⊞ Leo Koenigsberger, *Hermann Von Helmholtz* (1906)

Helmont, Johannes Baptista van 1579–1644
Flemish chemist, physiologist and physician

Born in Brussels, he studied philosophy and theology at the University of Louvain, subsequently turning to science and medicine. He travelled and studied widely, and received an MD in 1609. Thereafter he lived a secluded life in his estate at Vilvorde, near Brussels, and during this period did most of his scientific work. Little of this was published in his lifetime, probably due to opposition from the Catholic Church. His collected works were published by his son in 1648 under the title *Ortus Medicinae vel Opera et Opuscula Omnia*. Van Helmont occupies a position on the border of the old and the new learning, bridging the gap between alchemy and chemistry. He accepted traditional beliefs in alchemy and in the intervention of supernatural agencies, and he developed a two 'element' theory of matter (water and air). In a more modern approach, he was the first to take the melting point of ice and the boiling point of water as standards for temperature. He also obtained much empirical knowledge of chemistry, medicine, and both human and plant physiology. Notably he distinguished the existence of different gases (a word he coined from the Greek for 'chaos') and he emphasized the importance of the balance in chemical work.

Helms, Jesse 1921–
US politician

Born in Monroe, North Carolina, he joined the US navy in World War II and later became a radio broadcasting executive, whose ultra-conservative radio editorials in the 1960s drew fans from the right-wing backlash and launched his political career. He has served in the US Senate as a Republican from North Carolina since 1973 and is known for his dogged advocacy of school prayer and the death penalty, and for his vehement attacks on the National Endowment for the Arts. He chaired the Senate agriculture committee from 1981 to 1986, and when his party gained a majority in Congress in 1994, he became chairman of the powerful Senate Committee on Foreign Relations.

Helms, Richard McGarrah 1913–
US intelligence officer

Born in Pennsylvania, he was educated in Switzerland and at Williams College, and was a journalist before joining the US navy in 1942. After World War II he was inducted into the newly-formed Central Intelligence Agency (CIA) and rose to become the organization's director in 1966. He was dismissed by President **Nixon** in 1973 and appointed ambassador to Iran (1973–76). In 1977 he was convicted of lying before a congressional committee, when he argued that his oath as head of the intelligence service required him to keep secrets from the public. In 1993 he was awarded the National Security Medal.

Héloïse c.1098–1164
French abbess
She was the niece of canon Fulbert of Notre Dame, who arranged for her to be educated by the theologian Peter Abelard. Héloïse and Abelard fell in love but had to flee to Brittany when Fulbert discovered their affair. Secretly married, they had a son, but Héloïse's family were angered at this. She sought safety at the convent at Argenteuil but Abelard was attacked one night and castrated. Filled with shame, he became a monk at St Denis and persuaded his wife to take the veil at Argenteuil. Later he gave her the Benedictine convent, the Paraclete, that he had founded and she became abbess there, despite her self-confessed devotion to Abelard rather than God. Abelard's account of their tragic story, *Letters to a Friend*, and their famous correspondence form the basis for a plethora of literature on the subject.

Helpmann, Sir Robert Murray 1909–86
Australian dancer, actor and choreographer
Born in Mount Gambier, South Australia, he was dancing professionally in Adelaide at the age of 18, studied with Anna Pavlova's touring company (1929) and moved to Great Britain to study under Ninette de Valois (1931). He was the first dancer of the newly founded Sadler's Wells Ballet (1933–50) and became known for his dramatic roles in de Valois's works. A master of mime, he created the role of Master of Tregennis in the *Haunted Ballroom* (1934). His choreographic work includes *Hamlet* (1942), *Miracle in the Gorbals* (1944), a modern parable set in Glasgow, and *Yugen* (1965), created in Australia. His acting roles were mainly in Shakespeare and George Bernard Shaw. He also danced in the ballet films *The Red Shoes* (1948) and *The Tales of Hoffman* (1950). He was joint artistic director of the Australian Ballet (1965–76) and in 1983 worked in all three of the Sydney Opera House auditoria simultaneously. ⬜ Elizabeth Salter, *Helpmann* (1988)

Helst, Bartholomaeus van der 1611–70
Dutch painter
Born in Haarlem, he was joint founder in 1653 of the painters' guild of St Luke in Amsterdam, where he flourished as a portrait painter in the manner of Frans Hals. His best-known picture is the group portrait in celebration of the Peace of Munster, in the Rijksmuseum.

Helvétius, Claude-Adrien 1715–71
French philosopher
Born of Swiss parents in Paris, he trained for a financial career and was appointed to the lucrative office of Farmer-General (1738). He subsequently became chamberlain to the queen's household where he met philosophers such as Diderot and Jean d'Alembert with whom he later collaborated on the *Encyclopédie*. In 1751 he retired to the family estate at Voré where he spent the rest of his life in philosophy, philanthropic work and educating his family. His controversial work *De l'esprit* (1758,'On the Mind'), advanced the view that sensation is the source of all intellectual activity and that self-interest is the motive force of all human action. The book was denounced by the Sorbonne in Paris, and condemned by parliament to be publicly burnt. As a result it was widely read, was translated into all the main European languages, and together with his posthumous *De l'homme* (1772) greatly influenced Jeremy Bentham and the British Utilitarians.

Hemans, Felicia Dorothea, *née* Browne
1793–1835
English poet
Born in Liverpool, she published three volumes of poems between 1808 and 1812, and when her husband deserted her in 1818, she began writing for a living. She produced a large number of books of verse of all kinds—love lyrics, classical, mythological, sentimental—such as *The Siege of Valencia* (1823) and *Records of Women* (1828). She is perhaps best remembered for the poem *Casabianca*, better known as 'The boy stood on the burning deck', and for 'The stately homes of England'. ⬜ H F Chorley, *Memories of Mrs Hemans* (1837)

Hemerken, Thomas See **Kempis, Thomas à**

Hemessen, Catharina van c.1528–c.1587
Flemish painter
She was born in Antwerp, Flanders, the daughter of the artist Jan Sanders van Hemessen (c.1500–c.1575), with whom she studied, collaborating on some of his best-known works. She painted many portraits of well-to-do men and women, examples of which now hang in the Rijksmuseum, Amsterdam, and the National Gallery, London. Her famous self portrait *I, Caterina de Hemessen, painted myself in 1548*, now hangs in Basle Museum. She enjoyed the patronage of Queen Mary of Hungary, Regent of the Low Countries, and when Mary resigned her regency in 1556, Catharina was invited to accompany her to Spain. She returned to Antwerp after Mary's death.

Hemingway, Ernest Millar See panel p865

Hench, Philip Showalter 1896–1965
US physician and Nobel Prize winner
He was born in Pittsburgh, Pennsylvania, and took his medical degree there. Head of the department of rheumatics at the Mayo Clinic in Rochester from 1926, and Professor of Medicine at Minnesota University from 1947, he discovered cortisone, widely hailed as a 'miracle drug', and shared with Edward Kendall and Tadeus Reichstein the 1950 Nobel Prize for physiology or medicine for their work on the biology and therapeutic uses of the supra-renal hormones. Several patients severely crippled by arthritis were demonstrated with much greater freedom of movement and suffering much less pain. Unfortunately, the early improvement often did not last and a variety of side-effects from high doses of steroids began to manifest themselves. The early reports of dramatic 'cures' of severe rheumatoid arthritis were thus premature, but 'steroids' such as cortisone have played an important part in modern treatments.

Henderson, Alexander c.1583–1646
Scottish Covenanter
Born in Creich, Fife, he was educated at St Andrews. In 1610, as an Episcopalian, he was made Professor of Rhetoric and Philosophy there, and in 1611 or 1612 was appointed to the parish of Leuchars. He was one of the authors of the National Covenant, and was Moderator of the General Assembly at Glasgow in 1638 which restored all its liberties to the Kirk of Scotland. Moderator again in 1641 and in 1643, he drafted the Solemn League and Covenant, and was a commissioner for three years to the Westminster Assembly. He was the author of *Bishop's Doom* (1638).

Henderson, Arthur 1863–1935
Scottish Labour politician and Nobel Prize winner
Born in Glasgow, he was brought up in Newcastle upon Tyne, where he worked as an iron-moulder and became a lay preacher. Several times chairman of the Labour Party (1908–10, 1914–17, 1931–32), he was elected an MP in 1903, served in the coalition Cabinets (1915–17), and became Home Secretary (1924) and Foreign Secretary (1929–31) in the first Labour governments. A crusader for disarmament, he was president of the World Disarmament Conference (1932), won the 1934 Nobel Peace Prize, and also helped to establish the League of Nations. ⬜ Mary Agnes Hamilton, *Arthur Henderson* (1938)

Henderson, Fletcher 1897–1952
US pianist, arranger and bandleader

Hemingway, Ernest Millar 1899–1961
US writer of novels and short stories, and Nobel Prize winner

Hemingway was born in Oak Park, a respectable suburb of Chicago. His father was a doctor and a keen sportsman who passed on his enthusiasm to his son, though he also inherited a melancholic, self-destructive personality. He was educated at grammar school and the palatial Oak Park and River Forest Township High School, where he distinguished himself only in English. His mother wanted him to become a violinist but, modelling himself on **Ring Lardner**, he was determined to become a journalist and a writer and got a job on the *Kansas City Star* as a cub reporter; there he was paid $15 a week and was given a copy of the style book which told him to write the simple declarative sentences that were to be characterstic of the mature Hemingway.

In April 1918 he resigned and joined the Red Cross, to be hurled into World War I as an ambulance driver on the Italian front, where he was badly wounded. Returning to the USA he began to write features for the Toronto *Star Weekly* in 1919 and married Hadley Richardson, the first of four wives, in 1921. That same year he went to Europe as a roving correspondent and covered several large conferences. In Paris he moved easily and conspicuously among other émigré artists and came into contact with **Gertrude Stein**, **Ezra Pound**, **James Joyce** and **F Scott Fitzgerald**. *A Moveable Feast* (1964) records this time, reliving the struggle he and his new wife had to make ends meet. *Three Stories and Ten Poems* was given a limited circulation in Paris in 1923, and in 1924 he published *In Our Time*, which met with critical approval in America a year later. *The Sun Also Rises* (1926) and a volume of short stories, *Men Without Women* (1927), confirmed his reputation, and in

1928, divorced from Hadley and re-married to Pauline Pfeiffer, he moved to Key West, Florida.

Disentangling fact from myth in the years that followed is not easy. Drinking, brawling, posturing, big-game hunting, deep-sea fishing and bull-fighting all competed with writing. Nevertheless the body of Hemingway's work is impressive, if uneven. In 1929 he published *A Farewell to Arms*, and in 1932 the bull-fighting classic, *Death in the Afternoon*. *Green Hills in Africa* (1935) tells of tension-filled big-game hunts. Perhaps his most popular book is *For Whom the Bell Tolls*, published in 1940, about the Civil War in Spain to which he went as a journalist. He continued to work as a war correspondent during World War II, and in 1945 he settled in Cuba, where he wrote *Across the River and Into the Trees* (1950) and *The Old Man and the Sea* (1952). He won the Pulitzer Prize in 1953 and the Nobel Prize for literature in 1954. He cheated death more than once and had the strange pleasure of reading his own obituary twice; however he suffered from depression and shot himself in the mouth at his home in Ketchum, Idaho.

📖 H S Villard and J Nagel, *Hemingway in Love and War* (1989); R E Hardy and J G Cull, *Hemingway: A Psychological Portrait* (2nd edn 1987); M Reynolds, *The Young Hemingway* (1986); S Donaldson, *By Force of Will* (1977); C Baker, *Ernest Hemingway: A Life Story* (1969).

'I had learned already never to empty the well of my writing, but always to stop when there was still something there in the deep part of the well, and let it refill at night from the springs that fed it.' Hemingway on himself in *A Moveable Feast* (1964).

Born in Cuthbert, Georgia, he graduated in chemistry from the all-black Atlanta University, but on moving to New York in 1920 to continue his studies, he became diverted into a musical career, starting as house pianist for publishing and recording companies. In 1924 he put together a big band for what was supposed to be a temporary engagement, but stayed at the head of an orchestra until the mid-1930s, attracting the finest instrumentalists and arrangers of the time. His own orchestrations, and those of **Don Redman**, set the standard for the swing era. However he lacked business acumen, lost the initiative and remained in relative obscurity. His performing career was cut short by a stroke in 1950.

Henderson, Hamish 1919–
Scottish folklorist, composer and poet

He was born in Blairgowrie, Perthshire. One of his early poetic works, 'Ninth Elegy for the Dead in Cyrenaica' (1948), won him the **Somerset Maugham** award, but his literary output has been overshadowed by his impressive contributions to folk-song. Through his researches for the School of Scottish Studies, he was largely responsible for bringing to the fore great but little known traditional singers, like **Jeannie Robertson**, thereby ensuring the survival of the Scots ballad tradition. Many of his own compositions—notably 'Freedom Come All Ye', 'Farewell to Sicily' and 'The John Maclean March'—have become part of the traditional singer's repertoire. A selection of his writings, *Alias MacAlias* was published in 1992 followed by a collection of his letters in 1996 entitled *The Armstrong Nose*. 📖 P Orr (ed), *The Poet Speaks* (1966)

Henderson, Joe (Joseph) 1937–
US jazz saxophonist, bandleader and composer

Born in Lima, Ohio, he studied music before going into the army (1960–62), but established his reputation as a sideman, notably with Horace Silver (1964–66) and

Herbie Hancock (1969–70). He recorded under his own name for Blue Note from 1963, and appeared on many other albums for the label. He played briefly with the rock group Blood, Sweat and Tears, and made a number of fusion-influenced recordings for Milestone. He concentrated on teaching for a time, but his acclaimed *State of the Tenor* (1985) effected a revival of interest in his work, and he became a highly creative force in the 1990s making award-winning records for the jazz label Verve.

Henderson, Mary See **Bridie, James**

Henderson, Thomas 1798–1844
Scottish astronomer

Born in Dundee, he was intended for a law career, but devoted his leisure hours to astronomical calculations. In 1831 he was appointed director of the Royal Observatory at the Cape of Good Hope. In 1832 he succeeded in determining the parallax of the star Alpha Centauri. In 1834 he became Professor of Practical Astronomy at the University of Edinburgh and the first Astronomer Royal for Scotland. He was an indefatigable observer who in his 10 years in Edinburgh measured, with the help of only one assistant, no fewer than 60,000 positions of planets and stars.

Hendrix, Jimi (James Marshall) 1942–70
US black rock guitarist and singer

One of rock music's most innovative and influential instrumentalists, he was born into a poor black neighbourhood of Seattle, Washington, and taught himself to play the guitar. After being invalided out of the army in 1962 he moved to Nashville and played in numerous groups, including a period with **Little Richard**'s road band. However it was not until he moved to Great Britain in 1966 and formed the Jimi Hendrix Experience (with Noel Redding and Mitch Mitchell) that his true potential was realized. The band's first single, 'Hey Joe', was an immediate British success and his adventurous first album, *Are You Experienced?*, was an unexpected international success which paved the way for other psychedelic and experimental rock acts. The two subsequent albums—*Axis: Bold As Love* and *Electric Ladyland*—helped make 1968 his most commercially successful year. However the pressures of success also helped to destroy him both professionally and personally. The Jimi Hendrix Experience broke up in 1969 and a subsequent group, The Band Of Gypsies, disbanded after recording only one album. He died after mixing barbiturates and alcohol. 📖 C Welch, *Hendrix* (1972)

Hendry, Stephen 1969–
Scottish snooker player

Born in Edinburgh, he started playing at the age of 12, and turned professional at 16. He showed his exceptional talent by becoming the youngest-ever winner of a professional title with his 1987 victory in the Rothmans Grand Prix. In 1989 he won a host of titles, among them the British Open and, with Mike Hallett, the Fosters World Doubles. The following year he became the youngest winner of the Embassy world championship, which he won again five times (1992–96); he lost the title to Ken Doherty in 1997. Self-deprecating and apparently nerveless, he has improved with maturity, and now has a virtually flawless all-round game.

Hengist d.488AD and Horsa d.455AD
Semi-legendary Jutish brothers

According to Nennius and the *Anglo-Saxon Chronicle*, they led the first Germanic invaders to Britain. They landed from Jutland at the Isle of Thanet in AD449 to help King Vortigern against the Picts, and were rewarded with the gift of Thanet. Soon after they turned against Vortigern, but were defeated at Aylesford, where Horsa was killed. Hengist, however, is said to have conquered Kent. Both names mean 'horse'.

Heng Samrin 1934–
Cambodian (Kampuchean) politician

He served as a political commissar and commander in Pol Pot's Khmer Rouge (1976–78) but, alienated by his brutal tactics, led an abortive coup against him, then fled to Vietnam, where he established the Kampuchean People's Revolutionary Party (KPRP) and became head of the new Vietnamese-installed government. He has remained in effective control of Cambodia since 1979 but his influence began to wane after Vietnam's withdrawal of its troops from Cambodia in 1979, with the country's more accommodating prime minister, Hun Sen, growing in stature. In 1991 Heng Samrin stepped down in favour of Prince Sihanouk pending elections supervised by the UN, and a ceasefire was declared.

Henie, Sonja 1912–69
US ice-skater

She was born in Oslo, Norway. After winning the gold medal in figure-skating at the Olympics of 1928, 1932 and 1936, she turned professional and starred in touring ice-shows, and later went to Hollywood where she made several films. She became a US citizen in 1941. She died on an aeroplane ambulance while flying to Oslo.

Henle, Friedrich Gustav Jakob 1809–85
German anatomist

Born in Fürth, Bavaria, he studied in Bonn and Berlin under Johannes Müller and held professorships at Zurich, Heidelberg and Göttingen. He discovered the tubules in the kidney which are named after him, and wrote treatises on systematic anatomy. His influence in histology is comparable to that of Andreas Vesalius in anatomy.

Henley, John, *known as* Orator Henley 1692–1756
English clergyman

Born in Melton Mowbray, Leicestershire, he studied at St John's College, Cambridge, and was ordained in 1716. In 1726, he set up an 'oratory', to teach universal knowledge in weekday lectures and primitive Christianity in Sunday sermons, but his addresses were a mixture of ribaldry and solemnity, wit and absurdity. He compiled a grammar of seven languages, *The Complete Linguist* (1719–21), and his *Oratory Transactions* contain a life of himself. He was caricatured by Hogarth, and ridiculed by Alexander Pope in his *Dunciad* (1728).

Henley, W(illiam) E(rnest) 1849–1903
English poet, playwright, critic and editor

Born in Gloucester, he suffered from tuberculosis as a boy, had a leg amputated, and spent nearly two years in Edinburgh Infirmary (1873–75), where he wrote several of the poems in *A Book of Verses* (1888). In Edinburgh he became a close friend of Robert Louis Stevenson, with whom he collaborated on four plays, *Deacon Brodie* (1880), *Beau Austin* (1884), *Admiral Guinea* (1884) and *Macaire* (1885), and whose character of Long John Silver he inspired. His verse was notable for its unusual rhymes and esoteric words, and several other volumes followed, including *The Song of the Sword* (1892), *Collected Poems* (1898), *Hawthorn and Lavender* (1901), and *In Hospital* (1903), which contains his best-known poem, 'Invictus'. A pungent critic, he successfully edited the *Magazine of Art* (1882–86) and the *Scots Observer* (from 1889), which became *The National Observer* in 1891. He was joint compiler of a dictionary of slang (7 vols, 1894–1904). 📖 J Flora, *W E Henley* (1970)

Hennebique, François 1842–1921
French structural engineer

Born in Neuville-Saint-Vaast, he was one of the first to make extensive use of ferro-concrete (as reinforced concrete was then known). He patented his system in 1892. He built the first reinforced concrete bridge at Viggen in Switzerland (1894), the first grain elevator at Roubaix (1895), and the first multi-storey reinforced concrete framed building in Great Britain—Weaver's Mill at Swansea (1898). The popularity of his system was so great that by 1910 over 40,000 structures of various kinds had been completed, one of the most notable being the 15-storey Royal Liver Building in Liverpool (1909).

Henningsen, Charles Frederick 1815–77
Anglo-Swedish mercenary

Born in England, he served with the Carlists in Spain, with the Russians in Circassia, with Lajos Kossuth in Hungary, and with William Walker in Nicaragua. In the USA during the Civil War (1861–65), he commanded a Confederate brigade, and afterwards superintended the manufacture of Minié rifles. He wrote *The White Slave* (1845) and *The Past and Future of Hungary* (1852).

Henri I c.1008–60
King of France

The son of Robert II, he ascended the throne in 1031. He was involved in struggles with Normandy and with Burgundy, which he had unwisely granted to his younger brother, Robert. Several of his conflicts were with William of Normandy (the future William the Conqueror).

Henri II 1519–59
King of France

Born at St Germain-en-Laye, near Paris, he was the son of Francis I. In 1533, as Duke of Orléans, he married Catherine de Médicis, by whom he had seven surviving children, three of whom became kings of France (Francis II, Charles IX and Henri III). He became heir to the throne in 1536 on the death of his brother, the Dauphin Francis, and king in 1547. Dominated by his mistress, Diane de

Poitiers, and by Anne de Montmorency, Constable of France, he introduced reforms to curb extravagance at court and regularize the country's disordered finances. Through the influence of the **Guises** he formed an alliance with Scotland, declared war on England, and captured Boulogne (1550) and Calais (1558). He continued the war against the Holy Roman Emperor, **Charles V**, in alliance with the German Protestant princes, gaining Metz, Toul and Verdun, but his ambitions in Italy and the Low Countries were thwarted when he suffered reverses, including the annhilation of his army at St Quentin (1557), leading to the Treaty of Câteau-Cambrésis (1559). At home he began the persecution of Huguenots that would lead to the Wars of Religion (1562–98). He died of wounds received in a tournament, and was succeeded by his son as Francis II, husband of **Mary, Queen of Scots**. ⌨ Frederic J Baumgartner, *Henry II, King of France, 1547–1559* (1988)

Henri III 1551–89
King of France
Born in Fontainbleau, the third son of **Henri II** and **Catherine de Médicis**, he commanded the royal army as Duke of Anjou during the reign of his brother **Charles IX**, and won victories over the Huguenots at Jarnac and Moncontour (1569). With his mother was responsible for instigating the slaughter of Parisian Huguenots known as the St Bartholomew's Day Massacre (1572). He was elected King of Poland (1573), but had to return to France soon after his coronation in 1574, to ascend the French throne at his brother's death, and was deposed by his Polish subjects (1575). He was intelligent, but extravagant and unstable, and his reign in France was marked throughout by civil war between the Huguenots and Catholics, and between the sons of Catherine de Médicis. His brother François, Duke of Alençon, placed himself at the head of the Huguenots, while Henri aligned himself with the extreme Catholic League headed by Henri, Duke of **Guise**. After the death of François (1584), Henri joined forces with his brother-in-law, the Huguenot Henri of Navarre (the future **Henri IV**), heir presumptive to the throne, but had to capitulate to the Catholic rebels at Nemours in 1585. Caught amid the rivalry between Henri of Guise and Henri of Navarre, he was besieged in Paris (1588) by Henri of Guise (the Day of the Barricades), but managed to escape, and engineered the assassination of Guise (1589), which enraged the Catholic League. In 1589, soon after the death of his mother, he was assassinated by a fanatical priest, and with his death the Valois line of kings ended. ⌨ A Lynn Martin, *Henry III and the Jesuit Politicians* (1973)

Henri IV, *known as* Henri of Navarre 1553–1610
First Bourbon King of France
He was born in Pau, south-west France, the third son of Antoine de **Bourbon** and Jeanne d'Albret, heiress of Henri d'Albret (**Henri II**) of Navarre. Brought up by his mother as a Calvinist, he headed the Protestant forces in the Third Huguenot War (1569–72), but was defeated at the Battle of Jarnac (1569). In 1572 he succeeded his mother to the throne of Navarre as Henri III. After the peace of St Germain in 1572 he married **Margaret of Valois**, sister of **Charles IX** and **Henri III** of France, and was spared in the St Bartholomew Day Massacre (1572) on condition that he professed himself a Catholic. For three years he was virtually a prisoner at the French court, but in 1576 he escaped to Alençon, revoked his conversion, and by the 1580s had established himself as the leader of the French Protestants. The death in 1584 of the king's brother (François, Duke of Alençon) made him heir-presumptive to the French throne. In 1588 Henri, Duke of **Guise** was murdered by Henri III, and when Henri III was himself assassinated in 1589, Henri of Navarre claimed the throne and marched on Paris, which was in the hands of the

Catholic League. He was victorious in the war that followed, and in 1593 formally renounced Protestantism and declared himself a Catholic; he was crowned at Chartres in the following year. With the Edict of Nantes of 1598 guaranteeing the rights of the Huguenot minority, he brought an end to more than 40 years of religious wars in France, and the Treaty of Vervins ended nine years of war with **Philip II** of Spain. A great conciliator, he restored to France strong monarchy and stable government. He built up an efficient centralized bureaucracy, restoring the country's shattered economy, while his leading minister, the Duc de **Sully**, was responsible for drastically reducing the national debt. Although Henry showed favour to the Huguenots, he also patronized the Jesuits, and gave a positive lead to the revival in learning and the arts. In 1599 he divorced Margaret, and in 1600 married his second wife, **Marie de Médicis**; their children included the future Louis XIII and **Henrietta Maria**, queen consort of **Charles I** of Great Britain. In May 1610, with war threatening with Spain and the Empire, Marie was crowned formally to give more authority to her regency during Henri's absence on campaign. Three days before the king was due to leave Paris he was assassinated by a Catholic religious fanatic called François Ravaillac (1578–1610). ⌨ Desmond Seaward, *The First Bourbon: Henry IV, King of France and Navarre* (1971)

Henri of Navarre See **Henri IV**

Henri, Adrian Maurice 1932–
English poet
Born in Birkenhead, Merseyside, he has been saddled throughout his career with the 'Mersey Sound' tag. That was the title given to *Penguin Modern Poets 10* (1967), a very popular paperback compilation of his work (shared with **Roger McGough** and **Brian Patten**), which went through an unprecedented two revisions (1974, 1983), and has continued to sell well. Its success prompted him to try his luck as a performer, with the multi-media Liverpool Scene group (1968–70). His most substantial work, entitled simply *Autobiography* (1971), is searchingly honest and unaffected. Later works include *The Best of Henri* (1975), *From the Loveless Motel* (1980), *Penny Arcade* (1983), *Wish You Were Here* (1990) and *Not Fade Away* (1994). Henri is also a painter, whose canvases have the same immediacy and Pop imagery as his verse. ⌨ J Raban, *The Society of the Poem* (1971)

Henri, Florence 1893–1982
US pianist, artist and photographer
Born in New York City to a French father and a Silesian (Polish) mother, she studied music in Paris (1902), then in Italy and Berlin until 1914. She was a pianist until 1918, but she had studied painting in Berlin (1914) and returned to these studies in 1922–23. She married a Swiss man to facilitate her entry into France, and studied painting at the Académie Moderne in Paris (1925–26). Developing an interest in photography, she opened a photographic studio in Paris (1929), and her work was represented in influential exhibitions such as 'Film und Foto' (1929, Stuttgart). Best known for her explorations of abstract, Cubist and purist ideas, she also taught and published in journals such as *Vogue* and *Art et métiers graphiques*. A major retrospective of her art work was shown at the San Francisco Museum of Modern Art (1990–91).

Henri, Robert 1865–1929
US painter
Born in Cincinnati, Ohio, he first studied at the Pennsylvania Academy, then went to Paris to study at the École des Beaux-Arts (1888). Returning to Philadelphia, he taught at the Women's School of Design (1891–96) and became an ardent advocate of realism in art, establishing, in 1907, a group known as The Eight, in protest at the

conservatism of the National Academy. This was the start of the so-called Ash Can School of US Realists. Several of his students later became famous, including George Bellows, Edward Hopper, and Rockwell Kent. He also wrote a book, *The Art Spirit* (1923), which influenced many younger artists.

Henrietta Anne, Duchesse d'Orleans, *known as* Minette 1644–70
English princess

The youngest daughter of Charles I of Great Britain and Henrietta Maria, and sister of Charles II, she was born in Exeter during the English Civil Wars. Brought up as a Roman Catholic by her mother in France, she married Louis XIV's homosexual brother Philippe, Duc d'Orléans, but was also rumoured to have been the mistress of the French king himself. She played an important part in negotiating the Secret Treaty of Dover (1670) between Charles and Louis. There were rumours that her subsequent death was caused by poison, although it was more probably a case of a ruptured appendix.

Henrietta Maria 1609–69
French princess and Queen of England

Born at the Louvre, Paris, she was the youngest child of Henri IV of France. After his assassination (1610), she was brought up by her mother, Marie de Médicis. She was married in 1625 to Charles I of Great Britain, and after the death of the Duke of Buckingham in 1628 the marriage became a true love match. Her French attendants and Roman Catholic beliefs made her unpopular, especially as she meddled in politics. In 1642, under the threat of impeachment, she fled to Holland and raised funds for the Royalist cause. A year later she returned and met Charles near Edgehill. In 1644 she gave birth to Henrietta Anne at Exeter, but two weeks later she fled again to France, never seeing her husband again. She paid two visits to England after the Restoration (1660–61, 1662–65) but spent her remaining years in France. ⬚ Quentin Bone, *Henrietta Maria* (1972)

Henry (Kings of France) See Henri

Henry I 1068–1135
King of England and Duke of Normandy

The youngest and only English-born son of William the Conqueror, he was supposedly born in Selby, Yorkshire. When war broke out between his brothers, William II, Rufus and Robert Curthose, Henry helped the latter to defend Normandy, yet in the treaty which followed in 1091 he was excluded from the succession. Immediately after William's death, Henry seized the royal treasure, and was elected king by the Witan (1100). He issued a charter restoring the laws of Edward, the Confessor and William I, recalled Anselm, and set about reforming the administration of justice. He strengthened his position by a marriage with Eadgyth (Matilda), daughter of King Malcolm III, Canmore of Scotland and Queen Margaret, who was descended from the old English royal house. Robert had been granted a pension to resign his claim to the English Crown and concentrate his attentions on Normandy, but in 1105–06 Henry made war against his badly-governed duchy. Robert was defeated at Tinchebrai (1106), and was kept a prisoner for life (28 years). To keep Normandy Henry was obliged to wage nearly constant warfare. King Louis VI of France took part with William, Robert's son, but the first war ended in the favourable peace of Gisors (1113), and in 1114 Henry's daughter Matilda was married to the Emperor Henry V of Germany. The second war (1116–20) was marked by the defeat of the French king at Noyon in 1119, and Henry was able to satisfy the pope, who succeeded in bringing about a peace. In 1120 Henry's only legitimate son, William Adelin, was drowned on his way from Normandy to England. In 1126 Matilda, now a widow, returned from Germany. In 1127

Henry nominated her his heir, and in 1128 she was married to Geoffrey Plantagenet, son of the Count of Anjou. However, when Henry died the crown was seized by his sister Adela's son, Stephen of Blois. Henry I was posthumously styled Beauclerc, or the Scholar, in honour of his learning, which was, in fact, limited. He was able and crafty, consistent and passionless in his policy, but often guilty of acts of cold-blooded cruelty. His reign marks a milestone in the development of governmental institutions such as the Exchequer and the itinerant justices.

Henry II 1133–89
King of England

He was born in Le Mans, France, the son of Matilda, Henry I's daughter, and her second husband, Geoffrey Plantagenet, Count of Anjou. He was invested with the duchy of Normandy, his mother's heritage (1150), and became Count of Anjou on the death of his father (1151). His marriage with Eleanor of Aquitaine, the divorced wife of Louis VII, added Poitou and Guienne to his dominions. In January 1153 he landed in England, and in November was declared the successor of Stephen, founding the Angevin or Plantagenet dynasty of English kings, and ruling England as part of a wider Angevin empire. He was crowned in 1154. He repaired the chaos and disorder which had arisen during Stephen's reign, recovered the royal estates and spent much time dealing with problems arising from his Continental possessions. To help him in restricting the authority of the church in England he appointed his Chancellor, Thomas à Becket, as Archbishop of Canterbury, and compelled Becket and the other prelates to agree to the 'Constitutions of Clarendon', but Becket resisted, and the struggle between them ended only with Becket's murder (1170). In 1174 Henry did penance at Becket's tomb, but in many respects he managed to subordinate the Church in civil matters. Meanwhile he organized an expedition to Ireland (1171–72). Pope Adrian IV had given Henry authority over the entire island (1155), and a number of Norman–Welsh knights had gained a footing in the country—among them Richard de Clare, Earl of Pembroke, nicknamed Strongbow. Henry was jealous at the rise of a powerful feudal baronage in Ireland, and during his stay there he broke the power of Strongbow and the other nobles. By 1185 Prince John (the future King John) had been given some responsibility for Ireland, but in 1186 he was driven from the country, and all was left in confusion. The eldest of Henry's sons had died in childhood, and the second, Henry (b.1155), was crowned as his father's associate and successor in 1170. In 1173, encouraged by Queen Eleanor, John and his brother Richard I, Cœur de Lion rebelled—ultimately unsuccessfully—against their father, backed by the kings of France and Scotland. During a second, more limited, rebellion Henry the Younger died (1183), and in 1185 Geoffrey, the next son, was killed in a tournament at Paris. In 1188, while Henry was engaged in a war with Philip II of France, Richard joined the French king, and in 1189 Henry, having lost Le Mans and the chief castles of Maine, agreed a peace recognizing Richard as his sole heir for the Angevin empire, and granting an indemnity to his followers. Soon afterwards Henry died, and was succeeded by Richard. On the whole, Henry was an able and enlightened sovereign, a clear-headed, unprincipled politician, and an able general. His reign was one of great legal and financial reforms. His success can be judged by the fact that he kept intact an empire, stretching from the Scottish border to the Pyrenees, until the very last month of his life. ⬚ W L Warren, *Henry II* (1973)

Henry III 1207–72
King of England

Born in Winchester, the elder son of King John, he became king in 1216. He declared an end to his minority in 1227, and in 1232 he removed his regent, Hubert de Burgh, taking over the administration in 1234. A war with France cost him Poitou, but **Louis IX** allowed him the rest of his Continental possessions and he was granted the kingdom of Sicily in 1254. His arbitrary assertion of his royal rights conflicted with the principle of Magna Carta, and antagonized many of his subjects, so that in 1258 he was forced to agree to the far-reaching reforms of the Provisions of Oxford, transferring his power to a commission of barons. Louis IX supported him against the barons and **Simon de Montfort**, and the Provisions were annulled (1263). De Montfort and his party rebelled and imprisoned the king at Lewes (1264), and forced him to the humiliating agreement called the Mise of Lewes. However within a year Gilbert de Clare, 9th Earl of **Gloucester**, deserted de Montfort, and, with Prince Edward (later **Edward I**), defeated and killed him at Evesham (1265). The Dictum of Kenilworth (1266), though favourable to Henry, urged him to observe the Magna Carta. Organized resistance ended in 1267, and the rest of his reign was stable. He was succeeded by his elder son, Edward I. ☐ F M Powicke, *King Henry III and the Lord Edward* (1947)

Henry IV, *originally* Henry Bolingbroke c.1366–1413
First Lancastrian King of England

The son of **John of Gaunt**, he was surnamed Bolingbroke from his birthplace in Lincolnshire. His father was fourth son of **Edward III**, his mother a daughter of Duke Henry of Lancaster. In 1386 he married the co-heiress to the earldom of Hereford, Mary de Bohun (c.1394). In 1397 he supported **Richard II** against the Duke of Gloucester, and was created Duke of Hereford, but in 1398 he was banished, and in 1399, when his father died, his estates were declared forfeit to Richard. Henry landed at Ravenspur in Yorkshire then induced Richard, deserted and betrayed, to sign a renunciation of his claims. He had himself crowned king (1399), and four months later Richard died, possibly murdered. During Henry's reign rebellion and lawlessness were rife, and frequent descents were made upon the coast by expeditions from France, but his movements were constantly hampered for want of money. Under **Owen Glendower** the Welsh maintained a large degree of independence and although he invaded Scotland in 1400, besieging Edinburgh Castle, he was compelled by famine to retire. In 1402, while the king was engaged against the Welsh, the Scots invaded Northumberland, but they encountered and were defeated by Henry **Percy**, Earl of Northumberland, and his son **Harry Percy** (Hotspur), at Humbleton (or Homildon), where Archibald, 4th Earl of v **Douglas**, was taken prisoner. The Percys shortly after allied with Douglas and Glendower against Henry, but the king met them at Shrewsbury (1403), where they were utterly defeated, Hotspur slain, and Douglas again taken prisoner. In 1406 Prince James of Scotland (afterwards **James VI and I**) was captured on his way to France, and detained and educated in England. The civil wars in France gave Henry an opportunity to send two expeditions (1411–12) there, but in his later years his physical strength waned, and he became a chronic invalid, afflicted with epileptic fits. He chose to be buried in Canterbury, where he had often visited the shrine of **Thomas à Becket**, and his second wife, **Joan of Navarre**, was later buried there with him. ☐ J L Kirby, *Henry IV of England* (1970)

Henry V 1387–1422
King of England

Born in Monmouth, Wales, the eldest of the six children of **Henry IV** by Mary de Bohun, he was created Prince of Wales in 1399. He fought against **Owen Glendower** and the Welsh rebels (1401–08), and became Constable of Dover (1409), and Captain of Calais (1410). He was crowned king in 1413, and began his reign by freeing the young Earl of March, the true heir to the Crown, restoring lands and honours to his son, and arranging for **Richard II's** body to be buried at Westminster. His reign was marked by his attempt to claim the French Crown (from 1414). He apparently believed that he had a valid claim through his great-grandfather, **Edward III**, and he sailed (1415) with a great army, and took Harfleur. At Agincourt (1415) he won against such odds that his victory became known as one of the most notable in history. Two years later he again invaded France and regained Normandy (1418). By the 'perpetual peace' of Troyes (1420) Henry became Regent of France and was recognized as heir to the French throne. He married Charles VI's daughter, **Catherine de Valois**, and took his young queen to England to be crowned (1421), but a month later he was recalled to France by news of the defeat of his brother, Thomas, Duke of Clarence. Henry became ill, and died at Vincennes, leaving his baby son **Henry VI** to succeed him. Vigorous, efficient and autocratic, he was also devout and just, but his religion did not always make him merciful to the enemies he conquered, and he persecuted the Lollards, who had become the first group of English heretics to represent a political threat. ☐ C L Kingsford, *Henry V: The Typical Mediaeval Hero* (2nd edn, 1923)

Henry VI 1421–71
King of England

Born in Windsor, Berkshire, he was the son of **Henry V** and Catherine de Valois, and became king on the death of his father in 1422. During his minority, his uncle, John, Duke of **Bedford**, was regent in France, and another uncle, Humphrey, Duke of **Gloucester**, was Protector of England, with a council appointed by parliament. English power in France declined steadily from 1429, though Henry was crowned king of France in Paris (1431). After Bedford's death (1435), the English were gradually expelled from all France, except Calais (1453). Henry was obsessively pious, and from 1453 experienced bouts of insanity. In 1445 he married the strong-minded **Margaret of Anjou**, who had Gloucester arrested for treason (1447). Five days later he was found dead in his bed, but there is no proof that he was murdered. **Jack Cade** obtained temporary possession of London, but was soon captured and executed (1450). As a descendant of Lionel, Duke of Clarence, **Edward III's** third son, Richard, Duke of **York**, had a better claim to the crown than Henry and in 1454, during one of Henry's mental lapses, York was appointed Protector. On the king's recovery York raised an army to maintain his power, and took Henry prisoner at St Albans (1455). This was the first of many battles between the Houses of York and Lancaster in the Wars of the Roses. A return of Henry's illness made York Protector again (1455–56); and on his recovery Henry attempted to maintain peace between the factions. York was killed at the Battle of Wakefield (1460), but his heir, **Edward IV**, was proclaimed king (1461), and Henry was deposed (1461), imprisoned in the Tower of London, then exiled. Richard Neville, Earl of **Warwick** restored him to the throne (1470), but six months later he was again in Edward's hands. At Tewkesbury (1471) his son, Edward, was killed and his wife, Margaret, who had headed the Lancastrian forces, was taken prisoner. Edward returned to London, and that night Henry was murdered in the Tower of London. Henry, the 'royal saint', founded Eton and King's College, Cambridge. It was probably his inability to govern rather than the advent of bastard feudalism which was responsible for the so-called Wars of the Roses. ☐ Mabel E Christic, *Henry VI* (1922)

Henry VII 1457–1509
First Tudor King of England

Born in Pembroke Castle, Wales, he was the son of Edmund Tudor, Earl of Richmond, and **Margaret Beaufort**, and the grandson of Owen Tudor who married Catherine de Valois, widow of **Henry V**. His mother, a great-granddaughter of **John of Gaunt**, ranked as the lineal descendant of the House of Lancaster. After the Lancastrian defeat at Tewkesbury (1471), he was taken to Brittany, where several Yorkist attempts on his life and liberty were frustrated. On 1 August 1485, Henry landed, unopposed, at Milford Haven and defeated **Richard III** on Bosworth Field. As king, his undeviating policy was to restore peace and prosperity to a warworn and impoverished land, an aim which his marriage of reconciliation with Elizabeth of York (eldest daughter of **Edward IV**) materially advanced. Minor Yorkist revolts were firmly dealt with, but Henry's policy in general was mercantilist and pacific, as was demonstrated by his readiness to conclude peace with France for a promised indemnity of £149,000. He also subsidized shipbuilding to expand his mercantile marine while giving him first call on craft speedily convertible into warships. The marriage of Henry's heir, the future **Henry VIII**, to **Catherine of Aragon** cemented an alliance with Spain that largely nullified the soaring aspirations of France, while animosity with Scotland ended when **James IV** of Scotland married Henry's daughter **Margaret Tudor**. A widower after 1503, Henry's design to further his policy by remarriage was cut short by his death in 1509. His personal fortune of over £1.5 million reflected the commercial prosperity his prudent policy had restored to the realm. He had adopted the policies of **Edward IV** and had created a situation in which they could succeed. ⬜Michael Van Cleave Alexander, *The First of the Tudors: A Study of Henry VII and His Reign* (1980)

Henry VIII See panel p871

Henry I, King of Germany See **Henry the Fowler**

Henry III 1017–56
King of Germany and Holy Roman Emperor
The son of **Conrad II**, father of **Henry IV**, he became King of the Germans (1026), Duke of Bavaria (1027), Duke of Swabia (1038), and emperor (1039). One of the strongest German emperors in the Middle Ages, he encouraged the efforts of the Cluniac monks to reform the ecclesiastical system of Europe. In 1046 he deposed all three rival popes and elected Clement II in their stead. He compelled the Duke of Bohemia to acknowledge himself a vassal of the empire (1042), he established supremacy in Hungary (1044), and also extended his authority over the Norman conquerors of Apulia and Calabria. He promoted learning and the arts, founded numerous monastic schools, and built many churches.

Henry IV 1050–1106
King of Germany and Holy Roman Emperor
Elected King of the Germans in 1053, he succeeded his father, **Henry III**, in 1056. In 1070, once free of his mother Agnes of Poitou's regency, he tried to break the power of the nobles, but his measures provoked a rising of the Saxons. He defeated them at Hohenburg (1075), and then took action against the rebel princes. Pope **Gregory VII** took part in the dispute, and Henry declared him deposed (1076). Gregory then excommunicated Henry. Henry lost support, so submitted and the ban of excommunication was removed (1077). With Lombard support, he renewed the conflict and, having been excommunicated a second time, appointed a new pope, Clement III (the antipope), who crowned him emperor (1084). Henry defeated three rival German kings, but when he had crossed the Alps for the third time (1090) to support Clement III, and learned that his son Conrad had betrayed him and been crowned king at Monza, he retired to Lombardy. In 1097 he returned to Germany, and his second son, Henry, was elected King of the Germans and heir to the empire. Pope Pascal II (1099–1118) encouraged Prince Henry to take the emperor prisoner

(1105), and Henry IV was compelled to abdicate. He escaped and died in Liège. While his opponents considered him a tyrannical supporter of heresy, his friends saw him as pious and intelligent, a lover of justice and scholarship. He was succeeded by Prince Henry as **Henry V.**

Henry V 1081–1125
King of Germany and Holy Roman Emperor
In 1106 he allied himself with the nobility and dethroned his father, **Henry IV**. His reign was dominated by the issues involved in the Investiture Controversy and his power struggle with the princes, whose support he alienated by favouring the Ministeriales and the towns. In 1111 he agreed with Pope Pascal II to give up his rights to invest bishops in return for coronation as emperor and the return of the royal insignia. This agreement was rejected by the German bishops and princes, whereupon Henry took the pope prisoner and forced him to concede both coronation and rights of investiture. This concession was later withdrawn and Henry was excommunicated. Finally, negotiations with Pope Calixtus II led to the end of the Investiture Controversy in the Concordat of Worms, in which the princes, rather than the emperor, took the initiative.

Henry VI 1165–97
King of Germany and Holy Roman Emperor
The son of **Frederick I, Barbarossa**, he was born in Nmegen, the Netherlands, and married Constance, aunt and heiress of William II of Sicily (1186). He succeeded his father as King of Germany and emperor in 1190. He was opposed by the papacy, the **Guelfs**, **Richard I** of England and Constance's illegitimate brother **Tancred**, who had succeeded William in Sicily. This hostile coalition collapsed when Richard fell into the hands of **Leopold V** of Austria, who turned his captive over to Henry. When Tancred died (1194) Henry overran Sicily, where Constance bore him a son, **Frederick II**. Emperor (from 1191) and King of Sicily, Henry was extremely powerful, but failed to make the empire hereditary. He died young, of malaria, while preparing for a crusade.

Henry VII c.1274–1313
King of Germany and Holy Roman Emperor
Born in Valenciennes, Hainault, he was originally Count of Luxembourg, a French-speaking minor prince from the extreme west of the empire. He was elected emperor (1308) as an alternative candidate to **Charles of Valois**, mainly due to the skilful diplomacy of his brother Baldwin, Archbishop of Trier. His family soon rose to great power with the marriage in 1310 of his son John to Elizabeth, heiress of Bohemia. In the same year Henry led an army to Italy, where he remained with the aim of restoring imperial authority, but made little progress against the opposition of King Robert of Naples and the Guelf cities, and the imperialist cause collapsed when he died near Siena, probably of malaria.

Henry 1594–1612
Prince of Wales
Born at Stirling Castle, he was the eldest son of **James VI and I** and **Anne of Denmark**, and was appointed Prince of Wales in 1610. Dignified and athletic, interested in science and naval matters, he won national popularity by his support for a Protestant and anti-Spanish foreign policy, and he became the focus for the hopes of those at court with Puritan sympathies. His death from typhoid (rumoured to be a result of poison) led to the hopes of forward Protestants being centred increasingly upon Henry's sister, **Elizabeth** (the Winter Queen), and her husband, **Frederick V** of the Palatinate.

Henry of Blois 1101–71
English prelate

Henry VIII 1491–1547
King of England

Henry was born in Greenwich, the second son of **Henry VII**. His accession to the throne in 1509 was hailed by such men as **John Colet**, **Desiderius Erasmus** and **Thomas More**. Shortly after, he married **Catherine of Aragon**, his brother Prince **Arthur**'s widow, a step of tremendous consequence. As a member of the Holy League formed by the pope and Spain against King **Louis XII** of France, in 1512 he invaded France, and next year won the so-called Battle of Spurs, and captured Terouenne and Tournay. During his absence an English army won a greater triumph over the Scots at Flodden (1513). It was in this French war that Cardinal **Wolsey** became prominent. By 1514 he was, after the king, the first man in the country.

The chief aim of Henry's and Wolsey's foreign policy was to maintain a balance of power between France and Spain; at first they supported Spain, but when **Francis I** of France was brought to the verge of ruin by his defeat and capture at Pavia, they formed an alliance with France.

In 1521 the Duke of Buckingham was executed on a trumped-up charge of treason. The same year Henry published a defence of the Sacraments in reply to **Martin Luther**, and received from Pope **Leo X** the title borne by all Henry's successors, 'Defender of the Faith'. In order to finance their expensive foreign policy, Henry and Wolsey resorted to heavy taxation, and to the suppression of all monasteries having less than seven inmates, devoting the revenues to educational purposes.

The turning-point in Henry's reign is marked by his determination to end his marriage with Catherine of Aragon. All her children, except Mary Tudor (later **Mary I**), had died in infancy, and Henry professed to see in this the judgement of Heaven on an unnatural alliance. Henry had set his affections on **Anne Boleyn**, the niece of **Thomas Howard**, 3rd Duke of Norfolk. The pope, supported by the emperor, declined to support Henry. This proved the ruin of Wolsey, who now found himself without a friend at home or abroad. In 1529 he was stripped of his goods and honours, and dismissed in disgrace; next year he was summoned to London on a charge of high treason, but died on the way. He was succeeded as Chancellor by Sir Thomas More.

Henry remained determined on the divorce, and by humbling the clergy he thought he could bring the pope to terms. In 1531 the clergy were declared guilty of treason and only pardoned after payment of a large fine. The following year, the dues paid to the pope were cancelled. Thomas More asked to be relieved of the Great Seal. Meanwhile Henry was privately married to Anne Boleyn (1533), and in 1534 it was enacted that the king's marriage with Catherine was invalid, that the succession to the Crown should lie with the issue of Henry's marriage with Anne Boleyn, and that the king was the sole supreme head of the Church of England. To this last act Bishop **John Fisher** and Sir Thomas More refused to swear, and both were executed the following year.

The suppression of the monasteries continued, with the support of the new Chancellor **Thomas Cromwell**. An act was passed for the suppression of all monasteries with a revenue under £200 a year. This unpopular step, and other measures, caused a formidable insurrection in the northern counties, known as the 'Pilgrimage of Grace'. The revolt was crushed, and Henry next (1536) suppressed all the remaining monasteries. The bulk of the revenues passed to the Crown and to those who had made themselves useful to the king. In 1536 Queen Catherine died, and the same year Anne Boleyn herself was executed for infidelity.

The day after her execution Henry was betrothed to **Jane Seymour**, who later bore him a son (the future **Edward VI**), but died in childbirth. **Anne of Cleves** was chosen as the king's fourth wife, in the hope of attaching the Protestant interest of Germany. Anne's personal appearance proved so little to Henry's taste that he consented to the marriage only on the condition that a divorce should follow speedily. Cromwell had made himself as generally detested as Wolsey. It was mainly through his action that Anne had been brought forward, and his enemies used Henry's indignation to bring about his ruin. He was accused of high treason by the Duke of Norfolk, and was executed on a bill of attainder, without trial (1540). Henry married **Catherine Howard**, another niece of the Catholic Duke of Norfolk. Before two years had passed Catherine suffered the same fate as Anne Boleyn, on the same charge, and in July 1543 Henry married his sixth wife, **Catherine Parr**, widow of Lord Latimer, who survived him.

During all these years Henry's interest in the struggle between Francis I and Emperor **Charles V** had been kept alive by the intrigues of France in Scotland. Eventually Henry and Francis concluded a peace (1546), by which Scotland also benefited. The execution of Henry Howard, Earl of Surrey, son of the Duke of Norfolk, on a charge of high treason, completes the long list of the judicial murders of Henry's reign. Norfolk himself was saved from the same fate only by the death of Henry himself. Henry was succeeded by his son Edward VI.

📖 David Loaders, *The Politics of Marriage: Henry VIII and his Queens* (1994); Jasper Ridley, *Henry VIII* (1985); Marie Louise Bruce, *The Making of Henry VIII* (1977); J J Scarisbrick, *Henry VIII* (1968).

'We at no time stand so highly in our estate royal as in the time of Parliament, wherein we as head, and you as members, are conjoined and knit together into one body politic, so as whatsoever offence or injury is offered to the meanest member of the House is to be judged as done against our person and the whole Court of Parliament.' Address to a deputation from the House of Commons (31 March 1543).

He was Bishop of Winchester from 1129, and papal legate in England from 1139. He supported his younger brother, King **Stephen**, against the Empress **Matilda** (Maud), and went to France after Stephen's death (1154).

Henry of Huntingdon c.1084–1155
English chronicler

He was archdeacon of Huntingdon from 1109. In 1139 he visited Rome. He compiled a *Historia Anglorum*, which covered the years up to 1154.

Henry the Fowler c.876–936
King of Germany

The founder of the Saxon dynasty, he was Duke of Saxony from 912. As Henry I (from 919), he brought Swabia and Bavaria into the German confederation, regained Lotharingia (925), defeated the Wends (928) and the Hungarians in 933, and seized Schleswig from Denmark (934). He was about to claim the imperial Crown (936) when he died. He was succeeded by his son, **Otto I, the Great**. Another son was St **Bruno**.

Henry the Lion 1129–95
Duke of Saxony and Bavaria

He was head of the **Guelf** family. After Bavaria was restored to him by **Frederick I, Barbarossa** (1156) he became the most powerful prince in Germany, with domains stretching from the Baltic to the Adriatic. He expanded the frontiers of Saxony to the east against the Slavs, and did much to encourage the commerce of his lands, founding the city of Munich, and developing the towns of Lüneburg, Bremen, Lübeck and Brunswick, but his ambitions and growing power aroused the opposition of a league of Saxon princes (1166) and of Frederick I, who defeated him and deprived him of his lands (1180). Henry went into exile at the court of **Henry II** of England, whose daughter Mathilda he had married (1168). He finally returned to Germany after 1190 and was reconciled to Emperor **Henry VI** in 1194. His main achievements were steady colonization east of Saxony and keeping peace within Germany during Frederick's absence on his foreign interests. ◫ Karl Jordan, *Henry the Lion* (1986)

Henry the Navigator 1394–1460
Portuguese prince

The third son of John I, King of Portugal, and Philippa, daughter of **John of Gaunt**, he was born at Porto, and distinguished himself at the capture of Ceuta, North Africa (1415). He was made Governor of the Algarve (1419), and set up court at Sagres. During the war against the Moors his sailors reached previously unknown parts of the ocean. He founded an observatory and school of scientific navigation at Cape St Vincent, and sponsored many voyages of exploration, resulting in the discovery of the Madeira Islands (1418), the Azores and the Cape Verde Islands (1456). His school used classical and Arabic learning to help produce the caravel, a vessel especially fitted for long voyages. His pupils also explored, and established trading posts on the west coast of Africa, as far as Sierra Leone, thereby preparing the way for the discovery of the sea route to India. ◫ P E Russell, *Prince Henry the Navigator* (1960)

Henry, Carl Ferdinand Howard 1913–
US Protestant theologian

He was born in New York City, the son of German immigrants. In 1933, after conversion, he abandoned journalism to study and teach theology. He was the founding editor of the *Christianity Today* magazine (1956–68), and through it became widely recognized as a leading spokesman for conservative evangelicals. His many books include *The Uneasy Conscience of Modern Fundamentalism* (1948), which spurred evangelicals out of cultural isolation into social engagement, *Christian Personal Ethics* (1957), and *God, Revelation and Authority* (6 vols, 1976–82), which have been translated into Korean and Mandarin. He has taught at the Prison Fellowship Ministeries since 1990 and in 1993 was awarded the Religious Heritage Gold award for 50 years of religious service.

Henry, Joseph 1797–1878
US physicist

Born in Albany, New York, he studied at Albany Academy, and was appointed Professor of Mathematics there in 1826. In 1832 he became Professor of Natural Philosophy at Princeton University, and in 1846 first secretary of the Smithsonian Institution. An intuitive experimenter rather than a theoretician, he discovered electrical induction independently of **Michael Faraday**, constructed the first electromagnetic motor (1829) and also appreciated the effects of resistance on current, formulated precisely by **Georg Ohm** in 1827. He demonstrated the oscillatory nature of electric discharges (1842), and introduced a system of weather forecasting based on meteorological observations. The unit of inductance (the henry) is named after him. ◫ Patricia Jahns, *Joseph Henry: Father of American Electronics* (1969)

Henry, Lenny 1958–
English comic actor

Born in Dudley, West Midlands, he made his television debut as a winning contestant on *New Faces* (1975) and went on to appear in such series as *Tiswas* (1979–82) and *Three of a Kind* (1981, 1983). He showcased an array of characters such as Delbert Wilkins, 'love-god' balladeer Theophilus P Wildebeest and cleric Nathaniel Westminster. He also proved his dramatic worth in such television films as *Coast to Coast* (1988) and *Alive and Kicking* (1991), but made a somewhat lukewarm assault on Hollywood stardom with the film comedy *True Identity* (1991). He returned to television in 1993 with *Chef*, a character supposedly modelled on volatile, contemporary chefs. A leading figure in the charity Comic Relief, he is married to comedienne **Dawn French**.

Henry, O, *pseudonym of* William Sydney Porter 1862–1910
US short-story writer

Born in Greenboro, North Carolina, he was brought up during the depression in the South, and settled in Austin, Texas, where he became a bank-teller. In 1894 he 'borrowed' money from the bank to help his consumptive wife and to start a literary magazine, the *Rolling Stone*. He fled at the height of the scandal, but returned in 1897, to his wife's deathbed, and was found technically guilty of embezzlement, and spent three years in jail (1898–1901). There, he adopted his pseudonym and began to write short stories. From 1902, he roamed the back streets of New York, where he found ample material for his tales. His first of many collections was *Cabbages and Kings* (1904). His use of coincidence and trick endings, his purple phraseology and caricature have been criticized, but nothing can detract from the technical brilliance and boldness of his comic writing. ◫ D Stuart, *O. Henry: a biography* (1986)

Henry, Patrick 1736–99
American revolutionary and statesman

Born in Hanover County, Virginia, he trained as a lawyer after a career as shopkeeper and farmer. He entered the colonial Virginia House of Burgesses (1765–74), where his oratory won him fame. He was an outspoken opponent of British policy towards the colonies, particularly concerning the Stamp Act (1765), and he made the first speech in the Continental Congress (1774). In 1776 he became Governor of independent Virginia, and was four times re-elected. He opposed the Constitution on the grounds that the states did not need a strong central government, and when it was adopted he began to lobby for its amendment, arguing successfully for the addition of the Bill of Rights. He retired in 1791.

Henry, William 1774–1836
English physician and chemist

Born in Manchester, he studied medicine at Edinburgh University, but ill health forced him to give up practising medicine. Under the influence of his friend **John Dalton**, he turned to teaching and research in chemistry. His best-known work was the study of the influence of pressure and temperature on the solubility of gases in water, which resulted in the generalization that has become known as Henry's law, that the solubility of a gas at a given temperature is proportional to its pressure (1803). He also wrote the very successful *Elements of Experimental Chemistry* (1801), of which 11 editions were published. He was elected Fellow of the Royal Society in 1808 and was awarded its Copley Medal in the same year. He committed suicide.

Henryson, Robert c.1425–c.1508
Scottish medieval poet

He is usually designated 'schoolmaster of Dunfermline', and was certainly a notary in 1478. His work is part of the tradition of the Scottish 'makars' (as shapers of literary artifice), and his best-known poem is the *Testament of*

Cresseid, a sequel to Chaucer's *Troilus and Criseyde*. Of his 14 extant poems, *Robene and Makyne* is the earliest Scottish specimen of pastoral poetry. His other works include a metrical version of 13 *Morall Fabels of Esope the Phrygian*. ⊞R
L Kindrick, *Robert Henryson* (1979)

Henschel, Sir George 1850–1934
British composer, conductor, singer and pianist
Born in Breslau, Prussia (now Wrocław, Poland), he went to England in 1877. He composed operas, a requiem and chamber music, conducted the Boston Symphony Orchestra (1881–84), and became the first conductor of the Scottish Symphony Orchestra (1893–95). He was naturalized in 1890, and knighted in 1914.

Hensen, Christian Andreas Viktor 1835–1924
German physiologist
Born in Kiel, he studied medicine at Würzburg University, then returned to Kiel University, where he graduated. He remained in Kiel, teaching anatomy and histology, becoming full Professor of Physiology in 1868. He studied the organs of hearing, describing what are now known as Hensen's duct and Hensen's supporting cells, and publishing lengthy accounts (1880, 1902) of the physiology of hearing. In marine biology he investigated the marine fauna that he named 'plankton', calculating the quantity of plankton at different depths in the various oceans.

Henslowe, Philip c.1550–1616
English theatre manager
Born in Lindfield, Sussex, he was originally a dyer and starch-maker, but became lessee of the Rose Theatre on the Bankside, London, in 1584. From 1591 until his death he was in partnership with Edward Alleyn. Henslowe's business diary from 1593 to 1609, preserved at Dulwich College, was published in 1961 (eds RA Foakes and R T Rickert), and contains invaluable information about the stage of Shakespeare's day.

Henson, Jim (James Maury) 1936–90
US puppeteer and fantasy filmmaker
Born in Greenville, Mississippi, he studied commercial art before working in local television in Washington DC, later hosting his own show, *Sam and Friends* (1955–61). After he graduated from Maryland University, his endearing creations began to appear on national television, including *The Jimmy Dean Show* (1963–66). Intrigued by television technology and its potential, he continued to refine his characters and launched *Sesame Street* (1969), a series that entertained and educated pre-school children. Many of his long-established puppets, like Kermit the Frog and Miss Piggy, gained international popularity in the series *The Muppet Show* (1976–81) which reached an estimated 235 million viewers in more than 100 countries. The characters subsequently appeared in a string of films and a Grammy award-winning album of the same title (1979). He continued to make innovative television programmes combining live action and increasingly sophisticated puppetry, including *Fraggle Rock* (1983–88) and *The Storyteller* (1987) and received numerous Emmy awards for his work. His special-effects adventure films include *The Dark Crystal* (1982), *Labyrinth* (1986) and *The Witches* (1989).

Henson, Leslie 1891–1957
English comedian
Remembered for his facial elasticity, he took leading roles in *Lady Luck* (1927), *Funny Face* (1928), *It's a Boy* (1930), *Harvey* (1950), etc, and produced popular farces at the Aldwych Theatre, London, and many other plays. He published an autobiography, *Yours Faithfully* (1948).

Henty, G(eorge) A(lfred) 1832–1902
English novelist and journalist
Born in Trumpington, Cambridgeshire, and educated at Caius College, Cambridge, he became a special correspondent for the *Morning Advertiser* during the Crimean War and for the *Standard* in the Franco-Prussian War. He was best known, however, for his 80 historical adventure stories for boys, including *Under Drake's Flag* (1883), *With Clive in India* (1884) and *With Moore at Corunna* (1898). ⊞ G M Fenn, *G. A. Henty: The Story of an Active Life* (1907)

Henze, Hans Werner 1926–
German composer
Born in Gütersloh, he studied with Fortner at Heidelberg, and with René Leibowitz in Darmstadt and Paris. After early absorption of serial techniques Henze later reacted against the strictness and exclusiveness of the Darmstadt school and sought, in symphonic and theatre music, to communicate his aesthetic and social views directly with the public, without compromising either the personal or the contemporary qualities of his style. His political awareness was stimulated particularly by the Vietnam War and the student movements of 1967 to 1968, and his subsequent music reflects his socialist commitment to movements in Germany, Italy and Cuba. His stage works include nine full-length and three one-act operas, notably *Das Wundertheater* (1948, revised 1964, 'The Wonder Theatre'), *Boulevard Solitude* (1951), based on the theme of *Manon Lescaut*, *König Hirsch* (1955, 'King Stag'), *Elegy for Young Lovers* (1961), *The Bassarids* (1965), *We Come to the River* (1975), and *The English Cat* (1983). He has also written six full-length and five chamber ballets, and other music-theatre works. He has composed seven symphonies, five string quartets, concertos, and other orchestral, chamber, vocal and piano music. His collected writings from 1953 to 1981 were published as *Music and Politics* (1982). One of his recent posts was as Professor of Composition at the Royal Academy of Music (1987–91).

Hepburn, Audrey, *originally* Edda Van Heemstra Hepburn-Ruston 1929–93
Belgian actress
Born in Brussels, she trained in ballet in Amsterdam and London, making her film debut in *Nederland In 7 Lessen* (1948) and her London stage debut in the chorus of *High Button Shoes* (1948). She first appeared on Broadway in *Gigi* (1951), and won a Best Actress Academy Award for *Roman Holiday* (1953). An enchanting, pencil-slim actress of coltish grace, she had many film successes, including *Funny Face* (1957), *Breakfast At Tiffany's* (1961), *My Fair Lady* (1964), *Two for the Road* (1967) and *Wait Until Dark* (1967). In her later years she travelled extensively as a goodwill ambassador for UNICEF. She made her final appearance in *Always* (1989). ⊞ Barry Paris, *Audrey Hepburn* (1997)

Hepburn, James See Bothwell, 4th Earl of

Hepburn, Katharine Houghton 1907–
US film and stage actress
She was born in Hartford, Connecticut and educated at Bryn Mawr College. She made her professional stage debut in *The Czarina* (1928) in Baltimore and acted on Broadway, but from 1932 attained international fame as a film actress. Her many enduring films include *Bringing Up Baby* (1938), *The Philadelphia Story* (1940), *Woman of the Year* (1942), which saw the beginning of a 25-year professional and personal partnership with co-star Spencer Tracy, *Adam's Rib* (1949), *The African Queen* (1951), *Pat and Mike* (1952), and *Long Day's Journey Into Night* (1962). Noted for her distinctive New England diction, fine bone structure and versatile talent, she won Academy Awards for *Morning Glory* (1933), *Guess Who's Coming to Dinner?* (1967), *The Lion in Winter* (1968) and *On Golden Pond* (1981). On stage she has continued to tackle the classics and enjoyed enormous success in the musical *Coco* (1970). She continued to act despite suffering from Parkinson's Disease. Television

work includes *The Glass Menagerie* (1973), *Love Among the Ruins* (1975) and *Mrs Delafield Wants to Marry* (1986). ⚏ Charles Hignam, *Kate: The Life of Katharine Hepburn* (1975)

Hepburn, Mitchell Frederick 1896–1953
Canadian politician
A farmer who came to power as the Liberal premier of Ontario (1934–42) with the promise of a 'swing to the left' and a fight in favour of the 'dispossesed and oppressed', he soon began to fight the Congress of Industrial Organizations (CIO), which was asked in to help organize the General Motors plant at Oshawa in 1937, branding them as 'foreign agitators' and communists. After Mackenzie King refused to send in the Mounties, Hepburn organized his own anti-labour force, nicknamed 'Hepburn's Hussars' or the 'Sons of Mitch's' and attacked the federal government for its 'cowardice'. Although the strikers won company recognition, Hepburn gained increased electoral support, winning 75 per cent of the seats in the subsequent election. He continued his feud with the federal administration of Mackenzie King over both provincial rights (wrecking the 1941 conference on the recommendations of the Rowell–Sirois Commission) and its war policies, but this fight ruined his party and destroyed his health. Resigning from office in 1942, he lost his seat in the election of 1945 in which the Liberal Party was decimated.

Hepplewhite, George d.1786
English furniture designer
He seems to have trained as a cabinetmaker with the Lancaster firm of Gillow, and then set up a workshop in London, but no extant furniture is attributable to him. His simple and elegant designs, characterized by the free use of inlaid ornament and the use of shield or heart shapes in chair backs, only became famous with the posthumous publication by his widow of his *Cabinet-Maker and Upholsterer's Guide* (1788), containing nearly 300 designs. ⚏ F Lewis Hinckley, *Hepplewhite, Sheraton and Regency Furniture* (1987)

Hepworth, Dame Barbara See panel p875

Heracledies of Pontus and Ekphantus
c.388–c.315BC
Greek philosopher and astronomer
Born in Heraklea, he moved to Athens to become a pupil of Plato. It is reported that he was the first to propose that the Earth spins from west to east, thinking it highly improbable that the stars and planets could rotate once every 24 hours. It is also suggested that he took the first steps towards a heliocentric solar system, and that he considered the cosmos to be infinite, with the other planets being Earth-like with atmospheres.

Heraclitus d.460BC
Greek philosopher
Born in Ephesus, Asia Minor, of an old aristocratic family, he was criticized by his contemporaries for his oracular style, and was known as 'the obscure' and 'the riddler'. Only fragments remain of his book *On Nature*. He seems to have held that everything is in a state of flux ('you can never step into the same river twice') and that the apparent unity and stability of the world conceals a dynamic tension between opposites, which is somehow measured and controlled by reason (*Logos*) or its physical manifestation, fire. Fire is the ultimate constituent of the world, and the fire of the human soul is thus linked to the cosmic fire which virtuous souls eventually join. Philosophers as eminent as Hegel have claimed to have taken inspiration from him.

Heraclius c.575–641
Byzantine emperor
Born in Cappadocia, he revolted against Phocas, killed him, and took his throne (610). The empire was threatened to the north by the Avars, and to the east by the Persians under Chosroes II, who overran Syria, Egypt and Asia Minor. Heraclius carried out far-reaching reorganizations of the army, the provincial government, and the empire's finances, and made Greek its official language. These reforms enabled him to defeat the Persians in a series of campaigns which restored the lost territories (628–33). However, he failed to resolve the differences between the orthodox and monophysite parties in the Church, and from 634 the recent gains in the East were almost completely lost to the followers of Muhammad under the caliph 'Umar.

Herbart, Johann Friedrich 1776–1841
German philosopher and educational theorist
Born in Oldenburg, he taught in Switzerland (1797–1800), where he became interested in Pestalozzi's educational methods. He was Professor of Philosophy at Göttingen (1805–08), and at Königsberg as Kant's successor (1809–33), before returning to Göttingen (1833–41). His metaphysics posited a multiplicity of 'reals' (things which in themselves possess absolute existence independently of being perceived), and led to a psychology which rejected the notions of faculties and innate ideas and formed a basis for his pedagogical theories. His best-known works are *Psychologie als Wissenschaft neu gegrundet auf Erfahrung, Metaphysik und Mathematik* (2 vols, 1824–25, 'Psychology As Knowledge Newly Founded on Experience, Metaphysics and Mathematics'), and *Allgemeine Pädagogik* (1806, 'Universal Pedagogy').

Herbert
English noble family
Descended from Herbertus Camerarius, who came over from France with William the Conqueror, the Herberts later diverged into the Earls of Powis, the Lords Herbert of Cherbury, the Herberts of Muckross, and several untitled branches in England, Wales and Ireland. Sir William Herbert of Raglan Castle, Monmouth, was knighted (1415) by Henry V for his valour in the French wars. His descendants were Earls of Pembroke and Huntingdon, the Earls of Carnarvon descending from the 8th Earl of Pembroke.

Herbert, Sir A(lan) P(atrick) 1890–1971
English writer and politician
Born in Elstead, Surrey, he studied law at Oxford, then served in the navy during World War I. He was called to the Bar but never practised, having established himself in his twenties as a witty writer of verses, joining *Punch* in 1924. His first theatrical success, with Nigel Playfair in the revue *Riverside Nights* (1926), was followed by a series of brilliant libretti for comic operas, including *Tantivy Towers* (1930), a version of Jacques Offenbach's *Helen* (1932), *Derby Day* (1932) and *Bless the Bride* (1947). He was also the author of several successful novels, notably *The Secret Battle* (1919), *The Water Gipsies* (1930) and *Holy Deadlock* (1934). *What a Word* (1935) and many humorous articles he campaigned against jargon and officialese. Independent MP for Oxford University from 1935 to 1950, he introduced a marriage bill in the House of Commons that became law as the Matrimonial Causes Act 1938, and did much to improve divorce law in England. He was knighted in 1945. ⚏ *My Life and Times* (1970); S Glasspool, *Sir A P Herbert: A Short Guide to his Literary Work* (1973)

Herbert (of Cherbury), Edward Herbert, 1st Baron 1583–1648
English soldier, politician and philosopher
Born in Eyton-on-Severn, Shropshire, he was made a Knight of the Bath (1603) and as a member of the Privy Council was sent as ambassador to France in 1619, to

Hepworth, Dame (Jocelyn) Barbara 1903–75
English sculptor

Barbara Hepworth was born in Wakefield, and studied at the Leeds School of Art (with **Henry Moore**), the Royal College of Art, and in Italy. She married the sculptor John Skeaping (1901–80), and later the painter **Ben Nicholson** (by whom she had triplets). In 1939 she went to live in St Ives, Cornwall. She was one of the foremost non-figurative sculptors of her time, notable for the strength and formal discipline of her carving (eg the *Contrapuntal Forms* exhibited at the Festival of Britain, 1951).

Other works include *Pierced Form* (1931), *The Unknown Political Prisoner* (1953) and *Single Form* (1963). Until the early 1960s her works were mainly in wood, including *Forms in Echelon* (1938) and *Group II (People Waiting)* (1952). She then worked in stone, producing *Two Forms with White (Greek)* (wood and stone, 1963) and *Three Monoliths* (marble, 1964) and in metal, producing *Four Square (Walk Through)* (bronze, 1966). In all this work she developed a distinctive abstract style involving hollows with lengths of wire or string. Her representational paintings and drawings are of equal power. Created a DBE in 1965, she suffered from throat cancer in her later years, and died in a fire in her studio in Cornwall.

She published *A Pictorial Autobiography* in 1970.

> 'Carving is interrelated masses conveying an emotion: a perfect relationship between the mind and the colour, light and weight which is the stone, made by the hand which feels.' From *Unit One* (1934).

---

negotiate between **Louis XIII** and his Protestant subjects. In 1624 he was made a peer of Ireland, and in 1629 of England. When the English Civil War broke out he at first sided half-heartedly with the Royalists, but in 1644 surrendered to the Parliamentarians. Considered one of the finest deistical writers, his works include *De Veritate* (1624, 'On Truth'), and *De Religione Gentilium* (published posthumously in 1663, 'On the Religion of the Gentiles', Eng trans, 1709), which states that all religions recognize five main articles, from the acknowledgement of a supreme God to the concept that there are rewards and punishments in a future state. He also wrote poetry, contemporary histories and an autobiography. He was the brother of the poet **George Herbert**.

Herbert, Frank Patrick 1920–86
US science-fiction writer

Born in Tacoma, Washington, he was a journalist before turning to full-time fiction writing. His first novel, *The Dragon in the Sea* (1956), is an acute psychological study set on a submarine. He is best known for his series of novels about the desert planet *Dune* (1965), one of the most complex and fully realized examples of an alternative world in science fiction. Persistent themes of his work include the development of higher or artificial intelligence in human and non-human species, genetic engineering, ecology and overpopulation. Important titles include *The Green Brain* (1966), *The Santaroga Barrier* (1968) and *Hellstrom's Hive* (1973).

Herbert, George 1593–1633
English metaphysical poet and clergyman

He was the son of Lady Magdalen Herbert (to whom **John Donne** addressed his *Holy Sonnets*) and brother of **Edward Herbert** (of Cherbury). Educated at Westminster School and Trinity College, Cambridge, he was elected a Fellow there (1614) and Public Orator (1619), and was MP for Montgomery (1624–25). His connection with the court, and particularly the favour of King **James VI and I**, seemed to point to a worldly career, but in 1630, under the influence of Archbishop **Laud**, he took orders and spent his last years as a parish priest of Bemerton, in Wiltshire. Like his friend **Nicholas Ferrar**, he represents both in his life and works the counter-challenge of the Laudian party to the Puritans. He died of consumption at the age of 39. Practically all his religious lyrics are included in *The Temple, Sacred Poems and Private Ejaculations*, posthumously published in 1633. His chief prose work, *A Priest in the Temple*, containing guidance for the country parson, was published in his *Remains* (1652). J B Leishman, *The Metaphysical Poets* (1934); J J D Faniell, *The Life of George Herbert of Bemerton* (1902)

Herbert (of Lea), Sidney Herbert, 1st Baron 1810–61
English politician

Born in Richmond, Surrey, the son of the 11th Earl of Pembroke, he was educated at Harrow and Oriel College, Oxford. In 1832 he was elected Conservative MP for South Wiltshire, and was Sir **Robert Peel's** Secretary to the Admiralty from 1841 to 1845, when he became Secretary-at-War. He opposed **Richard Cobden's** motion for a select committee on the Corn Laws. In 1852 he was again Secretary-at-War under the Earl of **Aberdeen**, was largely blamed for the hardships of the army before Sebastopol, but sent **Florence Nightingale** to the Crimea. He was briefly Viscount **Palmerston's** Colonial Secretary in 1855, and his Secretary-at-War in 1859. Great improvements in the sanitary conditions and education of the forces, the amalgamation of the Indian with the imperial army, and the organization of the volunteer movement were results of his army administration.

Herbert, Victor 1859–1924
US composer

Born in Dublin, Ireland, he trained as a cellist, and played in the orchestras of **Johann Strauss**, the Younger, and the Stuttgart court before settling in New York City in 1886 as leading cellist of the Metropolitan Opera Company's orchestra. In 1893 he began his career as a band leader and conductor, and he composed his first successful operetta, *Prince Ananias* (1894), which was followed by a long series of similar works containing such popular songs as 'Ah, Sweet Mystery of Life' and 'Kiss Me Again'. Immensely prolific and possessed of accurate theatrical instincts, he wrote more than 40 operas, operettas and musical comedies, of which the best known are *Babes in Toyland* (1903), *The Red Mill* (1906) and *Naughty Marietta* (1910).

Herbert, Wally (Walter William) 1934–
British explorer

Brought up in South Africa and trained at the School of Military Survey, he spent two years in Egypt before joining the Falkland Islands Dependencies Survey in Antarctica (1955–57). This was followed by expeditions to Lapland, Svalbard and Greenland. He participated in the New Zealand Antarctic expedition (1960–62) which surveyed large areas of Queen Maud Range, and commemorated the 50th anniversary of **Roald Amundsen's** attainment of the North Pole by following his return journey. He made the first surface crossing of the Arctic Ocean (1968–69), a 464-day journey of 3,800 miles (6,115km) from Alaska to Spitsbergen via the Pole, the longest sustained sledge journey in history. He lived in the Arctic, filming the Inuit, and between 1978 and 1982 made several attempts to circumnavigate Greenland. He has written a number of books, including *The Noose of Laurels* (1989) on the Cook–Peary controversy.

Herbert, William, 3rd Earl of Pembroke
1580–1630
English poet
He was a patron of Ben Jonson, Philip Massinger and Inigo Jones, and a Lord Chamberlain of the Court (1615–30). He became Chancellor of Oxford in 1617 and had Pembroke College named after him. Shakespeare's 'W H', the 'onlie begetter' of the *Sonnets* has been taken by some to refer to him. ⬛ R Holzapfel, *Shakespeare's Secret* (1961); T Tyler, *The Herbert-Fitton Theory of Shakespeare's Sonnets* (1898)

Herbert, Xavier 1901–84
Australian novelist
Born in Port Hedland, Western Australia, he travelled extensively before settling in the Northern Territory. He is known mainly for his first novel, *Capricornia* (1938), and his last, *Poor Fellow My Country* (1975). The intervening years were spent drifting round Australia, a period which reinforced his sympathy with the treatment of Australia's Aboriginals. This sentiment is strongly evoked in his writing, especially in *Poor Fellow My Country*, a novel longer than *War and Peace*, and the longest novel then published in Australia.

Herbig, George Howard 1920–
US astronomer
Born in Wheeling, West Virginia, he studied astronomy at the University of California at Los Angeles in 1943, and then became a graduate student at the Lick Observatory, writing his thesis on T Tauri stars (very young stars which have not yet started to produce energy through nuclear fusion). Not only did Herbig discover many of these stars, but he also discovered one of the first 'Herbig–Haro' objects, small convoluted luminous nebulae that are intimately connected with newly formed stars. The unusually high abundance of lithium in T Tauri stars led Herbig to conclude that this value represents the original abundance of the element in the Milky Way. He also discovered the hotter, more massive stars of spectral class A and B, now known as Herbig emission stars, that are associated with T Tauri stars. In 1962 he suggested that the low- and intermediate-mass stars in clusters formed first, with the massive O stars forming later. Herbig was Professor of Astronomy at the University of California at Santa Cruz (1967–87), and currently works at the Institute of Astronomy at the University of Hawaii.

Herblock See Block, Herbert Lawrence

Herd, David 1732–1810
Scottish anthologist
Born in Marykirk in Kincardine, he was the son of a farmer. He worked for most of his life as an accountant in Edinburgh, collecting and faithfully transcribing songs and ballads in his spare time. He was the editor of *Ancient Scottish Ballads* (2 vols, 1776), which influenced Robert Burns.

Herder, Johann Gottfried 1744–1803
German critic and poet
Born in Mohrungen, East Prussia, he studied at Königsberg, and there made the acquaintance of Kant and Johann Hamann. In 1764 he became a schoolteacher and assistant pastor in a church in Riga. He met Goethe in Strasbourg (1769), was appointed court preacher at Bückeburg (1770), and first preacher in Weimar (1776). His belief that the truest poetry is the poetry of the people found expression in his collection of folksongs, *Stimmen der Völker in Liedern* (1778–79, 'Voices of the Peoples in Songs'), *Vom Geist der Ebraïschen Poesie* (1782–83, Eng trans

The Spirit of Hebrew Poetry, 1833), a treatise on the influence of poetry on manners (1778), in his version of the *Cid* (1805), and other works. The supreme importance of the historical method is fully recognized in these, and especially in *Ideen zur Geschichte der Menschheit* (1784–91, Eng trans *Outlines of a Philosophy of the History of Man*, 1800), which is remarkable for its anticipation of evolutionary theories. He is best remembered for the influence he exerted on Goethe and the developing German Romanticism. ⬛ H Reisiger, *Johann Gottfried Herder* (1942)

Heredia, José María 1803–39
Cuban poet
Born in Santiago de Cuba, he was the cousin of the French poet José María de Heredia. He was exiled to the USA for anti-government activities in 1823. He is remembered mainly for his patriotic verse and for his ode to Niagara (1824), but the earlier 'En el teocalli de Cholula' ('In the Pyramid of Cholula') is a significant philosophical poem. ⬛ A Harms, *Heredia* (1975)

Heredia, José María de 1842–1905
French poet
Born in Santiago de Cuba, he was the cousin of the Cuban poet José María Heredia. He went at an early age to France, where he was educated. One of the Parnassians, he achieved a great reputation with a comparatively small output, his most impressive work being found in his sonnets, which appeared in the collection *Les Trophées* (1893, 'The Trophies'). ⬛ C Utrera, *Heredia* (1939)

Hérelle, Felix d' 1873–1949
Canadian bacteriologist
Born in Montreal, he studied there and worked in Central America, Europe and Egypt before holding a chair at Yale from 1926 to 1933. A competitor of Frederick Twort, he was independently the discoverer in 1915 of bacteriophage, a type of virus which infects bacteria. Thereafter he tried to use 'phage' therapeutically, but without any significant successes. However, phage later proved of great value in research, and along with Twort he can be regarded as one of the founders of molecular biology.

Hereward, known as Hereward the Wake fl.1070
Anglo-Saxon thane and rebel
A Lincolnshire squire, he led a raid on Peterborough Abbey in 1070 as a protest against the appointment of a Norman abbot by William the Conqueror. He took refuge on the Isle of Ely with other rebels. When William succeeded in penetrating to the English camp in 1071, Hereward cut his way through to the swampy fens northwards and escaped. He was the hero of Charles Kingsley's romance, *Hereward the Wake* (1866). ⬛ Victor Head, *Hereward* (1995)

Hergé, pseudonym of Georges Rémi 1907–83
Belgian strip cartoonist
Born in Etterbeek, near Brussels, he drew his first strip, *Totor*, for a boy scouts' weekly in 1926. He created the Tin-Tin boy detective strip for the children's supplement of the newspaper *Le Vingtième Siècle*, using the pen name Hergé, a phonetic version of his initials, RG. *Tin-Tin in the Land of the Soviets* was quickly republished in album format (1930), as were all the adventures of the young detective (22 vols in all).

Heriot, George 1563–1624
Scottish goldsmith and philanthropist
Born in Edinburgh, he started business in 1586, and in 1597 was appointed goldsmith to Anne of Denmark, and then to her husband King James VI in 1603. He followed King James to London, where, as court jeweller and banker, he amassed considerable wealth. He bequeathed £23,625 to found a hospital or school in Edinburgh for

sons of poor burgesses, now an independent school known as George Heriot's. As 'Jingling Geordie' he features in Sir **Walter Scott**'s *Fortunes of Nigel*.

Herkomer, Sir Hubert von 1849–1914
British artist and film pioneer

Born in Waal, Bavaria, Germany, he studied art at Southampton, Munich and the College of Art in South Kensington, and in 1870 settled in London. As well as painting, he worked as an engraver, wood-carver, ironsmith, architect, journalist, playwright, composer, singer and actor. He was also a pioneer producer/director of British silent films, with his own studio at Bushey. He was Slade Professor of Fine Art at Oxford (1889–94). His paintings include portraits of **Richard Wagner**, **John Ruskin** and Lord **Kelvin**. He was an enthusiast for 'colour music', in which different colours instead of sounds are produced by a keyboard. He was knighted in 1907.

Herman, Woody (Woodrow Charles) 1913–87
US bandleader, alto saxophonist and clarinettist

He was born in Milwaukee, Wisconsin, and having learned to play saxophone at the age of nine, left home at 17 to begin his professional career. A member of the band led by Isham Jones, when this broke up in 1936, Herman took certain key members as the nucleus of his own first band, which established itself by the mid-1940s as a stylistic leader, particularly in its saxophone voicings. The Herman Orchestra was one of the very few to survive intact beyond the 1950s, continuing to tour until the 1980s.

Hermandszoon, Jakob See Arminius, Jacobus

Hermannsson, Steingrímur 1928–
Icelandic politician

He trained as an electrical engineer in the USA, returning to work in industry. He was director of Iceland's National Research Council (1957–78) and then made the transition into politics, becoming chairman of the Progressive Party (PP) in 1979. He became a minister in 1978 and then Prime Minister, heading a PP-Independence Party (IP) coalition (1983–87), after which he accepted the Foreign Affairs portfolio in the government of Thorsteinn Pálsson. He became Prime Minister again in 1988, but was defeated in the 1991 elections.

Hermes, Georg 1775–1831
German Roman Catholic theologian

Born in Dreyerwalde, Westphalia, he studied at the University of Münster and was ordained in 1799. He became a theological professor at Münster in 1807, and in 1819 at Bonn. In his works, for example his *Philosophische Einleitung in die Christkatholische Theologie* (1819, 'Introduction to Catholic Theology'), he sought to combine the Catholic faith and doctrines with Kantian philosophy. The Hermesian method became influential in the Rhineland, but his doctrines were condemned as heretical by a Papal Brief in 1835, and his followers were deprived of their professorships.

Hermes, Gertrude 1901–83
English printmaker and sculptor

Born in Bromley, Kent, she studied at the Beckenham School of Art before training at Leon Underwood's School in London alongside **Henry Moore** and her future husband Blair Hughes-Stanton, whom she married in 1926. Moving to Gregynog in 1930, she collaborated with Hughes-Stanton at the Gregynog Press. A highly skilled technical engraver, whose style is predominantly post-Cubist, she exhibited at the Paris and New York World Fairs and was chosen to represent Great Britain at the Venice Biennale in 1939. She was elected to the Royal Academy in 1971.

Hermite, Charles 1822–1901
French mathematician

Born in Dieuze, he received his degree in 1848, and was appointed to teaching posts at the École Polytechnique and the Collège de France. He later became professor at the École Normale (1869) and Professor of Higher Algebra at the Sorbonne (1870). He proved that the base of natural logarithms (e) is transcendental, ie cannot be a solution of a polynomial equation with rational coefficients. He published works on the theory of numbers, then on elliptic and Abelian functions, and in later life studied the applications of elliptic functions, and worked on invariant theory.

Hernández, José 1834–86
Argentine poet

Born near Buenos Aires, he founded the newspaper *Rio de la Plata* in 1869. He is known for his *gaucho* poetry of life on the pampas, where he had spent his early life among the cattlemen. His masterpiece is the epic *El gaucho Martín Fierro* (1872–79).

Hernández, Miguel 1910–42
Spanish poet and playwright

A goatherd's son, he was encouraged by **Juan Ramón Jiménez**, **Antonio Machado** and members of the Generation of '27 (**Federico García Lorca** and others) to publish his *Gongorista* early poetry. He fought against Franco, and died in a prison hospital of cold, starvation and tuberculosis. His poems were heavily censored when first published, and he has the reputation of another major poet-victim of 20th-century barbarism. His best work has been translated in *Songbook of Absences* (1972) and in *Miguel Hernández and Blas de Otero: Selected Poems* (1972). His poetry, though contemporary, is sombre and rooted in the past, and he is considered to be amongst the most original 20th-century Spanish poets and the last voice of the Generation of '27. 🕮 G Nichols, *Miguel Hernández* (1978)

Hero of Alexandria 1st century AD
Greek mathematician

He wrote on mechanics and invented many machines, including the aeolipile (the earliest known steam engine), a fire engine pump, and coin-operated devices. He also formulated an expression for the area of a triangle in terms of the lengths of its sides.

Herod, known as Herod the Great c.74–4BC
Ruler of Palestine in Roman times

The second son of the Idumaean chieftain, Antipater, procurator of Judea, he owed his initial appointment as Governor of Galilee (47BC) to **Julius Caesar**, his elevation to the kingship of Judea (37BC) to **Mark Antony**, and his retention in that post after Actium (31BC) to **Augustus**. He was a loyal Roman client king who ruthlessly kept all his subjects in check, but he also founded cities and fortresses and did much to develop the economic potential of his kingdom. He had 10 wives and 14 children, and life at his court was marked by constant and bloody in-fighting between the members of his family. His undoubted cruelty is shown in the Gospel account of the slaughter of the infants of Bethlehem (the Massacre of the Innocents).

Herod Agrippa I 10BC–AD44
Ruler of Judea

The son of Aristobulus and Berenice, and grandson of **Herod** the Great, he was educated at the court of the Emperor **Augustus** after his father was executed by Herod the Great, and lived there until his debts compelled him to take refuge in Idumea. From this period almost to the death of **Tiberius** he suffered a variety of misfortunes, but, having formed a friendship with **Caligula**, he received from him four tetrarchies, and, after the banishment of

Herod Antipas, that of Galilee and Peraea. Claudius added to his dominions Judea and Samaria. He showed some skill on conciliating the Romans and Jews, and produced a Roman-type coinage, but repressed the Christians, executing St James and imprisoning St Peter. 📖 A H Jones, *Herods of Judea* (1938)

Herod Agrippa II AD27–c.100
Ruler of Palestine in Roman times

The son of Herod Agrippa I, he was in Rome when his father died (AD44). Claudius detained him, and changed the kingdom back into a Roman province. In 53 he received nearly all his paternal possessions, which were subsequently enlarged by Nero (54). Agrippa spent great sums in adorning Jerusalem, and did all in his power to dissuade the Jews from rebelling. When Jerusalem was taken by the Jews he went with his sister to Rome, where he became praetor. It was before him that St Paul made his defence.

Herod Antipas 21BC–AD39
Ruler of Palestine in Roman times

The son of Herod the Great, by whose will he was named tetrarch of Galilee and Peraea, he divorced his first wife in order to marry Herodias, the wife of his half-brother Philip—a union against which John the Baptist remonstrated at the cost of his life. It was when Herod Antipas was in Jerusalem for the Passover that Jesus was sent before him by Pontius Pilate for examination. In AD39 he went to Rome in the hope of obtaining from Caligula the title of king; he not only failed, but, through the intrigues of his nephew Herod Agrippa I, he was banished to Lugdunum (now Lyons, France), where he died. 📖 A H Jones, *Herods of Judea* (1938)

Herodas See Herondas

Herodes Atticus, *in full* Vibullus Hipparchos Tiberius Claudius Atticus Herodes AD101–77
Greek orator and sophist

Born in Marathon, a friend of the Emperor Hadrian, he was summoned to Rome in AD140 by Antoninus Pius. He was consul in 143 with Marcus Cornelius Fronto, and a tutor to Marcus Aurelius. He is remembered as a prodigious benefactor of public buildings, including the Stadium and Odeum in Athens, a theatre in Corinth, a race-course at Delphi and a hospital at Thermopylae.

Herodian c.170–c.240AD
Greek historian

Born in Syria, he lived in Rome, and wrote a history of the Roman emperors in eight books, from the death of Marcus Aurelius (AD180) to the accession of Gordian III (AD238).

Herodotus c.485–425BC
Greek historian

He was born in Halicarnassus, a Greek colony on the coast of Asia Minor. When the colonies were freed from the Persian yoke, he travelled extensively in Asia Minor and the Middle East, and in 443BC joined the colony of Thurii, from where he visited Sicily and Lower Italy. On his travels, he collected historical, geographical, ethnological, mythological and archaeological material for his great narrative history, which included a record of the wars between Greece and Asia. Beginning with the conquest of the Greek colonies in Asia Minor by the Lydian king, Croesus, he gives a history of Lydia, Persia, Babylon and Egypt. He was the first to make the events of the past the subject of research and verification, and Cicero and others have called him 'the father of history'. 📖 A de Selincourt, *The World of Herodotus* (1962)

Hérold, Louis Joseph Ferdinand 1791–1833
French composer

Born in Paris, he composed many operas, and is best remembered for his comic operas, such as *Zampa* (1831) and *Le Pré aux clercs* (1832, 'The Field of Honour'). He also wrote several ballets and piano music.

Heron, Patrick 1920–
English painter, critic and textile designer

Born in Headingley, Leeds, he studied at the Slade School of Art, London (1937–39). A conscientious objector during World War II, he worked as a farm labourer. In St Ives (1944–45) he met Ben Nicholson, Barbara Hepworth and Adrian Stokes. He was art critic for the *New Statesman and Nation* (1947–50), and taught at the Central School of Art, London (1953–56). He has travelled and lectured in Australia, Brazil and the USA, and has held numerous one-man exhibitions worldwide. His paintings show a preoccupation with colour, and include *Scarlet, Lemon and Ultramarine* (1957) and *Cadmium with Violet, Scarlet, Emerald, Lemon and Venetian* (1969), both in the Tate Gallery, London. He has also designed for his family firm, Cresta Silks. Among his publications are *The Shape of Colour* (1973), *The Colour of Colour* (1978) and *Patrick Heron* (1988).

Herondas or Herodas 3rd century BC
Greek poet

He was a native of Cos or Miletus. His work *Mimiambi* ('Iambic Mimes'), pictures of Greek life in dialogue, comprising some 700 verses, was discovered on an Egyptian papyrus in 1891. 📖 F Will, *Herondas* (1973)

Herophilus c.335–c.280BC
Greek anatomist

Born in Chalcedon, he was the founder of the Alexandria school of anatomy. He was the first to dissect the human body to compare it with that of other animals. He described the brain, liver, spleen, sexual organs and nervous system, dividing the latter into sensory and motor, and was the first to measure the pulse, for which he used a water clock. 📖 Heinrich von Staden, *Herophilus: The Art of Medicine in Early Alexandria* (1989)

Héroult, Paul Louis Toussaint 1863–1914
French metallurgist

Born in Thury-Harcourt, Normandy, he studied at the École des Mines in Paris under Henri Le Chatelier. In 1886 he registered a patent for the extraction of aluminium by the electrolysis of cryolite in a carbon-lined crucible which served as a cathode, the method still used today. Charles Hall discovered the same process independently in the same year. In 1907 Héroult patented an arc furnace for melting iron and steel; the first arc furnaces for melting steel to be installed both in the USA and in Great Britain in the first decade of the 20th century were of his design.

Herrad of Hohenbourg, *also called* Herrad of Landsburg 1130–95
Alsatian abbess

She held the position of abbess at Hohenbourg, Alsace, from 1167. An energetic foundress, she was responsible for a priory, church, farm, hospital and hospice. She showed concern for her nuns' education and supervised their production of the *Hortus Deliciarum*, a major religious and scientific illustrated encyclopedia compiled between 1160 and 1170. The original was destroyed in the Siege of Strasbourg in 1870, but earlier tracings of many of the miniatures survive.

Herrera, Fernando de c.1534–1597
Spanish lyric poet

Born in Seville, he took holy orders and was known as 'El Divino'. Many of his love poems are remarkable for tender feeling, while his odes sometimes attain the grandeur of Milton. He wrote a prose history of the war in Cyprus

(1572), and translated Thomas Stapleton's biography of Sir Thomas More from Latin. ☐ M G Randel, *The Historical Prose of Fernando de Herrera* (1971)

Herrera, Francisco, *called* el Viejo (the Elder)
c.1576–1656
Spanish painter
Born in Seville, he painted historical pieces, and scenes from peasant life including wine shops, fairs, carnivals, and the like. His later work includes *St Basil Dictating* (c.1639, The Louvre, Paris), which shows his style developing towards the Baroque.

Herrera, Francisco, *called* el Mozo (the Younger)
1622–85
Spanish painter
Born in Seville, he was the son and pupil of Francisco Herrera, the Elder. He worked in Rome, and in 1656 moved back to Seville, where he helped to found the Academy there. In 1661 he became painter to Philip IV in Madrid. His best works are the design (later modified) of the church of El Pilar in Saragossa, a fresco, *The Ascension*, in the Atocha church in Madrid, and *St Francis*, in Seville Cathedral.

Herrick, Robert 1591–1674
English poet
Born in London, the son of a goldsmith, he was educated at Trinity Hall, Cambridge, ordained in 1623 and worked in Devon from 1629 until he was deprived of his living in 1647 for being a Royalist. His writing is mainly collected in *Hesperides: or the Works both Humane and Divine of Robert Herrick Esq* (1648), with a separate section of religious verse entitled *Noble Numbers*. He was at his best when describing rural rites as in *The Hock Cart* and *Twelfth Night*, and in well-known lyrics such as 'Gather ye rosebuds while ye may' and 'Cherry Ripe'. Youth and love and the pagan fields were his themes at a time when the West Country was devastated by the Civil War. He resumed his living in his Devon parish in 1662 after the Restoration. ☐ John Press, *Robert Herrick* (1961); M Chute, *Two Gentlemen: the lives of George Herbert and Robert Herrick* (1960)

Herriman, George 1880–1944
US strip cartoonist
Born in New Orleans, he started as office boy on the *Los Angeles Herald*, then migrated to the *New York World* in 1901, drawing a strip, *Lariat Pete* (1903). Becoming a sports cartoonist on the *New York Journal* (1904), he launched a daily strip, *Baron Mooch* (1907), replacing it with *The Dingbat Family* in 1910. The family cat eventually evolved into *Krazy Kat* (1913), the first comic strip to achieve intellectual acclaim with its originality of language and weird scenes, about an apparently bisexual cat and its unrequited love for a mouse named Ignatz.

Herring, John Frederick 1795–1865
English stagecoach driver turned painter
After driving local coaches, he devoted himself to painting racehorses, and moved to Doncaster where he depicted 33 winners of the St Leger. Moving to London, he exhibited at the Royal Academy (1818–46) and worked for both George IV and Queen Victoria. He was the most popular painter of sporting scenes in his day.

Herriot, Édouard 1872–1957
French radical-socialist statesman
Born in Troyes, he became professor at the Lycée Ampère, Lyons, and was mayor there from 1905 until his death. He was Minister of Transport during World War I, Premier (1924–25, 1926 (for two days), 1932) and several times President of the Chamber of Deputies, a post which he was holding in 1942 when he became a prisoner of Vichy and of the Nazis after renouncing his Legion of Honour,

in protest against the honour being conferred on collaborators with the Nazis. After the Liberation, he was President of the National Assembly (1947–53), and was then elected Life President. A keen supporter of the League of Nations, he opposed, however, the whole concept of the European Defence Community, especially German rearmament. He wrote a number of literary and biographical studies, the best known of which are *Madame Récamier* (1904) and *Beethoven* (1932).

Herschbach, Dudley Robert 1932–
US physical chemist and Nobel Prize winner
Born in San José, California, he studied mathematics and chemistry at Stanford University, and then chemical physics at Harvard. From 1959 to 1963 he was a member of the chemistry faculty of the University of California, Berkeley, before moving to Harvard where he was Professor of Chemistry (1963–76) then Baird Professor of Science (1976–). He shared the Nobel Prize for chemistry in 1986 with Yuan Tseh Lee and John Polanyi, for their respective contributions to chemical reaction dynamics. Reaction dynamics is concerned with the atomic and molecular motions which occur in chemical reactions, and with the energy states of reactant and product molecules. In 1959 Herschbach studied such details by adapting the technique of molecular beams, in which beams of atoms or molecules intersect at very low pressure, and special devices are used to detect the products. Among his many honours are the Polanyi Medal of the Royal Society of Chemistry (1982) and the Langmuir prize of the American Physical Society (1983).

Herschel, Caroline Lucretia 1750–1848
British astronomer
Born in Hanover, Germany, she was the sister of William Herschel. In 1772 her brother took her to England as assistant with his musical activities and she became his collaborator when he abandoned his first career for astronomy (1782). Between 1786 and 1797 she discovered eight comets. Among her other discoveries was the companion of the Andromeda nebula (1783). In 1787 she was granted a salary of £50 a year from the king as her brother's assistant at Slough. Her *Index to Flamsteed's Observations of the Fixed Stars* and a list of errata were published by the Royal Society (1798). Following her brother's death she returned at the age of 72 to Hanover where she worked on the reorganization of his catalogue of nebulae. For this unpublished work she was awarded the gold medal of the Royal Astronomical Society (1828). She was elected (with Mary Greig Somerville) an honorary member of the Royal Astronomical Society (1835), and a member of the Royal Irish Academy (1838). On her 96th birthday she received a gold medal from the King of Prussia.

Herschel, Sir John Frederick William 1792–1871
English astronomer
The only child of Sir William Herschel, he was born in Slough, and educated briefly at Eton, then at home and at St John's College, Cambridge, where he was Senior Wrangler and Smith's Prizeman (1813) and was made a Fellow of his college. His first award was the Copley Prize of the Royal Society for his mathematical research in 1821. In collaboration with Sir James South, he re-examined his father's double stars (1821–23) and produced a catalogue which earned him the Lalande Prize (1825) and the gold medal of the Royal Astronomical Society (1826). He reviewed his father's great catalogue of nebulae in Slough (1825–33), adding 525 new ones, for which he received the gold medals of the Royal Astronomical Society (1826) and the Royal Society (1836). To extend the survey to the entire sky he went to South Africa and in four years (1834–38) he completed a survey of nebulae and clusters in the southern skies, observing 1,708 of them,

the majority previously unseen. He also discovered over 1,200 pairs of double stars, catalogued over 1,000 objects in the Magellanic Clouds, and extended his father's star gauging exercise to southern fields. His southern observations, published as *Cape Observations* (1847) earned him the Copley Medal of the Royal Society (1847). Also interested in chemistry, he was a pioneer photographer, the inventor of the fixing process using hyposulphite of soda (1819) and independently of sensitized paper (1839), as well as the originator of the terms positive and negative in photography. He never occupied an academic post, supporting his research from his private means, his one official appointment being Master of the Mint (1850–55). He was made a baronet at Queen Victoria's coronation. Among his numerous honours were the Prussian Pour le Mérite and membership of the French Institute. 📖 Gunther Buttmann, *The Shadow of the Telescope* (1970)

Herschel, Sir (Frederick) William, originally Friedrich Wilhelm Herschel 1738–1822
British astronomer

Born in Hanover, Germany, he was the son of a musician who instructed his sons in the same profession. William joined the Hanoverian Guards band as an oboist and moved in 1755 to England where he built up a successful career in music, eventually settling in Bath in 1766, where his interest in astronomy began. He built his own telescopes, learning to cast his own metal discs for his mirrors. In 1781 he discovered the planet Uranus, the first to be found telescopically, which he named *Georgium Sidus* in honour of King George III, who a year later appointed him his private astronomer. At Slough, near Windsor, assisted by his sister Caroline Herschel, he continued his research and built ever larger telescopes. Herschel's discoveries included two satellites of Uranus (1787) and two of Saturn (1789), but his epoch-making work lay in his studies of the stellar universe. He drew up his first catalogue of double stars (1782), later demonstrating that such objects constitute bodies in orbit around each other (1802), and observed the Sun's motion through space (1783). His famous paper, *On the Construction of the Heavens* (1784), produced a model of the Milky Way as a non-uniform aggregation of stars; such studies occupied him for the rest of his life. Following the publication of Charles Messier's catalogue of nebulae and star clusters (1781), he began a systematic search for such non-stellar objects which revealed a total of 2,500, published in three catalogues (1786, 1789, 1802). He distinguished different types of nebulae, realizing that some were distant clusters of stars while others were nebulosities. Herschel was knighted in 1816. The epitaph on his tomb sums up his immense influence on the course of astronomy: *Coelorum perupit claustra* 'he broke the barriers of the heavens'. 📖 A Armitage, *William Herschel* (1962)

Hersey, John Richard 1914–93
US writer

Born in Tientsin, China, of US missionary parents, he was educated at Yale University in the USA, and became correspondent in the Far East for *Time* magazine. He began to write both fiction and non-fiction using the information he gathered as a journalist, producing the novel *A Bell for Adano* (1944, Pulitzer Prize winner; it was also dramatized and filmed), on the US occupation of Italy and the non-fiction work *Hiroshima* (1946), the first on-the-spot description of the effects of a nuclear explosion. Later works included *The War Lover* (1959), *Under the Eye of the Storm* (1967), *The Walnut Door* (1977) and *Antonietta* (1991). 📖 D Sanders, *John Hersey Revisited* (1990)

Hershey, A(lfred) D(ay) 1908–97
US biologist and Nobel Prize winner

Born in Owosso, Michigan, he studied at Michigan State College, and from 1950 to 1974 worked at the Carnegie Institution in Washington, where from 1962 he was director of the Genetics Research Unit. He became an expert on the viruses which infect bacteria (bacteriophage or 'phage'), and set up the Phage Group with Salvador Luria and Max Delbrück in the late 1940s, to encourage the use of phage as an experimental tool. At that time, it was not known whether the DNA or protein of this organism was its genetic information-carrying component. Oswald Avery had suggested in 1944 that DNA was the genetic material but experimental evidence was lacking. Working with Martha Chase in the early 1950s, Hershey provided firm evidence for the idea, and they and others later confirmed that the DNA of other organisms fulfils the same role. Hershey shared the 1969 Nobel Prize for physiology or medicine with Luria and Delbrück.

Herskovits, Melville J(ean) 1895–1963
US cultural anthropologist

Born in Bellefontaine, Ohio, he studied at Columbia University under Franz Boas and taught at Northwestern University, Illinois (1927–63), and set up the first US university programme in African studies (1951). He was an uncompromising advocate of cultural relativism, the view that all standards of judgement are culture-bound, and his most complete presentation of this is in *Man and His Works* (1948). His major interest in African cultures and his great knowledge of the continent gave rise to *The Human Factor in Changing Africa* (1962). He was also a pioneer in the field of economic anthropology, and published *The Economic Life of Primitive Peoples* in 1940. His other works include *Myth of the Negro Past* (1941), *Economic Anthropology* (1952) and *Cultural Dynamics* (1964).

Herter, Christian Archibald 1895–1966
US politician

Educated at Harvard, he was Governor of Massachusetts (1953–57), and Under-Secretary of State to John Foster Dulles, whom he succeeded as Secretary (1959–61). His background of diplomatic experience included being acting minister to Belgium at the age of 21, and personal assistant to Herbert Hoover (1921–24). A sincere if reticent internationalist, he tended to be overshadowed by Dulles.

Hertwig, Oscar Wilhelm August 1849–1922
German zoologist

Born in Freidberg, Hessen, he was professor at the universities of Jena and Berlin, and investigated early stages of development. He showed that it is necessary for the nuclei of egg cells and spermatozoa to fuse for fertilization to occur, and that only a single sperm cell is required. He also studied the effects of radioactivity on germ cells.

Hertz, Gustav Ludwig 1887–1975
German physicist and Nobel Prize winner

He was born in Hamburg, the nephew of Heinrich Hertz, and educated at the University of Berlin. In 1928 he was appointed Professor of Physics at the Technical University in Berlin, and later became director of the Siemens Research Laboratory. With James Franck, he showed that atoms would only absorb a fixed amount of energy, thus demonstrating the quantized nature of the atom's electron energy levels. For this work they shared the 1925 Nobel Prize for physics. The results provided data for Niels Bohr to develop his theory of atomic structure, and for Max Planck to develop his ideas on quantum theory. After World War II Hertz went to the USSR to become head of a research laboratory (1945–54), then returned to Germany to become director of the Physics Institute in Leipzig (1954–61).

Hertz, Heinrich Rudolf 1857–94
German physicist
Born in Hamburg, he was educated at the Johanneum Gymnasium before moving to Berlin where he studied under Gustav Kirchhoff and Hermann von Helmholtz, becoming the latter's assistant. In 1885 he was appointed Professor of Physics at Karlsruhe University, and in 1889 became professor at Bonn University. In 1887 Hertz confirmed James Clerk Maxwell's predictions by his fundamental discovery of 'Hertzian waves', now known as radio waves, which excepting wavelength, behave like light waves. Later he explored the general theoretical implications of Maxwell's electrodynamics, was widely honoured for his work on electric waves, and in 1890 he was awarded the Rumford Medal of the Royal Society.

Hertz, Joseph Herman 1872–1946
British Zionist leader and writer
Born in Rebrin, Hungary (now in Czechoslovakia), he studied at Columbia University, New York, and became rabbi at Johannesburg from 1898 to 1911 (with a temporary expulsion by President Kruger for his pro-British attitude during the Second Boer War). He was appointed Professor of Philosophy at Transvaal University College in 1906. In 1913 he became chief rabbi of the Hebrew Congregations of the British Empire. He wrote *The Jew in South Africa* (1905) and other works.

Hertzen, Aleksandr Ivanovich See Herzen, Aleksandr Ivanovich

Hertzog, J(ames) B(arry) M(unnik) 1866–1942
South African statesman
Born in Wellington, Cape Colony, he studied law at Stellenbosch and Amsterdam, became a Boer general (1899–1902), and in 1910 became Minister of Justice in the first Union government. In 1913 he founded the Nationalist Party, advocating complete South African independence from the British Empire, and in World War I opposed co-operation with Great Britain. As Prime Minister (1924–39), in coalition with Labour (1924–29), and with Jan Smuts in a United Party (1933–39), he pursued a programme which destroyed the African franchise, created reservation for whites, and tightened land segregation. He renounced his earlier secessionism, but at the outbreak of World War II declared for neutrality, was defeated, lost office, and in 1940 retired. 📖 L E Neame, *General Hertzog* (1930)

Hertzsprung, Ejnar 1873–1967
Danish astronomer
Born in Fredriksberg, Copenhagen, he graduated in chemical engineering from the Technical High School in Copenhagen and was employed for some years in this profession before entering astronomy (1902) and joining the staff of the university observatory in Copenhagen. He published in 1905 the principle of what was later to be called the Hertzsprung–Russell diagram, which became the key for the theory of stellar evolution. In 1909 he obtained a position under Karl Schwarzschild at the University of Göttingen, from where he moved with Schwarzschild to the Astrophysical Observatory in Potsdam. He was appointed director of the Leyden Observatory, where his enthusiasm and example were of great benefit to astronomy in the Netherlands. He was awarded the gold medal of the Royal Astronomical Society in 1929 and the Bruce Medal of the Astronomical Society of the Pacific in 1937.

Hervieu, Paul Ernest 1857–1915
French dramatist and novelist
He was born in Neuilly. His plays include *L'Énigme* (1901), *Le Dédale* (1903, 'The Labyrinth') and other powerful pieces, usually on family problems. He also wrote a successful drama about the Revolutionary period, *Théroigne de Méricourt* (1902), created for the famous actress Sarah Bernhardt. 📖 P Gaultier, *Maîtres de la pensée française* (1921)

Herzberg, Gerhard 1904–
Canadian physical chemist and Nobel Prize winner
Born in Hamburg, Germany, he was educated in Göttingen and Berlin, and taught at Darmstadt before emigrating to Canada in 1935, where he taught at the University of Saskatchewan (1935–45). From 1949 to 1969 he was director of the division of pure physics at the National Research Council in Ottawa. He greatly developed and used spectroscopic methods for a variety of purposes, including the detailed study of energy levels in atoms and molecules and the detection of unusual molecules both in laboratory work and in interstellar space. He was awarded the Nobel Prize for chemistry in 1971.

Herzen or Hertzen, Aleksandr Ivanovich 1812–70
Russian political thinker and writer
Born in Moscow, the illegitimate son of a nobleman, he was imprisoned in 1834 for his revolutionary socialism and exiled to the provinces. In 1847 he left Russia for Paris, and in 1851 settled in London, becoming a powerful propagandist through his novels and treatises, and by the smuggling into Russia of his journal *Kolokol* (1857–67, 'The Bell'). His most important writings are his memoirs, which were published in *Byloe i dumy* (1861–67, Eng trans *My Past and Thoughts*, 1924–27). 📖 E Acton, *Alexander Herzen and the Role of the Intellectual Revolutionary* (1979)

Herzl, Theodor 1860–1904
Hungarian Zionist leader
Born in Budapest, he moved to Vienna at the age of 18, where he trained as a lawyer and pursued a career as a journalist and author. In Paris as a newspaper correspondent (1891–95), he covered the Dreyfus trial (1894) and was deeply affected by its anti-Semitism. He became convinced that the only adequate Jewish response was a political one, and in 1895 published *Der Judenstaat* ('The Jewish State'), in which he argued that the Jews should have their own state. In 1897, in Basle, he convened the First Zionist Congress, which declared its goal to be the founding of a national Jewish home in Palestine and established the World Zionist Organization to that end. He spent his remaining years seeking support for the organization's aims from influential European leaders, and his name is inseparable from the emergence of political Zionism in the modern period.

Herzog, Émile See Maurois, André

Herzog, Roman 1934–
German Christian Democrat politician
Born in Landshut, he was educated at the University of Munich and the Free University of Berlin. A specialist in business studies, he is an honorary professor of the School of Management Studies at the University of Tübingen. In 1973 he was elected the representative for Rhineland-Palatinate and was appointed Minister of the Interior in 1980. He was president of the Federal Constitutional Court from 1987 to 1994, when he became President of Germany.

Heselrige, Sir Arthur See Haselrig, Sir Arthur

Heseltine, Michael Ray Dibdin 1933–
English Conservative politician
Born in Swansea, South Wales, and educated at Shrewsbury School and at Pembroke College, Oxford, after national service he established a successful publishing business, Haymarket Press, before entering the House of Commons in 1966, as MP for Tavistock, and, from 1974, Henley-on-Thames. After holding junior posts under Edward Heath, he joined Margaret Thatcher's Cabinet in

1979 as Secretary of State for the Environment and was made Defence Secretary in 1983. He resigned dramatically in 1986, claiming that he had been calumnied over the Westland Affair which involved the sale of the British helicopter manufacturer, Westland, to a US rather than a European company. Always popular at party conferences, he has long been seen as a potential Conservative leader, but was unsuccessful in the leadership contest which led to Margaret Thatcher's resignation in 1990. He returned to the Cabinet under John Major and again became Secretary of State for the Environment (1990–92), when he presided over the reform of the poll tax and the plans to replace it with a council tax. As President of the Board of Trade (1992–95) he announced the closure of 31 coal mines in 1992, and came under heavy public and political pressure to modify these cutbacks. First Secretary of State and deputy Prime Minister from 1995 to 1997, when the Conservatives were defeated in the general election, he declined to run in the ensuing leadership contest for health reasons. He was appointed Companion of Honour in 1997. His publications include *The Challenge of Europe* (1989). 📖 Michael Crick, *Michael Heseltine: A Life* (1997)

Hesiod c.8th century BC
Greek poet

Born in Ascra, Boeotia, he is one of the earliest known Greek poets. He wrote in a didactic style and is best known for the epics *Opera et dies* ('Works and Days'), which deals with the farmer's life and gives a realistic picture of a primitive peasant community, and *Theogonia* ('Theogony'), which teaches the origin of the universe and the history of the gods. 📖 A R Burn, *The World of Hesiod* (1966)

Hess, Germain Henri 1802–50
Russian chemist

Born in Geneva, Switzerland, he was taken to Russia in childhood. After studying medicine, chemistry and geology at the University of Dorpat (Tartu, Estonia), he worked briefly with Jöns Jacob Berzelius. He took part in a geological expedition to the Urals and practised medicine in Irkutsk, but from around 1830 devoted himself to chemistry. He was appointed Professor of Chemistry at the Technological Institute of St Petersburg. His earliest research was on mineral analysis and on the natural gas of Baku, but he then turned to thermochemistry. After extensive measurements of the heats of chemical reaction, he established the 'law of constant heat summation' (1838–40), which states that the heat developed in a given chemical change is constant, independent of whether the change is carried out in one stage or in several stages. This law, commonly called Hess's law, is a special case of the law of conservation of energy, but at the time this had not been clearly formulated.

Hess, Harry Hammond 1906–69
US marine geophysicist and geologist

Born in New York City and educated at the universities of Yale and Princeton, he returned to Princeton as instructor (1934), and later became Professor of Geology (1948) and Blair Professor (1964) there. During active service in the navy in 1941, he discovered flat-topped seamounts which he named guyots. Aware that such uniform ocean layers could only be formed by a uniform process, he described the oceans as young, ephemeral and with constant renewal by magma flowing into the mid-ocean ridges (1960). This sea-floor spreading process pushes the ocean floor away from the mid-ocean ridges through convection in the Earth's mantle, carrying the continental plates with it, and is thought to provide the power for continental drift.

Hess, Dame Myra 1890–1966
English pianist

Born in London, she studied under Tobias Matthay at the Royal Academy of Music, and was an immediate success on her first public appearance in 1907. She worked as a chamber musician, recitalist and virtuoso, achieving fame in North America as well as Great Britain. During World War II she organized the lunchtime concerts in the National Gallery, London, for which she was awarded the DBE in 1941. 📖 Denise Lassimonne (ed), *Myra Hess, By Her Friends* (1966)

Hess, (Walter Richard) Rudolf 1894–1987
German Nazi politician

Born in Alexandria, Egypt, and educated at Godesberg, he fought in World War I, after which he studied at Munich University, where he fell under Hitler's spell. He joined the Nazi Party in 1920, took part in the abortive Munich rising (1923) and, having shared Hitler's imprisonment and, it is said, taken down from him *Mein Kampf*, became in 1934 his deputy as party leader and in 1939 his successor-designate, after Hermann Goering, as Führer. In May 1941, on the eve of Germany's attack on Russia, he flew alone to Scotland (Eaglesham), supposedly to plead the cause of a negotiated Anglo-German peace, which prompted Churchill's comment: 'The maggot is in the apple'. He was temporarily imprisoned in the Tower of London, then placed under psychiatric care near Aldershot. At the Nuremberg Trials (1946) he was sentenced to life imprisonment. He spent the rest of his life in Spandau jail, Berlin, where after 1966 he was the sole remaining prisoner. 📖 W Schwartzwaller, *Rudolf Hess* (1988)

Hess, Victor Francis 1883–1964
US physicist and Nobel Prize winner

He was born in Waldstein, Austria, and while on the staff of Vienna University during 1911–12, he made a number of manned balloon flights carrying ionization chambers. He demonstrated that the radiation intensity in the atmosphere increased with height, and concluded that the high-energy cosmic radiation that was responsible must originate from outer space. He also helped to determine the number of alpha particles given off by a gram of radium (1918). For his work on 'cosmic radiation' he was awarded the 1936 Nobel Prize for physics, jointly with Carl Anderson. In 1938 he emigrated to the USA to become Professor of Physics at Fordham University, New York (1938–56).

Hess, Walter Rudolf 1881–1973
Swiss physiologist and Nobel Prize winner

Born in Frauenfeld, he studied medicine at Lausanne, Bern, Zurich, Berlin and Kiel universities, receiving his degree from Zurich in 1906. As Professor of Physiology and director of the Physiology Institute of the University of Zurich (1917–51), he studied the regulation of blood pressure and heart rate, and their relationship to respiration, and from 1925 worked on the function of structures at the base of the brain. He developed methods of stimulating localized areas of the brain by means of fine needle electrodes, which permitted major advances in the study of brain function. He was able to show that stimulating different parts of the hypothalamus causes changes in body temperature, blood pressure, respiration, and also anger, sexual arousal, and sleep. He was awarded the 1949 Nobel Prize for physiology or medicine with António Egas Moniz.

Hesse, Eva 1936–70
US sculptor

She was born in Hamburg, Germany, into a Jewish family, which emigrated to the USA in 1939 and settled in New York. There she attended the Pratt Institute, New York (1952–53), and Cooper Union (1954–57). From 1965 she worked in a variety of materials, such as rubber, plastic, string and polythene, creating objects designed to rest on the floor or against a wall or to be suspended from the ceiling, as in *Hang-up* (1965–66) and *Three Nets* (1960). Her unconventional techniques and imaginative work exerted a strong influence on later 'conceptual' artists. Her work is represented at the Tate Gallery in London.

Hesse, Hermann 1877–1962
Swiss novelist and poet, and Nobel Prize winner

Born in Calw, Württemberg, Germany, he was a bookseller and antiquary in Basle from 1895 to 1902, and published his first novel, *Peter Camenzind*, in 1904 (Eng trans 1961). From then on he devoted himself to writing, living in Switzerland from 1911 and becoming a naturalized citizen in 1923. Though he disclaimed any ruling purpose, the theme of his work might be stated as a musing on the difficulties put in the way of the individual in his efforts to build up an integrated, harmonious self. This is expressed in sensitive and sensuous language in such prose works as *Rosshalde* (1914, Eng trans 1970), *Knulp* (1915, Eng trans 1971), *Demian* (1919, Eng trans 1971), a psychoanalytic study of incest, *Narziss und Goldmund* (1930, Eng trans *Death and the Lover*, 1932), *Steppenwolf* (1927, Eng trans 1929) and *Das Glasperlenspiel* (1943, Eng trans *The Glass Bead Game*, 1949), a Utopian fantasy on the theme of withdrawal from the world. Hesse was awarded both the **Goethe** Prize and the Nobel Prize for literature in 1946. His poetry was collected in *Die Gedichte* in 1942 (a selection, Eng trans *Hours in the Garden and Other Poems*, 1979), and his letters, *Briefe*, appeared in 1951. His *Beschwörungen* (1955, 'Affirmations') confirmed that his powers were not diminished by age. 📖 J Mileck, *Hesse: his life and art* (1978)

Heston, Charlton, *originally* Charles Carter 1923–
US film actor

Born in Evanston, Illinois, he made his film debut in an amateur production of *Peer Gynt* (1941). After World War II service in the air force, and further theatre experience, he made his Broadway debut in *Antony and Cleopatra* (1947). His first Hollywood film was *Dark City* (1950), but his major early successes were the **Cecil B De Mille** films *The Greatest Show on Earth* (1952) and *The Ten Commandments* (1956). He also played the larger-than-life heroes for which his strapping physique suited him in *Ben Hur* (1959, Academy Award) and *El Cid* (1961). Other films include *Touch of Evil* (1958), *The War Lord* (1965) and *Will Penny* (1967). He has frequently returned to the stage, and has also directed *Antony and Cleopatra* (1972) on film and, for television, *A Man for All Seasons* (1988). He has published the autobiographies *The Actor's Life* (1978) and *In the Arena* (1995). 📖 M B Druxman, *Charlton Heston* (1976)

Hesychius fl.5th or 6th century
Alexandrian Greek scholar

He compiled a Greek lexicon in which are preserved many words and phrases found nowhere else. Of particular importance are the original rare words used by Greek poets which have later been replaced by commoner synonyms.

Heuss, Theodor 1884–1963
German statesman

Born in Brackenheim, Württemberg, he was educated in Munich and Berlin and became editor of the political magazine *Hilfe* (1905–12), professor at the Berlin College of Political Science (1920–33), and MP (1924–28, 1930–32). A prolific author and journalist, he wrote two books denouncing **Hitler**, and when the latter came to power in 1933, Heuss was dismissed from his professorship and his books were publicly burnt. Nevertheless, he continued to write them in retirement at Heidelberg under the pseudonym of 'Brackenheim' until 1946, when he became

founder member of the Free Democratic Party (FDP), and helped to draft the new federal constitution. He was the first President of the Federal Republic of Germany (1949–59) and in that capacity paid a state visit to Great Britain in October 1958, the first German head of state to do so since 1907. **Albert Schweitzer** officiated when Heuss in 1907 married Elly Knapp (1881–1951), social scientist and author. He published his autobiographical *Vorspiele* in 1954.

Hevelius, Johannes 1611–87
Polish astronomer

Born in Gdańsk, he studied law at the University of Leyden, and travelled in France and Germany. He constructed an observatory with a terrace for large quadrants and sextants, and high masts for the attachment of long telescopes in the 1640s. His *Selenographica* (1647) was a description of the Moon with 133 copper plates of lunar features made by his own hand. He named many details on the Moon after Earth features, and some of these names survive today. In the 1660s his interest turned to comets, resulting in his *Cometographia* (1668), a list of all comets observed up to that year. The first part of his major publication, *Machina Coelestis*, appeared in 1673, containing a detailed description of his observatory. In 1678 Hevelius was visited by the King of Poland, John III Sobieski, and in the following year by **Edmond Halley**. In 1879 the observatory, with all its instruments and manuscripts, was destroyed by fire. His last work, a catalogue of 1,564 stars with maps of the constellations, was published posthumously in 1690.

Hevesy, George Charles de 1885–1966
Hungarian chemist and Nobel Prize winner

He was born in Budapest, studied at Freiburg and held posts at the Technische Hochschule in Zurich and at Manchester University, where he worked with **Ernest Rutherford**. He moved to Vienna in 1912 and after service in the Austro-Hungarian army during World War I, he moved to the Institute of Theoretical Physics in Copenhagen to join **Niels Bohr**. There he and **Dirk Coster** discovered hafnium in 1923. In 1935 he returned to Freiburg where he began to calculate the relative abundances of the elements in the universe. In World War II he fled to Sweden, where he became professor at Stockholm. His work on isotopes has been very influential in physics, chemistry and medicine. From 1934 onwards he pioneered the use of radioactive tracers to study chemical processes, particularly in living organisms. This work won him the Nobel Prize for chemistry in 1943. 📖 Hilde Levi, *George de Hevesy: Life and Work* (1985)

Hewish, Antony 1924–
English radio astronomer and Nobel Prize winner

Born in Fowey, Cornwall, he studied at Cambridge and spent his career there, becoming Professor of Radio Astronomy (1971–89), then Emeritus Professor. In 1967 he began studying the scintillation ('twinkling') of astronomical radio sources. This led him and his student **Jocelyn Bell Burnell** to discover the first radio sources emitting radio signals in regular pulses now known as pulsars; many others have since been discovered. They are believed to be very small and dense rotating neutron stars. He shared the Nobel Prize for physics in 1974 with his former teacher Sir **Martin Ryle**.

Hewlett, Maurice Henry 1861–1923
English novelist, poet and essayist

Born in London, he was the keeper of land revenue records (1896–1900), and made his name with his historical romance *The Forest Lovers* (1898). He wrote several more novels on historical themes, and a trilogy of novels featuring the character John Maxwell Senhouse, a scholar-gypsy. He also wrote nature sketches and several volumes of poetry, of which the long poem *The Song of the Plow* (1916) is perhaps his best work. 📖 L. Binyon (ed), *The Letters of Maurice Hewlett. To Which is Added a Diary in Greece* (1926)

He Xiangning (Ho Hsiang-ning) 1880–1972
Chinese revolutionary and feminist

Educated in Hong Kong and Japan, she married fellow revolutionary **Liao Zhongkai** in 1905 and was an active advocate of links with the communists and Russia. Her husband was assassinated in 1925, and when two years later **Chiang Kai-shek** broke with the communists, she returned to Hong Kong and was an outspoken critic of his leadership. She returned to Beijing (Peking) in 1949 as head of the overseas commission. She was one of the first Chinese women publicly to advocate nationalism, revolution and female emancipation, and one of the first to cut her hair short.

Hey, James Stanley 1909–
English physicist

Born in the Lake District, he studied physics at Manchester University, and from 1940 to 1952 was on the staff of the Army Operational Research Group. He then moved to the Royal Radar Establishment (1952–69), where he was chief science officer from 1966. He was elected Fellow of the Royal Society in 1978. In 1942 he discovered that the Sun is a strong radio source in the 4–8 metre wavelength region, and that solar flares and sunspots are especially effective in this respect. In 1946 Hey and his colleagues identified that the radio waves coming from the constellation Cygnus originated in the small discrete source named Cygnus A. He was also a pioneer in the use of 5 metre wavelength radar for studying meteors, used to great effect in his detailed observations of the Giacobinid shower of 1946. His autobiography, *The Secret Man*, was published in 1992.

Heyden, Jan van der 1637–1712
Dutch painter

Born in Gorinchem, although he produced still-life paintings at the beginning and end of his career, he is best remembered for his novel and precise townscapes of Amsterdam, executed in the 1660s. In that city, where he lived from 1650 until his death, his financial success was mostly due to his mechanical inventions, especially of fire-fighting equipment and street lighting. These inventions were depicted in a series of engravings he did which were published in book form in 1690 under the title of *Brandspuiten-boek* ('Fire Engine Book').

Heydrich, Reinhard, *nicknamed* the Hangman 1904–42
German Nazi politician

Born in Halle, as a youth he joined the violent anti-Weimar Freikorps (Volunteer Corps) (1918). He served in the navy (1922–31) but quit to join the Nazi Party, and entered the SS (*Schutzstaffel*, protective force) rising to be second-in-command of the Gestapo. He was charged with subduing **Hitler**'s occupied countries, during which he ordered numerous mass executions. In 1941 he was made Deputy-Protector of Bohemia and Moravia, but the following year was killed by Czech assassins parachuted in from Great Britain. In the murderous reprisals, Lidice village was razed and every man put to death.

Heyer, Georgette 1902–74
English historical and detective novelist

Born in London, of partly South Slav descent, she studied at Westminster College, London, and after marriage in 1925 travelled in East Africa and Yugoslavia until 1929. By that time she had produced several well-researched historical novels from various periods, including *The Black Moth* (1921) and *Beauvallet* (1929). She also wrote fictional studies of **William the Conqueror**, **Charles II**, and the Battle of Waterloo. *Regency Buck* (1935) was the first of her novels on the Regency period, of which she made herself an outstanding authority. *My Lord John* (1976), on **Henry V**'s brother, was unfinished at her death. She also wrote modern comic detective novels such as *Behold, Here's Poison* (1936), and used detective and thriller plots with pace and irony in historical fiction such as *The Reluctant Widow* (1946) and *The Quiet Gentleman* (1951). 📖 J A Hodge, *The Private World of Georgette Heyer* (1984)

Heyerdahl, Thor 1914–
Norwegian anthropologist

Born in Larvik and educated at the University of Oslo, he served with the free Norwegian military forces during World War II. In 1937 he had led his first expedition to Fatu Hiva in the Marquesas Islands of the Pacific and during his year there developed the theory that certain aspects of the Polynesian culture owed their origins to settlers from the Americas, possibly the pre-Inca inhabitants of Peru. To prove this, in 1947 he and five colleagues sailed a balsa raft, *Kon-Tiki*, from Callao, Peru, to Tuamotu Island in the South Pacific, spending 101 days adrift. Although the academic community was initially slow to acknowledge his work, his success in this venture and on subsequent archaeological expeditions to the Galapagos in 1953 and Easter Island in 1955, won him popular fame and several distinguished awards. In 1970, to test the theory that ancient Mediterranean people could have crossed the Atlantic to Central America before **Christopher Columbus**, he sailed from Morocco to the West Indies in a papyrus-reed boat *Ra II*, reaching Barbados in 57 days. His subsequent journey (1977–78) from Iraq to Djibouti in the reed-ship *Tigris* was to show that these craft could be manoeuvred against the wind and so complete two-way journeys via the Persian Gulf and Arabian Sea. The political conflict in Ethiopia, Somalia and the Yemen and the appalling pollution, especially from oil, led them to burn the *Tigris* in protest at Djibouti. He went on to lead an archaeological expedition to the Maldive Islands (1982–84), jointly organized a Norwegian/Chilean expedition to Easter Island (1986–88) and in 1990 began to supervise an investigation into archaeological remains in Tenerife, Canary Islands. His books include *The Tigris Expedition* (1980), *The Maldive Mystery* (1986), *Easter Island: the mystery solved* (1989) and *Pyramids of Tucume* (1995). 📖 Arnold Jacoby, *Señor Kon-Tiki: The Biography of Thor Heyerdahl* (1967)

Heym, Stefan, *originally* Helmut Flieg 1913–
German novelist and journalist

He was born in Chemnitz, the son of a Jewish businessman, and fled Germany in 1937. He later served in the US army and took part in the Normandy landings of 1944, before settling in Munich when peace came. He moved to East Germany in 1953 and much of his writing has been concerned with a critique of capitalism and the deficiencies of the erstwhile Eastern bloc. His English novel *The Eyes of Reason* (1951) makes explicit Heym's support for the communist state and *Fünf Tage im Juni* (1974, 'Five Days in June') recounts the GDR workers' revolt of 1953 in a manner sharply at odds with the official version. He has recently been critical of the 'instant capitalism' which followed the fall of the Berlin Wall. In 1994, as a member of the Party of Democratic Socialism (the reformed Communist Party), he was elected to the Bundestag, becoming (at 81 years old) its oldest member.

Heymann, Lida Gustava 1867–1943
German feminist and political activist

Born in Hamburg, she was financially independent and during the 1890s organized a number of projects for women, including a day nursery, a women's home and training for apprentices. In 1898, with Minna Cauer, she campaigned against legalized prostitution, and together with **Anita Augspurg** they founded the women's suffrage society, *Deutscher Verband für Frauenstimmrecht* (1902). They then moved to Munich (1907), where they carried on a militant suffrage campaign. They joined the more radical *Deutscher Frauenstimmrechtsbund* in 1913, but their pacifism cost them support within the suffrage movement during World War I. The three colleagues then started a newspaper, *Die Frau im Staat*, in 1918. When Hitler gained power in 1933, Heymann and Augspurg fled to Zurich, continued to work for women's rights, and wrote their memoirs, *Erlebtes-Erschautes*.

Heymans, Corneille Jean François 1892–1968
Belgian physiologist and Nobel Prize winner

Born in Ghent, he studied medicine at the university there, where in 1922 he was appointed as a lecturer in pharmacology. After postgraduate work in Paris, Lausanne, Vienna, London and Cleveland, Ohio, he became director of the Institute of Pharmacology and Therapeutics in Ghent (1925). He developed the technique of 'cross circulation' to demonstrate that the rate of respiration is controlled by nerves, and showed that structures in the arteries contain special cells sensitive to blood pressure and blood chemicals which monitor the nervous mechanism by which respiration is controlled. He received the 1938 Nobel Prize for physiology or medicine.

Heyn, Piet See Heijn, Piet

Heyrovský, Jaroslav 1890–1967
Czech physical and analytical chemist and Nobel Prize winner

Born in Prague, he began to study chemistry, physics and mathematics at the Charles University, but in 1910 he moved to University College London. In 1913 he became a demonstrator there and might well have spent the rest of his career in London, but the outbreak of World War I caught him in Prague. He did war service as a dispensing chemist and radiologist in a military hospital and was able to continue his studies, obtaining his PhD in Prague in 1918. After the war he became an assistant at the Charles University and became Professor of Physical Chemistry by 1926. He invented the polarograph (1922–25) and his scientific effort for the rest of his life was devoted to the improvement of the polarographic technique and extending its applications. In 1950 he became director of the newly established Polarographic Institute, which was incorporated into the Czechoslovak Academy of Sciences in 1952. He received the Nobel Prize for chemistry in 1959, the first Czech national to gain a Nobel award. Among his numerous other honours were foreign membership of the Royal Society (1965) and honorary fellowship of the Chemical Society (1963).

Heyse, Paul Johann von 1830–1914
German writer and Nobel Prize winner

He was born in Berlin, and settled in Munich in 1854. He excelled as a short-story writer, his tales being marked by a graceful style, sly humour and frequent sensuality. They were collected in *Das Buch der Freundschaft* (1883–84, 'The Book of Friendship') and other volumes. He also wrote novels, plays and epic poems, and translations of Italian poets. He was awarded the 1910 Nobel Prize for literature. 📖 L Ferrari, *Paul Heyse und die literarische Strömungen seiner Zeit* (1939)

Heysen, Sir (Wilhelm Ernst) Hans (Franz) 1877–1968
Australian landscape painter

Born in Hamburg, Germany, of Austrian parentage, he emigrated to Adelaide, Australia, with his parents in 1884. He sold his first painting at the age of 16 for 10 shillings, and a local businessman paid for his tuition at the Adelaide School of Design. Other businessmen sponsored his trip to Europe (1899), where he studied in Paris and painted in Italy, Holland and the UK. Returning to Adelaide in 1903 to teach, the following year he won the Wynne Prize for landscape painting, a prize he won nine times between 1904 and 1932. Primarily a watercolourist, his first major exhibition was in Melbourne in 1908, and his success grew during the following 20 years. He was knighted in 1959. His daughter Nora Heysen (1911–) is a noted Impressionist painter of still lifes and portraits, and won the Archibald prize in 1938.

Heywood, John c.1497–c.1580
English epigrammatist, playwright and musician

He was born probably in London and studied at Oxford. Introduced at court by Sir **Thomas More** (a distant cousin by marriage), he made himself, by his wit and his skill in singing and playing on the virginals, a favourite with **Henry VIII** and with Queen **Mary I**, to whom he had been music teacher in her youth. He was a devout Catholic, and after the accession of **Elizabeth I** went to Belgium. He wrote several short plays or interludes, whose individual characters, such as 'the Pedlar', and 'the Pardoner', represent classes, and which thus form a link between the old moralities and the modern drama. He is remembered above all, however, for his collections of proverbs and epigrams. His wearisome allegorical poem, *The Spider and the Flie* (1556), contrasts Catholicism and Protestantism. He was the grandfather of **John Donne**. 📖 R C Johnson, *John Heywood* (1970)

Heywood, Thomas c.1574–1641
English dramatist, poet and actor

Born in Lincolnshire, he was educated at Cambridge, and in 1598 was engaged by **Philip Henslowe** as an actor with the Lord Admiral's Men. He contributed to the composition of 220 plays up to 1633, and he also wrote poetry, *Nine Bookes of Various History concerning Women* (1624), a volume of rhymed translations from **Lucian**, **Erasmus**, and **Ovid**, various pageants, tracts and treatises, and *The Life of Ambrosius Merlin* (1641). Of the 24 of his plays which have survived, the best are *A Woman Kilde with Kindnesse* (acted 1603, printed 1607), a domestic tragedy, and *The English Traveller* (1633). His work is usually distinguished by naturalness and simplicity. In the two parts of *The Fair Maid of the West* (1631), and in *Fortune by Land and Sea* (1655, with **William Rowley**), he gives some spirited descriptions of sea fights. *The Rape of Lucrece* (1608) is chiefly notable for its songs, *A Challenge for Beautie* (1636) for its tenderness. *The Royall King and Loyall Subject* (1637) stresses the doctrine of passive obedience to kingly authority. 📖 F S Boas, *Thomas Heywood* (1950)

Hezekiah 8th century BC
Biblical character

King of Judah, he was renowned for his religious reforms, including the re-establishment of Temple worship in Jerusalem (2 Chronicles 29–32), and for his political attempts to obtain independence from Assyrian domination (2 Kings 18–20; Isaiah 36–39).

Hiawatha, *originally* Haionhwat'ha ('He Makes Rivers') c.1570
Native American leader (perhaps legendary)

A chieftain of the Mohawk or of the Onondaga people, he is said to have been a founder of the League of the Five Nations of the Iroquois (known as the Iroquois Confederacy), uniting the Mohawk, Oneida, Onondaga, Cayuga, and Seneca tribes. According to legend, he joined Huron mystic Deganawida in a plan to end warfare among Native Americans in what is now New York State, travelling from tribe to tribe to negotiate the alliance and build a confederacy governed by elected representatives. **Henry Wadsworth Longfellow** used his name for the hero of his poem *The Song of Hiawatha* (1855).

Hibbert, Robert 1770–1849
British merchant and philanthropist

Born in Jamaica, where he became a slave-owner, he moved to England. In 1847 he founded the Hibbert Trust, whose funds, in 1878 applied to the Hibbert Lectures, also aided the *Hibbert Journal* (1920–70).

Hichens, Robert Smythe 1864–1950
English novelist

He studied music, but made his name as a novelist with books such as *The Green Carnation* (1894), a 'decadent' novel about London society, and the bestseller *The Garden of Allah* (1905), a desert romance set in North Africa. Later titles include *The Paradine Case* (1933) and *That Which is Hidden* (1939). ⌑ *Yesterday* (1947)

Hick, John Harwood 1922–
English theologian and philosopher of religion

He was born in Scarborough, Yorkshire. During a long teaching career in the USA and Cambridge, followed by professorships in Birmingham (1967–82) and at Claremont Graduate School, California (1979–92, now emeritus), he produced several standard textbooks and anthologies in the philosophy of religion, as well as studies such as *Faith and Knowledge* (1966), *Evil and the God of Love* (1966) and *Death and Eternal Life* (1976). His concern with questions about the status of Christianity among the world religions, raised in *God and the Universe of Faiths* (1973) and *The Myth of God Incarnate* (1977), is developed in *Problems of Religious Pluralism* (1985) and the expanded Gifford lectures, *An Interpretation of Religion* (1989). Later works include *The Metaphor of God Incarnate* (1993) and *The Rainbow of Faiths* (1995).

Hickok, Wild Bill, *originally* James Butler Hickok
1837–76
US frontier marshall

Born in Troy Grove, Illinois, he became a stagecoach driver on the Santa Fe and Oregon Trails, a fighter of Native Americans, and a Union army scout during the Civil War. He gained fame as the gambling, ready-to-kill marshall of Hays (1869) and Abilene (1871), Kansas. After touring briefly with **William F Cody**'s Wild West Show (1872–73), and teaming up with **Calamity Jane**, in Deadwood, Dakota, he was shot dead by Jack McCall during a poker game.

Hicks, Edward 1780–1849
US painter

Born in Attleboro (now Langhorne), Pennsylvania, he was apprenticed to a coachmaker at the age of 13 and later worked as a sign painter. For a time he was an itinerant Quaker preacher, but fearing that he took excessive pride in his ability to sway congregations, he left preaching for easel painting. He created naive, vivid landscapes and historical and religious paintings, which were characterized by flattened figures and rich colours, as well as by delicate detail and an almost mystical aura of religious faith. Between 1830 and 1840 he painted about 100 versions of the allegorical *The Peaceable Kingdom*, which showed wild and tame animals lying down with an infant in accordance with the prophecy in Isaiah. He is the best-known US primitive painter of the 19th century.

Hicks, Elias 1748–1830
US clergyman

Born in Hempstead, Long Island, he became a Quaker preacher in 1775, and was held responsible, because of his Unitarianism, for the split in the US Quakers into Orthodox and 'Hicksite' Friends in 1827.

Hicks, Sir John Richard 1904–89
English economist and Nobel Prize winner

Born in Leamington Spa, Warwickshire, he was educated at Clifton College and Balliol College, Oxford. He taught at the London School of Economics (1926–35), and was Professor of Political Economy at Manchester (1938–46) and Oxford (1952–65). He wrote a classic book on the conflict between business-cycle theory and equilibrium theory, *Value and Capital* (1939), and other works include *A Theory of Economic History* (1969) and *Causality in Economics* (1979). He shared the 1972 Nobel prize for economics with **Kenneth Arrow**.

Hicks, William, *known as* Hicks Pasha 1830–83
English soldier

After long service in India (1848–80) he commanded the Egyptian forces in the Sudan who were annihilated by the Mahdi (**Muhammad Ahmed**) at El Obeid (1883, The Battle of Kashgil).

Hidalgo (y Costilla), Miguel 1753–1811
Mexican priest and revolutionary

Born in Guanajuato state, Mexico, he was a priest in the village of Dolores and a member of a secret society that favoured independence from Spain. Threatened with arrest, he rang the bell of the village church on 16 September 1810 (now celebrated as Mexican independence day) and shouted the *grito de Dolores*—'Long live Our Lady of Guadalupe, death to bad government, death to the Spaniards!'—thus beginning the revolution. Although his untrained army of 80,000 Indians and mestizos initially was successful, winning victories at Guanajuato and Guadalajara, Hidalgo turned back on the verge of taking Mexico City, and the momentum was lost. His army was defeated by the Spanish (Jan 1811), and after fleeing northwards he was captured and executed. Hidalgo is known as the father of Mexican independence.

Hidayat, Sadiq 1903–51
Persian writer

Born in Teheran into a distinguished literary family, he studied in Paris in 1926, and then attempted, unsuccessfully, to train for dentistry and engineering. With a deep knowledge of ancient Iranian lore, and also foreign literature, he translated the work of many leading European writers into his own language. He also wrote short stories, parodies, novels, sketches, plays and collections of folk stories. His best work is the novel *Buf-i kur* (1936, Eng trans *The Blind Owl*, 1957), one of the dozen greatest works of the 20th century, in which the narrator investigates the subtle relationship between his external and his internal lives. Unable to get his life into any kind of order, an alcoholic and a drug addict, he finally gassed himself in despair in a Paris apartment. ⌑ H Kamshad, *Modern Persian Prose Literature* (1966)

Hide, Dubhighlas de See Hyde, Douglas

Hideyoshi Toyotomi 1536–98
Japanese soldier

He became the second of the three great historical unifiers of Japan, the others being Nobunaga and Ieyasu **Tokugawa**. Unusually, he was an ordinary soldier who rose to become Nobunaga's foremost general, and he became known as 'the Napoleon of Japan'. His law forbade all except samurai to carry swords (1588), and he banned Christianity for political reasons (1597). His armies invaded Korea (1592–98), but withdrew after his death.

Hiero or Hieron I d.467 or 466BC
King of Syracuse

He won a great naval victory over the Etruscans (474BC). Though reputedly violent and rapacious, in contrast with his idealized brother and predecessor Gelon (d.478), he had a keen interest in poetry, and was the patron of Simonides of Ceos, Aeschylus, Bacchylides, and Pindar.

Hieronymus, Eusebius See **Jerome, St**

Hieronymus Cardanus See **Cardano, Girolamo**

Higden, Ralph or **Ranulf** d.1364
English chronicler
A Benedictine monk of St Werburgh's monastery in Chester, he wrote a Latin *Polychronicon*, or general history from the creation to about 1342, which was continued by others to 1377. An English translation by John of Trevisa was printed by **William Caxton** in 1482.

Higgins, George V(incent) 1939–
US novelist
Born in Brockton, Massachusetts, he was admitted to the Massachusetts Bar in 1967, but worked in newspapers before becoming a successful attorney. He has used his experience of low-life and his observation of criminals at close quarters to telling effect in a spate of acclaimed literary thrillers. *The Friends of Eddie Coyle* (1972) was his first book and he has published many since, invariably told almost entirely in dialogue and using Boston as a backdrop. Titles include *Cogan's Trade* (1974), *Kennedy for the Defence* (1980), *Wonderful Years, Wonderful Years* (1988) and *Swan Boats at Four* (1995). ▦ G Daldry, in *Watching the Detective* (1990)

Higgins, Henry Bournes 1851–1929
Australian politician and judge
Born in Ireland, he emigrated with his family to Melbourne in 1870 and became a successful lawyer, entering the Victorian assembly in 1894. He was a state representative at the Federal Convention (1897–98), where he criticized the rigidity of the federal constitution. He lost his seat in the Victorian elections of 1900, as he supported Irish Home Rule and opposed both the terms of federation and Australian participation in the Boer War, but he remained popular with the Labor movement. In 1901 he entered Commonwealth politics as a Liberal, but became Attorney-General in the Labor administration of 1904. In 1906 he was appointed to the High Court, and in 1907 became president of the Commonwealth Conciliation and Arbitration Court. As president of the Arbitration Court he made the Harvester Judgement which established the principle of the minimum wage. He fought for the Commonwealth's right to arbitrate in the High Court, and resigned in protest against the interference of Prime Minister **William M Hughes** in 1921. By then arbitration had become an integral part of the Australian industrial system.

Higgins, Jack, *pseudonym of* **Harry Patterson** 1929–
English thriller writer
Born in Newcastle upon Tyne, he was educated at Roundhay School, Leeds, Beckett Park College for Teachers, and the London School of Economics. He was a teacher and college lecturer before becoming a bestselling author with the success of *The Eagle Has Landed* (1975, filmed 1976), set during World War II, in which the Germans plot to kidnap **Winston Churchill**. Higgins also writes as Martin Fallon, Hugh Marlowe and James Graham.

Higgins, Matthew James, *known as* **Jacob Omnium** 1810–68
Irish controversialist
Born in Benown Castle, County Meath, he earned his nickname from the title of his first published article. A prominent journalist, his humour and irony were directed against the abuses and minor evils of social and public life by means of letters and articles to the press. His *Essays on Social Subjects* was published in 1875.

Higgins, Rosalyn, *née* **Inberg** 1937–
English lawyer
Educated at Cambridge and Yale universities, she developed an interest in United Nations law. In 1961 she married Terence Higgins, an economist who became Conservative MP for Worthing in 1964. She was staff specialist in international law at the Royal Institute of International Affairs (1963–74). After an appointment as Professor of International Law at the University of Kent at Canterbury (1978), she moved to the chair at the London School of Economics (1981–95). She became the UK representative on the United Nations Committee on Human Rights in 1985 and was appointed QC the following year. In 1995 she became a judge in the International Court of Justice, the first woman to be so honoured. Her publications include *Problems and Process: International Law and How We Use It* (1995).

Higginson, Thomas Wentworth Storrow 1823–1911
US writer
Born in Cambridge, Massachusetts, he graduated from the divinity school at Harvard and became a Unitarian minister, preaching forcefully in favour of women's rights and abolitionism. He organized local opposition to enforcement of the Fugitive Slave Law of 1850, on one occasion leading a group in breaking down a courthouse door with axes and rescuing a slave, and was briefly indicted for the murder of a man killed during the attempt. He retired from the ministry in 1858, and during the Civil War he commanded (1862–64) the first Black regiment in the Union army, the 1st South Carolina Volunteers, which was raised from among former slaves. In 1880–81 he was a member of the Massachusetts legislature. His numerous books include, *Army Life in a Black Regiment* (1870), *Common-Sense about Women* (1881), and *Concerning All of Us* (1892). He corresponded for 20 years with **Emily Dickinson**, unfortunately discouraging her by judging her work 'too delicate—not strong enough to publish', but after her death he co-edited the first published selection of her works (1890). ▦ H N Meyer, *The Colonel of the Black Regiment* (1967)

Higgs, Peter Ware 1929–
British theoretical physicist
Born in Newcastle upon Tyne, he was educated at King's College London and appointed to a lectureship in mathematical physics at Edinburgh in 1960, where he became Professor of Theoretical Physics in 1980. He explained how the interactions which constitute the fundamental forces of nature take place via the exchange of massive gauge bosons. Building on **Chen Yang**'s simple gauge theories, which described interactions through the exchange of gauge bosons without mass, Higgs developed a field theory in which the gauge bosons could have mass. This was later used by **Steven Weinberg** and **Abdus Salam** to develop the electroweak theory of particle interactions. The so-called Higgs mechanism which allows massive gauge bosons does so by introducing another family of particles, the Higgs bosons. The detection of these particles is the goal of the next generation of particle accelerators. Higgs was awarded the Hughes Medal of the Royal Society in 1981 for this work and was elected FRS in 1983. In 1993 he was awarded the James Scott prize by the Royal Society of Edinburgh.

Highsmith, Patricia 1921–95
US novelist
Born in Fort Worth, Texas, she wrote 20 novels and seven collections of stories. She specialized in crime fiction and thrillers, and her first novel, *Strangers on a Train* (1950), was filmed by Alfred Hitchcock in 1951. Her best novels are generally thought to be the five describing the criminal adventures of her amoral psychotic anti-hero, Tom Ripley.

These include *The Talented Mr Ripley* (1956, filmed as *Plein Soleil*, 1960), for which she was awarded the **Edgar Allan Poe** Scroll by the Mystery Writers of America; *Ripley's Game* (1974, filmed as *The American Friend*, 1977); and *Under Water* (1991). Her final novel, *Small g: a Summer Idyll*, was completed a few weeks before her death. **Graham Greene** described the world she created as claustrophobic and irrational, one 'we enter each time with a sense of personal danger'. ⌑ F Cavigalli, *Über Patricia Highsmith* (1986)

Hightower, Rosella 1920–
US dancer and teacher

Born in Ardmore, Oklahoma, of Native American extraction, she studied in Kansas City, Missouri before beginning her long career as a leading ballerina with Ballet Russe de Monte Carlo (1938–41), American Ballet Theater (1941–45), and **Léonide Massine**'s Ballet Russe Highlights and the Original Ballet Russe (both 1945–46). She joined Nouveau Ballet de Monte Carlo in 1947 and, later, the Grand Ballet du Marquis de Cuevas (until 1961), touring the world and making guest appearances with various companies. She became founding director of the Centre de Danse Classique in Cannes in 1962, becoming ballet director of the Marseilles Opéra Ballet (1967–71), Ballet de Nancy (1973–74), and Paris Opera Ballet from 1980.

Hijikata, Tatsumi 1928–86
Japanese performance artist

Born in Akita province, Japan, he was a key figure in the Japanese avant-garde of the 1950s and 1960s, and closely linked with artists in many disciplines. His 1959 performance *Kinjiki* ('Forbidden Colours'), a rejection of both traditional Japanese and modern dance, shocked audiences because of its explicit sexuality. With Kazuo Ohno he is credited with the founding of the Butoh dance-theatre movement, that draws on and yet refutes traditional Japanese Kabuki and Noh theatre and such Western art forms as modern dance, German Expressionism and Pop Art. His company Ankoku Butoh ('Dance of Total Darkness') gave performances from 1963 to 1966. His 1968 piece *Nikutai No Hanran* ('Rebellion of the Body') is acknowledged as one of the most important productions in the development of Butoh.

Hilarion, St c.291–371AD
Palestinian hermit

Born in Tabatha, Palestine, he was educated at Alexandria, where he became a Christian. He lived as a hermit in the desert between Gaza and Egypt from AD306, and was founder of the first monastery in Palestine (329). His feast day is 21 October.

Hilary, St c.315–68AD
French prelate, and one of the Doctors of the Church

Born of pagan parents in Limonum (modern Poitiers), he was converted to Christianity quite late in life. He was elected Bishop of Poitiers c.350AD, and became a major opponent of Arianism. His principal work is that on the Trinity, but his three addresses to the Emperor **Constantius** are notable for their frankness. His feast day is 13 January, which also marks the beginning of a term at the universities of Oxford and Durham, and English law sittings, to which his name is applied.

Hilary of Arles, St c.403–49AD
French prelate

Born probably in Northern Gaul, he was educated in Lerins, and became Bishop of Arles in AD429. He presided at several synods, especially that of Orange in 441, whose proceedings involved him in a serious controversy with Pope **Leo I**. His feast day is 5 May.

Hilbert, David 1862–1943
German mathematician

Born in Königsberg, Prussia (now Kaliningrad, Russia), he studied and taught at the university there until he became professor at Göttingen University (1895–1930). His definitive work on invariant theory, published in 1890, removed the need for further work on a subject that had occupied so many 19th-century mathematicians, at the same time laying the foundations for modern algebraic geometry. In 1897 he published a report on algebraic number theory which was the basis of much later work. In 1899 he was the first to give abstract axiomatic foundations of geometry which made no attempt to define the 'meaning' of the basic terms but only to prescribe how they could be used. He then studied integral equations, the calculus of variations, theoretical physics (which he claimed was too difficult to be left to physicists), and mathematical logic. At the International Congress of Mathematicians in 1900 he listed 23 problems which he regarded as important for contemporary mathematics. The solutions of many of these have led to interesting advances, while others are still unsolved. ⌑ Constance Reid, *Hilbert* (1970) ·

Hilda, St 614–80
Anglo-Saxon abbess

Born in Northumbria, she was baptized at 13 by **Paulinus**. In 649 she became abbess of Hartlepool and in 657 founded the monastery at Streaneshalch or Whitby, a double house for nuns and monks, over which she ruled wisely for 22 years. It became an important religious centre and housed the Synod of Whitby in 664. Hilda was the daughter of a nephew of **St Edwin** of Northumbria. Her feast day is 17 November.

Hildebrand See **Gregory VII, St**

Hildebrand, Adolf 1847–1921
German sculptor

He was born in Marburg. He sought a renaissance of Classical Realism in his public monuments to **Brahms** at Meiningen, **Bismarck** at Bremen, **Schiller** at Nuremberg, and other works, and influenced the Heinrich Wöfflin school of art criticism by his *Das Problem der Form* (1893, Eng trans *The Problem of Form*, 1907). His best-known works are the Wittelsbach and Hubertus fountains in Munich.

Hildebrand, Joel Henry 1881–1983
US chemist

Born in Camden, New Jersey, he was educated at the University of Pennsylvania and did postdoctoral work in Berlin (1905–06) under **Walther Nernst** and **Jacobus van't Hoff**. He later moved to the University of California, Berkeley, becoming a full Professor of Chemistry by 1918. He was President of the American Chemical Society in 1955 and was awarded its Priestley Medal in 1962. He was also an honorary Fellow of the Royal Society of Edinburgh and of the Royal Society of Chemistry. His greatest scientific contribution was to the understanding of solubility. He devised influential concepts such as 'regular solutions', 'internal pressure' of liquids and the 'solubility parameter' (commonly prefaced with his name). One of the practical outcomes of his work was the use of a mixture of helium and oxygen as an atmosphere to be breathed by divers. He wrote the very influential book *Solubility* (1924).

Hildebrandt, Johann Lukas von 1668–1745
Austrian architect

Born in Genoa, Italy, he was a fortifications engineer in the Austrian army from 1695 to 1701. He trained in Genoa and then in Rome, and became court engineer in Vienna in 1701. A master of the Late Baroque, he was influenced by the work of **Andrea Palladio**, **Giacomo da Vignola**, **Francesco Borromini**, **Guarino Guarini** and **Carlo Fontana**. His earlier works were heavily influenced by the Italian school, as at the Mansfield Fondi garden palace (1697–1715) but he gradually developed a more mature style which was less classical and more intuitive, as seen in the Starhemborg-Schönberg garden palace (1705–06).

Hildegard of Bingen 1098–1179
German Benedictine abbess, mystical philosopher, healer and musician

She was born to a noble family in Böckelheim, but was brought up from the age of eight by a recluse named Jutta. At 15 she entered the convent at Diessenberg, where she succeeded Jutta as abbess in 1136. The community moved to Rubertsberg, near Bingen, sometime during the years 1147–52, and she undertook missions throughout the German states under the protection of **Frederick I Barbarossa**. In her youth, she experienced apocalyptic visions, 26 of which were collected in the *Scivias* (1141–52). Visions also prompted her *Liber vitae meritorum* (1158–63) and *Liber divinorum operum* (1163–74). Her other writings include saints' lives and studies in medicine and natural history. Her spiritual advice, given during travels and in many surviving letters, was widely sought, and she also wrote a body of religious music, which became widely known only in the 1980s. In parts of Germany she is treated as a saint. ▢ Sabina Flanagan, *Hildegard of Bingen: A Visionary Life* (1989)

Hill, Aaron 1685–1750
English poet, dramatist and speculator

Born in London, he wrote *Zaire* (1736) and *Mérope* (1749, adapted from **Voltaire**), and the scenario for **Handel's** opera *Rinaldo* (1711). He was one of **Pope's** victims in *The Dunciad*, and replied with *Progress of Wit* (1730). He left an epic poem, *Gideon* (1749), unfinished. He had a wide circle of literary friends, and launched the bi-weekly journal *The Plain Dealer* in 1724. ▢ D Brewster, *Aaron Hill, poet, dramatist, projector* (1913)

Hill, Alfred Francis 1870–1960
Australian composer

Born in Melbourne, he moved with his family to Wellington, New Zealand, and was appearing with the New Zealand Opera Orchestra by the age of 14. He studied at the Leipzig Conservatory from 1887. Returning to New Zealand in 1891 he became conductor of the Wellington Orchestral Society, and collected and recorded much Maori music, which influenced his music of the period. Returning to Australia in 1897, he worked in Sydney, where he conducted for the **J C Williamson** Company. For 20 years from 1915 he was Professor of Composition and Harmony at the New South Wales Conservatorium of Music. His work includes 13 symphonies, many of which are orchestrations of his earlier string quartets, 10 operas, a *Maori Rhapsody*, five concertos, and a considerable body of chamber music, keyboard and vocal music.

Hill, Anita Faye 1956–
US lawyer and teacher

Born in Morris, Oklahoma, she gained a law degree from Yale University (1977), then practised law in Washington DC in a private practice as well as for US government agencies, including the Equal Employment Opportunity Commission (EEOC). In 1983 she began teaching law at Oral Roberts University, then became professor at the University of Oklahoma College of Law. During her employment with the EEOC, she was special assistant to Clarence Thomas. During the televised hearings of his nomination to join the US Supreme Court (1991), she riveted the nation with charges of sexual harassment, which she denied. Although Thomas gained his appointment as an associate US Supreme Court Justice, Hill paved the way for future charges to be brought against men in high positions.

Hill, A(rchibald) V(ivian) 1886–1977
English physiologist and Nobel Prize winner

Born in Bristol, he was educated at Cambridge, where he began investigating the physiology of muscle and nerve tissue. He became professor at Manchester (1920), University College London (1923), and from 1926 to 1951 was Foulerton Research Professor of the Royal Society. He shared the 1922 Nobel Prize for physiology or medicine with **Otto Meyerhof** for his researches into heat production in muscle contraction. He organized air defence in World War II and was MP for Cambridge (1940–45). His works include *Muscular Movement in Man* (1927).

Hill, Benny, *originally* Alfred Hawthorne Hill 1924–92
English comedian

Born in Southampton, he was an enthusiastic performer in school shows. He was a milkman, drummer and driver before getting a job as an assistant stage manager. During World War II he appeared in *Stars in Battledress* and later followed the traditional comic's route of working men's clubs, revues and end-of-the-pier shows. An early convert to the potential of television, he appeared in *Hi There* (1949) and was named TV Personality of the Year in 1954. He made his film debut in *Who Done It?* (1955) but gained national, and eventually international popularity with the saucy *The Benny Hill Show* (1955–89). His few film appearances include *Light Up the Sky* (1960), *Those Magnificent Men in Their Flying Machines* (1965), *Chitty Chitty Bang Bang* (1968) and *The Italian Job* (1969). He enjoyed a hit record with 'Ernie (The Fastest Milkman in the West)' (1971).

Hill, Sir (Austin) Bradford 1897–1991
English medical statistician

Educated at Chigwell School and at University College London, he joined a statistical group at the National Institute for Medical Research, Mill Hill, in 1923. He later became Professor of Epidemiology and Medical Statistics at the London School of Hygiene and Tropical Medicine, then Dean from 1955 to 1957. He studied occupational hazards, the value of immunization against whooping cough and poliomyelitis, and the effects of smoking. This was set out in *Principles of Medical Statistics* (1937). Together with Richard Doll (1912–) he designed a case control study of patients with lung cancer (1950) which enabled him to conclude that smoking was one important cause of the disease. Hill devised and established the randomized controlled clinical trial which has transformed medical thinking.

Hill (of Luton), Charles Hill, Baron 1904–89
English physician, politician, broadcaster and administrator

Born in Islington, the youngest son of a piano-maker, he won scholarships to St Olave's Grammar School, Tower Bridge, and to Trinity College, Cambridge. In 1932 he became assistant secretary to the British Medical Association (BMA). As secretary during the postwar period when the National Health Service was being formed by the Labour government, he often clashed with Health Minister **Aneurin Bevan**. During World War II Hill had become the BBC's first 'Radio Doctor', and was an effective broadcaster, as he proved in his electioneering speech on radio in 1950. He left the BMA on being elected Liberal Conservative MP for Luton and became Postmaster General (1955–59), then Chancellor of the Duchy of Lancaster. Axed from **Harold Macmillan's** Cabinet (1962), he was appointed chairman of the Independent Television Authority (ITA) in 1963, and, to the astonishment and horror of those in Broadcasting House, appointed chairman of the BBC by **Harold Wilson** (1967). He decreased the influence of the director-general (**Ian Trethowan**) and increased that of the chairman, but maintained the BBC's independence from government.

Hill, Damon 1960–
English racing driver
Born in London, the son of twice world champion racing driver **Graham Hill**, he worked as a motorcycle despatch rider to fund his racing career (1982–85). Finance was often a problem for him but he became test driver for Williams's Grand Prix team in 1991. He finished 16th in his Grand Prix debut in 1992 and joined **Alain Prost** in Williams Grand Prix team in 1993. He finished third overall in his first full season and partnered **Ayrton Senna** in 1994 before Senna's death. He finished second to **Michael Schumacher** in 1994 and 1995. Williams terminated Hill's agreement in 1996, and he signed with TWR Arrows. His last race for Williams was the Japan Grand Prix, which he won; his 67th race of his Formula One career, it was his 21st win and made him world champion.

Hill, David Octavius 1802–70
Scottish photographer and painter
Born in Perth, he studied art in Edinburgh. In 1821 he issued probably the first set of lithographs published in Scotland, *Sketches of Scenery in Perthshire. The Land of Burns*, published in 1840, was illustrated by Hill, with text by Professor **John Wilson**. In 1843 he was commissioned to portray the founders of the Free Church of Scotland, and with the help of the Edinburgh chemist, **Robert Adamson** (1821–48), applied the calotype process of making photographic prints on silver chloride paper, newly invented by **William Henry Fox Talbot**. From 1843 to 1848 Hill and Adamson produced some 2,500 calotypes, mostly portraits but also landscapes. Hill was one of the founders of the Royal Scottish Academy in 1829. ◻Heinrich Schwarz, *David Octavius Hill, Master of Photography* (1932)

Hill, Geoffrey William 1932–
English poet
Born in Bromsgrove, Worcestershire, he was educated at Keble College, Oxford. He taught at the universities of Leeds and Cambridge, before becoming Professor of Literature and Religion at Boston University (1988). Brooding on death, sex and religion, his first collection of *Poems* was published in 1952. He also wrote *For the Unfallen: Poems 1952–1958* (1959), and *Preghiere* (1964), *King Log* (1968), *Mercian Hymns* (1971), *Somewhere is Such a Kingdom: 1952–1971* (1975), *Tenebrae* (1978) and *The Mystery of the Charity of Charles Péguy* (1983), which all won prestigious literary prizes, and a book of literary criticism, *The Enemy's Country* (1991). His *New and Collected Poems 1952–1992* were published in 1994. ◻V Sherry, *The Uncommon tongue: the poetry and criticism of Geoffrey Hill* (1987)

Hill, (Norman) Graham 1929–75
English racing driver
Born in London, he won the world championship in 1962 in a BRM (British Racing Motor), and was runner-up twice in the following three years. In 1967 he rejoined Lotus and won the world championship for a second time (1968). He won the Monaco Grand Prix five times (1963–65, 1968–69). In 1975 he started his own racing team, Embassy Racing, but was killed when the plane he was piloting crashed near London. His son **Damon Hill** also became a racing driver.

Hill, James Jerome 1838–1916
US railway magnate
Born near Guelph, Canada, he moved to St Paul, Minnesota, in 1856, where he entered the transportation business. He took over the St Paul-Pacific line (1878) and extended it to link with the Canadian system, becoming known for the sound management of his railroads and founding the Great Northern Railway Co in 1890 to unite all his properties. To reduce competition he acquired control of competing lines, including the Northern Pacific Railroad, which financier **Edward H Harriman**

tried in turn to wrest from him in a stock exchange battle that caused a panic on Wall Street in 1901. The same year Hill established an even larger holding company, the Northern Securities Co, which violated the Sherman Antitrust Act and was dissolved by the Supreme Court in 1904. He was later active in the construction of the Canadian Pacific Railroad.

Hill, Joe, originally Joel Emmanuel Hägglund or Joseph Hillstrom c.1872–1915
US labour organizer and songwriter
Born in Sweden, he was a seaman who went to the USA in about 1901 and became an active member of the radical labour union, the Industrial Workers of the World (IWW, nicknamed the 'Wobblies'). For them, he wrote popular pro-union songs such as 'Coffee An', 'The Rebel Girl', and 'The Preacher and the Slave' (which includes the phrase 'pie in the sky'). He became a legend and a martyr of the union movement after he was arrested for murder (1914), convicted on circumstantial evidence, and, despite calls for retrial by President **Woodrow Wilson** and the Swedish government, was executed.

Hill, Octavia 1838–1912
English reformer
She was born in London. Influenced by the Christian socialism of **F D Maurice**, and tutored in art by **John Ruskin**, she became an active promoter of improved housing conditions for the poor in London. From 1864, with Ruskin's financial help, she bought slum houses for improvement projects. With Maurice she founded the Charity Organization Society (1869). Her books include *Homes of the London Poor* (1875) and *Our Common Land* (1878). A leader of the open-space movement which advocated more public space and improved housing, she was a co-founder in 1895 of the National Trust for Places of Historic Interest or Natural Beauty. Her methods were imitated in Europe and the USA. She was the grand-daughter of **Thomas Southwood Smith**. ◻Gillian Darley, *Octavia Hill* (1990)

Hill, Rowland 1744–1833
English popular preacher
Born in Hawkstone Park, Surrey, he studied at St John's College, Cambridge, where he was influenced by the evangelist **George Whitefield**. From his ordination in 1773 until 1783 he was an itinerant preacher, afterwards making his headquarters at Surrey Chapel, Blackfriars Road, London, which he built himself. He helped to found the Religious Tract Society and the London Missionary Society, and it is said that the first London Sunday school was his. His *Village Dialogues* (1801) was very popular.

Hill, Sir Rowland 1795–1879
English originator of penny postage
He was born in Kidderminster, Worcestershire, and until 1833 was a teacher, noted for his system of school self-discipline. He interested himself in the socialistic schemes of **Robert Owen**, and took an active role in the colonization of South Australia. In his *Post-office Reform* (1837) he advocated a low and uniform rate of postage, to be prepaid by stamps, between places in the British Isles, and in January 1840 a uniform penny rate was introduced. In 1846 the Liberals made him Secretary to the Postmaster General and in 1854 Secretary to the Post Office. He established the book-post (1848), and reformed the money order office (1848) and the packet service. In a report of 1867 he advocated national ownership of railways.

Hill, Susan Elizabeth 1942–
English novelist, critic and broadcaster
Born in Scarborough, North Yorkshire, and educated at King's College London, she published her first novel, *The Enclosure* (1961), while still a student there. Her novels,

which tend to be formally-structured deliberations on the nature of loss and grief, deal with a wide range of themes, such as old age in *Gentleman and Ladies* (1969) and the bereavement of a young wife in *In the Springtime of the Year* (1974). Other novels include *Strange Meeting* (1971), set during World War I, and *Air and Angels* (1991), concerning the obsessive love of a middle-aged man for a young girl. *The Woman in Black* (1983) was adapted into a long-running West End stage play. She also writes plays and short stories and her books for children include *The Glass Angels* (1991) and *King of Kings* (1993). Later publications include *Mrs de Winter* (1993) and *Reflections from a Garden* (1995, with Rory Stuart).

Hillary, Sir Edmund Percival See panel p892

Hillel I, *also called* Hillel Hazaken (the Elder), *or* Hillel Hababli (the Babylonian) 1st century BC–1st century AD
Jewish teacher
He was born probably in Babylonia, and went to Palestine at about age 40. He founded a school of followers bearing his name which was frequently in debate with (and often presented more tolerant attitudes than) the contemporary followers of **Shammai**. Noted for his use of seven rules in expounding Scripture, he was one of the most respected teachers of his time, and influential on later rabbinic Judaism. 📖 N N Glatzer, *Hillel the Elder: The Emergence of Classical Judaism* (1956)

Hiller, Johann Adam 1728–1804
German composer
Born near Görlitz, Prussia, he studied law at Leipzig University, where he also performed as a singer and flautist. From 1763 he concentrated on composing, and wrote over 30 comic operas, practically creating this genre in Germany. He was also a noted conductor and teacher.

Hiller, Dame Wendy 1912–
English actress
Born in Bramhall, Cheshire, she was interested in dramatics as a child, and joined the Manchester Repertory Theatre in 1930. She made her London debut in *Love on the Dole* (1935) and her film debut in *Lancashire Luck* (1937). At the 1936 Malvern Festival she played both Saint Joan and Eliza Doolittle, a role she also played in the film of *Pygmalion* (1938) at the invitation of **George Bernard Shaw**. She is noted for her clear diction and spirited personality, and as one of Britain's leading stage performers. Her sporadic but distinguished film performances include *Major Barbara* (1940), *I Know Where I'm Going* (1945), *Sons and Lovers* (1960), *A Man for All Seasons* (1966) and *Separate Tables* (1958, Academy Award). Later credits include the films *Murder on the Orient Express* (1974) and *The Lonely Passion of Judith Hearne* (1987) and a stage version of *Driving Miss Daisy* (1988). She married the dramatist Ronald Gow in 1937, and was created DBE in 1975.

Hillery, Patrick (John) 1923–
Irish politician
Following his election as an MP (1951), he held ministerial posts in Education (1959–65), then Industry and Commerce (1965–66), and Labour (1966–69), then became Foreign Minister (1969–72). He served as the EEC Commissioner for Social Affairs (1973–76), and became President of the Irish Republic (1976–90).

Hilliard, Nicholas c.1547–1619
English court goldsmith and miniaturist
Born in Exeter, the son of a goldsmith, he worked for Queen **Elizabeth I** and **James VI and I** and founded the English school of miniature painting. His preference for firm contours was influenced by **Hans Holbein**, the Younger, who was working in England during his lifetime, but Hilliard developed his own exquisite linear style, with subtle fresh tints. This is evident in the miniature portrait of the Earl of **Essex**, *An Unknown Youth*

Leaning Against a Tree Among Roses (Victoria and Albert Museum, London). He also painted the portraits in miniature of **Mary, Queen of Scots**, **Elizabeth I**, **Sir Francis Drake** and **Sir Walter Raleigh** (National Portrait Gallery, London). He was the teacher of **Isaac Oliver**.

Hillier, James 1915–
US physicist
Born in Brantford, Ontario, in Canada, he was educated at the University of Toronto. He was a major contributor to the development of the electron microscope. **Louis-Victor de Broglie**'s theory that particles can behave like waves had led to the proposal of the electron microscope which would have much greater resolution than optical microscopes. While at Toronto, Hillier developed one of the first high-resolution electron microscopes produced. Later he moved to the USA (1940) and made his career with RCA (the Radio Corporation of America), giving him the resources to further develop the electron microscope, whose commercial availability after World War II revolutionized biology. He also maintained an interest in areas such as biology, medicine, chemistry and metallurgy, and he held visiting posts in the biology department of Princeton University and at the Sloan-Kettering Institute for Cancer Research.

Hillier, Tristram Paul 1905–83
British artist
Born in Beijing (Peking), China, he studied at the Slade School, London, and under **André Lhote** in Paris. He lived in France for a long time, particularly in Dieppe. Many of his paintings are of ships and beaches, the earlier ones of a Surrealist character, and his craftmanship and smooth handling of paint are such that his oil paintings are often mistaken for tempera. His works include *La Route des Alpes* (1937) and *Alcaniz* (1961).

Hilton, Conrad Nicholson 1887–1979
US hotelier
Born in San Antonio, New Mexico, he helped his father turn their house into an inn. He became a cashier in New Mexico State Bank in 1913, and was president and partner in A H Hilton and Son, General Store by 1915. He took over the family inn on the death of his father in 1918, and bought his first hotel, the Mobley Hotel in Cisco, Texas, in 1919, building up a chain of hotels in the major cities in the USA. After World War II he formed Hilton Hotels Corporation (1946), and Hilton International (1948). He continued to expand the company until his son, Barron Hilton, took over as president in 1966. He published his autobiography, *Be My Guest*, in 1957.

Hilton, James 1900–54
English novelist
Born in Leigh, Lancashire, he was educated both at school and university in Cambridge, before working as a freelance journalist. He quickly established himself as a writer, his first novel, *Catherine Herself*, being published in 1920. Many of his successful novels were filmed—*Knight without Armour* (1933), *Lost Horizon* (1933, awarded the Hawthornden Prize in 1934), *Goodbye Mr Chips* (1934) and *Random Harvest* (1941). He went to Hollywood during the 1940s to work as a scriptwriter, and died in California. 📖 *To You, Mr Chips* (1938)

Hilton, Roger 1911–75
English painter
Born in Northwood, Middlesex, he studied at the Slade School of Art, London (1929–31). After spending some time in Paris in the 1930s, he was captured at Dieppe in 1942 and was a prisoner of war until 1945. He produced his first abstract paintings, suggestive of landscape, in 1950, and from 1954 to 1956 taught at the Central School of Art, London. From 1961 the female figure often appears in his work, as in *Oi yoi yoi* (1963, Tate, London). He

Hillary, Sir Edmund Percival 1919–

New Zealand mountaineer and explorer, the first person to conquer Mount Everest

Edmund Hillary was born in Auckland. An apiarist by profession and climber by inclination, active both in New Zealand and in the Himalayas, he joined the 1953 British Everest Expedition, led by **John Hunt**, and with the sherpa **Tenzing Norgay** reached the summit of Mt Everest (at 8,850m/29,030ft) on 29 May 1953. He was knighted for this achievement.

During the International Geophysical Year (1957–58), Hillary was deputy leader under **Vivian Ernest Fuchs** of the British Commonwealth Antarctic Expedition, and made the first overland trip to the South Pole using tracked vehicles. He made further expeditions to the Everest area in 1960–61 and 1963–66, and led a geological expedition to Antarctica in 1967, during which he made the first ascent of Mt Herschel (3,335m/10,941ft).

Later, Hillary was appointed the New Zealand High Commissioner to India (1985–89), and he has raised funds in New Zealand to provide hospitals and schools in the Himalayan region. His son, Peter Edmund Hillary (1954–), is also an experienced explorer. He climbed the South Col of Mt Everest in 1989 and, with his father and New Zealanders Rob Hall and Gary Ball, reached the summit in 1990. He was also a member of the North Pole expedition of 1985 with his father.

📖 Hillary's publications include *High Adventure* (1955), *East of Everest* (with George Lowe, 1956), *The Crossing of Antarctica* (with Sir Vivian Fuchs, 1958), *No Latitude for Error* (1961), *High in the Thin Cold Air* (with Desmond Doig, 1963), *Schoolhouse in the Clouds* (1965), *Nothing Venture, Nothing Win* (autobiography, 1975), *From the Ocean to the Sky: Jet Boating up the Ganges* (with Peter Hillary, 1979) and *Two Generations* (with Peter Hillary, 1983).

'A symmetrical, beautiful snow-cone summit.' Thus Hillary described the summit of Everest to his teammates on return to their camp. It seems that everybody had expected a jagged pinnacle of rock, which is all that could be seen from below.

won first prize in the John Moores Liverpool Exhibition (1963) and the UNESCO Prize at the Venice Biennale (1964). From 1965 he settled permanently in Cornwall, working with the St Ives group. Bedridden for the last two years of his life, he worked in gouache, in a brighter range of colours.

Hilton, Walter d.1396

English mystic and writer

Born at Thurgarton Priory, Nottinghamshire, he was an Augustinian canon and the author of *The Ladder of Perfection* (1494) and possibly *The Cloud of Unknowing*, two books important in the history of English medieval prose, as their careful theological basis precedes the writings of St **John of the Cross**. Hilton remained popular during the 15th and early 16th centuries.

Himes, Chester Bomar 1909–84

US novelist

Born in Jefferson City, Missouri, and educated in Ohio, he spent nearly nine years in prison for armed robbery and after his release worked (1938–41) on a writers project as part of the New Deal's Works Progress Administration. His first novel, *If He Hollers Let Him Go* (1945), was an account of racial prejudice in the Californian shipyards and factories, while *Cast the First Stone* (1952) exorcized his prison experiences. He emigrated soon after to Europe, where his tough detective stories were welcomed as serious existential fiction. *For Love of Imabelle* (1957) was originally a story called 'La reine des pommes' and was republished (and subsequently filmed) as *A Rage in Harlem*. On its first appearance, it gained Himes the influential Grand Prix de Littérature Policière (1958). His subsequent Harlem thrillers, featuring two black detectives, Grave Digger Johnson and Coffin Ed Jones, were very popular and overshadowed his earlier work. 📖 *The Quality of Hurt* (1972); S F Miliken, *Chester Himes: A Critical Appraisal* (1976)

Himiko d.247AD

Queen of Japan

Traditionally thought to be the daughter of the emperor Suinin, she was originally ruler of the Yamato tribe, then extended her rule in the area around Nara (Kyushu) and became Japan's first known ruler. Chinese chronicles of the 3rd century describe her as a shamaness-ruler whose younger brother served as the non-spiritual ruler. She may have been killed by chieftains disillusioned with her waning religious powers in war, or else in battle. Her death sparked off civil war when her brother ignored the female right of inheritance and usurped the throne. Evidence of female rule at this time and the claim of Yamato rulers that they were descended from the Sun Goddess (Amaterasu) have led some historians to suggest that early Japan may originally have been a matriarchal society that was only gradually transformed into the strongly male-dominated family system of later times.

Himmler, Heinrich 1900–45

German Nazi leader and chief of police

Born in Munich and educated at the Landshut High School, he joined the army. In 1919 he studied at the Munich Technical College. He joined the Nazi Party in 1925. In 1929 **Hitler** made him head of the SS (*Schutzstaffel*, protective force), which he developed from Hitler's personal bodyguard into a powerful party weapon. With **Reinhard Heydrich**, he used it to carry out the assassination of **Ernst Röhm** (1934) and other Nazis opposed to Hitler. Inside Germany and later in Nazi war-occupied countries, he unleashed through his Gestapo (secret police) an unmatched political and anti-Semitic terror of espionage, wholesale detention, mass deportation, torture, execution and massacre. His systematic liquidation of whole national and racial groups initiated the barbarous crime of genocide. In 1943 he was given the post of Minister of the Interior to curb any defeatism. After the attempt on Hitler's life by the army in July 1944, he was made Commander-in-Chief of the home forces. His offer of unconditional surrender to the Allies (but excluding Russia) having failed, he disappeared but was captured by the British near Bremen. He committed suicide at Lüneburg by swallowing a cyanide phial concealed in his mouth, and thereby escaped being tried as the initiator of the horror of the gas oven and the concentration camp, and as the butcher of over seven million people. 📖 Peter Padfield, *Himmler: Reichsfuhrer-SS* (1990)

Hinault, Bernard, *known as* Le Blaireau ('the badger') 1954–

French cyclist

Born in Yffiniac, he won the Tour de France five times (1978–79, 1981–82, 1985). Only three others have ever won the race five times: **Jacques Anquetil**, **Eddy Merckx** and **Miguel Indurain**. He led a protest during the 1978 Tour in which all the riders walked across the finishing line pushing their bikes, complaining about the long days in the saddle. He has also won the Tour of Italy three times and the Tour of Spain twice. In 1985 he won his last Tour despite a fall midway through in which he broke his nose. He retired on his 32nd birthday and became technical adviser to the Tour de France. 📖 *Hinault by Hinault* (1987)

Hincmar of Reims c.806–82
French prelate

He was born probably in northern France, a descendant of the counts of Toulouse, and educated in the monastery of St Denis. He became abbot of Compiègne and St Germain, and in 845 was elected Archbishop of Rheims. He was party to the imprisonment and humiliation of the German theologian Gottschalk of Orbais (who died in 868 after 18 years' incarceration for his predestinarian views). He strenuously opposed Adrian II's attempts to compel obedience in imperial politics, and resisted the emperor's attempts to advance his favourites.

Hinde, Robert Aubrey 1923–
English ethologist and zoologist

Born in Norwich, Norfolk, he studied at Cambridge (1944–48) and Oxford (1950), before becoming curator of the ornithological field station of the Cambridge zoology department (1950–64). He held a Royal Society research professorship from 1963 to 1989 then was Master of St John's College (1989–94), before becoming a Fellow in 1994. His many scientific works have been in the area of ethology and human behaviour. While the early ethologists worked mainly with birds and lower vertebrates, Hinde has been concerned more with the application of ethological methods to the primates, including man. In particular he has used the comparative approach, in the belief that analysing primates' social behaviour can provide insights into that of humans. More recently, he has been concerned with human interpersonal relationships and the relations between biology, psychology and culture. He is the author of many research papers and books including *Animal Behaviour: A Synthesis of Ethology and Comparative Psychology* (1966), *Biological Bases of Human Social Behaviour* (1974) and *Individual Relationships and Culture* (1987). He was elected Fellow of the Royal Society in 1974 and made a CBE in 1988.

Hindemith, Paul 1895–1963
German composer

Born in Hanau, near Frankfurt am Main, he ran away from home aged 11 because of his parents' opposition to a musical career, and earned a living by playing his instruments in cafés, cinemas and dance halls. He studied at Hoch's Conservatory in Frankfurt, and from 1915 to 1923 was leader of the Frankfurt Opera Orchestra, which he often conducted. He also played the violin in the Rebner Quartet. In 1927 Hindemith was appointed a professor at the Berlin High School for music, and in 1929 gave the first performance in London of William Walton's Viola Concerto, which influenced his own 'Philharmonic' Concerto (1932). He pioneered *Gebrauchsmusik*, pieces written with specific utilitarian aims such as children's entertainment, newsreels and community singing, but the Nazis banned his politically pointed *Mathis der Maler* (1934, symphony, 1938, opera 'Matthias the Painter'). After a short time in the UK, where he composed the *Trauermusik* ('Mourning Music') for viola and strings (1936) on George V's death, and the ballet *Nobilissima Visione* (1938, 'Most Noble Vision'), he moved to the USA (1939). His later, mellower compositions include a requiem based on Walt Whitman's commemorative *For Those We Love* (1944). In 1947 he was appointed a professor at Yale and in 1953 at Zurich, where he composed his opera on Johannes Kepler's life, *Die Harmonie der Welt* (1957, 'The Harmony of the World'). In 1945 he published *Unterweisung im Tosatz* (Eng trans *The Craft of Musical Composition*). 📖 Geoffrey Skelton, *Paul Hindemith: The Man Behind the Music* (1975)

Hindenburg, Paul Ludwig Hans Anton von Beneckendorff und von 1847–1934
German soldier and statesman

Born in Posen of a Prussian Junker family, he was educated at the cadet schools at Wahlstatt and Berlin, fought at the battle of Königgrätz (1866), and in the Franco-Prussian War (1870–71) rose to the rank of general (1903), retiring in 1911. Recalled at the outbreak of World War I, he and General Ludendorff won decisive victories over the Russians at Tannenberg (1914) and at the Masurian Lakes (1915). His successes against the Russians were not, however, repeated on the Western Front, and in the summer of 1918 he was obliged to supervise the retreat of the German armies (to the 'Hindenburg line'). A national hero and father figure, he was the second President of the German Republic (1925–34). He did not oppose Gustav Stresemann's enlightened foreign policy, but neither did he oppose the rise of Hitler, whom he defeated in the presidential election (1932) and who became Chancellor in 1933. But such was his influence that Hitler was unable to overthrow constitutional government until his death. 📖 John W Wheeler-Bennett, *Wooden Titan: Hindenburg in Twenty Years of German History, 1914–1934* (1936)

Hindley, Myra 1942–
English murderess

Born in Gorton, near Manchester, she met Ian Brady while working as a typist. They became lovers and soon carried out a series of shocking murders. The couple lured children back to their house in Manchester and tortured them before killing them. David Smith, Hindley's brother-in-law, contacted the police on 7 October 1965 about the murders. Hindley and Brady were arrested, the body of 17-year-old Edward Evans was found at their house, and a search for other victims' bodies began. The graves and remains of 10-year-old Lesley Ann Downey and 12-year-old John Kilbride were found on Saddleworth Moor, and Hindley and Brady therefore became known as the 'Moors Murderers'. Hindley was convicted on two counts of murder and was sentenced to life imprisonment. She made a private confession to two other murders in 1986 and the body of Pauline Reade was found in August 1987, 24 years after her disappearance. The body of 12-year-old Keith Bennett has never been found. Her claims in recent years that she has reformed have not led to her release.

Hindmarsh, Sir John c.1782–1860
English naval officer and administrator

Born probably in Chatham, Kent, he was the son of a naval gunner. He joined HMS *Bellerophon* at the age of 14 and fought with the Channel fleet under Admiral Howe, and later in the Mediterranean under Lord Nelson at the Battle of the Nile in 1798 (when he was commended for action which saved his ship), and at Trafalgar (1805). In 1836 he was appointed the first Governor of South Australia. He objected strongly to William Light's plan for the site for the new town of Adelaide in the middle of a plain six miles from the sea, and tried to veto it, but met with strong objections from the settlers. The vagueness of Hindmarsh's powers led him into conflict with the resident commissioners, which set the tone for his period of office, and he was recalled to London in 1838. He was restored to favour two years later as Lieutenant-Governor of Heligoland, a small rocky island in the North Sea.

Hine, Lewis Wickes 1874–1940
US photographer

Born in Oshkosh, Wisconsin, he studied sociology in Chicago and New York (1900–07), making a photographic study of Ellis Island immigrants as an expression of his social concern. A similar record of child labour took him all over the USA (1908–15), and during World War I he recorded refugees for the US Red Cross. He photographed the construction of the Empire State Building in a survey entitled *Men at Work* (1932) and in the later 1930s registered the effects of the Depression for a US government project. This work left a detailed picture of the social life of industrial USA which spanned some three decades.

Hines, (Melvyn) Barry 1939–
English novelist

Born in Barnsley, Yorkshire, he worked as a physical education teacher before turning to writing. His novels are all set in his native Yorkshire, and deal with working-class life. He is best known for *A Kestrel for a Knave* (1974), also known as *Kes* following a successful film adaptation from his own screenplay, one of a number of collaborations with the filmmaker Ken Loach. Its story about an undersized, emotionally isolated young boy's love for a pet falcon is told with craft and sensitivity. His television scripts include *Born Kicking* (1992) and other novels include *The Blinder* (1966), about a young footballer, *The Gamekeeper* (1975), the industrial novel *The Price of Coal* (1979), *Unfinished Business* (1983) and *The Heart of It* (1994).

Hines, Earl Kenneth, *also called* Fatha 1903–83
US jazz pianist and bandleader

Born in Duquesne, Pennsylvania, he received his first piano lessons from his mother and began to play professionally as a teenager. Moving to Chicago in 1923, he worked under such leaders as Erskine Tate and Carroll Dickerson, then in association with trumpeter Louis Armstrong. His 1928 recording of 'Weather Bird' with Armstrong was a highly influential duet performance. He improvised single-note lines in the treble clef and punctuated them with internal rhythms in the bass, a style later known as 'trumpet piano' which began a significant development among jazz pianists. In 1928 Hines formed his own band, expanding it to a large orchestra, and a 12-year residency at the Grand Terrace Ballroom, Chicago, with national tours and recording engagements, brought him fame as one of the masters of the swing era. He led big bands until 1948, working thereafter in small groups, including a period (1948–51) with Louis Armstrong's All-Stars, as well as touring abroad. 📖 Stanley Dance, *The World of Earl Hines* (1977)

Hinkler, Bert (Herbert John Louis) 1892–1933
Australian pioneer aviator

Born in Bundaberg, Queensland, he went to England in 1913 and enlisted in the Royal Naval Air Service in World War I. After the war he bought an Avro 'Baby', and flew non-stop to Turin, but wars in the Near East prevented his flying on to Australia. In 1921, having shipped his plane to Sydney, he flew it non-stop 700 miles to Bundaberg, and in 1928 he created a new England–Australia record, arriving in Darwin, Northern Territory, 16 days after leaving England. He went to the USA in 1931 and bought a De Havilland Puss Moth, which he flew to England via Jamaica, Brazil and West Africa, creating another three records on the journey. He left England in his Puss Moth in January 1933 on a solo flight to Australia, but crashed in the Italian Alps.

Hinshelwood, Sir Cyril Norman 1897–1967
English physical chemist and Nobel Prize winner

Born in London, his education was interrupted by World War I, during which he served as a chemist at an explosives factory. In 1919 he went to Balliol College, Oxford and took his degree after only five terms of study. After a year as Research Fellow at Balliol, he became a Fellow and Tutor of Trinity College, an appointment he held until 1937, when he succeeded Frederick Soddy as Dr Lee's Professor of Chemistry. He retired from Oxford in 1964, becoming a Senior Research Fellow of Imperial College, London, where he was active until his death. His research work was largely in chemical kinetics. In the 1920s he carried out pioneering work in gas reactions and their interpretation in terms of the kinetic theory. He also studied heterogeneous catalysis and solution kinetics, but from 1936 onwards he was increasingly interested in the kinetics of bacterial growth. Some of his ideas generated much controversy with biologists. In 1956 he was awarded the Nobel Prize for chemistry, jointly with Nikolai Semenov, for his contributions to chemical kinetics. Hinshelwood was elected FRS in 1929 and was president of the Royal Society from 1955 to 1960. President of the Chemical Society from 1946 to 1948, he was knighted in 1948 and admitted to the Order of Merit in 1960. Hinshelwood was also an accomplished linguist, with a good knowledge of the classics, and in 1959 he served as president of the Classical Association.

Hinsley, Arthur 1865–1943
English prelate

He was born in Selby, Yorkshire. He studied at the English College in Rome, where he became rector (1917–28). He was made Archbishop of Westminster in 1935, and a cardinal in 1937. He was outspoken in his opposition to the Fascist powers in Germany and Italy.

Hinton (of Bankside), Christopher Hinton, Baron 1901–83
English nuclear engineer

Born in Tisbury, Wiltshire, he won a scholarship to Cambridge while working as an apprentice in a railway workshop, and rose to chief engineer of the alkali division of ICI at Northwich (1917–40). During World War II he supervised explosives filling stations. From 1946, as deputy director of atomic energy production, he constructed the world's first large-scale commercial atomic power station at Calder Hall, Cumbria, opened in 1956, which successfully combined the production of electricity with that of radioactive plutonium at the neighbouring gas-cooled atomic reactor at Windscale (now Sellafield), Cumberland. He was knighted in 1951 and given a life peerage in 1965.

Hipparchos or Hipparchus c.180–125BC
Greek astronomer and mathematician

Born in Nicaea, Bithynia, he made his observations from Rhodes where he spent a long time, and may also have lived in Alexandria. He compiled a catalogue of 850 stars (completed in 129BC) giving their positions in celestial latitude and longitude, the first such catalogue ever to exist, and this remained of primary importance up to the time of Edmond Halley. In comparing his observed star positions with earlier records he discovered the precession of the equinoxes. He observed the annual motion of the Sun, developed a theory of its eccentric motion and measured the unequal durations of the four seasons. He made similar observations of the Moon's more complex motion. Following the method of eclipse observations used by Aristarchos, he estimated the relative distances of the Sun and Moon and improved calculations for the prediction of eclipses. He developed the mathematical science of plane and spherical trigonometry required for his astronomical work. Hipparchos was the first to fix places on the Earth by latitude and longitude.

Hippias of Elis 5th century BC
Greek Sophist

A contemporary of Socrates, he was vividly portrayed in Plato's dialogues as a virtuoso performer as teacher, orator, memory-man and polymath. He is also credited with a mathematical discovery.

Hipper, Franz von 1863–1932
German naval officer

He commanded the German scouting groups at the battles of Dogger Bank (1915) and Jutland (1916). He succeeded as Commander-in-Chief of the German High Seas fleet in 1918.

Hippius, Zinaida Nikolayevna See Gippius, Zinaida Nikolayevna

Hippocrates d.c.485BC
Tyrant of Gela

He is remembered for making Gela the dominant city of Sicily. 📖 Owsei Temkin, *Hippocrates in a World of Pagans and Christians* (1991)

Hippocrates c.460–377/359BC
Greek physician

Known as the 'father of medicine', and associated with the medical profession's Hippocratic oath, this most celebrated physician of antiquity was born and practised on the island of Cos, but little is known of him except that he taught for money. Skilled in diagnosis and prognosis, he gathered together all the work of his predecessors which he believed to be sound, and laid the early foundations of scientific medicine. His followers developed the theories that the four fluids or 'humours' (blood, phlegm, yellow bile and black bile) of the body are the primary seats of disease. The Hippocratic writings contain many treatises which long exerted great influence. The Hippocratic oath, for example, has been seen as the foundation document of Western medical ethics, and is still occasionally used in a Christianized version. Of Hippocrates's works, *Airs, Waters, Places* contained shrewd observations about the geography of disease and the role of the environment in shaping the health of a community; *Epidemics III* examined epidemics in a population and offered case histories of patients with acute diseases; *The Sacred Disease* elaborated a rigorous defence of the naturalistic causes of diseases; and *Aphorisms* consisted of a series of short pithy statements, mostly about clinical situations, but beginning with the most famous, 'Life is short, the art is long'. 📖 Edwin Burton Levine, *Hippocrates* (1971)

Hippolyte See Delaroche, Paul

Hippolytus, St AD170–235
Christian leader and antipope in Rome

He defended the doctrine of the *Logos* and attacked the Gnostics. He was with Irenaeus in Gaul in AD194, was a presbyter at Rome, and in 218 was elected antipope in opposition to the heretical (Monarchian) Calixtus I. In 235, both Hippolytus and Calixtus were deported to work in the Roman mines in Sardinia, where they died as martyrs. Hippolytus is generally believed to be the author of a *Refutation of all Heresies* in 10 books, discovered in 1842 in a 14th-century manuscript at Mount Athos. He also wrote a smaller work against heretics extant in a Latin translation. The so-called *Canons of Hippolytus* are more probably Graeco-Egyptian in origin. His feast day is 13 August in the West, and 30 January in the East.

Hirata Atsutane 1776–1843
Japanese scholar and theologian

As an extreme chauvinist, he condemned Buddhist and Confucian influences in Japanese culture and insisted that the Japanese were superior to all other peoples. By elevating those Shinto beliefs in the divine character of the imperial institution, Hirata's teachings helped to undermine the legitimacy of the shogunate, influencing the imperial loyalist movement that was ultimately to overthrow the Tokugawa Shogunate.

Hird, Dame Thora 1911–
English actress

Born of theatrical parents in Morecambe, Lancashire, she was 'discovered' in repertory theatre at the age of 16 and given a film contract, making her screen debut in *Spellbound* (1940) and following it with 60 films, including *The Entertainer* (1960), *A Kind of Loving* (1962) and *Rattle of a Simple Man* (1964). On television, she starred in *Meet the Wife* (1964–66), *Ours is a Nice House* (1969) and *In Loving Memory* (1979–86), as well as the Alan Bennett *Talking Heads* monologue *A Cream Cracker Under the Settee* (1988, BAFTA Best Television Actress Award) and plays such as *Memento Mori* (1992), *Wide Eyed and Legless* (1993) and *Pat and Margaret* (1994). She has also presented religious series such as *Your Songs of Praise Choice*, *Praise Be!*, to accompany which she has published several books, and *Thora on the Straight and Narrow* (1993). She was created DBE in 1993. 📖 *Scene and Hird* (1976)

Hire, Philippe de la See La Hire, Philippe de

Hirn, Gustave Adolphe 1815–90
French physicist and engineer

Born in Logelbach, Alsace, he was educated privately until he was 19, when he entered the family calico firm as a colour chemist. He later became director of a mill, and there investigated steam-engine performance, aiming to increase efficiency by using mineral oil lubricants to reduce friction. Convinced that heat and work were interconvertible, he sought the 'exchange rate' and by 1847 had measured the mechanical equivalent of heat, independently of James Joule and Robert von Mayer. His re-determination of the mechanical equivalent in 1855 gained a prize from the Berlin Physical Society. Hirn's *Théorie Mécanique de la Chaleur* (1862, 'Mechanical Theory of Heat') was one of the earliest textbooks on thermodynamics.

Hiroa, Te Rangi See Buck, Sir Peter Henry

Hirohito 1901–89
Emperor of Japan

He was born in Tokyo, the eldest son of Crown Prince Yoroshito (Emperor Taisho 1912–26). The first Japanese prince to visit the West (1921), he was the 124th emperor in direct lineage. His reign was marked by rapid militarization and aggressive wars against China (1931–32, 1937–45) and Great Britain and the USA (1941–45), which ended after the two atomic bombs were dropped on Hiroshima and Nagasaki by the USA. Under US occupation, Hirohito in 1946 renounced his legendary divinity and most of his powers to become a democratic constitutional monarch. He was a notable marine biologist. 📖 Edward Behr, *Hirohito: Behind the Myth* (1989)

Hiroshige, Ando, *originally* Ando Tokutaro 1797–1858
Japanese Ukiyo-e painter and wood engraver

He was born in Edo (now Tokyo). He is celebrated for his impressive landscape colour prints, executed in a freer but less austere manner than those of his greater contemporary Hokusai. His *Fifty-three Stages of the Tokaido* (1832) had a great influence on western Impressionist painters, but heralded the decline of Ukiyo-e (wood block print design, 'passing of the floating world' art). His masterpieces are striking compositions of snow or rain and mist. 📖 Yone Noguchi, *Hiroshige* (2 vols, 1934–40)

Hirota Koki 1878–1948
Japanese diplomat and politician

He had close links with the ultra-nationalist Genyosha and served in diplomatic posts in China, Great Britain, the USA and the USSR before becoming Foreign Minister in various non-party cabinets (1933–34, 1934–36). He championed an assertive foreign policy to protect Japan's interests in China, and in 1935 laid down principles to guide Sino-Japanese relations: the formation of a Japan–China–Manchuria economic bloc, suppression of all anti-Japanese activities in China, and the creation of a Sino-Japanese front against communism. As Prime Minister (1936–37), he increased the military budget and signed the anti-Comintern pact with Germany and Italy. Appointed Foreign Minister again (1937–39), Hirota supported Japan's full-scale invasion of China in 1937. After World War II, he was tried as a Class A war criminal and executed in 1948, the only civilian to be so sentenced.

Hirsch, Moritz von Hirsch, Baron 1831–96
German financier and philanthropist
Born in Munich, he amassed a fortune in Balkan railroad contracts, and devoted his wealth to improving the lot of the Jews. He financed the Jewish Colonization Association to assist Jewish emigration to the USA.

Hirst, Damien, *originally* Damien Steven David Brennan 1965–
English painter and installation artist
Born in Bristol and brought up in Leeds, Yorkshire, he obtained a low grade in art at A-level and was rejected by St Martin's School of Art. However, he was accepted at Goldsmith's College, London University (1986–89). From 1988 he produced 'spot' paintings, or grids of coloured circles on white canvas, deliberately mechanistic and devoid of emotion. In his installations he employs controversial materials, such as blood, maggots, dying butterflies, dead animals, and fish in tanks, claiming to 'access people's worst fears'. Exploring the contradiction between life and the inevitability of death, in 1991 he began to compartmentalize space by means of perspex and steel chambers which emphasize the isolation and fragility of his subjects, such as the tiger shark in *The Physical Impossibility of Death in the Mind of Someone Living* (1991, Saatchi Collection, London). Also in 1991, his Tate Gallery installation *The Asthmatic Escaped* contrasted the hi-tech nature of police surveillance with the pathos of the victim, expressed through ragged clothing and an asthma inhaler. In 1993 Hirst caused a sensation at the Venice Biennale with his *Mother and Child, Divided*, where a cow and a calf, both sliced in half, expressed the severing of the closest of bonds. The following year he organized a touring exhibition entitled *Some Went Mad, Some Ran Away*, featuring a white lamb in formaldehyde, entitled *Away From the Flock*; this was vandalized with black ink by an intruder at the Serpentine Gallery in London. For this exhibition, and other work, Hirst was awarded the 1995 Turner Prize. His uncompromising imagery has made him one of the most influential artists of his generation.

Hirst, Sir Edmund Langley 1898–1975
English chemist
Born in Preston, Lancashire, he studied chemistry at St Andrews University and joined the staff there but left in 1923 and worked successively at the universities of Manchester, Durham and Birmingham. His first chair was at Bristol (1936) and he became professor at the University of Manchester in 1944. He ended his distinguished academic career as Forbes Professor of Organic Chemistry at the University of Edinburgh. Hirst made important contributions to the chemistry of carbohydrates, his most famous work being his collaboration with Norman Haworth in the laboratory synthesis of vitamin C, the first time a vitamin had been made artificially. He was elected FRS in 1934 and knighted in 1964.

His, Wilhelm 1831–1904
German anatomist and embryologist
Born in Basle, Switzerland, he studied medicine at the universities of Basle, Bern, Berlin and Würzburg, qualifying in 1855. He became Professor of Anatomy in Basle (1857–72) and later, from 1872, at Leipzig. He pursued valuable studies on the lymphatic system, and made

investigations into developmental processes and embryonic growth. One of his most important contributions lay in the development of the microtome (1866) for cutting very thin serial sections for microscopical purposes, which he used primarily in his examination of embryos. He also used photography for anatomical purposes, and furnished the first accurate description of the human embryo. His son, Wilhelm His (1863–1934), became a cardiologist and was Professor of Internal Medicine at Berlin (1907–26); he is credited with discovering the muscle fibres that connect the left and right chambers of the heart (now called bundle of His).

Hislop, Joseph 1884–1977
Scottish tenor
Born in Edinburgh, he went to work in Gothenburg, Sweden, where his voice was noticed in a male voice choir. After tuition in Stockholm he made his debut at the Royal Swedish Opera in 1914 as Faust in Gounod's opera. He subsequently appeared at the San Carlo Opera, Naples (1920), Covent Garden, London (in *La Bohème*), Chicago and New York Opera, Turin, Venice, Milan and Buenos Aires. In 1927 and 1931 he made an Empire concert tour of Australia, New Zealand and South Africa, and in 1928 sang Faust in a controversial production at Covent Garden, London opposite Chaliapin. In the 1930s he appeared in a film, *The Loves of Robert Burns* (directed by Herbert Wilcox). From 1937 to 1947 he taught at the Royal Academy and the Opera School in Stockholm, where his pupils included Birgit Nilsson and Jussi Björling, and later coached singers in London. From 1947 he was an adviser at the Royal Opera House, Covent Garden, and at Sadler's Wells, and later became a professor at the Guildhall School of Music.

Hispalensis, Isidorus See Isidore of Seville, St

Hiss, Alger 1904–96
US state department official
Born in Baltimore, Maryland, and educated at Johns Hopkins University and Harvard Law School, he began his career as secretary to Supreme Court Justice Oliver Wendell Holmes and joined the state department in 1936. He was actively involved in organizing the United Nations, attending the Dumbarton Oaks conference and advising President Franklin D Roosevelt at the Yalta Conference (1945). From 1946 to 1949 he served as president of the Carnegie Endowment for International Peace. He stood trial twice (1949, 1950) on a charge of perjury, having denied before the House Committee on Un-American Activities that he had passed secret state documents to *Time* magazine editor Whittaker Chambers, an agent for an international communist spy ring, in 1938. He was convicted at his second trial and sentenced to five years' imprisonment. The suspicions of the public, intensified by the subsequent Klaus Fuchs case in Britain, were fully exploited politically, not least by Senator Joseph McCarthy. In 1992, after the collapse of the USSR, a high-ranking Russian general and military historian announced that his examination of KGB files had discovered no evidence that Hiss had ever been a spy, though he later added that he could not claim to have examined the entire KGB archives.

Hitchcock, Sir Alfred Joseph 1899–1980
English filmmaker
Born in Leytonstone, London, he began as a film technician in 1920, and directed his first film in 1925. His films in Great Britain included *The Thirty-Nine Steps* (1935) and *The Lady Vanishes* (1938). His first Hollywood film, *Rebecca* (1940), won an Academy Award for Best Picture. Other films included *Spellbound* (1945), *Notorious* (1946), *Dial M for Murder* (1954), *Rear Window* (1955), *Psycho* (1960), *The Birds* (1963), and *Frenzy* (1972). He appeared briefly in many of his films, which were internationally recognized for his

unequalled mastery of suspense and innovative camera-work—the famous 'Hitchcock touch'. He received the American Institute's Life Achievement Award in 1979. ⌑ John Russell Taylor, *Hitch: The Life and Times of Alfred Hitchcock* (1978)

Hitchcock, Edward 1793–1864
US geologist

Born in Deerfield, Massachusetts, he began his career as a teacher and clergyman, became Professor of Chemistry at Amherst College (1825–45) and directed the first state-funded geological survey of Massachusetts (1830–33). He investigated dinosaur tracks in the Connecticut Valley, which he believed to be bird tracks. He co-founded the American Association of Geologists in 1840.

Hitchcock, Lambert 1795–1852
US furniture designer

Born in Cheshire, Connecticut, he established in 1818 a furniture factory in Barkhamsted (now Riverton), employing 100 workers for mass production of Hitchcock chairs, now considered collectors' items. He also made the first designer rocking-chair.

Hitchens, Ivon 1893–1979
English painter

Born in London, he studied at St John's Wood School of Art and at the Royal Academy, London, joining the Seven and Five Society (1922), the London Group (1931), and the Society of Mural Painters. Painting in a semi-abstract style with obvious roots in Cubism, he always retained a strongly expressive feeling for natural forms, especially in the wide, horizontal landscapes which he painted from 1936. His first retrospective exhibition was in Leeds in 1945, and since then he has had many one-man shows in Europe and the USA. His work for the Festival of Britain in 1951, *Aquarian Nativity*, won an Arts Council award. He painted murals for the English Folk Song and Dance Society (1952–54, Cecil Sharp House, London), Nuffield College, Oxford (1959), and Sussex University (1963).

Hitchings, George Herbert 1905–98
US biochemist and Nobel Prize winner

Born in Hoquiam, Washington State, he studied and worked at the University of Washington (1926–28), Harvard (1928–39) and Western Reserve University Medical School (1939–42) before moving to Burroughs Wellcome, North Carolina, where he became director (1968–77) and Scientist Emeritus and Consultant from 1975 to 1998. He was also Professor of Pharmacology at Brown University from 1968 to 1980. His early research involved the preparation and testing of RNA and DNA bases, and amino acids, as growth factors. In 1948 these investigations revealed the folic acid antagonist which paved the way for the discovery of drugs to alleviate gout, and combat cancer and malaria. In 1954 his team synthesized the very successful anti-leukaemia drug 6-mercaptopurine, followed by azathioprine (or Imuran ®), which suppresses the body's immune system to enable organ transplantation from an unrelated donor. His laboratory also produced the anti-viral acyclovir (Zovirax ®), active against herpes, and the anti-AIDS drug zidovudine (Retrovir ®). Hitchings shared with **Gertrude Elion** and **James Black** the 1988 Nobel Prize for physiology or medicine for these achievements.

Hite, Shere, *originally* Shirley Diana Gregory 1943–
US feminist writer

Born in St Joseph, Missouri, she studied history at the universities of Florida and Columbia and worked as a model before entering the feminist arena. She directed the feminist sexuality project at the National Organization for Women in New York (1972–78), and lectured at the universities of Harvard, McGill and Columbia. In 1976 she published *The Hite Report: A Nationwide Study of Female Sexuality*, which was the result of five years' research; it caused an uproar, exploding traditional attitudes to sex and was followed by *The Hite Report on Male Sexuality* (1981), *The Hite Report of Women* (1987) and *Good Guys, Bad Guys* (1989).

Hitler, Adolf See panel p898

Hittorf, Johann Wilhelm 1824–1914
German physicist and chemist

Born in Bonn, he studied at Bonn and Berlin, then became *Privatdozent* at the Münster Academy. When this became a university, he was appointed Professor of Physics and Chemistry and later became director of the physics laboratories. His earliest research was on the allotropy of phosphorus and selenium, but he is best remembered for his work on ion migration during electrolysis (1853–59). In association with **Julius Plücker**, he studied the conduction of electricity through gases and the discharge-tube spectra of gases.

Hitzig, Julius Eduard 1838–1907
German neurologist and psychiatrist

Born in Berlin, he studied medicine at the universities of Berlin and Würzburg, and moved to Zurich in 1875 as Professor of Psychiatry. Shortly afterwards he moved to Halle as Professor of Psychiatry (1881–85) and as director of a psychiatric clinic (1885–1903). Hitzig demonstrated in 1870 that electrical stimulation of the frontal cortex in animals caused movements of the extremities on the opposite side of the body. These early studies proved the existence of specific motor control areas and stimulated research in brain anatomy. Hitzig himself continued with experiments especially in the visual cortex, and he also postulated the localization of centres for mental processes. His major influence has been on the development of neurological and psychiatric studies, and their integration with morphological and physiological knowledge.

Hjartarson, Snorri 1906–86
Icelandic poet

Born in Borgarfjöröur, he studied art in Copenhagen and Oslo, but soon turned to writing and published a novel written in Norwegian, *Höjtflyver ravnen* (1934, 'High Soars the Raven'). He returned to Iceland in 1936 to become one of the most influential poets of his day, combining traditional and modern poetry with musical and painterly images. He published four volumes of poetry, including the innovative *Kvaeði* (1944, 'Poems') and *Haustrokkerið Yfirmer* (1979, 'The Autumn Mist Surrounds Me'), and was awarded the Nordic Council's Literary Award for 1981. ⌑ S Egilsson, *Ljóðmaeli Sveinbjarner Egilssonar* (1952)

Hjelmslev, Louis Trolle 1899–1965
Danish linguist

Born in Copenhagen, he founded the Linguistic Circle of Copenhagen in 1931, and was a co-founder of the journal *Acta Linguistica* in 1939. With associates in Copenhagen, he devised a system of linguistic analysis known as glossematics, based on the study of the distribution of, and the relationships between, the smallest meaningful units of a language (glossemes). This is outlined in his *Prolegomena to a Theory of Language* (1943, Eng trans 1953, 1961).

Hlinka, Andrei 1864–1938
Slovak priest and politician

As a young man he was attracted by the political stance of the Slovak National Party and by the concern for the peasants of the Magyar Populist Party. In 1905 he established the Slovak Populists Party as a compromise, but he was soon being harassed by the Hungarian authorities. In 1918 he supported the creation of Czechoslovakia but he

Hitler, Adolf, *originally surnamed* Schicklgrüber, *known as* Der Führer ('The Leader') 1889–1945
German dictator

Hitler was born in Braunau in Upper Austria, the son of a minor customs official. He was educated at the secondary schools of Linz and Steyr, and destined by his father for the civil service. Hitler, however, saw himself as a great artist and, perhaps deliberately, failed his school leaving examinations. After his father's death he attended a private art school in Munich, but failed to pass into the Vienna Academy. He lived on his wits in Vienna (1904–13), making a precarious living by selling bad postcard sketches, beating carpets, and doing odd jobs. He worked only fitfully and spent his time in passionate political arguments directed at the money-lending Jews and the trade unions. He dodged military service, and in 1913 emigrated to Munich, where he found work as a draughtsman.

In 1914 he volunteered for war service in a Bavarian regiment, where he rose to the rank of corporal, and was recommended for the award of the Iron Cross for service as a runner on the western front. At the time of the German surrender in 1918 he was lying wounded, and temporarily blinded by gas, in hospital. In 1919, while acting as an informer for the army, he had to spy on the activities of small political parties; he became a member of one of them, and changed its name to *National-sozialistische Deutsche Arbeiterpartei* (National Socialist German Workers' Party) in 1920. Its programme was a convenient mixture of mild radicalism, bitter hatred of the politicians who had 'dishonoured Germany' by signing the Versailles *Diktat*, and clever exploitation of provincial grievances against the weak federal government.

By 1923 Hitler was strong enough to attempt, with the support of General Ludendorff's and other extreme right-wing factions, the overthrow of the Bavarian government. On 9 November, the Nazis marched through the streets of Munich, Mussolini-style; but the police, despite a tacit agreement, machine-gunned the Nazi column. Hitler narrowly escaped serious injury, Hermann Goering was badly wounded, and 16 storm troopers were killed. Hitler spent nine months in Landsberg prison, during which time he dictated his autobiography and political testament, *Mein Kampf* (1925, 'My Struggle', Eng trans 1939), to

Rudolf Hess. He began, with Joseph Goebbels, to woo the Ruhr industrialists, Gustav Krupp and others, and although unsuccessful in the presidential elections of 1932 when he stood against Paul von Hindenburg, Hitler was made Chancellor in January 1933 on the advice of Franz von Papen, who thought that he could best be brought to heel inside the Cabinet.

Hitler, however, soon dispensed with constitutional restraints. He silenced all opposition, and, by plotting the burning of the *Reichstag* building (February 1933), and advertising it as a communist plot, succeeded in forcing a general election, in which the police, under Goering, allowed the Nazis full play to break up the meetings of their opponents. By these means the Nazi Party achieved a bare majority, and Hitler assumed absolute power through the Enabling Acts. He ruthlessly crushed opposition inside his own party by the purge of June 1934 (the Night of the Long Knives) in which his rival Ernst Röhm and hundreds of influential Nazis were murdered at the hands of Hitler's bodyguard, the SS, under Heinrich Himmler and Reinhard Heydrich. Hindenburg conveniently died in August, leaving Hitler sole master of Germany.

Under the pretext of undoing the wrongs of the Treaty of Versailles, and of uniting the German peoples and extending their living-space (*Lebensraum*), he openly rearmed (1935), sent troops into the demilitarized Rhineland zone, established the Rome–Berlin 'axis' (October 1936) with Mussolini's Italy, created 'Greater Germany' by the invasion of Austria (1938), and, by systematic infiltration and engineered incidents, engendered a favourable situation for an easy absorption of the Sudeten or German-populated border lands of Czechoslovakia, to which Great Britain and France acquiesced at Munich (September 1938). Renouncing further territorial claims, Hitler nevertheless seized Bohemia and Moravia, took Memel from Lithuania and demanded from Poland the return of Danzig and free access to East Prussia through the 'Corridor'. Poland's refusal, backed by Britain and France, precipitated World War II, on 3 September 1939.

cont

was subsequently disappointed with centralist rule from Prague and his own non-involvement in governing his countrymen. In the 1920s and 1930s he built up his party and secured some political concessions from Prague. In the middle of 1938 when President Eduard Beneš was in difficulties, Hlinka took the opportunity to demand autonomy for Slovakia, but died in August. He was replaced as leader of the party by the anti-Czech Jozef Tiso.

Hoagland, Mahlon Bush 1921–
US biochemist

Born in Boston, he studied medicine at Harvard, and was a visiting researcher at the universities of Copenhagen and Cambridge before returning to the bacteriology and immunology department of Harvard Medical School (1952–67). He later became Professor of Biochemistry at Dartmouth Medical School (1967–85), and from 1970 to 1985 was scientific director of the Worcester Foundation for Experimental Biology. He worked on the causes of cancer, liver regeneration and growth control, but his major scientific contribution was his confirmation that in protein synthesis the carrier for each amino acid is identified by an RNA transcript. Hoagland went on to illustrate the role played by amino acids in protein synthesis and the formation of ester links.

Hoare, Sir Richard 1648–1718
English banker

Born in London, he became a Lombard Street goldsmith (c.1673) and moved (c.1693) to Fleet Street, where he founded the bank which still bears his name. He was Lord Mayor of London in 1713.

Hoare, Sir Samuel John Gurney, 1st Viscount Templewood of Chelsea 1880–1959
English Conservative politician

Born in London and educated at Harrow and New College, Oxford, he became an MP in 1910, and held Colonial Office appointments in Russia and Italy. He was Secretary of State for Air (1922–29), and as Secretary of State for India (1931–35), helped draft its constitution, and piloted the 1935 India Act through the Commons. As Foreign Secretary in 1935, he made a memorable speech to the League of Nations on collective security, but was criticized for his part in the Hoare–Laval Pact, by which large parts of Abyssinia were ceded to Italy, and resigned the following year. He was made First Lord of the Admiralty in 1936, and during World War II was Lord Privy Seal, Secretary of State for Air again, and ambassador to Spain. His strong opposition to capital punishment was argued in *The Shadow of the Gallows* (1952), and an autobiographical work entitled *Nine Troubled Years* was published in 1954.

Hitler, Adolf cont

Meanwhile Hitler's domestic policy was one of thorough Nazification of all aspects of German life, enforced by the Secret State Police (*Gestapo*), and the establishment of concentration camps for political opponents and Jews, who were sytematically persecuted. Strategic roads or *Autobahnen* were built, **Hjalmar Schacht**'s economic policy expanded German exports up to 1936, and then Goering's 'Guns before Butter' four-year plan boosted armaments and the construction of the Siegfried Line. Hitler entered the war with the grave misgivings of the German High Command, but as his 'intuitions' scored massive triumphs in the first two years, he more and more ignored the advice of military experts.

Peace with Russia was secured by the Molotov–Ribbentrop pact (August 1939). Hitler invaded Poland, and after three weeks' *Blitzkrieg* ('lightning war') divided it between Russia and Germany. In 1940 Denmark, Norway, Holland, Belgium and France were occupied and the British repelled from Dunkirk; but Goering's invincible *Luftwaffe* was heavily defeated in the Battle of Britain (August–September 1940). Hitler then turned to the east; he entered Romania (October 1940), invaded Yugoslavia and Greece (April 1941), and, ignoring his pact of convenience with **Stalin**, attacked Russia. As an ally of Japan, he was soon also at war with the USA (December 1941).

The *Wehrmacht* penetrated to the gates of Moscow and Leningrad, to the Volga, into the Caucasus and, with Italy as an ally from 1940, to North Africa as far as Alexandria. But there the tide turned. **Montgomery**'s victory over **Rommel** at El Alamein (October 1942), and **Friedrich Paulus**'s grave defeat, through Hitler's misdirection, at Stalingrad (November 1942), heralded the Nazi withdrawal from North Africa pursued by the British and Americans (November 1942–May 1943). There followed the Allied invasion of Sicily, Italian capitulation (September 1943) and overwhelming Russian victories (1943–44); then the Anglo-American invasion of Normandy and the breaching of Rommel's 'Atlantic Wall' (June 1944). Using the newly developed V1 and V2 guided missiles, Hitler responded with attacks on southern England.

But these developments came too late, and the Allies made steady progress. Opposition to Hitler was growing, and several attempts were made on his life. In July 1944 Hitler miraculously survived the explosion of a bomb placed at his feet by Colonel **Stauffenberg**; he purged the army of all suspects, including Rommel, who was given the choice of committing suicide. In December, **Karl Rundstedt**'s counter-offensive against the Allies in the Ardennes was a failure, and the invasion of Germany followed. Hitler lived out his fantasies, commanding non-existent armies from his Berlin bunker. With the Russians only several hundred yards away, he went through a marriage ceremony with his mistress, **Eva Braun**, in the presence of the Goebbels family, who then poisoned themselves. The available evidence suggests that Hitler and his wife committed suicide and had their bodies cremated on 30 April 1945.

Hitler's much-vaunted *Third Reich*, which was to have endured for ever, ended ingloriously after 12 years of unparalleled barbarity, in which 30 million people lost their lives, 12 million of them far away from the battlefields, by mass shootings, in forced labour camps and in the gas ovens of Belsen, Dachau, Auschwitz, Ravensbrück and other concentration camps in accordance with Nazi racial theories and the 'New Order', not forgetting the indiscriminate torture and murder of many prisoners of war, or the uprooting and extermination of entire village communities in Poland, France and Russia. Such horror prompted the international trial at Nuremberg (1945–46), at which 21 of the leading living Nazis were tried and 11 executed for war crimes.

📖 Alan Bullock, *Hitler and Stalin: Parallel Lives* (1992) and *Hitler: A Study in Tyranny* (1952, rev edn 1964); Martin Broszat, *Hitler and the Collapse of Weimar Germany* (1987); Robert G L Waite, *The Psychopathic God: Adolf Hitler* (1977); Hugh Trevor-Roper, *The Last Days of Hitler* (1947).

> *Die breite Masse eines Volkes ... einer groen Lüge leichter zum Opfer fällt als einer kleinen.*
> 'The broad mass of a nation ... will more easily fall victim to a big lie than to a small one.' From *Mein Kampf*, ch.10 (1925).

Hoban, James c.1762–1831

US architect

Born in County Kilkenny, Ireland, he emigrated to the USA after the American Revolution and worked as an architect in Philadelphia. After he designed the capitol of South Carolina, he won the design competition for the White House in Washington DC, supervising its construction as well as that of the US Capitol. He rebuilt the White House after it was burned in the War of 1812.

Hoban, Russell Conwell 1925–

US writer

Born in Lansdale, Pennsylvania, he began by writing successful children's books, beginning with *Bedtime For Frances* (1960), the first of several picture books about a young badger. *The Mouse and His Child* (1967) was one of his most successful works for children, but two years later he moved to England and turned to adult writing. Much of his subsequent work has a fantasy or science-fictional strand to it, and includes *The Lion of Boaz-Jachin and Jachin-Boaz* (1973), *Riddley Walker* (1980, stage adaption 1986) and *The Medusa Frequency* (1987). He was made a Fellow of the Royal Society of Literature in 1988.

Hobart-Hampden, August Charles
See **Hobart Pasha**

Hobart Pasha, *properly* August Charles Hobart-Hampden 1822–86

English naval commander and adventurer

He was born in Waltham-on-the-Wolds, Leicestershire. He served in the Royal Navy (1835–63) during the American Civil War as 'Captain Roberts', repeatedly ran the blockade of the Southern ports, and afterwards became naval adviser to Turkey (1867) and was made pasha and admiral. In the Russo-Turkish war (1878) he commanded the Turkish Black Sea fleet. He wrote *Never Caught* (1867) and *Sketches from My Life*.

Hobbema, Meindert 1638–1709

Dutch landscape painter

Born probably in Amsterdam, he studied under **Jacob van Ruïsdael**, but lacked his master's brilliance and range, contenting himself with florid, placid and charming watermill scenes. Nevertheless his masterpiece, *The Avenue, Middelharnis* (1689), in the National Gallery, London, is a striking exception and has greatly influenced modern landscape artists. Through marriage, he became collector of the city's wine customs.

Hobbes, Thomas 1588–1679
English political philosopher

He was born in Malmesbury, Wiltshire, prematurely, as he liked to explain, when his mother heard news of the approaching Spanish Armada. He was the son of a wayward country vicar, brought up by an uncle, and was educated at Magdalen Hall, Oxford (1603–08). He had numerous notable patrons, in particular the **Cavendish** family, the Earls of Devonshire, with whom he travelled widely as family tutor, thereby making the acquaintance of many leading intellectual figures of his day: **Francis Bacon, John Selden** and **Ben Jonson** in England, **Galileo** in Florence, and the circle of **Marin Mersenne** in Paris, including **René Descartes** and **Pierre Gassendi**. But the first real intellectual turning-point of his life was his introduction at the age of 40 to Euclidean geometry, and he conceived the ambition of extending this compelling deductive certainty to a comprehensive science of man and society. His interest in political theory had already been indicated in his first published work, a translation of **Thucydides's** *History* (1629), and, becoming increasingly concerned with the civil disorders of the time, he wrote the *Elements of Law Natural and Politic* (completed in 1640 but not properly published until 1650), in which he attempted to set out in mathematical fashion the rules of a political science, and went on to argue in favour of monarchical government. When the Long Parliament assembled (1640) he quickly departed for France, to be followed by other Royalists who helped him to the position of tutor (1646) in mathematics to the exiled Prince of Wales (the future **Charles II**) in Paris. By then he had completed a set of 'Objections' (1641) to Descartes's *Meditations*, which Mersenne had commissioned from him (as from other scholars), and the *De Cive* (1642), a fuller statement of his new science of the state or 'civil philosophy'. His next work was his masterpiece, *Leviathan* (1651), which presented and connected his mature thoughts on metaphysics, psychology and political philosophy. He was a thorough-going materialist, seeing the world as a mechanical system consisting wholly of bodies in motion, driven by the forces of attraction and repulsion, which could be seen also to govern human psychology and to determine what we call 'good' and 'evil'. Human beings are wholly selfish. Enlightened self-interest explains the nature and function of the sovereign state: we are forced to establish a social contract in which we surrender the right of aggression to an absolute ruler, whose commands are the law. The *Leviathan* offended the royal exiles in Paris and the French government by its hostility to Church power and religious obedience, and in 1652 Hobbes returned to England, made his peace with **Cromwell** and the Parliamentary regime, and settled in London. He continued to write and to arouse controversy. *De Corpore* appeared in 1655, *De Homine* in 1658. At the Restoration Charles II gave his old tutor a pension and helped quash a bill aimed at Hobbes, whose enemies in the clergy were claiming that the Plague and the Great Fire of London of 1665–66 revealed God's wrath against England for harbouring such an atheist. He was banned from publishing in England in 1666 and his later books were published in the Netherlands first. He wrote on tirelessly into his eighties, and amongst other things published *Behemoth: a history of the causes of the Civil Wars of England* (completed 1668, published 1682), an autobiography in Latin verse (1672), and verse translations of the *Iliad* (1675) and *Odyssey* (1676). 📖 George C Richardson, *Hobbes* (2nd edn, 1967)

Hobbs, Jack, *properly* Sir John Berry Hobbs
1882–1963
English cricketer

Born in Cambridge, he became one of England's greatest batsmen. He first played first-class cricket for Cambridgeshire in 1904, but joined Surrey the following year and played for them for 30 years (1905–35). He played in 61 Test matches between 1907 and 1930, when he and Herbert Sutcliffe (1894–1978) established themselves as an unrivalled pair of opening batsmen, and he captained England in 1926. In his first-class career he made 197 centuries, and scored 61,237 runs (including the highest score at Lord's with 316 in 1926). He also made the highest ever score in the Gentlemen v. Players match, 266 not out; 98 of his 197 centuries were made after he attained the age of 40. An immensely popular figure, he was the first English cricketer to be knighted, in 1953. 📖 John Arlott, *Jack Hobbs: Profile of the Master* (1981)

Hobhouse, John Cam, 1st Baron Broughton
1786–1869
English politician

He was educated at Westminster and Trinity College, Cambridge, and became a friend of Lord **Byron**. His *Journey through Albania with Lord Byron* was published in 1813. He entered parliament as a Radical in 1820, succeeded as baronet in 1831, and from 1832 to 1852 held various Cabinet offices. He coined the term 'His Majesty's opposition'.

Hobhouse, Leonard Trelawney 1864–1929
English social philosopher and journalist

Born in St Ives, Cornwall, he was a Fellow of Merton College, Oxford (1894), before joining the editorial staff of the *Manchester Guardian* (1897). He became editor of the *Sociological Review* (1903) and during the same period (1903–05) he was secretary of the Free Trade Union, and later political editor of *Tribune* (1906–07). From 1907 he was Professor of Sociology at London University. His best-known works are *Labour Movement* (1893), *Theory of Knowledge* (1896), *Morals in Evolution* (1906), and *Development and Purpose* (1913). 📖 John E Owen, *Hobhouse, Sociologist* (1975)

Hobson, Sir Harold 1904–92
English drama critic

He was born into a mining family in Thorpe Hesley, South Yorkshire. Paralyzed in the right leg when he was seven, he was unable to attend school until he was 16. He won a scholarship to Sheffield University, but chose instead to go to Oxford. He was drama critic of the *Sunday Times* (1947–76) and became one of the most influential critics in Great Britain. He was also drama critic of the Christian Science Monitor (1931–74). An authority on French theatre and the French avant-garde, he hailed *Waiting for Godot* by **Samuel Beckett** on its London première in 1955, and would often discover plays on their first performance in France and recommend them to impresarios in Great Britain. He wrote a number of books on British and French theatre, an autobiography (*Indirect Journey*, 1978), and a personal history, *Theatre in Britain* (1984).

Hobson, John Atkinson 1858–1940
English economist

Born in Derby, he graduated at Oxford. An opponent of orthodox economic theories, he believed that 'under-consumption' was the main cause of unemployment. He wrote *The Science of Wealth* (1911) and an autobiography, *Confessions of an Economic Heretic* (1938).

Hobson, Thomas c.1544–1631
English livery-stable keeper and innkeeper

He kept a stable of horses to rent out to students at Cambridge, and required each customer to take the horse nearest the stable door, whatever its quality. From this comes the expression 'Hobson's choice', meaning no choice at all.

Hochhuth, Rolf 1931–
German dramatist

Born in Eschwege, he studied history and philosophy at Munich and Heidelberg, and worked as an editor before turning to documentary drama. His controversial play, *Der Stellvertreter* (1963, Eng trans *The Representative*, 1963) accused Pope **Pius XII** of not intervening to stop the Nazi persecution of the Jews. It caused a furore, as did the implication in his second play, *Soldaten* (1967, Eng trans *Soldiers*, 1968), that **Winston Churchill** was involved in the assassination of the Polish wartime leader, General Sikorski. He also wrote a novel, *Eine Liebe in Deutschland* (1978, 'German Love Story'), about Nazi atrocities. 📖 M E Ward, *Hochhuth* (1977)

Ho Chi Minh, *originally* Nguyen That Thanh 1890–1969
Vietnamese statesman

Born in Annam region, the son of a mandarin, from 1912 he worked in London and the USA, and in France from 1918, where he was a founder-member of the French Communist Party. From 1922 until 1930 he was often in Moscow. He founded the Viet Minh Independence League in 1941, and between 1946 and 1954 directed the successful military operations against the French, becoming Prime Minister (1954–55) and President (1954) of North Vietnam. Re-elected in 1960, with Chinese assistance he was a leading force in the war between North and South. Despite huge US military intervention in support of South Vietnam between 1963 and 1975, Ho Chi Minh's Viet Cong retained the initiative, and forced a ceasefire in 1973, four years after his death. The civil war continued until 1975, when Saigon fell and was renamed Ho Chi Minh City. 📖 David Halberstam, *Ho* (1971)

Hockney, David 1937–
English artist

He was born in Bradford, Yorkshire. His paintings began to attract interest while he was studying at the Royal College of Art. Associated with the Pop Art movement, his early paintings are a juxtaposition of artistic styles and fashions, with graffiti-like figures and words, as in *We 2 Boys Together Clinging* (1961, Arts Council, London), and a technique ranging from the broad use of heavy colour to a minute delicacy of line. A visit to the USA inspired his series of etchings, *The Rake's Progress* (1963), based on his adventures in New York, and while he was in California (1963–67) he began to develop his celebrated 'swimming-pool' paintings, such as *The Sunbather* (1966, Museum Ludwig, Cologne). He edited and illustrated *14 Poems of C P Cavafy*, and produced a series of etchings, *Six Fairy Tales from the Brothers Grimm* (1970). His later work, often double portraits, is more representational, such as *Mr and Mrs Clark and Percy* (1970–71, Tate, London). He also designed for several operas, including **Mozart**'s *Magic Flute* at Glyndebourne (1978), and for the New York Metropolitan Opera. In 1982, rejecting one-point perspective, he began a series of photo-collages (*Cameraworks*), composed from myriad separate shots. He has also experimented with computer technology and digital inkjet printings, as in 'The Studio March 28th 1996', and has transmitted huge murals to exhibitions by fax. His ability to deal with his homosexuality through his painting has contributed to greater tolerance and understanding. He was made an RA in 1991 and published his autobiography *That's the Way I See It* in 1993. An exhibition of his work from 1982 to 1995 was held at the Manchester City Art Galleries in 1996. 📖 Peter Webb, *Portrait of David Hockney* (1989)

Hoddinott, Alun 1929–
Welsh composer

He was born in Bargoed, Mid Glamorgan, and studied piano under Arthur Benjamin. He has held several academic posts in Wales, and was appointed Professor of Music at the University College of South Wales (1967–87). He has written a great deal of largely tonal romantic music that is influenced by serialism, including operas, orchestral music, songs and choral music, and chamber music. He co-founded the Cardiff Festival in 1967.

Hodge, Charles 1797–1878
US theologian

Born in Philadelphia, he studied at Princeton University, where he became a professor of biblical literature in 1822. He founded and edited the *Princeton Review*, and wrote a history of the Presbyterian Church in the USA (1840), and the well-known *Systematic Theology* (1871–72). His son, Archibald Alexander (1823–86), who succeeded his father at Princeton in 1878, wrote *Outlines of Theology* (1860).

Hodgkin, Sir Alan Lloyd 1914–98
English physiologist and Nobel Prize winner

Born in Banbury, Oxfordshire, he studied natural sciences at Trinity College, Cambridge, and has spent almost his entire career in Cambridge. Master of Trinity College from 1978 to 1984, he was a lecturer and assistant director of research at the Physiological Laboratory (1945–52), Royal Society Research Professor (1952–69) and president (1970–75), and Professor of Biophysics (1970–81). During World War II he worked on airborne radar research, and then on the conduction of nerve impulses. With **Andrew Huxley**, he described in physico-chemical and mathematical terms, the mechanisms by which nerves conduct electrical impulses by the movement of electrically charged particles across the nerve membrane. The techniques they developed have enabled scientists to study and understand many different kinds of excitable membranes. The two men shared the 1963 Nobel Prize for physiology or medicine with Sir **John Eccles**. Hodgkin's other honours and awards include the Order of Merit (1973). In 1992 he published his autobiography *Chance and Design: Reminiscences of Science in Peace and War*.

Hodgkin, Dorothy Mary See panel p902

Hodgkin, Sir Howard 1932–
English painter

Born in London, he trained at Bath Academy of Art and taught at Chelsea School of Art. His highly personal style has not followed any of the major art movements of recent decades. Although apparently abstract, his paintings are in fact representational, capturing a particular moment in time, as in *Rain* (1959, Tate, London). He spent some time in India, and his interest in the traditional painting of that country is reflected in the decorative features of his compositions and his use of brilliant colour as well as his preference for working on a small scale. He is also a celebrated printmaker, and there is a collection of his work in the Tate Gallery, London. Hand colouring applied to his prints is a feature of his work, as in the Indian balcony scene, *For Bernard Jacobson* (1979, Tate, London). In 1992 he painted a black and white mural of the banyan tree on the new British Council headquarters in New Delhi. He won the Turner Prize for contemporary British art in 1985. A new exhibition of his work was displayed at the Hayward Gallery, London, in 1996.

Hodgkin, Thomas 1798–1866
English physician and pathologist

Born in Tottenham, Middlesex, he was educated at Edinburgh, and held various posts at Guy's Hospital, London. He described the glandular disease, later named 'Hodgkin's disease', in which spleen, liver and lymph nodes become enlarged. 📖 Michael Rose, *Curator of the Dead: Thomas Hodgkin (1798–1866)* (1981)

Hodgkins, Frances Mary 1869–1947
New Zealand artist

Hodgkin, Dorothy Mary, *née* Crowfoot 1910–94
British crystallographer and Nobel Prize winner

Dorothy Hodgkin was born in Cairo, Egypt. She studied chemistry at Somerville College, Oxford, moved to Cambridge to study for her PhD and became a tutor and Fellow at Somerville (1935–77). She married Thomas Hodgkin (d.1982), a specialist in African studies, in 1937. After various appointments within the university, she became the first Royal Society Wolfson Research Professor at Oxford (1960–77).

In X-ray crystallography studies at Cambridge, Irish crystallographer John Bernal (1901–71) introduced her to the complex and demanding study of biologically interesting molecules. With him she began work on sterols, which she continued after her return to Oxford. Her detailed X-ray analysis of cholesterol was a milestone in crystallography, but an even greater achievement was the determination of the structure of penicillin (1942–45), especially since some of the best chemists in the UK and USA had been unable to find its constitution using chemical rather than physical techniques.

After World War II computational facilities increased, and Hodgkin was the first to apply them to the analysis of complex chemical structures; even so, the determination of the structure of vitamin B_{12e} (used to fight pernicious anaemia), which was her real triumph, occupied eight years (1948–56). For her later work on insulin, an even more complicated molecule, more advanced computing techniques were used.

A cheerful, caring woman, she served as Chancellor of Bristol University from 1970 to 1988, and was noted for her regular visits to the Students' Union, and for taking a personal interest in many individual students. Among her many honours she was elected FRS (1947), and in 1964, 'for her determination by X-ray techniques of the structures of biologically important molecules', she was awarded the Nobel Prize for chemistry; she was only the third woman to receive it (the first two being **Marie Curie** and **Irène Joliot-Curie**) and the first British woman to receive a Nobel science prize. In 1965 she was admitted to the Order of Merit, the first woman to be so honoured since **Florence Nightingale**, and in 1987 she was awarded the Lenin Peace Prize for her contribution as president from 1975 of the 'Pugwash' Conferences on Science and World Affairs.

Her best-known fourth-year student of X-ray crystallography was then called Margaret Roberts, later **Margaret Thatcher**.

When Dorothy Hodgkin explained what she had discovered the constitution of penicillin to be, **John Cornforth** exclaimed: 'If that's the formula of penicillin, I'll give up chemistry and grow mushrooms.' (Quoted in *The Independent*, 1 August 1994.) However, Cornforth ate his words and later he too won a Nobel Prize.

On being asked whether she felt handicapped in her career by being a woman, she replied: 'As a matter of fact, men were always particularly nice and helpful to me because I was a woman.' Quoted in *The Independent*, 1 August 1994.

Born and educated in Dunedin, she travelled extensively in Europe, with long visits to Paris and England. Her paintings, examples of which are in the Tate Gallery, and the Victoria and Albert Museum, London, are characterized by a harmonious use of flat colour reminiscent of **Matisse**. Though older than most of her circle, she was ranked as a leader of contemporary Romanticism.

Hodgkinson, Eaton 1789–1861
English engineer

Born in Anderton, Cheshire, he had little formal higher education, but became one of the foremost authorities on the strength of materials. As a result of tests carried out in the engineering works of Sir **William Fairbairn**, he proposed, in 1830, the famous 'Hodgkinson's beam' as the most efficient form of cast-iron beam, and after a further series of experiments he published a paper *On the Strength of Pillars of Cast Iron and other Materials* (1840). Hodgkinson also collaborated with Fairbairn and **Robert Stephenson** on the design of the rectangular wrought-iron tubes within which trains crossed the Menai Strait in four continuous spans, two of 460ft (138m) and two of 230ft (69m). His Britannia Bridge, opened in 1850, constituted a significant advance in the theory and practice of structural engineering at the time. He was elected FRS in 1840, and in 1847 was appointed Professor of the Mechanical Principles of Engineering at University College London.

Hodgson, Brian Houghton 1800–95
English Orientalist

Born near Macclesfield, Cheshire, he entered the East India Company's service in 1818, was resident in Nepal (1820–43), and settled in England in 1858. He wrote some 170 very valuable papers on the technology, languages and zoology of Nepal and Tibet, sent home 354 manuscripts, on which our knowledge of northern Buddhism is mainly based, and made a collection of 10,500 birds.

Hodgson, Leonard 1889–1969
English Anglican theologian

Born in London, he taught at Magdalen College, Oxford, and the General Theological Seminary, New York, before returning to Oxford as Professor of Moral and Pastoral Theology (1938–44) and then Professor of Divinity (1944–58). He was also theological secretary to the Commission on Faith and Order of the World Council of Churches, Geneva (1933–52), and Warden of William Temple College, Rugby (1954–66). He wrote some 20 books, including *The Doctrine of the Trinity* (1943) and *The Doctrine of the Atonement* (1951). His Gifford Lectures, *For Faith and Freedom* (2 vols, 1956–57), aimed to show that 'the Christian faith, while it forbids us to claim knowledge we have not got, gives us light enough to walk in the way that leads to knowing more'.

Hodgson, Ralph Edwin 1871–1962
English poet

Born in Yorkshire, he became a journalist in London. He published three volumes of Georgian poems with the recurring theme of nature and England: *The Last Blackbird* (1907), *Eve* (1913) and *Poems* (1917), containing 'The Song of Honour', 'The Moor', 'The Journeyman', and a passionate protest against man's cruelty to animals in 'To Deck a Woman'. He lectured in Japan (1924–38), and then made his home in Ohio, USA. An anthology of his works appeared as *The Skylark and Other Poems* (1958). He was awarded the Order of the Rising Sun (1938) and the Queen's Gold Medal (1954). His *Collected Poems* appeared in 1961.
📖 G B Saul, in *Withdraw in Gold: three portraits of genius* (1970)

Hodler, Ferdinand 1853–1918
Swiss painter

Born in Berne, he developed a highly decorative style of landscape, historical and genre painting with strong colouring and outline, sometimes using parallel motifs for effect. His works, in a Symbolist style influenced by the Rosicrucians in Paris, include *The Return from Marignano* (1896), *William Tell*, *Night* (1890), *Day* (c.1900), and many others at Berne, Zurich and elsewhere.

Hodja, Enver See **Hoxha, Enver**

Hoe, Richard Marsh 1812–86
US inventor and industrialist

Born in New York City, he joined his father's printing-press firm when he was 15 years old and took over the business with his cousin Matthew three years later when his father retired. Like **Augustus Applegath** in London, he saw the advantages of printing on a cylinder instead of a flat plate, and the 'Hoe rotary press' was first used by the *Philadelphia Public Ledger* in 1847. In 1865 William Bullock installed for the *Philadelphia Inquirer* a rotary press that printed on a continuous roll of newsprint, but by 1871 Hoe had produced a new design incorporating all the main features introduced by his rivals which was very commercially successful.

Høegh-Guldberg, Ove 1731–1808
Danish politician

Born in Jutland into a humble family, he studied theology at the University of Copenhagen and was appointed Professor at the Noble Academy in Sorø (1761). In the same year, he also became the tutor of Prince Frederick, son of the late King Frederick V and his second wife, the powerful Queen Dowager, Juliane Marie. In 1772 Juliane Marie was the leader of a palace revolution that overthrew the self-appointed, progressive-minded dictator, Count Johann Friedrich Struensee, who since the summer of 1770 had filled the power gap created by the mental illness of King Kristian VII. After the palace revolution, Høegh-Guldberg became Denmark's most influential politician, for 12 years pursuing his cautious policies from his power base, the King's 'court cabinet', of which he was the Secretary. In 1784 his regime was overturned by another coup led by Crown Prince Frederick VI, and by Høegh-Guldberg's principal political adversary, Andreas Peter Bernstorff. Høegh-Guldberg then became a civil servant in the provincial town of Aarhus, where he loyally implemented the progressive policies of the new regime.

Hofer, Andreas 1767–1810
Austrian political leader

Born in St Leonhard, in 1808 he called the Tyrolese to arms to expel the French and Bavarians, and defeated the Bavarians at the Battle of Iusel Berg (1809). He retook Innsbruck from the French, and for the next two months was ruler of his native land. Subsequently, however, he was forced to disband his followers and take refuge in the mountains. Two months later he was betrayed, captured and taken to Mantua, where he was tried by court martial and shot.

Hofer, Karl 1878–1955
German artist

Born in Karlsruhe, he studied there, and spent many years in France and Italy. He spent three years in an internment camp in Paris in World War I. In World War II, the Nazis condemned his work as degenerate. In 1943 his studio was bombed and most of his work destroyed. His severe style and harsh, brilliant colours, much influenced by his war experiences, express the bitterness of the times.

Hoff, Jacobus Henricus van't 1852–1911
Dutch physical chemist and Nobel Prize winner

Born in Rotterdam, he was educated at the universities of Leyden, Bonn, Paris and Utrecht. He became Professor of Chemistry, Mineralogy and Geology at the University of Amsterdam (1878), and in 1896 moved to Berlin as a member of the Prussian Academy of Sciences and as professor at the university there. His first work was in organic chemistry, where his research on the four bonds

of carbon provided a basis for explaining the optical activity of certain organic compounds. From 1877 he began to devote himself to physical chemistry, developing the principles of chemical kinetics and applying thermodynamics to chemical equilibria. The equation for the effect of temperature on equilibria is commonly called the Van't Hoff isochore. His important work on osmotic pressure was published in 1886, and was further developed in the next decade. He later studied the phase relationships of salt deposits. He was awarded the first Nobel Prize for chemistry in 1901, was elected a Foreign Member of the Royal Society in 1897, and became an honorary Fellow of the Chemical Society in 1888. He is regarded as one of the founders of physical chemistry.

Hoffa, Jimmy (James Riddle) 1913–75
US labour leader

He was born in Brazil, Indiana. He was a grocery warehouseman when he joined the International Brotherhood of Teamsters, Chauffeurs, Warehousemen and Helpers of America (the Teamsters' Union) in 1931. He proceeded to reorganize it, strengthening central control, and was elected president in 1957. In the same year the Teamsters were expelled from the American Federation of Labor and Congress of Industrial Organizations (AFL-CIO) for repudiating its ethics code. Hoffa negotiated the Teamsters' first national contract in 1964, but, following corruption investigations by the Attorney-General, Robert F Kennedy, was imprisoned in 1967 for attempted bribery of a federal court jury. His sentence was commuted by President Nixon and he was given parole in 1971, on condition that he resigned as Teamster' leader. In 1975 he disappeared and is thought to have been murdered.

Hoffman, Dustin 1937–
US actor

Born in Los Angeles, he studied music at the Santa Monica City College, and acting at the Pasadena Playhouse (1956–58), before beginning a career on stage and television in New York, interspersed with a variety of odd jobs. He made his Broadway debut in *A Cook for Mr. General* (1961) and achieved recognition with his performance in *Journey of the Fifth Horse* (1966). Following a modest film debut in *The Tiger Makes Out* (1967), he received an Academy Award nomination for his first leading role in *The Graduate* (1967). Similar anti-hero roles followed in *Midnight Cowboy* (1969), *Little Big Man* (1970), and *Marathon Man* (1976). A notorious perfectionist, he has displayed his versatility in such films as *All The President's Men* (1976), *Kramer vs Kramer* (1979, Academy Award), *Tootsie* (1982), *Rain Man* (1988, Academy Award), and *Hook* (1991). He returned to Broadway in *Death of a Salesman* (1984), winning an Emmy Award for the same role on television the following year. He tackled his first Shakespearean role on the London stage as Shylock in *The Merchant of Venice* (1989). Later films include *Accidental Hero* (1993), *American Buffalo* (1995) and *Sleepers* (1996).

Hoffman, Malvina 1887–1966
US sculptor

Born in New York City, she was trained under Rodin in Paris, who sent her to study anatomy at the local medical school. She created busts and full figures, using her social circle of artistic and literary people, such as Anna Pavlova. In 1929, she was commissioned by the Field Museum of Natural History in Chicago to sculpt figures of ethnic types observed all over the world. She duly produced the series of over 100 bronze figures (1930–33) for which she remains best known. She published the books *Heads and Tales* (1936), about her travels researching the ethnic types, and *Sculpture Inside and Out* (1937), on the techniques of sculpture.

Hoffman, Samuel Kurtz 1902–
US rocket propulsion engineer

Born in Williamsport, Pennsylvania, he graduated in mechanical engineering from Pennsylvania State University (1925), and after working in the aviation industry returned there as Professor of Aeronautical Engineering (1945–49). From 1949 he led the team developing rocket engines at North American Aviation, raising their power from an initial 75,000 pounds of thrust to 1.5 million pounds by the mid-1960s. Eight of these engines powered the multi-stage Saturn 5 launching vehicle which in July 1969 took US astronauts on the first stage of their journey to the moon.

Hoffmann, August Heinrich See Hoffmann von Fallersleben

Hoffmann, E(rnst) T(heodor) W(ilhelm),
known as **Amadeus** 1776–1822
German writer, music critic and caricaturist

Born in Königsberg, Prussia (now Kaliningrad, Russia), he trained as a lawyer and in 1816 attained a high position in the Supreme Court in Berlin. His shorter tales were mostly published in the collections *Fantasiestücke* (1814, 'Fantasies'), *Nachtstücke* (1817, 'Night-time Tales') and *Die Serapionsbrüder* (1819–21, Eng trans *The Serapion Brothers*, 1886–92). His longer works include *Elixiere des Teufels* (1816, Eng trans *The Devil's Elixirs*, 1824), and the partly autobiographical *Lebensansichten des Katers Murr* (1821–22, 'Opinions of the Tomcat Murr'). Three of his stories provided the basis for Jacques Offenbach's opera, *Les Contes d'Hoffmann* (1880, Eng trans *Tales of Hoffmann*, 1881), and another for **Léo Delibes's** *Coppelia* (1870). As a composer his most important opera was *Undine* (1816), a precursor of the scores of **Carl Weber** and **Richard Wagner**. He also composed vocal, chamber, orchestral and piano works. He was an influential writer on music, notably in his reviews of **Beethoven's** works, and the archpriest of ultra-German Romanticism. 🕮 H D Daemmrich, *The Shattered Self* (1973)

Hoffmann, Josef 1870–1956
Austrian architect

Born in Pirnitz, he was a leader of the Vienna 'Secession' group (1899—seceding from the traditional Viennese style), and in 1903 founded the *Wiener Werkstätte* (Vienna Workshops), devoted to arts and crafts. He himself designed metalwork, glass and furniture. His main architectural achievements were the white-stuccoed Purkersdorf Sanatorium (1903–05) and Stociet House (1905–11) in Brussels. He was city architect of Vienna from 1920, and designed the Austrian pavilion for the 1934 Venice Biennale.

Hoffmann, Roald 1937–
US chemist and Nobel Prize winner

Born in Złoczow, Poland, he arrived in New York City in 1949. In 1955 he went to Columbia University and obtained a PhD from Harvard in chemical physics in 1962, having spent nine months at the University of Moscow. He was elected a Junior Fellow at Harvard and in 1964 began a collaboration with **Robert Woodward**, in which factors controlling the way in which cyclization reactions occur when bond breaking and making occur simultaneously were established. The results of these considerations became known as the Woodward–Hoffmann rules for the conservation of orbital symmetry. It was for this work that, along with **Kenichi Fukui**, he received the 1981 Nobel Prize for chemistry. In 1965 Hoffmann moved to Cornell University and in 1974 he was appointed John A Newman Professor of Physical Science. His most recent work concerns the synergism of molecular orbital calculation and experiment in a number of areas of inorganic chemistry. He also writes popular articles on science and

has hosted a TV programme on chemistry. He has received many other awards and honours, including the Priestley Medal of the American Chemical Society. His publications include *Chemistry Imagined* (1993) and *The Same and Not the Same* (1995), as well as two volumes of poetry, *The Metamict State* (1987) and *Gaps and Verges* (1990).

Hoffmann von Fallersleben, *properly* August Heinrich Hoffmann 1798–1874
German poet and philologist, and composer

Born in Fallersleben, Lüneburg, he was keeper of the library of Breslau University (1823–38), and Professor of German there (1830–42). A popular writer of light lyrics, he published *Lieder und Romanzen* ('Songs and Romances') in 1841, but the publication of his *Unpolitische Lieder* ('Apolitical Songs') in 1842 cost him his chair. In 1860 he became librarian to the Duke of Ratibor at Korvei. He is best known for his popular and patriotic *Volkslieder* (1842, 'Folk Songs'), including 'Alle Vögel sind schon da' and the song 'Deutschland, Deutschland über Alles' (1841), which became the German national anthem in 1922. He also published several works on philology and antiquities, including *Horae Belgicae* (1830–62, 'Belgian Hours'). 🕮 K H de Raaf, *Heinrich von Fallersleben* (1943)

Hoffnung, Gerard 1925–59
British cartoonist and musician

Born in Berlin, he was taken to England as a boy. His first cartoon was published in *Lilliput* magazine while he was still at school (1941). After studying art at Highgate School of Arts, he became art master at Stamford School (1945) and Harrow (1948). He was staff cartoonist on the London *Evening News* (1947) and after a brief time in New York (1950) returned in 1951 to freelance for *Punch* and others. His interest in music led to his creation of the Hoffnung Music Festivals at the Royal Festival Hall in which his caricatures came to life and sound. They were also animated by **Halas-Batchelor** in the television series, *Tales From Hoffnung* (1965).

Hofmann, August Wilhelm von 1818–92
German chemist

He was born in Giessen, and his most successful post was as professor at the College of Chemistry in London. His pupils and assistants included some of the most significant chemists of the century, notably **William Henry Perkin, Snr**. He and his students had considerable success in extracting from coal tar some of its most valuable constituents (eg aniline) in pure form, and in exploring the chemistry of these compounds, thus preparing the way for the development of the dyestuffs industry. He supported **Charles Gerhardt's** theory of chemical types, later to be discredited, and described the ammonia type. He developed the process of exhaustive methylation for the conversion of amines into the corresponding olefin. Elected FRS in 1851, in 1865 he succeeded **Eilhard Mitscherlich** as professor in Berlin, where he continued to exercise a profound influence over European chemistry. He was raised to the rank of nobleman of Prussia (von Hofmann) on his 70th birthday.

Hofmann, Hans 1880–1966
US painter

Born in Weissenberg, Germany, he studied painting in Munich and from 1904 to 1914 lived in Paris, where he met **Henri Matisse** and the Cubists. He returned to Germany in 1914, opening an art school in Munich. In 1932 he emigrated to the USA, settling in New York where, again, he opened an art school. He took US nationality in 1941. Around 1940 he developed an abstract style, dripping paint on to the canvas and applying bright colour in broad strokes. These works had a significant impact on the development of abstract painting in the USA.

Hofmannsthal, Hugo von 1874–1929
Austrian poet and dramatist
He was born in Vienna into a banking family of Austro-Jewish-Italian origins, and while still at school he attracted attention by his 'lyrical dramas' such as *Gestern* (1896, 'Yesterday'), *Der Tod des Tizian* (1901, Eng trans *The Death of Titian*, 1920) and *Leben* (1894, 'Life'). An emotional and intellectual crisis precipitated the *Ein Brief des Lord Chandos* (1901, 'A Letter from Lord Chandos'), in which he conveys his reasons for abandoning poetry, his new hatred for abstract terms, and his doubts of the possibility of successful communication. Thenceforth he devoted himself to drama, most of his works being based on that of other dramatists: *Das gerettete Venedig* (1905, translated from **Thomas Otway**'s *Venice Preserved*), and the morality plays *Jedermann* (1911, Eng trans *The Salzburg Everyman*, 1930) and *Das Salzburger grosse Welttheater* (1922, 'The Great World Theatre of Salzburg', based on **Calderón de la Barca**'s *El gran teatro del mundo*). One of his major works is the comedy, *Der Schwierige* (1921, Eng trans *The Difficult Man*, 1963). Having renounced **Stefan George** and his circle, Hofmannsthal turned to the composer **Richard Strauss**, for whom he wrote the libretti for *Der Rosenkavalier* (1911, 'Knight of the Rose'), *Ariadne auf Naxos* (1912), and other works. With Strauss and **Max Reinhardt**, he was instrumental in founding the Salzburg Festival after World War I. His statue there was demolished by the Nazis in 1938.

Hofmeister, Wilhelm Friedrich Benedikt
1824–77
German botanist
Born and educated in Leipzig, he combined botanical research with a full-time career in music publishing. He became an authority on embryology and was one of the first to observe chromosomes, although he did not appreciate their significance. His most epoch-making discovery was of the alternation of generations in plants (in which a generation that reproduces sexually alternates with one that reproduces asexually), which marked the transition of botanical science from the medieval to the modern period. This discovery has been considered 'the greatest broad evolutionary treatise in botany'.

Hofstadter, Richard 1916–70
US historian
Born in Buffalo, New York, he was educated at Buffalo University and Columbia, where he taught from 1946 to 1970. His doctoral thesis was published as *Social Darwinism in American Thought 1860–1915* (1944), and *The American Political Tradition and the Men Who Made It* (1948) similarly examined ideological rationale and disguise in studying the impulses behind the careers of major American politicians and statesmen. Other works include *The Age of Reform* (1955, Pulitzer Prize), *Anti-Intellectualism in American Life* (1963, Pulitzer Prize), *The Development of Academic Freedom in the United States* (1955) and *The Paranoid Style in American Politics* (1965).

Hofstadter, Robert 1915–90
US physicist and Nobel Prize winner
Born in New York City, he was educated at City College, New York, and Princeton University. He then worked at the Norden Laboratory Corporation (1943–46) and at Princeton University, before moving to Stanford University where he became professor in 1954. He was also director of the Stanford High Energy Physics Laboratory (1967–74). In 1948 he developed a scintillation counter for X-ray detection. Later at Stanford, he used the linear accelerator to probe nuclear structure, investigating nuclear charge distribution and revealing that protons and neutrons also contain inner structure (now known to be due to quarks). For this work, he shared the 1961 Nobel Prize for physics with **Rudolf Mössbauer**.

He retired in 1985 but continued to pursue research, including his construction of a gamma ray observatory due to be sent aloft in a space shuttle in 1991.

Hogan, Ben (William Benjamin) 1912–97
US golfer
Born in Dublin, Texas, he began his career at the age of 11 as a caddie. A professional at various country clubs, he fought his way to the top despite financial difficulties. In 1948 he became the first man in 26 years to win all three US major titles; despite a bad car accident in 1949, he returned to win three of the four major golf titles in 1953 (US Open, US Masters, and British Open). He won the US Open four times (1948, 1950–51, 1953) before retiring in 1970.

Hogarth, David George 1862–1929
English archaeologist
He was born in Barton-upon-Humber, Lincolnshire. Keeper of the Ashmolean Museum, Oxford (1909–27), he excavated in Asia Minor, Syria and Egypt. In 1915 he was sent by the British government to Cairo to organize an Arab revolt against Turkish rule.

Hogarth, William 1697–1764
English painter and engraver
He was born in Smithfield, London, the son of a teacher. Early apprenticed to a silverplate engraver, he studied painting under Sir **James Thornhill**, whose daughter he married, after eloping with her, in 1729. By 1720 he already had his own business, engraving coats-of-arms, shop-bills, book illustrations and bookplates, and painting conversation pieces and portraits, including that of *Sarah Malcolm*, the triple murderess (1732–33). Tiring of conventional art forms, he resurrected the 'pictured morality' of medieval art by his 'modern moral subjects', often comprising several pictures in a series, but, unlike the modern strip cartoon, each artistically and representationally self-sufficient. The first of these was *A Harlot's Progress* (1730–31), destroyed by fire (1755). With an unerring eye for human foibles, he was often forthright to the point of coarseness, but although his didactic purpose was unmistakable, seldom indulged in melodrama. Single works such as *Southwark Fair* and the successfully captured atmosphere of a stag party entitled *A Midnight Modern Conversation* (both 1733) precede his eight pictures of *A Rake's Progress* (1733–35, Soane Museum, London). In 1735 he opened his own academy in St Martin's Lane. Two pictures in the conventional style, *The Pool of Bethesda* and *The Good Samaritan* (1735), he presented to St Bartholomew's Hospital in the hope of attracting commissions. He later returned to moral narrative, of which his masterpiece is the *Marriage à la mode* series (1743–45, National Gallery, London), and then extended his social commentaries to 'men of the lowest rank' by drawing attention to their typical vices in prints such as the *Industry and Idleness* series (1747), *Gin Lane*, and *Beer Street* (1751). He later ventured into politics with a cartoon of **John Wilkes**, the Earl of **Chatham** and Richard Grenville, 1st Earl Temple (1711–79) as warmongers (1762). His liberating influence upon the art of portraiture may be gathered from the informal treatment of *Captain Coram* (1740, Foundling Hospital, London), his *Self-Portrait* (c.1758) and an early undated study in impressionism, *The Shrimp Girl* (c.1759, National Gallery, London). He explained his artistic theories in *The Analysis of Beauty* (1753). 📖 Jenny Uglow, *Hogarth* (1997)

Hogben, Lancelot 1895–1975
English physiologist and writer
Born in Southsea and educated at Cambridge, he held academic appointments in zoology in England, Scotland, Canada and South Africa before becoming Mason Professor of Zoology at Birmingham (1941–47),

and Professor of Medical Statistics (1947–61). He wrote several popular books on scientific subjects, including *Mathematics for the Million* (1936) and *Science for the Citizen* (1938), and edited *The Loom of Language* (1943) in which he set out his version of an international auxiliary language, *Interglossa*.

Hogendorp, Gijsbert Karel 1762–1834
Dutch politician

A member of a patrician family, he studied law and became active in politics as a champion of the House of Orange during the revolutionary Patriot Movement in the 1780s. He became Pensionary of Rotterdam, but was out of office during the period of French domination of the Netherlands (1795–1813). As the French were withdrawing in 1812, he was instrumental in arranging the return of William of Orange (who became King William I), and chaired the committee which drew up the new Dutch constitutions in the post-Napoleonic period. He was Foreign Minister (1813–14), and Vice-President of the Council of State (1814–16), but disagreed with King William and spent the years 1816–25 as an MP highly critical of the government. His writings on political economy had considerable impact in the Netherlands, promoting both political and economic liberalism.

Hogg, Douglas Martin 1945–
English Conservative politician

Born in London, the son of the distinguished Conservative politician Lord **Hailsham**, he was educated at Eton and at Christ Church, Oxford. After graduation he trained as a barrister and was appointed Queen's Counsel in 1990. He entered parliament in 1979 as Conservative MP for Grantham and was parliamentary private secretary to **Leon Brittain** (1982–86). His ministerial appointments include Trade and Industry (1989–90) and the Foreign and Commonwealth Office (1990–95). As Minister for Agriculture, Fisheries and Food (1995–97), he was given the difficult task of directing Britain's agricultural policy in Europe following a crisis over the safety of British beef in 1996.

Hogg, James, *also called* the Ettrick Shepherd
1770–1835
Scottish poet and novelist

He was born on Ettrickhall Farm in the Ettrick Forest, Selkirkshire. He inherited a rich store of oral ballads from his mother, and in 1790 became shepherd to **William Laidlaw**, who encouraged him to write. He published *The Mountain Bard* in 1803, and on the proceeds of it dabbled unsuccessfully in farming then eventually settled in Edinburgh. A volume of poems, *The Queen's Wake* (1813), gained him cordial recognition, and a bequest of a farm at Altrive Lake (now Edinhope) enabled him to marry in 1820 and turn his attention to writing. A regular contributor to *Blackwood's Magazine*, and the 'Ettrick Shepherd' of **John Wilson's** *Noctes Ambrosianae*, he described himself as 'the King of the Mountain and Fairy School'. His poems of the supernatural are at their best when he avoids Gothic elaboration and relies on the suggestive understatement of the ballad style, as in 'Kilmeny'. 'The Aged Widow's Lament' shows the influence of the Scottish vernacular tradition, and his debt to **Robert Burns** is apparent in the riotous 'Village of Balmaquhapple'. Of Hogg's prose works, the most remarkable is *Private Memoirs and Confessions of a Justified Sinner* (1824), a macabre novel which anticipates **Robert Louis Stevenson's** *Dr Jekyll and Mr Hyde*. In 1834 he published his *Domestic Manners and Private Life of Sir Walter Scott*, against the wishes of **Scott's** family. 📖 A Strout, *James Hogg: a biography* (1946)

Hogg, Quintin 1845–1903
English philanthropist

Born in London, he was educated at Eton. He joined first tea merchants, then sugar merchants in the City of London, where he became prominent and very prosperous. In 1864 he founded a 'ragged school' at Charing Cross for the homeless, then a Youths' Christian Institute, and in 1882 opened Regent Street Polytechnic to permit the members to gratify, as he wrote, 'any reasonable taste, whether athletic, intellectual, spiritual, or social'. This initiated the polytechnic movement in London, but the intensity of voluntary work (he also organized holiday tours and a labour bureau) affected his health and he actually died in the Polytechnic.

Hogg, Quintin McGarel See **Hailsham, 2nd Viscount**

Hogg, Dame Sarah Elizabeth Mary, *née* Boyd-Carpenter 1946–
English economist and journalist

Educated at Oxford, she began her journalistic career at *The Economist* in 1967. She gained a reputation as a top-ranking journalist through her writing for *The Economist*, the *Sunday Times*, the *Independent*, the *Telegraph* and *Sunday Telegraph*, and as presenter on *Channel 4 News*. She was governor of the Centre for Economic Policy Research (1985–92) before becoming head of the political advisers in Prime Minister **John Major's** policy unit in 1990. She remained in her post through two successful Conservative general elections, and although she received some blame for the failure of Major's 1993 'back to basics' campaign, she was praised for her wise advice. She resigned in 1994 and was appointed DBE in 1995.

Hohenstaufen
German royal dynasty

Named after the castle of Staufen in north-east Swabia, dukes of Swabia from 1079, from 1138 to 1254 its members were Holy Roman Emperors, starting with **Conrad III** and ending with Conrad IV, and including **Frederick I, Barbarossa** and **Frederick II**. They were also kings of Germany and of Sicily. The Hohenstaufen period is associated with a flowering of German courtly culture.

Hohenzollern
German dynasty

They ruled in Brandenburg-Prussia from 1415 to 1918. The name is derived from the ancestral 9th-century castle of Zollern in Swabia. In 1415 a member of the family was made Elector of Brandenburg by Emperor **Sigismund**, thus founding the Prussian dynasty. The last elector, Frederick III (1688–1713) became the first King of Prussia as **Frederick I** (1701). The kings of Prussia were German emperors from 1872 to 1918 (**Wilhelm I, Frederick III** and **Wilhelm II**). Another branch of the family were kings of Romania from 1881 to 1947 (**Carol I, Ferdinand I** and **Carol II**). World War I ruined Hohenzollern militarism, and forced the abdication of the last emperor, Wilhelm II (1918).

Hohfeld, Wesley Newcomb 1879–1918
US jurist and law teacher

Interested in the analysis of the legal concept of a 'right', he tried to develop a theory of law based on legal relations, and his work stimulated much later thinking on the subject.

Hohner, Matthias 1833–1902
German mouth-organ manufacturer

In 1857 he established his firm at Trossingen, Württemberg. His five sons added music publishing (1931), the manufacture of accordions, harmonicas, saxophones and (from 1945) electrical musical instruments, established an accordion school at Trossingen in 1931, and made the family business the biggest of its kind.

Ho Hsiang-ning See **He Xiangning**

Hokusai, Katsushika 1760–1849
Japanese artist and wood-engraver

Born in Edo (modern Tokyo), he was apprenticed to a wood-engraver under whom he mastered the conventional surimono or commemorative paintings and book illustrations. He soon abandoned the traditional styles of engraving for the coloured woodcut designs of the ukiyo-e ('pictures of the floating world') school, which treated commonplace subjects in an expressionist manner, and of which he became the acknowledged master. His 15 volumes of *Mangwa* or *Random Sketches* depict most facets of Japanese life. His best-known works are his landscapes, an innovation to the ukiyo-e movement; they include his *36 Views of Mount Fuji* (c.1826–33). His work greatly influenced the French Impressionists.

Holbein, Hans, the Younger 1497–1543
German painter

Born in Augsburg, he was the son of Hans Holbein, the Elder (c.1460–1524), who was also a painter of merit. He studied under his father, and was influenced by the work of Hans Burgkmair. He worked in Basle in about 1516, but did not settle there till 1520. During this interval he was painting portraits at Zurich and Lucerne, including those of Burgomaster Meier and his wife, Erasmus and Philip Melanchthon. In 1519, he painted his *Noli Me Tangere* (c.1522, Royal Collection) and his portrait of *Erasmus* (1523, on loan to National Gallery, London), but he largely concentrated on designs for woodcuts, including illustrations for various editions of Martin Luther's Old and New Testaments (1522 and 1523). His most important woodcuts, however—the *Dance of Death* series and the *Old Testament* cuts—were not issued till 1538. He visited England at the end of 1526, where he began his great series of portraits of eminent Englishmen of the time, such as *Sir Thomas More* (1527, Frick Collection, New York). On his return to Basle (1529) he painted the group of his wife and two children, now in the museum there, and in 1530 resumed work in the council hall (pictures now destroyed). In 1532 he again visited London, where he painted several portraits for the German merchants of the Hanseatic League, including the exquisite *Derick Born* (1533, Royal Collection). The portrait group, *The Ambassadors* (1533, National Gallery, London), the portraits of Thomas Cromwell, and the miniatures of Henry and Charles Brandon, sons of the Duke of Suffolk, are attributed to this period. In 1536 he was appointed painter to Henry VIII, and executed a mural painting of him and Queen Jane Seymour with Henry VII and Elizabeth of York, destroyed in the Whitehall fire of 1698 (cartoon in the National Portrait Gallery, London) and miniatures of outstanding quality, such as *Mrs Pemberton* (1536, Victoria and Albert Museum, London). He also painted Kristina of Denmark (a prospective wife for Henry) in 1538 (National Gallery, London), and Anne of Cleves, at Cleves in 1539 (miniature in the Victoria and Albert Museum, London). One of the most charming of his paintings, *Lady with a Squirrel and a Starling* (of uncertain date) is now in the National Gallery, London. His last work was *Henry VIII granting a Charter to the Barber-Surgeons*, still in their guildhall. He died of the plague in London. 📖 Alfred Woltmann, *Holbein and His Times* (1872)

Holberg, Ludvig, Baron 1684–1754
Norwegian poet, playwright and philosopher

Born in Bergen, he was educated in Copenhagen, then settled in Denmark after travelling widely in Europe (1714–16). In 1717 he was appointed Professor of Metaphysics at Copenhagen University, later becoming Professor of Eloquence (1720), and History (1730). His poetical works include the satirical epics, *Peder Paars* (1719–20) and *Nicolai Klimii Iter Subterraneum* (1741, 'Niels

Klim's Subterranean Journey'). He also wrote a series of more than 30 classic comedies for the newly-opened Danish theatre in Copenhagen (1722–27). Thereafter he concentrated on historical books, including biographies and histories of Denmark, the Church, and the Jews, and reflective and philosophical works. 📖 F J Billeskev Hansen, *Holberg* (1974)

Holbøll, Einar 1855–1927
Danish postmaster

He originated the idea of special stamp issues for charitable purposes by his *Julemaerket* stamp (1904) for a tuberculosis prevention fund. The idea has since been adopted by countries all over the world.

Holbrooke, Josef Charles 1878–1958
English composer

Born in Croydon, Surrey, he studied at the Royal Academy of Music, was an accomplished pianist, and composed the symphonic poems *Queen Mab* (1904), *The Bells* (1906) and *Apollo and the Seaman* (1908). He also wrote a trilogy of operas based on Welsh legends, the first of which, *The Children of Don* (1912), was performed at Salzburg in 1923. His variation of 'Three Blind Mice' was his most popular composition.

Holcroft, M(ontague) H(arry) 1902–93
New Zealand writer, critic and historian

Born in Rangiora, Canterbury, he was editor of the influential periodical *The Listener* from 1949 to 1967. From this, he drew *The Eye of the Lizard* (1960) and *Graceless Islanders* (1970), both reissued as *A Voice in the Village: The Listener Editorials of M H Holcroft* (1989). He wrote three novels in the late 1920s, beginning with *Beyond the Breakers* (1928), and became a prolific essayist on literature and life. *The Deepening Stream* (1940), which won first prize in the New Zealand Centenary literary competition, followed by *The Waiting Hills* (1943) and *Encircling Seas* (1946), were collected as *Discovered Isles: A Trilogy* in 1950. He wrote a study of Ursula Bethell (1975) and autobiographical works including *Dance of the Seasons* (1952), *Reluctant Editor: the 'Listener' Years, 1949–67* (1969) and *The Way of a Writer* (1984).

Holcroft, Thomas 1745–1809
English playwright and novelist

Born in London, he worked as a stable boy, shoemaker, schoolmaster, and servant-secretary to Granville Sharp, before in 1770 becoming a strolling player. He then settled in London (1778), where he became a friend of William Godwin, Tom Paine and Charles Lamb, and took to writing. *Alwyn, or the Gentleman Comedian* (1780) was the first of four novels. He also wrote nearly 30 plays, mostly melodramas, of which *The Follies of a Day* (1784) and *The Road to Ruin* (1792) are the best. An ardent democrat, he was tried for high treason in 1794 with Sir Thomas Masterman Hardy (1769–1839), John Tooke and others and acquitted, but the adverse publicity reduced him to poverty and forced him abroad (1799–1801). His entertaining Memoirs were continued by William Hazlitt in 1816. 📖 R Baine, *Thomas Holcroft and the Revolutionary Novel* (1965)

Holden, Sir Edward Wheewall 1896–1978
Australian car manufacturer

He was born in Adelaide, South Australia and was educated at Prince Albert College, Adelaide and at the University of Adelaide. He joined his father's business of carriage-building and car body trimming, with the production of body panels and motorcycle sidecar bodies. Eventually Holdens became the major Australian producer of bodies for imported chassis, especially from General Motors in the USA. He had studied automation methods in the USA and rapidly expanded the productivity of the company. By 1929 Holdens had become the biggest car-body builder in the British Empire. However, through a downturn in demand during the Depression, General Motors acquired Holdens, and Edward Holden became chairman in 1931.

Hölderlin, (Johann Christian) Friedrich
1770–1843
German poet

Born in Lauffen, north of Stuttgart, he studied theology at Tübingen, and philosophy with Schelling and Hegel under Johann Fichte at Jena. With a growing enthusiasm for poetry, he developed an aversion to the 'snug parsonage' for which he was intended. As family tutor in Frankfurt am Main (1796–98) he found the wife of his employer, Susette Gontard, (the 'Diotima' of his works), the feminine embodiment of all he venerated in Hellenism. His early poetry owed much to Friedrich Klopstock and to Schiller, but 'Diotima' helped him to discover his true poetical self; he also wrote a philosophical novel, *Hyperion* (1797–99, Eng trans 1965). He went on to write fragments for a verse drama on the death of Empedocles, elegiac odes and the elegy 'Menon's Laments for Diotima', which examines the discrepancy between the actual and the ideally possible. After tutoring in Switzerland (1801), he wrote 'Brot und Wein' ('Bread and Wine') and 'Der Rhein' ('The Rhine'), but not long after was suffering from schizophrenia, aggravated by the news of 'Diotima's' death. After a period in an asylum (1806–07) he lived out his life in the charge of a Tübingen carpenter. It was the admiration of Rainer Maria Rilke and Stefan George which first established Hölderlin as one of Germany's greatest poets, 80 years after his death. ⌑ R Ungar, *Hölderlin's Major Poetry* (1975)

Holiday, Billie, *originally* Eleanora Fagan 1915–59
US jazz singer

Born in Baltimore, Maryland, she was one of the most influential singers in jazz, and one of the first to really employ the subtleties of jazz phrasing in a serious manner. She had an insecure childhood and was jailed for prostitution while a teenager. Insecurity and exploitation in personal relationships became a recurring theme in her life. In the early 1930s, she was working as a singer in New York clubs, and her wistful voice and remarkable jazz interpretation of popular songs led to work with Benny Goodman and recording sessions with such leading soloists as Teddy Wilson and Lester Young, who bestowed her familiar nickname, Lady Day. Her memorable ballads include 'Easy Living' (1937), 'Yesterdays' (1939) and 'God Bless the Child' (1914). In the late 1930s she worked with the big bands of Count Basie and Artie Shaw. During the 1940s she appeared in several films (including *New Orleans*, with Louis Armstrong) but by the end of that decade she was falling victim to drug addiction. Although her voice deteriorated in the 1950s, she continued to make absorbing recordings until late in her career, without ever recapturing the glorious freshness and spontaneity of her pre-war music. Her self-serving autobiography, *Lady Sings The Blues* (1956, actually written by William Dufty), was turned into a spurious film in 1972. ⌑ John White, *Billie Holiday: Her Life and Times* (1987)

Holinshed, Raphael d.c.1580
English chronicler

Born apparently of a Cheshire family, he went to London early in Elizabeth I's reign, and became a translator in a printing office. He compiled *The Chronicles of England, Scotland, and Ireland* (2 vols, 1577), which together with its predecessor, Edward Hall's *Chronicle*, was the source for many of Shakespeare's plays.

Holland, Agnieszka 1948–
Polish film director

Born in Warsaw, she graduated from the Polish Film School in 1971, and worked as assistant director on Zanussi's *Illuminations* in 1973. Her directing debut came with *Evening At Abdan's* the following year, and she became a leading figure in the Polish New Wave during the 1970s, her film *Provincial Actors* tying for the International Critics Prize at Cannes in 1980. She also worked as a screenwriter for the leading Polish director, Andrzej Wadja. She left Poland for Paris in 1981 to escape political repression, but returned after the political changes of 1989. Her work is marked by a strong sense of political and historical engagement. Later films include *Europa, Europa* (1991), *The Secret Garden* (1993) and *Washington Square* (1997).

Holland, Henry 1746–1806
English architect

The pupil and son-in-law of Lancelot ('Capability') Brown, he designed old Carlton House in London, Brook's Club (1776–78), the original Brighton Pavilion (1786–87) and many other buildings.

Holland, Henry Richard Fox, 3rd Baron
1773–1840
English Liberal politician

Born at Winterslow House, Wiltshire, the nephew of Charles James Fox, he succeeded to the title when he was a year old. Educated at Eton and Christ Church, Oxford, he was Lord Privy Seal in the Grenville ministry (1806–07). He worked for reform of the criminal code, attacked the slave trade, although he was himself a West Indian planter, and was involved in the Corn Law struggle. He was Chancellor of the Duchy of Lancaster from 1830 to 1834. He wrote biographies of Guillén de Castro and Lope de Vega, translated Spanish comedies and prepared a biography of his uncle. Holland's wife was the beautiful and autocratic Elizabeth Vassall (1770–1845), the daughter of a wealthy Jamaica planter. She had married Sir Godfrey Webster in 1786, but the marriage was dissolved in 1797 for her adultery with Holland, who immediately married her. Holland House became the meeting place of the most brilliant wits and distinguished statesmen of the time.

Holland, John Philip 1840–1914
US inventor

Born in Liscannor, County Clare, Ireland, and educated in Limerick, he was a school teacher in Ireland (1852–72), and, after emigrating to the USA in 1873, in Paterson, New Jersey. He offered a submarine design to the US navy which was rejected in 1875 as impracticable, but he continued his experiments with a practical submarine, the *Fenian Ram* (financed by the Fenian Society), which was launched on the Hudson River in 1881. In 1898 he launched the *Holland VI* and successfully demonstrated it on and under the Potomac River. It had almost all the features of a modern non-nuclear submarine, including an internal-combustion engine on the surface and an electric motor when submerged, hydroplanes and ballast tanks to regulate the depth, torpedo tubes, and a retractable periscope, and convinced the navies of the world that the submarine must be taken seriously as a weapon of war.

Holland, Jools (Julian) 1958–
English pop musician and television presenter

Born in London, he learned piano as a child, and played with the successful band Squeeze from 1974 to 1980. He formed The Millionaires, then went solo in 1983. He rejoined Squeeze (1985–90), and formed his Rhythm and Blues Orchestra in 1994. His piano style is rooted in the New Orleans boogie-woogie tradition, and he is a fine exponent of it. His high profile owes more to his success as a presenter of music programmes on television, including *The Tube* (where he caused a furore by swearing on air), *Juke Box Jury* and *Later*.

Holland, Josiah Gilbert 1819–81
US editor and novelist

Born in Belchertown, Massachusetts, he became assistant editor of the Springfield *Republican* and part proprietor in 1851. In 1870, with Roswell Smith and the Scribners, he founded *Scribner's Monthly*, which he edited, and in which appeared some of his novels, including *Arthur Bonnicastle* (1873), *The Story of Sevenoaks* (1875) and *Nicholas Minturn* (1876). ☐ H H Peckham, *Josiah Gilbert and his Times* (1940)

Holland, Philemon 1552–1637
English scholar

Born in Chelmsford and educated at Trinity College, Cambridge, from about 1595 he practised medicine in Coventry, and in 1628 became headmaster of the free school there. He translated Livy, Pliny's *Natural History*, Suetonius, Plutarch's *Morals*, Ammianus Marcellinus, Xenophon's *Cyropaedia* and William Camden's *Britannia*, becoming the best-known translator of his age. His son, Henry (1583–c.1650), a bookseller in London, published *Baziliologia* (1618) and *Heroologia Anglica* (1620).

Holland, Sir Sidney George 1893–1961
New Zealand politician

Born in Greendale, Canterbury, he was managing director of an engineering company before taking up politics. Entering parliament as a member of the National Party in 1935, he was Leader of the Opposition (1940–49), and then premier (1949–1957), resigning to become Minister without Portfolio.

Hollar, Wenzel or Wenceslaus 1607–77
Bohemian engraver and etcher

Born in Prague, he went to London with Thomas Howard, Earl of Arundel and Surrey in 1637, served in a Royalist regiment, and was taken prisoner at Basing House. From 1645 to 1652 he lived in Antwerp. Returning to London at the Restoration he was appointed 'His Majesty's designer'. He produced two magnificent plates of costume, entitled *Severall Habits of English Women* (1640) and *Theatrum Mulierum* (1643), as well as maps, panoramas, etc, preserved in the British Museum, London, and the Royal Library, Windsor. His panoramic view of London from Southwark after the Great Fire is one of the most valuable topographical records of the 17th century.

Hollerith, Herman 1860–1929
US inventor and computer scientist

Born in Buffalo, New York, he graduated in 1879 from the School of Mines at Columbia University, and worked as a statistician on the processing of data relating to the manufacturing industries for the US census of 1880. Realizing the need for automation in the recording and processing of such a mass of data, he devised a system based initially on cards with holes punched in them (similar to that invented by Joseph Jacquard in 1801 to produce a variety of complicated patterns on his loom). Hollerith used electrical contacts made through the holes in his cards to actuate electromechanical counters. He developed his system while employed first at the Massachusetts Institute of Technology, and then in the US Patent Office (1884–90), and won a competition for the most efficient data-processing equipment to be used in the 1890 US census. He established his own company in 1896, and later merged with two others to become the International Business Machines Corporation (IBM) in 1924. ☐ Geoffrey D Austrian, *Herman Hollerith, Forgotten Giant of Information Processing* (1981)

Holles (of Ifield), Denzil Holles, 1st Baron 1599–1680
English statesman

Born in Houghton, Nottinghamshire, he entered parliament in 1624, and in 1629 was one of the members who held the Speaker in his chair while resolutions were passed against Arminianism, tonnage and poundage. For this he was fined a thousand marks, and lived seven or eight years in exile. A leader of the Presbyterians, he was one of the five members whom Charles I attempted to arrest in 1642. During the Civil War, he was an advocate of peace. For proposing, in 1647, to disband the army he was accused of treason, but fled to Normandy. In 1660 he was the spokesman of the commission delegated to recall Charles II at Breda, and in 1661 he was created Baron Holles of Ifield in Sussex. His last important public duty was the negotiation of the treaty of Breda in 1667.

Holley, Robert William 1922–93
US biochemist and Nobel Prize winner

Born in Urbana, Illinois, he worked mainly at Cornell Medical School. He was a member of the team which first synthesized penicillin in the 1940s. In 1962 he identified two distinct transfer RNAs, and later secured the first pure transfer RNA (t-RNA) sample. In 1965 he published the full molecular structure of this nucleic acid—Crick's 'adaptor molecule', which plays a central role in the cellular synthesis of proteins. He shared the 1968 Nobel Prize for physiology or medicine with Har Gobind Khorana and Marshall Nirenberg. The same year he became a resident Fellow at the Salk Institute for Biological Studies in La Jolla, California, where he remained until his death.

Holliday, Judy, *originally* Judith Tuvim 1922–65
US comic actress

Born in New York, she became a telephonist for Orson Welles's Mercury Theatre, and performed as part of the Revuers cabaret group (1939–44). An engagement in Los Angeles earned her a contract with Twentieth Century-Fox and some minor film roles. As an understudy for *Born Yesterday* (1946), she replaced the original star and enjoyed a long-running Broadway triumph in the role of Billie Dawn, a dumb blonde with a heart of gold. The 1950 film version earned her the Best Actress Academy Award. She made a scene-stealing appearance in *Adam's Rib* (1949) and starred in such comedy classics as *It Should Happen To You* (1954) and *The Solid Gold Cadillac* (1956). A further Broadway success in *Bells Are Ringing* (1956) became her final film role in 1960.

Hollis, Sir Roger Henry 1905–73
English civil servant

Educated at Clifton and Worcester College, Oxford, he travelled extensively in China before joining the British counter-intelligence service MI5 in the late 1930s. He was appointed deputy director-general in 1953 and director-general (1956–65). In his memoirs *Spycatcher* (1987), Peter Wright argued that Hollis, with Anthony Blunt, Guy Burgess, Donald Maclean and Kim Philby, was a Soviet spy.

Holloway, Stanley 1890–1982
English entertainer

Born in London, he was variously an office boy, choir soloist and World War I army lieutenant before making his London stage debut in *Kissing Time* (1920) and his first film appearance in *The Rotters* (1921). He was an original member of The Co-Optimists revue group (1921–30). Popular on radio and in pantomime, he created the monologue characters of Sam Small and the Ramsbottom family, while his hearty, down-to-earth manner and booming tones made him a genial comedy actor in Ealing film classics like *Passport to Pimlico* (1948), *The*

Lavender Hill Mob (1951) and *The Titfield Thunderbolt* (1952). He made his New York debut in *A Midsummer Night's Dream* (1954) and created the role of Alfred Doolittle in *My Fair Lady* on Broadway (1956–58) and later on film (1964). An active performer until his death, he also had his own television series *Our Man Higgins* (1962) and published an autobiography, *Wiv a Little Bit of Luck* (1969).

Holloway, Thomas 1800–83
English manufacturer and philanthropist

Born in Devonport, Devon, he produced patent medicines which made him a fortune. He founded an asylum for the insane and a women's college in Egham, near Virginia Water, Surrey.

Holly, Buddy, *originally* Charles Hardin 1936–59
US rock singer, songwriter and guitarist

Born in Lubbock, Texas, and originally from a country and western background, he was also influenced by hillbilly, Mexican and Black music. Despite the fact that his recording career lasted less than two years, he is one of the most influential pioneers of rock-and-roll. He was the first to add drums and a rhythm-and-blues beat to the basic country style. With his band The Crickets he was the first to use what was to become the standard rock-and-roll line-up of two guitars, bass and drums, and he was also the first to use double-tracking and over-dubbing on his recordings. Splitting from The Crickets in 1958, he was forced by financial commitments to undertake an arduous touring schedule, and he died when a plane carrying him between concerts crashed. At the time he had released only three US albums. Only after his death was the full significance of his contribution to rock music realized; he became an important cult figure and much of his material was released posthumously. His most popular records include 'That'll Be The Day', 'Not Fade Away', 'Peggy Sue' and 'Oh Boy'.

Holm, Hanya, *originally* Johanna Eckert 1893–1992
US dancer, choreographer and teacher

Born in Worms, Germany, she was a pupil of Émile Jaques-Delcroze. Starting in 1921 she worked as both teacher and dancer with Mary Wigman, who sent her to New York in 1931 to establish the US branch of her school. In 1936 she founded her own studio, developing a technique that fused the disciplines of Wigman's approach to movement with more emphasis on speed and rhythm. She became a key figure in the field of modern dance, dividing her time between concert work and the staging of dances for such Broadway musicals as *Kiss Me Kate* (1948), *My Fair Lady* (1956) and *Camelot* (1960). She became a naturalized US citizen in 1939.

Holm, Sir Ian, *originally* Ian Holm Cuthbert 1931–
English actor

Born in Goodmayes, Essex, he was a member of the Shakespeare Memorial Theatre company at Stratford-upon-Avon (1954–55) and toured Europe with Laurence Olivier in *Titus Andronicus* (1955). His subsequent Royal Shakespeare Company roles included the title roles in *Richard III* (1963–64), *Henry V* (1964) and *Romeo and Juliet* (1967). He has also acted in Harold Pinter's *The Homecoming* (1965), Edward Bond's *The Sea* (1973), and in 1993 gave a highly acclaimed performance in Pinter's *Moonlight* at the Almeida in Islington. His film appearances include *Chariots of Fire* (1981), *Dance with a Stranger* (1984), *Henry V* (1989), *Hamlet* (1990), *Naked Lunch* (1992) and *Mary Shelley's Frankenstein* (1994). On television, his many roles include Zerah in *Jesus of Nazareth* (1977), Bernard Samson in *Game, Set & Match* (1988) and F R Leavis in *The Last Romantics* (1992). He was knighted in 1998.

Holmes, Arthur 1890–1965
English geologist

Born in Hebburn-on-Tyne, Tyne and Wear, he was awarded a scholarship to attend Imperial College, London, where he studied physics and geology under Lord Rayleigh. Rayleigh encouraged Holmes to develop the uranium–lead dating method, and Holmes's first book *The Age of the Earth* (1913) was a review of the history of attempts to ascertain the age of the Earth. He was appointed as a demonstrator in geology at Imperial College (1912–20) and then became chief geologist for an oil company operating in Burma. He returned to Great Britain to become Professor of Geology at the University of Durham (1924–43) and then Regius Professor of Geology at Edinburgh (1943–56). A pioneer of geochronology, he determined the ages of rocks by measuring their radioactive constituents and played a large part in gathering age data for the Precambrian, allowing a picture to emerge of how ancient orogenies gradually built up cratonic shields and continental nuclei. He was an early scientific supporter of Alfred Wegener's continental drift theory and his predictions of the amount of heat generated by radioactive decay in the Earth revealed a mechanism for continental plate movement. He used lead isotopes to demonstrate that lead ores were not generated from granitic magmas as generally supposed, undertook important petrological studies, particularly with reference to basalt and alkali volcanics, and with his wife, Doris Reynolds, he worked on the metasomatic origin of certain igneous rocks. He also wrote *Principles of Physical Geology* (1944), one of the most successful textbooks ever written.

Holmes, Sir Frank Wakefield 1924–
New Zealand economist and writer

He was born in Oamaru, Coromandel Peninsula, and educated at Otago, Auckland and Victoria (Wellington) universities. A British Commonwealth Fellow at Chatham House, London, he then became Fulbright Fellow at Brookings Institution, Washington DC, until 1964. Returning to Wellington University in 1952, he became Professor of Economics (1959–67) and Professor of Money and Finance (1970–77). He chaired the New Zealand Planning Council (1977–82) and has written books on monetary policy.

Holmes, Larry, *nicknamed* the Easton Assassin 1949–
US boxer

Born in Cuthbert, Georgia, he beat Ken Norton for the World Boxing Council heavyweight title in 1978, and held it until 1985, when he lost to Michael Spinks. He lost the return contest with Spinks, and in 1988 challenged Mike Tyson for the title, but was defeated in four rounds. Holmes staged a comeback in 1995 but after his defeat by Anthony Willis in 1996, his 43-year career came to an end.

Holmes, Oliver Wendell 1809–94
US physician and writer

Born in Cambridge, Massachusetts, he graduated at Harvard College in 1829, and, giving up law for medicine, spent two years in hospitals in Europe. He was Professor of Anatomy and Physiology at Dartmouth College (1839–40), and in 1842 discovered that puerperal fever, which killed mothers and newborns in huge numbers, was contagious. From 1847 to 1882 he was Professor of Anatomy at Harvard. Although he began writing verse while an undergraduate, it was 20 years later that *The Autocrat of the Breakfast Table* (1857–58) made him famous. This was followed by *The Professor at the Breakfast Table* (1858–59) and *The Poet at the Breakfast Table* (1872). *Elsie Venner* (1859–60) was the first of three novels, foreshadowing modern 'Freudian' fiction. He published several volumes of poetry, starting with *Songs in Many Keys* (1862), and also wrote *Our Hundred Days in Europe* (1887), an account of a visit made in 1886. 📖 E P Hoyt, *The Improper Bostonian* (1979); J T Morse (jnr), *Life and Letters of Oliver Wendell Holmes* (1896)

Holmes, Oliver Wendell, *nicknamed* the Great Dissenter 1841–1935
US jurist

Born in Boston, he was educated at Harvard Law School and served in the Union army during the Civil War (1861–65). He practised law in Boston from 1867 and edited Kent's *Commentaries* (1873), became co-editor of the *American Law Review*, and Weld Professor of Law at Harvard (1882). He made his reputation with a fundamental book on *The Common Law* (1881), which was revolutionary in its willingness to address the pragmatic and accidental aspects of the law as opposed to its invincible logic. Associate Justice (1882–99) and Chief Justice (1899–1902) of the Supreme Court of Massachusetts, he became Associate Justice of the US Supreme Court (1902–32). He earned his nickname, 'the Great Dissenter', because he frequently dissented from his conservative colleagues' majority opinions, especially as the Court moved to dismantle social legislation. Eschewing liberal activism, however, he argued eloquently in favour of judicial restraint, particularly relating to regulation of the economy. The force and clarity of his arguments and his polished literary style gave him a stature on the Supreme Court unmatched by any justice other than **John Marshall**, and he is considered one of the great judicial figures in US history. He was the son of the writer, **Oliver Wendell Holmes**.

Holmes, William Henry 1846–1933
US archaeologist and museum director

Born near Cadiz, Ohio, he trained as an artist, and became interested in archaeology in 1875 when exploring ancient cliff dwellings in the Southwest with the US Geological Survey. A visit to the Yucatán while he was curator of anthropology at the Field Museum of Natural History, Chicago, stimulated a major contribution to Mesoamerican archaeology, his magnificently illustrated *Archaeological Studies among the Ancient Cities of Mexico* (1895–97). Outstanding too were his classificatory studies of prehistoric ceramics and stone technology in North America, notably *Aboriginal Pottery of the Eastern United States* (1903) and the *Handbook of Aboriginal American Antiquities* (1919). He worked at the Smithsonian Institution, Washington DC, for much of his career, acting as chief of the Bureau of American Ethnology (1902–09) and director of the National Gallery of Art (1920–32).

Holroyd, Michael de Courcy Fraser 1935–
English biographer

He was born in London, and studied sciences at Eton, and literature at Maidenhead Public Library. His first book was *Hugh Kingsmill: a critical biography* (1964). His two-volume life of **Lytton Strachey**, *The Unknown Years* (1967) and *The Year of Achievement* (1968), is recognized as a landmark in biographical writing as it revived interest in the genre and in the Bloomsbury Group. He is the official biographer of **George Bernard Shaw**, with *The Search for Love* (1988), *The Pursuit of Power* (1989), *The Lure of Fantasy* (1991), *The Last Laugh* (1992) and *The Shaw Companion* (1992). He is married to **Margaret Drabble**. 📖 *Unreceived Opinions* (1973)

Holst, Gustav Theodore, *originally* Gustav Theodore von Holst 1874–1934
English composer

Born in Cheltenham, Gloucestershire, of Swedish origin, he studied under **Charles Stanford**, at the Royal College of Music, but neuritis in his hand prevented him from becoming a concert pianist. He taught music at St Paul's School, Hammersmith (1905–57), and then became

musical director at Morley College (1907) and at Reading College (1919). He shared **Ralph Vaughan Williams'** interest in the English folksong tradition, which inspired his *St Paul's Suite for Strings* (1913) and many charming arrangements of songs. Economy and clarity became his hallmark. He emerged as a major composer with the seven-movement suite *The Planets* (1914–16). Among his other major works are *The Hymn of Jesus* (1917), his comic operas *The Perfect Fool* (1922) and *At the Boar's Head* (1924), and his orchestral tone-poem *Egdon Heath* (1927), inspired by **Thomas Hardy's** *Return of the Native*. His daughter Imogen (1907–84), like him, was a musical educationist, conductor and composer of folk-song arrangements, and was associated with **Benjamin Britten** in the Aldeburgh Festivals.

Holt, Harold Edward 1908–67
Australian politician

Born in Sydney, the son of an impresario, he studied law at Melbourne University, joined the United Australia Party, which was to be replaced by the Liberal Party of Australia, and entered the House of Representatives in 1935. He became deputy leader of his party in 1956, and leader and Prime Minister, when Sir **Robert Menzies** retired, in 1966. During the Vietnam War he strongly supported the USA with the slogan 'all the way with LBJ'. He died in office, lost at sea while swimming at Portsea.

Holt, Sir John 1642–1710
English judge

Born in Thame, Oxfordshire, he was educated at Winchester and at Oriel College, Oxford, and was called to the Bar in 1663. He was a counsel in most of the state trials of that period, and in 1686 was made Recorder of London and King's Serjeant. In 1689 he became Lord Chief Justice of the King's Bench. Holt was a Whig, but his judicial career was entirely free from party bias or intrigue, and he was noteworthy for his recognition of the rights of accused persons and the liberties of the subject.

Holtby, Winifred 1898–1935
English novelist and feminist

Born in Rudston, Yorkshire, she was educated at Oxford, and served in France with the Women's Auxiliary Army Corps. She was a prolific journalist, and was a director from 1926 of *Time and Tide*. She wrote a number of novels with strong-willed women as her heroines, including *The Crowded Street* (1924) and *The Land of Green Ginger* (1927), but is chiefly remembered for her last and most successful, *South Riding* (1935). 📖 V Brittain, *Testament of Friendship* (1940)

Holtei, Karl von 1798–1880
German actor and dramatic poet

He was born in Breslau (now Wrocław, Poland), and wrote musical plays, such as *Der alte Freiherr* (1825, 'The Old Baron') and *Lenore* (1829), as well as novels and the autobiographical *Vierzig Jahre* (8 vols, 1843–50, 'Forty Years').

Holtzmann, Adolf 1810–70
German philologist

Born in Karlsruhe, he became Professor of German at Heidelberg in 1852. He wrote on the connection between Greek and Indian fables (1844–47). He also wrote on Celts and Germans (1855), maintaining that the two races were originally identical, and on the *Nibelungenlied* (1854). His son, Heinrich Julius (1832–1910), a German theologian, became Professor of Theology at Heidelberg (1861) and at Strasburg (1874), and was ultimately a leading representative of modern New Testament criticism.

Holub, Miroslav 1923–98
Czech poet and scientist

Born in Plzen, he studied immunology and had a distinguished career in medicine, doing much to popularize science through his editing of the magazine *Vesmír*.

He published several collections, many of which have been translated into English. His *Selected Poems* were published in 1967; other collections include *Sagittal Section* (1980) and *On the Contrary* (1982). He published a collection of essays, *The Dimension of the Present Moment*, in 1990. *Immunology of Nude Mice* (1989) is one of his scientific publications.

Holyfield, Evander 1962–
US boxer

Born in Alabama, he was described by his trainer, Don Turner, as 'rich enough to air-condition hell'. His earnings exceed $100 million. His three fights against **Riddick Bowe** are considered to be the fiercest and best of modern heavyweight boxing. He first won the heavyweight title in 1990 against Buster Douglas, beat Bowe in 1993 but lost in 1992 and 1995 (a non-title fight). He was the undisputed heavyweight world champion in 1990–92 and 1993–94. Worries over a heart condition caused him to say he would retire at the end of 1996; nonetheless, he beat **Mike Tyson** that year to regain the heavyweight title.

Holyoake, George Jacob 1817–1906
English social reformer

He was born in Birmingham. He taught mathematics for some years at the Mechanics' Institution in Birmingham, lectured on **Robert Owen's** socialist system, was secretary to **Garibaldi's** British contingent, edited the *Reasoner*, and promoted the bill legalizing secular affirmations. He was the last person imprisoned in England on a charge of atheism (1842). He wrote histories of the co-operative movement, works on secularism, *Sixty Years of an Agitator's Life* (1892) and *Public Speaking and Debate* (1895).

Holyoake, Sir Keith Jacka 1904–83
New Zealand politician

The son of a shopkeeper and farmer, he worked on the family farm at Scarborough, near Pahiatua, on North Island, and then bought and successfully expanded it. He joined the Reform Party, which was to be superseded by the New Zealand National Party, and entered the House of Representatives (1932–38) as its youngest member. Re-elected in 1943, he became deputy leader of the National Party in 1946, deputy Prime Minister in 1949, and party leader and Prime Minister, on the retirement of Sir **Sydney Holland**, in 1957. He was Prime Minister again from 1960 to 1972, and later served as Governor-General of New Zealand (1977–80).

Holz, Arno 1863–1929
German author and critic

Born in Rastenburg, East Prussia, he first produced lyric poetry, but he is best known for his criticism. *Die Kunst, ihr Wesen und ihre Gesetze* (1890–92, 'The Nature and Laws of Art') inaugurated the German Impressionist school. *Revolution der Lyrik* (1899, 'Revolution in Lyric') rejected all metrical devices, and *Phantasus* (1898–99) was written on this theory. *Papa Hamlet* (1899) and the drama *Die Familie Selicke* (1890, 'The Selicke Family'), both written in collaboration with Johannes Aschaf, are influenced by **Zola**.

Hom, Ken(neth) 1949–
US chef and cookery writer

Born of Cantonese parents, he has become an international populariser of Chinese cooking, earning renown as a food consultant. After revamping the menus of the airline Cathay Pacific in 1990, in 1993 he supervised the opening of London's Imperial City restaurant, where he remains the consulting chef. He has also organized promotions for hotels, including the Oriental in Bangkok and the Regent in Sydney. He has contributed to the *New York Times* and *Australian Vogue*, and his television series include BBC's *Hot Wok*, for which he produced the book *Hot Wok* (1996).

Home (of the Hirsel), Alec (Alexander Frederick) Douglas-Home, 14th Earl of Home, Baron 1903–95
Conservative politician and Prime Minister

Born in London, heir to the Scottish earldom of Home, he was educated at Eton and Christ Church, Oxford, entered parliament in 1931 and was **Neville Chamberlain's** secretary during the latter's abortive negotiations with **Hitler** and **Mussolini** (1937–39). He became Minister of State at the Scottish Office (1951–55), succeeded to the peerage as 14th Earl in 1951, was Commonwealth-Relations Secretary (1955–60), Leader of the House of Lords and Lord President of the Council (1957–60), and Foreign Secretary (1960–63). After **Harold Macmillan's** resignation, he was his party's surprise choice as leader (1963). He made history by renouncing his peerage and fighting a by-election at Kinross, during which, although Prime Minister, he was technically a member of neither House. A similar situation was depicted in the play, *The Reluctant Peer* (1964), by his brother, **William Douglas-Home**. Although a man of enormous political integrity and ability, his rather distant manner and aristocratic image did not serve him well in comparison with the streetwise and charismatic Labour leader, **Harold Wilson**, and the Conservatives lost the 1964 election by only 20 seats. The following year, he was replaced as party leader by **Edward Heath** under a new selection procedure that Douglas-Home had sponsored. He was Foreign Secretary in Heath's government (1970–74) and in 1974 he was made a life peer and retired from active politics. His publications include the autobiographical *The Way the Wind Blows* (1976), *Border Reflections* (1979) and *Letters to a Grandson* (1983). 📖 D R Thorpe, *Alec Douglas-Home* (1996); Kenneth Young, *Sir Alec Douglas-Home* (1970)

Home, Daniel Dunglas 1833–86
Scottish spiritualist

Born near Edinburgh, he went to the USA in the 1840s to live with an aunt, who became so alarmed at the unexplained noises and other phenomena associated with his presence that she turned him out of her house. He became well-known as a medium, and his séances were attended by high society in London (1855) and on the Continent. The subject of **Robert Browning's** sceptical poem, *Mr Sludge, the Medium* (1864), he nonetheless persuaded scientists like Sir **William Crookes**, under electric light, that he was genuine. He published an autobiography, *Incidents of My Life* (2 vols, 1863, 1872).

Home, Henry See **Kames, Henry Home, Lord**

Home, John 1722–1808
Scottish clergyman and dramatist

Born in Leith, Edinburgh, he graduated at Edinburgh, fought on the government side in the 1745 Jacobite Rising, and in 1747 became minister of Athelstaneford. His play *Douglas* (1754), produced in the Canongate Theatre, Edinburgh in 1756, met with brilliant success, and evoked the oft-quoted and possibly apocryphal 'whaur's yer Wullie Shakespeare noo?' from an over-enthusiastic member of the audience. However, it gave such offence to the Edinburgh Presbytery that Home resigned his ministry (1757), and became tutor to the Prince of Wales (later **George III**). The success of *Douglas* induced **David Garrick** in London to produce Home's tragedy, *Agis*, and to accept his next play, *The Siege of Aquileia* (1760). His other works are *The Fatal Discovery* (1769), *Alonzo* (1773), *Alfred* (1778), occasional poems and, in prose, *A History of the Rebellion of 1745* (1802). 📖 H Mackenzie, *An account of the life and feelings of John Home* (1822)

Homer See panel p913

Homer, *Greek* **Homeros** c.8th century BC

Greek epic poet, a major figure of Ancient Greek literature

Homer was regarded in Greek and Roman antiquity as the author of the *Iliad* (dealing with episodes in the Trojan War) and the *Odyssey* (dealing with Odysseus's adventures on his return from Troy). He was thought to be a blind poet, and was traditionally associated with Ionia, directly across the Aegean from mainland Greece, where four city-states had claims to be his birthplace: the mainland cities of Smyrna, Colophon and Ephesus, and the island of Chios.

It is now believed that the poems were developed from orally transmitted poems, which were much modified and extended by several hands. They are usually dated to the 8th century BC, although the *Odyssey* is probably later than the *Iliad*. The texts were further modified at a later

date, especially sections of the *Iliad* such as the 'Catalogue of Ships' in Book II, which underwent changes to suit the political aspirations of Athens. The 33 so-called 'Homeric Hymns' are almost certainly from a later age, and are no longer attributed to Homer.

📖 P Vivante, *Homer* (1985); W A Camps, *An Introduction to Homer* (1980); Jasper Griffin, *Homer* (1980); Alan J B Wace and Frank H Stubbings (eds), *A Companion to Homer* (1962)

> 'Tribeless, lawless, homeless is he who loves the horror of civil war.' *Iliad*, Bk 9, lines 63–64 (c.700BC), translated by Martin Hammond.

Homer, Winslow 1836–1910
US painter

Born in Boston, after apprenticeship to a lithographer (1855–57), he began his career as an illustrator for magazines such as *Harper's Weekly* (1859–67), and specialized in watercolours of outdoor life painted in a naturalistic style which, in their clear outline and firm structure, were opposed to contemporary French Impressionism. He spent two years (1881–83) at Cullercoats, a rugged fishing port near Tynemouth, England, and on his return to the USA continued to depict the sea, living at Prouts Neck, an isolated fishing village on the coast of Maine, where he spent the rest of his life. His work was highly original and is often considered to be an expression of the American pioneering spirit. 📖 William Howe Downs, *Life and Works of Winslow Homer* (1911)

Honda, Soichiro 1906–91
Japanese motor-cycle and car manufacturer

Born in Iwata Gun, he started as a garage apprentice in 1922 and opened his own garage in 1928. By 1934 he had started a piston-ring production factory. He began producing motor cycles in 1948, and became president of Honda Corporation in the same year, until 1973. He stayed on as a director, and was appointed 'supreme adviser' in 1983.

Honda Toshiaki 1744–1821
Japanese political economist and navigator

Born in Echigo Province, he learned Dutch in order to acquire knowledge of the West, especially of western mathematics. After surveying Japan's northern island of Hokkaido in 1801, he advocated a programme to bring about wealth and power focusing on the manufacture of gunpowder and metals, the encouragement of shipping, and the colonization of Hokkaido. Honda's programme envisaged an end to the traditional policy of isolation and the promotion of state-sponsored foreign trade, thus anticipating developments after the Meiji Restoration (1868).

Hondius, Jodocus, *Latin name of* Joost de Hondt 1563–1612
Flemish cartographer

He emigrated to London c.1584 and moved from there to Amsterdam c.1593. In addition to his own maps of the world and the hemispheres, he engraved much of John Speed's work.

Hondt, Joost de See Hondius, Jodocus

Honecker, Erich 1912–94
German politician

Born in Neunkirchen in the Saarland, the son of a miner, he joined the German Communist Party in 1929 and was imprisoned for anti-Fascist activity between 1935 and

1945. After World War II, he was elected to the East German parliament (Volkskammer) in 1949, and served as a 'candidate' member of the Socialist Unity Party (SED) politburo and security force worker during the 1950s. In 1958 Honecker became a full member of the SED politburo and secretariat, and in 1961 oversaw the building of the Berlin Wall. During the 1960s he was Secretary of the National Defence Council, before being appointed head (first secretary) of the SED in 1971. Following **Walter Ulbricht**'s death in 1973, Honecker became the country's effective leader, and was elected Chairman of the Council of State (Head of State) in 1976. He proceeded to govern in an outwardly austere and efficient manner and, while favouring East–West détente, closely followed the lead given by the USSR. Following a wave of pro-democracy demonstrations he was replaced in 1989 as SED leader and head of state by **Egon Krenz** who, himself, was forced to resign two months later. Honecker was arrested in 1990 and faced trial on charges of treason, corruption, and abuse of power, but in 1993 he was judged too ill to attend trial and he retired to Chile.

Honegger, Arthur 1892–1955
French composer

Born in Le Havre, of Swiss parentage, he studied in Zurich and at the Paris Conservatory, and after World War I became one of the group of Parisian composers known as Les Six. His dramatic oratorio *Le Roi David* (1921, 'King David') established his reputation, and amongst his subsequent works, *Pacific 231* (1923), a musical picture of a locomotive, won considerable popularity. He composed five symphonies, and these, like a second dramatic oratorio, *Jeanne d'Arc au bûcher* (1935, Eng trans, *Joan of Arc at the Stake*, 1936), are works of considerable depth and power. 📖 Harry Halbreich, *Arthur Honegger, un musicien dans la cité des hommes* (1992)

Hong, Ge See Ko Hung

Hongwu (Hung-wu), *originally* Zhu Yuanzhang (Chu Yuan-chang) 1328–98
Emperor of China and founder of the Ming dynasty

The son of a peasant, he became a leader of the Red Turbans, one of a number of Buddhist and Daoist-inspired millenarian sects that rose in revolt against the Mongol Yuan dynasty during the 1340s. In 1356 he captured Nanjing and during the next few years disposed of his rivals to establish his own dynasty, the Ming. His reign (1368–98) was marked by the consolidation of imperial power; he abolished the post of Senior Chancellor and all central government organs were placed directly under the emperor. He also introduced low land taxes, reforestation, and the resettlement of abandoned land, and intimidated the landed and scholarly elites, a reflection of his peasant origins.

Honorius I d.638
Italian pope
Born in Roman Campania (Italy), he was pope from 625 to 638. He was involved with the paschal controversy in Ireland and with the Anglo-Saxon Church. In the Monothelite controversy he abstained from condemning the new doctrines, and for so doing was stigmatized as a heretic at the Council of Constantinople (680). The three other popes of that name, all Italians, were Honorius II (1124–30, an antipope), III (1216–27) and IV (1285–87).

Honorius III, *original name* Cencio Savelli d.1227
Italian pope
Unanimously elected in 1216 as successor to Innocent III, his pontificate was at first dominated by the need to involve Emperor Frederick II in crusade. Concessions to achieve this aim were exploited by the emperor for his own ends. Honorius then devoted his energies to the suppression of heresy within the boundaries of Christendom and the extension of those boundaries in the Baltic and Spain.

Honorius, Flavius AD384–423
Western Roman emperor
He was the second son of Theodosius I, the Great, at whose death (AD395) the empire was divided between his sons Arcadius and Honorius, the latter (only 10 years old) receiving the western half. Stilicho was the de facto ruler of the western empire until 408, and after his death Alaric I, the Goth, overran Italy, and took Rome (410). Honorius died at Ravenna, which he had made his capital in 403.

Hontheim, Johann Nikolaus von, *pseudonym* Justinius Febronius 1701–90
German ecclesiastic
Born in Trier, he travelled throughout Europe, and was ordained in Rome in 1728. Becoming bishop of his home town in 1748, he wrote two works on the history of Trier (1750–57), but is remembered chiefly for a theological essay (1763) under his pseudonym. In this, he propounded a system of church government combining an exaggerated Gallicanism with the democratic element of Congregationalism (Febronianism).

Honthorst, Gerrit or Gerard van 1590–1656
Dutch painter
Born in Utrecht, he studied under Abraham Bloemaert and formed his style in Italy (1610–20). He worked in Utrecht and in Rome, and twice visited England (1620, 1628), where he painted portraits of Charles I and Henrietta Maria. He was fond of painting dimly illuminated interiors, earning him the nickname Gherardo della Notte (Gerard of the Night Scenes). From 1637–52 he was court painter at The Hague. His brother William (1604–66), a historical and portrait painter, worked for the court of Berlin (1650–64).

Hooch or Hoogh, Pieter de c.1629–1684
Dutch genre painter
Born in Rotterdam, by 1654 he was living in Delft and probably came under the influence of Carel Fabritius and the latter's pupil, Jan Vermeer. His *Interior of a Dutch House* (National Gallery, London) and the *Card Players* in the Royal Collection are among the outstanding examples of the Dutch School of the 17th century, with their characteristically serene domestic interior or courtyard scenes, warm colouring and delicate light effects. Other works include *Courtyard of a House in Delft* (1658, National Gallery, London). About 1665 he moved to Amsterdam, but his later work became increasingly artificial.

Hood, Alexander, 1st Viscount Bridport
1727–1814
English naval commander
The brother of Samuel, 1st Viscount Hood, he joined the navy in 1741. In 1761 he recaptured from the French the *Warwick*, a 60-gun ship, and during the French Revolutionary Wars he served under Richard, 1st Earl Howe in the English Channel and the Strait of Gibraltar. He took part in the defeat of the French off Ushant, at the Battle of the Glorious First of June (1794) and later became Commander-in-Chief of the Channel fleet from 1797 to 1800.

Hood, John B(ell) 1831–79
US Confederate soldier
Born in Owingsville, Kentucky, he graduated from West Point in 1853 and served in the US army until the outbreak of the Civil War, when he resigned his commission. He commanded the Texas Brigade in the Confederate army, leading his troops into action at Gaines's Mill, Manassas, and Antietam, and winning praise for his tenacity and courage. He was severely wounded at Gettysburg and again at Chickamauga, after which his right leg was amputated. In 1864 he was sent to assist Joseph Johnston in opposing General Sherman's advance through Georgia, and in July succeeded Johnston in command of the army of Tennessee. Besieged for five weeks in Atlanta, he was forced to evacuate the city in September, leaving the road free for Sherman's march to the sea. He afterwards pushed as far north as Nashville but, defeated by George H Thomas, was relieved of command in January 1865 at his own request. He later went into business in New Orleans.

Hood, Raymond M(athewson) 1881–1934
US architect
Born in Pawtucket, Rhode Island, and educated in Massachusetts, he trained at the Massachusetts Institute of Technology before moving to the École des Beaux-Arts, Paris, in 1905. In 1922, with John Mead Howells (1868–1959), he won the competition for the Chicago Tribune Tower, designed with Gothic details. He became the leading designer of skyscrapers in the USA in the following decade. The American Radiator Building, New York (completed 1924), again demonstrated his focus on historicist styles. Later works in New York City were designed in a modern, rationalist style, such as the Daily News Building (1929–30), the Rockefeller Center (1930–40) and the McGraw-Hill Building (1931).

Hood (of Whitley), Samuel Hood, 1st Viscount 1724–1816
English naval commander
The brother of Alexander Hood, he was born in Thorncombe, Dorset. He joined the navy in 1741, and, in command of the *Vestal* frigate, he took the French frigate *Bellona* (1759). In 1780, promoted to flag rank, he was sent to reinforce Admiral George Rodney on the North American and West Indian stations, and took part in the battle in Chesapeake Bay (1781). In the West Indies in 1782 he defeated the French off St Kitts, and played a part in the decisive victory off Dominica for which he was made a baron in the Irish peerage. In 1784, standing against Charles Fox, he was elected to parliament, and in 1788 he became a Lord of the Admiralty. In the French Revolutionary Wars he captured Toulon (1793) and Corsica (1794). He was created a viscount in 1796.

Hood, Thomas 1799–1845
English poet and humorist
Born in London, the son of a bookseller, he was sent in 1815 to Dundee, where he wrote for local newspapers and magazines. In 1818 he returned to London, and in 1821 was appointed sub-editor of the *London Magazine*, and met Thomas De Quincey, William Hazlitt, Charles Lamb and other literary men. Encouraged by John Hamilton Reynolds, he began to write poetry, publishing such poems as 'Lycus the Centaur' and 'Two Peacocks of

Bedfont', in the *London Magazine*. In 1825 he published (anonymously, with J H Reynolds) a volume of *Odes and Addresses to Great People* which was an instant success. In the first series of *Whims and Oddities* (1826) he exhibited his graphic talent in 'picture-puns', of which he seems to have been the inventor. He produced the *Comic Annuals* yearly and single-handedly from 1830 to 1839. In 1834 the failure of a publisher plunged Hood into serious difficulties. From 1835 he spent five years in Koblenz and Ostend, and on his return to England he became editor of the *New Monthly Magazine* (1841) and started *Hood's Monthly Magazine* in 1844. His only surviving son, Tom (1835–74), also a writer and illustrator, published poems and humorous novels, and in 1865 became editor of *Fun*. 📖 J C Reid, *Thomas Hood* (1963)

Hooft, Gerard 't See 't Hooft, Gerard

Hoogh, Pieter de See Hooch, Pieter de

Hook, Sidney 1902–89
US philosopher and educationist
Born in New York City, he gained his PhD from Columbia University. He was professor at New York University (1932–72). An expositor of the work of **John Dewey** and **Karl Marx**, he was politically active, first as a spokesman for Marxism, but latterly as a leading social democrat. Among his many books are *Towards an Understanding of Karl Marx* (1933), *From Hegel to Marx* (1936), *John Dewey: an intellectual portrait* (1936), *Heresy, yes. Conspiracy, no* (1953) and *Revolution, Reform and Social Justice* (1976).

Hook, Theodore Edward 1788–1841
English writer
Born in London, the son of the composer James Hook (1746–1827), he was educated at Harrow School, and achieved early fame as the author of 13 successful comic operas and melodramas (1805–11). He was well known as a maker of puns and as a practical joker. In 1812 he was appointed Accountant General of Mauritius, but he was dismissed five years later, after a large deficiency was discovered in the accounts, and was later imprisoned (1823–25). Meanwhile, in 1820, he had started the Tory journal *John Bull*. He wrote a number of short stories and fashionable novels, such as *Maxwell* (1830), *Gilbert Gurney* (1936) and *Jack Brag* (1837). 📖 M Brightfield, *Theodore Hook and his novels* (1928)

Hooke, Robert 1635–1703
English experimental philosopher and architect
He was born in Freshwater, Isle of Wight, educated at Christ Church, Oxford, and worked as an assistant to **John Wilkins** on flying machines and **Robert Boyle** on the construction of his air-pump. In 1662 he was appointed the first curator of experiments at the newly founded Royal Society of London (secretary 1677–83), and in 1665 he became Professor of Physics at Gresham College, London. In that year he published his *Micrographia*, an impressive account of his microscopic investigations in botany, chemistry and other branches of science. One of the most brilliant and versatile scientists of his day, he was also an argumentative individual who became involved in a number of controversies, including several priority disputes with **Isaac Newton**. He anticipated the development of the steam engine, discovered the relationship between the stress and strain in elastic bodies known as 'Hooke's law', and formulated the simplest theory of the arch, the balance-spring of watches, and the anchor-escapement of clocks. He also anticipated Newton's law of the inverse square in gravitation (1678), constructed the first Gregorian or reflecting telescope, with which he discovered the fifth star in Orion and inferred the rotation of Jupiter, and materially improved or invented the compound microscope, the quadrant, a marine barometer, and the universal joint. After the Great Fire of London (1666) he was appointed city surveyor, and designed the new Bethlehem Hospital (Moorfields) and Montague House. 📖 Margaret Espinasse, *Robert Hooke* (1956)

Hooker, John Lee 1920–
US blues singer and guitarist
Born in Clarksdale, Mississippi, he learned blues guitar as a child, and worked as a street musician in the South before moving to Detroit in 1943, where he established himself as a leading blues artist. Unlike the slicker Chicago school, he drew on the raw emotion of early blues styles for his inspiration, set in the characteristic insistent boogie rhythm which most clearly defined his work. His music was very influential on the UK blues boom of the 1960s, but went into relative decline in the 1980s. He has bounced back in the 1990s with successful recordings (often with rock star guests queuing up to be involved) and live performances.

Hooker, Joseph, *nicknamed* Fighting Joe 1814–79
US Union soldier
Born in Hadley, Massachusetts, he served in the Mexican War (1846–48). During the Civil War, he commanded a division of the 3rd Corps in the Peninsular Campaign of 1862, and compelled the enemy to evacuate Manassas. In command of the 1st Corps, he opened the battle at Antietam (1862). In January 1863 he succeeded General **Burnside** in the command of the army of the Potomac, but was defeated at the Battle of Chancellorsville and superseded by **George G Meade** in June. In November he carried Lookout Mountain, and took part in the attack on Missionary Ridge. He accompanied General **Sherman** in his invasion of Georgia, and served until the fall of Atlanta in 1864.

Hooker, Sir Joseph Dalton 1817–1911
English botanist
Born in Halesworth, Suffolk, he was the second child of Sir **William Jackson Hooker**, and educated at Glasgow University, where he studied medicine. His first post was as assistant surgeon and naturalist on HMS *Erebus* in the Southern Ocean, and led to the six-volume *The Botany of the Antarctic Voyage*, comprising *Flora Antarctica* (1844–47), *Flora Novae-Zelandiae* (1853–55) and *Flora Tasmaniae* (1855–60). In 1846 he was appointed to the Geological Survey and in 1855 became assistant director of the Royal Botanic Gardens, Kew. Between 1848 and 1851 he explored Sikkim, Darjeeling, eastern Nepal and Assam, introducing many species to cultivation. His monumental *Genera Plantarum* (3 vols, 1862–83), formed the basis of a new classification system still used, with modifications, at Kew and elsewhere. His *Flora of British India* (7 vols, 1872–97) remains the standard Flora for the whole Indian subcontinent. On becoming director of Kew in 1865, Hooker instigated the compilation of a list of all scientific names of flowering plants, *Index Kewensis* (1892), which continues to be compiled today. President of the Royal Society from 1872 to 1877, he was knighted in 1877 and received the Order of Merit in 1907. 📖 Mea Allen, *The Hookers of Kew 1785–1911* (1967)

Hooker, Richard 1554–1600
English theologian
Born near Exeter, Devon, he studied at Corpus Christi, Oxford, where he became a Fellow in 1577. He took orders in 1581, and in 1584 became rector of Drayton-Beauchamp near Tring. After a lengthy controversy over his appointment as Master of the Temple in 1585, he resolved to set forth the basis of Church government, and in 1591 accepted the living of Boscombe near Salisbury, where he began his eight-volume work *Of the Laws of*

Ecclesiastical Polity (1594, 1597, 1648, 1662). It is mainly to this work that Anglican theology owes its tone and direction.

Hooker, Sir Stanley George 1907–84
English aero-engine designer

Born in the Isle of Sheppey, Kent, he studied mathematics and aeronautics at Imperial College, London, then, gaining the Busk Studentship (1928), went to Oxford where he published several papers for the Royal Society on compressible fluid flow. After a spell as a scientific civil servant he joined Rolls-Royce (1938), investigating the performance and design of superchargers for the Merlin aero-engine. He led Rolls-Royce into the production of the jet engine in 1943, and as chief engineer produced the Welland, Nene, Derwent, Avon and Trent engines. In 1949 he moved to the aero-engine division of the Bristol Aeroplane Company, working on Proteus, Olympus (for Concorde), Orpheus, and Pegasus (Harrier) jet engines. He returned from retirement in 1970 to Rolls-Royce to resolve the problems of the RB-211. His autobiography, *Not Much of an Engineer*, was published in 1984.

Hooker, Thomas c.1586–1647
English nonconformist clergyman

Born in Markfield, Leicestershire, he was a Puritan, and became a Fellow of Emmanuel College, Cambridge, conducting a four-year teaching ministry at Chelmsford (1625–29). In 1631 his nonconformist views forced him to flee to Holland, and in 1633 he sailed for Massachusetts, and became a pastor in Cambridge. In 1636 he moved with his congregation to Connecticut, and founded the town of Hartford. He was the author of the Fundamental Orders of Connecticut (1638), the first political constitution in North America, which was the forerunner of the US Constitution and the reason for Connecticut being called the 'Constitution State'.

Hooker, Sir William Jackson 1785–1865
English botanist

Born in Norwich, Norfolk, he collected specimens in Scotland in 1806, and later in Iceland. His first five botanical works dealt mostly with mosses but his *British Jungermanniae* (22 parts, 1812–16) established hepaticology (the study of liverworts) as an independent discipline. In 1820 he became Regius Professor of Botany at Glasgow and in 1841 became first director of the Royal Botanic Gardens, Kew. While at Kew he published several still standard works on ferns, including *Genera Filicum* (12 parts, 1838–42), *Species Filicum* (5 vols, 1846–64) and *Synopsis Filicum* (1865). He was knighted in 1836.

Hooks, Benjamin Lawson 1925–
US civil rights leader

Born in Memphis, Tennessee, he became a lawyer, banker, and minister. He was appointed by President Richard Nixon to the Federal Communications Commission (1972) and was its first black member. From 1977 to 1993 he served as executive director of the National Association for the Advancement of Colored People (NAACP).

Hooper, John 1495–1555
English prelate

Born in Somerset, he was educated at Oxford, and entered a Cistercian monastery at Gloucester in 1518. He became a supporter of the Reformist teachings of Huldreich Zwingli which forced him to flee to the Continent in 1539, where he settled in Zurich. After his return in 1549 he became a popular preacher in London, and in 1550 was appointed Bishop of Gloucester, but was imprisoned for some weeks in the Fleet prison for his scruples over the oath and the episcopal vestments, which he considered idolatrous. In 1552 he was also made Bishop of Worcester. Under Mary I, he was again imprisoned in the Fleet (1553), and was burned for heresy at Gloucester.

Hooton, Earnest A(lbert) 1887–1954
US physical anthropologist

Born in Clemansville, Wisconsin, he studied classics at Lawrence College and Wisconsin University, but his interests turned to anthropology while studying at Oxford. From 1913 to 1954 he taught anthropology at Harvard, and his laboratory became the main US centre for training physical anthropology specialists. In his many popular writings, including *Up From the Ape* (1931) and *Apes, Men and Morons* (1937), he introduced the subject to a wide readership. In his research he concentrated on the racial classification of the human species, and on relationships between body-build and behaviour, as in *The American Criminal* and *Crime and Man* (both 1939).

Hoover, Herbert Clark 1874–1964
31st President of the USA

Born of Quaker parentage in West Branch, Iowa, and orphaned at the age of 9, he was trained in mining engineering at Stanford University. He worked in this field in the USA, Australia, China (during the Boxer rising) and founded his own successful mining firm in 1908. He became involved in relief activities in Europe during World War I, supervising the evacuation of stranded Americans, raising private funds to aid war-devastated Belgium, and directing voluntary rationing in the USA. His skilful administration of these ambitious projects made him a popular public figure and opened the way to a political career. As Secretary of Commerce (1921–29) under Warren Harding and Calvin Coolidge, he promoted regulation of the radio and aviation industries and helped initiate such engineering projects as the St Lawrence Seaway and the Boulder (later Hoover) Dam. He became the Republican presidential nominee in 1928, defeating Democratic candidate Al Smith to win the presidency. His administration (1929–33) was overshadowed by the Great Depression, beginning with the stock market crash in October 1929. His call for private relief rather than large-scale government programmes and his reserved, formal demeanour led to the perception that he lacked compassion for the sufferings of the US people. His popularity plummeted, and the shanty towns that sprang up around the country were called Hoovervilles after him. Though he did initiate some public relief efforts later enlarged in Franklin D Roosevelt's New Deal, notably the Reconstruction Finance Corporation, he was defeated in his re-election bid by Roosevelt in 1932. He retired to private life until World War II, when he organized civilian relief operations in Europe. He later headed the Hoover Commissions (1947–49, 1953–55), which studied the executive branch of government and suggested many administrative and policy reforms later adopted. 📖 David Burner, *Herbert Hoover* (1979)

Hoover, J(ohn) Edgar 1895–1972
US law enforcement official

Born in Washington DC, he supported his family after the premature death of his father, graduating in law at George Washington University in 1917, after taking evening classes. He then entered the Justice Department, becoming special assistant to the Attorney-General in 1919 and assistant director of the Federal Bureau of Investigation (FBI) in 1921. He became FBI director in 1924 and remained in charge of the Bureau until his death, remodelling it to make it more efficient and adding such improvements as a national fingerprint file and a crime laboratory. He campaigned against city gangster rackets in the inter-war years and communist sympathisers in the postwar period, but in his later years in office he was criticized for abusing his power by persecuting liberal and civil-rights activists, notably **Martin Luther King**. His 48-year term as head of the FBI, possible because President **Lyndon B Johnson** exempted him from Civil Service retirement regulations, has been interpreted both as a tribute to his national importance in the fight against crime and as a recognition that he had learned too much about the politicians.

Hoover, William Henry 1849–1932
US industrialist
He was born in Ohio. He ran a tannery business (1870–1907), then bought the patent of an electric cleaning machine from a janitor, James Murray Spangler, and formed the Electric Suction Sweeper Co in 1908 to manufacture and market it throughout the world. The company was renamed Hoover in 1910.

Hope, A(lec) D(erwent) 1907–
Australian poet and critic
Born in Cooma, New South Wales, he graduated from Sydney University and took up a scholarship at Oxford. He returned to Australia in 1931 and became a distinguished academic, teaching English at several Australian colleges, before retiring in 1972 to concentrate on poetry. Pre-eminent among his contemporaries, he has received many Australian awards since the appearance of his first collection, *The Wandering Isles*, in 1955. Subsequent volumes of new and collected poems include *A D Hope* (1963), *Collected Poems 1930–1965* (1966, expanded edition 1972), *A Late Picking* (1975), *A Book of Answers* (1978), *The Drifting Continent* (1979), *The Tragical History of Dr Faustus* (1982) and *Orpheus* (1991). He has also won international awards such as the Levinson Prize (1968) and the **Robert Frost** Award (1976). He talked humorously on literature as 'Anthony Inkwell' in a long-running 1940s radio programme for children. 📖 L Kramer, *A D Hope* (1979)

Hope, Anthony, *pseudonym of* Sir Anthony Hope Hawkins 1863–1933
English novelist
Born in London, the son of a clergyman, he was educated at Balliol College, Oxford, and was called to the Bar in 1887. He wrote several plays and novels in his spare time, and made his name as writer with a collection of sketches, *The Dolly Dialogues* (1894). But he is chiefly remembered for his 'Ruritanian' romances, *The Prisoner of Zenda* (1894; dramatized 1896) and its sequel, *Rupert of Hentzau* (1898). 📖 C Mallet, *Anthony Hope and His Books* (1935)

Hope, Bob (Leslie Townes) 1903–
US comedian
Born in Eltham, London, and raised in Ohio in the USA from 1907, he became a US citizen in 1920. He began as a vaudeville dancer and comedian on the US stage, making his Broadway debut in *The Sidewalks of New York* (1927), and his first film appearances in a string of shorts, beginning with *Going Spanish* (1934), before appearing in the full-length *The Big Broadcast of 1938* (1938). Famed for his ski-slope nose, lop-sided grin and impeccable timing, he had a string of hit films, including *The Cat and the Canary* (1939), *My Favourite Blonde* (1942), *The Princess and the Pirate* (1944) and *Paleface* (1948). In partnership with **Bing Crosby** and Dorothy Lamour (1914–96) he appeared in the seven highly successful *Road to…* comedies (1940–61). During World War II and the Korean and Vietnam wars he spent much time entertaining the troops in the field. He received a Special Academy Award on five occasions, and has written many books, including *I Owe Russia 1200* (1963) and *Confessions of a Hooker* (1985).

Hope, Sir Charles, 1st Earl of Hopetoun
1681–1742
Scottish nobleman
Elected Privy Councillor and a peer (1703), he was a supporter of the Union with England (1707), and became Lord Lieutenant of Linlithgow (1715). He had Hopetoun House built, near Queensferry, the building being completed in 1753 by the Scottish architects, William and his son **Robert Adam**.

Hope, Laurence, *pseudonym of* Adela Florence Nicolson, *née* Cory 1865–1904
English poet
Born in Stoke Bishop, Gloucestershire, she lived in India and wrote poems, influenced by **Algernon Charles Swinburne** and coloured by her life abroad. Some of her *Indian Love Lyrics* are best known in their musical settings by Amy Woodford Finden.

Hope, Thomas 1769–1831
English connoisseur and antiquary
Born in London, he travelled widely in Europe and the Near East in his youth, collecting marbles and making drawings of buildings and sculptures. He pioneered a Neoclassical Regency style and introduced the vogue of Egyptian and Roman decoration in his mansion in Duchess Street, London. He wrote *House Furniture and Interior Decoration* (1807), and a novel, *Anastasius, or Memoirs of a Modern Greek* (1819), a picaresque tale of an unscrupulous Greek adventurer which was popular in its time.

Hope, Thomas Charles 1766–1844
Scottish chemist
Born in Edinburgh, he studied medicine there, and afterwards taught chemistry at Glasgow and from 1795 at Edinburgh, where he worked with, and then succeeded, **Joseph Black**. Hope confirmed the earlier but neglected observations that water has a maximum density close to 4°C, an important result in biology, climatology and physics. He recognized and described a new mineral from Strontian in Scotland (1793); he even described the characteristic red flame colour of the new element present in it (strontium) which was isolated by Sir **Humphry Davy** in 1808. Hope was a successful teacher (his lectures were attended by 575 students in 1825) and was probably the first in Great Britain to teach the new ideas derived from the work of **Antoine Lavoisier**.

Hopf, Heinz 1894–1971
German mathematician
Born in Breslau (now Wrocław, Poland), he studied at the universities of Berlin and Göttingen, where he met the Russian topologist **Pavel Aleksandrov** with whom he wrote the influential *Topologie* (1935). In 1931 he became professor at Zurich University. One of Europe's leading topologists, he worked on many aspects of combinatorial topology, including homotopy theory and vector fields.

Hopkins, Sir Anthony 1937–
Welsh film and stage actor
He was born in Port Talbot, Wales, and after graduating from RADA, made his stage debut in *The Quare Fellow* (1960) at Manchester. A period in regional repertory was followed by his London debut in *Julius Caesar* (1964). Very successful on stage, and a member of the National Theatre company (1966–73), his mastery of timing and technique have allowed him to portray a vast variety of characters, from the saturnine to the heroic. Later stage appearances include *Equus* (1974) and three triumphant National Theatre performances, in *Pravda* (1985), *King Lear* (1986) and *Antony and Cleopatra* (1987). Film appearances include *The White Bus* (1967), his first film, *The Lion in Winter* (1968), *Audrey Rose* (1977) and *The Elephant Man* (1980). Television work includes *War and Peace* (1972, BAFTA award), *The Lindbergh Kidnapping Case* (1976, Emmy), *The Bunker* (1981, Emmy) and *The Hunchback of Notre Dame* (1982). He won a Best Actor Academy Award as cannibalistic serial killer

Hannibal Lector in *The Silence of the Lambs* (1991) and received further nominations for *The Remains of the Day* (1993) and *Nixon* (1995). Other recent films include *Howards End* (1992), *Shadowlands* (1993), *Surviving Picasso* (1996) and *Bookworm* (1997). Knighted in 1993, he made his directorial debut with the film *August* (1995).

Hopkins, Sir Frederick Gowland 1861–1947
English biochemist and Nobel Prize winner

Born in Eastbourne, Sussex, he learned chemistry in a pharmaceutical firm before commencing a brilliant career at Guy's Hospital, where he received the University of London gold medal in chemistry and qualified in medicine. Following his publication on estimating uric acid in urine, he became the first lecturer in chemical biology at Cambridge (1897). He was appointed professor there in 1914 and served as Sir William Dunn Professor from 1921 until his retirement in 1943. He discovered accessory food factors, now called vitamins, associated lactate production in muscle with muscle contraction (1907), and discovered glutathione (1921). He was elected a Fellow of the Royal Society in 1905, was awarded its Royal (1918) and Copley (1926) medals, and became the Royal Society's president (1931). Knighted in 1925, he shared with **Christiaan Eijkman** the 1929 Nobel Prize for physiology or medicine.

Hopkins, Gerard Manley 1844–89
English poet

Born in London, he was educated at Highgate School and Balliol College, Oxford, where he was a pupil of **Benjamin Jowett** and **Walter Pater** and a disciple of **Edward Pusey**, and met his lifelong friend **Robert Bridges**. Having followed **John Henry Newman** into the Roman Catholic Church in 1866, he was ordained a Jesuit priest in 1877. He taught at Stoneyhurst (1882–84) and became Professor of Greek at University College, Dublin (1884). None of his poems was published in his lifetime, but his friend Bridges brought out a full edition in 1918. His best-known poems include 'The Wreck of the Deutschland' (1876), 'The Windhover' and 'Pied Beauty', in which he used what he called 'sprung rhythm'. 📖 A G Sulloway, *Gerard Manley Hopkins and the Victorian Temper* (1972)

Hopkins, Harold Horace 1918–94
British optical physicist

Born in Leicester, he was educated at the universities of Leicester and London, and worked on optical design. He held the basic patents on zoom lenses, and was one of the originators of fibre-optic technology, which allows optical signals to be transmitted over great distances in fine-drawn glass fibres. He also invented the rod–lens system which is now used universally in medical endoscopes. His special interests included aberration theory, optical coherence and the diffraction theory of imaging. He was appointed Professor of Applied Optics at the University of Reading (1967–84, then emeritus), elected FRS (1973) and was Ives medallist of the Optical Society of America in 1978.

Hopkins, Harry L(loyd) 1890–1946
US administrator

Born in Sioux City, Iowa, he was Federal emergency relief administrator in the Depression of 1933, and under President **Franklin D Roosevelt** headed the 'New Deal' projects in the Works Progress Administration (1935–38). He became Secretary of Commerce (1938–40), and was supervisor of the Lend-Lease programme in 1941. As Roosevelt's closest confidante and special assistant, he undertook several important missions to Russia, Great Britain, and other countries during World War II, and helped to set up the Potsdam Conference (1945).

Hopkins, Johns 1795–1873
US businessman

He was born in Anne Arundel County, Maryland. He set up a grocery business in 1819 in Baltimore, and retired in 1847 with a large fortune. Besides a public park for Baltimore, he endowed an orphanage for black children, a free hospital, and gave over $3 million to found the Johns Hopkins University.

Hopkins, Lightnin' (Sam) 1912–82
US blues singer and guitarist

Born in Centerville, Texas, he began to perform blues as a child, and toured the south with his cousin, singer Texas Alexander. He cut his first record in 1946, and is thought to be the most recorded of all blues artists, although his use of pseudonyms to avoid contractual problems has made an accurate count difficult. He was 'rediscovered' singing in clubs in 1959, and his acoustic country blues style won favour with the folk revival audiences of the early 1960s. He was an inimitable raconteur as well as an idiosyncratic singer and guitarist, and he is one of the most important artists to have worked in the country blues tradition.

Hopkins, Matthew d.1647
English 'witchfinder-general'

He is said to have been a lawyer in Ipswich. Appointed witchfinder in 1644, he caused the deaths of scores of victims, and discharged his duties so conscientiously that he himself became suspect, and, being found guilty by his own test in that he floated, bound, in water, was hanged. His *The Discovery of Witches* was published in 1647.

Hopkins, Patty, née Wainwright c.1942–
English architect

She was born in Staffordshire and trained at the Architectural Association, London, where she met her husband and partner Michael Hopkins (1935–). They set up a practice in 1976, and since then Patty has worked on their major projects, including the Mound Stand at Lords Cricket Ground and the extension to Glyndebourne Opera House (1987–). Their designs, which combine high-tech design with traditional materials, gained them the 1994 RIBA (Royal Institute of British Architects) gold medal, and the honour of being the first British couple to win the award.

Hopkins, Samuel 1721–1803
American Congregational theologian

Born in Waterbury, Connecticut, he studied at Yale, and was pastor of Housatonick (now Great Barrington), Massachusetts, from 1743 to 1769, and then of Newport (1770–1803). A close friend of **Jonathan Edwards**, his *System of Doctrines* (1793) maintains that all virtue consists of disinterested benevolence, and that all sin is selfishness (Hopkinsianism). He was a vigorous opponent of slavery.

Hopkinson, Sir Tom (Henry Thomas) 1905–90
English writer and journalist

Educated at St Edward's School, Oxford, and Pembroke College, Oxford, he sold advertising and encyclopedias before becoming assistant editor of *Weekly Illustrated*. He then set up *Picture Post* with its editor Stefan Lorant (1901–97) in 1938, taking over as editor in 1940. The magazine, which used the new craft of photo-journalism, was the first picture magazine to appeal to 'popular' taste. He also edited the small, sister magazine, *Lilliput* (1941–46). His politics differed from those of the *Picture Post*'s owner, **Edward Hulton**, and when Hulton refused to run an exposée of the South Korean dictator **Syngman Rhee**, Hopkinson resigned. He went to South Africa as editor of *Drum* magazine for three years. At the age of 61 he began a new career as teacher, first on the new Press Studies course at the University of Sussex (1967–69), then at University College, Cardiff (1971–75). His publications include the novel *Shady City* (1987), and the auto-biographical works *Of This Our Time* (1982) and *Under the Tropic* (1984).

Hopman, Harry (Henry Christian) 1906–85
Australian tennis player

He was born in Sydney. Despite being a talented singles player, he specialized almost exclusively in doubles. He is, however, best known for his captaincy of the Australian Davis Cup side. He was briefly in charge before World War II and his return to the post in 1950 saw Australia dominate world men's tennis. In the next 17 years Australians won Wimbledon 10 times and the Davis Cup 15 times as Hopman produced a stream of talented players, from Ken Rosewall and Lew Hoad to **Rod Laver** and John Newcombe. A strict disciplinarian, he demanded total commitment. Willing to take a chance with young players, he often had players representing Australia in the Davis Cup before they were 20 years old. His wife Nell was a noted legislator in women's tennis.

Hopper, Dennis 1936–
US film actor and director

Born in Dodge City, Kansas, he first appeared in *Johnny Guitar* (1954), though *Rebel Without a Cause* (1955) is more often cited as his film debut. He played several hotheaded young malcontents and whingeing weaklings during the late 1950s, and was the villain in westerns such as *True Grit* (1969), before making his directorial debut with the highly successful *Easy Rider* (1969, with Peter Fonda). During the 1980s he emerged as a hard-working character actor and in 1986 played the drug-crazed hermit in *River's Edge*, the vengeful Texas ranger in *Texas Chainsaw Massacre 2* and the town drunk in *Hoosiers* (UK: *Best Shot*). He was a notable villain in *Blue Velvet* (1986), and he also continues to direct (eg *Colors*, 1988; *True Romance*, 1990).

Hopper, Edward 1882–1967
US painter

Born in Nyack, New York, he studied under **Robert Henri** (1900–06), and between 1906 and 1910 made several trips to Europe. His style of painting, however, owed little to contemporary European art movements and, in later years, was similarly unaffected by US Abstraction. His paintings of commonplace urban scenes are characterized by a sense of stillness and isolation, as in *Early Sunday Morning* (1930, Whitney Museum, New York), and figures are anonymous and uncommunicative, as in *Nighthawks* (1942, Art Institute of Chicago). He gave up painting for a time (1913–23) to work as a commercial illustrator, but received official recognition with a retrospective exhibition at New York's Museum of Modern Art in 1933, and is regarded as a master of 20th-century US figurative art.

Hopper, Grace Murray 1906–92
US computer programmer

Born in New York City, she was educated at Vassar College, where she taught in the mathematics department between 1931 and 1944. She then joined the Naval Reserve and was drafted to join **Howard Aiken's** team at Harvard as a coder for the Mark I. She gradually developed a set of built-in routines and was eventually able to use the machine to solve complex partial differential equations. In 1951 she conceived of a new type of internal computer program called a compiler, which was designed to scan a programmer's instructions and produce (compile) a set of binary instructions that carried out the programmer's commands. Hopper's ideas spread and were influential in setting standards for software developments, such as for COBOL. She was one of the few women to make a major impact on the history of computing.

Hopper, Hedda, *originally* Elda Furry 1885–1966
US actress and gossip columnist

Born in Hollidaysburg, Pasadena, the daughter of a butcher, she studied piano and voice in Pittsburgh before making her stage debut in 1907 with the Aborn Light Opera Company. She went on to the New York stage before moving to Hollywood, where she established a successful silent film career, appearing in as many as 50 productions a year. When her acting career waned, she found work as a gossip columnist in 1938 and was built up as a rival to **Louella Parsons**. Her Hollywood gossip column was syndicated to an estimated 3,000 daily newspapers and 2,000 weeklies, and her luxurious Beverly Hills mansion was called 'The House That Fear Built'. A vociferous right-wing supporter, she appeared frequently on radio and published two bestselling books, *From Under My Hat* (1952) and *The Whole Truth and Nothing But* (1963).

Hoppe-Seyler, Felix, *in full* Ernst Felix Immanuel Hoppe-Seyler 1825–95
German physiological chemist

Born in Freiburg im Breisgau, he was a pioneer in the application of chemical methods to understand physiological processes. He showed how the haemoglobin in the red blood cells binds oxygen, and investigated the chemical composition and functions of chlorophyll as well as the chemistry of putrefaction. He taught in Berlin, Tübingen and Strassburg and founded in 1877 *Zeitschrift für physiologische Chemie*, the first biochemical journal.

Hoppner, John c.1758–1810
English portrait painter

Born in Whitechapel of German parents, he was at first a chorister in the Chapel Royal, then received an allowance from **George III** to study at the Royal Academy schools in 1775. After the death of Sir **Joshua Reynolds** he became Sir **Thomas Lawrence's** only rival as a fashionable portrait painter. *The Countess of Oxford* is his masterpiece.

Hopwood, Sir David Alan 1933–
English geneticist

Born in Kinver, Staffordshire, he was educated at Cambridge, and later moved to a lectureship at the University of Glasgow (1961). In 1968 he became the first John Innes Professor of Genetics at the University of East Anglia and head of the genetics department at the John Innes Institute. Elected Fellow of the Royal Society in 1979, he is a member and fellow of many international scientific academies, institutes and universities. His major contribution has been in understanding the genetics of the bacteria which produce most of the antibiotics used in human and veterinary medicine. His work has led to the ability to manipulate genes for antibiotic production, enabling the development of new antibiotics by genetic engineering. He was knighted in 1994.

Horace, *in full* Quintus Horatius Flaccus 65–8BC
Roman poet and satirist

Born near Venusia, southern Italy, the son of a freed slave, he was educated in Rome and Athens, and was still there when the murder of **Julius Caesar** (44BC) rekindled civil war. The same year he joined **Brutus's** army and fought (and, he says, ran away) at the Battle of Philippi (42), then went back to Italy and began writing. His earliest verses were chiefly satires and lampoons, but some of his first lyrical pieces made him known to **Virgil**, who around 38BC introduced him to **Maecenas**, a generous patron who gave Horace a farm in the Sabine Hills. As the unrivalled lyric poet of the time he became Poet Laureate. His first book of *Satires* (35BC) was followed by a second, and a small collection of lyrics, the *Epodes* (c.30BC). In 23BC he produced his greatest work, three books of *Odes*, and in about 20BC his *Epistles*. These, together with his later *Carmen Seculare*, a fourth book of *Odes*, and three more epistles, including *Ars Poetica*, had a profound influence on poetry and literary criticism in the 17th and 18th centuries. 📖 G Wilson, *Horace* (1972); G Showerman, *Horace and his Influence* (1922)

Hordern, Sir Michael Murray 1911–95
English actor

He was born in Berkhamsted, Hertfordshire, and studied at Brighton College. He was an amateur actor with the St Pancras People's Theatre before making his first professional appearance as Lodovico in *Othello* at the People's Palace (1937). Following World War II, he appeared at Stratford-upon-Avon as Mr Toad in *Toad of Toad Hall*. He joined the Stratford Memorial Theatre company (1952) to play a number of roles, and the Old Vic (1953–54) as Polonius in *Hamlet*, King John, Prospero in *The Tempest*, and a much-acclaimed Malvolio in *Twelfth Night*. He played in both classical and modern roles, such as the philosopher in Tom Stoppard's *Jumpers* (1972) and the judge in Howard Barker's *Stripwell* (1975), and made numerous film and television appearances, notably in the television adaptation of John Mortimer's *Paradise Postponed* (1986). A formidable classical actor, he also cornered the market in amiable, elderly eccentrics.

Hore-Belisha, Leslie Hore-Belisha, 1st Baron 1893–1957
English barrister and politician

Born in Devonport and educated at Clifton College and Oxford, he became a London journalist after service in World War I, and in 1923, the year he was called to the Bar, Liberal MP for Devonport. In 1931 he became first Chairman of the National Liberal Party. In 1934, as Minister of Transport, he gave his name to the 'Belisha' beacons at pedestrian crossings, drafted a new highway code and inaugurated driving tests for motorists. As Secretary of State for War (1937–40) he carried out several far-ranging and controversial reforms to modernize and democratize the army. He was Minister of National Insurance in the 1945 caretaker government, but lost his seat at the July election. 📖 R J Minney, *The Private Papers of Hore-Belisha* (1991)

Horkheimer, Max 1895–1973
German philosopher and social theorist

Born in Stuttgart, he studied at Frankfurt, and became a leading figure (together with Theodor Adorno and Herbert Marcuse) at the Frankfurt School as well as Director of the Institut für Sozialforschung there (1930). He moved with the school to New York City when the Nazis came to power (1933). He returned to Frankfurt in 1950 as professor of the university. He published a series of influential articles in the 1930s, later collected in two volumes under the title *Kritische Theorie* (1968, 'Critical Theory'), which expound the basic principles of the school in their critique of industrial civilization and epistemology and the key tenets of their critical theory. His other major works include *Dialektik der Aufklärung* (with Adorno, 1947) and *Eclipse of Reason* (1947). 📖 Zvi Rosen, *Max Horkheimer* (1995)

Horn, Charles Edward 1786–1849
English singer and composer

Born in London, of German parentage, his works include the songs 'Cherry Ripe' and 'I know a bank', as well as glees and piano-pieces.

Hornblower, Jonathan Carter 1753–1815
English engineer

Born in Chacewater, Cornwall, he was the son of Jonathan Hornblower (1717–80), also an engineer. As a young man he was employed with his father and three brothers by Matthew Boulton and James Watt to build one of their engines. He determined to improve Watt's design and by 1781 had obtained a patent for a single-acting compound engine with two cylinders, in which the steam

acted expansively and much more efficiently. He was judged, however, to have infringed Watt's patent of the separate condenser, and had to abandon further development of his engine. He later patented a rotary type of steam engine which was never built.

Hornby, A(lbert) S(idney) 1898–1978
English teacher, grammarian and lexicographer

Born in Chester, he went to Japan in 1923 to teach English. In the 1930s he became involved in the preparation of an English dictionary for Japanese students of English, published in Japan in 1942, and printed in 1948 by Oxford University Press as *A Learner's Dictionary of Current English* (retitled in 1952 *The Advanced Learner's Dictionary of Current English*). Although he wrote many other books—textbooks, grammars and dictionaries—it is for this dictionary that he is best known. It has been said of him that 'no man has ever done more to further the use of English as an international language'.

Hornby, Sir Geoffrey Thomas Phipps 1825–95
English naval commander

The son of Sir Phipps Hornby, he was present at the bombardment of Acre (1840), and became Commander-in-Chief in the Mediterranean (1877–80). In the Russo-Turkish war of 1878 he took the fleet through the Dardanelles to Constantinople (Istanbul). In 1888 he was promoted Admiral of the Fleet.

Hornby, Sir Phipps 1785–1867
English naval commander

Born in Winwick, Lancashire, he joined the navy in 1797, and commanded a frigate in Sir William Hoste's victory of Lissa (1811). He was Commander-in-Chief in the Pacific (1847–50), and was appointed a Lord of the Admiralty (1851–52). He was promoted admiral in 1858.

Horne, Lena Calhoun 1917–
US singer and actress

Born in Brooklyn, New York, she made her debut at the legendary Cotton Club, aged 16, but gradually switched from dancing to band singing. In 1942, she became the first black singer to win a contract from a major Hollywood company (MGM), appearing in *Cabin in the Sky* (1943) and *Stormy Weather* (1943). The latter became her signature song, and provided the perfect vehicle for her deep, sensuous voice, with its bluesy edge. She has bravely confronted racism throughout her career and describes its impact in her two memoirs, *In Person* (1950) and *Lena* (1965).

Horne, Marilyn Bernice 1934–
US mezzo-soprano

Born in Bradford, Pennsylvania, she made her debut in Bedřich Smetana's *The Bartered Bride* (*Prodaná nevěsta*), Los Angeles (1954), at Covent Garden, London as Marie in *Wozzeck* (1964), and at the New York Metropolitan as Adalgisa in *Norma* (1970). She is also a noted recitalist.

Horne, Richard Henry or Hengist 1803–84
English writer

He was trained at Sandhurst, served in the Mexican navy, and fought at Vera Cruz, San Juan Ulloa and elsewhere. Having survived yellow fever, sharks, broken ribs, shipwreck, mutiny and fire, he returned to England and took up writing. He was the author of the epic *Orion* (1843), which he published at the price of one farthing to show his contempt for a public that would not buy poetry. In 1852 he went to Australia as commissioner for Crown lands, became well-known in Victoria, and published *Australian Facts and Prospects* and *Australian Autobiography* (both 1859). He returned to England in 1869. Among his other books are *A New Spirit of the Age* (1844), in which Elizabeth Barrett Browning helped him, and two tragedies, *Cosmo de' Medici* (1837) and *The Death of Marlowe* (1837). 📖 A Blainey, *The Farthing Poet: Richard Hengist Horne* (1968)

Horner, Arthur Lewis 1894–1968
Welsh politician and trade unionist

Born in Merthyr Tydfil, Glamorgan, he abandoned his studies at a Baptist College to enter politics and work in a Rhondda coalmine. A founder-member of the British Communist Party, he stood unsuccessfully for parliament a number of times. He was elected president of the South Wales miners' union in 1936 and general secretary of the National Union in 1946. He was a likeable character, with friends who had little sympathy with his communist views.

Horniman, Annie Elizabeth Fredericka
1860–1937
English theatre manager and patron

She was born in Forest Hall, London, the daughter of a wealthy Quaker tea-merchant. She developed a secret passion for the theatre in her teens, studied at the Slade School of Art, and travelled widely, especially in Germany. She failed with a play on the London stage (1894), and went to Ireland in 1903. She later financed the first staging of W B Yeats's *The Land of Heart's Desire* and George Bernard Shaw's *Arms and the Man*, and even acted a little, for example as the Gipsy Woman in Shaw's *The Gadfly* (a curtain-raiser) in 1898. She sponsored the building of the Abbey Theatre in Dublin (1904), and although she later quarrelled with Yeats, Shaw never failed to pay her tribute. In 1908 she purchased the Gaiety Theatre in Manchester, which she called 'the first theatre with a catholic repertoire in England' and her company put on over 100 new plays by the so-called 'Manchester School', mostly directed by Lewis Casson. They disbanded in 1917 due to lack of financial success. In Great Britain, the Repertory Theatre movement and the reputations of many playwrights and actors are her legacy; in Ireland, perhaps Irish national theatre itself.

Hornung, E(rnest) W(illiam) 1866–1921
English novelist

He was born in Middlesbrough, Cleveland, and was educated at Uppingham. He was the brother-in-law of Sir Arthur Conan Doyle. He is best remembered as the creator of 'Raffles', the gentleman burglar, hero of *The Amateur Cracksman* (1899), *Mr Justice Raffles* (1909) and many other adventure stories.

Horowitz, Vladimir, *originally* Vladimir Gorowicz
1904–89
US pianist

Born in Kiev, Ukraine, he studied at the Conservatory there, and with Sergei Tarnowsky and Felix Blumenfeld. He made his debut at Kharkov, 1921, and made his US debut, under Sir Thomas Beecham, in 1928. He settled in the USA in 1940, and became a US citizen in 1944. He retired from public playing for long periods, but played in Russia again in 1986. One of the most skilful players of the century, his technique and interpretation were highly accomplished in music ranging from Scarlatti to Liszt, Scriabin, and Prokofiev. In 1933 he married Wanda Toscanini (1907–98), daughter of Arturo Toscanini. 📖 Harold Schonberg, *Vladimir Horowitz* (1992)

Horrocks, Sir Brian Gwynne 1895–1985
English soldier

He was born in Raniket, India, and educated at Uppingham and Sandhurst. He joined the army in 1914, then served in France (1914–18) and in Russia (1919). During World War II he commanded the 9th Armoured Division and then the 13th and 10th Corps against Rommel in North Africa. His 30th Corps struggled unsuccessfully to link up with the airborne troops in Arnhem (1944). On retirement Horrocks was made Gentleman Usher of the Black Rod. He later made a reputation as a military journalist and broadcaster, and wrote *A Full Life* (1960) and *Corps Commander* (1977). 📖 Philip Warner, *Horrocks: The General Who Led from the Front* (1984)

Horrocks, Jeremiah 1619–41
English astronomer

Born in Toxteth, Liverpool, he went to Emmanuel College, Cambridge in 1632 and in 1639 became curate of Hoole, Lancashire, where he made the first observation of the transit of Venus (24 November 1639 according to the Julian calendar), deduced the solar parallax, corrected the solar diameter and made tidal observations. He was an enthusiastic admirer of Johannes Kepler and made considerable improvements to the equation of motion of the Moon. He also noticed irregularities in the motion of Jupiter and Saturn. Erroneously, Horrocks believed that comets were blown out of the Sun, their velocities decreasing as they receded, but increasing again when they started to fall back. He was the first person to undertake a continuous series of tidal observations, hoping eventually to understand the underlying causes of these variations.

Horsley, Sir Victor Alexander Haden 1857–1916
English physiologist and surgeon

Born in Kensington, London, he studied medicine at University College there, becoming Professor of Physiology in 1893. He was elected FRS in 1886, and served as Fullerian Professor at the Royal Institution (1891–93). Knighted in 1902, he volunteered for military service at the outbreak of World War I in 1914 and died of heat exhaustion in Mesopotamia. He was an early pioneer of brain surgery, and accomplished distinguished work on the localization of brain function. Studies of cretinism enabled him to advance thyroid research, and he was one of the first to attempt surgery on a pituitary tumour.

Horta, Victor, Baron 1861–1947
Belgian architect

Born in Ghent, he was influenced by the 1878 Paris World's Fair, and wanted to create a true modern western architecture. His works in Brussels include the Hôtel Tassel (1892–93), which was at the same time individual and contemporary but conscious of tradition; the Hôtel Solvay (1894–1900), a luxurious design full of light and movement; and the Maison du Peuple (1895–99), a masterpiece in metal, glass and stone (demolished in 1964). He also designed the first department store, l'Innovation (1901), in Brussels. His popularity declined after 1900 but he is now recognized as a master, and regarded as one of the earliest and most original exponents of Art Nouveau.

Horthy (de Nagybánya), Miklós 1868–1957
Regent of Hungary

Born in Kenderes, he rose to the post of naval aide-de-camp to Emperor Franz Joseph. After his victory at Otranto (1917) he became Commander-in-Chief of the Austro-Hungarian fleet (1918). He was Minister of War in the counter-revolutionary 'white' government (1919), opposing Béla Kun's Communist regime in Budapest and suppressing it with Romanian help (1920). His aim of restoring the Habsburg monarchy proved unpopular and so he allowed himself to be proclaimed regent. He regained parts of Czechoslovakia and Romania for Hungary (1938–40). During the 1930s he ruled virtually as a dictator, but allowed some parliamentary forms. He disliked Hitler, but supported his crusade against Bolshevism, backing Germany's invasion of Yugoslavia and Russia until Hungary itself was overrun (March 1944). In October 1944 Horthy defied Hitler in broadcasting an appeal to the Allied powers for an armistice, and was imprisoned in the castle of Weilheim, Bavaria, where he fell into US hands (1945), and was set free the following year. He died in Estoril, Portugal, where he had lived since 1949. ⬚ Mario D Fenyo, *Hitler, Horthy, and Hungary* (1972)

Horton, Lester 1906–53
US dancer, choreographer and teacher
Born in Indianapolis, Indiana, he studied ballet with **Adolph Bolm** and was greatly influenced by Japanese movement theatre and Native American dancing. He went to California in 1928, where he formed a dance company in 1932, designing sets and costumes as well as devising dances, and opened his own theatre in 1948. A neck injury forced him to retire from performing in 1944, but he continued to choreograph and teach. He also worked in films and nightclubs.

Horváth, Mihály 1809–78
Hungarian prelate and revolutionary
Professor of Hungarian at Vienna (1844), and Bishop of Csanad (1848), he took an active part in the revolution of 1848 and became Minister of Education. After the revolution was crushed (1849) he lived in exile, but returned under the amnesty of 1867. He was the author of a history of Hungary.

Horváth, Ödön von 1901–38
Austro-Hungarian, German-speaking dramatist
He was born in Fiume (now Rijeka in Yugoslavia). After being banned by the Nazis in the 1930s, his plays remained neglected in Germany until the 1950s and were almost unknown in Great Britain until **Christopher Hampton** began translating them during the 1970s. *Ges Chichten aus dem Wiener Wald* (1931, Eng trans *Tales from the Vienna Woods*, 1977) presents a wry and resigned picture of lower middle-class life, while *Don Juan kommt aus dem Kreig* (1936, Eng trans *Don Juan Comes Back From The War*, 1978), portrays Don Juan as a disillusioned warrior. Throughout his writing, Horváth paints a critical picture of bourgeois greed and what he suggests is the herd-like stupidity of those seduced by economic or political lures. One day, during his exile in Paris, he sheltered from a storm beneath a tree in the Champs Elysées. When a branch snapped and struck him on the head, he died instantly. ⬚ I Huish, *A Student's Guide to Horvath* (1980)

Hosea 8th century BC
Biblical character and prophet
The son of Beeri, he lived during the heyday of the Assyrian Empire, during the reign of King **Sennacherib**, when the Classical era in Greece had just begun. He was a contemporary of **Isaiah** and prophesied in very troubled times; in a period of 25 years there were six kings of Israel, four of whom were murdered by their successors. Despite clear statements of unrest and disaster, his message was one of hope, forgiveness and the prediction of rich and safe times to come for his people.

Hoskins, Bob (Robert William) 1942–
English actor
Born in Bury St Edmunds, Suffolk, he was employed as a market porter, circus fire-eater, steeplejack and seaman, among numerous other occupations, before alighting on acting and making his debut in *Romeo and Juliet* (1969) at Stoke-on-Trent. Notable stage performances include *Richard III* (1971), *King Lear* (1971), *Veterans* (1972), *The Iceman Cometh* (1976) and *Guys and Dolls* (1981). His ebullient personality and stocky build lend themselves to exuberant comedy or hardhitting drama, and he achieved widespread public recognition with the television series *Pennies From Heaven* (1978) and as the menacing hoodlum in the film *The Long Good Friday* (1980). After several busy years as a reliable supporting actor in films he acquired international stardom with performances in *Mona Lisa*

(1986) and *Who Framed Roger Rabbit?* (1988). A familiar face on television commercials, he has also directed the films *The Raggedy Rawney* (1988) and *Rainbow* (1995). He returned to the stage in *Old Wicked Songs* (1996–97).

Hosokawa, Morihiro 1938–
Japanese politician
Born in Tokyo, he was educated at the Sophia University and after graduating took up a career in journalism with the *Daily Asahi Shimbun*. He was elected to the House of Councillors in 1971 as a Liberal Democrat and was appointed Governor of Kumamoto in 1983. After he founded the Japan New Party in 1992, he became Prime Minister of a coalition government in 1993, ending 38 consecutive years of rule by the Liberal Democratic Pary. As a believer in devolution he attempted to end Japan's tradition of centrist government by giving more authority to the regions.

Hotchkiss, Benjamin Berkeley 1826–85
US inventor
Born in Watertown, Connecticut, he devised an improved type of cannon shell, the Hotchkiss revolving-barrel machine gun (1872), and a magazine rifle (1875) widely used in the USA, France and Britain.

Hotspur See **Percy, Sir Henry**

Hotter, Hans 1909–
German bass-baritone
He was born in Offenbach-am-Main, near Frankfurt, and studied at Munich, where he sang regularly. He was noted especially for his Wagnerian roles, above all Wotan in the *Ring des Nibelungen*, and was a fine exponent of the German Lied, especially of **Schubert** and **Brahms**. He retired in 1972, but continued to make occasional appearances on the stage and in recitals.

Hou, Miss See **Bennett, Louise Simone**

Houbraken, Arnold 1660–1719
Dutch portrait and historical painter and art historian
He was born in Dordrecht. He is known for his biographies of Netherlandish painters (3 vols, 1718–21), an important source of information on 17th-century Netherlandish arts. His son, Jakob (1698–1780), was a copper-engraver.

Houdin, (Jean Eugène) Robert 1805–71
French conjurer
Born in Blois, he worked in Paris for several years making mechanical toys and automata, and gave magical soirées at the Palais Royal (1845–55). In 1856 he was sent by the government to Algiers to destroy the influence of the dervishes by exposing their pretended miracles. He is considered the father of modern conjuring.

Houdini, Harry, originally Erich Weiss 1874–1926
US magician and escape artist
He was born in Budapest, Hungary, and after his family emigrated to the USA he became a trapeze performer. He later gained an international reputation as an escape artist, freeing himself from handcuffs, shackles, and other devices, even while imprisoned in a box underwater or hanging upside-down in mid-air. He was a vigorous campaigner against fraudulent mediums, and was president of the Society of American Magicians. He died from peritonitis following a stomach injury incurred when punched, unprepared, by a member of the public who wanted to test his famous ability to withstand any blow.

Houdon, Jean Antoine 1741–1828
French sculptor

Born in Versailles, he won the Prix de Rome in 1761, then spent several years in Rome, where he executed the huge classical sculpture of *St Bruno* in Santa Maria degli Angeli. In 1785 he visited the USA to execute a monument to George Washington (Virginia), a bronze copy of which stands outside the National Gallery, London. His most famous busts are those of Diderot (1771), Voltaire (foyer of the Théâtre Français, Paris, and the Victoria and Albert Museum, London), Napoleon, Catherine the Great and Jean Jacques Rousseau (Louvre, Paris). He was appointed professor at the École des Beaux-Arts in 1805.

Houedard, Dom Sylvester, *pseudonym* dsh
1924–92
British poet, priest, Benedictine monk and scholar
Born in Guernsey, he was the literary editor for the *New Testament Jerusalem Bible* (1967), and at his death was completing the late George Melhuish's *On Death and the Double Nature of Nothingness*. He instigated the annual Interfaith conferences at the Samye Ling Monastery, Dumfriesshire, Scotland, and founded, with Bob Cobbing, *The Association of Little Presses* (1965). Under the pseudonym 'dsh' he published over 1,000 'typetracts' during the 1960s and 70s. These include *12 Nahuatl Dancepoems from the Cosmic Typewriter* (1969) and *Begin Again: a book of reflections & reversals* (1975). Notorious for his appearance in *The Times* (1967) advertisement for the legalization of cannabis and his attacks on anti-homosexual legislation throughout the 1980s, he is justly famous for his work in both Concrete and Sound-Poetry. ▢ S Bann (ed), *Concrete Poetry: An International Anthology* (1967)

Houghton, Sir John Theodore 1931–
Welsh physicist and meteorologist
Born in Dyserth Clwyd, he studied at Oxford and became Research Fellow at the Royal Aircraft Establishment, Farnborough (1955–58), then was appointed professor at the Department of Meteorology at Oxford, and director of the Appleton Laboratory (1979). He became director-general of the Meteorological Office in 1983. His important contributions to meteorology include the design of the selective chopper radiometer which can assess the atmospheric temperature structure at high altitudes. Further research led to the pressure modulator radiometer (1975), and stratospheric and mesospheric sounder (1978) which obtained the first global information on the structure of the middle atmosphere, and greatly increased our knowledge of atmospheric chemistry, radiation properties and dynamics. Houghton was also involved in NASA's first Venus orbiter, Pioneer 12 (1978). In 1990 he acted as Chairman of the Scientific Assessment Working Group of the Intergovernmental Panel on Climate Change which had a substantial influence on government policies worldwide. Since 1992 he has been Chairman of the Royal Commission on Environmental Pollution. He was elected Fellow of the Royal Society (1972), president of the Royal Meteorological Society (1976–78), chairman of the Joint Scientific Committee for the World Climate Research Programme (1981–84) and was a Symons gold medallist in 1991. He was knighted in 1991.

Houghton, 1st Baron See Milnes, Richard Monckton, 1st Baron Houghton

Houghton, (William) Stanley 1881–1913
English playwright and critic
Born in Ashton-under-Lyne, Greater Manchester, he was a drama critic for the *Manchester Guardian* when his first play, *The Dear Departed*, was staged at Annie Horniman's Gaiety Theatre in 1908. In the wake of Ibsen and George Bernard Shaw he wanted to encourage a new 'Manchester School' of northern realism. The best of Houghton's plays, therefore, reflect Lancashire working-class life and reject contemporary ideas of social respectability. The best-known is *Hindle Wakes* (1912), the heroine of which is

Fanny Hawthorne, a weaver at a cotton mill. Houghton's sympathetic portrayal of a woman determined to make her own choices and lead her own life caused the play to be highly controversial.

Hounsfield, Sir Godfrey Newbold 1919–
English electrical engineer and Nobel Prize winner
Born in Newark, Nottinghamshire, he studied at the City and Guilds and Faraday House colleges in London. He worked as a radar lecturer in the RAF during World War II, joined Thorn/EMI in 1951 and became head of medical systems research in 1972. He headed the team which, independently of Allan MacLeod Cormack, developed the technique of computer-assisted tomography (CAT scanning), which enables detailed X-ray pictures of slices of the human body to be produced. The first scanners were produced by EMI in the early 1970s. Hounsfield shared the 1979 Nobel Prize for physiology or medicine with Cormack, and was knighted in 1981.

Houphouët-Boigny, Felix 1905–93
Côte d'Ivoire (Ivory Coast) politician
Born in Yamoussoukro, he studied medicine in Dakar, Senegal, and practised as a doctor (1925–40). He then entered politics, sitting in the French Constitutional Assembly (1945–46) and the National Assembly (1946–59). During this period he served in the Cabinets of Pierre Pflimlin, de Gaulle and Michel Debré. When the Côte d'Ivoire achieved full independence in 1960, he became its first President. His paternalistic rule, which also combined close relations with France and support for capitalist enterprises, saw Côte d'Ivoire initially develop more successfully than most other West African countries, but economic decline and profligacy, especially the building of a palace and cathedral at Yamoussoukro, reduced his popularity.

Houseman, John, *originally* Jaques Haussman
1902–88
US stage director, producer, teacher and actor
He was born in Bucharest, Romania, and educated in England. He first worked as a producer in New York City (1934) and joined the Federal Theater Project in 1935. With Orson Welles, he founded the Mercury Theater in New York (1937), becoming editor of the Mercury Theater of the Air, and producing Welles's famous adaptation of H G Wells's *The War of the Worlds* (1938). He was artistic director of the US Shakespeare Festival at Stratford, Connecticut (1956–59), artistic director of the University of California Professional Theater Group (1959–64), and became producing director of APA Phoenix, New York (1967–68), director of the drama division of the Juilliard School of the Performing Arts, New York (1968–76), and artistic director of the City Center Acting Company, New York (1972–75). He made many film appearances, notably in *The Paper Chase* (1973), and wrote three volumes of autobiography: *Run-Through* (1972), *Front and Center* (1981) and *Final Dress* (1983).

Houshiary, Shirazeh 1955–
British sculptor
Born in Shiraz, Iran, she went to London in 1975, trained at the Chelsea School of Art, and became a junior Fellow at Cardiff College of Art (1979–80). She exhibited at the Venice Biennale in 1982 and in 1993, in the Art against Aids section. Her work shows the influence of Sufi poetry, especially that of Jalal ad-din Rumi, the 13th-century mystic, as in *The Earth is an Angel* (1987, Tate, London). Later work is more austere, focusing on geometric shapes, as in *The Enclosure of Sanctity* (1993, Tate). In 1994 she was shortlisted for the Turner Prize for her exhibitions in Newcastle, London, Canada and the USA.

Housman, A(lfred) E(dward) 1859–1936
English scholar and poet

Born in Fockbury, Worcestershire, he was the brother of **Laurence Housman**. Educated at Bromsgrove School and St John's College, Oxford, he failed his degree, but became a distinguished classical scholar, and was appointed Professor of Latin at University College London (1892), and at Cambridge (1911). He published critical editions of the Roman poet Marcus Manilius (1903–30), **Juvenal** (1905) and **Lucan** (1926). He is known primarily for his own poetry, notably *A Shropshire Lad* (1896), *Last Poems* (1922) and *More Poems*, published posthumously in 1936.
📖 l Kilvert, *A E Housman* (1955)

Housman, Laurence 1865–1959
English novelist and dramatist

He was born in Bromsgrove, Worcestershire, the younger brother of **A E Housman**. He studied art at Lambeth and South Kensington, and attracted attention by his illustrations of **George Meredith**'s poem 'Jump-to-Glory Jane'. He is best known for his *Little Plays of St Francis* (1922) and his Victorian biographical 'chamber plays', notably *Angels and Ministers* (1921) and *Victoria Regina* (1937). His novels included *Trimblerigg* (1924), a satire on **Lloyd George**, and he also published books of verse, including *An Englishwoman's Loveletters* (1900). His autobiography, *The Unexpected Years* (1937), reveals a conservative radical, who espoused pacifism and votes for women.

Houssay, Bernardo Alberto 1887–1971
Argentine physiologist and Nobel Prize winner

Born in Buenos Aires, he graduated from the school of pharmacy of the University of Buenos Aires aged 17. From 1909 he was Professor of Physiology at the veterinary school and later took on a private practice and the directorship of a municipal hospital service. He was Professor of Physiology at the medical school from 1919, but was dismissed after **Juan Perón** became President in 1946. He continued his research privately until reinstated in 1955. Houssay studied interactions between the pituitary gland and insulin, showing that the gland produces a hormone with the opposite effect to insulin, and that removing the gland from a diabetic animal reduces the severity of the diabetes. This work produced fundamental insights into the working of the endocrine system. He shared the 1947 Nobel Prize for physiology or medicine with **Carl** and **Gerty Cori**.

Houston, Edwin J(ames) 1847–1914
US electrical engineer

He was born in Alexandria, Virginia, and with **Elihu Thomson** invented the Thomson–Houston arc lighting, patented in 1881, which led to great improvements in lighting systems.

Houston, Sam(uel) 1793–1863
US soldier and politician

Born near Lexington, Virginia, he lived for three years among the Cherokee as a teenager, fought in the War of 1812 under **Andrew Jackson** and later studied law. He was elected a member of Congress in 1823 and 1825 as a Democrat from Tennessee, and in 1827 became Governor of Tennessee. In 1829 he returned to the Cherokee, being adopted into their nation and operating a trading post in their territory until 1832, when President Jackson sent him to negotiate with tribes in Texas. Caught up in the Texan struggle for independence, he led the force that overwhelmed the Mexican army under **Santa Anna** at San Jacinto (1836), and achieved Texan independence. He was elected the first President of the Republic of Texas (1836–38), was re-elected in 1841, and on the annexation of Texas, in 1845, returned to the US Senate (1846–59) and was elected Governor of Texas in

1859. He opposed secession, was deposed in 1861 for refusing to swear allegiance to the Confederacy, and retired to private life. Houston, Texas is named after him.

Houston, Whitney 1963–
US pop and soul singer

She was born in Newark, New Jersey, the daughter of singer Cissy Houston, and cousin of **Dionne Warwick**. She began her career as a gospel singer and partner to her mother, supplementing her income with modelling. Her debut album, *Whitney Houston* (1985), was a huge seller and helped her cross over to the pop market. In 1988 she had her seventh US number one with 'Where Do Broken Hearts Go', thus breaking the **Beatles**' record of six. 'I Will Always Love You' (1990), written by **Dolly Parton**, is her biggest success to date, boosted by her role in *The Bodyguard*, the film featuring the song. In 1996 she released a gospel-orientated album, recorded as a soundtrack to the film *The Preacher's Wife* (1996).

Howard
English Catholic family

It was founded by Sir William Howard, Chief Justice of Common Pleas (d.1308). His grandson, Sir John Howard, was a captain of the king's navy and sheriff of Norfolk, and Sir John Howard's grandson married the daughter of the 1st Duke of Norfolk and co-heiress of the House of Mowbray. In one or other of their widespead branches, the Howards have had, or still have, the earldoms of Carlisle, Suffolk, Berkshire, Northampton, Arundel, Wicklow, Norwich and Effingham, and the baronies of Bindon, Howard de Walden, Howard of Castle Rising, and Howard of Effingham.

Howard, Catherine See **Catherine Howard**

Howard, Charles, 1st Earl of Nottingham and 2nd Baron Howard of Effingham 1536–1624
English admiral

The son of Sir William Howard (c.1510–1573), he succeeded to his father's title in 1573 and became Lord High Admiral in 1585. A cousin of Queen **Elizabeth I**, he was Commander-in-Chief of the English fleet against the Spanish Armada (1588). In 1596 he led the expedition (with Robert Devereux, 2nd Earl of **Essex**) that sacked Cadiz. He was a commissioner at the trial of **Mary, Queen of Scots** (1586), and in 1601 quelled Essex's rebellion.

Howard, Sir Ebenezer 1850–1928
English town-planner and reformer

He emigrated to Nebraska in 1872 but returned to England in 1877 and became a parliamentary shorthand-writer. He later became the founder of the garden city movement; his *Tomorrow* (1898), later republished as *Garden Cities of Tomorrow* (1902), envisaged self-contained communities with both rural and urban amenities and green belts, and led to the formation in 1899 of the Garden City Association and to the laying out of Letchworth (1903) and Welwyn Garden City (1919) as prototypes. 📖 John Moss Eccardt, *Ebenezer Howard* (1973)

Howard, Henry See **Surrey, Henry Howard, Earl of**

Howard, Sir John, 1st Duke of Norfolk, *known as* Jack of Norfolk c.1430–1485
English nobleman

Edward IV made him Constable of Norwich Castle (1462), Sheriff of Norfolk and Suffolk, Treasurer of the Royal Household, and Lord Howard (1470). He was created Duke of Norfolk, Earl Marshal of England (a distinction still borne by his descendants), and Lord Admiral of England, Ireland and Aquitaine by **Richard III** (1483). He was killed at the Battle of Bosworth and his honours were attainted.

Howard, John 1726–90
English philanthropist and reformer

Born in Hackney, London, the son of an upholsterer, he was captured by the French and spent some time in Brest as a prisoner of war (1756). In 1773, as High Sheriff of Bedfordshire, he was appalled by conditions in Bedford gaol and undertook a tour of British prisons that led to two Acts of Parliament in 1774, one enforcing standards of cleanliness, and the other replacing prisoners' fees for jailers with official salaries. He travelled widely, and wrote *The State of Prisons in England and Wales, with an Account of some Foreign Prisons* (1777), and *An Account of the Principal Lazarettos in Europe* (1780). He died of typhus contracted while visiting a Russian military hospital at Kherson in the Crimea. The Howard League for Penal Reform, founded in 1866, was named after him. ◻ Joyce Godber, *John Howard the Philanthropist* (1977)

Howard, John Winston 1939–
Australian Liberal politician

Born in Sydney, he was educated at the University of Sydney. After graduating he worked as a lawyer, becoming a solicitor to the Supreme Court of New South Wales in 1962. In 1974 he entered politics as Liberal MP for Bennelong, New South Wales, and was appointed Minister for Business and Consumer Affairs in 1975. When in 1983 the Liberals lost power, he became deputy Leader of the Opposition and then its Leader (1985–89, 1995–96). In 1996 he became Prime Minister of Australia, leading the Liberal–National coalition government, and announced plans in 1997 to allow the country to vote on abolishing the Queen as head of state.

Howard, Leslie, *originally* Leslie Howard Stainer
1893–1943
English actor

Born in London, of Hungarian origin, he made his film debut in *The Heroine of Mons* (1914). Invalided home during World War I, he made his stage debut in *Peg o' My Heart* (1917), and concentrated on theatre work over the next decade, including appearances on Broadway. From 1930 he turned to films, often portraying scholarly and archetypically tweedy Englishmen. His many film successes include *Of Human Bondage* (1934), *Pygmalion* (1938), which he co-directed, and his best-known performance as Ashley Wilkes in *Gone With the Wind* (1939). He returned to Great Britain during World War II and produced and directed patriotic films, including *The First of the Few* (1942). Returning from Lisbon in 1943, his plane was shot down by the Nazis, who had believed Winston Churchill to be on board. Both his son, Ronald Howard (1918–), and nephew Alan Howard (1937–) also became actors.

Howard, Michael 1941–
British Conservative politician

Born in Gorseinon, South Wales, he was educated at Llanelli Grammar School and Peterhouse, Cambridge. After graduating he trained as a barrister and was appointed Queen's Counsel in 1982. In 1983 he was elected Conservative MP for Folkestone and Hythe. Following a number of successful junior ministerial appointments he became Secretary of State for Employment in 1990 and Secretary of State for the Environment in 1992. As Home Secretary (1993–97), he promoted controversial policies for stricter sentencing of offenders and the privatization of prison facilities. Following the Conservatives' defeat in the general election of 1997, he entered the contest for leadership of the party.

Howard, Oliver Otis 1830–1909
US Union soldier

Born in Leeds, Maine, he graduated from West Point in 1854. At the outbreak of the Civil War he took command of a regiment of Maine volunteers (1861). In 1864 he commanded the army of Tennessee, and led the right wing of General Sherman's army on the march to the sea. He was Commissioner of the Freedmen's Bureau (1865–74), and also first President of Howard University in Washington DC, which was named after him (1869–74). Later he returned to military service, and conducted two campaigns against the Native Americans (1877–78). He was superintendant at West Point (1880–82).

Howard, Thomas, 2nd Duke of Norfolk and 1st Earl of Surrey 1443–1524
English nobleman, soldier and politician

Born in Stoke-by-Nayland, Suffolk, the son of John Howard, 1st Duke of Norfolk, he fought for Richard III and was wounded and captured at Bosworth (1485), but after three years' imprisonment in the Tower of London, he was released and restored to his estates. Modest and humane, he was mainly a soldier. He put down a serious revolt in Yorkshire (1489) and, as Lieutenant-General of the North for Henry VIII, he decisively defeated the Scots at Flodden (1513) and was created Duke of Norfolk (1514). He distrusted the policies of Cardinal Wolsey and presided over the trial of Edward Stafford, Duke of Buckingham (1521).

Howard, Thomas, 3rd Duke of Norfolk
1473–1554
English nobleman and politician

The son of Thomas Howard, 2nd Duke of Norfolk, he married (1495) Anne (d.1512), daughter of Edward IV and sister-in-law of Henry VII. His second marriage (1513) was to Elizabeth (d.1558), daughter of Edward Stafford, 3rd Duke of Buckingham, who was executed by Henry VIII (1521). He held several high offices, including Lord High Admiral (1513), and Lord Lieutenant of Ireland (1520). As Lord Steward he presided over the trial for adultery of the queen, his niece Anne Boleyn (1536). He also put down the Pilgrimage of Grace (1536) and opposed Thomas Cromwell. He lost influence at court when another niece, Catherine Howard, Henry VIII's fifth wife, was also beheaded for adultery (1542). He was saved from death for treason by Henry VIII's own death (1547), but throughout the reign of Edward VI he was kept in prison; his eldest son, Henry Howard, Earl of Surrey, was executed by Henry VIII (1547). He was released by Mary I in 1553.

Howard, Thomas, 4th Duke of Norfolk
1536–72
English nobleman

The son of Henry Howard, Earl of Surrey, he succeeded his grandfather, the 3rd Duke, as duke and Earl Marshal (1554). After the death of successive wives, as a commissioner appointed to inquire into Scottish affairs, he was imprisoned (1569–70) for attempting to marry Mary, Queen of Scots. He was also involved in the Ridolfi plot with Philip II of Spain to free Mary, and was executed.

Howard, Trevor Wallace 1916–88
English actor

Born in Cliftonville, Kent, he studied at RADA, making his stage debut in *Revolt in a Reformatory* (1934). Exclusively a theatre performer until World War II, he was invalided out of the Royal Artillery, enjoyed West End success in *A Soldier for Christmas* (1944), and made his film debut in *The Way Ahead* (1944). His performance in *Brief Encounter* (1945) made him one of the most popular British actors, a position he held for some years. A dependable leading man, he was occasionally asked to portray cynicism or weakness, as in *The Third Man* (1949) and *The Heart of the Matter* (1953). Developing into a character actor of international stature, he was nominated for an Academy Award in *Sons and Lovers* (1960), but spent his later years largely in cameo roles in such films as *Mutiny on the Bounty* (1962), *Ryan's Daughter* (1970), *Conduct Unbecoming* (1975) and *White*

Mischief (1987). He reminded audiences of his under-used talents in television work such as *Catholics* (1973), and *Staying On* (1980), in which he starred with Celia Johnson, his co-star in *Brief Encounter*.

Howe, Clarence Decatur 1886–1960
Canadian businessman and politician

In 1936 he was appointed Minister of Transport in the Liberal government of Mackenzie King and played a major role in establishing Trans-Canada Airlines (later Air Canada). He proved his ability as an administrator during World War II as director of the Wartime Prices and Trade Board and Minister for Munitions and Supply. Faced with the refusal by private companies to produce synthetic rubber, he set up the Polymer Corporation as a Crown company. Its success, both financial and in research and development, enabled the government to refuse its competitors' demands to close it down. Although he always had little patience for politics and politicians, he became Minister of Reconstruction in Saint Laurent's administration in 1951, when the Defence Production Act gave him such wide economic powers that he became known as the 'Minister of Everything'. However, his management of the Trans-Canada Pipeline project, which he rammed through parliament in 1956 over outspoken opposition and charges that he had sold out the public interest to private US companies, marked the beginning of the end of more than 20 years of Liberal federal government and allowed the Conservatives a platform of reform on which they won the 1957 election.

Howe, Elias 1819–67
US inventor

Born in Spencer, Massachusetts, he worked as a mechanic in Lowell and Boston, where he constructed and patented (1846) the first sewing-machine. He made an unsuccessful visit to England to introduce his invention, and, returning in 1847 to Boston, found his patent had been infringed. Harassed by poverty, he entered on a seven years' war of litigation to protect his rights, was ultimately successful (1854), and amassed a fortune.

Howe (of Aberavon), (Richard Edward) Geoffrey Howe, Baron 1926–
British Conservative politician

Born in Port Talbot, Glamorgan, he was educated at Cambridge. He was called to the Bar in 1952 and first elected to parliament as a Conservative MP in 1964. Knighted in 1970, he was Solicitor-General from 1970 to 1972. In his four years as Chancellor of the Exchequer (1979–83), he successfully engineered a reduction in the rate of inflation. He became Foreign Secretary after the 1983 general election. In 1989, in a major Cabinet reshuffle, he was moved from the Foreign Office to the leadership of the House of Commons (with the title of Deputy Prime Minister) following policy disagreements with Margaret Thatcher over European monetary union. A year later, he resigned in protest at her continuing intransigence, and his highly critical speech to the House in October 1990 heightened the party split that contributed to Thatcher's downfall and replacement by John Major. In 1991, he announced his decision not to continue as an MP after the next general election. He was made a life peer in 1992 and his memoirs, *Conflict of Loyalties*, were published in 1994.

Howe, Gordie (Gordon) 1928–
Canadian ice-hockey player

He was born in Floral, Saskatchewan. During his career in the National Hockey League (NHL), he set records for scoring the most goals (801) and most points (1,850), playing the most seasons (26) and most games (1,767). He was the first player to score 1,000 career major league goals but his all-time goals-scoring record was broken by

Wayne Gretzky in 1994. He began playing with the Detroit Red Wings (1946–71), joined the World Hockey Association Houston Aeros (1973–77) and New England (then Hartford, NHL) Whalers (1977–80), and was a six-time winner of the Hart Trophy as the NHL's Most Valuable Player (1952–53, 1957–58, 1960, 1963).

Howe, Irving 1920–93
US critic

Born in New York City, the son of Ukrainian immigrants, he grew up speaking Yiddish and learned English as a second language on the streets and in school. He graduated from the College of the City of New York in 1940 and was Professor of English at several universities, including Brandeis (1953–61), Stanford (1961–63) and the City University of New York (1963–86). He came to prominence in the 1950s as a social and literary critic and a member of the anti-Communist left, and after co-founding the political magazine *Dissent* in 1953, served as its editor for four decades. His best-known book is *World of Our Fathers* (1976), a classic study of Eastern European Jewish immigrants in the USA. He also produced such critical works as *Politics and the Novel* (1957), edited anthologies of Yiddish literature, and wrote an autobiography, *Margin of Hope* (1982).

Howe, Joseph 1804–73
Canadian statesman

Born in Nova Scotia, he was proprietor and editor of the Halifax *Nova Scotian*. He became premier of Nova Scotia (1863–70), and after federation entered the first Canadian government at Ottawa.

Howe, Julia Ward, *née* Ward 1819–1910
US feminist, reformer and writer

Born in New York, a wealthy banker's daughter, she became a prominent suffragette and abolitionist, and founded the New England Woman Suffrage Association (1868) and the New England Women's Club (1868). She published several volumes of poetry, including *Passion Flowers* (1854) and *Words for the Hour* (1857), as well as travel books and a play. She also wrote the 'Battle Hymn of the Republic' (1862, published in *Atlantic Monthly*), and edited *Woman's Journal* (1870–90). In 1908 she became the first woman to be elected to the American Academy of Arts and Letters. She was married to Samuel Gridley Howe.
📖 L Richards, *Julia Ward Howe* (1916)

Howe, Richard Howe, 1st Earl 1726–99
English admiral

Born in London, the brother of William, 5th Viscount Howe, he joined the navy at 13, and distinguished himself in the Seven Years War (1756–63). He became a Lord of the Admiralty (1763), Treasurer of the Navy (1765), First Lord of the Admiralty (1783), and earl (1788). In 1776 he was appointed commander of the British fleet during the American Revolution and, in 1778, defended the North American coast against a superior French force. On the outbreak of war with France (1793), he took command of the Channel fleet, defeating the French off Ushant at the Battle of the Glorious First of June (1794).

Howe, Samuel Gridley 1801–76
US reformer and philanthropist

He was born in Boston. In the Greek War of Independence (1821–31) he organized the medical staff of the Greek army (1824–27), went to the USA to raise contributions and, returning with supplies, formed a colony on the Isthmus of Corinth. Swamp fever drove him from the country in 1830. In 1831 he went to Paris to study the methods of educating the blind, and, becoming involved in the Polish insurrection, spent six weeks in a Prussian prison. On his return to Boston he established the Perkins School for the Blind, and taught Laura Bridgman, among others. Also concerned with the education of the mentally ill, he was a prison reformer and an abolitionist, and from 1851 to 1853 edited the antislavery *Commonwealth*. He was the husband of Julia Ward Howe.

Howe, William Howe, 5th Viscount 1729–1814
English soldier

Brother of Richard, 1st Earl Howe, he served under Wolfe at Louisburg (1758) and at Quebec (1759), where he led the famous advance to the Heights of Abraham. In the American Revolution (1776–83) he won the victory at Bunker Hill (1775) and became Commander-in-Chief. Supported from the sea by his sailor-brother, in 1776 he captured Brooklyn, New York, and, after the victory of White Plains, Washington, the following year defeated the Americans at Brandywine Creek. He was replaced by Sir Henry Clinton in 1778 after failure at Valley Forge. 📖 Ira D Gruber, *The Howe Brothers and the American Revolution* (1972)

Howell, James c.1593–1666
Anglo-Welsh writer

Born probably in Abernant, Carmarthenshire, he studied at Oxford, travelled abroad on business, and in 1627 entered parliament. From 1632 to 1642 he was a Royalist spy, and during the Civil War was imprisoned by parliament (1642–50). At the Restoration he became Historiographer Royal. As well as translations from Italian, French and Spanish, and works on history, politics and philosophy, he wrote *Instructions for Forreine Travell* (1642), a supplement to Randle Cotgrave's French–English dictionary, and the witty *Epistolae Ho-Elianae; or Familiar Letters* (1645–55).

Howells, Herbert 1892–1983
English composer

Born in Lydney, Gloucestershire, he studied under Charles Stanford at the Royal College of Music, where he became Professor of Composition (1920) after a short time as sub-organist of Salisbury Cathedral. In 1936 he followed Gustav Holst as director of music at St Paul's Girls' School, and in 1952 became Professor of Music at London University, retiring in 1962, though he continued to teach there until well into his eighties. He is best known for his choral works, especially the *Hymnus Paradisi* (1938, 'Hymn of Paradise'), which combine an alert sense of 20th-century musical developments with a firm foundation in the English choral tradition.

Howells, William Dean 1837–1920
US novelist and critic

Born in Martin's Ferry, Ohio, the son of an itinerant printer, he worked as a compositor for the *Ohio State Journal* (1856–61). Stimulated by the works of Cervantes, Pope and Heinrich Heine, he began to write poetry, some of which was published in the *Atlantic Monthly*, of which he later became editor (1871–81). His biography of Abraham Lincoln (1860) procured for him the post of US consul in Venice (1861–65). His editorship at *Harper's Magazine* (1886–91) made him the king of critics in the USA, and his 'Easy Chair' column for the magazine (1900–20) was also widely read. A champion of Realism in US literature, he wrote numerous novels, of which the best remembered are *A Modern Instance* (1882), *The Rise of Silas Lapham* (1885) and *A Hazard of New Fortunes* (1890). His theories of fiction, which influenced Mark Twain, Henry James and Stephen Crane, were expounded in *Criticism and Fiction* (1891). He also wrote the autobiographical *Years of my Youth* (1915) and *Literary Friends* (1900). 📖 K S Lynn, *William Dean Howells: an American life* (1971)

Howerd, Frankie, *originally* Francis Alex Howard 1917–92
English comedian and actor

Born in London, he made his debut at the Stage Door Canteen, Piccadilly, London, in 1946, and appeared in revues in London during the 1950s, including *Out of This World* (1950), *Pardon My French* (1953), and *Way Out In Piccadilly* (1960). He occasionally acted in plays and gave a notable performance in Stephen Sondheim's musical, *A Funny Thing Happened on the Way to the Forum* (1963). He appeared in the radio show *Variety Bandbox* (1946–47) and on television in the *Howerd Crowd* (1952), *Frankie Howerd* (1964–65), *The Frankie Howerd Show* (1969) and, most memorably, as Roman slave Lurcio in *Up Pompeii!* (1969–70), which spawned three film spin-offs, *Up Pompeii* (1971), *Up the Chastity Belt* (1971) and *Up the Front* (1972). His other films included *The Ladykillers* (1955), *The Fast Lady* (1962), *The Mouse on the Moon* (1963), *Carry On Doctor* (1967) and *The House in Nightmare Park* (1973).

Howlin' Wolf, *stage name of* Chester Arthur Burnett 1910–76
US blues singer, guitarist and harmonica player

Born in West Point, Mississippi, he began playing blues as a child, and was able to amalgamate several strains of country and urban blues into a distinctive, individual style. He was already a mature artist before recording his first record in Memphis in 1951, and settled in Chicago in 1953, where he was a giant (physically as well as metaphorically) of the emerging electric blues scene. He was one of the most intensely exciting of all blues performers, and recorded a number of classics of the genre, many of which were later covered by rock bands like The Rolling Stones and The Doors in the 1960s. Despite failing health after a car crash in 1970, he continued to perform until shortly before his death.

How-Martyn, Edith, *née* How c.1875–1954
English suffragette

Born in Cheltenham, she was educated at the North London Collegiate School for Girls, at University College, Aberystwyth, and London University. She was the secretary of the Women's Social and Political Union (1906–07), but left to co-found the Women's Freedom League with Charlotte Despard and Teresa Billington-Greig. She stood unsuccessfully for parliament as an independent candidate representing feminist issues (1918) when the franchise was extended to include property-owning women over the age of 30. In 1919 she became the first woman member of Middlesex Council. As founder of the Birth Control International Information Centre (1929) she travelled widely lecturing on women's issues, and published *The Birth Control Movement in England* (1931).

Hoxha *or* Hodja, Enver 1908–85
Albanian politician

Born in Gjirokastër and educated in France, he founded and led the Albanian Communist Party (1941) in the fight for national independence when the country was overrun by Germans and Italians during World War II, adopting a guerrilla warfare strategy. In 1946 he deposed King Zog (who had fled in 1939) and became effective head of state, holding the positions of Prime Minister (1944–54), Foreign Minister (1946–53) and Supreme Commander of the Armed Forces (1946–54). From 1954, Hoxha controlled the political scene through his position as First Secretary of the Albanian Party of Labour (Communist Party), and instituted a rigid Stalinist programme of thorough nationalization and collectivization which left Albania with the lowest per capita income in Europe on his death. A major secularization drive was also launched, while, in its external relations, an isolationist policy, independent of both Soviet and Chinese communism, was pursued. 📖 Jon Halliday (ed), *The Artful Albanian: Memoirs of Enver Hoxha* (1986)

Ho Xuan Huong fl.c.1780–c.1820
Vietnamese poet

Her precise identity is unknown—we know from her work that Ho is her real family name, but Xuan Huong is a pseudonym. An educated, cultured woman, she produced some of the most sensuous, witty and readable verse to come out of Asia in the 19th century. Typically, a poem by Ho will pretend to be about a harmless domestic activity (weaving or making rice cakes), which will make it seem innocent, but there is a second level of meaning, usually sexual. She argues in her verse that the sexes should be more equal, and often comes out against marriage, saying that love between men and women should be freely given.

Hoyland, John 1934–
English painter

Born in Sheffield, he studied at the Art College there (1951–56) and at the Royal Academy schools in London (1956–60), and has held numerous teaching posts, including principal lecturer at the Chelsea School of Art. He won an international Young Artists prize in Tokyo in 1964. In the USA in the same year he met 'Colour Field' painters like **Morris Louis** and turned to hard-edge abstraction, using broad, freely-painted rectangles of rich flat colour, often untitled, but dated, as in *28.5.66* (1966, Tate, London) and *17.7.69* (1969, Waddington Galleries, London). From the late 1970s he explored the physical nature of paint, employing heavy impasto to create a three-dimensional canvas, with geometric shapes, as for example in *Billy's Blues, 6.7.79* (private collection). He was made an RA in 1991. ⌨ Mel Gooding, *John Hoyland* (1990)

Hoyle, Edmond 1672–1769
English authority on card games, the 'Father of Whist'

His popular *A Short Treatise on the Game of Whist* (1742) systematized the rules of the game and remained the standard until the rules were changed in 1864. In 1748 he added manuals on backgammon, brag, quadrille, piquet and chess into an omnibus volume, *Hoyle's Standard Games*. The weight of his authority gave rise to the expression 'according to Hoyle' as an idiom for correct usage.

Hoyle, Sir Fred 1915–
English astronomer and mathematician

Born in Bingley, Yorkshire, he was educated at Bingley Grammar School and Emmanuel College, Cambridge. He taught mathematics at Cambridge (1945–58), was Plumian Professor of Astronomy and Experimental Philosophy there (1958–72), and was professor-at-large at Cornell University (1972–78). He is currently the Honorary Resident Professor at both Manchester University (1972–) and University College, Cardiff (1975–). In 1948, with **Hermann Bondi** and **Thomas Gold**, he propounded the influential but now descredited 'steady state' theory of the universe, which proposed that the universe is uniform in space and unchanging in time. He also suggested the currently accepted scenario of the build-up to supernovae, in which a chain of nuclear reactions in a star is followed by a massive explosion, in which matter is ejected into space, and recycled in second-generation stars which form from the remnants. His books include *Nature of the Universe* (1952) and *Frontiers of Astronomy* (1955). He also wrote science fiction, including *The Black Cloud* (1957), *A is for Andromeda* (1962, with J Elliot), and *The Molecule Men* (1971, with G Hoyle), and has written stories for children and two volumes of autobiography, *The Small World of Fred Hoyle* (1986) and *Home is Where the Wind Blows* (1994).

Hoyte, (Hugh) Desmond 1929–
Guyanese politician

Born in Georgetown, he studied at London University and the Middle Temple, taught in a boys' school in Grenada (1955–57) and then practised as a lawyer in Guyana. He joined the socialist People's National Congress Party (PNC) and in 1968, two years after Guyana achieved full independence, was elected to the National Assembly. He held a number of ministerial posts before becoming Prime Minister under **Forbes Burnham**. On Burnham's death, in 1985, he succeeded him as President, remaining in office until 1992.

Hrawi, Elias 1930–
Lebanese statesman

A Maronite Christian, he was born in Zahle in the Bekaa Valley. He became a businessman and a deputy of the National Assembly, until in 1989 he succeeded Rene Mouawad as President of Lebanon under the Lebanese constitutional arangement of 1943 which provides for a Maronite Christian President and Sunni Moslem Prime Minister. Mouawad had been assassinated after only 17 days in office. In 1995 the term of the presidency (six years) was extended by a further three years to allow Hrawi to continue.

Hrdlička, Aleš 1869–1943
US physical anthropologist

Born in Humpolec, Bohemia, he studied medicine in the USA and was on the staff of the American Museum of Natural History, New York City (1899–1903), and then the National Museum, Washington DC (1903–43). His anthropological studies of Native Americans led to his being one of the first to propose that their racial origins lay in Asia.

Hromadka, Josef Luki 1889–1969
Czech Reformed theologian

Born in Hodslavice, Moravia, he studied at Basle, Heidelberg, Vienna, Prague, and at the United Free Church College, Aberdeen, and was theological professor at Prague (1920–39) and at Princeton Theological Seminary (1939–47). Thereafter, he returned to Czechoslovakia and became dean of the Comenius faculty, Prague, in 1950. Active in the World Council of Churches from its inception, he contributed much to Christian–Marxist dialogue, and received the Lenin Peace Prize in 1958. He died a few months after the Russians invaded his homeland, an act against which he protested, causing his resignation from the Christian Peace Conference which he had founded. His major writings in English include *Masaryk* (1930), *Christianity in Thought and Life* (1931), *Luther* (1935), *Calvin* (1936), *The Gospel for Atheists* (1958) and *My Life between East and West* (1969).

Hrostwitha, also Roswita, Roswitha, Hroswita or Hroswitha fl.10th century
German playwright

A Benedictine nun of Gandersheim, near Göttingen, she wrote six comedies in Latin (*Gallicanus*, *Dulcitus*, *Callimachus*, *Abraham*, *Pafnutius*, and *Sapientia*) which are closely modelled on the work of **Terence**, but are Christian in theme. As the first known plays by a woman, they are of great historical importance. The verse in which they are written is lively and witty, and revival of her works is long-overdue.

Hrozny, Bedřich 1879–1952
Czech orientalist and archaeologist

Born in Lissa, he became a professor at Vienna (1905–19) and Prague (1919–52), and was the first to decipher the Hittite language. He excavated Hittite sites at Boğazköy, Turkey, and wrote *Die Sprache der Hethiter* (1917, 'Language of the Hittites').

Hsia Kuei See **Xia Gui**

Hsiao-p'ing, Teng See **Deng Xiaoping**

Hsüan Tsang See **Xuan Zang**

Hsü Pei-hung See **Xu Beihong**

Hua Guofeng (Hua Kuo-feng) 1920–
Chinese politician

Born in Hunan province into a poor peasant family, he fought under Zhu De during the liberation war of 1937–49, before later rising up the official ranks of the Communist Party (CCP) during the 1950s and 1960s in Mao Zedong's home province of Hunan, eventually becoming local first secretary in 1970. Viewed as an orthodox and loyal Maoist, Hua, despite his relative inexperience, was selected to succeed Zhou Enlai as Prime Minister in January 1976, and succeeded Mao as party leader on the latter's death in September 1976. He dominated Chinese politics during 1976–77, seeking economic modernization along traditional 'extensivist' lines, although also aiming at a greater opening-up of the country to external Western contacts. From 1978, however, he was gradually eclipsed by the reformist Deng Xiaoping, being replaced as Prime Minister and CCP Chairman by the latter's protégés, Zhao Ziyang and Hu Yaobang, in 1980 and 1981 respectively.

Huang-Ti See Shih Huang Ti

Huang Zongxi (Huang Tsung-hsi) 1610–95
Chinese scholar

He was celebrated for his opposition to the Manchu Qing (Ch'ing) Dynasty and in 1644 joined the resistance movement in the south loyal to the previous Ming Dynasty. However, he retired to a life of scholarship after 1649, refusing to accept an official position from the new dynasty. His critique of imperial absolutism, written in 1662, exerted a considerable influence on early 20th century Chinese reformers and revolutionaries.

Hubbard, L(afayette) Ron(ald) 1911–86
US science-fiction writer and founder of the Church of Scientology

He was born in Tilden, Nebraska, and from the age of 16 travelled extensively in the Far East before completing his education at George Washington University. He became a professional writer of adventure stories, turning to science fiction in 1938, with such classics as *Slaves of Sleep* (1939) and *Typewriter in the Sky* (1940). He served in the US navy during World War II, and in 1950 published *Dianetics: The Modern Science of Mental Health*, followed by *Science of Survival* (1951), which formed the basis of the Scientology philosophy which has made a significant impact on many US artists. The first Church of Scientology was founded by a group of adherents in Los Angeles in 1954 and Hubbard became the executive director of the Founding Church, Washington (1955–66). From 1959 to 1966 his base was in East Grinstead, England. He resigned his position as executive director of the church in 1966. In 1982 he returned to science fiction with an epic bestseller, *Battlefield Earth: A Saga of the Year 3000*, followed by a 10-volume series under the composite title *Mission Earth* (1985–87). 📖 R Miller, *Bare-Faced Messiah: the true story of L Ron Hubbard* (1987)

Hubble, Edwin Powell 1889–1953
US astronomer

Born in Marshfield, Missouri, he studied mathematics and astronomy at the University of Chicago and law as a Rhodes scholar at Oxford (1910–13). He returned to Chicago University, and to astronomy, and held a research position at its Yerkes Observatory (1914–17). Following military service during World War I, he moved in 1919 to the Carnegie Institution's Mount Wilson Observatory, where he began his fundamental investigations of the realm of the nebulae. He found that spiral nebulae are independent stellar systems and that the Andromeda nebula in particular is very similar to our own Milky Way galaxy. In 1929 he announced his discovery that galaxies recede from us with speeds which increase with their distance. This was the phenomenon of the expansion of the universe, the observational basis of modern cosmology. The linear relation between speed of recession and distance is known as Hubble's law. Hubble remained on the staff of Mount Wilson until his death. The 2.4m aperture Hubble Space Telescope, launched in 1990 in the space shuttle Discovery, was named in his honour.

Hubel, David Hunter 1926–
US neurophysiologist and Nobel Prize winner

Born in Windsor, Ontario, in Canada, he studied medicine at McGill University in Montreal, and was naturalized in 1953. After holding positions at Johns Hopkins Medical School (where he met Torsten Wiesel) he worked at the Walter Reed Army Research Institute in Washington DC, examining the electrical activity of the brain (1955–58). In 1959 he went to Harvard, where he held the posts of Professor of Neurophysiology (1965–77), Professor of Physiology and Chemistry (1967–68), and Professor of Neurobiology (1968–82). Since 1982 he has been John Franklin Enders University Professor. With Wiesel at Harvard Medical School, he investigated the mechanisms of visual perception, and they shared the 1981 Nobel Prize for physiology or medicine with Roger Sperry. Working on anaesthetized animals Hubel and Wiesel implanted electrodes into the brain, and then analysed individual cell responses to different types of visual stimulation, providing a complex picture of the sophisticated analysis of visual information by brain cells. His published work includes *Eye, Brain and Vision* (1987).

Huber, Eugen 1849–1923
Swiss jurist

A professor of law at Basle from 1880 and at Bern from 1892, he wrote *System und Geschichte des schweizerische Privatrechts* (1886–93) and other works on law. He was draftsman of the Swiss Civil Code which came into force in 1912.

Huber, Robert 1937–
German biophysicist and Nobel Prize winner

He was born and received his early training in Munich, remaining there as a lecturer (1968–76) and associate professor from 1976. Since 1972 he has been director of the Max Planck Institute for Biochemistry in Martinsried. A specialist in the high-resolution X-ray crystallography of biological macromolecules, he demonstrated that enzyme activation is not associated with a marked structural change (1972), and in 1974 helped elucidate the antibody structure proposed by Rodney Porter, including the molecular arrangement of the antigen binding site. In 1978 he performed a high-resolution analysis of the interaction between the digestive protease trypsin and the pancreatic trypsin inhibitor. Since 1979 he has studied the enzyme glutathione peroxidase, and contributed to the understanding of protein–DNA interactions. He has also collaborated with Hartmut Michel and Johann Deisenhofer (from 1982) to determine the structure of the reaction centre of the purple bacterium *Rhodopseudomonas viridis*, work for which they shared the 1988 Nobel Prize for chemistry.

Huber, Ulricus 1636–94
Dutch judge and jurist

Professor at Franeker, Utrecht and Leyden, and a judge in Friesland, he wrote *De jure civitatis* (1682), *Heedendaagse Rechtsgeleertheyt* (1686, Eng trans *Jurisprudence of My Time*, 1939), *Praelectiones juris civilis* (1687) and other works, many of which have been influential in South Africa.

Hubert, St 656–727
Frankish prelate
He was the son of the Duke of Guienne. He lived a luxurious life, but was converted to Christianity and in 708 became Bishop of Liège. Patron saint of hunting, in art he is a hunter converted by the apparition of a crucifix between the horns of a stag. This story may have been borrowed from St Eustace. His feast day is 3 November.

Huc, Evariste Régis 1813–60
French missionary
Born in Toulouse, he joined the mission of the Lazarist Fathers to China in 1839, and in 1844, with Père Gabet and a single native convert, he set out for Tibet. They reached Lhasa in January 1846, but had only just started a mission there when an order for their expulsion was obtained by the Chinese imperial commissioners, and they were escorted back to Canton. Huc's health broke down, and he returned to France in 1852. He wrote *Souvenirs d'un voyage dans la Tartarie, le Tibet et le Chine* (1850, 'Memories of a Journey in Tartary, Tibet and China').

Huc, Phillippe See Derème, Tristan

Huch, Ricarda 1864–1947
German novelist, historian and feminist
Born in Brunswick, she studied history at Zurich and taught at a girls' school there, then travelled extensively in Italy, married (unhappily) twice, and finally settled in Munich in 1910. A neo-Romantic, she rejected naturalism, and wrote novels including the semi-autobiographical *Erinnerungen von Ludolf Ursleu dem Jüngeren* (1893, 'Memoirs of Ludolf Ursleu the Younger') and *Aus der Triumphgasse* (1902, 'Out of Triumph Lane'). Her criticism includes *Die Blütezeit, Ausbreitung und Verfall der Romantik* (1899–1902, 'The Blossoming, Spread and Decline of Romanticism'), and she wrote social and political works, such as *Der Grosse Krieg in Deutschland* (1912–14, 'The Great War in Germany'). She also wrote on religious themes, in *Luthers Glaube* (1915, 'Beliefs of Luther') and *Das Zeitalter der Glaubenspaltung* (1937, 'The Age of Schism'). The first woman to be admitted to the Prussian Academy of Literature in 1931, she resigned in 1933 over the expulsion of Jewish writers. She lived in Jena during World War II. 📖 H Baumgarten, *Ricarda Huch* (1968)

Hückel, Erich 1896–1980
German physicist and theoretical chemist
Born in Berlin-Charlottenburg, he studied physics and mathematics at the University of Göttingen from 1914 to 1921, before becoming assistant to Peter Debye in Zurich. He then became successively instructor in physics at the Technische Hochschule, Stuttgart, Extraordinary Professor at Phillips University, Marburg (1935–37), and Professor of Theoretical Physics there (1937–61). Hückel's research interests were almost entirely in chemical physics. After work on strong electrolytes and interionic forces (resulting in the Debye–Hückel theory, 1923), his interests moved to the quantum-mechanical treatment of organic molecules. In 1937 he developed a procedure for calculating electron distribution and other characteristics of unsaturated compounds, Hückel molecular orbital (HMO) theory, which still finds application today.

Hudd, Roy 1936–
English actor and comedian
Born in Croydon, Surrey, he grew up on music-hall entertainment, played banjo and sang in clubs, before becoming a holiday-camp entertainer. Fame came as half of the comedy duo Hudd and Kay. After turning solo, he became a regular on the radio show *Workers' Playtime* and has had a long career in radio with programmes such as *The News Huddlines* (1976–). His big break came in 1964 with the satirical BBC television series *Not So Much a Programme, More a Way of Life*. He has since had his own series, *Hudd*, and played character roles in the Dennis Potter serials *Lipstick on Your Collar* (1993) and *Karaoke* (1996).

Huddleston, (Ernest Urban) Trevor 1913–98
English Anglican missionary
Educated at Christ Church, Oxford, and ordained in 1937, he entered the Community of the Resurrection and in 1943 went to Johannesburg, where he ultimately became provincial of the order (1949–55). From 1956 to 1958 he was novice-master of the Community in Mirfield, Yorkshire, and then prior of its London House (1958–60). He was then Bishop of Masasi, Tanzania (1960–68), Bishop Suffragan of Stepney (until 1978), and Bishop of Mauritius and Archbishop of the Indian Ocean (1978–83). After his retirement he became chairman of the Anti-Apartheid movement (1981–94) and Chairman of the International Defence and Air Fund for Southern Africa (1983–98). He was distinguished by a passionate belief that the doctrine of the universal brotherhood of men in Christ should be universally applied. His book, *Naught for your Comfort* (1956), reflects this conviction in the light of his experiences in South Africa and its racial problems and policies. He also wrote *God's World* (1966), *I Believe: Reflections on the Apostles' Creed* (1986) and *Return to South Africa* (1991).

Hudson, George, *known as* the Railway King 1800–71
English businessman and politician
Born near York, he was a linen-draper there when, inheriting £30,000 in 1828, he went into local politics and invested heavily in the North Midland Railway, making York a major railway centre. He bought large estates, was three times Lord Mayor of York, and was elected MP for Sunderland (1845), but the railway mania of 1847–48 plunged him into ruin. He was accused of fraudulent accounting and of having paid dividends out of capital, and was prosecuted. Sunderland, however, continued to elect him as MP until 1859.

Hudson, Henry c.1550–1611
English navigator
In 1607 he set sail in the *Hopewell*, on his first voyage for the English Muscovy Company, to seek a north-east passage across the North Pole to China and the Far East. He reached Spitsbergen and (probably) Jan Mayen Island. On his second voyage (1608) he reached Novaya Zemlya. He undertook a third voyage in 1609 for the Dutch East India Company, on the *Half Moon*, discovered the Hudson River, and followed it for 150 miles (241.5km), to Albany. In April 1610 he set out on the *Discovery* with a crew of 20 and his 12-year-old son, and reached Greenland in June, arriving at the waters now named after him, Hudson Strait and Hudson Bay. However, in November his ship was trapped in ice on the south of Hudson Bay. During the winter he was accused of distributing food unfairly, and when the ice began to break up, the men mutinied. On 23 June, Hudson and his son, with seven others, were cast adrift in an open boat, and never seen again. 📖 Llewelyn Powys, *Henry Hudson* (1928)

Hudson, 'Sir' Jeffery 1619–82
English dwarf
Born a butcher's son in Oakham, Rutland, he was court dwarf to Queen Henrietta Maria, and served as Captain of Horse at the start of the Civil War. In the 1650s he spent some time as a slave of the Barbary pirates. He was imprisoned in 1679 as a Catholic over the Popish Plot, but was soon released.

Hudson, Manley Ottmer 1886–1960
US judge and jurist

Born in St Peters, Missouri, he was educated at West Jewell College and Harvard, and became a professor at Harvard. He was a member of the Permanent Court of Arbitration at The Hague (1933–45), a judge of the Permanent Court of International Justice (1936–46), and became chairman of the International Law Commission. His works include *The Permanent Court of International Justice* (2nd edn, 1943), and he edited many volumes of cases and legislation on international law, including the *American Journal of International Law* (1924–60).

Hudson, Thomas 1701–79
English portrait painter

Born in London, he was a fashionable artist, now best known as the teacher of Sir Joshua Reynolds. He was the busiest portrait painter in London from c.1745 until 1755, when he retired, probably due to the competition provided by his former pupil.

Hudson, William 1734–93
English botanist and apothecary

Born and educated in Kendal, Cumbria, he was apprenticed to a London apothecary before working from 1757 to 1758 as sub-librarian at the British Museum. In 1762, whilst an apothecary in Haymarket, London, he published his *Flora Anglica*, the first British botanical work to adopt the classification system of Carolus Linnaeus. Hudson was later *praefector horti* to the Apothecaries' Company at Chelsea Physic Garden (1765–67).

Hudson, Sir William 1896–1978
New Zealand hydro-electric engineer

Born in Nelson, South Island, he served in World War I, joined the Armstrong Whitworth Company and worked for five years on hydro-electric schemes in New Zealand, then worked in Australia until 1930. Between 1931 and 1937 he was in charge of the Galloway hydro-electric scheme in Scotland before returning to Sydney, eventually to head the Metropolitan Water Board. In 1949 he was appointed Commissioner of the Snowy Mountains Hydro-Electric Authority in southern New South Wales, one of the 'seven engineering wonders of the world'. This scheme involved the construction of 16 dams, seven power stations, and 93 miles (150km) of tunnels. That the project was completed ahead of time in 1973 was due to Hudson's leadership, although he had retired six years previously. He was knighted in 1955.

Hudson, W(illiam) H(enry) 1841–1922
British writer and naturalist

Born near Buenos Aires, of American parents who had moved to Argentina to farm, he settled in England in 1869 and became a British subject in 1900. His early writings such as *The Naturalist in La Plata* (1892), concerned the natural history of South America, but he is remembered for his delightful account of his rambles in the New Forest in *Hampshire Days* (1903) and his romantic novel *Green Mansions* (1904). Other books include *A Shepherd's Life* (1910). His ornithological works include *Birds in London* (1898), *Birds of La Plata* (1920), and *Rare, vanishing and lost British Birds* (1923). A bird sanctuary, containing Sir Jacob Epstein's sculpture of Rima (a character from *Green Mansions*), was erected to his memory in Hyde Park, London (1925).

Hueffer, Francis 1845–89
British music critic

Born in Westphalia, Germany, he became the son-in-law of Ford Madox Brown. He settled in London in 1869 and as music critic of *The Times* championed *Richard Wagner and the Music of the Future* (1874).

Huerta, Victoriano 1854–1916
Mexican dictator

Born in Colotlán, Jalisco state, he was a Huichol Indian who joined the Mexican army and advanced to the rank of general during the dictatorship of Porfirio Díaz. After Díaz went into exile, Huerta became an ally of liberal President Francisco Madero, commanding the federal forces that suppressed the uprisings of Emiliano Zapata (1911) and others. In 1913, however, he overthrew Madero's regime and declared himself President of Mexico, dissolving the legislature and violently suppressing all opposition. When the US government withdrew its support and revolutionaries such as Zapata, Venustiano Carranza and Pancho Villa joined together to fight him, Huerta was forced into exile (1914).

Hugensz, Lucas See Lucas van Leyden

Huggins, Charles B(renton) 1901–
US surgeon and Nobel Prize winner

Born in Halifax, Nova Scotia, Canada, he worked at Chicago University from 1927, where he became Professor of Surgery in 1936 and was head of the Ben May Laboratory for Cancer Research from 1951 to 1969. He has been a pioneer in the investigation of the physiology and biochemistry of the male urogenital tract, including the prostate gland. Research on benign and malignant tumours of the prostrate in dogs led him to the possibility of using hormones in treating such tumours in human beings. He also worked on the use of hormones in treating breast cancer in women. He shared the 1966 Nobel Prize for physiology or medicine with Peyton Rous.

Huggins, Godfrey Martin, 1st Viscount Malvern of Rhodesia and Bexley 1893–1971
Rhodesian politician

Born in England, in 1911–12 he emigrated to Southern Rhodesia (now Zimbabwe) as a doctor but was soon drawn into politics (1923). He was made premier of Southern Rhodesia in 1933, a post he held until he became premier of the Central African Federation (1953), of which he was one of the chief architects. He retired in 1956. Although the Central African Federation proved short-lived and Huggins' readiness to respond to nationalist pressures was too limited, he established a more liberal base in Southern Rhodesia where class was deemed more significant than race. The development of the state which Zimbabwe's politicians inherited owes a great deal to Huggins' leadership in difficult economic conditions in the 1930s, 1940s and 1950s.

Huggins, Sir William 1824–1910
English astronomer

Born in London, he went into the mercery business, while in his spare time studying the sciences. He later devoted himself entirely to astronomy, erecting an observatory (1856), later enhanced by instruments on loan from the Royal Society (1871), in the garden of his house in the suburbs of London where he lived and worked for the rest of his life. In collaboration with William Allen Miller (1817–70), Professor of Chemistry at King's College London, Huggins began observations of spectra of stars (1864). His pioneering work included spectroscopy of comets, and observations of the Doppler shift in the spectra of stars as a means of measuring their radial motion. He and his wife and co-worker Margaret Lindsay Murray (1848–1915) were the first to make serious use of dry plate photography in astronomy (1876). Huggins twice received the gold medal of the Royal Astronomical Society (1867, 1885) and was awarded the Royal (1866), Rumford (1880) and Copley (1898) medals of the Royal Society. He was knighted in 1897 and was among the 12 first recipients of the Order of Merit when it was instituted in 1902.

Hugh of Avalon, St, *also called* St Hugh of Lincoln
c.1135–1200
English prelate

He was born of a French noble family at Avalon in Burgundy. A priest at the Grande Chartreuse (1160–70), he was called to England by Henry II to found a Carthusian monastery at Witham in Somerset (1178). He became Bishop of Lincoln (1186), when he spoke against the draconian forestry laws in the royal forests and defended the Jews against rioting mobs. He also began the rebuilding of Lincoln Cathedral. He refused to pay taxes to finance French wars (money grant). He was canonized in 1220 and his feast day is 17 November.

Hugh of Lincoln, St See Hugh of Avalon, St

Hughes, Arthur 1830–1915
English painter

Born in London, he entered the Royal Academy schools in 1847, and, by 1852, had become associated with the Pre-Raphaelite Brotherhood and its principal members, Holman Hunt, J E Millais and D G Rossetti. Although he never formally joined the Brotherhood, he produced several paintings during the 1850s that rank as some of the finest of works executed in its typically precise and richly coloured style, such as *April Love* (1855, Tate Gallery, London) and *The Long Engagement* (1859, Birmingham). He also, from around 1855, pursued a successful career as an illustrator of the works of, amongst others, Alexander Munro and Christina Rossetti. He visited Italy in 1862 and the same year completed *Home from Sea* (Ashmolean, Oxford), but later lived a reclusive life and exhibited for the last time at the Academy in 1908.

Hughes, Charles Evans 1862–1948
US jurist and politician

Born in Glens Falls, New York, he was admitted to the Bar in 1884, and after exposing huge frauds in the insurance industry and establishing a reputation as a reformer, he became Governor of New York (1907–10). He served as an associate justice of the US Supreme Court from 1910, resigning to run against Woodrow Wilson as Republican candidate for the presidency in 1916. He later became Secretary of State (1921–25) in the Warren G Harding administration and was the chief organizer of the Washington Conference (1921–22), which sought to limit the naval arms race and stabilize the balance of power in the Pacific. After serving as a judge of the Permanent Court of International Justice (1928–30), he was appointed Chief Justice of the Supreme Court by Herbert Hoover in 1930; serving in that position until 1941, he favoured a loose construction of the Constitution and took a liberal stance on civil-rights cases. He denounced Franklin D Roosevelt's 'court-packing' plan in 1937 but later led the Court in approving several major pieces of New Deal legislation. He wrote *The Supreme Court of the United States* (1928).

Hughes, David Edward 1831–1900
US inventor

Born in London, he and his family emigrated to Virginia in the USA when he was seven years old. He became Professor of Music at Bardstown College, Kentucky (1850–53). In 1855 he invented a telegraph typewriter which he took around Europe in 1857, and which was widely adopted in Europe and the USA, and in 1878 a carbon microphone and an induction balance. He left a large fortune to London hospitals.

Hughes, Howard Robard 1905–76
US millionaire businessman, film producer and director, and aviator

Born in Houston, Texas, he inherited his father's oil-drilling equipment company at the age of 18, and in 1926 began to involve himself and his profits in Hollywood

films. During the next six years he made several films, including *Hell's Angels* (1930) and *Scarface* (1932). Already considered eccentric, he suddenly left Hollywood in 1932 and, after working for a short while as a pilot under an assumed name, turned his entire attention to designing, building and flying aircraft. He broke most of the world's air speed records (1935–38), was awarded a congressional medal from Washington, then returned to filmmaking, producing and directing his most controversial film, *The Outlaw* (1943), starring Jane Russell. He continued his involvement in aviation by designing and building an oversized wooden sea-plane, the 'Spruce Goose', that was completed in 1947, flew only once, but yielded valuable technical knowledge to the aviation industry. Severely injured in an air crash in 1946, his eccentricity increased, and he eventually became a recluse, living in complete seclusion from 1966 while still controlling his vast business interests from sealed-off hotel suites, and giving rise to endless rumour and speculation. In 1971 an 'authorized' biography was announced, but the authors were imprisoned for fraud, and the mystery surrounding him continued until his death. 📖 Harold B Hinton, *Citizen Hughes* (1985)

Hughes, Hugh Price 1847–1902
Welsh Wesleyan minister

Born in Carmarthen, he founded the *Methodist Times* (1885), and in 1886 he was chosen to pioneer the West London mission. In his preaching he combined Methodism and socialism, and turned public opinion against Charles Parnell.

Hughes, John 1942–
British pharmacologist

He studied at the universities of London and Yale, and was appointed Deputy Director of the Drug Research Unit at Aberdeen University (1973–77) before becoming Reader (1977–79) and Professor (1979–82) in Pharmacological Biochemistry, Imperial College, London. In 1983 he became director of the Parke–Davis Research Unit, Cambridge, and from 1989 has been Honorary Professor of Neuropharmacology at Cambridge. Whilst at Aberdeen, he discovered with Hans Kosterlitz the opiate-like chemicals, enkephalins, and his work since has concentrated on the pharmacology and biochemistry of many neuroactive compounds.

Hughes, (James Mercer) Langston 1902–67
US poet, fiction writer and dramatist

Born in Joplin, Missouri, he published his first poems while still in high school, and during his early adulthood spent several years drifting, travelling to Africa and Europe as a messman on a freighter. While working as a busboy in a Washington hotel he showed his poems to Vachel Lindsay, who championed his work, and he was awarded a scholarship to Lincoln University in Pennsylvania. Though initially rejected by black critics who saw his use of African-American idioms and speech patterns as a betrayal of their efforts to elevate the race, he was eventually recognized as a major figure in the Harlem Renaissance of the 1920s. *Weary Blues* (1926) was his first of several collections of verse, culminating in *Selected Poems* (1959). His memorable character 'Jesse B Simple' first appeared in racy newspaper sketches and thereafter appeared in several volumes, before the publication in 1957 of *The Best of Simple*. Hughes's lyrical verse, resonant of his vast knowledge of folk culture, jazz and the blues, had a profound influence on the development of African-American literature and later poets of the Beat generation. *The Big Sea* (1940) and *I Wonder as I Wander* (1956) are autobiographical. 📖 M Meltzner, *Langston Hughes* (1968)

Hughes, Richard Arthur Warren 1900–76
English novelist

Hughes, Ted (Edward James) 1930–98
English poet, Poet Laureate from 1984

Ted Hughes was born in Mytholmroyd, a mill town in West Yorkshire. When he was seven his family moved to Mexborough, Yorkshire, where his parents opened a stationery and tobacco shop. At Mexborough Grammar School he began to write poetry, usually bloodcurdling verses about Zulus and cowboys. He won a scholarship to Pembroke College, Cambridge, where he read English literature, but switched to archaeology and anthropology, subjects which were to form a major influence on his poetry. After graduating he had a number of colourful jobs, including zookeeper, gardener and nightwatchman, and occasionally published poems in university poetry magazines.

He married the US writer **Sylvia Plath** in 1956 and after two years in the USA they settled in Cambridge, where Hughes taught while Plath studied. That same year he won an American poetry competition, judged by **W H Auden**, Sir **Stephen Spender** and **Marianne Moore**, with the poems that were to form The Hawk in the Rain (1957); they displayed a striking treatment of animal subjects and a vivid sense of nature. For the next few years he lived in America, where he taught and was supported by a Guggenheim Foundation grant. Lupercal (1960), his second collection, won the **Somerset Maugham** award and the Hawthornden prize.

In 1963 Sylvia Plath committed suicide and for the next few years Hughes published no new adult poetry, although he did complete books of prose and poetry for children. Wodwo (1967) was his next major work, and among later volumes are Crow (1970), Cave Birds (1975), Season Songs (1976), Gaudete (a long prose poem on the theme of fertility rites, 1977), Moortown (1979, revised edition 1989), Remains of Elmet (1979), on which he collaborated with the photographer **Fay Godwin**, River (1983), Wolf Watching (1989) and Tales from Ovid (1997). The retrospective volume New Selected Poems: 1957–1994 was published in 1995. He edited Plath's collected poems in 1981, and in 1998 published Birthday Letters, poems about his relationship with her.

Of his books for children, the most remarkable is The Iron Man (1968, published in the USA as The Iron Giant), a fantasy story about a huge iron man who comes from nowhere and eats machines; this was followed later by a complemenary volume, The Iron Woman (1993). His verse for children includes Meet my Folks (1961), a series of comic family portraits, Season Songs (1975), and Ffangs the Bat Vampire and the Kiss of Truth (1986). He has also written plays for children, including the collection The Coming of the King (1970).

Drawn magnetically towards the primitive, he was a writer at one with nature, mesmerized by its beauty but not blind to its cruelty and violence. Much acclaimed and imitated, he was appointed Poet Laureate in 1984. He published the collection Rain-Charm for the Duchy and other Laureate Poems in 1992 and in 1995 wrote an admiring poem about **Elizabeth**, the Queen Mother on her 95th birthday, comparing her to a six-rooted tree. He was appointed to the Order of Merit in 1998.

Hughes also wrote reviews and essays; some of these have been collected in Shakespeare and the Goddess of Complete Being (1992), A Dancer to God: Tribute to T S Eliot (1992) and Winter Pollen: Occasional Prose (1994).

📖 T Gifford and N Roberts, Ted Hughes (1986); T West, Ted Hughes (1985); K Sagar, The Art of Ted Hughes (1978).

'The Iron Man came to the top of the cliff.
How far had he walked? Nobody knows. Where had he come from? Nobody knows. How was he made? Nobody knows.
Taller than a house, the Iron Man stood at the top of the cliff, on the very brink, in the darkness.'
From The Iron Man, ch.1, 'The Coming of the Iron Man.'

'But Oedipus he had the luck
For when he hit the ground
He bounced up like a jackinabox
And knocked his Daddy down.'
From 'Song for a Phallus' (1970).

'Black village of gravestones.'
From 'Heptonsstall' (1979).

Born in Weybridge, Surrey, of Welsh descent, he was educated at Oriel College, Oxford, and co-founded and directed the Portmadoc (Caernarvonshire) Players (1922–25). His one-act play, The Sister's Tragedy, and a volume of verse, Gypsy Night and Other Poems, were published in 1922, followed by Confessio Juvenis in 1925. He travelled widely in Europe, the USA and the West Indies, and eventually settled in Wales. He is best known for A High Wind in Jamaica (1929, US title The Innocent Voyage), a superior adventure yarn about a family of children captured by pirates while sailing to England. His later work includes The Fox in the Attic (1961), and The Wooden Shepherdess (1973), the first of an unfinished series covering the period from World War I to the rise of the Nazis and their aftermath. 📖 P Thomas, Richard Hughes (1973)

Hughes, Robert Studley Forest 1938–
US–Australian art critic

Born in Sydney, Australia, he studied art and architecture at Sydney University, then became a freelance writer. After travelling and living in Europe, he settled in New York City, and since 1970 has been art reviewer at Time magazine, becoming known for his irascible critical persona and his lucid, elegant prose. He has also written and narrated art documentaries for television, winning the Richard Dimbleby award for the series American Visions (1997). His books include The Shock of the New (1980), a history of 20th-century art, and The Fatal Shore (1987), an account of the settlement of Australia, Nothing if Not Critical (1990), Barcelona (1992) and The Culture of Complaint (1993).

Hughes, Shirley 1919–
English children's writer and illustrator

Born in Lancashire, she began as an illustrator of other people's works, but by 1960 she was writing her own books for young children. Lucy and Tom's Day, produced in that year, was the first of six volumes about those two children. There followed a number of works about Alfie, including Alfie's Feet (1982). Her other works, light and gleeful but realistic, include Here Comes Charlie Moon (1980), Bouncing (1993), Chatting (1994) and Hiding (1994).

Hughes, Ted See panel above

Hughes, Thomas 1822–96
English reformer and novelist

Born in Uffington, Berkshire, he was educated at Rugby and Oriel College, Oxford, before being called to the Bar in 1848, and becoming a county court judge in 1882. He was a Liberal MP (1865–74), was closely associated with the Christian Socialists, supported trade unionism, and helped to found the Working Men's College, of which he was principal from 1872 to 1883, and a model settlement in Tennessee, USA. He is primarily remembered as the author of the semi-autobiographical public school

Hugo, Victor Marie 1802–85
French poet and writer, a leading figure of the French Romantic movement

Victor Hugo was born in Besançon, the son of one of **Napoleon I**'s generals. He was educated in Paris at the Feuillantines, in Madrid, and at the École Polytechnique. He wrote a tragedy at the age of 14, and at 20, when he published his first set of *Odes et ballades* (1822), he had been victor three times at the Floral Games of Toulouse. In the 1820s and 1830s he produced further poetry and drama, establishing his place in the forefront of the Romantic movement, in particular with *Hernani* in 1830, the first of the five-act lyrics which are especially associated with him. In 1831 he produced one of his best-known novels, *Notre Dame de Paris*, an outstanding historical romance, later filmed as *The Hunchback of Notre Dame* (1924).

During the 1840s Hugo became an adherent of republicanism, and he was elected to the Constituent Assembly in 1848. After the *coup d'état* of Louis Napoleon (**Napoleon III**) he was sent into exile to Guernsey in the Channel Islands (1851–70), where he issued his satirical *Napoléon le petit* (1852). His greatest novel, *Les Misérables*, a panoramic piece of social history, appeared in 1862. He returned to Paris in 1870, and stayed through the Commune, but then departed for Brussels, protesting publicly against the action of the Belgian government in respect of the beaten Communists, in consequence of which he was again expelled. In 1872 he published *L'Année terrible*, a series of pictures of the war, and in 1874 his last romance in prose appeared, *Quatre-vingt-treize*. In 1876 he was made a senator. He was buried as a national hero in the Panthéon.

📖 Principal Works

Poems: *Odes et Ballades* (1822); second set of *Odes et ballades* (1826); *Les Orientales* (1828), which showed his mastery of rhythms; *Les Feuilles d'automne* (1832, 'Autumn Leaves'); *Chants du crépuscule* (1835, 'Songs of Twilight'); *Les Voix intérieures* (1837, 'Inner Voices'); *Les Rayons et les ombres* (1840, 'Sunlight and Shadows'), a

collection of sonorous verse; *Les Châtiments* (1853, 'Punishments'); *Les Contemplations* (1856, 'Contemplations'); the *Légende des siècles* (1859, 'Legend of the Centuries'); *Les Chansons des rues et des bois* (1865, 'Songs of the Street and the Forest', perhaps his greatest poetic achievement); a second part of the *Légende* (1876).

Dramas: *Cromwell* (1827), whose preface set out Hugo's poetical creed; *Hernani* (1830); *Marion Delorme* (1832); *Le Roi s'amuse* (1832), which was banned, is best known as the basis of **Verdi**'s opera *Rigoletto*; *Lucrèce Borgia* and *Marie Tudor* (1832); *Claude Gueux* (1834); *Ruy Blas* (1838), after *Hernani* the most famous of his dramatic works.

Novels: *Notre Dame de Paris* (1831, 'The Hunchback of Notre Dame'); *Les Misérables* (1862); *Les Travailleurs de la mer* (1866, 'Toilers of the Sea'), an idyll of passion, adventure and self-sacrifice, set in Guernsey; *Quatre-vingt-treize* (1874, 'Ninety-Three', a prose romance).

Criticism and other writing: *Littérature et philosophie mêlées* (1834, 'Literature and Philosophy Combined'), a collection of his youthful writings in prose; *Napoléon le petit* (1852); *William Shakespeare* (rhapsody, 1864); *L'Homme qui rit* (1869), a piece of fiction meant to be historical; *L'Histoire d'un crime* (1877).

📖 See also Joanna Richardson, *Victor Hugo* (1976); André Maurois, *Victor Hugo* (Eng trans, 1954); Elliott M Grant, *The Career of Victor Hugo* (1945).

> *Il n'y a ni règles ni modèles; ou plutôt il n'y a d'autres règles que les lois générales de la nature qui planent sur l'art tout entier, et les lois spéciales qui, pour chaque composition, résultent des conditions d'existence propres à chaque sujet.*
> 'There are no rules or models; that is, there are no rules except general laws of nature which hover over the entire earth and special laws which apply to specific conditions.'
> From the Preface to *Cromwell*.

classic, *Tom Brown's Schooldays* (1857), based on his school experiences at Rugby under the headmastership of Dr **Thomas Arnold**. The sequel, *Tom Brown at Oxford* (1861), was less successful. He also wrote a number of biographies and social studies. 📖 E C Mack and W H G Armytage, *Thomas Hughes* (1952)

Hughes, William Morris 1862–1952
Australian statesman

He was born in Pimlico, London, and lived in Llandudno, Wales, as a child. He emigrated to Australia in 1884 and settled in Sydney in 1886. He entered politics in the New South Wales Legislative Assembly in 1894 and moved in 1901 to the first federal House of Representatives, representing West Sydney. He rose to be a Minister in 1904, Attorney-General (1908–09, 1910–13, 1914–15), and deputy Prime Minister (1910), and in 1915 replaced **Andrew Fisher** as Prime Minister and Labor Leader. His attempts to introduce conscription were defeated but he survived at the head of various coalitions until 1922, when after the election the County Party held the balance of power and forced his retirement in favour of **S M Bruce**. A strong figure in the Allied war councils during World War I, at Versailles he irritated **Woodrow Wilson** by claiming to speak for Australia's 'sixty thousand dead' but secured an Australian mandate over the neighbouring German colony of New Guinea (later incorporated in Papua New Guinea). He remained active in parliament until his death; he engineered the overthrow of the Bruce–Page government in 1929, for which he was expelled from the

Nationalist Party, and in the **Menzies** administration of 1939 was Minister for the Navy (1940–41). 📖 Fitzhardinge, *William Morris Hughes* (vol 1 1964, vol 2 1979)

Hugo, Victor Marie See panel above

Huidobro, Vicente 1893–1948
Chilean poet

Born in Santiago, he once stood for the presidency of Chile. He wrote in Spanish and in French, and with Pierre Reverdy (1899–1960) invented the short-lived movement called Creationism, which demanded that poems should grow as naturally as trees. He resolutely lived out his private life in public, and when he met Ximena Amuntágui, a high school student, in 1925, he announced his intention to leave his wife and children in the nation's leading newspaper. One of the most influential figures in Latin-American literature, he is remember mainly as a lyric poet, especially for the prose poems *Temblor de cielo* (1928, 'Quivering Sky') and *Altazor* (1931, Eng trans 1988). There are many translations, including *Arctic Poems* (1974) *The Selected Poetry* (1981), and *The Poet is a Little God* (1990). 📖 R de Costa, *Vicente Huidobro: The Careers of a Poet* (1984); H A Holmes, *Vicente Huidobro and Creationism* (1933)

Hulanicki, Barbara 1936–
Fashion designer

Born in Palestine of Polish parents, she moved to Great Britain in 1948 and attended Brighton Art College. She won a design competition in the London *Evening Standard* in 1955 and became a fashion illustrator. In 1963 she launched Biba's Postal Boutique ('Biba' is her sister's name) in the *Daily Express* and the *Daily Mirror*. Success led to the opening of three Biba stores in London which became the fashion Mecca of the 1960s. Targeted at the young, her smocks, mini-dresses and trouser suits were all designed to look different from the 1950s 'adult' fashions, and her customers included **Cilla Black**, **Twiggy** and **Brigitte Bardot**. The mail-order catalogue was launched in 1968 and make-up range in 1970. Biba closed in 1973 and Hulanicki and her family moved to Brazil in 1976. Her autobiography, *From A to Biba*, was published in 1983.

Hull, Bobby, *full name* Robert Marvin Hull, Jnr
1939–
Canadian hockey player

He was born in Point Anne, Ontario. One of professional hockey's greatest scorers, he was the second player ever to score 1,000 goals. He played for both the National Hockey League (Chicago Black Hawks, 1957–72, Winnipeg Jets, 1979–80) and World Hockey Association (Winnipeg Jets, 1972–78).

Hull, Cordell 1871–1955
US politician and Nobel Prize winner

Born in Overton, Tennessee, he was educated at Cumberland University, Tennessee. Under **Franklin D Roosevelt**, he became Secretary of State in 1933 and served for the longest term in that office until he retired in 1944, having attended most of the great wartime conferences. He was a strong advocate of maximum aid to the Allies. One of the architects of 'bipartisanship', he also helped to organize the United Nations, for which he received the Nobel Peace Prize in 1944. ▢ Harold B Hinton, *Cordell Hull* (1942)

Hull, E(dith) M(aude) Early 20th century
English 'queen of desert romance'

Very little is known about her. Her real name was Winstanley and, according to her travel book, *Camping in the Sahara* (1926), she visited Algeria when she was young. It is known that she married a gentleman pig-farmer in Derbyshire and wrote *The Sheikh* (1919), her first and enormously popular desert romance, while her husband was away during World War I. It tells the story of an independent Englishwoman, 'proud Diana Mayo', who refuses offers of marriage in order to travel, is captured and raped by a sheik, whom she then marries. Transformed into film (1921), it provided **Rudolph Valentino** with one of his most popular roles. Hull swept on to write *The Sons of the Sheikh* (1925) and *The Lion-Tamer* (1928), equally pulsating stories of exotic romance.

Hull, Isaac 1773–1843
US naval officer

Born in Derby, Connecticut, he was the nephew of **William Hull**. He joined the navy in 1798 after commanding a ship in the West Indian trade. He served in the war against Tripoli (1803–04), and in 1806 he was appointed to the *Constitution* frigate, known as 'Old Ironsides'. In 1812 he captured the British frigate *Guerrière*, and afterwards commanded Mediterranean and Pacific squadrons.

Hull, William 1753–1825
American soldier

Born in Derby, Connecticut, he fought in the American Revolution (1775–83) and was Governor of Michigan territory (1805–12). In the war with Great Britain (1812) he was sent with 1,500 men to defend Detroit, was compelled to surrender, and was afterwards court-martialled for cowardice and sentenced to be shot, although this was commuted.

Hulme, Denny (Denis Clive) 1936–94
New Zealand motor-racing driver

He was born in Nelson. After being the New Zealand champion driver in 1960 and 1961, he turned in 1965 to Formula 1 (F1) with **Jack Brabham**'s team, and in 1967 became the first New Zealander to win the world F1 Championship. He started in 112 grand prix races, winning eight. He died in 1994 (probably from a heart attack) while competing in the 1,000km endurance race at Bathurst, New South Wales.

Hulme, Keri Ann Ruhi 1947–
New Zealand writer

Born in Otautahi, Christchurch, of mixed Maori, Orkney and English descent, she came to international notice by winning the Booker Prize with her first novel, *The Bone People* (1983), a spell-binding mixing of Maori myth and Christian symbolism. After another novel, *Lost Possessions* (1985), she published a collection of short stories, *Te Kaihau: The Windeater* (1986). Some of her verse in Maori and English is collected in *The Silences Between* (1982). Later works include *Strands* (1991), a volume of poetry, and *Bait* (1992).

Hulme, T(homas) E(rnest) 1883–1917
English critic, poet and philosopher

Born in Endon, Staffordshire, he was educated at Newcastle under Lyme High School and sent down from St John's College, Cambridge, for brawling. After a stay in Canada he taught in Brussels and developed an interest in philosophy. He joined **Ezra Pound**, **Wyndham Lewis** and **Jacob Epstein** as a champion of modern abstract art, of the poetic movement known as 'Imagism' (his own small number of surviving poems are in that style) and of the anti-liberal political writings of **Georges Sorel**, which he translated. Killed in action in France, he left a massive collection of notes, edited by his friend **Herbert Read** under the titles *Speculation* (1924) and *More Speculation* (1956), which expose philistinism and attack what he considered to be weak and outworn liberalism. Most of his poetry appeared in *The New Age* in 1912. He was described by **T S Eliot** as 'classical, reactionary and revolutionary'. ▢ M Roberts, *T. E. Hulme* (1982)

Hulse, Russell 1950–
US physicist and Nobel Prize winner

He studied astronomy at the University of Massachusetts in Amherst, and is now principal research physicist at Princeton University's Plasma Physics Laboratory. During a systematic search for pulsars, the rapidly rotating dense stars which appear on Earth to emit regular pulses of radio waves, he discovered with **Joseph Taylor** one interesting candidate whose pulse frequency changed periodically. These changes revealed that the object was a pulsar in orbit of another dense neutron star. For the discovery of the first 'binary pulsar', Hulse was awarded the 1993 Nobel Prize for physics jointly with Taylor.

Hulst, Hendrik Christoffell van de 1918–
Dutch astronomer

He was born in Utrecht, where he was educated and obtained his PhD in 1946. After several years at universities in the USA, he became Professor of Astronomy at Leyden and director of Leyden Observatory in 1970. In 1944 he suggested that interstellar hydrogen might be detectable at radio wavelengths. Such emissions were first detected by **Edward Purcell** and Harold Ewen in 1951. Van de Hulst was also an expert on the scattering and absorption of dust in the interstellar medium, and was the first to suggest that the diameter of a typical interstellar dust grain is around the same as the wavelength of visible light. With C Allen, he showed that the solar F (Fraunhofer) corona is due mainly to forward scattering by dust (1946), this dust being the innermost component of the zodiacal cloud.

Hulton, Sir Edward George Warris 1906–88
English magazine proprietor and journalist

Born in Harrogate, Yorkshire, he was educated at Harrow and Brasenose College, Oxford, and was called to the Bar, Inner Temple. He inherited his father's newspaper interests and became chairman of Hulton Press Ltd. In 1938 he founded *Picture Post*, a remarkable experiment in journalism which ceased in 1957.

Humason, Milton Lasell 1891–1972
US astronomer

Born in Dodge Center, Minnesota, he is best known for his association with **Edwin Hubble** in work on the recession of the galaxies. In 1954 he was appointed astronomer at the Mount Wilson and Palomar observatories, and his skilful observations of the radial velocities of hundreds of faint galaxies provided important material for the extension of Hubble's data. He was awarded the honorary degree of Doctor of Philosophy by the University of Lund in Sweden in 1950.

Humboldt, (Friedrich Heinrich) Alexander, Baron von 1769–1859
German naturalist

Born in Berlin, he was the brother of **Wilhelm von Humboldt**. He studied at the universities of Frankfurt an der Oder, Berlin, Göttingen, and under **Abraham Werner** in the Mining Academy at Freiburg. For five years (1799–1804) he and **Aimé Bonpland** explored unknown territory in South America, which led to his monumental *Voyage de Humboldt et Bonpland aux Regions Equinoxiales* (23 vols, 1805–34, Eng trans *Personal Narrative of Travels to the Equinoctial Regions*, 7 vols, 1814–29). In Paris he made, with **Joseph Louis Gay-Lussac**, experiments on the chemical constitution of the atmosphere, and he stayed in France until 1827. In 1829, he explored Central Asia with **Christian Ehrenberg** and the mineralogist Gustav Rose (1798–1873), and their examination of the strata which produce gold and platinum, magnetic observations, and geological and botanical collections are described in Humboldt's *Asie Centrale* (1843). Political changes led to his employment in political services, and during the following twelve years he made frequent visits to Paris, where he published his *Géographie du nouveau continent* (1835–38). His work of popular science, *Kosmos* (1845–62), gave a comprehensive physical description of the universe. 📖 L Kellner, *Alexander von Humboldt* (1963)

Humboldt, (Karl) Wilhelm von 1767–1835
German politician and philologist

He was born in Potsdam, the elder brother of **Alexander von Humboldt**. He travelled in Europe, then became a diplomat, but without official employment. A friend of **Schiller**, for some time he devoted himself to literature. In 1801 he became Prussian Minister at Rome, and was a patron of young artists and scientists. He returned to Prussia (1808) to become First Minister of Education, and founded the Friedrich Wilhelm (now Humboldt) University of Berlin. In 1810 he went to Vienna as minister plenipotentiary, and to London in 1817. He was the first to study the Basque language scientifically, and also worked on the languages of the East and of the South Sea Islands.

Hume, Allan Octavian 1829–1912
Scottish colonialist and naturalist

Son of **Joseph Hume**, he was educated at Haileybury Training College, studied medicine at University College Hospital in London and joined the Bengal Civil Service in 1849. He became commissioner of Customs for the North West Provinces, and also director-general of Agriculture. He built a huge library and museum for his vast collection of Asiatic birds at Simla, and in 1872 founded a quarterly journal on Indian ornithology. He retired in 1882, but in 1883 the manuscript of his projected book on Indian birds was stolen and sold as waste paper. In despair he presented his whole collection to the

British Museum. In 1885 he was founder and First Secretary (until 1908) of the first National Congress in Bombay. Hume's tawny owl, lesser whitethroat and wheatear are named after him.

Hume, (George) Basil 1923–
English Benedictine monk and cardinal

Born in Newcastle upon Tyne, and educated at Ampleforth College, St Benet's Hall, Oxford, and Fribourg University, Switzerland, he was ordained a priest in 1950, and returned to Ampleforth College as senior modern languages master in 1952. From 1957 to 1963 he was Magister Scholarum of the English Benedictine Congregation, and in 1963 he became abbot of Ampleforth, where he remained until he created Archbishop of Westminster and a cardinal in 1976. He published *Searching for God* (1977), *In Praise of Benedict* (1981), *To Be a Pilgrim* (1984), *Towards a Civilization of Love* (1988), *Light in the Lord* (1991) and *Remaking Europe* (1994).

Hume, David 1711–76
Scottish philosopher and historian

He was born in Edinburgh. His early years were unsettled: he studied but did not graduate at Edinburgh University. He took up law, but suffered from bouts of depression, and tried his hand instead at commerce as a counting-house clerk in Bristol. In 1734 he went to La Flèche in Anjou where he studied for three years and worked on his first, and most important, work, *A Treatise of Human Nature*, which he had published anonymously in London (1739–40) when he returned to Scotland. The subtitle is 'An attempt to introduce the experimental method of reasoning into moral subjects' and the book is in many ways a consolidation and extension of the empiricist legacy of **John Locke** and **George Berkeley**, with major, and still influential, discussions of perception, causation, personal identity and what became known as 'the naturalistic fallacy' in ethics. In political theory he argued for the 'artificiality' of the principles of justice and political obligation, and challenged the rationalistic 'natural law' and 'social contract' theories of **Thomas Hobbes**, **Richard Hooker**, Locke and **Jean Jacques Rousseau**. Bitterly disappointed at the initial reception of the *Treatise* he produced the more popular *Essays Moral and Political* (1741, 1742), which were immediately successful, and through which his views became more widely known. These essays heralded the new school of classical economics, of which his friend **Adam Smith** was to be the leader, advocating free trade and clearly stating the relationship between international specie flows, domestic prices and the balance of payments. Hume's atheism thwarted his applications for the professorships of moral philosophy at Edinburgh (1744) and logic at Glasgow (1751). He became tutor for a year (1745) to an insane nobleman, the Marquis of Annandale, then became secretary to General St Clair on an expedition to France (1746) and secret missions to Vienna and Turin (1748). In 1748 he published a simplified version of the *Treatise* entitled *Enquiry concerning Human Understanding*. Its translation was said to wake **Immanuel Kant** from his 'dogmatic slumbers' and provoked the Idealists to counter Hume's scepticism. The brilliant *Dialogues concerning Natural Religion* were written in 1750 but were prudently left unpublished, and appeared posthumously in 1779. He became keeper of the Advocates' Library in Edinburgh in 1752 and achieved real fame and international recognition with his *Political Discourses* (1752) and his monumental *History of England* (5 vols, 1754–62). From 1763 to 1765 he acted as secretary to the ambassador in Paris, and was received with great enthusiasm by the French court and literary society. He returned to London in 1766 with Rousseau, whom he had befriended but who was to provoke a bitter and famous quarrel with him, and became Under-Secretary of State for the Northern Department in 1767. He returned to

Scotland in 1768 to settle in Edinburgh where he died and was widely mourned, the equal in intellectual reputation to his contemporary Adam Smith. He has been a dominant influence on empiricist philosophers of the 20th century. 🕮 A J Ayer, *Hume* (1980)

Hume, David 1757–1838
Scottish jurist
Born in Ninewells, Berwickshire, he was educated at Edinburgh High School, and Edinburgh and Glasgow universities. He was Professor of Scots Law at Edinburgh (1786–1822), and Baron of the Scottish Court of Exchequer (1822–34). He wrote the classic text on Scottish criminal law, *Commentaries on the Law of Scotland respecting the Description and Punishment of Crimes* (2 vols, 1797), and *Commentaries on the Law of Scotland respecting the Trial for Crimes* (2 vols, 1800) later combined into one work. These were based on exhaustive investigation of court records. His *Lectures on Scots Law*, published posthumously, are also highly regarded. He was the nephew of the philosopher **David Hume**.

Hume, Fergus 1859–1932
English writer
Brought up in Dunedin, New Zealand, he was called to the New Zealand Bar and practised as a lawyer. He was a pioneer of the detective story in *The Mystery of a Hansom Cab* in 1887. He went to England the following year, and there published around 140 other detective novels, including *The Bishop's Secret* (1900) and *The Caravan Mystery* (1926).

Hume, (Andrew) Hamilton 1797–1873
Australian explorer
He was born in Parramatta, New South Wales, and from the age of 17 spent eight years exploring the Goulburn and Yass plains and Lake Bathurst in southern New South Wales, reaching the Clyde River, and receiving grants of land as reward. In 1824 he was encouraged by Governor **Brisbane** to find an overland passage from Lake George to the southern coast. The expedition discovered part of the Murray River, and made the first sighting of Australia's highest mountain, Mount Kosciusko, but ended up on the wrong side of Port Phillip Bay, an error which later provoked a pamphlet war between Hume and his navigator which continued for many years. In 1828 Hume joined an expedition led by Charles Sturt (1795–1869) which discovered the Darling River, but poor health prevented his continuing, and he settled down to farm his land grants near Yass.

Hume, John 1937–
Northern Ireland politician
Born in Londonderry and educated at the National University of Ireland, he was a founder member of the Credit Union Party, which was a forerunner to the Social Democratic and Labour Party (SDLP). He sat in the Northern Ireland parliament (1969–72) and the Northern Ireland assembly (1972–73) and became widely respected as a moderate, non-violent member of the Catholic community. He became SDLP leader in 1979 and in the same year was elected to the European parliament. He has represented Foyle in the House of Commons since 1983. In the 1990s he took part in the Northern Ireland peace talks and in particular conversed with Sinn Féin leader **Gerry Adams**. 🕮 *John Hume: personal views, politics, peace and reconciliation in Ireland* (1996)

Hume, Joseph 1777–1855
Scottish radical politician
Born in Montrose, Angus, he studied medicine at Edinburgh, and in 1797 became assistant surgeon under the East India Company (1797–1808). He learned several native languages, and in the Maratha War (1802–07) filled important offices. A political philosopher of the school of **James Mill** and **Jeremy Bentham**, after his return to England (1808) he sat in parliament (1812, 1819–55), where his arguments for reform included the legalizing of trade unions, savings banks, freedom of trade with India, the abolition of flogging in the army and of naval impressment (seizure for service) and imprisonment for debt, and the repeal of the act prohibiting export of machinery.

Hummel, Johann Nepomuk 1778–1837
Austrian pianist and composer
Born in Pressburg, he was taught by his father, the director of the School of Military Music at Pressburg, and when the family moved to Vienna his playing impressed **Mozart**, who gave him lessons. He began playing in public in 1787, and after a tour of Germany, Denmark, Great Britain and Holland, he studied composition in London under **Muzio Clementi**, and in Vienna under **Johann Albrechtsberger**, **Franz Joseph Haydn**, and **Antonio Salieri**. In 1804 he became kapellmeister to Prince Esterházy, Haydn's former employer, and later held similar appointments at Stuttgart (1816) and Weimar (1819–37). He wrote several ballets and operas, but was best known for his piano and chamber works, and wrote a manual of piano technique (1828) which had considerable influence.

Humperdinck, Engelbert 1854–1921
German composer
Born in Siegburg, near Bonn, he studied music at Cologne, Frankfurt am Main, Munich and Berlin, and travelled in France, Spain and Italy. He taught at Barcelona, Cologne, Frankfurt and Berlin, and became famous as the composer of the musical fairy play, *Hänsel und Gretel* (1893), which was highly successful. *Schneewittchen* ('Snow White'), *Königskinder* (1897, 'The King's Children'), *The Miracle* (1912) and others followed.

Humphrey, Doris 1895–1958
US dancer, choreographer and teacher
Born in Oak Park, Illinois, she started dancing at the age of eight, and after beginning her career as a teacher of ballroom dancing in Chicago (1913), altered course to become one of the founders of modern dance. From 1917 to 1927 she danced with **Ruth Saint Denis's** Denishawn Company, beginning to choreograph in 1920 with *Tragica*. With her partner **Charles Weidman**, she founded a company in New York (1928), which thrived until the early 1940s. She started the Juilliard Dance Theater (1935), and ran the Bennington College Summer School of Dance (1934–42). She choreographed highly original work often concerned with form and based on musical structures, including *The Shakers* (1931), the trilogy *New Dance* (1935), *Theatre Piece* (1935), *With My Red Fires* (1935–36) and *Day on Earth* (1947), building the foundations for the future vocabulary and philosophy of modern dance. Disabled by arthritis, she gave up dancing in 1944 but choreographed for the company set up by one of her most talented students, **José Limón**. She was artistic director of the Limón company from 1946 to 1958. She also wrote *The Art of Making Dances* (1959), a key text on dance composition in modern dance. 🕮 Marcia B Siegel, *Days on Earth: The Dance of Doris Humphrey* (1987)

Humphrey, Hubert H(oratio) 1911–78
US Democratic politician
He was born in Wallace, South Dakota, and educated at Minnesota and Louisiana universities. He entered politics as Mayor of Minneapolis in 1945, and was elected as Democratic senator in 1948. He built up a strong reputation as a liberal, particularly on the civil rights issue, but, as Vice-President from 1964 under the **Johnson** administration, alienated many by his apparent support for the continuation of the increasingly unpopular war in Vietnam. Although he won the Democratic presidential

nomination in 1968 at the first ballot, a substantial minority of Democrats opposed him, and the general mood of disillusion with Democratic policies and a compromise candidate led to **Richard Nixon's** election victory. ⏛ Carl Solberg, *Hubert Humphrey: A Political Biography* (1984)

Humphreys, Emyr Owen 1919–
Welsh novelist, poet and dramatist
He was born in Prestatyn, Clwyd, and educated at University College, Aberystwyth, where he read history, learned Welsh and became a nationalist. He has worked as a teacher and a BBC Wales drama producer. The author of 19 novels, he won the **Somerset Maugham** award for *Hear and Forgive* (1952), and the Hawthornden prize for *A Toy Epic* (1958). He has also published two collections of short stories and six volumes of verse. Some of his poems have been set to music by the composer Alun Hoddinott. Later publications include *Bonds of Attachment* (1991), which won the 1992 Welsh Arts Council Book of the Year Award, and *Unconditional Surrender* (1996).

Humphries, (John) Barry 1934–
Australian comedian and writer
Born in Camberwell, Melbourne, he studied at Melbourne University. He made his theatrical debut at the Union Theatre, Melbourne (1953–54), and also appeared with the Phillip Street Revue (1956). In Great Britain from 1959, he made his London debut in *The Demon Barber* (1959) and subsequently appeared in *Oliver!* (1960, 1963, 1968). He created the Barry McKenzie comic strip in *Private Eye* (1964–73), and wrote the screenplay for *The Adventures of Barry McKenzie* (1972), in which he appeared as Dame Edna Everage. His many stage shows include *A Nice Night's Entertainment* (1962), *A Load of Olde Stuffe* (1971), *An Evening's Intercourse with the Widely Liked Barry Humphries* (1981–82) and *Back With a Vengeance* (1987–89). His characters, including the repellent cultural attaché Sir Les Patterson and the acid-tongued superstar housewife Dame Edna Everage, have appeared in television shows such as *The Dame Edna Experience* (1987–89), *Dame Edna's Neighbourhood Watch* (1992–93), *Dame Edna in Hollywood* (1993) and *The Dame Edna Christmas Experience!* (1995). His straight roles on television have included appearances in *Doctor Fischer of Geneva* (1984) and playing **Rupert Murdoch** in *Selling Hitler* (1991). He has been in the films *Bedazzled!* (1967), *Barry McKenzie Holds His Own* (1975), *The Getting of Wisdom* (1977) and *Les Patterson Saves the World* (1987). His many humorous books, include *Treasury of Australian Kitsch* (1980) and *The Traveller's Tool* (1985). He was married for a time to Australian painter Diane Millstead (1948–).

Hung-wu See Hongwu

Hunt, E(verette) Howard 1918–90
US spy and detective novelist, and political operative
Born in Hamburg, New York, he graduated from Brown University in 1940, and served with the Air Force (1943–46) after writing scripts for the hugely influential *March of Time* newsreels. He was recruited as a political officer after World War II and saw diplomatic service in Paris, Vienna, Mexico, Tokyo and Montevideo. His first novel was called *Maelstrom* (1948), reissued seven years later as *Cruel is the Night*. Others include *Dark Encounter* (1950) and *The Judas Hour* (1951). He also used pseudonyms, writing as John Baxter, Robert Dietrich and David St John, and detective fiction as Gordon Davis. As an adviser to **Richard Nixon's** re-election committee he became embroiled in the Watergate scandal in 1972. Conspiracy theorists also claim that Hunt appears on photographs of the notorious 'grassy knoll' on Dealey Plaza, Dallas, where **John F Kennedy** was ambushed in November 1963, and among the mysterious 'tramps' arrested subsequent to the assassination. Following his release from prison in 1977, he resumed his writing career; his work provides a fascinating insight into the clandestine side of US politics from the end of World War II through the Bay of Pigs (in which he had a hand), to Vietnam and beyond. ⏛ *Undercover: Memoirs of an American Secret Agent* (1974)

Hunt, Geoff(rey) 1947–
Australian squash rackets player
Born in Victoria, he was the Australian amateur champion at the age of 17, the world amateur champion in 1967, 1969, and 1971, and the world Open champion in 1976–77 and 1979–80.

Hunt, Henry, called Orator Hunt 1773–1835
English radical
Born in Upavon, Wiltshire, he became a well-to-do farmer, but in 1800 his quick temper brought him six weeks in jail. He came out a staunch radical, and spent the rest of his life advocating the repeal of the Corn Laws and parliamentary reform. In 1819 he presided over the demonstration that ended in the Peterloo Massacre, and delivered a speech which cost him three years' imprisonment (1820–23). He was subsequently MP for Preston (1831–33). ⏛ John Belchem, 'Orator' *Hunt: Henry Hunt and English Working-Class Radicalism* (1985)

Hunt, (William) Holman 1827–1910
English painter
Born in London, he became a student of the Royal Academy in 1845. He shared a studio with **Dante Gabriel Rossetti**, and the pair, along with **John Everett Millais** and four others, inaugurated the 'Pre-Raphaelite Brotherhood', which aimed at painting a detailed and uncompromising truth to nature. The first of his Pre-Raphaelite works was *Rienzi* (1849); others include *The Hireling Shepherd* (1852), *Claudio and Isabella* (1853), *Strayed Sheep* (1853) and *The Light of the World* (1854, Keble College, Oxford). The result of several visits to the East appeared in *The Scapegoat* (1856, Port Sunlight) and *The Finding of Christ in the Temple* (1860). Among his most famous canvases are *Isabella and the Pot of Basil* (1867) and *May Morning on Magdalen Tower* (1891). His autobiographical *Pre-Raphaelitism and the Pre-Raphaelite Brotherhood* (1905) is a valuable record of the movement. ⏛ A C Gissing, *William Holman Hunt* (1936)

Hunt, James (Simon Wallis) 1947–93
English motor-racing driver
Born in London, and educated at Wellington College, he drove with the Hesketh and McLaren teams (1973–79), and was world motor racing Grand Prix champion in 1976. He retired in 1979 and was a BBC television broadcaster from 1980 until his death.

Hunt (of Lanfair Waterdine), (Henry Cecil) John Hunt, Baron 1910–
English mountaineer and social reformer
He was born in Marlborough, Wiltshire, and educated there and at Sandhurst. After a distinguished military career in India and Europe, he led the first successful expedition to climb Mount Everest (see Sir **Edmund Hillary**), and was knighted. He also led the British party in the British–Soviet Caucasian mountaineering expedition (1958), and has been involved in mountaineering expeditions in western Europe, the Middle East, Himalayas, Greenland, Russia, Greece and Poland. From its inception in 1956, he was director of the Duke of Edinburgh's award scheme and was created a life peer for services to youth on his retirement in 1966. He then became chairman of the Parole Board of England and Wales (1967–1974) and the National Association of Probation Officers (1974–1980). He became a Knight of the Garter in 1979. His publications include *The Ascent of Everest* (1953) and *In Search of Adventure* (1989).

Hunt, (James Henry) Leigh 1784–1859
English poet and essayist

Born in Southgate, Middlesex, the son of an immigrant American preacher, he was educated at Christ's Hospital. His first collection of poetry was privately printed as *Juvenilia* in 1801. With his brother, a printer, he edited (1808–21) *The Examiner*, which became a focus of liberal opinion and attracted leading men of letters, including **Byron, Thomas Moore, Shelley** and **Charles Lamb**. He was imprisoned with his brother for two years (1813–15) for a libel on the Prince Regent (the future **George IV**). *The Examiner* introduced Shelley and **Keats** to the public—Keats' sonnet *On First Looking into Chapman's Homer* first appeared there in 1816, the year in which Hunt published his own romance, *The Story of Rimini*. Hunt also founded and edited *The Indicator* (1819–21), habitually introduced authors to each other, and his *Autobiography* (1850) provides a valuable picture of the times. ⊞ E Blunden, *Leigh Hunt* (1930)

Hunt, Richard Morris 1827–95
US architect

Born in Brattleboro, Vermont, he studied art and architecture at the École des Beaux-Arts in Paris and supervised the construction of additions to the Louvre and the Tuileries. In 1855 he returned to the USA, where he worked on an extension to the US Capitol in Washington, DC, and established a studio in New York City (from 1858). His designs, which reflected the eclecticism of his Beaux-Arts training, include the Lenox Library, the Tribune Building, one of the first skyscrapers, and the great Fifth Avenue façade of the Metropolitan Museum of Art (all in New York City), the National Observatory in Washington, and the Yale Divinity School. He also designed many mansions for wealthy families, notably the **Vanderbilt** estate called The Breakers (1892–95) in Newport, Rhode Island. He was the brother of painter **William Morris Hunt**.

Hunt, William Morris 1824–79
US painter

Born in Brattleboro, Vermont, he spent three years at Harvard, then went to Europe and studied painting in Paris, where he became a close friend and admirer of **Jean François Millet**. He was also influenced by **Camille Corot** and other French landscape painters of the Barbizon school, whose work he introduced to the USA. He returned to his own country in 1856 and soon gained a great reputation for his portraits and landscape paintings. He was the brother of architect **Richard Morris Hunt**.

Hunter, Evan, *originally* Salvatore A Lambino, *pseudonym* Ed McBain 1926–
US novelist

Born and educated in New York City, he served in the US navy and taught before concentrating on his career as a novelist. Writing under his pseudonym Ed McBain, he is renowned for his '87th Precinct' thrillers. As Evan Hunter he is best known for *The Blackboard Jungle* (1954), about a young inner-city school teacher confronted with social problems and recalcitrant students. It was acclaimed for its realism and topicality. Later publications include *Criminal Conversation* (1994, written as Hunter) and *Romance* (1995, written as McBain).

Hunter, Holly 1958–
US actress

Born in Conyers, Georgia, the youngest of seven children, she studied at Carnegie Mellon University, Pittsburgh, and made her film debut in *The Burning* (1981). Thereafter mainly a stage actress, her role in *Places of The Heart* (1982) began a continuing association with the plays of the US dramatist Beth Henley (1952–). She established herself on screen with the comedies *Raising Arizona* (1987) and *Broadcast News* (1987). A diminutive figure, she won Best Actress Emmy awards for her roles as an unwed mother in *Roe Vs Wade* (1989) and an obsessive Houston housewife in *The Positively True Adventures Of The Alleged Texas Cheerleader-Murdering Mom* (1993), and received a Best Actress Academy Award for her performance in *The Piano* (1993). Other films include *The Firm* (1993), the controversial *Crash* (1996) and *Home for the Holidays* (1996).

Hunter, John 1728–93
Scottish physiologist and surgeon

He was born in Long Calderwood, East Kilbride, and from 1748 to 1759 assisted at the London anatomy school run by his elder brother, **William Hunter**, where he learned his dissecting skills. He then studied surgery at St George's and St Bartholomew's hospitals, London, and in 1760 entered the army as staff surgeon, serving on the Belleisle and Portugal expedition. In 1768 he became surgeon at St George's, in 1776 surgeon-extraordinary to King **George III**, and in 1790 surgeon-general to the army. An indefatigable researcher, he built up huge collections of specimens to illustrate the processes of plant and animal life and elucidate comparative anatomy. His museum grew to contain an astonishing 13,600 preparations, and on his death it was bought by the government and subsequently administered by the Royal College of Surgeons in London. In the field of human pathology, Hunter investigated a wide range of subjects, from venereal disease and embryology to blood and inflammation. He developed new methods of treating aneurysm, and was the first to apply pressure methods to the main trunk blood arteries. He also succeeded in grafting animal tissues. His *Natural History of Human Teeth* (1771–78) revolutionized dentistry. His biological studies included work on the habits of bees and silkworms, on hibernation, egg incubation and the electrical discharges of fish. He trained many of the leading doctors and natural historians of the next generation, including **Edward Jenner**, and is considered the founder of scientific surgery. ⊞ Jessie Dobson, *John Hunter* (1969)

Hunter, John 1737–1821
Scottish sailor and administrator

Born in Leith, he studied for the ministry at Aberdeen University, but left at the age of 17 to join the navy. In 1786 he was appointed second captain on the *Sirius*, flagship of the first fleet, which was to sail for Australia under the command of Captain **Arthur Phillip**. He arrived in New South Wales in 1788, then sailed round the Horn to Cape Town, eventually circumnavigating the globe, and on return to Sydney set off for Norfolk Island, where the ship was wrecked and the crew were marooned for 11 months. In 1792 he returned to England, but went back to New South Wales as its second governor in 1795. Here he found the military had effectively taken over the running of the colony, and he had great difficulty in restoring civil government, making such powerful enemies that he was recalled to London in 1800. During his governorship he encouraged the exploratory voyages of **George Bass** and **Matthew Flinders**, and as a keen natural scientist he promoted many valuable expeditions in search of botanical and zoological specimens.

Hunter, Russell 1925–
Scottish actor

Born in Glasgow, he began his career as an amateur with the Glasgow Unity Theatre, and turned professional in 1946. He has acted with the Royal Shakespeare Company and the Old Vic, in plays such as *The Servant O' Twa Maisters* (1965), *A Midsummer Night's Dream* (1966), *Hamlet* (1968), *Cocky* (1969) and *The Merchant of Venice* (1981). He is best known for his television role as Lonely in *Callan* (1967–72) but has also played a veteran Clydeside rebel in *Dunroamin' Rising* (1988) and appeared in series such as *Rab C Nesbitt* (1992) and *A Touch of Frost* (1996). Actress Una McLean became his third wife in 1991.

Hunter, William 1718–83
Scottish anatomist and obstetrician

Born in Long Calderwood, East Kilbride, he studied divinity for five years at Glasgow University, but in 1737 took up medicine with **William Cullen**, and was trained in anatomy at St George's Hospital, London. From about 1748 he confined his practice to that of midwifery. In 1764 he was appointed physician-extraordinary to Queen **Charlotte Sophia**, and in 1768 he became the first Professor of Anatomy to the Royal Academy. In 1770 he built a house with an amphitheatre for lectures, a dissecting room, and a museum. His Hunterian museum was bequeathed finally, with an endowment of £8,000, to Glasgow University. His massive contributions to anatomy and obstetrics included his chief work, *The Anatomy of the Human Gravid Uterus* (1774). He was the brother of John Hunter.

Hunter, Sir William Wilson 1840–1900
Scottish statistician

Born in Glasgow, he studied there and at the universities of Paris and Bonn, and in 1862 entered the Civil Service of India. His post as superintendent of public instruction in Orissa (1866–69) gave him the opportunity to write the *Annals of Rural Bengal* (1868) and *A Comparative Dictionary of the Non-Aryan Languages of India* (1868). Then, after being Secretary to the Bengal government and the government of India, in 1871 he became director-general of the statistical department of India, the Indian census of 1872 being his first work. In 1887 he retired and returned home to write books, mostly on Indian subjects.

Huntingdon, Selina Hastings, Countess of,
née Shirley 1707–91
English Methodist leader

Born in Staunton Harold, Leicestershire, the daughter of Earl Ferrers, she married the Earl of Huntingdon in 1728 but was widowed in 1746. Joining the Methodists in 1739, she made **George Whitefield** her chaplain in 1748, and assumed a leadership among his followers, who became known as 'The Countess of Huntingdon's Connection'. She established a training college for ministers at Trevecca in Brecknockshire (1768), and built or bought numerous chapels, the principal one at Bath. She died in London, bequeathing to four persons her 64 chapels, most of which have survived under Congregational management.

Huntington, Collis Potter 1821–1900
US railway pioneer

Born in Harwinton, Connecticut, he was a pedlar and shopkeeper. He went to California in 1849 and pioneered the Central Pacific Railway, which was completed in 1869, as well as the Southern Pacific (1881), of which he became president, together with the allied steamship companies. His nephew, Henry Edwards Huntington (1850–1927), also a railroad executive, acquired an immense art collection and library, which he presented to the nation in 1922, together with his estate at Pasadena, California.

Huntington, Ellsworth 1876–1943
US geographer and explorer

Born in Galesburg, Illinois, he taught at Euphrates College, Harput, Turkey, and took part in expeditions to Central Asia (1903–06). He then became a geography lecturer and research associate at Yale University in the USA. He wrote on Asiatic subjects and carried out research on the relations between climate and anthropology. His books include *The Pulse of Progress* (1926), *The Human Habitat* (1927) and *Mainsprings of Circulation* (1945).

Huntly, Shirley Barbara de la See de la Huntly, Shirley Barbara

Huntsman, Benjamin 1704–76
English inventor

Born in Barton upon Humber, Humberside, the son of Dutch immigrants, he was apprenticed to a clockmaker and in 1725 established a business in Doncaster making clocks, locks and scientific instruments. The high cost and variable quality of the steel he had to import from Germany and Sweden prompted him to improve on the cementation process then in use. By 1742 he had developed the crucible process, which produced a better and more uniform steel with less expenditure of labour and fuel, at a foundry he opened in Sheffield. Although a major advance, his crucible steel could be made only in relatively small quantities, and it required the advances of **William Kelly**, **Henry Bessemer**, **William Siemens** and **Pierre Émile Martin** in the mid-19th century before steel could become a major structural material. 🕮 Kenneth C Barraclough, *Benjamin Huntsman, 1704–1776* (1976)

Hunyady, János Corvinus or John c.1387–1456
Hungarian warrior and statesman

Born apparently in Wallachia (modern Romania), the Holy Roman Emperor **Sigismund** granted him Hunyad in Transylvania in 1409. He spent most of his life crusading against the Turks, whom he expelled from Transylvania (1442). Despite defeats at Varna (1444) and Kossovo (1448), in 1456 he routed the Turkish armies besieging Belgrade, thus securing a 70-year peace and becoming a national hero. During the reign of Ladislaus V (1446–53), he acted as Governor of the Kingdom. He left two sons, Ladislaus, who was beheaded on a charge of conspiracy, and Matthias Corvinus, who became King of Hungary as Matthias I. 🕮 Lajos Elekes, *Hunyadi* (1952)

Huppert, Isabelle 1955–
French film actress

Born in Paris, she studied acting at the Conservatoire National d'Art Dramatique in Paris, and made her film debut in *Faustine Et Le Bel Été* (1971, UK title *Faustine*). She won international acclaim for her performance in *La Dentellière* (1977, UK title *The Lacemaker*), which she followed by winning the Best Actress prize at the Cannes Film Festival for *Violette Nozière* (1978). Adept at capturing the mix of good and evil in one person, she continues to work prolifically, having won acclaim in her best performances of the 1980s, *Coup de foudre* (1983, *At First Sight*) and *Une Affaire de femmes* (1988, *Story of Women*). She went on to appear in *La Vengeance d'une Femme* (1990, *A Woman's Revenge*), *Madame Bovary* (1991), *Amateur* (1994) and *La Cérémonie* (1995). She made her British debut in *Mary Stewart* (1996).

Hurd, Cuthbert Corwin 1911–
US computer company executive and scientist

Born in Estherville, Ohio, he was educated at Drake University and Iowa State College, and was awarded a PhD at the University of Illinois. During World War II he was involved in large-scale computations that led him to join IBM in 1949, and by 1951 he was closely involved with development work on the IBM 701 (the Defense Calculator). Its delivery to Los Alamos in 1953 was a harbinger of IBM's future dominance in the field of electronic digital computers. By the following year, Hurd's department had delivered the IBM 650, which was inexpensive, practical, reliable and mass produced, and proved to be a runaway success. Hurd was later appointed director of control systems at IBM (1961–62).

Hurd, Douglas Richard Hurd, Baron 1930–
English Conservative politician

He was born in Marlborough, Wiltshire, the son of Baron Hurd, and educated at Eton and Trinity College, Cambridge before joining the diplomatic service in 1952. After posts in Peking (Beijing), New York and Rome, he joined the Conservative Party research department in 1966. Moving into active politics, he became private and then political secretary to **Edward Heath** (1968–74). As MP for Mid-Oxon (1974–83) then Witney (1983–97), he held junior posts in **Margaret Thatcher**'s government (1979–84). Resignations by senior Cabinet Ministers made Hurd's progress rapid, from Northern Ireland Secretary (1984–85) to Home Secretary in 1985 and, unexpectedly, Foreign Secretary (1989–95). He was unsuccessful in the leadership contest following Thatcher's resignation (1990). After leaving the Cabinet he turned to writing political thrillers and was awarded a life peerage in 1997.

Hurst, Sir Cecil James Barrington 1870–1963
English lawyer and judge
Born in Horsham Park, Sussex, he was educated at Westminster and Trinity College, Cambridge. In 1902 he became Assistant Legal Adviser to the Foreign Office and, in 1918, Legal Adviser. He worked on the Paris Peace Treaties of 1919 and proposed the Permanent Court of International Justice. From 1929 to 1946 he was a judge of this court, becoming president (1934–36), and in this capacity greatly strengthened the court's prestige and authority. He was president of the Institute of International Law and a founder of the *British Yearbook of International Law* in 1919.

Hurst, Sir Geoff(rey) Charles 1941–
English footballer
Born in Ashton-under-Lyne, Lancashire, he became famous as the only player ever to score three goals in a World Cup Final, against West Germany at Wembley in 1966. This achievement resulted in the commentator Kenneth Wolstenholme's comment: 'There are people on the pitch … they think it's all over … it is now!' Hurst scored 24 goals for England in 49 appearances. Most of his career was spent with West Ham United before he moved on to Stoke City. He was knighted in 1998.

Hurst, Margery 1913–89
English businesswoman
Educated in London at Kilburn High School and RADA, she was invalided out of the Auxiliary Territorial Service in 1943. Left by her husband with a new baby, she set up a secretarial company in Portsmouth, with herself as the sole employee. She moved to a one-room office in Brook Street, Mayfair, in 1946 and within 10 years had opened 20 offices providing 'temps' in London and the south-east. Expansion led to offices being opened all over the UK, in the USA, and in Australia. In 1970 she was one of the first women to be elected to the membership of Lloyds, and was also the first woman to be elected to the New York Chamber of Commerce. The Brook Street Bureau was sold to Blue Arrow for nearly £20 million in 1985 but Mrs Hurst continued as chairman until ill health forced her to resign in 1988.

Hurston, Zora Neale c.1901–1960
US novelist
She was born in Eatonville, Florida, and described her early life as 'a series of wanderings'. She did occasional work, and studied at Baltimore's Morgan Academy and at Howard University, Washington DC, where she began to write. She also studied cultural anthropology at Barnard College and Columbia University, worked under anthropologist **Franz Boas**, and became a prominent figure in the Harlem Renaissance. Her best known novel is *Their Eyes Were Watching God* (1937). Other works include *Jonah's Gourd Vine* (1934), *Moses, Man of the Mountain* (1939) and *Seraph on the Suwanee* (1948). In the 1950s she withdrew from public life, and was distanced from many contemporaries by her controversial attack on the Supreme Court's ruling

on school desegregation. She argued that pressure for integration denied the value of existing Black institutions. Her last years were plagued by ill health and she died in poverty. **Alice Walker**'s collection of her writings, *I Love Myself When I Am Laughing*, was published in 1979. Hurston was inducted into the National Women's Hall of Fame in 1994. ⊞ *Dust Tracks on a Road* (1942)

Hurt, John 1940–
English actor
Born in Chesterfield, Derbyshire, he trained as a painter at St Martin's School for Art and won a scholarship to study at RADA. He made his film debut in *The Wild and the Willing* (1962) and his stage debut in *Infanticide in the House of Fred Ginger* (1962). An incisive character actor, drawn to roles on the fringes of mainstream society, his notable film work includes *A Man for All Seasons* (1966), *Midnight Express* (1978), *Alien* (1979), *The Elephant Man* (1980), *Scandal* (1989) and *Rob Roy* (1995). His stage performances include *The Dwarfs* (1963), *Little Malcom and his Struggle Against the Eunuchs* (1966) and *Travesties* (1974). He portrayed Quentin Crisp in the television play *The Naked Civil Servant* (1974) and **Caligula** in the television series *I, Claudius* (1977).

Hurt, William 1950–
US actor
Born in Washington DC, he performed in amateur dramatics and studied at the Juilliard School in New York. Describing himself as a 'character actor in a leading man's body', he built a substantial reputation in the theatre, appearing in *Long Day's Journey into Night* (1975) at the Oregon Shakespeare Festival, winning an Obie award for *My Life* (1977) and starring in *Hamlet* (1980) before making his film debut in *Altered States* (1980). Testing himself with often unpredictable choices, he appeared in such films as *Body Heat* (1981) and *The Big Chill* (1983) and won an Academy Award as a homosexual prisoner in *Kiss of the Spiderwoman* (1985). He received further nominations for *Children of a Lesser God* (1986) and *Broadcast News* (1987). Frequently returning to the stage, he received a Tony nomination for his supporting performance as a drug addict in *Hurlyburly* (1984–85) and starred in *Beside Himself* (1989) and *Ivanov* (1990). Increasingly drawn to projects outside the Hollywood mainstream, he has appeared more recently in the films *The Plague* (1992), *Smoke* (1995) and *Jane Eyre* (1995).

Hurtado, Miguel De La Madrid See De La Madrid Hurtado, Miguel

Hus, Jan See Huss, John

Husain, Saddam See Hussein, Saddam

Husák, Gustáv 1913–91
Czechoslovak politician
Born in Bratislava in Slovakia, he trained as a lawyer at the Bratislava Law Faculty, and was a member of the Resistance movement during World War II. After the war he worked for the Slovak Communist Party (SCP) before being imprisoned, on political grounds, in 1951. Rehabilitated in 1960, he worked at the Academy of Sciences (1963–68) before becoming First Secretary of the SCP and deputy premier in 1968. After the 'Prague Spring' and the Soviet invasion of 1968, he replaced **Alexander Dubček** as leader of the Communist Party of Czechoslovakia (CCP) in 1969. His task was to restore order, cleanse the CCP and introduce a new federalist constitution. He became state President in 1975 and, pursuing a policy of cautious **Brezhnev**ite reform, remained the dominant figure in Czechoslovakia until his retirement in 1987. He was replaced as state President by **Vaclav Havel** in 1989 after the CCP regime was overthrown and expelled from the Communist Party in 1990.

Husayn, Taha 1889–1973
Egyptian writer

Born in Maghagha, he was blind from early in his life. He obtained in 1915 the first PhD to be granted in Egypt from the new University at Cairo, for his thesis on the Arabic poet Ahmed ibn Abdullah Abul-Ala. From 1950 until 1952 he was Minister of Education. His autobiography, *Al-Ayyam* (1925–67, Eng trans *An Egyptian Childhood*, 1932, *The Stream of Days*, 1948, *A Passage to France*, 1976), is both a classic account of how the blind react to sound, and an important record of the progress (and regress) of an unhappy country. He also published the novel *Shjarat al-bus* (1944, 'The Tree of Misery'), and the story collection *Al-Muadhdhabun fi al-ard* (1949, 'The Sufferers on Earth'). 📖 D Semah, *Four Egyptian Literary Critics* (1974); P Cacchia, *Taha Husayn: His Place in the Egyptian Literary Renaissance* (1956)

Husayni, Amin al- 1897–1974
Arab nationalist leader

Educated in Jerusalem, Cairo and Constantinople (Istanbul), he went on to serve in the Turkish artillery. In 1921 the British, under their Mandate for Palestine, appointed him Mufti of Jerusalem and Permanent President of the Supreme Muslim Council, the most important Palestinian Muslim body. In 1930, in an attempt to attract outside support for the Arab cause in Palestine and to avert the Peel Commission's recommendation of the partition of Palestine, he told the German representative in Jerusalem that the Palestinians were in sympathy with the new Germany. He spent his life in an unsuccessful attempt to avert the partition of Palestine. His collaboration with Nazi Germany, his call for Egyptian aid for German and Italian troops and his support of Japan after Pearl Harbor, were more than enough to cast him in the darkest light in the eyes of the Allies. In 1945 he was captured by the French and kept under house-arrest near to Paris. By mid-1946, however, he had escaped to Damascus and was welcomed in Egypt by the Prime Minister, Isma'il Sidqi. He continued to work for the Palestinian cause from Gaza as leader of the 'All Palestine Government', recruiting guerrillas for raids into Israel. After 1956, however, with the growing influence of al-Fatah, his own power declined.

Hu Shi (Hu Shih) 1891–1962
Chinese liberal scholar and reformer

Born in Jiqi (Chi-ch'i), Anhui (Anhwei) province, he went to school in Shanghai, and went on to study English literature, political science and philosophy at the universities of Cornell (1910–14) and Columbia (1915–17), where he became a disciple of the philosopher John Dewey and developed his ideas for the revitalization of Chinese culture and literature by the use of the vernacular. He became Professor of Philosophy at Beijing (Peking) University (1917–26) and at Shanghai (1927–31), and Dean of the College of Arts and Letters at Beijing (1932–37). He wrote extensively on Chinese philosophy, but is best known for his championing of *bai hua*, the new Chinese vernacular that would make literature accessible to the masses, and wrote poetry in *bai hua* (*Experimental Poems*, 1920). An opponent of Communism, he served the Nationalist government as ambassador to the USA (1938–42) and the United Nations (1957), and was President of the Academia Sinica on Taiwan (1958–62).

Huskey, Harry Douglas 1916–
US computer scientist

Born in Whittier, North Carolina, he was educated at the universities of Idaho and Ohio, before he became involved with J Presper Eckert and John W Mauchly on the Electronic Numerical Integrator And Calculator (ENIAC) in Philadelphia, working on input and output devices for the machine. He then moved to Great Britain to join the ACE project at the National Physical Laboratory under Alan Turing. On returning to the USA in 1948, he joined the National Bureau of Standards, which was developing both the serial SEAC (Standards' Eastern Automatic Computer) built in Washington DC, and the parallel SWAC (Standards' Western Automatic Computer) built in Los Angeles. In 1953 Huskey designed a 'minicomputer', built by the Bendix Corporation, whose speed made it a favourite for certain classes of engineering problem.

Huskisson, William 1770–1830
English politician

He was born in Birch Moreton Court, Worcestershire. He entered parliament for Morpeth in 1796 as a supporter of Pitt, the Younger; returned for Liskeard in 1804, he became Secretary of the Treasury, and held the same office under William Bentinck, 3rd Duke of Portland (1807–09). In 1814 he became commissioner of the Woods and Forests, in 1823 president of the Board of Trade and treasurer of the navy, and in 1827 Colonial Secretary, but resigned office finally in 1828. He obtained the removal of restrictions on the trade of the colonies with foreign countries, the removal or reduction of many import duties and relaxation of the navigation laws, and was an active pioneer of free trade. He received fatal injuries at the opening of the Liverpool and Manchester Railway.

Huss, John, *also called* Jan Hus c.1369–1415
Bohemian religious reformer

Born in Husinetz (now Husinec, Czech Republic), from which his name derives, he studied at Prague University. In 1398 he began to lecture on theology at Prague, where he was influenced by the writings of John Wycliffe. In 1408 he defied a Papal Bull which alleged heretical teaching by continuing to preach, and was excommunicated in 1411. After writing his main work, *De Ecclesia* (1413, 'On the Church'), he was called before a general council at Constance, but he refused to recant and was burned at the stake. The anger of his followers in Bohemia (Hussites) led to the Hussite Wars, which lasted until the mid-15th century.

Hussein or Husain, Saddam 1937–
Iraqi dictator

Born in Tikrit, near Baghdad, into a peasant family, and educated in Baghdad, he joined the Arab Ba'ath Socialist Party in 1957. In 1959 he escaped to Syria and Egypt after being sentenced to death for the attempted assassination of the head of state, General Kassem. He returned to Iraq in 1963 after the downfall of Kassem, but in 1964 he was imprisoned for plotting to overthrow the new regime. After his release (1966) he took a leading part in the 1968 revolution which ousted the civilian government and established a Revolutionary Command Council (RCC), of which he became Vice-President. Initially behind the scenes, and then more overtly, he strengthened his position, and in 1979 became RCC Chairman and state President. Ruthless in the pursuit of his objectives, he fought a bitter war against his neighbour, Iran (1980–88), to gain control of the Strait of Hormuz, and dealt harshly with Kurdish rebels seeking a degree of autonomy. In December 1989 an attempt on his life led to the summary execution of 19 senior army officers. In July 1990 his army invaded Kuwait, bringing about UN sanctions against Iraq and later the Gulf War in which he was opposed by a UN-backed Allied Force, involving US, European and Arab troops. Hussein's troops surrendered in February 1991 following Operation Desert Storm, commanded by General Norman Schwarzkopf. Hussein was immediately confronted with a civil war as his army retreated through southern Iraq, but managed to contain the uprising there. In accordance with the terms of the peace treaty agreed at the end of the Gulf War, a special UN delegation were sent to oversee the destruction and removal of all non-conventional weapons stocks. Initially Iraq refused to disclose all its nuclear sites, but when a resumed air offensive was threatened by the allies the Iraqis supplied the necessary information. Hussein later defied UN ceasefire resolutions and made further raids on Iran in 1993. In 1995 his two sons-in law, their wives and children defected to Jordan and were granted political asylum there. Later that year Hussein held a national referendum and was confirmed as President for seven more years. 1996 saw him renew his involvement in the Kurdistan civil war. ⌑ E Karsh and I Rautsi, *Saddam Hussein* (1991)

Hussein ibn 'Ali 1856–1931
King of the Hejaz, and founder of the modern Arab Hashemite dynasty

He was born in Constantinople (Istanbul) and was Emir of Mecca (1908–16). After first siding with the Turks and Germany in World War I, on the advice of T E Lawrence he went over to the side of the Allies, declaring for Arab independence (1916), and was chosen first King of the Hejaz. He refused to recognize the mandatory regimes imposed on Syria, Palestine and Iraq by the Allies (1919). He was defeated by the Wahhabi leader, Ibn Saud, was forced to abdicate (1924), and was exiled in Cyprus. He was the father of King Faisal I and great-grandfather of King Hussein of Jordan.

Hussein (ibn Talal) 1935–99
King of Jordan

He was born in Amman, the great-grandson of Hussein ibn Ali and cousin of King Faisal II of Iraq. He was educated at Victoria College, Alexandria, and in Great Britain at Harrow and Sandhurst. In 1952 he succeeded his father, King Talal, who was deposed because of mental illness. His marriage (1955) to Princess Dina was later dissolved, and in 1961 he married an English girl, Antoinette Gardiner, given the title Princess Muna, who in 1962 gave birth to an heir, Abdullah. In 1972 he divorced Princess Muna and married Alia Baha Eddin Toukan, who was killed in an air accident in 1977. The following year he married Lisa Halaby. The young king maintained a vigorous and highly personal rule in the face of the political upheavals inside and outside his exposed country, steering a middle course, on the one side favouring the western powers, particularly Great Britain, on the other pacifying Arab nationalism, as by his curt dismissal of the British general, Sir John Bagot Glubb (1956). His federation of Jordan with Iraq (1958) came to an unexpected end with the Iraqi military coup d'état in July of the same year. He lost the West Bank to Israel (1967) and had problems coping with Palestine Liberation Organization (PLO) guerrillas based in Jordan, who had no attachment to him and wanted a firmer anti-Israeli policy. From 1979 he was reconciled with Yasser Arafat, renounced Jordan's claim to the West Bank (1988) and attempted to prevent the outbreak of the Gulf War (1990). After the war he distanced himself from Saddam Hussein, and signed a peace treaty with Israel in Washington in 1994. In 1999, after undergoing months of chemotherapy in the USA for cancer of the lymphatic tissue, he returned to Jordan, where he died. He was succeeded by his son Abdullah. ⌑ James Gant, *Hussein of Jordan* (1989)

Husserl, Edmund Gustav Albrecht 1859–1938
German philosopher and founder of the school of phenomenology

Born of Jewish parents in Prossnitz in the Austrian empire, he studied mathematics at Berlin (under Karl Weierstrass), psychology at Vienna (under Franz Brentano) and taught at Halle (1887), Göttingen (1901) and Freiburg (1916). While at Göttingen he developed phenomenology (a philosophy concerned with describing personal experiences without seeking to arrive at metaphysical explanations of them). His works included

Logische Untersuchungen (1900–01, 'Logical Investigations'), which defended philosophy as fundamentally an *a priori* discipline, unlike psychology, and *Ideen zu einer reinen Phänomelogie und phänomenologischen Philosophie* (1913, Eng trans *Ideas: General Introduction to Pure Phenomenology*, 1913) in which he presented a programme for the systematic investigation of consciousness and its objects, which proceeded by 'bracketing off', or suspending belief in, the empirical world to gain an indubitable vantage-point in subjective consciousness. His approach greatly influenced philosophers in the USA and in Germany, particularly Martin Heidegger, and helped give rise to Gestalt psychology. ⌑ Maurice Natanson, *Edmund Husserl: Philosopher of Infinite Tasks* (1973)

Hussey, Marmaduke James Hussey, Baron 1923–
English manager and administrator

Educated at Rugby and Trinity College, Oxford, his Oxford career was interrupted by World War II, when he served as platoon commander in the Grenadier Guards. He was wounded at Anzio and had his leg amputated at a German field hospital. After his recovery he completed his degree at Oxford and in 1949 joined Associated Newspapers as a management trainee. He went to Times Newspapers in 1971 and presided over the confrontation with the print union that led to the year's closure of *The Times* and the *Sunday Times* (1978). In 1986 he was asked by the Home Secretary, Douglas Hurd, to be chairman of the BBC in a proposed overhaul of the organization. The BBC continued to have problems and questions remained about its future funding, especially in 1993 when he survived calls for his resignation following the revelation that John Birt had been employed as deputy director-general as a freelance.

Hussey, Obed 1792–1860
US inventor

Born in Exeter, Maine, he spent his life in the invention, improvement and manufacture of machines for use in agriculture and light engineering. He achieved his greatest success with his reaping machine which he patented in 1833, the year before a very similar machine was patented by Cyrus McCormick based on the earliest known mechanical reaper invented in 1826 by Patrick Bell in Scotland. Hussey's and McCormick's machines were both exhibited at the Great Exhibition of 1851 in London, and although Hussey won the gold medal it was eventually McCormick who became the leading manufacturer in the USA.

Hüssgen See Oecolampadius, Joannes

Huston, Anjelica 1951–
US film actress

Born in Los Angeles, California, the daughter of director John Huston and granddaughter of actor Walter Huston (1884–1950), she was brought up in County Galway, Ireland, and educated in London. Her film debut was in her father's *A Walk With Love And Death* (1969). Disparaged by critics, she turned to modelling instead and became the companion of actor Jack Nicholson. Returning to acting in the 1980s, she gained critical acclaim by winning a Best Supporting Actress Academy Award for her part in *Prizzi's Honor* (1985). Her films include *The Dead* (1987), *Crimes and Misdemeanours* (1989), *The Grifters* (1990) and *The Addams Family* (1991). In 1996 she moved behind the camera to direct *Bastard Out of Carolina* from a novel by Dorothy Allison and then *Terrible Beauty*, based on the life of Maud Gonne.

Huston, John Marcellus 1906–87
US film director

Born in Nevada, Missouri, son of the actor Walter Huston (1884–1950), his early career involved spells as a boxer in California, a competitive horseman in Mexico and a journalist in New York. He moved to Hollywood in 1930, where he acted in films like *The Storm* (1930), and wrote or co-wrote screenplays including *Murders in the Rue Morgue* (1932), *Juarez* (1939) and *High Sierra* (1941). His first film as director, *The Maltese Falcon* (1941), was followed by wartime documentaries and a series of successful films, including *Key Largo* (1948), *The African Queen* (1951), *Moulin Rouge* (1952), *The Misfits* (1960), *Fat City* (1972), *The Man Who Would Be King* (1975) and *The Dead* (1987). Particularly adept at high adventure and film noir, he showed a consistent interest in quests that proved fruitless, or in men beset by delusions of grandeur. Latterly a prolific actor, he displayed reptilian patriarchal menace in *Chinatown* (1974), for which he received an Academy Award nomination; he also won Best Director and Best Screenplay awards for *The Treasure of the Sierra Madre* (1947), in which his father acted. An Irish citizen from 1964, he married five times and his children Danny, Tony and **Anjelica** have followed in his footsteps. His autobiography, *An Open Book*, was published in 1980. ⌨ Stuart M Kaminsky, *John Huston: Maker of Magic* (1978)

Hutcheson, Francis 1694–1746
British philosopher

Born probably of Scottish parents in Drumalig, County Down, Ireland, he studied for the church at Glasgow (1710–16). He started a successful private academy in Dublin, where he was a popular preacher, and then returned to Glasgow as Professor of Moral Philosophy from 1729 until his death. His main works were *An Inquiry into the Original of Our Ideas of Beauty and Virtue* (1725), *An Essay on the Nature and Conduct of the Passions and Affections, with Illustrations on the Moral Sense* (1726) and *System of Moral Philosophy* (posthumously published in 1755). He developed the theory of 'moral sense' first stated by the 3rd Earl of **Shaftesbury**, by which moral distinctions are directly intuited rather than arrived at by reasoning, and he identified virtue with universal benevolence. In this he anticipated Utilitarianism, and his formula 'the greatest happiness for the greatest numbers' was taken up, slightly modified, by **Jeremy Bentham**.

Hutchins, William See **Tyndale, William**

Hutchinson, Anne, *née* Marbury c.1590–1643
New England colonist and religious leader

Born in Lincolnshire, England, the daughter of a dissenting clergyman, she became a follower of **John Cotton**, and in 1634 she emigrated with her husband and family to Boston, Massachusetts. By 1636 she was holding religious meetings in her home, discussing Cotton's sermons and expressing her own theological views, notably her belief that salvation could be obtained through grace alone, and not through moral conduct. The leaders of the Massachusetts Bay Colony, though believers in the notion of the elect, saw Hutchinson's emphasis on the passivity of the soul before the visitation of the Holy Spirit as heretical, and perceived her independence as an attack on the Puritan theocracy. Tried and convicted by the General Court and banished from the colony, she acquired territory from the Narragansett tribe of Inuit of Rhode Island in 1638 and set up a democracy with friends and family on the island of Aguidneck. After her husband's death (1642) she moved to a new settlement in what is now Pelham Bay in New York State, where she and all but one of her family of 15 were murdered by Native Americans. She was inducted into the National Women's Hall of Fame in 1994.

Hutchinson, Sir Jonathan 1828–1913
English surgeon

Born in Selby, Yorkshire, he became surgeon at the London Hospital (1863–83), and Hunterian Professor of Surgery at the Royal College of Surgeons (1879–83). He is best known for his lifelong study of syphilis, 'Hutchinson's triad' being the three symptoms of congenital syphilis first described by him.

Hutten, Ulrich von 1488–1523
German humanist

Born in the castle of Steckelberg, he was sent to the Benedictine monastery of Fulda in 1499, but left it in 1504. He studied at various universities, and then moved to Italy (1512). Returning to Germany (1517), he was made Poet Laureate by Emperor **Maximilian I**, entered the service of Albert, Archbishop of Mainz, and shared in the famous satires against the ignorance of the monks, the *Epistolae Obscurorum Virorum* ('Letters of Obscure Men'). Eager to see Germany free from foreign and priestly domination, he took part in the campaign of the Swabian League against Ulrich of Württemberg (1519). His support of **Martin Luther** and a set of dialogues (1520) containing a formal manifesto against Rome caused the pope to have him dismissed from the archbishop's service. He was given shelter by **Franz von Sickingen** in his castle of Ebernburg, where he engaged in virulent polemics against the papal party to rouse the German emperor, nobles and people. His earliest work in German, *Aufwecker der teutschen Nation* (1520), is a satiric poem. Driven to flee to Basle in 1522, and rejected by **Erasmus**, he finally found a resting place through **Huldreich Zwingli**'s assistance on the island of Ufnau in Lake Zurich. Hutten was the uncle of the explorer Philip von Hutten (c.1511–1546).

Hutton, James 1726–97
Scottish geologist

Born in Edinburgh, after a short period as lawyer's apprentice he turned to medicine, which he studied in Edinburgh before going to the Continent to complete his professional training in Paris and Leyden. He never practised medicine, and instead went to Norfolk in 1752 to devote his time to agriculture; it was there that he became interested in geology. In 1754 he moved back to his estate in Berwickshire. He returned to Edinburgh in 1768 and joined an active intellectual group which included **Joseph Black, Adam Ferguson, Sir James Hall** and **John Playfair**. Hutton developed his theories about the Earth over a number of years as a result of many journeys into Scotland, England and Wales, and finally presented his ideas before the Royal Society of Edinburgh in *A Theory of the Earth* (1785; expanded, vols 1 and 2 1795, vol 3 1799). In this he demonstrated that the internal heat of the Earth caused intrusions of molten rock into the crust and that granite was the product of the cooling of molten rock and not the earliest chemical precipitate of the primeval ocean as advocated by **Abraham Werner** and others. This 'Plutonist' versus 'Neptunist' debate raged on for a considerable time after Hutton's death. His system of the Earth recognized that most rocks were detrital in origin having been produced by erosion from the continents, deposited on the seafloor, lithified by heat from below and then uplifted to form new continents. The cyclicity of such processes led him to envisage an Earth with 'no vestige of a beginning and no prospect of an end'. These uniformitarian ideas attracted strong opposition from the Swiss geologist Jean André De Luc (1727–1817), **William Buckland** and associates from the 'English School' of geology, and from **Richard Kirwan**. Nevertheless, Hutton's ideas held firm to form the basis of modern geology. ⌨ E B Bailey, *James Hutton: The Founder of Modern Geology* (1967)

Hutton, Sir Leonard, *known as* Len Hutton 1916–90
English cricketer

Born in Fulneck, Yorkshire, he was a Yorkshire player throughout his career. He first played for England in 1937, scoring a century on his first Test against Australia in 1938, and in the Oval Test against Australia in 1938, he scored a world record of 364 runs, which stood for 20 years until it was exceeded by one run by **Gary Sobers**. Renowned for the perfection of his batting technique, he made 129 centuries in his first-class career. After World War II he captained England in 23 Test matches, the first professional cricketer to do so on a regular basis. Under his captaincy England regained the Ashes from Australia in the Test series of 1953, and retained them during the Australian tour of 1954–55, thus ending 20 years of Australian supremacy. He retired in 1956 and was knighted that year.

Huxley, Aldous Leonard 1894–1963
English novelist and essayist

Born in Godalming, Surrey, the grandson of **T H Huxley**, he was educated at Eton and Balliol College, Oxford, where he read English, not biology as he intended, because of an eye disease which made him nearly blind. It later compelled him to settle in the warmer climate of California (1937). His first novels were *Crome Yellow* (1921) and *Antic Hay* (1923), satires on postwar Great Britain. *Those Barren Leaves* (1925) and *Point Counter Point* (1928) were written in Italy, where he associated with **D H Lawrence**, who appears as Mark Rampion in the last named. In 1932, in his most famous novel, *Brave New World*, Huxley warned of the dangers of moral anarchy in a scientific age, by depicting a repulsive Utopia, achieved by scientifically breeding and conditioning a society of human robots, for whom happiness is synonymous with subordination. Despite the wit and satire, Huxley was in deadly earnest, as his essay *Brave New World Revisited* (1959) shows. From such pessimism Huxley took refuge in the exploration of mysticism. *Eyeless in Gaza* (1936) and *After Many a Summer* (1939, James Tait Black Memorial Prize) pointed the way to *Time must have a Stop* (1944), in which he attempted to describe a person's state of mind at the moment of, and just after, death. *The Doors of Perception* (1954) and *Heaven and Hell* (1956) explore a controversial short cut to mysticism, the drug mescalin. *Island* (1962) is a more optimistic Utopian novel. He also wrote numerous essays on related topics including *Proper Studies* (1927), biographies, and a famous study in sexual hysteria, *The Devils of Loudun* (1952). 📖 S Bedford, *Aldous Huxley, a biography* (2 vols, 1973–74)

Huxley, Sir Andrew Fielding 1917–
English physiologist and Nobel Prize winner

A grandson of **T H Huxley** and the half-brother of **Aldous** and **Julian Huxley**, he was born in London and studied natural sciences at Trinity College and at the Physiological Laboratory at Cambridge. He later became a Fellow (1941–60) and assistant director of research in physiology (1952–60) at Trinity College, Cambridge, simultaneously holding positions in the Physiological Laboratory. He moved to University College London, as Joddrell Professor of Physiology (1960–69) and as Royal Society Research Professor (1969–83), before returning to Cambridge as Master of Trinity College (1984–89), then Fellow (1990–). With **Alan Hodgkin** he provided a physico-chemical explanation for the conduction of impulses in nerve fibres, and (1950) changed direction to study muscle physiology, devising a special microscope with which to study the contraction and relaxation of muscle fibres. He postulated a 'sliding filament' theory to explain muscular contraction, in which different sections of the muscle fibre overlapped, thus generating force in the direction of the shortening. He served as president of the Royal Society (1980–85), was knighted in 1974 and

was awarded the Order of Merit in 1983. In 1963 he shared the Nobel Prize for physiology or medicine with Hodgkin and Sir **John Eccles**.

Huxley, Elspeth Josceline, *née* Grant 1907–97
English novelist

She was born in Kenya, and wrote many novels and essays on her native land, its history, and its problems. Her best-known novel is *The Flame Trees of Thika* (1959), which deals with her childhood, as do *The Mottled Lizard* (1962) and *Death of an Aryan* (1986, also known as *The African Poison Murders*). She published a biography of Sir **Peter Scott** in 1993 entitled *Peter Scott: Painter and Naturalist*. Her husband Gervas Huxley (1894–1971), was a grandson of **T H Huxley**. 📖 *Love Among the Daughters* (1968)

Huxley, Hugh Esmor 1924–
English biophysicist

Born in Birkenhead, Merseyside, he studied natural sciences at Christ's College, Cambridge, graduating in 1943. In 1948 he joined the Molecular Biology Unit of the Medical Research Council (MRC) at Cambridge, was awarded a Commonwealth Fund Scholarship to study biophysics at the Massachusetts Institute of Technology (1952–54), and was then appointed to the biophysics department of King's College London. He returned to Cambridge in 1961, to the MRC Laboratory of Molecular Biology, of which he became deputy director in 1977. From the 1950s he was a central figure in developing the model of muscle action in which muscle filaments slide past each other to produce contraction; during this work he also devised important X-ray diffraction and electron microscopy techniques. He defined the detailed structure of the muscle cell, and analysed the cellular location of the major proteins involved in contraction. He has been Professor of Biology at Brandeis University since 1987 and was director of the Rosenstiel Basic Medical Sciences Research Center there from 1988 to 1994.

Huxley, Sir Julian Sorell 1887–1975
English biologist and humanist

The grandson of **T H Huxley** and brother of **Aldous Huxley**, he was educated at Eton and Balliol College, Oxford, was professor at the Rice Institute, Texas (1913–16), and after World War I became Professor of Zoology at King's College London (1925–27), Fullerian professor at the Royal Institution (1926–29), and secretary to the Zoological Society of London (1935–42). His writings include *Essays of a Biologist* (1923), *Religion without Revelation* (1927), *Animal Biology* (with **J B S Haldane**, 1927), *The Science of Life* (with **H G Wells**, 1931), *Evolution: The Modern Synthesis* (1942), *Evolutionary Ethics* (1943), *Biological Aspects of Cancer* (1957), and *Towards a New Humanism* (1957). He extended the application of his scientific knowledge to political and social problems, formulating a pragmatic ethical theory of 'evolutionary humanism', based on the principle of natural selection. His influence was based on his capacity for synthesis stimulation rather than his own scientific accomplishments. He was the first director-general of UNESCO (1946–48). 📖 Ronald W Clark, *The Huxleys* (1968)

Huxley, T(homas) H(enry) 1825–95
English biologist

He was born in Ealing, Middlesex, the son of a schoolmaster. He studied medicine at Charing Cross Hospital, and entered the Royal Navy medical service. As assistant surgeon on HMS *Rattlesnake* on a surveying expedition to the South Seas (1846–50), he collected and studied specimens of marine animals, particularly plankton. From 1854 to 1885 he was Professor of Natural History at the Royal School of Mines in London, and made significant contributions to palaeontology and comparative anatomy, including studies of dinosaurs, coelenterates, and the relationship between birds and reptiles. He was best known as the foremost scientific supporter of **Charles Darwin's** theory of evolution by natural selection during the heated debates which followed its publication, tackling Bishop **Samuel Wilberforce** in a celebrated exchange at the British Association meeting in Oxford (1860), when he declared that he would rather be descended from an ape than a bishop. He wrote *Evidence as to Man's Place in Nature* (1863). He also studied fossils, and influenced the teaching of biology and science in schools as a member of the London Schools Board. Later he turned to theology and philosophy, and coined the term 'agnostic' for his views. He wrote *Lay Sermons* (1870), *Science and Culture* (1881), *Evolution and Ethics* (1893) and *Science and Education* (published posthumously in 1899). ⌨ *Cyril Bibby, T H Huxley, Scientist, Humanist, and Educator* (1959)

Huxtable, Ada Louise, *née* Landman 1921–
US critic of architecture
Born in New York, she started work for the *New York Times* in 1963 as an architectural critic, the first to be appointed by a newspaper. She stimulated an interest in preserving US heritage and had a powerful influence on decisions concerning zoning laws and historic building preservation. Her views have always been broad and flexible, even criticising the Modern Movement, which was accepted unequivocally by the majority of the architectural community. She has published a book, *Pier Luigi Nervi* (1960), and received the first Pulitzer Prize for distinguished criticism in 1970. In 1982 she left the *Times*, having been on its editorial board since 1973, and became an independent architectural consultant and critic.

Hu Yaobang (Hu Yao-pang) 1915–89
Chinese politician
Born into a poor peasant family in Hunan province, he joined the Red Army in 1929 and took part in the Long March (1934–36). He held a number of posts under **Deng Xiaoping** before becoming head of the Communist Youth League (1952–67). During the Cultural Revolution (1966–69) he was purged as a 'capitalist roader' and 'rusticated'. Briefly rehabilitated (1975–76), he did not return to high office until 1978, when, through his patron Deng, he joined the Communist Party's politburo. From head of the Secretariat, he was promoted to party leader in 1981, but dismissed in 1987 for his relaxed handling of a wave of student unrest. Popularly revered as a liberal reformer, his death triggered an unprecedented wave of pro-democracy demonstrations.

Huygens, Christiaan 1629–93
Dutch physicist
He was born in The Hague, the second son of the poet Constantyn Huygens (1596–1687). He studied at the universities of Leyden and Breda, and his mathematical *Theoremata* was published in 1651. In 1655 he discovered the rings and fourth satellite of Saturn, using a refracting telescope he constructed with his brother. He later constructed the pendulum clock, based on the suggestion of **Galileo** (1657), and developed the latter's doctrine of accelerated motion under gravity. In 1663 he visited England, where he was elected FRS. He discovered the laws of collision of elastic bodies at the same time as **John Wallis** and Sir **Christopher Wren**, and improved the air-pump. In optics he first propounded the undulatory theory of light, and discovered polarization. The 'principle of Huygens' is a part of the wave theory. He lived for some years in Paris, a member of the Royal Academy of Sciences (1666–81), but later returned to The Hague. He was, after **Isaac Newton**, the greatest scientist of the second half of the 17th century. ⌨ *Arthur E Bell, Christiaan Huygens and the Development of Science in the Seventeenth Century* (1947)

Huysmans, Cornelius, the Second 1648–1727
Dutch landscape and religious painter
Born in Antwerp, his religious paintings, a successful blend of Italian and Flemish styles, include *Christ on the Road to Emmaus*. He was a relative of **Jacob Huysmans**.

Huysmans, Jacob c.1636–96
Dutch portrait painter
Born in Antwerp, he was a relative of **Cornelius Huysmans**. He went to London about 1661 and became fashionable at the Restoration court.

Huysmans, J(oris) K(arl) 1848–1907
French novelist
He was born in Paris of Dutch descent, and his works reflect many aspects of the spiritual and intellectual life of late 19th-century France. His early ultra-realism is reflected in such works as *Les Sœurs Vatard* (1879, 'The Vatard Sisters'), and *À vau-l'eau* (1882, 'Downstream'). His best-known work, *À rebours* (1884, Eng trans *Against Nature*, 1959) deals with a decadent, aesthetic hero who turns his back on the real world and constructs his own world of extreme artifice; it was much admired by **Oscar Wilde** and his circle, and established Huysmans as a leading light in the Decadent movement of the period. Later works include *Là-bas* (1891, 'Down There') and *En Route* (1892). His *L'Art moderne* (1882, Eng trans *Certains*, 1889) is a superb study of Impressionist painting. ⌨ *R B Baldick, The Life of J K Huysmans* (1955)

Huysum, Jan van 1682–1749
Dutch painter
Born in Amsterdam, the son of the painter Justus van Huysum (1659–1716), he painted conventional landscapes. His fruit and flower pieces, however, are distinguished for exquisite finish and are represented in the Louvre, Paris, and Vienna. A brother, Jacob (1680–1740), also a painter, worked in London.

Huzhou, Wen See Weng T'Ung or Wen Tong

Hyacinthe, Père, *properly* Charles Loyson 1827–1912
French Carmelite preacher
He taught philosophy and theology at Avignon and Nantes, gathering audiences to the Madeleine and Notre Dame in Paris. He boldly denounced abuses in the Church and was excommunicated (1869). He married (1872), and continued to preach, protesting against the Infallibility dogma. In 1879 he founded a Gallican Catholic Church in Paris. His works include *Mon Testament, ma protestation* (1873, 'My Testament, My Protestation').

Hyatt, John Wesley 1837–1920
US inventor
Born in Starkey, New York State, he was apprenticed as a printer, but soon found his real vocation as an inventor. He invented a knife sharpener in 1861, followed by a water filter, a multiple-needle sewing-machine, an improved sugar cane mill and the 'Hyatt roller bearing', for the manufacture of which he established a factory in 1892. His most successful discovery was the result of his efforts to find a substitute for ivory in dominoes and billiard balls. In 1868 he added camphor to cellulose nitrate and called the resulting plastic 'celluloid', from which by 1875 he was making 'Hyatt billiard balls' and other articles. The same substance had been discovered independently in England in 1862 by **Alexander Parkes**, and christened 'Parkesine', but it failed to be a commercial success.

Hyde, Charles Cheney 1873–1952
US jurist
Born in Chicago, he was educated at Yale and Harvard, and taught law at Northwestern University, Illinois (1907–25), and Columbia University (1925–45). He served

as a solicitor for the US Department of State and was a member of the Permanent Court of Arbitration at The Hague (1951–52). His major work, *International Law, Chiefly as Interpreted and Applied by the United States* (1922, revised 1945) is of high authority.

Hyde, Douglas, *Irish* Dubhighlas de Hide, *pseudonym* An Craoibhin Aoibhinn 1860–1949
Irish poet, folklorist, academic and statesman

Born in Frenchpark, County Roscommon, he ostensibly studied law at Trinity College Dublin, while publishing poems under the pseudonym 'An Craoibhin Aoibhinn' ('The Agreeable Little Branch'), which he also used in his translations from the Gaelic of folk-tales and poems. He became president of the National Literary Society (1892) and of the faction-ridden Gaelic League (1893), was Professor of Irish at University College Dublin (1909–32), and was elected first President of the Republic of Ireland (1932–44). His works, in Irish and English, include *Abhran Gradh Chuige Connacht* (1893, Eng trans *Love Songs of Connacht*, 1893), *A Literary History of Ireland* (1899), his essay *The Necessity for De-Anglicising Ireland* (1892), and poems and plays. ⌨ *I Believed* (1950); D Daly, *The Young Douglas Hyde: The Dawn of Irish Revolution and Renaissance* (1974)

Hyde, Edward See Clarendon, 1st Earl of

Hyde, Ida Henrietta 1857–1945
US physiologist

Born in Ohio and educated at Cornell University, she moved to Strasbourg then to Heidelberg, becoming the first woman to be awarded a doctorate there in 1896. In 1898 she joined the University of Kansas, and became a full professor in 1905, retiring in 1920. In World War I she chaired the national Women's Commission on Health and Sanitation. Her work, centring on systems physiology in both vertebrates and invertebrates, pioneered the use of micro-electrode techniques in single cells. She later established the Ida H Hyde Woman's International Fellowship of the American Association of University Women. In 1902 she became the first woman to be elected to the American Physiological Society.

Hyder, Ali See Haidar Ali

Hyman, Libbie Henrietta 1888–1969
US zoologist

Born in Des Moines, Iowa, she studied zoology at the University of Chicago (1906–10) and remained there as a research assistant until 1931. Dissatisfied with the practical texts then available, she wrote *A Laboratory Manual for Elementary Zoology* (1919) and *A Laboratory Manual for Comparative Vertebrate Anatomy* (1929). Both these texts were a great success and later editions of them are still in use. Hyman was thus able to resign her position at Chicago, and took up residence near the American Museum of Natural History in New York, where she investigated many aspects of the biology of the lower invertebrates. Her *magnum opus* was a series of comprehensive volumes on the invertebrates (*The Invertebrates*, 6 vols, 1940–68) which dealt with the protozoa, coelenterates, flatworms, nematodes, echinoderma and molluscs.

Hyne, Charles John Cutcliffe Wright
1865–1944
English traveller and writer

He was born in Bibury, Gloucestershire, and educated in Bradford and at Cambridge. He travelled in Europe, Africa and the Americas and as far afield as Russian Lapland, the Canary Islands and Tunisia, and wrote many books, beginning with *The New Eden* (1892). However, he is remembered above all as the creator of the fictional character 'Captain Kettle' in several adventure stories.

Hypatia c.370–415AD
Greek philosopher

The first notable female astronomer and mathematician, she taught in Alexandria and became head of the Neoplatonist school there. She was the daughter of Theon, a writer and commentator on mathematics, with whom she collaborated, and was herself the author of commentaries on mathematics and astronomy, though none of these survives. She was renowned for her beauty, eloquence and learning, and drew pupils from all parts of the Greek world, Christian as well as pagan. Cyril, Archbishop of Alexandria, resented her influence and she was murdered by a Christian mob he may have incited to riot. ⌨ Maria Dzielska, *Hypatia of Alexandria* (1995)

Hyperides or Hypereides 389–322BC
Athenian orator and statesman

He became a professional speech-writer, and earned large sums. He opposed peace with Philip II of Macedonia, and so supported Demosthenes until after the death of Philip and during the early portion of Alexander the Great's career. In 324BC, however, in the corruption case involving Harpalus, he was one of Demosthenes' accusers. He promoted the Lamian War against Macedonia (323–322BC) after the death of Alexander, for which he was executed by the Macedonian general Antipater (398–319BC). Although Hyperides was admired and studied in Roman times, it was not until 1847 that papyri containing four of his speeches were discovered. In these Hyperides is clear, fascinating, witty and ironic.

Hyrcanus I, John c.134–104BC
High Priest of Israel and possibly Syrian subject king

He was the son of the High Priest Simon Maccabaeus (see Maccabees), and in the line of Hasmonean priestly rulers. Hyrcanus consolidated his own hold over Israel, destroyed the Samaritan temple on Mount Gerizim, and forced the Idumeans (the inhabitants of southern Judea) to adopt Judaism. Eventually he supported the Sadduceans against the Pharisees, who opposed his combination of political and religious leadership. He was a just and enlightened ruler, and of his five sons, Aristobulus and Alexander became king.

Hyrcanus II d.30BC
High Priest of Israel

He was the grandson of Hyrcanus I and son of Alexander. On the death of his father (76BC) he was appointed High Priest by his mother Alexandra, who ruled Judea till her death (67). He then warred for power with his younger brother Aristobulus, with varying fortune until Aristobulus was poisoned in 49. In 47 Julius Caesar made Antipater of Idumaea Procurator of Judea with supreme power, and a son of Aristobulus, with Parthian help, captured Hyrcanus, and took him to Seleucia. But when Herod, the Great, son of Antipater, came to power, the aged Hyrcanus was invited home to Jerusalem, where he lived in peace until, suspected of intriguing against Herod, he was put to death.

Hyrtl, Joseph 1810–94
Austrian anatomist

He studied medicine at Vienna University and became Professor of Anatomy at Prague University in 1837, before returning to Vienna as professor in 1845. He was an outstanding teacher of anatomy, and author of a highly influential *Handbook of Topographical Anatomy* (1845). His techniques of staining and making preparations were models for the time. His chief researches were on the anatomy of the mammalian ear (from mice and elephants) and the comparative anatomy of fish.

Iacocca, Lee (Lido Anthony)
1924–
US businessman

Born in Allentown, Pennsylvania, the son of Italian immigrants, he studied engineering at Lehigh and Princetown universities. He worked for the Ford Motor Company (1946–78), at first in sales, rising to become president in 1970. He joined Chrysler Corporation as president and chief operating officer in 1978, at a time when the company was in serious financial difficulties, with declining market share. As chief executive officer and chairman of the board (1979–92), he steered the company back to profitability and health. He published a best-selling autobiography (with William Kovak), *Iacocca* (1985), and a sequel, *Talking Straight* (1989). 📖 David Abodaher, *Iacocca* (1986)

Iamblichus d.c. 330AD
Syrian Neoplatonist philosopher

He studied under **Porphyry**, and founded his own school in Syrian Apameia. His principal works (in Greek) are *Protreptikos eis Philosophian* ('Summons to Philosophy'), which is valuable in including excerpts from earlier philosophers, and *De mysteriis* ('On Mysteries'), which defended the relevance of magic to philosophy. His commentaries on works of **Plato** and **Aristotle** are now lost.

Iamblichus 2nd century AD
Syrian–Greek writer

He was the author of a lost Greek romance, *Babyloniaca*. A summary by **Photius** is all that we have.

Ibáñez, Vicente Blasco 1867–1928
Spanish novelist

He was born in Valencia and studied law at Madrid University, and his works deal in realistic fashion with provincial life and social revolution. Notable among them are *La Barraca* (1899, Eng trans *The Cabin*, 1919), *Sangre y Arena* (1908, Eng trans *Blood and Sand*, 1913), and *Los Cuatro Jinetes del Apocalipsis* (1916, Eng trans *The Four Horsemen of the Apocalypse*; 1918, US; 1919, UK), which vividly portrays World War I and earned him international fame. 📖 A Day, *Vicente Blasco Ibáñez* (1972)

Ibarruri (Gómez), (Isidora) Dolores, *known as* La Pasionaria 1895–1989
Spanish writer, communist orator and politician

Born in Gallarta, in Vizcaya province, the daughter of a Basque miner, she worked as a maid-servant, then joined the Socialist Party in 1917 and worked as a journalist for the workers' press, using the pseudonym La Pasionaria (the passion flower). She helped to found the Spanish Communist Party in 1920, edited several communist newspapers, and was a member of the Central Committee from 1930. She was Spanish delegate to the Third International (1933, 1935), founded the Anti-Fascist Womens' League in 1934 and was elected to the Cortes in 1936. During the Civil War (1936–39) she became legendary for her passionate exhortations to the Spanish people to fight against the Fascist forces, declaring that 'It is better to die on your feet than to live on your knees'. When **Franco** came to power in 1939 she took refuge in the USSR, returning to Spain in 1977 after his death. As Communist deputy for Asturias she re-entered the National Assembly at the age of 81.

Ibert, Jacques François Antoine 1890–1962
French composer

Born in Paris, he studied there, winning the French Prix de Rome in 1919. In 1937 he was made director of the Académie Française in Rome. His works include operas, ballets, cantatas and chamber music, the orchestral *Divertissement* (1928), based upon his incidental music for **Eugène Labiche**'s play, *Un Chapeau de paille d'Italie* (1851, Eng trans *The Italian Straw Hat*) and *Escales* (1922, 'Ports of Call') suite.

Ibn al-'Arabi 1165–1240
Arab mystic poet

Born in Murcia, Spain, he was known as the 'sultan of the Gnostics'. Moving to Seville as a child, he studied there under Andualasian spiritual masters. Serious ill-ness, in which he encountered visions, made him abandon ordinary life, and his wife, and on his recovery he took to pilgrimage, travelling to Jerusalem and Mecca. In Mecca he wrote *The Interpreter of Longings*, poetry dedicated to a Persian sheik's daughter. He was introduced to Sufism, and became increasingly sought after for his wisdom. He settled eventually in Damascus. A great influence on Sufi philosophy, he was viewed with suspicion by some since his ideas went beyond the bounds of orthodox Islam. His many writings, which sometimes present in obscure language a form of pantheism, include a commentary on the Koran, *Kitab al-Futuhat al-Makkiyya* ('Meccan Revelations'), and *Kitab fusus al-hikam* (1229, 'The Wisdom of the Prophets'). 📖 R Landau, *The Philosophy of Ibn 'Arabi* (1959)

Ibn Battutah or Batuta 1304–68
Arab traveller and geographer

Born in Tangiers, North Africa, he spent 30 years (1325–54) travelling. He covered all the Muslim countries, visiting Mecca, Persia, Mesopotamia, Asia Minor, Bokhara, India, China, Sumatra, southern Spain and Timbuktu. He then settled in Fez, and dictated the entertaining history of his journeys, the *Rihlah* ('Travels'), published with a French translation in 1855–59. 📖 *Travels in Asia* (1929)

Ibn Daud, Abraham c.1100–c.1180
Spanish–Jewish philosopher

Born in Toledo, he was the first to draw systematically on **Aristotle**. His *Al-Aqida al Rafia* (1160, 'The Exalted Faith'), argues the essential harmony of philosophy and Torah, and his *Sefer hak-Kabbalah* (1161, 'Book of Tradition') was an influential history demonstrating the tradition of Rabbinic authority from **Moses** to his own day.

Ibn Gabirol See **Avicebrón**

Ibn Khaldun 1332–1406
Arab philosopher, historian and politician

Born in Tunis, he was widely involved in political intrigues before he turned to history, eventually becoming a college president and judge in Cairo. He wrote a monumental history of the Arabs, best known by its *Muqaddima*, or introduction, in which he explains the rise and fall of states by the waxing and waning of the spirit of *asabiya* ('solidarity').

Ibn Rushd See **Averroës**

Ibn Saud, *in full* Ibn Abd al-Rahman al-Saud 1880–1953
First King of Saudi Arabia

Born in Riyadh, he followed his family into exile (1890) and was brought up in Kuwait. In 1901 he succeeded his father and with a small band of followers set out to reconquer the family domains from the Rashidi rulers, an aim which he achieved with British recognition (1927). His ambitions against King **Hussein ibn Ali**, however, had

Ibsen, Henrik 1828–1906
Norwegian dramatist generally regarded as the founder of modern prose drama

Ibsen was born in Skien, the son of a wealthy merchant who went bankrupt in 1836. He took his first job as a chemist's assistant in Grimstad (1844–50), with the intention of studying medicine, and during this time he wrote his first play, *Catilina* (1850, Eng trans *Catiline*), which was rejected by the Christiania Theatre. He worked briefly on a student journal in Christiania (Oslo), then was given a post as stage director and resident playwright at Ole Bull's Theatre, Bergen (1851), for which he wrote five conventional romantic dramas.

In 1857 he was appointed director of the Norwegian Theatre in Christiania, having just begun work on what would be his first play of significance, *Kongsemnerne* (1863, Eng trans *The Pretenders*), based on a historical Norwegian theme, in the manner of **Schiller**. In 1862 he wrote *Kjaerlighedens Komedie* (Eng trans *Love's Comedy*), on a satirical theme of marriage as a millstone to idealism. The theatre went bankrupt the following year and, disillusioned with his homeland, Ibsen went into voluntary exile for 27 years, to Rome, Dresden and Munich (1864–91), where he wrote the bulk of his dramas.

He published the dramatic poem *Brand* in 1866, which gave him his first major success, as well as the award of a government pension. The existentialist *Peer Gynt* (also in rhyming couplets) followed in 1867, and a third historical drama, *Kejser og Galilaer* (Eng trans *Emperor and Galilean*), in 1873.

He then produced his realistic plays, concerned with social and political issues, which revolutionized European drama and on which his towering reputation rests: *Samfundets støtter* (1877, Eng trans *Pillars of Society*); *Et dukkehjem* (1879, Eng trans *A Doll's House*); *Gengangere*

(1881, Eng trans *Ghosts*); *En folkefiende* (1882, Eng trans *An Enemy of the People*); *Vildanden* (1884, Eng trans *The Wild Duck*), *Rosmersholm* (1886), *Fruen fra havet* (1888, Eng trans *The Lady from the Sea*) and *Hedda Gabler* (1890). These plays caused a major stir among critics and audiences: Ibsen refused to provide 'happy endings' (for example, Nora Helmer slams the door on her marriage and family at the end of *A Doll's House*) and was often controversial in his subject matter (eg his study of venereal, moral and societal disease in *Ghosts*).

He returned to Norway in 1891, where he wrote his last plays. These are characterized by a strong emphasis on symbolism and the unconscious, as in *Bygmester Solness* (1892, Eng trans *The Master Builder*), *Lille Eyolf* (1894, Eng trans *Little Eyolf*), *John Gabriel Borkman* (1896) and *Naar vi døde vaagner* (1899, Eng trans *When We Dead Awaken*). In 1900 he suffered a stroke which ended his literary career.

📖 G B Bryan *An Ibsen Companion* (1984); H Koht, *Life of Ibsen* (1971); M Meyer, *Ibsen* (3 vols, 1967–71).

> 'I almost think we're all of us Ghosts, Pastor Manders. It's not only what we have inherited from our father and mother that walks in us. It's all sorts of dead ideas, and lifeless old beliefs, and so forth. They have no vitality, but they cling to us all the same, and we can't get rid of them. Whenever I take up a newspaper, I seem to see Ghosts gliding between the lines. There must be Ghosts all the country over, as thick as the sand of the sea. And then we are, one and all, so pitifully afraid of the light.' Mrs Alving in *Ghosts*, Act 2.

been frustrated by British intervention (1921). He substituted patriarchal administration by the nationalistic *Ikhwan* colonies (brotherhoods) and made pilgrimages to Mecca safe for all Muslims. He changed his title from Sultan of Nejd (1922) to King of the Hejaz and Nejd (1927) and King of Saudi Arabia (1932). After the discovery of oil (1938) he granted substantial concessions to US oil companies. He remained neutral but friendly to the Allies in World War II. The economic boom produced by oil undermined the traditional spartan Wahhabi lifestyle of the royal family, much to his regret. He sired 45 sons and over 200 daughters. His son Saud succeeded his father in 1953, only to be deposed by his brother Faisal in 1964. 📖 David A Howarth, *The Desert King* (1964)

Ibn Sīnā See **Avicenna**

Ibn Zohr See **Avenzoar**

Ibrahim, Abdullah, *formerly* Dollar Brand 1934–
South African jazz pianist
Born in Cape Town of Bushman and Basuto parents, he began to play the piano as a child, and later formed the Jazz Epistles group which recorded the country's first black jazz album in 1960. He moved to Switzerland for political reasons and was heard there by **Duke Ellington** (1962), who invited him to work in the USA. In 1966 Brand had the unique honour of replacing Ellington at the piano when the orchestra was on tour. Since then, he has worked as a soloist and leader in the USA and Europe, notably in the 1980s with his septet Ekaya (Home). Ibrahim, who also plays cello, soprano saxophone and flute, adopted his Muslim name in the 1970s. He is remarkable for his jazz interpretations of the melodies and rhythms of his African childhood.

Ibsen, Henrik See panel above

Ibycus fl.mid-6th century BC
Greek poet
From Rhegium, Italy, he lived at the court of **Polycrates**, tyrant of Samos, and wrote choral lyrics in Doric anticipating **Pindar**. According to legend he was killed by robbers near Corinth, and as he was dying he called upon a flock of cranes to avenge him. The cranes then hovered over the theatre at Corinth, and one of the murderers exclaimed, 'Behold the avengers of Ibycus!' This was overheard, and the murderers were convicted. The story is told in **Schiller's** ballad, *Die Kraniche des Ibykus* (1797–98, 'The Cranes of Ibycus'). 📖 M Noethiger, *Die Sprache des Stresichorus und des Ibycus* (1971)

Icahn, Carl 1936–
US arbitrageur and options specialist
Born in New York City, he graduated from Princeton University in 1957 and studied at New York University's School of Medicine, before dropping out to become an apprentice broker with Dreyfus Corporation. An options manager by 1963, he formed his own company, Icahn and Company, in 1968, holding the posts of chairman and president since then. He has been chairman and chief executive officer of ACF Industries Inc since 1984, and chairman of the airline TWA since 1986. Later business ventures include his purchase of rival Ozark Airlines in 1986 and his buying and selling of stock in Texaco which was rumoured to have earned him an estimated $1 billion in cash.

Ichikawa, Fusaye 1893–1981
Japanese feminist and politician
Starting her working life as a teacher, she moved to Tokyo as a young woman and became involved in politics and feminism, and helped to found the New Women's Association (c.1920) which successfully fought for the right of women to attend political meetings. During her

time in the USA (1921–24) she was impressed by the US suffrage movement, and in 1924 formed the Women's Suffrage League in Japan. Following World War II she became head of the New Japan Women's League, which secured the vote for women in 1945, and went on to fight for their wider rights. She campaigned against legalized prostitution and served in the Japanese Diet (1952–71), where she continued to press for an end to bureaucratic corruption. After defeat in 1971 she was returned to parliament in 1975 and 1980.

Ickx, Jacky 1945–
Belgian racing driver
Born in Brussels, he won eight races from 116 starts in Formula One. He won 34 world sports car championship races, and was world champion in 1982–83 (both Porsche). He won the Le Mans 24-hour race a record six times (1969, 1975–77, 1981–82).

Ictinus 5th century BC
Greek architect
With Callicrates he designed the Parthenon in Athens (438BC). The work was supervised by Phidias. Ictinus was also architect of temples at Eleusis and near Phigalia.

Ida d.559
King of Bernicia (Northumbria)
According to the Venerable Bede he was an Anglian king who thrust northwards over the River Tees (547), landing at Flamborough, and established a fortified stronghold on the rock of Bamburgh as the capital of his new kingdom.

Idriess, Ion Llewellyn 1889–1979
Australian writer
He was born in Waverley, Sydney. After a wandering life as opal miner, rabbit exterminator and crocodile hunter, during World War I he served with the Australian Imperial Forces at Gallipoli and in the Near East, episodes that were to provide colour for his books, such as *Madman's Island* (1927), which was based on his own experiences while marooned. His first success was *Lasseter's Last Ride* (1931), the story of the search for a legendary gold reef. In the next 40 years he wrote a book almost every year, of which the best known are *Flynn of the Inland* (1932, about Rev John Flynn, founder of Australia's Flying Doctor Service), *The Cattle King* (1936), and *The Red Chief* (1953). His earlier experiences resulted in his being commissioned to write six survival guides for the Australian army during World War II. 📖 *The Silver City* (1957)

Idris Aloma d.c.1600
Ruler of Bornu
He was a warrior-king and the dominant figure in central Sudan. During his reign (1569–1600), and those of his sons, the Karini peoples of Bornu became a distinct, unified nation.

Iglesias, Pablo 1850–1925
Spanish politician and trade union leader
He was the founder and father figure of both the Spanish Socialist Party (PSOE) and its trade union movement, the UGT. The socialist movement was dominated by him until his later years when he was incapacitated by ill health. Moralistic, austere and cautious, he preached revolutionary ideas, while practising a pragmatic reformism. His twin obsessions were building up the Socialists' organizations and educating the working class. He became the Socialists' first Deputy to the Cortes through the alliance with the Republicans in 1910, though the PSOE never surpassed seven seats before his death in 1925.

Ignatiev, Nikolai Pavlovich 1832–1908
Russian diplomat

Born in St Petersburg, he entered the diplomatic service in 1856. In 1858 he induced China to give Russia much of the Amur province, including the site of present-day Vladivostok, and in 1860, while ambassador at Peking (Beijing), secured another large strip of territory for the Maritime Province. He concluded treaties with Khiva and Bokhara. In 1864 he was made ambassador at Constantinople (Istanbul). An ardent Panslavist, he encouraged the Balkan Slavs, and took a principal part in the diplomacy before and after the Russo-Turkish war of 1878, the treaty of San Stefano being mainly his work. Under Alexander III he was Minister of the Interior (1881), but was dismissed in 1882 for expressing excessively liberal ideas.

Ignatius of Antioch, St c.35–c.107AD
Syrian Christian prelate
He was one of the apostolic Fathers, reputedly a disciple of St John, the second Bishop of Antioch. According to Eusebius, he died a martyr in Rome under Trajan. The *Ignatian Epistles*, whose authenticity was long controversial, were written on his way to Rome after his arrest. They provide valuable information on the nature of the early Church. His feast day is 1 February.

Ignatius Loyola, St See panel p951

Ihimaera, Witi Tame 1944–
New Zealand author
Born in Gisborne, he became the first published Maori writer in English with his collection of short stories *Pounamu, Pounamu* (1972). In his following collections, *The New Net Goes Fishing* (1977) and *Dear Miss Mansfield: A Tribute to Kathleen Mansfield Beauchamp* (1989), he alludes to the Paheka (white settler) fantasy *The Wizard of Oz* in his exploration of Maori identity. He also wrote an epic novel, *The Matriarch* (1986), and with Don Long edited *Into the World of Light* (1982), an important anthology of Maori writing. He was for some years a diplomat with the New Zealand Department of Foreign Affairs.

Ihre, Johan 1707–80
Swedish philologist
Born in Lund, of Scottish extraction, he became Professor of Belles Lettres and Political Economy in 1748. His *Glossarium Suiogothicum* (1769) was the foundation of Swedish philology. He noted a number of the sound changes later developed by Rasmus Rask and Jacob Grimm into what has become known as Grimm's Law.

Ikeda Hayato 1900–65
Japanese politician and economist
Educated in Kyoto, he became Finance Minister (1949) of the Liberal-Democratic (Conservative) Party, and introduced an 'income doubling policy' of economic growth and higher living standards. As Prime Minister (1960–64), he was a supporter of the US–Japan Security Treaty (1960), and developed a low-key style in international relations during the postwar recovery period.

Iliescu, Ion 1930–
Romanian politician
Born in Oltenita, Ilfov, and educated at Bucharest Polytechnic and in Moscow, he joined the Communist Youth Union in 1944 and the Communist Party in 1953, and from 1949 to 1960 served on its central committee. In 1965 he began a three-year term as Head of Party Propaganda, and as a member of the central committee again from 1968 held office as First Secretary and Youth Minister (1967–71), and First Secretary of Jassy County (1974–79). In 1984, he withdrew from office to take up the directorship of a technical publishing company, but in the wake of the 1989 revolution and the execution of Nicolae Ceauşescu, he became president of the National Salvation Front later that year, and of its successor, the

Ignatius Loyola, St, *properly* Iñigo López de Recalde 1491–1556
Spanish soldier and founder of the Jesuits

Ignatius Loyola was born at his ancestral castle of Loyola in the Basque province of Guipúzcoa. He became a page in the court of **Ferdinand, the Catholic**, and then a soldier. In the defence of Pampeluna he was severely wounded in the leg, which he had to have re-broken and re-set. During his long convalescence, he read the lives of **Jesus Christ** and the saints, which inspired him with an intense spiritual enthusiasm. He renounced military life, and in 1522 set out on an arduous pilgrimage to the Holy Land, travelling on foot and stopping on the way to pursue a course of self-prescribed austerity.

He returned to Venice and Barcelona in 1524. He then resolved to prepare himself for the work of religious teaching, and at the age of 33 returned to the rudiments of grammar, followed up by courses at Alcalá, Salamanca and Paris. In 1534, with St **Francis Xavier** and four other associates, he founded the Society of Jesus. The original intention was to achieve the conversion of the Infidels, but as access to the Holy Land was cut off by war with the Turks, the associates sought to meet the new wants engendered by the Reformation.

Loyola went to Rome in 1539, and submitted his proposed rule to Pope **Paul III**. The rule was approved in 1540, and next year the association elected Loyola its first general. From this time he resided in Rome. He sent out missionaries to Japan, India and Brazil, and founded schools for training the young. He was beatified in 1609, and canonized in 1622. His feast day is 31 July.

📖 At Manresa he wrote the first draft of the *Spiritual Exercises*, a vital work in the training of Jesuits.

J Brodick, *St Ignatius of Loyola: The Pilgrim Years* (1956); T Maynard, *St Ignatius and the Jesuits* (1956); P Dudon, *St Ignace de Loyola* (1949).

'Teach us, good Lord, to serve Thee as Thou deservest:
To give and not to count the cost;
To fight and not to heed the wounds;
To toil and not to seek for rest;
To labour and not to ask for any reward
Save that of knowing that we do Thy will.
'Prayer for Generosity' (1548).

Provisional Council for National Unity. In 1990, he was elected President and resigned his party posts. Discontent with the economic situation resulted in protests against his government at the end of 1990 and early in 1991; nevertheless he was re-elected in 1992.

Ilyushin, Sergei Vladimirovich 1894–1977
Soviet aircraft designer

Born in the region of Vologda, he was drafted into the province army in 1914, then served as an aircraft mechanic and began flight training in 1917. He graduated from the North-East Zhukovsky Air Force Academy in 1926, leading to his appointment in 1931 as director of the aircraft construction section of the Scientific and Technical Committee, Main Air Force Board. His first successful design, the TSKB-30 (1936), gained several records and was extensively used as a bomber in World War II. His other designs included the IL-2 Shturmovik dive-bomber (1939), the twin-engined passenger-carrying IL-12 (1946), the IL-28 jet bomber (1948), the IL-18 Moskva turboprop airliner (1957), the 182-passenger IL-62 jet of 1957 and its wide-bodied successor, the IL-86 airbus (350 passengers). An impressive designer, and a leading Communist Party official, he became Professor of Aircraft Design at the Zhukovsky Air Force Engineering Academy in 1948.

Imhof, Eduard 1895–1986
Swiss cartographer

Born in Schiers, he was educated at the Swiss Federal Institute of Technology (ETH) (1914–19). He was elected to the first Swiss professorship in cartography (1925) and founded the Institute of Cartography at the ETH, which he directed until his retirement in 1965. He pioneered good design as the basis of the cartographic discipline and published classic texts on relief and thematic techniques. As a cartographic artist throughout his life, he produced 50 full-colour relief maps. He edited the *Atlas der Schweiz* (1961–78, 'Atlas of Switzerland').

Imhotep 27th century BC
Egyptian physician

He was adviser to King Zoser (3rd dynasty), and probably the architect of the so-called Step Pyramid at Sakkara, near Cairo. In time he came to be revered as a sage, and during the Saite period (500BC) he was worshipped as the life-giving son of Ptah, god of Memphis. The Greeks identified him with their own god of healing, Asclepius, because of his reputed knowledge of medicine. Many bronze figures of him have been discovered.

Immelmann, Max 1890–1916
German airman

He laid the foundation of German fighter tactics in World War I, and originated the 'Immelmann turn'—a half-loop followed by a half-roll. He was killed in action.

Immermann, Karl Leberecht 1796–1840
German dramatist and novelist

Born in Magdeburg, he entered the public service of Prussia in 1817, and served in Münster, Magdeburg and Düsseldorf. His fame rests upon his tales (*Miscellen*, 1830) and the satirical novels *Die Epigonen* (1836, 'Those who Follow After') and *Münchhausen* (1839). He also wrote plays, poetry, and autobiographical works. 📖 B V Wiese, *Karl Immermann* (1969)

Imran Khan 1952–
Pakistani cricketer

He was born in Lahore and educated in England at Oxford University. He played county cricket for Worcestershire and Sussex, and made his Test debut in 1971. In 1983 he became the second player to score a century and take 10 wickets in a Test match. He captained Pakistan on several occasions (1982–83, 1985–87, 1988–92), and led them to victory in the World Cup in 1992. He scored over 3,000 Test runs, and took over 325 wickets in Test matches, before announcing his retirement from cricket in 1992. His high-profile marriage to Jemima Goldsmith thrust him into the eye of the media again in 1995, the year he entered Pakistani politics. He launched the Tehreek-i-Insaaf Party in April 1996, but won no seats in the 1997 election.

Inchbald, Elizabeth, *née* Simpson 1753–1821
English novelist, playwright and actress

Born in Bury St Edmunds, the daughter of a farmer, she ran away to go on the stage and in 1772 married John Inchbald (d.1779), an actor in London. She made her debut at Bristol as Cordelia, and later appeared at Covent Garden, but from 1789 made her name as a playwright. She was the author of 19 sentimental comedies, including *The Wedding Day* (1794) and *Lover's Vows* (1798), the play which the Bertram children act in **Jane Austen**'s *Mansfield*

Park. She also wrote the novels *A Simple Story* (1791) and *Nature and Art* (1796), and edited the 24-volume *The British Theatre* (1806–09).

Indiana, Robert, *originally* Robert Clarke 1928–
US painter and graphic designer

Born in New Castle, Indiana, he studied art in Indianapolis (1945–46), in Ithaca, New York, and at the Art Institute of Chicago before travelling to Great Britain in 1953. Settling in New York in 1956, he began making hard-edged abstract pictures and stencilled wooden constructions, which fall into the early Pop Art movement. His best-known images are based on the letters LOVE, as featured in his first one-man show in New York (1962). His other word-paintings have included HUG, ERR, DIE, and the 20ft *EAT Sign* (1964, New York World Fair).

Indurain, Miguel 1964–
Spanish cyclist

Born in Villava, Navarre, he is only the fourth cyclist to win five Tours de France (1991–95). His second win of the Giro d'Italia in 1993 ranks him among only six other cyclists ever to have won both events in the same year. His phenomenal success is based on his invincibility in the Tour's time trials—racing alone against the clock. As the leader of the Banesto team, he became the richest man in cycle racing and a national hero in Spain. He announced his retirement in 1997.

Indy, Vincent d' 1851–1931
French composer

Born in Paris, he was a student, disciple and biographer of César Franck, and founded the Schola Cantorum in Paris in 1894. He published *Treatise of Composition* (1900) and composed operas, chamber music and, notably, the *Symphonie cévenole* (1886, 'Symphony on a French Mountain Song') in the spirit of French Romanticism.

Ine d.c.726
West Saxon king

According to the Venerable Bede, he came to power in 688. During his reign of nearly 40 years he put Church organization on a proper footing and promulgated the earliest extant code of West Saxon laws. Probably the most notable king of his time in northern Europe, he abdicated (726), and died on a pilgrimage to Rome.

Inge, William Motter 1913–73
US playwright and novelist

Born in Independence, Kansas, he was educated at Kansas University and George Peabody College for Teachers, and taught and wrote art criticism for the St Louis *Star-Times*. Outside the mainstream of US theatre, he is nevertheless important for his plays *Come Back, Little Sheba* (1950), *Picnic* (1953, Pulitzer Prize), *Bus Stop* (1955) and *The Dark at the Top of the Stairs* (first produced as *Farther off from Heaven* in 1947 and revised in 1957). 📖 R B Schuman, *William Inge* (1965)

Inge, William Ralph, *also known as* Dean Inge 1860–1954
English prelate and theologian

Born in Crayke, Yorkshire, and educated at Eton and King's College, Cambridge, he taught at Eton and was vicar of All Saints, Kensington, for two years before being appointed in 1907 Professor of Divinity at Cambridge. From 1911 to 1934 he was dean of St Paul's, earning for himself by his pessimism in sermons and newspaper articles the sobriquet of 'the Gloomy Dean'. Popular books include *Outspoken Essays* (1919, 1922) and *Lay Thoughts of a Dean* (1926, 1931); his more serious works examined, among other things, Neoplatonism and Christian mysticism.

Ingemann, Bernhard Severin 1789–1862
Danish novelist and poet

Born in Thorkildstrup, Falster, he is best known for the patriotic verse cycle *Holger Danske* (1837, 'Holgar the Dane') and his idealized romantic historical novels, *Valdemar Sejer* (1826), *Kong Erik* (1833) and *Prins Otto af Danmark* (1835). He also wrote the historical novels *Valdemar den store og hans Mænd* (1824, 'Waldemar the Great and his Men') and *Dronning Margrethe* (1836, 'Queen Margaret'), both in verse. From 1822 he lectured at the Royal Academy of Sorø, near Copenhagen, and he was headmaster there from 1842 to 1849. 📖 C Langballe, *Bernhard Severin Ingemann* (1949)

Ingenhousz or Ingen-Housz, Jan 1730–99
Dutch chemist and biologist

He was born in Breda and qualified as a doctor after attending the universities of Louvain, Belgium and Leyden. Around 1765 he moved to England where he studied the methods of smallpox inoculation pioneered by William Watson and Thomas Dimsdale. Ingen-Housz's early scientific work was on electricity and he was the first person to generate static electricity. He also devised apparatus for comparing the different heat conductivities of different metals. He is most famous for his work on photosynthesis. By 1796 he had also discovered that all parts of plants give off carbon dioxide both in darkness and light.

Ingersoll, Robert Green 1833–99
US lawyer and orator

He was born in Dresden, New York State. In the Civil War (1861–65) he was colonel of a Federal cavalry regiment, and in 1867 became State Attorney-General of Illinois. A successful Republican orator, he was also noted for his agnostic lectures attacking Christian beliefs, and wrote numerous books, including *The Gods, and Other Lectures* (1876) and *Why I Am An Agnostic* (1896).

Inglis, Elsie Maud 1864–1917
Scottish surgeon and reformer

Born in Naini Tal, India, she was one of the first women medical students at Edinburgh and Glasgow, and inaugurated the second medical school for women at Edinburgh (1892). In 1901, appalled at the lack of maternity facilities and the prejudice held against women doctors by their male colleagues, she founded a maternity hospital in Edinburgh, completely staffed by women. In 1906 she founded the Scottish Women's Suffragette Federation, which sent two women ambulance units to France and Serbia in 1915. She set up three military hospitals in Serbia (1916), fell into Austrian hands, was repatriated, but in 1917 returned to Russia with a voluntary corps, which was withdrawn after the revolution.

Inglis, John, Lord Glencorse 1810–91
Scottish judge

Born in Edinburgh, he established himself as a leading advocate by his celebrated defence of Madeleine Smith, who was charged with poisoning her lover in a sensational murder trial in 1857, and rose to be successively Lord Justice Clerk (1858) and Lord President of the Court of Session (1867–91). He also played a major role in the reform of the Scottish universities.

Ingold, Sir Christopher Kelk 1893–1970
English chemist

Born in London, he studied physics at London University and chemistry at Hartley University College, Southampton, and then went to Imperial College London. The brilliance of his research on organic reactions led to his appointment as professor at Leeds University (1924), where he remained until 1930, when he moved to University College London, turning it into one of the finest departments in the world. He developed models for the ways in which organic reactions occur, describing the ground state properties of molecules by the ways in which atoms attract or repel electrons. He classified organic reactions according to the transition state (the energy level which the molecules have to reach in order to react) which provided a convincing model for organic reactions and explained many experimental observations. During the 1930s and 1940s he undertook a massive study of the mechanism of aromatic nitration. Another reaction which received considerable attention was electrophilic addition to the olefinic double bond. A notable aspect of his work was his use of physical techniques not then normally used by organic chemists (isotope effects, molecular spectroscopy). His monumental work *Structure and Mechanism in Organic Chemistry* (1953) influenced chemists worldwide, and was said to head the 'English school' of organic chemists. His papers are models of clarity and precision, and can be read with as much interest today as when they were first written. Elected Fellow of the Royal Society in 1924 at the early age of 30, he received countless honours, including a knighthood in 1958.

Ingram, Collingwood, *known as* 'Cherry' Ingram
1880–1981
English ornithologist, botanist, gardener and traveller
The grandson of the newspaper proprietor **Herbert Ingram**, he had a garden at Bettenden, Kent, celebrated for its collection of Japanese ornamental cherries. His books include *The Birds of the Riviera* (1926), *Isles of the Seven Seas* (1936), *Ornamental Cherries* (1948), *In Search of Birds* (1966), *A Garden of Memories* (1970) and *The Migration of the Swallow* (1974).

Ingram, Herbert 1811–60
English journalist
Born in Boston, Lincolnshire, he founded the *Illustrated London News* (1842), and was MP for Boston from 1856. He was drowned in a boat collision on Lake Michigan in the USA.

Ingrams, Richard Reid 1937–
English journalist
Born in Westcliffe-on-Sea, Essex, he was educated at Shrewsbury School and University College, Oxford, where he met many of his future colleagues. In 1962 he founded with **Peter Cook, Willie Rushton** and other new-wave satirists, the satirical magazine *Private Eye*, becoming editor in the following year and retaining that post until 1986. He was television critic for the *Spectator* (1979–84), and has been a columnist for the *Observer* since 1988. At times a contradictory and controversial figure, he is inveterately disrespectful of reputations, but can also be very traditional, characteristics which were made manifest in 1992, when he founded and became editor of *The Oldie*. He is the author or co-author of numerous spin-off and other books, including *Dear Bill: the collected letters of Denis Thatcher* (1980), *You Might As Well Be Dead* (1986), *England: An Anthology* (1989) and a biography of **Malcolm Muggeridge** (1995).

Ingres, Jean Auguste Dominique 1780–1867
French painter
Born in Montauban, he studied at Toulouse Acadamy, then he went to Paris in 1796 to study under **Jacques Louis David**. In 1801 he won the Prix de Rome with *Achilles Receiving the Ambassadors of Agamemnon* (École des Beaux-Arts), but quarrelled with David and from 1806 to 1820 lived in Rome, where he began many of his famous nudes, including *La Grande Odalisque* (1814), *The Valpinçon Bather* (1808) and *La Source* (begun in 1807 but not completed until 1856), all in the Louvre, Paris. Many of the paintings he sent to Paris from Rome attracted vehement criticism, especially from **Eugène Delacroix**, whose work Ingres

detested. The leading exponent of the classical tradition in France in the 19th century, Ingres painted with superb draughtsmanship, but little interest in facial characteristics or colour. His motto was 'A thing well drawn is well enough painted'. He also painted historical subjects such as *Paolo and Francesca* (1819, Chantilly), and in Florence (1820–24) painted *The Oath to Louis XIII* for Montauban Cathedral, which appeased the rival schools of classicists and Romantics in France. He returned to Paris in 1826 and was appointed professor at the Academy. His *Apotheosis of Homer* (Louvre ceiling) was well received, but *The Martyrdom of St Symphorian* (1834, Autun Cathedral) was not, and Ingres went off again to Italy (1834–41), becoming director of the Académie Française in Rome. His *Stratonice* (Chantilly), *Vierge à l'hostie* (Louvre) and *Odalisque à l'esclave* re-established him in Paris and he returned in triumph, was awarded the Legion of Honour (1855) and made a senator (1862). 📖 Gaetan Picon, *Ingres* (trans, 1980)

Inness, George 1825–94
US landscape artist
Born near Newburgh, New York, he visited Italy and France and came under the influence of the Barbizon school. Among his best-known paintings are *Delaware Valley* (1865), *Peace and Plenty* (1865) and *Evening at Medfield, Massachusetts*, in the Metropolitan Museum of Art in New York, and *Rainbow after a Storm* in the Chicago Art Institute. His late style is typified by *Sunrise* (1887, Metropolitan Museum).

Innocent I, St AD360–417
Italian pope
He was born in Albano. His pontificate (AD402–417), next to that of **Leo I**, the Great, is the most important for the relations of Rome to the other churches. He enforced the celibacy of the clergy, he maintained the right of the Bishop of Rome to judge appeals from other churches, and his letters contain many assertions of universal jurisdiction. During his reign, Rome was sacked (410) by **Alaric I**. His feast day is 28 July.

Innocent III, *original name* Lotario de' Conti di Segni
1160–1216
Italian pope
Born at Agnagni, he studied theology in Paris and canon law in Bologna under the great canonist Huguccio of Pisa. He succeeded Pope **Celestine** III, and his pontificate (from 1198) is regarded as the culminating point of the temporal and spiritual supremacy of the Roman see. He judged between rival emperors in Germany and had **Otto IV** deposed. He put England under an interdict and excommunicated King **John** for refusing to recognize **Stephen Langton** as Archbishop of Canterbury. John's submission made England and Ireland satellites of the Holy See. In his time the Latin conquest of Constantinople (Istanbul) in the Fourth Crusade destroyed the pretensions of his Eastern rivals. He zealously repressed simony (the buying and selling of ecclesiastical benefices) and other abuses of the time. He promoted the spiritual movement in which the Franciscan and Dominican orders had their origin. Under him the famous fourth Lateran Council was held in 1215. His works embrace sermons, a remarkable treatise on the *Misery of the Condition of Man*, a large number of letters, and perhaps the 'golden sequence' 'Veni, sancte Spiritus'. 📖 L Elliot-Binns, *Innocent III* (1931)

Innocent IV, *original name* Sinibaldo Fieschi d.1254
Italian pope
Born in Genoa and trained in canon law at Bologna, he took a view of papal supremacy very similar to that of **Innocent III**. He was unscrupulous in using patronage to construct his own power network, and his pontificate

(from 1243) brought the struggle between the papacy and Emperor **Frederick II** to its climax. At Frederick's death (1250), Innocent sought to establish papal overlordship in Sicily. This was acknowledge by Frederick's illegitimate son **Manfred** who nevertheless led a revolt in 1254. Innocent also put the Inquisition on a permanent basis in Italy.

Innocent X, *original name* Giambattista Pamfili
1574–1655
Italian pope

An unscrupulous man, he was notorious for his nepotism. Shortly after his election (1644) he began systematic attacks on the Barbarini, relatives of his predecessor, **Urban VIII**. His victims fled to France and successfully appealed for protection to Cardinal **Mazarin**, who threatened to annex the papal enclave of Avignon, whereupon Innocent backed down. Innocent's condemnation of the Peace of Westphalia served only to demonstrate the growing impotence of the papacy, while his support for Spanish claims to Portugal (which had regained its independence again in 1640) proved equally fruitless. Even the Bull *Cum Occasione* (1653) condemning Jansenist views on grace, rather than restoring unity to the Church, merely sparked more than a century of internal religious controversy.

Innocent XI, *original name* Benedetto Odescalchi
1611–89
Italian pope

Born in Como, he studied law at the University of Naples. Elected pope in 1676 despite the opposition of **Louis XIV** of France, he embarked on a policy of retrenchment (including the abolition of many sinecures and a campaign against luxury) and tried, with some success, to end the practice of nepotism, also seeking financial aid from Catholic princes. The consequence of these reforms was that he was able to put papal finances on a sufficiently sound footing to aid **John III Sobieski** of Poland and the Holy Roman Emperor, **Leopold I**, to break the Turkish siege of Vienna (1683). His relations with Louis XIV, however, were poor, and further deteriorated because of his reluctance to see the implementation of Louis's edict of 1673 which allowed him to appropriate the revenue of vacant sees. Louis summoned a French synod, which affirmed the limitations of papal authority within France, and in retaliation, Innocent refused to confirm the promotion of any French clergy involved in the synod. In 1685 he further angered Louis by condemning his treatment of the Huguenots and, in 1688, by opposing his candidate for the archbishopric of Cologne. Louis's response was to occupy the papal enclave of Avignon. In theological matters, Innocent was far from unsympathetic to Jansenist views, but he drew the line at the Quietist doctrines of his friend, the Spanish priest and mystic Miguel de Molinos (1640–97), whom he had tried and imprisoned.

Innocent XII, *original name* Antonio Pignatelli
1615–1700
Italian pope

He was educated by Jesuits and was papal ambassador to Tuscany, Poland and Austria before becoming a cardinal in 1681. He became pope in 1691. He brought an end to the poor relations between **Louis XIV** of France and the papacy by persuading the latter to withdraw the Gallican Articles of 1682 and to relinquish the occupied papal enclave of Avignon. In return, Innocent championed the candidacy of Philippe of Anjou (Louis XIV's grandson, later **Philip V** of Spain) as the heir to the Spanish throne and acknowledged the French monarch's right to administer vacant sees. In theological matters, he condemned both Jansenism (1696) and Quietism (1699), while in

ecclesiastical and domestic affairs he carried on the struggle against nepotism which he condemned in the Bull *Romanum decet pontificem* (1692).

Innocent XIII, *original name* Michelangelo dei Conti
1655–1724
Italian pope

A former papal ambassador to Switzerland and Portugal and a cardinal from 1706, he became pope in 1721. He invested the Holy Roman Emperor Charles VI with sovereignty over Naples (1721), and recognized **James Edward Stuart** (the Old Pretender) as King of England and promised him subsidies if he returned England to Roman Catholicism. Although he was hostile towards the Jansenists, he was also distrustful of the Jesuits, taking particular issue with modified 'Chinese rites' which they employed with some success to attract converts in Asia.

Inönü, Ismet, *originally* Ismet Paza 1884–1973
Turkish soldier and politician

He was born in Smyrna (now Izmir), Asia Minor. After a distinguished army career in World War I he became **Kemal Atatürk's** Chief of Staff in the war against the Greeks (1919–22), defeating them twice at the village of Inönü, which he adopted as his last name. As the first Prime Minister of the new republic (1923–37) he signed the Treaty of Lausanne (1923), introduced many political reforms transforming Turkey into a modern state, and was unanimously elected President in 1938 on Atatürk's death. From 1950 he was Leader of the Opposition. He became Prime Minister again with General Gürsel as President in 1961, surviving repeated assassination attempts, an army coup and constitutional crisis in 1963, but resigned in 1965 after failing to govern effectively with minority support.

Inoue Kaoru 1836–1915
Japanese politician and genro (elder statesman)

From a samurai family in Choshu, he took an active part in the overthrow of the **Tokugawa** shogunate, purchasing arms from England and playing a key role in arranging the Chosu–Satsuma alliance (1866) against the Tokugawa regime. In the new Meiji government (1868–87) he served as Minister of Public Works, Minister of Agriculture and Commerce, Minister of Finance and Minister of Foreign Affairs. He was a keen advocate of economic modernization and developed close ties with business interests. As Foreign Minister (1879–87) he negotiated with Western powers over treaty revision, but was unable to obtain their agreement to end the foreign privilege of extraterritoriality in Japan.

Ionesco, Eugène 1912–94
French playwright

Born in Slatina, Romania, he was educated in Bucharest and Paris, where he settled in 1940. He pioneered a new style of drama that came to be called the Theatre of the Absurd, in which the absurdity of man's condition was mirrored in a dramatic form of unreal situations without traditional narrative continuity or meaningful and coherent dialogue. Many of Ionesco's plays are in one act: they include *La Cantatrice chauve* (1950, UK title *The Bald Prima Donna*, 1956; US title *The Bald Soprano*, 1958) and *Les Chaises* (1952, Eng trans *The Chairs*, 1957). Other plays include *Amédée* (1954, Eng trans *Amedee*, 1955), *Le Tableau* (1955, Eng trans *The Picture*, 1968) and *Rhinocéros* (1959, Eng trans *Rhinoceros*, 1960). His later plays received less attention outside France: they include *Jeux de massacre* (1970, Eng trans *Wipe-Out Game*, 1971), *Macbett* (1972, Eng trans 1973) and *Voyages chez les morts ou Thème et variations* (1980, Eng trans *Journey Among the Dead*, 1983). He also wrote essays, children's stories and a novel *Le Solitaire* (1973, Eng trans *The Hermit*, 1974, US; 1975, UK). 📖 R Hayman, *Ionesco* (1972); A Lewis, *Ionesco* (1972)

Iorga, Nicolae 1871–1940/1
Romanian politician and historian

As editor (1903–06) of *Sămănătorul* ('The Sower'), he advocated conservative and patriotic values. Active in political life, he was elected to the Romanian parliament (1907) and founded the National Democrat Party. As Prime Minister and Minister of Education (1931–32), he supported King Carol II of Romania. With the establishment of the Antonescu regime, Iorga was one of several leading figures in Romanian political and cultural life who were murdered in the years 1940–41.

Ipatieff, Vladimir Nikolayevich 1867–1952
US organic and industrial chemist

Born in Moscow, Russia, he was an officer in the Russian army. He later studied at the Mikhail Artillery Academy, St Petersburg, and was professor there from 1898 to 1906. He synthesized isoprene, the basic unit of natural rubber, in 1897. Around 1900 he began to study the decomposition of alcohols in the presence of a catalyst, obtaining in this way aldehydes, esters and olefins. He particularly investigated the catalytic properties of alumina, now widely used as an industrial catalyst. From 1904 he studied the effects of high pressures on catalytic reactions and showed that they greatly increased the speed and output of the reaction. He demonstrated that it was possible to catalyse more than one reaction at a time by using two-component catalysts, now standard practice in the petrochemical industry. During World War I he directed Russia's chemical warfare programme. He emigrated to the USA in 1930 and worked for the Universal Oil Products Company in Chicago, where he developed a process for making high-octane petrol.

Iqbal, Sir Mohammad 1875–1938
Indian poet and philosopher

Born in Sialkot, India (now in Pakistan), he was educated at Lahore, Cambridge (where he read law and philosophy) and Munich. On his return to India, he practised law, but achieved fame through his poetry, where his mysticism and nationalism caused him to be regarded almost as a prophet throughout the Muslim world. President of the Muslim League in 1930, his efforts to establish a separate Muslim state eventually led to the formation of Pakistan. He was knighted in 1923, and his works include *Reconstruction of Religious Thought in Islam* (1934).

Ireland, John Nicholson 1879–1962
English composer

Born in Bowdon, Cheshire, he studied composition under Charles Stanford at the Royal College of Music, London. His poetic feelings, inspired by ancient traditions and places, are in evidence in such works as the orchestral prelude *The Forgotten Rite* (1913) of the Channel Islands, and the rhapsody *Mai-dun* (1921) of the Wessex countryside. He established his reputation with his Violin Sonata in A (1917), and between the wars was a prominent member of the English musical renaissance. The piano concerto (1930) and *These Things Shall Be* (1937) for chorus and orchestra feature strongly among his later works, which include song settings of poems by Thomas Hardy, John Masefield, A E Housman and others.

Ireland, William Henry 1777–1835
English literary forger

He was born in London, the son of a dealer in rare books, and articled at the age of 17 to a London conveyancer, with access to old deeds and documents. Tempted by his father's enthusiasm for Shakespeare, he forged the poet's signature on a carefully copied old lease, and went on to fabricate private letters and annotated books. James Boswell was among the many who were duped, but Edmund Malone and others saw through the forgery and denounced it. Ireland then produced a deed of

Shakespeare's bequeathing his books and papers to a William-Henrye Irelaunde, an assumed ancestor. Next a new historical play, *Vortigern and Rowena*, was announced, and produced by Richard Brinsley Sheridan at Drury Lane (1796). It was damned at once, and Ireland, finally suspected by his father, was forced to confess. He published a statement in 1796, and expanded it in his *Confessions* (1805). He produced a dozen poems, four or five novels, and ten or more biographical and miscellaneous compilations, but ended his life in poverty.

Irenaeus, St c.130–c.200AD
Greek theologian, and one of the Christian fathers of the Greek church

Born of Greek parents in Asia Minor, he was a pupil of Polycarp who had been a disciple of John the Apostle. He became a priest of the Graeco-Gaulish church of Lyons under Bishop Pothinus, after whose martyrdom in AD177 he was elected bishop. Gregory of Tours says that Irenaeus met his death in the persecution under Severus in 202, but this has never been substantiated. Irenaeus was a successful missionary bishop, but he is chiefly remembered for his opposition to Gnosticism (especially the Valentinians), against which he wrote his invaluable work *Against Heresies*. A masterly expositor of Christian theology, he was a key figure also in the maintenance of contact between Eastern and Western sections of the church. His feast day is 3 July.

Irene c.752–803
Byzantine empress

She was a poor orphan of Athens, and her beauty and talents led the Emperor Leo IV to marry her (769). After his death (780) she ruled as regent for her son, Constantine VI. Powerful and resolute, she imprisoned and blinded him and her husband's five brothers, and ruled in her own right from 797, but in 802 she was banished to Lesbos. For her part in patronizing monasteries and restoring icon veneration she was recognized as a saint by the Greek Orthodox Church.

Ireton, Henry 1611–51
English soldier

He was born in Attenborough, Nottinghamshire. At the outbreak of the Civil War (1642–51) he offered his services to Parliament, fighting at Edgehill (1642), Naseby (1645) and the siege of Bristol. In 1646 he married Oliver Cromwell's daughter Bridget. In 1647 he proposed a solution to the conflict in the form of a constitutional monarchy (the manifesto known as the 'Heads of the Army Proposals'), but the proposals proved unacceptable, and he later signed the warrant for the king's execution (1649). He accompanied Cromwell to Ireland, and in 1650 became Lord-Deputy. He died of the plague after the capture of Limerick, and was buried in Westminster Abbey. At the Restoration (1660), his remains, along with those of Cromwell and others, were transferred to Tyburn, where they were ceremonially hanged and buried under the gallows. ⌨ Robert Ramsey, *Henry Ireton* (1949)

Iriarte (y Oropesa), Tomas de 1750–91
Spanish poet and writer of fables

Born in Orotava, Tenerife, he was the author of *Fábulas Literarias* (1782), in which a number of animals are made to speak out against the author's literary enemies. He also translated Horace. He loved music, and wrote a long poem on the subject, as well as a poetic tribute to Joseph Haydn. ⌨ R Cox, *Tomas de Iriarte* (1972)

Irigoyen or Yrigoyen, Hipólito 1850–1933
Argentine politician

Born in Buenos Aires, he became leader of the Radical Civic Union Party in 1896 and worked for electoral reform, which, when it came in 1912, brought him to power as the first Radical President (1916–22). He was re-elected in 1928, but deposed by a military coup in 1930.

Irons, Jeremy 1948–
English actor

Born in Cowes on the Isle of Wight, he was educated at Sherborne and the Bristol Old Vic Theatre School where he made his first professional appearance in 1971. He made his West End debut as John the Baptist in *Godspell* (1973). He appeared in many productions including the drama series *The Pallisers* (1975) before winning the Clarence Derwent award for *The Rear Column* (1977) and making his film debut in *Nijinsky* (1980). Widespread public recognition followed his performances in the television series *Brideshead Revisited* (1981) and the film *The French Lieutenant's Woman* (1981). He has favoured artistic challenge over commercial gain and proved particularly adept at portraying victims of emotional repression. His films include *The Mission* (1986), *Dead Ringers* (1988), *Reversal of Fortune* (1990, Best Actor Academy Award), *Damage* (1993), *Die Hard With A Vengeance* (1995) and *Stealing Beauty* (1996). Stage work includes *The Real Thing* (1984–85), for which he received a Tony award, and *The Winter's Tale* (1986). He is married to the actress Sinead Cusack.

Ironside, William Edmund Ironside, 1st Baron
1880–1959
Scottish field marshal

He was born in Ironside, Aberdeenshire. He served as a secret agent disguised as a railwayman in the Second Boer War (1899–1902) and held several staff appointments in World War I. He commanded the Archangel expedition against the Bolsheviks (1918) and the Allied contingent in North Persia (1920). He was Chief of the Imperial General Staff at the outbreak of World War II, was promoted field marshal (1940) and placed in command of the home defence forces (1940). The 'Ironsides', fast, light-armoured vehicles, were named after him.

Irvine, Andy (Andrew Robertson) 1951–
Scottish rugby player

Born in Edinburgh, he attended George Heriot's School and took up rugby. A full-back, he played club rugby for Heriot's Former Pupils, and played for Scotland 51 times. His running talent and attacking style made him one of the most exciting players Scotland has ever produced. He toured with the British Lions in 1974, 1977 and 1980, and during his international career he scored a world record total of 301 points for Scotland and the Lions, a record that he held until it was broken by Gavin Hastings.

Irving, Edward 1792–1834
Scottish clergyman and mystic

Born in Annan, Dumfriesshire, he studied at Edinburgh University, became a schoolmaster and in 1819 was appointed assistant to Thomas Chalmers in Glasgow. In 1822 he went to the Caledonian Church, Hatton Garden, London, where he enjoyed great success as a preacher. In 1825 he began to announce the imminent second coming of Jesus Christ, and was charged with heresy in 1828 for maintaining the sinfulness of Christ's nature. Convicted by the London presbytery in 1830, he was ejected from his new church in Regent's Square in 1832, and finally deposed in 1833. The majority of his congregation adhered to him, and a new communion, the Catholic Apostolic Church (known as Irvingite) developed. He wrote *Homilies on the Sacraments* (1828).

Irving, Sir Henry, originally John Henry Brodribb
1838–1905
English actor

He was born in Keinton-Mandeville, Somerset, and was for a time a clerk in London but made his first appearance at the Sunderland Theatre in 1856, thereafter acting in Edinburgh (1857–60), Manchester (1860–65) and Liverpool. In 1866 he made his London debut at the St James's Theatre, transferring to the Lyceum in 1871. His *Hamlet* (1874), *Macbeth* (1875) and *Othello* (1876) gained him his reputation as the greatest English actor of his time, although his striking presence and flair for interpreting the subtler emotions made him more successful in parts such as Shylock and Malvolio than in the great tragic roles of King Lear or Hamlet. In 1878 he began his famous theatrical partnership with Ellen Terry at the Lyceum (where he became actor-manager-lessee), when she played Ophelia to his Hamlet. The association lasted until 1902, and among their successes was William Wills's version of Goethe's *Faust* (1885), in which Ellen Terry played Marguerite to Irving's Mephistopheles. They gave a command performance of *The Bells* for Queen Victoria at Sandringham (1889), and produced Tennyson's play *Becket* in 1893. Irving toured the USA with his company eight times. The failure of his son's play and the loss by fire of the Lyceum's stock of scenery in 1898 forced him to sell the lease of the Lyceum, which was eventually turned into a music hall. In 1895 he became the first actor to receive a knighthood. His ashes were buried in Westminster Abbey. His publications include *The Drama* (1893) and an edition of Shakespeare's plays (1888). Of his sons, Laurence (1871–1914) was a novelist and playwright who was drowned in the *Empress of Ireland* disaster, and Henry Brodribb ('H B'; 1870–1919) was an actor. 📖 Laurence Irving, *Henry Irving, the Actor and His World* (1951)

Irving, Washington 1783–1859
US writer

Born in New York City, he studied law, visited Rome, Paris, the Netherlands and London, and on his return in 1806 was admitted to the Bar. *Salmagundi* (1808), a series of satirical essays, was followed by a characteristically boisterous work, *A History of New York, by Diedrich Knickerbocker* (1809). He served as an officer in the 1812 war, and from 1815–32 lived largely in Europe. Under the pseudonym 'Geoffrey Crayon' he wrote *The Sketch Book* (1819–20), a miscellany including the tales 'Rip Van Winkle' and 'The Legend of Sleepy Hollow'. Another miscellany, *Tales of a Traveller*, was published in 1824, and his stay in Spain (1826–29) prompted such studies as *The History of the Life and Voyages of Christopher Columbus* (1828) and *The Conquest of Granada* (1829). On his return to New York in 1832 the criticisms made by James Fenimore Cooper and others that he had written only about Europe resulted in *A Tour on the Prairie* (1835) and *The Adventures of Captain Bonneville, USA* (1837). From 1842 to 1846 he was US ambassador to Spain. 📖 S T Williams, *The Life of Irving* (1935)

Isaac I, Comnenus c.1005–61
Eastern Roman emperor

He ruled in Constantinople (Istanbul) from 1057 to 1059. He established the finances of the empire on a sounder footing, confiscated Church property to pay for strengthening his military defences, and repelled the Hungarians attacking his northern frontier. He then resigned the Crown, and retired to a monastery, where he died. He wrote commentaries on Homer.

Isaac II, Angelus c.1135–1204
Eastern Roman emperor

He ruled in Constantinople (Istanbul) from 1185. After a reign of war and tumult, during which he defeated the Serbians (1190), he was dethroned, blinded and imprisoned by his brother Alexius (1195). Restored in 1203, he reigned for six months, was again dethroned, and died in prison.

Isaacs, Alick 1921–67
Scottish biologist
Born in Glasgow, he studied medicine there, did research work at the universities of Sheffield and Melbourne, and in 1950 joined the virology division of the National Institute for Research, where he became chief in 1961. His research into the way influenza viruses interacted and impeded each other's growth led him and Swiss virologist Jean Lindemann in 1957 to isolate a substance now known as interferon; this protein is produced as part of the body's response to a viral infection, and has been shown to be of therapeutic use in some viral diseases and several forms of cancer.

Isaacs, Sir Isaac Alfred 1855–1948
Australian jurist and politician
Born in Melbourne, the son of a Jewish tailor, he became a barrister and, as Attorney-General for the colony of Victoria, helped prepare the federal constitution (1897–99). He sat in the federal parliament (1901–06), was a justice of the high court (1906–30), and Chief Justice (1930–31). From 1931 to 1936 he was Governor-General, the first Australian to hold that office.

Isaacs, Sir Jeremy Israel 1932–
Scottish television executive and arts administrator
Born in Glasgow, he was educated at Merton College, Oxford. He became a producer with Granada Television in 1958 on such current affairs series as *What the Papers Say* and *All Our Yesterdays* (1960–63). He later worked on the BBC's *Panorama* (1965) and at Thames Television (1968–78) where he produced the documentary *The World at War* (1975). His later programmes include *Ireland: A Television History* (1981) and the brutal drama *A Sense of Freedom* (1981). He served as the first chief executive of Channel 4 (1981–87), and from 1988 to 1997 was general director of the Royal Opera House in Covent Garden. He was knighted in 1996.

Isaacs, Susan Brierley, *née* Fairhurst 1885–1948
English educationist
Born in Bromley Cross, Lancashire, she studied philosophy and psychology at Manchester and Cambridge, and lectured in Manchester and London. A disciple of Sigmund Freud and believer in the enduring effects of early childhood experiences, she ran an experimental progressive school, Malting House, in Cambridge (1924–27), which aimed at letting children find out for themselves rather than by direct instruction, and at allowing them emotional expression rather than imposing a restrictive discipline. From 1933 to 1944 she was the influential head of the department of child development at the Institute of Education, London. She wrote *Intellectual Growth in Young Children* (1930) and *Social Development of Young Children* (1933). Some of her conclusions challenged the theories of Jean Piaget concerning the stages of children's intellectual development, before it was acceptable to question Piaget's work. She was a powerful influence on the theory and practice of the education of young children between the wars.

Isabella I, of Castile, *also known as* Isabella the Catholic 1451–1504
Queen of Spain
The daughter of King John II of Castile and Leon, she succeeded her brother, Henry IV of Castile (1474). In 1469 she had married Ferdinand, the Catholic, of Aragon, and when he succeeded to the Crown of Aragon (1479), they became joint sovereigns (as Isabella I and Ferdinand V of Aragon and Castile). Together they strengthened royal administration, curbed the privileges of the nobility and military orders, and introduced *corregidors* to govern the towns. Also during their reign the reconquest of Granada was completed (1482–92). Pious and orthodox in belief,

Isabella backed the Inquisition (introduced 1478) and was the main force behind the expulsion of the Jews (1492). She and Ferdinand sponsored the voyage of Christopher Columbus to the New World (1492). She was succeeded by her daughter Juana the Mad. ⌑ Felipe Fernandez-Armesto, *Ferdinand and Isabella* (1975)

Isabella II 1830–1904
Queen of Spain
Born in Madrid, she succeeded to the throne on the death of her father, Ferdinand VII (1833), with her mother, Queen María Cristina (1806–78), acting as regent. She attained her majority (1843), and in 1846 married her effete cousin, Francisco de Asis de Bourbon. Although popular with the Spanish people, her scandalous private life made her the tool of rival factions, and in 1868 she was deposed and exiled to France, where in 1870 she abdicated in favour of her son, Alfonso XII.

Isabella of Angoulême c.1188–1246
Queen of England
She was the consort of King John, whom she married in 1200. In 1214 she was imprisoned by John at Gloucester, and after his death (1216) she returned to France, where she married (1220) Hugh of Lusignan, Comte de la Marche, the son of a former fiancé. She retired to Fontevrault Abbey (1243). She was the mother of Henry III; her daughter by John, Isabella (1214–41), married the Emperor Frederick II.

Isabella of France 1292–1358
Queen of England
The daughter of Philip IV of France, she married Edward II at Boulogne (1308), but was treated badly by him, and returned to France (1325) when her brother, Charles IV, seized Edward's territories in France. She became the mistress of Roger de Mortimer (later Earl of March), with whom she invaded England (1326) and overthrew Edward, forcing him to abdicate in favour of her young son, Edward III, with herself and Mortimer as regents. They plundered the treasury and had Edward II murdered at Berkeley Castle (1327). However three years later, Edward III asserted his authority, and Isabella and Mortimer were arrested. Mortimer was hanged, drawn and quartered, while Isabella was sent into retirement at Castle Rising, near King's Lynn, Norfolk, for the rest of her life. ⌑ Jean Verdon, *Isabeau de Bavière* (1981)

Isabey, Jean Baptiste 1767–1855
French portrait painter and miniaturist
Born in Nancy, he trained under Jacques Louis David. He painted portraits of the notable figures of the French Revolution, and afterwards became court painter to Napoleon I and the Bourbons. His son, Eugène (1804–86), was a historical painter.

Isaeus 4th century BC
Athenian orator
Little is known of his life. A pupil of Isocrates, he was a professional speech writer, but barely a dozen of the 50 speeches he composed have survived.

Isaiah, *Hebrew* Jeshaiah 8th century BC
Old Testament prophet
Born in Jerusalem, he was the son of Amoz. He began to prophesy in c.747BC, and wielded much influence in the kingdom of Judah until the Assyrian invasion of 701. According to tradition, he was martyred.

Isherwood, Christopher William Bradshaw 1904–86
US novelist
Born in Disley, Cheshire, England, he was educated at Repton and Corpus Christi College, Cambridge, and studied medicine at King's College London (1928–29),

but gave it up to teach English in Germany (1930–33). His best-known works, *Mr Norris Changes Trains* (1935) and *Goodbye to Berlin* (1939), were based on his experiences in the decadence of post-slump, pre-**Hitler** Berlin. In collaboration with **W H Auden**, a school friend, he wrote three prose-verse plays with political overtones, which use Expressionist technique, music-hall parody and ample symbolism to portray the social climate: *The Dog beneath the Skin* (1935), *The Ascent of F6* (1937) and *On the Frontier* (1938). He travelled in China with Auden in 1938 and wrote *Journey to a War* (1939). In 1939 he emigrated to California to be a scriptwriter for MGM and in 1946 took US citizenship. The Broadway hit *I am a Camera* (1951), and the musical *Cabaret* (1968), were based on his earlier Berlin stories, especially *Sally Bowles* (1937). Later novels include *Prater Violet* (1945), *The World in the Evening* (1954) and *Meeting by the River* (1967). He also translated the Hindu epic poem the *Bhagavad Gita* (with Swami Prabhavananda, 1944) and **Baudelaire**'s *Intimate Journals* (1947), and wrote several autobiographical books. 📖 *Christopher and His Kind* (1963)

Ishiguro, Kazuo 1954–
British novelist

Originally from Nagasaki, Japan, he settled in Great Britain and came to notice as a student on a creative-writing course at the University of East Anglia. After working as a community worker in Glasgow in the late 1970s (and, more incidentally, as a grouse beater for the Queen Mother, an experience which may have fostered his later interest in the English ruling class), he published the delicate *A Pale View of Hill* (1982), which represented a highly personal approach to modern Japanese history and society. *An Artist of the Floating World* (1988) was much more mannered, and so too, in the most positive sense, was *Remains of the Day* (1989), which shifted the setting to England for the first time. An elegiac study of a vanishing class told through the eyes of a butler, it won Ishiguro the Booker Prize and was made into an award-winning film (1993) starring **Emma Thompson** and Sir **Anthony Hopkins**.

Ishiwara Kanji 1889–1949
Japanese army officer

He graduated from the prestigious Army War College in 1918 and later lectured there (1925–28). Influenced by the apocalyptic doctrines of the Japanese medieval Buddhist monk, Nichiren, Ishiwara believed in the inevitability of a final conflict between East and West, as represented by Japan and the USA. As a result, he maintained that Japan needed to harness resources in East Asia (especially Manchuria). After 1929, as an operations officer attached to the Japanese army (Guandong Army) that guarded south Manchuria and the South Manchuria railway, Ishiwara helped plan the campaign that resulted in the transformation of Manchuria into the Japanese puppet-state of Manzhuguo in 1931. On his return to Japan (1932), his independent views brought him into conflict with his military superiors. In 1937 he criticized Japan's invasion of China, fearing that a prolonged war would sabotage Japan's efforts in building a national defence state. He was forced out of the army in 1941.

Ishmael
Biblical character

He was the son of **Abraham** by **Hagar**, Abraham's second wife. He was expelled into the desert with his mother from Abraham's household after the birth of Isaac. He is purported to have fathered 12 princes, and is considered the ancestor of the Bedouin tribes of the Palestinian deserts (the Ishmaelites). **Muhammad** considered Ishmael and Abraham as ancestors of the Arabs, and therefore associated with the construction of the Kaba in Mecca.

Isidore of Seville, St, *also called* Isidorus Hispalensis c.560–636
Spanish prelate, Doctor of the Church, and the last of the Latin Fathers of the Church

Born in Seville or Cartagena, he was Archbishop of Seville in c.600, and his episcopate included the Councils at Seville (618 or 619) and Toledo (633). A voluminous writer, he is best known for his weighty encyclopedia of knowledge, *Etymologiae*, which was a standard work for scholars throughout the Middle Ages. He also wrote an introduction to the Old and New Testaments, a defence of Christianity against the Jews, books on ecclesiastical offices and the monastic rule; and a history of the Goths, Vandals and Suevi. He was canonized in 1598 and his feast day is 4 April.

Isla, José Francisco de 1703–81
Spanish satirist

Born in Vidanes, he joined the Jesuits, and became famous as a preacher, but still better known as a humorous and satirical writer. His novel *Fray Gerundio* (1758–70, 'Friar Gerundio'), and the *Cartas de Juan de la Encina* (1732, 'Juan de la Encina's Letters') are good examples of his style. What **Cervantes** had done with the sham chivalry and sentiment of the romances, Isla strove to do in *Fray Gerundio* with the vulgar buffooneries of the popular preachers. It was well received by all except the friars, but the Inquisition stopped the publication of the book. In 1767 he shared the fate of the Jesuits in their expulsion from Spain, and went to Bologna. He translated **Alain René Lesage**'s *Gil Blas*, which he humorously claimed to have restored to its native language.

Islam, Kazi Nazrul, *known as* the Rebel Poet of Bengal and the National Poet of Bangladesh 1899–1976
Bengali poet

Born in the West Bengali village of Churulia, into extreme poverty, he rose to fame in the 1920s as a poet and leader of the anti-British movement in India with his poem *The Rebel*. He published a bi-monthly radical magazine, *Dhumketu* ('The Comet'), which was revolutionary and anti-British, and he spent 40 days on hunger strike in jail. In the 1930s he concentrated more on composing music and songs—over 4,000 songs and lyrics in all— and became well known as an actor and radio personality. In 1942, brain disease left him bereft of his faculties, including his speech. After Partition, which he had always opposed, he lived in penury until he was brought home in honour to the newly independent state of Bangladesh and installed as the national poet. A Muslim, he married a Hindu and was a lifelong advocate of Muslim–Hindu unity, and wrote more than 500 devotional Hindu songs.

Ismail Pasha 1830–95
Khedive of Egypt

The second son of Ibrahim Pasha (1789–1848), and grandson of **Mehemet 'Ali**, he was born in Cairo and educated at St Cyr, France. He succeeded Sa'id Pasha (1822–63) as viceroy (1863), and assumed the hereditary title of khedive (1866). In 1872 the Ottoman sultan granted him the right (withdrawn in 1879) of concluding treaties and maintaining an army, which virtually gave him sovereign powers. He began a series of vast internal reforms: he built roads, railways and docks, reclaimed land, expanded cotton exports and hugely increased the number of schools. He annexed Darfur (1874), and endeavoured through Sir **Samuel Baker** and General **Charles Gordon**, governors of the Sudan, to suppress the slave trade. To provide funds for his vast undertakings he sold to Great Britain (1875) 177,000 shares in the Suez Canal for £4 million but so chaotic were Egyptian finances that dual control by England and France was established. Although he tried to lead the opposition of the army, the landowners and the religious leaders against foreign domination, he was deposed by the sultan (1879), and Prince Tewfik, his eldest son, was proclaimed khedive. He ultimately retired to Constantinople (Istanbul), where he died. 📖 Pierre Crabites, *Ismail: The Maligned Khedive* (1933)

Ismay (of Wormington), Hastings Lionel Ismay, 1st Baron, *nicknamed* Pug 1887–1965
English soldier
Born in Naini Tal, India, and educated at Charterhouse and Sandhurst, he joined the 21st Cavalry, Frontier Force, in 1907. He served on India's North-West Frontier in 1908 and in Somaliland in World War I. His appointment in 1926 as assistant secretary to the Committee of Imperial Defence led to his service as Chief of Staff to Winston Churchill. He later became Secretary of State for Commonwealth Relations (1951–52), and then Secretary-General to NATO (1952–1957).

Isocrates 436–338BC
Greek orator and prose writer
He was born in Athens, and after studying under Gorgias and Socrates, he worked briefly and unsuccessfully as an advocate. He then turned to speech writing, and became an influential teacher of oratory (c.390BC), presenting rhetoric as an essential foundation of education. Many of his writings, like the *Symmachicus* and the *Panathenaicus*, were meant to serve as model speeches, but were widely circulated as instructional or argumentative constitutional texts, thus becoming the first ever political pamphlets. He urged the Greek city-states to unite against the Persians, but that ambition was thwarted by the victory at Chaeronea by Philip II of Macedonia in 338BC. His style employs complex sentence structure and the frequent use of antithesis. It influenced Demosthenes and Cicero, through whom the example of Isocrates was passed on to European literature.

Issigonis, Sir Alec (Alexander Arnold Constantine) 1906–88
British automobile designer
Born in Smyrna in Turkey, he settled in Great Britain in 1923 and studied at Battersea Polytechnic. His early fascination for cars led him to use his talents in the motor industry, and a period as an enthusiastic sports driver in the 1930s and 1940s familiarized him with all aspects of car design. His greatest successes during a long association with Morris (later British Motor Company) were the Morris Minor, launched in 1948 and produced until 1971, and the revolutionary Mini launched in 1959. A version of the Mini is still in production, and more than five million have been manufactured. He became a Royal Designer for Industry in 1967, and was knighted in 1969. 📖 Andrew Nahum, *Alec Issigonis* (1988)

Itagaki Taisuke 1837–1919
Japanese politician
The leader of the Freedom and People's Rights Movement in the 1870s, he came from a samurai family in Tosa domain and was a participant in the Meiji Restoration (1868). Although he entered the government in 1869, he resigned in 1873 when proposals for a military expedition to Korea were rejected. Condemning the monopoly of power held by those from the former domains of Choshu and Satsuma, from 1874 he began calling for a national representative assembly, drawing on ideas from Western liberalism. In 1881 he formed Japan's first political party, the Jiyuto (Liberals), which attracted the support of former samurai and wealthy landowners. Due to government harrassment and internal rivalries, the party was disbanded in 1884, but was revived in time to contest the country's first elections for a national diet in

1890. In 1898 Itagaki, in alliance with the Shimpoto (Progressives) of Okuma Shigenobu, formed Japan's first party cabinet but it only lasted four months before internal bickering brought an end to the experiment. Thereafter Itagaki retired from active politics.

Ito, Hirobumi 1838–1909
Japanese statesman
He was born in Choshu province. As Prime Minister (1885–88, 1892–96, 1898, 1900–01), he visited Europe and the USA on several occasions, drafted the Meiji constitution (1889), and played a major role in abolishing Japanese feudalism and building up the modern state. He was assassinated in Harbin by a supporter of Korean independence.

Itten, Johannes 1888–1967
Swiss painter and teacher
Born in Sudern-Linden, he studied art in Stuttgart (1913–16) before moving to Vienna where he started his own art school. A leading theorist at the Bauhaus (1919–23), he wrote on the theory of colour (*Kunst der Farbe*, 1961) and developed the idea of a compulsory 'preliminary course', based on research into natural forms and the laws of basic design. This has been widely adopted in art schools.

Iturbide, Agustín de, *also known as* Agustin I 1783–1824
Mexican soldier and politician
Born in Valladolid (now Morelia), he favoured Mexican independence, but fought for the Crown because he opposed the social revolution of the independence movement of Miguel Hidalgo and José María Morelos. He defeated Morelos's army at Valladolid (1810) and was given command of the royalist army but, dissatisfied with the imposition of a constitutional monarchy in Spain, betrayed the royalists and joined with the Liberals to issue the Plan of Iguala declaring Mexico independent (1821). Then, betraying that movement, he created himself Emperor Agustin I in the style of Napoleon I (1822). He was unable to govern and his popularity plummeted, forcing him to abdicate (1823). He went into exile in Europe but returned the following year and was captured and executed. 📖 William S Robertson, *Iturbide of Mexico* (1952)

Ivan I, *also called* Ivan Kalita ('Moneybag') c.1304–41
Grand Prince of Moscow
He was a careful, financially shrewd administrator and skilful diplomat and reformer, who expanded Moscow's territory by purchase rather than conquest. He made Moscow the capital of Russia by transferring the metropolitan cathedral from Kiev (1326). He became Grand Prince of Moscow in 1328. His two sons, Simeon the Proud (reigned 1341–53) and Ivan II (reigned 1353–59) succeeded him.

Ivan III Vasilyevich, *called* Ivan the Great 1440–1505
Grand Prince of Moscow and Grand Duke of Russia
Born in Moscow, he ruled from 1462, and ended his city's subjection to the Tatars. He gained control over a number of Russian principalities, including Novgorod, and after he married (1472) Sophia, a niece of Constantine XI Palaeologus, he assumed the title Sovereign of all Russia, and adopted the emblem of the two-headed eagle of the Byzantine Empire. He was the first Russian prince to establish contact with the West and laid the administrative basis of a centralized Russian state. 📖 J L I Fennell, *Ivan the Great of Moscow* (1961)

Ivan IV See panel p960

Ivan the Great See Ivan III Vasilyevich

Ivan the Terrible See Ivan IV (panel)

Ivan IV, *known as* Ivan the Terrible 1530–84
Tsar of Russia from 1533

Ivan IV was the grandson of **Ivan III Vasilyevich** (Ivan the Great), and was only three years old at the death of his father, Grand Prince Vasili. Following a period when authority was in the hands first of his mother Elena, and then, following her murder in 1537, in the hands of the Russian boyars, Ivan assumed power in 1547, becoming the first ruler of Russia to adopt the title of 'tsar'.

He proceeded steadily to reduce the power of the upper nobility (princes and boyars) in favour of the minor gentry. He summoned a legislative assembly in 1549, inaugurating a period of reform in both State and Church that continued for the next decade, establishing a new code of law and a system of local self-government. In 1552 he wrested Kazan from the Tartars and in 1554 captured Astrakhan. In 1558 he invaded Livonia, capturing the important Baltic port of Narva. In 1565, suspecting that a boyar rebellion was imminent, he offered to abdicate, but he was brought back by popular demand with sweeping powers to take drastic measures against those who had opposed him. This led to a prolonged spate of arrests and executions.

In 1570 he ravaged the free city of Novgorod. In 1571 the Crimean Tartars invaded Russia and fired Moscow, but Ivan was able to inflict a punishing defeat upon them the following year. In the last years of his reign, he rehabilitated posthumously many of the victims of his middle years, but in a fit of anger in 1581 accidentally killed his own eldest son, so that the throne passed on his death to his sickly and feeble-minded second son, Fyodor, who ruled from 1584 to 1598.

📖 Benson Bobrick, *Fearful Majesty: The Life and Reign of Ivan the Terrible* (1987); Henri Troyat, *Ivan the Terrible* (1974, trans by Joan Pinkham); Steven Graham, *Ivan the Terrible* (1933).

> 'To shave the beard is a sin that the blood of all the martyrs cannot cleanse. It is to deface the image of man created by God.' Quoted in David Maland, *Europe in the Seventeenth Century* (1968).

Ivanov, Lev Ivanovich 1834–1901
Russian choreographer, teacher and dancer

Born in Moscow, he studied there and in St Petersburg, joining the Maryinsky Theater in 1850, and becoming principal dancer in 1869. Appointed rehearsal director by **Marius Petipa** in 1882, he became second ballet master under Petipa in 1885. This was the year of his choreographic debut, with a new version of *La Fille Mal Gardée* ('The Unchaperoned Girl') which, like much of his work, is now lost. His two most celebrated works have survived—**Tchaikovsky**'s *The Nutcracker* (1892), and the second and fourth acts of Tchaikovsky's *Swan Lake* (1895). His 'White Acts' are now considered among the masterpieces of classical ballet, creating the quintessential image of ballerina as swan. Despite his achievements, he lived in the shadow of Petipa and died in poverty.

Ivanov, Nikolai Veniaminovich 1952–
Soviet lawyer

He was the junior partner of **Telman Gdlyan** in proving corruption in high places during the last years of **Leonid Brezhnev**'s dictatorial rule. He helped Gdlyan in the 'Uzbek affair' and then in attacking senior Muscovite communists. With Gdlyan, he attracted both official disapproval and popular encouragement.

Ivanov, Vyacheslav Ivanovich 1866–1949
Russian poet and critic

He studied in Berlin and lived in Greece and Italy, where he was converted to Roman Catholicism. The publication of his first poems established him as a leading figure in the Symbolist movement, but his poetry was later enriched by mysticism and his philological interests, and he wrote studies on the cult of Dionysus, and on **Dostoevsky**, Byron and **Nietzsche**. 📖 C Tschoepel, *Vyacheslav Ivanov* (1968)

Ivanov, Vyacheslav Nikolayevich 1938–
Soviet oarsman

He was the first man to win three consecutive Olympic gold medals in single sculls (1956, 1960, 1964), an achievement matched by Finland's **Pertti Karpinnen** (1976, 1980, 1984). However, Ivanov secured his place in Olympic history after his first title win in Melbourne when he ecstatically threw his medal into the air, only to see it fall into Lake Wendouree. Although he dived in, he was unable to recover it. After the Games, the International Olympic Committee gave him a replacement.

Ives, Burl 1909–95
US folk singer

Born in Hunt, Illinois, he trained as a teacher, then travelled around the USA collecting folk songs. He became a leader of the US folk movement, and during his career as a ballad singer and banjo player, his songs 'Blue Tail Fly' and 'Foggy Dew' were as well known as his radio show signature ballad 'Wayfarin' Stranger'. He also performed in dramas and musicals on the Broadway stage (notably as Big Daddy in *Cat on a Hot Tin Roof*, 1955) and in films (*The Big Country*, 1958, Academy Award). He won Grammy awards for his recordings 'A Little Bitty Tear' (1961), 'Funny Way of Laughin'' (1962), 'Chim Chim Cheree' (1964), and 'America Sings' (1974).

Ives, Charles Edward 1874–1954
US composer

Born in Danbury, Connecticut, the son of a musician, he studied music at Yale, but followed a business career until forced to abandon it due to ill health. His music is firmly based in the US tradition, but at the same time he experimented with dissonances, polytonal harmonies, and conflicting rhythms, anticipating modern European trends. He composed five symphonies, chamber music (including the well-known 2nd Piano Sonata, the 'Concord' Sonata), and many songs. In 1947 he was awarded the Pulitzer Prize for his 3rd Symphony (*The Camp Meeting*, composed 1904–11).

Ives, Frederick Eugene 1856–1937
US inventor

Born in Litchfield, Connecticut, he became interested in photography as a boy apprentice at the *Litchfield Enquirer*. He experimented with the possibilities of photography as a means of illustration, and invented (1878) and improved (1885), the half-tone process. He later pioneered natural colours for motion pictures (1914).

Ives, James Merritt 1824–95
US lithographer

Born in New York City, he was technical director and a partner of **Nathaniel Currier** in the Currier & Ives firm. He directed the artists who produced popular hand-coloured engravings depicting scenes of 19th-century US life. Between 1840 and 1890 the firm issued over 7,000 different prints, which became prized by collectors.

Ivory, James 1928–
US film director

He was born in Berkeley, California. He formed Merchant–Ivory Productions with Bombay-born Indian producer **Ismail Merchant** and, frequently in collaboration with screenwriter and novelist **Ruth Prawer Jhabvala**, made several highly successful films. These are characterized by a literate, precise script, ironic humour, scrupulous attention to period detail and design, and impeccable performances and include *Shakespeare Wallah* (1965), *The Europeans* (1979), *Heat and Dust* (1982), *The Bostonians* (1984), *A Room With a View* (1985), *Maurice* (1987), *Howards End* (1992), *Remains of the Day* (1993) and *Surviving Picasso* (1997).

Iwasaki Yataro 1835–85
Japanese entrepreneur

Born in Tosa Province, of petty samurai descent, he became the financial agent for Tosa, taking over its interests in shipping and coal-mining. In 1873 he founded the Mitsubishi Trading Company and developed close personal links with the new Meiji government, receiving government subsidies and contracts. By 1877 Iwasaki owned over 80 per cent of all ships in Japan and monopolized the coastal trade, having successfully defeated his US and UK rivals. Mitsubishi became one of the largest *zaibatsu* (financial combines), with interests in banking, insurance and mining.

Iwasa Matabei, *originally* Araki c.1578–1650
Japanese painter

A master of the Tosa school, he is credited with founding the Ukiyo-e school.

Iwerks, U B, *originally* Ubbe Iwwerks 1901–71
US animated-cartoon director

Born in Kansas City, he began as an apprentice to the Union Bank Note Company (1916). In 1920 in partnership, he set up the Disney–Iwerks Studio, and produced *Laugh-O-Gram* cartoons, followed by *Alice in Cartoon-land* (1923). The animator who put life into **Walt Disney's** sketches of Mickey Mouse, Iwerks joined Disney in California to animate *Oswald the Lucky Rabbit* (1924), then animated the first film to star Mickey Mouse, *Plane Crazy* (1928). He produced *Flip the Frog* in Cinecolor (1930), *Willie Whopper* (1933) and *Comicolor Cartoons* (1933), *Porky and Gabby* (1937) and *Gran'pop* (1939). He won Academy Awards (1959, 1964) for his technical achievements. He also developed xerographic animation for *The 101 Dalmations* (1961) and directed special effects for **Alfred Hitchcock's** *The Birds* (1963).

Iyasu, the Great d.1706
Emperor of Ethiopia

He succeeded to the throne in 1682. A modernizer and patron of the arts, he tried to reunify the kingdom following the migration of Galla tribesmen into the empire, and to reform its institutions after a period of decline during the 17th century. He was known especially for his justice and prosecution of greedy tax gatherers. He was assassinated by a kinsman of his wife.

Izetbegovich, Alija 1925–
Bosnia and Herzogovinian politician

Born in Bosanski Samac, he was educated at the University of Sarajevo. In 1945, following the creation of the Yugoslav Federation, he was imprisoned for three years for promoting Bosnian nationalist policies. On his release he wrote several books on Islamic politics and in 1988 became leader of the Party of Democratic Action. With the breakup of Yugoslavia he became President of Bosnia-Herzegovina (1990) and the inspirational leader of the Bosnian Muslims in the civil war which followed.

Jabir ibn Hayyan, Abu Musa
c.721–c.815
Arab alchemist
He was court physician to caliph **Harun al-Rashid**, and wrote a number of works on alchemy and metaphysics which were widely circulated in the Middle Ages.

Jack the Ripper 19th century
Unidentified murderer
Between August and November 1888, six prostitutes were found murdered and mutilated in the East End of London. The murderer was never discovered. The affair roused much public alarm, provoking a violent press campaign against the CID and the Home Secretary, and resulting in some reform of police methods. He has been the subject of many novels and films, and speculation about his identity continues into the 1990s. ⬛ Paul Begg, *Jack the Ripper* (1990)

Jacklin, Tony (Anthony) 1944–
English golfer
Born in Scunthorpe, Humberside, he became in 1969 the first Briton since 1951 to win the Open championship. Within 11 months he became the first Briton, since Harry Vardon (who was Open champion in 1899 and 1900 US Open champion) to have held the Open and the US Open titles in the same 12 months. His US Open victory by seven strokes was the biggest winning margin since that of Jim Barnes in 1921. Unable to repeat his success in the majors for the rest of his playing career, Jacklin next achieved fame as the non-playing captain of Europe's Ryder Cup team. His record of two wins, one draw (the tied match meant Europe retained the cup) and one loss is second only to that of **Walter Hagen**. ⬛ Liz Kahn, *Tony Jacklin: The Price of Success* (1979)

Jackson, Alexander Young 1882–1974
Canadian painter
He was born in Montreal. A member of the circle of Toronto artists known as the Group of Seven, he created bold, colourful paintings that glorify the beauty and grandeur of the Canadian north country.

Jackson, Andrew, nicknamed Old Hickory
1767–1845
7th President of the USA
Born into an Irish immigrant family in Waxhaw, South Carolina, he was raised on the frontier and fought in the Revolution aged 13, losing almost all of his immediate family in the war. After studying law and heading west he became public prosecutor in Nashville in 1788. He helped to frame the constitution of Tennessee, and became its representative in Congress in 1796, its senator in 1797 and a judge of its Supreme Court (1798–1804). When war was declared against Great Britain in 1812, as major-general of the state militia he took the field against the Creek Indians (allies of the British) in Alabama, achieving a decisive victory at Horseshoe Bend in 1814. Created major-general in the regular army and appointed to the command of the South, 'Old Hickory' invaded Spanish soil, stormed Pensacola, being then used by the British as a base of operations, and successfully defended New Orleans against Sir Edward Pakenham (1815), who was killed in the attack. The victory at New Orleans made him a national hero, though a treaty ending the War of 1812 had in fact been signed shortly before the battle took place. In 1818 Jackson again invaded Florida, defeated the Seminoles and became the state's first governor. He soon resigned, and in 1823 was re-elected to the US Senate. In 1824 as a Democratic candidate for the presidency, he had the highest popular vote, but not a majority of electoral votes, and in the House of Representatives the election was decided in favour of **John Quincy Adams**. Strongly supported in the West and South, Jackson was elected President in 1828. Fearless and honest, he was prompt to decide everything for personal reasons, and replaced a great number of minor officials with his partisans. He relied heavily on a set of informal advisers (his 'Kitchen Cabinet') and he quarrelled with his Vice-President, **John C Calhoun**, on the issue of states' rights, with Jackson defending union at all costs and Calhoun resigning over South Carolina's right to nullify the protective tariff of 1828. He favoured extended suffrage and sought to limit the power of the monied élite, and so is said to have ushered in the era of 'Jacksonian Democracy', though paradoxically he had little respect for the checks and balances of the democratic system and was high-handed in his use of executive power. He vetoed legislation much more freely than any of his predecessors and was particularly vehement in opposing the effort to recharter the Bank of the United States, which he saw as the malignant agent of centralized money power. On this issue he was re-elected President by an overwhelming majority in 1832, and in his second term he pursued hard-money policies, transferring federal funds to state banks and issuing the Specie Circular, which helped bring about the financial panic of 1837. Throughout his presidency he pressed for Indian removal in order to free new lands for settlement on the frontier, and his most shameful act was his deliberate refusal to enforce the 1832 Supreme Court decision invalidating Georgia's effort to annex the territory of the Cherokee. As a plain-speaking champion of the common man, however, he won enormous and enduring popularity. In 1837 he retired to the Hermitage, his Tennessee plantation. ⬛ Marquis James, *Andrew Jackson: The Border Captain* (1933)

Jackson (of Lodsworth), Dame Barbara Mary Ward, Baroness 1914–81
English economist, journalist and conservationist
Born in Sussex, and educated in Paris, Germany and at Somerville College, Oxford, she became foreign editor of *The Economist* in 1939. After World War II she lectured in the USA, including Harvard (1957–68) and Columbia (1968–73). She was president of the International Institute for Environment and Development from 1973 to 1980, and was made a life peer in 1976. She was a prolific and popular writer on politics, economics and ecology. Her books include *The International Share Out* (1936), *The Rich Nations and the Poor Nations* (1962), *Spaceship Earth* (1966) and *Only One Earth—the Care and Maintenance of a Small Planet* (1972).

Jackson, Benjamin Daydon 1846–1927
English botanist and bibliographer
Born in London and educated at private schools, from an early age Jackson had strong botanical and especially bibliographical instincts. A born indexer, his greatest work was the compilation of *Index Kewensis*, an index of all names of flowering plants hitherto described (published 1892). An essential tool for the plant taxonomist, *Index Kewensis* continues to be updated regularly. Jackson also compiled an indispensable *Glossary of Botanical Terms* (1900), the *Catalogue of the Library of the Linnaean Society* (1925) and wrote two botanical bibliographies, *Guide to the Literature of Botany* (1881) and *Vegetable Technology* (1882). An authority on **Linnaeus**, at celebrations in Sweden to mark

the bicentenary of Linnaeus's birth in 1907, he received the Order of Knighthood of the Polar Star.

Jackson, Betty 1949–
English fashion designer

Born in Bacup, Lancashire, she studied fashion at Birmingham College of Art before becoming a freelance illustrator in London. In 1973 she joined Wendy Dagworthy as assistant designer, then joined Quorum as designer (1975–81). With her husband David Cohen she launched her own label in 1981 and quickly gained a reputation for flattering designs in bold patterned fabrics. She has won numerous awards, including British Designer of the Year in 1985, the year she launched her menswear collection. In 1987 she signed an agreement with Vogue Patterns/Butterick Co to produce Betty Jackson patterns for home dressmakers. She has since launched Betty Jackson Accessories, BJ Beachwear and BJ Knits.

Jackson, Glenda 1936–
English actress and Labour politician

She was born in Birkenhead, Cheshire, became a student at RADA, and made her theatrical debut in *Separate Tables* (1957) at Worthing and her London debut in the same year in *All Kinds of Men*. She made her film debut in *This Sporting Life* (1963) but remained primarily a stage actress in such productions as *Alfie* (1963), *Hamlet* (1965) and *Marat/Sade* (1965). Her films include *Women in Love* (1969, Academy Award), *A Touch of Class* (1973, Academy Award), *Sunday, Bloody Sunday* (1971), *Hedda* (1975), *Stevie* (1978) and *Business as Usual* (1987). Stage performances include *Hedda Gabler* (1975), *Rose* (1980), *Strange Interlude* (1984), *The House of Bernarda Alba* (1986), *Macbeth* (1988), and *Mother Courage* (1990). On television, she played the title role in the series *Elizabeth R* (1971) and appeared in the film *The Patricia Neal Story* (1981). Later turning to a career in politics, she was elected as Labour MP for Hampstead and Highgate, London (1992), and given special responsibility for local transport. When Labour came to power in 1997 she became a junior Environment and Transport Minister. 📖 Ian Woodward, *Glenda Jackson: A Study in Fire and Ice* (1985)

Jackson, Gordon Cameron 1923–90
Scottish actor

Born in Glasgow, he performed in BBC radio plays as a child before leaving school at 15 to become an engineering draughtsman with Rolls-Royce. He began his professional career as callow servicemen in such films as *The Foreman Went to France* (1942), *Millions Like Us* (1943) and *San Demetrio London* (1943). His later films included *Whisky Galore!* (1949), *Mutiny on the Bounty* (1962), *The Great Escape* (1963), *Those Magnificent Men in Their Flying Machines* (1965), *The Prime of Miss Jean Brodie* (1968) and *Kidnapped* (1971). On stage, he played Ishmael in Orson Welles's production *Moby Dick* (1955), Banquo to Alec Guinness's *Macbeth* (1966) and Horatio in *Hamlet* (1969). Television brought him lasting popularity as the butler Hudson in *Upstairs, Downstairs* (1971–75, Emmy award), and as CI5 boss Cowley in the action series *The Professionals* (1977–83).

Jackson, Helen Maria Hunt, *née* Fiske 1830–85
US writer

Born in Amherst, Massachusetts, she was a friend of Emily Dickinson and a writer of poems (*Verses*, 1870) and popular prose works. After settling in Colorado Springs in 1875, she became interested in the plight of Native Americans in the West, and in 1881 she won public attention with *A Century of Dishonor*, an indictment of the US government for its shameful record of broken treaties and barbarous treatment of Native Americans. The book resulted in her government appointment in 1882 to investigate conditions among California Mission Indians.

Her most popular novel, *Ramona* (1884), was a sentimental romance on Native American themes, written in the style of *Uncle Tom's Cabin*. 📖 R Odell, *A Life* (1939)

Jackson, (George) Holbrook 1874–1948
English bibliophile and literary historian

Born in Liverpool, he moved to Leeds to work in lace manufacture. He encountered a fellow Nietzschean in A R Orage, with whom he helped establish the political and literary periodical *New Age* (1907), winning support from the subject of his book *Bernard Shaw* (1907). Jackson was active in the Fabian Society, and his life-long devotion to William Morris was reflected especially in his Morris Anthology, *On Art and Socialism* (1947). His *The Eighteen Nineties* (1913) established the literary contours of the decade, and as a literary critic he produced work for *T.P.'s Weekly* and *Today*. After World War I he managed trade journals and gave himself up to bibliophilia, such as the enormous *Anatomy of Bibliomania* (1931) and the anthology, *Bookman's Holiday* (1945).

Jackson, Jesse Louis 1941–
US politician and clergyman

Born in Greenville, North Carolina, the adopted son of a janitor, he won a football scholarship to Illinois University before entering a Chicago seminary. He was ordained a Baptist minister in 1968 and as a charismatic preacher and black-activist politician, he worked with Martin Luther King, before establishing Operation PUSH (People United to Save Humanity, 1971) to promote the economic advancement of black people. He was a candidate for the Democratic 1984 presidential nomination, being the first black American to mount a serious campaign for the office and constructing what he termed a 'Rainbow Coalition' of liberal and minority groups, won a fifth of the delegates' votes. He lost the nomination to Walter Mondale. In 1986 he successfully campaigned for US disinvestment in South Africa. He came second to Michael Dukakis in the Democrats' 1988 presidential nomination contest, doubling his 1984 vote share. 📖 Ernest R House, *Jesse Jackson and the Politics of Charisma* (1989)

Jackson, John Hughlings 1835–1911
English neurologist

Born in Providence Green, Green Hammerton, Yorkshire, he qualified in medicine from St Bartholomew's Hospital, and became a lecturer in pathology at the London Hospital. He was appointed assistant physician to the London Hospital in 1863, and later became full physician (1874–94), and consulting physician (1894–1911). Simultaneously he was assistant (1862–67) and full physician (1867–1906) at the National Hospital for the Paralysed and Epileptic, Queen Square. Jackson contributed extensively to the development of neurology, suggesting that function could be localized in specific regions of the cerebral cortex, investigating unilateral epileptiform seizures and the physiology of speech, and he also postulated that the evolution of the nervous system proceeds from the simplest centres to the most complex.

Jackson, Laura Riding See Riding, Laura

Jackson, Mahalia 1911–62
US gospel singer

Born in New Orleans, Louisiana, she grew up in a strict Baptist environment, but was attracted to the blues of Bessie Smith and the evangelical fervour of the Holiness Church. She then moved north and sang in the choir of the Great Salem Baptist Church, Chicago (1927) and, from 1932, with the Johnson Gospel Singers. She collaborated with the hymn writer Thomas A Dorsey and scored chart successes with 'Move On Up a Little Higher' and other blues-inflected gospel themes. Despite commercial success, she refused all secular engagements,

---

Jackson, Michael 1958–
US pop singer

Michael Jackson was born in Gary, Indiana. He was something of a child prodigy, growing up in the hothouse atmosphere of a show business career. He formed part of The Jackson Five with his brothers, Jackie, Tito, Marlon and Jermaine, from about 1965, when the group began to win local talent competitions. His distinctive vocals attracted particular attention, and the band were eventually signed by Tamla Motown records. They delivered four consecutive number-one hits for the label in 1969–70, when Michael was still only 11.

Between 1972 and 1975 he also had six solo hits on the label, while the group clocked up some 16 chart hits in all. They moved to the Epic label in 1976, when they changed their name to The Jacksons, and continued to rack up hits until Michael left the group in 1986. By that stage, his own solo success had grown to mammoth proportions.

In 1977 he played the scarecrow in The Wiz, a Black remake of the film The Wizard of Oz. His collaboration with producer Quincy Jones on Off The Wall produced four hit singles in 1979, and he consolidated his career with the album, single, and extended horror film-style video for Thriller (1982), which has sold over 40 million copies, and established him as one of the major pop superstars of the 1980s.

Having been a celebrity since childhood, he developed a reclusive lifestyle as an adult, and is usually portrayed in the media as an eccentric introvert. Bizarre plastic surgery, an on-stage accident in which his hair caught fire, and an unlikely and short-lived 'showbiz dynasty' marriage to Lisa Marie Presley did nothing to ease such speculation. His grip on his creativity was also called into question in the grandiose HIStory (1995), an overblown album in which he seemed to cast himself as a kind of saviour of mankind.

♫ His most important albums as a solo performer are Off The Wall (1979), Thriller (1982), and Bad (1987).

▢ C Andersen, Michael Jackson Unauthorized (1994).

> Jackson's eccentricites are legendary, but Quincy Jones offered a different perspective in recalling their work on Off The Wall: 'Michael is one of the most professional musicians I have ever worked with, of any age. He is totally disciplined. He comes to work and he knows his material backwards, and you know it's in there, it's all the way in his heart'.

---

particularly nightclubs, but did, however, sing at John F Kennedy's inauguration, her emotional and fervid delivery underlining the social imperatives of Kennedy's ground-breaking proposals in social legislation.

Jackson, Michael See panel above

Jackson, Milt(on), nicknamed Bags 1923–
US vibraphone player

Born in Detroit, he learned the guitar and piano while at school, taking up xylophone and vibraphone in his teens. His discovery by Dizzy Gillespie in 1945 led to his emergence as the most important vibraphone player of the bebop era. In 1952 he was a founding member of the Modern Jazz Quartet which existed, with a change of drummer, until 1974, and re-formed in the 1980s. Jackson's lyrical interpretations, particularly of ballads, kept him in the forefront of jazz through periods of stylistic change.

Jackson, Reggie (Reginald Martinez), nicknamed Mr October 1946–
US baseball player

Born in Wyncote, Pennsylvania, he equalled Babe Ruth's 51-year-old record for hitting three home runs in one game in the 1977 World Series. He started his League career in 1967 with Kansas City Athletics, then Oakland, and also played for the Baltimore Orioles, the New York Yankees, and the California Angels (1982–86) before returning to Oakland again in 1987. He was elected to the Baseball Hall of Fame in 1992. ▢Robert Kraus(ed), Reggie Jackson's Scrapbook (1978)

Jackson, Sir Thomas Graham 1835–1924
English architect

He studied under Sir George Gilbert Scott and was responsible for many restorations of and additions to libraries, public schools and colleges including Eton, Harrow and Rugby, the Inner Temple, the Bodleian Library and the New Examination Schools at Oxford.

Jackson, Thomas Jonathan, known as Stonewall Jackson 1824–63
US Confederate soldier

Born in Clarksburg, West Virginia, in 1851 he became general professor at the Virginia Military Institute. At the outbreak of war in 1861 he took command of the Confederate troops at Harpers Ferry on the secession of Virginia, and commanded a brigade at Bull Run, where his firm stand earned him his nickname. In the campaign of the Shenandoah Valley (1862) he out-generalled Nathaniel Banks and John C Frémont, and drove them back upon the Lower Shenandoah. He turned the scale at Gaines's Mills (27 June), and returned to defeat Banks at Cedar Run in August. He then seized General John Pope's depot at Manassas. On 15 September he captured Harpers Ferry with 13,000 prisoners, and next day arrived at Sharpsburg, where his presence at the Battle of Antietam saved General Robert E Lee from disaster. As lieutenant-general he commanded the right wing at Fredericksburg (13 December), and at Chancellorsville (1 May 1863) he repulsed General Joseph Hooker. The next night he fell upon the right of the Federal army and drove it back on Chancellorsville, but was accidentally killed by his own troops. ▢ G F R Henderson, Stonewall Jackson and the American Civil War (2 vols, 1898)

Jackson, Sir William Godfrey Fothergill 1917–
English soldier and historian

Educated at Shrewsbury School, the Royal Military Academy, Woolwich, and King's College, Cambridge, he was commissioned in the Royal Engineers (1937). He served during World War II in Norway (1940), North Africa, Sicily and Italy (1942–43) and the Far East (1945). Assistant Chief of General Staff (1968–70), he was Commander-in-Chief Northern Command (1970–72), and Quartermaster-General at the Ministry of Defence (1973–76). He served as military historian in the cabinet office (1977–78 and 1982–87), and was Governor and Commander-in-Chief, Gibraltar (1978–82). His publications on military, historical and strategic subjects include Attack in the West (1953), Seven Roads to Moscow (1957), The Battle for Italy (1967) and Overlord: Normandy 1944 (1978). Later works include Salvador (1995), Britain's Triumph and Decline in the Middle East (1996) and As Nineveh and Tyre (1996).

Jackson, William Henry 1843–1942
US photographer

Born in Keesville, New York, he served in the Union army during the Civil War, then established a photographic studio in Omaha, Nebraska. Working for the US Geological and Geographical Survey of the Territories (1870–78), he travelled throughout the West, taking pictures of Native Americans, settlers, the Union Pacific Railroad route, and scenery. His photographs of the Yellowstone area helped influence Congress to establish the region as the first US national park (1872).

Jacob
Biblical character

The son of Isaac, he is the patriarch of the nation Israel. He supplanted his elder brother **Esau**, obtaining his father's special blessing and thus being seen as the inheritor of God's promises. He was re-named 'Israel' (perhaps meaning 'God strives' or 'he who strives with God') after his struggle with a divine being. By his wives Leah and Rachel and their maids he fathered 12 sons, to whom Jewish the 12 tribes of Israel are traced by tradition.

Jacob, François 1920–
French biochemist and Nobel Prize winner

Born in Nancy, he was educated at the University of Paris and the Sorbonne, and worked at the Pasteur Institute in Paris from 1950. In 1960 he became head of the Cellular Genetics Unit at the Pasteur, and then was Professor of Cellular Genetics at the Collège de France (1964–91). During the 1950s, he worked on the bacterium *Escherichia coli*, and suggested that genes are controlled by a system of other genes which regulate certain enzymes. He formulated the 'operon system', in which a regulator gene controls structural genes by manipulating sections of DNA. With **André Lwoff** and **Jacques Monod**, Jacob was awarded the 1965 Nobel Prize for physiology or medicine for research into cell physiology and the structure of genes. His publications include *La Logique du Vivant* (1970, Eng trans *The Logic of Life*, 1974) and *La Statue Intérieure* (1987, Eng trans *The Statue Within*, 1988).

Jacob, Mary Phelps, *also known as* Caresse Crosby fl.1913–14
US society lady

She has become legendary as a society lady who, one evening in 1913 while dressing for a ball, became so frustrated with the tightly-boned corset of her era that she dispensed with hers and, with the help of a maid, tied two silk handkerchiefs together. Thus she created the very first 'backless brassière' which gave support yet natural definition to the breasts. The following year, allegedly haven fallen on hard times, she reputedly sold the patent to Warner's for $1,500. They developed the concept of the bra as an item of underwear separate from the body-shaping, all-in-one corset, and marketed it in 1915 as the step-sister of the corset, which reduced in length as well as in popularity.

Jacob, Max 1876–1944
French Cubist writer, mystic, astrologer, artist and monk

He was born in Quimper, Brittany. Always on the vital edge of various avant-garde movements, in essence he belonged to none; but each owed a massive debt to his example. He knew everybody in the literary and artistic circles of his era, and was a noted conversationalist (some of his conversation is recorded in L Emié's *Dialogues avec Max Jacob*, 1956 'Dialogue with Max Jacob', and in his *Lettres*, ed S J Collier, 1966). Some of his best poetry is in his collection of prose-poems, *Le Cornet de dés* (1917, 'The Dice Cup'). He also wrote many mystical works, notably *L'Homme de cristal* (1946, 'The Crystal Man'). A Jew, he

entered semi-monastic retirement in 1921, was arrested during World War II, and died in Drancy concentration camp. 📖 J M Schneider, *Clown at the Altar* (1978)

Jacob, Violet *née* Kennedy-Erskine 1863–1946
Scottish poet and novelist

Born in Montrose, Angus, she lived for some years in India. Although she began her writing career as a historical novelist with *The Sheep-stealers* (1902), she is best known for poems in the Angus dialect, such as *Songs of Angus* (1915), *More Songs of Angus* (1918), *Bonnie Joan* (1922) and *The Northern Lights* (1927). Her partly autobiographical *Lairds of Dun* (1931) is a standard history of her native district. Her *Diaries and Letters from India* (edited by Carol Anderson) were published in 1990.

Jacoba of Bavaria See Jacqueline of Holland

Jacobi, Carl Gustav Jacob 1804–51
German mathematician

Born in Potsdam, he was educated at Berlin University, and became a lecturer at the University of Königsberg, where he was appointed Extraordinary Professor in 1827 and Ordinary Professor of Mathematics in 1829. His *Fundamenta nova* (1829) was the first definitive book on elliptic functions, which he and **Niels Henrik Abel** had independently discovered. He discovered many remarkable infinite series connected to elliptic functions, and made important advances in the study of differential equations, the theory of numbers, and determinants.

Jacobi, Sir Derek George 1938–
English actor

Born in London, he had acted while a student at Cambridge and with the National Youth Theatre before he made his professional debut in N F Simpson's *One Way Pendulum* at Birmingham Repertory Theatre (1961). Since then, he has become one of Great Britain's most notable classical actors. He joined the National Theatre's inaugural 1963 company, making his London debut that year as Laertes in *Hamlet*. In 1972 he joined the Prospect Theatre Company and in 1980 he made his New York debut in Nikolai Erdman's *The Suicide*. He joined the Royal Shakespeare Company in 1982. He made his debut as director in 1988, with his production of *Hamlet* for the Renaissance Theatre Company. He has made several film and television appearances, notably the title role in the television adaptation of *I, Claudius* (1977). He was nominated for an Academy Award for his role as a hypnotist in **Kenneth Branagh's** *Dead Again* (1991). He was knighted in 1994, and in 1995 became artistic director of Chichester Festival Theatre.

Jacobi, (J) Lotte 1896–1990
US photographer

Born in Thorn, Germany (now Torun, Poland), she became the fourth-generation member of her father's family to practise as a commercial photographer; her great grandfather Samuel Jacobi was a pupil of **Louis Daguerre**. She studied art history in Posen (1912–16) and Munich (1925–27), and photography and film at the Staatliche Höhere Fach Schule für Phototechnik. In 1927 she took over her father Sigismund Jacobi's Berlin photography studio, running it until the political situation in Germany made her move to the USA in 1935. She operated a studio in New York until 1955, when she went to Deering, New Hampshire, and practised there. She is known for her portraits, her dance photographs and her photogenic drawings.

Jacobi, Mary Corrinna Puttnam, *née* Puttnam 1842–1906
US physician

Born in London, England, she was educated at home in Yonkers, New York, and at private school, and graduated from the New York College of Pharmacy in 1863. Qualifying MD from the Female Medical College of Pennsylvania (1864), she worked in Marie Zakrzewska's clinic in Boston for a few months before she became the first woman to enter the École Médecine in Paris. On graduating she returned to New York and combined private practice with hospital, educational and professional activities, often in association with Elizabeth Blackwell at the Women's Medical College in New York (1871–89). She was active in social causes and women's suffrage.

Jacobs, Aletta 1851–1929
Dutch doctor and birth control pioneer

The daughter of a doctor, she was educated at home and at her local school, and wanted to study medicine but medical school was closed to women. After training as a dispenser, she petitioned the Prime Minister of the Netherlands for the right to study medicine and was granted a place at the University of Groningen, later becoming the first female medical doctor in Holland. Working with her father, she set up free clinics for the poor. In 1882 she established the world's first birth control clinic for women in Amsterdam and campaigned for improvements in health education, changes in marriage and prostitution laws, and for female suffrage.

Jacobs, Joseph 1854–1916
Australian scholar and folklorist

Born in Sydney, he graduated from Cambridge (1876), and devoted himself to the collection of fables and myths. He compiled several collections, and (from 1900) was the editor of the *Jewish Encyclopaedia* in the USA.

Jacobs, W(illiam) W(ymark) 1863–1943
English short-story writer

He was born in Wapping, London, and worked as a post-office official (1883–99). He wrote humorous yarns of bargees and tars, most of which were illustrated by Will Owen, such as *Many Cargoes* (1896), *The Skipper's Wooing* (1897) and *DeepWaters* (1919), and macabre tales, including his best-known story, *The Monkey's Paw* (1902).

Jacobsen, Arne 1902–71
Danish architect and designer

Born in Copenhagen, he was educated at the Royal Danish Academy. He won a House of the Future competition in 1929 and became a leading exponent of Modernism. His theory was 'economy plus function equals style'. In 1956 he became Professor of Architecture at the Royal Danish Academy. He designed many private houses in the Bellavista resort near Copenhagen and his main public buildings were the SAS skyscraper in Copenhagen (1959), and St Catherine's College, Oxford (1964). He also designed cutlery and textiles, and classic furniture, especially the 'Egg' and 'Swan' chairs for his Royal Hotel in Copenhagen. ⌂ Tobias Faber, *Arne Jacobsen* (1964)

Jacobsen, Jens Peter 1847–85
Danish novelist

He was born in Thisted, Jutland, and studied science at Copenhagen. He translated Charles Darwin and became, under the influence of Georg Brandes, the leader of the new Danish Naturalistic movement. Having contracted tuberculosis in Italy, he published some beautiful poems and short stories such as 'Mogens' (1872), and also two psychological novels, *Fru Marie Grubbe* (1876, Eng trans 1914) and *Niels Lyhne* (1880, Eng trans 1896). His deliberate, impressionist style found many disciples, Rainer Maria Rilke among them. Jacobsen's collected works were edited by Fredrik Nielsen in the early 1970s. ⌂ A Gustafson, in *Six Scandinavian Novelists* (1940)

Jacobsz, Lucas See Lucas van Leyden

Jacobus de Voragine See Voragine, Jacobus de

Jacopone da Todi See Todi, Jacopone da

Jacquard, Joseph Marie 1752–1834
French silk-weaver

He was born in Lyons. His invention (1801–08) of the Jacquard loom, which used perforated cards for controlling the movement of the warp threads, enabled an ordinary workman to produce the most beautiful patterns in a style previously accomplished only with patience, skill and labour. But though Napoleon I rewarded him with a small pension and the Legion of Honour, the silk weavers themselves were so violently opposed to his machine that on one occasion he narrowly escaped with his life. At his death his machine was in almost universal use.

Jacqueline of Holland, *also known as* Jacoba of Bavaria 1401–36
Dutch noblewoman

The only child of Count William VI of Zeeland and Holland and Duke of Bavaria, she was born at Le Quesney, Flanders. She married, first (1415), Prince John, Dauphin of France (d.1417). She waged war against John of Bavaria for the right to succeed to her father's title there, then (1418) married her weak cousin, Duke John IV of Brabant, who mortgaged Holland and Zeeland to John of Bavaria. Repudiating the marriage, she went to England, where she married (debatably illegally) Humphrey, Duke of Gloucester (1422). Deserted by him during an invasion to regain her lands in Hainault, she surrendered to Philip, the Good of Burgundy (1428), and relinquished to him her claims to sovereignty (1433). In 1434 she married (for the second time) Frans van Borsselen, a Zeeland noble.

Jacques, Hattie, *originally* Josephine Edwina Jacques 1924–80
English comic actress

Born in Sandgate, Kent, she was a factory worker and Red Cross nurse during World War II, and made her stage debut in 1944. She toured with the Young Vic in *The King Stag* (1947–48) and made the first of many film appearances in *Green for Danger* (1946). Frequently called upon to play bossy figures of authority, she was also a highly respected foil to many comedians, notably in *ITMA* (1948–50) and *Educating Archie* (1950–54) on radio, and on television with Eric Sykes. Later stage work included *Twenty Minutes South* (1955), which she directed, and *Hatful of Sykes* (1979). She also appeared in 14 of the *Carry On …* films.

Jacuzzi, Candido 1903–86
US inventor

Born in Italy, he was an engineer whose infant son suffered from arthritis, and in an attempt to relieve the pain by hydrotherapy Jacuzzi devised a pump that produced a whirlpool effect in a bath. When his invention became generally available it was known as a 'jacuzzi'.

Jaffrey, Madhur 1933–
US cookery writer and actress

Born and educated in Delhi, India, she went to London to study at RADA, then married and moved to the USA. There she collected the recipes sent in letters from her mother in India and succeeded in publishing them. Her authentic and interesting recipes have encouraged appreciation of the richness of Indian cooking, which she also promotes through television and radio appearances. As an actress, her film work includes roles in *Heat and Dust* (1982) and *Vanya on 42nd Street*, as well as directing, and she also writes children's books. Her cookery books include *Flavours of India* (1995).

Jagan, Cheddi Berrat 1918–97
Guyanese Socialist statesman and writer

He was born at Port Mourant, a sugar plantation in the county of Berbice, and in 1936 went to the USA where he qualified as a dentist at Northwestern University, Chicago. He returned to British Guiana (renamed Guyana in 1966 on becoming independent) in 1943. With **Forbes Burnham**, he led the nationalist People's Progressive Party (PPP) in demanding self-government in the early 1950s. The Jagan–Burnham alliance won the 1953 election but the governor, accusing Jagan of 'communist' policies, suspended the constitution, dismissed Jagan and his Cabinet and called in British troops. Jagan came to power with the PPP again in 1957, but an austerity budget and his desire to hasten the end of imperial rule led to racial rioting and a long general strike in Georgetown only ended by further British military intervention (1961–64). In the 1964 election Burnham's People's National Congress was victorious; Jagan was Leader of the Opposition for 28 years until he was elected President in 1992.

Jagger, Charles Sargeant 1885–1934
English sculptor

Born in Yorkshire, he studied at the Royal College of Art, London, and at Rome, and executed mainly mythological and historical subjects. His most famous work is the Portland stone Royal Artillery Memorial at Hyde Park Corner, London. He exhibited at the Venice Biennale in 1928, and his bronze statue of **Ernest Shackleton** (1932) is outside the Royal Geographical Society, London.

Jagger, Mick (Michael Philip) 1943–
English rock singer and songwriter

He was born in Dartford, Kent, and is best known as the lead singer of the **Rolling Stones**. He reinvented himself from a rather shy middle-class student to a strutting rock hero and leading anti-establishment figure in the British pop music of the 1960s. His songwriting partnership with his Dartford contemporary, the Rolling Stones's guitarist Keith Richards (1943–), is one of the most celebrated in rock music. He did not make his first solo album until *She's The Boss* (1985), but neither it nor its successors have rivalled his work with the Stones. He has also acted in a number of films. 📖 C Sandford, *Primitive Cool* (1993)

Jahangir, *originally* Salim 1569–1627
Mughal emperor

Born in Fatehpur Sikri, India, he was the son of **Akbar the Great** and took the title of Jahangir on his accession in 1605. He was a shrewd judge of men and tolerant in religion, with a dilettante interest in Christianity. His early reign saw peace and great prosperity for the empire, with a steady growth of trade and commerce, and a flowering of the arts under royal patronage. Later there were continual rebellions against his rule, principally on behalf of his sons, especially Khurram (who succeeded him as **Shah Jahan**), and he was only able to survive through the vigour of the Empress **Nur Jahan**.

Jahn, Frederick Ludwig, *known as the* Father of gymnastics (Turnvater) 1778–1852
Prussian physical educationist

Born in Lanz, in 1811 he started the first gymnasium (Turnplatz) in Berlin and his methods soon became very popular. An ardent nationalist, he commanded a volunteer corps in the Napoleonic Wars (1813–15), and after the peace of 1815 resumed his teaching, and published *Die deutsche Turnkunst* (1816, Eng trans *A Treatise on Gymnastics*, 1828), but the gymnasiums began to witness political gatherings too liberal to please the Prussian government, and they were closed in 1818. Jahn, who had taken a prominent part in the movement, was arrested in 1819, and suffered five years' imprisonment. He was elected to the Frankfurt National Assembly in 1848.

Jahn, Helmut 1940–
US architect

Born in Allersberg, near Nuremberg, Germany, he moved to the USA in 1966 and studied at Illinois Institute of Technology (IIT), Chicago. As chief executive officer of Murphy/Jahn Associates from 1983, he was appointed Chevalier, Ordre des Arts et des Lettres, Paris, in 1988, and won the IIT award for Outstanding Contribution to the Built environment in 1992. An established architect of office buildings, civic structures, corporate office towers (such as the Xerox Centre, Chicago, 1980), he has undertaken international commissions in Berlin, Frankfurt, Amsterdam and Singapore, and is now moving towards planning work (Munich Airport Centre, 1996). He describes skyscrapers as 'monuments, rich and heroic' (in *Architecture + Urbanism*, June 1986). 📖 Joachim Andreas Joedicke and Karl Kramer (eds), *Helmut Jahn: Design of a New Architecture* (1986)

Jahn, Otto 1813–69
German archaeologist and musicologist

Born in Kiel, he lectured there, and at Greifswald and Leipzig. Deprived of his chair in 1851 for political activities in 1848–49, he became in 1855 Professor of Archaeology at Bonn. He published works on Greek art (1846), representations of ancient life on vases (1861, 1868), and the evil eye (1850), besides a life of **Mozart** (4 vols, 1856–60) and essays on music.

Jaimini c.200BC
Indian founder of the Purva-Mimamsa school of Hindu philosophy

The Purva-Mimamsa system is also known as Vkyaśastra, a study of words, from its concern with correct methods of interpreting the Vedas. Little is known of Jaimini himself, but his *Mimamsa Sutra* emphasizes the need for right action and performing the duties required by the Vedas. Right action presupposes understanding how to acquire valid knowledge, one of the *Mimamsa Sutra*'s chief concerns.

Jakeš, Miloš 1922–
Czechoslovak politician

He was born in České Chalupy. Originally an electrical engineer, he joined the Communist Party of Czechoslovakia (CCP) in 1945 and studied in Moscow (1955–58). He supported the Soviet invasion of Czechoslovakia in 1968 and later, as the leader of the CCP's central control commission, oversaw the purge of reformist personnel. He entered the CCP secretariat in 1977 and the politburo in 1981, and in 1987 he replaced **Gustav Husak** as party leader. Although enjoying close personal relations with the Soviet leader **Mikhail Gorbachev**, he emerged as a cautious reformer who made it clear that restructuring ('prestavba') in Czechoslovakia would be a slow and limited process. He was forced to step down as CCP leader in 1989, following a series of pro-democracy rallies.

Jakobovits (of Regent's Park), Immanuel Jakobovits, Baron 1921–
British Rabbi

He was born in Königsberg, Prussia (now Kaliningrad, Russia), but moved with his family to Great Britain and was educated at Jews College, London, and London University. He served as rabbi in synagogues in London before being appointed Chief Rabbi of Ireland in 1949. He was rabbi of Fifth Avenue Synagogue, New York, from 1958 to 1967 before returning to Britain as Chief Rabbi of the United Hebrew Congregations of the British Commonwealth. He received a life peerage in 1987, and retired in 1991. His writings include *Jewish Medical Ethics* (1959), *Jewish Law faces Modern Problems* (1966) and *If Only My People—Zionism in my Life* (1985).

Jalal ad-Din ar-Rumi, *also called* **Mawlana** 1207–73
Persian lyric poet and mystic
Born in Balkh (in modern Afghanistan), he settled at
Iconium (now Konya) in 1226 and founded a sect. After
his death his disciples became a group referred to in the
West as the Whirling Dervishes. He wrote much lyrical
poetry, including a long epic on the Sufi mystical doc-
trine, *Masnaviy ma'navi*. ▣ A L Aristah, *Rumi, the Persian, the
Sufi* (1974)

James, St, the Great See **James, son of
Zebedee**

James, St, *also known as* St James, the Just
1st century AD
Early Christian
He is listed with **Joseph**, **Simon**, and **Judas** (Matthew
13.55) as a 'brother' of **Jesus** of Nazareth, and identified as
the foremost leader of the Christian community in
Jerusalem (Galatians 1.19, 2.9; Acts 15.13). He is not included in lists of the disciples of Jesus, and should not be
confused with **James**, son of Alphaeus or **James**, son of
Zebedee, but he did apparently witness the resurrected
Christ (1 Corinthians 15.7), at which point he was converted. He showed Jewish sympathies over the question
of whether Christians must adhere to the Jewish law. Most
theologians consider him the author of the Epistle of
James, although it has been ascribed to both others. The
first of the Catholic Epistles, it was put by **Eusebius** of
Caesarea among the list of controverted books (*Anti-
legomena*), and was finally declared canonical by the third
Council of Carthage (AD397). According to **Josephus**,
James was martyred by stoning (c.62AD). His feast day
is 1 May.

James, son of Alphaeus, *also known as* **St James,
the Less** 1st century AD
One of the 12 Apostles of Jesus Christ
He was possibly the James whose mother Mary is referred
to at the crucifixion of **Jesus Christ**. His feast day is 1 May.

James, son of Zebedee, *also known as* **St James,
the Great** 1st century AD
One of the 12 Apostles of Jesus Christ
Born in Galilee, Palestine, he is often listed with **John** (his
brother) and **Peter** in the group closest to **Jesus Christ**,
who were among the first to be called, and who were with
him at the Transfiguration and at Gethsemane. James and
John were called *Boanerges* ('sons of thunder'). According
to Acts 12.2, James was martyred under **Herod Agrippa I**
(c.44AD). His feast day is 25 July.

James I 1394–1437
King of Scotland
Born in Dunfermline, Fife, he was the second son of
Robert III. After his elder brother David, Duke of
Rothesay, was murdered at Falkland (1402), allegedly by
his uncle, the Duke of **Albany**, James was sent for safety to
France, but was captured at sea by the English in 1406
and imprisoned for 18 years. Albany meanwhile ruled
Scotland as governor until his death (1420), when his son,
Murdoch, assumed the regency and the country rapidly
fell into disorder. Negotiations for the return of James
were completed with the Treaty of London (1423) and
James resumed his reign in 1424. Also in 1424, James
married Joan Beaufort (d.1445), a daughter of the Earl of
Somerset, niece of **Richard II**, and they soon came to
Scotland, where James dealt ruthlessly with potential
rivals to his authority. Murdoch, his two sons and the 80-
year-old Earl of Lennox were all beheaded at Stirling, the
first state executions since 1320, and others were dealt
with almost as severely. By such methods he was able to
treble the royal estates. Finance and law and order were
the two other main domestic themes of his reign. The
series of parliaments called after 1424, while encouraging

attendance by lesser landowners, was dominated by the
king's need for increased taxation, partly to pay off the
ransom extracted for his release, and partly to meet increased expenditure on his court, artillery and building
work at Linlithgow. James, described by the chronicler
Boece as 'our lawgiver king', for the most part only refined, repeated or extended judicial enactments of previous kings and many of his activities, here as elsewhere,
had a fiscal motive. He was the nominal founder and
benefactor of St Andrews University. In foreign affairs,
he attempted to increase trade by renewing a commercial
treaty with the Netherlands, and also concluded treaties
with Denmark, Norway and Sweden. His relations with
the Church were abrasive and his criticisms of monastic
orders pointed. His murder in the Dominican friary at
Perth, the first assassination of a Scottish king for 400
years, was the work of a group of dissidents led by descendants of **Robert II**'s second marriage. James left one
surviving son (James, the future **James II**), and six
daughters; the eldest, Margaret (1424–45), who married
the Dauphin, later **Louis XI**, of France, was a gifted poet,
as was James himself, who wrote the tender, passionate
collection of poems, *The Kingis Quair* (c.1423–24 'king's
quire' or book) to celebrate his romance with Joan
Beaufort.

James I of England and VI of Scotland See
panel p970

James II 1430–60
King of Scotland
The son of **James I** and known as James of the fiery face
because of a birth mark, he was born at Roxburgh Castle,
and was six years old at his father's murder (1437). He took
shelter in Edinburgh Castle with his mother, and was put
under her charge and that of Sir Alexander Livingston.
The liaison with Livingston lasted until 1444 when the
Livingstons began to monopolize offices, power and access to the king. In 1449, shortly after his marriage to
Mary, daughter of the Duke of Gueldres, James took
control of the government and the Livingstons were
dismissed from office. He had also to curb the rising
power of the **Douglas** family. Opinions vary as to who was
aggressor and victim in the sharp tussle between them,
which came to a climax (1452) when James stabbed to
death William, the 8th Earl of Douglas, at Stirling Castle.
The king was allowed to get away with murder and
he eventually completely defeated the Douglases of
Arkinholm, Dumfriesshire (1455). This smoothed the
way for a series of grants of earldoms and lands to families
such as the **Campbells**, Gordons and Hamiltons. A
growing stability in domestic politics, helped by the
king's proclaimed concern for justice and a settled economy, was vitiated by his reckless involvement in the
English struggles between the houses of York and
Lancaster. In 1460 he marched for England with a powerful army and laid siege to Roxburgh Castle, which had
been held by the English for over a hundred years, but
was killed by the bursting of a cannon. ▣ F C Turner,
James II (1948)

James III 1452–88
King of Scotland
The eldest son of **James II**, whom he succeeded at the age
of eight (1460), he was brought up under the guardianship of Bishop Kennedy (c.1408–1465) of St Andrews,
while the Earl of Angus was made lieutenant-general.
James's tutor was the leading humanist scholar Archibald Whitelaw, who inspired him with a love of culture
and a sincere piety. The beginnings of the flowering
of vernacular literature that marked **James IV**'s court
began in this reign. His minority, although (from 1466)
marked by the rise of the Boyds at the expense of others,
did not see the degree of disturbance that had marked

previous reigns. By 1469, when parliament condemned the Boyds and James was married to Margaret, daughter of **Kristian I** of Denmark, bringing Orkney and Shetland in pledge as part of her dowry, the king was firmly in control, but he was unable to restore strong central government. Various aspects of his rule, however, created resentment: money was short, successive parliaments reluctant to grant taxes, and in the 1480s James resorted to debasement of the coinage, stigmatized as 'black money'. His efforts (1471–73) to engage in campaigns in Brittany and Gueldres fell on deaf ears, and his attempts (1474–79) to bring about a reconciliation with England were ahead of their time and almost as unpopular. In 1479 he confiscated the estates of his brothers, the Duke of Albany and the Earl of Mar, the latter dying suspiciously. The breakdown of relations with England brought war (1480), and the threat of English invasion resulted in a calculated political demonstration by his nobles, who hanged Robert Cochrane and other unpopular royal favourites at Lauder Bridge (1482). The rebellion which brought about his downfall and death at Sauchieburn (1488) resulted from a further crisis of confidence in the king but ironically was less widespread. His eldest son, who had fought against him, succeeded as James IV.

James IV 1473–1513
King of Scotland

He became king at the age of 15 after the murder of his father **James III** (1488), and was soon active in government. Much of the early 1490s was taken up with securing recognition for the new regime. As a result his council was composed of a far broader, and more stable, coalition than under his three predecessors. Athletic, warlike and pious, James has been called an ideal medieval king; his reign was probably the epitome and climax of Scottish medieval kingship rather than of new monarchy (he was the last Scottish king to speak Gaelic). His rising status, as a king popular at home and respected abroad, was confirmed by his marriage (1503) to **Margaret Tudor**, eldest daughter of **Henry VII**—an alliance which ultimately led to the union of Scotland and England (1603). During his reign, vast sums were spent on building work, as at Stirling Castle, and on military and naval ventures, and in his brilliant Renaissance court he encouraged musicians such as **Robert Carver** and poets such as **William Dunbar**. The king's popularity ironically increased with the scale of the disaster which ended his life. Despite his new alliance with England, he adhered to his old French alliance when **Henry VIII** invaded France (1513). He invaded England and was killed at Flodden (1513), when his army of 20,000 men, probably the largest ever in Scotland, was crushed. 📖 R L Mackie, *King James IV of Scotland* (1958)

James V 1512–42
King of Scotland

Born in Linlithgow, the son of **James IV**, he was less than two years old when his father's death (1513) gave him the Crown, leaving him to grow up among the quarrelling pro-French and pro-English factions, during which time Scotland was reduced to a state of anarchy. Imprisoned (1525–28) by his former stepfather, the Earl of Angus, he eventually made his escape, and as an independent sovereign began to carry out a judicious policy which was largely framed by the need to increase the revenues of his all-but bankrupt kingdom. He continued and greatly extended his father's policy of making the Church a virtual department of state, and raised taxes from the Scottish Church to finance his College of Justice (1532). The pope, assured of James's support and anxious to prevent the spread of the Reformation in Scotland, allowed the king the right to make ecclesiastical appointments. James later used this to appoint five of his six illegitimate sons to high ecclesiastical office. In 1536 he visited France and married first Madeleine, the daughter

of **Francis I** (1537), and after her death, **Mary of Guise** (1538). Both wives brought a substantial dowry and confirmed the Franco–Scottish alliance. Although reasonably popular with the common people and determined to end disorder on the frontier with England, his treatment of the nobility was increasingly brusque. Relations with England, which had been deteriorating from 1536, burst into open war after he failed to attend a conference with **Henry VIII** at York (1541). By 1542 the countries were at war and England invaded. After James's army was defeated at Solway Moss (1542), he retired to Falkland Palace and died, less because of illness than a lack of will to live, only a few days after the birth of his daughter, **Mary, Queen of Scots**, who succeeded him. Sometimes seen as the most unpleasant of all **Stuart** kings, who overstepped many unwritten conventions, he was also a highly talented Renaissance monarch. The monuments to his reign are the literary works produced at his glittering court, such as the poems and plays of Sir **David Lyndsay**, and the ambitious, costly architectural transformation of Stirling Castle and the palaces of Holyrood, Falkland and Linlithgow. 📖 Caroline Bingham, *James V King of Scots, 1512–1542* (1971)

James VI and I See panel p970

James VII and II 1633–1701
King of Scotland as James VII, and then of England and Ireland as James II

The second son of **Charles I**, and brother of **Charles II**, he was born at St James's Palace, London, and was created Duke of York. Nine months before his father's execution in 1649 he escaped to the Netherlands, served under the Vicomte de **Turenne** (1652–55), and in 1657 took Spanish service in Flanders. At the Restoration (1660) James was made Lord High Admiral of England, twice commanding the English fleet in the Dutch wars. In 1659 he had entered into a private marriage contract with Anne Hyde, daughter of the Earl of **Clarendon** and a professed Catholic, and the year after her death in 1671, he himself became a convert to Catholicism. In 1673 parliament passed the Test Act, and he was obliged to resign the office of Lord High Admiral. Shortly after, he married **Mary of Modena**, daughter of the Duke of Modena. The national unrest caused by the Popish Plot (1678) became so formidable that he had to retire to the Continent, and during his absence an attempt was made to exclude him from the succession. He returned at the close of 1679, and was sent to Scotland to manage its affairs. This period saw the beginnings of a remarkable cultural renaissance under his patronage. Meanwhile the Exclusion Bill was twice passed by the Commons, but in the first instance it was rejected by the Lords, and on the second was lost by the dissolution of parliament. After defeat of the bill the exiled James returned to England, and in direct violation of the law took his seat in the council, and resumed the direction of naval affairs. When Charles II died in 1685 James ascended the throne, and immediately proceeded to levy, on his own warrant, the customs and excise duties which had been granted to Charles only for life. He sent a mission to Rome, heard mass in public, and became, like his brother, the pensioner of the French king. In Scotland, parliament remained loyal, despite renewed persecution of the Covenanters, but in England the futile rebellion of the Duke of **Monmouth** was followed by the 'Bloody Assizes'. The suspension of the Test Act by the king's authority, his prosecution of the Seven Bishops on a charge of seditious libel, his conferring ecclesiastical benefices on Roman Catholics, his violation of the rights of the universities of Oxford and Cambridge, his plan for packing parliament, and numerous other arbitrary acts showed his fixed determination to overthrow the constitution and the Church. The indignation of the people was at length roused, and the interposition of William,

James VI and I 1566–1625
King of Scotland from 1567 and of England from 1603

James was born in Edinburgh Castle, the son of **Mary, Queen of Scots**, and Lord **Darnley**. He was baptized Charles James at Stirling Castle. On his mother's forced abdication in 1567 he was proclaimed king as James VI. During his infancy, power was exercised through a sequence of regents; eventually some stability was achieved by James Douglas, 4th Earl of **Morton**, who laid down the foundations for James's later personal reign. Morton was executed in 1581, largely at the instigation of James's relations, the Earl of Arran and the Duke of Lennox. An extreme Protestant reaction followed, and the king was seized in the so-called Ruthven Raid, led by **William Ruthven** (1582). Although presbyterian ministers were not involved, the General Assembly, by approving 'this late work of reformation', stamped a life-long suspicion of the aims of the kirk in the young king's mind.

Within 10 months James had escaped and a countercoup was organized by Arran. In 1584 a parliament reiterated the primacy of the Crown over all estates, including the Church; within days more than a score of radical ministers had fled into exile in England along with some of the Ruthven lords. The exiles returned by the end of 1585 and Arran was displaced from power, but the assertion of royal power, now under the guiding hand of the Chancellor, John Maitland of Thirlestane (1543–95), continued.

The execution of Mary, Queen of Scots, in 1587 drew a token protest from her son, but it was not allowed to disturb the agreement recently concluded with England by the Treaty of Berwick (1586). In 1589 James visited Denmark, and there married Princess **Anne of Denmark**, who was crowned queen in May 1590. During the early 1590s a careful playing-off took place of Roman Catholic and ultra-Protestant factions against each other, and by 1596 a new stability resulted.

On the death of **Elizabeth I** of England (1603), James succeeded to the throne of England as great-grandson of **James IV**'s English wife, **Margaret Tudor**. Although he promised to visit Scotland once every three years, he did not return until 1617. A joint monarchy became for Scotland an absentee monarchy, although the king's political skill and knowledge allowed him to govern Scotland 'by his pen'.

In England, he was at first well received by his English subjects. After the failure of the Gunpowder Plot (1605), severe laws were brought in against Roman Catholics. Eventually, growing dislike of the joint rule of two kingdoms, Puritan resentment of his high-church stance, his use of court favourites, and his friendship with Spain all embittered the fragile relations between Crown and parliament, especially after 1621. The death of the king's eldest son, Henry, Prince of Wales (1612), caused the succession to pass to his second son, the future **Charles I**, who became closely attached to the king's new favourite, George Villiers, 1st Duke of **Buckingham**.

James's achievements as King of England are still a matter of dispute, but he is widely recognized as one of the most successful kings of Scotland, where politics and society were transformed during his long reign.

📖 C Durston, *James I* (1993); A Fraser, *King James VI of Scotland, I of England* (1974).

Other biographies from the reign of James VI and I: *politicians* **Francis Bacon** (Viscount St Albans), George Villiers (Duke of **Buckingham**), Duke of **Cavendish**, **William Cecil**, **Edward Coke**, **John Davies**, James Douglas, Earl of **Morton**; *travellers* **Walter Raleigh**, **Henry Wotton**; *scholars* **George Buchanan**, humanist and reformer, and tutor to the boy King James VI, Earl of **Southampton**, soldier and dedicatee of Shakespeare's *Venus and Adonis*; *musicians* **John Bull**, court organist, **Alfonso Ferrabosco**; *painters* **Marcus Gheeraerts**, **Daniel Mytens**; *architects* **Inigo Jones**; *physicians* **William Harvey**.

Prince of Orange, James's son-in-law and nephew (the future **William III**), was formally solicited by seven leading politicians. William landed at Torbay, 4 November 1688, with a powerful army, and marched towards London. He was hailed as a deliverer, while James was deserted not only by his ministers and troops, but even by his daughter the Princess Anne (later Queen **Anne**). At the first sign of danger, James had sent his wife and infant son to France, and, after one futile start and his arrest at Faversham, he also escaped and joined them at St Germain. He was hospitably received by **Louis XIV**, who settled a pension on him. In 1689, aided by a small body of French troops, he invaded Ireland and made an unsuccessful attempt to regain his throne. He was defeated at the Battle of the Boyne (1690), and returned to St Germain, where he resided until his death. He left two daughters—**Mary II**, married to William III, and Anne, afterwards queen—and one son by his second wife, **James Francis Edward Stuart**, the 'Old Pretender'. He had several illegitimate children—one of them, James Fitzjames, Marshal **Berwick**.

James, Arthur Lloyd 1884–1943
Welsh phonetician
Born in Pentre, he graduated at Cardiff University and at Trinity College, Cambridge, became lecturer in phonetics at University College London in 1920, and in 1927 head (professor, 1933) of the Phonetics Department at the School of Oriental and African Studies. He is chiefly remembered for his *Historical Introduction to French Phonetics* (1929) and for his work with the BBC, whose adviser he was in all matters concerning pronunciation, and whose well-known handbooks on the pronunciation of place names he edited. He committed suicide after killing his wife, as a result of a depressive psychosis brought on by the war.

James, Clive Vivian Leopold 1939–
Australian broadcaster and writer
Born in Sydney, he studied at the universities of Sydney and Cambridge, and began his career as a television critic with the British newspaper the *Observer* (1972–82), later publishing some of his work and writing other nonfiction, fiction, and verse, and three volumes of autobiography. Known as a perceptive cultural commentator, his clever turn of phrase has been heard on television in *Saturday Night People* (1978–80), *Clive James on Television* (1982–84, 1988), *The Late Clive James* (1983–87), *Saturday Night Clive* and *Sunday Night Clive* (1989–94) and *The Clive James Show* (1995–). 📖 *Unreliable Memoirs* (1980); *Falling Towards England: Unreliable Memoirs II* (1985); *May Week was in June: Unreliable Memoirs III* (1990)

James, C(yril) L(ionel) R(obert) 1901–89
Trinidadian writer, lecturer, political activist and cricket enthusiast
He was born in Tunapuna, Trinidad, and won a scholarship to Queens Royal College, Trinidad. An autodidact and a useful cricketer, he was urged to leave Trinidad for England by Learie Constantine and it was there that *The Life of Captain Cipriani* was published in 1929 at O'Leary's expense. James repaid the kindness by acting as his mentor's amanuensis for his newspaper column and five books. An advocate for the freedom of the black races through Marxism and revolution, James was deported

from the USA for his political activities, and while in Trinidad his former pupil, **Eric Williams**, the Prime Minister, put him under house arrest. Perhaps his most influential book was *The Black Jacobins: Toussaint L'Ouverture and the San Domingo Revolution* (1938). He wrote only one novel, *Minty Alley* (1936), a study of the relationship between education and working-class West Indians. His popular *Beyond the Boundary* (1963) is in part autobiographical, and ingeniously combines anecdote, report, analysis and comment, on sport and politics. 📖 Autobiographical account in *Radical America* (1970)

James, Elmore, *originally* Elmore Brooks 1918–63
US blues guitarist and singer
Born in Richmond, Mississippi, he taught himself to play on a homemade guitar, and was profoundly influenced by meeting **Robert Johnson** in 1937. He began performing with Sonny Boy Williamson (originally Rice Miller, 1910–65), and went on to establish the most important slide guitar style in modern blues. He made his first recording in 1952, and had an immediate hit with his adaptation of a Robert Johnson song, 'Dust My Broom', which became his best-known record. He moved to Chicago, but always remained in touch with his roots in the Mississippi Delta. Ironically, he died just as blues music was beginning to find a wide new white audience.

James (of Rusholme), Eric John Francis James, Baron 1909–92
English educational administrator
Born in Derby and educated at Taunton's School, Southampton, and Queen's College, Oxford, he became assistant master at Winchester (1933–45), high master at Manchester Grammar School (1945–62) and Vice Chancellor of the University of York (1962–73). He was chairman of the Committee to Inquire into the Training of Teachers (1970–71) which reported in 1972 (*Teacher Education and Training*). The *James Report* recommended a restructuring of the pattern of teacher training and advocated an all-graduate entry to the profession. It was the first education report to emphasize the importance of systematic in-service education for teachers. A lack of available funding to a large extent precluded its implementation.

James, George Payne Rainsford 1799–1860
English novelist
He was born in London. Influenced by Sir **Walter Scott**, he wrote over a hundred historical romances, such as *Richelieu* (1829), *Henry Masterton* (1832), *Arabella Stuart* (1844) and *The Cavalier* (1859). His habit of opening his novels with two horsemen was parodied by **Thackeray** in *Barbazure*, where he is characterized as 'the solitary horseman'. He served as a British consul in Europe and the USA for many years. 📖 S Ellis, *The Solitary Horseman* (1927)

James, Henry 1843–1916
US novelist
He was born in New York City, of Irish and Scottish stock. Until his father's death he was known as Henry James, Junior. His father, Henry James (1811–82), was a well-known theological writer and lecturer, and an exponent of **Emanuel Swedenborg** and Sandemanism. After a roving youth in the USA and Europe (where he met **Ivan Turgenev** and **Gustave Flaubert**), and desultory law studies at Harvard, he began in 1865 to produce brilliant literary reviews and short stories. His work as a novelist falls into three periods. To the first, in which he is mainly concerned with the 'international situation', the impact of US life on the older European civilization, belong *Roderick Hudson* (1875), *The American* (1877), *Daisy Miller* (1879), *Washington Square* (1880), *Portrait of a Lady* (1881), *Princess Casamassima* (1886), in which he probes the shadier

aspects of European political life, and finally *The Bostonians* (1886). From 1876 he made his home in England, chiefly in London and at Lamb House in Rye, Sussex, where he struck up an oddly contrasted friendship with the science fiction pioneer and self-conscious reformer of mankind, **H G Wells**, a friendship which lasted until the latter's savage attack on the Jamesian ethos in the novel *Boon* (1915). His second period, devoted to purely English subjects, comprises *The Tragic Muse* (1890), *The Spoils of Poynton* (1897), *What Maisie Knew* (1897) and *The Awkward Age* (1899). James reverts to Anglo-American attitudes in his last period, which includes *The Wings of a Dove* (1902), *The Ambassadors* (1903), possibly his masterpiece, *The Golden Bowl* (1904) and two unfinished novels. Collections of his characteristic 'long short stories' include *Terminations* (1895), *The Two Magics* (1898) and *The Altar of the Dead* (1909). His well known ghost story, *The Turn of the Screw*, was published in 1898. The acknowledged master of the psychological novel, which has profoundly influenced the 20th-century literary scene, he sacrifices plot in the interests of minute delineation of character. Many seemingly insignificant incidents, however, subtly contribute allegorically or metaphorically to the author's intentions. He became a British subject (1915) and shortly before his death was appointed to the Order of Merit. He also wrote critical studies such as *French Poets and Novelists* (1878), and the essay 'On the Art of Fiction' (1884), travel sketches such as *The American Scene* (1906) and three volumes of memoirs, *A Small Boy and Others* (1913), *Notes of a Son and a Brother* (1914) and the unfinished *The Middle Years* (1917). He was the brother of the philosopher and psychologist **William James**. 📖 L Edel, *Henry James* (5 vols, 1953–72); F O Matthiessen, *Henry James: the major phase* (1944)

James, Jesse Woodson 1847–82
US Wild West outlaw
Born in Clay County, Missouri, he joined a band of pro-Confederate guerrillas as a teenager, and at the war's end he and his brother Frank (1843–1915) turned to robbery, leading a gang of outlaws from 1866. They carried out numerous bank and train robberies over a period of 15 years, until a large price was put on Jesse's head and he was shot by Robert Ford, a member of his own gang seeking the reward. Frank gave himself up and after his release lived the rest of his life on the family farm. Jesse became a legendary figure, celebrated in ballads and dime novels and latterly in Hollywood films. 📖 L C Bradley, *Jesse James* (1980)

James, M(ontague) R(hodes) 1862–1936
English writer and scholar
Born in Goodnestone, Kent, and educated at Eton and Cambridge, he had a distinguished career as an archaeologist, medievalist and palaeographer, becoming Provost of King's College, Cambridge (1905–18), director of the Fitzwilliam Museum (1894–1908) and then Provost of Eton (1918), and publishing numerous scholarly works. He also wrote *Ghost Stories of an Antiquary* (1904), which was followed by three more collections, in which erudite scholarly details, often invented, add an air of veracity, and evil manifestations tend to be hinted at rather than explicitly described. Among his best stories are 'Oh, Whistle, and I'll Come to You, My Lad' (1904) set, typically, in East Anglia, and 'Casting the Runes' (1911). He was appointed to the Order of Merit in 1930. 📖 M Cox, *M. R. James: An Informal Portrait* (1983)

James, P(hyliss) D(orothy), Baroness James of Holland Park, *née* White 1920–
English detective story writer
Born in Oxford, the eldest child of an official in the Inland Revenue, she was educated at Cambridge Girls' High School. She worked in the theatre and during the

war she was a Red Cross nurse and also worked in the Ministry of Food. Later she was employed in hospital administration before working in the Home Office, first in the police department, where she was involved with the forensic science service, thereafter in the criminal law department. Since 1979 she has devoted herself to writing. *Cover Her Face*, published in 1962, was her first novel, a well-crafted, but slight detective story. She has written steadily since, many of her works featuring the superior detective (and minor poet), Adam Dalgleish. These include *A Mind to Murder* (1963), *The Black Tower* (1975) and *Death of an Expert Witness* (1977). *A Taste for Death* (1986), a macabre, elegant and substantial story, enjoyed an international vogue and was followed by *Devices and Desires* (1989). *The Skull Beneath the Skin* (1982) featured a female private detective, Cordelia Gray. One of the new 'queens of crime', P D James was awarded the Crime Writers Association Diamond Dagger in 1987. She was made a life peer in 1991. Later works include *The Children of Men* (1992) and *Original Sin* (1994). ▥ H R F Keating, *P D James* (1989)

James, Sid 1913–76
British comedy actor
He was born in Johannesburg, South Africa, the son of Jewish music hall artistes, and his early professional life included spells as a coal heaver, diamond digger and boxer. After work in an entertainments unit, then an anti-tank regiment during World War II, he moved to London in 1946. His early film roles included appearances in *The Lavender Hill Mob* (1951) and *The Titfield Thunderbolt* (1952). He was Tony Hancock's foil in *Hancock's Half Hour* (radio 1954–59, television 1956–60) and starred in the television sit-coms *Citizen James* (1960–62), *George and the Dragon* (1966–68) and *Bless This House* (1971–76). He is best remembered for his performances in 19 *Carry On …* films.

James, William 1842–1910
US philosopher and psychologist
Born in New York City, he graduated in medicine from Harvard, where he taught comparative anatomy from 1872, then philosophy from 1882. Professor from 1885, he changed his professorial title in 1889 from philosophy to psychology. A pioneer psychologist, he influenced both branches of his subject, the behaviouristic and the introspective. In his *Principles of Psychology* (1890) he places psychology firmly on a physiological basis and represents the mind as an instrument for coping with the world. He transformed the complex and obscurely expressed opinions of the philosopher Charles Sanders Peirce into the popular philosophy of pragmatism and described himself as a 'radical empiricist', maintaining that metaphysical disputes can be resolved or dissolved by examining the practical consequences of competing theories. He expounded these ideas most famously in *The Will to Believe* (1907) and *Pragmatism* (1907), and he treated ethics and religion in the same practical, non-dogmatic way, as in *The Varieties of Religious Experience* (1902) and *The Meaning of Truth* (1909). James and Henri Bergson were responsible for the formulation of the concept of 'stream of consciousness', a term which James himself coined. In his sympathetic *Varieties of Religious Experience* (1902) he showed himself to be a master of literary style, and simultaneously encouraged his readers, in an age of loss of faith, not to be afraid of religious and mystical experiences. He exercised a great influence both on politicians (who, like Mussolini, often misunderstood him) and on writers, such as his pupil Gertrude Stein. He also helped to found the American Society for Psychical Research. He was the elder brother of Henry James. ▥ E de Bono (ed), *The Greatest Thinkers* (1976)

Jameson, Sir Leander Starr Jameson, 1st Baronet 1853–1917
South African politician
Born in Edinburgh, he studied medicine there and at London, and began to practise at Kimberley in 1878. Through Cecil Rhodes, 'Dr Jim', as he was called, engaged in pioneer work, was in 1891 made administrator for the South Africa Company at Fort Salisbury, and became very much one of the whites. During the troubles at Johannesburg between the Uitlanders and the Boer government, Jameson, who by order of Rhodes had concentrated the military forces of Rhodesia at Mafeking on the Transvaal frontier, started with 500 troopers to support the Uitlanders (The Jameson Raid, 29 December 1895). At Krugersdorp they were overpowered by an overwhelming force of Boers and, sleepless and starving, were after a sharp fight compelled to surrender (2 January 1896). Handed over to the British authorities, Dr Jameson was in July condemned in London to 15 months' imprisonment, but was released in December. In 1900 he was elected to the Cape Legislative Assembly, and in 1904–08 was (Progressive) premier of Cape Colony. He retired from politics in 1912. ▥ I D Colvin, *The Life of Jameson* (2 vols, 1922)

Jameson, (Margaret) Storm 1891–1986
English novelist
She was born in Whitby, North Yorkshire, and studied at Leeds University. Her first success was *The Lovely Ship* (1927), which was followed by more than 30 books that maintained her reputation as storyteller and stylist. These include *The Voyage Home* (1930), *The Delicate Monster* (1937), *The Black Laurel* (1948), *A Cup of Tea for Mr Thorgill* (1957) and *The White Crow* (1968). She also wrote poems, essays, criticism and biography, and several volumes of autobiography, including *No Time Like the Present* (1933) and *Journey from the North* (1969). ▥ *The Writer's Situation* (1950)

Jamet, Marie, *known as* Marie Augustine de la Compassion 1820–93
French religious
Born in St Servan, she was a founder in 1840 of the Little Sisters of the Poor.

Jami 1414–92
Persian poet
He was born in Jam, Khorasan. Among his poems were *Yusuf o Zalikha* (Eng trans by A Rogers *The Book of Joseph and Zuleika*, 1892) and *Salámán u Absál* (Eng trans by Edward Fitzgerald *Salámán and Absál: an Allegory*, 1856). He also wrote prose works. ▥ E Bertel, *Jami* (1949)

Jamieson, John 1759–1838
Scottish lexicographer and philologist
Born and trained in theology in Glasgow, he was an Anti-Burgher secessionist minister in Forfar (1781–97) and in Nicholson Street, Edinburgh (1797–1830). He wrote several scriptural treatises, but his chief work was his monumental *Etymological Dictionary of the Scottish Language* (2 vols 1808–09, supplement 1825). He also edited John Barbour's *The Brus* (1820) and Blind Harry's *Wallace* (1820).

Jamison, Judith 1943–
US dancer and choreographer
Born in Philadelphia, she studied piano and violin at the Judimar School there before making her New York debut as a guest dancer with American Ballet Theater in 1964. She joined Alvin Ailey's American Dance Theater the following year, becoming one of his top soloists. He choreographed the solo *Cry* for her in 1971, a showcase for her statuesque physique, musical sensitivity and dramatic stage presence. She also starred in the Broadway musical *Sophisticated Ladies* (1981). As director of the Alvin Ailey Dance Theater since 1990, she has choreographed such works as *Sweet Release* (with music by Wynton Marsalis), staged at the New York State Theater in 1996. She is married to the Puerto Rican dancer, Miguel Godreau.

Jammes, Francis 1868–1938
French writer

Born in Tournay in the Pyrenees, he was educated at Pau and Bordeaux. He then settled near Pau. He wrote poems of nature and religion, such as *De l'angélus de l'aube à l'angélus du soir* (1898, 'Between the Morning and the Evening Angelus Bells'), *Deuil des primevères* (1901, 'Primroses in Mourning'), *Triomphe de la vie* (1904, 'The Triumph of Life') and *Géorgiques Chrétiennes* (1911–12, 'Christian Georgics'). He was for a time one of a group of poets known as Naturistes (sometimes called Jammistes). His prose romance works include *Le Roman du lièvre* (1903, 'The Romance of the Hare') and his *Mémoires* (1922–23). 📖 R Mallet, *Francis Jammes* (1961)

Janáček, Leoš 1854–1928
Czech composer

Born in Hukvaldy, Moravia, at the age of 16 he was choirmaster in Brno, where he settled after studying at Prague and Leipzig, and became Professor of Composition (1919). Devoted to the Czech folk-song tradition, he matured late as a composer, principally of operas, of which *Jenufa* (1904, first performed 1912), *Osul* (1904), and perhaps *From the House of the Dead* (1928, 'Z Mrtvého Domu*), for which he wrote his own libretto based on Dostoevsky's autobiographical novel, are the most original in terms of rhythm and subtle melodic dependence upon language. His other works include *The Excursions of Mr Brouček* (1908–17, *Výletypana Broučka*), *Kátya Kabanová* (1921), *The Cunning Little Vixen* (1924, *Příhody lišky Bystroušky*) and *The Makropulos Case* (1925, *Věc Makropulos*); the *Glagolitic Mass* (1926, *Glagolská mše*), two string quartets (1923, 1928), *Sinfonietta* (1926) and *The Diary of One Who Disappeared* (1919–24, *Zápisník Zmizeleho*). Janáček's scientific study of the melodic shapes and rhythmic patterns of speech, enhanced by bold, idiosyncratic orchestration, his deep sense of nationalism and intimate choice of subject matter are easily distinguishable features of his work. 📖 C Susskind, *Janáček and Brod* (1985)

Jane Seymour c.1509–1537
English queen

The daughter of Sir John Seymour, and sister of Edward Seymour, Protector Somerset, she was lady-in-waiting to both of Henry VIII's former wives, Catherine of Aragon and Anne Boleyn. She became his third wife 11 days after Anne Boleyn's execution (1536), and gave birth to a son, Edward (the future Edward VI), but died 12 days later. She was the best loved of Henry's wives, and her portrait was painted by Hans Holbein, the Younger.

Jane, Frederick Thomas 1870–1916
British naval author, journalist and artist

Born in Upottery, Devon, he worked first as an artist, then as a naval correspondent on various periodicals. He founded and edited *Jane's Fighting Ships* (1898) and *All the World's Aircraft* (1909), the annuals by which his name is still best known. Inventor of the naval war game, his non-fiction works include *Heresies of Sea Power* (1906) and *The World's Warships* (1915). Among his novels are *Ever Mohun* (1901) and *A Royal Bluejacket* (1908).

Janet, Pierre 1859–1947
French psychologist and neurologist

Born in Paris, he studied under Jean Charcot, lectured in philosophy and became the director of the psychological laboratory at La Salpêtrière Hospital in Paris (1899), and Professor of Psychology at the Sorbonne (1898) and Collège de France (1902). His theory of hysteria, which linked 'dissociation' with a lowering of psychic energy, was described by Sigmund Freud as the first significant psychological theory, based as it was on sound clinical practice.

Janin, Jules Gabriel 1804–74
French critic and novelist

Born in St Etienne, Loire, and educated at Lyons and Paris, he abandoned his law studies for journalism, and his dramatic criticisms in the *Journal des Débats* made his reputation as an opponent of Romanticism and advocate of a classical revival. After 1835 he was solely responsible for the weekly dramatic feuilleton of the Journal des Débats, published later in 6 volumes as *Histoire de la littérature dramatique* (1858, 'History of Dramatic Literature'). His strange and at least half-serious story *L'Âne mort et la femme guillotinée* (1829, 'The Dead Donkey and the Guillotined Woman') was followed by *Barnave* (1831), half historical novel, half polemic against the Orléans family. He was elected to Charles Augustin Sainte-Beuve's chair in the Académie Française in 1870.

Jannings, Emil, *originally* Theodor Friedrich Emil Janenz 1885–1950
German actor

Born in Rorschach, Switzerland, he grew up in Görlitz, Austria. He acted in Max Reinhardt's company (from 1906), and was introduced to films by Ernst Lubitsch. In the USA (1926–29), he won Academy Awards for his performances in *The Way of All Flesh* (1928) and *The Last Command* (1928). Returning to Germany, he appeared with Marlene Dietrich in *Der Blaue Engel* (1930, *The Blue Angel*), his most famous film. Blacklisted by the Allies for his co-operation with the Nazi régime, he retired to Austria.

Jansen, Cornelius Otto 1585–1638
Dutch Roman Catholic theologian, and founder of the Jansenist reform movement

Born in Acquoi, near Leerdam, he studied at Utrecht, Louvain and Paris and became Professor of Theology at Bayonne and in 1630 at Louvain. In 1636 he was made Bishop of Ypres. He died just as he had completed his great work, the *Augustinus*, which tried to prove that the teaching of St Augustine against the Pelagians and semi-Pelagians on grace, free will and predestination was directly opposed to the teaching of the Jesuit schools. On its publication in 1640 the *Augustinus* caused an outcry, especially amongst the Jesuits, and it was prohibited by a decree of the Inquisition in 1641. In the following year it was condemned by Urban VIII in the Bull *In Eminenti*. Jansen's adherents included Antoine Arnauld, Blaise Pascal and the Port-Royalists. The controversy raged in France for nearly a century, when a large number of Jansenists emigrated to the Netherlands. The Utrecht Jansenists are in doctrine and discipline strictly orthodox Roman Catholics, known by their countrymen as Oude Roomsch (Old Roman).

Jansky, Karl Guthe 1905–50
US radio engineer

Born in Norman, Oklahoma, he studied at the University of Wisconsin, and joined the Bell Telephone Laboratories in 1928. While investigating the sources of interference on short-wave radio telephone transmissions, he built a high-quality receiver and aerial system, with which he detected a weak source of static, and concluded that the radiation originated from a stellar source. By 1932 he had pinpointed the source as being in the constellation of Sagittarius—the direction towards the centre of the Milky Way. His findings were published in December 1932 and allowed the development of radio astronomy during the 1950s. In 1973 the unit of radio emission strength, the jansky, was named after him.

Janssen, Cornelis, *originally* Cornelius Johnson 1593–c.1664
Dutch portrait painter

Born in London, England, he moved to Amsterdam in 1643. His portraits show the influence of Van Dyck, with whom he worked at the court of Charles I. He is represented in the National Gallery, London, and at Chatsworth, Derbyshire.

Janssen, Pierre Jules César 1824–1907
French astronomer
Born in Paris, he became head of the Astrophysical Observatory at Meudon in 1876, and greatly advanced spectrum analysis by his observation of the bright line spectrum of the solar atmosphere (1868). He established an observatory on Mont Blanc, and published a pioneering book of celestial photographs, *Atlas de photographies solaires* (1904, 'Atlas of Solar Photographs').

Janssens, Abraham c.1575–1632
Flemish painter
His most famous pictures are the *Entombment of Christ* and the *Adoration of the Magi* at Antwerp.

Jansson, Tove 1914–
Finnish writer and artist
She was born in Helsinki. Her 'Moomintroll' books for children (written in Swedish), starting with *Trollkarlens hatt* (1949, Eng trans *The Magician's Hat*) and illustrated by herself, are as much appreciated by adults. Set in the fantastic yet real world of the Moomins, the books emphasize the security of family life. They have reached an international audience and she has been the recipient of many literary prizes. She later wrote a number of books for adults, including *Sommarboken* (1972, 'The Summer Book') and a psychological thriller *Den ärliga bedragaren* (1982, 'The Honest Deceiver'). ⌂ W G Jones, *Tove Jansson* (1984)

Janszoon, Coesius, Willem See Blaeu

Janszoon, Laurens, *often called* Laurens Coster or Koster c.1370–1440
Dutch inventor
He was an official in Haarlem, and has been credited by some with the invention of printing before Johannes Gutenberg. He is supposed to have made his great invention between 1420 and 1426, to have been sacristan (Koster) at Haarlem, and is thought to have died of the plague.

Januarius, St, *Italian* San Gennaro d.c.305AD
Italian prelate, patron saint of Naples
He was Bishop of Benevento. According to tradition, he was martyred in Pozzuoli in AD305, during the persecutions of Diocletian. His body is preserved in Naples Cathedral, with two phials supposed to contain his dried blood, believed to liquefy on 19 September, his feast day, and other occasions.

Jardine, Douglas Robert 1900–58
English cricketer
He was born in Bombay, India. In 1927 he scored five centuries and was picked for the Test team that toured Australia in 1927–28, where he scored 341 Test runs. He returned to Australia as captain of England during the controversial 'bodyline' tour, where he employed Harold Larwood to bowl extremely fast at the batsman's body (the so-called 'leg theory'), causing severe injury to the Australian batsmen. He wrote a defence of his tactics in *In Quest of the Ashes* (1933).

Jarman, Derek 1942–94
English painter and filmmaker
Born in Northwood, Middlesex, he studied painting at the Slade School, London (1963–67), and had work exhibited at the Young Contemporaries' and John Moores exhibitions before moving into costume and set design for the Royal Ballet. Continuing to paint, he first worked in the cinema as a production designer for Ken Russell's

The Devils (1970). He directed his first feature film, *Sebastiane*, in 1976 and transferred his painterly instincts to the cinema in a succession of often controversial works exploring the decline of modern Great Britain, his homosexual sensibilities and artistic idols. His films include *Jubilee* (1977), *Caravaggio* (1985), *The Last of England* (1987), *The Garden* (1991), *Edward II* (1991), an adaptation of Christopher Marlowe's 1594 play, *Wittgenstein* (1993) and *Blue* (1994). He also directed pop videos and designed for opera and ballet. His writings include the autobiographical *Dancing Ledge* (1984) and *Modern Nature* (1991). ⌂ Michael O'Pray, *Derek Jarman: Dreams of England* (1996)

Järnefelt, Armas 1869–1958
Swedish composer of operas, and conductor
Born in Viipuri, Finland, he studied under Ferrucio Busoni and Jules Massenet, and conducted in Germany, Helsinki and Stockholm, taking Swedish citizenship in 1910. He is best known for his *Praeludium* (1907) and *Berceuse* for orchestra, and for choral music. He was the brother-in-law of Jean Sibelius.

Jarrell, Randall 1914–65
US poet and critic
Born in Nashville, Tennessee, he graduated from Vanderbilt University and served in the air force in World War II. Many of his early poems draw on his war experience, and his later work continues to focus on alienation and loss, often exploring these themes through dramatic monologues. He published several volumes of poetry, ranging from *Blood for a Stranger* (1942) to *The Lost World*, published posthumously in 1966. His *Complete Poems* appeared in 1969. A merciless reviewer of bad verse, he also wrote lucid and eloquent essays on writers he admired, and collections of his criticism such as *Poetry and the Age* (1953) and *Kipling, Auden & Co* (1980) are of unfading interest, as are his children's books, notably *The Animal Family* (1965), illustrated by Maurice Sendak. He taught English at a series of colleges and universities, satirizing a stint at Bennington College in his novel *Pictures from an Institution* (1954). Near the end of his life he was hospitalized for depression, and soon after being released he was hit by a car, probably a suicide, possibly as a result of his war experience. ⌂ K Shapiro, *Randall Jarrell* (1967)

Jarrett, Keith 1945–
US jazz and classical musician and composer
Born in Allentown, Pennsylvania, he was a child prodigy on piano, and gave his first recital at the age of seven. He played professionally while at school, and spent a year at Berklee College of Music in Boston. He moved to New York in 1965, played briefly with Art Blakey, then spent three years with saxophonist Charles Lloyd, and two with Miles Davis. Established as a leader in his own right, he began performing lengthy solo concerts from 1972; the recording of one such event, *The Koln Concert* (1975), has sold over 2 million copies. He has recorded jazz with groups of various sizes, but most often with his Standards trio featuring Gary Peacock and Jack DeJohnette, and plays drums and soprano saxophone as well as piano. A brilliant improviser, he has also recorded works by Bach and Dmitri Shostakovich , and has composed music for classical settings. ⌂ I Carr *Keith Jarrett* (1991)

Jarry, Alfred 1873–1907
French writer
He was born in Laval, Mayenne, and was educated at Rennes. His satirical farce, *Ubu roi*, an attack on bourgeois conventions, was first written when he was 15 and performed as a puppet-show called *Les Polonais*. He later revised it and it was produced in 1896 (Eng trans 1951). In a crude parody of Shakespeare's *Macbeth*, le père Ubu, the grotesque hero, symbolizes the bourgeoisie pushed to

absurd lengths by the lust for power. He wrote two se-quels, *Ubu enchaîné* (1900, Eng trans *Ubu Enslaved*, 1953) and *Ubu cocu* (1944, Eng trans *Ubu Cuckolded*, 1965), and a two-act musical version of *Ubu roi* for marionettes (1901), as well as short stories and poems and other plays. His belief that the writer should empty the mind of in-telligence in order to open it to the possibilities of hal-lucination anticipates Surrealism. He also invented a logic of the absurd, which he called 'pataphysique', and his work is considered a precursor of the Theatre of the Absurd. Almost as eccentric as his creation, Ubu, he lived a life of excess and died an alcoholic. 📖 R Shattuck, *The Banquet Years: the arts in France, 1885–1919* (1959)

Jaruzelski, Wojciech Witold 1923–
Polish soldier and politician
He was born near Lublin. After a long and distinguished military career (Chief of General Staff 1965, Minister of Defence 1968) he became a member of the politburo in 1971 and was appointed Prime Minister (1981–85) and Communist Party leader after the resignations of Pin-kowski and Kania in 1981. Later that year, in an attempt to ease the country's crippling economic problems and to counteract the increasing political influence of the free trade union Solidarity, Jaruzelski declared a state of martial law. Solidarity was declared an illegal organiza-tion and its leaders were detained and put on trial. Martial law was suspended at the end of 1982 and lifted in July of the following year. In November 1985 Jaruzelski resigned as Prime Minister to become state President, overseeing a transition to a new form of 'socialist pluralist' democracy in 1989. He was President of the Polish Republic until December 1991, when he was succeeded by Lech Wałesa.

Jasmin, *pseudonym of* Jacques Boé 1798–1864
French poet
Born in Agen, he was a barber by profession, and wrote homely verses in his local Gascon dialect. Among his best pieces (collected in *Las Papillôtos*, 1835, French trans *Las Papillôtos*, 1860) are the mock-heroic *Charivari* (1825), *L'Abuglo de Castèl-Cuillé* (1835, Eng trans by Henry Wadsworth Longfellow, *The Blind Girl of Castel-Cuillé*), *Françovneto* (1840), and *La Semaine d'un fils* (1848, 'A Son's Week'). 📖 J Andrieu, *Jasmin et son œuvre* (1881)

Jason, David, *originally* David John White 1940–
English actor
Born in London, he acted in amateur theatre while working as an electrician, then turned professional as an actor. One of his earliest television roles was in *Crossroads*, before playing Captain Fantastic in *Do Not Adjust Your Set* (1967–69). Teaming up with Ronnie Barker, he acted Dithers in *Hark at Barker* (1969–70), Blanco in *Porridge* (1974–77) and Granville in *Open All Hours* (1976–85). He then took the roles of Shorty Mestead in *Lucky Feller* (1976), Peter Barnes in *A Sharp Intake of Breath* (1978–81), Derek Trotter in *Only Fools and Horses* (1981–), Skullion in *Porterhouse Blue* (1987, BAFTA Best Actor award 1988), Ted Simcock in *A Bit of a Do* (1989), Pop Larkin in *The Darling Buds of May* (1991–93) and Det Insp Jack Frost in *A Touch of Frost* (1992–). 📖 Stafford Hildred and Tim Ewbank, *The David Jason Story—A Perfect Life* (1991)

Jaspers, Karl Theodor 1883–1969
German existentialist philosopher
Born in Oldenburg, he studied medicine at Berlin, Göttingen and Heidelberg, where he joined the psychi-atric clinic (1909–15), published a textbook on psycho-pathology, *Allgemeine Psychopathologie* (1913, *General Psycho-pathology*, 1965), and was Professor of Psychology (1916–20). From 1921 he was Professor of Philosophy at Heidel-berg until dismissed by the Nazis in 1937. His work was banned but he stayed in Germany and was awarded the Goethe prize in 1947 for his uncompromising stand. In

1948 he settled in Basle as a Swiss citizen, and was appointed professor. The most important of his many works is considered to be *Philosophie* (3 vols, 1932). In this he developed his own brand of existentialism whereby *Existenz* (Being) necessarily transcends and eludes or-dinary objective thought: at the limits of the intellect the 'authentic self' must make a leap of apprehension of a different kind. 📖 Leonard H Ehrlich, *Karl Jaspers: Philosophy as Faith* (1975)

Jaurès, (Auguste Marie Joseph) Jean
1859–1914
French Socialist leader, writer and orator
Born in Castres, Tarn, he was a deputy from 1885 to 1889, lectured on philosophy at Toulouse and became a deputy again from 1893. He founded the French Socialist Party, and in 1904 co-founded the Socialist paper *L'Humanité*, which he edited until his death. An advocate of Franco–German rapprochement in the crisis that followed the assassination of Archduke Franz Ferdinand, Jaurès was himself assassinated in July 1914 by a fanatical French patriot. 📖 Harvey Goldberg, *The Life of Jean Jaurès* (1962)

Javolenus Priscus c.AD60–125
Roman jurist and writer
He was consul, commander of several legions, Governor successively of Germany, Syria and Africa, and writer of legal texts. Particularly notable is his *Epistulae* (in 15 books), from which several excerpts are included in Justinian's *Digest*.

Jawara, Sir Dawda Kairaba 1924–
Gambian politician
He was born in Barajally. After qualifying at Glasgow University, he returned to The Gambia to work in the national veterinary service (1957–60). He entered politics in 1960 and progressed rapidly, becoming Minister of Education and then premier (1962–65). When full in-dependence was achieved in 1965 he became Prime Minister and when it chose republican status, in 1970, President. He was re-elected in 1972, 1977, 1982 and 1987, despite an abortive coup against him in 1981. The coup was thwarted by Senegalese troops and brought the two countries closer together into a confederation of Sene-gambia. His presidency ended in 1994.

Jawlensky, Alexei von 1864–1941
Russian painter
Born in Kuslovo, he began as an officer in the Imperial Guards but turned to painting in 1889, studying at the St Petersburg Academy under Ilya Repin. In 1896 he went to Munich where he met Wassily Kandinsky, and in 1905 to France where he was strongly influenced by the work of Van Gogh, Gauguin and Matisse, developing a personal style which combined traditional Russian icons and peasant art with the new Fauvist emphasis on strong, flat colours and harsh outlines. A founder member of the *Neue Künstlervereinigung* ('New Artists' Association', known as the NKV) in Munich in 1909, he was never a pure abstractionist. In 1924, with Kandinsky, Paul Klee and Lyonel Feininger, he founded the short-lived *Der Blaue Vier* (Blue Four association). From 1917 he con-centrated mainly on painting the human head.

Jay, John 1745–1829
American jurist and politician
Born in New York City, he was admitted to the Bar in 1768, elected to the Continental Congress (1774–77), and he drafted the constitution of New York state in 1777, of which he was appointed Chief Justice. He was elected president of Congress in 1778, and in 1779 was sent as Minister to Spain. From 1782 he was one of the most influential of the commissioners negotiating peace with Great Britain. He was Secretary for Foreign Affairs (1784–89), then became Chief Justice of the Supreme

Court (1789–95). In 1794 he concluded with Lord Grenville, the convention known as Jay's Treaty, which, though favourable to the USA, was denounced by the Democrats as a betrayal of France. He was Governor of New York from 1795 to 1801, when he retired.

Jayawardene, Junius Richard 1906–96
Sri Lankan politician

Born in Colombo into a well-connected (goyigama) family, he studied law at Colombo University before he entered the House of Representatives in 1947 as a representative of the Liberal–Conservative United National Party (UNP). He held a number of ministerial posts (1953–70), before becoming Leader of the UNP, and of the Opposition, in 1970. He so revitalized it that it returned to power in 1977. He introduced a new constitution in 1978, creating a republic, and became the country's first President (1978). He embarked on a new, free-market economic strategy but was confronted with mounting unrest between Tamil separatists and the indigenous Sinhalese, forcing the imposition of a state of emergency in 1983 and the postponement of new elections until 1989, when he stepped down as President and was succeeded by Ranasinghe Premadasa. ⎶ K M De Silva and W H Wriggins, *The Life and Times of J R Jayawardene of Sri Lanka 1906–1956* (vol 1, 1988)

Jazari, In al-Razzaz al- fl.c.1200
Islamic engineer in Mesopotamia

He developed many mechanical and hydraulic devices including a reciprocating water pump. Details of this, and the earliest surviving description of a crankshaft, are recorded in his *Book of Knowledge of Ingenious Devices*.

Jean, Mère Angélique de Saint See Arnauld, Angélique

Jean de Meung See Meung, Jean de

Jeanne d'Arc See Joan of Arc

Jeans, Sir James Hopwood 1877–1946
English physicist, astronomer and writer

Born in Ormskirk, near Southport, he taught at Princeton University and at Cambridge before becoming a research associate at Mt Wilson Observatory in Pasadena. One of his first important results was the development of a formula to describe the distribution of energy of enclosed radiation at long wavelength, now known as the Rayleigh–Jeans law. He also carried out important work on the kinetic theory of gases, giving mathematical proofs of the law of equipartition of energy and James Clerk Maxwell's law of the velocity distribution of the molecules of a gas. He made significant advances in the theory of stellar dynamics by applying mathematics to problems. His wide-ranging research included studies of the formation of binary stars, stellar evolution, the nature of spiral nebulae and the origin of stellar energy, which he believed to be associated with radioactivity. He was renowned as a popularizer of physical and astronomical theories and their philosophical bearings, in works such as *The Universe Around Us* (1929) and *The New Background of Science* (1933). He was knighted in 1928. ⎶ E A Milne, *Sir James Jeans* (1952)

Jeb See Stuart, James Ewell Brown

Jebb, Eglantyne 1876–1928
English philanthropist

Born in Ellesmere, Shropshire, she graduated from St Margaret Hall, Oxford, and taught for a year at an elementary school in Marlborough. Forced by ill health to leave the profession, she did some social work in Cambridge before going to Macedonia to administer the relief fund for the victims of the Balkan wars. After the end of World War I the plight of the 4 to 5 million children

starving in Europe prompted her to set up the Save the Children Fund (1919). She raised large sums of money by her tremendous efforts, and the Save the Children International Union was established in Geneva, where she remained and worked until her early death.

Jefferies, (John) Richard 1848–87
English naturalist and novelist

Born near Swindon, the son of a Wiltshire farmer, he started as a provincial journalist and became known by a letter to *The Times* (1872) on the Wiltshire labourers. His first real success, *The Gamekeeper at Home* (1878), was followed by other books on rural life, including *Wild Life in a Southern County* (1879), *Wood Magic* (1881), the autobiographical *Bevis: The Story of a Boy* (1882), and his last and most successful novel, *Amaryllis at the Fair* (1887). He also wrote *The Story of my Heart* (1883), a strange autobiography of inner life and *After London, or Wild England* (1885), a curious romance of the future. ⎶ P E Thomas, *Richard Jefferies: his life and work* (1972)

Jeffers, (John) Robinson 1887–1962
US poet and dramatist

Born in Pittsburgh, Pennsylvania, he was educated in Europe and settled in California in 1904. His first poetry collection, *Flagons and Apples*, was published in 1912. His principal themes derive from biblical stories and Greek and Roman legend concerning the corruption of moral values, evident in *Tamar and Other Poems* (1924). Other collections include *The Women at Point Sur* (1927), *Be Angry at the Sun* (1941) and *Hungerfield and Other Poems* (1954). He also wrote a version of *Medea* (1946).

Jefferson, Blind Lemon 1897–1929
US blues guitarist and singer

Born in Couchman, Texas, he was one of seven children, and was born blind. He performed locally in and around Worthman, Texas, then moved to Dallas in 1917, where he played on the streets for small change. His recorded legacy of almost 100 songs was made between 1926 and his death (including some gospel and spiritual material using the pseudonym Deacon L J Bates). He was the first blues singer to establish a repertoire of his own songs, rather than buying from commercial songwriters, and his performing style, notably his intricate, improvisational guitar playing, was enormously influential in the development of the music.

Jefferson, Joseph 1829–1905
US comic actor

He was born in Philadelphia into a theatrical family, his great-grandfather having belonged to David Garrick's company at Drury Lane, London, while his father and grandfather were well-known US actors. Jefferson appeared on the stage at the age of three, and had for years been a strolling actor, when, in New York, he made a hit as Doctor Pangloss (1857), and created the part of Asa Trenchard in *Our American Cousin* (1858). He visited London (1865), and at the Adelphi first played his famous part of Rip Van Winkle, a role he continued to play until he retired.

Jefferson, Thomas 1743–1826
3rd President of the USA

Born on his father's plantation, Shadwell, in Albemarle County, Virginia, he graduated from the College of William and Mary and was admitted to the Bar in 1767. Two years later he was elected to the Virginia House of Burgesses, where he joined the Revolutionary Party. He played a prominent part in the calling of the first Continental Congress in 1774, to which he was sent as a delegate, drafting the Declaration of Independence (signed 4 July 1776). He helped to form the Virginia state constitution, and became Governor of Virginia (1779–81). As a member of Congress in 1783 he secured the adoption of the decimal system of coinage. He was sent to France in 1784 with **Benjamin Franklin** and **Samuel Adams** as plenipotentiary, and succeeded Franklin as Minister in 1785. In 1789 **George Washington** appointed him Secretary of State. As leader of the Democratic–Republican Party, he advocated limited government and envisioned the USA as a republic of independent farmers, and he clashed repeatedly with **Alexander Hamilton** and the Federalist Party. After running second in the presidential election of 1796, he became Vice-President (1797–1801) under **John Adams**, playing little part in an administration dominated by Federalists and drafting the Kentucky Resolves of 1798 to protest the passage of the Alien and Sedition acts. A tie with **Aaron Burr** in the electoral college threw the election of 1800 into the House of Representatives, where Jefferson was chosen as President, taking office in 1801. The popular vote re-elected him by a large majority for the next presidental term. Among the chief events of his first term were the war with Tripoli, which subdued the Barbary pirates, and the Louisiana Purchase of 1803, which Jefferson sponsored, setting aside for once his insistence on a strict construction of the Constitution. He also planned the **Lewis** and **Clark** expedition to explore the lands to the west of the Mississippi. His second term saw the firing on the *Chesapeake* by the *Leopard*, the Embargo Act of 1807, the trial of Aaron Burr for treason, and the prohibition of the slave import trade (1808). In 1809 he retired to his Virginian estate, Monticello, and devoted much time to founding the University of Virginia and designing its campus. A man of letters as well as a gifted architect, he published several books of which the most valuable is his *Notes on Virginia* (1785), and in old age carried on a famous correspondence with his former political rival John Adams. He and Adams both died on 4 July 1826, the 50th anniversary of the Declaration of Independence. ꕯ Fawn Brodie, *Thomas Jefferson: An Intimate History* (1974)

Jeffrey, Lord Francis 1773–1850
Scottish judge and critic

Born in Edinburgh, he studied at Glasgow and Oxford, and in 1794 was called to the Scottish Bar. Acquiring a considerable reputation in the trials for sedition (1817–22), he was twice elected Lord Rector of Glasgow University (1820, 1832), and in 1829, Dean of the Faculty of Advocates. In 1830 he became MP for Perth, and on the formation of Earl **Grey**'s ministry became Lord Advocate. After the passing of the Reform Bill he became MP for Edinburgh, which he represented until 1834, when he was made a judge of the Court of Session. With **Sydney Smith**, Lord **Brougham** and others, he established (1802) the influential *Edinburgh Review*, of which he was editor until 1829. He was a prolific and distinguished contributor, and a great admirer of many writers, including **Keats**, but failed to appreciate the 'Lake Poets', notoriously beginning his review of **Wordsworth**'s *The Excursion* (1814) with the words 'This will never do'. A selection of his articles was published in 1844.

Jeffrey, John 1959–
Scottish rugby player

Born in Kelso, Roxburghshire, a farmer by profession, he was educated at Merchiston Castle School, Edinburgh, and Newcastle University. He first played for Scotland in 1984 and, once established as a first-choice backrow forward, he gained a reputation as one of the most dangerous players in this position in the world. He played in Scotland's World Cup teams of 1987 and 1991, announcing his retirement from international rugby after the latter campaign. Loyal to his home-town club, Kelso, he was one of the most important members of the Scotland team which won the Grand Slam in 1990.

Jeffreys, Sir Alec John 1950–
English molecular biologist

Born in Oxford, he graduated from university there, and later became European Molecular Biology Organisation Research Fellow at the University of Amsterdam (1975–77) where he worked on mammalian globin genes. He later moved to the department of genetics at the University of Leicester, where he has remained throughout his career, becoming Professor of Genetics in 1987. He was elected FRS in 1986 and became Wolfson Research Professor of the Royal Society in 1991. He developed the technique of 'DNA fingerprinting', in which DNA from an individual is broken down and the resultant DNA fragments separated. Each individual has a unique pattern of DNA fragments, and thus samples of blood or semen can conclusively identify an individual in much the same way as a fingerprint. This technology is now used widely in forensic work. He was knighted in 1994.

Jeffreys (of Wem), George Jeffreys, 1st Baron 1648–89
English judge

Born in Acton, Clwyd, Wales, he was called to the Bar in 1668. He rose rapidly, was knighted (1677), and became Recorder of London (1678). He was active in the Popish Plot prosecutions, became Chief Justice of Chester (1680), baronet (1681), and Chief Justice of the King's Bench (1683). In every state trial he proved a willing tool of the crown, and was raised to the peerage by **James II** (1685). Among his earliest trials were those of **Titus Oates** and **Richard Baxter**. His period in the West Country to try the followers of the Duke of **Monmouth** earned the name of the 'Bloody Assizes' for its severity. He was Lord Chancellor (1685–88), but on James's flight into exile was imprisoned in the Tower of London, where he died. ꕯ G W Keeton, *Lord Chancellor Jeffreys* (1965)

Jeffreys, Sir Harold 1891–1989
English mathematician, geophysicist and astronomer

Born in Fatfield, Durham, he was educated at Armstrong College, Newcastle upon Tyne, and St John's College, Cambridge, where was elected a Fellow in 1914. After working in dynamical astronomy he joined the Meteorological Office as an assistant to the director, working on the dynamics of the winds and oceans (1915–17). Returning to Cambridge in 1922, he held various teaching appointments and later became Plumian Professor of Astronomy and Experimental Philosophy (1946–58). In his application of classical mechanics to geophysical problems, he discovered the discontinuity between the Earth's upper and lower mantle, found evidence for the fluid nature of the core and did much pioneering theoretical work on the shape and strength of the Earth. His analysis of seismic traveltimes was published as the *Jeffreys–Bullen Tables* (1940, see also **Keith Bullen**), which remains a standard reference. This work led him to a Bayesian theory (see **Thomas Rogers**) of probability applicable to a wide range of sciences. He was elected FRS in 1925, and knighted in 1953.

Jeffries, John 1744–1819
American balloonist and physician

Born in Boston, he was a loyalist during the American Revolution (1775–83). He settled in England and made the first balloon crossing of the English Channel with the French aeronaut, **Jean Pierre François Blanchard**, in 1785.

Jeffries, Lionel 1926–
English actor and director

Born in London, he trained at RADA and made his film debut in **Alfred Hitchcock**'s *Stage Fright* (1949) but went on to become known as a comedy performer in films such as *Blue Murder at St Trinian's* (1957), *Up the Creek* (1958), *Two Way Stretch* (1960), *The Wrong Arm of the Law* 1962), *First Men in the*

Moon (1964) and *Chitty Chitty Bang Bang* (1968). As a director, he had great success with *The Railway Children* (1970), *The Amazing Mr Blunden* (1972), *Wombling Free* (1977) and *The Water Babies* (1978). On television, he acted as Major Langton in *Shillingbury Tales* (1981), the title role in the sitcom *Father Charlie* (1982), Thomas Maddison in *Tom, Dick and Harriet* (1982–83) and Grandpa Rudge in *Rich Tea & Sympathy* (1991).

Jehan See Clouet, Jean

Jehu 842–815BC
Hebrew general and King of Israel

He had been military commander under King **Ahab**, but after Ahab's death he led a military coup and slaughtered the royal family, including Ahab's wife **Jezebel**. Having seized the throne for himself, he founded a dynasty that saw a decline in the fortunes of Israel, which was forced to pay tribute to Assyria.

Jekyll, Gertrude 1843–1932
English horticulturist and garden designer

Born in London, she trained as an artist but was forced by failing eyesight to abandon painting, and she took up landscape design at her garden at Munstead Wood, Surrey. In association with the architect **Edwin Lutyens** she designed more than 300 gardens for his buildings that had a great influence on promoting colour design in garden planning. Her books include *Wood and Garden* (1899), *Home and Garden* (1900), *Wall and Water Gardens* (1901), *Colour in the Flower Garden* (1918) and *Garden Ornament* (1918).

Jellicoe, Sir Geoffrey Alan 1900–96
English landscape architect

He was educated at Cheltenham College and at the school of the Architectural Association in London, and later became its Principal. His best-known work includes the information centre at Cheddar Gorge (1934), the Kennedy Memorial at Runnymede, Berkshire (1965), the gardens at Sandringham and Chequers, and at Sutton Place, Sussex (1980–84), and town plans for Guildford and Hemel Hempstead. He also wrote extensively, notably *Italian Gardens of the Renaissance* (1925, with J C Shepherd), *Studies in Landscape* (3 vols, 1959–70) and *Landscape of Man* (1965, with Susan Jellicoe). President of the Institute of Landscape Architects (1939–49), he was knighted in 1979 and became a member of the Royal Academy in 1991.

Jellicoe, John Rushworth Jellicoe, 1st Earl
1859–1935
English admiral

Born in Southampton, he served in the Egyptian war of 1882, and was one of the survivors of the collision between HMS *Victoria* and HMS *Camperdown* in 1893. He was Chief of Staff on an international overland expedition to relieve the legations in Peking (Beijing) during the Boxer Rebellion (1900), where he was severely wounded. He played a major part in the modernization of the fleet under Admiral **Fisher**. At the outbreak of World War I he was appointed Commander-in-Chief of the Grand fleet and his main engagement was the inconclusive Battle of Jutland (1916) for which he was much criticized. Promoted First Sea Lord (1916–17), he organized the defences against German submarines, and was made Admiral of the Fleet (1919). He later became Governor of New Zealand (1920–24). He was created an earl in 1925. 📖 Alfred Temple Patterson, *Jellicoe: A Biography* (1969)

Jen, Pa Ta Shan See Chu-Ta

Jenkins, David Edward 1925–
English theologian and prelate

Born in Bromley, Kent, of devout Methodist parents, he was a lecturer at Birmingham and Oxford before being appointed director of *Humanum* studies at the World Council of Churches, Geneva (1969–73), director of the William Temple Foundation, Manchester (1973–78), and Professor of Theology at Leeds (1979–84). He became Bishop of Durham in 1984 amidst controversy over his interpretation of the Virgin Birth and the Resurrection, and his trilogy, *God, Miracle and the Church of England* (1987), *God, Politics and the Future* (1988) and *God, Jesus and Life in the Spirit* (1988), maintains the exploratory spirit of earlier books, which included *A Guide to the Debate About God* (1966), *Living with Questions* (1969) and *The Contradiction of Christianity* (1976). Later books include *Still Living with Questions* (1990) and *Free to Believe* (1991). He retired as Bishop of Durham in 1994 and has since served as assistant bishop in the diocese of Ripon.

Jenkins, Robert fl. 1731–48
English merchant captain

He was engaged in trading in the West Indies. In 1731 he alleged that his sloop had been boarded by a Spanish coastguard, and that, though there was no proof of smuggling, he had been tortured and had his ear torn off. He produced the alleged ear in 1738 in the House of Commons and so helped to force **Robert Walpole** into the War of Jenkins' Ear against Spain in 1739, which merged into the War of the Austrian Succession (1740–48). Jenkins served with the East India Company, and for a time as Governor of St Helena.

Jenkins, (John) Robin 1912–
Scottish novelist

Born in Cambuslang, Lanarkshire, he was educated at Hamilton Academy and Glasgow University. At various times an English teacher in Scotland, Afghanistan, Spain and Borneo, he has set many of his stories in these countries. A prolific writer, his works begin with *So Gaily Sings the Lark* (1950), carry on to *Willie Hogg* (1993), and fall into three main groups: those set in Scotland, those set in 'Norania', his fictional Afghanistan, and those dealing with 'Kalewentan', a far eastern sultanate. Interested in exploring human beings' moral possibilities, as in *Dust on the Paw* (1961), he looks at the paradoxes of society's values. His best-known novels are *The Cone-Gatherers* (1955) and *Fergus Lamont* (1979). 📖 F R Hart, *The Scottish Novel* (1985)

Jenkins (of Hillhead), Roy Harris Jenkins, Baron 1920–
Welsh Labour politician and author

Born in Abersychan, Monmouthshire, he was educated at the local grammar school and at Balliol College, Oxford. Elected MP for Central Southwark in 1948, he was the youngest member of the House. He was MP for the Stetchford division of Birmingham from 1950 to 1976. He introduced, as a Private Members' Bill, the controversial Obscene Publications Bill, strengthening the position of authors, publishers and printers *vis-à-vis* prosecutions for obscenity. After a successful spell as Minister of Aviation (1964–65) he was made Home Secretary, but was criticized for his alleged 'softness' towards criminals. In 1967 he changed posts with **James Callaghan** to become Chancellor of the Exchequer, introducing a notably stringent Budget in March 1968. In 1970–72 he was deputy Leader of the Labour Party in opposition, and was again appointed Home Secretary on Labour's return to power in 1974. He resigned as an MP in 1976, and became president of the European Commission (1977–81). He was a founder-member of the joint leadership of the Social Democratic Party (1981–82), became its first leader in 1982, but stood down after the 1983 election in favour of Dr **David Owen**. He returned to represent Glasgow (Hillhead) from 1982 until he was defeated in 1987, when he was made a life peer, and also elected Chancellor of

Oxford. He was appointed to the Order of Merit in 1993. A successful journalist and author, he has published *Mr Balfour's Poodle* (1954), *Sir Charles Dilke* (1958), *Asquith* (1964) and *W E Gladstone* (1995), which won the Whitbread Biography award.

Jenkinson, Robert See **Liverpool, 2nd Earl of**

Jenner, Edward 1749–1823
English physician, the pioneer of vaccination

Born in Berkeley vicarage, Gloucestershire, he was apprenticed to a surgeon at Sodbury, near Bristol, and in 1770 went to London to study under **John Hunter**. In 1773 he settled in Berkeley, where he acquired a large practice. He began to examine the truth of the traditions respecting cowpox (1775), and became convinced that it was efficacious as a protection against smallpox. In 1796 he vaccinated James Phipps, an eight-year-old boy, with cowpox matter from the hands of Sarah Nelmes, a milkmaid, and soon afterwards inoculated him with smallpox, and showed that the boy was protected. Jenner described his early series of vaccination experiments in *An Inquiry into the Causes and Effects of the Variolae Vaccinae* (1798), a short monograph which was privately published after being rejected by the leading scientific periodical of his day. The practice of vaccination met with brief opposition, until over 70 principal physicians and surgeons in London signed a declaration of their entire confidence in it, and within five years vaccination was being practised in many parts of the world. Jenner devoted the remainder of his life to advocating vaccination. Parliament rewarded him with two large grants and **Napoleon I** had a medal struck in his honour. 📖 Dorothy Fisk, *Dr Jenner of Berkeley* (1959)

Jenner, Sir William 1815–98
English physician

Born in Chatham, Kent, he was educated at University College London, where he was professor from 1848 to 1879. He became physician-in-ordinary to Queen **Victoria** in 1862, and to the Prince of Wales (later **Edward VII**) in 1863. He established the difference between typhus and typhoid fevers (1851).

Jennings, Herbert Spencer 1868–1947
US zoologist

He was born in Tonica, Illinois, and became Professor of Experimental Zoology (1906) and Zoology (1910–38) at Johns Hopkins University. He wrote the standard work *Contributions to the Study of the Behaviour of the Lower Organisms* (1919) and investigated heredity and variation of micro-organisms.

Jennings, Pat(rick) 1945–
Northern Irish footballer

Born in Newry, County Down, he started his career with Newry Town then played for Watford, Tottenham Hotspur and Arsenal, making a total of 747 Football League appearances and winning several cup-winner's medals. Britain's most capped footballer, he played 119 games for Northern Ireland. He retired in 1986.

Jennings, Waylon 1937–
US country music singer and songwriter

Born in Littlefield, Texas, he was a radio disc-jockey by the age of 12, and joined **Buddy Holly's** band The Crickets in 1958, narrowly missing the fatal plane crash which killed his boss after giving up his seat to The Big Bopper (J P Richardson). **Chet Atkins** signed him to RCA in 1965, where his fight for greater artistic control produced the classic *Honky Tonk Heroes* (1972). He was a part of the so-called Outlaws clique in the mid-1970s, and enjoyed great commercial success into the early 1980s. He formed The Highwaymen with **Willie Nelson**, **Johnny Cash** and Kris Kristofferson in 1985, and turned his autobiographical

album *A Man Called Hoss* (1987) into a successful one-man show. He continues to record and perform into the late-1990s, and is an outspoken campaigner against drugs and for high school education, having kicked the former and never had the latter. 📖 B Allen, *Waylon and Willie* (1979)

Jensen, Adolf 1837–79
German songwriter and composer for the piano

Born in Königsberg, Prussia (now Kaliningrad, Russia), he was a pupil of **Franz Liszt**. He was a musician successively at Posen, Copenhagen and Berlin from 1856 to 1868. His brother Gustav (1843–95) composed chamber music and edited earlier music.

Jensen, Georg 1866–1935
Danish silversmith

Having worked as a sculptor, he founded his silversmithy in Copenhagen in 1904, and revived the artistic traditions of Danish silver.

Jensen, (Johannes) Hans Daniel 1907–73
German physicist and Nobel Prize winner

Born in Hamburg, he studied physics, mathematics and philosophy at Hamburg University, and was awarded his PhD in 1933. He was appointed professor at Hamburg in 1936 and at Hanover University in 1941. In 1949 he was made Professor of Theoretical Physics at Heidelberg University. From the large amounts of data available on nuclei it had emerged that stable nuclides had a 'magic number' of neutrons and or protons, similar to the pattern observed in atoms where a filled shell of electrons corresponds to a stable element. Jensen used this similarity to apply the ideas of atomic physics to nuclei, leading to the nuclear shell model. This was done independently by **Maria Goeppert-Mayer** in Chicago, and for this work Jensen, Goeppert-Mayer and **Eugene Wigner** shared the 1963 Nobel Prize for physics.

Jensen, Johannes V(ilhelm) 1873–1950
Danish novelist, essayist and poet, and Nobel Prize winner

He was born in Farsø, Jutland, and his native land and its people are described in his *Himmerlandshistorier* (1898–1910). Many of his other works, such as *Madama d'Ora* (1904), are based on his extensive travels in the Far East and USA. However, the journey traced in *Den Lange Rejse* (1908–22, *The Long Journey*, 1922–24) is that of man through the ages, the three constituent novels being an expression of Jensen's **Darwinism**. His psychological study of **Kristian II** of Denmark, *Kongens Fald* (1933, 'The Fall of the King'), his short prose works, *Myter* (1904–44, 'Myths'), 14 of which were translated into English as *The Waving Rye* (1959), and his lyric poetry (1901–41), all serve to vindicate his high place in modern Scandinavian literature. He was awarded the Nobel Prize for literature in 1944. 📖 E O Gelsted, *Johannes Vilhelm Jensen* (1938)

Jeremiah 7th century BC
Old Testament prophet

Born in Anathoth, near Jerusalem, he was the son of Hilkiah the priest. He was in Jerusalem during the siege by **Nebuchadnezzar**, and is said to have been martyred at Tahpanhes in Egypt. The Book of Jeremiah warned of the impending fall of Jerusalem to Nebuchadnezzar and the Babylonian exile, and foretold the coming of a Messiah.

Jerne, Niels Kai 1911–94
English immunologist and Nobel Prize winner

Born in London of Danish parents, he studied physics at the University of Leicester for two years, before transferring to the University of Copenhagen, receiving his doctorate in medicine in 1951. He conducted research at the Danish State Serum Institute until 1956. He was Chief Medical Officer of the World Health Organization (1956–62), an administrator at the University of Pittsburgh (1962–66), and was founding director of the Basle

Institute of Immunology (1969–80). Jerne's research into the immune system examined the creation of antibodies, explained the development of T-lymphocytes, and formulated the network theory which views the immune system as a network of interacting lymphocytes and antibodies. He shared the 1984 Nobel Prize for physiology or medicine with Cesar Milstein and Georges Köhler.

Jeroboam I 10th century BC
First king of the divided kingdom of Israel
Solomon made him superintendent of the labours and taxes exacted from his tribe of Ephraim at the construction of the fortifications of Zion. The growing disaffection towards Solomon fostered his ambition, but he was obliged to flee to Egypt. After Solomon's death he headed the successful revolt of the northern tribes against Rehoboam, and, as their king, established idol shrines at Dan and Bethel to wean away his people from the pilgrimages to Jerusalem. He reigned for 22 years.

Jeroboam II 8th century BC
King of Israel
The son of Joash, he thrust back the Syrians, and reconquered Ammon and Moab.

Jerome, St, *originally* Eusebius Hieronymus
c.342–420AD
Christian ascetic and scholar, one of the four Latin Doctors of the Church
Born in Stridon, near Aquileia, Dalmatia, he studied Greek and Latin rhetoric, and philosophy at Rome, where he was also baptized. In AD370 he settled in Aquileia with his friend the theologian Rufinus (c345–410), but then became a hermit (374–78) in the desert of Chalcis. Ordained priest at Antioch by St Paulinus of Nola in 379, he went on a mission connected with the Meletian schism at Antioch to Rome in 382, where he became secretary to Pope Damasus (reigned 366–84), and where he enjoyed great influence. In 385 he led a pilgrimage to the Holy Land, and settled in Bethlehem in 386, where he wrote the first Latin translation of the Bible from the Hebrew (which became known as the Vulgate). He also wrote biblical commentaries, and vehement criticisms of Jovinian, Vigilantius and the Pelagians, and even of Rufinus and St Augustine. St Jerome was the most learned and eloquent of the four Latin Doctors. His feast day is 30 September. 📖 Charles C Mierow, *Saint Jerome: The Sage of Bethlehem* (1959)

Jérôme Bonaparte See Bonaparte, Jérôme

Jerome of Prague c.1365–1416
Czech religious reformer
Born in Prague, he was educated at Oxford. He became a convert there to John Wycliffe's doctrines, and taught them after his return home (1407). King Wladislaw V of Poland employed him to reorganize the University of Kraków in 1410, and King Sigismund of Hungary invited him to preach before him in Budapest. A friend of Jan Huss, Jerome vigorously promoted his theology. When Huss was arrested in Constance Jerome wanted to go and defend him, but, being refused a safe-conduct, he set out to return to Prague. He was arrested in Bavaria in 1415, and was brought back to Constance. He recanted, but withdrew his recantation and, branded as heretic, was condemned to burn at the stake.

Jerome, Jerome K(lapka) 1859–1927
English humorous writer, novelist and playwright
He was born in Walsall, Staffordshire, and brought up in London. Leaving school at the age of 14, he was successively a clerk, schoolmaster, reporter, actor and journalist. He became joint editor of *The Idler* in 1892 and started his own twopenny weekly, *To-Day*. His magnificently ridiculous *Three Men in a Boat* (1889), the account of a boat trip up the Thames from Kingston to Oxford, established itself as a humorous classic. Other books include *The Idle Thoughts of an Idle Fellow* (1889), *Three Men on the Bummel* (1900), *Paul Kelver* (1902), the morality play *The Passing of the Third-Floor Back* (1907), and his autobiography, *My Life and Times* (1926). 📖 Joseph Connolly, *Jerome K. Jerome, A Critical Biography* (1982)

Jerrold, Douglas William 1803–57
English writer, dramatist and wit
Born in London, he joined the navy as a midshipman in 1813, then worked as a compositor on the *Sunday Monitor* (1819) before becoming its dramatic critic. From 1841 he was one of the contributors to the newly-launched *Punch* magazine, writing under the pseudonym 'Q'. He also edited the *Illuminated Magazine* (1843–44), *Douglas Jerrold's Shilling Magazine* (1845–48), *Douglas Jerrold's Weekly Newspaper* (1846–48), and from 1852 *Lloyd's Weekly Newspaper*. His books include the novel *The Story of a Feather* (1844), *Cakes and Ale* (1852, essays and tales), and *Punch's Letters to his Son* (1843). Among his plays are *Black-ey'd Susan* (1829), and the comedies *The Bride of Ludgate* (1831), *Time Works Wonders* (1845) and *The Catspaw* (1850). *Other Times* (1868) is a selection from his political writings in *Lloyd's*. 📖 W Jerrold, *Douglas Jerrold* (1914)

Jervis, Sir John See Saint Vincent, Earl of

Jesenská, Miléna 1890–1944
Czech journalist
Born in Prague and educated at the Minerva Gymnasium for Girls, she married the Jewish writer Ernst Polak and moved with him to Vienna, despite her father's anti-Semitic opposition (he had her placed in a mental asylum to separate them). In Vienna she became a well-known journalist, and through her work she met the novelist Franz Kafka around 1920. They corresponded (1920–23) and fell in love, but Miléna refused to leave her husband. Kafka's letters to her (*Briefe an Miléna*) were published in 1952. An opponent of Nazism, she died in Ravensbrück in 1944.

Jespersen, (Jens) Otto Harry 1860–1943
Danish philologist
Born in Randers, he became Professor of English Language and Literature at Copenhagen University (1893–1925), and revolutionized the teaching of languages. In 1904 his *Sprogundervisning* was published in English as *How to Teach a Foreign Language*, and became perhaps the best-known statement of what is now called the 'Direct Method' reform. His other books include *Progress in Language* (1894), *Growth and Structure of the English Language* (1905), *A Modern English Grammar on Historical Principles* (1909), and *Philosophy of Grammar* (1924). He also invented an international language, 'Novial', with its own grammar and lexicon.

Jesse, F(riniwyd) Tennyson 1888–1958
English novelist and dramatist
She was born in Chislehurst, Kent, a great-niece of Alfred, Lord Tennyson, and studied painting, but during World War I took up journalism as one of the few female war correspondents, and after it served on Herbert Hoover's Relief Commission for Europe. In 1918 she married H M Harwood, and with him collaborated on a number of light plays and a series of wartime letters, *London Front* (1940) and *While London Burns* (1942). However she is best known for her novels set in Cornwall, such as *The White Riband* (1921), *Tom Fool* (1926) and *Moonraker* (1927), as well as *The Lacquer Lady* (1929), set in Burma and regarded by many as her best novel, and *A Pin to See a Peepshow* (1934), based on the Thompson–Bywaters murder case. She also published collected poems, *The Happy Bride* (1920), and edited several volumes of the *Notable British Trials* series, including remarkable accounts

of the trials of the alleged poisoner Madeleine Smith (1927), Timothy Evans and **John Christie** (1958). 🕮 *Sabi Pas, or I Don't Know* (1935)

Jessel, Sir George 1824–83
English judge

Born in London, he was educated at University College London, and served as a Liberal MP (1868–73), Solicitor General (1871–73), and then as Master of the Rolls (1873–83). Very learned, with a remarkable memory and penetrating intellect, he gave many judicial opinions of continuing value and made important contributions to legal principle by reshaping the older doctrines, especially that of equity. He was also active in the development of the University of London.

Jessop, William 1745–1814
English civil engineer

Born in Devonport, Devon, he became a pupil of **John Smeaton** at the age of 16 and worked with him on canals in Yorkshire and elsewhere. With others he founded the Butterley Iron Works in 1790 and began to manufacture fish-bellied cast-iron rails which marked an important advance in railway track technology. He was involved as chief engineer on the construction of the Grand Junction Canal with its mile-long tunnel at Blisworth, Northamptonshire, the Surrey Iron Railway (opened in 1802), the docks on the Avon at Bristol and the West India Docks on the Thames, London. His works put him alongside Smeaton, **Thomas Telford** and Sir **John Rennie** in the front rank of early British civil engineers.

Jesus Christ See panel p982

Jevons, William Stanley 1835–82
English economist and logician

Born in Liverpool, he studied chemistry and metallurgy at University College London, and became assayer to the Mint at Sydney, Australia (1854–59). He then returned to England and studied logic under **Augustus De Morgan** at London. In 1866 Jevons became Professor of Logic at Owen's College, Manchester, and in 1876 Professor of Political Economy at London. He introduced mathematical methods into economics, was one of the first to use the concept of final or marginal utility as opposed to the classical cost of production theories, and wrote *Theory of Political Economy* (1871) and the posthumous *Principles of Economics* (1905). He also wrote an important practical paper, *Investigations in Currency and Finance* (1884). In his *Pure Logic and other Minor Works* (1890) he wrongly deplored **George Boole**'s extensive use of algebraic methods in his calculus of classes, attacked **John Stuart Mill**'s inductive logic and expounded alternatives in *The Principles of Science* (1874), but is also remembered for his introductory textbook, *Lessons in Logic* (1870). A professorship in political economy at Manchester was endowed in his memory. He was the son-in-law of the journalist **John Edward Taylor**.

Jewel, John 1522–71
English prelate

Born in Berrynarbor, Devon, he was educated at Barnstaple and at Merton and Corpus Christi Colleges, Oxford. He absorbed Reformed doctrines early in his career, and therefore, on **Mary I**'s accession, went abroad to Frankfurt and Strasbourg amongst other places. He was appointed Bishop of Salisbury by **Elizabeth I**, however, in 1559. Considered to be a father of English Protestantism, his ability as a controversialist soon made him one of the foremost churchmen of his age, demonstrated in his *Apologia Ecclesiae Anglicanae* (1562, 'Defence of the Anglican Church') against Rome.

Jewett, (Theodora) Sarah Orne 1849–1909
US novelist and short-story writer

She was born in South Berwick, Maine, and in 1877 published a series of sketches, *Deephaven*. These were followed by a more structured fiction, *The Country of the Pointed Firs* (1896), which developed her interest in the psychology of small, remote communities. She also wrote romantic novels and stories based on the provincial life of her state, such as *A Country Doctor* (1884) and *A White Heron* (1886), and a historical novel, *The Tory Lover* (1901). She was the first president of Vassar College (1862–64), and an acknowledged influence on **Willa Cather**. 🕮 F O Matthiessen, *Sarah Orne Jewett* (1929)

Jewsbury, Geraldine Endsor 1812–80
English novelist

She was born in Measham, Derbyshire, and from 1854 lived in Chelsea, to be near her friend **Jane Welsh Carlyle**. She contributed articles and reviews to various journals, and wrote six novels, including *Zoë* (1845), *The Half Sisters* (1848), *Marion Withers* (1851) and *Right or Wrong* (1859). *A Selection from the Letters of Geraldine Jewsbury to Jane Carlyle* (1892) aroused controversy over the emotional nature of their relationship. 🕮 S Howe, *Geraldine Jewsbury* (1935)

Jex-Blake, Sophia Louisa 1840–1912
English physician and pioneer of medical education for women

Born in Hastings, Sussex, she studied at Queen's College for Women, London, and became a tutor in mathematics there (1859–61). From 1865 she studied medicine in New York under **Elizabeth Blackwell**, but since English medical schools were closed to women she could not continue her studies on her return. She fought her way into Edinburgh University, however, where with five other women she was allowed to matriculate in 1869, but the university authorities reversed their decision in 1873. She then waged a public campaign in London, opened the London School of Medicine for Women in 1874 and in 1876 won her campaign when medical examiners were permitted by law to examine women students. In 1886 she founded a medical school in Edinburgh, where women were finally allowed to graduate in medicine from 1894.

Jezebel d.842BC
Phoenician princess

She was the daughter of Ethbaal, King of Tyre and Sidon, and the wife of King **Ahab** of Israel. She introduced Phoenician habits and the worship of Baal and Ashera to the capital, Samaria, thus earning the undying hatred of the prophet **Elijah** and his successors. After Ahab's death, Jezebel was the power behind the throne of her sons until the usurper **Jehu** seized power in an army coup. He had Jezebel thrown from a window, and trampled her to death under his chariot. She has become the archetype of female wickedness.

Jhabvala, Ruth Prawer 1927–
British novelist, and short-story and screenplay writer

She was born in Cologne, Germany, of Polish parents, who emigrated to Great Britain in 1939. She graduated from Queen Mary College, London University, married a visiting Indian architect, and lived in Delhi (1951–75). Most of her fiction relates to India, taking the viewpoint of an outsider looking in. Significant novels include *Amrita, or To Whom She Will* (1955, re-published as *To Whom She Will*, 1985), *Esmond in India* (1958), *The Householder* (1960), and *Heat and Dust* (1975) which won the Booker Prize. In association with the film makers **James Ivory** and **Ismail Merchant**, she has written several accomplished screenplays, among them *Shakespeare Wallah* (1965), *A Room with a View* (1985, Academy Award for best adapted screenplay) and *Howards End* (1992).

Jiang Jieshi See **Chiang Kai-shek**

Jesus Christ c.6BC–c.30AD

The central figure of the Christian faith, believed to be both human and divine, and to have been raised from the dead

Our knowledge of the life of Jesus Christ comes almost exclusively from the Gospel accounts and from other early Christian writing, including the Acts of the Apostles and the letters of St Paul. There are few references to him in other ancient sources, although Tacitus refers to his death and he is also mentioned by Pliny (but with no hint of his importance) and Josephus; he is also mentioned in some Hebrew sources. Of the Gospel accounts, Mark is now generally held to be the earliest (despite arguments for Matthew), and to be a source of the other three, Matthew, Luke and John, which also appear to have used another source not known to Mark (conventionally called 'Q'). John, which is the latest of the four and includes later material, presents the life of Jesus in a much more dramatic way than the others. There are two aspects to a life of Christ: the establishing of historical facts, and the identification of parts of his ministry which are the basis for the development of the Christian faith. This article, as a biography, concentrates necessarily on Jesus as a historical figure.

According to the accounts in Matthew and Luke, Jesus was the first-born child of Mary, of the tribe of Judah and descendant of David. At the time of his birth she was engaged to be married to Joseph, a carpenter. They had travelled from Nazareth to Joseph's home town of Bethlehem in order to comply with the regulations of a Roman population census. The birth took place in a stable, for 'there was no room for them at the inn'. According to Matthew, the child was born shortly before the death of Herod the Great (4BC), although the Roman census referred to by Luke did not take place before AD6.

Little is known of the early life of Jesus. He is believed to have followed Joseph's trade of carpentry (and Mark 6.3 calls him a carpenter); at the age of 12 his mother was moved to see him discussing learned matters with the scribes, and was assured by him that he was about his 'father's business'. After nearly 18 years of obscurity, he was baptized in the River Jordan by his cousin John the Baptist, who had been proclaiming the coming of the Messiah. Christ's baptism marks the beginning of his public life.

After 40 days in the wilderness struggling against temptation, he gathered around him 12 disciples (called apostles) and undertook two missionary journeys through Galilee, mainly in the villages and countryside rather than the towns and cities, and culminating in the miraculous feeding of the five thousand (Mark 6.30–52). The Gospels relate how he performed miraculous healings, exorcisms, and some 'nature' miracles such as the calming of the storm. Jesus taught mainly in the synagogues, bringing his message primarily to the Jews and only later to the Gentiles, and continued John the Baptist's message of a coming kingdom. This, seen through the eyes of Herod Antipas, John the Baptist's executioner, had dangerous political implications. Furthermore, Jesus' association with 'sinners', his apparent flouting of traditional religious practices, the performance of miracles on the Sabbath, the driving of the money-lenders from the temple and the whole tenor of his revolutionary Sermon on the Mount (Matthew 5–8), emphasizing love, humility, meekness and charity, alarmed the Pharisees.

cont

Jiang Qing (Chiang Ch'ing) 1914–91
Chinese politician

Born in Zhucheng, Shandong (Shantung) Province, the daughter of a carpenter, she trained in drama before studying literature at Qingdao University, and became a stage and film actress in Shanghai. Having already come into contact with left-wing ideas at university, in 1936 she went to the Chinese Communist Party headquarters at Yenan to study Marxist–Leninist theory, and met the Communist leader, Mao Zedong, becoming his third wife in 1939. She was attached to the Ministry of Culture in 1950–54, but it was in the 1960s that she began her attacks on bourgeois influences in the arts and literature, and she became one of the leaders of the 1966–69 Cultural Revolution. In 1969 she was elected to the politburo, but after Mao's death in 1976 she was arrested with three others—the hated 'Gang of Four'—after having attempted to seize power through organizing militia coups in Shanghai and Beijing (Peking). She was imprisoned, expelled from the Communist Party, tried in 1980 with subverting the government and wrongly arresting, detaining and torturing numbers of innocent people. She was sentenced to death, though the sentence was later suspended for two years, commuted to life imprisonment in 1983. The notice issued by the government after her death reported that she had committed suicide. It also stated that she had been out of custody and undergoing medical treatment since May 1984. ▢ Ross Terrill, *The White-Boned Demon* (1984)

Jiang Zemin (Chiang Tse-min) 1926–
Chinese politician

Born in Yangzhou, in Jiangsu (Kiangsu) province, the son-in-law of former President Li Xiannian, after university he began a career as an electrical engineer and trained in the USSR. He was Commercial Counsellor at the Chinese Embassy in Moscow (1950–56) and during the 1960s and 1970s held a number of posts in the Heavy and Power Industry Ministries. Elected to the Chinese Communist Party (CCP)'s Central Committee in 1982, he was appointed Mayor of Shanghai in 1985. Here he gained a reputation as a cautious reformer, loyal to the party line. He was inducted into the CCP's politburo in 1987 and in June 1989, following the Tiananmen Square massacre and the dismissal of Zhao Ziyang, was elected party leader. Fluent in English and Russian, Jiang has, as a compromise figure, pledged to maintain China's 'open door' economic strategy.

Jibran, Kahlil See Gibran, Kahlil

Jiménez, Juan Ramón 1881–1958
Spanish lyric poet and Nobel Prize winner

He was born in Moguer, Huelva, which he made famous by his story of the young poet and his donkey, *Platero y Yo* (1914, Eng trans *Platero and I*, 1956), one of the classics of modern Spanish literature. Abandoning his law studies, he settled in Madrid. His early poetry, which echoed that of Paul Verlaine, includes *Almas de Violeta* (1900, 'Violet Souls'), *Arias Tristes* (1903, 'Sad Arias') and *Jardines lejanos* (1905, 'Far-off Gardens'). He also wrote *Sonetos espirituales* (1916, 'Spiritual Sonnets') and *El silencio de oro* (1922, 'The Silence of Gold'). In 1936 he left Spain because of the Civil War and settled in Florida, where he emerged as a major poet, using subtle vers libre. He was awarded the Nobel Prize for literature in 1956. ▢ D Fogelquist, *Jiménez* (1976)

Jimenez de Cisneros, Francisco See Ximenes de Cisneros, Francisco

Jiménez de Quesada, Gonzalo c.1495–1579
Spanish conquistador

Born in Córdoba or Granada, he trained as a lawyer in Granada and sailed to South America in 1535 to become chief magistrate for the colony of Santa Marta. The next year he led an expedition up the Magdalena River,

Jesus Christ *cont*

Christ and his disciples sought refuge for a while in the Gentile territories of Tyre and Sidon, where he secretly revealed himself to them as the promised Messiah, and hinted at his coming passion, death and resurrection. According to Mark, he returned to Jerusalem in triumph, a week before the Passover feast. After the famous Last Supper with his disciples, he was betrayed in the garden of Gethsemane by **Judas Iscariot**, who kissed him to single him out to his enemies, and after a hurried trial was condemned to death by the Sanhedrin. The necessary confirmation of the sentence from **Pontius Pilate**, the Roman prefect, was obtained on the grounds of political expediency and not through proof of treason implicit in any claim to territorial kingship by Christ.

Jesus was crucified, along with two criminals, early on the Passover or the preceding day (the 'preparation of the Passover'), although the precise chronology is uncertain. The year is thought to be AD30 or 33. He was buried on the same day. The following Sunday, Mary Magdalene, possibly accompanied by other women, visited the tomb and found it empty. Jesus himself appeared to her, and she told the disciples of her experiences. Jesus also appeared to groups of his disciples after his death, according to stories that are thought to be late insertions into the Gospel accounts (even in Mark). The story that Jesus ascended into heaven is described explicitly only twice, in Acts (1.9) and at the end of Mark (thought to be a 2nd-century insertion). The conclusion of Luke says only that Jesus parted from his disciples (24.50–53). According to the Acts of the Apostles, 50 days after Passover (10 days after Jesus' final appearance) the disciples were hiding in an upper room when the Holy Spirit descended on them, as Jesus had promised (John 14.15–16), enabling them to speak in tongues, and giving them the power to preach and prophesy, and to heal.

The cross, the instrument of the crucifixion, became the symbol of Christianity. The history of the church begins after the Resurrection with the Acts of the Apostles in the New Testament. The apostolic succession claimed by the Church begins with Christ's public declaration to Peter (Matthew 16.17–19) that on him and on his declaration of faith, 'Thou art the Christ, the Son of the living God', he would build his Church.

There has been much discussion, in both historical and theological terms, of what Jesus Christ claimed to be. He certainly regarded himself as a prophet (Mark 4.4; Luke 8.33), and he encouraged his disciples to say who they thought he was; Peter replied that he was the Christ or Messiah (Mark 8.27–30). Several titles are applied to him in the New Testament accounts, including Son of Man and Son of God (which may be simply a singular version of 'Sons of God', a common designation for the Jews).

📖 E P Sanders, *The Historical Figure of Jesus* (1993); A N Wilson, *Jesus* (1993); J D Crossan, *The Historical Jesus* (1991); H Kee, *Jesus in History* (1977).

The name *Jesus* means 'saviour', and is derived from an Aramaic form of the Hebrew name Joshua. It is used as a common first name now only in Spanish and Portuguese. *Christ* is a Greek word meaning 'anointed one' (from *khrio*, 'to anoint') and is a translation of the Hebrew word *Messiah*.

'I am the bread of life: he that cometh to me shall never hunger; and he that believeth in me shall never thirst.' John 6.35.

---

conquered the Chibcha and founded Bogotá (1538). He became an important citizen of New Granada (modern Colombia), and in 1569 led an expedition in search of legendary El Dorado, returning two years later after fruitless wanderings with only 25 of his original company of 500 men.

Jinnah, Fatima, *known as* Madar-i-Millat ('Mother of the Country') 1893–1967
Pakistani politician

Born in Karachi, she was educated at a mission school then studied dentistry. She moved to Bombay in 1901 to live with her brother **Mohammed Ali Jinnah**. Living with her brother in London (1929–34) affected her attitude to women's status, and on her return to India in 1934, she joined the Muslim League, arguing against traditional conservative attitudes towards women. The first leader of the All-India Muslim Women's Committee (founded 1938), she toured India campaigning on behalf of women's welfare, education and training. She founded the Fatima Jinnah Women's Medical College in Lahore. She retired from politics after her brother's death but during the 1950s resumed her work for the Muslim League, and emerged during the 1960s as a significant opponent of the East Pakistan government.

Jinnah, Muhammad Ali 1876–1948
Pakistani statesman

Born in Karachi, he studied at Bombay and Lincoln's Inn, London, and was called to the Bar in 1897. He ran a successful practice in Bombay, and in 1910 was elected to the Viceroy's legislative council. Already a member of the Indian National Congress, in 1913 he joined the Indian Muslim League and as its president brought about peaceful co-existence between it and the Congress Party through the Lucknow Pact (1916). Although Jinnah supported the efforts of Congress to boycott the Simon Commission (1928), he opposed **Mahatma Gandhi's** civil disobedience policy and resigned from the Congress Party, which he believed to be exclusively fostering Hindu interests. He continued to try to safeguard the right of Muslim minorities at the London Round Table Conference in 1931. By 1940 he was strongly advocating separate statehood for Muslims and he resisted all British efforts, such as the mission by Sir **Stafford Cripps** (1942), to retain Indian unity. On 15 August 1947, the Dominion of Pakistan came into existence and Jinnah, *Quaid-i-Azam* (Great Leader), became its first Governor-General.
📖 Hector Bolitho, *Jinnah, Creator of Pakistan* (1954)

Joachim of Floris or Fiore c.1135–1202
Italian mystic

Born in Calabria, he became abbot of the Cistercian monastery of Corazzo in 1177, and later founded a stricter order of monks, Ordo Florensis, at San Giovanni in Fiore (later absorbed by the Cistercians in 1505). His mystical interpretation of history, based on historical parallels or 'concordances' between the history of the Jewish people and that of the Church, was grouped into three ages, each corresponding to a member of the Trinity. The last, that of the Spirit, which was to bring perfect liberty, was to commence in 1260. This mystical historicism was widely accepted although condemned by the Lateran Council in 1215, but lost influence when its prophecies were not fulfilled.

Joachim, Joseph 1831–1907
Hungarian violinist and composer

Born in Kittsee, near Pressburg, he first appeared in public at the age of seven. In 1844, under the patronage of **Felix Mendelssohn**, he performed in London, making a great impact. Director of the Berlin Conservatory from

Joan of Arc, St, *French* Jeanne d'Arc, *known as* the Maid of Orleans c.1412–1431
French patriot and martyr

Joan was born the daughter of well-off peasants in Domrémy, on the border of Lorraine and Champagne. She had an argumentative nature and shrewd common sense, but received no formal education. At the age of 13 she thought she heard the voices of St Michael, St **Catherine** and St **Margaret** bidding her rescue Paris from English domination in the Hundred Years War; English soldiers had over-run the area in 1421 and withdrawn in 1424. She was taken across territory occupied by the English to the dauphin (the future **Charles VII**) at Chinon. She is said to have identified the dauphin, who was standing in disguise in a group of courtiers, an act which was interpreted as divine confirmation of his previously doubted legitimacy and claims to the throne. She was equally successful in an ecclesiastical examination to which she was subjected in Poitiers and was consequently allowed to join the army assembled at Blois for the relief of Orleans. Clad in a suit of white armour and flying her own standard, she entered Orleans with an advance guard on 29 April and by 8 May had forced the English to raise the siege and retire in June from the principal strongholds on the Loire.

To put further heart into the French resistance, she took the dauphin with an army of 12,000 through English-held territory to be crowned Charles VII in Reims Cathedral. She set out on her own to relieve Compiègne from the Burgundians, was captured in a sortie (1430) and sold to the English by John of Luxembourg for 10,000 crowns. She was put on trial (1431) for heresy and sorcery by an ecclesiastical court of the Inquisition, presided over by Pierre Cauchon, Bishop of Beauvais. She was found guilty, taken out to the churchyard of St Ouen on 24 May to be burnt, but at the last moment broke down and made a wild recantation. This she later abjured and suffered her martyrdom at the stake in the market place of Rouen on 30 May, faithful to her 'voices'. In 1456, in order to strengthen the validity of Charles VII's coronation, the trial was declared irregular.

📖 Anne Barstow, *Joan of Arc* (1986); Edward Lucie-Smith, *Joan of Arc* (1977); V Sackville-West, *Joan of Arc* (1936).

> Most of the available facts concerning Joan's life are those preserved in the records of the trial. One of the first in history to die for a Christian-inspired concept of nationalism, she was designated Venerable in 1904, declared Blessed in 1908 and finally canonized in 1920. Her feast day is 30 May.

> 'And as for you, archers, soldiers, gentlemen, and all others who are besieging Orleans, depart in God's name to your own country… I assure you that wherever I find your people in France I shall fight them, and pursue them, and expel them from here, whether they will or not.' From a letter to the English at Poitiers, 22 March 1429. Quoted in *Les Procès de Jeanne d'Arc* (translated by C Larrington).

1869, he founded the Joachim Quartet which was renowned for its performances of **J S Bach**, **Mozart** and **Beethoven**. He also composed three violin concertos and overtures to *Hamlet* and *Henry IV*.

Joad, C(yril) E(dwin) M(itchinson) 1891–1953
English philosopher and controversialist

Born in Durham, and educated at Blundell's School and Balliol College, Oxford, he was a civil servant (1914–30), then became head of the philosophy department at Birkbeck College, London. He wrote 47 books in all, notably a *Guide to Philosophy* (1936) and a *Guide to the Philosophy of Morals and Politics* (1938). He was best-known for his appearances on the BBC radio programme *The BrainsTrust* and for his catchphrase 'It all depends what you mean by …'. 📖 Geoffrey Thomas, *Cyril Joad* (1992)

Joan, *also known as* Pope Joan
Fictitious religious figure

Born, according to one legend, in Mainz, Germany, she was said to have been so well educated by her lover, a monk, that she in due time became a cardinal and pope (John VIII, 855–58). Her reign was allegedly ended when she died on giving birth to a child during a papal procession between St Peter's and the Lateran, a route since avoided on such occasions. 📖 Rosemary and Darroll Pardoe, *The Female Pope: The Mystery of Pope Joan* (1988)

Joan of Arc, St See panel above

Joan of Navarre, *also called* Joanna of Navarre c.1370–1437
Queen of England

She married first John, Duke of Brittany (1386), by whom she had eight children. After his death (1399), she married **Henry IV** (1402) and became stepmother of **Henry V**. After Henry's death (1413), she was imprisoned for three years (1419) on specious allegations of witchcraft.

Joanna the Mad See **Juana**

Job Date unknown
Biblical character, a wealthy landowner

There is no objective evidence as to the authorship or date of the text describing this man who is referred to as 'the greatest man in all the East' in wealth, and blameless, upright and god-fearing in character. He was a partly nomadic sheik in the time before Israel's priesthood or organized religion. His writings, possibly translated from Aramaic, are regarded as great Hebrew poetry and placed among the masterpieces of world literature. The subject-matter of his writing is timeless, dealing with the probability of undeserved suffering, the question of why God allows suffering, the need to fight suffering, and God's vindication of and forgiveness for his righteous servant.

Jobs, Steven 1955–
US computer inventor and entrepreneur

Born in San Francisco, he was educated at Reed College, Portland, before becoming a computer hobbyist. Together with Stephen Wozniak (1950–) he set up the Apple Computer Company, in a garage, in 1976. Their brainchild, the Apple II computer (1977), helped launch the personal computer and made their company the fastest-growing in US history. In 1985 he left Apple and founded a new company, NeXT Inc.

Jochum, Eugen 1902–87
German conductor

He was born in Babenhausen in Bavaria and studied at Munich. After working in opera and concert life in Hamburg (1934–49), he founded the Bavarian Radio Symphony Orchestra, of which he was chief conductor from 1949 to 1961. He was later joint chief conductor of the Amsterdam Concertgebouw Orchestra and chief conductor of the Bamberg Symphony Orchestra. Towards the end of his life he worked frequently with London orchestras. His repertory ranged from the Viennese classics to **Bruckner** and **Wagner**, and he recorded several works of his contemporary **Carl Orff**.

Jochumsson, Matthías 1835–1920
Icelandic poet and clergyman

Born in Skógar, Thorskafjörður, he trained as a merchant in Copenhagen, then was a Lutheran pastor (1865) at various places in Iceland. Best known as a lyric poet, he was inspired by the historic traditions of the sagas and by the dramatic natural scene. He composed the words of the choral anthem written for the millennial celebrations of 1874 (Ó, Guð vors lands—'God of our Land') which is now the national anthem, and was regarded as unofficial Poet Laureate. He also wrote plays, including a historical drama about Bishop Jón Arason (1900), and translated Byron, Ibsen and Hitler's major tragedies. 📖 D Ostlund, *70th Birthday Essays* (1905)

Jodelle, Étienne, Sieur de Lymodin 1532–73
French poet and dramatist

He was the only Parisian member of the Pléiade, and he wrote the first French tragedy, *Cléopâtre captive* (1552, 'Cleopatra the Prisoner'), based on classical models. He also wrote the comedy, *Eugène* (1552) and another verse tragedy, in alexandrines, *Didon se sacrifiant* (1558, 'Dido's Sacrifice'), based on Virgil's story of Dido. 📖 E H Balmas, *Un poeta del Rinascimento francesca* (1962)

Jodl, Alfred 1890–1946
German general

He was born in Aachen. He served in World War I and became a general of artillery in 1940. For the remainder of World War II he was the planning genius of the German High Command and Hitler's chief adviser. He condemned the anti-Hitler plot (1944), counselled the terror bombing of English cities and signed orders to shoot commandos and prisoners of war. From January 1945 he was Chief of the Operations Staff. He was found guilty of war crimes on all four counts at Nuremberg (1946) and executed. A Munich denazification court posthumously exonerated him on charges of being a 'major offender' in 1953. 📖 Bodo Scheurig, *Alfred Jodl: Gehorsam und Verhagnis* (1991)

Joffre, Joseph Jacques Césaire 1852–1931
French soldier

Born in Rivesaltes, he entered the army in 1870, rose to be French Chief of Staff (1914), and planned the victory in the Battle of the Marne (1914). Silent, patient, mathematical, he carried out a policy of attrition or 'nibbling' against the Germans. He was Commander-in-Chief of the French armies from 1915 to 1916, but resigned after the French failure at Verdun (1916), and was made a Marshal of France. In 1917 he became president of the Allied War Council.

Joffrey, Robert, *originally* Abdullah Jaffa Anver Bey Kahn 1930–88
US dancer, choreographer, teacher and ballet director

Born in Seattle, Washington, of Afghan descent, he studied at the School of American Ballet and New York's High School of Performing Arts, making his debut in Roland Petit's Ballets de Paris in 1949. He choreographed his first ballet in 1952 and by 1954 had formed his own school and company, which began touring the USA. Working closely with dancer–choreographer Gerald Arpino, he created a young and energetic image for his company, helping to usher in the US ballet revival of the 1960s which used topical themes, rock music and multimedia techniques alongside contemporary classics.

Johan III 1537–92
King of Sweden

The second son of Gustav I Vasa and his second wife Margareta Leijonhufvud, he was born at Stegeborg Castle, and created Duke of Finland by his father (1556). Seized and imprisoned (1563–67) by his unbalanced brother Erik XIV, he rebelled against Erik and deposed him (1568). As king, he brought the Seven-Year War with Denmark to an inconclusive end with the Treaty of Stettin (1570), and formed an alliance with Poland (1578–83) in a war against Russia. He also tried, unsuccessfully, to impose on Sweden his own synthesis of Lutheranism and Catholicism. He married Katarina Jagellonica, sister of Sigismund II Augustus of Poland, and their Catholic son Sigismund III Vasa was crowned King of Poland (1587). After Katarina's death (1583) he married Gunilla Bielke. Scholarly and cultured, he was inept at control of finance and a poor administrator. He was succeeded by his brother Karl IX.

Johann Strauss II See Strauss, Johann, the Younger

Johannes Secundus, *Latin name of* Jan Everts or Everaerts 1511–36
Dutch poet, writing in Latin

Born in The Hague, he studied law at Bourges, and was secretary to the Archbishop of Toledo, the Bishop of Utrecht and the Emperor Charles V. His famous work is *Basia*.

Johannes von Saaz, *also known as* Johannes von Tepl c.1350–1415
German writer

He was born in Schüttwa. He wrote *Der Ackermann aus Böhmen* (c.1400, 'The Bohemian Peasant'), a classic piece of German prose in which the author, in the character of a peasant, reproaches Death for the loss of his wife, Margarete, before the heavenly Judge, but eventually accepts that God has ordained these events.

Johanson, Donald Carl 1943–
US palaeoanthropologist

Born in Chicago of Swedish immigrant parents, he graduated from Chicago University and worked at the Cleveland Museum of Natural History from 1972, serving as curator from 1974 to 1981. His spectacular finds of fossil hominids 3–4 million years old at Hadar in the Afar Triangle of Ethiopia (1972–77) generated worldwide interest. They include 'Lucy', a unique female specimen that is half complete, and the so-called 'first family', a scattered group containing the remains of 13 individuals. He suggested that these remains belong to a previously discovered species, which he named *Australopithecus afarensis* (Afar ape-man). In 1981 Johanson founded the Institute of Human Origins, Berkeley, California, and became president there. His publications include *Lucy: The Beginnings of Humankind* (with Maitland Edey, 1981), which describes the discovery of Lucy and reflects on her significance, *Lucy's Child: The Discovery of a Human Ancestor* (1989, with James Shreeve), and *Ancestors: In Search of Human Origins* (1994, with Lenora Johanson and Blake Edgar).

Johanssen, Wilhelm Ludwig 1857–1927
Danish botanist and geneticist

Born in Copenhagen, through his apprenticeship to a pharmacist he developed a knowledge of chemistry, and later learned botany. He began teaching in the late 1880s, and in 1905 became Professor of Plant Physiology at the University of Copenhagen. He postulated the pure line theory of genetics, which states that 'pure lines' are genetically identical, and that variation within them is due entirely to environmental forces. He introduced the term 'gene' for the unit of heredity, as symbols or units of calculation, and defined the genotype and the phenotype. His *Elements of Heredity* was published in 1909 and became an influential genetics text for around 20 years.

John, St, *also called* John the Evangelist
1st century AD
One of the 12 Apostles of Jesus Christ

John, surnamed Lackland 1167–1216
King of England from 1199

John was born in Oxford, the youngest son of **Henry II**. During the captivity of his brother **Richard I** in Austria, he attempted to seize the Crown, but was pardoned and nominated as successor by Richard on his deathbed. John was crowned at Westminster (27 May 1199), despite the claims of his nephew **Arthur**, supported by **Philip II** of France, whom John temporarily bought off. In the same year he obtained a divorce from his cousin Isabella of Gloucester, and married **Isabella of Angoulême**. In the war in France Arthur was taken prisoner, and before Easter 1203 was murdered. Philip at once marched against John until by March 1204 John had only Aquitaine and a few other small areas left.

In 1205 John found himself at odds with the church, when he refused to accept **Stephen Langton** as Archbishop of Canterbury. In 1208 the kingdom was placed under an interdict; John retaliated by confiscating the property of the clergy who obeyed it. He was excommunicated in 1209, and in 1212 the pope issued a bull deposing him; Philip of France was charged with the execution of the sentence. John, finding his position untenable, was compelled to make abject submission to Rome; in 1213 he agreed to hold his kingdom as a fief of the papacy, and to pay a thousand marks yearly as tribute. Meanwhile, in 1209 John compelled the Scots king,

William I, who had joined his enemies, to do him homage, put down a rebellion in Ireland (1210), and subdued Llewellyn, the independent Prince of Wales (1212).

John's oppressive rule led to demands by the barons, clergy, and people that he should keep his oath and restore the laws of **Henry I**. When these were scornfully rejected, preparations for war began on both sides. The army of the barons assembled at Stamford and marched to London; they met the king at Runnymede, and on 15 June 1215 the Great Charter (Magna Carta) was signed. It had little immediate effect. In August the pope annulled the charter, and the war broke out again. The first successes were all on the side of John, until the barons called over the French dauphin (the future **Louis VIII**) to be their leader. Louis landed in May 1216, and John's fortunes had reached a desperate state, when he died at Newark on 19 October.

📖 Deborah T Curren-Aquino (ed), *King John* (1988); W L Warren, *King John* (1961); Sidney Painter, *The Reign of King John* (1949).

> Despite his reputation for oppressive government, his reign was marked by improvements in the civil administration, the Exchequer and the law courts.

Born probably in Bethsaida, Galilee, he was the son of Zebedee and the younger brother of **James**. Formerly a fisherman, he was one of those closest to **Jesus**, among the first to be called, and with him at the Transfiguration and at Gethsemane. In Acts and Galatians he is described as one of the 'pillars' of the early Jerusalem Church. Some traditions claim he was slain by the Jews or **Herod Agrippa I**, but he may have spent his closing years at Ephesus. He wrote the Revelation, the Gospel, and the three Epistles which bear his name (although his authorship of these works has been disputed by modern scholars). His feast day is 27 December.

John, King See panel above

John II known as John the Good 1319–64
King of France

Born near Le Mans, the son of **Philip VI**, of Valois, he succeeded his father in 1350. He was taken prisoner by **Edward**, the Black Prince at Poitiers (1356) and taken to England. After the Treaty of Brétigny (1360), which surrendered most of south-west France to **Edward III**, he returned home, leaving his second son, the Duke of Anjou, as a hostage. When the duke broke his parole and escaped (1363), John chivalrously returned to London, where he died.

John II Casimir 1609–72
King of Poland

The son of King **Sigismund III Vasa** of Sweden, he was born in Kraków and became a cardinal before being elected king to succeed his brother, Ladislas IV (1648–68). A successful Swedish invasion forced him to take refuge in Silesia while moves were made to elect **Karl X Gustav** of Sweden in his place. John Casimir returned to Poland (1656) but hostilities continued until the peace of Oliva (1660), when he had to renounce his claim to the Swedish throne. The king tried to alleviate the plight of the Polish serfs and to introduce constitutional reform (1660–61), but noble opposition, led by Jerzy Lubomirski, produced a rebellion (1665–66). Frustrated in all his efforts, and forced to cede Kiev, Eastern Ukraine and Byelorussia to Russia, John Casimir abdicated (1668) and ended his life as a pensioner of **Louis XIV** in Paris.

John III Sobieski 1624–96
King of Poland

A native Pole of noble blood, he was born in Olesko, the son of senator Jacob Sobieski. Appointed Commander-in-Chief in 1668, he fought successful campaigns (1671–73) against Cossack and Tatar invaders, and against a superior Turkish army in Moldavia. He was elected king in 1674, and his queen, Maria Kazimiera, played an important part in directing his prodigious energies and ambitions. Both monarchs were patrons of the arts, and though pious Catholics, pursued a tolerant policy towards the non-Catholic peoples of Poland. His entire reign was spent campaigning. In 1683, in alliance with the Holy Roman Emperor **Leopold I**, he led the army that defeated the Turks before Vienna, but subsequent campaigns (1686, 1691) were less successful. He failed to extend Poland to the Black Sea and to rouse the nobility to any sort of patriotism.

John IV 1604–56
King of Portugal and Duke of Braganza

Born in Vila Viçosa, he was the great-grandson of **Manoel I** and the leading aristocrat and greatest landowner in Portugal. When the country bloodlessly freed itself from Spanish rule (1640), the duke became king of the newly independent Portugal (1640). Despite alliances with France, Sweden, the Dutch (expelled from Brazil and Angola), and with Portugal's ancient ally, England, he was unable to secure Spanish recognition of independent Portugal during his lifetime. His daughter, **Catherine of Braganza**, married **Charles II** of England.

John II Comnenus 1088–1143
Byzantine emperor

He succeeded his father **Alexius I Comnenus** in 1118. In government he relied on trusted servants rather than his immediate family, some of whom, such as his sister Anna and brother Isaac, intrigued against him and were deprived of their positions. Apart from an abortive attempt to curtail the trading privileges of the Venetians, his energetic rule was distinguished by military and diplomatic success. In the Balkans his victory over the Patzinaks (1122) effectively ended a long-standing threat to the empire and in the east he recovered territory in Cilicia and asserted Byzantine overlordship over the Normans of Antioch (1137). He was killed in a hunting accident while on campaign.

John XII *originally* Octavian c.937–964
Italian pope

Born in Rome, the grandson of Marozia, he was elected pope by the dominant party when he was only 18. A synod of the clergy in 963 deposed him for reasons of immorality, at the instigation of the Emperor Otto I, and elected Leo VIII in his place. In the next year John drove out Leo but died suddenly.

John XXII *originally* Jacques Duèse c.1245–1334
French pope

Born in Cahors, he studied canon and civil law at Paris and Orleans, and was the second Pope of Avignon (1316–34). Following his persecution of the Franciscan Spirituals who did not agree with his support of the Franciscan Conventuals, he intervened in the contest for the Crown of the Holy Roman Empire between Louis the Bavarian and Frederick of Austria, in support of the latter. A long conflict ensued both in Germany and Italy between the Guelf (papal) Party and the Ghibelline (imperial) Party. In 1327 Louis entered Italy, was crowned emperor at Rome, deposed John, and set up an antipope, Nicholas V (1328).

John XXIII *originally* Angelo Giuseppe Roncalli 1881–1963
Italian pope

He was born in Sotto il Monte, near Bergamo in northern Italy, the son of a peasant. Ordained in 1904, he served as sergeant in the medical corps and as chaplain in World War I, and subsequently as apostolic delegate to Bulgaria, Turkey and Greece. In 1944 he became the first papal nuncio to liberate France and championed the controversial system of worker-priests. Patriarch of Venice in 1953, he was elected pope in October 1958 on the twelfth ballot, and at once began attempts to modernize and reinvigorate the Roman Catholic Church. He convened the second Vatican Council in order to seek unity between the various Christian sects and broke with tradition by leaving the Vatican for short visits to hospitals and prisons in Rome. In 1963 he issued the celebrated encyclical *Pacem in Terris* ('Peace on Earth'), advocating reconcilation between East and West. His diary was published in English in 1965 as *The Journal of a Soul*.

John Chrysostom, St See Chrysostom, St John

John of Austria, Don, *Spanish* Don Juan 1547–78
Spanish soldier

The illegitimate son of Emperor Charles V, he defeated the Moors in Granada (1570) and the Turks at the Battle of Lepanto (1571). In 1573 he took Tunis, and was then sent to Milan and, in 1576, to the Spanish Netherlands as viceroy. He planned to marry Mary, Queen of Scots, but died of typhoid at Namur. 📖 Sir William Stirling-Maxwell, *Don John of Austria* (1883)

John of Beverley, St d.721
English prelate

Born in Harpham, Humberside, he was educated at Canterbury, and became a monk at St Hilda's double monastery (for nuns and monks) at Whitby in Yorkshire. In 687 he became Bishop of Hexham and in 705 was consecrated Bishop of York. During his ministry he took a special interest in the poor and disabled. In 717 he retired to the Monastery of Beverley, which he had founded while Bishop of York. His feast day is 7 May.

John of Capistrano, St, *properly* Giovanni da Capistrano 1386–1456
Italian prelate

Born in Capistrano in the Abruzzi, he entered the Franciscan Order at the age of 30, having been Governor of Perugia from 1412, and was employed as a legate by several popes, acting as inquisitor against the Fraticelli. In 1450 he preached a crusade in Germany against Turks and heretics, and opposed the Hussites in Moravia. His fanaticism led to many cruelties, such as the racking and burning of forty Jews in Breslau. When Belgrade was besieged by Mehmet II in 1456, he helped to raise and lead an army of 60,000 against him, but died of the plague on the journey back. He was canonized in 1690. His feast day is 28 March.

John of Damascus, St c.676–c.754
Greek theologian and hymnwriter of the Eastern Church

Born in Damascus of Greek parents, he was carefully educated by the learned Italian monk Cosmas. He replied to the Iconoclastic measures of Emperor Leo III, the Isaurian, with two addresses in which he vigorously defended image worship. His later years were spent in the monastery of Mar Saba near Jerusalem. There, ordained a priest, he wrote his hymns, an encyclopaedia of Christian theology (*Fount of Wisdom*), treatises against superstitions and Jacobite and Monophysite heretics, homilies, and *Barlaam and Joasaph*, now known to be a disguised version of the life of Buddha. His feast day is 4 December.

John of Gaeta See Gelasius II

John of Gaunt, Duke of Lancaster 1340–99
English prince

Born in Ghent, Flanders, the fourth (but third surviving) son of Edward III, he married his cousin, Blanche of Lancaster (1359), and was created duke (1362). His son by Blanche became Henry IV. After Blanche died (1369), he married (1372) Constance, daughter of Pedro the Cruel of Castile, and assumed the title of King of Castile, though he failed in his expeditions to oust his rival, Henry of Trastamare. Reserved, haughty and conventional, in England he was the most influential person during the reign of his father, and was thought to be aiming at the Crown. He was largely responsible for crushing the Peasants' Revolt (1381). He opposed the clergy and protected John Wycliffe. Edward's successor, Richard II, distrusting him, sent him on another attempt to secure a treaty for the marriage of his daughter Catherine to the future King of Castile (1386). After his return to England (1389) he became an influential peacemaker, was made Duke of Aquitaine by Richard (1394), and went on several embassies to France. On his second wife's death (1394) he married his mistress, Catherine Swynford (1396), by whom he had three sons, legitimized in 1397, from the eldest of whom Henry VII of England was descended. 📖 S Armitage-Smith, *John of Gaunt* (1904)

John of Halifax See Sacrobosco, Johannes de
John of Holywood See Sacrobosco, Johannes de

John of Leyden, *originally* Jan Beuckelson or Bockhold 1509–36
Dutch Anabaptist

Born in Leyden, he worked as a journeyman tailor, then settled in his native city as merchant and innkeeper, and became noted as an orator. Turning Anabaptist, he went to Münster in 1534, and led a Protestant rebellion, setting up a 'kingdom of Zion', with polygamy and community of goods. In 1535 the city was taken by the Bishop of Münster, and John and his followers were executed.

John of Nepomuk, St c.1345–93
Bohemian cleric and patron saint of Bohemia

Born in Pomuk, near Pilsen (now Plzén, Czech Republic), he studied at the University of Prague, and became vicargeneral to the Archbishop of Prague. For refusing to betray the confession of Queen Sophia to her husband Wenceslas IV, he was tortured and drowned in the Vltava. He was canonized in 1729 as part of the Habsburg and Jesuit campaign to ensure that there was an appropriate Catholic martyr to set against popular support for the Reformist martyr, **Jan Huss**. His feast day is 16 May.

John of Salisbury c.1115–80
English prelate and scholar

Born in Salisbury, he studied at Paris, under Abelard. He was a clerk to Pope **Eugenius III** and to Archbishop **Theobald** at Canterbury, but fell into disfavour with **Henry II** and retired to Rheims. He returned to England and witnessed **Thomas à Becket's** murder at Canterbury (1170). In 1176 he became Bishop of Chartres. A learned classical writer, he wrote biographies of Becket and Anselm, *Polycraticus* on Church and State diplomacy, *Metalogicon*, and *Entheticus, Historia Pontificalis* on logic and Aristotelian philosophy.

John of the Cross, St, *also called* Juan de la Cruz, *originally* Juan de Yepes y Álvarez 1542–91
Spanish mystic, poet and Doctor of the Church

Born in Fontiveros, Ávila, he was a Carmelite monk. He founded the ascetic order of Discalced Carmelites with St **Teresa of Ávila** in 1568. He accompanied St Teresa to Valladolid, where he lived an ascetic life until she appointed him to a convent in Ávila, where he was arrested (1577) and imprisoned in Toledo, where he wrote some of his finest poetry. After escaping in 1578, he became Vicar-Provincial of Andalusia (1585–87). His surviving poetry is some of the greatest in the Spanish language. It includes the lyrical and mystical *Cántico espiritual* (1577, 'Spiritual Canticle') and *Noche oscura del alma* (1577, 'Dark Night of the Soul'). He was canonized in 1726, and declared a Doctor of the Church in 1926. His feast day is 14 December. 🕮 E A Peers, *St John of the Cross* (1932)

John Paul I *originally* Albino Luciani 1912–78
Italian pope for 33 days

Born near Belluno, the son of a labourer in a Venice glass factory, he was educated at the Gregorian University in Rome. Ordained in 1935, he became a parish priest and teacher in Belluno, vicar-general of the diocese of Vittorio Veneto (1954), a bishop (1958), patriarch of Venice (1969) and a cardinal (1973). He was elected pope in August 1978 on the death of **Paul VI**, and died only 33 days later, being succeeded by **John Paul II**. The first pope to use a double name (from his two immediate predecessors, **John XXIII** and **Paul VI**), his was the shortest pontificate of modern times.

John Paul II *originally* Karol Jozef Wojtyła 1920–
Polish pope

Born in Wadowice, he was educated in Poland, ordained in 1946, and became Professor of Moral Theology at Lublin and Kraków. Archbishop and Metropolitan of Kraków (1964–78), he was created cardinal in 1967 and pope in 1978, the first non-Italian pope in 450 years. Noted for his energy and analytical ability, his pontificate has seen many foreign visits, in which he has preached to huge audiences. In 1981 he survived an assassination attempt, when he was shot and wounded in St Peter's Square by a Turkish national, Mehmet Ali Agca, possibly at Bulgarian instigation. A champion of economic justice and an outspoken defender of the Church in communist countries, he has been uncompromising on moral issues. In the 1980s his visits to Poland and his meetings with **Mikhail Gorbachev** were of great assistance to Solidarity in promoting Polish independence, achieved in 1989. In 1995 he participated in historic meetings aimed at discussing relations between the Orthodox and Roman Catholic Churches and other concerns. 1996 was a year of poor health but he continued performing his public duties. He has written a play and several books, including *The Freedom of Renewal* (1972) and *The Future of the Church* (1979), and his *Collected Poems* appeared in 1982. 🕮 Andre Frossard, *Portrait of John Paul II* (1990)

John Randolph of Roanoke See **Randolph, John**

John the Baptist, *also called* St John 1st century AD
Jewish prophet and ascetic

Born in Judaea, he was the son of the priest Zechariah. His mother was Elizabeth, cousin of **Mary**, the mother of **Jesus Christ**. He baptized many, including Jesus, at the River Jordan, and preached repentance and forgiveness of sins and about the coming of the Lord. He was executed by **Herod, Antipas**, but the circumstances differ in the accounts of **Josephus** and the Gospels. In the New Testament, he is portrayed as Christ's forerunner, and sometimes as a returned Elijah (Matthew 11.13–14). His feast day is 24 June. 🕮 Carl H Kraeling, *John the Baptist* (1951)

John the Blind 1296–1346
King of Bohemia

The son of Count Henry III of Luxembourg (afterwards Emperor **Henry VII**), he was born in Luxembourg, and married (1310) Elizabeth, the heiress of Bohemia, being crowned King of Bohemia in 1311. In the struggle between Austria and Bavaria for the Imperial Crown he contributed to the Bavarian victory at Mühldorf (1322), and he campaigned in Italy for the **Guelf** Party (1333–35). In 1334 he married a **Bourbon** and became an ally of the French king. He increased his Bohemian lands in Lucatia, Saxony and Lombardy, but his heavy taxes and constant absences on campaign increased the power of the Bohemian nobles at his expense. By 1340 he had become completely blind, but continued his military career, and fought at Crécy (1346) with conspicuous gallantry until he fell in a last hopeless charge; his motto *Ich Dien* (I serve), was adopted by **Edward**, the Black Prince, on the request of his father, **Edward III**, who commanded the English army in the battle.

John the Fearless 1371–1419
Duke of Burgundy

The eldest son of **Philip, the Bold**, he was born in Rouvrer, Burgundy, and married Margaret of Bavaria (1385). His father's death (1404) left him in possession of Burgundy, Flanders and Artois. He opposed Louis, Duc d'Orléans, his assassination of whom (1407) led to civil war. John gained, lost and regained control of Paris, the king, and the government, but was murdered at Montereau-Faut-Yonne, probably at the instigation of the Dauphin, the future **Charles VII**. Although violent, cunning and hypocritical, he brought peace and prosperity to his own Burgundian territories.

John the Good See **John II**

John the Scot See **Erigena, John Scotus**

John, Augustus Edwin 1878–1961
Welsh painter

Born in Tenby, Pembrokeshire, he studied at the Slade School in London (1896–99) with his sister **Gwen John**, and in Paris, and made an early reputation for himself by his etchings (1900–14). His favourite themes were gipsies, fishing folk and wild, yet naturally regal women, as in *Lyric Fantasy* (1913). In his portraits of women, including many of his wife Dorelia, he is concerned more with unique items of individual beauty or dignity than with portrayal of character, as shown in the beautifully caught posture of the scarlet-gowned cellist *Madame Suggia* (1923).

However, he could portray character as shown in the studies of **George Bernard Shaw** (c. 1914), **Thomas Hardy** (1923) and **Dylan Thomas**. 📖 Michael Holroyd, *Augustus John: The New Biography* (1996) and *Augustus John: A Biography* (1974–75)

John, Barry 1945–

Welsh rugby player

He was born in Cefneithin, Gwynedd. He played 25 times for his country, scoring a record 90 points, before retiring at the early age of 27. He was a devastating player with Llanelli and Cardiff at club level, and his elusiveness and skill at dropping goals made him equally effective at international level. On the British Lions tour of New Zealand in 1971 he scored 180 points.

John, Sir Elton Hercules, *originally* Reginald Kenneth Dwight

1947–

English pop singer, songwriter and pianist

He was born in Pinner, Middlesex. One of the most successful pop-rock stars of the 1970s, he began his career as pianist with the group Bluesology, which he left after their 1967 hit 'Let The Heartaches Begin'. Teaming up with lyricist Bernie Taupin, he launched his solo career with the undistinguished album *Empty Sky* in 1969. *Elton John* (1970), which included the single 'Your Song', brought his first solo success. A self-styled 'ultimate rock fan', he synthesized current popular styles which he forged into a durable hybrid of pop and rock. In a prolific career his albums have included *Tumbleweed Connection* (1970), *Don't Shoot Me I'm Only The Piano Player* (1973), the autobiographical *Captain Fantastic And The Browndirt Cowboy* (1975), *A Single Man* (1978), *Too Low for Zero* (1983), *Breaking Hearts* (1984) and *Sleeping with the Past* (1989). In the mid-1970s he developed a highly flamboyant stage image and an extravagant piano style. He formed his own record label, Rocket Records, and in 1979 became the first Western rock star to play in Moscow, an event documented in the film *To Russia With Elton* (1979). In 1976 he became owner and chairman of Watford Football Club, but sold most of his shares in 1990. He returned as director until 1993, when he became life president. He contributed five songs to *The Lion King* soundtrack in 1993, followed by a strong album, *Made In England* (1995). 📖 P Norman *Elton John* (1993)

John, Gwen 1876–1939

Welsh painter

Born in Haverfordwest, Pembrokeshire, she was the elder sister of **Augustus John**. She lived in Tenby, Pembrokeshire, before studying at the Slade School of Art (1895–98). On moving to Paris in 1904, she worked as an artist's model, becoming **Auguste Rodin**'s mistress in c.1906. After converting to Roman Catholicism in 1913 she lived at Meudon, where she became increasingly religious and reclusive. She painted some landscapes, but most of her paintings are of single female figures, nuns or young girls, cats and interiors. She exhibited with the New English Art Club from 1900–11, and her work was included in the Armory Show of 1913. Her only one-woman show during her lifetime was in London in 1926.

John, Otto 1909–97

German lawyer

Chief legal adviser to the German civil aviation company Lufthansa, in 1944 he played, with his brother Hans, a prominent role in the abortive anti-**Hitler** plot of 20 July, after which he escaped to Great Britain via Spain and worked for the British Psychological Warfare Executive. At the end of the war, he joined a London legal firm and appeared as a prosecution witness in the Nuremberg and **Erich von Manstein** trials. In 1950 he was appointed to the newly-formed West German Office for the protection of the constitution. Attending the annual commemorative ceremony of 20 July in West Berlin in 1954, he mysteriously disappeared and later made broadcasts for the East German Communists. In 1956 he returned to the West, was arrested, tried, and sentenced to four years' hard labour for treasonable falsification and conspiracy. He claimed that he was held a prisoner and forced to make broadcasts until he managed to escape. Released in 1958, he always protested his innocence. 📖 *Twice Through the Lines* (1972)

John, Patrick 1937–

Dominican politician

In the period before full independence he served in the government of Chief Minister Edward LeBlanc and succeeded him in 1974. On independence in 1978 he became the country's first Prime Minister. His increasingly authoritarian style of government led to the loss of his assembly seat in 1980 and his replacement as Prime Minister by **Eugenia Charles**. The following year he was arrested for alleged complicity in a plot to overthrow Charles but was acquitted of the charge. A subsequent trial, in 1985, found him guilty and he was given a 12-year prison sentence.

Johns, Jasper 1930–

US painter, sculptor and printmaker

Born in Allendale, South Carolina, he studied for a year at the University of South Carolina in Columbia (1947–48). He moved to New York City in 1949 and worked first as a commercial artist. In the mid-1950s, after meeting **Robert Rauschenberg**, he began to create bold pictorial images such as flags, targets and numbers, using heavily textured wax-based print in a manner derived from the Abstract Expressionists and often incorporating plaster casts. This work became an important source for the development of Pop Art in the USA. In the 1960s and 1970s he produced increasingly complex paintings, frequently with objects like brushes and rulers attached, and in recent years he has continued to create semi-abstract works, which incorporate tracings of images from sources as various as the Isenheim Altarpiece and architectural blueprints. From 1960 he worked extensively with lithography. His sculptures are of banal items, executed with detailed realism. The Museum of Modern Art in New York mounted a retrospective of his work in 1996.

Johns, W(illiam) E(arl) 1893–1968

English aviator and children's author

He was born in Hertford, Hertfordshire. He served in the Norfolk Yeomanry and when commissioned in 1916, transferred to the Royal Flying Corps where he served with some distinction before being shot down by **Ernst Udet** and sent to a prison camp. He retired from the Royal Air Force in 1930, edited *Popular Flying* and *Flying* in the 1930s, and served in the Ministry of Information (1939–45). His wartime marriage broke up after 1918 and he lived for many years with a woman his publishers prevented him from marrying, considering that his status as a children's author forbade his divorce. His stories are strikingly good flying yarns, mostly based on his experiences in World War I. The 'Biggles' series reflects unspoken anger at the expendability of airmen in bureaucratic thinking, while his World War II female pilot, 'Worrals', is savagely contemptuous of male self-satisfaction and chauvinism towards women. He later tried his hand, less successfully, at space exploration stories. 📖 P B Ellis and P Williams, *The Life of Captain W. E. Johns* (1981)

Johns Hopkins See **Hopkins, Johns**

Johnson, Alexander Bryan 1786–1867

US philosopher

Born of Dutch–Jewish ancestry in Gosport, Hampshire, England, he settled in 1801 in Utica, New York, where he enjoyed a successful career in business. He published three philosophical works, *The Philosophy of Human Knowledge* (1828), *A Treatise on Language: or the relation which Words bear to Things* (1836) and *The Meaning of Words* (1854), which can now be seen to anticipate views familiar to the logical positivists and linguistic philosophers of the 20th century. He also published works on politics, economics and banking.

Johnson, Amy 1903–41
English aviator

Born in Hull, Humberside, she became a pilot in 1929. In 1930 she flew solo from England to Australia (the first woman to do so) in her aircraft *Jason*, winning £10,000 from the London *Daily Mail*. In 1931 she flew to Japan via Moscow and back, and in 1932 made a record solo flight to Cape Town and back. With her husband **James Mollison**, she crossed the Atlantic Ocean in a De Havilland biplane in 39 hours (1933) and flew to India in 22 hours (1934). In 1936 she set a new record for a solo flight from London to Cape Town. She joined the Air Transport Auxiliary as a pilot in World War II, and was lost after baling out over the Thames estuary. ▭ Constance Babington Smith, *Amy Johnson: A Biography* (1977)

Johnson, Andrew 1808–75
17th President of the USA

Born in Raleigh, North Carolina, he went to Laurens, South Carolina, in 1824 to work as a journeyman tailor, and in 1826 emigrated to Greenville, Tennessee. In 1841 he was elected to the state senate, and in 1843 to Congress. In 1853 and 1855 he was Governor of Tennessee, and in 1857 US senator. A moderate **Jackson**ian Democrat, Johnson was alone among Southern senators in standing by the Union during the Civil War and was made military Governor of Tennessee (1862) and elected to the vice-presidency (March 1865). On **Abraham Lincoln's** assassination (14 April 1865) he became President. He sought to carry out the conciliatory policy of his predecessor, but the assassination had provoked a revulsion of public feeling, and Johnson's policy was denounced as showing disloyalty. He urged the readmission of Southern representatives, but the Radical Republican majority insisted that the Southern states should be kept for a period under military government. His removal of Secretary **Stanton** from the war department precipitated a crisis. He claimed the right to change his 'constitutional advisers', but was charged with violation of the 'Tenure of Office Act', in doing so without the consent of the Senate. He was impeached and brought to trial, and acquitted by a single vote. He retired from office in 1869, and was elected to the Senate in 1875. ▭ Robert W Winston, *Andrew Johnson, Plebeian and Patriot* (1928)

Johnson, Ben 1961–
Canadian track athlete

He was born in Falmouth, Jamaica. In the mid-1980s he was the world's fastest sprinter with **Carl Lewis**. He was unbeaten in 21 consecutive starts over 100 metres and at the 1988 Seoul Olympics set a new world 100 metres record. Later he had his medal withdrawn, was stripped of his world record, and was suspended after allegations that he had used steroids. His life ban from the Canadian team was lifted in 1990, but in March 1993 he was banned for life by the IAAF (International Amateur Athletic Federation) after he failed a drugs test in Montreal.

Johnson, Dame Celia 1908–82
English actress

Born in Richmond, Surrey, she was a student at RADA before making her stage debut in *Major Barbara* (1928) at Huddersfield and her London debut in *A Hundred Years Old* (1929). She made her first New York appearance as Ophelia in *Hamlet* (1931) and enjoyed a long run in *The Wind and the Rain* (1933–35) in London. She was often cast as a well-bred English lady, and her career ranged from exquisitely modulated portraits of quiet despair to sophisticated high comedy and her many theatrical successes included *The Three Sisters* (1951), *The Reluctant Debutante* (1955), *Hay Fever* (1965) and *The Kingfisher* (1977). *Dirty Work* (1934) was the first of her rare screen appearances, although she had leading roles in **Noël Coward's** films *In Which We Serve* (1942) and *This Happy Breed* (1944), and created an unforgettable impression as the sad suburban housewife in *Brief Encounter* (1945). She won a British Film award for *The Prime of Miss Jean Brodie* (1969) and continued in the theatre and on television until her death. ▭ Kate Fleming, *Celia Johnson: A Biography* (1991)

Johnson, Dorothy M (arie) 1905–84
US novelist

Born in Iowa, she grew up in Montana. A journalist, she worked as a magazine editor in New York for 15 years before returning to Montana and joining the staff of a local paper. She was the author of two classic western stories, 'The Man Who Shot Liberty Valance' and 'A Man Called Horse' (filmed but not published until 1984 in *The Reel West* and *The Western Hall of Fame* respectively). She also wrote full-length novels. *Warriors For A Lost Nation* (1969) was a biography of **Sitting Bull**.

Johnson, Eyvind Olof Verner 1900–76
Swedish novelist, short-story writer and Nobel Prize winner

He was born of working-class parents in Svartbjörnsbyn, near Boden, and after a number of years in mainly manual occupations he spent most of the 1920s in Paris and Berlin. His four-part *Romanen om Olof* (1934–37, 'The Story of Olof') is the finest of the many working-class autobiographical novels written in Sweden in the 1930s. He was much involved in anti-Nazi causes, and produced a number of novels, especially the *Krilon* series (1941–43), castigating totalitarianism. The same humanitarian values are evident in his later historical novels, particularly *Strändernas svall* (1946, 'Return to Ithaca'), *Drömmar om rosor och eld* (1949, 'Dreams about Roses and Fire') and *Hans nådes tid* (1960, 'The Days of his Grace'). He shared the 1974 Nobel Prize for literature with fellow Swede, **Harry Martinson**. ▭ G Orton, *Eyvind Johnson* (1972)

Johnson, Hewlett, *nicknamed* the Red Dean 1874–1966
English prelate

Born of a capitalist family in Macclesfield, and educated at Manchester and Oxford universities, he underwent an engineering apprenticeship, did welfare work in the Manchester slums and joined the Independent Labour Party, resolving to become 'a missionary engineer'. He was ordained in 1905. In 1924 he became dean of Manchester and from 1931 to 1963 was dean of Canterbury. In 1938 he visited Russia and with the publication of *The Socialist Sixth of the World* began his years of praise for Sovietism. In 1951 he received the **Stalin** Peace Prize. Though he was not a member of the Communist Party, his untiring championship of the Communist states and Marxist policies involved him in continuous and vigorous controversy in Great Britain. His sobriquet was a self-bestowed title when, during the Spanish Civil War, he said 'I saw red—you can call me red'. His other publications include *Christians and Communism* (1956) and the autobiographical *Searching for Light* (1968).

Johnson, J J (James Louis) 1924–
US jazz trombonist and composer

He was born in Indianapolis, Indiana, and took up the trombone at the age of 14 after studying piano. While working professionally in New York in the 1940s, he was inspired by the bebop movement; his recordings of the period with **Charlie Parker** and others show him to be the first slide trombonist to answer the demands of the style for speed, articulation and harmonic sophistication. From the 1960s he worked largely as a composer for films and television, but his playing continues to influence modern jazz trombonists.

Johnson, James P(rice) 1894–1955
US pianist and composer

Born in New Brunswick, New Jersey, he was given rudimentary piano instruction by his mother. The family moved to New York in 1908 and, while still at school, Johnson participated in informal after-hours sessions with other pianists, mainly ragtime performers. In 1912 he began a series of piano-playing jobs in movie-houses, cabarets and dance-halls, gradually becoming the most accomplished player in the post-ragtime 'stride' style. A prolific performer in the 1920s and during the traditional jazz revival of the 1940s, he wrote more than 200 songs (including 'The Charleston') as well as several stage shows, and was a strong influence on such later pianists as **Fats Waller** and **Art Tatum**.

Johnson, James Weldon 1871–1938
US writer

Born in Jacksonville, Florida, he practised at the Bar there (1897–1901), and later served as US consul at Puerto Cabello, Venezuela (from 1906), and at Corinto, Nicaragua (1909–12). He was secretary of the National Association for the Advancement of Colored People (1916–30), and from 1930 he was Professor of Creative Literature at Fisk University. His numerous works include his novel *The Autobiography of an Ex-Coloured Man* (1912) and his collection of free-verse folk sermons, *God's Trombones* (1927). He also wrote and edited books on African–American history and culture. ▢ E D Levy, *James Weldon Johnson: Black Leader, Black Voice* (1973)

Johnson, Linton Kwesi 1952–
Jamaican reggae poet and performer

He has lived in Great Britain since the age of nine, and studied sociology at London University. His verdict on British culture was most succinctly expressed in the title of a 1980 book and recording, *Inglan is a Bitch*. He writes powerful, committed verse which follows the cadences of Caribbean speech and the rhythmic values of reggae and dub. He wrote *Voices of the Living and the Dead* (1974) and became part of a revived poetry/performance movement in Britain, adopted by the Anti-Nazi League in its crusade against British racism. His most powerful work is the sombre rumble of *Dread Beat an' Blood* (1975), which is almost as effective on the page as it is on the record that followed.

Johnson, Lionel Pigot 1867–1902
English poet and critic

Born in Broadstairs, Kent, he was brought up in Wales, and educated at Winchester and New College, Oxford. After graduating, he moved to London, and made a living in literary journalism. He converted to Roman Catholicism in 1891 and fell under the spell of the Celtic Twilight, as *Poems* (1895) and *Ireland and Other Poems* (1897) testify. His most famous and frequently anthologized poem, however, is *By the Statue of King Charles at Charing Cross*. He was a member of the Rhymers' Club, and a friend of **Oscar Wilde** and **W B Yeats**, and as an influential critic he did much to promote an appreciation of **Thomas Hardy**. ▢ A W Patrick, *Lionel Johnson: poète et critique* (1939)

Johnson, Lyndon B(aines), *known as* L B J 1908–73
36th President of the USA

Born near Stonewall, Texas, into a Baptist family which was involved in state politics, he worked his way through college to become a high school teacher, then a congressman's secretary before being elected a strong 'New Deal' Democrat representative in 1937. He joined the US navy immediately after Pearl Harbor, and was decorated. He was elected senator in 1948 and became Vice-President under **John F Kennedy** in 1960, having earlier contested the party's nomination. A professional politician, he had been majority leader in the Senate since 1955. After Kennedy's assassination in Dallas, Texas, in 1963, he became President and was returned as President in the 1964 election with a huge majority. Under his administration the Civil Rights Act (1964), introduced by Kennedy the previous year, and the Voting Rights Act (1965) were passed, making effective, if limited, improvements to the position of blacks in the USA. He also introduced, under the slogan the 'Great Society', a series of important economic and social welfare reforms, including a Medicare programme for the aged and measures to improve education. However, the ever-increasing escalation of the war in Vietnam led to active protest and growing personal unpopularity for Johnson, and in 1968 he announced his decision to retire from active politics. ▢Paul K Conkin, *Big Daddy From Pedernales* (1986)

Johnson, Magic, *real name* Earvin Johnson 1959–
US basketball player

Born in Lansing, Michigan, he began his career in college basketball at Michigan State University, then played with the Los Angeles Lakers (1979–91, 1996) and was a member of the gold medal-winning US Olympic basketball team ('Dream Team') in 1992. He was a member of National Basketball Association (NBA) All-Star team (1980, 1982–92), and was named NBA Most Valuable Player in 1987, 1989 and 1990. During his years with the Lakers the team won five NBA championships (1980, 1982, 1985, 1987–88). He retired in 1992 after revealing that he had been diagnosed HIV positive, and had a brief comeback the following year. He coached the Lakers briefly in 1993–94. In 1996 he again played for the team, returning as a forward rather than, as previously, guard. His publications include *Magic* (1983) and *What You Can Do to Avoid AIDS* (1992).

Johnson, Michael 1967–
US track athlete

Born in Dallas, he attended Baylor University in Waco, Texas. He won world championship races in the 200 metres in 1991 and 1995 and in the 400 metres in 1993 and 1995. After missing the 1992 Olympics in Barcelona because of food poisoning, he competed at the 1996 Olympics in Atlanta, tempting fate by wearing gold running shoes but nevertheless winning gold medals in both the 200-metre and 400-metre events, the first man ever to do so. At the same time he set a new world record in the 200 metres, breaking the world record he himself set at the Olympic trials.

Johnson, Pamela Hansford See Hansford Johnson, Pamela

Johnson, Philip Cortelyou 1906–
US architect and theorist

Born in Cleveland, Ohio, he graduated from Harvard in 1927. He came late to architecture after working as critic, author and as director of the department of architecture at the Museum of Modern Art, New York (1930–36, 1946–54). He became renowned for his publication *The International Style* (1932, with Henry-Russell Hitchcock), which coined the popular term and helped promote architecture in the USA. From 1940 to 1943 he studied architecture at Harvard under **Walter Gropius** and **Marcel Breuer**. He designed his own home, the Glass House, New Canaan, Connecticut (1949–50), on principles of space unification derived from **Ludwig Mies van der Rohe**, with whom he collaborated on the Seagram Building, New York City (1956–58). Further works include the Amon Carter Museum of Western Art, Texas (1961) and the New York State Theater, Lincoln Center (1964). In mid-career he began to move away from the sleek simplicity of modernism, instead drawing inspiration and borrowing details from a variety of past architectural styles, and he was eventually recognized as one of the most prominent architects of the post-modern movement. In 1978–84 he designed the granite American Telephone and Telegraph Building in New York City, following the structure and classical form of early skyscrapers. Works in progress in 1996 included the Trump International Hotel and Tower in New York and the Cathedral of Hope in Dallas, Texas. 📖 Robert A M Stern (ed), *Philip Johnson, Writings* (1978)

Johnson, Richard Mentor 1781–1850
US politician

Born near Louisville, Kentucky, he was a member of Congress from 1807 to 1819, of the US Senate until 1829, and of Congress until 1837. He was elected Vice-President (1837–41) by the Senate after the elections had not thrown up a majority in the electoral college for any one candidate.

Johnson, Robert 1911–38
US blues singer and guitarist

Born in Hazelhurst, Mississippi, he is perhaps the most famous name in blues, and his story has attained a semi-legendary status in the mythology of the music. He was a virtuoso self-taught guitarist, and although he recorded only 29 songs, their impact on the development of blues has been incalculable. Little is known of his life, but the legend that he acquired his skills by selling his soul to the Devil has taken root in blues mythology. His real impact is due not only to his musical skills, but also to the passionate, haunted intensity of his singing and playing. Most of his surviving songs, recorded in only two sessions in 1936 and 1937, have acquired classic status. 📖 P Guralnick, *Searching for Robert Johnson* (1989)

Johnson, Samuel See panel p993

Johnson, Virginia E(shelman) 1925–
US psychologist and sexologist

She was born in Springfield, Missouri. Educated at Missouri University, she joined the research group of **William Masters** in 1957, and achieved fame through their investigations of the physiology of sexual intercourse, using volunteer subjects under laboratory conditions at their Reproductive Biology Research Foundation in St Louis (established 1970). She and Masters (who were married from 1971 to 1993), co-authored *Human Sexual Response* (1966), which became an international bestseller. Their other works include *Human Sexual Inadequacy* (1970), and *On Sex and Human Loving* (1986).

Johnson, Sir William 1715–74
Irish merchant and colonial administrator

Born in County Meath, he emigrated to America in 1737, and became a fur trader in the Mohawk Valley (now in New York State). By his fairness he acquired great influence with the Native Americans. In the Anglo-French Wars he often led the Six Nations (the Iroquois Confederacy) against the French, especially at Lake George. He was appointed superintendent of Indian Affairs (1756–64) and built Johnson Hall on the Mohawk River. After the death of his wife he took into his house Molly Brant, a sister of the Mohawk chief **Joseph Brant**, and had eight children with her. She was known as 'the Indian Lady Johnson'.

Johnson, William Eugene, nicknamed Pussyfoot
1862–1945
US reformer and temperance propagandist

Born in Coventry, New York, he became a journalist, and later a special officer in the US Indian Service (1908–11), where he received his nickname from his methods in raiding gambling saloons in Indian Territory. He was prominent during the prohibitionist movement in the USA and lectured for the cause all over Europe. In 1919 he lost an eye when he was struck and dragged from a lecture platform in London by medical students.

Johnston, Albert Sidney 1803–62
US general

Born in Washington, Kentucky, he graduated from West Point in 1826 and served in the US army until 1834. After the death of his wife he enlisted as a private in the army of Texas (1836), rising to the rank of general within a year and assuming command of the army in 1837; he was Secretary of War of the Republic of Texas from 1838 to 1840. He served in the Mexican War (1846–48) under General **Zachary Taylor**, who in 1849 appointed him paymaster in the US army. From 1857 to 1859 he was sent to 'pacify' the Mormons in Utah, and as brigadier-general commanded in Utah and on the Pacific. In 1861 he resigned his commission to become a Confederate general in the Civil War (1861–65). Appointed to the command of Kentucky and Tennessee, he fortified Bowling Green, and held the Northern army in check until February 1862, when he retreated to Nashville and later to Corinth, Mississippi. Here he attacked **Ulysses S Grant** at Shiloh in 1862. The Union army was taken by surprise, and the advantage lay with the Confederates until Johnston was mortally wounded.

Johnston, Brian Alexander 1912–94
English commentator and broadcaster

Educated at Eton and New College, Oxford, he helped in the family coffee business for five years before serving in the army during World War II. He joined the BBC in 1945 and remained there for 27 years, becoming a specialist in cricket commentary. He was also commentator for many significant royal occasions, such as the coronation of Queen **Elizabeth II** (1953), her silver jubilee (1977) and several royal weddings. After retiring from the BBC, he continued in radio broadcasting, and won various awards, including *Daily Mail* Radio Sports Commentator of the Year in 1988. His books include *Armchair Cricket* (1957), *Views From the Boundary* (1990) and *Someone Who Was* (1992).

Johnston, (William) Denis 1901–84
Irish playwright

He was born in Dublin, and educated at Cambridge and Harvard, then joined the English (1925) and Irish (1925) Bars. His impressionist play, *Shadowdance*, was rejected by **Lady Gregory** for the Abbey Theatre, Dublin, but, retitled *The Old Lady Says 'No'*, became a major success at the city's Gate Theatre in 1929. It was followed by a further triumph with *The Moon on the Yellow River* (1931) and several others over the next three decades. He also wrote two autobiographical works, *Nine Rivers from Jordan*, (1953) which recounts his experiences as a war correspondent, and *The Brazen Head* (1977), and a book about **Jonathan Swift**, *In Search of Swift* (1959). His daughter is the novelist Jennifer Johnston (1930–). 📖 J Ronsley, *Denis Johnston, a retrospective* (1981)

Johnston, Edward 1872–1944
British calligrapher

Born in Uruguay, of Scottish parents, he studied medicine at Edinburgh, then virtually taught himself the art of calligraphy by studying medieval manuscripts, and discovering how to prepare and use reeds and quills. From

Johnson, Samuel, *known as* Dr Johnson 1709–84
English writer, critic, lexicographer, and conversationalist

Dr Johnson was born in Lichfield, Staffordshire, the son of a bookseller, and he read voraciously in his father's shop. He was educated at Lichfield Grammar School and Pembroke College, Oxford, but left in 1731 without taking a degree. He taught briefly at a school in Market Bosworth, and then moved to Birmingham where he turned to writing. In 1735 he married Elizabeth ('Tetty') Porter, a widow 20 years older than himself, and they opened a school at Edial, near Lichfield; one of the pupils was the future actor **David Garrick**. The school failed, and in 1737, accompanied by the young Garrick, the Johnsons moved to London where he finished writing a tragedy, *Irene* (not staged for 12 years), and earned a living writing parliamentary reports for *The Gentleman's Magazine*. In it he published (anonymously) his first poem, *London: A Poem in Imitation of the Third Satire of Juvenal*.

In 1744 he produced a topical and successful *Life* of his friend **Richard Savage**. Meanwhile he had been cataloguing the great library of Edward Harley, 2nd Earl of Oxford (1689–1741), and was able further to indulge his huge appetite for reading. In 1747 he issued a prospectus of a *Dictionary of the English Language*, which was to take him eight years to complete. During this time he published a long didactic poem, *The Vanity of Human Wishes* (1749), based on another of **Juvenal**'s satires. Garrick fulfilled a boyhood promise by producing his *Irene* at Drury Lane Theatre (1749), and Johnson himself wrote and edited, practically single-handed, a bi-weekly periodical, *The Rambler*, which ran for 208 issues (1750–52), full of moral essays written (anonymously) by himself. In 1752 his wife died, plunging him into lasting depression.

His great Dictionary appeared in 1755, which gave rise to a celebrated letter in which Johnson disdained an offer of patronage from Lord **Chesterfield**. Johnson was awarded an honorary degree at Oxford, but he had to continue literary hack-work to earn a living, contributing reviews for the *Literary Magazine*, and *The Idler* series of papers in *The Universal Chronicle* (1758–60). During this time his mother died, and he wrote his moral fable, *Rasselas: The Prince of Abyssinia* (1759), in a week to defray the funeral expenses. With the accession of **George III** in 1760, Johnson was granted a pension of £300 for life, which brought him financial security for the first time. In 1763 he met the young Scot, **James Boswell**, who would become his biographer, and with whom he would share a delightful tour of the Hebrides in 1773 (*A Journey to the Western Isles of Scotland*, 1775).

In 1764 he founded the Literary Club with a circle of friends, including **Joshua Reynolds, Edmund Burke** and **Oliver Goldsmith**; later members were Boswell, Garrick and **Charles James Fox**. In 1765 he published his critical edition of **Shakespeare**'s plays (8 vols), with its classic Preface, and then set to work on his monumental *Lives of the Most Eminent English Poets* (10 vols, 1779–81). In that year his friend, the brewer Henry Thrale, died; his widow, Hester Thrale (see **Hester Piozzi**), who had looked after Johnson for many years, fell in love with an Italian musician, Gabriele Piozzi, and Johnson's wounded fury at their marriage in 1784 provoked a total estrangement. He died in dejection, and was buried in Westminster Abbey.

📖 Paul Fussell, *Samuel Johnson and the Life of Writing* (1977); D J Greene, *Samuel Johnson* (1970); James Boswell, *The Life of Samuel Johnson* (1791).

> Johnson's Dictionary contains many memorable definitions and quotations, including the following:
> *Lexicographer.* A writer of dictionaries, a harmless drudge.
> *Network.* Anything reticulated or decussated at equal distances, with interstices between the intersections.
> *Oats.* A grain, which in England is generally given to horses, but in Scotland supports the people.
>
> Johnson invented the spelling *despatch*. Before his dictionary was published, the spelling was uniformly *dispatch*. In his entry, he spelt it with an e, although all the quotations he gives used an *i*.

1899 to 1912 he taught, at **W R Lethaby**'s invitation, at the Central School of Arts and Design, London, where one of his students was **Eric Gill**, and he also taught at the Royal College of Art. His books, *Writing and Illuminating, and Lettering* (1906) and *Manuscript and Inscription Letters* (1909), were landmarks in the revival and development of calligraphy. When **Frank Pick** required a letter form for London Transport in 1913, Johnston produced his classic sans-serif alphabet which is still in use.

Johnston, Frances Benjamin 1864–1952
US photographer

Born in Grafton, West Virginia, she studied painting and drawing at the Académie Julian in Paris (1883–85), then at the Art Students League in Washington DC (1885). She studied photography with Thomas William Smillie of the Smithsonian Institution, and opened a professional studio in Washington DC in 1890. She and **Jessie Tarbox Beals** were two of the first women press photographers. Johnston worked first as a magazine correspondent (c.1889) then operated a studio in New York with a partner, specializing in architectural photography (1913–17). In 1900 she organized an important exhibition of work by 28 American women photographers, timed to coincide with the Exposition Universelle in Paris. After 1917 she photographed mainly gardens, architecture and estates. She became known as a champion of women and was best known for her careful social documentary work.

Johnston, George Henry 1912–70
Australian author and journalist

Born in Malvern, Victoria, he studied commercial art. He then worked as a journalist, and during World War II his syndicated dispatches from New Guinea, India, Burma, Italy and the North Atlantic were widely read. He wrote five books on his experiences, published between 1941 and 1944. Returning to journalism after the war, he worked in London as European editor of the Sydney *Sun*, before going to the Greek islands with his wife and fellow-author, **Charmian Clift**. With her he wrote three novels, and she described their life in the islands in short stories and essays. Johnston wrote short stories, plays and many novels, several under the pseudonym 'Shane Martin'. His novels include *Monsoon* (1948), *The Cyprian Woman* (1955) and *Closer to the Sun*, which won the US Literary Guild award in 1960. He also wrote a semi-autobiographical trilogy: *My Brother Jack* (1964, Miles Franklin award), *Clean Straw for Nothing* (1969, Miles Franklin award) and the unfinished *A Cartload of Clay* (1971).

Johnston, Sir Harry H(amilton) 1858–1927
English administrator, explorer, writer and artist

He was born in Kennington, London. He played a significant part in the partition of Africa. Trained as an artist, he also developed scientific and linguistic interests, learning many African languages, and in 1879 he went to Tunis to paint and explore. Later he travelled in Angola, the Congo and (in 1884) led the Royal Society's expedition to the Kilimanjaro region of East Africa, where he collected treaties with local chiefs. He subsequently served the Foreign Office in West Africa (1885–89),

Lisbon (1889), Mozambique (1889–91), British Central Africa (Malawi, 1891–96), Tunis (1897–99) and Uganda (1899–1901). He wrote books on the Congo and zoology, novels, and an autobiography, *The Story of My Life* (1923), and is generally credited with inventing the phrase 'Cape to Cairo'.

Johnston, Joseph Eggleston 1807–91
US general

Born near Farnville, Virginia, he fought in the Seminole War, became captain of engineers in 1846, served in the war with Mexico, and in 1860 was quartermaster-general. At the outbreak of the Civil War (1861–65) he entered the Confederate service, and as brigadier-general took command of the army of the Shenandoah. He supported P G T Beauregard at the first Battle of Bull Run, and in 1864 stubbornly contested General Sherman's progress towards Atlanta, but, driven back, was relieved of his command. Reinstated and ordered to 'drive back Sherman', he nevertheless was forced to surrender to Sherman on 26 April 1865. He later engaged in railway and insurance business, was elected to Congress in 1877 and was a US commissioner of railroads.

Johnston, Tom (Thomas) 1881–1965
Scottish Labour politician

Born in Kirkintilloch, Strathclyde, he was educated at Lenzie Academy and Glasgow University. After working as a journalist he joined the Independent Labour Party and in 1906 founded *Forward*, a Socialist weekly of considerable influence in the west of Scotland. He served as Labour MP for West Stirling (1922–24, 1929–31, 1935–45), and for Dundee (1924–29). Appointed Secretary of State for Scotland (1941–45), he did much to plan for postwar developments. In 1942 he set up the Scottish Council (Development and Industry) to attract new industries, and in 1945 became chairman of the North of Scotland Hydro-Electric Board.

Johnstone, (Christian) Isobel, pseudonym Meg or Margaret Dods 1781–1857
Scottish cookery writer, novelist and journalist

Born in Fife, she married her second husband, John Johnstone, in 1812, writing for the *Inverness Courier* when he was its owner and editor. Whilst in Inverness she wrote *Clan Albyn, A National Tale* (1815) and followed this with *Elizabeth de Bruce* (1827), both historical novels which enjoyed considerable popularity. She made her name, however, with *The Cook and Housewife's Manual*, by Mistress Margaret Dods (1826), popularly known as *Meg Dod's Cookery*. Using characters from Sir Walter Scott's *St Ronan's Well*, it was purportedly written by the landlady of the Cleikum Inn, St Ronan's. It remains an invaluable sourcebook for modern cooks. Isobel Johnstone also maintained a successful career as a literary journalist, writing for the *Schoolmaster*, *Johnstone's Magazine*, and *Tait's Magazine*.

Johnstone, William 1897–1981
Scottish painter

Born in Denholm, Roxburghshire, he studied at Edinburgh College of Art and subsequently in Paris. His work in the late 1920s and 1930s shows the influence of Surrealism, in its use of rounded semi-abstract images suggestive of dreamlike landscapes and human forms. He held a series of teaching posts in London, latterly as principal of the Central School of Arts and Crafts (1947–60). It was in the last decade of his life that he produced what is arguably his best work: large, free abstract paintings and ink drawings which have something of the feeling of Eastern calligraphy, but are still evocative of the natural world.

Joinville, François Ferdinand d'Orléans, Prince de 1818–1900
French naval officer and author

Born in Neuilly, the third son of Louis Philippe, he served in the French navy (1834–48), and was on George B McClellan's staff during the Virginian campaign in the American Civil War (1862). Exiled from France in 1870, he returned incognito in 1871 and served in the war against Prussia. From 1871 to 1875 he sat in the National Assembly. His works included *Essais sur la marine française* (1852, 'Essays on the French Navy') and *Vieux Souvenirs* (1894, 'Ancient Memories').

Joinville, Jean, Sire de c.1224–1319
French historian

Born in Joinville, Champagne, he became seneschal to the Count of Champagne and King of Navarre. He took part in the unfortunate Seventh Crusade (1248–54) of Louis IX, shared his captivity, and returned with him to France, and lived partly at court, partly on his estates. At Acre in 1250 he composed a Christian manual, his *Credo*, and throughout the crusade he took notes of events and wrote down his impressions, which he fashioned at the age of almost 80 into the entertaining *Histoire de saint Louis* (1309, 'Life of Saint Louis').

Jókai, Maurus or Mór 1825–1904
Hungarian novelist

He was born in Komárom, and was an active partisan of the Hungarian struggle in 1848. As well as dramas, humorous essays and poems, he wrote many novels and romances, including *Egy magyar nábob* (1853, Eng trans *An Hungarian Nabob*, 1898) and its continuation *Kárpáthy Zoltán* (1854), *Az uj földesur* (1862, Eng trans *The New Landlord*, 1868), *A fekete gyémántok* (1870, Eng trans *Black Diamonds*, 1896), *Egy ember a ki mindent tud* (1875, 'The Modern Midas') and *A lőcsei fehér asszony* (1884, 'The White Woman of Leutschau'). He was editor of several newspapers, and conspicuous as a Liberal parliamentarian. 📖 M Nágy, *Jókai* (1968)

Joliot-Curie, Frédéric, originally Jean-Frédéric Joliot 1900–58
French physicist and Nobel Prize winner

Born in Paris, he studied under Paul Langevin at the Sorbonne, and in 1925 he joined the Radium Institute under Marie Curie, where he studied the electrochemical properties of polonium. He married Marie's daughter Irène Joliot-Curie in 1926, and in 1935 he shared with his wife the Nobel Prize for chemistry for making the first artificial radio isotope. Professor at the Collège de France (1937), he became a strong supporter of the Resistance movement during World War II, and a member of the Communist Party. After the liberation he was director of scientific research and (1946–50) High Commissioner for atomic energy, a position from which he was dismissed for his political activites. He succeeded his wife as head of the Radium Institute, and as president of the Communist-sponsored World Peace Council, he was awarded the Stalin Peace Prize (1951). Commander of the Legion of Honour, he was given a state funeral by the Gaullist government when he died from cancer, caused by lifelong exposure to radioactivity. 📖 Maurice Goldman, *Frédéric Joliot-Curie* (1976)

Joliot-Curie, Irène, née Curie 1897–1956
French physicist and Nobel Prize winner

She was born in Paris, the daughter of Pierre and Marie Curie, and in 1918 she joined her mother at the Radium Institute in Paris, beginning her scientific research in 1921. In 1926 she married Frédéric Joliot, and they collaborated in studies of radioactivity from 1931. Their work on the emissions of polonium was built on by Sir James Chadwick in his discovery of the neutron. In 1933–34 the Joliot-Curies made the first artificial radioisotope, and it was for this work that they were jointly awarded the Nobel Prize for chemistry in 1935. Similar methods led them to make a range of radioisotopes, some of which have proved indispensable in medicine, scientific research and industry. Irène Joliot-Curie became director of the Radium Institute in 1946 and a director of the French Atomic Energy Commission. She died from leukaemia due to long periods of exposure to radioactivity. 📖 Eugénie Cotton, *Les Curie* (1963)

Jolley, (Monica) Elizabeth 1923–
Australian writer
Born in Birmingham, England, she settled in Western Australia in 1959. Her first publication, *Five Acre Virgin* (1976), received immediate critical praise and was followed by *The Travelling Entertainer* (1979). Often using lesbianism as a major theme, she also wrote *Palomino* (1980), *The Newspaper of Claremont Street* (1981), and *Mr Scobie's Riddle* (which won the Melbourne *Age* Book of the Year award in 1982). Her later books *My Father's Moon* (1989) and *Cabin Fever* (1990) and *The Georges' Wife* (1993) are a semi-autobiographical trilogy set in postwar England. She has also written a number of plays, mostly for radio. With her translator Françoise Cartano she won the inaugural 1993 France–Australia award for Literary Translation for her novel *The Sugar Mother* (1988, as *Tombe du Ciel*).

Jolliet or Joliet, Louis 1645–1700
French explorer
Born in Quebec, Canada, he studied at the Jesuit college there and served as an organist and music master before entering the fur trade in 1667. He first met Father **Jacques Marquette** at a Seneca village on the shore of Lake Ontario, and in 1673 the two men were commissioned to investigate Native American accounts of a great river called the Mississippi, which the French believed to empty into the Pacific. With five companions they travelled by canoe westward on the Fox and Wisconsin rivers and then down the Mississippi to the mouth of the Arkansas River. Determining from local Native Americans that the river probably emptied into the Gulf of Mexico, and fearing to encroach on Spanish territory, Jolliet and Marquette turned back, ascending the Illinois River and on to the site of present-day Chicago on Lake Michigan. Jolliet's journal and papers were lost when his canoe overturned on the St Lawrence River, but for his role in the expedition—the first European exploration of the Mississippi—he was rewarded with the island of Anticosti.

Jolson, Al, *originally* Asa Yoelson 1886–1950
US actor and singer
Born in Srednike, Lithuania, the son of a rabbi, he emigrated to the USA in 1893 and lived in Washington DC and New York City. He made his stage debut in *The Children of the Ghetto* (1899) and toured with circus and minstrel shows. His sentimental songs such as 'Mammy' (1909) and 'Sonny Boy' moved vaudeville audiences in the 1920s but he is best known as the star of the first talking picture *The Jazz Singer* (1927). His recorded voice featured in the commemorative films *The Jolson Story* (1946) and *Jolson Sings Again* (1949). 📖 Michael Friedland, *Jolson* (1972)

Joly, John 1857–1933
Irish geologist and physicist
Born in Offaly, King's County, he was educated at Trinity College, Dublin, where he was appointed assistant to the Professor of Engineering (1882). He invented several pieces of scientific apparatus, including the meldometer with which he produced artificial crystals, a hydrostatic balance for density determination, a steam calorimeter and in 1888 a photometer. He became Professor of Geology and Mineralogy in 1897. From 1899 he became involved in the debate about the age of the Earth, and his calculation of its age (as 80–90 million years) by measuring the sodium content of the sea (1899) was influential.

He was the first geologist to recognize the significance of radioactive atoms in maintaining the heat of the Sun and in directly moulding the history of the Earth (1903), and realized that pleochroic haloes in some minerals were the product of radioactivity and could be used for dating (1907–14). In 1914, at his suggestion, the Radium Institute was founded in Dublin; there Joly became involved in developing pioneering methods in radiotherapy, including the radium treatment of cancer using emanation-filled needles. He was also a pioneer of colour photography. His publications included *An Estimate of the Age of the Earth* (1899), *Radium and the Geological Age of the Earth* (1903), *Radioactivity and Geology* (1909) and *The Surface History of the Earth* (1924).

Jolyot de Crébillon, Claude Prosper See Crébillon, Claude Prosper Jolyot de

Jolyot de Crébillon, Prosper See Crébillon, Prosper Jolyot de

Jomini, (Antoine) Henri, Baron de 1779–1869
French general and strategist
He was born in Payerne, Switzerland. After commanding a Swiss battalion he attached himself to Marshall **Ney**, to whom he became Chief of Staff. He was created baron after the Peace of Tilsit (1807). He attracted **Napoleon I**'s notice by his *Traité des grandes opérations militaires* (5 vols, 1805, Eng trans *Treatise on Grand Military Operations*, 1865). He distinguished himself at Jena (1806), in the Spanish campaigns (1808) and during the retreat from Russia; but, offended at his treatment by Napoleon, he entered the Russian service (1813), and fought against Turkey (1828). He wrote a history of the wars of the Revolution (1806), a life of Napoleon (1827) and *Précis de l'art de guerre* (1838, Eng trans *Summary of the Art of War*, 1868).

Jonah 8th century BC
Hebrew prophet
From the Nazareth area, he probably knew the prophets **Elijah** and **Elisha**. He was sent to Nineveh, the capital of the powerful Assyrian Empire and the enemy of Israel, to urge the people to abandon their evil ways and injustices and ask God to forgive them. Reputedly delivered to the city by a large fish, he predicted the territorial expansion of **Jeroboam II**, King of Israel. He is later mentioned by **Jesus Christ** in his teaching.

Jonathan 11th century BC
Biblical character
The son and heir of **Saul** (the first King of Israel), he was a loyal friend of **David**. He was a cunning soldier (1 Samuel), but faced conflicting loyalties when he continued his friendship with David despite his father's mounting hostility. Jonathan was killed in the battle of Gilboa against the Philistines, and David succeeded Saul as King of Israel.

Jonathan, Chief (Joseph) Lebua 1914–
Lesotho chief and politician
Educated in mission schools before working in South African mines and then in local government in Basutoland, he entered politics in 1952. He joined the Basutoland National Council in 1956 and in 1959 founded the Basutoland National Party, which favoured a free enterprise economy and cordial relations with South Africa. He was elected to the Legco in 1960 and became Prime Minister in 1965 but he suspended the constitution in 1970. Parliamentary government was restored in 1973 and elections held regularly until 1985, when they were cancelled. He was overthrown in a military coup in 1986.

Jones, Allen 1937–
English painter, sculptor and printmaker

Born in Southampton, he studied at Hornsey Art School (1955–59), and at the Royal College of Art (1959–60). His first one-man show was held in London in 1962. An early Pop Artist, he won several prizes including the Paris Biennale (1963) and from c.1965 specialized in slick, fetishistic images (high-heeled shoes, stockings, etc) taken from pornographic or glossy fashion magazines. He was made a member of the Royal Academy in 1986.

Jones, Ann (Adrianne Shirley), *née* Jordan
c.1940–
English tennis player, table tennis player and broadcaster
Educated at King's Norton Grammar School in Birmingham, she was a finalist in the World Table Tennis championships (1954 and 1959), and won her first tennis title at the French Open in 1961. Seven times a semifinalist at Wimbledon, she won the Ladies Singles title in 1967. Since 1970 she has been a tennis commentator for the BBC, and director of Women's Tennis, Lawn Tennis Association, since 1990.

Jones, Bob (Robert Reynolds) 1883–1968
US evangelist
Born in Dale County, Alabama, he conducted revival meetings from the age of 13, and was licensed by the Methodist Church to preach at the age of 15. Educated at Southern University, Greensboro, South Carolina, he began full-time evangelistic work in 1902, and is estimated to have preached more than 12,000 'down-to-earth gospel messages'. In 1939 he left the Methodist Church, which he charged with theological liberalism, and broke also with other evangelists, notably **Billy Graham**, who displayed ecumenical tendencies. To further his brand of fundamentalism, in 1927 he founded Bob Jones University which from small beginnings in Florida was in 1947 established in Greenville, South Carolina, with several thousand students. The school is known for its biblical theology, its Puritanical code which is binding on its students, and tends towards right-wing politics. He once drew unwelcome attention to himself by a pamphlet entitled 'Is Segregation Scriptural?', to which he answered yes. His son, Bob Jones Jnr (b.1911), succeeded him as president of Bob Jones University.

Jones, Bobby (Robert Tyre) 1902–71
US amateur golfer
Born in Atlanta, Georgia, he studied law and was called to the Georgia Bar in 1928. He won the US Open four times (1923, 1926, 1929, 1930), the British Open three times (1926, 1927, 1930), the US Amateur championship five times and the British Amateur championship once. In 1930 he achieved the staggering feat of winning the Grand Slam of the US and British Open and Amateur championships in the same year. Thereafter, at the age of 28, he retired from competitive golf, regarded as one of the greatest golfers in the history of the game. He was responsible for the founding of the US Masters in Augusta.

Jones, Chuck (Charles) 1912–
US animated cartoon director
Born in Spokane, Washington, he became an animator in the early 1930s and later joined the cartoon department at Warner Brothers. His early work included *Daffy and the Dinosaur* (1939), the Inki series (*Inki and the Minah Bird*, 1943) and fast-paced duels between Wile E Coyote and the Road Runner (*Fast and Furry-ous*, 1949, etc). Pepe le Pew, the amorous skunk, won him his first Academy Award with *For Scentimental Reasons* (1951). His Bugs Bunny cartoons include the classic *What's Opera Doc* (1957) and the stereoscopic *Lumber Jack Rabbit* (1954). He won another Academy Award with *The Dot and the Line* (1965). For television he created many specials including **Rudyard Kipling**'s *Rikki-Tikki-Tavi* and *How the Grinch Stole Christmas*. He co-directed the live action/animated feature *The Phantom Tolbooth* (1969) and has contributed to feature films *Gremlins 2* (1990) and *Stay Tuned* (1992). He published an autobiography *Chuck Amuck* (1989) and in 1996 received a Special Academy Award for his contribution to the film industry.

Jones, Daniel 1881–1967
English phonetician
He was called to the Bar in 1907, when he was also appointed lecturer in phonetics at University College London (Professor 1921–49). He collaborated with others in compiling Cantonese (1912), Sechuana (1916) and Sinhalese (1919) phonetic readers. He wrote *Outline of English Phonetics* (1916), and compiled an *English Pronouncing Dictionary* (1917, 14th edn 1977). His other works included *The Phoneme* (1950), and *Cardinal Vowels* (1956). He was secretary (1928–49) and president (1950–67) of the International Phonetic Association.

Jones, David Michael 1895–1974
English poet and artist
He was born in Kent, England, but his Welsh father gave him a strong sense of identity with Wales. After art school he served in World War I, which gave him a lasting interest in martial matters. He became a Roman Catholic in 1921, and in 1922 he met **Eric Gill**, the beginning of a long association. His war experience is central to *In Parenthesis* (1937), the first of his two major literary works. *The Anathemata* (1952) draws heavily on his religious influences. He published a series of fragments of another large religious work as *The Sleeping Lord* (1974), but never finished it. He is less well known for his paintings, watercolours, drawings and inscriptions. He was noted for his book illustrations, such as those for the Golden Cockerel Press. ▭ K Raine, *David Jones, Solitary Perfectionist* (1974)

Jones, Ebenezer 1820–60
English poet
Born in Islington, London, he was brought up a strict Calvinist and, despite long hours as a clerk, completed *Studies of Sensation and Event* (1843), which was admired by **Robert Browning** and **Dante Gabriel Rossetti**. In his *Land Monopoly* (1849) he anticipated the economic theory of **Henry George** by 30 years. ▭ T Mardy Rees, *The Neglected Poet* (1909)

Jones, Eli Stanley 1884–1973
US missionary to India
Born in Baltimore, Maryland, he went to India as a missionary of the Methodist Episcopal Church in 1907, but later became an itinerant evangelist, declining a bishopric in 1928. Concerned equally for social justice and spirituality, he supported Indian aspirations for independence and was sensitive to Indian religious traditions, founding two Christian *ashrams*, one at Sat Tal and the other in Lucknow (where he also founded a psychiatric centre). He worked outside India for part of each year and wrote nearly 30 books, although none became better-known than *The Christ of the Indian Road* (1925). *Christ at the Round Table* (1928) and *Mahatma Gandhi: An Interpretation* (1948) were also significant in their day.

Jones, Ernest 1819–69
English poet and political leader
Born in Berlin, he was the son of the equerry to William, Duke of **Cumberland** and went to England in 1838. In 1841 he published his romance *The Wood Spirit*, was called to the Bar in 1844, and the next year became leader of the Chartist movement, issuing *The Labourer*, *Notes of the People* and *The People's Paper*. He rejected a legacy of nearly £2,000 per annum left to him on condition that he should abandon the Chartist cause. For his part in the Chartist proceedings at Manchester in 1848 he got two years' solitary confinement, and in prison composed an epic, *The*

Revolt of Hindostan. After his release he wrote *The Battleday* (1855), *The Painter of Florence* and *The Emperor's Vigil* (1856), and *Beldagon Church* and *Corayda* (1860). He made several unsuccessful efforts to enter parliament.

Jones, (Alfred) Ernest 1879–1958
Welsh psychoanalyst
Born in Llwchwr, Glamorgan, he studied at Cardiff University College and qualified as a physician in London. Medical journalism and neurological research brought him into contact with the work of **Sigmund Freud** and his new approach to neurosis. He learned German in order to study Freud's work more closely and in 1908 became his lifelong disciple and personal friend. He introduced psychoanalysis into Great Britain and North America, and in 1912 formed a committee of Freud's closest collaborators to uphold the Freudian theory. He founded the British Psycho-Analytical Society in 1913, and the *International Journal of Psycho-Analysis* in 1920, which he edited until 1933. He was Professor of Psychiatry at Toronto (1909–12) and director of the London Clinic for Psycho-Analysis. Among his numerous works and translations is a psychoanalytical study of *Hamlet and Oedipus* (1949). He also wrote authoritative biography of Freud (1953–57).

Jones, Freddie (Frederick Charles) 1927–
English actor
Born in Stoke-on-Trent, he gave up work as a laboratory assistant after winning a scholarship to train at the Rose Bruford College of Speech and Drama. In films, he played the Monster in *Frankenstein Must Be Destroyed* (1969), Professor Keeley in *The Satanic Rites of Dracula* (1973), Cranford in *All Creatures Great and Small* (1974) and Bytes in *The Elephant Man* (1980). On television, he won acclaim for his performance as Claudius in *The Caesars* (1968) and has since acted Sir George Uproar in *The Ghosts of Motley Hall* (1976–78), Dr Emlyn Isaacs in *District Nurse* (1987) and Tobias in *Mr Wroe's Virgins* (1993), as well as guest-starring in dozens of series.

Jones, George (Glenn) 1931–
US country music singer
Born in Saratoga, Texas, he began by imitating early idols like Roy Acuff and **Hank Williams**, but soon developed his own characteristic voice, one which eventually saw him recognized as the greatest of the 'honky tonk' style country singers. His career was interrupted at periods by well-publicized problems with alcohol, which also led to some unevenness in his recorded output, but much of his work has deservedly attained classic status. He married his third wife, **Tammy Wynette**, in 1969, and they recorded several hit duets, even after their divorce in 1975, and reunited to make *One* in 1995. A fourth marriage in 1983 brought some stability to his life and habits, and he later settled into an uncharacteristic elder-statesman role as the greatest surviving exponent of his hard-core style of country singing. 📖 B Allen, *The Life and Times of a Honky Tonk Legend* (1994)

Jones, Gwyn 1907–
Welsh scholar and writer
Born in Blackwood, Gwent, and educated at Tredegar Grammar School and the University of Wales, he was a schoolmaster and lecturer before becoming Professor of English Language and Literature at the University College of Wales, Aberystwyth (1940–64) and at University College, Cardiff (1965–75), where he became a Fellow in 1980. His works on Norse history and literature include *The Norse Atlantic Saga* (1964) and *A History of the Vikings* (1968), and various translations including *The Vatsndalers' Saga* (1942) and *Egil's Saga* (1960). His Welsh studies include a translation of the *Mabinogion* (1948), *Welsh Legends and Folk-Tales* (1955), and editing *Welsh Short Stories*

(1956) and *The Oxford Book of Welsh Verse in English* (1977). He has also published several novels and collections of short stories.

Jones, Dame Gwyneth 1936–
Welsh soprano
Born in Pontnewynydd, Gwent, she studied at the Royal College of Music, and made her Covent Garden debut in London in 1963. She first sang at the Vienna State Opera in 1966, and then performed at Bayreuth, Munich and Milan, amongst other great houses. She is a distinguished interpreter of the heroines of **Wagner** and **Strauss** operas. She became a DBE in 1986 and a Commandeur, L'Ordre des Arts et des Lettres, in 1992.

Jones, Sir Harold Spencer 1890–1960
English astronomer
Born in Kensington, London, he won a scholarship from Latymer Upper School to Jesus College, Cambridge (1908), where he obtained first-class honours degrees in mathematics (1911) and physics (1912) and was awarded the Isaac Newton studentship (1912) and second Smith prize (1913). He was chief assistant at the Royal Observatory, Greenwich (1913–23), and HM Astronomer at the Royal Observatory at the Cape of Good Hope (1923–33), before he returned to Greenwich as the tenth Astronomer Royal (1933–55). At the Cape he organized an international project to improve the value of the Earth–Sun distance utilizing the close approach of the asteroid Eros, and co-ordinated the reductions, which took 10 years. He was awarded the gold medal of the Royal Astronomical Society for this work in 1943. At Greenwich, following his analysis of the motions of the Sun, Moon and planets, he discovered long-term and irregular variations in the rate of the Earth's rotation (1939). This led to the concept of ephemeris time (1950), an independent system of measuring time which was adopted in the universal system of units in 1956. In 1948 he initiated the removal of the Royal Observatory from Greenwich to a country site at Herstmonceux, Sussex. The move was completed in 1958, but the Royal Greenwich Observatory was again moved in 1989 and is now in Cambridge. He was elected FRS in 1930, and knighted in 1943.

Jones, Henry, pseudonym Cavendish 1831–99
English physician and writer
He was born in London. The author of manuals on several games, he is mainly remembered for his codification of the rules of whist (1862). His pseudonym derives from the name of the first whist club he went to in London.

Jones, Henry Arthur 1851–1929
English dramatist
Born in Grandborough, Buckinghamshire, he was in business until 1878, when *Only Round the Corner* was produced at Exeter. His first major success was a melodrama, *The Silver King* (1882). This was followed by a series of social comedies, including *Saints and Sinners* (1884), *Rebellious Susan* (1894), *The Philistines* (1895), *Mrs Dane's Defence* (1900) and *Mary Goes First* (1913), many of which deal with serious social issues. He was a highly popular writer in his day and together with **Arthur Wing Pinero** founded the 'realist problem' drama in Great Britain. 📖 R A Cordell, *Jones and the Modern Drama* (1932)

Jones, Sir Henry Stuart 1867–1939
English classical scholar
Born in Hunslet, Leeds, he studied at Balliol College, Oxford, and in Greece and Italy, and became Camden Professor of Ancient History at Oxford and Principal of University College, Aberystwyth, in 1927. He contributed to archaeological studies and ancient history, edited

Thucydides (1898–1900) and edited the Greek lexicon of Robert Scott (1811–87) and **Henry Liddell** (9th edn 1925–40).

Jones, Inigo 1573–1652
English architect and stage designer

Born in London, he studied landscape painting in Italy, where he became a lifelong admirer of **Andrea Palladio**, and from Venice introduced the Palladian style into England. In Denmark, he is said to have designed the palaces of Rosenborg and Frederiksborg. In 1606 **James I of England** employed him in arranging the masques of **Ben Jonson**. He introduced the proscenium arch and movable scenery to the English stage. From 1613 to 1614 he revisited Italy and on his return in 1615 was appointed Surveyor-General of the royal buildings. In 1616 he designed the Queen's House at Greenwich, completed in the 1630s. Other commissions included the rebuilding of the Banqueting House at Whitehall (1619–22), the nave and transepts and a large Corinthian portico of old St Paul's, Marlborough Chapel, the Double Cube room at Wilton (1649–52), and possibly the York Water Gate. He laid out Covent Garden and Lincoln's Inn Fields. He is regarded as the founder of classical English architecture. 📖 J M Summerson, *Inigo Jones* (1964)

Jones, James 1921–77
US novelist

He was born in Robinson, Illinois, and educated at the University of Hawaii. He served in the US army as a sergeant (1939–44), boxed as a welterweight in Golden Gloves tournaments, and was awarded a Purple Heart. His wartime experience in Hawaii led to *From Here to Eternity* (1951), a classic novel dealing with the period before Pearl Harbor, for which he received a National Book award. Later work was disappointing, with the exception of the sequel *The Thin Red Line* (1962). 📖 F McShane, *Into Eternity—James Jones: the life of an American writer* (1985)

Jones, James Earl 1931–
US actor

Born in Arkabutla, Mississippi, he was raised by his grandparents on a farm in Michigan, and overcame a severe stammer to study acting at the University of Michigan and later with **Lee Strasberg** in New York. He made his Broadway debut in *Sunrise at Campobello* (1958) and won a Tony award for his performance as the black boxer Jack Jefferson in *The Great White Hope* (1968). He acted with the New York Shakespeare Festival in roles such as Othello and Caliban, starred in new plays by **Athol Fugard**, including *Boesman and Lena* (1970) and *A Lesson from Aloes* (1980) and appeared in **August Wilson's** *Fences* (1985). Noted for his resonant bass voice and commanding physical presence, he has starred in numerous films and provided the voice of the villain Darth Vader in *Star Wars* (1977) and its sequels.

Jones, John Paul, *originally* John Paul 1747–92
American naval officer

Born in Kirkbean, Kirkcudbrightshire, Scotland, he was apprenticed as a sailor boy, made several voyages to America, and in 1773 he inherited a property in Fredericksburg, Virginia. At about the same date he assumed the name Jones. At the outbreak of the American Revolution in 1775 he joined the navy. In 1778 in the *Ranger* he made a daring descent on the Solway Firth, Scotland. As commodore of a small French squadron displaying American colours, he threatened Leith (1779) and won an engagement on the *Bon Homme Richard* against the British Frigate *Serapis*. In 1788 he entered the Russian service and, as rear admiral of the Black Sea fleet, fought in the Russo-Turkish war of 1788–89. 📖 S E Morison, *John Paul Jones, a Sailor's Biography* (1959)

Jones, Lois Mailou 1905–
US painter

Born in Boston, she won a scholarship to the School of the Museum of Fine Arts in 1923, then worked as a textile designer and took advanced courses at Harvard, Howard and Columbia universities. She travelled to Paris to study at the Académie Julian, and on her return had work exhibited in the Vose Gallery in Boston. She began to paint works like *Mob Victim* (1944), dealing explicitly with her own background as a black American. Inspired by several trips to Africa, her later work became more abstract, as in *Moon Masque* and *Magic of Nigeria*, which combine the stylized forms of African art with her powerful flat design shapes. Regarded as the first black female painter of great importance, she was Professor of Art at Howard University in Washington DC for 45 years and a Fellow of the Royal Society of Arts in London.

Jones, Mary Harris, *known as* Mother Jones, *née* Harris 1830–1930
US labour agitator

Born in County Cork, Ireland, she migrated to the USA via Canada, and lost her family to an epidemic in 1867, and her home to the Chicago fire of 1871. Thereafter, she devoted herself to the cause of labour, travelled to areas of labour strife, especially in the coal industry, and was imprisoned in West Virginia on a charge of conspiracy to murder in 1912, aged 82. Freed by a new governor, she returned to labour agitation, which she continued almost until her death. She wrote *The Autobiography of Mother Jones* (1925).

Jones, Owen 1809–74
Welsh architect and designer

He was born in London, the son of the antiquary Owen Jones (1741–1814). He was superintendent of works for the Great Exhibition of 1851 in London, and director of decoration for the Crystal Palace when it was re-erected at Sydenham. He also designed St James's Hall in London. He wrote a monumental *Grammar of Ornament* (1856), magnificently illustrated with decorative patterns and motifs from many cultures and periods.

Jones, Thomas 1870–1955
Welsh administrator and writer

Born in Rhymney, Monmouthshire, he became an academic economist at Glasgow and Belfast. He was special investigator for the Royal Commission on the Poor Law (1903–09), assistant (later deputy) Secretary of the Cabinet from (1916–30), and played an important role in the negotiation of the Irish Treaty (1922) and the General Strike (1926). Appointed by **Lloyd George**, he served under four Prime Ministers. In 1930 he was appointed first secretary of the Pilgrim Trust, from which he promoted the Council for the Encouragement of Music and Arts (CEMA) in 1939 which became the Arts Council of Great Britain. In 1927 he founded the only adult residential college in Wales, Coleg Harlech. He was chairman of Gregynog Press (fine printed books), and wrote an account of his work as a civil servant in *Whitehall Diaries* (1969).

Jones, Sir William 1746–94
English jurist and Orientalist

Born in London and educated at Harrow and University College, Oxford, he was called to the Bar in 1774 and in 1776 became Commissioner of Bankrupts. He published a *Persian Grammar* (1772), Latin commentaries on Asiatic poetry (1774), and a translation of seven ancient Arabic poems (1780). From 1783 until his death he was judge in the Supreme Court of Judicature in Bengal. He devoted himself to Sanskrit, and in 1787 was the first to point out its striking resemblance to Latin and Greek, thus becoming a pioneer of comparative philology. In 1784 he established the Asiatic Society of Bengal, and was its first president. He completed a translation of *Sakuntala* (1789), the *Hitopadesa*, parts of the Vedas, and Manu, and wrote some important legal works. 📖 Garland Cannon, *Oriental Jones: A Biography* (1964)

Jongen, Joseph 1873–1953
Belgian composer

Born in Liège, he won the Belgian Prix de Rome and was a professor at the Liège Conservatory until the outbreak of World War I, when he went to England. Director of the Brussels Conservatory from 1920 to 1939, he composed piano, violin and organ works, the symphonic poem *Lalla Roukh*, an opera and a ballet.

Jonson, Ben (jamin) 1572–1637
English dramatist

He was born in Westminster, London, probably of Border descent, and educated at Westminster School under **William Camden**. After working for a while with his stepfather, a bricklayer, he volunteered for military service in Flanders before joining **Philip Henslowe**'s company of players. He killed a fellow player in a duel, became a Catholic in prison, but later returned to Anglicanism. His *Every Man in his Humour*, with **Shakespeare** in the cast, was performed at the Curtain in 1598 to be followed not so successfully by *Every Man Out of His Humour* in 1599. The equally unpopular *Cynthia's Revels* (1600), largely allegorical, was succeeded by *The Poetaster* (1600–01) which was helped by a personal attack on **Thomas Dekker** and **John Marston**. He then tried Roman tragedy, but his *Sejanus* (1603) and his later venture, *Catiline* (1611), are so padded with classical references as to be merely closet plays and poor imitations of Roman tragedy. His larger intent of discarding romantic comedy and writing realistically (though his theory of 'humours' was hardly comparable with genuine realism) helped to produce his four masterpieces—*Volpone* (1606), *The Silent Woman* (1609), *The Alchemist* (1610) and *Bartholomew Fair* (1614). *Volpone* is an unpleasant satire on senile sensuality and greedy legacy hunters. *The Silent Woman* is farcical comedy involving a heartless hoax. **John Dryden** praised it for its construction, but *The Alchemist* is better with its single plot and strict adherence to the unities. *Bartholomew Fair* is livelier, salted by his anti-Puritan prejudices, though the plot is lost in the motley of eccentrics. After the much poorer *The Devil is an Ass* (1616), Jonson turned again to the masque (he had already collaborated with **Inigo Jones** in *The Masque of Blacknesse* in 1605)—and produced a number of those glittering displays down to 1625 when **James I**'s death terminated his period of court favour. His renewed attempt to attract theatre audiences left him in the angry mood of the ode 'Come leave the loathed stage' (1632). Only his unfinished pastoral play *The Sad Shepherd* survives of his declining years. He attracted and influenced the learned and courtly, to several of whom his superb verse letters are addressed. His lyric genius was second only to Shakespeare's. His *Timber; or Discoveries*, printed in the folio of 1640, proves him also a considerable critic. He is buried in Westminster Abbey, London, with the words 'O Rare Ben Jonson' inscribed on his tombstone. 📖 D Riggs, *Ben Jonson, a life* (1989)

Jonsson, Ásgrímur 1876–1958
Icelandic landscape painter

Born on the farm of Rútsstaða-Suðurkot, he was the first artist to portray the Icelandic landscape in all its vivid variety and ethereal colour. In 1907 he was given a generous state grant to travel and study abroad, where he came into contact with the Impressionists. Back home in Iceland he travelled all over the country, seeking fresh landscapes and subject matter to paint. He also turned to watercolours and to interpreting Icelandic folk-tales. He

bequeathed his home in Reykjavík and his private collection of 500 of his own paintings to the nation, as an art gallery.

Jónsson, Bólu-Hjálmar 1796–1875
Icelandic folk-poet

Born in Eyjafjörður, he lived on a peasant croft and struggled with poverty all his life, making a meagre living from woodcarving. He was an eloquent and natural poet. His verses, whether railing against the Church and authority or revelling in poetic imagery, were recited throughout the country, but were only collected and published after he died. 📖 Gislason, in *Lögrétta 27* (1932)

Jónsson, Einar 1874–1954
Icelandic sculptor

Born on the farm of Galtafell, he went to Copenhagen to study art, and after exhibiting his powerful realistic work *Outlaws* (1901, now in Reykjavík), was given a grant by the Icelandic government to study in Rome. In 1903 he received the Grand Grant of the Copenhagen Academy, and after extensive travel he settled in Copenhagen in 1905. However, in 1909 he offered all his works to the Icelandic nation on condition that they were housed properly. The offer was accepted, and in 1914 he returned to Iceland, hailed as its national sculptor. He spent two years in the USA making a statue of the first European settler in North America, Thorfinn Karlsefni, for a new sculpture park in Philadelphia. Thereafter he lived in increasing isolation in Reykjavík, producing works replete with allegory and symbolism, like *Evolution* and *New Life*. The temple-like studio home built for him by the state in Reykjavík is now the Einar Jónsson Museum.

Jónsson, Finnur 1858–1934
Icelandic scholar and philologist

Born in Akureyri and educated in Reykjavík and at Copenhagen, he was appointed Professor of Old Icelandic studies there in 1898. He published a number of critical editions of sagas and histories, including *Hauksbók (1892–96)*, *Heimskringla* (4 vols, 1893–1901), and *Egils saga* (1886–88). He also compiled a monumental history of Old Norse literature (*Den oldnorske og oldislenske litteraturs historie*, 1894–1902), and a pioneering edition of all known Old Icelandic skaldic poetry, *Den norsk-islandske skjaldedigtning*, 4 vols, 1908–15).

Jónsson, Finnur 1892–1989
Icelandic Modernist painter

Born in Strýta, he worked first as a seaman, then as an apprentice goldsmith, and went to study in Copenhagen (1921), where he discovered a vocation for painting. He went to Berlin, where he joined the Modernist group at Der Sturm Gallery, and Dresden, where he was much influenced by **Oskar Kokoschka**. Back in Iceland, he held the first-ever exhibition of Abstract art in Reykjavík in 1925, causing something of a scandal, and thereafter worked in more traditional styles, painting landscapes and scenes from fishing life. His later paintings showed a return towards abstraction. He was the younger brother of the sculptor Ríkarður Jónsson (1888–1977).

Jooss, Kurt 1901–79
German dancer, choreographer, teacher and director

Born in Wasseralfingen, he was a student at the Stuttgart Academy of Music, and became the star pupil of the theoretician **Rudolf von Laban**. While working as a ballet master in Münster, he co-founded the Neue Tanzbühne (New Dance Stage) for which he choreographed his first works. In 1927 he was appointed director of the dance department at the Essen Folkwang School where he founded the Folkwang Tanztheatre in 1928 which finally became the Folkwang Tanzbühne. *Le Bal* (1930), *The Prodigal Son* (1931), *Pulcinella* (1932), and two of his most memorable works, *The Green Table* (1932) and *The Big City*

(1932), were made during this productive period. He left Germany during the Nazi years and toured the world, basing his company in Great Britain. He returned to Essen in 1949, and was ballet master of Düsseldorf Opera from 1954 to 1956. He was one of the first choreographers to blend classical technique with modern theatrical ideas to create dance for 'the common man'.

Joplin, Janis 1943–70
US rhythm and blues singer

Born in Port Arthur, Texas, she was a rebellious teenager. She developed a powerful blues voice and sang in clubs in the mid-1960s in Houston, before joining Big Brother and the Holding Company in San Francisco, with whom she recorded two albums (1967–68). She became a national star after a sensational appearance at the epochal Monterey Pop Festival in 1967. She formed the Kozmic Blues Band (1969), and then the Full Tilt Boogie Band, with whom she recorded the unfinished *Pearl* (released 1971), which included the earlier 'Ball and Chain' and 'Piece of My Heart' in addition to her famous version of Kris Kristofferson's 'Me and Bobby McGee'. Always given to excess, she died of an apparently accidental drugs overdose. ⨆ E Amburn, *Pearl* (1993)

Joplin, Scott 1868–1917
US pianist and composer

One of the originators of 'ragtime' music and one of its foremost exponents, he was born in Texas and largely self-taught. He became a professional musician in his teens, but later studied music at George Smith College, Sedalia. In the 1890s he formed and led a travelling vocal ensemble, and began to compose. His first major published work—the 'Maple Leaf Rag', named after a club in which he had played—proved to be the turning point in his career, and the resulting prosperity enabled him to concentrate on composing and teaching rather than playing. Although he was responsible for several famous and popular tunes, he was disheartened by the lack of commercial success of his two operas. When ragtime experienced a revival in the 1970s, due in part to the film *The Sting* (1973), his music became more widely known. ⨆ J Haskins and K Benson, *Scott Joplin* (1978)

Jordaens, Jacob 1593–1678
Flemish painter

Born in Antwerp, he became a member of an Antwerp guild in 1616 and from 1630 came under the influence of Rubens, who obtained for him the patronage of the kings of Spain and Sweden. His early paintings such as the *Four Evangelists* (1632) show him to be deficient in the handling of chiaroscuro effects and colour generally, but he improved greatly in such later canvases as *The Triumph of Frederick Henry* (1652), although he never achieved the delicacy of Rubens. He also designed tapestries and painted portraits.

Jordan, Barbara C(harline) 1936–96
US politician, lawyer, and educator

Born in Houston, Texas, she was educated at Texas Southern and Boston universities, becoming the first black student at Boston University Law School. Admitted to the Bars of Massachusetts and Texas in 1959, she later served in the Texas Senate (1966–72) as the only woman and the only black person, and in the US Congress (1972–78). She impressed the nation with her eloquence during the Watergate impeachment hearings concerning President Richard M Nixon in 1974. At the University of Texas, she was a Lyndon Johnson public services professor (1979–82), then was appointed to the Lyndon Johnson Centennial Chair in National Policy. She became a member of the House Judiciary Committee and in 1991 was appointed special counsel on ethics by the Governor of Texas. She received numerous awards and honours, including induction into the Texas Women's Hall of Fame (1984), the National Women's Hall of Fame (1990) and the African-American Hall of Fame (1993). Her autobiography, *Barbara Jordan: A Self-Portrait*, was published in 1979.

Jordan, (Marie-Ennemond) Camille 1838–1922
French mathematician

Born in Lyons, he was professor at the École Polytechnique and at the Collège de France, and as the leading group theorist of his day did much to establish the central ideas in the subject. His *Traité de substitutions* (1870, 'Treatise on Substitutions') remained a standard work for many years. He applied group theory to geometry and linear differential equations, and in the 1890s his *Cours d'analyse* was an influential textbook for the French school of analysts.

Jordan, Dorothy or Dorothea, *née* Bland 1762–1816
Irish actress

She was born near Waterford, Ireland, and made her debut in Dublin (1777). She soon became popular, and was engaged by Tate Wilkinson at Leeds in England (1782). Moving to London, she appeared with great success at Drury Lane in *The Country Girl* in 1785 and was well known for playing mainly comic tomboy roles for nearly 30 years. From 1790 to 1811 she had a liaison with the Duke of Clarence (the future William IV), by whom she had 10 of her 15 children. After playing in London and in the provinces until 1814, she is said to have been forced to retire to France for a debt of £2,000. In 1831 King William made their eldest son Earl of Munster. ⨆ Clare Tomalin, *Mrs Jordan's Profession: The Story of a Great Actress and a Future King* (1994)

Jordan, Michael Jeffrey 1963–
US basketball player

Born in Brooklyn, New York City, he began his career in college basketball at the University of North Carolina, then joined the Chicago Bulls (1984–93, 1995–). Perhaps the finest all-round player in the history of the game, he set numerous records, including most consecutive seasons leading the league in scoring (from the 1986–87 season through the 1992–93 season). He was a member of the US Olympic gold medal-winning basketball teams in 1984 and 1992. A member of the NBA All-Star team (1985–93, 1996), he was named the NBA Most Valuable Player (MVP) in 1988, 1991, 1992 and 1996. He retired in 1993, but after a quixotic effort to play minor-league baseball for the Birmingham Barons, he rejoined the Bulls in the 1994–95 season and led them to a 1996 NBA championship in a reprise of their 1991–93 wins. With an average of 32.2 points per game, he holds the NBA highest career scoring average.

Jordan, Neil 1950–
Irish filmmaker and writer

Born in Sligo, Ireland, he studied history and literature at University College, Dublin, and worked at various jobs in London before returning to Ireland and helping to form the Irish Writers Co-operative (1974). His first collection of stories, *Night in Tunisia* (1976), earned the Guardian Fiction prize and was followed by the acclaimed novels *The Past* (1980) and *The Dreams of the Beast* (1983). Interested in exploring cinema as a visual means of story-telling, he was given the opportunity to work as a script consultant on *Excalibur* (1981). He made his directorial debut with the thriller *Angel* (1982) and has boldly emphasized the fairy-tale and fantasy elements of such challenging works as *The Company of Wolves* (1984) and *Mona Lisa* (1986). Recently, he has turned his hand to comedy with *High Spirits* (1988) and *We're No Angels* (1989), but returned to serious drama with *The Crying Game* (1992), winning an

Academy Award for Best Original Screenplay. His subsequent films include *Interview with the Vampire* (1994), *Michael Collins* (1996) and *The Butcher Boy* (1997).

Jordan, (Ernst) Pascual 1902–
German theoretical physicist

Born in Hanover, he was educated there and in Göttingen before obtaining a post at the University of Rostock. He was subsequently appointed Professor of Physics at the universities of Berlin (1944–52) and Hamburg (1951–70). He worked with Max Born and Werner Heisenberg, and helped to formulate the theory of quantum mechanics in the matrix representation, showing how light could be interpreted as being composed of discrete quanta of energy. He also contributed to the theories which laid the foundations for the relativistic quantum field theory of electromagnetism, which are now known as quantum electrodynamics.

Jordan, Vernon Eulion, Jnr 1935–
US lawyer and civil rights activist

Born in Atlanta, Georgia, he became an attorney influential in the civil rights movements of the 1960s, working for voter registration in Georgia with the National Association for the Advancement of Colored People. He also served as executive director of the United Negro College Fund (1970–72) and president of the National Urban League (1972–81). Shot by an unknown assailant in 1980, he recovered and returned to practising law the next year, but he maintains his political involvement. He is an advisor to President Bill Clinton, and in 1992 he served as head (with Warren Christopher) of Clinton's post-election transition team.

Jordanus de Nemore fl.c.1220
Medieval French or German physicist

Almost nothing is known of his life, except that he lived and wrote in the first half of the 13th century. Some 12 books in Latin allegedly written by him were recorded by 1260, dealing with'the science of weights', ie statics. Here he invented the idea of component forces, studied inclined planes, made the principle of mechanical work less vague, and moved towards the concept of static moment. His approach linked Aristotle's ideas in physics with the more exact mathematical approach of Archimedes. His ideas in mechanics must have influenced Galileo, and he also wrote (or at least has ascribed to him) treatises on geometry, algebra and arithmetic.

Jörgensen, Johannes 1866–1956
Danish novelist and poet

Born in Svendborg, he lived most of his life in Italy, in Assisi, where he became a Roman Catholic (1896), but he returned to his birthplace shortly before his death. He published several volumes of poetry, as well as biographies of saints Francis of Assisi (1907), Catherine of Siena (1915), and Birgitta of Sweden (1941–43), and an autobiography, *Mit livs Legende* (1916–28, 'Legend of my Life'). 💷 W G Jones, *Johannes Jörgensen* (1969)

Jörmunrekkr See Ermanaric

Jorn, Asger Oluf, *original surname* Jørgensen 1914–73
Danish painter

Born in Vejrum, West Jutland, he studied art in Paris from 1936 with Fernand Léger and Le Corbusier, and in 1948–50 founded the 'Cobra' group (Co[penhagen], Br[ussels], A[msterdam]), which aimed to exploit fantastic imagery derived from the unconscious.

Joseph, St 1st century BC–1st century AD
Biblical character

He was a carpenter in Nazareth, and the husband of the Virgin Mary. He last appears in the Gospel history when Jesus is 12 years old. He is never mentioned during Jesus's ministry, and must be assumed to have already died. His feast day is 19 March.

Joseph
Old Testament character

He was the 11th son of Jacob, and the first by his wife Rachel. He is depicted as Jacob's favourite son (marked by the gift of a multicoloured coat), but was sold into slavery by his jealous brothers. The stories (Genesis 37–50) show him using his wisdom and God's help to rise to high office in Pharaoh's court, and he was reconciled with his brothers when they arrived in Egypt seeking food during a famine. His sons, Ephraim and Manasseh, were blessed by Jacob, and became ancestors of two of the tribes of Israel.

Joseph I 1678–1711
Holy Roman Emperor

Born in Vienna, he was the eldest son of Leopold I and became emperor in 1705. Musically talented and worldly, he helped reorganize Austrian finances. He defeated the Hungarian rebels under Francis II Rákóczi (1711), while Prince Eugène of Savoy led the Imperial army in alliance with the British forces under the Duke of Marlborough in the continuing struggle against Louis XIV of France.

Joseph II 1741–90
Holy Roman Emperor

Born in Vienna, the son of Francis I and Maria Theresa, he was elected King of the Romans in 1764, and after his father's death (1765) Holy Roman Emperor. Until his mother's death (1780) his power was limited to the army and foreign affairs. Although he failed to add Bavaria to the Austrian dominions, he acquired Galicia, Lodomeria and Zips, at the first partition of Poland (1772), and he appropriated a great part of Passau and Salzburg (1780). He declared himself independent of the pope, and prohibited the publication of any new papal Bulls without his permission. He suppressed 700 monasteries, displacing 36,000 monks, prohibited papal dispensations on marriage, and published an Edict of Toleration for Protestants and Greeks in 1781. He also abolished serfdom, freed the press and the theatre, emancipated the Jews, reorganized taxation, and curtailed the feudal privileges of the nobles. In 1788 he engaged in an unsuccessful war with Turkey, and in the same year there were outbreaks of insurrection within his non-German territories, Hungary and the Austrian Netherlands. Although intellectually gifted and well read, he was unworldly, short-tempered and autocratic, and naïve in his idea of a monarch's capacity for wholesale change. 💷 Saul K Padover, *The Revolutionary Emperor: Joseph the Second 1741–1790* (1934)

Joseph of Arimathea, St 1st century AD
New Testament councillor

Born in Arimathea, Samaria, he was a wealthy Samaritan who went to Pontius Pilate and asked for the body of Jesus Christ after the Crucifixion, and buried it in his own tomb. According to later Christian literature he visited England after the Crucifixion, with the Holy Grail, and built a church at Glastonbury. His feast day is 17 March (Western Churches) or 31 July (Eastern Churches).

Joseph, Chief, *originally* Hinmatonyalatkit ('thunder coming up over the land from the water') c.1840–1904
Nez Percé chief

Born in Wallowa Valley, Oregon, the ancestral territory of the Nez Percé, he was the son of a chief who had converted to Christianity. In the early 1860s gold was discovered on Nez Percé lands, and the US government attempted to renegotiate earlier treaties to deprive Joseph's people of their homeland. In 1871, on the death of his father, Joseph became one of the leaders of a Nez Percé band that refused to accept the new treaty. He counselled peace, but when his braves killed several white settlers, US troops were sent to capture the band (1877). After a series of battles and skirmishes the Nez Percé were forced to retreat. Joseph led about 750 of his people on a 1,500-mile journey across four states, fighting off pursuing US troops who greatly outnumbered them and twice crossing the Rockies. He nearly completed his plan of leading them into safety in Canada, but when they stopped to rest 30 miles from the border, they were surrounded by fresh troops under General Nelson A Miles. Joseph's dignified speech of surrender ('I will fight no more forever') is famous. He and his people were sent to Indian Territory (Oklahoma), and he died in the Colville Indian Reservation, Washington.

Joseph, Keith (Sinjohn) Joseph, Baron
1918–94
English Conservative politician

Born in London and educated at Oxford, he was called to the Bar (1946) before becoming a Conservative MP in 1956. A former Secretary of State for Social Services (1970–74) and Industry (1979–81), he held the education and science portfolio from 1981 to 1986. He was given an overall responsibility for Conservative policy and research in 1975 and was a close political adviser to Margaret Thatcher with whom he founded the Centre for Policy Studies. He succeeded to the baronetcy in 1943, and was made a life peer in 1987 when he retired from active-politics.

Joseph, Père, *also called* Eminence Grise ('Grey Eminence'), *originally* François Joseph le Clerc du Tremblay 1577–1638
French diplomat and mystic

Born in Paris, he became a Capuchin in 1599, and secretary to Cardinal Richelieu in 1611. His byname derives from his contact with Richelieu (the 'Eminence Rouge'), for whom he became adviser and agent, undertaking many diplomatic missions, notably during the Thirty Years War.

Joséphine de Beauharnais See Beauharnais, Joséphine de

Josephson, Brian David 1940–
Welsh physicist and Nobel Prize winner

Born in Cardiff, he studied at Cambridge, where he received his PhD in 1964, and has spent his career there, as Professor of Physics from 1974. In 1962, while a research student, he deduced theoretically the possibility of the 'Josephson effect' on electric currents in superconductors separated by a very thin insulator. He demonstrated that a current can flow between the superconductors with no applied voltage, and that an applied DC voltage produces an AC current of a proportional frequency. The effect was soon observed experimentally by Philip W Anderson, and Josephson junctions have since been much used in research, in fast switches for computers and in SQUIDs (superconducting quantum interference devices) used in geophysical measurements. The AC Josephson effect has been used to determine the constant e/h and led to a quantum standard of voltage. Josephson shared the 1973 Nobel Prize for physics with Leo Esaki and Ivar Giaever. He has an interest in the physics and theory of intelligence, and co-edited *Consciousness and the Physical World* in 1980.

Josephus, Flavius, *originally* Joseph ben Matthias
AD37–c.100
Jewish historian and general

Governor of Galilee, he took part in the Jewish revolt against the Romans (AD66) and, under the patronage of Vespasian and then Titus, he went to Rome after the fall of Jerusalem. His works (in Greek) include *History of the Jewish War*, *Antiquities of the Jews*, a history of the Jews to AD66, and *Against Apion*.

Joshua, *Hebrew* Yehoshua
Biblical character

The son of Nun, of the tribe of Ephraim, he was successor to Moses as leader of the Israelites. He was one of the 12 spies sent to collect information about the Canaanites, and during the 40 years' wanderings acted as minister or personal attendant of Moses. After 'the Lord was angry with Moses' Joshua, a charismatic warrior, was expressly designated to lead the people into Canaan. *The Book of Joshua* is a narrative of the conquest and settlement of Canaan under his leadership. 📖 Albert McShane, *Joshua: Possessing the Land* (1994)

Josiah 649–609BC
King of Judah

He succeeded his father Amon (641BC) at the age of eight. He re-established the worship of Jehovah, and instituted the rites in the newly discovered Book of the Law. He is credited with destroying pagan cults and attempting to centralize worship in Jerusalem and the Temple. He died in battle against the Egyptians at Megiddo.

Jósika, Miklós, Baron von 1794–1865
Hungarian novelist

He was involved in the revolution of 1848, and had to live in exile in Brussels and Dresden. His best-known novel is his first, *Abafi* (1836). He introduced the historical novel into Hungarian literature, and is sometimes referred to as the Hungarian Sir Walter Scott, from his adherence to the romantic tradition of that writer. 📖 F Szinnyei, *Jósika Miklós* (1915)

Josquin des Prez or Desprez c.1440–1521
Franco-Flemish composer

Born probably in Condé, he may have been a pupil of Johannes Okeghem. Composer to the Sforza family in Milan and Rome, Louis XII of France and the Duke of Ferrara, he was an expert in polyphony, and left several valuable masses, motets and secular vocal works. Charles Burney called him the 'father of modern harmony'.

Joubert, Joseph 1754–1824
French writer and moralist

Born in Montignac, Périgord, he studied and taught at the college of Toulouse, then went to Paris, where he lived through all the fever of the Revolution. In 1809 he was nominated by Napoleon I to the council of the new university. His friend René de Chateaubriand edited a small volume from his papers, and Joubert found fame with his *Pensées* (1838, 'Thoughts'), which are in the best French tradition of La Rochefoucauld, Pascal, La Bruyère and Vauvenargues. 📖 I Babbitt, *Masters of Modern French Criticism* (1912)

Joubert, Piet (Petrus Jacobus) 1834–1900
Afrikaner soldier and politician

Born in Cango, Cape Colony, he was a farmer in the Transvaal from 1840, and was elected to parliament in 1860, becoming Attorney-General in 1870 and acting President in 1875. In the First Boer War (1880–81) he commanded the Transvaal's forces, and defeated Colley in 1881. He negotiated the Pretoria Convention (1881), became Vice-President in 1883, and opposed Paul Kruger for the presidency. In the Second Boer War (1899–1902) he held command at the outset, but resigned from ill health and died soon afterwards.

Joule, James Prescott 1818–89
English natural philosopher
Born in Salford, Greater Manchester, he was educated by private tutors, notably the chemist **John Dalton**, and became famous for his experiments on heat. The 'Joule effect' (1840) asserted that the heat produced in a wire by an electric current was proportional to the resistance and to the square of the current, and in a series of notable researches (1843–78) he showed experimentally that heat is a form of energy, determined quantitatively the amount of mechanical (and later electrical) energy to be expended in the propagation of heat energy and established the mechanical equivalent of heat. Between 1853 and 1862 he collaborated with Lord **Kelvin** on the 'porous plug' experiments showing that when a gas expands without doing external work its temperature falls (the Joule–Thomson effect), and he was also the first to describe the phenomenon of magnetostriction. Recognition came with the award of the Royal Society's Royal (1852) and Copley (1870) medals. During the 1850s his ideas were recast in terms of the principle of the conservation of energy. The joule, a unit of work or energy, is named after him. 🕮 D S Cardwell, *James Joule* (1989)

Jourdan, Jean-Baptiste, Comte 1762–1833
French soldier
Born in Limoges, he joined the Revolutionary army and defeated the Austrians at Wattignies (1793), won the victory of Fleurus (1794), and then drove the Austrians across the Rhine, took Luxembourg, and besieged Mainz. But in 1795 he was defeated at Höchst, and then by the Archduke **Charles** of Austria. **Napoleon I** employed him in 1800 in Piedmont; in 1804 he was made marshal, and in 1806 Governor of Naples. In 1813 he was defeated by the Duke of **Wellington** at Vitoria, and in 1814 transferred his allegiance to **Louis XVIII**, who made him a count. He supported the Revolution of 1830.

Jouvet, Louis 1887–1951
French actor and theatre director
Born in Crozon, he became director of the Comédie des Champs Elysées (1924), and was the first to recognize **Jean Giraudoux**, all but one of whose plays he produced. In 1934 his company transferred to the Théâtre de l'Athénée, and he became professor at the Paris Conservatoire. The films in which he acted include *Topaze* (1933), *Les Bas-Fonds* (1936, 'The Lower Depths'), and *Hôtel du Nord* (1938). 🕮 Bettina Knapp, *Louis Jouvet, Man of Theatre* (1957)

Jouy, (Victor Joseph) Étienne (de) 1764–1846
French playwright, librettist and writer
He was born in Jouy-en-Josas, near Versailles, and until 1797 served as a soldier in India and at home. His stage works include a tragedy, *Tippo-Saïb* (1813), and several comedies and vaudevilles. As a librettist at the Paris Opéra, he collaborated with some of the most successful composers of the day. He contributed to the libretto for **Rossini**'s *Guillaume Tell* (1829), and to the composer's revision of *Mosè in Egitto* as the grand opera *Moïse et Pharaon, ou Le Passage de la mer rouge* (1827, 'Moses and Pharaoh, or The Crossing of the Red Sea'). Jouy thoroughly enjoyed the sensational and spectacular, as did the composer **Gasparo Spontini**, with whom he worked on *Fernand Cortez* (1809), an extravagant historical epic which includes in its effects a cavalry charge and the burning of the entire Spanish fleet.

Jowett, Benjamin 1817–93
English scholar
Born in Camberwell, London, and educated at St Paul's School and Balliol College, Oxford, he was elected a Fellow there in 1838, and tutor from 1840. He was elected Master of Balliol in 1870 and from 1855 to 1893 he was Regius Professor of Greek. From 1882 to 1886 he was Vice-Chancellor of Oxford. Jowett belonged to the Broad Church party. For his article 'On the Interpretation of Scripture' in *Essays and Reviews* (1860) he was tried but acquitted by the Vice-Chancellor's court. He is best known for his fine translations of the *Dialogues* of **Plato** (1871), **Thucydides** (1881), the *Politics* of **Aristotle** (1885), and Plato's *Republic* (1894). 🕮 G Faber, *Jowett: A Portrait with a Background* (1957)

Joyce, Eileen Alannah 1912–91
Australian pianist
Born in Zeehan, Tasmania, she was discovered by **Percy Grainger** when she was a child and was sent at the age of 15 to study at Leipzig Conservatory under Teichmuller and **Artur Schnabel**. In 1930 she was introduced to Sir **Henry Wood**, who arranged her debut at one of his Promenade Concerts. She became a prolific broadcaster and during World War II frequently visited the blitzed towns of Great Britain with **Malcolm Sargent** and the London Philharmonic. She also toured all over the world, and played with many major orchestras, having a repertoire of over 50 piano concertos and numerous recital programmes. She is particularly known for her work on film soundtracks, especially of *Brief Encounter* and *The Seventh Veil*, and the film of her childhood, *Wherever She Goes*. She retired prematurely in 1960 but returned to the concert platform in 1967.

Joyce, James Augustine Aloysius See panel p1004

Joyce, William, *also known as* Lord Haw-Haw 1906–46
British traitor
Born in Brooklyn, New York City, of Irish parentage, he lived in Ireland as a child and in 1922 emigrated to England with his family. In 1933 he joined Sir **Oswald Mosley**'s British Union of Fascists and secured a British passport by falsely claiming to have been born in Galway. Expelled from Mosley's party in 1937, he founded his own fanatical British National Socialist league and fled to Germany before World War II broke out. From September 1939 to April 1945, he broadcast propaganda against Great Britain from Radio Hamburg, gaining his nickname from his pretentious drawling accent. He was captured by the British at Flensburg, tried at the Old Bailey in 1945, and executed. His defence was his US birth, but his British passport, valid until July 1940, established nine months of treason. 🕮 J A Cole, *Lord Haw-Haw: The Full Story of William Joyce* (1987)

Joyner-Kersee, Jackie (Jacqueline), *née* Kersee 1962–
US athlete
Born in East St Louis, Illinois, she is a track and field competitor who has won five Olympic medals, including gold medals for the heptathlon (1988, 1992) and the long jump (1988). She was world champion of the long jump in 1991 and 1993 and of the heptathlon in 1993. She holds the world record for the heptathlon and the US record for the long jump. Participating in the 1996 Olympics, she won the bronze medal in the long jump.

Juana, *known as* Juana the Mad ('La Loca') 1479–1555
Countess of Flanders and Queen of Castile
The daughter of **Ferdinand**, the Catholic, and **Isabella** of Spain, she was born in Toledo, and married **Philip I, the Handsome**, of Flanders (1495). The couple settled in Ghent, and had several children, of whom the eldest was the future Holy Roman Emperor, **Charles V**. On her mother's death (1505), she became Queen of Castile. She and Philip moved to Spain in 1506, the year Philip died, and Juana, who suffered from severe depression which

Joyce, James Augustine Aloysius 1882–1941
Irish writer and poet

James Joyce was born in Dublin, which despite his long exile provides the setting for most of his work. He was educated by Jesuits at Clongowes Wood College and Belvedere College, and then at University College, Dublin, where he studied modern languages. A capable linguist and voracious reader, he corresponded with **Henrik Ibsen**. Among other influences were **Dante**, **George Moore** and **W B Yeats**.

He rejected Catholicism, and in 1902 went to Paris for a year, living in poverty and writing poetry. His mother's death prompted his return to Ireland, when he stayed briefly in the Martello Tower which features in the early part of *Ulysses*; he then left Ireland with Nora Barnacle, who was to be his companion for the rest of his life. He taught English for a spell in Trieste and Rome, and had two children, but he had to scrounge to make ends meet.

After a war spent mainly in Switzerland the couple settled in Paris. By now Joyce was the author of two books: *Chamber Music* (1907) and *Dubliners* (1914), a collection of short stories that includes among other celebrated items, 'The Dead'. The stories were greeted enthusiastically, and Joyce was championed by **Ezra Pound** and by Harriet Shaw Weaver, editor of *The Egoist*, in which the autobiographical *A Portrait of the Artist as a Young Man* appeared in instalments (1914–15). The support of friends, and of his brother Stanislaus, also did much to mitigate the difficulties of these years. Petitioned by Yeats and Pound on his behalf, the Royal Literary Fund in 1915 made him a grant and shortly afterwards the civil list followed suit. But his health was failing, his eyesight deteriorating and he was deeply disturbed by his daughter Lucia's mental illness.

In 1922 his seminal novel, *Ulysses*, was published in Paris on 2 February. Its explicit stream-of-consciousness description of the thoughts and happenings of everyday life immediately provoked violent reactions, and it was not published in the UK until 1936. But the story of Leopold Bloom's day-long perambulation through Dublin is now regarded as a major advance for fiction. Meanwhile Joyce and Nora Barnacle were married during a trip to London in 1931. Lucia was diagnosed as schizophrenic the following year. Although troubled by worsening glaucoma, Joyce supervised the publication of *Finnegans Wake*, which moved on from the consciousness of *Ulysses* to the semi-consciousness of a dream-world, in 1939. On the outbreak of World War II he returned to Zurich, where he underwent an operation for a duodenal ulcer, but he failed to recover.

Much critical energy has been spent trying to analyse Joyce's work, but readers continue to delight in his word play, comedy and irrepressible power of invention. He exercised a major influence on his contmporaries, especially **Virginia Woolf** and **Samuel Beckett**, and on later generations of writers, among whom **Saul Bellow**, **Thomas Pynchon**, **John Updike** and **Anthony Burgess** have acknowledged their debt.

📖 Joyce's letters have been published by S Gilbert, *The Letters of James Joyce* (vol 1, 1957) and by R Ellmann (vols 2 and 3, 1966); see also R Ellmann, *James Joyce* (2nd edn, 1982); A Burgess, *Joysprick: An Introduction to the Language of James Joyce* (1975).

'History, Stephen said, is a nightmare from which I am trying to awake.' *Ulysses*.

---

had been aggravated by her husband's infidelities, was declared unfit to govern and was kept under close watch in Tordesillas, while her father became Regent of Castile. Although Ferdinand died in 1516, her son, Charles, by then King of Spain, did not release her and Juana remained incarcerated, along with her youngest daughter, Catalina, until her death.

Juan Carlos I 1938–
King of Spain

Born in Rome, Italy, the grandson of **Alfonso XIII**, he spent his childhood in Rome and Spain. In 1954 Don Juan de Borbón (his father and third son of Alfonso) and General Franco agreed that Juan Carlos should take precedence over his father as pretender. He trained in the armed forces (1957–59) and was formally named by Franco as the future king (1969). He became king on Franco's death (1975), and has presided over a gradual return to democracy, despite internal political difficulties reflected in two attempted coups. In 1962 he married Sofia (1938–), elder daughter of King **Paul** of the Hellenes. They have two daughters, Elena (1963–) and Cristina (1965–), and a son, Felipe (1968–), Prince of the Asturias. 📖 Charles T Powell, *Juan Carlos of Spain: Self-Made Monarch* (1996)

Juan de La Cruz See John of the Cross, St

Juárez, Benito (Pablo) 1806–72
Mexican national hero and statesman

A Zapotec Indian, he was a clerk and lawyer and then Governor of Oaxaca (1847–52). Exiled by Conservatives under **Santa Anna** (1853–55), he then returned to join the new Liberal government. Proposing fundamental change, he abolished the fueros, seized control of Church lands, and passed the anticlerical and Liberal constitution of 1857. During the civil war of 1857–60 he assumed the presidency, upholding a free Church in a free State. He

was elected President on the Liberal victory (1861), a post he held until his death. The French invasion under **Maximilian** forced him to the far north, from where he directed resistance until Maximilian's defeat in 1867. He then restored republican rule, creating the basis for the regime of **Porfírio Díaz**. 📖 Ralph Roeder, *Juárez and His Mexico* (2 vols, 1947)

Judah
Old Testament figure

The fourth son of **Jacob** and Leah, he founded the greatest of the 12 tribes of Israel.

Judas or Thaddeus, St 1st century AD
One of the 12 Apostles

Judas (not Iscariot) is mentioned in the book of the Acts of the Apostles. He is referred to as 'Judas Son of James'. Also called Thaddeus, he may have come from a party of zealots, a Jewish nationalist movement from before 70AD. He is often paired with **Simon the Zealot**, for tradition holds that they were missionaries, first in Egypt and later in Persia where they were finally martyred. His becoming the patron saint of desperate causes originated in the 18th century in France and Germany. His feast day is 28 October (Western Churches) or 21 August (Greek Orthodox).

Judas Iscariot 1st century AD
One of the 12 Apostles

Born probably in Kerioth, in the tribe of Judah, he usually appears last in the lists in the synoptic Gospels (Mark 3.19). He is identified as the one who betrayed **Jesus Christ** for 30 pieces of silver by helping to arrange for his arrest at Gethsemane by the Jewish authorities (Mark 14.43–46). Other traditions indicate his role as treasurer (John 13.29) and his later repentance and suicide (Matthew 27.3–5). The meaning of Iscariot is uncertain: it may mean 'man of Keriot', 'assassin' or 'man of falsehood'. He was replaced by Matthias (Acts 1.26). 📖 G Buchheit, *Judas Iskarioth* (1954)

Judd, Donald 1928–94
US artist

Born in Excelsior Springs, Missouri, he studied at the College of William and Mary, Williamsburg, Virginia (1948–49), Columbia University (1949–53) and at the Art Students' League, New York (1947–48, 1950–53), and had his first one-man show in New York in 1964. A Minimalist, he has metal boxes manufactured to his specification, spray-painted one colour and stood or stacked on the floor, thus creating works with which he has had only 'minimal' contact, and which are deliberately non-imitative, non-expressive and not 'composed' in any traditional sense, such as *Untitled* (1980, Tate, London).

Jude, St 1st century AD
Early Christian

He was probably the Judas who was listed as one of the brothers of **Jesus Christ** (Matthew 13.55, Mark 6.3), and perhaps a brother of St **James**, the Just. A New Testament letter bears his name, but its authorship is disputed. It is said to be directed against the Gnostics of the 2nd century. According to tradition he was martyred in Persia with St **Simon**, who shares his feast day of 28 October (Western Churches) and 19 June or (Eastern Churches) 21 August.

Judith
Old Testament Jewish heroine

In the Apocryphal Book of Judith, she is portrayed as a widow who went to the tent of Holofernes, general of **Nebuchadnezzar**, cut off his head, and so saved her native town of Bethulia.

Judson, Adoniram 1788–1850
US missionary

Born in Malden, Massachusetts, he was educated at Andover Theological Seminary. In 1812, he went to Burma as a Baptist missionary, and was a prisoner during the Anglo-Burmese War (1824–26). His Burmese translation of the Bible (1833) was followed by a Burmese–English dictionary (1849).

Judson, E(dward) Z(ane) C(arroll), *pseudonym* Ned Buntline 1823–86
US writer and adventurer

Born in Stamford, New York, he ran away to sea as a boy and began a tumultuous life that included involvement in a murder and two riots. A writer of action stories, he started the popular sensationalist magazine *Ned Buntline's Own* (1845) and published his fiction in cheap pamphlets (dime novels), including a series about frontiersman **William F Cody**, whom he named 'Buffalo Bill'. He also wrote a play, *The Scouts of the Plains* (1872), which toured with Cody and **Wild Bill Hickok** as stars. His writing often reflected his jingoism and nativist sentiments, and he was an organizer of the 1850s anti-Catholic American (Know-Nothing) Party. 📖 J Monaghan, *The Great Rascal* (1952).

Jugnauth, Sir Aneerood 1930–
Mauritian politician

After qualifying as a barrister in London in 1954, he returned to Mauritius and was elected to the legislative council in the period before full independence in 1968. In 1970 he co-founded the socialist Mauritius Militant Movement (MMM), from which he later broke away to form his own Mauritius Socialist Party (PSM). In 1982 he became Prime Minister at the head of a PSM–MMM alliance. In 1983 his party was reconstituted as the Mauritius Socialist Movement (MSM) with a pledge to make the country a republic within the Commonwealth. He failed to obtain legislative approval for this change in the constitution but retained his control of a MSM-led coalition in elections in 1983, 1987, and 1991. In 1995 he was succeeded as Prime Minister by Navin Ramgoolam. He was made Grand Officer of the French Legion of Honour in 1990.

Jugurtha d.104BC
King of Numidia

By the murder of his cousin, Hiempsal, he secured a part of the kingdom of his grandfather **Masinissa**, and, according to **Sallust**, bribed the Roman senate to support him (116BC). He soon invaded his surviving cousin Adherbal's part of the kingdom, besieged him in Cirta (112BC), and put him, and the Romans who were with him, to death, thus beginning the Jugarthine War, in which the Romans twice attempted to defeat him, until finally, in 106BC, Jugurtha had to flee to the King of Mauretania, who delivered him to **Sulla**. He was left to die in prison in Rome.

Juin, Alphonse Pierre 1888–1967
French general

Born in Bône, Algeria, he passed out top of his class, which included **Charles de Gaulle**, at the Saint-Cyr military academy. He fought in World War I, and as divisional commander in the 1st French Army he was captured by the Germans in 1940, but was later released. He declined the post of Vichy Minister of War, but became Military Governor of Morocco. After the Allied invasion of Tunisia, he changed sides, helped to defeat Baron von Arnim's Afrika Corps remnants and distinguished himself in the subsequent Italian campaign. He was resident general in Morocco (1947–51) and served in senior NATO commands. He broke with de Gaulle in 1960 over his Algerian policy, and retired.

Julia 39BC–AD14
Roman noblewoman

The daughter of the Emperor **Augustus** and Scribonia, she was married at the age of 14 to her cousin **Marcellus**, a nephew of Augustus. After his death (23BC) she married (21BC) **Marcus Vipsanius Agrippa**, to whom she bore three sons and two daughters. He died (12BC), whereupon Julia was married to **Tiberius** (11BC). The marriage was unhappy and in 2BC, when her father learned of her adulteries, she was banished to the isle of Pandataria, and from there to Reggio, where she died of starvation. Her mother shared her exile.

Julian, *in full* Flavius Claudius Julianus, *also known as* Julian the Apostate c.331–363AD
Roman emperor

Born in Constantinople (Istanbul), he was the youngest son of **Constantius**, and half-brother of **Constantine I, the Great**. Only Julian and his elder half-brother Gallus survived a massacre of the Flavians on Constantine's death (AD337). Julian subsequently rejected Christianity, now an established religion. In 355 he became caesar, and married Helena, the sister of the Emperor Constantius II (his cousin). He then served in the army, overthrowing the Alemanni near Strasbourg, and also subduing the Frankish tribes along the Rhine. He endeared himself to the soldiers by his personal courage, his success in war, and the severe simplicity of his life. In 360 the jealous emperor ordered him to serve against the Persians, but his soldiers protested and proclaimed him Augustus. He took his army to Constantinople, and declared himself a pagan. His cousin died in 361 and as emperor, Julian embarked on public reform, tolerating Christians and Jews while restoring the old religion. He spent 362–363 at Antioch, and became unpopular by increasing the price of corn in order to prevent a threatened famine. In 363 he invaded Persia (Iran), but was forced to retreat and was killed. His extant writings are a series of *Epistles*, nine

Orations, Caesares, satires on past Caesars, and the *Misopogon*, a satire on the people of Antioch. His chief work, *Kata Christianon*, is lost.

Julian of Norwich c.1342–c.1413
English mystic

Born probably in Norwich, Norfolk, she is thought to have lived in isolation outside St Julian's Church, Norwich. She had a series of visions in May 1373, and her account of these and meditations on their significance have survived in mid-15th and mid-16th-century manuscript copies, published in modern versions as the *Showings* or *Revelations of Divine Love*. Her thoughts have had lasting influence on theologians stressing the power of the love of God.

Juliana, *in full* Juliana Louise Emma Marie Wilhelmina 1909–
Queen of the Netherlands

She was born in The Hague and was educated at Leyden University where she took a law degree. She married (1937) Prince **Bernhard Leopold** of Lippe-Biesterfeld, and they have four daughters: Queen **Beatrix**; Princess Irene (1939–), who married (1964) Prince Hugo of Bourbon-Parma (1939–), son of the Carlist pretender to the Spanish throne, Prince Xavier, (against her parents' wishes, and forfeiting her right of succession); Princess Margriet (1943–), who married Pieter van Vollenhoven (1967); and Princess Marijke (1947–), who married Jorge Giullermo (1975). On the German invasion of Holland (1940) Juliana escaped to Great Britain and later resided in Canada. She returned to Holland (1945), and in 1948, on the abdication of her mother Queen **Wilhelmina**, became Queen of the Netherlands. Her use of a faith healer in the 1950s aroused public concern, as did her husband's involvement in the Lockheed Aircraft Corporation scandal (1976). She herself abdicated (1980) in favour of her eldest daughter, Beatrix.

Julius II *originally* Giuliano della Rovere 1443–1513
Italian pope

Born in Albizula, Genoa, he became pope in 1503 and his public career was mainly devoted to political and military enterprises for the re-establishment of papal sovereignty in its ancient territory, and for the ending of foreign domination in Italy. To compel Venice to restore the papal provinces on the Adriatic, he entered into the League of Cambrai with the Emperor **Maximilian**, **Ferdinand the Catholic**, of Aragon, and **Louis XII** of France, and placed the republic under the ban of the Church. The French king ineffectually attempted to enlist the Church against the pope, and the fifth Lateran Council, assembled by Julius, completely frustrated Louis's plans. He is best remembered as a patron of the arts. He employed **Donato Bramante** for the design of St Peter's, begun in 1506, had **Raphael** brought to Rome to decorate his private apartments and commissioned **Michelangelo** for the frescoes on the ceiling of the Sistine chapel and for his own tomb. His military exploits inspired **Erasmus's** satire *Julius Exclusus*.

Julius III *originally* Gianmaria del Monte 1487–1555
Italian pope

Born in Rome, he became pope in 1550 and was one of the three delegates to the Council of Trent, which he reopened after his election. He sent Cardinal **Reginald Pole** to organize with **Mary I** the reunion of England with the Church of Rome.

Jumblat, Kemal 1919–77
Lebanese socialist politician and hereditary Druze chieftain

He was born in the Chouf Mountains. He founded the Progressive Socialist Party (1949), held several Cabinet posts (1961–64), and was Minister of the Interior (1969–70). The increasing power of his authority in partnership

with the Palestinians resulted in the Syrian intervention on the side of the Christians (1976). He was assassinated in an ambush outside the village of Baaklu in the Chouf Mountains, after which his son Walid became leader of the Druze.

Jung, Carl Gustav 1875–1961
Swiss psychiatrist

Born in Kesswil, he studied medicine there and worked under **Eugen Bleuler** at the Burghölzli mental clinic at Zurich (1900–09). His early *Studies in Word Association* (1904–09, in which he coined the term 'complex') and *The Psychology of Dementia Praecox* (1906–97) led to his meeting **Sigmund Freud** in Vienna in 1907. He became Freud's leading collaborator and was elected president of the International Psychoanalytical Association (1910). His independent researches, making him increasingly critical of Freud's insistence on the psychosexual origins of the neuroses, which he published in *The Psychology of the Unconscious* (1911–12), caused a rift in 1913. From then onwards he went on to develop his own school of 'analytical psychology'. He introduced the concepts of 'introvert' and 'extrovert' personalities, and developed the theory of the 'collective unconscious' with its archetypes of man's basic psychic nature as a 'self-regulating' system. He held professorships at Zurich (1933–41) and Basle (1944–61). His other main works were: *On Psychic Energy* (1928), *Psychology and Religion* (1937), *Psychology and Alchemy* (1944), *Aion* (1951), *The Undiscovered Self* (1957) and his autobiographical *Memories, Dreams, Reflections* (1962). He was regarded by many as a religious leader and is seen as the founder of a new humanism. 📖 Gerhard Wehr, *Jung: A Biography* (1987)

Jung, Johann Heinrich, *pseudonym* Jung Stilling 1740–1817
German mystic and writer

Born in Grund, Westphalia, he was a schoolteacher before qualifying in medicine and becoming Professor of Political Economy first at Marburg (1787–1804), then at Heidelberg. He wrote semi-mystical, pietistic romances and works on political economy, as well as a charming autobiography which began with *Heinrich Stillings Jugend* ('Heinrich Stilling's Youth'), and had grown to five volumes when edited by **Goethe** (1777–1804). A sixth volume was published in 1817. 📖 H Müller, *Jung Stilling* (1965)

Jung Bahadur 1816–77
Nepali statesman

He was Prime Minister and virtual ruler of Nepal from 1846 to 1877. He visited Great Britain (1850–51) and provided the British with a body of Gurkhas during the Indian Uprising of 1857–58; this led to the tradition of Gurkha military service in the British army. He was the founder of the Rana Dynasty, which provided a line of Prime Ministers for the country until 1951, when the last hereditary Prime Minister, Mohun, retired.

Jüngel, Eberhard 1934–
German Protestant theologian

Born in Magdeburg, he was a student in Naumberg, Berlin, Zurich and Basle, and lectured in East Berlin before becoming Professor of Systematic Theology in Zurich (1966–69), and then at Tübingen (1969–). He has been Dean of the Faculty of Evangelical Theology there since 1992, a post he held previously from 1970 to 1972. He has written widely in German on the death of **Jesus Christ** and the doctrine of justification, on problems of religious language, and on natural theology. His works available in English include *Death* (1975), *The Doctrine of the Trinity* (1976), *God as the Mystery of the World* (1983) and *Theological Essays* (1987).

Jünger, Ernst 1895–1998
German novelist

He served in the German army in World War I, winning the medal Pour le Mérite in 1918, and his postwar fiction conveys the spirit of Prussian militarism and, increasingly, the mystique of technological advance. His initial Nazi support disappeared on the Nazi accession to power and he enlisted again, serving in France during World War II, where he influenced the French right-wing. Controversy surrounds the intention of his novels, *Marmorklippen* (1939, 'On the Marble Cliffs') and *Heliopolis* (1949), both of which have been seen as deutero-fascist texts as well as texts of resistance. He himself complicated the issue by remaining silent on it, while continuing to write in a not dissimilar vein. The 50th anniversary celebrations of the end of the World War II in 1995 were given greater resonance by the occasion of Jünger's 100th birthday. ⌨Thomas Nevin, *Ernst Jünger and Germany: into the abyss, 1914–1945* (1997).

Junius, Franciscus or Francis, *properly* François du Jon c.1591–1677
Dutch philologist and antiquary
Born in Heidelberg in Germany, he was brought up in Holland, and from 1621 to 1651 he was tutor in England to the family of Thomas Howard, Earl of Arundel (1586–1646). He collected and edited Anglo-Saxon manuscripts now in the Bodleian Library, and edited works associated with Caedmon. He later came back to England in 1674, and died near Windsor.

Junker, Wilhelm Johann 1840–92
German traveller
Born in Moscow, Russia, he studied medicine in Germany, then travelled in Iceland in 1869 and in North Africa in 1873. From 1876 to 1878 he explored the western tributaries of the Upper Nile. He set off again in 1879, spent four years among the Monbuttu and Niam-Niam peoples, and met up with Emin Pasha, returning in 1877.

Junkers, Hugo 1859–1935
German aircraft engineer
Born in Rheydt, he became Professor of Mechanical Engineering at Aachen (1897–1912). After World War I he founded aircraft factories at Dessau, Magdeburg and Stassfurt, which produced many famous planes, both civil and military, including the Ju 87 'Stuka' dive bomber used in World War II.

Junot, (Jean-)Andoche, Duc d'Abrantès, *nicknamed* La Tempête ('The Tempest') 1771–1813
French soldier
Born in Bussy-le-Grand, he was adjutant under Napoleon I in Egypt. In 1806 he was made Military Governor of Paris, and in 1807 was appointed to the command of the army for Portugal. He was created Duc d'Abrantès and appointed Governor of Portugal but, defeated by the Duke of Wellington at Vimeiro (1808), was obliged to sign the Convention of Cintra and leave Portugal. He served in Germany and Russia, and after defeat at Smolensk (1812) was sent to govern Illyria. Mentally ill, he threw himself from a window of his father's house near Dijon. His wife Laure Permon, Duchesse d'Abrantès (1785–1838), wrote her *Mémoires* (1831–35), depicting the society of the time.

Junqueiro, Ablio Manuel Guerra 1850–1923
Portuguese lyric poet and satirist
Born in Freixo, he became a deputy in 1872, opposed the Braganzas (the ruling Portuguese dynasty) and was tried for *lèse majesté* in 1907. After the revolution, when a republic was established, he was Minister to Switzerland (1910). His poetry shows the influence of Victor Hugo, and is concerned with social and political reform, rather than more traditional subjects. His work was very popular in his own day.

Juppé, Alain Marie 1945–
French politician
Born in Mont-de-Marsan, Landes, he was educated in Paris at the Lycee Louis-le-Grand and the Institute for Political Studies. His first political appointment was in the office of the Prime Minister Jacques Chirac in 1976, but he made his reputation in local politics in Paris. In 1980 he was appointed the city's Director of Finance and in 1983 became a member of the city council. Between 1984 and 1986 he was a member of the European Parliament. In 1995 he won the general election during a period of trade union unrest following cutbacks in public spending and became the country's Prime Minister (1995–97). ⌨ Isabelle Dath, *Alain Juppé: La Tentation du Pouvoir* (1995)

Jussieu, Antoine Laurent de 1748–1836
French botanist
Born in Lyons, he studied at Paris University and became professor at the Jardin des Plantes (1793–1826), which he reorganized as the National Museum of Natural History. He elaborated in his *Genera Plantarum* (1778–89) his uncle's system of 'natural' classification. He adopted family names from Carolus Linnaeus and Bernard Jussieu amongst others, finishing with over 100 family names, of which 76 are still in current use. He was the nephew of Bernard Jussieu.

Jussieu, Bernard c.1699–1777
French botanist
Born in Lyons, he was educated at the universities of Montpellier and Paris, became a demonstrator at the Jardin des Plantes (1722), and created a botanical garden for Louis XV in 1759 using a system which became the basis of modern natural botanical classification. He first suggested that polyps were animals. His support for the principle of natural classification had a decisive influence on botanical history. He associated similar floral genera into families, although it was left to his nephew Antoine Laurent de Jussieu to elaborate and make explicit these relationships.

Justin, St, *known as* the Martyr c.100–c.165AD
Greek theologian, and one of the Fathers of the Church
Born of Greek parents in Sichem, Samaria, he was successively a Stoic and a Platonist. After his conversion to Christianity in Ephesus (c.130AD) he travelled about on foot defending its truths. At Rome between 150 and 160 he wrote the *Apologia* of Christianity addressed to the Emperor Marcus Aurelius, followed by a second one, and a *Dialogue with Trypho*, defending Christianity against Judaism. He is said to have been martyred. His feast day is 14 April.

Justin I c.450–527AD
Byzantine emperor
He was born in Illyria of peasant stock. He became commander in the imperial bodyguard, and in AD518 was raised to the Byzantine throne by the army. He resigned the civil administration to the quaestor Proclus. In 519 he entered into an arrangement with the pope, and in 523 resigned to Theodoric, King of Italy, the right of appointing consuls in Rome. In the same year he became involved in a war with the Persians. He was succeeded by his nephew Justinian I, who had given him significant help throughout his reign.

Justin II d.578
Byzantine emperor
He succeeded his uncle, Justinian I, in 565 and married and was ruled by Sophia, the unscrupulous niece of the Empress Theodora. He yielded part of Italy to the Lombards, was unsuccessful against the Persians and Avars, and became insane.

Justinian I *called* the Great, *in full* Flavius Petrus
Sabbatius Justinianus c.482–565AD
Emperor of the East Roman Empire

He was born in Tauresium in Illyria, the son of a Slavonic
peasant and the nephew of **Justin I**. Educated in
Constantinople (Istanbul), he was named consul in 521,
and in 527 was proclaimed by Justin his colleague in the
empire. Justin died the same year, and Justinian, proclaimed sole emperor, was crowned along with his wife
Theodora. His reign is the most brilliant in the history of
the late empire. He selected the ablest generals, and under
Narses and **Belisarius** his reign may be said to have largely
restored the Roman Empire to its ancient limits, and to
have reunited the East and West. His first war—that with
Persia—ended in a favourable treaty. The conflict of the
Blue and Green factions in 532 was an outburst of political discontent and led to the election of a rival emperor,
but Narses, Belisarius and Theodora repressed the rebellion relentlessly and 35,000 victims fell in a single day.
Through these generals, the Vandal kingdom of Africa
was reannexed to the empire, the imperial authority was
restored in Rome, Northern Italy and Spain, and Justinian
constructed or renewed a vast line of fortifications along
the eastern and south-eastern frontier of his empire. It
was as a legislator that Justinian gained his most enduring
renown. He collected and codified the principal imperial
constitutiones or statutes in force at his accession, and the
Codex, by which all previous imperial enactments were
repealed, was published in 529. The writings of the jurists
or commentators on Roman law were streamlined, and
published under the title *Digesta* or *Pandectae* in 533. The
direction of this work was entrusted to Tribonianus the
jurist (c.470–c.544) with a committee of professors and
advocates, who also prepared a systematic and elementary
treatise on the law—the *Institutiones* (533), based on the
Institutiones of **Gaius**. A new edition of the *Codex* was issued in 534. During the subsequent years of his reign
Justinian promulgated many new laws or constitutions,
known as *Novellae*. The Institutes, Digest, Code and
Novels together make up what is known as the *Corpus Juris
Civilis*, a work which was immensely influential on the law
of nearly all European countries down to modern times.
📖 P N Ure, *Justinian and his Age* (1951)

Justus of Ghent, *originally* Joos van Wassenhove
fl.c.1460–c.1480
Netherlandish painter

He became a member of the painters' guild in Antwerp in
1460, and in 1464 was a master in Ghent. There he was an
associate of **Hugo van der Goes**. He left Ghent some time
after 1469, and in the mid-1470s is recorded at the court of
Federigo da Montefeltro, Duke of Urbino. His only surviving documented work is *The Institution of the Eucharist*
(1472–74), though he is also thought to have painted a
series of 28 *Famous Men* for the Ducal Palace (c.1476). His
work was an important source of knowledge of the
Netherlandish oil technique for contemporary Italian
painters.

Juvarra or **Juvara, Filippo** 1678–1736
Italian architect

Born in Sicily, he studied under **Carlo Fontana** in Rome.
Influenced by the Roman Baroque, **Gian Lorenzo Bernini**
and French planning, he is regarded as a principal exponent of Rococo design. His major works include the
Palazzo Madama in Turin (1718–21), of which only the
staircase block was built, of proportions and magnificence hitherto unknown in Italy. Other works include the
hunting lodge at Stupinigi, outside Turin (1729), a country palace with wings radiating from and encompassing a
central *grande salone*, a masterpiece in which he briefly
eclipsed even the splendours of **Guarini**.

Juvenal, *in full* Decimus Junius Juvenalis
c.55–c.140AD
Roman lawyer and satirist

He was probably born in Aquinum in the Volscian country. Almost nothing is known of his life except that he
lived in Rome, was poor and was a friend of **Martial**. His
16 brilliant verse satires of Roman life and society (c.100–
c.128), written from the viewpoint of an angry Stoic
moralist, range from savage attacks on the vices and
extravagance of the ruling classes and the precarious
makeshift life of their hangers-on, to his hatred of Jews,
foreigners and society women. **Dryden's** versions of five
of Juvenal's satires are amongst the best of his work, and
Dr Johnson imitated two in his *London* and *Vanity of
Human Wishes*. 📖 G Highet, *Juvenal the Satirist* (1954)

Kabalevsky, Dmitri Borisovich 1904–87
Russian composer

Born in St Petersburg, he was educated at the Moscow Conservatory, studying composition with Nikolai Myaskovsky, and taught there himself from 1932. His prolific work output included four symphonies, operas, concertos, film scores, and a large amount of chamber and piano music.

Kádár, János 1912–89
Hungarian politician

Born in Kapoly in south west Hungary, he began life as an instrument-maker. Attracted to the Communist Party from an early age, he was a member of the central committee of the underground party during World War II, escaping from capture by the Gestapo. He emerged after the war as First Party Secretary and as one of the leading figures of the Communist regime. In 1950, as Minister of the Interior, he was arrested for 'Tito-ist' sympathies. He was freed in 1953, was rehabilitated in 1954 and became secretary of the party committee for Budapest in 1955. When the Hungarian anti-Soviet revolution broke out in October 1956 he was a member of the 'national' anti-Stalinist government of Imre Nagy. On 1 November he declared that the Communist Party had been dissolved as it had 'degenerated into perpetuating despotism and national slavery'. But as Soviet tanks crushed the revolution, he formed a puppet government which in the closing months of 1956 held Hungary in a ruthless reign of terror. The majority of his countrymen regarded him as a traitor, although a few saw him as a victim of forces beyond his control. He resigned in 1958, but became Premier and First Secretary of the Central Committee in 1961. In 1965 he lost the premiership, but remained First Secretary. He proceeded to introduce a series of 'market socialist' economic reforms which helped raise living standards, while continuing to retain cordial political relations with the Soviet Union. In 1988 he stepped down as Communist Party leader, moving to the new titular post of party president. He was removed from the Communist Party's central committee in 1989, shortly before his death.

Kael, Pauline 1919–
US film critic

Born in Petaluma, California, she was educated at the University of California at Berkeley. A waspish, insightful reviewer, she was movie critic of the *New Yorker* from 1968 to 1991. She has published several anthologies of her articles: *Kiss Kiss Bang Bang* (1968), *When the Lights Go Down* (1980), *5001 Nights at the Movies* (1982) and *Movie Love* (1991).

Kafka, Franz 1883–1924
Austrian novelist

Born of German–Jewish parents in Prague, he graduated in law there, and although overwhelmed by a desire to write, found employment (1907–23) as an official in the accident prevention department of the government-sponsored Workers' Accident Insurance Institution. A hypersensitive, introspective person with a very strong attachment to his father, he eventually moved to Berlin to live with Dora Dymant in 1923, his only brief spell of happiness before succumbing to a lung disease. He published several short stories and essays, including, 'Der Heizer' (1913, 'The Boilerman'), 'Betrachtungen' (1913, 'Meditations') and 'Die Verwandlung' (1916, Eng trans 'The Transformation', 1933; more widely known as 'Metamorphosis'). His three unfinished novels, *Der Prozess* (1925, Eng trans *The Trial*, 1937), *Das Schloss* (1926, Eng trans *The Castle*, 1937) and *Amerika* (1927, Eng trans

America, 1938), were published posthumously, through his friend Max Brod, and translated by Edwin Muir and Willa Muir. Literary critics have interpreted *Das Schloss* variously as a modern *Pilgrim's Progress* (however, there is literally no progress), as a literary exercise in Kierkegaardian Existentialist theology, as an allegory of the Jew in a Gentile world, or psychoanalytically as a monstrous expression of Kafka's Oedipus complex, but his solipsism primarily portrays society as a pointless and irrational organization into which the bewildered individual has strayed (Kafkaesque). He has exerted a tremendous influence on Western literature, not least on such writers as Albert Camus, Rex Warner and Samuel Beckett. As *The Trial*, *Der Prozess* has been memorably filmed by Orson Welles (1962) and staged by Steven Berkoff (1970). A number of his other writings have been published posthumously, including *Briefe an meinem Väter* (1919, Eng trans *Letters to my Father*, 1954), *Briefe an Milena* (1952, Eng trans *Letters to Milena*, 1967) and *Briefe an Felice* (1967, Eng trans *Letters to Felice*, 1974), and his diary and other correspondence. ▣ J P Stern, *The World of Kafka* (1980); A Thorlby, *Franz Kafka* (1972)

Kaganovich, Lazar Moiseyevich 1893–1991
Soviet politician

He joined the Communist Party in 1911 and, after participating in the 1917 Russian Revolution, became First Secretary of the Ukrainian Party in 1925. In 1928 he moved to the secretariat of the All-Union Party and in 1930 became a full member of the politburo, as well as serving as First Secretary of the Moscow Party. He played a prominent role in the brutal, forced collectivization programme in the early 1930s, and in the great purges of 1936–38. He also served as Commissar for Railways and was responsible for building the Moscow metro. A close ally of Stalin, he survived the latter's death in 1953 but, having fallen foul of Nikita Khrushchev and participated in the Anti-Party Plot, was dismissed in 1957 and posted to a managerial position in a Siberian cement works.

Kagawa, Toyohiko 1888–1960
Japanese social reformer and evangelist

A convert to Christianity, he was educated at the Presbyterian College in Tokyo, and Princeton Theological Seminary in the USA. Returning to Japan, he became an evangelist and social worker in the slums of Kobe. He became a leader in the Japanese labour movement, helping found the Federation of Labour (1918) and Farmer's Union (1921), and a system of agricultural collectives. He founded the Anti-War League in 1928. After World War II he helped to promote democratization and women's suffrage. He wrote numerous books, including the autobiographical novel *Before the Dawn* (1920).

Kagel, Mauricio Raúl 1931–
Argentine composer

Born in Buenos Aires, he became prominent in the avant-garde movement. Evolving a complex serial organization of elements of music, he combined these with aleatory components drawn from random visual patterns, linguistic permutations, electronic sounds and unconventional percussion instruments. His work often had a strong visual or theatrical aspect. Since 1957 he has lived mainly in Cologne.

Kahlo, Frida 1907–54
Mexican artist

Born in Coyoicoán, Mexico City, she was the daughter of a Jewish–German immigrant photographer and a Catholic Mexican mother. A serious road accident at the age of 15 destroyed her dreams of a career as a doctor, but during her convalescence she started painting, and sent her work to the painter Diego Rivera, whom she married in 1928; it was a colourful but tortured marriage. They divorced, but ultimately remarried. Characterized by vivid imagery, many of her pictures were striking self-portraits. Pain, which dogged her all her life, and the suffering of women are recurring themes in her surrealistic and often shocking pictures. She and Rivera mixed in a well-known circle of artists, photographers and politically controversial figures including Leon Trotsky. The surrealist poet and essayist André Breton likened her paintings to 'a ribbon around a bomb' (1938). In 1940 she participated in the International Exhibition of Surrealism in Mexico City, and in 1946 won a prize at the Annual National Exhibition at the Palace of Fine Arts. The Frida Kahlo Museum was opened in her house in Coyoicoán in 1958. 🕮 Martha Zamora, *Frida Kahlo* (1990)

Kahn, Gustave 1859–1936
French Symbolist poet and essayist

He was born in Metz, Lorraine. The self-proclaimed inventor of *vers libre*, he was one of the first, along with Jules Laforgue, to use the techniques of free verse, and was an influential theoretician of the new form of prosody, which he defended in a preface to *Premieres Poèmes* (1897), a republication of earlier work. Probably his most lasting impact was as co-founder of two important journals—*Le Symboliste* and *Vogue*. Later work appeared posthumously in *Poèmes 1921–1935* (1939). 🕮 J C Ireson, *L'Œuvre poétique de Gustave Kahn* (1962)

Kahn, Louis I(sadore) 1901–74
US architect

Born in Osel (now Saaremaa), Estonia, he emigrated to the USA in 1905 (naturalized 1917). A graduate of Pennsylvania, he taught at Yale (1947–57) and Pennsylvania (1957–74). He was a pioneer of functionalist architecture, expressed in a New Brutalist vein, clearly demonstrated in the Richards Medical Research Building, Pennsylvania (1957–61). Buckminster Fuller's geodesic designs influenced his City Tower Municipal Building, Philadelphia (with Anne Tyng, 1952–57). Further works include the Yale University Art Gallery (with Douglas Orr, 1953), the Salk Institute in La Jolla, California (1959–65), the Indian Institute of Management, Ahmedabad (with Balkrishna Doshi, 1962–74), and the Paul Mellon Center, Yale (1969–72).

Kaifu, Toshiki 1932–
Japanese politician

He was born in Nagoya and studied law at university. After entering the House of Representatives in the 1960s as a Liberal Democrat, he was re-elected five times and served as Labour Minister, and between 1974 and 1976 in a number of other senior posts under Takeo Miki. He was subsequently appointed deputy Cabinet Secretary, then chairman of the party's Diet policy committee, and was Education Minister (1976–77, 1985–86) and Prime Minister (1989–91). He was widely criticized for Japan's 5.5 billion yen contribution to the 1991 Gulf War and his (later abandoned) decision to send uniformed members of Japan's self-defence forces there.

Kain, Karen 1951–
Canadian dancer

Born in Hamilton, Ontario, she trained with the Canadian National Ballet School and joined the company in 1969, becoming principal dancer in 1970 and one of Canada's best known ballerinas. She has danced the major classical leads as well as interpreting roles in works by

contemporary choreographers. She partnered Rudolf Nureyev in New York, and, as guest artist at the Ballet National de Marseille, she created a leading role in Roland Petit's *Les Intermittences du Cœur* (1974).

Kaiser, Georg 1878–1945
German Expressionist dramatist, poet and novelist

He was born in Magdeburg. He wrote 78 plays, and was thus the most prolific, as he was the most influential and gifted, of the Expressionist playwrights. His own life had more than an Expressionist tinge (it included a six-month spell in jail for stealing and pawning a landlord's furniture: his defence—supposed to annoy the judges, which it did—was that he needed the money to maintain the high standards of his youth and his artistic requirement for luxuries and immunity from bourgeois pseudo-morality). *Von Morgens bis Mitternacht* (1916, Eng trans *From Morn to Midnight*, 1920), originally produced by Max Reinhardt, features a non-character, The Bank Cashier, the deadness of whose inner life is exposed and revealed by presenting it in the form of fantasy. Other plays include *Gas I* (1918) and *Gas II* (1920). His work was banned by the Nazis, and he left Germany in 1938. Later he wrote romantic dramas, and, finally, a *Hellenic Trilogy* (1948). He wrote two libretti for Kurt Weill, and a now neglected novel, *Es ist genug* (1932, 'It is Enough'), about incest.

Kaiser, Henry John 1882–1967
US industrialist

Born in New York State, from 1914 to 1933 he worked on major civil engineering projects in the USA, Canada and the West Indies. As manager of seven highly productive shipyards on the Pacific coast of the USA during World War II, he developed revolutionary methods of prefabrication and assembly in shipbuilding—enabling his ships to be constructed and launched within six days. His considerable industrial empire included a motor, a steel, and an aluminium and chemical corporation.

Kalashnikov, Mikhail Timofeyevich 1919–
Soviet military designer

Born of peasant stock in the Altai area, he joined the army in 1938. Seriously wounded in 1941, he began experimenting with what was to be the famous AK-47 assault rifle taken into Soviet service in 1949. Other versions were produced later. The rifle has also been extensively used by foreign armies and international terrorists, a fact deplored by Kalashnikov in later life. He was a Deputy of the USSR Supreme Soviet (1950–54, 1966–69).

Kaldor (of Newnham), Nicholas Kaldor, Baron 1908–86
British economist

Born in Budapest, Hungary, and educated in Budapest and at the London School of Economics (LSE), where he taught from 1932 to 1947. During World War II he served on both the British and US Strategic Bombing Surveys. In 1947 he became director of the research and planning commission of the Economic Commission for Europe, and was Professor of Economics at Cambridge from 1966 to 1975. He held a variety of senior United Nations appointments, and was fiscal adviser to the Treasury and to several overseas governments. He wrote *An Expenditure Tax* (1955), advocating expenditure taxes as opposed to income tax, and *The Scourge of Monetarism* (1982).

Kalecki, Michal 1899–1970
Polish economist and economic journalist

Born in Łódź, he studied engineering in Warsaw and Gdansk, and taught himself economics. He worked at the Institute of Statistics, Oxford (1940–45), becoming a United Nations economist (1946–54), and then a government economist and teacher of economics in Poland (1955–67). A Marxist, he was critical of both capitalism and socialism. He developed a theory of macroeconomic dynamics and introduced the new western methods in economics to the Soviet bloc. His books include *Essays in the Theory of Economic Fluctuations* (1939) and *Studies in Economic Dynamics* (1943).

Kálidása fl.450AD
Indian dramatist

He is best known through his drama *Śākuntala* (Eng trans by Sir **William Jones**, 1789), and is considered India's greatest dramatist. 📖 H H Wilson, *The Hindu Theatre* (1871)

Kalinin, Mikhail Ivanovich 1875–1946
Soviet politician

Born in Tver (which was renamed Kalinin after him from 1932 to 1991), he was a peasant and a metal-worker when young, and became head of the Soviet state after the 1917 revolution and during the years of **Stalin**'s dictatorship (1919–46). He entered politics as a champion of the poor classes, and won great popularity, becoming President of the Soviet Central Executive Committee (1919–38), and of the Presidium of the Supreme Soviet (1938–46). On his death Königsberg, East Prussia, was renamed Kaliningrad in his honour.

Kaltenbrunner, Ernst 1902–46
Austrian Nazi leader

Born in Reid im Innkreis, Austria, he was head of the SS at the time of the Anschluss. After **Reinhard Heydrich**'s assassination, he became head of the security police in 1943, sent millions of Jews and political suspects to the concentration camps, and was responsible for orders sanctioning the murder of prisoners of war. He was condemned by the Nuremberg Tribunal and hanged.

Kamb, (Walter) Barclay 1931–
US glaciologist

Born in San José, California, he studied physics and geology at the California Institute of Technology (Caltech), where he has remained throughout his career, becoming Professor of Geology in 1962 and Professor of Geology and Geophysics in 1963. Since 1990 he has been Rawn Professor there. He was also vice-president and provost of Caltech from 1987 to 1989. As well as leading glacial expeditions to Alaska, Antarctica and the Alps, his contributions to glacial research include work on ice-streaming phenomena in the polar ice sheets and their role in climatic change. He determined the structure of crystals in high-pressure forms of ice from 1960, and made the first detailed observations of a glacier in full surge (1985).

Kamen, Martin David 1913–
US biochemist

Born in Toronto, Canada, he studied in Chicago and held posts in several US universities. In 1960 he was appointed Professor of Biochemistry at the University of California, San Diego, where he was the first to isolate the carbon isotope ^{14}C, later widely used as a biochemical tracer. Studying photosynthesis, he confirmed that the oxygen released comes from water and not from carbon dioxide, determined the initial fate of the 'fixed' carbon dioxide, and demonstrated that illumination increases the phosphorus turnover. Kamen also studied nitrogen fixation and bacterial ferridoxins. He published *Radioactive Tracers in Biology* (1947) and *Primary Processes in Photosynthesis* (1963).

Kamenev, Lev Borisovich, *originally* Lev Borisovich Rosenfeld 1883–1936
Russian revolutionary and politician

Born of Jewish parentage in Moscow, he was an active revolutionary throughout Russia and abroad from 1901 onwards, associating with **Lenin**, **Trotsky** and **Stalin**, and was exiled to Siberia in 1915. Liberated after the February Revolution, he was active as a Bolshevik throughout 1917,

became the first chairman of the Central Executive Committee of the All Russian Congress of Soviets and subsequently held various party, government and diplomatic appointments. Expelled from the party as a Trotskyist in 1927, he was readmitted the next year but again expelled in 1932. The same happened in 1933–34. He was finally executed for allegedly conspiring with Trotsky and **Grigori Zinoviev** against Stalin. Like many others falsely accused, he was posthumously rehabilitated in 1988 during the **Gorbachev** years.

Kamerlingh Onnes, Heike 1853–1926
Dutch physicist and Nobel Prize winner

Born in Groningen, he studied physics and mathematics at the university there, and continued his studies at Heidelberg University. He later became Professor of Physics at the University of Leyden (1882–1923), where he established his famous low-temperature laboratory. He tested the ideas of **Johannes van der Waals**, studying liquids and gases over a wide range of temperatures and pressures. His most noteworthy achievements were the first liquefaction (1908) and later solidification of helium, and his discovery (1911) that the electrical resistance of metals cooled to near absolute zero disappears, a phenomenon later called 'superconductivity'. In 1913 he was awarded the Nobel Prize for physics, and he was elected a Foreign Member of the Royal Society in 1916.

Kames, Henry Home, Lord 1696–1782
Scottish judge, legal historian and philosopher

Born in Kames, Berwickshire, he was called to the Bar in 1723 and was raised to the bench as Lord Kames in 1752. A leading figure in the Scottish Enlightenment, he wrote notable works on Scots Law and philosophy, and his best-known book, *Elements of Criticism* (1762), was a major aesthetic work of its time. His other publications include *Historical Law Tracts* (1759), *Principles of Equity* (1760), *Essays on Morality and Natural Religion* (1751) and *An Introduction to the Art of Thinking* (1761).

Kammerer, Paul 1880–1926
Austrian zoologist

Born in Vienna, he was educated at the University of Vienna and later joined the Institute of Experimental Biology there. His experimental work appeared to support the view of **Jean-Baptiste Lamarck** that characteristics acquired during life can be transmitted through subsequent generations. The best known of these results concerned the apparent acquisition of nuptial pads on the forefeet of midwife toads. However, in 1926 G K Noble and H Przibram of the American Museum of Natural History examined material preserved from Kammerer's work in Vienna and showed that the dark swellings, which Kammerer claimed to be nuptial pads inherited through three generations, were due to injections of ink. Kammerer shot himself a few months later.

Kamp, Peter van de See **Van de Kamp, Peter**

Kamprad, Ingvar 1926–
Swedish businessman

Born in Pjätteryd, he is reputed to be the third richest man in Sweden. He is the founder (1943) and owner of the IKEA furniture company, whose products have established themselves as a life-style for many Swedes. Even though the company now has many outlets worldwide and has diversified into the financial and insurance sectors, its centre remains the Småland village of Ämhult.

Kanada c.300BC
Indian founder of the Vaiśeshika school of Hindu philosophy

He is sometimes identified with the legendary sage Kaśyapa. Kanada, meaning 'eater of atoms', may just be a descriptive name for the otherwise unknown author of the *Vaiśeshika Sutra*, a work which holds that things are made of invisible eternal atoms of earth, water, light or air. Although Kanada himself does not mention God, later commentators saw a need for a supreme being to regulate the atoms and account for the existence of the world.

Kanaris, Constantine 1790–1877
Greek sailor and statesman

He was one of several merchant-captains who provided their own ships for service in the struggle for Greek independence. He used fireships to blow up the Turkish flagship in the Strait of Chios (1822), repeated the feat in the harbour of Tenedos, and burnt a Turkish frigate and some transport ships in 1824. He held high commands, and was made a senator in 1847. He was Prime Minister of Greece on three occasions between 1848 and 1877, and took part in the revolution that put **George I** on the throne in 1863.

Kandinsky, Wassily, *Russian* Vasili Vasilyevich Kandinsky 1866–1944
French painter

Born in Moscow, Russia, he was the originator of Abstract painting. After studying law in Moscow, he went to Munich to study art, and at the age of 30, he began painting. A watercolour he produced in 1910 is considered to be the first 'abstract' work of art, but all representational elements were not banished from his work until the 1920s. In Paris he absorbed the influence of the Nabis and the Fauves, but Russian icon painting and folk-art were equal influences on him. In this he was at one with his Russian contemporaries. In 1912 he published his famous book *Über das Geistige in der Kunst* (Eng trans *On the Spiritual in Art*, 1947) and in the same year was a co-founder with **Franz Marc** and **Paul Klee** of the Blaue Reiter Group, editing with Marc the *Blaue Reiter* almanac. He returned to Russia to teach in 1914, and after the Russian Revolution became head of the Museum of Modern Art (1919) and founded the Russian Academy of Artistic Sciences (1921). In 1922 he left Russia and was eventually put in charge of the Weimar Bauhaus School. From 1920 his paintings are predominantly geometric, in line with the Suprematist and Constructivist work he had left behind in Moscow, which was eventually to fall out of favour there. In 1933 he moved to France (he became a naturalized citizen in 1939), and came under the influence of **Joán Miró**. As a painter and as a theoretician he has exerted considerable influence. ⌨ Will Grohmann, *Wassily Kandinsky: Life and Work* (1959)

Kane, Bob, *originally* Robert Kahn 1915–98
US cartoonist and animator, creator of Batman

Born in New York, he studied art at Cooper Union, joined the **Max Fleischer** Studio as a trainee animator in 1934, and entered the comic-book field with *Hiram Hick* in *Wow* (1936). His early strips were humorous, but mystery and menace entered his serial, *Peter Pupp*, in *Wags* (1937), where a cartoon hero battled a one-eyed super-villain. Working to scripts by his partner, Bill Finger (1917–74), he created *The Batman* for No.27 of *Detective Comics* (May 1939), which caught on rapidly. Kane then returned to animation to create *Courageous Cat* (1958) and *Cool McCool* (1969) for television.

Kane, Elisha Kent 1820–57
US explorer

Born in Philadelphia, he joined the US navy as surgeon and visited China, the East Indies, Arabia, Egypt, Europe, the west coast of Africa, and Mexico. In 1850 he sailed to the Arctic as surgeon and naturalist with the first expedition financed by **Henry Grinnell** in search of Sir

John Franklin (1850–51). He was commander of a second Arctic expedition (1853–55), and his account of it, *Arctic Explorations* was published in 1856.

Kane, Martin See Ó Cadhain, Máirtín

Kang Keqing (K'ang K'o-ch'ing) 1911–
Chinese political leader

Born in Wan'an, Jiangxi (Kiangsi) province, she studied at Jinggangshan Red Army College, and the Anti-Japan Military and Political Academy. She joined the Chinese Youth League in 1927, and organized Red Army guerrilla units. After her marriage in 1929 to General **Zhu De** she became Commander of the Red Army's Women's Department, and was one of the few women on the Long March (1934–35). After studying she held important posts in the Red Army's political department. In 1957 she was elected to the committee of the Chinese Democratic Women's Federation, becoming its president (1978), then honorary president (1988). Since her election in 1977 to the 11th Central Committee, she has held influential political posts, including membership of the Praesidium of the National People's Congress since 1980.

Kang Sheng (K'ang Sheng) 1899–1975
Chinese politician

He studied Soviet security and intelligence techniques in Moscow during the early 1930s. A prominent member of the Chinese Communist Party during the 1960s, he exercised considerable influence behind the scenes in his capacity as Head of Party Security. During the Cultural Revolution he was associated with the radical left group led by **Mao Zedong**'s wife, **Jiang Qing**. Since Mao's death in 1976, Kang's role in the persecution of party members and intellectuals during the Cultural Revolution has been condemned.

Kania, Karin, *née* Enke 1961–
German figure and speed skater

She began her career as a figure skater and, competing for East Germany, finished ninth in the 1977 European championships. Believing that she would be unable to better that performance, she took up speed skating and quickly showed a high level of aptitude. After only weeks of training, she produced an excellent 1,500 metres time and went on to win her first East German national title in 1980, the same year she won the world sprint championship and the Olympic 500 metres gold. She won another 14 national titles, another five world sprint championship titles and the overall world championship title a record five times. She also won another two Olympic golds, as well as a further four silvers and a bronze.

Kano Motonobu 1476–1559
Japanese painter

Born in Kyoto, he was the son of the painter Kano Masanobu (1434–1530), who had introduced the Kano style of painting which was directed at the feudal lords and warriors and not, as before, at the monks and priests. Borrowing from Buddhist and Chinese sources, the new style nevertheless had a nationalistic character. The latter was exemplified by Motonobu, who achieved a synthesis of Kanga (ink painting in the Chinese style) with the lively colours of Yamato-e (the Japanese style), arriving at a dynamic style of decorative art. Under him the Kano school established itself, both artistically as well as socially, and became a virtual academy. His most famous works, originally in various sanctuaries and monasteries in Kyoto, now preserved in its National Museum, show the decorative treatment of nature, which became standard for the Kano school.

Kant, Immanuel 1724–1804
German philosopher

The son of a saddler, he was born in Königsberg, Prussia (now Kaliningrad, Russia), and stayed there all his life. He studied and then taught at the university, becoming Professor of Logic and Metaphysics in 1770. He lived a quiet, orderly life and local people were said to set their watches by the time of his daily walk. His early publications were in the natural sciences, particularly geophysics and astronomy, and in an essay on Newtonian cosmology (*Allgemeine Naturgeschichte und Theorie des Himmels*, 1755) he anticipated the nebular theory of **Pierre Laplace** and predicted the existence of the planet Uranus before its actual discovery by **William Herschel** in 1781. He published extensively, but his most important works were produced relatively late in his life: the *Kritik der reinen Vernunft* (1781, 'Critique of Pure Reason'), *Kritik der praktischen Vernunft* (1788, 'Critique of Practical Reason'), and *Kritik der Urteilskraft* (1790, 'Critique of Judgement'). The first of these is a philosophical classic, albeit very difficult, which he himself described as 'dry, obscure, contrary to all ordinary ideas, and prolix to boot'. In it he responds to **David Hume's** empiricism and argues that the immediate objects of perception depend not only on our sensations but also on our perceptual equipment, which orders and structures those sensations into intelligible unities. He likened his conclusions to a Copernican revolution in philosophy, whereby some of the properties we observe in objects are due to the nature of the observer, rather than the objects themselves. There exist basic concepts (or 'categories'), like cause and effect, which are not learned from experience but constitute our basic conceptual apparatus for making sense of experience and the world. The second *Critique* deals with ethics, and his views are developed in the *Grundlagen zur Metaphysik der Sitten* (1785, 'Groundwork to the Metaphysic of Morals') where he presents the famous Categorical Imperative, 'Act only on that maxim which you can at the same time will to become a universal law'. The third *Critique* deals with aesthetics or judgments of 'taste', for which he tries to provide an objective basis and which he connects with our ability to recognize 'purposiveness' in nature. He also wrote on political topics, and his *Perpetual Peace* (1795) advocates a world system of free states. Kant described his philosophy as 'transcendental' or 'critical' idealism, and he exerted an enormous influence on subsequent philosophy, especially the idealism of **Johann Fichte, Hegel** and **Friedrich von Schelling**. He is regarded as one of the great figures in the history of western thought. ⌨ H W Cassiret, *Kant's Life and Thought* (1981)

Kantor, Tadeusz 1915–90
Polish theatre director and designer

He designed stage sets for the Stary Theatre, Kraków (1945–55) before founding his own experimental theatre company, Cricot 2. In Kraków he gave performances of several Surrealist plays by Stanisław Witkiewicz, some of which he staged for the first time. The world tour of his own play, *Dead Class* (1975), a largely silent piece with actors portraying corpses in a school classroom, brought him international acclaim. Another of his plays, the partly autobiographical *Wielopole, Wielopole*, was seen in Florence, Italy in 1979, and at the Edinburgh Festival and London a year later.

Kantorovich, Leonid Vitalevich 1912–86
Soviet economist, mathematician and Nobel Prize winner

Born and educated in St Petersburg, he was a professor at Leningrad (now St Petersburg) State University (1934–60) and later was director of the mathematical economics laboratory at the Moscow Institute of National Economic Management (1971–76) and the Institute of System Studies at the Moscow Academy of Sciences (from 1976). He shared the 1975 Nobel Prize for economics with **Tjalling Koopmans**.

Kao Kang See **Gao Gang**

Kapila 7th century BC
Indian founder of the Samkhya school of Hindu philosophy

An almost legendary figure, said to have spent the latter half of his life on Sagar Island at the mouth of the Ganges, he is held to be the originator of the philosophical system presently expounded in the commentary of Íśvarakrishna (3rd–5th century AD) and the *Samkhya Sutra* (c.1400AD). It is notable for parallels with Buddhist thought and a theory of evolution or constant 'becoming' of the world.

Kapil Dev, (Nihanj) 1959–
Indian cricketer

Born in Chandigarh, Punjab, an all-rounder, he made his first-class debut for Haryana at the age of 16, and played county cricket in England for Northamptonshire and Worcestershire. He led India to victory in the 1983 World Cup, and set a competition record score of 175 not out against Zimbabwe. In 1983 he became the youngest player (at 24 years 68 days) to perform a Test double of 2,000 runs and 200 wickets (surpassing **Ian Botham**). In February 1992 he became only the second player in Test history to take 400 wickets. In February 1994 he set a new world record of 432 Test wickets, surpassing the record (431 wickets) held by Sir **Richard Hadlee**.

Kapitza, Peter, *Russian* Pyotr Leonidovich Kapitsa 1894–1984
Soviet physicist and Nobel Prize winner

Born in Kronstadt, he studied at Petrograd (now St Petersburg) and under **Ernest Rutherford** at Cambridge, where he became assistant director of magnetic research at the Cavendish Laboratory (1924–32). He returned to the USSR in 1934, and was appointed director of the Institute of Physical Problems where he engineered a helium liquefier to investigate the extraordinary 'superfluid' properties of helium-2. He was dismissed in 1946 for refusing to work on the atomic bomb, but was reinstated in 1955. He is known for his work on high-intensity magnetism, on low temperature, and on the liquefaction of hydrogen and helium, and was awarded the Nobel Prize for physics, jointly with **Robert Wilson** and **Arno Penzias**, in 1978. In the 1970s he defended dissident physicist **Andrei Sakharov** from expulsion from the Soviet Academy of Sciences. ⌨ F Zedrov, *Kapitsa: zhizn i otkrytiia* (1979)

Kaplan, Mordecai Menahem 1881–1983
US rabbi and philosopher

Born in Svencionys, Lithuania, he emigrated to the USA with his family in 1889 and studied theology at various institutions in New York City, including Columbia University, before being ordained a rabbi in 1902. He was the founder of the Jewish Center in New York City (1916) and the Society for the Advancement of Judaism (1922), and he originated the Reconstructionist movement in Judaism, which celebrated the richness of Jewish culture but questioned some of its religious traditions, notably the belief that the Jews are a chosen people. He carried out his reassessment of the culture in books such as *Judaism as a Civilization* (1934) and in his journal *The Reconstructionist* (founded 1935). Though controversial, his views greatly influenced contemporary Reform Judaism, which answered his call for a more equal role for women in Jewish life.

Kaplan, Viktor 1876–1934
Austrian inventor

Born in Murz, he was educated as a mechanical engineer at the Technische Hochschule in Vienna, and from 1903 taught at the equivalent institution in Brunn. In his research he experimented with a propeller turbine working at very low heads of water, and found that its efficiency was greatly improved if the angle of the blades could be varied to suit the operating conditions. He patented the 'Kaplan turbine' in 1920 and it has since been used in most of the world's low-head (less than about 98 feet, 30 metres) hydropower schemes, as well as in the world's first major tidal power scheme on the estuary of the River Rance in Brittany.

Kapodístrias, Ióannis Antónios See Capo d'Istria, Giovanni Antonio, Count

Kapoor, Anish 1954–
British sculptor

Born in Bombay of Jewish–Indian parentage, he moved to Britain in 1972 and trained at Hornsey College of Art and Chelsea School of Art. His work is brightly coloured, consisting of disembodied shapes covered in powdered pigment, as used in Hindu worship. This often spills over onto the floor and around the form, as in *As if to Celebrate, I Discovered a Mountain Blooming with Red Flowers* (1981, Tate, London). He was appointed artist-in-residence in 1982 at the Walker Art Gallery, Liverpool. He exhibited at the Venice Biennale in 1982, and again in 1990, when he won the Premio Duemila for a young artist, with his 'voids', including a *Madonna* clothed in pigment of an intense blue shade.

Kaprow, Allan 1927–
US avant-garde artist and theorist

Born in Atlantic City, New Jersey, he studied art under the influential painter and theorist **Hans Hofmann** (1947–48), and music under **John Cage** (1956–58). Rejecting such traditional values as craftsmanship and permanence, he instead promoted 'happenings', involving the participation of spectators, and welcoming unplanned, chance developments. He had many exhibitions, at Amsterdam and Stockholm (1961), Paris (1963), Boston and New York (1966), and elsewhere.

Kapteyn, Jacobus Cornelius 1851–1922
Dutch astronomer

Born in Barnefeld, the Netherlands, he studied mathematics at the University of Leyden (1869–75), joined the staff of Leyden Observatory, and was appointed (1877) to a new chair of astronomy at the University of Groningen. His best-known work was the reduction of photographic plates obtained at the Cape Observatory in South Africa, which exhibited 455,000 stars. His investigations of the motions as well as the distribution of stars in space led to the discovery in 1904 of apparently preferred directions of motion or 'star-streams', later understood in terms of the differential rotation of our galaxy around a distant centre. Kapteyn was one of the founders of modern stellar statistics.

Kapwepwe, Simon 1922–89
Zambian nationalist leader and politician

Educated in mission schools before becoming a teacher, he helped found the Northern Rhodesian African National Congress in 1946. After a period of study in India, he returned to be Treasurer and then helped form the breakaway United National Independence Party (UNIP) of which he became Treasurer (1960–67). After holding several ministerial posts in the early days of independence (1964), including the vice-presidency, he resigned from UNIP to form his own party, the United Progress Party, in 1971 in order to oppose **Kenneth Kaunda**. The party was banned in 1972, when Zambia became a one-party state and Kapwepwe was detained. He rejoined UNIP in 1977.

Karadžić or Karadjic, Radovan Birthdate unknown
Bosnian-Serb politician

Born in Montenegro, he came to Sarajevo as a teenager after World War II. Formerly a psychiatrist and poet he became prominent in politics in 1990 on the creation of the Serbian Democratic Party (SDS), the main Serbian party in Bosnia. As the self-styled President of Serb-controlled Bosnia from 1992 to 1996, he signed the Vance–Owen Peace Plan in May 1993, and the Dayton Peace Agreement in December 1995. However, with the aim of uniting all the Serbs in the former Yugoslavia into one Greater Serbia, his militias drove over one million Muslims from their homes, killing many thousands, and he was indicted by the UN war crimes tribunal in 1996.

Karadžić, Vuk Stefanović 1787–1864
Serbian poet and philologist

Born in Trsić in western Serbia, he allegedly learned to write with ink made from gunpowder and water, and rose to lead the Serb national revival. During the first Serbian Uprising (1804), he was secretary to a leader of the Hajduks. The next year he studied briefly at Sremski Karlovci, then in southern Hungary. He returned to teach in Belgrade, but fled to Vienna when the Turks reoccupied the city and crushed the uprising of 1813. Influenced by the ideas of **Johann Herder**, he was persuaded by **Goethe** to collect Serbian folk poetry and folklore. Among his many literary and scholarly achievements, he tried, using a simplified Cyrillic alphabet, to create a standard Serbian orthography, grammar and dictionary based on the dialect used in Herzegovina in order to produce literature in the vernacular. He also compiled a Serbian–German dictionary (1818) and translated the New Testament into Serbian, published in 1869.

Karajan, Herbert von 1908–89
Austrian conductor

Born in Salzburg, he studied there and in Vienna. His career began at the opera houses of Ulm (1928–33) and Aachen (1934–38), and his fame grew when he was conductor at the Berlin Staatsoper (1938–42). He joined the Nazi Party in 1933 and after World War II was not permitted to work until 1947, but in 1955 was made principal conductor of the Berlin Philharmonic Orchestra with which he was mainly associated. He also frequently conducted at the Vienna State Opera, the Vienna Gesellschaft der Musikfreude, and at many major festivals, and was artistic director of the Salzburg Festival (1956–60) and of the Salzburg Easter Festival (from 1967). His passion for the theatre and for acoustical research was evident in his production of operas, in his idiosyncratic casting, the refined, impressive (often controversial) quality of his recordings, and in the films he directed and conducted.

Karamanlis or Caramanlis, Konstantinos 1907–98
Greek politician

He was born in Próti, Macedonia. A former lawyer, he held several government posts before being called upon by King **Paul I** to form a government in 1955. He remained Prime Minister almost continuously for eight years, during which time Greece signed a treaty of alliance with Cyprus and Turkey. He formed the National Radical Union Party. After his party's election defeat in 1963 he left politics and lived abroad, but he returned to become Prime Minister in 1974, supervising the restoration of civilian rule after the collapse of the military government. He then served as President (1980–85, 1990–95).

Karami, Rashid d.1987
Lebanese politician

The son of Abd al-Hamid Karami, he succeeded to the leadership, albeit disputed, of the Muslims in the Tripoli area of Lebanon while still a young man. Pro-**Nasser** in the 1950s, he became a member of the newly-formed National Front, in opposition to **Camille Chamoun**. After Chamoun's departure following the disturbances of 1958, and **Fuad Chehab**'s assumption of the presidency, Karami formed a predominantly National Front cabinet. A subsequent Christian strike drove home the fact that some

Phalange and pro-Christian elements would have to be included and, accordingly, a new and more representative cabinet was formed. During the civil war in the 1970s, he became Prime Minister, and later headed the coalition government formed by President **Amin Gemayel** in 1984. Karami, who was amongst those Lebanese politicians who strove to save the country, was assassinated in 1987.

Karamzin, Nikolai Mikhailovich 1766–1826
Russian historian and novelist

He was born in Mikhailovka, Orenburg. Among his writings are *Pisma ruskovo putishestvenika* (1790–92, 'Letters of a Russian Traveller'), an account of his travels in western Europe, several novels, including *Bednaya Lisa* (1792, 'Poor Lisa') and *Natalia, boyarskaya doch* (1792, 'Natalia, the Boyar's Daughter'), and a great unfinished *Gosudarstvo rossuskovo* (1816–29, 'History of Russia') down to 1613. His influence on the literature of Russia and its development was considerable. He modernized the literary language by his introduction of western idioms and his writing as a whole reflected western thought. 📖 H Nebel Jr, *Nikolai Mikhailovich Karamzin: a Russian sentimentalist* (1967)

Karan, Donna 1948–
US designer

Born in Donna Faske, New York, she dropped out of Parson's School of Design to work for **Anne Klein**, becoming her successor in 1974. In 1984 she launched her own company, featuring luxurious, user-friendly clothes that appeal to successful working women. Her collections include her own-label jewellery, accessories, shoes, lingerie, hosiery and eyewear. She launched the cheaper DKNY label in 1988, followed by DKNY Jeans (1990), Menswear (1991), the Beauty Company and DKNY Menswear (1992), the Shoe company (1992), and DKNY Kids (1993). She won the Coty award in 1977, 1981 and 1984 and now employs around 1,000 people worldwide.

Karavelov, Lyuben 1835–79
Bulgarian revolutionary and writer

Born in Koprivshtsa, he lived most of his life abroad: in Russia, Serbia, Hungary and Romania. Influenced by the Russian Slavophiles and radical socialists he met while studying in Odessa, he joined the Bulgarian revolutionary organizations active in Serbia (1867) and founded the Bulgarian Revolutionary Committee with Khristo Botev and Vasil Levski in Bucharest (1871). He published the émigré revolutionary journals *Freedom* (1869–72) and *Independence* (1873–4). His masterly stories created the prototype of the obstinate old Bulgarian peasant still known and appreciated in Bulgaria. He just lived to see his aim, Bulgarian independence, realized. 📖C Manning and R Smal-Stocki, *The History of Modern Bulgarian Literature* (1960)

Kardelj, Edvard 1910–79
Yugoslav (Slovene) politician

A schoolteacher, he joined the Communist Party and was among the many imprisoned during the dictatorship of **Alexander I**. He lived in the USSR and joined **Tito** as a partisan during World War II, becoming vice-president of his anti-Fascist council (AVNOJ) and in 1946 Foreign, and Deputy Prime Minister. With **Milovan Djilas** he went to Moscow in 1948 to face **Stalin**'s criticism of Yugoslavia's independent foreign policy and stood firm with Tito in demonstrating that Yugoslavia would not become merely a Soviet satellite. He was the prominent theoretician of Tito's postwar regime, drawing up the federal constitution and leading the search for a Marxism purified of all Stalinist accretions.

Karl VIII, *also known as* Karl Knutsson 1408–70
King of Sweden and of Norway

A powerful Swedish magnate, he was appointed Guardian of the realm (1438–40). During the reign of Kristofer of Bavaria (Christopher III of Denmark) he was given large fiefs in Finland, but was brought back and elected King as Karl VIII on Christopher's death (1448), and was also elected King of Norway (1448). He lost the Norwegian throne (1450) to **Kristian I** of Denmark, and in 1457 was driven out of Sweden by an insurrection in favour of Kristian, but was twice recalled to the throne (1464–65, 1467–70) by factions opposed to the Kalmar Union.

Karl IX 1550–1611
King of Sweden

Born in Stockholm, he was the youngest son of **Gustav I Vasa**, half-brother of **Erik XIV**, and uncle of King **Sigismund III Vasa** of Poland and Sweden. In 1568, as Duke Karl, he led a rebellion against Erik XIV which deposed him and brought their brother, **Johan III**, to the throne (1568–92). A defender of Lutheranism, he resisted the Counter-Reformation promoted by Johan III and Sigismund III. He called the Convention of Uppsala (1593) which renounced Catholicism before the Catholic Sigismund arrived from Poland for his coronation, then took over as regent. When Sigismund returned (1598) to reclaim his kingdom, Duke Karl defeated and deposed him. Although personally unattractive, he was a good administrator, and sponsored industrial development. Proclaimed king in 1604, he fought a long inconclusive war with Poland (1600–10), intervened ineffectively in Russia, and Sweden was invaded by Denmark (1611–13). He was succeeded by his young son, **Gustav II Adolf**.

Karl X Gustav 1622–60
King of Sweden

The son of John Casimir of Zweibrücken, Count Palatine, and of Catherine, daughter of **Karl IX** and sister of **Gustav II Adolf**, he was born at Nyköping Castle, and trained at the military academy in Sorö, Denmark. Decisive, energetic and ruthless, he took part in the Thirty Years War as generalissimo of the Swedish forces in Germany (1648). He was appointed Crown Prince (1650), and succeeded to the throne in 1654 on the abdication of his cousin Queen **Kristina**, whom he failed in his efforts to marry. He overran Poland in 1655, forcing the Elector of Brandenburg to acknowledge his lordship over Prussia, and crushed the Polish forces at Warsaw (1656). In war with the Danes (1657–58), he crossed the Little and Great Belt on the ice, seized Jutland and Zealand, and extorted from the Danes through the Treaty of Roskilde (1658) the southern parts of the Scandinavian peninsula, which they had held for centuries. Under him Sweden reached the limit of her territorial expansion. At home he imposed a policy of repossessing Crown lands from the nobles (*Reduktion*) in 1655. Dying suddenly, he was succeeded by his four-year-old son, **Karl XI**.

Karl XI 1655–97
King of Sweden

He was born in Stockholm, the son and successor in 1660 of **Karl X Gustav**. After regency rule by the nobility, he assumed power in 1672, and in 1675 helped stop a Danish invasion at Lund, winning favourable terms in the peace treaty (1679). Thereafter he followed a neutral foreign policy. He severely moderated the power of the nobility by reviving the *Reduktion* (repossession) of their Crown lands, and reorganized the armed forces and the administration. He was granted almost absolute monarchical power in 1693. Although shy and narrow-minded, he was abstemious and conscientious, and made bureaucratic promotion depend on merit rather than birth. He was succeeded by his adolescent son, **Karl XII**.

Karl XII (Charles XII) See panel p1016

Karl or Charles XII 1682–1718
King of Sweden from 1697, one of Sweden's greatest warrior kings

Karl was the son and successor of **Karl XI** and Ulrika Eleonora 'the Elder' of Denmark. He assumed the throne at the age of 15, having been declared of age. In 1700 the Great Northern War broke out, with a joint invasion of Swedish territory by Denmark and Saxony. Karl initially had no desire for war himself, but when Russia joined the alliance later in the year he counter-attacked by invading Denmark, forcing them to sue for peace. He defeated a Russian army at Narva, and in the following year gained a costly victory over the Saxons on the river Dvina. Next he defeated the Saxons at Kliszow in 1702, and dethroned King **Augustus II** of Poland in 1704 in favour of his ally Stanisław Leszczyński. His victories were consolidated at the Peace of Altanstrādt in 1706.

Karl's grand design for total Swedish dominion of the Baltic was not realized. A surprise invasion of Russia in 1707, although he almost captured the tsar, **Peter I, the Great**, resulted in a heavy defeat at Poltava in June 1709. The Swedish army surrendered and Karl escaped. Later that year he made an incognito journey across half of Europe, covering 1,250 miles (2,000km) on horseback in 15 days to the Baltic port of Stralsund. Cornered there

by a ring of enemies for a year, he escaped in December 1715 to Lund in Sweden, 15 years after he had left his homeland.

Undaunted, he raised a new army to keep the Russians at bay, and in 1716 launched a preliminary attack on Norway. He now formed an ambitious plan: he would be given freedom by Russia to conquer Norway in exchange for the Baltic provinces of Sweden, and then land in Scotland to put the Jacobite **James Edward Stuart**, the 'Old Pretender', on the British throne. But having made his treaty with the Russians and invaded Norway again in 1718, he was shot dead at the siege of the border fortress of Fredriksten, near Frederikshald.

A man of great ability, circumstances had made him a military adventurer, and by the end of his life he had become a futile victim of his own glittering legend. He died unmarried, and was succeeded by his younger sister, Queen **Ulrika Eleonora**.

📖 R H Hatton, *Charles XII of Sweden* (1968); Frans G Bengtsson, *Karl XII* (1935–36, Eng trans *The Life of Charles XII*, 1960).

Karl XIII 1748–1818
King of Sweden and of Norway

He was the younger brother of **Gustav III**, and uncle and successor to **Gustav IV Adolf**. As Duke of Södermanland he commanded the Swedish fleet against Russia (1788–90). He was made regent during the minority of his nephew (1792–96), and was elected king (1809), when he signed a new constitution limiting the powers of the monarchy. In 1810, the French Marshal Bernadotte was elected Crown Prince and adopted by him as **Karl Johan**; he took over the reins of power when the king's health failed (1811), and in 1814 secured the Crown of Norway for Sweden. Karl XIII was married to Charlotte of Oldenburg (d.1818), whose diary is an important source for the history of her time.

Karl XIV Johan, *originally* Jean Baptiste Jules Bernadotte 1763–1844
King of Sweden and Norway

Born a lawyer's son in Pau, France, he joined the French army as a soldier (1780), became an ardent partisan of the Revolution and rose to become Marshal (1804). In 1798 he married Desirée (Desideria) Clary, daughter of a wealthy Marseilles merchant. For his gallantry at the Battle of Austerlitz (1805) he was created prince and Duke of Pontecorvo. In 1810 he was elected Crown Prince of Sweden and Norway and heir to the elderly, childless **Karl XIII**; he turned Protestant, and assumed the name of Karl Johan. When the king's health failed (1811), he took command of affairs, helped defeat **Napoleon I** in the Battle of Nations (1813), attacked Denmark (1814) and secured a union between Norway and Sweden which lasted until 1905. He succeeded to the throne on the king's death (1818), and throughout his reign tried with some success to resist the growing tide of liberalism which wanted to curtail the autocracy of the Crown. He became the founder of the House of **Bernadotte**, the present royal dynasty of Sweden. He was succeeded by his son **Oskar I**.

Karl XV 1826–72
King of Sweden and Norway

He was the son and successor of **Oskar I**. He was an enthusiastic supporter of the idea of a united Scandinavia until his accession (from 1859). He promised to support Denmark in her border disputes with Germany, but when Denmark declared war on Germany in 1864 over Schleswig-Holstein, the Swedish government refused to

honour his pledge. During his reign the old Riksdag (parliament) of the four Estates was replaced (1865–66) by a Riksdag of two chambers with equal rights. A cheerful and flamboyant character, he was also a poet and artist of ability. Married to Lovisa of the Netherlands, he left no son and was succeeded by his younger brother, **Oskar II**.

Karl Ludwig Johann (of Austria) See Charles

Karle, Isabella Helen, *née* Lugoski 1921–
US chemist and crystallographer

Born in Detroit, Michigan, into a Polish immigrant family, she was educated at the University of Michigan, where in 1942 she married her fellow student **Jerome Karle**. They both accepted positions at the Naval Research Laboratories in Washington, and their new techniques of studying electron diffraction led Isabella Karle to study living structures by X-ray diffraction. Among the many important chemical structures she has discovered is that of enkephalin, a naturally occurring analgesic found in the brain, which is a class of chemicals co-discovered by **Candace Pert**. Isabella Karle has been honoured by scientific academies around the world.

Karle, Jerome 1918–
US physicist and Nobel Prize winner

Born in New York City, he studied at the City College of New York (CCNY), Harvard and Michigan University, where in 1942 he married his fellow student Isabella Lugoski (**Isabella Karle**). After working briefly on the Manhattan Project to develop the atomic bomb in the 1940s, he spent his career at the US Naval Research Laboratories in Washington, specializing in diffraction methods for studying the fine structure of crystalline matter. Since 1968 he has been Chief Scientist at the Laboratory for the Structure of Matter there. He shared the 1985 Nobel Prize for chemistry with his fellow CCNY student **Herbert Hauptman** for the development of the 'direct method' for interpreting raw data from X-ray crystallography measurements. He later investigated the use of high-speed computers to produce real-time images of crystals and complex biomolecules.

Karlfeldt, Erik Axel 1864–1931
Swedish lyric poet and Nobel Prize winner

Born in Folkärna, Dalarna, he published several volumes of highly individual nature poetry reflecting the traditional language and customs of peasant life in his native province. In *Fridolins visor* (1898, 'Fridolin's Songs') he introduced a peasant character who reappeared in *Fridolins lustgård* (1901, 'Fridolin's Pleasure Garden'). Critics have not been kind to his poetry, but it proved popular until the appearance of erotic volumes like *Flora och Bellona* (1918). He was secretary of the Swedish Academy from 1912. He was posthumously awarded the 1931 Nobel Prize for literature. ☐ T Fogelquist, *Erik Axel Karlfeldt* (1941)

Karloff, Boris, *originally* William Henry Pratt
1887–1969
English actor

Born in Dulwich, London, he was educated Uppingham and Merchant Taylors' schools. He emigrated to Canada in 1909 and became involved in acting. He spent 10 years in repertory companies, then went to Hollywood, and after several silent films made his name as the monster in *Frankenstein* (1931). His career was mostly spent in popular horror films, such as *The Bodysnatchers* (1945), though his performances frequently transcended the crudity of the genre. He returned to the stage in *Arsenic and Old Lace* (1941), and was a particularly effective Captain Hook in *Peter Pan* (1951). In 1955 he moved back to England, returning to Hollywood only to work. He continued to appear in films and on television and the stage until his death. ☐ Cynthia Lindsay, *Dear Boris: The Life of William Henry Pratt aka Boris Karloff* (1975)

Karmal, Babrak 1929–96
Afghan politician

The son of an army officer, he was educated at Kabul University, where he studied law and political science. He was imprisoned for anti-government activity during the early 1950s. In 1965 he formed the Khalq (masses) Party and, in 1967, the breakaway Parcham (banner) Party. These two groups merged in 1977 to form the banned People's Democratic Party of Afghanistan (PDPA), with Karmal as deputy leader. After briefly holding office as President and Prime Minister in 1978, he was forced into exile in eastern Europe, returning in 1979, after the Soviet military invasion, to become head of state. Karmal's rule was fiercely opposed by the mujahadeen guerrillas and in 1986 he was replaced as President and PDPA leader by Sayid Mohammad Najibullah.

Kármán, Theodore von 1881–1963
US physicist and aeronautical engineer

Born in Budapest, Hungary, he graduated as an engineer from Budapest Technical University (1902), gained a PhD under Ludwig Prandtl at Göttingen, and in 1912 became Professor of Aeronautics and Mechanics at the University of Aachen and head of the Aeronautical Institute there. After visits to the USA in 1926, he became director of the Guggenheim Aeronautical Laboratories (1930–49) and the Jet Propulsion Laboratory (1942–45) at the California Institute of Technology. He became a US citizen in 1936. He founded the Aerojet Engineering Corporation in the early 1940s and in 1951 the major international aerospace research organization AGARD (Advisory Group for Aeronautical Research and Development) as part of NATO. He was the first recipient of the National Medal of Science in 1963, and published major works in many fields. Several theories bear his name, such as the Kármán 'vortex street' (1911), a double line of vortices formed when air flows over a cylindrical surface. After the dramatic collapse of the Tacoma Narrows suspension bridge in the USA in 1940, he proved that oscillations due to vortex shedding in a moderate 42 mph wind were the cause of its destruction. He is sometimes called the 'father of modern aerodynamics'.

Karolyi, Mihalyi, Count 1875–1955
Hungarian politician

In 1901 he classified himself a liberal, but from 1906 an independent. Despite his aristocratic background he struggled for democratic reforms, and during World War I he opposed the alliance with Germany. In 1918 he was briefly Prime Minister, and President from January to July 1919. His well-known willingness to accommodate the subject nationalities won him the wrath of most of his fellow Magyars and he was forced into exile. Before and during World War II he won an international reputation as a champion of democratic Hungary, and he served as ambassador in Paris (1947–49). With the formation of a communist government in 1949, he was once more compelled to go into exile.

Karp, David 1922–
US writer

Born in New York, of Russian–Jewish descent, he served in the US army, and then worked as a journalist, and a radio, television and paperback writer. He emerged as a serious novelist with *One* (1953), an Orwellian condemnation of totalitarianism. Other works include *The Day of the Monkey* (1955), on British colonialism, *All Honourable Men* (1956), *The Sleepwalkers* (1960) and *Last Believers* (1964).

Karpinnen, Pertti 1953–
Finnish oarsman

Born in Parsio, he is a fireman, six feet seven inches (2m) tall, who won the first of his three individual Olympic gold medals in 1976. Finland's first gold medal, it was achieved when he rowed through both the German world champion Peter Kolbe, and the co-favourite Joachim Dreifke. Karpinnen retained his medal in 1980 and in 1984 he won his third, consecutive gold in the Los Angeles Olympics. With one of his famous finishing bursts, he powered past Kolbe in the final 25m of the 2,000m race. He shares his record of three individual golds with Vyacheslav Ivanov.

Karpov, Anatoli Yevgenevich 1951–
Soviet chess player

Born in Zlatoust, in the Urals, he received early chess tuition from former world champion Mikhail Botvinnik, winning the 1969 world junior championship. After Bobby Fischer refused to defend his title, he became world champion by default in 1975, defending his title successfully against Viktor Korchnoi in 1978 and 1982, in acrimonious matches. His 1984–85 defence against Gary Kasparov was controversially halted by FIDE (Fédération Internationale des Échecs) when he led but showed signs of cracking under the physical and psychological pressure. Kasparov won the title when the match was resumed from scratch in 1985. Karpov made at least two attempts to regain his title, eventually succeeding in 1993. In 1994, two chess world championships were held. Karpov played and won the FIDE title. Kasparov elected to play, and eventually won, the Professional Chess Association (PCA) version. Karpov's autobiography, *Karpov on Karpov*, was published in 1990.

Karr, (Jean Baptiste) Alphonse 1808–90
French novelist and journalist

He was born in Paris, and his *Sous les tilleuls* (1832, 'Under the Linden Trees') by its originality and wit found its author an audience for a long series of novels, of which *Geneviève* (1838) is probably the best. In 1839 he became editor of *Le Figaro*, and started issuing the bitterly satirical monthly pamphlets *Les Guêpes* (1839–47, 'The Wasps'). His *Voyage autour de mon jardin* (1845, Eng trans *A Tour Around My Garden*, 1855) is his best-known book. He also published his reminiscences, *Livre de bord* (4 vols, 1879–80, 'Logbook'). The best known of his epigrams is 'Plus ça change plus c'est la même chose' (of revolutions). ☐ L Bauthier, *Portraits du 19ième siècle* (1894)

Karrer, Paul 1889–1971
Swiss chemist and Nobel Prize winner

Born in Moscow, Russia, he was educated in Switzerland and studied chemistry under **Alfred Werner** at the University of Zurich. After graduating he worked with organo-arsenic compounds, and this interest led him in 1912 to move to Frankfurt to work with **Paul Ehrlich**. In 1919 he succeeded Werner as professor at Zurich. All his chemical studies involved natural products. During the 1920s he developed an interest in plant pigments and elucidated the structure of carotene, which then led to important discoveries concerning vitamin A. He also elucidated the structures of vitamins E, K and B$_2$ (riboflavin). For these achievements and for important studies of the chemistry of vitamin C and biotin, he shared the 1937 Nobel Prize for chemistry with **Norman Haworth**. Karrer's later studies included important work on the coenzyme nicotinamide-adenine dinucleotide, carotenoids and the curare-like alkaloids. He was the Rector of the University of Zurich from 1950 to 1952 and published the textbook *Lehrbuch der organischen Chemie* in 1928.

Karsavina, Tamara Platonovna 1885–1978
British dancer

Born in St Petersburg, Russia, she trained with **Enrico Cecchetti** at the Imperial Ballet School there and joined the Maryinsky Theatre in 1902. In 1909 she became one of the original members of **Diaghilev's** company, creating roles in ballets by **Michel Fokine** with **Nijinsky** (1909–13). She moved to London in 1918 with her husband, an English diplomat, though she continued to make guest appearances with Diaghilev's Ballets Russes and later advised on revivals of Diaghilev productions. She was vice-president of the Royal Academy of Dancing from 1920 to 1955 and wrote several books, including the autobiographical *Theatre Street* (1930), *Ballet Technique* (1956), and *Classical Ballet* (1962).

Karsh, Yousuf, *known as* Karsh of Ottawa 1908–
Canadian photographer

Born in Turkish Armenia, he emigrated to Canada in 1924, and was educated at the Boston School of Art and Design. He was apprenticed to a Boston portraitist (1928–31), and in 1932 opened his own studio in Ottawa, being appointed official portrait photographer to the Canadian government in 1935. His wartime studies of **Winston Churchill** and other national leaders were reproduced widely, and he continued to portray statesmen, artists and writers throughout the world. He became a Canadian citizen in 1947. His publications include the autobiography *In Search of Greatness* (1962) and *American Legends* (1992).

Kartini, Raden Adjeng 1879–1904
Javanese aristocrat

Born in Majong, she was one of the first to advocate equal opportunities for Indonesian women and her ideas and aspirations, as expressed in letters to a Dutch pen-friend, were published posthumously as *Door duisternis tot licht* (1911, 'Through Darkness Into Light'). She set up a school in her house (1903), with the blessing of the country's Education Minister. She later started another school with her husband, the Regent of Renbang, but died soon after giving birth to her first child. Her birthday was made a national holiday.

Karume, Sheikh Abeid 1905–72
Zanzibari and Tanzanian politician

A sailor, he became active in local politics in the 1940s, was elected a town councillor in 1954 and helped found the Afro-Shirazi Party in 1957. Following the 1964 coup which deposed the Sultan of Zanzibar, Karume became President of the Revolutionary Council. When Zanzibar united with Tanganyika in 1964 to form Tanzania, he became Vice-President, but his expressed opposition to democratic changes made him enemies and in 1972 he was assassinated.

Kasavubu, Joseph 1910–69
Congolese politician

Educated in a seminary, he worked as a teacher and civil servant in the colonial Belgian administration before entering politics. He was Mayor of Leopoldville (now Kinshasa, Democratic Republic of Congo) in 1957 and, supported by the UN in his struggle for power against **Patrice Lumumba**, became President of the Republic of the Congo in 1960. In the ensuing civil war he first defeated General **Sese Mobutu's** challenge and recaptured the presidency, but was later deposed by Mobutu, whom he had appointed as Commander-in-Chief.

Käsebier, Gertrude, *née* Stanton 1852–1934
US photographer

Born in Fort Des Moines (now Des Moines), Iowa, and raised in Golden, Colorado Territory, and later in Brooklyn, she began photographing her family in the late 1880s after she and her husband had moved to New Jersey, where they had three children. Opening her own portrait studio in Manhattan (1897–98), she built up a successful business, and her portraits were first exhibited in New York in 1897 at the Pratt Institute. She went on to become one of the first women members of the Linked Ring group in 1900 and a founder-member of Photo-Secession in 1902. She was represented in **Frances Benjamin Johnston's** exhibition of US women photographers (1900–01), and **Alfred Stieglitz** devoted the first issue of his influential magazine *Camera Work* to her in 1903. In 1916 she became co-founder with Alvin Langdon Coburn (1882–1966) and Clarence White (1871–1925) of the Pictorial Photographers of America.

Kasparov, Gary Kimovich, *originally* Gary Weinstein 1963–
Soviet chess player

Born in Baku, Azerbaijan, his surname was changed by the authorities after his father died in a road accident. He won the USSR under-18 championship at the age of 12 and became world junior champion at 16. His 1984–85 match with **Anatoli Karpov** for the world title was the longest in the history of chess—after 48 games, played over six months in Moscow, he had recovered from 0–5 to 3–5, with Karpov requiring only one more win, but showing signs of cracking under the physical and psychological pressure. In one of the most controversial decisions ever made in chess history, the match was abandoned by FIDE (Fédération Internationale des Échecs), and the players were given six months to recuperate. On resumption from scratch Kasparov won the title, which he defended successfully against Karpov in 1986 and 1987. Long-term friction between him and FIDE resulted in his establishing the Grandmasters' Association in 1987. He successfully defended his title in 1993 against Nigel Short, and is the highest-ranked active player. In 1994, two chess world championships were held. Kasparov elected to play, and eventually won, the Professional Chess Association one, but his great rival, **Anatoli Karpov**, played and won the FIDE title. In an autobiography, *Child Of Change* (1987), Kasparov portrayed himself as a chess product of the revolution of Soviet life instituted under Gorbachev's policy of *glasnost*.

Kassem, Abdul Karim 1914–63
Iraqi soldier and revolutionary

He was born in Baghdad. He joined the army and in 1958 he led the coup which resulted in the overthrow of the monarchy and the deaths of King **Faisal II**, his uncle Prince Abdul Ilah, and the pro-western Prime Minister General **Nuri Es-Sa'id**. Kassem attempted to suspend the constitution and established a left-wing military regime with himself as Prime Minister and head of state, but soon found himself increasingly isolated in the Arab world. He survived one assassination attempt, but failed to crush a Kurdish rebellion (1961–63) and was killed in a coup led by Colonel Salem Aref, who reinstated constitutional government.

Kastler, Alfred 1902–84
French scientist and Nobel Prize winner
Born in Guebwiller (then in Germany), he taught physics at lycées in Mulhouse, Colmar and Bordeaux, before leaving to join the University of Bordeaux in 1931, where he later became Professor of Physics. He moved to the École Normale Supérieure in Paris in 1941 where he led a research group in Hertzian spectroscopy, becoming professor in 1952. He obtained precise information about atomic structures by probing energy levels within atoms, using visible light and radio waves to excite electrons in atoms, which then emitted radiation as they returned to lower energy states. He also used optical techniques to develop 'optical pumping', which laid the foundations for the subsequent development of masers and lasers, and for which he was awarded the 1966 Nobel Prize for physics.

Kästner, Erich 1899–1974
German writer
He was born in Dresden, and his writing career began with two volumes of verse, *Herz auf Taille* (1928, 'Heart on Waistline') and *Lärm im Spiegel* (1929, 'Noise in the Mirror'), both cleverly satirical. In 1933 his books were publicly burnt by the Nazis, but he continued to live in Germany. His novels include *Fabian: Die Geschichte eines Moralisten* (1931, Eng trans *Fabian: The Story of a Moralist*, 1932) and *Drei Männer im Schnee* (1934, Eng trans *Three Men in the Snow*, 1935). However, he is best known for his delightful children's books, including *Emil und die Detektive* (1928, Eng trans *Emil and the Detectives*, 1930), *Annaluise und Anton* (1929, Eng trans 1932) and *Das fliegende Klassenzimmer* (1933, Eng trans *The Flying Classroom*, 1934), which gained him worldwide fame. Among his later writings is the autobiographical *Als ich ein kleiner Junge war* (1957, Eng trans *When I was a Little Boy*, 1959). ⊞ L Enderle, *Erich Kästner Bildbiographie* (1960)

Katayama Tetsu Dates unavailable
Japanese politician
A Christian socialist, he helped form the Socialist People's Party (Shakai Minshuto) in 1926, one of a number of 'proletarian parties' founded during the 1920s. In 1945 he emerged as the leader of the newly-created Japan Socialist Party, which achieved a plurality of votes in the first elections held under the 1947 Peace Constitution. He headed a coalition government in 1947–48, the country's first and, to date, only socialist Prime Minister. His government created a new Ministry of Labour, enacted the Anti-Monopoly Law, and presided over the dissolution of the pre-war financial combines (zaibatsu), but became increasingly unpopular when economic crisis forced it to impose price and wage controls. After his resignation (1948), he became identified with the party's right wing, and later (1960) helped to form the moderate Democratic Socialist Party, which supported the 1951 Security Treaty with the USA.

Katherine Parr See Catherine Parr

Katkov, Mikhail Nikiforovich 1818–87
Russian journalist
He was Professor of Philosophy at Moscow from 1845 to 1850, when the teaching of philosophy was stopped, and after 1861 editor of the *Moscow Gazette*. He was at first an advocate of reform, a vaguely Pan-Slavic liberal, but was converted by the Polish rising of 1863 into a chauvinist Russian, increasingly supportive of reactionary

Tsarist government. Because of his success as a publicist, he did great damage to the cause of moderate reform in 19th-century Russia.

Kato Takaaki (Komei) 1860–1926
Japanese politician
He initially worked for the firm of Mitsubishi, marrying the daughter of its founder, Yataro Iwasaki. He studied in England (1883–85) and was to remain an enthusiastic Anglophile throughout his life. As Minister to Britain (1894–1900), he supported the idea of an Anglo–Japanese Alliance. Elected to the Diet (1902) he joined the Constitutional Association of Friends (Doshikai) political party (1913), soon becoming its leader. While Foreign Minister (1914–16) he attempted to follow a policy free from the interference of the elder statesmen (genro). He engineered Japan's entrance into World War I on the side of the Allies in 1914 as a means of expanding Japan's influence in China. As leader of the moderately progressive Kenseikai, which became the largest single party in the 1924 elections, he became Prime Minister (1924–26). During his premiership, universal manhood suffrage was enacted (1925), but attempts to reform the Upper House (House of Peers) failed. In order to placate conservative critics, his government also enacted the Peace Preservation Law (1925) to restrict left-wing thought. He died in office.

Katsura Taro 1847–1913
Japanese army general and politician
A member of the Choshu clique, he was a general in the Sino–Japanese War (1894–95), Governor-General of Japan's colony of Taiwan (1896–98) and Army Minister, before serving as Prime Minister on three occasions (1901–06, 1908–11, 1912–13). He helped reorganize the army on the German model, and during his terms as Prime Minister, Japan became a major imperialist power, forging an alliance with Great Britain (1902), defeating Russia (1905) and annexing Korea (1910). In 1912 he came under increasing attack in and outside the Diet for his increased military expenditures and his attempts to stay in power by creating his own party (Doshikai) to rival the majority party, the Seiyukai. He resigned in Feb 1913 and died shortly afterwards.

Katz, Alex 1927–
US painter
Born in New York, he studied painting at Cooper Union there (1946–49) and at Skowhegan School, Maine (1949–50). From 1959 he began making portraits of his friends in a deliberately gauche, naïve style, simplifying forms and using a limited palette. These large-scale portraits, which have a directness bordering on kitsch, have been likened to cinematic images of film idols, as in *The Red Smile* (1963, Cologne). In recent years he has also painted landscapes, rendered in a style which is reminiscent of Japanese art and characterized by an air of unreality.

Katz, Sir Bernard 1911–
British biophysicist and Nobel Prize winner
Born and educated in Leipzig, Germany, he left Nazi Germany in 1935, and began physiological research at University College London. After work at the Kanematsu Institute in Sydney, Australia, where he collaborated in neurophysiological experiments with Sir John Eccles, in 1946 he returned to University College, where he remained for most of his career, although he spent a large part of the late 1940s in Cambridge and Plymouth working on the mechanisms by which the nerve impulse is transmitted. For the next three decades he focused on the mechanisms of neural transmission, showing that chemical neurotransmitters are stored in nerve terminals and released in specific portions called quanta when stimulated by the arrival of the neural impulse. For this work he

shared the 1970 Nobel Prize for physiology or medicine with Julius Axelrod and Ulf von Euler. He was elected FRS in 1952, and knighted in 1969.

Kauffer, Edward McKnight See McKnight Kauffer, Edward

Kauffmann, (Maria Anna Catharina) Angelica 1741–1807
Swiss painter

Born in Chur in the Grisons, Switzerland, and trained in Italy, she was painting portraits of notables in Italy at the age of 11 and in 1766 was persuaded by Sir Joshua Reynolds (a close friend) to go to London. There she became famous for her wit and intellect, and as a painter of classical and mythological pictures and of portraits, and was a founder member of the Royal Academy. In the 1770s she executed decorative paintings for houses built by the Adam brothers, and others. Her ceiling depicting *Painting* (c.1780) is now in Burlington House, London, and her self-portrait (c.1770–75) is in the National Gallery, London. Following her marriage to the Venetian painter, Antonio Zucchi, with whom she worked closely in England, she returned to Italy in 1781. Her work became internationally known from engravings by Francesco Bartolozzi, and included Shakespearean scenes commissioned by John Boydell for his Shakespeare Gallery (1789) in Pall Mall.

Kaufman, George S(imon) 1889–1961
US playwright and director

Born in Pittsburgh, Pennsylvania, he began his career as a newspaper columnist and drama critic, then turned to writing comedies for the stage in the early 1920s, working with a series of collaborators and producing a Broadway hit nearly every year for two decades. With Moss Hart he wrote such plays as *You Can't Take It With You* (1936, Pulitzer Prize) and *The Man Who Came to Dinner* (1939). Other well-known works include *Of Thee I Sing* (1931, Pulitzer Prize) with Morrie Ryskind and Ira Gershwin (1896–1983), as well as *Dinner at Eight* (1932) and *Stage Door* (1936), both with Edna Ferber. He also worked on two Marx Brothers vehicles, the *Cocoanut* (1925) and *Animal Crackers* (1928), which were later made into films. Another notable collaboration was with Howard Teichmann on *The Solid Gold Cadillac* (1953). He was an excellent humorist and theatrical craftsman. 🕮 S Meredith, *George S. Kaufman and his Friends* (1974, revised as *Kaufman and the Algonquin Round Table*, 1977)

Kaufman, Henry 1927–
US economist and banker

Born in Wenings, Germany, he moved to the USA in 1937 and attended New York and Columbia universities. From 1957 to 1961 he was assistant chief economist in the research department of the Federal Reserve Bank, New York. He joined Salomon Bros in 1962, became a partner in 1967 and managing director in 1981. He is chief economist in charge of (among other interests) bond market research and bond portfolio analysis, and a member of the board of governors of Tel Aviv University. In 1986 he published *Interest Rates, the Markets, and the New Financial World*.

Kaufmann See Mercator, Nicolaus

Kaunda, Kenneth David 1924–
Zambian statesman

Born in Lubwa, he became a teacher then entered politics and founded the Zambian African National Congress (1958). Subsequently he was imprisoned and the movement banned. In 1960 he was elected president of the United National Independent Party (UNIP) and played a leading part in his country's independence negotiations. After the break up of the Federation of Rhodesia and Nyasaland he was elected Prime Minister of Northern Rhodesia (Zambia) in January 1964, and was elected President when the country obtained independence in October that year. His long rule emphasized economic and social development for Zambia. He was re-elected six times before being defeated in 1991 in the first multiparty election for 19 years. 🕮 Richard S Hall, *The High Price of Principles: Kaunda and the White South* (1969)

Kaunitz(-Rietberg), Wenzel Anton, Prince von 1711–94
Austrian statesman

He was born in Vienna. He distinguished himself at the Congress of Aix-la-Chapelle (1748), and as ambassador at the French court (1750–52). As Chancellor (1753–92), he instigated the Diplomatic Revolution and directed Austrian politics for almost 40 years under Maria Theresa and Joseph II. He was also a liberal patron of arts and sciences. 🕮 Franz A J Szabo, *Kaunitz and Enlightened Absolutism, 1753–1780* (1994)

Kavanagh, Patrick Joseph 1905–67
Irish poet and novelist

He was born near Inniskeen, County Monaghan, and farmed before leaving for Dublin in 1939 to pursue a career as a writer and journalist. Perhaps his greatest achievement is *The Great Hunger* (1942), a passionate poem about the harsh reality of life for a frustrated Irish farmer and his sister. In *Tarry Flynn* (1948), an autobiographical novel, he depicts the countryside where he was brought up. His unorthodox, antisocial lifestyle in Dublin led to a savage anonymous profile (by the poet, Valentin Iremonger). In his libel action, *Kavanagh v The Leader* (1953), Kavanagh was the victim of a brutal cross-examination by opposing counsel John A Costello, from which he never recovered. His *Collected Poems* was published in 1964, and the *Complete Poems* followed in 1972.

Kawabata, Yasunari 1899–1972
Japanese writer and Nobel Prize winner

Born in Osaka, he was educated at Tokyo University (1920–24), reading English and then Japanese literature. In 1922 he published a collection of short stories, *Tales to hold in the Palm of your Hand*. His first novel, *Izu no odoriko* (Eng trans *The Izu Dancer*, 1955), was published in 1925. He experimented with various Western novel forms, but by the mid-1930s had returned to traditional Japanese ones. Later novels, which are typically melancholy, include *Yukiguni* (1935–47, Eng trans *Snow Country*, 1957), *Sembazuru* (1949, Eng trans *Thousand Cranes*, 1959) and *Yama no oto* (1949–54, Eng trans *The Sound of the Mountain*, 1971). He won the 1968 Nobel Prize for literature, the first Japanese writer to win the award. He died by committing suicide. 🕮 G B Peterson, *The Moon in the Water: on Tanizaki, Kawabata and Mishima* (1979)

Kawakubo, Rei 1942–
Japanese fashion designer

Born in Tokyo and educated at Keio University in 1964, she became a fashion stylist and designed her own clothes, founding her own company, Commes des Garçons, in 1969. The label meaning 'like boys', emphasizes her conviction that her clothes are for modern women 'who do not need to assure their happiness by looking sexy to man, by emphasizing their figures'. Her early 1980s collections shocked European critics with their lack of colour and androgynous shapes. However, her controversial 1980s 'ripped' sweater is now in the clothing collection at the Victoria and Albert Museum, London, recognized as an important 20th-century style development. She now has around 450 employees, 254 CDG stores in Japan, eight stores and 87 outlets worldwide, and also designs her own store interiors and furniture.

Kawawa, Rashidi Mfaume 1929–
Tanzanian trade unionist, nationalist leader and politician

Born in Songea and educated at Tabora secondary school, from an early age he was involved in labour politics, becoming president of the Tanganyika African Civil Servants' Association. He joined the Tanganyika African Association (1951–56) and was a founder member, and later secretary-general and president, of the Tanganyika Federation of Labour. From 1957 he was a member of the Tanganyika Legislative Council and, when Julius Nyerere resigned as Prime Minister in 1962, Kawawa briefly replaced him. He became the first Vice-President (1962–64) and was re-elected after the amalgamation of Tanganyika and Zanzibar (1964, named United Republic of Tanzania) until 1972, when he was once again appointed Prime Minister. As a result of his overly zealous commitment to the TANU Guidelines which were set down in the Arusha Declaration, he was demoted to Minister of Defence and National Service (1977), and became a Minister without Portfolio in 1980. He lost status in government when Ndugu Mwinyi replaced Nyerere (1985), but he was re-elected almost unanimously as Secretary-General of Chama Cha Mapundizi (CCM) in the 1987 Congress, a position he held until 1993.

Kay, John 1704–c.1780
English inventor

Born near Bury in Lancashire, he may have been educated in France. He was certainly back in Bury by 1730 when he patented an 'engine' for twisting and cording mohair and worsted. Three years later he patented his flying shuttle, one of the most important inventions in the history of textile machinery. Output and quality were both substantially improved, and Kay's new shuttle was adopted by the Yorkshire woollen manufacturers, but they were reluctant to pay the royalties due to him and the cost of court actions against defaulters nearly ruined him. In 1753 his house at Bury was ransacked by angry textile workers who feared that his machines would destroy their livelihood. He left England soon after for France, where he is believed to have died a pauper.

Kaye, Danny, *professional name of* David Daniel Kominski 1913–87
US stage, radio and film actor

Born in Brooklyn, New York City, he toured as a singer and dancer in the 1930s, and made his film debut in the short *Dime a Dance* (1937). Further work on stage in New York was followed by his first feature film, *Up in Arms* (1943). *Wonderman* (1944) made his reputation as a film comedian and was followed by international success in *The Secret Life of Walter Mitty* (1947). Other films include *The Inspector General* (1950), *Hans Christian Andersen* (1952) and *The Court Jester* (1956), as well as the television film *Skokie* (1981). He received a Special Academy Award in 1955, and in later years worked for international children's charities, especially UNICEF. ▣ M Freeland, *The Secret Life of Danny Kaye* (1986)

Kaye, Nora, *originally* Nora Koreff 1920–87
US dancer

Born in New York, she studied at the School of American Ballet and the New York Metropolitan Opera Ballet School, dancing with the latter and also at Radio City Music Hall. She joined American Ballet Theater (ABT) at its inception in 1939 and soon became one of the most acclaimed dramatic ballerinas of her generation, creating the role of Hagar in Antony Tudor's *Pillar of Fire* (1942), and appearing in other modern ballets as well as the classics. She was a member of New York City Ballet (1951–54), and then returned to ABT until her retirement in 1961. In 1961 she co-founded Ballet of Two Worlds with her film director and choreographer husband Herbert Ross

(1927–), and assisted him in his stage and film work, including *The Turning Point* (1977), which featured Mikhail Baryshnikov.

Kay-Shuttleworth, Sir James Phillips, *originally* James Phillips Kay 1804–77
English physician and educationist

Born in Rochdale, Lancashire, he studied and practised medicine. As secretary to the committee of the Privy Council on education he was instrumental in establishing a system of government school inspection. The pupil-teacher system, whereby especially gifted pupils between the ages of 13 and 18 simultaneously taught at primary schools while receiving a secondary education, originated with him and he founded his own training college which later became St John's College, Battersea. In 1842 he married the heiress of the Shuttleworths of Gawthorpe, and assumed her surname.

Kazan, Elia, *originally* Elia Kazanjoglou 1909–
US stage and film director

Born in Constantinople (Istanbul), Turkey, he emigrated to the USA in 1913. He studied at Williams College and Yale, then acted in minor roles on Broadway and in Hollywood before becoming a theatre director. He was co-founder of the Actors Studio (1947), in New York, and his Broadway productions include the works of Arthur Miller and Tennessee Williams. He began as a film director in 1944, and many of his films show his social or political commitment, such as *Gentleman's Agreement* (1948, Academy Award), on anti-Semitism, *Pinky* (1949), on racism, *Viva Zapata* (1952), *On the Waterfront* (1954, Academy Award), and *Face in the Crowd* (1957). Other notable films include Tennessee Williams's *A Streetcar Named Desire* (1951) and *Baby Doll* (1956), John Steinbeck's *East of Eden* (1954), William Inge's *Splendor in the Grass* (1962), *America, America* (1964) and *The Arrangement* (1969), based on his autobiographical novels (1963 and 1967), *The Visitors* (1972) and *The Last Tycoon* (1976). He continues to write novels and has published an autobiography, *My Life* (1988). ▣ Thomas H Pauly, *An American Odyssey: Elia Kazan and American Culture* (1983)

Kazankina, Tatyana Vasilevna 1951–
Soviet athlete

She was born in Petrovsk, and in 1976 won an Olympic double at 800 metres and 1,500 metres, the only woman to have done so to date. During the same year, she became the first woman to run the 1,500 metres in under four minutes, which was one of a total of three world records at that distance that she set during her career. She also set world records at 2,000 metres and 3,000 metres. She was suspended from competition in 1984 for failing to take a drugs test after running a personal best time for the 5,000 metres in Paris, but returned to competition in 1986.

Kazantzakis, Nikos 1883–1957
Greek novelist, poet and dramatist

He was born in Heraklion, Crete, and after studying law at Athens University spent some years travelling in Europe and Asia. He published his first novel *Toda Raba* in French in 1929 (Eng trans 1964), but is best known for the novel *Vios kai Politeia tou Alexi Zorba* (1946, Eng trans *Zorba the Greek*, 1952) and the epic autobiographical narrative poem, *Odyseia* (1938, Eng trans *The Odyssey, a Modern Sequel*, 1958). He wrote several other novels, including *O Christos Xanastavronetai* (1954, Eng trans *Christ Recrucified*, 1954), *O Kapetan Michalis* (1953, Eng trans *Freedom or Death*, 1955) and *O Teleftaios Peirasmos* (1955, Eng trans *The Last Temptation of Christ*, 1960), and translated many literary classics into modern Greek. He spent his last decade living in Antibes, France. ▣ P Bien, *Nicos Kazantzakis* (1968)

Kazinczy, Ferenc 1759–1831
Hungarian writer

Born in Érsemlyén, he published a radical journal, and was imprisoned (1794–1801) for his membership of a Jacobin society. He was a leading figure in the Hungarian literary revival and a strong advocate of the reform of the language, and is often referred to as 'the father of Hungarian criticism'. He translated many European classics and wrote poetry, including the first sonnets in Hungarian. There are 22 volumes of his letters. He died of cholera. 📖 J Váczy, *Kazinczy Ferences Kora* (1915)

Kean, Charles John 1811–68
English actor

Born in Waterford, Ireland, and educated in England at Eton, he was the son of Edmund Kean. To support his mother and himself he became an actor. He first appeared at Drury Lane (1827) as Young Norval, with little success, but developed and improved his performance in the provinces. In 1842 he married the actress, Ellen Tree (1805–80), who played opposite him in many of his major productions. In 1850 he became joint-lessee of the Princess's Theatre, where he produced a long series of spectacular, lavishly costumed revivals. He virtually retired from the London stage in 1859, although he continued to play in the USA and the provinces to within seven months of his death.

Kean, Edmund c.1789–1833
English actor

Born in London, it is likely he was the illegitimate son of Anne Carey, an actress and entertainer, and grand-daughter of Henry Carey. His father is thought to have been Edmund Kean, a thespian and drunk, who committed suicide when his son was an infant. He was taken into care by actress Charlotte Tidswell, formerly a mistress of Edmund's uncle, Moses, a ventriloquist. He was said to have been taught singing, dancing, fencing and elocution, and by the age of eight had made several appearances on the Drury Lane stage. Around 1804 he became an itinerant player and in 1808 married a mediocre actress, Mary Chambers, by whom he had two sons. He finally appeared at Drury Lane in a major role in 1814, playing Shylock in *The Merchant of Venice*. A delighted audience acclaimed his unconventional interpretation as a dark, desperate, bitter rogue brandishing a cleaver. Villainous parts suited him best and he continued to delight his public, but lost some popularity with poor performances as Lear, Romeo and Hamlet. His Macbeth, however, was magnificent, and he excelled as Richard III and Iago. His debauched and profligate life, excessive drinking and philandering finally lost him public approval when he was successfully sued for adultery in 1825. He charmed back public favour, only to lose it repeatedly. In the USA, where he first went in 1820, there was a similar pattern. After his US tour of 1825 he returned to England but he was visibly failing. His last performance was with his son Charles Kean at Drury Lane on 25 March 1833, where he collapsed while playing Othello to his son's Iago, and died a few weeks later. 📖 G W Playfair, *Kean* (1939)

Keane, Molly, *originally* Mary Nesta Skrine, *pseudonym* M J Farrell 1904–96
Irish novelist

She was born in County Kildare, into 'a rather serious Hunting and Fishing and Church-going family', and when young wrote only to supplement her dress allowance, adopting the pseudonym 'M J Farrell'. *The Knight of the Cheerful Countenance*, her first book, was written when she was 17. Between 1928 and 1952 she wrote 10 novels, including *The Rising Tide* (1937), *Two Days in Aragon* (1941) and *Loving Without Tears* (1951), drawing her material from the foibles of her own class. She also wrote spirited plays,

such as *Spring Meeting* (1938), *Treasure Hunt* (1949) and *Dazzling Prospect* (1961). When her husband died at 36, she stopped writing for many years, but *Good Behaviour* (1981), shortlisted for the Booker Prize, led to the reprinting of many of her books and a revival of critical appreciation. *Loving and Giving* (1988) is a bleak comedy, describing the break-up of a marriage through the eyes of the couple's eight-year-old daughter. 📖 B O'Toole, in *Across a Roaring Hill: The Protestant Imagination in Modern Ireland* (1985, Gerald Dawe and Edna Longley, eds)

Kearny, Philip 1814–62
US general

Born in New York City, he began his military career as a second lieutenant of cavalry on the Western frontier under the command of his uncle, Colonel Stephen Watts Kearny. He later fought in the Mexican War, losing an arm, and in 1859 he went to France to serve with Napoleon III. He became the first American to earn the cross of the French Legion of Honour but returned to the USA at the outbreak of the Civil War and became a brigadier-general of Union forces. A popular commander, he played an important role in the Peninsular Campaign, earning him promotion to major-general. He was killed during a reconnoitring mission in Virginia.

Kearny, Stephen Watts 1794–1848
US general

Born in Newark, New Jersey, he enlisted in the US army at the outbreak of the War of 1812, and spent much of the next 35 years on frontier duty. As brigadier-general of the army of the West during the Mexican War, he used diplomacy to occupy Sante Fe, New Mexico, in 1846, then proceeded with a small force to California, which was thought to have been pacified by Commodore Robert F Stockton but which was in fact still the scene of vigorous resistance by the Mexican-Californians. A conflict of authority with Stockton led to the arrest of John C Frémont, who had been appointed Governor of California by Stockton, and Kearny remained as military governor of the territory. He then became Governor-General of Vera Cruz and Mexico City (1848).

Keating, Geoffrey *Gaelic name* Seathrún Céitinn c.1570–c.1645
Irish historian

Born in Burges, County Tipperary, of Norman–Irish stock, he was educated for the priesthood at Bordeaux, and returned to Ireland as a doctor of theology in 1610. He served as Tipperary parish priest, apparently causing offence to local landowners for reproof of their living in concubinage, and became nomadic and for a time fugitive. Writing in his Gaelic name, his chief work was *Foras Feasa ar Éirinn* ('History of Ireland'). He wrote many songs, hymns and poems, and a spiritual essay translated as *The Three Shafts of Death*. In 1634 he once more obtained a parish, at Cappoquin, County Waterford, and was ultimately caught up in the Irish phase of the civil wars of 1640. According to legend, he was killed in a church in Clonmel, County Tipperary, by Cromwellian soldiers.

Keating, Paul John 1944–
Australian Labor politician

Born in Sydney, he was educated at De La Salle College and entered politics in 1969 as Labor MP for Blaxland. A committed republican, he opposed Australia's continuing links with the British Royal family and made it his party's policy to end them. In 1991 he was elected Prime Minister and produced proposals which would turn Australia into a republic by the end of the century. Although the policy attracted wide support he was defeated in the 1996 general election and announced that he was leaving politics. 📖 John Edwards, *Keating: The Inside Story* (1996)

Keating, Tom (Thomas Patrick) 1917–84
English art restorer and forger

Born in London, he won a box of paints at the age of 10 and became fascinated with painting. Invalided out of the navy in 1947, he took a course at Goldsmiths' College in London, where failing his exams left him with a lifelong grudge against what he saw as an elitist art world. He took up work restoring paintings. He also created fake paintings. His aim was not profit but the exposure of the fallibility of art experts. The scandal broke in 1976, when an art expert writing in *The Times* suggested that a work by Samuel Palmer, sold at auction, was not genuine. Keating admitted that a series of nine pictures, bearing imitations of Samuel Palmer's signature, were in fact drawn by him, and estimated that there were some 2,500 of his fakes in circulation. In 1979 he was put on trial at the Old Bailey for forgery, but charges were eventually dropped because of his deteriorating health. In 1982 Keating was given his own award-winning television art show and in 1983 sold paintings under his own name. 📖 *The Fake's Progress* (1978)

Keaton, Buster (Joseph Francis) 1895–1966
US film comedian

Born in Piqua, Kansas, he joined his parents in vaudeville ('The Three Keatons') at the age of three, developing great acrobatic skill. His Hollywood film debut was in *The Butcher Boy* (1917), the start of a prolific career. Famous for his deadpan expression in all circumstances, he starred in and directed such classics as *The Navigator* (1924) and *The General* (1926). His reputation declined with the advent of talking films until the 1950s and 1960s, when many of his silent masterpieces were re-released, and he himself began to appear in character roles in films like *Sunset Boulevard* (1950) and *Limelight* (1952). He received a Special Academy Award in 1959.

Keaton, Diane, *originally* Diane Hall 1946–
US actress

Born in Los Angeles, she won a scholarship to study at The Neighbourhood Playhouse in Manhattan, New York, and began her association with Woody Allen with her Broadway appearance in *Play It Again, Sam* (1969–70). Though she appeared in several films during the 1970s, her range as an actress was not explored fully until her performances in Allen's *Annie Hall* (1977), which won her a Best Actress Academy Award and in *Looking For Mr Goodbar* (1977). She also appeared in the Allen films *Interiors* (1978), *Manhattan* (1979), and *Manhattan Murder Mystery* (1993) among others, and dramas such as *Reds* (1981) and *Marvin's Room* (1996), but has been most commercially popular in such comedies as *Father of the Bride* (1991) and *The First Wives Club* (1996). One of her best dramatic roles was as Kay in all three parts of *The Godfather* (1972, 1974, 1990). A noted photographer, she has also directed television programmes and pop videos and made the feature *Unstrung Heroes* (1995).

Keats, Ezra Jack 1916–83
US illustrator and children's writer

Born in Brooklyn, New York City, his books often explored the emotional lives of young children in city apartment blocks. *My Dog is Lost* (1960) was his first book, but *The Snowy Day* (1962) about a small black boy's adventure in the snow, is the one for which he is best known. Later books include *Peter's Chair* (1967) and *Apt. 13* (1971). In his final books his style was becoming increasingly impressionistic.

Keats, John 1795–1821
English poet

He was born in London, the son of a livery-stable keeper, and went to school in Enfield. In 1811 he was apprenticed to a surgeon at Edmonton, and later (1815–17) was a medical student in the London hospitals, but took to writing poetry. Leigh Hunt, his neighbour in Hampstead, introduced him to other young Romantics, including Percy Bysshe Shelley, and published his first sonnets in *The Examiner* (1816). His first volume of poems (1817) combined 'Hymn to Pan' and the 'Bacchic procession' which anticipate the great odes to come. He published the long mythological poem *Endymion* in 1818. He returned from a walking tour in Scotland (1818), which exhausted him, to find the savage reviews of *Endymion* in *Blackwood's Magazine*, by John Gibson Lockhart, and the *Quarterly*. In addition, his younger brother Tom was dying of consumption, and his love affair with Fanny Brawne seems to have brought him more pain than comfort. It was under these circumstances that he published the volume of 1820, *Lamia and Other Poems*, a landmark in English poetry. Except for the romantic poem 'Isabella or The Pot of Basil', based on a story in Boccaccio's *Decameron*, and the first version of his epical poem, 'Hyperion', all the significant verse in this famous volume is the work of 1819, such as the two splendid romances 'The Eve of St Agnes' and 'Lamia', and the great odes—'On a Grecian Urn', 'To a Nightingale', 'To Autumn', 'On Melancholy' and 'To Psyche'. In particular, 'The Eve of St Agnes' displays a wealth of sensuous imagery almost unequalled in English poetry. In 'Lamia', the best told of the tales, he turns from stanza form to the couplet as used by Dryden in his romantic *Fables*. Keats's letters are also greatly admired, and throw light on his poetical development no less than on his unhappy love affair with Fanny Brawne. It is clear that he was both attracted and repelled by the notion of the poet as teacher or prophet. Having prepared the 1820 volume for the press, Keats, now seriously ill with consumption, sailed for Italy in September 1820, reached Rome and died there attended only by his artist friend Joseph Severn (1793–1879). The house in which he died (26 Piazza di Spagna), at the foot of the Spanish steps, is now known as the Keats-Shelley house, a place of literary pilgrimage with an outstanding library of English Romantic literature.

Keble, John 1792–1866
English Anglican churchman and poet

Born in Fairford, Gloucestershire, he was elected a scholar of Corpus Christi College, Oxford at 15, and in 1810 took a double first. He was elected a Fellow of Oriel in 1811. Ordained in 1816, he became a college tutor (1818–23). In 1827 his book of poems *The Christian Year* was widely circulated, and his theory of poetry was delivered as Oxford Professor of Poetry (1831–41). The Oxford Movement was inspired by his sermon on 'National apostasy' (1833), which encouraged a return to High Church ideals, and his circle (which originated the Tractarian movement) issued the 90 *Tracts for the Times* (ending in 1841). Other works are a Life of Bishop Thomas Wilson, an edition of Richard Hooker, the *Lyra Innocentium* (1846), a poetical translation of the Psalter (1839), *Letters of Spiritual Counsel*, 12 volumes of parochial sermons, and *Studia Sacra*. Keble College, Oxford, was founded in his memory (1870).

Kee, Robert 1919–
English broadcaster and writer

He studied history at Magdalen College, Oxford, then joined the RAF and spent four years in a POW camp during World War II. His first novel, *A Crowd is Not Company* (1947), reflected this experience and won him the Atlantic Award for literature. Other novels include *The Impossible Shore* (1949) and *A Sign of the Times* (1955). As a print journalist, he worked for *Picture Post* (1948–51), and was a special correspondent for the *Observer* (1956–57) and the *SundayTimes* (1957–58). Joining the BBC, he worked on *Panorama* from 1958 to 1962. The recipient of the Richard Dimbleby BAFTA Award (1976), his other major television work includes the series *Ireland* (1981), co-founding the breakfast programme *TV-am* (1983), and *Seven Days* (1984–88). His non-fiction books include *The Green Flag* (1972), *Ireland: A History* (1980), *Trial and Error* (1986) and *The Laurel and the Ivy: Parnell and Irish Nationalism* (1993).

Keegan, Kevin Joseph 1951–
English footballer and manager

He was born in Armthorpe, Yorkshire. He played for several English sides, notably for Liverpool (1971–77) and Newcastle (1982–84), and also for Hamburg (1977–80); while playing abroad he was twice voted European Footballer of the Year. He played many times for England (1972–82, as captain 1976–82), and was awarded an OBE in 1982. After retiring in 1984 he lived in Spain, until he was appointed manager of Newcastle United in 1992. He enjoyed much success; but despite great popularity he resigned unexpectedly in 1997.

Keeler, Christine 1942–
English former model and show girl

After an unhappy childhood spent mainly in the Thames Valley, at Wraysbury, she left home at 16 and went to London, where she worked at Murray's Cabaret Club. Here she met Mandy Rice-Davies, who was to become a close friend. Stephen Ward, an osteopath, was a frequent visitor to the club and he and Keeler formed a relationship and eventually lived together, although there were frequent rifts between them. Ward introduced her and Rice-Davies into his circle of influential friends, including the Conservative Cabinet minister, John Profumo, with whom Keeler had an affair, while being involved at the same time with a Soviet diplomat. This led to Profumo's resignation from politics (1963), the prosecution of Ward for living on immoral earnings, and Ward's eventual suicide. Keeler herself served a prison sentence for related offences. In the late 1980s, her autobiography, studies of the Ward trial and its aftermath, and the film *Scandal* (1988), in which she collaborated, revived interest in the events and raised doubts about the validity of the charges made against her and Ward.

Keeler, James Edward 1857–1900
US astronomer

Born in La Salle, Illinois, he was educated at Johns Hopkins University. He became assistant to Samuel Langley at Allegheny Observatory (1881–83) doing solar research which included observations at high altitudes on Mount Whitney. After a year at universities in Germany and a further year at Allegheny, he joined the newly founded Lick Observatory in California (1885–91), where he established his reputation as an outstanding spectroscopist from his work on nebulae with bright emission lines. He was director of the Allegheny Observatory (1891–98) and in 1898 became director of Lick Observatory. He established the composition of Saturn's rings (as James Clerk Maxwell had postulated), and carried out important spectroscopic work on nebulae of the kind now known as galaxies. Through long-exposure photography he was able to record very faint ones, and estimated that there were 120,000 nebulae in the sky capable of being photographed with the instrument.

Keersmaeker, Anne Teresa de See De Keersmaeker, Anne Teresa

Kefauver, (Carey) Estes 1903–63
US political leader

Born near Madisonville, Tennessee, he was elected by his home state to the House of Representatives (1939–49) and the US Senate (1949–63). A Democrat, he supported the New Deal and fought monopolies. He was noted for conducting televised Senate hearings concerned with the investigation of organized crime (1950–51).

Keightley, Thomas 1789–1872
Irish writer

He was born in Dublin, and settled in London in 1824. His *Fairy Mythology* (1850) and his Life and annotated edition of Milton (1855–59) are among his best works, and his histories of Rome, Greece and England long held their place as school textbooks.

Keilin, David 1887–1963
British biochemist

Born in Moscow, Russia, he was educated in Warsaw, Liège and Paris, and spent the rest of his career at Cambridge, where he was director of the Molteno Institute from 1931 and Quick Professor of Biology (1931–52). In 1925 he reinvestigated earlier spectrophotometric studies and discovered the pigment cytochrome. In 1929, with Edward Hartree, he found a cytochrome compound in heart muscle and defined the role of cytochrome in biochemical oxidation. He also investigated the enzymes catalase and peroxidase, based on a study of ethanol. A keen entomologist, Keilin used insects in many of his experiments in animal biochemistry.

Keillor, Garrison (Gary Edward) 1942–
US humorous writer and radio performer

He was born in Anoka, Minnesota, and graduated from Minnesota University in 1966, already writing for the *New Yorker*. He hosted the live radio show, *A Prairie Home Companion* (1974–87), delivering a weekly monologue set in the quiet, fictional mid-western town of Lake Wobegon. He has been a frequent contributor to the *New Yorker* throughout his career and has been described as 'the best humorous writer to have come out of America since Thurber'. His books include *Happy to be Here* (1981), *Lake Wobegon Days* (1985), *Leaving Home* (1987), *We Are Still Married* (1989), the novel *WLT: A Radio Romance* (1991) and the *Book of Guys* (1993).

Keino, Kip(choge) 1940–
Kenyan athlete

Born in Kipsamo, he was the first Kenyan to set a world record, with 7 minutes 39.6 seconds at 3,000 metres, and was the first black man to run a mile in under four minutes (3:54.2). In the 1968 Olympic Games at Mexico City he won a silver medal in the 5,000 metres and in 1972 at Munich he won the gold medal for the 3,000 metre steeplechase. His uninhibited long stride was distinctive and his achievements inspired some world class Kenyan runners such as Moses Kiptanui and Yobes Ondieki.

Keir, James 1735–1820
Scottish chemist and industrialist

Born in Edinburgh, he was educated at Edinburgh High School and at Edinburgh University, where he studied medicine. He joined the army and served in the West Indies, resigning with the rank of captain in 1768. In 1770 he settled at West Bromwich, outside Birmingham, joining Erasmus Darwin's circle of friends and becoming a member of the Lunar Society, an informal but influential club whose members met to exchange ideas in science and technology. He helped Joseph Priestley with some of his experiments, and unlike Priestley, was quick to accept Antoine Lavoisier's ideas on combustion. He set up a glass-making business at Stourbridge (1771), and observing what happens when glass cools very slowly, suggested that basalt cools in a similar manner and therefore must be igneous. In 1776 he translated the new chemical dictionary written by Pierre Joseph Macquer. Two years later he and Alexander Blair founded the Tipton Chemical Works, which manufactured alkali from the sulphates of potash and soda, preceding Nicholas Leblanc's more famous process by 40 years. He was elected FRS in 1785.

Keita, Modibo 1915–77
Mali politician
Educated at William Ponty School, Dakar, he helped to found the Rassemblement Democratique Africaine (RDA) in 1946 and was elected to the territorial assembly in 1948. He was a deputy in the French Assembly (1956–59) before becoming President of the Mali Federation (1959–60) and President of Mali (1960–68). A radical who looked to Kwame Nkrumah for leadership, he was overthrown by the military in 1968 and was imprisoned until his death.

Keitel, Harvey 1941–
US actor
Born in Brooklyn, New York, he joined the Marine Corps straight from school and later studied at the Actor's Studio and performed off-Broadway before making his film debut in *Who's That Knocking At My Door?* (1968), which began a long association with director Martin Scorsese. An intense performer who has illuminated all shades of human agony and ecstasy, he has worked extensively throughout world cinema in such films as *Mean Streets* (1973), *Taxi Driver* (1976), *The Duellists* (1977), *Deathwatch* (1979), *Bad Timing* (1980) and *Ulysses' Gaze* (1995). Nominated for an Academy Award for *Bugsy* (1991), he has been one of the most prolific film actors of the past decade, alternating supporting performances and starring roles in films such as *Thelma and Louise* (1991), *Reservoir Dogs* (1992), *Bad Lieutenant* (1992), *The Piano* (1993) and *Smoke* (1995).

Keitel, Wilhelm 1882–1946
German soldier
He joined the army in 1901 and served in World War I. In the 1930s he became an ardent Nazi, and was appointed Chief of the Supreme Command of the armed forces (1938). In 1940 he signed the Compiègne armistice with France and was Hitler's chief military adviser throughout the war. In May 1945, he was one of the German signatories of unconditional surrender to Russia and the Allies in Berlin. He was executed in October 1946 for war crimes.

Keith, Sir Arthur 1866–1955
Scottish physical anthropologist
Born in Aberdeen, he became a doctor in science, medicine and law, and was Professor of the Royal College of Surgeons, London (1908) and Professor of Physiology at the Royal Institution, London (1918–23). He wrote *Introduction to the Study of Anthropoid Apes* (1896), *Human Embryology and Morphology* (1901) and works on ancient man, including *Concerning Man's Origin* (1927) and *New Theory of Human Evolution* (1948).

Keith, Penelope, *originally* Penelope Hatfield 1940–
English actress
Born in Sutton, Surrey, she trained at the Webber Douglas Academy and made her London stage debut with the Royal Shakespeare Company in *The Wars of the Roses* (1964). Her subsequent West End plays include *Suddenly at Home* (1971), *The Norman Conquests* (1974), *Donkey's Years* (1976), *The Apple Cart* (1977), *The Millionairess* (1978), *Moving* (1986) and *Hobson's Choice* (1986). She starred on television as Margo Leadbeatter in *The Good Life* (1975–78), Audrey fforbes-Hamilton in *To the Manor Born* (1979–81), Jean Price in *No Job for a Lady* (1990–92), Phillippa Troy in *Law and Disorder* (1994) and Maggie Prentice in *Next of Kin* (1995–).

Keith, Thomas 1827–95
Scottish doctor, surgeon and amateur photographer
He was born in Kincardineshire. His photographs were mainly taken in Edinburgh, where he spent most of his life, and on Iona, and he was particularly active as a photographer from 1852 to 1857. His photographs are salted paper prints, made using the method invented by Gustave Le Gray, and he may have worked closely with other amateur photographers. His subject matter, for the most part, was architectural. His work, which is notable for its technical and compositional authority, was 'discovered' by the US photographer Alvin Langdon Coburn, who exhibited examples of it at the Royal Photographic Society in London (1914). Keith has since been recognized as one of the masters of early British photography.

Keith, Viscount See Elphinstone, George Keith

Keith-Falconer, Ion See Falconer, Ion Keith

Kekkonen, Urho Kaleva 1900–86
Finnish statesman
Born in Pielavesi, after studying law at Helsinki University and fighting against the Bolsheviks in 1918, he entered the Finnish parliament as an Agrarian Party deputy, holding ministerial office from 1936 to 1939 and in 1944. He was Prime Minister four times in the early 1950s before being elected President in 1956, in succession to Juo Paasikivi, a position he retained for 25 years. Although Kekkonen had always been hostile to Stalinist Russia, as President he encouraged a policy of cautious friendship with the USSR. At the same time his strict neutrality ensured that he retained the confidence of his Scandinavian neighbours. He supported Finland's membership of the European Free Trade Association (1961) and in 1975 was host to the 35-nation European Security Conference in Helsinki. Five years later he accepted a Lenin Peace Prize. His popularity in Finland led to the passage of special legislation enabling him to remain in office until 1984, but he resigned because of ill health in 1981.

Kekule von Stradonitz, (Friedrich) August, *originally surnamed* Kekulé 1829–96
German chemist
Born in Darmstadt, he was educated there and at the University of Giessen, where he switched from studying architecture to chemistry after hearing Justus von Liebig's lectures. During 1850 he worked in Liebig's laboratory, but soon moved to Paris, where he familiarized himself with Charles Gerhardt's type theory of organic chemistry. He later became assistant to John Stenhouse at St Bartholomew's Hospital in London, where he began to speculate about the structure of organic molecules. He began his teaching career in Heidelberg (1856) and built a private laboratory in his own house, then became professor at the University of Ghent (1858). During this time, he solved the apparent irreconcilability of his views on the tetravalency of carbon with the known formula of benzene (C_6H_6)—the cyclic nature of the benzene molecule. In 1867 he moved to Bonn, where he proposed delocalized rather than fixed double bonds. Despite his ill health from 1875, his work in 1890 on the structure of pyridine (a compound analogous to benzene) is an important landmark in the development of structural organic chemistry. Although some of his new ideas on structural organic chemistry were also put forward by others, Kekule made an important contribution to the development of organic chemistry.

Keller, Gottfried 1819–90
Swiss poet and novelist

Born near Zurich, he studied landscape painting at Munich (1840–42), but turned to literature. From 1861 to 1876 he was State Secretary of his native canton. His chief works are *Der grüne Heinrich* (1854, Eng trans *Green Henry*, 1960), *Die Leute von Seldwyla* (1856, which includes *A Village Romeo and Juliet*), *Sieben Legenden* (1872, Eng trans with the previous work as *Seven Legends* and *The People of Seldwyla*, 1929), *Züricher Novellen* (1878, 'Zurich stories') and *Martin Salander* (1886, Eng trans 1963). He excelled as a writer of short stories, and his powers of characterization and description and his sense of humour are best illustrated in his volumes of *Novellen*. ⌨ J M Lindsay, *Gottfried Keller: his life and works* (1968)

Keller, Hans 1919–85
British musicologist
Born in Vienna, Austria, he settled in England in 1938, becoming a British citizen in 1948. He co-founded the magazine *Music Survey*, wrote for many other journals, served on the BBC staff from 1959 and frequently broadcast. Highly analytical and eloquent, he wrote influential criticism of contemporary music and chamber music, and articles on sport.

Keller, Helen Adams 1880–1968
US writer
Born in Tuscumbia, Alabama, she became deaf and blind at 19 months, and was unable to communicate through language until the age of 7, when she was put under the tuition of Anne M Sullivan (later Mrs **Macy**), who taught her to associate words with objects and to read and spell through touch. She later learned to use sign language and to speak, and she graduated from Radcliffe College in 1904. She became a famous lecturer and crusader for the handicapped and published several books based on her experiences, notably *The Story of My Life* (1902).

Kellermann, François Étienne Christophe, Duc de Valmy 1735–1820
French soldier
Born in Wolfsbuchweiler, Alsace, he served in the Seven Years War (1756–63). In 1792 he repelled the forces of the Duke of Brunswick, and helped General **Dumouriez** in the famous 'cannonade of Valmy', but was suspected of treason, and imprisoned by **Robespierre**. He later served in Italy, and under the Empire was made a marshal and duke. In 1809 and 1812 he commanded the reserves on the Rhine. At the Restoration he attached himself to the **Bourbons**. His son, François Étienne (1770–1835), led the charge at the Battle of Marengo (1800).

Kelley, Florence 1859–1932
US feminist and social reformer
Born in Philadelphia, she was educated at Cornell University and at Zurich, where she became a socialist. From 1891 to 1899 she worked at **Jane Addams**'s Hull House Settlement and subsequently became the first woman factory inspector in Illinois, successfully fighting to reduce working hours and improve methods and conditions of production. After obtaining a law degree from Northwestern University (1895), she moved to New York in 1899, becoming general secretary of the National Consumers' League. In 1910 she was one of the founders of the National Association for the Advancement of Colored People, and in 1919 she helped establish the Women's International League for Peace and Freedom. Her works include *Some Ethical Gains Through Legislation* (1905) and a translation of **Friedrich Engels**'s *Condition of the Working Classes in England in 1844* (1887).

Kellgren, Johan Henric 1751–95
Swedish poet and journalist
He was born in Floby, and was editor from 1780 of the journal *Stockholmsposten*, where he acquired a reputation as a satirist. He was librarian (1780), and later secretary and

literary adviser to King **Gustav III**, with whom he collaborated on a tragedy, *Gustav Wasa* (1782), and he became a member of the newly founded Swedish Academy in 1786. As a poet he excelled in patriotic and lyrical verse, and, although a representative of the Enlightenment, he was not unsympathetic to the new ideas of Romanticism. Ek and Sjöding edited a nine-volume collected works (1923–70). ⌨ O Sylwan, *Johan Henric Kellgren* (1939)

Kellogg, Frank B(illings) 1856–1937
US jurist, statesman and Nobel Prize winner
He was born in Potsdam, New York, practised law in Minnesota, became senator (1917–23), ambassador in London (1923–25), and Secretary of State (1925–29). With **Aristide Briand** he drew up the Kellogg-Briand Pact (1928) outlawing war as an instrument for national policy, which became the legal basis for the Nuremberg Trials (1945–46). He was a judge of the Permanent Court of Justice at the Hague (1930–35), and was awarded the 1929 Nobel Peace Prize.

Kellogg, John Harvey 1852–1943 and W(ill) K(eith) 1860–1951
US inventors
Brothers, they were born in Tyrone and Battle Creek, Michigan. John Kellogg graduated from Bellevue Hospital Medical College in 1875. They joined forces, as physician and industrialist respectively, at Battle Creek Sanitarium to develop a process of cooking, rolling and toasting wheat and corn into crisp flakes that made a nourishing breakfast cereal for their patients. Soon their corn flakes were being sold through the mail, and in 1906 the W K Kellogg Company was founded. The new product was extensively advertised and the result was a revolution in the breakfast eating habits of North Americans, and before long the rest of the western world. In 1930 the W K Kellogg Foundation took its place as one of the leading philanthropic institutions in the USA.

Kelly, Ellsworth 1923–
US artist
Born in Newburgh, New York, he studied in Boston (1946–48) and at the Académie des Beaux-Arts in Paris (1948–49), and lived in France until 1954. Concerned with the essence of form, from the late 1950s he made his name as a 'hard-edge' abstract painter with his wide, flat areas of strong colour, such as in *Blue Curve* (1982, Stedelijk, Amsterdam). He is also a sculptor, and made a screen for the Philadelphia Transport Building in 1956.

Kelly, Emmett 1898–1979
US clown
He was born in Sedan, Kansas, and began his career as a professional cartoonist, then drifted into circus jobs. Portraying the clown 'Weary Willie', a sad-faced tramp with a ragged suit and bulbous nose, he performed in the Ringling Brothers–**Barnum** & Bailey Circus and in the film *The Greatest Show on Earth* (1952).

Kelly, Gene (Eugene Curran) 1912–96
US actor, dancer, choreographer and film director
Born in Pittsburgh, Pennsylvania, he graduated in economics from the University of Pittsburgh before turning to a career as a dancer. He made his New York debut in the chorus of *Leave it to Me* (1938) but it was his lead performance in *Pal Joey* (1939) that led to his film debut in *For Me and My Gal* (1942). An athletic, muscular dancer and choreographer, he would revolutionize the screen musical in films like *Cover Girl* (1944), *Anchors Aweigh* (1945, Academy Award nomination), *On The Town* (1949), *An American in Paris* (1951), and *Singin' in the Rain* (1952). He received a special Academy Award in 1951 for his 'brilliant achievements in the art of choreography on film'. With the demise of the original screen musical, he turned to dramatic acting in films like *Marjorie Morningstar* (1958)

and *Inherit the Wind* (1960), and directed a number of films, including *Hello Dolly!* (1969). Active in the theatre, cinema and television, he was the 1985 recipient of the American Film Institute Life Achievement award. 📖 Clive Firschhorn, *Gene Kelly: A Biography* (1975)

Kelly, George A 1905–66
US psychologist
Born in Kansas, he studied at several universities, including Edinburgh and Iowa. He taught at Fort Hays Kansas State College prior to World War II, during which he was an aviation psychologist with the US navy. From 1946 he worked at the Ohio State University, leaving to take up a post at Brandeis University in 1965. Best known for his novel approach to understanding personality, he devised the repertory grid test, an open-ended method for exploring an individual's 'personal constructs' (categories in terms of which one perceives and which construes others). The interrelations of these constructs can then be used in psychotherapy to help infer (and change) the ways in which subjective 'theories' are used by the individual in dealing with others.

Kelly, Grace Patricia, *married name* Grimaldi, Princess Grace of Monaco 1929–82
US film actress and princess
Born in Philadelphia, Pennsylvania, the daughter of a wealthy Irish businessman, she acted in television and on Broadway, before making her film debut in *Fourteen Hours* (1951). Her short but highly successful film career as a coolly elegant beauty included leading roles in *High Noon* (1952), *Rear Window* (1954), *The Country Girl* (1954, Academy Award), *To Catch a Thief* (1955), and *High Society* (1956). In 1956 she married Prince **Rainier III** of Monaco, and retired from the screen. She was killed in a motor accident.

Kelly, Howard Atwood 1858–1943
US surgeon and gynaecologist
Born in Camden, New Jersey, he practised surgery and gynaecology for several years before accepting a post at Pennsylvania University. In 1889 he became one of four original professors at the Johns Hopkins Medical School, where he remained until his retirement in 1919. He pioneered the use of cocaine anaesthesia, developed a number of operations for the kidney and bladder, and played an important role in the development of gynaecology as a surgical speciality separate from obstetrics. His textbooks (*Operative Gynecology*, 1898, and *Medical Gynecology*, 1908) dominated the field and described many of his technical innovations. During his long retirement he wrote on botany and medical history.

Kelly, Ned 1855–80
Australian bushranger
Born in Wallan, Victoria, he was the son of an Irish convict father. After minor brushes with the law he was imprisoned briefly in 1870 then took up livestock stealing. In 1878 he and his gang ambushed a group of policemen; Kelly shot three. Two bank robberies followed; a reward of £8,000 was offered for their capture and aboriginal trackers were brought in to help. The failed hold-up of a train at Glenrowan in Victoria led to the death of three gang members and the capture of Kelly, dressed in his home-made suit of armour. He was hanged in November 1880. Kelly became a folk-hero and the paintings of him in his armour by **Sidney Nolan** are an enduring Australian symbol.

Kelly, Petra, *originally* Petra Karin Lehmann 1947–92
German politician
Born in Günzburg, Bavaria, she moved with her mother to the USA at the age of 13. After studying political science and international relations at the American University, Washington, she worked for the EEC in Brussels. In 1979 she co-founded The Green Party (Die Grünen) and in 1983 they entered the Bundestag with 28 seats. However, in the 'unification election' of 1990, they lost all their parliamentary seats and were dogged by internal divisions. She died in an apparent suicide pact along with her partner, Gert Bastian, but subsequent reports have cast a shadow on this finding, by linking his name with the *Stasi*, the secret police of the former East Germany. Kelly's biography, written by Sara Lamb Parkin, appeared in 1994.

Kelly, Walt(er Crawford) 1913–73
US animator and strip cartoonist
Born in Philadelphia, Pennsylvania, he joined the **Walt Disney** studio in Hollywood as an animator in 1935. He moved to comics in 1941, creating his most famous characters, Albert Alligator and Pogo Possum of Okefenokee Swamp. He became art editor of the *New York Star* (1948), and introduced *Pogo* as a daily strip. The serial uniquely embraced slapstick, fantasy and influential political comment.

Kelly, William 1811–88
US inventor
Born in Pittsburgh, Pennsylvania, the son of a wealthy landowner, he developed an early interest in metallurgy, and at the age of 35, when he acquired an interest in iron-ore deposits and a nearby furnace, he became involved in the manufacture of wrought-iron articles. He soon discovered that an air blast directed onto, or blown through, molten cast iron can remove much of the carbon in it, so that the resulting metal becomes a mild steel, strong and ductile, suitable for a much wider range of applications than relatively brittle cast iron. He built seven of his 'converters' between 1851 and 1856, when he heard that **Henry Bessemer** had been granted a US patent for the same process. He convinced the Patent Office of his prior claim, but was almost immediately bankrupted in the 1857 financial panic. Although he continued to improve his process and made it in every way as effective as that of Bessemer, he never achieved commercial success, and his invention has come to be known as the 'Bessemer converter'.

Kelman, James 1946–
Scottish novelist, short-story writer and playwright
Born in Glasgow, he left school aged 15 to become an apprentice compositor, but abandoned this two years later when his family decided to emigrate to the USA. Returning to Scotland soon after, he was unemployed for long periods, but was determined to be a writer. His first publication, *Not Not While the Giro*, a collection of laconic stories, was published in 1983, and was followed by *The Busconductor Hines* (1984), *A Chancer* (1985), and *Greyhound for Breakfast* (1987), which evoked comparisons with **Chekhov** and **Beckett**. *A Disaffection*, his third novel, found a wide audience through its shortlisting for the Booker Prize in 1989. He has carved a niche as the spokesman for the disaffected, downtrodden and disenfranchised, and his fourth novel, *How late it was, how late* (1994), won the Booker Prize. Further stories were collected in *The Burn* (1991), and three plays are included in *Hardie and Baird & Other Plays* (1991). 📖 I Bell, in *Planet* (1986–87)

Kelsen, Hans 1881–1973
US jurist and legal theorist
He was born in Prague, and became Professor at Vienna (1911–30), and at Cologne (1930–33), then returned to Prague (1933–38). His early work was on constitutional and international law. He worked on the Austrian constitution of 1920 and until 1929 was a judge of the Austrian constitutional court. He went to the USA in 1938, where he continued his work teaching law and became a US

Kelvin (of Largs), WilliamThomson, 1st Baron 1824–1907
Scottish physicist and mathematician

Kelvin was born in Belfast and brought to Glasgow in 1832 when his father was appointed Professor of Mathematics there. He entered Glasgow University at the age of 10, went to Cambridge at 16, and after graduating was elected a Fellow of Peterhouse. He went to Paris to study under **Henri Victor Regnault**, and at the age of 22 was appointed Professor of Mathematics and Natural Philosophy (1846–99), and turned his mind to physics. In a career of astonishing versatility, he brilliantly combined pure and applied science. In an early paper (1842) he solved important problems in electrostatics. He proposed the absolute, or Kelvin, temperature scale in 1848. Simultaneously with **Rudolf Clausius** he established the second law of thermodynamics.

He investigated geomagnetism, and hydrodynamics (particularly wave-motion and vortex-motion). He was chief consultant on the laying of the first submarine Atlantic cable (1857–58), and became wealthy by patenting a mirror galvanometer for speeding telegraphic transmission. He improved ships' compasses, and invented innumerable electrical instruments (his house in Glasgow was the first to be lit by electric light); these instruments were manufactured by his own company, Kelvin & White. He was created 1st Baron Kelvin of Largs in 1892. He is buried in Westminster Abbey, beside Sir **Isaac Newton**.

📖 C W Smith and M N Wise, *Energy and Empire: A Biographical Study of Lord Kelvin* (1989); Silvanus P Thompson, *The Life of Lord Kelvin* (1977); Andrew Gray, *Lord Kelvin: An Account of his Scientific Life and Work* (1908).

'At what point does the dissipation of energy begin?' Kelvin's comment on his wife's proposal of an afternoon walk. Quoted in A Fleming, *Memories of a Scientific Life.*

citizen. He is mainly known as a legal theorist and creator of the 'pure theory of law' (*Reine Rechtslehre*, 1934), and his work has exerted great influence. Important translated works are *General Theory of Law and the State* (1949) and *Pure Theory of Law* (1967).

Kelvin, WilliamThomson, 1st Baron See panel above

Kemal Atatürk, Mustafa See Atatürk, Mustafa Kemal

Kemble, Charles 1775–1854
English actor

Born in Brecon, Wales, he made his first appearance at Sheffield in 1792. In 1794 he played Malcolm to his brother's Macbeth at Drury Lane, London. He retired from the stage in 1840, when he was appointed examiner of plays. Although he was not at first a good actor, he became more admired later in his career, and he distinguished himself in comedy and romantic roles. He was the brother of **Sarah Siddons**, **John Philip Kemble** and **Stephen Kemble**, and the father of both **Fanny Kemble** and the historian and philologist John Mitchell Kemble (1807–57).

Kemble, Fanny (Frances Anne) 1809–93
English actress

She was born in London, the daughter of **Charles Kemble**. A beautiful young woman, and a skilful actress, she made her debut at Covent Garden in 1829, when her Juliet created a great sensation. For three years she played leading parts in London, and went with her father to the USA (1832), where she married Pierce Butler (1834), a Southern planter. They were divorced in 1848 and after some years she returned to London. Resuming her maiden name, she gave Shakespearean readings for 20 years. She published dramas, poems, and also eight volumes of autobiography.

Kemble, John Philip 1757–1823
English actor

He was born in Prescot, Lancashire, the brother of **Sarah Siddons**, **Charles Kemble** and **Stephen Kemble**, and the eldest son of **Roger Kemble**. His father intended him for the Catholic priesthood, and sent him to a seminary at Sedgley Park, Staffordshire, and to the English college at Douai (France), but the life of a priest did not appeal to him and he became an actor. His first appearance was at Wolverhampton (1776). He joined the York circuit under Tate Wilkinson and he played in Ireland. The success of his sister, Mrs Siddons, gave him the opportunity to come to London, and in 1783 he made his London debut, as Hamlet at Drury Lane. He continued to play leading tragic characters at Drury Lane for many years, steadily improving his art, and in 1788 became **Richard Brinsley Sheridan's** manager. He bought a share in Covent Garden Theatre (1802), became manager, and made his first appearance there as Hamlet (1803). In 1808 the theatre was burned, and on the opening of the new building (1809) the notorious OP (Old Price) Riots broke out. Kemble retired in 1817, and afterwards settled in Lausanne, Switzerland.

Kemble, Roger 1721–1802
Travelling English theatre manager

He married the actress Sarah Ward (d.1807). Their children included the actors the father of **Charles**, **John Philip** and **Stephen Kemble**, and **Sarah Siddons**.

Kemble, Stephen 1758–1822
English actor

He was born in Kington, Herefordshire, and was the brother of **Sarah Siddons**, **John Philip Kemble** and **Charles Kemble**. He was chiefly remarkable for his enormous bulk, which enabled him to play Falstaff without padding. He was manager of the Edinburgh Theatre (1792–1800), where he was always involved in lawsuits and other troubles.

Kemnitz, Martin See Chemnitz, Martin

Kemp, George Meikle 1795–1844
Scottish draughtsman

Born in Hillriggs, near Biggar, the son of a shepherd, he was a carpenter by trade. He worked in England and France and made a study of Gothic architecture there. In 1838 his second design for the **Walter Scott** Monument in Edinburgh was accepted, but before its completion he was drowned in an Edinburgh canal.

Kemp, Jack French 1935–
US politician

Born in Los Angeles, he graduated from Occidental College with a degree in physical education in 1957 and was a professional football quarterback until 1969, most notably with the Buffalo Bills in New York. Elected as a US representative from New York in 1970, he remained in Congress until 1989, becoming known as a conservative who championed supply-side economics and tax cuts and argued for deregulation. As Secretary of Housing and Urban Development (1989–93) under President **George Bush**, he advocated 'urban enterprise zones' to stimulate inner-city neighborhoods but failed to secure sufficient funding for his plans. He ran unsuccessfully for Vice-President on the Republican ticket with **Bob Dole** in 1996.

Kemp, Lindsay 1939–
Scottish mime artist, actor, dancer, teacher and director

He was born on the Isle of Lewis. He grew up in Bradford, England, and studied at Bradford Art College before beginning his dance training with Ballet Rambert. His teachers included **Marie Rambert**, **Charles Weidman** and mime artist **Marcel Marceau**. His colourful career was launched at the 1964 Edinburgh Festival, and he has had his own company in various forms since the early 1960s. Since then, he has created his own work in extravagant, camp style, including *The Parade's Gone By* (1975) and *Cruel Garden* (1977, in collaboration with **Christopher Bruce**), both for Ballet Rambert, *Flowers* (based on the writings of **Jean Genet**, 1973), *Midsummer Night's Dream* (1979) and *The Big Parade* and *Onnagata* (1991) for his own company. He taught rock star **David Bowie** mime and appeared in **Ken Russell**'s films *Savage Messiah* (1972) and *Valentino* (1977) and **Derek Jarman**'s *Sebastiane* (1975) and *Jubilee* (1977). More recent film appearances include *Italian Postcards* (1986) and *Travelling Light* (1993). □ David Haughton, *Lindsay Kemp* (1982)

Kempe, Margery, née Brunham c.1373–c.1440
English mystic

Born in Lynn, Norfolk, she married a burgess there and had 14 children. Following a period of insanity she experienced a conversion and undertook numerous pilgrimages. Between 1432 and 1436 she dictated her spiritual autobiography, *The Book of Margery Kempe*. It recounts her persecution by devils and men, repeated accusations of Lollardism (following the teaching of **John Wycliffe**), and her journeys to Jerusalem and to Germany, and is regarded as a classic.

Kempe, Rudolf 1910–76
German conductor

He was born near Dresden, and studied with **Fritz Busch**. He became principal oboist of the Leipzig Gewandhaus Orchestra (1929–36), and made his conducting debut in 1935; he also worked with the Leipzig opera. He established a reputation as an opera conductor, especially of **Wagner**, conducting *Ring* cycles at Bayreuth and Covent Garden (1955–59), and in the music of **Richard Strauss**, much of which he recorded. He succeeded Sir **Thomas Beecham** as chief conductor of the Royal Philharmonic Orchestra in 1961, and was appointed principal conductor of the BBC Symphony Orchestra (1975–76).

Kempe, Will(iam) c.1550–c.1603
English comedian

A leading member of **Shakespeare**'s company, he left the stage when the Chamberlain's Men moved to the Globe Theatre, London. In 1600, he performed in a nine-day Morris dance from London to Norwich. He wrote *Nine Daies Wonder* (ed by Dyce, Camden Society).

Kempenfelt, Richard 1718–82
English naval officer

He served in command of HM ships in the West Indies (1739) and in the East Indies during the Seven Years War (1756–63). Promoted rear admiral (1780), he won a great action against a French convoy off Ushant in 1781. He was drowned when his flagship, HMS *Royal George*, capsized off Spithead. He is remembered for his progressive ideas on signalling, health at sea (he supported the findings of **James Lind**), and organization. His recommended divisional system survived in the Royal Navy in modern times.

Kempis, Thomas à, *also called* Thomas Hemerken or Hämmerlein 1379–1471
German religious writer

He was named after his birthplace, Kempen, near Cologne. In 1400 he entered the Augustinian convent of Agnietenberg near Zwolle in the Netherlands, took holy orders in 1413, was chosen sub-prior in 1429, and died as Superior. He wrote sermons, ascetical treatises, pious biographies, letters and hymns, and in particular the influential devotional work *Imitatio Christi* (c.1415–24, *The Imitation of Christ*).

Kemsley, James Gomer Berry, 1st Viscount 1883–1968
Welsh newspaper proprietor

Born in Merthyr Tydfil, he became chairman of Kemsley Newspapers Ltd in 1937, controlling the *Sunday Times* and other newspapers. He was created a baronet in 1928, raised to the peerage in 1936, and received a viscountcy in 1945. He published *The Kemsley Manual of Journalism* in 1950.

Ken, Thomas 1631–1711
English prelate and hymnwriter

Born in Little Berkhampstead, Hertfordshire, he held several livings and in 1666 was elected a Fellow of Winchester where he prepared his *Manual of Prayers for Scholars of Winchester College* (1674), and wrote his morning, evening, and midnight hymns, the first two of which, 'Awake, my soul', and 'Glory to Thee, my God, this night', are among the best known. In 1679 he was appointed by **Charles II** chaplain to Princess **Mary**, wife of William of Orange (later **William III**), but offended William, and returned home in 1680, when he became a royal chaplain. In 1683, on Charles II's visit to Winchester, Ken refused to give up his house for the accommodation of **Nell Gwyn**. In the same year he went to Tangiers as a chaplain, and in 1685 was consecrated Bishop of Bath and Wells. The chief event of his bishopric was his trial and acquittal among the Seven Bishops in 1688 for refusing to read the Declaration of Indulgence. At the Glorious Revolution of 1688 he refused to take the Oath of Allegiance to William, and was deprived of his bishopric in 1691.

Kendal, Felicity Anne 1946–
English actress

Born into a theatrical family in Olton, Warwickshire, she made her London debut in 1967 in *Minor Murder* at the Savoy and has since played the title role in *The Second Mrs Tanqueray* (1981–82), Louise in *Hidden Laughter* (1990) and Ariadne Utterwood in *Heartbreak House* (1992), as well as leading roles in the **Tom Stoppard** plays *The Real Thing* (1982), *Jumpers* (1985), *Hapgood* (1988) and *Arcadia* (1993). On television, she acted Barbara Good in *The Good Life* (1975–78), Helena Cuthbertson in *The Camomile Lawn* (1992) and Nancy Belasco in *Honey for Tea* (1994).

Kendal, Dame Madge, *stage name of* Margaret Brunton Grimston, *née* Margaret Shafto Robertson 1849–1935
English actress

She was born in Cleethorpes, Humberside, and was the sister of the dramatist **T W Robertson**. By the 1870s she was leading lady at the Haymarket Theatre where she acted principally in the plays of **Shakespeare**. In 1869 she married the actor William Hunter Kendal, properly Grimston (1843–1917), with whom she appeared in many productions. She was created a DBE in 1926.

Kendall, Edward Calvin 1886–1972
US chemist and Nobel Prize winner

Born in South Norwalk, Connecticut, he trained in Canada then joined the firm of Park, Davis (1910) and was asked to isolate the active principle of the thyroid gland. He left in 1911, going first to St Luke's Hospital in New

York and then to the Mayo Foundation, Rochester (1914), where he was made professor and head of biochemistry. In 1914 he isolated thyroxine. Its structure was elucidated partly by Kendall and partly by Sir **Charles Robert Harington**. In collaboration, Kendall isolated cortisone and 29 related steroids from the adrenal cortex. He prepared synthetic corticosterone in 1944 and cortisone (active against Addison's disease) in 1947. With **Philip Hench**, he found that cortisone was effective against rheumatic fever and that cortisone plus adrenocortical trophic hormone was effective against rheumatoid arthritis. Kendall, Hench and **Tadeus Reichstein** shared the 1950 Nobel Prize for physiology or medicine.

Kendall, (Thomas) Henry 1839–82
Australian pastoral and lyric poet
Born in Milton, Ulladulla, New South Wales, he spent his youth in the countryside, then settled in Sydney and contributed verse to local newspapers and journals, first collected in *Poems and Songs* (1862). He moved to Melbourne in 1868 where a second book, *Leaves from Australian Forests*, was published (1869). Despite continuing problems with debt and alcohol, he won the International Exhibition poetry competition in 1879, and the following year he published his last collection, *Songs from the Mountains*. Renowned for his ceremonial and patriotic verse, Kendall was a significant poet of the colonial period, reflected in the definitive *The Poetical Works of Henry Kendall* (1966).

Kendall, Henry Way 1926–
US physicist and Nobel Prize winner
Born in Boston and educated at the Massachusetts Institute of Technology (MIT), he later worked at Stanford University and MIT, where he was appointed professor in 1967 and J A Stratton Professor of Physics in 1991. Around 1970, with **Jerome Friedman** and **Richard Taylor**, he led a research team working at the Stanford Linear Accelerator, where they accelerated electrons towards a target and measured the energies and angles of the scattered electrons to obtain convincing experimental evidence of the existence of quarks. In conjunction with experiments at the European nuclear research centre, CERN in Geneva, they also confirmed predictions regarding the charges on quarks. For this work Kendall was awarded the W K H Panofsky prize (1989) and the Nobel Prize for physics (1990) jointly with Friedman and Taylor.

Kendrew, Sir John Cowdery 1917–97
English molecular biologist and Nobel Prize winner
Born in Oxford, he was educated at Clifton College, Bristol, and Trinity College, Cambridge. Elected a Fellow of Peterhouse College, Cambridge (1947–75), he was a co-founder (with **Max Perutz**) and deputy chairman of the Medical Research Council Unit for Molecular Biology at Cambridge (1946–75). He was also Scientific Advisor to the Ministry of Defence (1960–64). He carried out researches in the chemistry of the blood and determined by X-ray crystallography the structure of the muscle protein myoglobin. He was awarded the 1962 Nobel Prize for chemistry jointly with Perutz. He wrote *The Thread of Life* (1966), was elected FRS in 1960 and knighted in 1974. He was President of St John's College, Oxford from 1981 to 1987 when he became an honorary Fellow and was editor-in-chief of *The Encyclopaedia of Molecular Biology* (1994).

Keneally, Thomas Michael 1935–
Australian novelist
Born in Sydney, New South Wales, he studied for the priesthood and the law, served in the Australian Citizens' Military Forces, and has taught and lectured in drama. He would like, he has said, to disown his first two novels—*The Place at Whitton* (1964) and *The Fear* (1965). His third novel, *Bring Larks and Heroes* (1967), was followed by *Three*

Cheers for a Paraclete (1968) and *The Survivor* (1969), character studies in the English tradition, but it was the publication of *The Chant of Jimmy Blacksmith* (1972), based on the slaughter of a white family by an Aboriginal employee, that marked the beginning of his mature fiction. As gifted as he is prolific, Keneally is a born storyteller whose sympathies lie with the oppressed and the outcast. His reputation grew steadily until he published *Schindler's Ark* (1982), which tells how a German industrialist helped over 1,000 Jews survive the Nazis. A controversial winner of the Booker Prize because it blurred the boundary between fact and fiction, it was memorably filmed, as *Schindler's List*, in 1994. Recent books include *A Family Madness* (1985), *The Playmaker* (1987), *By the Line* (1989), *Flying Hero Class* (1991), *Woman of the Inner Sea* (1992) and *A River Town* (1995). His writings include travel and political commentary, but later novels have been criticized for apparent haste. ☐ P Quartermaine, *Thomas Keneally* (1991)

Kenilorea, Sir Peter (Kauona Keninarais'Ona) 1943–
Solomon Islands statesman
Born in Takataka on Malaita Island, after training in New Zealand, he worked as a teacher before entering the Solomon Islands' Civil Service in 1971. He then moved into politics, eventually leading the Solomon Islands United Party (SIUPA). He became Chief Minister in 1976 and Prime Minister after independence in 1978. His opposition to decentralization led to his departure in 1981, but he returned in 1984, leading a coalition government. He resigned the premiership in 1986, but remained Foreign Minister and Deputy Premier until the SIUPA coalition was defeated in the 1989 general election.

Kennan, George F(rost) 1904–
US diplomat and historian
Born in Milwaukee, Wisconsin, he graduated from Princeton in 1925 and joined the US Foreign Service, working in listening posts around the USSR. During World War II he served in the US legations in Berlin, Lisbon and Moscow, and in 1947 was appointed director of policy planning by Secretary of State **George C Marshall**. He advocated the policy of containment of the USSR, a strategy which was adopted by secretary of state **Dean Acheson**, whom he served as principal adviser (1949–52), and **John Foster Dulles**. Kennan subsequently served as US ambassador in Moscow (1952–53) and Yugoslavia (1961–63). From 1956 to 1974, as Professor of History at the Institute for Advanced Study in Princeton, he revised his strategic views and called for US disengagement from Europe. His books include *Realities of American Foreign Policy* (1954), *Russia Leaves the War* (1956), *The Nuclear Delusion* (1982), *Sketches from a Life* (1989) and *Around the Cragged Hill* (1993).

Kennaway, James 1928–68
Scottish novelist
He was born in Auchterarder, Perthshire, and did national service before going to Trinity College, Oxford, after which he worked for a London publisher and began to write in earnest. He married in 1951, and *The Kennaway Papers* (1981), edited by his wife Susan, gives an insight into his mercurial character and their turbulent relationship. *Tunes of Glory* (1956) was his first novel and remains his best known. He wrote the screenplay for the film of it, which starred **Alec Guinness** and **John Mills** in a class confrontation set in a military barracks in Scotland. *Household Ghosts* (1961) was equally powerful, and was made into a stage-play (1967) and a film (1969) under the title *Country Dance*. Later books of note include *Some Gorgeous Accident* (1967) and the autobiographical *The Cost of Living Like This* (1969). The novel *Silence* was published posthumously (1972).

Kennedy, John F(itzgerald) 1917–63
35th President of the USA

John F Kennedy was born in Brookline, Massachusetts, a son of **Joseph P Kennedy**. He graduated from Harvard in 1940 and the same year published *Why England Slept*, a bestselling analysis of Great Britain's unpreparedness for war. He served as a torpedo boat commander in the Pacific during World War II and was decorated for his courageous conduct when the boat was hit and sunk.

Elected to the US House of Representatives as a Democrat from Massachussetts in 1946, he won a Senate seat in 1952 and the next year married Jacqueline Lee Bouvier (see **Jackie Kennedy Onassis**). While convalescing from spinal operations he wrote *Profiles in Courage* (1956), which won a Pulitzer Prize. Though he failed in his effort to gain the Democratic vice-presidential nomination in 1956, he won his party's presidential nomination in 1960, defeating Republican **Richard Nixon** by a narrow margin in the popular vote and becoming the first Catholic and, at the age of 43, the youngest person to be elected President. He introduced a legislative programme, the 'New Frontier', which aimed to extend civil rights and to provide funding for education, medical care for the elderly and the space programme, but much of it stalled in Congress. Through his brother **Robert F Kennedy** he supported federal desegregation policy in schools and universities.

He faced a series of foreign policy crises, including the unsuccessful invasion of **Fidel Castro**'s Cuba at the Bay of Pigs (April 1961), the building of the Berlin Wall (August 1961) and the Cuban Missile Crisis (October 1962). At the risk of nuclear war, he induced the Soviet Union to withdraw its missiles from Cuba, and he achieved a partial nuclear test ban treaty with the USSR in 1963. He also founded the Peace Corps and increased the US military involvement in Vietnam.

On 22 November 1963, he was assassinated by rifle fire while being driven in an open car through Dallas, Texas. The alleged assassin, **Lee Harvey Oswald**, was himself shot and killed at point-blank range by Jack Ruby two days later. Kennedy's eloquent idealism and youthful glamour had won him much popularity in the USA and abroad, and though the legislative achievements of his brief administration were modest, his martyrdom enabled his successor, **Lyndon B Johnson**, to promote the social reforms of the 'Great Society' as his legacy.

📖 A M Schlesigner, Jnr, *A Thousand Days* (1965); T Sorenson, *Kennedy* (1965); T H White, *The Making of a President 1960* (1961).

> 'Let every nation know, whether it wishes us well or ill, that we shall pay any price, bear any burden, meet any hardships, support any friend, oppose any foe to assure the survival and success of liberty.' From Kennedy's Inaugural Address, 20 January 1961.

Kennedy, Edward M(oore), *also called* Ted Kennedy 1932–
US politician

Born in Brookline, Massachusetts, the youngest son of **Joseph Kennedy** and brother of **John F Kennedy** and **Robert F Kennedy**, he was educated at Harvard and Virginia University Law School and admitted to the Massachusetts Bar in 1959. He was elected as a Democratic senator to fill John F Kennedy's old Massachusetts seat in 1962. In 1969 he became the youngest-ever majority Whip in the US senate, but his involvement the same year in a car accident on Chappaquidick Island in which a young campaign worker, Mary Jo Kopechne, was drowned dogged his subsequent political career, and was still a major liability during his unsuccessful campaign to win the Democratic presidential nomination in 1980. Despite the apparent disorder of his personal life, he has been one of the most influential members of the Senate for more than three decades, focusing on issues such as health care and serving as an advocate for the working class and middle class. 📖 William H Honan, *Ted Kennedy: Portrait of a Survivor* (1972)

Kennedy, Helena Kennedy, Baroness 1950–
Scottish barrister, broadcaster and writer

Born in Glasgow into a working-class family, she studied law in London and set up practice with several colleagues, taking on a variety of radical cases. Renowned for her persuasive charm in court, she has represented clients as diverse as anarchists, a member of the Guildford Four and **Myra Hindley**. She achieved public recognition with her appearance on the BBC documentary series *The Heart of the Matter* and with *Blind Justice*, a television drama loosely based on her own legal experiences. Overtly left-wing and feminist, she has hastened changes in attitudes within the English legal profession. In 1991 she was made a QC and was appointed to the Bar Council. Her publications include *Eve Was Framed* (1992).

Kennedy, Jackie See **Onassis, Jackie Kennedy**

Kennedy, John F(itzgerald) See panel above

Kennedy, Joseph P(atrick) 1888–1969
US businessman and diplomat

Born in Boston, grandson of an Irish Catholic immigrant and the son of a Boston publican, he was educated at Harvard. He married Rose Fitzgerald in 1914, daughter of a local politician, John F Fitzgerald ('Honey Fitz', twice Mayor of Boston), also of Irish immigrant descent. They had nine children, including **John F**, **Robert F** and **Edward Kennedy**. He made a large fortune in the 1920s through business ventures and stock market speculation, and during the 1930s was a strong supporter of **Franklin D Roosevelt** and the 'New Deal', being rewarded with minor administrative posts, and the ambassadorship to Britain (1938–40). After World War II he concentrated on fulfilling his ambitions of a political dynasty through his sons and placed his large fortune at their disposal for that purpose. His eldest son, Joseph Patrick (1915–44), was killed in a flying accident while on naval service in World War II, but the others achieved international fame. 📖 David E Koskoff, *Joseph P Kennedy: A Life and Times* (1974)

Kennedy, Louise St John 1950–
Australian architect

Educated at the University of Western Australia and the University of Melbourne, she began her own practice in Cottlesloe, Australia, designing mostly smaller-scale buildings, and won an award for the most outstanding piece of domestic architecture in Australia. Inundated with clients, she designed 24 houses in an eight-year period. In 1986 her design for tearooms jutting out over Mosman Bay caused an uproar among the wealthy residents of this exclusive area, but after much wrangling they were built and gained acclaim from the public, the architectural press and even the residents themselves.

Kennedy, Sir Ludovic Henry Coverley 1919–
Scottish broadcaster and writer

Born in Edinburgh, and educated at Christ Church, Oxford, he served in the Royal Navy (1939–46) before becoming a librarian, lecturer and later editor of the BBC's *First Reading* (1953–54). In 1950 he married the ballerina Moira Shearer. On television, he introduced *Profile* (1955–56), was an ITN newscaster (1956–58), was the host of *This Week* (1958–60) and contributed to the BBC's *Panorama* (1960–63), and has devoted himself to setting the record straight on the falsely accused and wrongly convicted. His many notable series include *Your Verdict* (1962), *Your Witness* (1967–70) and *A Life With Crime* (1979). He hosted *Face the Press* (1968–72), *Tonight* (1976–78) and *Did You See?* (1980–88), among many others. His books include *Ten Rillington Place* (1961), *The Trial of Stephen Ward* (1964), *A Presumption of Innocence: The Amazing Case of Patrick Meehan* (1975), *Euthanasia: the good death* (1990), two volumes of autobiography, *On My Way To The Club* (1989) and *In Bed With An Elephant* (1995), and *Truth to Tell* (1991), his collected writings. He was knighted in 1994.

Kennedy, Nigel Paul 1956–
English violinist
Born in Brighton, he trained at the Yehudi Menuhin School, London, and the Juilliard School of Performing Arts, New York, and was the subject of a five-year BBC television documentary on the development of a soloist after his debut in 1977. He won international acclaim for his concerts and recordings, notably his award-winning performance of the Elgar *Violin Concerto* (1985). He has recorded concertos by Tchaikovsky, Sibelius, Bruch, Mendelssohn, Walton, Brahms and Beethoven, and a bestselling disc of Vivaldi's *The Four Seasons*. His insistence that classical music should not be exclusive, together with his punk image and attitude, seemed increasingly at odds with the classical establishment. In 1992 he 'retired' to concentrate on chamber music and music by living composers, and to develop his interest in jazz and rock, but returned to the concert stage in 1997. He published an autobiography, *Always Playing*, in 1991, and the first album of his own music, *Kafka*, appeared in 1996.

Kennedy, Robert F(rancis) 1925–68
US politician
Born in Brookline, Massachusetts, the third son of Joseph Kennedy, he was educated at Harvard and University of Virginia Law School and was admitted to the Massachusetts Bar in 1951. As Chief Counsel of the Senate Select Committee on Improper Activities (1957–59), he prosecuted David Bech and Jimmy Hoffa of the Teamster's Union, who were charged with corruption. He was an efficient manager of his brother John F Kennedy's presidential campaign, and was an energetic Attorney-General (1961–64) under the latter's administration, notable in his efforts to promote civil rights. He resigned after President Kennedy's assassination, and was elected Senator from New York in 1965. After much hesitation he declared his candidacy for the Democratic presidential nomination in 1968, quickly winning as an idealist reformer. On 5 June 1968, after winning the California primary election, he was shot by a Jordanian immigrant, Sirhan Sirhan, and died the following day. ⌨ Arthur M Schlesinger, Jnr, *Robert Kennedy and His Times* (1978)

Kennedy, William Joseph 1928–
US novelist and screenwriter
Born in Albany, New York, he was educated at Siena College, in Loudonville, New York, and served in the US army (1950–52) before becoming a journalist and eventually a full-time writer. *The Ink Truck* (1969) is distinct from subsequent novels in that it does not use the locale of his hometown as a backdrop. *Legs* (1975), which combines fact and fiction to retell the story of Legs Diamond, the notorious gangster, is the first of the 'Albany novels', followed in 1978 by *Billy Phelan's Greatest Game*. *Ironweed* (1983), his best known novel, describes the homecoming of a fallen baseball star, now down-and-out, drunk and maudlin. Jack Nicholson gave an accurate film portrayal of the character, and the book won a Pulitzer Prize. Later

novels in the Albany cycle include *Quinn's Book* (1988), *Very Old Bones* (1992) and *The Flaming Corsage* (1996). ⌨ E C Reilly, *William Kennedy* (1991)

Kennelly, Arthur Edwin 1861–1939
US engineer
Born in Bombay, India, he went to the USA in 1887, and worked as assistant to Thomas Edison. He became a professor at Harvard (1902–30), and in 1902 suggested, almost simultaneously with Oliver Heaviside, the existence of an ionized E-layer in the atmosphere known as the Kennelly-Heaviside layer, or Heaviside layer.

Kenneth I *called* Kenneth MacAlpin d.858
King of the Scots
He seems to have succeeded his father Alpin as king (841), and to have won acceptance by the Picts by 843. His reign marked a decisive step in the making of a united kingdom north of the rivers Forth and Clyde, and also saw the shift of the centre of the Church from Iona to the court at Dunkeld.

Kenney, Annie 1879–1953
English suffragette
Born in Springhead, near Oldham, she was a full-time worker from the age of 13. She started a union, then began a correspondence course at Ruskin College, Oxford. When she met Christabel Pankhurst, she became involved in the struggle for women's suffrage, the only working-class woman in the leadership. In 1905 she and Pankhurst were arrested for interrupting a meeting in Manchester, and again the next year for interrupting a speech by the Prime Minister, Sir Henry Campbell-Bannerman. She took over the leadership during Pankhurst's exile in Paris, crossing the Channel every week to receive instructions. She withdrew from public life in 1926. ⌨ *Memories of a Millhand* (1924)

Kennington, Eric Henri 1888–1960
English painter and sculptor
Born in London, he was an official war scultor in both world wars, and designed many memorials. *Costermongers* (1913) is an example of his early paintings of Cockney characters and London scenes. From his World War I paintings, *The Kenningtons at Levantie* is most impressive. His memorials include the British memorial at Soissons, France (1927–8) and the bronze head of Thomas Hardy at Dorchester (1929).

Kenny, Elizabeth, *known as* Sister Kenny 1886–1952
Australian nurse
She began practising as a nurse in the bush-country in Australia (1912), and then joined the Australian army nursing corps (1915–19). She developed a new technique for treating poliomyelitis by muscle therapy rather than immobilization with casts and splints. She established clinics in Australia (1933), Great Britain (1937) and the USA (Minneapolis, 1940), and travelled widely in order to demonstrate her methods. She published her autobiography, *And They Shall Walk*, in 1943.

Kent, Prince George, Duke of, *in full* George Edward Alexander Edmund 1902–42
English duke
The son of King George V and Queen Mary of Teck, he was born at Sandringham. He passed out of Dartmouth (1920), but because of delicate health served in the Foreign Office and inspected factories for the Home Office, the first member of the British royal family to work in the Civil Service. In 1934 he was created Duke of Kent, and married Princess Marina of Greece and Denmark (1906–68), a first cousin of King George I of Greece and a great-niece of Queen Alexandra. He was appointed Governor-General of Australia (1938) but was prevented

from taking up the post by the outbreak of World War II. He was killed on active service, as chief welfare officer of RAF Home Command, when his Sunderland flying-boat on its way to Iceland crashed into a mountain in the north of Scotland. Their three children are Edward, Duke of Kent, Princess Alexandra and Prince Michael of Kent (1942–), who married (1978) Baroness Marie-Christine von Reibnitz, and whose children are Lord Frederick Michael George David Louis Windsor (1979–) and Lady Gabriella Marina Alexandra Ophelia, or 'Ella', Windsor (1981–).

Kent, Bruce 1929–
British cleric and peace campaigner
He was born in London, and after education in Canada and at Oxford, he was ordained in 1958 and then served as a curate in Kensington, London (1958–63). He was subsequently secretary in the Archbishop's House, Westminster, Catholic chaplain to London University and a parish priest. He became increasingly involved in the Campaign for Nuclear Disarmament (CND), becoming its general secretary in 1980, its vice-chairman in 1985 and its chairman (1987–90). He resigned his ministry in 1987 and stood unsuccessfully as Labour Party candidate for Oxford West and Abingdon in 1992. He published *Undiscovered Ends* in 1992.

Kent, Edward, Duke of 1767–1820
British nobleman
The fourth son of George III, he was born at Buckingham Palace, London. At Gibraltar, first as colonel (1790–91), and then as governor (1802), his martinet discipline caused continual mutinies, ending in bloodshed and his recall. In 1818 he married Victoria Mary Louisa (1786–1861), daughter of the Duke of Saxe-Saalfeld-Coburg, and widow of the Prince of Leiningen. For the sake of economy they lived at Leiningen, and went to England (1819) for the birth of their child, the Princess Victoria. His three elder brothers, George IV, the Duke of York, and William IV, died leaving no children and Princess Victoria succeeded to the throne (1837).

Kent, Edward, Duke of, *in full* Edward George Nicholas Paul Patrick 1935–
English duke
The son of George, Duke of Kent, he was born in London and commissioned in the army in 1955. In 1961 he married Katharine Worsley (1933–), and they have three children, George Philip Nicholas Windsor, Earl of St Andrews (1962–), Lady Helen Marina Lucy (1964–), who married Timothy Verner Taylor in 1992, becoming Lady Helen Taylor, and Lord Nicholas Charles Edward Jonathan Windsor (1970–). He retired from the army in 1976.

Kent, James 1763–1847
US lawyer and judge
He was born in Fredericksburgh, New York, and after serving in the New York legislature he became Professor of Law in Columbia College (1794–98). In 1798, he was appointed Justice of the Supreme Court of New York. In 1804 he became Chief Justice, and from 1814 to 1823 was State Chancellor. His *Commentaries on American Law* (1826–30), modelled on Sir William Blackstone's work, was the USA's first classic legal text and was influential for many years.

Kent, Rockwell 1882–1971
US artist
Born in Tarrytown, New York, he studied with William Merritt Chase in 1900, and dropped out of Columbia University to begin a life of wandering. In 1917 he went to Alaska, where he painted and made woodcuts later published in his book *Wilderness* (1920), and he chronicled a voyage around Cape Horn and a trip to Greenland in

subsequent works. A member of the radical Left, he was awarded the Lenin Peace Prize in Moscow in 1967. He is best remembered for the bold and angular illustrations he created for books such as **Herman Melville's** *Moby Dick* and **Voltaire's** *Candide*.

Kent, William 1684–1748
English architect and landscape designer
Born in Bridlington, Yorkshire, he studied painting in Rome (1709–19), and played a leading part in introducing the Palladian style of architecture into Great Britain. He designed many public buildings in London, including the Royal Mews in Trafalgar Square, the Treasury buildings and the Horse Guards block in Whitehall. As an interior designer he decorated Burlington House and Chiswick House in London. As a landscape designer he liberated gardens from strict formality and introduced romantic settings, as at the garden of Stowe House in Buckinghamshire. A versatile artist, he also designed the Gothic screens in Westminster Hall and Gloucester Cathedral. 📖 John Dixon Hunt, *William Kent, Landscape Garden Designer* (1987)

Kentigern, St, *also called* St Mungo, *known as* the Apostle of Cumbria c.518–603AD
Celtic churchman
Born in Culross, Fife, Scotland, he was, according to legend, the son of a Princess Thenew, who was cast from Traprain Law, then exposed on the Firth of Forth in a coracle. It carried her to Culross, where she bore a son. Mother and child were baptized by St Serf, who educated the boy in his monastery, where he was so beloved that his name Kentigern (chief lord) was often exchanged for Mungo (dear friend). He founded a monastery at Cathures (now Glasgow), and in 543 was consecrated Bishop of Cumbria. In 553 he was driven to seek refuge in Wales, where he visited St David, and where he founded another monastery and a bishopric, which still bears the name of his disciple, St Asaph. In 573 he was recalled by a new king, Rederech Hael, and about 584 was visited by Columba. He was buried in Glasgow Cathedral, which is named after him as St Mungo's. A fragment of a Life, and the *Vita Kentigerni* ('Life of Kentigern') by Joceline of Furness both belong to the 12th century. His feast day is 13 January.

Kentner, Louis Philip 1905–87
British pianist
Born in Karwin, Silesia, he studied from the age of six at the Budapest Royal Academy and made his debut in Budapest in 1916. An acclaimed interpreter of Chopin and Liszt, he also gave first performances of works by Bartók, Zoltán Kodály, Sir Michael Tippett, William Walton and others. He settled in England in 1935, becoming a British citizen in 1946, and was a frequent chamber-music partner of his brother-in-law, Yehudi Menuhin.

Kenton, Stan(ley Newcomb) 1912–79
US pianist, composer and bandleader
Born in Wichita, Kansas, and brought up in Los Angeles, he studied piano privately before beginning his professional career in 1934 with a succession of lesser-known big bands. He first formed his own orchestra in 1941, but is more immediately associated with the big band 'progressive' jazz style of the 1950s, using dissonant ensemble writing. His later orchestras were unusual for their five-member trombone sections; and although some aspects of progressive jazz were dismissed as pretentious, Kenton's innovations, employing adventurous arrangers and outstanding soloists, have stood the test of time.

Kenyatta, Jomo, *originally* Kamau Ngengi c.1889–1978
Kenyan nationalist and political leader

Born in Mitumi, orphaned, and educated at a Scots mission school, he worked as a herd boy. He joined the Kikuyu Central Association (1922), and became its president. He visited Britain (1929, 1931–44) to lobby government, and studied for a year at London University under **Bronisław Malinowski**, who wrote the preface to his book *Facing Mount Kenya* (1938). He visited Russia three times, and was president of the Pan African Federation with **Kwame Nkrumah** as secretary. He worked on the land during the war and married an Englishwoman in 1942. On returning to Kenya in 1946 he was elected president of the Kenyan African Union, which advocated total independence in a unitary state. On the outbreak of the Mau Mau uprising, he was sentenced to seven years' hard labour in 1952, released in 1958, but exiled first to a remote northern area, then to his native village. Chosen in absentia to be president of the new KANU Party, and elected MP in 1961, he became Prime Minister in June 1963, retaining the post after Kenya's independence in December of that year, and becoming President of the republic of Kenya in December 1964. A remarkable mixture of Kikuyu nationalist, pragmatic politician and father figure (he was known as *Mzee* or 'old man'), he surprised observers by leading Kenya into a period of economic growth and unexpected tribal harmony. 📖 Jeremy Murray-Brown, *Kenyatta* (2nd edn, 1979)

Kenyon, Dame Kathleen Mary 1906–78
English archaeologist

Born in London, the daughter of a director of the British Museum, she was educated at Somerville College, Oxford. She was lecturer in Palestinian archaeology at London University (1948–62), Principal of St Hugh's College, Oxford (1962–73), and director of the British School of Archaeology in Jerusalem from 1951 to 1966. Her most notable books are *Digging up Jericho* (1957), *Archaeology in the Holy Land* (1965), and *Digging up Jerusalem* (1974).

Kenzo, *in full* Kenzo Takada 1940–
Japanese fashion designer

He was born in Kyoto. After studying art in Japan, he moved to Paris and produced freelance collections from 1964. He started a shop called Jungle Jap in 1970, and is known for his innovative ideas and use of traditional designs. He creates clothes with both oriental and western influences and is a trendsetter in the field of knitwear.

Keokuk 1788–c.1848
Sauk leader

Born near Rock Island, Illinois, he became a war chief of the Sauks, and a rival of **Black Hawk** for tribal leadership. Known for his accommodation to the US government, in contrast to Black Hawk, he aligned with the US cause and did not fight during the Black Hawk War (1832), in which the Illinois Sauks were defeated by US forces and sent to a reservation in Iowa. After speaking in Washington for peace between the Sauks and Sioux (1837), he was named chief of the united Sauk clans. He continued to support the US government, which moved the tribe farther west into Kansas.

Kepler, Johannes 1571–1630
German astronomer

Born in Weilderstadt, Württemberg, he was educated at the University of Tübingen where he obtained a master's degree in theology in 1591. He became Professor of Mathematics at Graz in 1594. Among his duties at Graz was the publication of almanacs to forecast the weather and to predict favourable days for various undertakings with reference to the rules of astrology. For a time he was astrologer to Duke Albrecht of **Wallenstein**. He recorded in his first major publication, the *Mysterium Cosmographium*

(1596), that the distances from the Sun of the six planets including the Earth could be related to the five regular solids of geometry, of which the cube is the simplest. He sent copies of his book to **Galileo** and **Tycho Brahe**, the greatest astronomers of the day, who responded favourably. When Kepler was later in difficulties in Graz, the latter invited him to join him at Prague. Kepler arrived in Prague in 1600, and when Brahe died in 1601 he was appointed to succeed him as imperial mathematician by the Emperor **Rudolf II**. His chief interest was the study of the planet Mars and he found that its movement could not be explained in terms of the customary cycles and epicycles. In this he broke with the tradition of more than 2,000 years by demonstrating that the planets do not move uniformly in circles, but in ellipses with the Sun at one focus and with the radius vector of each planet describing equal areas of the ellipse in equal times (Kepler's first and second laws). He completed his researches in dynamical astronomy 10 years later by formulating his third law, which connects the periods of revolution of the planets with their mean distances from the Sun. In 1627 he published the *Tabulae Rudolphinae*, which contained the ephemerides of the planets according to the new laws, and also an extended catalogue of 1,005 stars based on Tycho's observations. 📖 Max Caspar, *Kepler* (1959)

Keppel, Augustus Keppel, 1st Viscount
1725–86
English naval commander

He served under **Edward Hawke** in the Seven Years War (1756–63), captured Gorée in 1758, commanded a ship in the Battle of Quiberon Bay in 1759, and in the capture of Belleisle in 1761, and was second in command at the capture of Havana in 1762. In 1778, as Commander-in-Chief of the Grand Fleet, he encountered the French fleet off Ushant, but the French escaped. He was tried by court martial for neglect of duty, but was acquitted. He became First Lord of the Admiralty (1782–83).

Keppel, Sir Henry 1809–1904
English naval commander

He served during the war against China (1842), in the naval brigades before Sebastopol in the Crimea (1854), and in Chinese waters (1857). He also commanded a seven-nation force against pirates in the area from 1867 to 1869. He was promoted admiral in 1869, and Admiral of the Fleet in 1877. He wrote *A Sailor's Life under Four Sovereigns* (3 vols, 1899).

Ker, W(illiam) P(aton) 1855–1923
Scottish scholar

Born in Glasgow and educated at Glasgow and at Balliol College, Oxford, he was Professor of English at Cardiff (1883) and University College London (1889), and Professor of Poetry at Oxford (1920). He wrote *Epic and Romance* (1897), *The Dark Ages* (1904), *Essays on Medieval Literature* (1905) and *The Art of Poetry* (1923).

Kerekou, Mathieu Ahmed 1933–
Benin soldier and politician

Born in Natitingou, he trained in France and served in the French army before joining the army of what was then Dahomey. He took part in the 1967 coup which removed the civilian government but returned to military matters the following year and became army deputy chief. In 1972 he led the coup which deposed Justin Ahomadegbe, and established a National Council of the Revolution (CNR), intended to lead the country towards 'scientific socialism'. He renamed the country Benin; gradually social and economic stability returned, the CNR was dissolved and a civilian administration installed. Kerekou was elected President in 1980 and re-elected in 1984. He resigned from the army in 1987 as a gesture of his commitment to genuine democracy. He announced his abandonment of

Marxism in 1991, and his intention to stand in open elections to be held that year. Defeated, he handed over power to a national conference but was re-elected President in 1996.

Kerensky, Aleksandr Fyodorovich 1881–1970
Russian revolutionary leader

Born in Simbirsk, he was the son of a high school principal. He studied law in St Petersburg and made a name for himself as counsel for the defence in Tsarist times in several leading political trials. He was a critical but reasonable member of the Third and Fourth Dumas. In the 1917 Revolution he became Minister of Justice in March, Minister of War in May, and Prime Minister in July in the Provisional Government. Though crushing the military revolt of **Lavr Georgevich Kornilov** in August, he found it increasingly difficult to put through moderate reforms in a deteriorating political situation, and in October was swept away by the Bolsheviks, and fled to France. In 1940 he went to Australia and in 1946 to the USA where he taught at Stanford University from 1956. His writings include *The Prelude to Bolshevism* (1919), *The Catastrophe* (1927), *The Road to Tragedy* (1935), and *The Kerensky Memoirs* (1966). He died in New York City. 📖 R Abraham, *Alexander Kerensky* (1987)

Kerguélen-Trémarec, Yves Joseph de 1745–97
French aristocrat and naval officer

He was born in Quimper, Brittany. On an unsuccessful voyage of exploration seeking Terra Australis, he discovered a group of islands in the South Indian Ocean to which he gave the name Kerguélen's Islands (1772).

Kern, Jerome David 1885–1945
US composer

Born in New York City, he studied music there and in Heidelberg, Germany. He spent the years of his theatrical apprenticeship in New York and London, writing songs that were interpolated into musicals by other composers. His first complete score for a musical play was *The Red Petticoat* (1912), which first brought a 'Western' setting to Broadway, followed by numerous successful Broadway shows. *Show Boat* (1928, book and lyrics by **Oscar Hammerstein II**) is considered his greatest musical, and *Roberta* (1933) included three of his finest songs: 'Smoke Gets In Your Eyes', 'Yesterdays' and 'The Touch of Your Hand'. He also wrote songs for films, winning Academy Awards for 'The Way You Look Tonight' and 'The Last Time I Saw Paris'.

Kerner, Justinus Andreas 1786–1862
German poet

He was born in Ludwigsburg, Württemberg, became a physician at Wildbad, and settled finally in Weinsberg in 1818. He published several volumes of poetry between 1811 and 1852. He studied animal magnetism, believed in occultism, and wrote *Die Seherin von Prevorst* (1829, 'The Clairvoyant of Prevorst'), a study of a psychic case. 📖 H Buttiker, *Justinus Kerner* (1952)

Kerouac, Jack (John Louis) 1922–69
US novelist

He was born in Lowell, Massachusetts. His parents, devout Roman Catholics, came from rural communities in the French-speaking part of Quebec, so French was spoken in the home and he did not learn to speak English until he was six. His childhood was happy, but various disasters upset the family, including the death of an older brother and floods which destroyed his father's print shop and press. He was educated at Lowell High School before accepting a football scholarship at Columbia University, but he turned his back on that and spent the early years of World War II working as a grease monkey in Hartford before returning to Lowell, where he worked as a sports journalist on the *Lowell Sun*. His major energies were spent working on an autobiographical novel that was never published. In 1942 he went to Washington, DC, where he worked briefly on the construction of the Pentagon before joining the US merchant marines, subsequently enlisting in the US navy (1943). After only a month he was discharged and branded an 'indifferent character'. His friends included **Allen Ginsberg**, **Gary Snyder** and Neal Cassady, whom Kerouac portrayed as Dean Moriarty in his most famous novel, *On the Road* (1957). He was identified as leader and spokesman of the Beat Generation, a label he coined then came to regret and repudiate. *The Town and the City* (1950), his first novel, showed the scars of his reading of **Thomas Wolfe**. *On the Road*, his second novel, is loose, apparently structureless and episodic. It follows two friends as they weave their way across the USA. It has been much imitated (on film as well as in fiction) and made Kerouac a cult-hero. In later books, such as *The Dharma Bums* (1958), *Doctor Sax* (1959) and *Big Sur* (1962), he flirted with Zen Buddhism. 📖 A Charters, *Jack Kerouac: a biography* (1973)

Kérouaille, Louise de See **Portsmouth, Duchess of**

Kerr, Deborah, *originally* Deborah Jane Kerr-Trimmer, *married name* Viertel 1921–
Scottish actress

Born in Helensburgh, Strathclyde, she trained as a dancer, before deciding to take up acting. Work on stage was followed by roles in *Major Barbara* (1940), and other British films, notably *The Life and Death of Colonel Blimp* (1943) and *Black Narcissus* (1947). Moving to Hollywood, she was almost invariably cast in ladylike roles, and played numerous governesses and nuns, sensationally straying from her established image to play a nymphomaniac in *From Here to Eternity* (1953) for which she received an Academy Award nomination. She received further nominations for *Edward My Son* (1949), *The King and I* (1956), *Heaven Knows Mr Allison* (1957), *Separate Tables* (1958) and *The Sundowners* (1960). She retired from the screen in 1969 but continued to appear on the stage in such plays as *The Day After the Fair* (1972), *Seascape* (1975), *Candida* (1977) and *The Corn Is Green* (1985). She appeared in the films *Witness for the Prosecution* (1982) and *Reunion At Fairborough* (1985) and made a one-off return to the cinema in *The Assam Garden* (1985). In 1994 she received a special Academy Award and in 1998 was appointed a CBE.

Kerr, Graham Victor 1934–
New Zealand cookery writer

He was born in London, England, and became a successful sportsman (Uffa Fox Trophy Cup, 1950; British Army épée champion, 1955). After working as catering adviser to the British Army (1952–56) and to the Royal New Zealand Air Force (1958–63), he launched his highly popular television show *The Galloping Gourmet*, which was screened in the UK, Ireland, USA, Canada and in Asia. From this series came a number of books including *Entertaining with Kerr* (1963), the *Graham Kerr Cookbook* (1966) and *Galloping Gourmets* (1969). Kerr is also an active lay preacher with an Evangelical Church fellowship.

Kerr, John 1824–1907
Scottish physicist

Born in Ardrossan, Ayrshire, he was educated at Glasgow University in theology and became a lecturer in mathematics. He was one of the first research students of Lord Kelvin. In 1876 he discovered the magneto-optic effect named after him in which a beam of plane polarized light will become elliptically polarized when reflected from an electromagnet. The theoretical implications were later elucidated by **George Fitzgerald**. Kerr was the author of *An Elementary Treatise on Rational Mechanics* (1867), and was elected FRS in 1890.

Kerr, Sir John Robert 1914–91
Australian administrator

Born in Sydney, the son of a boilermaker, he graduated from Sydney University and was admitted to the New South Wales Bar in 1938. Following war service, he became a QC in 1953 and after a number of senior legal and judicial appointments, became Chief Justice of New South Wales in 1972, and lieutenant-governor in the following year. He was sworn in as Governor-General of the Commonwealth of Australia in 1974, and the next year made Australian constitutional history. The coalition opposition had refused to pass the government's budget bill unless a federal election was called. The private banks declined to release funds to enable the business of government to be conducted. To resolve this impasse he exercised his vice-regal 'reserve powers' and dismissed of the Prime Minister, Gough Whitlam, asking the leader of the Opposition, Malcolm Fraser, to form a caretaker government and to call an immediate election. At that election, Kerr's actions were endorsed by the voters, who elected a new coalition government, led by Fraser. Stepping down as Governor-General in 1977, he was named Australian ambassador to UNESCO in 1978, but the ensuing controversy obliged him to resign without taking up the appointment.

Kerr, Roy Patrick 1934–
New Zealand mathematician

Born in Kurow, he was educated in New Zealand and at Cambridge, then returned to New Zealand to become Professor of Mathematics at the University of Canterbury, Christchurch. His main contribution has been in the field of astrophysics. In 1916, Karl Schwarzschild had introduced the idea that a star could contract under gravity to form a black hole. However, Schwarzschild's mathematical description of the phenomenon assumed that the black hole is not rotating, an unrealistic condition, as almost all stars are found to rotate. Kerr discovered a new solution to Albert Einstein's equations, taking account of the resulting angular momentum to give the 'Kerr metric', an expression which completely describes the properties of any black holes which physicists expect to exist. In later work, he formulated the Kerr–Schild solutions, which were very useful in exact solution of the equations of general relativity.

Kertész, André 1894–1985
US photographer

Born in Budapest, Hungary, he served as a photographer with the Hungarian army in World War I. He emigrated to France in 1925 and then to the USA in 1936, and became a US citizen in 1944. Acknowledged as a recorder of the 'human condition', he strongly influenced Brassaï and Henri Cartier-Bresson, and was one of the first serious users of the Leica miniature camera in 1928. His work in New York in the 1940s and 1950s for Condé-Nast publications and like magazines became more conventional, and he did not return to a more individual creative style until 1962. A major retrospective exhibition at the New York Museum of Modern Art in 1964 was followed by numerous international presentations which brought him awards and belated official recognition in the 1970s.

Kesey, Ken Elton 1935–
US writer

He was born in La Junta, Colorado. Associated with the 1950s 'Beat' movement, he also worked as a ward attendant in a mental hospital, an experience he used to telling effect in *One Flew Over the Cuckoo's Nest* (1963). Filmed in 1975 by Miloš Forman it won five Academy Awards, including that for Best Film. *Sometimes a Great Notion* (1966) was a complete failure and he relinquished 'literature' for 'life'. He served a prison sentence for marijuana possession and formed the 'Merry Pranksters', whose exploits are described at length in *The Electric Kool-Aid Acid Test* (1967) by Tom Wolfe. *Sailor Song* (1990) confirmed the underlying Green values of *Demon Box* (1987), a collection of stories and pieces, and returned to something like the roistering fantasy of the earlier books. 📖 S Tanner, *Ken Kesey* (1983)

Kesselring, Albert 1885–1960
German air commander and field marshal

Born in Markstedt, Bavaria, he led the Luftwaffe attacks on France and (unsuccessfully) on Britain. He was made Commander-in-Chief in Italy (1941), and in the West (1945). Condemned to death as a war criminal in 1947, he had his sentence commuted to life imprisonment, but was released in 1952.

Ketch, Jack d.1686
English executioner

A hangman and headsman from about 1663, he was notorious for his barbarity and bungling, particularly at the executions of William, Lord Russell (1683), and the Duke of Monmouth (1685). His name became synonymous with the hangman's job.

Ketèlbey, Albert William, *pseudonym of* Anton Vodorinski 1875–1959
British composer and conductor

He was born in Birmingham. Success came early with, for example, a piano sonata written at the age of 11, and he won a scholarship to Trinty College, London, to study composition. His light, colourful and tuneful orchestral pieces had great popularity, and include *In a Monastery Garden* (1915), *In a Persian Market* (1920) and *Sanctuary of the Heart* (1924), among many others.

Kett, Robert d.1549
English rebel

He was a landowner of Wymondham, Norfolk, who in July 1549 headed 16,000 insurgents in an uprising against common land enclosures. The rebels twice captured Norwich, on the second occasion holding it until they were driven out by John Dudley, Earl of Warwick. Kett was captured and hanged.

Kettenfeier, Petri (P K) See Rosegger, Peter

Kettering, Charles Franklin 1876–1958
US engineer

Born near Loudonville, Ohio, he studied mechanical and electrical engineering at Ohio State University. Among his inventions were the electric cash register, the electric self-starter for automobiles, and the high-compression automobile engine. He also worked on fast-drying lacquer finishes, engine-oil coolers, leaded gasoline and high-octane fuels, and variable-speed transmissions. He was a co-founder of the Sloan-Kettering Institute for Cancer Research, New York City.

Kettlewell, Henry Bernard David 1907–79
English geneticist and entomologist

Born in Howden, Yorkshire, and educated at Charterhouse School and in Paris, he studied medicine at Gonville and Caius College, Cambridge, and St Bartholomew's Hospital, London. From 1952 he held various posts in the genetics unit of the zoology department, Oxford. His best known research was concerned with the industrial melanism of the peppered moth (*Biston betularia*). This common moth developed a dark colouration in areas where industry and dense populations caused atmospheric carbon pollution. He then demonstrated the survival value of the dark coloration in industrial regions and the original light coloration in rural areas, thus demonstrating the effectiveness of natural selection as an evolutionary process.

Keulen, Ludolph van See **Ceulen, Ludolph van**

Key, Ellen Karolina Sophia 1849–1926
Swedish reformer and educationist
Born in Sundsholm, Småland, she became a teacher in Stockholm (1880–99) when her father lost his fortune. She made her name as a writer on the feminist movement, child welfare, sex, love, and marriage, in *Barnets århundrade* (1900, Eng trans *The Century of the Child*, 1909) and *Lifslinjer* (1903–06, 'Life-lines'). Although her radical and liberal values were controversial, her writings were influential and widely translated.

Key, Francis Scott 1780–1843
US lawyer and poet
Born in Carroll County, Maryland, he practised law in Washington, DC. During the British bombardment of Fort McHenry, Baltimore, in September 1814, which he witnessed from a British man-of-war while on a mission to gain the release of a US citizen, he wrote a poem about the lone US flag seen flying over the fort as dawn broke. It was published as *The Defence of Fort McHenry*, and later set to a tune by the English composer, John Stafford Smith (*To Anacreon in Heaven*). In 1931 it was adopted as the US national anthem as 'The Star-Spangled Banner'.

Keyes (of Zeebrugge and of Dover), Roger John Brownlow Keyes, 1st Baron 1872–1945
English naval commander
He joined the navy in 1885, and served at Witu (1890) and in the Boxer Rebellion (1900). In World War I he was Chief of Staff Eastern Mediterranean (1915–16) and in 1918 commanded the Dover Patrol, leading the raids on German U-boat bases at Zeebrugge and Ostend (1918). He was Commander-in-Chief Mediterranean (1925–29) and commander Portsmouth (1929–31). He was MP for Portsmouth (1934–43), was recalled in 1940, as director of combined operations (1940–41), and became liaison officer to the Belgians. He wrote *Naval Memoirs* (2 vols, 1934–35), *Adventures Ashore and Afloat* (1939), and *Amphibious Warfare and Combined Operations* (1943). His son, Lieutenant-Colonel Geoffrey Keyes, MC and posthumous VC, was killed in the historic commando raid on Rommel's HQ in 1941.

Keyes, Sidney Arthur Kilworth 1922–43
English poet
Born in Dartford, Kent, he was educated at Tonbridge School and Oxford, where he co-edited *Eight Oxford Poets* (1941), which included his own work. His first book of poems, *The Iron Laurel*, was published in 1942, and his second, *The Cruel Solstice*, in 1944 (Hawthornden prize), after his death in action in Libya. His *Collected Poems* were published in 1945. 📖 J Guenther, *Sidney Keyes: a biographical enquiry* (1967)

Keynes, John Maynard, 1st Baron See panel p1038

Keyser, Hendrik de 1565–1621
Dutch architect and sculptor
Born in Utrecht, he trained with the sculptor **Abraham Bloemaert** in 1591. His designs in a Mannerist vein were often tempered with traditional Dutch details. In 1596 he engineered an opening bridge, and from 1612 he produced an imitation marble. Notable sculptural commissions were the Tomb of the Silent Delft (1614–21) and the bronze statue of **Desiderius Erasmus** in Rotterdam (1621). His three Amsterdam churches form a group: Zuiderkerk (1603–14), Westerkerk (1620–38) and Noorderkerk (1620–22). Between 1608 and 1611, with Cornelis Danckerts, he designed the Amsterdam Exchange (derived from the London Royal Exchange). In 1615 he produced designs for Haarlemmerpoort gates. Some of his later works were published in *Architectura Moderna* (1631, 'Modern Architecture'), which served as a pattern book for succeeding generations.

Khalid, *in full* Khalid ibn 'Abd al-'Aziz ibn 'Abd ar Rahman al Sa'ud 1913–82
King of Saudi Arabia
Born in Riyadh, he was the fourth son of **Ibn Saud**, the founder of the Saudi dynasty. A quiet and unspectacular monarch who had been troubled by ill health for many years, he ascended the throne after the assassination of his brother King **Faisal** (1975). Khalid's caution and moderation served as a stabilizing factor in the volatile Middle East and won international respect. His personal influence was evident at the halting of the Lebanese civil war (1975–76) and in Saudi Arabia's disagreement with the other members of the Organization of Petroleum Exporting Countries (OPEC) over oil price increases. He was especially esteemed by the Bedouin tribesmen, who shared with him a religious outlook and a fondness for the traditional pursuits of falconry and hunting.

Khama, Sir Seretse 1921–80
African politician
Born at Serowe, Bechuanaland (now Botswana), he was nephew of Tshekedi Khama (1905–59), who was chief regent of the Bamangwato from 1925. Seretse was educated in Africa and Balliol College, Oxford. Whilst a student at the Inner Temple in 1948 he married an Englishwoman Ruth Williams, and in 1950, with his uncle, was banned from the chieftainship and the territory of the Bamangwato. Allowed to return in 1956, he became active in politics, and was restored to the chieftainship in 1963. He became first Prime Minister of Bechuanaland (1965) and first President of Botswana (1966–80). 📖 Michael Dutfield, *A Marriage of Inconvenience: The Persecution of Ruth and Seretse Khama* (1990)

Khan, Imran See **Imran Khan**

Khan, Jahangir 1963–
Pakistani squash rackets player
Born in Karachi, he won three world amateur titles (1979, 1983, 1985), a record six World Open titles (1981–85, 1988), and 10 consecutive British Open titles (1982–91). He was undefeated from April 1981 to November 1986, when he lost to Ross Norman of New Zealand in the World Open final. He has mastered both soft and hardball squash.

Khan, Jinghit See **Genghis Khan**

Khan, Ra'ana Liaquat Ali, *née* Ra'ana Pant 1905–90
Pakistani politician
Born in Almora, North India, she studied economics from Lucknow University before becoming lecturer in economics at Indraprastha College for Women in New Delhi. In 1933 she married politician Zada Liaquat Ali Khan. On partition (1947) her husband became Prime Minister and she was one of the first to organize assistance for refugees during the mass transit. Following his assassination at Rawalpindi in 1951, she devoted herself to social work, but remained politically active. In 1952 she was appointed UN delegate, and between 1954 and 1966 represented her country as the first woman ambassador to Holland, Italy and Tunisia. In 1973 she became the first woman governor of Sind and was given the 1979 Human Rights Award.

Khatchaturian, Aram Ilyich 1903–78
Russian composer
Born near Tbilisi, Georgia, he was a student of folk-song, and an authority on oriental music. His compositions include symphonies, concertos, ballets, instrumental and film music.

Keynes (of Tilton), John Maynard Keynes, 1st Baron 1883–1946
English economist, pioneer of the theory of full employment

John Maynard Keynes was born in Cambridge, the son of the Cambridge logician and political economist John Neville Keynes (1852–1949). He was educated at Eton and King's College, Cambridge, where he lectured in economics and became one of the 'Bloomsbury group'. He was at the India Office (1906–08) and in 1913, as a member of the Royal Commission on Indian Finance and Currency, published his first book on this subject. In both world wars he was an adviser to the Treasury, which he represented at the Versailles Peace Conference, although he strongly opposed the terms of the draft treaty and thus resigned.

He set out his views against the harsh economic terms imposed on Germany in the Versailles Treaty in *The Economic Consequences of the Peace* (1919), written with the encouragement of **Jan Smuts**. In 1921 *Treatise of Probability* appeared, in which he explored the logical relationships between calling something 'highly probable' and a 'justifiable induction'. In 1923 he became chairman of the Liberal periodical *Nation*, and pamphleteered his controversial views on European reconstruction, strongly attacking **Winston Churchill**'s restoration of the gold standard (1925).

The unemployment crisis inspired his two great works, *A Treatise on Money* (1930) and the revolutionary *General Theory of Employment, Interest and Money* (1936). He argued that full employment was not an automatic condition, expounded a new theory of the rate of interest, and set out the principles underlying the flows of income and expenditure. He also fought the Treasury view that unemployment was incurable. His views on a planned economy influenced **Franklin D Roosevelt**'s 'New Deal' administration.

He married Lydia Lopokova, a ballerina with the **Diaghilev** company, and with her helped to found the Vic-Wells ballet. He also financed the establishment of the Arts Theatre in Cambridge. In 1943 he proposed the international clearing union, and in 1944–46 he played a leading part in the formulation of the Bretton Woods agreements, the establishment of the International Monetary Fund, and the troublesome, abortive negotiations for a continuation of American Lend-Lease. He died just prior to being appointed to the Order of Merit. He also wrote *Essays in Persuasion* (1931) and *Essays in Biography* (1933).

Robert Skidelsky, *John Maynard Keynes* (vol 1, 1983; vol 2, 1992); Hyman P Minsky, *John Maynard Keynes* (1975); Roy F Harrod, *The Life of John Maynard Keynes* (1951).

'England still stands outside Europe. Europe's voiceless tremors do not reach her. Europe is apart, and England is not of her flesh and body.' From *The Economic Consequences of the Peace* (1919).

'I believe that there is social and psychological justification for significant inequalities of incomes and wealth, but not for such large disparities as exist today.' From *The General Theory of Employment, Interest and Money* (1936).

Khayyám, Omar See **Omar Khayyám**

Khazini, al- fl.c.1115–30
Arab mathematician
Born in Merv' Iran (now Mary, Turkmenistan), he was a Byzantine slaveboy (possibly a castrato) who was well educated by his owner in mathematics and became a notable maker of scientific instruments. He also devised astronomical tables and wrote on mechanics, especially on specific gravity and its use in analysis.

Khinchin, Aleksandr Yakovlevich 1894–1959
Soviet mathematician
Born in Kondrovo, he studied at Moscow University, and became professor there in 1927. With **Andrei Kolmogorov** he founded the Soviet school of probability theory, and also worked in analysis, number theory, statistical mechanics and information theory.

Khomeini, Ayatollah Ruhollah, *originally* Ruholla Hendi 1900–89
Iranian religious and political leader
He was born in Khomeyn, became a religious scholar and was recognized as an ayatollah. A Shiite Muslim who was bitterly opposed to the pro-Western regime of Shah **Muhammad Reza Pahlavi**, Khomeini was exiled to Turkey, Iraq and France from 1964. He returned to Iran amid great popular acclaim in 1979 after the collapse of the Shah's government, and became virtual head of state. Under his leadership, Iran underwent a turbulent Islamic Revolution in which a return was made to the strict observance of Muslim principles and traditions, many of which had been abandoned during the previous regime. He endeavoured to rid Iran of Western influence, and his denunciation of US influences led to the storming of the US embassy in Teheran and the holding of 53 US hostages. In 1989 he provoked international controversy by publicly commanding the killing of **Salman Rushdie**, author of the novel *The Satanic Verses*. Hossein Musavian, *Imam Khomeini: His Life and Leadership* (1990)

Khorana, Har Gobind 1922–
US molecular chemist and Nobel Prize winner
Born in Raipur, India (now in Pakistan), he studied at Punjab University, was awarded a PhD in organic chemistry by Liverpool University, and was a Research Fellow at Cambridge before moving to Vancouver as head of the department of organic chemistry (1952–60). From 1960 to 1970 he was professor and co-director of the Institute of Enzyme Research at the University of Wisconsin, and since 1970 has been Professor of Biology and Chemistry at Massachusetts Institute of Technology. He determined the sequence of the nucleic acids, also known as 'bases', for each of the 20 amino acids in the human body. His work on nucleotide synthesis at Wisconsin was a major contribution to the elucidation of the genetic code. In the early 1970s he was one of the first to artificially synthesize a gene, initially from yeast, then later from the bacterium *Escherichia coli*. He shared the 1968 Nobel Prize for physiology or medicine with **Marshall Nirenberg** and **Robert Holley**.

Khosrow See **Chosroes**

Khrushchev, Nikita Sergeyevich 1894–1971
Soviet politician
Born in Kalinovka, near Kursk, he was a shepherd boy and a locksmith and is said to have been almost illiterate until the age of 25. Joining the Bolshevik Party in 1918, he fought in the Civil War and rose rapidly in the party organization. In 1939 he was made a full member of the politburo and of the Presidium of the Supreme Soviet. In World War II he organized guerrilla warfare in the Ukraine against the invading Germans and took charge of the reconstruction of devastated territory. In 1949 he launched a drastic reorganization of Soviet agriculture. In 1953, on the death of **Stalin**, he became First Secretary of the All Union Party and three years later, at the 20th congress of the Communist Party, in a speech that had far-reaching results, denounced Stalinism and the 'personality cult'. In 1957 he went on to demote **Vyacheslav**

Molotov, Lazar Kaganovich and Georgi Malenkov—all possible rivals. Among the events of his administration were the 1956 Poznan riots that he quietened down, the Hungarian uprising that he crushed, and the failed attempt to install missiles in Cuba (1962). Khrushchev, who did much to enhance the ambitions and status of the USSR abroad, was nevertheless deposed in 1964 and forced into retirement, being replaced by Leonid Brezhnev and Aleksei Kosygin. He died in retirement in Moscow. He has been substantially rehabilitated during recent years, with the text of his 'secret speech' to the 20th Communist Party congress being officially published for the first time in 1989. ▭ Edward Crankshaw, *Khrushchev: A Career* (1966)

Khwarizmi, Muhammad ibn Musa al-
c.800–c.850
Arab mathematician

He wrote in Baghdad on astronomy, geography and mathematics, and produced an early Arabic treatise on the solution of quadratic equations, synthesizing Babylonian solution methods with Greek-style proofs for the first time. His writings in Latin translation were so influential in transmitting Indian and Arab mathematics to medieval Europe that the methods of arithmetic based on the Hindu (or so-called Arabic) system of numeration became known in medieval Latin, by corruption of his name, as 'algorismus', from which comes the English 'algorithm'. The word 'algebra' is derived from the word *al-jabr* in the title of his book on the subject.

Kidd, Captain See Kidd, William

Kidd, Carol 1944–
Scottish jazz singer

Born in Glasgow, she began to sing with traditional jazz bands whilst still at school, later joining the Glasgow-based band of Jimmy Feighan. She married pianist George Kidd at the age of 17 and formed her own permanent trio. In the late 1970s she became known in London clubs and later appeared on radio and television, as a singer and presenter, and began her recording career. During the late 1980s she gave performances with specially assembled larger orchestras, and won various awards. By 1990 she had moved to England to develop her career, working and recording with a regular trio of London-based musicians, and was chosen to support Frank Sinatra at his Ibrox Stadium concert (1990).

Kidd, Dame Margaret Henderson 1900–88
Scottish pioneering lawyer

The daughter of a Linlithgow solicitor, she determined to go to the Bar and became the first woman member of the Scottish Bar (1923), the first woman QC (1948) and the first woman (part-time) sheriff of a county (Dumfries 1960–66, Perth 1966–74). She also served as keeper of the Advocates' Library (1956–69), and was vice-president of the British Federation of University Women. On her death she was described by a colleague as having 'paved the way for women in the legal profession and in the Scottish Bar in a way no one else could have done'. She was made a DBE in 1975.

Kidd, Michael 1919–
US dancer, choreographer and director

Born in Brooklyn, New York City, he studied privately and at the School of American Ballet, appearing on Broadway in 1937 and dancing with American Ballet the same year. He later danced with Ballet Caravan (1937–40), Dance Players (1941–42) and American Ballet Theater (1942–47) for which he choreographed *On Stage I* (1945). He then became a successful choreographer of Broadway and Hollywood musicals, including *Finian's Rainbow* (1947), *Guys and Dolls* (1951), *Can-Can* (1953), *Seven Brides for*

Seven Brothers (1954) and *Hello, Dolly!* (1969). He also appeared in the 1955 film *It's Always Fair Weather* with Gene Kelly.

Kidd, William, known as Captain Kidd c.1645–1701
Scottish merchant and privateer

Born in Greenock, Strathclyde, he worked as a successful sea captain with a small fleet of trading vessels, based in New York, in the 1680s. During the War of the League of Augsburg against France (1688–97) he fought as a privateer to protect Anglo-American trade routes in the West Indies. In 1695 he went to London and was given command of an expedition against pirates in the Indian Ocean. He reached Madagascar early in 1697, but instead of attacking pirates began to sanction attacks on merchant ships. After a two-year cruise he returned to the West Indies to find that he had been proclaimed a pirate. He sailed to Boston, where he surrendered on promise of a pardon (1699), but was sent as a prisoner to London, where he was convicted of piracy and hanged. ▭ Robert C Ritchie, *Captain Kidd and the War Against the Pirates* (1986)

Kidder, Alfred Vincent 1885–1963
US archaeologist

Born in Marquette, Michigan, he was educated at Harvard, where he came under the influence of the Egyptologist George A Reisner, whose systematic approach to fieldwork he adopted with notable success in Utah, Colorado, and New Mexico (1907–14). He was a pioneer of stratigraphic methods on a large scale in the USA, and his extensive excavations (1915–29) at Pecos, New Mexico, an Indian pueblo inhabited from AD1000 to the 19th century, revolutionized American settlement archaeology and allowed him to develop a chronological sequence for the cultures of the region. His *Introduction to the Study of Southwestern Archaeology* (1924) remains an important work. He subsequently became involved in Maya archaeology, from 1929 undertaking major work for the Carnegie Institution of Washington, at Kaminaljuyu and at Uaxactun in Guatemala. He later joined the faculty of the Peabody Museum at Harvard (1939–50).

Kidman, Sir Sidney 1857–1935
Australian pastoralist

Born near Adelaide, South Australia, he left home at the age of 13, with five shillings in his pocket and riding a one-eyed horse. He bought his first grazing station in 1886 and 30 years later he controlled lands greater in area than the whole of England. By judicious dealing in horses and cattle he gradually built up sufficient capital to purchase many more stations. The resultant ability to move stock to well-watered areas in times of drought, and selling in the best markets, enabled Kidman to withstand the Depression years of the 1890s and the Great Drought of 1902. During World War I he gave fighter planes to the forces and made large gifts to charities and the Government.

Kido Koin (Takayoshi) 1833–77
Japanese samurai politician

He played a prominent part in the Meiji Restoration (1868) and helped cement the anti-Tokugawa alliance between his own domain of Choshu and that of Satsuma in 1866. After 1868, he became one of the architects of the new centralized state. He was a member of Iwakura Tomomi's mission to the West (1871–73) and, when he returned, became the first Japanese leader to propose a constitution for Japan, based on the German model.

Kiefer, Anselm 1945–
German artist

Born in Donaueschingen, Baden, he held his first one-man show in Karlsruhe, in 1969. A pupil of Joseph Beuys in Düsseldorf (1970–72), he lives and works in Hornbach, producing Expressionist paintings steeped in German myths reworked to comment on Germany's Fascist past, as in *Parsifal III* (1973, Tate, London, painted in oil and blood), and often depicting the architecture of Fascism, such as in *Innenraum* (1982, 'Interior Space', Stedelijk, Amsterdam). From the late 1980s he was concerned with the disintegration of the planet, as in his cityscapes, such as *Lilith* (1989, Tate).

Kiehtreiber, Albert Conrad See Gütersloh, Albert Paris von

Kielland, Alexander L(ange) 1849–1906
Norwegian novelist

He was born in Stavanger, and studied law before buying and managing a brickyard. He became a follower of the Danish man of letters Georg Brandes (1842–1927) and an exponent of the Realist school. His stylish novels of social satire include *Garman og Worse* (1880, Eng trans *Garman and Worse*), *Skipper Worse* (1882) and *Tales of Two Countries* (1891). He also wrote plays and short stories. Despite intense lobbying by Bjørnson and Jonas Lie, he was not awarded a state literary pension, and in 1891 he became burgomaster of Stavanger. He later returned to writing, but disappointment drove him to reject the literary world.
📖 J Lunde, *Alexander Lange Kielland* (1970)

Kienholz, Edward 1927–94
US artist

Born in Fairfield, Washington, the son of farmers of Swiss descent, he was a self-taught artist who worked as a handyman in Los Angeles. He opened the Now Gallery in Los Angeles in 1956, and the next year co-founded the Ferus Gallery, which became the centre of the Los Angeles art scene. His own works are room-sized assemblages or tableaux that incorporate dummies, bones, furniture and household objects. His best known works include *Roxy's* (1961), a re-creation of a Las Vegas bordello; *Back Seat Dodge '38* (1964), in which a chicken-wire man and a plaster woman tryst in an automobile; and *The Beanery* (1965), a dingy Santa Monica bar in which the patrons have clocks for faces. His misanthropic and inventive art was calculated to shock, and his final outrageous act was his own funeral, at which, according to his request, he was buried upright in a 1940 Packard while a tape of Glenn Miller hits played in the background.

Kierkegaard, Søren Aabye 1813–55
Danish philosopher and theologian

He was born in Copenhagen and studied theology at the university there, though he was more interested in literature and philosophy. He suffered anguish and emotional disturbances which his later writings sometimes reflect: he was particularly oppressed by his father's death (1838) and by the burden of guilt he felt he had thereby inherited. He became engaged after leaving university (1840), but broke that off because he felt his domestic responsibilities were incompatible with his personal mission from God to be a writer. His philosophy represents a strong reaction against the dominant German traditions of the day, and in particular against Hegel. Kierkegaard attempted to reinstate the central importance of the individual and of the deliberate, significant choices we each make in forming our future selves. His philosophical works tend to be unorthodox and entertaining in a literary and determinedly unacademic style: *The Concept of Irony* (1841), *Enten-Eller* (1843, 'Either-Or'), *Philisophiske Smuler* (1844, Eng trans *Philosophical Fragments*, 1936) and *Afsluttende uvidenskabelig Efterskrift* (1846, 'Concluding Unscientific Postscript'). He was also opposed to much in organized Christianity, again stressing the need for individual choice against prescribed dogma and ritual in such works as *Frygt og Baeven* (1843, Eng trans *Fear and Trembling*, 1939), *Kjerlighedens Gjerninger* (1847, Eng trans *Works of Love*, 1946, 1962), *Christelige Tales* (1848, Eng trans *Christian Discourses*) and

Sygdommen til Döden (1849, Eng trans *The Sickness unto Death*, 1941). Regarded as one of the founders of Existentialism, he achieved real recognition only in the 20th century and has been a great influence on such thinkers as Karl Barth, Martin Heidegger, Karl Jaspers and Martin Buber.

Kiesinger, Kurt Georg 1904–88
West German politician

Born in Ebingen, he practised as a lawyer (1935–40). Having joined the Nazi Party in 1933, although not an active member in the following years, he served during World War II at the Foreign Office making radio propaganda. Interned after the war until 1947, he was released by the Allies as a 'fellow traveller' and exonerated by a German court in 1948. The next year he became a member of the Bundestag until 1958, when he became a Minister-President of his native Baden-Württemberg until 1966. He was President of the Bundesrat from 1962 to 1963, and in 1966 succeeded Ludwig Erhard as Chancellor after economic crisis had forced the latter's resignation. Long a convinced supporter of Konrad Adenauer's plans for European unity, he formed with Willy Brandt a 'grand coalition' government which combinined the Christian Democratic Union and the Social Democrats, until in 1969 he was succeeded as Chancellor by Brandt. He remained in the Bundestag until 1980.

Kieslowski, Krzysztof 1941–96
Polish film director

Born in Warsaw, he studied at the School of Cinema and Theatre in Łódź, making his directorial debut with the television documentary *Urzad* (1967, *The Job*). He worked extensively in television, before moving to such cinema features as *Blizna* (1976, *The Scar*), *Amator* (1979, *Camera Buff*) and *Bez Konka* (1984, *No End*). His international reputation was enhanced with *Dekalog* (1988–89, *The Ten Commandments*), a series of films for Polish television, each of which dramatically illustrated one of the Ten Commandments. Released to cinemas, *Krotki Film O Zabijaniu* (1988, *A Short Film About Killing*) earned an Academy Award as Best Foreign Film. Hailed as one the most trenchant and humanistic of European auteurs, he subsequently directed *La Double vie de Véronique* (1991, *The Double Life of Véronique*) and *Trois Couleurs: Blue* (1993), *Blanc* (1993), *Rouge* (1994) (*Three Colours: Blue, White* and *Red*), a triptych inspired by the French Revolution ideals of Liberty, Equality and Fraternity that proved to be the crowning glory of his career. He had announced his retirement but was working on a further three-film series, *Heaven, Hell* and *Purgatory*, at the time of his death.

Kilburn, Tom 1921–
English computer scientist

Born in Dewsbury, West Yorkshire, and educated at Sidney Sussex College, Cambridge, he became Professor of Computer Science at Manchester (1964–81) and one of the dominant figures in British computer design. He worked with Sir Frederic Williams to build the world's first operational stored-program computer in 1948, helping to perfect the storage device (the world's first electronic random access memory), and directed a series of collaborative ventures with Ferranti Ltd. His design for the ATLAS computer (1962) pioneered many modern concepts in paging, virtual memory and multiprogramming. He was elected FRS in 1965.

Kilby, Jack St Clair 1923–
US electrical engineer

Born in Jefferson City, Montana, the son of an electrical engineer, he went to the University of Illinois to study electrical engineering and then the University of Wisconsin, where he received a master's degree. In 1948 he joined Centrelab, a large radio and television parts manufacturer in Milwaukee, where he gained valuable experience with miniaturization and automation. In 1958 he joined Texas Instruments, an innovative Dallas firm, and almost immediately created the first monolithic integrated circuit, known as a phase-shift oscillator (a device that oscillates signals at a given rate), patented in 1959. Further development work by **Robert Noyce** at Fairchild resulted in the introduction of the first commercial integrated circuits in the early 1960s. A freelance inventor since 1970, Kilby has registered some 50 patents for his work on integrated circuits. In 1978 he became Distinguished Professor of Electrical Engineering at Texas Agricultural and Mechanical University.

Kilian, St See **Cilian, St**

Killigrew, Thomas 1612–83
English playwright and theatre manager
He was born in London, the brother of the dramatist Sir William Killigrew (1606–95). First a page in the household of **Charles I**, he later became a companion to **Charles II** in exile, and his groom of the bedchamber after the Restoration. In 1664 he published a collection of nine indifferent plays, written, so he claimed, in nine different cities. The most popular was *The Parson's Wedding*, probably derived from **Pedro Calderón de la Barca**'s *La dama duende* (c.1629), and most probably produced in 1640. After a later production, **Samuel Pepys** put in his diary that it was 'an obscene, loose play'. Killigrew did much to revive the energy of the English theatre after the Restoration and the reopening of the theatres in 1660. He introduced actresses into the theatre, and it was at Vere Street, where he had been awarded a patent to open The King's House, a theatre in a disused tennis court, in January 1661, that Pepys records seeing women as part of the acting company, apparently for the first time. Two years later Killigrew founded the Theatre Royal, Bridges Street. It was here that **Nell Gwyn** sold oranges in his auditorium before becoming an actress in 1665. When the theatre burned down in 1672, a second was built on the site, and opened as the Theatre Royal, Drury Lane, in 1674. Killigrew also founded one of the first training schools for actors, at the Barbican, London. 📖 A Harbage, *Killigrew: Cavalier dramatist* (1930)

Killy, Jean-Claude 1944–
French ski racer
Born in St-Cloud and brought up in Val d'Isère, he won the downhill and combined gold medals at the world championship in Chile in 1966. In 1968, when the Winter Olympics were held almost on his own ground at Grenoble, he won three gold medals for slalom, giant slalom and downhill. He turned professional immediately afterwards and pursued a career as an endorser and later manufacturer of winter sports equipment. 📖 Michel Clare, *Jean-Claude · Killy: essai sur un champion* (1967)

Kilmer, (Alfred) Joyce 1886–1918
US poet
Born in New Brunswick, New Jersey, he became a writer and poetry editor of the *Literary Digest* and *Current Literature* in New York City. He is best known for his poem 'Trees', in *Trees and Other Poems* (1914), inexplicably chosen for immortality by popular taste ('I think that I will never see/A poem lovely as a tree'). He joined the US army in World War I and was killed in France.

Kilmuir, Sir David Patrick Maxwell Fyfe, 1st Earl of 1900–67
Scottish jurist and politician
Born in Aberdeen, he was educated at George Watson's College, Edinburgh, and Balliol College, Oxford. In 1934, he became the youngest KC since the time of **Charles II**. He was Conservative MP for West Derby (Liverpool) from 1935 to 1954, becoming Solicitor-

General (1942–45). He was Deputy Chief Prosecutor at the Nuremberg trial of the principal Nazi war criminals. Home Secretary and Minister for Welsh Affairs in the 1951 government, he advised on a heavy programme of controversial legislation. Lord Chancellor from 1954 to 1962, he was knighted in 1942, created Viscount 1954, and Earl and Baron Fyfe of Dornoch in 1962. He wrote *Monopoly* (1948) and *Political Adventure* (1964).

Kilvert, (Robert) Francis 1840–79
English clergyman and diarist
He was a curate at Clyro in Radnorshire and later vicar of Bredwardine on the Wye. His *Diary (1870–79)*, giving a vivid picture of rural life in the Welsh marches, was discovered in 1937 and published in three volumes (1938–40). 📖 F Grice, *Kilvert: priest and diarist* (1975)

Kimberley, John Wodehouse, 1st Earl of 1826–1902
English Liberal statesman
He was Lord Privy-Seal (1868–70), Colonial Secretary (1870–74, 1880–82), Secretary for India (1882–85, 1886), Secretary for India and Lord President of the Council (1892–94), and then Foreign Secretary (1894–95). Kimberley in South Africa was named after him.

Kim Chong-II See **Kim Jong II**

Kimhi or Kimchi, David c.1160–1235
French Jewish grammarian and lexicographer
He was born in Narbonne. His chief work is the *Book of Completeness*, which comprises a Hebrew grammar and a lexicon, subsequent Hebrew grammars and lexicons being based on this. He also wrote biblical commentaries, the most interesting of which is his work on the *Psalms* with its polemics against the Christian interpretation of them, and his commentary on *Genesis* in which biblical stories are explained as visions. His father Joseph Kimhi (c.1105–1170) and brother Moses (d.c.1190) are also noted for their work on the Hebrew language and their biblical commentaries.

Kim-Il Sung, *originally* Kim Song-ju 1912–94
North Korean soldier and political leader
He was born near Pyongyang. He founded the Korean People's Revolutionary Army in 1932 and led a long struggle against the Japanese. He proclaimed the Republic in 1948, three years after founding the Workers' Party of Korea, and he has effectively been head of state ever since, as Premier until 1972, then as President. Kim was re-elected President in 1982 and 1986, and 1990, and has established a unique personality cult welded to an isolationist, Stalinist political-economic system. He has sought to establish his son, **Kim Jong II**, as his designated successor. 📖 Baik Bong, *Kim Il Sung: Biography* (3 vols, 1969–70)

Kim Jong II (Kim Chong-il) 1942–
North Korean politician
The eldest son and chosen heir of the North Korean communist leader **Kim-Il Sung**, he was born in a secret camp on Mount Paekdu in the USSR where his mother had retreated from the Korean anti-Japanese guerrilla base in Manchuria. Kim Jong Il has played a leading part in ideological and propaganda work, helping to create the cult that surrounds his father. In 1980 he became First Secretary of the party's Central Committee. Since 1982, frequently referred to as the 'dear leader', he has been virtual heir-apparent. Supreme Commander of the Korean People's Army since 1991, he was given the title Marshal in 1992, and has chaired the National Defence Committee since 1993. He succeeded his father after his death in 1994 but reportedly had already been running the nation's day-to-day operations for some time.

Kim Young Sam 1927–
South Korean politician

Born in Geoje District, in South Kyongsang province, and educated at Seoul National University, after election to the National Assembly in 1954, he was a founder member of the opposition New Democratic Party (NDP), becoming its president in 1974. His opposition to the Park Chung-Hee regime resulted in his being banned from all political activity. In 1983 he staged a 23-day pro-democracy hunger strike and in 1985 his political ban was formally lifted. In that year he helped form the New Korea Democratic Party (NKDP) and in 1987 the centrist Reunification Democratic Party (RDP). In his 1987 bid for the presidency he came second, behind the governing party's candidate, Roh Tae Woo. In 1990 he merged the RDP with the ruling party to form the new Democratic Liberal Party (DLP). He was elected President in 1993 and immediately launched an anti-corruption campaign but his popularity suffered and in the historic election of 1995, in which government officials were elected rather than appointed for the first time since 1961, the DLP won only five of the top 15 posts.

Kincaid, Jamaica, *originally* Elaine Potter Richardson 1949–
US novelist and journalist

Born in St John's, Antigua, she is known for her novels *At the Bottom of the River* (1983) and the semi-autobiographical *Lucy* (1991), the tale of a young West Indian girl who, having fled to New York, grows more eager to return to her own land. She has also published a non-fictional account of her home island, *A Small Place*. She is currently a staff writer for the *New Yorker*.

Kincaid-Smith, Priscilla 1926–
Australian physician

Born in Johannesburg, South Africa, she trained in medicine there and, after junior medical positions, relocated to London as registrar at the Royal Postgraduate Medical School, and at the Hammersmith Hospital (1953–58). Specializing in kidney diseases, she moved to the University of Melbourne as a Research Fellow in 1958 and became Professor of Medicine and the Director of Nephrology there in 1967.

Kinck, Hans E(rnst) 1865–1926
Norwegian novelist and dramatist

He was born in Øksfjord, and studied at King Frederick's University, Christiania (now Oslo), developing an interest in Norwegian folklore. His works illustrate his deep love of nature and his interest in the lives of peasants. They include *Sneskavlen brast* (1918–19, 'The Avalanche Broke') and *Driftekaren* (1908, 'The Drover'), a verse play. *Ungtfolk* (1893, Eng trans *A Young People*, 1929) introduced the problematic question of social betterment, taken up again in *Emigranter* (1904, 'Emigrants'). 📖 E Beyer, *Hans Ernst Kinck* (1956–65)

Kindi, al- c.800–c.870
Arab philosopher

Born in Kufa, he became tutor at the court in Baghdad and was a prolific author. He was one of the first to spread Greek thought (particularly that of Aristotle) into the Arab world and to synthesize it with Islamic doctrine. He was known as 'the philosopher of the Arabs'.

King, B B, *originally* Riley B King 1925–
US blues singer and guitarist

He was born into a black sharecropping family in Itta Bena, Mississippi. One of the best-known blues performers and an important consolidator of blues styles, he has had a considerable influence on rock as well as blues players with his economical guitar style. As a disc-jockey on the radio station WDIA in the 1940s he became known as the 'Beale Street Blues Boy', later shortened to B B.

In 1950 he signed a recording contract with Modern Records which led to a string of rhythm-and-blues hits over the next 10 years. In 1961 he moved to ABC Records, who released what is probably his finest album, *Live At The Regal* (1965). His reputation grew considerably in the late 1960s as the blues influence on rock music came to be acknowledged by white audiences. In the late 1970s he became the first blues artist to tour the USSR. Albums released during his prolific recording career have included *Confessin' The Blues* (1966), *Indianola Mississippi Seeds* (1970), the Grammy award-winning *There Must Be A Better World Somewhere* (1981), *Six Silver Strings* (1985) and *There Is Always One More Time* (1991). The retrospective, *King of the Blues* (1992), covers 40 years of his work.

King, Billie Jean, *née* Moffitt 1943–
US tennis player

She was born in Long Beach, California. She won the ladies doubles title at Wimbledon in 1961 (with Karen Hantze) at her first attempt, and between 1961 and 1979 won a record 20 Wimbledon titles, including the singles in 1966–68, 1972–73, and 1975, and four mixed doubles. She also won 13 US titles (including four singles in 1967, 1971–72, and 1974), four French titles (one singles in 1972), and two Australian titles (one singles in 1968). Towards the end of her playing career she became involved in the administration of tennis, and as president of the Women's Tennis Association (1980–1981) she played a prominent role in working for the improvement of remuneration and playing conditions for women in professional tennis. In 1973 she challenged the male player Bobby Riggs in a Houston Astrodome, watched by a crowd of 30,472, the biggest for a tennis match; a further 50 million television viewers witnessed her 6–4, 6–3, 6–3 victory. Her publications include *Tennis to Win* (1970), *Billie Jean* (1974), *Secrets of Winning Tennis* (1975) and *Billie Jean King* (1982).

King, Carole, *née* Klein 1942–
US composer and singer

Born in Brooklyn, New York, she co-wrote numerous songs with her future husband Gerry Goffin, including 'Will You Still Love Me Tomorrow', which was a number-one single for the Shirelles. Her other songs include 'Natural Woman', 'The Locomotion', 'Up on the Roof' and 'It's Too Late'. In 1971 her solo album *Tapestry* won four Grammy awards, including Album of the Year; it has since sold over 10 million copies worldwide. She was inducted into the Rock & Roll Hall of Fame in 1990, and in 1994 appeared on Broadway in *Blood Brothers*.

King, Cecil Harmsworth 1901–87
British newspaper proprietor

Educated at Winchester and Christ Church, Oxford, he joined the *Daily Mirror* in 1926. Appointed a director in 1929, he became chairman of Daily Mirror Newspapers Ltd and Sunday Pictorial Newspapers Ltd (1951–63) and chairman of the International Publishing Corporation and Reed Paper Group (1963–68). He was the nephew of the Harmsworth brothers.

King, Coretta Scott, *née* Scott 1927–
US singer, civil rights campaigner and writer

Born in Marion, Alabama, and trained in music at the New England Conservatory, she made her concert debut in 1948. She married Martin Luther King, Jnr in 1953. Two years later, the Montgomery (Alabama) bus strike led the couple into the struggle for civil rights for black Americans. After her husband's assassination in 1968, Coretta continued her husband's legacy of non-violent resistance by fighting (successfully) for a national holiday in his honour and by establishing the Martin Luther King, Jnr Center for Nonviolent Social Change. She currently serves as its president.

King, Don 1932–
US boxing promoter

He was born in Cleveland, Ohio, and his colourful and contentious style, clothes, hair and monologues fascinate the sports world. Now so powerful that he is considered by some to have personal control of the boxing world, since he became a boxing promoter in 1972 his clients have included **Muhammad Ali**, **Sugar Ray Leonard** and **Mike Tyson**. He has enjoyed great success despite a notorious past which includes having served a prison sentence in the 1970s for homicide.

King, Ernest Joseph 1878–1956
US naval officer

Born in Lorain, Ohio, of British parents, he was a graduate of the US Naval Academy, Annapolis. During World War I he served on the staff of Commander-in-Chief US Atlantic fleet (1916–19). Qualified in submarines, he commanded the submarine base at New London (1923–25); he also qualified in naval aviation (1927). He was Commander-in-Chief of the Atlantic Fleet (January–December 1941), and Commander-in-Chief of the US fleet (December 1941). As chief of Naval Operations (1942–45) he masterminded the carrier-bases campaign against the Japanese.

King, Jessie M(arion) 1875–1949
Scottish designer and illustrator

Born in New Kilpatrick (Bearsden), near Glasgow, she studied at Glasgow School of Art (1895–99), and won a travelling scholarship to Italy and Germany. She was an internationally renowned book illustrator, designed jewellery and wallpaper, and was interested in batik and pottery. In 1908 she married the designer **Ernest Taylor**. She participated in the decoration of **Charles Rennie Mackintosh**'s Scottish Pavilion at the Exposizione Nazionale in Turin, and won a gold medal for a book-cover design. She also worked designing fabric with Liberty & Co, but returned to Scotland at the outbreak of World War I; she lived in Kirkcudbright and exhibited up to the time of her death.

King, John 1838–72
Australian traveller

Born in Moy, County Tyrone, Ireland, he was a member of **Robert Burke** and **William Wills**'s expedition which set out from Melbourne in 1860 to cross Australia. King, Burke, Wills and another man reached the tidal marshes of the Flinders River at the edge of the Gulf of Carpentaria, but on the return journey all except King died of starvation. He was helped by the Aboriginals and was found emaciated but alive, by a relief party six months later. He was thus the first white man to cross the continent from south to north and survive. He married in 1871 but died the following year from tuberculosis.

King (of Wartnaby), John Leonard King, Baron 1917–
English industrialist

He founded his own companies after World War II, running the businesses until 1969. He became chairman of Dennis Motor Holdings in 1970, then chairman of the engineering group Babcock and Wilcox Ltd (later known as Babcock International) in 1972 and president in 1994. His other chairmanships and directorships in industry include the British Nuclear Association and the National Enterprise Board (1980–81). A believer in free enterprise, he was appointed chairman of British Airways in 1981, with a specific remit to prepare the company for sale to private investors. He gave up his chairmanship in 1993. He was made a life peer in 1983.

King, (William Lyon) Mackenzie 1874–1950
Canadian Liberal politician

Born in Kitchener, Ontario, he studied law at Toronto, and won a fellowship in political science at Ontario. He accepted the newly created post of Deputy Minister of Labour (1900–08), when he left the Civil Service and became an MP, being appointed Minister of Labour (1909–14). He became director of industrial relations in 1914 in the Rockefeller Foundation for industrial problems, publishing an important study on the subject, *Industry and Humanity* (1918). He became Liberal leader (1919) and was several times Prime Minister (1921–26, 1926–30, 1935–48). His view that the dominions should be autonomous communities within the British Empire and not form a single entity as **Jan Smuts** advocated, materialized in the Statute of Westminster (1931). He opposed sanctions against Italy over Ethiopia and on the eve of World War II wrote to **Hitler**, **Mussolini** and President Mosicki of Poland urging them to preserve the peace, but declared war on Germany with the other dominions once Poland was attacked. He opposed conscription, except eventually for overseas service, signed agreements with **Franklin D Roosevelt** (1940–41) integrating the economies of the two countries, and represented Canada at the London and San Francisco foundation conferences of the United Nations (1945).

King, Martin Luther, Jnr See panel p1044

King, Micki (Maxine) 1944–
US air force officer and champion diver

Born in Pontiac, Michigan, she displayed an early talent for diving, but could not afford to train after graduation. She joined the US air force and in 1969 entered the World Military Games, competing against men and performing dives that no other woman had done in competition. She finished fourth in the platform event and third overall in the springboard event. Between 1969 and 1972 she won 10 national springboard and platform diving championships, and at the 1972 Olympics won a springboard gold medal. In 1973, now a captain, she became the first woman to hold a faculty position at the Air Force Academy when she became the diving coach.

King, Phillip 1934–
British sculptor

Born in Kheredine, near Carthage, in Tunisia, he went to England in 1946 and attended Mill Hill School, London. From 1954 to 1957 he studied modern languages at Christ's College, Cambridge, while making sculpture. He then studied under **Anthony Caro** at St Martin's School of Art and became a teacher there in 1959. He worked as an assistant to **Henry Moore** in 1959–60 before travelling to Greece. In 1962 he began using fibreglass, with colour an essential component, as in *And the Birds Began to Sing* (1964, Tate, London), one of a series of works exploring the cone. In 1968 and 1988 he exhibited at the Venice Biennale. In 1969 he set up a studio at Clay Hall Farm, near Dunstable, for making large-scale steel sculpture for international commissions, and in 1980 he was appointed Professor of Sculpture at the Royal College of Art.

King, Rufus 1755–1827
US political leader

Born in Scarboro, Maine (then part of Massachusetts), he graduated from Harvard in 1777 and was a delegate to the Continental Congress (1784–87), where he argued for the prohibition of slavery in the Northwest Territory, and the Constitutional Convention (1787), where he argued influentially for a strong central government. A Federalist and a strong supporter of **Alexander Hamilton**, he was elected to the US Senate from New York (1789–96, 1813–25). He also served as Minister to Great Britain (1796–1803, 1825–27). He is regarded as a founding father of the USA.

King, Martin Luther, Jnr 1929–68
US clergyman and civil rights leader, and Nobel Prize winner

Martin Luther King was born in Atlanta, Georgia, the son of an African-American Baptist pastor. He studied at Morehouse College in Atlanta and Crozier Theological Seminary in Chester, Pennsylvania, and earned a PhD from Boston University in 1955. Shortly after he had become pastor of the Dexter Avenue Baptist Church in Montgomery, Alabama, the arrest of **Rosa Parks** sparked off the Montgomery bus boycott (1955–56), and King came to national prominence as its eloquent and courageous leader.

In 1957 he founded the Southern Christian Leadership Conference, which organized civil rights activities throughout the country. A brilliant orator, he galvanized the movement and in 1963 led the great march on Washington, where he delivered his memorable 'I have a dream' speech. Inspired by the example of **Mahatma Gandhi**, he espoused a philosophy of non-violence and passive resistance which proved effective as the spectacle of unarmed black demonstrators being harassed and attacked by white segregationists and police exposed the moral shabbiness of the opposing side.

King's efforts were instrumental in securing passage of the Civil Rights Act of 1964 and the Voting Rights Act of 1965, and in 1964 he received an honorary doctorate from Yale, the Kennedy Peace Prize, and the Nobel Peace Prize. He was assassinated in Memphis, Tennessee, while on a civil rights mission. His white assassin, James Earl Ray, was apprehended in London, and in 1969 was sentenced in Memphis to 99 years. King's widow **Coretta Scott King** has carried on his work. The third Monday in January is celebrated as Martin Luther King Day in the USA.

📖 S E Pyatt, *Martin Luther King, Jr: An Annotated Bibliography* (1986); S B Oates, *Let The Trumpet Sound: The Life and Times of Martin Luther King, Jr* (1982); L Davis, *I Have A Dream* (1969).

> 'He stood in that line of saints which goes back from Gandhi to Jesus; his violent end, like theirs, reflects the hostility of mankind to those who annoy it by trying hard to pull it one more painful step further up the ladder from the age to the angel.' I F Stone, *The Fire Has Only Just Begun* (1979).

King, Sir (Frederic) Truby 1858–1938
New Zealand physician and psychologist

He was born in Taranaki and educated at Edinburgh University. A man of wide-ranging interests, he was concerned especially with motherhood and nutrition, psychological medicine and the care of the mentally ill, and his methods and teaching were adopted worldwide. In 1907 he inaugurated the Royal New Zealand Society for the Health of Women and Children, or the Plunket Society (named after the then Governor of New Zealand, Sir William Lee, fifth Baron Plunket, 1864–1920). In 1917 he went to England to set up the Plunket system there, and on his return to New Zealand in 1921 he was appointed director of Child Welfare, retiring in 1927. In the 30 years to 1937 King's teachings had reduced the rate of infantile mortality in New Zealand from 88.8 to 30.9 per 1,000 births. When he died he was accorded a State funeral in recognition of his contribution to the nation's health.

King, William Rufus 1786–1853
US politician

Born in North Carolina, he was a member of the state legislature for three years. He entered Congress in 1810, was senator for Alabama (1820–1844), Minister to France (1844–46), senator again (1846–53), and, just before his death, Vice-President of the USA.

Kingdon-Ward, Frank (Francis) 1885–1958
English plant collector, geographer and author

The son of the botanist Harry Marshall Ward, he was born in Manchester and educated at Christ's College, Cambridge, and in 1911 he became a professional plant collector for Bees of Liverpool. He made a total of 24 expeditions, mainly to the remote borderlands of India, Burma (Myanmar) and China. He introduced many beautiful plants into cultivation, and through his intimate knowledge of Burma he developed some novel theories on the geography and palaeogeography of the Himalayas. His 25 books include *On the Road to Tibet* (1910), *The Land of the Blue Poppy* (1913), *In Farthest Burma* (1921), *Plant Hunter's Paradise* (1937), *Assam Adventure* (1941) and *Pilgrimage for Plants* (1960).

Kinglake, Alexander William 1809–91
English historian

Born in Wilton House, near Taunton in Somerset, he was educated at Eton and Trinity College, Cambridge. He was called to the Bar in 1837, but retired in 1856 to devote himself to literature and politics. After a tour about 1835 he wrote *Eothen* (1844), a popular book of eastern travel. In 1854 he went to the Crimea. He became MP for Bridgwater as a Liberal in 1857, took a prominent part against Lord **Palmerston**'s Conspiracy Bill, and denounced the French annexation of Savoy. His *History of the War in the Crimea* (8 vols, 1863–87) is one of the best-known historical works of the 19th century.

Kingo, Thomas Hansen 1634–1703
Danish poet and prelate

Born in Slangerup, of Scottish descent, he became Bishop of Fyn in 1677. He wrote collections of hymns, *Aandeligt sjungekor* (1674, 1681, 'Spiritual Chorus') and *Vinterparten* (1689, 'The Winter Part'), and much secular and religious poetry. His complete works were published in seven volumes between 1939 and 1975. He is considered the greatest Baroque poet in Denmark's literary history.
📖 J Simonsen, *Thomas Kingo* (1970)

Kingsford, Anna, *née* Bonus 1846–88
English doctor and religious writer

Born in Stratford, Essex, she married a Shropshire clergyman, Algernon Kingsford, in 1867 and three years later converted to Catholicism. She was an antivivisectionist, MD of Paris (1880), a vegetarian, and a theosophist, and in 1884 she founded the Hermetic Society to reconcile Christianity with Eastern religions.

Kingsford Smith, Sir Charles Edward
1897–1935
Australian pioneer aviator

Born in Hamilton, Queensland, he enlisted on his 18th birthday in the Australian Imperial Force, later transferring to the Royal Flying Corps with whom he won the Military Cross in 1918. Returning to Australia in 1921, he joined the pioneering West Australian Airways, flying a mail route. In 1927 he made a record-breaking flight round Australia with **Charles Ulm**. In the USA they bought a Fokker Tri-motor, which they named *Southern Cross*, and flew it to Australia in 10 days, making the first air crossing of the Pacific Ocean. They also made the first aerial circumnavigation of the globe (1929–30). In November 1935 he set off with another pilot from

Allahabad, India, on the second leg of an attempt at the England–Australia record, but the plane went missing over the Bay of Bengal.

Kingslake, Rudolf 1903–
US optical designer

Born and educated in London, England, he moved to the USA in 1929 to help set up the Institute of Optics at the University of Rochester. In 1937 he became director of the optical design department at the Eastman Kodak Company, where his team of optical designers devised a wide range of optical systems, including zoom telescopes for tanks and a famous range of aerial camera lenses for survey work and mapping. In 1967 he returned to Rochester University, where he became emeritus professor. He holds many patents on the design of specific optical systems, and continues to work and to publish books and papers; his *Lens Design Fundamentals* (1978) is a classic. He was Ives medallist of the Optical Society of America in 1973.

Kingsley, Ben, *originally* Krishna Bhanji 1943–
English actor

Born in Snaiton, near Scarborough, Yorkshire, he was originally a laboratory research assistant, but after joining an amateur dramatic group, turned professional in 1964. He made his London stage debut in *A Smashing Day* (1966) then joined the Royal Shakespeare Company from 1967, gaining acclaim for his *Hamlet* (1975–76). Associated with the work of South African dramatist and director **Athol Fugard**, he appeared on stage in *Baal* (1979), *Nicholas Nickleby* (1979) and *Edmund Kean* (1981 and 1983), a one-man tour de force. His television work includes *Coronation Street* (1966) and *The Love School* (1974). He had made one previous film appearance in *Fear is the Key* (1972) prior to starring in *Gandhi* (1982), a film that earned him a Best Actor Academy Award and which established his international reputation. Subsequent films include *Betrayal* (1983), *Turtle Diary* (1985) and *Without a Clue* (1988). Concentrating latterly on US cinema, he earned a Best Supporting Actor Academy Award nomination for his performance in *Bugsy* (1991). Subsequent films include *Schindler's List* (1993), *Death and the Maiden* (1994) and *Species* (1996).

Kingsley, Charles 1819–75
English writer

Born at Holne vicarage, Dartmoor, he entered Magdalene College, Cambridge in 1838, and took a classical first in 1842. As curate and then rector (1844) he spent the rest of his life at Eversley in Hampshire. His dramatic poem, *The Saint's Tragedy, or The True Story of Elizabeth of Hungary* (1848), was followed by *Alton Locke* (1850) and *Yeast* (1851), brilliant social novels which had enormous influence at the time. A Christian Socialist, he had thrown himself into various schemes aimed at the improvement of the working classes, and as 'Parson Lot' published an immense number of articles on current topics, especially in the *Christian Socialist* and *Politics for the People*. *Hypatia* (1853) concerns early Christianity in conflict with Greek philosophy in Alexandria, and *Westward Ho!* (1855) presents a realistic picture of Elizabethan England and the Spanish Main. His later novels include *Two Years Ago* (1857) and *Hereward the Wake* (1866). He also wrote a number of popular songs and ballads, including 'Airly Beacon' and 'The Sands of Dee'. He was appointed Professor of Modern History at Cambridge in 1860, but he resigned in 1869 and was appointed canon of Chester. He made a voyage to the West Indies the following year, and was appointed canon of Westminster and chaplain to Queen **Victoria**. The collected works of this combative, enthusiastic and sympathetic apostle fill 28 volumes (1879–81), and include *Glaucus* (1855), *The Heroes* (1856),

his children's classic *The Water Babies* (1863), *Town Geology* (1872), *Prose Idylls* (1873) and *Health and Education* (1874).
📖 S Chitty, *The Beast and the Monk* (1974)

Kingsley, Henry 1830–76
English novelist

Born in Barnack, Northamptonshire, he was the brother of **Charles Kingsley**, and was educated at Worcester College, Oxford. From 1853 to 1858 he worked as a gold prospector in Australia, and on his return he published a vigorous picture of colonial life in *Recollections of Geoffry Hamlyn* (1859). After this came *Ravenshoe* (1861), his masterpiece, followed by *Austin Elliot* (1863), and then *The Hillyars and the Burtons*, another novel of Australian life (1865). In 1869–70 he edited the *Edinburgh Daily Review*.
📖 J S D Mellick, *The Passing Guest: a life of Henry Kingsley* (1983)

Kingsley, Mary Henrietta 1862–1900
English traveller and writer

Born in Islington, London, she was not formally educated, but was a voracious reader in her father's scientific library. After her parents died, in 1893 she made the first of two remarkable journeys to West Africa, where she lived among the native peoples. Returning from her second journey in 1895, she wrote *Travels in West Africa* (1899), which was based on her diaries. *West African Studies* also appeared in 1899. She was subsequently consulted by colonial administrators for her wide understanding of African culture. Serving as a nurse in the Second Boer War, she died of enteric fever. She was the niece of the author **Charles Kingsley**.

Kingsley, Mary St Leger, *pseudonym* Lucas Malet 1852–1931
English novelist

She was the daughter of **Charles Kingsley**. In 1876 she married the Rev W Harrison, rector of Clovelly. She adopted the pen-name Lucas Malet to avoid association with her father and completed his *Tutor's Story* in 1916. She wrote over 20 works, among them such novels as *Mrs Lorimer* (1882), *Colonel Enderby's Wife* (1885), *The Wages of Sin* (1890), *The Carissima* (1896) and *Sir Richard Calmady* (1901). Her style is reminiscent of the 19th century in its characterization and is now considered sentimental, but she was awarded a civic pension in 1930 for her contribution to literature.

Kingsmill, Hugh, *originally* Hugh Kingsmill Lunn 1889–1949
English biographer and anthologist

He was educated at Oxford and Dublin. As a writer he was initially criticized for iconoclasm, but after the failure of his *Matthew Arnold* (1928), he recovered himself with the satirical fantasy *The Return of William Shakespeare* (1929), *Frank Harris* (1932) and elegant essays such as *The Progress of a Biographer* (1949). He produced several anthologies, including *Johnson Without Boswell* (1940) and *Invective and Abuse* (1944), and with **Hesketh Pearson** he published conversational literary journeys such as *Skye High* (1937), *This Blessed Plot* (1942) and *Talking of Dick Whittington* (1947).
📖 M Holroyd, *The Collected Hugh Kingsmill* (1964, revised edition 1971)

Kingston, Charles Cameron 1850–1908
Australian politician

A lawyer, he entered South Australian politics in 1881, and was state Attorney-General (1884–45, 1887–89), Chief Secretary (1892) and Premier (1893–99). His ministry was the first in Australia to give votes to women (1894), and to introduce state conciliation and arbitration (1894). He was a leading figure in the federation movement, and attended the National Australasian Convention in 1891 and the Federal Convention of 1897–98, at which, with **Henry Bournes Higgins**, he included Conciliation and

Arbitration powers in the federal constitution. He was Minister of Trade and Customs in **Edmund Barton**'s government (1901–03). Disputes with his colleagues over the scope of his Conciliation and Arbitration Bill led to his resignation in 1903.

Kingston, William Henry Giles 1814–80
English writer

He was the son of a merchant in Oporto, Portugal, where he spent much of his youth. He wrote over 150 children's adventure stories including such favourites as *Peter the Whaler* (1851) and *The Three Midshipmen* (1862). ⌨ M R Kingsford, *The Life, Work and Influence of William Kingston* (1947)

Kingston Trio
US folk group

With the exception of **Pete Seeger**, the Kingston Trio did more than anyone else to popularize the nascent folk revival of the late 1950s in the USA. The original group, consisting of Bob Shane, Nick Reynolds and Dave Guard, came together in San Francsico in 1957, and had a hit with the ballad 'Tom Dooley' in 1958. Their boyish, all-American looks and clean, fresh-sounding harmonies appealed to a wide audience, and they enjoyed considerable success in concert and with albums, thereby paving the way for the more radical departures of the 1960s generation. John Stewart, later a significant singer-songwriter in his own right, replaced Guard (1961–67), but the group eventually disbanded in 1968, overtaken by musical changes around them. Occasional reunions have followed, instigated by Shane.

Kinkel, Gottfried 1815–82
German poet

Born in Oberkassel, near Bonn, he lectured at Bonn on theology, poetry, and the history of art. Involved in the revolutionary movement of 1848, he was imprisoned in Spandau (1850), but escaped. He taught German in London until 1866, when he was appointed Professor of Archaeology and Art at Zurich. As a poet his fame rests upon *Otto der Schütz* (1846, 'Otto the Hunter'), *Der Grobschmied von Antwerpen* (1872, 'The Blacksmith of Antwerp'), *Tanagra* (1883, Eng trans *Tanagra: an idyll of Greece*, 1893), *Gedichte* (1843–68, 'Poems') and a drama, *Nimrod* (1857). He also wrote a history of art (1845), and monographs on **Ferdinand Freiligrath** (1867) and **Rubens** (1874). His first wife, Johanna (1810–58), a distinguished musician, wrote a novel, *Hans Ibeles in London* (1860), and, with her husband, the story collection *Erzählungen* (1849, 'Tales').

Kinkel, Klaus 1936–
German Free Democrat politician

Born in Metzingen, he was educated at the universities of Bonn, Cologne and Tubingen, and after graduating pursued a career as a lawyer. Between 1983 and 1987 he was head of Germany's External Intelligence Service. As a politician his first appointments were in the Justice Ministry and he was appointed Minister in 1991. The following year he became Foreign Minister and was responsible for promoting a more expansionist foreign policy.

Kinnaird, Alison 1949–
Scottish studio glass artist and engraver

Born in Edinburgh, she was educated at George Watson's Ladies College, Edinburgh, and studied Celtic history and archaeology at Edinburgh University. Since 1971 she has worked as a glass artist on a freelance basis, specializing in copper-wheel engraving as a decorative technique. Her pieces are inspired by myths and legends, music, naturalism and personal experiences. She was awarded the Worshipful Company of Glass Sellers of London prize for artistic achievement in glass in 1987 and has exhibited widely in Britain and abroad. Some examples of her work are in the National Museum of Scotland, Edinburgh, Glasgow Museum and Art Gallery, and in the Corning Museum of Glass in New York.

Kinnock, Neil Gordon 1942–
Welsh Labour politician

Born in Tredegar, Monmouthshire, and educated at University College Cardiff, he became Labour MP for Bedwellty in 1970, and leader of the British Labour Party in 1983. He was a member of the Labour Party's National Executive Committee from 1978 and chief Opposition spokesman on education from 1979. He was at the centre of a controversy in 1981 when he headed a group of left-wing MPs who refused to support **Tony Benn** during elections for the deputy leadership of the party. A skilful orator, Kinnock was the left's obvious choice in the Labour leadership contest of 1983, being regarded by many as the favoured candidate of the outgoing leader, **Michael Foot** (he was former Parliamentary Private Secretary to Foot). He was elected party leader by a large majority and re-elected in 1988. He succeeded in isolating the extreme elements within the party and persuaded it to adopt more moderate policies, better attuned to contemporary conditions. Nevertheless, the party was unsuccessful in the 1992 general election, following which Kinnock resigned and was replaced by **John Smith**. He was MP for Islwyn from 1983 until 1995, and became a member of the European Commission in 1995. His publications include *Making Our Way* (1986) and *Thorns and Roses* (1992). ⌨ Michael Leapman, *Kinnock* (1987)

Kinsey, Alfred Charles 1894–1956
US sexologist and zoologist

Born in Hoboken, New Jersey, he studied at Bowdoin Colleg and at Harvard. He was Professor of Zoology at Indiana University from 1920, and in 1942 was the founder director of the Institute for Sex Research there. He published *Sexual Behavior in the Human Male* in 1948, the Kinsey Report, which was based upon 18,500 interviews and attracted much attention from the general public as well as from fellow scientists. It appeared to show a greater variety of sexual behaviour than had previously been suspected, although the report was much criticized for the interviewing techniques used. *Sexual Behavior in the Human Female* followed in 1953. ⌨ Cornelia V Christensen, *Kinsey: A Biography* (1971)

Kipling, (Joseph) Rudyard 1865–1936
English writer and Nobel Prize winner

Born in Bombay, India, he was the son of John Lockwood Kipling (1837–1911), Principal of the School of Art in Lahore. He was educated at the United Services College, Westward Ho!, in Devon, England, but returned in 1880 to India, where he worked as a journalist on the Lahore *Civil and Military Gazette*. His mildly satirical verses *Departmental Ditties* (1886), and the short stories *Plain Tales from the Hills* (1888) and *Soldiers Three* (1889), won him a reputation in England. He returned in 1889 and settled in London, where *The Light that Failed* (1890), his first attempt at a full-length novel, was not altogether successful. In London he met Wolcott Balestier, the US author-publisher, with whom he collaborated on *The Naulakha* (1892), and whose sister Caroline he married (1892). A spell of residence in his wife's native Vermont ended abruptly in 1899 through incompatibility with in-laws and locals, and the remainder of his career was spent in England. Meanwhile he had written the brilliantly successful *Barrack Room Ballads* (1892) and *The Seven Seas* (1896), both collections of verse, and further short stories published as *Many Inventions* (1893) and *The Day's Work* (1899). The two *Jungle Books* (1894–95) have gained a place among the classic animal stories, and *Stalky and Co* (1899) presents semi-autobiographical but delightfully uninhibited episodes based on his schooldays. *Kim* appeared in 1901, and the children's classic *Just So Stories* in 1902. The verse collection *The Five Nations* (1903) included the highly successful 'Recessional', written for Queen Victoria's diamond jubilee in 1897. Later works include *Puck of Pook's Hill* (1906), *Rewards and Fairies* (1910), *Debits and Credits* (1926), and the autobiographical *Something of Myself* (1937). Kipling's real merit as a writer has tended to become obscured in recent years and he has been accused of imperialism and jingoism, but this ignores not only the great body of his work which was far removed from this sphere, but also his own criticisms and satire on some of the less admirable aspects of colonialism. He was awarded the Nobel Prize for literature in 1907. ▣ C Carrington, *Rudyard Kipling: his life and work* (1955)

Kipp, Petrus Jacobus 1808–64
Dutch chemist
Born in Utrecht, he started a business in laboratory apparatus in Delft in 1830. He invented 'Kipp's apparatus', a form of generator for the continuous and automatic production of certain gases such as carbon dioxide, hydrogen and hydrogen sulphide. A representation of it appears in the arms of the Dutch Chemical Society. He also invented a method of fixing carbon and pastel drawings.

Kipping, Frederick Stanley 1863–1949
English chemist
Born in Manchester, after completing his degree he worked first for the Manchester Gas Department, then moved to Munich (1886) to work for a PhD in Johann Baeyer's laboratory. His supervisor was William Henry Perkin Jnr (1860–1929) and they became close friends. After graduation he worked with Perkin at Heriot-Watt College in Edinburgh and moved to what is now Imperial College, London, in 1890. In 1897 he became professor at University College in Nottingham (now Nottingham University) and it was there that he published a series of pioneering papers on the organic compounds of silicon. He retired in 1936, expressing the view that his work on silicon compounds could have no practical value. Within a few years the value of silicones as inert, water-repellent polymers had been recognized and silicones are now important commercial materials. He was elected FRS in 1897 and became well known to generations of students through his book, co-written with Perkin, *Organic Chemistry* (1894).

Kirchhoff, Gustav Robert 1824–87
German physicist
He was born in Königsberg, Prussia (now Kaliningrad, Russia), and while still a student, he devised 'Kirchhoff's laws' for electrical circuits. Professor at Heidelberg University (1854–75) and Berlin University (1875–86), he distinguished himself in electricity, heat, optics and especially (with Robert Bunsen) spectrum analysis, which led to the discovery of caesium and rubidium (1859). More importantly it resulted in his explanation of the Fraunhofer lines in the solar spectrum as the absorption of the corresponding spectral wavelengths in the Sun's atmosphere. He formulated Kirchhoff's law of radiation, the key to the whole thermodynamics of radiation which, in the hands of his successor Max Planck, would later be developed into the concept of quanta. His electromagnetic theory of diffraction is still the most commonly used in optics.

Kirchner, Ernst Ludwig 1880–1938
German artist
Born in Aschaffenburg, he studied architecture at Dresden, but became the leading spirit in the formation in Dresden, with Erich Heckel and Karl Schmidt-Rottluff, of Die Brücke (1905–13), the first group of German Expressionists, whose work was much influenced by primitive German woodcuts. His work was characterized by erotic, vibrant colours and angular outlines. He moved to Switzerland in 1914. Many of his works were confiscated as degenerate by the Nazis in 1937, and he committed suicide in 1938.

Kirk, Alan Goodrich 1888–1963
US naval officer and diplomat
Born in Philadelphia, he was educated at the US Naval Academy, Annapolis, and was commissioned in the US navy in 1909. He served as naval attaché London from 1939 to 1941 and was promoted rear admiral in 1941. He commanded the amphibious forces in the invasion of Sicily (1943) and the Western Task Force in the 1944 Normandy landing. He was ambassador to Belgium (1946–49), the USSR (1949–52) and Taiwan (1962).

Kirk, Norman Eric 1923–74
New Zealand politician
Born on South Island at Waimate, Canterbury, he began his career as a driver of stationary engines. He joined the Labour Party and became involved in local, then national politics, becoming president of the party in 1964. He entered parliament in 1957, was Leader of the Opposition (1965–72) and became Prime Minister in 1972, at a time when his country's economy was in difficulties. Forced by Britain's entry into the EEC and the USA's disengagement in Asia, he sought a more independent regional role for New Zealand, opposed French nuclear testing in the Pacific and sent ships into the test area. He died in office in 1974 and was succeeded by the Finance Minister Wallace Rowling.

Kirkeby, Per 1938–
Danish painter
A professor at the Staatliche Hochschule für Bildende Künste, Frankfurt, since 1988, he has been a prominent representative of new, experimental Danish painting for several years. He has also published poetry, essays and novels, directed several documentary films, and taken part in two Greenland expeditions in the 1960s. He was awarded the Thorvaldsen Medal in 1987.

Kirkland, Gelsey 1952–
US dancer
Born in Bethlehem, Pennsylvania, she studied at the School of American Ballet, and joined New York City Ballet in 1968, becoming a principal in 1972. Roles were created for her by George Balanchine (1970, *The Firebird*), Jerome Robbins (1971, *The Goldberg Variations* and 1973, *An Evening's Waltzes*), and by Antony Tudor in his last two ballets, *The Leaves Are Fading* (1975) and *The Tillers in the Fields* (1978). In 1975 she moved to American Ballet Theater, where she began a highly successful partnership with Mikhail Baryshnikov. A troubled personal life hampered her career in the early 1980s, but she achieved a successful comeback in *Swan Lake* with the Royal Ballet in London, where she settled. Her controversial autobiographies, *Dancing on My Grave* (1986) and *The Shape of Love* (1990) document her career.

Kirkpatrick, Jeane Duane Jordan 1926–
US academic and diplomat
Born in Duncan, Oklahoma, she was educated at Columbia University and Paris University. She worked as a research analyst for the State Department (1951–53), then taught at Trinity College and became Professor of Government at Georgetown University, Washington, DC, in 1978. Noted for her 'hawkish', anti-communist defence stance and advocacy of a new Latin-American and Pacific-orientated diplomatic strategy, in 1981 she was made Permanent Representative to the United Nations

by President **Ronald Reagan**, remaining there until 1985. Formerly a Democrat, she joined the Republican Party in 1985.

Kirkup, James 1923–
English poet

He was born in Sunderland and educated in South Shields, and at Durham University. He has held academic posts in England (Leeds University, 1950–52), then, from the early 1960s, in Japan, where he became Professor of English Literature at Kyoto University. His collections include *A Correct Compassion* (1952) and *Zen Contemplations* (1978). His poem 'The Love that dares to speak its name', was the subject of a prosecution for blasphemous libel in 1977, the first for more than 50 years. He has also published plays, fiction, translations, and five volumes of autobiography: *The Only Child* (1957), *Sorrows, Passions and Alarms* (1987), *I, of All People* (1990), *A Poet Could Not But be Gay* (1991) and *Me All Over* (1993).

Kirkwood, Daniel 1814–95
US astronomer

Born in Harford County, Maryland, he became a teacher in 1833 and later Principal of Lancaster High School (1843–49). He was appointed Professor of Mathematics at Delaware (1851) and at Indiana (1856). In 1891 he became a lecturer at the University of Stanford. He is famous for explaining, in 1866, the unequal distribution in the semi-major axes of asteroid orbits. Asteroids with semi-major axes of 2.5, 2.95 and 3.3 astronomical units are missing, these orbits being in resonance with Jupiter; Jovian gravitational perturbation has moved the asteroid orbits away from these 'Kirkwood gaps'. Kirkwood also used his theory to explain the gaps in the rings of Saturn, the perturbers this time being the Saturnian satellites.

Kirov, Sergei Mironovich 1886–1934
Russian revolutionary and politician

He was born in Urzhun. In and out of prison from 1905 onwards, he played an active part in the October Revolution (1917) and the civil war which followed, and during the 1920s held a number of leading provincial Party posts. He had been elected a full member of the Central Committee by 1923, and became a full member of the politburo at the 17th Party Congress (1934) and was elected as a secretary of the Central Committee (1934). Later that year he was assassinated at his Leningrad (now St Petersburg) headquarters, possibly at the instigation of **Stalin**, who then used his death as the pretext for a widespread campaign of reprisals.

Kirstein, Lincoln 1907–96
US ballet director and writer

Born in Rochester, New York, he was educated at Harvard. He is best known for recognizing the talents of **George Balanchine** and taking him to the USA to co-found the School of American Ballet in 1934. Their school became attached to the Metropolitan Opera in 1935, at which time Kirstein was also running the touring company Ballet Caravan. In 1946 he and Balanchine founded the Ballet Society and in 1948 moved to New York as the directors of what has become one of the USA's most influential companies, New York City Ballet. He served as general director of the New York City Ballet (at the New York State Theater in Lincoln Center) from 1964 and president of the School of American Ballet until 1989, when he retired. He was founder-editor of *Dance Index Magazine* (1942–48), and wrote many books, including *Dance* (1935) and *Movement and Metaphor* (1970), and some poetry, including *Rhymes of a PFC* (1964) and *The Poems of Lincoln Kirstein* (1987).

Kirwan, Richard 1733–1812
Irish chemist

Born in Galway, he was educated at the University of Poitiers with the idea of becoming a Jesuit. After practising briefly as a lawyer, he spent 10 years in London and was elected FRS in 1780. On his return to Ireland he helped to found the Royal Irish Academy, presiding over it from 1799 to his death. He did valuable work on chemical affinity and the composition of salts, publishing the first systematic work on mineralogy in English in 1784. He is best known, however, for his opposition to the discoveries of **Antoine Lavoisier**. He also challenged the revolutionary views of the Scottish geologist **James Hutton**.

Kisfaludy, Karoly 1788–1830
Hungarian dramatist

Born in Tét, he turned his back on his noble upbringing, and lived the life of a bohemian artist. He was the regenerator of the national drama, and became famous for his *A' Tatárok Magyar Országban* (1819, 'Tartars in Hungary'). He also wrote *A Kérök* (1817, 'The Suitors'), a comedy, and *Iréne* (1820), a tragedy. ◫F Szinnyei, *Kisfaludy Karoly* (1927)

Kishi Nobusuke 1896–1991
Japanese politician

The brother of **Sato Eisaku**, he took the name of Kishi when he was adopted into his uncle's family. He entered the Ministry of Agriculture and Commerce (1920) and during the interwar years was identified as one of the new bureaucrats (shinkanryo), who championed more extensive economic planning. While he served in the Japanese puppet-state of Manzhuguo (1936–39), he worked closely with the military in developing heavy industry. On returning to Japan, he became a vice-minister of Commerce and Industry, helping to place the economy on a war footing. He then served in the wartime cabinet of **Tojo Hideki**. After the war, he was imprisoned by the US occupation authorities but was released in 1948. In 1955 he helped to create the Liberal Democratic Party (LDP), formed when the two major conservative parties merged. A controversial Prime Minister (1957–60), he ensured ratification of the renewed Security Treaty with the USA (1960) in the face of an opposition boycott in the Diet and massive public demonstrations. He resigned shortly afterwards, but remained influential within the LDP.

Kissinger, Henry Alfred 1923–
US political scientist, diplomat and Nobel Prize winner

Born in Fürth, Germany, his family emigrated to the USA in 1938 to escape Nazi persecution of the Jews. After war service he worked for a number of public agencies before he joined the Harvard faculty as Professor of Government (1962–71). He became President **Richard Nixon**'s adviser on national security affairs (1969), was the main US figure in the negotiations to end the Vietnam War, for which he shared the 1973 Nobel Peace Prize with the Vietnamese statesman **Le Duc Tho**, and the same year became Secretary of State. He played a major role in the improvement of relations (détente) with both China and the USSR during the early 1970s and in the peace negotiations between the Arabs and Israelis (1973–75) which continued during the **Ford** administration and resulted in a notable improvement in Israeli–Egyptian relations, emerging as the arch exponent of 'shuttle diplomacy'. He ceased to be Secretary of State in 1977 when **Jimmy Carter** became President, but later, in 1983, was appointed by President **Reagan** to head a bipartisan commission on Central America.

Kitaj, R(onald) B(rooks) 1932–
US painter

Born in Cleveland, Ohio, of Russian-Jewish descent, he was a sailor from 1951 to 1955 and travelled extensively. Following army service, he studied art at Oxford, then entered the Royal College of Art, London (1960) where he met, and influenced, fellow student **David Hockney**. Since 1960, apart from brief periods of residence in France, Spain and the USA, he has lived in London. His oil paintings and pastels demonstrate a mastery of figure drawing, while his economic use of line and flattened colour recall oriental art, as in *If Not, Not* (1976, National Gallery of Scotland, Edinburgh) and *Cecil Court, London WC2 (The Refugees)* (1984, Tate Gallery, London). There was a retrospective of his work at the Tate Gallery in 1996. Its cool reception by the critics, followed by the death of his second wife, the American painter, Sandra Fisher, was the subject of his sole contribution to the Royal Academy Summer Exhibition of that year, *The Critic Kills*.

Kitasato, Baron Shibasaburo 1852–1931
Japanese bacteriologist

Born in Oguni, after graduating from the Imperial University of Tokyo (1883), he moved to Berlin, and later founded in Japan an institute for infectious diseases. Kitasato succeeded in isolating the first pure culture of tetanus (1889), and he made the invaluable discovery of antitoxic immunity (1890), which led to the development of treatments and immunization for both tetanus and diphtheria. He later discovered the bacillus of bubonic plague and isolated the bacilli of symptomatic anthrax (1889) and dysentery (1898).

Kitchener (of Khartoum and of Broome), Horatio Herbert Kitchener, 1st Earl 1850–1916
British soldier and statesman

Born near Ballylongford, County Kerry, Ireland, he was educated in Switzerland and the Royal Military Academy, Woolwich. He entered the Royal Engineers in 1871, and served on the Palestine survey (1874–78), the Cyprus survey till 1882, and in the Sudan campaign (1883–85). In 1898 he won back the Sudan for Egypt by the final rout of the Khalifa at Omdurman, and was made a peer. Successively Chief of Staff and Commander-in-Chief in South Africa (1900–02), he brought the Second Boer War to an end. He was then made Commander-in-Chief in India (1902–09), and agent and consul-general in Egypt (1911). He was appointed field marshal and Secretary for War on 7 August 1914, and had recruited a great army (the 'Kitchener armies') for World War I before he was lost with HMS *Hampshire* (mined off Orkney) on 5 June 1916. 📖 Philip Magnus, *Kitchener: Portrait of an Imperialist* (1958)

Kitt, Eartha Mae c.1928–
US entertainer

Born in North, South Carolina, she graduated from the New York School of the Performing Arts, making her New York debut as a member of **Katherine Dunham's** dance troupe in *Blue Holiday* (1945). She was subsequently cast by **Orson Welles** in his production of *Dr Faustus* (1951). Her theatrical credits include *New Faces of 1952*, *Shinbone Alley* (1957) and *The Owl and the Pussycat* (1965–66). Since her debut in *Casbah* (1948), her film appearances have included *New Faces* (1954), *St Louis Blues* (1957), *Anna Lucasta* (1958), the documentary *All By Myself* (1982), and *Erik the Viking* (1989). On television from 1953, she received the Golden Rose of Montreux for *Kaskade* (1962) and was appropriately cast as Catwoman in the series *Batman* (1966).

Kitzinger, Sheila Helen Elizabeth, *née* Webster 1929–
British childbirth educationist

Educated at Bishop Fox's School, Taunton, and at Ruskin and St Hugh's colleges, Oxford, she conducted research into social anthropology from 1952 to 1953, and has worked with the Open University and the National Childbirth Trust. She has long been a campaigner for more natural childbirth procedures and her 1980 book *Pregnancy and Childbirth* sold over one million copies. Her other books, which cover all aspects of pregnancy and childbirth, include *The Good Birth Guide* (1979), *Birth over Thirty* (1982), *Homebirth* (1991), *Ourselves as Mothers* (1992) and *The Year After Childbirth* (1994).

Kivi, Aleksis, *pseudonym of* Aleksis Stenvall 1834–72
Finnish playwright and novelist

Born in Nurmijärvi or Palojoki, the son of a poor tailor, he managed to gain a place at Helsinki University but did not graduate. He wrote in Finnish not Swedish, establishing the western dialect as the modern literary language of Finland, and is considered the father of the Finnish theatre and novel. He wrote the first Finnish novel, *Seitsemän veljestä* (1870, Eng trans *Seven Brothers*, 1929), and a collection of Finnish poems, *Kanervala* (1866). As a dramatist he wrote rural comedies like *Nummisuutarit* (1864, 'The Cobblers on the Heath'), and a tragedy, *Kullervo* (1864), based on one of the central figures in the national epic, the *Kalevala*. 📖 V Tarkiainen, *Alexis Kivi* (1950)

Kjarval, Jóhannes Sveinsson 1885–1972
Icelandic Symbolist painter

Born on the remote farm of Efri-Ey, he was one of the pioneers of modern Icelandic art. He worked as a farm labourer and a deck-hand for some years, then went to Reykjavík where he was taught by **Ásgrímur Jónsson**, and held a one-man show in 1908. Eventually he realized his dream of becoming a professional painter when his friends held a lottery to raise funds for his schooling abroad. He went to London in 1911, where he was refused admission to the Royal Academy schools but came under the influence of the works of **J M W Turner**, and studied instead at the Royal Academy in Copenhagen (1912–18). From 1918 he lived in Iceland but travelled widely. Essentially an eccentric Romantic with strong mystical and Symbolist tendencies, he had a powerful sense of historical nationalism, and often featured the 'hidden people' of Icelandic folklore. His output was astonishing in its range and eclecticism; long before his death he had become the best-loved painter in Iceland.

Kjeldahl, Johan Gustav Christoffer Thorsager 1849–1900
Danish chemist

Born in Jagerpris, he studied chemistry at the Technical Institute in Copenhagen and was appointed as an instructor at the Agricultural College. In 1875 he set up a laboratory for the Carlsberg brewery and, in 1876 when the laboratory was transformed into a research institute, he became its director. His work was mostly in agricultural chemistry and his major contribution was to discover a method of estimating the nitrogen content of organic substances which was quicker, cheaper and more reliable than former methods. This method is known by his name.

Klammer, Franz 1953–
Austrian alpine skier

Born in Mooswald, he was the Olympic downhill champion in 1976, and the World Cup downhill champion five times (1975–78, 1983). Between 1974–84 he won a record 25 World Cup downhill races.

Klaproth, Martin Heinrich 1743–1817
German analytical chemist

He was born in Wernigerode and grew up in poverty, training as an apothecary. He moved to Berlin in 1768 and married the niece of **Andreas Sigismund Marggraf**, who brought him some scientific connections and enough money to set up his own shop. From 1792 he held various lectureships, becoming Germany's leading chemist and, on the foundation of the University of Berlin in 1810, the Professor of Chemistry there. Between 1789 and 1803 Klaproth discovered six new elements. His analytical techniques were as important as his discoveries: he found ways of treating particularly insoluble compounds, made adjustments to overcome contamination from his apparatus, and insisted on reporting discrepant as well as consistent results. He was also one of the first scientists outside France to propagate the revolutionary ideas of Antoine Lavoisier.

Kléber, Jean Baptiste 1753–1800
French general

Born in Strasbourg, he served in the Austrian army (1776–82), became an architect, and joined the National Guard (1792). He commanded in the Vendean War (1793), but was recalled for leniency. He later won victories at Fleurus (1794) and Altenkirchen (1796). He accompanied Napoleon I to Egypt, was wounded at Alexandria, and won the Battle of Mount Tabor (1799). When Napoleon left Egypt, Kléber was left in command. He attempted to reconquer Egypt, but was assassinated by a Turkish fanatic at Cairo.

Klee, Paul 1879–1940
Swiss artist

Born in Münchenbuchsee near Bern, he studied at Munich and settled there (1906), and was associated with Franz Marc and Wassily Kandinsky in the Blaue Reiter group (1911–12). From 1920 to 1931 he taught at the Bauhaus in Weimar and Dessau, with his *Pädagogisches Skizzenbuch* being published in 1925, and then taught in Düsseldorf (1931–33). After he had returned to Bern in 1933, many of his works were confiscated by the Nazis and 17 of them were included in the 1937 'Degenerate Art' exhibition in Munich. His work has been called Surrealist, but in his fantastic, small-scale, mainly abstract pictures he created, with supreme technical skill in many media, a very personal world of free fancy, expressed with a sly wit and subtle colouring and giving the effect of inspired doodling, for example the well-known *Twittering Machine* in the Museum of Modern Art, New York.
📖 Will Grohmann, *Paul Klee* (1954)

Kleiber, Erich 1890–1956
Argentine conductor

Born in Vienna, he became Director of the Berlin State Opera at the age of 33, holding this post for 12 years until forced by the Nazis to leave Germany. In 1938 he became a citizen of the Argentine. After World War II he was again appointed director of the Berlin State Opera, until his resignation in 1955. He gave the first performance of Alban Berg's *Wozzeck* (1925).

Klein, Anne Hannah, *née* Hannah Golofski
c.1921–1974
US fashion designer

She was born in New York City and in 1938 started as a sketcher on Seventh Avenue there. In 1948, Junior Sophisticates was launched, and Anne Klein & Co was established in 1968. She was a noted leader in designing sophisticated, practical sportswear for young women. She recognized early a need for blazers, trousers, and separates, and her designs were popular in the USA.

Klein, Calvin Richard 1942–
US fashion designer

Born in New York City, he graduated from New York's Fashion Institute of Technology in 1962, and set up his own firm (Calvin Klein Ltd) in 1968. He quickly achieved recognition and is known for understatement and the simple but sophisticated style of his clothes, including 'designer jeans'.

Klein, (Christian) Felix 1849–1925
German mathematician

Born in Düsseldorf, he studied at the University of Bonn (1865–68), and became Professor of Mathematics at Erlangen University (1872–75). He later accepted professorships at the universities of Leipzig (1880–86) and Göttingen (1886–1913), where he did much to make Göttingen University the world centre of mathematics. His 'Erlanger Programm' (published 1872) showed how different geometries could be classified in terms of group theory. His subsequent work on geometry included studies of non-Euclidean geometry, function theory and elliptic modular and automorphic functions. An influential teacher and organizer, he encouraged links between pure and applied mathematics and engineering, promoted general mathematical education, and organized the *Encyklopädie der Mathematischen Wissenschaften*, (23 vols, 1890–1930).

Klein, Lawrence Robert 1920–
US economist and Nobel Prize winner

Born in Omaha, Nebraska, he was educated in California, at the Massachusetts Institute of Technology, and at Oxford, and he has been professor at the universities of Chicago (1944–47), Michigan (1949–54) and Pennsylvania (from 1958). He was economic adviser to President Jimmy Carter (1976–81), and was awarded the Nobel Prize for economics in 1980 for his work on forecasting business fluctuations and portraying economic interrelationships.

Klein, Melanie 1882–1960
British psychoanalyst

Born in Vienna, Austria, she studied medicine at first, but when she was in Budapest she was analyzed by Sigmund Freud's follower Sandor Ferenczi, and she trained with him in his children's clinic. She studied under Karl Abraham in Berlin, then moved to London in 1926. She pioneered the now widely used techniques of play therapy and was the first to apply psychoanalysis to small children. Her belief that neuroses are fixed in the earliest months of life was always controversial and caused dissent among her colleagues. Her ideas and methods are expressed in her books, among them *The Psychoanalysis of Children* (1932).

Klein, Yves 1928–62
French artist

Born in Nice, he was a judo expert (he lived in Japan from 1952 to 1953), musician and leader of the postwar European neo-Dada movement. His monochrome (usually blue) canvases date from 1946. His *Anthropométries* involved girls covered with blue paint being dragged across canvases to the accompaniment of his *Symphonie monotone* (one-note symphony, composed in 1947).

Kleist, Ewald von 1881–1954
German military commander

He joined the army in 1900 and served as a cavalry officer during World War I. During World War II he commanded an armoured group in the French campaign (1940) and an army group on the Russian front (1942–44). Promoted field marshal in 1943, he was later dismissed by Hitler and was subsequently taken prisoner by the Allies. He died in captivity in the USSR.

Kleist, (Bernd) Heinrich (Wilhelm) von
1777–1811
German dramatist and poet

He was born in Frankfurt an der Oder. His family had a long military tradition, but he left the army in 1799 to study, and soon devoted himself to literature. His work is marked by a sometimes anguished struggle to come to terms with his doubts over man's ability to shape his own fate and destiny amid the political and personal upheavals of the age. His best plays are still popular, notably *Prinz Friedrich von Homburg* (1811, Eng trans *The Prince of Homburg*, 1959), and his finest tale is *Michael Kohlhaas* (1808–10). He committed suicide. ⌨ W Silz, *Heinrich von Kleist* (1961)

Klemperer, Otto 1885–1973
German conductor
Born in Breslau (now Wrocław, Poland), he studied at the Hoch Conservatory in Frankfurt am Main and in Berlin and first appeared as a conductor in 1907. He made a name as a champion of modern music and was appointed director of the Kroll Opera in Berlin (1927), which was closed down in 1931. Nazism drove him to the USA in 1933, where he was director of the Los Angeles Symphony Orchestra until 1939. In spite of continuing ill health, he was musical director of Budapest Opera (1947–50). In his later years he concentrated mainly on German classical composers, and was particularly known for his interpretation of **Beethoven**. His compositions included a mass and lieder.

Klerk, F W de See de Klerk, F(rederik) W(illem)

Klimt, Gustav 1862–1918
Austrian painter and designer
Born in Vienna, from 1883 to 1892 he worked in collaboration with his brother and another artist as a painter of grandiose decorative schemes. Under the influence of contemporary movements such as Impressionism, Symbolism and Art Nouveau, he became a founder and the first president (1898–1903) of the Vienna Secession, dedicated to furthering the avant-garde. His murals for Vienna University (1900–03) were considered pornographic and aroused official condemnation. He produced a number of portraits, mainly of women, as well as large allegorical and mythological paintings; typically, these combine a naturalistic though highly mannered delineation of the figure with an elaborately patterned, richly decorative treatment of the background or clothing, creating a luxuriant, languidly decadent effect. ⌨ Frank Witford, *Klimt* (1990)

Kline, Franz Joseph 1910–62
US artist
Born in Wilkes-Barre, Pennsylvania, he studied at Boston University before going to London, where he studied at Hetherley School of Art. Throughout the 1940s he worked in a traditional style, painting urban scenery, but after c.1950 his art became abstract, employing black, irregular shapes on white canvases, and becoming a leader of the 'action painting' Abstract Expressionists. He added colour to later works such as *Orange and Black Wall* (1939). Much of his life was spent in New York City, where he taught at such schools as the Pratt Institute and Cooper Union.

Klingenstierna, Samuel 1698–1765
Swedish mathematician and scientist
Born in Linköping, he studied law at Uppsala University, but turned to mathematics and physics. He was appointed secretary to the Swedish Treasury, and given a scholarship to travel and study. He studied under **Christian von Wolff** at Marburg University, and **Jean Bernoulli** at Basle University. He was appointed Professor of Mathematics, and Professor of Physics (1750), at Uppsala University, and tutor (1756) to the crown prince (later **Gustav III**). He showed that some of **Isaac Newton**'s views on the refraction of light were incorrect, and designed lenses free from chromatic and spherical aberration. By communicating his findings to **John Dollond** he contributed also to Dollond's success in constructing achromatic compound lenses, valuable in telescope and microscope construction.

Klinger, Friedrich Maximilian von 1752–1831
German playwright and novelist
Born in Frankfurt am Main, he was an officer in the Russian army (1780–1811), and curator of Dorpat University (1803–17). The 19th-century 'Sturm und Drang' school of German writing was named after one of his tragedies, *Der Wirrwarr* ('Confusion'), about the American Revolution, published as *Sturm und Drang* (literally 'Storm and Stress') in 1776. He wrote several other plays and some novels. ⌨ M Rieger, *Friedrich Maximilian Klinger* (3 vols, 1880–96)

Klinger, Max 1857–1920
German painter and sculptor
Born in Leipzig, he studied in Karlsruhe, Brussels and Paris, and excited hostility as well as admiration by his pen drawings and etchings, which were audaciously original in concept and often imbued with macabre realism. Later he turned to painting and did much work in coloured sculpture, including a chryselephantine sculpture of **Beethoven** (1902), modelled on the Zeus of **Phidias**.

Klint, Kaare 1888–1954
Danish architect and furniture designer
Born in Copenhagen, he was the son of P V Jensen Klint (1853–1930), the architect of Gruntvig's Church in Copenhagen, which Kaare completed in 1940. His furniture was based upon dimensional and anthropometric research as exemplified by his standardized, modular storage units. His admiration of English 18th-century furniture, together with his analytical approach, led him to design in a rational, modern idiom. He was one of the initiators of Denmark's prominence in the field of design, partly through his teaching at the Royal Danish Academy of Fine Arts, which he helped to found in 1924. He was made an honorary Royal Designer for Industry in the UK in 1949.

Klitzing, Klaus Von See Von Klitzing, Klaus

Klopstock, Friedrich Gottlieb 1724–1803
German poet
Born in Quedlinburg, he was inspired by **Virgil** and **Milton**, and began his religious epic, *Der Messias* ('The Messiah') as a student at Jena (1745), completing it in 1773. He settled in Hamburg in 1771 with a sinecure appointment, and pensions from Frederik V of Denmark (from 1751) and the Margrave of Baden. He wrote a number of plays, works on language, and a series of lyrical odes, collected in *Oden* ('Odes', 1771). ⌨ G Kaiser, *Klopstock* (1962)

Kluckhohn, Clyde Kay Maben 1905–60
US cultural anthropologist
Born in Le Mars, Iowa, he studied at Princeton, Wisconsin, Vienna and Oxford, and was appointed to the faculty of Harvard in 1935, where he remained for the rest of his career. His abiding research interest was in the culture of the Navaho, and his classic monograph *Navaho Witchcraft* (1944) was outstanding both for its ethnographic depth and for its combination of social structural and psychoanalytical approaches. He was a major contributor to culture theory, in which he collaborated closely with A L Kroeber. He set out his views on culture patterns and value systems in the popular work *Mirror for Man* (1949).

Klug, Sir Aaron 1926–
English biophysicist and Nobel Prize winner
Born in Zelvas, Lithuania, he moved to South Africa as a young child and studied physics at the universities of Witwatersrand and Cape Town. He became a research student in the Cavendish Laboratory of Cambridge (1949–52) before moving to London to John Bernal's department at Birkbeck College (Nuffield Research Fellow,

1954–57) where he worked with **Rosalind Franklin** and became particularly interested in viruses and their structure. Following Franklin's death in 1958, he became head of the virus structure research group at Birkbeck (1958–61) and returned to Cambridge in 1962 as a Fellow of Peterhouse and member of staff at the Medical Research Council's Laboratory of Molecular Biology, becoming its director in 1986. His studies employed a wide variety of techniques to elucidate the structure of viruses. From the 1970s he applied these methods to the study of chromosomes and other biological macromolecules such as muscle filaments. He was elected FRS in 1969, awarded the Nobel Prize for chemistry in 1982, knighted in 1988 and appointed to the Order of Merit in 1995.

Kluge, (Hans) Günther von 1882–1944
German soldier
He was born in Poznan, Poland. In 1939 he carried out the Nazi occupation of the Polish Corridor, commanded the German armies on the central Russian front (1942) and in July 1944 replaced **Karl von Rundstedt** as Commander-in-Chief of the Nazi armies in France confronting the Allied invasion, but was himself replaced after the Falaise gap débâcle. He committed suicide after being implicated in the failed plot to kill **Hitler**.

Kneale, Nigel 1922–
Manx writer and dramatist
Born on the Isle of Man, he worked in a lawyer's office, and first gained attention with the collection of short stories, *Tomato Cain* (1949), which won the **Somerset Maugham** Award. After a spell at RADA he joined the drama department of the BBC in a general capacity and progressed to writing the serial *The Quatermass Experiment* in 1953. An imaginative science-fiction drama, reflecting the paranoia of the day, its immense popularity led to *Quatermass II* (1955), *Quatermass and the Pit* (1959), *Quatermass* (1978) and three feature films. His early television adaptations also include *Curtain Down* (1952), *Wuthering Heights* (1953) and *1984* (1954). More recently he adapted **Kingsley Amis**'s *Stanley and the Women* and **Susan Hill**'s *The Woman in Black* (both 1991). His film scripts include *The Abominable Snowman* (1957), *First Men in the Moon* (1964) and *Halloween III* (1983). He also wrote television plays, such as *The Year of the Sex Olympics* (1968), *Beasts* (1975) and *Kinvig* (1981).

Kneller, Sir Godfrey, originally Kniller 1646–1723
German portrait painter
Born in Lübeck, he studied in Holland and Italy. In 1676 he went to London, and in 1680 was appointed court painter. In 1691 **William III** knighted him, and in 1715 **George I** made him a baronet. His best-known works are the *Beauties of Hampton Court* (painted for William III), and his 48 portraits of the 'Kit-Cat Club' and of 10 reigning monarchs (**Charles II** to George I, **Louis XIV, Peter the Great**, and the emperor Charles VI). His brother, John Zacharias (1644–1702), architectural and portrait painter, also settled in England.

Knight, Gladys 1944–
US soul and r'n'b singer
Born in Atlanta, Georgia, she began singing in the Maurice Brown and Wings Over Jordan gospel choirs. At the age of eight, she won a television talent competition, and the same year formed a close-harmony group called the Pips with her brother and two cousins. They began to record in 1958 and in 1966 switched to the Tamla Motown label where a string of hits followed. In 1972 she scored a huge hit with 'Help Me Make It Through the Night'. She left Motown in 1973 and had further success on the Buddah label with 'Midnight Train to Georgia' and 'The Way We Were'. Her activity since then has been sporadic, but she remains extremely popular.

Knight, Dame Laura, née Johnson 1877–1970
English artist
Born in Long Eaton, she travelled widely. She produced a long series of oil paintings of the ballet, the circus and gipsy life, in a lively and forceful style, and also executed a number of watercolour landscapes. 📖 Janet Dunbar, *Laura Knight* (1975)

Knollys, Sir Francis 1514–96
English statesman
From 1572 he was treasurer of **Elizabeth I**'s household. In 1568–69 he had charge of **Mary, Queen of Scots**.

Knopfler, Mark 1949–
British rock singer and guitarist
Born in Glasgow, he worked as a journalist and teacher before forming the phenomenally successful rock band Dire Straits in London in 1976 (his brother, David Knopfler, was also a founder-member). The success of 'Sultans of Swing' launched the band onto a world platform, and the album *Brothers In Arms* (1985) confirmed their commercial standing. He has pursued many other projects between Dire Straits albums and tours, including working with **Bob Dylan, Chet Atkins, Eric Clapton, Randy Newman** and **Tina Turner**, and issued his first official solo album, *Golden Heart*, in 1996. He has written several film soundtracks, beginning with *Local Hero* (1983). 📖 M Palmer, *Mark Knopfler: An Unauthorised Biography* (1992)

Knopoff, Leon 1925–
US geophysicist
Born in Los Angeles, he was educated at the California Institute of Technology, where he graduated in electrical engineering (1944) and physics (1949). Since 1950 he has worked at the University of California at Los Angeles (UCLA) where he became Professor of Geophysics in 1959 and Professor of Physics in 1961. From 1972 to 1986 he was also associate director of their Institute of Geophysics and Planetary Physics. He devised the first representation theorem for the full seismic wave equation (1956) and made important advances in work on the diffraction of seismic waves, eg by the core of the Earth (1959). In 1967 he pioneered numerical models to simulate seismicity and geological faulting, later describing the universal power law for the spatial distribution of earthquakes (1980), which has implications for the geometry of faults.

Knott, Alan Philip Eric 1946–
English cricketer
He was born in Belvedere, Greater London. One of a trio of noted Kent wicket-keepers (with **Leslie Ames** and **Godfrey Evans**), he played in 95 Test matches, and his 269 dismissals are exceeded only by Rodney Marsh of Australia. He was a genuine wicketkeeper-batsman whose 4,389 runs included five centuries. He kept wicket for England in 65 consecutive Test matches.

Knowles, (James) Sheridan 1784–1862
Irish dramatist
Born in Cork, the cousin of **Richard Brinsley Sheridan**, he served in the militia, then studied medicine at Aberdeen, but took to the stage. He did not achieve distinction, however, and subsequently opened a school in Belfast, then one in Glasgow (1816–28). His tragedy, *Caius Gracchus* (1815), was first performed in Belfast. *Virginius*, his most effective play, had been a success in Glasgow before **William Macready** produced it at Covent Garden in 1820. Other successful plays were *William Tell* (1825), *The Hunchback* (1832), *The Wife* (1833) and *The Love Chase* (1837). He also acted in many of his own pieces. In about 1844 he became a Baptist preacher. 📖 L H Meeks, *Sheridan Knowles and the theatre of his time* (1933)

Knox, Archibald 1864–1933
Manx designer
Born on the Isle of Man, he studied at Douglas School of Art, and worked part-time in an architectural office. In 1899 he designed silverwork and metalwork for Liberty & Co. By 1900 he was their main designer and the inspiration behind the Celtic revival. Apart from the Cymric (silver) and Tudric (pewter) ranges, he also designed carpets, textiles, jewellery and pottery, as well as teaching for Liberty's.

Knox, Edmund George Valpy, *pseudonym* Evoe 1881–1971
English humorist
He was the brother of Ronald Arbuthnott Knox. He joined the staff of *Punch* in 1921 and became editor from 1932 to 1949, contributing articles under his pseudonym. His best work was republished in book form and includes *Fiction as She is Wrote* (1923), *Quaint Specimens* (1925) and *Folly Calling* (1932).

Knox, Henry 1750–1806
US soldier
Born in Boston, Massachusetts, he ran his own bookshop there until the outbreak of the Revolutionary War. He commanded the Continental Army artillery and was a close friend and adviser to General George Washington throughout the war, wintering at Valley Forge and serving almost all the important engagements of the war. He became a major-general, followed Washington as commander of the army (1783–84), and was named US Secretary of War (1785–94).

Knox, John See panel p1054

Knox, Robert 1791–1862
Scottish anatomist
Born in Edinburgh, he studied medicine at Edinburgh University, in London, and later in Paris, prior to setting up an extramural anatomy school in Edinburgh. His need for a substantial supply of cadavers for dissection was met through the services of the disreputable William Burke and William Hare, who, unknown to Knox, obtained their corpses not by grave-robbing but by murder. Cold-shouldered by the medical establishment, Knox never obtained university employment but late in life succeeded in gaining employment as pathologist to the London Cancer Hospital, settling in Hackney. He published extensively on anatomy and physical anthropology.

Knox, Ronald Arbuthnott 1888–1957
English theologian and writer
Born in Birmingham, the son of an Anglican bishop, and educated at Eton and Balliol College, Oxford, he became a Fellow and lecturer at Trinity College, Oxford, in 1910, but resigned in 1917 when being converted to Catholicism. He was Catholic chaplain at Oxford from 1926 to 1939. He produced numerous works of apologetics, and his modern translation of the Bible, widely used by Roman Catholics, is especially noteworthy. He also wrote essays, and was a noted journalist and broadcaster. His autobiographical *A Spiritual Aeneid*, which describes his conversion, was published in 1918. He also wrote several detective novels, including *Still Dead* (1934), and *Let Dons Delight* (1939). He was the brother of Edmund George Knox, and a close friend of Evelyn Waugh.

Knox-Johnston, Sir Robin (William Robert Patrick) 1939–
English yachtsman
He was the first person to sail non-stop and singlehanded around the world in *Suhaili*—in 312 days from 14 June 1968 to 22 April 1969. The holder of the 1986 British Sailing Trans Atlantic Record (10 days, 14 hours and 9 minutes), he has since competed in many international races, and has won the Round Britian Race in both the two-man and crewed sections. In 1994 he was co-skipper with Peter Blake on *Enza NZ*, and achieved the world's fastest circumnavigation under sail—in 74 days, 22 hours, 17 minutes and 22 seconds. He has written over 13 books, and was knighted in 1995.

Knussen, (Stuart) Oliver 1952–
English composer and conductor
Born in Glasgow, of English parents, he showed early flair for composition, conducting the London Symphony Orchestra in his first symphony in 1968. Two symphonies have followed, together with numerous orchestral, chamber and vocal works, and operas (including, 1979–83, *Where the Wild Things Are*). He became co-director of the Aldeburgh Festival in 1983.

Knut Sveinsson, *also known as* Canute or Cnut the Great c.995–1035
King of England, Denmark and Norway
The son of Svein I Haraldsson, 'Fork-Beard', he accompanied his father on his attempted conquest of England (1013–14), but on his father's death withdrew to Denmark where his elder brother Harald had inherited the throne. The English recalled Ethelred II, the Unready, from refuge in Normandy to be their king again, but in 1015 Knut challenged him and gained all of England except London. When Ethelred died in 1016, Knut challenged his son and successor Edmund Ironside, defeated him at the Battle of Assandun in Essex (1016), and then concluded a treaty sharing the kingdom between them. Edmund died a month later, and Knut then became undisputed King of all England, banishing or executing all possible claimants to the throne from the royal dynasty of Wessex. He discarded his English mistress, Ælgifu of Northampton, and summoned Ethelred's widow, Emma, from Normandy to be his wife (their son was Hardaknut, King of Denmark and also, briefly, of England). He inherited the throne of Denmark from his brother (1018) and went to Denmark the following year to consolidate his power there. Later he helped to overthrow Olaf II Haraldsson (St Olaf) of Norway, and seized the throne there in 1030, installing his son Svein (by Ælgifu) as a puppet ruler. As King of England he brought firm government, justice and security from external threat, and showed reverence and generosity to the Church and its native saints. The story of his apparent attempt to turn back the tide has been totally misconstrued in folklore: in fact, he was trying to demonstrate to his courtiers that only God could control the tide, not man. When he died, his Anglo-Scandinavian Empire quickly disintegrated. He was succeeded in England by Harold I Knutsson, Harefoot, his younger son by Ælgifu, and then by Hardaknut, and in Norway Svein was immediately deposed by Magnus I Olafsson, who also inherited Denmark on the death of Hardaknut. Knut is regarded as one of the most effective early kings of England.

Knutsson, Karl See Karl VIII

Koch, C(hristopher) J(ohn) 1932–
Australian novelist
Born in Hobart, Tasmania, he published his first novel, *Boys in the Island*, in 1958 (rev edn 1974). It was followed by *Across the Sea Wall* (1965, rev edn 1982), a novel which moves between India and Australia and describes the betrayal of innocence. Koch's exotic thriller *The Year of Living Dangerously* (1978), set in Indonesia just before the downfall of Sukarno in the 1960s, became immensely popular through Peter Weir's 1982 film in which symbol, in the shape of Javanese 'Wayang' puppets, punctuates the action. He wrote *Crossing the Gap: A Novelist's Essays* appeared in 1993, and in the novel *Highways to a War* (1995) Koch returns to the theme of the journalist in a conflict.

Knox, John c.1513–1572
Scottish Protestant reformer, founder of the Church of Scotland

John Knox was born in or near Haddington, Lothian. He was educated there and probably at the University of St Andrews. From 1540 to 1543 he was a Catholic priest and acted as notary in Haddington. In 1544 he came into contact with **George Wishart**, now full of zeal for the Lutheran reformation, and Knox identified with him. Wishart was burned by Cardinal **David Beaton** in March 1546, and Beaton was murdered in May. The cardinal's murderers held the castle of St Andrews and Knox joined them with his pupils (1547). Here he was formally called to the ministry. A few months later the castle surrendered to the French, and for 18 months Knox remained a prisoner on the French galleys.

He was freed in February 1549, on the intercession of **Edward VI**, and for four years he made his home in England. In 1551 he was appointed one of six chaplains to Edward VI, and in 1552 declined an offer of the bishopric of Rochester. Knox was consulted by **Thomas Cranmer** regarding his 42 articles, and largely on Knox's re-presentation the thirty-eighth article was so couched as to commit the Church of England to the Genevan doctrine of the Eucharist. On the accession of **Mary I**, Knox fled to the Continent, where in Geneva he found a congregation of his own way of thinking; he remained there for the next two years, much influenced by **John Calvin**.

Knox returned to Scotland in 1559, now known for his *First Blast of the Trumpet Against the Monstrous Regiment of Women* (1558). He won over Perth and St Andrews to his cause, and won much support in Edinburgh. To counteract the influence of the regent, **Mary of Guise**, who was subsidized by France with money and soldiers, the Reformers, mainly through the efforts of Knox, sought the assistance of England; by the treaty of Leith and the death of the regent (1560) they became masters of the country, and the Church of Scotland was established. Ministers drew up the *First Book of Discipline*

(1561), with suggestions for the religious and educational organization of the country.

The return of **Mary, Queen of Scots** (1561) introduced new elements into the strife of parties; and during the six years of her reign Knox's attitude towards her amounted to open antagonism. The celebration of mass in Holyrood Chapel first roused his anger; and a sermon delivered by him in St Giles High Kirk led to the first of his famous interviews with Mary. After the murder of **David Rizzio**, Knox withdrew to Ayrshire, where he wrote part of his *History of the Reformation in Scotland*. During the later ascendancy of the Catholic party, he moved to St Andrews for safety.

In November 1572 he made his last public appearance at St Giles. He was buried in the churchyard then attached to St Giles. His first wife, Marjory Bowes, died in 1560, leaving him two sons. By his second wife, Margaret Stewart, daughter of Lord Ochiltree, whom (then not above 16) he married in 1564, he had three daughters.

Knox is the pre-eminent type of the religious Reformer: single-minded of purpose, and indifferent or hostile to every interest of life that did not advance his cause. He combined a shrewd worldly sense with an ever-ready wit and native humour. The impress of his individuality is stamped on every page of his *History of the Reformation in Scotland* (published 1586).

📖 J Ridley, *John Knox* (1968).

'To promote a woman to bear rule, superiority, dominion, or empire above any realm, nation, or city, is repugnant to nature, contumely to God, a thing most contrarious to his revealed will and approved ordinance; and, finally, it is the subversion of good order, of all equity and justice.' From *First Blast of the Trumpet against the Monstrous Regiment of Women* (1558).

Koch, Ed(ward) 1924–
US politician

Born in New York City, he practised law and became a member of the City Council (1967). Elected to Congress as a Democrat in 1969, he became Mayor of New York in 1978, and in the 1980s was a widely known political figure in the USA.

Koch, Ludwig 1881–1974
German naturalist, author, and lecturer

He followed a musical career in Paris and Milan, first as a violinist, then as a lieder and oratorio singer. He organized the 'Music in the Life of the Nations' exhibition (1927), and joined the staff of a recording company in 1928. He made the first outdoor recordings of songs of wild birds, and, coming to England in 1936, became known as a pioneer collector of bird and animal sounds. His joint publications include *Songs of Wild Birds* (1936) and *Animal Language* (1938).

Koch, Marita 1957–
German athlete

She was born in Wismar and studied paediatric medicine. Competing for East Germany, she won the Olympic 400 metres title in 1980 and the European title three times, remaining undefeated over 400 metres between 1977 and 1981. In the 200 metres race she won three indoor European championship titles and a world Student Games title. Dominating these two events for over a decade, she set the world 400 metres record seven times and the 200 metres four times, and succeeded in setting

16 world records in total. She retired in 1986 and married her coach, Wolfgang Meier. Her 400 metres record still stands.

Koch, (Heinrich Hermann) Robert 1843–1910
German physician, pioneer bacteriologist and Nobel Prize winner

Born in Klausthal in the Harz, he entered the University of Göttingen, and received his medical degree in 1866. He practised medicine at Hanover and elsewhere, and his work on wounds, septicaemia and splenic fever gained him a seat on the Imperial Board of Health in 1880. Koch proved that the anthrax bacillus was the sole cause of the disease, publishing his findings in 1876 and 1877, and discovered in 1882 the tubercle bacillus that causes tuberculosis. In 1883 he led a German expedition to Egypt and India, where he discovered the cholera bacillus, and in 1890 he produced a drug named tuberculin to prevent the development of tuberculosis. It proved to be ineffective as a cure, but useful in diagnosis. He became professor at Berlin and director of the Institute of Hygiene in 1885, and first director of the Berlin Institute for Infectious Diseases in 1891. He was awarded the Nobel Prize for physiology or medicine in 1905 for his work on tuberculosis. His formulation of essential scientific principles, known as 'Koch's postulates', established clinical bacteriology as a medical science in the 1890s.

Köchel, Ludwig Ritter von 1800–77
Austrian musicologist

Born in Stein, he compiled the famous catalogue of Mozart's works, arranging them in chronological order, and giving them the 'K' numbers now commonly used to identify them.

Kocher, Emil Theodor 1841–1917
Swiss surgeon and Nobel Prize winner

He was born and educated in Bern, where he became a professor (1871). He developed general surgical treatment of disorders of the thyroid gland, including goitre and thyroid tumours. His observations of patients suffering the long-term consequences of removing the thyroid gland helped elucidate some of its normal functions, and by the 1890s the isolation of one of the active thyroid hormones made replacement therapy possible. Kocher's clinic in Bern attracted many young surgeons from all over the world, and his textbook *Operative Surgery* (1894) went through many editions and translations. He also pioneered operations of the brain and spinal cord, and during World War I did experimental work on the trauma caused by gunshot wounds. He was the first surgeon to be awarded the Nobel Prize for physiology or medicine (1909).

Kock, Charles Paul de 1794–1871
French novelist

Born in Passy, he worked as a bank clerk at the age of 15, but turned to writing soon afterwards. He produced an enormously long series of novels about Parisian life. Vivacious and piquant, they were highly popular at the time, in both France and Great Britain. Titles include *Georgette* (1820, Eng trans 1843), *Mon voisin Raymond* (1822, Eng trans *My Neighbour Raymond*, 1903) and *L'Amant de la lune* (1847, 'The Lover of the Moon'). ▣ T Trimm, *Paul de Kock* (1877)

Kodály, Zoltán 1882–1967
Hungarian composer

Born in Kecskemét, he studied at the Budapest Conservatory where he became a professor. Among his best-known works are his *Háry János* suite (1926, 'John Háry'), *Dances of Galanta* (1933), and his many choral compositions, especially his *Psalmus Hungaricus* (1923, 'Hungarian Psalm') and *Te Deum* (1936). In 1913 he and Béla Bartók drafted a plan for a Hungarian folk-music collection, but the first volume was not published until 1951. He carried out important reforms in the field of musical education and developed an evolutionary system of training and sight-singing. ▣ P M Young, *Zoltán Kodály: A Hungarian Musician* (1964)

Koechlin, Charles Louis Eugène 1867–1950
French composer and writer on music

Born in Paris, he studied under Jules Massenet and Gabriel Fauré at the Paris Conservatory. Colourful and inventive in his orchestration, he composed symphonies, symphonic poems, choral-orchestral works (including seven based on Rudyard Kipling's *Jungle Book*), film music and works inspired by Hollywood, such as the *Seven Stars Symphony* (1933), and wrote prolifically and eclectically for a wide range of vocal and chamber combinations. His writings included studies of French music and treatises on music theory.

Koehler, Florence 1861–1944
US artist-craftswoman and jeweller

She lived and worked in Chicago, which became one of the two centres for the Arts and Crafts Movement, Boston being the other. The Chicago Arts and Crafts Society, which was founded in 1897, helped to promote Koehler's work. From around 1900 her jewellery designs became extremely popular in aesthetic and intellectual circles. Her designs for jewellery in the Art Nouveau style owed more to France than England. Along with the work of L C Tiffany, the craft jewellery produced by Koehler is considered to be the best of the period.

Koestler, Arthur 1905–83
British writer and journalist, political refugee and prisoner

Born in Budapest, he studied pure science at Vienna, worked on a collective farm in Palestine in 1926, then became a political correspondent and later a scientific editor for a German newspaper group. Dismissed as a Communist, he travelled in Russia (1932–33), but became disillusioned, breaking with the party finally in 1938, as described in *The God that Failed* (1950). He reported the Spanish Civil War (1936–37), was imprisoned under sentence of death by General Franco, as retold in *Spanish Testament* (1938) and *Dialogue with Death* (1942), and again by the French (1940). He escaped from German-occupied France via the French Foreign Legion and eventually joined the Pioneer Corps. These experiences provided the background for his first novel in English, *Arrival and Departure* (1943). The degeneration of revolutionary idealism in Roman times under Spartacus he portrayed in *The Gladiators* (1939), which was followed by the striking modern equivalent, *Darkness at Noon* (1940), Koestler's masterpiece and one of the great political novels of the century. *The Act of Creation* (1964) and *The Case of the Midwife Toad* (1971) were among his later works. *Bricks to Babel* (1980) is a selection from his non-fiction writings. He and his wife, active members of the Voluntary Euthanasia Society, committed suicide together when he became terminally ill. Under the terms of his will, the Koestler Chair of Parapsychology was established at the University of Edinburgh (1985). ▣ I Hamilton, *Koestler: a biography* (1982)

Koetsu, Honnami 1558–1637
Japanese calligrapher and decorative artist

Born in Kyoto, he started his career as a tea-master, and became famous for his Raku and lacquer ware, but his numerous interests made him one of the most creative figures in the history of Japanese art. He collaborated with the master of the later decorative style, Nonomura Sotatsu (1576–1643), founding the Kōrin school of Japanese painters. In 1615 he founded Takagamine, a community of artists and craftsmen in northern Kyoto which infused the Japanese art world with new vigour. He was considered one of the three best calligraphists of his day, and invented a new kind of poem scroll.

Koffka, Kurt 1886–1941
German psychologist, co-founder of the Gestalt school of psychology

He was born in Berlin. At the University of Geissen he took part in experiments in perception with Wolfgang Köhler, conducted by Max Wertheimer, and founded with them the Gestalt school of psychology, based on the concept that the organized whole is something more than the sum of the parts into which it can be logically analysed. He later taught at Oxford, England, and at Smith College, USA. He was the author of *Principles of Gestalt Psychology* (1935).

Kohl, Helmut 1930–
German statesman

The son of a tax official, he was born in Ludwigshafen am Rhein and studied law, attending the Universities of Frankfurt and Heidelberg, after a brief career in the chemical industry. He joined the Christian Democrats after the war, and became chairman for the Rhineland-Palatinate in 1956, and minister-president of the state in 1969. He moved to Bonn as a member of the federal parliament (1976) and was chosen to run as Christian Democrat and Christian Social Union candidate for the chancellorship. Although Helmut Schmidt retained power through his coalition with the Free Democratic

Party, Kohl made the CDU/CSU the largest party in parliament. In 1980 he was replaced as chancellor candidate by **Franz-Josef Strauss**. Schmidt again won, but the sudden collapse of his coalition in 1982 led to Kohl's installation as interim Chancellor, and in the elections of 1983 the CDU/CSU increased its number of seats, and formed a government. Very conservative, yet not in favour of an economy uncontrolled by state intervention, and anti-Soviet though by no means unquestioningly pro-USA, Kohl maintained an essentially central course between political extremes. From 1984 to 1986 Kohl was implicated in the 'Flick bribes scandal' concerned with the illegal business funding of political parties, but he was cleared of all charges of perjury and deception in 1986 and was re-elected as Chancellor in the 1987 Bundestag elections and again in 1990 and 1994. He played a decisive part in the integration of the former East Germany into the Federal Republic. In 1991, six weeks after united Germany's first national elections, he announced a coalition Government that, while maintaining CDU/CSU dominance in the key defence and Labour and Social Affairs Ministries, reflected the strength of the vote for the Free Democrats, with the FDP's **Hans-Dietrich Genscher** remaining as Foreign Secretary. The Kohl era ended in 1998 with the election victory of the Social Democrats, led by Gerhard Schröder.

Köhler, Georges Jean Franz 1946–95
German immunochemist and Nobel Prize winner

Born in Munich, he studied at the University of Freiburg and joined **Cesar Milstein** at the Medical Research Council Laboratory in Cambridge, where they discovered how to produce hybridomas—hybrid cells created by fusing an antibody-generating cell with a cancer cell. Hybridomas possess infinite life and are used to produce a single type of antibody against a specific antigen (foreign body). Their use opened the way to a precise examination of antibody structure. Köhler moved to the Basle Institute of Immunology in 1976, and in 1984 he became one of three directors of the **Max Planck** Institute of Immune Biology in Freiburg. He continued his research, studying the pattern of inheritance of hybridoma cells, and demonstrated that structural mutants of immunoglobulins could be formed by hybridomas (1980). More recently he has studied the carbohydrate component of immunoglobulins. Commercially produced monoclonal antibodies, derived from Köhler's hybridoma research, now provide an unambiguous and sensititive way of identifying and quantifying a wide range of substances, and are used in pregnancy and drug testing, and in the diagnosis and treatment of cancer and other diseases. For this outstanding contribution to the wellbeing of humans, Köhler shared with Milstein and **Niels Jerne** the 1984 Nobel Prize for physiology or medicine.

Köhler, Wolfgang 1887–1967
German psychologist, co-founder of the Gestalt school of psychology

Born in Estonia, he was director of the anthropoid research station in the Canary Islands (1913–20), where he became an authority on problem-solving in animals. He later held chairs of psychology at Berlin, and at Swathmore and Dartmouth colleges in the USA. He was the co-founder with **Kurt Koffka** of Gestalt psychology.

Kohlrausch, Friedrich Wilhelm Georg 1840–1910
German physicist

He was born in Rinteln, Niedersachen, the son of a well-known physicist, Rudolph Kohlrausch (1809–58), and held professorships of physics successively at the universities of Göttingen (1866–70), Zurich (1870–71), Darmstadt (1871–75), Würzburg (1875–88) and Strassburg (1888–95). In 1895 he succeeded **Hermann von Helmholtz** as president of the Physikalisch Technische Reichsanstalt in Charlottenburg, Berlin. Noted for his researches on magnetism and electricity, his most important contribution was his investigation of the conductivity of electrolytic solutions, which led to 'Kohlrausch's law' of independent ion migration. He published *Leitfaden der praktischen Physik* (1870), one of the first textbooks on physical laboratory methods, which was translated into English.

Koivisto, Mauno 1925–
Finnish politician

A Social Democrat, he served as Minister of Finance (1966–67) and Prime Minister (1968–70, 1979–81). As Governor of the Bank of Finland after 1968 (retaining office while serving as Prime Minister, with another politician serving as acting governor), he presided over a period of tight monetary policy which helped to consolidate the country's economic growth. President from 1982 to 1994, he had a more relaxed political style than his predecessor, **Urho Kekkonen**, although he maintained the latter's policy of close cooperation with the USSR until its demise in 1991.

Kokoschka, Oskar 1886–1980
British artist and writer

Born in Pöchlarn, Austria, of Czech and Austrian parentage, he studied from 1904 to 1908 in Vienna. In Berlin he painted portraits and worked for the avant-garde periodical *Der Sturm*, as well as making striking posters and lithographs. Seriously wounded in World War I, he afterwards taught at the Dresden Academy of Art (1919–24); thereafter he travelled widely, and painted many Expressionist landscapes in Spain, France and England. In 1938 he fled to England for political reasons, becoming naturalized in 1947, and painted a number of politically symbolic works, as well as portraits and landscapes. In the 1920s he also wrote a number of Expressionist dramas, including *Orpheus und Eurydike*. He lived in Switzerland from 1953.

Kolbe, (Adolph Wilhelm) Hermann 1818–84
German chemist

Born in Elliehausen, near Göttingen, he studied chemistry under **Friedrich Wöhler** (1838). He was assistant to **Robert Bunsen** in Marburg (1842) and to **Lyon Playfair** (1845) at the Museum of Economic Geology in London. In 1847 he returned to Marburg, and succeeded Bunsen in the chair in 1851. In 1865 he went to Leipzig where he remained until his retirement. He was a successful teacher, a brilliant experimentalist and he accomplished a number of important syntheses; he is best known for his electrolytic procedure for the preparation of alkanes.

Kolchak, Aleksandr Vasilevich 1874–1920
Russian naval commander

In World War I he was in command of the Black Sea fleet. After the Russian Revolution of 1917, he went to Omsk as War Minister in the anti-Bolshevik government, and cleared Siberia, in co-operation with General **Anton Denikin**, as leader of the White Army. In 1919 Omsk fell to the Bolsheviks, and Kolchak was betrayed and shot. ⌑K
A Bogdanov, *Admiral Kolchak: biograficheskaia porest-khronika* (1993)

Koldewey, Robert 1855–1925
German archaeologist

Born in Blankenburg am Harz, Brunswick, he excavated several sites in Asia Minor and Turkey, including Baalbek in East Lebanon. His major work was his excavations of the remains of the city of Babylon (1899–1917), where his discoveries included the Processional Street, the Ishtar Gate, and the site of the Tower of Babel.

Kolff, Willem Johan 1911–
US physician, developer of the artificial kidney

He was born in Leyden, the Netherlands, and studied medicine there, receiving his MD in 1946 from Groningen University. Kolff constructed his first rotating drum artificial kidney in the wartime Netherlands and treated his first patient with it in 1943. This dialysis machine used a series of membranes to remove impurities from the blood which would ordinarily be filtered out by the healthy kidney. From 1950, when he moved to the USA, he worked primarily at the Cleveland Clinic and Utah University, developing the artificial kidney further. He was also involved in research on the heart–lung machine used during open-heart surgery.

Kolingba, André Birthdate unavailable
Central African Republic general and politician

As chief of the armed forces of the Central African Republic, Kolingba became President of Central Africa following the overthrow of President David Dacko in a coup in 1981; he also held the posts of Minister of Defence and of War Veterans (1981–83, 1984–91), and of Prime Minister (1981–91). In 1985 the Cabinet became largely civilian and in 1986 Kolingba created and was first leader of the Central African Democratic rally (RDC). Constitutional change in 1992 allowed multi-party elections, and his presidency ended in 1993 when he lost in the presidential elections.

Kollár, Ján 1793–1852
Slovak poet

He was born in Mosovce, Slovakia, and educated at the University of Jena. He became Protestant pastor at Pest (1813–49), and then Professor of Slavonic Archaeology at Vienna. He was a proponent of a cultural Pan–Slavic union, urging the Slavonic peoples to co-operate with each other. He wrote a cycle of sonnets, which eventually rose to over 600 in number, and compiled an edition of Slovakian folk-songs. 📖 A Mráz, *Ján Kollár Literarna tudia* (1952)

Kölliker, Rudolph Albert von 1817–1905
Swiss anatomist and embryologist

He was born in Zurich, and attended the university there before proceeding to Bonn and Berlin. He became Professor of Anatomy in Zurich in 1845, and later moved to Würzburg University (1847). His early researches examined the spermatozoa of invertebrates, and later he worked on cell structure, employing cell theory for interpreting embryonic development. His *Manual of Human Histology* (1852) set new standards of exactitude for the subject, and his special emphasis upon the significance of the nucleus in cell physiology helped to establish cytology as a specialization.

Kollontai, Aleksandra Mikhailovna, *née* Domontovich 1872–1952
Russian feminist and revolutionary

Born in St Petersburg into an upper-class family, she rejected her privileged upbringing and became interested in socialism. Married to an army officer, she nevertheless joined the Russian Social Democratic Party, and for her revolutionary behaviour was exiled to Germany in 1908. In 1915 she travelled widely in the USA, begging the nation not to join World War I, and urging the acceptance of socialism. In 1917, following the Revolution, she returned to Russia, becoming Commissar for Public Welfare. In this post she agitated for domestic and social reforms, including collective childcare and easier divorce proceedings. Although her private liaisons shocked the party, she was appointed minister to Norway (1923–25, 1927–30), Mexico (1926–27) and Sweden (1930–45), becoming ambassador in 1943, the world's first woman ambassador. She played a vital part in negotiating the end of the Soviet–Finnish war (1944). Her writings, like *The New Morality and the Working Class* (1918), and a collection of short stories, *Love of Worker Bees* (1923), aroused much controversy because of their open discussion of sexuality and women's place in society and the economy. Her autobiography, written in 1926, was not published in Russia.

Kollwitz, Käthe, *née* Schmidt 1867–1945
German graphic artist and sculptor

Born in Königsberg, East Prussia (now Kaliningrad, Russia), she was educated in Königsberg and in Berlin, where she studied drawing and married a medical student, Karl Kollwitz, who went on to work in a poor quarter of the city. Although she has been called an Expressionist, she was uninterested in the fashions of modern art. Influenced by **Max Klinger**'s prints, she chose serious, tragic subjects, with strong social or political content, for example her early etchings, the *Weavers' Revolt* (1897–98) and the *Peasants' War* (1902–08). From c.1910 she preferred lithography, and after being expelled by the Nazis in 1933 from the Prussian Academy (of which she was the first woman member) she made a moving series of eight prints on the theme of *Death* (1934–35). Her sculpture also shows compassion for suffering, as in *The Complaint* (1938, Munich, in bronze). In 1932 she executed the bronze war memorial at Dixmuiden, Flanders.

Kolmogorov, Andrei Nikolayevich 1903–87
Soviet mathematician

Born in Tambov, he studied at Moscow State University and remained there throughout his career, as professor from 1931 and director of the Institute of Mathematics from 1933. He worked on a wide range of topics in mathematics, including the theory of functions of a real variable, functional analysis, mathematical logic, and topology. He is particularly remembered for his creation of the axiomatic theory of probability. His work with **Aleksandr Khinchin** on **Markov** processes, in which he formulated the partial differential equations which bear his name, was of lasting significance. He also worked in applied mathematics, on the theory of turbulence, on celestial mechanics, on information theory, and in cybernetics.

Komenský, John Amos See **Comenius, John Amos**

Komorowski-Bór, Tadeusz 1895–1966
Polish soldier

He was born in Lwów. As 'General Bór' he led the heroic but unsuccessful Warsaw rising against the occupying Germans in 1944, and settled in England after World War II.

Konev, Ivan Stepanovich 1897–1973
Soviet military commander

Born in Lodeyno, he was drafted into the Tsarist army in 1916, and joined the Red Army and the Communist Party in 1918. After graduating from the Frunze Military Academy in 1934 he held various commands, including in the Far East, before the USSR was drawn into World War II, during which he commanded several different fronts against the Germans, then became Commander-in-Chief, Ground Forces (1946–50), first Deputy Minister of Defence, and Commander-in-Chief of the Warsaw Pact forces (1956–60).

König, Friedrich 1774–1833
German printer, inventor of the steam printing-press

He was born in Eisleben, and in 1810, through the support of a printer in London, obtained a patent for a press. A second patent was obtained in 1811 for a cylinder-press, improved and in 1814 adopted by *The Times*. He also made steam printing-presses near Würzburg.

Koninck, Philips de 1619–88
Dutch painter

Born in Amsterdam, he was possibly a pupil of Rembrandt, and certainly a member of the same artistic circle. He painted portraits, religious subjects and scenes of everyday life, but his best paintings by far were panoramic landscapes with large areas of sky. (He was also the captain of a barge which crossed from Leyden to Rotterdam.)

Konoe Fumimaro 1891–1945
Japanese politician

From an aristocratic family, he inherited the title of prince from his father, and became a prominent member of the Upper House (House of Peers). He favoured the growth of Japanese influence in Asia, criticizing what he felt was an Anglo-American attempt to preserve the status quo. During his first term as Prime Minister (1937–39) he led Japan into full-scale war with China in an attempt to create a New Order in East Asia. During his second term (1940–41), Japan's relations with the USA worsened, especially after his government signed a military alliance with the Axis powers (Tripartite Pact) in 1940. He resigned when his offer of having a summit meeting with President Franklin D Roosevelt was rebuffed. Although Konoe was a member of the first post-war government (1945), he was indicted as a war criminal by the US occupation authorities. He committed suicide on the day he was to turn himself in for confinement and trial.

Konstantin Nikolayevich See Constantin Nikolayevich

Konstantinov, Aleko 1863–97
Bulgarian story writer and satirist

An inveterate traveller with a keen sense of the division in his country between East and West, he invented the most famous of all Bulgarian characters, Bay Ganyu (*Bay Ganyu*, 1895), a 'partisan thug' who travels about at home and abroad selling various articles. Konstantinov called himself 'the lucky one'—until his sharp and irreverent pen got him murdered. ▯ C Manning and R Smal-Stocki, *The History of Modern Bulgarian Literature* (1960)

Konwicki, Tadeusz 1926–
Lithuanian dissident writer and filmmaker

After fighting with guerrilla forces in Lithuania against both German and Russian occupation in World War II he moved to Poland, where he has made his home. In the 1950s, his *Przy budowie* (1950, 'At the Construction Site') was a much-prized novel of the Party as an engineer of souls. He was denounced in 1968, and *Mala apokalipsa* (1979, Eng trans *A Minor Apocalypse*, 1983) was banned. *Wschody i zachody księzyca* (1982, Eng trans *Moonrise, Moonset*, 1988) is about the early struggles of the Solidarity movement. His films include *Salto* (1965) and *Ostatni dzień lata* (1958, 'The Last Day of the Summer'). ▯ J Wegner, *Konwicki* (1973)

Koons, Jeff 1955–
US sculptor

Born in York, Pennsylvania, he trained at the Maryland Institute College of Art, Baltimore, and the School of Art Institute of Chicago. He chooses banal subjects, such as pet animals or vacuum cleaners, and instructs traditional silversmiths or porcelain manufacturers to re-create them, as in *Rabbit* (1986, Saatchi Collection, London). His *Michael Jackson and Bubbles* (1988, Sonnabend Gallery, New York) and *Ushering In Banality* (1988, Stedelijk Museum, Amsterdam) are also typical examples. From 1989 until they separated he worked with his wife Llona (La Cicciolina) on *Made In Heaven*, a series of explicitly erotic sculptures and posters which blur the distinction between pornography and innocence and challenge contemporary ideas about art, as in *Bourgeois Bust* (1991).

Koopmans, Tjalling Charles 1910–85
US economist and Nobel Prize winner

Born in 's-Graveland in the Netherlands, and educated at Utrecht and Leyden universities, he emigrated to the USA in 1940, and worked for a shipping firm, devising a system to optimize transport costs. He was Professor of Economics at Chicago (1948–55) and Yale (1955–81). He shared the 1975 Nobel Prize for economics (with Leonid Kantorovich) for his contributions to the theory of optimal allocation of resources.

Köpfel, Wolfgang Fabricius See Capito, Wolfgang Fabricius

Kopp, Hermann Franz Moritz 1817–92
German chemist and historian of chemistry

Born in Hanau, Hesse, he studied chemistry at Heidelberg, Marburg and Giessen. In 1841 he became *Privatdozent* at Giessen, where he was promoted to Extraordinary Professor in 1843. When Justus Liebig moved to Munich in 1852, Kopp became Ordinary Professor jointly with Heinrich Will, but resigned after one year. However, he continued to work in Giessen until he was appointed professor at Heidelberg (1863), where he remained until his death. He became an Honorary Fellow of the Chemical Society in 1849. His research work was largely concerned with the relationship between the physical properties of elements or compounds and their chemical composition. He published a notable work on the history of chemistry, *Geschichte der Chemie*, (4 vols, 1843–47).

Koppel, Herman D(avid) 1908–98
Danish composer and pianist

Born in Copenhagen, he was educated at the Royal Danish Academy of Music, and became a professor there in 1955. He made his debut as a composer in 1929 and as a pianist in 1930. His many compositions include seven symphonies, four piano concertos, six string quartets, an opera (1970, *Macbeth*), a ballet, and music for theatre, film and radio. He won the Ove Christensen honorary prize in 1952 and the Carl Nielsen prize in 1958. His son, Thomas Herman Koppel (1944–), is also a composer.

Köprülü late 17th century
Turkish politicians

The name of four Turkish grand viziers who effectively controlled the Ottoman government for most of the late 17th century. Mehmet Köprülü (d.1661) was an Albanian by birth, who rose from working in the imperial kitchen to become grand vizier (1656), when he was in his seventies. He ruthlessly consolidated his power and rebuilt the Ottoman fleet for service against the Venetians. He retired shortly before his death in 1661 in favour of his son, Fazil Ahmed Köprülü (d.c.1676), who built on the foundation laid down by his father. He led the army against Austria, securing advantageous terms at the peace of Vasvar (Eisenberg) in 1664, and against Crete, which was taken in 1669. On his death his place was taken by his foster-brother Kara Mustafa, who led the Ottomans to the gates of Venice. Fazil Ahmed's younger brother, Fazil Mustafa Köprülü (d.1691), became grand vizier in 1689. Like his predecessors, he reformed the administration and reorganized the army. He showed particular concern for non-Muslim subjects in the Balkans. He was killed in battle near Karlowitz.

Korbut, Olga Valentinovna 1956–
Soviet gymnast

Born in Grodno, Belorussia, she captivated the world at the 1972 Olympics at Munich with her supple grace, and gave gymnastics a new lease of life as a sport. She won a gold medal as a member of the winning Soviet team, as well as individual golds in the beam and floor exercises and silver for the parallel bars. After retiring, she became a coach.

Korda, Sir Alexander, *originally* Sándor Laszlo Kellner 1893–1956
British film producer

Born in Pusztatúrpáztó, Hungary, he began as a newspaperman in Budapest. He became a film producer there, then in Vienna, Berlin and Hollywood, where he directed for First National, before moving to the UK where he founded London Film Productions and Denham studios (1932). His many films as producer include *The Private Life of Henry VIII* (1932) which he also directed, *Rembrandt* (1936), *The Thief of Baghdad* (1940), *The Third Man* (1949), *The Red Shoes* (1948) and *Richard III* (1956). He was knighted in 1942. 📖 Karol Kulik, *Alexander Korda: The Man Who Could Work Miracles* (1975)

Koresh, David, *originally* Vernon Howell 1959–93
US cult leader

Born in West Texas, he founded the Branch Davidian sect, a breakaway from the Seventh Day Adventist Church. A self-proclaimed Messiah, he attracted a following of largely vulnerable and insecure people to his compound at Mount Carmel. His apocalyptic pronouncements led to growing concern and the authorities laid siege to the heavily armed compound, the affair ending tragically with the deaths of many cult members, including Koresh himself.

Korin, Ogata 1658–1716
Japanese calligrapher and designer of pottery and lacquer ware

Born in Kyoto, a relative of **Honnami Koetsu**, he first trained in the Kano school, but he later followed the style initiated by Nonomura Sotatsu. His artistic career only fully started in 1697 when he went virtually bankrupt. He first made designs for his younger brother's pottery, but eventually devoted himself entirely to painting. He became the greatest master of the decorative style of painting of his generation, a style which is associated with the new wealthy and cultured merchant class of the Tokugawa period, into which he was born. His work is characterized by simplified composition, an emphasis on decorative power in spacing and patterning of forms, and the use of dramatic colour contrast.

Kornberg, Arthur 1918–
US biochemist and Nobel Prize winner

Born in Brooklyn, New York City, he graduated in medicine from Rochester University, becoming director of enzyme research at the National Institutes of Health (1947–52) and head of the microbiology department of Washington University (1953–59). He was appointed professor at Stanford University in 1959. In studies of *Escherichia coli*, Kornberg discovered DNA polymerase, the enzyme that synthesizes new DNA. For this work he was awarded the 1959 Nobel Prize for physiology or medicine jointly with **Severo Ochoa**. Kornberg became the first to synthesize viral DNA (1967) and wrote *DNA Replication* (1980). 📖 *For the Love of Enzymes: The Odyssey of a Biochemist* (1993)

Kornberg, Sir Hans Leo 1928–
British biochemist

Born in Herford, Germany, he studied at the University of Sheffield, spent two years in postdoctoral work at Yale and in New York, and then joined **Hans Krebs**'s Medical Research Council Cell Metabolism Research Unit in Oxford (1955). He later moved on to the chair of biochemistry at Cambridge (1975–95), before becoming Professor of Biology at Boston University (1995–). He has worked mainly in microbial metabolism and is particularly noted for the discovery of the glyoxylate

cycle, which explains how bacteria grow on fatty acids, and how seeds convert fats to carbohydrates during germination. Elected Fellow of the Royal Society in 1965, he has received many honorary degrees and awards, and has been a member of several research councils, Chairman of the Royal Commission on Environmental Pollution, and a trustee of the Nuffield Foundation and the Wellcome Trust. He was knighted in 1978.

Körner, Karl Theodor 1791–1813
German lyric poet

Born in Dresden, he wrote plays and fiery patriotic songs such as *Leier und Schwert* (1814, 'Lyre and Sword'), which contained the *Schwert-Lied* ('Sword Song'), written shortly before his death in battle during the Napoleonic Wars, a patriotic end which inflated his literary reputation. 📖 K Bergens, *Theodor Körner* (1912)

Korngold, Erich Wolfgang 1897–1957
US composer

Born in Brno, Moravia, (now in Czech Republic), his teachers included **Alexander von Zemlinsky** in Vienna. From the age of 12, he achieved success there and throughout Germany as a composer of chamber, orchestral and stage works in late-Romantic vein. His most distinguished operas were *Violanta* (1916) and *Die tote Stadt* (1920, 'The Dead City'). A professor at the Vienna State Academy of Music from 1930, he emigrated to Hollywood in 1934 (becoming a US citizen in 1943), and composed a series of film scores, two of which, *Anthony Adverse* (1936) and *Robin Hood* (1938), received Academy Awards. His postwar works included a violin and a cello concerto and a symphony. He was the son of the eminent music critic Julius Korngold (1860–1945).

Kornilov, Lavr Georgiyevich 1870–1918
Russian general

Born in western Siberia, he was a Cossack. With previous intelligence and diplomatic experience, he was a divisional commander in World War I, tried to turn the tide against the Germans by an offensive in June 1917 and in August 1917 marched on Petrograd (now St Petersburg), in an attempt to set up a military directorate. He was forced to surrender by **Aleksandr Kerensky**, but subsequently escaped. Kornilov then organized a Cossack force against the Bolsheviks, but fell in battle.

Korolenko, Vladimir Galaktionovich 1853–1921
Russian novelist

He was born in Zhitomir, Ukraine, and was exiled in Siberia (1879–85) for revolutionary activities. On his return, he published his most famous story, *Son Makara* (1885, 'Makar's Dream'), and earned a reputation as a supporter of the underprivileged. He was involved in the Populist Movement, and opposed the Bolshevik Revolution in 1917. He is best known for his short stories, but left an epic autobiography, *Istoriya moyego sovremennika* (1905–21,'The History of my Contemporary'), unfinished at his death. 📖 M Comtet, *Vladimir Korolenko, 1853–1921: l'homme et l'oeuvre* (1975)

Korolev, Sergei Pavlovich 1907–66
Soviet aircraft engineer and rocket designer

Born in Zhitomir, Ukraine, he graduated from the Moscow Higher Technical School in 1929. He became a pilot and designed successful gliders and a light plane (SK-4) in 1930. In 1931 he formed the Moscow Group for Investigating Jet Propulsion, which launched the USSR's first liquid-propelled rocket in 1933. During World War II he worked on aircraft jet-assisted take-off systems. By 1949 he was engaged in high-altitude sounding flights employing rockets. As chief designer of Soviet spacecraft he directed the USSR's space programme with historic · 'firsts' such as the first orbiting Sputniks in 1957 and the first manned space flight (Yuri Gagarin) in 1961, the *Vostok* and *Voskhod* manned spacecraft, and the *Cosmos* series of satellites.

Korošec, Anton 1872–1940
Slovene politician

He studied theology at Maribor and was ordained priest, taking a leading role in the Slovene People's Party before World War I. He became president of the coalition of South Slav members in the Austrian parliament (1917) and president of the National Council of Slovenes, Croats and Serbs in Zagreb (1918). After the creation of the Kingdom of Serbs, Croats and Slovenes (later Yugoslavia), he served as Vice-Premier (1919). Conservative and opportunistic, he continued to represent the interests of the Slovenes and was the only non-Serb inter-war Prime Minister and Minister of the Interior (1928–29). During the dictatorship of Alexander I, he was interned on the island of Hvar (1933) but was released during the regency to serve again as Minister of the Interior (1935–38).

Korzybski, Alfred Habdank Skarbek 1879–1950
US scholar and philosopher of language

Born in Warsaw, Poland, he was sent by the Russian army on a military mission to North America during World War I. He remained there, becoming a US citizen in 1940. He is best known as the originator of general semantics, a system of linguistic philosophy concerned with the study of language as a representation of reality, which aims to increase people's ability to analyse the meanings and uses of words in order to promote mutual understanding between individuals and the accurate transmission of ideas from one generation to another. He was founder and director of the Institute of General Semantics in Chicago. His major work on general semantics is *Science and Sanity: An Introduction to Non-Aristotelian Systems and General Semantics* (1933). He also wrote *Manhood of Humanity: the Science and Art of Human Engineering* (1921).

Kościuszko, Tadeusz Andrzej Bonawentura 1746–1817
US–Polish soldier and patriot

Born near Slonim, Lithuania, he was trained in the military academies in Warsaw and Paris. In 1776 he went to North America, where he fought for the colonists in the American Revolution (1775–83) and became a US citizen. He returned to Poland in 1784, and when Russia attacked his country in 1792 held Dubienka for five days, with 4,000 men against 18,000. In 1794, he took charge of a national uprising in Kraków, being appointed dictator and Commander-in-Chief. Despite defeating a greatly superior force of Russians at Racławice, he had to withdraw to Warsaw, winning popular support by suspending serfdom. He defended the city but, overpowered in the Battle of Maciejowice (10 October 1794) and wounded, was taken prisoner. Emperor Paul of Russia freed him in 1796. He went first to England, then to the USA, and in 1798 to France. In 1806 he refused to support Napoleon I's plan for the restoration of Poland, the Grand Duchy, because it would not secure genuine independence. Similarly in 1815 he refused to support Alexander I's so-called Congress Poland. He settled in Switzerland in 1816.

Kosinski, Jerzy Nikodem 1933–91
US novelist

Born in Łódź, Poland, into a Jewish family, he evaded victimization during the Nazi Holocaust. He was educated in political science at Łódź University, and taught there (1955–57) before emigrating to the USA (1957). His novels espouse a belief in survival at all costs, his characters machinating to make the most of a given situation. He wrote two polemical books, *The Future is Ours, Comrade* (1960) and *No Third Path* (1962), under the pseudonym Joseph Novak. The trauma of war had rendered him

(literally) speechless and his novels, particularly the quasi-autobiographical *The Painted Bird* (1965), is a classic of Holocaust literature. Later works include *Being There* (1971), *Blind Date* (1977) and *Passion Play* (1979). A compulsive story teller who invented many myths surrounding his own life, he committed suicide in 1991. 🕮 P R Lilly Jnr, *Words in Search of Victims* (1988)

Kossel, Albrecht 1853–1927
German physiological chemist and Nobel Prize winner

Born in Rostock, Germany, he studied medicine at the University of Strassburg and worked under Felix Hoppe-Seyler. In 1895 he became Professor of Physiology and director of the Physiological Institute, Marburg, and he was later professor at Heidelberg (1901–23). He investigated the chemistry of cells and proteins. He was able to explain that in a blood leukaemia, the 'guanide' found in the blood in large amounts derived from decomposed young nucleated erythrocytes. He also discovered histidine in spermatozoa (1896). In 1910 he was awarded the Nobel Prize for physiology or medicine.

Kossel, Walther 1888–1956
German physicist

The son of Albrecht Kossel, he became Professor of Physics at the universities of Kiel (1921) and Danzig (1932), did much research on atomic physics, especially on Röntgen spectra, and was renowned for his physical theory of chemical valency.

Kossoff, Leon 1926–
English painter

Born in London, he studied at St Martin's School of Art, at the Borough Polytechnic, under David Bomberg (1949–53), and at the Royal College of Art (1953–56). Painting figures in interiors and views of London from the age of 12, he follows Bomberg and Chaim Soutine in his expressive style, using very thick impasto to portray bomb sites, building sites, railways, churches, schools, and even swimming pools. He often repeats subjects, such as *Christ Church, Spitalfields*, and his brother *Chaim*. In 1995 he exhibited at the Venice Biennale and had a major retrospective of his work at the Tate Gallery, London, in 1996.

Kossuth, Lajos 1802–94
Hungarian revolutionary

Born in Monok, near Zemplin, he practised law for a time, in 1832 was a deputy at the Diet of Pressburg, and edited a journal. The issue of a lithographed paper led, in 1837, to his imprisonment. Liberated in 1840, he became editor of the *Pesti Hirlap*, advocating extreme Liberal views. In 1847, sent by *Pesti* to the Diet, he became Leader of the Opposition, and after the French Revolution of 1848 demanded an independent government for Hungary. In April 1849 he induced the National Assembly at Debrecen to declare that the Habsburg dynasty had forfeited the throne. Appointed Provisional Governor of Hungary, he tried unsuccessfully to secure the intervention of the Western Powers, and he resigned his dictatorship in favour of Artúr Görgey. After the defeat at Temesvár, he fled to Turkey. Freed in 1851, he went to England, where, as subsequently in the USA, he was respectfully received. When, in 1867, Francis Deák effected the reconciliation of Hungary with the dynasty, Kossuth retired from active political life, and afterwards lived mostly in Turin.

Kosterlitz, Hans Walter 1903–96
Scottish pharmacologist

Born in Germany, he was educated at Heidelberg, Freiburg and Berlin universities. From 1928 until 1933 he worked in Berlin as a radiologist under Wilhelm His. With the rise of the Nazis he moved to the department of physiology, University of Aberdeen, gained British medical qualifications, and stayed in the department for many years. His researches concentrated on carbohydrate biochemistry, although in the early 1950s he turned to the physiology and pharmacology of the autonomic nervous system, and began examining the effects of morphine and other opiate-like drugs. In 1968 he was appointed Professor of Pharmacology (1968–73) and later became director of the university's drug addiction research unit (1973–96). Here he was joined by **John Hughes**, with whom he discovered the existence of naturally occurring opiates by comparing the physiological effects of known opiates with extracts made from brain tissue. They discovered that the two materials had the same effects. Further analysis revealed two almost identical chemicals which they named enkephalins, and quickly proved that they were powerful analgesics. Their work has been an important stimulus in recent studies in brain chemistry and pharmacology. He was elected FRS in 1978.

Kosuth, Joseph 1945–
US artist

Born in Toledo, Ohio, he trained at Toledo, Cleveland, and New York, where he also studied philosophy and anthropology at the New School for Social Research. Around 1965 he conceived the series which included *One and Three Chairs* (Museum of Modern Art, New York), where an object, a photograph of an object, and its dictionary definition were juxtaposed, the first of many such installations involving texts and neon lighting to address aspects of an idea and its presentation. Since the early 1980s he focused on the writings of **Ludwig Wittgenstein** and **Sigmund Freud**. In 1991 he exhibited *The Play of the Unmentionable* (Brooklyn Museum), on the subject of censorship, followed in 1993 by *The 'Herald Tribune', News from Kafka and a Quote* (Smithsonian Institute). Also in 1993 he exhibited *A Grammatical Remark* in Stuttgart. He has had a considerable influence on Conceptual artists.

Kosygin, Aleksei Nikolayevich 1904–80
Soviet politician

He was born and educated in St Petersburg. A textile-worker by training, he owed his advancement in the 1930s to the vacancies resulting from **Stalin's** purges. Elected to the Supreme Soviet (1938), he held a variety of political industrial posts, and became a member of the Central Committee in 1939 and of the politburo in 1948. He had a chequered career in the post-World War II period, falling in and out with both Stalin and **Nikita Khrushchev**. It was only really when, in 1964, he succeeded the latter as Chairman of the Council of Ministers (or Prime Minister) that he could attempt serious, if decentralizing, reforms. However, he was blocked in the late 1960s by the party machine and the caution of **Leonid Brezhnev**. He soldiered on until 1980, when he resigned because of ill health, and he died soon after, having failed to rescue the economy from over-centralization and over-planning.

Kotzé, Sir John Gilbert 1849–1940
South African judge

Born in Cape Town, he studied law in London, and then practised at the Cape Bar. In 1877, when the South African Republic was annexed by Great Britain, he was appointed first judge of the new Supreme Court of the Transvaal, and became Chief Justice in 1881 after the First Boer War. He tried to improve the standard of the administration of justice and to apply Roman-Dutch legal principles to circumstances which were radically different from those for which they were originally devised. In 1897 he held that laws of the Volksraad conflicting with the constitution would be invalid, and was consequently dismissed by President **Kruger**. After 1901 he continued to serve as a judge, although not in the Transvaal, and was a Judge of Appeal from 1922 to 1927. He was a vigorous advocate of codification.

Kotzebue, August Friedrich Ferdinand von 1761–1819
German dramatist

Born in Weimar, he held various offices in the service of Russia, as well as writing plays, tales, satires and historical works. He quarrelled with **Goethe** and satirized the leaders of the Romantic school. Among his 200 lively poetic dramas are *Menschenhass und Reue* (1788, Eng trans *The Stranger*, 1798), *Die Hussiten vor Naumburg* (1801, Eng trans *The Patriot Father*, 1830) and *Die beiden Klingsberge* (1799, Eng trans *Father and Son*, 1814). It was while on a mission from Emperor **Alexander I** to report on Western politics that he was stabbed to death by a Jena student. ▭H N Fairchild, *The Noble Savage* (1928)

Kotzebue, Otto 1787–1846
Russian explorer and naval officer

He was born in Reval (now Tallinn), Estonia, the son of the dramatist **August von Kotzebue**. He accompanied Baron **von Krusenstern** round the world in 1803–06. From 1815 to 1818 he tried to find a passage across the Arctic Ocean, and during this voyage discovered the Sound near Bering Strait which was named after him. He later made two voyages of exploration in the Pacific Ocean, and commanded another round-the-world voyage (1823–26).

Koufax, Sandy (Sanford) 1935–
US baseball player

Born in Brooklyn, New York City, he played for the Dodgers there, then in Los Angeles and his short career (1955–66) reached its peak in the 1960s, and in 1963 he was named Most Valuable Player (MVP) as the Dodgers beat the New York Yankees in the World Series. In 1965 he again helped the Dodgers to a World Series victory over Minnesota with two consecutive 'shut-outs' (where the opposition fail to score a single run). During his career he pitched four no-hitters, including a perfect game, and won the Cy Young award three times (1963, 1965, 1966). In 1966, aged only 31, he had to retire from baseball with arthritis of the left elbow, which impeded his throwing. He is considered one of the greatest pitchers in the history of the game.

Kountche, Seyni 1931–87
Niger soldier and politician

After military training in France he served in the French army before Niger achieved full independence in 1960, with **Hamani Diori** as its first President. Opposition to Diori grew during the severe drought of 1968–74 and Kountche, as army Chief-of-Staff, was the reluctant leader of the coup which overthrew him. He established a military government and started to restore the country's economy, aiming to return it to civilian rule, but died while undergoing surgery in a Paris hospital.

Koussevitzky, Serge, *originally* Sergei Alexandrovich Koussevitsky 1874–1951
US conductor, composer and double-bass player

Born in Vishny-Volotchok, Russia, he founded his own orchestra in Moscow in 1909, and after the Revolution was director of the State Symphony Orchestra in Leningrad (now St Petersburg). He left the Soviet Union in 1920, worked in Paris, and settled in 1924 in Boston, where he was the conductor of its symphony orchestra for 25 years. Throughout his life he championed new music; in Russia he performed and published **Nikolai Medtner, Prokofiev, Rachmaninov, Scriabin**, and **Stravinsky**; in the USA he commissioned and premiered many works which became 20th-century classics. He established the Berkshire Symphonic Festival (1934) and the Berkshire Music Center (1940) at Tanglewood, Massachusetts.

Kouwenhoven, William Bennett 1886–1975
US electrical engineer

Born in New York City, he studied at the Brooklyn Polytechnic, where he later taught physics. He moved to Washington University in 1913 and the following year to Johns Hopkins University where he became Professor of Electrical Engineering in 1930. In the 1930s he developed the first practical electrical defibrillator which has come into general use for the treatment of heart-beat irregularities. In 1959 he introduced the first-aid technique of external heart massage.

Kovács, Margit 1902–
Hungarian potter

Born in Györ, she began studying art in 1924, and went to Budapest to study ceramics. She left Hungary in 1926 and worked with H Bucher in Vienna, then studied modelling under the sculptor Karl Miller and ceramics under A Niemeyer in Munich (1928–29). Returning to Hungary in 1929, she had a successful exhibition in Budapest. She won an honorary diploma at the Paris International Exhibition in 1937, and the major prize at the Brussels Exhibition in 1958. Her work includes figures and relief panels both modelled, or sculpted, and thrown, or made on a pottery wheel. Among her later works is a series of figures entitled *Mourning Women*, large murals depicting figures in scenes from folklore and country life. A museum has been established at Szentendre, near Budapest in recognition of her work as a ceramic sculptor.

Kovalevskaya, Sofya Vasilevna 1850–91
Russian mathematician and novelist

Born in Moscow, she received a private education in mathematics, and studied at the University of Heidelberg under Hermann von Helmholtz (1869) and at Berlin University under Karl Weierstrass (1871–74). In 1884 she was appointed to a lectureship at the University of Stockholm, where she became professor in 1889. She first worked on the theory of partial differential equations, and studied Abelian integrals, their use in analysis of the motion of a top (or any other rotating body), and the structure of Saturn's rings. She was also a talented novelist and playwright whose works include *Véra Brantzova* (1895).

Kovalevsky, Aleksandr Onufrievich 1840–1901
Russian embryologist

Born in Dünaburg (now Daugavpils, Latvia), he was professor at the universities of St Petersburg, Kassan, Kiev and Odessa, and studied the embryological development of primitive animals which possess a flexible rod-like structure supporting the embryo, such as *Balanoglossus*, *Sagitta*, the *Brachiopoda* and *Amphioxus*. He established for the first time that there are common elements in the patterns of development in many animals and that it is possible to use these patterns to elucidate evolutionary relationships. His work provided evidence for Ernst Haeckel's now discredited theory of recapitulation. He was elected to the Russian Academy of Sciences in 1890.

Kovalskaya, Yelizaveta Nikolayevna, *née* Solntseva 1851–1943
Russian revolutionary worker

Born in Kharkov, she began her revolutionary work there by organizing a study group which was closed by the police in 1869. After 13 years of work in the revolutionary movement she founded the Southern Russian Workers' League in Kiev (1880), which committed terrorist acts against officialdom. She was arrested and sentenced to hard labour in Siberia. On her release in 1903 she went to Switzerland and returned to Russia in 1917 to become a distinguished historian of the Russian Revolution at the Petrograd Archives of Revolutionary History. In 1926 she published *The 1880-81 Southern Russian Workers' League*.

Kozlov, Ivan Ivanovich 1779–1840
Russian poet

Born in St Petersburg, he translated Byron and Thomas Moore. He turned to poetry at the age of 42, having gone blind at the age of 30. His romantic poems include *Chernets* (1824) and *Knyaginya Natalya Dolgarukiya* (1828). 📖 G R V Barratt, *Ivan Kozlov* (1972)

Kozlov, Peter, *Russian* Pyotr Kuzmich 1863–1935
Russian traveller and archaeologist

He explored the Altai Mountains, the Gobi Desert, and the head-waters of the great Chinese rivers. In 1909 he discovered the ancient city of Khara Khoto in the Gobi, with its library.

Kraepelin, Emil 1856–1926
German psychiatrist

Professor at Dorpat, Heidelberg and Munich, he was a pioneer in the psychological study of serious mental diseases (psychoses), which he divided into two groups, manic-depressive and dementia-praecox. He did research on brain fatigue and on the mental effects of alcohol.

Krafft-Ebing, Richard, Freiherr von 1840–1902
German psychiatrist

Born in Mannheim, he was professor at Strasbourg and at Vienna. Much of his work was on forensic psychiatry and on sexual pathology (*Psychopathia Sexualis*, 1876).

Kramer, Jack (John Albert) 1921–
US tennis player

Born in Las Vegas, he played for the USA against Australia in the last Davis Cup before World War II. He won the Wimbledon doubles title in 1946 and the year after won both the singles and doubles titles. He began his professional career in 1947 and became a founder of the Kramer Pro Tour, a forerunner to the Association of Tennis Professionals (ATP)—the modern-day men's professional tennis circuit. As executive director of the ATP from 1972, he oversaw the 1973 boycott of Wimbledon by 90 professionals.

Kramer, Dame Leonie Judith 1924–
Australian academic, writer and administrator

She was born in Melbourne and educated at Melbourne University and at St Hugh's College, Oxford. In 1968 she was appointed Professor of Australian Literature at Sydney University, the first ever to hold such a post. As a scholar and critic she has held positions on a number of influential bodies, being a member of the board of the Australian Broadcasting Commission since 1977 (chairman 1981–83), member of the Universities Council (1977–86), and council member of the Australian National University, Canberra, from 1984. Her published works include three critical volumes on the Australian author H H Richardson. She has co-authored two books on language and literature, edited the *Oxford History of Australian Literature* (1981) and co-edited the companion *Oxford Anthology of Australian Literature* (1985). She became Chancellor of the University of Sydney in 1991. Created DBE in 1983, she became a Companion of the Order of Australia in 1993.

Kraszewski, Józef Ignacy 1812–87
Polish novelist and poet

Born in Warsaw, he studied at the University of Vilna. He was one of the most prolific of all Polish authors, producing more than 300 works. His best-known novel is *Jermola: obrazki wiejskie* (1857, Eng trans *Jermola*, 1891), a tale of peasant life. In 1884 he was imprisoned at Magdeburg for treason.

Kray, Ronnie (Ronald) 1933–95 and Reggie (Reginald) 1933–
English murderers and gang leaders

Twin brothers, they were born in the East End of London, where they ran a criminal Mafia-style operation in the 1960s. Their gang or 'firm' collected protection money, organized illegal gambling and drinking clubs and participated in gang warfare. Ronnie Kray, nicknamed 'Colonel', was the dominant twin, who modelled himself on Chicago gangsters. An early attempt to convict the brothers of murder failed. In the late 1960s, Ronnie Kray shot dead a member of a rival gang and Reggie stabbed another to death. The twins were tried at the Old Bailey in 1969, found guilty and sentenced to imprisonment of not less than 30 years. A campaign to free them in 1987 failed. Ronnie Kray died in prison.

Krebs, Sir Edwin Gerhard 1918–
US biochemist and Nobel Prize winner
Born in Lansing, Iowa, he joined the Howard Hughes Medical Institute (1977) and department of pharmacology at the University of Washington School of Medicine (1983), where he and **Edmond Fischer** built on **Carl Cori's** work on the activation of glycogen enzymes to show that conversions to and from phosphorus compounds are involved, catalysed by two enzymes. These initial findings led to the discovery of the cascade of enzymes that switches on glycogen phosphorylase and other enzymes under the influence of hormones such as glucagon and adrenaline (epinephrine). Similar systems controlled by other activators were also subsequently discovered. His later work covered the structure of the kinases and the properties of the phosphatases. With Fischer, Krebs was awarded the 1992 Nobel Prize for physiology or medicine. He was elected FRS in 1947 and knighted in 1958.

Krebs, Sir Hans Adolf 1900–81
British biochemist and Nobel Prize winner
Born in Hildesheim, Germany, he worked first at the Kaiser Wilhelm Institute for Cell Physiology, Berlin, before emigrating to Great Britain in 1934, where he worked with **Frederick Gowland Hopkins** on redox reactions. He was a lecturer in pharmacology (1935–45) and Professor of Biochemistry at Sheffield University (1945–54), then Whitley Professor of Biochemistry at Oxford (1954–67). In 1932 he described the urea cycle whereby carbon dioxide and ammonia form urea in the presence of liver slices. Leading on from his earlier work, he elucidated the citric acid cycle (Krebs' cycle) of energy production (c.1943). He also carried out studies on acid oxidase, L-glutamine synthetase, purine synthesis in birds, and ketone bodies. In 1953 he shared with **Fritz Lipmann** the Nobel Prize for physiology or medicine for his discovery of the citric acid cycle. He was elected a Fellow of the Royal Society in 1947 and was awarded the society's Royal (1954) and Copley (1961) medals. ⌨ Frederic Lawrence Holmes, *Hans Krebs* (1991)

Krebs, Sir John Richard 1945–
English zoologist
Born in Sheffield, he was educated at Oxford (1963–69) and taught at the universities of British Columbia, Vancouver (1970–73), Bangor, North Wales (1973–74) and Oxford, where he was Royal Society Research Professor (1988–94). He is also director of the Agricultural and Food Research Council Unit of Ecology and Behaviour and chief executive of the Natural Environment Research Council Unit of Behavioural Ecology in Oxford (1994–). Interested in ecology and animal behaviour, he has investigated the strategies adopted by animals which maximize their fitness, studying aspects of foraging for food, territoriality and sexual behaviour. He has developed predictive mathematical models to account for these behavioural patterns. His book *An Introduction to Behavioural Ecology* (1981) is the standard text in its field. He was elected Fellow of the Royal Society in 1984 and knighted in 1998.

Kreisky, Bruno 1911–90
Austrian politician
Born in Vienna and educated at Vienna University, he joined the Social Democratic Party of Austria (SPO) as a young man and was imprisoned for his political activities from 1935 until he escaped to Sweden in 1938. He then returned to Austria and served in the Foreign Service (1946–51) and the Prime Minister's office (1951–53). He was increasingly active in party politics and in 1970 became Prime Minister in a minority SPO government. He steadily increased his majority in subsequent elections but in 1983, when that majority disappeared, he refused to serve in a coalition and resigned.

Kreisler, Fritz 1875–1962
US violinist
Born in Vienna, Austria, he studied medicine and became an Uhlan officer. One of the most successful violin virtuosos of his time, he also composed violin pieces, a string quartet and an operetta, *Apple Blossoms* (1919), which was a Broadway success. He became a US citizen in 1943.

Krenek, Ernst 1900–91
US composer
Born in Vienna, Austria, to Czech parents, he worked with various German theatres as a conductor–director, and began to compose, making his name with *Jonny spielt auf* (1927, 'Johnny Strikes Up the Band!'), a jazz opera. In Vienna he joined **Arnold Schoenberg's** circle and produced serialist works, such as *Karl V* (1930–33). He emigrated to the USA in 1938, was naturalized in 1945, and settled in California, where he continued to compose in avant-garde idioms, producing operas, orchestral and chamber music and choral works.

Krenz, Egon 1937–
German politician
Educated at Putbus Teacher Training Institute in Germany and Moscow University, he joined the Freie Deutsche Jugend (FDJ) in 1953 and the Socialist Unity Party (SED) in 1955, holding several posts in both (1957–64). He was Secretary-General of the Ernst Thälman Pioneer Organization (1967), and was chairman from 1971 when he also entered the Volkskammer. He was FDJ First Secretary (1974–83), continued his membership from 1969 of the Council of National Front, served as a candidate member of the SED central committee (1971–73), and was appointed Secretary in 1989. Having been admitted to the politburo as a candidate in 1976, he became a full member in 1983, and its General Secretary in 1989, in which year he was elected head of state, a position he held only until 1990.

Kreps, Juanita, *née* Morris 1921–
US economist
Born in Lynch, Kentucky, and educated at Berea College and Duke University, she taught economics at Denison College (1945–50), then returned to Duke University (1958), becoming professor there (1967) and its first woman vice-president (1973). She became director of the New York Stock Exchange (1972–77), and under President **Jimmy Carter** served as Secretary of Commerce (1977–79). She continues to serve on the boards of several major companies. Her political interests have principally focused on sexual and racial equality in business, and the economic consequences of women's patterns of work. Her works include *Lifetime Allocation of Work and Income* (1971), *Sex in the Marketplace: American Women at Work* (1971) and *Women and the American Economy* (1976).

Kretzer, Max 1854–1941
German novelist

He was born in Posen (Poznań), and went to work in a factory at the age of 13. Wholly self-taught, his books include *Die Betrogenen* (1882, 'The Duped'), which concerns poverty and prostitution, *Die Verkommenen* (1883, 'The Fallen'), *Meister Timpe* (1888) and *Das Gesicht Christi* (1897, 'The Face of Christ'). Essentially a writer on social problems and working people, he has, on account of his naturalism, been called the German Zola.

Kreuger, Ivar 1880–1932
Swedish industrialist and financier

Born in Kalmar, he trained as a civil engineer, emigrated to the USA and worked as a real-estate salesman and building contractor. He went to South Africa before returning to Sweden in 1907. In 1913 he founded the United Swedish Match Company and began a series of acquisitions and combinations which brought him control of three-quarters of the world's match trade. He lent large sums to governments in return for monopolistic concessions. In 1931 he was in difficulties and in March 1932, unable to meet a bank demand, he committed suicide. Irregularities in his financial dealings over seven years were revealed after his death.

Kripke, Saul 1940–
US philosopher and logician

Born in Bay Shore, New York, he was educated at Harvard and has taught at Rockefeller University (1968–76) and Princeton University (since 1976). As a youthful prodigy he made remarkable technical advances in modal logic, whose wider philosophical implications were later explored in such famous papers as 'Naming and Necessity' (1972).

Krishna Menon, V (engalil) K (rishnan) 1896–1974
Indian politician and diplomat

Born in Calicut, Malabar, he was educated at the Presidency College, Madras, and at London University. He worked as a history teacher and a London barrister. In 1929 he became secretary of the India League and the mouthpiece of Indian nationalism in Britain. When India became a Dominion in 1947 he became India's High Commissioner in London. In 1952 he became leader of the Indian delegation to the United Nations, bringing Jawaharlal Nehru's influence to bear on international problems as leader of the Asian 'uncommitted' and 'neutralist' bloc. As Defence Minister (1957–62) he came into conflict at the United Nations with Britain over Kashmir. ⬚ T J S George, *Krishna Menon* (1964)

Krishnamurti, Jiddu 1895–1986
Indian theosophist

Born in Madras, he was educated in England by Annie Besant, who in 1925 proclaimed him the Messiah. Later he dissolved The Order of the Star in the East (founded by Besant), and travelled the world teaching and advocating a way of life and thought unconditioned by the narrowness of nationality, race and religion. ⬚ Mary Lutyens, *Krishnamurti: His Life and Death* (1991)

Kristeva, Julia 1941–
French theorist and critic

Born in Bulgaria, she became a practising psychoanalyst and, influenced by Sigmund Freud and Jacques Lacan, she was led to question Western claims concerning philosophy, literary criticism, linguistics and politics. Her work focuses on language, literature and cultural history. *Desire in Language* (1977, Eng trans 1980) applies semiotics to literature and art. *Revolution in Poetic Language* (1974, Eng trans 1984) paved the way for a sociology of literature based on language. Her books *About Chinese Women* (1975, Eng trans 1976) and *Polylogue* (1977, Eng trans 1980) have brought her work to the forefront of feminist criticism.

Kristian I 1426–81
King of Denmark, of Norway and of Sweden

The founder of the Oldenburg royal line, he was the son of Dietrich, Count of Oldenburg, and Hedvig, heiress of Schleswig and Holstein. Improvident and spendthrift, he maintained a splendid court in Copenhagen, but was always chronically short of money; to provide part of a dowry for the marriage of his daughter Margaret to James III of Scotland, he mortgaged Orkney and Shetland—a pledge that was never redeemed. In Denmark he founded the University of Copenhagen in 1478. He was succeeded by his son, Johan I (1455–1513), who ruled from 1481 to 1513.

Kristian II 1481–1559
King of Denmark and Norway, and of Sweden

Born in Nyborg, Denmark, he succeeded his father, Johan I, as King of Norway and Denmark from 1513. He overthrew Sten Sture, the Regent of Sweden, and became King of Sweden (1520), but his treacherous massacre of the leading men of Sweden in the infamous Stockholm Bloodbath (1520) caused such hostility towards him that he was driven out by Gustav I Vasa (1523). He was also expelled from Denmark, largely because of his sweeping legal reforms in favour of the burghers and peasants, and fled to the Netherlands. An attempt to regain his lost territories (1531) was totally defeated, and he spent his remaining years in prison. His death marked the end of the Kalmar Union (1397–1523) of Denmark, Norway and Sweden.

Kristian III 1503–59
King of Denmark and Norway

Born in Gottorp, Schleswig, the son and successor of Frederik I, he was an ardent Lutheran, imposed the Reformation on Denmark, Norway and Iceland, and established the Lutheran State Church. His reign began in 1534, during the civil war (1533–36) between Catholic supporters of the ex-king, Kristian II, and the Protestant son of Frederik. After the capitulation of Copenhagen (1536), Kristian confiscated Church lands, encouraged agriculture and trade, made Denmark more aware of its national identity, and hugely strengthened the monarchy. He also brought out a Danish translation of the German Bible (1550).

Kristian IV 1577–1648
King of Denmark and Norway

Born at Frederiksborg Castle, the son of Frederik II, he acceded in 1588 and ruled under regents until 1596. Blunt, dissolute and hard-drinking, he won the affection of his nation. He strengthened the Danish navy, encouraged industry, enhanced Copenhagen with magnificent new buildings, and founded new towns, including Kristiania (now Oslo). Against his councillors' advice, he invaded Sweden (1611), but failed to capture Stockholm and made peace (1613) by the Treaty of Knäred. In the Thirty Years War (1618–48) he joined the Protestant Union (1625) to protect Danish and Lutheran interests in North Germany, but was defeated at Lutter by Count von Tilly and Albrecht von Wallenstein (1626). He withdrew from the war by the Treaty of Lübeck (1629). In a second war with Sweden (1643–45), he lost an eye and dominion of the Baltic. He was succeeded by his son, Frederik III.

Kristian VII 1749–1808
King of Denmark and Norway

Born in Copenhagen, the son and successor (1766) of Frederik V, he married his cousin Caroline Matilda, sister of King George III of Great Britain (1766), and toured Europe (1768), accompanied by his court physician, Count Johann Struensee (1737–72). Struensee was appointed Privy Councillor (1770), became the queen's lover, and seized effective power, but in 1772 he was charged with treason and executed, while the queen was divorced and exiled to Hanover. The king was judged insane in 1784, and relinquished control to his son, Crown Prince Frederik, who later succeeded as **Frederik VI**.

Kristian VIII 1786–1848
King of Denmark
Born in Copenhagen, the son and successor of **Frederik VI**, he was elected King of Norway (1814), but was ousted by **Karl XIV Johan** (Bernadotte) of Sweden. As King of Denmark (from 1839) he allowed freedom of trade with Iceland and revived the ancient Althing (parliament) of Iceland as an Icelandic consultative assembly (1843). He signed an order early in 1848 abolishing monarchical absolutism, which was implemented by his son and successor, **Frederik VII**, the following year.

Kristian IX 1818–1906
King of Denmark
A prince of Glücksburg, he was born in Gottorp, Schleswig, and confirmed as Crown Prince of Denmark by the Protocol of London, signed by all the great powers (1852) when it became clear that the old Oldenburg line would become extinct. He became king in 1863 in succession to the childless **Frederik VII**, and was immediately obliged to sign the November Constitution incorporating Schleswig into the Danish kingdom, an act which led to war with Prussia and Austria and the loss of both Schleswig and Holstein (1864). In 1874, on the 1,000th anniversary of the settlement of Iceland, he paid the first royal visit by a reigning monarch, and granted Iceland's first constitution, of limited autonomy under a governor. In Denmark, he presided over the move to full parliamentary government. He was succeeded in 1906 by his elder son as **Frederik VIII**, while his younger son became King **George I** of Greece. His elder daughter, **Alexandra**, married the future King **Edward VII** of Great Britain, and his younger daughter, Mari Dagmar, married the future Tsar **Alexander III** of Russia.

Kristian X 1870–1947
King of Denmark, and of Iceland
Born in Charlottenlund, the son of **Frederick VIII**, he was revered as a symbol of resistance during the German occupation in World War II. He signed a new constitution granting the vote to women (1915), and in 1918 signed the Act of Union with Iceland which granted Iceland full independence in personal union with the Danish sovereign (this ended in 1944). During World War II he elected to stay on in Denmark, riding on horseback through Copenhagen, and he was put under house arrest by the Germans (1943–45). He married Alexandrine, Duchess of Mecklenburg-Schwerin, and was succeeded by their son, **Frederik IX**.

Kristiansen, Ingrid, *née* Ingrid Christensen 1956–
Norwegian athlete
A former cross-country skiing champion, and then a long-distance runner, in 1985–86 she ran world best times for the 5,000m, 10,000m (surpassed in 1993 by **Wang Junxia** of China), and marathon. In 1986 she knocked 45.68 seconds off the world 10,000m record, and won the European title. She has won most of the world's major marathons, including London (1984–85, 1987–88), and was the world cross-country champion in 1988.

Kristina 1626–89
Queen of Sweden
She was born in Stockholm, the daughter and successor in 1632 of **Gustav II Adolf**. At her orders she was educated like a prince during her minority. The affairs of the kingdom were managed by her father's Chancellor, **Axel Oxenstjerna**, who continued Swedish military involvement in the Thirty Years War. When Kristina came of age (1644), she brought to an end the war against Denmark

with the Peace of Westphalia (1648). She recklessly dispensed Crown lands to the nobles and patronized the arts, attracting **Hugo Grotius**, **Claudius Salmasius** and **René Descartes** to her court. Headstrong, vain and intelligent, she was hunchbacked and bisexual by nature; she refused to marry her cousin, **Karl X Gustav**, but proclaimed him Crown Prince. Having secretly turned to Catholicism, and impatient of the personal restraints imposed on her as a ruler, she stunned Europe in 1654 by abdicating. She went into exile, was received into the Catholic Church and settled in Rome. When Karl X Gustav died (1660) she returned to Sweden, but failed to have herself reinstated. In 1667 she aspired to the throne of Poland. For the rest of her life she lived in Rome as a pensioner of the pope, collecting Venetian paintings and sponsoring the sculptor **Gian Lorenzo Bernini** and the composers **Corelli** and **Scarlatti**.

Kroeber, Alfred Louis 1876–1960
US cultural anthropologist
Born in Hoboken, New Jersey, he studied under **Franz Boas** at Columbia University, and went on to build up the anthropology department at the University of California at Berkeley (1901–46, professor from 1919). His extensive studies of the native Californians were compiled in his *Handbook of the Indians of California* (1925). However his primary influence lies in his concept of cultures as patterned wholes, each with its own 'configuration' or 'style', and undergoing a process of growth or development analogous to that of an organism. His view of culture-history was replete with biological metaphor, as in *Cultural and Natural Areas of Native North America* (1939), which correlates cultural areas, defined by complexes of traits, with ecological areas defined by associations of species, and *Configurations of Culture Growth* (1944) which documents the rise, flourishing and eventual decay of civilizations in terms of cultural life-cycles. His most influential work, *Anthropology* (1923), is a monument to the establishment of anthropology as a professional academic discipline. Many of his papers are collected in *The Nature of Culture* (1952).

Krogh, (Schack) August (Steenberg)
1874–1949
Danish physiologist and Nobel Prize winner
Born in Grenaa, he graduated with a PhD from Copenhagen University and worked there for the rest of his career, serving as Professor of Animal Physiology from 1916 to 1945. He worked on problems of respiration, then on the capillary system. He showed that blood flow through capillaries is determined by the activity of the surrounding muscle, rather than simply by blood pressure. He won the Nobel Prize for physiology or medicine in 1920 for this discovery, and later showed that the capillaries are under nervous and hormonal control.
📖 Bodil Schmidt-Nielson, *August and Marie Krogh: Lives in Science* (1995)

Krone, Julie 1963–
US jockey
She was born in Benton Harbor, Michigan, and became the first woman to win a racing title when she won the riding title at Atlantic City in 1982. Until the 1970s few women had made their living as jockeys, and in 1988 Krone became the leading female jockey in history on winning her 1,205th race. She rode in the annual Breeders' Cup races at Churchill Downs, the first woman ever to race in that event, and in 1991 became the first woman to race in the Belmont Stakes. By that year, with $31 million dollars in purses and 2,000 wins, she had become the most successful female jockey of all time.

Kronecker, Leopold 1823–91
German mathematician

Born in Liegnitz, he obtained his doctorate at Berlin University (1845), where he was taught by P Lejeune Dirichlet and Ernst Kummer, and then returned to Berlin in 1855 where, as an active member of the Berlin Academy of Sciences, he lived as a private scholar. He worked in algebraic number theory, elliptic functions and the foundations of analysis, and lectured widely. He was involved in a controversy with Karl Weierstrass and Georg Cantor over the use of the infinite in mathematics, as he believed that mathematics should be essentially based on the arithmetic of the whole numbers. At one point he declared that 'God made the integers; all the rest is the work of man'.

Kropotkin, Prince Peter, Russian Knyaz Pyotr Alekseyevich Kropotkin 1842–1921
Russian geographer and revolutionary

Born in Moscow, he was educated at the Corps of Pages, St Petersburg (1857). After five years of service and exploration in Siberia, he returned to Moscow to study mathematics, while he also worked as secretary to the Geographical Society. In 1871 he explored the glacial deposits of Finland and Sweden. In 1872, critical of the limited nature of reform in Russia, he began to associate himself with the extremist section of the International Workingmen's Association. Arrested and imprisoned in 1874 in Russia, he escaped to England in 1876 and then to Switzerland and France. He was condemned at Lyons in 1883 to five years' imprisonment for anarchism, but, released in 1886, he settled in England then returned to Russia in 1917. Well-known for his *Memoirs of a Revolutionist* (1900), he wrote widely on anarchism, social justice, and many topics in biology, literature and history. ⌸ George Woodcock and Ivan Avakumovic, *The Anarchist Prince* (1950)

Kroto, Sir Harold Walter 1939–
English chemist and Nobel Prize winner

Born in Wisbech, Cambridgeshire, and educated at the University of Sheffield, he then moved to the National Research Council, Ottawa, where he continued his studies in the electronic spectroscopy of free radicals and in microwave spectroscopy. In 1966 he moved to Bell Telephone Laboratories, New Jersey, where he carried out Raman spectroscopic studies of liquids and quantum chemistry calculations. Kroto is noted for his work in detecting unstable molecules through the use of methods such as microwave and photoelectron spectroscopy. His studies extend to molecules which exist in space, notably discovering interstellar poly-yne molecules, the most complex and heaviest interstellar molecules known. In 1985, together with his co-workers Robert Curl and Richard Smalley at William Marsh Rice University, Texas, he discovered the third allotrope of carbon C_{60}, known as 'buckminsterfullerene' (familiarly 'buckyballs'), because its 'football' shape resembles the buildings designed by the architect Buckminster Fuller. Kroto was elected FRS in 1990 and became Royal Society Research Professor at the University of Sussex in 1991, having been appointed Professor of Chemistry there in 1985. In 1996 he was joint recipient of the Nobel Prize for chemistry, and was awarded a knighthood.

Krüdener, Barbara Juliana von 1764–1824
Russian mystic

She was born in Riga, and briefly married to Baron von Krüdener, Russian ambassador at Venice, but they separated in 1785, and from 1789 she lived in Riga, St Petersburg and Paris. She published a remarkable novel, *Valérie* (1803), supposed to be autobiographical, then gave herself up to an exaggerated mysticism. Expelled in 1817–18 from Switzerland and Germany, and repulsed by her former admirer, Emperor Alexander I, she retired to her paternal estates near Riga, where she entered into relations with the Moravian Brethren.

Kruger, Paul, *in full* Stephanus Johannes Paulus Kruger 1825–1904
South African politician

Born in Colesberg in Cape Colony, he was a Boer. He trekked to Natal, the Orange Free State, and the Transvaal, and won such a reputation for cleverness, coolness, and courage that in the First Boer War (1880–81), he was appointed head of the provisional government. He was elected President of the Transvaal or South African Republic in 1883, and again in 1888, 1893 and 1898. 'Oom Paul' (Uncle Paul) governed the Second Boer War of 1899–1902, but after the tide had turned against the Boers, went to Europe to seek (in vain) alliances against Great Britain. He made his headquarters at Utrecht, and published *The Memoirs of Paul Kruger, told by Himself* (1902). ⌸ D W Kruger, *Paul Kruger* (2 vols, 1961-63)

Krupp, Alfred 1812–87
German arms manufacturer

Born in Essen, at the age of 14 he succeeded his father Friedrich (1787–1826), who had founded a small iron forge there in 1810, and began manufacturing arms in 1837. At the Great Exhibition in London (1851) he exhibited a solid flawless ingot of cast steel weighing 4,000 kg. He established the first Bessemer steel plant and became the foremost arms supplier not only to Germany but to any country in the world, his first steel gun being manufactured in 1847. He acquired large mines, collieries and docks, and became a dominating force in the development of the Ruhr territories.

Krupp (von Bohlen und Halbach), Alfried Alwin Felix 1907–67
German industrialist

Born in Essen, he graduated from Aachen Technical College, became an honorary member of Hitler's SS, and in 1943 succeeded his father, Gustav Krupp, to the Krupp empire. He was arrested (1945) and convicted (1947) with 11 fellow-directors by a US military tribunal for plunder in Nazi-occupied territories and for employing slave labour under inhuman concentration camp conditions. He was sentenced to 12 years' imprisonment and his property was to be confiscated. By an amnesty (1951) he was released and his property restored with the proviso that he should sell his iron and steel assets for a reasonable offer within five years. This, however, was extended yearly from 1958 with diminishing prospect of fulfilment. Meanwhile he actually increased these assets by the acquisition of the Bochumer Verein (1958). Krupp played a prominent part in the West German 'economic miracle', building factories in Turkey, Pakistan, India and the Soviet Union. In 1959 he belatedly agreed to pay some compensation to former victims of forced labour, but only to those of Jewish origin. His son Arndt succeeded him.

Krupp, Friedrich Alfred 1854–1902
German arms manufacturer

The son of Alfred Krupp, he incorporated shipbuilding, armour-plate manufacture (1890) and chrome nickel steel production into the Krupp empire and became a personal friend of the Prussian emperor.

Krupp, Gustav, *originally* Gustav von Bohlen und Halbach 1870–1950
German industrialist and arms manufacturer

He was born in The Hague. In 1906 he married Bertha Krupp (1886–1957), daughter of Friedrich Alfred Krupp and granddaughter of Alfred Krupp, and by special imperial edict he was allowed to adopt the name 'Krupp' (inserted before the 'von'). He took over the firm, gained the monopoly of German arms manufacture during

Kublai Khan, *also spelt* Kubla or Khublai 1214–94
Great Khan of the Mongols from 1260 and Emperor of China from 1271

Kublai Khan was the grandson of **Genghis Khan**. He was an energetic ruler, and completed his grandfather's conquest of northern China. He suppressed his rivals, adopted the Chinese mode of civilization, encouraged men of letters, and made Buddhism the state religion. An attempt to invade Japan ended in disaster. He established himself at Cambaluc (modern Beijing), the first foreigner ever to rule in China. His dominions extended from the Arctic Ocean to the Straits of Malacca, and from Korea to Asia Minor and the confines of Hungary. The splendour of his court inspired the graphic pages of **Marco Polo**, who spent 17 years in the service of Kublai, and at a later date fired the imagination of **Samuel Taylor Coleridge**.

📖 M Rossabi, *Khublai Khan* (1988); D Morgan, *The Mongols* (1987).

> 'In Xanadu did Kubla Khan
> A stately pleasure-dome decree:
> Where Alph, the sacred river, ran
> Through caverns measureless to man
> Down to a sunless sea.'
> S T Coleridge, opening lines of 'Kubla Khan' (1816).

World War I and manufactured the long-range siege gun nicknamed 'Big Bertha'. Turning to agricultural machinery and steam engines after the war, he backed first **Paul von Hindenburg** against **Hitler**, but then supported the latter's party financially and connived in secret rearmament, contrary to the Versailles Treaty, after Hitler's rise to power in 1933. Hitler's *Lex-Krupp* (1943) confirmed exclusive family ownership for the firm. After World War II, the Krupp empire was split up by the Allies, but Gustav was too senile to stand trial as a war criminal at Nuremberg.

Krupskaya, Nadezhda Konstantinova
1869–1939
Russian revolutionary

A Marxist activist, she met **Lenin** in 1894. She was sentenced to exile about the same time as he was and allowed to join him in Siberia in 1898 on condition that they got married. Thereafter they were inseparable, and she acted as his agent, organizer and fellow-thinker in both Europe and Russia. She disliked the political limelight and, following the Bolshevik Revolution, she was mainly active in promoting education and the status of women. As Lenin's widow she at first opposed **Stalin** but later supported some of his policies, and was accordingly exploited. She left a rather brief *Reminiscences of Lenin*.

Krusenstern, Adam Johann, Baron von
1770–1846
Russian admiral

Born in Haggud, Estonia, he served (1793–99) in the British Royal Navy, and was commissioned by Tsar **Alexander I** to command a Russian exploring expedition in the North Pacific, which ultimately became a voyage round the world (1803–06), the first by a Russian.

Krylov, Ivan Andreyevich 1768–1844
Russian fable writer

He was born in Moscow, and he started writing at the age of 20. After serving as secretary to a prince, and then travelling aimlessly through Russia, he obtained a government post in 1806, and, settling down, wrote nine collections of fables, published between 1809 and 1843. He also translated **Jean de la Fontaine's** *Fables*.
📖 N Stepanov, *Ivan Andreevich Krylov* (1973)

Kubelik, Rafael (Jeronym) 1914–96
Swiss conductor

Born in Bychory, Czechoslovakia, he was the son of the violin virtuoso Jan Kubelik (1880–1940). He studied at the Prague Conservatory, and first conducted the Czech Philharmonic Orchestra before he was 20. By 1939 he had established an international reputation, and settled first in England (1948), then moved to Switzerland, where he gained citizenship in 1967. He was conductor of the Chicago Symphony Orchestra (1950–53), at Covent Garden (1955–58) and from 1961 with the Bavarian Radio Orchestra. He has composed two operas, *Veronika* (staged in 1947) and *Cornelia Faroli* (staged in 1972), symphonies, concerts, and other works.

Kubin, Alfred 1877–1959
Austrian painter and engraver

Born in Leitmeritz, he exhibited in Munich with the Blaue Reiter group in 1911. He was also influenced by **Goya** and **Odilon Redon** in his drawings and engravings of dreamlike subjects, and he illustrated many books in this style.

Kubitschek (de Oliveira), Juscelino 1902–76
Brazilian politician

He was born in Diamantina, Minas Gerais, the grandson of a Czech immigrant. He studied medicine in Belo Horizonte, Minas Gerais, and went on to become mayor of the city (1940–45). He was elected to Congress by the Social Democratic Party (PSD) in 1945 and was Governor of Minas Gerais in 1951–55. As President (1956–61), his ambitious programme emphasized transportation, energy, manufacturing and the building of a new capital, Brasília, rather than social measures, and was the blueprint for subsequent programmes during military rule. The political necessity for high gross domestic product (GDP) growth-rates hampered any effective counterinflationary policies, leaving massive problems for the subsequent **Quadros / Goulart** and **Castelo Branco** administrations. He was a candidate for the presidency in 1965 when he was exiled by Castelo Branco.

Kublai Khan See panel above

Kübler-Ross, Elisabeth 1926–
US physician

She was one of a set of triplets born in Zurich, and after studying medicine at the university there, she settled in the USA (1958) and was naturalized (1961). She became known for her pioneering work in counselling the terminally ill, and in her book *On Death and Dying* (1969) she examined the process of dying, identifying five stages of emotion: denial, anger, bargaining with God, preparatory grief/depression, and acceptance. Other works include *Living with Death and Dying* (1981) and *On Life after Death* (1991). Since 1977 she has led the Shanti Nilaya Growth and Health Center in Escondido, California.

Kubrick, Stanley 1928–
US screenwriter, film producer and director

Born in the Bronx, New York City, he became a staff photographer with *Look* magazine at the age of 17. He made his directorial debut with the documentary *Day of the Fight* (1950). His first feature film was *Fear and Desire* (1953) and he established his reputation with the thriller *The Killing* (1956) and the anti-war drama *Paths of Glory* (1957). He has tackled a wide variety of subjects, painstakingly preparing each new film and shrouding his work in secrecy. Noted for his mastery of technique and visual composition, he is often criticized for an increasingly extravagant approach to his material and a lack of humanity. Resident in England from 1961, notable films include *Lolita* (1962), *Dr. Strangelove* (1963), *2001: A Space Odyssey* (1968), *A Clockwork Orange* (1971), *Barry Lyndon* (1975), *The Shining* (1980) and *Full Metal Jacket* (1987). After a ten year absence, he returned to films with *Eyes Wide Shut* (1997). 📖 Thomas Allan Nelson, *Kubrick: Inside a Film Artist's Maze* (1982)

Kučan, Milan 1941–
Slovenian politician

He was born in Krizevci and educated at Ljubljana University. During the late 1980s, as the communist President of Slovenia, he resisted pressure from Belgrade to stifle the emergence of opposition parties in his republic, long the most liberal in the Yugoslav federation. In 1990, after the Slovenes held the first free elections anywhere in Yugoslavia since World War II, he was re-elected as non-party President of Slovenia. He declared Slovenia's secession from the Yugoslav Federation in July 1991. With the backing of Serbia's President, **Slobodan Milošević**, Yugoslav Federal army units attacked Slovenia, but Milošević was obliged to withdraw and to accept Slovenia's independence.

Kuenen, Philip Henry 1902–76
Dutch geological oceanographer

Born in Dundee, Scotland, of a Dutch father and an English mother, he was educated at Leyden University, where the establishment of an experimental laboratory for the study of geological problems influenced Kuenen to remain until 1934. In 1929–30 he participated in the Snellius expedition to the Netherlands Indies (now Indonesia), conducting surveys complimentary to **Felix Vening Meinesz**'s work on gravity. He was professor at Groningen University from 1946 to 1972. Kuenen's main investigations concerned the deposition of coarse sediments from turbidity currents, and the downbuckling of the crust with compressive stresses.

Kuffler, Stephen William 1913–80
US neurobiologist

Born in Tap, Hungary, he was educated in Vienna, and graduated from its medical school in 1937. Shortly afterwards he moved to the Kanematsu Institute in Sydney, Australia, where he worked with Sir **Bernard Katz** and Sir **John Eccles**. In 1945 he moved to the Johns Hopkins School of Medicine until 1959, and then went to Harvard as Professor of Neurobiology (1959–66) and John Franklin Enders University Professor (1966–80). He contributed extensively and significantly to many areas of neurobiology. In Australia he studied the mechanisms of synaptic transmission, which provided important guidelines for the mechanisms of excitatory and inhibitory transmission. In 1953 Kuffler began working on retinal physiology, using the light sensitive cells of the retina to study the higher functions of the brain. However he discovered that cells had 'receptive fields', some of which were excited if light fell in the centre of their field, while others were inhibited under the same conditions. This pioneering work influenced the later research of **David Hubel** and **Torsten Wiesel**. He also initiated an innovative study of the most numerous cells in the nervous system, from which he and his co-authors concluded that the role of these cells raised a variety of tantalizing questions.

Kuhlmann, Quirinus 1651–89
German poet and mystic

Born in Breslau (now Wrocław, Poland), he was burned at the stake upon the orders of the Sultan of Turkey (for political rather than religious reasons) after preaching his **Böhme**- and Quaker-influenced notion of the Kingdom of God upon Earth. He was an erotico-religious poet of

immense gifts and technical ability, but was regarded as egocentric. However, he appears to have had a sense of humour, reflected in some of his bizarre and complex titles. A few translations of his work are in *The German Lyric of the Baroque in English Translation* (1962). 📖 W Dietze, *Quirinus Kuhlmann, Ketzer und Poet* (1963)

Kuhn, (Franz Felix) Adalbert 1812–81
German philologist and folklorist

Born in Königsberg, Prussia (now Kaliningrad, Russia), he was a teacher and director (from 1870) of the Kollnisches Gymnasium, Berlin, and he founded a new school of comparative mythology based on comparative philology. He published collections of German folk-tales, but is best known for his work on the Indo-European languages. He was founder and editor (from 1851) of the *Zeitschrift für vergleichende Sprachforschung*, now entitled *Historische Sprachforschung*.

Kuhn, Richard 1900–67
German chemist and Nobel Prize winner

Born in Vienna-Döbling, Austria, he studied at the University of Vienna then worked for his doctorate with **Richard Willstätter** in Munich. In 1926 he moved to Zurich, and in 1929 to the Kaiser Wilhelm Institute for Medical Research in Heidelberg, where he remained for the rest of his life. His early work on enzymes led to an interest in problems of stereochemistry and work on conjugated polyenes led to important studies on carotenoids and vitamin A. Later work on vitamins B_2 and B_6 and on 4-aminobenzoic acid earned him the 1938 Nobel Prize for chemistry. He was forbidden by the Nazi government to accept the award, but it was presented to him after World War II. His research continued actively after the war, when he worked on resistance factors effective in preventing infections in both plants and animals.

Kuhn, Thomas Samuel 1922–96
US philosopher and historian of science

Born in Cincinnati, Ohio, he studied physics at Harvard and worked first as a physicist, but became interested in the historical development of science. He published his celebrated work *The Structure of Scientific Revolutions* in 1962, which challenged the idea of cumulative, unidirectional scientific progress. His theory of 'paradigms', as sets of related concepts which compete for acceptance in times of rapid scientific change or revolution, has been influential in many other fields of enquiry. His other works include *The Copernican Revolution* (1957) and *Sources for the History of Quantum Physics* (1967). He held several academic posts at Harvard, Boston University, Berkeley (1958–64), Princeton (1964–79) and Massachusetts Institute of Technology (1979–91).

Kühne, Wilhelm 1837–1900
German physiologist

Born in Hamburg, he trained in medicine, and in 1871 became Professor of Physiology at Heidelberg University. He achieved fame through his study of the chemistry of digestion. He proposed the expression 'enzyme' to describe organic substances that actuate chemical changes. He devoted much attention to proteins, finding rigor mortis to result from the action of the protein myosin, and from 1876 studied the retina in animals, revealing that the retina works like a renewable photographic plate.

Kuiper, Gerard Peter 1905–73
US astronomer

Born in Harenkarspel, the Netherlands, and educated in Leyden, he moved to the USA in 1933. He took an appointment at the Lick Observatory in California, then taught at Harvard (1935–36) and then joined the Yerkes Observatory before going to work at the McDonald Observatory in Texas in 1939. From 1960 he worked at the

Lunar and Planetary Laboratory of the University of Arizona. In 1941 Kuiper pioneered the study of contact binary stars and he also suggested a system of spectroscopic classification of white dwarf stars. He discovered two new satellites: Miranda, the fifth satellite of Uranus; and Nereid, the second satellite of Neptune (1948–49). In 1951 he proposed that there is a flattened belt of some thousand million comets (now known as the Kuiper belt) just beyond the orbit of Pluto. He was the first to realize that the planets probably formed from a nebulous cloud. In 1944 he was the first to confirm that a planetary satellite had an atmosphere, detecting methane on Titan. A Lockheed C-141 jet aircraft fitted with an infrared telescope has been named the Kuiper Airborne Observatory and his name has also been given to the 7,500 angstrom bands in the spectrum of Neptune and Uranus. He was involved with the early US space flights, including the *Ranger* and *Mariner* missions.

Kumaratunga, Chandrika Bandaranaike
1945–
Sri Lankan politician
Born in Colombo, she was educated at St Bridget's Convent and the University of Paris. With her family connections—her father was leader of the Sri Lankan Freedom Party and her mother was **Sirimavo Bandaranaike**, the world's first female prime minister—it was inevitable that she too would enter politics and in 1974 she was elected to the Women's League of the Sri Lankan Freedom Party. In 1986 she became leader of the People's Party and was elected President of Sri Lanka in 1994. Although she was able to institute a number of land reforms her period of office was marred by the bitter civil war fought by Tamil separatists in the north.

Kumazawa Banzan 1619–91
Japanese samurai administrator and Confucian scholar
The son of a masterless samurai (ronin), he entered the service of the daimyo (feudal lord) of Bizen, where he was instrumental in promoting administrative reforms. His writings stressed the importance of empirical knowledge of the external world and of the need to adopt practical solutions to changing circumstances. His thought influenced later dissatisfied samurai activists of the early 19th century aiming to fight the rigidities of the status quo.

Kumbel See **Hein, Piet**

Kummer, Ernst Eduard 1810–93
German mathematician
Born in Sorau, he studied theology, mathematics and philosophy at the University of Halle, and then taught at the gymnasium in Liegnitz (1832–42). He became known to **Carl Jacobi** and **P Lejeune Dirichlet** through his work on the hypergeometric series, and was elected a member of the Berlin Academy of Sciences in 1839. He was later appointed Professor of Mathematics at Breslau University (1842–55) and subsequently at Berlin University (from 1855). He worked in number theory, where he gained a significant insight on **Pierre de Fermat**'s last theorem, proving it rigorously for many new cases, and in the process introduced the 'ideal numbers' which was later to became one of the fundamental tools of modern algebra. He also worked on differential equations and in geometry, where he discovered the quartic surface now named after him.

Kun, Béla 1886–c.1937
Hungarian political leader and revolutionary
Born in Szlágycseh, Transylvania, he was a journalist, soldier and prisoner in Russia, and in 1918 founded the Hungarian Communist Party. In March 1919 he organized a communist revolution in Budapest and set up a Soviet republic which succeeded **Karolyi**'s government. It failed to gain popular support, and he was forced to flee for his life in August of that year. After escaping to Vienna he returned to Russia. He is believed to have been killed in a Stalinist purge. ⚏ Rudolf L Toakes, *Béla Kun and the Hungarian Soviet Republic* (1967)

Kunaev, Dimmukhamed Akhmedovich
1912–93
Kazakh politician
He was born in Verny (now Almaty), Kazakhstan. A metallurgist by occupation and communist by inclination, he worked his way up the Kazakh party ladder in the 1940s and 1950s, coming into close contact with **Leonid Brezhnev** and being made First Secretary (1960). He was demoted by **Nikita Khrushchev** (1962), but reappointed in 1964 by Brezhnev who also brought him into full membership of the politburo. This inevitably meant his dismissal by **Mikhail Gorbachev** in 1986. His ousting led to riots in Alma Ata but these were countered by charges of extensive corruption.

Kundera, Milan 1929–
French novelist
Born in Brno, Czechoslovakia, he was educated in Prague at Charles University and the Academy of Music and Dramatic Arts Film Faculty, and worked as a labourer and a jazz musician before devoting himself to literature. For several years he was a professor at the Prague Institute for Advanced Cinematographic Studies. *Zert* (Eng trans, *The Joke*, 1969), his first novel, was published in 1967. After the Russian invasion in 1968 he lost his post and his books were proscribed. In 1975 he settled in France and took French citizenship. *Zert* and the stories in *Směšné lásky* (1970, Eng trans *Laughable Loves*, 1974) are his only books to have been published in his homeland. The publication in 1979 of *Kniha smíchu a zapomnění* (Eng trans *The Book of Laughter and Forgetting*, USA, 1980; UK, 1982) prompted the revocation of his Czech citizenship. Once described as 'a healthy sceptic whose novels are all anti-something', in exile he has emerged as one of the major European writers of the late 20th century. Other novels include *Nesnesitelná lehkost bytí* (1984, Eng trans *The Unbearable Lightness of Being*, 1984) and *Immortality* (1991). He has also published a critical work, *Umění romanu* (1960, Eng trans *Art of the Novel*, 1988). ⚏ R Porter, *Kundera: a voice from Central Europe* (1981)

Küng, Hans 1928–
Swiss Roman Catholic theologian
Born in Sursee, Lucerne, he became a professor at Tübingen in 1960, and has written extensively for fellow theologians and for lay people. His questioning of received interpretations of Catholic doctrine, as in *Rechtfertigung* (1965, Eng trans *Justification*), *Die Kirche* (1967, Eng trans *The Church*), and *Hufehlbar?* (1971, Eng trans *Infallible?*), and his presentations of the Christian faith, as in *Christ sein* (1977, Eng trans *On Being a Christian*), *Existiert Gott?* (1980, Eng trans *Does God Exist?*), and *Eniges Leben?* (1984, Eng trans *Eternal Life?*), aroused controversy both in Germany and with the Vatican authorities, who withdrew his licence to teach as a Catholic theologian in 1979. He defended himself in *Why I am still a Christian* (1987).

K'ung, H H *in full* K'ung Hsiang-hsi 1881–1967
Chinese politician and banker
He came from a family of traditional bankers and received a missionary education in China before studying in the USA (1901–07). Through marriage, he developed close ties with both **Sun Yat-sen** and **Chiang Kai-shek** (their wives were sisters), joining the Guomindang (Kuomintang) in 1924 and becoming Minister of Industry and Commerce of the new Nationalist government in 1928. As Governor of the Bank of China and Minister of Finance (1933–44), he attempted to increase the government's financial control of the modern sector.

Through control of the four major banks, the government floated more bond issues to finance its military projects. K'ung's abandonment of the silver standard in favour of a managed paper currency in 1935 was to lead ultimately to hyperinflation in the 1940s. During the war against Japan, he was instrumental in obtaining US loans and was China's representative at the UN Bretton Woods Conference (1944). He moved to the USA permanently in 1948.

Kunigunde or Cunegund, St c.978–1033
German empress

She was the daughter of Count Siegfried of Luxemburg, and wife of Emperor Henry II of Germany. According to legend, when her virtue was impugned she vindicated herself by walking barefoot over hot ploughshares. After the emperor's death (1024) she retired into the convent of Kaufungen, near Kassel, and died there. She was canonized in 1200, and her feast day is 3 March.

Kunitz, Stanley Jasspon 1905–
US poet

Born in Worcester, Massachusetts he was educated at Harvard University. A literature academic, he taught poetry at the New School for Social Research in New York City (1950–57) and Columbia University (from 1963). His first collection of verse was *Intellectual Things* (1930). *Selected Poems 1928–1958* was awarded a Pulitzer Prize in 1959. Subsequent books include *The Testing-Tree* (1971), *The Terrible Threshold: Selected Poems 1940–1970* (1974) and *Passing Through* (1995). He has also published literary reference books and translated several volumes of Russian poetry. 📖 G Orr, *Stanley Kunitz: an introduction to the poetry* (1985)

Kuo Mo-jo See Guo Morno

Kupka, Frank (Frantisek) 1871–1957
Czech painter

Born in Opocno, East Bohemia, he studied art at the Kunstgewerbeschule at Jaromer (1888), and entered the Academy of Prague in 1889. In 1892 he went to Vienna, at that time a centre of the European avant-garde. Moving to Paris in 1895, he worked as an illustrator and pursued his interest in theosophy and the occult, before meeting the Cubists. With **Wassily Kandinsky**, he was one of the pioneers of pure abstraction, a style called Orphism.

Kuprin, Aleksandr Ivanovich 1870–1938
Russian writer

Born in Narovchak, he joined the army, but left to devote himself to literature. As a teller of short tales he ranks next to **Chekhov**, although his work is uneven in quality. Those translated include *Poedinok* (1905, 'The Duel'), *Reka zhizni* (1906, 'The River of Life'), *Slavyanskaya dusha* ('A Slav Soul'), *Granatovyi braskyet* ('The Bracelet of Garnets') and *Sasha*. He left Russia and settled in France after the Revolution of 1917, but returned to his homeland in 1937. 📖 N Loker, *Alexander Kuprin* (1978)

Kurchatov, Igor Vasilevich 1903–60
Soviet physicist

Born in Sim, Russia, and educated at the University of Crimea, he was appointed director of Nuclear Physics at the Leningrad (now St Petersburg) Physical-Technical Institute (1938) and, before the end of World War II, of the Soviet Atomic Energy Institute. After early research into dielectrics, he became interested in the study of the atomic nucleus around 1932 in work at the Leningrad Physical-Technical Institute, where he supervised the construction of a cyclotron particle accelerator. He carried out important studies of neutron reactions and was the leading figure in the building of the USSR's first nuclear fission (1949) and hydrogen bombs (1953), and the world's first industrial nuclear power plant (1954). He became a member of the Supreme Soviet in 1949.

Kuropatkin, Aleksei Nikolayevich 1848–1925
Russian soldier

He was born in Pskov. He was Russian Chief of Staff under Mikhail Skobeleff (1843–82) in the Turkish war (1877–78), Commander-in-Chief in Caucasia (1897), Minister of War (1898), and Commander-in-Chief in Manchuria (1904–05) against the victorious Japanese. He commanded the Russian armies on the Northern Front February–August 1916, and then was Governor of Turkestan until the Revolution in 1917.

Kurosawa, Akira 1910–98
Japanese film director

Born in Tokyo, his first feature film was *Sanshiro Sugata* (1943, *Judo Saga*). He often adapted the techniques of the Noh theatre to filmmaking, such as in *Rashomon* (1950), which won the Venice Film Festival prize, *Living* (1952) and *The Seven Samurai* (1954), an uncompromisingly savage view of the samurai code. Also characteristic are his literary adaptations, such as *The Throne of Blood* (1957, from **Shakespeare's** *Macbeth*). He also adapted **Dostoevsky** (*The Idiot*, 1951) and **Maxim Gorky** (*The Lower Depths*, 1957) for the screen, and his Siberian epic *Dersu Uzala* (1975) won an Academy Award as Best Foreign Film. Later films include *Kagemushi* (1980, 'Shadow Warrior'), *Ran* (1985, 'Chaos'), and *Rhapsody in August* (1991).

Kurtén, Björn 1924–88
Finnish palaeontologist

Born in Vaasa, he studied zoology and geology at the universities of Helsinki and Uppsala, Sweden, and from 1955 was a lecturer at the University of Helsinki, where he became Professor of Palaeontology in 1972. His 1953 doctoral thesis *On the variation and population dynamics of fossil and recent mammal populations*, laid the foundations of his pioneering work on evolution in Ice Age mammal fossils. His biological approach to palaeontology made him one of the first to explore genetical and developmental aspects of fossil populations, such as growth patterns, polymorphisms and evidence for natural selection. His *Pleistocene Mammals of Europe* (1968) became a standard work, and he produced numerous publications on the evolution of Carnivora, including *The Cave Bear Story* (1976). He loved writing and was a committed popularizer, producing countless newspaper and magazine articles and a series of semi-popular books. In 1988 he was awarded UNESCO's Kalinga prize for the popularization of science.

Kurtzman, Harvey 1924–93
US strip cartoonist and scriptwriter

Born in Brooklyn, New York City, he studied art at Cooper Union, and entered comics drawing *Magno* (1943). He created *Silver Linings* for the *Herald Tribune*, then *Hey Look* one-pagers for *Marvel* comic. He became editor of *Frontline Combat* and *Two-Fisted Tales*, and in 1952 created *Mad* as a parody of comic books and characters, later converting it to magazine format. He also created the humour magazines *Trump*, *Humbug* and *Help*, then the colour strip *Little Annie Fanny* for *Playboy* (1962).

Kusano Shimpei 1903–
Japanese poet

He has achieved his enormous reputation within Japan by articulating a closeness to nature, considered by Japanese people to be a national trait, and (a quality highly unusual in Japanese poetry) a sense of humour. One of the most accessible Japanese poets, he is also highly regarded in the West, especially in the USA. Some of his work can be found in *Frogs and Others* (translated by C Corman, 1969).

Kusch, Polykarp 1911–93
US physicist and Nobel Prize winner

Born in Blankenburg, Germany, he became a naturalized US citizen in 1922, graduated from the Case Institute of Technology, Cleveland, and obtained his PhD from Illinois University. Later he became Professor of Physics at Columbia University (1937–72) and at the University of Texas (1972–82). With Isidor Rabi, Kusch investigated Samuel Goudsmit and George Uhlenbeck's theory that the electron has a magnetic moment. The large discrepancy they found between the observed and predicted values when measuring the hyperfine splitting in atomic hydrogen led US physicist Gregory Breit (1899–1981) to suggest that the electron's magnetic moment might be different from the previously accepted value. With the experimental results of Willis Lamb, this led to the reformulation of quantum electrodynamics by Richard Feynman, Julian Schwinger and Sin-Itiro Tomonaga. Kusch shared with Lamb the 1955 Nobel Prize for physics for his precise determination of the electron's magnetic moment. He retired in 1982.

Kushner, Tony 1956–
US playwright
Born in New York City, and raised in Lake Charles, Louisiana, he was educated at Columbia University and New York University. His plays are highly political in both content and intention, and are informed by an acute sense of historical awareness. *Yes, Yes, No, No* (1985) was followed by several more plays before the appearance of his epic *Angels in America*, which tells of the catastrophic effects of AIDS in New York, and was awarded the 1993 Pulitzer Prize for drama. Its two parts, running to almost seven hours, are *Millenium Approaches* (1991) and *Perestroika* (1992). Subsequent works include *Slavs!* (1995) and *Henry Box Brown* (1997).

Kutuzov, Mikhail Harionovich, Prince of Smolensk 1745–1813
Russian soldier
He fought in Poland and in the Turkish wars, and from 1805 to 1812 commanded against the French. In 1812, as Commander-in-Chief he fought Napoleon I at Borodino, and later obtained a great victory over Davout and Ney at Smolensk. His army pursued the retreating French out of Russia into Prussia. 🕮 Roger Parkinson, *Fox of the North* (1976)

Ku Yen-wu See Gu Yanwu

Kuyper, Abraham 1837–1920
Dutch theologian and politician
Born in Maassluis, he was a pastor and founder of the Free University of Amsterdam (1880). He became a member of the Dutch parliament and Prime Minister (1900–05) and sought to develop a Christian world-view of society. He founded two newspapers and wrote numerous books, few of which have been translated into English, apart from *Lectures on Calvinism* (1898), *Principles of Sacred Theology* (1898), and *The Work of the Holy Spirit* (1900). His theology of common grace, the kingdom of God, and the 'sphere-sovereignty' of the Church and other social institutions, offered a Calvinistic version of Christian Socialism. In the Netherlands he is remembered as the emancipator of the orthodox Calvinists and also as the founder of the Anti-Revolutionary Party.

Kuznets, Simon Smith 1901–85
US economist statistician and Nobel Prize winner
Born in Pinsk, Ukraine, he emigrated to the USA in 1922, studied at Columbia, and studied business cycles for the National Bureau of Economic Research from 1927. He was Professor of Economics at Pennsylvania (1930–54), Johns Hopkins (1954–60) and Harvard (1960–71). In his work he combined a concern for facts and measurement with creative and original ideas on economic growth and social change, such as the 20-year 'Kuznets cycle' of economic growth. His major publication was *National Income and its Composition, 1919–1938* (2 vols, 1941). He was awarded the Nobel Prize for economics in 1971.

Kyan, John Howard 1774–1850
Irish inventor
Born in Dublin, he worked in a brewery in England, and in 1832 invented a patent method of preserving wood, known as the 'kyanizing' process. He died in New York, where he was planning the filtering of the water supply.

Kyd, Thomas 1558–94
English dramatist
Born in London, he was probably educated at Merchant Taylors' School, and was most likely brought up as a scrivener under his father. His tragedies early brought him a reputation, especially *The Spanish Tragedy* (c.1587). Kyd translated from the French (1594) a tedious tragedy on Pompey's daughter Cornelia, and perhaps produced *Solyman and Perseda* (1592) and *Arden of Faversham*. He has been credited with a share in other plays, and some claim he wrote the lost original *Hamlet*. Imprisoned in 1593 on a charge of atheism (Unitarianism), which he tried to shift on to Christopher Marlowe's shoulders, Ben Jonson's 'sporting Kyd' died in poverty. 🕮 A Freeman, *Kyd: facts and problems* (1967)

Kylian, Jiri 1947–
Czech dancer and choreographer
Born in Prague, he trained at the Prague Conservatory, and was given a scholarship (1967) to study in London at the Royal Ballet School. A year later he joined Stuttgart Ballet, starting his prolific choreographic career in 1970. After a short period as assistant artistic director at Netherlands Dance Theater (NDT), he became director of the company in 1978 and has been associated with it ever since. His works include *Sinfonietta* with music by Janáček (1979), *Symphony of Psalms* (1978), the all-male *Soldiers' Mass* (1980), *Return to the Strange Land* (1975), *L'Enfant et les Sortileges* (1984), *Kaguya-Hine* (1988) and, based on Aboriginal culture, *Nomads* (1981), *Stamping Ground* (1982) and *Dreamtime* (1983). 1995 saw the 35th anniversary of NDT and the 20th anniversary of Kylian's directorship. To mark the occasion, the three companies making up NDT joined to stage *Arcimboldo*.

Kyprianou, Spyros 1932–
Cypriot politician
Born in Limassol, where he attended the Greek Gymnasium, he continued his education at the City of London College, and was called to the Bar in 1954. During that period he founded the Cypriot Students' Union and became its first secretary. He became secretary to Archbishbop Makarios in London in 1952, and returned with him to Cyprus in 1959. He was Foreign Minister (1961–72), and in 1976 founded the Democratic Front (DIKO). On Makarios's death in 1977 he became Acting President, and then President. He was re-elected in 1978 and 1983, but was defeated by the independent candidate Georgios Vassilou in 1988 having failed to find a peaceful solution to the divisions in Cyprus. In 1993 his party formed a coalition under President Glafkos Clerides.

Laar, Pieter van, *known as* **l Bamboccio ('the Cripple')** c.1590–c.1658
Dutch artist
Born in Haarlem, he is noted for his paintings of country scenes, weddings, wakes and fairs. He gave his name to the term 'bambochades' for genre paintings of bucolic themes.

Labadie, Jean de 1610–74
French Protestant reformer
He was born in Bourg, and joined a Jesuit Order in Bordeaux. He then became a Calvinist convert in 1650.

He preached a return to primitive Christianity in the Netherlands, and was excommunicated from the Reformed Church in 1670, when he moved his Labadist colony to Germany.

Laban, Rudolf von 1879–1958
Hungarian dancer, choreographer and dance theoritician
Born in Pozsony (Bratislava, Slovakia), he studied ballet, acting and painting in Paris and later danced in Vienna all over Germany, and toured Europe and Northern Africa. In 1910 he founded a school in Munich, and went on to work as a choreographer and teacher throughout Germany. He started many European schools, theatres and institutions as well as heading an organization of amateur 'movement choirs' throughout Germany. He was ballet director of Berlin State Opera (1930–34) and created dances for the Berlin Olympic Games in 1936. He moved to England (1938), where he developed his ideas about modern educational dance and movement in industrial settings. Considered the leader of the central European dance movement, he was instrumental in the development of modern dance as a theatre form. He established the Art of Movement Studio in 1946, now known as the Laban Centre and part of Goldsmiths College, London University. As early as 1920 he published the first of several volumes of his influential system of dance notation, now known as Labanotation. ⌨ John Hodgson, *Rudolf Laban: An Introduction to his Work and Influence* (1990)

Labé, Louise, *nicknamed* **la Belle Cordière ('the Lovely Ropemaker')** c.1520–1566
French poet
She was born in Parcieux, Ain, and educated in the Renaissance manner, learning Latin, music and riding. In 1542 she fought, disguised as a knight, at the Siege of Perpignan. In 1550 she married a wealthy rope manufacturer, Ennemond Perrin, at Lyons, hence her nickname. In 1555 she published her *Œuvres* ('Works'), which included three elegies and 23 sonnets in the Petrarchan style. She also wrote a prose work, *Débat de Folie et d'Amour* (1555, 'Debate Between Folly and Love'), and was noted for her love affairs, which are reflected in her work. ⌨ F Zameron, *Louise Labé, sa vie et son œuvre* (1945)

la Beche, Sir Henry Thomas de See **De la Beche, Sir Henry Thomas**

Labiche, Eugène 1815–88
French playwright
Born in Paris, he studied law but soon turned to writing as a career. He wrote one novel, *La Clef des champs* (1838, 'Key of the Fields'), and was the author of over 150 skilfully observed and crafted comedies, farces and vaudevilles, which dominated the light theatre of his day in France. His *Frisette* (1846) was the original of John Maddison Morton's *Cox and Box*, and his *Le Voyage de M. Perrichon* (1860) is a perennial favourite. ⌨ P Soupault, *Eugène Labiche, sa vie et son œuvre* (1945)

Lablache, Luigi 1794–1858
Italian bass
Born in Naples, he studied violin and cello at the Conservatorio della Pietra de' Turchini, but then concentrated on singing. He became the most famous bass of his time, his impressive voice ranging across three octaves from E flat to e' flat. He sang in Milan, Vienna, London and Paris, and had songs especially written for him, notably by Schubert. He was also a talented actor, equally at ease in tragedy or comedy.

La Bourdonnais, Bertrand François Mahé, Comte de 1699–1753
French naval officer
Born in St-Malo, he had distinguished himself by 1723, as captain in the naval service of the French Indies. In 1734 he became Governor of Île de France (Mauritius) and Île de Bourbon (Réunion) and was featured in the novel *Paul et Virginie* by Jacques Henri Bernardin de Saint Pierre. In 1740, in command of a fleet during the war between Great Britain and France, he inflicted great losses upon England. In 1746 he compelled Madras to capitulate, but granted terms on payment of 9 million livres. Accused by Joseph Dupleix of betraying the French East Indies Company's interests, he returned to Paris (1748) and languished in the Bastille until 1752, when he was declared guiltless.

Labrouste, (Pierre François) Henri 1801–75
French architect
Born in Paris, he studied at the École des Beaux-Arts and in Rome. Described as a romantic rationalist he was able to balance functional and imaginative forces to produce effective buildings. His two most influential works are the Bibliothèque Sainte Geneviève (1838–50) and the Bibliothèque Nationale reading room (1860–67), both in Paris. The former consists of a monumental stone rectangle encasing the closed book stacks supporting an ironwork structure for the reading rooms above; the latter is a fantasy shoe-horned into a restricted site in the old Palais Mazarin, where an innovatory tightly fitted cage of iron and glass, topped with skylit domes, creates a delicate feeling of movement and light.

La Bruyère, Jean de 1645–96
French writer
Born in Paris, he was educated by the Oratorians, and was chosen to aid Jacques Bossuet in educating the Dauphin. For a time he was treasurer at Caen. He became tutor to the Duc de Bourbon, grandson of the great Condé, and received a pension from the Condés until his death. His *Caractères* (1688), which gained him a host of implacable enemies as well as an immense reputation, consists of two parts, the one a translation of Theophrastus, the other a collection of maxims, reflections and character portraits of men and women of the time. He found a powerful protector in the Duchesse de Bourbon, a daughter of Louis XIV. His *Dialogues sur le quiétisme* (1699, 'Dialogues on Quietism') were directed against François Fénelon. A writer rather than a thinker of any real depth, his insight into character is shrewd rather than profound. ⌨ E Gosse, in *Three French Moralists* (1918)

Lacaille, Nicolas Louis de 1713–62
French astronomer
Born in Rumigny, he became a deacon before taking up astronomy. At the age of 26 he became Professor of Mathematics at the Collège Mazarin (now the Institut de France, Paris). As a geodesist he worked on the problem of the Earth's shape. From 1750 to 1754 he visited the Cape

of Good Hope, where he was the first to measure a South African arc of the meridian. He charted 14 new constellations and compiled the first list of 42 'nebulous stars'. His extensive catalogue of southern stars and positional data was published as *Coelum Australe Stelliferum* in 1763 ('Star Catalogue of the Southern Sky').

La Calprenède, Gautier de See Calprenède, Gautier de La

Lacépède, Bernard de Laville, Comte de
1756–1825
French naturalist

Born in Agen, he became curator in the Royal Gardens at Paris in 1785, and at the Revolution he became Professor of Natural History in the Jardin des Plantes. He was made senator in 1799, Minister of State in 1809, and in 1814 a peer of France. Besides continuing George-Louis Buffon's *Histoire Naturelle*, he wrote most of *Histoire naturelle des poissons* (1798–1803, 'The Natural History of Fishes'), *Les Âges de la nature* (1830, 'The Ages of Nature'), and other works.

Lacey, Janet 1903–88
English philanthropist

Raised in Sunderland, she worked for the YWCA in Kendal, Dagenham, and at the end of World War II with BAOR (British Army of the Rhine) in Germany. She joined the British Council of Churches as Youth Secretary in 1947, moving to the Inter-Church Aid department, which she directed from 1952 to 1968. Christian Aid Week was started in 1957, the name Christian Aid being adopted in 1964. Lacey moved on from Christian Aid to the Family Welfare Association and the Churches' Council for Health and Healing. She was the first woman to preach in St Paul's Cathedral and received an honorary Lambeth Doctor of Divinity in 1975. Her views on aid are expressed in *A Cup of Water* (1970).

Lachaise, François d'Aix 1624–1709
French Jesuit

Born in Aix, Forez, he was selected by Louis XIV to be his confessor in 1675—a post he retained until his death in spite of the difficulties of his position. The cemetery Père Lachaise was called after him.

Lachaise, Gaston 1882–1935
US sculptor

He was born in Paris, the son of a cabinetmaker, and studied at the École des Beaux-Arts in Paris from 1898 to 1903. With Isabel Nagel, an American who later became his wife, he left for Boston, arriving in January 1906. He worked initially for the jeweller René Lalique and from 1912 as an assistant to the sculptor Paul Manship in New York, and became a naturalized US citizen in 1916. He is chiefly known for his voluptuous, anatomically simplified, bronze statues of women, for example *Standing Woman* (1912–27, Whitney Museum, New York City). He also executed sculptures for the Rockefeller Center, New York City.

La Chaussée, Pierre Claude Nivelle de
1692–1754
French playwright

Born in Paris, he began writing after he was 40, and produced several sentimental plays which enjoyed great popularity. *La Comédie larmoyante* ('Tearful Comedy'), as his work was named by critics, had some influence on later writers, including Voltaire. Among his plays were *Le Préjugé à la mode* (1735, 'Fashionable Prejudice'), *Mélanide* (1741) and *L'École des mères* (1744, 'School for Mothers'). 📖 G Lanson, *Nivelle de la Chaussée et la Comédie larmoyante* (1903)

Lachmann, Karl Konrad Friedrich Wilhelm
1793–1851
German philologist

Born in Brunswick, he was professor successively at Königsberg and Berlin. A founder of modern textual criticism, he edited the *Nibelungenlied*, Walther von der Vogelweide, Propertius, Lucretius, and others. In his *Betrachtungen* (1837–41) he maintained that the *Iliad* consisted of 16 independent lays enlarged and interpolated. The smaller edition of his New Testament appeared in 1831 and the larger in 1842–50. Both were based mainly on uncial manuscripts.

Lack, David 1910–73
English ornithologist

Born in London and educated at Cambridge, he became director of the Edward Grey Institute at Oxford in 1945. His popular book, *The Life of the Robin* (1943) formed the basis of his reputation, but he also published *Darwin's Finches* (1947) on the finches of the Galapagos Islands, and *Swifts in a Tower* (1956), which contained the results of his long-term studies of great tits, swifts and a number of other species. He was a dominant influence in the transformation of ornithology from an observational to a scientific discipline. His most important books were *National Regulation of Numbers* (1954), *Population Studies of Birds* (1966), *Ecology Adaptations for Breeding in Birds* (1968) and *Ecology Isolation in Birds* (1971). He was elected FRS in 1951.

Lackland, John See John, King (panel)

Laclos, Pierre Ambroise François Choderlos de
1741–1803
French novelist and politician

Born in Amiens, he spent nearly all his life in the army but saw no active service until he was 60 and ended his career as a general. He is remembered by his one masterpiece, *Les Liaisons dangereuses* (1782, Eng trans *Dangerous Connections*, 1784). This epistolary novel reveals the influence of Jean Jacques Rousseau and Samuel Richardson and is a cynical, detached analysis of personal and sexual relationships, influenced by both Clauswitz and his own profound feminism. He also wrote *De l'éducation des femmes* (1785, 'On the Education of Women'). 📖 R Vaillant, *Laclos par lui-même* (1953)

Lacombe, Claire 1765–c.1795
French actress

Born in Pamiers, she became a professional actress in provincial theatre but took up residence in Paris in 1792. She was awarded a civic crown for her part in helping to storm the Tuileries on 10 August that year, and she was later nicknamed 'Red Rosa' for her red cap as she became recognized as a leading member of a left-wing group known as the *Enragés*. Her demand that women should be allowed to bear arms made her enemies in the new power structures evolving in Paris, and when her group was proscribed in 1794, she was imprisoned for nearly a year. Her later fate is unknown.

Lacondamine, Charles Marie de 1701–74
French mathematician, traveller and scientist

Born in Paris, he served in the army, travelled extensively, and was sent to Peru (1735–43) to measure a degree of the meridian. He explored the Amazon, and brought back the poison curare and definite information on India rubber and platinum. He wrote in favour of inoculation.

Lacoste, Robert 1898–1989
French socialist politician

Born in Azerat, he began his career as a civil servant, becoming a trade-union official. In World War II he formed the first trade-union Resistance group. In 1944 he was Minister of Industrial Production, and was Minister for Industry and Commerce in 1946–47 and again in 1948. From 1956 to 1958 he was resident minister in Algeria, and was accused of allowing the military authorities to use torture and other ruthless measures against the rebels. He was senator for the Dordogne (1971–80).

Lacroix, (François-Antoine-)Alfred 1863–1948
French mineralogist, petrologist and structural geologist
Born in Mâcon, he wen to the Sorbonne and the Collège de France in Paris, and also attended courses in mineralogy at the Museum of Natural History, where in 1893 he became Professor of Mineralogy. He recognized the importance to research of an excellent mineral collection, and devoted considerable time to building up a systematic collection from around the world. He carried out wide-ranging research on eruptive rocks, studying the eruptions of the Mont Pelée volcano in 1902, and recognized the 'nuée ardente', a glowing cloud type of eruption that he was first to witness. His studies during a visit to Madagascar in 1911 resulted in the three-volume *Minéralogie de Madagascar* (1922–23, 'Mineralogy of Madagascar'), one of his best works. He also worked on the igneous and volcanic rocks of the Massif Central, Etna, Vesuvius, and elsewhere, and on meteorites.

Lacroix, Christian 1951–
French couturier
He was born in Arles, Provence, the son of an engineer who sketched women and their clothes. He started sketching as a child and studied Classics in Montpellier, specializing in French and Italian painting and the history of costume. He studied fashion history, from 1973, intending to become a museum curator, but obtained employment at Hermès, the leather firm, and with Guy Paulin, the ready-to-wear designer. In 1981 he joined Jean Patou, who showed his first collection in 1982, but in 1987 he left to open The House of Lacroix in Paris. He made his name with ornate and frivolous clothes. In 1991 he was made Chevalier, L'Ordre des Arts et des Lettres and in 1992, published his autobiography *Pieces of a Pattern* (1992).

Lactantius, Lucius Caelius, *also called* Firmianus Caecilius 4th century AD
North African Christian apologist
Born and brought up in North Africa, he was a teacher of rhetoric in Nicomedia in Bithynia, where he was converted probably after witnessing the constancy of the Christian martyrs under the persecution of Diocletian. About AD313 he was invited to Gaul by Constantine I to act as tutor to his son Crispus. His principal work is his *Divinarum Institutionum libri vii*, a systematic account of Christian attitudes to life.

Ladenis, Nico (Nicholas Peter) 1934–
Kenyan chef and restaurateur
He went to Great Britain in 1955 to study economics at Hull University, and after graduation worked on the *Sunday Times* magazine, analysing advertising sales. He met his wife there, and after they married in 1963, travelled for a year with her in Provence, following the Michelin stars. He taught himself to cook and then opened his first restaurant in Dulwich in 1981. After many years, the coveted third Michelin star continued to elude him, and in 1992 he moved to new premises, Nico at Ninety, at the Grosvenor House Hotel on Park Lane, where the menu presents all the luxuries traditional to French cuisine. He has written *My Gastronomy* (1987).

Ladislas See Władysław IV

Laënnec, René Théophile Hyacinthe 1781–1826
French physician, inventor of the stethoscope
Born in Quimper, Brittany, he was an army doctor from 1799. In 1814 he became editor of the *Journal de Médecine* and physician to the Salpêtrière, Paris, and in 1816 chief physician to the Hôpital Necker, also in Paris, where he invented the stethoscope in the same year. In 1823 he succeeded Jean Nicholas Corvisart-Desmarets at the Hôpital de la Charité, Paris. His stethoscope consisted of a simply hollowed tube of wood, with adaptations at the end to help transmit sound more easily. The familiar binaural stethoscope, with rubber tubing going to both ears, was not developed until after his death. Regarded as the father of chest medicine, he demonstrated the importance of the instrument in diagnosing diseases of the lungs, heart and vascular systems, and introduced the basic vocabulary to describe heart and lung sounds. He died of tuberculosis, one of the chest diseases he had described so brilliantly in his *Traité de l'auscultation médiate* (1819, 'On Mediate Auscultation'). 📖 R Kervran, *Laënnec* (1960)

Laestadius, Lars Levi 1800–61
Swedish priest and botanist
Born in Arjeplog, he became in 1826 the parson in Karesuando, where he continued his botanical work. After a profound spiritual crisis in the early 1840s he began the ecstatic revivalist preaching that had great influence among the Lapps. Today there are some 300,000 Laestadians in Finland and 20,000 in Sweden.

La Farge, John 1835–1910
US artist and writer
Born in New York City of French parentage, he travelled widely in Europe, and painted pre-Impressionist landscapes and flowers from 1860 to 1876. He was commissioned (1876) by the architect H H Richardson to decorate Boston's Trinity Church with murals. Thereafter he concentrated on ecclesiastical art, designing opalescent stained-glass windows that contributed to a revival of the craft, and painting murals such as *The Ascension* in the Church of the Ascension in New York (1857). He wrote *Considerations on Painting* (1895) and *An Artist's Letters from Japan* (1897).

La Farina, Giuseppe 1815–63
Italian revolutionary and writer
Born in Messina, he was forced to leave his native Sicily in 1837 and settled in Florence. He returned when revolution broke out in 1848 and joined the Provisional Government. After the failure of the Revolutions of 1848–49, he went to live first in Paris and then in Turin. By 1853 he had come to believe in the idea of Italian unification under the King of Sardinia-Piedmont and in 1856 he founded the Italian National Society. In 1859 he helped to instigate and orchestrate a number of liberal/nationalist revolutions in central Italy which were used by the Conte di Cavour as a pretext for subsequent annexation by Piedmont. The following year he was sent by Cavour to Sicily to try to prevent Garibaldi exerting too much influence over the course of events on the island, but poor relations with the great military hero led to his withdrawal.

Lafayette, Marie Joseph Paul Yves Roch Gilbert du Motier, Marquis de 1757–1834
French soldier and revolutionary
Born in Chavagnac, into an ancient noble family, he spent a period at court before going to America, where he fought against the British during the American Revolution (1777–79 and 1780–82) and became a hero and a friend of George Washington. A liberal aristocrat, in the National Assembly of 1789 he presented a draft of a Declaration of the Rights of Man, based on the US Declaration of Independence. Hated by the Jacobins for his moderation, he defected to Austria, returning to France during the Consulate. During the Restoration he sat in the Chamber of Deputies (1818–24), became a

radical Leader of the Opposition (1825–30), and commanded the National Guard in the 1830 July Revolution.
📖 W Woodward, *Lafayette* (1939)

La Fayette, Marie Madeleine Pioche de Lavergne, Comtesse de, *known as* Madame de La Fayette 1634–93
French novelist and reformer of French romance-writing
She was born in Paris, the daughter of the Governor of Le Havre. Having married the Comte de La Fayette in 1655, and in her 33rd year formed a liaison with **François La Rochefoucauld** which lasted until his death in 1680, she played a leading part at the French court right up to her own death, as was proved by her *Lettres inédites* (1880, 'Unabridged Letters'); prior to their publication it was believed that her last years were given to devotion. Her novels are *Zaïde* (1670, Eng trans *Zayde: A Spanish History*, 1678) and her masterpiece *La Princesse de Clèves* (1678, Eng trans *The Princess of Cleves*, 1679), a study in conflict between love and marriage in the court life of her day, which led a reaction against the long-winded romances of **Gautier Calprenède** and **Madeleine de Scudéry**. 📖 M J Durry, *Madame de la Fayette* (1962)

La Follette, Robert Marion 1855–1925
US politician
Born in Primrose, Wisconsin, he graduated from the University of Wisconsin and was admitted to the Bar in 1880. He began his political career by winning election as a district attorney after exposing corruption in the local Republican Party machine. From 1885 to 1891 he served in the US House of Representatives. As Governor of Wisconsin (1901–06), he reformed the primary election process and the Civil Service, strengthened the railroad commission and introduced measures for workers' compensation and the conservation of natural resources. His widely publicized and imitated reforms became known as the 'Wisconsin Idea'. He served in the US Senate from 1906 to 1925, and though nominally a Republican he often voted independently and in keeping with his progressive views. He would have been the Progressive Party presidential candidate in 1912 but for the re-entry into politics of ex-President **Theodore Roosevelt**. In 1924 he became that party's nominee and, although he failed in his presidential bid, he received nearly 5 million votes.

La Fontaine, Jean de 1621–95
French poet
Born in Château-Thierry, Champagne, he devoted himself to studying the old writers and to verse writing. In 1654 he published a verse translation of the *Eunuchus* of **Terence**, and then went to Paris, where **Nicolas Fouquet** became his patron. He is best known for *Contes et nouvelles en vers* (1665–74, 'Stories and Tales in Verse') and *Fables choisies mises en vers* (1668–93, Eng trans *Fables*, 1804). In 1684 he presented *Discours en vers* ('An Oration in Verse') on his reception by the Academy. 📖 L Roche, *La vie de La Fontaine* (1913)

Lafontaine, Sir Louis Hippolyte 1807–64
Canadian statesman
Born in Boucherville, Quebec, he became a leader of French-Canadians and a champion of Canadian self-government. As the head of the Reform Party in Lower Canada (Quebec), he joined with **Robert Baldwin** to form a coalition government (1842–43, 1848–51). He also served as Chief Justice of Lower Canada (1853–64).

Lafontaine, Oskar 1943–
German Social Democrat politician
Born in Saarlouis and educated at Bonn University, he was chairman of the Saarland regional branch of the Social Democratic Party (SPD) from 1977 to 1996 and served as Mayor of Saarbrücken (1976–85). He gained a reputation for radicalism and was variously dubbed 'Red

Oskar' and the 'Ayatollah of the Saarland'. He began to mellow, however, after his election as Prime Minister of the Saarland regional parliament in 1985. An unsuccessful candidate for the chancellorship in 1990, he has been leader of the SPD since 1995, and was president of the SPD-controlled Bundesrat, or upper chamber (1995–96).

Laforgue, Jules 1860–87
French Symbolist poet
Born in Montevideo, Uruguay, and educated largely in Paris, he was brilliantly precocious. Up to the time of his marriage (1886), he worked as reader to the Empress Augusta of Germany. *Les Complaintes* (1885, 'The Complaints'), *L'Imitation de Notre-Dame la Lune* (1886, 'The Imitation of Our Lady the Moon') and *Le Concile féerique* (1886) were published during his lifetime. *Moralités légendaires* (1887, posthumous, 'Legendary Moralities') was a collection of satirical reworkings of folk materials. However, it was the mere dozen poems in his posthumous *Les Derniers vers* (1890) that had an enormous impact, validating free verse (he had translated **Walt Whitman**) and suggesting that poetry could be as abstract or impressionist as music or painting. A *Poésies complètes* appeared in 1894, but it was not until Pascal Pia's two-volume edition of 1979 that an authoritative text was available. His influence on French literature is almost equivalent to that of **Arthur Rimbaud**. His work also influenced Modernist poets, especially **Ezra Pound** and **T S Eliot**. 📖 M Collie, *Jules Laforgue* (1977)

Lagerkvist, Pär Fabian 1891–1974
Swedish novelist, poet, playwright and Nobel Prize winner
He was born in Växjö, and educated at Uppsala. He began his literary career first as a prose writer and then as an Expressionist poet with *Ångest* (1916, 'Angst') and *Kaos* (1918, 'Chaos'), in which he emphasizes the catastrophe of war. Later, in the face of extremist creeds and slogans, he adopted a critical humanism with the (later dramatized) novel *Bödeln* (1933, 'The Hangman') and the novel *Dvärgen* (1944, 'The Dwarf'), which explored the problems of evil and human brutality. His novel *Barabbas* (1950) concerns the thief in whose place **Jesus Christ** was crucified. Man's search for God was also explored in the play *Mannen utan själ* (1936, 'The Man without a Soul'). An ideological play, *Lät människan leva* (1949, 'Let Man Live'), was a study of political terrorism in which Christ, **Socrates**, **Bruno**, **Joan of Arc** and a US Negro appear as victims. He was awarded the Nobel Prize for literature in 1951. 📖 L Sjöberg, *Pär Lagerkvist* (1976)

Lagerlöf, Selma Ottiliaa Lovisa 1858–1940
Swedish novelist, the first woman winner of the Nobel Prize for literature
Born in Värmland, she taught at Landskrona (1885–95), and first sprang to fame with her novel *Gösta Berlings saga* (1891, 'The Story of Gösta Berling'), which was based on the traditions and legends of her native countryside, as were many of her later books, such as her trilogy on the Löwensköld family (1925–28, Eng trans *The Rings of the Löwenskolds*, 1931). She also wrote the children's classic *Nils Holgerssons underbara resa genom Sverige* (1906–07, 'The Wonderful Adventures of Nils'). Although she was a member of the Neo-Romantic generation of the 1890s, her work is characterized by a social and moral seriousness, as in *Antikrists Mirakler* (1897, 'The Miracles of Antichrist') and *Bannlyst* (1918, 'The Outcast'). She was awarded the 1909 Nobel Prize for literature, and in 1914 became the first woman member of the Swedish Academy. 📖 V Edström, *Selma Lagerlöf* (1984)

Lagrange, Joseph Louis de, Comte 1736–1813
French mathematician

Born in Turin, Italy, he succeeded **Leonhard Euler** (1766) as director of the mathematical section of the Berlin Academy, having gained a European reputation by his work on the calculus of variations, celestial mechanics and the nature of sound. While in Prussia he read before the Berlin Academy some 60 dissertations on celestial mechanics, number theory, algebraic and differential equations. He returned to Paris in 1787 at the invitation of **Louis XVI**. Under **Napoleon I** he became a senator and a count and taught at the École Normale and the École Polytechnique. In 1788 he published *Traité de mécanique analytique*, one of his most important works, in which mechanics is based entirely on variational principles, giving it a high degree of elegance. His work on the theory of algebraic equations was one of the major steps in the early development of group theory, considering permutations of the roots of an equation.

La Guardia, Fiorello H(enry) 1882–1947
US lawyer and politician

Born in New York City of Italian-Jewish origin, he became deputy Attorney-General of New York (1915–17), served with the US air force in Italy and sat in Congress (1917–21, 1923–33) as a Republican. A popular Mayor of New York (re-elected three times, 1933–45) he initiated housing and labour safeguards schemes, was one of the early opponents of **Hitler**'s anti-Semitic policies—he had his ears boxed in public by enraged US Fascists—and was civil administrator of Allied-occupied Italy. In 1946 he was appointed director-general of the United Nations Relief and Rehabilitation Agency. One of New York's airports is named after him.

Laguerre, Louis 1663–1721
French artist

Born in Paris, he went to London in 1683, where he carried out schemes of elaborate, allegorical decoration at Chatsworth, Petworth, Blenheim and elsewhere.

La Hire, Philippe de 1640–1718
French engineer, astronomer and mathematician

Born in Paris, he was employed for some years on geodesic survey work before joining the Collège Royal in 1682 where he taught mathematics. Five years later he became professor at the Royal Academy of Architecture, Paris. His most notable work was the *Traité de Méchanique* (1695) in which he correctly analysed the forces acting at various points in an arch, making use of geometrical techniques now generally known as graphic statics. Among his many inventions were improvements to the astrolabe, the sundial and the surveying level, to which he added a telescopic sight. He also devised a machine capable of showing the configurations of past and future eclipses. In 1678 he was admitted to the French Royal Academy of Sciences.

Lahr, Bert, *originally* Irving Lahrheim 1895–1967
US comic actor

Born in New York City, he left school at 15 and toured in vaudeville and burlesque before winning stardom on Broadway in the late 1920s. For nearly four decades he was a celebrated comedian on stage and in Hollywood, appearing in many farces and musicals as well as works by **Shakespeare** and **Aristophanes**. His jowly, expressive face and instinctive grasp of the comedy of fear and megalomania ideally suited him for his role as the Cowardly Lion in the film *The Wizard of Oz* (1939). He played Estragon in the original production of **Samuel Beckett**'s *Waiting for Godot* (1956), winning praise for his performance despite his protestations that he did not understand either the play or the role.

Laidlaw, William 1780–1845
Scottish poet

Born in Blackhouse, Selkirkshire, he wrote lyrics, but is best known as the friend and copying secretary of Sir **Walter Scott**, for whom he was also factor at Abbotsford (1817–26). His shepherd for 10 years was **James Hogg**, and together they helped Scott prepare his *Minstrelsy of the Scottish Border* (1802–03).

Laine, Dame Cleo, *originally* Clementina Dinah Campbell 1927–
English jazz musician and actress

Born in Southall, Middlesex, she began by singing with the big band of her husband-to-be **John Dankworth** (1927–), who was a founder-member of the legendary Club 11 (1948). She became a highly successful singer, with her wonderfully distinct delivery that has opened up opportunities in musical theatre and in straight acting. Dankworth later acted as her musical director and assumed a less prominent public role, concentrating on composition and arrangement. Although they opted to work apart for a short time, they have remained a significant musical partnership for over 30 years, running an annual workshop/festival for young musicians near their home at Wavendon, Buckinghamshire, since 1970.

Laing, Alexander Gordon 1793–1826
Scottish explorer

He was born in Edinburgh. Having served seven years as an officer in the West Indies, in 1825 he was sent to explore the Niger's source, which he found. He was murdered after leaving Timbuktu.

Laing, R(onald) D(avid) 1927–89
Scottish psychiatrist

Born in Glasgow, he graduated in medicine from Glasgow University (1951), and then practised as a psychiatrist in the city (1953–56). He joined the Tavistock Clinic, London, in 1957 and the Tavistock Institute for Human Relations in 1960, and was chairman of the Philadelphia Association (1964–82). He sprang to prominence with his revolutionary ideas about mental disorder with the publication of *The Divided Self* (1960). His principal thesis was that psychiatrists should not attempt to cure or ameliorate the symptoms of mental illness (itself a term which he repudiated) but rather should encourage patients to view themselves as going through an enriching experience. In expounding this doctrine of 'antipsychiatry', he implied in his writings that the primary responsibility for psychiatric breakdown lies with society and/or with the patient's immediate family. His writings extended from psychiatry into existential philosophy, and later into poetry. His other books include *The Politics of Experience* (1967), *Knots* (1970), *The Politics of the Family* (1976), *Sonnets* (1980) and *The Voice of Experience* (1982). 📖 Adrian C Laing, *R D Laing: A Biography* (1994)

Laing, Samuel 1780–1868
Scottish writer

Born in Orkney, he travelled, and wrote on Norway, Sweden, Russia and France. His major achievement was his monumental translation of *Heimskringla* by **Snorri Sturluson** (*History of the Kings of Norway*, 1844).

Laio Chung-k'ai See Liao Zhongkai

Laird, MacGregor 1808–61
Scottish explorer and merchant

Born in Greenock, Renfrewshire, he first travelled to the lower Niger with **Richard Lander**'s last expedition (1832–34), and was the first European to ascend the Benue River. In 1837 he started a transatlantic steamship company, for which the *Sirius*, in 1838, became the first ship to cross entirely under steam. In 1854 he financed a second expedition to the Niger, led by **William Balfour Baikie**.

Laïs
The name of two Greek courtesans

The elder was born in Corinth and flourished during the Peloponnesian War. The younger, born in Sicily, went as a child to Corinth, and sat as a model to **Apelles**. Both were famous for their beauty.

Laithwaite, Eric Roberts 1921–97
English electrical engineer and inventor

Born in Atherton, Yorkshire, he studied at Regent Street Polytechnic and Manchester University, where after war service in the RAF he remained until 1964, when he was appointed Professor of Heavy Electrical Engineering at the Imperial College of Science and Technology of the University of London. His principal research interest was in the linear motor, a means of propulsion utilizing electromagnetic forces acting along linear tracks. By incorporating magnetic levitation or air cushion suspension, high-speed experimental vehicles have been constructed without either wheels or conventional rotating electric motors. He was a professor of the Royal Institution (1967–76), and received the Nikola Tesla award from the Institution of Electrical and Electronic Engineers in 1986. His publications include *An Investor in the Garden of Eden* (1994).

Lajpat Rai, Lala 1865–1928
Indian politician and writer

He was a follower of the militant Hindu sect the Arya Samaj (Society of Nobles) and when, in 1893, it split, he and Hans Raj led the moderate 'college faction' which concentrated on building up a chain of 'Dayanand Anglo-Vedic colleges'. He also developed a somewhat sporadic interest in Congress politics, as well as a more sustained involvement in Swadeshi enterprises, a boycott of foreign-made goods, initiated in protest against the partition of Bengal. His published articles advocated technical education and industrial self-help and criticized the Congress as being a gathering of English-educated élites. Arguing that Congress should openly and boldly base itself on the Hindus alone, he led a wave of nationalism in Punjab (1904–07). The Congress split in the Surat session in 1907 and he formed the famous 'extremist' trio of Lal, Pal and Bal, with **B G Tilak** and **Bipin Chandra Pal**. Deported on charges of inciting the peasants, he led the Non-Co-operation Movement in Punjab in 1921.

Lakatos, Imre 1922–74
Hungarian philosopher of mathematics and science

Born in Debrecen, Hungary, he moved to England in 1956 after the Hungarian uprising. He taught at the London School of Economics from 1960 and became professor there in 1969. His best-known work is *Proofs and Refutations* (1976), a collection of articles in dialogue form demonstrating the creative and informal nature of real mathematical discovery. In philosophy of science he propounded a 'methodology of scientific research programmes' as an alternative to the theories of **Karl Popper** and **Thomas Kuhn** to explain scientific change. Two volumes of *Philosophical Papers* were published in 1978.

Laker, Sir Freddie (Frederick Alfred) 1922–
English business executive

Born in Kent and educated at Simon Langton School, Canterbury, he started his career in aviation with Short Brothers. He was a member of the Air Transport Auxiliary (1941–46) and a manager with British United Airways (1960–65). He was chairman and managing director of Laker Airways Ltd (1966–82), then chairman of Laker Airways (Bahamas) Ltd (1992–). His career suffered on the failure of the 'Skytrain' project in 1982, but in 1995 he founded Laker Airways Inc, which by 1997 ran a daily transatlantic flight (Gatwick–Miami). 📖 Howard Banks, *The Rise and Fall of Freddie Laker* (1982)

Laker, Jim (James Charles) 1922–86
English cricketer

He was born in Frizinghall, West Yorkshire. His outstanding achievement was to take 19 Australian wickets in the Fourth Test at Old Trafford in 1956. His figures for the match were 9 for 37 and 10 for 53. This is the only time a bowler has taken more than 17 wickets in first-class cricket and the only time a bowler has taken all 10 wickets in a Test innings. As a spin bowler he played 46 Tests for England, and at county level represented Surrey and Essex. He retired in 1964 to become a television commentator.

Lakshmi Bai 1835–58
Maratha Rani (Queen) of Jhansi

She was married to Gangadhar Roa, the Raja of Jhansi in northern India. The marriage was childless, however, so they adopted an heir who was entrusted to the regency of Lakshmibai on the Raja's death (1853). The British refused to recognize the adopted boy as heir and immediately absorbed the state of Jhansi under the annexation policy which stated that all 'dependent' Indian states without direct heirs were to lapse to the British. A brutal rebellion against the British took place in Cawnpore (1857) and Jhansi was besieged and taken despite the Rani's resistance. She fled to the fortress of Kalpi and persuaded the Indian leaders, including **Tantia Topee**, to seize the fortress of Gwalior where she proclaimed the **Nana Sahib** as Peshwa. She died fighting.

Lalande, Joseph Jérôme le François de 1732–1807
French astronomer

Born in Bourg-en-Bresse, Rhône-Alpes, he was sent to Berlin in 1751 by the Académie Française to determine the Moon's parallax. From 1762 he was Professor of Astronomy at the Collège de France, and from 1768 director of the Paris Observatory. His chief work is *Traité d'astronomie* (1764, 'Treatise of Astronomy').

Lalanne, Maxine 1827–86
French etcher and lithographer

Born in Bordeaux, he went to Paris in 1852 and executed his first lithograph in 1853. From 1853 to 1863 he worked mainly with charcoal drawings, prior to his debut as an engraver when he exhibited 32 works for the Society of Engravers. In 1866 he began a highly successful collaboration with the 'House of Cadart', who published his treatise on acid engraving, which ran to seven editions. A prolific artist whose plates of town and landscape were drawn from life, he transcribed his impressions of the troubles of 1870 to 1871 in a series of plates such as *The Siege of Paris* and *Bastion '66*.

Lalique, René 1860–1945
French jeweller and designer

Born in Ay, he established a jewellery firm (1885) in Paris, producing Art Nouveau styles. He was also an artist-craftsman in glass, which he decorated with relief figures, animals and flowers. 📖 Patricia Bayer and Mark Waller, *The Art of René Lalique* (1988)

Lalo, (Victor Antoine) Édouard 1823–92
French composer and viola player

He was born in Lille. His compositions include *Symphonie espagnole* (1875, 'Spanish Symphony') and other violin works, and operas, the best-known being *Le Roi d'Ys* (1888, 'The King of Ys'), and the ballet *Namouna* (1882).

Lam, Wilfredo 1902–82
Cuban painter

Born in Sagua la Grande, he held his first one-man show in Madrid in 1928. In 1938, in Paris, he met **Picasso**, who became his friend, and in 1940 the Surrealist **André Breton**. Lam fused Latin-American, African and Oceanic elements with the forms and conventions of the European modern movement, eg in *The Jungle* (1943). His numerous exhibitions included one in New York (with Picasso, 1939), Havana (1951) and Caracas (1955). He won the Guggenheim International award in 1964.

Lamarck, Jean-Baptiste Pierre Antoine de Monet Chevalier de 1744–1829
French naturalist and evolutionist

He was born in Bazentin. He became interested in Mediterranean flora, and while holding a post in a Paris bank began to study medicine and botany. In 1773 he published a *Flore française* ('French Flora'). In 1774 he became keeper of the royal garden (afterwards the nucleus of the Jardin des Plantes), and from 1794 he was keeper of invertebrates at the newly formed Natural History Museum. He lectured on zoology, originating the taxonomic distinction between vertebrates and invertebrates. About 1801 he had begun to think about the relations and origin of species, expressing his conclusions in his famous *Philosophie zoologique* (2 vols, 1809, Eng trans *Zoological Philosophy*, 1963) in which he postulated that acquired characters can be inherited by later generations. His *Histoire naturelle des animaux sans vertèbres* ('Natural History of Invertebrates') appeared in 1815–22. Lamarck broke with the old notion of immutable species, recognizing that species needed to adapt to survive environmental changes, and preparing the way for the now accepted theory of evolution. 📖 Richard W Burkhardt, *The Spirit of System: Lamarck and Evolutionary Biology* (1977)

La Marmora, Alfonso Ferrero 1804–78
Italian soldier and statesman

Born in Turin, he fought in the campaign against Austria in 1848 and was involved in the suppression of the Genoese revolt of 1849. During the 1850s he was instrumental in reforming the Piedmontese army, which formed the basis of the Italian army after 1860. In 1855 he commanded the Italian contingent in the Crimean War (1854–56), and in 1860 became Prime Minister on the resignation of the Conte di Cavour. In 1860 he was made Governor of recently annexed Milan and the following year Governor of Naples. He was Prime Minister again in 1864 and, as Foreign Minister, concluded the 1866 alliance with Prussia which was to lead to the Italian acquisition of Venetia. In 1870 he was once again made a royal governor, this time of Rome, just seized from the papacy.

Lamartine, Alphonse Marie Louis de 1790–1869
French poet, politician and historian

Born in Mâcon, he was brought up on ultra-royalist principles, spent much of his youth in Italy, and on the fall of Napoleon I joined the garde royale. His first, and probably his best-known and most succesful volume of poems, the *Méditations*, was published in 1820. He was successively secretary of legation at Naples and chargé d'affaires at Florence. In 1829 he declined the post of Foreign Secretary in the Bourbon ministry of the Prince de Polignac and, with another series of poems, *Harmonies poétiques et religieuses* (1829, 'Poetical and Religious Harmonies'), achieved his unanimous election to the Academy. Lamartine, still a royalist, disapproved of the revolution of 1830. A tour to the East produced his *Souvenirs d'Orient* (1841, Eng trans *Recollections of a Pilgrimage to the Holy Land*, 1850). Recalled to France in 1833, he became deputy for Mâcon. Between 1834 and 1848 he published his poems, *Jocelyn* (1836, Eng trans 1837) and *La Chute d'un ange* (1838, 'The Fall of an Angel'), and the celebrated *Histoire des Girondins* (1846, Eng trans *History of the Girondins*, 1847–48). He did not support the Orléanist regime and became a member of the Provisional Government (1848) and, as Minister of Foreign Affairs, its ruling spirit. In the presidential election of December 1848 he was defeated by Louis-Napoleon, on whose accession to power as Napoleon III Lamartine devoted

himself to literature, publishing *Confidences* (1849 and 1851, Eng trans *Memoirs of My Youth*, 1849 and 1851), *Raphaël* (1849, Eng trans 1849) (both autobiographical), *Geneviève*, *Le Tailleur de pierres de St-Point* (1851, Eng trans *The Stonecutter of St Point*, 1851), and *Histoire de la Restauration* (1850). He wrote on Joan of Arc, Cromwell, Madame de Sévigné and others, and issued monthly *Entretiens familiers* ('Intimate Conversations'). 📖 M F Guyard, *Alphonse de Lamartine* (1956)

Lamb, Lady Caroline 1785–1828
English writer

She was the daughter of Frederick Ponsonby, 3rd Earl of Bessborough, and spent her early childhood in Italy. She married William Lamb (later Viscount Melbourne) in 1805, and had a passionate affair with Byron (1812–13), of whom she famously wrote that he was 'mad, bad, and dangerous to know'. The affair is reflected in her Gothic novel *Glenarvon,* published anonymously in 1816, which contains a caricature portrait of Byron. Her mental instability, which her father had noticed when she was a child, intensified, and her condition was worsened by a chance encounter of Byron's funeral procession on its way to Newstead in 1824. She was separated from her husband the following year.

Lamb, Charles 1775–1834
English essayist and poet

Born in the Temple, London, the son of a clerk, he was educated at Christ's Hospital (1782–89), where he formed a lasting friendship with Coleridge. In 1792 he took a post at India House, where he remained for more than 30 years. In 1796 his sister Mary (1764–1847), in an attack of mania, stabbed their invalid mother to death. Her brother's guardianship was accepted by the authorities and to this trust Charles devoted his life. His early attempts at writing included poetry, a little prose romance entitled *The Tale of Rosamund Gray and Old Blind Margaret* (1797), and in 1801 *John Woodvil*—the result of his study of Elizabethan dramatic poetry, in whose revival he was to play so large a part. However, it was only with the joint publication with Mary of *Tales from Shakespeare* (1807), for William Godwin's 'Juvenile Library', that he achieved success. They went on to write several more books for children, then in 1818 Charles collected his scattered verse and prose in two volumes as the *Works of Charles Lamb*, and was invited to join the staff of the new *London Magazine*. His first essay, in August 1820, 'Recollections of the old South Sea House', was signed 'Elia', the name of a foreigner who had been a fellow-clerk. Collected as the *Essays of Elia* (1823–33), these became his best-known works. In 1825 he resigned his post in the India House due to poor health, and with Mary eventually moved to Edmonton. The separation from his friends and the now almost continuous mental alienation of his sister left him companionless, and with the death of Coleridge in 1834 the chief attractions of his life were gone. One of the most subtle and original critics and prose writers, he is familiar through his works, composed in the form of personal confidences, and through his letters, some of the most fascinating correspondence in the English language. 📖 E V Lucas, *Life of Charles Lamb* (2 vols, 1905, 1921)

Lamb, Hubert Horace 1913–97
English climatologist

Born in Bedford, Bedfordshire, he was educated at Cambridge, where he obtained a degree in natural science and geography, and went on to join the Meteorological Office. Throughout World War II he produced weather forecasts for transatlantic flights, and in 1946 he had a spell of duty on whaling ships in the southern ocean. From these two experiences he gained expertise in analysing weather charts, and this proved crucial to his two greatest achievements, namely the production of a daily weather classification for Great Britain for each day from 1861, and a study of major volcanic eruptions since 1500. This work has been invaluable in climate change studies. He helped to establish the Climatic Research Unit at the University of East Anglia in 1973, which uncovered much detail about past climates and the way people lived in those times. Lamb believed that climate had a great bearing on history and published *Climate, History and the Modern World* in 1982. His major publication, however, has been *Climate, Present, Past and Future* (2 vols, 1972, 1977).

Lamb, William See **Melbourne, 2nd Viscount**

Lamb, Willis Eugene 1913–
US physicist and Nobel Prize winner
Born in Los Angeles and educated at the University of California, he later became professor at Columbia University in New York (1938–51), before being appointed to similar posts at Stanford University (1951–56), Oxford (1956–62) and Yale (1962–74). He moved to the University of Arizona as Professor of Physics in 1974, and Regents' Professor in 1990. His studies of the structure of the hydrogen spectrum found the two possible hydrogen energy states to differ in energy by a very small amount. This 'Lamb shift' led to a revision of the theory of interaction of the electron with electromagnetic radiation, and ultimately to the theory of quantum electrodynamics. Lamb shared with **Polykarp Kusch** the 1955 Nobel Prize for physics for this research.

Lambert, Constant 1905–51
English composer, conductor and critic
Born in London, he had his first success when, as a student at the Royal College of Music, he was commissioned by **Sergei Diaghilev** to write a ballet, *Romeo and Juliet*, first performed in 1926. For several years he worked as a conductor for the Camargo Society and later of Sadler's Wells Ballet, where his musicianship and understanding of the problems of ballet had a lasting influence. He was also active as a concert conductor and music critic. Of his compositions, *The Rio Grande* (1929), a highly successful jazz concert work, is perhaps the most famous, but his lyrical gifts are apparent in the ballets *Pomona* (1927) and *Horoscope* (1938) as well as the cantata *Summer's Last Will and Testament* (1936). His concerto for piano and chamber orchestra was composed in memory of **Peter Warlock**. His book *Music Ho!* (1934) is enlivened by his understanding of painting, his appreciation of jazz, his devotion to Elizabethan music and the works of such composers as **Franz Liszt** and **Hector Berlioz**, and by its acidly witty, polished style. He was the son of the Austrialian artist **George Washington Lambert**.

Lambert, George Washington Thomas 1873–1930
Australian painter and sculptor
He was born in St Petersburg, Russia, where his US father was a railway engineer. His mother took him to Warren, New South Wales, in 1887 and in 1889 he was working in Sydney and attending art classes run by **Julian Ashton**. He returned to Sydney two years later after a time working as a station-hand in the country. He was soon contributing drawings to magazines and illustrating books. From 1894 he was exhibiting paintings, and in 1899 he won the Wynne prize for landscape painting. The next year Lambert went to England, then studied briefly in Paris, and returned to live in Chelsea where his principal work was in portraiture. His portrait subjects included Sir **George Reid** and an equestrian King **Edward VII**. In World War I he was an official war artist for Australia, and went to the Near East front, later visiting Gallipoli to make sketches with **C E W Bean**, the war historian. He returned to Australia in 1921, was involved in the contemporary arts movement, and took up sculpture.

Lambert, Johann Heinrich 1728–77
Swiss mathematician, scientist and philosopher
Born in Mulhouse, Alsace, he was largely self-taught. He first showed how to measure scientifically the intensity of light in his *Photometria* (1760), and his philosophical work *Neues Organon* (1764) was greatly valued by **Immanuel Kant**, with whom he shares early honours for work on the Milky Way. He wrote a successful popular book on cosmology, and in mathematics he proved that the numbers π and e are irrational. He also studied the mathematics of map projections and proved several theorems in what was later accepted as non-Euclidean geometry. Elected a member of the Berlin Academy of Sciences, he was the only scientist to present papers in all of its sections.

Lambert, John 1619–84
English general
He was born in Calton, near Settle, Yorkshire, and studied law before joining the Parliamentary army in the English Civil Wars, commanding **Thomas Fairfax**'s cavalry at Marston Moor in 1641 and participating in several victories, including helping **Cromwell** defeat the Scots at Preston (1648). He headed the cabal which overthrew **Richard Cromwell** in 1659, suppressed the Royalist insurrection in Cheshire in August 1659, and virtually governed the country with his officers as the 'committee of safety'. He was sent to the Tower, tried in 1662, and kept prisoner on Drake's Island, Plymouth, until his death.

Lambton, John George See **Durham, 1st Earl of**

Lamennais, Félicité Robert de 1782–1854
French priest and writer
Born in St-Malo, he was ordained as a priest in 1816. With his brother, Jean Marie Robert (1780–1860), also a priest, he retired to their estate at La Chesnaie, near Dinan, where he wrote *Réflexions sur l'état de l'Église* (1808, 'Reflections on the State of the Church') which was suppressed by **Napoleon I**. He wrote his famous *Essai sur l'indifférence en matière de religion* (1818–24, 'Essay on Indifference Toward Religion'), a denunciation of private judgement and toleration, which was favourably received in Rome. However, notions of popular liberty began to change his outlook, and *L'Avenir* ('The Future'), a journal founded by him in 1830 with **Charles de Montalembert** and others, was condemned by the pope in 1832. The *Paroles d'un croyant* (1834, 'The Words of a Believer') brought about complete severance with the Church, and he was imprisoned for the revolutionary doctrines in his later work. Active in the 1848 February Revolution, he sat in the Assembly until the coup d'état. At his death he refused to make peace with the Church. He also wrote *Esquisse d'une philosophie* (1840–46).

La Mettrie, Julien Offroy de 1709–51
French philosopher and physician
Born in St-Malo, he first studied theology, then switched to medicine and became surgeon to the Guards in Paris (1742). His materialistic philosophy held that all psychical phenomena were to be explained as the effects of organic changes in the brain and nervous system. His first exposition of this in *L'histoire naturelle de l'âme* (1745, 'Natural History of the Soul') provoked such hostility that the book was publicly burned and he was forced to flee to Leyden, Holland. He further developed these theories in *L'Homme machine* (1747, *A Study in the Origins of an Idea*, 1960) and had to move on again to escape arrest, finding refuge in Berlin under the protection of **Frederick II, the Great** of Prussia. He worked out the ethical implications of his materialism in such works as *Discours sur le bonheur* (1748, 'Discourse on Happiness'), *Le Petit Homme à longue queue* (1751, 'The Small Man in a Long Queue') and *L'Art de jouir* (1751) where he argued that the only real pleasures are

those of the senses, that pleasure is the only goal of life, that virtue is just enlightened self-interest and that the soul perishes with the body. He seems to have lived a life of carefree hedonism according to these precepts, and died of food poisoning. Frederick himself wrote a memoir of his life.

Lamming, George Eric 1927–
Barbadian novelist
Born in Carrington Village, he was a teacher in Trinidad and in Venezuela before going to England in 1950, where he worked as a factory labourer and hosted a book programme for the BBC West Indian Service. Beginning with *In the Castle of My Skin* (1953), he has explored the West Indian experience in a complex and highly textured way, but the unfamiliarity to many readers of the background and argot of his first novels meant they received a lukewarm reception. *Season of Adventure* (1960) articulates his own dilemma as an artist, and *Natives of My Person* (1972), with its archaic vocabulary and mythic roots, is perhaps his tour de force. ⌨ S P Paquet, *George Lamming* (1982)

Lamond, Frederic 1868–1948
Scottish pianist and composer
Born in Glasgow, he was a pupil of **Hans Bülow** and **Franz Liszt**. He made his debut in Berlin in 1885 and followed this by touring in Europe and the USA, earning a distinguished reputation as an exponent of **Beethoven**. Among his compositions are an overture *Aus dem schottischem Hochlande*, a symphony, and several piano works.

Lamont, Johann von 1805–79
German astronomer and geophysicist
Born in Braemar, Aberdeenshire, Scotland, he was educated at the Scottish monastery in Regensburg, Germany. In 1827 he went to work at the observatory at Bogenhausen, near Munich, under Johannes von Soldner, whom he succeeded as director in 1835. In 1852 he was appointed to the chair of astronomy at the University of Munich which he held, jointly with the directorship of the observatory, until his death. He published a number of star catalogues and determined the mass of the planet Uranus. In 1840 he equipped a magnetic observatory at Bogenhausen for comprehensive terrestrial magnetism surveys. In 1850, as a result of reviewing German magnetic records since 1835, he discovered a 10.5-year magnetic cycle subsequently shown to correlate with the sunspot cycle.

Lamont, Norman Stewart Hughson Lamont, Baron 1942–
Scottish Conservative politician
He was born in Lerwick, Shetland. He entered parliament in 1972 as MP for Kingston-upon-Thames. In the Thatcher administrations he rose to be Under-Secretary of State for Energy (1979–81) and Trade and Industry Minister (1981–85), before he entered the Treasury. As Financial Secretary (1986–89), then Chief Secretary, he supported the then Chancellor, **John Major**, in his successful bid for the premiership (1990), and was appointed Chancellor (1990–93). With the economy increasingly troubled, he withdrew Great Britain from the European Exchange Rate Mechanism (September 1992), which led to the effective devaluation of sterling. He resigned in 1993, and was replaced by **Kenneth Clarke**. When his seat was abolished in boundary changes he was accepted in 1996 as candidate for the apparently 'safe' seat of Harrogate and Knaresborough, but failed to be elected in 1997. He was created a life peer in 1998.

La Motte, Antoine Houdar de 1672–1731
French poet and playwright
He was born in Paris, and translated the *Iliad* into French verse (1714). Of his other writings, perhaps the best known is the play *Inès de Castro* (1723). ⌨ P Du Pont, *Antoine La Motte* (1898)

L'Amour, Louis 1908–88
US novelist
Born in Jamestown, North Dakota, he grew up riding and hunting in the West, and earned his living in a variety of ways—as prize-fighter, tugboat deckhand, lumberjack, gold prospector and deputy sheriff. The first of his crude, but effective novels about the Wild West, *Hondo* (1953), was an instant success. He followed it with another 80 titles, including *Hopalong Cassidy and the Riders of High Rock* (1951), *High Lonesome* (1962), *Ride the Dark Trail* (1972) and *The Iron Marshall* (1979). He received the 1984 Presidential Medal of Freedom. ⌨ *Education of a Wandering Man* (1989)

Lampedusa, Giuseppe Tomasi di 1896–1957
Italian novelist
He was born in Palermo, Sicily, the son of the Duke of Parma and grandson of the Prince of Lampedusa. His family had once been rich but indolence, divided inheritance and apathy had reduced its circumstances. As a youth he was wild but he turned bookish and scholarly and, despite his family's disapproval, buried himself in his library where he read voraciously and eclectically in several languages. His mother, born Beatrice Mastrogiovanni Tasca, was a dominant influence in his life and it was not until she died that he felt free to embark on the novel that is his memorial, his only book, *Il Gattopardo* (1958, Eng trans *The Leopard*, 1960). Set in Sicily in the latter half of the 19th century it is a historical novel, violent, decadent and nostalgic. It was rapturously received then vilified by the Italian literary establishment, including **Alberto Moravia**, but has subsequently come to be regarded as one of the greatest Italian novels of the 20th century. ⌨ A Vitello, *I Gattopardi di Donnafugata* (1963)

Lancaster, Duke of See **John of Gaunt**

Lancaster, Burt, *originally* **Stephen Burton Lancaster** 1913–94
US film actor
Born in New York City, he was a circus acrobat before making his Broadway debut in *A Sound of Hunting* (1945). Signed to a Hollywood contract, his film debut followed in *The Killers* (1946). Tall and muscular, he was cast in a succession of swashbuckling tough-guy roles. One of the first actors to form his own production company, he increasingly sought opportunities to test his dramatic abilities, earning Academy Award nominations for *From Here to Eternity* (1953), for his winning role as *Elmer Gantry* (1960), and for *Birdman of Alcatraz* (1962) and *Atlantic City* (1980).

Lancaster, G B, *pseudonym of* **Edith Joan Lyttleton** 1873–1945
Australasian author of novels and short stories
Born in Clyne Vale, Tasmania, of Scottish–Canadian descent, she was brought up on a sheep station outside Canterbury, New Zealand, but lived in London between 1909 and 1925. A prolific author, she wrote hundreds of short stories and 13 novels, from *Sons o' Men* (1904) to *Grand Parade* (1943). She travelled extensively in Europe and North America, and only three of her novels have an identifiably Australian origin, of which the most significant is *Pageant* (1933), the tale of a Tasmanian family, in which she drew extensively upon her family history. She was always more popular in Britain than in either of her homelands, being seen there as an 'expatriate' writer.

Lancaster, Sir James c.1554–1618
English navigator
A soldier and merchant, he served under **Francis Drake** in the Armada battle (1588), went on the first English trading expedition to the East Indies (1591–94), and in 1595 captured Pernambuco. He commanded the first fleet of

the East India Company that visited the East Indies (1600–03), and on his return was knighted. He later promoted voyages in search of the Northwest Passage.

Lancaster, Joseph 1778–1838
English educationist and Quaker

In 1798 he opened a school in London based on a monitorial system which was taken up by the Nonconformists, while **Andrew Bell** and his rival system were supported by the Church of England. The Lancasterian schools were non-denominational, and the Bible formed a large part of the teaching. The Royal Lancasterian Society, afterwards known as the British and Foreign School Society, was formed in 1808. Lancaster left the Society in anger in 1818, and went to the USA, where he gave lectures and founded several schools.

Lancaster, Sir Osbert 1908–86
English cartoonist and writer

Born in London, he studied art at Byam Shaw and the Slade School of Art, and worked on *Architectural Review* (1934–39), writing and illustrating humorous articles. For some time he designed posters for London Transport, book jackets, hotel murals, etc, before joining the *Daily Express* (1939) for a long series of front page *Pocket Cartoons*, witty comments for which he created Lady Maudie Littlehampton and friends. He also designed sets and costumes for ballet (*Pineapple Poll*, etc) and opera (*Rake's Progress*, etc) and wrote many books, including his autobiography, *All Done From Memory* (1953). 📖 Richard Boston, *Osbert: A Portrait of Osbert Lancaster* (1990)

Lanchester, Frederick William 1868–1946
English engineer, inventor and designer

Born in Lewisham, London, he won a scholarship to what is now Imperial College, London, then joined the Forward Gas Engine Company in Birmingham (1889), and in 1893 set up his own workshop next to theirs. He built the first experimental motor car in Great Britain (1895) and founded the Lanchester Engine Company in 1899, which produced the first Lanchester car in 1901. Over the next four years almost 400 of his cars were sold. Turning his attention to aeronautics, he laid the theoretical foundations of aircraft design in *Aerial Flight* (2 vols, 1907–08), which was ahead of its time in describing boundary layers, induced drag and the dynamics of flight. *Aircraft in Warfare* (1914), which quantified the numerical strength of contending military forces, was an early essay in operational analysis. He was elected president of the Institute of Automobile Engineers in 1910, Fellow of the Royal Aeronautical Society in 1917 and FRS in 1922.

Lancret, Nicolas 1690–1743
French painter

Born in Paris, he was renowned for his fête-galante paintings of balls, fairs and village weddings in the style of **Antoine Watteau**.

Land, Edwin Herbert 1909–91
US inventor and physicist

He was born in Bridgeport, Connecticut, and left his studies at Harvard University to study the principles of light polarization. He is known especially for his invention of the 'Polaroid' camera, which takes and processes photographs on the spot, and for research on the nature of colour vision. 📖 Ernest V Heyn, *Fire of Genius* (1976)

Landau, Lev Davidovich 1908–68
Soviet physicist and Nobel Prize winner

Born in Baku, he went to Baku University aged 14, and received his PhD from Leningrad (now St Petersburg) University in 1927. He studied with **Niels Bohr** in Copenhagen, and became Professor of Physics at Moscow University in 1937. He explained the 'superfluidity', or zero viscosity, of helium in terms of the collective, rather than individual, behaviour of the atoms in the liquid, work which was later developed by **Richard Feynman**. Landau received the 1962 Nobel Prize for physics for his work on theories of condensed matter, particularly helium.

Landells, Ebenezer 1808–60
English wood-engraver

Born in Newcastle upon Tyne, he originated the humorous magazine *Punch* in 1841, worked under **Thomas Bewick**, and in 1829 settled in London. He contributed wood-engravings to both *Punch* and the *Illustrated London News*.

Lander, Harald, *originally* Alfred Bernhardt Stevnsborg 1905–71
French dancer, choreographer and teacher

Born in Copenhagen, Denmark, he trained at the Royal Danish Ballet School (RDBS) and then joined the company (1923) to become a distinguished character soloist. He studied and danced in the USA, South America and the USSR (1926–29), returning to the RDBS as ballet master and, in 1932, becoming director. Under him the company flourished. He preserved the works of **August Bournonville** while developing a new repertoire (some 30 ballets of his own, including his most famous, *Études*, 1948) of contemporary European works and encouraging new dancers. From 1950 to 1966 he was married to the Danish dancer Toni Pihl Petersen (1931–). They moved to Paris in the early 1950s, where he became ballet master and director of the Opera's school, taking the company and his works all over the world. He became a French citizen in 1956.

Lander, Richard 1803–34
English explorer

Born in Truro, Cornwall, he accompanied the explorer **Hugh Clapperton** as his servant to Sokoto in 1825. There Clapperton died, and Lander published an account of the expedition. The British government sent him and his brother John (1807–39) to make further researches along the lower Niger, and in 1830 they proved that the Niger flows through many channels into the Bight of Benin. During a third expedition (1832–34), organized by **Macgregor Laird**, Lander was wounded by Niger people, and died in Fernando Pó.

Landers, Ann, *pseudonym of* Esther Pauline (Eppie) Lederer, *née* Friedman 1918–
US newspaper columnist

Born in Sioux City, Iowa, she won a competition in 1955 to take over an advice-to-the-lovelorn column in the *Chicago Sun-Times*. In her popular column, which is still published in newspapers throughout the USA, she replies to readers and gives advice and information on topics such as family life, marriage, social issues, and health. Her twin sister, **Abigail Van Buren** (Mrs Morton Phillips), also writes an advice column, 'Dear Abby'.

Landis, Kenesaw Mountain 1866–1944
US jurist and baseball commissioner

Born in Millville, Ohio, he was educated at the university of Cincinnati and the Union College of Law, Chicago. As a district judge in Illinois in 1907 he imposed a fine of $29m on the Standard Oil Company over rebate cases (the decision was reversed on appeal). After the bribery scandal in the World Series of 1919, when the Chicago White Sox were accused of deliberately losing a game to the Cincinnati Reds, he was appointed first commissioner of organized baseball (1920). He banned eight Chicago players from the game, although they had been acquitted in court, and his firm line was influential in restoring the credibility of baseball.

Landon, Alf(red Mossman) 1887–1987

US politician

Born in West Middlesex, Pennsylvania, he graduated from the University of Kansas in 1908 and soon made a fortune in the oil business. He entered state politics as a progressive Republican and served as Governor of Kansas (1933–37), garnering praise for his balanced state budgets and becoming the only Republican gubernatorial candidate to win in the elections of 1934. Nominated as the Republican candidate for President in 1936, Landon endorsed much of the New Deal, promising only to administer relief for the poor and unemployed more economically. His stinging defeat by incumbent **Franklin D Roosevelt**—he won only two states and eight electoral votes—ended his career in national politics.

Landor, Walter Savage 1775–1864

English writer

Born in Warwick, he was expelled from Rugby and Trinity College, Oxford, and spent a large part of his life in France and Italy. *Gebir* (1798), a poem showing the influence of **Milton** and **Pindar**, was the occasion of his lifelong friendship with **Robert Southey**, but it was a failure. He wrote other poems and plays, and his best-known work is *Imaginary Conversations* (2 vols, 1824–29), a collection of prose dialogues. He wrote the *Examination of Shakespeare* (1834), then quarrelled with his wife and moved to Bath, England, where he wrote *Pericles and Aspasia* (1836), *Pentameron* (1837), *Hellenics* (1847) and *Poemata et Inscriptiones* (1847). In 1858 an unhappy scandal (see his *Dry Sticks Fagoted by Landor*, 1858), involving a libel action, drove him back to Italy and he lived in Florence until his death. ▫ R H Super, *Landor, a biography* (1954)

Landowska, Wanda 1879–1959

Polish pianist, harpsichordist, and musical scholar

Born in Warsaw, she went to Paris in 1900, and in 1912 became Professor of the Harpsichord at the Berlin Hochschule. After World War I, when she was detained in Germany, she toured extensively, and in 1927 established her École de Musique Ancienne at Saint-Leu-la-Forêt, near Paris, where she gave specialized training in the performance of old works. When Germany invaded France in 1940, she fled first to the south of France, then to Switzerland, and finally in 1941 to the USA. A distinguished interpreter of **J S Bach** and **Handel**, she renewed interest in the harpsichord, and **Manuel de Falla** wrote his harpsichord concerto for her. She herself composed songs, and piano and orchestral pieces.

Landsberg, Helmut Erich 1906–85

US climatologist

Born in Frankfurt am Main, Germany, he studied there before carrying out research at Pennsylvania State University from 1934 to 1941. During the period 1941–43, he provided climatological knowledge for military planning. He produced climatological charts for the National Atlas of the USA and undertook a study of the results of urbanization of the natural environment. He did much to establish climatology as a physical science, being instrumental in establishing the National Climate Centre at Asheville. In 1946 he was on the Joint Research and Development Board of the USA which coordinated research activities nationally. At the Air Force Research Center in Cambridge, Massachusetts (1951–54), he organized the first numerical weather prediction efforts. He was director of the Climatology Weather Bureau (1954–65), president of the World Meteorological Organisation Commission for Climatology (1969–78), and the recipient of the International Meteorological Organisation prize and many other major awards.

Landsbergis, Vytautas 1932–

Lithuanian politician and musicologist

Born in Kaunas, he trained in music at the Vilnius Conservatory, where he later became Professor of Musicology. In 1988 he became founding-president of the Lithuanian separatist movement Sajudis, which took control of the government the following year. On becoming President when Lithuania declared its independence from Moscow in 1990, he was immediately confronted by economic sanctions imposed by Moscow. Landsbergis's refusal to back-track resulted in Russian troops occupying Vilnius and seizing several public buildings in 1991 on the pretext of rounding up Lithuanian conscripts to the Soviet army. His presidency came to an end in the elections of 1992 and he became leader of the Opposition party.

Landseer, Sir Edwin Henry 1802–73

English animal painter

Born in London, he was trained by his father, the engraver John Landseer (1769–1852), to sketch animals from life, and he began exhibiting at the Royal Academy when only 13 years old. His animal pieces were generally made subservient to some sentiment or idea, but did not lose their correctness and force of draughtsmanship. The scene of several fine pictures is laid in the Scottish Highlands, which he first visited in 1824. His *Monarch of the Glen* was exhibited in 1851, and the bronze lions at the foot of **Nelson's** Monument in Trafalgar Square were modelled by him (1859–66). He was buried in St Paul's Cathedral. Most of Landseer's pictures are well known from the excellent engravings of them by his elder brother Thomas (1796–1880). ▫ Ian B Hill, *Landseer* (1973)

Landsteiner, Karl 1868–1943

US pathologist, the discoverer of blood groups, and Nobel Prize winner

Born in Vienna, Austria, he was a research assistant at the Pathological Institute there, and Professor of Pathological Anatomy from 1909. He later went to the USA to work in the Rockefeller Institute for Medical Research, New York City (1922–39). He won the 1930 Nobel Prize for physiology or medicine, especially for his valuable discovery of the four major human blood groups (A, O, B, AB) which he discovered in 1901, and the M and N groups (discovered in 1927). In 1940 he also discovered the rhesus (Rh) factor.

Lane, Sir Allen, *originally* Allen Lane Williams 1902–70

English publisher and pioneer of paperback books

Born and educated in Bristol, he was apprenticed in 1919 to the Bodley Head publishing house under its founder and his relative John Lane (1854–1925). He resigned as managing director in 1935 in order to form Penguin Books Ltd, a revolutionary step in the publishing trade. He began by reprinting novels in paper covers at sixpence each, expanding to other series such as non-fictional Pelicans and children's Puffins, establishing a highly successful publishing concern. ▫ J E Monpurgo, *Allen Lane, King Penguin: A Biography* (1979)

Lane, Sir (William) Arbuthnot 1856–1943

Scottish surgeon

Born in Fort George, Inverness-shire, he was educated in Scotland and joined Guy's Hospital, London, in 1872. He was the first to join fractures with metal plates instead of wires. Other important contributions to medicine were his treatment of the cleft palate and of 'chronic intestinal stasis'. In 1925 he founded the New Health Society.

Lane, Edward William 1801–76

English Arabic scholar

Born in Hereford, the son of a cleric, he trained as an engraver in London, but went to Egypt for his health. There he was given a Greek slave, Anastasia, whom he later married. He wrote *Manners and Customs of the Modern Egyptians* (1836), followed by the annotated translation of the *Thousand and One Nights* (1838–40), which was the first accurate rendering, and by *Selections from the Koran* (1843). The great work of his life was the *Arabic-English Lexicon* (8 vols, 1863–93), of which the last three volumes were completed by his great-nephew, Stanley Lane-Poole (1854–1931).

Lane, Dame Elizabeth, *née* Coulbourn 1905–88
English lawyer

Educated privately and at Malvern Girls College, she married a barrister, Henry Lane (d.1975), in 1926. The death of her only child led her to study for the Bar and become a barrister in 1940. In 1960 she was the third woman to be appointed QC, and she became a Master of the Bench in 1965. She was assistant Recorder of Birmingham (1953–61) before becoming Recorder of Derby and Commissioner of the Crown Court at Manchester (1961–62). She was then the first woman circuit court judge until 1965, when she became the first woman to be appointed a High Court judge, working in the Family Division. In 1971–73 she chaired the committee on the working of the Abortion Act, continuing to serve at the High Court until her retirement in 1979. She was created DBE in 1965.

Lane (of St Ippollitts), Geoffrey Dawson, Lord 1918–
English judge

Appointed a judge in 1966, he became a Lord Justice of Appeal (1974–79) then Lord-of-Appeal-in-Ordinary (1979–80) and Lord Chief Justice of England (1980–92), in which capacity he proved a vigorous leader of the courts. He was made a life peer in 1979.

Lane, Sir Hugh Percy 1875–1915
Irish art collector and critic

Born in Ballybrack, Cork, he founded a gallery of modern art in Dublin at the beginning of the 20th century by his encouragement of contemporary artists, such as Jack B Yeats and William Orpen, and by his own gifts of pictures. Director of the National Gallery of Ireland in 1914, he was drowned the following year when the *Lusitania* was torpedoed. The disposition of his collection of French Impressionists caused a dispute between London and Dublin that was only settled in 1959 when it was decided to share them.

Lane, Richard James 1800–82
English engraver

Born in Berkeley Castle, Gloucestershire, he became an associate engraver of the Royal Academy, London (1827), then turned to lithography, reproducing works by Sir Thomas Lawrence, Thomas Gainsborough, Charles Robert Leslie, Sir Edwin Landseer and George Richmond (1809–96). He was also a sculptor. He was the brother of Edward William Lane.

Lane, William 1861–1917
Australian socialist and utopian

He was born in Bristol, England. In 1889 he became involved in the formation of the Australian Labour Federation (ALF) but when its maritime and shearers' strikes of 1891 collapsed and the ALF turned to political action, he decided to build his own socialist dream. Influenced by Edward Bellamy's popular utopian novel *Looking Backward* (1888), he sailed for Paraguay with his growing family and 220 colonists. There, on a strange mix of socialist, religious and racist principles, he founded 'New Australia'. This settlement eventually split and Lane created an even more rigid colony nearby, named 'Cosme'. When this broke up, he went to New Zealand and edited the conservative daily *New Zealand Herald*, in which he denounced industrial strife and advocated military training.

Lanfranc c.1005–89
Italian prelate

Born in Pavia, he studied law, and founded a school at Avranches c.1039. In 1041 he became a Benedictine at Bec, and in 1046 was chosen prior. He contended against Berengar of Tours in the controversy over transubstantiation. At first condemning the marriage of William of Normandy (William I) with his cousin, he went to Rome in 1059 to procure the papal dispensation. In 1062 William made him prior of St Stephen's Abbey at Caen, and in 1070 Archbishop of Canterbury. His chief writings are commentaries on the Epistles of St Paul, a treatise against Berengar's *De Corpore et sanguine Domini* (1079), and sermons.

Lanfranco, Giovanni c.1581–1647
Italian religious painter

Born in Parma, he was one of the first Italian Baroque painters. His work, the best of which can be seen on the dome of S Andrea della Valle in Rome and in his paintings for the cathedral at Naples, was widely copied by later painters.

Lang, Andrew 1844–1912
Scottish writer

Born in Selkirk, in the Borders, he was educated at St Andrews and Glasgow universities and Balliol College, Oxford, and was a Fellow of Merton College, Oxford (1868–74), studying myth, ritual and totemism. He moved to London in 1875 to take up journalism, and took part in a celebrated controversy with Max Müller over the interpretation of folk-tales, arguing that folklore was the foundation of literary mythology. The author of books such as *Myth, Ritual and Religion* (1887) and *Modern Mythology* (1897), he was also known as an indifferent and cantankerous critic. His other works include a *History of Scotland* (3 vols, 1899–1904), a *History of English Literature* (1912), studies of many literary figures, including *Letters to Dead Authors* (1886), a translation of Homer, and several volumes of verse. ▣ R L Green, *Andrew Lang, a critical biography* (1946)

Lang, Cosmo Gordon 1864–1945
Scottish Anglican prelate and Archbishop of Canterbury

Born in Fyvie, Aberdeenshire, he was the third son of John Marshall Lang (1834–1909), Principal of Aberdeen University. Entering the Church of England in 1890, he was a curate at Leeds, became Dean of Divinity at Magdalen College, Oxford, Bishop of Stepney (1901–08) and canon of St Paul's. In 1908 he was appointed Archbishop of York and in 1928 Archbishop of Canterbury. He retired in 1942. A man of wide interests, he was accepted by all parties in the Church of England and was both counsellor and friend to the royal family.

Lang, Fritz 1890–1976
US film director

Born in Vienna, Austria, he was educated there at the College of Technical Sciences and the Academy of Graphic Arts, intending to become a painter. Instead he joined the Decla Film Company (1919). In Berlin he directed two *Dr Mabuse* films (1926), and, also in 1926, his most famous film, *Metropolis*, a nightmare vision of the future where a large section of the population is reduced to slavery. When Hitler came to power in 1933, Goebbels offered Lang the post of head of the German film industry, but he refused and the same night fled to Paris and later to the USA. Among his many films of this period, *Fury* (1936) was acclaimed as a masterpiece for its portrayal of mob rule. His many other films include *Halbblut* (1919, 'The Half Caste'), *Liliom* (1933), *You Only Live Once*

(1937), *The Return of Frank James* (1940), *Hangmen Also Die* (1943), *Secret Beyond the Door* (1948), *The House By the River* (1949), *Clash by Night* (1951), *Human Desire* (1954), *While the City Sleeps* (1955) and *Beyond a Reasonable Doubt* (1956). Back in Germany in 1960 he directed a third *Dr Mabuse* film.
🕮 Lotte Eisner, *Fritz Lang* (1977)

Lang, Ian Lang, Baron 1940–
Scottish Conservative politician

Born in Glasgow and educated at Rugby and Sidney Sussex College, Cambridge, he was an insurance broker and Lloyds' underwriter before entering parliament at the third attempt, becoming Conservative MP for Galloway (1979). He retained his seat, by then called Galloway and Upper Nithsdale, in 1983, 1987 and 1992, but lost it in 1997. Minister of State for Scotland from 1987, he was promoted to Secretary of State for Scotland (1990–95), faced with the task of administering a country in which only one in eight members of parliament belonged to the party of government, and then served as President of the Board of Trade (1995–97).

Lang, John Dunmore 1799–1878
Australian clergyman and politician

Born in Greenock, Scotland, he was educated at Glasgow University, and went to New South Wales in 1823 with a mission to establish Presbyterianism in the new colony. The foundation stone of Scots Church, Sydney, was laid in the following year. With the support of Lord Bathurst, Secretary of State for the Colonies, the church opened in 1826. Lang started a weekly newspaper in 1835 and was soon involved in lawsuits as a result of his outspoken comments, being imprisoned on four occasions. Concerned about education, he was energetic in assisting the emigration of skilled workers. He was elected a member of the Legislative Council for three periods and of the Legislative Assembly from 1859 to 1869.

lang, k.d., *properly* Kathy Dawn Lang 1962–
Canadian singer and lesbian icon

Born in Consort, Alberta, she played piano and guitar as a child, and later attended drama college in Vancouver. She formed her group 'the reclines' (in memory of **Patsy Cline**) by the age of 21, and made a big impact with her magnificent voice and raw, unrestrained take on country music. She recorded *Shadowland* with the leading Nashville producer Owen Bradley in 1988, but after the successful *Absolute Torch and Twang* (1989), turned to sophisticated pop on the brilliant *Ingenue* (1992) and the less convincing *All You Can Eat* (1995). She was banned by US country radio for her outspoken anti-meat views in 1990.
🕮 V Starr, *All You Get Is Me* (1994)

Langdell, Christopher Columbus 1826–1906
US legal scholar

He was born in Hillsborough, New Hampshire, and educated at Harvard. As Dane professor (1870–75) and Dean of the Harvard Law school (1875–95), he raised the school's standards and exercised a powerful influence on legal education throughout the USA. Initiating the 'case method' of teaching in which real cases are cited in the text as examples, he compiled the first *Casebook on Contracts* (1871) which established a national trend.

Langdon, Harry Philmore 1884–1944
US comedian

Born in Council Bluffs, Iowa, he appeared in amateur shows as a child and joined *Dr Belcher's Kickapoo Indian Medicine Show* in 1897. He continued to gain experience in circuses, vaudeville and burlesque, developing the character of an innocent, bemused by the wider world. He made his film debut in the serial *The Master Mystery* (1918) and was signed by **Mack Sennett** for a series of short comedies, beginning with *Picking Peaches* in 1924. He made some popular features, including *Tramp Tramp Tramp*

(1926), *The Strong Man* (1926) and *Long Pants* (1927). After a failed attempt at making his own films, he had supporting roles in films like *Hallelujah, I'm a Bum* (1933) and *Zenobia* (1939), and worked behind the scenes on such **Laurel** and **Hardy** films as *Blockheads* (1938) and *Saps at Sea* (1940).

Lange, Carl Georg 1834–1900
Danish physician and psychologist

As Professor of Pathological Anatomy at Copenhagen University, he advanced a theory of emotion which was independently developed by William James and is now known as the James–Lange theory. He also wrote a history of materialism.

Lange, David Russell 1942–
New Zealand politician

After studying law at Auckland University and qualifying as a solicitor and barrister, he worked as a crusading lawyer for the underprivileged in Auckland. His election to the House of Representatives in 1977 changed the direction of his life and he rose rapidly to become deputy Leader of the Labour Party in 1979 and Leader in 1983. He won a decisive victory in the 1984 general election on a non-nuclear defence policy, which he immediately put into effect, despite criticism from other Western countries, particularly the USA. He and his party were re-elected in 1987, but, following bouts of ill health and disagreements within his party, he resigned the premiership in 1989. He was then Attorney-General and Minister of State until 1990.

Lange, Dorothea, *originally* Dorothea Nutzhorn 1895–1965
US photographer

Born in Hoboken, New Jersey, she studied at Columbia and established a studio in San Francisco in 1919, but became dissatisfied with the role of a society photographer. She is best known for her social records of migrant workers, sharecroppers and tenant farmers throughout the south and west of the USA in the Depression years from 1935, and especially for her celebrated study, 'Migrant Mother' (1936). With her husband, economist Paul Taylor, she collaborated on a book, *An American Exodus: A Record of Human Erosion* (1939). After World War II she worked as a freelance photo-reporter in Asia, South America and the Middle East (1958–63).

Lange, Jessica 1949–
US film actress

Born in Minnesota, she travelled across the USA and Europe with her first husband Paco Grande, settling for a time in Paris to study at the Opéra Comique before returning to New York. Her film debut was in the 1976 remake of *King Kong*, but public indifference to the film damaged her aspirations. She continued to find work, however, and won critical acclaim for her performances in *The Postman Always Rings Twice* (1981), *Frances* (1982), and *Tootsie* (1982, Best Supporting Actress Academy Award). Drawn to parts that reflect some of her political and environmental concerns, she has played diverse roles including *Country* (1984), *Sweet Dreams* (1985), *The Music Box* (1989), *Cape Fear* (1991), *Blue Sky* (1994, Best Actress Academy Award) and *Rob Roy* (1995). She made her Broadway debut in *A Streetcar Named Desire* (1992), repeating her role for a cable production in 1995 and at the Haymarket Theatre, London (1996–97).

Langer, Bernhard 1957–
German professional golfer

Born in Anhausen, he is regarded as the professional's professional, due to his course management and record 67 tournaments without missing a cut. He turned professional at the age of 15, won the US Masters twice and by 1995 had amassed 34 victories on the PGA (Professional Golfers' Association) European Tour—one title a year for

16 years. His putting problems led him to develop a unique style, which is largely successful, though he may go down in history for having missed a six-foot (2m) putt and lost Europe the 1991 Ryder Cup. The following week he won the German Masters.

Langer, Susanne K(nauth) 1895–1985
US philosopher
Born in New York City, she studied at Radcliffe College, where she taught (1927–42), later holding positions at the University of Delaware, Columbia University and Connecticut College. She was greatly influenced by **Ernst Cassirer**, and published important works in aesthetics and linguistic analysis, including *Philosophy in a New Key* (1942), *Feeling and Form* (1953), *Problems of Art* (1957) and *Mind: An Essay on Human Feeling* (3 vols, 1967–82).

Langevin, Paul 1872–1946
French physicist
Born in Paris, he was educated at the École Normale Supérieure, spent a year in Cambridge, and came to the notice of **J J Thomson**. He returned to Paris to take his doctorate and study with **Pierre Curie**. In 1909 he was appointed Professor of Physics at the Sorbonne. Studying magnetic phenomena, he related the paramagnetic movement of molecules to their absolute temperature (1905), and predicted the paramagnetic saturation discovered by **Heike Kamerlingh Onnes** in 1914. He worked on the molecular structure of gases, and during World War I applied sonar techniques to the detection of submarines. He was elected a Foreign Member of the Royal Society in 1928, and was awarded its Hughes Medal. Imprisoned by the Nazis, he managed to escape to Switzerland, and after the liberation returned to Paris. 📖 Bernadette Bensaude-Vincent, *Langevin: 1872–1946: Science et vigilance* (1987)

Langham, Simon d.1376
English prelate
He was born in Langham, Rutland, and became prior and abbot of Westminster (1349), Treasurer of England (1360), Bishop of Ely (1362), Chancellor (1363), Archbishop of Canterbury (1366) and a cardinal (1368).

Langland or Langley, William c.1332–c.1400
English poet
Born possibly in Ledbury, Herefordshire, he is thought to have been the illegitimate son of the rector of Shipton-under-Wychwood in Oxfordshire. Educated at the Benedictine school at Malvern, he became a clerk and may have earned a poor living in London from 1362 by singing in a chantry and by copying legal documents. In 1362 he began his famous *Vision of William concerning Piers the Plowman*, a medieval alliterative poem on spiritual pilgrimage. 📖 William M Ryan, *William Langland* (1968)

Langley, John Newport 1852–1925
English physiologist
Born in Newbury, Berkshire, he was educated at St John's College, Cambridge, initially in mathematics, and later in natural sciences. He remained in the Physiological Laboratory, Cambridge, for his entire career, as demonstrator (1875–84), Trinity College lecturer in natural science (1884–1903), university lecturer in histology (1884–1903) and Professor of Physiology (1903–25). His main contributions were in the physiology of secretion, and in elucidating the anatomy and physiology of the nervous system. Much of his research was summarized in his book *The Autonomic Nervous System, Part One* (1921); part two was never published. He played an influential role in the shaping of British physiology as owner and editor of the *Journal of Physiology* from 1894 until his death.

Langley, Samuel Pierpont 1834–1906
US astronomer and aeronautical pioneer

Born in Roxbury, Massachusetts, he first trained and practised as an engineer and architect. At the age of 30 he began his astronomical career as an assistant at the Harvard College Observatory (1865–66), followed by a year teaching mathematics at the US Naval Observatory at Annapolis. In 1867 he was appointed Professor of Astronomy at Western University of Pennsylvania and director of the Allegheny Observatory, where he stayed for over 20 years. His chosen field was solar physics: he was the inventor of the bolometer (1880), an instrument which recorded the infrared radiation of the Sun quantitatively in terms of an electric current. In 1881 he mounted an expedition to Mount Whitney in the Sierra Nevada, California, to examine the absorbing effects of the Earth's atmosphere on the Sun's radiation. His last appointment was as secretary of the Smithsonian Institution in Washington in 1887. A celebrated pioneer of heavier-than-air mechanically propelled flying machines, he built in 1896 a steam-driven pilotless airplane which flew a distance of 42,000 feet (12,802m) over the Potomac River. 📖 J Gordon Vaeth, *Langley: Man of Science and Flight* (1966)

Langley, William See **Langland, William**

Langmuir, Irving 1881–1957
US physical chemist and Nobel Prize winner
Born in Brooklyn, New York City, he studied metallurgical engineering at Columbia University, New York, and worked on chemical research with **Walther Nernst** at Göttingen. From 1906 to 1909 he taught chemistry at Stevens Institute of Technology in Hoboken, New Jersey, and then joined the General Electric Company (GEC) laboratories at Schenectady, New York, from which he retired as associate director in 1950. His first work at GEC was on extending the life of the tungsten filament in an electric light bulb. The mathematical formulation of adsorption which he devised, now known as the Langmuir isotherm, is still of importance in the study of catalysis by surfaces. He also invented atomic hydrogen welding and contributed to the further development of the electronic theory of the atom and of chemical bonding. Langmuir investigated films on liquid surfaces and devised a useful piece of apparatus which became known as the Langmuir trough; he also invented the Langmuir pump for high vacuum work. From 1940 he worked on gas masks, aircraft icing and the generation of artificial fogs, and after World War II his work led to techniques for cloud seeding to produce rain. He received the Nobel Prize for chemistry in 1932. Langmuir was elected an Honorary Fellow of the Chemical Society in 1929 and received its Faraday Medal in 1939. He became a Foreign Member of the Royal Society in 1935. 📖 John C Hylander, *Irving Langmuir: American Scientist* (1935)

Langton, Stephen c.1150–1228
English prelate
He was educated at the University of Paris. In 1206 his friend and fellow-student, Pope **Innocent III**, gave him a post in his household and made him a cardinal. On the disputed election to the see of Canterbury in 1205–07, Langton was recommended by the pope and, having been elected, was consecrated by Innocent at Viterbo in 1207. His appointment was resisted by King **John**, and Langton was kept out of the see until 1213. He sided with the barons against John and his name is the first of the subscribing witnesses of Magna Carta. Although the pope excommunicated the barons, Langton refused to publish the excommunication, and was suspended from his functions in 1215. He was reinstated in 1218.

Langtry, Lillie (Emilie Charlotte), *née* Le Breton, *nicknamed* the Jersey Lily 1853–1929
English actress

She was born in Jersey, Channel Islands, the daughter of the dean of the island. She married Edward Langtry in 1874, and made her first major stage appearance in 1881. Her nickname originated in the title of Sir **John Millais's** portrait of her. Her beauty brought her to the attention of the Prince of Wales, later **Edward VII**, and she became his mistress. She managed the Imperial Theatre which was never successful. Widowed in 1897, she married Hugo Gerald de Bathe in 1899, and became well known as a racehorse owner. She wrote *All at Sea* (as Lillie de Bathe, 1909) and her reminiscences, *The Days I Knew* (1925). 📖 James Brough, *The Prince and the Lily* (1975)

Lanier, Sidney 1842–81
US poet

Born in Macon, Georgia, he was a Confederate private in Virginia, an advocate in Macon, a flute player with the Peabody Orchestra, Baltimore, and a lecturer in English literature at Johns Hopkins University (1879). Among his writings are a novel, *Tiger Lilies* (1867), critical studies such as *The Science of English Verse* (1880), and poetry. He believed in a scientific approach to poetry writing, breaking from the traditional metrical techniques and making it more like a musical composition, as in 'Corn' and 'The Symphony'. 📖 A H Starke, *Sidney Lanier* (1933)

Lankester, Sir Edwin Ray 1847–1929
English zoologist

Born in London, he was a tutor at, and Fellow of, Exeter College, Oxford, professor at London University and at Oxford, and from 1898 to 1907 director of the British Museum (Natural History). His research embraced a wide range of interests including comparative anatomy, protozoology, embryology and anthropology. The parasite which is related to the causative agent of malaria is named Lankesterella after him, and his work led to an understanding of this disease. His studies of the invertebrates led him to support **Charles Darwin's** theory of evolution through natural selection. His anthropological studies included the discovery of flint implements, and thus the presence of early man, in the Pliocene sediments from Suffolk. Largely responsible for the founding of the Marine Biological Association in 1884, he became its president in 1892. His many books include *Comparative Longevity* (1871), *Advancement of Science* (1890) and *Science from an Easy Chair* (1910–12), and from 1900 to 1909 he edited the *Treatise on Zoology*. He was knighted in 1907.

Lansbury, Angela 1925–
US actress

Born in London, she was evacuated to the USA in 1940. Signed to a contract with MGM, she made her film debut in *Gaslight* (1944), for which she received a Best Supporting Actress Academy Award nomination. A versatile and talented performer, she subsequently appeared in such films as *National Velvet* (1944), *The Picture of Dorian Gray* (1945) and *State of the Union* (1948). She made her Broadway debut in *Hotel Paradiso* (1957) and later emerged as a leading stage star in the musical *Mame* (1966, Tony award). Her subsequent stage work includes *Dear World* (1969, Tony), *Prettybelle* (1971), *Gypsy* (1974, Tony), *Hamlet* (1975) and *Sweeney Todd* (1979, Tony). On film, she became a scene-stealing character in the likes of *All Fall Down* (1961), *The Manchurian Candidate* (1962), *Death on the Nile* (1978) and *The Company of Wolves* (1984), in which she played 'Granny'. She found her greatest popularity on television as the star of the mystery series *Murder She Wrote* (1984–96). She has also appeared in numerous television films and mini-series including *Mrs 'Arris Goes to Paris* (1992) and *Mrs Santa Claus* (1996).

Lansbury, George 1859–1940
English politician

Born near Lowestoft, Suffolk, he worked for the reform of the conditions of the poor for many years before entering parliament. He was first elected Labour MP for Bow and Bromely in 1910, resigning in 1912 to stand again as a supporter of women's suffrage. He was defeated and was not re-elected until 1922. Meanwhile he founded the *Daily Herald*, which he edited until 1922, when it became the official paper of the Labour Party. In 1929 he became first Commissioner of Works and Leader of the Labour Party (1931–35). As a pacifist, he resigned in 1935 over Labour's hostile response to the Italian invasion of Ethiopia, but remained an MP until his death. Besides his help to the poor, he opened up London's parks for games and provided a bathing place on the Serpentine. He wrote *My Life* (1928). The actress **Angela Lansbury** is his daughter.

Lansdowne, Henry Petty-Fitzmaurice, 3rd Marquis of 1780–1863
English politician

He graduated from Cambridge in 1801, and became MP for Calne the next year. He led the attack on Lord Melville (**Henry Dundas**) in 1805, and succeeded **William Pitt** as member for Cambridge University in 1806 and as Chancellor of the Exchequer in the **Grenville** administration. In 1809, by the death of his half-brother, he became marquis. A cautious Liberal, in 1826 he entered the Canning Cabinet, and in the **Goderich** administration (1827–28) presided at the Foreign Office. Under Lord Grey (1830) he became president of the Council, and helped to pass the Reform Bill of 1832. He held office, with a short interval, until 1841. In 1846, under Lord Russell, he resumed his post, taking with it the leadership of the Lords. Requested to form an administration in 1852, he preferred to serve without office in the **Aberdeen** coalition and in 1855 again declined the premiership. He formed a great library and art collection.

Lansdowne, Henry Charles Keith Petty-Fitzmaurice, 5th Marquis of 1845–1927
English statesman

The great grandson of Sir **William Petty**, he became marquis in 1866, and from 1868 held minor offices in the Liberal administration. From 1872 to 1874 he was Under-Secretary for War, in 1880 for India, joining the Liberal Unionists. Governor-General of Canada (1883–88) and of India (1888–94), he was War Secretary from 1895 to 1900. From 1900 to 1905 as Foreign Secretary he promoted arbitration treaties with the USA, the *Entente Cordiale*, and the Japanese alliance. As Unionist leader in the Lords from 1903, he sat (without portfolio) in H H **Asquith's** coalition Cabinet (1915–16), advocating peace by negotiation in 1917.

Lansing, Robert 1864–1928
US lawyer and politician

Born in Watertown, New York, he became an attorney in 1889, and made a name as US counsel in arbitration cases, including the Bering Sea arbitration (1892), the Alaskan boundary tribunal (1903) and the North Atlantic fisheries tribunal (1909–10). An authority on international law, he became counsellor for the Department of State (1914), and succeeded **William Jennings Bryan** as President **Woodrow Wilson's** Secretary of State (1915). He arranged for the purchase (1917) of the Danish West Indies (now the US Virgin Islands) and negotiated the Lansing-Ishii agreement with Japan (1917). He attended the Versailles Peace Conference (1919) but came into conflict with Wilson over the League of Nations, which he felt should be treated as secondary to the signing of a treaty, and was forced to resign as Secretary of State in 1920. He wrote *The Peace Negotiations* (1921) and *The Big Four and others of the Peace Conference* (1921).

Lansing, Sherry 1944–
US film executive

Born in Chicago, she taught in high school in Los Angeles before becoming an actress in 1970. Her real ambitions lay behind the camera, and she rose from script reader to vice-president in charge of production at Columbia. She was appointed president of Twentieth Century-Fox in 1980, becoming the first woman ever to head a Hollywood studio, and remained there until 1982. She then formed her own production company with Stanley R Jaffe; their highly successful films include *Fatal Attraction* (1987), *The Accused* (1988) and *Indecent Proposal* (1993). Appointed Chairman of Paramount Pictures in 1992, she has consolidated her status with such hits as *Forrest Gump* (1994).

Lanston, Tolbert 1844–1913
US inventor

Born in Troy, Ohio, he patented the Monotype, 'a type-forming and composing machine', in 1887. It was first used commercially in 1897 and revolutionized printing processes.

Lantz, Walter 1900–94
US cartoonist and film animator

Born in New Rochelle, New York, he worked as an office boy on the *New York American* (1914), studied cartooning by correspondence course and joined William Randolph Hearst's animation studio in 1916. He became writer/director and 'star' of his own *Dinky Doodle* cartoons, then went to Hollywood, where he took over *Oswald the Lucky Rabbit* (1928) after Walt Disney left Universal Pictures, and remained with that studio for over 50 years. The most popular of his many characters is *Woody Woodpecker*, who first appeared on the screen in *Knock Knock* (1940), and whose characteristic laugh is supplied by Lantz's wife, the actress Grace Stafford.

Lanyon, Peter 1918–64
English painter

Born in St Ives, Cornwall, he trained at Penzance School of Art and at the Euston Road School, London, before serving in the RAF during World War II. From 1950 to 1957 he taught at the Corsham Academy in Bath. In paintings such as *Porthleven* (1950, Tate, London) he evolved a way of capturing the Cornish landscape that was both abstract and a living experience, urging his students to literally feel the earth before painting it. He also made constructions 'to establish the illusion of space' and in 1959 he took up gliding; this brought an extra dimension to his work, as in *Turn Around* (1963–64, Tate) and *Glide Path* (1964). He died following a gliding accident in Somerset.

Lanza, Mario, *originally* Alfredo Arnold Coccozza 1921–59
US tenor and actor

Born in Philadelphia, he studied singing under Enrico Rosati and took part in opera and recitals before appearing in such films as *The Toast of New Orleans* (1950), which includes the song 'Be My Love', and *The Great Caruso* (1951). An alcohol problem and obesity contributed to his early death.

Laozi (LaoTzu), *literally* the old master 6th century BC
Chinese philosopher and sage, traditionally the founder of Taoism

He is probably a legendary figure and is represented as the older contemporary of Confucius, against whom most of his teaching is directed. The *Dao De Jing* (*Tao-Tê-Ching*, 'The Book of the Way and its Power'), one of the principle works of Taoism, compiled some 300 years after his death, is attributed to him. It teaches self-sufficiency, simplicity and detachment. Taoism venerates the 'feminine' qualities which promote longevity, equanimity and an instinctive unity with nature. 📖 Max Kaltenmark, *Lao Tzu and Taoism* (1969)

La Pasionaria See Ibarruri (Gomez), Dolores

La Pérouse, Jean François de Galaup, Comte de 1741–88
French navigator

Born in Guo, near Albi, he distinguished himself in the naval war against Great Britain (1778–83) by destroying the forts of the Hudson's Bay Company. In 1785, in command of an expedition of discovery, he visited the north-west coast of the USA, explored the north-eastern coasts of Asia, and sailed through La Pérouse Strait between Sakhalin and Yezo. In 1788 he sailed from Botany Bay, Australia, and his two ships were wrecked north of the New Hebrides.

Laplace, Pierre Simon, Marquis de 1749–1827
French mathematician and astronomer

Born in Beaumont-en-Auge, Normandy, he studied at Caen, went to Paris and became Professor of Mathematics at the École Militaire, where he gained fame by his research on the inequalities in the motion of Jupiter and Saturn and the theory of the satellites of Jupiter. In 1799 he entered the Senate, becoming its Vice-President in 1803. He was created marquis by Louis XVIII in 1817. His astronomical work culminated in the publication of the five monumental volumes of *Mécanique céleste* (1799–1825), the greatest work on celestial mechanics since Isaac Newton's *Principia*. His *Système du monde* (1796, Eng trans in 2 vols, *The System of the World*, 1830) is a non-mathematical exposition of all his astronomical theories, and his famous nebular hypothesis of planetary origin occurs as a note in later editions. In his study of the gravitational attraction of spheroids he formulated the fundamental differential equation in physics which bears his name. He also made important contributions to the theory of probability. 📖 Roger Hahn, *Laplace as a Newtonian Scientist* (1967)

La Plante, Lynda 1946–
English actress and writer

Born in Formby, Lancashire, she began her acting career in 1972, touring with Brian Rix, and working in both theatre and television, including roles in the popular television series *The Sweeney* (1974–78) and *Minder* (1979–86). She switched to writing, and her television successes have included *Widows* (1982), the award-winning *Prime Suspect* (1991–96), the controversial and violent drama about soldiers returning to civilian life, *Civvies* (1992), *Framed* (1992), *Comics* (1993), *She's Out* (1995) and *The Governor* (1995–96). She has also written a feature film, *The Profiler* (1996), starring Sean Connery. Her novels include *Bella Mafia*, which was adapted for television (1996).

Lapworth, Arthur 1872–1941
Scottish chemist

Born in Galashiels, Selkirkshire, he was educated at Birmingham University and the City and Guilds College, London, where he worked with Henry Armstrong. After work at the School of Pharmacy and Goldsmiths' Institute he moved to Manchester, where he became Professor of Organic Chemistry in 1913 and Professor of Inorganic and Physical Chemistry in 1922. He was one of the founders of physical organic chemistry and his ideas influenced the views of Robert Robinson and Christopher Ingold on reaction mechanisms in organic chemistry. He also developed a number of important ideas on acid–base catalysis, emphasizing the role of protons.

Lapworth, Charles 1842–1920
English geologist

Born in Faringdon, Oxfordshire, he undertook important work in elucidating the geology of the south of Scotland and the north-west Highlands. He was Professor of Geology at Birmingham (1881–1913) and wrote especially on graptolites, which he used to unravel the geological structure of the Southern Uplands of Scotland. He introduced the term Ordovician (1879), thereby ending a dispute involving the upper parts of Adam Sedgwick's Cambrian system and the lower parts of Sir Roderick Murchison's Silurian system, which Lapworth showed to be one and the same. His investigations in the north-west Highlands of Scotland helped resolve the controversy about the nature of the junction between the Cambrian and Ordovician sedimentary rocks and the overthrust Moinian. He published a memoir on southern Scotland in 1899 and his major *Monograph of British Graptolites* (1901–18).

Lara, Brian Charles 1969–
West Indies cricketer

Born in Santa Cruz, Trinidad, he was one of 11 children. His early promise of high run-scoring was developed by Joey Carew, the former West Indies opener and selector. Lara was only 24 when he made 375 runs for the West Indies against England in the fifth Test in Antigua in 1994. That was the highest individual score in 117 years of Test cricket. Seven weeks later the left-handed Lara recorded 501 for Warwickshire against Durham at Edgbaston, overtaking Mohammed Hanif to become the highest scorer in first-class cricket.

Larbaud, Valéry-Nicolas 1881–1957
French poet, essayist, critic and translator

Born in Vichy, he inherited a fortune and used it to further the cause of good writing. He corresponded with André Gide (published 1948) and Léon-Paul Fargue (published 1971) and wrote such influential and varied works as *Journal de A O Barnabooth* (1913, Eng trans *A O Barnabooth, His Diary*, 1924) and the poems of this same young American, *Poèmes par un riche amateur* (1908, Eng trans *Poems of a Multimillionaire*, 1955), which owe much in form to Walt Whitman, whom Larbaud translated. He also wrote translations of James Joyce. He published his own *Journal 1912–1935* in 1955. His biography (1950) was written by G Jean Aubry, French biographer of Joseph Conrad, but it has not been translated into English. 📖 M Raymond, *From Baudelaire to Surrealism* (1950)

Lardner, Dionysius 1793–1859
Irish science writer

He was born in Dublin. He attracted attention by his works on algebraic geometry (1823) and calculus (1825), and was elected Professor of Natural Philosophy and Astronomy at London University (1827), but is best known as the originator and editor of *Lardner's Cabinet Cyclopaedia* (133 vols, 1829–49), followed by the historical *Dr Lardner's Cabinet Library* (9 vols, 1830–32), the *Edinburgh Cabinet Library* (38 vols, 1830–44) and *Museum of Science and Art* (12 vols, 1854–56). He lectured in the USA and Cuba from 1840 to 1845, and after his return to Europe settled in Paris.

Lardner, Ring (gold Wilmer) 1885–1933
US short-story writer and journalist

Born in Michigan, he was a successful sports writer and newspaper columnist in Chicago, St Louis and New York, and drew on his sporting background in his first collection of stories *You Know Me Al: A Busher's Letters* (1916). His cynical humour marks him out as a distinctive voice, and his story collections include *Gullible's Travels* (1917), *Treat 'Em Rough* (1918), *The Love Nest* (1926) and *First and Last* (1934). He also wrote one novel, *The Big Town* (1921),

satirical verse, a satirical pseudo-autobiography, *The Story of a Wonder Man* (1927), and a musical comedy, *June Moon* (1929). 📖 D Elder, *Ring Lardner* (1956)

Largillière, Nicolas 1656–1746
French portrait painter

Born in Paris, he lived for some years in England where he was Sir Peter Lely's assistant. He was one of the most popular portraitists of his day.

Largo Caballero, Francisco 1869–1946
Spanish trade union and Socialist leader

He was born in Madrid and joined the Socialist Party in 1894. His corporativist aspirations as Secretary-General of the party's trade union federation, the Unión General de Trabajodores or UGT (1918–36), led him to collaborate with the dictatorship of Primo de Rivera (1923–30). As Minister of Labour (1931–33) under the Second Republic, he altered the exploitative economic and social relations of rural Spain. He was the leader of the Socialists' increasingly revolutionary left wing (1934–35) as the Right reversed the reforms of 1931 to 1933. Appointed Prime Minister in 1936 after the Spanish Civil War broke out, he proved a conservative and rigid war leader, curtailing the social revolution and re-establishing state authority. However, he was ousted by the Communists in 1937 for opposing the suppression of the CNT (National Confederation of Labour) and the POUM (Workers Party of Marxist Unification). First detained in exile by the Vichy French and then, in 1943, by the Gestapo, he was liberated from a concentration camp in April 1945.

Larionov, Mikhail Fyodorovich 1881–1964
Russian painter

Born in Tiraspol, Ukraine, he studied architecture and sculpture at the Moscow Institute of Painting until 1908. Beginning as a Russian Post-Impressionist, influenced by Pierre Bonnard and the Fauves, he gradually took to a more 'primitive' approach based on Russian folk-art. He worked closely with his future wife, Natalia Goncharova, and together they developed Rayonism (1912–14), a style akin to Italian Futurism. They held a joint exhibition in Paris in 1914. From 1915 they worked on ballet designs for Sergei Diaghilev.

Larivey, Pierre c.1550–1612
French dramatist

Born in Champagne, he was of Italian descent, and introduced Italian-style comedy to the French stage, foreshadowing Molière and Jean Regnard. His licentious *Comédies facétieuses* (2 vols, 1579, 1611, 'Facetious Comedies') were adaptations of existing Italian pieces. 📖 L Morin, *Les trois Pierre de Larivey* (1937)

Larkin, Philip Arthur 1922–85
English poet, librarian and jazz critic

Born in Coventry, Warwickshire, he was educated at King Henry VIII School, Coventry, and St John's College, Oxford. He worked in a number of libraries and in 1955 became librarian at the University of Hull. His early poems appeared in the anthology, *Poetry from Oxford in Wartime* (1944), and in a collection, *The North Ship* (1945). W B Yeats, Thomas Hardy and Dylan Thomas influenced him, and he became a friend of Kingsley Amis. Other collections of poems include *XX Poems* (1950), *The Less Deceived* (1955), *The Whitsun Weddings* (1964) and *High Windows* (1974). His *Collected Poems* was published posthumously in 1988 and became a bestseller. He wrote two novels, *Jill* (1946) and *A Girl in Winter* (1947), and his articles on jazz were collected in *All What Jazz?* (1970), and his essays in *Required Writing* (1983). Larkin also edited *The Oxford Book of Twentieth Century English Verse* (1973). 📖 A Motion, *Philip Larkin* (1993)

Laroche, Guy 1923–89
French fashion designer

He was born in La Rochelle, near Bordeaux, into a cattle-farming family. He worked in millinery, first in Paris, then New York, before returning to Paris where he worked for Dessès for eight years. In 1957 he started his own business and showed a small collection. By 1961 he was producing both couture and ready-to-wear clothes, achieving a reputation for skilful cutting. From 1966 his designs included menswear.

La Rochefoucauld, François, 6th Duc de
1613–80
French writer

He was born in Paris. Having devoted himself to the cause of the queen, **Marie de Médicis**, in opposition to Cardinal **Richelieu**, he became entangled in a series of amorous and political intrigues and was forced to live in exile from 1639 to 1642. He joined in the Fronde revolts (1648–53) and was wounded at the Siege of Paris. He retired to the country in 1652, but on Cardinal **Mazarin's** death in 1661 returned to the court of **Louis XIV**. A surreptitious edition of his *Mémoires* (1664), written in retirement, was published in 1662, but as it gave wide offence he denied its authorship. *Réflexions, ou sentences et maximes morales* (1665) demonstrates his brevity and clarity, and his remorseless analysis of character. 📖 W G Moore, *La Rochefoucauld* (1969)

Larousse, Pierre Athanase 1817–75
French publisher, lexicographer and encyclopedist

Born in Toucy in Yonne, he was educated in Versailles. He founded a publishing house and bookshop in Paris in 1852 and issued educational textbooks, several grammars and dictionaries. He also founded a journal for teachers, *École Normale*, in 1859. His major work was his *Grand dictionnaire universel du XIXe siècle* (17 vols, 1866–76), a combined dictionary and encyclopedia.

Larra, Mariano José de 1809–37
Spanish poet, satirist and political writer

He was born in Madrid. As a journalist he was unequalled and he published two periodicals between 1828 and 1833, but it was as a satirist that he became well known. His stylistically masterly prose writings include *El Doncel de Don Enrique el Doliente* (1834,'Don Enrique's Manservant'), a novel, *Macías* (1834), a play, and adaptations of French plays. 📖 R B Moreno, *Mariano Larra* (1957)

Larrieu, Daniel 1957–
French dancer and choreographer

Born in Marseilles, he began performing professionally in 1978, and in 1982 formed a three-member company called Astrakan that won the Bagnolet international choreographic competition that year. His most successful works include the underwater modern ballet *Waterproof* (1986), commissioned by Centre National de Danse Contemporaine in Angers and performed in swimming pools to video accompaniment. A witty choreographer who challenges audience expectations of what dance and theatre can be, he has received commissions from London Contemporary Dance Theatre, Netherlands Dance Theater and the Frankfurt Ballet.

Larsen, Henning 1925–
Danish architect

Educated at the Royal Danish Academy, Copenhagen, the Architectural Association, London, and Massachusetts Institute of Technology, Boston, he became a lecturer at the Royal Danish Academy in 1959 and has been Professor of Architecture since 1968. He was a visiting professor at Yale University in 1964 and at Princeton University in 1965. His buildings include the University of Trondheim (Norway), university institutes at the Free University of Berlin (Germany), houses at Milton Keynes (England), and the Foreign Ministry and the Danish Embassy in Riyadh (Saudi Arabia). The Foreign Ministry in Riyadh has been described as one of the first buildings successfully to combine eastern and western architectural traditions. Larsen was chosen as architect of the 1,100-seat Compton Verney opera house, near Stratford-upon-Avon, in England.

Larsson, Carl 1853–1919
Swedish artist

Born in Stockholm, he was a talented draughtsman and financed his studies at the Academy of Arts (1869–76) by illustrating newspapers and magazines. He visited Paris in 1877 and lived from 1882 to 1884 in Grez-sur-Loing, where he was the centre of the Scandinavian artists' colony. He abandoned oils for impressionistic water-colours of rural life. In 1885 he returned to Sweden and, after some years teaching in Gothenburg, settled in the idyllic province of Dalarna (1898). The series of 26 watercolours entitled *A Home* (1894–99) won him international renown and great popularity in Sweden, and influenced Swedish interior design. He also produced large historical paintings and was an outstanding illustrator of books.

Lartet, Édouard Arman Isidore Hippolyte
1801–71
French palaeontologist, stratigrapher and prehistorian

Born in St Guiraud, Gers, he went to Toulouse to study law, but later chose to research French Tertiary and Quaternary vertebrates, and discovered the fossil jawbone of an ape, *Pliopithecus*, in the Tertiary formations near Auch in southwestern France (1834). His studies in 1860 at the prehistoric sites of Massat and Aurignac yielded conclusive proof that man and extinct animal species existed at the same time. He published *Reliquiae Aquitanicae* (1865–75) with **Henry Christy**, with whom he had worked from 1863.

Lartigue, Jacques-Henri 1894–1986
French photographer and painter

Born in Courbevoie, he was given his first plate-camera in 1901 and from the age of eight used a Brownie No.2 hand-camera for candid family snapshots. He continued to adopt an informal approach to the photography of everyday subjects, including experiences in World War I, and was an early user of Autochrome, the Lumière system of colour photography, especially in recording the life of the leisured classes of the 1920s. Subsequently more interested in painting, he continued with creative photography throughout his life and a one-man show at the New York Museum of Modern Art in 1963 aroused wide interest. His 1970 collection, *Diary of a Century*, is particularly evocative of the elegance of the *belle époque* and the interwar years in France.

Larwood, Harold 1904–95
English cricketer

He was born in Nuncargate. His career was comparatively brief and he played in only 21 Test matches, but with his Nottinghamshire colleague Bill Voce he constituted an opening attack of blistering speed. He was employed by **Douglas Robert Jardine** to bowl 'Bodyline' (hard and fast towards the body of the batter) in the controversial 1932–33 tour of Australia when several of the home batsmen were seriously hurt, and diplomatic relations between the two countries were imperilled. On his return, feeling that he had not been supported in official quarters, he retired from Test cricket and in later life settled happily in Australia. He published two memoirs, *Bodyline* (1933) and *The Larwood Story* (1965).

La Salle, St Jean Baptiste Abbé de 1651–1719
French educational reformer

Born in Rheims into a noble family, he was ordained in 1678. He set up schools for the poor, reformatories, and training colleges for teachers, and was the founder in 1684 (with 12 companions) of the Brothers of the Christian Schools, known as Christian Brothers. He was canonized in 1900 and his feast day is 15 May.

La Salle, René Robert Cavelier, Sieur de
1643–87
French explorer and pioneer of Canada
Born in Rouen, he later settled as a trader near Montreal, Canada, and descended the Ohio and Mississippi to the sea (1682), claiming lands for France which he named Louisiana after Louis XIV. In 1684 an expedition set out to establish a French settlement on the Gulf of Mexico, but La Salle spent two years in fruitless journeys searching for the Mississippi Delta. His followers mutinied, and he was murdered.

Las Casas, Bartolomé de, *known as* the Apostle of the Indians 1474–1566
Spanish Dominican missionary
He was born in Seville. He sailed in the third voyage of Christopher Columbus (1498), and in 1502 went to Hispaniola as a planter. Eight years later he was ordained to the priesthood, and in 1511 accompanied Diego Velazquez to Cuba. His desire to protect and defend the natives from slavery led him to visit the Spanish court on several occasions. After missionary travels in Mexico, Nicaragua, Peru and Guatemala, he returned to devote four years to the cause of the Indians. Appointed Bishop of Chiapa, he was received (1544) with hostility by the colonialists, returned to Spain, and resigned his see (1547). He contended with the authorities in favour of the Indians until his death in Madrid, writing his *Veynte Razones* and *Brevísima Relación de la destrucción de las Indias* (1552, 'A Brief Report on the Destruction of the Indians'). His most important work is the unfinished *Historia de las Indias* (1875–76, 'History of the Indians'). 📖 Lewis Hanke, *Bartolomé de las Casas: An Interpretation of His Life and Writings* (1951)

Lasdun, Sir Denys Louis 1914–
English architect
Born in London, he was educated at Rugby School and trained at the Architectural Association School. He worked with Wells Coates (1935–37), and joined the Tecton partnership (1938–40). He partnered Lindsey Drake (1949–50), and in 1960 began the Denys Lasdun partnership. He was professor at Leeds from 1962 to 1963. His architecture follows the modern tradition, with horizontal emphasis, forceful articulation of mass and respect for urban context, and the occasional reference to the works of Le Corbusier is apparent. His early works include flats on the Paddington Estate, London, and at St James's Place, London. He is renowned particularly for the Royal College of Physicians (1958–64) in London, the University of East Anglia, Norwich (1962–68), the National Theatre, London (1965–76), European Investment Bank, Luxembourg (1975), and the Institute of Education (1970–78) in London. He was awarded the Royal Gold Medal of the RIBA in 1977. His publications include *A Language and a Theme* (1976) and *Architecture in an Age of Scepticism* (1984). He was knighted in 1976 and made a Companion of Honour in 1995.

Lashley, Karl Spencer 1890–1958
US psychologist
Born in Davis, Virginia, he was professor at the universities of Minnesota (1920–26) and Chicago (1929–35), and Research Professor of Neuropsychology at Harvard (1935–55). In 1942 he also became director of the Yerkes Laboratory for primate biology at Orange Park, Florida.

He made valuable contributions to the study of localization of brain function, and is regarded as the 'father' of neuropsychology.

Lasker, Emanuel 1868–1941
German chess player
Born in Berlinchen (Barliner), Brandenburg, he gained a doctorate in mathematics from Erlangen University, and his theorem of vector spaces is still known by his name. He defeated Wilhelm Steinitz in 1894 for the world title before he reached his chess prime. Consequently, his tournament record as champion was greater than any other until Anatoli Karpov, and his reign was the longest in the history of chess. He was the first chess Master to treat the game as a war of psychological attrition. His tenure was extended by the intervention of World War I, and he lost the championship in 1921 to José Raúl Capablanca. He was driven out of Germany and had his property confiscated in 1933 because of his Jewish birth, and lived the remainder of his life in England, the USSR and the USA.

Laski, Harold Joseph 1893–1950
English political scientist and socialist
Born in Manchester, he was educated at Manchester Grammar School and New College, Oxford, and lectured at McGill University (1914–16), Harvard (1916–20), Amherst (1917) and Yale (1919–20, 1931). In 1920 he joined the staff of the London School of Economics, and in 1926 became Professor of Political Science. He was chairman of the Labour Party in 1945–46. A brilliant speaker, as lecturer at the London School of Economics he had a great influence over his students. His political philosophy was a modified Marxism. He had a strong belief in individual freedom, but the downfall of the Labour government in 1931 forced him to feel that some revolution in Great Britain was necessary. His works include *Authority in the Modern State* (1919), *A Grammar of Politics* (1925), *Liberty in the Modern State* (1930) and *The American Presidency* (1940). 📖 Kingsley Martin, *Harold Laski, 1893–1950: A Biographical Memoir* (1953)

Laski, Marghanita 1915–88
English novelist and journalist
Born in Manchester, the niece of Harold Joseph Laski, she was educated at Oxford, and her first novel, *Love on the Supertax*, appeared in 1944. She wrote extensively on newspapers and reviews. Her later novels include *Little Boy Lost* (1949) and *The Victorian Chaise-longue* (1953). She also wrote a play, *The Offshore Island* (1959), as well as editing and writing various studies and critical works.

Lassalle, Ferdinand 1825–64
German revolutionary and political writer
Born in Breslau (now Wrocław, Poland), the son of a rich Jewish merchant, he was a disciple of Hegel. He wrote a work on Heraclitus (1858), and in Paris made the acquaintance of Heinrich Heine. On his return to Berlin, in 1844 he met the Countess Sophie Hatzfeld (1805–81), a lady at odds with her husband, prosecuted her cause, and after eight years of litigation forced the husband to accept a compromise favourable to her. He took part in the revolution of 1848, during which he met Karl Marx, and for an inflammatory speech got six months in prison. At Leipzig he founded the Universal German Working-men's Association (the forerunner of the Social Democratic Party) to agitate for universal suffrage. In 1863–64 he tried to win the Rhineland and Berlin to his cause. He died shortly after a duel with Count Racowitza of Wallachia over the hand of Helene von Domiges. 📖 Eduard Bernstein, *Ferdinand Lassalle as a Social Reformer* (1893)

Lassell, William 1799–1880
English astronomer

Born in Bolton, Lancashire, he built an observatory at Starfield, near Liverpool, where he constructed and mounted an equatorial reflecting telescope. The mount of this telescope completely relegated the clumsy mechanism used by Sir **John Herschel** and made reflecting telescopes easy to use. He discovered several planetary satellites, including Triton (1846) and Hyperion (1848, simultaneously with **William Bond** at Harvard). He also discovered Ariel and Umbriel, satellites of Uranus (1851). He realized the importance of good observing sites and moved his telescope to Malta in 1852. In 1860 he built a telescope of four times the capacity and with it discovered 600 new nebulae.

Lassus, Orlandus or **Orlando di Lasso**
c.1532–1594
Netherlandish musician and composer
Born in Mons (now in Belgium), he wrote many masses, motets and other works, and travelled widely, visiting Italy, England and France. In 1570 he was ennobled by **Maximilian II**. Unlike his contemporary, **Palestrina**, he wrote not only church music but also a large number of secular works. He was a highly distinguished composer of early music.

László, Sir Philip, *properly* Philip Alexius László de Lombos 1869–1937
British portrait painter
Born in Budapest, Hungary, he worked in England and gained an international reputation as a painter of royalty and heads of state.

Latham, John 1740–1837
English ornithologist
Born in Eltham, London, he was one of the founders of the Linnaean Society, and wrote *A General History of Birds* in 11 volumes (1821–28), for which he designed, etched and coloured all the illustrations. He lived from 1796 in Romsey.

Lathrop, Julia Clifford 1858–1932
US social reformer
Born in Rockford, Illinois, and educated at Vassar College, she joined **Jane Addams's** Hull House Settlement in Chicago in 1880. She was active in promoting welfare for children and the mentally ill. One of the founders of the Chicago Institute of Social Science (1903–04), she was associated with the Chicago School of Philanthropy from 1908 to 1920, and was first head of the Federal Children's Bureau (1912). She was a member of the Child Welfare Committee of the League of Nations from 1925 to 1931.

Latimer, Hugh c.1485–1555
English Protestant reformer
Born in Thurcaston, Leicestershire, he was sent to Cambridge. A Roman Catholic, he was elected a Fellow of Clare College in 1510, and in 1522 was appointed a university preacher. Converted to Protestantism, he was one of the divines appointed to examine the lawfulness of **Henry VIII's** marriage to **Catherine of Aragon**. He declared on the King's side, and was made chaplain to **Anne Boleyn** and rector of West Kington in Wiltshire. In 1535 he was appointed Bishop of Worcester and at the opening of Convocation in June 1536 preached two powerful sermons in favour of the Reformation. He opposed Henry's Six Articles, for which he was imprisoned in 1536, 1546 and 1553. At **Edward VI's** accession he declined to resume his episcopal functions, but devoted himself to preaching and good works. Under **Mary I** he was found guilty of heresy, with **Nicholas Ridley** and **Thomas Cranmer**, and on 16 October 1555 was burned with Ridley opposite Balliol College. 🕮 H S Darby, *Hugh Latimer* (1953)

La Tour, Georges de 1593–1652
French artist
Born in Vic-sur-Seille, Lorraine, he worked from 1620 at Lunéville in the same province and achieved a notable reputation. The Duke of Lorraine became his patron and later King **Louis XIII** himself accepted a painting by him, liking it so much he had all works by other masters removed from his chambers. He was entirely forgotten until his rediscovery in 1915, and in the meantime works by him were attributed to **Le Nain** and followers of **Caravaggio**. He specialized in candlelit scenes, using a palette of warm, glowing reds and browns to obtain eerie effects. Of the 40 works by him which have been positively identified, most are of religious subjects, such as *St Joseph the Carpenter* (Louvre, Paris) and *The Lamentation over St Sebastian* (Berlin).

La Tour, Maurice Quentin de 1704–88
French pastellist and portrait painter
Born in St Quentin, he settled in Paris, where he became immensely popular. His best works include portraits of Madame de **Pompadour**, **Voltaire** and **Jean Jacques Rousseau**.

La Tour d'Auvergne, Henri de See **Turenne, Henri de La Tour d'Auvergne, Vicomte de**

La Tour d'Auvergne, Théophile Malo Corret de, *known as* the First Grenadier of France
1743–1800
French soldier
Born in Carhaix, Finistère, he fought at Port Mahon in 1782, firmly refused advancement beyond captain and was killed at Oberhausen in Bavaria. His remains were interred in the Panthéon in 1889. French biographies are full of instances of his bravery, Spartan simplicity and chivalrous affection. He wrote a book on the Breton language and antiquities.

Latreille, Pierre Andrezac 1762–1833
French entomologist
Born in Brive, Corrèze, he was an ordained priest and became Professor of Natural History at Paris University. He is best known for his pioneering work on the classification of insects and crustaceans, and is described as the father of modern entomology.

Latrobe, Benjamin Henry 1764–1820
US civil engineer
Born in Fulneck, Yorkshire, England, he was the son of a Moravian minister. He was trained as an architect and a civil engineer before emigrating to the USA in 1796. He introduced the Greek Revival style to the USA and was surveyor of public buildings in Washington DC (1803–15). When this project failed he was ruined financially, but soon returned to Washington to make good the damage sustained by the Capitol and the White House, burned by the British in 1814. In 1817 his son Henry died of yellow fever while building the New Orleans waterworks. Latrobe went there in 1820 to complete the works but soon died of the same cause. Another son, Benjamin Henry (1806–78), and a grandson Charles Hazlehurst (1834–1902), were both noted US railway civil engineers.

Lattimore, Owen 1900–89
US sinologist and defender of civil liberties
Born in Washington DC, the son of a US trader in China, he spent his early childhood in China, was educated in England and Lausanne, and worked in China in business and journalism in the 1920s. He travelled in Mongolia and Manchuria, and returned to the USA to study at Harvard, where his proficiency led to his being sent back for research work. He published outstanding narratives of his journeys and observations in central Asia such as *The Desert Road to Turkestan* (1928), *High Tartary* (1930), *Mongol*

Journeys (1941), and his masterpiece, *Inner Asian Frontiers of China* (1940). He was made political adviser to **Chiang Kai-shek** by President **Franklin D Roosevelt** in 1941–42, but resigned because of his inability to persuade Chiang to follow a programme of social justice. He was director of Pacific Operations in the office of war information, edited *Pacific Affairs* (1934–41), published important syndicated columns on Far Eastern questions (summed up in his *Solution in Asia*, 1945, and *The Situation in Asia*, 1949), and held major academic posts in Johns Hopkins University and in Leeds. While on a UN mission to Afghanistan in 1950 he was named as the top Russian agent in the USA by Senator **Joseph McCarthy**: the five-year struggle to clear his name of this utterly baseless charge was carried out with great courage by himself and his wife Eleanor (1895–1970), and its initial phase was brilliantly described in his *Ordeal by Slander* (1950). He settled in England, and later in Paris, playing a major part in the development of Chinese studies in Europe, stressing a Chinese rather than a Western perspective.

Lattre de Tassigny, Jean de 1889–1952
French soldier

He was born in Mouilleron-en-Pareds. He served during World War I and World War II, and was then sent by the Vichy government to command in Tunisia. He was recalled for sympathy with the Allies and arrested in 1942 for resisting the Germans. He escaped to London in 1943, to become commander of the French 1st Army and take part in the Allied liberation of France (1944–45), signing the German surrender. He reorganized the French Army and was appointed Commander-in-Chief of Western Union Land Forces under **Montgomery** in 1948. In 1950 as Commander-in-Chief in French Indo-China, for a time he turned the tide against the Vietminh rebels. He was posthumously made a Marshal of France in 1952.

Latynina, Larissa Semyonovna, *née* Diril 1935–
Soviet gymnast

Born in Kharsan, Ukraine, she collected 18 Olympic medals in 1956 and 1964, a record for any sport, winning nine golds. During her 13-year career she gained 24 Olympic, world and European titles, including that of individual world champion in 1958 and 1962. She retired in 1966.

Laubach, Frank Charles 1884–1970
US missionary and pioneer of adult basic education

He was born in Benton, Pennsylvania. Discovering that the Moro tribespeople of the Philippines (whom he had been sent to evangelize in 1915) were unable to read or write, he devised a simple way to combat illiteracy. His method and its application in Southern Asia, India and Latin America are described in *India shall be Literate* (1940), *Teaching the World to Read* (1948) and *Thirty Years with the Silent Billion* (1961); and his spiritual motivation in *Letters by a Modern Mystic* (1937) and *Channels of Spiritual Power* (1955).

Laube, Heinrich 1806–84
German playwright and manager

Born in Sprottau, Silesia (now in Poland), he was one of the leaders of the 'Young Germany' movement and editor of *Die elegante Welt* ('The Elegant World'), its literary organ. He was director of Vienna's Burgtheater (1850–67), and among his writings are works on the theatre, on historical themes, novels such as *Das junge Europa* (1833–37, 'Young Europe'), *Die Karlsschüler* (1847, 'The Boys of the Karls-School'), a drama of the young **Schiller**, and a biography of **Franz Grillparzer**. 📖 M Dürst, *Heinrich Laube* (1951)

Laud, William 1573–1645
English prelate

He was born in Reading, Berkshire, the son of an affluent clothier. Educated at Reading Free School, he went to St John's College, Oxford, at the age of 16, becoming a Fellow four years later. Ordained in 1601, he made himself unpopular with the university authorities by his open antipathy to the dominant Puritanism, but his solid learning, amazing industry, administrative capacity, and sincere and unselfish churchmanship, soon won him friends and patrons. One of these was Charles Blount, Earl of Devonshire, whom in 1605 Laud married to the divorced Lady Rich; another was George, 1st Duke of **Buckingham**, to whom he became confessor in 1622. Meanwhile he rose steadily—incumbent of five livings (1607–10), president of his old college and king's chaplain (1611), prebendary of Lincoln (1614), archdeacon of Huntingdon (1615), dean of Gloucester (1616), prebendary of Westminster and Bishop of St Davids (1621), Bishop of Bath and Wells, dean of the Chapel Royal, and a privy councillor (1626), Bishop of London (1628), Chancellor of Oxford (1630), and finally Archbishop of Canterbury (1633). He was also offered two cardinalships. After Buckingham's assassination, he had virtually become the first Minister of the Crown, working with **Thomas Strafford** and **Charles I** towards absolutism in Church and State. He was to raise the Church of England to its rightful position as a branch of the Church Catholic, to root out Calvinism in England and Presbyterianism in Scotland. In England he drew up a list of 'Orthodox' and 'Puritan' ministers, whom he proceeded to separate by scolding, suspending and depriving. Freedom of worship was withdrawn from Walloon and French refugees, Englishmen abroad were forbidden to attend Calvinistic services, and at home 'gospel preaching', justification by faith, and Sabbatarianism were superseded by an elaborate ritual, by the doctrine of the real presence, celibacy and confession, and by the Book of Sports—changes rigorously enforced by the court of High Commission and the Star Chamber. In Scotland, his attempt (1635–37) to anglicize the Church led to the 'Bishops' war', and this to the meeting of the Long Parliament, which in 1640 impeached the Archbishop of treason, and 10 weeks later sent him to the Tower. He would not escape (**Grotius** urged him to do so), and at last, in December 1644, he was voted 'guilty of endeavouring to subvert the laws, to overthrow the Protestant religion, and to act as an enemy to Parliament'. The judges declared that this was not treason, but under an unconstitutional ordinance of attainder, he was beheaded on Tower Hill. 📖 H R Trevor-Roper, *Archbishop Laud, 1573–1645* (1962)

Lauda, Niki (Nikolas Andreas) 1949–
Austrian racing driver

He was born in Vienna. World-champion racing driver in 1975, 1977 and 1984, he suffered horrific burns and injuries in the German Grand Prix at the Nürburgring (1976). Despite a series of operations he returned and was runner-up in the world championship in that year. He won again in 1977. Going on to drive for Brabham meant a two-year absence from Grand Prix racing, before he crowned his comeback with McLaren by winning his third and last Grand Prix championship in 1984. He retired in 1985, and became the proprietor of Lauda-Air.

Lauder, Estée, *née* Mentzer 1908–
US entrepreneur and beautician

Born in New York City, the daughter of poor Hungarian immigrants, she worked her way up in the cosmetics industry by selling a face cream made by her uncle. She founded Estée Lauder Inc in 1946 and had great success with Youth Dew bath oil in the 1950s. She later multiplied the profits from Estée Lauder products by introducing deliberately competing lines, for example Aramis and

Clinique. Her husband and partner, Joe Lauder, died in 1982. She published her autobiography, *Estée: A Success Story*, in 1985.

Lauder, Sir Harry (Henry)
1870–1950
Scottish comic singer
He was born in Portobello, near Edinburgh, and started his career on the music-hall stage as an Irish comedian, but made his name as a singer of Scottish songs, many of which he wrote himself, such as 'Roamin' in the Gloamin'. He was knighted in 1919 for his work in organizing entertainments for the troops during World War I. His appeal was not just confined to Scottish audiences; some of his biggest successes were on the stages of London's famous music halls and his popularity abroad was immense, especially in the USA and the Commonwealth countries, which he toured almost annually after 1907. He wrote volumes of memoirs, the best known of which is *Roamin' in the Gloamin'* (1928). 📖 William Wallace, *Harry Lauder In The Limelight* (1988)

Lauder, Robert Scott 1803–69
Scottish painter
Born in Silvermills, Edinburgh, he lived in Italy and in Munich from 1833 to 1838, then in London until 1849, when he returned to Edinburgh. Sir Walter Scott's novels provided him with subjects for his most successful historical paintings.

Lauder, William c.1680–1771
Scottish scholar and charlatan
From 1747 to 1750 he sought to prove, by blatant forgeries, that Milton's *Paradise Lost* had plagiarized various 17th-century poets writing in Latin. He was exposed by Bishop John Douglas, and died poor in Barbados.

Lauderdale, John Maitland, Duke of 1616–82
Scottish statesman
Born in Lethington (now Lennoxlove), East Lothian, he ardently supported the Covenanters (1638), and in 1643 became a Scottish Commissioner at Westminster. He was taken prisoner at Worcester in 1651, and spent nine years in the Tower, at Windsor and at Portland. At the Restoration he became Scottish Secretary of State, and aimed to bring about the absolute power of the Crown in Church and State. A member of the Privy Council, he had a seat in the so-called Cabal ministry and was created a duke in 1672. Many of his harsher measures, especially against the Episcopal Church in Scotland, were probably the result not so much of personal ambition but of an inability to tolerate the follies of less astute contemporaries.

Laue, Max Theodor Felix von 1879–1960
German physicist and Nobel Prize winner
Born near Koblenz, he held university posts in Zurich (1912), Frankfurt (1914) and Berlin (1919), before being appointed as advisor to the Physikalisch Technische Reichsanstalt, and deputy director of the Kaiser Wilhelm Institute for Physics. At the age of 71 he was appointed director of the former Kaiser Wilhelm Institute for Chemistry and Electrochemistry in Berlin-Dahlhem (1951). He applied the concept of entropy to optics, and demonstrated that the formula for the velocity of light in flowing water followed from Albert Einstein's theory of special relativity. In 1912 he discovered how X-rays are diffracted by the atoms in crystals, for which he was awarded the 1914 Nobel Prize for physics.

Laughton, Charles 1899–1962
English actor
Born in Scarborough, Yorkshire, he worked in his family's hotel business before turning to the stage (1926). Major parts included Ephikhodov in *The Cherry Orchard*, and

William Marble in *Payment Deferred*. He also appeared with the Old Vic Company (1933), played in and produced George Bernarnd Shaw's *Don Juan in Hell* and *Major Barbara*, and gave many renowned Shakespearean performances. He began to act in films in 1932 and gave memorable performances as Henry VIII in *The Private Life of Henry VIII* (1933, Academy Award), Mr Barrett in *The Barretts of Wimpole Street* (1934), Captain Bligh in *Mutiny on the Bounty* (1935) and Quasimodo in *The Hunchback of Notre Dame* (1939). He was married to the actress Elsa Lanchester (1902–86), and became a US citizen in 1950. 📖 Simon Callow, *Charles Laughton* (1988)

Laurana, Luciano da c.1420–1479
Italian architect
Born in Dalmatia, he was working in Urbino c.1465, and by 1468 had been appointed chief architect at the ducal palace, a member of the humanist court of Federigo da Montefeltro. The design of the palace courtyard showed his familiarity with recent Renaissance masterpieces in the field, particularly Filippo Brunelleschi's Foundling Hospital, Florence.

Laurati, Pietro See Lorenzetti, Pietro

Laurel, Stan, originally Arthur Stanley Jefferson
1890–1965
US comic actor
Born in Ulverston, Lancashire, England, he was a teenage member of Fred Karno's touring company and sometime understudy to Charlie Chaplin, and first went to the USA in 1910. After gaining his first film part in 1917, he appeared in many of the early silent comedies and had tried producing and directing before his partnership with Oliver Hardy began in 1926. Though Laurel is usually described as the more creative partner, the team was much funnier and more successful than its individual parts. They made many full-length feature films, including *Bonnie Scotland* (1935) and *Way Out West* (1937), but their best efforts are generally reckoned to be their early (1927–32) shorts, one of which, *The Music Box* (1932), won an Academy Award. They survived the advent of the 'talkies' better than many others, though their style was basically silent. Purveying good honest slapstick, they deliberately avoided any attempt at subtlety. Ollie—fat, pretentious and blustering—fiddled with his tie and appealed to the camera for help, while Stan—thin, bullied and confused—scratched his head, looked blank and dissolved into tears. Their contrasting personalities, their general clumsiness and stupidity, and their disaster-packed predicaments made them a universally popular comedy duo. 📖 Fred L Guiles, *The Life of Stan Laurel* (1980)

Lauren, Ralph, originally Ralph Lipschitz 1939–
US fashion designer
Born in the Bronx, New York City, he attended night school for business studies and worked as a salesman in Bloomingdales. In 1967 he joined Beau Brummel Neckwear and created the Polo range for men, later including womenswear. He is famous for his US styles, such as the 'prairie look' and 'frontier fashions'.

Laurence, (Jean) Margaret, née Wemyss
1926–87
Canadian novelist
She was born in the prairie town of Neepawa, Manitoba, of Scots–Irish descent, and educated at United College (now Winnipeg University), from which she graduated in 1947, the same year she married John Laurence, a civil engineer. His job took them to England, Somaliland and, in 1952, to Ghana, where they spent five years. *A Tree for Poverty* (1954), a collection of translated Somali poetry and folk-tales, and the travel book *The Prophet's Camel Bell* (1963), resulted from her East African experience. *This Side Jordan* (1960), her first novel, was set in Ghana. In 1962 she

moved to England, where she wrote her famous 'Manawaka series' based on her home town: *The Stone Angel* (1964), *A Jest of God* (1966), *The Fire-Dwellers* (1969), *A Bird in the House* (1970) and *The Diviners* (1974). One of Canada's most potent novelists, she received Governor-General's awards in 1967 and 1975, and in 1972 was made a Companion of the Order of Canada. ▯ W H New, *Margaret Laurence: the writer and her critics* (1977)

Laurencin, Marie 1885–1957
French artist

She was born in Paris, and exhibited in the Salon des Indépendants in 1907. Best known for her portraits of women in misty pastel colours, she also illustrated many books with watercolours and lithographs.

Laurens, Henri 1885–1954
French graphic artist and sculptor

He was born in Paris, and was a leading exponent of three-dimensional Cubism, evident in such work as *The Bottle of Beaune* (1918, Pompidou Centre, Paris) and *Man with a Pipe* (1919, New York). He also created coloured reliefs and collages, but in the 1920s reintroduced curvilinear shapes into his work. During the depressed 1930s he worked in terracotta; he became interested in mythological subjects, and produced the series of *Sirens* (1937–45), *Oceanides* and *Ondines*. His bronze *Autumn* (1948, Pompidou Centre) represents the full flowering of his work using organic forms.

Laurens, Henry 1724–92
American Revolutionary leader

Born in Charleston, South Carolina, he made a fortune in the import-export business, then bought land and became active in South Carolina politics. He was president of the South Carolina Council of Safety (1775) and a delegate to the Continental Congress (1777–79), succeeding **John Hancock** as president of the Congress (1777–78). Captured by the British when travelling on a diplomatic mission to the Netherlands, he was imprisoned in the Tower of London until he was exchanged for General **Charles Cornwallis** (1782). He returned to France and England with **John Jay**, **John Adams** and **Benjamin Franklin** to negotiate the Treaty of Paris (1783).

Laurent, Auguste 1807–53
French chemist

Born in St Maurice, he went to the École des Mines in Paris in 1826. From 1832 to 1834 he worked as a chemist at a porcelain factory in Sèvres, then worked for a perfumery after having published a doctoral thesis on the topic of 'radicals' in organic chemistry. In 1838 he was appointed to the newly created chair in Bordeaux and in 1843 he met **Frédéric Gerhardt**, and together they incorporated Laurent's idea of a radical into the 'type' theory of organic chemistry. In 1850 he applied for the chair at the Collège de France, but was rejected by a vote in the Academy of Sciences, probably because of his strong republican views.

Laurentius, St See Lawrence, St

Laurie, John 1897–1980
Scottish actor

Born in Dumfries, he made his stage debut in J M Barrie's *What Every Woman Knows* (1921), and for the remainder of the decade he made valuable contributions to some of Britain's most prestigious classical theatre companies, including the Old Vic and the Shakespeare Memorial Theatre, where he played *Hamlet* in 1927. His notable stage roles include *John Knox* (1947), *MacAdam and Eve* (1951), and a performance as **William McGonagall** in *The Hero of a Hundred Fights* (1968). He made his film debut in *Juno and the Paycock* (1929), and followed it with films such as *The 39 Steps* (1935), *The Edge of the World* (1937), *Henry V* (1944),

I Know Where I'm Going! (1945), *Hamlet* (1948) and *Richard III* (1955). His greatest popularity, however, was achieved on television as Private Frazer, the prophet of doom, in the comedy series *Dad's Army* (1968–77) and the spin-off film (1971).

Laurier, Sir Wilfrid 1841–1919
Canadian statesman

He was born in St Lin, Quebec. He was a highly successful barrister and journalist, and became a member of the Quebec Legislative Assembly and entered federal politics in 1874, becoming Minister of Inland Revenue (1877). In 1887 he became Leader of the Liberal Party and Prime Minister in 1896. He was the first French–Canadian and also the first Roman Catholic to be premier of Canada. In 1911 his government was defeated on the question of commercial reciprocity with the USA, but he remained Liberal Leader. Though he had a strong feeling for Empire, Laurier was a firm supporter of self-government for Canada. During World War I he was against conscription though entirely in agreement with Canada's entering the war. In his home policy he was an advocate of free trade, passed many reforms to benefit the working classes and helped to plan a transcontinental railway, the Grand Trunk.

Lauterpacht, Sir Hersch 1897–1960
British lawyer and judge

Born near Lemberg, Poland, and educated in Vienna, he went to England in 1923 and eventually became a British citizen. He taught law in London, and became Whewell Professor of International Law at Cambridge (1938–55). Acting for Great Britain in many international disputes, he ultimately became a judge of the International Court of Justice (1954–60). He wrote extensively on international law, his works including *The Function of Law in the International Community* (1933), *Recognition in International Law* (1947) and *International Law and Human Rights* (1950).

Lautréamont, Comte de, *pseudonym of* Isidore Lucien Ducasse 1846–70
French prose poet

Born in Montevideo, Uruguay, the son of a consular officer, he went to France for his education, studying at both Pau and Tarbes, going to Paris in 1867. In 1868, the first instalment of his lyrical prose poem *Les Chants de Maldoror* ('The Songs of Maldoror') was published under his pseudonym of Lautréamont, borrowed from the title of a novel by **Eugène Sue**; it seems, however, that the printer refused to distribute the pamphlets, either because he was shocked by their contents or because he had not been paid. The work first appeared in Belgium and Switzerland. The author believed he would find there a more sympathetic audience for his 'poetry of revolt', which combines nightmarish blasphemy and sexual obscenity with a profusion of lyrical and hallucinatory imagery. His writing caused the Surrealists to claim him as their precursor, and it exercised an enormous influence on **André Breton**, **Alfred Jarry**, and other writers. Shortly before his premature death, Ducasse published *Poésies* (1870, under his own name). *Les Chants de Maldoror* was published in 1890 with an additional five fragments. ▯ P Zweig, *Lautréamont: The Violent Narcissus* (1972)

Laval, Carl Gustaf Patrik de 1845–1913
Swedish engineer

Born in Orsa, he invented a centrifugal cream separator in 1878 and made important contributions to the development of the steam turbine and many other devices.

Laval, François Xavier, de Montmorency 1622–1708
French prelate and missionary

Born in Montigny-sur-Avre, he was ordained to the priesthood in 1647, and took a degree at the Sorbonne in canon law. He was sent as vicar apostolic to Quebec in 1659, and became the first Bishop of Quebec (1674–88). In 1663 he founded the seminary of Quebec, which in 1852 was named Laval University after him.

Laval, Pierre 1883–1945
French politician
He was born in Châteldon, Puy-de-Dôme. He became an advocate, deputy (1914), senator (1926) and premier (1931–32, 1935–36). At first a Socialist, he moved to the Right during the late 1930s, and in the Vichy government was **Philippe Pétain**'s deputy (1940), rival and Prime Minister (1942–44), when he openly collaborated with the Germans. After the liberation he fled from France to Germany and Spain, was brought back, charged with treason and executed. 🕮 David Thompson, *Two Frenchmen: Pierre Laval and Charles de Gaulle* (1951)

La Vallière, Louise Françoise de la Baume le Blanc, Duchesse de 1644–1710
French aristocrat
Born in Tours, she was brought to court by her mother. She became **Louis XIV**'s mistress (1661–67) and bore him four children. When the Marquise de **Montespan** superseded her she retired to a Carmelite nunnery in Paris (1674). *Réflexions sur la miséricorde de Dieu par une dame pénitente* (1680, 'Reflections on God's mercy by a penitent woman') is attributed to her. 🕮 Jean Christian Petitfils, *Louise de la Vallière* (1990)

Lavater, Johann Kaspar 1741–1801
Swiss physiognomist, theologian and poet
Born in Zurich, he took Protestant orders in 1769. He became known by a volume of poems, *Schweizerlieder* (1767, 'Swiss Songs'), and his *Aussichten in die Ewigkeit* (1768–78, 'Prospects of Eternity') is characterized by religious enthusiasm and mysticism. He attempted to elevate physiognomy into a science in his *Physiognomische Fragmente* (1775–78, Eng trans *Essays on Physiognomy designed to promote the knowledge and the love of mankind*, 5 vols, 1789–98). While tending the wounded at the capture of Zurich by **André Masséna** (September 1799) he received a wound, from which he later died. 🕮 T Hasler, *Johann Lavater* (1942)

Lavenson, Alma Ruth 1897–1989
US photographer
Born in San Francisco, she graduated in psychology from the University of California, Berkeley, in 1919, and began taking photographs on tour of Europe in 1922. Her work was first exhibited in pictorialist salons in the 1920s. In 1932 her work was represented in San Francisco in the inaugural exhibition of the influential Group f/64. She began photographing California Gold Rush ghost towns (c.1933) and was represented in the 1955 'Family of Man' exhibition at the Museum of Modern Art, New York, organized by **Edward Steichen**. She had a retrospective at the California Museum of Photography in 1979, and was exhibited at the Friends of Photography in 1987 and 1990.

Laver, James 1899–1975
English writer and art critic
Born in Liverpool, he won the Newdigate prize for verse at Oxford in 1921; later books of verse include *His Last Sebastian* (1922) and *Ladies' Mistakes* (1933). From 1922 to 1959 he was assistant keeper, and then keeper, at the Victoria and Albert Museum, London. He wrote several books of art criticism, including *French Painting and the 19th century* (1937) and *Fragonard* (1956), and made a substantial contribution to the history of English costume with such books as *Taste and Fashion* (1937), *Fashions and Fashion Plates* (1943) and *Children's Costume in the 19th Century* (1951).

Laver, Rod (Rodney George) 1938–
Australian tennis player
He was born in Rockhampton, Queensland. A powerful and swift left-handed player, he won the Wimbledon singles title both as an amateur and as a professional. He first won the Wimbledon title in 1961, and won it again in 1962 in the course of a Grand Slam of all the major titles (British, US, French and Australian). He turned professional in 1962 and won the professional world singles title five times between 1964 and 1970. When Wimbledon allowed professionals to participate in 1968, he won it in that year, and won again in the course of another Grand Slam the following year. 🕮 *The Education of a Tennis Player* (1971)

Laveran, Charles Louis Alphonse 1845–1922
French physician, parasitologist and Nobel Prize winner
Born and educated in Paris, he became Professor of Military Medicine and Epidemic Diseases at the military college of Val de Grâce (1874–78, 1884–94). He studied malaria in Algeria (1878–83), discovering in 1880 the blood parasite which causes the disease. He suggested that the parasite was spread through mosquito bites, but the experimental demonstration of this was not provided until the late 1890s, by **Ronald Ross** and other investigators. Laveran also did important work on other tropical diseases including sleeping-sickness, leishmaniasis and kala-azar, which he summarized in important monographs. From 1896 until his death he worked at the Pasteur Institute in Paris. He was awarded the 1907 Nobel Prize for physiology or medicine for his discovery of the malaria parasite, and donated half his money to equip a laboratory for tropical medicine at the Pasteur Institute.

Lavery, Sir John 1856–1941
Irish painter
Born in Belfast, he studied in Glasgow, London and Paris. A portrait painter of the Glasgow school, his work enjoyed great popularity, especially his conversation pieces and paintings of women.

Lavigerie, Charles Martial Allemand 1825–92
French prelate
Born in Bayonne, he studied at Saint-Sulpice in Paris and was ordained in 1849. As primate of Africa and Archbishop of Algiers (1884) he became well-known for his missionary work, and founded the order of the White Fathers in 1868. In 1888 he founded the Anti-Slavery Society. In 1890 his 'toast of Algiers' launched Pope **Leo XIII**'s campaign to persuade French Catholics to rally to the Republic.

Lavin, Mary 1912–96
Irish short-story writer and novelist
She was born in East Walpole, Massachusetts, but returned to Ireland with her parents when she was nine, studied English at University College, Dublin, and thereafter lived in County Meath. 'Miss Holland', her first short story, was published in the *Dublin Magazine* where it was admired by Lord **Dunsany**, who encouraged her and later wrote an introduction to her first collection, *Tales from Bective Bridge* (1942), which was awarded the James Tait Black Memorial Prize. Apart from two early novels—*The House in Clewe Street* (1945) and *Mary O'Grady* (1950)—she concentrated on the short story. Her many collections include *Collected Stories* (1971), *A Memory and Other Stories* (1972), *The Shrine and Other Stories* (1977), *A Family Likeness* (1985) and *The House in Clewe Street* (1987). She was awarded the **Katherine Mansfield** prize (1961), two Guggenheim awards and the Gregory Medal, founded by **W B Yeats** as 'the supreme award of the Irish nation'. 🕮 R Peterson, *Mary Lavin* (1978)

Lavoisier, Antoine Laurent 1743–94
French chemist

Born in Paris, he accepted the office of farmer-general of taxes (1768) to finance his investigations. As director of the government powder mills (1776), he greatly improved gunpowder, its supply and manufacture, and successfully applied chemistry to agriculture. He discovered oxygen, by rightly interpreting **Joseph Priestley's** facts, its importance in respiration, combustion and as a compound with metals. His *Traité élémentaire de chimie* (1789, 'Treaty of Elementary Chemistry') was a masterpiece. Politically liberal, he saw the great necessity for reform in France but was against revolutionary methods. Despite a lifetime of work for the state, inquiring into the problems of taxation (which he helped to reform), hospitals and prisons, he was guillotined as a farmer of taxes. 📖 V Grey, *The Chemist Who Lost His Head* (1982)

Law, (Andrew) Bonar 1858–1923
Scottish statesman
Born in Kingston, New Brunswick, Canada, of Scottish descent, he became an iron merchant in Glasgow, and a Unionist MP from 1900. In 1911 he succeeded **Arthur Balfour** as Unionist Leader in the House of Commons. He was Colonial Secretary (1915–16), then a member of the War Cabinet, Chancellor of the Exchequer (1916–18), Lord Privy Seal (1919), and from 1916 Leader of the House of Commons. He retired in March 1921, but was recalled to serve as Prime Minister (1922–23), when the Conservatives withdrew from the coalition, forcing **David Lloyd George** to resign. Law resigned seven months later from ill health and died the same year. 📖 Robert N W Blake, *The Unknown Prime Minister* (1955)

Law, Denis 1940–
Scottish footballer
He was born in Aberdeen. One of the greatest of Scottish footballers, he never played at senior level in his own country, all his career being spent in England with the exception of a brief and unsuccessful spell in Italy. He made his international debut when only 18 years old and shortly afterwards moved to Manchester City. After the Italian failure with Turin, he returned to Manchester United, the club with which he is indelibly associated. With them he won every major domestic honour, although injury excluded him from the European Cup success of 1968. Law shares with **Kenny Dalglish** the record of 30 goals scored for Scotland.

Law (of Lauriston), John 1671–1729
Scottish financier
He was born in Edinburgh, the son of a goldsmith and banker, and educated at the Royal High School there. He became a successful gambler and speculator and went to London to make his fortune, but in 1694 was imprisoned for killing a man in a duel over a lady. In 1695 he escaped and fled to the Continent. He visited Amsterdam, Genoa (where he eloped with a Frenchman's wife) and Venice, making money as he went, and in 1703 returned to Edinburgh, a zealous advocate of a paper currency; but his proposals to the Scottish parliament on this subject, outlined in his *Money and Trade Considered* (1705), were unfavourably received. In Paris he and his brother William (1675–1752) set up in 1716 a private bank, the Banque Générale. Its success was so great that the regent, Philippe, Duc d'Orléans, adopted Law's plan of a national bank in 1718. In 1719 Law originated a joint-stock company, the Compagnie d'Occident, to fund the 'Mississippi scheme' for reclaiming and settling lands in the Mississippi valley, which made him a paper millionaire. He became a French citizen and a Roman Catholic, and in 1720 was made Comptroller-General of Finance for France. However the scheme collapsed that year due to over-issue of stock and Law fled; he died in poverty in Venice.

Law, William 1686–1761
English churchman and writer
Born in Kingscliffe, Northamptonshire, he studied at Emmanuel College, Cambridge, and became a Fellow in 1711. Unwilling to sign the Oath of Allegiance to **George** I, he lost his fellowship. About 1727 he became tutor to the father of **Edward Gibbon**, and for 10 years was 'the much-honoured friend and spiritual director of the whole family'. About 1733 he had begun to study **Jakob Böhme**, and most of his later books are expositions of his mysticism. Law won his first triumphs against controversy with his *Three Letters* (1717). His *Remarks on Mandeville's Fable of the Bees* (1723) is a work of great caustic wit. His most famous work remains the *Serious Call to a Devout and Holy Life* (1729), which greatly influenced **Dr Johnson** and the **Wesleys**.

Lawes, Henry 1596–1662
English composer
Born in Dinton, Wiltshire, he set **Milton's** *Comus* (1633) to music (1634) and also **Robert Herrick's** verses. He was highly regarded by Milton, who praised him in a sonnet, and his adaptation of music to verse and rhythm was impressive. His half-brother, William Lawes (d.1645), was also a composer, one of **Charles I's** court musicians.

Lawes, Sir John Bennet 1814–1900
English agriculturist
Born in Rothamstead, near St Albans, he was educated at Oxford. In 1834 he inherited the estate of Rothamstead. Noticing that rock phosphate was only effective as a fertilizer on acid soils, he found that it was insoluble in alkaline soils and that by treating it with acid it became useful on all types of land. In 1843 he began to manufacture this 'superphosphate' at Deptford Creek. The same year he founded the first agricultural research station in the world at Rothamstead, and asked **Henry Gilbert** to take charge of his laboratory. Lawes and Gilbert worked together for 50 years and earned Rothamstead an international reputation. They studied animal feeding, grasslands and manures, and during the course of their experiments introduced a system of randomly selected trial plots. This has been almost universally adopted and gives agricultural trials their characteristic chequer-board appearance. Lawes was elected FRS in 1854 and created a baronet in 1882. Rothamstead Experimental Station remains at the forefront of agricultural research. 📖 G V Dyke, *John Bennet Lawes: The Record of His Genius* (1991)

Lawler, Ray(mond Evenor) 1921–
Australian playwright
Born in Melbourne, he began writing plays in his teens while working as a factory hand, but it was not until his ninth play *The Summer of the Seventeenth Doll* (1955) that he achieved success. Lawler himself played Barney in the original production and in the London première (1957) which won the *Evening Standard* award. The play was filmed in 1960 and Lawler followed it with two 'prequels', *Kid Stakes* (1975) and *Other Times* (1976). The three plays are now published as *The Doll Trilogy* (1978), and in 1996 *Seventeenth Doll* transferred successfully to the operatic stage with music by Australian composer Richard Mills.

Lawrence or Laurentius, St d.258AD
Spanish Christian
Born possibly in Huesca, he became a deacon in Rome. In the persecution of Valerianus he was martyred by broiling. His feast day is 10 August.

Lawrence, Abbott 1792–1855
US merchant and politician
Born in Groton, Massachusetts, he became a prominent merchant in Boston, in partnership with his brother Amos. He promoted the expansion of New England railroads (Boston and Albany), founded and developed

the textile manufacturing city of Lawrence, Massachusetts (from 1845), and was known for his philanthropy, including generous contributions to Harvard University, where the Lawrence Scientific School was named for him. He served in the US House of Representatives (1835–37, 1839–40) and was US Minister to Great Britain (1849–52).

Lawrence, D(avid) H(erbert) 1885–1930
English novelist, poet and essayist

He was born in Eastwood, Nottinghamshire, the son of a miner. With his mother's encouragement, he became a schoolmaster and began to write, encouraged by the notice taken of his work by **Ford Madox Ford** and **Edward Garnett**. In 1911, after the success of his first novel, *The White Peacock*, he decided to write full-time. In 1912 he eloped with Frieda Weekley (*née* von Richthofen), a cousin of the German war ace Baron **Manfred von Richthofen** and wife of Ernest Weekley, and a professor at Nottingham University. They travelled in Europe for a year, and married in 1914 after her divorce. Lawrence had made his reputation with the semi-autobiographical *Sons and Lovers* (1913). They returned to England at the outbreak of World War I and lived in an atmosphere of suspicion and persecution in Cornwall. In 1915 he published *The Rainbow*, an exploration of marital and sexual relations, and was horrified when prosecuted for obscenity. He left England in 1919, and after three years' residence in Italy, where he produced another exploration of sex and marriage, *Women in Love* (1921), he went to the USA, settling in New Mexico until the tuberculosis from which he suffered drove him back to Italy where his last years were spent. He was again shocked by further prosecutions for obscenity over the private publication in Florence of *Lady Chatterley's Lover* in 1928 and over an exhibition of his paintings in London in 1929. *Lady Chatterley's Lover* was not published in the UK in unexpurgated form until after a sensational obscenity trial in 1961. Opinion is still divided over his literary worth but his effect on the younger intellectuals of his period is certain. He challenged them by his attempt to interpret human emotion on a deeper level of consciousness than that handled by his contemporaries. This provoked either sharp criticism or an almost idolatrous respect. His descriptive passages are sometimes superb, but he had little humour, and this occasionally produced unintentionally comic effects. His finest writing occurs in his poems, where all but essentials have been pared away, but most of his novels have an enduring strength. His other major novels include *Aaron's Rod* (1922), *Kangaroo* (1923, reflecting a visit to Australia) and *The Plumed Serpent* (1926, set in Mexico). His collected poems were published in 1928, and his *Complete Poems* in 1957. A *Complete Plays* appeared in 1965, and his other writings include vivid travel narratives, essays, works of literary criticism, including *Studies in Classic American Literature* (1923), and two studies of the unconscious. Over 5,000 of his letters have been published (7 vols, 1979). 📖 K Sagar, *The Life of D H Lawrence* (1980)

Lawrence, Ernest Orlando 1901–58
US physicist and Nobel Prize winner

Born in Canton, South Dakota, he graduated from the universities of South Dakota, Minnesota and Yale, and in 1929 he constructed the first cyclotron for the production of artificial radioactivity, fundamental to the development of the atomic bomb. He was professor at the University of California at Berkeley from 1930, and in 1936 was appointed first director of the radiation laboratory there. He was awarded the Nobel Prize for physics in 1939. 📖 Herbert Childs, *An American Genius: The Life of Ernest Orlando Lawrence, Father of the Cyclotron* (1968)

Lawrence, Geoffrey, 3rd Baron Trevithin and 1st Baron Oaksey 1880–1971
English lawyer

He graduated at Oxford and was called to the Bar in 1906. He became a judge of the High Court of Justice (King's Bench Division) in 1932, a Lord Justice of Appeal in 1944, and a Lord-of-Appeal-in-Ordinary (1947–57). As president of the international tribunal for the trial of war criminals at Nuremberg in 1945, he was distinguished for his fair and impartial conduct of the proceedings. Created Baron Oaksey in 1947, he succeeded his brother in the title of Trevithin in 1959.

Lawrence, Gertrude, *originally* Gertrud Alexandra Dagmar Lawrence Klasen 1898–1952
English actress

Born in London, she became one of the great stars of the Broadway musical stage, although she was an undistinguished dancer and technically indifferent singer. She had huge successes with musicals like *Oh, Kay!* (1926) and *Lady in the Dark* (1944). A highly acclaimed comic actress, she became particularly associated with the work of **Noël Coward**, beginning with *Private Lives* in 1931. Her last stage appearance came in one of her most famous productions, *The King and I* (1951).

Lawrence, Sir Henry Montgomery 1806–57
British soldier and administrator

Born in Matara, Ceylon (Sri Lanka), he took part in the first Burmese War (1828), the first of the Afghan Wars (1838), and the Sikh Wars (1845, 1848). In 1857 he was appointed to Lucknow, and did all he could to restore contentment there, but the Indian Uprising broke out in May. It was owing to his foresight that it was possible for 1,000 Europeans and 800 Indians to defend the Residency for nearly four months against 7,000 rebels. He was mortally injured during this defence.

Lawrence, Jacob 1917–
US painter

Born in Atlantic City, New Jersey, the son of a railroad cook, he moved to New York City in 1930 and studied at the Harlem Art Workshop and the American Artists School. Influenced by Social Realism, Cubism and by primitive art, he began to paint scenes from African-American life in a bold, angular style. He prefers water-based paints to oil and has often executed a series of works on a single theme, notably *Frederick Douglass* (1938–39), *Harriet Tubman* (1939–40) and *The Migration of the Negro* (1940–41). He has taught at numerous institutions, notably the Art Students League and the New School for Social Research in New York City, and since 1970 has been Professor of Art at the University of Washington in Seattle (emeritus since 1983). He is an important figure in contemporary US art and the most famous of African-American painters.

Lawrence (of the Punjab and of Grately), John Laird Mair Lawrence, 1st Baron 1811–79
English colonial administrator

He was born in Richmond, Yorkshire, the brother of Sir Henry Lawrence. His first years in the Indian Civil Service were spent at Delhi. Successively Commissioner and Lieutenant-Governor of the Punjab, he used every effort to curb the oppression of the people by their chiefs, devised a system of land tenure, and devoted his energy to restoring peace and prosperity. The once restless Sikhs had become so attached to his rule that he was able to disarm the mutineers in the Punjab, to raise an army of 59,000 men, and to capture Delhi from the rebels after a siege of over three months. In 1863 he succeeded Lord **Elgin** as Governor-General of India. He did not believe in British interference in Asia beyond the frontier of India, and was especially opposed to intriguing in Afghanistan, devoting the last days of his life in parliament (1878) to an exposure of the policy which led up to the disastrous Afghan War (1878–80).

Lawrence, Marjorie Florence 1908–79
Australian soprano

Born in Deans Marsh, Victoria, she won a singing competition in nearby Geelong in 1928, and her parents were persuaded by the operatic singer John Brownlee to let her study overseas. She made her debut in 1932 with the Monte Carlo Opera, and the following year appeared in Paris. In 1935 she became a member of the Metropolitan Opera, New York, where for four years she was a leading Wagnerian soprano. In 1941, while touring in Mexico, she contracted poliomyelitis. Returning to the USA she was treated there by Sister Elizabeth Kenny, and by the end of the following year was making guest appearances at 'The Met' in a wheelchair. During World War II she travelled extensively to entertain the troops, including visits to the Pacific and to Europe. Her autobiography, *Interrupted Melody* (1949), was filmed in 1955. Later she took up teaching at the University of Southern Illinois.

Lawrence, Sir Thomas 1769–1830
English painter

Born in Bristol, as a child he was famed for his portraits and at the age of 12 he had his own studio in Bath. His full-length portrait of Queen Charlotte Sophia (now in the National Gallery, London) which he painted at the age of 20, was remarkable for its maturity and is one of his best works. In 1792 he was appointed limner to George III and in 1820 he succeeded Benjamin West as president of the Royal Academy. He was buried in St Paul's. Lawrence was the favourite portrait painter of his time, and had an immense European practice.

Lawrence, T(homas) E(dward), *known as* Lawrence of Arabia 1888–1935
Anglo-Irish soldier and writer

Born in Tremadoc, Caernarvonshire, North Wales, he was brought up in Oxford. He joined the archaeological team under Sir Flinders Petrie at Carchemish, on the Euphrates (1911–14), where he first met the Bedouins. In World War I he worked for army intelligence in North Africa (1914–16). In 1916 he was British liaison officer to the Arab revolt against the Turks led by Faisal I, the son of Hussein ibn Ali. He co-operated with General Allenby's triumphal advance and entered Damascus in October 1918. He was an adviser to Faisal at the Paris Peace Conference and a member of the Middle East Department at the Colonial Office (1921). His account of the Arab Revolt, *Seven Pillars of Wisdom*, abridged by himself as *Revolt in the Desert*, became one of the classics of war literature. To escape his subsequent fame he enlisted in the ranks of the RAF (1922) as J H Ross, in the Royal Tank Corps (1923) as T E Shaw, and again in the RAF in 1925. He retired in 1935, and was killed that year in a motor-cycling accident in Dorset. 📖 Basil H Liddell Hart, *T E Lawrence, in Arabia and After* (1934)

Lawrence of Arabia See Lawrence, T E

Laws, Richard Maitland 1926–
English mammalogist and Antarctic scientist

Born in Whitley Bay, Northumberland, he was educated at Cambridge, from 1947 to 1953 was employed by the Falkland Islands Dependencies Survey, and later moved to the National Institute of Oceanography (1954–61). After a period as director of the Nuffield Unit of Tropical Animal Ecology in Uganda (1961–68), he was appointed as head of the Life Sciences Division of the British Antarctic Survey (1969–87), for which he served as director from 1973 to 1987. Laws made a precise population study of large mammals, ageing individuals on the basis of growth rings in the teeth and tusks. Through his leadership of the British Antarctic Survey, he was a dominant figure in changing the early phase of Antarctic research into a co-ordinated scientific endeavour. He was elected FRS in 1980 and was appointed Master of St Edmund's College, Cambridge, in 1985.

Lawson, Henry Hertzberg 1867–1922
Australian poet and short-story writer

He was born near Grenfell, New South Wales, the son of a Norwegian sailor and gold miner, and Louisa Lawson, a founder of the movement for women's suffrage in New South Wales. From his mother and her friends Henry acquired the radical opinions which coloured his own writing. He travelled widely in Australia and New Zealand and contributed to the Australian weekly *Bulletin*, but his first collection, *Short Stories in Prose and Verse* (1894), was published by his mother. It was followed by the volume of verse *In the Days When the World Was Wide* (1896) and the short-story collection *While the Billy Boils* (1896). He then moved with his wife and son to London, where he prepared for *Blackwood's Magazine* a collection of his earlier stories, and worked on the tales which were to appear the same year as *Joe Wilson and His Mates*. Returning to Australia in 1902, he separated from his wife. His later years were marred by ill health and alcoholism. The definitive seven-volume edition of his work edited by Colin Roderick (1967–72) includes letters and autobiographical writings. 📖 M Clark, *In Search of Lawson* (1978)

Lawson, Louisa, *née* Albury 1848–1920
Australian writer, social reformer and suffragist

She was born in Guntawang, near Mudgee, New South Wales, and in 1866 married a Norwegian, Niels Hertzberg Larsen. The family name was anglicized to Lawson after the birth of their son, the later famous Henry Lawson. Louisa left her husband in 1883 and took her five children to Sydney, where she worked as a seamstress. Soon involved in radical and feminist politics and social reform, she bought the *Republican* in 1887, editing it with Henry until 1888, then founded the journal *Dawn*, which she edited for 17 years, offering household advice, stories and reports on women around the world. In 1889 she founded the Dawn Club, a group that campaigned through *Dawn* mainly for female suffrage but also for 'health, temperance, social purity, education, dress reform and physiological matters'. In 1900 Lawson was thrown from a train and suffered physical and psychological injuries from which she never fully recovered. Australian women were given the vote in 1902, but she lived the rest of her life in poverty and died in a hospital for the insane.

Lawson, Nigel Lawson, Baron 1932–
English Conservative politician

Educated at Westminster and Christ Church, Oxford, he embarked on a career as a journalist after Royal Navy national service (1954–56). From *The Financial Times* he moved to the *Sunday Telegraph*, where he was city editor, and then gradually entered politics, unsuccessfully fighting the Slough seat for the Conservatives in 1970 and then becoming MP for Blaby, Leicestershire, in 1974. Margaret Thatcher appointed him Financial Secretary to the Treasury in 1979, from where he rose to Energy Secretary (1981–83) and Chancellor of the Exchequer in 1983, from which post he dramatically resigned in 1989, being replaced by John Major. Though at first one of Margaret Thatcher's closest Cabinet colleagues, by the late 1980s they had become increasingly estranged over Lawson's advocacy of lower interest rates to cure industrial stagnation and of Great Britain's full membership of the European monetary system. His sudden resignation marked the beginning of a party split that widened during the following year and saw Thatcher dropped as party leader in November 1990. He resigned from the Commons in 1992 and was awarded a life peerage the same year. Following his dramatic weight loss, he published *The Nigel Lawson Diet Book* in 1996. His other publications include *The Coming Confrontation* (1978), *The Power Game* (1979) and *The New Conservatism* (1980).

Lawton, John Hartley 1943–
English ecologist

Born in Preston, Lancashire, he was educated at Durham University, taught at the universities of Oxford and York, and since 1989 has been director of the Natural Environmental Research Council's Centre for Population Biology at Imperial College, London. His early studies on ecology energetics concerned energy use by animal populations, the structure of their food chains and the ratios of predator and prey species. He recognized that plant structural complexity plays a part in the control of insect species, and this work led to questions on the structuring of the insect communities on plants. He suggested that subtle, plant-mediated competitive effects, as well as vertical interactions such as enemy-free space, play important roles. In his studies of bracken and its herbivores Lawton has directed his findings towards the biological control of this worldwide weed. He was elected FRS in 1989.

Laxness, Halldór Kiljan, *pseudonym of* Halldór Guðjónsson 1902–98
Icelandic novelist and Nobel Prize winner

He was born in Reykjavík, and brought up on a farm near there. After World War I he steeped himself in Expressionism in Germany, Catholicism in a monastery in Luxembourg, and Surrealism in France, before going to Canada and the USA (1927–30), where he was converted to Socialism. In his fiction he explored the reality of Iceland, past and present, and rejuvenated Icelandic prose, in a series of incomparable epic novels like *Salka Valka* (1931–32), *Sjálfstætt fólk* (1934–35, Eng trans *Independent People*, 1945–46), *Heimsljós* (1937–40, Eng trans *World Light*, 1969) and *Íslandsklukkan* (1943–46, 'Iceland's Bell'). After World War II he continued to turn out a stream of brilliantly executed novels on Icelandic life: *Atómstöðin* (1948, Eng trans *The Atom Station*, 1961), *Gerpla* (1952, Eng trans *The Happy Warriors*, 1958), *Brekkukotsannáll* (1957, Eng trans *The Fish Can Sing*, 1966), *Paradísarheimt* (1960, Eng trans *Paradise Reclaimed*, 1962) and *Kristnihald undir Jökli* (1968, Eng trans *Christianity at Glacier*, 1972) which was filmed in 1989. He also wrote a number of plays, seven volumes of autobiography (1963–87) and adapted some of his own novels for the stage. 📖 P Hallberg, *Laxness* (1971)

Layamon fl. early 13th century
English poet and priest

He lived at Ernley (Areley), Worcestershire. In c.1200 he wrote an alliterative verse chronicle, the *Brut*, a history of England which was an amplified imitation of Robert Wace's *Brut d'Angleterre*. It is the first poem written in Middle English, and contains the first English versions of the stories of Arthur, Lear, Cymbelene and others. 📖 J S P Tetlock, *The Legendary History of Britain* (1950)

Layard, Sir Austen Henry 1817–94
English archaeologist and politician

Born in Paris, he excavated (1845–47, 1849–51) at Nimrud, near Mosul in Iraq, identifying it as the ancient city of Nineveh and finding the remains of four palaces of the 7th–9th centuries BC. He brought several large sculptures to London in 1848, and wrote books on Assyrian civilization. He became an MP in 1852, Under-Secretary of Foreign Affairs (1861–66), chief commissioner of works (1868–69), and British ambassador in Spain (1869) and Istanbul (1877–80). 📖 Gordon Waterfield, *Layard of Nineveh* (1963)

Laye, Camera 1928–80
Francophone novelist

Born in French Guinea of a Malinke family, he grew up away from the influence of colonialism; his father was a smith, a master of both metalwork and magic. His two masterpieces are his first two novels: the autobiographical *L'Enfant noir* (1953, Eng trans *The Dark Child*, 1954), and *Le Regard du roi* (1954, Eng trans *The Radiance of the King*, 1956). Sick and weak for the last years of his life, in 1965 he left his own country in disgust, for Senegal. President Touré had him condemned to death *in absentia*. Later work includes *Le Maître de la parole* (1978, 'The Wordmaster'). 📖 W Cartey, *Whispers from a Continent* (1969); A C Brench, *The Novelists' Inheritance in French Africa* (1967)

Lazarsfeld, Paul Felix 1901–76
US sociologist

Born in Vienna, he studied mathematics and law at Vienna University, then taught mathematics and physics in a Viennese secondary school. He also taught statistics at the university where he set up a social psychology research centre in 1927. In 1933 the Rockefeller Foundation awarded him a scholarship to the USA, where he settled, working at Newark University, then at Princeton. In 1940 he joined the department of sociology at Columbia, where he established the Bureau of Applied Social Research (1945). He is best known as a quantitative methodologist, but he also wrote about popular culture in mass communications, political sociology and applied sociology.

Lazarus, Emma 1849–87
US poet and essayist

Born in New York, she published volumes of poems and translations, including *Admetus and other poems* (1871), *Songs of a Semite* (1882) and *By the Waters of Babylon* (1887). She also wrote a prose romance, *Alide: An Episode of Goethe's Life* (1874), and a verse tragedy, *The Spagnaletto* (1876). A champion of oppressed Jewry, she is best known for her sonnet, 'The New Colossus' (1883), inscribed on the Statue of Liberty in New York harbour. 📖 H E Jacob, *The World of Emma Lazarus* (1949)

Leach, Bernard Howell 1887–1979
English potter

Born in Hong Kong, he studied at the Slade School of Art, London, and went to Japan at the age of 21 to teach. He studied pottery and became the sole pupil of Ogata Kenzan. He returned to England with his family in 1920 and, together with Shoji Hamada, established the pottery at St Ives, Cornwall. He produced stoneware and raku-ware using local materials and also turned to the 17th century as inspiration to produce English slipware. One of his aims was to provide sound handmade pots sufficiently inexpensive for people of moderate means to take into daily use. From 1922 to 1924 he began to take on student apprentices, among whom were Michael Cardew and Katherine Pleydell-Bouverie. A leading figure in the development of studio pottery in the UK, he had regular exhibitions of his work and began teaching at Dartington Hall, Devon, in 1932. His written works include *A Potter's Book* (1940).

Leach, Sir Edmund Ronald 1910–89
English social anthropologist

Born in Sidmouth, Devon, he studied mathematics and engineering at Clare College, Cambridge, then travelled in China before returning to England in 1937 to study anthropology under Bronisław Malinowski at the London School of Economics. Soon after he left to carry out fieldwork among the Kachin of Burma, World War II broke out. He spent the war serving in Burma, then took a post in anthropology at the London School of Economics (1947–53), and in 1954 published his first major monograph, *Political Systems of Highland Burma*. This overturned orthodox notions of social structural equilibrium, demonstrating the complex and fluctuating relationship between ideal models and political conduct. Leach's attack on structural-functional theory continued in *Pul Eliya* (1961), a study of a village in Ceylon (Sri Lanka). He became Reader in Social Anthropology at Cambridge (1957–72), and Professor (1972–78), and provost of King's College (1966–79). In later years his major interest shifted to structuralism, and the analysis of myth and ritual, as in *Genesis as Myth and other essays* (1969). His other publications include *Rethinking Anthropology* (1961), *Lévi-Strauss* (1970), *Culture and Communication* (1976) and *Social Anthropology* (1982). His considerable influence both within and outside anthropology was mainly as a provocative and polemical critic of prevailing orthodoxies.

Leacock, Stephen Butler 1869–1944
Canadian humorist and economist

He was born in Swanmore, Hampshire, England, and brought up and educated in Canada. He studied at the University of Toronto, and became first a teacher, then a lecturer at McGill University, and in 1908 head of the economics department there. He wrote several books on his subject, including *Elements of Political Science* (1906), *Practical Political Economy* (1910) and *The Economic Prosperity of the British Empire* (1931). But it is as a humorist that he became widely known. Among his popular short stories, essays and parodies are *Literary Lapses* (1910), *Nonsense Novels* (1911), *Behind the Beyond* (1913), *Winsome Winnie* (1920) and *The Garden of Folly* (1924). He also wrote biographies of **Mark Twain** (1932) and **Dickens** (1933). *The Boy I Left Behind Me*, an autobiography, appeared in 1946. ▢ D M Legate, *Stephen Leacock: a biography* (1970)

Leadbelly or Lead Belly, *originally* Huddie William Ledbetter 1888–1949
US folk and blues singer and guitarist

He was born in Mooringsport, Louisiana. Little is known of his early life, but at 15 he could play several instruments. He was twice sentenced to long prison terms, for murder in 1917 and intent to murder in 1930, but received an early pardon on each occasion. While serving the second sentence, he was heard by folk researcher Alan Lomax (see **John Avery Lomax**), who helped secure his release. He moved to New York, where he became a seminal figure in the burgeoning folk scene, alongside **Woody Guthrie** and **Pete Seeger**. His rough-hewn vocals and blues-soaked 12-string guitar style was hugely influential into the rock era, while songs like 'Good Night Irene' and 'The Midnight Special' became folk-blues standards. ▢ C Wolfe and K Larnell, *The Life and Legend of Leadbelly* (1993)

Leadbetter, David 1955–
English golf teacher

Born in Worthing, he took up teaching when he realized he would never succeed as a touring professional. He worked with **Tom Watson**, Curtis Strange and **Sevy Ballesteros** but not until he changed **Nick Faldo's** swing did he gain international cult status. Despite considerable success, Faldo went to him in 1985, radically changed his swing and won the Open in 1987. Leadbetter's gift is designing training drills so the player repeats the swing until the movement is instinctive. His teaching school is in Lake Nona, near Orlando, Florida.

Leakey, Louis Seymour Bazett 1903–72
British archaeologist and physical anthropologist

He was born of British missionary parents in Kabete, Kenya, where he grew up with the Kikuyu tribe. Educated at St John's College, Cambridge, he took part in several archaeological expeditions in East Africa, made

a study of the Kikuyu and wrote widely on African anthropology. He was curator of the Coryndon Memorial Museum at Nairobi (1945–61). His great discoveries of early hominid fossils took place at Olduvai Gorge in East Africa, where in 1959, together with his wife **Mary Leakey**, he unearthed the skull of *Zinjanthropus*, subsequently reclassified as a form of *Australopithecus* and now thought to be about 1.75 million years old. In 1960–63 at Olduvai Gorge he found remains of *Homo habilis*, a smaller species some 2 million years old, which led him to postulate the simultaneous evolution of two different species, of which *Homo habilis* was the true ancestor of man, while *Australopithecus* became extinct. In 1967 he discovered *Kenyapithecus africanus*, fossilized remains of a Miocene ape, c.14 million years old. He also unearthed evidence of human habitation in California more than 50,000 years old. ▢ Sonia M Cole, *Leakey's Luck: The Life of Louis Seymour Bazett Leakey, 1903–1972* (1975)

Leakey, Mary Douglas, *née* Nicol 1913–96
English archaeologist

She was born in London, and her interest in prehistory was roused during childhood trips to south-west France where she collected stone tools and visited the painted caves around Les Eyzies. She met **Louis Leakey** while preparing drawings for his book *Adam's Ancestors* (1934), became his second wife in 1936, and moved soon afterwards to Kenya where she undertook pioneering archaeological research. In 1948, at Rusinga Island, in Lake Victoria, she discovered *Proconsul africanus*, a 1.7 million-year-old dryopithecine (primitive ape) that brought the Leakeys international attention. From 1951 she worked at Olduvai Gorge in Tanzania, initially on a modest scale, but more extensively from 1959 when her discovery of the 1.75 million-year-old hominid *Zinjanthropus* (later reclassified as a form of *Australopithecus*), filmed as it happened, captured the public imagination and drew vastly increased funding. *Homo habilis*, a new species contemporary with, but more advanced than, *Zinjanthropus* was found in 1960–63 and published amidst much controversy in 1964. Perhaps most remarkable of all was her excavation in 1976 at Laetoli, 30 miles (48.3km) south of Olduvai, of three trails of fossilized hominid footprints which demonstrated unequivocally that our ancestors already walked upright 3.6 million years ago. Her books include *Olduvai Gorge: My Search for Early Man* (1979) and *Laetoli: a Pliocene site in Northern Tanzania* (1987, co-edited with Kevin O'Farrell). ▢ *Disclosing the Past* (1984)

Leakey, Richard Erskine Frere 1944–
Kenyan palaeoanthropologist

He was born in Nairobi, the second son of British archaeologists **Louis** and **Mary Leakey**, and from an early age worked in the field with his parents, finding his first fossil bone at the age of six. He left school at 16 and trapped animals for zoos, collected animal skeletons for zoologists, and ran a safari company before organizing his first research expedition, to Peninj on Lake Natron (1964), Lake Baringo (1966), and the Omo Valley in Ethiopia (1967). From 1969 to 1975 he worked with the archaeologist Glynn Isaac at Koobi Fora, part of a vast fossil site covering 500 square miles (1,300 sq km) on the eastern shores of Lake Turkana, and discovered well-preserved hominid remains that drew worldwide publicity. Of particular note are crania of *Australopithecus boisei* (found 1969), of *Homo habilis* dated 1.9 million years (found 1972), and of *Homo erectus* dated 1.5 million years (found 1975). He was appointed administrative director of the National Museum of Kenya in 1968 (director in 1974) and in 1995 co-founded and became Secretary-General of the Safina Party. His publications include *Origins* (1977), *People of the Lake* (1979) and *Origins Reconsidered* (1992), all with Roger Lewin; *The Making of Mankind* (1981); and *Man-Ape Ape-Man* (1993, with L Jan Slikkerveer). ▢ *One Life* (1984)

Lean, Sir David 1908–91
English film director

Born in Croydon, London, he began in the film industry as a clapperboard boy, and gradually progressed from camera assistant to assistant editor to editor. He was an editor for *Gaumont Sound News* (1930) and *British Movietone News* (1931–32) before moving on to fictional features such as *Escape Me Never* (1936) and *Pygmalion* (1938). His co-direction, with Noël Coward, of *In Which We Serve* (1942) and *Blithe Spirit* (1945) led to a full-scale directorial career in which his craftsmanship and compositional acumen were combined with a strong sense of narrative in films like *Brief Encounter* (1945), *Great Expectations* (1946) and *Oliver Twist* (1948). Increasingly drawn towards works of an epic and grandiose scale, he won Academy Awards for *Bridge on the River Kwai* (1957) and *Lawrence of Arabia* (1962). *Dr Zhivago* (1965) was followed by *Ryan's Daughter* (1970) and his last film, after a gap of 14 years, *A Passage to India* (1984). His sparse output has been attributed to exacting artistic standards. ⌨ Kevin Brownlow, *David Lean—A Biography* (1996); M A Anderegg, *David Lean* (1984)

Leander, St d.c.600
Spanish prelate

He was born probably in Seville. A friend of Pope Gregory I, the Great, he laid the foundations of church organization in Spain, and converted the Visigoths from Arianism. He was the elder brother of Isidore of Seville, and his predecessor as Archbishop of Seville (c.577–c.600).

Lear, Edward 1812–88
English artist, humorist and traveller

He was born in London, the youngest of 20 children, and was educated at home, mainly by his sister, Anne. In 1832 he was engaged by the 13th Earl of Derby to make coloured drawings of the rare birds and animals in the menagerie at Knowsley Hall (Merseyside). Under the Earl's patronage he travelled widely in Italy and Greece, making landscape sketches and oil paintings which he published in several travel books, including *Sketches of Rome* (1842) and *Illustrated Excursions in Italy* (1846). He became a friend of his patron's grandchildren, whom he entertained with nonsense limericks and other verse which he illustrated with his own sketches and first published (anonymously) as *A Book of Nonsense* in 1846. Later he published *Nonsense Songs, Stories, Botany, and Alphabets* (1870), *More Nonsense Rhymes* (1871) and *Laughable Lyrics* (1876). He spent most of his latter years in Italy. ⌨ S Chitty, *That Singular Person Called Lear* (1988)

Lear, William Powell 1902–78
US inventor and electronic engineer

Born in Hannibal, Missouri, he joined the US navy aged 16 and studied radio and electronics. His 150 or more patents in the fields of radio, electronics, aviation and automobile engineering included the first practical car radio, the first commercial radio compass for aircraft, and an automatic pilot for jet aircraft. In 1962 he founded Lear Jet Corp., which became the largest manufacturer of small private jet planes. Lear Motors Corp. (1967) tried unsuccessfully to introduce steam-powered cars and buses.

Leavis, F(rank) R(aymond) 1895–1978
English literary critic

Born in Cambridge and educated at the University there, he fought against literary dilettantism in the quarterly, *Scrutiny* (1932–53), which he founded and edited, as well as in his *New Bearings in English Poetry* (1932). From 1936 to 1962 he was a Fellow of Downing College, Cambridge. He developed I A Richards's ideas about practical and close criticism into a kind of crusade against industrialization and 'mass culture', and his sociological study, *Culture and Environment* (1933, with D Thomson), deploring the separation of culture and environment in modern times and stressing the importance of impressing critical standards upon the young, has become a classic. Other works include *Revaluation* (1936), *The Great Tradition* (1948), *The Common Pursuit* (1952), *D H Lawrence* (1955), *Two Cultures?* (1962), in which he challenged the theories of C P Snow on literature and science, *Anna Karenina and Other Essays* (1967) and *Dickens the Novelist* (1970). The oft-repeated judgement that he was 'the most important English-speaking critic of his time' is a debatable point—chiefly because of his unwillingness to see the virtues of those poets and novelists he disliked. ⌨ M Bell, *F R Leavis* (1988)

Leavitt, Henrietta Swan 1868–1921
US astronomer

Born in Lancaster, Massachusetts, she attended Radcliffe College where she became interested in astronomy. She was a volunteer research assistant at Harvard College Observatory and joined the staff there in 1902, quickly becoming head of the department of photographic photometry. Whilst studying Cepheid variable stars, she noticed that the brighter they were the longer their period of light variation. By 1912 she had succeeded in showing that the apparent magnitude decreased linearly with the logarithm of the period. This simple relationship proved invaluable as the basis for a method of measuring the distance of stars.

Lebed, Alexander 1930–
Russian soldier and politician

Born in Novocherkassk, he attended military school before joining the USSR's airborne forces. In the early 1980s he served with the Soviet forces which had been sent to restore order in Afghanistan and made his reputation as a forceful and forthright commander. Between 1986 and 1988 he was Deputy Commander of the Airborne Forces and in 1992 commanded the 14th Army during the war between Moldova and Transdnestr separatists. His success made him a popular public figure and he was elected to parliament in 1996. Although he stood unsuccessfully against Boris Yeltsin in the presidential election, he was appointed Security Minister but was sacked shortly afterwards. He remains a potentially powerful force in Russian politics.

Lebedev, Pyotr Nikolayevich 1866–1912
Russian physicist

Born in Moscow, he studied from 1887 at Strassburg University under August Kundt, returning to Moscow University in 1891 to teach. He completed his PhD there and subsequently became Professor of Physics. His interests included the effects of light waves on molecules, hydrodynamics and acoustic waves. He generated electromagnetic waves much shorter than those previously studied by Heinrich Hertz and Augusto Righi, and used these short waves to observe the double refraction of electromagnetic waves in crystals. James Clerk Maxwell's theory of electromagnetism had predicted that light exerts a pressure on bodies, and in 1898 Lebedev began experimental work on this radiation pressure overcoming many difficult practical problems to prove conclusively that it did indeed exist. He progressed to work on the origins of the terrestrial magnetic field, attempting to link it to the Earth's rotation.

Le Bel, Joseph Achille 1847–1930
French chemist

Born in Pechelbronn, Alsace, he was educated at the École Polytechnique before managing the family oil business for some years. He then sold his share of the business and studied chemistry at the Sorbonne. He held no academic post, but became an industrial consultant and continued research on his private estate. In 1874 he published his account of the asymmetrical carbon atom two months after Jacobus van't Hoff's identical but independent work, giving van't Hoff the priority in this fundamental stereochemical concept.

Lebesgue, Henri Léon 1875–1941
French mathematician

Born in Beauvais, he studied at the École Normale Supérieure, and taught at Rennes, Poitiers, the Sorbonne and the Collège de France. Following the work of Émile Borel and René Baire (1874–1932), he developed the theory of measure and integration which bears his name, and applied it to many problems of analysis, in particular to the theory of Fourier series. Overcoming the defects of the Riemann integral, this theory has proved indispensable in all subsequent modern analysis. Lebesgue's work found important applications in complex analysis, and in many areas where continuous but not differentiable functions dominate.

Leblanc, Nicholas 1724–1806
French industrial chemist

He was born near Issoudun and trained as a physician, becoming private surgeon to the future Duc d'Orléans (Philippe Égalité). At that time soda (sodium carbonate), which was essential in the manufacture of glass, porcelain, paper and soap, was made from the ashes of wood or seaweed, both in short supply. In 1755 the French Academy of Sciences had offered a prize for a method of converting common salt (sodium chloride), which was plentiful, into soda. Leblanc devised such a process, subsequently known by the name of its inventor, which was perfected by 1790, but by then the French Revolution had begun and he never received the prize. In 1791 he was granted a patent, and with finance from the Duc d' Orléans, built a factory at St-Denis for its production. After his patron was guillotined in 1793, the factory was confiscated. Napoleon I returned it to Leblanc in 1802 but he had no capital to revive it, and shot himself in Paris four years later. His process was widely used in the 19th century, despite its environmental offensiveness. Soda is now manufactured by the method due to Ernest Solvay.

Lebrun, Albert 1871–1950
French politician

He was born in Mercy-le-Haut, Meurthe-et-Moselle. He studied mining engineering, became a Left Republican deputy in 1900, and was Minister for the Colonies (1911–14), for Blockade and Liberated Regions (1917–19), senator (1920), and President of the Senate (1931). The last President of the Third Republic, he surrendered his powers to Philippe Pétain in 1940, and went into retirement from which he did not re-emerge, although consulted by General De Gaulle in 1944. His health was affected by a period of internment after arrest by the Gestapo in 1943.

Le Brun, Charles 1619–90
French historical painter

Born in Paris, he studied in Rome for four years under Nicolas Poussin, and for nearly 40 years (1647–83) exercised a despotic influence over French art and artists, usually being considered the founder of the French school of painting. He helped to found the Academy of Painting and Sculpture in 1648 and was the first director of the Gobelins tapestry works (1662). From 1668 to 1683 he was employed by Louis XIV in the decoration of Versailles.

Le Carré, John, *pseudonym of* David John Moore Cornwell 1931–
English novelist

Born in Poole, Dorset, he was educated at Sherborne School, Berne University, and, after military service in Austria, at Oxford. He taught French and German for two years at Eton school in England, before going into the British Foreign Service as Second Secretary in Bonn, and consul in Hamburg, from which post he resigned in 1964 to become a full-time writer. His novels present the unglamorous side of diplomacy and espionage, a world of boredom, squalor and shabby deceit. His settings and characters have a compelling authenticity and he questions the morality of present-day diplomacy and traditional patriotic attitudes. His first published novel, *Call for The Dead* (1961), introduced his 'anti-hero' George Smiley, who appears in most of his stories. *A Murder of Quality* was published in 1962, followed the next year by the very successful *The Spy Who Came In From The Cold*. After *The Looking-Glass War* (1965) and *A Small Town in Germany* (1968), *The Naive and Sentimental Lover* (1971), a departure from his usual subject and style, was not well received. He returned to his former world with *Tinker, Tailor, Soldier, Spy* (1974), *The Honourable Schoolboy* (1977), *Smiley's People* (1980), *The Little Drummer Girl* (1983), *A Perfect Spy* (1986), *The Russia House* (1989) and *The Secret Pilgrim* (1992), in which Smiley takes his final bow. His recent novels include *The Night Manager* (1993) and *Our Game* (1995). Many of his books have been successfully filmed or televised, although the presumed end of the Cold War may have removed his most fertile subject-matter. 📖 E Homberger, *John Le Carré* (1986)

Le Châtelier, Henri Louis 1850–1936
French chemist and metallurgist

Born in Paris, he was educated at the École Polytechnique and the École des Mines, where in 1877 he became Professor of General Chemistry and in 1887 Professor of Industrial Chemistry. From 1898 to 1908 he held the chair of mineral chemistry at the Collège de France and, from 1907 onwards, the chair at the Sorbonne. His awards and honours included the Davy Medal of the Royal Society (1916), of which he became a Foreign Member in 1913. His earliest researches on the nature and setting of cements led him to consider the fundamental laws of chemical equilibrium, and in 1884 he formulated the principle named after him, which states that if a change is made in pressure, temperature or concentration of a system in chemical equilibrium, the equilibrium will be displaced in such a way as to oppose this change. He devised a thermocouple for measuring high temperatures, studied gaseous explosions, and researched the metallurgy of steel and other alloys. He also invented the inverted stage metallurgical microscope.

Lecky, William Edward Hartpole 1838–1903
Irish historian and philosopher

Born near Dublin, he was educated at Trinity College, Dublin. He was a Unionist but sympathetic to the Irish problems, and became MP for Dublin University in 1895, and a privy councillor in 1897. He published anonymously *The Leaders of Public Opinion in Ireland* (1861), four essays on Johnathan Swift, Henry Flood, Henry Grattan and Daniel O'Connell. He is considered one of the most unbiased historians. His other works include the *History of Rationalism* (1865), *History of England in the 18th Century* (1878–90), *Democracy and Liberty* (1896) and *The Map of Life* (1899).

Leclair, Jean Marie 1697–1764
French composer and violinist

Born in Lyons, he wrote many fine sonatas for the violin, and also the opera *Scylla et Glaucus* (1746). He was murdered in a suburb of Paris.

Leclanché, Georges 1839–82
French chemist

Born in Paris and an engineer by training, he is remembered for the galvanic cell invented by him and given his name.

Leclerc or Le Clerc (de Hauteclocque), Jacques Philippe, *properly* Philippe Marie, Vicomte de Hauteclocque 1902–47
French soldier
Born in Belloy-Saint-Léonard, he had a prestigious military training at St Cyr and Saumur and served in Morocco before returning to St Cyr as an instructor. In World War II he served with the French army in France (1939–40), was captured and escaped twice during the German invasion, and joined the Free French forces under Charles De Gaulle in England. He became Military Commander in French Equatorial Africa, and led a force across the desert to join the British 8th Army, in 1942. He commanded the French 2nd Armoured Division in Normandy, and liberated Paris in 1944.

Lecocq, Alexandre Charles 1832–1918
French composer of comic operas
Born in Paris, he studied at the Paris Conservatoire (1849–54), where he took many prizes, and won a considerable reputation as an organist. His many operettas, in the style of Jacques Offenbach, include *Le Docteur Miracle* (1857, 'Doctor Miracle'), *Giroflé-Girofla* (1874) and *L'Égyptienne* (1890), but although he dominated the French stage in this genre, his more serious music was never appreciated.

Leconte de Lisle, Charles Marie René 1818–94
French poet
Born in Saint-Paul, Réunion, he travelled for some years, then settled in Paris. He influenced all the younger poets, headed the school called *Parnassiens*, and succeeded to Victor Hugo's chair at the Academy in 1886. His early poems appeared as *Poésies complètes* (1858), and other volumes include *Poèmes barbares* (1862) and *Poèmes tragiques* (1884). He also translated many classics. □ P Flottes, *Leconte de Lisle* (1954)

Lecoq, Jacques 1921–98
French mime artist, teacher and director
Born in Paris, he began his career as an actor with the Compagnie des Comédiens in Grenoble (1945), becoming responsible for the group's physical training. In 1948 he joined the Padua University Theatre, Italy, as a teacher and director, where he produced his first pantomimes. He became a member of the Piccolo Theatre in Milan (1951), returned to Paris (1956) and established his own school, the École Internationale de Mime et de Théâtre. He formed his own company (1959), and began his research into the various theatrical disciplines of the clown, the buffoon, commedia, tragedy and melodrama, in terms of the actor's physical movement on the stage.

Le Corbusier, *pseudonym of* Charles Édouard Jeanneret 1887–1965
French architect
Born in La Chaux-de-Fonds, Switzerland, he worked in Paris with the architect Auguste Perret, then associated with Peter Behrens in Germany (1910–11). In 1919 he published in Paris (with Amédée Ozenfant) the Purist manifesto, and began to work on his theory of the interrelation between modern machine forms and the techniques of contemporary architecture. His books, *Vers une architecture* (1923), *Le Modulor* (1948) and *Le Modulor 2* (1955), have had worldwide influence on town-planning and building design. His first building, based on the technique of the Modulor (a system using standard-sized units, the proportions of which are calculated according to those of the human figure), was the *Unité d'habitation*, Marseilles (1945–50), which was conceived as one of a number of tall buildings which, when the overall scheme

('la Ville radieuse') had been completed, would form a pattern projecting from the 'carpet' of low buildings and open spaces. This was his favourite type of town-planning concept, used again in designing Chandigarh, the new capital of the Punjab. Some of his buildings are raised on stilts or *pilotis*, an innovation first used by him in the Swiss Pavilion in the Cité Universitaire in Paris. In the 1920s, in collaboration with Charlotte Perriand, he designed furniture, especially chairs, which used tubular metal in their construction.

Lecouvreur, Adrienne 1692–1730
French actress
She was born near Chalons, and made her debut at the Comédie Française in 1717. She soon became famous for her acting and her admirers, who included Marshal de Saxe, Voltaire and Lord Peterborough. Some ascribed her death to poisoning by a rival, the Duchesse de Bouillon, and this was the plot of the play based on her life written by Augustin Scribe and Legouvé, *Adrienne Lecouvreur* (1849).

Ledbetter, Huddie William See Leadbelly

Leder, Philip 1934–
US geneticist
Born in Washington DC, he was educated at Harvard University, and held posts at the National Heart Institute, the National Cancer Institute, and the National Institute for Child Health and Human Development (1972–80). In 1980 he became Professor of Genetics at Harvard University Medical School, and he is currently John Emory Andrus Professor of Genetics at Harvard, and a senior investigator at the Howard Hughes Medical Institute. He has worked extensively on the structure and function of the globin genes, discovering how they are arranged on the chromosome, and more recently has worked on the function of oncogenes, normal cellular genes which can be activated to become carcinogenic. Using activated oncogenes injected into mouse eggs to create transgenic mice, Leder has shown that the introduction of cancer to transgenic mice requires the co-operative action of more than one oncogene. He received a US National Medal of Science in 1989.

Lederberg, Joshua 1925–
US biologist, geneticist and Nobel Prize winner
Born in Montclair, New Jersey, he studied biology at Columbia University, and became professor at the universities of Wisconsin (1947–59) and Stanford (1959–78), then president of Rockefeller University (1978–90), and University Professor (1990–). With Edward Tatum, he showed that bacteria can reproduce by a sexual process known as conjunction, in which a new strain has the characteristics of both parents. He made a further fundamental contribution with his description of 'transduction' in bacteria, whereby the bacterial virus transfers part of its DNA into the host bacterium. This study led to the development of techniques for manipulation of genes. He has been director and consultant to several biotechnology companies, served as a consultant to the US space programme in the early 1960s, and was also a consultant to the World Health Organisation on biological warfare. In 1958 he was awarded the Nobel Prize for physiology or medicine, jointly with Tatum and George Beadle, and in 1989 won a US National Medal of Science.

Lederman, Leon Max 1922–
US physicist and Nobel Prize winner
Born in New York City, he was educated at Columbia University, where he became professor in 1958. He was also director of the Fermi National Accelerator Laboratory, Batvia, Illinois (1979–89), now emeritus. In 1989 he became Frank L Sulzberger Professor of Physics

at the University of Chicago and since 1992 has been Pritzker Professor of Science at the Illinois Institute of Technology. It was suspected that the muon was composed of two sub-particles, the 'electron charge' being carried by the electron neutrino and the 'muon charge' being carried by the muon neutrino. After an experiment performed at Brookhaven by Lederman, Melvin Schwartz and Jack Steinberger, they announced in 1962 that they had observed 20 muon events confirming the existence of the two distinct neutrino types. This was the basis for the idea that fundamental particles come in generations, with the electron, the muon and the tau-lepton all having associated neutrinos. Lederman went on to discover the long-lived neutral kaon and the 'bottom' quark. In 1988 he was awarded the Nobel Prize for physics together with Schwartz and Steinberger. His publications include *The God Particle* (1992).

Ledoux, Claude Nicolas 1736–1806
French architect

Born in Dormans-sur-Marne, he was one of the great artists of neoclassicism, and was architect to Louis XVI. His major works include the Château at Louveciennes for Madame du Barry (1771–73), acclaimed by Jean Fragonard. The Saltworks at Arc-et-Senans (1775–80) expressed his Jean Jacques Rousseau-inspired philosophy that human happiness is found in the rational exploitation of nature and the healthy organization of labour. The theatre at Besançon (1771–73) is another of his works. In 1785 he was employed by the Fermes-Général to erect 60 tax buildings around Paris; of the few that were built, La Villette, a rotunda, is the best. In 1804 he published *L'Architecture considérée sous le rapport de l'art des mœurs et de législation* ('Architecture Studied in Relation to Art, Moral Tendencies and the Law').

Ledru-Rollin, Alexandre Auguste 1807–74
French politician

Born in Fontenay, he was elected Deputy for Le Mans in 1841. At the February Revolution (1848) he became Minister of the Interior in the Provisional Government. As candidate for the presidency against Louis Napoleon (Napoleon III) he was beaten, and an unsuccessful attempt to provoke an insurrection in June 1849 drove him to England. He was amnestied in 1870, and after his return was elected to the National Assembly (1871).

Le Duc Tho, *originally* Phan Dinh Khai 1911–90
Vietnamese politician

Born in Ninh Province, he joined the Communist Party of Indo-China (1929) and was exiled to Con Dia by the French (1930). Released in 1937, he became head of the Nam Dinh revolutionary movement but was re-arrested and imprisoned (1939–44). After World War II, he entered the politburo of the Vietnam Workers' Party (1955), which later became the Communist Party of Vietnam (CPV). For his actions as leader of the Vietnamese delegation to the Paris Conference on Indo-China (1968–73), he was awarded the 1973 Nobel Peace Prize, jointly with Henry Kissinger, but declined to accept it. He retired from the politburo in 1986.

Led Zeppelin
English heavy rock band

Singer Robert Plant (1948–) and guitarist Jimmy Page (1944–) were the key members of the band, although bassist and organist John Paul Jones (originally John Baldwin, 1946–) and the aggressive drumming of John Bonham (1948–80) were integral to their sound. Despite a reputation as the founding fathers of heavy rock, nurtured by the orgiastic frenzy of 'Whole Lotta Love' or 'Stairway To Heaven' and a reputation for off-stage excess, there was an undoubtedly respectful blues side and an increasingly folksy, semi-mystical aspect to their music.

The group split up after Bonham's death, but the three surviving members reunited for a one-off concert in 1988. Plant and Page then toured and recorded their *Unledded* project in 1994. 🕮 R Yorke *Led Zepplin* (1993)

Lee, Ann, *known as* Mother Ann 1736–84
American mystic and religious leader

Born in Manchester, England, she was the illiterate daughter of a blacksmith. In 1758 she had joined the 'Shaking Quakers', or 'Shakers', and married Abraham Stanley, also a blacksmith, in 1762. She gave birth to four children, all of whom died in infancy, and in c.1770 she experienced a spiritual crisis, did penance and began to proclaim a new gospel drawn from divine revelations. She rejected marriage and sexual relationships as sinful and asserted Christ was to appear in the second coming as a woman, a prophecy that the Shakers came to believe was realized in her. Imprisoned in 1770 for street-preaching, she emigrated with a handful of followers to America in 1774, and in 1776 founded the parent Shaker settlement at Niskayuna, 7 miles (11km) north-west of Albany, New York. Her preaching and the peaceable communal life she helped to establish had attracted thousands of converts to the Shakers by the time of her death.

Lee, Brenda, *née* Brenda Mae Tarpley 1945–
US singer

Born in Lithonia, Georgia, she began her career in 1956 as a child country star regularly appearing on the country-and-western television show *Ozark Jubilee*. During the 1950s she became a rock 'n' roll star and was nicknamed 'Little Miss Dynamite' because of her small stature and very powerful voice. She is best known for the song 'I'm Sorry'. She moved to country music in the 1970s and had virtually retired by the 1980s.

Lee, Charles 1731–82
American Revolutionary soldier

Born in Dernhall, Cheshire, England, he went to America in 1773 and joined the Continental army as a major-general at the outbreak of the American Revolution in 1775. Captured by the British in 1776, he proposed to them a secret plan for defeating the Americans. He was released in an exchange of prisoners in 1778, and rejoined the army just before the Battle of Monmouth, at which he was supposed to lead the attack but instead ordered a retreat, obliging General Washington to intervene. This action, either treasonous or reflective of his incompetence, led to his court-martial and suspension from command, and in 1780 he was dismissed from service.

Lee, Christopher Frank Carandini 1922–
English actor

Born in London, he turned to acting in 1947 after distinguished service as an RAF flight-lieutenant, making his film debut in *Corridor of Mirrors* (1947). A tall, sinister-looking figure, he often appeared as a villain before his role as the monster in *The Curse of Frankenstein* (1956) began a long and profitable association with Hammer Films. His portrayal of *Dracula* (1958) as an elegant and chilling sexual predator established him at the forefront of fantasy film making and he quickly became one of the cinema's most prolific if less discriminating actors. His notable films include *Rasputin — The Mad Monk* (1965), *The Devil Rides Out* (1968), *The Creeping Flesh* (1972) and *The Wicker Man* (1973). A concerted attempt to widen his range resulted in a succession of character parts and star villains in such films as *The Private Life of Sherlock Holmes* (1970), *The Three Musketeers* (1973), *The Man with the Golden Gun* (1974), *1941* (1979) and *Serial* (1980), but he continues to be most closely associated with the horror genre. More recent work includes *Gremlins 2* (1990) and the television series *Ivanhoe* (1997). 🕮 *Tall, Dark and Gruesome* (1977).

Lee, David Morris 1931–
US physicist and Nobel Prize winner

Born in Rye, New York, he was educated at Harvard, the University of Connecticut and Yale. After serving in the US army (1952–54) he became an instructor of physics at Cornell University (1959–60), then was made assistant Professor of Physics (1963–68) and Professor (1968–). He was jointly awarded the 1996 Nobel Prize for physics with Douglas Osheroff and Robert Richardson for their discovery in 1971 of the superfluid helium-3 (3He), which they froze to the temperature at which atomic motion stops. The fluid showed behaviour usually found only in subatomic particles, and registered motion to the point of rising over the rim of its container. Further research on 3He has supported the theory that just after the 'Big Bang' structures made up of superfluids formed to make the galaxies.

Lee, Gypsy Rose, *stage name of* Rose Louise Hovick 1914–70
US burlesque dancer and actress

Born in Seattle, Washington, she performed in a vaudeville routine with her sister June as a child (1922–28), and by the age of 17 had joined the striptease troupe at Minsky's Burlesque in New York. She developed a sophisticated song style to accompany her suggestive, teasing dancing, and became the first burlesque artist to achieve widespread fame. She was also the first to transfer her act to the legitimate Broadway stage when she played in the *Ziegfeld Follies* (1936), as well as in other prominent venues. She was the author of plays and stories, and her autobiography, *Gypsy* (1957), was adapted for the stage as a musical comedy.

Lee, (Nelle) Harper 1926–
US writer

Born in Monroeville, Alabama, the daughter of a lawyer, she was a descendant of Robert E Lee and a childhood friend of Truman Capote. She won a Pulitzer Prize for fiction (1961) for her only novel, *To Kill a Mockingbird* (1960), which deals with racial injustice in the South and depicts the characters of a small Southern town through the eyes of a young girl. The successful film version (1962) starred Gregory Peck.

Lee, Henry, *known as* Light-Horse Harry Lee 1756–1818
American Revolutionary soldier and politician

Born into a wealthy family in Prince William County, Virginia, he joined the cavalry at the outbreak of the Revolution and rose to the rank of lieutenant-colonel, becoming a hero through victories at Paulus Hook, New Jersey, and in the South. He later was a member of the Virginia legislature (1785–88, 1789–91) and the Continental Congress (1785–88) and was Governor of Virginia (1792–95). After commanding troops to suppress the Whiskey Rebellion (1794), he served in the US House of Representatives (1799–1801). He eulogized President George Washington with the famous description 'First in war, first in peace, and first in the hearts of his countrymen'. He was the father of Confederate General Robert E Lee.

Lee, James Paris 1831–1904
US inventor

Born in Hawick, Scotland, he emigrated with his parents to Canada, later moving to Hartford, Connecticut. The 'Lee–Enfield' and 'Lee–Metford' rifles are based in part on his designs.

Lee (of Asheridge), Jennie Lee, Baroness 1904–88
Scottish Labour politician

Born in Lochgelly, Fife, the daughter of a miner, she graduated from Edinburgh University with degrees in education and law, and at the age of 24, as a Labour MP for North Lanark, became the youngest member of the House of Commons. An ardent socialist, she campaigned with great wit and intelligence. In 1934 she married Aneurin Bevan and, despite her feminist principles, consciously stepped to one side as he rose within the Labour Party. Appointed Great Britain's first Arts Minister in 1964, she doubled government funding for the arts and was instrumental in setting up the Open University. She published two autobiographies, *Tomorrow is a New Day* (1939) and *My Life with Nye* (1980). She retired from the Commons in 1970 and was made a life peer.

Lee, Laurie 1914–97
English poet and writer

He was born in Slad, Gloucestershire, and educated locally. He worked as a scriptwriter for documentary films in the 1940s and his travels in many parts of the world are the subject of much of his writing. He was a nature-poet of great simplicity, whose works include *The Sun My Monument* (1944), *The Bloom of Candles* (1947) and *My Many-Coated Man* (1955). *A Rose For Winter* (1955) describes his travels in Spain, and his autobiographical books, *Cider With Rosie* (1959), *As I Walked Out One Midsummer Morning* (1969) and *I Can't Stay Long* (1975) are widely acclaimed for their evocation of a rural childhood, and of life in the numerous countries he visited. *A Moment of War* (1991, reprinted in 1992 as *Red Sky at Sunset*) takes up from the end of *As I Walked Out*, and recounts his experiences in Spain during the Civil War.

Lee, Nathaniel c.1649/53–1692
English playwright and actor

Born possibly in London, he attended Westminster School, then went to Trinity College, Cambridge. When nervousness caused him to abandon an acting career, he turned to writing and produced about 10 tragedies between 1674 and 1682. The early ones, such as *Nero* (1674), *Sophonisba* (1675) and *Gloriana* (1676), are written in heroic couplets. His finest, *The Rival Queens or, The Death of Alexander the Great* (1677), is written in blank verse, and is representative not only of Lee's gift for dramatic rhetoric, but also his grasp of character and political psychology. He collaborated with John Dryden on *The Duke of Guise* (1682). His plays were both popular and wildly sensational, containing many killings and several scenes of madness. Lee himself was not altogether a stable personality and was known to be one of the dissolute circle surrounding the notorious Earl of Rochester. His health subsequently broke down to the extent that he was confined in Bedlam from 1684 to 1689.

Lee, Richard Henry 1732–94
American Revolutionary leader

Born in Westmoreland County, Virginia, he served in the Virginia House of Burgesses (1758–75), led the Patriot cause in Virginia with Patrick Henry and Thomas Jefferson, and co-ordinated several colonies' efforts toward independence. He was a member of the Continental Congress (1774–79, 1784–89) and signed the Declaration of Independence, although he opposed the new Constitution. He was also a US senator (1789–92).

Lee, Robert 1804–68
Scottish theologian

Born in Tweedmouth, Northumberland, he was educated at Berwick and St Andrews. In 1846 he was appointed Professor of Biblical Criticism at Edinburgh University and a Queen's chaplain. He began his reform of the Presbyterian church service in 1857, restoring the reading of prayers, kneeling at prayer and standing during the singing. In 1863 he introduced a harmonium, and in 1865

Lee, Robert E(dward) 1807–70
US soldier, one of the greatest of the Confederate generals in the American Civil War

Robert E Lee was born in Westmoreland County, Virginia, and educated at the US Military Academy at West Point. He received a commission in the Engineer Corps, fought in the Mexican War (1846–48), and later became Superintendent of West Point. He commanded the US troops that captured **John Brown** at Harpers Ferry. When the Southern states seceded from the Union, he resigned from the US army so he would be free to serve his native state of Virginia, and in 1861 he accepted the position of Commander-in-Chief of the Confederate Army of Virginia.

Lee's achievements are central to the history of the American Civil War (1861–65). He was in charge of the defences at Richmond, and halted Federal forces in the Seven Days Battles (1862). His forces were victorious in the second Battle of Bull Run (1862). At the Battle of Antietam (1862) his first northern invasion was stopped, but his troops repulsed the Union side in the Battle of

Fredericksburg (1862) and were victorious at the Battle of Chancellorsville (1863). However his second northern invasion ended in defeat at the Battle of Gettysburg (1863), and in the Wilderness Campaign (1864) Lee's forces were badly battered.

In February 1865 Lee became Commander-in-Chief of all of the Southern armies, but the Confederate cause was hopeless at that point and two months later he surrendered his army to General **Ulysses S Grant** at Appomattox Court House, Virginia. After the war, Lee became president of Washington College at Lexington.

📖 Gene Smith, *Lee and Grant* (1984); Clifford Dowdey, *Lee* (1965); D S Freeman, *R E Lee* (4 vols, 1935–36).

'It is well that war is so terrible. We should grow too fond of it.' Attributed remark after the Battle of Fredericksburg, December 1862.

---

an organ, into his church. These 'innovations' provoked bitter attacks upon him. His works include a *Handbook of Devotion* (1845) and *Prayers for Public Worship* (1857).

Lee, Robert E See panel above

Lee, Sir Sidney 1859–1926
English scholar and critic

Born in London, he was educated at the City of London School and Balliol College, Oxford. He became assistant editor of the *Dictionary of National Biography* in 1883, editor in 1891, and Professor of English at East London College in 1913. He wrote a standard *Life of Shakespeare* (1898) and other works on Shakespeare. He also wrote Lives of Queen **Victoria** (1902) and **Edward VII** (1925–27).

Lee, Sophia 1750–1824
English writer

She enjoyed greater success as a dramatist than her sister Harriet Lee (1757–1851), notably with her play *The Chapter of Accidents* (1780), the success of which enabled her to open a girls' school in Bath, and the verse tragedy *Almeyda, Queen of Grenada* (1796). Her historical novel *The Recess* (1783–85) was well received, and she also wrote a lengthy ballad, *The Hermit's Tale* (1787). Her epistolary novel *The Life of a Lover* (1804) has autobiographical elements. 📖 K Rogers, *Feminism in 18th century England* (1982); D Punter, *The Literature of Terror* (1980)

Lee, Spike, originally Shelton Jackson Lee 1957–
US filmmaker

Born in Atlanta, Georgia, the son of a jazz musician and a school teacher, he grew up in Brooklyn, New York City. He developed an interest in Super-8 filmmaking while at Morehouse College (1975–79), and his early amateur efforts include *Last Hustle to Brooklyn* (1977). At New York University's Institute of Film and Television he gained artistic recognition and a student Academy Award for his graduation film *Joe's Bed-Stuy Barbershop: We Cut Heads* (1982). Struggling to support himself, he sank his energies into the low-budget independent feature *She's Gotta Have It* (1986) which established him internationally. Determined to explode Hollywood's racial clichés and to express the texture and variety of African-American life, he sparked controversy with *School Daze* (1988) and *Do The Right Thing* (1989), a blistering assault on racism. An engaging actor in his own productions, he has also directed music videos and assisted in the 1988 presidential campaign of **Jesse Jackson**. Later films include *Mo' Better Blues* (1990), *Jungle Fever* (1991), *Malcolm X* (1992), *Crooklyn* (1994) and *Girl 6* (1996).

Lee, Tsung-Dao 1926–
US physicist and Nobel Prize winner

He was born in Shanghai, China, and was educated at Jiangxi (Kiangsi) and at Zhejiang (Chekiang) University. He won a scholarship to Chicago in 1946, became a lecturer at the University of California, and from 1956 was professor at Columbia University, as well as a member of the Institute for Advanced Study (1960–63). With **Chen Ning Yang** he disproved the parity principle, till then considered a fundamental physical law, and they were awarded the Nobel Prize for physics in 1957. *Particle Physics* was published in 1981 and in 1986 Lee was appointed to the Italian Order of Merit.

Lee, Vernon, pseudonym of Violet Paget 1856–1935
English aesthetic philosopher, critic and novelist

Born of English parents in Boulogne, France, she travelled widely in her youth and settled in Florence. Studies of Italian and Renaissance art were followed by her philosophical study, *The Beautiful* (1913), one of the best expositions of the empathy theory of art. She also wrote two novels and a dramatic trilogy, *Satan the Waster* (1920), giving full rein to her pacifism.

Lee, Yuan Tseh 1936–
US physical chemist and Nobel Prize winner

Born in Hsinchu, Taiwan, he later moved to the USA, where he studied chemistry under **Dudley Herschbach** at the University of California, Berkeley. He remained at Berkeley as a postdoctoral Fellow until 1968. Between 1968 and 1974 he rose from assistant professor to full professor at the University of Chicago, and then returned to Berkeley as Professor of Chemistry. He shared the Nobel Prize for chemistry in 1986 with Herschbach and **John Polanyi**. In 1986 he also received the Debye award of the American Chemical Society. His main research area is chemical reaction dynamics, with Herschbach's successful development of the molecular beam technique owing much to Lee's experimental skill.

Leech, John 1817–64
English caricaturist

Born in London of Irish descent, he was educated at Charterhouse with **Thackeray** (with whom he had a lifelong friendship) and then studied medicine, but turned to art after publishing, at the age of 18, *Etchings and Sketchings, by A. Pen, Esq.* (1835). From 1841 he contributed hundreds of sketches of middle-class life and political cartoons to *Punch*, and also woodcuts to the *Illustrated London News* (1856) and *Once a Week* (1859–62). He illustrated several books, including **Dickens's** *Christmas Carol* and the sporting novels of **Robert Smith Surtees**. He also drew several lithographed series, particularly *Portraits of the Children of the Mobility* (1841). He was buried close to Thackeray at Kensal Green in London.

Leeds, Thomas Osborne, 1st Earl of Danby and Duke of 1631–1712
English statesman

He became MP for York in 1665. After opposition to the Earl of **Clarendon**, he was appointed Treasurer of the Navy (1668) and Privy Councillor (1673). He became Lord Treasurer in 1673, succeeding Thomas Clifford (1630–73) as King **Charles II**'s Chief Minister until his fall during the Exclusion Crisis (1679). Under Charles, he increased the yield from taxes and thus the king's financial independence. He arranged for the marriage of Princess Mary (**Mary II**), daughter of James, Duke of York, to William of Orange (**William III**) (1677), but was impeached on charges of secret financial dealings with **Louis XIV** of France on Charles's behalf, and imprisoned in the Tower (1684). During **James VII and II**'s reign, he opposed the king's Catholic policies, and negotiated William of Orange's assumption of the Crown (1688). He was rewarded with the marquisate of Carmarthen and the presidency of the Council (1689–99) and created Duke of Leeds (1694) but further impeachment proceedings, for taking a bribe to secure a charter for the new East India Company (1695), ended his career as Chief Minister. In semi-retirement during Queen **Anne**'s reign, he supported the Tories, especially defending the Church of England.

Leeghwater, Jan Adrianszoon 1575–1650
Dutch hydraulic engineer and millwright

Born in De Rijp, near Amsterdam, he was largely self-educated in many fields including mechanics, building, linguistics and sculpture. In 1608 he contracted to drain the largest lake in the north of the Netherlands, 17,000 acres in extent and up to 10ft (3m) in depth. After four years' work he was successful, having made extensive use of multi-stage scoop-wheel water-lifting systems, and thereafter he was involved in many drainage projects in Holland, France, Germany, Denmark and Poland. He also devised a modified type of windmill sail which was able to cope better with sudden changes in wind direction.

Lee Kuan Yew 1923–
Singaporean statesman

Born in Singapore into a wealthy Chinese family, he studied law at Cambridge and qualified as a barrister in London before returning to Singapore in 1951 to practise. He founded the moderate, anti-communist People's Action Party (PAP) in 1954 and entered the Singapore Legislative Assembly in 1955. He became the country's first Prime Minister in 1959 and acquired a reputation for probity and industry and overseeing the implementation of a successful programme of economic development. He remained in power until November 1990, when his deputy **Goh Chok Tong** took over. However, he still wields considerable influence as a senior Minister in the Cabinet.

Leese, Sir Oliver William Hargreaves 1894–1978
English soldier

He won the Distinguished Service Order in World War I, and in 1939 became deputy Chief of Staff of the British Expeditionary Force in France. In 1942 he was promoted to lieutenant-general and commanded an army corps from El Alamein to Sicily, where he succeeded **Montgomery** to the command of the 8th Army during the Italian campaign. In November 1944 he commanded an army group in Burma. He was appointed Lieutenant of the Tower of London in 1954.

Leeson, Nick See **Baring**

Lee Teng-Hui 1923–
Taiwanese politician

Born in Tamsui, Taiwan, and educated at universities in the USA and Japan, he taught economics at the National Taiwan University before becoming Mayor of Taipei in 1979. A member of the ruling Guomindang (Kuomintang) Party and a protégé of **Chiang Ching-Kuo**, he became Vice-President of Taiwan in 1984 and State President and Guomindang leader on Chiang's death in 1988. The country's first island-born leader, he is a reforming technocrat who has significantly accelerated the pace of liberalization and 'Taiwanization'. In 1995 he was allowed to enter the USA, after the reversal of a decade-old policy keeping him from setting foot there, to receive an honorary degree from his alma mater, Cornell University, Ithaca, New York.

Leeuwenhoek, Antoni van 1632–1723
Dutch amateur scientist

Born in Delft, he was educated as a businessman, and became skilled in grinding and polishing lenses to inspect cloth fibres. With his microscopes, each made for a specific investigation, he discovered the existence of protozoa in water everywhere (1674) and bacteria in the tartar of teeth (1676). Independently, he discovered blood corpuscles (1674), blood capillaries (1683), striations in skeletal muscle (1682), the structure of nerves (1717) and plant microstructures, among endless other observations. He was elected FRS in 1680. ⊞ Clifford Dobell, *Antony van Leeuwenhoek and His Little Animals* (2nd edn, 1958)

Le Fanu, (Joseph) Sheridan 1814–73
Irish novelist and journalist

Born in Dublin, he was a grand-nephew of **Richard Sheridan**. Called to the Bar in 1839, he soon abandoned law for journalism. He became editor and proprietor (1869) of the *Dublin University Magazine*, and later bought three Dublin newspapers. His novels include *The House by the Churchyard* (1863) and *Uncle Silas* (1864), his short stories are collected in *In a Glass Darkly* (1872), and he wrote 14 other works, remarkable for their preoccupation with the supernatural. His *Poems* were edited by **Alfred Percival Graves** (1896) and *Madam Crowl's Ghost* (1923) was edited by **M R James**. ⊞ I Melada, *Sheridan Le Fanu* (1987)

Lefauchaux, Marie-Helene, née Postel-Vinay 1904–64
French Resistance fighter

Born in Paris, she is best remembered for the part she played, along with her husband Pierre Lefauchaux, in the French Resistance of World War II. A woman of great resourcefulness as well as courage, she succeeded in having her husband released from Buchenwald, and her service during the war earned her the Croix de Guerre and Chevalier of the Legion of Honour. Before and after the war she became prominent in the municipal administration of Paris, then she became a professional diplomat for women's rights and showed a particular concern for students in French colonial Africa. She was a member of France's United Nations delegation (1946–59), and was president of the International Council of Women (1957–63). She died in a plane crash in the USA.

Lefebvre, Marcel 1905–91
French schismatic Roman Catholic prelate

Born in Tourcoing, he studied at the French Seminary in Rome and was ordained in 1929. In the 1930s he was a missionary in Gabon, and he later became Archbishop of Dakar, Senegal (1948–62). As a clerical traditionalist he opposed the liberalizing liturgical and spiritual reforms of the Second Vatican Council (1962–65), and in 1970 formed the 'Priestly Cofraternity of **Pius X**' to oppose them. He was suspended 'a divinis' in 1976 by Pope **Paul VI** for his refusal to stop the ordination of priests at his headquarters in Switzerland without papal permission. He defied the suspension and continued to ordain a further 216 priests before being formally excommunicated by Pope John Paul II in 1988, thus producing the first formal schism within the Roman Catholic Church since 1870.

Lefschetz, Solomon 1884–1972
US mathematician

Born in Moscow, Russia, he studied engineering in Paris before emigrating to the USA, where he worked as an engineer. He abandoned engineering for mathematics, taking his doctorate in 1911, and teaching at Kansas University (1913–25), where he soon made a reputation by his work in algebraic geometry when he developed a theory of complex algebraic varieties in n dimensions. This led him into the study of topology, and in 1925 he moved to Princeton where he remained until his retirement in 1953, when he became visiting professor at Brown University. Lefschetz became the leading topologist of his generation in the USA and an important theorem on the existence of fixed points of mappings bears his name. Interested in differential equations, he worked on their qualitative theory, and directed US mathematicians to the extensive Russian literature on the subject.

Le Gallienne, Eva 1899–1991
English actress on the US stage

She was born in London, the daughter of Richard Le Gallienne, and brought up in Paris. She made her debut in London in *Mona Vanna* (1914), before studying for a year under Herbert Beerbohm Tree and moving to New York. She was the founder (1926) and director of the Civic Repertory Theater of New York, acting in and directing most of the 37 plays produced there before it closed in 1935. She was then co-founder and director of the American Repertory Theater (1946–48). She acted until the early 1980s, and was renowned for her Chekhovian roles.

Le Gallienne, Richard 1866–1947
English writer

Born in Liverpool, of Guernsey ancestry, he became a journalist in London in 1891, but later lived in New York. He published many volumes of prose and verse from 1887, when his first collection, *My Ladies Sonnets*, was published. He was an original member of the Rhymers Club with W B Yeats, Oscar Wilde and others. His best books are *Quest of the Golden Girl* (1896), *The Romantic Nineties* (1926) and *From a Paris Garret* (1936).

Legat, Nikolai Gustavovich 1869–1937
Russian dancer, teacher, ballet master and choreographer

Born in St Petersburg, he studied with his father at the Imperial Ballet School, graduating in 1888. He joined the Maryinsky Theatre, where he spent 20 years as a principal, dancing in major works including the first performance of Lev Ivanov's *The Nutcracker* (1892). He took over the directorship of the company in 1905, dropping choreography for teaching. His pupils there included Tamara Karsavina, Michel Fokine and Nijinsky. In 1923 he moved to the USA to become Ballet Master of Sergei Diaghilev's company, but finally settled in London where he opened his own school and taught Alexandra Danilova, Margot Fonteyn, Ninette de Valois, Anton Dolin and Serge Lifar. His school continues to function at Mark Cross, Sussex.

Legendre, Adrien-Marie 1752–1833
French mathematician

Born in Paris, he studied at the Collège Mazarin, and became Professor of Mathematics at the École Militaire and a member of the French Academy of Sciences (1783). In 1787 he was appointed as one of the commissioners to relate the Paris and Greenwich meridians by triangulation

and in 1813 he succeeded Joseph de Lagrange at the Bureau des Longitudes. He proposed the method of least squares in 1806 (independently of Carl Gauss). His classic work *Essai sur la théorie des nombres* (1798, 'Essay on the Theory of Numbers') includes his discovery of the law of quadratic reciprocity, and his *Traité des fonctions elliptiques* (1825, 'Treatise on Elliptical Functions') became the definitive account of elliptic integrals prior to the work of Niels Henrik Abel and Carl Jacobi. His *Éléments de géométrie* (1794), translated into English by Thomas Carlyle, reintroduced rigour to the teaching of elementary geometry in France.

Léger, Fernand 1881–1955
French painter

Born in Argentan, he was a major force in the Cubist movement. Between 1903 and 1907 he studied at various Paris studios and initially painted in a diffuse Neo-Impressionist manner. He then discovered Paul Cézanne and began 'constructing' his pictures with volumetric shapes. His pictures differ from those of the fellow members of the avant-garde in being more 'tubist' than Cubist. By 1912, in pictures like *La Femme en Bleu* ('Woman in Blue'), Léger was nearing pure abstraction, but after World War I he returned to primarily figurative work in which the working man is combined with machinery in monumental patterns made up of heavy black outlines and primary colour infill. He also designed theatre sets, taught at Yale University, and executed murals for the United Nations building in New York (1952). He collaborated on the first 'art-film', *Le Ballet mécanique*, in 1923. There is a museum dedicated to his work at Biot on the Côte d'Azur in the south of France.

Legge, James 1815–97
Scottish missionary and sinologist

Born in Huntly, Aberdeenshire, he graduated from Aberdeen University in 1835. He ran the Anglo-Chinese missionary college in Malacca, followed by 30 years in Hong Kong. In 1876 he became the first Professor of Chinese at Oxford. His greatest work was a weighty edition of *Chinese Classics* (28 vols, 1861–86).

Legge, Walter 1906–79
British music impresario

He was born in London and became recording manager with HMV in 1927, and later with Columbia. He was largely responsible for engaging a number of musicians who went on to become internationally famous, notably Herbert von Karajan, Dietrich Fischer-Dieskau and Elizabeth Schwarzkopf, whom he married in 1953. He founded the Philharmonia Orchestra in 1945, managing it until 1964 when he tried without success to disband it. He was a lifelong devotee of the music of Hugo Wolf, and undertook the extensive recording of his songs.

Le Gray, Gustave See Gray, Gustave Le

Legros, Alphonse 1837–1911
British painter

Born in Dijon, France, he adopted England as his home. On the advice of James McNeill Whistler, he went to London in 1863 and by 1875 was in charge of the etching class at the Royal College. Appointed Slade Professor to the University College in 1875–76, he exercised a strong traditional influence. He produced over 750 etchings and was noted for his revival of original portraiture which had been in decline for many years. His landscape and figure studies particularly mark him as an influential figure in the British etching movement.

Le Guin, Ursula K(roeber), *née* Kroeber 1929–
US science-fiction writer

She was born in Berkeley, California, the daughter of the anthropologist **Alfred Louis Kroeber**, and educated at Radcliffe College and Columbia University. Much of her work focuses on subjective views of a universe incorporating numerous habitable worlds, some spawned by beings from the 'Hain'. The Hain trilogy consists of *Rocannon's World* (1966), *Planet of Exile* (1966) and *City of Illusions* (1967), and other novels include *The Left Hand of Darkness* (1969), *The Word for World is Forest* (1976) and *Dancing at the Edge of the World* (1989). In a prodigious work for children, known as the 'Earthsea' trilogy—*A Wizard of Earthsea* (1968), *The Tombs of Atuan* (1971) and *The Farthest Shore* (1972)—she depicts a magical but threatening world, in which every village has its small-time sorcerer and the forces of evil are uncomfortably close. She continued this trilogy in an overtly feminist vein with *Tehanu* (1990). A prolific and skilled writer, she has demonstrated that it is possible to work in genre and be taken seriously. Later works include the novels *Searoad* (1991) and *Fish Soup* (1992). 📖 E C Cogell, *Understanding Ursula K. Le Guin* (1990)

Lehár, Franz 1870–1948
Hungarian composer
Born in Komárom, he became a military band conductor in Vienna. He wrote a violin concerto but is best known for his operettas which include his most popular *The Merry Widow* (1905, *Die lustige Witwe*), *The Count of Luxembourg* (1909, *Der Graf von Luxemburg*), *Frederica* (1928, *Friederike*) and *The Land of Smiles* (1929, *Das Land des Lächelns*).

Lehmann, Beatrix 1903–79
English actress
She was born in Bourne End, Buckinghamshire, the daughter of journalist Rudolph Chambers Lehmann (1856–1929) and sister of **John** and **Rosamond Lehmann**. She first appeared on the stage in 1924 at the Lyric, Hammersmith, and subsequently appeared in many successful plays, including *Family Reunion*, **Peter Ustinov's** *No Sign of the Dove*, and *Waltz of the Toreadors*. In 1946 she became director-producer of the Arts Council Midland Theatre Company. She has also appeared in films and wrote two novels and several short stories.

Lehmann, Inge 1888–1993
Danish geophysicist
Born in Copenhagen, she went to Copenhagen University in 1907 to read mathematics. She spent a year at Cambridge (1910–11), pursued a career in insurance and then resumed her studies in 1918. From 1928 she was chief of the seismological department of the newly founded Danish Geodetic Institute, taking responsibility for the seismological stations in Greenland. Involved in the interpretation of seismic events, she discovered that the presence of a distinct inner core of the Earth was required to explain the observed data. In collaboration with **Beno Gutenberg** she found a low-velocity layer at 200 kilometres depth which fitted well with the seismic data, and became generally accepted.

Lehmann, John Frederick 1907–87
English writer and publisher
He was born in Bourne End, Buckinghamshire, the son of journalist Rudolph Chambers Lehmann (1856–1929), and educated at Trinity College, Cambridge. He founded the periodical in book format, *New Writing* (1936–41), was managing director of the Hogarth Press with **Leonard** and **Virginia Woolf** (1938–46), and ran his own firm, John Lehmann Ltd, with his sister, **Rosamond Lehmann**, as co-director from 1946 to 1953. In 1954 he inaugurated *The London Magazine*, which he edited until 1961. His first publications were volumes of poetry, including *A Garden Revisited* (1931) and *Forty Poems* (1942). He also wrote a novel, *Evil was Abroad* (1938), and studies of *Edith Sitwell*

(1952), *Virginia Woolf and her World* (1975) and *Rupert Brooke* (1980). He wrote his autobiography in three volumes, *The Whispering Gallery* (1955), *I am my Brother* (1960) and *The Ample Proposition* (1966).

Lehmann, Lotte 1888–1976
US soprano
Born in Perleberg, Germany, she studied in Berlin, made her debut in Hamburg (1910), and sang at the Vienna Staatsoper (1914–38), and at the New York Metropolitan Opera (1934–45). She was noted for her performances of **Schumann's** songs and her roles in **Richard Strauss's** operas, including the Marschallin in *Der Rosenkavalier* and for the premières of his *Die Frau ohne Schatten* (1919, *The Woman without a Shadow*) and *Intermezzo* (1924). She took US nationality, and retired to teach in Santa Barbara, California, in 1951.

Lehmann, Rosamond Nina 1901–90
English novelist
She was born in High Wycombe, Buckinghamshire, the daughter of journalist Rudolph Chambers Lehmann (1856–1929) and sister of **Beatrix** and **John Lehmann**. She was educated at Girton College, Cambridge, which provided the background for her first novel, *Dusty Answer* (1927). Among her other titles are *A Note in Music* (1930), *An Invitation to the Waltz* (1932) and its sequel *The Weather in the Streets* (1936), *The Echoing Grove* (1953), and *A Sea-Grape Tree* (1970), her last novel. They show a fine sensitive insight into character and her women especially are brilliantly drawn. She also wrote a play, *No More Music* (1939), and a volume of short stories, *The Gypsy's Baby* (1946), and in 1967 published the autobiographical *The Swan in the Evening*. She later developed a belief in spiritualism, and became president of the College of Psychic Studies. 📖 G Tindall, *Rosamond Lehmann: an appreciation* (1985)

Lehn, Jean-Marie 1939–
French chemist and Nobel Prize winner
Born in Rosheim, Bas-Rhin, he studied at the University of Strasbourg, where he worked on terpene chemistry, then collaborated with **Robert Woodward** at Harvard on vitamin B_{12} synthesis. He later joined the University of Strasbourg, becoming professor in 1970 and simultaneously professor at the Collège de France from 1979. Studying the mechanism of transport of metal ions across cell membranes, he built on **Charles Pedersen's** work to show that metal ions can exist in a non-polar environment if contained within the cavity of a large organic molecule. Such structures are known as cryptates, and similar compounds play an important role in the transport of metal ions across biological membranes. His research has initiated a new branch of organic chemistry—supramolecular chemistry—and earned him, along with Pedersen and **Donald Cram**, the Nobel Prize for chemistry in 1987. He was created Chevalier (1983) and later Officer (1988) of the Legion of Honour, and also Officer of the National Order of Merit (1993).

Leibl, Wilhelm 1844–1900
German artist
Born in Cologne, he studied in Paris, being much influenced by **Gustave Courbet's** realism, and later worked in Munich. Most of his paintings are genre scenes of Bavaria and the lower Alps, although he also painted a number of portraits.

Leibniz, Gottfried Wilhelm See panel p1110

Leicester, Robert Dudley, Earl of c.1533–1588
English nobleman

Leibniz, Gottfried Wilhelm 1646–1716
German philosopher and mathematician

Leibniz was born in Leipzig, the son of a professor of moral philosophy. In 1667 he obtained a position at the court of the Elector of Mainz on the strength of an essay on legal education. There he codified laws, drafted schemes for the unification of the churches, and studied the work of **René Descartes**, **Isaac Newton**, **Blaise Pascal**, **Robert Boyle** and others.

In London he came into contact with mathematicians of Newton's circle, causing a dispute later as to whether he or Newton was the inventor of the infinitesimal calculus; both had published systems in the 1680s. The Royal Society formally declared for Newton in 1711, but the matter was never fully settled. In 1676 Leibniz visited **Spinoza** in The Hague on his way to take up a new, and his last, post as librarian to the Duke of Brunswick at Hanover. Here he continued to elaborate his mathematical and philosophical theories, without publishing them, and maintained a huge learned correspondence.

He also travelled in Austria and Italy in the years 1687–90 to gather materials for a large-scale history of the House of Brunswick, and went in 1700 to persuade **Frederick I** of Prussia to found the Prussian Academy of Sciences in Berlin, of which he became the first president. He was disliked by George of Hanover and was left behind in 1714 when the Elector moved the court to London to become King of Great Britain (as **George I**). Leibniz died in Hanover two years later, without real recognition and with almost all his work unpublished. Remarkable for his encyclopedic knowledge and diverse accomplishments outside the fields of philosophy and mathematics, he was perhaps the last universal genius, spanning the whole of contemporary knowledge.

His best-known doctrine is that the world is composed of an infinity of simple, indivisible, immaterial, mutually isolated 'monads' which form a hierarchy, the highest of which is God; the monads do not interact causally but constitute a synchronized harmony with material phenomena. Leibniz is recognized as one of the great rationalist philosophers but he had perhaps his greatest influence (for example, on **Bertrand Russell**) as a mathematician and a pioneer of modern symbolic logic.

Leibniz made original contributions to optics, mechanics, statistics, logic and probability theory; he conceived the idea of calculating machines, and of a universal language; he wrote on history, law and political theory; and his philosophy was the foundation of 18th-century rationalism. His *Essais de théodicée sur la Bonté de Dieu, la liberté de l'homme et l'origine du mal* (the *Theodicy*, 1710), was a relatively popular work in theology, expressing his optimism and faith in enlightenment and reason, which **Voltaire** satirized brilliantly in *Candide* ('all is for the best in this best of all possible worlds'). The metaphysics and more technical philosophy are to be found in his response to **John Locke**, the *New Essays on Human Understanding* (completed in 1704 but not published until 1765), the *Discours de Métaphysique* (1846), the correspondence with **Antoine Arnauld** and with **Samuel Clarke**, and numerous short papers.

Stuart Brown, *Leibniz* (1984); Nicholas Rescher, *Leibniz: An Introduction to his Philosophy* (1979); C D Broad and C Lewy, *Leibniz: An Introduction* (1975).

> *C'est Dieu qui est la dernière raison des choses, et la connaissance de Dieu n'est pas moins la principe des sciences, que son essence et sa volonté sont les principes des êtres.*
> 'It is God who is the ultimate reason of things, and the knowledge of God is no less the beginning of science than his essence and will are the beginning of beings.'
> From 'Letter on a General Principle Useful in Explaining the Laws of Nature' (1687) in *Leibniz: Philosophical Papers and Letters* (Eng trans by L E Loemker, 1969).

He was the grandson of the notorious **Edmund Dudley** beheaded by **Henry VIII**, and the son of John Dudley, Earl of **Warwick**, who was executed for his support of Lady **Jane Grey**. Robert Dudley himself was sentenced to death, but, pardoned (1554), became a favourite of Queen **Elizabeth I**, who made him Master of the Horse, Knight of the Garter, a Privy Councillor, High Steward of the University of Cambridge, Baron Dudley, and finally (1564) Earl of Leicester. It was rumoured that he had poisoned Amy Robsart (1560), whom he had married in 1550, in order to be free to marry the queen. He was unpopular at court, and Elizabeth suggested him as a husband for **Mary, Queen of Scots** (1563). He made a secret marriage to the Dowager Lady Sheffield, but he remained popular with Elizabeth, who was magnificently entertained by him at his castle of Kenilworth (1575). She was only temporarily offended when he bigamously married (1578) the widow of Walter Devereux, Earl of **Essex**. He supported the Puritans in their opposition to Catholicism. Sent in 1585 to command the expedition to the Low Countries in which Sir **Philip Sidney**, his nephew, died at Zutphen, he was recalled for incompetence in 1587, and his arrogance and touchiness were counterproductive, but he was nonetheless appointed as leader of the forces assembled at Tilbury to defend England against the Spanish Armada (1588). He died suddenly at Cornbury, in Oxfordshire, probably of malaria, but some alleged he had taken poison originally intended for his wife. E Rosenberg, *Leicester, Patron of Letters* (1958)

Leicester (of Holkham), Thomas William Coke, Earl of 1752–1842
English agriculturist

One of the first agriculturists of England, by his efforts north-west Norfolk was converted from a rye-growing into a wheat-growing district, and more stock and better breeds of sheep, cattle and pigs were kept on the farms. He represented Norfolk as a Whig MP for periods during 1776–1833, and in 1837 was created Earl of Leicester of Holkham. He was a descendant of Sir **Edward Coke**.

Leichhardt, (Friedrich Wilhelm) Ludwig 1813–c.1848
Australian naturalist and explorer

Born in Trebatsch, Prussia, he studied at the universities of Berlin and Göttingen but obtained no formal qualifications. He became interested in natural history, and after arriving in Sydney mounted an expedition which set out from Brisbane north-west for Port Essington, a settlement on the coast of Arnhem Land. They reached it 15 hard months later, and the party's arrival back in Sydney in March 1846, when they had been presumed lost, caused great excitement. In December of the same year he set out to attempt an east–west crossing of the northern part of the continent, but was forced to turn back. On his return to Sydney he learned he had been awarded gold medals by the Geographical Societies of Paris and London. In February 1848 he set off on another transcontinental journey but nothing was heard of him or the expedition after April 1848.

Leif the Lucky, *real name* Leifur heppni Eiríksson
fl.1000
Icelandic explorer

He was the son of **Erik the Red**. Just before the year 1000 he set sail from Greenland to explore lands to the west, reaching Baffin Land, Labrador, and an area he called 'Vínland' (Wineland) because of the wild grapes he found growing there. The location of Vínland has defied precise identification, but incontrovertible remains of a Norse settlement have been found on Newfoundland. Other Icelandic settlers, led by **Thorfinn**, tried to establish a colony in 'Vínland', but withdrew in the face of hostility from the native Indians. Two Icelandic sagas, *Eiríks saga rauða* ('Saga of Eric') and *Grænlendinga saga* ('Tale of the Greenlanders'), tell the story of the Norse discovery and attempted colonization of North America, 500 years before **Christopher Columbus** discovered the New World.

Leigh, Mike 1943–
English film and theatre director

Born in Salford, Greater Manchester, he trained as an actor at RADA in London and subsequently studied at the Camberwell Art School, the Central School of Arts and Crafts, and London Film School. Associate director of the Midlands Arts Centre For Young People (1965–66) and an assistant director with the Royal Shakespeare Company from 1966, he began to develop his own style of reflecting the bittersweet ironies of everyday lives through pieces improvised in collaboration with hand-picked actors. He made his film debut with *Bleak Moments* (1971) and created acutely observed social comedies for television including *Nuts in May* (1976) and *Abigail's Party* (1977). His stage work includes *Goose Pimples* (1981) and *Smelling a Rat* (1988). He returned to the cinema with *High Hopes* (1988) and has subsequently created a body of work reflecting the extraordinary dramas to be found in ordinary lives. His films include *Life is Sweet* (1990), *Naked* (1993) and *Secrets and Lies* (1996), which gained the Palme D'Or at the Cannes Film Festival, five Academy Award nominations and three BAFTA awards.

Leigh, Vivien, *originally* Vivian Mary Hartley 1913–67
British actress

She was born in Darjeeling, India, and after training at RADA, her first contract was with **Alexander Korda**, playing in *Fire Over England* (1936) with **Laurence Olivier**, whom she later married (1940–60). In Hollywood she played her best-known part, Scarlett O'Hara in *Gone With the Wind* (1939), which won her an Academy Award. Other major film roles were in *Anna Karenina* (1948) and *A Streetcar Named Desire* (1951), which gained her another Academy Award. 📖 Hugo Vickers, *Vivien Leigh: A Biography* (1989)

Leigh-Mallory, Sir Trafford 1892–1944
English air force officer

Born in Cheshire, he was educated at Haileybury and Magdalen College, Oxford. He served with the Royal Flying Corps in World War I, and in World War II he commanded Groups in Fighter Command in the Battle of Britain. He was Commander-in-Chief of Fighter Command (1942–44) and of Allied Expeditionary Air Forces for the Normandy landings (1944). Appointed Commander-in-Chief of Allied Air Forces in South East Asia, he was killed in an air crash during the journey there.

Leigh-Pemberton, Robin (Robert) 1927–
English banker

Born in Sittingbourne, Kent, he practised at the Bar from 1954 to 1960, and in 1965 he qualified as a chartered accountant. He was chairman of Kent County Council (1975–77) and chairman of the National Westminster Bank from 1977 to 1983, when he became Governor of the Bank of England. During his time of office there (1983–93), the Bank of England was criticized for inadequate supervision of BCCI (Bank of Credit and Commerce International) and co-ordinated its closure in 1991.

Leighton, Clare Veronica Hope 1901–89
US artist

Born in London, England, into a literary family, she trained at the Brighton School of Art and the Slade School of Art, London, prior to learning engraving at the Central School of Arts and Crafts in London. She wrote several books on engraving, then moved to the USA in 1939, becoming a US citizen in 1945. She continued to paint but became famous for her wood engravings which use large areas of dark, defined by finely engraved lines often depicting labourers, farm workers or the fishermen of Cape Cod. She held many titles, including vice-president of both the National Institute of Arts and Letters and the Society of American Graphic Art. Boston Public Library lists some 789 engravings by her as well as work in other media such as stained glass and mosaic.

Leighton (of Stretton), Frederic Leighton, Baron 1830–96
English painter

Born in Scarborough, Yorkshire, he studied and travelled extensively in Europe and had immediate success with *Cimabue's Madonna carried in Procession through Florence* (1855)—a picture purchased by Queen **Victoria**. Also from his early period is his masterpiece *Songs without Words* (1860–61, Tate, London). Among his later works were *Paolo and Francesca* (1861), *The Daphnephoria* (1876) and *The Bath of Psyche* (1890). An aesthete and idealist, he was also a distinguished sculptor, and in 1877 his *Athlete struggling with a Python* was purchased out of the **Chantrey** Bequest. Several of his paintings, for example *Wedded* (1882), became mass bestsellers in photogravure reproduction. His *Addresses* were published in 1896. A president of the Royal Academy, London, and the consummate Academic artist, his final words are said to have been 'Give my love to the Academy'.

Leighton, Kenneth 1929–88
English composer and pianist

Born in Wakefield, Yorkshire, he studied at Oxford, and then took composition lessons with Goffredo Petrassi in Rome. He in turn taught composition at Edinburgh University from 1956, and from 1970 was Reid Professor of Music there. His compositions showed vigorous and individual grasp of traditional forms and contrapuntal disciplines. A skilful and rewarding composer of choral music, he also wrote extensively for the piano (including three concertos) as well as three symphonies, other concertos, an opera *Columba* (1981), and organ and chamber music.

Leighton, Margaret 1922–76
English actress

Born near Birmingham, she was the leading lady in many stage plays and films, and became one of the best-known actresses of her era. She trained for the stage as a teenager, joined the Old Vic under **Laurence Olivier** and **Ralph Richardson** in the 1940s, and made her Broadway debut in 1946. Her major plays include **Terence Rattigan's** *Separate Tables* (1956) and **Tennessee Williams's** *The Night of the Iguana* (1961). She was nominated for an Academy Award for the film *The Go-Between* (1971).

Leighton, Robert 1611–84
Scottish prelate

Born probably in London, he studied at Edinburgh and spent some years in France. He became a minister in 1641, signed the Covenant two years later and in 1653 was appointed Principal of Edinburgh University. Soon after the Restoration he was induced by **Charles II** to become one of the new bishops, and chose Dunblane. His aim was to preserve what was best in episcopacy and presbyterianism as a basis for comprehensive union, but he succeeded only in being misunderstood by both sides. The continued persecution of the Covenanters drove him to resign his see (1665), but Charles persuaded him to return. In 1669 he became Archbishop of Glasgow. His conferences at Edinburgh (1670–71) with leading Presbyterians were failures and, disillusioned, he retired in 1674.

Leino, Eino, *pseudonym of* **Armas Eino Leopold Lönnbohm** 1878–1926
Finnish poet and novelist
He published his first poetry collection, *Maaliskuun lauluja* (1896, 'Spring Songs'), aged 18. He developed the metre of the *Kalevala*, or national epic, into a distinctive, sombrely lyrical style of his own, best exemplified in the two volumes of *Helkavirsiä* (1903, 1916, 'Whitsongs'), the second of which is shadowed by his reaction to World War I. He also wrote novels, and translated works of **Dante**, **Racine**, **Corneille**, **Goethe** and **Schiller**. 📖 P Saarikoski, *Eino 'Leino'* (1974)

Leinsdorf, Erich 1912–93
US conductor
He was born in Vienna, Austria, and was assistant to **Bruno Walter** in Vienna and to **Toscanini** in Salzburg. He performed opera (notably Wagner) in New York and conducted several US orchestras, including the Cleveland Orchestra (1943–44), the Rochester Philharmonic Orchestra (1957–55) and the Boston Symphony Orchestra (1962–69). He was guest conductor of many other orchestras.

Leiris, Michel 1901–90
French anthropologist, writer and poet
He was born in Paris. After an early involvement with the Surrealist movement (1925–29), he joined the trans-African Dakar–Djibouti expedition of 1931–33. He took up anthropology as a profession and travelled in Africa and the Caribbean. His writings, many of them autobiographical, like *L'Âge d'homme* (1939, Eng trans *Manhood*, 1966) and *La Règle du jeu* (4 vols, 1948–76, 'The Rules of the Game'), are marked by a consuming interest in poetry, and he combined anthropology with a distinguished career as a literary and art critic. His major works include *L'Afrique fantôme* (1934, 'Phantoms of Africa') and *Afrique Noire: La création plastique* (1967, with Jacqueline Delange, Eng trans *African Art*, 1968). 📖 M Nadeau, *Michel Leiris et la quadrature du cercle* (1963)

Leishman, Sir William Boog 1865–1926
Scottish bacteriologist
Born in Glasgow, he obtained his MD from the University of Glasgow in 1886, and later became Professor of Pathology at the Army Medical College in Millbank (1903–13) and director-general of the Army Medical Service (1923). In 1900 he discovered the protozoan parasite (*Leishmania*) responsible for the disease known variously as kala-azar and dumdum fever. He went on to develop the widely used 'Leishman's stain' for the detection of parasites in the blood. He also made major contributions to the development of various vaccines, particularly those used against typhoid, and it was as a result of his work that mass vaccination was introduced in 1914 for the British army. He was knighted in 1909, and elected FRS in 1910.

Leith, Emmett Norman 1927–
US optical scientist and electrical engineer
Born in Detroit and educated at Wayne State University, he has been Professor of Electrical Engineering at the University of Michigan since 1968. In 1961 he suggested that applications of holography could be achieved by using an inclined reference beam, which led to separation of the twin images produced in **Dennis Gabor's** optical arrangement. This, coupled with Leith's production of

the first laser hologram, quickly led to important applications. In 1985 he was awarded the Ives Medal of the Optical Society of America.

LeJeune, Eddie 1951–
Cajun accordion player and singer
He was born in Lacassine, Louisiana. His father was the great Cajun accordionist Iry LeJeune (1928–55), who was killed in a road accident, leaving an all too scant recorded legacy. Eddie was brought up by his mother and grandmother, fully immersed in the Cajun musical tradition. He is a virtuoso accordionist, and has remained faithful to the authentic acoustic tradition and emotional honesty of that music. He leads his own trio, and has also worked extensively with another key Cajun musician of the modern era, the singer and guitarist D L Menard.

Leland, Charles Godfrey, *pseudonym* **Hans Breitmann** 1825–1903
US writer
Born in Philadelphia, he graduated at Princeton in 1845, and afterwards studied at Heidelberg, Munich and Paris. He was admitted to the Philadelphia Bar in 1851, but turned to journalism. From 1869 he resided chiefly in England and Italy, and investigated the gypsies, on which he published four valuable works (1873–91). He is best known for his poems in 'Pennsylvania Dutch', the famous *Hans Breitmann Ballads* (1871, continued in 1895). Other similar volumes gained him great popularity during his lifetime. He also translated the works of **Heinrich Heine**. 📖 *Memoirs* (1893)

Leland, John c.1506–1552
English antiquary
Born in London, he was educated at St Paul's School under **William Lilye**, then at Christ's College, Cambridge, and All Souls College, Oxford. After a stay in Paris he became chaplain to **Henry VIII**, who in 1533 made him 'king's antiquary', with power to search for records of antiquity in the cathedrals, colleges, abbeys and priories of England. His church preferments were the rectories of Peuplingues, near Calais, and Haseley in Oxfordshire, a canonry of King's College (now Christ Church), Oxford, and a prebend of Salisbury. Most of his papers are in the Bodleian and British Museums. Besides his *Commentarii de Scriptoribus Britannicis*, his chief works are *The Itinerary* and *De Rebus Britannicis Collectanea*.

Leland, John 1691–1766
English Presbyterian minister
Born in Wigan, Manchester, he was educated at Dublin, where from 1716 he was a minister. He wrote against **Matthew Tindal** (1733) and Thomas Morgan (1739–40). His chief work is an attack on deists in *A View of the Principal Deistical Writers* (1754–56).

Leloir, Luis Frederico 1906–87
Argentine biochemist and Nobel Prize winner
Born in Paris, France, and educated in Buenos Aires and at Cambridge, he worked mainly in Argentina where he set up his own Research Institute in 1947. He discovered a number of glucose enzymes and studied their reactions. In the 1950s Leloir linked these reactions to the formation of the energy storage material glycogen in the body. For this work, of medical significance and complementing that of **Carl Cori**, he was awarded the Nobel Prize for chemistry in 1970, becoming the first Argentine to be so honoured.

Lely, Sir Peter, *originally* **Pieter van der Faes** 1618–80
British painter
Born probably in Soest, Westphalia, he worked in Haarlem before he settled in London in 1641 as a portrait painter. He was patronized by **Charles I** and **Oliver**

Cromwell, and in 1661 was appointed court painter to Charles II, for whom he changed his style of painting. His *Windsor Beauties* series is collected at Hampton Court. The 13 Greenwich portraits of *Admirals* are among his best works. These, depicting the English admirals who fought in the Second Dutch War, are outstanding for their depth and sincerity of characterization. They present a marked contrast to his very popular and often highly sensuous court portraits which sometimes have a hasty, superficial appearance.

Lemaître, Antoine Louis Prosper, *stage name* Frédérick 1800–76
French actor

He was born in Le Havre, and his first success was in *Richard Darlington*, a play based on Sir Walter Scott's *The Surgeon's Daughter*. This was followed by a succession of triumphs including *Hamlet, Kean, ou Désordre et Génie* ('Kean or Disorder and Genius'), *Ruy Blas*, and the greatest of all, Victor Hugo's *L'Auberge des Adrets* and its sequel, *Robert Macaire*, much of which he wrote himself. He was admired by contemporary writers; Alexandre Dumas called him the French Kean, Gustave Flaubert called his Macaire the greatest symbol of the age and Victor Hugo wrote *Ruy Blas* for him. He visited London four times and was a favourite with Queen Victoria although she was offended by his performance of *Ruy Blas* in 1852. He suffered ill health in his later years and died in poverty.

Lemaître, Georges Henri 1894–1966
Belgian astrophysicist and cosmologist

He was born in Charleroi, and studied engineering at the University of Louvain. After voluntary service in World War I, he turned to mathematical and physical sciences and obtained his doctorate in 1920. Three years later he was ordained as a Catholic priest and obtained a travelling scholarship from the Belgian government, which took him to Cambridge, Harvard and Massachusetts Institute of Technology (MIT). In Cambridge he came under the strong influence of Sir Arthur Eddington. In 1927 he published his first major paper on the model of an expanding universe and its relation to the observed red shifts in the spectra of galaxies. In the 1930s he developed his ideas on cosmology, and from 1945 onwards he put forward the notion of the 'primeval atom' which is unstable and explodes, starting what is now called the Big Bang, the beginning of the expanding universe. Lemaître received many honours from all over the world. He was the first recipient of the Eddington Medal of the Royal Astronomical Society (1953) and in 1960 became the president of the Pontifical Academy of Sciences.

Lemaître, (François Élie) Jules 1853–1914
French playwright and critic

He was born in Vennecy, Loiret, and was educated at the École Normale Supérieure. His articles, written first for the *Journal des débats*, were issued in book form as *Impressions de théâtre* (1888–98, 'Impressions of a Theatregoer'), and those written for *Revue bleue* on modern French literature became *Les Contemporains* (1886–99, 'Our Contemporaries'). A masterly critic with a lucid style, he also wrote *Rousseau* (1907), *Racine* (1908), *Fénelon* (1910) and *Chateaubriand* (1912).

Lémery, Nicolas 1645–1715
French chemist and pharmacist

Born in Rouen, he studied as an apothecary there but because he was a Protestant could not join the Guild of Apothecaries. In 1764 he bought the office of Apothecary to the King, thereafter establishing a lucrative pharmaceutical business specializing in patent medicines. He also gave popular lectures on chemistry which were attended by fashionable society as well as by pharmaceutical

apprentices. Religious persecution drove him out of Paris in 1683. Having qualified as a doctor at Caen and converted to Roman Catholicism in 1685, after Protestants lost all their legal rights with the Edict of Nantes, he reopened his shop. He published two books on pharmacy and a monograph on antimony, and was admitted to the Academy of Sciences in 1699. Although he discovered little that was new, his influence as a teacher was considerable. His book *Cours de chymie* (1675, 'Chemistry Course Book') had run to 31 editions by 1756 and was translated into most European languages. It gave a lucid account of chemical methods and of the pharmaceutical compounds known at the time.

Le Mesurier, John, *originally* John Elton Halliley 1912–83
English actor

Born in Bedford, he started working life as a solicitor's articled clerk before training as an actor and touring in shows until World War II. After the war, he found success in British comedy films such as *Private's Progress* (1955), *Brothers in Law* (1956), *I'm All Right, Jack* (1959), *The Pure Hell of St Trinian's* (1960), *The Punch and Judy Man* (1960) and *The Pink Panther* (1963). He was also a regular on television with Tony Hancock in *Hancock's Half Hour* (1956–61) and followed that with the sitcom *George and the Dragon* (1966–68), before finding fame as Sergeant Wilson in the long-running *Dad's Army* (1968–77). 📖 *A Jobbing Actor* (1984, posthumous)

Lemmon, Jack (John Uhler) 1925–
US film and stage actor

Born in Boston, he graduated from Harvard and served in the navy in World War II. An appearance on the Broadway stage (1953) brought him to the attention of Hollywood, where he appeared in *It Should Happen to You* (1954), and he soon became established as one of the screen's most skilled comedy performers. *Some Like It Hot* (1959) began a successful seven-film collaboration with director Billy Wilder. Other acclaimed performances include *Days of Wine and Roses* (1962) and *The China Syndrome* (1979). His long association with Walther Matthau began in 1966 with *The Fortune Cookie* and included *The Odd Couple* (1968) and many others. He has periodically returned to the stage and directed one film, *Kotch* (1971). Nominated eight times for an Academy Award, he won Best Supporting Actor for *Mister Roberts* (1955) and Best Actor for *Save the Tiger* (1973). Recent films include *Glengarry Glen Ross* (1992), *Short Cuts* (1993), *The Grass Harp* (1995) and *Hamlet* (1996).

Lemnitzer, Lyman Louis 1899–1988
US general

Born in Honesdale, Pennsylvania, he was educated at West Point and commissioned into the artillery in 1920. After graduating from Staff College in 1936, he held a number of senior staff appointments in the US army and by the end of World War II was Deputy Chief of Staff to the Allied forces in Italy. He joined the Joint Chiefs of Staff in 1946 and was appointed its chairman in 1960. Although he had operational command of US forces in Korea and the Pacific, he was best known as a military planner and in 1963 became the Supreme Allied Commander of NATO Forces in Europe. He retired from the army in 1969.

Lemon, Mark 1809–70
English author and journalist

Born in London, he wrote a farce in 1835, followed by several melodramas, operettas, novels (the best of which is, perhaps, *Falkner Lyle*, 1866), children's stories, a *Jest Book* (1864) and essays. In 1841 he helped to establish

Punch, becoming first joint editor (with **Henry Mayhew**), then sole editor from 1843. ⌼ A A Adrian, *Mark Lemon: first editor of Punch* (1966)

LeMond, Greg(ory James) 1961–
US cyclist

Born in Lakewood, California, he began cycling in 1975 and dropped out of high school to race professionally. In 1986 he became the first American to win the Tour de France, winning it again in 1989 and 1990. His 1989 victory captivated the sporting world. After 23 days and 1,400 miles (2,253km), LeMond rode the race's fastest ever time-trial to beat French favourite Laurent Fignon by just eight seconds. His win was all the more miraculous as he had been accidentally shot in a hunting trip in 1987 and had not fully recovered his strength. He retired after contracting a rare muscular wasting disease.

Lemonnier, Antoine Louis Camille 1844–1913
Belgian writer

Born in Ixelles, near Brussels, he took up art criticism in 1863. By his novels (written in French) *Un Mâle* (1881, Eng trans *A Male*, 1917), *Happe-Chair* (1888) and other works, full of strong Flemish realism and mysticism, he won fame as one of Belgium's leading prose writers. His books on art include *Gustave Courbet* (1878), *Alfred Stevens et son œuvre* (1906, 'Alfred Stevens and his Work') and *L'École Belge de la peinture* (1906, 'The Belgian School of Painting'). ⌼ B M Woodridge, in *Le roman belge contemporain* (1930)

Lemonnier, Pierre Charles 1715–99
French astronomer

Born in Paris, he became professor at the Collège Royale in 1746. He greatly advanced astronomical measurement in France and made 12 observations of Uranus before it was recognized as a planet.

Le Moyne, François 1688–1737
French painter

Born in Paris, he specialized in mythological subjects, especially for the Salon d'Hercule at Versailles. **François Boucher** was his pupil.

Le Nain, Antoine c.1588–1648 and Louis c.1593–1648 and Mathieu c.1607–1677
French painters and brothers

Born in Laon, all three were resident in Paris by 1630. Mathieu became painter to the city in 1633, and they all became founder-members of the Académie Française. They each painted scenes of peasant life but, as they tended to sign their work without initials, any individual attribution has to be made on purely stylistic grounds.

Lenard, Philipp Eduard Anton 1862–1947
German physicist and Nobel Prize winner

Born in Pozsony, Hungary (Bratislava, Slovakia), and educated at the University of Heidelberg, he was a researcher at the universities of Bonn and Breslau before returning to Heidelberg as professor (1896–98). He then moved on to Kiel University (1898–1907) before returning to the University of Heidelberg until his retirement in 1931. His observations of the photoelectric effect were explained by **Albert Einstein** in 1905, and his studies of the magnetic deflection of cathode rays and their electrostatic properties, led him to suggest that atoms contain units of both positive and negative charge. For these studies he was awarded the Nobel Prize for physics in 1905. He was also awarded the Royal Society Rumford Medal (1904) and the Franklin Medal from the Franklin Institute (1905).

Lenau, Nikolaus, *in full* Nikolaus Niembsch von Strehlenau 1802–50
German poet

Born in Czatad, Hungary, he studied law and medicine at Vienna. He suffered from severe depression, became insane in 1844, and died in an asylum near Vienna. His poetic power is best shown in his short lyrics, collections of which appeared in 1832, 1838 and 1844. His longer pieces include *Faust* (1836), *Savonarola* (1837) and *Die Albigenser* (1842, 'The Albigensians'). ⌼ E Castle, *Nikolaus Lenau* (1902)

Lenbach, Franz 1836–1904
German portrait painter

Born in Schrobenhausen, Bavaria, he worked mostly in Munich. For some time he copied the great masters, including **Titian**, **Rubens** and **Velázquez**, before becoming one of the greatest 19th-century German portrait painters. His portraits of **Bismarck** are particularly famous.

Lenclos, Anne, *known as* Ninon de Lenclos 1620–1705
French courtesan, poet and feminist

Born of a good family in Paris, she started her long career at the age of 16, founding a salon which favoured Jansenists. Among her lovers were two marquises, two marshals, the great **Condé**, and the Dukes of **La Rochefoucauld** and **Sévigné**. Her behaviour cost her a spell in a convent in 1656 at the behest of **Anne of Austria**, but her popularity ensured a swift release, and afterwards she wrote *La Coquette vengée* (1659, 'The Avenger's Coquette') in her own defence. She was celebrated almost as much for her manners as for her beauty, and respectable women sent their children to her to acquire taste, style and politeness. She had two sons, one of whom, not realising who she was, fell in love with her. Informed of their relationship, he killed himself. ⌼ Edgar H Cohen, *Mademoiselle Libertine* (1970)

Lenclos, Ninon de See Lenclos, Anne

Lendl, Ivan 1960–
US tennis player

He was born in Ostrava, Czechoslovakia (now Czech Republic). He won the singles title at the US Open (1985–87), French Open (1984, 1986–87), and Australian Open (1989), and was the Masters champion (1986–87) and the World Championship Tennis champion (1982, 1985). He was runner-up at Wimbledon in 1986–87. He became the first official world champion in 1987. His powerful service and clinically efficient execution of shots make him a formidable clay-court player. Lendl became a US citizen in 1992.

L'Enfant, Pierre Charles 1754–1825
US architect

Born in Paris, France, the son of one of the royal painters, he studied art at the Royal Academy of Painting and Sculpture, then went to America in 1776 to serve as a soldier and engineer in the Continental Army. At the invitation of **George Washington**, he designed (1791) a grand plan for the city of Washington DC, with wide radiating boulevards, formal parks, and monumental public buildings. An autocrat in aesthetic matters, he disregarded all other authority, even that of the President, in directing the construction of the capital, and he promptly overspent the budget. In 1792 he was dismissed as chief engineer, and building was halted. He continued to work as an architect in private practice, but his volatile temperament and extravagant spending led to the interruption of several projects, and at his death in 1825 he was penniless and living on a friend's estate. The country later caught up with L'Enfant's grand ambitions, and after 1901, when a Senate-appointed commission approved the revival of his Washington plan, much of the city was developed according to his designs.

Lenin, Vladimir Ilyich, *originally surnamed* Ulyanov 1870–1924
Russian revolutionary

Lenin was born into a middle-class family in Simbirsk. He was educated at Kazan University and in 1892 began to practise law in Samara (Kuibyshev). In 1894, after five years' intensive study of **Karl Marx**, he moved to St Petersburg, which was renamed Leningrad after his death in 1924, until reverting to being called St Petersburg in 1991. Lenin organized the illegal 'Union for the Liberation of the Working Class', was arrested for his opinions, and spent several years in exile, first in Siberia and then in the west. In 1900 in Switzerland, he edited the political newspaper *Iskra* ('The Spark') and developed, with **Georgi Plekhanov**, an underground Social Democratic Party, to assume leadership of the working classes in a revolution against Tsarism. His evolving ideas were set out in *What is to be done?* (1902), in which he advocated a professional core of party activists to spearhead the revolution. This suggestion was adopted by the party's majority, Bolshevik wing at the congress in London in 1903, but was opposed by the 'bourgeois reformism' Mensheviks (minority wing).

Lenin returned to Russia in 1905, and blamed the failure of the rising of that year on lack of support for his own programme. He determined that when the time came 'Soviets' (councils of workers, soldiers and peasants) should be the instruments of total revolution. Lenin left Russia in 1907 and spent the next decade strengthening the Bolsheviks against the Mensheviks, interpreting the works of Marx and **Friedrich Engels** and organizing underground work in Russia. In April 1917, a few days after the deposition of Tsar **Nicholas II**, Lenin, with German connivance, made a fateful journey in a sealed train from Switzerland to Petrograd (the name of St Petersburg from 1914 to 1924). He told his followers to prepare for the overthrow of the shaky provisional government and the remaking of Russia on a Soviet basis.

In the October revolution the provisional government collapsed and the dominating Bolshevik 'rump' in the second Congress of Soviets declared that supreme power rested in them. Lenin inaugurated the 'dictatorship of the proletariat' with the formal dissolution of the Constituent Assembly. For three years he grappled with war and anarchy. In 1922 he began his 'new economic policy' of limited free enterprise to give Russia respite before entering the era of giant state planning. His health having been in progressive decline since an assassination attempt in 1918, he died on 21 January 1924, and his body was embalmed for veneration in a crystal casket in a mausoleum in Red Square, Moscow.

Lenin was a charismatic figure. Shrewd, dynamic, implacable, pedantic, opportunist, and ice-cold in his economic reasoning, he lived only for the furtherance of Marxism.

📖 Ronald Clark, *Lenin* (1988); Christopher Hill, *Lenin and the Russian Revolution* (1978); Adam Ulam, *Lenin and the Bolsheviks* (1965).

> 'Communism is Soviet power plus the electrification of the whole country.' (1920). Quoted in *Collected Works* (5th edn) vol. 42, p.30.

> 'Liberty is precious—so precious that it must be rationed.' Quoted in **Sidney** and **Beatrice Webb**'s *Soviet Communism: A New Civilization* (1935).

Leng, Virginia, *née* Holgate 1955–
British three-day eventer

Born in Malta, she was the European junior champion in 1973. She then won the team gold at the senior championship in 1981, 1985 and 1987, and individual titles in 1985, 1987 and 1989. She won the world championship team gold in 1982 and 1986, and the individual title in 1986 on Priceless. She has also won at Badminton (1985, 1989, 1993) and at Burghley (1983–86, 1989). She has co-authored such books as *Training the Event Horse* (1990).

L'Engle, Madeleine 1918–
US novelist

Born in New York City, she was educated at Smith College, Northampton, and at the New School for Social Research in New York. A prolific writer for children as well as adults, she imbues her work with explicitly Christian ideas and morals. Her most popular titles include *A Wrinkle in Time* (1962, Newbery Medal) and *The Young Unicorns* (1968), both of which combine elements of fantasy with tough ethical concerns.

Lenglen, Suzanne 1899–1938
French tennis player

Born in Compiègne, she was trained by her father, and became famous in 1914 by winning the women's world hard-court singles championship at Paris at the age of 15. She was the woman champion of France (1919–23, 1925–26), and her Wimbledon championships were the women's singles and doubles (1919–23, 1925), and the mixed doubles (1920, 1922, 1925). She won the singles and doubles gold medals at the 1920 Olympic Games. She became a professional in 1926, toured the USA, and retired in 1927 to found the Lenglen School of Tennis in Paris. She published *Lawn Tennis, the Game of Nations* (1925) and a novel, *The Love-Game* (1925). 📖 Alan Little, *Suzanne Lenglen, Tennis Idol of the Twenties* (1988)

Lenin, Vladimir Ilyich See panel above

Lenk, Timur See **Timur**

Lennard-Jones, Sir John Edward, *originally* Jones 1894–1954
English physicist and theoretical chemist

Born in Leigh, Lancashire, he graduated in mathematics at Manchester University in 1915, and then became a pilot in the Royal Flying Corps. After World War I he held posts at Manchester and at Cambridge before becoming Reader in Theoretical Physics at Bristol in 1925 and Professor in 1927. In 1932 he was appointed Plummer Professor of Theoretical Chemistry at Cambridge. From 1939 to 1946 he was engaged in war work, notably as director-general of Scientific Research (Defence) in the Ministry of Supply. He was appointed Principal of the University College of North Staffordshire in 1953. He was elected Fellow of the Royal Society in 1933, and received its Davy medal in 1953. From 1948 to 1950 he was president of the Faraday Society. At Cambridge he devised a mathematical expression for intermolecular forces which bears his name, and which is still widely used in statistical mechanics. During a year in Göttingen in 1929, he began his part in the development of the molecular orbital theory introduced by **Robert Mulliken**, of which he became a leading exponent.

Lennon, John (Winston) 1940–80
English songwriter, vocalist and rhythm guitarist

Born in Liverpool, he first found fame as a member of the **Beatles**, and pursued a solo career after the group disbanded in 1970. His marriage to Japanese conceptual artist **Yoko Ono** sharpened his social conscience and refocused the surreal wit that was part of his Lancashire Catholic inheritance. Their work together produced songs of mild protest like 'Give Peace a Chance' (1969), 'Cold Turkey' (1969) and 'Working Class Hero' (1970), a rare balance of the personal and political. His most successful albums were *Imagine* (1971) and *Mind Games* (1973). He was shot dead in New York.

Lennox, Annie 1954–
Scottish pop singer

Born in Aberdeen, she was working as a waitress in Hampstead, London, when she met musician and composer Dave Stewart in 1977. They formed The Tourists, and recorded three albums before disbanding in 1980. The pair then formed The Eurythmics, and continued the group even after their personal relationship ended in 1981. The combination of his intricate pop hooks and her strong, soulful vocals made them one of the most successful pop bands of the decade, but each decided to pursue solo careers. She took a break from music in 1990, but returned in 1992 to launch her lavish solo album *Diva*, and sidestepped the trauma of songwriting in *Medusa* (1995), a collection of cleverly arranged cover versions of songs originally sung by men. ▢ L O'Brien, *Annie Lennox* (1991)

Lennox, Charlotte, *née* Ramsay c.1729–1804
British novelist and playwright

She was born in New York City. Sent to England, where her father was posted, when she was 15, she found herself unprovided for when her father died, and supported herself as an actress and writer. Her first novel, *The Life of Harriot Stuart* (1750), is a romantic adventure yarn, but her next and most famous work, *The Female Quixote* (1752), is a satirical romp through the life of Arabella, a young lady besotted with French romantic novels. She also wrote *Shakespeare Illustrated* (1753–54), an examination of the playwright's sources, translated many French works, and was much admired by Dr Johnson, who cites her under Talent in his Dictionary.

Leno, Dan, *originally* George Galvin 1860–1904
English comedian

He began his career at the age of four, singing and dancing in public houses, and by 18 had become a champion clog-dancer. Ten years later he joined the Augustus Harris management at Drury Lane, where he appeared for many years in the annual pantomime. Leno was a slight man and his foil was the bulky Herbert Campbell (1844–1904). When Campbell had a fatal accident in 1904, Leno pined and died six months later. He will be remembered for his realistic 'dames' with their blend of Cockney humour and sentiment.

Lenoir, Jean Joseph Étienne 1822–1900
French inventor and engineer

Born in Luxemburg City, he invented the first practical internal-combustion gas engine (c.1859) which was fuelled by coal gas and air, and later built the first car to use it (1860). He also constructed a boat driven by his engine (1886).

Lenormand, Henri-René 1882–1951
French dramatist

Born in Paris, he studied at the university there. He was the author of *Les Possédés* (1909, 'The Possessed'), *Le Mangeur de rêves* (1922, 'The Eater of Dreams'), a modern equivalent of *Œdipus Rex*, *L'Homme et ses fantômes* (1924, 'Man and his Phantoms'), and several other plays in which Sigmund Freud's theory of subconscious motivation is adapted to dramatic purposes. He discusses the aesthetics of his dramatic style in *Confessions d'un auteur dramatique* (1949, 'Confessions of a Playwright'). ▢ P Blanchart, *Le théâtre de Lenormand* (1947)

Lenormant, François 1837–83
French archaeologist

He was born in Paris. At the age of 20 he won the prize in numismatics of the Académie des Inscriptions, and at 23 he was digging at Eleusis, near Athens. He continued his explorations, between working in Paris as sub-librarian at the Institute (1862–72) and Professor of Archaeology at the Bibliothèque Nationale (1874–83), until his health broke down from overwork and a wound received during the siege of the city (1870–71). His chief work was *Les Origines de l'histoire d'après la Bible* (1880–84, 'The Origins of History According to the Bible').

Le Nôtre or Lenôtre, André 1613–1700
French landscape architect

Born in Paris, he studied the laws of perspective and optics under the painter François Vouet and the principles of architecture under François Mansard. The creator of French landscape-gardening, he designed many celebrated European gardens, including those at Versailles and Fontainebleau, and St James's Park and Kensington Gardens in London.

Lenya, Lotte, *originally* Karoline Wilhelmine Blamauer 1898–1981
Austrian actress and cabaret singer

Born in Hitzing, Vienna, she studied dancing in Zurich (1914–20) and moved to Berlin (1920), where she took up acting and married Kurt Weill (1926). Her international reputation was made by her roles in his works, notably as Jenny in *Die Dreigroschenoper* (1928, *The Threepenny Opera*). In 1933 the couple fled to Paris and then settled in the USA (1935), where her stage appearances included *The Firebrand of Florence* (1945), *Brecht on Brecht* (1962) and *Mother Courage* (1972). Her rare film roles included *The Threepenny Opera* (1931) and *From Russia With Love* (1963). After Weill's death she became the public custodian of his legacy, and supreme interpreter of his work. ▢ D Spoto, *Lenya: A Life* (1989)

Lenz, Heinrich Friedrich Emil 1804–65
German physicist

Born in Dorpat, Russia, he first studied theology, but became Professor of Physics at St Petersburg (1836) and a member of the Russian Academy of Sciences. He was the first to state Lenz's law governing induced current, and is credited with discovering the dependence of electrical resistance on temperature (Joule's law).

Lenz, Jakob Michael Reinhold 1751–92
German writer

Born in Livonia, he was one of the young authors who surrounded Goethe in Strasbourg. He first wrote two plays which were well received, *Der Hofmeister* (1774, 'The Steward') and *Die Soldaten* (1776, 'The Soldiers'). Like all the Sturm und Drang poets he was a fervent admirer of Shakespeare, and this was expressed in his *Anmerkungen übers Theater* (1774, 'Remarks on the Theatre'). He was a gifted writer of lyrics, some of them being at first attributed to Goethe, and also wrote several novels, but of lesser quality. He suffered a mental breakdown while still young, and died in poverty.

Leo I, St, *known as* the Great c.390–461AD
Italian pope

Born possibly in Tuscany, he was one of only two popes (the other being Gregory I) to take the title 'the Great'. Pope from AD440 to 461, he was one of the most eminent of the Latin Fathers. He summoned the Council of Chalcedon (451), which accepted his doctrine of the Incarnation as defined in his 'Dogmatical Letter'. He made treaties with Attila the Hun (452) and with the Vandals (455) in defence of Rome, and consolidated the primacy of the Roman see.

Leo III, *called* the Isaurian c.680–741
Byzantine emperor

Born in northern Syria, near Isauria, he raised the Byzantine Empire from a very low condition, after seizing the crown from Theodosius III (717). He reorganized the army and financial system, produced a new legal code, and repelled a formidable attack by the Saracens (718). In 726 he prohibited the use of images (ie, pictures or mosaics; statues were hardly known as yet in churches) in public worship. In Italy, however, the Iconoclasts ('Image-Breakers') caused resistance by the people, and the subsequent controversy split the empire for over a century. In 728 Ravenna was lost, and the eastern provinces became the prey of the Saracens, over whom, however, Leo won a great victory at Phrygia.

Leo III c.750–816

Byzantine pope

He saw during his pontificate (795–816) the formal establishment of the Empire of the West. In the 8th century the popes, through the practical withdrawal of the Eastern emperors, had exercised a temporal supremacy in Rome, under the protectorate of the Frankish sovereigns. Leo was obliged to flee to Spoleto in 799, from where he went to Paderborn to confer with **Charlemagne**. On his return to Rome he was received with honour. In 800 Charlemagne, having come to Rome, was crowned emperor by Leo, and the temporal sovereignty of the pope over the Roman city and state was formally established, under the suzerainty of the emperor.

Leo X, *originally* Giovanni de' Medici 1475–1521

Italian pope

He was born in Florence. The second son of **Lorenzo de' Medici**, the Magnificent, and the brother of **Piero de' Medici**, he was created a cardinal at 13. Elected pope in 1513, he is best remembered as a patron of learning and the arts. He founded a Greek college in Rome and established a Greek press. His project for the rebuilding of St Peter's made it necessary to preach an indulgence in order to raise funds to do so and this provoked **Martin Luther**'s 95 theses. Leo's failure to respond either promptly or effectively helped to increase the Reformation's early momentum. With his election as pope, the rule of Florence passed first to his younger brother, Giuliano, and then to his nephew, Lorenzo, Duke of Urbino. The real power of the family, however, remained with the pope and his cousin, Guilio, grandson of **Cosimo de' Medici**, who succeeded to the papacy in 1523 as **Clement VII**. 📖 William Roscoe, *The Life and Pontificate of Leo the Tenth* (2 vols, 1853)

Leo XIII, *originally* Vincenzo Gioacchino Pecci 1810–1903

Italian pope

He was born in Carpineto, the son of Count Ludovico Pecci. After taking a degree in law he was appointed by **Gregory XVI** a domestic prelate in 1837, sent to Belgium as nuncio in 1843, nominated Archbishop of Perugia in 1846, and in 1853 created a cardinal by **Pius IX**. Elected to the papacy on the death of Pius IX in 1878, he restored the hierarchy in Scotland, resolved the difficulty with Germany, and in 1888 denounced the Irish Plan of Campaign. He held some enlightened views, but regarded himself as the despoiled sovereign of Rome, and persistently declined to recognize the law of guarantees. In 1883 he opened the archives of the Vatican for historical investigations, and he made himself known as a poet, chiefly in the Latin tongue. He affirmed that the only solution to the socialistic problem was the influence of the papacy, and in 1894 he constrained the French clergy and the monarchists to accept the republic. In 1896 he issued an encyclical pronouncing Anglican orders invalid.

Leo Africanus, *properly* Alhassan ibn Mohammed Alwazzan c.1494–c.1552

Arab traveller and geographer

He was born in the kingdom of Granada, and from c.1512 travelled in northern Africa and Asia Minor. Falling into the hands of Venetian corsairs, he was sent to Pope **Leo X** in Rome, where he lived for 20 years, and accepted Christianity. He later returned to Africa and (perhaps) his old faith, and died in Tunis. He wrote *Descrittione dell'Africa* (1550, Eng trans *A Geographical Historie of Africa*, 1660), an account of his African travels in Italian and for long the chief source of information about the Sudan.

Leochares fl. c.350–330BC

Greek sculptor

With his master **Scopas**, he decorated the Mausoleum of Halicarnassus. The marble *Demeter* in the British Museum (c.350BC) has been attributed to him. He also executed the official likenesses of **Philip II** of Macedon and **Alexander the Great**.

Leon, Daniel de See De Leon, Daniel

León, Ernesto Zedillo Ponce de See Zedillo Ponce de León, Ernesto

León, Juan Ponce de See Ponce de León, Juan

León, Luis Ponce de See Ponce de León, Luis

Leonard, Elmore John 1925–

US thriller writer

He was born in New Orleans, and lived in Dallas, Oklahoma City and Memphis before his family settled in Detroit in 1935. He served in the US navy during World War II, and afterwards he studied English literature at Detroit University. Throughout the 1950s he worked in advertising as a copywriter, but since 1967 he has concentrated on screenplays and novels, remarkable for their relentless pace and vivid dialogue. He is regarded as the foremost crime writer in the USA, and his numerous books include *Unknown Man No. 89* (1977), *Gold Coast* (1980), *Stick* (1983), *La Brava* (1983) *Touch* (1987), *Get Shorty* (1990), *Pronto* (1993) and *Out of Sight* (1996). 📖 D Geherin, *Elmore Leonard* (1989)

Leonard, Graham Douglas 1921–

English prelate

Born in London, he was appointed Bishop of Willesden in 1964, Bishop of Truro in 1973, and became Bishop of London in 1981. He is known more for his traditional Anglo-Catholic theological position than for his long-standing concern for the Church's role in education or his chairmanship of the Church of England Board for Social Responsiblility (1976–83). He opposed the 1970s Anglican-Methodist unity scheme (see *Growing into Union*, 1970), and as Bishop of London became the focus of theological opposition to the ordination of women to the priesthood. His offer of pastoral support to a congregation in Tulsa, Oklahoma, in 1986 caused controversy over the role of bishops outside their own dioceses. He retired as Bishop of London in 1991 and was received into the Roman Catholic Church in 1994. His books include *Is Christianity Credible?* (1981), *The Price of Peace* (1983) and *Tradition and Unity* (1991).

Leonard, Sugar Ray 1956–

US boxer

Born in South Carolina, he won an Olympic gold in Montreal in 1976, starting a professional career in which he fought 12 world title fights at various weights and won world titles in each weight. In 35 fights between 1977 and 1987, he was beaten only once, by Roberto Duran, who took the welterweight title from him on points in 1980. Leonard became the undisputed world welterweight

Leonardo da Vinci 1452–1519
Italian painter, sculptor, architect and engineer

Leonardo was born in Vinci, between Pisa and Florence, the illegitimate son of a Florentine notary and Caterina, a young peasant woman. He showed unusual gifts at an early age, and about 1470 he was sent to study in the studio of **Andrea del Verrocchio**, where **Botticelli** and **Perugino** were also pupils. To this period belong the *Baptism of Christ* and the unfinished *Adoration of the Magi*, now in the Uffizi Gallery in Florence. In 1482 he settled in Milan in the service of Duke **Ludovico Sforza**. His famous *Last Supper* (1498), commissioned jointly by Ludovico and the monks of Santa Maria delle Grazie, was painted on a wall of the refectory of the convent of Santa Maria delle Grazie. Because of dampness, and the method of tempera painting (neither oil nor fresco) upon plaster, it soon showed signs of deterioration; yet it is still regarded as a masterpiece. Among other paintings in Milan were portraits of two mistresses of the duke, one of them perhaps *La Belle Ferronnière* of the Louvre. He also devised a system of hydraulic irrigation of the plains of Lombardy and directed the court pageants.

After the fall of Duke Ludovico in 1500 Leonardo retired to Florence, and entered the service of **Cesare Borgia**, then Duke of Romagna, as architect and engineer. In 1503 he returned to Florence, and began work on a *Madonna and Child with St Anne*, of which only the cartoon now in the Royal Academy, London, was completed. Both he and **Michelangelo** received commissions to decorate the Sala del Consiglio in the Palazzo della Signoria with historical compositions. Leonardo dealt with *The Battle of Anghiari*, a Florentine victory over Milan, and finished his cartoon; but he employed a method of painting on the plaster which proved a failure, and abandoned the work in 1506.

About 1504 he completed his most celebrated easel picture, *Mona Lisa*. Another work portrayed the celebrated beauty Ginevra Benci; and Pacioli's *De divina Proportione* (1509) contained 60 geometrical figures from Leonardo's hand. In 1506 he was employed by **Louis XII** of France. **Francis I** bestowed on him in 1516 a yearly allowance, and assigned to his use the Château Cloux, near Amboise, where he lived until his death.

Among his later works are *The Virgin of the Rocks*, now in the National Gallery, London, a figure of *St John the Baptist*, and *Saint Anne*. There is no surviving sculpture which can positively be attributed to him, but he may well have designed or been closely associated with three works: the three figures over the north door of the Baptistery at Florence, a bronze statuette of horse and rider in the Budapest Museum, and the wax bust of Flora.

In his art Leonardo was hardly at all influenced by the antique; his practice was founded on the most patient and searching study of nature and in particular of light and shade. He occupies a supreme place as an artist, but so few of his works have survived that he may be most fully studied in his drawings, of which there are rich collections in Milan, Paris, Florence and Vienna, as well as in England in the British Museum and at Windsor Castle.

His celebrated *Trattato della Pittura* was published in 1651; but a more complete manuscript, discovered by Manzi in the Vatican, was published in 1817. Voluminous manuscripts by him in Milan (*Codice-Atlantico*), Paris, Windsor, and elsewhere have been reproduced in facsimile. Leonardo was the outstanding all-round genius of the Renaissance. He had a wide knowledge and understanding far beyond his times of most of the sciences, including biology, anatomy, physiology, hydrodynamics, mechanics and aeronautics, and his notebooks, written in mirror writing, contain original remarks on all of these.

📖 Robert Payne, *Leonardo* (1978); Kenneth Clark, *Leonardo da Vinci* (1959).

'The span of a man's outspread arms is equal to his height.' Quoted in Irma A Richter (ed), *Selections from the Notebooks of Leonardo da Vinci* (1977).

'Perspective is the bridle and rudder of painting.' Ibid.

---

champion in 1981 when he beat **Tommy Hearns** and earned a record fee of more than $10 million. He declared his retirement four times during his career, but it was finally a detached retina in 1991 that caused him to give up boxing.

Leonard, Tom 1944–
Scottish poet

He was born in Glasgow and educated at Glasgow University. He is a dedicated experimenter with poetic form, attempting everything from strict metres and forms to linguistic 'found objects', complex word association to snippets of conversation heard in bus queues. His first published collection was the slim *Six Glasgow Poems* (1969). Other volumes include *A Priest Came On at Merkland Street* (1970), and *Poems* (1973), for which he provided a parallel text translation of his phoneticized dialect into standard English. The best of his early work was collected as *Intimate Voices: Writing 1965–83* (1984). He edited *Radical Renfrew: Poetry from the French Revolution to the First World War* (1990).

Leonardo da Vinci See panel above

Leonardo of Pisa See **Fibonacci, Leonardo**

Leoncavallo, Ruggiero 1858–1919
Italian composer

Born in Naples, he studied at the Naples Conservatorio and, while touring Europe as a pianist, is thought to have been encouraged in his career by **Richard Wagner**. He produced *I Pagliacci* (1892, 'Clowns'), traditionally staged with **Pietro Mascagni's** *Cavalleria Rusticana* (1890, 'Rustic Chivalry'). He followed this with other less successful operas, including a *La Bohème* (1897, 'Bohemian life') which failed where **Puccini's** (1896), on the same theme, was a success.

Leoni, Leone 1509–90
Italian goldsmith, medallist and sculptor

Born in Arezzo, he worked in Milan, Genoa, Brussels and Madrid, and was the rival of **Benvenuto Cellini** in talent, vice and violence. His fine medals often depicted well-known artists, such as Titian and **Michelangelo**, and his sculpture which was mostly in bronze included busts of **Charles V** and **Philip II of Spain**, both of whom he served for some time.

Leonidas d.c.480BC
King of Sparta

He succeeded his half-brother, **Cleomenes I** (491BC). When the Persian king **Xerxes I** approached with a large army, Leonidas opposed him at the narrow pass of Thermopylae (480) with his 300 Spartans and 700 Thespians, and there all of them died heroically.

Leonov, Aleksei Arkhipovich 1934–
Soviet astronaut

Born in Listvyanka, he was the first man to walk in space. In 1955 he went to the Chuguyev Air Force Flying School in the Ukraine, graduating with honours in 1957, thereafter serving with air force units. He specialized in parachute training and joined the astronaut corps in 1959. On

18 March 1965 he made the first 'extra-vehicular-activity' (EVA) from the spacecraft *Voskhod 2* in orbit round the Earth, 'walking' in space for 10 minutes. In 1975 he took part in the joint US–USSR Apollo–Soyuz space mission.

Leontief, Wassily 1906–
US economist and Nobel Prize winner

Born in St Petersburg, Russia, and educated at Leningrad (now St Petersburg) and Berlin universities, he went to the USA in 1930. He taught at Harvard from 1931 to 1975 (professor from 1946), and from 1975 to 1985 was director of the Institute of Economic Analysis at New York University. His most important work was an analysis of US industry, *The Structure of the American Economy, 1919–29* (1941). He was awarded the 1973 Nobel Prize for economics for developing the input-output method of economic analysis, used in more than 50 industrialized countries for planning and forecasting. In 1985 he was made Commandeur, L'Ordre des Arts et des Lettres.

Leopardi, Giacomo 1798–1837
Italian poet

Born in Recanati, by the age of 16 he had read all the Latin and Greek classics, could write French, Spanish, English and Hebrew, and wrote a commentary on **Plotinus**. He devoted himself to literature, and although an invalid, travelled widely, and lived successively in Bologna, Florence, Milan and Pisa. In 1833 he accompanied his friend Ranieri to Naples and settled there. His works, which show his pessimistic views on life, include lyrics, collected under the title *I Canti* (1831, Eng trans *The Poems*, 1893), dialogues and essays classed as *Operette Morali* (1827, translated in a bilingual edition under original title, 1983), *Pensieri* (7 vols, 1898–1900, 'Thoughts') and letters. 📖 H H Whitfield, *Giacomo Leopardi* (1954)

Leopold I 1790–1865
King of Belgium

Born in Coburg, he was the son of Francis, Duke of Saxe-Coburg, and uncle of Queen **Victoria**. A general in the Russian army, he served at Lützen, Bautzen and Leipzig (1813). He married (1816) Princess **Charlotte** of Great Britain (d.1817). He declined the Crown of Greece (1830) and in 1831 he was elected King of the Belgians. He married Marie-Louise, daughter of **Louis Philippe**, in 1832. He conducted himself with prudence and moderation, with constant regard to the principles of the Belgian constitution, and by his policy did much to prevent Belgium becoming too involved in the revolutions which were raging in other European countries in 1848. 📖 Joanna Richardson, *My Dearest Uncle: A Life of Leopold I, King of the Belgians* (1961)

Leopold II 1835–1909
King of Belgium

The son of **Leopold I**, he was born in Brussels. Energetic and well-travelled, his chief interest was the expansion of Belgium abroad. In 1885 he became king of the independent state of the Congo, but the exposure of atrocities to natives working in rubber production (1904) led to it being annexed to Belgium (1908). At home he strengthened his country by military reforms (especially the introduction of conscription) and established a system of fortifications. He was not popular as a king, but under him Belgium flourished, developing commercially and industrially, especially during the later part of his reign. He was succeeded by his nephew, **Albert I**. 📖 Neal Ascherson, *The King Incorporated: Leopold II in the Age of Trusts* (1964)

Leopold III 1901–83
King of Belgium

Born in Brussels, he was the son of King **Albert I** and became king in 1934. On his own authority he ordered the capitulation of his army to the Nazis (1940), and remained a prisoner in his own palace at Laeken and in Austria. After the war he remained in Switzerland (1945–50), pending solution of the 'royal question', but although 58.1 per cent of voters favoured his return in a plebiscite (1950), continued unrest persuaded him to abdicate in favour of his son **Baudouin I** in 1951. 📖 James Page, *Leopold III: The Belgian Royal Question* (1961)

Leopold I 1640–1705
Holy Roman Emperor

Born in Vienna, he was the second son of Emperor **Ferdinand III** and the Infanta Maria Anna of Spain (daughter of **Philip III**). He became King of Hungary (1655) and Bohemia (1656), and was elected emperor (1658) in succession to his father. For most of his reign he was at war either with the Ottoman Turks over Hungary, or with the France of **Louis XIV**. The first war with Turkey (1661–64) ended in victory at St Gotthard. The second war (1682–99) involved the siege of Vienna (1683), relieved by **John III Sobieski** of Poland, and ended with the Treaty of Karlowitz, giving Leopold control of virtually all of Hungary. In 1686 he had combined with England and the Dutch Stadtholder William of Orange (later **William III** of Great Britain) to resist French expansionism in Europe, culminating in the War of the Spanish Succession (1701–14) which attempted to prevent the succession of the **Bourbon** House in Spain. A pious lover of the arts, and originally destined for the Church, Leopold strove to extend Habsburg power, the imperial Crown being declared hereditary in the family at the Diet of Pressburg (1687), and to repress Protestantism. Under him the Baroque flourished, and Vienna became renowned as a cultural centre. In 1703 his refusal to respect the traditional rights of the Hungarian nobles led to an uprising under **Francis II Rákóczi**. By his third wife, Eleanora of Neuburg, he had two sons who both succeeded him as emperor, **Joseph I** and Charles VI. 📖 John P Spielman, *Leopold I of Austria* (1977)

Leopold II 1747–92
Holy Roman Emperor

Born in Vienna, the third son of **Francis I** and **Maria Theresa**, he succeeded his father as Grand Duke of Tuscany (1765), and his brother, **Joseph II**, as emperor (1790). He was enlightened in his views and continued the policy of emancipating peasants and giving toleration to non-Catholics. He pacified the Netherlands and Hungary, and after the downfall of his sister, **Marie Antoinette**, he formed an alliance with Prussia against France, but died before war broke out.

Leopold V 1157–94
European nobleman and crusader

He was Duke of Austria from 1177 and of Styria from 1192, and captor of King **Richard I** of England. A crusader, he became a bitter enemy of Richard on the Third Crusade (1189–92), and took him prisoner in his dominions as he made his way home to England (1192).

Lepage, Jules Bastien See **Bastien-Lepage, Jules**

Le Parc, Julio 1928–
Argentine artist

Born in Mendoza, he trained in Buenos Aires, then moved to Paris in 1958, embarking on a career which placed him at the forefront of experimental art. He was associated, for a time, with **Viktor Vasarely**, and helped found the Groupe de Recherche d'Art Visuel in 1960. Increasingly interested in the artistic exploitation of movement and light, he constructed coloured mobiles using transparent prisms and cubes, for example in *Continual Mobile, Continual Light* (1963, Tate Gallery, London). Considerable controversy was aroused when he was awarded the Painting prize at the 1966 Venice Biennale.

After 1968 his art became for a time overtly political, involving the representation of personifications of capitalists, imperialists and the military, but his main importance is as a leading proponent of the Op and Kinetic art movements of the 1960s.

Le Pen, Jean-Marie 1928–
French politician

The son of a Breton fisherman, he graduated in law at Paris before serving in the 1950s as a paratrooper in Indo-China and Algeria, where he lost an eye during a violent street battle. In 1956 he won a National Assembly seat as a right-wing Poujadist. During the 1960s he was connected with ·the extremist Organisation de l'Armée Secrète (OAS), before forming the National Front in 1972. This party, with its extreme right-wing policies, emerged as a new 'fifth force' in French politics, winning 10 per cent of the national vote in the 1986 Assembly elections. A controversial figure and noted demagogue, he was barred from public office for two years in 1998 due to his riotous behaviour during the 1997 general election campaign.

Lepidus, Marcus Aemilius d.13BC
Roman politician

He declared for Julius Caesar against Pompey during the civil war (49–31BC), and became Caesar's deputy at Rome (46). He supported Mark Antony, and became one of the triumvirate with him and Octavian (Emperor Augustus), with Africa for his province (40–39). Outmanoeuvred by Octavian in the power struggle of the 30s BC, he retired from active politics, but remained head of state religion (Pontifex Maximus) until his death.

Le Play, (Pierre Guillaume) Frédéric 1806–82
French political economist and engineer

Born in Honfleur, he lived in Paris, where he was professor in the École des Mines. He was one of the first to realize the importance of sociology and its effect on economics, and stressed the need for co-operation between employer and employee without intervention from government. His works included *Les Ouvriers européens* (1855, 'European Workers') and *Réforme sociale en France* (1864 'Social Reform in France').

Lepsius, Karl Richard 1810–84
German Egyptologist

He was born in Naumburg. His first work on palaeography as an instrument of philology (1834) won the Volney prize of the French Institute, and in 1836 at Rome he studied Egyptology, Nubian, Etruscan and Oscan. From 1842 to 1845 he headed an antiquarian expedition sent to Egypt by Frederick William IV of Prussia, and in 1846 he was appointed professor in Berlin. His *Denkmäler aus Aegypten und Aethiopien* (12 vols, 1849–60, 'Egyptian and Ethiopian Monuments') remains an important work, and his *Chronologie der Aegypter* (1849, 'Egyptian Chronology') laid the foundation for a scientific treatment of early Egyptian history. Other works include his letters from Egypt, Ethiopia and Sinai (1852), the *Todtenbuch* (1867)—the Egyptian Book of the Dead—and writings on Chinese, Arabic and Assyrian philology. He was director of the Egyptian section of the Royal Museum and of the Royal Library at Berlin (1873).

Lerdo de Tejada, Sebastián 1827–89
Mexican statesman

Born in Jalapa, Mexico, he served in the Supreme Court (1855–57) and in various administrative positions and supported Benito Juárez during the French invasion. After the French withdrew he became Chief Justice (1867–72) of the Supreme Court. Following Juárez as President of Mexico (1872–76), he instituted reform laws in the constitution (1874), then was overthrown and forced into exile by Porfirio Díaz.

Lerma, Don Francisco Gómez de Sandoval y Rojas, Duke of 1553–1625
Spanish politician

The Minister and confidant of Philip III of Spain, he played an important role in government policy during the period 1598–1618. A peaceful foreign policy was being pursued at this time. Treaties were signed with the French (1598), English (1604), and Dutch (1609, the Twelve Years' Truce), and there was a rapprochement with France (the marriage, in 1615, of Philip to Elizabeth of France). In domestic affairs, he was notable in having influenced the transfer of the court from Madrid to Valladolid (1601–06), and the decree expelling the Moriscos (1609). Created cardinal in 1618, he was dislodged by a palace coup the same year, and forced to give up some of his accumulated wealth.

Lermontov, Mikhail Yuriyevich 1814–41
Russian poet

Born of Scottish parents in Moscow, he attended Moscow University and then the military cavalry school of St Petersburg, where he received a commission in the guards. A poem written in 1837 on the death of Alexander Pushkin caused his arrest and he was sent to the Caucasus. Reinstated, he was again banished following a duel with the son of the French ambassador. Another duel was the cause of his death in 1841. He wrote from an early age, but much of his work was not published until his last years and his fame was posthumous. The scenery of the Caucasus inspired his poetry, but he is best known for his novel *Geroy nashevo vremeni* (1839, Eng trans *A Hero of Our Times*, 1854). He also wrote the romantic verse play *Maskarad* (1842, 'Masquerade'). ▢ J Garrard, *Mikhail Lermontov* (1982)

Lerner, Alan Jay 1918–86
US librettist, lyricist and playwright

Born in New York City, he worked with Frederick Loewe, whom he met in 1942, and they collaborated to produce several successful Broadway musicals, including *Brigadoon* (1947), *Paint Your Wagon* (1951), and *My Fair Lady* (1956), and the film *Gigi* (1958). Lerner also wrote the script for the film *An American in Paris* (1951) and (with composer Burton Lane (1912–97) produced the musical *On a Clear Day You Can See Forever* (1965, filmed 1970).

Lerroux, Alejandro 1864–1949
Spanish politician and journalist

An innovative and charismatic populist leader in Barcelona, known as the 'Emperor of the Parallel' (a working-class thoroughfare), he founded the first modern party in Spain, the Radical Republican Party (1908). He afterwards became increasingly conservative, even offering in 1923 to become the civilian figurehead of Miguel Primo de Rivera's dictatorship. During the Second Republic, he led the Radicals as the principal source of opposition to the progressive Republican–Socialist coalition of 1931–33. He was crucial to the formation of the alliance with the non-Republican Right, which ruled Spain from 1933 to 1935 and which polarized the regime to an unprecedented degree. During this period he headed five administrations before falling from power because of a bribery scandal. Despite backing the Nationalists during the Spanish Civil War, he was prevented from returning to Spain from his exile in Portugal until 1947, because of his earlier involvement with freemasonry.

Lesage or Le Sage, Alain René 1668–1747
French novelist and dramatist

He was born in Sarzeau, Brittany, and in 1692 went to Paris to study law, but an early marriage drove him to seek his fortune in literature. The Abbé de Lionne, who had a good Spanish library, allowed Lesage free access to it, with a pension of 600 livres, and in 1700 he published two plays in imitation of Rojas and **Lope de Vega**. In 1707 *Don César Ursin*, from **Pedro Calderón de la Barca**, was played with success at court, and the following year the Théâtre Français showed interest in the play which later became his famous *Turcaret*. As a novelist his reputation rests on *Gil Blas* (4 vols, 1715–35). Later works include *Bachelier de Salamanque* (1736–38, 'The Bachelor of Salamanque') and a volume of letters, *La Valise trouvée* (1740, 'A Suitcase Discovered'). The death of his son (1743), a promising actor, and his own increasing infirmities, made him abandon Paris and literary life, and he retreated to Boulogne, where he lived until his death. Some critics deny originality to one who borrowed ideas, incidents and tales from others as Lesage did, but he was a great raconteur and the first to perceive the capabilities of the picaresque novel. ⌷ E Lintilhac, *Alain Le Sage* (1893)

Lesage, Jean 1912–80
Canadian politician

He became the Liberal premier of Quebec in 1960, carried into power on a wave of nationalist fervour, although the Liberals won only 50 out of the 95 seats. He then introduced the Quiet Revolution against corruption, the Catholic Church's involvement in lay issues such as education, welfare and health, and against the economic domination of the USA and of anglophone Canadians in Quebec. His demands for a more active governmental role in the province, because of its special situation within the Confederation, began to cause unease among other Canadian provinces, especially when he asked for an increased share of tax revenue. In 1966 his government was defeated by the Union Nationale. He remained leader of the Provincial Party until his retirement in 1970.

Lescot, Pierre c.1510–1578
French Renaissance architect

Born in Paris, he was one of the greatest architects of his time. Among his works are the screen of St Germain l'Auxerrois, the Fontaine des Innocents and the Hôtel de Ligneris, all in Paris. His masterpiece was the Louvre, one wing of which he completely rebuilt.

Lese, Benozzo di See **Gozzoli, Benozzo**

Leslie, Alexander, 1st Earl of Leven c.1580–1661
Scottish general

The illegitimate son of the captain of Blair Atholl Castle, he became a field marshal of Sweden under **Gustav II Adolf**. Recalled to Scotland in 1638, he commanded the Covenanting army against **Charles I**. In 1641 he was made Earl of Leven and Lord Balgony, but from 1644 he led the Covenanting army into England on behalf of the Parliamentarians. He fought at Marston Moor (1644) and the storming of Newcastle. He accepted the surrender of Charles I at Newark in 1646 and handed him over to parliament in 1647. He joined the Royalists in 1649, fought **Cromwell** in Scotland in 1650–51, was captured and imprisoned, but released on parole in 1654.

Leslie, Charles Robert 1794–1859
British genre painter

Born in London of US parentage, he was educated in Philadelphia from 1800, but in 1811 returned to England and studied at the Royal Academy. His paintings were mostly scenes from famous plays and novels. He was Professor of Drawings at West Point, New York (1833), and from 1848 to 1852 Professor of Painting at the Royal Academy. His lectures were published in the *Handbook for Young Painters* (1855). He wrote a Life of **John Constable** (1843), and began one of Sir **Joshua Reynolds**, completed by **Tom Taylor**, who also edited his *Autobiographical Recollections* (1860).

Leslie, Frank, *originally* Henry Carter 1821–80
English illustrator and journalist

Born in Ipswich, Suffolk, he entered a London mercantile house at 17, and the success of his sketches led him to join the staff of the *Illustrated London News*. In 1848 he went to the USA, assumed the name of Frank Leslie, and in 1854 founded the *Gazette of Fashion* and the *New York Journal*. *Frank Leslie's Illustrated Newspaper* began in 1855, the *Chimney Corner* in 1865; he also started the *Boys' and Girls' Weekly*, the *Lady's Journal* and other publications.

Leslie, Sir John 1766–1832
Scottish natural philosopher and physicist

Born in Largo, Fife, he studied at St Andrews and Edinburgh, and travelled as a tutor in the USA and on the Continent, meanwhile engaging in experimental research. He invented a differential thermometer, a hygrometer and a photometer, and wrote *An Experimental Inquiry into Heat* (1804). In 1805 he was appointed to the chair of mathematics at Edinburgh. In 1810 he succeeded in creating artificial ice by freezing water under an air pump. Transferred to the chair of natural philosophy (1819), he also invented the pyroscope, the atmometer and the aethrioscope.

Leslie, Sir Shane (John Randolph) 1885–1971
Irish writer

He was born in Glaslough, County Monaghan, into a conservative Irish Protestant landed family, and educated at Paris University and King's College, Cambridge. In 1907 he visited Russia, where he met **Leo Tolstoy**. The following year he converted to Roman Catholicism, and in 1910 he unsuccessfully contested Londonderry in the Irish Nationalist interest. He produced a brilliant analysis of the pre-war generation in *The End of a Chapter* (1916), followed by *The Celt and the World*, intended to attract the anglophobe Irish–Americans to the Allied cause: it influenced the young **F Scott Fitzgerald** but was otherwise forgotten and was never published in Great Britain. He also wrote several impressive novels based on his boyhood and youth, poetry, some good short stories on supernatural themes, and investigated the relations of **George IV** and **Mrs Fitzherbert** (from whom he was descended).

L'Esperance, Elise, *née* Strang 1878–1959
US physician and founder of women's cancer clinics

Born in Yorktown, New York, she studied at the Women's Medical College in New York, established by **Elizabeth Blackwell**, receiving her MD in 1900. She worked in paediatrics for some years, then in 1910 she moved to the department of pathology at Cornell University, remaining there until 1932, and becoming the first woman assistant professor in 1920. Her research on cancer stimulated her to found the Kate Depew Strang clinics in memory of her mother. Important work carried out at the Strang clinics included the development by **Dr George Papanicolaou** of the 'Pap' smear to detect cervical cancer. L'Esperance was active in many women's organizations, medical and non-medical, and was widely honoured for her work.

Lespinasse, Julie Jeanne Eléonore de 1732–76
French salon hostess

She was born in Lyons, an illegitimate daughter of the Countess d'Albon. At first a teacher, in 1754 she became companion to the ailing salon hostess, Marquise du Deffand (1697–1780), and whilst living with her formed a deep platonic relationship with the philosopher **Jean le Rond d'Alembert**. From 1764 she broke with the Marquise and created a brilliant salon of her own for the literary figures of her day. She also formed liaisons with the Marquis de More and the Comte de Guibert, to whom she wrote ardent love-letters that have since been published.

Lesseps, Ferdinand, Vicomte de 1805–94
French diplomat and entrepreneur

Born in Versailles, he was a cousin of the Empress Eugénie, wife of Napoleon III. From 1825 he held diplomatic posts in Lisbon, Tunis, Cairo, and other cities. In 1854 he began his campaign for the construction of a Suez Canal, and in 1856 obtained a concession from the viceroy. The works were begun in 1860 and completed in 1869. In 1881 work began on his over-ambitious scheme for a sea-level Panama Canal, but had to be abandoned in 1888. In 1892–93 the management was charged with breach of trust, and sentenced to five years' imprisonment for embezzlement, but the sentence was reversed. He wrote *Histoire du canal de Suez* (1875–79) and *Souvenirs de quarante ans* (1887, 'Forty Years of Memories'). ▢ Charles R L Beatty, *De Lesseps of Suez: The Man and His Time* (1956)

Lessing, Doris May, *née* Tayler 1919–
Rhodesian writer

She was born in Kermanshah, Iran, the daughter of a British army captain, and her family moved to Southern Rhodesia (Zimbabwe) in 1924. From 1937 to 1949 she lived in Salisbury, where she became involved in politics and helped to start a non-racist left-wing party. She went to London in 1949, and her experiences of working-class life there are described in *In Pursuit of the English* (1960). She joined the Communist Party briefly, and left it in 1956, in which year Rhodesia declared her a 'prohibited immigrant'. Her first published novel was *The Grass is Singing* (1950), a study of the sterility of white civilization in Africa. In 1952 *Martha Quest* appeared, the first novel in her sequence *The Children of Violence* (completed in *A Proper Marriage*, 1954, *A Ripple from the Storm*, 1958, *Landlocked*, 1965, and *The Four-Gated City*, 1969). Partly autobiographical, the sequence tells the life story of Martha, discussing contemporary social and psychological problems, and particularly the unattainable ideal of a city where there is no violence. Other works include *The Golden Notebook* (1962) and *Briefing for a Descent into Hell* (1971), both fictional studies of so-called 'mental breakdown', and the short-story collection, *The Story of a Non-marrying Man* (1972). Latterly, she has also attempted science fiction, but her commitment to exploring political and social undercurrents in contemporary society has never wavered and can be seen to potent effect in *The Good Terrorist* (1985). More recent publications include *London Observed* (1992), a collection of short stories, and the autobiographical *Under My Skin* (1994). ▢ R Whittaker, *Doris Lessing* (1988)

Lessing, Gotthold Ephraim 1729–81
German writer

Born in Kamenz, Saxony, he studied theology at Leipzig (1746), then went on to Berlin, where his chief means of support was the *Vossische Zeitung*, to which he contributed criticisms. In 1751 he went to Wittenberg, took his Master's degree, and produced a series of *Vindications* of unjustly maligned or forgotten writers, such as Cardan and Lemnius. He returned to Berlin, and in 1755 produced his classic tragedy *Miss Sara Sampson* (1755). It was based on English rather than French models, and in his contributions to a new critical Berlin journal, '*Briefe, die neueste Literatur betreffend* (1758, 'Letters Concerning the Latest Literature'), he protested against the dictatorship of French taste, combated the inflated pedantry of the Gottsched school, and extolled Shakespeare. His famous critical treatise defining the limits of poetry and the plastic arts, *Laokoon; oder, Über die Grenzen der Malerei und Poesie* (1766, Eng trans *Laocoon; or, The Limits of Poetry and Painting*, 1853), was written while he was secretary to the Governor of Breslau (Wrocław, Poland). It was followed in 1767 by his major dramatic work, the comedy *Minna von Barnhelm* (Eng trans *The Disbanded Officer*, 1786). In 1769 he was appointed Wolfenbüttel librarian by the Duke of Brunswick, and between 1774 and 1778 he published the *Wolfenbüttelsche Fragmente eines Ungennanten* ('Anonymous Fragments from Wolfenbüttel'), a rationalist attack on orthodox Christianity from the pen of the theologian Hermann Reimarus (1694–1768) which, universally attributed to Lessing, provoked a storm of refutations. The best of Lessing's counter-attacks were *Anti-Goeze* (1778) and the fine dramatic poem, *Nathan der Weise* (1779, Eng trans *Nathan the Wise*, 1868), a noble plea for toleration. ▢ H B Garland, *Lessing, founder of modern German criticism* (1937)

L'Estrange, Sir Roger 1616–1704
English journalist and pamphleteer

Born in Hunstanton, Norfolk, he narrowly escaped hanging as a Royalist spy for a plot to seize Lynn, in Norfolk, in 1644, and was imprisoned in Newgate, but escaped after four years. Pardoned by Cromwell in 1653, he lived quietly until the Restoration (1660) made him licenser of the press. He produced pamphlets contributing to the debates of his day, and his papers *The Public Intelligencer* (1663–66) and *The Observator* (1681–87) are of journalistic value. He also translated Aesop's Fables, Seneca's *Morals*, Cicero's *Offices*, the *Colloquies* of Erasmus, Quevedo's *Visions*, and Josephus.

Le Sueur, Eustache 1617–55
French painter

He was a pupil of Simon Vouet, whose style he imitated until, about 1645, he came under the influence of Nicolas Poussin's classical style. His most important early work was the decoration of two rooms in the Hôtel Lambert in Paris, while paintings of the life of St Bruno for the Charterhouse of Paris exemplify his late manner. The Louvre possesses 36 religious and 13 mythological pictures by him. He was one of the founders and first professors of the French Royal Academy of Painting (1648).

Le Sueur, Hubert c.1580–c.1670
French sculptor

He was born in Paris, and moved to England about 1628. His best-known work is the equestrian statue of Charles I at Trafalgar Square (formerly Charing Cross) in London (1633). He worked in the Italianate style and in 1631 was sent to Rome to make copies of classical sculpture. He also popularized the portrait bust. His bronze bust of Charles I is in the National Portrait Gallery, London, and he is also known for his monument to the Duke of Buckingham in Westminster Abbey (1628).

Lethaby, William Richard 1857–1931
English architect, designer and teacher

Born in Barnstaple, Devon, he trained as an architect, then worked (1877–87) in the London practice of Norman Shaw. He was a founder of the Art Workers' Guild (1884) and the Arts and Crafts Exhibition Society (c.1886). He was associated with Ernest Gimson in Kenton & Co during the period when he designed his most important building, Avon Tyrrell, near Salisbury, with Gimson plaster ceilings and Kenton furniture. In 1891 he became active in the Society for the Protection of Ancient Buildings, in which Philip Webb was a major influence. The Central School of Arts and Crafts, London, was founded in 1896 with Lethaby and the sculptor, George Frampton, as joint principals. Lethaby was sole principal from 1900 to 1912 and he also taught at the Royal College of Art, London. The emphasis he placed upon workshop practice at the Central School set a precedent for design education, including that at the Bauhaus in Germany.

Lethington, Lord See Maitland, Sir Richard

Lettow-Vorbeck, General Paul Emil von 1870–1964
Prussian officer

He commanded the German forces in East Africa during World War I. Early on in the war, he expanded and reorganized his troops and raided the Uganda railway. He failed to hold the Kilimanjaro area, where most German settlers were located, and fell back to the Tanganyika Central Railway. In 1916 the railway was captured by forces led by General **Jan Smuts** and Lettow-Vorbeck moved south to the Rufiji. He subsequently invaded Portuguese East Africa and Northern Rhodesia and surrendered after the Armistice at Abercorn (now Mbala, Zambia) on 25 November 1918.

Letts, Thomas 1803–73
English bookbinder
He was born in Stockwell, London. After his father's death in 1803 he began to manufacture diaries, and by 1839 was producing 28 different types.

Leucippus 5th century BC
Greek philosopher
Born in Miletus, Asia Minor (or in Elea, Lucania), he was the originator of the atomistic cosmology which **Democritus** later developed and which is most fully expounded in **Lucretius's** great poem *De Rerum Natura*. Leucippus is thought to have written two books, *The Great World System* and *On the Mind*, but his theories and writings are not reliably separable from those of Democritus.

Leuckart, Karl Georg Friedrich Rudolf
1822–98
German zoologist
Born in Helmstedt, he studied at the University of Göttingen, and became Professor of Zoology at the universities of Giessen (1850) and Leipzig (1869). A pioneer of parasitology, he described the complex life cycles of many parasites such as tapeworms and liver flukes, and was able to demonstrate that the disease trichiniasis in man was due to infection by a roundworm. He also showed that the radiata did not comprise a natural group and that the radial symmetry found both in the coelenterates and echinoderms (starfish) did not imply a close evolutionary relationship. Between 1863 and 1876 he wrote his great parasitological treatise *Parasites of Man* (translated 1886).

Leutze, Emanuel 1816–68
US painter
Born in Gmünd, Wüttemberg, Germany, but brought up in the USA, he studied in Europe from 1841 to 1859, then settled in New York City in 1859. His paintings were mainly scenes from American history, the best known of which is *Washington crossing the Delaware*.

Le Vau or Levau, Louis 1612–70
French architect
He was born in Paris, and headed a large studio of artists and craftsmen, producing outstanding Baroque designs for the aristocracy. Among his early works, the Hôtel Lambert, Paris, stands out particularly for the ingenious use of space. His masterful design of Vaux-le-Vicomte (1657–61), with formal landscape by **André Lenôtre**, constituted an influential milestone in French architecture, leading to his Baroque masterpiece of Versailles (from 1661, again with Lenôtre), designed on a palatial scale for court and government. Further works include the Collège des Quatre Nations, Paris (1661), where the Greek Cross plan of the church followed precedents in Rome.

Leven, 1st Earl of See Leslie, Alexander

Levene, Phoebus Aaron Theodor, *originally* Fishel Aaronovich Lenin 1869–1940
US biochemist
Born in Sasar, Russia, he qualified in medicine in St Petersburg in 1891 and emigrated to New York in 1892. His interest soon moved to chemistry, and in 1905 he became a founder-member of the Rockefeller Institute in New York, applying chemistry to biological problems, and spent his career there. The most important of his many biochemical studies is his pioneer research on the nucleic acids. His work established the nature of the sugar component which defines the two types of nucleic acid (RNA, ribonucleic acid; and DNA, deoxyribonucleic acid) before 1930, although it was not until 1953 that newer methods allowed **James Dewey Watson** and **Francis Crick** to deduce the complete structure of the nucleic acids. Levene also published extensively on the chemistry of the sugar phosphates and the optical isomerism of organic substances.

Lever, Charles James 1806–72
Irish novelist
Born in Dublin, of English parentage, he graduated from Trinity College, Dublin, in 1827, and then went to Göttingen to study medicine. His most popular work, *Charles O'Malley* (1841), is a description of his own college life in Dublin. About 1829 he spent some time in the backwoods of Canada and North America, and he later related his experiences in *Arthur O'Leary* (1844) and *Con Cregan* (1849). He practised medicine in various Irish country towns, and in 1840 in Brussels, then returned to Dublin, where he published *Jack Hinton* (1843), and was editor of the *Dublin University Magazine* (1842–45). From 1845 he was again in Europe, where he wrote such novels as *Roland Cashel* (1850), and, completely changing his style, *The Daltons* (1852) and the *Fortunes of Glencore* (1857). He was appointed British vice-consul in Spezia in 1858, and continued to write, producing *Luttrel of Arran* (1865), and some racy essays in *Blackwood's* by 'Cornelius O'Dowd'. In 1867 he was promoted to the consulship in Trieste. He wrote brilliant, rollicking sketches of a phase of Irish life which was passing away, but no doubt his caricatures created a false idea of Irish society and character.
📖 E Donney, *Charles Lever: his life in his letters* (1906)

Leverhulme, William Hesketh Lever, 1st Viscount 1851–1925
English soapmaker and philanthropist
Born in Bolton, Greater Manchester, he worked in his father's grocery business. He then opened new shops and in 1886 with his brother, James, started the manufacture of soap from vegetable oils instead of tallow, and founded the model industrial new town of Port Sunlight. Among his many benefactions, he endowed at Liverpool University a school of tropical medicine and gave Lancaster House to the nation. After World War I he attempted to develop the economy of the Western Isles of Scotland by purchasing the Islands of Lewis and Harris and planning a huge fishing and fish-producing industry there, but withdrew in 1923 after local opposition from the crofters of Lewis. 📖 W P Jolly, *Lord Leverhulme: A Biography* (1976)

Leverrier or Le Verrier, Urbain Jean Joseph
1811–77
French astronomer
Born in St Lô, Normandy, he became teacher of astronomy at the Polytechnique in 1836. His *Tables de Mercure* and several memoirs gained him admission to the Academy in 1846. From disturbances in the motions of planets he inferred the existence of an undiscovered planet and calculated the point in the heavens where, a few days afterwards, Neptune was actually discovered by **Johann Gottfried Galle** at Berlin (1846). Elected in 1849 to the Legislative Assembly, he became counter-revolutionary.

In 1852 Louis Napoleon (Napoleon III) made him a senator and in 1854 he succeeded François Arago as director of the observatory of Paris.

Leverson, Ada 1865–1936
English novelist and journalist

She was born in London. After being educated privately, she became a member of the circle which included Max Beerbohm and Oscar Wilde, whom she bravely supported during his trial in 1895. Wilde referred to her as 'The Sphinx'. Having published literary parodies in *Punch*, she contributed stories for *The Yellow Book* and, as 'Elaine', wrote over 100 columns for *The Referee*. Her six novels, written between 1907 and 1916, include *Love's Shadow* (1908), *Tenterhooks* (1912) and *Love at Second Sight* (1916). Domestic stories of difficult marriages (not unlike her own to the gambler Ernest Leverson), they were republished in one volume as *The Little Ottleys* in 1962. 📖 J Speedie, *Wonderful Sphinx: The Biography of Ada Leverson* (1993)

Levertov, Denise 1923–97
US poet

Born in Essex, England, of a Welsh mother and a Russian Jewish father who became an Anglican clergyman, she was educated privately, and emigrated to the USA in 1948. She was appointed poetry editor of *The Nation* in 1961. *The Double Image* (1946) was her first collection of verse and others appeared regularly. She was outspoken on many issues (including Vietnam and feminism), and her poetry was similarly questioning. Her attachment to the 'Black Mountain' poets like Charles Olson and William Carlos Williams is palpable but her voice is distinctive. *With Eyes at the Back of Our Heads* (1959), *Relearning the Alphabet* (1970), *Footprints* (1972) and *Evening Train* (1992) are particularly notable. Her *New and Selected Essays* were published in 1992. 📖 L Wagner, *Denise Levertov* (1967)

Lévesque, René 1922–88
Canadian statesman

Born in New Carlisle, Quebec, he became a journalist and television commentator and was elected to the Quebec National Assembly in 1960. In 1967 he helped to found the separatist group called Mouvement Souveraineté-Association, which became the Parti Québecois. As president of the party, then premier of Quebec (1976), advocated establishment of a French country which would be independent from English-speaking Canada and, under his plan of 'sovereignty-association', would have its own laws, taxes, and foreign relations programme while maintaining economic unity with the rest of Canada. Although the people of Quebec rejected Lévesque's plan in a popular referendum vote in 1980, he was re-elected premier the following year. He resigned in 1985 due to failing health.

Levi, Primo 1919–87
Italian writer and chemist

He was born of Jewish parents in Turin. He enrolled at Turin University to study chemistry for, as he wrote in *Il sistemo periodico* (1984, Eng trans *The Periodic Table*, 1984), he believed that 'the nobility of Man ... lay in making himself the conqueror of matter'. During World War II he fled into the mountains and tried to help set up a small guerrilla force, but this 'deluge of outcasts' was accidentally discovered and in December 1943 Levi was arrested, turned over to the SS, and despatched to Auschwitz. He was one of the few to survive, partly, after it was discovered he was Jewish because he contracted scarlet fever when the Germans evacuated the camp as the Russians approached. Those 10 months in Auschwitz haunted him for the rest of his life and may have prompted his suicide. His first book, *Se questo è un uomo* (Eng trans *If This Is a Man*, 1959), was completed soon after his return to Turin and

was published in 1947. A graphic account of life in a concentration camp, it is written with a chemist's detached sensibility, making it all the more powerful. He continued to combine his career as a chemist with that of a writer. His best-known book is *Il sistemo periodico*, a volume of memoirs and autobiographical reflections. He was one of the 20th century's most incisive commentators, and his other titles include *La chiave a stella* (1978, Eng trans *The Wrench*, 1987), *Se non ora, quando?* (1982, Eng trans *If Not Now, When?*, 1985) and *Altrui mestiere* (1985, Eng trans *Other People's Trades*, 1985). 📖 Mirna Cicioni, *Primo Levi: Bridges of Knowledge* (1995)

Levi-Civita, Tullio 1873–1941
Italian mathematician

Born in Padua, he studied and became professor there in 1897. From about 1900 he worked on the absolute differential calculus (or tensor calculus) which became the essential mathematical tool in Albert Einstein's general relativity theory. From 1918 to 1938 he was professor in Rome, but was forced to retire by Fascist laws against Jews.

Levi-Montalcini, Rita 1909–
Italian neuroscientist and Nobel Prize winner

She was born and educated in Turin, where she studied medicine, but from 1939 onwards she was prevented, as a Jew, from holding an academic position, and had to continue her studies on nerve growth from a home laboratory. In 1947 she was invited by Viktor Hamburger to Washington University in St Louis, where she was professor from 1958 until 1981, when she moved to Rome. Primarily studying chemical factors that control the growth and development of cells, she isolated a substance now called nerve growth factor that promoted the development of sympathetic nerves. Her work on the factor continued, revealing it had many diverse sources, that it was chemically a protein, and that cells are most responsive to its effects during the early stages of differentiation. This work has provided powerful new insights into processes of some neurological diseases and possible repair therapies, into tissue regeneration, and into cancer mechanisms. In 1986 she shared the Nobel Prize for physiology or medicine with Stanley Cohen. Her autobiography *In Praise of Imperfection* was published in 1988.

Levin, (Henry) Bernard 1928–
English journalist and writer

He has written for various newspapers and magazines in Great Britain and overseas, including *The Times*, the *Observer*, the *Spectator*, the *Daily Mail*, and the *International Herald Tribune*, as well as for radio and television. His books include *The Way We Live Now* (1984), *All Things Considered* (1988), *A Walk Up Fifth Avenue* (1989) and *If You Want My Opinion* (1992).

Levine, James 1943–
US pianist and conductor

Born in Cincinnati, Ohio, he was a child prodigy who made his piano debut with the Cincinnati Symphony Orchestra aged 10, and he studied at the Juilliard School of Music in New York. Finding that he preferred the sociability of conducting to the isolation of solo performance, he became apprentice conductor to George Szell at the Cleveland Symphony Orchestra in 1964 and was soon appointed assistant conductor. In 1971 he made his debut at the Metropolitan Opera in New York, conducting Puccini's *Tosca*, and a year later was named the Met's principal conductor. He became artistic director in 1986; he also makes guest appearances as conductor and pianist throughout the USA and Europe. He specializes in Italian opera, and his conducting style is brilliant but self-effacing—an attempt to draw out the essential qualities of the music rather than to impose his signature on it.

Levison, Mary 1923–
Scottish Presbyterian reformer and minister

Born in Oxford, she studied philosophy at Oxford, and theology at Edinburgh, Heidelberg and Basel, beginning work as a deaconess of the Church of Scotland in 1954. She was assistant chaplain to Edinburgh University before she petitioned the General Assembly in 1963 to be ordained, setting in motion a process of debate which culminated in the Assembly's historic decision of 1968 to permit the ordination of women. Although not herself the first woman minister of the Church of Scotland, Levison had made such a possibility a reality, and earned wide respect for the integrity and intelligence with which she had made her case. She was finally ordained to serve as the assistant minister at St Andrew's and St George's Parish Church in Edinburgh in 1978, and served as the first female chaplain to the Queen (1991–93). She published *Wrestling with the Church* in 1992.

Lévi-Strauss, Claude 1908–
French social anthropologist and philosopher

Born in Brussels, Belgium, he was a graduate in law and philosophy, and became interested in anthropology while lecturing (1934–39) at São Paulo University, Brazil. He subsequently worked in the New School for Social Research in New York before becoming director of studies at the École Pratique des Hautes Études in Paris (1950–74). Since the publication of *Les Structures élémentaires de la parenté* (1949, Eng trans *The Elementary Structures of Kinship*, 1969), he has exerted a considerable influence on contemporary anthropology, establishing a new approach to analysing various collective phenomena such as kinship, ritual and myth. In his extensive four-volume study *Mythologiques* (1964–72, 'Mythologics') he reveals the systematic ordering behind codes of expression in different cultures, and argues that myths are not 'justifications' but are instead attempts to overcome 'contradictions'. *Anthropologie structurale* (vol 1, 1958, Eng trans *Structural Anthropology*, 1963) shows the influence of the structural linguistics of **Ferdinand de Saussure**, Roman Jakobson (1896–1982) and others on Lévi-Strauss's work, and confirms his outstanding contribution to the philosophy of structuralism. More recent publications include *Le Regard éloigné* (1983, Eng trans *The View from Afar*, 1985), *La Potière jalouse* (1985, Eng trans *The Jealous Potter*, 1988) and *Regarder, écouter, lire* (1993, 'Look, Listen, Read'). 📖 R A Champagne, *Claude Lévi-Strauss* (1987)

Levitt, Helen 1913–
US photographer

Born in Brooklyn, New York, she worked for a portrait photographer in the Bronx in 1931, then studied at the Art Students League in New York (1956–57). She was strongly influenced by photographer **Henri Cartier-Bresson**. She began small-camera street photography in 1936, and in 1938 she assisted the photographer **Walker Evans** with his exhibition 'American Photographs' at the Museum of Modern Art, New York. Her photographs have been widely published in such journals as *Time*, the *New York Post* and *Harper's Bazaar*. She has also worked in film, as assistant film cutter with director **Luis Buñuel**, and with **James Agee** and painter and art historian Janice Loeb, she made the films *In the Street* (1945–46) and *The Quiet One* (1946–47). She returned to still photography in 1959 and taught at the Pratt Institute, Brooklyn, in the mid-1970s.

Lévy-Bruhl, Lucien 1857–1939
French philosopher and anthropologist

Born in Paris, he studied at the École Normale Supérieure in Paris and was appointed to a chair in the history of modern philosophy at the Sorbonne in 1904. His early work was in moral philosophy, and he published *La Morale et la science des mœurs* in 1903 (Eng trans *Ethics and Moral Science*, 1905). He went on to develop a theory of

'primitive' mentality in *La mentalité primitive* (1922, Eng trans *Primitive Mentality*, 1923) and several later books. He believed that the mentality of 'primitive' people was essentially mystical and prelogical, differing in kind from the rational and logical thought of the modern West. This view drew him into a sharp exchange with **Émile Durkheim**, and has few adherents today.

Lewald, Fanny 1811–89
German novelist

She was born in Königsberg, Prussia (now Kaliningrad, Russia). Jewish by birth, she became a Lutheran convert in 1828 to marry a young theologian, who died just before the wedding. She was an enthusiastic champion of women's rights, which were aired in her early novels, *Clementine* (1842), *Jenny* (1843) and *Eine Lebensfrage* (1845, 'A Question About Life'). In 1845 she met Adolf Stahr (1805–76), a Berlin critic, with whom she lived until he was free to marry in 1855. Her later works were family sagas, like *Von Geschlecht zu Geschlecht* (1863–65, 'From Generation to Generation') and *Die Familie Darner* (3 vols, 1887, 'The Darner Family'). She wrote records of travel in Italy (1847) and Great Britain (1852), and published an autobiography, *Meine Lebensgeschichte* (1861–63, 'The Story of my Life').

Lewes, G(eorge) H(enry) 1817–78
English writer

Born in London, and educated at Greenwich and in Jersey and Brittany, he went to Germany in 1838, and spent nearly two years there, studying the life, language and literature of the country. On his return to London he started writing for the *Penny Encyclopaedia* and *Morning Chronicle*, and was subsequently a contributor to numerous journals, reviews and magazines, and editor of the *Leader* (1851–54), and of the *Fortnightly* (1865–66), which he himself founded. He was unhappily married, with a family, when in 1854 he began his lifelong affair with **George Eliot**. His other works include two novels, *Ranthorpe* (1847) and *Rose, Blanche and Violet* (1848), and 10 plays, but he is best known for his writings on biography, the theatre, and later the sciences, and in particular his *Life and Works of Goethe* (1855). 📖 A R Kaminsky, *George Henry Lewes as literary critic* (1968)

Lewis, Alun 1915–44
Welsh soldier-poet and short-story writer

He was born in Cwmaman, near Aberdare, educated at the University College of Wales, Aberystwyth, and at Manchester University, and became a lieutenant in the army. His first work, a volume of short stories about army life, was *The Last Inspection* (1942), followed by a volume of poetry, *Raiders' Dawn*, in the same year. He died of gunshot wounds at Chittagong during the Burma campaign. Another volume of verse, ironically entitled *Ha! Ha! Among the Trumpets*, was published posthumously in 1945, followed by a collection of short stories and letters, *In the Green Tree* (1948). 📖 A John, *Alun Lewis* (1970)

Lewis, Sir (William) Arthur 1915–91
British economist and Nobel Prize winner

Born in St Lucia, the West Indies, he was Professor of Economics at Manchester University from 1948 to 1958, during which time he published three works that established his reputation: *Economic Survey 1918–1939*, *The Principles of Economic Planning* and *Overhead Costs* (all 1949). He then became first president of the University of the West Indies (1959–63). From 1963 until his retirement in 1983 he held a chair in economics at Princeton. In 1979 he was awarded the Nobel Prize for economics, with **Theodore Schultz**, for work on economic development in the Third World.

Lewis, Carl 1961–
US track and field athlete

Born in Birmingham, Alabama, he was a brilliant all-round athlete at Houston University (1979–82). He won four gold medals at the 1984 Los Angeles Olympics (100m, 200m, 4×100m relay and long jump), emulating the achievement of Jesse Owens at the 1936 Berlin Olympics. At the 1988 Seoul Olympics he won a gold medal in the long jump and was awarded the 100 metre gold medal after Ben Johnson was stripped of the title. In 1992 at the Barcelona Olympics he acquired two more golds in the long jump and the 4×100 metres relay, and in the 1996 Atlanta Olympics he earned the ninth and final gold medal of his career in the long jump, only the fourth Olympian to win as many.

Lewis, C Day See Day-Lewis, Cecil

Lewis, C(live) S(taples) 1898–1963
British novelist, literary scholar and religious writer
Born in Belfast, he won a scholarship to Oxford in 1916, but served in World War I before entering University College in 1918. His first book of poems, *Spirits in Bondage*, was published in that year. In 1925 he was made a Fellow of Magdalen College, where he headed an informal group of writers known as 'The Inklings', which included J R R Tolkien and Charles Williams. He became a distinguished teacher, and was appointed to the newly created chair of Medieval and Renaissance English at Cambridge in 1954. Having lost his faith at school, he returned to Christianity in the period 1929–31 and won a wide popular audience during World War II for his broadcast talks (collected as *Mere Christianity*, 1952) and his books on religious subjects, notably *The Screwtape Letters* (1940). His most important adult novels are the science-fiction trilogy *Out of the Silent Planet* (1938), *Perelandra* (1939) and *That Hideous Strength* (1945). His series of seven books for children, *The Chronicles of Narnia*, which began with *The Lion, The Witch and The Wardrobe* (1950) and ended with *The Last Battle* (1956, Carnegie Medal), is similarly suffused with Christian allegory and ethics, and is among the most important writing of the 20th century for children. 📖 A N Wilson, *C. S. Lewis: A Biography* (1990); C S Lewis, *Surprised By Joy* (1955)

Lewis, Daniel Day- See Day-Lewis, Daniel

Lewis, Gilbert Newton 1875–1946
US physical chemist
Born in Weymouth, Massachusetts, he was educated at Nebraska University and Harvard and then studied in Germany for two years before taking a post as government chemist in the Philippines. From 1905 to 1912 he taught at the Massachusetts Institute of Technology (MIT), then moved to California University (1912–45). He was a pioneer in taking ideas from physics and applying them to chemistry; his ideas focused on the arrangement of electrons around atomic nuclei. He assumed that all but the lightest elements (H and He) had a pair of electrons surrounding the nucleus, with further electrons (in number to balance the nuclear charge) in groups, a group of eight being especially stable (the noble gases). Bonding between atoms of the lighter elements occurred in such a way that atoms gained or lost outer electrons to create octets, either by transfer (electrovalence) or by sharing (covalence). Noting that nearly all chemical compounds contain an even number of electrons, he concluded that the electron pair is especially important, and a shared electron pair can be equated with a covalent bond. He also defined a *base* as a substance which has a pair of electrons which can be used to complete the stable shell of another atom; and an *acid* as a substance able to accept a pair from another atom, to form a stable group of electrons.

Lewis, Hywel David 1910–92
Welsh philosopher of religion

Born in Llandudno, Gwynedd, he succeeded **Charles Arthur Campbell** as Professor of Philosophy at University College, Bangor. Professor of the History and Philosophy of Religion at King's College London (1955–77), he championed the subject against 'fashions' that might have eliminated it. He was president of Mind and other learned societies, founder-editor of *Religious Studies* (1965–84), and author of many works, including *Our Experience of God* (1959), *The Self and Immortality* (1973), *Persons and Life after Death* (1978), and a trilogy based on his Gifford Lectures: *The Elusive Mind* (1969), *The Elusive Self* (1982), and *Freedom and Alienation* (1985). He also published several books in Welsh, including a volume of poems.

Lewis, Ida 1842–1911
US lighthouse keeper
She was born in Newport, Rhode Island, the daughter of a sea captain who was the lighthouse keeper on Lime Rock in Newport Harbour. She took over her father's duties when he suffered a stroke and she manned the lighthouse for 50 years, performing many rescues which began in 1858 when she saved four men whose boat had capsized. Lewis won public recognition in 1869 and **Susan B Anthony** reported her exploits in her suffrage journal *The Revolution*. She was awarded a gold medal by Congress and a pension by the Carnegie Hero Fund.

Lewis, Jerry, *originally* Joseph Levitch 1926 –
US entertainer
He was born in Newark, New Jersey, into a showbusiness family, and worked on a nightclub act before forming a partnership with singer and straight man **Dean Martin**. They made their film debut in *My Friend Irma* (1949) and became the USA's favourite double-act of the 1950s. A solo performer from 1956, Lewis wrote, produced and often directed a series of anarchic comedies that indulged his love of visual humour and crude slapstick. The most successful of these include *The Bellboy* (1960) and *The Nutty Professor* (1963). A top cabaret performer and tireless fundraiser for muscular dystrophy, he gave a strong dramatic performance in *The King of Comedy* (1982). He continues to make occasional film appearances and starred in a record-breaking tour of the musical *Damn Yankees* (1995–96).

Lewis, Jerry Lee 1935–
US rock and country singer and pianist
He was born in Ferriday, Louisiana. His powerful, energized style and driven personality quickly established him as one of the great originals of rock and roll, and brought him the nickname The Killer. After working as a session musician at Sun Studios in Memphis he was invited to record by the label's founder, Sam Phillips. His 1957 recordings 'Whole Lotta Shakin' and 'Great Balls of Fire' became classics of rock and roll, copied by successive generations of musicians. In 1958 he had further success with 'Breathless' and 'High School Confidential' (the title track to a film in which he appeared). After he married his 14-year-old (some sources say 13-year-old) cousin Myra in 1958 he was effectively boycotted by television and the pop radio stations. In the late 1960s he returned to country music, where he had begun, and was a huge success, but his personal behaviour continued to be erratic, and he had problems compounded by personal tragedies, including the deaths of his son, Jerry Lee Jnr, and two of his wives. Undaunted, he has continued to tour intermittently and record into the 1990s, and made one of the strongest of his many records, *Young Blood*, in 1995. His cousin is the disgraced US television evangelist, Jimmy Lee Swaggart; another cousin, Mickey Giley, is a country singer. 📖 J Lewis and C White, *Killer!* (1993)

Lewis, John L(lewellyn) 1880–1969
US labour leader

Born in Lucas County, Iowa, the son of a Welsh coal-miner, he entered the mines at the age of 15 and rose in union ranks to become president of the Union of United Mine Workers (UMW, 1920–60). When its membership fell to 150,000 in 1933, during the Great Depression, he feared a communist takeover and led a vigorous recruitment drive which succeeded in increasing the membership to 500,000. When, in 1935, he was unsuccessful in his attempts to change the American Federation of Labor's traditional exclusion of unskilled industrial workers, Lewis founded the Committee for Industrial Organizations, which became the Congress of Industrial Organizations (CIO) after its expulsion from the AFL in 1938. He took the coal miners out on several strikes during World War II, and his fiery personality and stubborn drive led to clashes with Presidents **Franklin D Roosevelt** and **Harry S Truman**. As the coal industry declined in the 1950s he adopted a more conciliatory style of negotiation.

Lewis, John Robert 1924–
English marine ecologist
Born in Wallasey, Merseyside, he was educated at the University College of Wales, Aberystwyth, and was appointed to the staff of the zoology department of Leeds University in 1954. In 1965 he took charge of the University of Leeds Wellcome Marine Laboratory, being appointed director in 1972. His major contributions to marine biology included the publication in 1964 of *Ecology of rocky shores*, a descriptive and analytical text which is still considered an essential text in marine ecology worldwide. The book stresses the importance of adaptations to physical factors in determining species' abundance, and distribution and community structure. Lewis also successfully developed and chaired COST 47, a European Community-funded long-term international monitoring project.

Lewis, Lennox 1965–
British boxer
Born in London, he won a gold medal at the 1988 Olympics for Canada, his home country since boyhood. Having turned professional in 1989, he went back to Great Britain and became the European heavyweight champion in 1990. In 1991, he took the British heavyweight title from Gary Mason, and in 1992, after a victory over Donovan 'Razor' Ruddock, was established as the number-one challenger for the world title. In December 1992, he was awarded the World Boxing Council (WBC) title by default (thus becoming Britain's first world heavyweight champion of the century), when Riddick Bowe, the then champion, refused to fight him and was stripped of the title. He retained his title when he defeated Tony Tucker in May 1993.

Lewis, M(atthew) G(regory), *nicknamed* Monk Lewis 1775–1818
English novelist
Born in London, he was educated at Westminster School and Christ Church, Oxford, and in Germany, where he met **Goethe**. In 1794 he was an attaché to The Hague and it was there he wrote *Ambrosio, or the Monk* (1796), a Gothic novel now generally known as *The Monk*, which was influenced by his formative reading of tales of witchcraft and the supernatural, and **Ann Radcliffe**'s *Mysteries of Udolpho*, and which inspired his nickname. Many others in a similar vein followed, including a musical drama, *The Castle Spectre* (1798). He published several volumes of verse, but his best-known poem, 'Alonzo the Brave and the Fair Imogine', appeared in *The Monk*. Concerned about the treatment of the slaves on the estates he had inherited in the West Indies, he went there in 1817, but died of yellow fever on the way home. His *Journal of a West Indian Proprietor* was published in 1834. ▢ L F Peck, *A Life of Monk Lewis* (1961)

Lewis, Meriwether 1774–1809
US explorer
Born near Charlottesville, Virginia, he joined the army and in 1792 led an unsuccessful expedition up the Missouri River. In 1801 he became personal secretary to President **Thomas Jefferson**, and was invited with his long-time friend **William Clark** to lead an expedition (1804–06) to explore the vast unknown lands to the west of the Mississippi. It was to become the first overland journey across North America to the Pacific coast, and one of the longest transcontinental journeys ever undertaken. Considered a triumph for the young nation, the Lewis and Clark expedition strengthened US claims to the Oregon Territory and spurred settlement of the West. Lewis was appointed Governor of the Louisiana Territory in 1806, but only three years later while travelling to Washington he died in a shooting incident in a cabin in Tennessee. ▢ John Logan Allen, *Lewis and Clark and the Image of the American Northwest* (1991); Richard H Dillon, *Meriwether Lewis: A Biography* (1965);

Lewis, Richard, *known as* Dic Penderyn 1807/8–1831
Welsh folk hero
Born near Aberavon, Glamorganshire, he was accused of wounding a soldier during the Merthyr Tydfil riots of 1831, found guilty and publicly executed at Cardiff on 31 August 1831. Many were convinced of his innocence and he became a folk hero in South Wales.

Lewis, Saunders 1893–1985
Welsh dramatist, poet and nationalist
Born in Cheshire, he studied English and French at Liverpool University, became a lecturer in Welsh at University College, Swansea, in 1922, and in 1924 published a study of English influences on classical Welsh 18th-century poetry, *A School of Welsh Augustans*. He was co-founder of the Welsh Nationalist Party (later Plaid Cymru) in 1925, and became its president in 1926. He became a Roman Catholic in 1932. Imprisoned in 1936 for a token act of arson against building materials for construction of an RAF bombing school at Penyberth, he was dismissed from Swansea and made his living by journalism, teaching and farming until his appointment as lecturer (later senior lecturer) in Welsh at University College, Cardiff, in 1952. He published many essays, 19 plays in Welsh and English, poems, novels, and historical and literary criticism, chiefly in Welsh. He retired from public life in 1957, but continued publishing plays, his last being *Excelsior* (1980). ▢ P Davies, *Saunders Lewis* (1950)

Lewis, (Harry) Sinclair 1885–1951
US novelist and Nobel Prize winner
He was born in Sauk Center, Minnesota, the son of a doctor. Educated at Yale University, he became a journalist and wrote several minor works before *Main Street* (1920), the first of a series of bestselling novels satirizing the arid materialism and intolerance of US small-town life. *Babbitt* (1922) still lends its title as a synonym for middle-class US philistinism. Other titles of this period are *Martin Arrowsmith* (1925), *Elmer Gantry* (1927) and *Dodsworth* (1929). From then on he tended to exonerate the ideologies and self-sufficiency he had previously pilloried, but the shift of attitude did nothing to diminish his popularity. His later novels include *Cass Timberlane* (1945) and *Kingsblood Royal* (1947). He refused the Pulitzer Prize for *Arrowsmith*, but accepted the Nobel Prize for literature in 1930, becoming its first US laureate. ▢ M Schorer, *Sinclair Lewis: an American life* (1961)

Lewis, Sir Thomas 1881–1945
Welsh cardiologist and clinical scientist

Born in Cardiff, he received his preclinical training at University College, Cardiff. In 1902 he went to University College Hospital, in London, where he remained as student, teacher and consultant until his death. Ernest Henry Starling stimulated his interest in cardiac physiology and the physician Sir James MacKenzie awakened his curiosity about diseases of the heart. He was the first to master completely the use of the electrocardiogram, and he and his students established the basic parameters which still govern the interpretation of electrocardiograms. Using animal experiments he was able to correlate the various electrical waves recorded by an electrocardiograph with the sequence of events during a contraction of the heart. This enabled him to use the instrument as a diagnostic aid when the heart had disturbances of its rhythm, damage to its valves or changes due to high blood pressure, and other conditions. During his later years he turned his attention to the physiology of cutaneous blood vessels and the mechanisms of pain. He fought for full-time clinical research posts to investigate what he called 'clinical science', and in 1933 changed the name of the journal he had founded in 1909, from *Heart* to *Clinical Science* (1933). His textbooks of cardiology went through multiple editions and translations. He was knighted in 1921.

Lewis, (Percy) Wyndham 1882–1957
English novelist, painter and critic
He was born on a yacht off Amehurst, Nova Scotia, his father being American and his mother English, and he was educated at the Slade School of Art, London. With Ezra Pound he instituted the Vorticist movement and founded *Blast* (1914–15), the magazine which expounded their theories. From 1916 to 1918 he served on the Western Front, as a bombardier, then as a war artist. In the early 1930s, his right-wing sympathies were out of vogue. He emigrated to Canada at the beginning of World War II, returning to London in 1945. In 1951 he went blind. His novels, *Tarr* (1918), *The Childermass* (1928), and *The Apes of God* (1930) are powerful, vivid satires. Other important novels are *The Revenge for Love* (1937) and *Self Condemned* (1954), which is partly autobiographical. *The Human Age* (1955), a trilogy which was conceived with *The Childermass* and continued with *Monstre Gai* and *Malign Fiesta* (both 1955), was modelled in part on Dante and Milton. He also wrote political and critical essays, short stories, and the autobiographies *Blasting and Bombardiering* (1937) and *Rude Assignment* (1950). As a writer he has been ranked by some critics alongside James Joyce, and as a painter, he was one of the foremost experimentalists of his time in British art, and a highly skilled portraitist, painting, among others, Ezra Pound (1938–39), Edith Sitwell and T S Eliot. 📖 J Meyers, *The Enemy: a biography* (1980)

Lewitt, Sol 1928–
US artist
Born in Hartford, Connecticut, he graduated from Syracuse University in 1949 and worked for an architect before emerging as an abstract artist in the early 1960s. Given to abstract 'philosophy' in the 1970s, he made Minimalist sculptures (or 'structures'), but he was already declaring that the concept was more important than the work, the planning more than the execution. His exhibited wall-drawings are therefore afterwards obliterated, but he has given many of them a second life in lithographs and etchings, characterized by geometric shapes and bands of colour. The Musem of Modern Art, New York, mounted a retrospective of his prints in 1996.

Lewontin, Richard Charles 1929–
US geneticist
Born in New York City, he studied at Columbia University, and subsequently held positions at the universities of Rochester, Chicago and Harvard, where he was appointed Professor of Zoology in 1973. He has contributed substantially to the theoretical and experimental dimensions of population genetics. The central theme to his research is how to explain the distribution of variation within and among natural populations. His empirical work has involved detailed studies of the genetics of natural populations of the fruit fly species, and has been dominated by what he has termed 'the struggle to measure variation'. He synthesized much of this work in his influential 1974 book, *The Genetic Basis of Evolutionary Change*. The widespread application of his 1966 gel electrophoresis technique resulted in the discovery of large amounts of variation, and indirectly led to the neutral theory of molecular evolution—that at the molecular level, most evolutionary changes result from mutations with no selective advantages. He has continued to apply technological developments to population genetic problems, carrying out the first study of nucleotide sequence polymorphism in 1983. He has also published widely on human genetics. He was one of the major figures in the development of population genetics in the second half of the 20th century.

Leyster, Judith 1609–60
Dutch painter
Born in Haarlem, she was an exceptionally talented child. She married an artist, Jan Molenaer, in 1636. Probably the best-known 17th-century female painter, she produced lively paintings of revellers including *The Jolly Toper*, which was attributed to Frans Hals (c.1580–1666) until her own monogram was revealed during cleaning. Her self portrait (c.1635) hangs in the National Gallery of Art in Washington, and many of her genre scenes of everyday Dutch life hang in the leading museums of Europe.

Lezama Lima, José 1910–76
Cuban novelist and poet
Brought up against a militaristic background, he was one of Cuba's leading intellectuals in the 1930s, first known as a poet and prose poet. His acknowledged masterpiece is his novel *Paradiso* (1966, Eng trans 1974), which is now required reading for all students of the Latin-American novel in its middle phase. His stature in Cuba was so great that he was left alone, though isolated, when confronted with evidence of his negative sentiments about Fidel Castro's Cuba. 📖 R S Minc (ed), *Latin-American Fiction Today* (1980)

Lhévinne, Josef 1874–1944
US pianist
Born in Oryel, Russia, he studied at the Moscow Conservatory and at the age of 15 played Beethoven's Emperor Concerto with Anton Rubinstein conducting. After playing and teaching in Russia he made his US debut in 1906, and after a period in Berlin (1907–19), emigrated to the USA, where he taught music. He often played two-piano recitals with his pianist wife Rosina (1880–1976).

Lhote, André 1885–1962
French artist, teacher, and writer on art
Born in Bordeaux, he associated with the Cubists and in his painting he combined classic precision of composition and a free, sensitive use of colour. His greatest influence, however, was exerted through his writings, such as *Treatise on Landscape* (1939) and *Treatise on the Figure* (1950), and through his teaching in Paris, where he established the Académie Montparnasse in 1922.

Li, Choh Hao 1913–
US biochemist
Born in Canton, China, he studied at Nanjing University and from 1935 at the University of California at Berkeley, where he became Professor of Biochemistry in 1950. His main work was on the pituitary hormones, isolating

adrenocorticotrophic hormone (ACTH) and by 1956 establishing its molecular structure. Ten years later he had similar success with the growth hormone, somatotropin, which he synthesized in 1970.

Li, Florence Tim Oi 1906–92
Hong Kong Christian and the first Anglican woman priest
She was ordained priest in 1944 to minister to the Anglican congregation in Macao, where she already served as deacon, during the Japanese occupation of South China. This extraordinary wartime measure by the Anglican Bishop of Hong Kong, R O Hall, was disowned by the Archbishop of Canterbury, Geoffrey Fisher, in 1945. Hall refused to suspend Li, so to save him from having to resign, she voluntarily gave up her priestly ministry. Li was appointed a teacher at Canton Theological Seminary. Later, since Hong Kong had made its own decision (1971) to ordain women priests, she was able to celebrate the fortieth anniversary of her ordination in Westminster Abbey in 1984.

Liadov or Lyadov, Anatoli Konstantinovich
1855–1914
Russian composer
He was born in St Petersburg, and trained under **Rimsky-Korsakov**. His works include music for the piano and the vivid nationalist symphonic poems *Baba-Yaga*, *Kikimora* and *The Enchanted Lake*. He also made collections of Russian folk-songs, conducted, and was a professor at St Petersburg.

Liao Zhongkai (Liao Chung-k'ai) 1878–1925
Chinese politician
Born into a Chinese family in the USA, he studied in Japan before becoming the leading financial expert of the Guomindang (Kuomintang) after 1912. Associated with its left wing, he supported the United Front with the communists in 1923, advocating a planned economy along socialist lines. In 1924 he played an important role in setting up both the workers and peasant departments under Guomindang auspices as part of its new strategy of mass mobilization. As the leading Guomindang representative at the Whampoa Military Academy, he also laid the basis for the political commissar system that was to be used throughout the National Revolutionary Army. He aroused opposition from right-wing members of the Guomindang who opposed the United Front, and who may have been involved in his assassination.

Libau or Libavius, Andreas c.1560–1616
German alchemist
Born in Halle, Saxony, he studied at Jena University, taught history and poetry there, and then in the 1590s moved to Rothenberg an der Taube, where he began to teach and write (voluminously) on alchemy. His main work was *Alchemia* (1597), a richly illustrated book which has a claim to be the first chemical textbook; it gives accounts of a range of chemical methods and substances, and vigorously attacks the ideas of **Paracelsus**. However, his philosophical, diffuse and mystical style limited its influence; his *Alchemia* was not translated out of Latin, was more quoted than used, and is more appreciated now as a step from alchemy towards chemistry than it was in his own time.

Libavius, Andreas See **Libau, Andreas**

Libby, Willard Frank 1908–80
US chemist and Nobel Prize winner
Born in Grand Valley, Colorado, he studied and lectured at the University of California at Berkeley, where he became associate professor in 1945. He carried out atom-bomb research (1941–45) on the separation of the isotopes of uranium at Columbia, and from 1945 to 1954 was Professor of Chemistry at Chicago. From 1954 to 1959 he served on the US Atomic Energy Commission. He was awarded the 1960 Nobel Prize for chemistry for his part in the invention of the carbon-14 method of determining the age of an object. He was Professor of Chemistry at California University from 1959 to 1976.

Liberace, *properly* Wladziu Valentino Liberace
1919–87
US entertainer
Born in West Allis, a suburb of Milwaukee, Wisconsin, he was playing piano by ear at the age of four. He appeared as a soloist with the Chicago Symphony Orchestra at 14 and earned a living in nightclubs and at student dances using the stage name Walter Busterkeys. He gradually developed an enduringly successful act of popular piano classics, which he performed with lavish showmanship. He made his film debut in *East of Java* (1949) but his one starring role in *Yours Sincerely* (1955) was not well received. *The Liberace Show* (1952–57), his television series, won him an Emmy as Best Male Personality. Liberace broke all box-office records at the Radio City Music Hall in New York during 1985. His books include *Liberace Cooks! Recipes From His Seven Dining Rooms* (1970) and *The Things I Love* (1976).

Li Bo (Li Po), *also known as* Li Tai Bo (Li T'ai-po)
701–762
Chinese poet
Born in Sichuan (Szechwan) Province, he led a dissipated life at the emperor's court and later became one of a wandering band calling themselves 'The Eight Immortals of the Wine Cup'. Regarded as the greatest poet of China, he wrote colourful verse of wine, women and nature. It is believed that he was drowned while attempting to grasp the Moon's reflection. *Li Tai Bo Juanji* ('The Complete Works') were published in three volumes in 1977. Collections of Li Bo's translated work were published in 1922 and 1973. ▢ A Waley, *The Poetry and Career of Li Po* (1950)

Lichfield, (Thomas) Patrick John Anson, 5th Earl of 1939–
English photographer
Educated at Harrow and Sandhurst, he served in the Grenadier Guards from 1959 to 1962, when he decided to become a professional photographer. After working as an assistant for many years he opened his own studio and since 1981 has achieved success in travel and publicity photography as well as with his many royal portraits. His publications include *The Most Beautiful Women* (1981), *Elizabeth R: a photographic celebration of 40 years* (1991) and his autobiography, *Not the Whole Truth* (1986).

Lichtenstein, Roy 1923–97
US painter
Born in New York City, he studied painting at the Art Students' League in New York, and at Ohio State University, Columbus (1940–43). He served in the US army from 1943 to 1946 before returning to Ohio, where he taught (1946–51). In the mid-1950s he worked in an Abstract Expressionist style, but by 1961, influenced by **Claes Oldenburg**, he was painting enlarged versions of popular magazine advertisements and violent cartoon strips. He duplicated the dot patterns of crude newspaper reproductions in brightly coloured, enlarged form. Regarded as one of the major figures of the Pop Art Movement, his works include *Whaam!* (1963, Tate, London), *As I Opened Fire* (1964, Stedelijk, Amsterdam) and *Little Big Painting* (1965, Whitney Museum of American Art, New York). He was also a sculptor, elevating banal objects to monumental works of art, as with his *Dinnerware Objects* of the 1960s and bronze *Sculptures* of the 1970s.

Lick, James 1796–1876
US financier and philanthropist
Born in Fredericksburg, Virginia, he became a piano-maker. He went to California (c.1848), made a fortune in real-estate investment and founded the Lick Observatory on Mount Hamilton.

Li Dazhao (Li Ta-chao) 1888–1927
Chinese revolutionary
He was one of the founders of the Chinese Communist Party, and his interpretation of Marxism as applied to China had a profound influence on Mao Zedong. Appointed head librarian of Beijing (Peking) University in 1918 and Professor of History in 1920, he had the young Mao as a library assistant, and founded one of the first of the communist study circles which in 1921 were to form the Communist Party. In 1927, when the Manchurian military leader, Zhang Zuolin (Chang Tso-lin), then occupying Beijing, raided the Soviet Embassy, Li was captured and executed.

Liddell, Eric Henry, *known as* the Flying Scotsman 1902–45
Scottish athlete and missionary
Born in Tientsin, China, of Scottish missionary parents, he was educated at Eltham College, London, and at Edinburgh University. At the 1924 Olympics in Paris he would have been favourite to win the 100 metres had he not refused to take part on religious grounds because the heats were to be run on a Sunday (the gold medal was eventually won by Harold Abrahams). Instead, he won the bronze medal in the 200 metres, and then caused a sensation by winning the gold medal in the 400 metres (at which he was comparatively inexperienced) in a world record time of 47.6 seconds. In 1925, having completed his degree in science and a degree in divinity, he went to China to work as a Scottish Congregational Church missionary. During World War II he was interned by the Japanese at Weihsien camp, and there, not long before the war ended, he died of a brain tumour. The story of his athletic triumphs was told in the film *Chariots of Fire* (1981).

Liddell, Henry George 1811–98
English classical scholar
Educated at Charterhouse and Christ Church, Oxford, he was ordained in 1838 and appointed Professor of Moral Philosophy at Oxford. Then headmaster of Westminster School (1846–55), he returned to Christ Church as dean, was Vice-Chancellor of the university (1870–74), and re-signed the deanship in 1891. He is renowned for the *Greek-English Lexicon* (1843), based on the dictionary of German scholar Franz Passow (1786–1883), with Robert Scott (1811–87), Master of Balliol College (1854–70). Liddell also wrote a *History of Rome* (1855). His daughter, Alice, was the little girl for whom **Lewis Carroll**, his colleague at Christ Church, wrote *Alice in Wonderland*.

Liddell Hart, Sir Basil Henry 1895–1970
English military journalist and historian
Born in Paris, he was educated at St Paul's and Cambridge, and served in World War I, retiring from the army in 1927. He was responsible for various tactical developments during the war, and wrote the postwar official manual of Infantry Training (1920). He was military correspondent to the *Daily Telegraph* (1925–35) and *The Times* (1935–39). In 1937 he relinquished his position as personal adviser to the Minister of War to publicize the need for immediate development of air power and mechanized warfare. He wrote more than 30 books on warfare, as well as biographies of **Ferdinand Foch**, **T E Lawrence** and others. He was knighted in 1966.

Liddon, Henry Parry 1829–90
English theologian

Born in North Stoneham, Hampshire, he graduated from Oxford in 1850. Ordained in 1852, he was Vice-Principal of Cuddesdon Theological College from 1854 to 1859. In 1864 he became a prebendary of Salisbury, in 1870 a canon of St Paul's, and Ireland Professor of Exegesis at Oxford (until 1882). An able and eloquent exponent of liberal High Church principles, he was a strong opponent of the Church Discipline Act of 1874, and as warmly supported **William Gladstone's** crusade against the Bulgarian atrocities of 1876. His *Analysis of the Epistle to the Romans* was published in 1893.

Lidman, Sara 1923–
Swedish writer
She was born in Missenträsk, in the far north of the country, and that area was the setting for her early novels such as *Tjärdalen* (1953, 'The Tar Still') and *Hjortronlandet* (1955, 'Cloudberry Land'). She began writing after her studies at the University of Uppsala were ended due to illness. The support for the underdog visible in these novels became more overt as her politics developed in the 1960s after visits to South Africa, Kenya and Vietnam. In the highly acclaimed series of novels beginning with *Din tjänare hör* (1977, 'Thy Servant Heareth'), she returns to her roots and takes as her theme the building of the railways of the north. She has experimented with documentary forms of writing and has also written plays. ▣ J Mawby, in *Writers and Politics in Modern Scandinavia* (1978)

Lie, Jonas Lauritz Idemil 1833–1908
Norwegian novelist and poet
He was born in Eker, near Drammen, and trained as a lawyer, but abandoned law for literature. Like Sir **Walter Scott**, he saw writing first and foremost as a means of paying off debt. His novels, which present realistic portrayals of fisher-life in Norway, include *Den fremsynte* (1870, 'The Visionary'), *Lodsen og hans Hustru* (1874, 'Lodsen and his Wife'), *Livsslaven* (1883, 'One of Life's Slaves') and *Kommandørens Døtre* (1886, 'The Commander's Daughters'). He also wrote fairytales like *Trold* (1891–92, 'Trolls'), and some poetry and plays. He was enormously popular and influential in Scandinavia. ▣ A Garborg, *Jonas Lie* (1925)

Lie, Marius Sophus 1842–99
Norwegian mathematician
Born in Nordfjordeide, he studied at Oslo University, then supported himself by giving private lessons. After visiting **Felix Klein** in Berlin, a chair of mathematics was created for him in Oslo. In 1886 he succeeded Klein at Leipzig University, but returned to Oslo in 1898. His study of contact transformations arising from partial differential equations led him to develop an extensive theory of continuous groups of transformations, now known as Lie groups. This theory has become a central part of 20th-century mathematics and has important applications in quantum theory.

Lie, Trygve Halvdan 1896–1968
Norwegian politician
He was born in Oslo. He was a Labour member of the Norwegian parliament and held several posts, including Minister of Justice and Minister of Supply and Shipping, before fleeing with the government to Great Britain (1940), where he acted as its Foreign Minister until 1945. He was elected first Secretary-General of the UN in 1946, but resigned in 1952 over Soviet opposition to his policy of intervention in the Korean War. He was Minister of Industry (1963–1964) and of Commerce and Shipping from 1964. He wrote *In the Cause of Peace* (1954).

Lieber, Francis 1800–72
US political scientist

Born in Berlin, he went to the USA in 1827 for political reasons and became a naturalized US citizen. He was Professor of History and Political Economy at South Carolina College, Columbia, and Columbia Law School. His *Code for the Government of the Armies of the US* was widely accepted. He also created *Encyclopaedia Americana* (13 vols, 1829–33).

Liebermann, Felix 1851–1925
German legal historian

Born in Berlin, he worked for many years to settle the texts of the Anglo-Saxon legal codes and to elucidate them. His major work, *Die Gesetze der Angelsachsen* (3 vols, 1903–16, 'The Laws of the Anglo-Saxons'), is indispensable for early English legal history.

Liebermann, Max 1847–1935
German painter and etcher

Born in Berlin, he studied at Weimar and in Paris, where he first won fame. In Germany from 1878 he painted open-air studies and scenes of humble life which were often sentimental. Later, however, his work became more colourful and romantic, and, influenced by the French Impressionists, he became the leading painter of that school in his own country.

Liebig, Justus von 1803–73
German chemist

Born in Darmstadt, he studied in Bonn, receiving his doctorate for work at Erlangen (1822). This was followed by two years' study in Paris where he learned techniques of analysis from Joseph Louis Gay-Lussac. In 1824 he was appointed Extraordinary Professor at the University of Giessen, where he set up an institute for training chemists based on his experiences in France. During this period he studied the phenomenon of isomerism and he and Friedrich Wöhler became close friends. He developed improved procedures for the elemental analyses of organic compounds. In his book *Die organische Chemie in Ihre Anwendung auf Agricultur und Physiologie* (1840, Eng trans *Organic Chemistry in its Applications to Agriculture and Physiology*, 1840), he described the process we now know as photosynthesis and considered the value of fertilizers. His book attracted great interest and led to a number of improvements in agricultural practice, including the use of ammonium salts as fertilizers. In 1852 he left Giessen for Munich, where he remained until his retirement.

Liebknecht, Karl 1871–1919
German barrister, politician and revolutionary

The son of Wilhelm Liebknecht (1826–1900), he was a member of the Reichstag from 1912 to 1916. In World War I he was imprisoned as an independent, anti-militarist, social democrat. He was a founder-member with Rosa Luxemburg of the German Communist Party (KPD) in 1918 and led an unsuccessful revolt in Berlin, the 'Spartacus Rising', in January 1919, during which he and Rosa Luxemburg were killed by army officers.

Liebrecht, Felix 1812–90
German writer

Born in Namslau, Silesia, he was Professor of German at Liège (1849–67), and made himself known by articles on the origin and diffusion of folk-tales, and by translations enriched with annotations. Among these are *Basile's Pentamerone* (1846), *Barlaam und Josaphat* (1847) and Dunlop's *Geschichte der Prosadichtungen* (1851, 'History of Prose Writing').

Lieven, Princess Dorothea, *née* von Benkendorf 1784–1857
Russian princess and salon hostess

She married Prince Lieven (1774–1857), the Russian Ambassador in Great Britain, and from 1837 lived mostly in Paris where her salon was much visited by diplomats. Her life is detailed in her *Correspondence with Earl Grey* (1891), *Letters from London* (1902) and *Unpublished Diary* (1925). ⌨ Parry, *The Correspondence of Lord Aberdeen and Princess Lieven* (1939)

Lievensz or Lievens, Jan 1607–74
Dutch historical painter and etcher

Born in Leyden, he was a friend of Rembrandt and shared a studio with him there. He visited England and lived in Antwerp before returning to Holland, where his paintings of allegorical subjects and his portraits became very successful.

Lifar, Serge 1905–86
French dancer and choreographer

Born in Kiev, Ukraine, he became a student and friend of Sergei Diaghilev, whose Ballets Russes he joined in 1923. Following his first important appearance in *La Boutique fantasque*, he danced with Anna Pavlova, Tamara Karsavina and Spessirtzeva, and was critically acclaimed for his roles in, amongst others, Bronislava Nijinska's *Les Fâcheux* (1924), Léonide Massine's *Ode* (1928), and George Balanchine's *Apollon* (1925) and *The Prodigal Son* (1929). He scored his first triumph as a choreographer in Paris with *Créatures de Prométhée* in 1929, the year he became artistic director of the Paris Opera. ⌨ *Ma Vie from Kiev to Kiev: an autobiography* (1970)

Ligachev, Yegor Kuzmich 1920–
Soviet politician

He was born in Novosibirsk. After graduating as an engineer in 1943, he worked in the Urals region before joining the Communist Party in 1944. As party chief (1957) of the new 'science city' of Akademgorodok, he gained a reputation as an austere opponent of corruption. He was brought to Moscow by Nikita Khrushchev in 1961 but, after the latter was ousted in 1964, he was sent to Tomsk, where he was regional party boss for 18 years. However, he became a full member of the Central Committee in 1976, and in 1983 he was promoted to the Secretariat by Yuri Andropov, becoming Ideology Secretary in 1984. With the accession to power of Mikhail Gorbachev in 1985, he was brought into the politburo. He initially served as Gorbachev's deputy, but they became estranged over the issue of reform and, in 1988, he was demoted to the position of Agriculture Secretary. As Gorbachev became more radical, Ligachev became conservative, and in 1990 he was expelled from the Central Committee as well as the politburo. He remained an anti-reform critic even after the USSR collapsed.

Ligeti, Györgi Sándor 1923–
Austrian composer

Born in Dicsöszentmárton, Hungary, he studied and later taught at the Budapest Academy of Music (from 1950). He researched Hungarian folk music and wrote some folksong arrangements, but not until he left Hungary in 1956 did he become seriously interested in composition. After working for a time at the electronics studio in Cologne, he settled in Vienna, developing an experimental approach to composition. His first large orchestral work, *Apparitions* (1958–59), made his name widely known. *Atmosphères* followed in 1961, demonstrating his technique of chromatic complexes, and in *Aventures* (1962) and *Nouvelles Aventures* (1962–65) he used his own invented language of speech sounds. Other works are the choral *Requiem* (1963–65) and *Lux Aeterna* (1966), the orchestral *Lontano* (1967), the Double Concerto for flute, oboe and orchestra (1972), the 'music theatre', *Le Grand Macabre* (1978), *The San Francisco Polyphony* (1996), and music for harpsichord, organ and wind and string ensembles. He has held academic posts in Stockholm, California and

Hamburg, and is a member of the Royal Academy of Arts and the Hamburg Free Academy of Arts. He became an Austrian citizen in 1967.

Light, William 1784–1839
English soldier and surveyor

Born in Kuala Kedah, Malaysia, where his father was the first British superintendent of the protectorate of Penang, he was educated privately in England. He joined the navy and later served as a dragoon in the Peninsular Wars, where his skills were employed in preparing battle maps. In 1824 he married and, with the aid of his wife's wealth, bought a yacht and travelled round the Mediterranean where he made sketches, some of which were later published. In 1834 he took command of the paddle-steamer *Nile* on its voyage to join the new navy of his friend the Pasha of Egypt. At this time he first met John Hindmarsh who later took over the vessel and who also beat Light to the vacant governorship of South Australia. Light was, however, appointed as surveyor-general to the new colony, and laid out the plan for Adelaide. The city was planned with squares and wide streets, the whole surrounded by the first 'green belt' of open spaces and parkland; an early and enduring example of town-planning.

Liguori, St Alfonso Maria de 1696–1787
Italian prelate

Born in Naples, he studied law before taking orders in 1726. He founded the order of Liguorians or Redemptorists with 12 companions in 1732. Bishop of Sant' Agata de' Goti from 1762, he resigned in 1775, and returned to his order. He was canonized in 1839, and declared a Doctor of the Church in 1871. His voluminous writings embrace divinity, casuistry, exegesis, history, canon law, hagiography, asceticism and poetry.

Li Hongzhang (Li Hung-chang) 1823–1901
Chinese statesman, soldier and scholar

Born in Hefei (Hofei), Anhui (Anhwei) Province, he joined the Imperial Army as secretary in 1853, was appointed a provincial judge, and in 1862 Governor of Jiangsu (Kiangsu), out of which, in conjunction with 'Chinese Gordon' (Charles George Gordon), he drove the rebels in 1863. Made a hereditary noble of the third class, he was appointed Governor-General of the Jiang provinces in 1864, and of Zhili (Chihli) in 1870, when he was also appointed Senior Grand Secretary. An advocate of 'Self Strengthening', he founded the Chinese navy and promoted a native mercantile marine. On the outbreak of the war with Japan (1894), Li, in supreme command in Korea, was thwarted by the incompetence, dishonesty and cowardice of inferior officers. The Chinese were swept out of Korea, and Li, whose policy was that of peace, was deprived of his honours and summoned to Beijing (Peking). The disastrous course of events soon compelled the emperor to restore him to honour. Through his efforts the war was brought to a termination in 1895, China ceding Formosa (Taiwan) and paying a war indemnity of £35 million.

Li Hsien-nien See Li Xiannian

Li Hung-chang See Li Hong zhang

Lilburn, Douglas Gordon 1915–
New Zealand composer

Born in Wanganui, he studied under Ralph Vaughan Williams at the Royal College of Music, London, and in 1936 his tone-poem *Forest* won the PdsStg 25 first prize in a competition offered by Percy Grainger. In 1949 Lilburn was appointed lecturer at Victoria University, Wellington. In 1950 he turned to electronic music and in 1970 became Professor of Music and Director of Electronic Music Studies. In his works for voice he collaborated with such leading New Zealand writers as Allen Curnow (1911–),

Robin Hyde (1906–39) and Denis Glover (1912–80). In 1967 he pioneered a series of autograph scores by New Zealand composers and was active in setting up the Archive of New Zealand Music.

Lilburne, John c.1614–1657
English revolutionary

He was born in Greenwich, London. Imprisoned by the Star Chamber in 1638 for importing Puritan literature, he rose in the Parliamentary army, but resigned from it in 1645 over the Covenant. He became an indefatigable agitator for the Levellers during the English Civil Wars, regarded Cromwell's republic as too aristocratic, and demanded greater liberty of conscience and numerous reforms. He was repeatedly imprisoned for his treasonable pamphlets. ▢ Pauline Gregg, *Free-born John* (1961)

Liliencron, Detlev von 1844–1909
German poet and novelist

Born in Kiel, he fought in the Prussian army in 1866 and 1870. He went to the USA but returned to Holstein in 1882, where for a time he held a Civil Service post. He is best known for his lyrics, which are lively and musical. His first volume, *Adjutantenritte* ('The Adjutant's Rides'), appeared in 1883, and others included *Der Heidegänger* (1890, 'The Moors Walker'), *Neue Gedichte* (1893, 'New Poems') and *Gute Nacht* (1909, 'Good Night'). He also wrote novels and a humorous epic poem, *Poggfred* (1896). A selection of translations of his poems was published in 1914 as *Selected Poems*. ▢ O J Bierbaum, *Detlev von Liliencron* (1892)

Lilienthal, Otto 1849–96
German aeronautical inventor, pioneer of gliders

Born in Anklam, he was educated at the trade school at Potsdam and the Berlin Trade Academy. He studied bird-flight in order to build heavier-than-air flying machines resembling the birdman designs of Leonardo da Vinci. He made hundreds of short flights in his gliders, but crashed to his death near Berlin.

Liliuokalani, *also* Lydia Kamakaeha Paki 1838–1917
Last monarch of the Hawaiian Islands

Born in Honolulu, she attended the Royal School conducted by US missionaries and married John Owen Dominis, the son of a Boston sea captain, in 1862, despite her earlier engagement to a Hawaiian prince. She became queen in 1891 on the death of her brother, King David Kalakaua, and attempted to restore the power of the monarchy which had been weakened by the 1887 US-sponsored constitution. In 1893 she proclaimed a new constitution by royal edict and was promptly deposed by wealthy sugar planters (who were mainly from the USA). She wrote songs, including the well-known 'Aloha Oe', and a memoir, *Hawaii's Story by Hawaii's Queen*, published in 1898, the year of Hawaii's annexation by the USA.

Lillee, Dennis Keith 1949–
Australian cricketer

Born in Perth, Western Australia, and hostile in bowling and temperament, he epitomized the move towards the more combative approach to international cricket. An automatic choice for his country when fit, he took 355 wickets in 70 Tests. His attempts to introduce a metal bat (illegal) into Test matches led to well-publicized clashes with the Australian cricketing authorities. He retired in 1984 and his publications include *Over and Out* (1984).

Lillehei, Clarence Walton 1918–
US thoracic and cardiovascular surgeon

Born in Minneapolis, Minnesota, he received his training in medicine, physiology and surgery at Minnesota University. Most of his professional career was spent in the department of surgery there, although he spent seven years (1967–74) at Cornell University Medical Center in

New York City. His pioneering work on open-heart surgery was begun in the early 1950s, before the development of the pump oxygenator made such procedures more reliable. He remained an international figure in cardiac surgery throughout the 1960s and 1970s.

Lilley, Peter 1943–
English Conservative politician

He was born in Kent and educated at Dulwich College and Clare College, Cambridge. After graduating he worked as an economic consultant in industry and was elected Conservative MP for St Albans in 1983. A right-winger, he came to prominence in 1990 when he was appointed Secretary of State for Trade and Industry. In 1992–97 he was Secretary of State for Social Security and introduced controversial proposals for ending the 'dependency culture' of state aid for the unemployed. Following the Conservatives' defeat in the 1997 general election and **John Major**'s resignation, he entered the leadership contest.

Lillie, Beatrice Gladys, *by marriage* Lady Peel
1894–1989
Canadian comic actress

She was born in Toronto and educated in Ontario. Her stage career began in London in 1914 at the Chatham Music Hall. She had begun as a serious singer of drawing-room ballads but turned to comedy, encouraged by André Charlot, and from 1914 she was renowned in music hall and the new vogue of 'intimate revue'. She entertained the troops on leave in World War I, worked with **Noël Coward** in London, and made her debut in the USA in 1932. She entered cabaret in London at the Café Royal (1938). During World War II she entertained the troops and was decorated by General **Charles de Gaulle**. During the 1950s she developed her own television series in the USA. She also appeared in films, such as *Thoroughly Modern Millie* (1967), but was at her best with a live audience.

Lillo, George 1693–1739
English dramatist and jeweller

He was born in London, of mixed Dutch and English Dissenting parentage, and wrote seven plays, including *The London Merchant, or the History of George Barnwell* (1731) and *Fatal Curiosity* (1736), both tragedies. His *Arden of Feversham*, which was published posthumously in 1759, is a weak version of the earlier anonymous play of that title (1592). Among the first to put middle-class characters on the English stage, he had a considerable influence on European drama. 📖T Drucker, *The Plays* (1979)

Lilly, William 1602–81
English astrologer

He was born in Diseworth, Leicestershire, and in 1620 he went to London, where for seven years he served an ancient citizen, whose widow he married. On her death in 1633 he inherited £1,000. He took up astrology, and soon acquired considerable fame and fortune. In 1634 he obtained permission to search for hidden treasure in the cloisters of Westminster, but was driven from his midnight work by a storm which he ascribed to demons. From 1644 till his death he annually issued his *Merlinus Anglicus, Junior*, containing prophecies. In the Civil War he attached himself to the Parliamentary Party as soon as it promised to be successful, and was rewarded with a pension. After the Restoration he was imprisoned for a time, and was reapprehended on suspicion of knowing something about the Great Fire of London in 1666. He wrote nearly 20 works on astrology.

Lily, John See Lyly, John

Lilye or Lily, William c.1466–1522
English grammarian

He was born in Odiham, Hampshire, and after studies at Magdalen College, Oxford, he visited Jerusalem, Rhodes and Italy, learning Greek from refugees from Constantinople (Istanbul). After he had taught for a while in London, Dean **John Colet** appointed him the first headmaster of his new school of St Paul's (1512)—perhaps the first man to teach Greek in London. He had a hand in Colet's *Brevissima Institutio*, which, as corrected by **Erasmus**, and redacted by Lilye himself, was known as the *Eton Latin Grammar*. Besides this he wrote Latin poems (1518) and a volume of Latin verse against a rival schoolmaster (1521).

Limann, Hilla 1934–
Ghanaian diplomat and politician

He was educated in Ghana and then at the London School of Economics and the Sorbonne, Paris, where he gained a doctorate. He was a teacher before joining the Ghanaian diplomatic service as Head of Chancery at Lome (1968–71). He attended many international gatherings while being his country's counsellor at its permanent mission to the UN in Geneva (1971–75) and senior officer in the Ministry of Foreign Affairs (1975–79). In 1979 he was chosen to lead the People's National Party and elected President. He was removed from office as a result of a military coup led by **Jerry Rawlings** (1981).

Limburg or Limbourg, Pol and Jehanequin and Hermann de fl.early 15th century
Flemish miniaturists

They were three brothers, who were taken prisoner as youths in Brussels in wartime, on their way home from Paris. They were released by the Duke of Burgundy and attached to his household as painters. In 1411 they became court painters to the Duke of Berri and produced 39 illustrations for his celebrated manuscript, *Très Riches Heures du Duc de Berri*, one of the greatest masterpieces of the international Gothic style. Other works have been attributed to Pol de Limburg, including *Heures d'Ailly*, two pages of the Turin-Milan Hours and several in a book of Terence.

Limón, José 1908–72
US dancer, choreographer and teacher

Born in Culiacan, Mexico, he went to New York, where he decided to become a dancer. Studies with **Doris Humphrey** and **Charles Weidman** led to his joining their company as a dancer (1930–40). He formed his own group in 1946, appointing his mentor, Doris Humphrey, as artistic director. In 1950 the José Limón Company was the first US modern dance group to tour Europe. Throughout the 1950s and 1960s it was one of the USA's most impressive modern dance companies, and toured the world. His choreography includes *La Malinche* (1949), *The Moor's Pavanne* (1949, one of his most well-known works), *The Traitor* (1954), *There is a Time* (1956), *Missa Brevis* (1958), the all-male *The Unsung* (1970) and *Carlotta* (1972). His company survived after his death and is still based in New York.

Limousin or Limosin, Léonard c.1505–1577
French painter in enamel

Born in Limoges, he was court painter from 1530 to **Francis I**, who appointed him head of the royal factory at Limoges.

Lin, Maya Ying 1959–
US architect

Born in Athens, Ohio, into a family of artists and intellectuals who had immigrated from China, she studied architecture at Yale. While still a student she entered and won the design competition for the Vietnam Veterans Memorial in Washington DC. Her design consisted of two black granite walls inscribed with the names of the dead, built into the earth and joining in a shallow V, and it

Lincoln, Abraham 1809–65
16th President of the USA

Abraham Lincoln was born in a log cabin near Hodgenville, Kentucky, the son of a restless pioneer. The family eventually settled in south-west Indiana in 1816. Two years later Abraham's mother died and his father remarried shortly afterwards. His stepmother encouraged education, although there was little schooling in the backwoods country. In 1830 the Lincolns moved on to Illinois and Abraham went to work as a clerk in a store at New Salem. He already had political ambitions, and saw the need to study law and grammar. He won election to the legislature in 1834, and began the practice of law in 1836. At Springfield, in 1842, he married Mary Todd (1818–82).

In 1846 he sat in congress; but professional work was distracting him from politics when in 1854 **Stephen A Douglas** repealed the Missouri Compromise of 1820, and reopened the question of slavery in the territories. The bill roused intense feeling throughout the North, and Douglas defended his position in a speech at Springfield in October. Lincoln delivered in reply a speech which first fully revealed his power as a debater. He was then elected to the legislature. When the Republican Party was organized in 1856 to oppose the extension of slavery, Lincoln was its most prominent leader in Illinois, and the delegates of his state presented him for the vice-presidency.

In 1858 he stood as candidate for the Illinois seat against Douglas. Lincoln lost, but his views attracted the attention of the whole country. In May 1860 the Republican convention on the third ballot nominated him for the presidency. The Democratic Party was divided between Douglas and **John Cabell Breckinridge**. After an exciting campaign Lincoln won a comfortable majority. At his inaugural address on 4 March, he declared the Union perpetual, argued the futility of secession, and expressed his determination that the laws should be faithfully executed in all the states. South Carolina had left the Union, and the six gulf states had formed the Confederate States of America. Not even Lincoln's oratorical skills and conciliatory efforts could prevent the impending conflict and

on 12 April 1861, the Civil War began with the Confederate attack on Fort Sumter in Charleston harbour. Lincoln defined the issue of the war in terms of national integrity, not antislavery, a theme he restated in the Gettysburg Address of 1863. Nonetheless, the same year he proclaimed freedom for all slaves in areas of rebellion, and he continued the theme in his re-relection campaign of 1864.

In the Republican Convention in June, Lincoln was unanimously nominated for a second term, and in November was re-elected. In his second inaugural address, in March 1865, he set forth the profound moral significance of the war. On Good Friday, 14 April, at Ford's Theatre, Washington, he was shot by **John Wilkes Booth**, an actor, and he died the next morning.

Lincoln was fair and direct in speech and action, steadfast in principle, sympathetic and charitable, a man of strict morality, abstemious and familiar with the Bible, though not a professed member of any church.

📖 Lincoln's *Collected Works* are to be found in several editions. These include his eloquent speeches: the *Emancipation Proclamation* of 1862, the *Gettysburg Address* of 1863 when first were heard these words, 'government of the people, by the people, for the people', and the *Inaugural Address* of 1865.

📖 Dwight G Anderson, *Abraham Lincoln: The Quest for Immortality* (1982); Lord Longford, *Abraham Lincoln* (1974); Albert J Beveridge, *Abraham Lincoln, 1809–1958* (2 vols, 1928).

> 'With malice toward none, with charity for all, with firmness in the right, as God gives us to see the right, let us strive on to finish the work we are in, to bind up the nation's wounds, to care for him who shall have borne the battle, and for his widow and his orphan, to do all which may achieve and cherish a just and lasting peace among ourselves, and with all nations.' From his second inaugural address, 4 March 1865, a month before the end of the Civil War.

was denounced by veterans'groups who called it a 'wall of shame'. Dedicated in 1982, it subsequently became, as she conceived it, a place of pilgrimage, where mourners, who leave tokens and messages, are reflected in the polished stone. Her design for the Civil Rights Memorial (1989) in Montgomery, Alabama, is almost as powerful, and uses flowing water to illustrate Martin Luther King's biblical invocation: 'justice rolls down like waters and righteousness like a mighty stream'.

Linacre, Thomas c.1460–1524
English humanist and physician

Born in Canterbury, he studied at Oxford, was elected Fellow of All Souls in 1484, and went to Italy, where he learned Greek, and took his MD at Padua. **Erasmus** and Sir **Thomas More** were both taught Greek by him. Around 1500 **Henry VII** made him tutor to Prince **Arthur**. As king's physician to Henry VII and **Henry VIII** he practised in London. In 1518 he founded the Royal College of Physicians, of which he became the first president. Late in life he took holy orders. Linacre was one of the earliest champions of the 'New Learning'. He translated several of **Galen's** works into Latin, and wrote grammatical treatises. 📖 Francis Maddison, Margaret Pelling and Charles Webster (eds), *Essays on the Life and Work of Thomas Linacre* (1977)

Lin Biao (Lin Piao) 1908–71
Chinese soldier and politician

Born in Wuhan, Hubei (Hupeh) Province, he was the son of a factory owner. In 1926 he joined the Communists to fight the Guomindang (Kuomintang), becoming Commander of the Northeast People's Liberation Army in 1945. He became Defence Minister in 1959 and emerged from the Cultural Revolution of 1966 as second-in-command to **Mao Zedong**, being appointed a party Vice-Chairman and formally designated as Mao's heir and successor at the congress of 1969. However, in 1971, Lin formulated 'Project 571'designed to assassinate Chairman Mao and seize power in a military coup. This plot was uncovered and Lin was killed in 1971 in a plane crash over Outer Mongolia while attempting to flee to the Soviet Union.

Lincoln, Abraham See panel above

Lincoln, Benjamin 1733–1810
American Revolutionary general

Born in Hingham, Massachusetts, he became major-general in the Continental Army, reinforcing **Washington** in 1776 after the defeat on Long Island. In 1777 he received command of the southern department. In 1780, besieged by **Henry Clinton** in Charleston, he was compelled to capitulate. After his release in an exchange of prisoners, he took part in the Siege of Yorktown (1781) and was Secretary of War (1781–83). He later commanded the soldiers suppressing **Daniel Shays's** Rebellion in Massachusetts (1787).

Lincoln, Mary Todd 1818–82
US First Lady, wife of President Abraham Lincoln

Born in Lexington, Kentucky, she was courted by Lincoln while living with her sister in Springfield, Illinois, and though their engagement was once broken, she married him in 1842. She was a sensitive, vivacious woman with a streak of neurosis, and although tales of the Lincolns' incompatibility as a married couple may be apocryphal, it is certain that the deaths of three of their four sons, especially 12-year-old Willie in 1862, brought them much unhappiness. During their years in the White House she was attacked for her extravagance and unfairly accused of disloyalty to the Union because of her Kentucky origins and brothers fighting on the Confederate side, and her husband's assassination, which occurred as she sat next to him in Ford's Theatre (1865), unhinged her completely. For much of the remainder of her life she was plagued by the paranoiac conviction that she was in dire poverty and at the same time by the compulsion to shop constantly. She was committed to a mental institution (1875) by her surviving son, Robert Todd Lincoln, but then was declared sane the following year.

Lind, James 1716–94
Scottish physician

Born in Edinburgh, he served in the navy as a surgeon's mate, then after qualifying in medicine at Edinburgh, became physician at the Royal Naval Hospital at Haslar. In 1747 he conducted a classic therapeutic trial, dividing 12 patients suffering from scurvy into six groups of two, treating each group with a different remedy. The two sailors given two oranges and a lemon each day responded most dramatically. His work on the cure and prevention of scurvy helped induce the Admiralty in 1795 at last to issue the order that the navy should be supplied with lemon juice, and during the Napoleonic Wars the British navy suffered far less scurvy than the French. Lind also stressed cleanliness in the prevention of fevers, and wrote major treatises on scurvy, fevers and the diseases encountered by Europeans in tropical climates.

Lind, Jenny, *originally* Johanna Maria Lind 1820–87
Swedish soprano

Born in Stockholm, she went to the court theatre school of singing at the age of nine. After lessons in Paris, she made her debut in Stockholm (1838) and attained international popularity. Known as the 'Swedish nightingale', she founded and endowed musical scholarships and charities in Sweden and in England, where she lived from 1856, and became Professor of Singing at the Royal College of Music (1883–86).

Lindau, Paul 1839–1919
German writer

Born in Magdeburg, he founded the journals *Die Gegenwart* (1872, 'The Present') and *Nord und Süd* (1877, 'North and South'), and wrote books of travel and works of criticism. However, he is better known as a writer of plays and novels. The most successful of the former is perhaps *Maria und Magdalena* (1872, Eng trans 1874). The novels include *Herr und Frau Bewer* (1882) and *Berlin* (1886–87).

Lindbergh, Charles Augustus 1902–74
US aviator

Born in Detroit, he worked as an airmail pilot on the St Louis–Chicago run. In May 1927 he made the first nonstop solo transatlantic flight from New York to Paris in a Ryan monoplane named *Spirit of St Louis* in 33 hours, for which he was awarded the Congressional Medal of Honour. During World War II he advocated US neutrality. His autobiography, *The Spirit of St Louis* (1953), won the Pulitzer Prize in 1954. His wife, Anne Morrow

Lindbergh (b.1906), wrote *North to the Orient* (1935), *Listen, the Wind* (1938), *Gift from the Sea* (1955), *Earthshine* (1970) and others. 📖 Brendan Gill, *Lindbergh Alone* (1977)

Lindblad, Bertil 1895–1965
Swedish astronomer

Born in Örebro, he studied at the University of Uppsala, where he started his work on the problem of distinguishing giant and dwarf stars of the same spectral type. From 1920 to 1922 he worked on two-dimensional stellar classification, leading to valuable results on the space density of common stars, and in 1925 he proposed the idea that our galaxy rotates around a distant centre. He then embarked on the study of external spiral galaxies. He was appointed director of the Observatory of the Swedish Academy in Stockholm in 1927 and established a magnificent new observatory in Saltsjöbaden (1931). His many honours included three honorary doctorates and gold medals from the Royal Astronomical Society (1948) and the Astronomical Society of the Pacific (1954). He was a highly esteemed president of the International Astronomical Union between 1948 and 1952.

Lindemann, Frederick Alexander See Cherwell, 1st Viscount

Linden, Johannes van der 1756–1835
Dutch judge and jurist

He practised in Amsterdam, where he became a judge, and is remembered in South Africa for his *Rechtsgeleerd Practicaal en Koopmans-Handboek* (1806). Sometimes called *The Institutes of the Law of Holland*, in 1852 it was made the official law book of the South African Republic. He also wrote a supplement to Books 1–11 of Johannes Voet's *Commentarius*, and prepared a code of civil law for the Netherlands in which he attempted to codify Roman-Dutch law, but which was not adopted.

Linderstrøm-Lang, Kaj Ulrik 1896–1959
Danish biochemist

Born in Copenhagen, he trained at the city technical college before joining the Carlsberg Laboratory as assistant to Søren Sørensen, who he succeeded as professor and head of the chemistry department. He first titrated the dissociable protons from proteins using the hydrogen electrode to measure pH, and in 1927 used organic solvents to lower the dissociation constant (pK) of an ionizing group. His work on digestive enzymes led him into a major study of protein structure. He found that the rate at which the protons of a polypeptide exchanged with the medium reflected the protein's inherent structural instability, and he subsequently classified globular protein structure into three divisions (1951): primary (amino acid-based bridges), secondary (based on hydrogen bonding) and tertiary (folding to form the active protein) which has become the basis of all modern teaching on this subject. In 1935 Linderstrøm-Lang was elected to the Danish Royal Society as its youngest member. He became a Foreign Member of the Royal Society in 1956.

Lindgren, Astrid 1907–
Swedish children's novelist

She was born in Vimmerby, and established her reputation with *Pippi Långstrump* (1945, Eng trans *Pippi Longstocking*, 1954). She wrote at least 50 more books, including *Mästerdetektiven Blomkvist* (1946, Eng trans *Bill Bergson Master Detective*, 1951), but none has eclipsed its popularity. *Samuel August från Seudstorp och Hanna: Hult* (1975) portrays her parents, who raised the illegitimate child she had at 18. 📖 V Edström, *Astrid Lindgren* (1987)

Lindley, John 1799–1865
English botanist and horticulturist

Born in Catton, near Norwich, Norfolk, he was the son of George Lindley, a nursery gardener and author of *Guide to Orchard and Kitchen Garden* (1831). He was appointed assistant secretary to the Horticultural Society of London in 1827, and was Professor of Botany at University College London (1829–60). In 1828 he prepared a report on the royal gardens at Kew which saved them from destruction and led to the creation of the Royal Botanic Gardens. The most important of his many publications were those on orchids, and *The Vegetable Kingdom* (1846).

Lindrum, Walter 1898–1960
Australian billiards player
Born in Kalgoorlie, Western Australia, he set the current world break record of 4,137 while playing Joe Davis in 1932, at Thurston's Hall, London. He competed in only two world championships (1933–34) and won both. He retired from competitive play in 1950.

Lindsay, Sir David See Lyndsay, David

Lindsay, Jack 1900–90
Australian poet, novelist, historian and translator
Born in Melbourne, the eldest son of artist and writer Norman Lindsay and brother of Philip Lindsay, he published his first book of verse, *Fauns and Ladies*, in 1923. He co-founded the Fanfrolico Press for which he translated many classics with his father contributing illustrations. He went to live in England in 1926 where the Press prospered. During World War II he published more verse, *Second Front* (1944), and war novels such as *We Shall Return* (1942). He achieved international respect as an historian and produced impressive critical studies of artists such as J M W Turner and Paul Cézanne in the 1960s. Well-known for historical novels such as *Light in Italy* (1941), he also wrote novels of contemporary life, like *Rising Tide* (1953), further verse including *Peace is Our Aim* (1950), and three volumes of autobiography, *Life Rarely Tells* (1958), *The Roaring Twenties* (1960) and *Fanfrolico and After* (1962). *Blood Vote*, his World War I novel set in Brisbane, was written in 1937, mislaid by the author, rediscovered and eventually published in 1987.

Lindsay, (John) Maurice 1918–
Scottish poet, critic and editor
Born in Glasgow, he was educated at Glasgow Academy and trained as a musician at the Scottish National Academy of Music. He worked as drama and music critic for the *Bulletin*, Glasgow (1946–60), then worked with Border Television (1961–67), first as programme controller and latterly as chief interviewer. He was director of the Scottish Civic Trust (1967–83), then consultant (1983–), and in 1983 was made honorary Secretary General of Europa Nostra. His major works are his critical treatments of Robert Burns and his *History of Scottish Literature* (1977). His own poetry was first published in *The Advancing Day* (1940) and the best of his work is brought together in *Collected Poems* (1979). Later publications include *Thankyou for Having Me: a personal memoir* (1983) and *Glasgow 1837* (1989).

Lindsay, Norman Alfred William 1879–1969
Australian artist and writer
Born in Creswick, Victoria, into a celebrated family of Australian artists, his diverse (and now dated) novels mostly portray aspects of a Rabelaisian Melbourne peopled by drunken but lovable artists and disapproving clergy. They include *A Curate in Bohemia* (1913), the rollicking *A Cautious Amorist* (1932), *Age of Consent* (1938) and *The Cousin from Fiji* (1945). His children's book *The Magic Pudding* (1918) stars hero Bunyip Bluegum, a perennial favourite with adults too. Some of his novels were banned and his art too was highly controversial. An eloquent champion of the pleasures of the flesh and of artistic freedom, he joined battle with middle-class Australia

through his writings, book illustrations, fine pen drawings and paintings. His sons were the writers Jack and Philip Lindsay.

Lindsay, Philip 1906–58
Australian historian, biographer, novelist and film writer
The son of Norman Lindsay and brother of Jack Lindsay, he published an early collection of verse then followed Jack to England to pursue a journalistic career. He began a series of picaresque novels with a tale of the buccaneer Captain Henry Morgan in *Panama is Burning* (1932). His books, that mainly deal with various periods of British history, include *Gentleman Harry Retires* (1936), *Pudding Lane* (1940), *The Devil and King John* (1942) and his last, *Rusty Sword* (1946). A respected medievalist, he also wrote the Lives of English kings Henry V (1934) and Richard III (1939), and of Australian batsman Don Bradman (1951).
📖 *I'd Live the Same Life Over* (1940)

Lindsay, Robert, *originally* Robert Lindsay Stevenson 1949–
English actor
Born in Ilkeston, Derbyshire, he trained at RADA and took over David Essex's role of Jesus in the London musical *Godspell* (1972). His subsequent stage roles include Bill Snibson in *Me and My Girl* (West End and Broadway, 1985–87, winning him a Tony award), Henry II in *Becket* (1991–92) and the title role in *Cyrano de Bergerac* (1992–93). On television, he played Jakey Smith in *Get Some In* (1975–76), Wolfie Smith in *Citizen Smith* (1977–80), Pete Dodds in *Seconds Out* (1981–82), Micky Noades in *Give Us a Break* (1983), Edmund in *King Lear* (1984), Michael Murray in *G.B.H.* (1991) and Jamie Diadoni in *Jake's Progress* (1995). He was also in the films *That'll Be the Day* (1973), *Bert Rigby, You're a Fool* (1988) and *Loser Takes All* (1989).

Lindsay, (Nicholas) Vachel 1879–1931
US poet
Born in Springfield, Illinois, into an evangelical family, he studied painting in Chicago and New York, and from 1906 travelled the USA like a troubadour, reciting his poems in exchange for hospitality. He won fame during the World War I era and began to attract large audiences to his readings. Highly rhythmic and influenced by ragtime, band music and the cadences of evangelical preaching, his best work appears in *General William Booth Enters Into Heaven* (1913) and *The Congo* (1914). His later volumes of verse were less successful, and, suffering from depression, he returned to Springfield and committed suicide.
📖 E Ruggles, *The West-Going Heart* (1959)

Lindwall, Ray (mond Russell) 1921–96
Australian cricketer
He was born in Sydney. A classic fast bowler, with Keith Miller he formed an invincible Australian opening attack in the five years after World War II. He took 228 wickets in 61 Tests, and also scored more than 1,500 runs including two Test centuries.

Lineker, Gary Winston 1960–
English footballer and commentator
Born in Leicester, he turned professional with Leicester City in 1978. He made his debut for England in 1984, moved to Everton the following year, and then, another year on, to Barcelona. In 1989 he came back to the UK when he signed for Tottenham Hotspur, and then made the last move of his playing career with his transfer to Grampus Eight of Nagoya, Japan, in 1993. He was the top scorer in the 1986 World Cup, and by the time of his retiral from international football in 1991 had scored 48 goals for England, one short of Bobby Charlton's record 49. In 1992 he was voted Footballer of the Year by the Football Writers Association and regularly appears presenting BBC Sports programmes on television.

Ling, Per Henrik 1776–1839
Swedish author and fencing master

Born in Ljunga, Småland, he produced many now-forgotten romantic works on Norse themes but his gymnastic system, developed in Lund from 1804, achieved worldwide popularity as the 'Swedish System'. He founded the Gymnastic Institute in Stockholm in 1813 and became a member of the Swedish Academy in 1835.

Lingen, Ralph Robert Wheeler Lingen, Baron 1819–1905
English civil servant

Born in Birmingham and educated at Trinity College, Oxford, he became a Fellow of Balliol College, Oxford, (1841) and honorary Fellow of Trinity College, Oxford (1886). He studied law at Lincoln's Inn and was called to the Bar in 1847. He was Secretary to the Education Office (1849–69) and Permanent Secretary of the Treasury (1869–85). The controlling executive force during the creation of the elementary education system, he was always a vigilant guardian of the public purse. He issued the code implementing 'payment by results' as proposed by the Newcastle Commission on Elementary Education (1858–61) and was held by contemporaries to be responsible for the revised Code of 1862. The Revised Code was considered by many to have had deleterious, restricting effects on education in Great Britain far into the 20th century.

Linh, Nguyen Van See Nguyen Van Linh

Lini, Walter Hadye 1942–
Vanuatuan politician and priest

Born on Pentecost Island, he trained for the Anglican priesthood in the Solomon Islands and New Zealand, and then joined the New Hebrides National Party, later renamed the Vanuaaku Pati (VP), campaigning for the return of land to the Aboriginal population. He became Chief Minister in 1979 and, on independence in 1980, Prime Minister of the new republic of Vanuatu. On the bases of a controversial non-aligned foreign policy and a 'Melanesian socialist' domestic programme, he was re-elected in 1983 and 1987, and survived an unconstitutional challenge to his leadership, engineered by the now imprisoned President Sokomanu, in 1988. The Vanuaaku Pati split in 1991 and were defeated in elections that year, when a coalition government was formed. Jean Marie Leye was elected President in 1992, and in 1995 Lini was created deputy Prime Minister. He published *Beyond Pandemonium* in 1980.

Linklater, Eric 1899–1974
Scottish novelist

He was born in Penarth, Wales, the son of a shipmaster. His paternal ancestors were Orcadian and he spent much of his childhood on the islands, returning there in later life. He was educated at the grammar school and university in Aberdeen, and served in World War I as a private in the Black Watch. In the mid-1920s he worked as a journalist on the *Times of India*, returning to Aberdeen as assistant to the Professor of English (1927–28). A Commonwealth fellowship took him to the USA from 1928 to 1930, after which he had a varied career as a broadcaster and a prolific writer of novels, popular histories, books for children (*The Wind on the Moon* was awarded the Carnegie Medal in 1944), plays and memoirs. *Juan in America* (1931), a picaresque classic, is his most enduring novel. His other novels include *White Maa's Saga* (1929), *Magnus Merriman* (1934), *Juan in China* (1937), *Private Angelo* (1946), *The Ultimate Viking* (1955) and *The Voyage of the Challenger* (1972). *The Man on My Back* (1941), *A Year of Space* (1953) and *Fanfare for a Tin Hat* (1970) are autobiographical. 📖 M Parnall, *Eric Linklater: a critical biography* (1984)

Linley, Thomas 1732–95
English composer

Born in Wells, Somerset, he taught singing and conducted concerts at Bath early in his career. In 1775 **Richard Brinsley Sheridan** induced him to set his comic opera *The Duenna* to music. In 1776 they and a successful physician, James Ford, bought **David Garrick**'s share of Drury Lane Theatre, London. During the next 15 years Linley was its musical director, composing songs, operas, cantatas and madrigals. Of his sons, Thomas (1756–78), a friend of **Mozart**, possessed great musical talent, and William (1767–1835) composed glees and songs. His daughter, Elizabeth Ann (1754–92), a singer, married **Sheridan**.

Linna, Väinö 1920–92
Finnish novelist

Born in Vrjala, he worked in a factory at Tampere before starting to write. His best-known works are *Tuntematen sotilas* (1954, Eng trans *The Unknown Soldier*, 1957), a controversial novel about the Russo-Finnish War, and his trilogy *Tä ällä Pohjantähden alla* (1959–62, 'Here Under the North Star'), about Finnish independence in 1918. He gave up fiction writing in the early 1960s. 📖 N Stormbom, *Väinö Linna* (1963)

Linnaeus, Carolus, *originally* Carl von Linné 1707–78
Swedish naturalist and physician

Born in Råshult, he studied botany at Uppsala University, where he was appointed lecturer in 1730. He explored Swedish Lapland (1732), publishing the results in *Flora Lapponica* (1737), then travelled in Sweden and went to Holland to study medicine (1735). In Holland he published his system of botanical nomenclature in *Systema Naturae* (1735), followed by *Fundamenta Botanica* (1736), *Genera Plantarum* (1737) and *Critica Botanica* (1737), in which he used his so-called 'sexual system' of classification based on the number of flower parts, for long the dominant system. His major contribution was the introduction of binomial nomenclature of generic and specific names for animals and plants, which permitted the hierarchical organization later known as systematics. He returned to Sweden in 1738 and practised as a physician in Stockholm, and in 1741 became Professor of Medicine and Botany at Uppsala. In 1749 he introduced binomial nomenclature, giving each plant a Latin generic name with a specific adjective. His other important publications included *Flora Suecica* and *Fauna Suecica* (1745), *Philosophia Botanica* (1750), and *Species Plantarum* (1753). His manuscripts and collections are kept at the Linnaean Society in London, founded in his honour in 1788. The founder of modern scientific nomenclature for plants and animals, in his time he had a uniquely influential position in natural history. 📖 Wilfred Blunt, *The Compleat Naturalist: A Life of Linnaeus* (1971)

Linney, Romulus 1930–
US playwright

Born in Philadelphia and raised in the South, he was educated at Oberlin College and trained at the Yale School of Drama. He has taught at numerous institutions, including the universities of Pennsylvania, Princeton and Columbia. A dramatist whose works are too various to be easily classified, he has written a series of historical plays such as *The Sorrows of Frederick* (1966), *Childe Byron* (1977) and *'2'* (1990), which paint real and immediate portraits of Frederick-William II of Prussia, Lord **Byron** and Hermann Goering respectively. Other plays, notably *Holy Ghosts* (1977) and *Heathen Valley* (1988), focus on life in the South. He has won two Obie awards, the first in 1980 for his play *Tennessee* and the second in 1992 for sustained excellence in playwriting.

Linowitz, Sol Myron 1913–
US lawyer, diplomat and businessman

He was born in Trenton, New Jersey. After graduating from Cornell University Law School, he worked in the Office of Price Administration in Washington (1942–44) and in the Office of the General Council Navy Dept (1942–46). He then joined the Xerox Corporation and became its chairman (1958–66). In the 1970s he served as US ambassador to the OAS (Organization of American States), and was a co-negotiator of the Panama Canal Treaties of 1977. He was personal ambassador for President Jimmy Carter during the Middle East negotiations (1979–81). His autobiography, *The Making of a Public Man —a Memoir*, was published in 1985.

Lin Piao See **Lin Biao**

Linton, Ralph 1893–1953
US cultural anthropologist

He was born in Philadelphia, and studied at Pennsylvania, Columbia and Harvard. His early work was in North American archaeology, but his fieldwork in Polynesia (1920–22) turned his interest towards contemporary peoples. On his return he joined the Museum of Natural History in Chicago, and became Professor of Sociology at Wisconsin (1928–37), Columbia (1937–46) and Yale (1946–53). During his years at Wisconsin, he developed wide interests in the study of human behaviour, culture and social organization. He pioneered the use of the terms 'status' and 'role' in social science, and exercised an important influence on the development of the culture-and-personality school of anthropology. His major work was *The Study of Man* (1936). He also wrote *The Tanala, A Hill Tribe of Madagascar* (1933), *The Cultural Background of Personality* (1945) and *The Tree of Culture* (1955).

Lin Tse-hsü See **Lin Zexu**

Lin Yutang (Lin Yü-t'ang) 1895–1976
Chinese author and philologist

Born in Zhangzhou, Fujian (Fukien), he studied at Shanghai, Harvard and Leipzig. He became Professor of English at Beijing (Peking) (1923–26) and Secretary of the Ministry of Foreign Affairs (1927). He lived mainly in the USA from 1936, and was Chancellor of Singapore University (1954–55). He is best known for his numerous novels and essays on, and anthologies of, Chinese wisdom and culture, and as co-author of the official romanization plan for the Chinese alphabet. 📖 *My Country and My People* (1935)

Lin Zexu (Lin Tse-hsü) 1785–1850
Chinese politician

He was appointed Imperial Commissioner to deal with the problem of the increase in illegal imports of opium. At Guangzhou (Canton) he held members of the British community hostage at their warehouses until they surrendered their stocks of opium, thus precipitating a British punitive expedition. When China suffered defeat, he was exiled to Chinese Turkestan, but later recalled. He was regarded in China as the first great patriot to resist the incursions of foreign powers into China.

Lionheart, Richard the See **Richard I**

Liouville, Joseph 1809–82
French mathematician

Born in St Omer, he was educated at the École Polytechnique and the École des Ponts et Chaussées, where he trained as an engineer. He taught at the École Polytechnique (1831–51), and then at the Collège de France and the University of Paris. In 1836 he founded the *Journal de Mathématiques*, still one of the leading French mathematical journals. His work in analysis continued the study of algebraic function theory begun by **Niels Abel** and **Carl Jacobi**, and he studied the theory of differential equations, mathematical physics and celestial mechanics. In algebra he helped to publicize the work of **Évariste Galois**, and in number theory he introduced new methods of investigating transcendental numbers.

Lipatti, Dinu 1917–50
Romanian pianist and composer

Born in Bucharest of a musical family, he studied in Paris with **Alfred Cortot**, **Paul Dukas** and **Nadia Boulanger**. After World War II he established an international reputation as a skilled player of sensitive phrasing and clear, delicate tone quality, particularly known for his interpretation of J S **Bach** and Frédéric **Chopin**. His career was cut short by a rare form of cancer called lymphogranulomatosis.

Lipchitz, Jacques 1891–1973
French sculptor

He was born in Druskieniki, Lithuania, of Polish Jewish parents, and studied engineering before moving to Paris (1909), where he started producing Cubist sculpture in 1914. He became a naturalized French citizen in 1925. In the 1920s he experimented with abstract forms he called 'transparent sculptures', such as *Reclining Nude with Guitar* (1928, New York). Later he developed a more dynamic style which he applied with telling effect to bronze figure and animal compositions, in works like *Mother and Child* (1930, Cleveland Museum of Art, Cleveland, Ohio) and *Benediction* (1942, private collection, New York). From 1941 he lived in the USA. He worked on the *Hagar* theme (Art Gallery of Toronto) from 1948 and on the *Spirit of Enterprise* (Philadelphia, bronze sketch in the Tate Gallery, London) during the 1950s.

Li Peng (Li p'eng) 1928–
Chinese politician

Born in Chengdu, Sichuan (Szechwan) Province, the son of the radical communist writer Li Shouxun (Li Shouhsün) who was executed by the Guomindang (Kuomintang) in 1930, he was adopted by **Zhou Enlai** on his mother's death in 1939. He trained as a hydro-electric engineer and was appointed minister with responsibility for the power industry in 1981. He became a vice-premier in 1983, was elevated to the politburo in 1985 and made Prime Minister in 1987. As a cautious, orthodox reformer, he sought to retain firm control of the economy and favoured improved relations with the Soviet Union. In 1989, he imposed martial law to counter widespread student agitation triggered by the failure of the leadership to honour promises made by party chief **Zhao Ziyang** to implement a measure of liberalizing reform. His refusal to make any concessions prompted the peaceful student occupation of Tiananmen Square, and Li Peng's action to use army units to bring the demonstration violently to an end, with the loss of around 3,000 lives, earned him international condemnation.

Lipman, Maureen Diane 1946–
English actress and writer

Born in Hull, East Yorkshire, she first appeared in London's West End in *Candida* (1976), won a Laurence Olivier award for her role as Miss Skillen in *See How They Run* (1984) and enjoyed success as Joyce Grenfell in her one-woman show *Re: Joyce* (1988–91, 1993–94). Her films include *Up the Junction* (1967), *Educating Rita* (1983), *National Lampoon's European Vacation* (1985) and *Carry On Columbus* (1992). On television, she appeared in her writer husband **Jack Rosenthal**'s plays *The Evacuees* (1975), *The Knowledge* (1979) and *Eskimo Day* (1996), and the comedy series *Agony* (1979–81), *All at No 20* (1986–87), *About Face* (1989–90) and *Agony Again* (series, 1995). She won a BAFTA advertising award for her memorable Beattie in the British Telecom commercials. Her books include *How Was it for You?* (1985), *You Got an 'Ology?* (1989) and *When's It Coming Out?* (1992).

Lipmann, Fritz Albert 1899–1986
US biochemist and Nobel Prize winner

Born in Königsberg, Prussia (now Kaliningrad, Russia), he studied medicine at Berlin University, and worked in biochemistry at the Carlsberg Institute, Copenhagen (1932–39), before emigrating to the USA. He joined the research staff at the Massachusetts General Hospital (1941–57) and became professor at Harvard Medical School (1949–57), and at Rockefeller University, New York, from 1957. He studied the role of phosphorus compounds in providing the energy for respiration, and identified the relationship with electron transfer potential. He demonstrated in 1950 the formation of citric acid from oxaloacetate and acetate (the first step in the **Hans Krebs** cycle) and found that a previously unidentified thiol cofactor is required—coenzyme A. He then isolated and partially elucidated the molecular structure of coenzyme A, for which he shared the 1953 Nobel Prize for physiology or medicine with Hans Krebs.

Li Po See **Li Bo**

Lippershey, Hans c.1570–c.1619
Dutch optician

Born in Wesel (now in Germany), he was one of several spectacle-makers credited with the discovery that the combination of two separated long-focus and short-focus convex lenses can make distant objects appear nearer, and applied for a patent on this type of telescope in 1608. He also showed that if this combination is reversed it becomes a microscope.

Lippi, Filippino c.1458–1504
Italian painter

Born in Prato, Florence, he was the son of **Fra Filippo Lippi**, and was apprenticed to **Botticelli**, who almost certainly was a pupil of his father. In c.1484 he completed the frescoes in the Brancacci Chapel in the Carmine, Florence, left unfinished by **Masaccio**. Other celebrated series of frescoes were painted by him between 1487 and 1502, one in the Strozzi Chapel in S Maria Novella and one in the Caraffa Chapel, S Maria sopra Minerva, in Rome. Easel pictures painted by him are *The Virgin and Saints* (c.1485, National Gallery, London), *The Adoration of the Magi* (1495, Uffizi, Florence) and *The Vision of St Bernard* (1481–86, Badia, Florence). ▢ Katherine B Nielson, *Filippino Lippi* (1938)

Lippi, Fra Filippo, *called* Lippo c.1406–1469
Italian religious painter

He was born in Florence. An orphan, he was sent to the monastery of S Maria del Carmine in Florence where he became a Carmelite monk. In 1424 he became a pupil of **Masaccio**, who was painting the frescoes in the Brancacci Chapel there. The style of his master can be seen in his early work, eg the frescoes *The Relaxation of the Carmelite Rule* (c.1432). Of his stay in Padua (c.1434) no artistic record has survived. The *Tarquinia Madonna* (1437), his first dated painting, shows Flemish influence. His greatest work, on the choir walls of Prato Cathedral, was begun in 1452. Between 1452 and 1464 he abducted a nun and was released from his monastic vows by Pope **Pius II** in order to marry her. She was the model for many of his Madonnas and the mother of his son, **Filippino Lippi**. His later works are deeply religious and include the series of *Nativities*. He was working in the cathedral at Spoleto when he died. He was immortalized in **Robert Browning's** poem 'Fra Lippo Lippi' in *Men and Women* (1855). ▢ C Strutt, *Fra Filippo Lippi* (1901)

Lippincott, Joshua Ballinger 1813–86
US publisher

He was born in Juliustown, New Jersey, had a bookseller's business in Philadelphia (1834–36), and then founded his well-known publishing firm. He founded *Lippincott's Magazine* in 1868.

Lippmann, Gabriel Jonas 1845–1921
French physicist and Nobel Prize winner

Born in Hollerich, Luxembourg, he was appointed Professor of Mathematical Physics at the Faculty of Sciences in Paris in 1883, Professor of Experimental Physics at the Sorbonne in 1886, and director of the Laboratory of Physical Research. His research in electrocapillarity in the laboratory of **Gustav Kirchhoff** led to his invention of a very sensitive mercury capillary electrometer. His many contributions to instrument design include an astatic galvanometer, the coelostat with which a region of the sky can be photographed for an extended period without apparent movement, and a new form of seismograph. For his technique of colour photography based on the interference phenomenon, subsequently also used by Lord **Rayleigh**, he was awarded the 1908 Nobel Prize for physics. He was elected FRS the same year.

Lippmann, Walter 1889–1974
US journalist

Born in New York, he was educated at Harvard, and was on the editorial staff of the *New York World* until 1931, then became a special writer for the New York *Herald Tribune*. His daily columns became internationally famous and he won many awards, including the Pulitzer Prize for international reporting (1962). Among his best-known books are *The Cold War* (1947) and *Western Unity and the Common Market* (1962). ▢ Larry Adams, *Walter Lippmann* (1977)

Lippo See **Lippi, Fra Filippo**

Lipscomb, William Nunn 1919–
US inorganic chemist and Nobel Prize winner

Born in Cleveland, Ohio, he studied at Kentucky and the California Institute of Technology (Caltech), and was appointed Professor of Chemistry at Harvard in 1959. He deduced the molecular structures of a curious group of boron compounds by X-ray crystal diffraction analysis in the 1950s and then went on to develop novel theories of chemical bonding in these compounds. His ingenious experimental and theoretical methods were later applied by him and others to a variety of related chemical problems. He received the 1976 Nobel Prize for chemistry.

Lipton, Sir Thomas Johnstone 1850–1931
Scottish businessman and philanthropist

Born in Glasgow of Irish parents, he began work as an errand-boy at the age of nine, and in 1865 went to the USA, where he worked successively on a tobacco plantation, in the rice fields and in a grocer's shop. Returning to Glasgow, he opened his first grocer's shop (1870, in Finnieston), which was rapidly followed by many others. They prospered and made him a millionaire at the age of 30. He bought tea plantations and rubber estates, factories and packing houses, and made generous donations to various charities.

Li Shih-chen See **Li Shizen**

Li Shizen (Li Shih-chen) 1518–93
Chinese pharmaceutical naturalist and biologist

A talented physician, he was appointed to the Imperial Medical Academy. He decided to produce, single-handed and without imperial authority, an encyclopedia of pharmaceutical natural history. The work took 30 years and involved much travelling to collect and study specimens. He compiled the *Ben Cao Gang Mu* ('Great

---

Lister, Joseph Lister, 1st Baron 1827–1912
English surgeon, the 'father of antiseptic surgery'

Lister was born in Upton, Essex, the son of the microscopist Joseph Jackson Lister. After graduating from London University in arts (1847) and medicine (1852), he became house surgeon at Edinburgh Royal Infirmary. After holding chairs in Glasgow, Edinburgh and London, he was elected president of the Royal Society (1895–1900). In addition to important observations on the coagulation of the blood and the microscopical investigation of inflammation, his great work was the introduction of his antiseptic system (1867), which revolutionized modern surgery.

His system was a development of the work of Louis Pasteur. Lister began soaking his instruments and surgical gauzes in carbolic acid, a well-known disinfectant. His early antiseptic work was primarily concerned with the treatment by surgery of compound fractures and tuberculous joints; both conditions would previously have been dealt with by amputation.

The procedures Lister developed made it possible for surgeons to open the abdominal, thoracic and cranial cavities without fatal infections resulting. He worked later in his life on the causes of wound infection and was an ardent advocate of the value of experimental science for medical and surgical practice. He was the first medical man to be elevated to the peerage.

📖 Martin Goldman, *Lister Ward* (1987), Richard B Fisher, *Joseph Lister, 1827–1912* (1977); Rickman John Godlee, *Lord Lister* (1917).

Pharmacopoeia'), completed in 1578 and published in 1596. It gives an exhaustive description of 1,000 plants and 1,000 animals, and includes more than 11,000 prescriptions. It is much more than a pharmacopoeia, however, as it treats mineralogy, metallurgy, physiology, botany and zoology as sciences in their own right. By categorizing diseases, it also forms a system of medicine. He recorded many instances of the sophistication of Chinese medicine, for example the use of mercury–silver amalgam for tooth fillings, not introduced to Europe until the 19th century. He adopted a system of priority in naming plants and animals, assigning the first name as the standard term, and treating later names as synonyms.

Li Si (Li Ssu) c.280–208BC
Chinese adviser to the state of Qin (Ch'in)

As chief counsellor to the first Emperor Shi Huangdi from 221 to 210BC, he was the principal architect of the harsh system of centralized control imposed throughout the empire. Laws, weights and measures, and the written script were all standardized. He was also associated with the notorious 'burning of the books and burial of the scholars' in 213, when Confucian texts were destroyed and many scholars were executed. As a result of factional rivalries at court, Li Si himself was executed two years after the death of Shi Huangdi.

Lisle, Alicia, *née* Beckenshaw c.1614–1685
English Parliamentarian

The widow of one of Cromwell's lords, she was beheaded at Winchester by order of Judge Jeffreys for sheltering two of the Duke of Monmouth's rebels after the Battle of Sedgemoor. At Charles I's execution she said that her 'blood leaped within her to see the tyrant fall'.

Lisle, Claude Joseph Rouget de See Rouget de Lisle, Claude Joseph

L'Isle, 1st Viscount de See De L'Isle, William Philip Sidney, 1st Viscount

Lissajous, Jules Antoine 1822–80
French physicist

He was professor at the Collège St Louis, Paris, and in 1857 invented the vibration microscope which showed visually the *Lissajous figures* obtained as the resultant of two simple harmonic motions at right angles to one another. His researches extended to acoustics and optics. His system of optical telegraphy was used during the Siege of Paris (1871).

Lissauer, Ernst 1882–1937
German poet and dramatist

He was born in Berlin, and much of his writing had a strong nationalist flavour. The poem cycle *1813* (1913), is a eulogy on the Prussian people in their fight to remove Napoleon I from their land, as is the successful drama *Yorck* (1921) about the Prussian general. The poem *Hassgesang gegen England* (1914,'Hate-Song against England') achieved popularity in wartime Germany with its well-known refrain 'Gott strafe England' ('God Punish England'). Other works include a play about Goethe, *Eckermann* (1921); poems on Anton Bruckner, *Gloria Anton Bruckners* (1921); a critical work, *Von der Sendung des Dichters* (1922, 'The Vocation of a Poet'); and some volumes of verse.

Lissitzky, El(iezer Markovich) 1890–1941
Russian painter and designer

Born in Smolensk, he trained in engineering and architecture. In 1919 Marc Chagall appointed him Professor of Architecture and Graphic Art at the Art School in Vitebsk, where he came under the influence of his colleague Kasimir Malevich, then at the forefront of the avant-garde. Lissitzky produced a remarkable series of abstract works, called collectively *Proun*, in which he combined flat rectilinear forms with dramatic architectonic elements. During the 1920s he lived and travelled in Germany and Switzerland, transmitting Russian ideas to the West through exhibitions, writings, and contact with leading painters, architects and teachers, most importantly László Moholy-Nagy.

Li Ssu See Li Si

Lister, Joseph, Lord See panel above

Lister (of Masham), Samuel Cunliffe Lister, 1st Baron 1815–1906
English inventor

Born in Bradford, he worked for a Liverpool firm of merchants, then in 1837 he and his brother were put in charge of a worsted mill built by their father at Manningham. Samuel applied himself to the improvement of textile machinery, inventing in 1845 a woolcomber. He subsequently bought up all his competitors and made a fortune, at the same time bringing prosperity to Bradford and the wool trade of Australia and New Zealand. Later he spent a quarter of a million pounds developing a machine to spin waste silk and was nearly bankrupt by the time it was commercially successful, making him a second fortune. Among his 150 other inventions were a swivel shuttle, a velvet loom, and in 1848, anticipating the patent of George Westinghouse by 21 years, a compressed air brake for railways. A determined business man, he was also a generous benefactor, presenting Bradford with, amongst other gifts, Lister Park.

Liszt, Franz 1811–86
Hungarian composer and pianist

Born in Raiding, he first played in public aged nine, then studied and played in Vienna and Paris, touring widely in Europe as a virtuoso pianist. In the late 1830s he lived with the Comtesse d'Agoult, by whom he had three children (Cosima married Richard Wagner), and in 1847 met Princess Carolyne zu Sayn-Wittgenstein with whom he lived until his death. In 1848 he went to Weimar, where he directed opera and concerts, composed, and taught, making it the musical centre of Germany. He later received minor orders in the Catholic Church (1865) and was known as Abbé. His works include 12 symphonic poems, masses, two symphonies, and a large number of piano pieces. All his original compositions have a very distinct, sometimes a very strange, individuality. In his 12 Weimar symphonic poems he created a new form of orchestral music. As a teacher of a new generation of pianists and the mentor of many young composers he was generous. The vocal and piano works of his last years were experimental and prophetic of 20th-century developments. His literary works on music include monographs on his friends Frédéric Chopin and Robert Franz (1815–92), and the music of the gypsies.

Li Ta-chao See Li Dazhao

Lithgow, Sir James 1883–1952
Scottish shipbuilder

Born in Port Glasgow, Strathclyde, he was educated locally, then at Glasgow Academy and in Paris. Both he and his brother Henry chose to enter the family engineering firm in Port Glasgow. They became partners in 1907 and a year later, on their father's death, assumed full joint ownership and control. There followed a remarkable collaboration between the brothers which led to the creation of the greatest industrial and financial power ever seen in Scotland. By 1920 they had forged a diversified and integrated empire with interests in coal, iron and steel, marine engineering and shipowning, as well as shipbuilding. Their shipyards on the lower Clyde remained, however, the fulcrum. Lithgow was also central to the rationalization of the shipbuilding industry in the late 1920s and 1930s, and played an influential role in the steel industry. During a term as president of the Federation of British Industries (1930–32) he formed the Scottish National Economic Development Council (1931–39), acting as chairman. He was continuously involved on the national and international scene, and may be regarded as one of Scotland's greatest industrialists.

Little, Alistair 1950–
British chef

He was educated at Cambridge and in 1985 became chef/proprietor of the London restaurant Alistair Little, winner of the *Times* Restaurant of the Year 1993. Little has regularly judged on BBC television's *Masterchef*, and during the summer months he teaches at La Cacciata, near Orvieto in Italy. His book *Keep It Simple* (1993) won the 1994 Glenfiddich award for Best Food Book.

Little, Clarence Cook 1888–1971
US pioneer of mammalian and cancer genetics

Born in Brookline, Massachusetts, he was educated at an agricultural college of Harvard University, where he established the first inbred strain of laboratory mice. Later he worked at Cold Spring Harbor (1918–22), where he began inbreeding several other strains of mice. He was appointed president of the University of Maine (1922–25) and of the University of Michigan (1925–29), then established Roscoe B Jackson Memorial Laboratory on Mount Desert Island, Maine, where he served as director from 1929 to 1956. The use of inbred mouse strains was an essential preliminary to much biomedical discovery. Without the work of Little our understanding of cancer, transplantation, drug action and multigenic conditions would have been much delayed.

Little Richard, *real name* Richard Wayne Penniman 1935–
US rock-and-roll singer and pianist

He was born in Macon, Georgia. His early recordings epitomized the hedonistic, sexually potent facets of rock and roll, and his wild piano style and manic songs were a model for many later performers, as was his overtly homosexual visual style, including wearing outrageous clothes and make-up. Raised as a Seventh-day Adventist, he sang in church choirs throughout his childhood, and screams and yells derived from gospel music were to become an important part of his recorded sound. He left home at 14, and started singing professionally with a series of itinerant medicine shows, becoming well known on the southern vaudeville circuit. He began his recording career with 'Every Hour' (1952) but it was 'Tutti Frutti' (1955), a salacious drinking song with its lyrics cleaned up by writer Dorothy La Bostrie, that really launched his career. In the late 1950s he decided that religion was more important than rock, and most of his recordings from 1958 to 1964 were of gospel songs. In the mid-1960s he recorded with a succession of labels and 'Whole Lot Of Shaking Goin' On' and 'Lawdy Miss Clawdy' are among the better songs from this period. His real come-back came in 1970 with the release of *The Rill Thing* album, which was followed by several more strong releases. He survived a serious car accident in 1985, and was still performing into the 1990s. ▫ C White, *The Life and Times of Little Richard* (1984)

Littleton or Lyttleton, Sir Thomas c.1415–1481
English judge and jurist

He was born in Bromsgrove, Worcestershire. He was appointed Recorder of Coventry (1450), King's Sergeant (1455), Judge of Common Pleas (1466), and in 1475 was made a Knight of the Bath. His reputation rests on his treatise on *Tenures*, written in law French, first printed in London (c.1481), translated into English about 1500 and the first book giving an authoritative account of landholding. This was the text on which Sir Edward Coke commented in his *Coke upon Littleton* (1628).

Littlewood, Joan Maud 1914–
English theatre director

Having trained at RADA, she co-founded Theatre Union with Ewan MacColl. An experimental company in Manchester (1935), it became the Theatre Workshop (1945), and opened at the Theatre Royal in Stratford East, London, with *Twelfth Night* (1953). The group quickly won acclaim and was invited to represent Great Britain at the Théâtre des Nations in Paris (1955, 1956), and played at the Moscow Art Theatre. Littlewood also directed the first British production of Brecht's *Mother Courage* in Barnstaple (1955), in which she played the title role. The ideology of Theatre Workshop company was aggressively left-wing, and their artistic policy revolved around a fresh, political approach to established plays and the staging of new, working-class plays, notably Brendan Behan's *The Quare Fellow* (1956), Shelagh Delaney's *A Taste of Honey* (1958), and *Fings Ain't Wot They Used T'Be* (1959). In 1963 she directed the musical *Oh, What a Lovely War!* and in 1986 was made Commandeur, L'Ordre des Arts et des Lettres. She received the Arts Council of Great Britain Woman of Achievement in the Arts award in 1993 and her autobiography, *Joan's Book*, was published in 1994.

Littlewood, John Edensor 1885–1977
English mathematician

Born in Rochester, Kent, he was educated at Trinity College, Cambridge, and after lecturing in Manchester (1907–10) he returned to Cambridge as a Fellow of Trinity and remained there for the rest of his life. At this time he started to collaborate with **Godfrey Hardy**, and a stream of joint papers on summability theory, Tauberian theorems, Fourier series, analytic number theory and the **Riemann** zeta function followed over the next 35 years. Littlewood was elected to the Rouse Ball chair of mathematics at Cambridge in 1928. He retired in 1950, but was still publishing mathematical papers at the age of 85. His reminiscences, *A Mathematician's Miscellany*, were published in 1953.

Littré, Maximilien Paul Émile 1801–81
French lexicographer and philosopher

Born in Paris, he became a doctor but abandoned medicine for philology, and his translation of **Hippocrates** procured his election in 1839 to the Academy of Inscriptions. An ardent democrat, he fought on the barricades in 1830, was one of the principal editors of the *National* down to 1851, and became an enthusiastic supporter of **Auguste Comte**, after whose death in 1857 he became the leader of the positivist school. *La Poésie homérique et l'ancienne poésie française* (1847) was an attempt to render Book I of the *Iliad* in the style of the trouvères. In 1854 he became editor of the *Journal des savants*. His splendid *Dictionnaire de la langue française* (1863–72, 'Dictionary of the French Language') did not prevent the Academy from rejecting its author (1863), whom Bishop Félix Dupanloup (1802–78) denounced as holding impious doctrines. In 1871 **Léon Gambetta** appointed him Professor of History and Geography at the École Polytechnique. He was chosen representative of the Seine department in the National Assembly, and in December 1871 the Academy at last admitted him.

Litvinov, Maksim Maksimovich 1876–1951
Soviet politician and diplomat

Born, a Polish Jew, in Bielostok, Russian Poland, he joined the Social Democratic Party in 1898 but in 1903 joined in revolutionary activities with **Lenin**. He was exiled to Siberia, but escaped. At the Revolution he was appointed Bolshevik ambassador in London (1917–18). He became deputy People's Commissar for Foreign Affairs in 1921 and Commissar (1930–39), achieving US recognition of Soviet Russia in 1934. He was dismissed in 1939 before the German–Soviet non-aggression pact, but reinstated after the German invasion of Russia. As ambassador to the USA (1941–43) and Vice-Minister of Foreign Affairs (1943–46), he strongly advocated co-operation between the USSR and the West, and world disarmament.

Liu Shaoqi (Liu Shao-ch'i) 1898–?1969
Chinese political leader

Born in Yinshan, Hunan Province, into a land-owning family, he went to school with the future leader, **Mao Zedong**. Educated at Changs'a and Shanghai (where he learned Russian), he went to Moscow to study (1921–22), joined the Chinese Communist Party, and returned to China to become a party labour organizer in Shanghai. He was elected to the politburo in 1934, and became its foremost expert on the theory and practice of organization and party structure, and wrote *How to be a Good Communist* (1939, originally a series of lectures). In 1943 he became Secretary-General of the Party, Vice-Chairman (1949), and Chairman of the People's Republic of China in 1958, second only to Mao Zedong. He advocated a freer market economy and financial incentives, but during the Cultural Revolution (1966–69) he was denounced as a bourgeois renegade, stripped of all positions in 1967 and

banished to Henan (Honan) Province, while **Lin Biao** emerged as Mao's heir-apparent. He reportedly died in detention. He was posthumously rehabilitated in 1980.

Liutprand of Cremona, *also spelt* Luitprand
c.922–972
Italian prelate and historian

Born in Pavia, he passed from the service of **Berengar II**, King of Italy, to that of the Emperor **Otto I**. Otto made him Bishop of Cremona, and sent him on an embassy to Constantinople (Istanbul). His *Antapodosis* ('Revenge') discusses history from 886 to 950. *De Rebus Gestis Ottonis* covers 960–64, and *Relatio de Legatione Constantinopolitana* ('Story of a Mission to Constantinople') is a satire on the Greek court.

Lively, Penelope 1933–
English novelist and children's author

She was born in Cairo, Egypt, and read history at Oxford. A preoccupation with the relation of the present and the past, and a vivid sense of time and place, form the central thread of much of her writing, notably in her children's books *The Ghost of Thomas Kempe* (1973) and *A Stitch in Time* (1976). Novels written for adults include *The Road to Lichfield* (1977), *Judgement Day* (1980), *Moon Tiger* (1987, Booker Prize), about the reminiscences of an intellectual old lady, and *Cleopatra's Sister* (1992), set in a fictitious country on the North African coast. Her short stories were collected in *Pack of Cards* (1986). She has also written *The Presence of the Past: An Introduction to Landscape History* (1976) and *Oleander, Jacaranda* (1994), an autobiography of her early years in Egypt.

Livermore, Mary Ashton, *née* Rice 1820–1905
US reformer

She was born in Boston. A teacher by training, she married the Rev Daniel P Livermore in 1845, and became active in the women's suffrage movement. She was founder-editor of *The Agitator* (1869), which was later merged into the *Woman's Journal*.

Liverpool, Robert Banks Jenkinson, 2nd Earl of 1770–1828
English politician

Born in London, he was the son of the 1st Earl (1727–1808). Educated at Charterhouse and Christ Church, Oxford, he entered parliament in 1790 as member for Rye. A Tory with Liberal ideas on trade and finance, he became a member of the India Board in 1793, and in 1801 as Foreign Secretary negotiated the unpopular Treaty of Amiens. In 1803 he was created Lord Hawkesbury, and on **William Pitt's** return to power he went to the Home Office (1804–06). In 1807 he again took the Home Office, and the next year succeeded his father as Earl of Liverpool. In **Perceval's** ministry of 1809 he was Secretary for War and the Colonies. In 1812 he formed an administration, regarded as reactionary, which lasted for nearly 15 years. He was a Free Trader, and ultimately sought to liberalize the tariff. He united the old and the new Tories at a critical period.

Livia, Drusilla, *later called* Julia Augusta 58BC–AD29
Roman empress

She was the third wife of Emperor **Augustus**, whom she married in 38BC after divorcing her first husband **Tiberius Claudius Nero**. From her first marriage she had two children, **Tiberius** the future emperor (who succeeded Augustus), and **Nero Claudius Drusus**, but none from her marriage with Augustus. She was believed to have influence over Augustus, cunningly promoting the interests of her sons at the expense of Augustus's kinsmen, by fair or foul means. She was adopted into the Julian family by Augustus at his death in AD14, and changed her name to Julia Augusta. Relations with her son Tiberius after his accession became strained, as she sought to exert influence, and when she died he did not execute her will or allow her to be deified. She was deified (AD42) by her grandson Claudius. 📖 Hugo Willrich, *Livia* (1911)

Livingston
US political dynasty
The family was descended from the 5th Lord Livingston, guardian of **Mary, Queen of Scots**, and from his grandson, John Livingstone (1603–72), a minister of Ancrum who was banished for refusing the Oath of Allegiance to **Charles II**, and who from 1663 was pastor of the Scots kirk at Rotterdam. His son Robert (1654–1728) went to America in 1673, settled at Albany, and received land. Of his grandsons, Philip (1716–78) signed the Declaration of Independence, and William (1723–90) became the first Governor of New Jersey (1776–90) and had a son who became a justice of the Supreme Court. Robert R Livingston (1746–1813), great-grandson of the first Robert, was born in New York, and admitted to the Bar in 1773. Sent to Congress in 1775, he was one of the five charged with drawing up the Declaration of Independence, and until 1801 was the Chancellor of New York state. As minister plenipotentiary at Paris he negotiated the cession of Louisiana. He enabled **Robert Fulton** to construct his first steamer, and introduced to the USA the use of sulphate of lime as a manure, and the merino sheep. Edward Livingston (1764–1836), also a great-grandson of the first Robert, was born at Clermont, New York, and called to the Bar in 1785. He sat in Congress from 1795 until 1801, when he became US district attorney for New York, and Mayor of New York, but in 1803, owing to a subordinate's misappropriations, he found himself in debt to the federal government. He handed over his property to his creditors, and in 1804 settled in New Orleans, where he obtained lucrative practice at the Bar. During the second war with Great Britain he was aide-de-camp to General **Jackson**, and from 1822 to 1829 he represented New Orleans in Congress. In 1823–24 he systematized the civil code of Louisiana. His criminal code was completed, but not directly adopted. In 1829 Livingston was elected to the Senate, and in 1831 appointed Secretary of State. In 1833 he went to France as plenipotentiary.

Livingstone, David 1813–73
Scottish missionary and traveller
He was born in Blantyre, Lanarkshire, and from 10 till 24 years of age he worked in a cotton factory there. A pamphlet by German missionary Karl Gutzlaff (1803–51) kindled his desire to become a missionary. After studying medicine in London he was attracted to Africa by **Robert Moffat**, whose daughter Mary he married in 1844. He was ordained under the London Missionary Society in 1840, and for several years worked in Bechuanaland (now Botswana). Repulsed by the Boers in an effort to plant native missionaries in the Transvaal, he travelled northwards, discovered Lake Ngami, and determined to open trade routes east and west. The journey (1852–56) was accomplished with a handful of followers, amid great difficulties, but a vast amount of valuable information was gathered respecting the country, its products and the native tribes. He discovered the Victoria Falls of the Zambezi. He was welcomed home with extraordinary enthusiasm, and published his *Missionary Travels* (1857). In 1858 he was appointed chief of a government expedition for exploring the Zambezi and explored the Zambezi, Shiré and Rovuma, discovered Lakes Shirwa and Nyasa, and concluded that Lake Nyasa and its neighbourhood was the best field for commercial and missionary operations, though he was hampered by the Portuguese authorities, and by the discovery that the slave trade was extending in the district. The expedition was recalled in 1863. At his own cost he journeyed 100 miles westwards

from Lake Nyasa, then navigated his little steamer to Bombay and returned to England in 1864. His second book, *The Zambesi and its Tributaries* (1865), was designed to expose the Portuguese slave traders, and to find means of establishing a settlement for missions and commerce near the head of the Rovuma. The Royal Geographical Society asked him to return to Africa and settle a disputed question regarding the watershed of central Africa and the sources of the Nile. In 1866 he started from Zanzibar, pressed westwards amid innumerable hardships, and in 1867–68 discovered Lakes Mweru and Bangweulu. Obliged to return for rest to Ujiji, he struck westwards again as far as the River Lualaba, thinking it might be the Nile, which afterwards proved to be the Congo. On his return after severe illness to Ujiji, Livingstone was found there by **Henry Morton Stanley**, sent to look for him by the *New York Herald*. Determined to solve the problem, he returned to Bangweulu, but died in Old Chitambo (now in Zambia). His faithful followers embalmed his body, and carried it to the coast. It was taken to England, and buried in Westminster Abbey. 📖 George Seaver, *David Livingstone: His Life and Letters* (1957)

Livingstone, Ken(neth) 1945–
English politician
He was born in London and educated at Tulse Hill Comprehensive School and Phillipa Fawcett College of Education. He worked as a technician at the Chester Beatty Cancer Research Institute from 1962 until devoting himself to a political career. After joining the Labour Party in 1969, he worked as a London regional executive (1974–86) and served as a Lambeth and Camden local councillor (1971–78). In 1973, he was elected to the Greater London Council (GLC), becoming leader in 1980. He transformed the GLC from being a significant but largely administrative element in the capital's political infrastructure into an instrument of left-wing policies and a key weapon in the party's barracking of national Conservative policies. The government in 1986 introduced legislation to dismantle the highest tier of Great Britain's regional political administration. The following year, Livingstone won election to parliament as MP for Brent East, but failed to gain the Shadow Cabinet post for which he once seemed pre-ordained. His publications include *Livingstone's Labour* (1989).

Livius Andronicus fl.3rd century BC
Roman writer
He was probably a Greek by birth, from Tarentum. He was taken prisoner at the Roman capture of the city and sold as a slave in Rome in 272BC, but later freed by his master. He translated the *Odyssey* into Latin Saturnian verse, and wrote tragedies, comedies and hymns based on Greek models. Only fragments are extant. He is regarded as the father of Roman dramatic and epic poetry. 📖 S Mariotti, *Livio Andronico e la traduzione artistica* (1952)

Livy, properly Titus Livius 59BC–AD17
Roman historian
Born in Patavium (Padua), he settled in Rome in about 29BC and was admitted to the court of **Augustus**, but took no part in politics. His history of Rome from her foundation to the death of **Nero** Claudius Drusus (9BC) comprised 142 books, of which 35 have survived and of these three are imperfect. Livy can be placed in the forefront of Latin writers, and his work was a major influence on subsequent historical writing. 📖 P G Walsh, *Livy, his historical methods* (1961)

Li Xiannian (Li Hsien-nien) 1905–92
Chinese politician
Born into a poor peasant family in Hubei (Hupeh) Province, he worked as a carpenter before serving with the Nationalist Guomindang (Kuomintang) forces in

1926–27. After joining the Communist Party (CCP) in 1927 he established the Oyuwan Soviet (people's republic) in Hubei, participated in the Long March (1934–36) and was a military commander in the war against Japan and in the civil war. He was inducted into the CCP politburo and secretariat in 1956 and 1958, but fell out of favour during the 1966–69 Cultural Revolution. He was rehabilitated, as Finance Minister, by Zhou Enlai in 1973, and later served as State President under Deng Xiaoping (1983–88). He was also a member of the Communist Party Political Bureau Standing Committee (1982–87) and chairman of the People's Political Consultative Conference, a post he held until the time of his death.

Llewellyn, Richard, *pseudonym of* Richard Doyle Vivian Llewellyn Lloyd 1907–83
Welsh writer

He was born in St David's, Pembrokeshire. After service with the regular army and a short spell as a film director, he established himself as a bestselling novelist with *How Green was my Valley* (1939), a novel about a Welsh mining village. Later works include *None but the Lonely Heart* (1943), *The Flame of Hercules* (1957), *Up into the Singing Mountain* (1963), *Green, Green My Valley Now* (1975) and *I Stand On A Quiet Shore* (1982).

Lliboutry, Louis Antonin François 1922–
French Earth scientist and glaciologist

Born in Madrid, Spain, he studied mathematics and physics at the École Normale Supérieure in Paris, then worked on pizomagnetism at Grenoble, and became associate professor at the University of Chile, Santiago (1951–56). He mapped all the unknown glaciers of the Chilean Andes before returning to Grenoble, where he studied field glacier dynamics and mass balances, with particular interest in the critical physical conditions necessary for the formation of glaciers and ice sheets. In plate tectonics he derived a predictive theorem for plate velocities relative to the mantle. He campaigned for the establishment of the Laboratory of Glaciology and Environmental Geophysics, of which he became head (1964–83).

Llorente, Juan Antonio 1756–1823
Spanish priest and historian

Born in Rincón del Soto, he became secretary to the Inquisition in 1789 and was made canon of Toledo in 1806. In 1809, when the Inquisition was suppressed, Joseph Bonaparte placed all its archives in his hands and he went to Paris, where the *Histoire critique de l'inquisition d'Espagne* (1817–18) appeared. Its value was recognized at once, but it provoked bitter feeling, and Llorente was ordered to quit France.

Llosa, Mario Vargas 1936–
Peruvian novelist

Born in Arequipa, he studied law and literature in Peru, then spent many years abroad as a student in Paris and Madrid, building up a reputation as a writer. He eventually returned to Lima shortly before the restoration of democratic government in Peru in 1980. *The Time of the Hero* (1962), his first novel, is a powerful social satire and so outraged the authorities that a thousand copies were publicly burned. *The Green House* (1965) brings to life Peruvian society in the days of the rubber boom, while the later *The Perpetual Orgy* (1975) is an expression of his obsession with Gustave Flaubert's *Madame Bovary*. Subsequent novels include his masterpiece *Aunt Julia and the Scriptwriter* (1977, trans 1982), an energetic, inventive comedy with an autobiographical inspiration: the novelist's first wife, Julia, was his aunt by marriage. He has also written *The War at the End of the World* (1981), *The Real Life of Alejandro Mayta* (1984), *Who Killed Palomino Molero?* (1987) and *In Praise of the Stepmother* (1990). He is recognized as one

of the world's great contemporary novelists. Formerly president of PEN (1976–79), an international organization for poets, playwrights, editors, essayists and novelists, he has won many honours, including the Ritz Paris Hemingway award, and he has been actively involved in politics, running unsuccessfully for the presidency of Peru in 1990, having declined an offer of the premiership in 1984.

Lloyd, Clive Hubert 1944–
West Indian cricketer

Born in Georgetown, Guyana, he was educated on a scholarship to Chatham High School, Georgetown. He worked as a hospital clerk until his first West Indies Test cap in 1966, then went to England to play for Haslingden in the Lancashire League before joining Lancashire (1968–86). A magnificent batsman and fielder, he played in 110 Test matches (captain 1974–85), scoring 7,515 runs and making 19 centuries. He captained the West Indies in 18 Test matches, losing only two, which makes him the most successful Test captain. He also captained the West Indies sides which won the World Cup in 1975 and 1979. He later became a British citizen.

Lloyd, Edward d.c.1730
English coffee-house keeper

From 1688 until 1726 he owned a coffee house in Lombard St, London, after which is named 'Lloyd's', the London society of underwriters. His coffee house became a haunt of merchants and ship-owners, and for them Lloyd started his *Lloyd's News*, later to become *Lloyd's List*.

Lloyd, George Walter Selwyn 1913–
English composer and conductor

He was born in St Ives, Cornwall, and his 3rd Symphony and two operas (*Iernin*, 1935, and *The Serf*, 1938) received London performances before he served during World War II in the Royal Marines Band. He was shell-shocked in 1942. Another opera, *John Socman*, followed (1951), but owing to illness he retired to Devon as a market gardener, and for a time composed only intermittently. With improved health he produced a large body of concertos and symphonies (No 12, 1990) in a colourful if conventional style. His publications include *English Heritage* (1990) and *Floating Cloud* (1993).

Lloyd, Harold Clayton 1893–1971
US film comedian

Born in Burchard, Nebraska, he was stagestruck from an early age and worked extensively as an extra from 1913. Gradually, he created his own character of the shy, sincere, bespectacled boy-next-door, developing a reputation for highly demanding stunts in works like *High and Dizzy* (1920) and, most famously, *Safety Last* (1923). He enjoyed a run of hits such as *Why Worry?* (1923) and *Speedy* (1928), but was less successful in the sound era and retired after *Mad Wednesday* in 1947. He published an autobiography, *An American Comedy*, in 1928 and received an honorary Academy Award in 1952. ▣ Adam Reilly, *Harold Lloyd: The King of Daredevil Comedy* (1977)

Lloyd, Henry Demarest 1847–1903
US journalist and reformer

Born in New York City, he was a graduate of Columbia University. He became a school lecturer in economics, studied law and was called to the Bar in 1869. From 1872 he worked on the Chicago *Tribune* as a reporter and on the editorial staff. He was reviled for pointing to the injustice of the trials of the Haymarket anarchists, four of whom were hanged for supposedly throwing a bomb on 4 May 1886. He became dedicated to exposure of capitalist abuses and his masterpiece, *Wealth Against Commonwealth* (1894), was a searing indictment of how John D Rockefeller built up Standard Oil. A strong advocate of co-operative methods, he visited New Zealand, reporting on it in *A Country without Strikes* (1900), and supported the Populist Party, denouncing its fusion with the Democrats and the 'free silver' movement under William Jennings Bryan.

Lloyd, Marie, *originally* Matilda Alice Victoria Wood
1870–1922
English music-hall entertainer
Born in London, she made her debut as Bella Delmare at the Royal Eagle Music Hall, London (later The Grecian), in 1885. After choosing a new stage name, she had her first success with the song 'The Boy I Love Sits Up in the Gallery'. She went on to become one of the most popular music-hall performers of all time, specializing in witty portrayals of working-class Londoners. She appeared in music halls throughout the country, and in the USA, South Africa and Australia, performing until a few days before her death. Among her most famous songs were 'Oh, Mr Porter','My Old Man Said Follow the Van'and 'I'm One of the Ruins that Cromwell Knocked About a Bit'. ◻ Richard Anthony Baker, *Marie Lloyd: Queen of the Music Halls* (1991)

Lloyd, Selwyn Brooke See **Selwyn-Lloyd, Baron**

Lloyd-George (of Dwyfor), David Lloyd George, 1st Earl 1863–1945
Welsh Liberal statesman
He was born in Manchester of Welsh parentage. At the age of two when his father died, his family were taken to Llanystumdwy, near Criccieth, Wales, the home of his uncle Richard Lloyd who recognized the latent brilliance in the young Lloyd George, and took responsibility for his education. Lloyd George thus acquired his religion, his industry, his vivid oratory, his radical views and his Welsh nationalism. He became a solicitor and in 1890 was elected as an advanced Liberal for Caernarvon Boroughs. From 1905 to 1908 he was president of the Board of Trade and was responsible for the passing of three important Acts—the Merchant Shipping Act and the Census Production Act (1906), and the Patents Act (1907). As Chancellor of the Exchequer from 1908 to 1915, he reached the heights as a social reformer with his Old Age Pensions Act (1908), the National Insurance Act (1911), and the momentous 'people's budget' of 1909–10, whose rejection by the Lords led to constitutional crisis and the Parliament Act of 1911 which removed the Lords' power of veto. Although a pacifist, he strongly believed in the national rights of a smaller country and saw the parallel between the Welsh and the Boers. His condemnation of the Boer War had been loud and the threat of invasion of Belgium by Germany in 1914 dispelled all pacifist tendencies. In 1915 he was appointed Minister of Munitions, in 1916 became War Secretary and superseded H H Asquith as coalition Prime Minister (1916–22). By his forceful policy he was, as Hitler later said of him, 'the man who won the war'. He was one of the 'big three' at the peace negotiations, which he handled brilliantly although he was inclined to pay too much attention to the demands of the small countries. This later, as with Greece, led Great Britain into difficulties. At home there was a split in the Liberal Party which never completely healed. In 1921 he negotiated with Sinn Féin and conceded the Irish Free State. This was very unpopular with the Conservatives in the government and led to his downfall and the downfall of the Liberals as a party at the 1922 election. Following the 1931 general election he resigned as leader of the party and led a group of Independent Liberal MPs. He retained his seat until the year of his death, in which year he was made an earl. He wrote his *War Memoirs* (1933–36) and *The Truth about the Peace Treaties* (1938). ◻ Thomas Jones, *Lloyd George* (1951)

Lloyd-George (of Dwyfor), Gwilym, 1st Viscount Tenby 1894–1967
Welsh politician
Born in Criccieth, he was the second son of David Lloyd-George. He entered parliament as Liberal MP for Pembrokeshire (1922, 1929–50). He was Parliamentary Secretary to the Board of Trade (1939–41) and Minister of Fuel and Power (1942–45). In 1951 he was returned as Liberal-Conservative member for Newcastle North and was Minister of Food until 1954. He was Minister for Welsh Affairs until 1957, when he was created Viscount Tenby of Bulford.

Lloyd-George (of Dwyfor), Lady Megan
1902–66
Welsh politician
Born in Criccieth, the younger daughter of David Lloyd George, she was elected Liberal MP for Anglesey in 1929 and was Independent Liberal between 1931 and 1945. Defeated in the election of 1951, she joined the Labour Party in 1955 and was MP for Carmarthen from 1957.

Lloyd-Jones, David Martyn 1899–1981
Welsh preacher and writer
Born in Newcastle Emlyn, he trained in medicine at London but in 1926 gave up a promising career in Harley Street to enter the Christian ministry. After 11 years in Aberavon he became colleague and successor to G Campbell Morgan at Westminster Chapel, London, and for 30 years made it virtually the heart of English Nonconformity, with his expository preaching based on Reformed theology. His published works include *Truth Unchanged, Unchanging* (1951), *From Fear to Faith* (1953), *Conversions: Psychological and Spiritual* (1959) and *Studies in the Sermon on the Mount* (2 vols, 1959–60).

Lloyd-Webber, Andrew Lloyd Webber, Baron 1948–
English popular composer
Born in London, he was educated at Westminster School and Magdalen College, Oxford, and at the Royal College of Music, London. He met Tim Rice in 1965, and together they wrote a 'pop oratorio' *Joseph and the Amazing Technicolor Dreamcoat* (1968) which was extended and staged in 1973 and revived in 1991. Their greatest success was the 'rock opera' *Jesus Christ Superstar* (staged 1970, filmed 1973), the long-playing record of which achieved record-breaking sales. He composed the music for *Jeeves* (1975), *Evita* (1978), which was the basis for the 1996 Alan Parker film of the same name, *Tell Me on a Sunday* (1980) and *Cats* (1981). His most recent successes include *The Phantom of the Opera* (1986), based on the 1911 novel by Gaston Leroux, *Aspects of Love* (1989), based on the novella (1955) by David Garnett, and *Sunset Boulevard* (1993), based on the 1950 film directed by Billy Wilder. He was knighted in 1992 and made a life peer in 1997. His brother Julian (1951–) is a cellist, and his father, Dr William Lloyd Webber (1914–82) was a notable organist, a choirmaster and director of the London College of Music from 1964 till his death. ◻ Gerald Mantle, *Andrew Lloyd Webber* (1984)

Llywelyn Ap Iorwerth, *called* the Great
1173–1240
Prince of Gwynedd
He seized power from his uncle David (1194), and soon had most of northern Wales under his control. In 1205 he married Joan (d.1237), the illegitimate daughter of King John of England. Welsh poetry and culture flourished under him, and there was harmony between him and the Church. He successfully maintained his independence against King John and Henry III, and extended his kingdom over most of Wales, before retiring to the Cistercian

monastery at Aberconway (Aberconwy), where he died and was buried. He was probably the ablest of all the medieval Welsh princes.

Loach, Ken(neth) 1936–
English filmmaker

Born in Nuneaton, Warwickshire, he acted before becoming a television director. He directed *Z Cars* (1962) before making his name in the Wednesday Play series, with productions such as *Cathy Come Home* (1966). His first feature film, *Poor Cow* (1967), was followed by the popular *Kes* (1969) and *Family Life* (1971). He has continued to explore social issues in such television work as *Days of Hope* (1975) and *The Price of Coal* (1977), and the film *Looks and Smiles* (1981). Subsequent films have included *Hidden Agenda* (1990), *Riff-Raff* (1990), *Raining Stones* (1993), *Land and Freedom* (1995) and *Carla's Song* (1997).

Lobachevski, Nikolai Ivanovich 1792–1856
Russian mathematician

Born in Nizhny Novgorod, he became professor at the University of Kazan in 1814, where he spent the rest of his life. From the 1820s he developed a theory of non-Euclidean geometry in which Euclid's parallel postulate (that there is only one straight line which passes through a given point and is parallel to another given line) did not hold. A similar theory was discovered almost simultaneously and independently by János Bolyai. Despite publication in various languages, his theory was too novel and its presentation too obscure to find acceptance in his lifetime. He also wrote on algebra and the theory of functions. 📖 F Veniamin, *N Lobachevsky and His Contributions to Science* (1957)

L'Obel or Obel or Lobel, Matthias de 1538–1616
Flemish naturalist

Born in Lille, he became botanist and physician to King James VI and I of Scotland and England, and gave his name to the *Lobelia*.

Lobo, Francisco Rodrigues c.1580–1622
Portuguese writer

He was born in Leiria, and wrote *Primavera* (1601, 'Spring') and other remarkable prose pastorals and verse. He was drowned in the River Tagus. His lyrics are of great beauty and his work holds a valuable place in Portuguese literature. 📖 R Jorge, *Francisco Lobo* (1920)

Lochhead, Liz 1947–
Scottish poet and dramatist

Born in Motherwell, Lanarkshire, she studied at Glasgow School of Art and worked as an art teacher before becoming a full-time writer in 1979. A frank and witty poet, she has published several collections, including *Dreaming Frankenstein and Collected Poems* (1984) and *True Confessions and New Clichés* (1985). Her most powerful work has been written for the stage, and includes *Mary Queen of Scots Got Her Head Chopped Off* (1987), and a version of Bram Stoker's *Dracula* (1985), which restored the serious intent of the original. She translated Molière's *Tartuffe* (1985) into demotic Glaswegian, and has written for radio and television. She wrote the text for the epic music theatre production *Jock Tamson's Bairns* in Glasgow in 1990.

Lochner, Stefan c.1400–1451
German painter

Born in Meersburg on Lake Constance, he was the principal master of the Cologne school, marking the transition from the Gothic style to naturalism. He may have studied in the Netherlands under Robert Campin, and settled in Cologne c.1430. The influence of Netherlandish art, particularly Jan van Eyck, shows in his work, eg the *Madonna with the Violet* (c. 1443, Cologne). His best-known work is the triptych in Cologne Cathedral.

Locke, Alain Leroy 1886–1954
US educationist and critic

Born in Philadelphia, he graduated from Harvard and became the first black Rhodes scholar at Oxford (1907–10). Professor of Philosophy at Howard University from 1917, he published numerous works that explored black culture in the USA and its African antecedents, notably *The New Negro* (1925), *The Negro in America* (1933) and *The Negro in Art* (1941). He was a leading figure in the Harlem Renaissance.

Locke, Bessie 1865–1952
US pioneer of kindergarten education

Born in West Cambridge (Arlington), Massachusetts, she herself attended a private kindergarten (then a recent importation from Germany), and went on to Brooklyn public schools and Columbia University, but took no degree. She is said to have been deflected from business to education by her observation of a friend's kindergarten in a slum area of New York City. She founded the National Association for the Promotion of Kindergarten Education (National Kindergarten Association) in 1909, and was head of the kindergarten division of the US Bureau of Education (1913–19), working to improve kindergarten teacher training. From 1917 she published home education articles for parents which became very influential. She helped to open over 3,000 kindergartens, serving over 1.5 million children.

Locke, Bobby, properly Arthur D'Arcy Locke 1917–87
South African golfer

He was born in Germiston. A slow, methodical player, he won four British Open championships (1949, 1950, 1952, 1957), and between 1947 and 1950 won 11 events on the US tour circuit.

Locke, John 1632–1704
English empiricist philosopher

He was born in Wrington, Somerset, and educated at Westminster School and Christ Church, Oxford. He reacted against the prevailing scholasticism at Oxford and involved himself instead in experimental studies of medicine and science, making the acquaintance of Robert Boyle, John Wilkins and others. In 1667 he joined the household of Anthony Ashley Cooper, later 3rd Earl of Shaftesbury, as his personal physician and became his adviser in scientific and political matters generally. Through Ashley he made contact with the leading intellectual figures in London and was elected FRS (1668). When Ashley became Earl of Shaftesbury and Chancellor (1672), Locke became secretary to the Council of Trade and Plantations, but retired to France (1675–79), partly for health reasons and perhaps partly from political prudence. In Paris he became acquainted with the circle of Pierre Gassendi and Antoine Arnauld. After Shaftesbury's fall and death in 1683, Locke felt threatened and fled to the Netherlands, where he joined the English supporters of William of Orange (the future William III) and remained until after the Glorious Revolution of 1688. His *Two Treatises of Government* published, anonymously, in 1690, constitute his reply to the patriarchal, Divine Right theory of Sir Robert Filmer and also to the absolutism of Thomas Hobbes. The *Treatises* present a social contract theory which embodies a defence of natural rights and a justification for constitutional law, the liberty of the individual and the rule of the majority. If the ruling body offends against natural law it must be deposed, and this sanctioning of rebellion had a powerful influence on American and the French revolutions. Locke returned to England in 1689, declined an ambassadorship and became Commissioner of Appeals until 1704. His health declined and he spent his remaining years at Oates, Essex, at the home of Sir Francis and Lady Masham (the daughter of Ralph Cudworth). Locke's major philosophical work was the *Essay concerning Human Understanding*, published in 1690 though developed over 20 years. The *Essay* is a systematic enquiry into the nature and scope of human reason, very much reflecting the scientific temper of the times in seeking to establish that 'all knowledge is founded on and ultimately derives from sense…or sensation'. The work is regarded as the first and probably the most important statement of an empiricist theory of knowledge in the British tradition which led from Locke to **George Berkeley** and **David Hume**. His other main works were *A Letter concerning Toleration* (1689), *Some Thoughts concerning Education* (1693) and *The Reasonableness of Christianity* (1695), and they are all characterized by the same tolerance, moderation and common sense. ▢ Richard I Aaron, *John Locke* (3rd edn, 1951)

Locke, Joseph 1805–60
English civil engineer

Born in Attercliffe, near Sheffield, he left school at the age of 13 and eventually became articled to **George Stephenson** in 1823 and began to learn the art of railway civil engineering. After almost 10 years with Stephenson he broke away and built a large number of important railways in England, Scotland, France and elsewhere on the Continent of Europe. His lines were noted for their straightness and avoidance of expensive tunnelling, but in adopting such a system he was forced in some places to adopt gradients that were too steep for economical running.

Locke, Matthew c.1621–1677
English composer

Born in Exeter, he collaborated with **James Shirley** on the masque *Cupid and Death* (1653), winning a reputation as a theatre composer. After writing the music for **Charles II**'s coronation procession, he was made Composer-in-Ordinary to the King. He was a champion of the 'modern' French style of composition, and his works include much incidental music for plays (though that for *Macbeth*, long attributed to him, is of doubtful authenticity), Latin church music, songs and chamber works.

Locke, William John 1863–1930
English novelist

Born in Demerara, British Guiana (Guyana), and educated in Trinidad and at Cambridge, he taught (1890–97) at Clifton and Glenalmond, but disliked teaching, and became the secretary of the Royal Institute of British Architects in London (until 1907). In 1895 he published the first of a long series of novels and plays which, with their charmingly written sentimental themes, enjoyed a huge success in Great Britain and the USA. *The Morals of Marcus Ordeyne* (1905) and *The Beloved Vagabond* (1906) assured his reputation. His other popular romances include *The Joyous Adventures of Aristide Pujol* (1912) and *The Wonderful Fear* (1916). His plays, some of which were dramatized versions of his novels, were produced with success on the London stage.

Lockhart, John Gibson 1794–1854
Scottish biographer, novelist and critic

Born in Cambusnethan, Lanarkshire, the son of a Church of Scotland minister, he spent his boyhood in Glasgow, and aged 13 won a Snell exhibition to Balliol College, Oxford. In 1813 he graduated with a first in classics. Then, after a visit to the Continent to see **Goethe** in Weimar, he studied law at Edinburgh, and in 1816 was called to the Bar. From 1817 he turned increasingly to writing, and with **John Wilson** ('Christopher North') became the chief mainstay of *Blackwood's Magazine*. There he exhibited the criticism and caustic wit that made him the terror of his Whig opponents. In 1819 he published *Peter's Letters to His Kinsfolk* (3 vols), a clever skit on Edinburgh intellectual society. He married Sophia, eldest daughter of Sir **Walter Scott**, in 1820, and went on to write four novels—*Valerius*

(1821), *Adam Blair* (1822), *Reginald Dalton* (1823) and *Matthew Wald* (1824). His other works include biographies of **Robert Burns** (1828) and **Napoleon I** (1829), and his masterpiece *The Life of Sir Walter Scott* (7 vols, 1837–38). In 1825 he moved to London to become editor until 1853 of the *Quarterly Review*. He also became auditor of the Duchy of Cornwall (1843). His closing years were clouded by illness and deep depression. He visited Italy for the sake of his health, but, like Scott, came back to Abbotsford in Scotland to die. ▢ A Lang, *Life and Letters of John Gibson Lockhart* (1896)

Lockwood, Belva Ann, *née* Bennett 1830–1917
US lawyer and reformer

Born in Royalton, Niagara County, New York, and educated at Genesee College, she graduated from the National University Law School in Washington (1873) and was admitted to the Bar. In 1868 she married Ezekiel Lockwood, her second husband (her first died in 1853). A skilled and vigorous supporter of women's rights, she became the first woman to practise before the Supreme Court, and helped to promote various reforms, such as the Equal Pay Act for female civil servants (1872). In 1884 and 1888, as a member of the National Equal Rights Party, she was nominated for the presidency. Holding strong pacifist views, she was a member of the nominating committee for the Nobel Peace Prize.

Lockwood, Margaret 1911–90
English actress

Born in Karachi, India, she studied at the Italia Conti School, then made her stage debut as a fairy in *A Midsummer Night's Dream* (1928). She subsequently studied at RADA before making her film debut in *Lorna Doone* (1934). Gaining a long-term contract with British Lion, she made a spirited young heroine in films like *Midshipman Easy* (1935) and *The Beloved Vagabond* (1936) before achieving stardom in *The Lady Vanishes* (1938) and *Bank Holiday* (1938). She was briefly in Hollywood before World War II, then returned to Great Britain and starred in costume melodramas like *The Man in Grey* (1943) and *The Wicked Lady* (1945). By 1946 she was judged to be Great Britain's favourite female star, but subsequent role choices failed to sustain her stardom and she played her last leading role in *Cast a Dark Shadow* (1955). She returned to the cinema for a final appearance as the wicked stepmother in *The Slipper and the Rose* (1976) and spent her last years as a publicity-shy recluse.

Lockyer, Sir (Joseph) Norman 1836–1920
English astronomer

Born in Rugby, Warwickshire, he became a clerk at the British War Office to which he remained technically attached (1857–75), devoting as much time as he could spare to science. In 1868 he designed a spectroscope for observing solar prominences outside of a total eclipse and succeeded in doing this independently of **Pierre Jules César Janssen**, who had used the same principle a few months earlier. In the same year he postulated the existence of an unknown element which he named helium (the 'Sun element'), an element not found on Earth until 1895 by **William Ramsay**. He also discovered and named the solar chromosphere. In 1875 he became a member of the staff of the Science Museum in South Kensington, London. His research gave rise to unconventional ideas such as his theory of dissociation, whereby atoms were believed to be capable of further subdivision, and his meteoritic hypothesis which postulated the formation of stars out of meteoric material. Among other activities, he took part in eclipse expeditions and made surveys of ancient temples for the purpose of dating them by astronomical methods. The founder (1869) and first editor of the scientific periodical *Nature*, he was knighted in 1897. His solar physics observatory at South Kensington was transferred to Cambridge University in 1911, but he remained active in a private observatory which he set up in Sidmouth, Devon, until his death. 📖 A J Meadows, *Science and Controversy: A Biography of Sir Norman Lockyer* (1972)

Lodge, David John 1935–
English novelist and literary critic

Born in Dulwich, Greater London, he was educated at University College London, and at the University of Birmingham, where he was Professor of Modern English Literature (1976–87) then Honorary Professor (1987–). His critical and theoretical writing (most of which is concerned with contemporary fiction) has been influential, notably *Language of Fiction* (1966), *The Novelist at the Crossroads* (1971), *Working with Structuralism* (1981) and *The Art of Fiction* (1992). Several of his novels have an academic setting, including the best-known of them, *Changing Places* (1975) and its sequel, *Small World* (1984). He moved away from the academic into the industrial world with *Nice Work* (1988, adapted for television 1989). *Paradise News* (1991) moves the scene to Honolulu. His most recent novel is *Therapy* (1995). He was made a CBE in 1998.

Lodge, Edmund 1756–1839
English writer

A biographer, and author of several works on heraldry, he is best known by his *Portraits of Illustrious Personages* (1821–34) and *The Genealogy of the Existing British Peerage* (1832, enlarged 1859).

Lodge, Henry Cabot 1850–1924
US politician, historian and biographer

Born in Boston into a socially prominent family, he earned a PhD in political science from Harvard, and while serving the US House of Representatives (1887–93) as a Republican he also pursued a scholarly career, publishing historical studies and biographies of US statesmen. He was a US senator from 1893 until his death and is best remembered for leading Senate opposition to the League of Nations. 📖 John A Garraty, *Henry Cabot Lodge: a Biography* (1953)

Lodge, Henry Cabot, Jnr 1902–85
US politician and statesman

Born in Nahant, Massachusetts, the grandson of **Henry Cabot Lodge**, he began a political career in the Massachusetts legislature (1932–36) and served as US Republican senator (1937–44, 1947–53). As manager of General **Dwight D Eisenhower**'s presidential campaign, he lost his senate seat to the Democratic challenger, **John F Kennedy**, but was appointed US ambassador to the United Nations (1953–60). Unsuccessful in a run for US Vice-President (with **Richard Nixon**) in 1960, he was chosen by President Kennedy to be ambassador to South Vietnam (1963), and he returned to this post under President **Lyndon B Johnson** (1965–67). Ambassador to West Germany (1968), he resigned to become chief US negotiator (1969) at the Vietnam peace talks in Paris, then served as special envoy to the Vatican (1970–77).

Lodge, Sir Oliver Joseph 1851–1940
English physicist

Born in Penkhull, Staffordshire, he studied at the Royal College of Science and at University College London, and in 1881 became Professor of Physics at Liverpool University. In 1900 he was appointed first Principal of the new university at Birmingham. He discredited the ether theory in 1893, thus preparing the way for the theory of relativity. Specially distinguished in electricity, he was a pioneer of wireless telegraphy. His scientific writings include *Signalling across Space without Wires* (1897), *Talks about Wireless* (1925) and *Advancing Science* (1931). He gave much time to psychical research and on this subject wrote *Raymond* (1916) and *My Philosophy* (1933). *Past Years: An*

Autobiography appeared in 1931. He was elected Fellow of the Royal Society in 1887, awarded the Society's Rumford Medal (1898), and knighted in 1902.

Lodge, Thomas c.1558–1625
English dramatist, romance writer and poet

Born in West Ham, London, he went to Trinity College, Oxford, and then to Lincoln's Inn (1578). He published a *Defence of Poetry* anonymously in 1580, and an attack on abuses by moneylenders, *An Alarum against Usurers*, in 1584, along with his first romance, *The Delectable Historie of Forbonius and Priscilla*. This was followed by *Scillaes Metamorphosis* in 1589. About 1588 he took part in a buccaneering expedition to the Canaries, and wrote another romance, *Rosalynde* (1590), his best-known work, which supplied **Shakespeare** with many of the chief incidents in *As You Like It*. He went on a second freebooting expedition to South America in 1591. *The Wounds of the Civil War* and *A Looking-glass for London and England* (with **Robert Greene**) appeared in 1594. He turned Catholic and is believed to have taken a medical degree at Avignon (1600), and to have written a *Treatise of the Plague* (1603). Among his remaining writings are a collection of poems, *Phillis* (1593), *A Fig for Momus* (1595), and translations of **Josephus** (1602) and **Seneca** (1614). 📖 W D Roe, *Thomas Lodge* (1967)

Loeb, Jacques 1859–1924
US biologist

Born in Mayen, Germany, he was educated in philosophy at Berlin University, and in medicine at Strassburg University, and in 1886 was appointed to an assistantship at Würzburg University. He began to publish on animal behaviour in 1888, showing that certain caterpillars move towards light even when their food is in the opposite direction. He emigrated to the USA in 1891, and held various university appointments before becoming head of the general physiology division at the Rockefeller Institute for Medical Research (1910–24). He conducted pioneering work on artificial parthenogenesis, and he became a champion of materialism in philosophy, of mechanistic explanations in science, and a socialist in politics. His writings include *Dynamics of Living Matter* (1906) and *Artificial Parthenogenesis and Fertilisation* (1913).

Loeb, James 1867–1933
US banker

Born in New York City, he founded the Institute of Musical Art in New York (1905) and a mental clinic in Munich. A classical scholar himself, in 1910 he provided funds for the publication of the famous Loeb Classical Library of Latin and Greek texts with English translations.

Loesser, Frank Henry 1910–69
US songwriter and composer

Born in New York City, he studied for a short time at the City College of New York. He published his first lyric in 1931, and in 1937 went to Hollywood as a contract writer. With a succession of collaborators he turned out several hit songs including *See What the Boys in the Backroom Will Have*, *Two Sleepy People* (with **Hoagy Carmichael**), and *Baby, It's Cold Outside*. He branched out into writing his own music with *Where's Charley*, a musical version of *Charley's Aunt* (1948), but he is best known for writing the music and lyrics for *Guys and Dolls* (1950). His other musicals include *The Most Happy Fella* (1956), and *How to Succeed in Business Without Really Trying* (1961), for which he shared the Pulitzer Prize for drama in 1962.

Loewe, Frederick 1904–88
US composer

Born in Berlin, he went to the USA in 1924, and worked as a composer on a number of Broadway musicals. Those he wrote in collaboration with **Alan Jay Lerner** were particularly successful, including *Brigadoon* (1947), *My Fair Lady* (1956) and the film score for *Gigi* (1958).

Loewe, (Johann) Karl Gottfried, *also* Karl Löwe
1796–1869
German composer

Born near Halle, he studied music and theology there, and in 1822 became a music teacher at Stettin. In 1847 he sang and played before the court of Queen **Victoria** in London. He composed operas (of which only one, *The Three Wishes*, was performed), oratorios, symphonies, concertos, duets, and other works for piano, but his ballads, including the *Erlkönig* (1818, 'The Erl-King') are his most impressive achievements. He published his autobiography in 1870.

Loewi, Otto 1873–1961
German pharmacologist and Nobel Prize winner

Born in Frankfurt am Main and educated at Strassburg and Munich, he was appointed Professor of Pharmacology at Graz (1909–38). Forced to leave Nazi Germany in 1938, he became research professor at New York University College of Medicine in 1940. From 1901 he worked for a time alongside **Henry Dale**, in the laboratories of **E H Starling** at University College London, on nerve impulses and their chemical transmission. He subsequently identified several possible transmitter substances and distinguished acetylcholine. He shared with Dale the 1936 Nobel Prize for physiology or medicine for investigations on the chemical transmission of nerve impulses. He was elected a Foreign Member of the Royal Society in 1954.

Loewy, Raymond Fernand 1893–1987
US industrial designer

Born in Paris, France, he emigrated to the USA in 1919. After a period of varied work as a commercial artist, he was commissioned to redesign the casing for the Gestetner duplicator, after which he designed products and graphics for major industrial corporations worldwide. Clients included Shell, BP, Coca Cola, Studebaker, BMW, Sud Aviation, and the National Aeronautics and Space Administration (NASA). Loewy was the archetypal US entrepreneurial designer, and was associated with the 'stylist' school of design, and with the 'streamlined' style in particular. He was the author of *Never Leave Well Enough Alone* (1951).

Löffler, Friedrich August Johann 1852–1915
German bacteriologist

Born in Frankfurt an der Oder, he began his career as a military surgeon, became professor at Greifswald (1888) and from 1913 was director of the Koch Institute for Infectious Diseases in Berlin. He first cultured the diphtheria bacillus (1884), discovered by Edwin Klebs and called the 'Klebs–Löffler bacillus', discovered the causal organism of glanders and swine erysipelas (1886), isolated an organism causing food poisoning, and prepared a vaccine against foot-and-mouth disease (1899). He also presented the first evidence for the occurrence of the pathogens which we now call filterable viruses. In 1887 he wrote an unfinished history of bacteriology.

Lofting, Hugh John 1886–1947
English children's novelist

He was born in Maidenhead, Berkshire. The 'Dr Dolittle' books (1920–53), for which he is famous (despite slurs that they are racist and chauvinistic), had their origins in the trench warfare of World War I, of which he had firsthand experience. The idea of the doctor who learns animal languages came to him from his reflections on the part that horses were playing in the war. There were a dozen Doolittle books, which he also illustrated, and though he tired of his eponymous hero—on one occasion attempting to abandon him on the Moon—his popularity with readers kept him alive. From 1912 Lofting was resident mainly in the USA.

Logan, George 1866–1939
Scottish furniture designer

Born in Beith, Ayrshire, he served a traditional cabinet-maker's apprenticeship before working for an established firm of Glasgow cabinetmakers, where he worked with **Ernest Archibald Taylor** and John Ednie (1876–1934). Gaining critical acclaim at home and abroad, he exhibited at the International Exhibition, Turin, and was greatly influenced by the work of **Jessie King**, Herbert Macnair (1868–1955) and **Charles Rennie Mackintosh**. He exhibited his watercolours regularly at the Royal Glasgow Institute.

Logan, James, *also called* Tah-gah-jute c.1725–1780
Native American leader

Born in Shamokin (now Sunbury), Pennsylvania, he was a prominent member of the Mingo, of the Ohio and Scioto rivers. He was friendly toward whites until his family was slaughtered at the Yellow Creek massacre, an event that resulted in Lord Dunmore's War (1774). He refused to participate in a peace treaty meeting, sending instead an eloquent speech expressing anger at his undeserved loss, and he spent the rest of his life seeking revenge by killing white settlers.

Logan, John Alexander 1826–86
US soldier and legislator

Born in Illinois, he served in the Mexican War, was called to the Bar in 1852, and was elected to Congress as a Democrat in 1858. He raised an Illinois regiment in the Civil War (1861–65), and retired at its close as major-general. Returned to Congress as a Republican in 1866, he was repeatedly chosen as a US senator.

Logan, Sir William Edmund 1798–1875
Canadian geologist

Born in Montreal, he was educated at Edinburgh University and spent 10 years in a London counting house before becoming book-keeper in Swansea to a copper smelting company (1828). There he made a map of the coal basin which was incorporated into the geological survey. In 1842 he was appointed first director of the Geological Survey of Canada, a post which he retained until 1869. He undertook studies of the coalfields of Nova Scotia and New Brunswick, and carried out important work on the copper-bearing rocks of the Lake Superior region. His discovery in 1841 of the animal tracks at Horton Bluff, Nova Scotia, provided the first demonstration of the existence of land animals in the Upper Palaeozoic. He was knighted in 1856.

Loisy, Alfred Firmin 1857–1940
French theologian

Born in Ambrières, Haute-Marne, he was ordained priest in 1879 and in 1881 became Professor of Holy Scripture at the Institut Catholique, where by his lectures and writings he incurred the disfavour of the Church and was dismissed. In 1900 he was appointed lecturer at the Sorbonne, but resigned after his works on biblical criticism were condemned by Pope **Pius X** in 1903 as too advanced. These books, proving him to be the founder of the Modernist movement, were *L'Évangile et l'Église* (1902, Eng trans *The Gospel and the Church*), *Quatrième Évangile* (1903, Eng trans *The Fourth Gospel*) and *Autour d'un petit livre* (1903, 'Around a Small Book'). For subsequent works of the same kind he was excommunicated in 1908. He was Professor of History of Religion in the Collège de France from 1909 to 1932.

Lollobrigida, Gina 1927–
Italian actress

Born in Subiaco, the daughter of a carpenter, she studied to become a commercial artist and made a living as a model before entering the film industry in 1946. Her curvaceous figure and ability to attract publicity made her a popular sex symbol in the glamour-starved Europe of the immediate postwar years. An actress of limited range, she enjoyed a prolific career in such Italian films as *Pane, Amore E Fantasia* (1953, *Bread, Love and Dreams*) and *La Donna Piò Bella Del Mondo* (1955, *Beautiful but Dangerous*). Under contract to Howard Hughes from 1949, she appeared in US films including *Beat the Devil* (1954), *Trapeze* (1956) and *Never So Few* (1959). A less frequent performer from the 1970s onwards, she appeared in the television series *Falcon Crest* (1984). She directed the documentary *Portrait of Fidel Castro* (1975) and has enjoyed some success as a photographer.

Lomax, Alan See Lomax, John Avery

Lomax, John Avery 1867–1948
US folklorist and musicologist

Born in Goodman, Mississippi, he was brought up in Texas and studied at Harvard, but turned to field research into cowboy songs. He worked in teaching and banking for 15 years, then returned to field work, this time in black folk-songs, blues, spirituals and work chants. Among his many publications are *Cowboy Songs and Other Frontier Ballads* (1910), *Plantation Songs of the Negro* (1916) and *Songs of the Cattle Trail and Cow Camp* (1919). He and his son, Alan Lomax (1915–), toured the South with basic recording equipment in the early 1930s, amassing a collection of some 10,000 invaluable recordings for the Library of Congress (where John was curator of American Folksong), and discovering the singer Leadbelly along the way. Together they published *American Ballads and Folk Songs* (1934) and *Negro Folk Songs as Sung by Lead Belly* (1936). Alan continued his father's work, and made a series of important recordings with jazz pioneer Jelly Roll Morton in 1938, and Muddy Waters in 1942. He later extended his researches beyond the USA, and produced an acclaimed documentary, *American Patchwork*, in the late 1980s.

Lombard, Carole, *originally* Jane Alice Peters 1908–42
US actress

Born in Fort Wayne, Indiana, she moved to California, where she was spotted by director Allan Dwan and cast as a tomboy in the film *A Perfect Crime* (1921). After completing her studies she returned to films (1925) where her blond beauty made her a decorative addition to many Mack Sennett comedies. She signed to a long-term contract with Paramount in 1930, saw her roles gradually improve and revealed her comic flair in *Twentieth Century* (1934). Glamorous, sophisticated and effervescent, she was the perfect heroine of screwball comedies like *My Man Godfrey* (1936), *Nothing Sacred* (1937) and *To Be or Not to Be* (1942), whilst her dramatic potential was glimpsed in *They Knew What They Wanted* (1940). Married to Clark Gable (1939), she was one of Hollywood's most popular stars at the time of her death in an air crash.

Lombard, Peter c.1100–1160
Italian theologian

Born near Novara, Lombardy, he studied at Bologna, Rheims, and (under Abelard) at Paris. After holding a chair of theology there, he became Bishop of Paris in 1159. He was generally styled *Magister Sententiarum* or the 'Master of Sentences', from his collection of sentences from Augustine of Hippo and other Fathers on points of Christian doctrine, with objections and replies. The theological doctors of Paris in 1300 denounced some of his teachings as heretical, but his work was the standard textbook of Catholic theology down to the Reformation.

Lombardi, Vince(nt Thomas) 1913–70
US football coach

Born in Brooklyn, New York City, he was a noted defensive guard in his playing days with Fordham University, although he was better known as a coach. He started in professional leagues by coaching offence for the New York Giants (1954–59), despite having been a defender, but his best work was done with the Green Bay Packers from Wisconsin (1959–69). With this comparatively small-town team he lifted five league titles and took them successfully to two Super Bowls (1967–68).

Lombardo, Pietro c.1433–1515
Italian sculptor and architect

Born in Corona, Milan, he worked in Padua, and probably Florence, then settled with his family in Venice c.1467 and became the head of the major sculpture workshop of the day. With the assistance of his sons, Tullio (c.1455–1532) and Antonio (c.1458–1516), he was responsible for both the architecture and sculptural decoration of S Maria dei Miracoli (1481–89), one of the finest Renaissance buildings in Venice. Amongst the many monuments he designed was the tomb of Dante in Ravenna.

Lombos, Philip Alexius László de See László, Sir Philip

Lombroso, Cesare 1836–1909
Italian physician and criminologist

He was born in Verona. After acting as an army surgeon, he became Professor of Mental Diseases at Pavia (1862), and director of an asylum at Pesaro, then Professor of Forensic Medicine (1876), of Psychiatry (1896) and of Criminal Anthropology (1906) at Turin. His theory postulated the existence of a criminal type distinguishable from the normal man. His great work is *L'uomo delinquente* (1875, 'The Criminal Man').

Lomonosov, Mikhail Vasilevich 1711–65
Russian scientist and writer

Born in Kholmogory, near Archangel, he ran away to Moscow in search of an education and later studied at St Petersburg, at Marburg in Germany under the philosopher Christian von Wolff, and finally at Freiburg, where he turned to metallurgy and glass-making. He became Professor of Chemistry at the St Petersburg Academy of Sciences in 1745 and set up Russia's first chemical laboratory there. His experiments led to the establishment of a glassworks making coloured glass for mosaics. He also made important contributions to Russian literature. Because he advocated popular education and freedom for the serfs, he always had to fight against prejudice, sometimes amounting to persecution. Although he came to be revered by many people in his own day, his papers were confiscated by Catherine II, the Great after his death.

Lomu, Jonah 1975–
New Zealand rugby football player and athlete

Born in Mangere, he is the youngest-ever capped All Black. He made his international debut for New Zealand against France in 1994. Although not yet a record holder, his early potential as an outstanding world-class winger is clear. He scored four tries against England in 1995, ending their World Cup hopes. This performance made him a household name worldwide and attracted lucrative offers from both rugby league and American football, but so far he has chosen to remain with rugby union. He is 19 stone (121kg) and 6 feet 5 inches (1.96m) tall, and has run 100 metres in 10.7 seconds.

London, Fritz Wolfgang 1900–54
US physicist

He was born in Breslau, Germany (Wrocław, Poland), brother of **Heinz London** and son of a professor of mathematics in Bonn. He studied classics at the universities of Frankfurt and Munich and did research in philosophy leading to a doctorate at Bonn. Later he was attracted to theoretical physics and worked with **Arnold Sommerfeld** at Munich and **Erwin Schrödinger** at Zurich University in 1927, and published on the quantum theory of the chemical bond with Walter Heitler. In 1930 he calculated the non-polar component of forces between molecules, now called van der Waals or London forces. He and his brother fled from Germany in 1933 to Oxford where they joined Sir **Francis Simon**'s group at the Clarendon Laboratory. Together they published major papers on conductivity giving the London equations (1935). Fritz moved to Duke University in the USA (1939–54) and continued to work on superconductivity, and on superfluidity. ◻ Kostas Gavroglu, *Fritz London: A Scientific Biography* (1995)

London, Heinz 1907–70
British physicist

He was born in Bonn, Germany, the younger brother of **Fritz London**, and was educated at the universities of Bonn, Berlin, Munich and Breslau, where he worked for his PhD with Sir **Francis Simon**. He fled Germany in 1933 with Fritz, and they joined Simon's group at the Clarendon Laboratory, Oxford, working together on conductivity. Heinz introduced a theory for the confinement of currents in a superconductor to a surface layer, and with his brother he published the London equations describing the electromagnetic behaviour of superconductors (1935). Briefly interned as an enemy alien in 1940, he was released to work with Simon and others on the development of the British atomic bomb. After two years at Birmingham University he transferred to the Atomic Energy Research Establishment at Harwell (1946), where he worked on isotope separation.

London, Jack, *pseudonym of* John Griffith Chaney
1876–1916
US writer

Born in San Francisco with the double handicap of illegitimacy and poverty, he was successively sailor, tramp and gold miner before he began his career as a writer. He used his knowledge of the Klondike in his highly successful novels *The Call of the Wild* (1903), *The Sea-Wolf* (1904) and *White Fang* (1905), all of them reflecting his preoccupation with the struggle for survival. Among his later works are novels inspired by his socialist political beliefs, notably *The Iron Heel* (1907) and *Martin Eden* (1909), and his autobiographical tale of alcoholism, *John Barleycorn* (1913). With his creative powers failing and his health undermined by illness, accidents and heavy drinking, he died at the age of 40. ◻ Alex Kershaw, *Jack London: A Life* (1997)

Lonergan, Bernard Joseph Francis 1904–85
Canadian Jesuit theologian and philosopher

He was born in Buckingham, Quebec, and joined the Society of Jesus in 1922. As Professor of Systematic Theology at the Gregorian University, Rome (1954–1965), his main concern was to discover precisely how theology develops, following an analysis of the way human understanding in general proceeds. The findings of his massive and seminal studies in *Insight: A Study of Human Understanding* (1957) and *Method in Theology* (1972) are summarized in *Philosophy of God, and Theology* (1973) and *Understanding and Being* (1980). His other interests in theology and the history of ideas were explored in occasional papers, assembled in three collections (1967, 1974, 1985).

Long, Crawford Williamson 1815–78
US physician

Born in Danielsville, Georgia, he practised in nearby Jefferson. In 1842, while operating on a neck tumour, he was the first to use diethyl ether as an anaesthetic, but did not reveal his discovery until 1849, after **William Morton** had demonstrated it publicly in 1846.

Long, Earl K(emp) 1895–1960
US politician

Born near Winnfield, Louisiana, the brother of **Huey Long**, he continued his brother's method of corrupt administration coupled with sound social legislation, as Lieutenant-Governor (1936–38) and Governor (1939–40, 1948–52, 1956–60) of Louisiana. Suffering from paranoid schizophrenia, he was at his wife's request placed in a mental hospital in 1959 and forcibly detained there with police help, until, using his powers as Governor, he dismissed the mental hospital's superintendent and appointed politically favourable medical officers.

Long, George Washington de See De Long, George Washington

Long, Huey Pierce, *known as* the Kingfish
1893–1935
US politician

Born near Winnfield, Louisiana, he was the brother of **Earl K Long**. He was admitted to the Bar in 1915 and headed the state's Public Service Commission. Styling himself as an advocate for the poor and rural folk of Louisiana, he became Governor (1928–31) and proceeded to build one of the most effective political machines in the history of US politics. His programme of extensive public spending not only reformed and developed Louisiana's public services, but also reduced the impact of the Depression upon the state. In 1931 he became a Democratic US senator. Notorious for corruption and demagoguery, he secured the support of the poor by his intensive 'Share the Wealth' social services and public works programmes, but also squandered public funds on extravagant personal projects, including the construction of a marble and bronze statehouse at Baton Rouge. At first a supporter of the New Deal and President **Franklin D Roosevelt**, he became a critic of the President and planned to stand against him in 1936, but was assassinated in the state capitol at Baton Rouge.

Long, Richard 1945–
English land artist

Born in Bristol, he trained at St Martin's School of Art, London. He takes country walks which he considers works of art in themselves, sometimes marking a place with a simple 'sculpture', such as a circle of stones or a shallow trench. Afterwards he exhibits these or, more often, photographs, maps and texts to document his actions, as with *A Hundred Mile Walk* (1971–72). He held his first one-man show in Düsseldorf in 1968, and has had a hundred since, worldwide. He won the 1989 Turner prize.

Longchamp, William de d.1197
English prelate

He was a low-born favourite of **Richard I**, who in 1189–90 made him Chancellor, Bishop of Ely, and joint Justiciar of England. In 1191 he was made papal legate, but because of his arrogant behaviour, was forced to withdraw to Normandy. He regained Richard's favour by raising his ransom, and was made Chancellor again.

Longfellow, Henry Wadsworth 1807–82
US poet

Born in Portland, Maine, he graduated at Bowdoin College in Brunswick, Maine, where one of his classmates was **Nathaniel Hawthorne**. He spent three years in Europe (1826–29) before becoming Professor of Foreign

Languages at Bowdoin (1829–35). After another visit to Europe, when he met **Thomas Carlyle**, he became Professor of Modern Languages and Literature at Harvard (1836–54). He visited Europe again in 1842 and 1868. *Voices of the Night* (1839), his first book of verse, made a favourable impression, as did *Ballads* (1841), which included 'The Wreck of the Hesperus' and 'The Village Blacksmith'. His most popular works are *Evangeline* (1847), a tale (in hexameters) of the French exiles of Acadia, and *The Song of Hiawatha* (1855), which is based on the legends of Native Americans, using a metre borrowed from the Finnish epic, the *Kalevala*. His gift of simple, romantic story-telling in verse brought him enduring popularity as a poet. ⌨ N Arvin, *Longfellow, his life and works* (1963)

Longford, Francis Aungier Pakenham, 7th Earl of 1905–
English politician
Educated at Eton and New College, Oxford, he worked as a lecturer before joining Conservative Party headquarters as a research assistant in 1930, then returned to lecturing at Christ Church, Oxford. After being forced to resign his 1940 army commission because of ill health, he was personal assistant to Sir **William Beveridge** (1941–44), and between 1947 and 1965 held office in Labour Governments as Chancellor of the Duchy of Lancaster, Minister of Civil Aviation, First Lord of the Admiralty, Lord Privy Seal, and Secretary of State for the Colonies. In 1964 he became Leader of the House of Lords, and was Lord Privy Seal from 1966 to 1968. His distinguished public and ministerial service over nearly three decades has been eclipsed by the famous campaigns against sexual liberalism (which won him the sobriquet 'Lord Porn') and for prison reform that the earl (a Catholic convert) has conducted since the 1960s. He has been widely criticized for his attempts to secure the release of the convicted multiple murderess **Myra Hindley**, who was sentenced to life imprisonment in 1966. He has written numerous works on the prison system, politics and religion, and his notable biographies, include works on **Abraham Lincoln** (1974), **John F Kennedy** (1976) and **Richard Nixon** (1980). He has also published four volumes of autobiography namely, *Born to Believe* (1953), *Five Lives* (1964), *The Grain of Wheat* (1974) and *Avowed Intent* (1994).

Longhi, Pietro, *originally* Pietro Falca 1702–85
Italian painter
Born in Venice, he was a pupil of Antonio Balestra (1666–1740), and excelled in small-scale satiric pictures of Venetian life. Most of his work is in Venetian public collections, but the National Gallery, London, has three, of which the best known is *Rhinoceros in an Arena* (1751). His son Alessandro (1733–1813) was also a painter, and some of his portraits are now attributed to his father.

Longimanus See Artaxerxes I

Longinus probably 1st century AD
Greek literary critic
Nothing certain is known of his life, but he is author of *On the Sublime* (about two-thirds of which survives), which analyses the qualities of great literature and has been enormously influential, particularly among Romantic critics.

Longman, Evelyn Beatrice 1874–1954
US sculptor
Born near Winchester, Ohio, she attended evening classes at the Chicago Art Institute and Mount Oliver College in Michigan, before returning to Chicago where she graduated with honours in 1900. She became **Daniel French's** only female assistant before opening her own studio and gaining a series of monumental commissions, such as *Victory* for the St Louis exposition and her most famous sculpture, *Genius of Electricity*, originally installed on top of a Manhattan building. She also executed many portrait commissions in a decorative classical style. Considered to be the most successful woman sculptor of her time, she collected many awards, including the honour of being the first woman elected to the National Academy of Design.

Longman, Thomas 1699–1755
English publisher and founder of the Longman firm
He was born in Bristol, the son of a merchant. He bought a bookselling business in Paternoster Row, London, in 1724, and shared in publishing Robert Ainsworth's *Latin Dictionary*, **Ephraim Chambers's** *Cyclopaedia*, and Dr **Johnson's** *Dictionary*.

Longo, Jeannie 1958–
French cyclist
She was born in Annecy. Her numerous wins include the Women's Tour de France three times, the Colorado equivalent four times and the world title a record eight times. She was French Women's Champion on the road 11 times between 1979 and 1989 and won the Tokyo and Osaka Grand Prix events and set numerous world records indoors and out. Her career was never highlighted by an Olympic gold medal, although she came out of retirement for the Barcelona Olympics in 1992 and won a silver in the road race that year. Widely considered the best female road cyclist of all time, she is married to her coach Patrice Ciprelli, who was a former Alpine skiing internationalist.

Longstreet, James 1821–1904
US soldier
He was born in Edgefield District, South Carolina. He fought in the Mexican War (1846–48), but resigned from the US army at the outbreak of the Civil War (1861–65) to join the Confederate army as a brigadier-general. He fought in both battles of Bull Run (1861–62) and at Gettysburg (1863), and surrendered with **Robert E Lee** at Appomattox Courthouse (April 1865).

Longuet-Higgins, (Hugh) Christopher 1923–
English theoretical chemist
Born in Lenham, Kent, he studied chemistry at Balliol College, Oxford, where he was a Research Fellow from 1946 to 1948. From 1948 to 1952 he was lecturer and then Reader in Theoretical Chemistry at the University of Manchester, before briefly holding the chair of theoretical physics at King's College London, and then in 1954 becoming Plummer Professor of Theoretical Chemistry at Cambridge. From 1968 to 1974 he was Royal Society Research Professor in the department of artificial intelligence at the University of Edinburgh and from 1974 to his retirement in 1988 he held a similar position at the University of Sussex. He made fundamental contributions to the molecular orbital theory of organic and inorganic chemistry and used symmetry arguments to predict the course of various electrocyclic reactions. Following his move to Edinburgh in 1968, he embarked on a second phase of research in which he has worked on problems of the mind, including language acquisition, music perception and speech analysis. He was elected FRS in 1958 and a foreign associate of the US National Academy of Sciences in 1968, and gave the Gifford Lectures in 1972.

Longus c.3rd century AD
Greek writer
He was a native probably of Lesbos. He was the author of the pastoral romance *Daphnis and Chloë*. ⌨ B P Reardon, *Les courants littéraires grecs* (1971)

Lönnbohm, Armas Eino Leopold See Leino, Eino

Lönnrot, Elias 1802–84
Finnish philologist and folklorist
Born in Sammatti, Nyland, he studied medicine, and was district medical officer for 20 years in Kajana. As a result of his folklore researches, he was appointed Professor of Finnish at Helsingfors (Helsinki) (1853–62). His major achievement was the collection of oral popular lays, which he organized into a long epic poem of ancient life in the far north, the *Kalevala* (the shorter *Old Kalevala* in 1835, the longer version in 1849). Having standardized the national epic, he compiled a great Finnish–Swedish dictionary (1866–80), which helped establish a literary Finnish language. ◫ W Wilson, *Folklore and Nationalism in Modern Finland* (1976)

Lonsdale, Frederick, *originally* **Frederick Leonard** 1881–1954
British playwright
Born in Jersey, he was known for his witty and sophisticated society comedies, among them *The Last of Mrs Cheyney* (1925), *On Approval* (1926) and *Canaries Sometimes Sing* (1929). He collaborated on operettas, including *Maid of the Mountains* (1916). ◫ F Donaldson, *Frederick Lonsdale* (1957)

Lonsdale, Hugh Cecil Lowther, 5th Earl of 1857–1944
English sportsman
A landowner in Cumberland, he was a noted huntsman, steeplechaser, yachtsman and boxer. As president of the National Sporting Club he founded and presented the 'Lonsdale belts' for boxing.

Lonsdale, Dame Kathleen, *née* **Yardley** 1903–71
Irish crystallographer
Born in Newbridge, County Kildare, she went to Bedford College, London, to study mathematics, but changed to physics at the end of her first year. On graduating in 1922 she was invited by **William Bragg** to join his crystallography research team, first at University College London (UCL) and then at the Royal Institution, where she remained until 1946, apart from a short period when she worked at Leeds (1929–31). In 1945, when the Royal Society agreed to admit women Fellows, she was one of the first two women to be elected FRS; she was awarded the society's Davy Medal in 1957. She became Reader in Crystallography in the chemistry department of UCL (1946) and was promoted to Professor of Chemistry in 1949. She was appointed DBE in 1956, and retired in 1968. Of her many contributions to crystallography, the most celebrated was her X-ray analysis of hexamethylbenzene and hexachlorobenzene in 1929, which showed that the carbon atoms in the benzene ring are coplanar and hexagonally arranged. She also made important contributions to space-group theory and to the study of anisotropy and disorder in crystals. She became a Quaker in 1935 and later worked tirelessly for various causes including peace, penal reform and the social responsibility of science.

Lonsdale, William 1794–1871
English geologist
Born in Bath, he served in the army, but left in 1815 and took up geology. He became assistant secretary and curator of the Geological Society of London (1829–42), and spent a good deal of time studying the fossil corals in the vicinity of Bath. He also made a study of the fossils in north and south Devon in 1837, placing them between the Silurian and Carboniferous. This subsequently led to the establishment of the Devonian system by **Roderick Murchison** and **Adam Sedgwick** (1839). Lonsdale employed the evolutionary concepts that **Charles Darwin** was to champion subsequently.

Loon, Hendrik Willem Van See **Van Loon, Hendrik Willem**

Loos, Adolf 1870–1933
Austrian architect and writer on design
Born in Brno, Moravia (now in Czech Republic), he studied architecture in Dresden, spent three years in the USA, then settled in Vienna in 1896. One of the major architects of the modern movement, he is particularly important for articulating in his own short-lived journal *Das Andere* (1903), and in other articles, the view that ornament is 'wasteful', 'decadent' and against modern 'civilized' design. His buildings and other designs such as furniture, glass and metalwork, reflect this view, but possess an elegance and visual interest which is derived from their functional form.

Loos, Anita 1893–1981
US writer
Born in Sisson (now Mount Shasta), California, she began writing screenplays for **D W Griffith** in 1912. Her comic novel about Hollywood, *Gentlemen Prefer Blondes* (1925), with its naïve, gold-digging heroine Lorelei Lee, was enormously popular and was made into both a movie and a musical, though readers failed to recognize it as a satire. A prolific and successful screenwriter, Loos also adapted **Colette**'s *Gigi* for the stage (1952) and wrote two gossipy Hollywood memoirs, *A Girl Like I* (1966) and *Kiss Hollywood Goodbye* (1974). ◫ G Carey, *Anita Loos, A Biography* (1988)

Lopes, Francisco Higino Craveiro 1894–1964
Portuguese statesman
Born in Lisbon of a distinguished military family, he was educated at the Military School there and fought in the expeditionary force in Mozambique in World War I. As a full colonel in 1942 he entered negotiations for co-operation with the Allies and was responsible for the modernization of the Portuguese air force. He entered parliament in 1944, was promoted to general in 1949, and was President of Portugal from 1951 to 1958.

López, Francisco Solano 1827–70
Paraguayan statesman
Born in Asunción, a grand-nephew of **Francia**, he succeeded his father as President of Paraguay in 1862. In 1864 he provoked war with Brazil and was faced with an alliance of Brazil, Uruguay and Argentina. The war lasted for five years, during which Paraguay was completely devastated and López himself, having fled, was shot by a soldier.

Lopez, Nancy 1957–
US golfer
Born in Torrance, California, she competed as an amateur in high school and college, winning the national championships of the Association for Intercollegiate Athletics for Women in 1976. Two years later she joined the professional tour and by 1991 had taken 44 LPGA (Ladies Professional Golf Association) victories and won more than $3.2 million. Her powerful play, impeccable putting, and impressive poise in pressurized situations, is considered to be one of the reasons that women's professional golf has attracted large purses and corporate sponsorship. Inducted into the LPGA Hall of Fame (1987) and the PGA (Professional Golfers Association) Hall of Fame (1989), she was selected by the Associated Press as Female Athlete of the Year (1978, 1985), and she has been the LPGA Player of the year four times—in 1978, 1979, 1985 and 1988.

López Portillo y Pacheco, José 1920–
Mexican politician

Born into a socially prominent family in Mexico City, he practised law until 1959, when he entered government service. He rose to become Finance Minister (1971–75), then succeeded Luis Echeverría as President of Mexico (1976–82). He sought to stimulate economic growth through tax concessions, foreign investment, and the exploitation of oil resources, but his administration was plagued by corruption and a mounting foreign debt.

Lopéz Rodó, Laureano 1920–
Spanish politician, academic and lawyer

As Secretary-General of the Presidency and Commissar of the Plan of Development, he formed part of the Opus Dei group (dubbed 'the Holy Mafia' for its power under the Franco regime). The group undertook the economic modernization of Spain from the late 1950s onwards. An intimate ally of Admiral Carrero Blanco, he became one of Franco's closest associates, being the dominant minister in the Cabinet from 1965 to 1973. He was also Minister of Foreign Affairs (1973–74) and ambassador to Austria (1974–77). He played an important role in persuading Franco to accept the candidacy of Juan Carlos I as heir to the throne. After Franco's death, he joined the Alianza Popular on its foundation in 1976, being elected as a deputy for Barcelona in 1977. He left the party in 1979.

López Velarde, Ramón 1888–1921
Mexican poet and impressionistic prose writer

Born in Zacatecas, he wrote supposedly patriotic poems to his country, which although full of love, are also full of a subtle irony which, however, for the most part has not been perceived by critics. He was one of the greatest love poets of his age in any language, and perhaps the most ironic of all. His posthumous prose sketches, which can be found in his complete poems, *Poesías completas* (1957), are remarkable. His influence upon Latin-American poetry as a whole, as well as on Mexican, has been unobtrusive but absolute, and he contributed greatly towards bringing poetry out of the *modernista* phase in which it was beginning to stultify. ⊞ A W Phillips, *Ramón López Velarde* (1962, in Spanish)

Lopukhov, Fyodor Vasilevich 1886–1973
Russian dancer, choreographer and teacher

Born in St Petersburg, he studied at the Imperial Ballet Academy there before joining the Maryinsky Theatre, where he established himself as a character dancer. He started choreographing in 1916, becoming one of the leading ballet experimentalists of his generation. He set the foundation of neoclassical and modern dance in Russia, introducing acrobatics into the academic vocabulary, and developing an interest in plotless, abstract ballets as a reaction against the literary, realist traditions of the 19th century. His most influential ballet was *Dance Symphony* (1923). He was artistic director of the Kirov (1923–30, and in the mid-1940s and 1950s), and of the Maly Theatre and Bolshoi Ballet companies (both in the mid-1930s).

Lorca, Federico García See García Lorca, Federico

Loren, Sophia, *originally* Sofia Scicolone 1934–
Italian film actress

Born in Rome, and brought up in poverty near Naples, she was a teenage beauty queen and model, before entering films as an extra in *Cuori sul Mare* (1950). As the protégée of the producer Carlo Ponti, later her husband, she gained the lead in *The Pride and the Passion* (1957) and other US productions. An international career followed and she won an Academy Award for her performance in De Sica's *La Ciociara* (1960, *Two Women*). Very beautiful, with a talent for earthy drama and vivacious comedy, she has attempted a wide range of characterizations with varying degrees of success. Among her many films are *The*

Millionairess (1961), *Matrimonia all' Italiana* (1964, *Marriage Italian Style*), *C'Era una Volta* (1967, *Cinderella Italian Style*) and *Una Giornata Speciale* (1977, *A Special Day*). She published *Sophia Loren: Living and Loving* (1979, with A E Hotchner) which was filmed for television as *Sophia: Her Own Story* (1981) with the actress playing both herself and her mother. Her career continues with television films like *Aurora* (1984) and *Courage* (1986). She received a Special Academy Award in 1991. Recent films include *Prêt-à-Porter* (1994) and *Grumpier Old Men* (1995). ⊞ A E Hotchner, *Sophia, Living and Loving: Her Own Story* (1979)

Lorente de No, Rafael 1902–
US neurophysiologist

He was born in Zaragoza, Spain, and studied medicine at the University of Madrid. After a period as a research assistant in the Cajal Institute in Madrid (1921–29) he was appointed head of the department of otolaryngology in Santander (1929–31) before travelling to the USA. From 1936 he worked at the Rockefeller Institute in New York (associate, 1936–38; associate member, 1938–41; member and professor, 1941–74). His research covered a wide range of neurophysiological and neuroanatomical problems, including the co-ordination of eye movements, the functional anatomy of neuron networks, and the neurophysiology of synaptic transmission.

Lorentz, Hendrik Antoon 1853–1928
Dutch physicist and Nobel Prize winner

Born in Arnhem, he studied at the University of Leyden and at the age of 25 was offered at Leyden (1878) the first chair of theoretical physics which had been created for Johannes van der Waals. He remained there until 1912 when he was appointed director of Teyler's Institute in Haarlem. His major contribution to theoretical physics was his electron theory. His derivation in 1904 of a mathematical transformation, the 'Fitzgerald–Lorentz contraction', explained the apparent absence of relative motion between the Earth and the (supposed) ether, and prepared the way for Albert Einstein's theories of relativity. In 1902 he was awarded, with Pieter Zeeman, the Nobel Prize for physics. He served as president of the League of Nations' International Committee of Intellectual Co-operation, was made a Foreign Member of the Royal Society in 1905, and was awarded its Copley Medal in 1912. ⊞ G L De Haas-Lorentz (ed), *H A Lorentz: Impressions of His Life and Work* (1957)

Lorenz, Edward Norton 1917–
US mathematician and meteorologist

Born in West Hartford, Connecticut, he was educated at Dartmouth College and Harvard University. He became an assistant meteorologist at the Massachusetts Institute of Technology (MIT) in 1946, and was appointed professor in 1962. He introduced a simplified model of the general circulation of the atmosphere, demonstrating that the equations possessed one or two steady-state solutions, one or two stable but periodic solutions, and also aperiodic (irregular) solutions. He concluded that the real atmosphere could probably jump from one major mode to another. It contains periodic motions (eg the annual cycle), but there are also irregular motions introduced by atmospheric conditions. He went on to demonstrate how weather systems produced from slightly different initial conditions diverge with time, and proved the limit of predictability of useful forecasts to be about 10–14 days. He was awarded the Symons gold medal of the Royal Meteorological Society in 1973.

Lorenz, Konrad Zacharias 1903–89
Austrian zoologist, ethologist and Nobel Prize winner

Born in Vienna, he studied there and founded, with Nikolaas Tinbergen in the late 1930s, the science of ethology (the study of animal behaviour under natural

conditions). Rather than studying animal learning in laboratories, Lorenz and his colleagues favoured the investigation of instinctive behaviour by animals in the wild. They mainly studied the behaviour of birds, fish and some insects whose behaviours contain a relatively high proportion of stereotyped elements or 'fixed action patterns', and made comparisons between species. His studies have led to a deeper understanding of behaviour patterns. In 1935 he published his observations on imprinting in young birds (the discovery for which he is chiefly known), by which hatchlings 'learn' to recognize substitute parents at the earliest stages in life. In his book *On Aggression* (1963) he argued that while aggressive behaviour in man is inborn it may be modified or channelled into other forms of activity, whereas in other animals it is purely survival-motivated. His books *King Solomon's Ring* (1949), *Man Meets Dog* (1950), and *Evolution and Modification of Behaviour* (1961) also enjoyed wide popularity. He shared the 1973 Nobel Prize for physiology or medicine with Nikolaas Tinbergen and **Karl von Frisch**.
📖 Alec Nisbett, *Konrad Lorenz* (1976)

Lorenz, Ludwig Valentin 1829–91
Danish physicist

Born in Elsinore, he trained as a civil engineer at the Technical University of Denmark in Copenhagen, going on to became professor at the Danish Military Academy in 1866. He investigated many areas of optics, heat and the electrical conductivity of metals. In his search for a phenomenological description of the way light passes through matter, he advanced a mathematical description for light waves (1863), showing that under certain conditions double refraction will occur. His work on relating refraction and specific densities of media (1869) was combined with that of **Hendrik Lorentz** to produce the Lorentz–Lorenz formula. From observations of the scattering of sunlight he made the first fairly accurate estimate of **Amedeo Avogadro's** number (1890), and without knowledge of **James Clerk Maxwell's** results, he published his own theory of electromagnetism.

Lorenzetti, Ambrogio c.1290–1348
Italian painter

Born in Siena, he worked in Cortona and Florence. He is best known for his allegorical frescoes in the Palazzo Pubblico at Siena, symbolizing the effects of good and bad government. An *Annunciation* (1344) is also at Siena. He was the younger brother of **Pietro Lorenzetti**.

Lorenzetti, Pietro, *also called* Pietro Laurati
c.1280–c.1348
Italian painter

He was born in Siena. Probably a pupil of **Duccio di Buoninsegna**, he was one of the liveliest of the early Sienese painters, and he also worked at Arezzo (the polyptych in S Maria della Pieve) and Assisi, where he painted dramatic frescoes of the *Passion* in the Lower Church of S Francis. A *Madonna* (1340) is in the Uffizi Gallery, Florence. He was the elder brother of **Ambrogio Lorenzetti**.

Lorenzo, Monaco, *originally* Piero di Giovanni
c.1370–c.1425
Italian painter

Born in Siena, he became a monk of the Camaldolese order in 1391 and lived and worked in Florence. (Lorenzo Monaco means 'Laurence the Monk.') He began as a painter of miniatures in the monastery of S Maria degli Angeli, but later executed many notable altarpieces, especially the *Coronation of the Virgin*. His pictures are represented in both the Uffizi and Louvre galleries.

Lorenzo, Piero di See **Piero di Cosimo**

Lorimer, Sir Robert Stodart 1864–1929
Scottish architect

He was born in Edinburgh, the son of jurist James Lorimer (1818–90), and educated at The Edinburgh Academy and Edinburgh University. He left without a degree and was articled to an architect's office first in Edinburgh and then in London. He set up on his own in Edinburgh in 1892, working on Scottish country houses like Hill of Tarvit in Fife (1904) and creating a distinctive Scottish form of the Arts and Crafts tradition of his English contemporary **Edwin Lutyens**. He built or totally remodelled some 50 country houses in Great Britain, like Rowallan in Ayrshire (1902), Ardkinglas in Argyll (1906), and the classical Marchmont in Berwickshire (1914). His most notable public works were the Thistle Chapel in St Giles, Edinburgh (1909–11), and the Scottish National War Memorial in Edinburgh Castle (1923–28). He also restored many castles, mansions and churches, including Balmanno House in Perthshire, Dunrobin Castle in Sutherland, Paisley Abbey and Dunblane Cathedral. His elder brother, John Henry Lorimer (1856–1936), was a noted artist, and produced the celebrated painting *Ordination of Elders in a Scottish Kirk*.

Lorimer, William Laughton 1885–1967
Scottish classicist

Born in Strathmartine, near Dundee, and belonging to a long tradition of Free Church of Scotland ministers, he was educated at Dundee High School, Fettes College, Edinburgh, and Trinity College, Oxford. He became assistant lecturer and subsequently lecturer in Greek (1910–29), Reader in Humanity (1929–53) and Professor of Greek (1953–55) at University College, Dundee. He was chairman of the Executive Council and a member of the editorial committee of the *Scottish National Dictionary*. He is best-known for his translation of the New Testament from Greek into Scots, necessarily recreating much of Scots prose in the process. His work dominated the last years of his teaching life and all of his retirement, involving the study of 180 translations in more than 20 languages, as well as the study of all known linguistic sources, and all significant commentaries. His manuscripts were revised after his death by his son, R L C Lorimer, and published in 1983 and 1985.

Lorjou, Bernard 1908–
French artist

Born in Blois, he was without formal training. He was the founder of L'Homme Témoin group of Social Realist painters in 1949 and among a number of large satirical paintings is his *Atomic Age* (1951). He later developed a violently expressive style with bold black outlines against a light background.

Lorraine, Claude See **Claude**

Lorre, Peter, *originally* Laszlo Löwenstein 1904–64
Hungarian actor

Born in Rosenberg, he studied in Vienna, where he acted in repertory theatre and gave one-man performances and readings. His early theatre appearances include *Pionier in Inoplastadt* (1928) in Berlin. He also appeared as the pathetic child murderer in **Fritz Lang's** classic *M* (1931), and thereby set the seal on much of his subsequent career. A diffident, sad-eyed figure with a whispering, wheedling voice, he was generally typecast as smilingly sinister villains and outcasts. He moved to Hollywood (1934), where his many successes included *Casablanca* (1942) and *The Beast With Five Fingers* (1946). A rare excursion to the right side of the law saw him cast as **John P Marquand's** Japanese detective Mr Moto in eight films, and he also formed an unholy alliance with Sydney Greenstreet (1879–1954) that was seen to particular advantage in *The Maltese Falcon* (1941) and *The Mask of Dimitrios* (1944). He wrote and directed one film in Europe, *Der Verlorene* (1951, *The Lost One*).

Lorris, Guillaume de fl.13th century
French poet

He wrote, before 1260, the first part (c.4,000 lines) of the *Roman de la Rose* (completed c.1280, Eng trans *The Romaunt of the Rose* by **Chaucer**, c.1370), which was later continued by **Jean de Meung**. Nothing certain is known of his life.

Lortzing, Gustav Albert 1801–51
German musician

Born in Berlin, the son of an actor, he took to the stage as a young boy, and learned about the main orchestral instruments. In 1824 he produced his first operetta, *Ali Pascha von Janina* ('Ali Pasha of Ioannina'). He became first tenor with the Leipzig Theatre (1833–43), and conducted and composed operas such as *Zar und Zimmermann* (1837, 'Tsar and Carpenter') for which he also wrote the libretti.

Losey, Joseph (Walton) 1909–84
US film director

He was born in La Crosse, Wisconsin, studied English literature at Harvard and wrote arts reviews and directed for the New York stage before making his film debut with the marionette short *Pete Roleum and His Cousins* (1939). His short film *A Gun in His Hand* (1945) received an Academy Award nomination. He directed *Galileo* (1947) in Los Angeles and New York before turning to film full time with *The Boy with Green Hair* (1945) and *The Prowler* (1951). Falling foul of the **McCarthy** witchhunts, he moved to the UK in 1951 and gained lasting acclaim for his collaborations with **Harold Pinter** on such films as *The Servant* (1963) and *Accident* (1967). *The Go-Between* (1971) won the Palme D'Or at the Cannes Film Festival. His later films include *Don Giovanni* (1979) and *Steaming* (1984), which was completed shortly before his death.

Lo Spagnoletto See Ribera, Jusepe de

Loti, Pierre See Viaud, Louis Marie Julien

Lotto, Lorenzo c.1480–1556
Italian religious painter

Born in Venice, he was a brilliant portrait painter whose subjects are vivid and full of character. He worked in Treviso, Bergamo, Venice and Rome, finally becoming a lay brother in the Loreto monastery.

Lotze, Rudolf Hermann 1817–81
German philosopher

Born in Bautzen, Saxony, he studied philosophy and medicine at Leipzig and became Professor of Philosophy at Leipzig (1842–44), Göttingen (1844–80) and Berlin (1880–81). He first became known as a physiologist, opposing the then popular doctrine of 'vitalism'. He also helped to found the science of physiological psychology, but he is best known for his religious philosophy, called 'Theistic Idealism', which is most fully expounded in *Mikrokosmos* (3 vols, 1856–58).

Loudon, John Claudius 1783–1843
Scottish horticultural writer, dendrologist and designer

Born in Cambuslang, Strathclyde, he worked in England and travelled in Europe, and founded and edited *The Gardener's Magazine* (1826–43). He also compiled an *Encyclopaedia of Gardening* (1822), in which he illustrated a wrought-iron sash bar he had invented in 1816, which could be bent in any direction but still maintain its strength. This paved the way for spectacular edifices like the Palm House in Kew Gardens and the Crystal Palace. In Porchester Terrace, London, he designed the prototype semi-detached house. He founded and edited the *Architectural Magazine* (1834), and published an influential *Encyclopaedia of Cottage, Farm and Villa Architecture and Furniture* (1833). His major work was *Arboretum et Fruticetum Britannicum* (8 vols, 1838), devoted to trees and shrubs.

Louganis, Greg 1960–
US diver

Born in El Cajon, California, of Samoan and Swedish ancestry, he took a BA in drama at the University of California. He won the gold medal in both the springboard and platform diving competitions at the 1984 Los Angeles Olympics, and won the world championship at both events in 1986. At the Seoul Olympics in 1988 he won gold medals in the same two categories despite receiving a head injury during the competition. In 1995 he revealed that he was infected with the HIV virus, and in the same year he published an autobiography, *Breaking the Surface*, which became a bestseller.

Loughlin, Dame Anne 1894–1979
English trade unionist

Born in Leeds, she became involved in union affairs after working in a clothing factory, and was a full-time organizer by the time of the Hebden Bridge strike by 6,000 clothing workers in 1916. In 1920 she was appointed women's officer of the Tailors and Garment Workers Union, and worked tirelessly to improve working conditions and to increase union strength. In 1948 she became general secretary of the National Union of Tailors and Garment Workers. She served on many government committees, as well as the Royal Commission on Equal Pay. In 1943 she became the first trade unionist to be created DBE, and also the first woman president of the Trades Union Congress.

Louis I, *known as* Louis the Pious 778–840
King of Aquitaine, King of the Franks and Emperor of the Western or Carolingian Empire

Born near Poitiers, he was the sole surviving son of **Charlemagne**. He was King of Aquitaine from 781 to 814, and Carolingian Emperor from 814 until his death. In 817 he attempted to secure his succession by dividing his territories between his three sons, Lothair (d.855), Pepin (d.838) and Louis 'the German' (d.876), with Lothair to be the emperor. In 829 a further share was given to a fourth son, Charles the Bald (**Charles I** of France). Louis I collaborated with St Benedict of Aniane to reform the Church, was a distinguished patron of scholarship, and defended the north-west from the raids of the Norsemen. It is greatly debated how far the proliferation of hereditary countships and of the institutions of vassalage, often thought to result from these raids, caused a general decline in imperial authority. After his death the empire disintegrated as his sons fought for supremacy.

Louis II, *known as* Louis the Stammerer 846–79
King of the Franks

He was the second son of **Charles I**, the Bald. King of Maine (856) and Aquitaine (867), he was often in revolt against his father, whom he succeeded with great difficulty as King of the Franks (877).

Louis III 863–82
King of France

He was the eldest son of **Louis II**, on whose death (879) he was proclaimed joint king with his brother **Carloman**. He took Francia and Neustria as his territories. He defeated the pagan Norsemen at Saucourt (881), and was succeeded by Carloman.

Louis IV, d'Outremer 921–54
King of France

He was the son of **Charles III**, the Simple, himself the posthumous son of **Louis II**. His early life was spent in exile in England but he was recalled on the death of King Raoul by Hugh the Great (father of **Hugo Capet**) from whose political domination he successfully escaped. Nevertheless, during his reign (936–954) many territorial princes in France consolidated their power to his cost. He was succeeded by his son, Lothair IV, and his grandson **Louis V**.

Louis V, le Fainéant 967–87
King of France

The son of Lothair IV, he was associated with Lothair's kingship (978). He ruled France from 986, but died heirless and was thus the last Carolingian ruler of France. The throne passed to **Hugo Capet**, the first of the Capetian line.

Louis VI, *known as* Louis the Fat 1081–1137
King of France

He succeeded his father **Philip I** in 1108. For most of his reign he campaigned incessantly against the turbulent and unruly nobility of the Île-de-France and eventually re-established his royal authority. Despite an inclination to gluttony and a corpulence which left him unable to mount a horse after the age of 46, he was one of the most active of the House of **Capet**, and greatly increased the power and prestige of the monarchy.

Louis VII c.1120–1180
King of France

The second son of **Louis VI**, he was originally educated for a Church career, but became heir on the death of his brother Philip (1131). In 1137 he became king, married **Eleanor of Aquitaine**, and continued the consolidation of royal authority begun by his father. He participated in the Second Crusade (1147), and had his marriage annulled (1152), whereupon Eleanor married Henry Plantagenet, Count of Anjou, who became King of England in 1154 as **Henry II**. Against such a vast mass of power on both sides of the Channel, Louis enlisted papal support and instigated discord within Henry's family.

Louis VIII, *known as* Louis the Lion 1187–1226
King of France

Born in Paris, the son of **Philip II** and Isabella of Hainault, he participated during his father's reign in attacks on the English (1214, 1216) and led two brief crusades against the heretics of the County of Toulouse (1215, 1219). He ruled France from 1223, acquired the de Montfort claim to the County of Toulouse (1224) and resumed the Albigensian Crusade in the south (1226). Despite his dubious death in the autumn of that year (variously attributed to poisoning, dysentery and sexual starvation) this royal crusade led to the submission of Count Raymond VII to his widow, Blanche of Castile (1229), and the eventual absorption of all Languedoc into the royal domain.

Louis IX, *also called* St Louis 1214–70
King of France

In 1226 he succeeded his father, **Louis VIII**; his mother, the pious Blanche of Castile, was his regent until 1234. Making Blanche regent again, he joined the Seventh Crusade (1248–54), but was defeated and captured, and ransomed for one million marks in 1250. He remained in Palestine, fortifying Christian strongholds, until his mother's death (1252). His long and peaceful reign strengthened the Capetian dynasty. He founded the Abbey of Royamount (1228), built the Sainte-Chapelle in Paris to hold the crown of thorns relic he acquired from Constantinople (Istanbul), determined by the Pragmatic Sanction the relations between the French Church and the Pope, countenanced the Sorbonne, set up in the provinces royal courts of justice or parliaments, and authorized a new code of laws. By the Treaty of Paris (1259) he made peace with England, recognizing **Henry III** as Duke of Aquitaine in exchange for French suzerainty elsewhere. In 1270 he embarked on a new crusade, but

died of plague in Tunis. He was canonized by Pope **Boniface VIII** in 1297, and his feast day is 25 August.
📖 William C Jordan, *Louis IX* (1979)

Louis X, *known as* Louis the Quarrelsome 1289–1316
King of Navarre and of France

The son of **Philip IV**, the Fair, he was King of Navarre (1305–16) and King of France (1314–16). During his brief reign, which was marked by unrest among his barons, he was guided in his policy by **Charles of Valois**.

Louis XI 1423–83
King of France

The son of **Charles VII** and Mary of Anjou, he was born in Bourges, and as Dauphin of France he married Margaret of Scotland (daughter of King **James I**) in 1436. He made two unsuccessful attempts to depose his father, but eventually succeeded to the throne on his father's death (1461). Though able and intelligent, his craftiness and treachery earned him the title 'spider-king'. He survived a coalition against him (1465) and broke the power of the nobility, led by **Charles, the Bold** of Burgundy, who was killed in 1477. By 1483 Louis had succeeded in uniting most of France under one Crown (with the exception of Brittany), and laid the foundations for absolute monarchy in France. He actively encouraged trade and industry, cherished the arts and sciences, and founded three universities, but he spent his latter years in great misery, suffering superstitious terrors and excessive fear of death.

Louis XII, *known as* the Father of the People 1462–1515
King of France

Born in Blois, the son of Charles, Duc d'Orléans, he succeeded his cousin **Charles VIII** (the Affable) in 1498, and married his widow **Anne of Brittany** (he had previously been married to a daughter of **Louis XI**). His military ambitions failed when his forces were driven from Italy (1512) and he was also defeated at the Battle of the Spurs by **Henry VIII** (1513). To guarantee peace, Louis married Mary Tudor, sister of Henry VIII, in 1514. Popular at home, he was responsible for continuing the trend towards centralized absolution and was concerned with providing justice and avoiding oppressive taxation.
📖 Frederic J Baumgartner, *Louis XII* (1994)

Louis XIII 1601–43
King of France

The eldest son of **Henri IV** of France and his second wife **Marie de Médicis**, he was born at Fontainebleau, and was only nine years old when his father was assassinated. In 1615 his mother, as regent, arranged his marriage to **Anne of Austria** (daughter of Philip III of Spain). Their eldest son, not born until 1638, succeeded him as **Louis XIV**. In 1617 he overthrew the regency of his mother, exiling her to the provinces, and assumed power. A devout Catholic, he attempted with moderate success to subdue the French Huguenots, and supported Emperor **Ferdinand II** in his struggle with the German Protestants. Conscientious, deeply religious and reserved, he had a strong sense of his royal position. In 1624 he appointed as his Chief Minister Cardinal **Richelieu**, who became the dominating influence of his reign. Richelieu subdued Huguenot resistance with the capture of La Rochelle (1628), while he supported the Protestants in Germany to prevent Habsburg domination of Europe. In 1629 Louis led a campaign in Italy to prevent Spanish expansion there. Although Richelieu was largely responsible for the centralization of administration and systematic patronage of the arts, the king was no cipher, and defended his minister against various plots, especially on the Day of Dupes (1630). On the death of Richelieu (1642) he turned to Cardinal **Mazarin**, who became his widow's favourite during her regency for Louis XIV. 📖 E W Marvick, *Louis XIII* (1987)

Louis XIV, *known as* Le Roi Soleil ('The Sun King') 1638–1715
King of France from 1643

Louis was born in St Germain-en-Laye, the son of **Louis XIII** and **Anne of Austria**, and came to the throne at the age of five. During his minority (1643–51), the government was carried on by his mother and her Chief Minister and lover, Cardinal **Jules Mazarin**, and Mazarin continued to exercise control until his death in 1661. Then Louis was his own Chief Minister, working with unremitting energy and making all the important decisions himself (*L'état, c'est moi*: '*I* am the state'). Pious and conservative, he was able to present himself within France and throughout Europe as the model of royal absolutism. In 1660 Louis married the Infanta Maria Theresa of Spain (1638–83), daughter of **Philip IV**.

Louis' reign is characterized by aggressive foreign policies, especially against the Dutch and Spanish, and by artistic and architectural splendour at home. The maintenance of high tax levels enabled him to build great palaces, especially Versailles (1676–1708). He built up a navy and remodelled the French army into the most formidable fighting force in Europe. After the death of his father-in-law in 1665, Louis laid claim to part of the Spanish Netherlands and launched the War of Dutch Devolution (1667–68) under the command of **Turenne** and **Condé**, which provoked a triple alliance between Great Britain, Holland and Sweden and ended with the Treaty of Aix-La-Chapelle.

In the Second Dutch War (1672–78), Louis had Britain as an ally, having bribed **Charles II** with the secret Treaty of Dover (1670); his assault was only halted when William of Orange (later **William III** of Britain) opened the sluices and inundated the country, but France did well out of the Peace of Nijmegen that ended the war in 1678. In the 1680s he secured Strasbourg and Luxembourg. His wife, Maria Theresa, died in 1683, and in 1685 Louis privately married one of his mistresses, the Marquise de **Maintenon**, under whose Catholic influence he passed the Revocation of the Edict of Nantes (1685) which led to

a bloody persecution of Protestants and mass emigration of French Huguenots to Holland and England.

In 1689 the opponents of French expansionism formed the Grand Alliance, which was strengthened by the addition of William III in England. The French were victorious at Mons (1691), Steenkirk (1692) and Neerwinden (1693), and defeated an Anglo-Dutch fleet off Cape St Vincent (1693); but the allies maintained a stubborn resistance, and by the Treaty of Ryswick (1697) Louis had to yield most of his territorial gains.

In 1700 **Charles II** of Spain died; in his will he bequeathed his throne to Louis's grandson, Philip of Anjou (**Philip V** of Spain). The prospect of a union of the Crowns of Spain and France so alarmed the other European powers that it gave rise to the War of the Spanish Succession (1701–14), which proved disastrous for France with crushing defeats at Blenheim (1704) and Ramillies (1706). Peace was only finally achieved with the Treaty of Utrecht (1713), two years before Louis' death, leaving France practically bankrupt.

📖 John B Wolf, *Louis XIV* (1968); Nancy Mitford, *The Sun King* (1966); Jacques Roujon, *Louis XIV* (1943).

> The reign of Louis, 'The Sun King', had been the longest in European history, a reign of incomparable brilliance; it was the Augustan Age of French literature and art, the age of **Corneille, Molière, Racine, Lully, Poussin** and **Claude**. His only son, Louis, died in 1711, and the Dauphin (his grandson, Louis of Burgundy) had died in 1712; so Louis XIV was succeeded by his great-grandson, the five-year-old **Louis XV**.

> 'How could God do this to me after all I have done for him?' Louis' reaction to hearing the news of the French defeat at Blenheim, August 1704. Quoted in L Norton, *Saint-Simon at Versailles* (1958).

Louis XIV See panel above

Louis XV, *known as* le Bien-Aimé ('the Well-Beloved')
1710–74
King of France

Born in Versailles, he succeeded his great-grandfather, Louis XIV, in 1715, aged only five. His regent, Philippe, Duc d'Orléans, a tolerant and liberal man, created much scandal by his private life and on his death in 1723 he was replaced briefly by the Duc de Bourbon. Louis came of age in 1723, married Maria, the daughter of the deposed King of Poland, Stanisłas I Leszczyński in 1725, and in 1726 replaced Bourbon by his former tutor, the Cardinal de Fleury. Fleury governed France well until his death in 1744 at the age of 90 but in 1740 France became embroiled, against his wishes, in the War of the Austrian Succession, in which Louis took part, falling seriously ill while at Metz in 1744. A popular king, the evident relief of his subjects at his recovery led to his being nicknamed '*le Bien-Aimé*'. Faced with his responsibilities as head of state, Louis was well intentioned but lacked Louis XIV's interest in politics or administration. He concentrated on preserving the royal autocracy to which he had succeeded and defending it from orthodox Catholics but was unable to effect any real reform of the system he had inherited. The heavy losses incurred under his command at Fontenoy left him with a marked distaste for warfare. In addition, he allowed his personal life to interfere with state matters as one particular mistress, Madame de Pompadour, who became 'reigning mistress' in 1745, used her position to exert considerable influence over government policy. However, fiscal reform advocated by the

comptroller-general Machault was blocked and local bureaucracies increased in power, notably the *Intendants* who were the king's principal representatives in the provinces. Peace in Europe had been temporarily achieved in 1748 but in 1756 renewed hostilities in Europe involved France in the Seven Years War. A series of military disasters abroad led to the replacement of the Foreign Minister, Bernis, by the Duc de Choiseul, a liberal and a friend and ally of Madame de Pompadour, who achieved peace with the *Pacte de famille* (1761), a permanent alliance with Spain, and rebuilt the weakened French navy. Choiseul regarded the Treaty of Paris (1763), which established British hegemony in India and North America, as little more than a truce in the continuing struggle between France and Great Britain, but Louis favoured a general European peace and worked behind Choiseul's back to promote diplomatic initiatives with this aim. Abroad Choiseul was able to incorporate the Duchy of Lorraine into France (1766) and conquer Corsica, a former Genoese colony (1770). At home, he was largely responsible, in alliance with the Parlements, for the suppression of the French Jesuits, despite the misgivings of Louis. Madame de Pompadour died in 1764, the Dauphin the following year and the queen in 1768. Louis found a new mistress and companion in Madame du Barry. The new Dauphin, Louis's grandson, the future Louis XVI, was married in 1770 to Marie Antoinette, the youngest daughter of the Habsburg Empress Maria Theresa, cementing the alliance between France and the Empire. In the same year, Choiseul, at Madame du Barry's insistence, was dismissed. To the growing displeasure of the Parlements all future projects for reform were abandoned. Louis and his new Chancellor, Maupeou, attempted to curb the Parlements' power, replacing the hereditary magistracy with a new body of royal nominees. However, the old system was reinstated after Louis's death. His last years were ones of peace abroad and deceptive calm at home, but the prestige of the royal government had never been lower and the France Louis left to his grandson remained in the grip of the same antiquated autocracy he had inherited, weakened but unreformed. ⌑ G P Gooch, *Louis XV: The Monarchy In Decline* (1956)

Louis XVI 1754–93
King of France

He was born at Versailles, the third son of the Dauphin Louis and Maria Josepha of Saxony. He became Dauphin by the death of his father and his elder brothers, and succeeded his grandfather **Louis XV** in 1774. He was married in 1770 to **Marie Antoinette**, youngest daughter of the Habsburg Empress **Maria Theresa**, to strengthen the Franco-Austrian alliance. When he ascended the throne the treasury was empty, the state was in debt to 4,000 million livres, and taxation levels were excessive. Reforms proposed by **Chrétien Malesherbes** and **Anne Robert Turgot** were accepted by the king, but rejected by the court, aristocracy, parliaments and Church. Louis managed to make some reforms and to relieve some of the fiscal problems and was for a time extremely popular. In 1777 **Jacques Necker** was made director-general, and succeeded in bringing the finances to a more tolerable condition, but through France's outlay in the American Revolution he was obliged to propose the taxation of the privileged classes, which led to his resignation. He was replaced by **Charles Calonne** (1783) who renewed for a while the splendour of the court, and advised the calling together of an Assembly of Notables. His successor, Brienne, obtained some new taxes, but the parliament of Paris refused to register the edict. The convening of the Estates General was universally demanded. Louis registered the edicts and banished the councillors of parliament, but had to recall them. In May 1788 he dissolved all the parliaments and established a *Cour plénière*. In August he ordered that the Treasury should cease all cash payments except to the army. The Estates General, in abeyance since 1614, met in May 1789 at Versailles. The *tiers-état* (third estate) formed themselves into a National Assembly, thereby commencing the Revolution, and called themselves the Constituent Assembly. The resistance of Louis to the demands of the deputies for political independence and equal rights led to their declaration of inviolability. Louis deployed troops, dissolved the Ministry and banished Necker. With revolutionary outbreaks in Paris on 12 July 1789, the National Guard of Paris was called out. On 14 July the people stormed the Bastille and the unrest spread to the provinces. On 4 August feudal and manorial rights, which declared the equality of human rights, were abrogated by the Assembly. The royal princes and all the nobles who could escape sought safety in flight. The royal family remained at Versailles and tried to conciliate the people by the feigned assumption of republican sentiments, but on 5 October the palace was attacked, compelling them to return to Paris, where the Assembly also moved. For two years Louis alternately made concessions to the republicans, and devised schemes for escape. The Constituent Assembly was succeeded in 1791 by the Legislative Assembly and in April 1792 Louis was compelled by the Girondins to a war (ultimately unsuccessful) with Austria. After the advance of the Prussians under the Duke of Brunswick into Champagne the Assembly dissolved itself, the National Convention took its place, and the Republic was proclaimed. In December the king was brought to trial, and called upon to answer for repeated acts of treason against the Republic. On 20 January 1793 sentence of death was passed, and next day he was guillotined in the Place de la Révolution, ending 1,025 years of monarchy. ⌑ S K Padover, *Life and Death of Louis XVI* (1939)

Louis XVII 1785–95
Titular King of France

Born Louis Charles at Versailles, the second son of **Louis XVI**, he became Dauphin on the death of his brother (1789). He became king (but only in name) in prison on the execution of his father (1793). He died, probably of tuberculosis, but rumour suggested by poison. Many persons subsequently claimed to be the Dauphin.

Louis XVIII, *in full* Louis Stanislas Xavier, Comte de Provence 1755–1824
King of France

Born at Versailles, he was the younger brother of **Louis XVI**. He fled from Paris to Belgium (1791), and eventually took refuge in England (1807). He declared himself king in 1795, following the death of his nephew, the Dauphin **Louis XVII**, and became the focal point for the Royalist cause. On **Napoleon I**'s downfall (1814) he re-entered Paris, and promised a Constitutional Charter. His restoration to the throne was interrupted by Napoleon's return from Elba until after Waterloo (1815). His reign was marked by the introduction of parliamentary government with a limited franchise, but after 1820 the hardline ultras, who favoured no concessions to Revolution principles, increased their control.

Louis (Lajos) I, *known as* Louis the Great 1326–82
King of Hungary and of Poland

He succeeded his father, **Charles Robert** (as King of Hungary in 1342), and campaigned unsuccessfully (1344–56) against Queen Giovanna of Naples, who was implicated in the murder of her husband Andrew, Louis's brother. He conquered Dalmatia, including the port of Dubrovnik, from Venice (1358), and also became King of Poland (1370) on the death of his uncle Casimir III. A notable patron of the arts, Louis founded the first Hungarian university at Pécs in 1367.

Louis IV, *known as* Louis the Bavarian c.1283–1347
Holy Roman Emperor

The son of Louis, Duke of Upper Bavaria, he was born in Munich, and was elected King of Germany (1314), in opposition to Frederick II, Duke of Austria, whom he eventually defeated at Mühldorf (1322). Pope **John XXII**, however, refused to recognize his title, referring to him only as Louis the Bavarian, a name which stuck. In 1328 he received the imperial crown from the people of Rome, but was forced to leave Italy the next year. Thereafter Louis remained mostly in Germany, maintaining his position against internal opposition with the financial support of the cities. He waged a war of propaganda against the papacy with the help of **Marsilius of Padua**, William of **Ockham**, and the Spiritual Franciscans; he invaded Italy (1327–30), captured Rome and set up an antipope, Nicholas V (1328–30), in opposition to Pope John. In 1338, at the Diet of Rhens, the electoral princes precipitated a Church/State division by declaring that the emperor did not require papal confirmation of his election. His energetic policy of family aggrandizement, however, cost him his alliance with the House of Luxembourg, who raised up a rival emperor, **Charles IV**, a year before Louis met his death while hunting.

Louis Philippe, *known as* the Citizen King
1773–1850
King of the French

Born in Paris, he was the eldest son of the Duc d'Orléans, and was brought up by Madame de Genlis. He joined the National Guard, and, like his father, renounced his titles and assumed the surname 'Égalité'. He fought in the wars of the republic, but deserted to the Austrians. For a time he lived in exile, mainly in Twickenham, London (1800–09). In 1809 he married Marie Amélie, daughter of Ferdinand I of the Two Sicilies and on the Restoration he recovered his estates. After the Revolution of 1830 he was appointed lieutenant-general, and then elected king. The country prospered under the rule of the 'citizen king', which saw victory of the upper bourgeoisie over the aristocracy, but their political corruption united all extremists in a cry for electoral reform. Louis Philippe took a middle course between the extreme right-wing Legitimists and socialists and republicans. Numerous rebellions and assassination attempts led him to more repressive actions like muzzling newspapers and tampering with trial by jury. Agricultural and industrial depression (1846) caused widespread discontent, and when the Paris mob rose (February 1848), he was forced to abdicate, and escaped to England as 'Mr Smith'. He died in Claremont, Surrey.

Louis the Bavarian See Louis IV

Louis, Joe, professional name of Joseph Louis Barrow 1914–81
US boxer

Born in Lexington, Alabama, he won the US amateur light-heavyweight title in 1934 and turned professional. In 1936 he was defeated for the first time, by the German champion Max Schmeling, with a knock-out in the 12th round (but he took merciless revenge with a first round knock-out in a return bout). He won the world championship by beating James J Braddock in 1937, and held it for a record 12 years, defending his title 25 times. He retired in 1949, but later made unsuccessful comebacks against Ezzard Charles in 1950 and Rocky Marciano in 1951. A boxer of legendary swiftness, power and grace, he won 68 of his 71 professional fights. ⌑ Gerald Astor, *And a Credit to His Race: The Hard Life and Times of Joseph Louis Barrow, a.k.a. Joe Louis* (1974)

Louis, Morris, originally Morris Bernstein 1912–62
US painter

Born in Baltimore, he was influenced in the early 1950s by Jackson Pollock and the New York Action Painters, but more decisive was the impact of Helen Frankenthaler, whose *Mountains and Sea* (1952) inspired him to throw acrylic paint on to unprimed canvases to create brilliant patches of abstract colour, forms without depth.

Louis, Pierre See Louÿs, Pierre

Louis, Pierre-Charles-Alexandre 1787–1872
French clinician and pathologist

Born in Ai, Champagne, he trained in medicine in Paris and practised for seven years in Russia, where his powerlessness in the face of a diphtheria epidemic convinced him that his medical knowledge was woefully inadequate. He returned to Paris and immersed himself in a hospital for seven years, collecting thousands of case histories and performing hundreds of autopsies. This resulted ultimately in his important publications on tuberculosis and typhoid fever, and in his introduction of the 'numerical method' for evaluating the effects of therapy. Louis's numerical method was a forerunner of the modern drug trial.

Louisa 1776–1810
Queen of Prussia

She was born in Hanover, where her father, Duke Karl of Mecklenburg-Strelitz, was commandant. Married to the Crown Prince of Prussia (afterwards Frederick William III)

in 1793, she was the mother of Frederick William IV and Wilhelm I. She endeared herself to her people by her spirit and energy during the period of national calamity that followed the Battle of Jena (1806), and especially by her patriotic and self-denying efforts to obtain concessions at Tilsit (1807) from Napoleon I, though he had shamelessly slandered her.

Loutherbourg, Philippe Jacques de 1740–1812
British painter, stage designer and illustrator

Born in Germany, he was educated at Strasbourg. His work, exhibited at the Paris Salon, attracted the attention of Diderot. In 1771 he moved to London and was hired by David Garrick as artistic adviser for his Drury Lane theatre, and he became a British subject. He devised many innovatory stage design techniques, including dramatic transparent backdrops, which influenced contemporary English landscape painting. In 1781 he invented his celebrated *Eidophusikon*, a moving panorama complete with lighting and sound effects which fascinated many artists, including Thomas Gainsborough. He illustrated, among other works, an edition of Shakespeare. One of the most versatile artists of the Romantic period, he later retired to Hammersmith and took up faith healing.

L'Ouverture See Toussaint Louverture

Louvois, François Michel le Tellier, Marquis de 1641–91
French statesman

Born in Paris, he was an energetic War Minister under Louis XIV from the War of Devolution (1668). His work reforming and strengthening the army bore fruit in the Dutch War, which ended with the Peace of Nijmegen (1678). He took a leading part in the capture of Strasbourg (1681) and in the persecution of Protestants. Recognized as a brilliant administrator, he was the king's most influential minister in the years 1683–91.

Louÿs, Pierre, pseudonym of Pierre Louis 1870–1925
French poet and novelist

He was born in Ghent, Belgium. In 1891 he founded a review in Paris called *Le Conque* to which Henri Régnier, André Gide and Paul Valéry were contributors. It also featured his first poems, before they appeared in *Astarté* (1891). His lyrics, based on the Greek form and popular in their time for their eroticism, are masterpieces of style. Other volumes are *Poésies de Méléagre de Gédara* (1893), *Scènes de la vie des courtisanes de Lucien* (1894, 'Scenes from Lucien's Life of Courtesans') and *Les Chansons de Bilitis* (1894), poems about Sapphic love which he claimed to have translated from the Greek. In 1896 his novel *Aphrodite* was published with great success, and a psychological novel *La Femme et le pantin* appeared in 1898 (Eng trans, *Woman and Puppet*, 1908).

Lovat, Simon Fraser, 11th Lord c.1667–1747
Scottish chief

Born in Tomich, Ross-shire, he graduated from Aberdeen in 1695. In 1696 his father, on the death of his great-nephew, Lord Lovat, assumed that title, and the next year Simon, after failing to abduct the late lord's nine-year-old daughter and heiress, forcibly married her mother, a lady of the Atholl family—a crime for which he was found guilty of high treason and outlawed. He succeeded his father as 11th Lord Lovat (1699), fled to France (1702), but returned to Scotland (1703) as a Jacobite agent and became involved in the abortive Queensberry plot, and again escaped to France, where he was a captive for 10 years. In 1715 he supported the government and obtained a full pardon, with possession of the Lovat title and estates. In the 1745 Jacobite Rebellion he sent his son and clan to fight for the Young Pretender (Charles Edward

Stuart), while he protested his loyalty to the government. After Culloden he fled, but was captured, taken to London for trial, and beheaded.

Love, Augustus Edward Hough 1863–1940
English geophysicist

Born in Weston-super-Mare, Avon, he studied at Cambridge from 1882, and in 1899 became Sedleian Professor of Natural Philosophy at Oxford. His research interests included fluids and solids, theoretical geophysics, the theory of electric waves, and ballistics. His *Treatise on the Mathematical Theory of Elasticity* (2 vols, 1892–93) was a standard textbook for nearly 50 years. He introduced the concept of 'Love waves' (Rayleigh waves transmitted over the surface of an elastic solid) and also related the periods and group velocities of surface waves, which led to the first evidence for the different crustal thicknesses of continents and oceans.

Love, Nat, *known as* Deadwood Dick 1854–1921
US cowboy

Born into slavery in Davidson County, Tennessee, he left home at 15 and became a cowboy near Dodge City, Kansas, working in cattle drives until 1889 and winning a reputation for his horsemanship and knowledge of cattle brands. He later became a railway porter (1890) and wrote stories about many legendary Western characters in his autobiography, *The Life and Adventures of Nat Love, Better Known in the Cattle Country as Deadwood Dick* (1907).

Lovecraft, H(oward) P(hillips) 1890–1937
US science-fiction writer and poet

He was born in Providence, Rhode Island, where he lived all his life, was educated at local schools, and as a young man supported himself by ghost writing and text revising. From 1923 he was a regular contributor to *Weird Tales*, and his cult following can be traced to the 60 or so stories first published in that magazine. He created what has come to be known as the 'Cthulhu Mythos', which holds that the Earth was originally inhabited by fish-like beings called the 'Old Ones' who worshipped the gelatinous Cthulhu. Among his various collections are *The Shadow over Innsmouth* (1936), *The Outsider and Others* (1939), *Dreams and Fancies* (1962) and *Dagon and Other Macabre Tales* (1965); the posthumous volumes were edited by August Derleth. His novellas include *The Case of Charles Dexter Ward* (1928) and *At the Mountains of Madness* (1931). 📖 A Derleth, *H P Lovecraft: A Memoir* (1945)

Lovejoy, Arthur Oncken 1873–1963
US philosopher and historian of ideas

Born in Berlin, Germany, he studied in the USA at Berkeley and Harvard and in France at the Sorbonne, Paris. After holding various teaching positions in the USA he became Professor of Philosophy at Johns Hopkins University (1910–38). He was co-founder (1938) and first editor of the *Journal of the History of Ideas* and effectively invented the discipline under that title. His method of detailed 'philosophical semantics' investigating the history of key terms and concepts is best exemplified in *The Great Chain of Being: a Study of the History of an Idea* (1936) and *Essays in the History of Ideas* (1948).

Lovelace, (Augusta) Ada, Countess of, *née* Byron 1815–52
English writer and mathematician

The daughter of Lord **Byron**, she taught herself geometry, and was educated in astronomy and mathematics. Acquainted with many leading figures of the Victorian era, she owes much of her recent fame to her friendship with **Charles Babbage**, the computer pioneer. She translated and annotated an article on his Analytical Engine written by an Italian mathematician, L F Menabrea, adding many explanatory notes of her own. The 'Sketch of the Analytical Engine' (1843) is an important source on Babbage's work. The high-level universal computer programming language, ADA, was named in her honour, and is said to realize several of her insights into the working of a computer system. 📖 Doris Langley Moore, *Ada, Countess of Lovelace: Byron's Legitimate Daughter* (1977)

Lovelace, Richard 1618–57
English Cavalier poet

Born in Woolwich, near London, or perhaps in Holland, he was educated at Charterhouse and Gloucester Hall, Oxford. He entered the court and went on the Scottish expedition in 1639. In 1642 he was imprisoned for presenting to the House of Commons a petition from the royalists of Kent 'for the restoring the king to his rights', and was released on bail. He spent his estate in the king's cause, assisted the French in 1646 to capture Dunkirk from the Spaniards, and was sent to jail on returning to England (1648). There he revised his poems, including 'To Althea, from Prison', and in 1649 published the collection *Lucasta*. He was freed at the end of 1649. In 1659 his brother published a second collection of his poems, *Lucasta: Posthume Poems*. 📖 C S Ker, *Richard Lovelace* (1949)

Lovell, Sir (Alfred Charles) Bernard 1913–
English astronomer

Born in Oldham Common, Gloucestershire, he graduated from Bristol University then became a physics lecturer at Manchester University. During World War II he worked for the Air Ministry Research Establishment, where he developed airborne radar for blind bombing and submarine defence. In 1951 he became Professor of Radio Astronomy at Manchester University and director of Jodrell Bank Experimental Station (now the Nuffield Radio Astronomy Laboratories). He gave the radio Reith Lectures in 1958. Lovell was a pioneer in the use of radar to detect meteors and day-time meteor showers. In 1950 he discovered that the rapid oscillations in the detected intensity (or 'scintillations') of signals from galactic radio sources were produced by the Earth's ionosphere, and were not intrinsic to the sources. He was the energetic instigator of the funding, construction and use of the radio telescope at Jodrell Bank, Cheshire. Plans to use the telescope to track Sputnik 1 and 2 attracted the funding which solved financial problems associated with its construction, and it was completed in 1957. From 1958 Lovell has collaborated with **Fred Whipple** in the study of flare stars. He has written several books on radio astronomy and on its relevance to life and civilization today. Elected FRS in 1955, he was knighted in 1961. 📖 Dudley Saward, *Bernard Lovell: a biography* (1984)

Lovelock, James Ephraim 1919–
English chemist

Born in Letchworth, Hertfordshire, he was educated at the universities of Manchester and London before he joined the National Institute for Medical Research in London (1941–61). He then held various posts in the USA, and since 1964 has pursued a career as an independent scientist. He is currently Visiting Fellow at Green College, Oxford (1994–). He invented the 'electron capture detector' (1958), a high-sensitivity device which was used in the first, and most subsequent, measurements of the accumulation of CFCs (or chlorofluorocarbons) in the atmosphere. In 1972 he put forward his controversial 'Gaia' hypothesis, which proposes that the Earth's climate is constantly regulated by plants and animals, to maintain a life-sustaining balance of organic substances in the atmosphere. Gaia is now regarded as an evolving system comprising the atmosphere, oceans, surface rocks and the biota, which behaves as a superorganism. Lovelock's theories are expounded in the popular books *Gaia* (1979), *The Ages of Gaia* (1988) and *The Practical Science of Planetary Medicine* (1991).

Lover, Samuel 1797–1868
Irish writer, artist and songwriter

He was born in Dublin, and he established himself there in 1818 as a marine painter and miniaturist. One of the founders of the *Dublin University Magazine*, he published *Legends and Stories of Ireland* in 1831 with his own illustrations. In 1835 he moved to London, where he wrote two popular novels, *Rory O'More* (1836) and *Handy Andy* (1842). He helped Dickens found *Bentley's Miscellany* and in 1844 started an entertainment, called 'Irish Evenings', which was hugely popular both in England and the USA (1846–48) with songs like 'The Low-Backed Car' and 'Molly Bawn'. 📖 W B Samuel, *The Life of Samuel Lover* (1874)

Lovett, Lyle 1956–
US country music singer, guitarist and songwriter

Born in Klein, Texas, he began performing while a student, and was encouraged by Nanci Griffith. He became a leading figure in the 'new country' movement of the late 1980s with the release of his eponymous debut album in 1986, and consolidated his reputation as a huge but idiosyncratic talent with the blues-inflected *Pontiac* (1987), followed by the jazzier *And His Large Band* (1989), *Joshua Judges Ruth* (1992) and *I Love Everybody* (1994). While clearly rooted in country, his original musical conception is not limited by generic boundaries. He married the actress Julia Roberts in 1993; their subsequent break-up is reflected in *The Road To Ensenada* (1996)

Lovino, Bernardino See Luini, Bernardino

Low, Bet 1924–
Scottish artist

Born in Gourock, Strathclyde, she trained at Glasgow School of Art and at Hospitalfield under James Cowie. She married fellow artist Tom MacDonald, and exhibited with him at the Blythswood Gallery, Glasgow (1969). In 1963 she became a co-founder of the New Charing Cross gallery. Her subtle use of colour and form in her watercolours enable her to capture the spirit of a place. She has exhibited widely and has works in many public and private collections. She was later elected to the Royal Scottish Water Colour Society and to the Royal Glasgow Institute of Artists, and became an Associate of the Royal Scottish Academy.

Low, Sir David Alexander Cecil 1891–1963
British political cartoonist

Born in Dunedin, New Zealand, he worked for several newspapers in New Zealand and for the *Bulletin of Sydney*, then joined the *Star* in London (1919). In 1927 he started to work for the *Evening Standard*, for which he drew some of his most successful cartoons. His art ridiculed all political parties, and some of his creations will never die, notably Colonel Blimp, who has been incorporated into the English language. From 1950 he worked for the *Daily Herald*, and from 1953 with *The (Manchester) Guardian*. He produced volumes of collected cartoons, including *Lloyd George and Co* (1922), *Low and I* (1923), *A Cartoon History of the War* (1941), *Low's Company* (1952), *Low's Autobiography* (1956) and many more.

Lowe, Arthur 1914–82
English actor

Born in Hayfield, Derbyshire, he became an actor while serving in the armed forces during World War II, appearing with the army entertainments division. His many stage appearances included *Larger Than Life* (1950), *Pal Joey* (1954) and *The Pajama Game* (1955), but it was television that brought him his greatest popularity, notably as the

irascible Mr Swindley in *Coronation Street* (1960–65), and as the pompous patriot Captain Mainwaring in *Dad's Army* (1968–77). His later stage work included *Inadmissible Evidence* (1964), *The Tempest* (1974) and *Bingo* (1974). He appeared in films from 1948 in supporting roles, and he took more substantial film roles in *The Ruling Class* (1972) and *O Lucky Man* (1973).

Löwe, Karl See Loewe, (Johann) Karl Gottfried

Lowell, Abbott Lawrence 1856–1943
US political scientist

Born in Boston into distinguished Massachusetts industrial and cultural dynasties, he was the brother of Percival Lowell and Amy Lowell. He graduated from Harvard in 1877, qualified in law in 1880, and practised law in Boston from 1880 to 1897, after which he lectured in law at Harvard and was made Professor of Government there in 1900. He was president of Harvard from 1909 to 1933. His publications include *Essays on Government* (1889), *Government and Parties in Continental Europe* (1897), *The Influence of Party Upon Legislation in England and America* (1902), *The Government of England* (1908), *Public Opinion and Popular Government* (1913), *Public Opinion in War and Peace* (1923), *Conflicts of Principle* (1932), *At War with Academic Traditions* (1934) and *What a College President Has Learned* (1938).

Lowell, Amy 1874–1925
US Imagist poet

Born in Brookline, Massachusetts, she was the sister of Abbott Lowell and Percival Lowell. She travelled extensively with her parents in Europe, and bought the parental home, 'Sevenals', in 1903. She wrote volumes of *vers libre* which she named 'unrhymed cadence', starting with the conventional *A Dome of Many-coloured Glass* (1912) and *Sword Blades and Poppy Seeds* (1914). She also wrote 'polyphonic prose'. Her other works include *Six French Poets* (1915), *Tendencies in Modern American Poetry* (1917) and a biography of Keats (1925). She was posthumously awarded the Pulitzer Prize in 1926 for *What's O'Clock* (1925). 📖 F C Flint, *Amy Lowell* (1969)

Lowell, Francis Cabot 1775–1817
US industrialist

Born in Newburyport, Massachusetts, he built a cotton spinning and weaving mill in Waltham, Massachusetts, during the War of 1812, taking advantage of the interruption in English imports and the consequent demand for domestic goods. Based on his observations of textile mills in England, he constructed, with the help of mechanical designer Paul Moody, a cotton factory which was the first in the world to process raw cotton and manufacture it into finished cloth under a single roof. Its establishment and Lowell's successful bid to win tariff protection in 1816 were fundamental in the creation of an industrial economy in New England. Lowell, Massachusetts, is named after him.

Lowell, James Russell 1819–91
US poet, essayist and diplomat

Born in Cambridge, Massachusetts, he graduated from Harvard in 1838. In 1843 he helped to edit *The Pioneer*, with Nathaniel Hawthorne, Edgar Allan Poe and John Whittier as contributors, and in 1845 he published his *Conversations on the Old Poets*. At the outbreak of war with Mexico (1846), he wrote a satiric poem in the Yankee dialect, out of which grew the *Biglow Papers* (1848). Many serious poems, written about 1848, formed a volume, and *A Fable for Critics* (1848) is a series of witty sketches of US authors. He visited Europe (1851–52), and in 1855 he was appointed Professor of Modern Languages and Literature at Harvard, later returning to Europe to finish his studies. He edited the *Atlantic Monthly* from 1857, and with **Charles Eliot Norton** the *North American Review* (1863–67). His prose writings include *Among my Books* (1870) and *My Study Windows* (1871). The second series of *Biglow Papers* appeared during the Civil War, in 1867. An ardent abolitionist, he gave himself unreservedly to the cause of freedom. He was appointed US Minister to Spain in 1877, and was transferred in 1880 to Great Britain, where he remained until 1885. 🕮 H E Scudder, *James Russell Lowell* (2 vols, 1901)

Lowell, Percival 1855–1916
US astronomer

Born into a prominent Boston family, the brother of **Abbott** and **Amy Lowell**, he was educated at Harvard and established the Flagstaff (Lowell) Observatory in Arizona (1894). He is best known for his observations of Mars, which resulted in a series of maps showing linear features crossing the surface. In 1907 he led an expedition to the Chilean Andes which produced the first high-quality photographs of Mars. He popularized his ideas in a series of books which include *Mars and its Canals* (1906) and *Mars as the Abode of Life* (1910). He is known for his prediction of the brightness and position of a planet that was supposedly responsible for the orbital perturbation of Neptune and Uranus. This he called planet X. In 1930, 14 years after his death, Pluto was found (discovered by **Clyde William Tombaugh**).

Lowell, Robert Traill Spence, Jnr 1917–77
US poet

Born in Boston, the great-great-nephew of **James Russell Lowell**, he attended St Mark's School and Harvard, but left to go to Kenyon College to study poetry, criticism and classics under **John Crowe Ransom**, then attended Louisiana State University. During World War II he was a conscientious objector and was imprisoned for six months (1944). In 1940 he married the writer **Jean Stafford** and became a Roman Catholic. His first collection, *Land of Unlikeness* (1944), contained biographical poems, and his widely acclaimed second volume, *Lord Weary's Castle* (1946), won him the Pulitzer Prize in 1947. *Life Studies* (1959), *For the Union Dead* (1964) and *Near the Ocean* (1967) were also 'confessional'. During the Vietnam years, he wrote *Notebook* (1968), and in *The Dolphin* (1973), he made public personal letters and anxieties. 🕮 I Hamilton, *Robert Lowell: a biography* (1985)

Lower, Richard 1631–91
English physician and physiologist

Born in Tremeer, near Bodmin, he studied at Oxford, where he came under the influence of **Thomas Willis** and several others soon to achieve prominence in the Royal Society of London. Gaining his MD in 1665, Lower followed Willis to London, setting up in medical practice and joining the Royal Society. He carried out early experiments on blood transfusion between dogs, and his *Tractatus de Corde* (1669, 'Treatise on the Heart') provides a fine account of contemporary knowledge in pulmonary and cardiovascular anatomy and physiology. Following **William Harvey**, Lower recognized that the heart acts as a muscular pump. He went on to investigate the colour change between dark venous blood and red arterial blood, and with **Robert Hooke** deduced that the red colour resulted from the mixing of dark blood with inspired air in the lungs. Lower thus established that the function of respiration lay in adding something to the blood. After the 1670s, he concentrated on his medical practice.

Lowie, Robert Harry 1883–1957
US cultural anthropologist

Born in Vienna, Austria, he went to the USA in 1893 and grew up in New York City. He studied anthropology at Columbia University under **Franz Boas**. From 1907 to 1917 he was on the staff of the American Museum of Natural History in New York City, following which he worked at the University of California, Berkeley (1917–50). He made several ethnographic studies of Native American societies, especially the Crow, publishing his *Social Life of the Crow Indians* in 1912 and *The Crow Indians* in 1935. His most influential general works were *Primitive Society* (1920), *Primitive Religion* (1924), *The History of Ethnological Theory* (1937) and *Social Organization* (1948), in which his theoretical position reflected that of the Boasian school of culture-history.

Lowry, L(aurence) S(tephen) 1887–1976
English painter

Born in Manchester, he worked as a clerk until 1952, but trained at Manchester College of Art in the evenings (1905–15). From 1915 to 1925 he attended Salford School of Art, and from 1918 the life class at Manchester Academy of Fine Arts. He produced numerous pictures of the Lancashire industrial scene, mainly in brilliant whites and greys, often filled with uncommunicative matchstick antlike men and women, in a deliberately naïve style. He lived at home nursing his mother until her death in 1939. Their claustrophobic relationship is the subject of a ballet. His work is represented in many major collections (Tate, London; Museum of Modern Art, New York, etc) and in the Lowry Gallery in Salford, and a Lowry Centre is to be built in the docklands area of Manchester (1997–).

Lowry, (Clarence) Malcolm 1909–57
English novelist

Born in New Brighton, Merseyside, he left public school to become a deck-hand on a ship bound for China, but returned to take a degree at St Catherine's College, Cambridge. He wrote about the voyage in his first novel, *Ultramarine* (1933), but completed only one more book, *Under the Volcano* (1947), for which he is best known. In later life a wanderer and alcoholic, he lived in Mexico, then in British Columbia, where he died 'by misadventure', choking in his sleep. Posthumous publications include stories, poems, letters, and three novels: *Lunar Caustic* (1963), *Dark as the Grave Wherein my Friend is Laid* (1968) and *October Ferry to Gabriola* (1970). 🕮 G Bowker, *Pursued by Furies* (1993); D Day, *Malcolm Lowry* (1974)

Lowry, (Thomas) Martin 1874–1936
English chemist

Born in Bradford, West Yorkshire, he studied chemistry under **Henry Armstrong** at the City and Guilds Institute, South Kensington, and in 1912 moved to Guy's Hospital Medical School, where from 1913 he was head of the chemistry department. In 1920 he became the first to hold a chair of physical chemistry at Cambridge. His earliest researches were on the changes in optical rotation (mutarotation) which occur when camphor derivatives are treated with acids or bases, leading ultimately to his redefinition of the terms acid and base (1923). He also worked extensively on optical rotatory dispersion, foreshadowing its importance many years later as a structural tool in organic chemistry. He was elected FRS in 1914, and from 1928 to 1930 was president of the Faraday Society.

Lowth, Robert 1710–87
English prelate and scholar

Born in Winchester, Hampshire, he became Professor of Poetry at Oxford in 1741, Bishop of St Davids and of Oxford in 1766, and of London in 1777. He published *De Sacra Poesi Hebraeorum* (1753), a *Life of William of Wykeham* (1758) and a new translation of Isaiah. He was one of the first to treat the Bible poetry as literature in its own right.

Lowther, Hugh Cecil See **Lonsdale, 5th Earl of**

Loy, Myrna, *originally* Katerina Myrna Adele Williams 1905–93
US film actress and comedienne

Born in Radersburg, Montana, of Welsh ancestry, she moved with her family to Los Angeles in 1919 and was performing in a movie house chorus when she was spotted by Rudolph Valentino. She made her debut in *Pretty Ladies* (1925) and then appeared in scores of silent features. After her role as the sadistic daughter in *The Mask of Fu Manchu* (1932), she moved to comedy and made her first of 13 appearances opposite William Powell (1892–1984) in *The Thin Man* (1934) as husband-and-wife detectives. She was successful also in *Test Pilot* (1938), *The Rains Came* (1939) and *The Best Years of Our Lives* (1946). She latterly became a character actress and made a belated Broadway debut in 1974, ending her acting career opposite Henry Fonda in the television film *Summer Solstice* (1981). Her autobiography, *Being and Becoming*, was published in 1987.

Loyola, St Ignatius See Ignatius Loyola, St

Loyson, Charles See Hyacinthe, Père

Lü d.180BC
Empress of China

The wife of Liu Bang (Liu Pang) or Gaozu (Kao tsu) who was the founder of the Han dynasty, she was virtual regent for 15 years after his death in 195BC, first for her son Hui Ti and then, after his death (188), for two other infants. By the time of her death, she had firmly established the authority of the ruling Liu family, although Chinese historiography condemns her for her resort to nepotism and employment of eunuchs at court.

Lubbers, Rudolf Franz Marie 1939–
Dutch politician

After graduating from Erasmus University, Rotterdam, he joined the family engineering business of Lubbers Hollandia. He made rapid progress after entering politics, becoming Minister of Economic Affairs (1973) and, at the age of 43, Prime Minister (1982), leading a Christian Democratic Appeal (CDA) coalition.

Lubbock, Sir John, 1st Baron Avebury
1834–1913
English politician and biologist

Born in London, he was the son of the astronomer Sir J W Lubbock (1803–65). From Eton he went into his father's banking house at the age of 14, becoming a partner in 1856. He served on several educational and currency commissions, and in 1870 was returned for Maidstone as a Liberal MP, and then in 1880 for London University—from 1886 to 1900 as a Liberal-Unionist. He succeeded in passing more than a dozen important measures, including the Bank Holidays Act (1871), the Bills of Exchange Act, the Ancient Monuments Act (1882) and the Shop Hours Act (1889). He was Vice-Chancellor of London University (1872–80), president of the British Association (1881), vice-president of the Royal Society, president of the London Chamber of Commerce, chairman of the London County Council (1890–92), and much else. Scientifically, he is best known for his researches on primitive man and on the habits of bees and ants; he published *Prehistoric Times* (1865, revised 1913), *Origin of Civilisation* (1870) and many books on natural history. He was a neighbour of Charles Darwin, and a friend and counsellor over many years. He was a member of the 'X' Club (together with T H Huxley, Joseph Dalton Hooker and others) which conspired to replace the ecclesiastical establishment with a scientific one.

Lubbock, Percy 1879–1965
English critic and biographer

Born in London and educated at Eton and King's College, Cambridge, he was librarian of Magdalene College, Cambridge, from 1906 to 1908. Among his writings are *The Craft of Fiction* (1921), *Earlham* (1922), a book of personal childhood memories, and studies of Samuel Pepys (1909) and Edith Wharton (1947). He was the grandson of Sir John Lubbock.

Lubetkin, Berthold 1901–90
English architect

Born in Tiflis (now Tbilisi), Georgia, he studied under Aleksandr Rodchenko, and Vladimir Tatlin in Moscow, and then at Atelier Perret in Paris, where he was influenced by Le Corbusier. In 1931 he emigrated to England, and set up his own firm, Tecton, with six students from the Architectural Association, London. His major works include the Penguin Pool at London Zoo (1933) and Highpoint I Hampstead (1935), a block of high-rise flats which was praised by Le Corbusier as a redevelopment of his own *urbanisme* and utopian ideals, creating a new quality for high-rise housing. His Finsbury Health Centre (1938), a social experiment, is still in use as intended today. Very influential in the development and practice of high quality modernism, he largely retired from architecture in 1939.

Lubitsch, Ernst 1892–1947
German film director

Born in Berlin, he was a teenage actor in Max Reinhardt's theatre company, then starred as 'Meyer' in a popular slapstick series before beginning his directorial career with *Fraülein Seifenschaum* (1914). A specialist in comedies, and costume epics like *Madame Dubarry* (1919), he was invited to Hollywood by Mary Pickford, whom he directed in *Rosita* (1923). He stayed to become an acknowledged master of sophisticated light comedies graced with 'the Lubitsch touch': a mixture of wit, urbanity and visual elegance. His many films include *Forbidden Paradise* (1924), *The Love Parade* (1929), *Trouble in Paradise* (1932), *Ninotchka* (1939, with Greta Garbo) and *Heaven Can Wait* (1943). He became a US citizen in 1936, and received a Special Academy Award in 1947. 📖 Herman G Weinberg, *The Lubitsch Touch: A Critical Study* (1968)

Luca Della Robbia See Della Robbia, Luca

Lucan, *in full* Marcus Annaeus Lucanus AD39–65
Roman poet

Born in Corduba (Córdoba), Spain, he was the nephew of the philosopher Seneca, the Younger. He studied in Rome and in Athens, and became proficient in rhetoric and philosophy. He was recalled to Rome by the Emperor Nero, who made him quaestor and augur. In AD60 he won the poetry competition in the first Neronia games. In 62 he published the first three books of his epic *Bellum Civile* (*Pharsalia*) on the civil war between Pompey and Julius Caesar. Nero, perhaps jealous of Lucan's literary successes, forbade him to write poetry or plead in the courts, and in 65 Lucan joined the conspiracy of Piso against Nero, but was betrayed and compelled to commit suicide. He was a precociously fluent writer in Silver Latin, but *Pharsalia* is all that has survived of his work. 📖 M P O Morford, *Lucan the Poet* (1967)

Lucan, George Charles Bingham, 3rd Earl of
1800–88
English field marshal

He was born in London. He accompanied the Russians as a volunteer against the Turks in 1828 and succeeded as 3rd Earl of Lucan in 1839. As commander of cavalry in the Crimean War (1854–56) he passed on the disastrous and ambiguous order from Lord Raglan which resulted in the Charge of the Light Brigade at Balaclava (1854). He later fought at Inkermann and was promoted field marshal in 1887.

Lucan, Richard John Bingham, 7th Earl of,
known as **Lord Lucan** 1934–
English alleged murderer

He disappeared on the evening of 7 November 1974. On that night, his estranged wife Veronica Lucan ran into a pub close to her London home with blood on her face, claiming that she had just escaped from a murderer. Shortly after, police found the body of the Lucan family's nanny, Sandra Rivett, in a mailbag in the basement of Lady Lucan's house. Lady Lucan told police that she had gone downstairs to find the nanny when a man, whom she identified as her husband, attacked her. When challenged, he claimed that he had mistaken the nanny for her and had killed her. The police failed to trace Lucan, who had large gambling debts and who had fought for and lost custody of his children. In June 1975 the coroner's jury charged Lord Lucan with the murder. Speculation about Lucan's whereabouts and about events that night continues to this day.

Lucaris or Lukaris, Cyril or Cyrillus 1572–1638
Greek Orthodox prelate and theologian

Born in Crete, he studied in Venice, Padua and Geneva, where he was influenced by **Calvin**ism. He rose by 1621 to be patriarch of Constantinople (Istanbul), and opened negotiations with the Calvinists of England and Holland with a view to union and the reform of the Greek Church. He corresponded with **Gustav II Adolf** of Sweden, and Archbishops Abbot and **Laud**, and he presented the Alexandrian Codex to **Charles I**. The Jesuits five times engineered his deposition, and are supposed by the Greeks to have instigated his murder by the Turks. The *Eastern Confession of the Orthodox Church*, of strong Calvinistic tendency, issued in 1629, may not have been written by him after all.

Lucas, Colin Anderson 1906–
English architect

Born in London, he studied at Cambridge. In 1930 he designed a house at Bourne End, Buckinghamshire, which was the first English example of the domestic use of monolithic reinforced concrete. Subsequent designs (1933–39) played an important part in the development in England of the ideas of the European modern movement in architecture. He was a founder-member of the MARS group of architects.

Lucas, Edward Verrall 1868–1938
English essayist and biographer

Born in Eltham, Kent, he became a bookseller's assistant, a reporter, contributor to and assistant editor of *Punch*, and finally a publisher. He compiled anthologies, and was the author of novels (the best of which is probably *Over Bemerton's*, 1908), books of travel and about 30 volumes of light essays. An authority on **Charles Lamb**, he wrote a Life of him in 1905. 📖 *Reading, Writing and Remembering* (1932)

Lucas, F(rank) L(awrence) 1894–1967
English critic and poet

Born in Hipperholme, Yorkshire, he became a Fellow and Reader in English at King's College, Cambridge. He wrote many works of criticism, including *Seneca and Elizabethan Tragedy* (1922) and *Eight Victorian Poets* (1930), volumes of poetry, such as *Time and Memory* (1929) and *Ariadne* (1932), and plays including *Land's End* (1938). He also wrote novels and popular translations of Greek drama and poetry.

Lucas, George 1944–
US filmmaker

Born in Modesto, California, he studied film at the University of Southern California where his short film *THX-1138: 4EB/Electronic Labyrinth* (1965) won first prize at the National Student Film Festival. A protégé of Francis Ford Coppola, he made his feature-length debut as a director with the science-fiction drama *THX-1138* (1971). He received Best Director Academy Award nominations for both *American Graffiti* (1973) and *Star Wars* (1977); the latter became one of the most commercially succesful films ever made. Lucas subsequently produced but did not direct a succession of big-budget adventure films including the *Star Wars* sequels *The Empire Strikes Back* (1980) and *Return of the Jedi* (1983), and the *Indiana Jones* series. He has also extended the boundaries of cinematic special-effects through his company Industrial Light And Magic (ILM) and developed the THX Sound System. He received the **Irving Thalberg** award in 1992, and planned to begin production on a trilogy of *Star Wars* prequels in 1997.

Lucas Van Leyden, *also known as* Lucas Jacobsz or Hugensz 1494–1533
Dutch painter and engraver

Born in Leyden, he practised almost every branch of painting, and his most notable works include the triptych of *The Last Judgement* (1526) and *Blind Man of Jericho Healed by Christ* (1531). As an engraver he is believed to have been the first to etch on copper, rather than iron. He was much influenced by **Albrecht Dürer**. 📖 Rik Vos, *Lucas Van Leyden* (1978)

Luce, Henry R(obinson) 1898–1967
US magazine publisher and editor

He was born in Shando Province, China, to a missionary family and was educated at a boarding school in Chefoo, north China, before going to the USA to study at Yale. He founded *Time* (1923), *Fortune* (1930) and *Life* (1936) magazines. He also inaugurated the radio programme 'March of Time' in the 1930s, which became a film feature. He married Clare Boothe Luce (1903–87) in 1935. 📖 James L Baughman, *Henry R Luce and the Rise of the American News Media* (1987)

Lucian c.117–c.180AD
Greek satirist, rhetorician and writer

Born in Samosata, Syria, he practised as an advocate in Antioch, and wrote and recited show speeches for a living, travelling through Asia Minor, Greece, Italy and Gaul. Having made his name and fortune, he settled in Athens, and there produced a new form of literature, the humorous dialogue. The old faiths, philosophy and literature were all changing, and Lucian found many targets for his satire. The absurdity of retaining the old deities without the old belief is brought out in such works as the *Deorum Dialogi* ('Dialogues of the Gods'), *Mortuorum Dialogi* ('Dialogues of the Dead') and *Charon*. Whether philosophy was more disgraced by the shallowness or the vices of those who now professed it, is discussed in his *Symposium*, *Halieus*, *Biōn Prasis*, *Drapetae* and others. *Vera Historia* ('True History') parodies the fantastic adventure tales of the 'new' literature. His style, which is notable for the purity of his Attic Greek, is straightforward and elegant. A *Selected Works* was published in 1965, edited by B P Reardon. 📖 J Bompaire, *Lucian écrivain* (1958)

Luciani, Sebastiano See Sebastiano del Piombo

Luciano, Lucky, *properly* Charles Luciano 1897–1962
US gangster

Born in Sicily, Italy, he emigrated with his family to the USA in 1907. Luciano, who earned his nickname by avoiding imprisonment and prosecution for many years, was a Mafia 'godfather' who operated successfully and profitably in the 1920s and 1930s. His business included narcotics-peddling, extortion, prostitution and networks of vice dens. When three prostitutes finally agreed to give evidence against him, he was arrested (1936) and found guilty of compelling women to become prostitutes. Even from prison, he retained control of his Family, setting up the Crime Syndicate of Mafia Families. In 1946 he was released and then deported to Italy as an undesirable alien. He was refused entry to various European cities and eventually found refuge in Italy. He was only post-humously allowed to return to the USA, where he was buried at St John's Cemetery in New York.

Lucilius, Gaius c.180–c.102BC
Roman satirist

Born in Suessa Aurunca, Campania, he wrote 30 books of *Satires*, of which only fragments remain. These *saturae* (or medleys), written in hexameters, are on a mixture of miscellaneous subjects, everyday life, politics, literature, travel. Their occasionally mocking and critical tone gave the word 'satire' its modern meaning. ▢ G C Fiske, *Lucilius and Horace* (1920)

Lucretia 6th century BC
Roman matron

She was the wife of Lucius Tarquinius Collatinus. According to legend she was raped by Sextus Tarquinius (son of Tarquinius, Superbus), then summoned her hus-band and friends, and, making them take an oath to drive out the Tarquins, plunged a knife into her heart. The tale has formed the basis of several works, for example Shakespeare's *Rape of Lucrece* (1594) and the opera *The Rape of Lucretia* by Benjamin Britten. The Tarquins were later expelled by Lucius Junius Brutus. ▢ Ian Donaldson, *The Rapes of Lucretia: A Myth and its Transformations* (1982)

Lucretius, *in full* Titus Lucretius Carus c.99–55BC
Roman poet and philosopher

Little is known of his life, though he is said to have gone mad and committed suicide after drinking a love potion given to him by his wife Lucilia. His great work is the didactic poem *De rerum natura* ('On the Nature of Things'), in six volumes of hexameters, in which he sets out the theories of Democritus and Epicurus on the origin of the universe, and attempts to eradicate superstition and religious belief, which he savagely denounces as the source of man's wickedness and misery. Freedom from fear, and a calm and tranquil mind were his goals, the way to them being through a materialistic philosophy. His poem abounds in strikingly picturesque phrases, epis-odes of exquisite pathos and vivid description, rarely equalled in Latin poetry.

Lucullus, Lucius Licinius c.110–57BC
Roman soldier

His origins were humble, but after service with Sulla he commanded the fleet in the First Mithridatic War (88BC). As consul he defeated Mithridates in the Third Mith-ridatic War (74), and introduced reforms into Asia Minor. He twice defeated Tigranes of Armenia (69 and 68), but his legions became mutinous, and he was superseded by Pompey (66). He attempted to check Pompey's power, and was one of the first triumvirate, but soon withdrew from politics. He had become very wealthy and spent the rest of his life in such luxury that the term 'Lucullan' has been used as an epithet for extravagant food. He was a notable patron of writers and artists.

Lucy, St d.303AD
Sicilian Christian martyr

According to tradition, she was born into a wealthy Sicilian family. She was a virgin denounced as a Christian by a rejected suitor, and martyred under Diocletian at Syracuse. She is patron saint of Syracuse and of the blind, and her feast day is 13 December.

Lucy, Sir Thomas 1532–1600
English country gentleman

A Warwickshire squire, MP, and Justice of the Peace, he is said to have prosecuted Shakespeare for stealing deer from Charlecote Park, and to have been the inspiration for Justice Shallow (*Henry IV, Part 2*; *Merry Wives of Windsor*).

Ludd, Ned fl.1779
English farm labourer

He worked in Leicestershire. About 1782 he destroyed some stocking frames, and it is from him that the 'Luddite' rioters (1812–18) took their name.

Ludendorff, Erich von 1865–1937
German soldier

He was born near Posen. In 1914 he was appointed Chief of Staff in East Prussia, and masterminded the annihila-tion of the Russians at Tannenberg (August 1914). When Paul von Hindenburg superseded Erich von Falkenhayn in 1916, Ludendorff sent August von Mackensen (1849–1945) to the Dobruja to defeat the Romanians. On the Western Front in 1918 he planned the major offensive that nearly won the war for Germany. In 1923 he was a leader in the Hitler putsch at Munich, but he was acquitted of treason. He was a Nazi member of the Reichstag from 1924 to 1928, but as a candidate for the presidency of the Reich in 1925 he polled few votes. Strongly opposed to Jews, Jesuits and freemasons, he later became a pacifist.

Ludlow, Edmund c.1617–1692
English Parliamentarian

He was born in Maiden Bradley, Wiltshire, and during the Civil War served under Sir William Waller and Thomas Fairfax. Elected to the Council of State, he was sent to Ireland as Lieutenant-General of Horse in 1651, but re-fused to recognize Cromwell's protectorate. He urged the restoration of the Rump Parliament, commanded again for a while in Ireland, was nominated by John Lambert to the Committee of Safety, and strove in vain to reunite the Republican Party. After the Restoration he made his way to Vevey in Switzerland. In 1689 he came back, but re-turned to Vevey when the House of Commons demanded his arrest.

Ludmilla, St d.921
Bohemian religious and patron saint of Bohemia

Born near Melník, Bohemia, the wife of Bohemia's first Christian duke, she was murdered by her heathen daughter-in-law, Drahomira.

Ludovicus See Vives, Juan Luis

Ludwig I 1786–1868
King of Bavaria

Born in Strasbourg, the eldest son of Maximilian I, he was king from 1825 to 1848. By his lavish expenditure on pictures, public buildings and favourites, and by taxes and reactionary policy, he provoked active discontent in 1830 and 1848, and abdicated in favour of his son, Maximilian II.

Ludwig II, *also known as* Mad King Ludwig 1845–86
King of Bavaria

The son of Maximilian II, he was born at Nymphenburg Palace. He succeeded in 1804 and devoted himself to patronage of Richard Wagner and his music. In 1870 he threw Bavaria on the side of Prussia, and offered the Imperial Crown to Wilhelm I, though he took no part in the war, and lived the life of a morbid recluse. He was almost constantly at odds with his ministers and family, mainly on account of his vast outlays on superfluous palaces, like the fairy-tale Neuschwanstein, and was declared insane (1886). A few days later he was found drowned, with his physician, in the Starnberger Lake, near his castle of Berg. It is not known whether his death was suicide, murder or accidental.

Ludwig, Emil, *originally* Emil Cohn 1881–1948
Swiss writer

Born in Breslau, Germany (Wrocław, Poland), he wrote some novels and plays, but made his name as a biographer of the intuitive school. His accounts of **Goethe, Napoleon I, Wilhelm II, Bismarck, Jesus Christ, Abraham Lincoln** and others, assemble carefully researched sources in a manner more appropriate to fiction narrative. He lived in Switzerland, and became a Swiss citizen in 1932, but settled in the USA in 1940.

Ludwig, Karl Friedrich Wilhelm 1816–95
German physiologist

Born in Witzenhausen, he became a medical student in Marburg in 1834. In 1840 he returned to Marburg and was teaching there by 1846, later teaching in Zurich, Vienna and Leipzig, where in 1865 he helped establish the famous Institute of Physiology. Ludwig's work proved fundamental to modern physiology. He devised many medical instruments, notably the kymograph (1846), which he used to study circulation and respiration, and the mercurial blood-pump (1859), which allowed examination of blood gases and respiratory exchange. His research focused on the operation of the heart and kidneys, on the lymphatic system, and on salivary secretion. He also studied the circulation of the blood, and investigated the relations of blood pressure to heart activity.

Lugard, Frederick John Dealtry Lugard, Baron 1858–1945
British soldier and colonial administrator

He was born in Madras, India. He was commissioned as an army officer (1878), and served in the Sudan against **Mohammed Ahmed**, the Mahdi (1885), and in Burma after the fall of King Thibaw (1886), and commanded an expedition against slavers in Nyasaland (1888). His work made Uganda a British protectorate in 1894. He was appointed commissioner in the Nigerian hinterland by **Joseph Chamberlain** (1897) and High Commissioner for the North (1900–07). He was Governor of Hong Kong from 1907, helping to establish its University in 1911. He returned to Nigeria as Governor of the Northern and Southern protectorates, becoming Governor-General (1914–19) on their amalgamation. His principle was one of use of existing tribal institutions as the infrastructure for British rule.

Lugosi, Bela, *originally* Bela Ferenc Denzso Blasko 1882–1956
US actor

Born in Lugos, Hungary (now in Romania), he studied in Budapest, and appeared on stage (from 1902) and on film (from 1917), before moving to the USA in 1921. He enjoyed his greatest success on Broadway as *Dracula* (1927), a role he repeated on film (1931). Heavily accented, he made a memorably menacing, aristocratic vampire but soon found himself typecast. His films include *Murders in the Rue Morgue* (1932), *Son of Frankenstein* (1939) and *Abbott and Costello Meet Frankenstein* (1948). After becoming a drug addict and successfully undergoing treatment, he appeared in low-quality films and died during the production of *Plan 9 from Outer Space* (1956), frequently voted the worst film ever made.

Lu Hsün See Lu Xun

Luini or Lovino, Bernardino c.1481–1532
Italian painter

Born in Luino on Lake Maggiore, Lombardy, he was trained in the school of **Leonardo da Vinci**, to whom many of his works have been attributed. He painted much at Milan. His *Virgin and Child with St John* is in the National Gallery, London, and his *Dream of Joseph* is in the Brera, Milan.

Luitprand See Liutprand of Cremona

Lukacs, Georg, *properly* György Szegedy von Lukacs 1885–1971
Hungarian Marxist philosopher and critic

Born in Budapest into a wealthy Jewish family, he studied in Budapest, Berlin and Heidelberg. He published two important early works on literary criticism, *Soul and Form* (1910) and *The Theory of the Novel* (1916). In 1918 he joined the Hungarian Communist Party, but after the defeat of the uprising in 1919 he lived abroad in Vienna (1919–29) and Moscow (1930–44). He returned to Hungary after World War II as professor at Budapest and joined **Imre Nagy**'s short-lived revolutionary government in 1956 as Minister of Culture. After the Russian suppression he was briefly deported to Romania and interned but returned to Budapest in 1957. He was a prolific writer on literature and aesthetics. His major book on Marxism, *History and Class Consciousness* (1923, Eng trans 1971), was repudiated as heretical by the Russian Communist Party and later, in abject public confession, by Lukacs himself.

Lukaris, Cyril See Lucaris, Cyril

Lukas, D(arrell) Wayne 1935–
US racehorse trainer

Born in Antigo, Wisconsin, he was the first trainer to top the US winnings list for eight consecutive years (1984–91) but his $17.8 million record winnings in 1989 did not last long. He lost some investors and then, two years later, lost millions when Calumet Farms went bankrupt. In 1993 his son, and chief assistant, nearly died after he was kicked by a horse. Undaunted, Lukas trained it into a champion and Tabasco Cat became his first Triple Crown winner in 1994. He went on to make history as the first trainer to win five consecutive Triple Crown races, winning them, sensationally, with different horses (Tabasco Cat, Thunder Gulch, and Timber County).

Luke, St 1st century AD
New Testament evangelist

Born possibly in Antioch, Syria, he may have been the 'beloved physician' and companion of **St Paul** (Colossians 4.14, Philippians 24). It is said that he was martyred. He was first named as author of the third Gospel in the 2nd century, and tradition has since ascribed to him both that work and the Acts of the Apostles. He is the patron saint of doctors and artists, and his feast day is 18 October.

Luks, George Benjamin 1867–1933
US painter

Born in Williamsport, Pennsylvania, he studied art in Philadelphia, London and Paris. From 1908 he was a member of the Eight, painting realistic works of New York City scenes. He also was a graphic artist, a portrait painter, and originator of the comic strip 'Hogan's Alley' in the *New York World*. His paintings, which show his adventurous spirit and vitality, include *The Spielers* (1905, Addison Gallery, Andover, Massachusetts) and *The Wrestlers* (1905, Museum of Fine Arts, Boston).

Lula, *properly* Luis Inácio Lula da Silva 1944–
Brazilian labour leader

He came to national prominence as the leader of the Metalworker's Union of São Bernardo, a São Paulo industrial zone housing key industries, especially in motor vehicles. Forced by the military regime's labour legislation to concentrate on local issues, Lula led strikes in the Saab-Scania plant in 1978 and 1979, involving 500,000 workers and making the employers concede higher wages through direct negotiations rather than via government-led labour courts. In October 1979 he founded the PT (Partido dos Trabalhadores), to achieve representation for workers in Congress; it has drawn support from a range of traditional radical movements and the left wing of the

Church. Elected to Congress in 1986, he narrowly defeated **Leonel Brizola** as the candidate for the Left against **Fernando Collor de Mello** in the 1989 presidential race.

Lully, Jean Baptiste, *originally* Giovanni Battista Lulli 1632–87
French composer

Born in Florence of Italian parents, he went as a boy to Paris, and was finally, after much ambitious intriguing, made operatic director by **Louis XIV** (1672). With Philippe Quinault as librettist, he composed many operas, in which he made the ballet an essential part. Most popular were *Thésée* (1675), *Armide et Rénaud* (1686), *Phaéton* (1683) and *Acis et Galatée* (1686). He also wrote church music, dance music and pastorals.

Lully or Lull, Raymond or Ramón, *known as* the Enlightened Doctor c.1232–1315
Spanish theologian and mystic

Born in Palma, Majorca, he served as a soldier and led a dissolute life, writing lyrical troubadour poetry, but from 1266 became an ascetic and resolved on a spiritual crusade for the conversion of the Muslims. To this end, after some years of study, he produced his *Ars Magna*, the 'Lullian method', a mechanical aid to the acquisition of knowledge and the solution of all possible problems by a systematic manipulation of certain fundamental notions (the Aristotelian categories, etc). He also wrote a book against the Averroists, and in 1291 went to Tunis to convert the Muslims, but was imprisoned and banished. After visiting Naples, Rome, Majorca, Cyprus and Armenia, he again sailed (1305) for Bugia (Bougie) in Algeria, and was again banished. At Paris he lectured against the principles of **Averroës**, and returning to Bugia, was stoned and died a few days afterwards. The Lullists combined religious mysticism with alchemy, but it has been disproved that Lully himself ever dabbled in alchemy. He was the first to use a vernacular language for religious or philosophical writings. He also wrote impressive poetry.

Lulu, *real name* Marie McDonald McLaughlin Lawrie 1948–
Scottish singer and actress

Born in Lennoxtown, near Glasgow, she had the first Scottish hit of the Beat era with a cover of the Isley Brothers' 'Shout' in 1964 and subsequently had a hit in the USA with the title song from the film *To Sir With Love* (1967), in which she had also acted. She was joint winner of the 1969 Eurovision Song Contest with *Boom Bang-a-Bang* and her albums have included *New Routes* (1969) and *Lulu* (1981). During the 1970s she became better known as an entertainer and television personality than as a pop singer, and she had her own BBC series *It's Lulu*. On television, she acted Adrian's mother Pauline in *The Growing Pains of Adrian Mole* (1987) and appeared in *Absolutely Fabulous* (1995). She was married to Maurice Gibb of The Bee Gees from 1969 to 1973.

Lumière, Auguste Marie Louis Nicolas and Louis Jean See panel p1169

Lumley, Joanna 1946–
English actress

Born in Srinagar, Kashmir, of British parents, she worked as a model before switching to acting. She was a Bond girl in the film *On Her Majesty's Secret Service* (1969) and acted in *The Trail of the Pink Panther* (1982), *Curse of the Pink Panther* (1983) and *Shirley Valentine* (1989). She made her name on television, playing Samantha Ryder-Ross in the comedy series *It's Awfully Bad for Your Eyes, Darling* (1971), Purdey in *The New Avengers* (1976–77), Sapphire in *Sapphire and Steel* (1979–82), Victoria Cavero in *Lovejoy* (1992), Patsy in *Absolutely Fabulous* (1992–95, winning her an Emmy award) and Kate Swift in *Class Act* (1994–95).

On stage, she has starred in *Noel and Gertie* (1983), *Blithe Spirit* (1986) and *The Revengers' Comedies* (1991). Her autobiography, *Stare Back and Smile*, was published in 1989.

Lummer, Otto Richard 1860–1925
German physicist

Born in Breslau (Wrocław, Poland), he became an assistant to **Hermann von Helmholtz**, and in 1904 was appointed Professor of Physics at Breslau University. His main field of research was optics. He was one of the discoverers of the interference effect which became known as the 'Lummer fringes' (1884), and designed various optical instruments, including a high-resolution spectroscope, a photometer (1889), and a bolometer (1892). His most important theoretical contribution was his investigation of certain properties of black-body radiation, an essential step on the road to **Max Planck's** quantum theory.

Lumumba, Patrice (Hemery) 1925–61
Congolese politician

Born in Katako Kombe and educated at mission schools, both Catholic and Protestant, he became a post office clerk and then director of a brewery. He helped form the *Mouvement National Congolais* in 1958 to challenge Belgian rule and, when the Congo became an independent republic, he was made its first Prime Minister (1960). A major symbolic figure in the African history of the period, he sought a unified Congo and opposed the secession of Katanga under Moise Tshombe. He was arrested by his own army in 1960, handed over to the Katangese and murdered. His name, however, remains significant as the embodiment of African nationalism and the opponent of balkanization manipulated by ex-colonial countries and their allies. 📖 Robin McKown, *Lumumba: A Biography* (1969)

Lunardi, Vicenzo 1759–1806
Italian aeronaut

Born in Lucca, he made, from Moorfields in London on 15 September 1784, the first hydrogen balloon ascent in England.

Lundy, Benjamin 1789–1839
US abolitionist

Born in Hardwick, New Jersey, a saddler to trade, he moved to Ohio where he organized one of the first antislavery societies, the Union Humane Society. An itinerant campaigner, he founded *The Genius of Universal Emancipation* (1831–36) and in 1836 *The National Enquirer* in Philadelphia (later called the *Pennsylvania Freeman*).

Lunn, Sir Arnold Henry Moore 1888–1974
English Roman Catholic apologist and Alpine ski pioneer

He was born in India, the son of the travel-bureau pioneer Sir Henry Lunn (1859–1939) and the brother of the writer **Hugh Kingsmill**. His first books were on the Alps and skiing, but he began studying Roman Catholicism from his father's Methodist perspective in *Roman Converts* (1924), *John Wesley* (1929), *The Flight from Reason* (1930) and, in debate with **Ronald Arbuthnott Knox**, *Difficulties*. Converted to Catholicism, he produced a classic of triumphalist Catholicism in *Now I See* (1933), and continued his dual-authorship debates, now from Knox's camp against **C E M Joad**, **J B S Haldane** and **George Gordon Coulton**. His *Spanish Rehearsal* (1937) defended General Franco. An accomplished skier, he invented slalom gates and obtained Olympic recognition for the modern Alpine slalom race and downhill races. He founded and edited the *British Ski Year Book* in 1919.

Lunny, Donal 1945–
Irish folk musician, composer and record producer

Lumière, Auguste Marie Louis Nicolas 1862–1954 and Louis Jean 1865–1948
French industrial and physiological chemists, pioneers of motion photography

The Lumière brothers were born in Besançon, the sons of a photographer and manufacturer of photographic materials. Auguste was educated at the University of Bern, Switzerland, and Louis at the École Technique, La Martinière. At the age of 17 Louis invented a dry-plate process which transformed the fortunes of the family business Lumière and Jougla. In 1894, after seeing a demonstration of **Thomas Alva Edison**'s kinetoscope, which could record movement, Louis determined to invent a method by which moving pictures could be projected; together the brothers invented the *cinématographe* (cinematograph), the first machine to project images on a screen, in 1895. The same year they built the first cinema, in Lyons, and produced the first film newsreels and the first motion picture in history, *La Sortie des ouvriers de l'usine Lumière* (Eng trans *Workers Leaving the Lumière Factory*). On 28 December 1895, which has since been regarded as the birthday of world cinema, the first film was projected to a paying public; this took place at the Grand Café on the Boulevard des Capucines in Paris.

During the next five years the Lumières amassed a huge catalogue of newsreel shot all over the world by their team of skilled photographers, and Louis directed 60 and produced about 2,000 films, including dramatizations of *Faust* and *The Life and Passion of Jesus Christ*. After 1900 they worked to improve colour photography, inventing the Autochrome screen plate for colour photography in 1903, and studied colloidal substances in living organisms. Auguste also carried out research into cancer, vitamins, and oral vaccination. Both were elected to the French Academy of Sciences. Louis died in Bandol and Auguste in Lyons.

📖 Bernard Chardère, *Les Lumière* (1985).

> *Mon frère en une nuit, avait inventé le cinématographe.*
> 'My brother, in one night, had invented the cinema.'
> Auguste Lumière on his brother's flash of inspiration which resulted in the 'Kinetoscope de projection'. Quoted in C W Ceram, *Archaeology of the Cinema* (1965).

He was born in Newbridge, County Kildare. His first instrument was drums, but he switched to guitar and then to bouzouki, as well as keyboards. He was a founder-member of Planxty with **Christy Moore**, Andy Irvine and Liam O'Flynn, then of The Bothy Band in 1975, and later Moving Hearts in 1981, three of the most important and influential groups in Irish music. Although self-effacing, he made a crucial contribution to all three, and he also ran an important record company, Mulligan, in Dublin. He continued to perform in the 1980s and 1990s, but devoted much of his time to producing records, and has been instrumental in developing the crossover success of Irish music, reflected in the eclectic *Common Ground* project (1996). His brother, Manus Lunny, is also a musician, and is a member of the Scottish folk-rock group Capercaillie.

Luns, Joseph Marie Antoine Hubert 1911–
Dutch politician

After studying law, he joined the Dutch diplomatic service (1940–52). In 1952 he became Minister without Portfolio for the Dutch Catholic People's Party, and from then on was inextricably bound up with Dutch foreign affairs. For the whole of the period between 1957 and 1971 he was Foreign Minister, and from 1971 to 1984 he was Secretary-General of NATO. He was integrally involved in the formation and consolidation of the European Communities, and was a central figure in international relations during the days of the Cold War.

Lunt, Alfred 1892–1977
US actor

He was born in Milwaukee, Wisconsin, and educated at Carroll College, Waukesha. He abandoned plans to be an architect, making his stage debut with the Castle Square Theatre Company in Boston (1912). He made his New York debut in *Romance and Arabella* (1917) and had his first major success in *Clarence* (1919–21). In 1922 he married actress Lynn Fontanne (1887–1983) and the couple seldom performed separately thereafter. He appeared in such plays as *The Guardsman* (1924), *Elizabeth, The Queen* (1930), *Design for Living* (1933), *Idiot's Delight* (1936) and *The Seagull* (1938). He made his film debut in *Backbone* (1923) and also recreated *The Guardsman* (1931), but the couple appeared primarily on stage. Their last performance in New York and London in *The Visit* (1958–60) was an unqualified success. Broadway's Lunt Fontanne Theatre, opened in 1958, was named in their honour.

Lupescu Magda 1902–
Mistress and second wife of King Charles II of Romania

Her Jewish descent as much as her dissolute behaviour earned her the disapproval of Romanian society, itself notorious for its profligacy. Because of the scandal surrounding their affair, Charles renounced his claim to the throne and when he returned to Romania in 1930 it was on condition that she remained abroad. When she also returned and took up residence in the palace, the Prime Minister, Iuliu Maniu, resigned. Upon her marriage in 1947 to Charles, she took the name Princess Elena and lived in exile with the former king.

Lupino, Ida 1918–95
English film actress and director

Born in London, the daughter of popular comedian Stanley Lupino (1893–1942), she trained at RADA and was still a teenager when she made her leading role debut in *Her First Affaire* (1932). Moving to Hollywood in 1933, she rose to stardom as the adulterous murderess in *They Drive By Night* (1940). Under contract to Warner Brothers, she appeared in musicals and comedies, but was most successful in roles expressing inner torment, repression and malevolence. Her films include *High Sierra* (1941), *Ladies in Retirement* (1941), *The Hard Way* (1943) and *Road House* (1948). She left Warner Brothers in 1947 to form her own company, producing, co-writing and directing *Not Wanted* (1949). She continued to act, but focused increasingly on direction with *Outrage* (1950) and *The Bigamist* (1953). With the formation of Four Star Productions (with Charles Boyer, **David Niven** and Dick Powell), she worked extensively for television, and also appeared in *Mr Adams and Eve* (1957–58) with her third husband Howard Duff (1917–90).

Lupton, Thomas Goff 1791–1873
English mezzotint engraver

Born in London, he was one of the first to use steel in engraving. Among his works are **J M W Turner**'s *Ports and Rivers*.

Lurçat, Jean 1892–1966
French painter and tapestry designer

Born in Bruyères, Vosges, he went to Paris in 1912 and trained at the École des Beaux-Arts and the Académie Colarossi. His achievement was to revive the art of tapestry in France. By 1940 no fewer than 40 of his designs were being woven by Aubusson, and in 1956 his tapestry *Hommage aux Morts de la Résistance et de la déportation*

('Homage to Those Who Died in the Resistance and After Transportation') was exhibited in Paris. In 1945 he bought an 11th-century fortress overlooking Saint-Céré, from which he transmitted calls to the Resistance. His best-known works also include *The Apocalypse* for the church at Assy (1948); tapestries for the Palais de L'Europe in Strasbourg (1951–54); the vast *Le Chant du Monde* (1957–65, 'The Song of the World', Angers), inspired by the medieval *Apocalypse* at Angers; *La Flamme et l'Océan* (1962, 'The Flame and the Ocean', Musée Unterlinden, Colmar); and *Tout Feu Tout Flamme* (1963, 'Full of Enthusiasm', Lyons).

Luria, Aleksandr Romanovich 1902–77
Soviet psychologist
Born in Kazan, he began his studies at the Moscow Medical Institute under the influential child psychologist Lev Semyonovich Vygotsky. From 1945 he taught at Moscow State University, and carried out extensive researches into the effects of brain injuries that had been sustained by people during World War II. He established, and became head of, the neuropsychology section of the department of psychology at the university in 1967. His contributions to the field of neuropsychology (the application of the theories and methods of experimental psychology to the understanding of neurological disorders) have been both empirical and theoretical, his influence being particularly felt by researchers concerned with understanding the effects of damage to the frontal lobes, and of damage to those regions of the left hemisphere of the brain that are concerned with language. His books include *The Man with a Shattered World* (Eng trans 1972) and *The Working Brain* (Eng trans 1973).

Luria, Salvador Edward 1912–91
US biologist and Nobel Prize winner
Born in Turin, Italy, he graduated in medicine at Turin University in 1935, and went on to the Radium Institute in Paris to study medical physics, radiation and techniques of working with phage, the bacterial virus. Later he emigrated to the USA, where he worked at Indiana University. With Max Delbrück, he showed that bacteria and phage genes can mutate, and that different strains of phage can exchange and recombine genes. With A D Hershey and Delbrück, Luria founded the Phage Group, committed to using phage to investigate genetics. In 1969 he was awarded the Nobel Prize for physiology or medicine, jointly with Delbrück and Hershey, for discoveries related to the role of DNA in bacterial viruses. He wrote *General Virology* (1953), which became a standard textbook.

Lurie, Alison 1926–
US novelist
She was born in Chicago and educated at Radcliffe College, Massachusetts. Since 1968 she has taught at Cornell University, since 1976 as Professor of English, and academic life became the backdrop for her first books, the ironically titled *Love and Friendship* (1962), *The Nowhere City* (1965) and *Foreign Affairs* (1984)—the last of which won her the Pulitzer Prize. She has increasingly turned to non-fictional commentary, brilliantly in *The Language of Clothes* (1981), often contentiously in *Don't Tell the Grown-ups: Children's Literature* (1990).

Lusignan, Guy of See Guy of Lusignan

Lusinchi, Jaime 1924–
Venezuelan politician
Born in Clarines, in Anzoategui state, he joined the Democratic Action Party (AD) while a medical student but was exiled during the repressive regime of General Jimenez, spending the time in Argentina, Chile and the USA (1952–58). The revival of democratic government saw his return and he became politically active again,

entering parliament and eventually becoming AD leader. In 1984 he succeeded the Christian Social Party (COPEI) leader, Luis Herrera, as President but the austere policies he followed in an effort to solve his country's economic problems proved unpopular and he lost the 1988 election to his AD rival, Carlos Andres Perez.

Luska, Sidney See Harland, Henry

Lussigny, Baron de See Ancre, Baron de Lussigny, Marquis d'

Luta, Mahpiua See Red Cloud

Luther, Martin See panel p1171

Luthuli or Lutuli, Albert John Mvumbi 1898–1967
South African black resistance leader and Nobel Prize winner
Born in Rhodesia, the son of a Zulu Christian missionary, and educated at a US mission school near Durban, he spent 15 years as a teacher before being elected tribal chief of Groutville, Natal. Deposed for anti-apartheid activities, he became President-General of the African National Congress (1952–60), in which capacity he dedicated himself to a campaign of non-violent resistance and was a defendant in the notorious Johannesburg treason trial (1956–57). He was awarded the 1960 Nobel Peace Prize for his unswerving opposition to racial violence in the face of repressive measures by the South African government and impatience from extremist Africans. He was elected Rector of Glasgow University (1962) but severe restrictions imposed by the South African government (in 1961, and for another five years in 1964), prevented him from leaving Natal. In 1962 he published *Let My People Go*. □ Mary Benson, *Chief Albert Lutuli of South Africa* (1963)

Lutosławski, Witold 1913–94
Polish composer and conductor
Born in Warsaw, he has travelled and taught widely in western Europe and the USA. The recipient of many awards, he is a prolific writer. His orchestral works are his most impressive—*Symphonic Variations* (1938), four symphonies (1947, 1967, 1983, 1993), *Concerto for Orchestra* (1954), *Livre pour orchestre* (1968), his Cello Concerto (1970), *Mi-parti* (1976), *Chain 3* (1986) and his *Piano Concerto for Piano and Orchestra* (1988). He has also composed chamber, vocal and piano music. The BBC Symphony Orchestra staged a festival of his work in 1997 at the Barbican Centre, London.

Lutuli, Albert John Mvumbi See Luthuli, Albert John Mvumbi

Lutyens, Sir Edwin Landseer 1869–1944
English architect
He was born in London. His designs ranged from the picturesque of his early country houses, including Marsh Court, Stockbridge, and the restoration of Lindisfarne Castle, which owed much to the Arts and Crafts Movement, to those in the Renaissance style such as Heathcote, Ilkley and Salutation, Sandwich. He finally evolved a classical style exhibited in the Cenotaph, Whitehall, and which reached its height in his design for Liverpool Roman Catholic Cathedral. Other prominent works were his magnificent Viceroy's House, New Delhi, a masterpiece in classical design, the British Pavilion at the Rome Exhibition of 1910 and the British Embassy in Washington. □ Christopher Hussey, *The Life of Sir Edwin Lutyens* (1950)

Lutyens, (Agnes) Elizabeth 1906–83
English composer

Luther, Martin 1483–1546
German religious reformer, and founder of the Reformation

Luther was born in Eisleben, the son of a worker in the copper mines. He went to school at Magdeburg and Eisenach, and went to the University of Erfurt in 1501, taking his degree in 1505. He was also interested in the study of the Scriptures, and spent three years in the Augustinian monastery at Erfurt. In 1507 he was ordained a priest, and in 1508 went to lecture and preach at the University of Wittenberg. On a mission to Rome in 1510–11 he was appalled by the corrput practices he found there, in particular the sale of indulgences by the Dominican Johann Tetzel and others to raise funds for building and other purposes. From this experience, Luther's career as a Reformer began.

As Professor of Biblical Exegesis at Wittenberg (1512–46), he began to preach the doctrine of salvation by faith rather than works; and in 1517 he drew up a list of 95 theses on indulgences, denying to the pope all right to forgive sins, and nailed them on the church door at Wittenberg. Tetzel published a set of counter-theses and burnt Luther's, and the Wittenberg students retaliated by burning Tetzel's. In 1518 Luther was joined by **Philip Melanchthon**. The pope, **Leo X**, at first took little notice of the disturbance, but in 1518 summoned Luther to Rome to answer for his theses. His university and the elector interfered, and ineffective negotiations were undertaken by Cardinal **Cajetan** and by Miltitz, envoy of the pope to the Saxon court. **Johann von Eck** and Luther held a memorable disputation at Leipzig (1519).

Luther meanwhile attacked the papal system as a whole more boldly. **Erasmus** and **Ulrich von Hutten** now joined in the conflict. In 1520 Luther published his famous address to the *Christian Nobles of Germany*, followed by a treatise *On the Babylonian Captivity of the Church of God*, which works attacked also the doctrinal system of the Church of Rome. A papal bull containing 41 theses was issued against him, and he burned it before a crowd of doctors, students and citizens in Wittenberg. Germany was convulsed with excitement; and Luther was summoned to appear before the first Diet at Worms, which

Charles V had convened in 1521. Finally he was put under the ban of the empire; on his return from Worms he was seized, at the instigation of the Elector of Saxony, and lodged (mostly for his own protection) in the Wartburg. During the year he spent there he translated the Scriptures and composed various treatises.

Civil unrest called Luther back to Wittenberg in 1522; he rebuked the unruly elements, and made a stand against lawlessness on the one hand and tyranny on the other. In this year he published his acrimonious reply to **Henry VIII** on the seven sacraments. Estrangement had gradually sprung up between Erasmus and Luther, and there was an open breach in 1525, when Erasmus published *De Libero Arbitrio*, and Luther followed with *De Servo Arbitrio*. In that year Luther married **Katherine von Bora**, one of nine nuns who had withdrawn from convent life. In 1529 he engaged in his famous conference at Marburg with **Zwingli** and other Swiss theologians, determinedly maintaining his views as to the real (consubstantial) presence in the Eucharist.

The drawing up of the Augsburg Confession, with Melanchthon representing Luther, marks the culmination of the German Reformation in 1530. Luther died in Eisleben, and was buried at Wittenberg. He possessed the power of kindling other souls with the fire of his own convictions.

📖 Luther's voluminous works include *Table-talk, Letters* and *Sermons*. His commentaries on Galatians and the Psalms are still read; and he was one of the great leaders of sacred song, his hymns having an enduring power. See also H A Oberman, *Luther* (1990); James Atkinson, *Martin Luther and the Birth of Protestantism* (1968); Roland Bainton, *Here I Stand: A Life of Martin Luther* (1951).

> *Esto peccator et pecca fortiter, sed fortius fide et gaude in Christo.*
> 'Be a sinner and sin boldly, but more boldly believe and rejoice in Christ.' From a letter to Melanchthon (1521).

Born in London, the daughter of Sir **Edwin Lutyens**, she studied in Paris and at the Royal College of Music, and had a setting of **Keats's** poem *To Sleep* (1819) performed while still attending the College. She was one of the first British composers to adopt the twelve-note technique, and the Chamber Concerto No 1 (1939), composed in her own interpretation of this style, was a highly original work. Her compositions were, in general, not immediately well received—the chamber opera *Infidelio* (1954) and cantata *De Amore* (1957) were not performed until 1973—but she later became accepted as a leading British composer. Her work includes *O Saisons, O châteaux* (1946), the chamber opera *The Pit* (1947), *Concertante* (1950), *Quincunx* (1959), *The Country of the Stars* (1963), *Vision of Youth* (1970) and *Echoi* (1979). She published her autobiography, *A Goldfish Bowl*, in 1972.

Luwum, Janani 1922–77
Ugandan bishop

Born in East Acholi, the son of a Christian, he became a teacher and was converted in 1948. He was ordained into the Anglican Church and, despite an evangelicanism which disturbed more conventional Christians in Uganda, became a theological college principal, Bishop of Northern Uganda and was elected Archbishop of Uganda in 1974. He spoke out fearlessly against the atrocities committed during **Idi Amin's** period of rule, as a result of which he was murdered. The Amin government forbade a memorial service for him.

Luxembourg, François Henri de Montmorency-Bouteville, Duc de 1628–95
French soldier

Born in Paris, he was brought up by his aunt, mother of the Great **Condé**. After 1659 he was pardoned by **Louis XIV**, who made him Duc de Luxembourg (1661). In 1667 he served under Condé in Franche-Comté. In 1672 himself successfully invaded the Netherlands although he was driven back in 1673. During the war he stormed Valenciennes and twice defeated the Prince of Orange. Made a marshal in 1675, soon after the peace (1678) he quarrelled with the Marquis de **Louvois**, and was not employed for 12 years. In 1690 he commanded in Flanders and defeated the Allies at Fleurus, and later he twice more routed his old opponent, now King **William III** of Great Britain, at Steinkirk (1692) and Neerwinden (1693).

Luxemburg, Rosa 1871–1919
German left-wing revolutionary

She was born in Zamość in Russian Poland. Converted to Communism in 1890, she took part in underground activities in Poland and founded the Polish Social Democratic Party (later the Polish Communist Party). A German citizen from 1895, she emigrated to Zurich in 1898, where she studied law and political economy. She moved to Berlin and became a leader of the left-wing movement, writing tracts such as *Sozialreform oder Revolution*. At the outbreak of World War I she formed, with **Karl Liebknecht**, the Spartakusbund (Spartacus League), later the core of the German Communist Party

(KPD), and spent most of the war in prison. After her release in 1919 she took part in an abortive uprising, and was murdered with Liebknecht in Berlin. 🕮 J P Nettl, *Rosa Luxemburg* (2 vols, 1966)

Lu Xun (Lu Hsün) 1881–1936
Chinese writer

He was born in Shaoxing, Zhejiang (Chekiang), into a family of scholars, and by 1913 had become Professor of Chinese Literature at the National Peking University and National Normal University for Women. In 1926 he went as professor to Amoy University in Xiamen and he was later appointed Dean of the College of Arts and Letters at Sun Yat-sen University, Guangzhou (Canton). His career as an author began with a short story, *Diary of a Madman* (1918). *The True Story of Ah Q* (1921, Eng trans 1941) is considered his most successful book, and has been translated into many languages. Between 1918 and 1925 he wrote 26 short stories and these appear in two volumes entitled *Cry* and *Hesitation*. 🕮 Huang Sung-k'ang, *Lu Hsün and the New Culture Movement in Modern China* (1957)

Lvov, Prince Georgi Yevgeniyevich 1861–1925
Russian politician

Born in Popovka, he was head of the first and second provisional governments after the February Revolution of 1917, but his moderate policies and popular opposition to Russia's war effort led to the collapse of his government. He was succeeded by Aleksandr Kerensky, and arrested by the Bolsheviks, but escaped to Paris.

Lwoff, André Michel 1902–94
French microbiologist and Nobel Prize winner

Born in Ainy-le-Château, of Russian-Polish extraction, he worked at the Pasteur Institute in Paris from 1921, becoming departmental head there in 1938. From 1959 to 1968 he was Professor of Microbiology at the Sorbonne. He researched the genetics of bacterial viruses (phage) and showed that when phage enters a bacterial cell, it becomes part of the bacterial chromosome and divides with it (lysogeny), in which form it protects the bacterium against further invasion by the same type of virus. These findings have had important implications for the development of drug resistance and for cancer research. In 1965 Lwoff was awarded the Nobel Prize for physiology or medicine jointly with François Jacob and Jacques Monod, for their discoveries concerning genetic control of enzyme and virus synthesis. He was elected a Foreign Member of the Royal Society in 1958 and was appointed director of the Cancer Research Institute at Villejuif, France, a position he held until his retirement in 1972. His writings include *Biological Order* (1962) and *Jeux et combats* (1981, 'Games and Combats').

Lyadov, Anatoli Konstantinovich See Liadov, Anatoli Konstantinovich

Lyapunov, Aleksandr Mikhailovich 1857–1918
Russian mathematician

Born in Yaroslavl, he studied at St Petersburg University, where he came under the influence of Pafnutii Chebyshev, and then taught at Kharkov University, until he returned to St Petersburg as professor in 1901. He is principally associated with important methods in the theory of the stability of dynamical systems, related to Jules Henri Poincaré's work. He committed suicide after his wife's death from tuberculosis.

Lyautey, Louis Hubert Gonzalve 1854–1934
French soldier and colonial administrator

Born in Nancy, he held administrative posts in Algeria, Tongking and Madagascar (under Joseph Galliéni), where he reformed the administration. But his most brilliant work was done in Morocco, where he was the resident commissary-general from 1912 to 1925, with a break as French Minister of War in 1916–17. He established firm French authority, and developed Casablanca as a seaport.

Lycurgus
Traditional, possibly legendary, law-giver of Sparta

He is said to have instigated the Spartan ideals of harsh military discipline.

Lydgate, John c.1370–c.1451
English monk and poet

He was born in Lydgate, Suffolk, and became a Benedictine monk. He may have studied at Oxford and Cambridge. He travelled in France and perhaps Italy, and became prior of Hatfield Broadoak, Essex, in 1423. A court poet, he wrote *The Troy Book* (1412–20), based on Colonna's Latin prose *Historia Trojana*, *The Siege of Thebes* (1420–22), represented as a new Canterbury tale, and the *Fall of Princes* (1431–38), based on Boccaccio. Other works include the *Daunce of Machabre*, from the French, *Temple of Glas*, a copy of Chaucer's *House of Fame*, and *London Lickpenny*, on London. 🕮 D Pearsall, *John Lydgate* (1970)

Lydiard, Arthur Leslie 1917–
New Zealand running coach and popularizer of jogging

Born in Auckland, he was a member of the New Zealand marathon team at the Empire Games there in 1950, and won the national championships in 1955 and 1957. He was the successful coach of many world-class distance- and middle-distance runners, such as Murray Halberg and Peter Snell, coached the New Zealand team for the Olympic Games in Tokyo (1964) and for the Commonwealth Games in Christchurch (1974), and has also coached national teams in Mexico, Venezuela, Finland and Denmark. In 1960 he introduced 'jogging' groups for cardiac rehabilitation, lecturing worldwide and writing on this popular activity.

Lyell, Sir Charles 1797–1875
Scottish geologist

Born in Kinnordy, Forfarshire, he was educated at Ringwood, Salisbury and Midhurst, studied law at Exeter College, Oxford, and was called to the Bar. William Buckland interested him in geology at Oxford, and he later became secretary to the Geological Society of London. He decided to give up law during an excursion to France in 1828 with Roderick Murchison, and on his return he completed the first volume of his *Principles of Geology* (1830). He had been appointed Professor of Geology at King's College London, by 1832. His authoritative *Principles of Geology* (1830–33) was very influential, as was his memoir *Consolidation of lava upon steep slopes of Etna*, in which he refuted the elevation crater theory of Leopold von Buch. He made two long geological tours of the USA and published his observations as *Travels in North America* (1845) and *A Second Visit to the United States* (1849). His 'uniformitarian' principle taught that the greatest geological changes might have been produced by the forces in operation now, given sufficient time. His interest was primarily in the biological side of geology, and his work had as great a contemporary influence as Charles Darwin's *Origin of Species*. Lyell's other publications include *The Elements of Geology* (1838) and *The Geological Evidence of the Antiquity of Man* (1863), a study discussing the nature and significance of worked flints found in the valley of the Somme, and which startled the public by its unbiased attitude towards Darwin. He was knighted in 1848. 🕮 L G Wilson, *Charles Lyell, The Years to 1841: The Revolution in Geology* (1972)

Lyle, Sandy, *properly* Alexander Walter Barr Lyle 1958–
Scottish golfer

Born in Shrewsbury, Shropshire, England, of Scottish parents, he started his golfing career by representing England at boys, youth and full international levels. In 1980 and 1982 he was a narrowly beaten finalist in the World Match-Play Championship. His major championship successes have been the European Open in 1979, the French Open in 1981, the British Open in 1985 and the US Masters Championship in 1988. An extremely long hitter with an admirably phlegmatic temperament, with **Nick Faldo** he has largely been responsible for the revival of British professional golf at world level. In 1986 he published *Learning Golf the Lyle Way.*

Lyly or Lily, John c.1554–1606
English dramatist and novelist, 'the Euphuist'
Born in the Weald of Kent, he took his BA at Magdalen College, Oxford, in 1573, and studied also at Cambridge. **William Cecil, Lord Burghley**, gave him some post of trust in his household, and he became vice-master of the St Paul's choristers. Having in 1589 taken part in the Marprelate controversy, he became MP for Aylesbury and Appleby (1597–1601). His *Euphues*, a romance in two parts—*Euphues, The Anatomie of Wit* (1578) and *Euphues and his England* (1580)—was received with great applause. It lead to the term 'euphuism', referring to an artificial and extremely elegant language, with much use made of complex similes and antitheses. His other works include the comedy *The Woman in the Moon*, produced in or before 1583, *Campaspe* and *Sapho and Phao* (both 1584), *Endimion* (1591), *Gallathea* and *Midas* (both 1592), *Mother Bombie* (1594) and *Love's Metamorphosis* (1601). 📖 J D Wilson, *John Lyly* (1905)

Lyman, Theodore 1874–1954
US physicist
Born in Boston, he studied at Harvard where he remained for the majority of his career, being appointed director of the Jefferson Physical Laboratory (1910–47). He addressed the problems of using diffraction gratings to measure wavelengths in the extreme ultraviolet region of the spectrum, and published his first accurate measurements for wavelengths below 2,000 angstroms in 1906, extending the known extreme ultraviolet region significantly. He analysed the spectra and optical properties of many materials, and in 1914 discovered the hydrogen spectral lines which bear his name, a result which made an important contribution to **Niels Bohr**'s development of quantum theory.

Lynagh, Michael Patrick 1963–
Australian rugby union player
Born in Queensland, he holds the record for the most points scored in international rugby (911), as well as the record for the most conversions (140 points) in his 72 international matches (1984–95). With 72 caps, he is second behind Campese for the record number for Australia, and, with 177 points, he holds the record for the most penalty goals in international rugby. He retired from the competitive international scene as Australia's captain after the 1995 World Cup. Having spent his summers playing for Italian Treviso, he has since signed for English club Saracens.

Lynch, David 1946–
US film director
He was born in Missoula, Montana. His first full-length feature film, *Eraserhead* (1976), about a sensitive daydreamer who hurls his offspring against a wall, testified to Lynch's dark originality. It was followed by *The Elephant Man* (1980), a bleak, if more conventional, narrative about carnival freak Joseph Merrick, which earned Lynch a Best Director Oscar nomination, as did the surrealistic thriller *Blue Velvet* (1986). After a lengthy absence, during which

he masterminded the cult television series *Twin Peaks* (1989–), he returned with the sensational love story *Wild at Heart* (1990).

Lynch, Jack (John) 1917–
Irish statesman
Educated at Cork and Dublin, he joined the Civil Service in the Department of Justice in 1936, continued his legal studies, and was called to the Bar in 1945. He then entered politics and represented Cork for Fianna Fáil (1948–81). He served in education, industry and commerce, and finance before he assumed the Fianna Fáil leadership and became Taoiseach (Prime Minister) in 1966. He was replaced by the Fine Gael leader, **Liam Cosgrave**, in 1973 but was re-elected in 1977. He resigned in 1979, to be succeeded by **Charles Haughey**, and he retired from politics in 1981.

Lynd, Robert 1879–1949
Irish essayist and critic
He was born in Belfast, studied there at Queen's University, then went to London (1901) and was from 1912 literary editor of the *Daily News* (later the *News Chronicle*). He also contributed to the *New Statesman* (1913–45), signing himself 'Y Y'. His intimate, witty essays, of which he wrote numerous volumes, are on a wide variety of topics. Titles include *The Art of Letters* (1920), *The Blue Lion* (1923) and *In Defence of Pink* (1939).

Lynd, Robert Staughton 1892–1970
US sociologist
Born in New Albany, Indiana, he studied at Princeton University and Union Theological Seminary. He collaborated with his wife, Helen Merrell (1896–1982), to write the well-known *Middletown: A Study in Contemporary American Culture* (1929) and *Middletown in Transition* (1937), which examine the culture of an ordinary US midwestern city (Muncie, Indiana). He was a professor at Columbia University (1931–60), and she taught at Sarah Lawrence College (1929–64).

Lynden-Bell, Donald 1935–
English astrophysicist
Born in Dover, Kent, he studied at Cambridge, and spent two years with **Allan Sandage** at the California Institute of Technology working on the dynamics of galaxies. He then returned to Cambridge and since 1972 has been Professor of Astrophysics and director of the Institute of Astronomy (1972–77, 1982–87, 1992–94). In 1962 Lynden-Bell identified the Population II stars which contain few metals and have little net motion around the centre of our galaxy. He pioneered the study of the dynamic evolution of the centres of globular clusters, and in 1969 was the first to propose that the cores of galaxies might contain supermassive black holes. His 1985 review of galactic structure meant that the distance to the centre of the galaxy was changed from 100,000 to 85,000 parsecs. The Royal Astronomical Society awarded Lynden-Bell the Eddington Medal in 1984. He was elected Fellow of the Royal Society in 1978 and was awarded its gold medal in 1993.

Lyndsay or Lindsay, Sir David c.1486–1555
Scottish poet
Born probably at The Mount, near Cupar, Fife, or at Garmylton (Garleton), near Haddington, East Lothian, he was appointed 'usher' (1512) of the newborn prince who became **James V**. In 1538 he appears to have been Lyon King-of-Arms. He went on embassies to the Netherlands, France, England and Denmark, and he (or another David Lyndsay) represented Cupar in parliament (1540–46). The earliest and most poetic of his writings is the allegorical *The Dreme* (1528), followed by *The Complaynt of the King* (1529) and *The Testament and Complaynt of Our Soverane Lordis Papyngo* (1530). He also wrote a satire on

court life called *Ane Publict Confession of the Kingis Auld Hound Callit Bagsche* (1536), *The Historie of Squyer Meldrum*, and *Ane Satyre of the Thrie Estaitis*, his most remarkable work, which was performed at Linlithgow in 1540 and revived at the Edinburgh Festival. 📖 W Murison, *Sir David Lindsay* (1938)

Lynen, Feodor Felix Konrad 1911–79
German biochemist and Nobel Prize winner

Born and educated in Munich, he joined the department of chemistry at the University of Munich (1942), and later became professor there (from 1947) and director of the Max Planck Institute for Cell Chemistry and Biochemistry (1954–79). In 1951 he isolated coenzyme A and showed that it formed acetyl-S-CoA, an important intermediate in lipid metabolism. In 1953, with Severo Ochoa, he substituted compounds of ethanolamine for the full coenzyme A molecule in the study of the pathway of fatty acid degradation. At the same time as Konrad Bloch, Lynen contributed towards elucidating the biosynthesis of cholesterol, for which he shared the Nobel Prize for physiology or medicine in 1964 jointly with Bloch.

Lynn, Loretta, *née* Webb 1935–
US country singer

She was born into rural poverty in Butcher's Hollow, Kentucky, married at the age of 14 and had four children by 18. Her first single, 'Honky-Tonk Girl', became a minor hit and earned her an invitation to perform in the prestigious *Grand Ole Opry* country music show in Nashville in 1960. She matured into a major country singer and songwriter with a string of hits, including a celebrated series of duets with Conway Twitty (1933–93) in the 1970s. She composes both the melodies and lyrics of her songs which often focus on the troubles of rural women and feature defiant parentheses such as 'Don't Come Home A-Drinkin' (with Lovin' on Your Mind)' and 'You Ain't Woman Enough (to Take My Man)'. Her career cooled after 1980, but she remained a big name, and her collaboration with Tammy Wynette and Dolly Parton on *Honky Tonk Angels* (1993) was a success. Her autobiography *Coal Miner's Daughter* (1976) became a bestseller, and was filmed in 1979. Her sister, Crystal Gayle (1951–), is a well-known country-pop singer.

Lyon, John d.1592
English philanthropist

A yeoman landowner of the estate of Preston, in Middlesex, he was relatively prosperous but childless and used his money for the endowment of local charities. In 1572 he obtained a royal charter from Queen Elizabeth I for the pre-Reformation school at Harrow, which he supported with endowments to guarantee its continuation. In 1590 he drew up statutes and a course of classical education for the school, and is regarded as the founder of the public school there.

Lyon, Mary Frances 1925–
English biologist

Born in Norwich, Norfolk, she studied at Cambridge, and in 1950 joined the UK Medical Research Council's staff, working from 1955 at their Radiobiology Unit, Harwell/Chilton (head of genetics division from 1962, deputy director from 1986). She has published on many aspects of mammalian genetics, but her name is particularly associated with the 'Lyon hypothesis' which she propounded in 1961. This proposed that one of the two X chromosomes in female mammals is inactivated in early development, so that females are made up of different genetic cell lines (characterized by which of the X chromosomes is switched off). This idea, widely confirmed, has greatly helped studies on clinical genetics and imprinting. She has a wide knowledge of the mammalian X chromosome and the mouse genomes, and has demonstrated the value of mouse genetics in helping us to understand the mammalian genome and to tackle the problems of hereditary disease. A foreign associate of the US National Academy of Sciences and foreign honoraria member of the Genetics Society of Japan, she was elected a Fellow of the Royal Society in 1973, and was awarded its royal medal in 1984. She retired in 1990.

Lyon, Mary Mason 1797–1849
US educator

Born in Buckland, Massachusetts, she was an early advocate of higher education for all women and founded Mount Holyoke Female Seminary in South Hadley, Massachusetts. She served as its president for 12 years, operating on a shoestring budget, and her students included Emily Dickinson in 1848. The seminary later became Mount Holyoke College, the first women's college in the USA.

Lyons, Edmund Lyons, 1st Baron 1790–1858
English naval commander

Born near Christchurch, Hampshire, he joined the navy in 1803, and served in the passage of Dardanelles (1807) and in the Dutch West Indies (1810–11). Promoted rear admiral in 1850, he served in the Mediterranean as Commander-in-Chief (1855–58).

Lyons, Dame Enid Muriel See Lyons, Joseph Aloysius

Lyons, Francis Stewart Leland 1923–83
Irish historian

Born in Derry, he was educated in Tunbridge Wells, at High School, Dublin, and Trinity College, Dublin, where he taught until becoming Professor of History at the University of Kent in 1964. He progressed from his technical doctoral thesis, subsequently published, on *The Irish Parliamentary Party 1890–1910* (1951), to a series of works embodying detailed research and judicious assessment of modern scholarship, notably *The Fall of Parnell* (1960), *John Dillon* (1968), *Ireland Since the Famine* (1971), *Charles Stewart Parnell* (1977) and *Culture and Anarchy in Ireland 1890–1939* (1978). He was provost of Trinity College, Dublin, from 1974 to 1981, and was working on a historical biography of W B Yeats when he died.

Lyons, Sir Joseph 1848–1917
English businessman

Born in London, he first studied art, and invented a stereoscope before joining with three friends to establish what was to become J Lyons and Co Ltd. Starting in Piccadilly with a teashop, he became head of one of the largest catering businesses in Great Britain.

Lyons, Joseph Aloysius 1879–1939
Australian statesman

Born in Stanley, Tasmania, and educated at Tasmania University, he was a teacher before entering politics in 1909 as a Labour MP in the Tasmanian House of Assembly. He held the post of Minister of Education and Railways (1914–16) and was premier (1923–29). In the federal parliament he was in turn Postmaster-General, Minister of Public Works and Treasurer. In 1931 he broke away as a protest against the government's financial policy, he himself being in favour of reduced public expenditure, and founded and led an opposition party, the United Australian Party. He became Prime Minister (1932–39) after the 1931 election. His wife, Dame Enid Muriel Lyons (1897–1981), was born in Leesville, Tasmania, and was very active in her husband's career. In 1943, after his death, she won the Federal seat of Darwin, Tasmania, becoming the first woman member of the House of Representatives and later the first woman member of the Federal Cabinet. She was created GBE in

1937. She wrote entertainingly of her marriage in *So we take Comfort* (1965) and of her life in parliament in *Among the Carrion Crows* (1972).

Lyot, Bernard Ferdinand 1897–1952
French astronomer and inventor
Born in Paris and trained as an engineer at the École Supérieure d'Électricité, he joined the staff of the Paris Observatory at Meudon (1920), where his early researches were concerned with the measurement of polarization of light from the moon and planets. In 1931 he succeeded in observing the solar corona from the summit of the Pic du Midi using his new coronagraph, an instrument in which scattered light was reduced to an absolute minimum. Previously such observations had only been possible during a total solar eclipse. Two years later he started photography of the sun through monochromatic polarizing filters: his pioneer cinematographic films of the movements of solar prominences taken in the light of the red hydrogen Hα line created a sensation. He was awarded the gold medal of the Royal Astronomical Society (1939) and the Bruce Medal of the Astronomical Society of the Pacific (1946). He died in Egypt on his return from an expedition to Khartoum where he had observed the total solar eclipse of February 1952.

Lysander d.395BC
Spartan naval commander
He commanded the fleet which defeated the Athenians at the Battle of Aegospotami in 405BC, and in 404 took Athens, thus ending the Peloponnesian War. He died while unsuccessfully besieging Haliartus in Boeotia.

Lysenko, Trofim Denisovich 1898–1976
Soviet geneticist and agronomist
Born in Karlovka, Ukraine, he graduated from Uman School of Horticulture (1921) and the Kiev Agricultural Institute (1925). During the famines of the early 1930s, he promoted 'vernalization', suggesting that plant growth could be accelerated by short exposures to low temperatures. His techniques seemed to offer a rapid way of overcoming the food shortages then prevailing, and gained him political support. In 1935 he developed a theory of genetics which suggested that environment can alter the hereditary material. As director of the Institute of Genetics of the Soviet Academy of Sciences (1940–65), he pronounced the **Mendel**ian theory of heredity to be wrong, ruthlessly silencing scientists who opposed him. After **Stalin**'s death in 1956, Lysenko increasingly lost support and was forced to resign in 1965. He was awarded the Stalin prize in 1949 for his book *Agrobiology* (1948). ▢ Zhores A Medvedev, *The Rise and Fall of T D Lysenko* (1969)

Lysias c.458–c.380BC
Greek orator
The son of a rich Syracusan, he was educated at Thurii in Italy, and settled in Athens about 440BC. The Thirty Tyrants in 404 stripped him and his brother Polemarchus of their wealth, and killed Polemarchus. The first use to which Lysias put his eloquence was, on the fall of the Thirty (403), to prosecute Eratosthenes, the tyrant chiefly to blame for his brother's murder. He then practised with success as a writer of speeches for litigants. From his surviving speeches Lysias emerges as delightfully lucid in thought and expression, and strong in character-drawing. The family home in Athens is portrayed in **Plato**'s *Republic*.

Lysimachus d.281BC
Macedonian general, King in Thrace
He served **Alexander the Great** until he became king in Thrace, to which he later added north-west Asia Minor and Macedonia. He was defeated and killed at Koroupedion by **Seleucus I Nicator**.

Lysippus of Sicyon 4th century BC
Greek sculptor
He was a prolific worker, said to have made more than 1,500 bronzes, and introduced a new naturalism, reducing the size of the head and making the limb more slender. There is a Roman marble copy of his bronze *Apoxyomenos* (*Man using a Strigil*), which shows an awareness of space as part of sculpture, in the Vatican Museum, Rome (c.330BC). He made several portrait busts of **Alexander the Great**.

Lyte, Henry Francis 1793–1847
Scottish hymnwriter
Born in Ednam, near Kelso, he studied at Trinity College, Dublin, and took orders in 1815. His *Poems, chiefly Religious* (1833, reprinted as *Miscellaneous Poems*, 1868), are not as well known as his hymns, amongst which are 'Abide with me' and 'Pleasant are thy courts'.

Lyttelton, Humphrey (Richard Adeane) 1921–
English jazz trumpeter and bandleader
He was born in Eton, Berkshire. He taught himself to play the cornet while at Eton (where his father was a housemaster), and after attending Camberwell School of Art and serving throughout World War II in the Grenadier Guards, he played trumpet with George Webb's Dixielanders, before forming his own band in 1948. He has led a band continuously since then, and maintains a high musical standard. He was one of the first 'trad' bandleaders to move towards mainstream jazz, replacing the banjo with a guitar and introducing an alto saxophone into the line-up. He founded his own record label, Calligraph, in 1984, and recorded for the first time with another veteran English jazz musician, clarinettist Acker Bilk (1929–), in 1992. He is also well known as a jazz broadcaster and writer.

Lyttelton, Oliver See Chandos, 1st Viscount

Lyttleton, Sir Thomas See Littleton, Sir Thomas

Lytton, Bulwer, *pseudonym of* Edward George Earle Bulwer-Lytton, 1st Baron Lytton (of Knebworth) 1803–73
English novelist, playwright, essayist, poet and politician
He was born in London, the youngest son of General Earle Bulwer (1776–1807) by Elizabeth Barbara Lytton (1773–1843), the heiress of Knebworth in Hertfordshire, and educated at Trinity Hall, Cambridge (1822–25), where he won the Chancellor's gold medal for a poem, but left with only a pass degree. His marriage (1827), against his mother's wishes, to the Irish beauty Rosina Wheeler, ended in separation (1836), and the temporary estrangement from his mother forced him to support himself by writing. His enormous output, vastly popular during his lifetime, but now forgotten, includes *Eugene Aram* (1832), *The Last Days of Pompeii* (1834) and *Harold* (1843). Among his plays are *The Lady of Lyons* (1838), *Richelieu* (1839) and *Money* (1840), and his poetry includes an epic, *King Arthur* (1848–49). MP for St Ives (1831–41), he was created a baronet in 1838, and in 1843 he succeeded to the Knebworth estate and assumed the surname of Lytton. He re-entered parliament as MP for Hertfordshire in 1852, and in the **Derby** government (1858–59) was Colonial Secretary. He was raised to the peerage in 1866.

Lytton, Sir Henry Alfred 1867–1936
English actor
He was born in London and first appeared on stage with the D'Oyly Carte Opera Company in Glasgow in 1884. Until 1932 he played leading parts in **Gilbert** and **Sullivan** opera. He wrote *Secrets of a Savoyard* (1927) and *A Wandering Minstrel* (1933).

Lytton, (Edward) Robert Bulwer-Lytton, 1st Earl of, *pseudonym* Owen Meredith 1831–91

English poet, diplomat and politician

Born in London, he was educated at Harrow school and at Bonn. In 1849 he went to Washington as attaché and private secretary to his uncle, **Henry Bulwer**, and subsequently was appointed attaché, secretary of legation, consul or chargé d'affaires at Florence (1852), Paris (1854), The Hague (1856), St Petersburg and Constantinople (now Istanbul, 1858), Vienna (1859), Belgrade (1860), Constantinople again (1863), Athens (1864), Lisbon (1865), Madrid (1868), Vienna again (1869) and Paris (1873). In the last year he succeeded his father, **Bulwer Lytton**, as 2nd Baron Lytton, and in 1874 became Minister at Lisbon. From 1876 to 1880 he was Viceroy of India, where he effected reform but failed to prevent the Second Afghan War (1878), and in 1880 he was made Earl of Lytton; in 1887 he was sent as ambassador to Paris. His works, published mainly under his pseudonym, include novels, poems (eg the epic *King Poppy*, 1892), and translations from Serbian. His *Indian Administration* (1899) and his *Letters* (1906) were both edited by his daughter, Lady Betty Balfour.

Lyubimov, Yuri Petrovich 1917–

Russian theatre director

He joined the Vakhtangov Theatre Company in Moscow after World War II, and after the tremendous success of his production of **Bertolt Brecht**'s *The Good Person of Setzuan*, was appointed director of the Taganka Theatre, Moscow, in 1964. At the Taganka he staged a series of provocative productions (both dramatically and politically), including an adaptation of *Ten Days That Shook The World* (1967), **Molière**'s *Tartuffe* (1969) and a modern-dress *Hamlet* (1974). He fell from favour, and while he was in England in 1983 he was fired from his theatre, expelled from the Party and deprived of his Soviet citizenship. He subsequently worked on several productions outside the Soviet Union, but returned to his native country in 1988, directing *Self-Murderer* (1990) and *Electra* (1992), both in Moscow.

Ma, Yo-Yo 1955–
US cellist

Born in Paris, the son of Chinese immigrants who were professionals in classical music, he was a prodigy on the cello, an instrument he took up because his older sister already played the violin. He moved to New York City with his family at the age of seven and two years later made his debut at Carnegie Hall. After studying at the Juilliard School of Music and graduating from Harvard in 1976, he achieved international fame as a cello virtuoso, playing both as a soloist and in chamber music ensembles. He has won 10 Grammy awards for his recordings.

Maazel, Lorin Varencove 1930–
US conductor and violinist

He was born in Neuilly, France, and went to the USA as a child prodigy on the violin. He studied at the University of Pittsburgh and became leader of a number of US orchestras, including the New York Philharmonic Orchestra and the Chicago and Cleveland orchestras. In 1960 he became the first US conductor to appear at Bayreuth, and he was later appointed musical director of the Deutsche Oper (1965–71), musical director of the Cleveland Orchestra (1972–82), and director of the Vienna Staatsoper (1982–84). Since 1986 he has worked with the Pittsburgh Symphony Orchestra, and since 1988 with the Orchestre National de France. In 1992 he was appointed chief conductor of the Bavarian Radio Symphony Orchestra.

Mabillon, Jean 1632–1707
French scholar

Born in St Pierremont in Champagne, he became a Benedictine monk in 1654, and from 1664 worked in the abbey of St Germain-des-Prés in Paris. Considered the founder of Latin palaeography, he edited the works of **Benedict of Nursia** (1667), and wrote a history of the Benedictine order (9 vols, 1668–1702) and *De re diplomatica* (1681; supplement 1704).

Mabon See Abraham, William

Mabuse, Jan, *real name* Gossaert c.1470–1532
Flemish painter

Born in Maubeuge (Mabuse), he entered the painters' guild of St Luke in Antwerp in 1503, and was influenced by **Hans Memlinc** and **Quentin Matsys**. In 1508–09 he accompanied Philip of Burgundy to Italy, where he adopted the High Renaissance style, which he introduced to Holland. He later lived in Middelburg.

McAdam, John Loudon 1756–1836
Scottish inventor and engineer

Born in Ayr, he went to New York in 1770, where he made a fortune in his uncle's counting-house. On his return to Scotland in 1783 he bought the estate of Sauchrie in Ayrshire, and started experimenting with a revolutionary method of road construction. In 1816 he was appointed surveyor to the Bristol Turnpike Trust, and remade the roads there with crushed stone bound with gravel, raising them to improve drainage—the 'macadamized' system. His advice was widely sought, but the cost of his experiments had impoverished him. He petitioned parliament in 1820, was voted £2,000 in 1825, and two years later was made surveyor-general of metropolitan roads.

McAliskey, (Josephine) Bernadette, *née* Devlin 1947–
Irish political activist

Born into a poor Catholic family, she was brought up in Dungannon, County Tyrone, and educated at St Patrick's Girls' Academy, Dungannon, and Queen's University, Belfast. While at university she became the youngest MP in the House of Commons since **William Pitt**, the Younger, when she was elected as an Independent Unity candidate in 1969, at the age of 21. Her aggressive political style led to her arrest while leading Catholic rioters in the Bogside, Belfast, and she was sentenced to nine months' imprisonment. In 1971 she lost Catholic support when she gave birth to an illegitimate child. She married two years later and did not stand in the 1974 general election. In 1979 she unsuccessfully sought a seat in the European Parliament, and in 1981 actively supported the IRA hunger strikers, making a dramatic appearance in Spain after her recovery from an attempted assassination in which she and her husband were shot. She was a co-founder of the Irish Republican Socialist Party in 1975. She published her autobiography, *The Price of My Soul*, in 1969. 📖 G W Target, *Bernadette: The Story of Bernadette Devlin* (1975)

Macalpin See Kenneth I

McAlpine, Sir Robert 1847–1934
Scottish building contractor

Born in Newarthill, Lanarkshire, he left school at the age of 10 to work in the pits, after which he was apprenticed as a bricklayer. In 1868 he set up a building business in the Hamilton area and began to win contracts nationally. He rebuilt his operations after a threat of bankruptcy in 1877, winning the crucial contract to build the Singer's factory at Kilbowie, Dunbartonshire. A rapid expansion as a contractor followed, in which McAlpine made use of new building techniques, such as concrete, and labour-saving machinery. In the postwar period he won large contracts from local authorities, especially for roads, and it was his company that built Wembley Stadium. He was created a baronet in 1918.

McAnally, Ray(mond) 1926–89
Irish actor

Born in Buncrana, Donegal, he made his professional debut in *A Strange House* (1942). A member of Dublin's Abbey Theatre from 1947, he had appeared in some 150 productions there by 1963 and attributed his versatility to a philosophy of 'five lines one week, King Lear the next'. His many celebrated performances include *The Shadow of a Gunman* (1951) and *The Country Boy* (1959). Performances in London include *A Cheap Bunch of Nice Flowers* (1962), *Who's Afraid of Virginia Woolf?* (1964) and *The Best of Friends* (1988). He frequently returned to the Abbey Theatre to direct and teach. Active in the cinema from 1957, his many films include *The Mission* (1986, BAFTA award) and *My Left Foot* (1989). A veteran of over 500 television productions after 1959, he also won BAFTA awards for *A Perfect Spy* (1988) and *A Very British Coup* (1989).

Macan t-Saoir, Donnachadh Ban See McIntyre, Duncan Ban

MacArthur, Charles Gordon 1895–1956
US playwright

Born in Scranton, Pennsylvania, he became a heavy drinker and prankster. While working as a journalist in Chicago he managed to convince the Chief of Police that one **Henry Wadsworth Longfellow** had been wrongly charged with rape. During World War I he is said to have dropped empty whisky bottles over Berlin—friends suggested he might simply have leaned out of the plane

MacArthur, Douglas 1880–1964
US soldier

Douglas MacArthur was born in Little Rock, Arkansas, the son of lieutenant-general Arthur MacArthur (1845–1912). He was educated at West Point, commissioned in the Corps of Engineers in 1903, and went to Tokyo in 1905 as aide to his father. In World War I he commanded the 42nd (Rainbow) Division in France, and was decorated 13 times and cited seven additional times for bravery. In 1919 he became the youngest-ever superintendent of West Point, and in 1930 he was made a general and Chief of Staff of the US army. In 1935 he became head of the US military mission to the Philippines.

In World War II he was appointed commanding general of the US armed forces in the Far East in 1941. In March 1942, after a skilful but unsuccessful defence of the Bataan Peninsula, he was ordered to evacuate from the Philippines to Australia, where he set up HQ as supreme commander of the South West Pacific Area. As the war developed he carried out a brilliant 'leap-frogging' strategy which enabled him to recapture the Philippine Archipelago from the Japanese. He completed the liberation of the Philippines in July 1945, and in September 1945, as supreme commander of the Allied powers, formally accepted the surrender of Japan on board the *Missouri*. He then exercised in the occupied Empire almost unlimited authority, giving Japan a new constitution and carrying out a programme of sweeping reform.

When war broke out in Korea in June 1950 President Truman ordered MacArthur to support the South Koreans in accordance with the appeal of the UN Security Council. In July he became Commander-in-Chief of the UN forces. After initial setbacks he pressed the war far into North Korea, but after the Chinese entered the war in November, MacArthur demanded powers to blockade the Chinese coast, bomb Manchurian bases and to use Chinese nationalist troops from Formosa against the communists. This led to acute differences with the US Democratic administration and in April 1951 President Truman relieved him of his commands. He failed to be nominated for the presidency in 1952.

A brilliant military leader and a ruler of Japan imbued with a deep moral sense, MacArthur became a legend in his lifetime. Equally, he inspired criticism for his imperious belief in his own mission and his strong sense of self-dramatization.

📖 W Manchester, *An American Caesar: Douglas MacArthur; 1880–1964* (1978); R Rovere and A Schlesinger, *The MacArthur Controversy and American Foreign Policy* (1965); J Gunther, *The Riddle of MacArthur: Japan, Korea, and the Far East* (1952; reprint 1974).

> 'But in the coming of my memory, always I come back to West Point. Always there echoes in my ear—Duty – Honour – Country.' Farewell address to the cadets of West Point, 12 May 1962.

and breathed over the city. He is best known for his collaborations with **Ben Hecht**: *The Front Page* (1928) for the stage, and the films *Barbary Coast* (1935) and *The Scoundrel* (1935), plus their enduring adaptation of *Wuthering Heights* (1939).

MacArthur, Douglas See panel above

Macarthur, Elizabeth, *née* Veale 1766–1850
Australian pioneer

Born in Bridgerule, Devon, England, she married **John Macarthur** in 1788 and sailed with him and their son to New South Wales in 1789. In 1793 John received a grant of land near Parramatta, New South Wales, which he named Elizabeth Farm. During her husband's prolonged absences from the colony, she was left, with their seven surviving children, to manage Macarthur's involved business ventures. Supported by her husband's nephew Hannibal Hawkins Macarthur (1788–1861), she introduced the merino sheep to Elizabeth Farm and to their new grant of land at Camden, New South Wales, and successfully carried out experiments in the breeding of sheep for fine wool which led to the establishment of the Australian wool industry.

Macarthur, John 1767–1834
Australian pioneer and wool merchant

Born in England, he joined the army at the age of 15. In 1789 he became a lieutenant in the New South Wales Water Corps, and emigrated to Australia with his wife **Elizabeth Macarthur**, becoming leader of the settlers in New South Wales. He inspired the Rum Rebellion (1808–10), in which the British soldiers mutinied and imprisoned the governor, **William Bligh** of *Bounty* fame. Macarthur was banished to England in 1810, but returned in 1816 and made a fortune in the wool trade. He was a member of the New South Wales Legislative Council (1825–32).

MacArthur, Robert Helmer 1930–72
US ecologist

Born in Toronto, Canada, he moved to the USA at the age of 17 and studied mathematics. While working for his PhD at Yale he changed to zoology; he became Professor of Biology at Princeton University in 1965. His mathematical training led him to develop quantitative models of the relative abundances of species in different habitats, showing the importance of the balance between immigration and extinction. One of his most influential ideas was the categorization of animals into two groups, one group exhibiting rapid growth followed by catastrophic decline, with fast rates of population increase (r-selected species, eg lemmings), and the other k-selected species having stable populations and slow intrinsic growth rates (eg tigers).

Macartney, George, 1st Earl 1737–1806
Irish diplomat

Born in Lissanoure, near Belfast, and educated at Trinity College, Dublin, he was sent as an envoy to Russia in 1764. From 1769 to 1772 he was Chief-Secretary of Ireland, and in 1775 was appointed Governor of Grenada, where he was taken prisoner by the French in 1779. Later Governor of Madras (1781–85), he was made an earl in 1792 and headed the first diplomatic mission to China (1792–94). After a mission to **Louis XVIII** at Verona (1795–96), he went out as Governor of the new colony of the Cape of Good Hope (1796), but returned in ill health in 1798.

Macaulay, Dame (Emilie) Rose 1881–1958
English novelist and essayist

She was born in Rugby, Warwickshire, and educated at Somerville College, Oxford, where she read history. Her first novel was *Abbots Verney* (1906), followed by *Views and Vagabonds* (1912) and *The Lee Shore* (1920), winner of a £1,000 publishers' prize. Her later novels include *Dangerous Ages* (1921), which won the Femina Vie Heureuse prize, *Crewe Train* (1926), *They Were Defeated* (1932) and *And No Man's Wit* (1940). After World War II she wrote two further novels, *The World My Wilderness* (1950), and *The Towers of Trebizond* (1956), which won the James Tait Black Memorial Prize. Her travel books include *They Went to*

Portugal (1946), *Fabled Shore* (1949) and *The Pleasure of Ruins* (1953). She also wrote collections of essays, such as *A Casual Commentary* (1925) and *Catchwords and Claptrap* (1926). She was created DBE in 1958. □ C B Smith, *Rose Macaulay, a biography* (1972)

Macaulay (of Rothley), Thomas Babington Macaulay, 1st Baron 1800–59
English writer and politician
Born Rothley Temple, Leicestershire, and educated at Trinity College, Cambridge, he was called to the Bar in 1826, and then combined his legal career with writing. His article on Milton in the August 1825 issue of the *Edinburgh Review* had gained him recognition, and for nearly 20 years he was one of the most prolific and popular of the writers on the magazine. He became MP for the borough of Calne in 1830, and took part in the Reform Bill debates. He was legal adviser to the Supreme Council of India (1834–38) and on his return in 1839 became MP for Edinburgh, and later Secretary of War under Lord Melbourne. He received a peerage in 1857. His *History of England from the Accession of James II* (5 vols, 1848–61) enjoyed unprecedented popularity for a work of its kind. He has been convicted of historical inaccuracy, but as a picturesque narrator he has few rivals. □ J Millgate, *Macaulay* (1973)

McAuley, Catherine Elizabeth 1787–1841
Irish religious
Born in Dublin, she was left money by her adoptive parents to buy a site for a school for poor children and a residence for working women, to be called House of Our Blessed Lady of Mercy. In 1831 she founded the order of the Sisters of Mercy.

McAuley, James 1917–76
Australian poet, critic and writer
Born in Lakemba, Sydney, he spent much time during and after World War II in Papua New Guinea, where he likened the destruction of traditional social structures there to the larger upheavals of the western world. His verse is of a classical and visionary style, and was first collected in *Under Aldebaran* (1946). His second volume, *A Vision of Ceremony*, did not appear until 1956, followed by *Captain Quiros* in 1964. In 1955 he started a controversy which lasted for 40 years by sending the collected works of a fictitious dead poet, 'Ern Malley', to the editor of the modernistic broadsheet *Angry Penguins*, thus hastening the demise of that periodical. McAuley founded the conservative literary and political journal *Quadrant* and edited it from its inception in 1956 to 1963. He also published some books of critical writing and compiled *A Map of Australian Verse: The Twentieth Century* (1975).

McBean, Angus Rowland 1904–89
Welsh stage photographer
Born in Newbridge, Monmouth, he was educated at Monmouth Grammar School. After a number of jobs, including the design of theatrical masks and scenery, he started as a full-time theatrical photographer in 1934. He became noted for his individual approach to portraiture (where he often used elaborate settings designed for the individual sitter) and for his use of photographic montage, collage and double exposure to achieve a surreal effect. In later years he worked in the field of pop music, but withdrew from professional photography after 1969.

Macbeth c.1005–1057
King of Scotland
He was Mórmaer (chief) of Moray (c.1031) and married Gruoch, granddaughter of Kenneth III. He became king in 1040 when he defeated and killed King Duncan I and drove Duncan's sons, Malcolm and Donald Bán, into exile. He seems to have represented a Celtic reaction against English influence and he ruled for over a decade. Malcolm

III, Duncan's son, ultimately defeated and killed him at Lumphanan. The conventional, Shakespearean view of Macbeth as a villainous usurper has little historical basis. His usurpation was a normal feature of Celtic succession struggles, his reign was a period of plenty, he was a friend to the Church and went on pilgrimage to Rome. Shakespeare took his material from the *Chronicles* of Holinshed, who drew on Hector Boece. □ R J Steward, *Macbeth: Scotland's Warrior King* (1988)

MacBeth, Ann 1875–1948
English embroiderer
Born in Little Bolton, she studied at Glasgow School of Art (1897–1900) and was a member of staff there from 1901 to 1920, latterly as head of the embroidery department. She was influential in advocating new methods of teaching embroidery through lecturing, teaching and through several books, including the instruction manual, *Educational Needlecraft*. She executed a number of ecclesiastical commissions and her embroidered panels decorate many Glasgow interiors. She was a member of the famous Glasgow School and received the Lauder award in 1930.

MacBeth, George Mann 1932–92
Scottish poet and novelist
Born in Shotts, Lanarkshire, he was educated at King Edward VII School in Sheffield and New College, Oxford, and produced poetry programmes at the BBC (1955–76). Associated with the informal coterie known as The Group (and represented in *The Group Anthology*, 1963), and with performance poetry in the 1960s, he published 20 books of verse, some of it experimental in form and violent in matter, although his later work was more traditional in form. A *Collected Poems 1958–70* appeared in 1971, and was later updated as *Collected Poems 1958–82*. He also published children's books and 10 novels, the last of which *The Testament of Spencer* (1992), appeared shortly after his death. □ *A Child of the War* (1987)

McBey, James 1883–1959
Scottish artist and etcher
Born in Newburgh, Aberdeenshire, he worked in a bank but left to become an artist and was entirely self-taught, producing his first etching in 1902. He travelled extensively in the UK, Spain, Holland, North Africa, Central and North America, and as a war artist in France and with the Australian Camel Patrol in Egypt and Palestine during World War I. His etched work has great spontaneity and strength.

MacBride, Maud See Gonne, Maud

MacBride, Seán 1904–88
Irish statesman and Nobel Prize winner
The son of Maud Gonne and Major John MacBride, he carried on his parents' commitment to Irish nationalism and served in the Irish Republican Army before entering the government of independent Ireland. He became involved in international human rights and was chairman of Amnesty International (1961–75). In 1974 he shared the Nobel Peace Prize with Sato Eisaku.

McBride, Willie (William) John 1940–
Northern Irish rugby player
Born in Toomebridge, County Antrim, he played mostly with the Ballymena team from 1962. A lock forward, he won 45 caps and went on four British Lions tours in 10 years. He made a record 17 appearances for the British Lions on five tours, and played for Ireland 63 times. When he retired from top-class rugby he became interested in the management of international teams.

MacBryde, Robert 1913–66
Scottish artist

Born in Ayrshire, he worked in industry for five years before studying at the Glasgow School of Art. He worked with **Robert Colquhoun**, painting brilliantly-coloured Cubist lifes, and, later, brooding Expressionist figures.

Maccabees
Jewish family
The founder of the dynasty, Mattathias, a priest, was the first to make a stand against the persecutions of the Jewish nation and creed by **Antiochus IV Epiphanes**. He was the great-great-grandson of Hasmon and the family is often known as the 'Hasmoneans'. Mattathias and his five sons, Jochanan, Simon, Jehudah, Eleazer and Jonathan, together with a handful of faithful men, attacked the national enemy, destroyed heathen worship, and fled into the wilderness of Judah. They soon increased in number and were able to restore the ancient worship of Jehovah in some of the major settlements. At the death of Mattathias (166BC) his son Jehudah or Judas, now called Makkabi (*Makkab*,'hammerer') or Maccabaeus, took command of the patriots, reconquered Jerusalem, purified the temple, and re-inaugurated the holy service (164). Having concluded an alliance with the Romans, he died in battle (160). His brother Jonathan renewed the Roman alliance and acquired the dignity of high priest, but was assassinated by the Syrians. Simon, the second brother, completely re-established the independence of the nation (141), and 'Judah prospered as of old'. He was murdered (135) by his son-in-law, **Ptolemy**.

MacCaig, Norman Alexander 1910–96
Scottish poet
Born in Edinburgh, he was educated at the Royal High School and the university there. He was a primary school teacher for almost 40 years, became the first Fellow in creative writing at Edinburgh University (1967–69), then lectured in English Studies at Stirling University (1970–79). With *Far Cry* (1943) and *The Inward Eye* (1946), he was labelled a member of the New Apocalypse school. His *Collected Poems* was first published in 1985, and other collections include *Riding Lights* (1955), *The Sinai Sort* (1957), *A Round of Applause* (1962), *Rings on a Tree* (1968), *A Man In My Position* (1969), *The White Bird* (1973), *The Equal Skies* (1980) and *Voice-Over* (1988). He was awarded the Queen's Gold Medal for poetry in 1986. A new edition of *Collected Poems* appeared in 1990. 🕮 R Fulton, in *Contemporary Scottish Poetry* (1974)

MacCarthy, Denis Florence 1817–82
Irish writer
Born in Dublin, he trained for the priesthood, but wrote poetry, much of it in a historical and patriotic vein. He also published highly regarded translations of a number of plays by **Pedro Calderón de la Barca**, and published *Shelley's Early Life* (1872).

MacCarthy, Sir Desmond 1878–1952
English writer and critic
Born in Plymouth and educated at Eton and Trinity College, Cambridge, he entered journalism and was successively editor of *New Quarterly* and *Eye Witness* (later *New Witness*). By 1913 he was writing for the *New Statesman*, of which he became literary editor in 1920, and later drama critic. He was also editor of *Life and Letters*, book reviewer for the *Sunday Times*, and a broadcaster of repute. His criticism, collected in book form, is represented by *Portraits* (1931), *Experience* (1935), *Drama* (1940), *Humanities* (1954) and *Theatre* (1955).

McCarthy, Eugene J(oseph) 1916–
US politician
He was born in Watkins, Minnesota. A teacher of political science, he entered the House of Representatives as a Democrat (1949) and in 1958 was elected senator from Minnesota. In 1968 he challenged President **Johnson** for the presidential nomination, on a policy of opposition to the Vietnam War. Johnson stood down, but McCarthy did not gain the nomination and he left the Senate in 1970 to devote himself to teaching and writing, although he mounted an independent presidential campaign in 1976. His publications include *Required Reading* (1988) and *Colony of the World* (1993).

McCarthy, John 1957–
English journalist
Born in Barnet, London, brought up in Hertfordshire and educated at Haileybury and Hull University, he worked as an advertising salesman for a shipping journal, then became a freelance journalist. Having worked for Worldwide Television News since 1981, he went to Lebanon as acting bureau chief. After only 32 days there, on 17 April 1986 he was abducted by the revolutionary fundamentalist group Islamic Jihad. He was held as a hostage for 1,943 days until his release on 8 August 1991. He wrote *Some Other Rainbow* (1993) with Jill Morrell about the experience.

McCarthy, Joseph Raymond 1909–57
US politician
Born in Grand Chute, Wisconsin, he studied at Marquette University, Milwaukee, became a circuit judge in 1939, and after war service was elected senator in 1946. He became known for his unsubstantiated accusations in the early 1950s that communists had infiltrated the State Department, and in 1953 became chairman of the House Committee on Un-American Activities. By hectoring cross-examination and damaging innuendo he arraigned many innocent citizens and officials, overreaching himself when he came into direct conflict with the army. This kind of anti-communist witchhunt became known as 'McCarthyism'. His power diminished after he was formally censured for his methods by the Senate in 1954.

McCarthy, Mary Thérèse 1912–89
US novelist and critic
She was born in Seattle, Washington, and at the age of eight won a state prize for an article entitled 'The Irish in American History'. Educated at Vassar College, New York, she wrote book reviews for the *Nation* and the *New Republic* and was an editor for *Covici Friede* in 1936–37. She was an editor and theatre critic for the *Partisan Review* (1937–48), during which period she wrote articles, stories and novels. Her voice has often been described as scathing, yet although she brought little emotional warmth to her work, she was a highly intelligent, observant novelist. Her best-known fiction includes *The Company She Keeps* (1942), *The Groves of Academe* (1952) and *The Group* (1963), a bestseller about eight Vassar graduates and their sex lives. She also wrote the documentary denunciations of US involvement in the Vietnam War, *Vietnam* (1967) and *Hanoi* (1968). Other works include *A Charmed Life* (1955), *Sights and Spectacles* (1956), the autobiographical *Memories of a Catholic Childhood* (1957) and *Cannibals and Missionaries* (1979). 🕮 C Gerlderman, *Mary McCarthy* (1988)

McCartney, Sir (James) Paul 1942–
English songwriter, vocalist and bass guitarist
Liverpool-born and a former member of the **Beatles**, he is one of the most distinctive lyricists in popular music. Following his first solo album, *McCartney* (1970), and a second, *Ram* (1971), recorded with his wife, Linda Eastman (1941–98), he recruited guitarist Denny Laine (1944–) to form Wings in 1971. Critics detected a lack of direction in the banned political single 'Give Ireland Back to the Irish' (1972) and its sequel 'Mary Had a Little Lamb' (1972), but the albums *Band on the Run* (1973) and *Venus & Mars* (1975) partially restored his reputation, while 'Mull of Kintyre' (1977) was a huge hit. His autobiographical film *Give My Regards to Broad Street* appeared in 1984.

Subsequent albums include *Tripping the Light Fantastic* (1990) and *Off The Ground* (1992), and he co-composed his *Liverpool Oratorio* with Carl Davis in 1991. He was knighted in 1997. 📖 Barry Miles, *Many Years From Now* (1997)

McCauley, Mary Ludwig Hays, *known as* Molly Pitcher 1754–1832
American Revolutionary war heroine
Born near Trenton, New Jersey, she earned her nickname by carrying water to her husband, John Hays (or Heis), and the other men of the 7th Pennsylvania Regiment during the Battle of Monmouth on 28 June 1778. When her husband collapsed from the heat, like (or perhaps confused with) Margaret Corbin, she took his place at his cannon for the remainder of the battle. For this act of bravery she was rewarded with a government pension in 1822.

McCay, Winsor Zezic, *also called* Silas 1867–1934
US cartoonist and film animator
He was born in Spring Lake, Michigan. His first newspaper illustrations were for the *Times-Star* (1893), and he created his first strip, *Tales of the Jungle Imps*, in 1903. He joined the *New York Herald* to make his first successful strip, *Dreams of a Rarebit Fiend* (1904), which was filmed by Thomas Edison. He drew under the pen name 'Silas', but used his own name for the explosive *Little Sammy Sneeze* (1904) and his masterpiece, *Little Nemo in Slumberland* (1905), which owed its success to McCay's mastery of perspective. From 1909 he began experimenting in animation, his films including *Gertie the Dinosaur* (1914), and *The Sinking of the Lusitania* (1918), the first dramatic/documentary cartoon.

McClellan, George Brinton 1826–85
US general
He was born in Philadelphia. In the Civil War in 1861, as major-general in the US army, he drove the enemy out of West Virginia, and was called to Washington to reorganize the army of the Potomac. He advanced near to Richmond, but was compelled to retreat, fighting the Seven Days Battles (25 June to 1 July 1862). After the disastrous second Battle of Bull Run (29–30 August), followed by a Confederate invasion of Maryland, he reorganized the army at Washington, marched north, met Robert E Lee at Antietam, and compelled him to recross the Potomac. He followed the Confederates into Virginia, too slowly for Abraham Lincoln, who replaced him with Ambrose E Burnside. In 1864, as Democratic candidate for the presidency he was defeated by Lincoln, and in 1878 was elected Governor of New Jersey.

McClelland, William 1889–1968
Scottish educationist
Born in Newton Stewart, Wigtownshire, and educated at Edinburgh University, he held various lecturing posts at Edinburgh and Aberdeen from 1921 before becoming concurrently Professor of Education at St Andrews and director of studies at Dundee Training College in 1925. Deeply interested in improving methods of teacher training, he was executive officer for the National Committee for Training Teachers in Scotland (1941–59) and chairman of the Advisory Council on Education in Scotland (SACE) (1947–51), being generally credited with the 1946 SACE report on training of teachers, which exercised a decisive influence within the training system. A specialist on statistical methods and educational psychology, he also wrote *Selection for Secondary Education* (1942), a pioneering study of the 11-plus examination.

McClintock, Barbara 1902–92
US geneticist and Nobel Prize winner
Born in Hartford, Connecticut, she received a PhD in botany from Cornell University, where she worked from 1927 to 1935. Later she held posts at the University of Missouri (1936–41) and Cold Spring Harbor (1941–92). Her work on the chromosomes of maize provided the ultimate proof of the chromosome theory of heredity. In the 1940s she showed how genes can control other genes, and can be copied from chromosome to chromosome. It was not until the 1970s that her work began to be appreciated, and finally in 1983 she was awarded the Nobel Prize for physiology or medicine. 📖 Evelyn Fox Keller, *A Feeling for the Organism* (1983)

McClure, Sir Robert John Le Mesurier 1807–73
Irish explorer and admiral
Born in Wexford, he joined the navy in 1824, and served in Sir George Back's Arctic expedition in 1836, and Sir John Ross's Franklin expedition in 1848. As commander of a ship in another Franklin expedition (1850–54), he penetrated eastwards to the north coast of Banks Land. He received a parliamentary award for the discovery of the Northwest Passage which is now credited to Sir John Franklin.

McClure, Samuel Sidney 1857–1949
US editor and publisher
Born in County Antrim, Ireland, he went to the USA with his family at the age of nine. While studying at Knox College in Illinois, he established (1884) the McClure Syndicate, the first newspaper syndicate in the USA, which allowed newspapers across the country to reprint previously published stories for a fee. Later he also bought novels from writers such as Rudyard Kipling and Robert Louis Stevenson and offered them for serialization. In 1893 he founded *McClure's Magazine,* and as its editor he assembled a staff that included Ida M Tarbell, Lincoln Steffens and other gifted journalists, whose 'muckraking' exposés of social and political corruption led to legislative reforms and made *McClures* the most influential US periodical of its era.

McColgan, Liz (Elizabeth) 1964–
Scottish athlete
Born in Dundee, she studied at the University of Alabama. She won the 10,000 metres gold medal in the 1986 Commonwealth Games, then won the silver medal at the Seoul Olympics of 1988. She retained her Commonwealth title in Auckland in 1990, and won a bronze in the 3,000 metres. Not long after the birth of her daughter, she won the 1991 New York Marathon in 2 hours, 27 minutes, the fastest female marathon debut. Also that year she won the 10,000 metres at the world championship in Tokyo. In 1993 she had two knee operations and was advised to give up racing, but returned to racing in 1995, when she came fifth in the London Marathon and finished fourth in the 10,000 metres in European Cup. In 1996 she won the British Half Marathon. She has been the Athletics Development Officer of Dundee District Council since 1987.

MacColl, Dugald Sutherland 1859–1948
Scottish painter and art historian
Born in Glasgow, he studied at London and Oxford, and after travelling Europe studying works of art, he established a reputation as a critic and brought out his *Nineteenth Century Art* in 1902. As Keeper of the Tate Gallery (1906–11) and of the Wallace Collection (1911–24), he instituted many reforms and improvements. He wrote *Confessions of a Keeper* (1931).

MacColl, Ewan, *originally* James Miller 1915–89
Scottish folk-singer, composer, collector, author, playwright and socialist
He was born in Auchterarder, Perthshire, and raised in industrial Lancashire. As a playwright, he collaborated with Joan Littlewood in forming the experimental Theatre Workshop in the 1940s and played an important

role in reviving street theatre. By the turn of the 1950s however, his musical interests were prominent; he combined music and drama in his opera *The Lost Factory Chimneys* (1955). To some extent this anticipated his series of 'Radio Ballads', begun in 1957 and recorded with his second wife Peggy Seeger, which combined contemporary social comment with traditional musical forms and had a powerful influence on songwriting and performing in subsequent decades. He founded the Ballads and Blues Club, subsequently known as the Singers Club, a bastion of his purist (but never reactionary or nostalgic) belief that folk music was a direct expression of everyday life, not high art and never mere 'entertainment'. He was one of the most influential pioneers of the British folk-music revival, and his best-known songs include 'Dirty Old Town' (1946), 'The Ballad of Springhill' (1958, co-written with Peggy Seeger) and 'The First Time Ever I Saw Your Face' (1958, hauntingly recorded by Roberta Flack in 1972). He published several anthologies of folk-song, and an autobiography, *Journeyman* (1990).

McColl, Robert Smyth 1876–1959
Scottish footballer and businessman

Born in Glasgow, he began playing for the amateur club Queen's Park in 1894. He moved to Newcastle seven years later, eventually turning professional. Returning to Scotland on signing for Rangers (1904), he went back to Queen's Park in 1907, thus becoming the only professional to rejoin the club. A centre-forward, he won 13 caps for Scotland between 1896 and 1908, the high point being a hat-trick against England in 1900. After retiring from football he established a successful chain of confectioners, R S McColl's.

McCollum, Elmer Verner 1879–1967
US biochemist

Born in Fort Scott, Kansas, he studied at the universities of Yale, Cincinnati and Manitoba, and became Professor of Biochemistry at Johns Hopkins University, Baltimore (1917–44). In 1913 he published the first description of a vitamin, and distinguished between vitamins A (fat-soluble) and B (water-soluble). In 1922 he discovered the 'rickets-preventative factor', vitamin D, by testing more than 1,000 different diets on rats. His A, B and D were later shown to consist of separable constituents (eg A_1 and A_2). He was a prolific writer, and his works include the popular *The Newer Knowledge of Nutrition* (1918) and *A History of Nutrition* (1957). He received numerous awards and was elected a Foreign Member of the Royal Society in 1961.

McCormack, John 1884–1945
US tenor

Born in Athlone, Ireland, he made his London debut in 1905, sang at Covent Garden, London (1906–07), and also appeared in oratorio and as a lieder singer. As an Irish nationalist, he lost British support during World War I and took US citizenship in 1919, turning to popular sentimental songs. He returned to England in 1924, and toured widely until he retired from the stage (1938). During World War II, however, he continued to sing on the radio. He was raised to the papal peerage as a count in 1928.

McCormick, Cyrus Hall 1809–84
US inventor and industrialist

Born in Rockbridge, Virginia, and educated locally, he was the son of Robert McCormick (1780–1846) who patented several agricultural implements but had in 1831 abandoned an attempt to build a mechanical reaper. Cyrus took up the challenge successfully, but did not patent his machine until 1834, the year after the reaper invented by **Obed Hussey** had been patented. US agriculture had entered a period of rapid expansion, and

there was intense competition between the two men and with other manufacturers, but in the end the McCormick Harvesting Machine Company emerged as the leader. In 1902 it became the International Harvester Company, with his son Cyrus Hall McCormick, Jnr (1859–1936) as first president and chairman of the board. 📖 Herbert N Casson, *Cyrus Hall McCormick: His Life and Work* (1909)

McCormick, Eric Hall 1906–
New Zealand cultural historian

Born in Taihape, he was secretary of, and later editor to, the National Historical Committee which commissioned publications to mark the centenary of European settlement in 1840. For this series he wrote *Letters and Art in New Zealand* (1940), the first critical conspectus of New Zealand writing, later expanded as *New Zealand Literature: A Survey* (1959). His other critical works include *Alexander Turnbull: His Life, His Circle, His Collections* (1974), *The Expatriate, a Study of Frances Hodgkins* (1954), *Portrait of Frances Hodgkins* (1981), and the autobiographical *The Inland Eye: a Sketch in Visual Autobiography* (1959). He contributed greatly to the recognition of New Zealand literature from 1940.

MacCormick, John MacDonald 1904–61
Scottish nationalist politician

Born in Glasgow and a graduate of Glasgow University, he initially became active in the Scottish movement for self-government through the Independent Labour Party, and, from its foundation, the National Party of Scotland (1928). He was chairman of the Scottish National Party from its foundation in 1934 until 1942 when the party refused his request that it seek all-party support for independence and cease fighting elections. He thereupon founded and became chairman of the Scottish Convention, and chairman of the National Assembly, organizing the Scottish Covenant in 1949 which ultimately attracted two million signatures but achieved nothing. He wrote *The Flag in the Wind* (1955).

McCowen, Alec (Alexander Duncan) 1925–
English actor

Born in Tunbridge Wells, Kent, he trained at RADA and has won most acclaim as a theatre actor, performing the classics with the Old Vic and the Royal Shakespeare Company in the 1950s and 1960s; acting on Broadway in *Antony and Cleopatra* (1951), *The Comedy of Errors* (1964), *King Lear* (1964) and *The Misanthrope* (1975); and staging his one-man shows *St Mark's Gospel* (since 1978) and *Kipling* (since 1984). His films include *The Loneliness of the Long Distance Runner* (1962), *The Witches* (1966), *Frenzy* (as Chief Inspector Oxford, 1972), *Cry Freedom* (1987) and *Henry V* (1989). On television, he took the title role in *Mr Palfrey of Westminster* (1984–85). 📖 *Young Gemini* (1979)

McCracken, James 1927–88
US tenor

Born in Gary, Indiana, he became a steelworker and joined the US navy, where his potential as a singer was spotted. A large, powerfully-built man with great stage presence, he made his operatic debut as Rodolfo in Puccini's *La Bohème* ('Bohemian Life') in 1952, but his Otello, first performed in Europe in 1959, marked a turning point in his career. In 1963 he returned to the USA to become the first native US citizen to sing Otello at the Metropolitan Opera, and he became one of their leading tenors. He wrote about his operatic experience with his wife (the mezzo-soprano Sandra Warfield) in *A Star in the Family* (1971).

McCrae, John 1872–1918
Canadian poet

Born in Guelph, Ontario, he graduated from the University of Toronto in 1898, served in the South African War, and practised medicine in Montreal until the outbreak of World War I. He served as an army medical officer from 1914 until his death in France, and he is best remembered for his war poem 'In Flanders Fields' (1915).

McCrea, Sir William Hunter 1904–
Irish theoretical astrophysicist and mathematician

Born in Dublin, he was educated at Cambridge, lectured in mathematics at Edinburgh University and at Imperial College, London, and later became the Professor of Mathematics at Queen's University, Belfast (1936). After World War II he moved to Royal Holloway College, London, and then to the University of Sussex (1966). In 1934, with Edward Milne, McCrea was the founder of modern Newtonian cosmology, applying classical physics to the primordial gas cloud that condensed to form the galaxies. He also extended Ernst Mach's viewpoint, suggesting that Werner Heisenberg's uncertainty principle applies to light as it travels. He emphasized the effect of turbulence in condensing gas clouds and its role in the formation of planets and stars, and made important contributions to relativity and the low-probability transitions of electrons between atomic energy states. In 1975 McCrea proposed that comets may have been formed in the galactic spiral arms, and that the Earth, Moon and Mars were formed from a single body that differentiated and then split up. He was elected FRS in 1952, and knighted in 1985.

MacCready, Paul 1925–
US aeronautical engineer and inventor

Born in New Haven, Connecticut, he studied physics at Yale University (1947) and aeronautics at the California Institute of Technology (1952). He designed the ultralight aircraft *Gossamer Condor* which in 1977 made the first man-powered flight over a one-mile (1.6km) course. In 1979 its successor, *Gossamer Albatross*, crossed the 23 miles (37km) of the English Channel in just under three hours at a height of only a few metres, propelled and piloted by US racing cyclist, Bryan Allen. In 1981 his *Solar Challenger* flew from Paris to London at an average speed of 37mph (59.5kph), powered by 16,000 solar cells, and in 1985 he built a powered reproduction of a pterodactyl.

McCubbin, Frederick 1855–1917
Australian landscape painter

Born in Melbourne, Victoria, where he lived and worked for most of his life, he taught drawing at the National Gallery of Victoria's Art School from 1886 until his death. The previous year, with other painters including Tom Roberts, he had established the first of the artist camps which grew into the Heidelberg school of Australian painting. From his romantic depictions of bush life he turned to an Impressionistic style, and he exhibited in London and Paris in 1897. Although principally known for his landscapes, he also executed many successful portraits during his later years.

McCullers, (Lula) Carson, *née* Smith 1917–67
US novelist

She was born in Columbus, Georgia, and attended classes at Columbia University, New York, and New York University. After marrying in 1937, she moved to Charlotte, North Carolina, then in 1941 to Greenwich Village, New York. *The Heart is a Lonely Hunter*, her first book, about a character who could neither see nor hear, appeared in 1940, distinguishing her immediately as a novelist of note. She wrote the best and the bulk of her work in a six-year spell during World War II. Along with William Faulkner, Tennessee Williams and Truman Capote she is credited with fashioning a type of fiction labelled by critics as Southern Gothic. Fusing, in her own words, 'anguish and farce', she peopled her work with grotesque characters who are expressionistic extensions of normal, universal human problems. Her books include *Reflections*

in a Golden Eye (1941), *The Member of the Wedding* (1946), *The Ballad of the Sad Cafe* (1951) and *Clock Without Hands* (1961), a last ironic look at the South. ☒ V S Carr, *The Lonely Hunter* (1975)

McCullough, Colleen 1937–
Australian novelist

Born in Wellington, New South Wales, she is best known for her novel *The Thorn Birds* (1977), a saga of sex, religion and disaster, later produced as a televison series. Her earlier book *Tim* (1974) was also filmed, as was *An Indecent Obsession* (1981). A delicate novella, *The Ladies of Missalonghi* (1987) showed that she is capable of some fine writing, and her recent books, including a series of six novels set in ancient Rome, demonstrate a concern for historical detail. Later publications include *The Grass Crown* (1991) and *Fortune's Favorites* (1993).

MacCunn, Hamish 1868–1916
Scottish composer

Born in Greenock, near Glasgow, he studied at the Royal College of Music in London, and from 1888 to 1894 was Professor of Harmony at the Royal Academy of Music. His works, largely Scottish in character and subject, include the overtures *Cior Mhor* (1887), *Land of the Mountain and the Flood* (1887) and *The Dowie Dens of Yarrow*, choral works, such as *The Lay of the Last Minstrel*, the operas *Jeanie Deans* (1894) and *Diarmid* (1897), and songs.

MacDiarmada, Seán, *English* John MacDermott 1884–1916
Irish revolutionary

Born in Kiltyclogher, County Leitrim, he worked as barman and tram conductor in Glasgow and Belfast, where he became involved in the Ancient Order of Hibernians. He participated in the Sinn Féin by-election defeat in 1908, but had already entered the moribund Irish Republican Brotherhood (IRB) which he now regalvanized as agent for Thomas J Clarke. Appointed IRB organizer, he infiltrated the Gaelic Athletic Association, the Gaelic League, and later the Irish Volunteers with his agents, and edited the IRB paper *Irish Freedom*. Crippled by polio in 1912, his intransigence increased, and he ensured the hijack of the John MacNeill wing of the Irish Volunteers in an ultimate insurrection which was finally achieved in Easter 1916. He was afterwards courtmartialled and shot.

MacDiarmid, Hugh, *pseudonym of* Christopher Murray Grieve 1892–1978
Scottish poet

Born in Langholm, Dumfriesshire, he was educated at Langholm Academy, and became a pupil-teacher at Broughton Higher Grade School, Edinburgh, before turning to journalism. He served with the Royal Army Medical Corps in Greece and France during World War I, and was a munitions worker in World War II. A foundermember of the National Party of Scotland (which became the Scottish National Party) in 1928, and intermittently an active communist, he stood as a Communist candidate in 1964. He became the leader of the Scottish Renaissance and dedicated his life to the regeneration of Scots as a literary language, repudiated by his fellow Scottish poet, Edwin Muir, in 1936. As a journalist in Montrose, he edited anthologies of contemporary Scottish writing, such as *Northern Numbers* (1920–22) and *The Scottish Chapbook* (1922–23), in which he published his own early poetry. His early lyrical verse appeared in *Sangschaw* (1925) and *Penny Wheep* (1926), but he is best known for *A Drunk Man Looks at the Thistle* (1926). Other publications include *To Circumjack Cencrastus* (1930), the three *Hymns to Lenin* (1931, 1932, 1957), *Scots Unbound* (1932), *Stony Limits* (1934), *A Kist o' Whistles* (1947) and *In Memoriam James Joyce* (1955). He wrote numerous essays, such as *Albyn* (1927) and *The*

Islands of Scotland (1939), and his autobiography was published in *Lucky Poet* (1943) and *The Company I've Kept* (1966).
📖 A Bold, *Hugh MacDiarmid: a biography* (1985)

MacDonagh, Donagh 1912–68
Irish dramatist

He was born in Dublin and orphaned by the execution of his father, **Thomas MacDonagh**, in 1916 and the drowning of his mother during an attempt to plant the tricolour on an island in Dublin Bay in 1917. Educated at Belvedere College and University College, Dublin, he became a barrister in 1935 and was made a district justice in 1941. He won success as a writer with the exuberant *Happy as Larry* (1946), and other plays such as *God's Gentry* (1951, a study of tinker life) and *Step-in-the-Hollow* (1957). He was also a highly acclaimed broadcaster, and edited with **Lennox Robinson** *The Oxford Book of Irish Verse* (1958), which drew criticism for its loose interpretation of Irishness. He published poems, *The Hungry Grass* (1947) and *A Warning to Conquerors* (1968), and a perceptive essay on his father.
📖 Introduction to *The Oxford Book of Irish Verse* (1958)

MacDonagh, Thomas 1878–1916
Irish poet, critic and nationalist

He was born in Cloughjordan, County Tipperary, and later lived in Dublin, where he helped **Patrick Pearse** to found St Enda's College (1908), and published several volumes of delicate and sardonic poems, original works and translations from the Irish. In 1914 he founded the Irish Theatre with Joseph Plunkett and Edward Martyn (1859–1923). He was also an outstanding critic of English literature, and his aspirations for Irish literature derived from his deep love of English and his recognition of comparable possibilities, as may be seen by his *Literature in Ireland* (posthumous, 1916) and *Thomas Campion* (1913), and by his articles in the *Irish Review*. An Irish Volunteer, he was very belatedly drawn into preparations for the Easter Rising of 1916, commanded at Jacob's Factory in the fighting, and was executed. The poet **James Stephens** wrote an introduction to *Poetical Works* (1917) after his death, and **W B Yeats** wrote his epitaph in 'Easter 1916'.
📖 A W and E Parks, *Thomas MacDonagh, the Man, the Patriot and the Writer* (1967)

MacDonald, Alexander, *Gaelic* Alasdair Mac Maighstir Alasdair c.1695–c.1770
Scottish poet

Born in Islandfinnan, where his father was minister, and educated in Glasgow, he was the foremost Gaelic literary figure of the 18th century, and his poems reflect the turbulent times in which he lived. He took part in the 1745 rebellion on the Jacobite side, and his best verse is inspired by the subsequent upheavals in and diminution of Gaelic culture. His masterwork is *Birlinn Chlann Raghnaill* (c.1780), a long poem about Clan Ranald, lamenting the fate of Gaeldom after the '45. A translation of the poem by **Hugh MacDiarmid** was published in 1935.

Macdonald, Dwight 1906–82
US writer and film critic

He was born in New York City. While still a student at Yale he became a literary editor and also a Troskyite while working for the business magazine *Fortune* (1929–36). A penetrating social and political commentator, he wrote regularly for *Partisan Review*. He was a staff writer for the *New Yorker* (1951–71) and film critic for *Esquire* (1960–66). His essays were collected in several books, including *The Memoirs of a Revolutionist* (1957), *Against the American Grain* (1963) and *Discriminations: Essays and Afterthoughts* (1974).

McDonald, Elaine 1943–
Scottish dancer

Born of Scottish parents in Tadcaster, Yorkshire, she trained at the Royal Ballet School in London, joining Western Ballet Theatre in 1964 and moving with the company to Glasgow when it became Scottish Ballet in the late 1960s. Remaining with the company for the whole of her dancing career, she became a dancer of international repute and created many roles for the choreographer/director Peter Darrell, including *Sun Into Darkness* (1966), *Beauty and the Beast* (1969), *Tales of Hoffman* (1972), *Mary Queen of Scots* (1976) and *Five Ruckert Songs* (1978). She was made artistic controller of the company in 1988, and left the company in 1990, becoming associate director of Northern Ballet Theatre in 1991. 📖 J S Dixon (ed), *Elaine McDonald* (1983)

Macdonald, Flora 1722–90
Scottish Jacobite heroine

Born in South Uist in the Hebrides, she was adopted by Lady Clanranald. After the Battle of Culloden (1746) which finally broke the 1745 Jacobite rebellion, she took the Young Pretender, **Charles Edward Stuart**, disguised as her maid 'Betty Burke', from Benbecula to Portree. In 1750 she married the son of Macdonald of Kingsburgh, where in 1773 she entertained Dr **Johnson**. In 1774 she emigrated to North Carolina with her husband, who fought in the American Revolution. She returned to Scotland in 1779, followed by her husband two years later, and they settled at Kingsburgh. 📖 Alexander MacGregor, *Life of Flora MacDonald* (1882)

MacDonald, Frances 1873–1921
Scottish painter and designer

Born in Glasgow, the sister of **Margaret MacDonald**, she became the wife of Herbert MacNair (1868–1955). These three, together with **Charles Rennie Mackintosh**, comprised the Glasgow 'Group of Four', the prime exponents of Art Nouveau in Scotland, whose influence was international. Frances MacDonald's paintings and decorations are generally strongly poetic, incorporating insubstantial figures in symbolic settings.

MacDonald, George 1824–1905
Scottish novelist, lecturer and poet

Born in Huntly, Aberdeenshire, he was educated at King's College, Aberdeen, and Highbury Theological College, and became a Congregationalist pastor at Arundel. However, his unorthodox views—especially his belief in purgatory, and in a place in heaven for everyone, even animals—caused conflict with his parishioners, and finally brought about his resignation. After the successful publication of his poem 'Within and Without' (1856), he turned to writing and lecturing, publishing the allegorical novel *Phantastes* (1858), which met with a cold reception. He followed this with a series of novels, including *David Elginbrod* (1863), *Robert Falconer* (1868) and *Lilith* (1895), confessing that he used his books as his pulpit. He is now best known for his children's books, among them *At the Back of the North Wind* (1871) and *The Princess and Curdie* (1888), but his adult works have enjoyed a revival, especially among evangelical Christians. 📖 W Raeper, *George MacDonald* (1987)

Macdonald, Sir Hector Archibald 1857–1903
Scottish soldier

Born on the Black Isle, Easter Ross, he was apprenticed to a draper in Inverness before joining the Gordon Highlanders and serving in India and Afghanistan. Promoted from the ranks in 1880, he transferred to the Egyptian army and served with **Horatio Kitchener** in the Sudan campaign which ended in 1898. At the Battle of Omdurman his tactical awareness prevented a dervish counter-attack on the Anglo-Egyptian army in its moment of victory. He was promoted major-general and was knighted in 1901. During the Boer War he commanded the Highland Brigade and in 1902 he became commander of the British forces in Ceylon (now Sri Lanka). His career ended in disgrace when he committed suicide rather than face charges of paederasty.

Macdonald, Jacques Étienne Joseph Alexandre, Duc de Tarrente 1765–1840
French soldier

Born in Sedan, the son of a Scottish Jacobite schoolmaster, he fought in the cause of the Revolution and rapidly rose to high rank. In 1798 he was made Governor of Rome and subjugated Naples, but Count **Suvorov** defeated him after a bloody contest on the Trebbia (1799). In 1805 he lost the favour of **Napoleon I** but, restored to command in 1809, took Laibach (now Ljubljana), fought at Wagram, and was created marshal and Duc de Tarrente (Taranto). He held a command in Spain in 1810, and in the Russian campaign, and in 1813 he contributed to the successes of Lützen and Bautzen, but was routed by **Blücher** at the Katzbach. After Leipzig he helped to cover the French retreat. The **Bourbons** made him a peer, and from 1816 he was Chancellor of the Legion of Honour.

Macdonald, Sir John Alexander 1815–91
Canadian statesman

Born in Glasgow, Scotland, he emigrated with his parents in 1820. He was called to the Bar in 1836 and appointed QC. Entering politics he became leader of the Conservatives and premier in 1856, and in 1867 formed the first government for the new Dominion. Minister of Justice and Attorney-General of Canada until 1873, he was again in power from 1878 until his death. He was instrumental in bringing about the confederation of Canada and in securing the construction of the intercolonial and Pacific railways.

MacDonald, Margaret, *married name* Mackintosh
1865–1933
Scottish artist

Born in Staffordshire, the sister of **Frances MacDonald**, she studied at the Glasgow College of Art, and in 1900 married **Charles Rennie Mackintosh**. Best known for her work in watercolours and stained glass, she exhibited widely on the Continent, winning the Diploma of Honour at the Turin International Exhibition of 1902. She collaborated with her husband in much of his work.

MacDonald, (James) Ramsay 1866–1937
Scottish Labour statesman

He was born in Lossiemouth, Morayshire, and educated at a board school. He joined the Independent Labour Party in 1894 and was secretary (1900–11) and Leader (1911–14, 1922–31) of the Labour Party. A member of the London County Council (1901–04) and of parliament from 1906, he became Leader of the Opposition in 1922, and from January to November 1924 was Prime Minister and Foreign Secretary of the first Labour government in Britain—a minority government at the mercy of the Liberals. He was Prime Minister again from 1929 to 1931. He met the financial crisis of 1931 by forming a predominantly Conservative 'National' government (opposed by most of his party), which he rebuilt and led (1931–35) after a general election. In 1935 **Stanley Baldwin** took over the premiership and MacDonald became Lord President. He died shortly after his retirement in 1937.

Macdonald, Ross, *pseudonym of* Kenneth Millar
1915–83
US thriller writer

Born in Los Gatos, California, of Canadian parentage, and raised in Ontario, he took a PhD at the University of Western Ontario, and became a college teacher. From the 1950s he lived in southern California. His 'Lew Archer' series, a chip off the **Raymond Chandler** and **Dashiell Hammett** block, is sustained by tough and witty dialogue and rare intelligence, and many of his novels have been adapted for Hollywood. One of the finest writers in the genre, he is the author of such durable titles as *The Moving Target* (1949), *The Barbarous Coast* (1956), *The Underground Man* (1971) and *The Blue Hammer* (1976). He also wrote as 'John Macdonald' and 'John Ross Macdonald'. ⌨ J Speir, *Ross Macdonald* (1978)

McDonald, Trevor 1939–
Trinidadian television newscaster

Born in San Fernando, Trinidad, he began his career reporting for local radio stations there and went on to become an announcer, sports commentator and assistant programme manager. He joined Trinidad Television in 1962, where he presented the news and interviewed for current affairs programmes. Moving to London seven years later, he joined the BBC World Service and, in 1973, ITN. After general reporting assignments, including Northern Ireland, he became sports correspondent (1978–80) and diplomatic correspondent (1980–87), before a stint as diplomatic editor of *Channel Four News* (1987–89). He switched to newscasting in 1989 and, three years later, became the main presenter of *News at Ten*. ⌨ *Fortunate Circumstances* (1993)

Macdonell, Alastair Ruadh c.1724–1761
Scottish Jacobite

Born in Glengarry, Inverness-shire, he joined the French Scots brigade (1743) and was sent to Scotland to support the 1745 Jacobite rebellion, but was captured and imprisoned in the Tower of London (1745–47). He succeeded his father (1754) as 13th Chief of Glengarry. **Andrew Lang** proved that he had become a government spy in *Pickle the Spy* (1897).

McDonnell, James Smith 1899–1980
US aircraft manufacturer and pioneer in space technology

Born in Denver, Colorado, he graduated from Princeton before taking a master's degree in aeronautical engineering at the Massachusetts Institute of Technology (MIT) in 1925. He had a varied career as test pilot, stress analyst and chief engineer to several US companies, and set up his own company in 1928. By 1938 he had organized the McDonnell Aircraft Corporation and embarked on a series of successful military and naval aircraft, including the Banshee, Demon, Voodoo, and the famous F-4 Phantom, of which over 5,000 were built. He took his company into space technology and constructed the Mercury and Gemini manned satellite capsules.

McDougall, William 1871–1938
US psychologist

He was born in Chadderton, Lancashire. After studying at Weimar in Germany, and at Manchester and Cambridge, he trained in medicine at St Thomas's Hospital, London, and in 1898 accompanied an anthropological expedition to the Torres Strait. He held academic posts at both Oxford and Cambridge, and in 1920 went to Harvard as Professor of Psychology. In 1927 he transferred to Duke University, North Carolina, where he conducted experiments in parapsychology. He preached purposive psychology as opposed to behaviourism and his chief works are *Physiological Psychology* (1905), *Body and Mind* (1911), *Outlines of Psychology* (1923) and *The Energies of Man* (1933).

MacDowell, Edward Alexander 1861–1908
US composer and pianist

Born in New York City, he studied in Paris, Wiesbaden and Frankfurt, and in 1881 was appointed head teacher of piano at the Darmstadt Conservatory. At the invitation of **Franz Liszt**, he played his first piano concerto in Zurich in 1882. He returned to the USA in 1888, and was head of the newly organized department of music at Columbia University from 1896 to 1904, when he suffered a mental breakdown. He composed extensively for voices, piano and orchestra, and is best remembered for some of his small-scale piano pieces, such as *Woodland Sketches* (1896) and *Sea Pieces* (1898).

Maček, Vladko 1879–1964
Croatian politician

A doctor of law, he served in the Austrian army during World War I. As a member of the Croatian Peasant Party (HSS), he was imprisoned in 1924 with its leader, Stjepan Radić, becoming party leader himself in 1928. Again imprisoned in 1933, on charges of treason, he was released the following year under the regency of Prince Paul Karadjordjević. In 1939 he signed an agreement with Dragiša Cvetković, securing Croatian participation in government. He became Vice-President of Yugoslavia, continuing in this position under General Dušan Simović who seized power in a coup in 1941. He refused Joachim von Ribbentrop's offer of assistance in creating an independent Croatia and at first urged the Croats to support the Fascist regime of Aute Pavelić. He retired from political life shortly afterwards and was interned on his farm until the end of World War II when he went into exile in France and the USA.

McEnroe, John Patrick 1959–
US tennis player

He was born in Wiesbaden, Germany. He reached the semi-final at Wimbledon as a pre-qualifier in 1977, turned professional in 1978, and was runner-up to Björn Borg in the 1980 Wimbledon final. He won the Wimbledon title three times (1981, 1983–84), the US Open singles four times (1979–81, 1984), and eight Grand Slam doubles events, seven of them with Peter Fleming, and one at Wimbledon in 1992, with Michael Stich. He was Grand Prix winner in 1979 and 1984–85, and world championship winner in 1979, 1981 and 1983–84. Throughout his professional career, his outbursts on court resulted in much adverse publicity.

McEwan, Geraldine, *originally* McKeown 1932–
English actress

Born in Windsor, she received attention for *Member of the Wedding* in 1957, and went on to appear at the Shakespeare Memorial Theatre in Stratford-upon-Avon, playing such roles as Jean Rice in *The Entertainer* (1957), Olivia in *Twelfth Night* (1957, 1960), Beatrice in *Much Ado About Nothing* (1961) and Ophelia in *Hamlet* (1961). On television, she played the title role in *The Prime of Miss Jean Brodie* (1978), Emmeline Lucas in *Mapp & Lucia* (1985–86), Mother in *Oranges Are Not the Only Fruit* (1990) and Miss Farnaby in *Mulberry* (1992–93). Her films include *Foreign Body* (1986) and *Robin Hood: Prince of Thieves* (1991).

McEwan, Ian Russell 1948–
English writer of novels, short stories and screenplays

He was born in Aldershot, Hampshire, and educated at the universities of Sussex and East Anglia. His first collections of stories, *First Love, Last Rites* (1975) and *In Between the Sheets* (1978), attracted notoriety for their preoccupation with the erotic and the macabre, still a distinguishing feature of his writing. Less obtrusive but equally consistent is the nature of romantic love, a theme explored in the novels *The Comfort of Strangers* (1981) and *The Innocent* (1990), and the screenplay *The Ploughman's Lunch* (1985). McEwan's 1987 novel, *The Child in Time*, won the Whitbread award. His later novels, including *Black Dogs* (1992) build on the theme of the nature of human understanding and man's relationship with history and contemporary society. Recent publications include *The Daydreamer* (1994) and *The Short Stories* (1995).

McEwen, Sir John Blackwood 1868–1948
Scottish composer

Born in Hawick, Roxburghshire, he taught music in Glasgow, and was Professor of Composition and Harmony at the Royal College of Music in London (1898–1924), and Principal from 1924 to 1936. His particular interest was to promote a revival of composition for chamber orchestras.

Macewen, Sir William 1848–1924
Scottish neurosurgeon

He was born and educated in Glasgow, where he worked throughout his life. His interest in surgery was stimulated by Joseph Lister, then Regius Professor of Surgery at Glasgow University, and he adopted and then extended Lister's antiseptic surgical techniques and pioneered operations on the brain for tumours, abscesses and trauma. In 1879 he successfully removed a tumour involving the meninges of the brain, the first time this had been performed with the survival of the patient. He developed a new procedure for repairing hernias and published work on the treatment of aneurysms by acupuncture. In addition, he operated on bones, introducing methods of implanting small grafts to replace missing portions of bones in the limbs. In 1892 he was appointed to the chair which Lister had held when Macewen was a student, and he was knighted in 1902. 📖 Hugh Allan MacEwen, *The Man in the White Coat: An Account of the Forebears and Early Life of Sir William Macewen, Surgeon* (1975)

McGee, Thomas D'Arcy 1825–68
Canadian writer and politician

Born in Carlingford, County Louth, Ireland, he was influenced by the mass movements of the Rev Theobald Mathew and Daniel O'Connell against drink and the Union. In 1842 he left for Quebec and Boston, where he worked on the local Catholic *Boston Pilot*. He became its editor at the age of 19, wrote fiction and supported a variety of romantic causes, returning to Ireland in 1845 where he was identified with the Young Ireland Party's journal, the *Nation*. After the abortive rebellion of 1848 he returned to the USA, where he argued for US annexation of Canada in his New York *Nation*. He lost Catholic ecclesiastical support by sympathy for Giuseppe Mazzini's anti-papal Roman Republic, and started the *American Celt* in Boston, publishing high-flown Romantic poems and *A History of the Irish settlers in North America* (1851). He moved to Montreal in 1857, founded the *New Era* newspaper, took Canadian citizenship and became an MP in 1858, and was Minister of Agriculture (1864–68). A strong advocate of Canadian Confederation, he was assassinated in Ottawa for his opposition to a threatened Fenian invasion of Canada. His published works include *A Popular History of Ireland* (1862–69) and *Poems* (1869). 📖 I M Skelton, *The Life of Thomas McGee* (1925)

McGeechan, Ian 1946–
Scottish rugby player and coach

Having moved to Yorkshire as a teenager, he played club rugby for Headingley, and made his international debut in 1972 in the same match as Andy Irvine. He played 32 times for Scotland between then and 1979, 12 at fly-half and 20 as centre. He also played eight times for the British Lions, on the 1974 tour of South Africa and the 1977 series in New Zealand. Scotland's assistant coach in the inaugural World Cup of 1987, he took over as head coach the following year, and was also coach of the British Lions in 1989. In 1990, his crucial role in Scotland's Grand Slam win heightened his reputation as one of the best coaches in world rugby. He announced his retirement from the game in 1993.

McGill, Donald, *originally* Fraser Gould 1875–1962
English comic-postcard artist

Born in Blackheath, West Midlands, he was a junior to a naval architect, then studied cartooning with **John Hassall**'s correspondence course. In 1905 he drew his first comic card for Asher's Pictorial Postcards, for whom one popular card sold two million copies. Famous for his outsize women in bathing costumes, paddling alongside weedy henpecked husbands, and for the double meanings in his captions, McGill did not receive critical attention until **George Orwell**'s *Horizon* article (1941). He is estimated to have drawn 500 cards a year for 50 years.

McGill, James 1744–1813
Canadian entrepreneur and philanthropist
Born in Glasgow, Scotland, he emigrated to Canada in the 1770s, and made a fortune in the northwest fur trade and in Montreal. He bequeathed land and money to found McGill College, Montreal, which became McGill University in 1821.

MacGill, Patrick 1890–1963
Irish navvy, novelist and poet
Born in the Glenties, County Donegal, and sold into servitude by his farming parents, he escaped to Scotland, working as a farm labourer and a navvy. His early verses attracted the attention of patrons, and he got a job on the London *Daily Express*, and was then adopted as secretary by Canon **John Dalton** of Windsor. His brilliantly naturalistic novel of migrant navvy life, *Children of the Dead End*, was published in 1914, followed a year later by a powerful feminist parallel narrative of the forcing of female Irish labour into prostitution, *The Rat-Pit*. He volunteered when war broke out, and wrote a kaleidoscopic account of the troops before embarkation, *The Amateur Army* (1915), then *The Red Horizon* (1916) and *The Great Push* (1916), describing action in France in which he was wounded. Later works include *Glenmornan* (1919), *Lanty Hanlon* (1922), *Moleskin Joe* (1923), and *Black Bonar* (1928). He went to the USA in 1930, where he declined into poverty and developed multiple sclerosis.

McGillivray, Alexander 1759–93
Creek leader
Born in Alabama, the son of a Scots trader and a French-Creek mother, he became a chief of the Creek nation and served as a British agent during the American Revolution. He accepted Spanish aid in resisting US westward expansion, leading attacks on American settlers. In 1790, under the Treaty of New York, he acknowledged US sovereignty, but two years later he resumed Spanish-subsidized attacks.

MacGillivray, James Pittendrigh 1856–1938
Scottish sculptor and poet
He was born in Inverurie, Aberdeenshire, the son of a sculptor, and studied under William Brodie and John Mossman. His major sculptures, in a naturalistic style, included the huge statue of **Robert Burns** in Irvine, the Scottish National Memorial to **William Gladstone** in Coates Crescent Garden, Edinburgh, the great statue to the third Marquess of Bute in Cardiff, the statue of **Byron** in Aberdeen, and the **John Knox** statue in St Giles Cathedral, Edinburgh. His most notable publications were verse (*Pro Patria*, 1915, and *Bog Myrtle and Peat Reek*, 1922) and various papers of professional significance. He was appointed the king's sculptor-in-ordinary for Scotland in 1921.

McGonagall, William 1830–1902
Scottish doggerel poet and novelist
The son of an immigrant Irish weaver, he spent some of his childhood on the island of South Ronaldsay in the Orkneys, settled with his family in Dundee at the age of 11, and became a handloom weaver with his father. He acted at Dundee's Royal Theatre and in 1878 published his first collection of poems, including 'Railway Bridge of the Silvery Tay'. He then travelled in central Scotland,

giving readings and selling his poetry in broadsheets, becoming idolized in Edinburgh by the legal and student fraternity. His poems are characterized by a disarming naïveté and a calypso-like disregard for metre. His *Poetic Gems* were published in 1890 and *More Poetic Gems* in 1962, and his *Collected Works* were most recently published in 1992.

McGoohan, Patrick 1928–
Irish–US actor
Born in Long Island, New York, his Irish–American parents returned to the family farm in County Leitrim when he was six months old and later moved to Sheffield, South Yorkshire, where he joined Sheffield Repertory. He made his West End debut in *Serious Charge* (1953). After his film debut in *The Dam Busters* (1954), he appeared in pictures such as *Hell Drivers* (1957), *Ice Station Zebra* (1968) and *Escape from Alcatraz* (1979). He became best known on television as secret agent John Drake in *Danger Man* (1960–67) and Number Six in the surrealistic cult classic *The Prisoner* (1967–68). He also appeared in and directed episodes of the US detective series *Columbo* (1971–78).

McGough, Roger 1937–
English poet, playwright and performer
Born in Liverpool, Merseyside, and educated at Hull University, he worked as a schoolteacher and art college lecturer. He became associated for ever with the 'Mersey Sound', a title used for the hugely successful *Penguin Modern Poets No. 10* (1967, 1974, 1983), which he shared with the other 'Liverpool Poets', **Adrian Henri** and **Brian Patten**. He enjoyed brief, bizarre pop success with the performing group The Scaffold. He shares the lugubrious self-ironizing wit and runaway punning that **John Lennon** brought to **Beatles** interviews, with something of the same faintly adolescent desire to shock. Much more of a 'street' poet than either Henri or Patten, he uses the rhythms of speech in a curiously subversive way. This was evident in the novel-plus-poems *Frinck, A Life in the Day of, and Summer with Monika* (1967), and it saw service again in collections like *Gig* (1973), *In the Classroom* (1976) and the acclaimed *Waving at Trains* (1982). McGough has written many plays, often with music, and a number of funny children's books such as *The Magic Fountain* (1995). A recent novel is *Defying Gravity* (1992).

McGovern, George Stanley 1922–
US politician
Born in Avon, South Dakota, the son of a Methodist minister, he served in the US air force during World War II, and became a Professor of History and Government at Dakota Wesleyan University. He served as a Democratic congressman (1956–61) and senator (1963–81) from South Dakota and was an early opponent of the Vietnam War. In July 1972, following a campaign expounding his new radicalism, he was chosen as Democratic candidate to oppose **Richard Nixon** in the presidential election but was heavily defeated, largely due to his wholly unsuccessful attempts to negotiate with Hanoi. In 1984 he failed to secure a second nomination, with his party favouring **Walter F Mondale** instead, and his effort to win the 1992 nomination was likewise unsuccessful. His autobiography, *Grassroots*, was published in 1978. ▢ Robert Sam Anson, *McGovern* (1972)

McGowan, Harry (Henry) Duncan, 1st Baron 1874–1961
Scottish chemical manufacturer
Born in Glasgow, he joined **Alfred Nobel**'s Explosives Company as an office boy in 1889. Twenty years later he had risen to assistant manager, and was sent to Canada where Nobel, **Pierre Du Pont** and others were in competition for a share of the market. He recommended a merger of all the manufacturers into one company and,

when that proved to be successful, he pursued a policy of mergers and marketing agreements for the rest of his life. In 1918, by which time he was managing director of Nobel's, he combined all the British explosives manufacturers into one group of companies, and began to diversify into other industries, becoming a director of the British Dyestuffs Corporation in 1919. In 1926 he persuaded **Alfred Mond** and others to join him in forming Imperial Chemical Industries, of which he was chairman and sole managing director from 1930 to 1950. He received a baronetcy in 1937.

McGrath, John Peter 1935–
English writer, director and filmmaker

Born in Birkenhead, Cheshire, he did National Service before studying at St John's College, Oxford, where his early plays were performed. Moving into television, he was one of the creators of the innovative police drama *Z Cars* in 1962. His work for the cinema includes the screenplays for *Billion Dollar Brain* (1967), *The Bofors Gun* (1968) and *Robin Hood* (1991). He has also produced such films as *The Dressmaker* (1988) and *Carrington* (1995). As founder and artistic director of the 7:84 Scotland theatre company (1973–88) he wrote many plays exploring the cultural and political struggles within Scotland, including *The Cheviot, The Stag and The Black, Black Oil* (1973) and *The Game's A Bogey* (1974). His books include *The Bone Won't Break: On Theatre and Hope in Hard Times* (1990). 📖 A Bold, 'The Impact of 7:84', in *Modern Scottish Literature* (1983)

Macgregor, Douglas 1906–64
US industrial psychologist

He took a doctorate in psychology at Harvard University (1935) and taught there before moving to the Massachusetts Institute of Technology (MIT), to help set up an industrial relations section in 1937. He was president of Antioch College (1948–54), and then returned to MIT to become the first Sloan Fellows Professor (1962). His highly regarded book *The Human Side of Enterprise* (1960) discussed two contrasting theories of motivation at work, which he called 'Theory X and Theory Y'. His unfinished book *The Professional Manager* was published posthumously in 1969.

McGregor, Sir Ian Kinloch 1912–98
US business executive

He was born in Kinlochleven, Scotland, and educated at Glasgow University and the Royal College of Science and Technology (now Strathclyde University). He went to the USA in 1940, when he was seconded to work with the US army. He developed his career in business in the USA, but in 1977 he returned to the UK as deputy chairman of British Leyland, working with Sir **Michael Edwardes**. In 1980 he was appointed chairman of the British Steel Corporation, and then became chairman of the National Coal Board (1983–86). Both industries required drastic cut-backs to survive and he faced strong trade union opposition, particularly from the miners in 1984–85. He published *The Enemies Within* in 1986 and was knighted the same year.

MacGregor, John, pseudonym Rob Roy 1825–92
English writer and traveller

Born in Gravesend, Kent, he was educated at Trinity College, Cambridge. He travelled widely in Europe, the Middle East and Russia, but is best remembered as the pioneer and popularizer of canoeing in Great Britain and designer of the 'Rob Roy' type canoe. His travel books include *A Thousand Miles in a Rob Roy Canoe* (1866).

MacGregor, Robert See Rob Roy

MacGregor, Sue (Susan Katriona) 1941–
English radio presenter

She was born in Oxford and educated mainly in South Africa. Her first job was as an announcer and producer with the state-run South African Broadcasting Corporation (1962–67). Moving to London in 1967, she joined the BBC as a reporter (1967–72), working on *World at One*, *World this Weekend* and *PM*, before beginning her 15-year position as presenter of *Woman's Hour* for Radio 4 (1972–87). She also worked on *Tuesday Call* (1973–86) and has her own radio series, *Conversation Piece* (1978–). A presenter of BBC Radio 4's *Today* programme since 1984, she also presented the television programme *Around Westminster* (1990–92).

MacGregor, William York 1855–1923
Scottish painter

Born in Glasgow, he studied at the Slade School of Art in London. A leading figure, along with Sir **James Guthrie**, of the so-called 'Glasgow Boys', whose paintings were based on a realistic approach to subject matter, he painted mostly human figures, although his masterpiece, *The Vegetable Stall* (1884) is an unusually large still life. Painted in rich, solid chunks of colour, and remarkably modern in style, it is one of the great Scottish paintings of the late 19th century.

McGuffey, William Holmes 1800–73
US educator

Born near Claysville, Pennsylvania, he was a Presbyterian minister and university professor who is remembered for compiling four of the six *Eclectic Readers*, known as *McGuffey's Readers*. His first two readers, published in 1836, extolled religion and patriotism and constituted a guide to social and moral conduct; his second pair, issued the following year, contained lessons on elocution as well as literary selections in which virtue was rewarded and vice was punished. The books were used as standard texts for nearly a century in the Mid-West, and through them McGuffey helped shape the American character.

McGuire, Edward 1948–
Scottish musician and composer

Born in Glasgow, he studied flute at the Royal Scottish Academy of Music and composition in London and Stockholm. When he joined the Whistlebinkies folk group in Glasgow in 1973 he was still essentially a classical instrumentalist, but folk music soon made its mark on his playing, and his first major composition, 'Trilogy', in the late 1970s, showed the influence of folk themes. His 'Rant' was the test piece for the 1978 Carl Flesch International Violin Competition in 1978, and his string quartet was performed in 1983 at an anniversary concert of the Society for the Promotion of New Music at the Barbican in London. Later compositions include the music for Scottish Ballet's *Peter Pan* (1989), 'A Glasgow Symphony' for the National Youth Orchestra of Scotland (1990) and a three-act opera, *The Loving of Etain*, for Paragon Opera's production in Glasgow (1990). The Paragon Ensemble also recorded his *Songs of New Beginnings* (1991).

Mach, David 1956–
Scottish sculptor

Born in Methil, Fife, he studied at Duncan of Jordanstone College of Art, Dundee, and the Royal College of Art, London. He has attracted both critical and popular attention, through his choice of materials and his working methods. Working to a time limit, often in public view, he has created monumental structures from society's surplus materials, which include a military tank constructed from car tyres and enormous classical columns from magazines. In 1992 he was awarded the City of Glasgow Lord Provost prize.

Mach, Ernst 1838–1916
Austrian physicist and philosopher

Born in Turas, Moravia, he studied at Vienna University, and became Professor of Mathematics at Graz in 1864, of Physics at Prague in 1867, and of Physics again at Vienna in 1895. He carried out much experimental work on supersonic projectiles and on the flow of gases, obtaining some remarkable early photographs of shock waves and gas jets. His findings have proved of great importance in aeronautical design and the science of projectiles, and his name has been given to the ratio of the speed of flow of a gas to the speed of sound (Mach number) and to the angle of a shock wave to the direction of motion (Mach angle). In the field of epistemology he was determined to abolish idle metaphysical speculation. His writings greatly influenced Albert Einstein and laid the foundations of logical positivism. He wrote *Mechanik in ihrer Entwicklung* (1883, Eng trans *The Science of Mechanics*, 1893) and *Beiträzur Analyse der Empfindung* (1897, 'Contributions to the Analysis of Sensation'). ◻ John T Blackmore, *Ernst Mach: His Life, Work and Influence* (1972)

Machado, Antonio 1875–1939
Spanish writer
Born in Seville, he was educated at the University of Madrid and the Sorbonne. He wrote lyrics characterized by a nostalgic melancholy, among them *Soledades, Galerias y otros poemas* (1907, 'Loneliness, Galleries and Other Poems') and *Campos de Castilla* (1912, 'Fields of Castille'). His brother Manuel (1874–1947), also a poet, collaborated with him on several plays.

Machado de Assis, Joaquim Maria 1839–1908
Brazilian novelist
Born in Rio de Janiero, he was an epileptic from a humble family background who became a high-ranking official in the Civil Service. The co-founder of the Brazilian Academy of Letters in 1896, he became its president from 1897. His novels dissect the minutiae of Brazilian upper-class life in cunningly ambiguous prose, and include *Mémorias pósthumos de Brás Cubas* (1881, Eng trans *Epitaph of a Small Winner*, 1952), *Quincas Borba* (1891, Eng trans *Philosopher or Dog?*, 1954), *Dom Casmurro* (1900, Eng trans 1953) and *Esaúe Jacó* (1904, Eng trans *Esau and Jacob*, 1966). He also wrote several volumes of short stories. A complete edition of his works in Portuguese was issued in 1959. ◻ H Caldwell, *Machado de Assis: the Brazilian master and his novels* (1970)

Machar, Josef Svatopluk 1864–1942
Czech poet
Born in Kolin, he became a bank official in Vienna. The author of satirical and political verse, he was known for the trilogy *Confiteor* (1887, 'I Confess'), the verse romance *Magdalena* (1893), and the epic *Warriors of God* (1897). His nine-volume *Svědomim věku* (1902–26, 'The Conscience of the Age') is a pessimistic epic of humanity's progress, or lack of it. He became inspector-general of the Czechoslovak army in 1919, having been imprisoned by the Austrians during World War I. ◻ V Martinek, *Josef Svatopluk Machar* (1948)

Machaut, Guillaume de See **Guillaume de Machaut**

Machel, Samora Moises 1933–86
Mozambique nationalist leader and politician
He trained as a medical assistant before joining FRELIMO (Front for the Liberation of Mozambique) in 1963, soon becoming active in the guerrilla war against the Portuguese colonial power. Commander-in-Chief in 1966, he succeedeed Eduardo Mondlane on the latter's assassination in 1969 and was President of Mozambique from its independence in 1975 until his own death in an air crash. Avowedly a Marxist, his success at politicizing the peasantry in northern Mozambique during the liberation war led him to believe in the dominant role of the

party but, after the flight of white Portuguese in 1974 and the economic failure of his policies, he became more pragmatic, turning to the West for assistance, advising Robert Mugabe to temper principle with prudence, and establishing more harmonious relations with South Africa.

Machen, Arthur 1863–1947
English novelist
Born in Carleon-on-Usk, Wales, of English parentage, he was popular with readers, but never gained much critical praise. His books include *The Great God Pan* (1894), *The Hill of Dreams* (1907), and *Things Far and Near* (1923), an interesting volume of recollections. He wrote many well-executed tales of the uncanny, collected in *Tales of Horror and the Supernatural* (1964), and his autobiography (1951, edited by Morchard Bishop).

Machiavelli, Niccolò See panel p1190

Macià, Francesc or Francisco 1859–1933
Spanish Catalan leader
He was born in Villa nueva y Geltrú. Elected to parliament in 1905, he was the leader and founder, in 1922, of Estat Català, the Catalan nationalist party, and a central figure in the Catalan struggle to achieve autonomy. After Miguel Primo de Rivera's dictatorship collapsed, Macià forged a coalition of the Catalan Republican Party and Estat Català, creating the Republican Left of Catalonia. He was the first President of Catalonia under the autonomy statute of 1932 granted by the Second Republic. His Republican Left was defeated in the elections of 1933 and Macià died a few weeks later.

McIlvanney, William Angus 1936–
Scottish novelist and poet
Born in Kilmarnock, Ayrshire, he was educated at Kilmarnock Academy and Glasgow University and taught from 1960 to 1975, when he took up writing full-time. His first novel was *Remedy is None* (1966), a paean to working-class values, and it was followed in 1968 by *A Gift from Nessus*. Other novels include *Docherty* (1975), about an Ayrshire miner, which won the Whitbread award, *The Big Man* (1985) and *The Kiln* (1996). His thrillers featuring the Glasgow detective Jack Laidlaw, such as *Laidlaw* (1977), *The Papers of Tony Veitch* (1983) and *Strange Loyalties* (1991), evoke comparisons with Raymond Chandler. Volumes of poetry include *The Longships in Harbour* (1970) and *These Words* (1984). His short stories are collected in *Walking Wounded* (1989), and his essays and journalism in *Surviving the Shipwreck* (1991).

MacIndoe, Sir Archibald 1900–60
New Zealand plastic surgeon
He was born in Dunedin. Educated at Otago, at the Mayo Clinic in the USA, and at St Bartholomew's Hospital, London, he was the most eminent pupil of Sir Harold Gillies. He won fame during World War II as surgeon-in-charge at the Queen Victoria Hospital, East Grinstead, where the faces and limbs of injured airmen ('MacIndoe's guinea-pigs') were remodelled with unsurpassed skill.

MacInnes, Hamish 1930–
Scottish mountaineer, writer and broadcaster
Born in Gatehouse of Fleet, Kirkcudbrightshire, he has climbed in Scotland, the European Alps, New Zealand, the Caucasus and the Himalayas, and has been a member of two expeditions to Everest (spring and autumn 1972). He was deputy leader of the successful south-west face of Everest expedition in 1975. He made the first ascent of the Great Prow on Mount Roraima, Guyana, in 1973. A leading authority on mountain rescue, he has been founder and leader of the Glencoe Mountain Rescue Team (1960–94), honorary secretary of the Mountain Rescue Committee of Scotland, and was founder and honorary

Machiavelli, Niccolò 1469–1527
Italian statesman, writer and political philosopher

Machiavelli was born in Florence, but nothing much is known of his early life. He was among those who rapidly rose to power in 1498, despite his lack of political experience, when **Savonarola's** regime in Florence was overthrown. He was appointed head of the Second Chancery and Secretary to the Council of Ten (the main foreign relations committee in the republic). He served on a variety of diplomatic missions over the next 14 years and met many important political leaders including **Louis XII** of France, **Cesare Borgia,** Pope **Julius II** and Emperor **Maximilian I.** His reports and correspondence demonstrate a shrewd appraisal of people and events and enabled him to try out ideas he was later to develop in his political works.

In 1512, when the **Medici** family, in exile since 1494, returned to run the city and the republic was dissolved, Machiavelli was dismissed from his post (for reasons that are unclear) and the following year was arrested on a charge of conspiracy against the new regime. He was tortured, and although soon released and pardoned, was obliged to withdraw from public life and devote himself to writing. To console himself, as he explained in a famous letter to his friend Francesco Vettori, he studied ancient history, pondered the lessons to be learned from his experiences in government service, and drafted 'a little book' on the subject. That was his masterpiece, *The Prince,* which was written in 1513 and circulated in manuscript form before being published in 1532. It was intended to be a handbook for rulers, advising them what to do and what to say to achieve political success, and its main theme is that rulers must always be prepared to do evil if they judge that good will come of it.

Machiavelli's admirers have praised him as a political realist; his (rather more numerous) critics have denounced him as a dangerous cynic and amoralist. He dedicated the book to the Medici, hoping to secure their sympathetic attention, but he was never offered any further political offices and he spent his last 15 years as a man of letters. He died among family and friends, and was buried in Santa Croce, Florence.

▥ In addition to *The Prince,* he wrote a series of *Discourses* on *Livy* (a full-scale analysis of republican government, completed in about 1518), a treatise on *The Art of War* (published 1521), *Mandragola,* a comic play about a seduction (completed in about 1518), and several minor literary and historical works. See also Q Skinner, *Machiavelli* (1981); P Bondanella and M Musa, *The Portable Machiavelli* (1979); M Fleisher, *Machiavelli and the Nature of Political Thought* (1973); R Ridolfi, *The Life of Machiavelli* (1963).

> 'One can make this generalization about men: they are ungrateful, fickle, liars, and deceivers, they shun danger and are greedy for profit; while you treat them well they are yours. They would shed their blood for you, risk their property, their lives, their children, so long as danger is remote, but when you are in danger they turn against you.'
> From *The Prince,* ch.17.

president of the Search and Rescue Dog Association. His publications include *Climbing* (1964), *West Highland Walks* (4 vols, 1979–88) and *Land of Mountain and Mist* (1989).

Macintosh, Charles 1766–1843
Scottish industrial chemist and inventor

He was born in Glasgow and studied at the university there and in Edinburgh. By 1786 he had started a chemical works, and in 1799 he and **Charles Tennant** developed bleaching powder, which was used industrially to bleach cloth and paper until the 1920s. In 1823 Macintosh succeeded in bonding two pieces of woollen cloth together with a solution of dissolved india-rubber, and thus produced the first waterproof cloth. He patented the process that year and, joining forces with **Thomas Hancock,** began making waterproof garments at a factory in Manchester. The rubber was difficult to sew and tended to crumble in cold weather and become sticky in hot weather. These difficulties were largely overcome with the invention of vulcanization in the late 1830s, following which the production of waterproof clothing ('mac(k)intoshes') and outdoor equipment expanded rapidly.

McIntosh, Genista Mary, *née* Tandy 1946–
English arts administrator

Born in London and educated at the University of York, she began her career working with the York Festival of the Arts before joining the Royal Shakespeare Company, where she was casting director (1972–77), planning controller (1977–84), senior administrator (1984–90) and associate producer in 1990. She was executive director of the Royal National Theatre from 1990 to 1997, when she became the first woman chief executive of the Royal Opera House, Covent Garden.

MacIntyre, Alasdair Chalmers 1929–
Scottish philosopher

Born in Glasgow and raised in Ireland, he was educated at Oxford and London. Unusually broad in his intellectual sympathies, he wrote about and taught a wide range of subjects, holding posts in sociology and in philosophy of religion at, among others, Sussex, Manchester, Boston and Nashville universities. His time in the USA helped him address a more general audience with some revision of his earlier views in his trilogy *After Virtue* (1981), *Whose Justice? Which Rationality?* (1986) and *Three Versions of Moral Enquiry,* the last of these being the 1989 Gifford Lectures at Edinburgh. He values 18th/19th-century Scottish philosophy, and places some importance on studies in Greek thought and language. A figure of considerable international reputation, he is considered by some to be the most famous living philosopher in the English language. Since 1995, he has been Arts and Sciences Professor of Philosophy at Duke University in Durham.

McIntyre, Duncan Ban, *English name of* Donnachadh Ban Macan t-Saoir 1724–1812
Scottish poet

Born in Glenorchy, Argyll, he worked as a forester and gamekeeper, fought as a Hanoverian at Falkirk in 1746, and from 1799 to 1806 was one of the City Guard of Edinburgh. He composed a great deal of nature poetry which, since he was illiterate, was written down by the minister's son at Killin and published in a collection in 1768. Some of it has been translated into English by Hugh MacDiarmid and Iain Crichton Smith, including his long poem 'Moladh Beinn Dòbhrainn' ('The Praise of Ben Doran'). He also wrote formal occasional verse, love poems, satires and songs.

Mack, Connie, *originally* Cornelius Alexander McGillicuddy 1862–1956
US baseball player and manager

Born in East Brookfield, Massachusetts, he was closely involved in the early days of US baseball. He was catcher with various teams from 1886 to 1916, and began his managerial career as player/manager at Pittsburgh (1894–96). He moved on to Philadelphia in 1901 and stayed for 50 years. He holds the record for most years managing (53), most games won (3,776), and most games lost (4,025). He won world championships in 1910–11, 1913 and 1929–30, and in 1930 he was also honoured (unusually for a sportsman) with the Edward P Bok prize for distinguished service to Philadelphia. In 1937 he was elected to the Baseball Hall of Fame.

Mack, Karl, Freiherr von 1752–1828
Austrian soldier

Born in Nennslingen, Franconia, after fighting the Turks and the French republicans, he was created field marshal (1797). He occupied Rome for the King of Naples, but had to conclude an armistice with the French, and was driven by riots in Naples to seek safety with them. He was carried as a prisoner to Paris, but escaped in 1800. Having surrendered with his army to the French at Ulm in 1805, he was tried by court martial and condemned to death, but the sentence was commuted to 20 years' imprisonment. In 1808 he was freed and in 1819 fully pardoned.

Mack, (Marie) Louise Hamilton 1874–1935
Australian novelist, journalist and war correspondent

She was born in Hobart, Tasmania. Her first juvenile novel, *The World is Round*, appeared in 1896. She moved to London in 1901 and wrote the popular *An Australian Girl in London* (1902); nine other adult novels include *The Red Rose of Summer* (1909) and *The Music Makers* (1914). She spent some years in Florence during which she edited the English-language *Italian Gazette* (1904–07). In 1914 she went to Belgium for the London *Daily Mail* and *Evening News* as the first woman war correspondent; her adventures were published in 1915 as *A Woman's Experiences in the Great War*. Her sister was the Australian naturalist and children's writer Amy Mack (1876–1939).

Mackarness, (Guy) Richard 1916–96
English physician and diet reformer

He was born in Pakistan of English parents and went to England at the age of six. After World War II he took up general practice and also wrote a medical column for the *News Chronicle* and its successor the *Daily Mail*. In 1958 he wrote the bestseller *Eat Fat and Grow Slim*, the first popular dietary book, proposing a diet of protein and fat. He became known worldwide as an advocate of 'clinical ecology' as a control for allergies and certain mental illnesses, as described in his book *Not All in the Mind* (1976). He co-founded the charity Action against Allergies and from 1981 lived in partial retirement in Australia, where he wrote *A Little of What You Fancy* (1985).

McKay, Claude, *originally* Festus Claudius 1890–1948
US writer

Born in the mountains of central Jamaica, he published two books of verse in dialect before emigrating to the USA in 1912. Radicalized by his experiences of racial hatred in America, he wrote poems such as his sonnet 'If We Must Die', urging blacks to fight for their freedom and dignity. A leading figure in the Harlem Renaissance, he became the first bestselling black author with his novel *Home to Harlem* (1928), the story of a black soldier returning to New York after World War I, and although the vogue for black literature ended with the coming of the Depression, he continued to write fiction, including *Gingertown* (1932) and *Banana Bottom* (1933). He lived in Russia and Europe from 1922 to 1934 but returned to the USA and was naturalized in 1940. His autobiography is entitled *A Long Way from Home* (1937). 📖 W F Cooper, *Claude McKay: Rebel Sojourner in the Harlem Renaissance* (1987)

Mackay, Fulton 1922–87
Scottish actor

Born in Paisley, Renfrewshire, he began his stage career in 1947, and was a member of the Citizens' Theatre, Glasgow (1949–51, 1953–58), and of the Old Vic company (1962–63). At the Royal Court Theatre in 1969 he appeared in David Storey's *In Celebration*. He then became a director of the Scottish Actors Company. He made several television and film appearances, but is probably best remembered for playing the role of the officious prison warden Mr Mackay in the 1970s television series *Porridge*.

McKay, Heather Pamela, *née* Blundell 1941–
Australian squash player

Born in Queanbeyan, New South Wales, she played hockey for Australia as a schoolgirl, then at the age of 18 was Queanbeyan tennis champion. Having taken up squash at 17 to keep fit for hockey, she won 14 Australian titles (1960–73), won the British Open in 16 successive years (1962–77), and was world champion in 1976 and 1979. She was unbeaten between 1962 and 1980. She married another top squash player, Brian McKay, in 1965 and 10 years later moved to Canada, where she became Canadian racketball champion.

Mackay (of Clashfern), James Peter Hymers Mackay, Baron 1927–
Scottish judge and jurist

Born in Scourie, Sutherland, the son of a railway signalman, he was educated at George Heriot's School and Edinburgh University. After teaching mathematics at St Andrews University he switched to law, and was called to the Bar in 1955. As a QC, specializing in tax law, he was unexpectedly made Lord Advocate for Scotland, and a life peer, by Margaret Thatcher, in 1979. He took the title of his peerage from the name of a shepherd's cottage he knew as a boy. As Lord High Chancellor of Great Britain in succession to Lord Havers (1987–97), he created consternation proposing radical reform. His personal affairs also aroused controversy when, in 1989, he clashed with the Calvinist elders of his Church, the Free Presbyterians, for attending the funeral of a Roman Catholic colleague. He was succeeded in 1997 by Lord Irvine of Lairg (1940–). He is Chancellor of Heriot-Watt University in Edinburgh (1991–).

Mackay, John Alexander 1889–1983
US scholar and ecumenist

Born into a Free Presbyterian family in Inverness, Scotland, he was educated at Aberdeen, Princeton, and in Spain, where he developed a lifelong love of Hispanic culture. He became the first Protestant to become Professor of Philosophy at Peru's National University (1915–25), served the YMCA in Uruguay and Mexico (1925–32), and later became president of Princeton Theological Seminary (1936–59). A leader in the ecumenical movement, he was president of the World Alliance of Reformed Churches (1954–59). His works include *The Other Spanish Christ* (1932), *The Presbyterian Way of Life* (1960) and *Ecumenics: The Science of the Church Universal* (1964).

Mackay, Mary See **Corelli, Marie**

Mackay, Robert, *English name of* Rob Donn MacAoidh 1714–78
Scottish Gaelic poet

Born in Strathmore, Sutherland, he became a herdsman for the Mackay chief, Lord Reay. He became known as 'Rob Donn', an oral bard who described rural life in his area and the disintegration of clan society on Strathnaver and Strathmore after the 1745 Jacobite rebellion. His poetry was later collected and written down by local ministers, and a first edition appeared in 1828.

Macke, August 1887–1914

German painter

Born in Meschede in the Rhineland, he studied at Düsseldorf and designed stage scenery. Profoundly influenced by **Henri Matisse**, whose work he saw in Munich in 1910, he founded the Blaue Reiter group with **Franz Marc**. He was a sensitive colourist, bright but not garish, working in watercolour as well as oil, and remained attached to the kind of subject matter favoured by the Impressionists: figures in a park, street scenes, children and animals (as in *The Zoo*, 1912). He was killed fighting in World War I in Champagne, France.

Mackellar, Dorothea 1885–1968

Australian poet

She was born in Sydney, and her fame rests solely on 'My Country', a poem first published in the London *Spectator* in 1908. Later revised and included in her first collection *The Closed Door* (1911), its opening lines 'I Love a Sunburnt Country,/A Land of Sweeping Plains —' evoke an emotional response from Australians the world over. Three further volumes of verse were published between 1914 and 1926, all in pastoral and patriotic vein, and three novels, two of which were in collaboration with another Australian, Ruth Bedford (1882–1963): *The Little Blue Devil* (1912) and *Two's Company* (1914).

McKellen, Sir Ian Murray 1939–

English actor

Born in Burnley, Lancashire, he made his London debut in *A Scent of Flowers* (1964) and, with the actor Edward Petherbridge, founded the Actors Company (1972), run along democratic lines. His many plays for the Royal Shakespeare Company include the title roles in *Faustus* (1974), *Romeo and Juliet* (1976), *Macbeth* (1976–77) and *Richard III* (1990). On television, he has acted the title role in *Walter* (1982), Iago in *Othello* (1989) and Amos Starkadder in *Cold Comfort Farm* (1995). His film roles include **John Profumo** in *Scandal* (1989). He is an active campaigner for equal rights for homosexuals in the UK and a member of the Stonewall lobbying group. In 1996 he directed and starred in the leading role in the film of *Richard III*.

Mackendrick, Alexander 1912–

US film director

Born in Boston of Scottish origin, he was educated at the Glasgow School of Art, then worked as an animator and commercial artist before joining the script department at Pinewood Studios. During World War II he made documentaries, newsreels and propaganda films for the Ministry of Information, and after the war he joined Ealing Studios, making his directorial debut on *Whisky Galore* (1948). A master of the Ealing comedy and a gifted children's director, he had success with *The Man In The White Suit* (1951), *Mandy* (1952) and *The Maggie* (1954). Embarking on international projects, he created a memorable portrait of greed in *Sweet Smell of Success* (1957). He retired as an active filmmaker after *Don't Make Waves* (1967) and lectured at the California Institute of Arts, where he was Dean of the Film Department (1969–78).

Mackenzie, Sir Alexander 1764–1820

Scottish explorer and fur-trader

Born in Stornoway, Isle of Lewis, he joined the Northwest Fur Company in 1779, and in 1788 established Fort Chipewayan on Lake Athabasca, in Canada. From there he discovered the Mackenzie River (1789), followed it to the sea, and in 1792–93 became the first European to cross the Rocky Mountains to the Pacific Ocean.

Mackenzie, Alexander 1822–92

Canadian statesman

Born in Logierait, Perthshire, Scotland, he went to Canada in 1842 and found work as a mason and contractor. In 1852 he became editor of a Reform paper, and in 1861 he was elected to parliament, leading the Liberal Opposition to **John Macdonald**'s government from 1867. As the first Liberal Prime Minister (1873–78), he sought to strengthen the provincial governments and encourage immigration. His go-slow public construction of the Canadian Pacific Railway (for which he took personal responsibility as Minister of Public Works) nearly lost British Columbia to the USA, while his inability to deal with the severe depression and his refusal to raise the tariff lost him the election of 1878. In 1880 the party threatened to rebel and he was succeeded by Edward Blake.

Mackenzie, Sir Alexander Campbell 1847–1935

Scottish composer

Born in Edinburgh, he studied music at Sondershausen, Germany, and at the Royal Academy of Music, London. From 1865 to 1879 he was a teacher, violinist and conductor in Edinburgh, and later Principal of the Royal Academy of Music (1887–1924). *The Rose of Sharon* (1884), an oratorio, contains some of his best work. Other compositions include operas, cantatas, Scottish rhapsodies, a concerto and a suite for violin, chamber music and songs. He also wrote *A Musician's Narrative* (1927).

Mackenzie, Sir (Edward Montague) Compton 1883–1972

English writer

Born in West Hartlepool, Cleveland, he was educated at St Paul's School and Magdalen College, Oxford, then studied for the Bar but stopped in 1907 to work on his first play, *The Gentleman in Grey*. His first novel, *The Passionate Elopement*, was published in 1911. There followed his successful story of theatre life, *Carnival* (1912), and the autobiographical *Sinister Street* (2 vols, 1913–14) and *Guy and Pauline* (1915). In World War I he served in the Dardanelles, and in 1917 became director of the Aegean Intelligence Service in Syria, an experience described in his book on the Secret Service, *Extremes Meet* (1928). In 1923 he founded *The Gramophone* (now *Gramophone*), the oldest surviving record magazine in the world. His considerable output includes *Sylvia Scarlett* (1918), *Poor Relations* (1919), *Rich Relatives* (1921), *Vestal Fire* (1927), *The Four Winds of Love* (4 vols, 1937–45), *Aegean Memories* (1940), *Whisky Galore* (1947), *Eastern Epic* (1951) and *Rockets Galore* (1957). His monumental autobiography, *My Life and Times* (1963–71), came out in 10 *Octaves*. 🕮 Andro Linklater, *Compton Mackenzie: A Life* (1987)

McKenzie, Dan Peter 1942–

English geophysicist

Born in Cheltenham, Gloucestershire, he studied physics and geophysics at Cambridge, and since 1984 has been Professor of Earth Sciences there. In 1966 McKenzie became convinced of the importance of the new hypothesis of **Harry Hess**, **Frederick J Vine** and **Drummond H Matthews** on sea-floor spreading, and wrote a paper on the relationships of oceanic heat flow and gravity (1967). He developed a theory of plate tectonics (1967, with Robert L Parker) which he used in further work on plate geometries, and plate motions (1969). Plate tectonic theory at last provided a plausible mechanism for continental drift, and proved the key to understanding crustal tectonics. McKenzie also worked on problems of convection within the mantle (1966–83), the tectonics of continental mountain belts (1978–81) and on melting within the mantle and its relation to the generation of continents (from 1984). He was elected FRS in 1976.

Mackenzie (of Rosehaugh), Sir George
1636–91
Scottish lawyer

Born in Dundee, he studied at St Andrews, Aberdeen and Bourges, and was called to the Bar at Edinburgh in 1656. He entered parliament for Ross-shire in 1669, and in 1677 was made King's Advocate. He became known as 'Bluidy Mackenzie' for his vigorous prosecution of the Covenanters. In 1682 he founded the Advocates Library in Edinburgh (now the National Library of Scotland). A prolific author and an aficionado of Scottish literature, he wrote works of fiction, politics, history and law. His law writings include *Laws and Customs of Scotland in Matters Criminal* (1674), *Institutions of the Law of Scotland* (1684) and *Observations on the Acts of Parliament* (1686), which are still important. His *Memoirs of the Affairs of Scotland* was published in 1821.

Mackenzie, Henry 1745–1831
Scottish writer

Born in Edinburgh, and educated at Edinburgh University, he became a crown attorney in the Scottish Court of Exchequer (1765), and in 1804 comptroller of taxes. For more than half a century he was 'one of the most illustrious names connected with polite literature in Edinburgh', and a regular contributor to the *Scots Magazine and General Intelligencer*. His sentimental, but highly influential, novel *The Man of Feeling* was published in 1771, followed by *The Man of the World* (1773) and *Julia de Roubigné* (1777). He also wrote two tragedies, *The Spanish Father* (1773, never performed) and *The Prince of Tunis* (1773). One of the founders of the Royal Society of Edinburgh (1783), he is also remembered for his recognition of **Robert Burns**, and as an early admirer of **Gotthold Lessing** and **Schiller**. His memoirs were published as *Anecdotes and Egotisms* (1927).

MacKenzie, Sir James 1853–1925
Scottish physician and cardiologist

Born in Scone, Perthshire, he studied medicine in Edinburgh before settling in Burnley, Lancashire, as a general practitioner, where he developed a 'polygraph' for recording the pulse and its relationship to cardiovascular disease. He described several irregularities of the heartbeat and acquired through his writing an international reputation. His work was particularly important in the diagnosis and treatment of atrial fibrillation. His *Diseases of the Heart* (1908) summarized his vast experience. In 1918 he left London to establish the Institute of Clinical Research at St Andrews, designed to establish better guidelines for the treatment of common diseases. In 1915 he was elected FRS and knighted in the same year.

McKenzie, Joseph 1929–
Scottish photographic artist and teacher

Born in London, he served in the RAF as a photographer (1947–52), then studied at the London College of Printing. He taught photography at St Martin's School of Art in London and then at the Duncan of Jordanstone College of Art in Dundee until 1986. From 1974 to 1980 he operated the Victoria House Gallery of Photography from his home in Tayport, Fife. His wide-ranging photographs are seen in his *Pages of Experience: Photography 1947–87* (1987). His work relates more closely to the American rather than to the European tradition of photography, and he is probably best known for his photographic essays of people, often children, in mainly urban environments in Scotland and Ireland.

McKenzie, Julia Kathleen 1941–
English actress and singer

Trained at the Guildhall School of Music and Drama, London, she is a noted interpreter of the work of US musicals composer **Stephen Sondheim**. Her London appearances include *Maggie May* (1965), *Mame* (1969), Sondheim's *Company* (1972); the anthologies *Cowardy Custard* (1973), *Cole* (1974), and *Side by Side by Sondheim* (1977); **Frank Loesser**'s *Guys and Dolls* (1982), and Sondheim's *Follies* (1987). She has interspersed musicals with plays, notably **Brecht**'s *Schweyk in the Second World War* (1982); and three plays by **Alan Ayckbourn**: *The Norman Conquests* (1974), *Ten Times Table* (1979), and *Woman in Mind* (1986). She has also appeared in television films such as *Adam Bede* (1992) and in the feature film *Shirley Valentine* (1989). Following her directorial debut, *Stepping Out* (1984), she has directed such plays as *Steel Magnolias* (1989) and *Putting It Together* (1992).

Mackenzie, William Forbes 1801–62
Scottish politician

He was born in Portmore, Peeblesshire. As MP for Peeblesshire (1837–52), he introduced a liquor Act for Scotland; it was passed in 1853 and imposed Sunday closing and other controls.

Mackenzie, William Lyon 1795–1861
Canadian politician

Born in Dundee, Scotland, he emigrated to Canada in 1820, and published the *Colonial Advocate* in Toronto (1824–34), in which he attacked the government continually. In 1828 he was elected to the provincial parliament for York, but was expelled in 1830 for libel on that assembly. He was Mayor of Toronto in 1834. In 1837 he published in his paper a declaration of independence for Toronto, headed a band of 800 insurgents and attacked the city (5 December). Repulsed, he fled across the border, and on 13 December seized Navy Island in the Niagara River, where he declared a provisional government. A Canadian force promptly crossed the river (29 December) and burned the US steamer *Caroline*, which had been supplying the rebels, precipitating an international incident. Mackenzie fled to New York (1838), where he was sentenced by the US authorities to 12 months' imprisonment. He returned to Canada in 1849, and became an MP (1850–58). He was the grandfather of **Mackenzie King**.

Mackenzie Stuart (of Dean), Lord Alexander John 1924–
Scottish judge

Born in Aberdeen, he was educated at Fettes College, Edinburgh, Sidney Sussex College, Cambridge, and at Edinburgh University. After practising at the Scottish Bar, he became a judge of the Court of Session (1972), and then the first British judge appointed to the Court of Justice of the European Communities (1973–88), serving as president of that court from 1984 to 1988. He published *The European Communities and the Rule of Law* (1977).

McKern, Leo, *originally* Reginald McKern 1920–
Australian actor

Born in Sydney, Australia, he worked as a commercial artist before making his stage debut in *Uncle Harry* there (1944) and moving to London in 1946, where he made his debut with the Old Vic Company in *Love's Labour's Lost* (1949). On television, he played Number Two in *The Prisoner* (1967–68) and, most famously, the eccentric barrister Horace Rumpole in **John Mortimer**'s *Rumpole of the Bailey*, first as a BBC Play for Today (1975) and then as an ITV series (1978–92). He also appeared in *Rumpole's Return* (1980), and acted Basil Zaharov in *Reilly—Ace of Spies* (1983) and Sancho in *Monsignor Quixote* (1985).

Mackerras, Sir (Alan) Charles (MacLaurin) 1925–
Australian conductor

Born in Schenectady, New York, of Australian parents, he played the oboe with the Sydney Symphony Orchestra (1943–46), was a staff conductor at Sadler's Wells Opera

(1949–53), and returned there as musical director (1970–77), gaining an international reputation. Subsequent conducting posts have included the BBC Symphony Orchestra, Sydney Symphony Orchestra, Royal Liverpool Philharmonic Orchestra and Welsh National Opera (musical director 1987–92). In 1993 he became principal guest conductor of both the San Francisco Opera and the Royal Philharmonic Orchestra. He is a noted scholar of the music of Leoš Janáček and was knighted in 1979. 📖 Nancy Phelan, *Charles Mackerras: a musician's musician* (1987)

MacKillop, Mary Helen, known as Mother Mary of the Cross 1842–1909
Australian nun, the country's first saint
She was born in the Fitzroy district of Melbourne, Victoria, of Scottish parents. With Father Tenison-Woods she founded the Society of the Sisters of St Joseph of the Sacred Heart in Penola, South Australia, in 1866. Although the Society quickly grew, establishing 170 schools and 160 Josephite convents, diocesan rivalry caused Mother Mary to be excommunicated in 1871; however she was reinstated two years later by Pope Pius IX, who approved the Sisterhood in the same year. In 1875 she was confirmed as superior-general of the order, which is popularly known as the 'Little Joeys'. Its work is highly regarded, and it is devoted to the education of poorer children and care of orphans and unmarried mothers. The case for the beatification of Mother Mary, the first step towards canonization, was made in 1925, and in 1975 her cause was formally introduced by the Vatican. She was beatified by Pope John Paul II in 1995.

McKim, Charles Follen 1847–1909
US architect
Born in Chester County, Pennsylvania, he studied architecture at the École des Beaux-Arts in Paris, returning to the USA in 1870 and working in the office of H H Richardson. In 1879 he and William Rutherford Mead (1846–1928) joined up with Stanford White to found McKim, Mead, & White, which became the nation's leading architectural firm and remained so for decades. Working co-operatively, McKim and his partners designed buildings influenced by Classical and Renaissance models, helping to establish the neoclassical revival in the USA. The firm's best-known buildings include the Boston Public Library (1887–95) and, in New York City, the old Madison Square Garden (1891), the Morgan Library (1903) and Pennsylvania Station (1904–10). McKim also took on special projects such as the restoration of the White House and the revival (1901) of Pierre L'Enfant's plan for Washington DC. Convinced that young US architects needed training in the European tradition, he was instrumental in founding the American Academy in Rome, which he supervised from 1894.

Mackinder, Sir Halford John 1861–1947
English geographer and politician
Born in Gainsborough, Lincolnshire, he was educated at Epsom College and Christ Church, Oxford. He became the first Reader in Geography at Oxford (1887–1905) and established the first university school in the subject in 1899 (director, 1899–1904). He thus laid the foundations of British academic geography at Oxford, and later at Reading and the London School of Economics. He held numerous senior university appointments, was an MP (1910–22) and also British High Commissioner for South Russia (1919–1920). In *Democratic Ideals and Reality* (1919), he expounded his famous Eurasian 'Heartland' concept. He also wrote *Britain and the British Seas* (1902) and *The Nations of the Modern World* (1911).

McKinley, William 1843–1901
25th President of the USA
Born in Niles, Ohio, he served in the Civil War, retiring with the rank of major in 1865 and later practising law in Canton, Ohio. He was elected to Congress as a Republican in 1876, and repeatedly re-elected. In 1891, with business community support, he was made Governor of Ohio, his name being identified with the high protective tariff carried in the McKinley Tariff Act of 1890. Chosen Republican candidate for the presidency in 1896 and 1900, he conducted exciting contests with W J Bryan who advocated the cause of free silver, denounced trusts, high tariffs, and imperialism, and was understood to favour labour at the expense of capital. McKinley, a conservative and an advocate of the gold standard, had the backing not only of Republicans but of the so-called 'Gold Democrats' or 'Sound Money Democrats', in spite of their dislike of his policy on many points. His administration (1897–1901) saw the adoption of the highest tariff rate in US history and the rise of US imperialism. In his first term the Spanish–American War (1898) brought the USA possession of Puerto Rico, Guam and the Philippines, and its colonial empire was further increased by the annexation of Hawaii. The domain of US trade was likewise protected and extended by the proclamation of the Open Door Policy in China. Less than a year into his second term, McKinley was shot by an anarchist, Leon F Czolgosz, in Buffalo, New York, and died eight days later. 📖 M K Leech, *In the Days of McKinley* (1959)

MacKinnon, Catherine 1946–
US feminist writer and legal scholar
Born in Minneapolis, Minnesota, she studied at Smith College and Yale Law School before studying for a PhD in political science at Yale. Her first publication arose from an extended student essay, *Sexual Harassment of Working Women: A Case of Sex Discrimination* (1979). In 1986 her fight for equality in the workplace bore fruit, when the Supreme Court decreed that sexual harassment was sex discrimination. With feminist writer Andrea Dworkin, she formulated an ordinance which classified pornography as a human rights violation; it was, however, rejected in the courts. McKinnon has also lectured and written extensively on the related issues of rape and abortion, as well as working with Croatian and Muslim women demanding justice for Serbian sexual atrocities. Her publications include *Feminism Unmodified: A Discourse on Life and Law* (1987) and *Only Words* (1994).

Mackinnon, Donald Mackenzie 1913–94
Scottish philosopher of religion
Born in Oban, Argyll, he was Professor of Moral Philosophy at Aberdeen (1947–60) and of Philosophy of Religion at Cambridge (1960–78). He explored the relations between theology, metaphysics and moral philosophy, championing realism over idealism. His wide concerns, ranging from the theory of knowledge to moral freedom and political action, and from Marxist-Leninism to a theological basis for unilateral disarmament, are evidenced in numerous essays, some of which are collected in *Borderlands of Theology* (1968), *Explorations in Theology 5* (1979) and *Themes in Theology* (1988). His 1965–66 Gifford Lectures were published as *The Problem of Metaphysics* (1974).

Mackintosh, Charles Rennie 1868–1928
Scottish architect, designer and watercolourist
Born in Glasgow, he attended Allan Glen's School before starting his architectural apprenticeship and in 1900 marrying Margaret MacDonald. His architectural output, though not large and mostly within the Glasgow region, exercised very considerable influence on European design and he was both a leader of the 'Glasgow Style', a movement related to Art Nouveau, and the outstanding exponent of Art Nouveau in Scotland. His works include the Glasgow School of Art (1897–1909), the Cranston

tearooms, and houses like Hill House in Helensburgh (1903–04). His style contrasted strong rectilinear structures and elements with subtle curved motifs, and in his houses there are deliberate references to traditional Scottish architecture. His designs also included detailed interior design, textiles, furniture and metalwork. His work was exhibited at the Vienna Secession Exhibition in 1900, where it was much admired. In 1914 he left Scotland and did no further major architectural work. In his later years he turned to painting, and produced a series of exquisite watercolours, chiefly in France (1923–27).

Mackintosh, Elizabeth See Tey, Josephine

Mackintosh, Hugh Ross 1870–1936
Scottish theologian
He was born in Paisley, Renfrewshire. As Professor of Systematic Theology at New College, Edinburgh (1904–36) and Moderator of the General Assembly of the Church of Scotland (1932), he sought to spread understanding of developments in Continental theology, which he had studied at Marburg. He helped produce translations of Albrecht Ritschl's *Justification and Reconciliation* and Friedrich Schleiermacher's *The Christian Faith*, and his 1933 Croall Lectures on trends from Schleiermacher to Karl Barth, described by John Baillie as 'a fine mingling of generous appreciation with stern rebuke', were published posthumously as *Types of Modern Theology* (1937). Earlier books of note include *The Doctrine of the Person of Jesus Christ* (1912) and *The Christian Experience of Forgiveness* (1927).

Mackintosh, Sir James 1765–1832
Scottish writer
Born in Aldourie, Inverness-shire, he studied medicine at Aberdeen, then settled in London as a journalist. His *Vindiciae Gallicae* (1791) was written as a defence of the French Revolution in reply to Edmund Burke's *Reflections on the French Revolution* (he later recanted his views in *On the State of France*, 1815). He was called to the Bar in 1795, and in 1806 was appointed judge of Bombay's Admiralty Court. On his return he became Whig MP for Nairn (1813). He published a number of works on history and philosophy.

Macklin, Charles, *originally* Charles McLaughlin
c.1697–1797
Irish actor
He was born in the North of Ireland and after a wild, unsettled youth, he acted in Bristol and Bath, and at Drury Lane from 1733. His popularity grew and in 1741 he appeared in his greatest role, Shylock. From then on he was considered one of the best actors of his day, successful in both tragedy and comedy. In 1735 he killed a fellow actor in a quarrel over a wig, was tried for murder and found guilty of manslaughter, but seems to have escaped punishment. He wrote a tragedy and several farces and comedies, of which *Love à la Mode* (1759) and *The Man of the World* (1781) were printed. His last performance was at Covent Garden in 1789.

Mackmurdo, Arthur Heygate 1851–1942
English architect and designer
Born in London, he studied architecture, then came under the influence of his friends John Ruskin and William Morris, and became a central but very individual member of the Art and Crafts movement. In 1875 he set up in architectural practice and in 1882 was a founder of the Century Guild, a group which designed for all aspects of interiors. He himself designed furniture, textiles, metalwork and for print. The title page of his book, *Wren's City Churches* (1883), an inexplicably free, linear design for a book on classical architecture, but which does resemble other examples of his decorative work, is often seen as a forerunner of Art Nouveau.

McKnight Kauffer, Edward 1890–1954
US poster designer, illustrator and artist
Born and educated in the USA, where he trained as a painter, he went to England in 1914. In 1921 he gave up painting for commercial art and designed posters for the Underground Railway Co, London Transport Board, Shell-Mex, BP, Great Western Railway, General Post Office, The Orient Line, Gas Light and Coke Co, and many others. He also illustrated a number of books including *Don Quixote* (1930) and T S Eliot's *Triumphal March* (1931). He designed a wrapper for the *Studio* and a number of book jackets. In addition, he designed sets and costumes for various productions, including the ballet *Checkmate* in 1937.

MacLaine, Shirley, *originally* Shirley McLean Beaty 1934–
US actress
Born in Richmond, Virginia, she entered showbusiness as a teenager and made her film debut in Alfred Hitchcock's black comedy *The Trouble With Harry* (1955). Adept at light comedy, she had an impish good-humour and waif-like appearance that made her an unconventional leading lady, and Hollywood struggled at first to showcase her talent. She won the first of five Best Actress Academy Award nominations for her role opposite Frank Sinatra in *Some Came Running* (1958), and a second for her heart-rending performance in Billy Wilder's *The Apartment* (1960). She appeared in several lavish 1960s productions, was acclaimed in the musical *Sweet Charity* (1968), and has starred in such successful films as *Being There* (1979), *Terms of Endearment* (1983) for which she finally won her coveted Best Actress Academy Award, *Steel Magnolias* (1989), *Postcards From The Edge* (1990) and *The Evening Star* (1996). Her numerous volumes of soul-searching autobiography include *Don't Fall Off The Mountain* (1971), *Out on a Limb* (1983), *Going Within* (1989) and *My Lucky Stars* (1995). She is the sister of the actor Warren Beatty.

McLaren, Dame Anne Laura 1927–
Welsh developmental biologist and geneticist
Raised in Tal-y-cafn, near Conwy, she obtained a PhD from Oxford, and later joined the Agricultural Research Council's Unit of Animal Genetics in Edinburgh (1959). She was director of the Medical Research Council's Mammalian Development Unit (1974–92) and became a principal research associate at the Wellcome Trust/Cancer Campaign Research Institute in Cambridge. She has published extensively and is best known for her discovery and isolation of the embryonal carcinoma cell line. This cell type can develop into many different cell types, thus enabling the study of the environmental and genetic factors which cause cells to develop in a particular way; it is also of great value in studying the nature of cancer growth. She received the Scientific Medal of the Zoological Society of London in 1967, was elected FRS in 1975 (foreign secretary 1991 and vice-president 1992, the first woman to serve as an officer of the Royal Society), receiving its gold medal in 1990, and was created DBE in 1993.

McLaren, Bill 1923–
Scottish rugby broadcaster and writer
Born in Hawick, Roxburghshire, he was a wing-forward for Hawick, and was selected for a Scottish trial, but injury prevented him from playing. After retiring from the game he combined a career as a physical education teacher with journalism, starting off with a local paper before making his first broadcast in 1953. As the BBC's chief rugby union commentator, his love and knowledge of the game have given him an unrivalled reputation as a sports broadcaster of warmth, intelligence and integrity, a

reputation enhanced by his loyalty to the BBC despite a lucrative offer to move to the independent network for the 1991 World Cup.

Maclaren, Charles 1782–1866
Scottish writer and editor

Born in Ormiston, East Lothian, he was the co-founder (1817) and first editor of *The Scotsman* (1820–45), editor of the *Encyclopaedia Britannica* (6th edn 1820–23) and wrote *Geology of Fife and the Lothians* (1839).

Maclaren, Ian, *pseudonym of* John Watson
1850–1907
Scottish clergyman and writer

He was born in Manningtree, Essex, England, and was a Presbyterian minister in Liverpool from 1880 to 1895. After the success of *Beside the Bonnie Brier Bush* (1894), he gave the stories the motto 'kailyard' (meaning cabbage patch) which gave rise to the 'Kailyard School' of Scottish writers; *Days of Auld Lang Syne* (1895) and others followed. He also wrote religious works, such as *Children of the Resurrection* (1912). 🕮 W R Nicoll, *Ian Maclaren* (1908)

McLaren, Norman 1914–87
Scottish animator

Born in Stirling, he studied interior design at the Glasgow School of Art and became an avid cineaste, mixing live action and drawn animation in his own first films like *Camera Makes Whoopee* (1934) and *Hell Unlimited* (1934). Later employed at the General Post Office Film Unit, he emigrated to Canada in 1941, ultimately running the animation department at the National Film Board. An innovator and experimentalist, he worked in many different forms from hand-drawn works like *Hoppity Hop* (1946) to the three-dimensional *Around is Around* (1952), and *Rhymetic* (1956), a paper cut-out film. He also devised a pixillation technique for animating human actors. Later, he made further advances in matching sound and visuals with *Synchrony* (1971) and created a trio of live-action dance studies that culminated in *Narcissus* (1981–83) before his retirement in 1983.

McLaughlin, John 1942–
English jazz guitarist and composer

He was born in Doncaster. He played with British blues, rock and free jazz groups in the 1960s, and recorded two classic records, *Extrapolation* (1969) and *My Goal's Beyond* (1970). He played on Miles Davis's seminal jazz-fusion albums *In A Silent Way* (1969) and *Bitches Brew* (1970), before forming his own fusion group, The Mahavishnu Orchestra, in 1971. His interest in Indian music and culture was manifest both in that band, and more overtly in Shakti, a collaboration with Indian musicians. Since the late-1970s, he has alternated between acoustic and electric guitars, most often in a trio setting, and has written classical works, including a guitar concerto. He returned directly to jazz roots with imaginative tributes to John Coltrane and Bill Evans in the mid-1990s.

McLaughlin, (Mary) Louise 1847–1939
US artist

After studying at the McMicken School of Design in Cincinnati, she began to experiment with slip-painting and was influenced by the Limoges ceramics; her work with the underglazing techniques known as faience; led her style to be known as 'Cincinnati Limoges' or 'Cincinnati faience' ware. However, she was forced to abandon this work in 1885 due to a lack of facilities. She founded the Cincinnati Art Pottery Club in 1879 with Clara Newton and Laura Ann Fry to encourage other women, and fired their work at the Coultry Pottery. In 1895 she patented a new method of decoration called 'American faience'. Her most successful work, produced around 1901, was named 'Losanti' (the original name for

Cincinnati being Losantiville), a high-fired translucent porcelain carved and filled with delicate glazes. McLaughlin abandoned ceramics entirely in 1906.

MacLaurin, Colin 1698–1746
Scottish mathematician

Born in Kilmodan, Argyll, he graduated from the University of Glasgow (1713), and became professor at Aberdeen (1717). In 1725 he was appointed to the chair of mathematics at Edinburgh University on Isaac Newton's recommendation. He published *Geometria organica* in 1720, and his best-known work, *Treatise on fluxions* (1742), gave a systematic account of Newton's approach to the calculus, taking a geometric, rather than analytical, point of view. This is often thought to have contributed to the neglect of analysis in 18th-century Great Britain.

MacLaurin, Richard Cockburn 1870–1920
New Zealand mathematician and academic

He was born in Scotland and his family emigrated to New Zealand when he was four. He read mathematics at Auckland University and Cambridge, and became president of the Massachusetts Institute of Technology (MIT). During his presidency the MIT became a leading scientific and educational body.

MacLean, Alistair 1922–87
Scottish author

Born in Glasgow, he was educated at Glasgow University and served in the Royal Navy (1941–46). In 1954, while a schoolteacher, he won a short-story competition held by the *Glasgow Herald*, contributing a tale of adventure at sea. At the suggestion of William Collins, the publishers, he produced a full-length novel, *HMS Ulysses*, the next year, and this epic story of wartime bravery became an immediate bestseller. He followed it with *The Guns of Navarone* (1957), and turned to full-time writing. He preferred the term 'adventure story' to 'novel' in describing his work. His settings are worldwide, including the China Seas (*South by Java Head*, 1958), Greenland (*Night Without End*, 1960), Florida (*Fear is the Key*, 1961), the Scottish islands (*When Eight Bells Toll*, 1966), a polar scientific station (*Ice Station Zebra*, 1963) and the Camargue (*Caravan to Vaccares*, 1970). As well as two secret service thrillers (written as 'Ian Stuart'), *The Dark Crusader* (1961) and *The Satan Bug* (1962), he wrote a Western (*Breakheart Pass*, 1974) and biographies of T E Lawrence and Captain Cook. Other titles include *Where Eagles Dare* (1967), *Force Ten From Navarone* (1968) and *Athabasca* (1980). Most of his stories were made into highly successful films. 🕮 Jack Webster, *Alistair MacLean: A Life* (1991)

McLean, Bruce 1944–
Scottish artist

Born in Glasgow, he attended Glasgow School of Art and St Martin's School of Art, London. In 1971 he became a lecturer at Maidstone College of Art and formed The Pose Band, Nice Style, a group of performance artists. The aim of his performance art was to parody the self-regard of the art establishment. Although continuing to produce performances, he has also turned to painting and other forms of visual art, including ceramics.

Maclean, Donald Duart 1913–83
English double-agent

Born in London, the son of Liberal cabinet minister, Sir Donald Maclean, he was educated at Gresham's School and studied at Trinity College, Cambridge, at the same time as Anthony Blunt, Guy Burgess and Kim Philby. Similarly influenced by communism, he joined the diplomatic service in 1935, working in Paris, Washington (1944–48) and Cairo (1948–50), and from 1944 was a Soviet agent. After a 'nervous breakdown' in 1950, he became head of the American department of the Foreign Office, but by 1951 was a suspected traitor, and in May of that year, after Philby's warning, disappeared with Burgess to the USSR. He was joined in 1953 by his wife, Melinda (b.1916) and children, but she left him to marry Philby in 1966. Maclean became a respected Soviet citizen, working for the Foreign Ministry and at the Institute of World Economic and International Relations. In 1970 he published *British Policy Since Suez, 1956–68*. 📖 Robert Cecil, *A Divided Life: A Biography of Donald Maclean* (1988)

Maclean, Sir Fitzroy Hew 1911–96
Scottish diplomat and soldier

He was educated at Eton and Cambridge, served with the Foreign Office from 1933, and in World War II distinguished himself as commander of the British military mission to the Yugoslav partisans (1943–45). Conservative MP for Lancaster from 1941, and for Bute and North Ayrshire from 1959, he was Under-Secretary for War from 1954 to 1957. His *Eastern Approaches* (1949) *Disputed Barricade* (1957), *A Person from England* (1958), and *Back from Bokhara* (1959) gained him a considerable reputation.

McLean, John 1785–1861
US jurist

Born in Morris County, New Jersey, he was trained as a lawyer in Ohio and served as a member of Congress (1812–16) and a judge of the Ohio supreme court. As Postmaster-General (1823–29), he reformed the entire US postal system and instituted a system of appointments based on merit. He served on the Supreme Court from 1829 and is remembered for his dissenting opinion in the **Dred Scott** case, in which he argued that slavery has no fundamental legal sanction in the USA.

Maclean, John 1879–1923
Scottish Socialist politician

He was born in Pollokshaws, Glasgow, and educated at Pollokshaws Academy and Queen's Park School. Sacked from his post as a schoolteacher in Govan in 1915, he became a full-time Marxist educator and organizer. His classes recruited many working men, and in 1916 he formed the Scottish Labour College. A member of the British Socialist Party before the World War I, he became Soviet consul on the Clyde after the Russian Revolution. When the Communist Party was formed he refused to join, instead setting up the Scottish Workers' Party, which promoted a more nationalistic message. He was arrested six times between 1916 and 1923 on various charges of sedition and incitement to strike. His health was badly broken during these prison sentences and he died young.

MacLean, Sorley, Gaelic Somhairle MacGill-Eain 1911–96
Scottish Gaelic poet

Born on the island of Raasay, off Skye, he attended school there and on Skye before reading English at Edinburgh University. He began writing as a student, and by the end of the 1930s he was an established Scottish literary figure. In 1940 he published *Seventeen Poems for Sixpence*, which he produced with **Robert Garioch**, and in 1943, after his recovery from wounds sustained during active service at El Alamein, came *Dàin do Eimhir* ('Poems to Eimhir'), which contained many of his love lyrics addressed to the legendary Eimhir of the early Irish sagas. Influenced by the metaphysical poets as well as the ancient and later Celtic literature and traditional Gaelic song, he reinvigorated the Gaelic literary language and tradition, much as his friend **Hugh MacDiarmid** was reinstating Scots as a serious literary language. A teacher and headmaster until his retirement in 1972, he produced his major collection of poems, *Reothairt is Contraigh* ('Spring Tide and Neap Tide'), in 1977. His work has been translated and issued in bilingual editions all over the world. In 1989 his *Collected*

Poems appeared and in 1990 he received the Queen's Gold Medal for poetry. 📖 T McCaughey, in *The History of Scottish Literature* (vol 4, 1987, ed Cairns Craig)

Maclehose, Agnes, née Craig 1759–1841
Scottish literary figure

She was born in Edinburgh, the daughter of a surgeon. In 1776 she married a Glasgow lawyer, from whom she separated in 1780. She met **Robert Burns** at a party in Edinburgh in 1787, and subsequently, under the name 'Clarinda', carried on a remarkable correspondence with him. A number of Burns's poems and songs were dedicated to her.

MacLeish, Archibald 1892–1982
US poet and librarian

Born in Glencoe, Illinois, and educated at Yale and the Harvard Law School, he taught constitutional law briefly at Harvard College, but moved to Europe in 1923 to concentrate on writing. He was Librarian of Congress (1939–44), assistant Secretary of State (1944–45), co-founder of UNESCO, and Boylston Professor of Rhetoric and Oratory at Harvard University (1949–62). His many works include *The Happy Marriage* (1923), *The Pot of Earth* (1925) and *The Hamlet of A. MacLeish* (1928). For *Conquistador* (1932) he was awarded the 1932 Pulitzer Prize for poetry; for *Collected Poems 1917–1952* he was awarded a second Pulitzer Prize, the Bollingen prize and a National Book award in 1953 and for *J.B.*, a verse play, he won the Pulitzer Prize in drama and the Antoinette Perry ('Tony') award for best play in 1959. 📖 G Smith, *Archibald MacLeish* (1971)

McLennan, John Cunningham 1867–1935
Canadian physicist

Born in Ingersoll, Ontario, and educated at the University of Toronto, where he later became professor (1907–31), he did much research on electricity and the superconductivity of metals. He succeeded in liquefying helium in 1923. An early investigator of atomic and molecular energy levels, he used spectrographic techniques over a broad range of wavelengths, and often at low temperatures in the region of 20 kelvin. During the 1920s he published widely on the spectra of many materials including silicon, tin, gold, lead and hydrogen. He also made some of the earliest studies of the effect of temperature on the photoelectric effect.

McLennan, John Ferguson 1827–81
Scottish lawyer and theorist of social evolution

Born in Inverness, he was educated at King's College, Aberdeen. He then studied at Cambridge before being called to the Scottish Bar in 1857. He became parliamentary draftsman for Scotland in 1871. He is chiefly remembered for his theories of totemism and the evolution of familial organization. In *Primitive Marriage* (1865) he proposed an evolution from primitive promiscuity, through a stage of matriarchy, to patrilineal descent. He coined the terms 'exogamy' and 'endogamy', which are still in use today. He also wrote *The Patriarchal Theory*, published posthumously in 1885.

Maclennan, Robert Adam Ross 1936–
Scottish politician

Born in Glasgow, the son of an eminent gynaecologist, he attended the Glasgow Academy, Balliol College, Oxford, Trinity College, Cambridge and Columbia University, New York, before being called to the Bar in 1962. He entered parliament as Labour MP for Caithness and Sutherland in 1966 and has represented it ever since. He held junior posts in the governments of **Harold Wilson** and **James Callaghan** and was a founder-member of the Social Democratic Party (SDP) in 1981. He came to prominence in 1987 when, after **David Owen** had resigned the SDP leadership, Maclennan became a 'caretaker' leader until the terms of the merger had been agreed. He then became a leading member of the new party, the Liberal Democrats, under **Paddy Ashdown**, where he has been president, and spokesman on constitutional affairs and national heritage, since 1994.

MacLeod (of Fuinary), George Fielden MacLeod, Baron 1895–1991
Scottish Presbyterian clergyman

The second son of Sir John MacLeod, 1st Baronet, a Glasgow MP, he was educated at Winchester and Oriel College, Oxford, won the MC and Croix de Guerre in World War I, and studied theology at Edinburgh, becoming minister of St Cuthbert's there (1926–30) and at Govan in Glasgow (1930–38). He founded the Iona Community, which set about restoring the ruined abbey and monastic buildings on the historic island of Iona. As Moderator of the General Assembly of the Church of Scotland (1957–58), he created controversy by supporting the unpopular scheme to introduce bishops into the kirk in the interests of Church unity. Well known as a writer and broadcaster, he was strongly left-wing, as his *Only One Way Left* (1956) testifies. He succeeded to the baronetcy in 1924, but preferred not to use the title, and he was created a life peer in 1967. In 1986 the General Assembly finally accepted as official Church of Scotland policy the position he had argued for so long—that nuclear weapons were so immoral that their use should never be countenanced by the Church.

Macleod, Iain Norman 1913–70
British politician

Born in Skipton, Yorkshire, and educated at Fettes College, Edinburgh, and Gonville and Caius College, Cambridge, he fought in France during World War II, and after working as a member of the Conservative Party secretariat, he became an MP in 1950. He was Minister of Health (1952–55) and of Labour (1955–59), before being appointed Secretary of State for the Colonies in 1959, in which office he oversaw the granting of independence to many British territories in Africa. He was Chancellor of the Duchy of Lancaster and Leader of the House of Commons and party chairman (1961–63), then edited the *Spectator* for two years. When **Edward Heath** became leader, MacLeod was appointed shadow Chancellor (1965–70) and after the Conservative victory in 1970 he became Chancellor of the Exchequer, until his death a month later. One of the most popular figures in his party, and a gifted orator, he had been considered a leading contender for the premiership. 📖Robert Shepherd, *Iain Macleod: a biography* (1994)

Macleod, John James Rickard 1876–1935
Scottish physiologist and Nobel Prize winner

Born in Cluny, Fife, he studied at Aberdeen, Leipzig and Cambridge, and became Professor of Physiology at Western Reserve University, Cleveland (1903), and at Toronto University (1918). He published many papers on the control of respiration, and on aspects of carbohydrate metabolism, but his fame rests upon his involvement with the discovery of insulin. In 1921 he accepted **Frederick Grant Banting** into his department for research on the pancreas with **Charles Best**, and they succeeded in purifying a pancreatic extract which lowered blood sugar levels. The extract was insulin, and insulin therapy soon became the main treatment for diabetes. In 1923 Macleod and Banting were awarded the Nobel Prize for physiology or medicine. Macleod returned to Scotland in 1928 as Professor of Physiology at Aberdeen.

Mac Liammóir, Mícheál, *originally* Alfred Wilmore 1899–1978
Irish actor, painter and writer

Born in Cork, Ireland, he moved with his family to London, and became a child actor as Michael Darling in **Beerbohm Tree's** production of *Peter Pan*, with **Noël Coward** as Lost Boy. He studied art at the Slade School, becoming a distinguished painter and designer, and a proficient linguist after residence abroad. With his lifelong friend Hilton Edwards, he founded the Gate Theatre Company in Dublin (1928), having toured Ireland with the Shakespearean company of Anew McMaster (1894–1962). His company's work made the most of dramatic possibilities of Irish writing, drew in much European drama using his translations, adaptations, design and lighting, and offered bold productions of classical material. He wrote fiction, plays and memoirs in Irish and in English, and in the 1960s his one-man shows brought him an international reputation, in *The Importance of Being Oscar* (1960), about the life of **Oscar Wilde**, *I Must Be Talking to My Friends* (1963), on Irish history and literature, and *Mostly About Yeats* (1970). His film performances include Iago in **Orson Welles's** *Othello* (1949, brilliantly described in his *Put Money in Thy Purse*, 1954), and the narrator in *Tom Jones* (1963).

Maclise, Daniel 1806–70
Irish painter

Born in Cork, he made pencil portraits in Cork, and in 1827 went to London, where he studied at the school of the Royal Academy. His most notable works are his frescoes in the Royal Gallery of the House of Lords, *The Meeting of Wellington and Blücher* (1861) and *The Death of Nelson* (1864). He was also known as an illustrator of books for **Tennyson** and **Dickens**. His sketches of contemporaries in *Fraser's Magazine* (1830–38) were published in 1874 and 1883.

McLuhan, (Herbert) Marshall 1911–80
Canadian writer

Born in Edmonton, he studied English literature at the universities of Manitoba and Cambridge, and in 1946 became a professor at St Michael's College, Toronto. In 1963, having directed two surveys into culture and communication media, he was appointed director of the University of Toronto's Centre for Culture and Technology. He held the controversial view that the invention of printing, with its emphasis on the eye rather than the ear, can lead to the destruction of a cohesive, interdependent society, since it encourages humans to be more introspective, individualistic and self-centred. His publications include *The Mechanical Bride* (1951), *The Gutenberg Galaxy* (1962), *Understanding Media* (1964), *The Medium is the Message* (with Q Fiore, 1967) and *Counter-Blast* (1970). 📖D Duffy, *Marshall McLuhan* (1969)

Maclure, William 1763–1840
US geologist

Born in Ayr, Scotland, he was educated privately and soon made a large fortune as a merchant and entrepreneur. He travelled widely in Europe, Russia and the USA, and lived at times in London, Spain and Mexico. He settled in the USA around 1800. On his travels he always studied the geology and met leading geologists, and he employed a personal cartographer–naturalist (Charles Lesueur, 1778–1846) and organized expeditions with others. His work as an observer and writer in geology made him influential and he helped to found the Academy of Natural Sciences in Philadelphia, serving as its president from 1817 to 1840. His *Observations on the Geology of the United States* (1817) gives the first full account of the subject, and he went on to study the West Indies and Mexico. Maclure's later writing supported the ideas on evolution offered by **Jean-Baptiste Lamarck**. He believed that primitive rocks had diverse origins, and opposed **Abraham Werner's** theory of their exclusively sedimentary origin.

MacMahon, Marie Edmé Patrice Maurice de
1808–93
French soldier and statesman
Born in Sully near Autun, he was descended from an Irish Jacobite family. He served in Algeria and at Constantine (1837), and for his services in the Italian campaign (1859) was made marshal and Duke of Magenta. He became Governor-General of Algeria in 1864. In the Franco-Prussian War (1870–71) he commanded the 1st Army Corps, but was defeated at Wörth, and captured at Sedan. After the war, as commander of the army of Versailles he suppressed the Commune (1871). In 1873 he was elected President of the Republic for seven years, and was suspected of reactionary and monarchical leanings. He resigned in 1879.

McMahon, Sir William
1908–88
Australian politician
Born in Sydney, he studied at the university there and then qualified and practised as a solicitor. After service in World War II he became active in the Liberal Party and was elected to the House of Representatives in 1949. Under Harold Holt he became Treasurer and Deputy Leader. Precluded from the leadership on Holt's death by the veto of the Liberals' coalition partner, the Country Party, he became Prime Minister on John Gorton's resignation in 1971, but was defeated at the 1972 election. He remained Liberal leader until 1973 and retired from parliament in 1982.

McManus, Mark
1935–94
Scottish actor
Born in Hamilton, Lanarkshire, he emigrated to Australia and was briefly a professional boxer before finding some employment at the docks in Sydney. Performances with the Dockers' Amateur Theatre Group gave him a taste for acting and he turned professional in 1964, touring in Shakespeare, co-starring in the film *Ned Kelly* (1970) and appearing in such television series as *Skippy*, before returning to London in 1971. He then worked with the Royal Court and National Theatre companies and achieved television fame in *Sam* (1973–75). He was best known in the title role of *Taggart* (1985–94), a character first seen in *Killer* (1983). His many theatre appearances included *No Man's Land* (1975), *Julius Caesar* (1977) and *Macbeth* (1983).

McMaster, John Bach
1852–1932
US historian
Born in Brooklyn, New York, he studied civil engineering, but from 1883 to 1920 was Professor of American History at Pennsylvania University. He wrote a *History of the People of the US* (8 vols, 1883–1913), *Franklin as a Man of Letters* (1887) and other works.

Macmillan, Chrystal
1882–1937
Scottish feminist, pacifist and lawyer
Born in Edinburgh, she was educated at St Leonard's School in St Andrews, and at Edinburgh University where, as one of its first women graduates, she obtained a first-class degree before further study in Berlin. Called to the Bar in 1924, she never practised, but immersed herself in feminist causes. As the first woman to address the House of Lords (1908), she appealed for the right of female graduates to vote and served on a variety of committees, as well as being a leader of the National Union of Suffrage Societies, secretary of the International Women's Suffrage Alliance, and the founder of the Open Door Council (1929) which opposed legal restraints on women. As a pacifist, she was an instigator of the International Women's Congress at the Hague (1915) and Secretary of the International Alliance of Women (1913–23).

Macmillan, Daniel
1813–57
Scottish bookseller and publisher
He was born in Upper Corrie, Arran, and was apprenticed to a bookseller in Irvine at the age of 10. In 1843 he and his brother Alexander opened a bookshop in London, then moved to Cambridge. By 1844 he had branched out into publishing, first educational and, religious works and by 1855, English classics such as Charles Kingsley's *Westward Ho!* and Thomas Hughes's *Tom Brown's Schooldays*. In 1858, the year of his death, the firm opened a branch in London and by 1893 had become a limited liability company with Daniel's son, Frederick (1851–1936), as chairman. His other son, Maurice, father of Harold Macmillan, was also a partner.

MacMillan, Donald Baxter
1874–1970
US explorer
He was born in Provinceton, Massachusetts. A member of the Robert Peary Arctic expedition of 1908–09, he later carried out anthropological research among the Inuit of Labrador, and led expeditions to Greenland (1913–17). He also led expeditions to Baffin Island (1921–22), North Greenland (1923–24) and the North Pole (1925).

McMillan, Edwin Mattison
1907–91
US atomic scientist and Nobel Prize winner
Born in Redondo Beach, California, he was educated at the California Institute of Technology (Caltech) and at Princeton University, where he took his doctorate in 1932. He joined the staff of the University of California at Berkeley, moving to the Lawrence Radiation Laboratory when it was founded within the university in 1934. In 1940, following up the work of Enrico Fermi who had split the uranium atom by bombarding it with low-velocity neutrons, McMillan and Philip Hauge Abelson synthesized an element heavier than uranium by bombarding uranium with neutrons in the Berkeley cyclotron. They called this new silvery metal 'neptunium' and the synthesis of this first 'transuranic' element marked the beginning of a new epoch in science and in world affairs. The following year Glen Theodore Seaborg, also working at Berkeley, synthesized plutonium, leading on to the development of the atomic bomb. McMillan spent the rest of World War II working on radar and sonar, and on the atomic bomb at Los Alamos. He was appointed to the chair at Berkeley in 1946 and to the directorship of the Lawrence Radiation Laboratory in 1958, retiring in 1973. From 1968 to 1971 he was chairman of the US National Academy of Sciences. He was awarded the Nobel Prize for chemistry, jointly with Seaborg, in 1951.

Macmillan, (Maurice) Harold, 1st Earl of Stockton
1894–1986
English Conservative statesman
Born in London, he was educated at Eton, and at Balliol College, Oxford, his studies having been interrupted by service with the Grenadier Guards during World War I, in which he was seriously wounded. In 1919–20 he was in Canada as aide-de-camp to the Governor-General, the Duke of Devonshire, whose daughter Lady Dorothy (d.1966) he married. Returning to Britain, he partnered his brother Daniel in the family publishing firm, but preserved his interest in politics and stood successfully as Conservative MP for Stockton-on-Tees in 1924; he was defeated in 1929, but re-elected in 1931. Not always willing to conform to the party line, he remained a backbencher until 1940, when Churchill made him Parliamentary Secretary to the Ministry of Supply. After a brief spell as Colonial Under-Secretary, in 1942 he was sent to North Africa to fill the new Cabinet post of Minister Resident at Allied Headquarters where he showed great acumen and proved his ability as a mediator in the many clashes of factions and personalities. Defeated in the Labour landslide of 1945, he was returned later the same year for Bromley, which he held until he retired in 1964. He was Minister of Housing (1951–54), silencing general doubts

by achieving his promised target of 300,000 houses in a year. He was Minister of Defence from autumn to spring 1954–55, and thereafter Foreign Minister to the end of 1955, when he was appointed Chancellor of the Exchequer. On **Anthony Eden**'s resignation in 1957 he emerged, in **R A Butler**'s words, as 'the best Prime Minister we have', his appointment being received without enthusiasm, for as an intellectual and a dyed-in-the-wool aristocrat he was regarded with suspicion by many. Nevertheless, his economic expansionism at home, his resolution in foreign affairs, his integrity, and his infectious optimism inspired confidence, and his popularity soared. Having told the people in 1957 that most 'have never had it so good', he embarked upon a new term as Prime Minister in 1959. His 'wind of change' speech in Cape Town (1960) acknowledged the inevitability of African independence. In 1962, after some electoral setbacks, he carried out a drastic 'purge' of his government, involving seven Cabinet Ministers. Further setbacks followed, such as the **Profumo** scandal (1963), and ill health brought about his reluctant resignation in 1963. He wrote *Winds of Change* (1966), *The Blast of War* (1967), *Tides of Fortune* (1969), *Riding the Storm* (1971), *Pointing the Way* and *At The End of the Day* (both 1972). An earldom was bestowed upon him on his 90th birthday in 1984 and he took the title Earl of Stockton. ▣ Nigel Fisher, *Harold Macmillan* (1982)

Macmillan, Sir Kenneth 1929–92
Scottish ballet-dancer and choreographer

Born in Dunfermline, Fife, he was one of the original members of the Sadler's Wells Theatre Ballet (1946–48). In 1953 he began to choreograph with the Royal Ballet (*Somnambulism*), and, after three years as director at the Berlin Opera (1966–69), returned to the Royal Ballet in 1970 as artistic director. In 1977 he became the company's principal choreographer. His works include *Romeo and Juliet* (1965), *The Seven Deadly Sins* (1973), *Élite Syncopations* and *Manon* (both 1974), *Mayerling* (1978), *Isadora* (1981) and *The Judas Tree* (1992). As well as creating ballets for many of the world's foremost companies, he worked on theatre, television, and musical shows. ▣ Edward Thorpe, *Kenneth Macmillan, the Man and the Ballets* (1985)

Macmillan, Kirkpatrick 1813–78
Scottish inventor

Born near Thornhill, Dumfriesshire, he was a farm labourer and a coachman before becoming a blacksmith in Keir. Having caught sight of a hobby-horse being ridden in the neighbourhood he made one himself. After a while he began to experiment with pedals and cranks as a means of propulsion. He applied pedals to a tricycle in 1834, and in 1840 succeeded in building the world's first primitive bicycle, riding it as far afield as Dumfries and, in two days, to Glasgow, some 70 miles (112.6km) to the north. He never patented his invention and it was widely copied, to such an extent that for many years afterwards it was usually credited to one of his imitators, Gavin Dalzell of Lesmahagow.

McMillan, Margaret 1860–1931
British educational reformer

Born in New York in the USA, and brought up near Inverness, Scotland, she was educated in Frankfurt, Geneva and Lausanne, but returned to Great Britain and campaigned ceaselessly in the industrial north of England for medical inspection and school clinics. In 1902 she joined her sister Rachel (1859–1917) in London, where they opened the first school clinic (1908), and the first open-air nursery school (1914). After Rachel's death, the Rachel McMillan Training College for nursery and infant teachers was established as a memorial.

MacMurrough, Dermot, *Irish Gaelic* Diarmaid Mac Murchadha Uí, *surname usually anglicized as* Murphy 1110–71
Irish ruler

He was a subject of **Henry II**. Succeeding his father as King of Leinster in 1126, he was ousted by the King of Connaught for eloping with Devorgilla, wife of Tiernan O'Rourke (or O'Ruark), King of Breifne. Henry II permitted him to recruit allies among the Normans of Wales, and their principal leader, Richard de Clare (2nd Earl of Pembroke, nicknamed Strongbow, c.1130–1176) arrived in 1170. He took Waterford, married Dermot's daughter Aoife, and with the Normans and Leinstermen captured the Norse city of Dublin. Strongbow succeeded Dermot (1171) as ruler of Leinster but was forced to resubmit to Henry II. Posterity cast Dermot as the archetypal traitor, as in **W B Yeats**'s play, *The Dreaming of the Bones* (1921).

McMurtry, Larry Jeff 1936–
US novelist

Born in Wichita Falls, Texas, and educated at North Texas State College, Denton, and Rice University, Houston, he helped to establish the Western as a serious contemporary genre through his vision of the history of Texas. Hollywood's interest in his work consolidated his reputation: *Horseman, Pass By* (1961) was successfully filmed, as was *Hud*. McMurtry also wrote the screenplay for Peter Bogdanovich's prize-winning movie of his third novel, *The Last Picture Show* (1966). Later books also dealt with the opposition of freedom and rootedness, and a kind of heroic resistance to circumstance. These include *All My Friends are Going to be Strangers* (1972), *Terms of Endearment* (1975), the basis of a third successful film, and *Cadillac Jack* (1982). Subsequent works include *Lonesome Dove* (1985), the epic story of a cattle drive from Texas to Montana, *Some Can Whistle* (1989) and *Buffalo Girls* (1990). ▣ C D Peavy, *Larry McMurtry* (1977)

Macnaghten, Edward Macnaghten, Baron 1830–1913
English judge

Born in London, he was educated at Trinity College, Dublin, and Cambridge. He became an MP in 1880, declined to be Home Secretary or a judge and was then appointed direct from the Bar in 1887 to be a Lord-of-Appeal-in-Ordinary and a life peer. His writings were impressive for their literary quality and their wit, but also for his ability to extract a leading principle from a mass of authority. He was also a leader in reforming professional legal education.

McNair (of Gleniffer), Arnold Duncan McNair, 1st Baron 1885–1975
English legal scholar and judge

Born in London, he was educated at Aldenham School and Gonville and Caius College, Cambridge. He taught law at London and Cambridge and served as Vice-Chancellor of Liverpool University. A judge of the International Court of Justice (1946–55), and its president (1952–55), he then became president of the European Court of Human Rights (1959–65). He was also president of the Institute of International Law (1949–50). His writings include *Law of Treaties* (1961), *International Law Opinions* (3 vols, 1956) and he edited **Lassa Oppenheim**'s *International Law* (1905–06).

Macnamara, Dame (Annie) Jean 1899–1968
Australian physician

Born in Beechworth, Victoria, and educated at Melbourne University, she worked in local hospitals where she developed an interest in 'infantile paralysis'. During the poliomyelitis epidemic of 1925, she tested the use of immune serum and, convinced of its efficacy, visited England, the USA and Canada with the aid of a Rockefeller scholarship. With **Macfarlane Burnet**, she found that there was more than one strain of polio virus, a discovery which led to the development of the 'Salk vaccine' (named after US virologist **Jonas Salk**). She also supported the experimental treatment developed by **Elizabeth Kenny**, and introduced the first artificial respirator (iron lung) into Australia. She was created a DBE in 1935, and later became involved in the controversial introduction of the disease myxomatosis as a means of controlling the rabbit population of Australia. In the early 1950s it was estimated that as a result of her efforts the wool industry had saved over £30 million.

McNamara, Robert Strange 1916–
US Democrat politician and businessman
Born in San Francisco, he served in the US air force (1943–46), then worked his way up in the Ford Motor Company to be president by 1960. In 1961 he joined the **Kennedy** administration as Secretary of Defense, in which post he was an early influential advocate of the escalation of the Vietnam War. By 1967 he was convinced that the war was unwinnable, but his pleas to seek a diplomatic solution went unheeded, and he resigned to become president of the World Bank (1968–81). In the 1980s he emerged as a critic of the nuclear arms race. He reawakened the Vietnam controversy with his 1995 memoir *In Retrospect: The Tragedy and Lessons of Vietnam*, which examined the blunders of the US government and expressed regret for his role.

McNaught, William 1813–81
Scottish mechanical engineer and inventor
Born in Paisley, Strathclyde, he was apprenticed to **Robert Napier** at the age of 14 and attended classes at the Andersonian Institution in Glasgow. Eight years later he joined his father in the manufacture of steam-engine components, and became aware of the need felt by many industrialists for an increase in the power of the single-cylinder low-pressure beam engines they had already installed in their factories. He conceived the idea in 1845 of adding a second smaller cylinder operating at a higher pressure which emitted its spent steam into the original cylinder where its remaining energy could be utilized. For many years the process of adding an extra cylinder to an existing engine was called 'McNaughting'.

McNaughton, Andrew George Latta
1887–1966
Canadian soldier
He was born in Moosomin, Saskatchewan. Educated at McGill University, he became a lecturer in engineering after obtaining a commission in the artillery arm of the Canadian militia. He served in World War I, and attained the rank of brigadier-general. Chief of General Staff (1929–35), he was president of the National Research Council from 1935 to 1939, and during World War II commanded the 1st Canadian Division (1939), Canadian Corps (1940) and 1st Canadian Army (1942–43) as lieutenant-general.

McNaughton, Daniel 19th century
English murderer
He was tried in 1843 for the murder of Edward Drummond, private secretary to Sir **Robert Peel**. The question arose whether he knew the nature of his act. The criminal responsibility of the insane is now embodied in the judges' 'answers', known as the McNaughton Rules. They are that (a) every man is presumed sane until the contrary is proved and (b) it must be clearly proved that at the time of committing the act, the accused's reason was impaired so as not to know the nature of the act, or that he was doing wrong.

Macnee, (Daniel) Patrick 1922–
English actor

Born in London, a cousin of the actor **David Niven**, he chose acting as a career after being expelled from Eton College. He followed his film debut in *Sailors Three* (1940) with appearances in such films as *The Life and Death of Colonel Blimp* (1943), *Hamlet* (1948), *Les Girls* (1957), *The Sea Wolves* (1980) and *A View to a Kill* (1985), and often appeared as cowboys in Hollywood Westerns. On television, he appeared in the Canadian series *The Moonstone* and played a sheriff in the US Western series *Rawhide*, but it was as the archetypal Englishman John Steed in the 1960s fantasy espionage series *The Avengers* (1961–69) and its sequel, *The New Avengers* (1976–77), that he became best known. 📖 *Blind in One Ear* (1988)

MacNeice, (Frederick) Louis 1907–63
Northern Irish poet
Born in Belfast, he was educated at Marlborough and at Merton College, Oxford, and became a lecturer in classics at Birmingham (1930–36) and in Greek at Bedford College, University of London (1936–40). He was closely associated with the British left-wing poets of the 1930s, especially **W H Auden**, with whom he wrote *Letters from Iceland* (1937). Among his volumes of poetry are *Blind Fireworks* (1929), *Autumn Journal* (1938), *Collected Poems* (1949), *Autumn Sequel* (1954), and *Eighty-Five Poems* and *Solstices* (both 1961). He was the author of a novel, *Round about Way* (1932, under the pseudonym of Louis Malone), and several verse plays for radio, notably *The Dark Tower* (1947), as well as translations of **Aeschylus** and of **Goethe's** *Faust*. He also produced several volumes of literary criticism. A volume of autobiography, *The Strings Are False*, appeared posthumously in 1965, and his *Collected Poems* in 1966.

McNeill, Billy (William), *known as* Caesar 1940–
Scottish footballer and manager
Born in Bellshill, Lanarkshire, he was the backbone of the highly successful Glasgow Celtic side between 1965 and 1975. He received the European Cup after Celtic's victory at Lisbon in 1967, and had nine championship and seven Scottish Cup medals. He was capped 29 times. Appointed to succeed **Jock Stein** as manager of his old club in 1978, he left after a quarrel with the board, but following comparatively unsuccessful spells with Manchester City and Aston Villa he returned in 1987; in his first season he guided Celtic to League and Cup victory in the club's centenary year. They also won the 1989 Scottish Cup before McNeil was forced to leave the club in 1991.

McNeill, F(lorence) Marian 1885–1973
Scottish folklorist
Born in Saint Mary's Holm, Orkney, she was educated there and at the universities of Glasgow and Edinburgh, becoming active as a suffragette. She worked for the Association for Moral and Social Hygiene, then as a tutor in Athens and as a freelance journalist in London. Returning to Scotland in 1926, she worked on the *Scottish National Dictionary*, but remains best known for her work as a folklorist. Her reputation is based upon *The Scots Kitchen* (1929), a study of Scottish culinary history. *The Silver Bough* (1957–68) is a four-volume study of the folklore, festivals and traditions of Scotland, and *Hallowe'en* (1970) uses photographs and illustrations to explore the origins of the rites and ceremonies associated with this occasion in Scotland.

MacNeill, John, *pen name* Eoin 1867–1945
Irish historian and nationalist
Born in Glenarm, County Antrim, and educated at St Malachy's College, Belfast, he made himself an authority on Old Irish. He ultimately became Professor of Early Irish history at University College, Dublin (1908–45), and

his pioneer work in Irish history strongly asserted the strength of its legal and cultural civilization, exhibited in the inspirational lectures *Phases of Irish History* (1919), and the more formal works *Celtic Ireland* (1921) and *Early Irish Laws and Institutions* (1935). In 1913 he inspired and led the Irish Volunteers. His organization was taken over by John Redmond, who persuaded most of its members to support the Allied cause in 1914 after the outbreak of World War I. Irish Republican Brotherhood manipulation steered MacNeill's Volunteers towards insurrection in 1916 without his knowledge. In the end he accepted the insurrection with reluctance but countermanded it when it became clear German aid would fail. After the Dublin Rising MacNeill was interned, and played a part in organizing the new Sinn Féin Party and its abstentionist body Dáil Éireann where, as MP for Derry, he was given Cabinet status. He supported the Anglo-Irish Treaty and was Minister for Education in the first Irish Free State government. He was delegate for his government to the Boundary Commission which shattered Irish nationalist hopes of a revision of Irish partition in the Catholics' favour; he resigned rather than accept its verdict, and the boundary was left unchanged.

Maconchy, Dame Elizabeth Violet 1907–94
English composer

Born in Broxbourne, Hertfordshire, of Irish parentage, she studied under Ralph Vaughan Williams at the Royal College of Music and in 1929 went to Prague, where her first major work, a piano concerto, was performed (1930). Her suite, *The Land*, was performed at the London Proms the same year, and her early works were often written for festivals of the International Society for Contemporary Music. Her most characteristic work is in the field of chamber music, and among her best-known compositions are her *Symphony* (1953) and overture *Proud Thames*, also written in Coronation Year, a carol cantata *A Christmas Morning* (1962), a choral and orchestral work *Samson and the Gates of Gaza* (1963), an opera for children, *The King of the Golden River* (1975), *Heloise and Abelard* (1978) and *My Dark Heart* (1981). She also wrote a group of one-act operas, 12 string quartets and songs. She was made a DBE in 1987. Her daughter, Nicola Frances LeFanu (1947–), is also a composer.

Macphail, Agnes Campbell, *née* Campbell 1890–1954
Canadian suffragette and politician

She was born in Grey County, Ontario, and became a schoolteacher. She became involved with the women's suffrage movement and was elected Canada's first woman MP for the United Farmers of Ontario (1921–40). She was a leader of the Co-operative Commonwealth Federation of Canada, which had been formed in 1933 and represented Canada in the Assembly of the League of Nations.

McPherson, Aimee Semple, *née* Kennedy 1890–1944
US Pentecostal evangelist

She was born near Ingersoll, Ontario, Canada, into a Salvation Army family. She became a Pentecostalist and married a preacher, Robert Semple. They went to China as missionaries but on his death in 1910, she returned to North America and subsequently embarked on a hugely successful evangelistic career. In 1918 she founded the Foursquare Gospel movement in Los Angeles, and for nearly two decades she conducted a preaching and healing ministry in the Angelus Temple, Los Angeles, which cost her followers $1.5 million to construct. She had her own radio station, bible school, magazine, and social service work. Considerable controversy surrounded her: she was continually embroiled in legal suits against her, and disappeared for five weeks in a bizarre and unexplained incident in 1926 (she claimed she was kidnapped but was later suspected to have been involved in a romantic liaison). Even her death raised questions: authorities differ on whether it was due to a heart attack or an overdose of barbiturates. Her books include *This is That* (1923), *In the Service of the King* (1927) and *Give Me My Own God* (1936).

Macpherson, James 1736–96
Scottish poet and 'translator' of Ossian

Born in Ruthven, Inverness-shire, he was educated at King's College and Marischal College, Aberdeen, and studied for the ministry, but in 1756 became a village schoolmaster in Ruthven. In 1758 he published an epic poem, *The Highlander*, and two years later published some fragments of Gaelic oral poetry *Fragments of Ancient Poetry Collected in the Highlands of Scotland* (1870). The introduction (by Hugh Blair) suggested that a poetic epic relating to the legendary hero Fingal, as told by his son Ossian, was still extant. In 1760 Macpherson was commissioned by the Faculty of Advocates in Edinburgh to tour the Highlands in search of this material, which he published in 1762 as *Fingal: an Ancient Epic Poem in Six Books*; it was followed by *Temora, an Epic Poem, in Eight Books* (1763). They were received with huge acclaim, but their authenticity was soon questioned and Macpherson was unable to produce the originals. He seems, in fact, to have used some original Gaelic poetry, greatly amended, and invented the rest. In 1763 he was appointed Surveyor-General of the Floridas, but soon returned to London and became a wealthy merchant with interests in the East India Company. He was MP for Camelford from 1780 and was buried, at his own request and expense, in Westminster Abbey.

Macpherson, Robert d.1872
Scottish artist and pioneering photographer

Born in Forfarshire, he studied medicine in Edinburgh, but left to pursue an artistic career and went to Italy (1840), living in Rome for the rest of his life. He made a living as a painter and picture-dealer for some years before taking up photography in 1851; he became one of the most prolific and successful photographers in Italy. He exhibited internationally and is regarded as one of the greatest architectural photographers, and was also the inventor of a photo-lithographic process.

McQuaid, John Charles 1895–1973
Irish prelate

Born in Cootehill, County Cavan, and educated there, and in Dublin and Rome, he was ordained priest in the Holy Ghost Fathers in 1924, becoming dean of studies in 1925, and then president at his order's Blackrock College in 1931. An influential commentator on social and moral questions, he was credited with strong links to Éamon de Valera, whose sons were his pupils, and this may have accounted for his being named Archbishop of Dublin by Pope Pius XII in 1940, the only Irish bishop from a religious order during his papacy. He fell foul of de Valera through championing the cause of striking schoolteachers in 1947, and was reduced thereafter to opposing state policy. He played a leading part in the Irish bishops' successful objection to a national health proposal, the Mother and Child Scheme of Dr Noël Browne, whose consequent resignation from the first Costello government led to its fall in 1951. He also banned Catholics from attending Trinity College, Dublin, from 1944, being bitterly hostile to mixed religious education. He retired in 1972.

Macquarie, Lachlan, *known as* the Father of Australia 1761–1824
Scottish soldier and colonial administrator

Born on the island of Ulva, off Mull, he joined the Black Watch in 1777, and after service in North America, India and Egypt was appointed Governor of New South Wales following the deposition of Captain **William Bligh**. The colony, depressed and demoralized, populated largely by convicts and exploited by influential land-grabbers and monopolists, was raised by his energetic administration and firm rule to prosperity: its population trebled, extensive surveys were carried out, and many roads were built. In 1821 the monopolists' political manoeuvering and his own ill health compelled him to return to Great Britain. He gave his name to the Lachlan and Macquarie rivers, and to Macquarie Island.

Macquarrie, John 1919–

Scottish theologian and philosopher of religion

He was born in Renfrew, Strathclyde. A lecturer at Glasgow (1953–62), and professor at Union Theological Seminary, New York (1962–70) and at Oxford (1970–86), he has written extensively across the whole field of theology. While the influence of **Rudolf Bultmann** and **Paul Tillich** may be traced in *An Existentialist Theology* (1955) and *Principles of Christian Theology* (1966), his catholic interests may be discerned in *Paths in Spirituality* (1972), *In Search of Humanity* (1982), the Gifford Lectures *In Search of Deity* (1984), and *Theology, Church and Ministry* (1986). Students have also appreciated successive revisions of *Twentieth Century Religious Thought* (1963–88), and his editing of *A Dictionary of Christian Ethics* (1967), revised, with J F Childress, as *A New Dictionary of Christian Ethics* (1986). Later publications include *Heidegger and Christianity* (1994) and *Invitation to Faith* (1995).

McQueen, (Terence) Steve(n) 1930–80

US actor

Born in Indianapolis, Indiana, after a delinquent youth he took up acting on stage and television, and by 1955 was a film star with a reputation as a tough, unconventional rebel, both on and off the screen. He co-starred in *The Magnificent Seven* (1960), a role which helped to create his image as a laconic loner, and became the archetypal 1960s cinema hero/rebel with his performances in *The Great Escape* (1963), *The Cincinnati Kid* (1965) and *Bullitt* (1968). He attempted **Ibsen** in *An Enemy of the People* in 1977 before returning to action roles in two final films. He was married to actress Ali McGraw (1973–78), and died after a long struggle with cancer. ◫ Grady Ragsdale, *Steve McQueen: The Final Chapter* (1983)

Macquer, Pierre Joseph 1718–84

French chemist and physician

Born in Paris, he qualified in medicine in 1742. Elected to the Academy of Sciences in 1745, he studied dyes, arsenic, platinum and the properties of milk. He began lecturing at the Jardin du Roi in 1770 and was appointed professor in 1777. After helping Jean Hellot, scientific adviser to the famous porcelain factory at Sèvres, to study the effects of firing on hundreds of clays from different parts of France, he succeeded him as adviser in 1766. Macquer is best known as the author of two widely read textbooks and the first dictionary of chemistry–*Élémens de chymie théorique* (1749, 'Elements of Theoretical Chemistry') and *Élémens de chymie pratique* (1751, 'Elements of Practical Chemistry)–which provided much-needed, straightforward accounts of the state of knowledge at the time and were particularly popular in their English translations. Macquer's greatest work, *Dictionnaire de chymie* (1766), was translated into German, English, Danish and Italian. He was sympathetic to the revolutionary ideas of **Antoine Lavoisier** but died, in Paris, before he could incorporate them into a new edition of the *Dictionnaire*.

Macrae, (John) Duncan 1905–67

Scottish actor

He was born and educated in Glasgow, and taught before becoming a full-time actor. He made his first London appearance in 1945, and became known and respected in a broad range of roles, but particularly as a Scottish actor. His long association with the Citizens' Theatre in Glasgow dated from its opening production in 1943, and, in partnership with the Scottish playwright and critic T M Watson, he ran a company to present plays on tour in Scotland (1952–55). His many performances included Sir **David Lyndsay**'s *Ane Satyre of the Thrie Estaitis* (1948), Robert McLellan's *Jamie the Saxt* (1955) and Robert Kemp's Scots translation of **Molière**'s *L'École des Femmes* (1956, *Let Wives Tak Tent*). The best known of his many films is *Whisky Galore* (1948), and he also appeared in numerous television productions.

Macready, William Charles 1793–1873

English actor and theatre manager

He was born in London. After making his debut at Birmingham in 1810, he appeared at Covent Garden in London (1816), but it was not until 1837 that he became known as the leading English actor of his day. In that year he became manager of Covent Garden, where he produced **Shakespeare**. After two seasons he moved to Drury Lane (1841–43), then played in the provinces, Paris and the USA. His last visit to the USA was marked by riots (10 May 1849) in which 22 people died, following the hissing of his Macbeth by supporters of US actor **Edwin Forrest**. He made his last appearance on the stage at Drury Lane in 1851. He wrote *Reminiscences and Diaries* (1875) and *Diaries* (ed W Toynbee, 1912). ◫ Alan S Dower, *The Eminent Tragedian William Charles Macready* (1959)

Macrobius, Ambrosius Theodosius 5th century

Roman writer and neo-Platonist philosopher

Born probably in Africa, he wrote a commentary on **Cicero**'s *Somnium Scipionis* ('The Dream of Scipio'), and *Saturnaliorum Conviviorum Libri Septem*, a series of historical, mythological and critical dialogues.

MacSwiney, Terence 1879–1920

Irish nationalist and writer

Born in Cork, he trained as an accountant, and wrote poetry and plays under the influence of **Daniel Corkery**. He was a major influence in forming the Irish Volunteers in Cork in 1913, and wrote for *Irish Freedom*, but accepted **John MacNeill**'s countermand of the Easter Rising in 1916. He was elected Sinn Féin MP for West Cork in 1918, sitting in Dáil Éireann and maintaining his work as volunteer recruiter and organizer. In March 1920 he was elected Lord Mayor of Cork after the murder of Mayor Tomás Mac Curtain by irregular British forces; he was arrested the following August, sentenced to two years' imprisonment. He declared his intention to hunger-strike, was transferred to Brixton prison, and died after a fast of 74 days which had aroused worldwide sympathy. Among others deeply influenced by his sacrifice was a Vietnamese kitchen-worker in the London Ritz hotel, the future **Ho Chi Minh**.

M'Taggart, John M'Taggart Ellis 1866–1925

English philosopher

Born in London, he was educated at Clifton College and at Trinity College, Cambridge, where he later taught (1897–1923). His early works were commentaries on **Hegel**'s philosophy and were effectively preliminaries to his own systematic metaphysics set out in *The Nature of Existence* (2 vols, 1921, and posthumously, 1927). He is regarded as the most important of the Anglo-Hegelian or Idealistic philosophers who dominated British and US thought in the late 19th and early 20th centuries.

McTaggart, William 1835–1910

Scottish painter

Born in Kintyre, he lived in or near Edinburgh for most of his life. In 1852 he entered the Trustees' Academy, where he studied under **Robert Scott Lauder**. He became the outstanding landscape painter of his time. His grandson **William MacTaggart** was also a painter.

MacTaggart, Sir William 1903–81
Scottish painter
Born in Loanhead, near Edinburgh, he was the grandson of **William McTaggart**. He attended Edinburgh College of Art (1918–21), where he later taught, and was the recipient of many honours. His main subject matter was landscape and seascape, painted in a richly coloured expressionistic manner, and he is remembered as a prominent representative of the modern Scottish school.

MacThómais, Ruaraidh See Thomson, Derick

McWilliam, F(rederick) E(dward) 1909–92
Northern Irish sculptor
Born in Banbridge, County Down, he studied at the Slade School of Art, London, before travelling in France on a scholarship (1931). On his return to England, he began to carve as well as paint. He held his first one-man show in 1939, but his career was interrupted by World War II and service in the RAF. He was sent to India where he was influenced by Indian sculpture, and after the war he taught at Chelsea School of Art (1946–47), then at the Slade School (1947–68). A highly individual artist, his continued to carve and also made bronze castings. His works include *Princess Macha* (1957) and *Women of Belfast* (1972–73). A major retrospective of his work was held at the Tate Gallery, London, in 1989.

Macy, Anne Mansfield Sullivan, *née* Sullivan
1866–1936
US educator
Born in Feeding Hills, Massachusetts, she lost most of her sight in childhood due to an infection and attended the Perkins Institute for the Blind in Boston. She regained some of her sight through operations, but nevertheless learned the manual alphabet in order to communicate with other disabled people. In 1887 she was chosen to teach **Helen Keller**, a girl who could not see, hear or speak. Using the manual alphabet and a method of touch-teaching in which she allowed the child to hold objects rather than have their properties explained, she was dramatically successful in instructing her. She later accompanied Keller to Radcliffe College and on worldwide lecture tours. In 1905 she married John Macy, a writer and critic, but continued in her work for the blind, championing the cause of the new American Foundation for the Blind during the 1920s.

Mad Anthony See Wayne, Anthony

Madariaga, Salvador de 1886–1978
Spanish writer, scholar and diplomat
He was born in La Coruña, and educated at the Instituto del Cardenal Cisneros, Madrid, and at the École Polytechnique, Paris. He was a London journalist (1916–21) and director of the disarmament section of the League of Nations Secretariat (1922–27). From 1928 to 1931 he was Professor of Spanish studies at Oxford, and was Spanish ambassador to the USA (1931) and to France (1932–34). A liberal opponent of the **Franco** regime, he lived in exile. His publications include *The Genius of Spain* (1923), *Theory and Practice of International Relations* (1938), *Portrait of Europe* (1952), *Democracy v. Liberty?* (1958) and *Latin America between the Eagle and the Bear* (1962).

Madar-i-Millat See Jinnah, Fatima

Madden, Sir Frederic 1801–73
English antiquary and palaeographer

Born in Portsmouth, he was keeper of manuscripts in the British Museum (1837–66). He edited *Havelok the Dane* (1833), *William and the Werewolf* (1832), the early English versions of the *Gesta Romanorum* (1838), the **Wycliffe** version of the Bible (1850), **Layamon**'s *Brut* (1847), and the works of **Matthew Paris** (1858).

Mademoiselle, La Grande See Montpensier, Anne Marie Louise d'Orléans, Duchesse de

Maderna, Bruno 1920–73
Italian composer and conductor
Born in Venice, he appeared from the age of seven as an infant prodigy violinist and conductor, and studied composition and conducting. Early in his musical career he composed for films and radio, and taught at the Venice Conservatorio. In 1955 he began to research the techniques and possibilities of electronic music, founding, with **Luciano Berio**, the Studio di Fonologia Musicale of Milan Radio in Italy (1955). He became music director of Milan Radio. His compositions are intellectual, based on a mathematical calculation of form rather than an emotional or inspirational approach, but much of the resulting music is surprisingly lyrical. He wrote pieces for combinations of live and taped music, such as the *Compositions in Three Tempi* and *Music in Two Dimensions* (1958) for flute and taped sounds, and a number of compositions for electronic music, such as *Dimensions II* (1960). His opera *Satyricon* appeared in 1973.

Maderna or Maderno, Carlo 1556–1629
Italian architect
Born in Capalago, he had moved to Rome by 1588, where he became assistant to his uncle, **Domenico Fontana**. He was the leading exponent of the early Baroque in Rome, producing bold and vigorous designs, divorced from the Mannerist style of the preceding generation. In 1603 he was appointed architect to St Peter's, where he lengthened the nave and added a massive façade (1606–12). Other notable works include S Susanna (1597–1603), and the Palazzo Barberini (1628–38), completed by **Francesco Borromini** and **Gian Lorenzo Bernini**, in Rome, the latter in a revolutionary design, dispensing with the traditional quadrangular courtyard in favour of an H-plan.

Madero, Francisco Indalecio 1873–1913
Mexican revolutionary and statesman
Born in San Pedro, Coahuila, the son of a wealthy landowner, and educated in Paris and the USA, he was no social revolutionary, although he greatly improved the *peons'* condition on his own estates. He unsuccessfully opposed **Porfirio Díaz**'s local candidates in 1904, and in 1908, when Díaz was quoted as saying that he would not seek another term, Madero took the dictator at his word and launched his own presidential campaign. A spiritualist, vegetarian, and practitioner of homeopathic medicine, he seemed an unlikely challenger, and at first was not taken seriously, but his popularity grew rapidly and Díaz turned to repression, imprisoning Madero and many of his supporters. He escaped to the USA, from where he directed a military campaign. His supporters, including **Pancho Villa**, captured Ciudad Juárez, where Madero formed his capital (May 1911), and the dictatorship crumbled. Once he had been elected President (Oct 1911), Madero's moderate political reform programme pleased no one and he faced a succession of revolts by **Emiliano Zapata** and others demanding land reform, as well as by supporters of the old dictatorship. On the night of 23 February 1913, he and his Vice-President were murdered following a military coup led by General **Victoriano Huerta**, planned with the assistance of US ambassador Henry L Wilson.

Madhva 14th century
Kanarese Brahmin philosopher

Born near Mangalore, South India, he studied in Trivandrum, Benares and elsewhere, settled in Udipi and is traditionally held to have vanished in mid-lecture in 1317 and retired to the Himalayas. Taking **Ramanuja**'s side against **Śankara**, he promoted *dvaita* or dualistic *Vedanta*, allowing for the separate existence of the Divine, human souls, and matter. His belief that some souls were eternally damned suggests a Christian influence on his thinking.

Madison, Dolley Payne Todd, *née* Payne
1768–1849
US society hostess and First Lady
Born in Guilford County, North Carolina, she was already a widow when she married **James Madison** in 1794. She became famous as a vivacious Washington hostess, especially after Madison had become Secretary of State (1801–09). Madison became 4th President of the USA in 1809, and as First Lady (1809–17), she restored formality to the White House and was considered a premier hostess and society figure. In 1814, when the British captured Washington and burned government buildings including the White House, she salvaged many important state documents and artistic artefacts.

Madison, James 1751–1836
4th President of the USA
Born in Port Conway, Virginia, he graduated from the College of New Jersey (now Princeton) and quickly became involved in revolutionary politics. In 1776 he was a member of the Virginian Convention, and he served in the Continental Congress (1780–83, 1787) and the Virginia legislature (1784–86). He was one of the most active delegates to the Constitutional Convention of 1787, and his capable management of the proceedings and ability to engineer compromises won him the title 'master builder of the constitution'. Among other contributions, he was the chief author of the 'Virginia plan', and he suggested the compromise by which, for taxation, representation, etc, slaves were regarded as population and not chattels, five being counted as three persons, thus securing the adoption of the Constitution by South Carolina and the other slave-holding states. He was influential in the campaign to win ratification of the Constitution, and he joined **Alexander Hamilton** and **John Jay** in writing the *Federalist Papers* (1787–88). As a congressman from Virginia (1789–97) he was an advocate of the Bill of Rights and was anxious to limit the powers of the central government. He was a leader of the Jeffersonian Republicans, joining **Thomas Jefferson** in opposing the Alien and Sedition Acts and drawing up the Virginia Resolves. When Jefferson was elected President in 1800, Madison was made Secretary of State, and in 1809 he succeeded Jefferson as President. His administration was dominated by concerns about the European wars of the period and the damage done to US commerce, and by the War of 1812, an unpopular conflict with Great Britain in which the USA gained none of its objectives. In 1817, at the close of his second term, Madison retired to Virginia.

Madoc, *properly* Madog ab Owain Gwynedd
fl.1150–80
Welsh prince
Probably legendary, he was long believed by his countrymen to have discovered America in 1170. The story is in **Richard Hakluyt**'s *Voyages* (1582) and Lloyd and Powell's *Cambria* (1584). An essay by Thomas Stephens, written in 1858 for the Eisteddfod (published 1893), proved it to be without foundation, but it provided the basis for **Robert Southey**'s poem *Madoc* (1805).

Madonna, *full name* Madonna Louise Veronica Ciccone 1958–
US pop singer and actress
Born in Rochester, Michigan, she trained as a dancer at Michigan University before moving to New York, where she began her professional career as a singer. Highly ambitious and commercially astute, her debut album in 1983 delivered five US hit singles. Her brash, overtly sexual stage persona, controversial fashions and often stormy personal life made her an influential role model for teenagers in the 1980s, and her success has been greatly enhanced by clever promotion and image-making. She maintained the controversy level surrounding her with her enormously successful photo-book *Sex* (1993). She has appeared in a number of films, including her own concert movie, *In Bed With Madonna* (1991) and the biopic of **Eva Perón**, *Evita* (1996). 📖 Robert Matthew-Walker, *Madonna: The Biography* (1991)

Maecenas, Gaius Cilnius d.8BC
Roman statesman
He was the trusted counsellor of **Augustus**, and his name has become a synonym for a patron of letters.

Maedoc, St Maol See **Malachy, St**

Maerlant, Jacob van c.1235–c.1300
Flemish didactic poet
He was the author of verse translations of French and Latin originals, including the *Roman de Troie* (c.1264, 'The Tale of Troy'), and **Vincent de Beauvais**'s *Speculum Majus* (1284) as *Spiegel Historiael*, a history of the world.

Maes, Nicolaes 1634–93
Dutch painter
Born in Dordrecht, from c.1648 he was a pupil of **Rembrandt** in Amsterdam. Painting in a style close to his master's he specialized in painting genre scenes, especially of single figures praying or sleeping. He travelled to Antwerp (c.1665) and there became influenced by Flemish art, especially that of **Van Dyck**. Upon his return to Holland in 1667 he began to paint portraits which, because of their very different style, were for a long time thought to have been by a different artist.

Maeterlinck, Maurice, Count 1862–1949
Belgian dramatist and Nobel Prize winner
Born in Ghent, he studied law there, but became a disciple of the Symbolist movement, and in 1889 produced his first volume of poetry, *Les Serres chaudes* ('The Greenhouses'). In the same year came his prose play, *La Princesse Maleine* (Eng trans *The Princess Maleine*, 1890), and in 1892 *Pelléas et Mélisande* (Eng trans *Pelleas and Melisande*, 1894), on which **Claude Debussy** based his opera. Other plays include *Joyzelle* (1903, Eng trans 1906) and *Marie-Magdeleine* (1910, Eng trans *Mary Magdalene*, 1910). *La Vie des abeilles* (1901, Eng trans *The Life of the Bee*, 1901) is one of his many popular expositions of scientific subjects, and he also wrote several philosophical works. He was awarded the Nobel Prize for literature in 1911. 📖 B Knapp, *Maurice Maeterlinck* (1975)

Maevius and Bavius 1st century BC
Roman poets
They were colleagues, and were lampooned by **Virgil** in his Eclogues, and also by **Horace**. Their names were used by **William Gifford** for the titles of his satires on the Della Cruscan school of poets ('The Baviad' and 'The Maviad').

Maffei, Francesco Scipione, Marchese di
1675–1755
Italian dramatist
Born in Verona, he fought in the War of the Spanish Succession (1703–04) under his brother Alessandro, a field-marshal. He was a leading reformer of Italian drama, and his tragedy *Merope* (1714, Eng trans 1740) ran through 70 editions; the comedy *Le Ceremonie* (1728) was also successful. He also wrote scholarly works, including

Verona illustrata (4 vols, 1731–32, Eng trans *A Compleat History of Verona*). 🕮 G Silvestri, *Un europeo del Settecento* (1954)

Magellan, Ferdinand c.1480–1521
Portuguese navigator

He was born near Villa Real in Tras os Montes, served in the East Indies and Morocco, then laid before Charles V a scheme for reaching the Moluccas by the west. Sailing from Seville on 10 August 1519 with five ships and 270 men, he coasted Patagonia, passing through the strait which bears his name (21 October–28 November), and reached the ocean which he named the Pacific. He was later killed by local people in the Philippine Islands, but his ship, the *Victoria*, was taken safely back to Spain by the Spanish captain, Juan Sebastian del Cano, on 6 September 1522, to complete the first circumnavigation of the world. The four other ships had been lost, and of the 270 men who had set out three years earlier, fewer than 20 returned. 🕮 Edouard Roditi, *Magellan of the Pacific* (1972)

Magendie, François 1783–1855
French physiologist

Born in Bordeaux, he graduated in medicine at Paris in 1808, was elected a member of the French Academy of Sciences in 1821, and became its president in 1837. In 1831 he was appointed Professor of Anatomy at the Collège de France. A pioneer of scientific pharmacology, he used vivisection to conduct trials on plant poisons, and through such researches he introduced into medicine the range of plant-derived compounds now known as alkaloids, many of which possess outstanding pharmacological properties. He investigated the role of proteins in human diet, was interested in olfaction and inquired into the white blood cells. He worked extensively on the nerves of the skull and the paths of the spinal nerves. His numerous works include the *Elements of Physiology* (1816–17). He is often regarded as the founder of experimental physiology.

Magician, Simon the See Simon Magus

Maginot, André Louis René 1877–1932
French politician

Born in Paris, he was first elected to the Chamber of Deputies in 1910. As Minister of War (1922–24, 1926–31) he pursued a policy of military preparedness, and ordered the construction on the Franco-German border of the famous Maginot line of fortifications, comprising concealed weapons, underground stores and living quarters. However, in World War II, the German strategy of invading through Belgium made the scheme redundant, and its name has since become a euphemism for a useless form of defence.

Magliabechi, Antonio 1633–1714
Italian bibliophile

Born in Florence, he was a goldsmith by trade but slowly turned to books. His learning and his memory were prodigious and precise. In 1673 he was appointed court librarian by the Grand Duke of Tuscany. His vanity and intolerance involved him in bitter literary squabbles. His library of 30,000 volumes, bequeathed to the Grand Duke, is now a free library named after him.

Magnus, St See Magnus Erlendsson

Magnus I Olafsson, *called* the Good 1024–47
King of Norway and of Denmark

The illegitimate son of King Olaf II Haraldsson (St Olaf), he was named after Emperor Charlemagne. After St Olaf's death at the Battle of Stiklestad (1030), the boy went to Prince Jaroslav the Wise in Kiev. In 1035 he assumed the Norwegian throne by popular acclaim. He inherited the Danish throne in 1042, and won a notable victory over the Wends in 1043 at Lürschau Heath in

southern Jutland. In 1045 he agreed to share the throne of Norway with his uncle Harald III Sigurdsson, and died two years later during a campaign in Denmark.

Magnus III Olafsson, *called* Barfot ('Barefoot') c.1074–1103
King of Norway

One of the last of the Norse Viking sea-kings bent on strengthening Norway's hold over her North Sea territories, he was the son of King Olaf III Haraldsson. He became king in 1093 and attacked the Hebrides, Orkney and Shetland (1098–99). In 1102–03 he led another punitive naval expedition west to Scotland and Ireland. He took Dublin, and built new fortifications in the Isle of Man, but was killed in an ambush in Ulster. He earned his nickname because he abandoned Norse trousers in favour of the Scottish kilt.

Magnus V Erlingsson 1156–84
King of Norway

The son of Earl Erling the Crooked, he became king in 1162 and was raised to the throne, under his father's regency, as a child. In 1164 he was crowned by Archbishop Eystein at a church ceremony in Bergen, the first religious coronation in Norway. After his father's death (1179) he was engaged in a long war against a rival claimant to the throne, the Faroese-born usurper Sverrir Sigurdsson and was forced to flee to Denmark for safety. He died in a naval battle in an attempt to regain his kingdom.

Magnus VI Haakonsson, *called* Lagabøter ('Law-Reformer') 1238–80
King of Norway

He was the son of Haakon IV Haakonsson, and succeeded to the throne (1263) when his father died in Orkney on his return to Norway after the Battle of Largs. He made peace with King Alexander III of Scotland and ceded the Western Isles and the Isle of Man. Under him the Church became virtually independent, and Norwegian maritime trade flourished. He revised and standardized the laws of the land in a series of legal codes, from which he earned his nickname, and which were based on the 'four sisters' of Mercy, Truth, Fairness and Peace.

Magnus VII (of Norway) See Magnus Eriksson

Magnus Eriksson 1316–74
King of Sweden, and King of Norway as Magnus VII

He was the son of Duke Erik Magnusson of Sweden and Ingeborg, the daughter of King Haakon V of Norway (1270–1319). He inherited the throne of Norway from his grandfather at the age of three (1319), and was elected to the Swedish throne the same year on the deposition of his treacherous uncle, Birger Magnusson (1280–1321). A regency controlled both kingdoms until 1332. In 1335 he married Blanche of Namur, by whom he had two sons. He handed over the Crown of Norway to his younger son, Haakon VI (1355), and was temporarily deposed in Sweden (1356) by his elder son, Erik (XII). After Erik's death (1359) he returned to power, but lost the strategic Baltic island of Gotland (1361) to an invasion by King Valdemar IV Atterdag of Denmark, and was again deposed (1364), in favour of his nephew, Albert of Mecklenburg. He was imprisoned from 1364 to 1371, and died in a shipwreck. He is associated with a code of law which covered the whole of Sweden and which remained in force until the 18th century.

Magnus Erlendsson, *known as* St Magnus c.1075–1116
Earl of Orkney

Early in the 12th century, the Norse earldom of Orkney was shared by Magnus and his cousin, Earl Haakon. After years of feuding, they agreed to hold a peace-meeting on the island of Egilsay in 1116. Haakon treacherously broke the terms of the truce, took Magnus prisoner, and had him executed. The manner of Magnus's death suggested martyrdom, and soon miracles were reported. In his honour, his nephew Earl Rognvald Kali built St Magnus's Cathedral in Kirkwall, where his relics were discovered in 1919. His feast day is 16 April.

Magnus Maximus d.AD388
Roman emperor
He was a Roman army commander in Britain who, after being proclaimed emperor by his troops in AD383, crossed to Gaul and overthrew the emperor of the West, **Gratian**. Recognized as emperor by the Emperor of the East, **Theodosius I, the Great**, who was then preoccupied with problems nearer home, Maximus proceeded to rule over Gaul, Spain and Britain. His attempts to add Italy to his empire backfired, as Theodosius defeated him in battle and had him executed.

Magnus, Heinrich Gustav 1802–70
German physicist
Born in Berlin, he went to the University of Berlin in 1822, was awarded a doctorate five years later for a dissertation on tellurium, and then moved to Sweden to work under **Jöns Berzelius**. He returned to Berlin in 1828 and turned towards physics, becoming Professor of Technology and Physics at the University of Berlin in 1845. He worked on a wide range of topics including thermoelectricity, electrolysis, optics, mechanics, magnetism, fluid mechanics and aerodynamics. Working in this last field in 1853, he discovered and evaluated the Magnus effect—the sideways force experienced by a spinning ball, which is responsible for the swerving of golf or tennis balls when hit with a slice.

Magnússon, Eiríkur 1833–1913
Icelandic philologist and scholar
Born in eastern Iceland, he became librarian of Cambridge University, England. Among the many classical Icelandic texts he edited and translated was **Jón Árnason**'s monumental collection of folk-tales (*Legends of Iceland*, 1864–66). He also collaborated with **William Morris** in a notable series of Saga translations, including *Grettis Saga* (1869), *Völsunga Saga* (1870) and *The Saga Library* (5 vols, 1891–95).

Magnusson, Magnus 1929–
Scottish journalist and broadcaster
Born in Reykjavík, Iceland, he was raised in Edinburgh and educated at The Edinburgh Academy and Oxford. He entered journalism in 1953 with the *Scottish Daily Express*, later becoming assistant editor of the *Scotsman* (1961–67). As a broadcaster, his wide historical and cultural interests have informed such television series as *Chronicle* (1966–80), *BC: The Archaeology of the Bible Lands* (1977) and *Vikings!* (1980), although he remains best known for acting as quizmaster of the long-running *Mastermind* (1972–97). A dedicated public servant, he was Rector of Edinburgh University (1975–78), chairman of the Ancient Monuments Board for Scotland (1981–89), and chairman of Scottish Natural Heritage (1992–96). His numerous publications and translations include *Introducing Archaeology* (1972) and *Treasures of Scotland* (1981). He was editor of the fifth edition of *Chambers Biographical Dictionary* (1990) and of *The Nature of Scotland* (1991). In 1989 he was awarded an honorary knighthood.

Magoun, Horace Winchell 1907–91
US neuroscientist
Born in Philadelphia, he studied at Rhode Island State College and received his PhD from Northwestern University Medical School in 1934, remaining there as Assistant Professor (1934–37) and Professor of Micro-Anatomy (1937–50). In 1950 he moved to the School of Medicine at UCLA as Professor of Anatomy. He demonstrated the important role of the hypothalamus, and was a pioneer in the development of the field of neuroendocrinology. Later he studied the factors which control sleep, wakefulness, awareness and other components of higher nervous activity, and his 1963 publication *The Waking Brain* summarizes much of his work on brain-endocrine interactions. He collaborated on many neurological and psychopharmacological projects and was one of the leaders in the creation of neuroscience, the multidisciplinary approach to the study of the nervous system.

Magritte, René François Ghislain 1898–1967
Belgian Surrealist painter
Born in Lessines, Hainault, he moved in 1913 to Charleroi after his mother committed suicide. He was educated at the Académie Royale des Beaux-Arts (1916–18) in Brussels. He became a wallpaper designer and commercial artist and in 1924 a leading member of the newly-formed Belgian Surrealist group. He made his name with *The Menaced Assassin* (1926, Museum of Modern Art, New York) but after a badly-received one-man show in Brussels (1927), he lived in Paris until 1930, and became associated with **André Breton** and others there. Apart from a brief Impressionist phase in the 1940s, Magritte remained faithful to Surrealism, using Freudian symbols and recurring motifs of dreamlike incongruity, as in *Rape*, in which he substitutes a torso for a face. His best-known paintings include *Man with a Newspaper* and *The Reckless Sleeper* (1928, Tate, London), *The Red Model* (1935, Pompidou Centre, Paris), *The Wind and the Song* (1928–29) and *The Human Condition* (1, 1934; 2, 1935). In 1957 he designed the mural *La Fée Ignorante* for the Palais des Beaux-Arts in Charleroi, and in 1961 the mural *Les Barricades Mystérieuses* for the Palais des Congrès, Brussels. He was acclaimed in the USA as an early innovator of the Pop Art of the 1960s. 🕮 Richard Calvocoressi, *Magritte* (1990)

Mahan, Alfred Thayer 1840–1914
US naval historian
Born in West Point, New York, he served in the US navy (1854–1896), and in 1906 was given the rank of rear admiral retired. In works such as *The Influence of Sea Power upon History, 1600–1812* (3 vols, 1890–92), he argued for the strategic importance of naval power in determining a nation's strength and position in international politics. His theories were greatly admired in the USA, Great Britain, Japan and Germany, and were a major cause of the worldwide naval build-up that preceded World War II. He also wrote biographies of **David Farragut**, **Horatio Nelson** and other naval figures.

Mahap, Walter See Map, Walter

Maharaj Ji, *originally* Prem Pal Singh Rawat 1957–
Indian guru
He was born in India and succeeded his father as Perfect Master of the Divine Light Mission when still a teenager. The movement has an ecstatic and erotic devotion to Krishna and attracted a large following in the West. On moving to the USA in 1971, he adopted an increasingly lavish lifestyle while the movement lost much of its original Hindu ethos. Many Eastern followers grew disillusioned and links with the Indian ashrams were severed in 1974. There remains a reduced but devoted following for the cult, now known as Elan Vital, based in the USA. 🕮 Ruth Tucker, *Strange Gospels* (1989)

Maharishi Mahesh Yogi, *originally* Mahesh Prasad Varma 1911–
Indian cult leader
He was born in Jabalpur and abandoned his scientific studies to become a follower of guru Dev. He founded the science of creative intelligence and, as an exponent of the relaxation technique called transcendental meditation, he became one of the first Eastern gurus to attract a

Western following. He first introduced his Hindu meditation technique, based on a literalist interpretation of yogic concepts and the use of mantras, to the West in 1958, and went on to found the Spiritual Regeneration movement, aimed at saving the world through meditation. This concept has developed into a worldwide network of meditation centres with an estimated four million practitioners.

Mahathir bin Mohamad, Datuk Seri 1925–
Malaysian politician
Born in Alur Setar, in Kedah state, he practised as a doctor (1957–64) before being elected to the House of Representatives as a United Malays' National Organisation (UMNO) candidate. He won the support of UMNO's radical youth wing through his advocacy of 'affirmative action' in favour of bumiputras (ethnic Malays) and a more Islamic social policy. After holding several ministerial posts he was appointed UMNO leader and Prime Minister in 1981, immediately launching a new 'look east' economic policy, which sought to emulate Japanese industrialization. Despite internal ethnic conflicts, he was re-elected in 1982, 1986, 1990 and 1995.

Mahdi, al- See Muhammad Ahmed

Mahfouz or Mahfuz, Naguib 1911–
Egyptian novelist and Nobel Prize winner
Born in the al-Gamaliyya old quarter of Cairo, the youngest son of a merchant, he studied philosophy at King Fuad I (now Cairo) University. An avid reader of French, British, Russian, US and Arab writers, he especially admired the critical writings of ostracized fellow Egyptians such as Taha Hasayn. He worked in university administration, then for the government's Ministry of Waqfs (religious foundations), and in journalism. He started writing as a boy and by 1939 had already written three novels, among them *Kifah Tiba* (1944, 'The Struggle of Thebes'). He later began work on *Al-Thulathiya* (1956–57, 'The Cairo Trilogy'), a monumental, partially autobiographical work. However, his early work was overshadowed by the notoriety surrounding *Awlad Haratina* (1967, Eng trans *The Children of Gebelawi*, 1981), serialized in the magazine *al-Ahram*. An allegorical work which shows his disillusionment with religion, it depicts average Egyptians living the lives of Cain and Abel, Moses, Jesus Christ and Muhammad, and portrays the decline of five communities towards futility and nihilism. It was banned throughout the Arab world, except in Lebanon. He subsequently became more interested in the plight of the individual, as in *Al-Liss wa-l-Kilab* (1961, 'The Thief and the Dogs'), *Al-Shahhadh* (1965, 'The Beggar') and *Miramar* (1967, Eng trans 1978). Described as 'a Dickens of the Cairo cafés' and the 'Balzac of Egypt', he won the Nobel Prize for literature in 1988, the first Arab to receive the award. His work is still unavailable in many Middle Eastern countries on account of his outspoken support for President Sādāt's Camp David peace treaty with Israel. 📖 S Somekh, *The Changing Rhythm: a study of Mahfuz's novels* (1973)

Mahler, Gustav See panel p1209

Mahmud II 1785–1839
Ottoman Sultan of Turkey
Born in Constantinople (Istanbul), he succeeded his brother Mustafa IV in 1808. His reign saw the loss to Russia of Bessarabia; the independence of Greece and Serbia; and the autonomy of Egypt under Mehemet 'Ali. At home he increased central control over the provinces, curbed the power of the religious leaders (ulama), and set up European-type schools. He suppressed the corps of janissaries, replacing it with a new regular army on the European model.

Mahmud of Ghazni 971–1030
Muslim Afghan conqueror of India
The son of Sebüktigin, a Turkish slave who became ruler of Ghazni (modern Afghanistan), he succeeded to the throne in 997. He invaded India 17 times (1001–1026), and created an empire that included the Punjab and much of Persia. A great patron of the arts, he made Ghazni a remarkable cultural centre.

Mahon, Derek 1941–
Northern Irish poet
Born in Belfast, he was educated at Belfast Institute and Trinity College, Dublin, and he taught before turning to journalism and other writing. He was associated with the Northern Poets in Belfast in the 1960s, with Seamus Heaney and Michael Longley (1939–). A poet drawn to squalid landscapes and desperate situations, he acknowledges Louis MacNeice and W H Auden among his influences. His works include *Twelve Poems* (1965), *Night-Crossing* (1968), *The Snow Party* (1975), *The Hunt by Night* (1982), *A Kensington Notebook* (1984) and *Antarctica* (1985). *Poems 1962–1978* (1979) contained some revised versions of earlier works, and a new *Selected Poems* appeared in 1991. 📖 Introduction to the *Penguin Book of Contemporary Irish Poetry* (1990)

Mahony, Francis Sylvester, *pseudonym* Father Prout 1804–66
Irish priest and humorist
Born in Cork, he became a Jesuit priest, but was expelled from the order for a late-night frolic and was ordained a priest at Lucca in 1832. He moved to London in 1834 and gave up the priesthood for journalism and poetry, and contributed to *Fraser's Magazine* and *Bentley's Miscellany*. He is remembered as author of the poems 'The Bells of Shandon' and 'The Lady of Lee'. 📖 C Kent, memoir in *Works* (1881)

Mahony, Marion Lucy, *married name* Griffin 1871–1961
US architect and designer
Born in New York of Irish parentage, she was one of the first two women to receive a degree in architecture from the Massachusetts Institute of Technology. She worked in Frank Lloyd Wright's Oak Park Studios until 1909 and became his chief draftsman, completing many of his commissions and designing several of her own. Wright's work was published in 1910, and of 27 attributable drawings, 17 were Mahony's and the other 10 were the joint work of Mahony and others. In 1911 Mahony married Walter Burley Griffin, a colleague in Wright's office, and it was she who produced the drawings with which her husband won the Canberra competition in 1912. In 1916 Wright included two Decatur Houses in an exhibition of his work which were entirely Mahony's work, but she was shunned by Wright in later years, though she did inherit some of his commissions when he left for Europe.

Maiden, Joseph Henry 1859–1925
Australian botanist
Born in London, England, he was educated at the University of London. In 1880 he emigrated to Australia, and from 1896 to 1924 was director of the Sydney Botanic Gardens and Government Botanist of New South Wales. A prolific writer, he published many scientific papers and books, including *The Useful Native Plants of Australia* (1889), *Australian Economic Botany* (1892), *The Forest Flora of New South Wales* (8 vols, 1902–24), *A Census of New South Wales Plants*, and his greatest work, *A Critical Revision of the Genus Eucalyptus* (1903–33).

Mailer, Norman Kingsley 1923–
US novelist and journalist

Mahler, Gustav 1860–1911
Czechoslovakian-born Austrian composer

Gustav Mahler was born in Kalist in Bohemia (now the Czech Republic). He began to learn the piano at an early age, and in 1875 he went to the Vienna Conservatory, where he studied composition and conducting. He became a follower of **Anton Bruckner**, although he was not his pupil. He wrote the cantata *Das klagende Lied* for the Beethoven Prize in 1881, but was unsuccessful. He then turned to conducting, rapidly reaching important positions in Prague, Leipzig, Budapest and Hamburg, where in 1891 he became chief conductor of Hamburg Opera. There he introduced several new works and took the company on tour, which resulted in his only visit to London (1892). In 1897 he became conductor and artistic director at the Vienna State Opera House, where he established the high standards for which that theatre has since become famous.

In 1902 Mahler married Alma Schindler, who played an important part in his life and published his letters and other documents and reminiscences after his death. They had two daughters, of whom the elder died in 1907 at the age of four. Mahler detested the intrigues of theatrical life and was much affected by the frequent personal attacks upon him for his Jewish birth, despite (or perhaps because of) his conversion to Roman Catholicism, and he resigned after 10 years to devote himself to composition and the concert platform. From 1908 to 1911 he was conductor of the New York Philharmonic Society, spending his summers composing in Austria.

His mature works consist entirely of songs and symphonies. He wrote nine numbered symphonies, one requiring a solo voice and three requiring choral forces, plus the song-symphony *Das Lied von der Erde*, which he did not include in the nine for superstitious reasons (**Beethoven**, **Schubert** and Bruckner having all died after completing nine); in the end he too left a tenth symphony unfinished. He also wrote songs with orchestral accompaniment, notably *Kindertotenlieder* (1901–04, 'Songs on the Death of Children'), based on poems by the German poet and scholar Friedrich Rückert (1788–1866).

In his lifetime and for many years after, Mahler was known principally as a conductor; more recently, his compositions have gained enormous popularity in Europe and the USA, and many of his works are now regarded as part of the central orchestral repertoire. He is an important bridge between the late romantic 19th-century style and the revolutionary works of **Schoenberg** and his followers.

📖 Alma Mahler's edition of documents has been published in an English edition by D Mitchell and K Hartner, *Alma Mahler: Memories and Letters* (3rd edition, 1975). There is an important memoir of Mahler written by his pupil, the conductor Bruno Walter, published in an English translation (New York, 1941). See also D Cooke, *Gustav Mahler, An Introduction to his Music* (1980); D Mitchell, *Gustav Mahler* (3 vols: I (2nd edition), 1980; II, 1975; III 1985); M Kennedy, *Mahler* (1974).

> 'A symphony must be like the world, it must embrace everything.' In conversation with **Sibelius**. Quoted in Ian Crofton and Donald Fraser, a *Dictionary of Musical Quotations* (1985).

Born in Long Branch, New Jersey, he was brought up in Brooklyn, educated at Harvard University, and during World War II served in the Pacific. His first novel *The Naked and the Dead* (1948), an anti-war blast and social satire, became a bestseller, establishing him as a leading novelist of his generation. He maintained his antagonism towards contemporary society in *Barbary Shore* (1951) and *The Deer Park* (1955), but the writing of the period documents his gradual ideological shift from liberal socialism to a kind of anarchist libertarianism. A proponent of the 'New Journalism', and one who helped define that solipsistic genre, he has created a vast body of work, impressive for its energy and its self-obsession. *Advertisements for Myself* (1959) is generally regarded as one of his more successful books. As a polemicist, campaigner and protester he was prominent throughout the 1960s, publishing *An American Dream* (1965), *Why Are We In Vietnam?* (1967) and *Armies of the Night* (1968, winner of a National Book award and the Pulitzer Prize). Subsequent books include *The Executioner's Song* (1979, Pulitzer Prize) and *Ancient Evenings* (1983). Later novels include *Harlot's Ghost* (1991), an account of the CIA from the end of World War II to the assassination of **John F Kennedy**. He published two biographical works in 1995, *Oswald's Tale*—a study of the life of **Lee Harvey Oswald**—and *Portrait of Picasso as a Young Man*. He has also been active as a screenwriter, film director and actor, with such works as *Maidstone* (1970) and *Tough Guys Don't Dance* (1987, from his 1984 thriller of the same title). 📖 H Mills, *Mailer: a biography* (1982)

Maillart, Ella Kini 1903–97
Swiss travel writer

Born in Geneva, she represented Switzerland in the 1924 Olympic Games in Paris in the single-handed sailing competition, captained the Swiss ladies hockey team in 1931 and skied for her country from 1931 to 1934. She crossed Russian Turkestan in 1932 and wrote of her tribulations in both French and English. In 1934, working as a journalist for *Petit Parisien*, she went to Mongolia to report on the Japanese invasion and returned via Peking (Beijing) across Tibet and into Kashmir with **Peter Fleming**, described in *Oasis interdites* (1937, Eng trans *Forbidden Journey*, 1937). She worked and journeyed in Iran and Afghanistan, and then spent the period 1939–45 living in an ashram in southern India under the tutelage of Sri **Ramana**. She was one of the first travellers into Nepal when it opened in 1949, and wrote *The Land of the Sherpas* (1955). She later worked as a travel guide, and spent six months of each year in Switzerland.

Maillart, Robert 1872–1940
Swiss civil engineer

Born in Berne, he studied at the Zurich Polytechnic (1890–94), worked with **François Hennebique**, then set up on his own in 1902. He was one of the first to realize the economic and aesthetic advantages of three-hinged reinforced-concrete arch bridges in the Swiss Alps, designing some remarkable examples, from the bridge over the Inn at Zuoz (1901) to the spectacular curving Schwandbach Bridge at Schwarzenburg (1933). He also designed many industrial buildings in which he employed the so-called 'mushroom' column supporting a flat two-way reinforced floor slab.

Maillol, Aristide Joseph Bonaventure
1861–1944
French sculptor

Born in Banyuls-sur-mer, he studied at the École des Beaux-Arts in Paris, and spent some years designing tapestries. The latter half of his life was devoted to sculpting female nudes, such as the *Three Graces*, *Mediterranean*, *Crouching Woman* (c.1901, Museum of Modern Art, New York) and *The Mountain* (1937), in a style of monumental simplicity and classical serenity. His torso for the monument in 1905 to Auguste Blanqui, *Chained Action*, is in the Tate Gallery, London.

Maiman, Theodore Harold 1927–
US physicist who constructed the first working laser

He was born in Los Angeles, and after military service in the US navy, studied engineering physics at Colorado and Stanford Universities, then joined the Hughes Research Laboratories in Miami in 1955. The maser (producing coherent microwave radiation) had been devised and constructed in 1953 by Charles Townes (and independently by Nikolai Basov and Aleksandr Prokhorov in the USSR in 1955). Maiman made some design improvements to the solid-state maser, and turned to the possibility of an optical maser, or laser (Light Amplification by Simulated Emission of Radiation). He constructed the first working laser in the Hughes laboratories in 1960. Lasers have found use in a variety of applications, including spectroscopy, surgical work, such as repair of retinal detachment in the eye, and in compact disc players. Maiman founded the Korad Corporation (1962) to build high-powered lasers and was a co-founder of the Laser Video Corporation (1972) to develop large-screen video displays.

Maimonides, Moses, *originally* Moses ben Maimon 1135–1204
Jewish philosopher

Born in Córdoba, Spain (then ruled by the Moors), he studied Greek medicine and Aristotelian philosophy. He moved to Egypt where he settled in Cairo about 1165 and became physician to Saladin, and head of the Jewish community. The foremost figure of medieval Judaism, he wrote an important commentary in Hebrew on the Mishna (Jewish code of law), but his other main writings are in Arabic. His greatest work is the *Guide to the Perplexed* (1190), which argued for the reconciliation of Greek philosophy and Judaism. He had an enormous influence on a range of philosophers and traditions, Jewish, Muslim and Christian. ▢ Solomon Zeitlin, *Maimonides* (2nd edn 1955)

Mainbocher, *originally* Main Rousseau Bocher c.1890–1976
US fashion designer

He was born in Chicago, where he studied and worked. After World War I, he stayed on in Paris, eventually becoming a fashion artist with *Harper's Bazaar* and, later, editor of French *Vogue* until 1929. He started his couture house in Paris in 1930. One of his creations was the wedding dress of Mrs Wallis Simpson, the Duchess of Windsor (1937). He opened a salon for ready-to-wear clothes in New York in 1940, but returned to Europe in 1971.

Maintenon, Françoise d'Aubigné, Marquise de, *known as* Madame de Maintenon 1635–1719
French queen

The second wife of Louis XIV and granddaughter of the Huguenot Théodore Agrippa d'Aubigné (1552–1630), she was born in Niort, Poitou. She was converted to Roman Catholicism in her teens, and in 1652 she married the crippled poet Paul Scarron, whose death (1660) left her penniless. In 1669 she was appointed governess of the two illegitimate sons of her friend the Marquise de Montespan by Louis XIV, and she became the king's mistress. In 1674, with his help, she bought the estate and marquisate of Maintenon. After the death of Queen Maria Theresa in 1683, Louis secretly married Madame de Maintenon, and she was accused of influencing him, particularly over the persecution of Protestants after the revocation of the Edict of Nantes (1685). She encouraged piety and dignity at court and her letters are still very interesting to read. After Louis's death (1715), she retired to a home for poor noblewomen which she had founded in 1680 at Saint-Cyr. ▢ Mme Saint-René Taillandier, *Madame de Maintenon* (1920, Eng trans 1922)

Mairet, Ethel 1872–1952
English weaver

After visiting Ceylon (now Sri Lanka) between 1903 and 1906, she worked with Charles Robert Ashbee and the Guild of Handicrafts. She started weaving in Devon in 1911 and, after marrying Philip Mairet (her second husband), established the workshop 'Gospels' based at Ditchling in Sussex. Gospels became a creative centre for many weavers from all over the world. Her writing revealed a desire for rethinking the educational approach to handweaving and a reassessment of its relationship to power loom production.

Maisonneuve, Paul de Chomeday, Sieur de 1612–76
French colonial administrator

Born in Neuville-sur-Vannes, France, he was chosen in 1641 by the Company of Notre-Dame de Montreal to establish a new settlement in Canada. As commander of a detachment of French soldiers, he landed on the island of Montreal in 1642 and founded the city of Ville Marie, later called Montreal. He served as the city's first governor (1642–63).

Maistre, Joseph Marie, Comte de 1753–1821
French political philosopher and diplomat

Born in Chambéry, he emigrated to Switzerland during the French Revolution (when Savoy was annexed), but became ambassador to St Petersburg (1803–17) for Victor Emmanuel I (King of Piedmont-Sardinia), and later Minister of State of Sardinia. He was hostile to all liberal and democratic thought and defended a doctrine of the divine right of kings. He was the brother of Xavier de Maistre.

Maistre, Xavier, Comte de 1763–1852
French novelist, painter and soldier

Born in Chambéry, he was exiled after the French occupation of Savoy (1798), and joined the Russian army, becoming a general. He spent most of the rest of his life in Russia, publishing several appealing works, such as *Voyage autour de ma chambre* (1794, 'Journey around my Room'), describing a period of imprisonment, and *Les Prisonniers du Caucase* (1825, 'The Prisoners of the Caucasus') and *La Jeune Sibérienne* (1825, 'The Young Siberian Woman'). He was the brother of the political philosopher Joseph Marie, Comte de Maistre. ▢ A Berthier, *Xavier de Maistre* (1921)

Maitland, Frederic William 1850–1906
English legal historian

Educated at Eton College and Trinity College, Cambridge, he became a barrister (1876), Reader in English law at Cambridge (1884) and Downing professor (1888). He wrote a *History of English Law before Edward I* (1895, with Sir Frederick Pollock), *Domesday Book and Beyond* (1897), and other works on legal antiquities and history, and edited several volumes of legal records. He was one of the creators of English legal history.

Maitland, Sir Richard, *known as* Lord Lethington 1496–1586
Scottish lawyer and poet

He studied at the University of St Andrews, became a Lord of Session in 1551, and (after losing his sight in 1561) Lord Privy Seal in 1562, becoming known for his moderation and integrity. His poems—mostly lamentations for the poor state of his country—were published in 1830 by the Maitland Club. He made a collection of early

Scottish poetry, now forming two manuscript volumes, which are in the Pepysian collection at Cambridge. He also wrote a *Historie of the Hous of Seytoun*.

Maitland, William, *known as* Secretary Lethington
c.1528–1573
Scottish politician

The son of Sir **Richard Maitland**, in 1558 he became Secretary of State to the queen-regent, **Mary of Guise**. He represented **Mary, Queen of Scots** at the court of **Elizabeth I**, but aroused her hostility by his connivance at **David Rizzio's** murder in 1566. He was also privy to the assassination of Lord **Darnley** and was one of the commissioners who presented to Elizabeth an indictment of Mary in 1568. Accused of plotting against his colleagues, he was jailed in Edinburgh Castle and died in prison at Leith.

Major, John 1943–
English Conservative statesman

He was born in Merton, south-west London, the son of a trapeze performer, and educated at Rutlish Grammar School. He started a career in banking but his interest in politics grew and he eventually won a Commons seat, as Conservative MP for Huntingdonshire, in 1979. He entered **Margaret Thatcher's** government as a junior Minister in 1981 and rose to become Treasury Chief Secretary, under Chancellor **Nigel Lawson**, in 1987. Thereafter, having caught the eye of the Prime Minister, his progress was spectacular. In the summer of 1989 he replaced Sir **Geoffrey Howe** as Foreign Secretary, in controversial circumstances, and in the autumn of the same year, even more surprisingly, returned to the Treasury as Chancellor of the Exchequer, when Lawson dramatically resigned. He remained loyal to Thatcher in the first round of the 1990 Conservative Party leadership election. When she stood down, he ran successfully against **Michael Heseltine** and **Douglas Hurd** to become Prime Minister, thus completing one of the swiftest rises to power of recent times. Despite the country's deepening recession and Labour's improving showing in the opinion polls, he remained in power after the 1992 general election. However when his party succumbed to the Labour landslide victory of 1997, Major immediately resigned the leadership. 📖 Terry Major-Ball, *Major Major: Memories of an Older Brother* (1994)

Major, Dame Malvina Lorraine 1943–
New Zealand operatic soprano

She was born in Hamilton and studied in Auckland with Dame Sister Mary Leo, teacher of **Kiri Te Kanawa**, and at the London Opera Centre. She won the **Kathleen Ferrier** Scholarship in 1966 and made her international debut as Rosina in the *Barber of Seville* in Salzburg in 1968. She went back to New Zealand in 1970, took leading roles around the country, including Constanze opposite Inia te Wiata in *Die Entführung aus dem Serail* ('The Abduction from the Seraglio'), and had two successful television series. Returning to the international scene in 1985 in *La Finta giardiniera* ('The Feigned Gardener') in Brussels, she then toured as Donna Anna in *Don Giovanni* with the Australian Opera (1987–88). She was made DBE in 1991.

Makarios III *originally* Mihail Christodoulou Mouskos 1913–77
Cypriot Orthodox archbishop and statesman

Born in Pano Panayia, he was ordained priest in 1946, elected Bishop of Kition in 1948, and became archbishop and primate in 1950. Suspected of collaborating with anti-British (EOKA) guerrilla forces, he was exiled to the Seychelles by the colonial government, later lived in Athens, but returned after a 1959 agreement that gave Cyprus independence and made Makarios head of state as the first President of the Republic of Cyprus. He had to cope with a restive Turkish Muslim minority, fellow bishops who critized his dual role, and a small but active Communist presence which Makarios was not above using for his own ends. A short-lived coup put his life in danger and removed him briefly from leadership in 1974, but he was reinstated in 1975. On his death the posts of archbishop and head of state were separated, thus closing a chapter of Byzantine history that had somehow lingered into the 20th century. 📖 Stanley Mayes, *Makarios* (1981)

Makarova, Natalia 1940–
Soviet dancer

Born in Leningrad (now St Petersburg), she studied there, joining the Kirov in 1959 and becoming one of their star dancers. She defected to the West in 1970, while on tour in London, and established herself as one of the best-known dancers of the 1960s and 1970s, particularly in the title role of *Giselle* (1961). Establishing herself with American Ballet Theater in New York from 1970, she often guested with the Royal Ballet, Covent Garden and other international companies. While specializing in the classics, she also created roles for contemporary choreographers like **Antony Tudor**, **George Balanchine** and **Glen Tetley**. Her work as producer includes *La Bayadère* (1980) for American Ballet Theater, and *The Kingdom of the Shades* (1985) and *Swan Lake* (1988), both for London Festival Ballet. In London in 1988 she became the first dancer in exile to guest with her home company, the Kirov. Her publications include *A Dance Autobiography* (1979) and *On Your Toes* (1984).

Makeba, Miriam 1932–
US singer

She was born in Johannesburg, South Africa, but was exiled because of her political views. After settling in the USA she became widely known in the 1960s as 'the empress of African song', making concert tours and recording several albums. She was the first African performer to gain an international following and played a vital role in introducing the sounds and rhythms of traditional African song to the West. Her marriage in the late 1960s to the militant black leader **Stokely Carmichael** effectively ended her career in the USA, as she was declared persona non grata; she moved to Guinea and virtually disappeared from the international concert arena, emerging only to take part in special, politically-oriented events.

Malachy, St, *also called* St Maol Maedoc
c.1094–1148
Irish prelate and reformer

Born in Armagh, he became abbot of Bangor (1121), Bishop of Connor (1125) and, in 1134, Archbishop of Armagh. He substituted Roman for Celtic liturgy, and renewed the use of the sacraments. In 1139 he went to Rome, visiting St **Bernard** at Clairvaux. On his return (1142), he introduced the Cistercian Order into Ireland. In 1148 he once more went to France, and died at Clairvaux in St Bernard's arms. The so-called 'Prophecies of St Malachy', first published in *Lignum Vitae* (1595) by the Flemish Benedictine Arnold Wion, are spurious. He was canonized in 1190—the first papal canonization of an Irishman. His feast day is 3 November.

Malamud, Bernard 1914–86
US novelist

He was born in Brooklyn, New York, and educated at Columbia University, then taught at Oregon State University (1949–61) and Bennington College (1961–86). One of the leading US writers of the later 20th century, he wrote fiction that mingled mysticism, pessimism and gentle humour, and drew on the idiom of Jewish America. *The Natural* (1952), his first novel, used baseball as an extended metaphor for life, following the fading career of a once-promising big-hitter. *The Assistant* (1957) was darker in mood, but had a warm critical reception. In

A New Life (1961) he abandoned the close urban setting of his previous novels for the mountainous western USA, where Seymour Levin arrives at a small college to teach and analyse happiness. *The Fixer* (1966), set in Tsarist Russia, is Malamud's bleakest and most potent book, streaked with self-deprecating humour. Later novels include *Dubin's Lives* (1979), and *God's Grace* (1982), a prophetic, apocalyptic allegory. He was also an accomplished short-story writer; *The Stories of Bernard Malamud* was published in 1983. He won the National Book award twice, in 1959 and 1967, and the Pulitzer Prize in 1967.
📖 J Helterman, *Understanding Malamud* (1985)

Malan, Daniel F(rançois) 1874–1959
South African politician

Born in Riebeek West, Cape Province, he was educated at Victoria College, Stellenbosch, and Utrecht University. On his return to South Africa in 1905 he became a predikant of the Dutch Reformed Church, but after 10 years abandoned his clerical career to become editor of *Die Burger*, the Nationalist newspaper. He became an MP in 1918, and in 1924 in the **Hertzog** Nationalist-Labour government he held the portfolios of the Interior, of Education and of Public Health. He introduced measures strengthening the Nationalist position—in particular, that making Afrikaans an official language. He was Leader of the Opposition (1934–39, 1940–48), and on becoming Prime Minister and Minister for External Affairs in 1940, embarked on the hotly controversial policies of apartheid with the aim of re-aligning South Africa's multi-racial society. The Group Areas Act divided the country into white, black and coloured zones. The apartheid legislation, which involved strongly-contested constitutional changes, was met by non-violent civil disobedience at home and vigorous criticism abroad. Malan resigned from the premiership in 1954. Crusty and austere, a scholar of profound convictions and an uncompromising manner, he was a back-veldt **Moses** to the Boers. He never wavered in his belief in a strict white supremacy, in a Heaven-sent Afrikaner mission and a rigidly hierarchical society. 📖 Eric Robins, *This Man Malan* (1953)

Malatesta, Enrico 1853–1932
Italian anarchist

Born in Campania of a wealthy family, he studied medicine at Naples University but was expelled for encouraging student unrest. To demonstrate his beliefs, he gave away his personal wealth and worked as an electrician in cities around Europe, at the same time preaching anarchism and spending numerous periods in prison. He became something of a legend because of his unusually small stature and ability to escape. He settled in London in 1900, advocating peaceful opposition to authority, and in 1911 survived an attempt to deport him for alleged complicity with the Sidney Street anarchists who had killed three policemen. He returned to Italy in 1913 and died peacefully 19 years later.

Malcolm I d.954
King of Scotland

He was the son of Donald II, and succeeded his cousin, Constantine II, in 943. He annexed Moray, but lost Northumbria, and was killed near Dunnottar.

Malcolm II c.954–1034
King of Scotland

He was the son of Kenneth II, and became king in 1005 after his slaughter of Kenneth III. He won a great victory over the Northumbrians at Carham (1018) and secured Strathclyde, but had to submit to the English King **Knut Sveinsson** (Canute) in 1032. He was succeeded by his grandson **Duncan I**.

Malcolm III *called* Canmore, *from Gaelic* Ceann-mor ('Great Head') c.1031–1093
King of Scotland

He was a child when his father, King **Duncan I**, was killed by **Macbeth** (1040). He stayed in Northumbria with his uncle, Earl Siward, who established him (1054) in Cumbria and Lothian. In 1057, after Macbeth was killed, Malcolm became King of all Scotland. In 1069 he married **Margaret**, sister of **Edgar the Ætheling**. He invaded England five times (1061–1093), and was killed at Alnwick. He left five sons, of whom four succeeded him, Duncan, Edgar, **Alexander** and David.

Malcolm IV, *called* the Maiden c.1141–1165
King of Scotland

He was the grandson and successor (1153) of **David I**. Compelled to restore the northern English counties to **Henry II** in return for the earldom and honour of Huntingdon (1157), he served on Henry's expedition to Toulouse (1159), and was then knighted. Malcolm continued to implement David I's Normanizing policies, despite native opposition. He defeated Fergus, Lord of Galloway (1161) and Somerled, Lord of Argyll (1164). His byname was coined in the 15th century, in recognition of his well-attested reputation for chastity.

Malcolm, George John 1917–97
English harpsichordist, pianist and conductor

He was born in London and studied at Oxford and the Royal College of Music. He was Master of Music at Westminster Cathedral (1947–59), where he conducted the first performance of the Missa Brevis which **Benjamin Britten** wrote specially for his choir. He acquired an international reputation as a harpsichordist, especially in the works of **Bach**.

Malcolm X, *originally* Malcolm Little, *Muslim name* el-Hajj Malik el-Shabazz 1925–65
US black nationalist leader

Born in Omaha, Nebraska, the son of a radical Baptist minister, he was brought up in Lansing, Michigan, and Boston. After an adolescence of violence, narcotics and petty crime, he came under the influence of **Elijah Muhammad** while in prison for burglary, changed his name, and after his release in 1952 became Muhammad's chief disciple within the Black Muslims; he greatly expanded the organization's following and became the most effective spokesman for Black Power. In 1963 Malcolm was suspended from the Nation of Islam after disagreements with Muhammad and gained the profound hatred of the leader's loyal followers. Malcolm founded the Organization for Afro-American Unity, dedicated to the alliance of American blacks and other non-white peoples. In the last year of his life, following a pilgrimage to Mecca, Malcolm announced his conversion to orthodox Islam and put forward the belief in the possible brotherhood between blacks and whites. Malcolm's extreme stance and the inflammatory nature of his oratory, which had scared many whites, appealed to many northern blacks in the urban ghettos, but had been met with criticism by moderate civil rights leaders who deplored his violent message. In 1965 Malcolm was killed in Harlem by Black Muslim assassins who retaliated against the man they viewed as a traitor.

Malebranche, Nicolas 1638–1715
French philosopher

Born in Paris, he studied theology and joined the Catholic community of Oratorians (1660), but became interested in philosophy, particularly the work of **René Descartes**. His own major work, *De la recherche de la vérité* (1674, Eng trans *Search for the Truth*), draws on Descartes's dualism of mind and body but explains all causal interaction between them by a theory of 'occasionalism' (divine intervention, governing our bodily movements and all physical events), and argues as a corollary that 'we see all things in God' since external objects cannot act directly upon us. His other works include *Traité de la morale* (1684, Eng trans *A Treatise of Morality*) and *Entretiens sur la métaphysique et la religion* (1688, 'Dialogues on Metaphysics and on Religion').

Malenkov, Giorgi Maksimilianovich 1901–79
Soviet politician

Born in Orenburg in Central Russia, he joined the Communist Party in 1920, began working for the Central Committee in Moscow in 1925 and was quickly selected by Stalin to serve as his personal secretary. He was involved in the collectivization of agriculture and Stalin's purges of the 1930s. From 1934 he headed the party's personnel department and during World War II was part of the five-man defence council which managed the Soviet war effort, being placed in charge of armaments. He was appointed deputy Prime Minister in 1946 and made a full member of the politburo, and on Stalin's death in 1953 took over as de facto party leader. This post, however, was soon assumed by Nikita Khrushchev and a power-struggle ensued. In 1955 Malenkov was forced to resign as Prime Minister, pleading inadequate experience and admitting responsibility for the failure of Soviet agricultural policy. He was succeeded by Marshal Nikolai Bulganin and relegated to the office of Minister for Electric Power Stations, but in 1957, having been accused, with Vyacheslav Molotov and Lazar Kaganovich, of setting up an 'anti-party' group, he was dismissed both from the government and the party's presidium and central committee, and was sent to Kazakhstan as manager of a hydroelectric plant. He retired in 1968 and died in obscurity.

Malesherbes, Chrétien (Guillaume de Lamoignon) de 1721–94
French statesman

He was born in Paris. In 1744 he became a Counsellor of the Parlement of Paris, and in 1750 he was made chief censor of the press; he allowed the publication of the *Encyclopédie* in Paris, despite the fact that its 'privilege' (licence) had been revoked. On Louis XVI's accession (1774) he was made Secretary of State for the royal household. He brought about prison and legal reforms alongside Anne Robert Jacques Turgot's economic improvements, but resigned on Turgot's dismissal (1776). Under the Convention he went to Paris to conduct the king's defence. Despite his integrity and reforming zeal, he was mistrusted as an aristocrat during the Revolution, arrested as a Royalist in 1794, and guillotined.

Malevich, Kasimir Severinovich 1878–1935
Russian painter and designer

Born and trained near Kiev, he worked in Moscow from c.1904. Around 1910 his work began to show Cubist and Futurist influences; however, he was above all interested in developing a totally non-objective art, and in Moscow c.1913 he launched Suprematism, a movement dedicated to the expression in painting of the absolute purity of geometrical forms. The austerity of the earliest Suprematist works had given way by 1917 to less rigid compositions, with a greater colour range and a suggestion of three-dimensional space; in 1918–19, however, he returned to his early ideals with the *White on White* series. After this he virtually stopped producing abstract paintings, and concentrated on expounding his theories through writing and teaching, first at Vitebsk, where he was highly influential, and later in St Petersburg, where he lived from 1922. In 1926 he published *Die gegenstandlose Welt* ('The Non-Objective World'), in which he outlined his theories.

Malherbe, François de 1555–1628
French poet

Born in Caen, he ingratiated himself with Henri IV, and received a pension. He founded a literary tradition, 'Enfin Malherbe vint', and led his countrymen to disdain the richly-coloured verses of Pierre de Ronsard, and to adopt a clear, refined, but prosaic style. He was an industrious writer, producing odes, songs, epigrams, epistles, translations and criticisms. ▣ R Fromilhague, *La vie de Malherbe* (1954)

Malibran, Marie Felicita, *née* Maria García 1808–36
Spanish mezzo-soprano

Born in Paris, she was the daughter of the Spanish singer Manuel Garcia, who was her most important teacher, and sister of Pauline Viardot. She made her operatic debut in London in 1825, and went on to become the most famous female singer of her time. Divorcing her first husband in 1836, she remarried, but died the same year following a fall from a horse.

Malik, Yakob Aleksandrovich 1906–80
Soviet politician

Born in the Ukraine, he was said to be one of Stalin's favourite 'juniors'. Ambassador to Japan (1942–45) and Deputy Foreign Minister (1946), he succeeded Andrei Gromyko as Soviet spokesman at UNO (1948) and was ambassador to Britain (1953–60). From 1960 he was again Deputy Foreign Minister, serving a second term as ambassador to the United Nations (1968–76).

Malinovsky, Rodion Yakovlevich 1898–1967
Russian soldier

He was born in Odessa. He fought in World War I and joined the Red Army after the Revolution (1917). A major-general at the time of the Nazi invasion in 1941, he commanded the forces which liberated Rostov, Kharkov and the Dnieper basin and led the Russian advance on Budapest and into Austria (1944–45). When Russia declared war on Japan, he took a leading part in the Manchurian campaign. In October 1957 he succeeded Marshal Georgi Zhukov as Nikita Khrushchev's Minister of Defence.

Malinowski, Bronisław (Kasper) 1884–1942
British anthropologist, a founder of modern social anthropology

Born in Kraków, Poland, he studied physics and mathematics at the Jagellonian University, and went on to study psychology under Wilhelm Max Wundt at Leipzig, and sociology under Edvard Westermarck at London. In 1914 he left on a research assignment to Australia, but with the outbreak of war was partially confined to the Trobriand Islands, off the eastern tip of New Guinea. Returning to London in 1920, he was appointed in 1927 to the first chair in social anthropology at the London School of Economics. In 1938 he moved to the USA, where he taught at Yale University and undertook field research in Mexico. He was the pioneer of 'participant observation' as a method of fieldwork, and his works on the Trobriand Islanders, especially *Argonauts of the Western Pacific* (1922) and *Coral Gardens and their Magic* (2 vols, 1935), set new standards for ethnographic description. His better-known writings on the Trobriands include *Crime and Custom in Savage Society* (1926) and *Sex and Repression in Savage Society* (1927). A major proponent of functionalism in anthropology, he set out his views in *A Scientific Theory of Culture* (1944). ▣ *Malinowski and the Work of Myth* (1992)

Malipiero, Francesco 1882–1973
Italian composer

Born in Venice, he became a professor at the Venice Conservatorio (1932) and its director (1939–52). He wrote much chamber and symphonic music in a characteristic style and edited **Monteverdi** and **Vivaldi**. He wrote *Claudio Monteverdi* (1930), *Igor Stravinsky* (1945) and the autobiographical *Cosi va lo mondo, 1922–45* (1946).

Mallarmé, Stéphane 1842–98
French Symbolist poet

Born in Paris, he taught English in various schools in Paris and elsewhere, and visited England on several occasions. He translated **Edgar Allan Poe**'s 'The Raven' as 'Le Corbeau' (1875), and in prose and verse he was a leader of the Symbolist school. *L'Après-midi d'un faune* ('A Faun's Afternoon'), which inspired the prelude by **Debussy**, is one of his best-known poems. His *Les Dieux antiques* (1880, 'The Ancient Gods'), *Poésies* (1899) and *Vers et prose* (1893) were other works admired by the 'decadents'. In the second half of the 20th century he has been much admired by the Structuralists. 📖 H Mondor, *La vie de Mallarmé* (2 vols, 1941)

Malle, Louis 1932–95
French film director

Born in Thumières to a wealthy sugar-producing family, he attended the Institut des Hautes Études Cinématographiques and began his career working as an assistant to the explorer **Jacques Cousteau**; they shared an Academy Award for the underwater documentary *Le Monde du silence* (1956, *The Silent World*). Malle made his directorial debut with the thriller *L'Ascenseur pour l'échafaud* (1957, *Frantic*) and was associated with the nouvelle vague through innovative features like *Les Amants* (1958, *The Lovers*) and *Zazie dans le métro* (1960, *Zazie in the Underground*). Interested in social issues, world affairs and the problems of adolescence, he was a sympathetic director of actors and a rare European filmmaker who was able to pursue his personal vision of cinema with equal success on both sides of the Atlantic. His later films include *Le Souffle au cœur* (1971, *Murmur of the Heart*), *Lacombe Lucien* (1974), *Atlantic City* (1980) and *Au Revoir les enfants* (1987, 'Goodbye Children'). He was married to US actress **Candice Bergen** from 1980 until his death.

Mallea, Eduardo 1903–82
Argentine novelist, essayist and editor

Born in Bahia Blanca, son to a self-sacrificing and humane country doctor who greatly influenced him, he was literary editor of the newspaper *La Nación* from 1931. His ambition in his fiction was always to explore the essence of Argentina. But he was an inveterate traveller, and his books drew intelligently from European models, including **Chekhov**, **William Blake**, **Miguel de Unamuno** and **Ramón Pérez de Ayala**. Like **Jorge Luis Borges**, he has been attacked by Marxists. His books include *Historia de una passión argentina* (1937, Eng trans *History of an Argentine Passion*, 1983) and *Todo verdor perecerá* (1941, Eng trans *All Green Shall Perish and Other Novels and Stories*, 1966). 📖 H E Lewald, *Edourdo Mallea* (1977); J H Richard, *The Writings of Edourdo Mallea* (1959)

Mallet, David, *originally* David Malloch
c.1705–1765
Scottish poet

Born near Crieff, Perthshire, he worked as the janitor at Edinburgh High School (1717–18), then studied at Edinburgh University. In 1720 he became a tutor, working from 1723 to 1731 in the family of the Duke of Montrose. Living mostly in London, he changed his name from Scots Malloch to English Mallet. *William and Margaret* (1723), developed from the fragment of an old ballad, gained him a reputation as a poet, which he enhanced by *The Excursion* (1728). He also wrote a play, *Mustapha*, which had a brief success in 1739. *Alfred, a Masque* (1740), was written in conjunction with **James Thomson**, and one of its songs, 'Rule Britannia', was claimed by both.

Mallon, Mary See **Typhoid Mary**

Mallowan, Sir Max Edgar Lucien 1904–78
English archaeologist

Born in London, he studied classics at New College, Oxford (1921–25). His apprenticeship in field archaeology was served with **Leonard Woolley** at Ur in Mesopotamia (1925–31), and it was at Ur that he met the novelist **Agatha Christie**, whom he married in 1930. He made excavations for the British Museum, London, at Arpachiyah near Nineveh (1932–33), and in Syria at Chagar Bazar (1935–36) and Tell Brak (1937–38). After service in the RAF in World War II he became Professor of Western Asiatic Archaeology at London University (1947–60). From this base he continued to excavate in the Near East for several months each year, principally at Nimrud, the ancient capital of Assyria (1949–60), with striking results described in detail in *Nimrud and Its Remains* (1970). Agatha Christie's *Come, tell me how you live* (1946) is a wry account of Mallowan's five seasons' digging in Syria (1934–38). His own autobiography, *Mallowan's Memoirs*, appeared in 1977.

Malmesbury, William of See **William of Malmesbury**

Malone, Edmund 1741–1812
Irish editor of Shakespeare

Born in Dublin, he graduated from Trinity College and was called to the Irish Bar in 1767, but from 1777 devoted himself to literary work in London, his first work being a 'supplement' to **George Steevens**'s edition of Shakespeare (1778). His own 11-volume edition of the great dramatist (1790) was warmly received. He had been one of the first to express his disbelief in **Thomas Chatterton**'s Rowley poems, and in 1796 he denounced the Shakespeare forgeries of **William Henry Ireland**. He left behind a large mass of materials for 'The Variorum Shakespeare', edited in 1821 by James Boswell the younger. The Malone Society was founded in his honour (1907).

Malory, Sir Thomas d.1471
English writer

In **William Caxton**'s preface to Malory's masterpiece, *Le Morte d'Arthur*, it states that Malory was a knight, that he finished his work in the ninth year of the reign of **Edward IV** (1469–70), and that he 'reduced' it from some French book. It is probable that he was the Sir Thomas Malory of Newbold Revel, Warwickshire, whose quarrels with a neighbouring priory and (probably) Lancastrian politics brought him imprisonment. Of Caxton's black-letter folio only two copies now exist. An independent manuscript was discovered at Winchester in 1934. *Le Morte d'Arthur* is a prose romance, which gives epic unity to the whole mass of French Arthurian romance. **Tennyson**, **Algernon Charles Swinburne** and many others took their inspiration from Malory. 📖 S Johnson, in *Lives of the Most Eminent English Poets* (10 vols, 1779–81)

Malouf, David 1934–
Australian novelist and librettist

He was born in Brisbane. A full-time writer since 1978, he has written some verse, collected in *Selected Poems* (1991) and *Poems 1959–1979*, and short stories in *Antipodes* (1985), but is best known for his novels, beginning with *Johnno* (1975). His second novel, *An Imaginary Life*, received wide acclaim when it was serialized by *New Yorker* in 1978; it went on to win the 1979 New South Wales Premier's Literary award. Other novels are *Harland's Half Acre* (1984), *Great World* (1991) and *Remembering Babylon* (1993, Dublin Literary award). He is interested in opera as a vehicle of expression, and has written librettos for **Richard Meale**'s *Voss* (1982), from **Patrick White**'s novel loosely based on Australian explorer Leichhardt, and the same composer's *Mer de Glace* on **Shelley** and **Byron**. His latest collaboration is with composer **Michael Berkeley** in *Baa Baa Black Sheep*, which was taken from **Rudyard Kipling's** autobiographical story, and premiered in 1993. The Conversations at Curlew Creek, between a bushranger about to be hanged and the police officer sent to supervise his execution, was published in 1996. ⚄ P Neilsen, *Imagined Lives: a study of the novels of David Malouf* (1990)

Malpighi, Marcello 1628–94
Italian anatomist and microscopist

Born near Bologna, where he studied philosophy and medicine, he later became professor at the universities of Pisa, Messina and Bologna (1666), and from 1691 served as chief physician to Pope **Innocent XII**. An early pioneer of histology, plant and animal, he conducted a remarkable series of microscopic studies of the structure of the liver, lungs, skin, spleen, glands and brain. He gave the first full account of an insect, the silkworm moth, and investigated muscular cells. ⚄ Howard Adelmann, *Marcello Malpighi and the Evolution of Embryology* (5 vols, 1966)

Malraux, André 1901–76
French writer

Born in Paris, he studied Oriental languages and spent much time in China, where he worked for the Guomindang (Kuomintang) and was active in the 1927 revolution. He also fought as a pilot with the Republican forces in the Spanish Civil War, and in World War II he escaped from a prisoner-of-war camp to join the French Resistance movement. He was Minister of Information in **de Gaulle's** government (1945–46), minister delegate from 1958 and Minister of Cultural Affairs (1960–69). He is best known for his novels, which are a dramatic meditation on human destiny and are highly coloured by his personal experience of war, revolution and resistance to tyranny. Among them are *Les Conquérants* (1928, Eng trans *The Conquerors*, 1929), *La Condition humaine* (1933, Eng trans *Man's Fate*, 1934, winner of the Prix Goncourt) and *L'Espoir* (1937, Eng trans *Man's Hope*, 1938). He also wrote *La Psychologie de l'art* (1947, Eng trans *The Psychology of Art*, 1949), *Les Voix du silence* (4 vols, 1951, Eng trans in 4 vols *The Voices of Silence*, 1953), and other books on art and museums. ⚄ A Madsen, *Malraux* (1979); C Malraux, *Le bruit de nos pas* (3 vols, 1965–69)

Malthus, Thomas Robert 1766–1834
English economist and clergyman

Born near Dorking, Surrey, he was educated at Jesus College, Cambridge, of which he was elected a Fellow in 1793, and in 1797 he was appointed curate at Albury, Surrey. In 1798 he published anonymously his *Essay on the Principle of Population*, with a greatly enlarged and altered edition in 1807. In it he maintained that the optimistic hopes of **Jean Jacques Rousseau** and **William Godwin** are rendered baseless by the natural tendency of population to increase faster than the means of subsistence. (Malthus gives no sanction to the theories and practices currently known as Malthusianism.) The problem had been handled by **Benjamin Franklin, David Hume** and many other writers, but Malthus crystallized the views of those writers, and presented them in systematic form with elaborate proofs derived from history, and he called for positive action to cut the birth-rate, by sexual abstinence or birth control. In 1805 he was appointed Professor of Political Economy at the East India College at Haileybury. His other works included *An Inquiry into the Nature and Progress of Rent* (1815), largely anticipating **David Ricardo**, and *Principles of Political Economy* (1820). **Charles Darwin** read Malthus in 1838, and was greatly influenced by him, seeing in the struggle for existence a mechanism for producing new species—natural selection. ⚄ J Ronar, *Malthus and His Work* (1885)

Malus, Étienne Louis 1775–1812
French physicist

Born in Paris, he was a military engineer in **Napoleon I's** army (1796–1801), and carried out research in optics, discovering the polarization of light by reflection in 1808. This phenomenon provided a very convincing demonstration of the transverse nature of light. Also in 1808 he discovered a fundamental theorem in geometrical optics, which generalizes **Christiaan Huygens** construction to determine the position of a wavefront after light originating from a point source has been reflected or refracted. His paper explaining the theory of double refraction in crystals won him the French Institute's prize in 1810.

Malvern, 1st Viscount See **Huggins, Godfrey Martin**

Mameli, Goffredo 1827–49
Italian poet and patriot

Born in Genoa, he was a volunteer in **Garibaldi's** forces. His patriotic poem 'Fratelli d'Italia' ('Brothers of Italy') was adopted as the Italian national anthem in 1946. He died in the defence of Rome against the French. ⚄ A Viviani, *Mameli* (1937)

Mamet, David Alan 1947–
US dramatist, screen writer and director

Born in Chicago, he graduated from Goddard College, Vermont, and studied acting in New York. His best-known plays, including *American Buffalo* (1975), *Glengarry Glen Ross* (1983, Pulitzer Prize, filmed 1992), *Speed-the-Plow* (1988) and *Oleanna* (1992), address the psychological and ethical issues that confront modern, urban society. Other plays include *Sexual Perversity in Chicago, The Water Engine* (both 1977), *A Life in the Theater* (1978), *Edmond* (1982), and *The Shawl* (1985). He has translated works by **Chekhov**, and his screenplays include a new adaptation of *The Postman Always Rings Twice* (1981), *The Untouchables* (1987) and *Vanya on 42nd Street* (1994), based on **Ibsen's** *Uncle Vanya*. He wrote and directed *House of Games* (1987), a look at seedy professional gambling, and published essay collections such as *Writing in Restaurants* (1986) and *Make-Believe Town* (1996). He won his third Obie award for *The Cryptogram* (1994), a play inspired by his childhood, featuring a small boy struggling to decipher the hostile and cryptic language of the adults around him. Other work includes *The Cabin* (1992) and *The Village* (1994). ⚄ C W E Bigsby, *David Mamet* (1985)

Mamluks
Egyptian sultans

They are commonly divided into the two lines of Kipchak (Bahris, 1250–1382) and Circassian (Burjis, 1382–1517) origin. Their name derives from that originally applied to the group from which they were drawn, a privileged caste of military slaves recruited from various non-Muslim peoples (especially Turks and Caucasians) and who, as converts, served in the armies of most Islamic powers from the 9th century onwards. In 1250 the Ayyubid Sultan of Egypt, Turan-Shah, was murdered by a group of Turkish Kipchak mamluks belonging to his military household, who later enthroned one of their number, thus inaugurating the *dawlat al-Atrak* ('state of the Turks'). The Mamluks defeated the Mongol invaders of Syria at 'Ayn Jalut and Hims (1260). One of the successful commanders in these campaigns was Baybars (1233–77), who murdered his predecessor to become sultan (1260) and went on to consolidate Mamluk rule, capturing Caesarea, Jaffa and Antioch from the Franks and reducing the crusader states to a coastal strip based around Acre. Although he secured religious legitimation by installing various members of the 'Abbasid family as caliphs in Cairo, Baybars was unable to establish a dynasty. In 1279 the throne was seized by al-Mansur Qalawun (d.1290) whose son al-Ashraf Khalil (d.1293) captured Acre, crushing the crusaders' kingdom (1291). Khalil's murder by a rival led to a period of turbulence from which his brother, al-Nasir Muhammad (d.1341), emerged victorious in 1310 after having been deposed twice. The sultanate remained in this family until 1382, when the last Qalawunid was dethroned by Barquq (d.1399), the representative of the Circassian element whose influence had come to outweigh that of the Kipchaks. After the deposition and death of Barquq's son Faraj (1389–1412), the succession ceased to be hereditary, but tended to be determined by the strongest Mamluk faction. In the 15th century the Mamluks failed to keep pace with developments in warfare, and consequently were no match for the technically superior Ottoman army. They were decisively defeated by Selim I, who incorporated Egypt into the Ottoman Empire (1516–17). While the sultanate thus ended with his execution of the last Burji, Tuman-Bay, the Mamluk class retained a privileged status under Ottoman rule until it was finally suppressed by Mehemet 'Ali in 1812.

Manasseh 7th century BC
Biblical King of Judah

He was the son of Hezekiah whom he succeeded as king (697–642BC). He earned notoriety for his idolatry and wickedness until, as a captive in Babylon, he repented. *The Prayer of Manasseh* is apocryphal.

Manasseh Ben Israel 1604–57
Dutch Jewish scholar

Born in Lisbon, Portugal, he was taken early to Amsterdam. He became chief rabbi there at the age of 18, and set up the first printing press in Holland (1626). From 1655 to 1657 he was in England, securing from Cromwell the readmission of the Jews to Great Britain. He wrote important works in Hebrew, Spanish and Latin, and in English a *Humble Address* to Cromwell, *A Declaration*, and *Vindiciae Judaeorum* (1656,'Vindication of the Jews').

Manby, George William 1765–1854
English inventor

He was barrack-master at Yarmouth from 1803. In 1807 he demonstrated a means of saving shipwrecked persons by firing a rope to the ship from a mortar on shore. He wrote on this method, on lifeboats, criminal law and other subjects.

Manchester, Edward Montagu, 2nd Earl of
1602–71
English soldier

In 1623 he accompanied Prince Charles (Charles I) to Spain on his abortive mission to woo the Infanta Maria, and in 1626 was raised to the House of Lords as Baron Montagu of Kimbolton, but was better known by his courtesy title of Viscount Mandeville. Siding with the Popular party, and an acknowledged leader of the Puritans in the Upper House, in 1642 he was impeached by the king for treachery, but was acquitted. He succeeded his father as 2nd Earl in the same year. At the outbreak of the Civil War he fought for the Parliamentarians. He served under the 3rd Earl of Essex at Edgehill, and then held the associated (eastern) counties against William Cavendish, Duke of Newcastle, took Lincoln (1644), and routed Prince Rupert at Marston Moor (1644). He then marched to oppose the Royalists in the south-west, and defeated them at Newbury (the second battle). Deprived of his command (1645), he opposed the trial of the king, and protested against the Commonwealth. Afterwards, having been active in promoting the Restoration, he was made Lord Chamberlain (1660), a step designed to conciliate the Presbyterians.

Manchester, William Raymond 1922–
US novelist and contemporary historian

Born in Attleboro, Massachusetts, he began his career as a newspaper reporter and foreign correspondent in the Middle East, India and Southeast Asia. His book *The Death of a President* (1967), written at the behest of the Kennedy family, was a landmark in reportage and sold in millions but has subsequently been superseded as new evidence on the assassination of President John F Kennedy has emerged. Among his other major works are *The Arms of Krupp* (1968), a history of the German munitions makers, and the biographies *American Caesar: Douglas MacArthur, 1880-1964* (1978) and *The Last Lion: Winston Spencer Churchill* (2 vols, 1983–87). Later publications include *This Is Our Time* (1989) and *A World Lit Only By Fire* (1992). ▭ *Controversy* (1976)

Mancini, Hortense, Duchesse de Mazarin
1646–99
Italian beauty

She was the sister of Marie Anne, Olympe, Laura and Marie Mancini. Married off by Cardinal Mazarin to Armand Charles de la Porte, who assumed the Mazarin title, she separated from him and became famous for her beauty at the court of Charles II in London.

Mancini, Laura, Duchesse de Mercoeur
1636–57
Italian beauty

The sister of Hortense, Marie Anne, Olympe, and Marie Mancini, she went to the French court and was married to Louis de Vendôme. Louis Joseph, Duc de Vendôme was their son.

Mancini, Marie, Princess de Colonna
1640–1715
Italian beauty

She was the sister of Hortense, Marie Anne, Olympe and Laura Mancini. She was a mistress of Louis XIV, who was prevented from marrying her by the machinations of Cardinal Mazarin. She lived in Spain for most of her life.

Mancini, Marie Anne, Duchesse de Bouillon
1649–1714
Italian noblewoman and alleged poisoner

She was the sister of Hortense, Laura, Marie and Olympe Mancini. She moved with them and their uncle Cardinal Mazarin to France and became renowned for her beauty, her literary salon and for her patronage of the French poet Jean de La Fontaine. She was banished in 1680, having been involved in the *cause célèbre* of the notorious sorceress La Voisin (real name Catherine Deshayes Monvoisin, burned 1680) known as the 'Affair of the Poisons'.

Mancini, Olympe, Comtesse de Soissons
1639–1708
Italian beauty

The sister of Hortense, Marie Anne, Laura and Marie Mancini, she was a mistress of Louis XIV. She was involved with her sister, Marie Anne, in the La Voisin intrigues and, accused of poisoning her husband and the Queen of Spain, she fled to the Netherlands. Her son was Prince Eugène of Savoy.

Mandela, Nelson See panel p1217

Mandela, (Nomzano) Winnie (Winifred)
Xhosa surname Madikizela 1934–
South African civil rights activist

Born in Bizana, she married Nelson Mandela in 1958, and became active in his work for the African National Congress (ANC). When he was put in prison by the South African government (1964–90), she too was banned, imprisoned (1969–70), and forced into internal exile (1977–85). In 1985 she returned to Soweto and became involved

Mandela, Nelson 1918–
South African lawyer, statesman and Nobel Prize winner

Nelson Mandela was born in Umtata, the son of a local chief in Transkei. He practised as a lawyer in Johannesburg, establishing the country's first black legal practice. In 1944 he joined the African National Congress (ANC), and for the next 20 years he directed a campaign of defiance against the South African government and its policy of apartheid or 'separate development'. The ANC was banned in 1960 after the Sharpeville massacre; the following year Mandela organized a three-day national strike, and in 1964 he was sentenced to life imprisonment for political offences that included sabotage and treason. From his prison cell, Mandela became a symbol of black resistance to apartheid, acquiring a charisma that was enhanced by his refusal to enter into any kind of deal with the authorities.

During the 1970s and 1980s, Mandela grew into an international figure and the focus of an increasingly powerful international campaign for his release, in which his second wife **Winnie Mandela** (married to him in 1958) played a leading part. In 1988 his seventieth birthday provided the opportunity for further intensifying demands for his release, and international alarm at reports of his declining health led to his being moved to a more comfortable confinement.

The liberalizing measures of **F W de Klerk** (President from 1989) began the process of dismantling apartheid; within months of his election, de Klerk visited Mandela in prison, and finally ordered his release in February 1990, after lifting the ban on the ANC, removing restrictions on political groups, and calling a halt to the executions. In 1991 Mandela was elected President of the ANC (his friend **Oliver Tambo** was elected chairman), and entered into talks with de Klerk about the country's future. He travelled extensively to win support for continued inter national pressure to abolish apartheid completely. In 1993 he was awarded the Nobel Peace Prize jointly with de Klerk for their work in the process of reform. On 10 May 1994 he was inaugurated as South Africa's first black President.

Nelson Mandela's marriage to Winnie came under increasing strain as a result of her controversial activities and associations, and they were separated in 1992 and divorced in 1996. He had appointed her to government office in 1994, but removed her the following year. This embarrassment, together with continued hostility between the ANC and the Zulu Inkatha movement, has only slightly tarnished Mandela's triumph as the new leader of his country, and he has continued to strengthen relations with South Africa's trading partners in Europe and America. His term as President ends in 1999.

📖 Mandela wrote *No Easy Walk to Freedom* (1965); his autobiography, *Long Walk to Freedom*, was published in 1994. See also Fatima Meer, *Higher than Hope: The Authorized Biography of Nelson Mandela* (1990) and M Benson, *Nelson Mandela* (1986).

Mandela's world renown was recognized when South Africa hosted the Rugby World Cup in 1995. Mandela himself, in acknowledgement of the importance of sport to international reputation, walked out on to the pitch wearing his country's shirt before the final, which South Africa won. As well as the Nobel Prize, Mandela has honorary degrees from over 50 universities throughout the world.

'During my lifetime I have dedicated my life to this struggle of the African people. I have fought against white domination, and I have fought against black domination. I have cherished the ideals of a democratic and free society in which all persons live together in harmony with equal opportunities. It is an ideal which I hope to live for, and to see realized. But My Lord, if needs be, it is an ideal for which I am prepared to die.' Speech in court when charged under the Suppression of Communism Act and facing the death penalty, 20 April 1964.

in the militant politics of the township. Throughout Nelson Mandela's 26-year incarceration (1964–90), she campaigned ceaselessly for black rights on his behalf and for his release. Her popularity declined in 1988–89 when her bodyguards were implicated in the kidnapping, beating and murder of a black youth. She was convicted of the kidnapping alone but her six-year sentence was commuted to a £9,000 fine. She was appointed head of the ANC's department of social affairs in 1994, but was removed the following year. Her marriage came under strain due to her controversial activities and associations and the couple separated in 1992 and divorced in 1996. She retained her position as president of the ANC Women's League, winning re-election in 1997.

Mandelstam, Osip Yemilevich 1891–1938

Russian poet, critic and translator

Born of Jewish parents in Warsaw, he grew up in St Petersburg and attended Heidelberg University. A classicist whose Russian 'sounds like Latin', he had a great love of Greek poetry. Three books of poems appeared during his lifetime—*Kamen* (1913, Eng trans *Stone*, 1981), *Tristia* (1922) and *Stikhotvoreniya* (1928, 'Poems')—and *Sobraniye sochineniy* (1964–71, Eng trans *The Complete Poetry*, 1973) appeared in 1973. He is regarded by some as the greatest Russian poet of the century. Arrested, exiled and re-arrested, he died on his way to one of **Stalin**'s camps. His wife Nadezhda Mandelstam wrote their story in *Hope Against Hope* (1970). 📖 N Struve, *Osip Mandelstam* (1982)

Mander, Karel van 1548–1606

Flemish portrait painter and writer

Born in Meulebeke, he lived mostly in Haarlem, and is chiefly remembered for his *Schilderbouck* (1604, 'The Book of Painters'), a collection of biographical profiles of painters, important as a source for the art history of the Low Countries.

Mandeville, Bernard 1670–1733

British satirist

Born in Dort, the Netherlands, he took his MD at Leyden in 1691, then practised medicine in London. He is known as the author of a short work in doggerel verse, *The Fable of the Bees* (1723, originally *The Grumbling Hive*, 1705). In it he argued that 'private vices are public benefits', and that every species of virtue is basically some form of gross selfishness. The book was widely attacked, and condemned by the grand jury of Middlesex. He also wrote several works arguing for an improvement in the status of women, including *The Virgin Unmasked* (1709), and *A Modest Defence of Public Stews* (1724), on the condition of brothels. 📖 J M Robertson, *Pioneer Humanists* (1907)

Mandeville, Viscount (Edward) See Manchester, 2nd Earl of

Mandeville, Sir Jehan de or John, also spelt Maundeville or Maundevylle 14th century

Unknown compiler of a travel book

This writer compiled a famous book of travels, *The Voyage and Travels of Sir John Mandeville, Knight*. The book was published apparently in 1366, and soon translated from the French into all European languages. It may have been written by a physician, Jehan de Bourgogne, otherwise Jehan à la Barbe, who died in Liège in 1372, and who is said to have revealed on his death-bed his real name of Mandeville (or Maundevylle), explaining that he had had to flee from his native England for a homicide. Some, however, attribute it to Jean d'Outremeuse, a Frenchman. 'Mandeville' claims to have travelled through Turkey, Persia, Syria, Arabia, North Africa and India, but much of the book is a compilation from various literary sources. 📖 J W Bennett, *The Rediscovery of Sir Jehan Mandeville* (1954)

Manen, Hans van 1932–
Dutch dancer, choreographer and director

Born in Nieuwer, Amstel, he joined Ballet Recital in 1952, moving to Amsterdam Opera Ballet in 1959. Later that year he became one of the founding members of Netherlands Dance Theater (NDT), of which he was appointed artistic director. In 1973 he joined the Dutch National Ballet as choreographer and ballet master but re-established his relationship with NDT. His work for NDT includes *Symphony in Three Movements* (1963), *Essay in Silence* (1965), *Five Sketches* (1966), *Squares* (1969), *Septet Extra* (1973) and *Songs Without Words* (1977).

Manet, Édouard 1832–83
French painter

Born in Paris, he was originally intended for a legal career, and sent on a voyage to Rio to distract his thoughts from art. Nevertheless, between 1850 and 1856 he studied under Thomas Couture (1815–79), and his *Spanish Guitar Player* was awarded an honourable mention at the 1861 Salon. Pursuing official recognition, he entered his *Déjeuner sur l'herbe* for the Salon of 1863 but it scandalized the jury with its portrayal of a nude female with clothed male companions, and was rejected. This was followed by the acceptance of his *Olympia* in 1865, but, being a stark depiction of a woman obviously modelled by a prostitute, it elicited a similar outcry from the public. Manet was influenced by conventional artists: *Olympia* owes a great deal to the nudes of Giorgione, Titian and Raphael. But the strong contrasts he learned from the Spanish masters—he was an ardent admirer of Velázquez—and his adherence to the advice of Gustave Courbet in always selecting subjects from contemporary life marked him out from the older Salon artists. In the 1870s he came under the influence of the Impressionists and, in particular, of Monet while painting at Argenteuil, and his technique became free and more spontaneous. He never exhibited with the group but became a father-figure to them because of his stand against the conventions of the Salon. His last major work was *Un Bar aux Folies-Bergères* (1881–82). In that year, official recognition finally arrived—he was appointed Chevalier of the Legion of Honour—but he died an embittered man.

Manetho 3rd century BC
Egyptian historian

He was high priest of Heliopolis. He wrote in Greek a history of the 30 dynasties from mythical times to 323BC, of which only portions have been preserved in the works of Julius Africanus (AD300), Eusebius of Caesarea, and George Syncellus (AD800).

Manfred 1232–66
King of Sicily

He was a natural son of Emperor Frederick II, and was made Prince of Taranto. He was regent in Italy for his half-brother, Conrad IV, and defended the empire's interests against Pope Innocent IV for his nephew Conradin of Swabia. The pope, however, compelled Manfred to flee for shelter to the Saracens, who helped him defeat the papal troops. In 1257 he became Master of Naples and Sicily, and on the (false) rumour of Conradin's death (1258) he was crowned king at Palermo. In spite of excommunication by Pope Alexander IV, he occupied Tuscany after victory at Montaperti (1260). Pope Urban IV renewed the excommunication and bestowed Manfred's dominions on Charles of Anjou, brother of Louis IX of France. Manfred fell in battle at Benevento, and was succeeded by Charles.

Mangan, James Clarence 1803–49
Irish poet

Born in Dublin, the son of a grocer, he worked as a lawyer's clerk, and later found employment in the library of Trinity College, Dublin. Although he knew no Irish, he published English versions of Irish poems in *The Poets and Poetry of Munster* (1849), notably 'My Dark Rosaleen', 'The Nameless One' and 'The Woman of Three Cows'. He also published translations from German poets in *Anthologia Germanica* (1845). 📖 D J O'Donaghue, *The Life and Writings of James Clarence Mangan* (1897)

Mangin, Noel 1931–95
New Zealand operatic bass

Born in Wellington, he trained as a tenor and sang thus in *The Merry Widow* in 1956. He made his operatic debut as a baritone in 1957 but by 1959 was singing the demanding bass role of Osmin in *Die Entführung aus dem Serail* ('The Abduction from the Seraglio') with the New Zealand Opera Company. He made his debut at Sadler's Wells in *Tosca* in 1963, and at the Hamburg Statsoper in 1967. In 1977 he went freelance with a repertoire of over 100 bass roles, and was always in demand as Osmin; as Dr Bartolo or Don Basilio in *Barber of Seville*; or as Baron Ochs in *Rosenkavalier*—the 'heavy comic' roles. In 1979 he sang the roles of Fafner, Hunding and Hagen in one complete *Ring* cycle.

Manichaeus or Mani c.215–276AD
Persian religious leader

Born in Ecbatana, he was the founder of the heretical sect of Manichaeism. About AD245 he began to proclaim his new religion at the court of the Persian King Sapor (Shahpur) I. He travelled widely, but eventually King Bahram I abandoned him to his Zoroastrian enemies, who crucified him.

Manin, Daniele 1804–57
Italian lawyer and statesman

Born in Venice of Jewish ancestry, he practised at the Bar, and became a leader of liberal opinion. As President of the Venetian republic (1848) he was at the centre of the heroic five months' defence against the Austrians. When Venice capitulated (1849), Manin, with 39 others, was excluded from the amnesty, but escaped to Paris, where he taught Italian. He shifted from his republican stance to support for a united Italy, and he supported Giuseppe La Farina in his creation of the Italian National Society. His bones were taken to Venice in 1868.

Maniu, Iuliu 1873–1953
Romanian politician

The leader of the National Party, he directed the provisional government in Transylvania which proclaimed union with Romania (1918). Later, as leader of the National Peasant Party, he served as Prime Minister and tried to carry out agrarian reform (1928–30) but resigned from office when King Carol II of Romania introduced his mistress, Magda Lupescu, into the Romanian court. He was again Prime Minister (1932–33) and his electoral alliance with the Iron Guard was an expediency aimed at curbing the king's power (1937). He played a major role in the coup of 1944 and was a minister without portfolio in

General Sănătescu's national government which declared war on Germany. The postwar Communist regime, in a move intended to destroy the Peasant Party, had him arrested, accused of conspiring with US intelligence agents. He received a life sentence (1947) and died in prison.

Mankiewicz, Herman Jacob 1897–1953
US screenwriter

He was born in New York. A member of the United States Marine Corps, he later worked in Europe for the Red Cross Press Service, as Isadora Duncan's publicity manager and as Berlin correspondent for the *Chicago Tribune*. Returning to the USA in 1922, he was assistant drama editor for the *New York Times* (1922–26) and wrote his first screenplay for *The Road To Mandalay* (1926). A prolific writer, he was also much in demand as a script doctor and in addition was the producer of a number of films, including the Marx Brothers comedies *Horse Feathers* (1932) and *Duck Soup* (1933). A member of the Algonquin Round Table set and a frequent contributor to the *New Yorker*, his move to Hollywood was widely seen as the prostituting of a fine, witty literary talent. His most significant contribution to the cinema came as the co-writer of Orson Welles's *Citizen Kane* (1941), for which he received an Academy Award. Other credited screenplays include *The Royal Family of Broadway* (1930), *Dinner At Eight* (1933), *It's A Wonderful World* (1939) and *The Enchanted Cottage* (1946). He was the brother of Joseph L Mankiewicz.

Mankiewicz, Joseph Leo 1909–93
US filmmaker

Born in Wilkes-Barre, Pennsylvania, he worked as a reporter before joining Paramount Pictures as a junior writer in 1929. As a screenwriter, he collaborated on such films as *If I Had A Million* (1932) and *Manhattan Melodrama* (1934). Under contract to MGM from 1933, he produced sophisticated comedies like *The Philadelphia Story* (1940) and *Woman Of The Year* (1942). He made his directorial debut with *Dragonwyck* (1946) and won Academy Awards for Direction and Screenwriting on both *A Letter to Three Wives* (1949) and *All About Eve* (1950). His best work is distinguished by the quality of its wit, the sharpness of its dialogue and the power of its performances. Among his films are *Julius Caesar* (1953), *Guys and Dolls* (1955) and the notorious failure *Cleopatra* (1963). He directed *Carol for Another Christmas* (1964) for television and made his final film, *Sleuth*, in 1972.

Mankowitz, (Cyril) Wolf 1924–
English author, playwright and antique dealer

He was born in Bethnal Green, London, and studied at Cambridge. An authority on Josiah Wedgwood, he published *Wedgwood* (1953) and *The Portland Vase* (1953), and was an editor of *The Concise Encyclopedia of English Pottery and Porcelain* (1957). Other publications include the novels *Make Me an Offer* (1952), *A Kid for Two Farthings* (1953) and *A Night With Casanova* (1991), and a collection of short stories, *The Mendelman Fire* (1957). Among his plays is *The Bespoke Overcoat* (1954), and his films, *The Millionairess* (1960), *The Long, The Short, and the Tall* (1961), *Casino Royale* (1967) and *The Hebrew Lesson* (1972), as well as his documentary on Yiddish cinema from 1929 to 1939, *Almonds and Raisins* (1984).

Manley, (Mary) Delarivier or de la Rivière
c.1672–1724
British writer

She was born either in Holland or in Jersey, the daughter of a future governor of Jersey. After her father's death (1688) she was lured into a bigamous marriage with her cousin, John Manley of Truro, MP, who soon deserted her. She went to England, where she had a success with the publication of her letters, and in 1696 wrote two plays, entitled *The Lost Lover* and *The Royal Mischief*. She also

wrote gossipy chronicles disguised as fiction, especially the scandalous anti-Whig *The New Atalantis* (1709), and in 1711 she succeeded Jonathan Swift as editor of *The Examiner*. She wrote a fictional account of her own early struggles in *The Adventures of Rivella* (1714). Her last work was *The Power of Love, in Seven Novels* (1720). 🕮 *Letters Written by Mrs Manley* (1696)

Manley, Michael Norman 1924–97
Jamaican politician

Born in Kingston, the son of Norman Manley, and educated in Jamaica, he served in the Royal Canadian Air Force in World War II, and then studied at the London School of Economics (1945–49). He spent some time in journalism in Britain before returning to Jamaica. He became a leader of the National Workers' Union in the 1950s, sat in the Senate (1962–67) and was then elected to the House of Representatives. He became leader of the People's National Party (PNP) in 1969 and Prime Minister in 1972. He embarked on a radical, socialist programme, cooling relations with the USA, and despite rising unemployment was re-elected in 1976. He was decisively defeated in 1980 and 1983 but returned to power in 1989, with a much more moderate policy stance. However, he was forced to resign in 1992 due to poor health. His publications include *The Politics of Change* (1994) and *The Poverty of Nations* (1991).

Manley, Norman Washington 1893–1969
Jamaican politician

He was born in Kingston. He studied law, was called to the Bar and became a respected QC. In 1938 he won fame by successfully defending his cousin, and political opponent, Alexander Bustamante, who was then an active trade unionist, on a charge of sedition. In the same year Manley founded the People's National Party (PNP) and in 1955, seven years before Jamaica achieved full independence, became Prime Minister. He handed over leadership of the PNP to his son Michael Manley in 1969.

Mann, Heinrich 1871–1950
German novelist

He was born in Lübeck, the brother of Thomas Mann. He began to be described as the German Zola for his ruthless exposure of pre-1914 German society in *Im Schlaraffenland* (1901, Eng trans *Berlin, the Land of Cockaigne*, 1925), and the trilogy describing the three classes of Kaiser Wilhelm II's empire, *Die Armen* (1917, 'The Poor'), *Der Untertan* (1918, 'The Subject') and *Der Kopf* (1929, 'The Head'). He is best known for the macabre, Expressionist novel, *Professor Unrat* (1904, 'Professor Nonsense'), describing the moral degradation of a once outwardly respectable schoolmaster, which was translated and filmed as *The Blue Angel* (1932). He lived in France (1933–40) and then escaped to the USA. Other works include *Die kleine Stadt* (1901, 'The Little Town'), set in a small Italian town, and a remarkable autobiography, *Ein Zeitalter wird besichtigt* (1945–46, 'Exposition of an Era'). His influence is evident in the works of Jakob Wasserman and Lion Feuchtwanger. 🕮 R N Lina, *Heinrich Mann* (1967)

Mann, Horace 1796–1859
US educationist

Born in Franklin, Massachusetts, he entered the Massachusetts legislature in 1827, and was president of the state senate (1827–37). As Secretary of the Massachusetts Board of Education (1837–48), he improved and reorganized the public school system and established the basis for universal, non-sectarian public education. His call for free public education as a bulwark of democracy had a national influence. He became a member of the House of Representatives (1848–53), and president of Antioch College, Ohio (1852–59). He is regarded as the 'father of American public education'.

Mann, Thomas 1875–1955
German novelist and Nobel Prize winner

Thomas Mann was born in Lübeck into a patrician family of merchants and senators of the Hanseatic League. His older brother was **Heinrich Mann**, also a novelist, and his mother was a talented musician of mixed German and Portuguese West Indian blood. The tensions between a conservative background and an artistic disposition, as well as between the Nordic and Latin temperaments inherent in his own personality, were to form the psychological basis of his subject matter.

At the age of 19, without completing school, he settled with his mother in Munich, and after a spell at the university he joined his brother in Italy, where he wrote his early masterpiece, *Buddenbrooks: Verfall einer Familie* (1901, Eng trans *Buddenbrooks: The Decline of a Family*, 1924), the saga of a family like his own, tracing its decline through four generations as business acumen gives way to artistic sensibilities. With this work, Mann was a leading German writer at the age of 25.

On his return to Munich he became a reader for the satirical literary magazine *Simplicissimus*, which published many of his early, remarkable short stories. The novelettes *Tonio Kröger* (1902), *Tristan* (1903) and *Der Tod in Venedig* (1913, Eng trans *Death in Venice*, 1925) all deal with the problem of the artist's salvation; in the last of these, the subject of an opera by **Benjamin Britten** (1973) and a film by **Luchino Visconti** (1971), a successful writer dies on the brink of perverted eroticism.

World War I precipitated a quarrel between the two novelist brothers, with Thomas's *Betrachtungen eines Unpolitischen* (1918, Eng trans *Reflections of a Non-political Man*, 1983) revealing his militant German patriotism, already a feature of his essay on **Frederick the Great**, and a distrust of political ideologies, including the radicalism of his brother. *Der Zauberberg* (1924, Eng trans *The Magic Mountain*, 1927), won him the Nobel Prize for literature in 1929. It was inspired by a visit to his wife at a sanatorium for consumptives in Davos in 1913 and tells the story of a patient, Hans Castorp, with the sanatorium representing Europe in its moral and intellectual disintegration.

The same year, Mann delivered a speech against the rising Nazis and in 1930 exposed Italian fascism in *Mario und der Zauberer* (1930, Eng trans *Mario and the Magician*, 1930). He left Germany for Switzerland after 1933 and in 1936 delivered an address for **Freud**'s eightieth birthday. Both shared an enthusiasm for the biblical patriarch, **Joseph**, and Mann wrote a tetralogy on his life (1933–43).

He settled in the USA in 1936 and wrote a novel on a visit to **Goethe** by an old love, Charlotte Buff, *Lotte in Weimar* (1939). During World War II, he delivered anti-**Hitler** broadcasts to Germany, which at the end of the war were collected under the titles *Achtung Europa!* (1938) and *Deutsche Hörer* (1942, Eng trans *Listen Germany! Twenty-Five Messages to the German People over the BBC*, 1943; augmented edition of 55 messages, 1945). In 1947 he returned to Switzerland and was the only returning exile to be fêted by both West and East Germany. His greatest work, a modern version of the medieval legend *Doktor Faustus* (1947), combines art and politics in the simultaneous treatment of the life and catastrophic end of a composer, Adrian Leverkühn, and German disintegration in two world wars.

His last unfinished work, hailed as Germany's greatest comic novel, *Bekenntnisse des Hochstaplers Felix Krull*, Part I (1922; 1953, Eng trans *Confidence Man*, 1955), written with astonishing wit, irony and humour and without the tortuous stylistic complexities of the *Bildungsroman*, commended itself most to English translators.

📖 Thomas Mann was essentially a 19th-century German conservative whose cultural landmarks disappeared in World War I, and he resorted in his work to a critique of the artistic. Other later works include *Der Erwählte* (1951, Eng trans *The Holy Sinner*, 1951), a retelling of the 12th-century legend of an incestuous pope named Gregory, *Die Betrogene* (1953, Eng trans *The Black Swan*, 1954) and *Last Essays*, on **Schiller**, **Goethe**, **Nietzsche** and **Chekhov**.

See also M Swales, *Thomas Mann: A Study* (1980); Thomas Mann, *Sketch of My Life* (1960); H Hatfield, *Thomas Mann* (1951).

> *Die Zeit hat in Wirklichkeit keine Einschnitte, es gibt kein Gewitter oder Drommetengetön beim Beginn eines neuen Monats oder Jahres, und selbst bei dem eines neuen Säkulums sind es nur wir Menschen, die schieen und läuten.*
>
> 'Time has no divisions to mark its passage, there is never a thunderstorm or blare of trumpets to announce the beginning of a new month or year. Even when a new century begins it is only we mortals who ring bells and fire off pistols.'
>
> From *Der Zauberberg*, ch.4, section 4 (translated by H T Lowe-Porter).

Mann, Thomas See panel above

Mannerheim, Carl Gustav Emil, Baron
1867–1951
Finnish soldier and politician

He was born in Villnäs, but fought in the Russian army during the Russo-Japanese War (1904–05) and World War I. When Finland declared her independence (1918), he became Supreme Commander and regent. Defeated in the presidential election of 1919, he retired into private life, but returned as Commander-in-Chief against the Russians in the Russo-Finnish War of 1939–40. He continued to command the Finnish forces until 1944, when he became President of the Finnish Republic, remaining in office until 1946. He died at Lausanne, Switzerland. 📖 S Jagerskjold, *Mannerheim* (1987)

Mannheim, Karl 1893–1947
German sociologist

Born in Budapest, Hungary, he was educated at the universities of Budapest and Strasbourg. In 1919, after the Hungarian revolution, he emigrated to Heidelberg, became a lecturer at the university (1925), and in 1930 was appointed Professor of Sociology and Political Economy at Frankfurt University. When he was expelled from Germany by the Nazis in 1933, he fled to England, where he joined the London School of Economics. In 1945 he became Professor of Sociology and Philosophy of Education at the London University Institute of Education. One of the founders of the sociology of knowledge, he also wrote about political planning and education. His books include *Ideology and Utopia* (1929, trans 1936), *Man and Society in an Age of Reconstruction* (1935, trans 1940), *Freedom, Power and Democratic Planning* (1950) and *Diagnosis of Our Time* (1943).

Manning, Henry Edward 1808–92
English Roman Catholic prelate

Born in Totteridge, Hertfordshire, he was educated at Harrow and Balliol College, Oxford. After taking a classical first in 1830, he was elected a Fellow of Merton (1832). An eloquent preacher and a High Churchman, in 1833 he became rector of Woollavington and Graffham, Sussex, and in 1840 archdeacon of Chichester. In 1851, he joined the Roman Catholic Church, and in 1865 succeeded Cardinal Wiseman as Archbishop of Westminster. At the Ecumenical Council of 1870 Manning was one of the most zealous supporters of the infallibility dogma, and, elected a cardinal in 1875, continued as a leader of the Ultramontanes. He was a member of the royal commissions on the housing of the poor (1885) and on education (1886), and took a prominent part in temperance and benevolent movements.

Manning, Dame (Elizabeth) Leah, *née* Perrett 1886–1977
English Labour politician
Born in Rockford, Illinois, she was strongly influenced by the legend of her great-grandmother (by marriage), the Methodist philanthropist Susan Tappin, who did good works among the poor of London's East End. She trained as a teacher at Homerton College, Cambridge, where she also began her involvement with the Fabian Society. She was an MP in the Labour Government (1929–31, 1945–50), and she tirelessly championed the Republican cause during the Spanish Civil War. Her publications include *What I Saw in Spain* (1933), in which she strongly advocates a policy of non-intervention, and her autobiography, *A Life for Education* (1970). She was created DBE in 1966.

Manning, Olivia 1908–80
English novelist
She was born in Portsmouth, but spent much of her youth in Ireland, and had 'the usual Anglo-Irish sense of belonging to nowhere'. She trained at art school, and then went to London, and in 1937 published her first novel, *The Wind Changes*. She married in 1939 and went abroad that year with her husband, Reggie Smith, a British Council lecturer in Bucharest. Her experiences there formed the basis of her 'Balkan trilogy', comprising *The Great Fortune* (1960), *The Spoilt City* (1962) and *Friends and Heroes* (1965). When the Germans approached Athens, she and her husband evacuated to Egypt, finally ending up in Jerusalem. She returned to London in 1946, where she lived until her death. Her prolific output includes *Artist Among the Missing* (1949), *A Different Face* (1953), and her 'Levant trilogy', comprising *The Danger Tree* (1977), *The Battle Lost and Won* (1978) and *The Sum of Things* (1980). The 'Balkan trilogy' and the 'Levant trilogy' form a single narrative entitled *Fortunes of War*, which Anthony Burgess described as 'the finest fictional record of the war produced by a British writer'. 📖 K Dick, *Friends and Friendship* (1974)

Manning, Thomas 1772–1840
English traveller
Born at Broome rectory, Suffolk, he went to Caius College, Cambridge, to study Chinese (1790), and in 1806 went to Canton as a doctor. In 1811–12 he was the first Englishman to visit Lhasa in Tibet. He returned to England in 1817, and later travelled to Italy (1827–29).

Mannix, Daniel 1864–1963
Australian Catholic archbishop
Born in Deerpark, Rathluirc, County Cork, Ireland, and ordained at Maynooth in 1890, he was appointed Coadjutor-Archbishop of Melbourne, Australia in 1912 and Archbishop in 1917, and campaigned strongly for the rights of Catholics in Australian society, especially state aid for Church schools. After the Easter Rising in Ireland (1916) he became an outspoken supporter of Irish Home Rule, and opposed William Morris Hughes's demands for

conscription in 1916–17. His position verged on a populist identification with the working classes, with whom he enjoyed an immense prestige which he never lost; the social establishment demanded his deportation. In 1920, after being fêted in the USA, he returned to Europe but was refused entry to Ireland by the British government. His social views involved a hostility to capitalism that for many years made him close to the Australian Labor Party, but increasingly he came to regard communism as the greater threat, and he supported the Democratic Labor Party after the Labor Party split of the mid-1950s. His involvement with the Catholic laity and his combative nature made him a powerful force in Australian society and politics for half a century.

Manns, Sir August 1825–1907
German musician
Born in Prussia, he became musical director at the Crystal Palace in London in 1855, and from 1883 to 1902 conducted the Handel Festivals.

Mannyng, Robert, *also known as* Robert of Brunne d.c.1338
English chronicler and poet
Born in Bourne, Lincolnshire, he entered the nearby Gilbertine monastery of Sempringham in 1288. His chief work is *Handlynge Synne* (c.1303), a free and amplified translation into English rhyming couplets of the *Manuel des Pechiez* of William of Wadington. It is a landmark in the transition from early to later Middle English, and a colourful picture of contemporary life. He also composed a rhyming translation of Robert Wace's *Brut d'Angleterre*, with a translation from French of a rhyming chronicle, *The Story of Ingeland*, by the Augustinian canon, Peter Langtoft. 📖 R Crosby, *Robert Mannyng of Brunne: a new biography* (1942)

Manoel I, *also spelt* Manuel *or* Emanuel I, *called* the Fortunate *or* the Great 1469–1521
King of Portugal
Born in Alcocheta, he was the grandson of John I, and succeeded John II (1495). His reign, marred by persecution of the Jews, consolidated royal power, and marked a golden age for Portugal: he prepared the code of laws which bears his name, and made his court a centre of chivalry and the arts. He also sponsored the voyages of Vasco da Gama, Pedro Cabral, Albuquerque and others, which helped to make Portugal the first naval power of Europe, opened up sea trade with India, discovered Brazil and consolidated Portuguese presence in the East.

Manrique, César 1919–92
Spanish artist and ecologist
Born in Arrecife, Lanzarote, Canary Islands, he fought in the Spanish Civil War in Catalonia in 1937. In 1945 he went to Madrid to study at the San Fernando Fine Art School, and in 1953 he defied General Franco by painting abstracts. Exhibitions in Europe, Japan, the USA, and at the 28th Venice Biennale brought him international recognition. Returning from a stay in New York in 1968, he became the arbiter of artistic taste on his island, and by prohibiting high-rise buildings he prevented some of the worst excesses of mass tourism. He was killed in a road accident, leaving as lasting monuments to his sense of design a unique cactus garden, a house containing his paintings (the Fundacion César Manrique), and public sculptures all over Lanzarote.

Manrique, Jorge 1440–79
Spanish poet
Born in Paredes de la Nava, he is best remembered for his elegy on his father's death, *Coplas por la muerte de su padre* ('Verses for the Death of his Father'). He also wrote love-

songs, satires and acrostic verses. He was killed in the civil wars. ⌑ A Serraro de Hero, *Personalidad y destino de Jorge Manrique* (1966)

Mansard or Mansart, François 1598–1666
French architect

Born in Paris, he was apprenticed to **Salomon de Brosse**. Considered to embody French 17th-century Classicism, his mastery is evident in his first major work, the north wing of the Château de Blois, which featured the double-angled high-pitched roof which bears his name. He designed churches such as Santa Marie de la Visitation and Val-de-Grâce, and built or remodelled several notable buildings in Paris and elsewhere, such as the Hôtel de la Vrillière and the Château de Maisons.

Mansard or Mansart, Jules Hardouin
1645–1708
French architect

Born in Paris, he became chief architect to **Louis XIV** and designed many notable buildings, especially part of the Palace of Versailles, including the Grand Trianon. He was the great-nephew by marriage of **François Mansard**.

Mansbridge, Albert 1876–1952
English adult educator

Born in Gloucester and educated at Board schools and Battersea Grammar School, he left school aged 14, and became a clerk and then cashier of the Co-operative Permanent Building Society. After attending extension classes at King's College London, he became an evening-class teacher under the London School Board. He proposed a scheme in 1903 which led to the formation of the Association to Promote the Higher Education of Working Men, later known as the Workers' Educational Association (WEA). In 1905 he became general secretary, encouraging the development of branches and setting great store by the three-year university tutorial classes which an Oxford conference on the WEA and the university advocated in 1907. After visits to the Commonwealth in 1913–14 he became seriously ill but was instrumental in founding the National Central Library (1916), and was a member of the adult education committee of the Ministry of Reconstruction which produced an important report in 1919. Among his publications is a biography of **Margaret McMillan**.

Mansell, Nigel Ernest James 1953–
English motor-racing driver

Born in Solihull, West Midlands, he made his Grand Prix debut in 1980, and had his first win in 1985, with the Williams team. He finished second in the 1986 world championship after a burst tyre forced his withdrawal in the last race. Following a spell with Ferrari, he returned to Williams in 1991, and in 1992 won the world championship. He did not defend his title, preferring to drive in the Indycar circuit in the United States. He won his first race in Australia in 1993, where he was the first driver to win his maiden race since **Graham Hill**'s victory at the Indianapolis 500 in 1966, and in 1993 he became the first man to win the Indycar world series championship in his rookie year. In 1996 he announced plans to return to Formula One racing.

Mansfield, Katherine, *pen name of* Kathleen Mansfield Beauchamp 1888–1923
New Zealand short-story writer

Born in Wellington, she was educated at Queen's College, London, returned briefly to New Zealand to study music, then left again for London in 1908, determined to pursue a literary career. Finding herself pregnant, she was installed by her mother in a hotel in Bavaria, but miscarried. The experience bore fruit in the stories collected as *In A German Pension* in 1911. That same year she met **John Middleton Murry**, and thereafter her work began to surface

in Murry's *Rhythm*. From 1912 the couple lived together (they married in 1918), mingling with the literati, particularly **D H Lawrence**, who portrayed them as Gudrun and Gerald in *Women in Love* (1921). Her first major work was *Prelude* (1917), a recreation of the New Zealand of her childhood. *Bliss, and other stories* (1920), containing the classic stories 'Je ne parle pas français' and 'Prelude', confirmed her standing as an original and innovative writer. The only other collection published before her premature death from tuberculosis was *The Garden Party, and other stories* (1922). Posthumous collections include *Something Childish and Other Stories* (1924, published in the USA as *The Little Girl and Other Stories*, 1924). *The Letters of Katherine Mansfield*, edited by Murry, appeared in 1928 and *Katherine Mansfield's Letters to John Middleton Murry 1913–1922*, detailing the couple's stormy but tender relationship appeared in 1951. Vincent O'Sullivan edited *Poems of Katherine Mansfield* (1988), and her work for the theatre was collected in *Katherine Mansfield: Dramatic Sketches* (1988). ⌑ A Alpers, *The Life of Katherine Mansfield* (1980)

Mansfield, William Murray, 1st Earl of 1705–93
English judge

Born in Perth, Scotland, the fourth son of Viscount Stormont, he was educated at Westminster and Christ Church, Oxford. He was called to the Bar in 1730 and soon acquired an extensive practice. He was appointed Solicitor-General in 1742, entered the House of Commons as MP for Boroughbridge, was appointed Attorney-General (1754), and became Chief Justice of the King's Bench (1756) and a member of the Cabinet, and was created Baron Mansfield. His judgements were influential, particularly by incorporating many principles of mercantile custom in rules of law and therefore developing the law of maritime contracts, insurance and bills. He also made important contributions to international law. He was impartial as a judge, but his opinions were unpopular. 'Junius' (Sir **Philip Francis**) bitterly attacked him, and during the Gordon riots of 1780 his house was burned. Made Earl in 1776, he resigned office in 1788.

Manship, Paul Howard 1885–1966
US sculptor

Born in St Paul, Minnesota, he studied in New York and Philadelphia, and attended the American Academy in Rome from 1908 to 1912. Returning to New York, he became renowned for his bronze figurative sculptures, which drew heavily on Roman and Greek sources. His subject-matter is taken principally from Classical mythology and treated in the stylized, decorative manner of the Art Deco period. From 1921 to 1927 he worked in Paris. His many important commissions include the gilded *Prometheus Fountain* (1934) for the Rockefeller Center, New York. In the 1930s he was widely regarded as the USA's greatest sculptor, but his mannered style later became unfashionable.

Manson, Charles 1934–
US hippy cult leader, and murderer

Born in Kentucky, the son of a prostitute, he committed his first armed robbery at the age of 13 and a homosexual rape at 17. In 1960 he was imprisoned for a variety of offences including procuring, fraud and theft. On his release in 1967 he set up a hippy commune, first in San Francisco and later at the Saphn ranch outside Los Angeles. It became a base for various criminal activities. The group was called 'the Family', and Manson was unquestionably the leader. He had enormous power over his followers and began drawing up a death list of 'Pigs'— people to be killed starting on a day code-named 'Helter Skelter'. He ordered his followers to carry out the killings. In 1979 he was found guilty of nine murders and sentenced to life imprisonment.

Manson, Sir Patrick, *known as* Mosquito Manson
1844–1922
Scottish physician
Born in Old Meldrum, Aberdeen, he studied medicine in Aberdeen and then practised in China (from 1871) and Hong Kong (from 1883), where he helped start and was the first Dean of a school of medicine that became the University of Hong Kong. In China, he studied a chronic disease called elephantiasis and showed that it is caused by a parasite spread through mosquito bites. This was the first disease to be shown to be transmitted by an insect carrier. In 1890 Manson set up practice in London, where he became the leading consultant on tropical diseases and was appointed medical adviser to the Colonial Office, and in 1899 he helped to found the London School of Tropical Medicine. He was the first to argue that the mosquito is host to the malaria parasite (1877), and encouraged Sir Ronald Ross's malaria research.

Manstein, Fritz Erich von 1887–1973
German soldier
At the outset of World War II he became chief of staff to Karl von Rundstedt in the Polish campaign and later in France, where he was the architect of Hitler's *Blitzkrieg* invasion plan. In 1941 he was given command of an army corps on the Eastern Front. After the disaster of Stalingrad, he successfully staged a counter-attack at Kharkov, though he failed to relieve Friedrich Paulus's 6th Army. After being captured in 1945 he was imprisoned as a war criminal but released in 1953.

Mansur, al-, *meaning the victorious* d.775
A title assumed by many Muslim princes
It was most notably assumed by the cruel and treacherous 'Abbasid caliph Abu-Jafar, who succeeded his brother al-Saffah in 754 and founded Baghdad in 764. He died while leading his fifth pilgrimage to Mecca.

Mantegna, Andrea 1431–1506
Italian painter
Born near Vicenza, he was apprenticed to the tailor-painter Francesco Squarcione (1396–c.1468) in Padua and seems to have been adopted by him. In 1453 he married a daughter of Jacopo Bellini and quarrelled with his master. In 1459 he was persuaded by Ludovico Gonzaga, Duke of Mantua, to work for him, and remained in Mantua in his service for the rest of his life with the exception of a two-year stay in Rome (1488–90) when he painted a fresco cycle (now destroyed) for the private chapel of Pope Innocent VIII. In Padua he had come under the influence of Donatello and his debt to him is evident in works such as his Saint Zeno Altarpiece and his *Saint Sebastian*. His style is very sculptural and ostentatious in its use of foreshortening. At Mantua his most important works were nine tempera pictures of *The Triumph of Caesar* (c.1486) which were later acquired by the English king Charles I and are now at Hampton Court Palace, and his decoration of the ceiling of the Camera degli Sposi. The latter is an illusionistic tour-de-force in which the ceiling is opened up to the heavens and putti look down from the painted balustrade. This is the first example of an effect which became common during the Baroque era. The other chief feature of his art was his incorporation of Classical motifs into his compositions. In this he strove for accuracy, and with this aim he built up a collection of Classical statuary which was the envy of the pope.

Mantell, Gideon Algernon 1790–1852
English palaeontologist
Born in Lewes, Sussex, he studied medicine in London and returned to Lewes as a practising surgeon. Busy and successful, he also took time to study the local geology and collected many fossils which were put on show to the public. He wrote *The Fossils of the South Downs* in 1822,

moved to Brighton in 1833 and was able to complete his *Geology of the South-east of England* by 1837. His collection was sold to the British Museum in 1838 and he followed it to London in 1844. He discovered several dinosaur types, including the first to be fully described; noting the similarity between the fossil teeth and those of the living iguana, he named it 'Iguanodon' (1825). In 1831 he introduced the notion of the 'age of reptiles', one of the earliest pictorial representations of which was produced by the celebrated artist John Martin (1789–1819) for Mantell's *The Wonders of Geology* (1838).

Manuel I, Comnenus c.1122–1180
Byzantine emperor
He was the youngest son of John II, whom he succeeded in 1143. Although he absorbed Croatia, Bosnia and Dalmatia into the empire (1167), his initial successes against the Turks and the Normans were halted by the catastrophic defeat of his army by the Seljuks at Myriokephalon (1176). This marked the beginning of the downfall of the empire.

Manuel II, Palaeologus 1350–1425
Byzantine emperor
The son of John V Palaeologus, he became emperor in 1391 (but reverted to being co-emperor 1399–1402 and 1421–25). For much of his reign he was besieged in Constantinople (Istanbul) by the Turks. At one point he was relieved by the advance of Timur into Asia Minor, but he failed to profit from this diversion and was overwhelmed, finally retiring to a monastery.

Manuel, Nikolaus, *called* Deutsch 1484–1530
Swiss painter, poet and reformer
Born in Bern, he began as a painter of stained glass but changed over to orthodox media and produced biblical and mythological pictures in the Renaissance style, often showing the influence of Hans Baldung in his tendency toward the macabre. He held several government offices, was a member of the Great Council, and wrote satirical verse.

Manuel, Peter 1931–58
Scottish criminal
Born in New York, of Scottish parentage, he emigrated with his family to Glasgow during the Depression. Between September 1956 and January 1958, in addition to committing a number of burglaries, he broke into the home of William Watt in Rutherglen and shot the three occupants dead, strangled and robbed a girl at Mount Vernon, robbed a house in Uddingston, killing all three of the family who lived there, and shot dead a Newcastle taxi driver. He was also accused of battering to death Ann Kneilands of East Kilbride, but was acquitted through lack of evidence. His trial at Glasgow High Court was one of the most highly publicized in legal history. Having already successfully defended himself against a former charge, he dismissed the counsel appearing on his behalf. Conducting his case with some skill, he brought in a special defence plea giving alibis and accusing William Watt himself, already a suspect, of the Rutherglen murders. Manuel, however, was found guilty of seven of the murders, and hanged. The Newcastle shooting was later officially attributed to him by an inquest jury.

Manutius, Aldus See Aldus Manutius

Manzoni, Alessandro 1785–1873
Italian novelist and poet
Born in Milan, of a noble family, he lived in Paris from 1805 to 1807, and published his first poems in 1806. Having married happily in 1810, he spent the next few years writing sacred lyrics and a treatise on the religious basis of morality. But the work which gave him European fame is his historical novel, *I promessi sposi* (1827, Eng trans

Mao Zedong (Mao Tse-tung) 1893–1976
Chinese Communist leader and first Chairman of the People's Republic

Mao Zedong was born in Shaoshan in Hunan province, the son of a peasant farmer. He was educated at Changsha, and in 1918 went to the University of Beijing (Peking), where as a library assistant he studied the works of **Marx** and others and helped found the Chinese Communist Party (CCP) in 1921. Seeing the need to adapt communism to Chinese conditions, and seeking a rural rather than urban-based revolution, he set up a commun ist 'people's republic' (soviet) at Jiangxi (Kiangsi) in south-east China between 1931 and 1934. The soviet de- fied the attacks of **Chiang Kai-shek**'s forces until 1934, when Mao and his followers were obliged to uproot themselves and undertake an arduous and circuitous 'Long March' (1934–36) to Shaanxi (Shensi) province in north-west China.

During the Long March, Mao was elected CCP chair- man at the Zunyi conference of February 1935. At the new headquarters of Yan'an, he set about formulating a unique communist philosophy which stressed the im- portance of ideology, re-education and 'rectification', and, in 1939, he married his third wife, **Jiang Qing**.

By employing the tactic of mobile, rural-based guerrilla warfare, Mao's communists successfully resisted the Japanese between 1937 and 1945, and on their collapse issued forth to shatter the Nationalist regime of Chiang Kai-shek and proclaim the People's Republic of China in Beijing in 1949, with Mao as chairman. Mao resigned the chairmanship of the Republic in 1959, but remained chairman of the CCP's politburo until his death.

During the early 1960s, an ideological rift developed between Mao and **Khrushchev**, with Mao opposing the latter's policy of peaceful co-existence with the West and the USSR's volte-face during the Cuban missile crisis (1962). This developed into a formal split in 1962 when the Soviet Union supplied fighter aircraft to India during the

brief Sino-Indian border war of that year. In China, Mao's influence waned during the early 1960s as a result of the failure of the 1958–60 'Great Leap Forward' experiment of rapid agricultural and industrial advance through the es- tablishment of massive communes. However, Mao re- established his dominance by implementing the 1966–69 'Cultural Revolution', a campaign of rectification directed against liberal, revisionist forces. This was the period of the Red Guard excesses, following which Mao, working closely with **Zhou Enlai**, oversaw a period of reconstruction from 1970.

During his final years, he was beset by deteriorating health, and his political grip weakened. Mao's writings and thoughts, set out in *New Democracy* (1940) and, most popularly, in his *Little Red Book*, dominated the function- ing of the People's Republic between 1949 and 1976. He stressed the need for reducing rural–urban differences and for 'perpetual revolution' to prevent the emergence of new elites. Overseas, after precipitating the Sino-Soviet split of 1960–62, Mao became a firm advocate of a non- aligned 'Third World' strategy.

On his death at the age of 83, there followed a power struggle that was briefly won by the so-called 'Gang of Four', who included Mao's widow, Jiang Qing. After 1978, the new Chinese leadership of **Deng Xiaoping** began to re- interpret Maoism and criticized its policy excesses. However, many of Mao's ideas remain influential in con- temporary China.

📖 Zhisui Li, *The Private Life of Chairman Mao* (1994); P Rule, *Mao Zedong* (1984).

'Politics is war without bloodshed; war is politics with bloodshed.' From a speech, 1938.

The Betrothed Lovers, 1828), a Milanese story of the 17th century, and one of the most notable novels in Italian literature. Despite his Catholic devoutness, he was a strong advocate of a united Italy, and became a senator of the kingdom in 1860. 📖 A Colquhoun, *Manzoni and His Times* (1954)

Manzú, Giacomo 1908–91
Italian sculptor

He was born in Bergamo, and was apprenticed to various craftsmen, including a woodcarver and a stuccoist, before studying at the Fantoni Trade School. In 1930 he was commissioned to make religious reliefs and saints for the Catholic University of Milan, and in 1936 he visited Paris, where he admired the work of **Auguste Rodin**. He held his first one-man exhibition in Rome in 1937, and subse- quently taught sculpture in Milan (1940) and Turin (c.1940–45). He revived Classical techniques of relief sculpture in bronze, and is particularly known for the bronze doors of St Peter's in Rome (1950) and of Salzburg Cathedral, Austria (1955). He also made a commissioned portrait bust of Pope **John XXIII** for the Vatican (1963) and a relief of *Mother and Child* in The Rockefeller Center in New York (1965).

Mao Dun (Mao Tun), *pseudonym of* Shen Yanbing (Shen Yen-ping) 1896–1981
Chinese writer

He was born in Wuzhen, Zhejiang (Chekiang) province, educated at Beijing (Peking) University, and became a founder-member of the Literary Research Society (1920), and editor of the *Short Story Monthly* (1921–23). Moving to Shanghai, he taught a course of fiction at Shanghai College, and became editor of the *Hankou (Hankow)*

National Daily, but in 1926 he had to go underground because of his Communist sympathies. He wrote a trilogy of novellas, published as *Shi* (1930, 'Eclipse'), a bestselling novel, *Ziye* (1932, 'Midnight'), about financial exploiters in the decadent Shanghai of the time, and a collection of short stories. In 1930 he helped to organize the influential League of Left-Wing Writers. After the Communists came to power in 1949 he was China's first Minister of Culture (1949–65), and founder-editor of the literary journal *People's Literature* (1949–53). During the Cultural Revolution he was kept under house arrest in Beijing (1966–78). 📖 M Galik, *Mao Tun and Modern Chinese Literary Criticism* (1969)

Mao Zedong (Mao Tse-tung) See panel above

Map or Mahap or Mapes, Walter c.1137–1209
British ecclesiastic and writer

Born probably in Herefordshire, England, he is some- times said to have been a Welshman. He studied at Paris, became a clerk to **Henry II** of England, went on a mission to Rome, and became canon of St Paul's and archdeacon of Oxford (1197). Although famous in his day as a writer and wit, the only work which can be attributed to him with certainty is the satirical miscellany *De Nugis Curialum* ('Of Courtier's Trifles'), a collection of anecdotes, reflec- tions and tales gleaned from history, romance and gossip. 📖 T Wright, *Latin Poems Commonly Attributed to Walter Map* (1879)

Mar, John Erskine, 6th or 11th Earl of 1675–1732
Scottish Jacobite

He was born in Alloa, Ayrshire. He began public life as a Whig, but his frequent changes of side earned him the nickname of 'Bobbing John'. He headed the Jacobite rebellion of 1715, was defeated at Sheriffmuir, and died in exile at Aix-la-Chapelle. His *Legacy* was published by the Scottish History Society in 1896.

Maradona, Diego 1960–
Argentine footballer
Born in Lanús, he played in the 1982 World Cup in Spain, but was sent off in the match against Brazil. He soon joined Barcelona from his home country club, Boca Juniors, but injury and illness kept him out of top-class football for two seasons. Restored to health, he captained the Argentine side to World Cup victory in Mexico in 1986, earning fame for apparently fisting his first goal against England, an action which he subsequently attributed to 'the hand of God'. He moved for £5 million to Naples, playing for the team from 1984 and helping them (1987) to their first-ever Italian championship. With his speed, phenomenal strength and balance he is one of the greatest players of his generation, but in recent years his career has been marred by repeated suspensions for drug use. He left Naples in 1991 after being suspended for 15 months following a drugs test, and in 1993 he returned to Argentina after being released by his club Seville. He was again suspended after failing a drugs test at the 1994 World Cup, and in 1995 he signed a contract with his old team, the Boca Juniors.

Marais, Marin 1656–1728
French composer and viol player
Born in Paris, he was in the Sainte Chapelle choir as a boy. A bass violist in the Royal Band and in the orchestra of the Paris Opera, he was appointed joint conductor of the Paris Opera. He studied with Jean Baptiste Lully, and wrote several operas, the most famous of which was *Alcyone* (1705), but his posthumous and growing reputation is based on his music for the viol.

Marat, Jean Paul 1743–93
French revolutionary, physician and journalist
Born in Boudry near Neuchâtel, Switzerland, he studied medicine and practised in London in the 1770s and in Paris from 1777. He was brevet-physician to the guards of the Comte d'Artois (afterwards Charles X) until 1786, and during that time worked in optics and electricity, and produced several scientific works. He became a member of the Cordeliers' Club, and in 1789 he established the radical paper, *L'Ami du Peuple*, inciting the 'sans-culottes' to violence. The hatred he inspired forced him into hiding several times, once in the sewers of Paris. His consequent loathing of constituted authority influenced the September Massacres. In 1792 he was elected to the Convention, and with Robespierre and Danton he overthrew the Girondins. A skin disease contracted in the sewers meant he could only write sitting in his bath, and on the evening of 13 July he was assassinated there by Charlotte Corday, a member of the Girondins.

Maratti, Carlo 1625–1713
Italian painter
Born in Camerano, as a leader of the 17th-century Baroque school he painted many notable canvases and frescoes in Rome, and several portraits.

Marbeck or Merbecke, John d.c.1585
English musician and theologian
Organist of St George's Chapel, Windsor, he was condemned to the stake in 1544 as a reformer, but pardoned by Bishop Gardiner. In 1550 he published his famous *Boke of Common Praier Noted*, an adaptation of the plainchant to the first prayer-book of Edward VI. He prepared the earliest concordance to the whole English Bible, and wrote several theological works.

Marc, Franz 1880–1916
German artist

Born in Munich, with Wassily Kandinsky he founded the Blaue Reiter Expressionist group in Munich in 1911. Most of his paintings were of animals (eg *Tower of the Blue Horses*, 1911 and *The Fate of the Animals*, 1913), portrayed in forceful colours, with a well-defined pictorial rhythm. He was killed in World War I at Verdun.

Marcantonio, *in full* Marcantonio Raimondi c.1488–1534
Italian engraver
Born in Bologna, he began as a goldsmith, but moved to Rome in 1510 and became an engraver of other artists' works, especially those of Raphael and Michelangelo. The capture of Rome by Charles Bourbon in 1527 drove him back to Bologna.

Marceau, Marcel 1923–
French mime artist
He was born in Strasbourg, and studied at the École des Beaux-Arts in Paris. In 1948 he founded and directed (1948–64) the Compagnie de Mime Marcel Marceau, specializing in and developing the art of mime, of which he has become the leading exponent. His white-faced character 'Bip' became famous worldwide from his appearances on stage and television. Among the many original performances he has devised are the mime-drama *Don Juan* (1964) and the ballet *Candide* (1971). He became head of the École Mimodrame Marcel Marceau in 1978. 📖 Ben Martin, *Marcel Marceau: Master of Mime* (1978)

Marcel, Gabriel Honoré 1889–1973
French existentialist philosopher and dramatist
Born in Paris, he was a Red Cross worker in World War I but made his living thereafter as a freelance writer, teacher, editor and critic. In 1929 he became a Catholic and came reluctantly to accept the label 'Christian Existentialist', partly in order to contrast his views with those of Jean-Paul Sartre. He emphasized the importance and possibility of 'communication' between individuals, as well as between the individual and God, but was suspicious of all philosophical abstractions and generalizations which misrepresented the freedom, uniqueness and particularity of each person. He was not himself a system-builder and his philosophical works tend to have a personal, meditative character, as in *Journal métaphysique* (1927, Eng trans *Metaphysical Journal*, 1952), *Être et avoir* (1935, Eng trans *Being and Having*, 1949), *Le Mystère de l'être* (1951, Eng trans *The Mystery of Being*, 1951), *Les Hommes contre l'humain* (1951, Eng trans *Men Against Humanity*, 1952) and *L'Homme problématique* (1955, Eng trans *Problematic Man*, 1967). His plays include *Un Homme de Dieu* (1925, 'A Man of God'), *Le Monde cassé* (1933, 'The Broken World'), *Ariadne: Le Chemin de Crête* (1936, Eng trans *Ariadne*, 1952) and *La Dimension Florestan* (1956, 'The Florestan Dimension'). 📖 S Keen, *Gabriel Marcel* (1967)

Marcello, Benedetto 1686–1739
Italian composer
Born in Venice, he is remembered for his *Estro poetico armonico* (1724–27), an eight-volume collection of 50 settings in cantata style of the Psalms of David, for his oratorio *Le Quattro Stagioni* (1731), and for his keyboard and instrumental sonatas. He also wrote the satirical *Il Teatro alla moda* (1720). A judge of the Venetian republic, he was a member of the Council of Forty, and afterwards held offices at Pola and Brescia. His brother Alessandro (c.1684–c.1750), philosopher and mathematician as well as composer, published a number of cantatas, sonatas and concertos under the pseudonym 'Eterico Stinfalico'.

Marcellus, Marcus Claudius, *known as* the Sword of Rome c.268–208BC
Roman general

His main exploits were the defeat of the Insubrian Gauls (222BC) and the capture of Syracuse (212). During the Second Punic War (218–201) he stopped **Hannibal** at Nola (216).

Marcellus, Marcus Claudius 42–23BC
Roman nobleman

He was a son of **Octavia**, the sister of the Emperor **Augustus**, and married his 14-year-old cousin **Julia** in 25BC. That same year Augustus adopted Marcellus, who served under him in Spain, and named him his first successor; his early death was widely regarded as a national calamity and was lamented by **Virgil** in the *Aeneid* (vi. 861–87).

March, Ausiàs 1397–1459
Catalan poet

Born in Valencia, he was a pioneer of the trend away from the lyricism of the troubadours towards a more metaphysical approach. Influenced by Italian models, he wrote chiefly on the themes of love and death. ⌑ A Pagès, *Ausiàs March et ses prédécesseurs* (1912)

March, Francis Andrew 1825–1911
US philologist

Born in Millbury, Massachusetts, he was educated at Amherst College, studied law in New York and was admitted to the Bar in 1850. After some years of teaching, he became Professor of English Language and Comparative Philology at Lafayette College, Easton, Pennsylvania (1857–1906), and came to be regarded as the founder of comparative Anglo-Saxon linguistics. Among his publications were the monumental *Comparative Grammar of the Anglo-Saxon Language* (1870) and *An Anglo-Saxon Reader* (1870). From 1879 to 1882 he was director of the American readers for the *New English Dictionary* (later named the *Oxford English Dictionary*).

March, Fredric, *originally* Frederick Ernest McIntyre Bickel 1897–1975
US actor

Born in Racine, Wisconsin, he served as an artillery lieutenant in World War I. He turned to acting in 1920, becoming a star in silent films and working extensively on stage. Under contract to Paramount he proved a versatile and subtle screen performer, whose work ranged from costume drama to screwball comedies. He won Best Actor Academy Awards for *Dr Jekyll and Mr Hyde* (1931) and as the homecoming veteran in *The Best Years of Our Lives* (1946). Other films in a long and distinguished career included *Les Misérables* (1935), *A Star Is Born* (1937), *Death of a Salesman* (1952) and *The Iceman Cometh* (1973). His many stage appearances included *The Skin of Our Teeth* (1942) and *Long Day's Journey Into Night* (1956). He was married to actress Florence Eldridge (1901–88) from 1927.

Marchais, Georges 1920–97
French Communist politician

Born in La Hoguette, Calvados, the son of a miner, he became a metal-worker, and joined the French Communist Party (PCF) in 1947, becoming its Secretary-General in 1972. Under his leadership the PCF pledged its commitment to the transition to socialism by democratic means, and joined the Socialist Party (PS) in a new 'Union of the Left'. This union was, however, severed by Marchais in 1977 and the party returned to an orthodox Moscow line, although PCF ministers participated in the **Mitterrand** government (1981–84). He unsuccessfully contested the 1981 presidential election and stepped down as PCF leader in 1994.

Marchand, Jean-Baptiste 1863–1934
French soldier and explorer

He joined the army at 20, explored the Niger, western Sudan and the Ivory Coast, and caused a Franco-British crisis by hoisting the tricolour at Fashoda in 1898. As a general he distinguished himself in World War I.

Marciano, Rocky, *originally* Rocco Francis Marchegiano 1923–69
US boxer

Born in Brockton, Massachusetts, he first took up boxing as a serviceman in Great Britain during World War II, and turned professional in 1947. He made his name in 1951 when he defeated the former world champion **Joe Louis**, who had been knocked out only once. He won the world title from Jersey Joe Walcott the following year, and when he retired in 1956 was undefeated as world champion with a professional record of 49 bouts and 49 victories. He resisted all attempts to talk him into a come-back, and died in an air-crash. ⌑ Everett Skehan, *Rocky Marciano* (1977)

Marcion c.100–c.165AD
Italian Christian Gnostic

A wealthy shipowner of Sinope in Pontus, in about AD140 he went to Rome, and founded the quasi-Gnostic Marcionites (144), which soon had churches in many eastern countries.

Marconi, Guglielmo, Marchese See panel p1227

Marco Polo See Polo, Marco

Marcos, Ferdinand Edralin 1917–89
Filipino politician

He was born in Ilocos Norte, and educated at the University of the Philippines. He was accused, in 1939, while a law student, of murdering a political opponent of his father, but secured his own acquittal. During World War II he served in a Philippines army unit (but his claims of being a resistance fighter against the Japanese were later proved to be false). After the war he sat in the Philippines' House of Representatives (1949–59) and Senate (1959–66) for the Liberal Party and then the Nationalist Party. Promising a new programme of industrial development, he was elected President. His regime as President (1965–86) was marked by increasing repression, misuse of foreign financial aid and political murders, such as that of **Benigno Aquino** (1983). With a declining economy, and faced with a growing communist insurgency, he declared martial law in 1972 and began to rule by decree. He was eventually overthrown in 1986 by a popular 'People's Power' front led by **Cory Aquino**. The ailing Marcos and his influential wife **Imelda Marcos** fled into exile in Hawaii. After his death his wife faced charges of fraud and corruption in the US courts. ⌑ Raymond Bonner, *Waltzing With a Dictator* (rev edn 1988)

Marcos, Imelda Romualdez c.1930–
Filipino politician

She was born in Manila and after her businessman father went bankrupt she was brought up in conditions of extreme poverty. In 1954 she married a young politician, **Ferdinand Marcos**, who was elected to the Senate and became President in 1965. Known to her fellow countrymen as the 'Iron Butterfly', she used her husband's power and position to build an extravagant financial empire, and served as Governor of Metropolitan Manila (1975–86) and Minister of Human Settlements and Ecology (1979–86). To maintain his rule Marcos turned his country into a dictatorship, but in 1986 he was deposed and fled with his wife into exile in Hawaii. In 1988 they were indicted in New York on corruption charges but she was acquitted in 1990. In 1989 Marcos died and she returned to the Philippines where in 1992 she was an unsuccessful presidential candidate. ⌑ Sterling Seagrave, *The Marcos Dynasty* (1989)

Marconi, Guglielmo, Marchese 1874–1937
Italian physicist, inventor and Nobel Prize winner

Marconi was born in Bologna into a wealthy family, of an Italian father and Irish mother. He was educated for a short time at the Technical Institute of Livorno, but mainly by private tutors, and started experimenting with a device to convert electromagnetic waves (recently discovered by **Heinrich Hertz**) into electricity. His first successful experiments in wireless telegraphy were made at Bologna in 1895, and in 1898 he transmitted signals across the English Channel.

In 1899 he erected a wireless station at La Spezia, but failed to win the support of the Italian government and decided to establish the Marconi Telegraph Co in London. In 1901 he succeeded in sending signals in Morse code across the Atlantic, from Cornwall, England to St John's, Newfoundland, and the following year he patented the magnetic detector. He later developed short-wave radio equipment, and established a worldwide radio telegraph network for the British government. From 1921 he lived on his yacht, the *Elettra*, and in the 1930s he was a strong supporter of the Italian Fascist leader **Mussolini**.

Marconi shared the 1909 Nobel Prize for physics with **Ferdinand Braun**.

📖 W P Jolly, *Marconi* (1972); W J Baker, *A History of the Marconi Company* (1970); Orrin E Dunlap, *Marconi: The Man and His Wireless* (1937).

Marcus Aurelius See panel p1228

Marcus Cocceius Nerva See **Nerva, Marcus Cocceius**

Marcus, George E 1946–
US cultural anthropologist

He was born in Brownsville, Pennsylvania, and studied at both Yale and Harvard. In 1980 he joined Rice University, Houston, as associate Professor of Anthropology, becoming Professor in 1986. From 1986 to 1991 he was editor of the journal *Cultural Anthropology*. His most influential work to date is *Writing Culture: The Poetics and Politics of Ethnography*, edited with James Clifford (1945–), in which he raises post-modernist concerns relating to ethnographic authority and the problems of cultural representation in the contemporary world. Publications on these and related topics include *Anthropology as Cultural Critique* (with Michael Fischer, 1986), and *Rereading Cultural Anthropology* (1992).

Marcus, Rudolph Arthur 1923–
US physical chemist and Nobel Prize winner

Born in Montreal, Canada, where he studied chemistry at McGill University, he joined the chemistry faculty of the Polytechnic Institute of Brooklyn, New York, advancing from assistant professor to professor between 1951 and 1964. From 1964 to 1978 he worked at the University of Illinois, and in 1978 he became Professor of Chemistry at the California Institute of Technology. He is celebrated for the 'Marcus theory' of electron transfer reactions, which considers in detail the role of solvent molecules and leads to quantitative expressions for rate coefficients. The theory is of importance in inorganic chemistry, organic chemistry and biochemistry. Marcus has also extended the theoretical treatment of unimolecular gas reactions in terms of molecular vibrations. He received the Nobel Prize for chemistry in 1992. In 1987 he was elected a Foreign Member of the Royal Society and in 1991 he became an honorary Fellow of the Royal Society of Chemistry.

Marcuse, Herbert 1898–1979
US Marxist philosopher

Born in Berlin, Germany, and educated at the universities of Berlin and Freiburg, he became an influential figure in the Frankfurt Institute of Social Research (the so-called 'Frankfurt School') along with **Theodor Adorno** and **Max Horkheimer**. After the Nazis closed the Institute (1933) he fled to Geneva and thence to the USA (1934), where the Institute was re-established in New York. He served as an intelligence officer for the US army during World War II, and when the Institute moved back to Europe in the early 1950s he remained in the USA as a naturalized citizen, taking a series of teaching posts at Columbia (1951), Harvard (1952), Brandeis (1954) and California, San Diego (1965–76). He had published *Eros and Civilization* in 1955, offering a Freudian analysis of the repressions imposed by the unconscious mind, but became a celebrity at the age of 66 with the publication of *One Dimensional Man* (1964), condemning the 'repressive tolerance' of modern industrial society which both stimulated and satisfied the superficial material desires of the masses at the cost of more fundamental needs and freedoms. He looked to students as the alienated élite who would initiate revolutionary change, but his hopes did not really survive the student riots of the 1960s at Berkeley and Paris. He expressed an equal hostility to bureaucratic communism in his *Soviet Marxism* (1958). 📖 Peter Lind, *Marcuse and Freedom* (1985)

Marden, Brice 1938–
US painter

Born in Bronxville, New York, he studied at Boston University and Yale before settling in New York in 1963. By 1965 he was producing minimalist uniformly coloured canvases of horizontal and vertical formats. From 1968 he made two- and three-panel canvases, each of contrasting monochromatic colour, such as *Vertical Horizontal* (1973, Stedelijk, Amsterdam). His paintings of the 1980s moved away from minimalism, and involved crossing diagonal and vertical lines, and the use of bright colour, as in *Thira* (1980, Pompidou Centre, Paris) with its explicit reference to ancient architecture.

Mare, Walter de la See **de la Mare, Walter**

Maréchal, André 1916–
French optical physicist

Born in La Garenne and educated at the University of Paris and the Institute of Optics, he became assistant professor at the university and institute in 1943, lecturer in 1950 and full professor in 1955. From 1968 to 1984 he was also director of the institute. He served as a member of the French National Committee for Scientific Research (1961–88), and was president of the International Commission of Optics (1962–65). His distinguished contributions to optics have included work on the diffraction theory of imaging systems, on geometrical optics, and on imagery in partially coherent light. He was awarded the Thomas Young Medal of the UK Institute of Physics in 1965 and the C K Mees Medal of the Optical Society of America in 1977.

Marets, Jean Nicolas, Baron de Corvisart des See **Corvisart-Desmarets, Jean Nicolas, Baron de**

Marett, Robert Ranulph 1866–1943
British anthropologist

After studying classics and philosophy at Oxford and German philosophy at Berlin, he was admitted to the Bar in Jersey (1891). However, he decided to pursue his developing interest in anthropology; by 1910 he was Reader

---

Marcus Aurelius, *surnamed* Antoninus, *originally* Marcus Annius Verus AD121–80
Roman emperor and philosopher

Marcus Aurelius was born in Rome, the son of M Annius Verus, a member of a consular family, and Domita Calvilla. At the age of 17 he was adopted by Antoninus Pius, who had in turn been adopted by Hadrian; Marcus Aurelius married Antoninus's daughter Faustina in 145. From 140, when he was made consul, until the death of Antoninus in 161, he discharged his public duties conscientiously, and maintained good relations with the emperor. At the same time he devoted himself to the study of law and philosophy, especially Stoicism; one of his teachers was the Stoic Apollonius of Chalcedon.

On his accession, he voluntarily shared the throne with his brother by adoption, Lucius Aurelius Verus, who in 161 was sent to take command against the Parthians. Despite the self-indulgence and dilatoriness of Verus, the generals were victorious, but the army brought back from the East a plague that ravaged the empire. Peaceful by temperament, Marcus Aurelius was nevertheless destined to suffer from constant wars throughout his reign, and although in Asia, Britain, and on the Rhine the invaders were checked, permanent peace was never secured. Rome was suffering from pestilence, earthquakes and inundations when the imperial colleagues led the Roman armies against the northern barbarians on the Danube. Verus died in 169; the Marcommani were subdued in 168 and 173; and the Quadi in 174.

Marcus Aurelius was next called to the East by a rebellion of the governor, Avidius Cassius (175), who was assassinated before Aurelius arrived. On his way home, he visited lower Egypt and Greece. At Athens he founded chairs of philosophy for each of the chief schools: Platonic, Stoic, Peripatetic, and Epicurean. Towards the end of 176 he reached Italy, and the following autumn he departed for Germany, where fresh disturbances had broken out. He was victorious once more, but died in 180 in Pannonia.

One of the few Roman emperors whose writings have survived, Marcus Aurelius wrote 12 books of *Meditationes* which record his innermost thoughts and form a unique document. They show his loneliness, but also that he did not allow himself to be embittered by his experiences of life. They were written during the military campaigns of the last 10 years of his life, and were published unedited only after his death.

He was retrospectively idealized as the model of the perfect emperor, whose reign and style of rule contrasted with the disastrous period that began with the accession of his son Commodus, the disturbed age of the Severan emperors, and the imperial anarchy that followed in the 3rd century.

📖 A R Birley, *Marcus Aurelius* (1987).

> 'Nowhere can a man find a quieter or more untroubled retreat than in his own soul.' From *Meditationes*, bk 4, no.3 (trans by M Staniforth).

---

in Anthropology at Oxford, where he founded the department of anthropology. He wrote a number of influential books, including *The Threshold of Religion* (1909), *The Birth of Humility* (1910), *Anthropology* (1912), *Psychology and Folklore* (1920), *Man in the Making* (1928), *The Raw Material of Religion* (1929), *Faith, Hope and Charity in Primitive Religion* (1932), *Sacraments of Simple Folk* (1933), *Head, Heart and Hands in Human Evolution* (1935) and *Tylor* (1936). He became famous for his theory of pre-animism or dynamism in which he went beyond Edward Tylor 's theory of animism and J G Frazer 's theory of magic, arguing that religion begins with a sense of awe in the face of a religious force that is felt and experienced rather than reasoned out. Thus religion starts with a supernatural stage, and Marett used the Melanesian term *mana* to describe the religious force at work.

Marey, Etienne-Jules 1830–1904
French physiologist

Born in Beaune, he developed ingenious mechanical devices, and used his skill to study and measure heart action. From the 1860s he introduced scientific photography, devising by 1881 a cine camera to analyse rapid movements through 'slow motion', and using time-lapse to speed up slow changes.

Margai, Albert Michael 1910–80
Sierra Leone politician

The son of a trader and the brother of Sir Milton Margai, he was educated in Roman Catholic schools before becoming a nurse and pharmacist. He studied law in London (1944–47) and was elected a member of Legco in 1951, when he was appointed Minister of Education, Welfare and Local Government. A member of the Sierra Leone People's Party from 1951–58, he helped found the People's National Party and became Minister of Finance on independence (1961). When his brother died, he succeeded him as party leader and Prime Minister (1964–67). Following the disputed election of 1967 and the military coup led by Siaka Stevens in 1968, he went into exile in London.

Margai, Sir Milton A S 1895–1964
Sierra Leone nationalist leader and politician

The elder brother of Sir Albert Margai, he was educated in Roman Catholic mission schools, Fourah Bay College and in the UK, where he qualified as a doctor. Appointed a member of the Protectorate Assembly in 1940, he was elected to Legco in 1951, when he helped found the Sierra Leone People's Party and played a major role in pressing for independence. He was Chief Minister (1954–58) and, on independence (1961), Prime Minister until his death.

Margaret, St c.1046–1093
Queen of Scotland

Born in Hungary, where her father Edward the Ætheling, was in exile, she later went to England, but fled to Scotland after the Norman Conquest with her brother, Edgar the Ætheling. The Scottish king, Malcolm III Canmore, married her at Dunfermline (c.1070). Much of her reputation comes from her confessor and biographer, Turgot. She refined and anglicized the court, brought Benedictine monks to Dunfermline, stimulated change in usages in the Celtic Church, but institutional change and the real influx of new orders were initiated by her sons. Canonized by Innocent IV (1251), she remains the only Scottish royal saint. Her feast day is 16 November.
📖 Mary Clayton and Hugh Magennis, *The Old English Lives of St Margaret* (1994).

Margaret, Maid of Norway 1283–90
Queen of Scotland

The granddaughter of Alexander III of Scotland, she was the only child of King Erik II of Norway. When Alexander III died (1286), she was the only direct survivor of the Scottish royal line. In 1289 she was betrothed to the infant Prince Edward (the future Edward II of England), son of Edward I, but she died at sea in Orkney the following year on her way from Norway to England.

Margaret (Rose), Princess 1930–
British princess

Born at Glamis Castle, Scotland, the younger daughter of King **George VI** and only sister of Queen **Elizabeth II**, she was the first scion of the royal house in the direct line of succession to be born in Scotland for more than three centuries. In 1955 she rejected a possible marriage to Group Captain Peter Townsend, on advice from the Church and the establishment, because his previous marriage had been dissolved. In 1960 she married Antony Armstrong-Jones, a photographer, who was created Earl of **Snowdon** in 1961. Their children are David, Viscount Linley (1961–), and Lady Sarah Armstrong-Jones (1964–). The marriage was dissolved in 1978. ▢ Theo Aronson, *Princess Margaret* (1997); Nigel Dempster, *H R H the Princess Margaret* (1981)

Margaret (Marguerite) of Angoulême, *also known as* Margaret of Navarre 1492–1549
Queen of Navarre, and writer

The sister of **Francis I** of France, she married first the Duke of Alençon (d.1525) and then (1527) Henry d'Albret (titular King of Navarre), to whom she bore Jeanne d'Albret (1528–72), mother of **Henri IV** of France. With a strong interest in Renaissance learning, Margaret also became influenced by **Erasmus** and the religious reformers of the Meaux circle, who looked to her for patronage and protection. Although she remained a Roman Catholic she was also influenced by the writings of **Martin Luther**, with which she had a certain sympathy. One of the most brilliant women of her age, she encouraged agriculture, learning and the arts, and her court was the most intellectual in Europe. The patron of men of letters, including the heretical poet **Clément Marot**, and **Rabelais**, she herself was a prolific writer. Her works included long devotional poems published as *Le Miroir de l'âme pécheresse* (1531, 'The Mirror of a Sinner's Soul') and her most celebrated work was *Heptaméron*, a collection of stories on the theme of love, modelled upon the *Decameron* of **Boccaccio**.

Margaret of Anjou 1430–82
Queen of England

The daughter of René of Anjou, she was married to **Henry VI** of England in 1445, but because of his madness she became involved in government, acting as virtual sovereign, and she was held responsible for the war of 1449, in which Normandy was lost. During the Wars of the Roses, Margaret was a leading Lancastrian, and after a brave struggle of nearly 20 years, was finally defeated at Tewkesbury (1471). She was imprisoned in the Tower of London for four years, until she was ransomed by **Louis XI**. She then retired to France. ▢ J J Bagley, *Margaret of Anjou, Queen of England* (1948)

Margaret of Austria 1480–1530
Duchess of Savoy and Regent of the Netherlands

The daughter of Emperor **Maximilian I** and Mary of Burgundy, she was born in Brussels, and married first (1497) the Infante Juan of Spain, who died within a few months, then (1501) Philibert II, Duke of Savoy (d.1504). Her father appointed her Regent of the Netherlands (1507–15) and guardian of her nephew, the future Emperor **Charles V**. In 1519 she was again appointed regent by Charles V (until 1530), and proved herself a wise and capable stateswoman. Under her the Netherlands were heavily taxed to finance **Habsburg** military activity elsewhere.

Margaret of Navarre See **Margaret of Angoulême**

Margaret of Parma 1522–86
Regent of the Netherlands

She was born in Oudenarde, the illegitimate daughter of Emperor **Charles V**. She married first (1536) Alessandro de' Medici and second (1538) Ottavio Farnese, later Duke

of Parma, to whom she bore **Alessandro Farnese** (also later Duke of Parma) in 1546. As Regent of the Netherlands (1559–67), she proved herself masterful, able, and a staunch Catholic. In 1567 she suppressed a Calvinist revolt, but was replaced by the Duke of Alva. When her son Alessandro became Governor of the Netherlands (1578–86), ruling as regent for **Philip II** of Spain, Margaret returned with him as head of the civil administration for a time, finally retiring to Italy in 1583.

Margaret of Valois 1553–1615
Queen of Navarre

Born at St Germain-en-Laye, she was the daughter of **Henri II** of France and **Catherine de Médicis**, and sister of **Francis II, Charles IX** and **Henri III**. Noted for her beauty, learning and licentiousness, in 1572 she married Henri of Navarre (later **Henri IV**). The marriage was childless, and was dissolved by the pope (1599) in order to allow Henri to marry Marie de Médicis. She became famous for her *Mémoires*, published in 1628.

Margaret Tudor 1489–1541
Queen of Scotland

Born in London, the eldest daughter of **Henry VII** of England, she married **James IV** of Scotland (1503), Archibald Douglas, the 6th Earl of Angus (1514), and, having divorced him, Henry Stewart, later Lord Methven (1527). She had a significant, enigmatic role in the conflict between pro-French and pro-English factions during the minority of her son, **James V** of Scotland, for whom she acted as regent. Her great-grandson, **James VI** of Scotland, inherited the English throne (1603). ▢ Patricia Hill Buchanan, *Margaret Tudor Queen of Scots* (1985)

Marggraf, Andreas Sigismund 1709–82
German chemist and agricultural scientist

He was born in Berlin and studied there and at several other German universities. He was elected to the Royal Prussian Academy in 1738 and became director of its laboratory (1753). In 1747 he extracted the juice from beet and, using a microscope, showed that the crystals which formed in the juice were identical to cane sugar. This discovery laid the basis for the sugar beet industry. Marggraf also used flame tests to distinguish between sodium and potassium and showed that magnesium salts burn with a green flame. He also isolated zinc from calamine and carried out valuable investigations of the alkaline earths.

Margrethe I, *also called* Margareta or Margaret 1353–1412
Queen of Denmark, of Norway and of Sweden

Born in Søborg, Denmark, she was married to King Haakon VI of Norway (1363) at the age of 10. She became Queen of Denmark (1375) on the death of her father, Valdemar IV Atterdag, holding the Crown in trust for her five-year-old son Olav, for whom she acted as regent. By Haakon's death (1380), she also became Regent of Norway for Olav, who died suddenly (1387), leaving her sole ruler of Denmark–Norway. In 1388 the Swedish nobles rose against their German king, Albert of Mecklenburg, and offered her his Crown, whereupon she invaded Sweden, took Albert prisoner, and became Queen of Sweden (1389). She had her seven-year-old great-nephew, **Erik VII**, adopted as her successor to the three Scandinavian kingdoms, and his coronation (1397) as king of all three kingdoms effected the Union of Kalmar, whereby the kingdoms should remain under one ruler each, retaining its separate laws. Nominally governed by Erik (as Erik VII), Margaret remained the ruler of Scandinavia until her death, recovering Crown land, and gaining

Gotland and much of Schleswig. ▣ Kristian Erslev, *Dronning Margrethe og Kalmarunionens Grundlaeggelse* (1882)

Margrethe II 1940–
Queen of Denmark

Born in Copenhagen, she was the daughter of Frederik IX, whom she succeeded in 1972, and she became the first reigning queen in Denmark for nearly 600 years. She was educated at the universities of Copenhagen, Aarhus and Cambridge, the Sorbonne, Paris, and the London School of Economics and became an archaeologist. In 1967 she married a French diplomat, Count Henri de Laborde de Monpezat, now Prince Henrik of Denmark. Their children are the heir apparent, Crown Prince Frederik (1968–) and Prince Joachim (1969–). She has published several books which include, in translation, *All Men Are Mortal* (1981, co-written with Prince Henrik) and *The Forest* (1989). ▣ Anne Wolden-Raethinge, *Dronning i Danmark: Margrethe den Anden fortaeller om sit liv* (1989)

Maria II, *known as* Maria Da Glória 1819–53
Queen of Portugal

Born in Rio de Janeiro, Brazil, the daughter of Peter I of Brazil and IV of Portugal, she became queen under a regency in 1834 following the renunciation by her father of his rights on the death of her grandfather, John IV. She was overthrown in 1828 by her uncle, Michael, and fled to England and Brazil. A civil war between Liberals and Absolutists ensued, which returned Maria to the throne in 1834. In 1836 she tried to engineer a coup d'état against a leftist government. Similarly, the civil war of 1846–47 was caused by Maria's imposition of the conservative Saldanha as Prime Minister. Although Maria was forced to abdicate, the English and Spanish enforced the Peace of Gramido (1847), which restored her to power until her death in childbirth. Through both her interference and her favouritism, she undoubtedly exacerbated the political instability of the years 1836–51.

Maria Theresa 1717–80
Holy Roman Empress, Archduchess of Austria, and Queen of Hungary and Bohemia

The daughter of the Emperor Charles VI, she was born in Vienna. By the Pragmatic Sanction, her father appointed her heir to his hereditary thrones. In 1736 she married Francis Stephen, Duke of Lorraine (afterwards Grand Duke of Tuscany (1737–65) and Holy Roman Emperor (1745–65) as Francis I), and at her father's death (1740) she became Queen of Hungary and of Bohemia, and Archduchess of Austria. Her claim to the hereditary Habsburg lands led to the War of the Austrian Succession (1740–48) when she lost Silesia to Prussia, and some lands in Italy, but her husband was recognized as Emperor Francis I. Aided by Haugwitz, she instituted financial reforms, fostered agriculture, manufactures and commerce, and nearly doubled the national revenues, while decreasing taxation. Marshal Daun reorganized her armies. With Prince von Kaunitz-Rietberg as her Foreign Minister and France as an ally, she renewed the contest with the Prussian King, Frederick II, the Great, but the Seven Years War (1756–63) confirmed Frederick in his possession of Silesia. After the peace she carried out a series of reforms: peasant serfdom was reduced, as was the power of the Church, law reform continued, and she set up the best educational system in Europe. After the death of her husband (1765), her son Joseph (Emperor Joseph II) co-operated with her in the government. She joined with Russia and Prussia in the first partition of Poland (1772), securing Galicia. Warm, friendly and spirited, she tempered her idealism with earthy common sense and won the affection and admiration of her subjects. Of her 10 surviving children, the eldest son, Joseph II, succeeded her, Leopold, Grand Duke of Tuscany, succeeded him as

Leopold II, Ferdinand became Duke of Modena, and Marie Antoinette married Louis XVI of France. ▣ Robert Pick, *Empress Maria Theresa* (1966)

Marianus Scotus d.c.1088
Irish monk and calligrapher

Born in Ireland, he went to Bamberg in 1067, became a Benedictine, and was founder and abbot of the monastery of St Peter's in Ratisbon (now Regensburg). He was a prolific calligrapher, copied the Bible many times, and left commentaries on Paul's Epistles and on the Psalms.

Maricourt, Peter the Pilgrim See Peregrinus, Petrus

Marie Antoinette, *in full* Josèphe Jeanne Marie Antoinette 1755–93
Queen of France

Born in Vienna, Austria, she was the fourth daughter of the Empress Maria Theresa and the Emperor Francis I, and in 1770 was married to the Dauphin of France, afterwards Louis XVI (from 1774). Young and inexperienced, she aroused criticism by her frivolity, extravagance and disregard for conventions, her devotion to the interests of Austria, and her opposition to all the measures devised by Turgot and Necker for relieving the financial distress of the country. The miseries of France became identified with her extravagance. She opposed all new ideas, and prompted Louis into a retrograde policy to his own undoing. She was, however, also capable of strength rising to the heroic, and possessed the power of inspiring enthusiasm. Amid the horrors of the march of women on Versailles (1789) she alone maintained her courage, but she consistently failed to understand the troubled times of the Revolution, and the indecision of Louis and his dread of civil war hampered her plans. She had an instinctive abhorrence of the liberal nobles such as the Marquis de Lafayette and the Comte de Mirabeau, and although she finally reached agreement with Mirabeau (July 1790) she was too independent to follow his advice, and his death in April 1791 removed the last hope of saving the monarchy. She and Louis tried to escape to the frontier, but were intercepted at Varennes. The storming of the Tuileries and slaughter of the Swiss guards, and the trial and execution of Louis (21 January 1793) quickly followed, and soon she herself was sent to the Conciergerie (2 August 1793). After eight weeks the 'Widow Capet' was herself arraigned before the Revolutionary Tribunal, where she bore herself with dignity and resignation. After two days and nights of questioning came the inevitable sentence, and she was guillotined on the same day, 16 October 1793. ▣ Charles Kunstler, *La Vie privée de Marie-Antoinette* (1938, Eng trans *The Personal Life of Marie-Antoinette,* 1940)

Marie de France fl.c.1160–c.1190
French poet

Born in Normandy, she spent much of her life in England. The *Lais* (sometime before 1167), her most important work, are dedicated to 'a noble king', probably Henry II of England, and comprise 14 romantic narratives in octosyllabic verse based on Celtic material. A landmark in French literature, they influenced a number of later writers. She also wrote *Fables* (sometime after 1170) and translated into French the *Tractatus de Purgatorio Sancti Patricii* (c.1190, 'St Patricius's Treatise on Purgatory'). ▣ H Hoepffner, *Les lais de Marie de France* (1935)

Marie de Médicis, *Italian* Maria de' Medici 1573–1642
Queen of France

Born in Florence, she was the daughter of Francis I, Grand Duke of Tuscany, second wife of Henri IV from 1600, and mother of Louis XIII. After Henri's assassination (1610), she became regent (1610–17) for her nine-year-old son. Squandering state revenues and adopting a pro-Spanish foreign policy, she dismissed her husband's Minister, the Duc de Sully, and relied on a circle of unscrupulous favourites, especially her Italian lover Concini, and his wife. At the Estates General (1614), she received support from the young Richelieu, Bishop of Luçon, who was in charge of foreign affairs from 1616. In 1615 she had arranged a marriage for her son Louis with the Infanta Anne of Austria (daughter of Philip III of Spain), and for her eldest daughter Elizabeth to the heir to the Spanish throne (the future Philip IV), thus bringing an end to the war with the Habsburgs. In 1617 Louis assumed royal power, arranged for the assassination of Concini, and exiled his mother to the provinces. With Richelieu's mediation she was reconciled to her son (1620), was readmitted to the council (1622), and persuaded Louis to make Richelieu his Chief Minister. She plotted tirelessly against her former protégé, Richelieu, but he broke her power on the Day of Dupes (1630) and she went into exile in Brussels. Her lasting achievement was the building of the Luxembourg Palace in Paris, whose galleries were decorated by Rubens. ▣ Louis Batiffol, *Marie de Medicis and the French Court in the Seventeenth Century* (1908)

Marie Louise 1791–1847
Empress of France

Born in Vienna, Austria, she was the daughter of Francis I of Austria. She married Napoleon I in 1810 (after his divorce from Joséphine), and bore him a son (1811), who was created King of Rome and became Napoleon II. On Napoleon's abdication (1814) she returned to Austria, and was awarded the duchy of Parma. In 1822 she contracted a morganatic marriage with Count von Neipperg (c.1829) and another with the Count of Bombelles (1834). ▣ Patrick Turnbull, *Napoleon's Second Empress* (1974)

Mariette, Auguste Édouard 1821–81
French Egyptologist

He was born in Boulogne, where he was made professor in 1841. In 1849 he joined the staff of the Louvre, Paris, and in 1850 was dispatched to Egypt, where he brought to light important monuments and inscriptions in Memphis, Sakkara and Giza. In 1858 he was appointed keeper of monuments to the Egyptian government, and excavated the Sphinx, the temples of Dendera and Edfu, and made many other discoveries. He was made a pasha in 1879. He died of diabetes and was buried at the door of his museum at Bûlâq, Cairo.

Marillac, Ste Louise de 1591–1660
French Catholic co-founder of the Sisters of Charity

Born in Ferrières-en-Brie, near Meaux, she lost both of her parents by the age of 15, and after marrying Antony Le Gras, was widowed in 1625. She took Vincent de Paul as her spiritual director, who saw her as the right person to train girls and widows to help the sick and the poor. In 1633 four girls started work in her Paris home. From this modest beginning sprang the Sisters of Charity, who ministered in hospitals, orphanages and schools in Paris and beyond. They did not take vows until 1642, and then only for a year at a time, a practice that continues today. Louise de Marillac was canonized in 1934 and named the patron of Christian social work in 1960. Her feast day is 15 March.

Marin, John 1872–1953
US artist

Born in Rutherford, New Jersey, he trained and worked as an architect before studying art at Pennsylvania Academy and at the Art Students League. From 1905 to 1910 he travelled in Europe. When he returned to New York he came into contact with avant-garde movements at the gallery of the Stieglitz circle. He became well known for his watercolours and etchings executed in an extremely

individual style. His early work was in the manner of James McNeill Whistler, but his later works are more expressive in style and draw on Cubist concepts.

Marin, Maguy 1951–
French dancer and choreographer

Born in Toulouse, she studied dance as a child and first worked with the Strasbourg Opera Ballet before continuing to train at the Mudra school in Brussels. This led to her joining Maurice Béjart's Ballet of the 20th Century in the mid-1970s. In 1978 she won first prize at the Bagnolet international choreographic competition and that same year founded her own troupe, which in 1981 became the resident company of Créteil, a Paris suburb. She has choreographed for major European companies including Paris Opera Ballet, Dutch National Ballet and, most notably, a 1985 version of *Cinderella* for Lyons Opera Ballet, which is in a style that encompasses theatre as much as dance.

Marinetti, Emilio Filippo Tommaso 1876–1944
Italian writer

He was born in Alexandria, Egypt, and studied in Paris and Genoa. One of the founders of Futurism, he published the original Futurist manifesto in *Figaro* in 1909. In his writings he glorified war, the machine age, speed and 'dynamism', and in 1919 he became a fascist. His publications include *Le Futurisme* (1911), *Teatro sintetico futurista* (1916, 'The Synthetic Futurist Theatre') and *Manifesti del Futurismo* (4 vols, 1920, 'Manifesto of Futurism'). He condemned all traditional forms of literature and art, and his ideas were applied to painting by Umberto Boccioni, Giacomo Balla and others. ▣ W Vaccari, *Vita e tumulti di Filippo Tommaso Marinetti* (1959)

Marini, Giambattista 1569–1625
Italian poet

Born in Naples, he was ducal secretary at Turin, and wrote his main work, the *Adone* (1622), at the court of France. His florid hyperbole and overstrained imagery were copied by the Marinist school.

Marini, Marino 1901–80
Italian sculptor and painter

Born in Pistoia, he studied in Florence, and from 1929 to 1940 taught at the Scuola d'Arte di Villa Reale, Monza, before moving to Milan, where he was professor at Brera Academy (1940–70). Never part of any modern movement, he remained an individual. His work was figurative and his best-known theme the horse and rider, which he explored in many versions over the years. He liked to combine different techniques, including colour, for example *Dancer* (1949–54), and executed portraits of Igor Stravinsky, Marc Chagall, Henry Miller and others. He won many prizes, including the Venice Biennale (1952). ▣ Alberto Busignani, *Marini* (1971)

Marino, Dan 1961–
US footballer

Born in Pittsburgh, he plays as quarterback with the Miami Dolphins, and in the 1984 season he gained 5,084 yards passing to create a National Football League record. He completed a record 29 passes in the 1985 Super Bowl, and in 1986 established a record for the most passes completed in a season (378).

Marion, Frances, *originally* Frances Marion Owens 1887–1973
US screenwriter and novelist

She was born in San Francisco. A reporter with the *San Francisco Examiner*, she had worked as a commercial artist and model before arriving in Hollywood in 1913 as the protégé of director Lois Weber. A prolific screenwriter during the silent era, she was associated with actress Mary

Pickford on such films as *Rebecca Of Sunnybrook Farm* (1918) and *Pollyanna* (1920). She was also one of the first female war correspondents during the latter stages of World War I. She later wrote star vehicles for the likes of Greta Garbo and Jean Harlow and received Academy Awards for *The Big House* (1930) and *The Champ* (1931). She retired from screenwriting in 1940 and subsequently wrote novels, including *Westward The Dream* (1948) and *The Powder Keg* (1954). ▭ *Off With Their Heads!* (1972)

Marion, Francis, *known as* the Swamp Fox
c.1732–1795
American Revolutionary general
Born in Winyah, South Carolina, he first saw action against the Cherokee in 1759, and he joined the Revolutionary army in 1776. After American forces were defeated at Charleston and Camden, South Carolina, the state was almost entirely in British hands, but Marion gathered a rough militia (1780) and led a series of guerrilla attacks on British troops. His nickname referred to his skill in retreating to seemingly impassable swamps where the British could not follow. He was promoted to brigadier-general in 1781, and in September of that year he won an important victory at Eutaw Springs.

Mariotte, Edmé c.1620–1684
French physicist and physiologist
Born probably in Chazeuil, Burgundy, he was prior of Saint-Martin-de-Beaumont-sur-Vingeanne and moved from Dijon to Paris in the early 1670s. Elected to the Paris Academy of Sciences (1666), he attracted attention as a physiologist, studied pendulums and falling bodies (1667–68), and published an exposition of the laws of elastic and inelastic collisions (1673). In 1679 he restated the law bearing his name in France (elsewhere attributed to Robert Boyle) and used it to estimate the height of the atmosphere. He also discussed scientific methodology, hydrology, optics (including the rainbow), astronomy and the strength of materials.

Maris
Dutch family of artists
There were three brothers, all painters, notably Jacob (1837–99), a landscape and genre painter, born in The Hague. He studied there, in Antwerp, and in Paris (1866–71), coming under the influence of Díaz de la Peña, Camille Corot and Jean François Millet. Matthijs (1839–1917) and Willem (1843–1910) Maris were also famous and worked chiefly in London.

Maritain, Jacques 1882–1973
French philosopher
Born in Paris and brought up a Protestant, he was educated in Paris and Heidelberg, and converted to Catholicism (1906). He was professor at the Institut Catholique in Paris (1914–40) and then taught mainly in North America, at Toronto, Columbia, Chicago and Princeton (1948–60). He was also French ambassador to the Vatican (1945–48) and later a strong opponent of the Vatican Council and the neo-Modernist movement. His best-known works are *Les Degrés du savoir* (1932, Eng trans *The Degrees of Knowledge*, 1937), in which he applied Thomas Aquinas's thought to contemporary philosophical canons in the theory of knowledge, and various writings on art and politics including *Art et scolastique* (1920, Eng trans *Art and Scholasticism*, 1930) and *Humanisme intégral* (1936), which were better known abroad than in France.

Marius, Gaius 157–86BC
Roman general and politician
He was born in Arpinum, and was consul seven times. He reformed the Roman army and had victories over Jugurtha of Numidia (105BC) in Africa, the Teutones (102) in Gaul, and the Cimbri (101) in north Italy. His final years were dominated by rivalry with the Roman

dictator Sulla over the command against Mithridates. Civil war followed, and Marius was forced to flee to Africa. He returned to capture Rome for the Roman politician Cinna from the forces backing Sulla (87) but died soon after.

Marius, Simon, *German surname* Mayr 1570–1624
German astronomer
A pupil of Tycho Brahe, in 1609 he claimed to have discovered the four satellites of Jupiter independently of Galileo. He named them Io, Europa, Ganymede and Callisto, but other astronomers merely numbered them as they did not recognize his claim to discovery. He was one of the earliest users of a telescope and the first to observe by this means the Andromeda nebula (1612).

Marivaux, Pierre Carlet de Chamblain de
1688–1763
French playwright and novelist
Born in Paris, he published *L'Homère travesti* ('Homer Burlesqued'), a burlesque of the *Iliad*, in 1716, and from then on wrote several comedies, of which his best is *Le Jeu de l'amour et du hasard* (1730, Eng trans *Love in Livery*, 1907). His best-known novel, *La Vie de Marianne* (1731–41, Eng trans *The Life of Marianne*, 1736–42), was never finished. It is marked by an affected, 'precious' style ('Marivaudage'). His other romances, *Pharsamon* (1737, Eng trans *Pharsamond*, 1950) and *Le Paysan parvenu* (1735–36, Eng trans *The Fortunate Villager*, 1765) are considerably inferior. ▭ E J H Greene, *Marivaux* (1965)

Mark, St, *also called* John Mark 1st century AD
New Testament evangelist
Born probably in Jerusalem, he is described as 'John whose surname was Mark' (Acts 12.12, 25), and commended in Colossians 4.10 and 2 Timothy 4.11. He helped the Apostles Barnabas and Paul during their first missionary journey, but caused a split between them over the question of his loyalty. Traditionally the author of the second Gospel, he was also described as the 'disciple and interpreter' of Peter in Rome. In medieval art, Mark is symbolized by the lion. His feast day is 25 April.

Markham, Beryl 1902–86
English–African aviator
Born in England, she moved with her father to East Africa in 1906, and she grew up playing with Murani children, learning Masai and Swahili. She apprenticed with her father as a horse trainer and breeder, until he left Africa for Peru in 1919. She decided to remain in her adopted homeland and later turned to aviation. From 1931 to 1936 she carried mail, passengers and supplies in her small plane to remote corners of Africa, including the Sudan, Tanganyika, Kenya and Rhodesia. In 1936 she became the first person to fly solo across the Atlantic from east to west, taking off in England and crash-landing in Nova Scotia 21 hours and 25 minutes later. Her autobiography *West With the Night* (1942) contains reflections on Africa and flying.

Markham, Sir Clements Robert 1830–1916
English geographer
Born in Stillingfleet, near York, he was educated at Westminster. He served in the Royal Navy (1844–51), and took part in the expedition that located the records of Sir John Franklin. He explored Peru (1852–54), introduced cinchona-bark culture from South America into India (1860), and was geographer to the Abyssinian expedition of 1867–68. As president of the Royal Geographical Society (1893–1905), he appointed Captain Robert Falcon Scott to lead his first Antarctic expedition. He wrote travel books and biographies and edited the *Geographical Magazine* from 1872 to 1878.

Markievicz, Constance Georgine, Countess,
née **Gore-Booth** 1868–1927
Irish nationalist and first British woman MP

Born in London, daughter of Sir Henry Gore-Booth of County Sligo, she was a society beauty, who studied art at the Slade School in London and in Paris, where she met and married (1900) Count Casimir Markievicz. They settled in Dublin in 1903, and in 1908 she joined Sinn Féin and became a friend of **Maud Gonne**. Her husband left in 1913 for the Ukraine and never returned. She fought in the Easter Rising in Dublin (1916) and was sentenced to death, but reprieved in the general amnesty of 1917. In 1918 she was elected Sinn Féin MP for the St Patrick's division of Dublin—the first British woman MP—but refused to take her seat. She was elected to the first Dáil Éireann in 1919 and became Minister for Labour, but was imprisoned twice. After the Civil War she was a member of the Dáil from 1923.

Markov, Andrei Andreyevich 1856–1922
Russian mathematician

Born in Ryazan, he studied at St Petersburg University, where he was professor from 1893 to 1905, before going into self-imposed exile in the town of Zaraisk. A student of **Pafnutii Chebyshev**, he worked on number theory, continued fractions, the moment problem, and the law of large numbers in probability theory, but his name is best known for the concept of Markov chain, a series of events in which the probability of a given event occurring depends only on the immediately previous event. This concept has since found many applications in physics and biology.

Markova, Dame Alicia, *stage name of* Lilian Alicia Marks 1910–
English ballerina

Born in London, she joined **Sergei Diaghilev's** Ballets Russes (1924–29), then returned to Britain to the Vic-Wells (later Sadler's Wells and Royal) Ballet. A period of partnership with **Anton Dolin** led to their establishment of The Markova-Dolin Company in 1935. As well as performing Dolin's choreography in the joint company they also made guest appearances together around the world and were famed for their interpretations of *Giselle*. Their touring group developed into the London Festival Ballet (1949) which became English National Ballet in 1988. She was created DBE in 1963, was a director of the Metropolitan Opera Ballet (1963–69), and has been a governor of the Royal Ballet since 1973 and president of the London Festival Ballet since 1986. Her books include *Markova Remembers* (1986). ▱ Maurice Leonard, *Markova, the Legend* (1995); Cyril W Beaumont, *Alicia Markova* (1935)

Marković, Ante 1924–
Yugoslav politician

He joined the Communist Youth Movement in Yugoslavia in 1940 and fought in **Tito's** partisans, becoming a member of the Communist League of Yugoslavia in 1943. He was a member of the Central Committee of the League of Communists of Croatia (1982–86) and, as Prime Minister of the Socialist Federal Republic of Croatia, introduced a programme of economic reform. A member of the Central Committee of the League of Communists of Yugoslavia since 1986, he succeeded Branko Mikulić as Prime Minister of Yugoslavia (1989). A liberal and pro-Western, he was hailed as 'man of the year' by the popular Croatian magazine *Danas* (1990). After six months of civil war between the Serbs and Croats, he announced his resignation as Prime Minister of Yugoslavia (1991).

Marks (of Broughton), Simon Marks, Baron 1888–1964
English businessman

Born in Leeds, he was educated at Manchester Grammar School. In 1907 he inherited the 60 Marks and Spencer 'penny bazaars', which his father Michael Marks and Thomas Spencer, had built up from 1884. In collaboration with **Israel** (later Lord) **Sieff**, his schoolfriend and brother-in-law, Marks expanded Marks and Spencer from a company with the policy of 'Don't ask the price—it's a penny' to a major retail chain. 'Marks and Sparks', as it became known, used their considerable purchasing power to encourage British clothing manufacturers to achieve demanding standards. The 'St Michael®' brand label became a guarantee of high quality at a reasonable price.

Marlborough, Duchess of See **Churchill, Sarah**

Marlborough, John Churchill, 1st Duke of
1650–1722
English soldier

Born in Ashe, Devon, he was the son of Sir Winston Churchill, an impoverished Devonshire Royalist. His first post was as page to the Duke of York (the future **James VII and II**). The patronage of **Barbara Villiers** (Duchess of Cleveland) enriched him, and brought him an ensigncy in the Guards (1667). Service in Tangier and the Netherlands, combined with the influence of his sister Arabella, mistress of the Duke of York, brought him promotion to colonel. His prospects were further enhanced by his secret marriage in 1677, to Sarah Jennings (see **Sarah Churchill**), an attendant to, and close friend of, the Princess, later Queen **Anne**. In 1678 his discreet handling of a confidential mission to William of Orange (**William III**) led to his ennoblement as Baron Churchill of Eyemouth (1682), and his wife was made Lady of the Bedchamber to Anne. In 1685 he crushed the rebellion led by the Duke of **Monmouth**, and was rewarded with an English barony. When William landed Churchill pledged his support to his cause. The value of his defection was recognized by his elevation to the earldom of Marlborough. Yet by 1692, despite his brilliant service in William's Irish campaign, the suspicion that he was still sympathetic to the Jacobites brought him into temporary disfavour, though Sarah maintained her close friendship with Anne, who succeeded as queen in 1702. In the War of the Spanish Succession (1701–14) Marlborough was given supreme command of the British and Dutch forces. His march to the Danube brought him the vital co-operation of Prince **Eugène of Savoy**, and ended in the victory of Donauworth and the costly but unequivocal triumph of Blenheim (1704), which earned him a palatial residence at Woodstock. He defeated **Louis XIV** in the campaign of 1706 at Ramillies and foiled the Duc de **Vendôme's** 1708 attempt to recover Flanders, which led to the surrender of Lille and Ghent. With their superior manpower, the French recovered from their failure of 1709 at Malplaquet; however in 1711 Marlborough displayed his military flair, when he forced the Duc de **Villars'** 'impregnable' lines and went on to capture Bouchain. But in England **Robert Harley** and the Tories had been conspiring for a compromise peace—the Treaty of Utrecht (1713), which sacrificed virtually everything for which the war had been fought—and for Marlborough's public overthrow, while Queen Anne had transferred her friendship from Sarah to **Abigail Masham**. In 1711 Marlborough, charged with embezzlement, was dismissed and then went abroad (1712). With the accession of **George I** (1714), however, he was restored to his honours, his advice being sought at the time of the Jacobite rebellion in 1715. ▱ Winston Churchill, *Marlborough: His Life and Times* (6 vols, 1933–38)

Marley, Bob (Robert Nesta) 1945–81
Jamaican singer, guitarist and composer of reggae music

Born in the rural parish of St Ann, he moved to Kingston at the age of 14, made his first record at 19, and in 1965, with Peter Tosh and 'Bunny' Livingstone, formed the vocal trio The Wailers. Together they became the first reggae artists to gain international success; Marley continued to build on this through a series of world tours after the departure of his original collaborators. By the 1970s, both through his music and his religious and political views (which made him, at one point, the victim of an assassination attempt), he became a national hero. A devout Rastafarian, Marley made reggae popular with white audiences through his warm, expressive voice, memorable compositions—from the lyrical 'No Woman, No Cry' to the fiercely political 'I Shot the Sheriff' and 'Exodus'—and a willingness to embrace rock styles and techniques. Although he suffered from cancer in his last years, his output was undiminished and he remained a major force in popular music. His albums include *Catch a Fire* (1972), *Rastaman Vibration* (1976) and *Uprising* (1980). 📖 Ian McCann, *Bob Marley* (1993)

Marlowe, Christopher 1564–93
English dramatist

He was born in Canterbury, Kent, a shoemaker's son, and educated at King's School and Benet (Corpus Christi) College, Cambridge. His *Tamburlaine the Great*, in two parts, was first printed in 1590, and probably produced in 1587. In spite of its bombast and violence it was infinitely superior to any tragedy that had yet appeared on the English stage. Earlier dramatists had used blank verse, but Marlowe was the first to discover its strength and variety. *The Tragical History of Dr Faustus* was probably produced soon after *Tamburlaine*; the earliest edition is dated 1604. *Faustus* is rather a series of detached scenes than a finished drama and some of the scenes are evidently not by Marlowe. *The Jew of Malta*, produced after 1588 and first published in 1633, is very uneven. *Edward II*, produced about 1590, is the most mature of his plays. It does not have the impressive poetry of *Faustus* and the first two acts of *The Jew of Malta*, but it is planned and executed with more firmness and solidity. *The Massacre at Paris*, his weakest play, survives in a mutilated state. It was written after the assassination of Henri III of France (1589) and was probably one of the latest plays. *The Tragedy of Dido* (1594), left probably in a fragmentary state by Marlowe and finished by Thomas Nashe, is of slight value. Marlowe doubtless contributed to the three parts of Shakespeare's *Henry VI*, and probably to *Titus Andronicus*. A wild, shapeless tragedy, *Lust's Dominion* (1657) may have been adapted from one of Marlowe's lost plays. The unfinished poem, *Hero and Leander*, composed in heroic couplets, was first published in 1598; a second edition, with Chapman's continuation, followed the same year. Marlowe's translations of Ovid's *Amores* and of the first book of Lucan's *Pharsalia* add nothing to his fame. The pastoral ditty, 'Come, live with me and be my love', to which Sir Walter Raleigh wrote an Answer, was imitated, but not equalled, by Robert Herrick, John Donne and others. It was first printed in *The Passionate Pilgrim* (1599), without the fourth and sixth stanzas. Another anthology, Allot's *England's Parnassus* (1600), preserves a fragment by Marlowe, beginning 'I walked along a stream for pureness rare'. He led an irregular life, kept dubious company, and was on the point of being arrested when he was fatally stabbed in a tavern brawl. In tragedy he prepared the way for Shakespeare, on whose early work his influence is evident. 📖 H Levin, *The Over-Reacher* (1954); F S Boas, *Christopher Marlowe* (1940)

Marmion, Simon 1425–89
French manuscript illuminator, and painter

Born probably in Amiens, he worked there and in Tournai and Valenciennes. His illuminations are among the finest in 15th-century manuscript art.

Marmont, Auguste Frédéric Louis Viesse de 1774–1852
French soldier

He went with Napoleon I to Italy, and fought at Lodi, in Egypt, and at Marengo (1800). He was sent to Dalmatia in 1805, defeated the Russians there, and was made Duke of Ragusa. He was Governor of the Illyrian Provinces, and in 1811 succeeded André Masséna in Portugal. In 1813 he fought at Lützen, Bautzen and Dresden. In 1814 he deserted to the Allies, compelling Napoleon to abdicate, and earned the title of traitor from the Bonapartists. In the July Revolution of 1830 he tried to reduce Paris to submission but failed, and finally retreating with a few faithful battalions, conducted Charles X across the frontier. Accused of treachery and forced into exile, he published his *Mémoires* in 1856–57.

Marmontel, Jean François 1723–99
French writer

Born in Bort, Limousin, he studied at a Jesuit college, settled in Paris in 1745 on the advice of Voltaire, and in 1753 got a secretaryship at Versailles through Madame de Pompadour. He wrote successful tragedies and operas, ran the official journal, *Le Mercure*, and was the main contributor on literature to the *Encyclopédie* (35 vols, 1751–80). He became secretary of the Académie Française in 1783, and was appointed royal historian of France. His most celebrated work was *Bélisaire* (1766, 'Belisarius'), a dull and wordy political romance, containing a chapter on toleration which excited furious hostility. 📖 S Lenel, *Jean François Marmontel* (1902)

Marmora, Alfonso Ferrero La See La Marmora, Alfonso Ferrero

Marnix, Philips van, Heer (Lord) van Sint Aldegonde 1538–98
Flemish statesman

Born in Brussels, he was active in the Reformation, and in 1566 in the revolt against Spain. An intimate friend of William I, the Silent, he represented him at the first meeting of the Estates of the United Provinces, held at Dort in 1572, and was sent on special missions to the courts of France and England. As burgomaster of Antwerp he defended the city for 13 months against the Spaniards, but after having surrendered he incurred so much ill-will that he retired from public life. He wrote the patriotic 'Wilhelmus' song, the prose satire *Den byencorf der H. Roomsche Kercke* (1569, 'The Roman Beehive'), a metrical translation of the Psalms (1580) and part of a prose translation of the Bible.

Marochetti, Carlo, Baron 1805–67
Italian sculptor

He was born in Turin, and trained in Rome, and in Paris where he later settled. At the Revolution of 1848 he went to London, where he produced many dramatic statues, such as the equestrian figures of Queen Victoria and Prince Albert (1849, Glasgow), and Richard I, Cœur-de-Lion (1860) outside the House of Lords. Highly regarded by Prince Albert and Queen Victoria, he was commissioned to execute the statue of Prince Albert for the Albert Memorial and produced the first full size model in 1867, but died unexpectedly.

Marot, Clément c.1497–1544
French poet

Born in Cahors, he entered the service of Margaret of Angoulême, Queen of Navarre. He was wounded at the Battle of Pavia in 1525, and soon after imprisoned for a few months on a charge of heresy. In 1535 he fled first to the court of the Queen of Navarre, and later to that of the Duchess of Ferrara, and returned to Paris in 1536, where he began to translate the Psalms into French in 1538. He had to flee again in 1543 when accused of heresy by the

Sorbonne. He made his way to Geneva, but left under a cloud (he is said to have played backgammon on a Sunday), and went to Turin. His poems consist of elegies, epistles, rondeaux, ballads, sonnets, madrigals, epigrams, nonsense verses and longer pieces. 📖 C A Mayer, *Marot* (1969)

Marozia d.938
Roman noblewoman
Of infamous reputation, she was married three times, was the mistress of Pope Sergius III, mother of Pope John XI, and grandmother of Pope John XII. She had sufficient influence to arrange the deposition of Pope John X, her mother's lover, and the election of her own son, John XI. She died in prison in Rome.

Marquand, John P(hillips) 1893–1960
US novelist
Born in Wilmingon, Delaware, he was educated at Newbury Port High School, Massachusetts, and at Harvard University. He served with the military, was a war correspondent and wrote advertising copy. He started as a writer of popular stories for magazines, featuring the Japanese detective Mr Moto, and went on to produce a series of notable novels gently satirizing affluent middle-class US life, in a vein similar to Sinclair Lewis, whom he admired. Key titles are *The Late George Apley* (1937), *Wickford Point* (1939) and *Point of No Return* (1949). 📖 M Bell, *John P Marquand: an American life* (1979)

Marquet, (Pierre) Albert 1875–1947
French artist
Born in Bordeaux, he studied under Gustave Moreau and was one of the original Fauves. After initial hardships he became primarily an Impressionist landscape painter and travelled widely, painting many pictures of the Seine (eg *Pont neuf*), Le Havre and Algiers in a cool restrained style. In his swift sketches he showed himself a master of line.

Marquette, Jacques 1637–75
French Jesuit missionary and explorer
Born in Laon, he was sent in 1666 to North America, where he took Christianity to the Ottawans living around Lake Superior, and went on the expedition which discovered and explored the Mississippi (1673).

Márquez, Gabriel García 1928–
Colombian novelist and Nobel Prize winner
Born in Aracataca, he was educated at a Jesuit school, and studied law and journalism at the National University of Colombia, Bogotá. He worked as a journalist from 1950 to 1965, when he devoted himself to fiction writing, becoming celebrated for his craft as well as his rhetorical exuberance and fecund imagination. One of Latin America's most formidable writers, he is a master of 'magic realism', the practice of representing possible events as if they were wonders and impossible events as if they were commonplace. His best-known work is *Cien años de soledad* (1967, Eng trans *One Hundred Years of Solitude*, 1970), a vast, referential 'total' novel charting the history of a family, a house and a town, from edenic, mythic genesis through the history of wars, politics, and economic exploitation to annihilation at a moment of apocalyptic revelation. It is regarded as one of the great novels of the 20th century. Many of his other novels have been translated, including *El otono del patriarca* (1975, Eng trans *The Autumn of the Patriarch*, 1976), *Crónica de una muerte anunciada* (1981, Eng trans *Chronicle of a Death Foretold*, 1982), *El amor en los tiempos del colera* (1985, Eng trans *Love in the Time of Cholera*, 1988), *Amores Difíciles* (1989, Eng trans *Of Love and Other Demons*, 1995) and *Doce cuentos peregrinos* (1992, Eng trans *Strange Pilgrims*, 1993). He was awarded the Nobel Prize for literature in 1982.

Marquis, Don(ald Robert Perry) 1878–1937
US novelist, playwright and poet
Born in Walnut, Illinois, he abandoned formal education at 15 and worked at various jobs before studying art for a spell. He had a varied career as a journalist and wrote serious plays and poems, but he became a celebrity as a comic writer with *The Old Soak's History of the World* (1924). *archy and mehitabel* (1927) and *archys life of mehitabel* (1933) follow the fortunes of Archy the cockroach who cannot reach the typewriter's shift key (hence the lower-case titles) and Mehitabel, an alley cat. 📖 E Antony, *O Rare Don Marquis* (1962)

Marriner, Sir Neville 1924–
English conductor and violinist
He was born in Lincoln, and studied at the Royal College of Music. He was a violinist in the Philharmonia Orchestra and the London Symphony Orchestra (1956–68), and in 1958 founded his own chamber orchestra, the Academy of St Martin-in-the-Fields, which he directed until 1978. He has also conducted the Los Angeles Chamber Orchestra and the Minnesota Orchestra (1979–86). Although principally associated with baroque and rococo music for small orchestra, he has also performed 20th century music and opera. He was knighted in 1985.

Marryat, Frederick, *known as* Captain Marryat 1792–1848
English naval officer and novelist
Born in London, the son of an MP, he sailed as midshipman under Lord Cochrane in 1806, and after service in the West Indies took command of a sloop cruising off St Helena to guard against the escape of Napoleon I. He also worked to suppress the Channel smugglers, and served in Burma. On his return to England (1826) he was given the command of the *Ariadne* (1828), but he resigned in 1830 to lead the life of a writer. He was the author of a series of novels on sea life, including *Frank Mildmay* (1829), *Peter Simple* (1833), *Jacob Faithful* (1834) and *Mr Midshipman Easy* (1834). In 1837 he set out for a tour through the USA, where he wrote *The Phantom Ship* (1839). Although it was a financial success, he was extravagant and unlucky in money matters, and eventually retired to his small farm of Langham, Norfolk, in 1843 and wrote the stories for children for which he is best remembered, including the once very popular *Children of the New Forest* (1847). 📖 O Warner, *Captain Marryat* (1953)

Mars, Anne Françoise Boutet Monvel, *known as* Mademoiselle Mars 1779–1847
French actress
She starred at the Comédie-Française from 1799, excelling in the plays of Molière and Beaumarchais, and retired in 1841. She published her autobiographical *Mémoires* (2 vols, 1849) and *Confidences* (3 vols, 1855).

Marsalis, Wynton 1961–
US trumpeter and composer
He was born in New Orleans. His father, Ellis Marsalis, is a distinguished jazz pianist and teacher, and his brothers, Branford, Delfayeo and Jason, are all musicians. He learned to play from the age of eight, and is unusual in his dual achievement in both classical and jazz music. He performed the first of many engagements as a classical virtuoso aged 14, but his major achievements have been in jazz. He played with Art Blakey's Jazz Messengers (along with Branford Marsalis, tenor and soprano saxophones) from 1980–82, before forming the first of many ensembles under his own leadership. He became the figurehead of the neo-bop jazz renaissance of the 1980s, and went on to absorb aspects of the jazz tradition, including the early New Orleans, blues and gospel styles, within modern treatments in a range of recordings and performance projects, including large-scale works at the

Lincoln Center in New York, where he directs the jazz orchestra. In 1983 he released *Think of One* (jazz) and *Trumpet Concertos* (classical), becoming the first musician to win (or even be nominated for) Grammy awards in both categories.

Marschner, Heinrich 1795–1861
German composer of operas

Born in Zittau, he was successively music director at Dresden, Leipzig and Hanover, and is remembered mainly for his opera *Hans Heiling* (1833).

Marsden, Samuel 1764–1838
Australian clergyman, magistrate and farmer

Born in Farsley, Yorkshire, England, he arrived in New South Wales as assistant chaplain in 1794. The chaplain to the colony, Richard Johnson, was at that time the only minister in New South Wales. Marsden farmed land at Parramatta, New South Wales, where he was also appointed magistrate. His harsh measures as magistrate, particularly in regard to the rising by Irish convicts in 1800, earned him the title 'The Flogging Parson'. However, he received praise for his farming skills and was a pioneer breeder of sheep for wool production. In 1807 he took to England the first commercial consignment of Australian wool. He made seven missionary journeys to New Zealand on behalf of the Church Missionary Society, and conducted New Zealand's first Christian service at Rangihoua, Bay of Islands, in 1814.

Marsé, Juan, originally Juan Fonseca 1933–
Spanish novelist

He was born in Barcelona and his mother died at his birth, so he was adopted by the Marsé family. After publishing his first novel, *Encarrados con un solo juguete* (1961, 'Locked in with a Single Toy'), as an opposer of the Franco regime he exiled himself to Paris where he knew other exiles such as Juan Goytisolo. Later he went into the cinema business. He began to make a reputation as an ironic critic of society with his novel *Ultimas tardes con Teresa* (1965, 'Last Evenings with Teresa'), which shows the influence of the techniques of Ramón Valle-Inclán, the extraordinary Catalan Josep Pla and the Castilian Luis Martín-Santos. Like Martín-Santos, Marsé flayed the submissiveness of post-Civil War Spanish society, and worked it further in *Si te dicenque caí* (1973, Eng trans *The Fallen*, 1979). His other novel, *La muchacha de las bragas de oro* (1978, Eng trans *Golden Girl*, 1981), mercilessly burlesques the memoirs of the Falangist Rector of Madrid University, Pedro Laín Entralgo.

Marsh, George Perkins 1801–82
US diplomat and philologist

Born in Woodstock, Vermont, he studied and practised law and was elected to Congress in 1842. He was US Minister to Turkey (1849–53) and to Italy (1861–82), where he died. His chief linguistic works are *A Compendious Grammar of the Old Northern or Icelandic Language* (1838), *Lectures on the English Language* (1861) and *The Origin and History of the English Language* (1862). Among his other writings are a treatise on the camel, one on saints and miracles, and *Man and Nature* (1864; rewritten and reissued as *The Earth as Modified by Human Action*, 1874).

Marsh, James 1789–1846
English chemist

Born in London, he worked at the Royal Arsenal in Woolwich and was subsequently assistant to Michael Faraday at the Royal Military Academy. His most significant work was on poisons; he is best known for devising a sensitive test for arsenic (the Marsh test) which was published in 1836. He also wrote on electromagnetism and invented a percussion tube for ship's cannon made from quills.

Marsh, Dame (Edith) Ngaio 1899–1982
New Zealand detective novelist and theatre director

Born in Christchurch, she had brief careers on stage and as an interior decorator, then introduced her detective-hero Roderick Alleyn in her first novel *A Man Lay Dead* (1934), which was followed by 30 more stories ending with *Light Thickens* (1982). In theatre, she toured with the Wilkie company during the early 1920s, and during the 1940s and 1950s devoted much time to theatrical production in New Zealand, founding the Little Theatre in Christchurch. She wrote on art, theatre, and crime fiction, and a libretto for the fantasy-opera *A Unicorn for Christmas* (1962), with music by New Zealand composer David Farquhar. Her autobiography, *Black Beech and Honeydew*, was published in 1966. She was made DBE in 1948.

Marsh, O(thniel) C(harles) 1831–99
US palaeontologist

Born in Lockport, New York, and wealthy by inheritance, he studied at Yale, at New Haven, and in Germany, and became first Professor of Palaeontology at Yale in 1866, without a salary or classes to teach. From 1870 to 1873 he led a series of expeditions through the western territories making spectacular discoveries of vertebrate fossils; this led him into bitter clashes with Edward Drinker Cope, who organized rival dinosaur collecting expeditions. Marsh discovered (mainly in the Rocky Mountains) over a thousand species of extinct American vertebrates, including dinosaurs and the mammals uintatheres and brontotheres. By 1874 he was able to establish an evolutionary lineage for horses using the fossil remains which he had assembled. He also contributed to the documentation of evolutionary changes with his discovery of Cretaceous birds with teeth. His major contribution to stratigraphic palaeontology was an early discussion of the Miocene–Pliocene boundary. Marsh was the first vertebrate palaeontologist of the US Geological Survey (1882–92). He published over 300 papers, including *Odontornites: a Monograph on the Extinct Toothed Birds of North America* (1880) and *Dinosaurs of North America* (1896).

Marsh, Reginald 1898–1954
US painter

Born in Paris, the son of American artists, he studied at Yale and at the Art Students League in New York. He supported himself as a newspaper and magazine illustrator in the 1920s and was an original staff member of the *New Yorker*. With egg tempera he was able to paint in the rapid, graphic style that came naturally to him, and he became known for his lively, humorous paintings of New York life, which often focused on subways, elevated trains, burlesque houses, and other crowded locales, celebrating the tawdry vitality of the city. Among his works are *'Why Not Use the 'L'?'* (1930, Whitney Museum, New York) and *Tattoo and Haircut* (1932, Art Institute of Chicago).

Marshal, William, 1st Earl of Pembroke and Strigul c.1146–1219
English nobleman, Regent of England

The nephew of the Earl of Salisbury, he supported Henry II against Richard I, Cœur de Lion. Pardoned by Richard, he married (1189) the heiress of Strongbow, which brought him his earldom. He became a marshal of England and after Richard died supported the new king, John. He advised John in his conflicts with the pope and his barons, and brought peace and prosperity to Ireland (1207–13). After John's death he was appointed regent (1216–19) for the nine-year-old Henry III, and concluded a peace treaty with the French.

Marshall, George Catlett 1880–1959
US soldier, politician, and Nobel Prize winner

He was born in Uniontown, Pennsylvania. He was commissioned in 1901, and as Chief of Staff (1939–45) he directed the US army throughout World War II. After two years in China as special representative of the President he became Secretary of State (1947–49) and originated the Marshall Aid plan for the postwar reconstruction of Europe (ERP). In 1950 he was made Secretary of Defense by President Truman. He was awarded the Nobel Peace Prize in 1953. 📖 Forrest C Pogue, *Organizer of Victory, 1943–45* (1973); *Ordeal and Hope, 1939–42* (1966); *Education of a General, 1880–1939* (1963)

Marshall, John 1755–1835
US jurist

Born near Germantown, Virginia, he served (1775–79) in the Continental army during the American Revolution and afterwards studied law and became active in Virginia state politics. He was a special envoy to France during the XYZ affair (1797–98), and he served briefly in Congress and as Secretary of State under President John Adams before being appointed by Adams as Chief Justice of the Supreme Court in 1801. During his 34-year tenure, he established the power and independence of the Supreme Court as well as the fundamental principles of constitutional law. He ended the practice by which each justice wrote a separate opinion, instead producing a single majority opinion that stood as the verdict of the Court. His most important decision was in the case of *Marbury* v. *Madison* (1803), which established the principle of judicial review, asserting the Court's authority to determine the constitutionality of legislation. He also wrote majority opinions in decisions that upheld the inviolability of contracts with states and the superiority of federal over state authority. He is the single most influential figure in US legal history. 📖 Albert J Beveridge, *The Life of John Marshall* (4 vols, 1916–19)

Marshall, Sir John Hubert 1876–1958
English archaeologist and administrator

Born in Chester, he studied classics at Cambridge and excavated in Greece before being appointed director-general of archaeology in India (1902–31). He reorganized the Indian Archaeological Survey, recruiting Indians for the first time, established an ambitious programme for the listing and preservation of monuments, expanded museum services, and excavated widely on early historic sites. The city of Taxila in the Himalayan foothills (occupied 420BC–AD500) was the subject of a 20-year campaign (1913–33), and he worked also at the Buddhist religious centres of Sanchi in Madhya Pradesh and Sarnath near Benares. Prehistoric research was established on an equal footing in the 1920s with extensive excavation at Mohenjo Daro and Harappa, the chief cities of the Indus civilization which flourished in the northwest of the subcontinent c.2300–1750BC. This revealed for the first time the unsuspected antiquity of Indian civilization. His publications included *Mohenjo Daro and the Indus Valley Civilization* (3 vols, 1931), *The Monuments of Sanchi* (3 vols, 1939) and *Taxila* (1951).

Marshall, Paule 1929–
US writer

She was born in Brooklyn, New York City, to parents who had emigrated from Barbados during World War I. She grew up during the Depression, and in 1948 enrolled at Hunter College, New York City, but she left prematurely because of illness. Later she graduated from Brooklyn College and worked for *Our World Magazine*. *Brown Girl, Brownstones* (1959), her first novel, is regarded as a classic of African-American literature, telling the story of the coming of age of Seling Boyce, the daughter of Barbadian immigrants living through the Depression

and World War I. Her subsequent novels are *The Chosen Place, the Timeless People* (1969), *Praisesong for the Widow* (1983) and *Daughters* (1992). She won a MacArthur award in 1992.

Marshall, Penny, *originally* Penny Marscharelli 1942–
US film director and comedienne

Born in Brooklyn, New York, she established her reputation as a comedy actress in television shows like *The Odd Couple* (1971–75) and *Laverne and Shirley* (1976–83). She made her debut as a film director with *Jumpin' Jack Flash* (1986) and scored a box office success with *Big* (1988). Her other films include *Awakenings* (1990), *A League of Their Own* (1992) and *The Preacher's Wife* (1996).

Marshall, Peter 1902–49
US Presbyterian clergyman

Born in Coatbridge, Scotland, and educated at the technical school and mining college there, he served in the navy before finding himself called to the ministry. Entry to a regular course of training in Scotland seemed barred because of his inadequate qualifications, so he went to the USA, graduated from Columbia Theological Seminary, Decatur, Georgia, and served pastorates in the South before his appointment in 1937 to the historic New York Avenue Presbyterian Church in Washington, DC. In 1948 he became chaplain to the US senate. He was much in demand as a speaker, and a collection of his sermons, *Mr Jones, Meet the Master*, edited by his wife Catherine (*née* Wood, 1914–83), was published in 1949. After his premature death he was himself the subject of a film, *A Man Called Peter*, based on his wife's 1951 biography of him.

Marshall, Thurgood 1908–93
US jurist

Born in Baltimore, Maryland, and educated at Lincoln and Howard universities, he joined the legal staff of the National Association for the Advancement of Colored People, and argued many important civil rights cases. He served as a judge of the US Court of Appeals (1961–65), and as Solicitor-General of the United States (1965–67), before becoming the first black Justice of the US Supreme Court (1967–91).

Marshall, William 1748–1833
Scottish fiddler and composer

Born in Fochabers, Moray, he was considered by Robert Burns 'the first composer of strathspeys of the age'. He set new standards of technical accomplishment in fiddle music and proudly claimed that he did not write for 'bunglers'. His two principal collections of compositions were published in 1781 and 1822, and among the many Marshall tunes that are still played are 'The Marquis of Huntly's Farewell' and 'Craigellachie Brig'.

Marshall, William Calder 1813–94
Scottish sculptor

He was born in Edinburgh, and trained in London at the Royal Academy Schools under Sir Francis Chantrey. As well as memorial statues, busts, etc, he did the group *Agriculture* on the Albert Memorial, London.

Marsilius of Padua c.1275–c.1342
Italian political theorist and philosopher

Born in Padua, he was Rector of the University of Paris from 1313. In 1324 he completed *Defensor Pacis*, a political treatise much influenced by Aristotle's *Politics*, which argued against the power of clergy and pope and developed a secular theory of the state based on popular consultation and consent and on natural rights. When the authorship of the work became known he was forced to flee Paris (1326). Excommunicated by Pope John XXII, he took refuge at the court of Louis of Bavaria in Munich, and remained there for the rest of his life.

Marston, John 1576–1634
English dramatist and satirist

Born in Wardington, Oxfordshire, the son of a Shropshire lawyer and an Italian mother, he attended Brasenose College, Oxford, and then studied law at the Middle Temple. His first work was *The Metamorphosis of Pygmalion's Image: and Certain Satires* (1598), a licentious poem which was condemned by Archbishop Whitgift. He began to write for the theatre in 1599, and in 1602 published *Antonio and Mellida* and *Antonio's Revenge*, two gloomy and ill-constructed tragedies, partially redeemed by some strikingly powerful passages. A comedy, *The Malcontent* (1604), more skilfully constructed, was dedicated to Ben Jonson, with whom he had many quarrels and reconciliations, and with Jonson and George Chapman he wrote the comedy *Eastward Ho* (1605), for which, due to some reflections on the Scots, the authors were imprisoned. Other plays include *The Dutch Courtesan* (1605, a comedy), *Parasitaster, or the Fawn* (1606), *Sophonisba* (1606, a tragedy) and *What You Will* (1607). He gave up play-writing, and took orders in 1609, and (1616–31) as a clergyman at Christchurch, Hampshire. The rich and graceful poetry of *The Insatiate Countess* (1613) is unlike anything else in Marston's work, suggesting the play may have been completed by another hand. 📖 A F Caputi, *John Marston, Satirist* (1961)

Marston, Philip Bourke 1850–87
English poet

He was born in London, the son of dramatic poet John Westland Marston (1819–90), and became blind at the age of three. He was grief-stricken at the death of his fiancée and then of his sisters, and his friends, Oliver Madox Brown and Dante Gabriel Rossetti. He is remembered for his friendship with Rossetti, Theodore Watts-Dunton and Algernon Swinburne rather than for his sonnets and lyrics. *Songtide, All in All* and *Wind Voices* were the three volumes of poetry he published between 1870 and 1883. A collection of his short stories appeared posthumously in 1887. 📖 C C Osborne, *Philip Bourke Marston* (1926)

Martel, Charles See Charles Martel

Martel, Sir Giffard le Quesne 1889–1958
English soldier

During World War I he aided in the development of the first tanks, and in 1925 was responsible for the construction of the first one-man tank. In 1940 he commanded the Royal Armoured Corps and in 1943 headed the British military mission in Moscow.

Martens, Conrad 1801–78
Australian landscape painter

Born in Crutched Friars, London, England, where his father was consul for Austria, he studied in London under the celebrated watercolourist Copley Fielding, and in 1833 was appointed by the commander of *The Beagle* as a topographer for the voyage with Charles Darwin from Rio de Janeiro to Valparaiso. The scientific interests of these two men greatly influenced Martens's future work, especially in the accurate depiction of natural detail. In 1835 he arrived, by way of Tahiti, in Sydney, where he set up a studio and began teaching. He travelled widely through New South Wales and southern Queensland, but his favourite subject was Sydney harbour, and a set of lithographs, *Sketches of Sydney*, was published in 1850 and 1851. In 1863 he obtained a post in the parliamentary library where he remained for the rest of his life.

Martens, Wilfried 1936–
Belgian statesman

Educated at Louvain University, he was adviser to two governments, in 1965 and 1966, before becoming Minister for Community Problems in 1968. He was president of the Dutch-speaking Social Christian Party (CVP) from 1972 to 1979, when he became Prime Minister at the head of a coalition. He continued in office until 1992, apart from a brief break in 1981, heading no fewer than six coalition governments. Since 1992 he has been Minister of State.

Martha 1st century AD
Biblical character

From Bethany, near Jerusalem, she was possibly the wife or widow of Simon the Leper. She was devoted to Jesus Christ, like her sister (purportedly Mary who anointed him) and brother, the Lazarus whom he raised from the dead (John 11). Perhaps unfairly, she is remembered for when Jesus rebuked her for fussing over domestic arrangements and being irked that Mary just sat listening to him (Luke 10.39–42). In later Christian tradition Mary and Martha have been taken as symbols for the two paths of contemplative and active spirituality and used in arguments about the superiority of one over the other.

Martí, José 1853–95
Cuban writer and patriot

Born in Havana, he was exiled at the age of 16 for associating with activists for Cuban independence from Spain. He lived in Mexico, Guatemala, Spain and the USA, and gained a reputation as a distinguished author and poet. His poetry is more direct in its expression of feelings than that of his contemporaries, and his prose contains many correct prophecies about race and integration. One of his poems was set to music as *Guantanamera*. In the USA, he organized a new revolutionary movement and abandoned his career as a writer to take part in the 1895 uprising, but within weeks was killed at the Battle of Dos Rios. 📖 I A Schulman, *Simbolo y color en la obra de José Martí* (1960)

Martial, *properly* Marcus Valerius Martialis c.40–c.104AD
Roman poet and epigrammatist

Born in Bilbilis, Spain, he went to Rome in AD64 and became a client of the influential Spanish house of the Senecas, through which he found a patron in Calpurnius Piso. The failure of the Pisonian plot to assassinate Cicero lost Martial his closest friends—Lucan and Seneca. When the Emperor Titus dedicated the Colosseum in 80, Martial's epigrams in *Liber Spectaculorum* ('Book of Spectacles') brought him equestrian rank. In 86 appeared the first 12 books of the *Epigrams*, satirical comments on contemporary events and society. His admirers included Pliny, the Younger, from whom he borrowed the means of returning to Bilbilis. 📖 P Nixon, *Martial and the Modern Epigram* (1927)

Martin, St c.316–c.400AD
French churchman, and a patron saint of France

Born in Savaria, Pannonia, he was educated at Pavia, serving in the army under Constantine I, the Great, and Julian. He became a disciple of St Hilary of Poitiers, and, returning to Pannonia, was forced, because of persecution by the Arian party, to go to Gaul, where he founded a monastery at Ligugé near Poitiers (c.360), the first in France. In 371–72 he was made Bishop of Tours. The fame of his good works and his reputation as a worker of miracles attracted crowds of visitors. To avoid distraction he established the monastery of Marmoutier near Tours, in which he himself lived. His military cloak, which he gave to a beggar, has become the symbol of charity, and he is the patron saint of publicans and inn-keepers.

Martin I, St d.655
Italian pope

Born in Tuscany, he held the first Lateran Council (against the Monothelites) in the first year of his reign (649), and was banished by Constans II in 654 to the Crimea.

Martin V, *originally* **Oddone Colonna** 1368–1431
Italian pope
Born in Genazzano, Papal States, he was elected during the Council of Constance in 1417. With this event, the Great Schism, which had begun in 1378, was finally ended. He died in Rome, just after calling the Council of Basle.

Martin, Agnes 1912–
Canadian painter
Born in Maklin, Saskatchewan, she studied at Columbia University in the 1940s, and began painting in a style called Biomorphic Abstraction. She lived in New Mexico from 1956 to 1957, and in 1959 began painting the barely visible grids of vertical and horizontal lines on pale monochrome backgrounds which characterize her work, and demand quiet concentration from the viewer. In 1967 she left New York and settled permanently in New Mexico, ceasing to paint for several years while she built a small adobe house and wrestled with a spiritual crisis, but she later returned to her former themes. The Whitney Museum of American Art, New York, held a retrospective of her work in 1992.

Martin, Archer John Porter 1910–
English biochemist and Nobel Prize winner
Born in London, he trained at Cambridge and then at the Lister Institute where he studied the vitamin deficiency disease pellagra (1937–38) and the significance of B vitamins. Martin then moved to the Wool Industry Research Association in Leeds (1938–46) where, with Richard Synge, he developed the technique of partition chromatography (the use of silica gel to separate amino acid derivatives from protein compounds) in the analysis of protein structure. Their technique revolutionized analytical biochemistry, and it earned him the 1952 Nobel Prize for chemistry, shared with Synge. Martin subsequently joined the staff of the Medical Research Council (1948–52), and became director of the Abbotsbury Laboratories (1959–70) and a consultant to the Wellcome Research Laboratories (1970–73). From 1953 he worked on analysis by gas–liquid chromatography. He was elected FRS in 1950. He then became Professorial Fellow at the University of Sussex (1973–78) and Robert A Welch Professor of Chemistry at the University of Houston, Texas (1974–79).

Martin, Dean, *originally* **Dino Paul Crocetti** 1917–95
US entertainer
Born in Steubenville, Ohio, he worked in a steel mill and boxed as a welterweight before starting to earn a living as a nightclub crooner. Teamed with comedian Jerry Lewis in 1945, he became part of one of the most successful double-acts in entertainment history, enjoying spectacular success as a nightclub attraction and in such films as *My Friend Irma* (1949), *The Stooge* (1953) and *Hollywood or Bust* (1956). A solo performer from 1956, he displayed his dramatic abilities and comic touch in films like *The Young Lions* (1958), *Rio Bravo* (1959) and *Kiss Me Stupid* (1964). He found enduring popularity as a booze-loving, mellow-voiced singer whose casual, lighthearted manner belied his consummate professionalism. He enjoyed chart success with songs like 'Volare', 'That's Amore' and his signature tune 'Everybody Needs Somebody', a number-one hit in 1964. Part of the Frank Sinatra Rat Pack, he starred in the long-running television series *The Dean Martin Show* (1965–74). Later film appearances include *Airport* (1969) and his last in *Cannonball Run II* (1983).

Martin, Frank 1890–1974
Swiss composer and pianist
Born in Geneva, he studied at the Conservatory there, and in 1928 was appointed a professor at the Jaques-Dalcroze Institute in Geneva. His works are refined and precise in style, and include the oratorios *Golgotha* (1945–48) and *In Terra Pax* (1944, 'On Earth Peace'), a mass and the cantata *Le Vin herbé* (1938–41), based upon the legend of Tristan and Isolde, as well as incidental music and works for orchestra and chamber combinations.

Martin, Glenn Luther 1886–1955
US aircraft manufacturer
He was born in Macksburg, Iowa, and educated at Kansas Wesleyan University in Salina. Influenced as a boy by the flights of the Wright brothers, he built his first glider in California in 1905, and by 1909 had built and flown his first powered aircraft. In 1912 he flew a Martin-built seaplane from near Los Angeles to Catalina Island and back (32 miles, 51.5km). He invented a bomb sight and a free-fall parachute in 1913 and produced his MB-1 bomber at a factory in Cleveland in 1918. In 1929 he moved to Baltimore, producing such famous aircraft as the B-10 bomber and the China Clipper flying boat. In World War II his factory created the B-26 Marauder, Mariner and Mars flying boats.

Martin, Homer Dodge 1836–97
US painter
He was born in Albany, New York, and his early work was in the style of the Hudson River School, emphasizing the grandeur of the landscape. During a stay in France (1882–86), he was influenced by French Impressionism. Despite failing eyesight his later years were a time of creative flowering, and the contemplative, often melancholy paintings he made in the late 1880s and 1890s, including *Westchester Hills*, *The Sun Worshippers*, and *Adirondack Scenery*, are his finest work.

Martin, John 1789–1854
English painter
He was born in Haydon Bridge, Northumberland. After a youth spent struggling in London (from 1806) as a heraldic and enamel painter, in 1812 he exhibited at the Royal Academy the first of his 16 grandiose biblical paintings which included *The Fall of Babylon* (1819), *Belshazzar's Feast* (1821) and *The Deluge* (1826).

Martin, Kenneth 1905–
English painter and sculptor
Born in Sheffield, he trained at Sheffield School of Art and the Royal College of Art. From abstract paintings he turned to kinetic constructions ('screw mobiles') in 1951, and through his teaching at Goldsmiths College (1946–67) he pioneered Constructivism in Great Britain. Commissions included the Peter Stuyvesant project in Sheffield (1972), the steel fountain in Gorinchem, Holland (1974), and the Kinetic Monument in Swansea. He was married to Mary Martin.

Martin, (Basil) Kingsley 1897–1969
English journalist
Born in London, he was educated at Mill Hill School and Cambridge, and also studied at Princeton, USA. After teaching at the London School of Economics (1923–27), he joined the *Manchester Guardian* (1927–31). As editor of the *New Statesman and Nation* (1932–62), he transformed it into a self-assured weekly journal of socialist opinion. He kept up socialist pressure on Labour under Clement Attlee and in the late 1950s Nikita Khrushchev and John Foster Dulles replied in its columns to an open letter it had published from Bertrand Russell on the Cold War. His books include *The Triumph of Lord Palmerston* (1924), *French Liberal Thought in the Eighteenth Century* (1929), a memoir of Harold Laski, *Critic's London Diary* (1960, a selection from his *New Statesman* column) and two autobiographical works, *Father Figures* (1966) and *Editor* (1968). 📖 C H Rolph, *Kingsley: The Life Letters and Diaries of Kingsley Martin* (1973)

Martin, Mary, née Balmford 1907–69
English painter and sculptor
Born in Folkestone, she trained at Goldsmiths College and the Royal College of Art. From rug design and abstract painting, she turned to construction in 1951. In 1969 she did the Wall Construction for Stirling University and won first prize (with Richard Hamilton) in the John Moores Liverpool exhibition. She was the wife of Kenneth Martin.

Martin, Paul 1864–1942
French photographer
Born in Herbenville, France, he went to England in 1872, but remained a French citizen throughout his life. First employed as a wood-engraver on magazine illustrations, he was an amateur photographer who made good use of a disguised camera (with glass plates). With this, he recorded working people in the streets of London and on holiday at the seaside (1888–98), perhaps the first use of 'candid camera' as a long-term social record. He turned professional in 1899 but produced no further work of significance. His *London by Gaslight* (1896) was recognized by the Royal Photographic Society and by Alfred Stieglitz, and his records have been much used this century to represent the realities of late-Victorian everyday life.

Martin, Pierre Émile 1824–1915
French metallurgist
Born in Bourges, he devised an improved bulk steel-making method in 1864. The open-hearth (or Siemens–Martin) process derived its name from the fact that molten metal lay in a comparatively shallow pool on the furnace hearth. The products of the process won a gold medal at the Paris Exhibition of 1867, and by World War I the open-hearth furnace had taken over from the Bessemer converter as the major source of the world's steel. Martin himself was crippled financially by unsuccessful litigation and spent his later years in poverty while others profited from his process, until in 1907 an international benefit fund restored his finances.

Martin, Richard 1754–1834
Irish lawyer and humanitarian
Born in Dublin, he was dubbed 'Humanity Martin' by George IV, who was his friend. He was educated at Harrow and Trinity College, Cambridge. As MP for Galway (1801–26) he sponsored a bill in 1822 to make the cruel treatment of cattle illegal, the first legislation of its kind. Through his efforts the Royal Society for the Prevention of Cruelty to Animals was formed. 📖 Shevawn Lynam, *Humanity Dick: A Biography of Richard Martin, MP, 1754–1834* (1975)

Martin, Steve 1945–
US film actor
Born in Waco, Texas, he began performing stand-up comedy as a student, when audiences of 20,000 witnessed the verbal dexterity and manic inventiveness that would eventually make him a star. As a comedy-writer, he won an Emmy award for *The Smithers Brothers Comedy Hour* (1968) for television, and he was awarded Grammys for his bestselling albums *Let's Get Small* (1977) and *Wild and Crazy* (1978). He made his big screen debut in the short *The Absent-Minded Waiter* (1977) and took the title role in the juvenile comedy *The Jerk* (1979). His films include the dramatic musical *Pennies From Heaven* (1981), *Dead Men Don't Wear Plaid* (1982), *The Man With Two Brains* (1983), *All Of Me* (1984), *Little Shop of Horrors* (1986) and *Dirty Rotten Scoundrels* (1988), the witty contemporary reinterpretation of *Cyrano de Bergerac* entitled *Roxanne* (1987), and *Parenthood* (1989) and *Father of the Bride* (1991), in which he portrays over-anxious father-figures.

Martin, Sir Theodore 1816–1909
Scottish writer and biographer
He was born in Edinburgh. His series of poetic parodies the *Bon Gaultier Ballads* (1855), written in conjunction with William Aytoun, were followed by verse translations from Goethe, Horace, Catullus, Dante and Heinrich Heine. He was requested by Queen Victoria to write the life of Prince Albert (5 vols, 1874–80), and he also wrote biographies of Aytoun (1867), Lord Lyndhurst (1883) and the Princess Alice (1885).

Martin du Gard, Roger 1881–1958
French novelist and Nobel Prize winner
He was born in Neuilly-sur-Seine. After studying history, he qualified as an archivist before turning to writing, publishing his first novel, *Devenir* ('Becoming'), in 1909. In that same year the *Nouvelle revue française*, with which he had a long and fruitful association, was founded. After serving in World War I he lived as a recluse and devoted himself to writing in various forms, including novels, plays and memoirs. His novels include *Jean Barois* (1913, Eng trans 1949), which deals, among other matters, with the Dreyfus affair, and *Vieille France* (1933, Eng trans *The Postman*, 1954), a study of a less-than-idyllic rural life. He is best known, however, for his eight-novel series *Les Thibault* (1922–40, Eng trans *The Thibaults*, 1939–41) dealing with family life during the first decades of the 20th century. He was awarded the Nobel Prize for literature in 1937. The correspondence (1913–51) between him and Gide was published in 1968. 📖 D L Schak, *Martin du Gard* (1967)

Martineau, Harriet 1802–76
English writer
She was born in Norwich, Norfolk, the daughter of a textile manufacturer of Huguenot descent. Her first article, for the (Unitarian) *Monthly Repository* (1821) was followed by the books *Devotional Exercises for the Use of Young Persons* and *Addresses for the Use of Families* (both 1826), and short stories about machinery and wages. A failed investment obliged her to earn her living from 1829. She became a successful author through her *Illustrations of Political Economy* and *Poor Laws and Paupers Illustrated* (1833–34), and settled in London. After a visit to the USA (1834–36) she published *Society in America* and the novels *Deerbrook* (1839), and *The Hour and the Man* (1840), about Toussaint Louverture. From 1839 to 1844 she was an invalid, suffering from heart disease and lack of hearing at Tynemouth, but she recovered after mesmerism (a type of hypnotism), her subsequent belief in which alienated many friends. She visited Egypt and Palestine, and wrote *Eastern Life* (1848). In 1851, in conjunction with H G Atkinson, she published *Letters on the Laws of Man's Social Nature*, which was so agnostic that it gave much offence, and in 1853 she translated and condensed Auguste Comte's *Philosophie positive*. She also wrote much for the daily and weekly press and the larger reviews. Her *Autobiographical Memoir* was published posthumously in 1877. She was the sister of James Martineau. 📖 V Wheatley, *Life and Work of Harriet Martineau* (1957)

Martineau, James 1805–1900
English Unitarian theologian
Born in Norwich, and educated there and at Bristol, he became a Unitarian minister at Dublin and Liverpool, until 1841, when he was appointed Professor of Mental and Moral Philosophy at Manchester New College. He left for London in 1857, after that institution had been transferred there, becoming also a pastor in Little Portland Street Chapel, and later principal of the College (1869–85). One of the profoundest thinkers and most effective writers of his day, he wrote *Endeavours after the Christian Life* (1843–47), *A Study of Spinoza* (1882), *Types of Ethical Theory* (1885), *A Study of Religion* (1888) and *The Seat of Authority in Religion* (1890). He was the brother of Harriet Martineau.

Martinelli, Giovanni 1885–1969
Italian tenor

He was born in Montagnana where he played clarinet in the town band and occasionally sang in concerts. The bandmaster was impressed by his voice and he was sent to Rome to study singing. In 1910 in Milan, he sang in Rossini's *Stabat Mater*. The performance was heard by Puccini who asked him to take the role of Dick Johnson in the European première of *La Fanciulla del West* ('The Girl of the Golden West') in 1911. Martinelli made his Covent Garden debut in 1912 in *Tosca*, and his US debut, also in *Tosca*, in Philadelphia in 1913. He continued singing in opera, mostly at the New York Metropolitan Opera, until 1946. He then taught voice in New York, where he gave a guest performance in *Turandot* at the age of 82.

Martinet, Jean d.1672
French army officer

He won renown as a military engineer and tactician, devising forms of battle manoeuvre, pontoon bridges, and a type of copper assault boat used in Louis XIV's Dutch campaign. He also achieved notoriety for his stringent and brutal forms of discipline, and was 'accidentally' killed by his troops at the siege of Duisberg.

Martínez Sierra, Gregorio 1881–1947
Spanish novelist and dramatist

Born in Madrid, he was a theatre manager and an original and creative producer as well as a prolific writer, publishing his first volume of poetry, *El poema del trabajo* (1898, 'The Poem of Work'), when he was only 17 years old. His plays *Canción de Cuna* (c.1910, Eng trans *The Cradle Song*, 1934), *El Reino de Dios* (1916, Eng trans *The Kingdom of God*, 1927) and *El Sueño de Una Noche de Agosto* (1918, Eng trans *The Romantic Young Lady*, 1929) were also popular in Great Britain and the USA. Much of his writing was done in collaboration with his wife Maria, whose feminist opinions find expression in some of the plays. ⊞ G Serrat, *Imager humana y literara de Gregorio Martínez Sierra* (1965)

Martini or Memmi, Simone c.1284–1344
Italian painter

Born in Siena, he was a pupil of Duccio di Buoninsegna. He was one of the major artists of the 14th-century Sienese school, notable for his grace of line and exquisite colour. He worked in Assisi from 1333 to 1339 and at the papal court at Avignon from 1339 to 1344. His works include the *Annunciation* (1333, Uffizi, Florence), and *Christ Reproved by his Parents* (1342, Walker Art Gallery, Liverpool).

Martins, Peter 1946–
Danish dancer

Born in Copenhagen, he trained at the Royal Danish Ballet School from the age of eight. Unusually tall for a dancer at 6ft 2in (1.88m), he made his debut in Edinburgh with New York City Ballet (NYCB) (1967). He joined the company two years later and created roles for George Balanchine. His partnership with NYCB's Kay Mezzo was to prove highly successful. In the late 1970s he returned to the Royal Danish Ballet, retiring from performance in 1983. In the same year, Balanchine died and Martins stepped into his place, sharing the directorship of the NYCB with Jerome Robbins. His autobiography, *Far From Denmark*, was published in 1982.

Martín-Santos, Luis 1924–64
Spanish novelist

Born in Larache, Morocco, he helped to revolutionize the form of the novel in his country during the Francoist period. He was a psychiatrist by profession and his first writings were technical. His only finished and influential novel, *Tiempo de silencio* (1962, Eng trans *Time of Silence*, 1965), deals with a man's unfulfilled life in the sick and submissive society of Madrid in 1949 and shows the influence

of the psychology of Karl Jaspers in its attempt to reconcile subjectivity with objectivity. Aesthetic innovations in his work combine with his wish to understand and relieve mental illness. His stories were collected in *Apólogos* (1970, 'Apologues'), and an attempt has been made to reconstruct his unfinished and pessimistic novel about a law student, *Tiempo de destrucción* (1975, 'Time of Destruction'). ⊞ J C Mainer (ed), Introduction to *Tiempo de destrucción* (1975)

Martinson, Harry Edmund 1904–78
Swedish poet, novelist and Nobel Prize winner

He was born in Jäshög, Blekinge, and after a harsh childhood as a parish orphan he went to sea as a stoker (1919), travelling worldwide. He made his poetic debut in 1929, and soon found an individual voice, particularly as a nature poet with such volumes as *Nomad* (1931) and *Natur* (1934) which established his reputation. During the 1930s he was married to the writer Moa Martinson (1890–1963). His masterpiece, the poetic space epic *Aniara* (1956), questions whether man possesses sufficient ethical maturity to control his own technological inventions, and was set to music as an opera by Karl-Birger Blomdahl. *Nässlorna blomma* (1935, 'Flowering Nettle') and *Vägen ut* (1936, 'The Way Out'), moving accounts of his childhood and youth, and his 'tramp' novel *Vägen till Klockrike* (1948, 'The Road to Klockrike'), contributed to the growing genre of working-class autobiographical novels in Sweden. He shared the 1974 Nobel Prize for literature with the Swedish novelist Eyvind Johnson, and a Harry Martinson Society was founded in 1984. ⊞ I Holm, *Harry Martinson* (1960)

Martinu, Bohuslav 1890–1959
Czech composer

Born in Policka, he began to compose at the age of 10, and in 1906 was sent by a group of fellow-townsmen to the Prague Conservatory, where disciplinary regulations and the routine course of studies irritated him. Expelled from there, he played the violin in the Czech Philharmonic Orchestra, and in 1920 attracted attention with his ballet *Ishtar*. Readmitted to the Conservatory, he studied under Joseph Suk until interest in the French Impressionist composers led him to work in Paris. In 1941 he escaped from Occupied France to the USA, where he produced a number of important works, including his 1st Symphony, commissioned by Serge Koussevitsky for the Boston Symphony Orchestra (1942). A prolific composer, he ranges from orchestral works in 18th-century style, including a harpsichord concerto, to modern programme pieces evoked by unusual stimuli such as football (*Half Time*, 1925) or aeroplanes (*Thunderbolt P.47*). His operas include the miniature *Comedy on a Bridge* (1935), written for radio and successfully adapted for television and stage.

Marty, Martin Emil 1928–
US church historian

Born in West Point, Nebraska, he had an extensive theological training before taking a PhD at Chicago University. Ordained in the Lutheran Church in 1952, he ministered in Illinois, then was appointed Professor of the History of Modern Christianity at Chicago in 1963. A versatile scholar, he was also one of the editors of the liberal *Christian Century* (1956–85), and a welcome lecturer in Roman Catholic and moderate evangelical circles. Among his many books are *A Short History of Christianity* (1959), *Second Chance for American Protestants* (1963), *Righteous Empire* (1970), *Protestantism in the United States* (1985) and *The Glory and the Power* (1992).

Martyn, Henry 1781–1812
English missionary

Born in Truro, Cornwall, he graduated from St John's College, Cambridge, and in 1802 became a Fellow. Through the influence of **Charles Simeon** he sailed for India in 1805 as a chaplain with the East India Company. He translated the New Testament into Hindustani, Hindi and Persian, as well as the prayer book into Hindustani and the Psalms into Persian.

Marvell, Andrew 1621–78
English metaphysical poet

Born in Winestead, Yorkshire, he was educated at Hull Grammar School and Trinity College, Cambridge. He travelled (1642–46) in Holland, France, Italy and Spain. After a period as tutor to Lord **Fairfax**'s daughter, when he wrote his pastoral and garden poems, he was appointed tutor to **Cromwell**'s ward, William Dutton. In 1657 he became **Milton**'s assistant and two years later, MP for Hull. In 1663–65 he accompanied Lord Carlisle as secretary to the embassy to Muscovy, Sweden and Denmark, but the rest of his life was devoted to his parliamentary duties, fighting against intolerance and arbitrary government. Marvell's works are divided by the Restoration into two very distinct groups. After 1660 he concentrated on politics—his last satires are a call to arms against monarchy—except when he produced the lines which prefixed the second edition of Milton's *Paradise Lost*. He wrote *The Rehearsal Transpos'd* (1672–73), against religious intolerance, and in 1677 his most important tract, the *Account of the Growth of Popery and Arbitrary Government*, was published anonymously. As a poet, he belongs to the pre-Restoration period, although most of his poetry was not published until 1681 as *Miscellaneous Poetry*. A subsequent volume was entitled *Poems on Affairs of State* (1689–97). 📖 J B Leishman, *The Art of Marvell's Poetry* (1966); P Legouis, *Andrew Marvell, poète, puritain, patriote* (1928)

Marx, Karl See panel p1243

Marx Brothers
US family of film comedians

They were born in New York City, the sons of German immigrants, and were called Julius Henry (Groucho, 1895–1977), Leonard (Chico, 1891–1961), Arthur (Harpo, 1893–1964) and Herbert (Zeppo, 1901–1979). They began their stage career in vaudeville in a team called the Six Musical Mascots that included their mother, Minnie (d.1929), and an aunt; another brother, Milton (Gummo, 1894–1977), left the act early on. They later appeared as the Four Nightingales and finally as the Marx Brothers. They appeared in musical comedy, but their main reputation was made in films such as *Animal Crackers, Monkey Business* (both 1932), *Horse Feathers* and *Duck Soup* (both 1933). Herbert retired from films in 1935 but the others scored further successes in *A Night at the Opera* (1935), *A Day at the Races* (1937), *A Day at the Circus* (1939), *Go West* (1940) and *The Big Store* (1941). *Love Happy* (1950) was the team's last film before they broke up to lead individual careers. Each had a well-defined role: Groucho with his over-sized moustache and wisecracks, Chico, the pianist with an individual technique, and Harpo, the dumb clown and harp maestro. Groucho Marx wrote *Many Happy Returns*, his autobiography, *Groucho and Me* (1959) and a serious study of American income tax. Harpo's autobiography, *Harpo Speaks!*, was published in 1961. 📖 Joe Adamson, *Groucho, Harpo, Chico and Sometimes Zeppo* (1973)

Mary, Mother of Jesus, *also entitled* the Blessed Virgin Mary d.c.63AD
Mother of Jesus Christ

The New Testament records the Annunciation, the conception of **Jesus** by the Holy Spirit (Matthew 1.18), her betrothal to **Joseph**, and the birth of Jesus. She only occasionally appears in Christ's ministry, but in John 19.25 she is at the Cross and is committed to the care of one of the Disciples. She has become a subject of devotion in her own right, especially in Roman Catholic doctrine and worship. The belief that her body ascended into heaven is celebrated in the festival of the Assumption, defined as Roman Catholic dogma in 1950. The Immaculate Conception has been a dogma since 1854. Belief in the appearances of the Virgin in such places as Lourdes, Fatima, and Medjugorje attracts many thousands of pilgrims each year. In Roman Catholic and Orthodox Christianity, she holds a special place as an intermediary between God and humanity.

Mary Magdalene, St, *also called* Mary of Magdala
1st century BC–1st century AD
Early follower of Jesus Christ

Mary Magdalene was born probably in Magdala on the west coast of the sea of Galilee, hence her name. Luke 8.2 reports that **Jesus** exorcized seven evil spirits from her, and throughout the Church's history she has epitomized the archetypal repentant sinner. She features also in the narratives of Jesus's passion and resurrection as, seemingly with other women, she was present at the Cross and later at the empty tomb. Most memorably, as related in John 20 and Mark 16, she was the first to encounter the risen Lord, who appeared to her in the garden of his burial; blinded by her tears, she at first supposed him to be the gardener. Her cult was influenced greatly by her identification with Mary the sister of **Martha** (John 11–12) and also with the woman in Luke 7 who anointed Jesus's feet and dried them with her hair. However, nowadays these are thought to be three separate people. One tradition holds that she accompanied St **John** the Evangelist to Ephesus where she later died and was buried. Her feast day is 22 July.

Mary I, Tudor 1516–58
Queen of England and Ireland

She was born in Greenwich, near London, the daughter of **Henry VIII** and his first wife, **Catherine of Aragon**. She was well-educated, a good linguist, fond of music and devoted to her mother and the Catholic Church. After her mother's divorce, Henry forced her to sign a declaration that her mother's marriage had been unlawful. During the reign of her half-brother **Edward VI** she lived in retirement, refusing to conform to the new religion. On his death (1553), being entitled to the Crown by her father's testament and the parliamentary settlement, she became queen. She upset the Duke of Northumberland's (Sir Thomas **Percy**) conspiracy to set Henry's will aside in favour of his daughter-in-law Lady **Jane Grey**, and, with the support of the whole country, entered London in triumph. Northumberland and two others were executed, but Lady Jane and her husband were, for the present, spared. Mary proceeded very cautiously to bring back Catholicism, reinstated the Catholic bishops and imprisoned some of the leading reformers, but dared not restore the pope's supremacy. In spite of national protests, she determined to marry **Philip II**, King of Spain. The unpopularity of the proposal brought about Sir Thomas **Wyatt**'s rebellion (1554), quelled mainly through Mary's courage and coolness. Lady Jane, her husband and father were executed, and the Princess Elizabeth (later **Elizabeth I**), suspected of complicity, was committed to the Tower of London. Ecclesiastical laws were restored to their state under Henry VIII. In 1554 Philip was married to Mary; Cardinal **Pole** entered England as papal legate, parliament petitioned for reconciliation to the Holy See, and the realm was absolved from the papal censures. Soon after, the persecution of Protestant opposition which gave Mary the name of 'Bloody Mary' began. In 1555 **Nicholas Ridley** and **Hugh Latimer** were brought to the stake, **Thomas Cranmer** followed the next year, and Pole, now Archbishop of Canterbury, was left supreme in the councils of the queen. How far Mary herself was responsible for the cruelties practised is doubtful, but

Marx, Karl 1818–83
German social, political and economic theorist

Karl Marx was born in Trier and brought up in a Jewish family which converted to Protestantism in order to escape anti-Semitism. He studied at the universities of Bonn (1835–36) and Berlin (1836–41), where he associated with the radical followers of **Hegel**, 'the young Hegelians', who were concerned particularly with the critique of religion.

In 1842 he worked for the liberal Cologne paper *Rheinische Zeitung*, until it was suppressed by the government the following year. Marx then emigrated to Paris, where he became a communist and first stated his belief that the proletariat must itself be the agent of revolutionary change in society. In Paris he wrote his first long critique of capitalism, usually called *Economic and Philosophical Manuscripts of 1844* (not published until 1932), which developed the important Marxist notion of the alienation of man under capitalism, and also in Paris he began his lifelong friendship with **Friedrich Engels**.

Under political pressure he moved on to Brussels in 1845, and in collaboration with Engels wrote the posthumously published *German Ideology*, a full statement of his materialist conception of history, and the famous *Communist Manifesto* (1848), a masterpiece of political propaganda which ends with the celebrated rallying-cry: 'The workers have nothing to lose but their chains. They have a world to win. Workers of all lands, unite!' With Engels he also reorganized the Communist League, which met in London in 1847.

After the 1848 Paris revolution, he returned to Cologne as editor of the radical *Neue Rheinische Zeitung*, but when that folded in 1849 he temporarily abandoned his political activism and took refuge with his family in London. They lived in some poverty, but in the reading room of the British Museum he began the researches which culminated in the publication of his major works

of economic and political analysis, *Grundrisse der Kritik der politischen Ökonomie* (1857–58, published in Moscow 1939–41), *Zur Kritik der politischen Ökonomie* (1859) and, most notably, his magnum opus *Das Kapital* (Vol 1 1867, Vols 2 & 3 posthumously 1884, 1894), one of the most influential works of the 19th century. In this last work, which remained unfinished at his death, he developed his mature doctrines of the theory of surplus value, class conflict and the exploitation of the working class, and predicted the victory of socialism over capitalism and the ultimate withering away of the state as the classless society of communism was achieved. Marx was supported in his research over these years by his collaborator, Engels, and he eked out his income by journalistic work from 1825 to 1862 as European correspondent for the *New York Daily Tribune*.

He later revived his political involvement and was a leading figure in the First International (Working-Men's Association) from 1864 until its effective demise in 1872, when the anarchist followers of **Mikhail Bakunin** broke away. The last decade of his life was marked by increasing ill health. He died in 1883 and was buried in Highgate cemetery, London. Despite the apparent failure of Marxian principles as practised in communist Europe, his theories still exert an enormous influence on social science, and his secular adherents continue to outnumber the followers of many other religious or political creeds.

📖 D McLellan, *Karl Marx: His Life and Thought* (1973); I Berlin, *Karl Marx* (1939).

'The philosophers have only interpreted the world in various ways; our task is to change it.' *Theses on Feuerbach*, no.11. (1845).

---

during the last three years of her reign 300 victims were burned. She died childless. 📖 H F M Prescott, *Mary Tudor* (1940)

Mary II 1662–94
Stuart Queen of Great Britain and Ireland

Born at St James's Palace, London, she was the daughter of the Catholic Duke of York (later **James VII and II**) and his first wife, Anne Hyde (1638–71), but was brought up a Protestant. She was married (1677) to her first cousin, William of Orange, Stadtholder of the Netherlands, who in 1688 landed in Torbay with an Anglo-Dutch army in response to an invitation from seven Whig peers hostile to the arbitrary rule of James II. When James fled to France, Mary went to London from Holland and was proclaimed queen (1689), sharing the throne with her husband, who became King **William III**. Mary left executive authority with William (except when regent during his frequent absences abroad), but she was largely responsible for raising the moral standard of court life, and she took great interest in church appointments. Naturally kind, gracious and sincere, she died, childless, of smallpox.

Mary, Queen of Scots See panel p1244

Mary of Guise, *also called* Mary of Lorraine
1515–60
French noblewoman and Scottish queen

The daughter of Claude of Lorraine, 1st Duke of **Guise**, she married Louis d'Orléans, Duke of Longueville (1534), and **James V** of Scotland (1538), at whose death (1542) she was left with one child, **Mary, Queen of Scots**. During the troubled years that followed, she acted with wisdom and moderation, but after she was made Regent

of Scotland (1554) she campaigned against Protestantism and allowed the Guises so much influence that the Protestant nobles raised a rebellion (1559), which continued until her death at Edinburgh Castle.

Mary of Hungary 1505–58
Queen of Hungary and Bohemia

The daughter of **Philip I**, the Handsome of Castile and **Juana** the Mad, she married Louis II of Hungary and Bohemia (ruled 1516–26) in January 1522, a month after he was declared of age. Their life of debauchery soon disqualified the king from affairs of state, and he is said to have drowned whilst fleeing from a battle in which his forces were routed by marauding Ottoman Turks. Hungary then became divided between the Turks and the Austrian Habsburgs. In 1531 Mary's brother, Emperor **Charles V**, asked her to act as regent in his Low Countries possessions, which she did from 1531 to 1555. Mary's rule subjugated the interests of the Netherlands provinces to those of Spain and the empire, which helped lay the ground for the Eighty Years War (1568–1648) by the Low Countries against Habsburg rule.

Mary of Lorraine See Mary of Guise

Mary of Magdala See Mary Magdalene, St

Mary of Modena, *née* d'Este 1658–1718
Queen of Great Britain and Ireland

Born in Modena, the only daughter of Alfonso IV, Duke of Modena, she married James, Duke of York (1672), later **James VII and II**. Proud, dignified and devout, after losing five children in infancy, she gave birth in 1688 to **James Francis Edward Stuart** (the future Old Pretender). This was received with scepticism, and the 'warming pan'

Mary, Queen of Scots 1542–87
Queen of Scotland 1542–67

Mary was the daughter of **James V** of Scotland by his second wife, **Mary of Guise**. She was born at Linlithgow, while her father lay on his deathbed at Falkland. She became queen when she was a week old, and was promised in marriage by the regent **James Hamilton**, 2nd Earl of Arran, to Prince **Edward** of England, son of **Henry VIII**, but the Scottish parliament declared the promise null. War with England followed, which resulted in defeat at Pinkie (1547), and Mary was sent to France to be betrothed to the dauphin (later **François II**) at St Germain.

Her next 10 years were spent in the splendour of the French court, where she was given a thorough French education. She was brought up as a member of the large, young family of **Henri II**; her special friend was Elizabeth of Valois, later the wife of **Philip II** of Spain. In 1558 she was married to the dauphin; the marriage treaty contained a secret clause by which, if she died childless, both her Scottish realm and her right of succession to the English Crown (as great-granddaughter of **Henry VII**) would pass to France.

In 1559 the dauphin succeeded to the throne as **Francis II**, but he died the following year, and power then shifted towards **Catherine de Médicis**, acting as regent for her son **Charles IX**. Mary became a dowager queen of France, with her own estates and a large income. Meanwhile her presence was increasingly needed in Scotland, where the death of her mother in 1560 had left a highly unstable situation. Effective power in the hands of the Protestant Lords of the Congregation, who had held an illegal parliament in 1560 to implement a Reformation and negate the authority of the pope.

On Mary's arrival, a Protestant riot threatened the first mass held in her private chapel at Holyrood and within days a proclamation issued by her privy council imposed a religious standstill, which in effect banned the mass to all but the queen and her household. Her chief advisers were Protestant, the talented diplomat, **William Maitland** of Lethington, and her illegitimate brother, James Stewart, Earl of **Moray**.

The question of Mary's remarriage arose, and a series of candidates was proposed (1562–65) including Robert Dudley, Earl of **Leicester**, but Mary decided unexpectedly on her cousin, Henry Stewart, Lord **Darnley**, who was a son of Lady Margaret Douglas, a granddaughter of **Henry VII**; Darnley therefore might strengthen her descendants' claim to the English throne. The immediate effect of the marriage was to cool relations with England and to undermine the position of **Moray** and the Hamilton family.

Darnley led a debauched life which soon appalled Mary. Eventually he became involved with **William Ruthven, James Morton** and other Protestant lords in a conspiracy that led to the murder of the queen's Italian private secretary, **David Rizzio**, in the queen's antechamber at the Palace of Holyroodhouse (1566). As a result, Darnley became an object of mingled abhorrence and contempt. Shortly before the birth of their son, the future **James VI and I** (June 1566), the queen's affection for her husband seemed briefly to revive, but Darnley refused to attend the child's Catholic baptism at Stirling Castle. Divorce was openly discussed, and Darnley spoke of leaving the country, but he was mysteriously killed while recovering from a bout of smallpox at Glasgow in January 1567, when the house in which he was sleeping was blown up by gunpowder.

cont

legend was born. When William of Orange (the future **William III**) landed in England later that year, she escaped to France with her infant son, to be joined there later by her deposed husband. She spent the rest of her life at St Germain.

Mary of Teck 1867–1953
Queen of Great Britain and Northern Ireland

Born at Kensington Palace, London, she was the only daughter of Francis, Duke of Teck, and Princess Mary Adelaide of Cambridge, and a granddaughter of **George III**. Princess May (as she was known) accepted a marriage proposal (1891) from the eldest son of the Prince of Wales, the Duke of Clarence, who within six weeks died from pneumonia. She then became engaged to his brother, the Duke of York, marrying him in 1893. After his accession (as **George V**) in 1910, Queen Mary accompanied him to Delhi as Empress of India for the historically unique Coronation Durbar (1911). Although by nature stiff and reserved, Mary was more sympathetic to changing habits than her husband, whom she helped to mould into a 'people's king'. After the abdication of her eldest son, **Edward VIII**, she applied her wide experience to strengthening once again the popular appeal of the monarchy throughout the reign of her second son, **George VI**, whom she survived by 13 months. She died at Marlborough House, London, less than three months before the coronation of her granddaughter, **Elizabeth II**.
📖 S W Jackman, *The People's Princess: A Portrait of H R H Princess Mary, Duchess of Teck* (1984)

Masaccio, *real name* Tommaso de Giovanni di Simone Guidi 1401–?1428
Italian painter of the Florentine school

In his short life he brought about a revolution in the dramatic and realistic representation of biblical events which was recognized by his contemporaries and had a great influence on **Michelangelo** and, through him, on the entire 16th century. In many ways Masaccio began where **Giotto** left off. He stripped away all the decorative affectations of the International Gothic style and concentrated on the drama of the situation. Line was not allowed to meander into graceful arabesques, but instead, the gestures and groupings of the figures were used to describe the action. His greatest work is the fresco cycle in the Brancacci Chapel of the church of S Maria del Carmine in Florence (1424–27). **Masolino da Panicale**, an inferior painter with whom Masaccio is associated, also worked there, as did **Filippino Lippi**.

Masaniello, *properly* Tommaso Aniello 1623–47
Neapolitan patriot

A fisherman from Amalfi, he led the successful revolt of the Neapolitans against their Spanish oppressors in July 1647, but the revolt deteriorated into murder and massacre, and he was assassinated by agents of the Spanish viceroy.

Masaoka Shiki 1867–1902
Japanese poet

He came from Ehime but lived in Tokyo. He worked with the traditional poetic forms, especially *waka* and *haiku*, refining them and devising new ways of seeing them, to the extent that there is good reason to think of him as the originator of the modern haiku (as a concise, beautiful and above all self-sufficient expression of some idea or feeling). Some of his most beautiful and poignant verse was written in the final stages of his drawn-out and agonizing death from spinal tuberculosis. His famous poem

Mary, Queen of Scots cont

The chief culprit in this incident was probably the Earl of Bothwell, who had recently enjoyed the queen's favour; and there were suspicions that the queen herself was not wholly ignorant of the plot. Bothwell was given a mock trial and acquitted; shortly after this he intercepted the queen on her way from Linlithgow to Edinburgh, and carried her, with scarcely a show of resistance, to Dunbar. Mary publicly pardoned his seizure of her, and created him Duke of Orkney; then, three months after her husband's murder, she married the man who was widely regarded as his murderer.

This fatal step united her nobles in arms against her. Her army melted away without striking a blow on the field of Carberry (15 June 1567); after that Mary had no choice but to surrender to the confederate lords. They led her to Edinburgh, where she suffered the insults of the mob. At Lochleven, she was compelled to sign an act of abdication in favour of her son, who within days was crowned as James VI at Stirling.

After escaping and suffering a further defeat, Mary crossed the Solway, and threw herself on the protection of Queen Elizabeth I of England, only to find herself a permanent prisoner in a succession of strongholds, ending up at Fotheringay. The presence of Mary in England was a constant source of disquiet to Elizabeth and her advisers, both as a descendant of Henry VII and because a significant minority naturally looked to her as the likely restorer of Catholicism. Her position, as guest or prisoner, was always ambiguous. A series of plots came to light, including the Ridolfi plot (1571), but Mary's complicity could not easily be established.

Finally, in 1586, the queen's secretary of state, Francis Walsingham, got wind of a plot by Anthony Babington, and contrived to implicate Mary. Letters apparently from her and seeming to approve of Elizabeth's death passed along a postal route to which Walsingham himself had access. Mary was brought to trial in 1586 and sentenced to death, although it was not until February 1587 that Elizabeth signed the warrant of execution. It was carried into effect a few days later, and she was buried at Peterborough. In 1612 her body was moved to Henry VII's chapel at Westminster, where it still lies.

Mary enjoyed great beauty and personal accomplishments, including a knowledge of six languages, a good singing voice, and an ability with various musical instruments. By 1567 she possessed a library of over 300 books, which included the largest collection of Italian and French poetry in Scotland. She is known to have been reponsible for a significant revival of Scots vernacular poetry, including the important collection, The Bannatyne Manuscript. The portraits and defences of her after 1571 largely fall into one of two moulds—Catholic martyr or papist plotter—making all the more difficult a proper assessment of Mary as Queen of Scots.

📖 I B Cowan, Mary, Queen of Scots (Saltire Society pamphlets, new series, no. 9, 1987); A Fraser, Mary, Queen of Scots (1969).

En ma fin git mon commencement.
'In my end is my beginning.'
Mary's embroidered motto.

Drop of Ink was composed when he was totally paralysed. 📖 'Masaoka Shiki and Tanka Reform' in D Shively (ed), Tradition and Modernisation in Japanese Culture (1971)

Masaryk, Jan 1886–1948
Czechoslovak diplomat and politician

Born in Prague, the son of Tómaš Masaryk, after a youth of travelling and developing a variety of skills, he entered the diplomatic service in 1918, and from 1925 to 1938 was Czechoslovak ambassador in London. There, his fluent English and personal charm won him many friends, but proved inadequate to prevent Neville Chamberlain imposing the Munich Agreement on his country. He became a popular broadcaster to his home country during World War II. In July 1941 he was appointed Foreign Minister of the Czechoslovak government-in-exile, returning with President Eduard Beneš to Prague in 1945 and remaining in office in the hope of bridging the growing gap between East and West in the developing Cold War. On 10 March 1948, following the Communist takeover of power in Czechoslovakia, his body was found beneath the open window of the Foreign Ministry in Prague, and it was assumed that he killed himself in protest at the Stalinization of his homeland.

Masaryk, Tomáš Garrigue 1850–1937
Czechoslovak statesman

Born in Hodonin in Moravia, the son of a coachman, half Czech and half Slovak, he received his university education in Vienna and Leipzig, read and travelled widely, and married Charlotte Garrigue, from Boston, USA, before becoming Professor of Philosophy at the newly authorized Czech University of Prague in 1882. Entering politics in the nationalistic atmosphere of the 1880s and 1890s, he made his name as an independent of courage and common sense through his many writings and his intervention in several fraught disputes. A deputy in the Czech and Austrian Imperial parliaments off and on after 1891, he was variously a 'realist' and a 'progressive', but his main political contribution came after 1914 when he travelled abroad to France, Britain, Russia and the USA to win support and recognition for an independent state, first Czech, then Czechoslovak. He became its first President in 1918 and was regularly re-elected until he retired in 1935 in favour of his right-hand man, Eduard Beneš. 📖 Emil Ludwig, Gespräche mit Masaryk: Denker und Staatsman (1935, Defender of the Democracy: Masaryk of Czechoslovakia, 1936)

Mascagni, Pietro 1863–1945
Italian composer

Born in Leghorn (Livorno), he produced the highly successful one-act opera Cavalleria Rusticana ('Rustic Chivalry') in 1890, now frequently performed with Leoncavallo's I Pagliacci (1892). His many later operas failed to repeat this success, though arias and intermezzi from them are still performed. These include L'Amico Fritz (1891), Guglielmo Ratcliffe (1895), Le Maschere (1901) and Londoletta (1917). 📖 David Stivender (ed), Mascagni (1988)

Mascall, Eric Lionel 1905–93
English Anglo-Catholic theologian, and author

He read mathematics for four years at Cambridge, but his interest in philosophy led him to theology, and he was ordained priest in 1932. After a few years in parish work he was appointed sub-warden of Lincoln Theological College, where he remained for eight years. He then became tutor in theology and university lecturer in the philosophy of religion at Christ Church, Oxford (1946–62), and Professor of Historical Theology at London University (1962–73). His books He Who Is (1943) and Existence and Analogy (1949) have become standard texts on natural theology. His other works include Christian Theology and Natural Science (Oxford Bampton Lectures, 1956) on the relations of theology and science, the ecumenical The Recovery of Unity (1958), The Christian Universe (1966), Nature and Supernature (1976), Whatever Happened to the Human Mind (1980) and The Triune God (1986).

Masefield, John Edward 1878–1967
English poet and novelist

Born in Ledbury, Herefordshire, and educated at the King's School, Warwickshire, he joined the merchant navy, then served his apprenticeship on a windjammer. Ill health drove him ashore, and after three years in New York he returned to England to become a writer in 1897, first making his mark as a journalist. His sea poetry includes *Salt Water Ballads* (1902) and *Dauber* (1913), and his best-known narrative poem is *Reynard the Fox* (1919). Other works are *The Everlasting Mercy* (1911), *The Widow in the Bye-Street* (1912), *Shakespeare* (1911) and *Gallipoli* (1916). He also wrote novels such as *Sard Harker* (1924), *Odtaa* (1926) and *The Hawbucks* (1929), and plays including *The Trial of Jesus* (1925) and *The Coming of Christ* (1928). He became Poet Laureate in 1930 and his final work was *Grace before Ploughing* (1966). ⬓ *So Long to Learn* (1952)

Masham, Lady Abigail, *née* Hill d.1734
English courtier

She was a cousin of **Sarah Churchill**, Duchess of Marlborough, through whose influence she entered the household of Queen **Anne**. In 1707 she married Samuel (later Baron) Masham. A Tory and a subtle intriguer, she gradually turned the queen against the Marlboroughs, and superseded her cousin (1710) as the queen's confidante and the power behind the throne. On Anne's death (1714) she withdrew into obscurity.

Masina, Giulietta, *originally* Giulia Anna Masina
1920–94
Italian actress

Born near Bologna, she met **Federico Fellini** whilst both students in Rome, and they married in 1943. She made her film debut in **Roberto Rossellini**'s *Paisà* (1946, *Paisan*), then worked briefly on the stage, but her reputation rests on her work with Fellini. As Italy's leading director, he regarded her as an inspiration, and together they created a number of memorable roles in films like *La Strada* (1954, *The Road*), *Giulietta degli Spiriti* (1965, *Juliet of the Spirits*), and *Ginger e Fred* (1986, *Fred and Ginger*).

Masinissa 238–149BC
King of Numidia

He helped the Carthaginians to subdue the Massaesylli or Western Numidians. He accompanied his allies to Spain, and fought valiantly against the Romans but, going over to them (206BC), he received as his reward Western Numidia and large portions of Carthaginian territory.

Masire, Quett Ketumile Joni 1925–
Botswana statesman

He began a journalistic career before entering politics, through the Bangwaketse Tribal Council and then the Legislative Council. In 1962, with **Seretse Khama**, he was a founder-member of the Botswana Democratic Party (BDP) and in 1965 became deputy Prime Minister. When Bechuanaland became the Republic of Botswana within the Commonwealth and full independence was achieved in 1966, Masire became Vice-President and, on Seretse Khama's death in 1980, President. He continued his predecessor's policy of non-alignment and helped Botswana become one of the most politically stable nations in Africa. He was elected for his third five year term in 1994.

Maskell, Dan(iel) 1908–92
English tennis player and commentator

Born in London, he began his tennis career as a ball boy at the Queen's Club, London. He captained Britain's Davis Cup, and was one of the leading professional players of the 1930s, winning 16 titles. He was also a coach, before becoming a television commentator on the sport in 1950. Working until 1991, he became one of Britain's best-loved broadcasters.

Maskelyne, Nevil 1732–1811
English astronomer

Born in London, after being educated at Westminster School he went on to study divinity at Trinity College, Cambridge. He joined the Royal Greenwich Observatory in 1755. In 1763 he produced the *British Mariner's Guide* and went to Barbados to test chronometers. In 1765 he was appointed Astronomer Royal. He improved methods and instruments of observation, invented the prismatic micrometer and made important observations. He went to St Helena to observe the transit of Venus, the aim being to make better estimates of the Earth–Sun distance. In 1767 he founded the *Nautical Almanac*. He also measured the Earth's density from the deflection of the plumb-line at Schiehallion in Perthshire (1774), obtaining a value between 4.56 and 4.87 times that of water. An ordained minister, he was rector from 1775 of Shrawardine, Salop, and from 1782 of North Runcton, Norfolk.

Maskelyne, (John) Nevil 1839–1917
English magician

Born in Wiltshire, he became a watchmaker, and built magic boxes, and automata which he used in his entertainments. He joined forces with George Cooke (d.1904) and they appeared together, first at Cheltenham and then at the Crystal Palace, London, in 1865. In 1873 they leased the Egyptian Hall for three months, but their tenancy lasted for 31 years. Maskelyne then moved his 'Home of Magic' to the St George's Hall in 1905 with David Devant as his partner. He devoted much energy to exposing spiritualistic frauds.

Masodi or Mas'udi, Abu al-Hasan Ali al- d.957
Arab traveller

Born in Baghdad, he became one of the most important writers on history and geography in the medieval world. He travelled extensively in Egypt, Palestine, the Caspian, India, Ceylon (Sri Lanka), Madagascar, and perhaps even China. He wrote a (lost) 30-volume work, *Reports of the Age*.

Maso di Banco fl.1325–50
Italian painter

He is recorded as working in Florence between 1343 and 1350. Although few works are ascribed to him, he was held in great esteem by later Italian artists, due to his realistic style in the manner of his famous predecessor **Giotto**. His best-known work is a fresco, in S Croce, Florence, of the legend of St Silvester who quelled a dragon which, by its foul breath, had terrorized Rome.

Masolino da Panicale, *properly* Thommaso di Cristoforo Fini c.1383–1447
Florentine painter

He is usually associated with **Masaccio** because of his work with him in the Brancacci Chapel of the church of S Maria del Carmine in Florence. Sixteenth-century sources say he was Masaccio's master but this seems unlikely (in the Brancacci Chapel the influence seems to be the other way around). Masolino was, however, a much older artist, trained in the International Gothic style in the **Ghiberti** and Starnina workshops. The strongest early influence on him was **Gentile da Fabriano**. Masolino's greatest work is the fresco cycle in the Baptistery and Collegiata of Castiglione d'Olona near Como (1430s). His influence is clear in the work of **Domenico Veneziano** and **Paolo Uccello**.

Mason, Alfred Edward Woodley 1865–1948
English novelist

Born in Dulwich, London, and educated at Oxford, he became a successful actor, and subsequently combined writing with politics, as Liberal MP for Coventry (1906–10). His first published novel was *A Romance of Wastdale*

(1895). The adventure novel *Four Feathers* (1902) captured the popular imagination and *The Broken Road* (1907) cemented his success. With *At the Villa Rose* (1910) he started writing detective novels and introduced his ingenious 'Inspector Hanaud'. From then on he alternated historical adventure and detective fiction. Several of his books have been filmed. □ R L Green, *Alfred Mason: the adventures of a story-teller* (1952)

Mason, Charles 1730–87
English astronomer

As an assistant at Greenwich Observatory, with the English surveyor Jeremiah Dixon, he observed the transit of Venus at the Cape of Good Hope in 1761. From 1763 to 1767 Mason and Dixon were engaged to survey the boundary between Maryland and Pennsylvania and end an 80-year-old dispute. They reached a point 224 miles west of the Delaware River, but were prevented from further work by Native Americans. The survey was completed by others, but the boundary was given the name 'Mason and Dixon Line'.

Mason, George 1725–92
American Revolutionary statesman

Born in Fairfax County, Virginia, he belonged to the wealthy planter class and was a neighbour to George Washington, whom he joined in opposition to the Stamp Act and the Townshend duties. He wrote the Virginia Declaration of Rights (1776), which was one of Thomas Jefferson's models for the Declaration of Independence. He helped draft the Constitution (1787) but opposed its ratification because it permitted slavery and failed to define the rights of citizens. The first 10 amendments to the Constitution were in part based on the bill of rights he advocated, and after their passage in 1791 he gave his support to the government but declined a seat in the Senate on the plea of ill health.

Mason, James 1909–84
English actor

Born in Huddersfield, West Yorkshire, he made his stage debut in *The Rascal* (1931) at Aldershot and appeared at the Old Vic, London, and with the Gate Company in Dublin before making his film debut in the 'quota quickie' *Late Extra* (1935). He attained stardom with his suave, saturnine villainy in costume dramas like *The Man in Grey* (1943), *Fanny By Gaslight* (1944) and *The Seventh Veil* (1945). Moving to Hollywood (1947), he became one of the most prolific, distinguished and reliable of cinema actors. He was nominated for an Academy Award for *A Star is Born* (1954), *Georgy Girl* (1966) and *The Verdict* (1982). Other respected performances from more than 100 films include *Odd Man Out* (1946), *Lolita* (1962) and *The Shooting Party* (1984). His autobiography, *Before I Forget*, was published in 1982.

Mason, Sir (Basil) John 1923–
English physicist and meteorologist

Born in Docking, Norfolk, he graduated from Nottingham University in 1948, and moved to Imperial College, London, where he set up his own section on cloud physics. He worked on the study of rain-making processes, electrification in thunderstorms, ice nucleation and other aspects of cloud physics. His book, *The Physics of Clouds* (1957), is a classic. Elected FRS in 1965, he became director-general of the Meteorological Office (1965–83), where he directed the first operational numerical weather predictions, and research on stratospheric gases using meteorological radar. From 1983 to 1989 he organized a thorough interdisciplinary study of acid rain which finally established the facts. He was also chairman of the Global Atlantic Tropical Experiment 1978 and chairman of the Joint Organising Committee of the World Climate Research Programme. Since 1994 he

has been Chancellor of the Institute of Science and Technology at Manchester University. Knighted in 1979, he received many awards including the royal medal of the Royal Society (1991). His published works include *Acid Rain* (1992).

Mason, Sir Josiah 1795–1881
English philanthropist and pen manufacturer

Born in Kidderminster, he was a hawker, but after 1822 manufactured split-rings. In 1829 he began to make pens for Perry & Co., and soon became the greatest penmaker in the world. He was a partner with his cousin George Elkington in electroplating (1842–65), and had smelting works for copper and nickel. He endowed almshouses and an orphanage at Erdington at a cost of £260,000, and gave £180,000 to found the Mason College (now Birmingham University).

Mason, Lowell 1792–1872
US musician

Born in Medfield, Massachusetts, he was organist of a Presbyterian church in Savannah, where he compiled a book of hymns, taking melodies from the works of Handel, Mozart and Beethoven. The success of this work led him to produce similar volumes for school use, and additional hymn books. In 1832 he founded the Boston Academy of Music, with the aim of giving free instruction to children, which he later extended to adults. The most famous of his compositions is probably the hymn tune 'From Greenland's icy mountains'.

Maspero, Sir Gaston 1846–1916
French Egyptologist

Born in Paris, of Italian parents, he became Professor of Egyptology at the Collège de France in 1874, and from 1881 to 1886 and 1899 to 1914 was keeper of the Bûlâq Museum, Cairo, and director of explorations in Egypt, making valuable discoveries at Sakkara, Dahshûr, and Ekhmim. He wrote many works on Egyptology.

Masséna, André 1758–1817
French general

The greatest of Napoleon I's marshals, he served for 14 years in the Sardinian army, and in the French Revolution rose rapidly in rank, becoming in 1793 a general of division. He fought in the campaigns in Upper Italy, defeating Count Suvorov's Russians at Zurich (1799), and became Marshal of the Empire in 1804. In Italy he kept the Archduke Charles in check, crushed him at Caldiero, and overran Naples. In 1807 he commanded the right wing, and was created Duke of Rivoli. In the campaign of 1809 against Austria he earned the title of Prince of Essling. In 1810 he compelled Wellington to fall back upon his impregnable lines at Torres Vedras, was forced to retreat after five months by lack of supplies, but was recalled. At the Restoration (1814) he adhered to the Bourbons and on Napoleon's return from Elba Masséna refused to follow him. □ James Marshall-Cornwall, *André Masséna* (1965)

Massenet, Jules Emile Frédéric 1842–1912
French composer

Born near St Étienne, he studied at the Paris Conservatoire, where he became a professor (1878–96). He made his name with the comic opera *Don César de Bazan* (1872). Other operas are *Hérodiade* (1884), *Manon* (1884), *Le Cid* (1885), *Werther* (1892) and *Thaïs* (1894), and among his other works are oratorios, orchestral suites, music for piano and songs. He wrote *Mes Souvenirs* (1912, Eng trans, 1919).

Massey, Gerald 1828–1907
English mystic and poet

Born near Tring, Hertfordshire, he became a Christian Socialist, edited a journal, lectured, and between 1851 and 1869 published several volumes of poetry, including *Babe*

Christabel and other Poems and *Craigcrook Castle*. He also wrote mystical and speculative theological or cosmogenic works, and claimed to have discovered a 'Secret Drama' in Shakespeare's sonnets.

Massey, (Charles) Vincent 1887–1967
Canadian politician and diplomat
Born in Toronto, he joined the Canadian Cabinet after World War I. In 1925 Mackenzie King invited him to join his Cabinet but he failed to win a seat in 1926 and he was appointed instead as Canada's first Minister to the USA. He was High Commissioner in London (1935–46) and chairman of the 1949 Royal Commission on National Development in Arts, Letters and the Sciences and the first Canadian Governor-General of Canada (1952–59).

Massey, William Ferguson 1856–1925
New Zealand statesman
Born in Ireland, he emigrated to New Zealand where he became a farmer. Elected to the House of Representatives (1894) he became Leader of the Opposition (1903) and, in 1912, Prime Minister, which office he held until his death. During World War I, he formed a coalition government (1915–19) with Sir Joseph Ward.

Massie, Allan 1938–
Scottish novelist, critic and journalist
Born in Singapore and brought up in Aberdeenshire, he was educated at Glenalmond and Cambridge, then taught in a private school before going to Italy, where he taught English as a foreign language. His first two novels, *Change and Decay In All Around I See* (1978) and *The Last Peacock* (1980), show a native sensibility and can be compared to the work of Evelyn Waugh. In both *The Death of Men* (1981) and *Augustus* (1986) he turned to Italy, while *Tiberius* (1990) and *Caesar* (1993) draw on his knowledge of the ancient world. Other novels include *A Question of Loyalties* (1989), *The Sins of the Father* (1991), *These Enchanted Woods* (1993), *The Ragged Lion* (1994) and *King David* (1995). As well as being a prolific novelist, Massie has written books on Muriel Spark, the Caesars and Lord Byron, and his other non-fiction publications include *Edinburgh* (1994). He is also a respected reviewer and a columnist, with trenchant political views.

Massine, Léonide, *originally* Leonid Fyodorovich Myassin 1896–1979
Russian dancer and choreographer
Born in Moscow, he trained with the Imperial Ballet School at St Petersburg, becoming principal dancer and choreographer with Sergei Diaghilev (1914–21, 1925–28) and developing his interests in choreography with ballets like *Parade* (1917) and *La Boutique fantastique* (1919), with music by Erik Satie and design by Picasso. He choreographed some controversial 'symphonic ballets', such as *Choreartium* (1933), which was danced to Brahms's 4th Symphony, and became principal dancer and choreographer for the Ballets Russes de Monte Carlo (1938–43). Though he worked periodically in the USA, Massine settled in Europe working freelance for companies like Sadler's Wells and Ballets des Champs Elysées. He appeared in the ballet films *The Red Shoes* (1948) and *The Tales of Hoffmann* (1950).

Massinger, Philip 1583–1640
English dramatist
He was born in Salisbury, Wiltshire, the son of a retainer of the Earl of Pembroke. After leaving Oxford without a degree he became a playwright and was associated with Philip Henslowe, who died in 1616. In later years he wrote many plays on his own, but much of his work was done in collaboration with others, particularly John Fletcher. Probably the earliest of Massinger's extant plays is *The Unnatural Combat*, printed in 1639. The first in order of publication is *The Virgin Martyr* (1622), partly written by

Thomas Dekker. In 1623 was published *The Duke of Milan*, a fine tragedy, but too rhetorical. Other plays include *The Great Duke of Florence* (1627) and *The Emperor of the East* (1631). Nathan Field joined Massinger in writing *The Fatal Dowry* (1632). *The City Madam* (licensed 1632), and *A New Way to Pay Old Debts* (1633), are Massinger's most masterly comedies—brilliant satirical studies, though without warmth or geniality. It is difficult to assess his contribution to the plays which appeared under the names of Francis Beaumont and Fletcher. 📖 A Dunn, *Massinger: the man and the playwright* (1957)

Massio, Niccolò di Giovanni di See Fabriano, Gentile da

Massys See Matsys

Master of Flémalle See Campin, Robert

Masters, Edgar Lee 1869–1950
US writer
Born in Garnett, Kansas, he was a successful lawyer in Chicago, then turned to writing poetry. He became famous with the satirical *Spoon River Anthology* (1915), a book of epitaphs in free verse about lives of people in Illinois. He published several more collections and some novels, and returned to his first success with *The New Spoon River* (1924), attacking the new style of urban life. *Across Spoon River* (1936) is an autobiography. 📖 H W Masters, *Edgar Lee Masters: a biographical sketchbook* (1978)

Masters, William Howell 1915–
US gynaecologist and sexologist
Born in Cleveland, Ohio, he received his MD from Rochester University in 1943. He joined the faculty of the Washington University School of Medicine (St Louis) in 1947, where his studies in the psychology and physiology of sexual intercourse were carried out using volunteer subjects under laboratory conditions. Much of his research has been done in collaboration with Virginia Johnson, whom he married in 1971, and with whom he published *Human Sexual Response* in 1966, which became an international bestseller. They also wrote *On Sex and Human Loving* (1986). They continued to work together at the Masters and Johnson Institute in St Louis after their divorce in 1993.

Mastroianni, Marcello 1923–96
Italian actor
Born in Fontana Liri, Italy, the son of a carpenter, he trained as a draughtsman, survived a wartime Nazi labour camp, and became a cashier in postwar Rome, pursuing amateur dramatics as a hobby. He made his film debut in *I Miserabili* (1947) and, from 1948, was employed by Luchino Visconti's theatrical troupe in productions including *A Streetcar Named Desire* and *Death of a Salesman*. *Peccato che sia una Canaglia* (1955, *Too Bad She's Bad*) began an enduring film partnership with Sophia Loren, while his performances in Visconti's *Le Notte Bianchi* (1957, *White Nights*) and Federico Fellini's *La Dolce Vita* (1960, *The Sweet Life*) established him as an international star. Stereotypically perceived as a 'Latin lover', in his prolific career he encompassed a wide variety of roles and worked with some of the most distinguished European film directors. He received Academy Award nominations for *Divorzio all'Italiano* (1961, *Divorce Italian Style*), *Una Giornata Particolare* (1977, *A Special Day*) and *Oci Ciornie* (1987, *Dark Eyes*). Other films include Fellini's *8½* (1962), *Città Delle Donne* (1979, *City of Women*) and *Intervista* (1987, *Interview*). He appeared in well over 100 films, making a belated American debut in *Used People* (1992).

Mas'udi, Abu al-Hasan Ali al- See Masodi, Abu al-Hasan Ali al-

Masur, Kurt 1927–
German conductor
He gained international fame in 1970 as the conductor of the Leipzig Gewandhaus Orchestra. He was a leader in public protests in Leipzig that helped bring down the Communist government of East Germany in 1989. In 1991 he became musical director of the New York Philharmonic Orchestra.

Masursky, Harold 1922–
US geologist
Born in Fort Wayne, Indiana, after graduating from Yale he joined the US Geological Survey, and later began working for NASA. His main work has been the surveying of lunar and planetary surfaces to select landing sites for space missions. He worked on the *Ranger 9* programme, the first to obtain close-up images of the lunar surface, progressed to the *Lunar Orbiter* and *Apollo* programmes, and also participated in the 1971 *Mariner Orbiter* and 1975 *Viking Lander* explorations of Mars. In 1978 Masursky joined the *Vénus Orbiter* Imaging Radar Science Group and was one of the chief scientists associated with the *Voyager* missions to the outer planets.

Mata Hari, *stage name of* Margaretha Gertruida MacLeod, *née* Zelle 1876–1917
Alleged Dutch spy
Born in Leeuwarden, she married a Scottish officer in the Dutch army in 1895 and travelled around with him before they separated in 1905 and she became a dancer in France. She was a beautiful woman with apparently few qualms about near-nudity on stage, and had many lovers, several in high military and governmental positions (on both sides before and during World War I); found guilty of espionage for the Germans, she was shot in Paris.

Mather, Cotton 1662–1728
American clergyman
Born in Boston, the son of Increase Mather, he studied at Harvard, and became the most prominent Puritan minister of his time in New England. A polymath, he reported on American botany, and was one of the earliest New England historians. However, his reputation was irrevocably harmed by his involvement in the Salem witchcraft trials of 1692. He published 382 books, including *Memorable Providences relating to Witchcraft and Possessions* (1685), *Wonders of the Invisible World* (1692) and *Christian Philosopher* (1721). He supported smallpox inoculation and other progressive ideas.

Mather, Increase 1639–1723
American theologian
Born in Dorchester, Massachusetts, he graduated at Harvard in 1656, and again at Trinity College, Dublin, in 1658. His first charge was Great Torrington in Devon, but in 1661, finding it impossible to conform, he returned to the USA, and from 1664 till his death was pastor of the Second Church, Boston. From 1685 to 1701 he was also President of Harvard. Sent to England in 1689 to lay colonial grievances before the king, he obtained a new charter from William III. He published 136 works, including *Remarkable Providences* (1684) and a *History of the War with the Indians* (1676), and his *Cases of Conscience Concerning Evil Spirits* (1693) helped to calm the atmosphere during the witchhunts of 1692.

Mathew, Theobald, *known as* Father Mathew 1790–1856
Irish temperance reformer
Born in Thomastown, Tipperary, he joined the Capuchin order in 1814, and became provincial of the Capuchins at Cork (1822–51). In 1838 he became an ardent advocate of total abstinence. He carried out crusades in Ireland, England and Scotland, and later in the USA (1849–51).

Mathews, Charles 1776–1835
English comedian
He made his debut as an actor at Richmond in 1793, but left the 'legitimate' stage in 1818 and achieved great success as an entertainer, visiting the USA twice. He was the father of Charles James Mathews.

Mathews, Charles James 1803–78
English comedian
His light style of comedy was considered graceful and delicate. In 1838 he married Lucia Vestris. He was the son of Charles Mathews.

Mathews, Harry Burchell 1930–
US writer
He was born in New York City and educated at Harvard and at the École Normale de Musique in Paris. In 1952 he moved to Europe, and began writing highly literary fiction; he has lived there, mainly in France, ever since. He is a member of the hermetic Ouvroir de Littérature Potentielle (Oulipo). In 1960, he joined John Ashbery, Kenneth Koch and James Schuyler in founding the influential magazine *Locus Solus*, which was based in France. His fictional writing includes *The Conversions* (1962), *Tlooth* (1966) and his masterpiece, *The Sinking of the Odradek Stadium* (1971–75), originally published in the *Paris Review*, which concerns the correspondence between a librarian and his Thai wife. Later work includes *Cigarettes* (1982). His collected verse was published as *Armenian Papers* (1987).

Mathias, William 1934–92
Welsh composer and pianist
He was born in Whitland, Dyfed, and studied at the University College of Wales, Aberystwyth, and the Royal College of Music, London. He held several academic posts, including a professorship at the University College of North Wales from 1970. His music includes an opera, *The Servants* (1980), concertos for piano, harp and organ, orchestral and chamber music, and sacred music. He wrote within the bardic and mythic traditions of ancient Wales and Cornwall, and he was influenced by the work of Bartók, as is reflected in the titles of some of his works, including the *Concerto for Orchestra* (1966). He wrote an anthem for the wedding of the Prince and Princess of Wales in 1981.

Mathieu, Georges 1921–
French painter
Born in Boulogne, he took a degree in literature, but began to paint in 1937 in a calligraphic style, using rapid strokes. He settled in Paris in 1947, exhibiting there and in New York. He has perfected a form of lyric, non-geometrical abstraction, in close sympathy with the US neo-Expressionists, such as Jackson Pollock, as in his *Battle of Bouvines* (1954). In 1956 he painted a 12ft (3.66m) canvas in the presence of an audience, anticipating the 'happenings' of US artists in the 1960s and in 1974 he designed the new 10 franc coin.

Matilda, *called* the Empress Maud 1102–67
English princess
The only daughter of Henry I, she was born in London and married (1114) Emperor Henry V. She returned to England as Empress Maud after his death (1125) and was acknowledged as the heir to the English throne. In 1128 she married Geoffrey Plantagenet of Anjou, by whom she had a son, Henry 'FitzEmpress', the future Henry II of England. When Henry I died (1135), his nephew Stephen of Blois seized the throne and Matilda invaded England from Anjou (1139) with her half-brother, Robert, Earl of Gloucester. After capturing Stephen, she was acknowledged as 'Lady of the English', but was never crowned. Lacking in judgement, she lost potential allies, especially the city of London, through her financial impositions.

Stephen regained control, while Matilda left England (1148) and returned to her son in Normandy, where she exerted influence over his continental territories.

Matilda of Tuscany, known as the Great Countess of Tuscany c.1046–1115
Italian noblewoman

The daughter of the Margrave Boniface II of Canossa, she was intelligent, well-educated and determined. She inherited much of northern Italy and married first Godfrey the Hunchback, Duke of Upper Lorraine (d.1076), and later, Welf V of Bavaria. She supported the papacy, particularly Pope Gregory VII (Hildebrand). It was at her stronghold of Canossa that the Emperor Henry IV did barefoot penance to the pope (1077). After Gregory's death in 1085 her lands were ravaged by Henry's allies, but she refused to make peace or recognize the antipope Clement III, supporting Pope Urban II until his death (1099). She died at the Benedictine monastery of Polirone, near Mantua. Her remains were reburied in St Peter's, Rome (1634), so high was the regard for her of succeeding popes.

Matilda, Anna See Cowley, Hannah

Matisse, Henri (Emile Benoît) 1869–1954
French painter

Born in Le Cateau, he studied law in Paris and then worked as a lawyer's clerk in St Quentin. In 1892 he began studying art seriously in Paris, first under Adolphe Bouguereau at the Académie Julian and then under Gustave Moreau at the École des Beaux-Arts, where he met Georges Rouault. Between 1899 and 1900 he was working at the Académie Carrière, where he met André Derain. In the 1890s he came under the influence of Impressionism and Neo-Impressionism and, in particular, of the Divisionism developed by Georges Seurat and Paul Signac, but this was eclipsed for a time by his admiration for Cézanne. Although poverty-stricken, he managed to buy Cézanne's small *Bathers* from the dealer Ambroise Vollard (1865–1939). In 1904 he returned to his Divisionist technique while working in the brilliant light of St Tropez and started using high-pitched colour, as in his celebrated *Woman with the Hat* (1905). From this departure grew the movement irreverently dubbed the Fauves (Wild Beasts) by critics. Matisse was the leader of this group, which also included Derain, Maurice Vlaminck, Raoul Dufy and Rouault. His most characteristic paintings display a bold use of luminous areas of primary colour, organized within a two-dimensional rhythmic design. The purity of his line drawing is seen in his many sketchbooks and book illustrations. Resident in Nice from 1914, he designed some ballet sets for Sergei Diaghilev. The art of Matisse owes a great deal to oriental influences and his sensuous art has been as influential in the 20th century as more cerebral movements such as Cubism. In his later years he began working with large paper cut-outs, creating abstract designs. He also designed the stained glass for the Dominican Chapelle du Rosaire at Vence, Alpes-Maritimes. His works include *Bonheur de vivre* (1906), *L'Escargot* (1953), and *La Liseuse* (1894, 'Woman Reading'). He also produced sculpture, and his works in this field include the bronze *The Back I–IV* (1909–30).

Matsuoka Yosuke 1880–1946
Japanese diplomat and politician

After studying in the USA, he joined the diplomatic service (1904) and attended the Paris Peace Conference (1919) as a member of the Japanese delegation. As vice-president, and later president, of the South Manchuria Railway, he supported the expansion of Japan's interests in Manchuria. He led the withdrawal of the Japanese delegation from the League of Nations in 1933 in response to the League's adoption of the Lytton Commission report, which had criticized the actions of the Japanese military in Manchuria. As Foreign Minister (1940–41), Matsuoka sought to strengthen Japan's position in the Far East and counter US hostility to its war in China by concluding the Tripartite Pact with Germany and Italy (1940) and signing a neutrality pact with the USSR (1941). Matsuoka's grand scheme ultimately failed since Hitler's invasion of the USSR brought the latter into the allied camp, while US hostility to Japan's war in China (1937–45) merely intensified. In 1946 he was indicted as a class-A war criminal, but died before the trial was concluded.

Matsys or Massys, Jan 1509–75
Flemish painter

An imitator of his father, Quentin Matsys, he worked in Antwerp. His brother, Cornelius (1513–79), was also a painter.

Matsys or Massys, Quentin c.1466–c.1531
Flemish painter

Born in Louvain, according to legend he was a blacksmith. In 1491 he joined the painters' guild of St Luke in Antwerp. His paintings are mostly religious and genre pictures, treated with a reverent spirit, but with decided touches of realism (as in *The Banker and His Wife*) and exquisite finish. He also ranks high as a portrait painter, notably for his portrait of Erasmus.

Matteotti, Giacomo 1885–1924
Italian politician

He was born in Fratta Polesine. A member of the Italian Chamber of Deputies, in 1921 he began to organize the United Socialist Party on a constitutional basis in opposition to Mussolini's Fascists. Matteotti's courageous protests against Fascist outrages led to his murder in 1924, which resulted in widespread hostility and disgust towards Mussolini and a wave of anti-fascist feeling, which briefly threatened to bring an end to his rule. ▭ Carlo Carini, *Giacomo Matteotti: idee giuridiche e azione politica* (1984)

Matthau, Walter, originally surnamed Matuschanskayasky 1920–
US actor

Born in New York City, he was a radioman-gunner on army airforce bombers before studying at the New School's Dramatic Workshop. He made his Broadway debut in *Anne of a Thousand Days* (1948) and appeared in such productions as *Will Success Spoil Rock Hunter?* (1955) and *A Shot in The Dark* (1961–62) before winning a Tony award for his role as the slobbish Oscar in *The Odd Couple* (1964–65), a part he recreated on film in 1968. He made his film debut in *The Kentuckian* (1955) and spent a decade as a valuable supporting actor before winning an Academy Award for *The Fortune Cookie* (1966) which began a long association with co-star Jack Lemmon. They subsequently appeared together in films like *The Front Page* (1974), *Buddy, Buddy* (1981) and *Grumpy Old Men* (1993). They also appeared on stage in *Juno and The Paycock* (1974) and Lemmon directed him in the film *Kotch* (1971). An unlikely star with a lugubrious manner and a sure comic touch, he has appeared in other films including *The Sunshine Boys* (1975), *The Bad News Bears* (1976) and *House Calls* (1978). Enjoying renewed popularity in the 1990s, he acted on television in *The Incident* (1990) and its two sequels, and in such cinema films as *I.Q.* (1994) and *I'm Not Rappaport* (1996). His son Charles (1964–), a filmmaker, directed him in *The Grass Harp* (1996).

Matthay, Tobias 1858–1945
English pianist and teacher

Born in London, he was Professor of Pianoforte at the Royal Academy of Music from 1880 to 1925, when he resigned to devote himself to his own school, which he had founded in 1900. His method of piano playing was described in *The Act of Touch* (1903) and in his subsequent publications.

Matthew, St 1st century AD
One of the 12 Apostles of Jesus Christ

He was a tax collector before his conversion, and he is called Levi (his name may have been Matthew the Levite) in Mark 2.14 and Luke 5.27. According to tradition, he was the author of the first Gospel, was a missionary to the Hebrews, and was martyred. His feast day is 21 September (West) or 16 November (East).

Matthews, Alfred Edward 1869–1960
English actor

Born in Bridlington, Yorkshire, he began his career in 1887, and played innumerable comedy roles from *Charley's Aunt* to *Quiet Weekend*. He was still a popular favourite at 90. He published his autobiography in 1952.

Matthews, Drummond H(oyle) 1931–97
English geologist and geophysicist

He was educated at Cambridge, and started his professional career as a geologist with the Falkland Islands Dependencies Survey (1955–57) before returning to Cambridge, where he became assistant director of research in the department of geophysics in 1966. He became Reader in Geology in 1971 and subsequently published many important papers in the realm of marine geophysics. He was elected FRS in 1974. He predicted in 1963 that Harry Hess's 'sea-floor spreading' theory should produce strips of normally and reversely magnetized oceanic crust on either side of the mid-ocean ridges, due to the periodic polarity changes of the Earth's magnetic field. By 1966 the accumulation of sufficient magnetic survey data yielded striking proof of the theory, causing a paradigm shift in geological thinking and the widespread acceptance of continental drift and the development of plate tectonic theory. From 1982 to 1990 he was scientific director of the British Institutions Reflection Profiling Syndicate at Cambridge University.

Matthews, Jessie 1907–81
English actress

Born in London, of a poor family, she made her stage debut at the age of 10, and danced in chorus lines as a teenager. She became a hugely popular star in musical revues in the 1920s, and in the 1930s made a successful transition into film roles. These films were largely undistinguished, but her appeal transcended their limitations. She chose to remain in Britain rather than enhance her career in Hollywood, and worked only sporadically after World War II. She directed the short film *Victory Wedding* in 1944.

Matthews, Sir Stanley 1915–
English footballer

Born in Hanley, he was the son of a notable featherweight boxer, Jack Matthews. He started his sporting career as a sprinter, but soon switched to football, and joined Stoke City as a winger in 1931. First picked for England at the age of 20, he won 54 international caps, spread over 22 years. He played for Blackpool from 1947 to 1961, winning an FA Cup Winner's medal in 1953 at the age of 38. He returned to Stoke in 1961, and continued to play First Division football until after the age of 50. He played for England 54 times, was twice the Footballer of the Year (1948, 1963), and was the inaugural winner of the European Footballer of the Year award in 1956. He was knighted in 1965. He later managed Port Vale, and became president of Stoke City Football Club in 1990. His autobiography was published in 1960 entitled *The Stanley Matthews Story.*

Matthias 1557–1619
King of Bohemia and of Hungary, and Holy Roman Emperor

Born in Vienna, the third son of Emperor Maximilian II, he was tolerant in religious matters, favouring a policy of moderation towards German Protestants, although, as Governor of Austria, he suppressed risings of Protestant peasants (1595–97). He ruled Bohemia (1611–17) and Hungary (1608–18), and after being elected emperor on the death of his brother Rudolf II (1612), he continued to pursue a conciliatory policy which aroused the antagonism of other Catholic princes, including his nephew and heir, Ferdinand (later Ferdinand II). An asthmatic, he increasingly withdrew from public life, leaving government to his minister Khlesh.

Matthias I Hunyadi, called Corvinus c.1440–90
King of Hungary

Born in Transylvania, the second son of János Hunyadi, he was elected king in 1458. He drove back the Turks, and made himself master of Bosnia (1462), Moldavia and Wallachia (1467), Moravia, Silesia, and Lusatia (1478), Vienna, and a large part of Austria proper (1485). He greatly encouraged the arts and letters, founded the Corvina Library and the Pozsony Academy (university), promoted industry, and reformed finances and the system of justice. However, his rule was arbitrary and his taxes heavy, and in the end he had to compromise with the nobility who feared for the loss of their privileges. He failed in his aim of becoming Holy Roman Emperor, and many of his achievements did not survive his death.

Matthias, Bernd Teo 1918–
US physicist

Born in Frankfurt am Main, Germany, he studied at Rome University and the Federal Institute of Technology, Zurich, before moving to the USA in 1947, becoming a naturalized citizen in 1951. After a period with Bell Telephone Laboratories he was appointed Professor of Physics at the University of California, San Diego, in 1961. He worked on ferroelectricity, measuring many ferroelectric materials and discovering some new ones. By the early 1950s he was also working on superconductivity, discovering that alloys of metals with five or seven valence electrons were the most effective superconductors. Higher temperature superconducting metal alloys discovered as a result of this work were used until superseded by ceramic materials in the late 1980s.

Matthiessen, F(rancis) O(tto) 1902–50
US literary critic

Born near Pasadena, California, and raised in Illinois, he espoused socialism, despite his wealthy background, due to his Christian ideals. He studied at Yale, Harvard and was a Rhodes Scholar at Oxford. His studies of Henry James (1944) and T S Eliot (1935, rev edn 1947) are direct and perceptive. Joining the faculty at Harvard, he supported civil liberties causes and trade unionism, and in *American Renaissance* (1941) argued that individualism was the bane of US life and culture. At the end of World War II, he became involved in Henry Wallace's Progressive third party movement and was widely reviled from left and right for either closet communism or 'accommodationism'. His journal *From the Heart of Europe* (1948) suggested growing introspection, and two years later, he threw himself from a hotel room window. He bequeathed his inheritance to the struggling journal *Monthly Review*. 📖 W Cain, *F O Matthiessen and the Politics of Criticism* (1988)

Matthiessen, Peter 1927–
US novelist, travel writer, naturalist and explorer

Born in New York City, he studied at the Sorbonne and at the University of Paris. He has made anthropological and natural history expeditions to Alaska, the Canadian Northwest Territories, Peru, New Guinea, Africa, Nicaragua and Nepal, out of which has come a number of eloquent ecological and natural history studies, which reflect the concerns of his cultish novel *At Play in the Fields of the Lord* (1965). He won the National Book Award with the bestselling *The Snow Leopard* (1978), one man's inner story of a mystical trek across the Tibetan plateau to the Crystal Mountain. Other novels include *Race Rock* (1954), *Partisans* (1955), *Far Tortuga* (1975), *Killing Mister Watson* (1990) and *African Silences* (1991). In recent years, he has taken up the cause of Native Americans, writing *In the Spirit of Crazy Horse* (1983), an account of a 1975 shoot-out with the FBI, the publication of which was delayed by litigation.

Maturin, Charles Robert 1782–1824
Irish dramatist and novelist

He was born in Dublin, and educated at Trinity College there, and became a curate in Loughrea and Dublin. He made his name with a series of extravagant novels in macabre vein that rivalled those of **Ann Radcliffe**. These include *The Fatal Revenge* (1807), *Melmoth the Wanderer* (1820), which influenced **Honoré de Balzac**, and *The Albigenses* (1824). His tragedy, *Bertram*, had a warm reception at Drury Lane, London, in 1816, but its successors, *Manuel* (1817) and *Fredolpho* (1819), were failures. 📖 W Scholten, *Charles Robert Maturin: the terror novelist* (1933)

Matuyama, Motonori 1884–1958
Japanese geophysicist

Born in Oita Prefecture, he graduated in physics from Kyoto University (1911), where he subsequently became an instructor and then assistant professor (1916). At the University of Chicago (1919) he studied the physics of ice movement before returning to Japan as Professor of Theoretical Geology at the Imperial University (1921). From 1926 he worked on the magnetism of basalts from Japan and Manchuria, and made the first successful link of magnetic reversals with the geological timescale. In 1934 he initiated a marine gravity survey of the Japan trench. He published numerous papers on the physics of the lithosphere and interior of the Earth, seismology and magnetism, and conducted research into physical methods of locating underground resources.

Mauchly, John W(illiam) 1907–80
US physicist and inventor

He was born in Cincinnati, Ohio, and graduated in physics at Johns Hopkins University. After a few years school-teaching, he joined **John Eckert** in 1943 at the University of Pennsylvania, where they developed the ENIAC (Electronic Numerical Integrator and Computer). This giant military calculator led to the pair's major contribution to computing: the design of a stored-program machine, the EDVAC (Electronic Discrete Variable Computer), which played a large part in launching the computer revolution in the second half of the 20th century. They founded in 1948 the Eckert–Mauchly Computer Corporation, but it was not a commercial success and had to be sold in 1950. Following EDVAC, they built UNIVAC, the Universal Automatic Computer, first used in 1951 by the US Census Bureau. Although Mauchly and Eckert relied to a certain extent on the work of others, notably **John Vincent Atanasoff** (who later was awarded priority by the courts for inventing the computer) and **John von Neumann**, it was their conviction that computers had a commercial market that launched the modern data-processing industry in the USA.

Maud, Empress See **Matilda**

Maude, Clementina, Lady Hawarden 1822–65
Scottish amateur photographer

She was born at Cumbernauld House, the daughter of the Hon Charles Elphinstone-Fleming (MP for Stirlingshire). Married in 1845 to Cornwallis Maude, 4th Viscount Hawarden, she spent the rest of her life in England, much of it in London. In 1864 she met and became a close friend of Charles Dodgson (**Lewis Carroll**). Her photographs, apparently made over relatively few years in the late 1850s and early 1860s, are mainly of women in country-house interiors. Romantic and sensuous, they are often conspiratorial in feeling, and are unusually light in comparison with the ponderous seriousness of much contemporary work.

Maudling, Reginald 1917–79
English Conservative politician

Born in London, he was educated at Merchant Taylors' and Merton College, Oxford, and was called to the Bar. He served in the air force during World War II and in 1945 became one of **R A Butler**'s 'backroom boys' in the Conservative central office. He was elected MP in 1950 and after two junior ministerial posts, became Minister of Supply (1953–57), Paymaster-General (1957–59), President of the Board of Trade (1959–61), Colonial Secretary (1961–62), Chancellor of the Exchequer (1962–64), and deputy Leader of the Opposition in 1964. In 1970 he became Home Secretary in the **Heath** government but resigned in 1972, when he became implicated in the bankruptcy proceedings of architect John Poulson. He published his memoirs in 1978. 📖 Michael Gillard, *A Little Pot of Money: The Story of Reginald Maudling and the Real Estate Fund of America* (1974)

Maudslay, Henry 1771–1831
English engineer and inventor

Born in Woolwich, Kent, he was apprenticed to **Joseph Bramah**, then set up on his own in 1797 and invented various types of machinery, including a screw-cutting lathe. He also invented a slide rule, and a method of desalinating sea water. With Joshua Field (1757–1863) he began producing marine engines and started the firm of Maudslay, Sons and Field (1810).

Maudsley, Henry 1835–1918
English psychiatrist

Born near Giggleswick, Yorkshire, he was physician to the Manchester Asylum, and Professor of Medical Jurisprudence at University College (1869–79). The Maudsley Hospital, Denmark Hill, London, is named after him. 📖 Michael Collie, *Henry Maudsley Victorian Psychiatrist* (1988)

Mauger, Ivan Gerald 1939–
New Zealand speedway rider

Born in Christchurch, he rode for Wimbledon, Rye House, Eastbourne, Newcastle, Belle Vue, Exeter, and Hull between 1957 and 1982, and won the world individual title a record six times (1968–70, 1972, 1977, 1979). He also won two pairs world titles, four team titles, and the world long track title twice.

Maugham, W(illiam) Somerset 1874–1965
British writer

Born in Paris, France, of Irish origin, he was educated at King's School, Canterbury, and read philosophy and literature at Heidelberg in Germany. He qualified as a surgeon at St Thomas's Hospital, London, and a year's medical practice in the London slums gave him the material for his first novel, the lurid *Liza of Lambeth* (1897), and the magnificent autobiographical novel, *Of Human Bondage*, eventually published in 1915. Initial attempts to have his plays accepted failed, but four of them ran simultaneously in London in 1908. In 1914 he served first with a Red Cross unit in France, then as a secret agent in Geneva and finally in Petrograd (St Petersburg), attempting to prevent the outbreak of the Russian Revolution. *Ashenden* (1928) is based on these experiences. He also visited Tahiti and the Far East, which inspired *The Moon and Sixpence* (1919) and such plays as *East of Suez* (1922). In 1928 he settled in the south of France, where he wrote his astringent, satirical masterpiece, *Cakes and Ale* (1930). A British agent again in World War II, he fled to the USA (1940–46), where he ventured into mysticism with *The Razor's Edge* (1945). He is best known for his short stories—several of which were filmed, including *Quartet* (1949)—although his sparse, careful prose has sometimes unjustly been mistaken for superficiality. Other works include essays on **Goethe**, **Chekhov**, **Henry James** and **Katherine Mansfield** in *Points of View* (1958). 📖 R Calder, *Willie: the life of Maugham* (1989); *Strictly Personal* (1941); *Summing Up* (1938)

Maunder, Edward Walter 1851–1924
English astronomer

He was born and educated in London, and in 1873 he became assistant for photography and spectroscopy at the Royal Greenwich Observatory, a post which he held for 40 years. One of his duties was daily photography of the sun and the recording of sunspot numbers, from which data he established the pattern of latitude drift in sunspots, demonstrated in his well-known 'butterfly diagram'. He also worked on correlations between solar and geomagnetic activity, and studied historical records of the low-sunspot period in the 16th century, the 'Maunder minimum'. He took part in several eclipse expeditions to photograph the solar corona. In 1890 he founded the still-flourishing British Astronomical Association for amateur astronomers.

Maundeville, Jehan de See Mandeville, Jehan de

Maung, Shu See Ne Win, U

Maupassant, Guy de 1850–93
French novelist

Born in the Norman château of Miromesnil, near Dieppe, he was educated at Rouen and spent his life in Normandy. After a short spell as a soldier in the Franco-Prussian war he became a government clerk, but encouraged by **Gustave Flaubert**, a friend of his mother's, he took to writing and mingled with **Zola** and other disciples of Naturalism. Free from sentimentality or idealism, his stories lay bare with minute and merciless observation the pretentiousness and vulgarity of the middle class of the period and the cunning and traditional meanness of the Norman peasant. He first achieved success with *Boule de suif* (1880, 'Ball of Tallow'), which exposes the hypocrisy, prudery and ingratitude of the bourgeois in the face of a heroic gesture by a prostitute, and went on to write nearly 300 short stories. *Le Horla* (1887, Eng trans 1890) and *La Peur* (posthumous 1925, 'The Fear') describe madness and fear with a horrifying accuracy, foreshadowing the insanity which beset Maupassant in 1892 and finally precipitated his death. He also wrote several full-length novels, including *Une Vie* (1883, Eng trans *A Woman's Life*, 1888) and *Bel-Ami* (1885, Eng trans 1891). 📖 F Steegmuller, *Maupassant* (1950)

Maupertuis, Pierre Louis Moreau de 1698–1759
French mathematician

Born in St Malo, he headed a group of French academicians sent to Lapland in 1736–37 to measure a degree of the meridian. **Frederick II, the Great** made him president of the Berlin Academy in 1746. He formulated the principle of least action in mechanics, which states that a mechanical system evolves in such a way that its action is as small as possible. Maupertuis also formed a theory of heredity which was a century ahead of its time.

Maura, Carmen 1945–
Spanish actress

Born in Madrid, her family were very conservative, and her decision to give up teaching in favour of acting caused a serious rift. She made slow progress at first, but became nationally known as the host of the television show *Esta Noche* (*Tonight*) in the 1970s. Her career took off internationally in the 1980s through her collaboration with the controversial Spanish director **Pedro Almodovar**, winning the Best Actress Award at the European Film Awards in 1988 for her performance in his *Woman on the Verge of a Nervous Breakdown*. Subsequent films include *Ay, Carmela* (1990) and *Le Bonheur (est dans le pré)* (1995).

Mauriac, François 1885–1970
French novelist and Nobel Prize winner

Born in Bordeaux, he was educated at the University of Bordeaux, then the École Nationale des Chartes in Paris in 1906, but left to become a poet, publishing his first volume of verse in 1909. He was of Roman Catholic parentage, and came to be regarded as the leading novelist of that faith. In his novels, his treatment of the themes of temptation, sin and redemption, set in the brooding Bordeaux countryside, show his art as cathartic, exploring the universal problems of sinful, yet aspiring, man. Major titles are *Le Baiser au lépreux* (1922, Eng trans *The Kiss to the Leper*, 1923), *Génitrix* (1923, Eng trans 1930), *Thérèse Desqueyroux* (1927, Eng trans 1928), and *Le nœud de vipères* (1932, Eng trans *Vipers' Tangle*, 1933). Also important is his play *Asmodée* (1938, Eng trans 1939). He was awarded the 1952 Nobel Prize for literature. 📖 M Alyn, *François Mauriac* (1960)

Maurice 1567–1625
Count of Nassau, Prince of Orange

Born in Dillenburg, Nassau, the second son of **William I, the Silent**, he was appointed stadtholder by the States General of the United Provinces upon his father's murder (1584), and took command of the republic's army in its struggle for independence from Spain. A master of siege warfare, with English aid he inflicted a series of defeats on the Spanish in the 1590s, leading to the Twelve Years' Truce (1609). His military reforms made the Dutch army the most advanced in Europe. He became Prince of Orange in 1618 on the death of his elder brother William and, after the execution of his rival, the veteran statesman Oldenbarnevelt (the only blot on his character), he established a virtually monarchical authority over the state, but left the constitution unchanged on his death. He died unmarried and was succeeded by his brother, Frederick Henry.

Maurice, (John) Frederick Denison 1805–72
English theologian and writer

He was born in Normanston, Suffolk, and attended Trinity College and Trinity Hall, Cambridge, but as a Dissenter, left in 1827 without a degree, and began a literary career in London. Influenced by **Coleridge**, he took orders in the Church of England, became chaplain to Guy's Hospital (1837) and to Lincoln's Inn (1841–60). In 1840 he became Professor of Literature at King's College London, where he was also Professor of Theology (1846–53), and from 1866 he was Professor of Moral Philosophy at Cambridge. The publication in 1853 of his *Theological Essays*, dealing with atonement and eternal life, lost him his professorship of theology. With **Thomas Hughes** and **Charles Kingsley** he founded the Christian socialism movement (1848). He also was the founder and first Principal of the Working Man's College (1854) and of the

Queen's College for Women. His other books include *Moral and Metaphysical Philosophy* (1850–62), *The Conscience* and *Social Morality* (1869).

Maurier, Daphne du See **du Maurier, Dame Daphne**

Maurier, George du See **du Maurier, George**

Maurier, Sir Gerald du See **du Maurier, Sir Gerald**

Maurois, André, *pseudonym of* **Émile Herzog** 1885–1967
French novelist and biographer
He was born in Elbeuf, one of a family of Jewish industrialists from Alsace who settled in Normandy after 1870. During World War I he was a liaison officer with the British army, and he began his literary career with two books of shrewd and affectionate observation of British character, *Les Silences du Colonel Bramble* (1918, 'The Silences of Colonel Bramble') and *Les Discours du Docteur O'Grady* (1920, 'The Speeches of Dr O'Grady'). His large output includes such distinguished biographies as *Ariel* (1923, on Shelley), *Disraeli* (1927), *Voltaire* (1935), *À la recherche de Marcel Proust* (1949, 'In Search of Marcel Proust'), and *La vie de Sir Alexander Fleming* (1959, Eng trans *The Life of Sir Alexander Fleming*, 1959). He also wrote several novels, fantasies, tales for children, and critical and philosophical essays. ◫ J Suffel, *André Maurois* (1963)

Mauroy, Pierre 1928–
French statesman
He was a teacher before becoming involved with trade unionism and socialist politics. He was prominent in the creation of a new French Socialist Party in 1971 and in the subsequent unification of the left. He became Mayor of Lille in 1973, the same year that he was first elected to the National Assembly, and held the post until President François Mitterrand made him Prime Minister (1981). He oversaw the introduction of a radical, but unsuccessful, reflationary programme and was replaced as Prime Minister by **Laurent Fabius** in 1984 when a major switch in policy became essential. A representative of the traditional left faction, he became First Secretary of the Socialist Party in 1988.

Maurras, Charles 1868–1952
French royalist journalist and political theorist
He was early influenced by the ideas of **Auguste Comte**. By 1894 he was established as an avant-garde journalist and a proponent of monarchism. From 1908, in the newspaper *Action française*, his articles wielded a powerful influence on the youth of the country. In 1936 he was imprisoned for violent attacks on the government. At the fall of France (1940), he supported the Vichy government. He was sentenced to life imprisonment in 1945, but was released on medical grounds in 1952. ◫ M Mourre, *Charles Maurras* (1958); C H Sisson, *The Avoidance of Literature* (1986)

Maury, Matthew Fontaine 1806–73
US hydrographer
Born in Spotsylvania, Virginia, he entered the US navy in 1825, and during a voyage round the world (1826–30) commenced his well-known *Navigation* (1834). Lamed for life in 1839, he was appointed superintendent in 1842 of the hydrographical office at Washington, and in 1844 of the observatory. There he wrote his *Physical Geography of the Sea* (1856), and his works on the Gulf Stream, ocean currents, and Great Circle sailing. He became an officer of the Confederate navy, and later Professor of Physics at Lexington University.

Mauser, Peter Paul von 1838–1914
German firearm inventor

He was born in Oberndorf, Neckar. With his brother Wilhelm (1834–82) he was responsible for the improved needle-gun (adopted by the German army in 1871) and for the improved breech-loading cannon. He produced the 'Mauser' magazine rifle in 1897.

Mauss, Marcel 1872–1950
French sociologist and anthropologist
Born in Épinal, he studied philosophy under his uncle **Émile Durkheim** at Bordeaux, and the history of religion at Paris. In 1901 he became professor in the philosophy and religion of 'non-civilized' peoples, and in 1925 was co-founder of the Institute of Ethnology at Paris University. From 1931 to 1939 he was at the Collège de France. Before World War I, he collaborated closely with Durkheim and other members of the *Année sociologique* school on studies of sacrifice, magic, collective representations and social morphology. After World War I, he edited the work of the *Année* school and his best-known work, *Essai sur le don* (1925), in which he demonstrated the importance of gift exchange in primitive social organization. His last significant work, a lecture on the concept of the person, appeared in 1938.

Mauve, Anton 1838–88
Dutch painter
Born in Zaandam, he was one of the greatest landscapists of his time. He was influenced by **Camille Corot** and **Jean François Millet**. From 1878 he lived in Laren, gathering other painters round him in a kind of Netherlandish Barbizon school.

Mawhinney, Sir Brian Stanley 1940–
English Conservative politician
Born in Belfast, he was educated at Queen's University there, and at the universities of Michigan and London, and became Assistant Professor of Radiation Research at the University of Iowa (1968–70). He lectured at the Royal Free Hospital School of Medicine from 1970 to 1984, and was elected MP for Peterborough in 1979 (Cambridgeshire North West from 1997). His government posts included Under-Secretary of State for Northern Ireland (1986–90), Minister of State in the Northern Ireland Office (1990–92) and Secretary of State for Transport (1994–95) before he became the blunt, no-nonsense Chairman of the Conservative Party (1995–97).

Mawlana See **Jalal ad-Din ar-Rumi**

Mawlay Isma'il 1672–1727
Sultan of Maghrib (Morocco)
He consolidated the authority of the state and took control of piracy, which he turned into a state enterprise. He also established an élite corps of black slaves (*abid al-Bukhari*).

Mawson, Sir Douglas 1882–1958
Australian explorer and geologist
Born in Bradford, Yorkshire, England, he was educated at Sydney University. In 1907 he joined the scientific staff of **Ernest Shackleton's** Antarctic expedition and discovered the South Magnetic Pole. From 1911 to 1914 he was leader of the Australasian Antarctic expedition, which charted 2,000 miles (3,220km) of coast. He was knighted on his return. In 1929–31 he led the Australian-British-New Zealand expedition to the Antarctic.

Max, Adolphe 1869–1939
Belgian politician and patriot
Born in Brussels, he was first a journalist and then an accountant. He became Burgomaster of Brussels in 1909, and when German troops approached Brussels in August 1914, he boldly drove to meet them and opened negotiations. He defended the rights of the Belgian population against the invaders, and was imprisoned by the

Germans, later refusing an offer of freedom on condition that he went to Switzerland and desisted from anti-German agitation. In November 1918 he returned to Belgium, was elected to the House of Representatives, and became a Minister of State.

Maxim, Sir Hiram Stevens 1840–1916
British inventor and engineer

Born in Sangersville, Maine, USA, he became a coach-builder in an engineering works in Fitchburg, Massachusetts in 1865, and from 1867 took out patents for gas apparatus and electric lamps, among other devices. He emigrated to England in 1881, where he perfected his 'Maxim' machine-gun in 1883. He also invented a pneumatic gun, a smokeless powder, a mousetrap, carbon filaments for light bulbs, and a flying machine (1894). He became a naturalized British citizen in 1900, and was knighted in 1901. ☐ P F Mottelay, *The Life and Work of H S Maxim* (1920)

Maximilian I 1459–1519
Holy Roman Emperor

He was born Archduke of Austria in Weiner Neustadt, the eldest son of **Frederick III, of Germany** and Eleanor of Portugal, and by his marriage with Mary, heiress of **Charles the Bold** (1477), he acquired Burgundy and Flanders. This involved him in war with **Louis XI** of France, and he was forced to give Artois and Burgundy to Louis (1482). Elected King of the Romans (1486), he drove out the Hungarians (1490) who, under **Matthias I Hunyadi** (Corvinus), had seized much of Austria. At Villach (1492) he defeated the Turks, and in 1493 he became Holy Roman Emperor. Having next married a daughter of the Duke of Milan (1494), he turned his ambition towards Italy, but after years of war he had to cede Milan to **Louis XII** (1504) and despite the League of Cambrai (1508), he was defeated by the Venetians, and the Swiss broke away from the German Empire. The peaceful acquisition of the Tyrol, however, increased his territory, and the marriage of his son Philip to the Infanta **Juana** united the Houses of Spain and Habsburg, Philip becoming **Philip I, the Handsome** of Spain. The marriage of his grandson Ferdinand to the daughter of Ladislas of Hungary and Bohemia brought both these kingdoms to Austria. Although full of wild schemes which he could not finance, he was genial, energetic and popular. He improved the administration of justice, greatly encouraged the arts and learning, and caused to be written both *Theuerdank* in verse and *Weisskunig* in prose, of both of which he himself is the hero, and probably part-author. He left his extended empire to his grandson **Charles V.** ☐ R W Setson-Watson, *Maximilian I, Holy Roman Emperor* (1902)

Maximilian II 1527–76
Holy Roman Emperor

Born in Vienna, the eldest son of Emperor **Ferdinand I** and Anne of Bohemia and Hungary, he became King of Bohemia (1548), King of Hungary (1563) and Holy Roman Emperor (1564). An intelligent, tolerant and cultivated man who considered himself 'neither Catholic nor Protestant but a Christian', he embarrassed his family by his Protestant leanings and was obliged (1562) to swear to live and die within the Catholic Church. As emperor he secured considerable religious freedom for Austrian Lutherans and deplored the intolerance of the Catholic reaction in Spain and France. Abroad, he fought unsuccessfully against the Turks, and continued to pay them tribute. A patron of the arts and sciences, he set out to make Vienna a centre of European intellectual life.

Maximilian I 1573–1651
Duke and Elector of Bavaria

The son of Duke William V, he was born in Munich and educated at the Jesuit college at Ingolstadt. From 1597 he instituted reforms of the country's legal system, army, inefficient bureaucracy and disordered finances. He placed himself at the head of the Catholic League (1609) and supported Emperor **Ferdinand II** in the Thirty Years War, obtaining as a reward the confiscated lands of **Frederick V** of the Palatinate. By the Peace of Westphalia (1648), the Lower Palatinate was returned to Frederick's heir, Charles Louis, but Maximilian retained the electoral title. Patient and worldly-wise, he was a keen defender of German liberties and resisted imperial attempts to turn the empire into a centralized Habsburg monarchy.

Maximilian II Emmanuel 1662–1726
Elector of Bavaria

Elector from 1679 to 1726, he was a military leader and distinguished himself at the capture of Belgrade (1688). He was Governor of the Spanish Netherlands (1692) while fighting for the **Habsburg**s against **Louis XIV** of France. He supported the French in the War of the Spanish Succession and lost his lands as a result (after Blenheim). He was restored to his former possessions after the Peace of Utrecht (1713).

Maximilian, Ferdinand Joseph 1832–67
Emperor of Mexico and Archduke of Austria

He was born in Vienna, the younger brother of Emperor Francis Joseph I. He married Carlota, daughter of **Leopold** I, King of the Belgians. He accepted the offer of the Crown of Mexico (1863), supported by France, and was crowned emperor (1864). He attempted liberal reforms, largely in the interest of the Indian peasants, but when **Napoleon III** withdrew his troops, he refused to abdicate, made a brave defence at Querétaro against **Benito Juárez**, and was betrayed and executed.

Maxton, James 1885–1946
Scottish politician

Born in Glasgow, he was educated at the university there and became a teacher in the east end of the city, where the poverty he witnessed converted him to socialism. A supporter of the Independent Labour Party, he became its chairman in 1926. He was MP for Glasgow Bridgeton from 1922 until his death. A man of strong convictions, he was a staunch pacifist, and suffered imprisonment for attempting to foment a strike of shipyard workers during World War I, in which he was a conscientious objector. One of the most turbulent 'Red Clydesiders', he was expelled from the House of Commons in 1923 for calling a minister a murderer. As chairman of the Independent Labour Party (1926–40), he led its secession from the Labour Party in 1932, and became increasingly isolated from mainstream Labour politics. His extreme views won few supporters, but his sincerity won the respect of all.

Maxwell, James Clerk, *surname also* Clerk-Maxwell 1831–79
Scottish physicist

Born in Edinburgh, at the age of 15 he devised a method for drawing oval curves which was published by the Royal Society of Edinburgh. He studied mathematics, physics and moral philosophy at Edinburgh University, and later graduated from Cambridge as Second Wrangler. He was appointed Professor of Natural Philosophy at Marischal College, Aberdeen University (1856) and King's College London (1860). In 1871 he was appointed the first Cavendish Professor of Experimental Physics at Cambridge, where he organized the Cavendish Laboratory. He published papers on the kinetic theory of gases, theoretically established the nature of Saturn's rings (1857), investigated colour perception and demonstrated colour photography with a picture of tartan ribbon (1861). He worked on the theory of electromagnetic radiation, and his *Treatise on Electricity and Magnetism* (1873) treated mathematically Michael Faraday's theory of electrical and magnetic forces and provided the first conclusive evidence that light consisted of electromagnetic waves. He suggested that electromagnetic waves could be generated in a laboratory—as Heinrich Hertz was to demonstrate in 1887. His work is considered to have paved the way for Albert Einstein and Max Planck. He was one of the greatest theoretical physicists the world has known. 📖 Ivan Tolstoy, *James Clerk Maxwell* (1982)

Maxwell, John 1905–62
Scottish painter
Born in Dalbeattie, Kirkcudbrightshire, he trained at Edinburgh College of Art (1921–26), then travelled to France and attended the Académie Moderne under Amédée Ozenfant and Fernand Léger. Contrary to the strict order evident in these artists' work, Maxwell developed a more loosely painted dreamlike style, composed of freely associated figures and objects. He taught alongside Sir William Gillies at Edinburgh College of Art for most of the period 1929–61.

Maxwell, (Ian) Robert, *originally* Jan Ludvik Hoch 1923–91
British publisher and politician
Born in Czechoslovakia and self-educated, he served in World War II (1940–45) before founding the Pergamon Press, a publishing company specializing in scientific journals and one of the first to use computerization. A former Labour MP (1964–70), Maxwell, who had many business interests including film production, rescued the large British Printing Corporation from financial collapse in 1980 and rapidly transformed it into the successful British Printing and Communications Corporation, which became the Maxwell Communication Corporation in 1985 and of which he became joint managing director in 1988. Despite a 1973 declaration by the Department of Trade and Industry that Maxwell was unreliable in handling money, by 1991 he was head of a considerable empire. However he was later revealed to have been involved in questionable transactions using money taken from the pension funds of some of his companies to buy shares in others to prop them up. The cause of his mysterious death when at sea on his luxury yacht has never quite been ascertained. 📖 Joe Haines, *Maxwell* (1988)

Maxwell Davies, Sir Peter 1934–
English composer
Born in Manchester, he studied in Manchester and Rome. After three years as director of music at Cirencester Grammar School he went to Princeton University in 1962 for further study. He has lectured in Europe, Australia and New Zealand, and was composer-in-residence at the University of Adelaide in 1966. Most of his music is written for chamber ensembles, often including a large percussion section. The Fires of London, a group founded by him (1970), is particularly associated with his work. He has a keen interest in early English music, in particular the 16th-century composer John Taverner, the subject of his opera *Taverner* (1972), and has always experimented with different orchestral combinations. In later works he introduced stereo tape and electronic sounds. The scoring of one of the parts in *Vesalii Icones* (1970) for a dancer-pianist exemplifies his idea of 'music theatre', with no artificial division between the forms of expression. His works include *Prolation* (1959), *Revelation and Fall* (1965), two *Fantasias on an In Nomine of John Taverner* (1962, 1964), *Eight Songs for a Mad King* (1969), *Our Lady's Juggler* (1978, *Le Jongleur de Notre Dame*), four symphonies, an opera, *The Lighthouse* (1979) and a ballet, *Caroline Mathilde* (1991). Since 1970 Maxwell Davies has done most of his work in

Orkney, frequently using Orcadian or Scottish subject matter. He directed the St Magnus Festival (1977–86), and in 1988 received a commission of 10 concertos for the Scottish Chamber Orchestra, for which he was associate conductor and composer from 1985 to 1994, and then Composer Laureate (1994–). 📖 Paul Griffiths, *Peter Maxwell Davies* (1981)

May, Elaine, *originally* Elaine Berlin 1932–
US screenwriter and film director
Born in Philadelphia, the daughter of a well-known Yiddish actor, Jack Berlin, she was a child actress, then met Mike Nicols while studying at the University of Chicago. They developed a successful writing partnership for the stage until their break-up in 1961. She continued to write for both stage and film, and shared an Academy Award nomination for Best Screenplay with Warren Beatty for *Heaven Can Wait* (1978). Her work as a film director includes *A New Leaf* (1971) and the notorious failure *Ishtar* (1987).

May, Phil(ip William) 1864–1903
English caricaturist
Born in Wortley, near Leeds, he was orphaned at the age of nine and endured years of poverty before he became poster artist and cartoonist of the *St Stephen's Review*. He went to Australia and on his return in 1890 established himself by his *Annual*, and contributions to *Punch* and other periodicals. He cleverly depicted East London types and brought a new simplicity of line to popular cartooning.

May, Robert McCredie 1936–
Australian physicist and ecologist
Born in Sydney, he studied physics at the university there, taught mathematics at Harvard (1959–61) and theoretical physics at Sydney University, where he held a personal chair (1961–73). He was Professor of Biology at Princeton University from 1973 to 1988 and subsequently Royal Society Research Professor at Oxford. He has worked on the dynamics of animal populations and has applied non-linear models to explain fluctuations in animal numbers. His realization of the widespread relevance of deterministic chaos has opened up fruitful areas of research. His investigations into the abundance and diversity of species have covered parasite–host relationships and the ways in which infectious diseases control the natural populations of animals and plants. He wrote *Stability and Complexity in Model Ecosystems* (1973) and *Infectious Diseases of Humans: Transmission and Control* (1991). Since 1995 he has been Chief Scientific Advisor to the Government and head of the Office of Science and Technology.

May, Sir Thomas Erskine, 1st Baron Farnborough 1815–86
English constitutional jurist
He was educated at Bedford School, became Assistant Librarian of the House of Commons in 1831, Clerk-Assistant in 1856, and Clerk of the House in 1871. He was created a baron in 1881 on his retirement, and his *Treatise on the Law, Privileges, Proceedings, and Usage of Parliament* (1844) has been translated into various languages and remains a standard work. He also wrote *Constitutional History of England 1760–1860* (1861–63).

Mayakovsky, Vladimir Vladimirovich 1894–1930
Russian poet and playwright
Born in Bagdadi (Mayakovsky), Georgia, he was involved in the Social Democratic movement during his youth, but when imprisoned for 11 months he renounced politics for art. Writing was his first love, however. He was an enthusiastic supporter of the 1917 Revolution, and both his play *Misteriya-Buff* (1918, Eng trans *Mystery-Bouffe*, 1968) and the long poem *150,000,000* (1919–20) are well-

known works of the period. The advent of the new conservative leaders in 1921 led him to write *Pro eto* (1923, 'About This'), poems pre-Revolution in sentiment, and satirical plays like *Klop* (1929, Eng trans *The Bedbug*, 1960) and *Banya* (1930, Eng trans *The Bath-House*, 1968). *Vladimir Ilyich Lenin* (1924), *Khorosho!* (1927, 'Good!') and the unfinished *Vo ves golos* (1929–30, translated into Scots by Edwin Morgan, 1972), made him famous in the former USSR. Towards the end of his life he was severely castigated by more orthodox Soviet writers and critics for his outspoken criticism of the bureaucracy and his unconventional opinions on art, and he committed suicide.
📖 E Brown, *Mayakovsky: a poet in the revolution* (1973)

Mayall, Nicholas Ulrich 1906–
US astrophysicist

Born in Moline, Illinois, and educated at the University of California, he worked at the Massachusetts Institute of Technology's Radiation Laboratory (1942–43) and the California Institute of Technology (1943–45), and in 1960 was appointed director of Kitt Peak Observatory in Arizona. Mayall's principal researches were in the field of optical observations of galaxies. In the early 1930s he collaborated with Edwin Hubble to study the galactic distribution in space, and later work included optical radial velocity measurements of the Andromeda galaxy, and the development of a system of classifying galaxies from their composite spectra (1957). In 1961 Mayall oversaw the building of a 4-metre telescope named the Mayall telescope.

Maybach, Wilhelm 1846–1929
German inventor and car manufacturer

Born in Heilbronn, he joined Gottlieb Daimler in 1869 as a draughtsman, and became his partner in 1882 when he established a factory at Cannstatt near Stuttgart. He devised the float-feed carburettor (1893), which was crucial to the development of high-speed petrol engines suitable for motor cars. He also made improvements in timing, gearing and steering, all of which played their part in the success of the Daimler car that won the first international road race in 1894. He left the Daimler firm in 1907 and set up his own works at Friedrichshafen (1909), where he made engines for Zeppelin airships, and (1922–39) luxury 'Maybach' cars.

Mayer, Louis B(urt), *originally* Eliezer Mayer 1885–1957
US film producer

Born in Minsk, Russia, his family emigrated to Canada when he was three. He was working as a scrap metal dealer at the age of eight and later expanded his activities to ship salvaging. In 1907 he bought a house in Haverhill in Massachusetts, refurbished it as a nickelodeon and opened one of the earliest custom-designed cinemas. He subsequently acquired a chain of movie theatres in New England and bought the regional rights to such popular attractions as *Birth of a Nation* (1915). He set up a film production company in Los Angeles in 1919, and in 1924 became vice-president of the newly merged group, Loew's Metro-Goldwyn-Mayer. He was instrumental in the creation of Hollywood as a dream factory and the establishment of the star system, wielding enormous power for more than two decades. He oversaw such successes as *Ben Hur* (1926), *Grand Hotel* (1932), the Andy Hardy series, *Ninotchka* (1939) and countless others. He was also involved in setting up the Academy of Motion Picture Arts and Sciences (1927), from whom he received an honorary Academy Award in 1950, before he retired in 1951.

Mayer, (Julius) Robert von 1814–78
German physician and physicist

Born in Heilbronn, Baden-Württemberg, he enrolled at the University of Tübingen in 1832 and received his medical doctorate in 1838. In 1842 physiological considerations convinced him that heat and motion were different manifestations of a single force. He estimated the mechanical equivalent of heat by examining the difference in the two principal specific heats of a gas, and enunciated a general principle of conservation for biological, magnetic, electrical and chemical processes (now interpreted as the conservation of energy), which led to a dispute with James Joule over priority. Mayer initially gained little recognition and became depressed; he attempted suicide in 1850 and spent years in asylums.

Mayhew, Henry 1812–87
English writer

Born in London, he ran away from Westminster School, and collaborated with his brother Augustus (1826–75) in writing numerous successful novels such as *The Good Genius that turns everything to Gold* (1847) and *Whom to Marry* (1848). Of his other works the best-known is the classic social survey, *London Labour and the London Poor* (1851–62). He was a co-founder and first joint editor of *Punch* (1841), with Mark Lemon. 📖 G S Jones, *Outcast London* (1971)

Mayhew (of Twysden), Patrick Barnabas Burke Mayhew, Baron 1929–
English Conservative politician

He was born in Cookham, Berkshire, and educated at Tonbridge School and Balliol College, Oxford. After National Service in the 4th/7th Royal Dragoon Guards he trained as a barrister and was appointed QC in 1972. In 1974 he became Conservative MP for Royal Tunbridge Wells (1974–97). Knighted in 1983, he served as Solicitor-General (1983–87), Attorney-General (1987–92), and Secretary of State for Northern Ireland (1992–97); it was a time of hope for a peaceful solution to the province's political troubles. He proved to be a firm and resolute leader, and was awarded a life peerage in 1997.

Mayling Soong See Chiang Kai-shek

Maynard Smith, John 1920–
English geneticist and evolutionary biologist

He was born in London, and educated at Eton and Cambridge, where he graduated as an aeronautical engineer (1941), and at University College London, where he received a degree in zoology in 1951. He taught at University College London (1951–65) before being appointed Professor of Biology at the University of Sussex (1965–85). After early work in collaboration with J B S Haldane, he went on to develop a new phase of the mathematical understanding of evolutionary processes, in particular the application of game theory to behavioural ecology (*Evolution and the Theory of Games*, 1983) where his development of the fitness concept of William Donald Hamilton has been immensely fruitful. His popular book, the *Theory of Evolution* (1958), was widely influential. Other publications include *Evolutionary Genetics* (1989) and *The Major Transitions in Evolution* (1995, with E Szathmáry). He was elected FRS in 1977.

Mayo, Charles Horace 1865–1939
US surgeon

Born in Rochester, Minnesota, the son of a doctor, he studied medicine at Chicago Medical College, and joined with his father William Worrall Mayo (1819–1911) and his brother William James Mayo to establish the clinic in St Mary's Hospital, Rochester, which was to become the Mayo Clinic in 1905. A specialist in the treatment of goitre, he co-founded the Mayo Foundation for Medical Education and Research in 1915. 📖 Helen B Clapesattle, *The Doctors Mayo* (2nd edn 1954)

Mayo, Katherine 1868–1940
US journalist

Born in Ridgeway, Pennsylvania, she is remembered for her books exposing social evils, especially *Isles of Fear* (1925), condemning US administration of the Philippines, and *Mother India* (1927), a forthright indictment of child marriage and other customs.

Mayo, Richard Southwell Bourke, Earl of 1822–72
Irish politician and administrator

Born in Dublin, he was educated at Trinity College. He entered the House of Commons as a Conservative in 1847, and was appointed Chief-Secretary of Ireland by Lord Derby in 1852, 1858 and 1866. Sent out in 1868 to succeed Lord Lawrence, he was eminently successful as Viceroy of India, but was fatally stabbed by a convict while inspecting the settlement at Port Blair on the Andaman Islands.

Mayo, William James 1861–1939
US surgeon

He was born in Le Sueur, Minnesota. A specialist in stomach surgery, with his brother Charles Horace Mayo and his father William Worrall Mayo (1819–1911) he established the clinic, in St Mary's Hospital, Rochester, Minnesota, which was to become the Mayo Clinic in 1905. He also helped Charles in 1915 to set up the Mayo Foundation for Medical Education and Research.

Mayow, John 1640–79
English chemist and physiologist

Born in Bray, Cornwall, he studied medicine at Oxford and thereafter practised as a physician. He noted the similarities between combustion and respiration, in particular that both use up only a small proportion of the available air. He also noted that the remainder of the air does not support life, extinguishes a lighted candle and is insoluble in water. He also suggested that respiration is the source of animal heat and pointed out that the foetus breathes through the placenta. Mayow's originality and the extent of his influence, if any, on Antoine Lavoisier, are the subject of debate.

Mayr, Ernst Walter 1904–
US zoologist

Born in Kempten, Germany, he studied at Berlin University and emigrated to the USA in 1932, serving as Professor of Zoology at Harvard from 1953 to 1975. His early work was on the ornithology of the Pacific Ocean, leading three scientific expeditions to New Guinea and the Solomon Islands (1928–30), but in his later career he became one of the most important proponents of the neo-Darwinian concepts of evolution. Mayr was also first to propose the 'founder effect', describing the genetic bottle-neck of a population 'founded' by a few individuals. The author of one of the key works on synthesis, *Systematics and the Origin of Species* (1942), he also wrote an influential history of biology, *The Growth of Biology Thought* (1982), complemented by *Towards a New Philosophy of Biology* (1988), followed by *One Long Argument* (1991).

Mayr, Simon See Marius, Simon

Mays, Willie Howard, Jnr 1931–
US baseball player

Born in Fairfield, Alabama, he played for the New York Giants (1951–57), who moved to San Francisco (1958–72), and the New York Mets (1972–73). A magnificent fielder, batter and base runner, only he and Hank Aaron have performed the baseball double of more than 3,000 hits and 600 home runs. He was voted the Most Valuable Player (MVP) in 1954 and 1965, and was voted the Baseball Player of the Decade (1960–69). He was elected to the National Baseball Hall of fame in 1979. 📖 J Grabowski, *Willie Mays* (1990)

Mazarin, Jules, *originally* Giulio Mazarini 1602–61
French cleric, diplomat and politician

Born in Pescina, Italy, he studied under the Jesuits in Rome, and at Alcala in Spain. He was Papal Nuncio to the French court (1634–36) and entered the service of Louis XIII in 1639, having become a naturalized Frenchman. Through the influence of Cardinal Richelieu he was elevated to cardinal, succeeding him as Chief Minister in 1642. After Louis's death (1643), he retained his authority under the Queen Regent, Anne of Austria, to whom it is said he was married. Blamed by many for the civil disturbances of the Frondes, he twice fled France, and returned to Paris in 1653 after the nobles' revolt had been suppressed. His foreign policy was more fruitful: he gained the alliance of Cromwell at the price of Dunkirk, concluded the Peace of Westphalia (1648), whose terms increased French prestige, and negotiated the Treaty of the Pyrenees (1659), ending the prolonged Franco-Spanish conflict. His impressive library was bequeathed to the Collège Mazarin, and his name is borne by the rare 'Mazarin Bible'. 📖 Arthur Hassall, *Mazarin* (1903)

Mazeppa, Ivan Stepanovich c.1644–1709
Russian nobleman, and hetman of the Cossacks

He became a page at the court of Poland, but was dismissed after an intrigue with a nobleman's wife. He joined the Cossacks, and was elected hetman of the Ukraine (1687). Peter I, the Great, made him Prince of the Ukraine, but when Peter curtailed the freedom of the Cossacks, Mazeppa entered into negotiations with Karl XII of Sweden. After the disaster of Poltava (1709), he fled with Karl to Bender in Turkey, where he died. His story is the theme of poems (notably that by Byron), plays, novels, opera and paintings.

Mazzini, Giuseppe 1805–72
Italian patriot and political leader

Born in Genoa, he was initiated into the Carbonari as a young man. He was arrested by the Piedmontese police and exiled to France, where in 1833 he founded his own movement, Young Italy. Expelled from France, he travelled widely in Europe, calling for republican insurrection. During the Revolution of 1848 he took part first in the Lombard revolt against Austrian rule and, subsequently, in the governing triumvirate of the Roman Republic established after Pius IX fled the city. A number of abortive Mazzinian insurrections during the 1850s (notably that of Pisacane) and a growing support for the moderate views embodied by the Italian National Society largely discredited him. In the final decade of his life he continued to preach republicanism and women's emancipation and played a small part in the establishment of the First International, but never managed to reconcile his ideas to those of socialism.

Mazzola, Girolamo Francesco Maria See Parmigiano

M'Ba, Leon 1902–67
Gabon statesman

Educated in Catholic schools, he was in turn accountant, journalist and administrator. He was elected for the Rassemblement Democratique Africaine (RDA) to the Gabon Assembly in 1952 and, in the French tradition, used the mayoral position (of Libreville) to enhance his political ambitions. He was head of government (1957–60) and President from Gabon's independence (1960) until his death.

Mbande, Jinga c.1582–1663
Angolan queen

Born in the West African kingdom of Kongo and Ndongo, the daughter of the King of Ndongo, she was committed to the struggle against the Portuguese who in

1576 had founded Luanda, beginning a lucrative trade exporting slaves to Brazil. In 1622 she entered into negotiations for Ndongo's independence from the Portuguese on behalf of her brother Ngola, apparently converting to Christianity to strengthen her cause. On Ngola's death (by murder or suicide), Jinga renounced her Christianity, seized power, and declared war on the Portuguese. Ousted from her country, she travelled east and conquered the kingdom of Matamba. She continued debilitating raids on the Portuguese until 1643, when they imprisoned her sister and recaptured Luanda. After hiding in the Matamba hills, she negotiated a peaceful settlement (1656) with the Portuguese, exchanging her sister for 130 slaves along with military protection when she required it. She returned to ruling the Jaga, converting them to Christianity.

Mbeki, Thabo 1942–
South African politician
He was born in Transkei, the son of Govan Mbeki (1910–) who was imprisoned in 1964, and was active in the African National Congress (ANC) from his student days; he was briefly imprisoned in 1962. After that he studied in England and the USSR. On his return to South Africa he took a leading role in the ANC and became its chairman in 1989. As such he played a significant part in the negotiations with F W de Klerk which led to the dismantling of apartheid.

Mbiti, John Samuel 1931–
Kenyan theologian
He was born in Kenya, and taught theology and comparative religion at Makere University College, Uganda, before becoming director of the World Council of Churches Ecumenical Institute, Bossey, Switzerland (1972–80). He then taught Christianity and African religions at Berne University and was a pastor in Burgdorf, Switzerland. His books, which include *African Religions and Philosophy* (1969), *Concepts of God in Africa* (1970), *The Prayers of African Religion* (1975) and *Bible and Theology in African Christianity* (1987), maintain that the African is naturally religious and that the Christian message should be seen as a fulfilment of traditional African beliefs rather than a rejection of them.

Mboya, Tom (Thomas Joseph) 1930–69
Kenyan trade unionist and politician
Born on a sisal estate in the white highlands of Kenya, he was educated at Holy Ghost College, Mangu and Ruskin College, Oxford. He was an employee of the Nairobi City Council when he became Treasurer of the Kenyan African Union in 1953. He was elected Secretary-General of the Kenyan Federation of Labour in 1955 and a member of Legco in 1957. He was a founder member, and Secretary-General (1960–69), of the Kenyan African National Union (KANU). His reformist instincts brought him into conflict with his fellow Luo, Oginga Odinga, but he eventually won out, forcing Odinga out of KANU after the party's conference at Limuru (1966), thus binding himself closer to Jomo Kenyatta. He was Minister of Labour (1962–63), Minister of Justice and Constitutional Affairs (1963–64), and Minister for Economic Planning and Development (1964–69), when his essentially Fabian philosophy established the 'free enterprise with state regulation' economic system which Kenya epitomizes. He was assassinated in 1969.

Mead, George Herbert 1863–1931
US social psychologist
Born in South Hadley, Massachusetts, he studied at Oberlin College, then at Harvard and the universities of Leipzig and Berlin. He taught at Michigan from 1891 to 1894 before moving to the philosophy department at Chicago (1894–1931). His main interest lay in the theory of the mind, and he was particularly concerned with the notion of the self, and how this is developed through communication with others. His work gave rise to symbolic interactionism, a social science tradition which is concerned with the meanings that people give to the world, and how these are worked out through interpersonal interaction. His books include *The Philosophy of the Present* (1932) and *Mind, Self and Society* (1934, based on his lecture courses).

Mead, Margaret 1901–78
US anthropologist
Born in Philadelphia, she studied with Franz Boas and Ruth Benedict at the graduate school of Columbia University from 1923, gaining her PhD in 1929. She was appointed assistant curator of ethnology at the American Museum of Natural History, New York City, in 1926, associate curator from 1942, and curator from 1964. After expeditions to Samoa and New Guinea, where she studied sexual behaviour and the rites of adolescence among primitive peoples, she wrote *Coming of Age in Samoa* (1928) and *Growing Up in New Guinea* (1930). In later books such as *Male and Female* (1949) and *Growth and Culture* (1951), she argued that personality characteristics, especially as they differ between men and women, are shaped by cultural conditioning rather than heredity. Her work often focused on the relativity of values from culture to culture and implicitly suggested the need to question social standards in the USA and other 'civilized' nations. Her writings proved very popular and made anthropology accessible to a wide public. She was accused of making colossal errors by Derek Freeman in *Margaret Mead and Samoa, The Making and Unmaking of an Anthropological Myth* (1983). 📖 Jane Howard, *Margaret Mead: A Life* (1984)

Meade, George Gordon 1815–72
US soldier
Born in Cadiz, Spain, he trained at West Point and served against the Seminoles and in the Mexican War (1846–48). In the American Civil War he fought at Bull Run and Antietam, after which he was promoted to major-general of volunteers. He led troops at Fredericksburg and at Chancellorsville, and in 1863 he was given command of the Army of the Potomac. He defeated Robert E Lee at Gettysburg but was criticized for failing to press his advantage.

Meade, James Edward 1907–95
English economist and Nobel Prize winner
Born in Swanage, Dorset, he worked for the League of Nations in the 1930s. He was a member (latterly director) of the economic section of the Cabinet Office (1940–46), then Professor of Economics at the London School of Economics (1947–57) and of Political Economics at Cambridge (1957–68) where he remained a resident Fellow until 1974. A prolific writer, his principal contributions have been in the area of international trade, including *The Theory of International Economic Policy* (2 vols, 1951–55), *Principles of Political Economy* (4 vols, 1965–76) and *The Intelligent Radical's Guide to Economic Policy* (1975). He shared the 1977 Nobel Prize for economics with Bertil Ohlin. In the 1980s he was an advisor to the Social Democratic Party (SDP).

Meade, Richard (John Hannay) 1938–
British three-day eventer
Born in Chepstow, Gwent, Wales, he won three Olympic gold medals: the Three Day Event team golds in 1968 and 1972, and the individual title in 1972, on Laurieston. He also won at Burghley (1964) and Badminton (1970, 1982), and won world championship team gold medals (1970, 1982) and European championship team gold medals (1967, 1971, 1981). He published *Fit for Riding* in 1984.

Meagher, Thomas Francis 1822–67
Irish nationalist and US politician
Born in Waterford, he became a prominent member of the Young Ireland Party and a founder-member (1847) of the Irish Federation, and in 1848 was transported for life to Van Diemen's Land ('Tasmania') after an abortive rising. He made his escape in 1852, and made his way to the USA, where he studied law and became a journalist. At the outbreak of the Civil War in 1861 he organized the 'Irish brigade' for the Federals, and fought at Richmond and elsewhere. While secretary of Montana territory he was drowned in the Missouri River.

Meale, Richard Graham 1932–
Australian composer, conductor and teacher
Born in Sydney, he studied at the New South Wales State Conservatorium for Music, and later at the University of California in Los Angeles (1960) where he researched the music of Japan, Java and Bali. Returning to Australia, he made an immediate impact with his compositions *Los Alboradas* (1963) and *Homage to Garcia Lorca* (1964). The influence of Japanese music on him is apparent in *Images: Nagauta* (1966) and *Clouds Now and Then* (1969). Later works, such as *Viridian* (1979) and his second string quartet reflect **Debussy**. His first opera *Voss* (1982, with a libretto by **David Malouf** based on the novel by **Patrick White**) demonstrates the strength of his orchestral and vocal writing. From 1969 he was Reader in Music at Adelaide University.

Meany, George 1894–1980
US labour leader
Born in New York City, he followed his father into the plumbing trade and rose through union ranks to become head of the American Federation of Labor in 1952. He worked to heal the breach with the Congress of Industrial Organizations, and when the two groups merged, he served as the first president (1955–79) of the new federation (the AFL-CIO). Under his leadership, and goaded by the Republican-controlled Congress's passage of the Taft-Hartley Act in 1947, the AFL-CIO abandoned the AFL's policy of political neutrality and made an alliance with the Democratic Party. Meaney became an influential figure on the national political scene, supporting civil rights and the Great Society legislation, as well as, to the dismay of liberals, the Vietnam War. In his administration of the AFL-CIO he was notable for preferring arbitration and lobbying to strikes and picket lines and for his efforts to end corruption among member unions, which led to the expulsion of the Teamsters in 1957.

Mears, Rick 1951–
US professional car racer
Born in Wichita, Kansas, he is four times winner of the Indianapolis 500 (1979, 1984, 1988, 1991), and winner of the Indy Car national championship three times (1979, 1981, 1982). In the 1984 Indy 500 he set a record average speed of 163.612mph (263.301kph). He comes closely behind **A J Foyt**, and Bobby and **Al Unser** in the list of number of wins in a career. His earnings exceed $11 million.

Mechnikov, Ilya Ilyich or Elie See Metchnikoff, Elie

Medawar, Sir Peter Brian 1915–87
British zoologist, pioneering immunologist and Nobel Prize winner
Born in Rio de Janeiro of English-Lebanese parents, he was educated in zoology at Magdalen College, Oxford. During World War II he studied skin grafting for burn victims, where he realized that rejection of a graft occurred by the same immunological mechanism as the response to foreign bodies. He was appointed Professor of Zoology at Birmingham University (1947–51), Jodrell Professor of Comparative Anatomy at University College London (1951–62), and director of the National Institute for Medical Research at Mill Hill from 1962. He investigated the problems of tissue rejection in transplant operations. In 1960 he shared the Nobel Prize for physiology or medicine with Sir **Macfarlane Burnet**, for researches into immunological tolerance. They showed that prenatal injection of tissues from one individual to another resulted in the acceptance of the donor's tissues. His writings include *The Uniqueness of the Individual* (1957), *The Art of the Soluble* (1967) and *Pluto's Republic* (1982). He was elected FRS in 1949 and knighted in 1965. ⨆ Jean Medawar, *A Very Decided Preference: Life with Peter Medawar* (1990)

Medici
Florentine banking family
During the 14th and 15th centuries, starting with Giovanni di Bicci de Médicis (1360–1429), they became public benefactors and patrons of the arts. The Medici remained rulers of Tuscany until its cession to Austria in 1737, but after **Cosimo I, the Great**, achieved little. Francis I (1541–87) began work on what is today the Uffizi gallery. Ferdinand I (1549–1609) developed the port of Livorno (Leghorn), and his daughter **Marie de Médicis** married Henri IV of France, while his son and successor Cosimo II (1590–1621) was the patron of **Galileo**. Both he and his sons, Ferdinand and Leopold, maintained Florence's reputation throughout the first half of the 17th century as a centre for art and learning.

Medici, Caterina de' See Catherine de Médicis

Medici, Cosimo de' 1389–1464
Florentine financier, statesman and philanthropist
His father, Giovanni de' Bicci Medici, appears to have created the Medici wealth, and Cosimo was to use it to fuel the machine of his own power in Florence. He was exiled by the ascendant Albizzi faction in 1433, having opposed the imposition of taxes for what proved a disastrous war. He returned in 1434 and stifled family faction while maintaining the façade of republican government with a mixture of ruthlessness and urbanity. He employed some of his wealth in patronage of the arts, including Europe's first public library, and made the city the centre of the new learning. He was posthumously commemorated as 'Pater Patriae'.

Medici, Cosimo I de', *called* the Great 1519–74
Florentine politician
Duke of Florence from 1537 and Grand Duke of Tuscany from 1569, he possessed the astuteness of his greater predecessors, but was cruel and relentless, though one of the ablest rulers of his century. A skilled soldier, he annexed the republic of Siena in 1555 and doubled the territory of Tuscany during his rule. He devoted his energies to developing the trade, agriculture and economic infrastructure of Tuscany, and to building up its armed forces. At the same time, he was a notable patron of artists and a great collector of Etruscan antiquities.

Medici, Giovanni Angelo de' See Pius IV

Medici, Lorenzo de', *called* the Magnificent 1449–92
Florentine ruler
The son of Piero I de' Medici and grandson of **Cosimo de' Medici**, he succeeded as head of the family upon the death of his father (1469), and was an able, if autocratic, ruler who made Florence the leading state in Italy. In 1478 he showed courage and judgement in thwarting an attempt by the malcontent Pazzi, rival bankers, to overthrow the Medici, with the encouragement of Pope **Sixtus IV**, although the rising led to the assassination of Lorenzo's

brother, Giuliano (1453–78). Lorenzo was a distinguished lyric poet as well as being, in the words of Machiavelli, 'the greatest patron of literature and art that any prince has ever been'. He aroused the criticism of Savonarola for his secular tastes during his later years.

Medici, Maria de' See **Marie de Médicis**

Medici, Piero de', *called* the Unfortunate 1471–1503
Florentine ruler
The eldest son of Lorenzo de' Medici, he succeeded his father (1492), but his disregard of republican forms made him unpopular. With the invasion of Italy by Charles VIII of France (1494), Piero was obliged to surrender key Florentine forces to the aggressor, a step strongly resented by the civic authorities, who banished the Medici from the state, placed a price on Piero's head and permitted the plundering of the Medici palace. Piero died fighting against the French. The Medici did not return to Florence until 1512, when the head of the family was Piero's brother, Giovanni de' Medici.

Medina-Sidonia, Alonzo Pérez de Gusmàn, Duque de 1550–1619
Spanish seaman
Captain-general of Andalusia and one of the wealthiest and most influential men in Spain, he was involved in the conquest of Portugal as well as being an important administrator. Appointed to command the Great Armada in the Enterprise of England on the death of the Marquis of Santa Cruz (1588), he led the Armada successfully up the English Channel to rendezvous with Parma off the Dutch coast, but was thwarted by the latter's failure to break out, by the action of the English fleet as well as by adverse weather.

Medlicott, William Norton 1900–87
English diplomatic historian
Born in Wandsworth, London, he was known especially for his studies of the Bismarck period in international relations, and British diplomacy in the 20th century. Educated at Aske's School, Hatcham, and University College London, he was Professor (later Principal) of History at Exeter University (1939–53) and Stevenson Professor of International History at the London School of Economics (1953–67). Amongst his many publications were *The Congress of Berlin and After* (1938), *British Foreign Policy since Versailles* (1940) and *Bismarck, Gladstone and the Concert of Europe* (1956), as well as a history of British economic warfare against Germany, *The Economic Blockade* (2 vols, 1952–59). He also edited 11 volumes of the multi-volume *Documents on British Foreign Policy, 1919–1939*. The Norton Medlicott Medal, awarded by The Historical Association, was instituted in his honour (1984).

Medtner, Nikolai 1880–1951
Russian composer and pianist
Born in Moscow, he went to live in western Europe in 1922. His classical-romantic compositions included three piano concertos, songs and much piano music.

Medvedev, Roy Aleksandrovich 1925–
Soviet historian, dissident and politician
Although remaining a Marxist, he was highly critical of Stalin and other communist leaders. In 1968 he was expelled from the Communist Party and denied employment in academic bodies. However, he continued writing as a private individual, helping to sustain ideological criticism of Leonid Brezhnev's regime. Under Mikhail Gorbachev he was readmitted to the party and elected to the Congress and the Supreme Soviet in 1989. His best book is considered to be *Let History Judge* (1971). He published *Brezhnev: A Political Biography* in 1991. His twin brother, Zhores Medvedev (1925–), also suffered as a critic of Brezhnev.

Medwall, Henry 1462–c.1505
English dramatist
He wrote *Fulgens and Lucrece*, the earliest extant English secular play written before 1500. Little is known of his life, but he was a chaplain to Cardinal Morton, and held various livings. His only other extant work is a morality play, *Nature*, printed in 1530. 📖 P Hogrefe, *The Thomas More Circle* (1959)

Mee, Arthur 1875–1943
English journalist, editor and writer
Born in Stapleford, Nottingham, he is best known for his *Children's Encyclopaedia* of 1908, which continued as a monthly for 25 years under the name *My Magazine*. He also produced a *Self-Educator* (1906), a *History of the World* (1907), both with Sir John Hammerton (1871–1949), a *Popular Science* (1912), a *Children's Shakespeare* (1926), and *The King's England* (1936–53), a series of topographical books describing the English counties.

Mee, Margaret Ursula 1909–89
English botanical artist and traveller
Born in Chesham, Buckinghamshire, she trained at the Camberwell School of Art, London, and first visited the Amazon forests when she was 47. Ten years later, having settled in Brazil, she began her impressive career as a botanical artist, travelling extensively in the Brazilian Amazonia and collecting new species and painting many others, some of which have since become extinct. She was well known for her outspoken anger at the destruction of the Amazonia, which she called 'a valley of death'. The Margaret Mee Amazon trust was set up in 1988 to draw attention to the area's ecological crisis.

Meegeren, Han or **Henricus van** 1889–1947
Dutch artist and forger
Born in Deventer, in 1945 he was accused of selling art treasures to the Germans. To clear himself he confessed to having forged the pictures, and also the famous *Supper at Emmaus*, 'discovered' in 1937 and accepted by the majority of experts as by Jan Vermeer. His fakes were subjected to a detailed scientific examination, and in 1947 their maker was sentenced to 12 months' imprisonment for forgery. He died a few weeks later, a popular hero.

Meehan, Patrick Connolly 1927–
Scottish criminal
Born in the Gorbals, Glasgow, he spent most of his teenage life in approved schools and in Borstal, for theft. In December 1947 he was arrested and charged with blowing up a safe. He was convicted and sentenced to three years' imprisonment in 1948. Other prison sentences followed. On 14 July 1969, after a routine interview with police in which Meehan admitted that he had been in Ayr on 6 July, two men, who called each other 'Jim' and 'Pat' broke into the Ayr home of Abraham and Rachel Ross. They assaulted the Rosses, and Rachel Ross died of her injuries shortly after. Ross identified Meehan's voice and Meehan was charged. Meanwhile, James Griffiths, a friend of Meehan, who had been on the run, was shot dead by the police, having killed one person and wounded others. Suspicions arose about some of the police evidence, but Meehan was nonetheless found guilty on 24 October. After years of failed appeals, new evidence, confessions from the real killer, and the publication of Ludovic Kennedy's book *A Presumption of Innocence* (1976), Meehan was pardoned.

Meer, Simon van der See **van der Meer, Simon**

Megasthenes fl.300BC
Greek historian

He was ambassador (306–298BC) at the Indian court of Sandrakottos or **Chandragupta**, where he gathered materials for his *Indica*, from which **Arrian, Strabo** and others borrowed.

Mège Mouriés, Hippolyte 1817–80
French chemist and inventor
He was born in Draguignan, and patented margarine in its original form in 1869 after several years of research into the food value of various animal fats. The French government had offered a prize for a satisfactory and economic substitute for butter, which had become very difficult to supply in adequate quantities to the rapidly increasing urban populations and armed forces. Mège Mouriés' margarine was manufactured from tallow, and although he was awarded the prize it was not until F Boudet patented a process for emulsifying it with skimmed milk and water in 1872 that it could be made sufficiently palatable to be a commercial success.

Mehemet 'Ali, *also known as* Muhammad 'Ali
c.1769–1849
Viceroy of Egypt
An Albanian military officer, he was sent to Egypt (1801) with a Turkish-Albanian force to counter the French invasion. After the departure of the French, he supported the Egyptian rulers in their struggles with the Mamluks and had himself proclaimed Viceroy by his Albanians (1805). He formed a regular army, improved irrigation, and introduced elements of European civilization. He reduced part of Arabia (1816), annexed Nubia and part of the Sudan (1820), and occupied various points in the Morea and Crete (1821–28) to aid the Turks in their war with the Greeks. His fleet was defeated at Navarino (1827), but in 1831 the conquest of Syria was begun, and the Ottoman army was defeated at Konya (1832), after which he was given Syria on condition of tribute. The victory at Nezib (1839) might have elevated him to the throne of Constantinople (Istanbul); but the Quadruple Alliance (1840), the fall of Acre to the British, and the consequent evacuation of Syria, compelled him to limit his ambition to Egypt. In 1848 he became insane and was succeeded, for two months, by his son Ibrahim Pasha (1789–1848).

Mehmet I c.1387–1421
Sultan of Turkey
The youngest son of **Bayezit I**, his short reign (from 1413) marks the beginning of the recovery from the devastating effects of the conquests of **Timur**. He made gains in Albania, re-established control over western Anatolia, and put down a religious revolt. He was the father of Sultan Murad II.

Mehmet II, the Conqueror, *also called* Mohammed 1432–81
Sultan of Turkey and founder of the Ottoman Empire
Born in Adrianople (Edirne), he succeeded his father, Murad II, in 1451, and took Constantinople (1453), rebuilding it into a prosperous Ottoman capital, popularly known as Istanbul, and thus extinguishing the Byzantine Empire and giving the Turks their commanding position on the Bosphorus. Checked by **János Hunyadi** at Belgrade (1456), he nevertheless annexed most of Serbia, all of Greece, and most of the Aegean Islands, threatened Venetian territory, was repelled from Rhodes by the Knights of St John (1479), took Otranto (1480) and died in a campaign against Persia (Iran).

Mehmet III 1566–1603
Sultan of Turkey
The son of Murad III, he was born in Manisa, and on his succession in 1595 he invoked the law of fratricide by which the sultan could have his brothers put to death. All

19, of whom the eldest was aged 11, were executed by strangulation. His reign involved wars with Austria and Russia, and revolts in Anatolia.

Mehmet IV 1642–93
Sultan of Turkey
Born in Constantinople (Istanbul), he succeeded his deposed father, Ibrahim I, as a child in 1648, during a war with Venice (1645–64). Anarchy was quelled by the grand viziers, Mohammed Kiuprili (1656) and his son Ahmed (1661). The Turks were defeated by the Austrians under Count Montecucculi at the Battle of St Gotthard (1664), and in a war with Poland (1672–76) they were twice defeated by King **John III Sobieski**, but gained Polish Ukraine, which they lost to Russia (1681). In 1683 under the Grand Vizier Kara Mustafa, they besieged Vienna, which was relieved by John Sobieski. After defeat at the second Battle of Mohacs (1687), Mehmet was deposed, and replaced by **Süleyman II**.

Mehmet VI 1861–1926
Sultan of Turkey
The brother of Mehmet V, he was the last Ottoman sultan (1918–22). Although clever and perceptive, he was unsuccessful in suppressing the nationalists led by Mustafa Kemal (**Kemal Atatürk**), who abolished the sultanate (1922). Mehmet fled to Malta, and after abortive attempts to become ruler in the Hejaz, he died in exile.

Mehta, Ved Parkash 1934–
US writer
He was born in Lahore. Blind from the age of eight, he went to the USA for his education when he was 15 and attended the Arkansas School for the Blind at Little Rock and Pomona College, before going on to Oxford and Harvard universities. While at Pomona he published his first book, the autobiography *Face to Face* (1957). He has had a distinguished career as a journalist, contributing chiefly to the *New Yorker*. Employing amanuenses he has written biographies (*Mahatma Gandhi and His Apostles*, 1977, and *Rajiv Gandhi and Rama's Kingdom*, 1995), stories, essays and portraits of India. His enduring achievement, however, is *Continents of Exile*, an acclaimed series of autobiographical books: *Daddyji* (1972), *Mamaji* (1979), *Vedi* (1982), *The Ledge Between the Streams* (1984), *Sound-Shadows of the New World* (1986), *The Stolen Light* (1989) and *Up at Oxford* (1993). He became a naturalized US citizen in 1975.

Mehta, Zubin 1936–
US conductor
Born into a Parsi family in Bombay, he was taught music by his father, a violinist and conductor of modest pretensions, and later studied at the Vienna Academy of Music, graduating in 1957. After conducting in Liverpool and Montreal, he became musical director of the Los Angeles Philharmonic (1962–78) and the New York Philharmonic (1978–91). Since 1968 he has also served as music director of the Israel Philharmonic, and in 1981 he was named its music director for life. He specializes in late Romantic and early modern music and is known for his flamboyant style and strong technique.

Méhul, Étienne Nicolas 1763–1817
French composer of operas
Born in Givet, he became a professor of the Paris Conservatoire in 1795. Of his numerous operas, *Joseph* (1807) is his most impressive.

Meidner, Ludwig 1884–1966
German painter and lithographer
Born in Bernstadt, Silesia, he moved to Berlin in 1905, and in 1906 visited Paris, where he first saw the work of **Van Gogh**, which impressed him deeply. Although he did not belong to any of the major artistic movements, most of his work has strong links with Expressionism in style

and subject matter. Shortly before the outbreak of World War I he produced a series of apocalyptic visions—scenes of disaster and chaos which were remarkable prefigurations of the horrors to come.

Meidre, Bryan Mac Giolla See Merriman, Bryan

Meighen, Arthur 1874–1960
Canadian politician

Born in Anderson, Ontario, he became a lawyer and sat in the Canadian House of Commons as a liberal Conservative (1908–26). In 1913 he became Solicitor-General in Robert Borden's Union government and was the architect of much of its strategy during World War I: railway nationalization, conscription and the deeply-resented Wartime Elections Act. It was Meighen who also orchestrated the government's draconian response to the Winnipeg General Strike (1919), insisting that organized labour was revolutionary. Both the Immigration Act and the criminal code were amended so that strike leaders would face either deportation or long prison sentences. In 1920 Meighen succeeded Borden as Prime Minister and his high tariff policy was a major factor in the defeat of the Conservative Party in 1921. He became Prime Minister again in 1925 but when the Progressives deserted him, the Governor-General allowed him to dissolve parliament, a mechanism which had not been afforded to Mackenzie King in a similar situation. King won the election by promising to prevent such imperial intervention. Meighen then resigned as Conservative leader a few months later, and was replaced by Richard Bennett. In 1940 the Conservatives invited him to lead the party again but he failed to win a seat and retired from politics.

Meikle, Andrew 1719–1811
Scottish millwright and inventor

Born at Houston Mill, near Dunbar, he inherited his father's mill and showed a keen interest and considerable talent in devising improvements to its machinery. He also turned his attention to the design of windmills, inventing the fantail which kept the sails rotating at right angles to the direction of the wind (1750), a machine for dressing grain (1768), and the 'spring' sail which counteracted the effect of sudden gusts of wind (1772). His most significant invention was a drum threshing machine which could be worked by wind, water, horse or (some years later) steam power. He obtained a patent in 1788 and built a factory to produce them, but as with all his other inventions he made very little profit, and in his old age £1,500 was raised by his friends to alleviate his poverty.

Mei Lanfang 1894–1961
Chinese opera singer and actor

He was born in Yanzhou, Jiangsu (Kiangsu), the son of an actor. He made his stage debut in Beijing (Peking) at the age of 10, and went on to study at the Xi liancheng Dramatic Training School before forming a professional troupe, and establishing his reputation in 1913 in Shanghai as a gifted performer of the 'dan' (female) role. He was the first Chinese actor to perform outside his own country when he appeared to great acclaim in Tokyo (1919), and following this travelled widely abroad. He made his first colour film *Sheng-si-gen* ('The Wedding is a Dream') in 1947, and from 1949 held various prestigious cultural posts. Best known for his female roles in opera, he became China's supreme theatrical performer in the first half of the 20th century and played a major role in preserving the essential heritage of Chinese dramatic art.

Meilhac, Henri 1831–97
French playwright

He was born in Paris, and from 1855 produced a long series of light comedies—some in conjunction with Ludovic Halévy, and some, including *La Belle Hélène*

(1864), well known through Jacques Offenbach's music. His masterpiece is *Frou-Frou* (1869). He also collaborated with Ludovic Halévy and Gille respectively on the libretti of the operas *Carmen* (1875) and *Manon* (1884). 📖 F Gaiffe, *Le rire et la scène française* (1932)

Meillet, Antoine 1866–1936
French philologist

Born in Moulins, he was a great authority on Indo-European languages, and was professor at the École des Hautes Études (1891–1906) and at the Collège de France from 1906. He wrote standard works on Old Slavonic, Greek, Armenian, Old Persian, etc, and on comparative Indo-European grammar and linguistic theory.

Meinhof, Ulrike Marie 1934–76
West German terrorist

Born in Oldenburg, the daughter of a museum director, she campaigned for the creation of a neutral, nuclear-free 'Greater Germany' while studying at Marburg University, and subsequently became a respected left-wing journalist. In 1961 she married the Communist activist, Klaus Rainer Röhl (divorced 1968), by whom she had twin daughters. After an interview with the imprisoned arsonist, Andreas Baader, she became committed to the use of violence to secure radical social change. In May 1970, she helped free Baader and they both then headed an underground urban guerrilla organization, the Red Army Faction, which conducted brutal terrorist attacks against the postwar West German 'materialist order'. As the Faction's chief ideologist, she was arrested in 1972, and in 1974 was sentenced to eight years' imprisonment. She committed suicide in Stammheim high-security prison.

Meinong, Alexius von 1853–1920
Austrian philosopher and psychologist

He was born in Lemberg, Galicia (Ukraine). A disciple of Franz Brentano in Vienna, he became professor at Graz in 1882 and founded there in 1894 Austria's first institute of experimental psychology. His main works were *Über Annahmen* (1902, 'On Assumptions') and *Untersuchungen zur Gegenstandstheorie und Psychologie* (1904, 'Investigation into the theory of objects and psychology'). In the latter he distinguishes sharply between the content and the objects of thoughts and makes further distinctions between different kinds of objects, to the point of paradox if not absurdity—as Bertrand Russell devastatingly demonstrated, wielding 'Ockham's razor'.

Meir, Golda, *née* Goldie Mabovich, *later* Goldie Myerson 1898–1978
Israeli politician

She was born in Kiev, and her family emigrated to Milwaukee, USA, when she was eight years old. She married in 1917 and settled in Palestine in 1921, where she took up social work and became a leading figure in the Labour movement. She was Israeli ambassador to the Soviet Union (1948–49), Minister of Labour (1949–56), and Foreign Minister (1956–66). She was elected Prime Minister in 1969, but her efforts for peace in the Middle East were halted by the fourth Arab–Israeli War (1973) and she resigned in 1974.

Mei Sheng d.140BC
Chinese poet

He is often credited with the introduction of the five-character line. For this reason he is sometimes called 'the father of modern Chinese poetry'. 📖 E von Zach, *Die chinesische Anthologie* (1958)

Meissonier, (Jean Louis) Ernest 1815–91
French painter

Melba, Dame Nellie, *née* Helen Porter Mitchell 1861–1931
Australian operatic soprano and pioneer recording artist

Dame Nellie Melba was born in Richmond, a suburb of Melbourne, Victoria. Her father, David Mitchell (1829–1916), was a building contractor, born the son of a tenant farmer in Forfarshire, Scotland. Helen, as she was called then, studied singing and piano under Madame Ellen Christian, a pupil of **Manuel García**, but after her mother's death the family moved to Queensland where Helen met and married Captain Charles Armstrong, the younger son of a baronet. A boy was born, but Helen grew bored with provincial domesticity and in 1884 she returned to Melbourne to study under Pietro Cecchi (c.1831–1897). She made her professional debut at Melbourne Town Hall in May of that year.

After a visit to London, Helen had an audition in Paris with Madame Mathilde Marchesi (1826–1913), the leading vocal teacher of her time, and took her stage name from her native city. Marchesi added the polish to the fine instrument Cecchi had trained, and tutored Melba in the social graces, removing the Australian rough edges—though Melba retained her forthrightness and earthy speech.

She made her operatic debut at the Théâtre Royal de la Monnaie in Brussels in October 1887 as Gilda in **Verdi**'s *Rigoletto*. Her Covent Garden debut was in May 1888, in the title role of **Donizetti**'s *Lucia di Lammermoor*. That opera's famous 'Mad Scene' was to become one of her popular successes, but her first appearance in London left the critics indifferent.

Her return to Covent Garden the following year was a different story. Under the patronage of society hostess Lady de Grey, Melba was idolized. Covent Garden was in its heyday and Melba sang alongside other great singers such as the Italian tenor **Enrico Caruso**. Melba was a welcome guest in the royal palaces of Europe, and had a brief relationship with the young Duke of Orléans, son of the Pretender to the French throne. Her international career was on its way.

With Caruso, she was one of the artists who made the recording industry, and who were made by it. She recorded on some early cylinders, but her first standard (78rpm) records were issued in 1904, on a special purple label, at the price of 21 shillings. She made her last recordings, in the new electrical process, at her Covent Garden farewell in 1926. Sustained by her strong physique and excellent early training, Melba's numerous 'Farewell' performances were often the cause of amusement.

📖 Melba's memoirs, *Melodies and Memories* (1925, reprinted Melbourne 1980) were ghost-written by the young Beverley Nichols, who later wrote the novel *Evensong* (1932) on the declining years of a prima donna, generally supposed to be based on Melba's career. See also Agnes G Murphy's *Melba, a biography*, with chapters by Madame Melba: 'The Selection of Music as a Profession' and 'The Science of Singing' (1909, reprinted New York 1977). The best modern biography is John Hetherington's *Melba, a biography* (1967).

'If you wish to understand me at all … you must understand first and foremost that I am an Australian.' From *Melodies and Memories*, Ch 1.

In 1901, on the eve of her first tour of Australia, the contralto Dame **Clara Butt** asked Melba's advice on appropriate repertoire. 'All I can say is, sing 'em muck!', Melba is reported to have replied, 'It's all they can understand'. This account was later repudiated by Melba, and became the cause of legal dispute.

Born in Lyons, he specialized in small genre and military scenes of the Napoleonic campaign, eg *Campagne de France 1814* (1864) and *Le Siège de Paris* (1870), both in the Musée d'Orsay, Paris, and *Napoleon and his Staff* (1868, Wallace Collection, London).

Meitner, Lise 1878–1968
Austrian physicist

Born in Vienna and educated at the University of Vienna, she became professor at Berlin University (1926–38) and a member of the Kaiser Wilhelm Institute for Chemistry (1907–38), where she set up a nuclear physics laboratory with **Otto Hahn**, with whom she had discovered the radioactive element protactinium in 1917. In 1938 she fled to Sweden to escape the Nazis, and shortly afterwards Hahn wrote to Meitner concerning his discovery of radioactive barium. With her nephew **Otto Frisch**, she proposed that the production of barium was the result of nuclear fission, later verified by Frisch. Meitner worked in Sweden until retiring to England in 1960. Nuclear physicists recently named the element of atomic number 108 after her. 📖 Deborah Crawford, *Lise Meitner, Atomic Pioneer* (1969)

Mela, Pomponius fl.40AD
Latin geographer

Born in Tingentera, southern Spain, he lived during the reign of the Emperor **Claudius I**. He was the author of an unsystematic compendium entitled *De Situ Orbis* (3 vols, 'A Description of the World').

Melanchthon, Philip, *Greek surname for original name* Schwarzerd ('Black Earth') 1497–1560
German Protestant reformer

Born in Bretten, in the Palatinate, he studied at Heidelberg (1509–11), then Tübingen (1512–14) universities. Appointed Professor of Greek at Wittenberg in 1516, he became **Martin Luther**'s fellow-worker. The Augsburg Confession (1530) was composed by him. After Luther's death he succeeded to the leadership of the German Reformation movement but lost the confidence of some Protestants by concessions to the Catholics. His conditional consent to the introduction of the stringent Augsburg Interim (1549) in Saxony led to painful controversies. His *Loci Communes* (1521) is the first great Protestant work on dogmatic theology.

Melba, Dame Nellie See panel above

Melbourne, William Lamb, 2nd Viscount
1779–1848

English statesman

Born in London and educated at Eton, Trinity College, Cambridge, and Glasgow, he became Whig MP for Leominster in 1805, but in 1827 accepted the chief-secretaryship of Ireland in **George Canning**'s government, and retained it under Viscount **Goderich** (the Earl of Ripon) and **Wellington**. Succeeding as second viscount (1828), he returned to the Whigs, became Home Secretary in 1830, for a few months of 1834, and in 1835, was premier. He was still in office at the accession of Queen **Victoria** (1837). In 1841 he passed the seals of office to **Peel**, and after that took little part in public affairs. His wife (1785–1828), a daughter of the Earl of Bessborough, wrote novels as Lady Caroline Lamb, and was notorious for her nine month's devotion (1812–13) to Lord **Byron**. 📖 Bertram Newman, *Lord Melbourne* (1930)

Melchett, 1st Baron See **Mond, Alfred Moritz**

Melchior, Lauritz Lebrecht Hommel 1890–1973
US tenor
Born in Copenhagen, Denmark, his career began as a baritone in *Pagliacci* ('Clowns') in 1913. From 1918 he appeared as a tenor, making his Covent Garden, London debut in 1924. One of the foremost Wagnerian singers of the century, he sang at Bayreuth (1924–31) and regularly at the New York Metropolitan (1926–50). He became a US citizen in 1947.

Meleager c.140–c.70BC
Greek poet and epigrammatist
From Gadara, Syria, he was the author of 128 exquisite short poems and epigrams included in his *Stephanos* ('Garland'), the first large anthology of epigrams. 📖 C Redinger, *Meleagros von Gadara* (1895)

Meléndez Valdés, Juan 1754–1817
Spanish poet
Born near Badajoz, he became a Professor of Classics at the University of Salamanca, fought for **Napoleon I** in the War of Independence, and held political office in Madrid. Considered the greatest Spanish poet of his time, he is remembered for his odes, ballads and romantic verses. 📖 R Froldi, *Un poeta illuminista* (1967)

Melgund, Viscount See **Minto, Gilbert John Murray Kynynmond-Elliot, 4th Earl of**

Melissus 5th century BC
Greek philosopher and politician
He commanded the Samian fleet which defeated the Athenians under **Pericles** in a battle in 441BC. He was probably a pupil of **Parmenides of Elea** and wrote a book entitled *On Nature* which elaborated Parmenides' views on the properties of reality and which most influenced the atomists, **Democritus** and **Leucippus**, in their response to Eleatic doctrines.

Mellanby, Sir Edward 1884–1955
English pharmacologist
Born in West Hartlepool, Cleveland, he was educated at Cambridge, and in 1907 moved to London to complete his clinical studies at St Thomas's Hospital Medical School, where he became a demonstrator in physiology. In 1913 he was appointed Professor of Physiology at King's College for women, and seven years later became Professor of Pharmacology at Sheffield University and Honorary Physician. He was elected FRS in 1925. He worked on several important biochemical aspects of nutrition at a time when the concept of vitamins was still not universally accepted. He identified vitamin D deficiency as a cause of rickets, and his advocacy of cod-liver oil as a sound source of the vitamin was soon applied, helping to eliminate the then prevalent disease. His studies revealed that lack of vitamin A during embryonic development could result in serious nerve and bone malformation. He was appointed secretary of the Medical Research Council (1933–49), and with his scientist wife **May Mellanby** he continued his laboratory research during and after this administrative period of his life.

Mellanby, Kenneth 1908–
Scottish entomologist and environmentalist
Born in Barrhead, Renfrewshire, and educated at King's College, Cambridge, he researched medical entomology at the London School of Hygiene and Tropical Medicine. During World War II he worked on the transmission of diseases spread in humans by parasitic mites. From 1947 to 1953 he was the first Principal of University College, Ibadan, Nigeria, returning to the UK to head the department of entomology at Rothamstead (1955–61) and to

become the first director of the Nature Conservancy's Monks Wood Experimental Station (1961–74). There he worked mainly on the problems concerned with the effects of agriculture and industry on the environment, particularly the role of pesticides such as DDT. His publications on this topic include *The Biology of Pollution* (1972) and *Waste and Pollution* (1991).

Mellanby, Lady May, *née* **Tweedy** 1882–1978
English nutritional scientist
She was born in London and after spending her early years in Imperial Russia, where her father worked in the oil industry, she entered Girton College, Cambridge, in 1902, and was permitted to attend several lectures not normally open to women. She was awarded the equivalent of a second class honours degree in 1906 and became a lecturer in physiology at Bedford College for women in London. In 1914 she married **Edward Mellanby**, and collaborated with him on several nutritional researches. She also developed an important research line on dental development, showing from animal experiments that vitamins A and D were essential for the proper development of teeth. She was the first woman to present a paper to the British Orthodontics Society (1919). She travelled widely, examining the teeth of adults and children and authored important special reports for the Medical Research Council on the relationship between diet, and dental structure and disease.

Mellis, Margaret 1914–
Scottish painter and constructivist artist
Born in China of Scottish parents, she studied at Edinburgh College of Art under **Samuel John Peploe** and won several awards, including a travelling scholarship that enabled her to visit Spain, France and Italy. Before World War II she studied in London with the Euston Road School. She moved to Cornwall in 1939, and was friendly with the artists **Ben Nicholson**, **Naum Gabo** and **Barbara Hepworth**. Originally a painter, she has also created constructivist collage (a work pieced together rather than moulded, cast or carved) and relief carving. Retrospectives were held in the Nottingham Art Gallery and elsewhere in 1987.

Mellon, Andrew W(illiam) 1855–1937
US financier, philanthropist and politician
Born in Pittsburgh, Pennsylvania, he trained as a lawyer and entered his father's banking house in 1874. He took over in 1882, soon establishing himself as a banker and industrial magnate. Entering politics, he was Secretary of the Treasury from 1921 to 1932 under presidents **Warren G Harding**, **Calvin Coolidge** and **Herbert Hoover** and made controversial fiscal reforms, drastically reducing taxation of the wealthy. He was ambassador to the UK from 1932 to 1933. He endowed the National Gallery of Art at Washington DC. 📖 F D Denton, *The Mellons of Pittsburgh* (1948)

Mellon, Harriot c.1777–1837
English actress
She was born in London and appeared at Drury Lane in 1795. In 1815 she married her elderly protector, **Thomas Coutts**, who left her all his money when he died (1822). In 1827 she married the Duke of St Albans.

Melo, Francisco Manuel de 1608–66
Portuguese writer
Born in Lisbon, he had an arduous and hazardous life as soldier, political prisoner, and exile in Brazil, whence he returned in 1657. He wrote in both Spanish and Portuguese, and is better remembered for his critical works and his history of the Catalan Wars than for his voluminous poetry. 📖 E Prestage, *Don Francisco Manuel de Melo* (1922)

Melvill, Thomas 1726–53
Scottish scientist

He was probably born in Glasgow and studied theology at Glasgow University. His detection of the yellow line of sodium when salt and sal ammoniac were introduced into burning alcohol made no impact on the scientific community, and no other serious investigations were carried out until William Wollaston discovered the dark lines in the Sun's spectrum in 1802. Melvill also attempted to explain why different colours of light bend by different amounts when passing from one medium to another, suggesting that they travel at different speeds. His early death at the age of 27 may explain his lack of influence.

Melville, Andrew, *nicknamed* the Blast 1545–c.1622
Scottish Presbyterian reformer

Born in Baldowie, Angus, he was educated at St Andrews and Paris. In 1568 he became Professor of Humanity at Geneva. On his return to Scotland he was appointed Principal of Glasgow University (1574–80), and did much to reorganize university education, introducing Greek for the first time to a Scottish university. He also had an important share in drawing up the *Second Book of Discipline* (1579). Chosen Principal of St Mary's College in St Andrews in 1580, he taught Hebrew, Chaldee and Syriac besides lecturing on theology. In 1582 he preached boldly against absolute authority before the General Assembly and advocated a presbyterial system of church government, and in 1584, to escape imprisonment, he went to London. He was repeatedly Moderator of the General Assembly of the Church of Scotland. In 1596 he headed a deputation to 'remonstrate' with King James VI (James VI and I), and in 1606, with seven other ministers, was called to England to confer with him. Having ridiculed the service in the Chapel Royal in a Latin epigram, he was summoned before the English Privy Council, and sent to the Tower. In 1611 he was released through the intercession of the Duke of Bouillon, who wanted his services as Professor of Theology in his university at Sedan. His nickname stems from his religious fervour.

Melville, George John Whyte See Whyte-Melville, George John

Melville, 1st Viscount See Dundas, Henry

Melville, Herman 1819–91
US novelist, short-story writer and poet

Born in New York City, he became a bank clerk but, in search of adventure, joined a whaling ship bound for the South Seas. His adventures in the Marquesas and Tahiti inspired his first two books, *Typee* (1846) and *Omoo* (1847). *White Jacket* (1850) drew on his experiences as a seaman on the man-of-war which eventually brought him home. He married in 1847, and after three years in New York took a farm near Pittsfield, Massachusetts, where Nathaniel Hawthorne was his neighbour and friend. It was during this period that he wrote his masterpiece, *Moby-Dick* (1851), a novel of the whaling industry, of extraordinary vigour and colour. Later novels include *Pierre* (1852), in a symbolic vein which was not appreciated by his readers, and *The Confidence Man* (1857). Melville also wrote short stories, most notably 'Benito Cereno' and 'Bartleby the Scrivener', which were collected, with others, in *The Piazza Tales* (1856). Now regarded as one of the USA's greatest novelists, he was not so successful during his life. Exhausted and disillusioned, he wrote only poetry after 1857, and from 1866 he was obliged to work as a New York customs official. Near the end of his life he returned tentatively to fiction with *Billy Budd* (1924), an unfinished but brilliant novella published posthumously. Recognition did not come until some 30 years after his death. 📖 E H Miller, *Herman Melville* (1975); C Olson, *Call Me Ishmael* (1947)

Memlinc or Memling, Hans c.1440–1494
Flemish religious painter

Born in Seligenstadt, Germany, of Dutch parents, he lived mostly in Bruges. A pupil of Roger van der Weyden, he repeated the types of his master. The triptych of the *Madonna Enthroned* at Chatsworth (1468), the *Marriage of St Catherine* (1479) and the *Shrine of St Ursula* (1489), both at Bruges, are among his best works. He was also an original and creative portrait painter.

Memmi, Simone See Martini, Simone

Menaechmus 4th century BC
Greek mathematician

One of the tutors of Alexander the Great, he was the first to investigate conics as sections of a cone.

Menander c.343–c.291BC
Greek comic dramatist and poet

He was born in Athens. His comedies were more successful with cultured than with popular audiences, but Quintilian praised him, and Terence imitated him closely. The greatest writer of Attic New Comedy, he wrote more than a hundred plays, but only a few fragments of his work were known until 1906, when Lefebvre discovered in Egypt a papyrus containing 1,328 lines from four different plays. In 1957, however, the complete text of the comedy *Dyskolos* (Eng trans 1960) was brought to light in Geneva. 📖 O Veh, *Beitrage zu Menander Protektor* (1955)

Menchu, Rigoberta Tum 1959–
Guatemalan activist and Nobel Prize winner

Born near San Marcos, she has worked as a domestic servant and as a cotton-field labourer. Her campaign for human rights began when she was a teenager and later she had to flee to Mexico when her brother and parents were killed by security forces in 1980. In 1983 her book *I Rigoberta Menchu* was published and her cause was taken up by Madame Danielle Mitterrand, wife of President Mitterrand of France. In 1986 Menchu narrated the film *When the Mountains Tremble*, which portrays the difficulties experienced by the native Quiche people. In 1992 she helped to organize opposition to the 500th anniversary of the arrival of Christopher Columbus in America and that same year was awarded the Nobel Peace Prize.

Mencius, *properly* Mengzi or Meng-tzu c.372–c.289BC
Chinese philosopher and sage

Born in Shandong (Shantung), he helped to develop and popularize Confucian ideas and founded a school to promote their study. For over 20 years he travelled China searching for a princely ruler who would put into practice his system of social and political reform. The search was unsuccessful but his conversations with rulers, disciples and others are recorded in a book of sayings which his pupils compiled after his death as the *Book of Mengzi*. His ethical system was based on the belief that human beings were innately and instinctively good but required the proper conditions and support for moral growth. Like Confucius he emphasized the cardinal virtues of magnanimity (*ren*), sense of duty (*yi*), politeness (*li*) and wisdom (*zhi*), and his detailed proposals included practical recommendations about taxes, road maintenance and poor law. 📖 W A Dobson, *Mencius* (1963)

Mencken, H(enry) L(ouis) 1880–1956
US journalist, editor, critic and historian of language

Born in Baltimore, Maryland, he became editor of the *Baltimore Herald*, then joined the *Sunpapers* in 1906. From 1908 to 1923 he worked with the *Smart Set*, and in 1924 he and George Jean Nathan founded the *American Mercury*. He attacked what he called the 'boo-joy' (bourgeois), became a major influence on the US literary scene of the 1920s and supported many writers such as Theodore

Dreiser and Sherwood Anderson. His main work is *The American Language* (1919). *The Vintage Mencken*, edited by Alistair Cooke, appeared in 1955. ▭ Carl Bode, *Mencken* (1969)

Mendel, Gregor Johann 1822–84
Austrian botanist

Born near Udrau, he was ordained a priest in 1847, and after studying science at Vienna University (1851–53), he became an abbot in 1868. In the experimental garden of the monastery, he researched the inheritance characteristics of plants between 1856 and 1863. He crossed species that produced tall and short plants, and the resulting numbers of tall and short plants in subsequent generations led him to suggest that each plant received one character from each of its parents, tallness being 'dominant', and shortness being 'recessive' or hidden, appearing only in later generations. His experiments led to the formulation of 'Mendel's law of segregation' and his 'law of independent assortment'. His concepts have become the basis of modern genetics. ▭ H Iltis, *Gregor Mendel: Leben, Werk und Wirkung* (1924, Eng trans *Life of Mendel*, 1932)

Mendel, Lafayette Benedict 1872–1935
US chemist

Born in Delhi, New York, he was professor at Yale (1897–1935) and did much original work on nutrition, discovering vitamin A (1913) and the function of vitamin C.

Mendeleyev, Dmitri Ivanovich 1834–1907
Russian chemist

He was born in Tobolsk, Siberia, and studied at St Petersburg and Heidelberg, Germany, where he collaborated briefly with Robert Wilhelm Bunsen and investigated the behaviour of gases, formulating the idea of critical temperature. He was appointed professor at the St Petersburg Technical Institute in 1863 and at the University of St Petersburg in 1866. In 1869 he tabulated the elements in ascending order of their atomic weight and found that chemically similar elements tended to fall into the same columns. Several attempts had already been made to group the elements by their chemical properties and to relate chemical behaviour to atomic weight but Mendeleyev's great achievement was to realize that certain elements still had to be discovered and to leave gaps in the table where he predicted they would fall. At first the periodic table was largely rejected by the scientific world, but as each new element that was subsequently discovered fitted into it perfectly, scepticism turned to enthusiasm. However, the underlying reason for the periodicity of the elements remained unexplained until the structure of the atom came to be understood. Mendeleyev continued to refine the table for the next 20 years, meanwhile continuing his work on gases, studying solutions and taking up aeronautical research (he made a solo ascent in a balloon in 1887). The transuranic element mendelevium (atomic number 101) is named in his honour. ▭ Mendeleyev, Daniel Q Posin, *Mendeleyev: The Story of a Great Scientist* (1948)

Mendelsohn, Erich 1887–1953
US architect

Born in Allenstein, Germany (Olszlyn, Poland), he was a leading exponent of functionalism. He designed the Einstein Tower in Potsdam (1919–21) and various factories and department stores. He fled to England in 1933, and designed hospitals. He also designed the Hebrew University at Jerusalem. He emigrated to the USA in 1941, where he designed synagogues and hospitals.

Mendelssohn(-Bartholdy), (Jakob Ludwig) Felix 1809–47
German composer

Born in Hamburg, he made his first public appearance as a pianist at the age of 10. Within the next few years he formed the acquaintance of Goethe, Carl Weber and Ignaz Moscheles, and composed his Symphony in C minor (1824) and the B minor Quartet (1824–25). His *Midsummer Night's Dream* overture (1826) was an early success, and a tour of Scotland in the summer of 1829 inspired the *Hebrides* overture (1830) and the 'Scotch' Symphony. He settled in Berlin in 1841 when the King of Prussia asked him to co-found an Academy of Arts, and in 1843 his new music school at Leipzig was opened, with Schumann and the violinist Ferdinand David among his associates. He produced his *Elijah* in Birmingham in 1846, one of 10 visits to England. His sister's death in 1847 affected him profoundly, and he never recovered. The grandson of Moses Mendelssohn, his father added the name Bartholdy.

Mendelssohn, Moses 1729–86
German Jewish philosopher and biblical scholar

Born in Dessau, he studied in Berlin and went on to become the partner to a silk manufacturer. He is an important figure in the history of Jewish philosophy and in the Enlightenment. His most important works, which reflect his commitment both to Judaism and rationalism, include *Phädon* (1767), an argument for the immortality of the soul, based on Plato's *Phaedo*; *Jerusalem* (1783), which advocates Judaism as the religion of reason; and *Morgenstunden* (1785, 'Morning Hours') which argues for the rationality of belief in the existence of God. He was a friend of Gotthold Lessing and the prototype of his *Nathan*. He was the grandfather of Felix Mendelssohn.

Menderes, Adnan 1899–1961
Turkish statesman

He was born near Aydin. Though trained as a lawyer, he became a farmer, then entered politics in 1932, at first in opposition, then with the party in power under Kemal Atatürk. In 1945 he became one of the leaders of the new Democratic Party and was made Prime Minister when it came to power in 1950. Re-elected in 1954 and 1957, in 1960 he was deposed and superseded by General Cemal Gursel following an army coup. He was put on trial, and hanged.

Mendès, Catulle 1841–1909
French writer

He was born in Bordeaux, of Jewish parentage. One of the Parnassians, a group of French poets advocating an austere and objective poetry, he founded the *Revue fantaisiste* (1859), and later recorded the history of the movement in *La légende du Parnasse contemporain* (1884, 'The Legend of *Le Parnasse contemporain*'). He subsequently turned to Romanticism and wrote poems, novels, dramas and libretti as well as articles and criticism. ▭ A Bertrand, *Catulle Mendès, une biographie critique* (1908)

Mendès-France, Pierre 1907–82
French statesman

Born in Paris, he entered parliament in 1932 as a Radical. In 1941 he made a daring escape from imprisonment in Vichy France and went to England to join the Free French forces. He was Minister for National Economy under de Gaulle in 1945, then opposed him as a prominent member of the Radical Party, and succeeded M Laniel as Prime Minister (1954–55). At a troubled period he handled France's foreign affairs with firmness and decision, but his government was defeated on its North African policy, and he resigned in 1955. A firm critic of de Gaulle, he lost his seat in the 1958 election. He returned to the Assembly in 1967, but retired due to ill health in 1973, later giving much attention to Israeli affairs. ▭ Jean Lacouture, *Pierre Mendès-France* (1981)

Mendoza, Iñigo López de See Santillana, Iñigo López de Mendoza, Marqués de

Menelik II, originally Sahle Miriam or Sahle Mariam 1844–1913
Emperor of Ethiopia
Born in Ankober, Shoa, he became King of Shoa (1865–89) and succeeded John IV as Emperor of Ethiopia (1889). He greatly expanded the Ethiopian empire. He signed the Treaty of Wachile or Uccialli (1889) with the Italians, who interpreted it as giving them a protectorate over Ethiopia. However Menelik defeated them at the Battle of Adowa (1896), perhaps the greatest success of Africans against Europeans in the Partition of Africa. From c.1906 Menelik suffered strokes and power passed eventually to his grandson, Lij Iyasu.

Menem, Carlos Saúl 1935–
Argentine statesman
Born in Anillaco, Argentina, the son of Syrian immigrants, he earned a law degree from Córdoba University in 1958. A follower of **Juan Perón** he was a provincial governor from 1973, and was imprisoned for five years after the military coup in 1976. Elected President in 1989, he addressed Argentina's economic crisis by introducing free-market policies and privatizing state-owned industries. He stabilized the economy and reduced inflation, and in 1995 he won re-election.

Mengistu, Haile Mariam 1941–
Ethiopian soldier and politician
He was born in Addis Ababa and trained at Guenet Military Academy. He took part in the attempted coup against Emperor **Haile Selassie** in 1960, but was not put on trial, and became one of the leaders of the bloody coup that successfully deposed the emperor in 1974 and later abolished the monarchy. He manipulated himself into the chairmanship of the Provisional Military Administrative Council (Dergue) and became undisputed leader and head of state in 1977. Allying himself with the USSR and modelling himself upon Cuba's **Fidel Castro**, he sought to create a Socialist state in Ethiopia, while retaining its territorial borders intact. Civilian rule was formally established in 1987, when he became Ethiopia's first President, but mismanagement, drought and internal war weakened his hold on the country and in 1991 he was overthrown by the Ethiopian People's Revolutionary Democratic Front (EPRDF). He resigned and fled to Zimbabwe, where he was offered political asylum. In 1994 he was tried *in absentia* in Ethiopia and found guilty of genocide and war crimes.

Mengs, Anton Raphael 1728–79
German painter
Born in Aussig in Bohemia, the son of a Danish artist, he eventually settled at Rome, turned Catholic and directed a school of painting. A close friend of **Johann Winckelmann**, he became the most famous of the early Neoclassical painters. In Madrid (1761–70 and 1773–76) he decorated the dome of the grand salon in the royal palace with the *Apotheosis of the Emperor Trajan*.

Mengzi See Mencius

Menken, Adah Isaacs, *née* Adah Bertha Theodore c.1835–1868
US actress
She was born near New Orleans and appeared on stage in New York in 1859. She later appeared in *Mazeppa* with immense success in Albany (1861), New York, London (1864) and elsewhere. She had many husbands, and many literary friends, including **Dickens**. No reports of her acting ability are extant and her reputation rests, apparently, on her stage appearance in *Mazeppa*, in a state of virtual nudity and bound to the back of a wild horse.

Mennin, Peter 1923–83
US composer
Born in Erie, Pennsylvania, he studied at the Eastman College of Music and rapidly established himself as a composer of large-scale works. He composed nine symphonies, including *The Cycle*, for which he wrote the text, concertos, choral and chamber music.

Menninger, Karl Augustus 1893–1990
US psychiatrist
He was born in Topeka, Kansas, where he and his father, Charles Frederick (1862–1953), founded the Menninger Clinic for psychiatric research and therapy in 1920. His brother, William Claire (1899–1966), joined the clinic in 1926, and it soon became one of the major psychiatric centres in the USA. The Menninger Foundation was established in 1941 to fund clinics and sponsor public education in psychiatry.

Menno Simons 1496–1561
Dutch Anabaptist leader, and founder of the Mennonite sect
Born in Friesland, and ordained a Catholic priest (1524), he left the Church after being influenced by the ideas of **Martin Luther** (1536). He was made an elder at Groningen (1537), and organized Anabaptist groups in northern Europe that were persecuted by Catholics and Protestants alike. Mainly resident in the USA, the evangelical Mennonite sect named after him practises adult baptism, excommunication, close adherence to the New Testament, restriction of marriage to members of the group, and refusal to hold civic office.

Menon, V(engalil) K(rishnan) Krishna See Krishna Menon, V(engalil) K(rishnan)

Menotti, Gian-Carlo 1911–
US composer
Born in Milan, he settled in the USA at the age of 17, achieving international fame with a series of operas that began with *Amelia goes to the Ball*, produced in 1937 at Philadelphia, where he was a student. He writes his own libretti, and his other works, including *The Medium* (1946), *The Consul* (1950, Pulitzer Prize), *Amahl and the Night Visitors* (1951) composed for television performance, *The Saint of Bleecker Street* (1954, Pulitzer Prize), *Maria Golovin* (1958) and *The Most Important Man* (1971) have great theatrical effectiveness, with a musical style derived from a wide variety of models. In 1958 he founded the Festival of Two Worlds in Spoleto, Italy. ▢ John Gruen, *Menotti: A Biography* (1978)

Menshikov, Aleksandr Danilovich c.1660–1729
Russian field marshal and statesman
Born of poor parents in Moscow, he entered the army, and accompanied **Peter I, the Great**, in his travels. He played an important part during the war with Sweden (1702–13), and at the capture of Marienburg found and introduced to the tsar the girl who became **Catherine I**. Menshikov lost favour towards the end of Peter's reign, but when Peter died he secured the succession of Catherine, and during her reign and that of her young successor, **Peter II**, he governed Russia with almost absolute authority. He was about to marry his daughter to the young tsar when the jealousy of the old nobility led to his banishment to Siberia and the confiscation of his estates.

Menshikov, Aleksandr Sergeyevich 1789–1869
Russian general
The great-grandson of **Aleksandr Danilovich Menshikov**, he rose to the rank of general in the Napoleonic campaigns of 1812–15. Seriously wounded at Varna in the Turkish campaign of 1828, he was made head of the Russian navy. His overbearing behaviour and incompetent diplomacy as ambassador at Constantinople (Istanbul) contributed greatly

to the outbreak of the Crimean War (1854–56). He commanded at Alma and Inkerman, and defended Sebastopol, but in 1855 was recalled because of illness.

Menuhin, Yehudi Menuhin, Baron 1916–99
British violinist

Born in New York, USA, he appeared as a soloist with the San Francisco Symphony Orchestra at the age of seven. In 1932 he recorded Elgar's Violin Concerto, conducted by the composer, and subsequently appeared all over the world. After 18 months' retirement for study he continued his career as a virtuoso, gaining an international reputation. During World War II he gave concerts to the troops, and after the war settled in England, beginning to conduct in 1957. In the same year, he set up the Gstaad Festival, and in 1963 he founded the Yehudi Menuhin School of Music for musically talented children. Noted also for raising the profile of Indian music in the West, he was awarded an honorary KBE in 1965 and Order of Merit in 1987. He published his autobiography in 1977. He took British citizenship in 1985 and was made a life peer in 1993. His sister Hephzibah (1920–81) was a gifted pianist. ▢ Robert Magidoff, *Yehudi Menuhin* (1955)

Menzel, Donald Howard 1901–76
US astrophysicist

Born in Florence, Colorado, and educated at the universities of Denver and Princeton, he joined the staff of the Lick Observatory in California and was appointed director of the Harvard College Observatory (1954–66). He did valuable work on planetary atmospheres and on the composition of the Sun.

Menzel, Wolfgang 1798–1873
German critic and historian

Born in Waldenburg, Silesia, he studied at Jena and Bonn, but from 1825 lived mainly in Stuttgart. He edited magazines, and wrote poems, novels, histories of German literature and poetry, a history of the world, literary criticism and polemics.

Menzies, John Ross 1852–1935
Scottish wholesale publisher and distributor

Born in Edinburgh, he joined his father's business in Princes Street, Edinburgh, and with his brother pushed the firm westwards, opening a branch in Glasgow in 1868. This was followed by establishing bookstalls in almost all towns of significance. He directed the creation of a huge network of railway station bookstalls, a lucrative development that raised the firm to a position second only to W H Smith in size. By the time of his death he had built up Scotland's leading organization in the book, periodical and newspaper retailing and wholesale trade, becoming, in the process, a household name.

Menzies, Sir Robert Gordon 1894–1978
Australian statesman

Born in Jeparit, Victoria, he practised as a barrister before entering politics, becoming a member of the Victoria parliament in 1928. He went to the Federal House of Representatives in 1934, sitting as MP for Kooyang. He was Commonwealth Attorney-General (1935–39), Prime Minister (1939–41), and Leader of the Opposition (1943–49), when he again took office as premier of the coalition government. He continued as Prime Minister, exploiting the factionalism of his Labor opponents, and held office for a record 16 years, during which time Australia's economy grew and prospered. In 1956 he headed the Five Nations Committee which sought to settle the Suez question with Gamal Nasser. His final years were marked by Australia's entry into the Vietnam War. A powerful orator and declared Anglophile, he succeeded Winston Churchill as Lord Warden of the Cinque Ports (1965), and retired from parliament in 1966.

Merbecke, John See Marbeck, John

Mercator, Gerardus, *originally* Gerhard Kremer
1512–94
Flemish geographer and map-maker

Born in Rupelmonde, Flanders, he graduated at Louvain in philosophy and theology. He studied mathematics, astronomy and engraving, and produced a terrestrial globe (1536) and a map of the Holy Land (1537). In 1544 he was imprisoned for heresy, but released for lack of evidence. In 1552 he settled at Duisburg in Germany, becoming cosmographer to the Duke of Cleves, and produced maps of many parts of Europe, including Great Britain. To aid navigators, in 1569 he introduced a map projection (Mercator's map projection), in which the path of a ship steering on a constant bearing is represented by a straight line on the map; it has been used for nautical charts ever since. In 1585 he published the first part of an 'Atlas' of Europe, said to be the first use of the word to describe a book of maps. It was completed by his son in 1595. On the cover was a drawing of Atlas holding a globe on his shoulders, hence 'atlas' became applied to any book of maps. ▢ A S Osley, *Mercator* (1969)

Mercator, Nicolaus, *German* Kaufmann
c.1620–1687
German mathematician and astronomer

As an engineer he planned the fountains at Versailles and as a mathematician he was one of the discoverers of the series for log $(1 + x)$. From 1660 he lived in England.

Mercer, David 1928–80
English dramatist

He was born in Wakefield, Yorkshire, and after studying painting at King's College, Newcastle, he moved to Europe and began to write. His first television play, *Where the Difference Begins* (1961), signalled his interest in fusing the personal and the political in work that challenged the conventions of television drama. Further plays, like *A Climate of Fear* (1962), *A Suitable Case for Treatment* (1962) and *In Two Minds* (1967), explored his fascination with mental health, psychiatry and his struggle to reconcile a belief in socialism with the repression he saw in Eastern Europe. His stage work includes *Ride A Cock Horse* (1965), *Flint* (1970) and *Cousin Vladimir* (1978). His film scripts include *Morgan* (1965) and *Providence* (1977). He continued to address issues of personal alienation and the class system in later television plays like *Huggy Bear* (1976), *The Ragazza* (1978) and *Rod of Iron* (1980). ▢ Paul Madden (ed), *Where the Difference Began* (1981)

Mercer, John 1791–1866
English dye chemist

He was born in Blackburn, Lancashire. Self-educated, he became a partner in a dye-works at the age of 16 and was subsequently employed in the colour shop of Fort Brothers printworks at Oakenshaw. In 1813 he discovered how to make a good orange dye for calico, using antimony, and he went on to develop or improve a number of other dyes. He became a partner in Fort Brothers and when the printworks was sold profitably, he devoted himself to research. He is chiefly known for inventing the process, named 'mercerization', which gives cotton a lustre resembling silk. It was patented in 1850, and in 1852 Mercer was elected FRS.

Merchant, Ismail 1936–
Indian film producer

Born in Bombay, he studied at St Xavier's College and earned a master's degree in business administration at New York University. He co-produced the short film *The Creation of Woman* (1960) and in 1961 teamed with director James Ivory to make a series of feature films reflecting aspects of Indian culture and the legacy of colonial rule. These include *Shakespeare Wallah* (1965), *Bombay Talkie*

(1970) and *The Autobiography of a Princess* (1975). One of the most successful and enduring independent production units, Merchant–Ivory have latterly become synonymous with sensitive literary adaptations like *A Room With a View* (1985), *Howards End* (1992) and *The Remains of the Day* (1993). Merchant has also published cookbooks and directed feature films, including *In Custody* (1993) and *The Proprietor* (1996).

Merckx, Eddy, *known as* the Cannibal 1945–
Belgian racing cyclist

He was born in Woluwe St Pierre, near Brussels. In the 1969 Tour de France he won the major prizes in all three sections: overall, points classification and King of the Mountains. He won the Tour de France five times (1969–72, and 1974), and now shares the record with **Jacques Anquetil, Bernard Hinault** and **Miguel Indurain**. He also won the Tour of Italy five times, and all the major classics, including the Milan–San Remo race seven times. He was the world professional road race champion three times. He won more races (445) and more classics than any other rider, before retiring in 1978.

Mercouri, Melina, *originally* Anna Amalia Mercouri 1923–1994
Greek film actress and politician

Born in Athens, she began her film career in 1955, and found fame in 1960 with *Never on Sunday*. Always politically involved, she was exiled from Greece (1967–74), so she played in British and US productions, such as *Topkapi* (1964) and *Gaily, Gaily* (1969). She returned to be elected to parliament in 1977, and was Minister of Culture and Sciences (1981–85) and of Culture, Youth, and Sports (1985–90).

Mercury, Freddie, *originally* Frederick Bulsara 1946–92
British pop singer

Born in Zanzibar, he became a naturalized British citizen. With guitarist Brian May (1947–), bassist John Deacon (1951–) and drummer Roger Taylor (originally Roger Meadows-Taylor, 1949–), he formed the group Queen. A darling of the fans yet seldom of the critics, Mercury developed an increasingly camp stage presence (ermine robes and crown, tight trousers) that obscured the forcefulness of his vocal delivery. The formula was successful first in the song 'Seven Seas of Rhye' on their second album *Queen II* (1974), and then on the number-two hit 'Killer Queen' (1974). 'Bohemian Rhapsody' (1975), a bizarre six-minute epic embracing opera, heavy metal and four-part harmony, has a permanent place in rock history, and started the pop video boom. Later work includes 'We Are the Champions' (1977) and 'Radio Gaga' (1984). Mercury disappeared from view in the early 1990s, eventually succumbing to AIDS.

Meredith, George 1828–1909
English novelist

Born in Portsmouth, Hampshire, he was educated privately in Germany. In London, after being articled to a solicitor, he turned to journalism and letters, his first venture appearing in *Chambers's Journal* in 1849, the year in which he married Mary Ellen Nicolls, daughter of **Thomas Love Peacock**. This disastrous marriage gave him an insight into relations between the sexes, which appear as largely in his work as his other great interest, natural selection as Nature's way of perfecting man. His writing did not bring him much financial reward and he had to rely on his articles in *The Fortnightly* and his work as a reader in the publishing house of Chapman and Hall. His prose works started with a burlesque Oriental fantasy, *The Shaving of Shagpat* (1855), followed in 1859 by *The Ordeal of Richard Feverel*, but he did not achieve general popularity

as a novelist until *Diana of the Crossways* appeared in 1885. Other popular titles include *Evan Harrington* (1860), *Harry Richmond* (1871), and best of all, *Beauchamp's Career* (1875), which poses the question of class and party and is well constructed and clearly written. This cannot be said of his later major novels, *The Egoist* (1879), a study of refined selfishness, and *The Amazing Marriage* (1895). These two powerful works are marred by the artificiality and forced wit which occurs in so much of his poetry. His main poetic work is *Modern Love* (1862), a novelette in pseudo-sonnet sequence form, based partly on his first marriage. *Poems and Lyrics of the Joy on Earth* (1883) again discussed his master themes—the 'reading of earth' and the sex duel. *A Reading of Life* (1901) adds little to the record. The modern revaluation of the Victorians has enhanced the fame of this very cerebral poet. ⊞ L Stevenson, *The Ordeal of Meredith* (1954)

Meredith, James Howard 1933–
US civil rights advocate

Born in Kosciusko, Mississippi, he served in the air force and began his undergraduate studies at Jackson State College, a black institution. After being rejected by the University of Mississippi, which had admitted only whites during its 114-year history, he filed a lawsuit against them with the aid of the NAACP (National Association for the Advancement of Colored People) and won admission for his senior year in the fall of 1962. His appearance on campus provoked rioting, but he completed the year under federal guard and became the university's first African-American graduate in 1963.

Meredith, Owen See Lytton, (Edward) Robert Bulwer-Lytton, 1st Earl of

Merezhkovsky, Dmitri Sergeyevich 1865–1941
Russian novelist, critic and poet

He was born in St Petersburg, and studied philology and history at the university there before turning to writing. He wrote a collection of poetry (1888), a historical trilogy *Khristos i Antikhrist* (1896–1905, 'Christ and Antichrist') and books on **Tolstoy, Ibsen**, and **Nikolai Gogol**. He opposed the Revolution in 1917 and fled to Paris in 1919, where he continued to write historical novels, including one on Jesus (1932–33) and another on **Dante** (1939). His wife was Zinaida Gippius (1870–1945). ⊞ C Bedford, *Dmitri Sergeyevich Merezhkovski and the Silver Age* (1975)

Mergenthaler, Ottmar 1854–99
US inventor

Born in Hachtel, Germany, he was a watchmaker's apprentice at the age of 14 and attended technical school in the evenings. He went to the USA in 1872 and became a US citizen in 1878. He invented the Linotype typesetting machine (patented in 1884).

Merikanto, Aarre 1893–1958
Finnish composer

Born in Helsinki, he was the son of the notable song-composer Oskar Merikanto (1868–1924). He studied in Helsinki, with **Max Reger** in Leipzig, and in Moscow (where **Aleksandr Scriabin**'s music influenced him). His compositions of the 1920s display great individuality, but they were largely unrecognized in his lifetime. His major work, the opera *Juha* (1922), was premiered only in 1963. From 1936 till his death he was an influential teacher at the Sibelius Academy.

Mérimée, Prosper 1803–70
French novelist

Born in Paris, the son of a painter, he studied law, visited Spain in 1830, and held posts under the ministries of the Navy, Commerce and the Interior. He was appointed Inspector-General of historical remains in France in 1833, and became a senator in 1853. He wrote novels, short stories, archaeological and historical dissertations, and travel stories, all of which display exact learning, keen observation, real humour, and an exquisite style. Among his novels are *Colomba* (1841, Eng trans 1856), *L'Abbé Aubain* (1846, Eng trans *The Abbé Aubain*, 1903), *Carmen* (1847, Eng trans 1878), *Arsène Guillot* (1852) and *La Chambre bleue* (1866, 'The Blue Room'). His letters include the famous *Lettres à une inconnue* (1873, 'Letters to an Unknown Woman'), the *Lettres à une autre inconnue* (1875, 'Letters to Another Unknown Woman') and the letters to the bibliographer **Anthony Panizzi** (1881). He also wrote some plays. His last years were clouded by ill health and melancholy, and the downfall of the Second Empire hastened his death. 📖P Léon, *Mérimée et son temps* (1962)

Merle, Jean Henri d'Aubigné 1794–1872
Swiss historian

Born in Eaux-Vives, near Geneva, he studied at Berlin under the German historian and theologian Johann Neander (1789–1850), and in 1818 became pastor of the French Protestant church in Hamburg. In 1823 he was appointed court preacher at Brussels. Returning to Geneva, he took part in the institution of the new Evangelical Church, and held its chair of church history until his sudden death. His works include *Histoire de la Réformation du XVIe siècle* (1835–53), *Germany, England, and Scotland* (1848), a vindication of **Cromwell** (1848), *Trois siècles de lutte en Écosse* (1849) and *Histoire de la Réformation en Europe au temps de Calvin* (1863–78).

Merleau-Ponty, Maurice 1908–61
French phenomenological philosopher

Born in Rochefort-sur-mer, Charente-Maritime, he studied in Paris, taught in various lycées, served as an army officer in World War II, and then held professorships at Lyons (1948) and the Sorbonne, Paris (from 1949). With **Jean-Paul Sartre** and **Simone de Beauvoir** he helped found the journal *Les Temps modernes* (1945), and he travelled with Sartre in the Communist Party during the early postwar years, becoming disillusioned and more detached after the Korean War. His philosophical works include *La Structure du comportement* (1942, 'The Structure of Behaviour') and *Phénoménologie de la perception* (1945, 'The Phenomenology of Perception'). They investigate the nature of consciousness, and reject the extremes of both behaviouristic psychology and subjectivist accounts; the world is neither wholly 'given' nor wholly 'constructed' for the perceiving subject, but is essentially ambiguous and enigmatic. 📖Albert Rabil, *Merleau-Ponty: Existentialist of the Social World* (1967)

Merman, Ethel Agnes, née Zimmerman 1909–84
US actress and singer

Born in Astoria, New York, she had no formal musical training, but her powerful, brassy voice and energy as a performer won her immediate success when she made her Broadway debut in **George Gershwin's** *Girl Crazy* in 1930, and she was a musical comedy star for the next three decades. She appeared in several **Cole Porter** shows, including *Anything Goes* (1934), and *Du Barry Was a Lady* (1939). She also starred in *Annie Get Your Gun* (1946), introducing the song 'There's No Business Like Show Business', which became her trademark, and won praise as the indomitable stage mother in *Gypsy* (1959).

Merovech or Merovius 5th century AD
Frankish ruler

The grandfather of **Clovis**, he fought against **Attila** the Hun and gave his name to the Merovingian dynasty.

Merovius See Merovech

Merriam, Clinton Hart 1885–1942
US naturalist, zoologist and conservationist

Born in New York City, he was a physician by training, but became interested in natural history and travelled with the Hayden Geological Surveys (1872–76). In 1888 he helped to found the National Geographical Society (which subsequently became the Fish and Wildlife Service) and was its head between 1885 and 1910. He is best known for devising a scheme of distinct life zones based upon temperature differences, which is described in *Life Zones and Crop Zones of the United States* (1898). He latterly joined the staff of the Smithsonian Institution (1919–37) and collected ethnographic data on Native American tribes.

Merrifield, (Robert) Bruce 1921–
US chemist and Nobel Prize winner

Born in Fort Worth, Texas, he obtained both his BA (1943) and PhD (1949) from the University of California at Los Angeles. He joined the Rockefeller Institute for Medical Research in 1949, and was appointed assistant professor at Rockefeller University in New York City in 1957, full professor in 1966 and John D Rockefeller, Jnr Professor in 1984. He devised (1959–62) the important 'solid-phase' method for synthesizing peptides and proteins from amino acids. This process has now been automated and computer controlled, allowing the ready synthesis of small quantities of quite large proteins. He was awarded the Nobel Prize for chemistry for this work in 1984.

Merrill, James Ingram 1926–95
US poet

Born into the upper class in New York City (his father was a partner in a wealthy brokerage firm), he was raised in Greenwich Village and attended Amherst College. Though he wrote two plays and two novels, he is best known for his poetry—metrically inventive meditations on memory and lost time, in which his own urbane and witty voice can be distinctly heard. His later work reflects his sometimes playful, sometimes genuine interest in the occult, which led him to use a Ouija board to communicate with the poets of the past. His collections include *Nights and Days* (1966), *Divine Comedies* (1976, Pulitzer Prize), and *The Changing Light at Sandover* (1982, revised 1992), an epic poem in three parts which records his interest in the spirit world. His book of memoirs, *A Different Person*, was published in 1993.

Merrill, Stuart Fitzrandolph 1863–1915
US Symbolist poet

Born in Hempstead, Long Island, New York, he was educated in Paris, where he lived from 1889. His French poems *Les gammes* (1895), *Les quatre saisons* (1900), and others developed the musical conception of poetry, and made full use of alliteration. *Une voix dans la Foule* (1909) espouses a strongly democratic sympathy which is unmistakably American. 📖M L Henry, *Stuart Merrill, sa vie, sa œuvre* (1929)

Merriman, Bryan, English name of Bryan Mac Giolla Meidre 1747–1805
Irish Gaelic poet

Born in Ennistymon, County Clare, he became a schoolteacher and small farmer in Feakle, later settling in Limerick as a mathematics teacher. His reputation depends on a 1,000-line mock-heroic epic, traditional in its use of dream-vision, but satirical and feminist in content: *Cúirt an Mheáin Oidhche* (c.1786, Eng trans *The Midnight Court* by **Frank O'Connor** in the *Penguin Book of Irish Verse*, 1970). It is an attack on Irish Catholic puritanism, greatly praised by O'Connor, one of its many translators. The poem was banned in all English translations after Irish independence, but the Irish language itself was deemed incapable of being a corrupting influence. Liberal Irish intellectuals have established an annual Merriman Summer School, convening in August in Clare.

Merritt, William H 1793–1862
Canadian entrepreneur

He built the Welland Canal, bypassing the Niagara cataract, to provide a major route for exports and imports into the American–Canadian interior. The canal was completed by 1829 but essential improvements were not completed until 1848, when the US railways provided a satisfactory alternative which Canadians were ready to use. Merritt was also one of the foremost proponents of reciprocity.

Mersenne, Marin 1588–1648
French mathematician and scientist

Born in Oize, Maine, he became a Minim Friar in 1611, and lived in Paris. Devoting himself to science, he corresponded with all the leading scientists of his day including Descartes, Pierre de Fermat, Pascal and Thomas Hobbes, acting as a clearing house for scientific information. He experimented with the pendulum and found the law relating its length and period of oscillation, studied the acoustics of vibrating strings and organ pipes and measured the speed of sound. He also wrote on music, mathematics, optics and philosophy.

Merton, Robert King 1910–
US sociologist

Born in Philadelphia, he was educated at Temple and Harvard universities. He taught at Harvard (1934–39) and Tulane University (1939–41), before joining the department of sociology at Columbia University (1941–79). He was also associate director of the Bureau of Applied Social Research, collaborating with Paul Lazarsfeld. His work emphasizes the connections between theory and empirical evidence, and he is regarded as the founder of the sociology of science in its modern form. His works include *Social Theory and Social Structure* (1949), *On Theoretical Sociology* (1967), *Science, Technology and Society in Seventeenth-Century England* (1938, 1970), *The Sociology of Science* (1973) and *The Sociology of Science in Europe* (1977).

Merton, Thomas 1915–68
US Cistercian monk

Born in Prades, France, of an English father and a US mother, he studied and taught English at Columbia, but in 1938 he became a convert to Roman Catholicism and in 1941 joined the Trappist order at Our Lady of Gethsemane Abbey, Kentucky. His bestselling autobiography, *The Seven Storey Mountain* (1946), prompted many to become monks, but Merton himself was to discover intense tensions between his hermitic inclinations and community living. However, ways were found for him to follow his vocation and at the same time keep up a voluminous correspondence and write many books, ranging from personal journals and poetry to social criticism, and some of the best popular books on Zen Buddhism. As a poet he is respected as a minor practitioner in the tradition of Thomas Traherne and Gerard Manley Hopkins. He was electrocuted in an accident.

Merton, Walter de d.1277
English prelate

Born probably in Surrey, he founded Merton College, Oxford (1264), the prototype of the collegiate system in English universities. He was Bishop of Rochester from 1274.

Mesdag, Hendrik Willem 1831–1915
Dutch marine painter

Born in Groningen, he settled at The Hague, where his personal collection is housed in the Mesdag Museum.

Meselson, Matthew Stanley 1930–
US molecular biologist

Born in Denver, Colorado, he studied chemistry at the California Institute of Technology (Caltech) and was Professor of Biology at Harvard from 1964. With F W Stahl in 1957 he carried out some ingenious experiments which both verified James Dewey Watson and Francis Crick's ideas on the way the double helix of the DNA molecule carries genetic information, and gave new information on the details.

Mesmer, Franz Anton 1734–1815
Austrian physician and founder of mesmerism

Born near Constance, he studied medicine at Vienna, and about 1772 claimed that there exists a power, which he called 'magnetism', that could be used to cure diseases. His treatment, activated by a magnetized object, aimed to facilitate the flow of an invisible fluid around the body; known as 'mesmerism', it was the forerunner of hypnotism. In 1778 he was accused of fraud and went to Paris, where he created a sensation. However, in 1785 a learned commission appointed by King Louis XVI reported unfavourably, and he retired into obscurity in Switzerland. 📖 Vincent Buranelli, *The Wizard From Vienna* (1976)

Messager, André Charles Prosper 1853–1929
French composer

Born in Montluçon, he composed largely operettas, of which *La Basoche* (1890) was his best. His works also, however, include several ballets and piano pieces. He was artistic director of Covent Garden Theatre, London (1901–07) and director of the Opéra Comique, Paris (1898–1903, 1919–20).

Messalina, Valeria c.25–c.48AD
Roman matron

She was the third wife of the Emperor Claudius I, whom she married at the age of 14. She bore him two children, Octavia (the wife of Nero) and Britannicus. Her name became a byword for avarice, lust and cruelty, to which only Claudius was blind. In the emperor's absence she publicly married one of her favourites, the consul-designate Silius, and the emperor had her executed.

Messerer, Asaf Mikhailovich 1903–92
Russian dancer, teacher and choreographer

Born in Vilnius, into a ballet family, he studied with Mikhail Mordkin and Gorsky at the Bolshoi Ballet School, graduating in 1921 to join the company. A versatile principal, he retired from dancing in 1954 to concentrate on teaching, the element of his work for which he is best known. His choreography includes *Football Player* (1924) and *Ballet School* (1962).

Messerschmitt, Willy (Wilhelm) 1898–1978
German aviation designer and engineer

Born in Frankfurt am Main, he studied at the Munich Institute of Technology, and in 1923 established the Messerschmitt aircraft manufacturing works. His ME-109 set a world speed record in 1939, and during World War II he supplied the Luftwaffe with its foremost types of combat aircraft. In 1944 he produced the ME-262 fighter, the first jet-plane flown in combat. From 1955 he continued his activities with the revived Lufthansa and later also entered the car industry. 📖 Anthony Pritchard, *Messerschmitt* (1974)

Messiaen, Olivier Eugène Prosper Charles 1908–92
French composer and organist

Born in Avignon, he studied under Duprè and Paul Dukas, and taught at the Schola Cantorum (from 1936). In 1941 he became Professor of Harmony at the Paris Conservatoire. He composed extensively for organ, orchestra, voice and piano, and made frequent use of new instruments such as the Ondes Martenot. He is best known outside France for the two-and-a-half-hour piano work, *Vingt regards sur l'enfant Jésus* (1944, '20 Looks at the Child Jesus'), and the *Turangalila* Symphony (1946–48), which makes use of Indian themes and rhythms. His music, which evolved new methods of pitch organization and intricate mathematical rhythmic systems, was often inspired by religious mysticism. His interest in birdsong provided the stimulus for several works including the *Catalogue d'oiseaux* for piano (1956–58). Other works include an oratorio *La Transfiguration de Notre Seigneur Jésus-Christ* (1965–69), an opera *St François d'Assise* (1975–83) and *Technique de mon language musical* (2 vols, 1944, Eng trans 1957).

Messier, Charles 1730–1817
French astronomer
Born in Badonville, Lorraine, he began his life as an astronomer in 1751 in Paris. He observed the return of Halley's comet in 1759 and from that time onwards was an avid searcher of comets, discovering independently a total of 13 of them. He mapped the faint unmoving nebulous objects in the sky which he could discard in comet-searching, and drew up a catalogue of 103 entries (1781) by which his name is perpetuated in astronomy. Messier's objects, known by the prefix M and their catalogue number, comprise nebulae, galaxies and star clusters. The 'ferret of comets', as he was nicknamed by Louis XV, was elected to the Royal Society (1764) and the Paris Academy of Sciences (1770).

Messmer, Otto 1894–1985
US animator
Born in New Jersey, he contributed joke cartoons to *Life* magazine (1914) and entered animation in 1916, scripting and animating many films including the *Charlie Chaplin* cartoons (1917). In 1920 he created *Feline Follies*, the first Felix the Cat cartoon, and Felix was the first cartoon film star to win international fame. One of the many spin-offs was a comic strip for newspaper syndication (1923) which he drew in his spare time. Felix failed to make the transition to sound, but Messmer continued the strip until 1954.

Messner, Reinhold 1944–
Austrian mountaineer
Born in the South Tyrol, he became one of the world's foremost solo climbers. He pursued the goal of becoming the first person to climb all the world's 14 peaks over 8,000 metres, and realized his dream in 1986, but not without cost. In 1970 he had joined an expedition to Nanga Parbat, in northern Pakistan, where his brother died in an avalanche. In 1978 Messner and his partner Peter Habelar became the first people to climb Everest without bottled oxygen and Messner later climbed Everest alone by the North Col route without oxygen or support. He also made the first crossing of Antarctica on foot since Sir Ernest Shackleton.

Meštrović, Ivan 1883–1962
US sculptor
He was born in Vrpolje, Slavonia (in Austria-Hungary, later part of Yugoslavia). A shepherd boy, he was taught stone-cutting and woodcarving by his father, eventually studying in Vienna and Paris, where he became a friend of Auguste Rodin. He designed the national temple at Kossovo (1907–12), and the colossal *Monument to the Unknown Soldier* in Belgrade (1934). He lived in England during World War II and executed many portrait busts, including that of Sir Thomas Beecham. After the war he emigrated to the USA, and from 1955 was Professor of Sculpture at the University of Notre Dame, Indiana. His work is naturalistic, emotionally intense and is characterized by an impressive simplicity.

Mesurier, John Le See Le Mesurier, John

Metastasio, Pietro, *originally* Pietro (Armando Domenico) Trapassi 1698–1782
Italian poet
Born in Rome, he had a gift for versifying which gained him a patron who educated him and left him a fortune (1718). He acquired his reputation with his masque, *The Garden of Hesperides* (1722), wrote the libretti for 27 operas, including Mozart's *Clemenza di Tito* (libretto Eng trans *The Clemency of Titus*, 1828), and became court poet at Vienna in 1729. ▭C Burney, *Life and Letters of Metastasio* (1796)

Metaxas, Yanni 1870–1941
Greek politician
He was born in Ithaka. He fought in the Thessalian campaign against the Turks in 1897, and helped reorganize the Greek army before the 1912–13 Balkan Wars, when he became Chief of the General Staff. A Royalist rival of the Republican Eleutherios Venizelos, he opposed Greek intervention in World War I. On King Constantine I's fall he fled to Italy, but returned with him in 1921. In 1923 he founded the Party of Free Opinion. In 1935 he became deputy Prime Minister after the failure of the Venizelist coup, and in April 1936 became Prime Minister, in August establishing an authoritarian government with a cabinet of specialist and retired service officers. His work of reorganizing Greece economically and militarily bore fruit in the tenacious Greek resistance to the Italian invasion of 1940–41.

Metcalf, John, *known as* Blind Jack of Knaresborough 1717–1810
English engineer
He lost his sight at the age of six, but became an outstanding athlete and horseman. During the 1745 Jacobite rising he fought at Falkirk and Culloden (1746), set up a stagecoach between York and Knaresborough, and from 1765 constructed 185 miles (296km) of road and numerous bridges in Lancashire and Yorkshire.

Metchnikoff, Elie, *Russian* Ilya Ilyich Mechnikov 1845–1916
Russian embryologist, immunologist and Nobel Prize winner
Born in Ivanovka, Ukraine, he graduated from the University of Kharkov in 1864, and studied invertebrate and fish embryology at several European centres. After spells of teaching and research at the universities of St Petersburg and Odessa, he took a research post at the University of Messina, Italy, where he began his immunological studies. Studying how mobile cells in starfish larvae attack foreign bodies, he called these cells phagocytes, and hypothesized that their role in vertebrate blood is to fight invasion by bacteria. In 1886 he became director of the Bacteriological Institute in Odessa, where he studied the action of phagocytes in animal infections, and in 1888 Louis Pasteur offered him a post at the Pasteur Institute in Paris. As the role of phagocytes became accepted, Metchnikoff turned to other problems, such as investigating ageing and death. He was awarded the 1908 Nobel Prize for physiology or medicine jointly with Paul Ehrlich.

Metford, William Ellis 1824–99
English engineer and inventor
He was born in Taunton, Somerset. Having invented an explosive rifle bullet which was outlawed by the St Petersburg Convention of 1869, he turned to the design of a breech-loading rifle (1871). It was adapted by James Paris Lee as the 'Lee-Metford' rifle, and adopted by the British War Office in 1888.

Methuen, Sir Algernon Methuen Marshall, *originally* Algernon Stedman 1856–1924
English publisher

He was born in London. A teacher of Classics and French (1880–95), he began publishing as a sideline with Methuen & Co in 1889 to market his own textbooks. His first publishing success was Rudyard Kipling's *Barrack-Room Ballads* (1892), and, amongst others, he published works of Hilaire Belloc, G K Chesterton, Joseph Conrad, John Masefield, Robert Louis Stevenson and Oscar Wilde.

Métraux, Albert 1902–63
US cultural anthropologist

Born in Lausanne, Switzerland, he spent much of his childhood in Mendoza, Argentina, returning to Europe to complete his education in Lausanne, Paris and Gothenburg. In 1928 he founded and directed the Institute of Ethnology at the University of Tucumán, Argentina, relinquishing his post in 1934 to join a Franco-Belgian expedition to Easter Island. In 1938–39 and 1940–41 he was visiting professor at Yale, and in the intervening year conducted field research in Argentina and Bolivia. After field studies in Haiti in 1941, he joined the Bureau of American Ethnology, Smithsonian Institution (1941–45), returning to Europe as part of the US Bombing Survey to investigate German responses to military defeat. From 1947 to 1962 he worked under the auspices of UNESCO, taking part in the Hylean Amazon project (1947–48), an education survey in Haiti (1948–50) and migration studies of the Aymara and Quechua Indians in Peru and Bolivia (1954). Métraux was arguably the foremost expert on South American Indians of his day, a prolific scholar with around 250 titles to his credit, and an exemplary figure in the fields of historical ethnology and applied anthropology. His books include *Ethnology of Easter Island* (1940), *The Native Tribes of Eastern Bolivia and Western Mato Grosso* (1942) and *Voodoo in Haiti* (1959).

Metsu, Gabriel 1630–67
Dutch painter

Born in Leyden, he settled in Amsterdam in 1650, and is known for his religious and domestic genre works.

Metternich, Prince Clemens Lothar Wenzel 1773–1859
Austrian politician

Born in Coblenz, Germany, he studied at Strasbourg and Mainz, was attached to the Austrian embassy at The Hague, and at 28 was Austrian Minister at Dresden, two years later at Berlin, and in 1805 (after Austerlitz) at Paris. In 1807 he concluded the Treaty of Fontainebleau. In 1809 he was appointed Austrian Foreign Minister, and as such negotiated the marriage between Napoleon I and Marie Louise. In 1812–13 he maintained a temporizing policy at first, but at last declared war against France. The Grand Alliance was signed at Teplitz, and he was made a Prince of the Empire. He took a prominent part at the Congress of Vienna, rearranging a German confederation and guarding Austria's interests in Italy. As the main supporter of autocracy and police despotism at home and abroad he was largely responsible for the tension that led to the upheaval of 1848. The French Revolution of that year, which overturned for a time half the thrones of Europe, was felt in Vienna, and the government fell. Metternich fled to England, and in 1851 retired to his castle of Johannesberg on the Rhine. He was a brilliant diplomat and a man of iron nerve and will. 📖 Alan W Palmer, *Metternich* (1972)

Mettrie, Julien Offray de la See La Mettrie, Julien Offray de

Meung, Jean de, *also called* Jean Clopinel c.1250–1305
French poet and satirist

He flourished in Paris under Philip IV, the Fair. He translated many books into French, and left a witty *Testament*. His major work is his lengthy continuation (18,000 lines) of the *Roman de la Rose* by Guillaume de Lorris, which substituted for allegory his own satirical pictures of actual life and an encyclopedic discussion of contemporary learning.

Mew, Charlotte Mary 1869–1928
English poet and short-story writer

Born in London, she was essentially self-educated and her work largely concerned the problems of women in a society that provided few reliable terms of reference or role models for female individuality. Her most famous poem is 'The Farmer's Bride' (1915), a vigorous narrative about an emotionally restricted life. Her reputation has been sustained by the critical support of those such as Walter de la Mare and Thomas Hardy, who predeceased her only briefly; the circumstances of Mew's suicide, following the death of her sister, has fostered a certain romantic cult around her. In the late 1970s, she was rediscovered by the feminist movement; her collected verse and prose, reissued by Virago Press, made a significant impact on a revisionist awareness of post-Victorian social and cultural attitudes. 📖 P Fitzgerald, *Charlotte Mew and her Friends* (1984)

Meyer, Adolf 1866–1950
US psychiatrist

He was born in Niederweningen, Switzerland. After medical and psychiatric training in Zurich and elsewhere, he emigrated to the USA in 1892, where he held posts in a number of universities and psychiatric hospitals, especially Johns Hopkins Medical School (1910–41). He was an eclectic at a time when psychoanalytical concepts dominated US psychiatry. Through his notion of 'psychobiology' he sought to integrate psychiatry and medicine, seeing mental disorder as the consequence of unsuccessful adjustment patterns. He also tried to improve the standards of patient record-keeping and long-term follow-up care in psychiatry, and lent his considerable prestige to the mental hygiene movement of Clifford Beers. His *Collected Papers* (1950–52) were published after his death. 📖 Annemarie Jaeggi, *Adolf Meyer, der zweite Mann* (1994)

Meyer, Conrad Ferdinand 1825–98
Swiss poet and novelist

He was born in Zurich and studied in Lausanne, Paris and Italy, but due to severe depression, spent time in an asylum throughout his adult life. After a period during which he concentrated mainly on ballads and verse romances, he composed the epic poem *Huttens Letzte Tage* (1871, 'Hutten's Final Days') and a number of historical novels such as *Jürg Jenatsch* (1876) and *Der Heilige* (1880, 'The Saint'), in which he excels in subtle and intricate psychological situations and in complex characters. 📖 H Mayne, *Conrad Ferdinand Meyer und sein Werk* (1925)

Meyer, Julius Lothar von 1830–95
German chemist

Born in Varel, Oldenburg, he qualified in medicine at Zurich and subsequently studied and taught at several German universities. In 1876 he was appointed the first Professor of Chemistry at Tübingen. He studied the physiology of respiration and by 1857 had recognized that oxygen combines chemically with haemoglobin in the blood. Independently of Dmitri Mendeleyev, he examined the relationship between the chemical reactivities of the elements and their atomic weights. In 1864 he showed that atomic volume is a function of atomic weight. Meyer was also a considerable organic chemist and made the revolutionary suggestion that the carbon atoms in benzene might be in the form of a ring; he missed only the fact that the ring contains double bonds.

Meyer, Viktor 1848–97
German chemist

Born in Berlin, he studied under **Robert Bunsen** in Heidelberg and Berlin, and was professor successively at Zurich, Göttingen and Heidelberg. He discovered a method for determining vapour densities and the apparatus he designed became standard laboratory equipment. He developed a method of synthesizing aromatic acids and investigated the nitroparaffins and their derivatives. He also discovered several new types of organic nitrogen compounds. He discovered oximes, studied their isomerism and introduced the term 'stereochemistry' for the study of molecular shapes.

Meyerbeer, Giacomo, *originally* Jakob Liebmann Meyer Beer 1791–1864
German composer of operas

Born in Berlin, he played **Mozart**'s D-minor Piano Concerto in public at seven. His earlier works were unsuccessful, but in Vienna he attracted attention as a pianist. After three years' study in Italy he produced operas in the new (**Rossini**'s) style, which were immediately well received. After a careful study of French opera, he wrote the popular *Robert le Diable* (1831, libretto by **Eugène Scribe**), and followed it in 1836 by the even more successful *Huguenots*. Appointed kapellmeister at Berlin, he composed several more well-received works, but was severely condemned by **Schumann** and **Richard Wagner** on the ground that he made everything subsidiary to theatrical effect.

Meyerhof, Otto Fritz 1884–1951
US biochemist and Nobel Prize winner

Born in Hanover, Germany, and trained in medicine at the University of Heidelberg, he was appointed to a position in clinical psychiatry at the Heidelberg Clinic in 1910, where **Otto Warburg**'s work on chemical reactions in living cells inspired Meyerhof to change direction and study biochemical mechanisms. He moved to the department of physiology at the University of Kiel and was then appointed director of the physiology department at the Kaiser Wilhelm Institute for Biology in Berlin (1924–29). He then moved to a similar position at the Kaiser Wilhelm Institute for Medical Research in Heidelberg (1929–38). His biochemical research was primarily on muscle contraction, and its related metabolic pathways, and he shared the 1922 Nobel Prize for physiology or medicine with **A V Hill** for this work. In 1938 he left Nazi Germany, first continuing his work in France, then briefly in Spain, and in 1940 he reached the USA, where he was professor at the University of Pennsylvania.

Meyerhold, Vsevolod Yemilevich 1874–c.1940
Russian actor and director

Born in Penza, he joined the Moscow Art Theatre when it opened in 1898. From 1902 to 1905 he toured Russia with his own company, the Society of New Drama, both acting and directing, and was appointed by **Stanislavsky** as the director of the new Studio on Povarskaya Street (1905). Later he founded his own studio in Moscow, where he developed his theories of a director's theatre, with the actor subservient to the director's vision. He became an ardent Bolshevik, and directed the first Soviet play, **Vladimir Mayakovsky**'s *Mystery-Bouffe* (1918). In 1920 he was provided with the former Sohn Theatre in Moscow in which to work (officially known as the Meyerhold Theatre from 1926). He was director of the Theatre of the Revolution (1922–24) and of the Meyerhold Theatre (1923–38). He directed several new and revolutionary works, including two more Mayakovsky plays, *The Red Bug*

(1929) and *The Bath House* (1930). During the 1930s, when Socialist Realism was decreed the official art form, he fell from favour. His theatre was closed in 1938 and he was arrested, and disappeared in prison.

Meynell, Alice Christiana Gertrude, *née* Thompson 1847–1922
English essayist and poet

Born in Barnes, London, she spent her childhood on the Continent, and converted to Catholicism. Her volumes of essays include *The Rhythm of Life* (1893), *The Colour of Life* (1896) and *Hearts of Controversy* (1917). She published several collections of her own poems, starting in 1875 with *Preludes*, and anthologies of **Coventry Patmore**, of lyric poetry, and of poems for children. In 1877 she married Wilfrid Meynell (1852–1948), author and journalist, with whom she edited several periodicals. 📖 A K Tuell, *Mrs Meynell* (1925)

Miall, Edward 1809–81
English clergyman

Born in Portsmouth, Hampshire, he was an Independent minister at Ware and Leicester, and a lifelong advocate of disestablishment of the Church of England. In 1841 he founded the weekly *Nonconformist* newspaper, and in 1842 tried to amalgamate with the Chartists. Later he was MP for Rochdale (1852–57) and Bradford (1869–74).

Micah 735–665BC
Old Testament minor prophet

He was born in Moresheth Gath, in south-west Judah. He prophesied during the reigns of Jotham, Ahaz and Hezekiah, being a younger contemporary of **Isaiah**, Hosea and **Amos**.

Michael 1921–
King of Romania

The son of the future **Carol II**, he was born in Sinaira, and first succeeded to the throne (1927) on the death of his grandfather Ferdinand I, his father having renounced his own claims (1925). In 1930 he was supplanted by Carol, but was again made king (1940) when the Germans gained control of Romania. In 1944 he played a considerable part in the overthrow of the dictatorship of **Ion Antonescu**. He announced the acceptance of the Allied peace terms, and declared war on Germany. His attempts after the war to establish a broader system of government were foiled by the progressive Communization of Romania. In 1947 he was forced to abdicate and has since lived in exile, finally in Switzerland.

Michael VIII Palaeologus c.1224–1282
Byzantine emperor

He was born into the Greek nobility and became a general in the empire of Nicaea. In 1258 he became regent and co-ruler with the eight-year-old emperor, John IV Lascaris, whom he later had blinded and imprisoned. Resourceful and a master of intrigue, he conquered Constantinople (Istanbul) in 1261, extinguishing the empire of **Baldwin II**, and was crowned sole emperor, thus founding the Palaeologan dynasty. The papacy and **Charles of Anjou**, who aimed to re-establish the Latin Empire, opposed Michael, and Byzantium survived only by his diplomatic skill. By reuniting the Orthodox Church with Rome he aroused discontent among his subjects but warded off attacks until 1281 when Pope Martin IV proclaimed a crusade against him. Michael prevented this by encouraging the Aragonese to invade Sicily. Although his concentration on Europe tended to ignore the Ottoman threat to the east, he helped prolong Byzantine independence for another two centuries, and presided over the beginnings of a revival of learning.

Michael Romanov 1596–1645
Tsar of Russia

The great-nephew of **Ivan IV**, the Terrible, he was the founder of the Romanov dynasty, which ruled Russia until the Revolution of 1917. He was elected tsar (1613–45) by the boyars after a successful revolt against the Poles, when Russia was threatened with invasion from Sweden, and he brought an end to the Time of Troubles (1605–13). He concluded peace with Sweden (1617) and Poland (1618). He left government to his father, the patriarch Filaret, who reorganized the army and industry, improved finances, consolidated the system of serfdom, and increased contacts with western Europe. Michael was succeeded by his son Alexis.

Michaelis, Leonor 1875–1949
US biochemist

Born in Berlin, Germany, he became professor at Berlin University (1908–22) and the Nagoya Medical School in Japan (1922–26), before settling in the USA at the Johns Hopkins (1926–29) and Rockefeller (1929–40) institutes. He studied the physical properties of enzymes and proteins, but is best remembered for the Michaelis–Menten equation, which defines the role played by enzyme concentration in enzyme-catalyzed reactions. Michaelis also contributed over 80 papers on the measurement of pH and electrolytic dissociation.

Michaelson, Sidney 1925–91
English computer scientist

Born in London and educated at the Imperial College there, from 1949 to 1963 he lectured at the College, pioneering the design of digital computers and the principles of microprogramming. In 1963 he moved to Edinburgh University, where he founded the department and held the chair of computer science (1966–91). There he initiated work to provide interactive, multiple-user access to computers, and led a range of research activities, from computational theory to VLSI (very large scale integration) design. A leader in the field of stylometry, the science of computer-based analysis of literary texts, he fought to promote the professional recognition of computer scientists.

Michel, Claude, *pseudonym* Clodion 1738–1814
French sculptor

He was born at Nancy. Perhaps the greatest sculptor of the Napoleonic era, he is famous for his small terracotta figures of classical subjects such as fauns, satyrs and nymphs. A fine example of his work is a vase in the Wallace Collection, London, of white marble carved with relief.

Michel, Hartmut 1948–
German biochemist and Nobel Prize winner

Born in Ludwigsburg, West Germany, he studied at the universities of Tübingen, Würzburg, Munich and the Max Planck Institute of Biochemistry, and was appointed director of the Max Planck Institute of Biophysics in Frankfurt in 1987. In 1981 he produced a crystal of the membrane-bound, photosynthetic reaction centre of the bacterium *Rhodopseudomonas viridis*, and collaborated with **Robert Huber** and **Johann Deisenhofer** to determine its structure by X-ray crystallography. By 1985 they were able to report the complete structure, which confirmed and elaborated predictions about how the energy transfer process in photosynthesis operates. For this discovery Michel shared the 1988 Nobel Prize for chemistry with Huber and Deisenhofer. He published *Crystallization of Membrane Proteins* in 1990.

Michelangeli, Arturo Benedetti 1920–95
Italian pianist

Born in Brescia, he studied there and in Milan, and won the Geneva International Music Competition in 1939. After war service in the Italian air force, he acquired a considerable reputation as a virtuoso, which was enhanced by the rarity of his public performances. He became a noted teacher and founded and directed the International Pianists Academy in Brescia (1964–69).

Michelangelo See panel p1277

Michelet, Jules 1798–1874
French historian

Born in Paris, he lectured on history at the École Normale, assisted **François Guizot** at the Sorbonne, worked at the Record Office, and was appointed Professor of History at the Collège de France (1838–51). The greatest of his many historical works are his monumental *Histoire de France* (24 vols, 1833–67) and his *Histoire de la Révolution* (7 vols, 1847–53). By refusing to swear allegiance to **Louis Napoleon** he lost his appointments, and henceforth worked mostly in Brittany and the Riviera. His second wife, Adèle Mialaret, collaborated with him on several nature books, including *L'Oiseau* (1856), *L'Insecte* (1857) and *La Mer* (1861). In his last years he set himself to complete his great *Histoire*, but lived to finish only three volumes (1872–75).

Michelin, André 1853–1931
French tyre manufacturer

Born in Paris, he established the Michelin tyre company in 1888 with his younger brother Edouard (1859–1940). They were the first to use demountable pneumatic tyres on motor cars, and became known for their road maps and Michelin guides. The guides were introduced by André Michelin to promote tourism by car and the first Red Guide, showing restaurant ratings, was published in 1900.

Michell, John 1724–93
English geologist and astronomer

Born in Nottinghamshire, he was a Fellow of Queen's College, Cambridge and Professor of Geology (1762–64), and became rector of Thornhill, Yorkshire (1767), where **William Herschel** was a regular guest. He published an important work on artificial magnets (1750), but is best known as the founder of seismology. He invented a torsion balance, a device to measure the strength of small forces, and with it intended to measure the value of the gravitational constant. However, he died before he had the opportunity—it was **Henry Cavendish** who finally carried this out in the famous 'Cavendish experiment' and derived from it the mean density of the Earth. Michell also made important contributions to astronomy: he demonstrated that many double stars must exist as binary systems and devised a method of calculating stellar distances.

Michelozzi, Michelozzo di Bartolommeo 1396–1472
Italian architect and sculptor

Born in Florence, he was associated with **Lorenzo Ghiberti** on his famous bronze doors for the baptistery there, and collaborated with **Donatello** in several major sculpture groups, including monuments to (the antipope) Pope John XXIII and Cardinal Brancacci (1427). He was court architect to **Cosimo de' Medici**, with whom he was in exile at Venice, where he designed a number of buildings. One of his finest works is the Ricardi Palace in Florence.

Michelson, Albert Abraham 1852–1931
US physicist and Nobel Prize winner

Born in Strzelno, Poland, he emigrated with his family to the USA and graduated from the US Naval Academy in 1873. After teaching at the Academy, the Case School of Applied Science in Cleveland and Clarke University, he became Professor of Physics at Chicago University in 1892. His lifelong passion was precision measurement in experimental physics, and he is chiefly remembered for

Michelangelo, *in full* Michelangelo di Lodovico Buonarroti 1475–1564
Italian sculptor, painter and poet

Michelangelo was born in Caprese in Tuscany, where his father Lodovico was mayor. He was brought up in Florence and placed in the care of a stonemason and his wife at Settignano, where Lodovico owned a small farm and marble quarry. At school he devoted his energies more to drawing than to his studies. In 1488, against his father's wishes, he was apprenticed for three years to **Domenico Ghirlandaio**. He was recommended by Ghirlandaio to **Lorenzo de' Medici**, and entered the school for which Lorenzo had gathered together a priceless collection of antiques (1490–92). To this period belong two interesting reliefs. In the *Battle of the Centaurs* the Classical influence of Lorenzo's garden is strikingly apparent, though the straining muscles and contorted limbs, which mark the artist's mature work, are already visible. A marvellous contrast to the *Centaurs* is the *Madonna of the Steps*, conceived and executed in the spirit of **Donatello**.

After Lorenzo's death in 1492, **Piero de' Medici**, his son and successor, is said to have treated the artist with scant courtesy; and Michelangelo fled to Bologna for three years, returning to Florence in 1495. During this time he made a marble *Cupid*, which was bought by Cardinal San Giorgio who recognized the talent of the sculptor and summoned him to Rome in 1496. The influence of Rome and the antique is easily discernible in the *Bacchus*, now in the National Museum in Florence. The *Pieta* (1497), now in St Peter's, shows a realism wholly at variance with the antique ideal. For four years the sculptor remained in Rome and then, returning to Florence, fashioned his *David* out of a colossal block of marble. *David* is the Gothic treatment of a classical theme; in pose and composition there is a stately grandeur, a dignified solemnity.

During the same period he painted the *Holy Family of the Tribune* and the *Madonna* now in the National Gallery in London, proving that he had not wholly neglected the art of painting. His genius, however, was essentially plastic, and he had more interest in form than in colour. In 1503 the new pope, **Julius II**, summoned Michelangelo back to Rome, where their dealings were continually interrupted by bitter quarrels and recriminations. The pope commissioned the sculptor to design his tomb, and for 40 years Michelangelo clung to the hope that he would yet complete the great monument; but other demands were continually made upon him, and the sublime statue of **Moses** is the best fragment that is left to us of the tomb of Julius.

Instead of being allowed to devote himself to the monument, he was instructed, despite Michelangelo's urgings to consider **Raphael**, to decorate the ceiling of the Sistine Chapel with paintings (1508–12). In the event, Michelangelo achieved a masterpiece of decorative design, depicting the Creation, the Fall and the Flood. Almost superhuman invention, and a miraculous variety of attitude and gesture, place this work among the greatest achievements of human energy. No sooner had he finished his work in the Sistine Chapel than he returned with eagerness to the tomb. But in 1513 Pope Julius II died, and the cardinals, his executors, demanded a more modest design.

Then Pope **Leo X**, of the Medici family, commissioned Michelangelo to rebuild the façade of the church of San Lorenzo in Florence and enrich it with sculptured figures. He reluctantly complied, and set out for Carrara to quarry marble; from 1514 to 1522 his artistic record is a blank, as the elaborate scheme was ultimately given up, although Michelangelo remained in Florence. In 1528–29 he devoted his energies to improving the fortifications of Florence, now under siege. After the surrender he completed the monuments to Giuliano and Lorenzo de' Medici, which are considered to be among the greatest of his works.

In 1533 yet another compact was entered into concerning Pope Julius's ill-fated sepulchre; Michelangelo was once again commissioned to adorn the Sistine Chapel with frescoes. After some years he began in 1537 to paint *The Last Judgement*. In 1547 he was appointed architect of St Peter's, and devoted himself to the work with loyalty until his death.

Michelangelo is by far the most brilliant representative of the Italian Renaissance. He was not only supreme in the arts of sculpture and painting, in which grandeur and sublimity rather than beauty was his aim, but was versed in all the learning of his age, and wrote copious poetry.

📖 Sidney Alexander, *Michelangelo the Florentine* (1985); Linda Murray, *Michelangelo: His Life, Work and Times* (1984); Robert J Clements (ed), *Michelangelo: A Self-Portrait* (1968); Gilbert Creighton, *Michelangelo* (1967).

> 'I've finished that chapel I was painting. The pope is quite satisfied.' From a letter written to his father after 18 months of painting the Sistine Chapel. Quoted in Robert J Clements (ed), *Michelangelo: A Self-Portrait* (1968).

---

the Michelson–**Morley** experiment to determine ether drift, the negative result of which set **Albert Einstein** on the road to the theory of relativity. The interferometer which he invented for this experiment was developed subsequently for spectroscopic studies, and he also developed a stellar interferometer for measuring the sizes and separations of celestial bodies. In 1898 he invented the echelon grating, an ultra-high-resolution device for the study and measurement of hyperfine spectra. Michelson became the first US scientist to win a Nobel Prize when he was awarded the Nobel Prize for physics in 1907. A member (1888) and president (1923–27) of the US National Academy of Sciences, his many honours included foreign membership of the Royal Society (1902), and the award of the Society's Copley Medal (1907). 📖 Dorothy Michelson Livingston, *The Master of Light* (1973)

Michie, Donald 1923–
British specialist in artificial intelligence

He was born in Rangoon, Burma (Myanma), and educated at Balliol College, Oxford. His work during World War II on the Colossus code-breaking project acquainted him with computer pioneers such as **Alan Turing**, with whom he discussed the mechanization of thought processes. After a biological career in experimental genetics, he developed the study of machine intelligence at Edinburgh University as director of experimental programming (1963–66) and Professor of Machine Intelligence (1967–84). He is editor-in-chief of the *Machine Intelligence* series, and became chief scientist at the Turing Institute in 1986, which he founded in Glasgow in 1984. In publications such as *The Creative Computer* (1984) and *On Machine Intelligence* (1974), he has argued that computer systems are able to generate new knowledge. His research contributions have primarily been in the field of machine learning.

Michurin, Ivan Vladimirovich 1855–1935
Russian horticulturist

He was born in Koslov. At his private orchard there, which became a state institution, he developed many new varieties of fruit and berries. His theory of crossbreeding ('Michurinism'), which postulated the idea that acquired characteristics were heritable, became state doctrine and influenced the pernicious anti-Mendelian doctrines of Trofim Lysenko. Koslov was renamed Michurinsk after him.

Mickiewicz, Adam Bernard 1798–1855
Polish poet

Born in Lithuania, he was educated in Vilna and published his first poems in 1822. He was arrested and exiled to Siberia for his revolutionary activities, and after the failure of the Polish revolt (1830–31) he had to flee to the West. After travelling in Germany, France and Italy he wrote his epic *Pan Tadeusz* (1834, Eng trans *Thaddeus*, 1886), about Lithuania. He taught at Lausanne and was Slavonic professor at Paris (1840). Generally he tried to keep the Polish spirit alive through his writings, and in 1852 **Louis Napoleon** appointed him librarian in the Paris Arsenal. He is considered the national poet of Poland. ▢ K Pruszynski, *Adam Mickiewicz: the life story of the greatest Polish poet* (1950)

Mickle, William Julius 1735–88
Scottish poet

Born in Langholm, Dumfriesshire, and educated at Edinburgh High School, he failed as a brewer, and became an author in London. In 1765 he published a poem, *The Concubine* (or *Syr Martyn*), and from 1771 to 1775 he wrote a version of the *Lusiad* of **Luis de Camoëns**. In 1779 he went to Lisbon as secretary to Commodore Johnstone, but his last years were spent in London. His ballad of *Cumnor Hall* (which suggested *Kenilworth* to Sir **Walter Scott**), and 'There's nae luck aboot the hoose' ensured his immortality, even if its authorship has been challenged.

Midas 8th century BC
King of Phrygia

He is mentioned in Assyrian records, and was the first non-Greek ruler to have made a dedication to the Oracle of Apollo at Delphi, thus anticipating **Gyges** of Lydia. Many stories were told about him (or about a namesake), notably that, in gratitude for his hospitality to the satyr Silenus, the god Dionysus gave him the power to turn to gold anything he touched. On discovering that this included food, he was relieved of the gift by washing in the Pactolus River.

Middleton, Thomas c.1580–1627
English dramatist

Born in Newington Butts, Surrey, the son of a bricklayer, he is first mentioned in **Philip Henslowe's** *Diary* in 1602, when he was engaged with Anthony Munday, **Michael Drayton** and **John Webster** on a lost play, *Cæsar's Fall*. *Father Hubbard's Tale* and *The Black Book*, exposing London rogues, were published in 1604, to which year belongs the first part of *The Honest Whore* (mainly written by **Thomas Dekker**, partly by Middleton). Other early works include *A Mad World, My Masters* (1608), from which **Aphra Behn** pilfered freely in *The City Heiress*. *The Roaring Girl* (1611, written with Dekker) idealizes the character of a noted cutpurse and virago. Middleton was repeatedly employed to write the Lord Mayor's pageant. *A Chaste Maid in Cheapside* was probably produced in 1613, as was *No Wit, No Help like a Woman's*. *A Fair Quarrel* (1617) and *The World Lost at Tennis* (1620) were written in conjunction with **William Rowley**. In 1620 Middleton was appointed city chronologer, and a manuscript Chronicle by him was extant in the 18th century. *A Game of Chess*, a curious and skilful play, was acted in 1624. Three posthumously-published plays, *The Changeling*, *The Spanish Gypsy* and *Women Beware Women*, include some of his best writing. *The Widow*, published in 1652, was mainly by Middleton, and he was also concerned in the authorship of some of the plays included in the works of **Francis Beaumont** and **John Fletcher**. ▢ R H Barker, *Thomas Middleton* (1958)

Midgley, Thomas, Jnr 1889–1944
US engineer and inventor

Born in Beaver Falls, Pennsylvania, he graduated in mechanical engineering at Cornell University in 1911. During World War I, on the staff of the Dayton (Ohio) Engineering Laboratories (1916–23), he worked on the problem of 'knocking' in petrol engines, and by 1921 found tetra-ethyl lead to be effective as an additive to petrol, used with 1,2-dibromoethane to reduce lead oxide deposits in the engine. He also devised the octane number method of rating petrol quality. As president of the Ethyl Corporation from 1923, he also introduced Freon 12 as a non-toxic non-inflammable agent for domestic refrigerators. Since 1980, however, there has been rising concern about the pollutant effects of both the lead emitted in vehicle exhausts, and of chlorofluorocarbons (CFCs), such as Freon. Midgley was a polio victim, and died by accidental strangulation through the failure of a harness he used to help him rise in the morning.

Midler, Bette 1945–
US comedienne, actress and singer

Born in Honolulu, Hawaii, she studied drama at the University of Hawaii, then was hired as an extra in the film *Hawaii* (1966). Moving to New York, she made her stage debut in *Miss Nefertiti Regrets* (1966). She then developed a popular but bawdy nightclub act. Her album *The Divine Miss M* (1974) won her a Grammy award as Best New Artist, and in the same year she received a Tony award for her record-breaking Broadway show. Midler's performance in the film *The Rose* (1979) earned her an Academy Award nomination and she has continued to enjoy commercial success in a series of film farces including *Down and Out in Beverly Hills* (1986), *Ruthless People* (1986), *Outrageous Fortune* (1987), *Big Business* (1988), *Beaches* (1988), *Stella* (1990), *Scenes from a Mall* (1991), *For the Boys* (1991), *Hocus Pocus* (1993) and *The First Wives Club* (1996). As a singer, her hit singles include 'The Rose' and 'Wind Beneath My Wings'. Her autobiographical *A View from A Broad* was published in 1980.

Mieris, Frans van 1635–81
Dutch painter

Born in Leyden, he excelled in small-scale, exquisitely finished genre paintings in the style of his teacher **Gerard Dou** and **Gerard Terborch**. His sons Jan (1660–90) and Willem (1662–1747) followed his example. Willem's son Frans (1689–1773) was less successful as a painter, but made his name as a writer of antiquarian works.

Mies van der Rohe, Ludwig 1886–1969
US architect

Born in Aachen, Germany, the son of a mason, he studied design under **Peter Behrens** and became a pioneer of glass skyscrapers. In pre-war Berlin he designed high-rise flats for the Weissenhof Exhibition (1927), and the German Pavilion for the Barcelona International Exposition in 1929. He also designed tubular-steel furniture, particularly the 'Barcelona chair'. He was director of the Bauhaus in Dessau (1930–33), and emigrated to the USA in 1937, where he became Professor of Architecture at the Armour (now Illinois) Institute of Technology in Chicago. He designed two glass apartment towers on Lake Shore Drive in Chicago and collaborated with **Philip Johnson** on the Seagram Building in New York (1956–58). His other works include the Public Library in Washington DC (1967), and two art galleries in Berlin (1968). He was a major figure in 20th-century architecture and a founder of the modern style. ▢ Arthur Drexler, *Ludwig Mies van der Rohe* (1960)

Mifsud Bonnici, Carmelo 1933–
Maltese statesman

A graduate of Malta University, he lectured in law at University College London and then in Malta. In 1969 he became legal consultant to the General Workers' Union and then moved more openly into politics, becoming deputy Leader of the Malta Labour Party (MLP) in 1980, under Dom Mintoff, and then Leader, and Prime Minister, on Mintoff's retirement in 1984. In the 1987 general election the MLP won 34 seats to the Nationalist Party's 31, but because they had won a larger share of the vote the Nationalists were, under the terms of the constitution, awarded four more seats, and Mifsud Bonnici went out of office.

Mignard, Pierre 1612–95
French painter
Born in Troyes, after studying under Simon Vouet he worked in Rome from 1636 to 1657, where he developed a classicizing style much influenced by Nicolas Poussin. He was summoned to Paris by Louis XIV and became a successful court portraitist and favourite of the king. Upon the death of his great rival Charles Le Brun, the king appointed him *premier peintre* as well as director and chancellor of the Académie. His brother, Nicolas (1608–68), was also a painter.

Mignault, Pierre-Basile 1854–1945
Canadian text-writer and judge
He taught civil law at McGill University, Montreal, before serving as a judge (1918–29) of the Supreme Court of Canada. He was a prolific writer, and his *Le droit civil canadien* (9 vols, 1895–1916, 'Canadian Civil Law') is still an important work. Through his writings and judgements he defended the integrity and distinction of Quebec civil law in the Canadian Supreme Court.

Miguel, *properly* Miguel Maria Evaristo de Bragança 1802–66
King of Portugal
Born in Lisbon, the third son of King John VI, he plotted (1824) to overthrow the constitutional government established by his father, but was banished with his mother, his chief abettor. His elder brother, Pedro I, resigned the throne to his daughter Maria, making him regent; but he summoned a *Cortes* (1828), which proclaimed him king. In 1832 Oporto and Lisbon were captured, and Charles Napier destroyed his fleet off Cape St Vincent (1833). Maria was restored in 1834, and he withdrew to Italy.

Mihailovich, Draza 1893–1946
Serbian soldier
After distinguished service in World War I, he rose to the rank of colonel in the Yugoslav army, and following the German occupation in 1941, headed the Chetniks mountain guerrilla movement. In exile from 1943, he was appointed Minister of War, but when Tito's Communist Partisans' resistance developed, Mihailovich allied himself with the Germans and then with the Italians in order to fight the communists. After the war he was captured and executed by the Tito government for collaboration with the occupying powers. ⌨ Nikola Milovanovic, *Kontra-revolucionarni pokret Draze Mihailovica* (1984)

Mikan, George Lawrence 1924–
US basketball player
Born in Joliet, Illinois, he graduated from De Paul University, Chicago, in 1946 and played with Minneapolis in the National Basketball Association from 1948 to 1956, winning the championship five times. He led the NBA in points-scoring three times. A trendsetter, he helped launch basketball into a new era and at 6ft 10in tall (2.08m), he set the stage for the big men who now dominate the sport.

Mikkola, Hannu 1942–
Finnish rally driver
Born on the eastern borders of Finland, he launched himself and the Ford Escort to popular status when he won a hat-trick of rallies in 1970: the 16,000-mile London–Mexico rally, the Arctic and the 1,000 Lakes. His immense versatility has been proved through a career of 19 wins (1970–94) in cars that have included Ford, Mercedes and Audi, and in rallies as varied as the Safari (winner 1972, with Gunnar Palm) to the Lombard RAC rally, which Mikkola has won four times. He has rallied more world championship miles than any other man, but has won the title only once, in 1983.

Mikoyan, Anastas Ivanovich 1895–1978
Soviet politician
Born in Sanain, Armenia, of poor parents, the brother of Artem Mikoyan, he studied theology and became a fanatical revolutionary. Taken prisoner in the fighting at Baku, he escaped and made his way to Moscow, where he met Lenin and Stalin. A member of the Central Committee in 1922, he supported Stalin against Trotsky, and in 1926 became Minister of Trade, in which capacity he did much to improve Soviet standards of living. He showed himself willing to learn from the West, for example, in the manufacture of canned goods and throughout the food industry generally. While other politicians came and went, Mikoyan's genius for survival enabled him to become a first vice-chairman of the Council of Ministers (1955–64), and president of the Presidium of the Supreme Soviet from 1964.

Mikoyan, Artem Ivanovich 1905–70
Soviet aircraft designer
Born in Sanain, Armenia, he worked as a metal-worker in Rostov-on-Don and Moscow and served in the Red Army before graduating from the NE Zhukovsky Air Force Academy (1936). His career began as an engineer at the NN Polikarpov Design Bureau where he worked on refinements to the I-16 monoplane and the development of the I-153 ('Seagull') fighter. He was best known for the fighter aircraft produced by the design bureau he headed with Mikhail Gurevich, the MiG (Mikoyan and Gurevich) series. The most notable of this series include: the MiG-1 (1940), and the MiG-3 (1941), both used in World War II, the MiG-9 (1946), one of the Soviet Union's first jet fighters, the MiG-15 and the MiG-17, which were deployed in the Korean War, the MiG-21 (1967) single-turbojet Mach 2 fighter-interceptor, on which design the world's first supersonic passenger aircraft, the Tu-144, was based, and the MiG-25 (1971) single-turbojet reconnaissance fighter. He was the brother of Anastas Mikoyan.

Milankovich, Milutin 1879–1958
Yugoslav geophysicist
Born in Dalj, he was educated at the Institute of Technology in Vienna, and then moved to the University of Belgrade, where he remained for the rest of his career. Studying the possible astronomical cycles which produce climatic variations, he realized that the key to past climates was the amount of solar radiation received by the Earth, which varies according to latitude and depends upon the Earth's orbit and the tilt of the Earth's rotational axis, both of which change over a long time period. Using this data he reconstructed the classic theoretical radiation curves for the past 650,000 years. These are known as the Milankovitch cycles and are still in use.

Miles, Bernard James Miles, Baron 1907–91
English actor, stage director and founder of the Mermaid Theatre
Born in Uxbridge, London, he made his London debut as an actor in 1930, and worked in several repertory theatres as a designer, scene-painter, carpenter, property-manager and character actor before touring with the Old Vic company as Iago in *Othello* (1941). He later rejoined the

company (1947–48), and went onto the music-hall stage, including the London Palladium (1950). Wanting to rid the theatre of snobbery and class distinctions, he founded the Mermaid Theatre (1951) as a small private theatre in the grounds of his home in St John's Wood, London. In 1953 the Mermaid was rebuilt in the City of London, and in 1959 a permanent, professional Mermaid Theatre, financed by public subscription, was built at Puddle Dock, Blackfriars; it was seen as the model of many theatres during the next two decades.

Milgram, Stanley 1933–84
US psychologist

Born in New York City, he was educated at Harvard, spending 1959–60 at the Institute for Advanced Study at Princeton. He was professor at Yale (1960–63) and later became Professor of Psychology at the City University of New York (1967–84). Like many other postwar social psychologists, he became concerned to understand how apparently ordinary people in Nazi Germany had committed the atrocities of the Holocaust against the Jews and other minority groups. In his most famous research programme, published in *Obedience to Authority: An Experimental View* (1974), he set out to examine what factors would influence the tendency of ordinary people to 'obey orders' in an artificial situation where they were given to believe (wrongly) that they were administering electric shocks to other experimental subjects. The most striking result of this controversial study was that the vast majority of people were apparently prepared to give huge shocks in the cause of 'science' when authorized to do so by an apparently respectable academic scientist.

Milhaud, Darius 1892–1974
French composer

Born in Aix-en-Provence, he studied under Vincent d'Indy. He frequently collaborated with the playwright Paul Claudel, as on the opera *Christopher Columbus* (1928). For a time he was a member of the group of young French composers known as Les Six. In 1940 he went to the USA, where he was made Professor of Music at Mills College, California (1940–47). He was one of the most prolific of modern composers, his work including several operas, much incidental music for plays, ballets (including the jazz ballet *La Création du monde*, 1923, 'The Creation of the World'), symphonies and orchestral, choral and chamber works. He wrote an autobiography, *Notes sans musique* (1948, Eng trans *Notes without Music*, 1952).

Milingo, Emmanuel 1930–
Zambian Catholic cleric

He was born in Zambia and educated in Malawi before studying in Ireland and Rome, specializing in pastoral sociology. He was Archbishop of Lusaka from 1969 to 1983, when he was appointed delegate to the Pontifical Council for the Pastoral Care of Migrants, Refugees and Pilgrims. He is concerned with the legitimate role of African culture in the Christianity of that continent. His books include *The World in Between: Christian Healing and the Struggle for Survival* (1984) and *The Demarcations* (1982).

Milk, Harvey 1931–78
US politician and gay rights activist

Born in Woodmere, New York, he settled in California and became an outspoken advocate of gay rights in an era when homosexuality was rarely acknowledged in public. After being elected to the San Francisco Board of Supervisors in 1977, he was assassinated (along with Mayor George Moscone) by a former city supervisor. He is a figure often invoked by the US gay rights movement.

Mill, Harriet Taylor, *née* Hardy 1807–58
English feminist philosopher, essayist and political theorist

She was born in London, but little else is known of her early life. She was one of the first writers in England to press for women's rights and suffrage, writing essays in the 1850s that authoritatively rejected the legal and political traditions subordinating women. Her suggested remedies for the improvement of women's position lay in education, law and politics. Advocating women's suffrage as early as 1851, she claimed full legal and political citizenship for women, and promoted equality in higher education. Unable to remain politically active due to bad health, she was able to pursue her cause through the activities of her second husband, the philosopher John Stuart Mill. She collaborated with him in particular on his classic expression of feminist thought, *The Subjection of Women* (1869). Among her works are the important *Essays on Sex Equality*.

Mill, James 1773–1836
Scottish philosopher, historian and economist

Born in Northwater Bridge, Logiepert, Tayside, he studied for the ministry at Edinburgh and was ordained in 1798. He moved to London (1802) and supported himself through journalism and editorial work for periodicals such as the *Edinburgh Review* and *St James's Chronicle*. He became a disciple and friend of Jeremy Bentham, an enthusiastic proponent of utilitarianism, and a prominent member of the circle of 'Philosophical Radicals' which included George Grote, David Ricardo, John Austin and in due course his eldest son John Stuart Mill. The group was active in social and educational causes and James Mill took a leading part in the founding of University College London (1825). His first major publication was the *History of British India* (1817–18) on which he had worked for 11 years and which led to a permanent position with the East India Company, where he rose to become head of the Examiner's Office (1830). He continued writing utilitarian essays for publications like the *Westminster Review* and the *Encyclopaedia Britannica*, and published three further important books: *Elements of Political Economy* (1821), which derived from Ricardo and was an important influence on Karl Marx; *Analysis of the Phenomenon of the Human Mind* (1829), his main philosophical work, which provides a psychological basis for utilitarianism; and *A Fragment on MacKintosh* (1835), which argues that morality is based on utility.

Mill, John Stuart See panel p1281

Millais, Sir John Everett 1829–96
English painter

Born in Southampton, he became the youngest ever student at the Royal Academy in 1840, and in 1846 exhibited his *Pizarro Seizing the Inca of Peru*. Along with Dante Gabriel Rossetti and Holman Hunt he was a founder-member of the Pre-Raphaelite Brotherhood, and was markedly influenced by them and by John Ruskin. His first Pre-Raphaelite picture, the banquet scene from *Isabella* by Keats, figured in the Academy in 1849, where it was followed in 1850 by *Christ in the House of His Parents*, which met the full force of the anti-Pre-Raphaelite reaction. The exquisite *Gambler's Wife* (1869) and *The Boyhood of Raleigh* (1870) mark the transition of his art into its final phase, displaying brilliant and effective colouring, effortless power of brushwork and delicacy of flesh-painting. The interest and value of his later works, largely portraits, lie mainly in their splendid technical qualities. A late painting, *Bubbles* (1886), achieved huge popularity. Millais executed a few etchings, and his illustrations in *Good Words*, *Once a Week*, *The Cornhill*, etc (1857–64) place him in the first rank of woodcut designers. He was buried in St Paul's Cathedral, London. 🕮 *Sir John Everett Millais* (1979)

Millan, Bruce 1927–
Scottish Labour politician

Mill, John Stuart 1806–73
English philosopher and social reformer

John Stuart Mill was born in London, the son of the Scottish philosopher **James Mill**, who was wholly responsible for his son's remarkable and rigorous education. He taught him Greek at the age of three, Latin and arithmetic at eight, logic at 12, and political economy at 13. He was shielded from association with other boys of his age, his only recreation being a daily walk with his father, during which he was tested with oral examinations. After a visit to France in 1820 he broadened his studies into history, law and philosophy and in 1823 began a career under his father at the India Office, where he advanced to become head of his department.

This forced education gave him an advantage, as he put it, of a quarter of a century over his contemporaries, and he began enthusiastically to fulfil the ambitions his father had for him to become the leader and prophet of the Benthamite utilitarian movement. He began publishing in the newspaper *The Traveller* in 1822; he helped form the Utilitarian Society, which met for reading and discussion in **Jeremy Bentham**'s house (1823–26), and with Bentham he helped found University College London in 1825; he was a major contributor to the *Westminster Review* and a regular performer in the London Debating Society; and he corresponded with **Thomas Carlyle** and met **Frederick Maurice**. He espoused **Malthus**ian doctrines, and was arrested in 1824 for distributing birth control literature to the poor in London.

In 1826 he suffered a mental crisis which he describes in his autobiography, and which has usually been seen as a result of his precocious but emotionally restricted development. For a while he was in 'a dull state of nerves', but the depression passed and he recovered, with his sympathies broadened and his intellectual position importantly modified, as his reviews of **Tennyson** (1835), **Carlyle** (1837), **Bentham** (1838) and **Coleridge** (1840) indicate. He effectively humanized utilitarianism by his recognition of the differences in the quality as well as the quantity of pleasures thereby restoring the importance of cultural and idealistic values.

In 1830 he had met Harriet Taylor, the bluestocking wife of a wealthy London merchant, and after a long, intense but apparently chaste romance he married her in 1851, two years after her husband's death. She took an active interest in his writing and contributed significantly to his essay *On Liberty* (1859), the most popular of all his works, which eloquently defines and defends the freedoms of the individual against social and political control. Her views on marriage and the status of women helped inspire *The Subjection of Women* (1869), which provoked great antagonism.

Remaining politically active in later life, he was elected to parliament in 1865. He campaigned for women's suffrage and generally supported the Advanced Liberals. In 1872 he became godfather, 'in a secular sense', to Lord Amberley's second son, **Bertrand Russell**. His last years were spent in France and he died in Avignon.

📖 Mill's major work, *A System of Logic* (1843), ran through many editions, establishing his philosophical reputation and greatly influencing **John Venn**, **John Neville Keynes**, **Gottlob Frege** and **Bertrand Russell**, particularly in its treatment of induction. His other works include *Principles of Political Economy* (1848), *Considerations on Representative Government* (1861), *Utilitarianism* (1863), *Examination of Sir William Hamilton's Philosophy* (1865), *Auguste Comte and Positivism* (1873) and *Three Essays on Religion* (1874). His *Autobiography* was published in 1873. See also A Ryan, *J. S. Mill* (1974).

'The only purpose for which power can be rightfully exercised over any member of a civilized community, against his will, is to prevent harm to others.' From *On Liberty*, ch.1.

Born in Dundee and educated at the Harris Academy, he qualified as a chartered accountant. MP for Glasgow Craigton (1959–83) and for Govan (1983–88), he held junior ministerial appointments (1964–70, 1974–76), mainly in the Scottish Office. Appointed Secretary of State for Scotland (1976–79), he proved a competent administrator in a period dominated by devolution legislation, sharply rising unemployment, and a weakening Scottish economy. He left parliament to become European Community Commissioner (1989–95), with responsibility for regional development.

Milland, Ray *originally* Reginald Truscott-Jones 1905–86

Welsh actor

Born in Neath, Glamorganshire, he was a member of the Household Cavalry before turning to acting. He performed in a dance team with **Anna Neagle** and made several modest film appearances in 1929. Venturing to Hollywood, he built a substantial career as a leading man in light comedies and adventure yarns like *Easy Living* (1937), *Beau Geste* (1939) and *Reap the Wild Wind* (1942). Cast against type as the chronic alcoholic in *The Lost Weekend* (1945), he won a Best Actor Academy Award and explored the darker side of his character further in *Alias Nick Beal* (1949) and *Dial M for Murder* (1954). He also proved an able director of off-beat subjects like the western *A Man Alone* (1955) and *Panic in Year Zero* (1962). He made a further career as cantankerous older figures after playing the role of the father in the phenomenally popular *Love Story* (1970). *Wide-Eyed in Babylon* (1976) is his autobiography.

Millar, John 1735–1801

Scottish jurist

He was born in Shotts, Lanarkshire, and educated at Hamilton Grammar School and Glasgow University. He became Professor of Law at Glasgow (1761). A friend of **Adam Smith** and Lord **Kames**, he had a distinguished reputation as a law teacher and a leading liberal. His main works are the *Origin of the Distinction of Ranks* (1771), a pioneer work on sociology; and *An Historical View of the English Government* (1787), the first constitutional history of Great Britain or England, and a work with many new and original insights. Both books were widely influential. An ardent Whig, he was regarded at the time as a radical, even a near-revolutionary.

Millay, Edna St Vincent 1892–1950

US poet

Born in Rockland, Maine, she published her first volume of poetry, *Renaissance and Other Poems*, on graduating from Vassar College in 1917. Moving to Greenwich Village, a popular meeting place for artists and writers, she published *A Few Figs from Thistles* (1920), which celebrated Bohemian life. In 1923 came *The Harp Weaver and Other Poems*, for which she was awarded the 1923 Pulitzer Prize. The popularity she enjoyed during her own time waned after her death, and she was dismissed as petulant and artificial, but the admiration of writers like **Maya Angelou** has caused her to be re-evaluated. 📖 N A Brittan, *Edna St Vincent Millay* (1967)

Mille, Agnes de See **De Mille, Agnes**
Mille, Cecil B de See **De Mille, Cecil B (lount)**

Miller, Arthur 1915–
US playwright

Born in New York City, he graduated from the University of Michigan in 1938. His first successful play, *All My Sons* (1947), focused on the family of an arms manufacturer and reflected the preoccupation with moral issues that was to characterize his work. His tragedy, *Death of a Salesman* (1949), won the Pulitzer Prize and brought him international recognition. *The Crucible* (1953) is probably, to date, his most lasting work, since its theme, the persecution of the Salem witches equated with contemporary political persecution, stands out of time. Other works include *A View from the Bridge* (1955), the film script of *The Misfits* (1960), *After the Fall* (1963), *Incident at Vichy* (1964), *The Creation of the World and Other Business* (1972), *Playing for Time* (1981), *Danger: Memory!* (1987), *The Ride Down Mount Morgan* (1991), *The Last Yankee* (1992) and *Broken Glass* (1994). His marriage to **Marilyn Monroe**, from whom he was divorced in 1961, and his brush with the authorities over early communist sympathies, brought him considerable publicity. Since the 1980s, almost all of Miller's plays have been given major British revivals, but the apparent spurning of serious work by Broadway has made it difficult for his voice to be heard in the USA. □ N Carson, *Arthur Miller* (1982)

Miller, Cheryl 1964–
US basketball player

Born in Riverside, California, she is noted as the first woman to 'dunk' a basketball in regulation play (ie to score by thrusting the ball downward through the basket). She holds the California Interscholastic Federation records for the most career points and the most points scored in one season. At the University of Southern California, she won nearly every major basketball award, including the Naismith Trophy (1984, 1985, 1986), the Broderick award as college player of the year (1984, 1985), and the Women's Basketball Coaches' Association Player of the Year (1985, 1986). Her number was retired by the university in 1986, marking the first time a basketball player had been so honoured. She now works as the women's basketball coach at USC. She was inducted into the International Women's Sports Hall of Fame in 1991.

Miller, Sir (Ian) Douglas 1900–96
Australian neurosurgeon

He was born in Melbourne and after graduating from Sydney University he worked at St Vincent's Hospital in Sydney. In 1934 he went to England to study the then new practice of neurosurgery, returning to St Vincent's in 1939. In World War II he went to the Western Desert and in 1942 took charge of the AIF (Australian Imperial Force) neurological centre in Cairo. Afterwards he worked in Asia, training surgeons in Singapore, Malaysia, Thailand and India. He founded the neurological centre at St Vincent's in 1939. Honorary neurosurgeon there until 1960, he became a member of the Board in 1954 and served as chairman until 1973, establishing 'Vinnie's' as one of the leading hospitals in Australia. □ *A Surgeon's Story* (1985)

Miller, (Alton) Glenn 1904–44
US trombonist and bandleader

He was born in Clarinda, Iowa, and educated at the University of Colorado, but before completing his studies he joined the Ben Pollack Band (1924), moving to New York in 1928 and working as a freelance musician and arranger. From 1937 he led a succession of popular dance orchestras and joined the US Army air force in 1942, forming another orchestra—the Glenn Miller Army Air Force Band—to entertain the troops. While they were stationed in Europe, Miller was a passenger in a small aircraft lost without trace over the English Channel. His music has continued to be performed since his death by orchestras rehearsed in his distinctive style. □ G T Simon, *Glenn Miller and His Orchestra* (1980)

Miller, Henry Valentine 1891–1980
US writer

He was born in New York, to German–American parents, and brought up in Brooklyn. With money from his father which was intended to finance him through Cornell University, he travelled in the south-west and Alaska. He then went to work in his father's tailor shop, left after trying to unionize the workforce, became employment manager for the Western Union Telegraph Co (1920), and ran a speakeasy in Greenwich Village (1927). From 1930 he spent nine years in France, during which time he published *Tropic of Cancer* (1934) and *Tropic of Capricorn* (1938), as well as *Black Spring* (1936). He returned to the USA in 1940 but travelled extensively both at home and abroad before settling in Big Sur, California. Much of his fiction is autobiographical and explicitly sexual, and he had to overcome many impecunious years and rebuffs from state censors. (US editions of the *Tropics* were not published until 1961 and 1962 respectively.) In his time, however, he became one of the most read US authors, solipsistic, surrealistic and blackly comic, empathizing with the outcast: prostitutes, hobos and artists. Important books are *The Colossus of Maroussi* (1941), a dithyrambic travel book, *The Air-Conditioned Nightmare* (1945), a bleak essay on contemporary USA, and *The Rosy Crucifixion* trilogy of novels: *Sexus* (1949), *Plexus* (1953) and *Nexus* (1960). A guru of the sexually liberated 1960s, he fell foul of feminist critics in the 1970s. □ J Martin, *Always Merry and Bright: the life of Henry Miller* (1978)

Miller, Hugh 1802–56
Scottish geologist and writer

Born in Cromarty, he was apprenticed to a stonemason at 16 and developed an interest in fossils and devoted his winter months to reading, writing and natural history. He became a bank accountant for a time (1834–39) and later became involved in the controversy over church appointments that led to the Disruption of the Church of Scotland (1843). At the same time he wrote a series of geological articles in the Scottish 'Evangelist' newspaper *The Witness*, later collected as *The Old Red Sandstone* (1841). He made important discoveries of fossil fish from the Devonian rocks of Scotland. Also a pioneer of popular science books, he combated Darwinian evolutionary theory with *Footprints of the Creator* (1850), *The Testimony of the Rocks* (1857) and *Sketchbook of Popular Geology* (published posthumously in 1859).

Miller, Jacques Francis Albert Pierre 1931–
Australian immunologist

Born in Nice, France, he graduated in medicine from the University of Sydney in 1955, before working in London at the Chester Beatty Research Institute (1958–65). He studied the development of leukaemia in mice, and in 1960 obtained his PhD in experimental pathology. Miller played a major part in discovering the function of the thymus gland, which had been removed from animals in previous experiments with no apparent effect. However, when he tried removing the thymus from newborn mice, he found that they failed to develop properly and died within a few months. He showed that these animals would accept skin grafts from unrelated mice and even rats, and concluded that the thymus gland is an important organ in the control of the immunity system. He went back to Australia in 1966 to become head of the experimental pathology (later thymus biology) unit of the Walter and Eliza Hall Institute, Melbourne. He was made an Officer of the Order of Australia in 1981.

Miller, Joaquin, *pseudonym of* Cincinnatus Heine Miller 1839–1913

US poet

Born in Liberty, Indiana, he became a miner in California, and fought in the Indian wars. After practising law in Oregon, he edited a paper suppressed for showing Confederate sympathies. He was a county judge in Oregon (1866–70) and, after a spell as a Washington journalist, he settled in California as a fruitgrower in 1877. His poems include *Songs of the Sierras* (1871). He also wrote a successful play, *The Danites of the Sierras* (1877), and his autobiography: *My Life among the Modocs* (1873) and *My Own Story* (new edition 1891). 🕮 M M Marberry, *Splendid Poseur: Joaquin Miller, American Poet* (1953)

Miller, Jonathan Wolfe 1934–

English theatre director and author

Born in London, he qualified as a doctor at Cambridge, and co-authored and performed in the revue, *Beyond the Fringe*, at the 1960 Edinburgh Festival. He made his directorial debut with *Under Plain Cover* (1962), a play by John Osborne, at the Royal Court Theatre, and was editor and presenter of the BBC Television arts programme, *Monitor* (1964–65). He has been responsible for many memorable productions, and from 1974 has also specialized in opera productions for the English National Opera and other major companies. He has written and presented two BBC television series related to the world of medicine, *The Body in Question* (1977) and *States of Mind* (1982). In 1985 he became Research Fellow in Neuropsychology at Sussex University. One of the most original of directors, he has written several books, including *Subsequent Performances* (1986), an illuminating and invigorating discussion of his views on the theatre and directing plays and operas. He became artistic director of the Old Vic in 1988 and in his first season staged Racine's *Andromache* and an 'anticolonialist' version of *The Tempest* with Max von Sydow playing Prospero, and produced *King Lear* the following year.

Miller, Keith Ross 1919–

Australian cricketer

He was born in Melbourne. He established himself as the world's leading all-rounder of the time, playing in the great Don Bradman Test side of 1948. Miller scored 2,598 runs in 55 Test matches including seven centuries, and took 170 wickets.

Miller, Lee 1907–77

US photographer

Born in Poughkeepsie, New York, she studied in Paris (1925) and at the Art Students League, New York (1927–29), during which time she also modelled for Edward Steichen. She studied with Man Ray in Paris (1929–32) before returning to the USA to run her own photography studio in New York. In 1947 she married the painter Roland Penrose in England, with whom she had a son, Anthony (b.1947), who was later to write her biography, *The Lives of Lee Miller* (1985). She was a photographer in London for *Vogue* from 1940, and in 1942 became official war correspondent for the US forces. She then returned to *Vogue* as a freelance journalist and photographer (1946–54). Retrospective exhibitions of her work were held at the Statey-Wise Gallery in New York (1985), the Photographers' Gallery, London (1986), and the San Francisco Museum of Modern Art (1987). Her publications include *Grim Glory: Pictures of Britain under Fire* (1941, with E Carter).

Miller, Max, *originally* Thomas Henry Sargent 1895–1963

English music hall comedian

Born in Brighton, he worked with the original Billy Smart's Circus and army concert parties during World War I. He subsequently pursued a solo career as a stand-up comedian, touring throughout Britain before making his London debut in 1922. By 1926 he was top of the bill at the Holborn Empire, a position he maintained for three decades. Traditionally attired in white trilby, two-tone shoes, kipper tie and rainbow-coloured plus-four suit, he turned innuendo into an art form, earning the nickname the 'Cheeky Chappie'. He made his film debut in *The Good Companions* (1933) and appeared in a host of modest British comedies during the next 10 years but remained at his best as a live performer—the highest paid variety artist in Britain—whose superb timing and raucous vulgarity reduced loyal audiences to helpless laughter.

Miller, Stanley Lloyd 1930–

US chemist

Born in Oakland, California, he studied at California University and taught there from 1960. His best-known work was carried out in Chicago in 1953 and concerned the possible origins of life on Earth. Inspired by the theories of Aleksandr Oparin and J B S Haldane, with Harold Clayton Urey, he passed electric discharges (simulating thunderstorms) through mixtures containing reducing gases (hydrogen, methane, ammonia and water) which Haldane had suggested were likely to have formed the early planetary atmosphere. The formation of the Oparin–Haldane 'primeval soup' is now accepted as the most plausible theory for the generation of complex organic molecules on Earth, although the probable subsequent path from these chemicals to a living system is still hotly debated.

Miller, William 1782–1849

US religious leader

Born in Pittsfield, Massachusetts, he became a farmer and underwent a religious conversion in c.1816. Believing that the Second Coming of Christ was imminent, he began preaching in 1831 and founded the religious sect of Second Adventists or Millerites. He attracted tens of thousands of converts, many of whom fell away when the event did not occur as predicted in 1843 or 1844. His remaining followers continued to meet and organized the Seventh Day Adventist Church in 1863.

Miller, William, *known as* the Laureate of the Nursery 1810–72

Scottish poet

Born in Glasgow, he was a woodturner by profession, having relinquished a medical career through ill health. In 1863, encouraged by his friends, he published a collection of poems which brought him some fame. Today, however, he is remembered only as the author of 'Wee Willie Winkie', one of his numerous dialect poems about children and childhood.

Milles, Carl Vilhelm Emil 1875–1955

US sculptor

Born near Uppsala, Sweden, he executed numerous monumental works, such as the Sten Sture monument near Uppsala and the Gustav I Vasa statue, and was especially renowned as a designer of fountains. Much of his work is in Sweden and the USA, where he settled in 1931, noteworthy examples being *Wedding of the Rivers* (1940) in St Louis, and *St Martin of Tours* (1955) in Kansas City, his last work.

Millet, Jean François 1814–75

French painter

Born in Grouchy near Gréville, he worked on the farm with his father, a peasant, but, showing a talent for art, he was placed under a painter at Cherbourg in 1832. In 1837 he went to Paris and worked under Paul Delaroche, achieving recognition in 1844 at the Salon. The 1848

Revolution and poverty drove him from Paris, and he settled with his wife and children at Barbizon, near the forest of Fontainebleau, living much like the peasants around him, and painting the rustic life of France with sympathetic power. His famous *Sower* was completed in 1850. His *Peasants Grafting* (1855) was followed by *The Gleaners* (1857), *The Angelus* (1859) and other masterpieces. He also produced many charcoal drawings of high quality, and etched a few plates. He received little public notice, and was never well off, but following the Great Exhibition of 1867 at Paris, in which nine of his best works were on show, he was awarded the Legion of Honour. 📖 Julia M Ady, *Jean François Millet: His Life and Letters* (1896)

Millett, Kate (Katherine) Murray 1934–
US feminist, writer and sculptor
Born in St Paul, she was educated at the University of Minnesota, St Hilda's College, Oxford, and at Columbia University, New York. Her PhD thesis became the bestseller and feminist classic, *Sexual Politics* (1970). Early in her career as a sculptor she spent some time in Tokyo (1961–63), and has exhibited in Tokyo, New York, Los Angeles and Berlin. She also founded the Women's Art Colony at Poughkeepsie, New York. Her other publications include *The Prostitution Papers* (1973), the autobiographical *Flying* (1974), *Going to Iran* (1982) and *The Loony Bin Trip* (1990).

Milligan, Spike (Terence Alan) 1918–
English humorist
Born in Ahmadnagar, India, he was a singer and trumpeter before doing war service. He made his radio debut in *Opportunity Knocks* (1949) and, along with Peter Sellers, Harry Secombe and Michael Bentine, co-wrote and performed in the *Goon Show* (1951–60). His unusual perspective on the world, allied to his sense of the ridiculous and the surreal, has had a great influence on British humour. On stage, he has appeared in *Treasure Island* (1961, 1973, 1974, 1975) and *The Bed-Sitting Room* (1963, 1967) which he also co-wrote. His many television programmes include *Paging You* (1947), *Idiot Weekly, Price 2d* (1956), *A Show Called Fred* (1956), *Son of Fred* (1956), *The World of Beachcomber* (1968–69) and the *Q* series (1969–80). He has appeared in films such as *The Bed Sitting Room* (1969), *The Magic Christian* (1969) and *Digby—The Biggest Dog in the World* (1973). He has published a variety of children's books, poetry, autobiography and comic novels including *Puckoon* (1963), *Adolf Hitler, My Part in His Downfall* (1971), *Where Have All the Bullets Gone?* (1985), *The Looney: An Irish Fantasy* (1987) and *Peacework* (1991). 📖 Pauline Scudamore, *Spike Milligan* (1985)

Millikan, Robert Andrews 1868–1953
US physicist and Nobel Prize winner
He was born in Illinois, and studied at Oberlin College and Columbia University, where he received his PhD in 1895. After working at the universities of Berlin and Göttingen, he became Albert Michelson's assistant at the University of Chicago, where he was appointed professor in 1910. In 1921 he moved to the California Institute of Technology (Caltech) where he established the experimental physics laboratory. At Chicago he refined J J Thomson's oil drop technique, and was able to show that the charge on each droplet was always a multiple of the same basic unit—the charge on the electron—which he measured very precisely. In studies of the photoelectric effect he confirmed Albert Einstein's theoretical equations and gave an accurate value for Planck's constant. For all these achievements he was awarded the 1923 Nobel Prize for physics. He also investigated cosmic rays, a term that he coined in 1925. 📖 Robert H Kargon, *The Rise of Robert Millikan: Portrait of a Life in American Science* (1982)

Mills, Dame Barbara Jean Lyon 1940–
English lawyer
Born in Chorley Wood, Hertfordshire, and educated at St Helen's School, Northwood, and Lady Margaret Hall, Oxford, she was called to the Bar in 1963. She became a recorder of the Crown Court in 1982, and a QC in 1986. She was a Junior Treasury Counsel to the Central Criminal Court in the 1980s, during which time she became known for prosecuting Michael Fagin for breaking into the bedroom of Queen Elizabeth II. She was made director of the Serious Fraud Office in 1990, and in 1992 became the first woman to be head of the Department of Public Prosecutions, at a time when its activities were under scrutiny following damaging revelations of earlier miscarriages of justice. She resigned in 1998.

Mills, C(harles) Wright 1916–62
US sociologist and academic
Born in Waco, Texas, he was educated at the universities of Texas and Wisconsin. He taught at Wisconsin and Maryland, and became professor at Columbia (1946–62). His two main contributions to social understanding were *White Collar* (1951), a critical account of the 'new' postwar middle classes, and *The Power Elite* (1956), a darker and more pessimistic study of social control by the military, politicians and corporate money. *The Causes of World War Three* (1958) had an important impact on the New Left in the USA; his last book was the highly prescient *Listen Yankee: The Revolution in Cuba* (1960). 📖 J Eldridge, *C Wright Mills* (1983)

Mills, Sir John Lewis Ernest Watts 1908–
English actor
Born in Felixstowe, Suffolk, into a theatrical family, he took an early interest in amateur dramatics which led to his London stage debut as a chorus boy in *The Five O'Clock Revue* (1927). More prestigious theatre work followed in *Cavalcade* (1931) and *Words and Music* (1932) before his film debut in *The Midshipmaid* (1932). He established himself as one of the hardest-working mainstays of the British film industry, portraying typically English roles in such films as *In Which We Serve* (1942), *Scott of the Antarctic* (1948) and *The Colditz Story* (1954). As a character actor his many credits include *Great Expectations* (1946) and *The History of Mr Polly* (1949). Later films include *Ryan's Daughter* (1970, Academy Award), *Ghandi* (1982) and *A Woman of Substance* (1986). Active in the theatre and on television, he also directed the film *Sky West and Crooked* (1965). Knighted in 1977, he published his autobiography, *Up in the Clouds, Gentlemen Please*, in 1980. Married to the playwright Mary Hayley Bell since 1941, both his daughters Juliet (1941–) and Hayley (1946–) are actresses. 📖 Robert Tanitch, *John Mills* (1993)

Mills, Robert 1781–1855
US architect
He was born in Charleston, South Carolina, and studied under important US architects such as Thomas Jefferson and Benjamin Latrobe, who taught him to look to classical models for inspiration. He became a leading exponent of the Greek revival, and in 1836 President Andrew Jackson appointed him architect of public buildings in Washington DC. His major works there include the Treasury Building (1836–42), the Patent Office (1836–40), and the Post Office (begun 1839). He also designed the Washington Monument in 1836, but it was not begun until 1848 (completed 1884).

Miln, James 1819–81
Scottish antiquary
A former naval officer and merchant in China and India, he made excavations on a Roman site at Carnac, Brittany, and published the results in *Excavations at Carnac* (1877 and 1881). Miln Museum, Carnac, contains his collection.

Miln, Walter See Mylne, Walter

Milne, A(lan) A(lexander) 1882–1956
English writer

Born in St John's Wood, London, he was educated at Westminster and Trinity College, Cambridge. He joined the staff of *Punch* as assistant editor, and became well known for his light essays and his comedies, notably *Wurzel-Flummery* (1917), *Mr Pim Passes By* (1919) and *The Dover Road* (1922). In 1924 he achieved world fame with his book of children's verse, *When We were Very Young*, written for his own son, Christopher Robin. Further children's classics include the enchantingly whimsical *Winnie-the-Pooh* (1926), *Now We are Six* (1927) and *The House at Pooh Corner* (1928), memorably illustrated by **E H Shepard**. He wrote an autobiography, *It's Too Late Now* (1939).
📖 A Thwaite, *A. A. Milne* (1990)

Milne, Edward Arthur 1896–1950
English astrophysicist

Born in Hull, Humberside, and educated at Hymer's College, Hull, and at Trinity College, Cambridge, he became assistant director of the Cambridge Solar Physics Observatory (1920–24), and then Professor of Mathematics at Manchester (1924–28) and Oxford (from 1928), making notable contributions to the study of cosmic dynamics. In 1923, with the English mathematician and physicist Ralph Fowler (1889–1944), he studied the ionization, temperature and energy flux of stellar surface material and was the first to estimate the electron pressure in a stellar atmosphere. He noticed that a decrease in luminosity might cause the collapse of the star, which could lead to the production of a nova. In 1932 he began to develop his theory of 'kinematic relativity'. One outcome of this was the prediction that the universe is 10,000 million years old.

Milne, John 1859–1913
English seismologist

Born in Liverpool, he was educated at King's College and the Royal School of Mines, London. He began his career as a mining engineer in the UK and Germany, then spent two years in Newfoundland, and travelled in Egypt, Arabia and Siberia. Always a keen traveller, he joined an expedition in 1874 to locate Mount Sinai and on being appointed Professor of Geology in Tokyo (1875–94), travelled there by camel across Mongolia. In Japan he took up an interest in earthquakes, becoming a supreme authority, for which he was awarded the Order of the Rising Sun. He pioneered modern seismology and introduced precise physical measurements. In 1892, with colleagues, he developed a seismometer to record horizontal components of ground motion which became used on a worldwide basis. Milne devised methods of locating distant earthquakes and early traveltime curves for seismic wave arrivals, initiated experiments using explosives, and compiled *A Catalogue of Destructive (Japanese) Earthquakes AD 7–AD 1899* (1912). On his retirement to the Isle of Wight (1895) he ran a private seismological observatory, regularly issuing a bulletin summarizing data from a worldwide network of seismological stations which he set up with his own instruments, a forerunner of the International Seismological Summary. A prolific writer, he published *Earthquakes and other Earth Movements* (1886) and *Seismology* (1898).

Milner (of St James's and Cape Town), Alfred Milner, 1st Viscount 1854–1925
English politician and colonial administrator

Born in Bonn, Germany, son of a university lecturer in English at Tübingen, and educated at Oxford, he established his reputation in Egypt and was appointed Governor of the Cape and High Commissioner in South Africa (1897). There he became convinced that the British position was endangered by the South African Republic (Transvaal), and set about the political rationalization of the region through the Boer Wars. He hoped to encourage sufficient English-speaking immigration to outnumber the Boers in a South African dominion. He additionally became Governor of the Transvaal and Orange River Colony in 1901, but was forced to resign in 1905 as a result of irregularities over Chinese labour he had introduced for the Rand gold mines. He was Secretary for War (1916–19) and Colonial Secretary (1919–21).

Milner, Brenda Atkinson, *née* Langford 1918–
Canadian psychologist

She studied at Cambridge and at McGill University, Montreal, then worked at the Ministry of Supply in England (1941–44) before emigrating to Canada. She taught at the University of Montreal (1944–1952), leaving to join McGill University (1952–), and then becoming head of the Neuropsychology Research Unit at the Montreal Neurological Institute (1970–91). Her contributions to neuropsychology have been mainly empirical, the best-known being a series of investigations of a man rendered profoundly amnesic following a radical brain operation for the relief of epilepsy. This work has formed the basis for a large body of subsequent research that has improved our understanding of the brain structures implicated in laying down a new memory, and their mode of function. Other important research by Milner has concerned the asymmetrical activities of the two sides of the brain, particularly in relation to the temporal and the frontal lobes, and has been used in the development of the surgical treatment of temporal-lobe epilepsy. One of the most significant figures in the growth of neuropsychology, she won the Distinguished Scientific Contribution award of the American Psychological Association (1973), and the Ralph W Gerard prize of the Society for Neuroscience (1987).

Milnes, Richard Monckton, 1st Baron Houghton 1809–85
English politician and writer

Born in London, he was a member of the Apostles Club at Cambridge along with **Tennyson** and **Thackeray**. He was MP for Pontefract from 1837 until he entered the House of Lords in 1863. A patron of young writers, he befriended **David Gray**, was one of the first to recognize **Algernon Charles Swinburne**'s genius, and secured the poet laureateship for Tennyson (1850). He was the 'Mr Vavasour' of **Disraeli**'s novel *Tancred*. A traveller, a philanthropist and an unrivalled after-dinner speaker, he went up in a balloon and down in a diving-bell. He was the first publishing Englishman who gained access to the harems of the East, he championed oppressed peoples and the rights of women, and carried a bill for establishing reformatories (1846). In addition to his poetry and essays he published *Life, Letters and Remains of Keats* (1848).
📖 J Pope-Hennessey, *Monckton Milnes* (1950–52)

Milnor, John W(illard) 1931–
US mathematician

He was born in Orange, New Jersey, and educated at Princeton University, where he has taught for most of his life. Chiefly a topologist, he discovered that familiar objects can be described in unfamiliar ways, so that, for example, functions on higher dimensional spheres are differentiable in one description but not in another. For this highly unintuitive result and others, he was awarded the Fields Medal (the mathematical equivalent of the Nobel Prize) in 1962. He has also worked on the topology of higher dimensional manifolds. Many of his books have provided introductions to current research, and he stimulated William Thurston to win the Fields Medal in 1978 for his work on three-dimensional manifolds.

Milo of Croton 6th century BC
Semi-legendary Greek wrestler

From the Greek colony of Croton in southern Italy, he was the best-known Greek athlete of ancient times. He won the wrestling contest at five successive Olympic Games and swept the board at all other festivals. A man of huge stature, he boasted that no one had ever brought him to his knees, and it is said that he carried a live ox upon his shoulders through the stadium at Olympia and then ate it all in a single day. He played a leading part in the military defeat of Sybaris in 511BC. Tradition has it that in his old age he tried to split a tree which closed upon his hands and held him fast until he was devoured by wolves.

Milošević, Slobodan 1941–
Serbian politician

He was born in Pozarevac and educated at Belgrade University. He joined the Communist League in 1959, was active in student affairs, and entered government service as an economic adviser to the Mayor of Belgrade in 1966. From 1969 to 1983 he held senior posts in the state gas and banking industries. He became president of the Serbian League of Communists in 1984, and President of Serbia in 1988. As a hardline party leader in the pre-perestroika mould, he won immediate popularity by disenfranchising the Albanian majority in Kosovo province, and survived the republic's 1990 multi-party elections that removed the communist leadership in Croatia and Slovenia. However, his continued efforts to dominate the affairs of the more liberal republics, his initial refusal to accept a Croat, Stipe Mesić, as President of Yugoslavia, and his action in appropriating £875 million of Yugoslav federal reserves to buttress Serbia's ailing economy without the consent of any of them, prompted Croatia and Slovenia to declare their independence in 1991. Bitterly opposed to the break-up of Yugoslavia, he agitated for the Yugoslav federal army to be sent into Slovenia and Croatia and later (1992) into Bosnia-Herzegovina. An unrepentant champion of a 'Greater Serbia', he has done nothing to prevent the fighting in Bosnia led by avowedly 'independent' Serbian militias bent on joining the greater part of the newly-independent Republic of Bosnia to the Republic of Serbia and eliminating all non-Serb residents through 'ethnic cleansing'. In 1995 he played a key role in the release of UN hostages who had been captured by Bosnian Serbs. Later that year he took part in the peace talks in Dayton, Ohio, negotiating on behalf of the Bosnian Serbs. A treaty was signed and US sanctions against the country were lifted. In 1996 Milošević was re-elected amidst furious accusations of electoral rigging.

Milosz, Czeslaw 1911–
Polish poet, novelist and essayist, and Nobel Prize winner

Born in Szetejnie, Lithuania, he worked for the Resistance during World War II, and became Professor of Slavic Languages and Literature at Berkeley in California (1961–78). He established a reputation with his first two volumes of poetry, *Poem on Time Frozen* (1933) and *Trzy zimy* (1936, 'Three Winters'). In 1945 he published *Ocadenie* ('Rescue'), a collection primarily of war poems. He spent nearly 35 years in exile, first in Paris, then in California. Later volumes include *Hymn of the Pearl* (1982), *The Unattainable Earth* (1986), *Provinces* (1991), *A Year of the Hunter* (1994) and *Facing the River* (1995), and his *Collected Poems* were published in 1988. He was awarded the Nobel Prize for literature in 1980.

Milstein, Cesar 1927–
British molecular biologist, immunologist and Nobel Prize winner

Born in Bahía Blanca, Argentina, he graduated in chemistry from Buenos Aires University in 1945, and worked on enzymes at Cambridge (1958–61), where he obtained a PhD in 1960. In 1961 he returned to Argentina to become head of the division of Molecular Biology at the National Institute of Microbiology, but following a military coup, he returned to Cambridge, where he has been on the staff of the Medical Research Council at the laboratory of Molecular Biology since 1963 and Fellow of Darwin College (1981–95). He has conducted important research into antibodies, developing the technique of 'monoclonal antibodies' by fusing together different cells to maintain antibody production. This technique has become widespread in the commercial development of new drugs and diagnostic tests, and in 1984 it won Milstein the Nobel Prize for physiology or medicine, shared with **Georges Köhler** and **Niels Jerne**.

Milstein, Nathan Mironovich 1904–
US violinist

Born in Odessa, Russia, he began his concert career there in 1919, soon playing with **Vladimir Horowitz** and **Gregor Piatigorsky**. He left the USSR in 1925, gave recitals in Paris, and made his US debut under **Leopold Stokowski** in 1929. He became a US citizen in 1942 and toured anually into his 80s. He received the Kennedy Center award for Lifetime Achievement in 1987 and published his memoirs *From Russia to the West* in 1990.

Miltiades, the Younger c.550–489BC
Athenian general and politician

He became a vassal of **Darius I** of Persia and accompanied him on his Scythian expedition (c.514BC). He returned to Athens in 493, and was the chief strategist in the Greek victory against the Persians at Marathon (490). The following year he attacked the island of Paros, but failed and was impeached, and died in prison. He was the father of **Cimon**, also an Athenian hero.

Milton, John See panel p1287

Min 1851–95
Queen of Korea

The leader of a powerful faction at court, mainly comprising members of her own family, she was strongly opposed to increased Japanese influence in Korea. Though her husband Kojong (or I T'aewang) was king from 1864–1907, she was the real holder of the ruling power. She struggled for power with her father-in-law Hungson (or Tai Wen Kun) who was official regent (1864–73) and remained a dominant political figure until his death (1898). Min was assassinated in a palace coup instigated by the Japanese Minister to Korea, Miura Goro, in an attempt to secure Japanese control over the Korean king. The plot misfired, however, as Miura was cashiered by his own government while King Kojong increasingly looked to China for protection.

Mindszenty, József 1892–1975
Hungarian Roman Catholic primate

Born in Mindszent, Vas, he became a priest in 1915, Archbishop of Esztergom and primate in 1945, and cardinal in 1946. He then acquired international fame in 1948 when he was charged with treason by the Communist government in Budapest. He was sentenced to life imprisonment the following year, but in 1955 was released on condition that he did not leave Hungary. At the end of the Hungarian Uprising in 1956 he was granted asylum in the US legation, where he remained as a voluntary prisoner until 1971, when conditions in Hungary eased and he was allowed to go abroad. He spent his last years in a Hungarian religious community in Vienna. ⌨ J Vecsey and P Schlafly, *Mindszenty the Man* (1972)

Minette See **Henrietta Anne, Duchesse d'Orléans**

Mingus, Charles 1922–79
US jazz bassist, composer and bandleader

Milton, John 1608–74
English poet

John Milton was born in Bread Street, Cheapside, the son of a scrivener and composer. He was educated at St Paul's School and Christ's College, Cambridge. His apprentice work at Cambridge includes the 'Nativity Ode', an epitaph on **Shakespeare** and 'At a Solemn Music'. In 1635 his father moved to Horton in Buckinghamshire; there Milton wrote *L'Allegro* and *Il Penseroso, Comus* and the pastoral elegy *Lycidas* (1637). For the next two years Milton visited Italy (1638–39). The fame of his Latin poems had preceded him and he was received in the academies with distinction.

His Italian tour was interrupted by news of the imminent outbreak of Civil War in England. This event, into which he threw himself with revolutionary ardour, silenced his poetic output for 20 years except for some Latin and Italian pieces and occasional sonnets, most of which were published in a volume of *Poems* in 1645. Two of these stand out: the noble 'On His Blindness' and 'On the Late Massacre in Piedmont'.

During the years after his return to London in 1639, he devoted himself to the cause of the revolution with political activity and a series of pamphlets defending civil and religious liberties. These included five pamphlets against episcopacy, including *Apology for Smectymnuus* (1642, *Smectymnuus* was an attack on episcopacy by five Presbyterians). In 1642 Milton married Mary Powell, the daughter of a Royalist; when she failed to return to him after a visit to her parents in Oxford, Milton published *The Doctrine and Discipline of Divorce* (1643), followed by three supplementary pamphlets against the opponents of his views; these occasioned a threat of prosecution by a parliamentary committee dominated by the Presbyterians, who were now to be reckoned his chief enemies after the episcopacy pamphlets. *Areopagitica, A Speech for the Liberty of Unlicensed Printing* (1644) was the famous vindication which is still quoted when the press finds itself in danger.

Meanwhile, in 1645 his wife returned to him, accompanied by her whole family as refugees after the Battle of Naseby, and two years later Milton inherited sufficient money to give up his schoolteaching. The execution of **Charles I** launched him on his third public controversy, now addressed however to the conscience of Europe. As Latin secretary to the new council of state to which he was appointed immediately after his defence of the republicans (*The Tenure of Kings and Magistrates*, 1649), he became official apologist for the Commonwealth. As such he wrote *Eikonoklastes* and two *Defensiones*, the first, *Pro Populo Anglicano Defensio* (1650), addressed to the celebrated humanist **Claudius Salmasius**. The second, also in Latin,

Defensio Secunda (1654), contains autobiographical matter and so supplements the personal matter in the *Apology for Smectymnuus.*

Meanwhile, his wife had died in 1652, leaving three daughters, and he now married Catherine Woodcock, whose death two years later is the theme of his beautiful sonnet 'Methought I saw my late espoused Saint'. Although blind from 1652 onwards, he retained his Latin secretaryship until the Restoration (1660), which he roused himself to resist in a last despairing effort as pamphleteer. But the fire had gone out of him, and *The Readie and Easie Way*, which pointed to dictatorship, became the target of the Royalist wits. After the Restoration Milton went into hiding for a short period, and then after the Act of Oblivion (August 1660) he devoted himself wholly to poetry with the exception of his prose *De Doctrina Christiana* (which did not appear until 1823).

He married his third wife, Elizabeth Minshull, in 1662. This was the period of his most famous works, beginning with *Paradise Lost* (completed 1665, published 1667), the theme of which had been in Milton's mind since 1641. It was originally to be a sacred drama; but when in 1658 his official duties were lightened so as to allow him to write, he chose the epic form. The first three books reflect the triumph of the godly, so soon to be reversed; the last books, written in 1663, are tinged with despair. God's kingdom is not of this world. Man's intractable nature frustrates the planning of the wise. In *Paradise Regained* (1671), the tone is more of resignation, and the theme is the triumph of reason over passion. *Samson Agonistes*, published with it in 1671, shows the reviving spirit of rebellion, due perhaps to the rise of Whig opposition about 1670. The parallel of his own fortunes, both in the private and the public sphere, with those of **Samson** made Milton pour out his spirit into this Greek play, which also formed the libretto of **Handel**'s oratorio.

His last years were spent in sociable comfort in Cripplegate, where he was buried next to his father in St Giles' Churchyard.

📖 A N Wilson, *The Life of John Milton* (1983); C Hill, *Milton and the Puritan Revolution* (1977).

> 'Lords and Commons of England, consider what nation it is whereof ye are, and whereof ye are the governors: a nation not slow and dull, but of a quick, ingenious, and piercing spirit, acute to invent, subtle and sinewy to discourse, not beneath the reach of any point the highest that human capacity can soar to.' From *Areopagitica.*

He was born in Nogales, Arizona, and brought up in Los Angeles. He was taught to play the cello at school, eventually performing with the LA Junior Philharmonic, but contact with jazz musicians led him to take up the double-bass. His first professional work as a bassist was with traditional-style bands. As a child, he had sung gospel music at the Holiness Church, and he drew on this background in his mature music, but in the context of modern and avant-garde ideas. He worked with big bands led by **Louis Armstrong** and **Lionel Hampton** in the 1940s, before moving to New York, where he played in smaller groups, notably with vibraphonist Red Norvo. He was recognized as a leading figure on his instrument, but his ambitions lay in composition. He launched a record label, Debut, in 1953, and became involved with the experimental Jazz Composers Workshop, before forming his own Jazz Workshop in 1955. Recordings like *Pithecanthropus Erectus* (1956) and *The Black Saint and the Sinner Lady* (1964)

attempted to stretch and redefine the boundaries of jazz and the relationship of composition to improvisation within it, and his huge musical legacy is among the most important in jazz. He wrote an inchoate, unfinished, semi-fictional 'autobiography', *Beneath The Underdog*, and was an emotional campaigner for black rights. He was crippled by sclerosis in 1978. His massive work *Epitaph*, for 31 instruments, was performed in complete form for the first time in 1989, under the supervision of **Gunther Schuller**. 📖 B Priestley, *Mingus* (1982)

Minkowski, Hermann 1864–1909
German mathematician

He was born near Kovno, Russia, and educated at the University of Königsberg. Appointed professor there (1895), he later became professor at the universities of Zurich (1896) and Göttingen (1902). He discovered a new branch of number theory, the geometry of numbers, and in his most important work he gave a precise mathematical description of space–time as it appears in Einstein's relativity theory. This four-dimensional 'Minkowski space' was described in *Space and Time* (1907).

Minnelli, Liza May 1946–
US singer and actress

Born in Los Angeles, the daughter of director Vincente Minnelli (1910–86) and Judy Garland, she first appeared on screen in her mother's film *In The Good Old Summertime* (1949) and acted in a school production of *The Diary of Anne Frank* (1960). She made her off-Broadway debut in *Best Foot Forward* (1963) and became the youngest actress to win a Tony award, for *Flora, the Red Menace* (1965). Seen on television and in cabaret, her vibrant voice and emotionally charged renditions brought comparisons with Garland. Roles in films like *Charlie Bubbles* (1967), *The Sterile Cuckoo* (1969) and *Tell Me That You Love Me, Junie Moon* (1970) revealed her dramatic skills. She won an Academy Award for *Cabaret* (1972), and a television special, *Liza with a Z* (1972), confirmed her versatility. Subsequent dramatic appearances include *New York, New York* (1977) and the television film *A Time to Live* (1985). Her private life has often seemed as volatile as her mother's but she remains a potent attraction as a recording artist and concert performer.

Minot, George Richards 1885–1950
US physician and Nobel Prize winner

He was born in Boston, and educated at Harvard College and Medical School with which, except for three post-doctoral years at Johns Hopkins, he was associated all his working life. Using special staining techniques on blood smears, he studied anaemia, and from 1925, working with William Murphy, he examined clinically George Whipple's observation that dogs made anaemic through repeated bleedings improved significantly when fed liver. Minot and Murphy established the importance of a liver diet for patients suffering from pernicious anaemia, at that time a fatal disease, and shared with Whipple the 1934 Nobel Prize for physiology or medicine. Minot, a diabetic, was one of the earliest patients to benefit from insulin therapy.

Minto, Gilbert John Murray Kynynmond-Elliot, 4th Earl of, *also called* Viscount Melgund 1845–1914
Scottish politician and colonial administrator

He was born in London and educated at Eton and Cambridge. He led an adventurous life as a soldier and journalist (including service in the Afghan Wars and a period as war correspondent for the *Morning Post*) before being appointed Governor-General of Canada (1898–1904). During this period he helped raise Canadian troops for the Boer War and settled a dispute over Alaska with the USA. As Viceroy of India (1905–10) he dealt with border friction with Russia over Persia (Iran), Tibet and Afghanistan. Within India he sternly repressed extremist nationalist elements after an attempt on his life in 1909. Simultaneously, together with Secretary of State John Morley, he attempted to secure better representation of important Indian interests and the enlargement of the powers of the existing legislative councils. The Indian Councils Act, the core of what is generally known as the Morley–Minto Reforms, became law in 1909. As a result of a campaign by a Muslim delegation for representation of Muslim interests through special constituencies this law introduced the principle of communal representation. Six special Muslim constituencies of land-holders were created for the Imperial Legislative Council, and others in some other provinces. This measure is considered as the official germ of Pakistan.

Mintoff, Dom(inic) 1916–
Maltese Labour statesman

Born in Cospicua, he was educated at Malta and Oxford Universities, afterwards becoming a civil engineer. In 1947 he joined the Malta Labour Party and in the first Malta Labour government that year he became Minister of Works and deputy Prime Minister. He became Prime Minister in 1955 and in 1956–57 undertook negotiations with Britain to integrate Malta more closely with the former. These broke down in 1958, when his demands for independence and political agitation over the transfer of the naval dockyard to a commercial concern led directly to the suspension of Malta's constitution in January 1959. Having resigned in 1958 to lead the Malta Liberation Movement, he became Leader of the Opposition in 1962. The country was granted full independence two years later, and Mintoff became Prime Minister in 1971. Three years later Malta became a republic within the Commonwealth. He continued as Prime Minister until 1984, and followed a policy of moving away from British influence.

Minton, (Francis) John 1917–57
English artist

Born in Cambridge, he studied in London and Paris, and from 1943 to 1956 taught at various London art schools. He was noted for his book illustrations and watercolours, and also as a designer of textiles and wallpaper.

Minton, Thomas 1765–1836
English pottery and china manufacturer

Born in Shrewsbury, Shropshire, he originally trained as a transfer-print engraver, working for Josiah Spode for a time, but in 1789 he set up the firm which bears his name in Stoke-on-Trent, producing copperplates for transfer-printing in blue underglaze. He is reputed to have invented the willow pattern (for which an original copper-plate engraved by him is in the British Museum). In 1793 he built a pottery works at Stoke, where he very soon produced a fine bone china (approximating to hard paste) for which the best period is 1798–1810. Much of it was tableware, decorated with finely painted flowers and fruit. His son, Herbert (his partner from 1817 to 1836), took over the firm at his death.

Minton, Yvonne Fay 1938–
Australian mezzo-soprano

Born in Earlwood, Sydney, she studied at the New South Wales Conservatorium of Music, and after winning a scholarship and the Shell aria contest, went to London where in 1961 she won the Kathleen Ferrier prize. She made her operatic debut in 1964 at the Royal Opera House, Covent Garden, London, where she has since been a resident artist. Minton has also been a guest member of the Cologne Opera since 1969, and a guest artist with the New York Metropolitan, the Chicago, Paris and Australian Opera Companies. She is noted for her Octavian in Richard Strauss's *Der Rosenkavalier* and for Wagnerian roles to which her voice is well suited.

Minuit, Peter 1580–1638
Dutch colonial official

Born in Wesel, Rhenish Prussia (now in Germany), probably to Dutch parents, he was sent to America by the Dutch West India Company to become the first director-general of New Netherland, and he bought (1626) Manhattan Island from Native Americans for trinkets worth $24. He later headed the colonists who founded (1638) New Sweden in present-day Delaware.

Mira Bai c.1498–1546
Indian bhakti poet and mystic, devoted to Krishna

She was born a Rajput princess, and was duly married to a prince before she was 20. However, even then she had already surrendered herself to Krishna and neglected her husband as a result. She constantly fought against the traditional roles ascribed to women in society, the crisis coming on the death of her husband when her father-in-law insisted that she become a suttee. She escaped to a community of bhakti devotees who supported her, eventually becoming a wandering ascetic attached to a temple in the holy city of Dwarka. Her poetry reflects her deep love for Krishna, especially in her use of the romantic symbolism of the 'mystical marriage' between herself and her Lord. Her notion of Krishna encompasses both his mythological and transcendent natures. As a result she is able to identify herself with him on the personal level and by seeing herself as being absorbed in him, which helps to explain her wide appeal.

Mirabeau, Honoré Gabriel Riqueti, Comte de
1749–91
French revolutionary politician and orator
Born in Bignon, he was dismissed from the cavalry for his disorderly behaviour, and wrote *Essai sur le despotisme* in hiding in Amsterdam, having eloped with a young married woman. In May 1777 he was imprisoned for three and a half years, during which he wrote *Erotica biblion*, *Ma conversion*, and his famous *Essai sur les lettres de cachet* (2 vols, 1782). In 1786 he was sent on a secret mission to Berlin, and there obtained the materials for his work *Sur la monarchie prussienne sous Frédéric le Grand* (4 vols, 1787). In 1789 he was elected to the States General by the Third Estate for both Marseilles and Aix. When the Third Estate constituted itself the National Assembly, Mirabeau's political acumen made him a great force, while his audacity and volcanic eloquence endeared him to the people. He advocated a constitutional monarchy on the English model but was distrusted both by the court and the extremists. Nonetheless he was elected president of the Assembly in January 1791, but died soon afterwards.

Miranda, Carmen, *professional name of* Maria do Carmo Miranda Da Cunha, *also known as* the Brazilian Bombshell 1909–55
Brazilian singer and actress
Born near Lisbon and raised in Rio de Janeiro, she became a film and radio personality before being taken to the USA by Lee Shubert in 1939. She became known as the 'Brazilian Bombshell', and made fun of her diminutive stature by wearing platform shoes and towering hats of fruits and flowers. Her US debut was in the Broadway show *The Streets of Paris* (1939) with George Abbott and Tom Costello. She went on to star in *Down Argentine Way* (1941) and *The Gang's All Here* (1943), which included the song 'The Lady in the Tutti Frutti Hat'. She died suddenly while preparing a television special with Jimmy Durante.

Miranda, Francisco de 1750–1816
Venezuelan revolutionary
Born in Caracas, Venezuela, he served in the Spanish army and the French Revolutionary Wars, then became a leader in the revolution against Spanish rule in Venezuela (1810). He ruled Venezuela briefly as dictator, but a royalist counterattack prompted him to sign an armistice (1812) yielding the country to the Spanish. He was arrested and sent to Spain, where he died in prison.

Mirandola, Giovanni See Pico Della Mirandola, Comte

Mirbeau, Octave 1850–1917
French dramatist, novelist and journalist
Born in Trévières (Calvados), he was a radical, and attracted attention by the violence of his writings. His play *Les Affaires sont les affaires* (1903, 'Business is Business') was adapted by Sidney Grundy (1905). Other works include *Le Jardin des supplices* (1898, Eng trans *Torture Garden*, 1931) and *Le Journal d'une femme de chambre* (1900, Eng trans *A Chambermaid's Diary*, 1934). ▭ M Renan, *Octave Mirbeau* (1924)

Miró, Joán 1893–1983
Spanish artist
Born in Montroig, he studied in Paris and Barcelona and exhibited with the Surrealists in 1925. In his early years he had great admiration for primitive Catalan art and the Art Nouveau forms of Antoni Gaudí's architecture. Before World War I he painted in Cézannesque and Fauve styles but in 1920 he settled in Paris and came into contact with Picasso and Juan Gris. Seduced by Surrealism he invented a manner of painting using curvilinear, fantastical forms which suggest all kinds of of dreamlike situations. Eventually, these pictures became almost entirely abstract and had a great influence on American Abstract Expressionist artists such as Maxim Gorky in the late 1940s and 1950s. His works include *Catalan Landscape* (1923–24, New York) and *Maternity* (1924). He also designed ballet sets, sculptures, murals, and tapestries.

Miró, Dr José Cardona 1903–74
Cuban politician
He was born in Havana and studied at Havana and Rome universities. He was among the academics who in exile engineered the movement against Fulgencio Batista's ruthless military dictatorship and his eventual downfall in 1958. He was the first Prime Minister of Fidel Castro's revolutionary government, but Castro stripped him of the premiership after only 45 days, appointing him ambassador to Spain and then to Washington. Instead of taking up the latter post, Miró found political asylum in the Argentine embassy in Havana, and then formed the Cuban National Revolutionary Council (CNRC) in exile in Miami, calling for an uprising against Castro and his replacement by an elected government with himself as provisional president. In the Bay of Pigs fiasco (1961), he felt that President Kennedy had betrayed his support by not committing sufficient forces to the adventure and failing to order a second invasion. He subsequently resigned his leadership of the CNRC and moved to Puerto Rico, where he worked as a professor of law until his death.

Miron, Gaston 1928–96
French–Canadian poet
Born in Saint-Agathe-des-Montes, Quebec, in the 1950s and 1960s he became a legendary personality in Quebec and Montreal, the author of long poems which he did not care if he published or not, and with a dramatically separatist stance. The best-known of these poems was 'La Vie agonique' ('The Anguished Life'). He reached the status of 'Miron le magnifique' with the publication of *L'Homme rapaillé* (1970), a collection of 57 poems on the theme of 'the present impossibility of writing a book'. Some of his poems are translated into English in *The Poetry of French Canada in Translation* (1970, ed John Glassco). ▭ J Brault, *Miron le magnifique* (1966, in French)

Mirren, Helen, *originally* Helen Lydia Mironoff
1945–
English actress
Born in Hammersmith, West London, she was a member of the National Youth Theatre and joined the Royal Shakespeare Company in 1967, where her performances included Ophelia in *Hamlet* (1970), the title role in *Miss Julie* (1971) and Lady Macbeth in *Macbeth* (1974–75). She made her film debut in *Herostratus* (1967) and won acclaim for her roles in *The Long Good Friday* (1979) and *Cal* (1984). Her subsequent pictures include *The Mosquito Coast* (1986), *The Cook The Thief His Wife & Her Lover* (1989), *Where Angels Fear to Tread* (1991), *The Madness of King George* (1994) and *Some Mother's Son* (1996). On television, she is best known as policewoman Jane Tennison in *Prime Suspect* (1991–96). Her other stage plays include a Broadway production of *A Month in the Country* (1995).

Mirrlees, James Alexander 1936–
Scottish economist and Nobel Prize winner

Born in Minnigaff, Dumfries and Galloway, he studied mathematics at Edinburgh and Cambridge before he became an adviser at the Massachusetts Institute of Technology Center for International Studies on the India Project, New Delhi (1962–63). He was a lecturer then a Fellow of Trinity College, Cambridge, from 1963 to 1968, when he became Edgeworth Professor of Economics at Oxford (1968–95). In 1995 he became Professor of Political Economy at Cambridge. His work in the 1960s concentrated on welfare economics under the assumption that no government can be certain of the future economic climate. For this work he was the joint recipient of the 1996 Nobel Prize for economics with William Vickrey, whose economic theories were similar. Mirrlees's later work has focused more on the economies of developing countries. His publications include *Models of Economic Growth* (with N H Stern, 1973) and *Project Appraisal and Planning for Developing Countries* (with I M D Little, 1974).

Mises, Richard von 1883–1953
US mathematician and philosopher

Born in Austria, he was professor at the universities of Dresden (1919), Berlin (1920–33), Istanbul, and from 1939 at Harvard. An authority in aerodynamics and hydrodynamics, he set out in *Wahrscheinlichkeit, Statistik und Wahrheit*, (1928, 'Probability, Statistics and Truth') a frequency theory of probability which has had a wide influence, even though not generally accepted.

Mishima Yukio, *pseudonym of* Hiraoka Kimitake 1925–70
Japanese writer

Born in Tokyo, he attended Tokyo University before becoming a civil servant and embarking on a prolific writing career which, as well as 40 novels, produced poetry, essays and modern Kabuki and Nō drama. His first major work was *Kamen no Kokuhaku* (1949, Eng trans *Confessions of a Mask*, 1958) which dealt with his discovery of his own homosexuality and the ways in which he attempted to conceal it. His great tetralogy, *Hojo no umi* (1965–70, Eng trans *The Sea of Fertility*, 1972–74), has a central theme of reincarnation, and spans Japanese life and events in the 20th century. Passionately interested in the chivalrous traditions of Imperial Japan, he believed implicitly in the ideal of a heroic destiny, the pursuit of an absolute ideal of beauty, and the concept of a glorious and honourable death in battle. He became an expert in martial arts, and in 1968 founded the Shield Society, a group of 100 youths dedicated to a revival of *Bushido*, the Samurai knightly code of honour. The most extreme expression of his élitist right-wing views was in an essay *Taiyo to tetsu* (1968, Eng trans *Sun and Steel*, 1970), and in the same year he committed suicide by performing *seppuku* following a carefully staged token attempt to rouse the nation to a return to pre-war nationalist ideals. ▣ H S Stokes, *A Life of Mishima* (1974)

Missoni, Tai Otavio 1921–
Italian knitwear designer

He was born in Yugoslavia, the son of an Italian father and a Serbian mother. He founded the Missoni company in Milan with his wife, Rosita, in 1953. At first manufacturing knitwear to be sold under other labels, they later created, under their own label, innovative knitwear notable for its sophistication and distinctive colours and patterns.

Mistinguett, *stage name of* Jeanne Marie Bourgeois 1874–1956
French dancer and actress

Born in a suburb of Paris, she was given her stage name by friends who thought that 'Miss' characterized her 'English' looks. She made her debut in 1895 and reached the height of her success with Maurice Chevalier at the Folies Bergères. A highly popular music-hall artiste for the next 30 years, she had a vivacious stage personality and made up for her weak voice by her remarkable versatility and originality in comedy. She also distinguished herself as a straight actress in *Madame Sans-Gène* and *Les Misérables*. Among her most famous songs are 'Mon Homme' and 'J'en ai marre'. She published her memoirs, *Toute ma vie* (*Mistinguett, Queen of the Paris Night*), in 1954.

Mistral, Frédéric 1830–1914
French poet and Nobel Prize winner

Born in Maillane, near Avignon, he studied law at Avignon, then returned home to work on the land and write poetry. He helped to found the Provençal renaissance movement (Félibrige school). In 1859 his epic *Mirèio* (Eng trans 1890) gained him the poet's prize of the Académie Française and the Legion of Honour. He was awarded the Nobel Prize for literature in 1904. Other works are an epic, *Calendau* (1861), poems *Lis Isclo d'or* (1876), a tragedy *La Reino Jano* (1890), and a Provençal–French dictionary (1878–86). ▣ L Larguier, *Mistral* (1930, in French)

Mistral, Gabriela, *pseudonym of* Lucila Godoy de Alcayaga 1889–1957
Chilean poet, diplomat and teacher, and Nobel Prize winner

Born in Vicuña, as a teacher she won a poetry prize with her *Sonetos de la muerte* (1914, 'Sonnets of Death') at Santiago in 1915. She taught at Columbia University, Vassar and in Puerto Rico, and was formerly consul at Madrid and elsewhere. The cost of publication of her first book, *Desolación* (1922, 'Desolation'), was paid by the teachers of New York. Her work is inspired by religious sentiments and a preoccupation with sorrow and death. Her career as a teacher led her to write for children, notably the songs in *Ternura* (1924); much of her children's writing is translated in *Crickets and Frogs* (1972). She was awarded the Nobel Prize for literature in 1945. ▣ M Arce de Vázquez, *Gabriela Mistral: the poet and her work* (1964)

Mita, Luigi Ciriaco de See De Mita, Luigi Ciriaco

Mitchel, John 1815–75
Irish patriot

Born near Dungiven, County Derry, the son of a Presbyterian minister, he studied at Trinity College, Dublin, practised as an attorney, and became assistant editor of the *Nation*. Starting the *United Irishman* (1848), he was tried for his articles on a charge of 'treason-felony' and sentenced to 14 years' transportation, but in 1853 he escaped from Van Diemen's Land (Tasmania) to the USA, and published his *Jail Journal* (1854). Returning in 1874 to Ireland, he was the next year elected to parliament for Tipperary, declared ineligible and re-elected, but died the same month.

Mitchell, Arthur 1934–
US dancer, choreographer and director

Born in New York City, he studied at the High School for Performing Arts and the School of American Ballet. In 1956 he joined New York City Ballet and created roles in George Balanchine's *Agon* (1957) and *A Midsummer Night's Dream* (1962). He was the first African-American principal dancer to join that company, and his dream, following the assassination of Martin Luther King in 1968, was to found his own group in order to develop opportunities for fellow black dancers. He immediately began laying foundations, and Dance Theatre of Harlem made its highly successful debut in New York in 1971. Quickly growing from a school in a garage, Dance Theatre of Harlem has become a company of international standing.

Mitchell, George 1933–
US Democrat politician

Born in Waterville, Maine, he worked part-time to gain his education as a lawyer and was called to the US Bar in 1960. In 1962 he became a special adviser to Senator **Edward Muskie** and began his own political career. An attempt to run for Governor of Maine failed in 1974 and he returned to private legal practice, but in 1980 he was elected Senator of Maine in succession to Muskie. In 1995, with the Democrats in power, he was appointed Special Adviser to President **Clinton** for Economic Initiatives in Ireland. The son of an Irishman, Mitchell had an interest in the country that led to his appointment as chairman of the Northern Ireland peace talks in 1996.

Mitchell, Sir James Fitzallen 1931–
St Vincent and the Grenadines statesman

He trained and worked as an agronomist (1958–65) and then bought and managed a hotel in Bequia, St Vincent. He entered politics through the St Vincent Labour Party (SVLP) and in the pre-independence period served as Minister of Trade (1967–72). He was then premier (1972–74), heading the People's Political Party (PPP). In 1975 he founded the New Democratic Party (NDP) and, as its leader, became Prime Minister in 1984, achieving re-election in 1989. His plan to retire before the next election has been shelved in the 'national' interest. He received a knighthood in 1995.

Mitchell, John Newton 1913–88
US Attorney-General

Born in Detroit, he was a law partner of **Richard M Nixon** in New York City, and he managed Nixon's successful presidential campaign in 1968. As Attorney-General (1969–72), he ordered wiretaps without court authorization and prosecuted antiwar protesters. He was chosen to run Nixon's 1972 re-election campaign but resigned at the outset of the Watergate affair, and in 1975 he was convicted of conspiracy, obstruction of justice, and perjury. After serving 19 months in prison he was released in 1979.

Mitchell, Joni (Roberta Joan), *née* Anderson 1943–
Canadian singer and songwriter

Born in McLeod, Alberta, she studied commercial art for a time, then turned to folk music as a teenager. A short-lived marriage to folk singer Chuck Mitchell in 1965 took her to the USA, where she made her first album, *Song of a Seagull* (1967). The original imagery of her songs established her as an important bridge between folk and pop, and she cut several highly regarded, and often highly confessional, albums. Her music became increasingly complex and jazz-influenced on later recordings like *The Hissing of Summer Lawns* (1975), culminating in her misjudged but sincere tribute *Mingus* (1979). She has continued to make intelligent pop music, but has also devoted increasing amounts of time and creative energy to her painting. She resumed touring after a 12-year gap in 1994, in support of her *Turbulent Indigo* album. 📖 L Fleischer, *Joni Mitchell* (1976)

Mitchell, Juliet 1934–
British feminist and writer

Born in New Zealand, she moved to Britain with her family in 1944 and was educated at King Alfred School, Hampstead, London, and at St Anne's College, Oxford. After studying for a PhD at Oxford, she subsequently lectured at the University of Leeds (1962–63) and at the University of Reading (1965–70). Since 1971 she has been a freelance writer and broadcaster and has lectured on psychoanalysis throughout the world. Her publications include *Women's Estate* (1972), *Psychoanalysis and Feminism* (1974) and *Women: The Longest Revolution* (1966). She has also co-authored *The Rights and Wrongs of Women* (1976) and co-edited *What is Feminism* (1986), both with **Ann Oakley**.

Mitchell, Margaret 1900–49
US novelist

Born in Atlanta, Georgia, she studied at Smith College, Northampton, Massachusetts, for a medical career, but turned to journalism. After her marriage in 1925, she began the 10-year task of writing her only novel, *Gone with the Wind* (1936), which won the Pulitzer Prize, sold over 25 million copies, was translated into 30 languages and was the subject of a celebrated film in 1939. 📖 A Edwards, *The Road to Tara* (1983)

Mitchell, Maria 1818–89
US astronomer

Born in Nantucket, Massachusetts, she worked as a librarian on the island while observing the skies at night. Upon discovering a new comet in 1847, she became the first woman to be elected to the American Academy of Arts and Sciences. Her first professional commission was the computing of tables of the planet Venus for the American Ephemerides and Nautical Almanac, a duty she performed for 20 years (1849–68). From 1865 to 1888 she was Professor of Astronomy at the newly founded Vassar College in Poughkeepsie.

Mitchell, Sir Peter Chalmers 1864–1945
Scottish zoologist and journalist

Born in Dunfermline, Fife, he began his career as a lecturer at the universities of Oxford and London, where he taught comparative anatomy. In 1903 he was elected secretary of the Zoological Society and inaugurated a period of prosperity at the London Zoo, being responsible for the Mappin terraces, Whipsnade, the Aquarium and other improvements. His books on zoology included *The Nature of Man* (1904) and *Materialism and Vitalism in Biology* (1930). He was elected FRS in 1906, and knighted in 1929.

Mitchell, Peter Dennis 1920–92
English biochemist and Nobel Prize winner

Born in Mitcham, Surrey, he graduated from Cambridge and taught there (1943–55) and at Edinburgh University (1955–63) before founding his own research institute, the Glynn Research Laboratories at Bodmin in Cornwall (1964), to extend his studies of energy generation in cells at the molecular level. In the 1960s he proposed a new theory of energy generation, in which electron transport causes the formation of a proton gradient, which alters molecular structures and releases energy. Although at first greeted with scepticism, his views became widely accepted, and his theory was formally acknowledged when he was awarded the Nobel Prize for chemistry in 1978.

Mitchell, Reginald Joseph 1895–1937
English aircraft designer

Trained as an engineer, he was led by his interest in aircraft to join the Vickers Armstrong Supermarine Co in 1916, where he soon became chief designer. He designed world-beating sea-planes for the Schneider trophy races (1922–31) and later the famous Spitfire, the triumph of which he did not live to see.

Mitchell, Silas Weir 1829–1914
US physician and writer

Born in Philadelphia, he was a surgeon in the Union army in the American Civil War. He specialized in nervous diseases and was a pioneer in the application of psychology to medicine. As well as a host of historical novels and poems he wrote medical texts, including *Injuries of Nerves* (1872) and *Fat and Blood* (1877).

Mitchell, Sir Thomas Livingstone 1792–1855
Scottish explorer

Born in Craigend, Stirlingshire, he served in the Peninsular War, and from 1828 was surveyor-general of New South Wales in Australia. In four expeditions (1831, 1835, 1836, 1845–47) he did much to explore Eastern Australia ('Australia Felix') and Tropical Australia, especially the Murray, Glenelg and Barcoo rivers.

Mitchell, Warren, *originally* Warren Misell 1926–
English actor

Born in London, he studied at Oxford and RADA and made his first appearance at the Finsbury Park Open Air Theatre (1950). His interpretation of Willy Loman in Arthur Miller's *Death of a Salesman* at the National Theatre (1979) was highly praised. He is best known for playing the character of Alf Garnett, a garrulous, foul-mouthed, right-wing Cockney in the television series *Till Death Us Do Part* (1966–78). The character returned in two films, *Till Death Us Do Part* (1968) and *The Alf Garnet Saga* (1972), a stage show, *The Thoughts of Chairman Alf* (1976), and a further television series, *In Sickness and In Health* (1985–92). Mitchell has also appeared in the series *So You Think You've Got Troubles* (1991) and the mini-series *Jackaroo* (1993). His many films include *Carry On Cleo* (1964), *The Spy Who Came in from the Cold* (1965), *Help!* (1965) and *Jack Rosenthal's The Chain* (1985).

Mitchell, William 1879–1936
US soldier and aviation pioneer

Beginning his army career in the signal service, he successfully commanded the US air forces in World War I, reaching the rank of brigadier-general by 1918. He foresaw the development and importance of air power in warfare, but his outspoken criticism of those who did not share his convictions resulted in a court martial (1925) which suspended him from duty. After his resignation he lectured and wrote in support of his ideas. He was posthumously promoted and decorated.

Mitchison, Naomi Margaret, *née* Haldane 1897–1999
Scottish writer

Born in Edinburgh, the daughter of the physiologist John Scott Haldane, and educated at the Dragon School, Oxford, she won instant attention with her brilliant and personal evocations of Greece and Sparta in a series of novels including *The Conquered* (1923), *Cloud Cuckoo Land* (1925) and *Black Sparta* (1928). The erudite *The Corn King and The Spring Queen* (1931) brought to life the civilizations of ancient Egypt, Scythia and the Middle East. She travelled widely, and in 1963 was made tribal adviser and 'mother' to the Bakgatla of Botswana. She wrote more than 70 books, among them her memoirs *Small Talk* (1973), *All Change Here* (1975) and *You May Well Ask* (1979). She married the Labour MP Gilbert Richard Mitchison (1890–1970, created life peer in 1964) in 1916, and from 1937 lived in Carradale on the Mull of Kintyre, Scotland. Later publications include *A Girl Must Live* (1990) and *The Oathtakers* (1991). 📖 J Benton, *A Century of Experiment* (1990)

Mitchison, Rosalind Mary, *née* Wrong 1919–
English historian

Born in Manchester, she was educated at Channing School, Highgate, London, and Lady Margaret Hall, Oxford, and became assistant lecturer in history first at Manchester University (1943–46), then at Edinburgh (1954–57). In 1970 she published *A History of Scotland*, which was conspicuous for its forthright language and integration of economic and social history with political history, and became a standard text for the next 20 years. She was Professor of Social History at Edinburgh (1981–86), and her many works include *British Population Change*

since 1869 (1977), *Lordship and Patronage: Scotland 1603–1745* (1983) and *People and Society in Scotland, 1760–1830* (1988). A vigorous and inspirational lecturer and teacher, she was the foremost authority on the Scottish poor law.

Mitchum, Robert 1917–97
US film actor

Born in Bridgeport, Connecticut, a youth spent as a travelling labourer, vagrant and professional boxer took him to Hollywood where he began his career in 1943. He was nominated for an Academy Award for his performance in *The Story of G.I. Joe* (1945) and became a prolific leading man especially noted for his association with the postwar film noir thriller. His laconic, heavy-lidded manner was deceptively casual, disguising a potent screen presence and thorough professionalism that enlivened many routine assignments. His many notable films include *Out of the Past* (1947), *The Night of the Hunter* (1955), *The Sundowners* (1960), *Ryan's Daughter* (1970), *The Friends of Eddie Coyle* (1973) and *Farewell My Lovely* (1975). His television performances include the epic mini-series *The Winds of War* (1983) and its sequel *War and Remembrance* (1989).

Mitford, Jessica Lucy 1917–96
English writer

She was born in Burford, Oxfordshire, the fifth of the six daughters of the 2nd Baron Redesdale, and sister of Diana Mitford, Nancy Mitford and Unity Mitford. She went to the USA in 1939 and joined the US Communist Party, her experiences of which were the subject for *A Fine Old Conflict* (1977). Her observation of various aspects of American society provided material for her works, such as her bestselling *The American Way of Death* (1963), an exposé of the funeral industry's unethical practices, a new edition of which she was working upon when she died. *The Trial of Dr Spock* (1970), based on the trials of anti-Vietnam War activists, was inspired by her interest in civil-rights cases. Other works include *Hons and Rebels* (1960), which is her autobiography and the story of the unconventional Mitford childhood, and *The Making of a Muckraker* (1979).

Mitford, Mary Russell 1786–1855
English novelist and dramatist

Born in Alresford, Hampshire, she won £20,000 in a lottery at the age of 10 and attended school in Chelsea. However, her father was a spendthrift, and as the family became more and more impoverished she had to write to earn money. She produced several plays, but her gift was for sketches of country manners, scenery and character, which after appearing in magazines were collected as *Our Village* (5 vols, 1824–32). She received a civil list pension in 1837 which was increased on her father's death from subscriptions raised to pay his debts. In 1852 she published her *Recollections of a Literary Life*. 📖 V Watson, *Mary Russell Mitford* (1949)

Mitford, Nancy Freeman 1904–73
English writer

Born in London, daughter of the 2nd Baron Redesdale, and educated at home, she established a reputation with her witty novels such as *The Pursuit of Love* (1945) and *Love in a Cold Climate* (1949), followed by *The Blessing* (1951) and *Don't Tell Alfred* (1960). After World War II she settled in France and wrote her major biographies *Madame de Pompadour* (1953), *Voltaire in Love* (1957), *The Sun King* (1966) and *Frederick the Great* (1970). As one of the essayists in *Noblesse Oblige*, edited by herself (1956), she helped to originate the famous 'U', or upper-class, and 'non-U' classification of linguistic usage and behaviour. She was the elder sister of Unity Mitford and Jessica Mitford. 📖 Charlotte Mosley (ed), *The Letters of Nancy Mitford and Evelyn Waugh* (1996); Selina Hastings, *Nancy Mitford* (1985)

Mitford, Unity Valkyrie 1914–48
English socialite
The daughter of the 2nd Baron Redesdale and sister of Diana Mitford, Jessica Mitford and Nancy Mitford, she was notorious for her attempted suicide on the outbreak of World War II and for her associations with leading Nazis in Germany, including Hitler. However she returned to Great Britain in 1940, suffering from a gunshot wound.

Mithridates VI *surnamed* Eupator, *called* the Great
c.132–63BC
King of Pontus
He succeeded to the throne (c.120BC) as a boy, but soon subdued the tribes who bordered on the Euxine as far as the Crimea, and made an incursion into Cappadocia and Bithynia, then Roman. In the First Mithridatic War (88), Mithridates, intially successful, was compelled to make peace with Sulla (85), relinquishing all his conquests in Asia. The aggressions of the Roman legate led to the Second Mithridatic War (83–81), which Mithridates won. In the Third Mithridatic War (74) he prospered with some Roman support until Lucullus compelled him to take refuge with his son-in-law, Tigranes I of Armenia (72), and defeated both of them at Artaxata (68). In 66 Pompey defeated Mithridates on the Euphrates, and his son's rebellion caused him to kill himself. He was cruel and sensual but energetic and determined, and his political skill enabled him to pose a serious threat to Rome; he was unlucky to meet able Roman generals.

Mitre, Bartolomé 1821–1906
Argentine politician
Exiled by General Juan Manuel de Rosas, he returned to the country as a follower of General Justo José de Urquiza after the Battle of Monte Caseros, which brought about Rosas's downfall. He became Governor of Buenos Aires in 1860. As President (1862–68), he created a national administrative structure in Buenos Aires, set about the construction of railroads and encouraged immigration. He was defeated by Domingo Sarmiento in the 1868 presidential elections. In 1870 he founded the newspaper *La Nación*, and in 1874 attempted a coup against Sarmiento's choice for President, Nicolas Avellanada. Mitre failed, however, to rally support among the estancieros (ranch owners), and was jailed. He made another bid for the presidency in 1891 as the candidate for the Union Civica, but withdrew in favour of the Conservative candidate.

Mitropoulos, Dimitri 1896–1960
US conductor and pianist
He was born in Athens and studied at the Athens Conservatory and under Ferruccio Busoni in Berlin. After working in Berlin and Paris, he went to the USA where he made his debut with the Boston Symphony Orchestra in 1937. He became a US citizen in 1946. He conducted the Minneapolis Symphony Orchestra (1937–49) and the New York Philharmonic Orchestra (1949–58), and conducted the first performance of Samuel Barber's opera *Vanessa*. He was renowned as an exponent of contemporary music, notably that of Shostakovich.

Mitscherlich, Eilhard 1794–1863
German physical and organic chemist
Born in Neuende, near Jeve, he studied Persian at Heidelberg and Paris, medicine at Göttingen, and geology, mineralogy, chemistry and physics in Berlin and in Stockholm under Jöns Jacob Berzelius. He became Professor of Chemistry at the Friedrich Wilhelm Institute in Berlin, and was elected to the Berlin Academy of Sciences in 1852. He contributed to many branches of chemistry, but is best known for his work in crystallography. He identified isomorphism and diamorphism in crystals. While visiting Paris (1823–24) he and Augustin

Jean Fresnel discovered that the optical axes of a biaxial crystal change with a change in temperature. Mitscherlich also investigated the decomposition products of benzaldehyde and benzoin, synthesized artificial minerals by fusing silica with various metallic oxides and wrote a number of successful textbooks.

Mitsugu, Akimoto See Chiyonfuji

Mitterrand, François Maurice Marie 1916–96
French statesman
Born in Jarnac in south-west France, the fifth child of a stationmaster, he attended the University of Paris during the mid-1930s, studying law and politics and immersing himself in French literature. During World War II he served with the French forces (1939–40), was wounded and captured, but escaped (on the third attempt) in December 1941 from a prison camp in Germany and became a network commander in the French Resistance. He was awarded the Légion d'Honneur, the Croix de Guerre and the Rosette de la Résistance. He was a Deputy in the French National Assembly almost continuously from 1946, representing the constituency of Nièvre (near Dijon), and held ministerial posts in 11 centrist governments between 1947 and 1958. A firm believer in the democratic traditions of Republican France, he opposed Charles de Gaulle's creation of the Fifth Republic in 1953 and, as a result, lost his Assembly seat in the 1958 election. He became radicalized, left the Catholic Church during the early 1960s, and began building up a strong new, left-of-centre anti-Gaullist alliance, the 'Federation of the Left'. After returning to the National Assembly in 1962, he performed creditably as the Federation's candidate in the 1965 presidential election against de Gaulle and in 1971 became leader of the new Socialist Party (PS). He embarked on a successful strategy of electoral union with the (then important) Communist Party, bringing major gains for the Socialists, establishing them as the single most popular party in France by 1978 and in 1981 was elected President, defeating Valéry Giscard d'Estaing. As President, Mitterrand initially introduced a series of radical economic and political reforms, including programmes of nationalization and decentralization. However, deteriorating economic conditions after 1983 forced a policy U-turn and in the 1986 election the Socialists lost their National Assembly majority, compelling him to work with a Prime Minister, Jacques Chirac, from the opposition 'right coalition'. Despite being forced to concede considerable executive authority to Chirac in this unique 'co-habitation' experiment, Mitterrand, nicknamed 'the fox', outmanoeuvred his younger rival, and comfortably defeated him in the presidential election of 1988. Following fresh National Assembly elections in which the conservative parties lost their majority, the moderate socialist, Michel Rocard, was appointed Prime Minister in a new left-of-centre administration. During the Gulf crisis of 1990 Mitterrand tried to find a diplomatic settlement but when this failed he demonstrated his commitment to the Atlantic alliance by sending French troops to the area. In 1992 the Socialist Party suffered a crushing defeat, with the right-wing parties winning 484 seats to the left's 92. Despite Mitterrand's peacemaking efforts in Bosnia the same year, the combination of France's recession and unemployment situation and the scandals which plagued the Socialists proved too much and in 1995 he lost the presidency to Jacques Chirac. 📖 Alan Clark (ed), *Anthologie Mitterrand* (1986); Denis MacShane, *François Mitterrand: A Political Odyssey* (1982)

Mivart, St George Jackson 1827–1900
English biologist

Born in London, although educated in law he devoted himself to zoological research. He became Professor of Zoology and Biology at the Roman Catholic University College in Kensington (1874–84) and in 1890 accepted a chair of philosophy of natural history at Leuven University. Although he supported the theory of evolution, he rejected natural selection as its mechanism and proposed in its place the idea of an innate plasticity which he called individuation, publishing books in support of his views such as *The Genesis of Species* (1871), *Nature and Thought* (1883) and *The Origin of Human Reason* (1889).

Miyake, Issey 1938–
Japanese fashion designer

He was born in Hiroshima, studied at Tama Art University in Tokyo, and spent six years in Paris and New York fashion houses. Although he showed his first collection in Tokyo in 1963, he founded his studio there only in 1971. His first subsequent show was in New York the same year, followed by a show in Paris in 1973. His distinctive style combines eastern and western influences in garments which have an almost theatrical quality. Loose-fitting but with dramatic often asymmetric outline, his clothes achieve richness by varied textures, weaves and patterns rather than by colour which is often subdued.

Mlynar, Zdenek 1930–97
Czechoslovak politician

He was born in Vysoke Myto, Bohemia. Coming of age in Communist Czechoslovakia, educated in law in Moscow in the last years of Stalin and the first years of Khrushchev, and then observing the slow stagnation of the Novotný years in Czechoslovakia, he became a reformer through disillusionment. However, during the period of the Prague Spring (1968), when he became a secretary of the purged Communist Party Central Committee, he made a major contribution to Alexander Dubček's action programme and was one of the leaders abducted to Moscow following the Soviet invasion. Released with the others, he quickly lost his party function and eventually, when he signed Charter '77 (1977), he went to Austria and taught politics at Innsbruck. He returned to Czech politics in the 1990s as a member of the reform Communist group Left Bloc.

Mnemon See Artaxerxes II

Mnouchkine, Arianne 1938–
French stage director, dramatist and founder of Théâtre du Soleil

She studied at Paris and London universities, and set up the Association Théâtrale des Étudiants de Paris with fellow students of the Sorbonne (1959), putting on plays, organizing workshops and lectures. In 1962 she travelled to Cambodia and Japan and on her return founded the Théâtre du Soleil as a theatre co-operative (1963). The early productions were influenced by the teachings of Stanislavsky, and their first major success came with a production of Arnold Wesker's *The Kitchen* (1967). After the student uprising of May 1968, the company performed a series of collective improvisations based on techniques of collage, circus and continuous and discontinuous narrative. One of the company's best-known works is *1789*, first produced in 1970.

Moberg, (Carl Artur) Vilhelm 1898–1973
Swedish writer

Born in Algutsboda, Småland, he came from a family of crofters and enlisted soldiers and remained loyal to his background in his writing. His best-known work is the series of novels that discuss with documentary accuracy the 19th-century mass migration of Swedes to the USA: *Utvandrarna* (1949, Eng trans *The Emigrants*, 1951), *Invandrarna* (1952, Eng trans *Unto a Good Land*, 1957), *Nybyggarna* (1956, 'The Settlers') and *Sista brevet till Sverige* (1959, 'Last Letter to Sweden'). His unfinished *Min svenska historia 1–2* (1970–71,

'My Swedish History') looks at history from the viewpoint of the common people. He was a popular dramatist and several of his novels, notably *The Emigrants*, have been filmed.

Möbius, August Ferdinand 1790–1868
German mathematician

Born in Schulpforta, he was professor at Leipzig University, where he worked on analytical geometry, statics, topology and theoretical astronomy. He extended Cartesian coordinate methods to projective geometry, and gave a straight-forward algebraic account of statics, using vectorial quantities before vectors as such entered mathematics. In topology he investigated which surfaces can exist, and became one of the discoverers of the 'Möbius strip' (a one-sided surface formed by giving a rectangular strip a half-twist and then joining the ends together). He also examined in detail the possible types of three-dimensional spaces which can be created by similar gluing constructions. 📖 John Fauvell, Raymond Flood and Robin Wilson (eds), *Möbius and His Band: Mathematics and Astronomy in Nineteenth-Century Germany* (1993)

Mobutu Sese Seko Kuku Ngbendu Wa Za Banga, *originally* Joseph-Désiré Mobutu 1930–97
Zairean soldier and politician

Born into a poor family in Lisala, he undertook army training and a period of study in Brussels, before joining the Force Publique in 1949. He joined Patrice Lumumba's Mouvement National Congolais in 1958 and was Chief of Staff in 1960 at the time of independence. He took over the government to deal with the problem of Katanga's secession but he handed power back to civilians within five months. After the 1963–65 civil war, he intervened again, this time permanently. He renamed the country Zaire in place of the Belgian Congo and imposed a degree of stability onto the country which had hitherto been unknown. Backed by US money and the power of the army, his regime became increasingly unpopular. By 1993 Zaire (now renamed the Democratic Republic of Congo) was in a state of financial collapse; meanwhile, Mobutu lived in splendour, having amassed a fortune from his country's resources. He was forced to abandon democratic elections and ruled through a military council. In May 1997, Laurent Kabila's army forced him into exile and brought his dictatorship to an end. His health already failing, Mobutu died four months later in Rabat, Morocco.

Modahl, Diane 1966–
British athlete

Born in Moss Side, Manchester, she finished fourth in the 800 metres world championship race in 1993. Previously she had won the 1990 Commonwealth title, but it was four years later that she hit the headlines. She returned home early from the 1994 Commonwealth Games when a Lisbon testing laboratory announced they had found evidence of massive testosterone abuse in her drugs test. Despite maintaining her innocence, she was banned for four years. At her own, enormous, financial cost, Modahl fought for her innocence through the courts. She was cleared in 1996 when the laboratory's evidence was found to be unreliable.

Model, Lisette, *née* Elise Amelie Felicie Stern 1901–83
US photographer

Born in Vienna of Austrian-Italian and French parentage, she studied music with composer Arnold Schoenberg (1918–20), and in Paris (1922). She began to paint in 1932 and to photograph in 1937, both for pleasure and in the hope of employment as a darkroom technician. Moving to New York in 1938, she worked as a freelance photographer for *Harper's Bazaar* and other publications (1941–57). She also taught photography at the New School for Social Research, New York (1951–82), where Diane Arbus was among her students. Her work was first exhibited in

1940 in the exhibition 'Sixty Photographs: A Survey of Camera Esthetics' at the Museum of Modern Art, New York. Retrospectives were held at the New Orleans Museum of Art (1981) and the National Gallery of Canada, Ottawa (1990).

Modersohn-Becker, Paula, *née* Becker
1876–1907
German painter
Born in Dresden, she joined an artists' colony at the village of Worpswede, and married a fellow artist, Otto Modersohn. She made several trips to Paris between 1900 and 1906 where she came under the influence of avant-garde painters such as **Paul Gauguin** and **Cézanne**. Her subsequent paintings, in which personal response in the form of simple forms and strong colour takes precedence over realistic portrayal, place her at the beginning of the German Expressionist movement.

Modigliani, Amedeo 1884–1920
Italian painter and sculptor
He was born in Leghorn (Livorno), Tuscany. His early work was influenced by the painters of the Italian Renaissance, particularly the primitives, and in 1906 he moved to Paris, where he was further influenced by **Toulouse-Lautrec** and 'les Fauves'. In 1909, impressed by the Romanian sculptor **Constantine Brancusi**, he took to sculpture and produced a number of elongated stone heads in African style. He continued to use this style when he later resumed painting, with a series of richly-coloured, elongated portraits—a feature characterizing all his later work. In 1918 in Paris he held one of his first one-man shows, which included some very frank nudes; the exhibition was closed for indecency on the first day. It was only after his death from tuberculosis that he obtained recognition and the prices of his paintings soared.
📖 William Fifield, *Modigliani* (1976)

Modigliani, Franco 1918–
US economist and Nobel Prize winner
Born in Rome, he took a law degree in Rome in 1939, then emigrated to the USA. After teaching at a number of smaller institutions, he held professorships at Illinois (1949–52), Carnegie-Mellon (1952–60) and Northwestern (1960–62) universities, and at Massachusetts Institute of Technology (1962–). He was awarded the 1985 Nobel Prize for economics for his work on two fundamental theories: personal saving and corporate finance.

Modjeska, Helena 1844–1909
Polish actress
Born in Kraków, she began to act in 1861, and became well known in her native city. She then became the leading actress in Warsaw (1868–76). After learning English, however, she achieved her greatest triumphs in the USA and Great Britain, in such roles as Juliet, Rosalind, and Beatrice, and in *La Dame aux camélias* ('The Lady with the Camellias'). She wrote *Memories and Impressions* (1910).

Modotti Mondini, Tina (Assunta Adelaide Luigia) 1896–1942
Mexican photographer, model and revolutionary
Born in Udine, Italy, she worked in a textile factory there before emigrating to San Francisco in 1913. In 1918 she went to Hollywood and became an actress. She met photographer **Edward Weston** around 1920 and, living with him in Mexico (1923–26), modelled for him and the muralists **Diego Rivera** and **José Orozco**. Learning photography there she became Weston's partner in a photographic studio, working on illustrations for books, newspapers and magazines. In 1927 she joined the Communist Party in Mexico and became increasingly involved with revolutionary politics, forming liaisons with the Cuban revolutionary Julio Antonio Mella (1928) and with the communist Vittorio Vidali (from c.1933).

Deported from Mexico in 1929, she moved to Berlin, then Moscow (1931–34) and Spain (1935–38), where she worked for the relief organization Red Aid. She returned with Vidali to Mexico in 1939, where she died.

Modrow, Hans 1928–
German politician
He was born in Jasenitz and after serving his apprenticeship as a locksmith, served in the German army from 1942 until the end of World War II. From 1949 he was active in the Socialist Unity Party (SED), taking office as a member of East Berlin city committee (1953–61) and city council (1953–71). A member of the Volkskammer from 1958 to 1990, in 1967–71 he was head of Agitprop. In 1973 he was elected First Secretary for Dresden, and elected to the party's Central Committee. In 1989, as demonstrations for a more liberal regime and the exodus to West Berlin continued, his reputation as a liberal and his personal popular support brought his appointment as Prime Minister of a new East German government pledged to reform and free elections. Shortly after his meeting with West Germany's Chancellor **Kohl** in 1989, Modrow announced a four-point plan to reunify Germany, and within months, hardliners such as **Erich Honecker**, Egon Krenz and Willi Stoph had resigned or been arrested. He headed the new GDR coalition formed in April 1990, and following unification of the two Germanys in October 1990, was one of five prominent former East German politicians who were sworn in as Ministers without Portfolio of the new federal government. In 1993 he was tried and found guilty of vote-rigging.

Moe, Jørgen Engebretsen 1813–82
Norwegian folklorist and poet
With **Peter Christian Asbjørnsen** he collected and edited *Norske Folkeeventyr* (1841–44, Eng trans *Norwegian Folk Stories*, 1859). He also published a book of Romantic verse (1850), and a children's classic, *I brønden og i kjærnet* (1851). From 1875 to 1881 he was Bishop of Christiansand.
📖 P C Asbjørnsen, *Mannen og livsverket* (1947)

Moeran, Ernest John 1894–1950
English composer
Born in Middlesex, he was a pupil at the Royal College of Music and, after service in World War I, studied under **John Ireland**. He first emerged as a composer in 1923, but left London to live in Herefordshire, where he worked prolifically in all forms. As well as a large number of songs, he composed a symphony and concertos for violin, piano and cello.

Moffat, Robert 1795–1883
Scottish missionary
Born in Ormiston, East Lothian, he turned from gardening to the mission field in 1815, and began his work in Great Namaqualand in 1818. He finally settled at Kuruman in Bechuanaland (1826–70), which soon became, through his efforts, a centre of Christianity and civilization. He printed both New (1840) and Old (1857) Testaments in Sechwana and published *Missionary Labours and Scenes in South Africa* (1842). **David Livingstone** married his daughter, Mary.

Moffatt, James 1870–1944
US theologian
Born in Glasgow, Scotland, he was ordained a minister of the Free Church of Scotland in 1896, then became professor at Mansfield College, Oxford (1911–14), and at the United Free Church College, Glasgow, (1914–27). In 1927 he went to the USA and became Professor of Church History at Union Theological Seminary, New York (1927–39). His most famous work is the translation of the Bible into modern English: his New Testament was published in 1913 and his Old Testament in 1924. He also wrote theological works, including *Presbyterianism* (1928).

Mohammed (Prophet) See **Muhammad** (panel)

Mohammed See **Mehmet II, the Conqueror**

Mohammad 'Ali See **Mehemet 'Ali**

Mohammad Reza Pahlavi See **Pahlavi, Mohammad Reza**

Mohammed Nadir Shah c.1880–1933
King of Afghanistan
The brother of Dost Mohammed, as Commander-in-Chief to **Amanullah Khan** (ruler and later King of Afghanistan from 1926) he played a prominent role in the 1919 Afghan War against Great Britain which secured the country's full independence (1922). He subsequently fell into disfavour and was forced to live in exile in France. In 1929, with British diplomatic support, he returned to Kabul and seized the throne, immediately embarking on a programme of economic and social modernization. These reforms, however, alienated the Muslim clergy and in 1933 he was assassinated. He was succeeded by his son, Mohammed Zahir Shah.

Mohl, Hugo von 1805–72
German botanist
Born in Stuttgart, he was Professor of Physiology at Bern University (1832–35) and Professor of Botany at Tübingen (1835–72). His most lasting researches lay in the field of plant cell structure and physiology, where his meticulous observations were the first attempts at cytochemistry. He differentiated the cell membrane, nucleus, cellular fluid, utricle, and was the first to use the term protoplasm in plant cell biology. He was also the first to clearly explain osmosis, and discovered that the secondary walls of plant cells are fibrous.

Moholy-Nagy, László 1895–1946
US artist and photographer
Born in Bucsborsod, Hungary, he trained in law in Budapest, and painted with Dada and Constructionist groups in Vienna and Berlin (1919–23). He produced his first 'photograms' (non-representational photographic images made directly without a camera) in 1923 and joined the Bauhaus under **Walter Gropius** in 1925. There he began to use a camera and was quickly recognized as a leading avant-garde artist in the New Photographers movement in Europe (1925–35), his work including filmmaking and typography integrated with photographic illustration. He left Germany in 1935 and after working as a designer in Amsterdam and London was invited to the USA in 1937 to head the new Bauhaus school in Chicago, later the Institute of Design. He taught photography there, and became a US citizen shortly before his death.

Mohorovičić, Andrija 1857–1936
Yugoslav seismologist and meteorologist
Born in Volosko, Croatia, he was educated in physics and mathematics at the University of Prague. He was later appointed to the Royal Nautical School at Bakar, where he taught meteorology and oceanography, and in 1887 founded the meteorological station at Bakar. Appointed as professor and director at the Zagreb Technical School (1891–1921), he campaigned for the independence of Zagreb Observatory from government control, making it a recognized centre for meteorology and geodynamics. Investigating the Croatian earthquake of 1909 in the Kulpa valley, he observed from some distance two distinct seismic wave arrivals. He deduced that the slower of the two arrivals followed the direct route from the earthquake focus to the observation point, while the faster wave is refracted from a discontinuity. From this he concluded that the Earth's crust must overlie a denser mantle and he calculated the depth to this transition. The

sharp discontinuity was subsequently found to exist worldwide, and became known as the Mohorovičić discontinuity or 'Moho'.

Mohs, Friedrich 1773–1839
German mineralogist
Born in Gernrode, Sachsen-Anhalt, and educated at the University of Halle, he became professor at Graz (1812), at Freiburg as successor to **Abraham Werner** (1818), and at Vienna (1826). He developed a mineralogical classification system based on a variety of mineral characters, rather than adopting the traditional purely chemical system. The Mohs scale of hardness which he introduced is still in use. Around 1820, he arrived at the concept of the six crystal systems; this mineral classification system was based on the different orientation of crystallographic axes, but the names which he applied were not widely used. His publications included *The Natural History System of Mineralogy* (1821) and *Treatise on Mineralogy* (3 vols, 1825).

Moi, Daniel Arap 1924–
Kenyan statesman
Born in Rift Valley Province, the son of a poor farmer, he was educated at the Mission School, Kabartonjo, and at the Government African School in Kapsabet. After entering the House of Representatives in 1963, he served as Minister for Local Government (1963–64), and for Home Affairs (1964–67). In 1967 he was appointed Vice-President by **Jomo Kenyatta** as his nominated successor. He was provincial President of the Kenyan African National Union from 1966, and after becoming KANU President and head of state on Kenyatta's death in 1978, he purged the army, launched an ambitious plan to develop Kenya's economy and infrastructure, and pre-empted political opposition by proclaiming KANU as the country's only legal party. He was re-elected head of state in 1983 and 1988. In 1992 he held elections and won amid controversy about the conduct of the elections.

Moinaux, Georges See **Courteline, Georges**

Moir, John Willam b.1851 and **Frederick Lewis Maitland** b.1852
Scottish explorers and traders
Brothers, they were born in Edinburgh and studied botany and natural history at the university there before training as chartered accountants. In 1878 they founded the African Lakes Company which pioneered the trade route from the east coast to Lakes Nyasa and Tanganyika. To exploit natural waterways, they had steamers built in sections to be carried overland. The *Lady Nyasa* was the first to ply the Zambezi and Shire rivers. Establishing an anti-slaving mission and trading post near Balantyre, they waged a two-year private war against Arab slave traders, which ended in 1889. This victory opened up an area which subsequently came under British rule as the Nyasaland Protectorate and Northern Rhodesia.

Moiseiwitsch, Benno 1890–1963
British pianist
Born in Odessa, Russia, he studied at the Imperial Academy of Music there, and won the **Rubinstein** prize at the age of nine. He subsequently worked in Vienna under Leschetizky, and rapidly became known as an exponent of the music of the Romantic composers. He first appeared in Great Britain in 1908, and took British nationality in 1937.

Moiseyev, Igor Aleksandrovich 1906–
Russian dancer, choreographer and ballet director
Born in Kiev, he studied privately and at the Bolshoi Ballet School, graduating in 1924 into the main company where he remained, as character soloist and choreographer, until 1939. Always interested in folk dance, he accepted an appointment in 1936 as director of the new

Molière, *pseudonym of* Jean Baptiste Poquelin 1622–73
French playwright

Molière was born in Paris, the son of a wealthy upholsterer. He studied with the Jesuits at the Collège de Clermont, and may have been called to the Bar. His mother died when he was young, and when he came of age he inherited some of her fortune. Instead of following his father's business, he embarked on a theatrical venture (1643) under the title of L'Illustre Théâtre, which lasted for over three years in Paris. The company then moved to the provinces from Lyons to Rouen, and had sufficient success to keep going from 1646 to 1658, eventually obtaining the patronage of the king's brother, **Philippe d' Orléans**.

In 1658 he played before the king, and organized a regular theatre, first in the Petit Bourbon, and later in the Palais Royal. As a theatre manager he had to perform tragedy as well as comedy, but he had little success with either **Corneille**'s *Nicomède* or with the works of **Racine**, despite their personal friendship. Molière soon realized his own considerable resources as a comic writer. *Les Précieuses ridicules* was published in November 1659, and every year until his death he produced at least one of his comic masterpieces, including *Tartuffe* in 1667, *Le Misanthrope* in 1666, *Amphitryon* in 1668, and *Le Bourgeois gentilhomme* in 1671.

In the spring of 1662 he married Armande Béjart, a young actress in his own company and the sister of Madeleine, with whom Molière is said to have had a love affair. In August 1665 the king adopted Molière's troupe as his own servants. In 1667 symptoms of lung disease were apparent. He died in his home in the Rue de Richelieu the night after having acted as the *Malade* in the seventh representation of his last play, *Le Malade imaginaire*.

📖 Molière's most important plays (with the conventional English titles) appeared as follows: in 1658 *L'Étourdi* (The Blunderers) and *Le Dépit amoureux* (The Amorous Quarrel, 1656 in the provinces); in 1659 *Les Précieuses ridicules* (The Conceited Young Ladies); in 1660 *Sganarelle* (The Picture); in 1661 *Don Garcie de Navarre* (Don Garcia of Navarre); in 1662 *L'Ecole des maris* (The School for Husbands), *Les Fâcheux* (The Impertinents) and *L'Ecole des femmes* (The School for Wives); in 1663 *La Critique de l'école des femmes* (School for Wives Criticised) and *Impromptu de Versailles* (The Impromptu of Versailles); in 1664 *Le Mariage forcé* (The Forced Marriage), *La Princesse d'Élide* (The Universal Passion) and *Tartuffe* (in part); in 1665 *L'Amour médecin* (The Quacks); *Le Misanthrope* (The Misanthrope); in 1666 *Le Médecin malgré lui* (The Dumb Lady); in 1667 *Tartuffe*; in 1668 *Amphitryon, George Dandin* and *L'Avare* (The Miser); in 1669 *Monsieur de Pourceaugnac*; in 1671 *Le Bourgeois gentilhomme* (The Citizen turned Gentleman) and *Les Fourberies de Scapin* (The Cheats of Scapin); in 1672 *Les Femmes savantes* (The Female Virtuosos); and in 1673 *Le Malade imaginaire* (The Imaginary Invalid). He collaborated with Philippe Quinault and **Pierre Corneille** to write *Psyché* (1671), and wrote farces, a few court masques, and some miscellaneous poems.

📖 F Lawrence, *Molière: The Comedy of Unreason* (1968).

On ne meurt qu'une fois et c'est pour si longtemps!
'We only die once; and it's for such a long time!'
From *Le Dépit amoureux*, act 5, scene 3.

Dance Department of the Moscow Theatre for Folk Art. He formed a professional folk dance company the following year, developing simple steps and primitive patterns into full theatrical expression. This ensemble has toured the world, including all 15 republics of the former USSR, meanwhile gathering a substantial repertoire of dances from other nations. As a choreographer, his greatest strength is creating scenes from daily life and genre pieces. In 1967 he founded the State Ensemble of Classical Ballet.

Moissan, (Ferdinand Frédéric) Henri
1852–1907
French chemist and Nobel Prize winner

Born in Paris, he studied chemistry and pharmacy in Paris and qualified as a pharmacist in 1879. He taught at the School of Pharmacy in Paris, becoming Professor of Toxicology and Inorganic Chemistry in 1886 and moving to the chair of inorganic chemistry at the University of Paris in 1900. He was noted for his teaching and experimental work. He was the first to isolate fluorine (1886). In 1892 he invented the electric arc furnace and, with the high temperatures that could be reached for the first time, he reduced the oxides of uranium and tungsten, prepared carbides, borides and hydrides, and synthesized rubies. Moissan is regarded as the founder of high-temperature chemistry, and both his furnace and his discoveries were soon shown to have many industrial applications. For his work on fluorine he was awarded the Nobel Prize for chemistry in 1906.

Moivre, Abraham de 1667–1754
French mathematician

Born in Vitry, Champagne, he left France for religious reasons and went to England around 1686, supporting himself by teaching. **Isaac Newton**'s *Principia* whetted his devotion to mathematics and he became known to the leading mathematicians of his time. Elected FRS in 1697, he helped the Royal Society to decide the famous contest between Newton and **Gottfried Leibniz** on the origins of the calculus. His principal work was *The Doctrine of Chances* (1718) on probability theory, but he is best remembered for the fundamental formula on complex numbers, known as de Moivre's theorem, that relates the exponential and trigonometric functions.

Mokanna, al-, *properly* Hakim ben Atta c.778
Arab prophet

He was the founder of a sect in the Persian province of Khorasan. Ostensibly to protect onlookers from being dazzled by his divine countenance, but actually to conceal the loss of an eye, he wore a veil ('Mokanna' means 'the Veiled One'). Claiming he was a reincarnation of God, he gathered enough followers to seize several fortified places, but the Caliph Almahdi, son of **al-Mansur**, eventually took his stronghold of Kash, when Mokanna took poison. His story is the subject of one of **Thomas Moore**'s poems in *Lalla Rookh*.

Molenaer, Jan Miense c.1610–1668
Dutch painter

Born in Haarlem, he was active there and in Amsterdam. In 1636 he married the painter **Judith Leyster**, and their work is similar. They probably trained together in the studio of **Frans Hals**, and later collaborated. Molenaer excelled at musical and peasant scenes, such as *A Young Man and Woman Making Music* (National Gallery, London), *Children Making Music* (National Gallery) and *Dutch Merrymaking* (Royal Collection, Hampton Court). He also painted portraits and religious pictures.

Molière See panel above

Molina, Luis de 1535–1600
Spanish Jesuit theologian

Born in Cuenca, he studied at Coimbra, and was Professor of Theology at Evora for 20 years. His views on predestination were seen as a revival of Pelagianism provoking the dispute between Molinists and Thomists. A papal decree in 1607 permitted both opinions. His principal writings are a commentary on the *Summa* of Thomas Aquinas (1593); a treatise, *De Justitia et Jure* (1592, 'On Law and Justice'); and the celebrated treatise on grace and free will, *Concordia Liberi Arbitrii cum Gratiae Donis* (1588, 'The Harmony of Free Will with Gifts of Grace').

Moll Cutpurse See Frith, Mary

Möller, Poul Martin 1794–1838
Danish writer

Born in Uldum, he graduated in theology at Copenhagen and later became a professor of philosophy, in Oslo, and then in Copenhagen. His chief work, *En dansk Students Eventyr* ('Adventures of a Danish Student'), which he finished in 1824, but which was published posthumously, is a light-hearted account of undergraduate life in Copenhagen. *Sceneri Rosenborg Slotshave* (1819–21, 'Scenes from the Garden at Rosenberg Castle') is a representative work, showing how he avoids the abstract and metaphysical, for his credo was 'all poetry that does not come from life is a lie'. He made the first Danish translation of *The Odyssey*, wrote philosophical essays and was a coiner of aphorisms. 📖 F Nielson, *Om Poul Möller* (1961)

Mollet, Guy Alcide 1905–75
French socialist politician

Born in Flers, Normandy, of working-class parentage, he joined the Socialist Party in 1923 and shortly afterwards became English master at the Arras Grammar School. In World War II he was a captain in the secret Resistance army. In 1946 he became Mayor of Arras, an MP, Secretary-General of the Socialist Party and a Cabinet Minister in the Blum government. A keen supporter of a Western European Federation, he was a delegate to the Consultative Assembly of the Council of Europe (1949) and was its president in 1955. He became Prime Minister in 1956. He survived the international crisis over the Anglo-French intervention in Suez later that year, but lost office in 1957 after staying in power longer than any French premier since the war. In 1959 he was elected a senator of the French Community.

Mollison, James Allan 1905–59
Scottish aviator

Born in Glasgow, he became a consultant engineer. He was commissioned into the RAF in 1923, and won fame for his record flight, Australia–England in 1931 in 8 days 19 hours and 28 minutes. He made the first solo east–west crossing of the North Atlantic in 1932, and in February 1933 the first England–South America flight. With his wife Amy Johnson he made the first flight across the Atlantic to the USA in 1933, and to India in 1934. He was awarded the Britannia Trophy in 1933.

Molnár, Ferenč, *originally* Ferenč Neumann 1878–1952
Hungarian playwright and novelist

He was born in Budapest, and changed his name to Molnár in 1896. He wrote 36 plays, mainly fantasies and romantic comedies, and there is probably no other Hungarian playwright more translated and performed outside his own country. Several light farces were followed in 1907 by *Az Ördg*, a variation on the *Faust* theme. As *The Devil*, this play opened in two rival productions on the same night in New York in 1908. *Liliom* (1909) later became the basis for the Rodgers and Hammerstein musical *Carousel* (1945). Subsequent plays include *A fehér felho*

(1916, 'The White Cloud') and *A hattyú* (1920, 'The Swan'). *Jétek a Kastélyban* (1926), a sophisticated social comedy, was translated by P G Wodehouse as *The Play's the Thing* for the New York production in 1927, and by Tom Stoppard as *Rough Crossing* for the National Theatre, London, in 1985. *Olimpia* (1928, 'Olympia') is a similarly well-made play, peopled by amiable, well-to-do hedonists, and recalling a more comfortable, elegant world. Molnár emigrated to the USA in 1940, becoming a US citizen seven years later. 📖 I Vécsei, *Molnár Ferenc* (1966)

Molotov, Vyacheslav Mikhailovich, *originally* Vyacheslav Mikhailovich Skriabin 1890–1986
Soviet politician

Born in Kukaida, Vyatka, he was educated at Kazan High School and Polytechnic. In the 1905 revolution he joined the Bolshevik section of Lenin's Social Democratic Workers' Party and in 1912 became the staunch disciple of Stalin when *Pravda* was launched. During the March 1917 revolution he was a member of the military revolutionary committee which directed the coup against Aleksandr Kerensky. In 1921 he became secretary of the Central Committee of the Russian Communist Party and the youngest candidate-member of the politburo. In 1928 his appointment to the key position of secretary of the Moscow committee of the all-Union Party marked the launching of the first Five-Year Plan. As chairman of the Council of People's Commissars (1930–41), he became an international figure in 1939 when he took on the extra post of Commissar for Foreign Affairs, shaping the policy which led to the non-aggression pact with Nazi Germany. In 1942 he signed the 20 years' Treaty of Alliance with Britain. He was Stalin's chief adviser at Teheran and Yalta and represented the Soviet Union at the 1945 founding conference of the United Nations at San Francisco and at the Potsdam Conference. After the war Molotov, who negotiated the pacts binding the satellite states to the Soviet Union, emerged as the uncompromising champion of world Sovietism. His '*niet*' at meetings of the United Nations and in the councils of foreign ministers became a byword. His attitude led to the prolongation of the Cold War and the division of Germany into two conflicting states. In 1949 he resigned as Foreign Minister but resumed the post in 1953. He resigned in 1956 and was appointed Minister of State Control. In 1957 Nikita Khrushchev called him a 'saboteur of peace', accused him of policy failures and appointed him ambassador to Outer Mongolia until 1960. He was expelled from the Communist Party in 1962 but reinstated in 1984. 📖 Bernard Bromage, *Molotov: The Story of an Era* (1956)

Moltke, Helmuth 1848–1916
German soldier

He was a nephew of Count Helmuth von Moltke. Like his uncle, he rose to be Chief of the General Staff (1906), but in World War I, after losing the Battle of the Marne in September 1914, was superseded by Erich von Falkenhayn. 📖 F E Whitton, *Moltke* (1921)

Moltke, Helmuth, Count von, *known as the* Silent 1800–91
Prussian soldier

In 1819 he became lieutenant in a Danish regiment, but in 1822 entered Prussian service. In 1832 he was appointed to the staff, and in 1835 obtained leave to travel. Asked by the Sultan to remodel the Turkish army, he did not return to Berlin until 1839. From 1858 to 1888 he was Chief of the General Staff in Berlin and reorganized the Prussian army. His strategical skill was displayed in the successful wars with Denmark in 1863–64, with Austria in 1866, and with France in 1870–71.

Moltmann, Jürgen 1926–
German Reformed theologian
He was born in Hamburg. A professor at Wuppertal (1958–63), Bonn (1963–67) and Tübingen (1967–), he is best known for his influential trilogies, *Theology of Hope* (1967), *The Crucified God* (1974) and *The Church in the Power of the Spirit* (1977); *The Trinity and the Kingdom of God* (1981); and the Gifford lectures *God in Creation* (1985) and *The Way of Jesus Christ* (1990). Probably the most significant Protestant theologian of the 20th-century since **Karl Barth**, he espoused a theology of hope which marked a reaction against the individualistic existential approach of **Rudolf Bultmann**, and a revival in Protestant theology of concern for the social nature of Christian faith in the modern world. He also wrote *Hope and Planning* (1971), *On Human Dignity* (1984) and *Creating a Just Future* (1989).

Molyneaux, James Henry Molyneaux, Baron 1920–
Northern Irish politician
Born in Seacash, Killead, County Antrim, and educated at Aldergrove School, Country Antrim, he served in the RAF from 1941 to 1946, and was a vice-chairman of hospital and mental-health management committees before becoming active in politics as Secretary of the South Antrim Unionist Association (1964–70) and Vice-President of the Ulster Unionist Council from 1974. In 1970 he entered the House of Commons as an Ulster Unionist MP, and from 1974 to 1977 served as leader of the Ulster coalition there. He was a member of the Northern Ireland assembly from 1982 to 1986. As deputy Grand Master of the Orange Order and a close political ally of **Ian Paisley**, he played a leading role in the 1991 efforts by Northern Ireland Secretary **Peter Brooke** to initiate new negotiations between loyalist leaders and the British and Irish governments to bring peace to the Province. He resigned in 1995 as leader of the Ulster Unionist Party after 16 years in the post. He received a knighthood in 1996 and a life peerage in 1997.

Molyneux, Edward Henry 1891–1974
English fashion designer
He was born in London, studied art, and worked for Lucile in London and abroad. After service as a captain in the British Army in World War I, in which he lost an eye, he opened his own couture house in Paris in 1919 with branches in London, Monte Carlo, Cannes and Biarritz, and became famous for the elegant simplicity of his tailored suits with pleated skirts, and his evening wear. He closed his salons in 1950 and retired to Jamaica. He reopened in 1965 but soon retired again.

Mommsen, (Christian Matthias) Theodor 1817–1903
German historian and Nobel Prize winner
Born in Garding, Schleswig-Holstein, he studied at Kiel for three years, examined Roman inscriptions in France and Italy for the Berlin Academy (1844–47), and in 1848 was appointed to a chair of law at Leipzig, of which he was deprived two years later for the part he took in politics. In 1852 he became Professor of Roman Law at Zurich, and in 1854 at Breslau, and in 1858 Professor of Ancient History at Berlin. He edited the monumental *Corpus Inscriptionum Latinarum*, helped to edit the *Monumenta Germaniae Historica*, and from 1873 to 1895 was permanent secretary of the Academy. In 1882 he was tried and acquitted on a charge of slandering **Bismarck** in an election speech. His greatest works include *Römische Geschichte* (3 vols, 1854–55, Eng trans *The History of Rome*). He abandoned the fourth volume, but the fifth was translated as *The Provinces of the Roman Empire* (1885). He was awarded the Nobel Prize for literature in 1902. Amongst his 920 separate publications were works on the Italic dialects (1845, 1850), Neapolitan inscriptions (1857), Roman coins (1850), Roman constitutional law (1871), and an edition of the Pandects (1866–70). ⌑ Wickert, *Theodor Mommsen: Eine Biographie* (3 vols, 1959–80)

Momoh, Joseph Saidu 1937–
Sierra Leone soldier and statesman
Born in Binkolo, in the Northern Province, he was trained at military schools in Ghana, Great Britain and Nigeria before being commissioned in the Sierra Leone army in 1963. By 1983 he was an army commander and a major-general. In 1985 President **Siaka Stevens** announced his retirement at the age of 80, and Momoh was endorsed by Sierra Leone's only political party, the All-People's Congress (APC), as the sole presidential candidate. After taking office he disassociated himself from the policies of his predecessor and pledged to fight corruption and improve the economy, but he was deposed in 1992 and now lives in Guinea.

Mompesson, William 1639–1709
English clergyman
He was rector of Eyam, Derbyshire, when in 1665–66 the plague (brought from London in a box of infected cloths) killed 267 of his 350 parishioners. He persuaded his people to confine themselves entirely to the parish, and the disease was not spread. In 1669 he became rector of Eakring, Nottinghamshire, and in 1676 was made a prebendary of Southwell.

Monash, Sir John 1865–1931
Australian soldier
He was born in Melbourne of German parentage. He practised as a civil engineer and also held a commission in the Australian Citizen Force (1887). He commanded the 4th Australian Brigade at Gallipoli (1914–15), the 3rd Australian Division in France (1916), and the Australian Corps as Lieutenant-General (1918). Recognized as one of the outstanding generals of World War I, he was noted for the meticulous preparation and planning of his operations. He retired in 1930 with the rank of general.

Monboddo, James Burnett, Lord 1714–99
Scottish judge and pioneer anthropologist
Born at Monboddo House, Kincardineshire, and educated at Aberdeen, Edinburgh and Gröningen, he was called to the Scottish Bar, and in 1767 was raised to the bench as Lord Monboddo. Highly respected as a judge, he nevertheless held a variety of bizarre views, for example, that babies are born with tails which are cut off by midwives before anyone has a chance to see them. He had a strong aversion to anything modern, such as sedan-chairs, and an ardent devotion to the ways of the ancient Greeks, whose simple lifestyle he tried to emulate. His *Of the Origin and Progress of Language* (6 vols, 1773–92) is learned but idiosyncratic, but his theory of human affinity with monkeys anticipated **Charles Darwin** and the modern science of anthropology. He also published, anonymously, *Antient Metaphysics* (6 vols, 1779–99).

Monck, George See **Monk, George**

Monckton, Lionel 1861–1924
English composer
He was born in London. Prominent as an amateur actor while at Oxford, he turned to composition and contributed songs to many of the shows of **George Edwardes**, at the Gaiety Theatre and elsewhere in London. His musical comedies *The Country Girl* (1902) and *The Quaker Girl* (1910) were very popular.

Monckton (of Brenchley), Walter Turner Monckton, 1st Viscount 1891–1965
English lawyer and politician

Born in Plaxtol, Kent, and educated at Harrow and Balliol College, Oxford, he was called to the Bar in 1919. He became Attorney-General to the Prince of Wales in 1932, in which capacity he was adviser to him (as **Edward VIII**) in the abdication crisis of 1936. He held many legal offices, and in World War II was Director-General of the Ministry of Information; in the 1945 caretaker government he was Solicitor-General. MP for Bristol West from 1951 until his elevation to the peerage in 1957, he was Minister of Labour (1951–55), of Defence (1955–56) and Paymaster-General (1956–57).

Mond, Alfred Moritz, 1st Baron Melchett
1868–1930
British industrialist and politician
Born in Farnworth, Cheshire, the son of **Ludwig Mond**, after some years in industry and as chairman of the Mond Nickel Co, he became a Liberal MP (1906–28). He was the first Commissioner of Works (1916–21) and was Minister of Health (1922). In 1926 he helped to form ICI (Imperial Chemical Industries Ltd), of which he became chairman. A powerful advocate of industrial co-operation, in 1927 he instituted the Mond–Turner conference with the TUC which suggested the formation of a national industrial council.

Mond, Ludwig 1839–1909
British chemist
Born in Kassel, Germany, he studied chemistry at Marburg and then under **Robert Wilhelm Bunsen** at Heidelberg. He settled in Great Britain in 1862, and, while working for John Hutchinson at Widnes, developed a process to retrieve sulphur from the waste products of the Leblanc process. In 1873 he joined John Brunner in setting up a factory at Winnington, Cheshire, to manufacture soda by the new ammonia process invented by **Ernest Solvay**. Brunner–Mond & Co eventually grew to be the largest soda plant in the world. Mond also developed a new fuel, producer gas. He is perhaps best known for the process he invented for purifying nickel. He noticed that nickel valves in a manufacturing plant were corroded by carbon monoxide and discovered that a compound new to science, nickel carbonyl, had been formed, and that it would yield pure nickel on further heating. He put this reaction to use on an industrial scale (the Mond process). He was succeeded in business by his son Robert (later Sir Robert) Mond (1867–1938). 📖 J M Cohen, *The Life of Ludwig Mond* (1956)

Mondale, Walter F(rederick) 1928–
US politician and lawyer
Born in the small town of Ceylon, Minnesota, he was the son of a Methodist preacher of Norwegian extract. After graduating from the University of Minnesota Law School, he made his reputation as a local Democrat 'machine politician' in his home state, before serving in the US senate between 1964 and 1976. He was selected as **Jimmy Carter's** running-mate in the 1976 presidential election and served as an active Vice-President between 1977 and 1980. In 1984 he was the Democratic presidential nominee, but was crushingly defeated by the Republican candidate, **Ronald Reagan**. Following this reverse, Mondale retired from national politics to resume his law practice, but in 1993 he was appointed US ambassador to Japan. 📖 Finlay Lewis, *Mondale: Portrait of an American Politician* (1980)

Mondlane, Eduardo 1920–69
Mozambique nationalist leader
Educated in mission schools, he furthered his training at Fort Hare College and Lisbon University and developed into a respected sociologist with research posts in the USA and with the UN. He returned to Mozambique in 1961 to form Frelimo (Mozambique Liberation Front) and

launched the guerrilla war against Portuguese colonialism in 1964. He was murdered by a parcel bomb in Dar es Salaam.

Mondrian, Piet, *properly* Pieter Cornelis Mondriaan 1872–1944
Dutch artist
Born in Amersfoort, he was associated with **Theo van Doesburg** in founding the De Stijl movement in architecture and painting. He began by painting landscape in a traditional sombre Dutch manner, but after moving to Paris in 1909 he came under the influence of **Henri Matisse** and Cubism. He then began painting still lifes— his early work included a series of abstracts, *Trees*—which are analysed in terms of the relationship between the outlines and the planes. In the hands of Mondrian these became increasingly abstract, so that eventually the patterns made become more important than the subject itself. During World War I he discarded the subject altogether and concentrated on constructing grids of simple black lines filled in with primary colours. These rectilinear compositions depend for their beauty on the simple relationships between the coloured areas. He was a great theoretician and published the pamphlet *Neo-Plasticism* in 1920, which inspired the Dutch philosopher Schoenmaekers. He went to London in 1938, and from 1940 lived in New York City. Later works include more colourful abstracts (eg *Broadway Boogie-Woogie*, 1942–43, New York). His work has been a major influence on all purely abstract painters.

Monet, Claude 1840–1926
French Impressionist painter
Born in Paris, he spent his youth in Le Havre, where he met **Eugène Boudin**, who encouraged him to work in the open air. Moving to Paris, he associated with **Renoir**, **Camille Pissarro** and **Alfred Sisley**, and exhibited with them at the first Impressionist Exhibition in 1874. One of his works at this exhibition, *Impression: soleil levant*, gave its name to the movement. Later he worked much at Argenteuil. Along with Pissarro, Monet is recognized as one of the creators of Impressionism, and he was one of its most consistent exponents. He visited England, Holland and Venice, and spent his life expressing his instinctive way of seeing its most subtle nuances of colour, atmosphere and light in landscape. Apart from many sea and river scenes, he also executed several series of paintings of subjects under different aspects of light, such as *Haystacks* (1890–91), *Rouen Cathedral* (1892–95) and the almost abstract *Waterlilies* (at the Orangerie, Paris). The last years of his life were spent as a recluse at Giverny. 📖 William C Seitz, *Claude Monet* (1960)

Monge, Gaspard 1746–1818
French mathematician and physicist
Born in Beaune, Burgundy, he became Professor of Mathematics at Mézières in 1768, and in 1780 Professor of Hydraulics at the Lycée in Paris. In 1783, independently of **James Watt** or **Henry Cavendish**, he discovered that water resulted from an electrical explosion of oxygen and hydrogen. He helped to found (1794) the École Polytechnique, and became Professor of Mathematics there. In 1795 his *Leçons de géométrie descriptive* stated his principles regarding the general application of geometry to the arts of construction (descriptive geometry). In 1805 he was made a senator and Count of Pelusium, but lost both dignities on the restoration of the **Bourbons**. 📖 René Taton, *Gaspard Monge* (1950)

Moniz, António Egas See **Egas Moniz, António**

Monk or Monck, George, 1st Duke of Albemarle 1608–70
English soldier

The second son of a Devonshire baronet of Loyalist sympathies, he was a volunteer in the Île de Rhé expedition of 1628. He campaigned for 10 years in the Low Countries (1629–38). In the Civil War (1642–51) he was at first a Royalist and fought in Ireland (1642–43), but he was captured at the Battle of Nantwich (1644). Following a two-year imprisonment in the Tower he supported the Commonwealth cause. His successful activities in Ireland brought him to the notice of Cromwell. He defeated the Scots at Dunbar in 1650, and was successful in pacifying Scotland. In the First Dutch War he speedily adapted his talents to sea fighting, and played a major part in the 1653 victory over Maarten Tromp off the Gabbard. Instrumental in bringing about the restoration of Charles II, he was rewarded with the dukedom of Albermarle, and was appointed lieutenant-general of the forces. He played a conspicuous and useful part in the Second Dutch War, defeating the Dutch at St James's Fight in 1666. In 1667, with Michiel de Ruyter raiding the Medway virtually unopposed, Monk took command of the defences. Thereafter he retired more and more into private life. He was buried in Westminster Abbey, London.

Monk, Maria 1816–49
Canadian impostor
Born in Saint-Jean-sur-Richelieu, Quebec, she became slightly brain-damaged after sticking a slate pencil in her ear. She turned to prostitution but was institutionalized in 1834, then escaped to New York and pretended not only to have witnessed cruel treatment in a nunnery at Montreal, but also to have become pregnant by a monk. She published *Awful Disclosures by Maria Monk* (1836) and *Further Disclosures* (1837) before being exposed as a fake.

Monk, Meredith Jane 1943–
US dancer, choreographer and musician
Born in Lima, Peru, she was the daughter of a professional singer. She took dance classes as a child and began composing music as a teenager. Briefly associated with the experimental Judson Dance Theatre in the mid-1960s, she broke away to develop multimedia music/theatre/dance events of her own. These are either solos or inventive group performances featuring her own company, The House (formed in 1968). Her works are frequently performed in unconventional venues (eg churches, museums, car parks) and utilize film, props, sound, gestures and other movement, public history and personal myth.

Monk, Thelonious Sphere 1917–82
US jazz pianist and composer
He was born in Rocky Mount, North Carolina, and brought up in New York. After childhood piano lessons, he began to perform at 'rent parties' in Harlem and to play in church. While in his twenties, he worked as a freelance musician and studied briefly at the Juilliard School of Music. Between 1939 and 1945 he worked under a succession of leaders in New York, including Kenny Clarke, Lucky Millinder, Cootie Williams and Kermit Scott. Monk first recorded while with the Coleman Hawkins Sextet in 1944. During this period the bebop style was causing a ferment among young jazz musicians in New York, and Monk was a key figure in these experiments at Minton's Playhouse. He joined Dizzy Gillespie's first big band in 1946, formed specifically to perform bebop-style arrangements. Monk formed his own small group in 1947, and from that time his performing and recording was done largely with small groups, latterly with a quartet using such tenor saxophone players as John Coltrane, Johnny Griffin and (for 11 years) Charlie Rouse. World tours from the 1960s brought wide recognition for Monk's percussive and harmonically iconoclastic style. He played little after the mid-1970s but many of his compositions, such as 'Round Midnight' and 'Straight No Chaser', are frequently performed.

Monkees, The
US pop group
The Monkees are the classic example of a manufactured pop group, although far from the only one. The band was put together by NBC television in 1966 to cash in on the success of the Beatles in a zany television series. The four chosen members were the English singer Davy Jones, Mike Nesmith (guitar), Peter Tork (bass) and Mickey Dolenz (drums). The series and the band, produced by the commercially astute Don Kirshner, were very successful, and produced some fine pop music. Tork left in 1968, and the band broke up when Nesmith, the most genuinely talented musician, formed his idiosyncratic First National Band in 1969. They re-formed without Nesmith for a tour and album in 1986–87. 1996, however, saw the complete reformation of the band and the recording of their album *Justus*. They toured Great Britain in 1997. 📖 E Lefowitz, *The Monkees Tale* (1987)

Monmouth, James Scott, Duke of 1649–85
English claimant to the throne
Born in The Hague (or Rotterdam), the illegitimate son of Charles II and Lucy Walter, he was committed by Charles to the care of Lord Crofts. In 1662 he went to England and was created Duke of Monmouth (1663), was wedded to a rich heiress, Anne, Countess of Buccleuch, and became captain-general (1670). Handsome, athletic, but a brainless libertine, he was popular because of his humanity towards the Scottish Covenanters at Bothwell Brig (1679), the Popish Plot and the Exclusion Bill, and his two semi-royal progresses (1680–82). The first Earl of Shaftesbury pitted the protestant Duke against the popish heir-presumptive (later James VII and II), and involved him in the Rye House Plot (1683), after which Monmouth fled to the Low Countries. At Charles's death, he landed at Lyme Regis, quickly raised 4,000 troops, branded James as a popish usurper, and asserted his own right to the Crown. At Taunton he was proclaimed King James II, and he attempted to surprise the king's forces at Sedgemoor. He was defeated and fled, but was captured and beheaded. His followers were persecuted in the 'Bloody Assizes' of Judge Jeffreys. 📖 Bryan Bevan, *James, Duke of Monmouth* (1973)

Monnet, Jean 1888–1979
French political economist and diplomat
Born in Cognac, he was educated locally, and in 1914 entered the Ministry of Commerce. A distinguished economist and expert in financial affairs, he became in 1947 Commissioner-General of the 'Plan de modernisation et d'équipement de la France' (Monnet plan). He was awarded the Prix Wateler de la Paix (1951), and he was president of the European Coal and Steel High Authority (1952–55). In 1956 he became president of the Action Committee for the United States of Europe.

Monod, André Théodore 1902–
French naturalist and explorer
Born in Rouen, he was educated at the Sorbonne, and went on to make extensive botanical and geological studies of remote regions of the Sahara. His most memorable trans-Saharan crossing, of 560 miles (902km), was by camel from Wadan, Mauritania to Arawan, Mali, made by laying down advance depots of food and water. He subsequently became director of the Institut Français d'Afrique Noire (1938–64), and Dean of the faculty of sciences of Dakar University, Senegal.

Monod, Jacques Lucien 1910–76
French biochemist and Nobel Prize winner
Born in Paris, he graduated from the university there (1931), and then left to work at Columbia University. He returned to France and received his PhD from the Sorbonne for his thesis on bacterial growth. After World

War II he began work at the Pasteur Institute in Paris, becoming head of the cellular biochemistry department in 1954 and director in 1971. From 1967, he was also Professor of Molecular Biology at the Collège de France. Monod worked closely with François Jacob on genetic control mechanisms, developing the theory of the operon system, whereby a regulator gene controls other genes by binding to a specific section of the DNA strand. In 1965 Monod and Jacob shared the Nobel Prize for physiology or medicine with **André Lwoff**. He published *Chance and Necessity* in 1970, a biologically-based philosophy of life.

Monophthalmos See Antigonus

Monro, Alexander, *known as* Monro Primus
1697–1767
Scottish anatomist
Born in London, he studied there, in Paris, and in Leyden (under **Hermann Boerhaave**). From 1719 he lectured at Edinburgh on anatomy and surgery, serving as professor from 1725 to 1759. He played a key part in founding the Edinburgh Royal Infirmary, and his energetic and well-organized teaching expedited the rise of Edinburgh as a popular centre for medical training. He founded a three-generation dynasty of anatomy professors that dominated anatomy teaching there for 126 years. His works include *Osteology* (1726), *Essay on Comparative Anatomy* (1744), *Observations Anatomical and Physiological* (1758) and *Account of the Success of Inoculation of Smallpox in Scotland* (1765), and it was partly through the orientation of his interests that the Edinburgh ideal of the practitioner integrated the physician and the surgeon.

Monro, Alexander, *known as* Monro Secundus
1733–1817
Scottish anatomist
The son of **Alexander Monro**, 'Monro Primus', he was educated at Edinburgh University, and groomed by his father to succeed him in the chair of Anatomy, which he formally did at the age of 21 in 1754, though his father continued to teach. Monro pursued his studies in London, under **William Hunter**, and in Paris, and in 1757 published his *De Venis Lymphaticis Valvulosis*, which demonstrated that the lymphatics were absorbents and quite separate from the circulatory system, and sparked a vitriolic priority dispute with Hunter. An energetic researcher, Monro made public some of his most important findings in *Observations on the Structure and Functions of the Nervous System* (1783). He is said to have taught 13,404 students, and he also built up a large anatomical and pathological collection which he bequeathed to the university.

Monro, Harold (Edward) 1879–1932
English poet and anthologist
Born in Brussels, he was educated at Cambridge. He subsequently travelled abroad and was involved with various progressive communities before taking up the promotion of English poetry. He founded the influential *Poetry Review* in 1912 and the Poetry Bookshop in London the following year. Generous to other poets, he published the Georgians and the Imagists; some of his own work is close to the former, including such popular pieces as the closely observed 'Milk for the Cat' (1914), but his best, least romantic and most original poems, mainly written in his later years, are bitter in tone, reflecting a loneliness related to his alcoholism and bisexuality. These include 'Strange Meetings' (1917), 'The One, Faithful …' (1933) and 'Bitter Sanctuary' (1933). His *Collected Poems* (1933) were edited by his second wife, Alida. ⌖ J Grant, *Harold Monro and the Poetry Bookshop* (1967)

Monroe, Bill (William Smith) 1911–96
US singer and mandolin player

Born on a farm near Rosine, Kentucky, he took up the mandolin in order to accompany his two older brothers, who were fiddlers, and performed with them before starting his own band, the Blue Grass Boys, in 1938. They first performed on the *Grand Ole Opry* radio show in Nashville in 1939, and continued to perform on it for more than half a century, in addition to touring widely. Monroe's syncopated rhythms, complex harmonies and tenor verging on falsetto (which he called his 'high, lonesome sound') inspired the genre of bluegrass music, and his group's combination of mandolin, fiddle, guitar, banjo and bass established its standard instruments. In 1951 he founded the Bean Blossom festival, a bluegrass festival in Indiana that still continues. Regarded as the 'father of bluegrass music', he continued to look for new ways to develop the music, and was still performing in the mid-1990s. ⌖ N Rosenberg, *Bill Monroe and His Blue Grass Boys* (1974)

Monroe, Harriet 1860–1936
US poet and critic
Born in Chicago, she founded (1912) the magazine *Poetry*, which was influential in publicizing the work of **Vachel Lindsay**, **T S Eliot**, **Ezra Pound** and **Robert Frost**, among others. She wrote the 'Columbian Ode' for the Chicago World's Columbian Exposition (1892), celebrating the 400th anniversary of the West's 'discovery' of the USA. In 1917 she edited the influential free-verse anthology, *The New Poetry*. Her own work was collected in *Chosen Poems* (1935). ⌖ *A Poet's Life* (1937)

Monroe, James 1758–1831
5th President of the USA
Born in Westmoreland County, Virginia, he served in the American Revolution, and was elected to the assembly of Virginia and in 1783 to Congress, where he sat for three years. As a member of the US Senate (1790–94) he opposed **Washington** and the Federalists; the government recalled him in 1796 from the post of Minister to France. He was Governor of Virginia (1799–1802), and in 1803 helped to negotiate the Louisiana Purchase. The next four years were spent in less successful diplomacy at London and Madrid. In 1811 he was again Governor of Virginia, from 1811 to 1817 Secretary of State, and from 1814 to 1815 also Secretary of War. In 1816 he was elected President of the USA, and in 1820 was re-elected overwhelmingly. His administration (1817–25) was a time of peaceful prosperity that became known as the 'era of good feeling'. He signed the Missouri Compromise of 1820, recognized the Spanish American republics and promulgated in a message to Congress (1823), the 'Monroe Doctrine', embodying the principle that 'the American continents … are henceforth not to be considered as subjects for future colonization by any European power', though existing colonies were not to be interfered with. ⌖ William P Cresson, *James Monroe* (1973)

Monroe, Marilyn See panel p1303

Monsarrat, Nicholas John Turney 1910–79
English novelist
Born in Liverpool, and educated at Trinity College, Cambridge, he abandoned law for literature and wrote three quite successful novels, and a play, *The Visitors*, which reached the London stage. During World War II he served in the navy, and out of his experiences emerged his best-selling novel *The Cruel Sea* (1951), which was subsequently filmed. *The Story of Esther Costello* (1953) repeated that success, followed by *The Tribe That Lost Its Head* (1956) and *The Pillow Fight* (1965). He settled in Ottawa, Canada, as director of the UK Information Office (1953–56) after holding a similar post in South Africa (1946–52).

Monson, Sir William 1569–1643
English naval commander

Monroe, Marilyn, *originally* Norma Jean Mortenson 1926–62
US film actress

Marilyn Monroe was born in Los Angeles. She had a disturbed childhood spent largely in foster homes on account of the mental illness suffered by her mother, Gladys Pearl Baker (*née* Monroe). She was married for the first time at the age of 16, and went on to have two more husbands: the baseball star **Joe DiMaggio**, and the playwright **Arthur Miller**. She became a photographer's model in 1946, and after several small film parts and a very high-powered studio publicity campaign, she starred as a sexy, beautiful dumb blonde in *How to Marry a Millionaire* and *Gentlemen Prefer Blondes* (both in 1953). She developed her flair for light comedy in **Billy Wilder**'s *The Seven Year Itch* (1955) and *Some Like It Hot* (1959).

Wanting more serious roles, she studied at **Lee Strasberg**'s Actors' Studio and appeared to critical acclaim in *Bus Stop* (1956) and *The Misfits* (1961), her last film, written for her by Arthur Miller. She came to London to make *The Prince and the Showgirl* (1957) with Sir **Laurence Olivier**, returning after two years to Hollywood. She was divorced from Arthur Miller in 1961, and the following year died of an overdose of sleeping pills. She had a close relationship with **John F Kennedy** and **Robert F Kennedy**, and famously sang 'Happy Birthday Mr President' in 1961. Since her death, she has become a symbol of Hollywood's ruthless exploitation of beauty and youth. Some accounts maintain that she was murdered, possibly for political motives, but these views remain unsubstantiated.

📖 Her autobiography, *My Story*, was published in 1974. See also D Spoto, *Marilyn Monroe: The Biography* (1993); Norman Mailer, *Marilyn* (1973).

'He's not a director, he's a dictator.' Attributed remark about Billy Wilder, after making *Some Like it Hot* (1959).

'He's the only person I know who's in worse shape than I am.' On **Montgomery Clift**, her co-star in *The Misfits* (1961).

'Marilyn Monroe was a legend. In her own lifetime she created a myth of what a poor girl from a deprived background could attain. For the entire world she became a symbol of the eternal feminine.' Lee Strasberg, at her funeral. Quoted in Ephraim Katz, *The Macmillan International Film Encyclopedia* (1994).

Born in South Carlton, Lincolnshire, he served at sea against the Spaniards (1585–1602), was taken prisoner and sentenced to the galleys (1591) but returned to active service with Lord **Essex**. He distinguished himself in the Cadiz expedition of 1596. He was imprisoned briefly on charges of treason and corruption, but was released and became Admiral of the Narrow Seas (1604–16). He wrote *Naval Tracts* which are partly autobiographical (5 vols, 1902–14, edited by M Oppenheim).

Montagna, Bartolomeo c.1450–1523
Italian painter

A native of Brescia, he probably studied at Venice under **Giovanni Bellini** and **Vittore Carpaccio**. He founded a school of painting at Vicenza and also worked in Verona and other places.

Montagnier, Luc 1932–
French molecular biologist

He was educated at the University of Poitiers and the University of Paris, became laboratory head of the Radium Institute (1965–71) in Paris, and since 1972 has worked at the Pasteur Institute, as head of the Viral Oncology Unit, professor (since 1985) and head of the department of AIDS and retroviruses (since 1990). Since 1974 he has also been director of research at the National Centre for Scientific Research. Montagnier has published widely in molecular biology and virology, and is now credited with the discovery of the HIV virus. He and his team first isolated the HIV virus from a Frenchman with AIDS in 1983, although it was only around 10 years after the discovery, when the US scientist Robert Gallo's (1937–) claim to have discovered the virus was discredited, that Montagnier was recognized as the discoverer. Montagnier holds the controversial view that mycoplasms (bacteria-like organisms) might play a crucial part in the progression from HIV infection to symptomatic AIDS.

Montagu, Ashley, *originally* Montague Francis Ashley Montague 1905–
US anthropologist

Born in London, England, he studied at London and Florence universities, and gained his PhD under **Franz Boas** in 1937 at Columbia University, New York City. Throughout his work on human biosocial evolution he has argued strongly against the view that cultural phenomena are genetically determined. His many influential publications, both scholarly and popular, include *Coming Into Being among the Australian Aborigines* (1937), *The Natural Superiority of Women* (1953), *Man's Most Dangerous Myth: the Fallacy of Race* (1964), *The Elephant Man* (1971), *The Nature of Human Aggression* (1976), *The Dehumanization of Man* (1983), *The Peace of the World* (1986) and *What We Know About Race* (1987). He has held posts at numerous universities, including the New School for Social Research, Rutgers University, New Jersey, and Princeton University.

Montagu, Edward See **Manchester, 2nd Earl of**

Montagu, Elizabeth, *née* Robinson 1720–1800
English writer and society leader

In 1742 she married Edward Montagu, grandson of the 1st Earl of Sandwich and cousin of Edward Wortley Montagu (husband of Lady **Mary Wortley Montagu**). The first of the blue-stockings, with £10,000 a year, she established a salon in Mayfair which became the heart of London social and literary life for people like Dr **Johnson, David Garrick, Joshua Reynolds** and many others. She wrote an essay on **Shakespeare** (1768).

Montagu, George 1753–1815
English naturalist and soldier

Born in Wiltshire, after a failed career in the army and a disastrous marriage that led to the loss of his estates, he turned his attention to ornithology. He moved to Devon, where he produced his notable *Ornithological Dictionary; or Alphabetical Synopsis of British Birds* (2 vols, 1802). Montagu's Harrier is named after him.

Montagu, Lady Mary Wortley 1689–1762
English writer

A colourful, eccentric feminist, the eldest daughter of the 5th Earl (later Duke) of Kingston, she was a well-known society hostess, who had a celebrated quarrel with **Alexander Pope**. From 1716 to 1718 her husband was ambassador in Constantinople (Istanbul) and her letters from there and from Vienna were the basis of her contemporary reputation. After seeing it in Turkey, she was instrumental in introducing vaccination against smallpox into Great Britain.

Montague, Charles Edward 1867–1928
English novelist and essayist

He was of Irish parentage, and studied at Balliol College, London. From 1890 to 1925 he was on the staff of *The Manchester Guardian*. His numerous writings include the novels *A Hind Let Loose* (1910), *Rough Justice* (1926) and *Disenchantment* (1922), an account of his experiences as a soldier in World War I.

Montaigne, Michel Eyquem de 1533–92
French essayist

He was born at the Château de Montaigne, Périgord, the third son of the Seigneur de Montaigne. As an experiment in humanist upbringing, he spoke no language but Latin until he was six. He then spent seven years at the Collège de Guienne in Bordeaux, boarding in the rooms of his famous teachers, **George Buchanan** and Marc-Antoine de Muret. He subsequently studied law, obtained a post in connection with the Parlement of Bordeaux, and for 13 years was a city counsellor. A translation (1569) of the *Natural Theology* of a 15th-century professor at Toulouse supplied the text for his *Apologie de Raymon Sebond* ('Apologia for Raymond Sebond'), in which he exhibited the full scope of his own sceptical philosophy. In 1571 he succeeded to the family estate at Château de Montaigne, and adopted the life of a country gentleman, varied only by visits to Paris and a tour in Germany, Switzerland and Italy. He also began his *Essais* (1572–80 and 1588, Eng trans *Essays*, 1603) on the ideas and personalities of the time, which introduced a new literary genre and provided a major contribution to literary history. Unanimously elected Mayor of Bordeaux (against his wishes), he performed his duties to the satisfaction of the citizens, serving two terms of office (1581–85). He was a fearless and all-questioning critic, seemingly inspired by the mere caprice of the moment, but highly original and capable of embracing and realizing the largest experience of life. **Pascal** among others acknowledged a debt to him. 📖 D M Frame, *Montaigne* (1965)

Montale, Eugenio 1896–1981
Italian poet and Nobel Prize winner

Born in Genoa, he worked as a journalist and critic, and was an early opponent of fascism. World War I left him with a pessimism which permeates his writing. He was the leading poet of the modern Italian 'Hermetic' school, and his primary concern was with language and meaning. His works include *Ossi di Seppia* (1925, 'The Cuttlefish Bones'), *Le occasioni* (1939, 'Opportunities'), *Finisterre* (1943, 'Finistère'), *La bufera e altro* (1956, 'The Storm and Other Things'), *Satura* (1962, Eng trans *Satura: Five Poems*, 1969) and *Xenia* (1966, Eng trans 1970). He was awarded the Nobel Prize for literature in 1975. 📖 S Ramat, *Eugenio Montale* (1965)

Montalembert, Charles René Forbes de, Comte de 1810–70
French historian and politician

Born in London, the eldest son of a noble French émigré and his English wife, he was educated at Fulham and the Collège Ste Barbe. In 1830 he eagerly joined the Abbé **Lamennais** and Henri Lacordaire in *L'Avenir*, a Catholic liberal newspaper. He pleaded the cause of religious liberty, in spite of the papal condemnation of *L'Avenir*. His great speech (1848) on Switzerland is a famous protest against tyranny. After the February Revolution (1848) he was elected a member of the National Assembly, and supported Louis Napoleon (**Napoleon III**) until the confiscation of the Orléans property, when he became a determined opponent of the imperial regime. He visited England in 1855, and wrote *De l'Avenir politique de l'Angleterre* (1856, 'The Political Future of England'), and

many other works on medieval church history and contemporary political topics in an attempt to reconcile Catholicism and liberalism.

Montana, Joe 1956–
US football player

Born in New Eagle, Pennsylvania, he joined the San Francisco 49ers in 1979, and played in their winning Super Bowl teams in 1982, 1985, 1989, and 1990. He won the Most Valuable Player award in 1982, 1985, and 1990. He joined the Kansas City Chiefs in 1993, after being unable to play for two years because of injury. In 1989 he co-authored *Cool Under Fire* with Alan Steinberg.

Montand, Yves, *originally* Ivo Livi 1921–91
French actor and singer

Born in Monsummano in Tuscany, Italy, he worked at a variety of jobs before performing as a singer and impressionist in Marseilles and Paris. A protégé of **Edith Piaf**, he made his film debut with her in *Etoile sans lumière* (1946, *Star Without Light*). He was a star attraction with his one-man show, and his film career temporarily blossomed with *Le Salaire de la peur* (1953, *The Wages of Fear*). An international cabaret star, he also appeared on stage in *The Crucible* (1954) and ventured abroad for films like *Let's Make Love* (1960). His acting reputation was enhanced by an association with the director Costa-Gavras and films such as *Z* (1968) and *L'Aveu* (1970, *The Confession*), which also reflected his sympathy for a variety of left-wing causes. Married to actress **Simone Signoret** from 1951 until her death in 1985, he became a distinguished elder statesman of the French film industry, in productions including *Jean de Florette* (1986), *Manon des Sources* (1986) and *IP5* (1991).

Montano See Arias, Benito

Montcalm, Louis Joseph, Marquis de Montcalm Gezan de Saint Véran 1712–59
French soldier

He was born near Nîmes. A soldier at 15, in the Seven Years War (1756–63) he commanded the French troops in North America in 1756, and captured the British post of Oswego, and also Fort William Henry, where the prisoners (men, women, and children) were massacred by the Native American allies. In 1758 he successfully defended Ticonderoga with a small force, won Louisburg and Fort Duquesne, and moved to defend Quebec against a British attack. In 1759 General **Wolfe** ascended the St Lawrence, and finally, in a battle on the Plains of Abraham, drove the French in retreat on the city. Montcalm tried to rally his force, but was mortally wounded.

Montefiore, Sir Moses Haim 1784–1885
British philanthropist

Born in Leghorn (Livorno), Italy, he retired with a fortune from stockbroking in 1824, and from 1829 was prominent in the struggle for removing discrimination against Jews. After a long exclusion and repeated re-election, he was made Sheriff of London in 1837. Between 1827 and 1875 he made seven journeys to Palestine in the interests of his oppressed co-religionists in Poland, Russia, Romania and Damascus. He endowed a hospital in Jerusalem in 1855 and a Jewish college in Ramsgate in 1865. 📖 Paul Goodman, *Montefiore* (1925)

Montemayor, Jorge de c.1515–1561
Portuguese novelist and poet

Born in Montemoro-Velho, Coimbra, he wrote, in Castilian, the (unfinished) pastoral romance *Diana* (1559), which influenced Sir **Philip Sidney** and **Shakespeare**. He was also a musician and singer. 📖 J B Auraille-Arce, *La novela pastoril española* (1959)

Montesi, Wilma 1932–53
Italian model

She was the daughter of a middle-class carpenter from Rome. The finding of her body on the beach near Ostia in April 1953 led to sensational allegations of drug and sex orgies in Roman society, and four years of debate, scandal, arrests, re-arrests and libel suits, culminating in the Venice trial in 1957 of three suspects, the son of a former Italian foreign minister, a self-styled marquis and a former Rome police chief, for complicity in her death. They were acquitted after many conflicts of evidence, but the trial exposed corruption in high public places and helped to bring about the downfall of the Scelba government in 1955.

Montespan, Françoise Athénaïs, Marquise de, known as Madame de Montespan 1641–1707
French courtier

Born in Tonnay-Charente, the daughter of the Duc de Mortemart, she married the Marquis de Montespan (1663), and became attached to the household of the queen. In c.1668 she became the mistress of Louis XIV. The marquis was exiled to Guyenne, and his marriage was annulled (1676). The Marquise de Montespan reigned supreme until 1682, and bore the king seven children, who were legitimized, but she was then replaced by Madame de Maintenon, the governess of her children. In 1691 she left the court, and retired to a convent. 📖 Jean Christian Petitfils, *Madame de Montespan* (1988)

Montesquieu, Charles-Louis de Secondat, Baron de la Brède et de 1689–1755
French philosopher and jurist

Born at the Château de la Brède, near Bordeaux, he became counsellor of the *parlement* of Bordeaux (1714), and its president (1716). He discharged the duties of his office faithfully, but until his poor eyesight hindered him, preferred scientific research. His first great literary success was the *Lettres persanes* (1721, 'Persian Letters'), a satirical description of French society. Weary of routine work, he sold his office (1726) and moved to Paris. For three years he travelled extensively in order to study political and social institutions. In England (1729–31), he mixed in society, visited the Houses of Parliament, studied the political writings of John Locke, and analysed the English constitution. *Causes de la grandeur des Romains et de leur décadence* (1734, 'Causes of the Greatness and Decadence of the Romans') is one of his best works. His best-known work, the monumental *Défense de l'esprit des lois* (1748, Eng trans *The Spirit of the Laws*, 1750), a dialogue on despotism, was published anonymously and put on the Index of prohibited books, but went through 22 editions in less than two years. A comparative study of legal and political issues, it had an immense influence. Other works include *Lysimaque* (1748) and *Arsace et Isménie* (Eng trans 1927), a romance, and an essay on taste (*Goût*) in the *Encyclopédie* (1751–80). A member of the Académie Française from 1728, he died totally blind. 📖 J Starobinksi, *Montesquieu par lui-même* (1953)

Montessori, Maria 1870–1952
Italian physician and educationist

Born in Rome, the first woman in Italy to receive a medical degree (1894), she founded a school for children with learning disabilities (1899–1901), and developed a system of education for children of three to six based on spontaneity of expression and freedom from restraint. The system was later worked out for older children, and applied in Montessori schools throughout the world. She opened the first Montessori school for children in the slums of Rome in 1907. 📖 E Mortimer Standing, *Maria Montessori, Her Life and Work* (1957)

Monteux, Pierre 1875–1964
US conductor

Born in Paris, he trained at the Paris Conservatoire, where he began his career as a viola player. From 1911 to 1914, and in 1917, he conducted Sergei Diaghilev's Ballets Russes in Paris, leading the world premières of Igor Stravinsky's *Petrushka* (1911) and *The Rite of Spring* (1913, *Vésna Svyashchennaya*) and Maurice Ravel's *Daphnis and Chloé* (1912). In 1914 he organized the 'Concerts Monteux' whose programmes gave prominence to new French and Russian music. After serving in the army in World War I he went to the USA where he conducted in New York and Boston before returning to Europe in 1924 to the Amsterdam Concertgebouw Orkest. After founding and directing the Orchestre Symphonique de Paris between 1929 and 1938, he took over the newly organized San Francisco Symphony Orchestra in 1936, and in 1941 established a summer school for student conductors at Hanover, New Hampshire. From 1960 until his death he was principal conductor of the London Symphony Orchestra, and was one of the 20th century's leading conductors, his interpretations equally admired in ballet, opera and symphonic music. He became a US citizen in 1942.

Monteverdi, Claudio 1567–1643
Italian composer

Born in Cremona, he became a proficient violist and learned the art of composition, publishing a set of three-part choral pieces, *Cantiunculae Sacrae*, at the age of 15. In about 1590 he was appointed court musician to the Duke of Mantua, who appointed him maestro di capella in 1602. In 1613 he took a similar post at St Mark's, Venice, where he remained until his death. By his efforts the musical reputation of that church, which had declined since the days of the Gabrielis, was restored to its former high position. Monteverdi left no purely instrumental compositions. His eight books of madrigals (1587–1638) contain some boldly experimental harmonies which brought criticism from academic quarters but underlined the composer's originality. His first opera, *Orfeo* (1607), with its programmatic use of orchestral sonorities, its dramatic continuity and the obbligato character of the accompaniment, marked a considerable advance in the evolution of the genre. The two surviving operas of his later period, *Il Ritorno d'Ulisse in patria* (1641, 'Ulysses's Return to his Native Land') and *L'Incoronazione di Poppea* (1642, 'The Coronation of Poppea'), both written when he was in his seventies, show further development towards the baroque style and foreshadow the use of the leitmotif. His greatest contribution to church music is the *Mass* and *Vespers* of the Virgin (1610), another innovative work. Other new features which he introduced were the orchestral ritornello, and the use of tremolo and pizzicato. 📖 Denis Arnold, *Monteverdi* (1975, rev edn)

Montez, Lola, originally Maria Délores Gilbert 1818–61
US dancer

Born in Limerick, Ireland, she became a dancer in London in 1843. While touring Europe, she went to Munich (1846), where she had an affair with the eccentric artist-king, Ludwig I of Bavaria, a great boost to her career as a dancer. After a tour of the USA (1848) she decided to settle in California.

Montezuma II 1466–1520
Aztec emperor

The ninth Aztec emperor to rule Mexico before the Spanish invasion, and a distinguished warrior and legislator, he succeeded to the title (1502) and became absolute monarch of a vast empire. When the Spanish conquistadors arrived under the leadership of Hernán Cortés, he gave them rich gifts in the belief that they might be incarnations of the white god Quetzalcoatl and reluctantly received them in his palace at Tenochtitlán.

They, in turn, imprisoned him and made themselves rulers instead. He died before their conquest of Mexico was complete. One of his descendants was Viceroy of Mexico (1697–1701). The last, banished from Spain for liberalism, died in New Orleans (1836). 📖 C A Burland, *Montezuma, Lord of the Aztecs* (1973)

Montfaucon, Bernard de 1655–1741
French scholar and monk

Born in Soulage, near Brioude, he became a Benedictine monk at Saint-Maur in 1676. He went to Paris to edit the Latin works of the Greek fathers of the church, and published *Palaeographia graeca* (1708, 'Greek Palaeography'), the first work to be based on a study of manuscript handwriting, becoming the founder of the science of palaeography. He also published editions of Athanasius and St John Chrysostom.

Montfort, Simon IV de, Earl of Leicester
c.1160–1218
Norman crusader

He took part in the Fourth Crusade (1202–04); he also undertook a crusade against the Albingenses (1208) and fell at the Siege of Toulouse.

Montfort, Simon de, Earl of Leicester
c.1208–1265
English soldier and politician

He married (1238) Henry III of England's youngest sister, Eleanor. In 1248, as King's Deputy in Gascony, he suppressed disaffection with a heavy hand. In 1253 he returned to England where famine and taxation had exhausted the country. Prince Edward (the future Edward I) intrigued with the subtenants, and the barons quarrelled among themselves until de Montfort became their leader against the king in 1261. After varying success, both sides sought an arbitrator in Louis IX of France, who decided for surrender to the royal authority. London and the Cinque Ports repudiated the agreement, and de Montfort defeated the king's army at Lewes (1264). De Montfort, the Earl of Gloucester, and the bishop of Hereford, were appointed to preside over a parliament in 1265. This, the Model Parliament, held the germ of modern parliaments. But the barons soon grew dissatisfied with the rule of 'Simon the Righteous' and Prince Edward combined with Gloucester to defeat Simon at Evesham, where he was killed. His father was Simon IV de Montfort. 📖 M W Labarge, *Simon de Montfort* (1962)

Montgolfier, Joseph Michel 1740–1810 and Jacques Étienne 1745–99
French aeronautical inventors

Brothers, they were born in Annonay, near Lyons, the sons of a paper manufacturer. Joseph developed an early interest in science, while his younger brother became a successful architect before joining the family firm. After some preliminary model experiments, they constructed a balloon (1782) whose bag was lifted by lighting a cauldron of paper beneath it, thus heating and rarifying the air it contained. The world's first manned balloon flight, of 7 miles (12.1km) in less than half an hour, at a height of 3,000 feet (915m), carrying Pilatre de Rozier and the Marquis d'Arlandes, took place in November 1783. Their achievement created great public interest, and many other inventors attempted to follow their example, not always with equal success. Further experiments were frustrated by the outbreak of the French Revolution, Étienne being proscribed, and his brother returning to his paper factory. Joseph later became interested in other applications of science, inventing a type of parachute, a calorimeter and the widely used hydraulic ram, a device for raising small quantities of water to a considerable height. He was subsequently elected to the French Academy of Sciences

and created a Chevalier of the Legion of Honour by Napoleon I. 📖 Léon Ronstaing, *La Famille de Montgolfier, ses alliances, ses decendants* (1910)

Montgomerie, Alexander c.1545–c.1611
Scottish poet

Born probably at Hessilhead Castle near Beith, Ayrshire, he was 'maister poet' to James VI and I. He was detained in a continental prison and was embittered by the failure of a lawsuit involving loss of a pension. His pro-Catholic sympathies led to his being denounced as a traitor in 1597, and he went into exile. His fame rests on the *Cherrie and the Slae*, published twice in 1597, and his love lyrics, especially 'To his Mistress'. 📖 R D S Jack, *Montgomerie* (1985)

Montgomerie, Colin Stuart 1963–
Scottish golf professional

Born in Glasgow, he turned professional in 1988 after an amateur career that included two Walker Cup appearances (1985, 1987), and victories in the 1985 Scottish Stroke-play Championship and the 1987 Scottish Amateur Championship. He was Europe's top golfer for 1993, 1994, 1995 and 1996, but has yet to win one of golf's major titles. However, he has come close, gaining third place in the 1992 US Open, and losing play-offs in both the 1994 US Open and the 1995 PGA Championship. He also played in the Ryder Cup teams of 1991, 1993 and 1995. His displays of temper prevent him from being more popular.

Montgomery (of Alamein), Bernard Law Montgomery, 1st Viscount 1887–1976
English soldier

He was born in London, the son of Bishop Montgomery, and was educated at St Paul's School and the Royal Military College, Sandhurst. He served with the Royal Warwickshire Regiment in World War I. In World War II he commanded the 3rd Division, with which he shared the retreat to Dunkirk. In North Africa in 1941 he commanded the 8th Army, restoring their bruised confidence and the will to win. Conforming to General Harold Alexander's strategic plans, he defeated Erwin Rommel at the Battle of El Alamein (October 1942). This was followed up by a series of victories that eventually drove the Axis forces back to Tunis. His subsequent activities in Sicily and Italy were solid if somewhat pedestrian. Appointed Commander for the Ground Forces for the Normandy invasion in 1944, his strategy was characterized by wariness and unflagging tenacity. By deliberately attracting the main weight of the German counter-offensive to the British flank, he freed the US armoured formations to inaugurate the joint drive across France and Belgium. His attempt to roll up the German right flank by way of Arnhem (September 1944) lacked co-ordination and the deployment of the proper means to ensure success and ended in disaster, but his timely intervention helped materially to frustrate Karl von Rundstedt's surprise offensive of December 1944. He accepted the German capitulation on Lüneburg Heath, and was commander of the British occupied zone in Germany (1945–46) and Chief of the Imperial General Staff (CIGS) in 1946–48. He was deputy Supreme Commander of NATO forces (1951–58). His publications include *Normandy to the Baltic* (1947), his controversial *Memoirs* (1958), *The Path to Leadership* (1961) and *History of Warfare* (1968). Controversial and outspoken, he was known as a 'soldier's general' and is regarded by some as the best British field commander since the Duke of Wellington. 📖 R W Thompson, *The Montgomery Legend* (1967)

Montgomery, L(ucy) M(aud) 1874–1942
Canadian novelist

She was born in Clifton, Prince Edward Island, and qualified as a schoolteacher from Prince of Wales College, Charlottetown. After studying at Dalhousie

College, Halifax, Nova Scotia, she returned to Cavendish to spend the next 13 years caring for her grandmother. Her first book was the phenomenally successful *Anne of Green Gables* (1908), the story of an orphan girl adopted in error for a boy by an elderly brother and sister. She followed it with several sequels, of which *Rilla of Ingleside* (1921) is an invaluable description of the impact of World War I on the island community. She married the Rev Ewan MacDonald in 1911, and moved to his manse at Leaskdale, Ontario. Her works are sometimes highly satirical, and at her best she captures memorably the mysteries and terrors of early childhood, as in *Magic for Marigold* (1929), while her later writing shows qualities which recall the work of **Guy de Maupassant**. 📖 H M Ridley, *The Story of Lucy Montgomery* (1956)

Montherlant, Henri Millon de 1896–1972
French novelist and playwright

Born in Neuilly-sur-Seine, he was severely wounded in World War I, after which he travelled in Spain, Africa and Italy. A man of athletic interests, he advocates, in both his plays and novels, the overcoming of the conflicts of life by vigorous action, and disdains the consolation of bourgeois sentiment. His stylish novels include the largely autobiographical *La Relève du matin* (1920, 'The Morning Relief'), *Les Bestiaires* (1926, Eng trans *The Bullfighters*, 1927), *Les Jeunes filles* (1935–39, 'The Young Girls') and *L'Histoire d'amour de la rose de sable* (1954, 'The Love Story of the Sandflower'). Among his plays are *Malatesta* (1946), *Don Juan* (1958) and *Le Cardinal d'Espagne* (1960, 'The Cardinal of Spain'). 📖 H Perruchot, *Henri de Montherlant* (1959)

Montholon, Charles Tristan, Marquis de 1783–1853
French general and diplomat

Born in Paris, he served in the navy and cavalry, was wounded at Wagram (1809), and in 1809 was made **Napoleon I**'s chamberlain. He was promoted general in 1811, and was Napoleon's aide-de-camp at Waterloo (1815). He accompanied him to St Helena, and published *Mémoires pour servir à l'histoire de France sous Napoléon, écrits sous sa dictée* (8 vols, 1822–25, 'Reports to be Used in the Writing of the History of France During Napoleon's Reign as Dictated by him'). Condemned in 1840 to 20 years' imprisonment for helping Louis Napoleon (**Napoleon III**) attempted seizure of power, he was liberated in 1848, having in 1846 published *Récits de la captivité de Napoléon à Ste Hélène* ('Accounts of Napoleon's Captivity in St Helena').

Montmorency, Anne, 1st Duc de 1493–1567
French soldier

He distinguished himself under his childhood friend **Francis I** at Marignano (1515), Mézières and Bicocca, was taken prisoner along with Francis at Pavia (1525), defeated **Charles V** at Susa (1536), and became Constable of France in 1538. Suspected by the king of siding with the Dauphin, he was banished from court in 1541. He was restored by **Henri II** (1547), commanded at the disaster of St Quentin (1557), and was taken prisoner by the Spaniards. He opposed the influence of **Catherine de' Médicis**, commanded against the Huguenots led by the Prince de **Condé** at Dreux (1562), and was taken prisoner a third time. In 1563 he drove the English out of Le Havre. He again engaged Condé at St Denis (1567), where he was fatally wounded.

Montpensier, Anne Marie Louise d'Orléans, Duchesse de, *known as* La Grande Mademoiselle 1627–93
French noblewoman

The niece of **Louis XIII**, she was born in Paris, and supported her father and the Prince de **Condé** in the second Fronde (1651–52), where she commanded an army that occupied Orleans and later the Bastille. After a period in exile she returned to the court and wished to marry M. de Lauzun, but the king refused his consent until 1670. Her marriage in the end was not successful and her last years were spent in religious duties. She wrote two novels and some literary portraits.

Montrose, James Graham, Marquis of 1612–50
Scottish general

After travelling in Italy, France and the Low Countries, he returned in the year (1637) of the 'Service-book tumults' in Edinburgh (see **Jenny Geddes**), and was one of the four noblemen who drew up the National Covenant in support of Presbyterianism. In 1638 he was dispatched to Aberdeen, which he occupied for the Covenanters. When **Charles I** invited several Covenanting nobles to meet him in Berwick, Montrose was among them, and the Presbyterians dated his 'apostasy' from that interview. In the General Assembly of 1639 he expressed misgivings about the Covenant. It leaked out that he had been communicating with the king; he was cited before a committee of the Scottish parliament, and in the next year was confined in Edinburgh Castle. In 1644 he made his way into Perthshire as lieutenant-general and Marquis of Montrose. At Blair Atholl he met 1,200 Scoto-Irish auxiliaries, and routed the Covenanters under Lord Elcho at Tippermuir, near Perth. Next he took Aberdeen, then laid waste the estates of the Covenanting nobles, devastated the Campbell country, and drove Argyll himself from his castle at Inveraray. The 'Estates' placed a fresh army under William Baillie of Letham, who was to take Montrose in front, while Argyll should fall on his rear; but Montrose instead surprised Argyll at Inverlochy (1645). Finally escaping into the Grampians, in July 1645 he marched southward with over 5,000 men. Baillie, following, was defeated with a loss of 6,000 at Kilsyth; this, the most notable of Montrose's six victories, seemed to lay Scotland at his feet. Entering the Border country with depleted forces, on 13 September he was surprised and routed by 6,000 troopers under David Leslie at Philiphaugh, near Selkirk. Escaping to Atholl, he sailed for Norway on 3 September 1646, and thence travelled to Paris, Germany and the Low Countries. When news of Charles's execution reached him, he swore to avenge it; he lost most of his army by shipwreck, but reached the borders of Ross-shire, where his dispirited remnant was defeated on 27 April 1650. He nearly starved to death in the wilds of Sutherland, was captured and taken to Edinburgh, where he was hanged in the High Street on 21 May 1650. Eleven years afterwards his mangled remains were collected and buried in St Giles' Cathedral, and a monument was erected to him there in 1888. Montrose's few passionately loyal poems are little known, save the one stanza beginning, 'He either fears his fate too much'; even its ascription to Montrose (first made in 1711) is doubtful. 📖 John Buchan, *Montrose* (1928)

Monts, Pierre du Gua, Sieur de c.1560–c.1630
French explorer and colonist

He was made lieutenant-general of Acadia (French America) by **Henri IV** in 1603, and with **Samuel de Champlain** he explored the coasts of New Brunswick and New England. In 1605 they founded Port Royal, the first French colony in Canada.

Moodie, Susanna 1803–85
English novelist and poet

Born in Bungay, Suffolk, she married and emigrated to Canada, where her husband took up farming with limited success. She began writing partly in order to contribute to the family income, publishing a collection of verse, *Enthusiasm and Other Poems*, in 1831. Her novels, sentimental in style, include *Mark Hurdlestone and the Gold Worshipper* (1853) and *Flora Lyndsay* (1854). Her most popular non-fiction books, *Roughing It in the Bush, or Life in Canada* (1852) and *Life in the Clearings Versus the Bush* (1853), are loosely based upon her own experiences.

Moody, Dwight L(yman) 1837–99
US evangelist

Born in Northfield, Massachusetts, he was a shoe salesman in Boston and in 1856 went to Chicago, where he gave up his job to engage in missionary work, and organized the North Market Sabbath School. In 1870 he was joined by Ira David Sankey (1840–1908), who was born in Edinburgh, Pennsylvania. In 1873 and 1883 they visited Great Britain as evangelists, Moody preaching and Sankey singing; afterwards they worked together in the USA. They published the *Sankey and Moody Hymn Book* (1873) and *Gospel Hymns* (1875). In 1899 he founded the Moody Bible Institute in Chicago. 💷 James F Findlay, Jnr, *Dwight L Moody, American Evangelist: 1837–1899* (1969)

Moody, William Vaughn 1869–1910
US dramatist and poet

He was born in Indiana. In his plays, he was among the first to move from popular adaptations of French farce in order to deal realistically with wholly US subject-matter and themes. *The Great Divide* (1906, originally *A Sabine Woman*), uses the story of a woman's abduction from Massachusetts by a man from Arizona, their tempestuous association and eventual marriage, to reflect the cultural differences between a settled, inflexible society on the one hand and the wild spirit of the frontier on the other. Moody also wrote an incomplete trilogy in verse, and several volumes of poems of which *Poems* (1901), containing the much-anthologized 'Gloucester Moors', is perhaps the most representative.

Moon, Sun Myung 1920–
South Korean religious leader

In 1954 he founded the Unification Church, an amalgam of Christianity and the teachings of its self-declared prophet, Moon. In 1973 he moved its headquarters from South Korea to Tarrytown, New Jersey. He and his followers have been accused of brainwashing converts and of financial misdealings, and in 1984 Moon was convicted of tax evasion under US law and was sentenced to 18 months in prison.

Moon, William 1818–94
English inventor

He was born in Kent. Partially blind from the age of four, he became totally blind in 1840 and began to teach blind children. Dissatisfied with existing systems of embossed type, he invented (in 1845) a system based on Roman capitals, and he later invented a stereotype plate for use with it. Although requiring more space, his type is easier to learn than Braille and is still widely used.

Mooney, Ria 1903–73
Irish actress and teacher

Born in Dublin, she began acting at the age of six, and first appeared at the Abbey Theatre in Dublin in 1924. She attracted significant attention in Sean O'Casey's *The Plough and The Stars* (1926), and made her US debut in 1927. After a short spell at the Gate Theatre in Dublin, she returned to the Abbey (1935), and was placed in charge of their experimental Peacock Theatre in 1937, where she directed her first play. In 1948 she became the first woman director of the Abbey Theatre, and served with distinction until her retirement in 1963.

Moorcock, Michael 1939–
English novelist

Born in Mitcham, Surrey, he became, at 17, editor of *Tarzan Adventures* and was a regular contributor to the *Sexton Blake Library*. From the mid-1960s onwards, he was editor (1964–71), then publisher, of the influential science fiction series *New Worlds*. He also wrote comic strips. Much of his fiction has been organized in cycles. The 'Elric' novels began with *Stormbringer* in 1965. Perhaps his best-known sequence, starring the morally and sexually ambiguous 'Jerry Cornelius', started with *The Final Programme* (1968). He introduced 'Karl Glogauer' in *Behold the Man* (1969), a controversial re-working of the Crucifixion. A further enormous mythic cycle began with *The Eternal Champion* in 1970. He has also written in non-sci-fi mode, including the sprawling, Dickensian *Mother London* (1988). This was followed by a complex, emotionally demanding cycle, beginning with *Byzantium Endures* (1981). 💷 M Moorcock, with C Greenland, *Michael Moorcock: Death is no Obstacle* (1991)

Moorcroft, William 1872–1945
English potter

Born in Staffordshire, he set up his own firm in 1913 in Burslem, producing a range of white-bodied ceramics decorated with stylized flowers and leaves, titled Florian ware. His Hazledene ware (landscape and trees) and Claremont ware (toadstools) were more colourful. His main interest, however, was the flambé glazes, and he won many prizes for his work in Paris, Brussels and the USA. In 1928 he was appointed potter to the Crown.

Moore, Albert Joseph 1841–93
English painter

The son of William Moore, and brother of the painter Henry Moore, he is best known for his Hellenic decorative paintings.

Moore, Archie, *originally* Archibald Lee Wright 1913–98
US boxer

Born in Benoit, Wisconsin, he became a professional boxer in 1936, and eventually, in 1952, won the world light-heavyweight title by defeating Joey Maxim. He held the title for 10 years (1952–62), when he retired at the age of 49. He also challenged for the heavyweight title, despite a lack of weight and height, and in 1955 gave Rocky Marciano a hard fight before being knocked out. He also fought Floyd Patterson for the title in 1956. Of his 229 fights he won more than half inside the distance, and ranks high in any list of the world's greatest-ever fighters.

Moore, Bernard 1850–1935
English potter

Born in Staffordshire, he joined Moore Brothers, where he traded with his brother until the sale of the business in 1905. That year he set up his own business where he was joined by his son in 1906. As a chemist he was particularly interested in glazes and his experiments led him to produce a series of red flambés, turquoise, sang-de-bœuf, crystalline and aventurine glazes, as well as fine lustres. He worked as a consultant with many British, European and US companies, assisting them with problems relating to technical production. He was greatly concerned with health risks to pottery workers and delivered an influential paper to the Ceramic Society in 1932 suggesting changes in production to minimalize lung disease.

Moore, Bobby (Robert) 1941–93
English footballer

Born in Barking, Essex, in a long career with West Ham (1958–74) and later Fulham (1974–77), he played 1,000 matches at senior level, winning an FA Cup-winner's medal in 1964 and a European Cup-winner's medal in 1965. He was capped a record 108 times (107 in succession), 90 of them as captain. He played in the World Cup finals in Chile in 1962, captained the victorious England side in the 1966 World Cup, and led the team with some success in Mexico in 1970 despite being the victim of a trumped-up charge of theft in Bogota in the run-up to the finals. He was sports editor for the *Sunday Sport* from 1986 to 1990, when he became a commentator. He died following a two-year-long battle against cancer. ⌨ Jeff Powell, *Bobby Moore: The Life and Times of a Sporting Hero* (1993)

Moore, Brian 1921–99
Canadian novelist

He was born in Belfast, Northern Ireland, and served with the British Ministry of War Transport during the latter stages of World War II. After the war he worked for the United Nations in Europe before emigrating to Canada in 1948, where he became a journalist and adopted Canadian citizenship. He spent time in New York before moving to California. Though he wrote thrillers under the pseudonym Michael Bryan, he is best known for novels like *The Feast of Lupercal* (1957), *The Luck of Ginger Coffey* (1960), *Catholics* (1972) and *The Temptation of Eileen Hughes* (1981). Particularly admired for his portrayal of women, he won the Author's Club First Novel award with *The Lonely Passion of Judith Hearne* (1955), though it was not, strictly speaking, his first novel. *The Great Victorian Collection* (1975) was awarded the James Tait Black Memorial Prize, and both *The Doctor's Wife* (1976) and *Black Robe* (1985, filmed 1991) were shortlisted for the Booker Prize. Later works include *No Other Life* (1993) and *The Statement* (1996). ⌨ H Dahlie, *Brian Moore* (1981)

Moore, Christy 1945–
Irish folk singer

Born in Dublin, he began as a solo singer, working the folk clubs and pubs between bouts of manual labouring in both Eire and England. He was a co-founder of Planxty in 1971, and then Moving Hearts in 1981, two of the most influential groups in Irish music, but on each occasion eventually chafed against the group setting, and returned to solo performance. He has taken a high-profile campaigning stance on controversial issues like nuclear power and the political situation in Northern Ireland (and elsewhere) in his music, mixed with a great deal of sometimes surreal humour. He is an imposing live performer, with a level of genuine artistry rare in the folk field, and which has proved difficult to capture fully on recordings.

Moore, Clement Clarke 1779–1863
US poet

Born in New York City, he attended Columbia College and became a Hebrew scholar and a professor of Oriental and Greek literature. He is now best remembered for his poem 'A Visit from St. Nicholas' (1823), popularly known as ''Twas the Night Before Christmas'.

Moore, Dudley Stuart John 1935–
English actor

Born in Dagenham, Essex, he studied music at Oxford. In 1960, he joined fellow Oxbridge graduates in the *Beyond the Fringe* at the Edinburgh Festival, then in London and on Broadway. He formed a satirical comedy partnership with Peter Cook that flourished on television in *Not Only … But Also* (1965–71) and in such films as *The Wrong Box* (1966) and *Bedazzled* (1967). He eventually went his own way and enjoyed belated Hollywood success as the middle-aged hero of comedies such as '*10*' (1979) and *Arthur* (1980). An acclaimed pianist and jazz performer, he has also composed the music score for some films and performed with some of the world's leading classical orchestras. On television, he presented the series *Concerto!* (1993). ⌨ Barbra Paskin, *Dudley Moore* (1997)

Moore, Edward 1712–57
English dramatist

Born in Abingdon, Berkshire, he became a draper in London, and took to writing plays to avoid going bankrupt. The comedy *Gil Blas* (1751), based on that of Alain René Lesage, and the prose tragedy *The Gamester* (1753), are his best-known productions. He also edited the weekly journal *The World* (1753–57). ⌨ J M Caskey, *The Life and Works of Edward Moore* (1927)

Moore, Francis 1657–1715
English astrologer

Born in Bridgnorth, Shropshire, he practised medicine in London, and in 1700 started 'Old Moore's' astrological almanac.

Moore, George Augustus 1852–1933
Irish writer

Born in Ballyglass, County Mayo, the son of a landed gentleman, he was educated at Oscott College, Birmingham, and intended for the army, but soon became an agnostic, abandoned a military career and lived a bohemian life in London and Paris, until Zola's example revealed to him his true métier as a novelist of the Realist school. Moore has been credited with introducing this type of fiction into Great Britain with his novels of low life, *A Modern Lover* (1883), *A Mummer's Wife* (1885), and others. During the Boer War he sought exile in Ireland where he wrote *Evelyn Innes* (1898) and *Sister Teresa* (1901), which reflect his increasing interest in love, theology and the arts, and the stories in *An Untilled Field* (1903), which mark a move away from his earlier 'sordid' realism. He returned to England early in the century and published his confessions, *Memoirs of My Dead Life* (1906) and the trilogy *Hail and Farewell — Ave* (1911), *Salve* (1912) and *Vale* (1914)—in which he wrote about his friends and his associates in setting up the Abbey Theatre in Dublin, particularly W B Yeats. His other later works include *The Brook Kerith* (1916), which relates an apocryphal story of Paul and Jesus Christ among the Essenes, and the mythical *Aphrodite in Aulis* (1930). ⌨ J Hone, *The Life of George Moore* (1936)

Moore, G(eorge) E(dward) 1873–1958
English empiricist philosopher

Born in London, he was educated at Dulwich College and Trinity College, Cambridge, where a fellow student, Bertrand Russell, helped persuade him to switch from classics to philosophy. After some years of private study in Edinburgh and London he returned to Cambridge to teach philosophy (1911) and became Professor of Mental Philosophy and Logic (1925–39). After a brief, early infatuation with the prevailing Hegelian idealism of John McTaggart and others, in 1903 he published an article 'The Refutation of Idealism' (in the journal *Mind*), and a book, the celebrated *Principia Ethica* ('Principal Ethics'). These marked an important change of direction and the effective revival, in a new form, of a British empiricist philosophical tradition, emphasizing in particular the intellectual virtues of clarity, precision and honesty, and identifying as a principal task of philosophy the analysis of ordinary concepts and arguments. Moore and Russell, and later their student Ludwig Wittgenstein, were the dominant figures in this tradition in the interwar years. *Principia Ethica* analysed the moral concept of goodness and commended the value of friendship and aesthetic experience; it was a major influence on the Bloomsbury Group, which included Leonard Woolf, Lowes Dickinson, John Maynard Keynes and E M Forster. Other works include *Ethics* (1916), an elaboration and restatement of these views, and three important collections of his influential articles and papers: *Philosophical Studies* (1922), *Some Main Problems of Philosophy* (1953) and *Philosophical Papers* (1959). He also edited the journal *Mind*

Moore, Henry Spencer 1898–1986
English sculptor

Henry Moore was born in Castleford, Yorkshire, the son of a coal miner. He studied at Leeds and at the Royal College of Art, London, where he taught sculpture (1924–31); from 1931 to 1939 he taught at the Chelsea School of Art. He travelled in France, Italy, Spain, USA and Greece, and was an official war artist from 1940 to 1942. During this time he produced a famous series of drawings of air-raid shelter scenes. In 1948 he won the International Sculpture prize at the Venice biennale.

He is recognized as one of the most original and powerful modern sculptors, producing figures and groups in a semi-abstract style based on the organic forms and undulating rhythms found in landscape and natural rocks, and influenced by primitive African and Mexican art. His interest lay in the spatial, three-dimensional quality of sculpture, an effect he achieved by the piercing of his figures. His principal commissions included the *Madonna and Child* in St Matthew's Church, Northampton (1943–44), the decorative frieze (1952) on the Time-Life building in London, and the massive reclining figures for the UNESCO building in Paris (1958) and the Lincoln Center in New York (1965).

📖 W Packer, *Henry Moore* (1985).

> 'Sculpture in stone should look honestly like stone... To make it look like flesh and blood, hair and dimples is coming down to the level of the stage conjuror.' From an article in *Architectural Association Journal* (1930).

(1921–47) and made it the major English-language journal in the field. 📖 D Rohatyn, *The Reluctant Naturalist* (1987)

Moore, Gerald 1899–1987
English piano accompanist
Born in Watford, Hertfordshire, he studied music at Toronto, Canada, and established himself as a skilful accompanist of the world's leading singers and instrumentalists. A constant performer at international music festivals, he was also a notable lecturer and television broadcaster on music. He wrote an engaging and instructive account of his art and experiences in *The Unashamed Accompanist* (1943, new edn 1959).

Moore, Henry 1831–95
English painter
He was the son of William Moore and brother of Albert Joseph Moore. Starting as a landscape painter, he later achieved great success as a sea painter.

Moore, Henry Spencer See panel above

Moore, Sir (John) Jeremy 1928–
English soldier
He joined the Royal Marines (RM) at the age of 19 and saw service in Great Britain, Brunei and Australia in a variety of roles, including that of commandant of the RM School of Music. He had reached the rank of major-general in the commando forces by 1979, and in 1982, when the decision was taken to recapture the Falkland Islands from Argentina, he was made Commander of Land Forces. His success in the brief campaign brought him unexpected fame as well as a knighthood. He retired from the forces in 1983 and took up a new career in the food and drinks industry.

Moore, Sir John 1761–1809
Scottish soldier
Born in Glasgow, he served in the American Revolution from 1779 to 1783, the Revolutionary War in France, the West Indies (1796), Ireland (1798) and Holland (1799). He was in Egypt in 1801, and in 1802 served in Sicily and Sweden. In 1808 he was sent to strengthen the English army in the Peninsula. In October he received instructions to co-operate with the Spanish forces in the expulsion of the French, and moved his army from Lisbon towards Vallodolid; but Spanish apathy, French successes elsewhere and the intrigues of his own countrymen soon placed him in a critical position. When news reached him that Madrid had fallen, and that Napoleon I was marching to crush him, he was forced to retreat. In December he began a disastrous march from Astorga to Coruña. His army reached Corrunna (La Coruña) in a lamentable state, and Nicolas Soult was waiting to attack as soon as the embarkation should begin. In a desperate battle on 19 January 1809, the French were defeated with the loss of 2,000 men. Moore himself was mortally wounded in the moment of victory, and his burial was immortalised in Charles Wolfe's poem 'The Burial of Sir John Moore'.

Moore, John Bassett 1860–1947
US lawyer and judge
Born in Smyrna, Delaware, he was educated at the University of Virginia. He served as a law clerk in the Department of State (1885–86), was Assistant Secretary of State (1886–91), and became Professor of International Law at Columbia (1891–1924). The author of a comprehensive *History and Digest of International Arbitrations* (6 vols, 1898), a *Digest of International Law* (8 vols, 1906), *International Adjudications* (7 vols, 1929–36) and other works on international law, he also served as a judge of the Permanent Court of International Justice (1921–28).

Moore, Marianne Craig 1887–1972
US poet
Born in St Louis, Missouri, she was educated at Bryn Mawr College, and Carlisle Commercial College in Pennsylvania. She taught commercial studies at Carlisle, tutored privately, and was a branch librarian in New York (1921–25). She contributed to the Imagist magazine, *The Egoist*, from 1915, and edited *The Dial* from 1926 until its demise in 1929. She was acquainted with seminal modernists like Ezra Pound and T S Eliot, but New York was her milieu, not Paris, and she was associated with the Greenwich Village group including William Carlos Williams and Wallace Stevens. She has supplied a much-quoted definition of the creative ideal as 'imaginary gardens with real toads in them'. Her first book, *Poems*, was published by friends in London in 1921. Idiosyncratic, a consummate stylist and unmistakably modern, she ranks high among the US poets of the 20th century. Other volumes include *Collected Poems* (1951, Pulitzer Prize) and *The Complete Poems* (1967). She also published *Predilections*, a collection of essays, in 1955. 📖 E P Sheehy and K A Lohf, *The Achievement of Moore, 1907–1957* (1958)

Moore, Mary Tyler 1936–
US actress
Born in Brooklyn, New York City, she trained as a dancer, and her first professional job was as the Happy Hotpoint Pixie in a series of television commercials in 1955. Small acting roles followed, and she was seen in the series *Richard Diamond, Private Eye* (1957–59) and *The Dick Van Dyke Show* (1961–66) which won her Emmy awards in 1964 and 1965. She starred on Broadway in *Breakfast at Tiffanys* (1966) but returned to television with the long-running *The Mary Tyler Moore Show* (1970–77). The series won her Emmy awards in 1973, 1974 and 1976. She went on

to win an Emmy for *First, You Cry* (1978), a Tony Award for *Whose Life Is It Anyway?* (1980) and an Academy Award nomination for the film *Ordinary People* (1980). Seldom offered good film roles, she had a rare chance to display her comic gifts on the large screen in *Flirting with Disaster* (1996).

Moore, Patrick Alfred Calderwell 1923–
English astronomer, author and broadcaster

Educated privately owing to illness, he served in the RAF during World War II as a navigator in Bomber Command (1940–45). He began his perennially popular television series, *The Sky at Night*, in 1957, and it has continued since that time. He was director of Armagh Planetarium (1965–68) and has written more than 60 books, including *Atlas of the Universe* (1970, revised 1981), *Guide to the Planets* (1976), *Guide to the Moon* (1976), *TV Astronomer* (1987), *A Passion for Astronomy* (1991), *The Starry Sky* (1994) and *Teach Yourself Astronomy* (1995).

Moore, Roger George 1927–
English actor

Born in London, he studied painting before making his film debut as an extra in *Perfect Strangers* (1945). He appeared in small roles on stage and in films prior to National Service in the army. Subsequently performing in the USA, he appeared on Broadway in *A Pin to See the Peepshow* (1953) and in the Hollywood film *The Last Time I Saw Paris* (1954). On television his boyish good looks, smooth manner and athletic prowess won him stardom as the action-man hero of such series as *Ivanhoe* (1957), *The Alaskans* (1959–60), *The Persuaders* (1971–72) and most especially, *The Saint* (1962–68). His own wittiest critic, he brought a lightweight insouciance to the role of James Bond in seven films between *Live and Let Die* (1973) and *A View to a Kill* (1985). Now a goodwill ambassador for UNICEF, he recently appeared in *The Quest* (1996).

Moore, Stanford 1913–82
US biochemist and Nobel Prize winner

Born in Chicago, he studied chemistry at Vanderbilt University and the University of Wisconsin, and spent his career at the Rockefeller Institute (1939–82). He is best known for inventing, with **William Stein**, a chromatographic method for the identification and quantification of amino acids in mixtures of proteins or from physiological tissues (1950). By 1958 they had also developed an ingenious automated analyser to carry out all the steps of the analysis of the structure of RNA on a small sample. In a study of streptococcus, Moore and Stein found the first example of convergent evolution—two enzymes of similar function arising by different evolutionary paths. They also complemented the structural studies of **Christian Anfinsen** (1954–56), and all three shared the Nobel Prize for chemistry in 1972.

Moore, Thomas 1779–1852
Irish poet and composer

Born in Dublin, he was educated at Whyte's School and Trinity College, Dublin, and became a lawyer. His translation of **Anacreon** (1800) proved a great success, followed by *Poems* (1801). In 1803, after being appointed registrar of the Admiralty Court in Bermuda, he arranged for a deputy, and returned and settled in Wiltshire. Meanwhile he had published the earlier of the *Irish Melodies* (1807–34) and *The Twopenny Postbag* (1812), and in 1817 *Lalla Rookh* appeared. His Bermuda deputy embezzled £6,000, and in 1819, to avoid arrest, Moore went to Italy and then to Paris. He returned in 1822 to Wiltshire, and published *The Loves of the Angels* (1823) and a novel, *The Epicurean* (1827), and wrote biographies of **Richard Brinsley Sheridan** and **Byron**. 📖 T de Vere White, *Tom Moore, the Irish Poet* (1977)

Moore, Thomas Sturge 1870–1944
English poet, critic and wood-engraver

Born in Hastings, Sussex, he was the brother of the philosopher **G E Moore**. He is known for his classical verse style, beginning with *The Vinedresser* (1899), his verse dramas, works on **Albrecht Dürer** and other artists, and as a distinguished designer of bookplates, including those of his friend **W B Yeats**. His *Collected Poems* appeared in four volumes between 1931 and 1933. 📖 F C Gwynn, *Moore and the life of art* (1951)

Moore, William 1790–1851
English painter

A well-known portrait painter in York, he was the father of 13 sons, several of whom also became well-known artists.

Moore Sitterly, Charlotte 1898–1990
US astronomer and spectroscopist

Born in Enciltoun, Pennsylvania, she graduated from Swarthmore College in 1920, was assistant to **Henry Russell** (1920–25) at Princeton University, and moved to Mount Wilson Observatory to revise and extend the table of wavelengths in the solar spectrum. In the revised table, published in 1928, over 58,000 wavelengths were tabulated, and a second revision under her direction (1966) added 10,000 more lines. She returned to Princeton (1931–45) where she produced her famous *Multiplet Tables of Astrophysical Interest* (1945), and in 1945 joined the Bureau of Standards, Washington (1945–68), where she published her *Ultraviolet Multiplet Tables* (1946) and *Atomic Energy Levels* (1949–58).

Mor or More or Moro, Anthonis 1519–75
Dutch portrait painter

Born in Utrecht, he entered the Antwerp guild of St Luke in 1547, visited Italy, Spain, and England, where he was knighted, and painted Queen **Mary I** for her bridegroom, **Philip II** of Spain. From about 1568 he lived in Antwerp.

Morandi, Giorgio 1890–1964
Italian painter

Born in Bologna, he studied at the Academy of Fine Arts, Bologna, where he later taught (1930–56). Although influenced (c.1918–19) by the Italian Metaphysical painters, he otherwise eschewed the changing fashions of the modern movement, concentrating on landscapes, portraits and above all still life. His arrangements of everyday objects on a tabletop were painted in subdued tones and with a monumental simplicity of form reminiscent of **Cézanne**. He won the Grand Prix for Painting at the Venice Biennale, 1948, and other honours followed.

Morant or Murrant, Harry Harbord, originally Edwin Henry Murrant 1865–1902
Australian adventurer and poet

Born probably in Bridgewater, Somerset, England, he went to northern Queensland in 1883 and the following year married Daisy May O'Dwyer, later **Daisy Bates**. He lived in Queensland and New South Wales, earning a living from his skills as a rider and horse-breaker. Under the pseudonym 'Breaker' he contributed ballads and bush verse to the Sydney magazine *The Bulletin*, writing some 60 poems from 1891. In 1899 he enlisted in the Australian contingent sailing for the Boer Wars. In South Africa, after the murder and mutilation by the Boers of a close friend, Morant and others of his patrol shot a number of Boers who were coming to surrender. Morant was also implicated in the murder of a British missionary who was witness to these events. After a lengthy and confused court-martial, Morant was found guilty, and executed by firing squad.

Morant, Sir Robert 1863–1920
English educationist and civil servant

Born in Hampstead, London, he was educated at Winchester and New College, Oxford, and became tutor to the Crown Prince of Siam and laid the foundation of public education there (1886–94). He joined the Department of Education in England in 1895, and became Permanent Secretary to the Board of Education in 1902, and First Secretary at the Ministry of Health (1919). He remodelled the English educational machinery and constructed the Ministry of Health. He devised the Balfour Education Act of 1902 which made county and county borough councils the local education authorities in place of the school boards, and brought voluntary schools under the new authorities. The act led to the development of the county grammar schools, but caused relentless political disputation for several years. His *Regulations for Secondary Schools* (1904), by ignoring the practical and quasi-vocational curriculums developed in the Higher Grade Schools of the School Board era, are now thought to have inhibited the development of vocational education in secondary schools.

Morata, Olympia 1526–55
Italian humanist scholar and poet

She was the daughter of the poet and scholar, Pellegrino Morato. She gave public lectures when 15, but, having married a German physician, Andreas Grundler, in 1548, she followed him to Germany, became a Protestant, and died penniless, leaving numerous Latin and Greek poems, a treatise on Cicero, dialogues and letters.

Moratin, Leandro de 1760–1828
Spanish dramatist and poet

Born in Madrid, he began as a designer of jewellery, and later held official and ecclesiastical positions. He wrote a number of successful comedies influenced by French ideas and especially by Molière, and translated *Hamlet*. He also wrote poetry, and a history of Spanish literature. His acceptance of the post of librarian to Joseph Bonaparte resulted in his exile to Paris in 1814.

Moravia, Alberto, *pseudonym of* Alberto Pincherle 1907–90
Italian novelist and short-story writer

He was born in Rome, of middle-class parents, and spent some years in a sanatorium as a result of a tubercular infection. Before the outbreak of World War II he travelled extensively and lived for a time in the USA when out of favour with the fascist government. His first novel, *Gli indifferenti* (1929, Eng trans *The Indifferent Ones*, 1932), which achieved popular success, contains many of the ingredients of his later novels and short stories. Without making an explicit moral judgement, he analyses the decadent bourgeois society of Rome, portraying their preoccupation with sex and money, their apathy, their lack of communication, and the total incapability of action of even the intellectuals who acknowledge the corruption but cannot break away from it. *La romana* (1947, Eng trans *The Woman of Rome*, 1949) also encompasses socio-economic problems of the working class, and in *Raconti romani* (1954, Eng trans *Roman Tales*, 1956) he turns his critical eye to the corruption of the lower middle class. His later works include *L'attenzione* (1965, Eng trans *The Lie*, 1966), *La vita interiore* (1978, Eng trans *Time of Desecration*, 1980) and *L'uomo che guarda* (1985, Eng trans *The Voyeur*, 1986). 📖 K Longobardi, *Alberto Moravia* (1970)

Moray, James Stewart, 1st Earl of 1531–70
Regent of Scotland

The second illegitimate son of James V of Scotland and Lady Margaret Douglas, he was made Prior *in commendam* of St Andrews (1538), and was educated at the university there. He emerged as one of the leaders of the Protestant Lords of the Congregation whose revolt produced the Scottish Reformation of 1560. In 1561 he visited his half-sister, Mary, Queen of Scots, in France and after she returned to Scotland he defended her right to attend mass in her private chapel, and fended off the protests of John Knox. He was granted the earldoms of Mar and Moray (1562), which resulted in the revolt of the Catholic dissident, the 4th Earl of Huntly. He remained the queen's chief adviser until her marriage to Lord Darnley (1565), which triggered an abortive coup by him and the Hamiltons and his flight to England. He returned to Edinburgh on the day after David Rizzio's murder (1566) and was rehabilitated. His foreknowledge of the plot to murder Darnley (1567) induced another diplomatic absence, and he was in France when Mary was overthrown and imprisoned at Lochleven. He returned to become regent for Mary's infant son, James VI. His regency was chequered: it saw for the first time a Protestant government, but little was done by it to advance the Reformation of the Church; the civil war continued, and he had few supporters and many influential enemies in Scotland. He was shot as he rode through Linlithgow by James Hamilton of Bothwellhaugh, and died of his wounds soon after. One of the few Protestant nobles who acted consistently for religious motives, it was he as much as any of the ministers, including Knox, who helped give a Calvinist tone to the Scottish Reformation. His reputation has ironically been obscured by the brilliance of the case put in his defence in the writings of George Buchanan. 📖 Maurice Lee, *James Stewart, Earl of Moray* (1953)

Mordaunt, Charles See Peterborough, 3rd Earl of

Mordecai c.5th century BC
Biblical character

He is described in the Book of Esther as a Jew in exile in Persia (Iran), who cared for his orphaned cousin Esther and gained the favour of King Xerxes I after uncovering a plot against him. He used his subsequent influence to protect Jews from an edict issued against them, an event commemorated by the annual Jewish feast of Purim.

Mordkin, Mikhail 1880–1944
US dancer, teacher and director

Born in Moscow, he graduated from the Bolshoi Ballet School in 1899, becoming first soloist with, and then ballet master of the company. His career in the West was launched with his appearance in Sergei Diaghilev's 1909 Paris season, from which he went on to work with Anna Pavlova. After touring the USA, he went back to the Bolshoi (1912), becoming director in 1917. The October Revolution that year forced his return to the USA, where he settled, becoming a pioneer of US ballet. He twice attempted to establish his own company, but these efforts were short-lived. Latterly he was best known for his teaching, with Judy Garland and Katharine Hepburn among his pupils.

More, Hannah 1745–1833
English playwright and religious writer

Born in Fishponds, near Bristol, she was educated at the boarding school in Bristol run by her elder sisters. She was engaged in 1767 to a Mr Turner, who eventually settled £200 a year on her and left her. In 1773 she published *The Search after Happiness*, a pastoral drama for schools. The following year she went to London, where she joined the 'Blue Stocking' coterie of Elizabeth Montagu and her friends, and wrote two tragedies for David Garrick, *Percy* (1777) and *The Fatal Secret* (1779). Led by her religious views to withdraw from society, she retired to Cowslip Green near Bristol, where she did much to help the poor. She published *Sacred Dramas* (1782) and *Estimate on the Religion of the Fashionable World* (1790), and her moral tracts for the poor, such as *Village Politics by Will Chip* (1793), led to the founding of the Religious Tracts Society. She also wrote a didactic novel, *Coelebs in Search of a Wife* (1809). ⌨M G Jones, *The Life of Hannah More* (1952)

More, Henry 1614–87
English philosopher and theologian

Born in Grantham, Lincolnshire, he was educated at Eton and Christ's College, Cambridge, where he remained all his life, becoming a leading figure in the circle of Cambridge Platonists which included **Benjamin Whichcote** and **Ralph Cudworth**. He devoted himself entirely to study, despite the turbulent political times in which he lived, and developed a particular affinity for **Plato**, **Plotinus** and **Descartes**, with the last of whom he corresponded enthusiastically at first, though his admiration for him later lessened as his interest in occultism and mysticism grew. His philosophy aimed to demonstrate the compatibility of reason and faith. He wrote in both prose and verse, and his best-known works were *Philosophical Poems* (1647), *An Antidote against Atheism* (1653), *The Immortality of the Soul* (1659), *Enchiridion Ethicum* (1666) and *Divine Dialogues* (1668). ⌨Richard Ward, *The Life of the Learned and Pious Dr Henry More* (1710)

More, Kenneth Gilbert 1914–82
English actor

Born in Gerrards Cross, Buckinghamshire, he turned to performing after working as a stage hand at the Windmill Theatre, London. A naval lieutenant during World War II, he appeared in the West End in *Power Without Glory* (1947) and gained extensive television and film experience as a reliable supporting performer. After receiving acclaim for his stage performances in *The Way Things Go* (1950) and *The Deep Blue Sea* (1952), he had more cinema roles, becoming one of the most popular British film stars of the 1950s. His films include *Genevieve* (1953), *Doctor in the House* (1954) and *Reach for the Sky* (1956). His career suffered with the decline of the British film industry, but he performed on television in *The Forsyte Saga* (1967–68) and *Father Brown* (1974) and had success on stage with the likes of *The Secretary Bird* (1968) and *Getting On* (1971). His volumes of autobiography include *Happy Go Lucky* (1959) and *More or Less* (1978).

More, Sir Thomas, St 1478–1535
English politician and scholar

He was born in London, the son of a judge. Educated at Oxford under **John Colet** and **Thomas Linacre**, he completed his legal studies at New Inn and Lincoln's Inn, was Reader for three years in Furnival's Inn, and spent the next four years in the Charterhouse in 'devotion and prayer'. During the last years of **Henry VII** he became Under-Sheriff of London and a member of parliament. Introduced to **Henry VIII** through **Thomas Wolsey**, he became Master of Requests (1514), Treasurer of the Exchequer (1521), and Chancellor of the Duchy of Lancaster (1525). He was Speaker of the House of Commons, and was sent on missions to the French courts of **Francis I** and **Charles V**. On the fall of Wolsey in 1529, More, against his own strongest wish, was appointed Lord Chancellor. He executed his office with a primitive virtue and simplicity but displayed particular harshness in his sentences for religious opinions. He sympathized with John Colet and **Erasmus** in their desire for a more rational theology and for radical reform in the manners of the clergy, but like them he felt no promptings to break with the historic Church. He saw with displeasure the successive steps which led Henry to the final schism from Rome. In 1532 he resigned the chancellorship. In 1534 Henry was declared head of the English Church and More's steadfast refusal to recognize any other head of the Church than the pope led to his sentence for high treason after a harsh imprisonment of over a year. Still refusing to recant, he was beheaded. By his Latin *Utopia* (1516, Eng

trans 1556), More takes his place with the most eminent humanists of the Renaissance. His *History of King Richard III* (1513) 'begins modern English historical writing of distinction', although it is actually a second-hand account taken from Richard's enemy, Archbishop **John Morton**. From Erasmus we realize the virtues and attractions of a winning rather than an imposing figure. He was canonized in 1935. His feast day is 9 July. ⌨R W Chambers, *Thomas More* (1935)

Moréas, Jean, *originally* Yannis Papadiamantopoulos 1856–1910
French poet

Born in Athens, he wrote first in Greek, then settled in Paris (1879) and became a leader of the Symbolist school, to which he gave its name in 1886. He gradually grew interested in a return to classical and traditional forms, however, and by 1891 had formed a new grouping under the name École Romane, dedicated to antiquity. His works include *Les Syrtes* (1884), *Cantilènes* (1886, 'Ballads'), *Le Pèlerin passioné* (1891, 'The Passionate Pilgrim') and *Les Stances* (1905, 'Stanzas'), the masterpiece of his classical period. ⌨R Niklaus, *Jean Moréas, poète lyrique* (1936)

Moreau, Gustave 1826–98
French painter and teacher

Born in Paris, he studied at the École des Beaux-Arts, Paris. An eccentric Symbolist, he painted colourful but usually rather sinister scenes from ancient mythology and the Bible (eg *Salome*, 1876, which inspired **Joris Huysmans** to write an enthusiastic description). In 1892 he was appointed Professor of Painting at the École des Beaux-Arts; his pupils included **Georges Rouault** and **Henri Matisse**.

Moreau, Jean Victor 1761–1813
French general

Born in Morlaix, he studied law, but at the Revolution in 1789 commanded the volunteers from Rennes, served under **Charles Dumouriez** in 1793, and in 1794 was made a general of division. He took part, under **Charles Pichegru**, in reducing Belgium and the Netherlands. He drove the Austrians back to the Danube, but was forced to retreat and later deprived of his command (1797). In 1798 he took command in Italy and skilfully conducted the defeated troops to France. The party of the Abbé **Sieyès**, which overthrew the Directory, offered him the dictatorship. He declined it, but lent his assistance to **Napoleon I** in the coup d'état of 18th Brumaire. Commanding the army of the Rhine, he repeatedly defeated the Austrians in 1800, drove them back behind the Inn, and at last won the decisive Battle of Hohenlinden. Napoleon, grown jealous of Moreau, accused him of sharing in the plot of **Georges Cadoudal** and sentenced him to two years' imprisonment (1804). The sentence was commuted to banishment, and Moreau settled in New Jersey. In 1813 he joined the Russian service and accompanied the Russian attack on Dresden, where he was fatally wounded by a French cannonball.

Moreau, Jeanne 1928–
French actress and director

Born in Paris, she studied at the Conservatoire National D'Art Dramatique, and made her stage debut with the Comédie Française in *A Month in the Country* (1948) and her film debut in *Dernier Amour* (1948, 'Last Love'). An association with the directors of the French Nouvelle Vague (New Wave) brought her recognition as an intense, hypnotic film actress, capable of immersing her own personality in a succession of generally world-weary, sensual characterizations. Her most famous films include *Les Amants* (1958, *The Lovers*), *La Notte* (1961), *Jules et Jim* (1961, 'Jules and Jim'), *Le Journal d'une Femme de Chambre* (1964, *Diary of a Chambermaid*) and *Viva Maria* (1965). Occasional

English-language ventures met with little acclaim but she proved herself a formidable director with *Lumière* (1976) and *L'Adolescente* (1978, 'The Adolescent').

Morecambe and Wise, *properly* Eric Morecambe, *originally* John Eric Bartholomew 1926–84 *and* Ernie Wise, *originally* Ernest Wiseman 1925–
English comedians
Eric was born in Morecambe and, having appeared in working men's clubs since the age of 11, teamed up in 1941 with fellow-entertainer Ernie in the touring stage 'discovery' show *Youth Takes a Bow*. They made their West End debut in the revue *Strike a New Note* in 1943. In 1947 they teamed up again and, as Morecambe and Wise, worked in music hall, summer shows, pantomimes, radio, films and television. They were the most successful double-act in the history of British television, known primarily for *The Morecambe and Wise Show* (1961–83), and hugely popular Christmas specials. Their films, *The Intelligence Men* (1965), *That Riviera Touch* (1966) and *The Magnificent Two* (1967), were not successful. The pair's autobiography, *Eric and Ernie*, was published in 1973. Since Eric's death in 1984, Ernie has acted in the West End stage shows *The Mystery of Edwin Drood* and *Run for Your Wife*, and the US television comedy series *Too Close for Comfort*. His own autobiography, *Still on My Way to Hollywood*, was published in 1990.

Morel See **Deschamps, Eustache**

Morelli, Giovanni 1816–91
Italian art critic
He was born in Verona. After studying natural philosophy and medicine at Munich University, he returned to Italy in 1846 and became active in the Italian liberation movement against Austrian rule. In 1861 he became a deputy for Bergamo in the first free Italian Parliament and later, in 1873, a senator. From that year he began writing art criticism and, in 1880, published *Die Werke Italienischer Meister in den Galerien von München, Dresden und Berlin* (Eng trans *Italian Masters in German Galleries*, 1883). This was followed, from 1890 to 1893, by *Kunstkritische Studien über Italienischer Maler* (Eng trans *Critical Studies of Italian Painters*). His criticism concentrated on attribution, which he claimed to have reduced to scientific principles by close analysis of the artist's depiction of details such as eyes, hands and ears—the so-called 'Morellian method'. He also promoted an Act, named after him, which gave state protection to important works of art.

Morelos (y Pavón), José María 1765–1815
Mexican revolutionary
Born in Michoacán, New Spain, he was a mestizo and spent his early life as a muleteer before entering the priesthood. He then joined Miguel Hidalgo in the struggle for Mexican independence, becoming the leader in the south and reorganizing the insurgents (1810–13). A brilliant guerrilla leader, he regrouped opposition to Spanish rule in 1811 under a supreme junta. In opposition to the Spanish Constitution of Cadiz, he convened a 'sovereign congress' at Chilpancingo which declared independence at Apatzingán (October 1814). This first Mexican constitution was republican, and abolished the fuero and slavery. Isolated and trapped by royalist forces under Viceroy Felix Calleja, he was captured and executed in Mexico City. He was one of the founders of the radical liberal tradition of Mexican politics.

Moresby, John 1830–1922
English naval commander and explorer
He was born in Allerton, Somerset. He conducted exploration and survey work in New Guinea, where he discovered the natural harbour now fronted by Port Moresby, which was named after him.

Moretto da Brescia, *properly* Alessandro Bonvicino 1498–1554
Italian painter
Born in Brescia, he painted for several churches there, and also became a fine portrait painter.

Morey, Samuel 1762–1843
US inventor
Born in Hebron, Connecticut, he built up a successful business in timber and sawmills, and acted as local consulting engineer for the construction of locks on the Bellows Falls Canal. After 1790 he and his older brother became interested in steam navigation and built a series of paddle-wheel steamboats, but in spite of financial support from Robert R Livingston none of them was commercially successful. Samuel took out more than 20 patents in all, some of them many years ahead of their time, such as his American Water Burner (1817–18) which was ridiculed when it appeared but was a precursor of the water-gas process widely used half a century later. His triple-pipe steam boiler of 1818 and a gasoline-powered internal combustion engine patented in 1826 likewise pointed to future technological developments.

Morgagni, Giovanni Battista 1682–1771
Italian physician
Born in Forli, he graduated in Bologna, and taught anatomy there and later in Padua. His great work *De Sedibus et Causis Morborum per Anatomen Indagatis* (1761, 'The Seats and Causes of Diseases Investigated by Anatomy') was not published until he was 80. It was based on over 600 postmortems, and written in the form of 70 letters to an anonymous medical colleague. Case by case, Morgagni described the clinical aspects of illness during the patient's life then detailed the postmortem findings, aiming to relate the course of the illness to the findings of the autopsy. The book may be seen as a crucial stimulus to the rise of morbid anatomy. Furthermore, Morgagni was the first to delineate syphilitic tumours of the brain and tuberculosis of the kidney. He grasped that where only one side of the body is stricken with paralysis, the lesion lies on the opposite side of the brain. His explorations of the female genitals, of the glands of the trachea, and of the male urethra also broke new ground.

Morgan, Augustus De See **De Morgan, Augustus**

Morgan, Barbara Brooks, *née* Johnson 1900–92
US photographer and writer
Born in Buffalo, Kansas, she studied art at the University of California, Los Angeles (UCLA). She then painted and taught art in San Fernando (1923–24) and at UCLA (1925–30). In 1930 she moved to New York City with her photographer husband Willard D Morgan. From 1935 she worked mainly in photography, setting up a studio in Scarsdale, New York, in 1941. She was co-owner of the publishing company Morgan and Morgan. She is best known for vibrant black-and-white photographs of dancers, especially Martha Graham and Merce Cunningham (1935–40), for experimental photomontages and light abstractions, and for portraits and photographs of children. Her publications include *Martha Graham: Sixteen Dances in Photographs* (1941) and *Barbara Morgan: Photomontage* (1980).

Morgan, Charles Langbridge 1894–1958
English writer
Born in Kent, the son of a civil engineer, he served in Atlantic and China waters as a midshipman (1911–13), but finding it uncongenial, resigned. He rejoined the navy in 1914 and was later interned in the Netherlands until 1917. On repatriation he went to Oxford University, where he published *The Gunroom* (1919) on his early experiences, and became a well-known personality. In 1921, he joined

the editorial staff of *The Times*, and he was their principal drama critic from 1926 to 1939. Under the pen-name of 'Menander' he also wrote for the *Times Literary Supplement* critical essays called *Reflections in a Mirror*, which were later (1944–45) collected in two series. His novels and plays show high professional competence, but lack vividness and urgency. *Portrait in a Mirror* (1929), which won the Femina Vie Heureuse prize in 1930, is his most satisfying novel. Later works seem unduly solemn, pompous and vaguely sentimental. Nonetheless, *The Fountain* (1932) won the Hawthornden prize and *The Voyage* (1940) won the James Tait Black Memorial Prize. His plays are *The Flashing Stream* (1938), *The River Line* (1952) and *The Burning Glass* (1953). 📖 H C Duffin, *The Novels and Plays of Charles Morgan* (1959)

Morgan, Edwin George 1920–
Scottish poet and critic

Born in Glasgow, he was educated at Glasgow University and served in the Royal Army Medical Corps during World War II, an option he chose as a conscientious objector. He became assistant lecturer in English at Glasgow University (1947), rising to titular Professor of English (1975–80), now emeritus. He published his first volume of poems, *The Vision of Cathkin Braes*, and a translation of *Beowulf*, in 1952. His verse from the 1950s is introspective and rather gloomy, but his later work contains optimism, and by the time of *A Second Life* (1968), he had embraced his homosexuality. An incomplete *Collected Poems* was published in 1990, followed by a collection of his influential essays and critical writings, *Crossing The Border* (1990). A skilled translator, he collected his translations of various writers, such as **Boris Pasternak**, **Alexander Pushkin** and **Federico García Lorca**, in *Rites of Passage* (1976). His adaptation of **Edmond Rostand**'s *Cyrano de Bergerac* into demotic Glaswegian in 1992 was highly acclaimed. 📖 R Fulton, *Contemporary Scottish Poetry* (1974)

Morgan, Sir Henry c.1635–88
Welsh buccaneer

Born in Llanrhymney, Glamorgan, he was kidnapped as a child and shipped to Barbados, where he joined the buccaneers. His many raids against the Spanish and Dutch in the West Indies and Central America included the famous capture of Porto Bello and Panama (1671). Transported to London under arrest to placate the Spanish (1672), he was subsequently knighted (1674) on the renewal of hostilities, and died a wealthy planter and deputy Governor of Jamaica.

Morgan, John Hunt 1825–64
US Civil War general

Born in Huntsville, Alabama, he grew up in Kentucky, fought in the Mexican War, and joined the Confederate army in 1861. He became famous for his daring cavalry raids behind Union lines in Tennessee and Kentucky, during which he avoided direct combat and focused on destroying telegraph and railroad lines, burning supplies, and taking prisoners. In 1862 he was promoted to brigadier-general and in 1863 he carried raids as far north as Ohio, where he was captured and briefly imprisoned before escaping from the Ohio State Penitentiary. He was killed by Union troops in Tennessee while attempting a final raid in 1864.

Morgan, J(ohn) Pierpont 1837–1913
US banker, financier and art collector

He was born in Harford, Connecticut, the son of the financier John Spencer Morgan (1813–90), and built his father's firm into the most powerful private banking house in the USA. His house financed the Federal Reserve system in the depression of 1895, and he acquired a controlling interest in many of the country's principal railroads. In 1901 he bought out **Andrew Carnegie** and formed the US Steel Corporation, the world's largest corporation, and in the public mind he came to represent the manipulative forces of the 'money trust'. He compiled one of the greatest private art collections of his day, which he bequeathed to the Metropolitan Museum of Art in New York. He was also noted for his extensive philanthropic benefactions. His son, John Pierpont Morgan Jnr (1867–1943), inherited his father's firm and fortune, raised loans for Great Britain during World War I and endowed the Pierpont Morgan Library in New York. 📖 Frederick Lewis Allen, *The Great Pierpont Morgan* (1949)

Morgan, Julia 1872–1957
US architect

She was born in San Francisco and trained in engineering at the University of California before becoming, at the age of 30, the first woman to graduate in architecture from the École des Beaux-Arts in Paris. Registered in 1904 as the first woman architect in California, she opened an office in 1906. Although a very reclusive architect, it is believed that in her career she completed 800 buildings. Her most famous works include the residences at San Simeon for **William Randolph Hearst**, the media magnate. A commission lasting from 1919 to 1937, it is a vast exotic complex, showing Morgan's mastery of light, space and scale. She also completed a large number of works for women's organizations, including the Berkeley Women's City Club (1930), which is still in use today.

Morgan, Lewis Henry 1818–81
US ethnologist

Born in Aurora, New York, he became a lawyer in Rochester, and served in the state assembly (1861) and senate (1868). He undertook extensive investigations of the cultures of Native Americans, publishing *The League of the Iroquois* (1851), and *Houses and House-Life of the American Aborigines* (1881). His *Systems of Consanguinity and Affinity* (1869) laid the foundations for the modern social anthropological study of kinship, but his best-known work is *Ancient Society* (1877). A treatise on the origins and evolution of the institutions of government and property, it was hailed by **Marx** and **Engels** as furnishing independent confirmation for their materialist theory of history. Morgan is also remembered as the author of an authoritative study on *The American Beaver and his Works* (1868), in which he argued that animals as well as humans possess powers of rational thought.

Morgan, Lady Sydney, *née* Owenson 1783–1859
Irish novelist

She was born in Dublin. Her father, a theatrical manager, got into financial problems and she supported the family, first as a governess, then as a writer of sentimental poems and novels. In 1812 she married a surgeon, Thomas Charles Morgan (1783–1843), who was later knighted. Her works—lively novels, verse and travels—were bestsellers of their day, and include *The Wild Irish Girl* (1806), *Florence Macarthy* (1816), *The O'Briens and the O'Flahertys* (1827) and *Memoirs* (1862).

Morgan, Thomas Hunt 1866–1945
US geneticist, biologist and Nobel Prize winner

Born in Lexington, Kentucky, he graduated in zoology from Kentucky State College in 1886, and received his PhD from Johns Hopkins University in 1890. He became Professor of Experimental Zoology at Columbia University (1904–28) and then at the California Institute of Technology (Caltech, 1928–45). In work on *Drosophila*, the fruit fly, he found that certain traits are linked, but that the traits are not always inherited together. This suggested that certain traits are carried on the X chromosome, that traits can cross over to other chromosomes, and that the rate of crossing-over could be used as a measure of distance along the chromosome. With C B Bridges he wrote *The Mechanism of Mendelian Heredity* (1915), which established the chromosome theory of inheritance in confirmation of **Mendel**'s work. Morgan was awarded the 1933 Nobel Prize for physiology or medicine. His many other books include *Evolution and Adaptation* (1911), *The Theory of the Gene* (1926) and *Embryology and Genetics* (1933). ⌑ Ian Shine and Sylvia Wrobel, *Thomas Hunt Morgan: Pioneer of Genetics* (1976)

Morganwg, Iolo See **Williams, Edward**

Mori Arinori 1847–89
Japanese politician
From a Satsuma samurai family, he studied in Great Britain and the USA and on his return in 1868 became a vigorous proponent of Westernization, advocating the abolition of traditional customs and even the replacement of the Japanese language by English. He was Japan's first envoy to the USA (1871–73) and Vice-Foreign Minister (1878–79) before heading the newly-established Education Ministry in 1885. He created a centralized and secular education system with emphasis on practical instruction and service to the state. A series of higher schools, culminating in the prestigious Tokyo Imperial University, were also founded to train a governing elite. He was assassinated by a religious fanatic on the same day the Meiji Constitution was promulgated (11 February 1889).

Moricz, Zsigmond 1879–1942
Hungarian novelist and dramatist
He was born of peasant stock. Influenced by the poetry of **Endre Ady** and by the novels of **Émile Zola**, he was the first prose writer to challenge the sentimentality of the peasant–landlord relationship, which had suited more conservative novelists to idealize. He saw his peasants with a clear eye, and thus anticipated such writers as **Roger Martin du Gard**, who were also to present country people as they really are. His most powerful novel is *Legy jó mindhalálig* (1920, Eng trans *Be Faithful unto Death*, 1962), about a child who struggles against the evil adult world. *A fáklya* (1917, Eng trans *The Torch*, 1931) is about an idealistic priest whose life is shattered by his parishioners. ⌑ *American Slavic Review*, 4 (1945)

Morihiro Hosokawa See **Hosokawa Morihiro**

Mörike, Eduard Friedrich 1804–75
German poet and novelist
Born in Ludwigsburg, he entered the theological seminary at Tübingen in 1822 and became vicar of Kleversulzbach in 1834, retiring in 1843. He produced a minor masterpiece in *Mozart auf der Reise nach Prag* (1856, 'Mozart on the Journey to Prague') and many poems of delicacy and beauty with something of the deceptive simplicity of **Heinrich Heine**. These were published collectively in 1838. ⌑ M More, *Mörike: the man and the poet* (1957)

Mori Ogai (Rintaro) 1862–1922
Japanese writer, aristocrat, soldier, doctor and bureaucrat
Born into a samurai family in Shimane, Mori (whose given name was Rintaro) studied medicine, rising to become director of the Army Medical Corps and being influential in the introduction of western medicine. He started writing by translating European literature (one of the first to do so), then produced his own historical fiction in a style strongly influenced by the directness and accessibility of the Europeans (again, one of the first to do so). His style was to supplant traditional literary forms. The best example of his fiction available in English translation is *Incident at Sakai and Other Stories*. ⌑ R J Bowring, *Mori Ogai and the Modernisation of Japanese Culture* (1979)

Morison, Robert 1620–83
Scottish botanist
Born in Aberdeen, he graduated from the university there in 1638. A Royalist during the reign of **Charles I**, he escaped to France and studied medicine at Angers University (1648). He managed the gardens of the Duc d'Orléans, travelled throughout France collecting plants, and returned to England with **Charles II**, who appointed him senior physician, king's botanist and superintendent of the royal gardens. In 1669 he became Professor of Botany at Oxford, shortly after publication of his *Praeludia Botanica* which contained the basis of his classification system. In 1672 he published the pioneering *Plantarum Umbelliferarum Distributio Nova*. The rest of Morison's life was spent compiling his great *Plantarum Historiae Universalis Oxoniensis* (1680–99).

Morison, Samuel Eliot 1887–1976
US historian
Born in Boston, he studied at Harvard from 1904 and received a PhD in 1913. His *History of US Naval Operations in World War II* (15 vols, 1947–62) was commissioned by President **Franklin D Roosevelt** and was based largely on firsthand observation in the Pacific theatre. His other works include *Admiral of Ocean Sea* (1942, Pulitzer Prize) and *John Paul Jones* (1959, Pulitzer Prize). He taught at Harvard for more than 35 years and wrote the university's official history (1929–36).

Morison, Stanley 1889–1967
English typographer
Born in Wanstead, Essex, he worked as a clerk in the London City Mission (1905–12), then gained typographical experience working on the periodical *The Imprint* (1912–13). He was typographical adviser to Cambridge University Press (1923–44, 1947–59) and to the Monotype Corporation from 1923. On the staff of the London *Times* from 1929, he designed the Times New Roman type, introduced in 1932. He edited *The Times Literary Supplement* (1945–47) and was the author of many works on typography and calligraphy. He also edited the history of *The Times* (1935–52). In 1961 he was appointed to the editorial board of the *Encyclopaedia Britannica*. ⌑ Nicholas Barker, *Stanley Morison* (1972)

Morisot, Berthe Marie Pauline 1841–95
French painter
The granddaughter of **Jean Fragonard**, she painted mainly women and children, and was the leading female exponent of Impressionism. Her early work shows the influence of **Camille Corot**, who was her friend and mentor, but her later style owes more to **Renoir**. She herself exercised an influence on **Édouard Manet**, whose brother she married.

Morita, Akio 1921–
Japanese businessman
Born in Nagoya, he was educated at Osaka Imperial University. After World War II he founded, with Masaru Ibuka (1908–97), the electronics firm which since 1958 has been known as Sony. He became chairman of the board in 1989 and has been awarded many international honours. Like many Japanese companies, Sony has been at the forefront of technological developments and has had a strong design policy. Among its most important products have been early tape recorders for the domestic market (c.1950), advanced television equipment and (one of the best examples of miniaturization) the 'Walkman' range of radios and cassette players, first produced in 1980. His autobiography was published in 1987 entitled *Made in Japan* and he became an honorary KBE in 1992.

Moritz, Karl Philipp 1756–93
German writer

He was born in Hameln, and was a hat-maker's apprentice, an actor, then teacher and professor. Self-educated, he travelled in England and Italy and wrote *Reisen eines Deutschen in England* (1783, 'Travels of a German in England'), and *Reisen eines Deutschen in Italien* (1792–93, 'Travels of a German in Italy'). His autobiographical novel, *Anton Reiser* (1785–90), influenced **Goethe**. He was a precursor of the German Romantic movement, and wrote *Versuch einer deutschen Prosodie* (1786, 'Essay on German Prosody'), which he dedicated to **Frederick II, the Great**.
📖 W Rose, *From Goethe to Byron* (1924)

Morland, George 1763–1804
English painter

Born in London, he was the eldest son and pupil of the painter Henry Morland (1712–97), who brought him up with extreme rigour. He exhibited sketches at the Royal Academy when only 10 years old, but his adult life was a downward course of drunkenness and debt. In the last eight years of his life he turned out nearly 900 paintings and over 1,000 drawings, many of them inferior in quality and hastily completed to bring in money. His strength lay in country subjects, such as pigs, gypsies, and stable interiors, and his best known work is *The Interior of a Stable* (1791).

Morley, Christopher Darlington 1890–1957
US novelist and essayist

He was born in Haverford, Pennsylvania, and was a Rhodes scholar at Oxford. He joined the editorial staff of Doubleday's from 1913 to 1917 and later contributed to numerous periodicals such as *Ladies' Home Journal*, the New York *Evening Post* and the *Saturday Review of Literature*. His chief works, whimsical and urbane, include *Parnassus on Wheels* (1917) and its sequel *The Haunted Bookshop* (1919), *Thunder on the Left* (1925), *Swiss Family Manhattan* (1932), *Kitty Foyle* (1939), *The Ironing Board* (1949) and a book of poems, *The Middle Kingdom* (1944). 📖 *John Mistletoe* (1931)

Morley, Edward Williams 1838–1923
US chemist and physicist

Born in Newark, New Jersey, he was educated at Williams College in Williamstown, Massachusetts, and from 1860 to 1864 at Andover Theological Seminary. He also continued scientific studies and when he became pastor of the Congregational Church at Twinsburg, Ohio (1868), he was invited to teach at the nearby Western Reserve College in Hudson. In 1882 this college transferred to Cleveland and became Adalbert College of Western Reserve University. He became Professor of Chemistry and Natural History, an appointment he held until his retirement in 1906. He was awarded the Davy Medal of the Royal Society in 1907. Morley had a passionate concern for precise measurement. In Hudson he analysed the oxygen content of the atmosphere with a precision of 0.0025 per cent, and endeavoured to correlate the results for samples taken at different times and places with meteorological records. In Cleveland, he measured the atomic weight of oxygen relative to hydrogen as 15.879, with an uncertainty of only one part in 10,000. His later research interests involved collaborative studies with physicists, notably with **Albert Abraham Michelson** on the velocity of light and the 'ether drift' problem.

Morley, Henry 1822–94
English writer and editor

Born in London, he studied medicine at King's College London, but after practising for a while he turned to journalism, and eventually became a lecturer (1857–65) and Professor of English (1865–89) at London University. He was assistant editor for **Dickens**'s *Household Words* and *All the Year Round* (1850–65), and edited *The Examiner*

(1859–65). A champion of adult education, he wrote biographical and critical works, and edited 'Morley's Universal Library' of English classics (63 vols, 1883–88), *Cassell's Library of English literature* (1875–81) and *Cassell's National Library* (214 vols, 1886–90). He also wrote the first 11 volumes of an ambitious history of English literature, *English Writers* (1864–95).

Morley, John Morley, 1st Viscount 1838–1923
English journalist, biographer, philosophical critic and statesman

Born in Blackburn, Lancashire, the son of a doctor, and educated at Cheltenham and Lincoln Colleges, Oxford, he was called to the Bar, but chose literature as a profession. From 1867–82 he edited the *Fortnightly Review* and he was editor of the 'English Men of Letters' series, writing the volume on **Edmund Burke**, while for the 'English Statesmen' series he wrote *Walpole* (1889). From 1880–83 he edited the *Pall Mall Gazette*. His articles and speeches in favour of Home Rule made him **Gladstone**'s most conspicuous supporter. In 1886 he was a successful Irish Secretary, and again from 1892 to 1895. He was MP for Newcastle (1883–95), and for Montrose Burghs from 1896 until his elevation to the peerage in 1908. He was Secretary for India (1905–10), repressing sedition and making the government more representative, and Lord President of the Council from 1910 until the outbreak of World War I. His other writings include a life of Gladstone (4 vols, 1903), and *Recollections* (1917).

Morley, Malcolm, formerly Malcolm Evans 1931–
English painter

Born in Highgate, London, he worked at sea and spent four years in Borstal and prison, where he took a correspondence course in art. He trained at Camberwell before emigrating to the USA in 1958, inspired by an exhibition of US art at the Tate Gallery. Working as a waiter, he met **Barnet Newman**, and began painting in horizontal bands, using a pastry gun. In the mid-1960s he painted in a super-realist style, later incorporating 'accidents', as in *Los Angeles Yellow Pages* (1971), where the image is ripped through. By the 1980s he was painting landscapes, animals, and mythological motifs, for example *Arizonac* (1981, Saatchi Collection, London) and *Macaws, Bengals, with Mullet* (1982, Saatchi). He was the first winner of the Turner Prize at its inauguration in 1984.

Morley, Robert 1908–92
English actor

Born in Semley, Wiltshire, he studied at RADA, then made his stage debut at Margate in *Dr Syn* (1928). He toured throughout Great Britain, establishing his own summer theatre in Cornwall, before a succession of London stage successes in *Oscar Wilde* (1936), *The Great Romancer* (1937) and *Pygmalion* (1937). His first film was the lavish Hollywood drama *Marie Antoinette* (1938) for which he received a Best Supporting Actor Academy Award nomination. He remained committed to the theatre, appearing in *The Man Who Came To Dinner* (1941), *Edward, My Son* (1947), which he co-wrote, and *The Little Hut* (1950). His films include *The African Queen* (1951), *Beau Brummell* (1954), *Oscar Wilde* (1960) and *Someone is Killing the Great Chefs of Europe* (1978). An entertaining wit and raconteur, he published numerous collections of droll observations including *A Musing Morley* (1974), *Robert Morley's Book of Bricks* (1978) and *The Pleasures of Ages* (1988).

Morley, Samuel 1809–86
English woollen manufacturer, politician and philanthropist

He was born in Homerton, the son of a hosier. By 1860 he had greatly extended his father's business with mills in Nottingham, Leicester and Derbyshire. Deeply religious, he was a conscientious employer, a supporter of the temperance movement and was a Liberal MP (1865–85). His son, Arnold (1849–1916), was Liberal Chief Whip and Postmaster General (1892–95).

Morley, Thomas 1557–1603
English composer and organist

Born in Norwich, Norfolk, he was a pupil of **William Byrd**. He became organist at St Paul's Cathedral, and from 1592 was a Gentleman of the Chapel Royal. Best known for his *A Plaine and Easie Introduction to Practicall Musicke* (1597), written in entertaining dialogue with the purpose of encouraging part-singing for pleasure, he also wrote madrigals and canzonets, which include such popular pieces as 'Now is the month of maying', 'My bonny lass she smileth' and 'It was a lover and his lass'. He was compiler of the collection, in honour of Queen **Elizabeth I**, called *The Triumphes of Oriana* (1603).

Mornay, Philippe de, Seigneur du Plessis-Marly, *also called* Philippe Duplessis-Mornay 1549–1623
French statesman and polemicist

He was born in Buhy. Converted to Protestantism in 1560, he was nicknamed the 'Pope of the Huguenots' for his role in the Wars of Religion (1562–98). A trusted counsellor of Henri de Navarre (**Henri IV**), he undertook many embassies for the Protestant cause. However, he lost the king's favour after Henry's conversion to Catholicism (1593) and played no further part in national affairs. His treatise on Christianity was translated into English in 1589 as had been requested by his dead friend, Sir **Philip Sidney**.
📖 David de Liques, *Histoire de la vie de messire Philippes de Mornay, seigneur du Plessis Marly* (1647)

Morny, Charles Auguste Louis Joseph, Duc de 1811–65
French nobleman

Born in Paris, he was believed to be the son of Hortense de **Beauharnais** and the Comte de **Flahaut**, and so half-brother of **Napoleon III**. He was adopted by the Comte de Morny, and served in Algeria, but soon left the army, and in 1838 became a manufacturer of beet sugar. From that time he was mixed up in a variety of speculations. Chosen a deputy (1842), he quickly became prominent in financial questions. After 1848 he supported Napoleon, took a leading part in the coup d'état, and became Minister of the Interior. He was president of the *corps législatif* from 1854 to 1865, was ambassador to Russia (1856–57), and was created a duke (1862). He is the 'Duc de Mora' in **Léon Daudet**'s *Nabab*.

Moro, Aldo 1916–78
Italian politician

A leading figure in the Christian Democrats (DC), he served twice as Prime Minister (1963–68, 1974–76) and was Foreign Minister (1970–72). During the 1970s he was one of the DC moderates who sought to cooperate with **Enrico Berlinguer**. He was one of several important figures to die at the hands of the Red Brigades.

Moro, Antonis See **Mor, Anthonis**

Moroni, Giovanni Battista 1525–78
Italian portrait and religious painter

Born in Bondo, near Albino, he painted altarpieces, but is best known for his portraits, especially *The Tailor* in the National Gallery, London.

Morphy, Paul Charles 1837–84
US chess player

Born in New Orleans, he had a meteoric chess career from 1857 to 1859, partly because he graduated early in law and could not practise before reaching the age of 21. During this time he won the US championship and beat the strongest masters in Europe, which established

him as unofficial world champion (the championship was not instituted until 1886). Foreshadowing the career of fellow US chess genius **Bobby Fischer**, he retired from competitive chess and returned to his native New Orleans to make abortive attempts to commence his legal career. His brilliantly conducted games, particularly his approach to attack, continued to exert a strong influence upon generations of chess players long after his death.

Morris, Desmond John 1928–
English ethologist and writer

Born in Wiltshire, he was educated at Birmingham University and at Oxford, where he held a research post from 1954 to 1956. He was head of Granada TV and the film unit at the Zoological Society of London (1956–59), and subsequently curator of mammals at the Zoological Society (1959–67). He then became the director of the Institute of Contemporary Arts, London (1967–68), and later a Research Fellow at Wolfson College, Oxford (1973–81). He carried out important research on the ethology of several animals, but it was his interest in primate behaviour which led to his best-known work, the popular *The Naked Ape* (1967). In this he described the behaviour of humans using the approach and techniques of ethology. He used the same formula in several books such as *Manwatching: A Field Guide to Human Behaviour* (1977), which dealt with non-verbal signals, and *The Soccer Tribe* (1981), a study of crowd behaviour. Later works include *Catwatching* (1986) and *The Human Animal* (1994), which was made into a television series. His books and films have popularized sociology and zoology. 📖 *Animal Days* (1979)

Morris, George Pope 1802–64
US journalist and poet

Born in Philadelphia, he founded the *New York Mirror* in 1823 (editor 1824–42), and later edited the *Evening Mirror* and the *Home Journal* (1846–64), publishing **Edgar Allan Poe**'s 'The Raven' in the former. He published many poems, including the celebrated 'Woodman, Spare that Tree!', which appeared in *The Deserted Bride* (1838).

Morris, Gouverneur 1752–1816
US politician

Born on the family estate in Morrisania, New York, he graduated from King's College (now Columbia) in 1768, and was admitted to the Bar in 1771. He lost a leg in an accident in 1780. A political moderate, he served in the Continental Congress (1777–79) and later was assistant in the finance department (1781–85) of the new government, proposing the system of decimal coinage for the national currency. As a delegate to the Constitutional Convention (1787), he advocated a strong central government and opposed slavery. He sailed for Europe in 1789 and witnessed the French Revolution in Paris, recording its progress in his diary. After spending the greater part of 1791 in England as **George Washington**'s agent, he served as US Minister to France (1792–94). Returning to the USA in 1798, he sat in the Senate as a Federalist from 1800 to 1803.

Morris, Jan, *formerly* James Morris 1926–
English journalist, historian, essayist and travel writer

Born in Somerset, and educated at Lancing College and Oxford, he began his career as a young journalist on the editorial staff of *The Times* (1951–56). In 1953 he was assigned to cover the expedition to climb Mount Everest, and reported the successful ascent on the day of Queen **Elizabeth II**'s Coronation. He underwent a gender change in 1972 and published under the name of Jan Morris from 1973. As a freelance travel writer, she has visited almost every major city in the world and produced a prolific number of books. Among her best-known books are

Venice (1960), *The Oxford Book of Oxford* (1978), the *Pax Britannica* trilogy, and her autobiography *Conundrum* (1974).

Morris, Sir Lewis 1833–1907
Welsh poet and barrister

Born in Carmarthen, he was educated at the town's Queen Elizabeth Grammar School, Sherborne, and Jesus College, Oxford. His main literary works were *Songs of Two Worlds* (3 vols, 1872–75), followed in 1876 by *The Epic of Hades* and more verse and drama, largely drawing on incidents in Welsh history and mythology. In the later stages of his career he campaigned for the fostering of higher education in Wales and the establishment of a National University. In 1895 he was made knight bachelor, and thereafter had fruitless hopes of becoming Poet Laureate.
📖 D Phillips, *Sir Lewis Morris* (1981)

Morris, Mark William 1956–
US dancer and choreographer

Born in Seattle, Washington, he trained in genres as various as ballet, flamenco and Balkan folk dance. He danced for several important modern choreographers (**Eliot Feld**, **Laura Dean**, and **Twyla Tharp**) before making an informal New York debut with his own company, The Mark Morris Dance Company, in 1981. Within a few years he had established an impressive reputation as an innovative and skilled choreographer. He has devised dances for his own and other companies, and for opera. From 1988 to 1991 the Mark Morris Dance Group was in residence at Théâtre de la Monnaie in Brussels, and in 1990 Morris created dances for the White Oak Dance Project with Mikhail Baryshnikov. Utterly original and profoundly unconventional, his works include *L'Allegro, Il Penseroso ed il Moderato* (1988, to **Handel**'s music), *Dido and Aeneas* (1989), and an irreverent version of *The Nutcracker* entitled *The Hard Nut* (1991).

Morris, Robert, *known as* the financier of the American Revolution 1734–1806
US financier and government official

Born in Liverpool, England, he emigrated from Lancashire to Philadelphia in 1747 and began working in the shipping business. A member of the Continental Congress (1775–78), he was a signatory of the Declaration of Independence. He organized the finances for **George Washington**'s military supplies, used his personal credit to keep the Revolution afloat, and in 1782 founded the Bank of North America. He later lost his money speculating in western lands, and he died bankrupt.

Morris, Talwin 1865–1911
English designer

Born in Winchester, Hampshire, England, he was educated at Lancing College and later became an architect's apprentice to his uncle, Joseph Morris of Reading. After a short spell as sub art editor for the journal *Black and White* (1891) he moved to Scotland with his wife to work as art director for the publishing firm Blackie and Sons. One of the best-known exponents of the Glasgow Style, he produced a wide range of designs in a variety of media, including book bindings, furniture, stained glass, metalwork and jewellery, was a personal friend of Francis and Jessie Newbery of the Glasgow School of Art, and was closely associated with **Charles Rennie Mackintosh** and his immediate circle. Morris's work earned regular comment in the artistic press, and the work he executed for his own home at Bowling was illustrated in *The Studio* (1897). His work was exhibited in Great Britain and abroad, and in 1902 his designs were shown at Budapest and Turin.

Morris, Thomas, *also called* Old Tom 1821–1908
Scottish golfer

Born in St Andrews, he served an apprenticeship as a golfball-maker there. He went to Prestwick as a greenkeeper in 1851, returning to St Andrews as a professional in 1861. He won the British championship belt four times, (1861, 1862, 1864, 1866). His son, **Thomas Morris** ('Young Tom'), became champion after him.

Morris, Thomas, *also called* Young Tom 1851–75
Scottish golfer

Precociously brilliant, he won the British championship three times in succession (1868, 1869, 1870), thereby winning the championship belt outright; there was no contest in 1871, but he won it again in 1872. His early death was said to have been caused by grief at the loss of his young wife. He was the son of **Thomas Morris** ('Old Tom').

Morris, William See panel p1320

Morrison, Arthur 1863–1945
English novelist

Born in Poplar, Kent, the son of an engine-fitter, he became clerk to the People's Palace in Mile End Road, then a journalist on the *National Observer*, for which he wrote a series of stories published as *Tales of Mean Streets* (1894). His reputation rests on his powerfully realistic novels of London life such as *A Child of the Jago* (1896) and *The Hole in the Wall* (1902). He also wrote detective stories featuring a private investigator, 'Martin Hewitt'. 📖 A Brome, *Four Realist Novelists* (1965)

Morrison (of Lambeth), Herbert Stanley Morrison, Baron 1888–1965
English politician

Born in Lambeth, London, he was educated at an elementary school and by intensive private reading. After being an errand-boy and a shop-assistant, he helped to found the London Labour Party and became its secretary in 1915. Mayor of Hackney (1920–21), he entered the London County Council (1922), becoming its leader (1934). He grouped together London's passenger transport system, and much of the credit for the 'Green Belt' was due to him. He was MP for South Hackney three times between 1923 and 1945, when he was elected for East Lewisham. In **Churchill**'s War Cabinet he was Home Secretary and Minister of Home Security. He was a powerful figure in the postwar social revolution, uniting the positions of deputy Prime Minister, Lord President of the Council, and Leader of a House of Commons which enacted the most formidable body of legislation ever entrusted to it. In 1955 he was defeated by **Hugh Gaitskell** in the contest for the leadership of the Labour Party. His *Autobiography* was published in 1960.

Morrison, Jim (James Douglas), *nicknamed* the Lizard King 1943–71
US rock singer and poet

He was born in Melbourne, Florida. He was the lead singer of The Doors, an important Los Angeles-based rock band of the late-1960s which also included Ray Manzarek (1939–), Robbie Kreiger (1946–), and John Densmore (1945–). He combined a poetic intensity with a rebellious non-conformism, but his attempts to push beyond conventional behaviour and states of consciousness brought him into conflict with the authorities, mainly over drugs, but also for outspoken political songs like 'When The Music's Over' or 'Five To One'. The band's output was uneven, but immensely powerful at its best. He died in Paris in slightly mysterious circumstances, adding fuel to a familiar rock legend, and his grave there became a shrine for fans. 📖 J Hopkins, *The Lizard King* (1993)

Morrison, Robert 1782–1834
Scottish scholar and missionary

Morris, William 1834–96
English craftsman, poet and socialist

William Morris was born in Walthamstow, near London, into a middle-class family. He was educated at Marlborough School and Exeter College, Oxford. He studied for holy orders, but renounced the Church and studied architecture, with his friends and fellow-members of the Pre-Raphaelite Brotherhood, particularly the painter Edward Burne-Jones. He studied architecture under George Edmund Street, but on the advice of Dante Gabriel Rossetti became a professional painter (1857–62).

In 1859 he married a model, Jane Burden, and moved into the Red House at Bexley Heath, which he designed and furnished with the architect Philip Webb. From the ideas expressed there, and with the help of his pre-Raphaelite associates, in 1861 he founded the firm of Morris, Marshall, Faulkner and Company, which soon revolutionized the art of house decoration and furniture in England.

His literary career began with a volume of poetry and longer narrative poems including The Earthly Paradise (1868–70), a collection of 24 classical and medieval tales in a Chaucerian mould. He developed a passionate interest in the heroic literature of Iceland, and worked with Eiríkur Magnússon on a series of saga translations. He visited Iceland twice, in 1871 and 1873, and was inspired to write Three Northern Love Songs (1875) and a four-volume epic, The Story of Sigurd the Volsung and the Fall of the Nibelungs (1876), regarded as his greatest literary work.

He founded a Society for the Protection of Ancient Buildings in 1877. His experience as a master-craftsman, and his devotion to the Gothic, persuaded him that the excellence of medieval arts and crafts sprang from the joy of free craftsmen, which was destroyed by Victorian mass-production and capitalism. He joined the Social Democratic Federation in 1883; his Utopian ideals did much to develop the philosophy of socialism, and when the Social Democratic Federation suffered disruption in 1884 he formed a breakaway Socialist League.

In 1890, in a further rejection of Victorian values, he founded a publishing house, the Kelmscott Press at Hammersmith, for which he designed clear typefaces and wide ornamental borders; it produced a stream of his own works as well as reprints of English classics.

📖 Morris's other publications include a verse morality, Love is Enough, or The Freeing of Pharamond (1872), and translations of Virgil's Aeneid (1875) and Homer's Odyssey (1887). His socialist zeal inspired two prose romances, The Dream of John Ball (1888) and News from Nowhere (1891). Further prose romances concentrated more on story-telling: The House of the Wolfings (1889), The Roots of the Mountains (1889) and The Story of the Glittering Plain (1891), all set in the far north. His last works were a book of verse (Poems by the Way, 1891), and further prose romances: The Wood beyond the World (1895), The Well at the World's End (1896), The Water of the Wondrous Isles and The Story of the Sundering Flood (published posthumously in 1897).

📖 J Lindsay, William Morris (1975); P Henderson, Morris, His Art, Writings and Public Life (1967); J W Mackail, William Morris (1899).

'The reward of labour is life.'
From News from Nowhere, ch.15.

He was born near Jedburgh, in the Scottish Borders, and after studying theology in his spare time was sent in 1807 to Canton by the London Missionary Society as the first Protestant missionary to China. From 1809 to 1814 he translated and printed the New Testament (1819) and, with some help, the Old Testament into Chinese. In 1823 he completed his great Chinese Dictionary. In 1818 he established an Anglo-Chinese College at Malacca.

Morrison, Toni, pen name of Chloe Anthony Morrison, née Wofford 1931–
US novelist, winner of the Nobel Prize for literature

Born in Lorain, Ohio, she was educated at Howard and Cornell universities, and taught at Howard before moving to New York in 1965. She worked in publishing as senior editor at Random House while becoming established as a fiction writer. Labelled as a black James Joyce or William Faulkner, she explores in rich vocabulary and cold-blooded detail the story of African-Americans. The Bluest Eye (1970) focuses on the incestuous rape of an 11-year-old girl; Sula (1974) again confronts a generation gap, but between a grandmother and the eponymous scapegoat; and Song of Solomon (1977) is a merciless study of genteel blacks. Her novels Tar Baby (1981), Beloved (1987) and Jazz (1992), formidable in their mastery of technique and courageous in their subject-matter, confirmed her as one of the most important US contemporary novelists. She was awarded the Nobel Prize for literature in 1993.
📖 W D Samuels and C Hudson, Toni Morrison (1990).

Morrison, Van (George Ivan) 1945–
Northern Irish rock singer and songwriter

Born in Belfast, he first came to attention as the lead singer with the Irish band Them, remembered for their epic pop hit 'Gloria' (1967). He moved onto a different plane of achievement with the haunting Astral Weeks (1968), the prelude to a classic period of his work in the early 1970s, which includes Moondance (1970), Saint Dominic's Preview (1972), and the electrifying live recording It's Too Late To Stop Now (1974). His highly original fusion of soul, rhythm and blues, jazz and folk influences has resulted in peaks and troughs in his output across the ensuing decades, both in the studio and on stage, but he has continued to confound conventional expectations. He moves easily between high-energy rock and Celtic mysticism, and remains one of the most original and powerful performers and writers in rock music. 📖 S Turner, It's Too Late To Stop Now (1993)

Morse, Samuel Finley Breese 1791–1872
US artist and inventor

Born in Charlestown, Massachusetts, he graduated at Yale in 1810, and went to England to study painting. On his return he was a founder and first president of the National Academy of Design in New York (1826) and became a professor at New York University (1832). He studied chemistry and electricity, and in 1832 conceived the idea of a magnetic telegraph, which he exhibited to Congress in 1837, and attempted in vain to patent in Europe. He struggled on with little financial backing until 1843, when Congress granted him $30,000 for an experimental telegraph line between Washington and Baltimore, built by Ezra Cornell, over which he sent the historic message, 'What hath God wrought?' on 24 May 1844. His system, widely adopted, at last brought him honours and rewards. The 'Morse code' (originally called the 'Morse alphabet') was evolved by him for use with his telegraph.

Morshead, Sir Leslie James 1889–1959
Australian soldier

He was born in Ballarat, Victoria. He commanded a company at Gallipoli, and later a batallion on the Western Front, where he won the Distinguished Service Order and the Legion of Honour. In World War II he commanded the 18th Brigade in the Middle East and led the 9th Division at Tobruk during the siege of 1941 and at the battles of El Alamein. He returned to Australia to lead the New Guinea Force and to become general officer commanding of the First Australian Corps, ending the war in 1945 as commander of the Australian and US Task Force in Borneo.

Mort, Thomas Sutcliffe 1816–78
Australian businessman and pioneer of refrigeration

Born in Bolton, Lancashire, England, he went to Sydney in 1838 as agent for an English firm and later established his own woolbroking business, for some years the largest in Australia. In 1854 he constructed a dry dock at Balmain, Sydney, a venture in which half of the company shares were held by his employees. Shipbuilding began there in 1855 and the first Australian railway locomotive was built there in 1870. He established a scientific farm at Bodalla on the south coast of New South Wales, building a model community for his workers. His experience there in the wastage of perishable foods led to an interest in refrigeration and to a large freezing plant being built at Darling Harbour, Sydney, in 1875.

Mortarà, Edgar 1852–1940
Italian monk

Born into a Jewish family, he became the unwitting principal in the celebrated 'Mortara' case. In 1858 he was carried off from his parents by the Archbishop of Bologna, on the grounds that he had been secretly baptized by a Catholic maid servant when he was a gravely ill infant. The refusal of the authorities to give him up to his parents excited much indignation in Great Britain. Eventually he was discovered in Rome in 1870, but he chose to retain his Christian faith, and became an Augustinian monk.

Mortensen, Erik 1926–
Danish fashion designer

Since 1948 he has been attached to the Balmain fashion house in Paris, becoming the artistic director in 1960. He took over the management of the house after the death of Pierre Balmain in 1982. He was awarded the Golden Thimble of the French Haute Couture in 1983 and 1987.

Mortimer, John Clifford 1923–
English dramatist, novelist and barrister

Born in London, he was called to the Bar in 1948, participated in several celebrated civil cases, and is a constant defender of liberal values. His series of novels featuring Horace Rumpole, an amiable, late-middle-aged defence barrister and frequenter of Pomeroy's bar, has been adapted for television as *Rumpole of the Bailey*. His other novels, including *Paradise Postponed* (1985) and *Summer's Lease* (1988), are highly popular, evoking, often savagely, what Mortimer perceives as the moral decline of the English middle class. His many plays and adaptations for the stage include *The Dock Brief* (1958), *The Wrong Side of the Park* (1960), *Two Stars for Comfort* (1962) and an autobiographical play, *A Voyage round My Father* (broadcast 1963, staged 1970), which was filmed for television in 1982 with **Laurence Olivier** as the father. He has published two autobiographical volumes, entitled *Clinging to the Wreckage* (1982) and *Murderers and Other Friends* (1994). He has made notable translations, especially of **Georges Feydeau**, and several TV screenplays including *Brideshead Revisited* (1981), from the novel by **Evelyn Waugh**, *The Ebony Tower* (1984) from the story by **John Fowles**, and his own *Paradise*

Postponed (1986). His recent novel *Under the Hammer* (1994) was televised. His first wife was the novelist Penelope Mortimer (1918–). ▢ J R Taylor, *Anger and After* (1962)

Morton, H(enry) V(ollam) 1892–1979
English travel writer and journalist

He was born and educated in Birmingham, and began his career on the staff of the *Birmingham Gazette* in 1910 and became assistant editor in 1912. He was the author of many informative and informal travel books, including *The Heart of London* (1925), *In Search of Scotland* (1929), *In the Steps of the Master* (1934), *Middle East* (1941), *In Search of London* (1951) and *A Wanderer in Rome* (1957).

Morton, James Douglas, 4th Earl of c.1516–81
Regent of Scotland

The younger son of Sir George Douglas of Pittendreich, near Edinburgh, he became Earl of Morton (1553), and although a Protestant, was made Chancellor by **Mary, Queen of Scots** (1563). Involved in the murders of both **David Rizzio** (1566) and Lord **Darnley** (1567), he joined the Protestant nobles who defeated the Earl of **Bothwell** and Mary, Queen of Scots, at Carberry Hill (1567), 'discovered' the 'Casket Letters', led the forces at Langside (1568) and, after the brief regencies of **Moray**, Lennox and Mar, took over himself as regent for **James VI** (1572). After the end of the civil war in Scotland (1573), he increased links with England, but his high-handed attempts to control ecclesiastical appointments and to bring the Church into conformity with England brought him into sharp conflict with the radical ministers, led by **Andrew Melville**. His regency brought a welcome restoration of law and order, especially to the Borders, but it was achieved at the cost of a monopoly of many offices by the **Douglas** family, which caused intense resentment. He fell briefly from power in 1578, but the arrival of the young king's cousin, Esmé Stuart, Earl of Lennox (1579) recast political expectations. His fall was engineered by Captain James Stewart, nominally for his part in Darnley's murder, and he was beheaded by the 'Maiden', a device he had himself introduced to Scotland, in Edinburgh's Grassmarket. His regency, though brief, was in many respects a turning-point, not least in the beginning of the restoration of royal power which was to be continued in James VI's personal reign. ▢ George R Hewitt, *Scotland Under Morton 1572–80* (1982)

Morton, Jelly Roll, originally Ferdinand Joseph La Menthe or Lamothe 1890–1941
US jazz pianist, composer and bandleader

Born into a Creole family in New Orleans, he worked as a gambler and pimp as well as a piano entertainer in 'sporting houses'. His status as a jazz pioneer comes from his recordings (1923–27) while living in Chicago, and his unaccompanied piano solos made bestsellers of such tunes as 'King Porter Stomp', 'Wolverine Blues' and 'Jelly Roll Blues'. In 1926 he formed the recording band the 'Red Hot Peppers', a collection of some of the finest New Orleans sidemen of the day, and probably the first in jazz to combine arranged ensemble passages with collective improvisation and improvised solos. In 1938 Morton made a series of recordings, including spoken recollections on his early years, for the American Library of Congress.

Morton, John c.1420–1500
English prelate and statesman

Born probably in Milborne St Andrew, Dorset, he trained as a lawyer. Faithful to **Henry VI** until after the Lancastrian defeat at the Battle of Tewkesbury (1471), he made his peace with **Edward IV**, and became Master of the Rolls (1473) and Bishop of Ely (1479). **Richard III** imprisoned him (1483), but he escaped, and after the accession of Henry VII was made Archbishop of Canterbury (1486), Chancellor (1487) and a cardinal (1493).

Morton, John Cameron Andrieu Bingham Michael 1893–1979
English author and journalist
After serving in World War I he took up writing and published many books of humour, fantasy and satire, as well as a number of historical works including several on the French Revolution. From 1924 to 1975 he wrote a regular humorous column, 'By the Way', under the name of 'Beachcomber', for the *Daily Express*.

Morton, John Maddison 1811–91
English dramatist
Born in Pangbourne, Berkshire, the son of Thomas Morton, he became a prolific writer of farces (mostly from French), but is best remembered as the author of *Cox and Box* (1847). The rise of burlesque was his ruin and he became a 'poor brother' of the Charterhouse. 🕮 F Wilson, *An Epistolary Remonstrance* (1887)

Morton, Lee See Boucicault, Dion (ysius Lardner)

Morton, Levi Parsons 1824–1920
US banker and politician
Born in Shoreham, Vermont, he began as a country storekeeper's assistant, and in 1863 founded banking-houses in New York and London. In 1878–80 he was returned to Congress as a Republican and in 1881–85 was minister to France. He was Vice-President of the USA to President Benjamin Harrison (1889–93), and Governor of New York State (1895–97).

Morton, Thomas 1764–1838
English dramatist
He was born in Durham, and abandoned his law studies at Lincoln's Inn, London, to write plays. His works include *Speed the Plough* (1798, with its invisible 'Mrs Grundy'), *The Blind Girl* (1801), *Town and Country* (1807), *School for Grown Children* (1826), and other popular plays. He was the father of John Maddison Morton.

Morton, William Thomas Green 1819–68
US dentist
Born in Charlton, Massachusetts, he practised in Boston from 1842. As a medical student at Harvard in 1846 he used sulphuric ether ('letheon') as an anaesthetic for the excision of a vascular malformation from a patient, and patented the process, which was hotly disputed by Crawford Long and other medical men.

Mosaddeq, Mohammad 1880–1967
Iranian statesman
Born in Teheran, he held office in Iran in the 1920s, and returned to politics in 1944. By his Oil Nationalization Act of 1951 (in which year he became Prime Minister), he claimed to have expropriated the Anglo-Iranian Oil Co. His government was overthrown by a royalist uprising in 1953, and he was imprisoned. He was released in 1956.

Mosby, John Singleton 1833–1916
US Confederate soldier
Born in Edgemont, Virginia, he fought at Bull Run in 1861 and served as a scout on General J E B Stuart's staff during the Peninsular Campaign. From 1863 to 1865 he commanded an independent cavalry unit known as Mosby's Rangers, which attacked Union outposts in Virginia and cut communications and supply lines. Their most famous exploit was the capture of Ben E H Stoughton and his staff behind Union lines at Fairfax Court House (1863). They operated without drills or camps and with minimal discipline, and they were declared outlaws by the Union army because they often confiscated private property as well as army supplies. Initially consisting of only nine men, the Rangers had grown to eight companies at the time of Mosby's promotion to colonel in 1864. After the Civil War ended he entered politics as a Republican and was a loyal supporter of his wartime adversary, Ulysses S Grant.

Moscheles, Ignaz 1794–1870
Bohemian pianist and composer
Born in Prague of Jewish parents, he was by 1808 the favourite musician and music-master of Vienna. From 1825 he taught in London, and from 1844 in Leipzig. He edited, in English, Anton Felix Schindler's *Life of Beethoven* (1841).

Moscíki, Igancy 1867–1946
Polish chemist and politician
Born in Mierzanów near Plock, he studied at the Polytechnical School in Riga, Latvia, and fled to Great Britain after being involved in an assassination attempt. In 1897 he was appointed Professor of Electrochemistry at Fribourg, Switzerland, and in 1912 became Professor of Electrochemistry at the Polytechnical School at Lvov, Poland. After the end of World War I he founded factories to manufacture fertilizers synthetically from nitric acid, derived from atmospheric nitrogen which had been fixed by electric arcs. In 1926, when the Polish national hero and former revolutionary Józef Piłsudski overthrew the government, Moscíki supported the move and became President of the Republic, a post he retained until 1939 when he fled from the Nazis and the Russians to spend the rest of his life in Switzerland.

Moseley, Harry (Henry Gwyn Jeffreys) 1887–1915
English physicist
He was born in Weymouth, Dorset, and educated at Oxford, where he graduated in 1910. He then joined Ernest Rutherford in Manchester before returning to work at Oxford in 1913. He measured the X-ray spectra of over 30 different metals, and suggested that the regular variance from element to element was related to the nuclear charge, allowing the atomic numbers of elements to be calculated. Discontinuities in the spectral series made it clear that a number of elements were missing from the periodic table and allowed prediction of their properties; these elements were sought and soon discovered. Moseley's work was an important step in advancing knowledge of the nature of the atom, firmly establishing that the properties of the elements are determined by atomic number rather than atomic weight. He was killed in action at Gallipoli. 🕮 J L Heilbron, *H G J Moseley: The Life and Letters of an English Physicist, 1887–1915* (1974)

Moser, George Michael 1704–83
Swiss gold chaser and enameller
Moving early to London, he became the head of his profession. A founder member of the Royal Academy, he was elected its first keeper.

Moser, Mary c.1744–1819
English flower painter
Daughter of George Michael Moser, she was one of the founder members of the Royal Academy, and an intimate friend of the royal family.

Moser-Pröll, Annemarie, *née* Pröll 1953–
Austrian alpine skier
Born in Kleinarl, she won a women's record 62 World Cup races (1970–79), and was overall champion (1979), downhill champion (1978, 1979), Olympic downhill champion (1980), world combined champion (1972, 1978), and world downhill champion (1974, 1978, 1980). She temporarily retired from 1975 to 1976, and finally retired after the 1980 Olympics.

Moses, Hebrew Môsheh 15th–13th century BC
Old Testament Hebrew prophet and lawgiver

Moses is the principal figure dominating the Old Testament books from Exodus to Deuteronomy. The sequence begins with his birth and ends with his death, and describes him as the leader of the Israelites in their Exodus from captivity in Egypt and as receiver of the Divine Law. He was the younger son of a Levite couple, and was hidden in a basket to avoid death at the hands of the Egyptians. He was discovered by a daughter of Pharaoh and raised as her son.

After killing an Egyptian who was beating a Hebrew, Moses fled to Midian, and there married Zipproah, the daughter of a Midianite priest. According to the biblical account, God appeared to Moses in a burning bush, and ordered him to lead his people out of Egypt. He returned to Egypt with his brother Aaron, and eventually persuaded Pharaoh to release the Hebrews by producing signs and visiting plagues on the country.

Moses led the Hebrews out of Egypt, pursued by Pharaoh's army, which was engulfed by the waters of the Red Sea after they had parted to allow the Hebrews through. After a long period in the wilderness, Moses took the people to Sinai, where he received the commandments from God in the mountain. On his return from the mountain, he interceded with God not to punish the Hebrews for adoring the golden calf. For 39 years Moses led his people in the wilderness, where they were fed with manna and quails. After failing to enter Canaan from the south, Moses settled the people in land north of Moab. After delivering a series of addresses, Moses died in the fortieth year after the Exodus, according to Deuteronomy (1.3).

In assessing the role of Moses in early biblical history, it should be noted that many of the stories told about him in the Pentateuch belong to a type that is also told elsewhere (for example, the threat to the child and its recovery). The pharaoh of the captivity is not named (he has commonly been identified with Rameses II), and Moses is never mentioned in any contemporary non-biblical sources, Egyptian or otherwise. He represents the ideal leader and wise judge of his people, but it is difficult to separate legend from history in the biblical accounts that have come down to us.

📖 R de Vaux, *The Early History of Israel* (1978).

> Moses has been depicted in art with horns growing out of his head. This tradition arose from a misassociation of the Hebrew word *qaran* (usually translated 'to shine') with *qeren* meaning 'horn'. It occurs in *Exodus* (34 .29): 'When he descended [from the mountain], he did not know that the skin of his face shone because he had been speaking with the Lord' (NEB).

Moses See panel above

Moses, Anna Mary, known as Grandma Moses
1860–1961
US primitive artist
Born in Washington County, New York, she was a farmer's wife in Staunton, Virginia, and in New York State, and did embroideries of country scenes. She began to paint at about the age of 75, mainly country scenes remembered from her childhood—'old, timey things ... all from memory'. From her first show in New York in 1940, she had great popular success in the United States.

Moses, Sir Charles Joseph Alfred 1900–88
Australian broadcaster and administrator
Born in Little Hulton, Lancashire, England, he trained as a soldier at the Royal Military College, Sandhurst, then emigrated to Australia in 1922. After a number of ventures, he became an announcer with the then Australian Broadcasting Company in 1930. On the formation of the Australian Broadcasting Commission (1934), he was appointed controller of talks and school broadcasts, and in 1935 became general manager of the ABC, a position he held for the next 30 years. He pioneered broadcasting to schools and to rural areas, introduced the ABC's own independent news service and national television, and established ABC symphony orchestras in each state. He joined the Australian Imperial Forces in 1940, and escaped after the fall of Singapore in 1942 to serve in New Guinea.

Moses, Ed(win Corley) 1955–
US track athlete
He was born in Dayton, Ohio. The greatest 400-metre hurdler ever, he was unbeaten in any race in this event from August 1977 to June 1987, and as Olympic champion in 1976 and 1984 and four times world record holder, he dominated this discipline for over a decade. He would have been favourite for the gold medal in the 1980 Moscow Olympics as well, but missed them because of the US boycott. His third place in the 1988 Olympic final marked the end of a unique era but he made a comeback in 1991.

Moses, Grandma See Moses, Anna Mary

Moses, Robert 1888–1981
US public official
He was born in New Haven, Connecticut, the son of a department-store owner, and was educated at Yale, Oxford, and Columbia universities. In 1919 he became Chief of Staff of the New York state reconstruction committee, and in 1924 was appointed president of the New York state council of parks and chairman of Long Island state park commission, thus giving him almost total supervision of the state park system. In 1934 he was appointed commissioner of the city parks, and became an eminent and committed spokesman for parks and limited-access roads. Widely known for his part in the constitution of the Triborough Bridge (which gave New Yorkers access to parkland), he also has the Jones Beach development and many other projects, such as slum clearance and housing estates, to his credit. He is considered to be responsible for much of the modern appearance of New York City.

Môsheh See Moses (panel above)

Moshoeshoe II, Constantine Bereng Seeiso
1938–96
King of Lesotho
Educated at Oxford, England, he was installed as Paramount Chief of the Basotho people (1960) and proclaimed King of Lesotho when the country became independent (1966). His desire for political involvement led to his being twice placed under house arrest, and in 1970 an eight-month exile in Holland ended when he agreed to take no further part in the country's politics. After a military coup in 1990, he was deposed and sent into exile in Britain (1990–92) and his eldest son, Letsie III, was put on his throne. Regional leaders led by Nelson Mandela later negotiated the restoration of constitutional rule and Moshoeshoe was returned to power in 1995. He died in a motor accident.

Mosley, Sir Oswald Ernald Mosley, 6th Baronet 1896–1980
English politician

Successively a Conservative, Independent and Labour MP, he was a member of the 1929 Labour government. He later resigned and became founder of the New Party (1931). After a visit to Italy he became founder and leader of the British Union of Fascists (1932) whose followers, the Blackshirts, provoked violent demonstrations by staging anti-Semitic marches through the traditionally Jewish east end of London. Detained under the Defence Regulations during World War II, he founded a new Union Movement in 1948. His vision of a politically and economically united Europe is embodied in his *Europe: Faith and Plan* (1958). He married Cynthia, 2nd daughter of Earl Curzon of Kedleston, in 1920. His second wife, the Honourable Diana Mitford whom he married in 1936, was the sister of Jessica, Nancy and Unity Mitford.

Mosquera, Tomás Cipriano de 1798–1878
Colombian politician

Born into a prominent colonial family, he served under Simón Bolívar as a boy and was a brigadier at the age of 30. Well-travelled and pragmatic, he was instrumental in repressing a revolt led by religious interests against constitutionalist measures (1839–42). By the time of his presidency of New Granada (1845–49), he had begun to move to the conservative camp, favouring centralist rule, supported by his brother, the Archbishop of Bogotá, and the army. Benefitting from increasing prosperity and international trade, he switched towards a conservative liberal view, becoming President of Colombia for a second time (July 1861). Architect of the anticlerical, liberal and ultra-federalist constitution of 1863, he manipulated a shifting alliance of Radicals, Liberals and Independents against the ever-present Conservatives. Elected to a further term in 1865, he assumed dictatorial powers, and was toppled and exiled in 1867.

Moss, Stirling 1929–
English racing driver

Born in London, he won many major races in the 1950s, including the British Grand Prix (1955, 1957), the Mille Miglia, and the Targa Florio. Between 1951 and 1961, he won 16 races from 66 starts. He retired in 1962 after a crash at Goodwood. He then became a journalist and broadcaster, and returned to saloon car racing in 1980. His publications include *All But My Life* (1963) and *My Cars, My Career* (1987). 🕮 Robert Raymond, *Stirling Moss* (1953)

Mössbauer, Rudolf Ludwig 1929–
German physicist and Nobel Prize winner

Born in Munich, he was educated at the Technical University in Munich, and carried out postgraduate research at the Max Planck Institute for Medical Research in Heidelberg before receiving his PhD from the Technical University in 1958. He has held professorships there and at the California Insititute of Technology (Caltech) since 1961. Before completing his PhD, he observed what is known as the 'Mössbauer effect', the narrow resonance in the energy spectrum produced when the whole of the nuclear lattice, rather than just one nuclei, recoils from gamma radiation. The effect has been used to test Albert Einstein's theory of general relativity, to study the properties of nuclei and as an analytical tool in chemistry and biology. Mössbauer shared the 1961 Nobel Prize for physics with Robert Hofstadter for research into atomic structure.

Mosseen, Annalena 1952–
Swedish architect

Trained at the Royal Academy of Technology, Stockholm, she initially worked with Ralph Erskine but turned down a partnership with him to start her own practice, Visby Arkitektgrupp, with three other architects in her native Gotland. In 1982 the Gothland housing association approached her to address the problem of unpopular housing estates. In discussion with tenants at Grabo housing estate, she drew up a four-year plan for improvements, providing a better social mix of housing and many individual physical improvements. Her practice also sought funding to renovate a medieval block of Visby town, known as the Triangle. Their work on this project won the prestigious Europa Nostra award in 1990.

Moszkowski, Moritz 1854–1925
Polish composer and pianist

Born in Breslau, Germany (now Wrocław, Poland), he taught at the Kullak Academy, Berlin, and later lived in Paris. A prolific composer for piano and orchestra, he is now remembered almost solely for his lively *Spanish Dances* (1876, *Spanische Tänze*).

Mota, Rosa 1958–
Portuguese athlete

She was born in Foz do Douro, and competed in her first marathon in Athens in 1982, when she won the European title. She improved her time on the next seven occasions she competed. Weighing in at just over seven stones (44kg), she possesses surprising reserves of stamina which helped her to win 10 of her first 13 marathons. She has had victories in Tokyo, Boston, Chicago, Rotterdam, London and Osaka, as well as a further two European titles, and the world championship title in 1987. In 1988, she won an Olympic gold medal, making her the first Portuguese woman to do so.

Mother Mary of the Cross See McKillop, St Mary Helen

Motherwell, Robert Burns 1915–91
US painter and writer

Born in Aberdeen, Washington, he briefly attended the California School of Fine Arts in San Francisco and read philosophy at Stanford, Harvard, Grenoble and, later, Columbia. He wrote a good deal on the theory of modern art and helped found the Abstract Expressionist group in New York in the 1940s. His images often resemble semi-automatic doodles of a kind that the Surrealists had explored, but enlarged to fill huge canvases. He is best known for *Elegy to the Spanish Republic*, a series of more than a hundred paintings. He was married to the artist Helen Frankenthaler from 1958 to 1971.

Motlana, Nthato 1925–
South African doctor and politician

Educated at Kilnerton High School and Fort Hare College where he came into contact with the ANC (African National Congress) Youth league, he qualified as a doctor at the University of the Witwatersrand. Involved in establishing a network of ANC branches on the Witwatersrand, he was banned in 1953 for five years. By the mid-1970s he had become a leading figure in Soweto and played a major role in the 1976 uprising, helping to establish the Soweto Committee of Ten, which developed into the Soweto Civil Association, of which he became chairman. One of the few figures to have lived in the townships and retained the respect of ordinary citizens, he became an articulate spokesman for black interests in the 1980s while the ANC was still banned.

Motley, John Lothrop 1814–77
US historian and diplomat

Born in Dorchester, Massachusetts, he studied at Harvard and several German universities, and began a diplomatic career. He soon turned to literature, however, and 10 years were spent on his *Rise of the Dutch Republic* (1856), which established his fame. This was enhanced by the *History of the United Netherlands* which appeared in 1860–69. He was Minister to Austria (1861–67), and to Great Britain (1869–70).

Motodo Eifu 1818–91
Japanese Confucian scholar
As tutor to the Meiji Emperor, he called for a return to traditional values during the 1880s and represented a conservative backlash against the westernizing trends of the 1870s. Appointed court adviser in 1886 and a member of the Privy Council in 1888, Motoda helped draft the Imperial Rescript on Education (1890), which emphasized the inculcation of patriotism and reverence for the emperor.

Motoori Norinaga 1730–1801
Japanese scholar
He championed the superiority of Japan's ancient culture and beliefs as a reaction against the influence of rational Chinese thought. Condemning Japan's deference to Chinese civilization, Motoori reaffirmed Shinto myths portraying Japan as the 'Land of the Gods' and highlighted the uniqueness of Japan's sacred imperial institution (an unbroken line of emperors descended from the gods) in contrast to the succession of dynasties that prevailed in China. Known as *Kokugaku* (National Learning), Motoori's ideas were to influence the imperial loyalist movement of the 19th century that overthrew the Tokugawa Shogunate and to provide the basis of ultranationalist ideology in the 1930s.

Mott, John Raleigh 1865–1955
US religious leader, social worker and Nobel Prize winner
He was born in Livingston Manor, New York. A Methodist layman, he became known the world over by his work for the Student Volunteer Movement (1888–1920), the Young Men's Christian Association (1915–31) and the World Missionary Council (1941–42). He shared the 1946 Nobel Peace Prize with Emily Balch.

Mott, Lucretia, *née* Coffin 1793–1880
US abolitionist and feminist
Born in Nantucket, Massachusetts, she was educated near Poughkeepsie, New York, where she later became a teacher. She first rose to prominence in 1817, as a speaker at Quaker meetings, and became an active campaigner for temperance, peace, women's rights and the abolition of slavery. She helped to organize the American Anti-Slavery Society (1833) and was president of the Philadelphia women's branch but was denied membership in the World Anti-Slavery Convention in London, for which Daniel O'Connell denounced it. She also took an active part in the Anti-Slavery Convention of American Women (1837). She was strongly supported by her husband James Mott, and under her influence he left his commission business because of its connection with slave-produced cotton, in which he had dealt throughout the 1820s. She and Elizabeth Cady Stanton organized the first Woman's Rights Convention in 1848. ⊞ Otelia Cromwell, *Lucretia Mott* (1958)

Mott, Sir Nevill Francis 1905–96
English physicist and Nobel Prize winner
Born in Leeds, he studied mathematics at Cambridge, where he became a lecturer and Fellow, working with Ernest Rutherford. He later became Professor of Theoretical Physics at Bristol University, where he studied the electronic behaviour of 'Mott transitions' between metals and insulators, and in 1954 was appointed Cavendish Professor of Physics at Cambridge, decisively shaping the Cavendish Laboratory's research activities. In 1965 he retired and returned to full-time research to work on the new area of noncrystalline semiconductors. He shared the 1977 Nobel Prize for physics (with Philip Anderson and John van Vleck) for his work on the electronic properties of disordered materials. Mott has been one of the major theoretical physicists of this century, opening new and difficult areas of solid-state physics and materials science. He was knighted in 1962 and his book *Can Scientists Believe?* was published in 1991. ⊞ *A Life in Science* (1986)

Motte, Antoine Houdar de La See La Motte, Antoine Houdar de

Motte, Friedrich Heinrich Karl de la See Fouqué, Friedrich Heinrich Karl de la Motte, Baron

Mottelson, Ben(jamin) Roy 1926–
Danish physicist and Nobel Prize winner
Born in Chicago, USA, he was educated at Purdue University and Harvard. From Harvard he moved to the Institute of Theoretical Physics in Copenhagen (now the Niels Bohr Institute), where he worked with Aage Bohr on the problem of combining the two models of the atomic nuclei. They secured experimental evidence in support of James Rainwater's collective model of the atomic nuclei and Bohr, Mottelson and Rainwater shared the 1975 Nobel Prize for physics. From 1953 to 1957 Mottelson held a research position in CERN (Conseil Européen pour la Recherche Nucléaire) before returning to Copenhagen where he became professor at Nordita (Nordic Institute for Theoretical Atomic Physics). He took Danish nationality in 1973.

Motteux, Peter Anthony 1660–1718
British writer
Born in Rouen, France, he went to London after the revocation of the Edict of Nantes (1685) and after a time took up journalism. He edited the *Gentleman's Journal* (1691–94), but is best known for his translations of Rabelais (1693–1708) and *Don Quixote* (1703).

Moule, Charles Francis Digby 1908–
English biblical scholar
Born in Hanchow, China, he graduated at Cambridge and was ordained into the Anglican church in 1933. After several curacies and theological appointments he returned to Cambridge as lecturer before becoming Professor of Divinity (1951–76). One of the most versatile scholars of his time, he has made substantial contributions to the *Encyclopaedia Britannica* and has written many books including *An Idiom Book of New Testament Greek* (1953), *The Origin of Christology* (1977), *The Holy Spirit* (1978), *The Birth of the New Testament* (1981), and *Essays in New Testament Interpretation* (1982).

Moulins, Master of c.1460–c.1529
French artist
He is so called from his principal work, the triptych in Moulins Cathedral of the *Virgin and Child*. He is regarded as the most accomplished French artist of the time. The influence of Hugo van der Goes can be seen in his vividly coloured and realistic paintings, and some authorities identify him with Jean Perreal or Jean de Paris, court painter to Charles VIII.

Mountbatten, *originally* Battenberg, Prince Louis Alexander, 1st Marquess of Milford Haven 1854–1921
British naval commander
Born in Austria, the son of Prince Alexander of Hesse, he became a naturalized British subject and joined the Royal Navy in 1868. He served with distinction as a commodore in the Mediterranean fleet, as director of naval intelligence and senior sea commands. He was First Sea Lord at the outbreak of World War I, but was forced to resign because of anti-German prejudice. By royal command he gave up his German titles in 1917 and changed the family name from Battenberg to Mountbatten, and was created Marquess of Milford Haven. He was promoted admiral in 1919.

Mozart, (Johann Chrysostom) Wolfgang Amadeus 1756–91
Austrian composer

Mozart was the son of Leopold Mozart, deputy kapell-meister to the Archbishop of Salzburg. He displayed early musical gifts, playing the keyboard confidently at the age of four, composing his first pieces for it at five, and soon mastering the violin. Leopold was keen to exhibit his son's extraordinary talents along with those of his pianist-daughter, Maria-Anna or 'Nannerl' (1751–1829), and he undertook a series of tours of the European courts with them.

In 1762 they played before the Elector of Bavaria in Munich and before Empress **Maria Theresa** in Vienna. In 1763 they gave concerts in Munich, Augsburg, Mainz and Frankfurt before a five-month stay in Paris, which included a visit to the court of **Louis XV** at Versailles. They then went to London for 15 months, where a friendship was formed with **J C Bach**. During the next six months in the Netherlands, both children became seriously ill. In 1766 they began the homeward journey, stopping in Paris for two months, and making many appearances throughout Switzerland and Germany. Accounts of this tour mention Mozart's precocity, spirited playing and rare talent for improvisation.

In September 1767 the family went for five months to Vienna, where he wrote an opera buffa, *La finta semplice* ('The Feigned Simpleton') and a singspiel, *Bastien und Bastienne*, the latter commissioned by Dr **Franz Anton Mesmer**. On returning to Salzburg Mozart was appointed honorary konzertmeister to the court. There followed three extended visits by father and son to Italy (1770–72). In Rome, Mozart heard the *Miserere* of Gregorio Allegri (1582–1652) and afterwards wrote out the parts from memory. His musical experiences on these tours helped mould his style, especially in dramatic music, although he was prolific also in writing sacred vocal pieces and in-strumental works: by 1772 he had written about 25 sym-phonies (of which some are lost) and his first quartets. Further quartets and symphonies followed during and after a visit to Vienna in 1772, during which Mozart came into contact with the music of **Haydn**.

The years 1775–76 saw two stage works, *La finta giardiniera* ('The Feigned Gardener Girl') and *Il rè pastore* ('The Shepherd King'), five violin concertos, the *Haffner* Serenade, and Masses for the Salzburg Court Chapel. Unhappy with the austere and unmusical Archbishop Colloredo of Salzburg, Mozart left his service in 1777 and, travelling with his mother, sought employment elsewhere. They stayed at Mannheim, and heard the orchestra there, but no post was offered. He wrote a number of piano concertos and flute quartets, and fell in love with a singer, Aloysia Weber. Then in Paris, where his mother died in July, Mozart wrote the *Paris* Symphony. His father persuaded him to return to Salzburg, and he reluctantly accepted the post of court organist. At this time he composed the Symphonies (K318–19), the *Coronation Mass*, and the Sinfonia Concertante for violin and viola. In 1780 he re-ceived an important commission from the Elector of Bavaria, for the opera seria *Idomeneo, rè di Creta* ('Idomeneo, King of Crete'), produced in Munich in January 1781.

In 1781 Archbishop Colloredo summoned Mozart to Vienna for the coronation of Emperor **Joseph II**. Again, after a stormy scene, he soon left the Archbishop's service but remained in Vienna, which became home for the rest of his short, crowded life. Here his reputation as composer and pianist was to reach its peak within a few years. Aloysia Weber had married a court actor, and Mozart turned his attentions to her sister Constanze, whom he married in 1782, shortly after the first performance of his opera *Die Entführung aus dem Serail* ('The Abduction from the Seraglio').

Mountbatten, Edwina Cynthia Annette, *née* Ashley, Countess of 1901–60
English philanthropist

The wife of **Louis, Earl Mountbatten of Burma**, whom she married in 1922, she rendered distinguished service dur-ing the London Blitz (1940–42) to the Red Cross and St John Ambulance Brigade, of which she became super-intendent-in-chief in 1942. As Vicereine of India (1947), her work in social welfare brought her the friendship of **Mahatma Gandhi** and **Jawaharlal Nehru**. She died sud-denly on an official tour of Borneo for the St John Ambulance Brigade.

Mountbatten (of Burma), Louis Francis Albert Victor Nicholas Mounbatten, 1st Earl 1900–79
English naval commander and statesman

Born near Windsor, Berkshire, the younger son of Prince **Louis Mountbatten** and great-grandson of Queen **Victoria**, he was known as Prince Louis Francis of Battenberg until 1917. Educated at Osborne and Dartmouth Royal Naval Colleges (1913–16), he served at sea in World War I in HMS *Lion* and HMS *Elizabeth*. In World War II he commanded the 5th destroyer flotilla (1939–41), and became chief of Combined Operations Command (1941–43). He was Supreme Allied Commander South-East Asia from 1943 to 1945, and was then appointed the last Viceroy of India (1947) to oversee the rapid transfer of power. He returned to service at sea as Fourth Sea Lord and commander of the Mediterranean fleet (1952–55), and was appointed First Sea Lord (1955–59) and Chief of Defence Staff (1959–65). His close friends included the Duke of Windsor (formerly **Edward** VIII) and **Noël Coward**, and he was a valued confidante to Prince **Charles**. He was murdered by an IRA bomb while sailing near his holiday home in County Sligo, Ireland.

Mountcastle, Vernon Benjamin 1918–
US neurophysiologist

Born in Shelbyville, Kentucky, he received his medical training at the Johns Hopkins University School of Medicine, where he later joined the faculty (Research Fellow in Physiology, 1946–49; Assistant Professor, 1949–59; Professor of Physiology, 1959–80). He has been University Professor of Neuroscience there since 1980. His research has been concerned with central nervous mechanisms in sensation and perception, and his dem-onstration that cells in the cerebral cortex respond speci-fically to particular types of skin stimulation proved to be a major stimulus to later work on the visual system. His research has led to a better understanding of the neuro-physiological basis of higher functions such as learning and memory, described in his 1978 book, *The Mindful Brain*.

Mountevans, Edward Ratcliffe Garth Russell Evans, 1st Baron 1881–1957
English naval commander

Educated at Merchant Taylors' School, he joined the navy in 1897. From 1910 to 1913 he was second-in-command to Captain **Robert Scott**'s Antarctic expedition. In World War I he fought at Jutland, and in command of HMS *Broke* he scored an impressive victory over four German destroyers. In 1929 he was appointed rear admiral com-manding the Royal Australian Navy. He later was Commander-in-Chief of the Africa station and deputy high commissioner of the British Protectorates, where his

Mozart, (Johann Chrysostom) Wolfgang Amadeus *cont*

Married life was happy, but insecure financially (they had six children, of whom two survived), and Mozart increased his meagre income by teaching. In 1784, the year he became a freemason, he produced six piano concertos; in 1785 a further three; in 1786 three more. This was the rich flowering of his maturity, along with six string quartets dedicated to Haydn (who had declared Mozart to be the greatest composer known to him), the *Linz* and *Prague* Symphonies and the three Italian comic masterpieces composed to libretti by **Lorenzo Da Ponte**: *Le Nozze di Figaro* (1786, *The Marriage of Figaro*, after **Beaumarchais**), *Don Giovanni* (first performed in Prague, 1787), and *Così fan tutte* (1790, 'Women are all Like That'). Productions of his operas were usually more successful in Prague than in Vienna. The String Quintets in C major and G minor (1787), the last three symphonies (1788), the quartets for the King of Prussia (K575, 589, 590), the serenade *Eine kleine Nachtmusik*, and the Clarinet Quintet mark the peak of his output of orchestral and chamber music. In 1787, Mozart's father Leopold died in Salzburg.

The letters to fellow masons in his last three years make sad reading, reflecting countless anxieties about finance or health. He hoped for new commissions or a court post on the accession of Emperor **Leopold II**, but none was forthcoming. In 1791 he applied unsuccessfully for the post of kapellmeister of St Stephen's Cathedral. His last works were the opera *Die Zauberflöte* (*The Magic Flute*), based on a fairy-tale with a libretto by Emanuel Schikaneder, and an opera seria, *La Clemenza di Tito* (also of 1791), a Clarinet Concerto and a Requiem. The last was written to an anonymous commission (now known to be from Count Walsegg) and was unfinished when he died on 5 December.

Mozart's apparently irresponsible way of life may have contributed to the troubles of his last years, and the childish humour exhibited in his surviving letters appears to be the antithesis of his music. For he was a universal genius of music, in its facility, grace and polish, his innate sense of phrasing and gift of melodic beauty, his mastery of form and the richness of his harmony, and his ability to portray the deepest human feelings with the most sublime and sincere musical expression.

📖 Of the many general biographies of Mozart, that by Alfred Einstein (English edition 1946) is still considered the finest. See also H C Robbins Landon, *Mozart and Vienna* (1991) and *Mozart's Last Year* (2nd edition, 1989, with further bibliography); W Hildesheimer, *Mozart* (translated by Marion Faber, 1983); H C Robbins Landon and D Mitchell, *The Mozart Companion* (1956). A documentary account is given by O E Deutsch, *Mozart: A Documentary Biography* (1965); a selection of letters in English translation is given in E Anderson, *The Letters of Mozart and His Family* (3rd edition, 1985). Mozart's works were catalogued by Ludwig von Köchel and are usually cited from this catalogue (with several revisions by Alfred Einstein and later editors, 1983) with the prefix 'K'. Eduard Mörike's novella *Mozart auf seine Reise nach Prag* (1855, 'Mozart's Journey to Prague') is a fictional romance based on Mozart's visit to Prague for the first production there of *Don Giovanni*.

'Melody is the very essence of music. When I think of a good melodist I think of a fine race horse. A contrapuntist is only a post-horse.' From a letter to Michael Kelly, 1786.

---

actions against the paramount chief Tshekedi Khama of Bechuanaland were criticized. Recalled in 1939, he served in World War II as London regional commissioner. He wrote *Keeping the Seas* (1920) and *South with Scott* (1921).

Mountford, Charles Pearcy 1890–1976
Australian ethnologist, writer and film director

He was born in Hallett, South Australia. During his early years as a mechanic for the post office he was brought into contact with the Aboriginals and became an expert on their way of life, although he had no formal training. In 1937 he led an expedition in search of the lost explorer **Ludwig Leichhardt**, and between 1938 and 1960 he led 10 expeditions into central Australia. In 1948 he was leader of expeditions into Arnhem Land and to Melville Island, for the National Geographic Society of the USA. Beginning with *Brown Men and Red Sand* (1948), he wrote a series of books, illustrated with his own photographs, about the Aboriginals and their culture. He received awards for his photography and went on to direct feature films on Aboriginal life from 1950.

Mountjoy, Lord See Blount, Charles

Moussorgsky, Modest Petrovich See Mussorgsky, Modest Petrovich

Mowlam, Mo (Marjorie) 1949–
English Labour politician

Educated in Coventry, and at Durham University and Iowa University, she lectured at Florida State University (1977–78) before moving to Newcastle upon Tyne (1979–83). In 1987 she was elected as MP for Redcar. Within a year she was an assistant front bench spokesperson on Northern Ireland (1988–89), then became deputy co-ordinator for Labour's successful European parliament campaign in 1989. Rising through the Labour Party ranks, she was the spokesperson for city and corporate

affairs (1989–92), for the Citizen's Charter and women (1992–93), for national heritage (1993–94) and for Northern Ireland (1994–97), before entering Tony Blair's Cabinet as Secretary of State for Northern Ireland after Labour's landslide win in the 1997 general election.

Moyne, François Le See Le Moyne, François

Moynihan (of Leeds), Berkeley George Andrew Moynihan, 1st Baron 1865–1936
British surgeon

Born in Malta, he held various posts at the Leeds General Infirmary, England, specializing in the techniques of abdominal, gastric and pancreatic operations, and became professor at Leeds in 1909. The driving impulse of his life was the promotion of scientific surgery, and he set out his doctrine in his *Abdominal Operations* (1905). He formed the Moynihan Chirurgical Club, and was active in starting the Association of Surgeons of Great Britain and Ireland and the *British Journal of Surgery* (1913).

Moynihan, Daniel Patrick 1927–
US politician

Educated at the City College of New York and Tufts University, he taught at Syracuse, Harvard, and the Massachusetts Institute of Technology. He served in the administrations of Presidents **Lyndon B Johnson** and **Richard Nixon**, acquiring notoriety as the author of *The Negro Family: The Case for National Action* (1965). He became ambassador to India (1973–74), and won a seat in the US Senate as a Democrat from New York in 1976. He also wrote *Pandaemonium: ethnicity in international politics* (1993).

Moynihan, Rodrigo 1910–
English painter

Born in Santa Cruz, Tenerife, he studied at the American School in Rome, then at the Slade School of Art, London, and joined the London Group in 1933. In 1934 he organized the Objective Abstraction exhibition at the Zwemmer Gallery, London. Most of his works are of an Impressionist nature, with soft tones (eg his portrait of Queen Elizabeth II as *Princess Elizabeth*). From 1943 to 1944 he was an official war artist, and was Professor of Painting at the Royal College of Art (1948–57), where he painted his Portrait Group (1951, Tate, London) of the editors of Penguin Books. In 1956 he returned to abstract painting, with a show at the Institute of Contemporary Arts. There was a major retrospective of his work at the Royal Academy in 1978. He has since become best known for his still lifes and portraits, such as *Margaret Thatcher* (1985, National Portrait Gallery, London).

Mozart, (Johann Chrysostom) Wolfgang Amadeus See panel p1326

Mravinsky, Yevgeni Aleksandrovich 1903–88
Russian conductor
Born in St Petersburg, he studied biology, but followed his considerable talent as a pianist to become a rehearsal pianist for the Imperial Ballet. He entered the Leningrad (now St Petersburg) Conservatory in 1924, and on graduating in 1931 immediately took over the Leningrad Theatre of Opera and Ballet. From 1938 until his death he was the principal conductor of the Leningrad Philharmonic Orchestra. Mravinsky believed in trying to give an audience exactly what the composer intended, and in so doing gave some electrifying performances. He gave the world premières of several symphonies by both Prokofiev and Shostakovich.

M'Taggart, John M'Taggart See entry following MacSwiney

Mu'Awiyah c.602–680
First Umayyad caliph
He opposed the prophet Muhammad until the conquest of Mecca (630), then became his secretary. Under the 2nd caliph, Omar, he took part in the conquest of Syria and was made governor (640). He rebelled against the 4th caliph, Ali, for the murder of his kinsman, the caliph 'Uthman, and fought him at the indecisive Battle of Siffin (657). With the help of Amr ibn al-'As he gained control of Egypt, and after the assassination of Ali (661) took over the caliphate, thus founding the Umayyad dynasty, and moved the capital to Damascus. He centralized control of the caliphate and extended it through conquests in North Africa and Afghanistan. He was succeeded by his son, Yazid (d.683).

Mubarak, (Mohammed) Hosni Said ?1928–
Egyptian statesman
Born in al-Minufiyah, he served as a pilot and flying instructor and rose to become Commander of the Egyptian Air Force. He was Vice-President under Anwar Sādāt from 1975 until the latter's assassination in 1981. The only candidate for the presidency, Mubarak was declared President and pledged to continue Sadat's domestic and international policies, including firm treatment of Muslim extremists, and the peace process with Israel. During the 1991 Gulf War, he was the Arab leader most critical of Saddam Hussein, and reasserted his credentials with Israel by strongly denouncing the Iraqi missile attacks on Tel Aviv and Haifa. In 1995, the year of his re-election, he survived an assassination attempt by Islamic fundamentalists and was involved in the events leading to the signing of a peace accord between the Palestinian Liberation Organization (PLO) and Israel.

Mucha, Alphonse, *originally* Alfons Maria Mucha 1860–1939
Czech graphic artist, painter and designer
Born in Ivancise, he studied in Munich, Vienna, and at the Académie Julian and the Académie Colarossi, Paris. He designed jewellery, wallpaper and furniture, but his best-known works are his posters for Sarah Bernhardt, in the rich curvilinear Art Nouveau style of the 1890s. He designed a shop for a jeweller in Paris in 1901, before devoting himself mainly to painting from c.1903. He returned to Prague in 1914, where he painted a series of 20 monumental pictures, *The Slav Epic*.

Muddy Waters See Waters, Muddy

Mueller, Erwin Wilhelm 1911–77
US physicist
Born in Berlin, he graduated in engineering from the Technical University in Berlin, and worked for industrial laboratories there and at the Fritz Haber Institute. In 1936 he invented the field-emission microscope, which could produce an image of up to one million times magnification, allowing the atomic structure of certain materials to be directly observed. He followed this in 1951 with the field-ion microscope, which gave the first photographs affording a direct view of individual atoms in some high-melting-point metals and alloys and some large organic heat-stable molecules. He emigrated to the USA in 1952, and joined the staff of Pennsylvania State University. He became a naturalized US citizen in 1962.

Mueller, Ferdinand Jakob Heinrich von, Freiherr See Müller, Ferdinand Jakob Heinrich von, Freiherr

Mugabe, Robert Gabriel 1924–
Zimbabwean nationalist leader and statesman
Born in Kutama, Southern Rhodesia, and educated in Catholic mission schools and Fort Hare College, he was a teacher successively in Southern Rhodesia (Zimbabwe), Northern Rhodesia (Zambia) and Ghana before returning to Southern Rhodesia in 1960 as Publicity Secretary to the National Democratic Party. He was Deputy Secretary-General of the Zimbabwe African People's Union (ZAPU) in 1961 before being detained and then imprisoned, but escaped to co-found the Zimbabwe African National Union (ZANU) in 1963. He was detained again (1964–74), during which period he replaced Ndabaningi Sithole as President of ZANU and qualified as a lawyer. Released in 1974, he went to Mozambique to oversee the guerrilla war against the white regime. United uncomfortably with Joshua Nkomo's ZAPU in the Patriotic Front to press for black majority rule, Mugabe essentially retained his independence and, to the surprise of many, led ZANU (PF), as the combined party was called, to a decisive victory in 1980; hence, he became Prime Minister in the first government of independent Zimbabwe. In 1987 he persuaded parliament to agree to combine the roles of head of state and head of government, and he became the country's first executive President. In 1988 ZANU and ZAPU merged to make Zimbabwe effectively a one-party state, under Mugabe's leadership. He was re-elected in the 1996 presidential election after each of his challengers had withdrawn from the running. He has been leading an anti-homosexual crusade for several years. 📖 David Smith and Colin Simpson, *Mugabe* (1981)

Muggeridge, (Thomas) Malcolm 1903–90
English journalist and sage
Born in Croydon, London, he lectured at the Egyptian University in Cairo (1927–30), then joined the *Manchester Guardian* (1930–33), serving as their Moscow correspondent. He was also assistant editor of the *Calcutta Statesman* (1934–35) and on the editorial staff of the *Evening Standard*. Serving with the Intelligence Corps during World War II, he received the Legion of Honour and the Croix de Guerre with Palm. He worked with *The Daily Telegraph* (1946–52), and was editor of *Punch* (1953–57) and also a television reporter and interviewer, making regular contributions to *Panorama* (1953–60). In his own series

---

Muhammad or Mohammed c.570–c.632
Arab prophet, and founder of Islam

Muhammad was the son of Abdallâh, a poor merchant of the powerful tribe of Quaraysh, hereditary guardians of the shrine in Mecca. He was orphaned at six, and brought up by his grandfather and uncle, Abu Tâlib, who trained him to be a merchant. At the age of 24 he entered the service of a rich widow, Khadija (c.595–619), whom he eventually married. They had six children, including their daughters **Fatima** and Umm Kulthum, who married '**Uthman**, the third caliph.

While continuing as a trader, Muhammad became increasingly drawn to religious contemplation. Soon after 600 (the traditional date is c.610) he began to receive revelations from the angel Jibra'el (Gabriel) of the word of Allah, the one and only God. This Qur'an (Koran), or 'reading', commanded that the numerous idols of the shrine should be destroyed and that the rich should give to the poor. This simple message attracted some support but provoked a great deal of hostility from those who felt their interests threatened.

When his wife and uncle died, Muhammad was reduced to poverty, but he began making a few converts amongst pilgrims to Mecca from the town of Yathrib, an agricultural community to the north. By 622 Muhammad and his small band of devoted followers could no longer remain in Mecca; they were saved by an invitation from the people of Yathrib, who wanted Muhammad to come and arbitrate in the feuds that racked their community. He migrated there, and this migration, the Hegira, marks the beginning of the Muslim era. The name of the town was changed to Medina, 'the city of the prophet'.

The most important act in the first year of the Hegira was Muhammad's permission to go to war with the enemies of Islam—especially the Meccans—in the name of God. In December 623 his Muslims defeated a Meccan force, but he was severely wounded in a battle at Ohod (January 625). In 627 he repelled a Meccan siege of Medina. By 629 he was able to take control of Mecca, which recognized him as chief and prophet. By 630 he had control over all Arabia. In March 632 he undertook his last pilgrimage to Mecca, and there on Mount Arafat fixed for all time the ceremonies of the pilgrimage.

He fell ill soon after his return and died on 8 June in the home of the favourite of his nine wives, **Aïshah**, the daughter of one of his first followers, **Abu Bakr**. His tomb in the mosque at Medina is venerated throughout Islam. 📖 M Cook, *Muhammad* (1983).

Appointment With... (1960–61) and *Let Me Speak* (1964–65), he quizzed the great figures of the day and challenged minorities to defend their beliefs. A controversial Rector of Edinburgh University (1967–68), he resigned over student liberalism and promiscuity. In 1982 he became a Roman Catholic. Later television appearances include the autobiographical *Muggeridge Ancient and Modern* (1981). Among his many books are *The Earnest Atheist* (1936), *Tread Softly for You Tread on My Jokes* (1966), *Chronicle of Wasted Time* (1982) and *Conversion: a spiritual journey* (1988). 📖 Gregory Wolfe, *Malcolm Muggeridge: a biography* (1995)

Muggleton, Lodowick 1609–98
English Puritan

Born in London, he founded the sect of Muggletonians (1652) with his cousin, John Reeve (1608–58). They held that the Devil became incarnate in **Eve**, and denied the Holy Trinity. He was imprisoned, and later fined for blasphemy, and published a *Spiritual Transcendental Treatise* (1652).

Muhammad See panel above

Muhammad, Abu Abdallah See Boabdil

Muhammad, Elijah, *originally* Elijah Poole
1897–1975
US religious leader

Born near Sandersville, Georgia, he left home at 16, married in 1919 and four years later took his family to Detroit, where he worked in a car factory and endured hard times, living on relief from 1929 to 1931. Like his father he was for a time a Baptist preacher, but in 1931 he became an assistant to Wali Farad, the founder of the Nation of Islam (known as the Black Muslims), a sect that favoured black separatism and rejected Christianity as a tool of oppressive whites. Abandoning his 'slave name' in favour of the name of the prophet, Elijah Muhammad embraced Farad's militant doctrines, seeking to win converts and to promote the movement's goal of African-American economic self-sufficiency. He founded the second mosque of the Nation of Islam in Chicago (1934) and organized business enterprises and parochial schools sponsored by the Black Muslims. On Farad's disappearance in 1934, Elijah Muhammad became the leader of the movement, which grew rapidly even during his six-year imprisonment for opposing military conscription in World War II. During the late 1950s and 1960s he was critical of the integrationist agenda and non-violent philosophy of the civil rights movement, but he benefited from the raising of African-American consciousness that accompanied it, and by 1962 there were an estimated 250,000 Black Muslims. A schism occurred in the Nation of Islam when his disciple **Malcolm X** broke away in 1965, and Malcolm's assassination was allegedly carried out by Black Muslims loyal to Elijah Muhammad. When Muhammad himself died in 1975, he was succeeded by his son Wallace D Muhammad (1933–), who moved the Black Muslims closer to orthodox Islam.

Muhammad Ahmed, *known as* al-Mahdi ('Divinely Guided One') 1844–85
Arab ascetic and rebel

Born in Dongola, Sudan, the son of a shipbuilder, he was the creator of an Islamic state and a religious movement (Mahdism). He was educated within a religious order rather than at university, and was for a time in the Egyptian Civil Service and a slave trader before beginning his relentless and successful campaign against Egyptian rule in eastern Sudan. He was motivated by a conviction that, due to their apparent desertion of the Islamic faith, the ruling class were unfit to govern Muslims. Believing himself to have been selected by God to destroy any government responsible for the defilement of Islam, he declared himself 'al-Mahdi' in 1881 and gathered together a group of virtually unarmed disciples as his *ansar* ('helpers'). By 1883 he had proclaimed El Obeid (now al-Ubayyid) his capital and had united the nation's diverse and discontented citizens into an army strong enough to defeat any army Egypt could muster, including the 8,000-strong force commanded by General **William Hicks** (Hicks Pasha). On 26 January 1885, al-Mahdi took Khartoum in the action in which (against al-Mahdi's orders) General **Charles Gordon** was killed. Following these successes he consolidated his religious empire, establishing a new capital at Omdurman, but was taken ill and died a few months later, probably of typhus. The Mahdists were defeated by British forces led by **Horatio Herbert Kitchener** at the Battle of Omdurman (1898).

Muhammed, Shams ed-Dín See Háfiz

Muir, Edwin 1887–1959
Scottish poet

Born in Deerness, Orkney, he migrated with his family to Glasgow at the age of 14, where he suffered the period of drab existence described in *The Story and the Fable* (1940), revised as *An Autobiography* in 1954. He spent much time reading Nietzsche, George Bernard Shaw, Ibsen, Heinrich Heine and Blatchford, and became interested in left-wing politics. When he married the novelist Willa Anderson (Willa Muir) in 1919, they settled in London, then travelled on the Continent (1921–24), where they collaborated in translations of Franz Kafka and Feuchtwanger and he wrote novels, notably *The Marionette* (1927). He spent most of the 1930s in Sussex and St Andrews. He also worked for the British Institute in Prague and Rome, and was appointed warden of Newbattle Abbey, near Edinburgh, in 1950. After a year as Eliot Norton Professor of Poetry at Harvard (1955–56), he retired near Cambridge. His poems appeared in eight slim volumes, including *First Poems* (1925), *The Voyage* (1946) and *The Labyrinth* (1949), and in *Collected Poems* (1952). Muir's critical work includes a controversial study of John Knox and *Scott and Scotland* (1936). A new *Collected Poems* was published in 1991. 📖 W Muir, *Belonging* (1968)

Muir, Frank 1920–98
English writer and broadcaster

Born in Ramsgate, Kent, he was educated at Chatham House, Ramsgate, and Leyton County High School. Following service in the RAF during World War II, he began a fruitful professional partnership with Denis Norden in 1947, which lasted until 1964. Together they wrote the radio comedy series *Take It From Here* (1947–58) and *Whack-O!* (1958–60) in which Jimmy Edwards appeared. He was also a well-known television personality, and his appearances include the long-running game show series *Call My Bluff*. His many publications include the bestselling *Oxford Book of Humorous Prose* (1989), which took 17 years to compile and edit.

Muir, Jean Elizabeth 1928–95
English fashion designer

She was born in London and educated at Dame Harper School, Bedford. She started as a salesgirl with Liberty's in London in 1950, then moved to Jaeger in 1956. In 1961 she started on her own as Jane & Jane. In 1966 she established her own company, Jean Muir. Her clothes are noted for their classic shapes and their softness and fluidity.

Muir, John 1810–82
Scottish Sanskrit scholar

He was born in Glasgow. After spending 25 years in the East India Company's Civil Service in Bengal, he settled in Edinburgh, where he founded a chair of Sanskrit. His great work was his *Original Sanskrit Texts* (5 vols, 1858–70). Another of his books is *Metrical Translations from Sanskrit Writers* (1878).

Muir, John 1838–1914
US naturalist

Born in Dunbar, Scotland, he emigrated to the USA in 1849, and studied at Wisconsin University. He concentrated his interest on natural history, exploring the western USA, especially the Yosemite area. He farmed very successfully in California, and also campaigned for a national park there. It needed a decade of Muir's vigorous oratory and article-writing, and President Theodore Roosevelt's support, before the idea of wildlife conservation became widely accepted. Muir wrote a number of books, including *The Mountains of California* (1894), *Our National Parks* (1901), *My First Summer in the Sierra* (1911) and *The Yosemite* (1912). The John Muir Trust to acquire wild land in Great Britain was established in 1984. He is regarded as the father of the modern environmental movement. 📖 William Frederick Bade, *The Life and Letters of John Muir* (1924)

Muir, Willa, *née* Anderson, *pseudonym* Agnes Neill Scott 1890–1970
Scottish novelist and translator

Born in Montrose, Angus, she studied at St Andrews University, then taught classics and educational psychology in London until she was forced to resign after marrying the 'atheist' Edwin Muir (1919). Travelling often, they lived for short periods in Prague, Rome and the USA. They translated jointly (although often only Edwin was credited), and were influential in popularizing Franz Kafka in the 1930s. Her essay *Women: An Enquiry* (1925) dealt with the demoralizing effects of Scottish smalltown life, a subject she returned to in her novel *Imagined Corners* (1931). *Mrs Grundy in Scotland* (1936) examined the role of women in Scottish culture. She also wrote of her partnership with Edwin Muir in *Belonging* (1968), and finished his project *Living With Ballads* (1965) after his death.

Muirhead, (Litellus) Russell 1896–1976
English editor and traveller

Educated at University College School and Christ's College, Cambridge, he became editor (1930) of the 'Blue Guides' to Europe. His other editorial work included scientific journals and the Penguin guides to England and Wales (1938–49). He was also author of numerous travel books and articles.

Mujibur Rahman, *known as* Sheikh Mujib 1920–75
Bangladesh statesman

Born in Tungipana, into a landowning family, he was educated in Calcutta and Dacca University, from which he was expelled for political activities. He co-founded (1949) the Awami (People's) League, campaigning for autonomy for East Pakistan (Bangladesh), became its leader in 1953, and led it to electoral victory in 1970. In 1972, after the civil war between East and West Pakistan, he became Prime Minister of newly independent Bangladesh. He introduced a socialist economic programme but became increasingly intolerant of opposition, establishing a one-party state. In August 1975 he and his wife were assassinated in a military coup.

Mulcaster, Richard c.1530–1611
English educationist

He was born in Cumberland. A brilliant Greek and Oriental scholar, he was head of Merchant Taylors' School, London, and one of the great Elizabethan schoolmasters, his ideas on education being well in advance of his time. In 1582 he published in *Elementaire* a list of 7,000 words in his proposed reformed spellings (eg 'guest' to be spelled 'gest' and 'guide' to be spelled 'gide'; an accent ˘ to show the short 'a' in, eg 'băbble').

Muldoon, Sir Robert David 1921–92
New Zealand statesman

Born in Auckland, he served as an infantryman in World War II before becoming an accountant. He was first elected to parliament (as a National Party MP) in 1960, and after five years as Minister of Finance became deputy Prime Minister. Though the government was defeated in elections later that year, Muldoon (having become party leader and Leader of the Opposition in 1974) led the National Party to victory in the 1975 elections. He was Prime Minister from 1974 to 1984, when he gave up leadership of the National Party. He resigned from parliament in 1991. 📖 *Muldoon* (1978)

Mulgan, Alan E(dward) 1881–1961
New Zealand writer and journalist

Born in Katikati, he was the author of *Maori and Paheka: A History of New Zealand* (1922, with A W Shrimpton), *The City of the Strait: Wellington and its Province: a Centennial History* (1939), *Literature and Authorship in New Zealand* (1943) and *Great Days in New Zealand Writing* (1962). He also published verse, a novel and a collection of plays, travel and history.
📖 *The Making of a New Zealander* (1958)

Mulgan, John Alan Edward 1911–45
New Zealand writer

The son of the writer **Alan E Mulgan**, he wrote only one novel, the sprawling Hemingwayesque *Man Alone* (1939). Through the struggles of his war-veteran hero, Johnson, in the Depression years, he analyses and criticizes the structure of contemporary New Zealand society. The novel is important in New Zealand literature for spawning other books on the theme of the 'isolated man', alone either by virtue of his nature, race or environment.
📖 *Report on Experience* (1949, posthumous)

Müller, (Karl) Alex(ander) 1927–
Swiss physicist

Born in Basle, he was educated at the Swiss Federal Institute of Technology, Zurich, where he received his PhD in 1958. After five years at the Battelle Institute in Geneva (1958–63) he joined the IBM Zurich Research Laboratory working in the area of solid-state physics. For the discovery of new low-temperature superconductors, Müller shared the 1987 Nobel Prize for physics with **Georg Bednorz** (1950–   ).

Müller or Mueller, Ferdinand Jakob Heinrich von, Freiherr 1825–96
Australian explorer and botanist

Born in Rostock, Germany, he emigrated to Australia in 1847, was appointed government botanist for the state of Victoria in 1853, and in the next few years built up a valuable collection of native flora. From 1857 to 1873 he was director of Melbourne Botanic Gardens, where a separate library and herbarium was set up for him. He explored Western Australia and Tasmania, promoted expeditions into New Guinea, and was a member of the first Australian Antarctic Exploration committee. He also sponsored a fund organized by Melbourne ladies for an expedition in search of the lost explorer **Ludwig Leichhardt**, and organized the 1875 trip into the central desert by **Ernest Giles**. He was responsible for the introduction of the blue gum tree (*Eucalyptus* species) into Europe, and published many scientific works on the plants of Australia.

Müller, Franz Joseph, Baron von Reichenstein 1740–1825
Austrian chemist and mineralogist

Born in Nagyszeben, Transylvania (now in Romania), he studied law in Vienna and metallurgy at Schemnitz, Hungary. He worked in the state-owned salt works in Transylvania, becoming the director of state mines in the Tirol from 1775 to 1778 and director of all mining in Transylvania from 1778 to 1802. During 1802–18 he headed the committee which controlled minting and mining in the Austro-Hungarian Empire and he was created a baron on his retirement. In 1784 he identified an impurity in a gold-bearing ore as a new element and described its semi-metallic properties. These findings were later confirmed by **Martin Heinrich Klaproth**, who named the element tellurium.

Müller, Gerd Birthdate unavailable
German footballer

He is the highest-scoring player in World Cup finals. He scored 14 goals for West Germany between 1966 and 1974, and scored against every country West Germany met in the competition. He scored twice in the 1972 final and secured the World Cup title for West Germany in 1974

with his goal against Holland. He also helped West Germany to be the first country to reach five World Cup finals by 1986. At club level he played for Bayern Munich.

Müller, Hermann Joseph 1890–1967
US geneticist and Nobel Prize winner

Born in New York City, he studied at Columbia University and spent the 1920s at the University of Texas at Austin, where he was appointed Professor of Zoology. In 1933 he moved to Leningrad (St Petersburg) to work at the Institute of Genetics there, joined a medical unit in Spain during the Spanish Civil War, and after a period at the Institute of Animal Genetics of the University of Edinburgh, he finally returned to the USA in 1940. From 1945 to 1967 he was Professor of Zoology at the University of Indiana. His major work was on the use of X-rays to cause genetic mutations, for which he was awarded the Nobel Prize for physiology or medicine in 1946. Concerned about the possible dangers of radiation-induced mutations, he campaigned for safety measures in hospitals and against the nuclear bomb tests.

Müller, Johannes Peter 1801–58
German physiologist

Born in Koblenz, he studied at Bonn University, was appointed to the chair of physiology there in 1826, and in 1833 moved to Berlin University. He won fame for his precocious researches in embryology, and also showed early interest in the eye and vision. His later work was wide-ranging, covering electrophysiology, the glandular system, the human embryo and the nervous system. He worked on zoological classification, dealing especially with marine creatures. In 1840 he proposed the law of specific nerve energies, that is, the claim that each sensory system will respond in the same way to a stimulus whether this is mechanical, chemical, thermal or electrical. Müller's *Handbuch der Physiologie des Menschen* (1833–40) was extremely influential, and he himself was probably the most significant life scientist and medical theorist in Germany in the first half of the 19th century.

Muller, Mary 1820–1902
New Zealand feminist

She was born in Britain, but little is known of her early life. Following the death of her first husband, a man named Griffiths, she went to New Zealand at the age of 30. She soon married S L Muller, whose disapproval of her feminist views led to her secretly publishing these anonymously through a local newspaper. Her feminist tract *An Appeal to the Men of New Zealand* won her international acclaim, and she was instrumental in having a women's property act passed in 1884, and in achieving female suffrage in her adopted homeland 10 years later.

Müller, (Friedrich) Max 1823–1900
British philologist and Orientalist

Born in Dessau, Germany, where his father, the poet Wilhelm Müller (1794–1827), was ducal librarian, he studied at Dessau, Leipzig and Berlin, taking the then novel subject of Sanskrit and its kindred sciences of philology and religion. In Paris, under Eugène Burnouf, he began to prepare an edition of the *Rig-Véda*, the sacred hymns of the Hindus. He went to England in 1846 to examine the manuscripts, and the East India Company commissioned him (1847) to edit and publish it at their expense (1849–74). He was appointed Taylorian Professor of Modern Languages at Oxford (1854) and Professor of Comparative Philology (1868 onwards), a study he did more than anyone else to promote in Great Britain. Among his most popular works were *Lectures on the Science of Language* (1861–64), *Auld Lang Syne* (1898), and *My Indian Friends* (1898), and he edited the *Sacred Books of the East* (51 vols, 1879–1910).

Müller, Otto Frederick 1730–84
Danish biologist
Born in Copenhagen, he was the first to describe diatoms (a class of unicellular algae) and bring to notice the animal kingdom of *Infusoria*. He was the inventor of the naturalist's dredge.

Müller, Paul Hermann 1899–1965
Swiss chemist and Nobel Prize winner
He was born in Olten and educated at the University of Basle. From 1925 onwards he worked at the experimental laboratory of the J R Geigy company, where he later became deputy head of pest control. He is known for his work on insecticides, particularly for discovering and developing DDT (dichlorodiphenyltrichloroethane) which was first marketed in 1942. DDT is extremely toxic to a wide variety of disease carriers and plant pests, and was used in tropical areas during World War II and after the war in many parts of the world. However, in the 1960s it became clear that many species quickly became resistant to it, and that its cumulative effects in the food chain are very destructive, so its use was discontinued. For the discovery of DDT, Müller was awarded the 1948 Nobel Prize for physiology or medicine.

Mulligan, Gerry (Gerald Joseph) 1927–96
US jazz saxophonist, bandleader and composer
Born in New York City, he grew up in Philadelphia, and learned piano as a child before specializing in the baritone saxophone. He began his career in jazz as an arranger for big bands. He moved to New York, and became involved in the **Miles Davis** sessions later known as *The Birth of the Cool* (1948–50). Moving to Los Angeles, he led a series of very popular small groups without the customary piano or guitar from 1952, in the cool west-coast style. His Concert Jazz Band transferred his ideas to a larger soundscape from 1960. He played with **Dave Brubeck** for a time (1968–1972), and continued to lead bands of various sizes into the 1990s. 🕮 J Klinkowitz, *Listen: An Aural Narrative in Jazz* (1986)

Mulliken, Robert Sanderson 1896–1986
US chemical physicist and Nobel Prize winner
Born in Newburyport, Massachusetts, he was educated at Massachusetts Institute of Technology and at the University of Chicago, where he took a PhD in chemistry in 1921. After holding a fellowship at Chicago and later at Harvard between 1921 and 1925, he became assistant Professor of Physics at Washington Square College of New York University (1926–28) and then joined the faculty of the University of Chicago, rising to full professor by 1937. From 1961 he was Distinguished Professor of Physics and Chemistry. During World War II he worked on the development of the atomic bomb. His earliest work was on the isotope effect in the band spectra of diatomic molecules, but he is best known for his share in the creation of molecular orbital theory in the 1930s. Mulliken also made important contributions to the development of the concept of hyperconjugation and a scale of electronegativity of the elements, and studied donor–acceptor interactions and charge transfer spectra. He became an Honorary Fellow of the Chemical Society in 1956 and was awarded the Nobel Prize for chemistry in 1966.

Mullis, Kary Banks 1944–
US biochemist and Nobel Prize winner
Born in Lenoir, North Carolina, he was educated at Georgia Institute of Technology and the University of California. In the early 1980s, while working for Cetus Corporation in California, he discovered a technique known as the 'polymerase chain reaction' (PCR), which allows tiny quantities of DNA to be copied millions of times to make analysis practical. It is now used in a multitude of applications, including tests for the HIV virus and the bacteria which cause tuberculosis, forensic science and evolutionary studies of the genetic material in fossils. For this work Mullis was awarded the 1993 Nobel Prize for chemistry (with **Michael Smith**). Since 1988 he has been an independent consultant for various laboratories.

Mulready, William 1786–1863
Irish painter
Born in Ennis, Country Clare, he studied at the Royal Academy, painting such subjects as *A Roadside Inn*, *Barber's Shop*, and *Boys Fishing* (1813). He also worked at portrait painting and book illustration, and designed the first penny postage envelope.

Mulroney, (Martin) Brian 1939–
Canadian statesman
Born in Baie Comeau, Quebec province, the son of an Irish immigrant, he attended St Francis Xavier University in Nova Scotia and studied law at Laval University, Quebec City. He practised as a labour lawyer in Montreal while becoming increasingly active in the Progressive Conservative Party. In 1976 he lost a party leadership contest against Joe Clark and returned to business as president of a US-owned iron ore company. In 1983 he replaced Clark and in 1984 became Prime Minister, with a landslide victory over the Liberals. He initiated a number of radical measures, including the Meech Lake Accords, which aimed at settling disputes between the provinces and the centre, but which later collapsed. He was decisively re-elected in 1988, and his efforts to bring about the free trade agreement with the USA were crowned with success in 1993. In the same year Mulroney resigned from office, returning to Montreal to practise law. He published *Where I Stand* in 1983.

Multatuli See Dekker, Eduard Douwes

Mumford, Lewis 1895–1990
US author, editor and critic
Born in Flushing, New York, he grew up in New York City and studied at several universities there, devoting much time to exploring the city and developing the fascination with urban society and architecture that was to characterize much of his work. *The Culture of Cities* (1938) and *The City in History* (1961) are perhaps the best known of his numerous writings, but the earlier *Technics and Civilisation* (1934) was also influential. In studying civilizations, his object was always to determine how they reflected the values of the societies that created them, and he argued eloquently against the domination of modern urban environments by technology. His works include *The Story of Utopias* (1922), *The Human Prospect* (1955), *The Myth of the Machine* (1967) and *The Pentagon of Power* (1971). 🕮 *My Works and Days: A Personal Chronicle* (1979).

Munch, Edvard 1863–1944
Norwegian painter
Born in Löten, he studied in Oslo, travelled in Europe and finally settled in Norway in 1908. In Paris he came under the influence of **Paul Gauguin**. He began working in a distinctly Expressionist style around the turn of the century and his work was widely disseminated in periodicals. His use of primary colours and tortuously curved designs were a great influence on German Expressionists in particular. He became obsessed by subjects such as death and love, and his mature paintings are really non-representative but evocative of these themes. His most characteristic work is *The Scream* (1913), depicting an anonymous figure on a bridge screaming, the swirling lines of colour contributing to the mood of desperation. Other works include many self-portraits (eg *Between the Clock and the Bed*, Oslo, 1940) and various woodcuts and engravings. Munch's work is represented in most major collections, and there is a Munch museum in Oslo.

Münchhausen, Karl Friedrich Hieronymus, Baron von 1720–97
German soldier

Born in Bodenwerder, he was a member of an ancient Hanoverian house. He was the narrator of ridiculously exaggerated exploits, and served in Russian campaigns against the Turks. A collection of stories attributed to him was first published in English as *Baron Munchausen's Narrative of his Marvellous Travels and Campaigns in Russia* (1785) by Rudolf Erich Raspe. *Munchausen* is based partly on 16th-century German jokes, partly as a satire on James Bruce and other travellers.

Munefusa, Matsuo See Basho, Matsuo

Mungo, St See Kentigern, St

Munk, Kaj, *originally* Kaj Harald Leininger Petersen 1898–1944
Danish playwright, priest and patriot

Born in Maribo, Laaland, he studied theology at Copenhagen University, and as priest of a small parish in Jutland wrote heroic and religious plays that led the Danish dramatic revival in the 1930s. His first play was *En Idealist* (1928, Eng trans *Herod the King*, 1953), followed by *Cant* (1931), *Henrik VIII* (1931, 'Henry VIII'), *Ordet* (1932, Eng trans *The Word*, 1955) and *Han sidder ved smeltedigien* (1938, Eng trans *He Sits by the Melting-Pot*, 1944). Though he had initially admired Mussolini and Hitler, their aggressive expansionism and repressive methods changed his views, and during World War II he was one of the spiritual leaders of the Danish Resistance. In 1942 he wrote a patriotic drama, *Niels Ebbeson*. Early in 1944 he was taken from his home by the Gestapo one night and found murdered in a ditch near Silkeborg next morning. 📖 B N Broust, *Kaj Munk—liv og død* (1984)

Munk, Walter Heinrich 1917–
US physical oceanographer and geophysicist

Born in Vienna, Austria, he travelled to the USA in 1932 and was educated at the California Institute of Technology and the University of California, where he studied oceanography. At Scripps Institution of Oceanography he was appointed assistant professor of geophysics (1947–49), associate professor (1954–59), and professor from 1954. He was also associate director of their Institute of Geophysics and Planetary Physics (1959–82). During World War II his tidal predictions were used in the allied landings in North Africa and in the Pacific, and probably saved many lives. He determined that a July day is two milliseconds shorter than a January day (1961), which he attributed to seasonal shifts in terrestrial air masses, ocean tides, the distribution of glaciers and changes within the Earth's core. He initiated the 'Mohole' deep drill project, and developed ocean acoustic tomography (three-dimensional modelling of the ocean temperature field), which is currently being applied in tests for global warming.

Munkácsy, Mihály von, *originally* Leó Lieb 1846–1900
Hungarian painter

Born in Munkács, he settled in Paris in 1872. His best-known pictures include *Christ before Pilate* (1881) and *Death of Mozart* (1884).

Munnings, Sir Alfred 1878–1959
English painter

Born in Suffolk, a specialist in the painting of horses and sporting pictures, he became president of the Royal Academy (1944–49). His work is in many public galleries and he was well known for his forthright criticism of modern art. 📖 Jean Goodman, *What a Go! The Life of Alfred Munnings* (1988)

Muñoz Marín, Luis 1898–1980
Puerto Rican statesman

Born in San Juan, Puerto Rico, the son of Puerto Rican nationalist Luis Muñoz Rivera, he spent much of his youth in Washington DC. After studying at Georgetown University and Georgetown Law School, he went to New York City, where he contributed political commentary to the *Nation* and other journals. At this time he was a socialist and an advocate of Puerto Rican independence, though he later came to believe that complete independence from the USA would be an economic disaster for his homeland. He returned to San Juan in 1926 and became editor of his father's newspaper, *La Democracia*, and from 1932 to 1936 he served in the Puerto Rican senate as a member of the Liberal Party, using his New Deal contacts to get millions of dollars in government aid for the impoverished island. Conflicts with the Liberal Party prompted him to found the Popular Democratic Party in 1938, and he served in the senate again from 1940 to 1948, originating an economic development strategy known as Operation Bootstrap, which was intended to attract US mainland investors and diversify the Puerto Rican economy. Appointed Puerto Rico's first native-born Governor by President Harry S Truman in 1947, he became the island's first elected Governor the following year and was re-elected three times before finally stepping down in 1964. His achievements included land redistribution of tens of thousands of acres and the establishment of commonwealth status for Puerto Rico in 1952.

Muñoz Rivera, Luis 1859–1916
Puerto Rican journalist and nationalist

Born in Barranquitas, Puerto Rico, he founded the newspaper *La Democracia* to campaign for Puerto Rican independence, and he helped win the Spanish charter for home rule (1897). He served as President of the first Puerto Rican cabinet but resigned in 1899, when the USA ended his country's short-lived autonomy. From 1910 to 1916 he was resident commissioner for Puerto Rico in Washington DC. Considered the father of Puerto Rican nationalism, he was instrumental in gaining US citizenship for Puerto Ricans under the Jones Act, which was passed by Congress a few months after his death.

Munro, Alice, *originally* Alice Anne Laidlaw 1931–
Canadian short-story writer and novelist

She was born and brought up in Wingham, Ontario, and attended the University of Western Ontario. She wrote short stories from an early age, waiting until she was 'ready' to write a great novel. Her only novel to date, *Lives of Girls and Women* (1971), accomplished though it is, cannot claim to be that. Her stories, however, published for many years without being collected, are recognized as among the finest of the day. They are often set in rural and semi-rural Ontario, the landscape of her childhood, or feature women who have escaped from such backgrounds. Her many collections of stories include *Dance of the Happy Shades* (1968), which won the Governor General's award for fiction, *Something I've Been Meaning to Tell You* (1974), *The Progress of Love* (1987) and *Selected Stories* (1996). 📖 'The Colonel's Hash Resettled', in J Metcalf, *The Narrative Voice* (1972)

Munro, Hector Hugh, *pseudonym* Saki 1870–1916
British novelist and short-story writer

He was born in Burma, the son of a police inspector. Educated in England at Bedford Grammar School, he returned to Burma and joined the police force in 1893, but went to London in 1896 and took up writing for the *Westminster Gazette*. From 1902 he was the Balkans correspondent for the *Morning Post*. He settled in London again in 1908. He is best known for his short stories, humorous and macabre, which are highly individual, and full of eccentric wit and unconventional situations. Collections of his stories are *Reginald* (1904), *The Chronicles of Clovis* (1911) and *Beasts and Superbeasts* (1914). His novels *The Unbearable Bassington* (1912) and *When William Came* (1913) show his gifts as a social satirist of the upper-class Edwardian world. He was killed on the Western Front during World War I.

Munro, Sir Hugh Thomas 1856–1919
Scottish mountaineer

Born in London, he inherited the family estate near Kirriemuir. Although a fanatically keen traveller, he is remembered for his contribution to mountaineering. A founding member of the Scottish Mountaineering Club in 1889, he served as its president from 1894 to 1897. He compiled the first authoritative list of what have come to be known as 'Munros' when he published his *Tables of Heights over 3000 Feet* in the first issue of the *SMC Journal* in 1891. While 'Munro-bagging' has become a commonplace pastime, Munro himself never achieved the distinction of climbing all the peaks he listed, remaining two short at his death.

Munro, Neil 1864–1930
Scottish novelist and journalist

Born in Inveraray, Argyll, he worked in a law office before taking up journalism in Glasgow, where he became editor of the *Glasgow Evening News* (1918–27). He wrote romantic Celtic tales such as *The Lost Pibroch* (1896) and *Gilian the Dreamer* (1899), and historical Highland novels, *John Splendid* (1898), *Doom Castle* (1901) and *The New Road* (1914). However, he is best known for his humorous tales about a Clyde puffer, published as *The Vital Spark* (1906) and collected as *Para Handy and Other Tales* (1931). His memoir, *Brave Days*, was published posthumously in 1931. 📖 G Blake, introduction to *The Brave Days* (1931)

Münter, Gabriele 1877–1962
German Expressionist painter

Born in Berlin, she studied at the Women's Academy in Düsseldorf (1897), before travelling across the USA for three years. On her return, she attended classes under **Wassily Kandinsky** at his Phalanx School in Munich and travelled with him throughout Europe (1903–08). Whilst in France she became influenced by Fauvism and the work of **Paul Gauguin**. She and Kandinsky settled in Murnau where she worked closely with two Russian artists, Von Werefkin and **Alexei von Jawlensky**. Her relationship with Kandinsky ended in 1916 but she returned to painting in the late 1920s, and from 1945 until her death she promoted the work of the *Blaue Reiter* (Blue Rider) group.

Müntzer or Münzer, Thomas c.1488–1525
German religious reformer and Anabaptist

Born in Stolberg, he studied theology, and in 1520 began to preach at Zwickau. As he travelled more widely, his socialism and mystical doctrines led to conflict with the authorities. In 1525 he was elected pastor of the Anabaptists of Mülhausen, where his communist ideas soon aroused the whole country. He joined the Peasants' Revolt of 1524–25, but was defeated at Frankenhausen, and executed. 📖 Eric W Gritsch, *Reformer Without a Church: The Life and Thought of Thomas Muentzer, 1488?–1525* (1967)

Muqaddasi 945–88
Arab geographer, and pioneer of fieldwork

Born in Jerusalem, he travelled widely and described Moslem lands in a geographical compendium (985).

Murad IV 1612–40
Ottoman sultan

Born in Constantinople (Istanbul), he succeeded in 1623 on the deposition of his father, Mustafa I, when the state was in political and financial anarchy. A savage disciplinarian, he crushed a serious revolt among the janissaries (1632), and eliminated corruption in administration and justice. In 1638 he led an expedition against Persia (Iran), recapturing Baghdad, which had been taken by **Abbas I, the Great**, in 1624.

Murakami Haruki 1949–
Japanese novelist

He was born in Kobe and educated in classics at Waseda University. He started his career in writing by translating the works of modern US writers (**Raymond Chandler** and **Truman Capote**) into Japanese, and his own highly original novels are remarkable for being more influenced by the Americans than by his Japanese predecessors. Wild, surreal, mystical and often extremely funny, he is a best-selling author in Japan. Of his works available in English, *A Wild Sheep Chase* (1982) is one of the best, and is a sort of detective novel in which a psychic detective searches for a war criminal, a woman with beautiful ears, and a supernatural sheep with a star on its back. He published a trilogy entitled *Nejimaki-dori kuronikura* ('The Chronicle of the "Screw-turning" Bird') in 1995.

Murasaki Shikibu c.970–c.1015
Japanese writer

She was a member of the Fujiwara family, one of the most powerful aristocratic dynasties in Japan, but her real name is unknown: 'Shikibu Murasaki' is a later fictive construction. She was responsible for the *Genji Monogatari* (Eng trans *The Tale of Genji*, 1925–35), the first great work in Japanese. Complex, delicate and often sublimely beautiful, it far outclasses anything produced elsewhere in its day. 📖 I I Morris, *The World of the Shining Prince* (1964)

Murat, Joachim 1767–1815
French soldier and King of Naples

He was born at La Bastide-Murat, Lot, the son of an innkeeper. He enlisted in the cavalry on the eve of the Revolution, and was promoted general during **Napoleon I**'s Egyptian campaign (1799). He helped Napoleon become First Consul, married his sister, and replaced his brother, **Joseph Bonaparte**, as King of Naples (1808). There he dismantled the huge landed estates, suppressed brigandage and encouraged cotton-growing. He commanded Napoleon's cavalry during the 1812 invasion of Russia, but resigned his commission (1812) to try and rescue Naples. He supported Napoleon after his defeat (1813) but, defeated by the Austrians at Tolentino (1815), he was eventually captured and executed by the troops of **Ferdinand I**. 📖 A Hilliard Atteridge, *Joachim Murat, Marshal of France and King of Naples* (1911)

Murchison, Sir Roderick Impey 1792–1871
Scottish geologist

Born in Tarradale, Ross-shire, he devoted himself to geology after leaving the army in 1816. He established the Silurian system (1835) and, with **Adam Sedgwick**, the Devonian system. From 1840 to 1845, with others, he carried out a geological survey of the Russian empire. Struck with the resemblance between the Ural mountains and Australian chains, he foreshadowed the discovery of gold in Australia (1844). Murchison Falls (Uganda) and Murchison River (Western Australia) are named after him. In 1855 he was made director-general of the Geological Survey and director of the Royal School of Mines. His principal works were *The Silurian System* (1839) and *The Geology of Russia in Europe and the Urals* (1845).

Murdoch, Dame Iris See panel p1335

Murdoch, (Keith) Rupert 1931–
US newspaper publisher

Murdoch, Dame (Jean) Iris 1919–99
Irish novelist, playwright and philosopher

Iris Murdoch was born in Dublin of Anglo-Irish parents. She was educated at Badminton School, Bristol, and Oxford, where she was Fellow and tutor in philosophy at St Anne's College (1948–63). She married the literary critic John Bayley in 1956, and was made a DBE in 1987.

She published a study of **Jean-Paul Sartre** (who was, like her, both a novelist and a philosopher) in 1953 and two important but unfashionable philosophical works, much influenced by **Plato**, *The Fire and the Sun* (1977) and *The Sovereignty of the Good* (1970). These deal with the relationships between art and philosophy, and between love, freedom, knowledge and morality. A later philosophical work is *Metaphysics as a Guide to Morals* (1992).

Her fiction, which was at first a secondary activity, is mostly concerned with the preoccupations of middle-class intellectuals and deals with the conflict of good and evil in the context of involved personal relationships, often attended by strange situations and incidents. The popularity of her work derives largely from her narrative skill in controlling tangled and shifting patterns of relationships, the ironic or even startling circumstances in which the characters find themselves, and the pervasive blend of realism and symbolism. One of the finest writers of her generation, she spent her final years suffering from Alzheimer's disease.

⌑ Her first novel, *Under the Net*, framed round a male narrator, appeared in 1954, and was followed by a further 26 titles in the next 45 years, including *The Sandcastle* (1957), about a schoolmaster's relationship with a young artist; *The Bell* (1958), about the consecration of a bell by a lay community; *A Severed Head* (1961), a black comedy; *An Unofficial Rose* (1962); *The Red and the Green* (1965); *The Nice and the Good* (1968); *The Black Prince* (1973); *The Sea, The Sea* (1978), about an obsession with a childhood sweetheart, which won the Booker Prize; *Nuns and Soldiers* (1980); *The Good Apprentice* (1985); *The Book and the Brotherhood* (1987), about a group of Oxford intellectuals; *The Message to the Planet* (1989); and *The Green Knight* (1993).

She also wrote several plays, including *A Severed Head* (adapted with **J B Priestley** from her novel in 1963); *Servants and the Snow* (1970); *The Two Arrows* (1972); and *Art and Eros* (1980); and a book of poetry, *The Year of the Birds* (1978).

⌑ D Johnson, *Iris Murdoch* (1987); A S Byatt, *Degrees of Freedom* (1965).

> 'All our failures are ultimately failures in love.' From *The Bell*.

He was born in Melbourne, Australia, and educated at Geelong Grammar School and Oxford, where he was active in Labour politics. His grandfather was a prominent Presbyterian minister in Scotland, and his father a celebrated World War I correspondent who later became chief executive of the Melbourne Herald newspaper group. When his father died in 1952 he inherited the Adelaide *News* and, employing shrewdly the experience gained at the *Daily Express* in London, he soon made it a success. He became in the space of a decade Australia's second largest publisher and began to set his sights on expansion abroad. First he acquired the *News of the World* in London in 1969, which at the height of the **Profumo** scandal had a circulation of six million. Then, at the end of the same year, he bought the *Sun*. Denounced for its puerile taste, including the introduction of daily 'page 3' girls, the *Sun* defied its critics and maintained its lead in the circulation war. In 1981 he struck at the heart of the English Establishment when his company, News International, acquired *The Times* and *The Sunday Times* after a bitter struggle. In 1989 he bought the book publishers Collins and inaugurated Sky Television (now BSkyB), a satellite television network. He moved into the US market in 1976 with the purchase of the New York *Post*, and then acquired numerous other US publications, including the Village Voice, New York magazine and TV Guide, as well as 20th Century Fox film studios. He created a successful television network, the Fox Network, and in 1996 bought New World Communications, becoming the owner of television stations that reached up to 40 per cent of US viewership. He has been a US citizen since 1985.
⌑ J Tucille, *Rupert Murdoch* (1989)

Murdock, George Peter 1897–1985
US cultural anthropologist

Born in Meriden, Connecticut, he studied history at Yale and taught there (1928–60), and was Mellon Professor of Anthropology at Pittsburgh University (1960–71). He initiated the cross-cultural survey, later known as the 'human relations area files', as an instrument of sociological and anthropological generalization. His best-known work is *Social Structure* (1949), which focuses on family and kinship organization, seeking sets of functionally interrelated traits in a wide range of societies.

Murdock, William 1754–1839
Scottish engineer

Born in Lugar, Ayrshire, he worked with his father, a millwright, and then with **Matthew Boulton** and **James Watt** of Birmingham, by whom he was sent to Cornwall to erect mining engines. At Redruth he constructed the model of a high-pressure engine to run on wheels (1784), introduced labour-saving machinery, a new method of wheel rotation, an oscillating engine (1785), and a steam-gun. He also improved Watt's engine. He was a pioneer of coal gas for lighting and his distillation of coal gas began at Redruth in 1792, when he illuminated his own home with it. Successful experiments were made at Neath Abbey in 1796, but it was not until 1803 that Boulton's engineering works at Soho were lighted with gas.

Mure, Sir William 1594–1657
Scottish poet

Born in Rowallan, Ayrshire, he was a staunch Protestant and Royalist. He was wounded at Marston Moor (1644), but later led his regiment at Newcastle (1644). He wrote a long religious poem, *The True Crucifixe for True Catholikes* (1629), a version of the Psalms (1639), and some love and courtly poems. *The Cry of Blood and of a Broken Covenant* (1650) is a poem on behalf of the Covenanters' cause. He also translated parts of **Virgil**'s *Aeneid*.

Murger, Henri 1822–61
French writer

Born in Paris, he began life as a notary's clerk, and, devoting his time to literature, led the life of privation and adventure described in his first and best novel, *Scènes de la vie de Bohème* (1845, Eng trans *The Bohemians of the Latin Quarter*, 1887), the basis of **Puccini**'s opera, *La Bohème*. During his later years he led a dissipated life and wrote slowly and fitfully. His other prose works include *La Vie de jeunesse* (1861, 'The Youthful Life') and *Le Pays Latin* (1861, 'Latin Country'). His poems, *Les Nuits d'hiver* (1862, Eng trans *Winter Nights*, 1923), are graceful and often deeply pathetic, and several were translated by **Andrew Lang** in his *Lays of old France*. ⌑ R Baldick, *The First Bohemian* (1961)

Murillo, Bartolomé Esteban 1618–82
Spanish painter

He was born in Seville and spent most of his life there. He painted 11 remarkable pictures for the convent of San Francisco in 1645, which made his name. In 1660 he founded the Academy of Seville, of which he became first president. He frequently chose the Immaculate Conception or the Assumption of the Virgin as a subject, and treated them much alike. In 1681 he fell from a scaffold when painting an altarpiece at Cadiz, and died soon afterwards. His pictures naturally fall into two groups—scenes from low life, such as gypsies and beggar children (mostly executed early in his life), and religious works.

Murnau, F W, originally Friedrich Wilhelm Plumpe
1888–1931
German film director
Born in Bielefeld, Germany, he studied philology in Berlin, and art history and literature at Heidelberg, and was briefly an actor with **Max Reinhardt's** theatre troupe before World War I. A combat pilot, he crash-landed in Switzerland during 1917. Returning to Germany two years later, he founded the Murnau Veidt Filmgesellschaft and made his directorial debut with *Der Knabe in Blau* (1919, 'The Boy in Blue'). Experimenting with the mobility of the camera, his expressive use of light and shade heightened the menace in such macabre works as *Der Januskopf* (1920, *Janus-Faced*, a version of *Dr Jekyll and Mr Hyde*), and *Nosferatu* (1922, a chilling and faithful rendition of the Dracula story). After a successful trio of films with actor **Emil Jannings**, including *Der Letzte Mann* (1924, *The Last Laugh*), he moved to the USA and made *Sunrise* (1927), a tale of a young rural couple whose love is threatened by the sophistication of the big city, which won three of the first-ever Academy Awards. He had just completed the much-praised South Seas documentary *Tabu* (1931) before his death in a car crash.

Murphy, Arthur 1727–1805
Irish actor and playwright
Born in Clomquin, Roscommon, he was educated at St Omer, and from 1747 to 1751 worked as a clerk in Cork and then London. From 1752 to 1774 he published the weekly *Gray's Inn Journal*, through which he met Dr **Johnson**. Murphy turned to the stage to pay off his debts, and in 1758 produced *The Upholsterer*, a successful farce. The previous year he had entered Lincoln's Inn, and in 1762 he was called to the Bar, but he continued to write farces and adaptations for the stage. His translation of **Tacitus** (1793) is excellent, unlike his *Essay on Johnson* (1792) and *Life of David Garrick* (2 vols, 1801). 📖 J P Murphy, *Arthur Murphy* (1946)

Murphy, Dervla 1931–
Irish travel writer
Born in Cappoquin, County Waterford, she attended the Ursuline Convent, Waterford, but left school early to look after her invalid mother. Reading avidly, after her mother's death (1962) she cycled to India to work with Tibetan refugees. Her first two books, *Full Tilt* (1965) and *Tibetan Foothold* (1966), financed further journeys to Nepal and Ethiopia. With her daughter Rachel (1968–) she subsequently made several long journeys in southern India, trekking through the Karakoram Mountains and 1,300 miles along the Andes. She has won several literary awards and has also written books on subjects closer to home, including Northern Ireland, racial conflict and the nuclear controversy.

Murphy, Eddie (Edward Regan) 1961–
US comedian and film actor
Born in the Bushwick section of Brooklyn, New York City, he became a stand-up nightclub comic in Long Island. He first came to national prominence on the television show *Saturday Night Live* (1980–84). His debut in the film *48 Hrs* (1982) was followed by several box-office

hits including *Trading Places* (1983) and *Beverly Hills Cop* (1984). Subsequent films include *Coming to America* (1988), *Harlem Nights* (1989), which he also directed, *Boomerang* (1992) and *The Nutty Professor* (1996). His popular recordings include *Eddie Murphy Comedian* (1982) and *How Could it Be?* (1984).

Murphy, Emily Gowan, *pseudonym of* Janey Canuck, *née* Ferguson 1868–1933
Canadian journalist and feminist
Born in Cookstown, Ontario, she was educated at Bishop Strachan School, Toronto. On moving to Edmonton, Alberta, in 1907, she became involved in the women's movement and campaigned with Nellie McClung for legal reform which would entitle a wife to one third of her husband's property (The Dower Act, 1911). In 1916 she became the first woman in the British Empire to be appointed magistrate but this was opposed on the grounds that she was a woman. She was the president of the Canadian Women's Press Club (1913–20) and was literary editor of *The Winnipeg Telegram* and *Edmonton Journal*. She published many books, including *The Impressions of Janey Canuck Abroad* (1902), *Open Trails* (1912) and *Black Candle* (1922).

Murphy, Graeme Lloyd 1950–
Australian dancer, choreographer and ballet director
Born in Melbourne, he trained at the Australian Ballet School, the youngest boy ever to enter, and subsequently joined the company. Dance studies in New York were succeeded by six months as a member of Sadler's Wells Royal Ballet. He worked as a freelance choreographer in 1975 before rejoining Australian Ballet as a dancer and resident choreographer. Appointed director of Sydney Dance Company in 1976, he has brought international status to this young contemporary ensemble by creating dances which feature an eclectic range of subjects and styles, all rooted in the classical idiom. Recognized internationally, he choreographed **Benjamin Britten's** *Death in Venice* for the Canadian Ballet in 1984, created *Vast*, an Australian bicentennial performance featuring Australian Dance Theatre, Queensland Ballet, West Australian Ballet and his own troupe in 1988, and toured the Sydney Dance Theatre to Taiwan and Japan in 1996.

Murphy, William Parry 1892–1987
US physician and Nobel Prize winner
He was born in Stoughton, Wisconsin, and educated at the University of Oregon and Harvard Medical School. Although postgraduate training encouraged his interest in clinical research, Murphy entered private practice, working part-time at Harvard with **George Richards Minot** (from 1925) in their investigation of the effect of raw liver in the diets of patients diagnosed as suffering from pernicious anaemia. He was awarded the 1934 Nobel Prize for physiology or medicine jointly with Minot and **George Whipple**, but his research career never flourished. He worked on the standardization of liver extract preparations, but continued in private practice and fell out with Minot over what he interpreted as the latter's lack of support for him.

Murrant, Harry Harbord See Morant, Harry Harbord

Murray, Andrew 1828–1917
South African religious leader and writer
Born in Graaf-Reinet, and educated in Aberdeen and Utrecht, he was ordained a minister in the Scottish Dutch Reformed Church and posted to a vast frontier parish. Later, prompted by a national religious revival that started in his Worcester, Cape Colony, pastorate in 1860, he became an evangelistic preacher, holding meetings throughout South Africa, Europe, and the USA, from 1879. His emphasis on prayer and personal holiness was

expounded in *With Christ in the School of Prayer* (1885), *The Spirit of Christ* (1888), *The Full Blessing of Pentecost* (1907), and numerous other books and pamphlets. He also took a keen interest in the welfare of Africans, opposed both to Afrikaner nationalism and British colonialism.

Murray, Lord George c.1700–1760
Scottish Jacobite soldier

Son of the Duke of Atholl, he took part in the Jacobite risings of 1715 and 1719 and fled to France, but was pardoned in 1726. In 1745 he joined the Young Pretender (Prince **Charles Edward Stuart**), and was one of his generals. He won a victory at Prestonpans (September 1745), and conducted a masterly retreat from Derby. He opposed the decision to fight at Culloden, but commanded the right wing. He resigned the next day, escaped abroad, and died in Holland.

Murray, George Gilbert Aimé 1866–1957
Australian classical scholar and writer

Born in Sydney, he went to England at the age of 11, and was educated at the Merchant Taylors' School and Oxford. He was Professor of Greek at Glasgow (1889–99) and Regius Professor of Greek at Oxford (1908–36). His work as a classical historian and translator of Greek dramatists brought him acclaim as the foremost Greek scholar of his time. His celebrated verse translations of Greek plays, including *The Trojan Women*, *Bacchae*, *Medea* and *Electra*, were performed at London's Court Theatre from 1902. His many works on classics include *History of Ancient Greek Literature* (1897), *The Rise of the Greek Epic* (1907) and *Five Stages of Greek Religion* (1913). He was president of the League of Nations Union (1923–38) and was appointed to the Order of Merit in 1941. His brother, Sir (John) Hubert Plunkett Murray (1861–1940) was Lieutenant-Governor of Australia from 1908 until his death. He was respected by the Papuans, and wrote *Papua, or British New Guinea* (1912) and *The Papua of Today* (1925). 📖 F West, *Gilbert Murray* (1984)

Murray, Sir James Augustus Henry 1837–1915
Scottish philologist and lexicographer

Born in Denholm in the Scottish Borders, he was for many years a schoolmaster at Mill Hill school. His *Dialects of the Southern Counties of Scotland* (1873) established his reputation. The great work of his life, the editing of the Philological Society's *New English Dictionary* (later called the *Oxford English Dictionary*), was begun at Mill Hill (1879), and completed (1928) at Oxford. Murray himself edited about half the work, and he created the organization and the inspiration for completing it. 📖 K M Elisabeth Murray, *Caught in the Web of Words: James A H Murray and the 'Oxford English Dictionary'* (1979)

Murray, Sir John, *known as* Murray of Broughton 1715–77
Scottish Jacobite soldier

He was born in Peeblesshire. Educated at Edinburgh and Leyden, he visited Rome and made contact with the Jacobite court. He was Prince **Charles Edward Stuart**'s secretary during the 1745 Rising, but, captured after Culloden, saved his life by betraying his fellow Jacobites. He succeeded as baronet in 1770.

Murray, John 1741–1815
US theologian

Born in Alton, Hampshire, England, he converted to Universalism in 1759. He went to America in 1770, where he preached the doctrine of universal salvation and became known as the 'father of American Universalism'. In 1779 he became the first pastor of the new Independent Church of Christ in Gloucester, Massachusetts.

Murray, John, *originally* John McMurray 1745–93
Scottish publisher

He was born in Edinburgh and in 1768 bought Sandy's bookselling business in London, and published the *English Review*, Disraeli's *Curiosities of Literature*, and other works. His son, John (1778–1843), carried the business from Fleet Street to Albemarle Street, launched the *Quarterly Review* which first appeared in 1809, and began the 'Family Library' in 1829. His grandson, John Murray the third (1808–92), issued the works of David Livingstone, George Borrow, Charles Darwin, Samuel Smiles, and *Handbooks for Travellers* (begun 1836). His great-grandson, Sir John Murray (1851–1928), absorbed Smith, Elder & Co. in 1917, edited Edward Gibbon's *Autobiography* and Byron's letters, and began the publication of the *Letters of Queen Victoria*, which was completed by his own son, also John (1884–1967).

Murray, Sir John 1841–1914
Canadian marine biologist

Born in Cobourg, Ontario, of Scottish parents, he was educated in Canada and at Edinburgh University. During visits to the Arctic islands on a whaler, he made collections of marine organisms, and was then appointed one of the naturalists to the *Challenger* expedition (1872–76) which explored all of the oceans of the world. He assisted in the editing of the *Challenger Reports*, and was in charge of the important biological collection from the expedition maintained at Edinburgh University. Among his publications are a narrative of the expedition and *The Depths of the Ocean* (1912, with J Hjort). Murray also surveyed the depths of the Scottish freshwater lakes. Knighted in 1898, he is considered one of the founders of oceanography.

Murray, Joseph Edward 1919–
US surgeon

He was born in Milford, Massachusetts, and educated at Harvard Medical School. He then joined the Peter Bent Brigham Hospital in Boston, where he became chief plastic surgeon (1951–86). In 1954 Murray and his colleagues first successfully transplanted a kidney between identical twins, which greatly stimulated the clinical and laboratory studies, and after testing X-rays and drugs in attempts to suppress the immunological reactions, successful transplants between non-identical twin brothers, and later using an unrelated kidney, took place. By 1962 the X-ray and drugs techniques were shown to be successful, and soon kidney transplants became common, with systems established for finding donors. He was also chief plastic surgeon at the Children's Hospital Medical Center in Boston (1972–85) and became Professor of Surgery at Harvard Medical School in 1970. He retired in 1985 and was awarded the 1990 Nobel Prize for physiology or medicine with Donnall Thomas.

Murray (of Epping Forest), Len (Lionel) Murray, Baron 1922–
English trade union leader

Born in Shropshire, he studied at London University but his studies were interrupted by World War II and completed at New College, Oxford, in 1947 when he joined the staff of the Trades Union Congress (TUC). He progressed from the economic department to become Assistant General Secretary (1969–73) and then General Secretary (1973–84). He played a major role in the 'social contract' partnership between the TUC and the Labour governments of Harold Wilson and James Callaghan (1974–78), but, from 1979, had an unhappy relationship with the new Conservative administration of Margaret Thatcher. He was made a life peer in 1985.

Murray, Les(lie Allan) 1938–
Australian poet, critic and editor

Born in Nabiac, New South Wales, he grew up on a dairy farm, then attended Sydney University, but left without graduating. He has worked as a translator and a freelance writer and his poetry, which has made him one of Australia's leading literary figures, is revered for its perceptive evocation of rural life. His verse includes *The Ilex Tree* (1965, with Geoffrey Lehmann), *The Weatherboard Cathedral* (1969), *Poems Against Economics* (1972), a verse-novel in 140 sonnets called the *Boys Who Stole the Funeral* (1980), and *The People's Otherworld* (1983), which won the 1984 Australian Literary Society's Gold Medal. His *Selected Poems: the Vernacular Republic* was published in 1976 and revised as *The Vernacular Republic: Poems 1961–1981* (1982). In 1993 he received his fifth National Book Council poetry prize for *Translations from the Natural World* (1992). His later verse includes *The Middle Sea: Book 1 of a Verse Novel in Progress*, published in the *Sydney Review* (1993), and *Subhuman Redneck Poems* (1996), which won Murray the T S Eliot prize for poetry in 1997. He compiled and edited the *New Oxford Book of Australian Verse* (1986). ⊞ P Nelson, *Study Notes on the Poetry of Les A Murray* (1978)

Murray, Lindley 1745–1826
US grammarian

Born in Swatara Creek, Pennsylvania, he practised law, made a fortune in New York during the American Revolution and then, for health reasons, retired to England in 1784 and bought an estate near York. His *English Grammar* (1795) was for long the standard text, and was followed by *English Exercises*, the *English Reader*, and various religious works.

Murray, Matthew 1765–1826
English inventor and mechanical engineer

Born near Newcastle upon Tyne, he was apprenticed to a blacksmith at the age of 14, and in 1788 moved to Leeds as a qualified mechanic. He devised and patented several improvements in flax-spinning machinery before establishing his own engineering works in 1795, where he manufactured textile machinery and also steam engines of his own design. When James Watt's master patent expired in 1800, Murray was one of the first to make significant improvements to the steam engine, his designs being smaller, lighter, more efficient and easier to assemble. His success and the rapid expansion of his firm led to an intense rivalry with the firm of Boulton & Watt. There is no doubt that he was a more versatile engineer than Watt himself, making use of the new powers of steam in locomotives and ships as well as stationary engines.

Murray, William Staite 1881–1962
English potter

He worked for 10 years on a bulb plantation in Holland, but returned to England in 1908. He studied pottery at Camberwell School of Art and began working as a potter at Yeoman's Row, South Kensington, in 1919. He worked at Brockley in Kent and Bray in Berkshire, and then taught at the Royal College of Art, where he became head of the Pottery School in 1926. He taught pottery as a fine art medium, placing on it as much importance as on painting and sculpture. He lived in Rhodesia from 1939.

Murrow, Edward R originally Egbert Roscoe Murrow 1908–65
US journalist and broadcaster

Born in Pole Creek, North Carolina, he first visited Europe as assistant director of the Institute of International Education (1932–35). Joining CBS in 1935, he returned to Europe in 1937 to report on cultural items, but he extended his brief to political matters and reported on wartime Great Britain. In postwar USA he became a producer and presenter of current affairs programmes such as *See It Now* (1951–58) and *Person to Person* (1953–60). His courageous questioning of Senator Joseph McCarthy

in 1954 contributed to the latter's fall from grace and he received five Emmy awards between 1953 and 1958. He later became director of the US Information Agency (1961–64). The recipient of numerous international distinctions, he was awarded an honorary KBE in 1964. ⊞ A M Spencer, *Murrow: His Life and Times* (1986)

Murry, John Middleton 1889–1957
British writer and critic

Born in Peckham, London, he was educated at Christ's Hospital and at Brasenose College, Oxford. He wrote some poetry and many volumes of essays and criticism which had a strong influence on the young intellectuals of the 1920s. In 1911 he met Katherine Mansfield, whom he married in 1918, and introduced her work in *The Adelphi*, of which he was founder and editor from 1923 to 1948. He also produced posthumous selections from her letters and diaries, and a biography in 1932. He edited the *Athenaeum* (1919–21). He became a pacifist and was editor of *Peace News* from 1940 to 1946. Towards the end of his life he became interested in agriculture, and started a community farm in Norfolk. His major works include critical studies on *Keats and Shakespeare* (1925), his friend *D H Lawrence* (1931), *William Blake* (1933) and *Swift* (1954). He also wrote religious works, including *The Life of Jesus* (1926). He published his autobiography, *Between Two Worlds*, in 1935. ⊞ F A Lea, *The Life of John Middleton Murry* (1959)

Musaeus 5th–6th century
Greek epic poet

He was the author of *Hero and Leander*, which has been translated into many languages. ⊞ M H Jellinek, *Die Sage in der Dichtung* (1890)

Musa ibn Nusayr or Nosair 640–717
Arab soldier

He conquered northern Africa from 699 to 709 and Spain in 712, fell into disfavour with the caliph of Damascus, and died in poverty in the Hejaz.

Musäus, Johann Karl August 1735–87
German writer

He was born in Jena, studied theology there, and in 1770 became professor at the Weimar gymnasium. His first book, *Der deutsche Grandison* (1760), was a parody of Samuel Richardson's *Sir Charles Grandison*, and in 1778–79 he satirized Johann Lavater in *Physiognomische Reisen* (Eng trans *Physiognomical Travels*, 1800). However, his fame rests on his German popular tales (*Volksmärchen der Deutschen*, 1782–86, Eng trans *Popular Tales of the Germans*, 1791), which claimed, falsely, to be a collection made from traditional stories told by old people; although artificially naive, they contain some satirical humour and graceful writing. ⊞ A Richli, *Johann Musäus* (1957)

Museveni, Yoweri Kaguta 1944–
Ugandan soldier and politician

After graduating at Dar-es-Salaam University he worked for President Milton Obote until his overthrow, in 1971, by Idi Amin. From exile in Tanzania he formed the Front for National Salvation and, fighting with the Tanzanian army, took part in the defeat and expulsion of Amin in 1979. He became Minister of Defence in the governments of Yusof Lule and Godfrey Binaisa (1979–80) but was in disagreement with Obote, who returned to the presidency in 1980 but only retained power with the help of Tanzanian troops. When these withdrew in 1982, a virtual civil war ensued and reasonable normalcy did not return until 1986 when Museveni became President, pledging himself to follow a policy of national reconciliation. In 1996 he restored tribal leaders 26 years after they were abolished but denied them their former political power. Later that year he was re-elected President.

Musgrave, Thea 1928–
Scottish composer

Born in Edinburgh, she studied at Edinburgh University, the Paris Conservatoire, and with **Nadia Boulanger**. Her early work was largely Scottish in inspiration: her *Suite o' Bairnsangs* (1953) and the ballet *A Tale for Thieves* (1953), were followed by *Cantata for a Summer's Day* (1954), a chamber opera, *The Abbot of Drimock* (1955) and her *Scottish Dance Suite* (1959). In the late 1950s her work became more abstract, and she began to use serial and aleatory devices. Her music includes two choral and orchestral works, *The Phoenix and the Turtle* (1962) and *The Five Ages of Man* (1963), a full-length ballet, *Beauty and the Beast* (1968), works for instruments and pre-recorded tapes, the chamber opera *The Voice of Ariadne* (commissioned for the Aldeburgh Festival of 1974), the operas *The Decision* (1964–65), *Mary, Queen of Scots* (1977), *A Christmas Carol* (1979), and *Simón Bolívar* (1993), the radio opera *An Occurrence at Owl Creek Bridge* (1981), and the orchestral works *The Seasons* (1988) and *Rainbow* (1990). Recent works include *On the Underground* (1994), for voice, and *Helios* (1995), an oboe concerto.

Mushet, David 1772–1847
Scottish ironmaster

He was born in Dalkeith, near Edinburgh. Like many of his contemporaries he was continually experimenting with new materials and processes in the search for better and cheaper iron and steel. He discovered black band ironstone at Calder ironworks near Glasgow (1801) and maintained against strong opposition that it was suitable for smelting. After the invention of the hot blast process by **James Beaumont Neilson** in 1828 it became widely used in the Scottish iron industry. He showed that non-phosphoric oxides of iron could be used to make better quality wrought iron, patented a process for making cast steel from wrought iron, and discovered the beneficial effects of adding manganese to iron and steel. He moved from Scotland (1805) to Derbyshire and later to the Forest of Dean.

Mushet, Robert Forester 1811–91
English metallurgist

Born in Coleford, Gloucestershire, he assisted with and continued the researches of his father, **David Mushet**, into the manufacture of iron and steel. In 1856 **Henry Bessemer** patented his new steel-making process, but he soon encountered a major problem with the over-oxidation or burning of the metal inside the converter, which removed most of the vital carbon. Working in the Forest of Dean, Mushet solved Bessemer's problem by adding his 'triple compound' (a type of high-carbon ferromanganese) and then later spiegeleisen. Only through his discovery (patented in 1856) did the Bessemer process become a commercial success. Ironically, Mushet's patent was allowed to lapse and his vital discovery became common property from which he derived little or no benefit. Bessemer repudiated the validity of Mushet's patent, and only later bestowed upon him a small pension. Mushet was much more successful with his invention of 'R Mushet's Special' steel in 1868, a self-hardening tungsten alloy steel which was later extensively produced in Sheffield, where it spawned a whole family of tool steels.

Musial, Stanley Frank, *known as* Stan the Man 1920–
US baseball player

Born in Domona, he was a talented left-handed hitter and played a record number of major league games (3,026) with the St Louis Cardinals (1941–63). He scored a record number of hits (3,360), and won the batting championship seven times. He was voted the Most Valuable Player (MVP) three times, and elected to the National Hall of Baseball Fame in 1969. There is a lifesize statue of him in the Busch Stadium, St Louis. 🕮 Bob Broeg, *The Man Stan: Then and Now* (1977)

Musil, Robert 1880–1942
Austrian novelist

He was born in Klagenfurt, and trained as a scientist (he invented a chromatometer) and as a philosopher. During World War I he was an officer, and he drew on this experience for *Die Verwirrungen des Zöglings Törless* (1906, Eng trans *Young Törless*, 1955), a terrifying, sadistic story of life inside a military academy. Memorable though it is, it is eclipsed by *Der Mann ohne Eigenschaften* (1930–43, Eng trans *The Man Without Qualities*, 1953–60), his unfinished tour de force, left as a confusion of final drafts when he died suddenly in Geneva. Portraying a society on the brink, through the eyes of Ulrich, the man who has dispensed with conventional qualities, its multi-layered narrative covers just one year, 1913–14. It is widely acknowledged as one of the great novels of the century. 🕮 K Dinklage, *Robert Musil: Leben, Werk, Wirkung* (1960)

Muskie, Edmund Sixtus 1914–96
US politician and lawyer

Born in Rumford, Maine, he trained as a lawyer at Cornell Law School in Ithaca, New York, and was admitted to the Bar in 1939. A former member of the Maine House of Representatives (1947–51) and Governor of Maine (1955–59), he represented his home state in the Senate (1959–80), and was the Democratic vice-presidential nominee in 1968. He served as Secretary of State in 1980–81 under President **Jimmy Carter**.

Muspratt, James 1793–1886
British chemist and industrialist

Born in Dublin, Ireland, of British parents, he was apprenticed to a druggist and then fought in the Peninsular War, writing a record of his dramatic experiences. Back in Dublin he began a small chemical manufacturing business, but when the British salt tax was lifted he moved to Liverpool and began manufacturing soda-ash by the **Leblanc** process. The Liverpool district offered every advantage as both salt and coal were available locally and there were ships and canals to take the soda-ash to the expanding industries of 19th-century Great Britain. Muspratt prospered and in 1828 he and Josias Gamble set up a new works at St Helens. In the mid-1800s Muspratt parted with Gamble and founded large new factories employing several thousands of people at Widnes and Flint.

Musschenbroek, Pieter van 1692–1761
Dutch physicist

He was born in Leyden. Professor of Physics at Duisburg, Utrecht, and Leyden (1740–61), he invented the pyrometer and in 1746 discovered the principle of the Leyden jar (an early form of capacitor).

Musset, (Louis Charles) Alfred de 1810–57
French poet and dramatist

Born in Paris, he found, after tentative study of law and medicine, that he had a talent for writing and at 18 published a translation of **Thomas De Quincey**'s *Confessions of an Opium Eater* (*L'Anglais mangeur d'opium*, 1828). His first collection of poems, *Contes d'Espagne et d'Italie* (1830, 'Tales of Spain and Italy'), won the approval of **Victor Hugo**. His first play, *La Nuit vénitienne* ('A Night in Venice'), failed at the Odéon in 1830, and from then on he conceived an 'armchair theatre' with plays intended for reading only. When *Un Caprice*, published in 1837, and several of his other 'armchair' plays were staged successfully more than 10 years later, he wrote *On ne saurait penser à tout* (1849, 'You Can Never Think of Everything'), *Carmosine* (1850, Eng trans 1865) and *Bettine* (1851) for actual performance. In 1833 Musset had met **George Sand**, and there began the

---

Mussolini, Benito Amilcare Andrea 1883–1945
Italian dictator 1925–43

Mussolini was born in Predappio, near Forli, Romagna. He was the son of a blacksmith, and first worked as a teacher and a journalist. In 1902 he travelled to Switzerland, where he developed revolutionary beliefs, and in 1904 he returned to Italy. After a brief period of imprisonment for his political activities, he edited a socialist publication from Trento (which was then in Austria) and in 1912 became editor of the influential nationalist newspaper *Avanti*. He broke with the socialists when he refused to support their neutral stance in World War I, and founded Popolo d'Italia to publicize his belief that only by supporting the Allies could Italy retrieve the disputed Austrian territories.

Mussolini fought in World War I and was injured. In 1919 he founded the *Fasci di Combattimento* (Fascist Movement), ostensibly to serve the interests of neglected ex-servicemen, but in reality to promote the extreme form of nationalism to which he was now committed. The groups of fascist Blackshirts whose creation he encouraged were turned to his advantage against the Communists, and in 1921 he exploited his growing personal popularity to win election to the Chamber of Deputies; the following year his Blackshirts marched on Rome. He presented himself as the only man capable of restoring order to a country that seemed to be slipping ever more rapidly into political chaos. In October 1922 he was asked by **Victor Emmanuel III** to form a government. In 1925 he took the title *Il Duce* ('the leader'). Using a mixture of intimidation, patronage and propaganda, he was able to turn Italy into a totalitarian state by 1929. Despite his early aggression over Corfu and his fierce nationalism, his foreign policy was not marked by overt expansionism or aggression until the mid-1930s. However,

in 1935 he launched the Conquest of Abyssinia which was followed by large-scale intervention in the Spanish Civil War on the side of General **Franco**. During this period he moved increasingly towards co-operation with **Hitler**, which culminated in the 1939 politico-military Pact of Steel (signed by **Joachim von Ribbentrop** and **Galeazzo Ciano**) and eventually in the invasion of France in 1940. In 1939 Mussolini annexed Albania but the following year he failed to seize Greece. The arrival of German troops to assist in the conquest of Greece signalled the beginning of his dependence on Hitler, and from then on his actions were dictated largely by the needs of Berlin.

Dissatisfaction with this policy and a realization of the likely victory of the Allies persuaded many of his supporters to oppose him. After the allied landings in Sicily in 1942, even Mussolini's own Fascist Council turned on him, and he had to be rescued by German paratroops and taken to northern Italy in a doomed attempt to re-establish his authority. When that failed, he tried to flee the country with his mistress disguised as a German soldier, but was caught and unmasked by a member of the Italian resistance and summarily executed. His corpse was mutilated by the people after it was hung upside down in a public square in Como.

📖 A translation of his *Autobiography* was published in 1928, and memoirs of his wife, Rachele, *My Life with Mussolini*, in 1959. See also D Mack-Smith, *Mussolini* (1981).

> 'If I advance, follow me. If I retreat, kill me. If I die, avenge me.' Said to senior officials after an attempt on his life, 6 April 1926.

---

stormy love affair (1833–35), which is traced in his four volumes of *Nuits* (1835–37). Other works include the autobiographical poem *Confessions d'un enfant du siècle* (1835, Eng trans *The Confessions of a Child of the Century*, 1892) and *L'Espoir en Dieu* (1838, 'Hoping in God'). 📖 Margaret Rees, *Alfred de Musset* (1971)

Mussolini, Benito Amilcare Andrea See panel above

Mussorgsky, Modest Petrovich, *also spelt* Moussorgsky or Musorgsky or Musorgski or Mussargsky 1835–81
Russian composer

Born in Karevo (Pskov), he was educated for the army but resigned his commission in 1858 after the onset of a nervous disorder, and began the serious study of music under **Mili Balakirev**. A member of the **Glinka**-inspired nationalist group in St Petersburg, which included **Aleksandr Dargomizhsky** and **Rimsky-Korsakov**, he first made a name with his songs, among them the well-known setting of **Goethe**'s satirical 'Song of the Flea' (1879). His most impressive work is the opera *Boris Godunov*, first performed at St Petersburg in 1874, and his piano suite *Pictures from an Exhibition* (1874, *Kartinki s vystavki*) has also maintained its standing in the concert repertoire. Other operas and large-scale works remained uncompleted as the composer sank into the chronic alcoholism which hastened his early death. His friend Rimsky-Korsakov undertook the task of musical executor, arranged or completed many of his unfinished works and rearranged some of the finished ones, sometimes to the detriment of their robust individuality.

Mustafa Kemal Atatürk See Atatürk, Mustafa Kemal

Muthesius, Hermann 1861–1927
German architect, writer and propagandist

Born in Gross-Neuhausen, Thuringia, he studied architecture in Berlin, practised in Tokyo, and from 1893 worked as a Prussian government architect and editor of the official architectural journal. Attached to the German embassy in London from 1896 to 1903, he studied the developments taking place in British architecture and design. His reports and articles of that period were followed, on his return, by the three-volume study *Das Englische Haus* (1904–05), which was influential in Germany and remains an invaluable document of that time. With **Henri van de Velde** he was one of the main initiators in 1907 of the Deutsche Werkbund, which, like the Bauhaus and its successors, led to the high design standards of contemporary German industry.

Mutsuhito 1852–1912
Emperor of Japan

He was born in Kyoto, the son of the titular emperor, Komei, whom he succeeded in 1867. Within a year he had recovered the full powers of the emperors when, after a brief civil war, he overthrew the last of the shoguns, who had exercised dictatorial authority in Japan for 700 years. He was intelligent and energetic, and his long reign saw the rapid political and military westernization of Japan, under the initiative of the emperor himself. The feudal system was abolished (1871), most restrictions on foreign trade were removed, a constitution providing for an advisory cabinet and an Imperial Diet was promulgated (1889), and a navy was created on the British model and an army on the German. Military success against China (1894–95) was followed by Japan's victories in the Russo-Japanese War (1904–05) and by the economic penetration of Korea and Manchuria. When Mutsuhito died he was succeeded by his only son, Crown Prince **Yoshihito**. Assigned a posthumous title, in accordance with Japanese custom, Mutsuhito was styled Meiji Tenno.

Muybridge, Eadweard, *originally* Edward James Muggeridge 1830–1904
US photographer and inventor

Born in Kingston upon Thames, England, he emigrated to California in 1852 and became a professional photographer, and eventually chief photographer to the US government. He invented a shutter which allowed an exposure of 1/500 seconds, and using a battery of between 12 and 24 cameras, was able in 1877 to show that a trotting horse had all of its feet off the ground at times. In 1880 he devised the zoopraxiscope, a precursor of cinematography, in which the photographs were printed on a rotating glass disc. He employed this to demonstrate the trotting horse and after exhibiting it in his Zoopraxographical Hall in Chicago (1893) went on tour in the USA and Europe. In 1884–85 he carried out an extensive survey of the movements of animals and humans for the University of Pennsylvania, publishing the results as *Animal Locomotion* (1887). In 1900 he retired to his birthplace. ▢ Gordon Hendricks, *Eadweard Muybridge: The Father of the Motion Picture* (1975)

Muzorewa, Abel (Tendekayi) 1925–
Zimbabwean cleric and politician

Born in Umtali, Southern Rhodesia (Zimbabwe) and educated in Methodist schools in Southern Rhodesia and at theological college in the USA, he was ordained in 1963 and became a bishop of the United Methodist Church in Southern Rhodesia in 1968. Founder president of the African National Council (ANC) in 1971, he failed to hold together the differing elements of the nationalist movement and chose the path of an 'internal settlement' rather than guerrilla war. After the ANC won the first universal suffrage election in 1979, he was Prime Minister of 'Zimbabwe–Rhodesia' for a few months before the 1980 election swept **Robert Mugabe** into power. He was detained between 1983 and 1984 then fled to the USA in 1985, returning to Zimbabwe a year later. His autobiography, *Rise Up and Walk*, was published in 1978.

Mwalimu See Nyerere, Julius Kambarage

Mwinyi, Ndugu Ali Hassan 1925–
Tanzanian politician

Born in Zanzibar and educated at Mangapwani School and Dole School, and at Zanzibar Teacher Training College and Durham University, England, he worked as a teacher and head teacher. He then joined the Ministry of Education and, after working in a parastatal trading corporation on the mainland, entered the government of **Julius Nyerere**. He was appointed Minister of State in the presidential office in 1972, and was later Minister for Health (1972–75), Minister for Home Affairs (1975–77), ambassador to Egypt (1977–81), and Minister for Natural Resources and Tourism (1982–83). In 1985 he succeeded Nyerere as President of the United Republic of Tanzania.

Myaskovsky, Nikolai Yakovlevich 1881–1950
Russian composer

Born in Novogeorgievsk, near Warsaw, he began a career as a military engineer, turning to music in 1907. His teachers included **Anatol Liadov** and **Rimsky-Korsakov**. After army service (1914–21) he became an influential Professor of Composition at the Moscow Conservatory. He composed 27 symphonies and other orchestral works, concertos for violin and cello, 13 string quartets and other chamber music, songs, nine piano sonatas and other works.

Myers, Frederic William Henry 1843–1901 ·
English poet and essayist

The brother of Ernest James Myers, he was a classical scholar, and a school inspector (1872–1900). In 1882 he was one of the founders of the Society for Psychical Research. He wrote poems (collected 1921), essays, *Wordsworth* (1881) and *Human Personality and its Survival of Bodily Death* (1903).

Myerson, Goldie See Meir, Golda

Myles, Lynda 1947–
Scottish film and television producer

Born in Arbroath, Angus, she became involved in the running of the Edinburgh International Film Festival whilst studying philosophy at Edinburgh University. She was its director from 1973 to 1980 and raised the event's international reputation through her championing of the New German Cinema, underappreciated Hollywood veterans, and the new generation of US directors. She worked as curator of the Pacific Film Archive in California (1980–82), then returned to the UK and worked for Channel 4 and Enigma Films, where she produced the political thriller *Defence of the Realm* (1985). She was senior vice-president of European Production for Columbia Pictures before working for the BBC. Returning to independent film production, she has had success with *The Commitments* (1991), *The Snapper* (1993) and *The Van* (1996). In 1981 she received a BFI Special award for services to the film industry.

Mylne, Robert 1734–1811
Scottish architect

Born in Edinburgh of a notable family of stonemasons, architects and engineers, he studied on the Continent and designed Blackfriars' Bridge (erected in 1769 and pulled down in 1868), and planned the Gloucester and Berkeley Ship Canal and the Eau Brink Cut for fen drainage at King's Lynn. His buildings, for example St Cecilia's Hall, Edinburgh (1763–65), show an elegance typical of the best late 18th-century work. His brother, William, designed the North Bridge in Edinburgh.

Mylne or Miln, Walter d.1558
Scottish Protestant reformer

While on a visit to Germany he was greatly influenced by Reformist doctrines, and later as priest of Lunan in Angus was denounced for heresy. Condemned by Cardinal **David Beaton** to be burnt, he fled the country, but returned after the cardinal's death. Taken prisoner at Dysart, he was tried at St Andrews, and although by this time over 80 years old, he was burned at the stake, the last Scottish Protestant martyr.

Mylonas, George 1898–1988
Greek archaeologist

Born in Smyrna, he taught for many years in the USA and became president of the Archaeological Society of America. He was also secretary-general of the Greek Historical Society. His main excavation was at the Outer Grave Circle at Mycenae, and before that the Neolithic material at Olyathus, and the small Bronze Age site at Ayios Kosmas, near Athens Airport. He was also responsible for the building of a new museum at Mycenae.

Myrdal, Alva, *née* Reimer 1902–86
Swedish sociologist, politician and peace reformer, and Nobel Prize winner

Born in Uppsala, she was educated at the universities of Uppsala, Stockholm, and Geneva. In 1924 she married **Gunnar Myrdal**. A proponent of child welfare and equal rights for women, she was director of the United Nations Department of Social Sciences (1950–56). Appointed Swedish ambassador to India, Burma and Ceylon from 1955 to 1961, she was elected to the Swedish parliament in 1962, and was on the UN Disarmament Committee (1962–1973). As Minister for Disarmament and Church

Affairs (1966–73) she played a prominent part in the international peace movement. Her works include *The Game of Disarmament: How the United States and Russia Run the Arms Race* (1977). She was awarded the 1980 Albert Einstein Peace prize, and in 1982 received the Nobel Prize for Peace, jointly with **Alfonso García Robles.**

Myrdal, (Karl) Gunnar 1898–1987
Swedish economist and politician, and Nobel Prize winner
He studied law, and then economics, at Stockholm, and taught economics at Stockholm from 1927 to 1950 and from 1960 to 1967. He wrote a classic study of race relations in the USA (*An American Dilemma*, 1944), then was Minister of Trade and Commerce in Sweden (1945–47), and then Executive Secretary of the UN Economic Commission for Europe (1947–57). His later works include *Beyond the Welfare State* (1960) and *The Challenge of Affluence* (1963). He was awarded the Nobel Prize in economics in 1974 (jointly with **Friedrich August von Hayek**), principally for his work on the critical application of economic theory of Third World countries. ⌨ Walter A Jackson, *Gunnar Myrdal and America's Conscience: Social Engineering and Racial Liberalism, 1938–1987* (1990)

Myron 5th century BC
Greek sculptor
He was born in Eleutherae, and lived in Athens. A contemporary of **Phidias**, he worked in bronze and is best known for the celebrated *Discobolos* (c.450BC, Roman marble copy from bronze original, Museo della Terme, Rome) and *Marsyas*.

Mytens, Daniel c.1590–1642
Flemish portrait painter
Born in The Hague, he worked for **James VI and I** and **Charles I**, who made him King's Painter. He painted portraits of many notable persons of the time.

Nabokov, Vladimir 1899–1977
US novelist

Born in St Petersburg, Russia, to aristocratic parents, he was educated at the relatively progressive Tenishev School, where he was accused of 'not conforming' to his surroundings. In 1919, following the Bolshevik Revolution, his family became émigrés, and he and his brother went to England to study, on scholarships to Cambridge. He then rejoined his family in Berlin (1922), where he lived for more than 15 years and published his first novels, among them *Korol, Dama, Valet* (1928, 'King, Queen, Knave') and *Otchayanie* (1936, 'Despair'). All were written in Russian, under the pseudonym V Sirin, the author himself later collaborating on English translations. From 1937 to 1940 he was in Paris, where he met **James Joyce**, and he then emigrated to the USA where he took citizenship in 1945. He taught at Wellesley College and Cornell University, and earned distinction as a lepidopterist. He began to write in English and published many short stories and novels, including *Bend Sinister* (1947) and *Pale Fire* (1962). *Lolita* (1959) was a succès de scandale and allowed him to abandon teaching and devote himself to writing full-time. From 1959 he lived in Montreux in Switzerland. Among 20th-century novelists he is regarded for his linguistic ingenuity and dazzling intellect. His other works include *Lectures on Literature* (1980) and a translation of **Alexander Pushkin**'s *Eugene Onegin* (1963). 📖 A Field, Vladimir Nabokov, the life and art (1977)

Nabuco (de Araújo), Joaquim Aurélio
1849–1912
Brazilian politician and abolitionist

Born into a major Liberal political dynasty, he was a diplomat, then became a deputy (1878–80, 1885, 1887–89). He founded the Brazilian Society for the Abolition of Slavery and led the campaign to abolish slavery through the legislature and the courts, rather than by extrajudicial means. He triumphed, largely as a result of the slave insurrections in São Paulo in 1887–88, the refusal of the Cabinet to face possible civil war, and the acceptance of abolition as a fait accompli by the Chamber of Deputies in 1888. An admirer of **Pedro II**, he left public life after the former's deposition (1889), returning as a special envoy and ambassador to the USA.

Nachtigal, Gustav 1834–85
German traveller

Born in Eichstedt, he studied medicine, served as an army surgeon, and in 1863 went to North Africa. He travelled across the Sahara Desert from Tripoli to Cairo (1869–74) via Tiberti and Lake Chad, which resulted in the first detailed description of the south-eastern Sahara. As German consul in Tunis, he went to annex Togo and Cameroon for Germany in 1884.

Nadar, *pseudonym of* Gaspard-Felix Tournachon
1820–1910
French journalist, artist and photographer

He was born in Paris, where he worked as a left-wing journalist from 1840, after studying medicine in Lupus. In 1852 he published a series of caricatures, some of which were based on his photographs, and soon afterwards opened a studio which became a meeting place for the intelligentsia. For many years he produced lively portraits of distinguished literary and artistic contemporaries, successfully capturing individual personalities in intimate and natural studies. Among other innovations, he proposed the use of aerial photographs for mapmaking and in 1858 took the first photographs from a balloon, of the city of Paris. In 1886 he produced the first 'photo-interview', a series of 21 photographs of the scientist **Michel Chevreul**, each captioned with the sitter's replies to Nadar's questions. In his later years he was active as a writer and journalist.

Nadel, Siegfried Frederick
1903–56
British social anthropologist

He was born in Vienna, Austria, and although his early interests were in music, he studied psychology and philosophy at Vienna University. In 1932 he moved to England to study anthropology under **Bronisław Malinowski** at the London School of Economics. He was Reader at Durham University (1948–50), and professor at Canberra University, Australia (1950–56). He carried out fieldwork among the Nupe in northern Nigeria (1934–36) and the Nuba of the Sudan (1938–40), which resulted in his three major monographs: *A Black Byzantium* (1942), *The Nuba* (1947) and *Nupe Religion* (1954). However, his major contribution to anthropology lay not in ethnography but in theory, in his *The Foundations of Social Anthropology* (1951) and *The Theory of Social Structure* (1957).

Nadelman, Elie 1882–1946
US sculptor

He was born in Warsaw and studied at the Art Academy there, but left Poland to settle in Paris (c.1902). His drawings and sculptures after 1906 reveal a simplification of forms and stylization close to Cubism, as in *Standing Bull* and *Wounded Bull* (both 1915, New York) but also show an affinity with antique sculpture. In 1914 he moved to the USA, took a studio in New York City, and began to produce a number of primitive painted figure sculptures in wood. He became a US citizen in 1927. From the 1930s he worked extensively in ceramics. Many of his sculptures were accidentally destroyed, but a memorial exhibition of his work was held in New York in 1948.

Nader, Ralph 1934–
US lawyer and consumer activist

He was born in Winsted, Connecticut, and educated at Princeton and Harvard Law School. Admitted to the Connecticut Bar in 1959, he campaigned for improved consumer rights and protection, encouraging the establishment of powerful 'civic interest lobbies' of which the US Congress, state legislatures and corporate executives were forced to take note. His bestseller about the automobile industry, *Unsafe at Any Speed* (1965), led to the passage of improved car safety regulations in 1966. He became head of the Public Citizen Foundation in 1980. His other books include *The Menace of Atomic Energy* (1977), *Who's Poisoning America?* (1981), and *Winning the Insurance Game* (1990). In 1996 he was nominated by the Green Party as a protest candidate for US President.

Nadir Shah 1688–1747
King of Persia

Born in Khurasan, of Turkish origin, he was king from 1736. A brigand leader who expelled the Afghan rulers of Persia (Iran), he forced Russia to hand over her Caspian provinces, defeated the Turks (1731), conquered Bahrain, Oman and Afghanistan, and ravaged the north-west of India, taking Delhi (1739) and capturing the Peacock Throne and Koh-i-noor diamond. His domestic policy led to revolts, especially on religious matters, and he was assassinated at Fathabad. Suspicious and cruel, he imposed harsh taxes that ruined the economy and he had few statesmanlike qualities.

Naevius, Gnaeus c.264–c.201BC
Roman poet and dramatist
Born probably in Campania, he served in the first Punic War (264–241BC), and started producing his own plays in 235. A plebeian who for 30 years satirized the Roman nobles in his plays, he was compelled to leave Rome, ultimately retiring to Utica in Africa. Fragments of an epic, *De Bello Punico* ('The Punic Wars'), are extant. 📖 M Barchiesi, *Nevio epico* (1962)

Nagano, Osami 1880–1947
Japanese naval officer
Educated at the Naval Academy, Etajima, he studied law at Harvard and served as naval attaché in Washington (1920–23). Promoted rear admiral in 1928, he was superintendent of the Naval Academy (1928–29). As head of the Japanese delegation to the second London Naval Conference (1935–36), he advocated the expansion of Japanese naval power. He was Navy Minister (1936–37), Commander-in-Chief of the combined fleet (1937), and Chief of Naval General Staff (1941–44). He planned and ordered the Japanese attack on Pearl Harbor in December 1941. He died while on trial for war crimes.

Nāgārjuna c.150–c.250AD
Indian Buddhist monk-philosopher
He was the founder of the Madhyamika or Middle Path school of Buddhism.

Nagel, Ernest 1901–85
US philosopher of science
Born in Nové Město, Bohemia (Czech Republic), he moved to the USA (1911) and became a naturalized US citizen in 1919. He taught philosophy at Columbia University (1931–70) and published widely on the philosophy of science. His best-known works are his *An Introduction to Logic and Scientific Method* (1934, with M R Cohen), *Logic without Metaphysics* (1957) and *The Structure of Science* (1961).

Nägeli, Karl Wilhelm von 1817–91
Swiss botanist
He was born in Kilchberg, near Zurich, became professor at Munich University (from 1858), and was one of the early writers on evolution. He investigated the growth of cells and originated the micellar theory relating to the structure of starch grains and cell walls. He originated the concept of cell organelles, describing the membrane surrounding chloroplasts, and their increase by division. He distinguished between two types of cell formation—vegetative and reproductive—and observed the cell nucleus dividing into two parts before the cell itself divided. He almost certainly made the first observation of chromosomes, but his most significant advance was probably the recognition of phloem as a fundamental tissue.

Nagy, Imre 1895–1958
Hungarian politician
Born in Kaposvar, he was captured while serving in the Austrian army in World War I, and sent to Siberia. At the revolution he escaped, joined the Bolshevik forces, and became a Soviet citizen in 1918. Back in Hungary in 1919, he had a minor post in the Kun revolutionary government, but later fled to Russia where he remained throughout World War II. Returning with the Red Army (1944), he became Minister of Agriculture in the provisional government, enforcing Communist land reforms. In 1947 he became Speaker of the Hungarian parliament, and in 1953 Prime Minister, introducing a 'new course' of milder political and economic control. In 1955 the regime of Mátyás Rákosi removed him from office as a 'right deviationist'. He returned to the premiership in 1956 on Rakosi's downfall. When the Hungarian Uprising broke out (October 1956) he promised free elections and a Russian military withdrawal. When, in November, Soviet forces began to suppress the revolution he appealed to the world for help, but was displaced by the Soviet puppet János Kádár and later executed. In 1989, following the overthrow of the Communists, he was given a hero's re-burial in Budapest. 📖 Peter Unwin, *Voice in the Wilderness: Imre Nagy and the Hungarian Revolution* (1991)

Nahayan, Sheikh Zayed bin Sultan al- 1918–
Emir of Abu Dhabi
He was Governor of the eastern province of Abu Dhabi, one of seven Trucial States on the southern shores of the Persian Gulf and the Gulf of Oman, which were under British protection, until he deposed his brother, Sheikh Shakhbut (1969), and became emir. When the States decided to federate as the United Arab Emirates (1971) he became president of its supreme council. He was unanimously re-elected in 1986. Under his rule the UAE ceased to be a collection of medieval emirates and emerged as an efficient modern state with one of the highest per capita incomes in the world.

Nahhas, Mustafa al- 1879–1965
Egyptian politician
He was the leader of the Wafd Party in Egypt in 1923 and became premier in 1928, 1930 and 1950. In addition, he acted as regent for King Farouk I in his early years and, despite their being dismissed by Farouk in 1938, the Wafd were brought back in 1941 at the request of Great Britain. The damage done to the reputation of the Wafd by their co-operation with the British was irreparable. Although al-Nahhas became premier again in 1950 after the Wafd's victory in the elections, and despite his endeavours to regain credibility for the Wafd by giving the party an anti-British bias, they were again dismissed by Farouk in 1952. Al-Nahhas then left the political stage, charged with, but not tried for, corruption. The Wafd Party was dissolved in 1953.

Nahum 7th century BC
Old Testament minor prophet
Born probably either in Israel or Judah, he may have been a captive in Nineveh. He prophesied the destruction of Nineveh by the Medes in 612BC.

Naidu, Sarojini, *née* Chattopadhyay, *known as* the Nightingale of India 1879–1949
Indian feminist and poet
Born in Hyderabad, she was educated at Madras, London and Cambridge. She published three volumes of lyric verse: *The Golden Threshold* (1905), *The Bird of Time* (1912) and *The Broken Wing* (1915). She organized flood-relief in Hyderabad (1908), and lectured and campaigned on feminism, in particular the abolition of purdah. Associated with Mahatma Gandhi, she was the first Indian woman to be president of the Indian National Congress (1925). She was imprisoned several times for civil disobedience incidents, and took part in the negotiations leading to independence. In 1947 she was appointed Governor of United Provinces (Uttar Pradesh). 📖 P Sengupta, *Sarojini Naidu* (1966)

Naipaul, Sir V(idiadhar) S(urajprasad) 1932–
Trinidadian novelist
Born in Chaguanas, he was educated at Queen's Royal College, Port of Spain, then left the Caribbean for England in 1950 to study at Oxford. The editor of 'Caribbean Voices' for the BBC, he dabbled in journalism before his first novel, *The Mystic Masseur* (1957), was published. *Miguel Street* (1959) collected sketches depicting lower-class life in Trinidad through the eyes of a growing boy. The book which made his name was *A House for Mr Biswas* (1961), a spicy satire spanning three Trinidadian

generations but focusing on its eponymous six-fingered sign-writer. Thereafter the Caribbean figured less prominently in his work, which grew steadily darker and more complex. *In a Free State* (1971) won the Booker Prize, and in 1979 he published *A Bend in the River*, a masterly recreation of what it is like to live under an African dictatorship. As well as novels he has written several trenchant 'travel' books, including *An Area of Darkness: An Experience of India* (1964) and *Among the Believers: An Islamic Journey* (1981). *Finding the Centre* (1984) is autobiographical. Later works include *The Enigma of Arrival* (1987) and *A Way in the World* (1994). He was knighted in 1990. His brother Shiva Naipaul was also a gifted writer. 🕮 S Kamra, *The Novels of V S Naipaul* (1990)

Nairn, Nick 1959–
Scottish chef

He began his working life with seven years' service in the merchant navy. A self-taught chef and cookery teacher, since 1986 he has been the joint owner, with his wife and business partner Fiona, of the Braeval restaurant in Aberfoyle, Scotland, where they also run a popular cookery school. Braeval was awarded a Michelin Star in 1991. In 1992 Nairn became a member of the Masterchefs of Great Britain. Television appearances include being a regular participant in *Ready Steady Cook*, and the presenter of the series *Nick Nairn's Wild Harvest*, for which he published the companion volume *Nick Nairn's Wild Harvest* (1995).

Nairne, Lady Carolina, *née* Oliphant 1766–1845
Scottish songwriter

She was born in Gask, Perthshire, the daughter of a Jacobite laird, and in 1806 married a cousin, Major Nairne (1757–1830), who became Lord Nairne in 1824. She lived in Edinburgh, but travelled widely in Ireland and Europe after her husband's death. She collected traditional airs and wrote songs to them under the pseudonym 'Mrs Bogan of Bogan', which were published in *The Scottish Minstrel* (1821–24), and posthumously as *Lays from Strathearn*. They include the lament for Prince Charles Edward Stuart, 'Will ye no' come back again', 'The Land o' the Leal', 'Caller Herrin'', 'The Laird o' Cockpen', 'The Rowan Tree', and 'The Auld Hoose', as well as the martial setting for 'The Hundred Pipers'.

Naismith, James 1861–1939
Canadian educationist

Born in Almonte, Ontario, he is regarded as being the originator of basketball in 1891 at the YMCA college in Springfield, Massachusetts, using peach baskets on a gym wall. The game was originally designed merely to bridge the gap between the baseball and American football season, but it soon became popular in its own right. He taught at the YMCA, Denver, Colorado (1895–98), and the University of Kansas (1898–1937). He attended the Berlin Olympics of 1936, at which basketball was elevated to the status of an Olympic sport.

Najibullah, Sayid Mohammad 1947–96
Afghan politician

Born in Paktia province and educated at Habibia Lycée and Kabul University, he became active in the Moscow-inspired People's Democratic Party of Afghanistan (PDPA) in the mid-1960s, and was twice imprisoned for his political activities. After King Mohammed Zahir Shah was deposed in a military coup (1973), he rose rapidly in the party hierarchy, and as a member of the PDPA's central committee, played a key role in the negotiations that led to the 1978 treaty of friendship with the USSR. The treaty served as a pretext for the Russian invasion the following year, when he was made Information Minister. He was admitted to the Afghan politburo in 1981, and became

President in 1987. Strong guerrilla resistance by the members of the National Islamic Front continued, and insistence by the Russian army, in the wake of continued attacks by Pakistani Mujahadeen guerrillas on the Kabul–Soviet border, that Najibullah's regime should continue to be funded despite the USSR's own economic difficulties was a factor in the resignation of Foreign Minister Eduard Shevardnadze (1990). In 1991, the United Nations renewed its call for elections in Mujahadeen-controlled territories with a view to replacing Najibullah's regime with a democratically-elected government. Najibullah finally resigned, handing over power to a coalition of Mujahadeen leaders in May 1992, and took refuge in a UN compound until his death.

Nakasone, Yasuhiro 1917–
Japanese politician

Born in Takasaki and educated at Tokyo Imperial University, he served in the Japanese navy in World War II, and afterwards entered politics as a member of the conservative Liberal Democratic Party (LDP), holding a number of ministerial posts from 1967 to 1982. He established his own faction within the LDP and was elected Secretary-General (1974–76), Chairman (1977–80) and, in 1982, LDP President, and thus Prime Minister. He introduced an innovative programme which combined greater economic liberalism at home with a more assertive posture abroad, and became Japan's most forceful and popular political leader for decades. The first LDP President to be re-elected for a second term since the 1960s, he stepped down as Prime Minister in 1987, and nominated Noboru Takeshita as his successor. He remained an influential figure in politics but was forced to resign from the LDP in 1989 after becoming involved in the Recruit scandal. Since 1988 he has been chairman and president of the International Institute for Global Peace.

Namath, Joe Willie (Joseph William), *known as* Broadway Joe 1943–
US football player

Born in Beaver Falls, Pennsylvania, he was noted for his high living off the field. An outstanding quarterback in Alabama University's unbeaten team of 1964, he turned professional in the American Football League with the New York Jets (1965). In a phenomenally successful career, he played for a total of 23 seasons, passing for a total of 27,663 yards and scoring 173 touchdowns. In 1967 he passed for a record 4,007 yards, and in 1969 inspired the Jets to an upset victory over the Baltimore Colts in the Superbowl. Since his retirement (1978) he has remained in the public eye with appearances in films and on television.

Namias, Jerome 1910–
US meteorologist

Born in Bridgeport, Connecticut, he was educated at the Massachusetts Institute of Technology (MIT), where his enthusiasm for meteorology helped him to become an assistant to Carl-Gustav Rossby. He realized that the persistence of the Rossby long waves in the upper atmosphere would allow weather forecasting for up to five days ahead. In 1936 Rossby offered him a teaching post at MIT, and he was made chief of the extended forecast division of the Weather Bureau. He held this position until 1971, and during this time forecasting was extended to monthly forecasts of temperature and rainfall for the northern hemisphere, and eventually to seasonal forecasts, although Namias was aware that the atmospheric Rossby waves could be modified by the underlying surface such as snow cover and deserts. His many scientific papers related anomalous sea temperature patterns to atmospheric phenomena, as he realized that ocean–atmosphere inter-actions were a two-way process. In 1971 he moved to the Scripps Institute of Oceanography at the University of California and continued his research, particularly into methods of seasonal forecasting.

Namier, Sir Lewis Bernstein, *originally surnamed* Bernstein 1888–1960
British historian

Born near Warsaw, Poland, of Russian origin, he went to England in 1906 and was educated at Balliol College, Oxford. He became a naturalized citizen in 1913, had a distinguished career in diplomacy and journalism, and was Professor of Modern History at the University of Manchester (1931–52). His influence created a Namier school of history, which emphasized the analysis of events and institutions, particularly parliament, so as to reveal the motivation of the individuals involved. He compelled a 're-thinking' of history through his *Structure of Politics at the Accession of George III* (1929) and *England in the Age of the American Revolution* (vol 1, 1930). 📖 Julia Namier, *Lewis Namier: A Biography* (1971)

Nanak, *also known as* Guru Nanak 1469–1539
Indian religious leader, and founder of Sikhism

Born near Lahore (Pakistan) he was a Hindu by birth and belief. He travelled widely to Hindu and Muslim centres where he taught spiritual truth. He settled in Kartarpur, in the Punjab, where he attracted many followers. His doctrine, set out later in the *Adi-Granth*, sought a fusion of Brahmanism and Islam on the grounds that both were monotheistic, although his own ideas leaned rather towards pantheism. 📖 W H McLeod, *Guru Nanak and the Sikh Religion* (1968)

Nana Sahib, *properly* Brahmin Dundhu Panth c.1820–59
Indian rebel

The adopted son of the ex-peshwa (head) of the Marathas, he became the leader of the Sepoys in Cawnpore at the outbreak of the Indian Mutiny (1857), and was held responsible for the massacre of the British residents. After the collapse of the rebellion he escaped into Nepal.

Nansen, Fridtjof 1861–1930
Norwegian explorer, biologist and oceanographer, and Nobel Prize winner

Born in Store-Frøen, he studied at Christiana (now Oslo) University and later at Naples. In 1882 he sailed into the Arctic regions in the sealer *Viking*, and in the summer of 1888 made an adventurous journey across Greenland from east to west. However, his great achievement was the partial accomplishment of his scheme for reaching the North Pole by letting his ship get frozen into the ice north of Siberia and drift with a current setting towards Greenland. He started in the *Fram*, built for the purpose, in August 1893, reached the New Siberian islands in September, made fast to an ice floe, and drifted north to 84° 4' in March 1895. There he left the *Fram* and pushed across the ice, reaching the highest latitude till then attained, 86° 14' N, on 7 April, and overwintering in Franz Josef Land. Professor of Zoology (1897) and of Oceanography (1908) at Oslo, he furthered the cause of Norwegian independence from Sweden, and was the first Norwegian ambassador in London (1906–08). In 1922 he was awarded the Nobel Peace Prize for Russian relief work, and he did much for the League of Nations. 📖 E E Reynolds, *Nansen* (2nd edn, 1949)

Naomi
Biblical character in the Old Testament

Naomi's name means 'my delight' in Hebrew. She is de-scribed in the stories of the Book of Ruth as the mother-in-law of Ruth and Orpah. After Naomi was widowed, and her two sons had also died, she persuaded Orpah to return to her own people. Ruth, however, made an oath to remain with Naomi and returned with her from Moab to Bethlehem, where Naomi helped to arrange the marriage of Ruth with Boaz, one of the secondary kinsmen of Naomi's deceased husband. Ruth and Boaz had a son called Obed, who was to be the father of Jesse, who in turn was the father of David.

Naoroji, Dadhabai 1825–1917
Indian politician

Born in Bombay, he became Professor of Mathematics at Elphinstone College there, and a member of the Legislative Council. From 1892 to 1895 he represented Finsbury in the British House of Commons—the first Indian MP—and was also president of the Indian National Congress.

Napier, Sir Charles 1786–1860
Scottish naval commander

Born at Merchiston Hall near Falkirk, he went to sea at the age of 13, received his first command in 1808, then served as a volunteer in the Peninsular army, inflicting great damage on the French in the Mediterranean. In the American War of 1812 he led the ascent of the Potomac River, and took part in the operations against Baltimore. In command of the loyalist Portuguese fleet (1831–33), he defeated the fleet of the pretender, Maria Evaristo Miguel, and restored Queen Maria II to the throne. Returning to the British navy in 1839, he stormed Sidon in the war between the Porte and Mehemet Ali, defeated Ibrahim Pasha in Lebanon, attacked Acre, blockaded Alexandria, and concluded a convention with Ali. He commanded the Baltic fleet in the Crimean War (1854–55). He twice sat in parliament, and worked to reform the naval administra-tion. He was a cousin of Sir Charles James Napier.

Napier, Sir Charles James 1782–1853
British general and colonial administrator

Born in London, he fought in the Peninsular War from 1808 to 1811 and against the USA in the War of 1812, and in 1842 was sent to India to take command of the war in Sind. He defeated the emirs at Miani (1843), and was made Governor of the province. In 1847 he returned to England, but went back to India before the end of the second of the Sikh Wars to command the army. He left India in 1851.

Napier, John 1550–1617
Scottish mathematician, inventor of logarithms

Born at Merchiston Castle, Edinburgh, he went to St Andrews University at the age of 13 but never graduated, travelled on the Continent, then settled down to a life of literary and scientific study. He described his famous invention of logarithms in *Mirifici Logarithmorum Canonis Descriptio* (1614, 'Description of the Marvellous Canon of Logarithms'). Formulated to simplify computation, his system used the natural logarithm base e, but was modified soon after by Henry Briggs to use the base 10. Napier also devised a calculating machine, using a set of rods, called 'Napier's bones', which he described in his *Rabdologiae* (1617, Eng trans *Study of Divining Rods*, 1667). A strict Presbyterian, he published religious works, such as the *Plaine Discovery of the whole Revelation of Saint John* (1593) and believed in astrology and divination. For defence against Philip II of Spain, he devised warlike machines (including primitive tanks). 📖 C G Knott (ed), *Napier Tercentenary Memorial Volume* (1915)

Napier, Robert 1791–1876
Scottish shipbuilder and engineer

Napoleon I, *also called* Napoleon Bonaparte 1769–1821
Emperor of France

Napoleon Bonaparte was born in Ajaccio in Corsica, the second son of **Charles Bonaparte**, a Corsican lawyer. He entered the military schools at Brienne (1779) and Paris (1784), and in 1785 he was commissioned in the regiment of la Fère as second-lieutenant of artillery, garrisoned at Valence. At Auxonne he saw the beginnings of the French Revolution, but, more concerned with Corsica than France, he went home on leave to organize a revolution and was temporarily struck off the army list for returning to his regiment late (1792). He was given command of the artillery at the Siege of Toulon (1793), where he served with distinction and was promoted to brigadier-general.

On the fall of **Robespierre** in 1794, Napoleon was arrested on a charge of conspiracy because of his friendship with the younger Robespierre, but the charges were not proven and he was released. In 1795 he helped to defeat supporters of the counter-revolution in Paris with the celebrated 'whiff of grapeshot' against the mob at the Tuileries, and was then appointed commander of the army of Italy (1796), in which role he was able to demonstrate his great military genius. Two days before his departure for Italy he married **Joséphine**, widow of General Vicomte de **Beauharnais**, who had been executed during the Reign of Terror.

On arrival in Nice he was appalled by the poverty and indiscipline of the French army. As his army was outnumbered by the combined Piedmontese–Austrian forces he determined to separate them. He finally routed the Piedmontese at Mondovi, after which Sardinia sued for peace, and the Austrians at Lodi, after which he entered Milan. He next broke through the Austrian centre and occupied the line of the Adige, taking Verona and Legnago from the neutral republic of Venice. The Austrians made attempts to recover Lombardy, but were defeated at Arcole and Rivoli.

When Napoleon's position in Italy was secured he advanced on Vienna, and reached Leoben in April 1797. Negotiations for a peace settlement with Austria began, but progressed slowly as Austria hoped to benefit from the political crisis in France, where the moderates and royalists were gaining power on the legislative councils. Napoleon, however, despatched General **Augereau** to assist the Directory in disposing of their opponents by force. In October 1797 Austria signed the Treaty of Campo Formio, by which France obtained Belgium, the Ionian Islands and Lombardy, while Austria received Istria, Dalmatia and Venetia; the treaty also set out plans for a congress at Rastatt to decide upon the future of Germany, though Austria had already secretly promised the left bank of the Rhine to France. It marked the end of the War of the First Coalition, the first stage of the French Revolutionary Wars.

The Directory, fearing Napoleon's power and ambition, hoped to keep him away from Paris by giving him command of the army of England. But Napoleon realized the impossibility of invading England while her fleet was supreme, and instead set out on an expedition to Egypt in the hope of damaging Britain's trade with India. He set sail in May 1798, captured Malta, managed to escape the British fleet, and arrived with his army at Alexandria on 30 June. He twice defeated the Mamluks and entered Cairo on 24 July, but the French fleet was destroyed by **Nelson** at the Battle of the Nile, producing an effective stalemate. Napoleon defeated the Turks at Mount Tabor but failed to capture St Jean d'Acre, which was defended by the British squadron under Sir **Sidney Smith**, and he was obliged to return to Egypt. There he heard reports of French reverses in Italy and on the Rhine, and secretly embarked for France (22 August 1799)

cont

Born in Dumbarton, he built the engines for the first four Cunard steamships. He also built some of the earliest ironclad warships, including the *Black Prince* in 1860, and helped in the development of the Clyde as a great shipbuilding centre. ⌑ Brian D Osborne, *Robert Napier 1791–1876: The Father of Clyde Shipbuilding* (1991)

Napier (of Magdala), Robert Cornelis Napier, 1st Baron 1810–90
British field marshal

Born in Colombo, Ceylon (Sri Lanka), he entered the Bengal Engineers in 1826. He served in campaigns in India, and during the Indian Mutiny (1857) he fought at the Siege of Lucknow. He received the thanks of parliament for his services in the Chinese war of 1860 and for leading the expedition in Abyssinia in 1868. In 1870 he became Commander-in-Chief in India and a member of the Indian Council; later he was Governor of Gibraltar, field marshal, and Constable of the Tower.

Napoleon I   See panel above

Napoleon II, *properly* François Charles Joseph Bonaparte 1811–32
French nobleman and titular King of Rome

Born in Paris, the son of **Napoleon I** and **Marie Louise**, he was styled King of Rome upon his birth at the Tuileries. From 1814 until his death he lived at the Austrian court and was created Duke of Reichstadt (1818) by his grandfather, **Francis I**. Loyal Bonapartists proclaimed him Napoleon II in Paris in 1815, but he was formally deposed five days later. He spent the rest of his life in Vienna. ⌑ Jean Tulard, *Napoleon II* (1992)

Napoleon III, *originally* Charles Louis Napoléon Bonaparte 1808–73
President of the second French Republic and Emperor of France

Born in Paris, he was the third son of **Louis Bonaparte**, and a nephew of **Napoleon I**. His mother was **Hortense de Beauharnais**, daughter of Napoleon's first wife, **Joséphine**. Brought up in Switzerland, he assisted the Romagna in Italy in its revolt against pontifical rule in 1831. On the death of the Duke of Reichstadt, (Napoleon II), in 1832, he considered himself the head of the Napoleonic dynasty. Between 1832 and 1836 he published his *Rêveries politiques, Projet de constitution*, and *Considérations politiques et militaires sur la Suisse*. Following an unsuccessful action against the French at Strasbourg in 1836 he went to the USA, returning to Europe after his mother's death (1837), and at the insistence of the French government he settled in London. In 1838 he published his *Idées napoléoniennes*. In 1840 he made a second and equally abortive attempt on the throne of France at Boulogne, and was imprisoned for life in the fortress of Ham, near Amiens. He continued his Bonapartist propaganda and helped to edit the *Dictionnaire de la conversation*. He escaped to England in 1846. The revolution of February 1848 was a victory for the workers, and he hurried back to France as a virtual nominee of the Fourth Estate, or working-classes. Elected Deputy for Paris and three other departments, he took his seat in the Constituent Assembly on 13 June 1848. Two days later he resigned and left France. His quintuple election recalled him in September, and he won a huge victory over General **Louis Cavaignac**, his genuinely Republican competitor. On 20 December he took the oath of allegiance to the Republic as President,

Napoleon I *cont*

In Paris, Napoleon formed an alliance of convenience with **Sieyès**, one of the Directory, and took part in the revolution of 18th Brumaire (9 November 1799); Sieyès, Roger Ducos and Napoleon drew up a new constitution, by which Napoleon was nominated first consul for 10 years. But before embarking on further military campaigns, Napoleon had to improve the poor state of the French Treasury. He drew up plans for a Bank of France, and sought to stabilize the franc and regulate the collection of taxes by employing paid officials. He also endeavoured to reform the system of local government and the judiciary.

Napoleon offered peace terms to England and Austria but these were rejected. He secretly collected an army, reached the plains of Italy, and occupied Milan. Further victories at Marengo and Hohenlinden (1800) led to the signing of the Treaty of Luneville (February 1801), consolidating the French gains of Campo Formio. France's power in Europe was further strengthened by a Concordat with Rome, by which Pope **Pius VII** recognized the French Republic, and by the Peace of Amiens with war-weary England (1802). England retained Ceylon and Trinidad but relinquished Egypt, Malta and the Cape of Good Hope. France agreed to evacuate Naples, and the independence of Portugal and the Ionian Islands was recognized.

In 1802 Napoleon was made first consul for life by a plebiscite, and continued his programme of domestic reforms by restoring the Church, improving secondary education and instituting the Légion d'Honneur. When hostilities were resumed between England and France because of difficulties in implementing the Peace of Amiens, Napoleon made preparations to invade England, at the same time seizing Hanover. England in turn sent support to a royalist plot against Napoleon's life, but Napoleon arrested the conspirators and rid himself of **Moreau**, his most dangerous rival.

On 18 May 1804 Napoleon assumed the hereditary title of emperor. In 1805 he had to face a coalition of Russia and Austria, as well as England. England's naval supremacy precluded any idea of invasion, and he suddenly led his armies from Boulogne to the Danube, leaving Admiral **Villeneuve** to face the English fleet. He succeeded in surprising the Austrians under **Mack** at Ulm and they surrendered (19 October), leaving him free to enter Vienna on 13 November. Meanwhile the French fleet had been destroyed by Nelson off Cape Trafalgar.

On 2 December he inflicted a disastrous defeat on the Russians and Austrians at Austerlitz. The Holy Roman Empire came to an end, the Confederation of the Rhine was formed under French protection, and Napoleon then entered into negotiations for peace with Russia and England. Prussia, afraid that an Anglo-French alliance would mean the loss of Hanover to England, mobilized a Prussian army in August 1806, but Napoleon crushed it at Jena and Auerstadt on 14 October. Russia, who had intervened, was defeated at Friedland (14 June 1807). By the Peace of Tilsit Prussia lost half her territory and Napoleon became the arbiter of Europe.

Napoleon was now master of an empire that extended from France to Italy and from the Pyrenees to the Dalmatian coast. He ruled his territories by installing his brothers as kings, including **Joseph Bonaparte** in Naples. The principal threat to his power remained the naval supremacy of England. Knowing England's reliance on trade, he tried to cripple her by the so-called Continental System, by which he ordered the European states under his control to boycott British goods. To enforce the
cont

---

but at the beginning of 1849 a struggle emerged between the President and the majority of the Assembly. He took command of the army and established his supporters in posts of influence. Hampered by the National Assembly in his efforts to make his power perpetual, he threw off the mask of a constitutional president and on 2 December 1851, with the help of the military, he dissolved the Constitution and imprisoned or deported those who rebelled. France appeared to acquiesce, for when the vote was taken in December, he was re-elected for 10 years by seven million votes. He assumed the title Emperor of France in 1852, a year after the coup d'état, in accordance with another plebiscite. Political parties were either demoralized or broken, he gagged the press, awed the bourgeoisie, and courted the clergy to win the peasantry. In 1853 he married Eugénie de Montijo (1826–1920), a Spanish countess, born in Granada. The emperor now proclaimed the right of peoples to choose their own masters, helping his own cause with the annexation of Savoy and Nice to France (1860), his Mexican intervention through **Maximilian** of Austria, and in his handling of the Italian question. He regulated the price of bread, encouraged public works for the enrichment of the working-class and peasantry, and prompted the complete remodelling of Paris under the direction of Baron **Georges Haussmann**. International exhibitions and treaties of commerce were a further inducement to internal peace. His foreign policies flourished with the Crimean War (1854–56), the campaign in Lombardy against Austria (1859), and the expeditions to China (1857–60). He monitored changing public opinion and when his *Vie de César*, written to extol his own methods of government, met with loud protests he reorganized his army, set himself up more proudly as an arbiter in Europe, and took a more conciliatory attitude to liberalism. In 1869 his Prime Minister Eugène Rouher, an advocate of absolutism, was dismissed, and new men were called into power to liberalize the Constitution. By another plebiscite the new parliamentary scheme was sanctioned by seven million votes (May 1870) but when 50,000 dissentient votes given by the army revealed an unsuspected source of danger he contrived a distraction by declaring war against Prussia (July 1870). By the end of July, Prussia had almost double the number of men in the field as the French had and the campaign ended in defeat for Napoleon, who surrendered on 2 September. On 4 September the Second Empire was ended. Until the conclusion of peace he was confined at Wilhelmshöle. In 1871 he joined the ex-empress at Chislehurst, Kent, and resided there in exile until his death. ⌺ F A Simpson, *The Rise of Louis Napoleon* (3rd edn, 1950)

Narayan, Jaiprakash, *also known as* JP 1902–79
Indian freedom fighter and politician

He was educated in a village primary school and abandoned his studies in 1921 to join the Non-Co-operation Movement. He later went to the USA on a scholarship to study at the University of Ohio. Influenced by Marxist ideas, he joined the communist movement, but accepted **Nehru**'s offer to take charge of the Labour Department in Congress. He joined the civil disobedience movement after the failure of the **Gandhi**–Irwin talks and was jailed. He was one of the founders of the Congress Socialist Party (1934). The author of a number of books and booklets on social, political and economic problems, he took an active part in the Quit India Movement of 1942, but gave up politics after India gained independence and joined the Bhoodan movement led by **Vinoba Bhave**.

Napoleon I *cont*

blockade, he sent armies to occupy Spain and Portugal, precipitating the Peninsular War. A British army, under Wellesley (**Wellington**), landed in Portugal, defeated the French at Vimeiro (1808), and forced them to evacuate Portugal under the terms of the Convention of Cintra. The war was to occupy a large part of the French army until 1813, when Wellington routed the French and forced them out of Spain.

In 1809 Austria took advantage of the French troubles in Spain to declare war on France. Napoleon drove the Austrians out of Ratisbon, entered Vienna (13 May) and was victorious at the Battle of Wagram on 5 and 6 July. By the Treaty of Schönbrunn (20 October 1809), France wrested the Illyrian provinces from Austria and secured a heavy money indemnity. In December Napoleon, who wanted an heir, divorced the childless Joséphine and married the archduchess **Marie Louise** of Austria. A son (the future **Napoleon II**) was born on 20 March 1811.

Napoleon now turned his attention to Russia, which he suspected of seeking an alliance with England. He invaded Russia, defeated the Russians at Borodino (6 September), and entered the deserted city of Moscow (1812). But his lines of communication were overstretched, and his army was tired and hungry. When the city was destroyed by fire, he was forced to retreat, encumbered by the sick and wounded and suffering from the harsh effects of the Russian winter which he had greatly underestimated. Only a fraction of the Grand Army that had set out for Russia reached Vilna.

Napoleon, now also defeated in Spain, hurried to Paris to raise a new levy, stem the rising panic and dispel rumours of his death. After initial successes against the allies (later joined by Austria), he was significantly defeated

at the Battle of the Nations near Leipzig. The allies invaded France and attacked Paris (1814), which capitulated. Napoleon fell back to Fontainebleau; but his position was desperate and Wellington had now led his army across the Pyrenees into France.

Napoleon was forced to abdicate, first in favour of his son, and then unconditionally (11 April). By the Treaty of Fontainebleau he was given the sovereignty of Elba, allowed to retain the title of emperor, and awarded a revenue from the French government. The Bourbons in the person of **Louis XVIII** were restored to the throne of France, but their return was unpopular, especially with the army. Napoleon hoped to take advantage of the situation and landed on the French coast on 1 March 1815. On 20 March he entered Paris at the start of the 'Hundred Days', with the support of the army.

Europe declared war against him. After an initial success against the Prussians under **Blücher**, he was defeated by the combined armies of Wellington and Blücher at Waterloo in Belgium. Napoleon fled to Paris, abdicated on 22 June, and surrendered to the British. He was banished by the British government to St Helena, where he died of a stomach illness on 5 May 1821.

📖 F Kafker and J Laux, *Napoleon and his Times* (1988).

C'est un fossé qui sera franchi lorsqu'on aura l'audace de le tenter.
'[The English Channel] is just a ditch, and will be crossed when someone has the nerve to try it.' From a letter of November 1803, in *Correspondance de Napoléon Ier* (1858–69), vol 9.

Later, he was closely involved in the protest movement against the Chinese policy on Tibet and also toured the tribal areas of Nagaland in an attempt to bring about a rapprochement between the rebel Nagas and the government of India. He organized famine relief for the affected people of Bihar in 1967 and persuaded several dacoits of Madhya Pradesh to surrender their arms in 1972. He led the movement for restoration of democracy and liberties after the imposition of the 'emergency' by **Indira Gandhi** (1975), for which he was arrested. Released in 1977, he led the Janata Party to victory in the general election of that year.

Narayan, Rasipuram Krishnaswamy 1906–
Indian novelist

Born in Madras, south India, he was educated there and at Maharaja's College in Mysore. His first novel, *Swami and Friends* (1935), and its successor *The Bachelor of Arts* (1937), are set in the enchanting fictional territory of 'Malgudi'. Other Malgudi novels are *The Dark Room* (1938), *The English Teacher* (1945)—a thinly veiled account of his own marriage and the event that most matured and shaped his character, the early death of his beloved wife—*Mr Sampath* (1949), *The Financial Expert* (1952), *The Man-Eater of Malgudi* (1961), *The Painter of Signs* (1977), *The Tiger for Malgudi* (1983), *Talkative Man* (1986) and *The World of Nagaraj* (1990). His novel *The Guide* (1958) won him the National Prize of the Indian Literary Academy. He has also published stories, travel books, books for children and essays, as well as *My Days: A Memoir* (1974). The best Indian novelist of his generation, he was first published in Great Britain through the influence of **Graham Greene**. 📖 C Vander, *R K Narayan* (1986)

Nares, Sir George Strong 1831–1915
Scottish naval commander and explorer

Born in Aberdeen, he was educated at the Royal Naval College, New Cross, and joined the navy in 1846. He served as mate on the *Resolute* during its Arctic expedition of 1852, in the Crimea, and as commander of the cadet sail-training ship *Britannia*, and worked on surveys of north-east Australia and the Mediterranean (1872–74). He commanded the *Challenger* (1872–74) on its oceanographic voyage around the world which resulted in a 50-volume report for its sponsors, the Admiralty and the Royal Society. In 1875 he was transferred to command the *Alert* and *Discovery* in the Arctic, and later, on the *Alert*, surveyed the Magellan Straits.

Narses c.478–573
Byzantine general

He was born in Armenia, and served **Justinian I** in Constantinople (Istanbul). In 552 he succeeded **Belisarius** in Italy, where he defeated the Ostrogoths, took possession of Rome, and completely extinguished the Gothic power in Italy. Justinian appointed him prefect of Italy in 554, and he administered its affairs with vigour and ability. He was charged with greed, and on Justinian's death the Romans complained to **Justin II**, who deprived him of his office in 567.

Narváez, Ramón María 1800–68
Spanish soldier and senator

Born in Loja, a supporter of **Isabella II**, he defeated the Carlists in 1836, then took part in an unsuccessful insurrection against Espartero in 1840 and fled to France, where he was joined by Maria Cristina. In 1843 he led a Republican insurrection in Madrid that drove Espartero from power, and became virtual dictator. He lost power temporarily in 1851, and was briefly exiled as special ambassador to France, but from 1856 he was premier again several times.

Nash, Heddle 1896–1961
English tenor

He was born in London where he was a chorister at Westminster Abbey. He studied first in London, then in Milan, where in 1924 he made his debut in the Italian opera *Il Barbiere di Siviglia (The Barber of Seville)*. Returning to England, he sang first at Sadler's Wells, then with the British National Opera Company, and from 1929 to 1948 had a long association with Covent Garden. Nash also built up a strong reputation in oratorio and made celebrated recordings of *The Messiah* and *The Dream of Gerontius*.

Nash, John 1752–1835
English architect

Born in London or Cardigan, Wales, he trained as an architect, but after coming into a legacy retired to Wales. Having lost heavily by speculations in 1792, he resumed practice in London and gained a reputation by his country house designs. He came to the notice of the Prince of Wales (later **George IV**), and was engaged (1811–25) to plan the layout of the new Regent's Park and its environs of curved terraces. He laid out Regent Street (1825) to link the Park with Westminster. He built Carlton House Terrace, and laid out Trafalgar Square and St James's Park. He recreated Buckingham Palace from old Buckingham House, designed the Marble Arch which originally stood in front of it (moved to its present site in 1851), and rebuilt Brighton Pavilion in oriental style. On the strength of a patent (1797) for improvements to the arches and piers of bridges, he claimed much of the credit for introducing steel girders. The skilful use of terrain and landscape featured in his layouts marks him as one of the greatest town planners. ⊞ John Summerson, *The Life and Work of John Nash, Architect* (1980)

Nash, (Frederic) Ogden 1902–71
US writer of light verse

Born in Rye, New York, he was educated at Harvard, and worked in teaching, editing, selling bonds and copywriting, before devoting himself to verse. He soon became a popular writer and frequently produced witty verse for the *New Yorker*. He used puns, parody, pastiche and alliteration to amuse as well as shock. He published many collections, including *Free Wheeling* (1931), *Hard Lines* (1931), *Parents Keep Out: Elderly Poems for Youngerly Readers* (1951), *The Private Dining Room and Other New Verses* (1953) and *Boy is a Boy* (1960). *I Wouldn't Have Missed It: Selected Poems of Ogden Nash* was published in 1983. ⊞ L B Axford, *An Index to the Poems of Ogden Nash* (1972)

Nash, Paul 1889–1946
English painter

Born in London, he became an official war artist in 1917 (remembered particularly for his poignant *Menin Road*, 1919). Developing a style which reduced form to bare essentials without losing the identity of the subject, he won renown as a landscape painter and also practised scene painting, commercial design and book illustration. For a while he taught at the Royal College of Art. Experiments in a near abstract manner were followed by a phase of Surrealism until, in 1939, he again filled the role of war artist, this time for the Air Ministry and the Ministry of Information, producing such pictures as *Battle of Britain* and *Tôtes Meer*. Shortly before his death he turned to a very individual style of flower painting. His autobiography, *Outline*, was posthumously published in 1949.

Nash, Richard, *known as* Beau Nash 1674–1762
Welsh dandy

Born in Swansea, he was educated at Carmarthen and Oxford, held a commission in the army, and in 1693 entered the Middle Temple. He then made a shifty living by gambling, but in 1704 became Master of Ceremonies at Bath, where he conducted the public balls with a splendour never before witnessed. His reforms in manners, his influence in improving the streets and buildings, and his leadership in fashion helped to transform Bath into a fashionable holiday resort.

Nash, Sir Walter 1882–1968
New Zealand politician

He was born in Kidderminster, England. He served on the national executive of the New Zealand Labour Party from 1919 to 1960, encouraging the adoption of a moderate reform programme in the Christian Socialist tradition. An MP from 1929, he held numerous ministerial appointments from 1936 onwards and in World War II was deputy Prime Minister to **Peter Fraser**, although from 1942 to 1944 he headed a special mission to the USA. He was Prime Minister from 1957 to 1960, but as his government possessed a majority of only one there were few political innovations.

Nashe, Thomas 1567–1601
English dramatist and satirist

Born in Lowestoft, Suffolk, he studied for seven years at St John's College, Cambridge, travelled in France and Italy, and then went to London. His first work was the *Anatomie of Absurditie* (1589), perhaps written at Cambridge. He plunged into the Marprelate controversy, showing a talent for vituperation which he expressed in such works as *Pierce Penilesse, his Supplication to the Divell* (1592), against Richard Harvey who had criticized Nashe's preface to **Robert Greene**'s *Menaphon*, and *Have with you to Saffron Walden* (1596), against Gabriel Harvey, who had by then assailed Greene's memory in *Foure Letters*. In 1599 the controversy was suppressed by the Archbishop of Canterbury. Nashe's satirical masque *Summer's Last Will and Testament* (1592) contains the song 'Spring the sweet Spring is the year's pleasant king'. *The Unfortunate Traveller* (1594) is a picaresque tale, one of the earliest of its kind. After **Christopher Marlowe**'s death, Nashe prepared his unfinished tragedy *Dido* (1596) for the stage. His own play *The Isle of Dogs* (1597), now lost, drew such attention to abuses in the state that it was suppressed, the theatre closed, and the writer himself thrown into the Fleet prison. His last work was *Lenten Stuffe* (1599), a panegyric on the red herring trade at Yarmouth. ⊞ M Schaluch, *Antecedents of the English Novel* (1963)

Nasmyth, Alexander 1758–1840
Scottish painter

Born in Edinburgh, he was a pupil of **Allan Ramsay**. The inventor Patrick Miller (1731–1815) partly financed his visit to Italy (1782–84), which had a considerable influence on his work. Back in Edinburgh he established a reputation as a portrait painter, his portrait of **Robert Burns** in the Scottish National Gallery being particularly famous. He later confined himself to landscape painting, and set up a school where his children also taught.

Nasmyth, James 1808–90
Scottish engineer

Born and educated in Edinburgh, the son of **Alexander Nasmyth**, he established the Bridgewater Foundry at Patricroft in 1836. His steam hammer was devised in 1839 for forging an enormous wrought-iron paddle-shaft. Three years later he came across an identical steam hammer in a works at Le Creusot in France—it had been adapted from his own scheme-book. Nasmyth patented his invention, and it was adopted by the Admiralty in 1843. His other inventions included a steam pile-driver, a planing machine, and a hydraulic punching machine. He published *Remarks on Tools and Machinery* (1858) and *The Moon* (1874). ⊞ J A Cantrell, *James Nasmyth and the Bridgewater Foundry* (1985)

Nasmyth, Patrick 1787–1831
Scottish landscape painter

Born in Edinburgh, the son of **Alexander Nasmyth**, he settled in England, painted many English scenes and became known as the 'English **Hobbema**'.

Nasser, Gamal Abd al- 1918–70
Egyptian statesman

He was born in Alexandria. As an army officer with bitter experience of the mismanaged Palestine campaign of 1948, he became dissatisfied with the inefficiency and corruption of the **Farouk** regime, and founded the military Junta which led to its downfall. Chief power behind the coup of 1952, he was mainly responsible for the rise to power of General **Mohammed Neguib**. Tension between the two grew and Nasser assumed the office of Prime Minister (April 1954) and then President (November 1954) by deposing Neguib. Nasser was officially elected President in 1956, and his nationalization of the Suez Canal in that year led to Israel's invasion of Sinai. When Anglo-French forces intervened, widespread differences of opinion in Great Britain and elsewhere, coupled with veiled Russian threats, enabled Nasser to turn an abject military débâcle into a political victory. His aim was to build an Arab empire stretching across North Africa, the first step being the creation, by federation with Syria, of the United Arab Republic of which Nasser was President in February 1958. In March 1958 the Yemen and the UAR formed the United Arab States. This was followed by a sustained effort to break up the Baghdad Pact and liquidate the remaining sovereign states in the Middle East, a policy which succeeded in Iraq, but was thwarted in Jordan and the Lebanon by the deployment of US and British forces. His plans for unity among the Arab states received a setback when Syria withdrew from the UAR and when the union with the Yemen was dissolved (1961). In 1964, however, the UAR formed joint presidency councils with Iraq and the Yemen. After the six-day Arab–Israeli War (1967), heavy losses on the Arab side led to Nasser's resignation, but he was persuaded to stay on , and he died in office, one year before the completion of one of his greatest projects, the Aswam High Dam. 📖 Robert St John, *The Boss* (1961)

Nast, Thomas 1840–1902
US cartoonist and illustrator

Born in Landau, Germany, he went to New York City in 1846 and became a staff artist for *Harper's Weekly* during the Civil War. He used his political cartoons to expose the corruption of the Tweed Ring in New York's Tammany Hall (1869–72), and his devastating caricatures of **William Marcy Tweed**, grotesquely swollen with graft but still recognizable, led to Tweed's discovery and arrest in Spain. Nast also originated the donkey and the elephant as symbols of the Democratic and Republican parties, and he helped to create the modern image of Santa Claus.

Nathan, George Jean 1882–1958
US writer, editor and critic

Born in Fort Wayne, Indiana, he was known for his caustic drama reviews and his satirical observations on US life and culture. He was a founder and editor (1924–30) of the *American Mercury* with **H L Mencken**.

Nathan, Isaac 1790–1864
Australian composer and music teacher

Born in Canterbury, Kent, England, he was musical librarian to King **George IV**, and a friend of the poet **Byron** whose *Hebrew Melodies* (1815) Nathan set to music inspired by Jewish chants. Moving with his family to Australia in 1841, he became choirmaster of St Mary's Cathedral, Sydney. He published *Australia the Wide and Free* in 1842, and the first opera to be composed and performed in Australia, *Don John of Austria* in 1847. He also composed a dramatic scena, *Leichhardt's Grave*, and in 1849 published *The Southern Euphrosyne*, which included the first harmonizations of Aboriginal music.

Nathans, Daniel 1928–
US microbiologist and Nobel Prize winner

Born in Wilmington, Delaware, of Russian–Jewish extraction, he studied at the University of Delaware and Washington University School of Medicine. From 1955 to 1957 he worked at the National Cancer Institute of the National Institutes of Health. As a guest at the Rockefeller University, New York (1959–62), he researched protein biosynthesis. Professor at Johns Hopkins University from 1962, he pioneered the use of restriction enzymes to fragment DNA molecules, enabling him to make the first genetic map and to identify the location of specific genes on the DNA. For this work he shared the 1978 Nobel Prize for physiology or medicine with **Hamilton Smith** and **Werner Arber**. In 1993 he was awarded a US National Medal of Science.

Nation, Carry Amelia, *née* Moore 1846–1911
US temperance crusader

She was born in Garrard County, Kentucky. As the widow of an alcoholic, she was adamantly opposed to the use of liquor, and conducted a series of raids on saloons in Kansas and other states (1899–1909), breaking bottles and destroying furniture with a hatchet. Her frequent arrests focused public attention on the cause of Prohibition, and she often appeared as a temperance lecturer.

Natta, Giulio 1903–79
Italian chemist and Nobel Prize winner

Born in Imperia, near Genoa, he first studied mathematics at the university there, but switched to chemical engineering at Milan Polytechnic Institute, where he later became assistant lecturer in chemistry. In 1933 he was appointed Professor of Chemistry at the University of Pavia, and two years later became director of the Institute of Physical Chemistry in Rome. He was appointed Professor of Chemistry in Turin in 1937 and from 1938 held the post of Professor and director of the Milan Institute of Industrial Chemistry until his retirement in 1973. His early work concerned heterogeneous catalysts used in a number of industrial processes and in 1938 he initiated a programme for the production of artificial rubber. His most important work used the organometallic catalysts developed by **Karl Ziegler** for the polymerization of propene to give polypropylene containing uniformly oriented methyl groups. In 1963 he shared the Nobel Prize for chemistry with Ziegler.

Nattier, Jean Marc 1685–1766
French artist

Born in Paris, he executed historical pictures and portraits, including those of **Peter the Great** and the empress **Catherine the Great** of Russia, but after losing his money in the **John Law** financial crisis he took up the fashionable stereotyped style of court portraiture now labelled 'le portrait Nattier' for the court of **Louis XV**.

Naughton and Gold, *properly* Charles Naughton 1887–1976 and Jimmy Gold, *originally* James McGonigal 1886–1967
Scottish comedians

Born in Glasgow, they first appeared as 'Naughton and Gold' at the Hippodrome, Glasgow, in 1908, and the same year made their London debut at the Brixton Empress. In the early 1930s they joined several other double acts to form the London Palladium Crazy Gang, which raised their prestige from routine comedy to star billing. Their burlesque on British builders gave them the immortal catchphrase, 'Turn it round the other way'. They appeared in many Royal Variety Performances, and from 1947 staged Crazy Gang revival shows at the Victoria Palace, London. Their films include *Okay for Sound* (1937) and *Gasbags* (1940).

Nauman, Bruce 1941–
US sculptor

Born in Fort Wayne, Indiana, he studied mathematics and art at Wisconsin University. In the 1960s he became a leading exponent of Conceptual Art, using neon lights and holograms in addition to producing minimalist sculptures from more conventional materials, as in *From Hand to Mouth* and *Six Inches of my Knee Extended to Six Feet* (both 1967). Since 1970 he has worked principally with wood and fibreglass, exploring the relationship between sculpture and the gallery space, producing installations such as *House Divided* (1983), *Room with my Soul Left Out/Room That Does not Care* (1984) and *Dream Passage with Four Corridors* (1984, Pompidou Centre, Paris).

Navier, Claude Louis Marie Henri 1785–1836
French civil engineer

He was born in Dijon. Educated at the École Polytechnique and the École des Ponts et Chaussées, he taught, for much of his life, at one or the other of these schools, being principally occupied in developing the theoretical basis of structural mechanics and the strength of materials, as well as the work done by machines. Recognizing the importance of being able to predict the limits of elastic behaviour in structural materials, his formulae represented one of the greatest single advances in structural analysis ever made. He was responsible for the construction of a number of elegant bridges over the River Seine, but one of his most ambitious designs, a suspension bridge in Paris, encountered both engineering and political problems, to such an extent that it was dismantled just before completion.

Navratilova, Martina 1956–
US tennis player

Born in Prague, Czechoslovakia (Czech Republic), she played for Czechoslovakia in the Federation Cup for three years. In 1975 she defected to the USA (US citizen 1981) and immediately turned professional. Her rivalry with Chris Evert was one of the great features of the game from 1975. She won a record nine singles titles at Wimbledon (1978–79, 1982–87, 1990) and the US Open four times (1983–84, 1986–87) and recorded over 100 tournament successes. She also won the Grand Slam twice. Her impressive number of wins makes her second only to Margaret Smith Court. In 1994, having reached the final at Wimbledon, she retired from regular competitive singles play. Her books include *Martina* (1985) and *Feet of Clay* (1996).

Nazarbaev, Nursultan Abishevich 1940–
Kazakhstan politician

Originally a metal worker, he turned to party duties in 1969 and rose steadily in the 1970s and dramatically in the 1980s. He was chairman of the Kazakhstan Council of Ministers by 1984, and was made first secretary of the Kazakh Communist Party in 1989. In 1990 he was chosen for the Soviet politburo and became President of the Kazakh Supreme Soviet. As elected President of Kazakhstan in 1991 he took his republic out of the USSR but kept it in the new Commonwealth of Independent States (CIS).

Nazianzus, Gregory of See Gregory of Nazianzus, St

Nazimova, Alla, *originally* Alla Leventon 1879–1945
US actress

Born in Yalta, Russia, she studied in Moscow under Stanislavsky, made her debut in St Petersburg (1904), and appeared in New York as Hedda Gabler (1905). In 1910 she took over the 39th Street Theatre, rechristening it 'The Nazimova', and became a highly popular dramatic actress, later specializing in the plays of Ibsen, Ivan Turgenev, Chekhov and Eugene O'Neill. She had a successful period in films, which included *The Brat, Camille, A Doll's House, The Red Lantern* and her own *Salomé*, based on the Beardsley illustrations to Oscar Wilde's play.

Nazor, Vladimir 1876–1949
Croatian poet

Born in Postire on the island of Brač, he wrote lyrics and ballads as well as epic poems and dramatic works in a style similar to the Symbolists. His works include *Slav Legends* (1900), *Lirika* (1910, 'Lyrics'), *Carmen Vitae*, an anthology (1922), and a diary of his experiences with the Yugoslav partisans in World War II.

Nazrul Islam, Kazi See Islam, Kazi Nazrul

N'Dour, Youssou 1959–
Senegalese singer, musician and composer

Born in Dakar, Senegal, into a musical family of griots, he developed a style based on the traditional music of the Wolof tribe of Senegal, but with added influences from Cuban, jazz, and later rock music. His Étoile de Dakar band became African superstars, and his magnificent singing voice brought him to the attention of Peter Gabriel and Paul Simon. His initial western albums were not a success, and many felt he had left too much of Senegal behind him, but he has gone on to become a major attraction on the concert circuit with a spectacular stage show, and is one of the major artists bringing African music to a wider global audience.

Neagle, Dame Anna, *originally* Marjorie Robertson 1904–86
English actress

Born in London, she studied and taught dance and was a chorus girl before graduating to leading roles, making her film debut in 1930. Under the tutelage of director Herbert Wilcox, whom she later married (1943), she emerged as a major star of historical film dramas, offering genteel portraits of inspiring heroines such as *Victoria, the Great* (1937) and *The Lady With the Lamp* (1951). A series of musicals made her Great Britain's top box-office attraction but later attempts to tackle contemporary subjects were ill-judged and she retired from the screen in 1958. She retained the affection of British audiences, later stage appearances including *Charlie Girl* (1965–71) and *My Fair Lady* (1979–79). Created DBE in 1969, she wrote two autobiographies, *It's Been Fun* (1949) and *There's Always Tomorrow* (1974).

Neal, John 1793–1876
US editor, poet, novelist and critic

Born in Falmouth, Maine, he went into business but failed, qualified as a lawyer, then became editor of *Portico*, a literary monthly published by the chauvinistic Delphian Club, Baltimore. He sometimes signed himself 'Jehu O'Cataract'. His melodramatic novel *Keep Cool* (1817), about a man's guilt over the death of his opponent in a duel, made him famous. Among his many other novels is *Logan, A Family History* (1822), about an (actual) Englishman who married the queen of a Native American tribe. Soon after its publication Neal went to England, where he acted as secretary to Jeremy Bentham. His finest novel, *Rachel Dyer*, about a Salem witch, was published in 1828. His *Wandering Recollections of a Somewhat Busy Life* (1869) is a useful source book.

Neal, Patricia (Patsy Louise) 1926–
US actress

Born in Packard, Virginia, she studied drama at Northwestern University in Evanston, Illinois, and worked as a model before making her Broadway debut in *The Voice Of The Turtle* (1946). Joining the New York Actors Studio, she won a Tony award for *Another Part Of The Forest* (1946) and made her film debut in *John Loves Mary* (1949). Hollywood squandered her talents on a succession of conventional roles, though she later proved her worth in films like *A Face In The Crowd* (1957), *Breakfast At Tiffany's* (1961) and *Hud* (1963, Best Actress Academy Award). Her brave fight to regain her health after several massive strokes was rewarded with the Heart of the Year award from President Lyndon B Johnson and a further Academy Award nomination for *The Subject Was Roses* (1968). Her more recent notable performances are in such television productions as *The Homecoming* (1971) and *Things In Their Season* (1974). She was married (1953–83) to the writer Roald Dahl and has written an autobiography *As I Am* (1988).

Neale, Edward Vansittart 1810–92
English social reformer
Born in Bath and educated at Oxford, he became a barrister, and from 1851 was a pioneer Christian Socialist and an advocate of co-operation. He founded the first co-operative shop in London, and became general secretary of the Central Co-operative Board (1875–91).

Neale, John Mason 1818–66
English hymnologist
Born in London, he studied at Trinity College, Cambridge, and from 1846 was warden of Sackville College, East Grinstead. He wrote many books on church history, but is remembered chiefly for his hymns, and many of his translations are cherished worldwide. Among his best-known pieces are 'Jerusalem the golden' and 'O happy band of pilgrims'. His *Collected Hymns* was published in 1914.

Nearchus 4th century BC
Macedonian general
Born in Crete, he settled in Amphipolis during the reign of Philip II of Macedon, and became the companion of the young Alexander the Great. In 330BC he was Governor of Lycia, and in 329 he joined Alexander in Bacria with a body of Greek mercenaries, and took part in the Indian campaigns. Having built a fleet on the Hydaspes (Jhelum), Alexander gave Nearchus the command. He left the Indus in 325, and, skirting the coast, reached Susa in 324. His narrative is preserved in the *Indica* of Arrian.

Neave, Airey 1916–79
British Army intelligence officer and politician
Born in London, he was educated at Eton and Merton College, Oxford. In World War II he was wounded at Calais (1940) and taken prisoner. He escaped from a Polish POW camp but was recaptured and sent to the maximum security prison at Colditz Castle, from which he was the first British officer ever to escape (1942). On his return to London he established new underground movements and trained air-crews in the means of escape in occupied territory. He was awarded many medals for his war service, including the Croix de Guerre. In 1943 he was called to the Bar, and as a lieutenant-colonel served charges on many of the war criminals who stood trial at Nuremberg. He entered parliament for the Conservatives at his third attempt, in 1951, held several junior government posts, survived a heart attack in 1959, and became Governor of Imperial College, London (1963–71). He was prominent in the group that deposed Edward Heath as party leader (1975) and replaced him with Margaret Thatcher, who rewarded Neave by appointing him head of her private office and, in 1979, Secretary of State for Northern Ireland. As an opponent of power-sharing and

of the withdrawal of British forces from the Province, Neave was killed by an INLA car bomb outside the House of Commons. His writings include *They Have Their Exits* (1953), *Saturday at MI9* (1969), and *The Flames of Calais* (1975), describing his wartime experiences.

Nebuchadnezzar or Nebuchadrezzar II
d.562BC
King of Babylon
He succeeded his father Nabopolassar and founded the New Babylonian Empire. He rebuilt Babylon and restored almost every temple in the land. He extended the Babylonian Empire as far as the Mediterranean, defeating the Egyptians at Carchemish (605BC) and gaining control of Syria. He captured Jerusalem in 597 and 586, when he destroyed the city and deported the Jews into exile in Babylon. 📖 D J Wiseman, *Nebuchadrezzar and Babylon* (1985)

Neckam or Nequam, Alexander 1157–1217
English scholar
Born in St Albans on the same night as Richard I, he was nursed by his mother along with the future king. Educated at St Albans and Paris (where he lectured), he returned to England to be schoolmaster at Dunstable. In 1213 he became abbot of Cirencester. In his *De naturis rerum* ('On the Nature of Things') and *De utensilibus* ('On Instruments') he was the first in Europe to describe the use of a magnetic needle by sailors.

Necker, Anne Louise Germaine See Staël, Madame de

Necker, Jacques 1732–1804
French politician and financier
Born in Geneva, he went to Paris as a banker's clerk when he was 15, and in 1762 established the London and Paris bank of Thellusson and Necker. In 1776 he was made the director of the Treasury, and next year director-general of Finance. Some of his remedial measures assisted France, but his most ambitious scheme—the establishment of provincial assemblies, one of whose functions should be the apportionment of taxes—proved a disastrous failure. His retrenchments were hateful to the Queen, and his famous *Compte rendu* (1781, 'Financial Report') prompted his dismissal. He retired to Geneva, but was recalled to Paris in 1788, where he won popularity by recommending the summoning of the Estates General. However, his proposals for reform displeased the king and he was dismissed. His dismissal contributed to the public mood which culminated in the storming of the Bastille. The king recalled him in 1789, but he retired the following year. He was the father of Madame de Staël.

Nedreaas, Torborg 1906–
Norwegian novelist
Born in Bergen, of Jewish extraction, she turned to writing late in life, after World War II. She is a left-wing feminist, and her books highlight social life and class struggle in Norwegian urban society. Especially powerful are *Musikk fra en blå brønn* (1960, Eng trans *Music from a Blue Well*) and *Ved neste nymåne* (1971, Eng trans *At the Next New Moon*), about a girl called Herdis growing up in Bergen between the wars. Her best stories were collected in *Stoppested* (1953, 'Stopping Place'). 📖 H Eriksen, *Nedreaas* (1979)

Needham, (Noël) Joseph (Terence Montgomery) 1900–95
English biochemist and historian of Chinese science
Born in London and educated at Cambridge, he was university demonstrator in biochemistry there (1928–33), working mainly to discover the process underlying the development of the fertilized egg into a differentiated

and complex organism, which he published in *Chemical Embryology* (1931). He was Reader from 1933 to 1966, and Master of Gonville and Caius College, Cambridge, from 1966 to 1976. His publications at first reflected philosophical problems in science, like *Man a Machine* (1927) and *The Sceptical Biologist* (1929), but these began to give way to historical preoccupations shown in *A History of Embryology* (1934) and *History is on Our Side* (1945). During World War II he became head of the British Scientific Mission in China and Scientific Counsellor at the British Embassy there. Adviser to the Chinese National Resources Commission, the Chinese Army Medical Administration and the Chinese Air Force Research Bureau, he became director of the department of natural sciences, UNESCO (1946–48), which he helped found. He published *Chinese Science* (1946), and *Science and Civilisation in China* (12 vols, 1954–84), a work of the foremost significance concerning the history of science and the Chinese historical achievement. He has also published on the history of acupuncture and Korean astronomy and clocks, as well as a vast body of other work. Needham was elected Fellow of the Royal Society (1941) and the British Academy (1971), and in 1992 was made Companion of Honour.

Néel, Louis Eugène Félix 1904–
French physicist and Nobel Prize winner

Born in Lyons, he graduated from the École Normale Supérieure, and later became Professor of Physics at Strasbourg University (1937–40). In 1940 he moved to Grenoble and helped to make it one of the most important scientific centres in France, becoming director of the Centre for Nuclear Studies there in 1956. His research has been concerned with magnetism in solids, predicting (1936) the existence of a special type of magnetic ordering called 'antiferromagnetism', which was experimentally confirmed in 1938, with full neutron diffraction confirmation in 1949. His work on ferromagnetic materials saw great application in the coating of magnetic tape, the permanent magnets of motors and the magnetic storage media used by computers. He shared the Nobel Prize for physics in 1970 with Hannes Alfvén. He has also studied the past history of the Earth's magnetic field.

Neer, Aert van der 1603/4–1677
Dutch painter

Born in Amsterdam, he specialized in moonlit canal and river scenes and, although these paintings are now regarded as major works of the Dutch school, received little recognition in his own time. In 1658 he gave up painting in order to open a wineshop. He was no more successful in this venture and returned to painting in 1662 after being declared bankrupt. Two of his sons, Eglon (1634–1703) and Jan (1638–65), became artists.

Neeson, Liam, *originally* William John Neeson
1952–
Northern Irish actor

Born in Ballymena, he was a boxer, architect's clerk and had studied to become a teacher before turning to acting and making his stage debut in *The Risen* (1976). He worked at the Lyric Players Theater and at the Abbey Theatre in Dublin before making his film debut in *Excalibur* (1981). Tall and physically imposing but capable of great sensitivity, he appeared in such films as *The Bounty* (1984), *Lamb* (1985) and *The Mission* (1986) before moving to Hollywood in 1987. He established his viability as a film star with such diverse roles as the mute Vietnam veteran in *Suspect* (1987), the iconoclastic sculptor in *The Good Mother* (1988) and the gentle editor in *Husbands and Wives* (1992). He received an Academy Award nomination for his powerful performance as the philanthropic industrialist in *Schindler's List* (1993). Subsequent films include *Nell* (1994), *Rob Roy* (1995) and *Michael Collins* (1996). He made

his Broadway debut in *Anna Christie* (1993) opposite actress Natasha Richardson (1963–), whom he married in 1994.

Nefertiti (Neferneferuaten) See panel p27 at Akhenaten

Negri, Ada 1870–1945
Italian poet

Born in Lodi, she became a teacher in a small primary school, and made her literary debut with *Fatalità* (1892, 'Destiny'), a derivative and idealistic collection of humanitarian poems. Her subsequent works, nine more volumes of verse and a number of prose works, refined the political, feminist and mystical basis of her work.
📖 M Magni, *L'opera di Ada Negri e la su umanità* (1961)

Neguib, Mohammed 1901–84
Egyptian leader

As general of an army division, he carried out a coup d'état in Cairo (1952) which banished King Farouk I and initiated the 'Egyptian Revolution'. Taking first the offices of Commander-in-Chief and Prime Minister, he abolished the monarchy in 1953 and became President of the republic. He was deposed in 1954 and succeeded by Colonel Gamal Abd al-Nasser.

Negus, Arthur George 1903–85
English broadcaster and antiques expert

Born in Reading, Berkshire, the son of a cabinet maker, he took over the family shop in 1920 and spent 20 years as an antique dealer. The shop was bombed during World War II, and in 1946 he joined the Gloucester firm of fine art auctioneers, Bruton, Knowles & Co, becoming a partner in 1972. Asked to expound on the merits and value of antiques, he became a regular panel member on the television series *Going for a Song* (1966–76), and his wry humour and expertise made him a popular broadcaster in such series as *Arthur Negus Enjoys* (1982) and *The Antiques Roadshow* (1982–83). His books include *Going for a Song: English furniture* (1969) and *A Life Among Antiques* (1982).

Nehemiah 5th century BC
Old Testament prophet

He was cupbearer to Artaxerxes I, who in 444BC made him Governor-Extraordinary of Judea. He had the walls of Jerusalem rebuilt, and repopulated the city by drafts from the surrounding districts. In 432BC he revisited Jerusalem, and either initiated or renewed and completed certain reforms which were among the most characteristic features of post-exilic Judaism. The canonical book of Nehemiah originally formed the closing chapters of the undivided work, Chronicles-Ezra-Nehemiah.

Neher, Erwin 1944–
German biophysicist and Nobel Prize winner

Born in Landsberg, he studied physics at the Technical University of Munich and the University of Wisconsin, joining the Max Planck Institute for Psychiatry in Munich (1970–72). He then moved to the Max Planck Institute for Biophysical Chemistry in Göttingen (1972), becoming director of the membrane biophysics department in 1983. In 1976, with Bert Sakmann, he succeeded in recording the electric currents through single ion channels in biological membranes, which had been predicted by Sir Alan Hodgkin and Sir Andrew Huxley. They developed the 'patch-clamp' technique, which isolated a small section of cell membrane and permitted precise biophysical measurements to be made over a discrete area, a method that has revolutionized cell physiology. In 1991 Neher and Sakmann shared the Nobel Prize for physiology or medicine for this work.

Nehru, Jawaharlal, *known as* Pandit ('teacher')
1889–1964
Indian statesman

Born in Allahabad, the son of **Motilal Nehru**, he was educated at Harrow and Trinity College Cambridge. He read for the Bar, returned home and served in the High Court of Allahabad. A persistent vision of himself as an Indian **Garibaldi** made him become a member of the Indian Congress Committee in 1918 and brought him, if with scientific reservations, under the spell of **Gandhi**. He was imprisoned by the British in 1921 and spent 18 of the next 25 years in jail. In 1928 he was elected president of the Indian National Congress, an office he often held afterwards, and was the leader of the movement's socialist wing. Although sympathetic to the Allied Cause in World War II, he, in common with other Congress Party leaders, did not co-operate and turned down the offer, brokered by **Stafford Cripps**, of dominion status for India in 1942. When India achieved independence in 1947, Nehru became her first Prime Minister and Minister of External Affairs. As democratic leader of the first republic within the Commonwealth, he followed a policy of neutralism and peace-making during the Cold War, often acting as a go-between between the Great Powers, and originated the theory of non-alignment. He committed India to a policy of industrialization, to a reorganization of its states on a linguistic basis and, although championing his people's claim to Kashmir, acted with restraint to bring this outstanding dispute with Pakistan to a peaceful solution. His many works include *Soviet Russia* (1929), *India and the World* (1936), *Independence and After* (1950) and an *Autobiography* (1936). His daughter **Indira Gandhi** was later Prime Minister.

Nehru, Motilal 1861–1931
Indian nationalist leader, lawyer and journalist

He became a follower of **Gandhi** in 1919, founded the *Independent* of Allahabad and became the first president of the reconstructed Indian National Congress. In the 1920s he co-headed the Swaraj Party (with **Chittaranjan Das**) in which members of the Congress entered the legislatures, and wrote a report as a basis for Indian constitutional development and to solve the political differences between Hindus and Muslims. The report was not, however, acceptable to members of the All-India Muslim League, led by **Muhammad Ali Jinnah**. He was the father of **Jawaharlal Nehru**.

Neil, Andrew Ferguson 1949–
Scottish journalist

Born in Paisley, Strathclyde, and educated at Glasgow University, he worked briefly in the Conservative Party's research department before joining *The Economist* magazine (1973–83), becoming UK editor. He was appointed editor of the *Sunday Times* in 1983 without any previous experience of national newspapers. In his position there, with the encouragement of its proprietor, **Rupert Murdoch**, he changed the paper's soft-left bias and strongly supported most of the key policies of **Margaret Thatcher**'s government. He identified himself publicly with Murdoch's coup against the unions at Wapping in 1986, which led to the introduction of new labour practices in the newspaper industry. Neil left the Sunday Times in 1994, becoming a freelance writer and broadcaster, fronting his own discussion television programme *The Midnight Hour*. In 1996 he published his autobiography *Full Disclosure* and became editor-in-chief of Scotsman Publications Ltd.

Neill, A(lexander) S(utherland) 1883–1973
Scottish educationist and author

Born in Kingsmuir, Tayside, the son of a village schoolmaster, he became a pupil-teacher there (1899–1903), and assistant master at Kingskettle School, Fife (1903–06) and Newport Public School, Fife (1906–08). After studying English at Edinburgh University and working briefly in publishing he became headmaster of Gretna Public School (1914–17) and after World War I he taught at King Alfred School, Hampstead (1918–20). He was editor of *New Era* (1920–21) and started a community school at Hellerau, near Salzburg, which eventually settled at Leiston, Suffolk, in 1927 as Summerhill School, a co-educational progressive school which 'began as an experiment and became a demonstration'. It was an attempt to provide an education free even of the authoritarian overtones of other progressive schools. He held with **Sigmund Freud** that 'emotions are more important than intellect'. Many pupils were 'difficult' and Neill spent a lot of time in psychotherapy, at first called 'Private Lessons'. He was the most extreme and radical of British progressive schoolmasters and a great publicist, publishing over 20 books from *A Dominie's Log* (1916) to *Neill! Neill! Orange Peel!* (1973).

Neill, Stephen Charles 1900–84
Scottish missionary and theologian

He was born in Edinburgh, and from 1924 worked in south India as an evangelist, theological teacher, and latterly as the Anglican Bishop of Tinnevelly (Tirunelveli). He became deeply concerned with producing Tamil Christian literature and promoting church union. Returning to Europe in 1944, he maintained his ecumenical interests through working with the World Council of Churches and lecturing in Hamburg, Nairobi, and elsewhere. His *Anglicanism* (1958), *Interpretation of the New Testament* (1962) and *History of Christian Missions* (1964) remain classics in their fields, as does the *History of the Ecumenical Movement* (1954, edited with Ruth Rouse).

Neilson, Donald, *originally* Donald Nappey 1936–
English murderer and kidnapper

Born near Bradford, he was convicted of four murders. Because of the black hood he wore as a disguise, he became known as 'the Black Panther'. Three murders were committed during burglaries early in 1974. Soon after, 17-year-old Lesley Whittle was abducted from her home, and a ransom demand of £50,000 was accompanied by a death-threat. Lesley's naked body was found at the foot of a ventilation shaft two months later. Neilson evaded the police until late 1975, when a security guard he had shot and wounded was able to provide a description. Disarmed by police in December 1975, he received life sentences for the murders and 21 years for kidnapping.

Neilson, James Beaumont 1792–1865
Scottish engineer

Born in Shettleston, Glasgow, he invented the hot-blast which revolutionized iron manufacture in 1828, and was chief engineer and manager of Glasgow Gasworks from 1817 to 1847.

Neilson, Julia 1868–1957
English actress

She was born in London and after a successful career at the Royal Academy of Music made her debut at the Lyceum in 1888. Her greatest success was as Rosalind in the record-breaking run of *As You like It* (1896–98). She married **Fred Terry**, who often appeared with her and who partnered her in management from 1900. Their children Dennis (1895–1932) and Phyllis (1892–1977) Neilson-Terry also became famous for their acting, the latter especially in the title role of *Trilby*, and also for their productions.

Neisser, Ulric Richard Gustav 1928–
US psychologist

Born in Kiel, Germany, he emigrated with his family to the USA in 1933. He gained his PhD at Harvard in 1956 and subsequently taught at Brandeis University (1957–66), Cornell University (1967–80, 1996–), and Emory University (1983–96). The modern growth of cognitive psychology received a major boost from the publication in 1967 of the first and most influential of his books, *Cognitive Psychology*. It synthesized a large body of experimental data on memory, attention, thought and perception in a timely theoretical package, setting the agenda and serving as a framework for much research in the area. However, in his later writings he has become critical of the methodology of much cognitive psychology, faulting it for being 'ecologically invalid'.

Nekola, Karel 1857–1915
Scottish pottery decorator

Originally a carpenter with his father in Bohemia, he was appointed decorator at the Fife Pottery of Robert Heron & Son, in Gallatown (now part of Kirkcaldy) in 1882. Wemyss Ware was one of the products of the pottery and Nekola was responsible for exerting a great deal of influence throughout its most popular period (1888–1915). Highly decorative and extremely colourful flowers, fruit, animals and birds were his main subject matter, which contrasted strikingly against the white body of each pot. He stayed with the firm for 30 years, painting and teaching others, including his sons Carl and Joseph.

Nekrasov, Nikolai Alekseyevich 1821–78
Russian lyrical poet

Born near Vinitza, Podolia, he worked as a journalist and critic. A poet of the Realistic school, he made his name with poems depicting the social wrongs of the peasantry, such as his unfinished narrative epic, *Komu na Rusi zhit khorosho?* (1879, Eng trans *Who Can Be Happy and Free in Russia?*, 1917). 📖 M Peppard, *Nikolai Alexeyevich Nekrasov* (1967)

Nelken, Margarita 1896–1968
Spanish politician and feminist

Born in Madrid, the daughter of German Jews, she did not achieve Spanish nationality until 1931. During her early years she was a painter, exhibiting her works in Paris and Vienna as well as Spain, but following a severe eye illness dedicated herself to literary criticism. She was also active on behalf of women's rights, publishing *The Social Condition of Women* (1922), as well as being involved in land reform movements in Estremadura and Andalucia. During the Second Republic (1931–36) she was successful in all three general elections as a deputy for the Socialist Party (PSOE). She agitated for land reform, was active in the national arbitration boards, and formed part of the National Committee of Women against War and Fascism. Her impatience with the parliamentary process led her to become one of the most radical Socialist deputies. During the Spanish Civil War (1936–39) she led various campaigns for the mobilization of women. She joined the Communist Party (PCE) in 1937. After the war, she was exiled in Paris, Moscow and finally Mexico, where she died.

Nelson, (John) Byron, Jnr 1912–
US golfer

Born in Fort Worth, Texas, he became one of the USA's most outstanding players, winning the US Open in 1939, the US Masters twice (1937, 1942), and the PGA (Professional Golfers' Association) title twice (1940, 1945). In 1945 he won a remarkable 11 consecutive US Tour events—an all-time record. He played in two Ryder Cup matches, and retired in 1955 to become a broadcaster and coach.

Nelson, George 1907–86
US designer, architect and writer

Born in Hartford, Connecticut, he graduated in architecture and travelled in Europe during the early 1930s, familiarizing himself with the work of the Modern movement. Its influence is evident in his design work, the best known being his range of storage furniture (1946) for the manufacturer Herman Miller, whose design policy he directed. He also commissioned Charles Eames to collaborate with the firm. He was editor of *Architectural Forum* from 1935 to 1944, and wrote widely on design and architectural subjects.

Nelson, Horatio Nelson, Viscount 1758–1805
English admiral

He was born in Burnham Thorpe rectory, Norfolk. He entered the navy in 1770, made a voyage to the West Indies, and served in the arctic expedition of 1773, and afterwards in the East Indies. As lieutenant of the *Lowestoft* frigate (1777) he went to Jamaica, and in 1779 was posted to the *Hinchingbrook* frigate. In 1780 he commanded the naval force in the expedition against San Juan. In 1781 he commissioned the *Albemarle* and joined the squadron under Samuel, 1st Viscount Hood in the USA. In 1784 he was appointed to the frigate *Boreas* for service in the West Indies, where he enforced the Navigation Act against the USA. Here he married a widow, Mrs Frances Nisbet (1761–1831), and in 1787 retired with her to Burnham Thorpe for five years. At the outbreak of the French Revolution (1792–1802) he commanded the *Agamemnon* and accompanied Lord Hood to the Mediterranean. When Toulon was given up to the Allies Nelson was ordered to Naples, where he first met Emma Hamilton, the wife of the British ambassador. In 1794 he commanded the naval brigade at the reduction of Bastia and of Calvi, where he lost his right eye. In 1796 he inflicted a signal defeat with John Jervis (Lord Saint Vincent) on the Spanish fleet off Cape St Vincent. Promoted to rear admiral, he was sent with an inadequate squadron to seize a richly-laden Spanish ship at Santa Cruz, where he lost his right arm. In 1798, commanding the *Vanguard*, he defeated the French fleet by his victory at the Battle of the Nile, off Aboukir Bay. He returned in triumph to Naples, to a hero's welcome from Emma Hamilton, who became his mistress. Nelson was raised to the peerage as Baron Nelson of the Nile, parliament voted him a pension of £2,000 a year, the East India Company awarded him £10,000 and the King of Naples conferred on him the title of Duke of Bronte, in Sicily. He resigned his command and went back to England with the Hamiltons, where Emma gave birth to a daughter, Horatia, and Nelson separated from his wife. In 1801 he was promoted to vice-admiral, and appointed second in command of the expedition to the Baltic, under Sir Hyde Parker (1739–1807). In the face of Parker's irresolution, Nelson disregarded orders and engaged in the Battle of Copenhagen, which he won decisively. In 1803, on the resumption of the war, he was made commander in the Mediterranean. In 1805 he won his greatest victory against the French and Spanish fleets at Trafalgar. He directed the engagement from the *Victory*, but was mortally wounded. His body was brought home and buried in St Paul's Cathedral. 📖 Robert Southey, *The Life of Nelson* (1813)

Nelson, Thomas 1780–1861
Scottish publisher

He was born in Edinburgh and the company of the same name was established in 1798. Specializing in tracts, educational books and affordable reprints, the company's authors included John Buchan.

Nelson, Willie (Hugh) 1933–
US country singer and songwriter

Born in Abbott, Texas, he began performing at the age of 10, and was a disc jockey for a time, but his initial success came as a songwriter in Nashville in the early 1960s. He continued to write and record throughout the decade, but reached a watershed of personal and professional frustration in 1970, and returned to Texas. His progressive, alternative country style found a new audience in Austin, and he became a major star, moving out from country to embrace both rock and jazz standards, but without losing his roots in the music. He launched his annual Farm Aid concerts in 1985, and continued to record and tour prolifically. 📖 *Willie: An Autobiography* (1988)

Nemerov, Howard 1920–
US poet, novelist and playwright
Born in New York City, he was based in England while serving with the Royal Canadian Air Force during World War II. He has written several novels, including *The Melodramatists* (1949), but has won greater acclaim as a poet. His relatively accessible verse, in which, as he has said, he 'writes of history from the point of view of the loser', includes *The Image and The Law* (1947) and *The Next Room of the Dream* (1962). His *Collected Poems* (1977) won the National Book Award.

Nenni, Pietro 1891–1980
Italian socialist politician
Born in Faenza, Romagna, he became an agitator at the age of 17. As editor of the socialist paper *Avanti!* he was exiled by the Fascists in 1926, and served as a political commissar for the International Brigade during the Spanish Civil War. He became Secretary-General of the Italian Socialist Party (PSI) in 1944, vice-premier in the **De Gasperi** coalition (1945–46) and Foreign Minister (1946–47). From 1963 to 1968 he once again served as vice-premier in the four-party left-centre coalition headed by **Aldo Moro**. In 1968 he accepted the post of Foreign Minister but resigned in 1969.

Nennius fl.769
Welsh writer
He is reputedly author of the early Latin compilation known as the *Historia Britonum*, which gives an account of the origins of the Britons, the Roman occupation, the settlement of the Saxons, and King **Arthur's** 12 victories. It contains much material of doubtful historical significance, and its real value lies in its preservation of material needed for the study of early Celtic literature in general, and the Arthurian Legend in particular. 📖 J F Kenney, *Sources for the Early History of Ireland* (1929)

Neot, St d.877
English monk
According to legend, he was a monk of Glastonbury who became a hermit in Cornwall. His relics were taken to Crowland about 1003. His feast day is 31 July.

Nepomuk, St John of See **John of Nepomuk, St**

Nepos, Cornelius c.99–c.24BC
Roman historian
A native of Pavia or Hostilia, northern Italy, he was the contemporary and close friend of **Cicero**, and **Catullus** dedicated his poems to him. His *De Viris Illustribus* ('Lives of Famous Men'), of which only some 25 (mainly on Greek warriors and statesmen) survive, are written in a clear, straightforward style. He was the first to adopt the pairing of Greek and Roman soldiers and statesmen, a form later followed by **Plutarch**.

Nequam, Alexander See **Neckam, Alexander**

Neri, St Philip 1515–95
Italian mystic
Born in Venice, he went to Rome at the age of 18, and spent many years in charitable works, and teaching and praying. In 1551 he became a priest, and later, with his followers, formed the Congregation of the Oratory (1564). The community was finally established at Vallicella, where Philip built a new church (Chiesa Nuova) on the site of Santa Maria. He was canonized with **Ignatius Loyola** and others in 1622, and his feast day is 26 May.

Nernst, Walther Hermann 1864–1941
German physical chemist and Nobel Prize winner
Born in Briesen, West Prussia, he studied physics at the universities of Zurich, Berlin, Graz and Würzburg, and in 1887 he became assistant to **Wilhelm Ostwald** at Leipzig. In 1891 he moved to Göttingen, first as associate professor and from 1894 as Professor of Physical Chemistry. He succeeded Hans Landolt in the chair of physical chemistry at the University of Berlin in 1905. During World War I he engaged in military activities, including gas warfare. From 1922 to 1924 he was president of the Physikalisch Technische Reichsanstalt, but then returned to the chair of physics at the university. He retired in 1933, being out of favour with the Nazi regime. Nernst is regarded as one of the co-founders of physical chemistry, along with Ostwald, **Jacobus Henricus van't Hoff** and **Svante August Arrhenius**. His earliest research was in electrochemistry and his development of the theory of electrode potential and the concept of solubility product were particularly important. He devised experimental methods for measuring dielectric constant, pH, and other physico-chemical quantities. The electrochemical work led to a special interest in thermodynamics and in 1906 he enunciated his heat theorem, which has come to be regarded as a statement of the third law of thermodynamics. This enables equilibrium constants for chemical reactions to be calculated from heat data. He later became concerned with the quantum theory and in particular with photochemistry. He received the Nobel Prize for chemistry in 1920. He was made an Honorary Fellow of the Chemical Society as early as 1911 and became a Foreign Member of the Royal Society in 1932. 📖 Kurt A G Mendelssohn, *The World of Walter Nernst* (1973)

Nero See panel p1358

Neruda, Jan 1834–91
Czech writer
Born in Prague, he was brought up in poverty, an experience reflected in some of his work, notably *Povídky malostranské* (1878, Eng trans *Tales of the Little Quarter*, 1957), and became a teacher before switching to a career in journalism. He suffered from persistent ill health. He was a disciple of Romanticism but developed into the foremost classical poet in modern Czech literature. He is also known for some prose and drama. 📖 M Novotný, *Zivot, Jana Nerudý* (4 vols, 1951–56)

Neruda, Pablo, *originally* Ricardo Eliecer Neftalí Reyes 1904–73
Chilean poet and Nobel Prize winner
Born in Parral and educated at Santiago, he made his name with *Veinte poemas de amor y una canción desesperada* (1924, Eng trans *Twenty Love Poems and a Song of Despair*, 1969). From 1927 he held diplomatic posts in East Asia and Europe (Spain during the Civil War) and in Mexico from 1940. On his way back to Chile from Mexico (1943) he visited the Inca city of Macchu Picchu, which was the inspiration of one of his best-known poems. Once settled in Chile again he joined the Communist Party and was elected to the senate in 1945. He travelled in Russia and China (1948–52), was awarded the Stalin Prize in 1953,

Nero AD37–68
Roman emperor from AD54 to AD68

Nero was born in Antium, son of Cnaeus Domitius Ahenobarbus and of **Agrippina**, the Younger, daughter of **Germanicus**. His mother became the wife of the Emperor **Claudius**, who adopted him in AD50. After the death of Claudius (54), the Praetorian Guard declared Nero emperor.

His reign began well, but the influence of his mother and his moral weakness and sensuality, soon plunged him into debauchery, extravagance and tyranny. He caused **Britannicus**, the son of Claudius, to be poisoned, and afterwards murdered his mother and his wife Octavia. After this **Seneca**, the Younger, was the main power behind the throne. In July 64 two-thirds of Rome was destroyed by fire. Nero is said to have been responsible, but this is doubtful, as is the story that he admired the spectacle from a distance while reciting his own verses about the sack of Troy. But he needed a scapegoat, and found one in the Christians, many of whom were cruelly put to death.

He rebuilt the city with great magnificence, and built a splendid palace on the Palatine hill; but in order to provide for his expenditure Italy and the provinces were plundered. A conspiracy against Nero in 65 failed, and Seneca and the poet **Lucan** fell victims to his vengeance. In a fit of passion he murdered his second wife **Poppaea Sabina**, by kicking her when she was pregnant. He then offered his hand to Antonia, daughter of Claudius, but was refused; whereupon he had her executed, and married Statilia Messallina, after murdering her husband. He also executed or banished many eminent persons.

Nero sought distinction as poet, philosopher, actor, musician and charioteer; as a poet he seems to have had some talent, and a few fragments survive from his poem on 'The Sack of Troy'. However, his patronage of the arts and promotion of musical and theatrical contests, in which he took part himself, caused much criticism and increased his unpopularity. In 68 the Gallic and Spanish legions, and after them the Praetorian Guards, rose against him to make **Galba** emperor. Nero fled to the house of a freedman, four miles from Rome, and saved himself from execution by suicide.

📖 M Griffin, *Nero: The End of a Dynasty* (1985); B W Henderson, *The Life and Principate of the Emperor Nero* (1903).

Nero took this name when he was adopted by Claudius, with whose family it was associated. It is said to be a Sabine word meaning 'courageous and energetic'.

Qualis artifex pereo!
'How great an artist dies in me!'
Attributed words on the point of taking his life, quoted in Suetonius, *Nero*, 49.1.

and was later the Chilean ambassador in Paris (1970–72). His works include *Residencia en la tierra I, II* and *III* (1933, 1935, 1947, 'Residence on Earth'), *Alturas de Macchu Picchu* (1945, Eng trans *The Heights of Macchu Picchu*, 1966), which later became part of *Canto General* (1950, Eng trans in part as *Poems from Canto General*, 1966), and *Odas elementales* (1954, Eng trans *Elementary Odes*, 1961). In 1971 he was awarded the Nobel Prize for literature. 📖 E Rodriguez Moregul, *El viajero immovil* (1967)

Nerva, Marcus Cocceius c.32–98AD
Roman emperor

He was elected (AD96) by the senate after the assassination of **Domitian**. He introduced liberal reforms after Domitian's tyranny, but lacked military support, and had to adopt **Trajan** as his successor.

Nerval, Gérard de, *properly* Gérard Labrunie
1808–55
French writer

Born in Paris, he was greatly influenced by reading his uncle's collection of occult books as a youth. At the age of 20, he published a translation of **Goethe**'s *Faust*, expanded as *Faust, et le second Faust* (1840), which **Hector Berlioz** drew on in his *La Damnation de Faust* (1846). He wrote in prose and verse, but his travels, criticism, plays and poems are less interesting than his fantastic short tales, the *Contes et facéties* (1852, 'Stories and Jests'), the partly autobiographical series *Filles du feu* (1854, Eng trans *Daughters of Fire*, 1923), and *La Bohème galante* (1855, 'Gallant Bohemian Life'). He is often seen as a precursor of both the Symbolist and Surrealist movements. 📖 L Cellier, *Gérard de Nerval* (1956)

Nervi, Pier Luigi 1891–1979
Italian architect and engineer

Born in Sondrio, he graduated as an engineer then set up as a building contractor. His many works include the Berta Stadium in Florence (1930–32) and a complex of exhibition halls in Turin (1948–50). He achieved an international reputation by his designs for the two Olympic stadia in Rome (1960), in which bold and imaginative use is made of concrete for roofing in the large areas. He also designed San Francisco cathedral (1970). He was professor at Rome from 1947 to 1961. 📖 Ada Louise Huxtable, *Pier Luigi Nervi* (1960)

Nesbit, Edith 1858–1924
English writer

Born in London, the daughter of an agricultural chemist who died when she was three, she was educated at a French convent, and began her literary career by writing poetry, having met the **Rossetti**s and their friends. In 1880 she married the Fabian journalist Hubert Bland, and to help with the family finances turned to popular fiction and children's stories about the Bastaple family, including *The Story of the Treasure Seekers* (1899), *The Would-be-Goods* (1901), *Five Children and It* (1902), *The New Treasure Seekers* (1904), *The Railway Children* (1906) and *The Enchanted Castle* (1907). She also wrote ghost stories, and a number of other novels, the last of which was *The Lark* (1922). 📖 N Streatfeild, *Magic and Magician* (1958)

Nesle, Blondel de See **Blondel**

Nesselrode, Karl Robert, Count 1780–1862
Russian diplomat

Born in Lisbon, the son of the Russian ambassador, he gained the confidence of **Alexander I**, and took a principal part in the negotiations which ended in the Peace of Paris and in the Congress of Vienna. He was also one of the most active diplomats of the Holy Alliance. Foreign Minister of Russia for over 30 years, he was partly responsible for bringing about the Crimean War (1853).

Nestorius d.451AD
Syrian ecclesiastic

Born in Germanicia, he became a priest. Well known for his zeal, ascetic life, and eloquence, he was selected as patriarch of Constantinople (Istanbul) in AD428. He defended the Presbyter Anastasius in denying that the Virgin **Mary** could be truly called the Mother of God, and so emphasized the distinction of the divine and human natures that antagonists accused him—falsely—of holding that there were two persons in **Jesus Christ**. A controversy ensued, and Nestorius was deposed by a general council in Ephesus (431). He was confined in a monastery near Constantinople, was banished to Petra in Arabia, and died after imprisonment in the Greater Oasis in Upper Egypt. There are still a few Nestorians in Kurdistan and Iraq, and a small body of Christians in India are nominally Nestorian.

Nestroy, Johann Nepomuk 1801–62
Austrian dramatist

Born in Vienna, he began life as an operatic singer, turned playwright and was director of the Vienna Carl-Theater (1854–60). His 60 or so plays, which include *Der böse Geist Lumpazivagabundus* (1833, 'The Wicked Ghost Lumpazivagabundus'), *Einen Jux will er sich machen* (1842, 'He Wants to Play Pranks') and *Judith und Holofernes* (1849), are mostly elaborate jibes at theatrical sentimentality characterized by deft play on words. His work revolutionized the Viennese theatre and influenced **Ludwig Wittgenstein**. 🕮 M Preisner, *Johann Nepomuk Nestroy* (1968)

Netanyahu, Binyamin 1949–
Israeli Likud politician

He was born in Israel and educated at the Massachusetts Institute of Technology in the USA. Between 1967 and 1972 he served as a soldier in the Israeli Defence Forces and in 1976 became a director of the Jonathan Institute, a foundation which studies counter-terrorism. In 1982 he was appointed Israel's ambassador to the United Nations and in 1988 was elected to the Knesset as a member of the right-wing Likud Party. Having served as deputy Foreign Minister (1988–91) and deputy Prime Minister (1991–92), he contested the 1996 general election and was elected Prime Minister. In contrast to his predecessor **Yitzhak Rabin**, who was assassinated in 1995, he has pursued a more cautious policy in implementing the 1993 peace accord with the Palestinian people.

Neto, (Antonio) Agostinho 1922–79
Angolan nationalist and politician

The son of a Methodist missionary, he was educated in a Methodist school in Luanda before studying medicine in Portugal. He returned to Angola to work in the colonial medical service and joined the MPLA. He was imprisoned several times (1952–62) but escaped from the Cape Verde Islands to Zaire (now the Democratic Republic of Congo) where he soon became president of the MPLA and its leader in the guerrilla war against Portuguese colonialism. His close ties with **Fidel Castro** gave him both Cuban and Soviet backing and this assistance enabled him to prevail in the civil war which followed the Portuguese retreat from Angola. He became the first President of Angola in 1974, holding the post until his death.

Neuberger, Julia Babette Sarah, *née* Schwab 1950–
British rabbi, writer and broadcaster

Born in London and educated at Cambridge, she took a Rabbinic Diploma at Leo Baeck College, where she later returned as lecturer in 1979. She became rabbi of the South London Liberal Synagogue (1977–89), becoming the first female rabbi in Britain, and was picked to front *Choices* on BBC1 (1986–87). Noted for her liberal and reasonable approach, she has often been involved in religious and secular advisory committees on such topics as health and human rights. In 1993 she became Chancellor of the University of Ulster, the second non-Royal female chancellor of a UK university (Dame **Margot Fonteyn** was the first, on becoming Chancellor of the University of Durham in 1982).

Neugebauer, Gerald 1932–
US astronomer

Born in Göttingen, Germany, he was educated at Cornell University and the California Institute of Technology. After working at Mount Wilson and Palomar observatories, he became Professor of Physics at the California Institute of Technology (1970) and director of Palomar Observatory in 1981. He produced the first extensive infrared map of the heavens in the 1960s, which had dramatic results. Many new infrared sources were discovered, most of which did not coincide with previously observed visible sources, and new and curious objects were revealed, such as objects thought to be stars in the process of formation. Working with E E Becklin, Neugebauer discovered a strange infrared source radiating intensely in the Orion nebula, which is now known as the 'Becklin–Neugebauer object' and is thought to be a young massive star blowing gases outwards at high speed. He has also played an important role in interplanetary missions such as the *Mariner* and *Viking* programmes, and in the design of new infrared telescopes.

Neumann, (Johann) Balthasar 1687–1753
German architect

Born in Eger, he was at first a military engineer in the service of the Archbishop of Würzburg, but soon found his true métier, and after visiting Paris and absorbing new ideas, he became Professor of Architecture at Würzburg. Many outstanding examples of the Baroque style were designed by him, the finest being probably Würzburg Palace and Schloss Bruchsal.

Neumann, St John Nepomucene 1811–60
US Roman Catholic bishop and saint

Born in Prachatice, Bohemia, he settled in the USA in 1836, entered the Redemptorist order, and was appointed Bishop of Philadelphia in 1852. He was responsible for building 80 churches and nearly 100 parochial schools, and he founded US branches of several orders of teaching nuns. Miracles were said to have occurred at his tomb, and in 1977 he became the first US male to be canonized.

Neumann, John Von See Von Neumann, John (Johann)

Neumann, Theresa 1898–1962
German mystic and stigmatic

She was born in Konnersreuth, Bavaria. Sickness and accident from 1918 onwards were followed by a string of illnesses up to 1925 that were cured without medical intervention. During Lent in 1926 she had visions of the Passion of Christ accompanied by stigmata on her hands, feet and left side. She is said to have had no food from 1927 onwards, apart from daily Holy Communion. Her life attracted much interest, but claims that miraculous healing and survival proved her a saint have not been accepted as reaching the standards required by Church authority.

Neumeier, John 1942–
US dancer, choreographer and artistic director

Born in Milwaukee, Wisconsin, he danced with the Stuttgart Ballet (1963–69) before assuming directorship of Frankfurt Ballet (1969–73) and Hamburg Ballet (since 1973). He creates acrobatically expressive contemporary ballets to match the grand themes and important composers he favours in his work.

Neurath, Baron Konstantin von 1873–1956
German administrator

He was born in Klein-Glattbach, Württemberg. After consular service, he joined the German Embassy in Istanbul and in 1921 became ambassador to Italy and in 1930 to Great Britain. Foreign Minister from 1932 to 1938, he then became Reich Protector of the Czech territories (1939–43). At the Nuremberg Trial he was sentenced to 15 years' imprisonment for war crimes, but was released in 1954.

Neurath, Otto 1882–1945
Austrian philosopher and social theorist

Born in Vienna, he was a member of the influential Vienna Circle which also included **Moritz Schlick**, **Kurt Gödel** and **Rudolf Carnap**. The group were logical positivists, generally hostile to metaphysics and theology and respectful of empirical science. Neurath is particularly associated with the radical version of positivism called 'physicalism', which aimed to establish an entirely materialist basis of knowledge. His best philosophical work was published in the group's journal *Erkenntnis*, but he also wrote books on sociology, education and social policy, including *International Picture Language* (1936) and *Modern Man in the Making* (1939), and was active in public affairs as an independent Marxist. He was an energetic organizer, and at different stages in his life was involved with bodies as diverse as the Carnegie Endowment for International Peace (1911–13), the Central Planning Office, Munich (1919), the Museum for House and Town Planning (1919–24), the Social and Economic Museum, Vienna (1924–34), the International Foundation for Visual Education (1933–40), and the International Unity of Science movement (1934–40). He was founding editor of the uncompleted *International Encyclopaedia of Unified Science*.

Nevelson, Louise, *née* Berliawsky 1900–88
US sculptor and printmaker

Born in Kiev, she emigrated with her family to Portland, Maine, in the USA, in 1905. She studied at the Art Students' League in New York (1929–33) and with the influential theorist **Hans Hofmann** in Munich. In 1932 she worked as an assistant to the Mexican mural-painter **Diego Rivera**. She is best known for her 'environmental' sculptures—abstract, wooden box-like shapes stacked up to form walls and painted white or gold, for example in *An American Tribute to the British People (Gold Wall)* (1959, Tate Gallery, London). In 1966 she began to use plexiglass and aluminium, as in *Transparent Sculpture VI* (1967, Whitney Museum, New York City). In the 1970s she received commissions for public sculptures, such as *Transparent Horizon* (1975, Massachusetts Institute of Technology) and *Bicentennial Dawn* (1976, Philadelphia Courthouse).

Neville, Richard See Warwick, Earl of

Neville-Jones, Dame (Lilian) Pauline 1939–
English diplomat

Educated in Leeds and at Oxford, she entered the Foreign Office in 1963. She worked her way through the diplomatic ranks, including postings in Rhodesia (Zimbabwe) in 1964–65, Singapore (1965–68) and Washington DC (1971–75). She worked in the Foreign and Commonwealth Office (FCO) in 1968–71 and 1975–77, as Chef de Cabinet for the European Commissioner for Budget (1977–82) and at the Royal Institute for International Affairs (1982–83) before becoming FCO Head of Planning Staff in 1987. She was also deputy in Bonn (1988–91). In 1994 she became the second-highest official in the FCO as political director and deputy Under-Secretary of State—a higher rank than any other woman in the Foreign Office. Her last FCO post was as head of the British delegation during the Bosnian peace talks in Dayton, Ohio (1995). In 1996, the year she was created DBE, she joined the NatWest bank as a European specialist.

Nevinson, Christopher Richard Wynne
1889–1946
English artist

Born in Hampstead, London, he was the son of the war correspondent Henry Wood Nevinson (1856–1941). He studied at the Slade School of Art in London, and for a brief period went into journalism before venturing back to painting and etching in Paris. He became a leader of the pre-1914 avant-garde, joining **Emilio Marinetti** as co-signatory of the Futurist Manifesto *Vital English Art* (1914, published in England). He volunteered for the Red Cross, was discharged (1916), but returned the following year as an artist attached to the Bureau of Information. Many of his best and most famous works reflect his experiences of World War I. He later moved away from Futurism to paint New York, Paris and the English landscape. In his etchings he maintained an assured Realist vein. In 1937 he published the autobiographical *Paint and Prejudice*.

Nevison, John, *nicknamed* Swift Nicks 1639–84
English highwayman

Born in Pontefract, Yorkshire, he enlisted in the Spanish army and fought in Flanders. Following the Restoration he decided to return to England and become a highwayman. He was renowned for his courteous manner and made it his policy only to rob the rich and to give some of his booty to the poor. He also ran a protection system for the farmers in his native Yorkshire, levying a charge on local drovers in return for protection from robbers. Escaping several times from capture, he was finally arrested by Captain Hardcastle and hanged in York in 1684. It is probable that it was he and not **Dick Turpin** who inspired the legend of the epic ride to York.

Newbery, John 1713–67
English publisher and bookseller

Born in Berkshire, a farmer's son, he settled in London around 1744 as a seller of books and patent medicines. He was the first to publish small books for children, and he was—perhaps with **Oliver Goldsmith**—part author of some of the best ones, notably *Goody Two-Shoes*. In 1758 he started the *Universal Chronicle*, or *Weekly Gazette*, in which the *Idler* appeared. Goldsmith's *Citizen of the World* appeared in the *Public Ledger* (1760). Since 1922 the Newbery medal has been awarded annually for the best US children's book.

Newbigin, (James Edward) Lesslie 1909–98
English missionary and theologian

Born in Newcastle, he went to Madras as a Church of Scotland missionary in 1936 and spent most of the next 38 years in south India, being appointed Bishop of Madura and Ramnad (1947–59) and bishop in Madras (1965–74), in the Church of South India. In his retirement he lectured at the Selly Oak Colleges, Birmingham, was appointed moderator of the United Reformed Church (1978–79), and became a parish minister in Birmingham (1980–88). His many writings on the uniqueness of Christianity and on Christian responses to secularism in modern western culture are put in context by his autobiography, *Unfinished Agenda* (1985). Other works include *The Gospel in a Pluralist Society* (1989) and *Truth to Tell* (1991).

Newbolt, Sir Henry John 1862–1938
English poet

Born in Bilston, Staffordshire, he studied at Clifton School and Oxford, and became a barrister. He published a novel, *Taken from the Enemy* (1892), followed by *Mordred: A Tragedy* (1895), but is best known for his sea songs—*Admirals All* (1897), which contained 'Drake's Drum', *The Island Race* (1898), *Songs of the Sea*, and others. In World War I he was controller of telecommunications and an official war historian, and in 1920 he published *The Naval History of the Great War*.

Newby, Eric 1919–
English travel writer

Born in London, he worked briefly in advertising before joining a Finnish four-masted bark in 1938, an adventure described in *The Last Grain Race* (1956). In 1942 he was captured off Sicily while trying to rejoin the submarine from which he had landed to attack a German airfield. For some years he worked in the clothing industry, which he eagerly left to take *A Short Walk in the Hindu Kush* (1958). In 1963, after some years as a fashion buyer to a chain of department stores, he made a 1,200-mile (1,931km) descent of the Ganges, described with typical aplomb and wit in *Slowly Down the Ganges* (1966). Later he became travel editor of the *Observer*. Other significant books are *The Big Red Train Ride* (1978), the story of a journey from Moscow to the Pacific on the Trans-Siberian Railway, his autobiography, *A Traveller's Life* (1982), and *Round Ireland in Low Gear* (1987), about a mountain-bike journey. Later works include *What the Traveller Saw* (1989) and *A Small Place in Italy* (1994).

Newby-Fraser, Paula 1962–
South African athlete

She was born in Zimbabwe and brought up in South Africa, and is the most outstanding female triathlete of the present day. She has won the women's event at the gruelling Hawaii Ironman Triathlon a record five times and is also the only woman to have won it more than once. She won the Nice Triathlon four years in a row and the US Triathlon series in 1990 and 1991. A regular challenger of the best male athletes, she achieved the fastest women's time ever for the triathlon, which is also among the top 10 times for the event, male or female. In 1990, she was voted athlete of the year by the Women's Sport Foundation.

Newcomb, Simon 1833–1909
US astronomer

Born in Wallace, Nova Scotia, Canada, he had little formal education but developed a talent for mathematics. He was employed as a computator at the American Nautical Almanac Office at Washington in 1857, achieving also a degree from the scientific school of Harvard in 1858. He became Professor of Mathematics in the US navy (1861–97) with charge of the naval observatory at Washington. From 1877 he edited the *American Nautical Almanac* and he was additionally Professor of Mathematics and Astronomy at Johns Hopkins University (1884–93, 1898–1900). Newcomb's major work, begun in 1879 and continued throughout his life, was the recalculation of the constants required for the preparation of ephemerides and the drawing up of immense tables of the motions of the planets. He was responsible for the worldwide adoption of a standard system of constants by almanac makers, which served until the middle of the 20th century.

Newcomen, Thomas 1663–1729
English inventor

He was born in Dartmouth, Devon. A blacksmith by trade, in 1698 he teamed up with **Thomas Savery**, who had just patented an atmospheric steam engine for pumping water from mines, and by 1712 he had constructed a practical working engine that was widely used in collieries.

Newdigate, Sir Roger 1719–1806
English antiquary

Born in Arbury, Warwickshire, he was MP for 36 years for Middlesex (1741–47) and Oxford University (1750–80). He built up a famous collection of antiquities and endowed the Newdigate prize for English verse at Oxford, winners of which have included **Frederick Faber, John Ruskin, Matthew Arnold, Laurence Binyon** and **John Buchan**.

Ne Win, U also known as Shu Maung 1911–
Burmese politician

Educated at Rangoon University, he was an active anti-British nationalist in the 1930s. In World War II he became Chief of Staff in the collaborationist army after the Japanese invasion of Burma, but joined the Allied forces later in the war. He held senior military and Cabinet posts after Burma's independence (1948), before becoming caretaker Prime Minister (1958–60). In 1962, following a military coup, he ruled the country as chairman of the revolutionary council and became state President in 1974. After leaving this office in 1981, he continued to dominate political affairs as chairman of the ruling Burma Socialist Programme Party (BSPP), following an isolationist foreign policy and a unique domestic 'Burmese Way to Socialism' programme, a blend of Marxism, Buddhism and Burmese nationalism. In 1988, with economic conditions rapidly deteriorating and riots in Rangoon, he was forced to step down as BSPP leader, although he remained a formidably powerful political figure.

Newlands, John Alexander Reina 1837–98
English chemist

Born in London, he spent a year at the Royal College of Chemistry. From 1868 to 1888 he was chief chemist to a sugar refinery at Victoria Docks, London, and later set up as an independent analyst and consultant. By 1863 he had begun to build on earlier observations by **Johann Döbereiner** and others that there was a relationship between the chemical properties of elements and their atomic weight. In 1865 he drew up a table of 62 elements arranged in eight groups in ascending order of atomic weight to illustrate what he described as the 'law of octaves'. **Dmitri Ivanovich Mendeleyev** made the critical leap forward when he realized that spaces should be left for undiscovered elements, thus allowing the known elements to fall into groups which demonstrated a true periodicity. After Mendeleyev published his periodic table, Newlands claimed priority and was eventually awarded the Davy Medal of the Royal Society in 1887.

Newman, Barnet 1905–70
US painter

He was born in New York City. Until c.1948 his art was Biomorphic in style, and he was always interested in the primitive, and in the psychiatrist **Carl Jung's** primordial archetypes. In 1948, with **William Baziotes, Robert Motherwell** and **Mark Rothko**, he founded the 'Subject of the Artist' school, and produced *Onement I*, the first of his stripe paintings, which consist of vertical bands of colour and look forward to his Minimalist works of the 1960s, such as *Vir Heroicus Sublimis* (1950–51) and *Station of the Cross* (1966).

Newman, Ernest 1868–1959
English music critic

Born in Liverpool, he was educated at Liverpool College and Liverpool University. He was successively music critic of the *Manchester Guardian*, the *Birmingham Post* and the *Sunday Times* (from 1920). His writings are noted for their wit and elegance, and for their strict factual accuracy. His works include studies of **Christoph Gluck** and **Hugo Wolf**, and of opera (for example *Opera Nights* and *Wagner Nights*), but it is for his far-reaching studies and deep understanding of **Richard Wagner** that he is best known—his four-volume biography of Wagner (1933–37) is the most complete and authoritative account of the composer in existence. In *A Musical Critic's Holiday* he vindicates music criticism as a valuable study.

Newman, Francis William 1805–97
English scholar

Born in London, he obtained a double first at Worcester College, Oxford in 1826, and was elected to a fellowship at Balliol College. After losing sympathy with Anglicanism, he withdrew from the university in 1830, declining subscription to the Thirty-nine Articles. He went as an unsectarian missionary to Baghdad (1830–33), then returned to England, becoming Classical tutor at Bristol College in 1834, professor at Manchester New College (1840) and Professor of Latin at University College London (1846–69). In religion he took a position directly opposite to his brother's, being eager for a belief system including whatever is best in all the historical religions. *Phases of Faith* (1853), the best known of his works, was preceded by *The Soul* (1849). His other works include a *History of the Hebrew Monarchy* (1847), and a small book on his brother, **John Henry Newman** (1891).

Newman, Sir George 1870–1948
English medical officer and pioneer in public health
Born in Leominster, Hereford and Worcester, he was educated at Bootham School, King's College London and Edinburgh University. After qualifying as a doctor, he became medical officer for Bedfordshire (1897–1900) and Finsbury (1900–1907), chief medical officer for the Board of Education (1907–19), and worked at the Ministry of Health (1919–35). He was responsible for drafting the 1907 Act which empowered local education authorities to provide medical treatment, and he pioneered school medical inspection, probably as influential in raising educational standards as any other factor between the wars. He advocated open-air schools for the delicate, and new techniques in physical education, and by 1935 Great Britain had a complex and universal school medical service. He was also influential in the establishment of the London School of Hygiene and Tropical Medicine. His annual reports, 15 to the Minister of Health, 26 to the Minister of Education, had a lasting effect on the development of public health and education in Great Britain.

Newman, John Henry 1801–90
English autobiographer, poet and religious writer
Born in London, he was appointed vicar of St Mary's, Oxford. He became celebrated as a preacher and leader of the Tractarian (or Oxford) Movement, but in the early 1840s drew closer to Roman Catholicism. Converted in 1845, he became a Catholic priest and established the Birmingham Oratory. He wrote extensively on the theological questions of the day, but is famous chiefly for the *Apologia pro Vita Sua* (1864), in which he set out the history of his religious views and defended himself forcefully against the charge of untruthfulness levelled against him by **Charles Kingsley**. This unusual autobiography established him as one of the great stylists in the history of English prose. His poem 'The Dream of Gerontius' (1865), provided the text of **Elgar's** oratorio, and his hymn 'Lead, kindly light' illustrates his gift for a memorable turn of phrase. Made a cardinal in 1879, Newman avoided public display and remained in Birmingham serving his congregation for the remainder of his life. His brother was **Francis William Newman**. 📖 M Trevor, *Newman's Journey* (1974)

Newman, Paul Leonard 1925–
US film actor
Born in Cleveland, Ohio, he turned to acting after a knee injury ended a promising sports career, studying at the Yale School of Drama and the Actors Studio in New York City. Starting in stage repertory and television, he made a disastrous film debut in *The Silver Chalice* (1954) but recovered to become one of the major film actors of his generation, combining blue-eyed masculinity with a rebellious streak in films like *Cat on a Hot Tin Roof* (1958), *The Hustler* (1961) and *Cool Hand Luke* (1967). Later films

include *Butch Cassidy and the Sundance Kid* (1969), *The Sting* (1973), *The Verdict* (1982), *The Color of Money* (1986), for which he won an Academy Award, *Blaze* (1989), *Mr and Mrs Bridge* (1990, with his wife, **Joanne Woodward**), *Nobody's Fool* (1994) and *Magic Hour* (1997). He also directed *Rachel, Rachel* (1968) and *The Glass Menagerie* (1987), among others, and has been active politically in liberal causes. He was given an Honorary Academy Award in 1986 and another in 1994 for his philanthropic donation of the profits from his food products to charity.

Newnes, Sir George 1851–1910
English publisher
He was the son of a Matlock Congregational minister, and was educated at Shireland Hall, Warwickshire, and the City of London School. He founded *Tit-Bits* (1881), *The Strand Magazine* (1891), *The Westminster Gazette* (1873), *Country Life* (1897), *The Wide World Magazine* (1898) and others. He was Liberal MP for Newmarket (1885–95).

Newton, Alfred 1829–1907
English zoologist
Born in Geneva, Switzerland, he was appointed the first Professor of Zoology and Comparative Anatomy at Cambridge in 1866. He made visits to Lapland, Spitsbergen, the West Indies and North America on ornithological expeditions, and was instrumental in having the first Acts of parliament passed for the protection of birds. His ornithological writings include *A Dictionary of Birds* (1893–96), and he was editor of *Ibis* (1865–70) and *Zoological Record* (1870–72).

Newton, Sir Isaac See panel p1363

Newton, John 1725–1807
English clergyman and writer
Born in London, the son of a shipmaster, he sailed with his father for six years, and for 10 years engaged in the African slave trade. In 1748 he was converted to Christianity, but still went on slave trading. He became tide surveyor at Liverpool in 1755, but in 1764 he was offered the curacy of Olney in Buckinghamshire and took orders. **William Cowper** went there four years later, and they became close friends. In 1779 Newton became rector of St Mary Woolnoth, London. His prose works are little read, apart from the *Remarkable Particulars in his own Life*, but some of his *Olney Hymns* (1779) are still sung, including 'Approach, my soul, the mercy-seat', 'How sweet the name of Jesus sounds', 'One there is above all others' and, most famous of all, 'Amazing Grace'.

Nexö, Martin Andersen 1869–1954
Danish novelist
Born in Copenhagen, he spent his boyhood in Bornholm, near Nexö (from where he took his surname), and worked as a shoemaker and bricklayer before turning to books and teaching. In 1906 he won European fame with *Pelle Erobreren* (4 vols, 1906–10, Eng trans *Pelle the Conqueror*, 1915–17), describing poor life and the growth of the Labour movement. He spent considerable time abroad, an experience that fostered his sympathy for the working class. *Morten hin Röde* (1945–47, 'Morten the Red') is an uncharacteristically dull, three-volume sequence. 📖 B Houmann, *Martin Andersen Nexö og hans samtid* (1981–82)

Ney, Michel 1769–1815
French general
Born in Saarlouis, he rose to be adjutant-general (1794) and general of brigade (1796). For the capture of Mannheim he was made general of division (1799), and under the Empire he was made marshal. In 1805 he stormed the entrenchments of Elchingen. He fought at Jena and Eylau and Friedland, gaining the grand eagle of the Légion

Newton, Sir Isaac 1642–1727
English scientist and mathematician

Newton was born in Woolsthorpe, Lincolnshire, and educated at Grantham Grammar School and Trinity College, Cambridge. He began his researches at an early date, but his work was interrupted by the outbreak of the Great Plague in 1664, when the university was closed down for several years. In 1665 or 1666 he contemplated the fall of an apple in his garden, which led him to begin formulating the law of gravitation.

He was also concerned with the nature of light and the construction of telescopes. By a variety of experiments upon sunlight refracted through a prism, he concluded that rays of light which differ in colour differ also in refrangibility—a discovery which suggested that the indistinctness of the image formed by the object-glass of telescopes was due to the different coloured rays of light being brought to a focus at different distances. He concluded (correctly for an object-glass consisting of a single lens) that it was impossible to produce a distinct image, and was led to the construction of reflecting telescopes, of a type that was later developed further by **William Herschel** and the Earl of **Rosse**.

Newton became a Fellow of Trinity College, Cambridge, in 1667, and was appointed Lucasian Professor of Mathematics in 1669. By 1684 he had demonstrated the whole gravitation theory, which he expounded first in *De Motu Corporum* (1684). Newton showed that the force of gravity between two bodies, such as the Sun and the Earth, is directly proportional to the product of the masses of the bodies and inversely proportional to the square of the distance between them. He described this more completely in *Philosophiae Naturalis Principia Mathematica* (1687, 'The Mathematical Principles of Natural Philosophy'), his greatest work, edited and financed by **Edmond Halley**, who had encouraged him to develop his theories.

In the *Principia* Newton stated his three laws of motion: (1) that a body in a state of rest or uniform motion will remain in that state until a force acts on it; (2) that an applied force is directly proportional to the acceleration it induces, the constant of proportionality being the body's mass ($F = ma$); and (3) that for every 'action' force which one body exerts on another, there is an equal and opposite 'reaction' force exerted by the second body on the first.

In the political domain, Newton defended the rights of the university against the illegal encroachments of **James VII and II**, and thereby won a seat in the Convention parliament (1689–90). In 1696 he was appointed Warden of the Mint, and was Master of the Mint from 1699. He again sat in parliament in 1701 for his university. He solved two celebrated problems proposed in June 1696 by **Jean Bernoulli**, as a challenge to the mathematicians of Europe; and performed a similar feat in 1716, by solving a problem proposed by **Gottfried Leibniz**.

Newton was involved throughout his life in controversies with other scientists, in particular with **John Flamsteed**, whose *Greenwich Observations* Newton published, and **Robert Hooke**, who claimed priority of discovery for some of Newton's work on the attraction of lunar bodies. The controversy between Newton and Leibniz over the discovery of the differential calculus and the method of fluxions is still disputed, but the general opinion of science is that the methods were invented independently, with a greater debt owing to Leibniz for the superior facility and completeness of his method.

Newton, who was knighted by Queen **Anne** in 1705, is buried in Westminster Abbey. Throughout his life he also devoted much time to the study of alchemy and theology, and he left substantial discourses on transmutation, a remarkable manuscript on the prophecies of **Daniel** and on the Apocalypse, a history of creation, and a large number of miscellaneous tracts.

📖 R S Westfall, *Never at Rest: A Biography of Isaac Newton* (1981).

'If I have seen further it is by standing on the shoulders of giants.' From a letter to Hooke, 1676.

Corpus omne perseverare in statu suo quiescendi vel movendi uniformiter in directum, nisi quatenus illud a viribus impressis cogitur statum suum mutare.
'Every body continues in its state of rest, or of uniform motion in a right line, unless it is compelled to change that state by forces impressed thereon.' First Law of Motion (1687). From *Philosophiae Naturalis Principia Mathematica* (translated by Andrew Motte, 1729).

---

d'honneur. Serving in Spain, he quarrelled with **André Masséna** and returned to France. In command of the 3rd Corps (1813) he fought at Smolensk and Borodino, received the title of Prince of the Moskwa, and led the rearguard in the disastrous retreat. In 1813 he was present at Lützen and Bautzen, but was defeated by Count Friedrich Bülow von Dennewitz (1775–1816) at Dennewitz. He fought at Leipzig, but submitted to Louis XVIII. Ney was sent against **Napoleon I** on his return from Elba, but went over to his old master's side and led the centre at Waterloo (1815). On Louis XVIII's second restoration he was condemned for high treason and shot. 📖 John B Morton, *Marshal Ney* (1958)

Ngata, Sir Apirana Turupa 1874–1950
New Zealand Maori lawyer and politician

Born at Te Araroa, East Cape, he was the first Maori graduate—from Canterbury University in 1893—and was admitted to the Bar in 1897. He was elected to parliament in 1905 and remained for 38 years, becoming Minister for Native Affairs three times. He researched Maori tribal history and wrote a number of books, including a two-volume work on Maori songs and chants.

Ngo Dinh Diem 1901–63
Vietnamese statesman

Born in Annam, the son of a mandarin and himself a Roman Catholic, he worked as a civil servant before becoming Minister of the Interior in 1933. Refusing to support **Ho Chi Minh** and **Bao Dai**, he was forced into exile in 1950, but returned to South Vietnam as Prime Minister in 1954, masterminded Bao's fall from power, and succeeded him as President in 1955. Although almost wholly dependent on US support for his country's economic survival and with hostilities with the North mounting, he refused to be counselled by the USA on his handling of the war and after causing further unrest by embarking on a campaign against militant Buddhists, he was murdered by dissident army officers.

Ngoyi, Lilian Masediba 1911–80
South African campaigner

Born near Pretoria, she received little education and worked in a variety of menial jobs, before marrying, bearing three children, and being widowed by the age of 40. Her experience of working conditions in clothing factories led her to campaign for a fair society in South Africa. She agitated against the infamous Pass Laws with such persistence that she was arrested and imprisoned for her beliefs. She was charged with treason in 1956 for further activities. Although acquitted, she was imprisoned again while awaiting trial, and endured 71 days in solitary confinement. A brilliant orator, she did not live to see the dismantling of apartheid, as she died under house arrest.

Nguyen Thi Binh 1927–
Vietnamese patriot
Born in South Vietnam into a family of Vietnamese pa-triots, she dedicated herself at an early age to carrying on the work of her father and grandfather. In 1951 she was imprisoned for her political activities until the French rule ended in 1954. Resuming the fight for independence, she fought against the Vietnamese dictator **Ngo Dinh Diem** and later the USA. When the provisional government was formed in 1969 she was appointed Foreign Minister and in 1973, as representative of the National Liberation Front, she signed the treaty that ended the war. In 1979 she was appointed Minister of Education in the United Government and she has been Vice-President of Vietnam since 1992.

Nguyen Van Linh 1914–98
Vietnamese politician
Born in northern Vietnam, he joined the anti-colonial Thanh Nien, a forerunner of the Communist Party of Vietnam (CPV), in Haiphong in 1929, and spent much of his subsequent party career in the south, gaining a re-putation as a pragmatic reformer. A member of CPV's politburo and secretariat (1976–81), his career suffered a temporary setback during the early 1980s when party conservatives gained the ascendancy. He re-entered the politburo in 1985, becoming CPV leader from 1986 to 1991. His leadership brought a new phase of economic liberalization and improved relations with the West, typified by his phased withdrawal of Vietnamese forces from Kampuchea (Cambodia) and Laos.

Nguyen Van Thieu 1923–
Vietnamese soldier and political leader
Born in Ninh Thuan, he was educated at a Catholic school and at the National Military Academy in Hue. His mili-tary career began in the 1940s and by 1963 he was Chief of Staff of the Armed Forces of the Republic of Vietnam (South Vietnam). That year he was a leader in the coup against **Ngo Dinh Diem**. He became deputy premier and Minister of Defence in 1964, and head of state in 1965. In 1967, as the war against the Vietcong escalated and US involvement increased, he became President of the Republic of Vietnam, and in early 1973 was a signatory to the peace treaty that formally ended hostilities. However, fighting between North and South continued until the communist victory in 1975 with the fall of Saigon (now Ho Chi Minh City), when Thieu took refuge first in Taiwan, and then in Surrey, England.

Niarchos, Stavros Spyros 1909–96
Greek ship-owner
Born in Athens, he graduated in law from Athens Uni-versity and became controller of one of the largest inde-pendent fleets in the world. He served during World War II in the Royal Hellenic Navy and then pioneered the construction of super-tankers, in competition with his brother-in-law **Aristotle Onassis**. He was also a major art collector and racehorse owner.

Niccolò, dell' Abbate See **Abbate, Niccolò dell'**

Nicholas, St 4th century AD
Christian prelate and patron saint of Greece and Russia
He was born, according to tradition, in the ancient Lycian seaport city of Patara. Allegedly the Bishop of Myra in Lycia (Turkey), he was imprisoned under **Diocletian** and released under **Constantine I, the Great**. In legend he gave gifts of gold to three poor girls for their dowries, which

gave rise to the custom of giving gifts on his feast day, still followed in the Netherlands and Germany. Elsewhere this has transferred to 25 December (Christmas Day). His identification with Father Christmas began in Europe and spread to the USA, where the name became Santa Claus. He is also the patron saint of children, scholars, merchants, sailors, travellers and thieves. His feast day is 6 December.

Nicholas I, St, *called* the Great c.820–867
Italian pope
Born in Rome, he was pope from 858 to 867. He asserted the supremacy of the Church against secular rulers such as Lothair, King of Lorraine (whose divorce he forbade) and church leaders like **Hincmar**, Archbishop of Rheims. He had problems with the Eastern Church, however, partic-ularly with **Photius**, whom he tried to depose as patriarch of Constantinople, leading to the Photian Schism. His feast day is 13 November.

Nicholas I 1796–1855
Emperor of Russia
The third son of **Paul I**, he married the daughter of **Frederick William III** of Prussia (1817) and became tsar on the death of his elder brother **Alexander I** in 1825. He suppressed the Decembrist Rebellion that year, which turned him against reform. He had a great sense of duty, but ruled by the ancient policy of the tsars—absolute despotism, supported by military power. Wars with Persia (now Iran) and Turkey gained Russia territory in Armenia and the Caucasus. He crushed a Polish rising (1830) and strove to extinguish the Polish nationality. He also at-tempted to Russianize all the inhabitants of the empire, and to convert Roman Catholics and Protestants to the Russian Orthodox Church. During the political storm of 1848–49 he assisted the Emperor of Austria in quelling the Hungarian insurrection, and tightened the alliance with Prussia. The re-establishment of the French Empire confirmed these alliances, but the opposition of Great Britain and France to his plans to dominate Turkey brought on the Crimean War, during which he died. 📖 W Bruce Lincoln, *Nicholas I* (1978)

Nicholas II 1868–1918
Emperor of Russia
The eldest son of **Alexander III**, he succeeded his father in 1894. He married a princess of Hesse (**Alexandra Fyodorovna**), who dominated him. Diffident and easily swayed by irresponsible favourites, he distrusted his ministers and lacked the strength of will to fulfil his self-appointed autocratic role. His reign was marked by alli-ance with France, entente with Great Britain, a disastrous war with Japan (1904–05), and the establishment (1906) of the Duma (parliament). He took command of the Russian armies against the Central Powers (1915). Forced to abdicate (1917) at the revolution, he was shot with his entire family at Yekaterinburg by the Red Guards in 1918. 📖 Robert K Massie, *Nicholas and Alexandra* (1967)

Nicholas of Cusa 1401–64
German philosopher, scientist and churchman
Born in Kues, Treves, he studied at Heidelberg (1416) and Padua (1417–23), received a doctorate in canon law, and was ordained about 1430. He was active in 1432 at the Council of Basle, supporting in his *De concordantia catholica* (1433, 'On Catholic Concordance') the 'conciliarists' who advocated the supremacy of Church councils against the pope. He later switched allegiance to the papal party, undertook various papal missions as a diplomat, and was created cardinal in 1448. His best-known philosophical work is *De docta ignorantia* (1440, 'On Learned Ignorance'), which emphasizes the limitations of human knowledge but at the same time argues that faith, science, theology and philosophy all pursue convergent though different

paths towards the ultimately unattainable goal of absolute reality. He also wrote on mathematics and cosmology and anticipated **Copernicus** in his non-geocentric theories.

Nicholas, Grand-Duke 1856–1929
Russian soldier
In World War I he was Russian Commander-in-Chief against Germany and Austria, and Commander-in-Chief in the Caucasus (1915–17). After 1919 he lived quietly in France. He was the nephew of **Alexander II**.

Nicholls, Sir Douglas Ralph 1906–88
Australian clergyman, activist and administrator
Born at Cummeragunja aboriginal station, southern New South Wales, he grew up on a mission station, and worked on the land until his Australian-rules football skills took him to Melbourne where, in 1935, he became the first Aboriginal to represent his state in football. As pastor, he established an Aboriginals' mission at Fitzroy in 1943 and worked actively for Aboriginal advancement. In 1972 he became the first Aboriginal to be knighted. In December 1976 he was appointed Governor of South Australia, but he was forced to relinquish the position four months later due to ill health.

Nichols, John Gough 1806–73
English writer and editor
He was the son of the printer and writer John Bowyer Nichols (1779–1863), and like his father edited the *Gentleman's Magazine*. He also made valuable contributions to English history and genealogy.

Nichols, Mike, *originally* Michael Igor Peschkowsky 1931–
US film and theatre director
Born in Berlin, Germany, he emigrated to the USA with his family in 1938 and was naturalized in 1944. He studied acting with **Lee Strasberg** before joining the improvisational theatre group, Compass Players, in Chicago (1955–57). He also became popular on radio, records and stage with **Elaine May**, dissecting the American psyche through offbeat, satirical duologues (1957–61). The partnership culminated in a year-long Broadway engagement, after which he turned to direction, showing a flair for comedy, a liking for literate scripts and an ability in eliciting polished performances from his casts. He has received seven Tony Awards for his theatre work which includes *Barefoot in the Park* (1963), *The Odd Couple* (1965), *The Prisoner of Second Avenue* (1971), *The Real Thing* (1984) and *Death and the Maiden* (1992). He also co-produced the hit musical *Annie* (1977). He directed his first film, *Who's Afraid of Virginia Woolf?*, in 1966 and received an Academy Award for *The Graduate* (1967). His films offer sardonic portraits of US life, social mores and sexual politics, and include *Catch 22* (1970), *Silkwood* (1983), *Working Girl* (1988), *Postcards from the Edge* (1990), *Wolf* (1994) and *The Birdcage* (1996).

Nicholson, Ben 1894–1982
English artist
Born in Denham, London, the son of Sir **William Nicholson**, he exhibited with the Paris Abstraction-Création group from 1933 to 1934 and at the Venice Biennale in 1954. He designed a mural panel for the Festival of Britain (1951) and in 1952 executed another for the Time-Life building in London. As one of the leading abstract artists he gained an international reputation and won the first Guggenheim award in 1957. Although he produced a number of purely geometrical paintings and reliefs, he generally used conventional still-life objects as a starting point for his finely drawn and subtly balanced variations. His second wife was **Barbara Hepworth**.

Nicholson, Jack 1937–
US film actor

Born in Neptune, New Jersey, he began his career as an office boy at MGM, and after studying and working with the Players Ring Theater, made his film debut in *Cry Baby Killer* (1958). He spent the next decade in a succession of low-budget exploitation films before his first major success in *Easy Rider* (1969). He won praise for his portrayals of explosive non-conformists in *Five Easy Pieces* (1970) and *The Last Detail* (1973). His intense charisma and acute sense of humour have illuminated a wide range of characters in such diverse films as *Chinatown* (1974), *The Shining* (1980), *Prizzi's Honor* (1985) and *Ironweed* (1987). He won Academy Awards for *One Flew over the Cuckoo's Nest* (1975), *Terms of Endearment* (1984), and *As Good as it Gets* (1997), and has appeared in *Batman* (1989), *Hoffa* (1992), *Wolf* (1994), *Blood and Wine* (1996) and *Mars Attacks!* (1996). He has also written scripts and occasionally directs.

Nicholson, (Edward) Max 1904–
English conservationist
Born in Ringwood, Hampshire, and educated at Oxford, he was director-general of Nature Conservancy (1952–66), in which role he stimulated and established conservation work in the UK and throughout the world. He received the John C Phillips Medal from the International Union of the Conservation of Nature in 1963. He was president of the Royal Society for the Protection of Birds (1980–85) and has also served on the boards of the Wildfowl Trust, World Wildlife Fund, and Common Ground International. He chaired the UK Standing Committee for World Conservation Strategy Programme (1981–83). His publications range from *Birds of England* (1926) to *The New Environmental Age* (1987). He was one of the founding fathers of modern wildlife conservation in Great Britain.

Nicholson, Seth Barnes 1891–1963
US astronomer
Born in Springfield, Illinois, he was on the staff of the Mount Wilson Observatory (1915–57) and discovered the ninth, tenth and eleventh satellites of Jupiter.

Nicholson, William 1753–1815
English physicist and inventor
He was born in London, educated in Yorkshire, and at the age of 16 entered the service of the East India Company. After returning to England in 1776, he settled in London where he opened a school of mathematics and from 1797 to 1815 published the *Journal of Natural Philosophy, Chemistry, and the Arts…* . He also worked as a patent agent, and as engineer to several water supply undertakings. Only a few months after the first primitive electric battery had been constructed in 1799 by Count **Alessandro Volta**, he built the first voltaic pile in England, and soon afterwards noticed that when the ends of the leads from the battery were immersed in water, bubbles of gas were produced. The results of his experiments were reported in 1800 in his journal and excited a great deal of interest. Among his many inventions were the hydrometer named after him, and a method for printing on linen and other materials, patented in 1790 but never put into practice.

Nicholson, Sir William Newzam Prior, *also called* J Beggarstaff 1872–1949
English artist
Born in Newark, Cambridgeshire, he studied in Paris and was influenced by **James McNeill Whistler** and **Édouard Manet**. He became a fashionable portrait painter, but is principally remembered for the posters produced (with his brother-in-law, **James Pryde**) under the name of J and W Beggarstaff, for his woodcut book illustrations, and for his glowing still-life paintings (for example the *Mushrooms* in the Tate Gallery, London).

Niepce, (Joseph) Nicéphore 1765–1833
French chemist, one of the pioneers of photography

Nicéphore Niepce was born in Chalon-sur-Saône, Burgundy. He served under **Napoleon I** and in 1795 became administrator of Nice. With enough inherited wealth to support himself, he was able to devote himself to research in chemistry from 1801 on. He experimented with the new technique of lithography, using a camera obscura to project an image on to a wall, then tracing round the image in the time-honoured fashion.

Being a poor draughtsman, he decided to look for ways of fixing the image automatically. In 1822, using silver chloride paper and a camera, he achieved a temporary image of the view outside his workroom window, but could not fix it. In 1826 he succeeded in making a permanent image using a pewter plate coated with bitumen of Judea,

an asphalt which hardens on exposure to light. This historic negative, which Niepce termed a 'heliograph', is now preserved at the University of Texas.

From 1829 Niepce collaborated with **Louis Daguerre** in the search for materials which would reduce the exposure time but he died, in Saint-Loup-de-Varennes, before any progress was made. Although Niepce is known principally for his photographic work, he was active in other fields; he invented a method to extract sugar from pumpkin and beetroot, and together with his brother Charles, built the Pyreolophore motor.

📖 Victor Fouque, *The Truth Concerning the Invention of Photography: Nicéphore Niepce—His Life, Letters and Works* (1935, trans by Edward Epstean).

Nicholson, (Rose) Winifred, *née* Roberts, *also known as* Winifred Dacre 1893–1981
English painter

Born in Oxford, she attended the Byam Shaw School of Art in London, and married the artist **Ben Nicholson** in 1920. She worked in Paris, Lugano, India and the Hebrides in Scotland then moved to Cumbria and became a member of the Seven and Five Society (1925–35). After 1931, the year her husband left her to live with **Barbara Hepworth**, she changed her style from the figurative to experiment with abstraction. From 1935 to 1945 she exhibited under her mother's surname of Dacre.

Nicias c.410–413BC
Athenian soldier and politician

A member of the aristocratic party, he opposed **Cleon** and **Alcibiades**. In 427–426BC he defeated the Spartans and the Corinthians. In 424 he ravaged Laconia, but in 421 made a short-lived peace between Sparta and Athens (the Peace of Nicias). He was appointed commander of the naval expedition against Sicily (418) despite his lack of sympathy with the mission. He laid siege to Syracuse (415), and was at first successful, but subsequently experienced a series of disasters; his troops were forced to surrender, and he was put to death.

Nicklaus, Jack, *known as* the Golden Bear 1940–
US golfer

Born in Columbus, Ohio, he won the US Amateur championships twice while still a student at Ohio State University and played in the Walker Cup twice before turning professional in 1962. His first professional victory was the US Open (1962), a tournament he won a further three times (1967, 1972, 1980). Of the other Majors, he won the Masters a record six times (1963, 1965–66, 1972, 1975, 1986); the Open championship three times (1966, 1970, 1978); and the US PGA (Professional Golfers' Association) a record-equalling five times (1963, 1971, 1973, 1975, 1980). His total of 20 Major victories (including his two US Amateurs) is also a record. Arguably the greatest golfer in history, he has earned more than $84 million from the game. He currently plays in seniors tournaments and designs golf courses around the world.

Nicks, Swift See Nevison, John

Nicol, William 1768–1851
Scottish geologist and physicist

Born in Edinburgh, he lectured in natural philosophy at the university there. In 1828 he invented the Nicol prism, which utilizes the doubly refracting property of Iceland spar, and which proved invaluable in the investigation of polarized light. It was also of fundamental importance in studies of minerals under the microscope. He devised

a new method of preparing thin sections of rocks for the microscope by cementing the specimen to the glass slide and then grinding it until it was possible to view it by transmitted light, thus revealing the mineral's properties and internal structure. The technique was initially developed to examine the minute details of fossil and recent wood, and Nicol himself prepared a large number of thin sections to this end. His reluctance to publish delayed the widespread use of thin sections for some 40 years until **Henry Clifton Sorby** and others introduced them into petrology.

Nicolai, (Carl) Otto (Ehrenfried) 1810–49
German composer and conductor

Born in Königsberg, Prussia (now Kaliningrad, Russia), he became court conductor in Vienna (1841) and kapellmeister of the Royal Opera in Berlin (1847), where his opera *Die Lustigen Weiber von Windsor* (1846–47, Eng trans *The Merry Wives of Windsor*) was produced just before his death.

Nicolini, Adelina See Patti, Adelina

Nicolle, Charles Jules Henri 1866–1936
French physician, microbiologist and Nobel Prize winner

Born in Rouen, he was educated there and in Paris. His aptitude for research was stimulated at the Pasteur Institute in Paris by **Émile Roux** and Elie Metchnikoff. He became director of the Pasteur Institute in Tunis (1902–32), which he and his colleagues turned into a leading research centre, working on the mode of spread, prevention and treatment of a number of diseases, including leishmaniasis, toxoplasmosis, Malta fever and typhus. His discovery that typhus is spread by lice (1909) had important implications during World War I and led to his award, in 1928, of the Nobel Prize for physiology or medicine. From 1932 he lectured each year at the Collège de France in Paris, but maintained his base in Tunis. He wrote novels, short stories and philosophical works.

Nicolson, Alexander 1827–93
Scottish Gaelic scholar

Born in Usabost in Skye, he was educated for the Free Church at Edinburgh. He became assistant to the philosopher Sir **William Hamilton** and became an advocate. A prolific writer in both English and Gaelic, he was a member of the Napier Commission that reported on crofting conditions in the Highlands and Islands (1884) and established the Crofters' Commission. He helped to revise the Gaelic Bible, and published *A Collection of Gaelic Proverbs and Familiar Phrases* (1881).

Nicolson, Sir Harold George 1886–1968
English diplomat, writer and critic

Nightingale, Florence 1820–1910
English nurse and hospital reformer

Florence Nightingale was named after the place of her birth in Italy. She trained as a nurse at Kaiserswerth (1851) and Paris and in 1853 became superintendent of a hospital for invalid women in London. In the Crimean War she volunteered for duty and took 38 nurses to Scutari in 1854. She organized the barracks hospital after the Battle of Inkerman (5 November) and by imposing strict discipline and standards of sanitation reduced the hospital mortality rate drastically. She returned to England in 1856 and a fund of £50,000 was subscribed to enable her to form an institution for the training of nurses at St Thomas's and at King's College Hospital.

She devoted many years to the question of army sanitary reform, to the improvement of nursing and to public health in India. Her main work, *Notes on Nursing* (1859), went through many editions.

📖 S Dengler, *Florence Nightingale* (1988); E Huxley, *Florence Nightingale* (1975).

'No *man*, not even a doctor, ever gives any other definition of what a nurse should be than this—devoted and obedient. This definition would do just as well for a porter. It might even do for a horse. It would not do for a policeman.' From *Notes on Nursing*.

He was born in Teheran, where his father (later 1st Baron Carnock) was British chargé d'affaires, and educated at Wellington College and Balliol College, Oxford. He had a distinguished career as a diplomat, entering the service in 1909, and holding posts in Madrid, Constantinople (Istanbul), Teheran and Berlin until his resignation in 1929, when he turned to journalism. From 1935 to 1945 he was National Liberal MP for West Leicester. He wrote several biographies, for example those of Tennyson, Algernon Swinburne and the official one of George V, as well as books on history, politics and, in *Good Behaviour* (1955), manners. He was highly regarded as a literary critic. He was married to Victoria Sackville-West.

Nicot, Jean 1530–1600
French diplomat and scholar

Born in Nîmes, he became French ambassador in Lisbon (1559–61), and in 1561 introduced the tobacco plant into France from Portugal, called after him *Nicotiana*. The word 'nicotine' derives from his name. He also compiled one of the first French dictionaries (1606).

Nidetch, Jean 1923–
US entrepreneur

Born in Brooklyn, New York, she embarked on a diet to lose five stone in 1961 and found it to be easier when she had the support of a group of overweight friends with a similar goal. From this simple idea grew an organization, Weight Watchers International, launched in 1963, which foreshadowed a major boom in the diet and fitness industries.

Niebuhr, Helmut Richard 1894–1962
US theologian

Born in Wright City, Missouri, he taught at Yale from 1931, becoming Professor of Theology and Christian Ethics and director of graduate studies. Like his brother, Reinhold Niebuhr, he had enormous influence on generations of students. His classic study *The Meaning of Revelation* (1941) was followed by *Christ and Culture* (1951), *Radical Monotheism and Western Culture* (1960) and *The Responsible Self* (1963): a series of books advocating critical reflection on the relation between faith and moral action and a quest for a Christian transformation of society. His concern that ministers be adequately trained for this task was reflected in his direction of a survey of American Protestant theological education (1954–56).

Niebuhr, Reinhold 1892–1971
US theologian

Born in Wright City, Missouri, the son of a clergyman, he was educated at Elmhurst (Illinois) College, Eden Theological Seminary and Yale Divinity School. He became an evangelical pastor in working-class Detroit (1915–28) and was Professor of Christian Ethics at the Union Theological Seminary, New York (1928–60). His

early liberalism and social idealism eventually gave way to a more pessimistic theology known as Christian Realism, which recognized man's sinfulness and propensity to abuse power and asserted that such a recognition was necessary if the struggle for social justice was to have any measure of success. He wrote *Moral Man and Immoral Society* (1932), *The Nature and Destiny of Man* (2 vols, 1941–43), *Faith and History* (1949), *The Irony of American History* (1952), *Structure of Nations and Empires* (1959), and many other books. He was the brother of Helmut Richard Niebuhr.

Niel, Cornelis Bernardus Kees Van See Van Niel, Cornelis Bernardus Kees

Nielsen, Carl August 1865–1931
Danish composer

Born in Nörre-Lyndelse, near Odense, he became a bandsman at Odense, and in 1883 entered the Copenhagen Conservatory. His compositions from this period —including the G minor quartet and oboe fantasias— are not revolutionary, but with his 1st Symphony (1894) his progressive tonality and rhythmic boldness become apparent, though still within a classical structure. His 2nd Symphony (1901–02, 'The Four Temperaments') shows the first use in Danish music of polytonality, along with the contrapuntal style which was to become characteristic of him. His other works include four other symphonies (1912, 1916, 1922, 1925), the tragic opera *Saul and David* (1902), the comic opera *Masquerade* (1906), chamber music, concertos for flute, clarinet and violin, and a huge organ work, *Commotio* (1931). In 1915 he was appointed director of Copenhagen Conservatory. He tried through new harmonies, rhythms and melodic ideas of Nordic character to rid Danish music of its prevalent Romanticism. Nielsen was also a distinguished conductor, and exerted a great influence on the musical development of Denmark.

Niemeyer, Oscar 1907–
Brazilian architect

Born in Rio de Janeiro, he studied at the National School of Fine Arts in Brazil and began work in the office of Lucio Costa (1935). From 1936 to 1943 he joined Costa and others to design the Ministry of Education and Public Health, Rio (1937–42, with Le Corbusier as consultant architect). With Costa he designed the Brazilian Pavilion at the New York World Fair (1939). He became architectural adviser to Nova Cap, serving as its chief architect (1957–59), and co-ordinating the development of Brasilia. His Expressionist powers are well displayed in a group at Pampúlha, including the Church of São Francisco (1942–44), where parabolic sections indicate the organic, antirationalist principles underlying his work. Further major works are the Exhibition Hall, São Paolo (1953), and the President's Palace, Law Courts and Cathedrals, Brasilia.

Nijinska, Bronislava or Bronisława 1891–1972
Russian ballet dancer and choreographer

Nijinska was born in Minsk, the sister of **Vaslav Nijinsky**. Her parents were professional dancers, and she, like her brother, studied at the Imperial Ballet School in St Petersburg, graduating in 1908 and going on to become a soloist with the Maryinsky company. She danced with **Sergei Diaghilev**'s Ballets Russes in Paris and London before returning to Russia during World War I, when she started a school in Kiev, but went back to Diaghilev in 1921, following **Léonide Massine** as principal choreographer.

Among the ballets she created for the company were her masterpieces *Les Noces* (1923, 'The Wedding') and *Les Biches* (1924, 'The Does'). After working in Buenos Aires and for Ida Rubinstein's company in Paris she briefly formed her own company in 1932. From 1935 she choreographed for many companies in Europe and the USA, but lived mainly in the USA and started a ballet school in Los Angeles (1938). She was persuaded to stage a revival of *Les Noces* and *Les Biches* at Covent Garden in 1964. ⌑ Her *Early Memoirs* were translated into English in 1981. See also Nancy Van Norman Baer, *Nijinska: A Dancer's Legacy* (1986); Richard Buckle, *Nijinska* (1972).

Niemöller, Martin 1892–1984
German theologian and resistance figure

Born in Lippstadt, Westphalia, he served as a U-boat commander in World War I, then entered the Lutheran Church and held various positions, most notably as pastor in Berlin-Dahlem from 1931. He was a prominent member of the anti-Nazi Confessing Church for which he was arrested in 1937 and sent to Sachsenhausen and Dachau concentration camps. Freed in 1945, he resumed his church career and adopted outspoken views on current affairs, most notably on German reunification and nuclear disarmament. In 1961 he became president of the World Council of Churches. He wrote *Vom U-Boot zur Kanzel* (1934, 'From U-Boat to the Pulpit'), and collections of his sermons include *Six Dachau Sermons* (1946, Eng trans 1959). ⌑ C Start-Davidson, *God's Man* (1959)

Niepce, (Joseph) Nicéphore   See panel p1366

Nietzsche, Friedrich Wilhelm 1844–1900
German philosopher, scholar and writer

Born in Röcken, Saxony, the son of a Lutheran pastor, he proved himself a brilliant classical student at the universities of Bonn and Leipzig. He was appointed Professor of Classical Philology at the University of Basle at the age of 24 and became a Swiss citizen, serving briefly as a medical orderly in 1870 in the Franco-Prussian War but returning to the university in poor health. His first book *Die Geburt der Tragödie* (1872, Eng trans *The Birth of Tragedy*, 1909), with its celebrated comparison between 'Dionysian' and 'Apollonian' values, was dedicated to **Richard Wagner**, who had become a friend and whose operas he regarded as the true successors to Greek tragedy. However, he broke violently with Wagner in 1876, nominally at least because he thought the Christian convictions expressed in *Parsifal* were 'mere playacting' and political expediency. In 1878 he was forced to resign his university position after worsening bouts of his psychosomatic illnesses and spent most of the next 10 years at various resorts in France, Italy and Switzerland writing and trying to recover his health. In 1889 he had a complete mental and physical breakdown, probably syphilitic in origin, and he was nursed for the next 12 years, first by his mother at Naumberg then by his sister Elizabeth at Weimar. He never recovered his sanity. In the 16 years from 1872 he had produced a stream of brilliant, unconventional works, often aphoristic or poetical in form, which have secured him an enormous, if sometimes cultish, influence in modern intellectual history. The best-known writings are: *Unzeitgemässe Betrachtungen* (1873–76, Eng trans *Thoughts Out of Season*, 1909), *Die Fröhliche Wissenschaft* (1882, Eng trans *The Joyful Wisdom*, 1910), *Also sprach Zarathustra* (1883–92, 'Thus Spake Zarathustra'), *Jenseits von Gut und Böse* (1886, Eng trans *Beyond Good and Evil*, 1907), *Zur Genealogie der Moral* (1887, Eng trans *A Genealogy of Morals*, 1897), and *Ecce Homo* (his autobiography, completed in 1888 but withheld by his sister and not published till 1908). One cannot derive systematic 'theories' from these often highly-wrought literary works but the characteristic themes are the vehement repudiation of Christian and liberal ethics, the detestation of democratic ideals, the celebration of the *Übermensch* (superman) who can create and impose his own law, the death of God, and the life-affirming 'will to power'. His reputation suffered when his views were taken up in a simple-minded and perverted form by the German Nazis, but he is now regarded as a major, though very individual, influence on many strands of 20th-century thought, including existentialism and psychoanalysis, and on figures as various as **Karl Jaspers, Martin Heidegger, Thomas Mann, W B Yeats, Karl Mannheim** and **Michel Foucault**. ⌑ Peter Bergman, *Nietzsche* (1987)

Nieuwland, Julius Arthur 1878–1936
US chemist

He was born in Hansbeke, Belgium, and after his parents emigrated to the USA he was educated at the University of Notre Dame, South Bend, Indiana. He then studied for the priesthood at the Catholic University of America, Washington DC. He spent his teaching career at Notre Dame, as Professor of Botany (1904–18) and Professor of Organic Chemistry (1918–36). While studying the reaction between acetylene and arsenic trichloride in the course of his doctoral work, Nieuwland had made a highly toxic gas and discontinued his research because of its deadly nature. It was subsequently developed into a poison gas (lewisite) and used in World War I. In the 1920s Nieuwland carried out further research into the reactions of acetylene, working from 1925 in collaboration with the chemists of Du Pont de Nemours. This research resulted (1929) in the synthesis of neoprene (at first known as Duprene), the first commercially successful synthetic rubber.

Nightingale, Florence   See panel p1367

Nijinska, Bronislava   See panel above

Nijinsky, Vaslav   See panel p1369

Nikisch, Arthur 1855–1922
Hungarian conductor and composer

Born in Lébényi Szentmiklós, he was conductor of the Boston Symphony Orchestra (1889–93), the Gewandhaus Orchestra of Leipzig from 1895, and the Berlin Philharmonic Orchestra from 1897. His compositions include a string quartet and a symphony.

Nikodim, Boris Georgiyevich, *originally* Rotov 1929–78
Russian prelate, and metropolitan of Leningrad

Born in Frolovo, he entered the Russian Orthodox monastery at Ryazan, and assumed the name of Nikodim on being made deacon in 1947. He combined parochial work with studies at Leningrad (now St Petersburg), and

Nijinsky, Vaslav 1890–1950
Russian dancer and choreographer

Nijinsky was born in Kiev into a family of dancers who had their own dance company. Considered to be the greatest male dancer of the 20th century, he was, like his sister **Bronislava Nijinska**, trained at the Imperial Ballet School in St Petersburg, and first appeared in ballet at the Maryinski Theatre. As the leading dancer in **Sergei Diaghilev**'s Ballets Russes, which performed in Paris in 1909, he became enormously popular, and in 1911 he appeared as Petrushka in the first perfomance of **Igor Stravinsky**'s ballet. His choreographic repertoire was small but had two exceptional high points, in **Claude** **Debussy**'s *L'Après-midi d'un Faune* (1912, 'Prelude to the Afternoon of a Faun') and in Stravinsky's *Sacre du Printemps* (1913, 'The Rite of Spring').

He married in 1913 and was interned in Hungary during the early part of World War I. He rejoined Diaghilev for a world tour, but was diagnosed a paranoid schizophrenic in 1917. Even before his death Nijinsky had become a legendary figure.
📖 Nijinsky's *Diary* was published in English in 1968. See also biographies by his wife Romola Nijinsky: *Nijinsky* (1933) and *The Last Years of Nijinsky* (1952).

---

was archimandrite in charge of the Russian Orthodox Mission in Jerusalem before being consecrated in 1960 as Bishop of Podolsk. He then became head of foreign relations for the Russian Church, which led into the World Council of Churches amid great acclaim in 1961. Two years later, still only 34, he was appointed metropolitan, and became known at ecumenical meetings all over the world. He collapsed and died during an audience with Pope **John Paul I** in the Vatican.

Nikolais, Alwin 1910–93
US dancer, choreographer, teacher and director

Born in Southington, Connecticut, he was, at first, a pianist for silent films and a puppeteer. After seeing **Mary Wigman** perform in 1933 he turned to dance and studied with **Hanya Holm**. He moved to New York City in 1948, where he produced children's theatre at the Henry Street Playhouse, out of which he founded his own dance company, Nikolais Dance Theatre. His style was idiosyncratic and uninhibited by conventional artistic boundaries. He designed his own sets with painted slides and tin cans punctured with holes to remarkable effect, and composed scores out of chopped tape. Always an innovator, he became, in 1963, the first artist to use the Moog synthesizer. His work includes *Noumenon* (1953), *Kaleidoscope* (1956), *Imago* (1963), *Sanctum* (1964), *Gallery* (1978) and for the Paris Opéra Ballet, *Schema* (1980) and *Arc-en-Ciel* (1987).

Niland, D'Arcy Francis 1919–67
Australian writer

He was born in Glen Innes, New South Wales. After his early years working in the bush, he went to Sydney and in 1942 married the New Zealand writer **Ruth Park**, after which he settled down to writing. Between 1949 and 1952 he won many prizes for short stories and novels, and in 1955 he achieved international fame with his novel *The Shiralee* (filmed 1957). This was followed by *Call Me When the Cross Turns Over* (1957), *Gold in the Streets* (1959) and perhaps his best novel, *Dead Men Running* (1969, later an ABC serial). He also wrote radio and television plays, and hundreds of short stories, some of which were published in four collections between 1961 and 1966. With Ruth Park he wrote the story of their early married life and writing careers in *The Drums Go Bang* (1956).

Niles, Daniel Thambyrajah 1908–70
Tamil Methodist, ecumenical leader and evangelist

Born near Jaffna, a fourth-generation Tamil Christian, he became increasingly involved in the developing ecumenical movement. The youngest delegate at the 1938 International Missionary Council Tambaram Conference, he was appointed a president of the World Council of Churches after Uppsala (1968), and at the time of his death was chairman of the East Asian Christian Conference and president of the Methodist Church in Ceylon.

He wrote 45 hymns for the *EACC Hymnal* (1963), and these, along with the posthumous *A Testament of Faith* (1972), convey the spirit of his many books.

Nilsen, Dennis 1945–
Scottish convicted murderer

He was born in Fraserburgh, Aberdeenshire, and after a period in the army and a year as a probationary policeman, he became a civil servant in 1974. While living in two rented flats in London, he invited a series of young men home, strangling, or attempting to strangle, several of them. He dissected the dead victims, disposing some of the remains by flushing them down the toilet. When, in 1983, the drains became blocked he was discovered, and arrested. He has admitted to 15 murders. Throughout the four years of his offending, he had sustained his employment, gained promotion and was an active trade unionist. He was at the centre of controversy in 1993 after he was interviewed on television about his crimes, showing no remorse.

Nilsson, (Märta) Birgit 1918–
Swedish soprano

Born near Karup, Kristianstadslaen, she studied at the Stockholm Royal Academy of Music, where her teachers included **Joseph Hislop**. Following her debut in 1946, she sang with the Stockholm Royal Opera (1947–51), and at the Bayreuth Festival from 1953 to 1970. She was the leading **Wagner**ian soprano of that period, having a voice of great power, stamina and intense personality. Well known in most of the great houses and festivals of the world, her repertoire included works by **Verdi**, **Puccini** and **Richard Strauss**. She retired from the stage in 1982 and is the only woman to have received the Swedish Gold Medal.

Nilsson, Lennart 1922–
Swedish photographer

He worked as a freelance press photographer, gaining respect for several portraits such as *Sweden in Profiles* (1954), but went on to pioneer microfilm showing the anatomy of plants and animals. He has since become best known for his microbiological and medical photography. Working in close contact with medical teams, he has successfully combined the techniques of photography and endoscopy. He perfected special lenses to film inside the human body, which enabled him to produce pictures of the human foetus in the womb from conception to birth. His pictorial record entitled *Ett barn blir till* (1965, 'The Everyday Miracle: A Child is Born'), which won him the American National Press Association Picture of the Year award, was syndicated and became well known internationally.

Nimeiri, Gaafar Mohamed el- 1930–
Sudanese soldier and politician

Born in Omdurman, he joined the army and continued his training in Egypt, where he became a disciple of **Gamal Abd al-Nasser**. In 1969, with the rank of colonel, he led the military coup which removed the civilian government and established a Revolutionary Command Council (RCC). In 1971, under a new constitution, he became President. Although he was twice re-elected, by the 1980s his regional policies and his attempts to impose strict Islamic law had made his regime unpopular and in 1985, while visiting the USA, he himself was deposed by an army colleague, General Swar al-Dahab.

Nimitz, Chester William 1885–1966
US naval commander

Born in Fredericksburg, Texas, he graduated from the US Naval Academy, Annapolis, in 1905, served mainly in submarines, and by 1938 was rear admiral. From 1941 to 1945 he commanded the US Pacific fleet and Pacific Ocean areas, contributing largely to the defeat of Japan. Made a fleet admiral in 1944, he signed the Japanese surrender documents for the USA on the USS *Missouri* in Tokyo Bay (1945). He became Chief of Naval Operations from 1945 to 1947 and Special Assistant to the Secretary of the Navy (1947–49), and led the UN mediation commission in the Kashmir dispute in 1949. ☐ E B Potter, *Nimitz* (1976)

Nin, Anaïs 1903–77
US writer

Born in Paris, to parents of mixed Spanish–Cuban descent, she spent her childhood in Europe until, at the age of 11, she left France to live in the USA. Ten years later, she returned to Paris, where she studied psychoanalysis under **Otto Rank**, became acquainted with many well-known writers and artists and began to write herself. Her first novel, *House of Incest*, was published in 1936 and was followed by volumes of criticism, among them *The Novel of the Future* (1968), and a series of novels including *Winter of Artifice* (1939), *A Spy in the House of Love* (1954) and *Collages* (1964). She also published an early collection of short stories, *Under a Glass Bell* (1944). Ultimately, however, her reputation as an artist and seminal figure in the new feminism of the 1970s rests on her seven *Journals* (1966–83). Spanning the years 1931–74 they are an engrossing record of an era and some of its most intriguing and avant-garde players, as well as a passionate, explicit and candid account of one woman's voyage of self-discovery. ☐ N Scholar, *Anaïs Nin* (1984)

Ninagawa, Yukio 1935–
Japanese stage director

He studied at the Seihari Theatre Company, and emerged as a leading light in Japanese avant-garde theatre with his work at Toyko's Small Basement Theatre. He staged *Romeo and Juliet* as his first production for the Toho Company (1974), followed by a series of classical works and numerous Japanese plays. In 1985 he created a sensation at the Edinburgh Festival with a vibrant, colourful, violent, Samurai-influenced production of *Macbeth*, followed by an open-air production in a Georgian courtyard of **Euripides**' *Medea* in 1986. Both productions were subsequently seen at the National Theatre in London, for which Ninagawa won the 1987 Olivier award for director of the year. In 1992 he produced a Noh-influenced version of *The Tempest* at the Barbican Theatre, London.

Ninian, St, *also known as* Nynia *or* Ringan fl.390AD
Scottish bishop, the earliest known Christian leader in Scotland

Born Ailred of Rievaulx, near the Solway Firth, according to his 12th-century biographer, he was also alleged to be the son of a Christian king. According to **Bede**, writing about 730, he was a bishop of the Old Welsh British, and studied in Rome. He was consecrated bishop by the pope (AD394) and sent as an apostle to the western parts of Great Britain. On his way home from Rome he visited St **Martin** of Tours, who supplied him with masons and to whom he later dedicated his church. He selected Wigtownshire for the site of a monastery and church, which was built around 400 (and named Candida Casa, or 'White House', according to Bede). Successful in converting the southern Picts, he died at Whithorn and was buried there, although other sources suggest he may have withdrawn to Ireland.

Nino See **Bixio, Girolamo**

Ninoy See **Aquino, Benigno**

Nipkow, Paul 1860–1940
German engineer

He was born in Lauenburg. One of the pioneers of television, he invented the 'Nipkow disc' in 1884, a mechanical scanning device consisting of a revolving disc with a spiral pattern of apertures. In use until 1932, it was superseded by electronic scanning.

Nirenberg, Marshall Warren 1927–
US biochemist and Nobel Prize winner

Born in New York City, he was educated at the universities of Florida and Michigan, and worked from 1957 at the National Institutes of Health in Bethesda, Maryland. It had been proposed that there are different combinations of three nucleotide bases (triplets or 'codons') in nucleic acid chains in DNA and RNA, with each triplet coded for a different amino acid in the biological synthesis of proteins, the fundamental process in the chemical transfer of inherited characteristics. The precise nature of the code remained unknown, with 64 possible combinations of bases, and only 20 amino acids to be coded. Nirenberg attacked the problem of the 'code dictionary' by synthesizing a nucleic acid with a known base sequence, and then finding which amino acid it converted to protein. With his success, **Har Gobind Khorana** and others soon completed the task of deciphering the full code. In 1968 Nirenberg, Khorana and **Robery Holley** shared the Nobel Prize for physiology or medicine for this work.

Niro, Robert De See **De Niro, Robert**

Nishtar, Shah Muhammad Birthdate unavailable
British Muslim 'Allama and educationist

Born in Pakistan, he took an MA in Arabic at the Punjab University, and moved to Bradford, Yorkshire, in the 1970s. He is Imam of a large Barelwi mosque and is responsible for the Islamic education of many young people in the community, including, unusually, the education in Arabic of girls. He emphasizes understanding, rather than rote learning, and has established a lending library of books in English, Urdu and Arabic. He is a member of the Imams and Mosques Council of Great Britain and an authority on Islamic law. ☐ Philip Lewis, *Islamic Britain* (1994)

Nithsdale, William Maxwell, 5th Earl of 1676–1744
Scottish Jacobite

A Catholic, he joined the English Jacobites in the 1715 Rising and was taken prisoner at Preston. He was tried for high treason in London and sentenced to death, but escaped from the Tower in his wife's clothes on the eve of his execution. They settled in Rome.

Ni Tsan See **Ni Zan**

Nitsch, Hermann 1938–
Austrian performance artist

Nixon, Richard Milhous 1913–94
37th President of the USA

Richard Nixon was born in Yorba Linda, California, into a lower-middle class Quaker family of Irish descent, and was educated at Whittier College and Duke University. After five years' practice as a lawyer, he served in the US navy (1942–46), then ran for Congress as a Republican in California in 1946, defeating his Democratic opponent by painting him as a Communist sympathizer, a strategy he would use often in his career.

His fearless outspokenness and tactical brilliance allowed him to rise swiftly in political circles, and he was particularly prominent as a member of the House Committee on Un-American Activities, working on the **Alger Hiss** case. After serving in the Senate (1951–53) he was elected Vice-President under **Dwight D Eisenhower** in 1952 and was re-elected in 1956. In May 1958 he and his wife were subjected to violent anti-American demonstrations in Peru and Venezuela, during a goodwill tour of Latin America, and in 1959 on a visit to Moscow he achieved notoriety by his outspoken exchanges with **Nikita Khrushchev**. As the Republican presidential candidate in 1960, he lost the election to **John F Kennedy** by a tiny margin. Standing for the governorship of California in 1962, he was again defeated.

Despite an emotional declaration that he was retiring from politics, he returned to win the presidential election in 1968 by a small margin, and he was re-elected in 1972 by a large majority. His administration (1969–74) was marked by continuing controversy over the Vietnam War, especially the invasion of Cambodia (1970) and the heavy bombing of North Vietnam, which ended with the eventual signing of a cease-fire in 1973. Other dramatic foreign policy events were Nixon's initiation of a strategic arms limitation treaty with the USSR, his reopening of US relations with the People's Republic of China (1972), and his visit there, the first by a US president.

During an official investigation into a break-in in June 1972 at the Democratic National Committee's headquarters in the Watergate building, Washington, Nixon lost credibility with the US people by at first claiming executive privilege for senior White House officials to prevent them being questioned, and by refusing to hand over tapes of relevant conversations. On 9 August 1974, after several leading members of his government had been found guilty of being involved in the Watergate scandal, he resigned, the first US president to do so, thus averting the threat of impeachment, and in September 1974 he was given a full pardon by President **Gerald Ford**. In his memoirs (1978) and other works written during his retirement he sought to salvage his damaged reputation and rebuild his image as a statesman.

📖 F Emery, *Watergate, the Corruption and Fall of Richard Nixon* (1994); S Ambrose, *Nixon: The Triumph of a Politician* (1989) and *Nixon: The Education of a Politician* (1987); C L Sulzberger, *The World of Richard Nixon* (1987); T H White, *Breach of Faith* (1975).

> 'So you are lean and mean and resourceful, and you continue to walk on the edge of the precipice because over the years you have become fascinated by how close you can walk without losing your balance.' Quoted in the *Washington Post*, 9 August 1979.

Born in Vienna, he lives and works in Prinzendorf. After reading **Arthur Schopenhauer** and **Nietzsche**, he decided that 'art was something similar to religion, and the performance of art corresponded to a ritual'. His work consists of 'installations' in which, for example, slaughtered cattle are hung up before naked men who lie on stretchers, spattered with blood, while music is played.

Nivelle, Robert 1857–1924
French soldier

Born in Tulle, he was an artillery colonel, and made his name when in command of the army of Verdun by recapturing Douaumont and other forts (1916). He was briefly Commander-in-Chief (1916–17), when his Aisne offensive failed and he was superseded by **Philippe Pétain**.

Niven, David, *originally* James David Graham Nevins 1910–83
English actor

Born in London, he was a graduate of the Royal Military College at Sandhurst, and took a variety of jobs before he arrived in Hollywood, where he joined the social set led by **Errol Flynn** and **Clark Gable**, and worked as an extra in *Mutiny on the Bounty* (1935). Signed by **Samuel Goldwyn**, he developed into a polished light-comedian and gallant hero in films like *Dodsworth*, *The Charge of the Light Brigade* (both 1936), *The Dawn Patrol* (1938) and *Bachelor Mother* (1939). After service as an army officer in World War II he spent 30 years as an urbane English-style leading man, perfectly cast as the gentlemanly voyager Phileas Fogg in *Around the World in 80 Days* (1956), and winning an Academy Award for *Separate Tables* (1958). An inimitable raconteur, he published two volumes of lighthearted autobiography, *The Moon's A Balloon* (1972) and *Bring on the Empty Horses* (1975).

Niven, Frederick John 1878–1944
Scottish novelist

Born in Chile, of Scots parentage, he was educated at Glasgow School of Art, then travelled widely in South America and worked as a journalist (1898–1914). After World War I he emigrated to Canada. He wrote more than 30 novels, mostly set in Glasgow or Canada, including *The Lost Cabin Mine* (1908), *The Justice of the Peace* (1914) and *The Staff at Simsons* (1937). His major work was a trilogy on Canadian settlement, comprising *The Flying Years*, *Mine Inheritance* and *The Transplanted* (1935–44). He also published an autobiography, *Coloured Spectacles* (1938).

Nixon, Richard Milhous   See panel above

Ni Zan or Ni Tsan 1301–74
Chinese landscape painter, calligrapher and poet

Born in Wui, Jiangsu (Kiangsu) Province, he may not be the greatest of the Four Great Masters of the Yuan period, but he is certainly the purest. A passionate lover of culture and aesthetics, he nevertheless spent the last 20 years of his life travelling the lakes of the lower Yangtze River with no possessions. His solitary temperament and search for purity, and an absolute spiritual certainty and technical discipline, permeate his work. Instead of showing the typical development from early to mature, his work consists of a rational, austere and disembodied assemblage of expressive forms, almost reduced to signs, which constituted a radical departure from all previous traditions.

Nkomo, Joshua (Mqabuko Nyongolo) 1917–
Zimbabwean nationalist and politician

He was born in Semokwe, Matabeleland, and educated in Natal and at Fort Hare College, where he joined the African National Congress (ANC). He returned to Bulawayo as a social worker and became general secretary of the Rhodesian Railway African Employees Association in 1951. Elected chairman of the (Southern Rhodesian) African National Congress in 1951, he became its

---

Nobel, Alfred Bernhard 1833–96
Swedish chemist and manufacturer, the inventor of dynamite and the founder of the Nobel prizes

Alfred Nobel was born in Stockholm, the son of an engineer. He moved in his childhood to Russia, where his father was working on an underwater mine he had devised. He studied chemistry in Paris, worked in the USA with the Swedish-born **John Ericsson**, and settled in Sweden in 1859. Like his father he was an explosives expert, and in 1866 he invented a safe and manageable form of nitroglycerin, which he called 'dynamite'; later, he invented smokeless gunpowder, and in 1875 gelignite.

On the strength of these inventions, he created an

industrial empire which manufactured many of his other inventions, from artificial gutta-percha to mild steel for armour-plating. He amassed a huge fortune, much of which he left to endow annual Nobel prizes (first awarded in 1901) for physics, chemistry, physiology or medicine, literature and peace (a sixth prize, for economics, was instituted in his honour in 1969). The synthetic transuranic element nobelium was named after him.

📖 Michael and Marjorie Evlanoff, *Alfred Nobel: The Loneliest Millionaire* (1969).

---

president in 1957, leaving the country for exile in 1959. When the ANC was banned, he became president of its successor, the National Democratic Party, but that, too, was banned. He then helped form the Zimbabwe African People's Union (ZAPU) of which he became president. His non-confrontationist tactics and tendency to spend time outside Rhodesia led to a more radical group breaking away to form the Zimbabwe African National Union (ZANU). ZANU, led by **Robert Mugabe**, and ZAPU, with different international patrons and separate military wings, competed for the representation of African opinion but were persuaded to unite to form the Patriotic Front in 1976. ZAPU, however, was increasingly an Ndebele Party and in the 1980 elections won only 20 seats. Mugabe became Prime Minister and Nkomo, who still saw himself as the father of Zimbabwean nationalism, was disappointed to be offered only the post of Minister of Home Affairs, from which he was dismissed in 1981. Violence in Matabeleland encouraged him into a period of further exile, but he returned and agreed to integrate his party into ZANU, the two merging to form ZANU-PF in 1988, making Zimbawe effectively a one-party state with Mugabe as President, and Nkomo as Vice-President from 1990. 📖 *Nkomo: The Story of My Life* (1984)

Nkrumah, Kwame 1909–72
Ghanaian politician

He was born in Nakroful, Gold Coast, and educated at Achimota College, Lincoln University, Pennsylvania, and the London School of Economics. He returned to Africa (1947) and in 1949 formed the nationalist Convention People's Party with the slogan 'self-government now'. In 1950 he was imprisoned for his part in calling strikes and was elected to parliament while still in jail. A year later he was released, and became virtual Prime Minister with the title of Leader of Business in the Assembly. He was confirmed in power at the 1956 election and in 1957 was appointed the first Prime Minister of the independent Commonwealth State of Ghana. Called the 'Gandhi of Africa', he was a significant leader, first of the movement against white domination, and then of Pan-African feeling. Ghana became a republic in 1960. Nkrumah was the moving spirit behind the Charter of African States (1961). Economic reforms sparked off political opposition and several attempts on his life. Legal imprisonment of political opponents for five years and more without trial, and interference with the judiciary in the treason trial (1963, when he dismissed the Chief Justice), heralded the successful referendum for a one-party state in 1964, in which the secrecy of the ballot was called into question. In 1966 his regime was overthrown by a military coup during his absence in China. He sought refuge in Guinea where he was appointed joint head of state. He died in Bucharest.

Noah
Biblical character

He is depicted as the son of Lamech. A 'righteous man', he was given divine instruction to build an ark in which he, his immediate family, and a selection of animals were saved from a widespread flood over the Earth (Genesis 6–9). In the Table of Nations (Genesis 10), Noah's sons Japheth, **Ham** and Shem are depicted as the ancestors of all the nations on Earth.

Noailles, Anna Elizabeth de Brancoven, Comtesse Mathieu de 1876–1933
French poet and novelist

She was born in Paris, of Romanian and Greek descent. With her first book, a collection of sensual and musical poems, *Le Cœur innombrable* (1901, 'The Innumerable Heart'), written under the influence of **Francis Jammes**, she won the hearts of the French poetry-reading public, and was acclaimed as 'Princesse des lettres'. This verse has now dated, but the best of it is still worthy of attention. However, her last poems show her at her most original. A friend to **Maurice Barrès**, she was greatly disliked by some French critics, and has hardly had her posthumous due. 📖 C Fournet, *Un Grand poète français moderne: la Comtesse de Noailles* (1950)

Nobel, Alfred See panel above

Nobile, Umberto 1885–1978
Italian aviator

Born in Lauro, he became an aeronautical engineer and built the airships *Norge* and *Italia*. He flew across the North Pole in the *Norge* with **Roald Amundsen** and **Lincoln Ellsworth** in 1926, but in 1928 he was wrecked in the *Italia* when returning from the North Pole, and was adjudged (1929) responsible for the disaster. In the USA from 1936 to 1942, he later returned to Italy and was reinstated in the Italian air service.

Nobili, Leopoldo 1784–1835
Italian physicist

Born in Trassilico, he served in the Italian army as an artillery captain, then was appointed Professor of Physics at Florence, and engaged in research into electricity. He developed the theory that an electric current is a flow of heat or caloric, an essential step towards the ultimate acceptance of **James Clerk Maxwell**'s electrodynamic theories. He invented the thermopile, which could be used in the measurement of radiant heat, and to measure very small electric currents more accurately he devised the astatic galvanometer.

Noble, Adrian Keith 1950–
English stage director

He studied at Bristol University and the Drama Centre in London, and worked for two years in community and young people's theatre in Birmingham. He became an associate director of the Bristol Old Vic (1976–79), and joined the Royal Shakespeare Company as a resident director (1980). He became an associate director in 1982, and succeeded **Terry Hands** as artistic director (1991), aiming to continue Hands's policy of using outside directors and expand training in the company. Among his recent productions are *Romeo and Juliet* and **Chekhov**'s *The Cherry Orchard* (both 1995).

Nocard, Edmond Isidore Étienne 1850–1903
French biologist

He made important discoveries in veterinary science, and showed that meat and milk from tubercular cattle could transmit the disease to man.

Noddack, Ida Eva Tacke, *née* Tacke 1896–1978 and Walter Karl Friedrich 1893–1960
German chemists

Ida Tacke was born in Lackhausen and educated at the University of Berlin-Charlottenburg. Walter Noddack was born in Berlin and educated at Berlin University. They worked together at the Physikalisch Technische Reichsanstalt and continued their collaboration after their marriage in 1926. In 1935 they moved to the Institute of Physical Chemistry at the University of Freiburg. Walter taught at the University of Strasbourg, France, during World War II and they both ended their careers at the Institute of Geochemical Research, Bamberg, Germany. In 1925 they discovered rhenium (atomic number 75) by X-ray spectroscopy. The same year they announced the discovery of element 43 which they called masurium. Its existence was debated until 1937 when Carlo Perrier and **Emilio Segrè** demonstrated its presence in a sample of molybdenum which had been bombarded with deuterons, and named it technetium. It is now known that technetium exists in minute quantities in the Earth's crust as a decay product of uranium, and in 1952 it was shown to exist in some stars. In photochemistry the Noddacks investigated the physical properties of sensitizing colouring substances, photochemical problems in the human eye and other subjects.

Nodier, Charles 1780–1844
French writer

Born in Besançon, he was persecuted for a pamphlet aimed against **Napoleon I** in 1803, and held a number of jobs, including editing a newspaper, before becoming a librarian in Paris (1824). His novels were widely known in his own day and he had a profound influence on the Romanticists of 1830, but only his short stories and fairytales are remembered, such as *Les Vampires* (1820) and *Le Chien de Brisquet* (1844, 'The Dog of Brisquet'). 📖 J Richer, *Charles Nodier* (1962)

Noel-Baker (of the City of Derby), Philip (John) Noel-Baker, Baron 1889–1982
English Labour politician

Born in London, he captained the British Olympic team (1912) after a brilliant athletic and academic career at Cambridge, and in World War I commanded a Friends' ambulance unit. He served on the secretariat of the Peace Conference (1919) and of the League of Nations (1919–22), and was MP for Coventry (1929–31), then for Derby from 1936. He was Cassel Professor of International Relations at London (1924–29) and Dodge lecturer at Yale (1934), where he was awarded the Howland Prize. He wrote a number of books on international problems, including *Disarmament* (1926), and a standard work, *The Arms Race* (1958). During and after World War II he held several junior ministerial posts and was Labour Secretary of State for Air (1946–47), of Commonwealth Relations (1947–50) and Minister of Fuel and Power (1950–51). He was awarded the Nobel Peace Prize in 1959 and created a life peer in 1977. His son, Francis Edward Noel-Baker (1920–), was a Labour MP from 1945 to 1950 and from 1955 to 1968.

Noether, (Amalie) Emmy 1882–1935
German mathematician

Born in Erlangen, she studied at the universities of Erlangen and Göttingen. Though invited to Göttingen in 1915 by **David Hilbert**, as a woman she could not hold a full academic post at that time. However, she worked there in a semi-honorary capacity until, expelled by the Nazis as a Jew, she emigrated to the USA in 1933 to Bryn Mawr College and Princeton University. She was one of the leading figures in the development of abstract algebra, working in ring theory and the theory of ideals. The theory of Noetherian rings has been an important subject of later research, and she developed it to provide a neutral setting for problems in algebraic geometry and number theory.

Noguchi, Hideyo 1876–1928
US bacteriologist

Born in Inawashiro, Japan, he graduated from Tokyo Medical College and worked in the USA from 1900. At the Rockefeller Institute in New York City, he successfully cultured the bacterium which causes syphilis, which enabled him to devise a diagnostic skin test for the disease using an emulsion of this culture. This earned him the Order of the Rising Sun in his home country in 1915. He went on to show the bacterial cause of Oroya fever, but in his later study of yellow fever in West Africa, where he proved it to be a viral disease, he contracted the disease and died shortly afterwards.

Noguchi, Isamu 1904–88
US sculptor

He was born in Los Angeles, to a Japanese father and a US mother, and from 1906 to 1917 he was brought up in Japan. He studied medicine at Columbia University, then moved to New York where he attended sculpture classes. A Guggenheim Fellowship enabled him to study with **Constantine Brancusi** in Paris from 1927 to 1929. After returning to New York he made stylized sculptures of sheet metal which owed much to his teacher, but from 1940 his work moved closer to Surrealism and he turned to slate and marble, for example in *Kouros* (1946, Metropolitan Museum of Art, New York City). From the mid-1940s he was one of the best-known US sculptors, gaining worldwide commissions for large-scale public sculptures, as in Peace Park, Hiroshima, and Fort Worth, Texas. Later work included the use of ceramics, as in *Centipede* (1952, Metropolitan Museum of Art), and stainless steel, as in *Iutetra* (1976, Palm Beach, Florida).

Noiret, Philippe 1930–
French actor

Born in Lille, he was encouraged to become an actor after appearing in a school play. He studied at the Centre Dramatique de l'Ouest and made his film debut in *Gigi* (1948). In 1953 he joined the Théâtre National Populaire and for a time was primarily a stage actor and cabaret performer. He embraced the cinema with a vengeance after 1960, playing key roles in such films as *Zazie dans le Métro* (1960), *Thérèse Desqueyroux* (1962), *Les Copains* (1964) and *Alexandre le Bienheureux* (1967). His rare, English-language films include *Lady L* (1965) and *Topaz* (1969). One of Europe's most distinguished and prolific film actors, he has won Best Actor César awards for *Le Vieux Fusil* (1976, *The Old Gun*) and *La Vie et rien d'autre* (1989, *Life And Nothing But*). He has appeared in more than 100 films, including *L'Horloger de Saint Paul* (1973, 'The Clockmaker of Saint Paul'), *Les Ripoux* (1984, *My New Partner*), *Cinema Paradiso* (1989) and *Il Postino* (1994).

Noke, Charles John 1858–1941
English ceramic specialist, modeller and designer

Born in Worcester, he was apprenticed to the Worcester Porcelain Factory at the age of 15. He joined Doulton & Co in 1889 as head modeller, and produced large vases, table services and ornamental centrepieces. He was later responsible for many Parian-ware figures, including the ivory glazed Henry Irving and Ellen Terry figures in theatrical costume in 1894, and was instrumental in introducing the Holbein and Rembrandt wares. In 1914 he succeeded John Slater as art director in Doulton's art department in Burslem, where he experimented with reproducing red rouge-flambé and sang-de-bœuf glazes from the Sung, Ming and early Ching dynasties.

Nolan, Sir Sidney Robert 1917–92
Australian painter
Born in Melbourne, he held his first exhibition in 1940. He made his name with a series of 'Ned Kelly' paintings begun in 1946, and followed this with an 'explorer' series based on the travels of Robert Burke and William Wills. He first came to Europe in 1950, and although he worked in Italy, Greece and Africa, he remains best-known for his Australian paintings. He was also a theatrical designer, and designed the Covent Garden productions *The Rite of Spring* (1962) and *Samson and Delilah* (1981), and illustrated books by Robert Lowell and Benjamin Britten. He published a volume of poems, drawings and paintings, *Paradise Garden* (1972). ▣ Jane Clark, *Sidney Nolan* (1988)

Noland, Kenneth 1924–
US painter
Born in Asheville, North Carolina, he trained under Ilya Bolotowsky (1907–81) and Josef Albers at Black Mountain College there (1946–48). He met Ossip Zadkine while studying in Paris (1948–49), and was influenced initially by Paul Klee and Henri Matisse, and the New York action painters. However, he had developed his own kind of hard-edge Minimalist abstract painting by the late 1950s. His style is characterized by large-scale circles, ovals or chevrons, and by horizontal stripes, as in *Via Blues* (1967, Rowan Collection, Pasadena). His 'plaid' paintings date from c.1971.

Nolde, Emil, *pseudonym of* Emil Hansen 1867–1956
German painter and printmaker
Born in Nolde, he was one of the most important Expressionist painters. He was briefly a member of the Expressionist group *Die Brücke* (1906–07), but produced his own powerful style of distorted forms in his violent religious pictures such as *The Life of Christ* (1911–12). He also produced a large number of etchings, lithographs and woodcuts.

Noli, Fan S 1882–1965
Albanian bishop and politician
Born into an Orthodox family in Thrace, he was educated in Greece and taught at a Greek school in Egypt, where he first encountered the Albanian national movement. After studying law at Harvard, he was ordained a priest and became a bishop in the Albanian Orthodox Church (1908). In 1920 he returned to Albania to represent the American Albanians at the National Assembly held in Lushnjë. Left-wing and known as the 'Red Bishop', he was Foreign Minister in the 1921 Popular Party regime, but he criticized the conservative policies of King Zog I and went on to form his own opposition party. After Zog fled (1924), Noli formed a government and tried to establish constitutional rule. He introduced agrarian reforms, tried to minimize Italian influence in Albania and made steps towards recognizing the Soviet regime. However, his government collapsed after only seven months, when Zog invaded the country. In 1930 he retired from political life and resumed his religious duties in the USA.

Nollekens, Joseph 1737–1823
English sculptor
He was born in London, and was a pupil of Pieter Scheemakers. From 1760 he spent 10 years in Rome. He sculpted neoclassical busts of most of his famous contemporaries, including Oliver Goldsmith (1774, Westminster Abbey), Dr Johnson (1784, Westminster Abbey), Charles James Fox (1791, Holkham Hall, Norfolk), George III (1773, Royal Society, London), and Dr Charles Burney (1802, British Museum). He is also known for his statues of goddesses, including *Vénus Tying her Sandal* (1773).

Nollet, Jean Antoine 1700–70
French abbé and physicist
He was born in Pimprez, Noyan, and became interested in science while following an ecclesiastical course of study at Paris. From 1730 he collaborated in electrical researches with Charles Dufay, René Réaumur and others, taking a leading part in the popularization of experimental science in France. In 1748 he became the first Professor of Physics at the Collège de Navarre, in Paris, and in the same year he discovered and gave a clear explanation of the phenomenon of osmosis. He invented an early form of electroscope, and improved the Leyden jar (an early form of capacitor) invented by Pieter van Musschenbroek.

Nonius Marcellus c.4th century AD
Latin grammarian
He is thought to have lived sometime between the 2nd and 5th centuries and was perhaps born in Numidia. He wrote *De compendiosa doctrina*, a sort of lexicon in 20 chapters, of no great merit in itself but valuable to scholars in that it preserves forgotten senses of many words and passages from ancient Latin authors now lost.

Nono, Luigi 1924–90
Italian composer
Born in Venice, he attended the Venice Conservatorio, studying under Francesco Malipiero and later Bruno Maderna. With Maderna, he and Luciano Berio helped to establish Italy in the forefront of contemporary music. Unlike them, however, Nono was a socially conscious and politically committed artist, which had a considerable influence on his music. He worked for a time at the electronic studio in Darmstadt, and though radically avant-garde in technique, his concern for artist-to-audience communication, and the readily understandable inspiration of pieces such as *La Victoire de Guernica* (1954), prevented his work from degenerating into obscurity. *Il Canto Sospero* (1956), based on the letters of victims of wartime oppression, brought him to international notice. His opera *Intolleranza* (1960–61, 'Intolerance'), an attack on the restrictions of freedom, aroused violent hostility at its first performance in Venice. Among his other compositions are *Variazioni canoniche* (1950), *Polyfonica-Monodia-Ritmica* (1951), *Canto per il Vietnam* (1973), the operas *Al gran sole carico d'amore* (1972–75, 'In the Great Sun of Blooming Love') and *Prometeo* (1981–85), *...sofferte onde serene...* (1976) for piano and tape, and a string quartet (1980). In 1955 he married Nuria, the daughter of composer Arnold Schoenberg.

Noonan, Robert See Tressel, Robert

Nordal, Sigurður (Jóhanneson) 1886–1974
Icelandic scholar
Born in Vatnsdalur, he studied philology at Copenhagen, and psychology and philosophy in Germany and at Oxford. A leading authority on classical Icelandic literature, he was Professor of Old Icelandic Literature at the new University of Iceland (1918–45), and Charles Eliot Norton Professor of Poetry at Harvard (1931–32). He was

appointed Icelandic ambassador to Denmark (1951–57) at the time when the return of the Árni Magnússon manuscript collection to Iceland was being negotiated. His seminal publications, on *Ólafs saga helga* (1914), *Snorri Sturluson* (1920), *Völuspá* (1923), *Hrafnkatla* (1940) and particularly *Íslenzk menning I* (1942, Eng trans *Icelandic Culture I*, 1942), had a profound impact. He founded the *Íslenzk Fornrit* series of literary editions of the sagas, to which he contributed *Egils saga* (1933) and *Borgfirðingar sögur* (1938). He also published some poetry, a play, and a collection of short stories (*Fornar ástir*, 1919).

Norden, Denis 1922–
English scriptwriter and broadcaster
Born in Hackney, London, he served in the RAF during World War II, and started his writing career in a variety agency before teaming up with Frank Muir to write comedy scripts and books. The early fruits of this 17-year partnership included the successful radio series *Take It From Here* (1947–58) and *Bedtime with Braden* (1950–54). Several other series were written with or for Jimmy Edwards. Later Norden presented selected film clips of media mishaps on *It'll Be All Right On The Night* (1977–), and in 1991 his *Laughter File* was listed among the most popular television programmes of the year.

Nordenskjöld, Nils Adolf Erik, Baron 1832–1901
Swedish Arctic navigator
He was born in Helsingfors (Helsinki), Finland. A naturalized Swede, he made several expeditions to Spitsbergen, mapping the south of the island. After two preliminary trips proving the navigability of the Kara Sea, he accomplished the navigation of the Northeast Passage (on the *Vega*) from the Atlantic to the Pacific along the north coast of Asia (1878–79). He later made two expeditions to Greenland.

Nordenskjöld, (Nils) Otto 1869–1928
Swedish explorer and geologist
Born in Småland, he accompanied a Swedish scientific expedition to Patagonia and in 1898 travelled through Klondike and Alaska. In 1900 he was a member of Georg Karl Amdrup's Danish expedition to Greenland and in 1901 he led a Swedish party on *Antarctic* to the Antarctic Peninsula. They reached the Weddell Sea and spent two winters on Snow Hill Island. *Antarctic* was crushed by ice, but they were rescued by an Argentinian gunboat. In 1920–21 he explored the Andes. He was appointed Professor of Geography at Gothenburg University in 1905, and Principal of Gothenburg University Business School in 1923. He was the nephew of Baron Nils Nordenskjöld.

Nørgård, Per 1932–
Danish composer
He was educated at the Royal Danish Academy of Music, and continued his studies in Paris. His compositions include operas, symphonies, and ballet and chamber music. He wrote the music for the Academy Award-winning Danish film *Babette's Feast* (*Babettes Gæstebud*), directed by Gabriel Axel in 1987.

Noriega, General Manuel Antonio Morena 1940–
Panamanian soldier and politician
Born in Panama City, he was commissioned in Panama's National Guard in 1962 and rose to become Head of Intelligence (1970) and Chief of Staff (1982). As commander of the National Guard (1982–89), he eventually became de facto ruler of the country, in which there was growing evidence of undemocratic practices. He had been recruited by the CIA in the late 1960s and was supported by the US government until 1987, but in 1988 his indictment by a US grand jury on charges of drug trafficking made that association embarrassing. In 1989, an attempted coup against him failed, and US President George Bush was criticized for not supporting it. However, later that year, with relations rapidly deteriorating, Bush sent troops into Panama to arrest him. Noriega initially took refuge in the Vatican embassy but eventually surrendered and was taken to Miami for trial. In 1992 he was convicted of drug trafficking and racketeering, and he is serving a 40-year prison sentence, though the verdict has been appealed against.

Norman, Barry Leslie 1933–
English journalist and broadcaster
Born in London, the son of film director Leslie Norman (1914–93), he worked for various newspapers before specializing in the world of show business and presenting such radio programmes as *Today* (1974–76), *Going Places* (1977–81) and *Breakaway* (1979–80). He made his name as an influential film critic through the television series that began with *Film '73* (1973–81, 1983–). A recipient of the BAFTA Richard Dimbleby award (1981), he made various documentary series, including *The Hollywood Greats* (1977–79, 1984–85) and *Talking Pictures* (1988). His publications include *The Matter of Mandrake* (1967), *The Birddog Tape* (1992), *100 Best Films* (1992) and *The Mickey Mouse Affair* (1995).

Norman, Greg 1955–
Australian golfer
Born in Mount Isa, Queensland, he is the richest golfer the game has ever seen, with numerous victories all over the world and winnings in excess of $16 million. He has won two major titles—the 1986 and 1993 Open championships—but ironically retains the reputation of the eternal runner-up. The only player of modern times to have competed in a Grand Slam of playoffs, unfortunately he lost them all. Perhaps his worst loss from a winning position came in the 1996 US Masters, when his final-day, six-stroke lead collapsed into a harrowing five-shot loss to Nick Faldo.

Norman, Jessye 1945–
US soprano
Born in Augusta, Georgia, she made her operatic debut at the Deutsche Oper, Berlin in 1969 and at both La Scala and Covent Garden, London, in 1972. Her US debut was at the Hollywood Bowl (1972). She is widely admired in opera and concert music for her beauty of tone, breadth of register and her dynamic range. She was made Commandeur, L'Ordre des Arts et des Lettres in 1984 and has won two Grammies (1984, 1988).

Norman, Montagu, 1st Baron 1871–1950
English banker
After serving in the South African War he entered banking and became associated with the Bank of England. He was elected Governor of the Bank in 1920 and held this post until 1944. During this time he wielded great infuence on national and international monetary affairs.

Noroyi, Ryoji 1937–
Japanese chemist
Educated at the universities of Kyoto and Harvard, he discovered the asymmetric reactions in homogeneous phases (1966), which are catalysed by transition metals, a discovery which has led to further research in the synthesis of chiral molecules. His widely applicable homogeneous asymmetric hydrogenation process allows different optical isomers to be specifically synthesized, a process of particular value in the pharmaceutical industry. The important aspect of these reactions is that the chirality (the optical isomerism) is passed on from catalyst to reaction product. This chemical multiplication of

chirality is a vital ingredient in the production of physiologically active compounds such as pharmaceuticals. Noroyi's discoveries have opened up efficient routes to such diverse compounds as terpenes, alkaloids and prostaglandins. He won the Chemical Society of Japan award in 1984.

Norris, (Benjamin) Frank(lin) 1870–1902
US novelist

Born in Chicago, he first studied art but later turned to journalism, and while a reporter for the *San Francisco Chronicle* (1895–96) was involved in the Jameson raid in South Africa. He was influenced by Émile Zola and was one of the first US naturalist writers, his major novel being *McTeague* (1899), a story of lower-class life in San Francisco, which formed the basis for the classic movie *Greed* (1924). He also wrote the first two volumes of an unfinished 'epic of the wheat' trilogy, *The Octopus* (1901) and *The Pit* (1903). The essay *The Responsibilities of the Novelist* also appeared posthumously, as did *Vandover and the Brute* (1914), the manuscript of which was at first believed lost during the San Francisco earthquake. 📖 F Walker, *Frank Norris: a biography* (1932)

Norris, George William 1861–1944
US politician

Born in Sandusky, Ohio, he obtained a law degree in what is now Valparaiso University, moving to Beaver City, Nebraska, in 1885. He became county prosecuting attorney, and served as district judge from 1895 to 1902. He was elected as a Republican to the House of Representatives (1902–12), was identified with the growing progressive movement for national reform, and under his leadership the House was democratized to the extent of breaking the virtually monarchical rule of the Speaker. He was senator for Nebraska (1912–42), voted against entry into World War I and was irreconcilably opposed to the Versailles Treaty. He maintained the progressive struggle in the cynical capitalist 1920s, sponsored the Norris–La Guardia anti-injunction Act (1932), restricting the use of legal injunctions in labour disputes, and broke with his party on the issue of public ownership of water power. His hopes were realized under the New Deal, and the Tennessee Valley Authority's first dam was named in his honour.

Norrish, Ronald George Wreyford 1897–1978
English physical chemist and Nobel Prize winner

Born in Cambridge, he studied at Emmanuel College, Cambridge, and carried out research under Sir Eric Keightley Rideal. Following various junior appointments at Cambridge, he became H O Jones Lecturer in Physical Chemistry in 1928, and in 1937 he was promoted to Professor of Physical Chemistry and head of department, a post he held until his retirement in 1965. He was one of the founders of modern photochemistry and also made advances in the area of chain reactions. His most important innovation (1945), in association with Sir George Porter, was flash photolysis. For this work Norrish was awarded the Nobel Prize for chemistry jointly with Porter and Manfred Eigen in 1967. He was elected a Fellow of the Royal Society in 1936 and received its Davy Medal in 1958. He received the Faraday Medal of the Chemical Society in 1965 and its Longstaff Medal in 1969, and served as president of the Faraday Society (1953–55).

North, Frederick, 2nd Earl of Guilford, *known as* Lord North 1732–92
English statesman

He entered parliament at the age of 22, became a lord of the treasury, Chancellor of the Exchequer and in 1770 Prime Minister. He was criticized both for failing to avert the Declaration of Independence by the North American colonies (1776) and for failing to defeat them in the subsequent war (1776–83). He resigned in 1782 and entered into a coalition with his former opponent, Charles James Fox, and served with him under the Duke of Portland (William Bentinck) in 1783. He succeeded to the earldom in 1790 on the death of his father Francis, 7th Baron North and 1st Earl of Guilford.

North, John Dudley 1893–1968
English applied mathematician, aircraft engineer and designer

Born in London, he went to Bedford School, took a brief marine apprenticeship and at the age of 20 became Claude Grahame-White's chief engineer at his flying school at Hendon, London. Thereafter he created a succession of highly original aircraft, both for his first company and then in 1917 for Boulton Paul Aircraft Ltd, of which he eventually became chairman and managing director. His aircraft included the Grahame-White Popular, Type XIII, and Charabanc, and for Boulton Paul the Bobolink, Bourges, Bugle, Phoenix, Sidestrand, Overstrand and Defiant. His company specialized in hydraulic gun turrets and, later, power controls. Renowned also for his advanced mathematical ideas on cybernetics, operational research and ergonomics, he contributed significant papers on these subjects to the Royal Aeronautical Society.

North, Marianne 1830–90
English flower painter

At the age of 40, after the death of her father, she set off to paint colourful and exotic flowers in many countries. With the encouragement of Sir Joseph Dalton Hooker she gave her valuable collection to Kew Gardens, where they can be seen in a gallery, opened in 1882, which bears her name.

North, Oliver 1943–
US soldier

Born into a military family in San Antonio, Texas, he graduated from the US Naval College, Annapolis. During the Vietnam War he led a counter-insurgency marines platoon, winning a Silver Star and Purple Heart, before returning home wounded. After working as an instructor and security officer, he was appointed a deputy director of the National Security Council by President Ronald Reagan in 1981. Here he played a key role in a series of controversial military and security actions. In 1986, when the Iran-Contra affair became public, he resigned. In 1989, despite appeals to patriotism, a Washington Court found him guilty on three of 12 charges arising from the affair. He was given a three-year suspended jail sentence and fined $150,000, but he successfully appealed against this conviction, and in 1991 all charges were dropped. He ran for the US Senate in Virginia in 1994 but was defeated. He published *Under Fire: An American Story* in 1991.

North, Robert, *originally* Robert North Dodson 1945–
British dancer and choreographer

Born in Charleston, South Carolina, USA, he joined the Royal Ballet School in 1965 and later took classes with the London Contemporary Dance School. Going on to become one of the founding members of London Contemporary Dance Theatre (1966), he spent 12 years with that company as a dancer and choreographer. His classical training with jazz elements has given him popular appeal. Early work includes *Still Life* (1975), *Scriabin Preludes and Studies* (1978) and *Troy Game* (1974). In 1981 he was made artistic director of Ballet Rambert, but was dismissed five years later. After working as a freelance choreographer for a time, and as ballet director of the Teatro Regio in Turin (1990–91), he was appointed ballet director of the Gothenburg Ballet in 1991. He has been married to the dancer Janet Smith since 1978.

North, Sir Thomas c.1535–c.1601
English translator
Born in London, he is known for his translation of Plutarch (1579), from which Shakespeare drew his knowledge of ancient history.

Northcliffe, Lord See **Harmsworth, Alfred Charles William**

Northrop, John Howard 1891–1987
US biochemist and Nobel Prize winner
Born in Yonkers, New York, and educated at Columbia University, he became Professor of Bacteriology at the University of California at Berkeley (1949–62). In 1930 he crystallized pepsin, the protein-digesting enzyme of the stomach, and went on to purify other macromolecules. He isolated the first bacterial virus, and was the first to equate the biological function of an enzyme with its chemical properties. His *Crystalline Enzymes* (1939) describes his important discovery of purifying proteins by 'salting out'. He also discovered the fermentation process used in the manufacture of acetone. For their studies of methods of producing purified enzymes and virus products, Northrop, **Wendell Stanley** and **James Sumner** shared the 1946 Nobel Prize for chemistry.

Northrop, John Knudsen 1895–1981
US aircraft manufacturer
Born in Newark, New Jersey, he began as a project engineer for the Loughead Aircraft Co in 1916, continued with Douglas Aircraft Co and was a co-founder and chief engineer of the Lockheed Aircraft Co of Burbank, California (1927–28). He was vice-president and chief engineer of The Northrop Corporation, a subsidiary of Douglas Aircraft (1933–37), and became president and director of engineering of Northrop Aircraft Inc (1939–52). He was an engineering consultant from 1953. His company built many famous aircraft, including two very large all-wing types, the first propeller driven and a later version jet-propelled.

Northumberland, Dukes of See **Percy**

Norton, Caroline Elizabeth Sarah, *née* **Sheridan** 1808–77
Irish writer and reformer
She was born in London, the granddaughter of **Richard Brinsley Sheridan**. In 1827 she married a dissolute barrister, the Hon George Chapple Norton (1800–75), and bore him three sons. She took up writing to support the family and published a successful book of verse, *The Sorrows of Rosalie* (1829). In 1836 she separated from her husband, who brought an action of 'criminal conversation' (adultery) against Lord **Melbourne**, obtained custody of the children and tried to obtain the profit from her books. Her spirited pamphlets led to improvements in the legal status of women in relation to infant custody (1839) and marriage and divorce (1857). She married the historian Sir William Stirling-Maxwell (1818–78) in 1877, but died soon afterwards. Her other books of verse include an attack on child labour in *Voice from the Factories* (1836), *The Dream* (1840) and *The Lady of Garaye* (1862), and she also published three novels. She was the model for **George Meredith's** central character in his novel *Diana of the Crossways* (1885).

Norton, Charles Eliot 1827–1908
US writer and scholar
Born in Cambridge, Massachusetts, he was joint editor (with **James Russell Lowell**) of the *North American Review* (1864–68), and was a co-founder of *The Nation* (1865). He then became Professor of Art at Harvard (1873–97), where he instituted a course in the history of fine arts as related to society and general culture. A personal friend

of **Thomas Carlyle**, **John Ruskin**, **Henry Wadsworth Longfellow**, **Ralph Waldo Emerson** and many other leading literary figures, he wrote on medieval church-building, translated **Dante's** *Divina Commedia* (1891–92), edited the poems of **John Donne** (1895) and **Anne Bradstreet** (1897), and the letters of Carlyle (1883–91).

Norton, Mary Teresa Hopkins, *née* Hopkins 1875–1959
US politician
Born in Jersey City, New Jersey, she formed a non-sectarian day-care centre for children of working women in 1912. She was its secretary for three years and president for 12 years. She became the first woman to serve on the New Jersey State Democratic Committee, serving as either vice-chair or chair from 1921 to 1944. From 1925 to 1951 she served in the US Congress, the first woman to be in that position on her own political strength. As the first woman to head a congressional committee, she chaired the District of Columbia Committee. She also chaired the Labor Committee in 1937, and fought successfully for the Fair Labor Standards Act.

Norton, Mary 1903–92
English children's novelist
She was born in Leighton Buzzard, Bedfordshire. Aiming to become an actress she joined the Old Vic Theatre Company, London, in the 1920s, but marriage took her to Portugal, where she first began to write, and later to the USA. Returning to Great Britain in 1943, she published her first book two years later. But it was *The Borrowers* (1952, Carnegie Medal), an enchanting story about tiny people living beneath the floorboards of a big house, which established her as one of the foremost children's writers of her generation. There were four sequels, the last being *The Borrowers Avenged* (1982).

Norton, Thomas 1532–84
English lawyer, and poet
Born in London, he was a successful lawyer and a zealous Protestant, and married a daughter of **Thomas Cranmer**. He translated **John Calvin's** *Christianae Religionis Institutio* (1561). With **Thomas Sackville** he was joint author of the tragedy *Gorboduc*, which was performed before Queen Elizabeth I in 1562, and has some claim to be considered the first proper English tragedy.

Norwich, 1st Viscount See **Cooper, (Sir Alfred) Duff**

Norwood, Sir Cyril 1875–1956
English educationist
Born in Whalley, Lancashire, he was educated at Merchant Taylors' School and St John's College, Oxford. He taught at Leeds Grammar School (1901–06) and became headmaster of Bristol Grammar School (1906–16), master at Marlborough College (1916–26), headmaster of Harrow (1926–34) and president of St John's College, Oxford (1934–46). He was chairman of the Committee on Curriculum and Examinations in Secondary Schools from 1941. The committee report contained a plan for the main features of a new secondary education for all children which incorporated a tripartite system of grammar schools and modern schools as proposed in the Hadow Report of 1926, and of technical schools as proposed in the Spens Report of 1938. It affected many of the development plans presented by local education authorities after the Education Act of 1944.

Nossal, Sir Gustav Joseph Victor 1931–
Australian immunologist
Born in Bad Ischl, Austria, he arrived in Australia in 1939 and was educated at the universities of Sydney and Melbourne. He was appointed Research Fellow at the

Walter and Eliza Hall Institute of Medical Research (1957–59), and worked as assistant Professor of Genetics at Stanford University (1959–61) before returning to the Hall Institute as deputy director (immunology) in 1961; he was director from 1965, when he also became Professor of Medical Biology at Melbourne University, until 1996. His research work has been on antibody response in immunity, discovering the 'one cell–one antibody' rule crucial to modern work in immunology. He has written several popular books on immunology, and also on the progress of medical science, including *Antibodies and Immunity* (1971), *Medical Science and Human Goals* (1975) and *Reshaping Life: Key Issues in Genetic Engineering* (1984). He was knighted in 1977, and elected FRS in 1982.

Nostradamus, *also called* Michel de Notredame
1503–66
French physician and astrologer
Born in St Rémy, Provence, he became doctor of medicine in 1529, and practised in Agen, Lyons, and other places. He set himself up as a prophet in c.1547. His *Centuries* of predictions in rhymed quatrains (two collections, 1555–58), expressed generally in obscure and enigmatic terms, brought their author a great reputation. Charles IX appointed him his physician-in-ordinary.
📖 Edgar Leoni, *Nostradamus and His Prophecies* (1982)

Nöth, Heinrich 1928–
German chemist
Born in Munich and educated at the University of Munich, he returned there as professor in 1969 after working at the University of Marburg. A main group chemist, he has made discoveries in boron–nitrogen chemistry and tetrahydroborate complexes, and has synthesized many ring and cage compounds of aluminium, phosphorus and arsenic. He was partly responsible for developing nuclear magnetic resonance (NMR) spectroscopy as a probe. He was awarded the Alfred Stock Medal of the German Chemical Society in 1976.

Notke, Bernt c.1440–1509
German painter and sculptor
He was born in Lübeck. A surviving reference in 1467 to his exemption from guild rules suggests that he enjoyed an unusually high social status amongst German artists. In 1477 he carved and painted the great cross for Lübeck Cathedral. He executed major works outside Germany, such as the high altar of Aarhus Cathedral in Denmark, and, during a period of several years spent in Sweden, produced a monument for the church of St Nicholas in Stockholm depicting St George killing the dragon.

Notman, William 1826–91
Canadian photographer
Born in Paisley, Scotland, he emigrated to Canada in 1856 after failing to save the family business from bankruptcy. By the 1860s he had built up a photographic business with branches in Montreal, Ottawa, Toronto and Halifax, and in the USA from the 1870s. Establishing a considerable studio practice in portraiture, he made a reputation for hunting and snow scenes, staged in the studio, and composite groups organized and painted by his studio assistants. Work outside the studio included landscape photography and the documenting of great engineering projects, such as the laying of the railways. In later years, Notman's studios effectively dominated North American photography.

Nott, Sir John William Frederick 1932–
English Conservative politician
Born in Bideford, Devon, he was commissioned in the 2nd Gurkha Rifles and served in Malaysia (1952–56). He left the army to study law and economics at Trinity College, Cambridge (1957–59), and was called to the Bar in 1959. He entered the House of Commmons in 1960 as Conservative MP for St Ives, Cornwall, and was a junior Treasury Minister (1972–74) in the government of Edward Heath. In Margaret Thatcher's administration he was Trade Secretary (1979–81), and then Defence Secretary during the Falklands War. He left the House of Commons, with a knighthood, in 1983 and became chairman and chief executive of Lazard Brothers, the merchant bankers (1985–90). Since 1993 he has been chairman of Hillsdown Holdings.

Nouri Said Pasha See Es-Sa'id, Nuri

Novák, Vitezslav 1870–1949
Czech composer
Born in Kamenitz, he was a pupil of Antonin Dvořák, studying at the Prague Conservatory, and later becoming a professor there (1909–20). His many compositions, which include operas and ballets, show the influence of his native folk melodies.

Novalis, *pseudonym of* Baron Friedrich Leopold von Hardenberg 1772–1801
German Romantic poet and novelist
Born in Oberwiederstadt, Saxony, he fell in love with a girl in 1795, in whose memory he wrote the prose lyrics of *Hymnen an die Nacht* (1800, Eng trans *Hymns to the Night*, 1948). He also published *Geistliche Lieder* (1799, Eng trans *Devotional Songs*, 1910). He left two philosophical romances, both incomplete, *Heinrich von Ofterdingen* (1802) and *Die Lehrlinge zu Sais* (1802, 'The Apprentices at Sais'). He was known as 'the Prophet of Romanticism'. 📖 F Hiebel, *Novalis* (1972, in German)

Novatian 3rd century AD
Roman Christian cleric
Born in Rome, he was converted to Christianity and ordained a priest. Formerly a Stoic, in the aftermath of the persecution of Decius (AD251), he challenged the papal policy of readmitting lapsed Christians to communion and formed instead his own sect (the Novatiani) with rigorous views on Christian purity. The first theologian at Rome to write in Latin, Novatian is believed to have died in the persecution of Valerian. His sect survived until the 6th century.

Novello, Ivor, *originally* David Ivor Davies
1893–1951
Welsh actor, composer, songwriter and dramatist
Born in Cardiff, the son of the singer Dame Clara Novello Davies (1861–1943), he was educated at Magdalen College School, Oxford, where he was a chorister. His song 'Keep the Home Fires Burning' was one of the best known of World War I. He first appeared on the regular stage in London in 1921 and enjoyed great popularity, his most successful and characteristic works being his 'Ruritanian' musical plays such as *Glamorous Night* (1935), *The Dancing Years* (1939) and *King's Rhapsody* (1949). 📖 James Harding, *Ivor Novello* (1987)

Novello, Vincent 1781–1861
English organist, composer and music publisher
Born in London of an Italian father and English mother, he arranged the publication in 1811 of two volumes of sacred music, which was the start of the publishing house of Novello & Co. He was a founder-member of the Philharmonic Society in 1813, and subsequently its pianist and conductor. His compositions include church music, and he was a painstaking editor of unpublished works. His son, Joseph Vincent Novello (1810–96), was also an organist and music publisher, and his daughter, Clara Anastasia Novello (1818–1908), had considerable success in Europe as a concert and operatic singer.

Noverre, Jean-Georges 1727–1810
French dancer, choreographer and ballet-master

Born in Paris, he studied dance with Louis Dupré of the Paris Opera, but opted for a career as a choreographer instead. He was ballet-master at the Paris Opera Comique (1754), the royal court theatre of Württemberg (now the Stuttgart Ballet, 1760–66) and the Paris Opera (under the patronage of Queen Marie Antoinette, 1776–79). He also worked extensively in Lyons, Vienna and Milan. In 1760 he published his important *Lettres sur la danse* ('Letters on Dance'). During the French Revolution he formed a company at the King's Theatre, London, where he staged his last of approximately 150 ballets, none of which has survived. He claimed invention of the notion of the *ballet d'action*, in which truthful movement expression was integrated with plot, music and décor. This theory has had a great influence on ballet as it is known and practised today.

Novotný, Antonín 1904–75
Czechoslovak politician

Born the son of a bricklayer in Letnany, near Prague, he became a Communist at the age of 17 and held various party jobs in the years before World War II. Arrested in 1941, he survived four years in a Nazi concentration camp. Following his release, he rose rapidly in the Czechoslovak Communist Party, becoming regional secretary in Prague in 1945 and a member of the Central Committee in 1946. He played a leading part in the Communist takeover of the Czechoslovak government in 1948. Novotný became all-powerful first secretary of the party in 1953 and from 1958 to 1968 he was also President of the republic. He was essentially a Soviet-style communist, so much committed to central planning and the needs of heavy industry that by 1961 there was an economic recession. His unpopularity forced him to make token concessions from 1962 onwards, especially in the hope of placating the Slovaks, but he failed to satisfy his critics within the party. He was forced out, and succeeded as first secretary by the reformist Slovak, Alexander Dubček (1968), and was also forced to resign the presidency. His negative and protracted tenure of office lost the Czechoslovak reform movement more time than it could make up in the course of the Prague Spring.

Noyce, Robert Norton 1927–90
US physicist and electronics engineer

Born in Burlington, Iowa, he studied at the Massachusetts Institute of Technology (MIT), and later joined William Shockley's semiconductor laboratory. In 1957 he was co-founder of Fairchild Semiconductor in Silicon Valley, where he developed the planar integrated circuit, which led directly to the commercially feasible integrated circuit. With Jack Kilby, who worked on the microchip independently, he is regarded as the co-inventor of the integrated circuit. In 1961 Fairchild introduced its first chips and Noyce's company prospered. He also co-founded the chip manufacturer Intel.

Noyes, Alfred 1880–1958
English poet

Born in Staffordshire, he began writing verse as an undergraduate at Oxford, and on the strength of having a volume published in his final year he left without taking a degree. This book, *The Loom of Years* (1902), which was praised by George Meredith, was followed by *The Flower of Old Japan* (1903) and *The Forest of Wild Thyme* (1905), both of which attracted some notice. The sea, and in particular its treatment in English poetry, was the subject of some of his most successful work, as in *Forty Singing Seamen* (1908) and the epic *Drake* (1908). He married an American, travelled in the USA and became visiting Professor of Poetry at Princeton (1914–23). His trilogy *The Torchbearers* appeared between 1922 and 1930, praising men of science.

He published literary essays, as in *Some Aspects of Modern Poetry* (1924), a defence of traditionalism, and also wrote plays, studies of William Morris and Voltaire, and an anecdotal memoir, *Two Worlds for Memory* (1953).

Noyes, Eliot 1910–77
US designer and architect

Born in Boston, he came under the influence of Walter Gropius, Marcel Breuer and Le Corbusier when studying architecture, and it is not surprising that he was the most 'European' of the prominent US designers working from the 1930s to the 1970s. In 1940 he set up and directed the department of industrial design at the Museum of Modern Art, New York. After working for the stage designer and architect Norman Bel Geddes, he established his own practice in 1947. He set high ethical standards, working only for clients who shared his approach to design and who allowed sufficient time and money for the proper execution of the project. This did not prevent his working for major companies such as Westinghouse, Mobil and, most notably, IBM, for which he became consultant design director.

Noyes, John Humphrey 1811–86
US social reformer

Born in Brattleboro, Vermont, he graduated from Dartmouth College in 1830 and studied law before undergoing a religious conversion at a revival meeting. His religious and social experiments were founded on his own unorthodox Christian beliefs, including his conviction that any person could attain a state of perfect sinlessness. He founded the Oneida Community in New York (1848), where he and his followers lived communally and practised free love. In 1879 he fled to Canada to avoid prosecution for adultery. The Oneida Community later reorganized itself as a joint-stock company and became a successful silverware manufacturer.

Nu, U *originally* Thakin Nu 1907–95
Burmese politician

Born in Wakema and educated at Rangoon University, he began his career as a teacher and in the 1930s joined the Dobhama Asiayone (Our Burma) Nationalist Organization. He was imprisoned by the British for sedition at the outbreak of World War II, during the Japanese occupation, and in 1942 was released to serve in Ba Maw's puppet government. However, he founded the Anti-Fascist People's Freedom League (AFPFL), which collaborated with the British against the Japanese in 1945, and on independence in 1948 he became Burma's first Prime Minister. He held this post until 1962, apart from short breaks (1956–57, 1958–60). In 1962, with regionalist discontent mounting, his parliamentary regime was overthrown by General Ne Win, and he was imprisoned until 1966 when he lived abroad, in Thailand and India, organizing exiled opposition forces. He returned to Burma (Myanma) in 1980, and in the same year became a Buddhist monk trainee in Rangoon. He helped found the National League for Democracy political movement (1988). That year he made an unsuccessful attempt to form a civilian government, and from 1990 to 1992 was placed under house arrest. 📖 Richard Buttwell, *U Nu of Burma* (rev edn, 1969)

Nudd, Bob *Birthdate unavailable*
English angler

Born in Chelmsford, Essex, he won three angling world championships in five years. Unknown as an amateur, he first entered the Fermanagh Festival in 1978, and landed one of fishing's top prizes when he caught 498 roach within five hours. Since then he has become the mainstay in a successful English team who have won the world team championship four times in 11 years. A unique sportsman, he has a sponsorship deal with a tackle company, has made a rap record about fishing, and, known for his calm temperament, relaxes by fishing for cod.

Nuffield, William Richard Morris, 1st Viscount 1877–1963
English motor magnate and philanthropist
Born in Worcestershire, he started in the bicycle repair business and by 1910 was manufacturing prototypes of Morris Oxford cars at Cowley, in Oxford. The first British manufacturer to develop the mass production of cheap cars, he received a baronetcy in 1929 and was raised to the peerage in 1934. He used part of his vast fortune to benefit hospitals, charities and Oxford University. In 1937 he endowed Nuffield College, Oxford, and established the Nuffield Foundation for medical, scientific and social research in 1943. ⊞ James Adeney, *Nuffield: a biography* (1993)

Nujoma, Sam Daniel 1929–
Namibian politician
Born in Ongandjern and educated at a Finnish missionary school in Windhoek, he entered active politics as a co-founder of the South West Africa People's Organisation of Namibia (SWAPO) in 1958. After being exiled in 1960 he set up a provisional headquarters for SWAPO in Dar es Salaam, and on his return to Namibia (1966) was again arrested and expelled. Feeling that peaceful opposition to South Africa's exploitation of his country was unproductive, he established a military wing, the People's Liberation Army of Namibia (PLAN), in the mid-1960s, and his long struggle for Namibia's independence eventually bore fruit in 1989. He was elected President of the new republic in 1990 and re-elected in 1994.

Numa Pompilius 8th–7th century BC
Second of Rome's early kings
According to tradition he ruled 715–673BC. He is described as a peaceful ruler, and was credited with organizing the religious life of the community.

Núñez, Rafael 1825–94
Colombian politician
Trained as a lawyer, he rose to prominence as a Liberal leader in the 1870s but, influenced by radical Spencerian ideas, such as the 'survival of the fittest', turned to conservatism. Governor of Bolivar, he was elected President (1880–82) with the support of moderate Liberals and Conservatives. Returned to office (1884–94), he fought the Liberals, assuring centralized government in the constitution of 1886, which lasted until 1936. He restored the power of the Church, and the Jesuits returned to dominate the education system. His governments were also marked by attempts at modernization. The secession of Panama in 1903 partially resulted from his centralization of administration in Bogota, and his concern for the interests of his birthplace, Cartagena, the historic rival to Panama.

Núñez de Arce, Gaspar 1834–1903
Spanish poet, dramatist and politician
Born in Valladolid, he held office in the government in 1883 and 1888, and received a national ovation at Toledo in 1894. As a lyric poet he may be styled 'the Spanish Tennyson', and among his poems are *Gritos del Combate* (1875, 'Cries of Battle'), *Última Lamentación de Lord Byron* (1879, 'Lord Byron's Last Lamentation'), *El vértigo* (1879, 'Vertigo'), *La Pesca* (1884, 'Fishing') and *La Maruja* (1886). His plays include *La Cuenta del Zapatero* (1859, 'The Countess of Zapatero') and *El Haz de Leña* (1872, 'The Bundle of Firewood'). ⊞ J Romano, *Gaspar Núñez de Arce* (1944)

Nunn, Sir (Thomas) Percy 1870–1944
English education administrator and teacher trainer
Born in Bristol, he was educated at his father's school at Weston-super-Mare and Bristol University College. He taught in Halifax and London grammar schools, becoming vice-principal of London Day Training College in 1905. Director from 1922 to 1936, he transformed it into the Institute of Education of the University of London (1932). His principal claim to fame is his book, *Education: its Data and First Principles* (1920), which derived its child-centred philosophy from the US educationist John Dewey, and which dominated English teacher training for more than 25 years. He was on the drafting committee of the Hadow Committee (1926) and on the curriculum sub-committee of the Spens Committee (1938). Both reports incorporated his views on the validity and liberality of vocational education.

Nunn, Trevor Robert 1940–
English stage director
Born in Ipswich, Suffolk, he graduated from Cambridge, and joined the Belgrade Theatre, Coventry, as a trainee director before joining the Royal Shakespeare Company (1965). In 1968 he succeeded Peter Hall as the company's artistic director, and was joined as co-artistic director by Terry Hands 10 years later. At the RSC he has directed many outstanding productions, and during his directorship (1968–86) the company took many strides forward, including the opening of two new theatres in Stratford-upon-Avon: The Other Place (1974) and The Swan (1986). He directed Andrew Lloyd Webber's musical *Cats*, followed by *Starlight Express* (1984), *Les Misérables* (1985), *Chess* (1986) and *Aspects of Love* (1989). He has also directed operas at Glyndebourne, including *Così Fan Tutte* (1991) and *Peter Grimes* (1992). In 1996 he directed a film version of *Twelfth Night* and it was announced later that year that he would be taking over from Sir Richard Eyre as artistic director of the National Theatre.

Nureddin, *properly* Nur ad-Din Abu al-Qasim Mahumd ibn 'Imad ad-Din Zangi, *also known as* al-Malik al-Adil ('the Just Ruler') 1118–74
Sultan of Egypt and Syria
He was the son of the Turkish atabeg Zangi, whom he succeeded as ruler of Aleppo (1146). He concentrated on the jihad, the holy war against the crusading Christian Franks, defeating and killing Prince Raymond of Antioch (1149) and completely extinguishing the most exposed Frankish state, the county of Edessa (1146–51). He aimed to unify the Muslim Middle East, conquering Damascus (1154) and Mosul (1170), while through his generals Shirkuh and Saladin he took control of Egypt and abolished the Fatimid caliphate. His empire began to disintegrate soon after his death, and it was left to Saladin, now independent, to carry on his mission.

Nureyev, Rudolf Hametovich 1938–93
Russian ballet dancer
Born in Irkutsk, Siberia, he trained first as a folk-dancer and then at the Kirov School in Leningrad (now St Petersburg), where he became principal dancer for the Kirov Ballet. While in Paris with them in 1961 he defected and obtained political asylum, later becoming a member of Le Grand Ballet du Marquis de Cuevas. An intelligent man with an impressive ability to express emotion through the body, he had many different roles, often appearing with Margot Fonteyn, with whom he made his Covent Garden debut in 1962. Theirs was a partnership which was to transform dance in the West. As a guest performer, he danced with most of the prominent companies of the world. He also had a successful career as a producer of full-length ballets and was artistic director of

the Paris Opera (1983–89). Films in which he appeared include *Swan Lake* (1966), *Don Quixote* (1974) and *Valentino* (1977). 📖 Clive Barnes, *Nureyev* (1982)

Nur Jahan, *originally* Mih-run-Nisha d.1645
Mughal empress
She was the daughter of Itimaduddaula, who was made joint diwan by **Jahangir**, the eldest son of Emperor **Akbar the Great**, in the first year of his reign. She married her first husband, Sher Afghan, in 1611, but he died in a clash with the Mughal Governor of Bengal. Her father was raised to the office of chief diwan, while her brother, Asaf Khan, was appointed Khan-i-saman, a post reserved for nobles in whom the emperor had full confidence. Along with her father and brother, and in alliance with Khurram (**Shah Jahan**), Nur Jahan formed a group or *junta* which 'managed' Jahangir (who may have had a tendency to drink) and his political activities. This led to the division of the court into two factions.

Nurmi, Paavo Johannes, *known as* the Flying Finn
1897–1973
Finnish athlete
Born in Turku, he dominated long-distance running in the 1920s, winning nine gold medals at three Olympic Games (1920, 1924, 1928). From 1922 to 1926 he set four world records at 3,000 metres, bringing the time down to 8 minutes 20.4 seconds. He also established world records at six miles (1921, 29:7.1), one mile (1923, 4:10.4) and two miles (1931, 8:59.5). Disqualified in 1932 for alleged professionalism, he nevertheless remained a Finnish national hero. His statue stands outside the stadium in Helsinki where, in 1952, he was given the honour of lighting the Olympic flame.

Nurse, Paul Maxime 1949–
English microbiologist
Born in Norwich, Norfolk, he studied at the universities of Birmingham, East Anglia and Edinburgh. In 1979 he moved to the University of Sussex, where he was on both the Science and Engineering and the Medical Research councils. In 1984 he became head of the Cell Cycle Control Laboratory at the Imperial Cancer Research Fund, London, and moved to Oxford in 1987 to take up the Chair of Microbiology. He was Napier Research Professor at Oxford (1991–93) and is currently director of laboratory research with the Imperial Cancer Research Fund (1993–). His major work has focused on yeast genetics, in particular the regulation of the cell division cycle. He was elected FRS in 1989.

Nuttall, Thomas 1786–1859
US naturalist
Born in Settle, Yorkshire, he emigrated to Philadelphia in 1808, where he took up botany, accompanied several scientific expeditions between 1811 and 1834, and discovered many new US plants. He wrote *Genera of North American Plants* (1818) and became curator of the botanical garden at Harvard (1822–32). While at Harvard he also turned his attention to ornithology, and published *A Manual of the Ornithology of the United States and Canada* (1832). His two-volume work *North American Silva* was published in 1842.

Nye, John Frederick 1923–
English physicist and glaciologist
Born in Hove, Sussex, he was educated at Cambridge, where he worked as a demonstrator in the department of mineralogy and petrology (1949–51) before joining Bell Telephone Laboratories in the USA (1952–53). In 1953 he became a lecturer in physics at the University of Bristol, later becoming emeritus professor (1988). At the Cambridge Cavendish Laboratory, he showed how the photoelastic effect (where solids exhibit optical changes due to compression or stress) could be used to study arrays of dislocations in crystals. His suggestion that glacier motion be treated as non-linear viscous flow explained many properties of mountain glaciers and ice sheets, work which provided the foundation for modern glacier mechanics. He also showed how fields of waves typically contain dislocations similar to crystal dislocations, and applied mathematical theory to explain the phenomena. In 1989 he was awarded the Charles Chree Medal by the Institute of Physics.

Nyerere, Julius Kambarage, *known as* Mwalimu ('teacher') c.1922–
Tanzanian politician
Born in Butiama, Lake Victoria, he qualified as teacher at Makerere College and, after a spell of teaching, studied history and economics at Edinburgh University. On his return, in 1954 he reorganized the nationalists into the Tanganyika African National Union of which he became president, entered the Legislative Council (1958) and in 1960 became Chief Minister. He became Prime Minister when Tanganyika was granted internal self-government (1961). During 1962 he retired for a while to reorganize his party, but was elected President in December when Tanganyika became a republic. In 1964 he negotiated the union of Tanganyika and Zanzibar (which became Tanzania in October of the same year). He had genuine hopes of bringing a unique form of African socialism to his country, based on rural values, but his efforts were largely frustrated by economic difficulties, particularly following the debilitating war against the Ugandan dictator, **Idi Amin** (1978–79). He gave up the presidency in 1985 but retained leadership of his party, Chama cha Mapinduzi (CCM, Revolutionary Party) until 1990, and remained one of Africa's most respected political figures. He has written a number of political works, as well as Swahili translations of the plays of **Shakespeare**. 📖 Shirley Graham, *Julius K Nyerere: Teacher of Africa* (1975)

Nykaenen, Matti 1964–
Finnish ski jumper
A world champion in 1982, he won the 90m jump in the Sarajevo Olympics (1984), but it was at the Calgary Olympics (1988), where he won a record three gold medals, that he became the first man to win both the 70m and 90m titles. He won the 70m by 17 points and his first jump in the 90m event set a new Olympic record of 118.5m. His second was even longer. He then achieved the longest jump in the 90m team event and won an unprecedented third gold.

Nyman, Michael 1944–
English pianist, composer and writer
Born in London, he studied at the Royal Academy of Music and King's College London, and became a music critic (1968–78). He formed his own ensemble in 1977 to play his music, written in a minimalist vein, often with allusions to Baroque music woven in. He became a very successful composer of film soundtracks, including a large number for the filmmaker **Peter Greenaway**. His evocative score for **Jane Campion**'s *The Piano* (1993) became a bestseller, and was turned into the more expansive large-scale work *The Piano Concerto*. He has arranged much of his film music in concert versions, and has also written many works for his ensemble, and for other chamber groups and symphony orchestras. His music for theatre includes the opera *The Man Who Mistook His Wife For A Hat* (1986).

Nynia, St See Ninian, St

Nzinga d.1663
Queen of Matamba

A royal princess of the Ndongo (a small kingdom adjoining the Portuguese colony of Angola), she fought to establish a kingdom independent of the Portuguese, free from war and the slave trade. In 1623, when she went to Angola to negotiate with the governor, she was baptized a Christian as Dona Aña de Souza. She became Queen of Ndongo on her brother's death in 1624. Driven out of Ndongo by Portuguese troops (1626), she created the new kingdom of Matamba, with herself as Queen of Matamba from 1630. There she trained military élites to resist the Portuguese, and allied herself with the Dutch after their capture of Luanda, the Angolan capital (1641). Although she had abandoned Christianity, she re-converted towards the end of her life, by which time Matamba was a thriving commercial kingdom (largely through the Portuguese slave trade).

Oakeshott, Michael Joseph
1901–90
English philosopher and political theorist

Born in Harpenden, Hertfordshire, he was educated at Cambridge where he taught from 1929 to 1949. In 1951 he became Professor of Political Science at the London School of Economics, retiring in 1969. His first and main philosophical work was *Experience and its Modes* (1933), written broadly from within the English idealist tradition. This view of human experience and conduct is developed in the political theory, which tends to be conservative, pragmatic and sceptical of systematization and ideology, as represented in *Rationalism in Politics* (1962), *On Human Conduct* (1975), and *On History, and other Essays* (1983).

Oakley, Ann, *née* Titmuss 1944–
British sociologist, writer, and feminist

Educated at Chiswick Polytechnic and Somerville College, Oxford, she has been Professor of Sociology and head of the Thomas Coram Research Unit at the Institute of Education, University of London, since 1991. She is a prolific writer and her work focuses largely on gender roles. Her best-known work in recent years is *The Men's Room* (1988) which was made into a BBC television serial. Other works include *Sex, Gender and Society* (1972), *The Sociology of Housework* (1974) and *Essays on Women, Medicine and Health* (1994), as well as two books on which she collaborated with Juliet Mitchell, *The Rights and Wrongs of Women* (1976) and *What is Feminism* (1986).

Oakley, Annie, *originally* Phoebe Anne Oakley Moses 1860–1926
US sharp-shooter and Wild West performer

She was born near Woodland, Ohio, into a Quaker family and learned to shoot at an early age, helping to provide food for her family after her father's death. She married Frank E Butler in 1880 after beating him in a shooting match. Together they formed a trick-shooting act, and from 1885 toured widely with Buffalo Bill's Wild West Show. A tiny woman just under five feet tall, she shot cigarettes from her husband's lips, and could shoot through the pips of a playing card tossed in the air (hence an 'Annie Oakley' for a punched free ticket). She retired in 1922. Her life was fictionalized in the Irving Berlin musical comedy *Annie Get Your Gun* (1946), starring Ethel Merman. 📖 Walter Havighurst, *Annie Oakley of the Wild West* (1954)

Oaksey, 1st Baron See Lawrence, Geoffrey

Oastler, Richard 1789–1861
English social reformer

Born in Leeds, as a Tory humanitarian he attacked the employment of children in factories and advocated a shorter working day; these campaigns resulted in both the Factory Act (1833) and Ten Hours Act (1847). He was a strong opponent of laissez-faire political economy, and campaigned against the implementation of the Poor Law Amendment Act (1834) which he believed reduced paupers to the status of slaves. His *Fleet Papers*, attacking the Poor Law and criticizing the government, were edited from prison, where he had been placed for debts to his former employer.

Oates, Joyce Carol 1938–
US writer

Born in Millersport, New York, and educated at Syracuse University and the University of Wisconsin, she taught English at the University of Detroit (1961–67), then was appointed Professor of English at the University of Windsor, Ontario (1967–87). A prolific fiction writer and essayist, she published her first novel, *With Shuddering Fall*, in 1964. Violent, and impressive in its social scope, her fiction challenges received ideas about the nature of human experience. *Them* (1969), her fourth novel, won a National Book award. Later novels include *Marya: A Life* (1986), *You Must Remember This* (1989) and *What I Lived For* (1994). Her interest in pugilism emerged in *On Boxing* (1987), first published in the *Ontario Review*, with which she has long had a connection. Since 1987 she has been a professor at Princeton University.

Oates, Lawrence Edward Grace 1880–1912
English explorer

Born in Putney, London, he was educated at Eton, but left school to serve in the South African War with the Inniskilling Dragoons. In 1910 he set out with Captain Robert Scott's Antarctic expedition, and was one of the party of five to reach the South Pole (17 January 1912). On the return journey the explorers were dangerously delayed and became weatherbound. Lamed by severe frostbite, Oates, convinced that his crippled condition would fatally handicap his companions' prospect of winning through, walked out into the blizzard, deliberately sacrificing his life to enhance his comrades' chances of survival. 📖 Louis Charles Bernacchi, *A Very Gallant Gentleman* (1933)

Oates, Titus 1649–1705
English conspirator

Born in Oakham, the son of an Anabaptist preacher, he took Anglican orders, but was dismissed from his curacy for misconduct. In 1677 he concocted the 'Popish Plot', in which he infiltrated Jesuit seminaries pretending to be Catholic. In 1678 he told a magistrate, later found dead, of a Catholic plot to massacre Protestants, burn London, and assassinate Charles II, replacing him with his brother James, Duke of York (James VII and II). Oates was considered a hero, and his evidence led to 35 judicial murders. But after two years a reaction set in. In 1683 Oates was fined £100,000 for calling the Duke of York a traitor, was imprisoned, and in May 1685 found guilty of perjury and imprisoned for life. He was set free in the Revolution of 1688.

Oatley, Sir Charles 1904–96
English electronic engineer and inventor

Born in Frome, Somerset, he graduated in physics from St John's College, Cambridge (1925), and shortly afterwards joined the staff of King's College London. During World War II he was a member of the Radar Research and Development Establishment, and in 1945 he returned to Cambridge where in 1960 he became Professor of Electrical Engineering. Efforts by Vladimir Zworykin and others in the early 1940s to construct a practical electron microscope had met with only limited success, but Oatley realized in 1948 that newly developed circuits and components might overcome at least some of the problems. One of his research students, D McMullan, produced a prototype instrument, and further development at Cambridge resulted in a scanning electron microscope being manufactured commercially in 1960. It was capable of producing three-dimensional images at magnifications of 100,000 or more. Oatley was elected FRS in 1969 and knighted in 1974.

Obasanjo, Olusegun 1937–
Nigerian soldier and politician

Educated at Abeokuta Baptist High School and Mons Officers' School, he joined the Nigerian army in 1958, training in both the UK and India, specializing in engineering. He served with the Nigerian unit in the UN Congo operations and was military commander of the federal forces during the Biafran War (1967–70). He was made Federal Commissioner of Works and Housing (1975) as well as Chief of Staff. After the short interim military rule led by Murtala Mohammed, he became head of state, (1976–79), overseeing the transfer back to civilian rule. Since then, he has played an important role on the international stage, especially within the Commonwealth, and as founder and leader of the African Leadership Forum. His publications include the autobiographical *My Command* (1980), and the *Challenge of Agricultural Production and Food Security in Africa* (1992).

Obel, Matthias de l' See L'Obel, Matthias de

Oberth, Hermann Julius 1894–1990
German astrophysicist

Born in Sibiu (Hermannstadt), Romania, he abandoned a medical career for mathematics and astronomy, and published his first book *By Rocket to Interplanetary Space* in 1923. In 1928 he was elected president of the German Society for Space Travel (Verein für Raumschiffahrt). He designed a manned rocket and space cabin for Fritz Lang's film *Woman in the Moon* in 1929. In World War II he worked at the experimental rocket centre at Peenemünde and later, from 1955 to 1961, he assisted Werner von Braun in developing space rockets in the USA.

Obote, (Apollo) Milton 1924–
Ugandan politician

Born in Lango, and educated in mission schools and Makerere College, Kampala, he worked in Kenya (1950–55), and was a founder-member of the Kenyan African Union. He kept his political links with his home country and was a member of the Uganda National Congress (1952–60), being elected to Legco (the Legislative Council) in 1957. He helped form the Uganda People's Congress (UPC) in 1960, became its leader and then Leader of the Opposition during the Kiwanuka government of 1961–62. The 1962 elections resulted in a coalition between Obote's UPC and the neo-traditionalist Kabaka Yekka, with Obote as Prime Minister. When fundamental differences between himself and the Kabaka could not be mediated, he staged a coup in 1966, deposing the Kabaka and establishing himself as executive President. In 1971, however, his government was overthrown in a military coup, led by Idi Amin. He went into exile in Tanzania and returned to Uganda with the Tanzanian army in 1979, regaining the presidency after elections in 1980. In 1985 he was once more overthrown by the military under Brigadier Basilio Okello (1918–90), and was granted political asylum in Zambia.

Obradović, Dositej 1743–1811
Serbian nationalist monk

Born to a Serbian family in the Banat of Temesvár, as an Orthodox monk he travelled widely in the Near East, England, France and Germany. On his travels he absorbed the ideas of the Enlightenment and became fiercely anticlerical. During the Serbian Uprisings, he was responsible for education in the administration of George Karageorge.

Obregón, Alvaro 1880–1928
Mexican general and politician

Born near Álamos, Mexico, he was a planter in Sonora who gained prominence fighting against the revolutionaries, first in the service of Francisco Madero in 1912, and then in aid of Venustiano Carranza against Pancho Villa and Emiliano Zapata in 1915. Five years later

he overthrew President Carranza and was himself elected as President of Mexico. In office from 1920 to 1924, he carried out agrarian, labour, and educational reforms, struggled against US oil companies, and sought to limit the power of the Catholic Church. Re-elected in 1928, he was assassinated by a fanatical Roman Catholic before his term began.

O'Brien, (Donal) Conor (Dermod David Donat) Cruise 1917–
Irish historian, critic and politician

Born into a strongly nationalist Dublin family, described in his *States of Ireland* (1973), he was educated at Trinity College, Dublin, and his doctoral dissertation was later published as *Parnell and his Party* (1957). Already his *Maria Cross* (1953) had made him a well-known critic. His finest work is *To Katanga and Back* (1962), an autobiographical narrative of the Congo crisis of 1961 which he had seen as UN Secretary-General Dag Hammarskjöld's representative in Katanga; the earlier tragedy of Patrice Lumumba formed the theme of his play *Murderous Angels* (1968). He was elected Irish Labour TD (MP) for Dublin Clontarf (1969), became Minister for Posts and Telegraphs in 1973, and was defeated in 1977. He was subsequently editor-in-chief of the *Observer* and a mordant political columnist, as well as the author of studies of Albert Camus and Edmund Burke (1992). A recent publication is *Ancestral Voices* (1994).

O'Brien, Edna 1932–
Irish novelist, short-story writer and playwright

Born in Tuamgraney, County Clare, she was educated at the Convent of Mercy, Loughrea, and at the Pharmaceutical College of Dublin, and practised pharmacy briefly before becoming a writer. Her dominant themes are loneliness, guilt and loss, articulated in musical prose. 'My aim', she has written, 'is to write books that in some way celebrate life and do justice to my emotions'. Among her celebrated books are *The Country Girls* (1960), *The Lonely Girl* (1962), *Girls in Their Married Bliss* (1964), *August is a Wicked Month* (1965) and *A Pagan Place* (1970). *The Collected Edna O'Brien*, containing nine novels, was published in 1978, and she has also published several collections of short stories. Recent novels include a collection of *The Country Girls Trilogy* with an epilogue (1986), and *The High Road* (1988). She has also written a number of plays and screenplays, a book of verse, *On the Bone* (1989), and some non-fiction. Recent publications include *Time and Tide* (1992) and *House of Splendid Isolation* (1994). 📖 G Eckley, *Edna O'Brien* (1974)

O'Brien, Flann, *pseudonym of* Brian O'Nolan 1911–66
Irish writer

He was born in Strabane, County Tyrone, and educated at Blackrock College and University College, Dublin, studying German, Irish and English, although much of his time was frittered away at billiards or in pubs. From 1933 to 1934 he was in Germany where there is speculation (but no proof) that he married a girl called Clara who died of consumption a month later. He returned to Dublin, finished his thesis, and founded *Blather*, whose six editions he wrote mainly himself. He gave talks on literature on Irish radio, completed his eccentric but brilliant novel *At Swim-Two-Birds* in 1936, and joined the Irish Civil Service, which occupied him until his premature retirement in 1953. The death of his father and the need to supplement his salary to support his kin led him reluctantly to submit *At Swim-Two-Birds* to publishers. Its publication in 1939 by Collins owed much to Graham Greene's enthusiasm and led to the birth of the Flann O'Brien pseudonym. A year later, in 1940, came the debut of 'Myles na Gopaleen', the pseudonym under which he contributed a column to the *Irish Times* for some 20 years.

His second novel *An Béal Bocht* was published in Irish in 1941 (*The Poor Mouth*, 1973), and *The Third Policeman*, written and rejected in 1940, was published posthumously in 1967. He is best known as an idiosyncratic newspaper columnist; various anthologies appeared after his death—*The Best of Myles* (1968), *The Various Lives of Keats and Chapman and the Brother* (1976) and *Myles From Dublin* (1985). ⌑ T O'Keeffe, *Myles* (1973)

O'Brien, James, *known as* Bronterre 1805–64
Irish journalist and politician
He was born in County Longford and educated at Edgeworthstown school and Trinity College, Dublin. He went to London and was admitted to Gray's Inn, where he met Henry ('Orator') Hunt and William Cobbett. He wrote extensively in the *Poor Man's Guardian* and the *Poor Man's Conservative* from 1831, signing himself 'Bronterre'. He studied and wrote on the French Revolution, especially on François-Noël Babeuf and Robespierre in *Bronterre's National Reformer* (1837) and *The Operative* (1838–39). He was prominent in London Chartism from its beginnings in 1838, and established links with Manchester and secretly advocated physical force. He was cleared of conspiracy at Newcastle, but was sentenced to 18 months' imprisonment at Liverpool for seditious speaking (1840). He became editor of the *British Statesman* (1842) and of the *National Reformer* (1845). He opposed physical force in 1848 and dissociated himself from the Chartist revival of that year.

O'Brien, Kate 1897–1974
Irish playwright and novelist
She was born in Limerick, County Limerick, and educated at University College, Dublin. At 30 she began a career in London as playwright and in 1931 she published her prizewinning *Without My Cloak*, followed by *Mary Lavelle* (1936), *The Land of Spices* (1941), *That Lady* (1946) and *As Music and Splendour* (1958), among others. A remarkable observer of life, she suffered a profoundly unhappy marriage to Gustaaf Johannes Renier, and her novels are best understood by appreciation of her consciousness of a lesbian sexual identity. *Farewell Spain* (1937) and *My Ireland* (1962), in particular, reflect her deep knowledge of those countries. ⌑ *English Diaries and Journals* (1943)

O'Brien, (Michael) Vincent 1917–
Irish horse-trainer
Born in Tipperary, he made an immediate impact on the postwar English National Hunt scene when he trained Cottage Rake, which won the Cheltenham Gold Cup in three consecutive years from 1948. Later he turned his attention to the Flat and on several occasions led the list of winning trainers. Two notably successful seasons were those of 1966, when he trained the winners of the Oaks, the 1000 Guineas, the Eclipse Stakes and the Champion Stakes, and 1977, when one of his horses, The Minstrel, won the Derby, the Irish Derby, the King George VI and Queen Elizabeth Stakes. On the Flat, he was closely associated with Lester Piggott, especially from 1968 to 1980. He retired from horse-training in 1994.

O'Brien, William 1852–1928
Irish journalist and nationalist
Born a Catholic in Mallow, County Cork, he was educated at the Protestant Cloyne Diocesan College and Queen's College, Cork. He became a journalist, founded the Land League journal, *United Ireland* (1881), sat in parliament as a Nationalist for Mallow (1883–95), founded the agrarian United Irish League (1898) and was nine times prosecuted, and imprisoned for two years. He retired from parliament in 1895 owing to dissensions in the party. He headed the Independent Nationalists, but returned to parliament (1900–18) for Cork. He withdrew from politics in 1918 when the Sinn Féin Party swept the polls. He

wrote *Recollections* (1905), *Evening Memories* (1920), *An Olive Branch* (on 'All-for-Ireland', 1910) and *The Irish Revolution* (1923).

O'Brien, William Smith 1803–64
Irish nationalist
Born in County Clare, and educated at Harrow and Cambridge, he was Conservative MP for Ennis (1825) and County Limerick (1835) and, though a Protestant, supported the Catholic claims as a Whig. In 1848 he urged the formation of a National Guard and a national rebellion. The sentence of John Mitchel for 'treason-felony' in 1848 hastened the projected rising, which ended ludicrously in an almost bloodless battle in the widow McCormack's cabbage garden at Ballingarry in County Tipperary. O'Brien was arrested, tried and sentenced to death, but the sentence was commuted to transportation for life. He served five years in Van Diemen's Land (Tasmania), and in 1854 he was released on condition of not returning to Ireland. In 1856 he received an unconditional pardon and returned to Ireland, but took no further part in politics.

Ó Bruadair, Dáibhidh (David) c.1625–1698
Irish Gaelic poet
Born in Cork, he was well-educated. The wars and proscriptions drove his FitzGerald patrons in Kerry into danger and exile, and the poet's later verses dramatically and lyrically convey his fall from places of patronage and honour to the status of farm labourer. His work, complex and resourceful, innovative as well as traditional, offers a bridge from the earlier, assured world of the Gaelic bards to the dark dispossession of the next century. The Irish Texts Society published a bilingual edition of his surviving poems, *Duanaire Dháibhidh Uí Bhruadair* (1913–17).

O'Bryan, William 1778–1868
English Nonconformist clergyman
He was the son of a Cornish yeoman. He quarrelled with the Methodists and in 1815 founded a new Methodist communion called the (Arminian) Bible Christians or Bryanites. In 1831 he went to the USA as an itinerant preacher.

Ó Cadhain, Máirtín, *anglicized name* Martin Kane 1906–70
Irish Gaelic short-story writer and novelist
Born in Spiddal, Connemara, the Gaelic-speaking area of Galway in the west of Ireland, he worked for a time as a schoolteacher. He was actively involved in the IRA and was interned during World War II. The second of five collections of short-stories, *An Braon Broghach* (1948, Eng trans *The Hare Lip*, in *The Field Day Anthology of Irish Writing*, 1991), established him as a stern critic of accepted social conventions. The novel *Cré Na Cille* (1949, 'The Clay of the Churchyard') is a commentary by the dead on the perfidies of the politicians in the 'fledgling Free State'. In 1969 he became Professor of Irish at Trinity College, Dublin. He was a staunch advocate of revolution, and had a strong influence on subsequent generations of writers, a role which has often detracted attention from the stylish, inventive originality of his writing. ⌑ *Páipéir Bhána Páipéir Bhreaca* (1969); A Titley, *Máirtín Ó Cadhain* (1975)

O'Casey, Sean 1884–1964
Irish playwright
Born in a poor part of Dublin, he picked up whatever education he could, and worked as a labourer and for nationalist organizations before beginning his career as a dramatist. His early plays, dealing with low life in Dublin—*Shadow of a Gunman* (1923) and *Juno and the Paycock* (1924)—were written for the Abbey Theatre, Dublin. Later he became more experimental and impressionistic. Other works include *The Plough and the Stars* (1926), *The Silver Tassie* (1929), *Cockadoodle Dandy* (1949) and *The Bishop's*

Bonfire (1955). He also wrote essays, such as *The Flying Wasp* (1936). He was awarded the Hawthornden Prize in 1926. His autobiography, begun in 1939 with *I Knock at the Door*, continued through six volumes to *Sunset and Evening Star* (1954). ☐ E O'Casey, Sean (1971)

O'Cathain, Detta O'Cathain, Baroness 1938–
Irish businesswoman

Educated in Limerick and at University College, Dublin, she became an expert in economics and marketing and worked her way up through the ranks of private-sector industry, from Aer Lingus through Tarmac, Rootes, Viyella, British Leyland and Unigate to the Milk Marketing Board, which she headed between 1985 and 1988. From 1990 to 1994 she was managing director of the Barbican Centre in the City of London, reputedly the biggest arts centre in Europe. During this time she procured enhanced funding for the London Symphony Orchestra, and won a £9.7 million refurbishment of the Centre. She was awarded a life peerage in 1991.

Occam, William of See Ockham, William of

Ochino, Bernardino 1487–1564
Italian Protestant reformer

Born in Siena, he joined the Franciscans, but in 1534 changed to the Capuchins, becoming Vicar-General of the order after four years. In 1542 he was summoned to Rome to answer accusations of evangelicism, but fled to John Calvin in Geneva. In 1545 he became preacher to the Italians in Augsburg. Archbishop Thomas Cranmer invited him to England, where he was pastor to the Italian exiles and a prebend in Canterbury. At Mary I's accession (1553) he went to Switzerland, and ministered to the Italian exiles in Zurich for 10 years. The publication of *Dialogi XXX* (1563, 'Thirty Dialogues'), one of which the Calvinists said contained a defence of polygamy, led to his being banished.

Ochoa, Severo 1905–
US geneticist and Nobel Prize winner

Born in Luarca, Spain, he graduated in medicine at Madrid in 1929 and worked at the universities of Heidelberg and Oxford before emigrating to the USA, where he accepted a post at the Washington University School of Medicine in St Louis. He later settled at the New York University School of Medicine, becoming full professor in 1946. Ochoa isolated two of the catalysts of the Hans Krebs cycle, and this led him to study the energetics of carbon dioxide fixation in photosynthesis from 1948. He studied the enzyme later used for the first synthesis of artificial RNA, and in 1961 adopted Marshall Nirenberg's approach to solving the amino acid genetic code, determining a number of base triplets. He also studied the direction of protein synthesis along the DNA (1965), and the first amino acid in a peptide sequence (1967). He left New York University in 1974 and became associated with the Roche Institute of Molecular Biology in Nutley, New Jersey (1974–85). For his contributions to the elucidation of the genetic code he was awarded the 1959 Nobel Prize for physiology or medicine, jointly with Arthur Kornberg.

Ochs, Adolph Simon 1858–1935
US newspaper publisher

Born of German–Jewish parents in Cincinnati, Ohio, he entered the newspaper business at age 11 as an office boy for the *Knoxville Chronicle* in Tennessee. At the age of 20 he bought control of the *Chattanooga Times*, which became one of the leading journals in the South. He bought the failing *New York Times* in 1896 and served as its publisher until his death almost 40 years later. His only bow to the competition of the yellow press was to lower the price of the newspaper to one cent, and by rejecting sensationalism in favour of accurate, non-partisan reporting, he turned the *Times* into one of the greatest newspapers in the world. He was also director of the Associated Press from 1900 to 1935.

Ochus See Artaxerxes III

Ockeghem, Johannes See Okeghem, Johannes

Ockham or Occam, William of, *nicknamed* the Venerable Inceptor c.1285–c.1349
English philosopher, theologian and political writer

Born in Ockham, Surrey, he entered the Franciscan order, studied theology at Oxford as an 'inceptor' (beginner), but never obtained a higher degree—hence his nickname. He was summoned to Avignon by Pope John XXII to answer charges of heresy, and became involved in a dispute about Franciscan poverty which the Pope had denounced on doctrinal grounds. He fled to Bavaria (1328), was excommunicated, and remained under the protection of Emperor Louis of Bavaria until 1347. He died in Munich, probably of the Black Death. He published many works on logic while at Oxford and Avignon, notably the *Summa Logicae*, *Quodlibeta Septem* and commentaries on the *Sentences* of Peter Lombard and on Aristotle. He also published several important political treatises in the period 1333–47, generally directed against the papal claims to civil authority, including the *Dialogus de potestate Papae et Imperatoris* and the *Opus nonaginta dierum* ('Work of 90 Days'). His best-known philosophical contributions are his successful defence of nominalism against realism, and the philosophical principle of 'Ockham's razor', a rule of ontological economy to the effect that 'entities are not to be multiplied beyond necessity', ie a theory should not propose the existence of anything more than is needed for its explanation. He was perhaps the most influential of later medieval philosophers. ☐ Gordon Leff, *William of Ockham: The Metamorphosis of Scholastic Discourse* (1975)

Oconaire, Pádraic, *in English* Patrick Conroy 1883–1928
Irish Gaelic writer

Born in Galway and educated in Gaelic-speaking Rosmuc, he went to sea, then spent many years in the London Civil Service. He left in 1913, having won prizes in 1904 and 1909 for stories in Gaelic. Famous as a novelist, essayist, travel writer and short-story writer of deceptive simplicity and fine construction, he sometimes worked in children's fiction, and took up themes of psychological complexity which worried the more puritanical elements in the Gaelic revival. His later years were spent in writing and teaching Irish, chiefly in Galway.

O'Connell, Daniel, *known as* the Liberator 1775–1847
Irish political leader

He was born near Cahirciveen, County Kerry. Called to the Irish Bar in 1798, he was a successful barrister. Leader of the agitation for the rights of Catholics, in 1823 he formed the Catholic Association which successfully fought elections against the landlords. Elected MP for County Clare in 1828, he was prevented as a Catholic from taking his seat, but was re-elected in 1830, the Catholic Emancipation Bill having been passed in the meantime. He denounced the ministry of Wellington and Robert Peel, but in the face of a threatened prosecution (1831) he temporized, saved himself, and was made KC. In 1830 the potato crop had been very poor, and under O'Connell's advice the people declined to pay tithes. At the general election of 1832 he became MP for Dublin. At this time he nominated about half of the candidates returned, while three of his sons and two of his sons-in-law composed his 'household brigade'. Of the 105 Irish members, 45—his famous 'tail'—were declared Repealers. He fought fiercely against the Coercion Act of 1833. By Feargus O'Connor, the *Freeman's Journal*, and his more ardent followers he was forced to bring the Repeal movement prematurely into parliament; a motion for inquiry was defeated by 523 to 38. For the next five years (1835–40) he gave steady support to the Whigs. The Earl of Mulgrave and Thomas Drummond governed Ireland so mildly that O'Connell was prepared to abandon the Repeal agitation. In 1836 he was unseated on petition for Dublin, and he was returned for Kilkenny. In 1837 the mastership of the rolls was offered to him but he declined. In August he founded his 'Precursor Society', and in April 1840 his famous Repeal Association, for repeal of the 1801 Union with Great Britain. Yet the agitation languished until the appearance of the *Nation* in 1842 brought him the aid of the nationalist John Blake (1816–66), Dillon, Charles Duffy, T O Davis, James Mangan and Daunt. In 1841 he lost his seat at Dublin, found another at Cork, and in November was elected Lord Mayor of Dublin. In 1843 he brought up Repeal in the Dublin corporation, and carried it by 41 to 15. The agitation now leaped into prominence, but the Young Ireland party began to grow impatient of his tactics, and O'Connell allowed himself to outrun his better judgement. Wellington ordered 35,000 men into Ireland and a meeting fixed at Clontarf for 8 October 1843 was abandoned. Early in 1844, with his son and five of his chief supporters, O'Connell was imprisoned and fined for a conspiracy to raise sedition. The House of Lords set aside the verdict on 4 September, but for 14 weeks O'Connell lay in prison. He opposed Peel's provincial 'godless colleges', and it soon came to an open split between him and Young Ireland (1846). Next followed the potato famine. A broken man, he left Ireland for the last time in January 1847, and died in Genoa on his way to Rome. ⌨ Dennis Rolleston Gwynn, *Daniel O'Connell, The Irish Liberator* (1930)

O'Connor, Feargus Edward 1794–1855
Irish politician

Born in Connorville, County Cork, he studied at Trinity College, Dublin, became a lawyer, and entered parliament for County Cork in 1832. Estranged from Daniel O'Connell, he devoted himself to the cause of the working classes in England. His Leeds *Northern Star* (1837) became the most influential Chartist newspaper. He attempted with little success to unify the Chartist movement via the National Charter Association (1840), and presented himself as leader of the Chartist cause. Elected MP for Nottingham in 1847, in 1852 he became insane. ⌨ James Epstein, *The Lion of Freedom: Feargus O'Connor and the Chartist Movement, 1832–1842* (1982)

O'Connor, (Mary) Flannery 1925–64
US novelist

Born in Savannah, Georgia, she was educated at Peabody High School, Midgeville, Georgia, graduating in 1942. Thereafter she attended Georgia State College for Women and the University of Iowa. She was brought up a Catholic in the 'Christ-haunted' bible-belt of the Deep South, and in her work she homed in on the Protestant fundamentalists who dominated the region. Her characters seem almost grotesque and freakish, but she was describing her reality, and her heightened depiction of it is unforgettable. *Wise Blood* (1952), the first of her two novels, is a bizarre tragi-comedy, and its theme of vocation is taken up again in her second, *The Violent Bear It Away* (1960). Regarded as one of the finest short-story writers of her generation, her work in that form can be found in *A Good Man Is Hard To Find and other stories* (1955, 'nine stories about original sin'), and in *Everything That Rises Must Converge*

(1965), affected by the pain she was suffering in the closing stages of chronic disseminated lupus. *The Habit of Being: Letters of Flannery O'Connor* was published in 1979. ⌨ L Getz, *Flannery O'Connor, her life and library* (1980)

O'Connor, Frank, *pseudonym of* Michael O'Donovan 1903–66
Irish writer

Born in Cork, County Cork, he was a member of the IRA in his teens (1921–22), fought in the civil war and was imprisoned. He then worked as a railway clerk in Cork, and later as a librarian in Wicklow, Cork and Dublin. Although he wrote plays and some excellent literary criticism—*Art of the Theatre* (1947), *The Modern Novel* (1956), *The Mirror in the Roadway* (1957)—his best medium was the short story. W B Yeats said of him that he was 'doing for Ireland what Chekhov did for Russia'. Representative titles are *Guests of the Nation* (1931), *Bones of Contention* (1936), *Crab Apple Jelly* (1944), *Travellers' Samples* (1956), and *My Oedipus Complex* (1963). He also wrote two volumes of memoirs, *An Only Child* (1961) and *My Father's Son* (1969), translations of Irish verse, a novel, *Dutch Interior* (1940), the critical studies *The Lonely Voice* (1963) and *Shakespeare's Progress* (1960), and a biography of Michael Collins, *The Big Fellow* (1937).

O'Connor, Sandra Day 1930–
US jurist

Born in El Paso, Texas, she studied law and was admitted to the Bar in California. Taking up practice in Arizona, she became Assistant Attorney-General there (1965–69) and then a state senator. She then became a Superior Court judge of Maricopa County (1974–79) and a judge of the Arizona Court of Appeals (1979–81) before being named an Associate Justice of the US Supreme Court (1981), the first woman to attain that office. A moderate conservative opposed to judicial activism, she has shown an independent spirit in the Court. ⌨ Mary Virginia Fox, *Justice Sandra Day O'Connor* (1983)

O'Connor, Thomas Power 1848–1929
Irish journalist and politician

Born in Athlone, West Meath, he was educated at Queen's College, Galway, and became a journalist for the *Saunders' Newsletter* in Dublin and the *Daily Telegraph* in London. Elected a Parnellite MP for Galway in 1880, he sat for Liverpool (Scotland division) in 1885, and was a conspicuous Irish Nationalist. He founded various Radical newspapers, including *TP's Weekly* (1902). He wrote *The Parnell Movement* (1886) and *Memoirs of an Old Parliamentarian* (1928). He became a privy councillor in 1924, and was regarded as the 'father' of the House of Commons for many years.

Octavia d.11BC
Roman matron

She was the sister of Emperor Augustus, distinguished for her beauty and womanly virtues. On the death of her first husband, Marcellus (40BC), she consented to marry Mark Antony, to reconcile him and her brother, but in 32 Antony divorced her for Cleopatra. Noble, loyal and kind, she brought up Mark Antony's children by Cleopatra alongside her own.

Ó Dálaigh, Muireadhach Albanach c.1180–c.1250
Irish poet

An outstanding character of his time, he is perhaps the only poet who has killed a tax-collector (with an axe). Owing to this indiscretion, he had to flee his home in County Sligo, and ended in Scotland (hence 'Albanach'). His poem on the death of his (probably Scottish) wife, beginning 'I was robbed of my soul last night', is one of the most famous in Irish literature. ⬚ R Flower, *The Irish Tradition* (1947)

Odets, Clifford 1906–63
US playwright and actor

Born in Philadelphia, and educated in New York City, he joined the Group Theatre, New York, in 1931, under whose auspices his early plays were produced. *Waiting for Lefty*, *Awake and Sing* and *Till the Day I Die* were all produced in 1935, and *Golden Boy* in 1937. The most important US playwright of the 1930s, his works are marked by a strong social conscience and grow largely from the conditions of the Depression of that time. He was also responsible for a number of film scenarios, including *The General Died at Dawn* (1936), *None but the Lonely Heart* (1944, which he directed) and *The Big Knife* (1949). ⬚ M B Gibson, *Odets, American Playwright: the years from 1906 to 1940* (1981)

Odinga, (Zaramogi) Oginga (Ajuma) 1916–94
Kenyan nationalist and politician

Educated at Alliance High School and Makerere College, he was a schoolteacher when he became active in local Luo politics. He was elected to Legco (the Legislative Council) in 1957 and was Vice-President of the Kenya African National Union (1960–66), during which period he pressed unflinchingly for independence, his apparent extremism being contrasted with the moderation of Tom Mboya. He was Minister of Home Affairs (1963–64) and then Vice-President (1964–66). At the Limuru Party Conference in 1966, Mboya managed to remove Odinga from positions of authority and he soon resigned to form the Kenya People's Union (KPU). He was re-elected on the KPU ticket in the Little General Election of 1966 and provided a charismatic figure round whom dissidents might congregate. Consequently, the party was soon banned and Odinga spent some of the next 25 years in and out of detention. He was expelled from the party and briefly imprisoned in 1982, and in 1991 helped found the opposition Forum for the Restoration of Democracy. He came third in Kenya's first multi-party presidential election. His autobiography, *Not Yet Uhuru*, was published in 1967.

Odling, William 1829–1921
English chemist

Born in London, he qualified in medicine at London University in 1851 and held various positions before becoming Professor of Chemistry at Oxford in 1872, retiring in 1912. He classified the silicates and developed a system of chemical notation which clarified the theory of valence. Because he discounted the advances made by Jöns Jacob Berzelius, and failed to recognize the significance of the distinction between atomic and molecular weight made by Stanislao Cannizzaro, much of his theoretical work has not endured.

Odo of Bayeux c.1036–97
Anglo-Norman prelate

He was Bishop of Bayeux. The half-brother of William the Conqueror, he fought at the Battle of Hastings (1066) and was created Earl of Kent. He played a conspicuous part under William in English history, and was regent during his absences in Normandy, but left England after rebelling against William II, Rufus. He rebuilt Bayeux Cathedral, and may have commissioned the Bayeux Tapestry.

Odoacer or Odovacar AD433–493
Germanic warrior, first barbarian king of Italy

He was the son of a tribal captain in the service of the western Roman Empire. A leader of the Heruli, he was the German commander of the imperial guard in Rome.

He participated in the revolution (AD476) which drove Julius Nepos from the throne and gave Orestes' son Romulus the title of Augustus (known as Romulus Augustulus). He marched against Pavia (476) and Romulus abdicated in his favour, ending the western Roman Empire, and making Odoacer King of Italy. His increasing power alarmed the Byzantine Emperor Zeno, who encouraged Theodoric the Great, King of the Ostrogoths, to invade Italy (489). Odoacer, defeated, retreated to Ravenna, which he defended for three years. Compelled by famine, he capitulated (493) and a fortnight later he was assassinated at a banquet by Theodoric.

O'Donnell, Leopoldo 1809–67
Spanish soldier and statesman

He was born in Tenerife of Irish descent. He supported the infant queen Isabella II against her uncle Don Carlos and later supported her mother, the regent María Cristina, but was forced into exile with her in 1840. In 1843 his intrigues against Baldomero Espartero were successful, and as Governor-General of Cuba he amassed a fortune. He returned to Spain in 1846, was made War Minister by Espartero in 1854, but in 1856 supplanted him as Prime Minister by a coup d'état. After only three months in office he was succeeded by Ramón Narváez, but in 1858 returned to power. In 1859 he led a successful campaign against the Moors in Morocco and was made Duke of Tetuan. He was Prime Minister again in 1863 and 1865, but in 1866 his government was upset by Narváez.

O'Donnell, Peadar (Peter) 1893–1986
Irish revolutionary and writer

Born in Meenmore, County Donegal, the son of a small farmer, he became a teacher, then labour organizer, and guerrilla Republican leader. He opposed the 1921 Anglo-Irish Treaty, was captured in civil war fighting, and escaped after a 41-day hunger-strike. A vigorous publicist and editor of *An Phoblacht*, the official IRA newspaper, he gave (and then withdrew) qualified support for Eamon de Valera in 1932, left the IRA in 1934, fought for the Spanish Republic in 1936–37 and wrote extensively on his experiences: the novel *Storm* (1925) on the Anglo-Irish War, *The Gates Flew Open* (1934) on his imprisonment, *Salud!* (1937) on the Spanish Civil War, and *There Will Be Another Day* (1963) on his campaign against land annuities which led to the Anglo-Irish Economic War of the 1930s. His editorship of the literary monthly, *The Bell* (1946–54), was invaluable in furthering Irish writing. His finest work is *Islanders* (1927), but his last novel, *The Big Windows* (1955), also demonstrates his power in social depiction.

O'Donovan, John 1809–61
Irish Gaelic scholar

Born in Kilkenny, he was educated in Dublin. He worked in the Irish Record Office and then with his brother-in-law Eugene O'Curry (1796–1862) on the Ordnance Survey, for which he visited every Irish parish to obtain accurate Irish place names. His authoritative *Letters* on these and allied questions proved an invaluable historical source when published (50 vols, 1924–32). He worked from 1836 on Irish MSS in Trinity College, Dublin, from which came his analytical catalogue, generally regarded as the first step in scientific Gaelic scholarship. Together with O'Curry he founded the Archaeology Society and prepared a seminal Irish grammar. Editor of many Irish texts, his masterpieces are his editions of annalist Michael O'Clery. He became Professor of Celtic Studies at Queen's College, Belfast in 1850, and collaborated in the translation of the *Senchus Mór*, a corpus of ancient Irish laws.

Odovacar See Odoacer

O'Duffy, Eimar Ultan 1893–1935
Irish satirical playwright and novelist

He was born in Dublin, educated at Stonyhurst (Jesuit) College in Lancashire and studied dentistry at University College, Dublin. He embraced the new Irish revolutionary cultural nationalism under the influence of **Thomas MacDonagh** and Joseph Plunkett, who published and produced his first play, *The Walls of Athens*, and whose Irish Theatre also staged his *The Phoenix on the Roof* (1915). He broke with them on the Easter Rising of 1916 during which, as an Irish volunteer loyal to **John MacNeill**, he was one of the couriers who tried to transmit the order countermanding it. His best play, *Bricriu's Feast* (1919), satirized neo-Gaelicism, and his first novel, *The Wasted Island* (1919, revised edition 1929), is a valuable source on the origins of the Rising. He was responsive to **James Joyce's** *Ulysses*, and wrote many novels, of which his Butlerian fantasies are the most noteworthy. Emigrating to England in 1925, he won some success with his autobiographical *Life and Money* (1932).

Odum, Eugene Pleasants 1913–
US ecologist
Born in Newport, New Hampshire, he was educated at the universities of North Carolina and Illinois, and was Professor Emeritus of Ecology and of Zoology at the University of Georgia. His research interests have included ecological energetics, and physiological and population ecology. He believes that ecosystem theory links man and nature and that neither can be considered in isolation, views expounded in his *Ecology and Our Endangered Life-support Systems* (1989). He is also the author of three widely used textbooks, *Fundamentals of Ecology* (1953), *Ecology* (1975) and *Basic Ecology* (1982).

Oecolampadius, Joannes, *Latinized Greek for* Hüssgen or Hausschein 1482–1531
German clergyman and scholar
Born in Weinsberg, Swabia, he studied at Heidelberg. He became tutor to the sons of the elector palatine, and subsequently preacher at Weinsberg (1510) and Basle (1515), where **Desiderius Erasmus** employed him on his Greek New Testament. In 1520 he entered a monastery at Attomünster, but under **Martin Luther's** influence became a reformer at Basle in 1522, where he was Professor of Theology. He gradually adopted the views of **Huldreich Zwingli** on the Lord's Supper, disputed with Luther at Marburg in 1529, and wrote treatises.

Oehlenschläger, Adam Gottlob 1779–1850
Danish poet and playwright
Born in Vesterbro, he was the founder of Danish Romanticism, and was much influenced by **Goethe** and the **Schlegel** brothers. He published his symbolic poem, *Goldhornene* (1802, 'The Golden Horns') and a verse fantasy, *Aladdin* (1805), but is best known for writing 24 blank-verse historical tragedies, starting with *Hakon Jarl* (1807, 'Earl Hakon'). He later wrote *Helge* (1814), a cycle of verse romances, and *Nordens Guder* ('Gods of the North'), an epic ballad cycle. He was appointed Professor of Aesthetics at Copenhagen in 1810. In 1829 he was crowned 'king of the Scandinavian singers' by **Elaias Tegnér** at Lund, and in 1849 was publicly proclaimed the national poet of Denmark. ⬚V Andersen, *Adam Oehlenschläger* (1899–1900)

Oë Kenzaburo 1935–
Japanese novelist and Nobel Prize winner
He was born in Shikoku and educated at Tokyo University, where he studied French literature. His earliest fiction, influenced by **Abe Kobo**, attempts to come to terms with the bleak cultural landscape of postwar Japan. His first three novels, including *Shisha no Ogori* ('The Arrogance of the Dead') and *Nip the Buds, Shoot the Kids* (Eng trans 1996), were all published in 1958, but it was not until 1963 that Oë found an effective personal voice. In that year he

visited Hiroshima and witnessed the delivery of his son, who was born with a major skull abnormality. Thereafter, his writing became more personal and engaged. *Kojinteki na taiken* (1964) was the first of his books to be published in English, as *A Personal Matter* (1968). His next book, perhaps his finest, followed—*Man'en gannen no futtuboru* (1967, Eng trans *The Silent Cry*, 1974), about two brothers' search for their roots—and won Oë the **Tanizaki** prize. Four of his short novels of the 1970s were collected in translation as *Teach Us to Outgrow Our Madness* (1977). In the 1980s he began to explore new principles of organization for his fiction, drawing on social anthropology and philosophy, and published *The Crazy Iris and Other Stories of the Atomic Aftermath* (Eng trans 1985). One of Japan's most remarkable contemporary novelists, he was awarded the Nobel Prize for literature in 1994. ⬚ Y Hisaaki, *The Search for Authenticity in Modern Japanese Literature* (1978)

Oersted, Hans Christian 1777–1851
Danish physicist
Born in Rudkøbing, Langeland, he had little formal education, but learned German, French, Latin and some chemistry, and passed the entrance examination at Copenhagen University. The idea that nature's forces had a common origin resulted in his epochal discovery in 1820, when professor at Copenhagen University, of the magnetic effect produced by an electric current. This paved the way for the electromagnetic discoveries of **André Ampère** and **Michael Faraday**, and the development of the galvanometer, in which Oersted also played a part. He made an extremely accurate measurement of the compressibility of water, and succeeded in isolating aluminium for the first time in 1825. ⬚ Bern Dibner, *Oersted and the Discovery of Electromagnetism* (2nd edn, 1963)

Oerter, Al(fred) 1936–
US athlete and discus-thrower
He was born in Astoria, New York State. An outstanding Olympic competitor, he won four consecutive gold medals for the discus, at Melbourne (1956), Rome (1960), Tokyo (1964) and Mexico (1968), breaking the Olympic record each time. No other athlete has dominated his event so overwhelmingly for so long.

O'Faolain, Sean 1900–91
Irish writer
He was born in Dublin, and educated at the National University of Ireland and at Harvard. He lectured for a period (1929) at Boston College, then took a post as a teacher in Strawberry Hill, Middlesex, and in 1933 returned to Ireland to teach. His first writing was in Gaelic, and he produced an edition of translations from Gaelic, *The Silver Branch*, in 1938. Before this, however, he had attracted attention with a novel, *A Nest of Simple Folk* (1933). He never quite repeated its success with later novels, and from then on wrote many biographies, including *Daniel O'Connell* (1938), *De Valera* (1939) and *The Great O'Neill* (1942). He edited the autobiography of **Wolfe Tone** (1937) and published one of his own, *Vive-moi!* (1964). His *Stories of Sean O'Faolain* (1958) cover 30 years of writing, and progress from the lilting 'Irishry' of his youth to the deeper artistry of his maturity. A later version was published as *Collected Stories* in 1981. His daughter is the novelist Julia O'Faolain (1932–). ⬚ P A Doyle, *Sean O'Faolain* (1968)

Offa d.796
King of Mercia
He succeeded his cousin Æthelbald (757), extended his dominion over Kent, Sussex, Wessex and East Anglia, and styled himself *rex Anglorum* in his charters. To protect his frontiers to the west against the Welsh, he built the great earthwork known as Offa's Dyke, stretching for 70 miles along the Welsh border. Overlord of all England south of the Humber, he was probably the most powerful

English monarch before the 10th century, and considered himself on an equal footing with **Charlemagne** in diplomatic correspondence. He founded a new archbishopric of Lichfield (788) with the sanction of Pope Hadrian I. His silver coinage remained standard until the 13th century. He had his son Ecgfrith anointed as King of Mercia (787), but Ecgfrith only survived him by a few months.

Offenbach, Jacques, *originally* Jakob Eberst
1819–80
German composer
Born in Cologne, he composed many light, lively operettas, but is best known as inventor of modern *opéra bouffe* (funny or farcical opera), examples of which are *Orphée aux enfers* (1858, 'Orpheus in the Underworld'), *La Belle Hélène* (1864), *Barbe-bleue* (1866, 'Bluebeard') and *La Vie Parisienne* (1866, 'Parisian Life'). His one grand opera *Les Contes d'Hoffmann* ('The Tales of Hoffmann') was produced posthumously in 1881.

Offiah, Martin 1966–
English rugby league player
Born in London, he began as a rugby union player with Rosslyn Park, representing England Students in the amateur code. He made the move to rugby league by signing for Widnes in September 1987, and by the following January had played for Great Britain. With his great strength and speed, he became an automatic choice at international level. In January 1992 he joined Wigan, reinforcing that club's dominant position in the British game.

O'Flaherty, Liam 1897–1984
Irish writer
Born on Inishmore, in the Aran Islands, he was educated at University College, Dublin, fought in the British army during World War I, and later travelled in North America and Latin America. He returned to Ireland in 1921 and fought on the Republican side in the Irish Civil War. He went to London in 1922 to become a writer, and soon published his first novels, *Thy Neighbour's Wife* (1923) and *The Black Soul* (1924). *The Informer* (1926) won the James Tait Black Memorial Prize and was a popular success. Other books, reflecting the intensity of his feeling and style, include *The Assassin* (1928), *Famine* (1937) and *Land* (1946). He also wrote three volumes of autobiography, *Two Years* (1930), *I went to Russia* (1931) and *Shame the Devil* (1934).

Ogarkov, Nikolai Vasilevich 1917–
Soviet military adviser and politician
Son of a peasant, he joined the Red Army in 1938 and rose through wartime experience and subsequent commands to become First Deputy Chief of the General Staff in 1968 and full member of the Communist Party Central Committee in 1971. From 1977 to 1984 he was Chief of Staff and Deputy Defence Minister. For over a decade he helped to strengthen and expand the Soviet forces, but his advocacy of further improving conventional forces met opposition even from **Leonid Brezhnev** and certainly from **Yuri Andropov**. His removal in 1984 got rid of one of the obstacles to East–West arms control talks.

Ogden, C(harles) K(ay) 1889–1957
English linguistic reformer
He was born in Fleetwood, Lancashire, and educated at Rossall School. He studied classics at Cambridge, where he was founder-editor of the *Cambridge Magazine* (1912–22) and founder in 1917 of the Orthological Institute. In the 1920s he conceived the idea of 'Basic English', a simplified system of English as an international language with a restricted vocabulary of 850 words, which he developed, with the help of **I A Richards**. Although by the

1940s it was attracting considerable interest, its popularity soon declined. With Richards he wrote *The Foundations of Aesthetics* (1921) and *The Meaning of Meaning* (1923).

Ogdon, John Andrew Howard 1937–89
English pianist and composer
Born in Mansfield Woodhouse, Nottinghamshire, he studied at the Royal Manchester College of Music. In 1962 he was the joint winner (with **Vladimir Ashkenazy**) of the Moscow Tchaikovsky Competition. He had a powerful technique, a remarkable memory and a large repertoire in the virtuoso pianist-composer tradition, notably of **Franz Liszt**, **Ferruccio Busoni**, **Ronald Stevenson** and **Kaikhosru Sorabji**. His own works, which include a piano concerto, are part of that distinguished line. His career was interrupted by the onset of mental illness. ⌨ Brenda Lucas Ogdon, *Virtuoso: The Story of John Ogdon* (1989)

Ogilby, John 1600–76
Scottish topographer, printer and map-maker
Born in Edinburgh, he became a dancing teacher in London and a tutor in the household of the Earl of **Strafford**. He lost everything in the Civil War, but after the Restoration obtained court recognition, became a London publisher, and was appointed king's cosmographer and geographic printer. His early productions include his own translations of **Virgil** and **Homer**, but his most important publications were the maps and atlases engraved in the last decade of his life, including Africa (1670), America (1671) and Asia (1673), and a road atlas of Great Britain (1675), unfinished at his death.

Ogilvie, St John c.1579–1615
Scottish Jesuit priest
Born in Banff, Aberdeenshire, he worked in Edinburgh, Glasgow and Renfrew, and was hanged at Glasgow Cross for his defence of the spiritual supremacy of the pope. Beatified in 1927 and finally canonized in 1976, he is the only officially recognized martyr in post-Reformation Scotland.

Ogilvie, Alan Grant 1887–1954
Scottish geographer
Born in Edinburgh and educated at Oxford, he had a distinguished military career before being appointed Reader in Geography at Manchester University. He was later established at Edinburgh in the first chair of geography in Scotland (1931). Other posts included head of the Hispanic American Division of the American Geographical Society of New York, president of the Royal Scottish Geographical Society (1946–50) and president of the Institute of British Geographers (1951–52). His awards included the Royal Scottish Geographical Society Research Medal and the Livingstone Gold Medal. He is known for establishing the fundamental importance of physical geography to the life of humankind.

Ogilvie, Bridget Margaret 1938–
Australian parasitologist
Born in Glen Innes, New South Wales, she studied agricultural science before obtaining a PhD at Cambridge. She then became a member of the scientific staff of the Institute for Medical Research in London, working in the Parasitology Division. Her work focused on the biology of intestinal parasites, in particular the worm *Nippostrongylus*, and the immune responses of their infected hosts. After secondment to the Wellcome Trust in 1979, her career changed direction towards scientific administration, and she joined the Trust full time, becoming its director in 1991. In 1993 she was the only woman appointed to the Council of Science and Technology.

Oglethorpe, James Edward 1696–1785
English general and colonial settler

Born in London, he served with Prince **Eugène** of Savoy, and from 1722 to 1754 sat in parliament. He suggested a colony in America for debtors from English jails and persecuted Austrian Protestants. Parliament contributed £10,000, while **George II** gave a grant of land, called Georgia after him, and in 1732 Oglethorpe went out with 120 emigrants and founded Savannah. In 1735 he took out 300 more, including **Charles** and **John Wesley**; and in 1738 he was back again with 600 men. After war with Spain was declared in 1739, Oglethorpe invaded Florida (1740), and in 1742 repulsed a Spanish invasion of Georgia. In 1743 he left the colony to repel charges for failing as major-general to overtake Prince **Charles Edward Stuart**'s army after the 1745 Jacobite Rising.

O'Gorman, Juan 1905–82
Mexican architect
Born and trained in Mexico City, he was apprenticed to Carlos Santacilia in 1927, and subsequently studied painting under **Diego Rivera**. Thereafter he worked as a draughtsman and as director of the Town-Planning Administration, beginning independent practice in 1934. He began as a functionalist, eschewing the ideas of **Le Corbusier**, apparent in early works such as the studio for Diego Rivera. He later rejected the purist simplicity of functionalism and, inspired by **Frank Lloyd Wright**, turned in the 1950s to the artistry of traditional Mexican architecture. His masterpieces include the Library of the National University of Mexico in Mexico City (1952, in collaboration), and his own house, San Angelo, Avenida San Jeronimo (1953–56). He also created many striking murals and frescoes for his buildings. In later years, disillusioned, he turned to painting.

O'Hara, John 1905–70
US novelist and short-story writer
He was born in Pottsville, Pennsylvania, which in his fiction becomes 'Gibbsville', the setting for *Appointment in Samarra* (1934). The book's naturalistic, fatalistic account of the last three days in the life of Julian English made him a success almost overnight. O'Hara was notoriously irascible and hypersensitive. Unable to attend Yale University due to his father's death, he went to New York City to work as a critic and reporter. 'Brash as a young man', wrote **John Updike**, 'he became with success a slightly desperate braggart'. Two of his works—*Butterfield 8* (1935) and *Pal Joey* (1940)—became film and stage successes. His short stories are obsessed with class, social privilege and feminist issues. 📖 F Farr, *John O'Hara: a biography* (1973)

O'Hara, Maureen, *originally* Maureen FitzSimons 1920–
Irish actress
Born near Dublin, she joined the Abbey Players there at the age of 14. She made her film debut in *Kicking The Moon* (1938) and her Hollywood debut as the gypsy Esmerelda in *The Hunchback of Notre Dame* (1939). Over the next three decades she appeared as a swashbuckling spitfire in such adventure films as *The Black Swan* (1942) and *At Sword's Point* (1952). Often cast as a fiery woman tamed by a man, she was a favourite co-star of **John Wayne**, with whom she starred in *The Quiet Man* (1952), *McLintock* (1963) and *Big Jake* (1971), among others. She returned to the screen, little changed after a 20-year absence, in *Only The Lonely* (1991).

O'Higgins, Bernardo 1778–1842
Chilean revolutionary
Born in Chillán, the illegitimate son of Ambrosio O'Higgins, an Irish-born Governor of Chile and Viceroy of Peru, he was educated in Peru and England. He played the major role in the Chilean struggle for independence, having been influenced by others involved in the struggle for Latin American independence, especially **Francisco de Miranda**. He became the first leader of the new Chilean state in 1817. However, his reforms aroused antagonism, particularly from the Church, the aristocracy and business community, and he was deposed and exiled in 1823.

O'Higgins, Kevin Christopher 1892–1927
Irish politician
Born in Stradbally, County Laois, he joined the newly emerging Sinn Féin Party after the Easter Rising of 1916. He became MP as abstentionist candidate in his family constituency (1918), and his formidable legal powers consolidated his ascendancy in Dáil Éireann. After the Dáil split on the Anglo-Irish Treaty issue in 1922, his cruel skill in debate and defence of hard policies of repression made him the most hated opponent of his former comrades now in arms against the Irish Free State. He was Minister for Justice when he was assassinated by unknown gunmen.

Ohlin, Bertil Gotthard 1899–1979
Swedish economist and politician, and Nobel Prize winner
Born in Klippan and educated in Sweden and at Harvard in the USA, he was professor at Copenhagen (1925–30) and at Stockholm (1930–65). He was a member of the Swedish parliament from 1938 to 1970 and leader of the Liberal Party from 1944 to 1967. He was awarded the 1977 Nobel Prize for economics, jointly with **James Meade**.

Ohm, Georg Simon 1787–1854
German physicist
Born in Erlangen, Bavaria, he completed his studies at the University of Erlangen, and later became professor at the universities of Nuremberg (1833–49) and Munich (1849–54). His 'Ohm's law', relating voltage, current and resistance in an electrical circuit, was published in 1827, although neither this nor his work on the recognition of sinusoidal sound waves by the human ear (1843) received immediate recognition. He was awarded the Royal Society's Copley Medal (1841) and was elected a foreign member of the Society in 1842. The unit of electrical resistance is named after him.

Oistrakh, David Fyodorovich 1908–74
Russian violinist
Born in Odessa, he studied at Odessa Conservatory, graduating in 1926. In 1928 he went to Moscow and began to teach at the Conservatory there in 1934, being appointed a professor in 1939. He made concert tours in Europe and the USA, and was awarded the Stalin Prize in 1945 and the Lenin Prize in 1960. His son Igor Davidovich (1931–), born in Odessa, is also a noted violinist.

Ojukwu, Chukwenmeka Odumegwu 1933–
Nigerian soldier and politician
Educated in church schools in Lagos and at Oxford, he joined the Nigerian Army in 1957. After attending military college in England, he served with the Nigerian force in the UN Congo operations and was named Military Governor of the mainly Ibo-speaking Eastern Region of Nigeria after the military coup of January 1966. He proclaimed the Eastern Region the independent Republic of Biafra in May 1967, thus precipitating the Biafran War, and for three years acted as head of government and supreme commander. When his forces were finally defeated in 1970, he fled to the Ivory Coast. He returned to Nigeria in 1982 but an attempt to return to politics led to his imprisonment. He was released two years later but was banned from standing for president in the 1993 elections.

Okawa Shumei 1886–1957
Japanese ultranationalist

He was involved in several right-wing plots against the civilian government. A fierce critic of Western colonialism in Asia, he founded societies to protect the Kokutai (national essence) and promote renovation of the state. Unlike Ikki Kita, he was willing to work with military and bureaucratic elites, and he lectured to the Army Academy on the need for Asian unity and struggle against the West. He was imprisoned in 1932 for his participation in an abortive military coup but was released in 1934. He was indicted by allied authorities as a class-A war criminal in 1945 (the only person to be so indicted who was not a military or government figure). Judged to be insane, however, he was never brought to trial.

Okazaki, Reiji 1930–75
Japanese biochemist
Born in Hiroshima, he graduated in science at Nagoya University, remained there as a lecturer, and was appointed professor in 1967. Working with bacteria and bacteriophage, Okazaki was the first to identify the DNA–RNA fragments named after him (1967). These units of DNA replication were used to show how continuous synthesis could occur on one DNA strand, while 'Okazaki fragments', subsequently joined together, built up on the other. With **Arthur Kornberg** he was the first to recognize the 'primer' function of the short RNA sequence to which the DNA is attached. He also studied the RNA-free, so-called pseudo-Okazaki fragments produced by certain bacterial mutants or derived by degradation of normal DNA. Okazaki was awarded the Asahi Prize in 1970.

O'Keeffe, Georgia 1887–1986
US painter
Born in Sun Prairie, Wisconsin, she studied at the Art Institute of Chicago, 1905–06 and at the Art Students' League in New York City, 1907–08, where she met **Alfred Stieglitz**, whom she married in 1924. As early as 1915 she pioneered abstract art in the USA (eg *Blue and Green Music*, 1919) but later moved towards a more figurative style, painting flowers and architectural subjects, frequently with a Surrealist flavour. After her husband's death in 1946 she lived in New Mexico (from 1949), but travelled extensively in Europe, Asia and the Middle East in the 1950s and 1960s.

Okeghem or Ockeghem, Johannes c.1430–1497
Flemish composer
Born probably in Termonde, he had become a court musician to **Charles VII** of France by 1452, and was in 1459 treasurer of the abbey of St Martin at Tours. He was also kapellmeister to **Louis XI**. Renowned as a teacher, he played an important part in the stylistic development of church music in the 15th century. **Josquin des Prez** was probably among his pupils.

O'Kelly, James 1845–1916
Irish war correspondent and politician
Born in Dublin, he seems to have studied at Trinity College, Dublin, and at the Sorbonne, Paris, before joining the French Foreign Legion in which he served against **Ferdinand Maximilian** in Mexico. He covered the Cuban revolt for the *New York Herald*, was captured by Spanish troops, sentenced to be shot, and respited in Spain partly through intervention by **Isaac Butt**. He reported on the Brazilian imperial tour of the USA and **Sitting Bull's** war (1876–77), but was drawn into Fenian negotiations with **Charles Stewart Parnell**. Converted to Parnell's cause, he became MP for Roscommon (1880–1916) but was ousted (1892–95) as Parnellite after the Parnell divorce scandal. Working for the *Daily News*, he covered the revolt of the Mahdi (**Muhammad Ahmed**) in the Sudan (1881).

O'Kelly, Sean Thomas, *properly* Seán Thomas Ó Ceallaigh 1882–1966
Irish statesman
Born in Dublin, he was a pioneer in the Sinn Féin movement and the Gaelic League. He fought in the Easter Rising (1916) and was imprisoned. Elected to the first Dáil in 1918, he became Speaker (1919–21). As an opponent of the Irish Free State, he became prominent in de Valera's Fianna Fáil Party, serving under him as Minister for Local Government (1932–39) and for Finance and Education (1939–45). He was President of the Irish Republic from 1945 to 1952, and again from 1952 to 1959.

Okri, Ben 1959–
Nigerian novelist, poet and short-story writer
He was born in Minna, but now lives in London, England. His first, precocious novel was *Flowers and Shadows* (1980), but it was not until 1987, and the publication of its successor, *Incidents at the Shrine*, that he achieved recognition in the form of the Commonwealth Writers' Prize for Africa. *Stars of the New Curfew* (1988), a volume of short stories, marked time, but his career began a new stage with his third novel, *The Famished Road* (1991), which won the Booker Prize; the sequel, *Songs of Enchantment*, followed in 1993. Subsequent novels are *Astonishing the Gods* (1995), *Birds of Heaven* (1995), *A Way of Being Free* (1996) and *Dangerous Love* (1996).

Okuma Shigenobu 1838–1922
Japanese politician
He came from a samurai family in Saga domain, one of the four domains (along with Choshu, Satsuma and Tosa) that took the lead in the overthrow of the **Tokugawa** Shogunate (1868). He became a councillor in the new Meiji government and was a keen advocate of industrial development. He aroused the ire of his government colleagues in 1881 when he proposed the immediate establishment of constitutional government based on the British parliamentary system. He was purged from government and, in the following year, he created Japan's second political party, the Constitutional Reform Party (Rikken Kaishinto), which gained support amongst the urban educated and mercantile classes. In 1898 he joined with **Itagaki Taisuke**, Leader of the Liberal Party (Jiyuto) to form Japan's first party Cabinet, but it collapsed within four months due to internal rivalries. In 1914 he was chosen by the genro (elder statesmen) to head a non-party Cabinet but his aggressive attempt to enhance Japan's influence in China brought him into conflict with the more cautious genro and he was forced to resign.

Olaf I Tryggvason c.965–1000
King of Norway
The great-grandson of **Harald I Halfdanarson** (Fair Hair), he was brought up in Novgorod at the court of Prince **Vladimir I**, and became a Viking mercenary in the Baltic. In the early 990s he took part in Viking expeditions to Britain, and was the leader of the Viking army that defeated the Anglo-Saxons at Maldon (991). He returned to harry England (994) under the King of Denmark, **Svein I Haraldsson** (Fork-Beard), and was converted to Christianity. He returned to Norway (995), where he seized the throne and attempted, with limited success, to convert Norway to Christianity by force. Five years later he was overwhelmed by a combined Danish and Swedish fleet at Svold (1000). When defeat became inevitable he leapt overboard and was never seen again.

Olaf II Haraldsson, St Olaf c.995–1030
King of Norway
He was the half-brother of King **Harald III Sigurdsson** (Hardraade). He became a Viking mercenary in the Baltic and attacked England, Frisia and Spain. In England

(1010) he took part in an attack on London when London Bridge was torn down by grappling irons ('London Bridge is falling down'). He was converted to Christianity in Normandy (1013), and returned to Norway (1014), where he seized the throne (1015) and tried to complete the conversion of Norway begun by **Olaf I Tryggvason**. In 1028 he fled to Russia from Danish-inspired rebellion, but returned in 1030, when he was defeated and killed at Stiklestad. Within 12 months he was regarded as a national hero and he was declared the patron saint of Norway in 1164. His feast day is 29 July.

Olaf III Haraldsson, *called* the Peaceful d.1093
King of Norway
The son of **Harald III Sigurdsson** (Hardraade), he was at the Battle of Stamford Bridge in Yorkshire (1066) when his father was defeated and killed by King **Harold II** of England. He was allowed to return to Norway, and, after ruling jointly with his brother, Magnus II, became sole ruler (1069). His long reign was marked by unbroken peace and prosperity in Norway. He built churches and founded the city of Bergen. He was succeeded by his illegitimate son, **Magnus III** Olafsson (Barefoot).

Olav V 1903–91
King of Norway
Born in England, he was the son and successor (1957) of **Haakon VII** and Maud, daughter of **Edward VII** of Great Britain. He was educated in Norway and at Balliol College, Oxford. An outstanding sportsman and Olympic yachtsman in his youth, he stayed in Norway when it was invaded by Germany (1940), and was appointed head of the Norwegian armed forces. Later he escaped with his father to England, returning in 1945. In 1929 he married Princess Martha of Sweden (1901–54). They had two daughters, and a son succeeded to the Norwegian throne as **Harald V**. 📖 Arvid Moller, *King Olav V, 1903–1991* (1991)

Olbers, Heinrich Wilhelm Matthäus 1758–1840
German astronomer
Born in Ardbergen, near Bremen, he studied medicine at Göttingen and Vienna, and in 1781 set up in medical practice in Bremen. Though a conscientious physician he was mainly interested in astronomy. He devised a method of calculating the orbits of comets (1779) and from the small observatory at his house at Bremen swept the sky whenever it was clear. He discovered the minor planets Pallas (1802) and Vesta (1807). His greatest discovery was of the comet of 1815 named after him; he found its period to be 70 years, similar to that of comet Halley.

Olbrich, Joseph Maria 1867–1908
German architect and designer
Born in Troppau, Silesia, he was a contemporary of **Josef Hoffmann** at the Vienna Academy of Fine Arts, where he won the Prix de Rome. He, too, was a prominent member of the Vienna Secession and in 1897–98 built its exhibition building. In 1899 he joined the Darmstadt Artists' Colony where **Peter Behrens** was also working. In Darmstadt he designed a number of buildings, including the impressive Wedding Tower (1907), as well as furniture, lighting, cutlery and graphics.

Olcott, Henry Steel 1832–1907
US theosophist
Born in Orange, New Jersey, he was a lawyer by training, but studied theosophy under Madame **Blavatsky** and was founder-president of the Theosophical Society in 1875. He travelled to India and Ceylon as her partner (1879–84), but fell out with her in 1885. He opened schools for untouchables (scheduled castes) in India, and became an associate of **Annie Besant**.

Oldcastle, Sir John, *also called* Lord Cobham
c.1378–1417
English Lollard leader and knight
Born in Herefordshire, he served under **Henry IV** on the Welsh marches. He acquired the title of Lord Cobham (1409) by marrying the heiress, and presented a remonstrance to the Commons on the corruptions of the Church. He had **John Wycliffe's** works transcribed and distributed, and paid preachers to propagate his views. He fought in the Scottish and Welsh wars, and in France earned a European reputation for chivalry. He became an intimate friend of the Prince of Wales, the future **Henry V**, but after Henry's accession he was condemned as a heretic (1413). A courageous man of principle, he was an able exponent of Lollard doctrine, and corresponded with the Hussites in Bohemia. He escaped from the Tower of London and conspired with other Lollards to capture Henry and take control of London (1414). He was captured, taken to London, and was eventually 'hanged and burnt hanging'. **Shakespeare's** Sir John Falstaff was based partly on him.

Oldenburg, Claes Thure 1929–
US sculptor
Born in Stockholm, Sweden, he emigrated to the USA in 1936, becoming a US citizen in 1953. He studied at Yale and the Art Institute of Chicago before moving to New York City (1956), where he became part of the milieu from which 'happenings' and Pop Art developed. In the early 1960s he worked on exhibitions inspired by New York street life, and in 1962 he began to make giant versions of foodstuffs such as hamburgers. The following year he introduced soft sculptures of normally hard objects like light switches, made of vinyl or canvas stuffed with kapok. His projects for colossal monuments in public places (eg giant lipsticks in Piccadilly Circus, London) have occasionally been realized, as in the *Giant Clothespin* (1975) in Philadelphia. Since 1976 he has collaborated with his wife, the writer Coosje van Bruggen, to stage events such as *The Course of the Knife* (1985, Venice) and to produce giant installations in 26 cities in Europe and the USA, for example *Match Cover* (1992, Barcelona). In 1989 he was awarded the Wolf Prize for the Arts. His publications include *Claes Oldenburg: Multiples in Retrospect* (1991).

Oldfield, Anne 1683–1730
English actress
Born in London, she made her debut in 1700, her reputation in *The Careless Husband* (1703), and by 1705 had become one of the most popular actresses of her time. She continued to act until the last year of her life.

Oldfield, Barney (Berna Eli) 1878–1946
US motor-racing driver
Born in Wauseon, Ohio, he specialized in short 'match' races on dirt-tracks at the beginning of the 20th century. He was chief driver from 1902 of **Henry Ford's** '999' racer. In 1903 he became the first American to race a mile in a minute (at Indianapolis), then in 1910 set records at one mile, two miles and one kilometre. An extrovert showman, he preferred the one-off challenges to organized races like the Indianapolis 500, but competed in them too with some success. He retired in 1918. His success in motor racing earned him a fortune, but he was reported to have lost $1 million in the Wall Street Crash.

Oldfield, Bruce 1950–
English fashion designer
Born in London, he taught art then studied fashion in Kent (1968–71) and in London (1972–73), after which he became a freelance designer. He designed for Bendel's store in New York and sold sketches to **Yves Saint Laurent**. He showed his first collection in 1975 in London. His

designs include evening dresses for royalty and screen stars, and ready-to-wear clothes. His publications include *Bruce Oldfield's Season* (1987, with Georgina Howell).

Oldham, Richard Dixon 1858–1936
Irish geologist and seismologist

Born in Dublin, he was educated at Rugby and the Royal School of Mines, was a member of the Geological Survey of India (1878–1903) and, for some of this time, director of the Indian Museum in Calcutta. His important report on the Assam earthquake of June 1897 distinguished for the first time between primary and secondary seismic waves and was able to characterize many other phenomena of earthquake activity. He proved the generality of his notions about the different types of seismic waves with reference to six other earthquakes in *On the Propagation of Earthquake Motion to Great Distances* (1900) and laid the foundations of what is now one of the principal branches of geophysics. In 1906 he established from seismographical records the existence of the Earth's core. He was the author of *Bibliography of Indian Geology* (1888), *Catalogue of Indian Earthquakes* (1883) and many other works on Indian geology.

Old Pretender, The See Stuart, Prince James Francis Edward

Oldys, William 1696–1761
English antiquary and bibliographer

He was the illegitimate son of Dr Oldys, Chancellor of Lincoln, and became librarian to the Earl of Oxford (1738–41), whose valuable collections of books and MSS he arranged and catalogued. He was appointed Norroy king-of-arms (1755–61). His chief works are a *Life of Sir Walter Raleigh*, prefixed to Walter Raleigh's *History of the World* (1736), and *The British Librarian* (1737). He worked with Samuel Johnson on a catalogue of the Harleian Library, and issued with him *The Harleian Miscellany* (1753).

Ole-Luk-Oie See Swinton, Sir Ernest Dunlop

Olga, St c.890–968
Russian princess and Regent of Kiev

The wife of Prince Igor of Kiev, as Regent (945–64) she ruled Kiev firmly during the minority of her son, Svyatoslav. She was baptized at Constantinople (Istanbul) in c.957 and, returning to Russia, worked hard for her new creed. She had little success in her lifetime but, subsequently sanctified, she played an important part in the development of Kievan Christianity. Her grandson was Vladimir I, the Great. Her feast day is 11 July.

Oliphant, Laurence 1829–88
English travel writer and mystic

He was born in Cape Town, South Africa, of Scottish descent, the son of the Attorney-General there. His first work, *A Journey to Khatmandu* (1852), was followed by *The Russian Shores of the Black Sea* (1853). As secretary to James Bruce, 8th Earl of Elgin, he travelled to China in 1857–58, thus finding material for further books. In 1861, while acting as chargé d'affaires in Japan, he was severely wounded by assassins. From 1865 to 1868 he sat for the Stirling burghs. His satirical novel, *Piccadilly* (1870), was a book of exceptional promise, full of wit and delicate irony. He joined the religious community of Thomas Lake Harris in the USA, and later settled in Haifa in Palestine. His mystical views he published in 1886 in *Sympneumata; or, Evolutionary Forces Now Active in Man* (written with his wife and advocating purity in one's sex life) and in *Scientific Religion* (1888). 📖 P Henderson, *Life of Oliphant* (1956)

Oliphant, Margaret, *née* Wilson 1828–97
Scottish novelist

She was born in Wallyford, Midlothian, and moved to England with her family when she was 10 years old. She took her name from her mother, and little is known about her father. Her first novel was written when she was just 16, but her first published work was *Passages in the Life of Mrs Margaret Maitland* (1849). In 1851 she began her lifelong connection with the Edinburgh publishers Blackwood and *Blackwood's Magazine*, culminating in a history of the firm (published posthumously, 1897). In 1852 she married her cousin, Frances Oliphant, an artist, but she was widowed in 1859, and found herself £1,000 in debt with an extended family to support and educate. She went on to write almost a hundred novels, the best known of which are collectively known as *The Chronicles of Carlingford* (1863–76) and earned her the sobriquet, a 'feminist Trollope'. She also wrote novels of Scottish life, including *Effie Ogilvie* (1886), and other notable works include *The Railway Man and His Children* (1891) and *Sir Robert's Fortune* (1895). She was awarded a Civil List pension in 1868, but continued her prolific output, producing a spate of biographies, literary histories, translations, travel books, tales of the supernatural, and an autobiography (1899). 📖 *Autobiography and Letters of Mrs Margaret Oliphant* (ed. Mrs Harry Coghill, 1899)

Oliphant, Sir Mark (Marcus Laurence Elwin) 1901–
Australian nuclear physicist

Born in Adelaide, he studied there and at Trinity College, Cambridge, where he received his PhD in 1929. Working at the Cavendish Laboratory in Cambridge with Ernest Rutherford and the Austrian-US physical chemist Paul Harteck (1902–85), he discovered the tritium isotope of hydrogen in 1934, and in 1937 he became professor at Birmingham University, where he designed and built a 60-inch cyclotron particle accelerator. He worked on the Manhattan Project at Los Alamos (1943–45) to develop the nuclear bomb, but at the end of hostilities strongly argued against the US monopoly of atomic secrets. In 1946 he became the Australian representative of the UN Atomic Energy Commission. He was later appointed research professor at Canberra University (1950–63) and designed a proton synchrotron accelerator for the Australian government. From 1971 to 1976 he served as Governor of South Australia. He was elected FRS in 1937, and knighted in 1959.

Olivares, Gaspar de Guzmán, Count-Duke of 1587–1645
Spanish nobleman and politician

He was born in Rome where his father was ambassador. He was the favourite (*valido*) of Philip IV of Spain, and his Chief Minister for 22 years (1621–43). Dynamic and swarthy, as in Velazquez's equestrian portrait, he alternated between euphoria and dejection as he toiled to defend Spanish interests in Europe, while at home he aimed to extend the centralizing power of Madrid over the non-Castilian provinces and to raise sufficient revenue. He achieved little abroad: the Dutch pushed back the Spaniards in Flanders, and captured Spanish colonies; he had little success in Italy, where Spain was overstretched; and France conquered Artois and defeated Spain at Rocroi (1643). At home his attempted reforms annoyed the nobles and his debasement of the currency produced a financial crisis (1639–40). This provoked rebellion in Catalonia and led to the secession of Portugal (1640). Under pressure from the nobles, the king dismissed him in 1643.

Olive, Princess, *assumed title of* Mrs Olivia Serres, *née* Wilmot 1772–1834
English impostor

Olivier, Laurence Kerr, Baron Olivier of Brighton 1907–89
English actor, producer and director

Laurence Olivier was born in Dorking. His first professional appearance was as the Suliot officer in Chapman's *Byron* in 1924, and he joined the Old Vic Company in 1937. He played all the great Shakespearean roles, while his versatility was underlined by a virtuoso display as a broken-down low comedian in *The Entertainer* (1957). After war service he became co-director of the Old Vic Company (1944); and he produced, directed and played in acclaimed films of *Henry V, Hamlet* and *Richard III*. He played memorable roles in several other films, including *Wuthering Heights* (1939), *Rebecca* (1940), *The Prince and the Showgirl* (which he directed, 1957), *Sleuth* (1972) and *Marathon Man* (1976).

Olivier was knighted in 1947. He was divorced from his first wife, Jill Esmond, in 1940 and in the same year married **Vivien Leigh**. They were divorced in 1960, and the following year he married **Joan Plowright**. In 1962 he undertook the directorship of a new venture, the

Chichester Festival, where he was highly successful; later the same year he was appointed director of the National Theatre, where among many successes he directed and acted a controversial but outstanding *Othello* (1964). He was director of the National Theatre until 1973, and then Associate Director for a year. After 1974 he appeared chiefly in films and in television productions (notably as Lord Marchmain in *Brideshead Revisited*, 1982, and as King Lear in 1983). He was made a life peer in 1970 and was awarded the Order of Merit in 1981.

📖 Olivier published his autobiography, *Confessions of an Actor*, in 1982, and there is a memoir of him, *My Father Laurence Olivier* (1992), written by his son Tarquin Olivier.

> 'Acting is a masochistic form of exhibitionism. It is not quite the occupation of an adult.' Quoted in *Time Magazine*, 3 July 1978.

She was born in Warwick, the daughter of a house painter. She became an artist and in 1806 was appointed landscape painter to George, Prince of Wales (later **George IV**). In 1817 she claimed to be an illegitimate daughter of the Duke of Cumberland, brother of **George III**, and in 1821 had herself rechristened as Princess Olive, legitimate daughter of the Duke and his first wife, Olive. The same year, arrested for debt, she produced an alleged will of George III, leaving £15,000 to her as his brother's daughter. However, in 1823 her claims were found to be baseless, and she died in prison.

Oliver, Isaac c.1560–1617
English miniature painter
Of French Huguenot origin, he was the pupil and later the rival of **Nicholas Hilliard**, and executed portraits of Sir Philip Sidney, Anne of Denmark, and others. His son and pupil, Peter (1594–1648), continued his work, and was employed by **Charles I** to copy old master paintings in miniature.

Oliver, King (Joe) 1885–1938
US cornettist, composer and bandleader
He was born in Abend, Louisiana, and raised in New Orleans. His first instrument was the trombone, and as a youth he played in various parade bands as well as in early jazz groups. He moved to Chicago where in 1922 he formed his 'Hot' Creole Jazz Band; featuring Oliver's cornet partnership with **Louis Armstrong**, the band made some of the finest recordings of the period. Although he worked as a musician until 1937, he made no recordings after 1931. Some of his compositions, such as 'Dippermouth Blues' and 'Dr Jazz', are part of the standard traditional repertoire.

Olivetti, Adriano 1901–60
Italian manufacturer
He was born in Ivrea. After a period in the USA assimilating the methods of mass-production, he returned to transform the manufacturing methods of the typewriter firm founded by his father Camillo Olivetti (1868–1943). As well as greatly increasing production, he established a strong design policy which embraced products, graphics and the architecture of the company's buildings. Many notable designers such as Marcello Nizzoli, Marco Zanuso and **Ettore Sottsass Jnr** are associated with Olivetti. His strong social concerns, for which he was widely noted, led him to provide housing and facilities of a high standard for his employees. He made the company the exemplary manufacturer of the 'Modern Movement'. The firm survived a period of stagnation in the 1970s to

regain its primacy by exploiting modern technological advances in office equipment. 📖 Saverio Santa Maita, *Educazione comunita sviluppo: l'impegno educativo di Adriano Olivetti* (1987)

Olivier, Laurence, Baron   See panel above

Olmsted, Frederick Law 1822–1903
US landscape architect and writer
Born in Hartford, Connecticut, he studied engineering and agriculture and published a notable series of travel books. In 1856 he was co-designer of Central Park, New York City, and he served as its chief architect. Among the other famous parks he created are Prospect Park in Brooklyn, the Emerald Necklace in Boston, and the grounds of the 1893 World's Columbian Exposition in Chicago (now Jackson Park). His object in park design was to provide the illusion of wildness and arcadian peace in the midst of the city, and his work is unequalled in US landscape architecture.

Olney, Richard 1835–1917
US Democratic politician
Born in Oxford, Massachusetts, he was educated at Harvard, and called to the Bar. In 1893 he became Attorney-General under **Grover Cleveland**, in 1895 Secretary of State, and within six months caused a crisis by his interference, in support of the Monroe Doctrine (see **James Monroe**), in the boundary question between British Guiana and Venezuela. In 1897 he returned to practise law in Boston. In 1913 he declined the ambassadorship to London.

Olsen, Kenneth Harry 1926–
US computer engineer and entrepreneur
Born in Bridgeport, Connecticut, of Scandinavian parentage, he studied electrical engineering at the Massachusetts Institute of Technology (MIT), and joined **Jay Forrester**'s pioneering computer group in 1950. Olsen then worked at IBM, but in 1956 established his own computer company, the Digital Equipment Corporation (DEC). DEC exploited a new niche in the growing computer industry—the market for minicomputers, or 'interactive' machines, that were less expensive and easier to use than mainframes. Aided by brilliant engineers, such as **Gordon Bell** from MIT, Olsen launched the PDP-8—the first successful minicomputer—in the early 1960s. In 1986 DEC was the second largest US computer company behind IBM, but by 1992 the company was suffering heavy losses and stagnating sales, and Olsen was forced to resign as the chief executive.

Olson, Charles John 1910–70
US poet

Born in Worcester, Massachusetts, he was educated at Wesleyan University, and at Yale and Harvard. During World War II he worked as a civil liberties activist, and in 1947 published *Call Me Ishmael*, ostensibly a study of Herman Melville, but one which strongly emphasizes Olson's concern for ethnic minorities and working-class solidarity. He published an essay called 'Projective Verse' in the magazine *Poetry New York* (1950), which drew on Walt Whitman and William Carlos Williams as advocates of a poetry governed by human speech and the rhythms of breath. As director of Black Mountain College near Asheville, North Carolina (1951–56), Olson became nominal head of the 'Black Mountain poets' (including Robert Creeley, Ed Dorn, and others). His most important work, *The Maximus Poems*, appeared in several volumes during his lifetime (1953–70, edited by George Butterick, 1983), but was left unfinished at his death. Olson's shorter verse was collected as *Archaeologist of Morning* (1970), and *The Complete Shorter Poems* appeared in 1985. 📖 Butterick, *A Guide to the Maximus Poems* (1978)

Olson, Harry Ferdinand 1901–82
US radio engineer and inventor

Born in Mount Pleasant, Iowa, he graduated from the University of Iowa and joined the RCA Laboratories in 1928, his first invention being a directional microphone, later developed into a true unidirectional microphone of the type still in use today. In the late 1940s he carried out a series of tests which established the standards for high-fidelity sound reproduction, and in 1955 he developed the first electronic music synthesizer. (Charles Wuorinen (1938–) used it to produce his composition *Time's Encomium*, which was awarded the Pulitzer Prize for music in 1970.) Olson held more than 100 US patents for acoustic devices and systems.

Olympias d.316BC
Macedonian queen

The wife of Philip II of Macedonia, and mother of Alexander the Great, she was the daughter of King Neoptolemus of Epirus. When Philip divorced her and married Cleopatra, niece of Attalus, she left Macedonia and ruled Epirus by herself, supposedly instigating the murder of Cleopatra. After Alexander's death (323BC) she returned to Macedonia, where she had his half-brother and successor killed, and made Alexander's posthumous son, Alexander IV, king. Eventually Cassander besieged her in Pydna, and on its surrender put her to death.

Olympio, Sylvanus 1902–63
Togolese politician

Educated at the London School of Economics, he returned to Africa as District Manager of the United Africa Company. He was President of the Togolese Assembly in 1946 and then led the country's government from 1958 to 1960 when, on independence, he became President. He was killed in a military coup.

O'Mahony, John 1816–77
Irish political leader

Born in Kilbeheny, County Limerick, he studied at Trinity College, Dublin, and in 1848 he joined in William Smith O'Brien's rebellion. He fled to France, and from there to the USA (1852), where he joined John Mitchel in New York. In 1858 he helped James Stephens found the Irish Republican Brotherhood, popularly known as the Fenians.

Oman, Sir Charles William Chadwick
1860–1946
English historian

Born in Muzaffarpur, India, he was educated at Winchester and New College, Oxford. He was made a Fellow of All Souls College in 1883, establishing his reputation with studies on Richard Warwick the Kingmaker (1891), Byzantine history (1892) and the art of war in the Middle Ages (1898). In 1902 appeared the first part of his great seven-volume history of the Peninsular War, which took him 28 years to complete. In 1905 he was elected Chichele Professor of Modern History at Oxford, and from 1919 to 1935 sat in parliament for the university. He also wrote *Things I have Seen* (1933), *On the Writing of History* (1939) and *Memories of Victorian Oxford* (1941).

Omar or Umar c.581–644
Second caliph

He was father of one of Muhammad's wives, and succeeded Abu Bakr in 634. Through his generals he built up an empire comprising Persia (Iran), Syria and all North Africa. He was assassinated in Medina by a Persian slave.

Omar Khayyám c.1048–c.1122
Persian poet, mathematician and astronomer

Born in Nishapuur, he was well educated in his home town and in Balkh, particularly in the sciences and philosophy. In Samarkand he completed a seminal work on algebra, and he made the necessary astronomical observations for the reform of the Muslim calendar, collaborating on an observatory in Isfahan. On his return from a pilgrimage to Mecca he served at the court as an astrologer. As a poet he had attracted little attention until Edward FitzGerald translated and arranged the collection of *robáiyát*, or quatrains, attributed to him, into *The Rubáiyát of Omar Khayyám*, first published anonymously in 1859. Though the authorship was questioned, it has been established that at least 250 *robáiyát* were the work of Omar. 📖 A Dashti, *In Search of Omar Khayyám* (1971)

Omar Pasha, *also spelt* 'Umar Pasha, *properly* Michael Latas 1806–71
Ottoman general

Born in Plasky, Croatia, he served in the Austrian army but in 1828 he deserted, fled to Bosnia, and became a Muslim. He was appointed writing-master to Abdul-Medjid, on whose accession to the Ottoman throne in 1839 he was made colonel, and in 1842 Governor of Lebanon. From 1843 to 1847 he suppressed insurrections in Albania, Bosnia and Kurdistan. On the invasion of the Danubian Principalities by the Russians in 1853 he defeated the Russians in two battles. In the Crimean War (1854–56) he repulsed the Russians at Eupatoria (1855). He was sent, too late, to relieve Kars. He was Governor of Baghdad from 1857 to 1859. In 1861 he again pacified Bosnia and Herzegovina, and overran Montenegro in 1862.

Omnium, Jacob See Higgins, Matthew James

Onassis, Aristotle Socrates 1906–75
Argentine–Greek ship-owner

He was born in Smyrna, Turkey, the son of a Greek tobacco importer. At the age of 16 he left Smyrna for Greece as a refugee, and from there went to Buenos Aires where he made a fortune in tobacco and was Greek consul for a time. In 1925 he took Argentine and Greek citizenship. Buying his first ships in 1932, he built up one of the world's largest independent fleets, and was a pioneer in the construction of super-tankers. His first marriage, to Athina, daughter of Stavros Livanos, a Greek ship-owner, ended in divorce (1960), and after a long relationship with Maria Callas, in 1968 he married Jacqueline Bouvier Kennedy (see Jackie Kennedy Onassis), widow of US president John F Kennedy. 📖 L J Davis, *Onassis: Aristotle and Christina* (1986)

O'Neill, Eugene Gladstone 1888–1953
US playwright

Eugene O'Neill was born in New York City, the third son of the popular actor James O'Neill (1847–1920) and his wife Ella. He arrived after the death of his brother Edmund, who had contracted measles from his elder brother Jamie. Following a fragmentary education and a year at Princeton University (1906–07), O'Neill took a clerical job then signed on as a sailor on voyages to Australia, South Africa and elsewhere.

He contracted tuberculosis while working as a reporter in Connecticut, and spent six months in a sanatorium (1912–13), where he began to write plays, the first being *The Web* (1914). He joined the Provincetown Players in 1915 and wrote a sequence of plays (eg *Bound East for Cardiff*, 1916), based on life aboard a steamship, the SS *Glencairn*. *Beyond the Horizon*, which was produced in New York in 1920 and published in the same year, was awarded the Pulitzer Prize. These works were followed during the next two years by *Exorcism* (1920), *Diff'rent* (1920), *The Emperor Jones* (1921), *Anna Christie* (1921; Pulitzer Prize) and *The Hairy Ape* (1922). *Desire Under the Elms*, a family tragedy set in New England and until then his most mature play, appeared in 1924.

O'Neill then began experimenting in new dramatic techniques; in *The Great God Brown* (1926) he used masks to emphasize the differing relationships between a man, his family and his soul. *Marco Millions* (1931) is a satire on tycoonery. *Strange Interlude* (1928; Pulitzer Prize), a marathon nine-act tragedy, lasting five hours, uses a stream-of-consciousness technique with dramatic asides and soliloquies. In the same year he wrote *Lazarus Laughed*, a humanistic affirmation of his belief in the conquest of death. His trilogy *Mourning Becomes Electra* (1931), set at the end of the American Civil War, is a restatement of the Orestean tragedy in terms of biological and psychological cause and effect. *Ah, Wilderness*, a nostalgic comedy, appeared in 1933, and *Days Without End* in 1934.

For 12 years he released no more plays but worked on *The Iceman Cometh* (first performed in New York 1946; London, 1958) and *A Moon for the Misbegotten* (1947). The former, set in a bar, is a gargantuan, repetitive parable about the dangers of shattering illusions, and is considered one of his most important plays. *Long Day's Journey into Night* (first performed posthumously in 1956; Pulitzer Prize 1957) is probably O'Neill's masterpiece. Set in 1912, it describes one day in the life of the tragic Tyrone family, and is closely based on the playwright's early life. *A Touch of the Poet* (1957) and *Hughie* (1959, first performed 1964) were also published posthumously. He was awarded the Nobel Prize for literature in 1936, the first US dramatist to be thus honoured, and is generally regarded as America's finest playwright.

📖 T Bogard and J R Bryer, *Selected Letters of Eugene O'Neill* (1988); L Sheaffer, *Eugene O'Neill: son and artist* (1973); *Eugene O'Neill: son and playwright* (1968).

> 'Oh, I know how you resent the way I have to show you up to yourself. I don't blame you. I know from my own experience it's bitter medicine, facing yourself in the mirror with the old false whiskers off. But you forget that, once you're cured. You'll be grateful to me when all at once you find you're able to admit, without feeling ashamed, that all the grandstand foolosopher bunk and the waiting for the Big Sleep stuff is a pipe dream. You'll say to yourself, I'm just an old man who is scared of life, but even more scared of dying. So I'm keeping drunk and hanging on to life at any price, and what of it?' Hickey in Act 2 of *The Iceman Cometh* (1946).

Onassis, Jackie (Jacqueline) Kennedy, *née* Lee Bouvier 1929–94
US First Lady

Born in Southampton, New York, she was a photographer with the Washington *Times–Herald* in 1952 before marrying John F Kennedy in 1953. During his presidency (1961–63), she supervised the restoration of the White House and wielded a powerful and widespread influence on fashion. After her husband's assassination she returned to private life, and in 1968 married the Greek shipping magnate Aristotle Onassis. She later worked with Viking Publications (1975–77), and Doubleday and Co as editor (1978–82).

Ondaatje, (Philip) Michael 1943–
Canadian poet and novelist

Born in Ceylon, he emigrated to Canada in 1962 in the footsteps of his brother. Two decades later, he portrayed his aristocratic and eccentric relatives in the beguiling memoir, *Running in the Family* (1982). His first poetry was *The Dainty Monsters* (1967), followed by *The Man With Seven Toes* (1969) and the prize-winning sequence *The Collected Works of Billy the Kid: Left Handed Poems* (1970). In that same year, he wrote a critical study of the lyricist and novelist Leonard Cohen, clarifying some of his own literary concerns. After his collected poems were published as *There's a Trick With a Knife I'm Learning to Do* (1979, published in the UK as *Rat Jelly and Other Poems*, 1980), he turned increasingly to prose. His novels include *Coming Through Slaughter* (1976), *In the Skin of a Lion* (1987) and the hauntingly lyrical *The English Patient* (1991, filmed 1996), for which he shared the Booker Prize with Barry Unsworth. Ondaatje has directed several films and is editor of the *Faber Book of Canadian Short Stories* (1990).

O'Neal, Shaquille Rashaun 1972–
US basketball player

Born in Newark, in his first season he transformed Orlando Magic into a top team and he was National Basketball Association (NBA) Rookie of the Year (1993). He played in the NBA All-Star team (1993, 1994) and the Dream Team II (1994). As centre for Orlando in 1995, he was the NBA leading scorer with 2,315 points from 79 games. His contract with Orlando Magic, signed in 1992, runs for seven years at $6 million a year. At 7 feet 1 inch (2.16m) tall and weighing 302lb (137kg), he has size 20 feet, which will earn him $30 million over five years from Reebok. He also has a $15 million deal with Pepsi. O'Neal's style and wealth fascinate.

O'Neill, Eugene Gladstone See panel above

O'Neill, Hugh, 2nd Earl of Tyrone c.1540–1616
Irish rebel

Born in Dungannon, the son of an illegitimate son of Conn O'Neill (c.1484–c.1559), a warlike Irish chieftain who was made Earl of Tyrone on his submission to Henry VIII in 1542, he was invested with the title and estates c.1597, but soon plunged into intrigues with the Irish rebels and the Spaniards against Elizabeth I. As 'the O'Neill' he spread insurrection all over Ulster, Connaught and Leinster (1587). Despite Spanish support he was defeated in 1601–02 by Charles Blount, 8th Lord Mountjoy, at Kinsale and badly wounded. He intrigued with Spain against James VI and I, and in 1607 fled to the Spanish Netherlands. He died in Rome.

O'Neill, Jonjo (John Joseph) 1952–
Irish National Hunt jockey

Born in Castletownroche, County Cork, he started as an apprentice jockey at The Curragh in Kildare, and was then briefly at the stable of Gordon Richards (1930–98). When this proved unsuccessful, he decided to become freelance, and concentrated on National Hunt racing. Establishing a reputation for utter fearlessness and an astonishing ability to endure pain, he suffered innumerable broken bones, but fought on to become champion jockey twice, in 1977–78 and 1979–80. He set the remarkable record of 148 winners in a season and won the Champion Hurdle on Sea Pigeon in 1980 and the Gold Cup on Dawn Run in 1986.

O'Neill (of the Maine), Terence (Marne) O'Neill, Baron 1914–90
Northern Irish statesman

Born in County Antrim, he was a member of the Northern Ireland parliament (1946–70), and became Minister for Home Affairs (1956), Finance (1956–63), and then Prime Minister (1963–69). A supporter of closer cross-border links with the Republic, he angered many Unionists, and his acceptance in 1969 of civil rights for the Roman Catholic minority forced his resignation. Made a life peer in 1970, he continued to speak out on Northern Ireland issues. He wrote *Ulster at the Crossroads* (1969) and *The Autobiography of Terence O'Neill* (1972).

O'Neill, Tip, *in full* Thomas Philip O'Neill, Jnr 1912–94
US politician

Born into an Irish Catholic family in Cambridge, Massachusetts, he was elected to the House of Representatives as a Democrat from Massachusetts in 1952. A canny and faithful member of his party, he became majority whip in 1971 and majority leader in 1973. He was Speaker of the House from 1977 to 1987.

Onetti, Juan Carlos 1909–94
Uruguayan novelist and short-story writer

Born in Montevideo, he left school early and, following several menial jobs, became a full-time writer in 1939, when he began working for the magazine *Marcha*. His highly regarded short novel *El Pozo* (1939, 'The Well') was published shortly before he moved to Buenos Aires. His next novel, *Tierra de Nadie* (1941, 'No Man's Land'), is an important landmark in the creation of a modern, urban Latin-American literature, in its setting in a fictional fusion of Buenos Aires and Montevideo. He returned to Uruguay in 1954, but left 20 years later for Spain after his imprisonment by the military government. His short-story collections include *Un Sueño Realizado y otros cuentos* (1951, 'A Dream Comes True and other stories').

Onions, Charles Talbut 1873–1965
English scholar and lexicographer

Born in Edgbaston, Birmingham, he was recruited to the staff of the *Oxford English Dictionary* by Sir **James Murray** in 1895. After the completion of that dictionary, he was commissioned to revise and complete the unfinished *Shorter Oxford English Dictionary*, which was published in 1933 and which he continued to revise and enlarge until 1959. He was Reader in English Philology at Oxford between 1927 and 1949, and editor of the journal *Medium Aevum* from 1932 to 1956. His last great work was the *Oxford Dictionary of English Etymology* (1966), produced with the collaboration of **Robert Burchfield** and G W S Friedrichsen.

Onnes, Heike Kamerlingh See Kamerlingh Onnes, Heike

Ono, Yoko 1933–
Japanese artist, writer, singer and campaigner

Born in Tokyo, she moved to the USA after World War II, and married the composer Toshi Ichiyanagi (later divorced). She established a reputation as an avant-garde filmmaker, occasionally branching out into experimental music. She married **John Lennon** in 1969, and was criticized for her role in the **Beatles'** break-up (1970). She subsequently became Lennon's collaborator in the Plastic Ono Band and in various well-publicized peace protests. Her book *Grapefruit* (1970) and album *Approximately Infinite Universe* (1972) suggest she was more talented than detractors still claim. Since Lennon's murder, she has protected his unpublished work and continued to campaign for peace.

Ono No Komachi c.810–c.880
Japanese poet

She was born probably in Kyoto, during the classical period of Japanese literature. Like many of the other great figures of classical literature in Japan, she was a court poet, writing in a rarefied form of the vernacular—it was more common for men to write in a form of Chinese, which is why so much surviving classical Japanese literature is by women (see **Murasaki Shikibu**). She is known in Japan as one of the Six Poetic Geniuses, the supreme writer of the verse form *tanka*. ▣ H C McCullough, *Ise Monogatari. Tales of Ise: Lyrical Episodes from Tenth Century Japan* (1968)

Onsager, Lars 1903–76
US chemical physicist and Nobel Prize winner

Born in Christiania (Oslo), Norway, he was trained at the Technical University of Norway as a chemical engineer, but pursued further studies in mathematics. He worked in Zurich with **Peter Joseph Wilhelm Debye** from 1926 to 1928 and then went to the USA, where he spent the rest of his life. After periods at Johns Hopkins University and Brown University, Rhode Island, he settled at Yale, where he advanced from assistant professor to associate professor between 1934 and 1945, when he became Gibbs Professor of Theoretical Chemistry. He held this position until 1972, when he moved to the University of Miami as Distinguished University Professor. Onsager's work with Debye was on strong electrolytes, for which he developed an extension of the Debye–Hückel theory. However, he is best known for his pioneering work on the thermodynamics of irreversible processes, which he put on a sound basis. The fundamental equations in this field are called the 'reciprocal relations' and are commonly known by his name. For this work he was awarded the Nobel Prize for chemistry in 1968.

Oodgeroo, Noonuccal Moongalba, *originally* Kath(leen Jean) Walker 1920–93
Australian Aboriginal artist and writer

She was born in Brisbane, Queensland, and brought up with the Noonuccal group on Stradbroke Island, Queensland. From the age of 13 she worked in domestic service in Brisbane, gaining her education mainly from the libraries of her employers. She joined the Australian Women's Army Service during World War II, and afterwards became involved in Aboriginal activism. In 1964 she became the first Aboriginal writer to be published, with her collection of poems *We are Going*, followed by *The Dawn is at Hand* (1966). With other works these were republished in 1970 as *My People, a Kath Walker Collection*. In 1972 she published a book of Aboriginal stories, *Stradbroke Dreamtime*. She won a number of awards, including the Mary Gilmore Medal. She visited the USA on a Fulbright Scholarship from 1978 to 1979, lecturing on Aboriginal rights, and was active on many Aboriginal interest committees including the Aboriginal Arts Board. In 1985 she published *Quandamooka, the art of Kath Walker*. She also ran a Centre for Aboriginal Culture, for children of all races, on Stradbroke Island. **Malcolm**

Williamson has set some of her poems for choir and orchestra: *The Dawn is at Hand* was premiered in 1989. In 1988 she adopted the Aboriginal name Oodgeroo of the Noonuccal group.

Oort, Jan Hendrik 1900–92
Dutch astronomer

Born in Franeker, he studied at the University of Groningen and then worked mainly at the Leyden Observatory (1924–70), becoming director there in 1945. He proved (1927) by observation that our galaxy is rotating and calculated the distance of the Sun from the centre of the galaxy, initially locating it 300,000 light years away. He also made the first calculation of the mass of galactic material interior to the Sun's orbit. In 1932 he made the first measurement that indicated that there is dark matter in the galaxy. In 1946 he realized that the filamentary nebulae called the Cygnus Loop is a supernova remnant. In 1950 he extended Ernst Öpik's suggestion concerning the huge circular reservoir of comets surrounding the solar system. These have maximum distances from the Sun of some 100,000 astronomical units and are thus susceptible to being perturbed by passing stars. This 'Oort cloud' was the suggested source of long-period comets. In 1956, with Theodore Walraven, he discovered the polarization of the radiation from the Crab nebula indicating that it was produced by synchrotron radiation from electrons moving at high speeds along magnetic field lines.

Oparin, Aleksandr Ivanovich 1894–1980
Russian biochemist

Born near Moscow, he was educated at Moscow State University, and became head of plant biochemistry at Moscow University in 1929, and then director of the Bakh Institute of Biochemistry of the USSR Academy of Sciences. His thoughts on the origin of life in his *Proiskhozhdenie Zhizny* (1924) received little attention until 1952, when Harold Urey used the Oparin–Haldane theory, that life slowly emerged from a primeval soup of biomolecules, as a basis for his generation of simple biomolecules. Oparin suggested that life was initiated by the slow binding together of molecules to form droplets, which then absorbed other biomolecules and spontaneously divided. His simulated living systems mimicked fermentation, electron transport and photosynthesis. His other major publications include *The Origin of Life on Earth* (1936) and *The Chemical Origin of Life* (1964).

Opechancanough d.1644
Native American chief of the Powhatan confederacy

He succeeded Powhatan, the father of Pocahontas in 1618. Less peaceable than his predecessor, cunning and bitter, he attacked the white settlers of Virginia (1622). Years of reprisals and crop stealing by the whites had all but destroyed the livelihood of the Native Americans when Opechancanough led a renewed attack on the settlements in 1644. The chief, then in his nineties, was captured and killed, and the confederacy ceased to exist.

Ophuls or Ophüls, Max, *originally* Max Oppenheimer 1902–57
French film director

Born in Saarbrücken, Germany, he chose French nationality in the plebiscite of 1934. He worked in films from 1930, in Germany, France, and the USA. These included *Liebelei* (1932), *The Exile* (1947), *The Reckless Moment* (1949), *La Ronde* ('The Round', 1950), and *Lola Montes* (1955).

Opie, John 1761–1807
English portrait and historical painter

He was born near St Agnes, Cornwall. His attempts at portrait painting interested John Wolcot (Peter Pindar), by whom he was taken to London in 1789 to become the 'Cornish Wonder'. He married the writer Amelia Opie (1769–1853) in 1798. He became renowned as a portraitist of contemporary figures, and also painted historical pictures like the well-known *Murder of Rizzio*, *Jephtha's Vow* and *Juliet in the Garden*. He wrote a Life of Sir Joshua Reynolds, and published his *Lectures on Painting* (1809) at the Royal Institution.

Opie, Peter Mason 1918–82 and Iona 1923–
British children's literature specialists

They married in 1943 and the birth of their first child prompted them to study the folklore of childhood. This culminated in *The Oxford Dictionary of Nursery Rhymes* (1951), acknowledged widely for its scholarship as well as its sense of humour. Through their work on this they amassed the peerless Opie Collection of children's books which is now housed in the Bodleian Library, Oxford. In 1993 Iona published *The People in the Playground*, based on the research she had done with her husband for their earlier books. She also collects publications by contemporary illustrators.

Öpik, Ernst Julius 1893–1985
Estonian astronomer

Born just north of Rakvere, he studied at Tartu State University, and worked at observatories in Tashkent, Moscow and Turkistan, before returning to Tartu. After World War II he moved to the Armagh Observatory in Northern Ireland, where he became the director, as well as holding a post at the University of Maryland. Öpik's research concentrated on comets and meteoroids in the solar system, and his theory on the burn-up and disintegration of meteoroids when they enter the Earth's atmosphere has been applied to space capsules and meteorite-dropping asteroids. He also studied the orbits of comets, and in 1932 was the first to predict that there is a huge cometary cloud surrounding the solar system. In 1934 he designed an ingenious rocking mirror device to improve the accuracy of meteor visual velocity measurements. He pioneered the measurement of meteoroid size distribution, and also suggested that Apollo asteroids were dormant cometary nuclei. Among his many awards was the Gold Medal of the Royal Astronomical Society (1975).

Opitz von Boberfeld, Martin 1597–1639
German poet

Born in Bunzlau, Silesia, he was the founder of the Silesian school of poets and wrote a plea for the purification of the German language in *Aristarchus sive de contemptu linguae Teutonicae* (1617, written in Latin) and other works. In 1620 he fled to Holland to escape war but still fell victim to the plague. His works include translations from classical authors (Sophocles and Seneca), the Dutch Daniel Heinsius and Hugo Grotius, and from the Bible. He also wrote a prose translation of Ottavio Rinuccini's *Daphne* (1627), which formed the basis of the first German opera in 1627. 📖 J Gellinek, *Martin Opitz* (1973)

Oppenheim, Edward Phillips 1866–1946
English novelist

Born in London, he worked in his father's leather business after leaving school at the age of 17. He wrote in his spare time, had his first book published in 1887 and went on to become a pioneer of the novel of espionage and diplomatic intrigue. Among his best are *Mr Grex of Monte Carlo* (1915), *Kingdom of the Blind* (1917), *The Great Impersonation* (1920) and *Envoy Extraordinary* (1937). 📖 R Standish, *The Prince of Story-Tellers* (1957)

Oppenheim, Lassa Francis Lawrence
1858–1919
German international lawyer
He was born near Frankfurt am Main, and educated at Frankfurt Gymnasium and Göttingen, Berlin, Heidelberg and Leipzig universities. He taught law in Germany, Switzerland and England, where he settled in 1895, holding a chair at Cambridge from 1908. His major work, *International Law: a Treatise* (1905–06, and later editions) is a standard British text. He stressed positive international law, based on the usages of and agreements between states rather than on theoretical principles, and the supremacy of national sovereignty and national laws over international law. He nevertheless accepted the necessity for—and indeed advocated—the League of Nations after World War I.

Oppenheimer, Sir Ernest 1880–1957
South African mining magnate, politician and philanthropist
Born in Friedberg in Germany, he was the son of a Jewish cigar merchant. At the age of 16 he worked for a London firm of diamond merchants and, sent out to Kimberley as their representative in 1902, soon became one of the leaders of the diamond industry. In 1917, with J Pierpont Morgan, he formed the Anglo-American Corporation of South Africa and at the time of his death his interests covered 95 per cent of the world's supply of diamonds. He was Mayor of Kimberley (1912–15), raised the Kimberley Regiment and, a friend of Jan Smuts, was MP for Kimberley (1924–38). He endowed university chairs and funded slum clearance schemes in Johannesburg.

Oppenheimer, Harry Frederick 1908–
South African industrialist
Born in Kimberley and educated at Oxford, he was the son of Sir Ernest Oppenheimer. He succeeded his father as chairman of Anglo-American from 1957 to 1983. As an MP (1947–88) he was a critic of the South African government's policy of apartheid. In 1990 he was awarded the gold medal by the American Institute of Mining and Metallurgy. His son, Nicholas Frederick (1945–), born in Johannesburg and educated at Oxford, was chairman of de Beers (1984–85).

Oppenheimer, (Julius) Robert 1904–67
US nuclear physicist
Born in New York City, he studied at Harvard, Cambridge and under Max Born at Göttingen University, Germany, where he received his doctorate in 1927. He returned to the USA and established schools of theoretical physics at Berkeley and the California Institute of Technology (Caltech). His work included studies of electron–positron pairs, cosmic-ray theory and deuteron reactions. During World War II he was selected as leader of the atomic bomb project, set up the Los Alamos laboratory and brought together a formidable group of scientists. After the war he became director of the Institute for Advanced Studies at Princeton University and continued to play an important role in US atomic energy policy from 1947, promoting peaceful uses of atomic energy and bitterly opposing development of the hydrogen bomb. In 1953 he was declared a security risk and was forced to retire from political activities. He delivered the BBC Reith Lectures in 1953, and received the Enrico Fermi award in 1963. 📖 Michel Rouze, *Oppenheimer* (1962, Eng trans *Robert Oppenheimer: The Man and His Theories*, 1965)

Opperman, Sir Hubert Ferdinand 1904–96
Australian cyclist and politician
Born in Rochester, Victoria, after leaving school he started work as a telegraph boy and it was this which developed his phenomenal cycling speed. Between 1924 and 1937 he held at various times every long-distance, track

and road record in Australia, and also competed with success in France, where in 1931 he was voted sportsman of the year. His paced record for 24 hours and for 1,000 miles, set in 1932, still stands. Opperman served with the Royal Australian Air Force in World War II, and was involved in federal politics from 1949 to 1967, during which time he held two ministerial posts and was government whip. From 1967 to 1972 he was Australian High Commissioner to Malta.

O'Rahilly, Little Hugh See below

Ó Rathaille, Aodhagán, *in English* Little Hugh O'Rahilly 1670–?1730
Classical Irish Gaelic poet
He was born in Kerry on lands formerly ruled by the MacCarthy earls of Clancarty, whose memory he idolized as a descendant of their hereditary bards. His poetry embodies the great Jacobite lament for the overthrow of Catholic Gaelic Ireland, much of it realized in rich lyrical and elegant development of the *Aisling* (patriotic dream-vision). Although essentially oral, his Gaelic poems survived in part and were edited for the Irish Texts Society bilingually (1900, revised edition 1911). His death date is unknown, usual estimates being based on a poem avowedly written on his death-bed. 📖 P Ua Duinnin, introduction to *Collected Poetry* (1900–11)

Orbach, Susie 1946–
British psychotherapist and feminist author
Born in London, she studied in both London and New York and became a psychotherapist in 1972, co-founding the Women's Therapy Centre in London (1976), and the Women's Therapy Centre Institute in New York (1981). Her book *Fat is a Feminist Issue* (1976) addresses women's feelings about food, fat and femininity, and argues that the obsession with food that dieting induces actually makes women fat. Her later works include *Understanding Women* (1982, co-authored) and *Hungerstrike* (1985). In 1991 she presented the BBC television programme *Behind the Headlines*, as well as becoming a columnist for *The Guardian* newspaper. The latter post gave her a platform for tackling topical issues and their relation to psychoanalysis.

Orbison, Roy 1936–88
US country-pop singer and songwriter
Born in Vernon, Texas, he began playing on local radio stations at the age of eight and was discovered in his early teens by the record producer Norman Petty. After moving to the Sun record label he had his first minor success with 'Ooby Dooby' (1956), but subsequently spent four years writing for other artists. He re-emerged with such hit singles as 'Only The Lonely' (1960) and 'O! Pretty Woman' (1964), which was used in the soundtrack for the 1990 film. The deaths of his wife Claudette (1966) and two of his sons (1968) coincided with a low period in his career and he spent 10 years in relative obscurity. However in the late 1970s and early 1980s, a series of successful cover versions of his songs by other artists, and the patronage of a younger generation of musicians, helped to reverse his fortunes. In 1988 he helped to form the ageing 'supergroup' The Travelling Wilburys, but he died of heart failure later that year.

Orcagna, *properly* Andrea de Cione c.1308–1368
Italian sculptor, painter, architect and poet
His tabernacle in Or San Michele at Florence is a remarkable piece of sculpture. His greatest paintings are frescoes, an altarpiece in S Maria Novella, and *Coronation of the Virgin* in the National Gallery, London. His brothers Nardo (active 1343/6–1365/6) and Jacopo (active 1365–98) were both painters who worked in his style.

Orchardson, Sir William Quiller 1832–1910
Scottish painter

Born in Edinburgh, he studied at the Trustees' Academy with the Scottish painter John Pettie (1839–93) and went to London in 1862. He painted portraits, but is best known for historical and social subject paintings; his most famous is the scene of **Napoleon I** on board the *Bellerophon* (1880) in the Tate Gallery. Among other well-known subjects are *Queen of the Swords* (1877), *Mariage de convenance* (1884) and *Her Mother's Voice* (1888).

Orczy, Baroness (Emma Magdalena Rosilia Marie Josefa Barbara) 1865–1947
British novelist and playwright
She was born in Tarna-Eörs, Hungary, the daughter of a musician. Educated in Paris and Brussels, she then studied art in London, where she exhibited some of her work in the Royal Academy. *The Scarlet Pimpernel* (1905) was the first success in her long writing career. It was followed by many popular adventure romances, including *The Elusive Pimpernel* (1908) and *Mam'zelle Guillotine* (1940), which never quite attained the success of her early work.
📖 *Links in the Chain of Life* (1947)

O'Reilly, John Boyle 1844–90
US journalist and political agitator
Born in Dowth Castle, near Drogheda, Ireland, he was apprenticed as a printer, and became a reporter on the *Manchester Guardian*. He joined the Fenians and returned to Dublin, where he enlisted in the 10th Hussars in 1863. In 1866 he was sentenced to 20 years' penal servitude and transportation for spreading Fenianism in the army. He escaped in 1869 from Western Australia to the USA, and settled as a journalist in Boston, where he became known as an author of songs and novels.

O'Reilly, Tony (Anthony John Francis) 1936–
Irish industrialist and rugby internationalist
Born in Dublin and educated at Belvedere College, University College, Dublin, and Bradford University, he was an outstanding wing-threequarter. He won 23 caps for Ireland, spanning 15 years (his last cap against England came after an interval of seven years). He was particularly in his element with the British Lions teams, for whom he scored a record number of tries touring in South Africa and New Zealand. After a busy and productive business career, he became chief executive and chairman of the Heinz International Corporation.

Orellana, Francisco de c.1500–1549
Spanish explorer
Born in Trujillo, he went to Peru with **Francisco Pizarro**. After crossing the Andes in 1541, he descended the Amazon River to its mouth. The river's original name was Rio Santa Maria de la Mar Dulce, but Orellana is said to have renamed it after an attack by a tribe in which he believed women were fighting alongside men.

Orff, Carl 1895–1982
German composer
Born in Munich, he studied under Kaminski and in 1925 helped to found the Günter school in Munich, where he subsequently taught. His aim, discussed in his didactic composition *Das Schulwerk* (1930–54), was to educate in the creative aspects of music. The influence of **Igor Stravinsky** is apparent in his compositions, which include three realizations of **Claudio Monteverdi**'s *Orfeo* (1925, 1931, 1941), an operatic setting of a 13th-century poem entitled *Carmina Burana* (1936, 'Songs of Beuren'), *Die Kluge*, (1943, 'The Prudent Woman'), *Oedipus* (1958) and *Prometheus* (1968).

Orfila, Mathieu Joseph Bonaventure 1787–1853
French chemist
Born in Mahón, Minorca, he studied at Valencia, Barcelona and Paris. In 1811 he lectured on chemistry, botany and anatomy, becoming a professor of medical jurisprudence in 1819 and of chemistry in 1823. His celebrated *Traité de toxicologie générale* ('Treatise of General Toxicology') appeared in 1813; it was the first systematization for the classification of toxicology and led to Orfila being named as its founder.

Orford, Earl of See **Walpole, Sir Robert**

Orhan or Orkhan 1288–1359
Sultan of Turkey
The son of Osman I, he took Brusa in his father's time, and as sultan (from 1324) reduced Nicaea and Mysia. He organized the state and established the Ottoman bridgehead in Europe, marrying the daughter of the Byzantine Emperor John V Palaeologus, minting the first Ottoman silver coins, creating a more permanent army, and building mosques and theological schools in the conquered towns.

Ó Riada, Seán, originally **John Reidy** 1931–71
Irish traditional and classical composer and teacher
Born in Cork, he was educated at University College there. He became assistant music director at Radio Éireann in Dublin (1954–55), then became music director of the Abbey Theatre, Dublin, until 1962, and taught at University College, Cork, from 1963 to 1971. He composed numerous works in contemporary idioms with no reference to traditional music, but is remembered for the powerful influence which he exerted in the revival of Irish music, both with his group Ceoltóirí Cualann (from which sprang **The Chieftains**) and in his experimental combinations of traditional and classical music.

Origen c.185–c.254AD
Christian scholar, theologian, and early Greek Father of the Church
Born of Greek parents probably in Alexandria, he studied at the catechetical school there, even though his parents may not have been Christians. He became head of the school (c.211–232AD), and was ordained in Palestine (c.230), but was denied the office of presbyter by an Alexandrian synod. He however returned to Palestine and established a new school of literature, philosophy and theology in Caesarea. He was imprisoned and tortured during the persecution under **Decius** in 250. His views on the unity of God and speculations about the salvation of the Devil were condemned by Church councils in the 5th and 6th centuries. His many writings extended over nearly the whole of the Old and New Testaments, and included a number of books on **Matthew** and **John** which are extant in Greek. His weighty *Hexapla*, the foundation of the textual criticism of the Scriptures, is mostly lost. His *Eight Books against Celsus*, preserved entire in Greek, constitute the greatest of early Christian apologies.

Orkhan See **Orhan**

Orlando di Lasso See **Lassus, Orlando**

Orlando, Vittorio Emanuele 1860–1952
Italian politician
Born in Palermo, Sicily, he became Professor of Law at Palermo University, and was elected to parliament in 1897. He served as Minister of Education, before becoming Minister of Justice in 1916. At the height of the crisis following the disastrous defeat of the Italian forces at the Battle of Caporetto (Kobavid) he became Prime Minister, remaining in office until June 1919. His inability to force **Woodrow Wilson** and **Clemenceau** to honour the terms of the Treaty of London (1915) at the Paris peace talks, in addition to postwar economic dislocation and growing political violence, brought about his downfall. He made

little attempt to resist **Mussolini** and was a supporter of the Fascists in the 1924 election, but adopted a more openly anti-Fascist stance in 1925. After World War II he became a senator, and served as the first president of the Constituent Assembly (1946–47); he ran unsuccessfully for the presidency in 1948.

Orléans, Charles, Duc d' 1391–1465
French nobleman, poet and soldier

Born in Paris, he married (1406) his cousin Isabella, widow of **Richard II** of England. In alliance with Bernard d'Armagnac, he did his best to avenge the murder of his father by the Duke of Burgundy. He held a high command at Agincourt (1415), and was captured and taken to England, where he lived for 25 years, composing courtly poetry in French and English, which was conventional, musical and graceful. Ransomed in 1440, he returned to France where he maintained a kind of literary court at Blois. His son became **Louis XII**.

Orléans, Jean Baptiste Gaston, Duc d'
1608–60
French nobleman and soldier

Born at Fontainebleau, he was the third son of **Henri IV** of France. He was heir to **Louis XIII** until 1638 and conspired against **Cardinal Richelieu** on behalf of the queen mother, **Marie de Médicis**. He was lieutenant-general of the kingdom during the minority of **Louis XIV**, but played a leading part in the Frondes. Spoilt, treacherous and unstable, he was exiled to his château at Blois, with its new wing, built by **François Mansard**.

Orléans, Louis Philippe Joseph, Duc d', *also called* Philippe Égalité 1747–93
French Bourbon prince

Born in Saint-Cloud, the cousin of **Louis XVI**, he succeeded to the title on his father's death (1785). His hostility to **Marie Antoinette** caused him to live away from court. He visited London frequently, and became a close friend of the Prince of Wales, afterwards **George IV**. In 1787 he showed his liberalism against the king, and was sent by a *lettre-de-cachet* to his château of Villers-Cotterets; as the Estates General drew near he circulated throughout France books and papers by **Emmanuel Sieyès** and other liberals. During the Revolution he was a forceful supporter of the Third Estate against the privileged orders, and in June 1789 he led the 47 nobles who seceded from their own order to join it. Although he joined the radical Jacobin Club (1791), he gradually lost influence and in 1792 renounced his title and adopted the name of Philippe Égalité. A member of the Convention, he voted for the death of Louis XVI. When his eldest son (afterwards King **Louis Philippe**) rode with **Charles Dumouriez**, his commander, into the Austrian camp, Égalité was arrested with all the **Bourbons** still in France, and was found guilty of conspiracy and guillotined. 📖 E S Scudder, *Prince of the Blood* (1938)

Orléans, Philippe, Duc d' 1674–1723
Regent of France

The son of the first Duke Philippe, and grandson of **Louis XIII**, he was born in Saint-Cloud. He showed courage at Steenkirk and Neerwinden (1692–93), and commanded successfully in Italy and Spain (1706–14). For some years he lived in exile from the court, spending his time in profligacy, the fine arts and chemistry. On **Louis XIV's** death he became Regent during the minority of **Louis XV** (1715–23), having married a daughter of **Louis XIV** and Madame de **Montespan**. He was popular, but his adoption of **John Law's** financial schemes led to disaster. His alliance with England and Holland (1717) was joined by the Emperor, and overthrew Alberoni in Spain. He

expelled **James Francis Stuart** from France, debarred the parliament of Paris from meddling with political affairs, and to appease the Jesuits sacrificed the Jansenists.

Orley, Bernard or Barend van c.1491–1542
Flemish painter

Born in Brussels, he became court painter to the regent, **Margaret of Austria**, and was one of the first Flemish painters to adopt the Italian Renaissance style. He executed a number of altarpieces and triptychs of biblical subjects, and in his later years designed tapestries and stained glass.

Orm or Ormin fl.1200
English monk and spelling reformer

Born probably in Lincolnshire, he invented an orthography based on phonetic principles, in which he wrote the *Ormulum* (meaning 'because Orm made it'), a series of homilies in verse on the gospel history.

Ormandy, Eugene, *real name* Jenö Blau 1899–1985
US conductor

He was born in Budapest, Hungary, and studied violin at the Royal Academy there. While still a teenager, he toured Europe as a child prodigy. Having emigrated to the USA in 1920, he became leader and then conductor of the Capitol cinema in New York, and in 1931, two years after becoming a US citizen, he was appointed conductor of the Minneapolis Symphony Orchestra. When Leopold **Stokowski** relinquished the baton of the Philadelphia Orchestra in 1936, Ormandy became conductor, remaining until shortly before his death. Temperamentally he was unsuited to the music of **Haydn**, **Mozart** and **Beethoven**, but he excelled in 'Romantic' scores and some from the 20th century. The last of his many recordings featured music by **Richard Strauss** and was released the year of his death.

Ormin See Orm

Ormond, John 1923–90
Welsh poet and film-maker

Born in Dunvant, near Swansea, he was educated at University College, Swansea. After training as a journalist he joined BBC Wales (1957) as a director and producer of documentary films, including studies of Welsh painters and writers such as **Ceri Richards**, **Dylan Thomas**, **Alun Lewis** and **R S Thomas**. He himself established a reputation as an accomplished Anglo-Welsh poet. 📖 Autobiography in M Stephens, *Artists in Wales* (1973)

Ormonde, James Butler, 12th Earl and 1st Duke of 1610–88
Anglo-Irish nobleman

Born in London, he was a member of the ancient family of Butler, and in 1632 he succeeded to the earldom and estates of Ormonde. Dignified and upright, he distinguished himself during the **Strafford** administration (1633–41), and in the Civil War he was the effective leader of the supporters of **Charles I** in Ireland. The armistice he concluded (1643) was condemned on both sides. Appointed Lord Lieutenant of Ireland (1643–47), he later (1649–50) led Irish resistance against **Oliver Cromwell**, but was forced into exile in France in 1650. At the Restoration he was rewarded by the ducal title of Ormonde, twice became Lord Lieutenant (1661–69, 1677–84), and attempted to encourage Irish trade and industry.

Ormonde, James Butler, 2nd Duke of
1665–1745
Irish nobleman

The grandson of James Butler, 1st Duke of **Ormonde**, he was born in Dublin, and as Earl of Ossory he served in the army against the Duke of **Monmouth**. After his accession to the dukedom (1688), he took his share in the

Revolution conflict and headed William III's lifeguards at the Boyne (1690). He commanded the troops in George Rooke's expedition against Cadiz (1702), and was appointed Lord Lieutenant of Ireland (1703–05, 1710–13), and Commander-in-Chief against France and Spain (1711). Under George I he fell into disgrace for maintaining Jacobite ties, and was impeached (1715) of high treason, his estates being attainted. He retired to France and spent years in the intrigues of the Old Pretender James Francis Stuart, dying abroad.

Orosius, Paulus 5th century
Spanish priest and historian
Born probably in Braga, he studied under Jerome at Bethlehem. He was the author of a seven-volume universal history called *Historiarum adversus Paganos*, from the Creation to AD417, a favourite textbook during the Middle Ages which was translated into Anglo-Saxon by King Alfred.

O'Rourke, Sir Brian-Na-Murtha d.1591
Irish chieftain
A leader in Galway, Sligo, and the west of Ulster, he was in frequent collision with the English authorities. He sheltered the Spaniards from the Armada wrecked on Irish coasts, and went to Scotland (1591) to seek support from James VI and I, who handed him over to the English. He was tried and executed at Tyburn, London.

Orozco, José Clemente 1883–1949
Mexican painter
Born in Zapotlán, Jalisco, he studied engineering and architectural drawing in Mexico City and from 1908 to 1914 studied art at the Academia San Carlos. His first exhibition was in Paris in 1925; a major retrospective was held in Mexico City in 1947. One of the greatest mural painters of the 20th century, he decorated many public buildings in Mexico and the USA. He was influenced by Byzantine mosaics (eg *The Coming of Quetzalcoatl* and *The Return of Quetzalcoatl*, 1932–34, in Dartmouth College), and his powerful realistic style, verging on caricature, was a vehicle for revolutionary socialist ideas. 📖 Alma Reed, *Orozco* (1956)

Orpen, Sir William 1878–1931
Irish painter
Born in Stillorgan, County Dublin, he did many sketches and paintings at the front in World War I, and was present at the Paris peace conference as official painter. The results may be seen at the Imperial War Museum. He is also known for Irish genre subjects, but is most famous for his portraits, whose vitality and feeling for character place them among the finest of the century.

Orr, Bobby (Robert Gordon) 1948–
US hockey player
He was born in Parry Sound, Ontario, Canada. The highest goal-scorer ever in North American National League hockey, he played mainly with Boston Bruins and became that city's greatest-ever sporting hero. During his career he changed the stategy of ice hockey by showing the defensive line could attack rather than just defend. By the time he moved to Chicago Black Hawks in the 1976–77 season (for a contract reputed to be worth $3 million), his career was already almost over. Six major leg operations had left him unable to stand the stress of major league hockey and he played only a few games for Chicago before being compelled to retire in 1979.

Orr, James 1844–1913
Scottish theologian
He was born in Glasgow. As a long-time parish minister, and Professor of Church History at the United Presbyterian Divinity Hall (from 1891) and Professor of Apologetics and Theology at the new Trinity College, Glasgow (1900–13), he defended and promoted conservative evangelical views against contemporary challenges. His books, including *The Christian View of God and the World* (1893), *The Ritschlian Theology and the Evangelical Faith* (1897), *The Virgin Birth of Christ* (1907) and *Revelation and Inspiration* (1910), gave him considerable influence in North America as well as Great Britain. His standing as a major representative of evangelical orthodoxy in the early 20th century was consolidated by his editorship of the *International Standard Bible Encyclopaedia* (1915).

Orr, John Boyd See Boyd Orr, John

Orrery, 1st Earl of See Boyle, Roger

Orsini, Felice 1819–58
Italian patriot and revolutionary
Born in Meldola, he was elected to the Roman Constituent Assembly in 1848 and took part in the defence of the city under the command of Garibaldi. In 1858 he went to Paris to try to assassinate Napoleon III, whom he considered to have betrayed the Italian cause: in the attempt, 10 people were killed but the Emperor survived. Orsini was sentenced to death, but before his execution he wrote a personal appeal to Napoleon begging him to assist the Italian struggle. It is possible that fear of further attempts on his life or the passion of Orsini's plea contributed to Napoleon's readiness to meet with the Conte di Cavour at Plombières and to declare war on Austria in 1859.

Ørsted Pedersen, Niels-Henning 1946–
Danish jazz musician.
Born in Osted, he learned piano, but turned to bass in order to play duets with his friend, pianist Ole Kock Hansen, who is also a leading jazz musician. He quickly established a reputation as one of the top jazz bass players in the world, and seemed at home in almost any style, from mainstream to avant-garde. His melodic approach to the instrument, combined with an impeccable harmonic and time sense, kept him much in demand with touring soloists, and his international reputation was sealed in an extended partnership with pianist Oscar Peterson. He has performed on several hundred recordings, and continues to be a major presence on his instrument.

Ortega Saavedra, Daniel 1945–
Nicaraguan politician
Born in La Libertad, Chontales, he became active in his teens in the resistance movement against the Somoza regime, and in 1963 joined the Sandinista National Liberation Front (FSLN), which had been founded in 1960. He became national director of the FSLN in 1966, was imprisoned for seven years for urban guerrilla bank raids, and then, in 1979, played a major part in the overthrow of Anastasio Somoza. In 1985 he became President, but counter-revolutionary forces, the 'Contras', with US support threatened his government's stability. By 1989, however, there were encouraging signs of peace being achieved. Surprisingly he lost the 1990 general election to Violetta Chamorro, and supervised the peaceful handover of power.

Ortega y Gasset, José 1883–1955
Spanish critic, journalist and philosopher
Born in Madrid, he studied at Madrid University (1898–1904), and was professor there from 1911. He also lived in South America and Portugal (1931–46). *Meditaciones del Quijote* (1914, Eng trans *Meditations on Quixote*, 1961) outlines national symbols in Spanish literature and compares them with those of others. In *Tema de nuestro tiempo* (1923, 'Modern Theme') he argues that great philosophies demarcate the cultural horizons of their epochs. His best-known work, *La Rebelión de Las Masas* (1930, Eng trans *The*

Revolt of the Masses, 1932), foreshadowed the Spanish Civil War. Often mistakenly taken as a right-wing and élitist document, it is a masterly analysis of the 20th-century situation, in which the masses have revolted against minorities. He corrected any possible ambiguities inherent in this book in his posthumous *El hombre y la gente* (1957, Eng trans *Man and People*, 1957). He introduced Marcel Proust and James Joyce to Spain and his writing has radically influenced the majority of Spanish writers of his time and after him. 📖 R McClintock, *Man and His Circumstances* (1971); J F Mora, *Ortega y Gasset* (1963)

Ortelius, Abraham Ortel 1527–98
Flemish geographer

Born of German parents in Antwerp, he produced *Theatrum Orbis Terrarum* (1570, Eng trans *Epitome of the Theater of the Worlde*), the first great atlas. 📖 C Koeman, *The History of Abraham Ortelius and his Theatrum orbis terrarum* (1964)

Orton, Joe, *originally* John Kingsley 1933–67
English dramatist

He was born in Leicester. After training as an actor at RADA in London, he turned to writing vivid, outrageous farces, beginning with *The Ruffian on the Stair* (1964) and *Entertaining Mr Sloane* (1964). Later plays include *Loot* (1966), *The Erpingham Camp* (1966) and *What the Butler Saw* (1969). He was murdered by his lover, Kenneth Halliwell, who subsequently killed himself. 📖 J Lahr, *Prick Up Your Ears* (1978)

Orwell, George, *pseudonym of* Eric Arthur Blair
1903–50
English novelist and essayist

Born in Motihari, Bengal, he was educated in England at Eton, served in Burma in the Indian Imperial Police from 1922 to 1927 (later recalled in 1935 in the novel *Burmese Days*), and then literally went *Down and Out in Paris and London* (1933), making an occasional living as tutor or bookshop assistant. In 1935 he became a small country shopkeeper, and published two novels, *A Clergyman's Daughter* (1935) and *Keep the Aspidistra Flying* (1936). *Coming Up for Air* (1939) is a plea for the small man against big business. He fought and was wounded in the Spanish Civil War and he developed his own brand of socialism in *The Road to Wigan Pier* (1937), *Homage to Catalonia* (1938) and *The Lion and the Unicorn* (1941). During World War II, he was war correspondent for the BBC and the *Observer*, and wrote for *Tribune*. His intellectual honesty motivated his biting satire of communist ideology in *Animal Farm* (1945), which was made into a cartoon film. It also prompted his terrifying prophecy for mankind in *Nineteen Eighty-Four* (1949): the triumph of the scientifically-perfected servile state, the extermination of political freedom by thought-control and an ideologically delimited basic language of *newspeak* in which 'thought crime is death'. Other penetrating collections of essays include *Inside the Whale* (1940) and *Shooting an Elephant* (1950). His *Collected Essays* appeared in four volumes in 1968. 📖 B Crick, *Orwell: a life* (1979)

Ory, Kid 1886–1973
US trombonist and bandleader

Born in Louisiana, one of the first polyinstrumentalists, singers, and composers in jazz, he formed Kid Ory's Sunshine Orchestra in 1922, played with Louis Armstrong's Hot Five and Jelly Roll Morton's Red Hot Peppers, and took part in the New Orleans Revival from 1942. His compositions include 'Muskrat Ramble'.

Osborn, Henry Fairfield 1857–1935
US palaeontologist and zoologist

Born in Fairfield, Connecticut, he studied at Princeton and became Professor of Zoology at Columbia University and concurrently Curator of Vertebrate Palaeontology at the American Museum of Natural History (1891–1910). Retaining a research professorship at Columbia, he was president of the American Museum of Natural History from 1908 to 1933. Although known as an autocratic leader, he revolutionized museum display with innovative instructional techniques and the acquisition of spectacular specimens, especially dinosaurs. He popularized palaeontology, mounting skeletons in realistic poses with imaginative backdrops. His many publications include *The Age of Mammals* (1910), *Man of the Old Stone Age* (1915) and *The Origin and Evolution of Life* (1917). His major scientific contribution was a vast monograph on *Proboscidea*, published posthumously in two volumes (1935–42).

Osborn, Sherard 1822–75
English naval officer

Born in Madras, he entered the navy in 1837. He took part in the Chinese War (1841–42), commanded vessels in two expeditions (1849 and 1852–55) in search of Sir John Franklin, was head of the British squadron in the Sea of Azov during the Crimean War, and took a leading share in the 1857–59 Chinese War. He was involved in laying a telegraph cable between the UK and Australia; hence Osborn Deep in the Indian Ocean bears his name. Promoted rear admiral in 1873, he helped to fit out the Arctic expedition of George Nares and Clements Markham (1875). He published *Arctic Journal* (1851), *Journals of McClure* (1856) and *Fate of Sir John Franklin* (1860).

Osborne, John (James) 1929–94
English playwright and actor

Born in London, he left Belmont College, Devon, at the age of 16 and became a copywriter for trade journals. Hating it, he turned actor (1948) and by 1955 was playing leading roles in new plays at the Royal Court Theatre, London. There his fourth play, *Look Back in Anger* (1956, filmed 1958), and *The Entertainer* (1957, filmed 1960), with Sir Laurence Olivier playing Archie Rice, established Osborne as the leading young exponent of British social drama. The 'hero' of the first, Jimmy Porter, the prototype 'Angry Young Man', and the pathetic, mediocre music hall joker Archie Rice, both echo the author's uncompromising hatred of outworn social and political institutions and attitudes. Among other works are *Luther* (1960), *Inadmissible Evidence* (1965), *Time Present* and *The Hotel in Amsterdam* (both 1968), and the filmscript of *Tom Jones*, which won him an Academy Award (1963). He wrote his credo in *Declarations* (1957), and three volumes of autobiography, *A Better Class of Person* (1981), *Almost a Gentleman* (1991) and *Damn You, England* (1994). 📖 S Trussler, *The Plays of John Osborne* (1969)

Osborne, Thomas See Leeds, Duke of

Osbourne, Lloyd 1868–1947
US writer

He was born in San Francisco, the son of Fanny Osbourne (*née* Vandegrift, 1840–1914) and stepson of Robert Louis Stevenson. He collaborated with Stevenson on several books, including *The Wrong Box* (1889), *The Wrecker* (1892) and *The Ebb Tide* (1894). He became US vice-consul in Samoa, and published several books of his own including *An Intimate Portrait of RLS* (1925). 📖 *Memoirs of Vailima* (1902)

Osceola c.1804–1838
Seminole leader

Born probably in present-day Georgia, he moved into Florida Territory with his mother and is thought to have fought as a teenager against General Andrew Jackson in the first of the Seminole Wars. In the early 1830s he denounced treaties that required Native Americans to move west, and when his warriors killed an Indian agent (1835), the second of the Seminole Wars began. For two years he served as the military leader of the Seminole, leading guerilla attacks on US troops in Florida and avoiding capture by retreating deep into the Everglades, where his people were hiding. Their resistance was so fierce that the USA lost 1,500 soldiers in the course of the war—and spent at least $20 million, the most costly Indian war in US history. Osceola's frustrated opponent, General Thomas S Jesup, at last tricked him into a meeting under a flag of truce and arrested him (1837). He died in prison at Fort Moultrie, South Carolina.

O'Shane, Pat(ricia) 1941–
Australian lawyer

Born in Mossman, Queensland, the daughter of an Irish father and Aboriginal mother, she trained at the University of New South Wales, the first Aboriginal to graduate in law there, and was called to the Bar in 1976. She was head of the Ministry of Aboriginal Affairs in New South Wales from 1981 to 1986, when she became a magistrate in the local courts. She is known for her progressive attitude, as shown especially in decisions concerning women and Aboriginal people.

O'Shaughnessy, Arthur William Edgar 1844–81
English poet

Born in London, he began work in the British Museum in 1861, moving to the natural history department in 1863. An associate of the Pre-Raphaelites, he published *An Epic of Women* (1870), *Lays of France* (1872), *Music and Moonlight* (1874) and *Songs of a Worker* (1881). His best-known poem is the often anthologized 'The Music-Makers'.

Osheroff, Douglas Dean 1945–
US physicist and Nobel Prize winner

Born in Aberdeen, Washington, he studied at the California Institute of Technology (Caltech) and at Cornell University. He worked as a member of the technical staff at Bell Laboratories, Murray Hill, New York (1972–82), where he became head of the department of solid state and low temperature physics (1982–87). He then moved to Stanford University (1987), and was made J G Jackson and C J Wood Professor of Physics in 1992. His co-discovery of the superfluid helium-3 (3He) and subsequent research on the superfluidity of matter near freezing point resulted in him being jointly awarded the 1996 Nobel Prize for physics with David Lee and Robert Richardson.

Oskar I 1799–1859
King of Sweden and Norway

Born in Paris, he was the only son and successor (1844) of Karl XIV Johan. A liberal by temperament, though increasingly conservative after 1848, he sought to conciliate nationalist feelings in Norway, encouraged social and economic reforms, developed schools, railways, banks and industry, and pursued a policy of Scandinavian unity and Swedish neutrality. He married Josephine of Leuchtenberg, the daughter of Eugène de Beauharnais, Duke of Leuchtenberg, and his wife Augusta Amalia of Bavaria.

Oskar II 1829–1907
King of Sweden and Norway

He was born in Stockholm, the younger son of Oskar I and brother of Karl XV, whom he succeeded in 1872. A vigorous, intelligent man of literary bent, his foreign policy was marked by admiration of the new German Empire of Bismarck, whose friendship he hoped would strengthen Sweden against Russia. He served as a mediator in international disputes, but found it impossible to keep the union of Norway and Sweden intact, and in 1905 surrendered the Crown of Norway to Prince Karl of Denmark, elected King of Norway as Haakon VII. He wrote a number of poems and historical works (including a *Life of Karl XII*), and translated German literature, including Goethe's *Faust*. Married to Sofia of Nassau (1836–1913), sister of Adolf, Grand Duke of Luxemburg, he was succeeded as King of Sweden by his son, Gustav V.

Osler, Sir William 1849–1919
Canadian–British physician

He was born in Bond Head, Ontario, and educated at Toronto and McGill universities. After graduating in medicine, he toured Great Britain and Germany for scientific training and in 1874 became Professor of Medicine at McGill. Chairs at the University of Pennsylvania (1884–89) and Johns Hopkins (1889–1904) followed, and he was subsequently appointed to the Regius Chair of Medicine at Oxford. His textbook *The Principles and Practice of Medicine* (1892) codified the scientific clinical practice of his time and was frequently revised and translated. An advocate of full-time clinical training and research, he was instrumental in founding the Association of Physicians of Great Britain and Ireland. He was an advocate of humane values in a world of science, and by the time of his death was revered throughout the English-speaking world as a kind of patron saint of patient-oriented scientific medicine. He was made a baronet in 1911. ▫Harvey W Cushing, *The Life of Sir William Osler* (2 vols, 1925)

Osman I c.1259–c.1326
Founder of the Ottoman Empire

Born in Bithynia, the son of a border chief, he founded a small Turkish state in Asia Minor called Osmanli (or Ottoman). On the overthrow of the Seljuk sultanate of Iconium in 1299 by the Mongols, he gradually subdued a great part of Asia Minor, his greatest success being the capture of Bursa.

Osman Nuri Pasha 1832–1900
Turkish general

Born at Tohat in Anatolia, he joined the cavalry in 1853 after graduating from the Military Academy in Constantinople. He fought in the Crimean War (1853–56), the Cretan Revolt (1866–68), the Serbo-Turkish War (1876) and the Russo-Turkish War (1877–78). In 1878 he was given the title Ghazi ('Victorious') for his resourceful defence of the fortress of Plevna during the war against Russia. His army's resistance held up three Russian attacks over the River Danube and prevented Russia from claiming an easy victory. Following his retirement from the army he served four terms as Turkey's War Minister.

Osmund, St d.1099
Norman prelate

He became Chancellor of England (1072) and helped to compile the *Domesday Book*. Nephew and chaplain to William the Conqueror, he was Bishop of Salisbury from 1078, where he established the so-called 'Use of Sarum' (a version of the Latin liturgy of worship). His feast day is 4 December.

Ossian or Oisín Mac Fhinn Mhic Cumhail Mhic Tréanmóir Uí Baoisne ?3rd century AD
Semi-legendary Irish Gaelic poet and warrior

The son of Fionn (Fingal), he served for many years in the *Fianna*, or sworn band of heroes, then he went to *Tír na n-Óg*, the land of perpetual youth, with its queen, Niamh Chinn Óir, from whom he returned after 300 years to be converted to Christianity by St Patrick. Oral ballads, lyrics and prose ascribed to him were circulated in Ireland and Scotland, but the texts are probably from the 2nd century. The *Ossian* of James Macpherson supposes a coherence and royal status lacking in the original and was probably of Macpherson's own devising, since after Ossian's departure his father Fionn and his followers were finally defeated by the actual King of Ireland (or Tara), Cairbre Lifeachar, son of the Fianna's former suzerain, Cormac Mac Airt.

Ossietzky, Carl von 1888–1938
German pacifist, writer, and Nobel Prize winner

He was a reluctant conscript in the German army in World War I. The co-founder of *Nie Wieder Krieg* ('No More War') in 1922, he became editor in 1927 of the weekly *Weltbühne*, in which his articles denounced German military leaders' secret rearmament activities. Convicted of treason in 1931, he had his 18-month imprisonment sentence commuted, but as he was again editor when Hitler became Chancellor, he was sent to Papenburg concentration camp. In prison hospital he was awarded the 1935 Nobel Peace Prize. He died of tuberculosis under prison conditions in a private hospital.

Ossoli, Marchioness See Fuller, (Sarah) Margaret

Ostade, Adriaan van 1610–85
Dutch painter and engraver

Born probably in Haarlem, he was a pupil of Frans Hals, and his use of chiaroscuro shows the influence of Rembrandt. His subjects are taken mostly from everyday life, and include tavern scenes, farmyards, markets and village greens. His *Alchemist* is in the National Gallery, London. His brother Isaac (1621–49) treated similar subjects, but excelled at winter scenes and landscapes.

Östberg, Raynor 1866–1945
Swedish architect

A leader of the quest for a modern national style, he designed Stockholm City Hall (1911–23), in which many Swedish influences combine to create not only a city hall but a national monument commanding a magnificent waterfront site. His other important work is the classical Swedish Patent and Registration Office (1921). Although his popularity declined with the rise of functionalism, he is now acknowledged as a modern master.

Ostrovsky, Aleksandr Nikolayevich 1823–86
Russian dramatist

Born in Moscow, he studied law, but joined the Civil Service. He became director of a school of drama in 1885 and was given the task of choosing the repertoire for the Moscow imperial theatres. His own dramas are mainly domestic in nature, although he also looked at the darker side of official life; his later work includes historical dramas, and a fairy tale, *Snegurochka* (1873, 'Snow Maiden'), which Rimsky-Korsakov later used as the basis for his opera. His best-known play is *Groza* (1859, Eng trans *The Storm*, 1899). ⬚ M Hoover, *Alexander Ostrovsky* (1981)

Ostrovsky, Yuri 1926–92
Soviet holographic scientist

Born in Baku, Azerbaijan, he was educated at Leningrad (now St Petersburg) University and became assistant professor at the Leningrad Institute of Mines in 1961, moving in 1964 to the USSR Academy of Sciences. Ostrovsky measured and interpreted atomic line spectra, and used holographic techniques to measure mechanical vibrations and the wear of surfaces. He also made optical studies of hydrodynamic processes such as cavitation and shock waves, and wrote many books on spectroscopy and holography.

Ostwald, (Friedrich) Wilhelm 1853–1932
German physical chemist and Nobel Prize winner

Born in Riga, Latvia, he studied chemistry at the University of Dorpat (Tartu), taking the *Candidat* examinations in 1875. After holding various posts as an assistant at Dorpat, he was appointed Professor of Chemistry at the Riga Polytechnic in 1881. In 1887 he moved to Leipzig as Professor of Physical Chemistry, taking early retirement in 1906. With Jacobus Henricus van't Hoff and Svante August Arrhenius, Ostwald is regarded as one of the founders of physical chemistry. At Dorpat he worked on the measurement of chemical affinity and during his Riga period he used rates of reaction to study chemical affinity and he measured the 'affinity coefficients' of many acids, particularly organic acids, through studies of their catalytic behaviour. His results were greatly illuminated by the electrolytic dissociation theory of Arrhenius, which Ostwald did much to promote. In Leipzig he built up a great school of physical chemistry, which attracted students from all over the world. His studies of electrolytic conductivity (resulting in Ostwald's dilution law) and of the electromotive force of cells were carried out in Leipzig. He founded the journals *Zeitschrift für physikalische Chemie* in 1887 and *Annalen der Naturphilosophie* in 1901. His various books were very influential, notably his *Lehrbuch der allgemeinen Chemie* (2 vols, 1883–87). In his long retirement he worked on the theory of colour perception. He became an Honorary Fellow of the Chemical Society in 1898 and received its Faraday Medal in 1904. For his work on catalysis, he was awarded the Nobel Prize for chemistry in 1909.

Ó Súilleabháin, Eoghan Ruadh, *in English* Red Owen O'Sullivan 1748–84
Irish Gaelic poet

Born in County Kerry, he was variously a teacher in proscribed Catholic ('hedge') schools, an itinerant labourer, a sailor serving with George Rodney in the West Indies, a British soldier, and at all times an insatiable lover. His work followed Irish patriotic poetic traditions, and symbolizes the last phase of native Irish vernacular poetry. Obvious parallels exist with his contemporary Robert Burns. W B Yeats's 'Red Hanrahan' was based on him, as is 'Owen MacCarthy' in Thomas Flanagan's *The Year of the French* (1979). ⬚ D Corkery, in *The Hidden Ireland* (1924)

O'Sullivan, Red Owen See above

O'Sullivan, Timothy H(enry) 1840–82
US photographer

Born in New York City, he trained in Mathew B Brady's gallery and was a key member of the team sent by Brady to make a photographic record of the Civil War. O'Sullivan's pictures of this period in US history include *Harvest of Death* (1863), depicting the dead after the Battle of Gettysburg. He left Brady in 1863 and joined Alexander Gardner, contributing many photographs to his *Photographic Sketchbook of the War* (1965). He was chief photographer on the US Geological Exploration of the 40th Parallel from Nevada to Colorado (1867–69) and in the early 1870s took part in the surveys of the Arizona and New Mexico deserts. He also took the first photographs of underground mines and in 1880 was appointed chief photographer for the treasury department. ⬚ J D Horan, *Timothy O'Sullivan, America's Forgotten Photographer* (1966)

Oswald, St c.605–642
Anglo-Saxon King of Northumbria

He was the second son of King Æthelfrith of Bernicia. He fled to Iona for safety when his father was overwhelmed by King Edwin (St Edwin) of Deira in 616, but after Edwin's death in 633, Oswald returned from Iona and fought his way to the throne of Northumbria (Deira and Bernicia) with a victory over King Cadwallon near Hexham in 634. He re-established Christianity in Northumbria with the help of the Celtic monk St Aidan whom he summoned from Iona to set up a bishopric on

Lindisfarne, the Holy Isle, but was later killed by **Penda** of Mercia at the Battle of Maserfelth (Old Oswestry). 📖 Peter Clemoes, *The Cult of St Oswald on the Continent* (1983)

Oswald, Lee Harvey 1939–63
US alleged assassin of President John F Kennedy
Born in New Orleans, he was a Marxist and former US marine who had lived for some time in the USSR (1959–62). On 23 November 1963 he was charged with the murder of President **Kennedy**, whom he was alleged to have shot from the sixth floor of the Texas School Book Depository, as the President passed by in a motor cavalcade. Two days later, Oswald was shot dead by Jack Ruby (1911–67), who claimed to be avenging Jacqueline Kennedy (**Jackie Kennedy Onassis**). Claims were made that Oswald had links with the US secret service and with the Mafia. In 1979, the House Assassination's Committee decided that Kennedy 'was probably assassinated as a result of a conspiracy'. 📖 Edward J Epstein, *The Secret World of Lee Harvey Oswald* (1978)

Otake, Eiko 1952– and Koma 1948–
Japanese dance-theatre artists
They met in 1971 as law and political science students who joined Butoh master **Tatsumi Hijikata**'s company in Tokyo. What began as an experiment developed into a partnership in which they perform and choreograph only their own work. They made their debut in 1972, and began studying with Kazuo Uhno, the other central figure of Japan's mid-20th-century avant-garde. That same year their interest in the roots of German modern dance took them to Hanover, where they studied with a disciple of **Mary Wigman**. They made their US debut in 1976, since when they have regularly toured North America and Europe with both short and full-length pieces.

Otho, Marcus Salvius AD32–69
Roman emperor
Formerly a close friend of Emperor **Nero** and ex-husband of Nero's consort, the Empress **Poppaea Sabina**, from AD58 until Nero's downfall (68), he governed in Spain, virtually as an exile from court. A supporter briefly of **Galba**, he rose against him (69) and became emperor in his place, only to find his own position immediately challenged by the governor of Lower Germany, **Aulus Vitellius**. In the brief civil war that followed, Otho was comprehensively defeated and committed suicide.

Otis, Elisha Graves 1811–61
US inventor
Born in Halifax, Vermont, he became a master mechanic in a firm making bedsteads, and was put in charge of the construction of their new factory at Yonkers. The factory had several floors connected by a hoist, and Otis, knowing of the many serious accidents caused by runaway lifting platforms, designed in 1853 a spring-operated safety device which would hold the platform securely if there was any failure of tension in the rope. He patented his 'elevator' and exhibited it in New York in 1854, after which orders came in rapidly for passenger as well as goods lifts. He patented a new type of steam-powered lift in 1861, just before he died, and his two sons continued the successful expansion of the business.

Otis, James 1725–83
American statesman
Born in West Barnstable, Massachusetts, he became a leader of the Boston Bar. He was Advocate-General in 1760, when the revenue officers demanded his assistance in obtaining from the superior court general search warrants allowing them to enter any man's house in quest of smuggled goods. Otis refused, resigned, and appeared in defence of popular rights. In 1761, elected to the Massachusetts assembly, he became a radical opponent of

British rule. In 1769 he was beaten by revenue officers and received a head injury from which he never fully recovered. His fame chiefly rests on *The Rights of the Colonies Asserted* (1764).

O'Toole, Peter Seamus 1932–
Irish actor
Born in Connemara, he was a journalist and member of the submarine service, and a student at RADA, before joining the Bristol Old Vic where he made his professional debut in *The Matchmaker* (1955). He made his film debut in *Kidnapped* (1959). West End success in *The Long and The Short and The Tall* (1959) and a season with the Royal Shakespeare Company (RSC) established his stage reputation, while his performance in *Lawrence of Arabia* (1962) made him an international film star. Adept at drama, comedy or musicals, he has tackled many of the great classical roles and is frequently cast as mercurial or eccentric characters. Stage work includes *Hamlet* (1963, London), *Waiting for Godot* (1971, Dublin), *Uncle Vanya* (1978, Toronto) and a critically roasted *Macbeth* (1980, London). He was nominated seven times for the Academy Award, and his films include *The Lion in Winter* (1968), *Goodbye Mr Chips* (1969), *The Ruling Class* (1972), *My Favourite Year* (1982) and *The Last Emperor* (1987). He has published two autobiographies, *Loitering With Intent* (1992) and *The Apprentice* (1996). 📖 Nicholas Wapshott, *Peter O'Toole: a biography* (1983)

Ottey, Merlene 1960–
Jamaican athlete
She has won a record 13 world championship outdoor medals—the most by any female athlete—although she has never won an Olympic gold. Beaten on the line in Atlanta 1996, she had earlier lost the 1993 world 100m title by 0.001 seconds. Fired up, she went on to take the 1993 200m title, setting a world-record time of 21.98 seconds. In 1996 she set a 100m record of 10.74 seconds. She was appointed a roving ambassador for Jamaica in 1993 and signed a modelling and clothing contract in 1996.

Otto I, the Great 912–73
Holy Roman Emperor
The son of **Henry, the Fowler** he was crowned King of Germany in 936 and Emperor in 962. Virtual founder of the kingdom of Germany, he brought the great tribal duchies under the control of the monarchy, and made the Church the main instrument of royal government. He was married (930) to Edith, daughter of **Edward, the Elder**, and sister of **Athelstan** of England, and later (951) to St **Adelaide**. He preserved Germany from the Hungarian invasions by his great victory on the Lechfeld, near Augsburg (955), and re-established imperial rule in Italy in a revival of the Carolingian tradition. He presided over a cultural revival, sometimes called the Ottonian renaissance. 📖 Rudolf Koepke and Ernst Duemmler, *Jahrbücher der deutschen Geschichte: Kaiser Otto der Grosse* (1876)

Otto II 955–83
Holy Roman Emperor
The son of **Otto I**, he became emperor in 973, successfully fought the Danes and Bohemians, and subdued Bavaria (974–78), which he reduced in size by splitting it up. In 972 he married **Theophano**, daughter of the Byzantine Emperor Romanus II. He invaded France, was defeated by the Arabs in southern Italy, and overreached himself in attempts on the Eastern Empire.

Otto III 980–1002
Holy Roman Emperor
The son of **Otto II**, he came to the throne at the age of three. His mother, Empress **Theophano**, ruled as Regent until her death (991); thereafter his grandmother

Adelaide, widow of Otto I, ruled as Regent until his accession (996). He made first his cousin (Gregory V) and then his tutor (Sylvester II) pope. He lived most of his short life in Rome and tried to make it the capital of the empire, but was driven out by the hostility of the people (1002). The Ottonian cultural revival reached new heights under his encouragement of scholars and artists.

Otto IV c.1178–1218
Holy Roman Emperor

The son of Henry the Lion, he grew up at the court of his uncle Richard I of England, who created him Count of Poitou and Duke of Aquitaine. He was elected king (1198) in opposition to Philip of Swabia, against whom he struggled for supremacy for 10 years. Philip's murder (1208) freed him to be crowned emperor (1209), but his subsequent invasion of Sicily lost him the support of Pope Innocent III who raised up Philip's nephew Frederick II as a rival. Otto's cause finally collapsed after his defeat by Philip II of France at Bouvines in 1214, and he was deposed in 1215.

Otto, Kristin 1966–
German swimmer

She was born in Leipzig, and between 1982 and 1986 won a total of seven world championship medals—three individual and four relay. Between 1983 and 1989 she won nine gold medals at the European Cup—four individual and five relay. She broke the record for the most medals won by any woman in one sport at the same Olympic Games by winning six gold medals in the 1988 Olympics. They were for the 50m freestyle, 100m freestyle, 100m butterfly, 100m backstroke, and two relay races. Otto was also the first woman to break the minute barrier for the 100m backstroke in a short course (25m) pool. She is now a coach and commentator.

Otto, Nikolaus August 1832–91
German engineer

Born near Schlangenbad, he invented in 1876 the four-stroke internal-combustion engine, the sequence of operation of which is named the 'Otto cycle'.

Otto, Rudolf 1869–1937
German Protestant theologian and philosopher

Born in Peine, Hanover, he became Professor of Systematic Theology at Göttingen (1904), and later held chairs at Breslau (1914) and Marburg (1917). His best-known work, *Das Heilige* (1917, 'The Idea of the Holy'), explores the non-rational aspect of religion, termed 'the numinous' (the deity or awareness of it), and was largely prompted by the work of both Kant and Friedrich Schleiermacher, and by his own study of non-Christian religions in the East. His other books include *Die Gnadenreligion Indiens und das Christentum* (1930, Eng trans *India's Religion of Grace and Christianity*) and *West-Östliche Mystik* (1926, Eng trans *Mysticism East and West*, 1932).

Otway, Thomas 1652–85
English dramatist

Born in Trotton, Sussex, he went to Christ Church, Oxford, in 1669, leaving without a degree in 1672. He failed utterly as an actor, but had some success with his tragedy *Alcibiades* (1675). In it the actress Elizabeth Barry made her first appearance, and Otway is said to have fallen in love with her. In 1676 Thomas Betterton accepted his *Don Carlos*, a good tragedy in rhyme. The following year Otway translated Racine's *Bérénice*, and Molière's *Les Fourberies de Scapin* as *Cheats of Scapin*. In 1678–79 he was in Flanders as a soldier. His coarse but diverting comedy, *Friendship in Fashion*, appeared in 1678, followed in 1680 by two tragedies, *The Orphan* and *Caius Marius*, and his one important poem, *The Poet's Complaint of his Muse*. His greatest work, *Venice Preserved, or a Plot Discovered* (1682), is a

masterpiece of tragic passion. Later works include *The Atheist*, a feeble comedy, and *Windsor Castle* (1685), a poem addressed to the new king, James VII and II. He died in poverty. In 1719 a badly edited tragedy, *Heroick Friendship*, was published as his. ▫ E Rothstein, *Restoration Tragedy* (1967)

Oud, Jacobus Johannes Pieter 1890–1963
Dutch architect

Born in Purmerend, he collaborated with Piet Mondrian and others in launching the review *De Stijl*, and became a pioneer of the modern architectural style based on simplified forms and pure planes. Appointed city architect at Rotterdam in 1918, he designed a number of striking buildings, including municipal housing blocks.

Oughtred, William 1575–1660
English mathematician

Born at Eton College, he was educated there and at Cambridge, was ordained as a minister and became Rector of Albury. He wrote extensively on mathematics, notably *Clavis Mathematicae* ('The Key to Mathematics', 1631), a textbook on arithmetic and algebra in which he introduced many new symbols including multiplication and proportion signs. He also invented the earliest type of slide rule, and wrote on trigonometry in *Trigonometria* (1657).

Ouida, *pseudonym of* Marie Louise de la Ramée 1839–1908
English novelist

She was born in Bury St Edmunds. Her mother was English, her father French, and she was educated in Paris, then settled in London in 1857. 'Ouida' was a childish mispronunciation of 'Louise'. Starting her career by contributing stories to magazines, in particular to *Bentley's Miscellany* (1859–60), her first success was *Held in Bondage* (1863), shortly followed by *Strathmore* (1865), both aimed at the circulating libraries. She was soon established as a writer of hot-house romances, often ridiculed for her opulent settings, preposterous heroes and improbable plots, but her narratives were full of energy, and until her popularity waned in the 1890s she was a bestselling author. From 1860 she spent much time in Italy and in 1874 she settled in Florence where she lived lavishly. She wrote almost 50 books, mainly novels, such as *Folle-Farine* (1871), which was praised by Edward Bulwer Lytton, and *A Village Commune* (1881)—but also animal stories, essays and tales for children. Latterly, her royalties dried up and she fell into debt; she spent her last years destitute in Viareggio. ▫ E Bigland, *Ouida* (1950)

Ouspensky, Peter 1878–1947
Russian philosopher

He became a student of Georgei Gurdjieff in 1914, but eventually broke off relations with him in order to teach his own version of Gurdjieff's doctrine in London and the USA. He works of fiction, in the mould of Vladimir Soloviev, include *Strange Life of Ivan Osokin* (1947). His *In Search of the Miraculous* (1949) has been one of the most widely read religious books of the postwar period. ▫ M Nicoll, *Living Time* (1949)

Outram, James, *known as* the Bayard of India 1803–63
English general and colonial administrator

Born in Derbyshire, he joined the Bombay native infantry in 1819, and became political agent in Gujarat (1835–38). He fought in the first of the Afghan Wars (1838–42) and took part in the relief of Lucknow (1857–58).

Overbeck, Johann Friedrich 1789–1869
German painter

Born in Lübeck, he settled in Rome, where he allied himself with the like-minded Peter von Cornelius, Johann Gottfried Schadow, Julius Schnorr and Philipp Veit, who, because of the stress they laid on religion and moral significance, were nicknamed the Nazarenes. In 1813 he became a Roman Catholic. He painted in fresco as well as oil, mainly religious and historical subjects.

Ovett, Steve 1955–
English athlete

Born in Brighton, Sussex, he launched, with Sebastian Coe, a new era of British dominance in middle distance athletics. Gold medallist in the 800 metres at the 1980 Olympics, he also won a bronze in the 1,500 metres. He broke the world record at 1,500 metres (three times), at one mile (twice) and at two miles. An outspoken and sometimes controversial figure, he occasionally upset the press but remained generally popular with his fellow athletes and the spectators. As his competitive career faded he began a new role as a television commentator.

Ovid, *in full* Publius Ovidius Naso 43BC–AD17
Roman poet

Born in Sulmo (Solmona), in the Abruzzi, he was trained as a lawyer in Rome, but devoted himself to poetry. Later acclaimed as the master of the elegiac couplet, he had his first literary success with a collection of love poems, the *Amores* ('Loves'), followed by *Heroides* ('Heroines'), imaginary love letters from ladies to their lords. The *Ars Amandi* or *Ars Amatoria* ('The Art of Love'), a handbook of seduction, appeared about 1BC, followed by the *Remedia Amoris* ('Cures for Love'). While writing his *Metamorphoses*, a collection of mythological tales in 15 books, he was banished by Augustus (AD8), for some unknown reason, to Tomis (Constanza) on the Black Sea. He also wrote the elegies which he published in five books, the *Tristia* ('Sorrows'), the four books of the *Epistolae ex Ponto* ('Letters from the Black Sea'), *Ibis*, written in imitation of Callimachus, and *Halieutica* ('Fishing Matters'), a poem extant only in fragments. 📖 H Fränkel, *Ovid, a Poet between Two Worlds* (1945)

Owain ap Gruffydd c.1109–70
Prince of Gwynedd

Succeeding his father Gruffydd ab Cyrain to the kingdom of Gwynedd in 1137, he fiercely resisted Henry II, and kept his independent position and a reputation for chivalry and shrewdness until his death.

Owen, David Anthony Llewellyn Owen, Baron 1938–
English politician

He was born in Plymouth, and trained as a doctor before becoming Labour MP for Plymouth in 1966. He was Minister of State at the Department of Health and Social Security (1974–76), and then at the Foreign and Commonwealth Office (1976–77) before becoming the youngest Foreign Secretary for over 40 years (1977–79). Owen was one of the so-called 'Gang of Four' who broke away from the Labour Party to found the Social Democratic Party (SDP) in 1981. He succeeded Roy Jenkins as SDP leader after the party's rather poor election performance in 1983. When the Liberal leader, Sir David Steel, called for a merger of his party with the SDP, immediately after the 1987 general election, Owen resigned the leadership and persuaded a minority of members to join him in a breakaway, reconstituted, SDP, but the party was dissolved in 1990. He retired from politics in 1991; the following year he was appointed co-chairman with Cyrus R Vance of the international peace conference on the former Yugoslavia, and he was made a life peer. 📖 *Time to Declare* (1992)

Owen, John c.1560–1622
Welsh epigrammatist

Born in Llanarmon, Pwllheli, he was educated at Winchester, and became a jurist Fellow at New College, Oxford, in 1584. He was later employed as a schoolmaster at Trelleck, Gwent, and in 1595 became headmaster of Warwick school. He published 10 books of *Epigrammata*, written in Latin, between 1606 and 1613. His epigrams were bestsellers in their day, and particularly popular on the Continent.

Owen, Sir Richard 1804–92
English zoologist and palaeontologist

Born in Lancaster, he studied medicine at Edinburgh and at St Bartholomew's Hospital, London, and became curator at the Royal College of Surgeons. In 1856 he was appointed superintendent of the natural history department of the British Museum and was instrumental in the establishment of the separate British Museum (Natural History), now the Natural History Museum, becoming its first director in 1881. He was the most prestigious zoologist of Victorian England and published 400 scientific papers as well as a number of important books, including *British Fossil Mammals and Birds* (1846), *A History of British Fossil Reptiles* (1849–84) and an influential essay on *Parthenogenesis*. He named and reconstructed numerous celebrated fossils, including the giant moa bird *Dinornis*, the dinosaur *Iguanodon*, and the earliest bird, the *Archaeopteryx*. He coined the term 'dinosaur' ('terrible lizard'). He studied in detail the homologies between apparently dissimilar structures in organisms and drew the crucial distinction between homologous and analogous organs. However, he remained implacably opposed to evolution; for him, homologies were variants on a divine plan or 'archetype', not evidence of common descent. Owen accepted a knighthood in 1884, having previously declined the honour in 1842.

Owen, Robert See panel p1410

Owen, Robert Dale 1801–77
US social reformer

Born in Glasgow, Scotland, he was the son of Robert Owen. In 1825 he accompanied his father to the USA to help set up the New Harmony colony in Indiana. He taught in the school there and edited the *New Harmony Gazette*. In 1829 he moved to New York City, where he edited the *Free Inquirer*. He returned to Indiana in 1832 and became a member of the Indiana legislature, and entered congress in 1843. He was US ambassador to India (1855–58). An advocate of emancipation of slaves, he became a spiritualist. He wrote *The Policy of Emancipation* (1863) and *The Wrong Slavery* (1864), and an autobiography, *Threading My Way* (1874).

Owen, Wilfred 1893–1918
English poet

Born near Oswestry, Shropshire, he was educated at the Birkenhead Institute and at Shrewsbury Technical School, and worked as a pupil-teacher at Wyle Cop School. In 1913 he left England to teach English in Bordeaux at the Berlitz School of Languages. During World War I he suffered concussion and trench fever and was sent to recuperate near Edinburgh, where he met Siegfried Sassoon, who helped him improve his poems. Posted back to France, he was killed in action a week before the Armistice was signed. Only five of his poems were published while he was alive. His work was first collected in 1920 by Sassoon, reappearing in 1931 with a memoir by Edmund Blunden, and *The Collected Poems* was published in 1963. His poetry expresses a horror of the cruelty and waste of war and individual poems such as

Owen, Robert 1771–1858
Welsh social and educational reformer

Robert Owen was born in Newtown, Montgomeryshire, the son of a saddler. At the age of 10 he was put into a draper's shop at Stamford, and by 19 had risen to be manager of a cotton mill in Manchester. In 1799 he married Anne Caroline, eldest daughter of **David Dale**, and bought from him the cotton-mills and manufacturing village Dale had established with **Richard Arkwright** at New Lanark in Scotland. Here he established a model community with improved housing and working conditions, and built an Institute for the Formation of Character, a school (including the world's first day-nursery and playground, and also evening classes) and a village store, the cradle of the co-operative movement. In 1813 he formed New Lanark into a new company with **Jeremy Bentham** and others.

In *A New View of Society* (1813) he argued that character was formed by the social environment, and went on to found several co-operative Owenite communities, including one at New Harmony in Indiana (1825–28), but they were unsuccessful. In 1825 he ceased to be manager at New Lanark after disagreements with his partners, and

in 1828 sold all his shares, after which the place went into obscurity. He organized the Grand National Consolidated Trades Union in 1833, and spent the rest of his life campaigning for various causes, including (later) spiritualism. He also wrote *Revolution in Mind and Practice* (1849). He died in his home town of Newtown.

Vigorous conservation and restoration work at New Lanark Village since the formation of the New Lanark Conservation Trust in 1973 has made it a living community again. It received a grant from the European Regional Development Fund in 1986, and was awarded a Europa Nostra Medal of Honour in 1988.

📖 Owen published a memoir, *The Life of Robert Owen Written by Himself*, in 1857. See also J Butt (ed), *Robert Owen, Prince of Cotton Spinners* (1971); G D H Cole, *Life of Robert Owen* (1930).

'All the world is queer save thee and me, and even thou art a little queer.' Attributed words said to his partner W Allen when they ended their business relationship.

'Dulce et Decorum Est' and 'Anthem for doomed Youth' have shaped the attitude of many. 📖 D S R Welland, *Wilfred Owen* (1960)

Owens, Jesse James Cleveland 1913–80
US athlete

He was born in Danville, Alabama. While competing for the Ohio State University team in 1935, he set three world records and equalled another (all within the space of an hour), including the long jump (26ft 8in), which lasted for 25 years. At the 1936 Olympics in Berlin he won four gold medals (100m, 200m, long jump, and 4 × 100m relay) which caused the German Nazi leader, **Adolf Hitler**, to leave the stadium, apparently to avoid having to congratulate a black non-Aryan athlete. Back in the USA, Owens gained no recognition for his feat and was reduced to running 'freak' races against horses and dogs. Later he held an executive position with the Illinois Athletic Commission, and attended the 1956 Olympics as President **Dwight Eisenhower**'s personal representative. In 1976 he was awarded the Presidential Medal of Freedom. He is considered the greatest sprinter of his generation. 📖 William J Baker, *Jesse Owens: An American Life* (1986)

Oxenstjerna or Oxenstern, Count Axel Gustafsson 1583–1654
Swedish statesman

Born near Uppsala into one of Sweden's great families, he entered royal service in 1605 and helped to achieve the smooth accession of **Gustav II Adolf** in 1611. From 1612 he was Gustav's chancellor, and showed outstanding administrative and diplomatic ability, negotiating favourable peace treaties with Denmark (1613), Russia (1617) and Poland (1629). During the Thirty Years War (1618–48) he governed Sweden when Gustav was absent on military expeditions, supporting the war effort despite his attempts to prevent the king from entering the war. After the king's death in 1632 he became director of the Protestant League (1633). He was regent for Queen **Kristina** (1636–44), and continued to exercise authority in policy-making after she came of age.

Oz, Amos 1939–
Israeli Hebrew-language writer

He was born in Jerusalem, and went to live in a kibbutz at the age of 14, where he taught in the school and wrote. His novels, which deal with historical and contemporary

themes of guilt and persecution, include *Makom aher* (1966, Eng trans *Elsewhere, Perhaps*, 1973), the collection *Har ha-etsah ha-raah* (1976, Eng trans *The Hill of Evil Counsel*, 1978) and *Menuhah nekhonah* (1984, Eng trans *A Perfect Peace*, 1985). *Mikha'el sheli* (1972, Eng trans *My Michael*, 1972), described by the *New York Times* as 'a modern Israeli *Madame Bovary*', is the book by which he is best known. *Kufsah shehorah* (Eng trans *Black Box*, 1988) appeared in 1988. His work has been widely translated (a process in which he has collaborated), and he has won many awards. In 1987 he became the writer-in-residence at Boston University.

Özal, Turgut 1927–93
Turkish politician

Born in Malatya and educated at Istanbul Technical University, he entered government service and in 1967 became Under-Secretary for State Planning. From 1971 he worked for the World Bank and in 1979 joined the office of prime minister **Bülent Ecevit**. In 1980 he was deputy to Prime Minister **Bülent Ulusu**, within the military regime of Kenan Evren. When political pluralism returned in 1983, Özal founded the Islamic, right-of-centre Motherland Party (ANAP) and led it to a narrow but clear victory in the elections of that year. In the 1987 general election he retained his majority, and in 1989 became Turkey's first civilian president for 30 years. He sought to secure Turkey's admission as a member of the European Union and to improve his country's reputation for human rights abuses. In the 1991 Gulf War, despite strong domestic criticism, he allowed Turkish bases to be used by the US air force in mounting attacks on Iraq and the occupation forces in Kuwait.

Ozawa, Ichiro 1942–
Japanese politician

Born in Iwate prefecture and educated at Keio University, he was elected a Liberal Democratic Party (LDP) member of the Japanese parliament (Diet) in 1969, following in his father's footsteps. He was Home Affairs Minister in 1985–87. He took over as Secretary-General of the LDP in 1989 and was subsequently its president until 1995. He formed and was first leader of the opposition New Frontier Party (Shinshinto) in 1995, outside the coalition government.

Ozawa, Seiji 1935–
US conductor

Born of Japanese parents in Manchuria, he studied piano in Tokyo and turned to composing and conducting after breaking both his index fingers in a rugby game. After further musical training in Paris and Berlin, he was appointed director of the Toronto Symphony (1965–69). The first Japanese conductor prominent in the West, he settled in the USA and served as director of the San Francisco Symphony (1970–76) and the Boston Symphony Orchestra (1973–).

Ozbeck, Rifat 1954–
Turkish fashion designer

Born in Istanbul, he began to study architecture at Liverpool University but, without completing the course, moved to St Martin's School of Art in London. Beginning with small collections, he now has a multimillion pound business and enjoys international acclaim, which has twice gained him the title of Designer of the Year (1989 and 1992). His vivid collections embrace myriad styles and display cross-cultural references.

Ozenfant, Amédée 1886–1966
French artist

Born in St Quentin, he was the leader of the Purist movement in Paris and published a manifesto of Purism with **Le Corbusier** in 1919. From 1921 to 1925 they published an avant-garde magazine, *Esprit nouveau*. They also collaborated in writing *Après le Cubisme* (1918, 'After Cubism') and *La Peinture moderne* (1925, 'Modern Painting'). Ozenfant's still lifes based on this theory reduce vases and jugs to a static counterpoint of two-dimensional shapes. He founded art schools in London

(1935) and New York City (1938); his publications include *Art* (1928) and his diaries for the years 1931–34.

Ozick, Cynthia 1928–
US novelist and short-story writer

Born in New York City, she was educated at New York University and Ohio State University. She has said she began her first novel, *Trust* (1966), an American writer and ended it six and a half years later a Jewish one. Powerfully and originally expressing the Jewish ethos, her slight but significant œuvre includes *The Pagan Rabbi and Other Stories* (1971), *Bloodshed* (1976), *Levitation* (1982), *The Cannibal Galaxy* (1983) and *The Messiah of Stockholm* (1987). She has also written lucid essays on life and literature, collected in volumes such as *Art and Ardor* (1983) and *Fame and Folly* (1996). ▢ J Lowin, *Cynthia Ozick* (1988)

Ozu, Yasujiro 1903–63
Japanese film director

Born in Tokyo, he was an inveterate cinema-goer as a youngster, joined the industry as an assistant cameraman, became an assistant director and made his directorial debut with *Gakuso O Idete* (1925, 'Out of College'). Adept at many popular genres, from comedies to thrillers, he began to specialize from the 1930s in 'home drama'. A precise and rigorous cinematic stylist, his films offered gentle, compassionate portraits of everyday family life laced with humour and, latterly, underlying tragedy. A prolific filmmaker, his most widely-seen work was made in the 1950s and includes *Ochazuke No Aji* (1952, *The Flavour of Green Tea Over Rice*), *Tokyo Monogatari* (1953, *Tokyo Story*) and *Ohayo* (1959, *Good Morning!*).

Paasikivi, Juo Kusti 1870–1956
Finnish statesman

He was born in Tampere. He became Conservative Prime Minister after the civil war in 1918. He recognized the need for friendly relations with the USSR, and took part in all Finnish–Soviet negotiations. He sought to avoid war in September 1939, conducted the armistice negotiations and became Prime Minister again in 1944. He succeeded Carl Mannerheim as President (1946–56).

Pabst, G(eorg) W(ilhelm)
1895–1967
German film director

Born in Raudnitz, Bohemia, Austro-Hungary, he began directing in 1923, and developed a darkly realistic, almost documentary style in *Die Liebe der Jeanne Ney* (1927, 'The Love of Jeanne Ney'). Other works, all examples of New Realism, include *Westfront 1918* (1930), *Kameradschaft* (1931, 'Comradeship'), and he recreated the last days of Hitler in *Der Letzte Akt* (1955, 'The Last Act').

Pacheco, Francisco 1564–1654
Spanish painter

Born in Seville, he was influenced by Raphael, painted portraits and historical subjects, and opened a school of art at Seville, where Velazquez was his pupil and became his son-in-law. He wrote a notable technical treatise, *Arte de la pintura* (1639).

Pachelbel, Johann c.1653–1706
German composer and organist

Born in Nuremberg, he held a variety of organist's posts before, in 1695, he returned to Nuremberg as organist of St Sebalds' Church. His works, which include six suites for two violins, and organ fugues, greatly influenced J S Bach.

Pacher, Michael c.1435–1498
Austrian painter and wood-carver

Born in the Tyrol, he was one of the earliest artists to import Italian Renaissance ideas into northern Europe. His paintings show the influence of Italian artists, especially the Paduan painter Andrea Mantegna, in their convincing foreshortening and perspective. Most of his work is still in the parish churches for which it was commissioned, including his high altar for the church of St Wolfgang on the Abersee (1481), depicting the life of the Virgin Mary and the legend of St Wolfgang.

Pa Chin See Ba Jin

Pachmann, Vladimir de 1848–1933
Russian pianist

Born in Odessa, he studied at Vienna, and became well known as an interpreter of Chopin. He was considered rather eccentric, sometimes talking to the audience as he played.

Pachomius, St 4th century AD
Egyptian hermit

Born probably in Upper Egypt, he superseded the system of solitary reclusive life by founding (c.318AD), the first monastery on the island of Tabenna on the Nile, with its properly regulated communal life and rule. He founded ten other monasteries, including two convents for women.

Pacino, Al(fred James) 1940–
US film actor

Born in East Harlem, New York City, he studied at the High School of Performing Arts and the Actors Studio, going on to win an Obie award for *The Indian Wants The*

Bronx (1966) and a Tony for *Does a Tiger Wear a Necktie?* (1969). He made his film debut in *Me, Natalie* (1969) and received the first of his numerous Academy Award nominations for *The Godfather* (1972). Drawn to characters on an emotional knife-edge, he has made appearances in films like *Serpico* (1973), *The Godfather Part II* (1974), *Dog Day Afternoon* (1975) and *Scarface* (1983). Absent from the screen after the failure of *Revolution* (1985), he returned in the thriller *Sea of Love* (1989) and has shown himself more at one with his fame, starring in such films as *Frankie and Johnny* (1991), *Glengarry Glen Ross* (1992), *Heat* (1995) and *Donnie Brasco* (1997). He finally won a Best Actor Academy Award for *Scent of a Woman* (1993) and made his directorial debut with *Looking for Richard* (1996). He has frequently returned to the stage.

Packer, Sir (Douglas) Frank Hewson 1906–74
Australian newspaper proprietor

He was born in Sydney and was educated at the Church of England Grammar School there. The son of Robert Clyde Packer (1879–1934), founder of *Smith's Weekly*, he became a cadet reporter on his father's *Daily Guardian* in 1923. He established the magazine *Australian Women's Weekly* in 1933, the success of which led to the formation of the Australian Consolidated Press group, which owned the (Sydney) *Daily Telegraph* (sold to Rupert Murdoch in 1972) and *The Bulletin* magazine, as well as television and radio interests. In 1962 and 1970 his racing yachts *Gretel I* and *Gretel II* unsuccessfully contested the America's Cup.

Packer, Kerry Francis Bullmore 1937–
Australian media proprietor

Born in Sydney, he was educated at Cranbrook School, Sydney, and Geelong Grammar School. He inherited the Australian Consolidated Press (ACP) group from his father, Sir Frank Packer. Packer created 'World Series Cricket' in the 1977–78 season, contracting the leading Test cricketers for a knock-out series of one-day matches and 'Super-Tests', played in colourful costume and often under floodlights, sole television rights for which were held by ACP's Channel Nine. This led to disputes with the Australian Cricket Board and other national cricket bodies, and provoked many legal battles, before a *modus operandi* was established. He sold his television *Channel Nine* to Alan Bond in 1987 for $1 billion (Australian) and bought it back three years later for $200 million when Bond's financial dealings collapsed. He successfully bought into, and then out of, the *Sydney Morning Herald* takeover consortium, Westpac Bank and Australian National Industries. He was made a Companion of the Order of Australia in 1983.

Paderewski, Ignacy Jan 1860–1941
Polish pianist, composer, and patriot

He was born in Kurylowka, Podolia. Beginning to play as a child of three, he studied in Warsaw, becoming a professor in the Warsaw Conservatory (1878), and a virtuoso pianist, appearing throughout Europe and the USA. During World War I he used his popularity abroad to argue the case, particularly in the USA, for Poland regaining its independence, and in 1919 he became for a time Prime Minister of Poland in order to establish a sense of political unity. But he soon retired from politics, lived in Switzerland, and resumed concert work. He was elected President of Poland's provisional parliament in Paris in 1940, though poor health prevented him pursuing an active role. 📖 Charlotte Kellogg, *Paderewski* (1956)

Padilla, Juan de 1490–1521
Spanish rebel

A leading noble of Toledo, he was commandant of Saragossa under **Charles V**. As a principal leader of the Revolt of the Comuneros (1520), he headed an insurrection against intolerable taxation, but was eventually defeated at the Battle of Villalar in 1521 and beheaded. His wife Maria (d.1531) held Toledo against the royal forces from 1521 to 1522, and then fled to Portugal.

Padmore, George 1902–59
Trinidadian international revolutionary and Pan-Africanist

He spent most of his life campaigning against colonialism in Africa and preaching African socialism and unity; his memory is revered in West Africa.

Páez, José Antonio 1790–1873
Venezuelan revolutionary and political leader

He was born near Aricagua, Venezuela, at the edge of the great plains. During the War of Independence he was chief Venezuelan commander under **Simón Bolívar**, winning victories that forced the withdrawal of the Spanish. When Venezuela separated from Colombia in 1830, he became its first President (1831), and he remained in control until 1846. He was a moderate dictator until his imprisonment (1847–50) and exile (1850–58), but when he returned to rule Venezuela again (1861–63) he was severely repressive.

Paganini, Niccolò 1782–1840
Italian violinist

Born in Genoa, he gave his first concert in 1793 (when his father reduced his age by two years in advertisements) and began touring professionally in Italy in 1805. He later visited Austria, Germany, Paris and London (1828–31), where his dexterity and technical expertise acquired him an almost legendary reputation. He revolutionized violin technique, among his innovations being the use of stopped harmonics. He published six concertos and (1820) the celebrated *24 Capricci*. 📖 L Day, *Paganini of Genoa* (1929)

Page, Sir Frederick Handley 1885–1962
English aircraft designer

Born in Cheltenham, Gloucestershire, he founded the first British aircraft manufacturing firm, Handley-Page Ltd in 1909. His 0/400 (1915) was the first twin-engined bomber, and saw service in World War I, and his Hampden and Halifax bombers were used in World War II. His civil aircraft include the Hannibal, Hermes and Herald transports. He was knighted in 1942.

Page, Geraldine 1924–87
US stage and screen actress

Born in Missouri and trained at the Goodman Theatre Dramatic School, Chicago, she made her New York debut in 1945, but it was not until her success in **Tennessee Williams**'s *Summer and Smoke* (1952) that she became established there. Credited with great versatility and sensitivity, her notable roles include Alexandra del Lago in Williams's *Sweet Bird of Youth* (1959) and Mother Miriam Ruth in *Agnes of God* (1982). She acted in many films, and won an Academy Award in 1985 for *The Trip To Bountiful*.

Page, Thomas Nelson 1853–1922
US novelist and diplomat

Born in Hanover County, Virginia, he practised law in Richmond, and wrote many stories, some in Negro dialect, the best of which are *Marse Chan* (1884) and *Ole Virginia* (1887). He was US Ambassador to Italy from 1913 to 1919. 📖 H Holman, *The Literary Career of Page, 1884–1910* (1978)

Pagels, Elaine 1943–
US theologian

As Professor of Religion at Princeton University and a former teacher at the California Institute for Integral Studies, which specializes in the comparative study of the religious traditions of East and West, Pagels is a recognized authority on the early Christian sect, the Gnostics. *The Gnostic Gospels* (1979) is a scholarly introduction to its ancient texts and in *The Gnostic Paul* (1992) she examines historical sources, including the Nag Hammadi documents, and challenges the assumption that the Pauline letters were written to counter Gnosticism. Her other works include *Adam and Eve and the Serpent* (1988) and *The Origin of Satan* (1995).

Paget, Sir James 1814–99
English physician and pathologist

Born in Great Yarmouth, Norfolk, he studied at St Bartholomew's Hospital, London, where he became full surgeon in 1861. One of the founders of modern pathology, he discovered the cause of trichinosis, and described 'Paget's disease' (an early indication of breast cancer) and 'Paget's disease of bone' (osteitis deformans, a bone inflammation). He published his *Lectures on Surgical Pathology* and *Clinical Lectures* in 1853. 📖 S Roberts, *James Paget: The Rise of Clinical Surgery* (1989)

Paglia, Camille 1947–
US academic, essay writer and media personality

Born in Endicott, New York, of Italian parentage, she studied at Yale before becoming a teacher at Bennington College (1972–80). She then lectured at Wesleyan University and Yale and became an assistant professor at the Philadelphia College of Performing Arts (now called the University of the Arts) in 1987. Remaining there, she was appointed associate professor (1987) then Professor of Humanities (1991). She has become renowned both for her powerful intellect, and for her attempt not only to pour scorn on modern feminism, but also to promote her theory of women as the powerful sex whose destiny is neither to serve nor to demean men, but to rule them. Her publications include *Sexual Personae: Art and Decadence from Nefertiti to Emily Dickinson* (1990), *Sex, Art, and American Culture: Essays* (1992) and *Vamps and Tramps* (1995).

Pagnol, Marcel 1895–1974
French dramatist, filmmaker and scriptwriter

He was born near Marseilles. His childhood in Provence informs his best work, the play trilogy *Marius* (1929, filmed 1931), *Fanny* (1931, filmed 1932) and *César* (1936, filmed two years earlier), each part being a comedy of Marseilles life. He first became widely known with the memoir *Topaze* (1928), a satirical study of bourgeois bad faith, which was filmed five years later by Louis Gasneur. Provence and its warmth, both literal and human, is at the centre of *La Gloire de mon père* (1957, filmed 1990, *My Father's Glory*) and his other memoirs. The film *Jean de Florette* (1986), also set in Provence, was based on one of his stories, as was its sequel *Manon des Sources* (1986, based on *L'eau des collines*). In turn, both stories were based on Pagnol's own earlier film, *Manon des Sources* (1952). He became a member of the Académie Française in 1946, the first filmmaker to be so honoured.

Pahlavi, Muhammad Reza 1919–80
Shah of Iran

He succeeded on the abdication of his father, **Reza Shah Pahlavi**, in 1941. His first two marriages, to Princess Fawzia, sister of **Farouk I**, and to Soraya Esfandiari, ended in divorce after the failure of either to produce a male heir. By his third wife Farah Diba, daughter of an army officer, he had two sons, Crown Prince Reza (1960–), Ali Reza (1966–), and two daughters, Princess Farahnaz (1963–) and Princess Leila (1970–). He had a daughter, Princess Shahnaz (1940–) from his first marriage. His reign was for many years marked by social reforms and a movement away from the old-fashioned despotic concept of the monarchy. Ambitious five-year plans (1963–72) enhanced agricultural and industrial development and increased literacy. Nationalization of the western oil consortium (1973) boosted export revenue as oil prices increased. But in the later 1970s the economic situation deteriorated, social inequalities worsened, and protest at western-style 'decadence' grew among the religious fundamentalists. After several attempts at parliamentary reform the shah, having lost control of the situation, left the country (1979), after which a revolutionary government was formed under Ayatollah **Khomeini**. The ex-shah having been admitted to the USA for medical treatment, the Iranian government seized the US embassy in Teheran and held many of its staff hostage for over a year, demanding his return to Iran. He made his final residence in Egypt at the invitation of President **Sādāt** and died there. ⌑ Ryszard Kapuscinski, *Shah of Shahs* (1985)

Pahlavi or Pahlevi, Reza Shah 1877–1944
Shah of Persia (Iran)

He was an Iranian army officer who led a successful coup in 1921. After serving as premier (1923–25), he deposed the last Kajar ruler and declared himself shah. He sought to modernize Iran, improving transportation and communications and emancipating women. He was forced to abdicate when British and Russian troops occupied the country in 1941, and was succeeded by his son, **Muhammad Reza Pahlavi**.

Paige, Elaine 1951–
English actress and singer

Born in Barnet, London, she joined the West End cast of *Hair* in 1969, but it was her performances in *Jesus Christ Superstar* (1972) and *Billy* (1974) that established her as an actress in musicals. She appeared at Chichester Festival Theatre and at Stratford East before she became a star as *Evita* (1978). In 1981 she played in *Cats*, followed by *Chess* (1986) and *Anything Goes* (1989–).

Paine, Tom (Thomas) 1737–1809
English radical political writer

He was born in Thetford, Norfolk, the son of a Quaker smallholder and corset-maker. He worked from the age of 13 as a corset-maker, then became a sailor and a schoolmaster. In 1771 he became an exciseman, but was dismissed as an agitator after fighting for an increase in pay. In London he met **Benjamin Franklin**, who in 1774 helped him to emigrate to America, where he settled in Philadelphia as a radical journalist. After the outbreak of the American Revolution (1775–83) he published a pamphlet, *Common Sense* (1776), which outlined the background to the war and urged immediate independence. He served in the continental army, and issued a series of pamphlets, *The American Crisis* (1776–83), urging the colonial cause, and became secretary to the Congress committee on foreign affairs (1777–79). He went to France in 1781, and published *Dissertations on Government* in 1786. He returned to England in 1787, where he published *The Rights of Man* (1791–92), a reply to **Edmund Burke**'s *Reflections on the French Revolution* (1790). In it he supported both the French Revolution and an overthrow of the British monarchy. He was indicted for treason, but escaped to Paris, was made a French citizen and became a member of the National Convention as the Deputy for Pas-de-Calais (1792–93). A supporter of the Girondins, he opposed the execution of the king, thus falling foul of **Robespierre**, who had his French citizenship rescinded and arrested him on the charge of being an enemy Englishman (1793–94). After the Terror, he was released on the plea that he was a US citizen. Just before his arrest he published Part I of his powerful attack on accepted religion, *The Age of Reason* (1794; Part II, written in prison,

was published in 1796), alienating most of his friends, including **George Washington**. Following his release he remained in Paris, but in 1802 he returned to the USA, where he was ostracized as an atheist and a freethinker. He died, alone and in poverty, on the farm at New Rochelle which the state of New York had once given him. His influence lay not in his originality of thought but in his passion and directness, which, if only very occasionally, cut through the elegance and intricacy of Burke, and cause it to look a little disingenuous. His defences of democracy have always been extremely persuasive. ⌑ R R Fennessey, *Burke, Paine and the Rights of Man* (1963); H Pearson, *Tom Paine, Friend of Mankind* (1937)

Painter, William ?1540–1594
English translator

He studied at Cambridge, was Master of Sevenoaks school, but in 1561 became clerk of ordnance in the Tower of London. His *Palace of Pleasure* (1566–67), composed largely of stories from **Giovanni Boccaccio**, **Matteo Bandello**, and **Margaret of Angoulême**, became popular, and was a major source for many dramatists, including **Shakespeare**.

Paish, Frank Walter 1898–1988
English economist

He was educated at Winchester and at Trinity College, Cambridge. Appointed lecturer at the London School of Economics in 1932, and Reader in 1938, he was Professor of Economics (with special reference to business finance) from 1949 until his retirement in 1965. In the 1960s he advocated an inbuilt level of 'therapeutic' unemployment (around 2½ per cent) as a government policy to keep inflation in check, and attacked the validity of incomes policy as an instrument of economic control. He published several books on his economic principles, in particular *Studies in an Inflationary Economy* (1962) and *The Rise and Fall of Incomes Policy* (1969).

Paisiello, Giovanni 1740–1816
Italian composer

Born in Taranto, he studied at Naples, writing at first only church music. Turning successfully to opera, he was court musician to Empress **Catherine II** at St Petersburg (1776–84). In 1799 he was appointed director of National Music by the republican government of France and later enjoyed the patronage of **Napoleon I**. He returned to Naples in 1804. He was the most successful Neapolitan opera composer of his time, and his *Barbiere di Siviglia* (1782, 'The Barber of Seville') was so popular that **Rossini**'s use of the same libretto met with considerable hostility. His 90-odd pieces are seldom staged today, possibly because of their comparative superficiality, though they contain many delightful tunes, one of which, *Nel cor più non mi sento*, was used by both **Beethoven** and **Paganini** as a theme for variations.

Paisley, Bob 1919–96
English football coach and manager

Born in Hetton-le-Hole, he is celebrated as perhaps the most successful club manager in British football history. After serving in the army in the desert campaigns of World War II, he joined Liverpool Football Club and won a championship medal in 1947. After his playing career finished, he was one of Liverpool's coaching staff for 20 years before succeeding Anfield legend **Bill Shankly** as manager. Under Paisley, Liverpool won the League championship six times, the European Cup thrice, the UEFA Cup once and also won three League Cups. Only the FA Cup eluded him. Loyal, quiet and determined, Paisley was also admired for remaining unspoiled by his extraordinary achievements and success.

Paisley, Ian Richard Kyle 1926–
Northern Ireland clergyman and politician, founder of the Free Presbyterian Church of Ulster

Born in Ballymena, and educated at South Wales Bible College and the Reformed Presbyterian Theological College, Belfast, he was ordained by his Baptist minister father in 1946 and founded his own denomination, the Free Presbyterian Church of Ulster, in 1951. In 1969 he entered the Northern Ireland parliament as Protestant Unionist MP for Bannside, becoming leader of the Opposition in 1972. He co-founded the Democratic Unionist Party, and since 1970 has been MP for Antrim North in the House of Commons and leader of the Democratic Unionists there, though he resigned briefly in protest at the Anglo-Irish Agreement. As a member of the European Parliament since 1979, he staged a well-publicized one-man protest there against the choice of the pope as a guest speaker in 1988. The Province's most vociferous opponent of Irish unification, he is the object of fanatical devotion from Ulster loyalists and participated in the all-party peace process of 1995–96 only with deeply held misgivings. His publications include *The Massacre of Bartholomew* (1974), *America's debt to Ulster Kidd* (1982) and *Those Flaming Tennents* (1983). 📖 Patrick Marrinan, *Paisley, Man of Wrath* (1973)

Paki, Lydia Kamakaeha See Liliuokalani

Pal, Bipin Chandra 1858–1932
Indian nationalist and freedom fighter

Though born into an orthodox Zamindar family in Sylhet (in Bangladesh), he opposed traditional orthodoxy and religious practices. He entered politics in 1877 and his association with the great reformist Brahma Samâj leader, Keshub Chunder Sen, drew him into this movement in 1880. He was also greatly influenced by Bal Gangadhar Tilak, Lala Lajpat Rai (with whom he formed the famous Congress trio 'Lal, Pal and Bal') and Aurobindo. In 1898 he went to England on a scholarship for theological studies and, on his return, launched a weekly journal, *Young India* (1902), through which he championed the cause of Indian freedom. He campaigned for the boycott of British goods and also advocated a policy of passive resistance and non-co-operation. He spent the years between 1908 and 1911 in England, where he worked for India's freedom and published *Swaraj*. In the later stages of the freedom movement, he withdrew from political life, although he continued to write on national matters.

Palach, Jan 1948–69
Czechoslovak philosophy student

As a protest against the August 1968 invasion of Czechoslovakia by the Warsaw Pact forces, he set fire to himself in Wenceslas Square, Prague, on 16 January 1969. After his death five days later he became a hero and symbol of hope, and was mourned by thousands. In 1989 there were huge popular demonstrations in Prague to mark the 20th anniversary of his death.

Palacký, František 1798–1876
Czech historian

A leading light in the Czech national revival, he argued the case before and during the 1848–49 revolutionary outburst in the Habsburg Empire for the restoration of Czech autonomy. Subsequently, and particularly after the Ausgleich of 1867 recognized the equality of Hungary alongside Austria, he became more radical in looking towards eventual independence. His mammoth *History of Bohemia* (1836–67) established the historical case for the burgeoning national movement.

Palade, George Emil 1912–
US cell biologist and Nobel Prize winner

Born in Iassy, Romania, he trained as a doctor in Bucharest and became Professor of Anatomy there, until he emigrated to the USA in 1946. He worked at the Rockefeller Institute, New York (1946–72), and from 1972 headed cell biology at Yale Medical School. Since 1990 he has been Professor of Cellular and Molecular Biology at the University of California, San Diego. In the 1950s Palade developed a method of separating cell components, known as 'cell fractionation'. He identified these components as the mitochondria, the endoplasmic reticulum, the Golgi apparatus and the ribosomes, and showed that protein synthesis occurs on strands of RNA in the ribosomes. For his work in cell biology he shared the 1974 Nobel Prize for physiology or medicine with Albert Claude and Christian de Duve.

Palestrina, Giovanni Pierluigi da c.1525–1594
Italian composer

Born in Palestrina, he learned composition and organ playing in Rome, and in 1544 he became organist and maestro di canto at the cathedral of St Agapit, Palestrina. He was master of the Julian choir at St Peter's, for which he composed many fine masses from 1551, the first of many important appointments. His works include over 100 masses and a large number of motets, hymns and other liturgical pieces, as well as madrigals. His compositions, unsentimental yet intense, show great skill in the handling of contrapuntal texture, but also contain examples of homophony and subtle dissonances which are extremely effective chorally. Having in its original form no division into bars, his music is free-flowing and unhampered by rhythmic conventions. His place as the most distinguished composer of the Renaissance remains unchallenged, and many generations of later composers, including J S Bach, Mozart, Richard Wagner, Franz Liszt and Debussy, have acknowledged their debt to him. 📖 Henry Coates, *Palestrina* (1938)

Paley, Grace, *née* Goodside 1922–
US short-story writer

Born in New York City, she was educated at Hunter College, New York, and has taught in several US colleges. Her fiction, usually set in New York, and often with Jewish settings and themes, has all been in the short-story form. Her talent for convincingly realistic dialogue is evident in all her stories. *Little Disturbances of Man* (1959) and *Enormous Changes at the Last Minute* (1974) share a common wit, compassion, and characteristic tone of voice. Her support of the peace movement is evident in *Later the Same Day* (1985), as well as in the non-fiction *365 Reasons Not to Have Another War* (1989). Other writings include *Begin Again: New and Collected Poems* (1992), and an essay collection, *Long Walks and Intimate Talks* (1991).

Paley, William 1743–1805
English theologian

Born in Peterborough, Cambridgeshire, he was Fellow and Tutor of Christ's College, Cambridge (1768–76), and became Archdeacon of Carlisle (1782) and Subdean of Lincoln (1795). He published *Principles of Moral and Political Philosophy* (1785), expounding a form of utilitarianism. In 1790 he published his most original work, *Horae Paulinae*, the aim of which is to prove the improbability of the hypothesis that the New Testament is a cunningly devised fable. It was followed in 1794 by his famous *Evidences of Christianity*. In 1802 he published perhaps the most widely popular of all his works, *Natural Theology, or Evidences of the Existence and Attributes of the Deity*.

Palgrave, Francis Turner 1824–97
English poet and critic

Born in Great Yarmouth, Norfolk, he was the eldest son of the historian Sir Francis Palgrave (1788–1861). He became a scholar of Balliol College, Oxford, and Fellow of Exeter College, was successively vice-principal of a training college, private secretary to George Leveson-Gower (Earl Granville), an official in the education department, and Professor of Poetry at Oxford (1886–95). His works include *Idylls and Songs* (1854), *Essays on Art* (1866), *Visions of England* (1881) and *Landscape in Poetry* (1897), but he is best known as the editor of the *Golden Treasury of Lyrical Poetry* (1875), *Sonnets and Songs of Shakespeare* (1877), selections from **Robert Herrick** (1877) and **Keats** (1885), and *Treasury of Sacred Song* (1889). 𝄞 R H Palgrave, in *Collected Works* (1919–22)

Palin, Michael Edward 1943–
English actor and writer

Born in Sheffield and educated at Oxford, he wrote for television shows such as *The Frost Report* (1966–67), *Do Not Adjust Your Set* (1967–69) and *Marty* (1968–69), before joining the innovative *Monty Python's Flying Circus* (1969–74). He appeared with fellow members of the group in such films as *Monty Python and the Holy Grail* (1975) and *Monty Python's Life of Brian* (1977–79) and has been among the most successful of the team with a wide variety of solo ventures that include the comedy show *Ripping Yarns* (1976–80), children's novels such as *Small Harry and the Toothache Pills* (1981) and *The Cyril Stories* (1986), and the globetrotting television documentary series *Around the World in 80 Days* (1989) and *Pole to Pole* (1992). His most memorable film appearances include *A Private Function* (1984), *A Fish Called Wanda* (1988), *American Friends* (1991) and *Fierce Creatures* (1996). He won further acclaim for a rare dramatic role in the television series *G.B.H.* (1991).

Palissy, Bernard c.1509–1589
French potter

Born in Agen, he became a glass-painter, then he settled in Saintes and devoted 16 years to experimentation on how to make enamels. From 1557 his ware, with its high relief plants and animals coloured to represent nature, made him famous. He was imprisoned as a Huguenot in 1562, but in 1564 was taken into royal favour and he established his workshop at the Tuileries, and was exempted from the St Bartholomew's Day massacre (1572). From 1575 to 1584 he lectured on natural history, physics and agriculture. In 1588 he was again arrested as a Huguenot and was thrown into the Bastille of Bucy, where he died.

Palladio, Andrea, *originally* Andrea di Pietro della Gondola 1508–80
Italian architect

He was born in Vicenza, and trained as a stonemason. He developed a modern Italian architectural style based on classical Roman principles, unlike the ornamentation of the Renaissance. This Palladian style was widely imitated all over Europe, in particular by **Inigo Jones** and **Christopher Wren**. Palladio started by remodelling the basilica in Vicenza, and extended his style to villas and palaces and churches, especially in Venice (San Giorgio Maggiore). His *Quattro Libri dell' Architettura* (1570, Eng trans *The Four Books of Architecture*, 1715) greatly influenced his successors. 𝄞 James J Ackerman, *Palladio* (2nd edn, 1979)

Palladius, Rutilius Taurus Aemilianus
4th century AD
Roman writer

He was the author of *De Re Rustica* ('On Agriculture'), in 14 books.

Pallas, Peter Simon 1741–1811
German naturalist

Born in Berlin, he studied medicine at the universities of Halle, Göttingen and Leyden, but his interests always tended towards natural history. He classified the Zoophytorum, the corals and sponges, and his comparative anatomical methods laid the foundation for modern taxonomy. He published *Miscellania Zoologica* (1766) and *Spicilegia Zoologica* (1767 onwards) and was elected FRS in 1763. Pallas was invited to St Petersburg by Empress **Catherine II, the Great**, as professor at the Academy of Sciences, and spent six years (1768–74) exploring the Russian interior. On his return he wrote on the geography, ethnography, geology, flora and fauna of the regions he had visited. His interest was not merely to catalogue specimens, as his observations led him to examine the relationships between the animals and their environment, so that he became the first zoogeographer. His major contribution was probably to geology, as he was the first to propose a modern view of the formation of mountain ranges. He made another expedition in 1793–94, subsequently remained in Russia, and wrote *Zoographica Russo-Asiatica* (3 vols, 1811–31).

Palma, Jacopo, *called* Palma Vecchio ('Old Palma') c.1480–1528
Italian painter of the Venetian school

He is particularly remembered for the ample blonde women who appear in many of his works. His pictures are sacred subjects or portrait groups; his brother's grandson, Jacopo (1544–1628), called Il Giovane (the Younger), was a prolific painter of poorish religious pictures in a style influenced by **Tintoretto** and late **Titian**.

Palma, Ricardo 1883–1919
Major Peruvian writer

He invented a new and unique genre, the *tradición,* based on some single fact or folk belief, expanded upon into an essay-fiction of some thousand words. His *Tradiciones peruanas* were collected in 1957, and a good selection from them was translated in 1945 as *The Knights of the Cape*. Palma was an ultra-critical lover of his country and its ways, and these ironic, racy, colloquial pieces cover almost every aspect of its life—and often anticipate events which have taken place since his death. He was director of the National Library. He wrote much else besides the *tradiciones*, including important books on Peruvian Spanish. His son, Clemente Palma (1872–1946), was also a writer. 𝄞 J M Oviedo, *Ricardo Palma* (1968, in Spanish); E M Aldrich, *The Modern Short Story in Peru* (1966)

Palme, (Sven) Olof 1927–86
Swedish politician

Born in Stockholm, he was educated in the USA at Kenyon College, and studied law at Stockholm University. He joined the Social Democratic Labour Party (SAP) in 1949 and became leader of its youth movement in 1955. After election to the Riksdag in 1956, he entered the government in 1963 and held several ministerial posts before assuming the leadership of the party, and becoming Prime Minister, in 1969. Although he lost his parliamentary majority in 1971, he managed to carry out major constitutional reforms, but was defeated in 1976 over taxation proposals to fund the welfare system. He was returned to power, heading a minority government, in 1982, and was re-elected in 1985, but was shot and killed in the centre of Stockholm while walking home with his wife after a visit to a cinema.

Palmen, Erik Herbert 1898–1985
Finnish meteorologist

Born in Vaasa, he was educated in both astronomy and meteorology at Helsinki University and joined the Marine Research Institute in Helsinki (1922), where he studied the effect of wind stress on water level changes and on the formation of water layers in the oceans. He was director there from 1939 to 1947. Interested in atmospheric dynamics, Palmen was one of the first to discover the jet stream and to realize that it is virtually a global phenomenon. His investigations led to original studies on how energy is converted from potential to kinetic energy in the atmosphere. He worked with **Carl-Gustaf Rossby** at the University of Chicago (1946–48) and later moved to the University of California at Los Angeles (1953–54). He later showed that tropical cyclones can only develop if the ocean temperature and the thermal structure of the atmosphere meet certain criteria, and worked out a satisfactory energy budget for the whole atmosphere.

Palmer, Arnold 1929–
US golfer

Born in Youngstown, Pennsylvania, he was one of the postwar golfing stars whose powerful, attacking golf introduced the game to millions throughout the world. He turned professional in 1955 after a brilliant amateur career, but won only eight Majors: the US Amateur (1954), US Masters (1958, 1960, 1962, 1964), US Open (1960) and the Open championship (1961, 1962). He was twice captain of the American Ryder Cup team. His participation in the Open is seen as being responsible for reviving Europe's only Major. 'Arnie's Army', as his fans became known, flocked to see him play and his back-to-back victories inspired his fellow Americans to travel and compete on the seaside courses of Great Britain. As a mark of his stature, fully 30 years after his prime, at the age of 66, he could command endorsements of $14 million dollars. ☐ James T Olsen, *Arnold Palmer* (1974)

Palmer, Daniel David 1845–1913
US osteopath and founder of chiropractic medicine

Born in Toronto, he was a self-educated businessman who took up 'magnetic healing' and evolved the theory that disease results from the pressure of misaligned skeletal structures on nerves in the spinal cord and elsewhere in the body. He settled at Davenport, Iowa, in 1895 and founded the Palmer School of Chiropractic in 1898. He also established a college of chiropractic in Portland, Oregon.

Palmer, Geoffrey Winston Russell 1942–
New Zealand politician

He was born in Nelson, South Island, and graduated from Victoria University, Wellington, becoming Professor of New Zealand Law and English there in 1974. He taught there and in the USA before going into politics, entering the House of Representatives in 1979 as Labour MP for Christchurch. By 1984 he had become Attorney-General and Deputy Prime Minister and in 1989, when Prime Minister **David Lange** resigned, he succeeded him but resigned one year later.

Palmer, Roundell See **Selborne, 1st Earl of**

Palmer, Samuel 1805–81
English landscape painter and etcher

Born in London, he produced mainly watercolours in a mystical style derived from his friend **William Blake** (eg *Repose of the Holy Family*, 1824). From 1826 to 1835 he lived in Shoreham, Kent, where he was surrounded by a group of friends who called themselves 'The Ancients'. Palmer later visited Italy and began producing more academic, conventional work in a completely different style. He was thereafter forgotten until the Neo-Romantics—**Graham Sutherland**, **John Minton** and **Paul Nash**—rediscovered him during World War II, seeing in his work something essentially English but with overtones of Surrealism.

Palmerston, Henry John Temple, 3rd Viscount 1784–1865
English statesman

He was born in Westminster, of the Irish branch of the ancient English family of Temple. He was educated at Edinburgh (1800) and Cambridge (1803–06) universities. In 1802 he succeeded his father as viscount and was elected MP in 1807 for Newport (Wight). He represented Edinburgh from 1811 for 20 years, but lost his seat when he supported the Reform Bill. Afterwards he was returned for South Hampshire, lost his seat in 1835, but found a seat for Tiverton. He was junior Lord of the Admiralty and Secretary at War under **Spencer Perceval**, the Earl of **Liverpool**, George Canning, Frederick Ripon and the Duke of **Wellington** (1809–28). His official connection with the Tory Party ceased in 1828 and he entered the Foreign Office in Earl **Grey**'s Whig government in 1830. With England and France acting in concert, Palmerston took a leading part in securing the independence of Belgium, establishing the thrones of Maria of Portugal and **Isabella II** of Spain, and endeavouring, in alliance with both Austria and Turkey, to check Russian influence in the East. In 1841 Palmerston and the Whigs lost office on the question of free trade in corn, and under Lord **John Russell** in 1846 he again became Foreign Minister. The Spanish marriages (see **François Guizot**), the revolutions in 1848, the rupture between Spain and Great Britain, the affair of Don Pacifico (a Gibraltar Jew living in Athens, who claimed the privileges of a British subject), and the consequent quarrel with Greece, combined with his self-assertive character, brusque speech, and interferences in foreign affairs, made him a controversial figure. He became known as 'Firebrand Palmerston' and a vote of censure on him was carried in the House of Lords (1850), but it was defeated in the House of Commons. In December 1851 Palmerston expressed to the French ambassador his approbation of the coup d'état of Louis-Napoleon (**Napoleon III**), without consulting either the premier or the queen, and Russell advised his resignation. He shattered the Russell administration soon after on a militia bill, refused office under the Earl of **Derby**, but was Home Secretary in the Earl of **Aberdeen**'s coalition (1852), whose fall (1855) brought him the premiership. Defeated in 1857 on **Richard Cobden**'s motion condemning the Chinese war, he appealed to the country, and met the House of Commons with a greatly increased majority, but fell in February 1858 over the Conspiracy Bill. In June 1859 he again became Prime Minister, remaining in office till his death. The chief events of his premiership were the American Civil War, Napoleon III's war with Austria, and the Austro-Prussian war with Denmark. It was his ambition to be the minister of a nation rather than of a political party, and his opponents admitted that he held office with more general acceptance than any minister since William Pitt, the Elder (1st Earl of **Chatham**). ☐ Jasper Ridley, *Lord Palmerston* (1970)

Palmiter, Richard de Forest 1942–
US molecular geneticist

Born in Poughkeepsie, New York, he was educated at Duke University and Stanford University, performed postdoctoral research at Stanford, at Searle Roche Laboratories in the UK and at Harvard University, and then joined the University of Washington, where he was made Professor of Biochemistry in 1981. Since 1976 he has also held the post of investigator at the Howard Hughes Medical Institute, Seattle, receiving the George Thorn Award there in 1982. Palmiter produced the first transgenic mice by injecting the human growth hormone gene into a mouse embryo and reintroducing the embryo into the mother's uterus. Such mice were found to be significantly larger than normal, indicating that the human growth hormone gene had been active. This technique has now been used for a variety of mammalian genes and is a vital tool in the investigation of the mechanisms which control gene expression.

Paludan-Müller, Frederick 1809–76
Danish poet

He wrote poems, dramas and romances, including the verse novel *Danserinden* (1833, 'The Dancer'). He became famous with *Adam Homo* (1841–49), a humorous, satiric, didactic epic about the worldly sin and moral decline of a successful man. ▢ S Møller Kristensen, *Digtning og livssyn* (1959)

Panaetius c.185–c.110BC
Greek Stoic philosopher
Born on the island of Rhodes, he taught in Athens and Rome, and became head of the Stoa in Athens in 129BC. His writings are now lost but he was an important figure in the popularization of Stoicism in Rome. He was a friend of Scipio Aemilianus, the Younger, and his ethical and political works were an important source for Cicero's influential treatise *De Officiis*.

Pan Chao See Ban Zhao

Pancras, St d.304AD
Greek Christian
Born in Phrygia of Greek parents, he was baptized in Rome, but was killed in the Diocletian persecutions while still a child. One of the patron saints of children, his feast day is 12 May.

Pander, Christian Heinrich 1794–1865
German anatomist
Born in Riga, Russia (now in Latvia), he studied at Dorpat University, and subsequently at the universities of Berlin, Göttingen and Würzburg. He researched embryo development in the egg, demonstrating the embryonic layers named after him. He spent much time travelling, in 1820 acting as a naturalist on a Russian mission to Bokhara, and in 1826 was elected a member of the St Petersburg Academy of Sciences. He was a crucial figure in modern embryology.

Pandit See Nehru, Jawaharlal

Pandit, Vijaya Lakshmi, *née* Swarup Kumari Nehru 1900–
Indian politician and diplomat
Born in Allahabad, the sister of Jawaharlal Nehru, she was educated privately. She entered Government service in 1935 and was Local Government and Health Minister (1937–39), and as a member of the Opposition was imprisoned in 1940 and 1941 for her nationalist campaigns. Leader of the Indian United Nations delegation (1946–48, 1952–53), she also held several ambassadorial posts (1947–51). She became the first woman President of the UN General Assembly in 1953, and then Indian High Commissioner in London (1954–61). She returned to parliament in 1964. In 1977 she opposed her niece Indira Gandhi's authoritarian policies and successfully campaigned against her party, for which she was reportedly never forgiven. She wrote *The Evolution of India* (1958), and her memoirs, *The Scope of Happiness*, were published in 1979.

Pandulf, Cardinal d.1226
Italian prelate
Born in Rome, he was the commissioner sent by Innocent III to King John of England after his excommunication to receive his submission (1213). He returned to England as papal legate (1218–21), was made Bishop of Norwich in 1218, and exercised great authority during the minority of Henry III (1299–1321).

Paneth, Friedrich Adolf 1887–1958
Austrian chemist
Born in Vienna, he studied at Munich, Glasgow and Vienna, and taught at Hamburg, Berlin and Königsberg, before moving to England in 1933. He worked at Imperial College, London, and Durham University, where he was appointed Professor of Chemistry (1939). In 1953 he returned to Germany and the directorship of the Max Planck Institute. With George von Hevesy he developed the concept of radioactive tracers (1912–13) and from the

1920s used them to establish the age of rocks and meteorites by their helium content, and to detect novel metal hydrides and short-lived free radicals.

Panhard, René 1841–1908
French engineer and inventor, a pioneer of the motor industry
He was born in Paris and studied at the École Centrale des Arts et Manufactures. With Émile Levassor, his partner from 1886, he was the first person to mount an internal-combustion engine on a chassis (1891). He founded the Panhard Company.

Panini 5th–7th century BC
Indian grammarian
He was the author of the *Astadhyayi* ('Eight Lectures'), a grammar of Sanskrit comprising 4,000 aphoristic statements which provide the rules of word formation and, to a lesser extent, sentence structure. His work has been reckoned by many to be the finest grammar ever written, but it is composed in a very condensed style and has required extensive commentary. It forms the basis of all later Sanskrit grammars.

Panizzi, Sir Anthony 1797–1879
Italian bibliographer
Born in Brescello in Modena, he was an advocate by training. He fled to Liverpool after the 1821 revolution, and in 1828 became Professor of Italian at University College London. He was appointed assistant librarian (1831), and later chief librarian (1856–66), of the British Museum, where he showed great administrative ability, undertook a new catalogue, and designed the famous Reading Room.

Pankhurst family See panel p1419

Pan Ku See Ban Gu

Pannenberg, Wolfhart 1928–
German Lutheran theologian
He was born in Stettin (now Poland), and became Professor of Systematic Theology at Wuppertal, Mainz, then Munich (1968–). His best-known work is *Jesus—God and Man* (1964, Eng trans 1968), which opposes Rudolf Bultmann's programme of demythologization with the claim that revelation and history *are* significant theological categories and that the resurrection of Jesus is the pivot on which everything turns. His other works, including *Basic Questions in Theology* (3 vols, 1970–73), *Theology and the Philosophy of Science* (1976) and *Anthropology in Theological Perspective* (1985), defend the place of reason in theology. He has also written on ethics, spirituality, the Church and secularization. Later works are *Metaphysics and the Idea of God* (1990) and *Systematic Theology* (1991).

Panofsky, Erwin 1892–1968
US art historian
Born in Hanover, Germany, he was classically educated in Berlin and at the universities of Munich, Berlin and Freiburg (Baden), where he took his doctorate in 1914. He taught at Hamburg (1926–33) and, from 1935, was professor at the Institute for Advanced Study at Princeton. He set new standards for the study of the meaning of works of art (iconology). His many books include seminal studies of Dürer, Titian and early Netherlandish painting, as well as his *Studies in Iconology* (1939) and *Meaning in the Visual Arts* (1955).

Panov, Valeri Matveyevich 1938–
Soviet dancer
Born in Vitebsk, he trained in Leningrad (now St Petersburg), and made his debut with the Maly Theatre Ballet in 1957, later moving to the Kirov (1964–72). There his reputation as a virtuoso performer grew as he created roles in both classical works and new ballets like *Gorianka*

The Pankhursts
English suffragettes

Pankhurst, Emmeline, *née* Goulden
1857–1928

Emmeline Pankhurst was born in Manchester. In 1879 she married Richard Marsden Pankhurst (d.1898), a radical Manchester barrister who had been the author of the first women's suffrage Bill in Britain and of the 1870 and 1882 Married Women's Property Acts.

In 1889 she founded the Women's Franchise League, and in 1903, with her daughter **Christabel Pankhurst**, the Women's Social and Political Union (WSPU), which fought for women's suffrage with extreme militancy. In 1894 she won the right for married women to vote in local elections, though not for Westminster offices. She was frequently imprisoned and underwent hunger strikes and forcible feeding. She later joined the Conservative Party. Her 40-year campaign reached a peak of success shortly before her death, when the Representation of the People Act of 1928 was finally passed, establishing voting equality for men and women. She wrote her autobiography in *My Own Story* (1914).

She had three daughters: **Christabel**, **Sylvia** and **Adela**.

Pankhurst, Christabel Harriette
1880–1958

Christabel was the eldest daughter of Emmeline Pankhurst. The militant campaigning that Christabel undertook with **Annie Kenney** in 1905 resulted in their arrest, and stimulated a wave of militant action throughout the country with large-scale imprisonment and forcible feeding of suffragettes. She encouraged such tactics until 1914, when her efforts were channelled into meetings and tours in support of World War I. With the end of the war in 1918 and the granting of the vote to women over the age of 30, Christabel turned to preaching on Christ's Second Coming.

▣ She edited *The Suffragette* from 1912 to 1920, and wrote her political memoirs, *Unshackled: The Story of How We Won the Vote* (1959), at the very end of her life.

Pankhurst, (Estelle) Sylvia 1882–1960

Sylvia was the second daughter of Emmeline Pankhurst. Scholarships enabled her to study at both the Manchester Municipal School of Art and the Royal College of Art in London; at the same time she worked in London's East End for the WSPU. However, her relations with the union deteriorated, and in 1913 she left the East End branch. A year later, her objections to involvement in World War I stood in sharp contrast to the support of Emmeline and Christabel.

▣ An irrepressible campaigner, she wrote extensively advocating not only woman suffrage but also Ethiopian independence, socialism, and international and domestic issues. Her works include *The Suffragette Movement* (1931) and *Ethiopia: A Cultural History* (1955).

Pankhurst, Adela Constantia 1885–1961

Adela was the youngest daughter of Emmeline Pankhurst. She too became involved in the movement for woman suffrage, but disagreements with her mother prompted her to sail for Australia. There she helped direct the socialist-feminist movement with **Vida Goldstein** of the Women's Political Association.

With the outbreak of World War I Adela threw herself into the anti-conscription campaign, holding talks and writing such polemics as *Put up the Sword!* (1915). In 1916 she travelled to New Zealand, where she married Tom Walsh, a militant socialist, joined the Victorian Socialist Party as an organizer, and took up a number of causes, including support for an alliance with Japan. This she renounced after the attack on Pearl Harbor, but was nonetheless interned. After the death of her husband in 1943, she took on work as a nurse for retarded children.

▣ B Castle, *Sylvia and Christabel Pankhurst* (1987); L Hoy, *Emmeline Pankhurst* (1985); R Pankhurst, *Sylvia Pankhurst: Artist and Crusader* (1979); D Mitchell, *The Fighting Pankhursts* (1967).

'Women had always fought for men, and for their children. Now they were ready to fight for their own human rights.' Emmeline Pankhurst, *My Own Story*, Ch.3.

'How long you women have been trying for the vote. For my part, I mean to get it.' Childhood remark of Christabel Pankhurst c.1890, quoted by her mother in *My Own Story* (1914), Ch.2.

(1968) by Vinogradov, *Hamlet* (1970) by Sergeyev and *Land of Miracles* (1967) by Iacobson. He became known internationally when he was refused emigration papers by the Soviet authorities, who eventually allowed him to resettle in Israel in 1974. From that time he made guest appearances with companies around the world. His choreography includes *Le Sacre du printemps* (1978, 'The Rite of Spring'), *The Idiot* (1979, for Berlin Opera Ballet) and *Cinderella* (1977). Since 1992 he has been artistic director of Bonn Ballet.

Panufnik, Sir Andrej 1914–94
British composer and conductor

Born in Warsaw of Polish origins, he had a father who made instruments and a mother who was a professional violinist. They sent him to the Warsaw Conservatory to study conducting and at the age of 23 he went to work with **Felix Weingartner** in Vienna. Panufnik returned to Poland at the start of World War II and worked with the underground movement there until 1945. For a few years he conducted in Kraków and Warsaw, but his hatred of the Communist regime forced him to leave Poland. He settled in the UK and became a naturalized British citizen in 1961. He conducted the City of Birmingham Symphony Orchestra (1957–59) but spent more and more time composing. During the Warsaw Uprising in 1944 all his early compositions were destroyed, but later he wrote many colourful and involving works, including the *Sinfonia Rustica* (1948, revised 1955) and the *Sinfonia Sacra* (1963). He was knighted in 1991. ▣ *Composing Myself* (1987)

Paoli, Pasquale de 1725–1807
Corsican patriot

Born in Stretta, he returned from exile in 1755 to take part in the struggle against the island's Genoese overlords. After Corsica's purchase by the French in 1768 he led a renewed rebellion, but was defeated and fled to England. With the French Revolution he was made Governor of Corsica. However, he again grew dissatisfied with French rule and then launched an insurrection against the Convention. This too failed and in 1796 he went to live in exile in England.

Paolo, Fra See **Sarpi, Pietro**

Paolozzi, Sir Eduardo Luigi 1924–
Scottish sculptor and printmaker

Born in Leith, Edinburgh, of Italian parentage, he studied at Edinburgh College of Art and at the Slade School in London. He has held many teaching posts (in London,

Hamburg and California, among other places). His first one-man show was at the Mayor Gallery, London, in 1947, and he has held many since, including those at the Museum of Modern Art, New York (1964) and the Tate Gallery, London (1971). His early collages were inspired by Surrealism, and his use of magazine cuttings in works such as *I Was a Rich Man's Plaything* (1947, Tate Gallery) made him a pioneer of Pop Art. In the 1960s he made large sculptures in brightly-painted metal, for example *The City of the Circle and the Square* (1963, Tate Gallery), and acrylic. Other works incorporate waste material, such as oil cans. From the late 1970s he received public commissions, as for the Tottenham Court Road Underground mosaics (exhibited at the Royal Academy in 1986). In 1984 he was elected to the committee of the Architectural Association and in 1985 his exhibition 'Lost Magic Kingdoms' at the Museum of Mankind in London gave a personal and unconventional view of ethnography. Since 1989 he has been Visiting Fellow at the Royal College of Art.

Papadopoulos, Georgios 1919–96
Greek soldier and politician

Born in Eleochorion, Achaia, he underwent army training in the Middle East and fought in Albania against the Italians before the German occupation of Greece in World War II. He was a member of the resistance during the occupation. In 1967 he led a coup against the government of King Constantine II and established a virtual military dictatorship. In 1973, following the abolition of the monarchy, he became President under a new republican constitution, but before the year was out he was himself ousted in another military coup. In 1974 he was arrested, tried for high treason and convicted, but his death sentence was commuted.

Papagos, Alexandros 1883–1956
Greek field marshal and politician

After a brilliant military career he was made Minister of War in 1935 and Chief of Staff the following year. In 1940, as Commander-in-Chief, he repelled the Italian attack on Greece, but was less successful against a German attack in April 1941, when he was captured. After his release at the end of World War II, he led the campaign in Greece against the communist guerrillas. In 1951 he resigned as Commander-in-Chief in order to concentrate on a political role. He formed a new political party, the Greek Rally, and was Prime Minister of an exclusively Greek Rally government from 1952 until his death in 1955.

Papandreou, Andreas George 1919–96
Greek politician

The son of George Papandreou, he was born on the island of Chios and educated at Athens University Law School, Columbia and Harvard. He became a US citizen in 1944 and served for two years in the US navy, but returned to Greece as director of the Centre for Economic Research in Athens (1961–64) and economic adviser to the Bank of Greece, and resumed his Greek citizenship. His political activities led to imprisonment and exile after the military coup led by Georgios Papadopoulos in 1967. He returned to Greece in 1974 and threw himself wholeheartedly into Greek national politics, founding the Pan-Hellenic Liberation Movement, which later became PASOK (the Pan-Hellenic Socialist Movement). He was leader of the Opposition from 1977, critical of the US bases in Greece and of the economic policy of Konstantinos Karamanlis. In 1981 he became Greece's first socialist Prime Minister. During his ministry inflation was reduced, and Greece benefited from its membership of the EEC. Re-elected in 1985, in 1988 a heart operation and his association with a young former air stewardess (whom he married following his divorce), created speculation and scandal, and PASOK was defeated. He was

brought to trial on corruption charges but cleared in 1992, and his party was returned to power in 1993. He was in poor health throughout his last premiership.

Papandreou, George 1888–1968
Greek politician

Born in Salonika, he became a lawyer and moved into politics in the early 1920s. The monarchy had been temporarily removed (1923) and reinstated by the army (1925) but Papandreou, a left-of-centre republican, held office in several administrations including the brief period when the monarchy was temporarily removed (1923–25) and in the following decade. In 1942 he escaped from Greece during the German occupation and returned in 1944 to head a coalition government, but, suspected by the army because of his socialist credentials, remained in office for only a few weeks. He remained an important political figure, founding the Centre Union Party in 1961, and returning as Prime Minister (1963, 1964–65). A disagreement with the young king Constantine II in 1965 led to his resignation, and in 1967, when a coup established a military regime, he was placed under house arrest. His son, Andreas Papandreou, then carried forward his political beliefs.

Papanek, Victor 1925–
US designer, teacher and writer

Born in Vienna, he has worked in many parts of the world including developing countries, where he has specialized in design appropriate to local materials and to the local level of technology, and on programmes to further such countries' interests. In the western world he has demonstrated particular concern for the handicapped. In the book for which he is best known, *Design for the Real World* (1971), he questioned the designer's role, and encouraged a sense of his responsibility towards humankind as a whole, and to ecological considerations, rather than simply to the interests of western commercial economies.

Papanicolaou, George Nicholas 1883–1962
US physiologist and microscopic anatomist, developer of the 'pap smear'

Born in Kimi, Greece, he received his MD from Athens University (1904) and a PhD from Munich University (1910). He moved to the USA in 1913, becoming assistant in pathology at the New York Hospital and, in 1914, assistant in anatomy at Cornell Medical College. All his research was conducted at these two institutions until 1961, when he was appointed director of the Miami Cancer Institute, although he died three months later. He became Professor of Clinical Anatomy at Cornell in 1924 and was Emeritus Professor from 1949. His research on reproductive physiology led him to the discovery that the cells lining the wall of the guinea pig vagina change with the oestrus cycle. Similar changes take place in women, but more importantly, he noticed that he could identify cancer cells from scrapings from the cervixes of women with cervical cancer. He subsequently pioneered the techniques, now known as the 'pap smear', of microscopical examination of exfoliated cells for the early detection of cervical and other forms of cancer.

Papen, Franz von 1879–1969
German politician

Born in Werl, Westphalia, he was military attaché in Mexico and Washington, Chief of Staff with a Turkish army, and took to centre party politics. As Chancellor to Paul Hindenburg in 1932 he suppressed the Prussian socialist government, and as Hitler's Vice-Chancellor (1933–34) he signed a concordat with Rome. He was ambassador to Austria (1936–38) and Turkey (1939–44) and was taken prisoner in 1945. He stood trial at Nuremberg in 1946 but was acquitted.

Papin, Denis 1647–c.1712
French scientist
Born in Blois, he studied medicine at the University of Angers, and by 1673 was in Paris assisting **Christiaan Huygens** in experiments with the new air-pump. He went to London in 1675 where he collaborated in similar investigations with **Robert Boyle** (1676–79), creating the 'steam digester' (a prototype pressure cooker). In 1681 he moved to Venice, where he lived and demonstrated experiments for three years, before returning to London in 1684 as Royal Society curator of experiments, meanwhile continuing his investigations in hydraulics and pneumatics. He settled in Marburg as Professor of Mathematics from 1687, and in about 1690 made a working model of an atmospheric condensing steam engine on principles later developed by **Thomas Newcomen** and **James Watt**.

Papineau, Louis Joseph 1789–1871
French–Canadian politician
Born in Montreal, he was Speaker of the House of Assembly for Lower Canada (1815–37). He opposed the union with Upper Canada, and agitated against the imperial government. At the rebellion of 1837 a warrant was issued against him for high treason. He escaped to Paris, but returned to Canada, amnestied, in 1847.

Papinianus, Aemilius c.140AD–212AD
Roman jurist
A distinguished thinker and praetorian prefect, he held offices at Rome under **Lucius Septimius Severus**, but was put to death by **Caracalla**. Nearly 600 excerpts from his legal works were incorporated in **Justinian I**'s *Pandects*.

Papp, Joseph, *originally* Yosl Papirofsky 1921–91
US stage director and producer
Born in Brooklyn, New York City, he studied acting and directing in Hollywood under the GI Bill, then returned to New York and founded the Shakespeare Workshop at the Emanuel Presbyterian Church on the Lower East Side (1952). They started performing free shows during the summer in Central Park (1954), which became the New York Shakespeare Festival (1960). A permanent open-air theatre, the Delacorte, was built in the Park for the company in 1962. In 1967 Papp founded the Public Theater, an off-Broadway house that staged classics as well as new works such as *Hair* (1967) and *A Chorus Line* (1975). He was director of the theatres at the Lincoln Center (1973–78).

Pappus of Alexandria 4th century AD
Greek mathematician
He wrote a mathematical *Collection* covering a wide range of geometrical problems, some of which contributed to the development of modern projective geometry. The work was of great importance for the historical understanding of Greek mathematics, covering the curves of a circle, the generalization of **Pythagoras**'s theorem to triangles that are not right-angled, and offering commentaries on **Euclid**'s *Elements* and **Ptolemy**'s *Almagest*.

Paracelsus, *real name* Philippus Aureolus Theophrastus Bombastus von Hohenheim 1493–1541
German alchemist and physician
He was born in Einsieden, Switzerland. His name referred to the celebrated Roman physician **Celsus** and meant 'beyond' or 'better than' Celsus. He is said to have graduated in Vienna and taken his doctorate in Ferrara. He then spent many years exploring Europe, Russia and the Middle East, studying contemporary medical practice and the medical lore of the common people. In 1526 he was appointed town physician in Basle and lecturer in chemistry at the university. He raged against medical malpractices and the fashion for patent medicines, criticized both the Catholic Church and the new Lutheran doctrines, and taught in German, not Latin, which displeased the authorities who preferred learning to be kept from the populace. Having antagonized all the vested interests in the town, he had to flee (1528), and spent most of the rest of his life as an itinerant preacher and physician. However, his work became enormously influential, particularly through the emphasis he laid on observation and experiment and the need to assist—rather than hinder—natural processes. He stated that diseases had external causes and that every disease had its own characteristics, thus reversing the traditional view that disease was generated within the patient and followed an unpredictable course. He undertook careful studies of tuberculosis and silicosis, recognized that there was a connection between goitre and the minerals in drinking water and was the first to recognize congenital syphilis. He discovered many techniques which became standard laboratory practice, such as concentrating alcohol by freezing it out of its solution, and prepared drugs with due regard to their purity and advocated carefully measured doses, both important steps forward in medicine. 📖 A Stoddart, *The Life of Paracelsus, Theophrastus von Hohenheim* (1911)

Parc, Julio Le See **Le Parc, Julio**

Pardee, Arthur Beck 1921–
US biochemist
Born in Chicago, he trained and worked at the University of California, Berkeley (1942–61), spending time at the California Institute of Technology (Caltech, 1943), the University of Wisconsin (1947–49) and the Pasteur Institute, Paris (1957–58), before becoming professor at Princeton University (1961–67). Since 1975 he has been Professor of Pharmacology at Harvard. After early work on biological oxidation, tumour metabolism and antibody reactions, he became interested in how cells control their own synthetic processes. He also discovered feedback control of amino acid synthesis, and his study of DNA led him to examine a range of specific inhibitors which regulate biochemical processes. From around 1980 Pardee investigated the effects of serum peptides, including insulin-like growth factor, and the ubiquitin system (1984).

Pardo Bazán, Emilia, Condesa de 1851–1921
Spanish writer
She was born in La Coruña, Spain, of an aristocratic Galician family and later settled in Madrid. She was strongly influenced by the French naturalist writers, and this can be seen in her first novel, *Pascual Lopez* (1879). Her best-known books in this genre are *Los Pazos de Ulloa* (1886, 'The Manors of Ulloa') and *La Madre Naturaleza* (1887,'Mother Nature'), both set in the rural decadence of her native Galicia. Later novels such as *La Quimera* (1905, 'The Chimera') and *La Sirena Negra* (1908, 'The Black Mermaid') are unmistakably modernist in atmosphere and psychology. Latterly she came under the influence of fin de siècle spiritualism and adopted more idealistic values. Besides her novels she published over 500 short stories, as well as poems, travel writing, and critical works on **Émile Zola** and naturalism, the revolution in Russia, and modern French literature. She ran a library for women and was the first Spanish woman of note to sustain a feminist campaign. 📖 M Hemingway, *Emilia Pardo Bazán: The Making of a Novelist* (1983)

Paré, Ambroise c.1510–1590
French surgeon, 'the father of modern surgery'
He was born near Laval. In 1537 he joined the army as a surgeon, and became surgeon to **Henri II**, **Charles IX** and **Henri III**. He improved the treatment of gunshot wounds, and substituted ligature of the arteries for cauterization

with a red-hot iron after amputation. His *Cinq Livres de chirurgie* (1562) and other writings exercised a great influence on surgery.

Parer, Damien 1912–44
Australian news photographer

Born in Malvern, Victoria, he trained for the priesthood, but instead developed an interest in cinematography and worked with the pioneer film director Charles Chauvel on *Heritage* (1933) and the epic *Forty Thousand Horsemen* (1940). He became an official cameraman with the 2nd Australian Imperial Forces in 1940 and went with the first troops to the Middle East, filming the action at the Siege of Tobruk, later working in Greece and Syria, and in New Guinea. He shot a number of documentary films of battle, and *Kokoda Front* (1942) was the first Australian film to win an Academy Award. In 1943 he joined the US troops for the liberation of the Pacific and was killed while filming their landing at Peleliu, Caroline Islands.

Pareto, Vilfredo 1848–1923
Italian economist and sociologist

Born in Paris, he was Professor of Political Economy at Lausanne from 1893, writing well-known textbooks on the subject in which he demonstrated a mathematical approach. In sociology his *Trattato di sociologica generale* (1916, Eng trans *The Mind and Society*) anticipated some of the principles of Fascism.

Paretsky, Sara 1947–
US crime writer

She was born in Eudora, Kansas and educated at the University of Kansas and the University of Chicago, where she received an MBA and a PhD in history. She worked for a research firm and as a marketing manager for an insurance company, before becoming a full-time writer in 1986. That same year she co-founded Sisters in Crime, an organization devoted to promoting women crime writers. Her novels feature the feisty female detective V I Warshawski (played on screen by Kathleen Turner in 1992), who faces such diverse problems as toxic waste and anti-abortionists. From these situations Paretsky looks at the nature of relationships between women, and at the line between the personal and professional as experienced by her outwardly tough but essentially warm-hearted heroine. Later works include *Burn Marks* (1990), *Guardian Angel* (1992) and *Tunnel Vision* (1995).

Parini, Giuseppe 1729–99
Italian poet

Born near Milan, he became a priest in 1754, and was professor at the Palatine and Brera schools (1769–99). He made his name as a poet by the sequence of poems collectively titled *Il Giorno* (1763–1803, 'The Day'), which satirized the daily round of a young nobleman. 📖 G Petronio, *Parini, storia della critica* (1957)

Paris, Louis Philippe, Comte de 1834–94
French nobleman and pretender to the French throne

He was born in Paris, the grandson of King Louis Philippe, Duc d'Orléans (Égalité). He went into exile in England (1848), served as a captain of volunteers on the staff of General George McClellan in the American Civil War (1861–62), and wrote *Histoire de la guerre civile en Amérique* (1874–89, 'History of the Civil War in America'). He returned to France (1871) and renounced his claim to the throne to the Comte de Chambord, but on his death (1883) he again became head of the Bourbon house. Exiled again by the French republican government in 1886, he retired to England.

Paris, Matthew c.1200–1259
English chronicler

He entered the monastery of St Albans as a Benedictine monk in 1217, and succeeded Roger of Wendover as the abbey chronicler in 1236. He made two journeys to France, and was sent on a mission to Norway on behalf of Pope Innocent IV. His *Chronica Majora* is a revision of the earlier work of Roger of Wendover, with an additional 23 years of his own work, which establishes him as the finest chronicler of the 13th century. He produced an abridged form for the years 1200 to 1250, known as the *Historia Anglorum sive Historia Minor*. He also wrote Lives of abbots, and a book of *Additamenta*.

Park, Maud May, née Wood 1871–1955
US suffrage leader

Born in Boston, Massachusetts, she was educated at Radcliffe College. She joined the Massachusetts Woman Suffrage Association, and was co-founder and leader of Boston Equal Suffrage Association for Good Government. With Inez Hayes Gillmore (Irwin) she founded the College Equal Suffrage League (from 1901), which aimed to involve young women in the fight for equality. An efficient, strong-minded campaigner, she helped to bring about the 19th Amendment (1920), which secured the vote for women. She became first president of the League of Women Voters (LWV) (1920–24), and shortly afterwards head of the Women's Joint Congressional Committee.

Park, Mungo 1771–1806
Scottish explorer

Born in Fowlshiels, in the Scottish Borders, he studied medicine at Edinburgh (1789–91), and through Sir Joseph Banks was made assistant surgeon on the *Worcester* bound for Sumatra (1792). In 1795 his services were accepted by the African Association. After leaving Mandingo at an English factory on the Gambia, he set off inland in December, finally reaching the Niger at Sego in July 1796. He pursued his way westwards along its banks to Bammaku, but fell ill, and was eventually brought back to the factory by a slave trader. Park told his adventures in *Travels in the Interior of Africa* (1799), which at last determined the direction of flow of the Niger. Marrying in 1799, he settled as a surgeon in Peebles, Scotland, but in 1805 undertook another journey to Africa. He started from Pisania on the Gambia, and reached Sansanding in November 1805. Battling against great dangers and difficulties he reached Boussa with four others, but they were attacked by local people, and drowned in the fight. 📖 R Tames, *Mungo Park* (1973)

Park, Nick 1958–
English animator

Born in Lancaster, he started making films in his attic as a teenager, one of which, *Archie's Concrete Nightmare* (1975), was screened on BBC television. A graduate in communication arts at Sheffield, he studied animation at the National Film and Television School. Using painstaking stop-motion techniques and investing his plasticine characters with a rare fluidity and humanity, he made the short film *Creature Comforts* (1989), which won an Academy Award. Created over a period of six years, *A Grand Day Out* (1990) introduced the characters of inventor Wallace and his faithful dog Gromit. Subsequently they appeared in *The Wrong Trousers* (1993) and *A Close Shave* (1995), both of which also won Academy Awards and secured Park an international following.

Park, Robert Ezra 1864–1944
US sociologist

Born in Luzerne County, Pennsylvania, he was educated at the universities of Minnesota and Michigan. From 1887 to 1898 he worked as a newspaper reporter, before he returned to study at Harvard, Strasbourg and Heidelberg universities. He worked as publicity officer from 1905 for the black leader, **Booker T Washington**. He taught at Chicago University (1913–33) and at Fisk University (1936–43). A founder of urban sociology, he also made important contributions to the study of race relations (*Race and Culture*, 1950). He created the Chicago school of sociology, which flourished in the 1920s and 1930s, and which used the participant observation methods that he pioneered.

Park, Ruth c.1923–
Australian writer

Born near Hamilton, New Zealand, and educated at Auckland University, she went to Australia in 1942 and married the author **D'Arcy Niland**. Her first success was in 1947 with the novel *The Harp in the South*, which won a newspaper competition. This story of Sydney slum life has been translated into 10 languages and forms a trilogy with *Poor Man's Orange* (1949) and the retrospective *Missus* (1986). *Swords and Crowns and Rings* (1977) won the **Miles Franklin** award for its sensitive tale of a society outcast. She also wrote some popular children's books based on ABC's series *The Muddle-Headed Wombat*, and novels for adolescent readers, including the two set in Victorian Sydney, *Come Danger, Come Darkness* (1978) and the haunting *Playing Beatie Bow* (1980, filmed 1987). The autobiographical *A Fence Round the Cuckoo* (1992) won Park the Foundation for Australian Literature Studies award. A second volume of autobiography was published in 1993 as *Fishing in the Styx*.

Park Chung-Hee 1917–79
South Korean soldier and politician

He was born in Sangmo-ri, in Kyongsang province, the son of a Buddhist farmer. He fought with the Japanese forces during World War II, but joined the South Korean army in 1946, becoming a major-general by 1961, when he ousted the civilian government of Chang Myon in a bloodless coup. He formed the Democratic Republican Party (DRP) and was elected state President in December 1963. He embarked on a programme of export-led industrial development, based on strategic government planning and financial support, which attained 'miracle' annual growth rates of 10 to 20 per cent during the 1960s and 1970s. However, he ruled in an austere and authoritarian manner, imposing martial law in October 1972 and introducing restrictive 'emergency measures' in May 1975. During a brief economic downturn in October 1979, he was assassinated by the head of the Korean central intelligence service.

Parker, Alan 1944–
English film director

He was born in London and worked as a scriptwriter and on television before making his feature-film debut with the musical gangster pastiche *Bugsy Malone* (1976). This was followed by *Midnight Express* (1978), a brutal account of a young American incarcerated in a Turkish jail, which with its controversially handled subject matter, glossy visuals and overwrought emotions, indicated the type of film Parker favoured and reflected his opposition to social realist traditions. He worked on *Birdy* (1985), *Angel Heart* (1987) and *Mississippi Burning* (1988) before moving into a lighter, more lyrical vein with the sentimental romance *Come See The Paradise* (1990) and the youth musical *The Commitments* (1991). Also a cartoonist and an irreverent critic of the British film establishment, he made the documentary, *A Turnip Head's Guide to the British Cinema*, in 1984. In 1996 he directed *Evita*, starring **Madonna** in the role of **Eva Perón**.

Parker, Bonnie 1911–34
US thief and murderess

Born in Rowena, Texas, she was the partner of **Clyde Barrow**. Despite their popular romantic image, they and their gang were responsible for a number of murders. The pair met in 1932 when Parker was working as a waitress. Shortly after, when Barrow was convicted of theft and sentenced to two years in jail, Parker smuggled a gun to him and he escaped. With their gang, Parker and Barrow continued to rob and murder until they were shot dead at a police roadblock in Louisiana on 23 May 1934. Their end was predicted by Parker in a poem, variously called *The Story of Bonnie and Clyde* and *The Story of Suicide Sal*.

Parker, Charlie See panel p1424

Parker, Dorothy, *née* **Rothschild** 1893–1967
US wit, short-story writer and journalist

She was born in West End, New Jersey, the daughter of a clothes salesman. Her mother died when she was five and her father re-married; Dorothy could barely contain her antipathy to her stepmother and refused to address her. She attended a private parochial school in New York City run by the Sisters of Charity, and Miss Dana's School in Morristown, New Jersey, where the typical girl was 'equipped with a restfully uninquiring mind'. She lasted only a few months and her formal education ended in 1908 at the age of 14. She was a voracious reader and, having read **William Thackeray** when she was 11, decided to make literature her life. In 1916 she sold some of her poetry to the editor of *Vogue*, and was subsequently given an editorial position on the magazine, writing captions for fashion photographs and drawings. She then became drama critic of *Vanity Fair* (1917–20), where she met **Robert Benchley** and **Robert Sherwood** and formed with them the nucleus of the legendary Algonquin Hotel Round Table luncheon group in the 1920s. Famed for her spontaneous wit and acerbic criticism, she has had attributed to her many cruel wisecracks and backhanded compliments. She was at her most trenchant in stories and book reviews in the early issues (1927–33) of the *The New Yorker*, a magazine whose character she did much to form. Her work continued to appear in the magazine at irregular intervals until 1955. Her reviews were collected in *A Month of Saturdays* (1971). She also wrote for *Esquire* and published poems and sketches. Her poems are included in *Not So Deep as a Well* (1930) and *Enough Rope* (1926), which became a bestseller. Her short stories were collected in *Here Lies* (1936). She also collaborated on several film scripts, including *The Little Foxes* and *A Star Is Born*. Her own last play was *Ladies of the Corridor* (1953). Twice married (1917 and 1933), she took her surname from her first husband. Her public persona was not mirrored in her personal life. Both marriages foundered and there was a string of lacerating love affairs, abortive suicide attempts, abortions, debts and drinking bouts. She died alone in a Manhattan apartment with Troy, her poodle, at her side.
📖 J Keats, *You Might As Well Live* (1971)

Parker, Matthew 1504–75
English prelate

Born in Norwich, Norfolk, he became chaplain to Queen **Anne Boleyn** (1535), Master of Corpus Christi College, Cambridge (1544), Vice-Chancellor (1545) and dean of Lincoln. Deprived of his preferments by Queen **Mary I**, he was made Archbishop of Canterbury in 1559 by **Elizabeth I**. He adopted a middle road between Catholic and Puritan extremes, and revised the Thirty-Nine Articles of Anglican doctrine. Parker also made a revised translation of the Scriptures known as 'the Bishops' Bible' (1572), and edited works by **Ælfric**, **Gildas**, **Asser**, **Matthew Paris**, **Thomas Walsingham** and **Giraldus Cambrensis**. He was a keen collector of books, and employed printers, transcribers and engravers. His *De Antiquitate Britannicae*

Parker, Charlie (Charles Christopher), *known as* Bird 1920–55
US alto and tenor saxophonist, bandleader and composer, the most influential performer in post-1940s modern jazz

Charlie Parker was born in Kansas City. He learnt to play baritone horn and alto saxophone while at school, frequenting the clubs and halls where jazz was played, and left school at 14 to practise and find casual work. In 1939 he went to New York, living by menial jobs but working out rhythmic and harmonic ideas which would form the basis of the bebop style. He worked from 1940 to 1942 with the Jay McShann Band, then joined the Earl Hines Band where he began an important musical association with trumpeter **Dizzy Gillespie**, another of the young adherents to the new jazz idiom. Both joined Billy Eckstine's orchestra in 1944, but the following year Parker led the first of his influential bebop quintets, with Gillespie on trumpet.

The harmonic and rhythmic advances of their music were rightly perceived as a major sea-change in jazz. Bebop was seen as a revolutionary style, although in retrospect it can be understood as more an evolution from the work of swing-era giants like **Lester Young**, **Coleman Hawkins** and **Charlie Christian**. His influence was not confined to saxophonists, but spread to players on every instrument. Despite addiction to heroin and alcohol and recurring mental illness, he continued to lead and record with the style-setting small groups of modern jazz, using trumpeters such as **Miles Davis** and Red Rodney, and pianists like Al Haig and Duke Jordan. He made two European tours (1949, 1950), which strengthened the development of modern jazz on the Continent and in Britain.

His style was fully developed by the end of the 1940s, and although he worked with strings for a time in the 1950s, he made no further major changes before his early death, hastened by the abuse of his lifelong addiction. His influence on the development of jazz cannot be overestimated, and many of his compositions, such as 'Now's The Time' and 'Ornithology', have become standard jazz works.

♫ His major recorded works fall into three distinct segments, collected as *The Complete Savoy Sessions* (1944–48), *Charlie Parker On Dial* (1946–47), and *Bird: The Complete Charlie Parker On Verve* (1946–54). Numerous live recordings are also extant, including the legendary *The Complete Dean Benedetti Recordings*, issued in 1990.

📖 Ross Russell's flawed biography *Bird Lives!* (1972) has still to be fully superseded. **Clint Eastwood**'s film *Bird* (1988) presented an entertaining but sanitized version of his life.

> Ross Russell quotes a famous Parker dictum in *Bird Lives!*: 'There is no boundary line to art. Music is your own experience, your thoughts, your wisdom. If you don't live it, it won't come out of your horn'. Sadly, too many musicians took him to mean his lifestyle rather than his musical experience, despite his frequent warnings not to emulate his addiction.

Ecclesiae (1572) is said to be the first privately printed English book. 📖 V J K Brooks, *A Life of Archbishop Parker* (1962)

Parker, Theodore 1810–60
US Unitarian clergyman

Born in Lexington, Massachusetts, he graduated at Harvard in 1836, and settled as Unitarian minister in West Roxbury (now in Boston). The rationalistic views which separated him from the conservative Unitarians were expounded in *A Discourse of Matters Pertaining to Religion* (1841), followed by *Sermons for the Times*. In 1845 he resigned his ministry and became pastor of a new free church, the 28th Congregational Society in Boston. From then on he wrote incessantly. He lectured throughout the USA, and became involved in social causes such as antislavery agitation.

Parkes, Alexander 1813–90
English chemist and inventor

Born in Birmingham, he was noted for his inventions in connection with electroplating, in the course of which he even electroplated a spider's web. He invented xylonite (a form of celluloid), first patented in 1855.

Parkes, Bessie Rayner 1829–1925
English feminist and editor

Born into a Unitarian family, the great-granddaughter of **Joseph Priestley**, she formed a lifelong friendship with **Barbara Bodichon**, with whom she was a founding member of the women's movement. This included supporting the unsuccessful Married Woman's Property Bill. In 1858 Parkes bought the *Englishwoman's Journal*, which she edited with the help of Bodichon, **Emily Faithfull** and Jessie Boucherett, the owner of The Englishwoman's *Review*. The journal became the voice of the woman's movement. In 1867 she married Louis Belloc, a French barrister, and became the mother of the future writers Marie Adelaide Belloc (1868–1947, later Mrs Lowndes) and **Hilaire Belloc**.

Parkes, Sir Harry Smith 1828–85
English diplomat

Born near Walsall, he went to China in 1841, served as consul at Canton, Amoy and Foochow, figured prominently in the *Arrow* episode, and in 1858 was appointed a commissioner after the capture of Canton. His seizure by the Chinese while he was acting as Lord **Elgin**'s envoy in 1860 led to the burning of the Summer Palace in Peking. He was British Minister in China from 1883.

Parkes, Sir Henry 1815–96
Australian politician

He was born near Kenilworth in Warwickshire, England. He fell under the influence of radical politics and, when his business failed, he sailed in 1839 with his first wife to New South Wales, Australia, where he involved himself in politics and contributed to various journals. His ivory shop in Sydney was a focus of radical dissidents, and in 1850 he founded the *Empire* newspaper, which he edited until 1858. By 1854 he had become a member of the New South Wales (NSW) Legislative Council and in the next 40 years he was rarely out of state parliament. He was NSW Colonial Secretary (1866–68), during which time he recruited, with the help of **Florence Nightingale**, the first trained nurses for the Colony. He first became premier of NSW in 1872, a position he was to hold in five ministries for a total of 15 years, despite marital and business troubles. In the late 1880s he saw in the federalist movement an opportunity to move to a larger stage and in 1889 delivered the famous 'Tenterfield Oration' which gave the necessary impetus to federalism. This led in 1891 to a meeting of the Australian colonies, which framed a draft constitution, but Parkes, 'the Father of Australian Federation', died before the establishment of the Commonwealth of Australia, having married three times and fathered 18 children.

Parkin, Sara Lamb 1946–
English environmentalist

Educated in Coventry and at Edinburgh Royal Infirmary, she began her working life as a nurse (1973–79). Her environmental career began when she became International Liaison Secretary for the newly-formed Green Party in 1983. She was co-secretary of European Green Coordination (1985–90) and became environmental spokesperson for the UK Green Party (1990–92). In 1994 she published *The Life and Death of Petra Kelly* about the co-founder of the German Green Party, **Petra Kelly**, and in 1996 she helped to found the Real World coalition of pressure groups.

Parkinson, Cecil Edward Parkinson, Baron
1932–

English Conservative politician

He was born in Carnforth, Lancashire, and educated at the Royal Lancaster Grammar School and Emmanuel College, Cambridge. He joined the Metal Box Company as a management trainee and then qualified as an accountant. His wife introduced him to local Conservative Party politics and in 1970 he entered the House of Commons as MP for Enfield West. He was elected MP for Herts South (1974–83), and Hertsmere in 1983. In 1979 he was made a junior minister at the Department of Trade by **Margaret Thatcher** and, two years later, Chairman of the Conservative Party. He became prominent as a close confidant of the Prime Minister and a member of her inner Cabinet during the Falklands War. After his successful direction of the 1983 general election campaign his political future seemed secure until the publicity about an affair with his former secretary, Sara Keays, which had resulted in her pregnancy, forced his resignation. After a period on the back benches he returned to the Cabinet as Secretary of State for Energy in 1987, and became Secretary of State for Transport in 1989. He surrendered office in the Cabinet reshuffle that followed **John Major**'s election as party leader and his succession to the premiership in 1990. In 1992 he retired from politics and was made a life peer, publishing his autobiography, *Right at the Centre*, the same year.

Parkinson, Cyril Northcote 1909–93

English political scientist, historian and writer

He graduated from Emmanuel College, Cambridge, of which he became a Fellow in 1935. Professor of History at the University of Malaya (1950–58), and visiting professor at Harvard (1958), Illinois and California (1959–60), he wrote many works on historical, political and economic subjects, but achieved wider renown by his serio-comic tilt at bureaucratic malpractices *Parkinson's Law, the Pursuit of Progress* (1957).'Parkinson's Law'—that work expands to fill the time available for its completion, and subordinates multiply at a fixed rate, regardless of the amount of work produced—has passed into the language. Subsequently he published several novels, and from 1989 worked on his autobiography, *A Law unto Myself*.

Parkinson, James 1755–1824

English physician and amateur palaeontologist

In 1817 he gave the first description of paralysis agitans, or 'Parkinson's disease' (shaking palsy, a disease characterized by shaking hands and rigidity of muscles). He had already (1812) described appendicitis and perforation, and was the first to recognize the latter condition as a cause of death.

Parkinson, John 1567–1650

English herbalist

Born probably in Nottinghamshire, he was apothecary to **James VI and I** and author of *Paradisus Terrestris* (1629) and *Theatrum Botanicum* (1640), for a long time the most comprehensive English book of medicinal plants.

Parkinson, Norman, *originally* Ronald William Parkinson Smith 1913–90

English photographer

Born in London and educated at Westminster School, he was apprenticed as a photographer. He opened his own studio in 1934 and became one of Great Britain's best-known portrait and fashion photographers. His style was primarily romantic but some of his later portraits of the famous gave a clear insight into the sitter's personality. In the 1950s his advertising work took him all over the world and he settled in Tobago in 1963, regularly returning to Great Britain and the USA for exhibitions and awards.

Parkman, Francis 1823–93

US historian

Born in Boston, he graduated at Harvard in 1844 and took a law degree two years later. He then set out on a journey to the Western frontier, which he chronicled in his first book, *The California and Oregon Trail* (1849). Though hampered by a nervous disorder and near-blindness, he became one of the most eminent US historians and an authority on the rise and fall of the French domination in America. His works include *The Pioneers of France in the New World* (1865), *La Salle and the Great West* (1869), *Frontenac and New France* (1877), *A Half-Century of Conflict* (1893) and *Montcalm and Wolfe* (1884).

Parks, Rosa Lee, *née* McCauley 1913–

US civil rights activist

Born in Tuskegee, Alabama, she worked as a seamstress and housekeeper and served as a secretary of the Montgomery, Alabama branch of the National Association for the Advancement of Colored People (NAACP) from 1943 to 1956. In December 1955 she was arrested and fined when she refused to give up her seat on a bus to a white man in Montgomery, choosing instead to disobey the segregated seating policies common in the South. This incident prompted **Martin Luther King, Jnr**, and the Montgomery Improvement Association to organize a city-wide boycott of the bus company and file a federal suit challenging the constitutionality of the segregation laws. The boycott continued until the following year, when the Supreme Court declared the city's segregated seating policies unconstitutional. Parks and her husband lost their jobs as a result of the boycott and were obliged to move to Detroit, where they remained active in civil rights but endured difficult times until 1965, when she began more than 20 years of employment as secretary to a congressman. Her refusal to yield her seat in 1955 and the events that followed are regarded as the beginning of the modern US civil rights movement.

Parmenides of Elea c.515–c.445BC

Greek philosopher

Born in Southern Italy, he founded the Eleatic school (which included his pupils **Zeno** and **Melissus**). Little is known of his life but he produced a remarkable philosophical treatise, *On Nature*, written in hexameter verse, of which substantial fragments have survived and which represents a radical departure from the cosmologies of his Ionian predecessors such as **Thales** and **Anaximander**. The first part is a sustained deductive argument about the nature of being, which argues for the impossibility of motion, plurality and change. He contrasts this 'way of truth' with the 'way of seeming' in the second part of the poem, which is very obscure but apparently presents a more traditional cosmology. This highly original work set an agenda of problems for the subsequent pre-Socratic philosophers, and in some ways foreshadows the dualism of **Plato**'s metaphysics. ▢ Scott Austin, *Parmenides: Being, Bounds and Logic* (1986)

Parnell, Charles Stewart 1846–91
Irish politician

Charles Parnell was born in Avondale, County Wicklow, the grandson of Sir John Parnell (1744–1801), who had been Chancellor of the Irish Exchequer. His father belonged to an old Cheshire family which had purchased land in Ireland, and his mother was the daughter of an American admiral. He studied for four years at Magdalene College, Cambridge, but took no degree. He became High Sheriff of County Wicklow (1874), and in 1875 he became an MP supporting home rule.

In 1877–78 he gained great popularity in Ireland by his audacious and deliberate obstruction of parliamentary tactics. In 1878 he devoted himself to agrarian agitation, and was elected president of the Irish National Land League, for whom he secured substantial donations from the USA. In 1880 he became chairman of the Irish Parliamentary Party. The Land League was later declared illegal, and was revived in 1884 as the National League, with Parnell as president.

In 1886, Parnell and his 85 fellow Irish MPs used their vote to help introduce **William Gladstone**'s Home Rule Bill, but failed to secure the legislation because of defections by Liberal MPs. When Salisbury took the issue to the country later the same year, he was returned with a Unionist majority of more than 100, causing Parnell to form an alliance with Gladstone. In 1889, Parnell was cleared of complicity in the murder of **Thomas Burke** and other organized outrages following the publication in *The Times* of letters purportedly written by him. His character restored, he was given the freedom of the city of Edinburgh the same year.

In 1890 Parnell was cited co-respondent in a divorce case brought by Captain William Henry O'Shea (1840–1905) against his wife Katherine, and a decree was granted with costs against Parnell. The Irish members met to consider his position a week later, and eventually elected **Justin McCarthy** chairman in his place. Parnell also lost support in Ireland, and at the general election of 1892, 72 anti-Parnellites were returned against nine of his supporters. Meanwhile, Parnell had died suddenly in Brighton, five months after his marriage to Katherine O'Shea; he is buried in Glasnevin cemetery, Dublin.

📖 P Bew, *Parnell* (1980).

'No man has a right to fix the boundary of the march of a nation. No man has a right to say to his country, Thus far shalt thou go and no further.' From a speech in Cork, 21 January 1885.

Parmigiano or Parmigianino, *properly* Girolamo Francesco Maria Mazzola 1503–40
Italian painter of the Lombard school

Born in Parma, he first worked as a painter in Parma, especially on the frescoes in S Giovanni Evangelista, but after 1523 worked in Rome, whence he fled to Bologna when the city was sacked in 1527. At Bologna he painted his famous Madonna altarpiece for the nuns of St Margaret before returning to Parma in 1531. His work there includes *Madonna of the Long Neck* (c.1535, Uffizi, Florence). His work shows the influence of **Correggio** and **Raphael**, and his *Vision of St Jerome* and *Self-Portrait in a Convex Mirror* are particularly well known.

Parnell, Charles Stewart See panel above

Parnell, Thomas 1679–1718
Irish poet and clergyman

Born in Dublin, he was educated at Trinity College, took holy orders in 1700, and received the archdeaconry of Clogher (1706) and the vicarage of Finglass (1716). He also owned property in Cheshire, and he lived much in London, where he met **Robert Harley**, **Jonathan Swift** and **Pope**. The year after Parnell's death, Pope published a selection of his poems, the best-known of which are 'The Hermit', 'The Nightpiece on Death' and 'Hymn to Contentment'. His *Complete Poems* were first published in 1985. 📖 O Goldsmith, *The Life of Parnell* (1770)

Parr, Catherine See **Catherine Parr**

Parr, Thomas, *known as* Old Parr c.1483–1635
English centenarian

He was born, according to tradition, in 1483. He was a Shropshire farm-servant, and when 120 years old married his second wife, and till his 130th year performed all his usual work. In his 152nd year his fame had reached London, and he was induced to journey there to see Charles I, where he was treated at court so royally that he died. John Taylor, the 'Water-poet', wrote his biography.

Parrhasius 4th century BC
Greek painter

He worked in Athens. According to tradition he was the greatest painter of ancient Greece, and reputedly the first to use shading.

Parrington, Vernon Louis 1871–1929
US literary historian

Born in Aurora, Illinois, he was a graduate of Harvard (1893), and he taught at Emporia, at Oklahoma University from 1897 to 1908, then at the University of Washington, Seattle. His main work was *Main Currents in American Thought* (1927), which charted American literature from colonial times. He also published *The Connecticut Wits* (1926) and a study of **Sinclair Lewis** (1927).

Parrish, Maxfield Frederick 1870–1966
US artist

Born in Philadelphia, he studied at the Pennsylvania Academy of the Fine Arts and was widely popular as an illustrator by the late 1890s. His sentimental, dreamlike illustrations, characterized by intricate detail and tastelessly heightened colour, often featured classical maidens and natural landscapes. They appeared in magazines and advertisements as well as in books such as *The Arabian Nights* and *Mother Goose*.

Parry, Sir (Charles) Hubert (Hastings) 1848–1918
English composer

Born in Bournemouth, Hampshire, he was educated at Eton and Oxford. He became a professor at the Royal College of Music in 1883, and Professor of Music at Oxford in 1900. The composer of three oratorios, five symphonies, an opera, and many other works, his best-known works are the anthem 'I Was Glad' (1902), and his unison chorus 'Jerusalem' (1916), sung as an unofficial anthem at the end of each season of Promenade Concerts in London. He published *Evolution of the Art of Music* (1896), a biography of **J S Bach** (1909) and *The Oxford History of Music*, vol 3 (1907).

Parry, Sir William Edward 1790–1855
English navigator

Born in Bath, he was the son of Caleb Hillier Parry (1755–1822), an eminent physician. Joining the navy as midshipman, he served against the Danes in 1808, and in 1810 was sent to the Arctic regions to protect the whale fisheries. He took command in five expeditions to the Arctic—in 1818 (under Sir **John Ross**), 1819–20, 1821–23, 1824–25 and 1827—the last an unsuccessful attempt to reach the Pole on sledges from Spitsbergen, but which travelled further north than anyone had done previously. In 1829 he was knighted, and in 1837 was made controller of a department of the navy. He was subsequently superintendent of Haslar (1846), rear-admiral (1852), and governor of Greenwich Hospital (1853).

Parsons, Sir Charles Algernon 1854–1931
Irish engineer

Born in London, fourth son of the 3rd Earl of **Rosse**, he was educated at Dublin and Cambridge. He became an engineering apprentice, and in 1884 developed the high-speed steam turbine. He also built the first turbine-driven steamship, the *Turbinia*, in 1897. This caused a sensation at Queen Victoria's Diamond Jubilee Naval Review with its top speed of 35 knots, much faster than any other ship at that time. He was elected FRS in 1898, knighted in 1911, and was the first engineer to be admitted to the Order of Merit (1927).

Parsons, Louella Oettinger 1881–1972
US gossip columnist

She was born in Freeport, Illinois. Little is known of her early years, a fact partly attributable to her embroidered accounts of the past. In 1910, she became a reporter for the *Chicago Tribune* and also wrote screenplays for silent films, publishing the book *How to Write for the Movies* in 1915. In New York from 1919 and Hollywood from 1926, she rose to prominence writing a daily, syndicated Hollywood movie star gossip column. Feared within the film community for her influence, in time she could make or break a career and was said to have 'ruled as a queen'. She also hosted a number of radio shows, including *Hollywood Hotel* (1934–38), and wrote the books *The Gay Illiterate* (1944) and *Tell It To Louella* (1961). She retired in 1964.

Parsons, Robert 1546–1610
English Jesuit

Born in Nether Stowey, Somerset, he became a Fellow and tutor of Balliol College, but was forced to retire from Oxford by his enemies (1574). He turned Catholic, and in Rome entered the Society of Jesus (1575), becoming a priest in 1578. With **Edmund Campion** he landed in disguise at Dover in 1580, and evaded capture for a year during which he had notable success. In 1581 he escaped to the Continent, and in 1582 was in Paris conferring with the Provincial of the French Jesuits and other interested parties concerning his own project for the invasion of England. He explained this plan to **Philip II** in Madrid, who supported it and began a series of political manoeuvres which culminated in the Armada of 1588. Rector of the college at Rome from 1588, he founded a number of Jesuit seminaries. His *Christian Directory* was published in 1585, and in *The Conference on the next Succession to the Crown* he insisted on the right of the people to set aside, on religious grounds, the natural heir to the throne.

Parsons, Talcott 1902–79
US sociologist

Born in Colorado Springs, he was educated at Amherst College, the London School of Economics and at Heidelberg. He taught economics at Amherst (1926–27) and at Harvard from 1927 until 1931 when he joined the newly created sociology department. In 1946 he set up the interdisciplinary department of social relations. He was a leading proponent of functionalism, which attempts to explain social practices in terms of the function they have in maintaining society; the functionalist school dominated US sociology from the 1940s to the 1960s. Of his empirical studies, the most influential have been those in the sociology of medicine. His books include *The Structure of Social Action* (1937), *The Social System* (1952), *Sociological Theory and Modern Society* (1968), and *Politics and Social Structure* (1969).

Pärt, Arvo 1935–
Austrian composer

Born in Paide, Estonia, he emigrated in 1980, and settled in West Berlin in 1982. His many compositions (orchestral, choral, piano and chamber works) demonstrate an eclectic range of musical techniques: neo-baroque, strict serialism, aleatory methods, minimalism, impressionism, polytonality, etc. In his religious works especially, he evokes old polyphonic forms, medieval harmonies and plainsong. His compositions include three symphonies (1964, 1966, 1971), *Meie* (1959, 'Our Garden'), *Nekrolog* (1960), *Credo* (1968), *Fratres* (1977) and *Te Deum* (1993). He emigrated to Vienna in 1980, became an Austrian citizen in 1982, and in 1996 became an honorary member of the American Academy of Arts and Letters.

Parton, Dolly 1946–
US country singer, songwriter and actress

Born in Sevier Country, Tennessee, the fourth of 12 children, she was a child television star, and moved to Nashville immediately after graduating from high school. Her breakthrough came when she joined singer Porter Wagoner (1927–) on his television show in 1967. A string of hits followed, but their duo ended acrimoniously in 1974. She had her first big solo hit in 1970, and the early 1970s saw her greatest musical achievements. She went on to become an international celebrity well beyond country music, as a pop singer, songwriter (her 'I Will Always Love You' became a record-breaking hit for **Whitney Houston**) and actress, and made the most of her physical endowments. She moved back into country music settings in the 1990s. She published her autobiography, *Dolly*, in 1995. Her marriage to builder Carl Dean has lasted since 1966, and remains intensely private.

Partridge, Eric Honeywood 1894–1979
British lexicographer

Born near Gisborne in New Zealand and educated at Queensland and Oxford universities, he was elected Queensland Travelling Fellow at Oxford after World War I. He was a lecturer at the universities of Manchester and London (1925–27), wrote on French and English literature, and later made a specialized study of slang and colloquial language. His works in this field include the standard *Dictionary of Slang and Unconventional English* (1937), *Usage and Abusage* (1947), *Dictionary of Forces Slang* (1948), and *A Dictionary of the Underworld, British and American* (1950).

Pascal, Blaise 1623–62
French mathematician, physicist, theologian and man-of-letters

He was born in Clermont-Ferrand, the son of the local president of the court of exchequer. When his mother died, the family moved to Paris (1630), where his father, a considerable mathematician, educated his children. Pascal was not allowed to begin a subject until his father thought he could easily master it, and by the age of 11 had worked out for himself in secret the first 23 propositions of **Euclid**, calling straight lines 'bars' and circles 'rounds'. Inspired by the work of **Girard Desargues**, at 16 he published an essay on conics which **René Descartes** refused to believe was the work of a youth. It contains his famous theorem on a hexagram inscribed in a conic. Father and son collaborated in experiments to confirm **Evangelista Torricelli**'s theory, unpalatable to the schoolmen, that nature does not, after all, abhor a vacuum. They carried up the Puy de Dôme two glass tubes containing mercury, inverted in a bath of mercury, and noted the fall of the mercury columns with increased altitude. This led on to the invention of the barometer, the hydraulic press and syringe. In 1647, he patented a calculating machine, later simplified by **Gottfried Leibniz**, built to assist his father in his accounts. In 1651 Pascal's father died, his sister, Jacqueline, entered the Jansenist convent at Port-Royal, and Pascal divided his time between mathematics and socializing. His correspondence with **Pierre de Fermat** in 1654 laid the foundations of probability theory. That year he had the first of two religious revelations, according to a note found sewn into his clothes. He joined his sister in her retreat at Port-Royal, gave up mathematics and society almost completely and joined battle for the Jansenists against the Jesuits of the Sorbonne who had publicly denounced **Antoine Arnauld**, the Jansenist theologian and mathematician, as a heretic. In 18 anonymous pamphlets, the *Lettres provinciales* (1656–57), Pascal attacked the Jesuits' meaningless jargon, casuistry and moral laxity. This early prose masterpiece in the French language, the model for **Voltaire**, failed to save Arnauld, but undermined for ever Jesuit authority and prestige. In 1669 Pascal's papers on the area of the cycloid heralded the invention of the integral calculus. Notes for a casebook of Christian truths were discovered after his death, and published as the *Pensées* in 1669. They contain profound insights into religious truths coupled with scepticism of rationalist thought and theology. Their style owes much to **Michel de Montaigne** and Pierre Charron. Morris Bishop, *Pascal, the Life of a Genius* (1936)

Pascoli, Giovanni 1855–1912
Italian poet and writer
Born in San Mauro di Romagna, he was Professor of Latin at Bologna from 1907. Much of his poetry, set in his native Romagna, is of a tragic nature. His volumes of verse include *Myricae* (1891), *In Or San Michele* (1903, 'For San Michele') and *Canti di Castelvecchio* (1903, 'Songs of Castelvecchio'). *Sotto il Velame* (1900, 'Beneath the Veil') and *La Mirabile Visione* (1902, 'Heavenly Vision') are critical studies of **Dante**'s *Commedia Divina*. P Mazzamuto, *Pascoli* (1966)

Pasha, Arabi See **Ahmed Arabi**

Pasha, Hicks See **Hicks, William**

Pasha, Nouri Said See **Es-Sa'id, Nuri**

Pashukanis, Yevgeni Bronislavich 1894–c.1937
Russian legal philosopher
He was the author of *General Theory of Law and Marxism* in 1924, which led to his appointment as People's Commissar for Justice (1936). He contended that law was a feature of societies which practised commodity exchange through markets. He argued that law embodied a concept of the individual which corresponded to the individual involved as buyer or seller in market exchange. This approach made him unpopular with **Stalin** and he disappeared in 1937. His work has been more influential outside Russia than that of any other Marxist legal philosopher.

Pasić, Nicola c.1846–1926
Serbian statesman
Born in Zajecar, he was condemned to death in 1883 for his part in the 'Revolution of Zajecar', a plot against King Milan, but escaped to Austria, and on the accession of King **Peter I** became Prime Minister of Serbia (1891–92, 1904–05, 1906, and from 1908 almost continuously until 1918). He was instrumental in the creation of Yugoslavia, and was Prime Minister from 1921 to 1924 and 1924 to 1926.

Pasionaria, La See **Ibarruri Gomez, Dolores**

Pasmore, (Edwin John) Victor 1908–98
English artist
Born in Chelsham, Warlingham, Surrey, he worked for the London County Council, attending evening classes at the Central School of Art, and was one of the founders of the Euston Road School of realist painters in London (1937). His *The Quiet River: The Thames at Chiswick* (1944, Tate, London) is typical of this period. He became an art teacher, and perfected a delicate style of landscape painting, as in *The Hanging Gardens of Hammersmith* (1947, Tate), in which he was already turning from realism to a highly abstract style, as in *The Coast of the Inland Sea* (1950, Tate), culminating in *Relief Construction in White, Black, Red and Maroon* (1957). In 1960 he exhibited at the Venice Biennale, and in 1966 took a house in Malta, reintroducing colour and freer forms into his work. Retrospectives were held in 1965 (Tate) and 1980 (Arts Council, London) and 1990 (Center for International Contemporary Art, New York).

Pasolini, Pier Paolo 1922–75
Italian critic, poet, novelist, film director and screenwriter
Born and educated in Bologna, most of his childhood was spent in Casara della Delizia, in his mother's birthplace of Friuli. He became a Marxist following World War II, moved to Rome, wrote novels and also worked as a film scriptwriter and actor. Unheard of until the 1940s, he became notorious in the 1950s, principally through the publication of the first two parts of a projected trilogy, *Ragazzi di vita* (1955, *The Ragazzi*, 1968) and *Una vita violenta* (1959, *A Violent Life*, 1968). Superficially works of protest, they exhibit a strong thematic continuity with his early youthful poetry, portraying the timeless innocence of Friuli. From 1961 he devoted himself to directing films, many based on literary sources including *Il Vangelo Secondo Matteo* (1964, *The Gospel According to Saint Matthew*), *Il Decamerone* (1971, *The Decameron*), *I Racconti di Canterbury* (1973, *The Canterbury Tales*) and *Salò, o, Le centoventi giornate di Sodoma* (1975, *Salo — The 120 Days of Sodom*). He was murdered during a sexual encounter with another man. E Sicialiano, *Pasolini* (1981, in Italian)

Passfield, Baron See **Webb, Sidney James**

Passmore, George See **Gilbert and George**

Passmore, John 1914–
Australian philosopher
Born in Manly, New South Wales, he studied at Sydney University under **John Anderson**, and held academic posts in philosophy there (1935–49), before becoming Professor of Philosophy at Otago University, New Zealand. In 1955 he returned as Reader in Philosophy at the Australian National University's Institute of Advanced Studies, Canberra, and held the chair (1959–79). He was also president of the Australian Academy of the Humanities (1975–77). He is regarded as a principal exponent of the 'Andersonian' school of philosophy, and his many books include the classic *A Hundred Years of Philosophy* (1957), the ABC's Boyer Lecture for 1981, *The Limits of Government*, and *Serious Art* (1991). Since 1983 he has been Visiting Fellow in History of Ideas at McMaster University, Canada.

Passy, Frédéric 1822–1912
French economist and author, and Nobel Prize winner
Born in Paris, he became a member (1881–89) of the Chamber of Deputies, was a founder-member of the International Peace League in 1867, and a member of the International Peace Bureau in Bern in 1892. In 1901 he shared the Nobel Peace Prize with **Jean Dunant**. His writings include *Mélanges économiques* (1857), *L'Histoire du travail* (1873, 'The History of Work') and *Vérités et paradoxes* (1894, 'Truth and Paradoxes').

Passy, Paul Édouard 1859–1940
French philologist and phonetician
Born in Versailles, he was the son of **Frédéric Passy**. An advocate of phonetic spelling, he was one of the founders of the Phonetic Teachers' Association (later called

Pasteur, Louis 1822–95
French chemist, the father of modern bacteriology

Pasteur was born in Dôle. He studied at Besançon and at the École Normale Supérieure, and held academic posts at Strasbourg, Lille and Paris, where in 1867 he became Professor of Chemistry at the Sorbonne. His principal work was in discovering that fermentations are essentially due to organisms, not spontaneous generation. He greatly extended **Theodor Schwann's** researches on putrefaction, and gave valuable rules for making vinegar and preventing wine disease, introducing in this work the technique of 'pasteurization', a mild and short heat treatment to destroy pathogenic bacteria.

After 1865 his research into silkworm disease revived the silk industry in southern France; he also investigated injurious growths in beer, splenic fever, and fowl cholera. His 'germ theory of disease' maintained that disease was communicable through the spread of micro-organisms, the virulence of which could be reduced by exposure to air, by variety of culture, or by transmission through various animals. He demonstrated that sheep and cows 'vaccinated' with the weakened bacilli of anthrax were protected from the harmful results of subsequent inoculation with the virulent virus; by the culture of antitoxic reagents, the prophylactic treatment of diphtheria, tubercular disease, cholera, yellow fever and plague was also found effective. In 1885 he introduced a similar treatment for hydrophobia (rabies).

The Pasteur Institute, of which he became first director, was founded in 1888 for his research.

📖 R Dubos, *Louis Pasteur* (1986).

> *Dans les champs de l'observation le hasard ne favorise que les esprits préparés.*
> 'Where observation is concerned, chance favours only the prepared mind.' Speech at the inauguration of the Faculty of Science, University of Lille, 7 December 1854.

the International Phonetic Association) in 1886, and was Assistant Professor of Phonetics at the Sorbonne. His publications include *Le Français parlé* (1886) and *Études sur les changements phonétiques* (1890).

Pasternak, Boris Leonidovich 1890–1960
Russian lyric poet, novelist and translator

Born in Moscow, the son of Leonid Pasternak (1862–1945), painter and illustrator of **Tolstoy's** works, he studied law at the university, then musical composition under **Aleksandr Scriabin**, abandoning both for philosophy at Marburg, Germany. A factory worker in the Urals during World War I, he was employed in the library of the education ministry in Moscow after the Revolution. He published three collections of verse between 1917 and 1923, and under the influence of his friend **Vladimir Mayakovsky** wrote the political poems *Devyat'sot pyaty god* (1927, 'The Year 1905'), on the Bolshevik uprising. *V toroye rozhdeniye* (1932, 'Second Birth') is autobiographical. Among his outstanding short stories are *Detstvo Lyuvers* (1922, Eng trans *The Childhood of Luvers*, 1945), a delicate presentation of a girl's first impressions of womanhood, and *Provest'* (1934, Eng trans *The Last Summer*, 1959), in which Pasternak's imagery is at its freshest and most unexpected. Under **Stalin**, Pasternak became the official translator into Russian of **Shakespeare, Paul Verlaine, Goethe** and **Heinrich von Kleist**, but with **Khrushchev's** misleading political 'thaw' he caused a political earthquake with his first novel, *Doktor Zhivago* (1957, Eng trans *Doctor Zhivago*, 1958), banned in Russia. A fragmentary, poet's novel, it describes with intense feeling the Russian revolution as it impinged upon one individual, both doctor and poet. Its strictures on the post-revolutionary events are those not of an anti-Marxist but those of a communist, disappointed that history has not conformed to his vision. Expelled by the Soviet Writers' Union, he had to take the unprecedented step of refusing the 1958 Nobel Prize for literature. 📖 R Hingley, *Pasternak, a biography* (1983)

Pasteur, Louis See panel above

Paston 15th–17th centuries
English family, authors of the Paston letters

They were named after the village of Paston, Norfolk, and their letters and papers, published in 1787, 1789 and 1823, shed a vivid light on domestic life from the 15th to 17th centuries. James Gairdner edited them with more fullness between 1872 and 1875, and again completely in 1904, after the recovery of two long lost volumes. The chief members of the family were William Paston (1378–1444), a justice of common pleas, his son John (1421–66), Clement (c.1515–1597), a sailor, and Sir Robert (1631–83), Earl of Yarmouth.

Patañjali fl.2nd century BC
Indian founder of the Yoga system of Hindu philosophy

The four books of his *Yoga Sutra*, extant versions dating from the 3rd century AD but drawing on earlier traditions, expound the moral and physical disciplines considered necessary for attaining absolute freedom of the self. He is not to be confused, according to modern scholarship, with Patañjali the Grammarian (c.140BC) who wrote a substantial commentary on *Astadhyayi* (4th century BC), the Sanskrit grammar of Panini.

Pataudi, Mansur Ali, Nawab of 1941–
Indian cricketer and captain

Born in Bhopal, he was the son of Iftikhar Ali Pataudi. Despite the loss of an eye in a car crash, he captained the Indian Test team. In all he made 2,793 runs, scoring six centuries, and his brisk energetic captaincy gave India the self-confidence which took it to a leading place among the world's cricketing nations.

Patel, Vallabhbhai Jhaverbhai, *also called* Sardar 1875–1950
Indian politician and lawyer

A staunch Hindu, conservative and broadly identified with the interests of the business community, he was a lawyer by training and began his political career in local government in Ahmadabad (1917). Soon after, he joined the Gujarat Sabha, a political body of great assistance to **Mahatma Gandhi** during his political campaigns. He played a leading role in the Kheda peasants' Satyagraha (1918) and the Bardoli Satyagraha (1928), both launched in opposition to the colonial government's attempts to raise the land tax on peasant farmers, for which he was given the honorific title, Sardar (Leader) by Gandhi. He joined the Salt Satyagraha of 1930, the individual civil disobedience movement of 1940–41 and the Quit India Movement of 1942, following each of which he spent long periods in prison. He was, with **Jawaharlal Nehru**, a key negotiator on behalf of the Indian National Congress during the talks leading to the transfer of power from the British (1947). He became deputy Prime Minister in the newly independent India, and tackled the problems of post-Partition India with a thoroughness and ruthless efficiency that has caused him to be greatly admired, both as a statesman and politician, by subsequent generations.

Patenier or Patinier or Patinir, Joachim
c.1485–1524
Flemish painter

He was probably born in Bouvignes, Belgium. Nothing is known of his early life, although it has been suggested that he studied under **Hieronymus Bosch**. In 1515 he is recorded as a member of the Antwerp painters' guild. He was arguably the first Western artist to paint scenes in which the natural world, although not the whole subject of the painting, clearly dominates the religious narrative. A drawing of him was made by **Albrecht Dürer** in 1521, who described him as a 'good landscape painter'.

Pater, Jean Baptiste Joseph 1695–1736
French genre painter

Born in Valenciennes, a talented pupil and follower of **Antoine Watteau**, he is known for paintings such as *La Balançoire* and *Conversation galante*.

Pater, Walter Horatio 1839–94
English critic and essayist

Born in London, he was educated at King's School, Canterbury, and Queen's College, Oxford, and became a Fellow of Brasenose College. His *Studies in the History of the Renaissance* (1873) displays the influence of the pre-Raphaelites with whom he associated. His philosophic romance, *Marius the Epicurean* (1885), appealed to a wider audience. His *Imaginary Portraits* (1887) and *Appreciations* (1889), followed by *Plato and Platonism* (1893), established his position as a critic, but already people were beginning to talk of his influence as being unhealthy, in the sense that he advocated a cultivated hedonism. That Pater's neo-Cyrenaism, as it might be called, involved strenuous self-discipline hardly occurred to his critics, who found in his style alone an enervating quality. His influence on Oxford, however, was profound. He died having left unfinished another romance, *Gaston de Latour* (1896). ▢ A C Benson, *Walter Pater* (1906)

Paterson, A(ndrew) B(arton), *also called* Banjo
1864–1941
Australian bush poet and balladeer

Born at Narrambla in Orange, New South Wales, he is best known for his verse 'Waltzing Matilda', which he set to an old Scottish melody to become the unofficial national anthem of Australia. Under the pseudonym 'The Banjo' (the name of a bush racehorse) he contributed verse such as *Clancy of the Overflow* (1889), and *The Man from Snowy River* (1890) to the Sydney periodical the *Bulletin*. His verses were collected as *The Man from Snowy River, and Other Verses* (1895), followed by *Rio Grande's Last Race, and Other Verses* (1902), and his popular bush character appeared in *Saltbush Bill JP, and Other Verses* in 1917. His first *Collected Verse* was published in 1923. He also wrote two novels and a collection of short stories, a book of verse for children, illustrated by **Norman Lindsay**, *The Animals Noah Forgot* (1933), and edited a pioneering collection of *Old Bush Songs* (1905). ▢ C Gemmler, *The Banjo of the Bush* (1966)

Paterson, Emma, *née* Smith 1848–86
English trade unionist

Born in London and educated by her father, she became an apprentice book-binder then assisted her mother as a teacher. In 1872 she became secretary of the Women's Suffrage Association and later founded the Women's Protective and Provident League to aid the establishment of trade unions on the model of the Umbrella Makers' Union in New York. She was the first woman to be admitted as a delegate to the Trades Union Congress (1875) and she co-founded and edited the *Women's Union Journal* (1876).

Paterson, Robert, *also known as* Old Mortality
1715–1801
Scottish stonecutter

Born near Hawick, in the Scottish Borders, he deserted his wife and five children in 1758, and for over 40 years he repaired or erected headstones to Covenanting martyrs.

Paterson, William 1658–1719
Scottish financier and founder of the Bank of England

He was born at Skipnayre farm in Tinwald parish, Dumfriesshire, and spent some years trading in the West Indies. Returning to Europe, he consolidated his fortune in London, and in 1691 proposed the establishment of the Bank of England. When it was founded in 1694 he became a director, but resigned in 1695. Instead he went to Edinburgh, where he promoted a scheme for establishing a new colony at Darien, on the Panama Isthmus. The Scottish parliament created the Company of Scotland to finance the enterprise, and the whole nation backed it. He sailed with the first expedition in a private capacity, shared all its troubles, and returned with its survivors a broken man in December 1699. His energy, however, remained unabated and he had a considerable share in promoting the Union of the Parliaments of Scotland and England in 1707. He was elected to the first united parliament by the Dumfries burghs. He prepared the scheme for **Robert Walpole's** Sinking Fund, and the conversion and consolidation of the National Debt (1717). In 1715 was awarded £18,000 as indemnity for his Darien losses.

Paterson, William 1745–1806
American Revolutionary leader

Born in County Antrim, Ireland, he emigrated to America with his family in 1747 and settled in New Jersey. As a delegate to the Constitutional Convention in 1787, he proposed the New Jersey Plan (favoured by small states) for giving equal representation to all states. Though the plan was rejected, it helped bring about a compromise between equal representation (in the Senate) and representation based on population (in the House). After serving in the Senate and as Governor of New Jersey, he was appointed to the Supreme Court (1793–1806).

Pathé, Charles 1863–1957
French film pioneer

Born in Paris, he founded the company Pathé Frères with his three brothers (1896), and introduced the newsreel to France (1909), the USA (1910) and Great Britain, and the screen magazine *Pathé Pictorial*. The company developed Pathécolor, a hand-colouring stencil process, and became one of the world's largest film production organizations. He produced the cliff-hanger series, *The Perils of Pauline*, with **Pearl White** (1914). In 1949 the company became Associated British Pathé Ltd.

Patinier, Joachim See Patenier, Joachim

Patkau, Patricia 1950–
Canadian architect

Born in Winnipeg, Manitoba, she trained at the University of Manitoba and at Yale, where she won six academic awards. With her husband John Patkau, she has run Patkau Architects in Edmonton and Vancouver since 1979. They have won prizes for their innovative designs, including the Governor-General's Medal for Architecture (1986) and the British Columbia Honour award (1988) for the Pyrch Residence in Victoria, British Columbia and The Canadian Clay and Glass Gallery in Waterloo, Ontario (1989). The Seabird Island Indian School in Aggasiz, British Columbia (1989), is another of their major projects. She has taught at the universities of British Columbia, Pennsylvania and California.

Patmore, Coventry Kersey Dighton 1823–96
English poet

Born in Woodford, Essex, he was an assistant librarian at the British Museum, and was associated with the Pre-Raphaelite Brotherhood, with whom his verse was popular. His best-known work is *The Angel in the House* (4 vols, 1854), a poetic treatment of married love. After the death of his first wife in 1862, he converted to Roman Catholicism and from then his works had mystical or religious themes as in *The Unknown Eros* (1877) and *The Rod, The Root and the Flower* (1895). ▭ J C Reid, *The Mind and Art of Coventry Patmore* (1957)

Paton, Alan 1903–88
South African writer and educator

Born in Pietermaritzburg, he was educated at the University of Natal, and spent 10 years as a schoolteacher, first at a native school and later at Pietermaritzburg College. From 1935 to 1948 he was principal of the Diepkloof Reformatory for young offenders, where he became known for the success of his enlightened methods. From his deep concern with the racial problem in South Africa sprang the novel *Cry the Beloved Country* (1948). His other novels were *Too Late the Phalarope* (1953) and *Ah, But Your Land is Beautiful* (1981). He also wrote *Hope for South Africa* (1958), a political study written from the Liberal standpoint, *Debbie Go Home* (1961, short stories), *Instrument of Thy Peace* (1968), *Apartheid and the Archbishop* (1973), and his autobiography, *Towards the Mountain* (1981). He was national president of the South African Liberal Party from 1953 to 1960. ▭ E Callan, *Alan Paton* (1968)

Paton, Sir Joseph Noël 1821–1901
Scottish painter

Born in Dunfermline, he studied at the Royal Academy, London, and became a painter of historical, fairy, allegorical and religious subjects in a style close to that of the Pre-Raphaelites. He was appointed Queen's Limner for Scotland from 1865. He also published two volumes of poems.

Paton, William 1886–1943
Scottish missionary and writer

Born in England of Scottish parents, he was educated at Oxford and Cambridge, and served in the Student Christian Movement (1911–21). Though a pacifist, he worked as an evangelist among British troops in India, and returned there to minister under ecumenical auspices (1922–27). He organized the international conferences in Jerusalem (1928) and Madras (1938), and was editor of the prestigious *International Review of Missions*. Among his numerous writings are *Jesus Christ and the World's Religions* (1916), *The Church and the New Order* (1941) and *The Ecumenical Church and World Order* (1942).

Patou, Jean 1880–1936
French fashion designer

He was born in Normandy, the son of a prosperous tanner, and he joined an uncle who dealt in furs in 1907. In 1912 he opened Maison Parry in Paris, and in 1913 sold his collection outright to an American buyer. After war service he successfully opened again as couturier in 1919. He was noted for his designs for sports stars, actresses and society ladies, and for his perfume 'Joy'. ▭ Meredith Etherington-Smith, *Patou* (1983)

Patrick, St 5th century
Christian apostle and patron saint of Ireland

Born perhaps in South Wales, less probably at Boulogne-sur-Mer, or Kilpatrick near Dumbarton, his father was a Romano-British deacon named Calpurnius. His own Celtic name or nickname was Succat. According to legend, he was sold by pirates to an Antrim chief called Milchu when he was 15. After six years he escaped, and went to France, where he became a monk, first at Tours and afterwards at Lérins. He was consecrated a bishop at 45, and in AD432 it is thought he was sent by Pope Celestine as a missionary to Ireland. He converted his old master Milchu, and other chiefs, and after 20 years spent in missionary work, he fixed his see at Armagh (454). The only certainly authentic literary remains of the Saint are his spiritual autobiography *Confession*, and a letter addressed to Coroticus, a British chieftain who had taken some Irish Christians as slaves. His feast day is 17 March.

Patrick, (James) McIntosh 1907–98
Scottish painter and printmaker

Born in Dundee, he studied at Glasgow School of Art and was part of a general revival of printmaking during the 1920s and 1930s. He mainly painted landscapes, seen from a high viewpoint, in an intensely detailed style. His work had a huge audience in the 1950s due to commissions from the then British Railways for prints to decorate railway stations. He was Fellow of Duncan and Jordanstone College of Art, Dundee (1987) and Glasgow School of Art (1994).

Patten, Brian 1946–
English poet and playwright

He was born in Liverpool, Merseyside, and educated at Sefton Park Secondary, after which he worked as a reporter. With Roger McGough and Adrian Henri he shared the oustandingly successful *Penguin Modern Poets 10* (1967). Patten was, perhaps, the closest of the three to the earlier English tradition. Some of his best work can be found in his early poems, gathered in *Walking Out: The Early Poems of Brian Patten* (1970), and in the fine sequence *Notes to the Hurrying Man* (1969). He is never academically sententious; the bizarrely titled *The Eminent Professors and the Nature of Poetry as Enacted Out By Members of the Poetry Seminar One Rainy Evening* (1972) neatly captures his view of the literary world's pretensions. Later volumes include *The Unreliable Nightingale* (1973), *Love Poems* (1981), *Storm Damage* (1988) and *Grinning Jack* (1990). In 1983, he joined McGough and Henri in an updated version of *The Mersey Sound*. He has also written for the theatre and for children; *Gargling with Jelly* (1985) is a small masterpiece.

Patten, Chris(topher Francis) 1944–
English Conservative politician

After Balliol College, Oxford, he joined the Conservative Party's research department, then, under Edward Heath, worked in the Cabinet and home offices and became personal assistant to the party chairman (1972–74). In opposition he was director of the research department (1974–79) and when the Conservatives returned to power in 1979, under Margaret Thatcher, he held a number of non-Cabinet posts, culminating in that of Minister for Overseas Development, in 1986. With Mrs Thatcher's sudden interest in ecological issues, Patten's 'green credentials' and valuable presentational skills made him the obvious choice to replace Nicholas Ridley as Secretary of State for the Environment in 1989. As chairman of the Conservative Party (1990–92) he organized a successful 1992 general election campaign but was not re-elected. In the same year he was made Governor of Hong Kong. During his period of office there were some sharp exchanges with the Chinese leadership over the type of government which would prevail after 1997, and in 1995 Beijing barred Patten from the official handover ceremony. He was created Companion of Honour in 1997.

Patterson, H Orlando 1926–
Jamaican novelist and sociologist

He is the author of *Children of Sisyphus* (1965), probably the most vivid and authentic study ever made of the Rastafarian cult in fictional form. Besides important sociological studies, he has written further novels, of which *An Absence of Ruins* (1967) and *Die the Long Day* (1972), stand out.

Patterson, P(ercival) J(ames) 1935–
Jamaican statesman and lawyer

He was born in St Andrew and educated at the University of the West Indies and London School of Economics, being called to the Bar in in 1963. Having joined the People's National Party (PNP) in 1958, he was nominated to the Senate in 1967 and held various government posts, including deputy Prime Minister (1978, 1989–92), before becoming Prime Minister when **Michael Norman Manley** resigned in 1992; he was elected to his first full term in 1993. Though he was a socialist earlier in his political career, he favoured free-market reforms in the 1990s.

Patteson, John Coleridge 1827–71
English bishop and martyr

He was born in London, the son of Sir John Patteson, judge in the King's Bench, and of a niece of **Coleridge**. He was educated at Eton and Balliol College, Oxford, and was a Fellow of Merton, and curate of Alfington in Devonshire. From 1855 he spent 16 years in missionary work in the New Hebrides, Banks, Solomon and Loyalty islands; and in 1861 he was consecrated Bishop of Melanesia. He was killed by natives.

Patti, Adelina, *later* Adelina Nicolini 1843–1919
British soprano

Born in Madrid, the daughter of a Sicilian tenor, she sang in New York at the age of seven, and made her debut there (1859), in the title role of *Lucia di Lammermoor* ('The Bride of Lammermoor'). Her voice was an unusually high, rich, ringing soprano. In 1866 she married the Marquis de Caux, and, on her divorce in 1886, the Breton tenor Ernesto Nicolini (1834–98), followed in 1899 by the Swedish Baron Cederström. In 1898 she was naturalized. Her sister Carlotta (1840–89) was also a fine soprano.

Pattison, Dorothy Wyndlow *known as* Sister Dora 1832–78
English philanthropist

Born in Hauxwell, she became schoolmistress at Little Woolston, near Bletchley, in 1861, and in 1864 joined the Sisterhood of the Good Samaritan at Coatham, near Redcar. She became a nurse at Walsall, and in 1877 became head of the Municipal Epidemic Hospital at Walsall (mainly for smallpox).

Patton, George Smith, *known as* Old Blood and Guts 1885–1945
US soldier

Born in San Gabriel, California, he graduated from West Point in 1909. In World War I he commanded a tank brigade on the western front. A major general by 1941, he became one of the most daring US combat commanders in World War II. He trained the 1st Armoured Corps and later led the first US troops to fight in North Africa, playing a key role in the Allied invasion. In 1943 he commanded the US 7th Army in the Sicilian campaign. At the head of the 3rd Army he swept across France and Germany in 1944–45 and reached the Czech frontier. He was fatally injured in a motor accident near Mannheim in occupied Germany. His memoirs, *War As I Knew It*, were published in 1947. 📖 H Essame, *Patton* (1974)

Pauker, Ana, *née* Rabinsohn 1893–1960
Romanian politician

The daughter of a Moldavian rabbi, she joined the Social Democrat Party in 1915 and took part in revolutionary movements in Romania (1917–18). She joined the Communist Party, and became a member of the Central Committee (1922). She was arrested in 1925, but escaped to the USSR where she worked for Comintern. She returned to Romania in 1934 and was again arrested. She spent World War II in the USSR then returned home after the overthrow of Ion Antonescu (1944). Summoned to Moscow with **Gheorghe Gheorgiu-Dej** (1945), she was instructed by **Stalin** to establish a government under the control of the National Democratic Front in Romania. She entered the Foreign Ministry in 1947 and took part in organizing the collectivization of all land. She was relieved of her offices in 1952.

Paul, St See panel p1433

Paul, St Vincent de See **Vincent de Paul, St**

Paul 1754–1801
Emperor of Russia

Born in St Petersburg, the second son of **Peter III** and **Catherine II, the Great**, he succeeded his mother in 1796. His father's murder and his mother's neglect had exerted an unfortunate influence on his character. His earliest measures were the exile of the murderers and the pardon of Polish prisoners, including **Tadeusz Kościuszko**, but he soon revealed his violent temper, capriciousness and inconsistency, and he irritated his subjects by vexatious regulations. He suddenly declared for the allies against France, and sent an army of 56,000 men under Count **Suvorov** into Italy (1799). He sent a second army to co-operate with the Austrians, retired from the alliance, quarrelled with England, and entered into close alliance with **Napoleon I**. After his convention with Sweden and Denmark, England sent a fleet into the Baltic under Lord **Nelson** to dissolve the coalition (1801). His own officers conspired to compel him to abdicate, and in a scuffle he was strangled.

Paul I 1901–64
King of Greece

The son of **Constantine I**, brother and successor of **George II**, he was born in Athens and educated at the naval academy there. He was in exile with his father during his first deposition (1917–20). In 1922 he served with the Greek navy in the campaign against the Turks, but went into exile again (1923) when his brother George was deposed and a republic was proclaimed. In 1935 he returned to Greece with his brother, as Crown Prince. At the start of World War II he served with the Greek general staff in the Albanian campaign, and was a member of the Greek government in exile in London for the rest of the war. He succeeded to the throne on the death of his brother (1947). He married (1938) his cousin, Princess Frederika, daughter of the Duke of Brunswick, whose political views aroused controversy, but his reign was seen as a symbol of Greek postwar recovery. He was succeeded by his son **Constantine II**.

Paul III, *originally* Alessandro Farnese 1468–1549
Italian pope

Born in Canino, in the Papal States, he was made cardinal-deacon in 1493, and was elected pope in 1534. The first of the popes of the Counter-Reformation, he issued the bull of excommunication and deposition against **Henry VIII** of England in 1538, and also the bull instituting the Order of the Jesuits in 1540. He summoned the Council of Trent in 1545. 📖 Carlo Capasso, *Paolo III, 1534–1549* (2 vols, 1923–24)

Paul IV, *originally* Giampietro Carafa 1476–1559
Italian pope

He was born in Carpriglio, Abruzzi. As Bishop of Chieti, he showed rigorous opposition to heresy and was instrumental in the re-establishment of the Inquisition in Rome and Italy at large. As pope (1555–59), he tried to enforce discipline among the clergy, established censorship and a full index of forbidden books. He was an opponent of the Jesuits, and declared war in 1555 on Emperor **Charles V** on the grounds that the emperor could not abdicate his title without papal permission. Defensive of papal authority, he was also opposed to a reconvening of the Council of Trent.

Paul, St, *also known as* Saul of Tarsus Died c.64/68AD
Christian missionary and martyr, the Apostle of the Gentiles

Paul was born of Jewish parents at Tarsus in Cilicia, and was brought up to be a rabbi by **Gamaliel** at Jerusalem; he also acquired the trade of tent-maker. A strenuous Pharisee, he took an active part in the persecution of Christians, including St **Stephen**. He was on his way to Damascus on this mission when a vision of **Jesus Christ** converted him into a fervent adherent of the new faith.

After three years spent mainly in Damascus and partly in Arabia, he visited Jerusalem again, where Barnabas persuaded the Apostles of the genuineness of his conversion. He began to preach, but opposition to him was strong and he was compelled to live in retirement in Tarsus. After 10 years, he was brought to Antioch by Barnabas, and began with him and **Mark** the first of three missionary journeys, this one to Cyprus, Pisidia, Pamphylia and Lycaonia. On his return to Antioch, he encountered controversy over the manner in which Gentiles and Jews were to be admitted to the Christian Church; this dispute led to the first apostolic council in Jerusalem (c.49 or 50). Paul opposed **Peter** during the debate, and once the question was finally settled by a compromise, he addressed himself mainly to the Gentiles. Thousands of people became Christians through the clarity of Paul's teaching and the power of the Holy Spirit.

Paul's second missionary journey took him, with Silas, again to Asia Minor and through Galatia and Phrygia to Macedonia and Achaia; he was especially well received in Corinth. A year and a half later he was again in Jerusalem and Antioch, and then he undertook a third journey, to Galatia and Phrygia. Driven from Ephesus, he visited Achaia and Macedonia again, and by way of Miletus returned by sea to Jerusalem. There the fanaticism of the Jews against him led to disturbances, whereupon he was brought to Caesarea to be tried before **Felix** the procurator, and after two years' imprisonment, before Felix's successor **M Porcius Festus**. Paul, invoking his right as a Roman citizen, 'appealed to Caesar', and in the spring of 56 arrived in Rome, where he spent two years a prisoner in his own hired house. Paul was executed under **Nero**, probably at the end of the two years' captivity, although according to tradition he escaped to visit Spain and other countries.

The ancient Church recognized 13 of the New Testament Epistles as Paul's, although it did not unanimously regard Hebrews as his. Most critics now accept the Epistles to the Galatians, Romans, Corinthians (1st and 2nd) and Galatians, but scholarly opinion is divided over the Pastoral Epistles, 2nd Thessalonians and Ephesians, and some also Colossians and Philippians. The order of the Epistles is certainly not chronological, although it is difficult to establish the correct order.

▦ The many important studies of the life of St Paul include G Ogg, *The Chronology of the Life of St Paul* (1966); A Schweitzer, *The Mysticism of St Paul the Apostle* (1931); and W M Ramsay, *St Paul the Traveller* (1908). The Epistles and the Acts of the Apostles are major sources.

> 'For when the Gentiles, which have not the law, do by nature the things contained in the law, these, having not the law, are a law unto themselves.' Romans 2.14.
> 'O death, where is thy sting? O grave, where is thy victory?' 1 Corinthians 15.15.

Paul V, *originally* Camillo Borghese 1552–1621
Italian pope

Born in Rome, he became a nuncio in Spain and a cardinal prior to his election as pope in 1605. In 1606 he issued a decree of excommunication against the Doge and Senate of Venice, and placed the republic under interdict. The crisis, and the fierce anti-papal propaganda of the Venetian Paolo Sarpi, prompted the English ambassador to suggest that Venice might become a Protestant state, but it ended in a messy compromise.

Paul VI, *originally* Giovanni Battista Montini
1897–1978
Italian pope

Born in Concesio, the son of the editor of a Catholic daily paper, he graduated at the Gregorian University of Rome, was ordained in 1920, and entered the Vatican diplomatic service, where he remained until 1944. He was then made Archbishop of Milan, in which important diocese he became known for his liberal views and support of social reform. Made a cardinal in 1958, he was elected pope on the death of **John XXIII** in 1963, many of whose opinions he shared. He travelled more widely than any previous pope, and initiated important advances in the move towards Christian unity. ▦ J L Gonzalez and T Perez, *Paul VI* (1964)

Paul, Alice 1885–1977
US feminist

Born into a Quaker family in Moorestown, New Jersey, she was educated at Swarthmore College and at Pennsylvania University. Involved with the British suffragette movement while living in England, she became, on her return to the USA, the leader of the National American Woman Suffrage Association (NAWSA) congressional committee. She organized a march in 1913 of several thousand women in Washington but although her tactics did much to publicize the cause, they proved too militant for her fellow NAWSA members and she left the organization, founding the National Women's Party shortly afterwards, of which she later became leader. She used civil disobedience, hunger strikes, and pickets in the struggle to gain the vote for women, and after this goal was realized in the 19th Amendment (1920), she continued to work for women's rights, founding the World Party for Equal Rights for Women (1928) and campaigning for the passage of an equal rights amendment from the 1920s through the 1970s.

Paul, Charles Kegan 1828–1902
English author and publisher

Born in White Lackington in Somerset, he was a graduate of Oxford, entered the Church and became a chaplain at Eton in 1852 and vicar at Sturminster Hall in 1862. During this time he wrote religious works and edited the *New Quarterly Magazine*. In 1874 he left the Church to settle in London, where he wrote *William Godwin, his Friends and Contemporaries* (1876) and in 1877 he took over a publishing firm which became C Kegan Paul & Co. Among his first publications were the monthly *Nineteenth Century*, and the works of G W Cox, **Tennyson**, **George Meredith** and R L **Stevenson**. He became a Roman Catholic and among his works were *Biographical Sketches* (1883), *Maria Drummond* (1891), works on religion and translations from **Goethe** and **Blaise Pascal**.

Paul, Jean See **Richter, Johann Paul Friedrich**

Paul, Lewis d.1759
English inventor

The son of a French Huguenot refugee, he invented a roller spinning-machine and opened two mills, one in Birmingham and one in Northampton. This machine was a failure commercially, although the idea was utilized later by **Richard Arkwright**. In 1738 he invented a carding-machine which was used in Lancashire after his death, and in 1758 patented another type of spinning-machine.

Paul, Wolfgang 1913–
German physicist

Born in Lorenzkirch, he studied in Munich and at the Technical University in Berlin, where he received his doctorate in 1939. He later joined the staff of the University of Göttingen (1944), and became professor there in 1950. He simultaneously held a teaching post at Bonn University from 1952. He developed the 'Paul trap' to constrain electrons and ions within a small space for study, a technique which advanced the accuracy with which atomic properties could be measured, and which has proved important in testing modern atomic theory. For this work he shared one-half of the 1989 Nobel Prize for physics with **Hans Dehmelt**, who had developed a similar technique (the other half of the prize was awarded to **Norman Ramsey**). He was involved in the European Organization for Nuclear Research (CERN) in Geneva and was president (1979–89) of the **Alexander von Humboldt** Foundation.

Paulding, James Kirke 1778–1860
US writer

He was born in Great Nine Partners (Putnam County), New York. He was a friend and associate of **Washington Irving** and they founded *Salmagundi* (1807–08), a satirical periodical, and during the 1812 war he published the *Diverting History of John Bull and Brother Jonathan*. A more serious work, *The United States and England*, in 1814, rewarded him with an appointment on the Board of Naval Commissioners. He also wrote *The Dutchman's Fireside* (1831), *Westward Ho!* (1832), a *Life of Washington* (1835), and a defence of *Slavery in the United States* (1836). From 1838 to 1841 he was Secretary of the Navy. ▢ A L Herold, *James Kirke Paulding: Versatile American* (1926)

Paulet or Poulet, Sir Amyas c.1536–1588
English courtier

He succeeded his father as Governor of Jersey, was ambassador to France (1576–79), and was keeper of **Mary, Queen of Scots** from 1585 till her death (1587).

Pauli, Wolfgang 1900–58
Austrian–Swiss theoretical physicist and Nobel Prize winner

Born in Vienna, he studied under **Arnold Sommerfeld** at Munich University, receiving his doctorate in 1921, then worked at Göttingen University (1921–22) and with **Niels Bohr** at his institute in Copenhagen (1922–23) before becoming professor at Hamburg University (1923–28). In 1928 he moved to Zurich, became a Swiss citizen and was given a professorship at the Federal Institute of Technology. Pauli demonstrated that a fourth 'spin' quantum number was required to describe the state of an atomic electron, and went on to formulate the 'Pauli exclusion principle' (1924), which states that no two electrons in an atom can exist in exactly the same state, with the same quantum numbers. This gave a clear quantum description of electron distribution within different atomic energy states, and earned him the 1945 Nobel Prize for physics. He suggested the existence of a low-mass neutral particle (1931), later discovered as the neutrino, and his studies in the early 1950s of quantum interactions paved the way for **Tsung-Dao Lee** and **Chen Ning Yang**'s discovery of parity non-conservation in 1956. He was visiting professor at Princeton University in 1935 and, at **Albert Einstein**'s invitation, again from 1939 to 1946, the same year that he became a naturalized US citizen.

Pauling, Linus Carl 1901–94
US chemist and Nobel Prize winner

Born in Portland, Oregon, he was educated at Oregon State College and California Institute of Technology (Caltech), receiving his PhD in 1925. After postdoctoral work in Munich, Zurich and Copenhagen, he was on the chemistry faculty at Caltech from 1927 to 1963, as full professor from 1931. His early work on crystal structures (1928) led to their rationalization in terms of ionic radii and greatly illuminated mineral chemistry. He then turned to the quantum-mechanical treatment of the chemical bond and made many important contributions, including the concept of the 'hybridization of orbitals', central to understanding the shapes of molecules. This period of his work generated two influential books: *Introduction to Quantum Mechanics* (1935, with E Bright Wilson) and *The Nature of the Chemical Bond* (1939). His interest in complex molecular structures led him to work in biology and medicine; he studied the structures of proteins and antibodies, and investigated the nature of serological reactions and the chemical basis of hereditary disease. During the past 20 years he has advocated the use of vitamin C in combating a wide range of diseases and infections, and his views have generated controversy. He has also been a controversial figure for his work in the peace movement and his criticism of nuclear deterrence policy. Pauling was awarded the Nobel Prize for chemistry in 1954 and the Nobel Peace Prize in 1962. He was elected an Honorary Fellow of the Chemical Society in 1943. He became a Foreign Member of the Royal Society in 1948 and was awarded its Davy Medal in 1947. ▢ Anthony Serafini, *Linus Pauling: A Man and His Science* (1989)

Paulinus d.644
Roman Christian

Born in Rome, he was a missionary to England in 601 with **Augustine of Canterbury**. Consecratated a bishop in 625, he went north with Princess Æthelburh of Kent on her marriage to the pagan King **Edwin** of Northumbria. He baptized Edwin and all his court in York at Easter, 627, and was made Bishop, and later the first Archbishop of York (633). Edwin's murder by the pagan **Penda** of Mercia and **Cadwallon** of Wales in 633 drove him back to Kent, where he was appointed Bishop of Rochester.

Paulinus of Nola, St, *also called* Pontius Meropius Anicius Paulinus AD353–431
French prelate

Born in Bordeaux, he was baptized a Christian (c.389AD) and settled in Nola in Italy, where he became known for his charity and his rigid asceticism. He was consecrated Bishop of Nola (c.409). He is remembered for his *Carmina* and for his epistles to **Augustine of Hippo**, **Jerome**, **Sulpicius Severus**, and **Ausonius**.

Paulinus, Pontius Meropius Anicius See Paulinus of Nola, St

Paullus, Lucius Aemilius d.216BC
Roman general and politician

The father of **Lucius Aemilius Paullus Macedonicus**, he is chiefly remembered for his disastrous generalship at the Battle of Cannae (216BC), where the Roman army, though numerically superior, was heavily defeated by **Hannibal** and the Carthaginians, and suffered one of its worst defeats ever. Paullus himself, consul at the time, died on the field of battle. His grandson, adopted by **Scipio**, was **Scipio Aemilianus**.

Paullus Macedonicus, Lucius Aemilius d.160BC
Roman general and politician

The son of **Lucius Aemilius Paullus**, he was famous primarily for his defeat of **Perseus**, King of Macedonia, at the Battle of Pydna (168BC), and for suppressing the

---

Pavarotti, Luciano 1935–
Italian tenor

Pavarotti was born in Modena, the son of Fernando Pavarotti, an amateur tenor, and Adele Venturi. He abandoned a career in school teaching to become a singer, and won the international competition at the Teatro Reggio Emilia in 1961, making his operatic début there as Rudolfo in *La Bohème* the same year. He performed with the La Scala tour of Europe 1963–64 and in 1965 toured Australia with **Joan Sutherland** in *Lucia di Lammermoor*. He made his American début at the Metropolitan Opera House, New York in 1968. His voice and performance are very much in the powerful style of the traditional Italian tenor, and he is also internationally known as a concert performer.

He has made many recordings, including joint performances with **José Carreras** and **Placido Domingo** as 'The Three Tenors', and he appeared in the film *Yes, Giorgio* (1981). That year he won the Grammy award for best classical vocal soloist. In 1990, at the time of the football World Cup, he recorded the aria *Nessun Dorma* ('Nobody is Sleeping') from **Puccini**'s *Turandot*, which was used as the theme tune for the event. The same year he toured the USSR. In 1991 he gave a mass concert in London, 'Pavarotti in the Park'.

💷 He wrote his autobiography (with W Wright) in 1981, which has been revised as *My World* (1995). See also Adua Pavarotti, *Life with Luciano* (1992) and Martin Mayer, *Grandissimo Pavarotti* (1986).

Macedonian monarchy, whence his title 'Macedonicus'. With Perseus's book collection, which fell to him as booty, he created the first private library at Rome. His second son, whom he gave in adoption to Publius Scipio, was the notorious destroyer of Carthage and Numantia, **Scipio Aemilianus**.

Paulus, Friedrich 1890–1957
German soldier and tank specialist
As commander of the 6th Army he capitulated to the Russians with the remnants of his army at the siege of Stalingrad in February 1943. Released from captivity in 1953, he became a lecturer on military affairs under the East German communist government.

Paulus, Julius c.190–c.225AD
Roman jurist
He was the legal councillor of the praetorian prefect **Papinianus** and Emperor **Septimius Severus**. A voluminous writer, many passages from his works are included in **Justinian**'s *Digesta*. His *Decrees*, reports of cases heard by Severus, are the only law reports surviving from classical times.

Paulus Aegineta 7th century
Greek physician
He wrote a compendium of all medical knowledge of his time, *Epitomae medicae libri septem*, which went through many editions and had a great influence on Arab physicians in particular.

Pausanias 5th century BC
Spartan soldier and Regent
The nephew of **Leonidas**, he commanded the Greek forces at Plataea (479BC), where the Persians were routed. He then compelled the Thebans to surrender the chiefs of the Persian party. Capturing the Cyprian cities and Byzantium (478), he negotiated with **Xerxes I** in the hope of becoming ruler under him of all Greece, and was twice recalled to Sparta for treachery. He tried to stir up the helots, was betrayed, and fled to a temple of Athena on the Spartan acropolis, where he was walled up and only taken out when dying of hunger (c.470).

Pausanias 2nd century AD
Greek geographer and historian
Born probably in Lydia, he travelled through almost all Greece, Macedonia and Italy, and through part of Asia and Africa. From his observations and researches he composed an *Itinerary* of Greece, describing the different parts of that country and the monuments of art. Intended as a guidebook, it is an invaluable source of information.

Pavarotti, Luciano See panel above

Pavel, Josef 1908–73
Czechoslovak soldier, politician and reformer

Joining the Communist Party in the depression in 1929, he studied with the Comintern in Moscow in 1935–37, fought in the Spanish Civil War in 1937–38 and in the West in 1939–45. He then rose to be commander of the people's militia that gave their backing to the February Revolution (1948) and acted as deputy to the Minister of the Interior until his arrest (1950). Because of his service in the West he was viewed as suspect by **Stalin**'s puppets in Prague and was sentenced to 25 years in prison. Released in 1955, he did little until he became Minister of the Interior during the Prague Spring (1968). His attempt to make the political police responsible won him enemies and soon after the Soviet invasion he was dismissed.

Pavese, Cesare 1908–50
Italian novelist, poet, critic and translator
Born in Piedmont, he was brought up in Turin where he worked for Einaudi, the publisher. Among his various translations, that of **Herman Melville**'s *Moby-Dick* (1932) is regarded as a classic. A leader of the Italian postwar Neorealist school, he was politically disillusioned and eventually committed suicide. His poetry is slight, and his finest work is in novels like *La casa in collina* (1949, Eng trans *The House on the Hill*, 1961) and *La luna e i falò* (1950, Eng trans *The Moon and the Bonfire*, 1952), which express precisely and categorically his abhorrence of war and fascism. 💷 D Lajolo, *Absurd Vice: a biography of Pavese* (1983)

Pavie, Auguste Jean Marie 1847–1925
French explorer and diplomat
He was born in Dinan. He served in the French Marines before joining the Telegraph Department in Cochin-China (southern Vietnam) and being posted to Kampot in Cambodia where he learned the language and explored locally. In 1880 he supervised the laying of the telegraph line between Phnom Penh and Bangkok, before being granted permission to explore French Indochina. The series of expeditions which he organized (1881–95), known as the Pavie Mission, surveyed 260,000 square miles (676,000 sq km), collected important scientific data, which was published in 11 volumes with accompanying maps (*Mission Pavie*, 1898–1919), and led to the French political domination over the Laotian states. He was vice-consul in Luang Prabang (1886–91) and consul-general in Bangkok (1891–93).

Pavlov, Ivan Petrovich 1849–1936
Russian physiologist and Nobel Prize winner
Born near Ryazan, he studied natural sciences, graduating from St Petersburg in 1875, and medicine, receiving his doctorate in 1879. From 1886 he worked at the Military Medical Academy in St Petersburg. He became Professor of Pharmacology (1890), Professor of Physiology (1895), and director of the Institute of Experimental Medicine (1913). His work was concerned with three main areas of

physiology: the circulatory system (1874–88), the digestive system (1879–97), and also higher nervous activity including the brain (1902–36). He studied digestion in dogs, investigating the nervous control of salivation and the role of enzymes, and for this work was awarded the Nobel Prize for physiology or medicine in 1904. His most famous research showed that if a bell is sounded whenever food is presented to a dog, it will eventually begin to salivate when the bell is sounded without food being presented. This he termed a 'conditioned' or acquired reflex, and it was the starting point for subsequent studies of experimental psychoses, human psychic disorders, and his theories of animal and human behaviour. ▭ Boris P Babkin, *Pavlov: A Biography* (1949)

Pavlova, Anna 1881–1931
Russian ballerina
Born in St Petersburg, she trained there at the Imperial Ballet School, and quickly became famous, creating roles in work by Michel Fokine, in particular *The Dying Swan* (1907). After travelling to Paris with Sergei Diaghilev's Ballets Russes in 1909, she began touring all over the world with her own company dancing reduced versions of the classics. She choreographed over a dozen works of which the best known are *Snowflakes* (1915) and *Autumn Leaves* (1919). She did much to create the stereotyped image of the ballerina which persists today. ▭ Victor Dandré, *Anna Pavlova* (1932)

Paxman, Jeremy 1950–
English journalist and broadcaster
Born in Leeds, he was educated at Cambridge and edited a student newspaper there. He became a journalist in Northern Ireland before entering television as a presenter on current affairs programmes including *Tonight* (1977–79), *Panorama* (1979–85), and *Newsnight* (1989–). He has also compered a revived version of the quiz game *University Challenge* (1994–). His publications include *A Higher Form of Killing* (1982), *Through the Volcanoes* (1985) and *Friends in High Places* (1990).

Paxton, Sir Joseph 1801–65
English gardener and architect
Born in Milton-Bryant, near Woburn, he became superintendent of gardens to the Duke of Devonshire at Chiswick and Chatsworth (from 1826). He remodelled the gardens and designed a glass and iron conservatory at Chatsworth (1836–40). This became the model for his design of the building for the Great Exhibition of 1851 (it was later re-erected as the Crystal Palace in Sydenham, and destroyed by fire in 1936). He was Liberal MP for Coventry from 1854.

Paxton, Steve 1939–
US experimental dancer and choreographer
Born in Tucson, Arizona, he was drawn to dance as a schoolboy gymnast, and after moving to New York in 1958 he made it his primary concern. His training there included three years with Merce Cunningham and a year with José Limón. An experimental composition course with musician Robert Dunn led to his involvement with the Judson Dance Theatre, with which he performed works by Yvonne Rainer, Trisha Brown and others. He was also a founding member of the experimental Grand Union. In 1972 he invented the dance form known as 'contact improvisation' which has now been absorbed into the choreography of dancers the world over. Contact relies only on the performer's own weight to determine the shape of the dance, without any reliance on set steps. Though an important dancer of his generation, he is one of the most reclusive, now choosing to live in the Vermont countryside and performing rarely and usually alone.

Paxton, Tom 1937–
US folk-singer and writer
He was born in Chicago, Illinois, and developed an interest in folk music as a student, beginning to perform in the Greenwich Village coffee house scene after moving to New York in 1960. He began to attract attention as a songwriter, and recorded *Ramblin' Boy* (1964), the first in a sequence of successful albums which took a traditional folk approach in the manner of Pete Seeger, to which he has remained largely constant. His songs mixed hard-hitting protest with evocative ballads and children's songs, and he developed the latter aspect of his work in a series of successful books for children.

Payne, John Howard 1791–1852
US actor and playwright
He was born in New York City and made his debut there in 1809, and in London in 1813. For 30 years he had a successful career as an actor and author of plays, chiefly adaptations. His play *Clari* contains the song 'Home, Sweet Home', the music being by Sir Henry Bishop. Payne was appointed US consul and in Tunis in 1841. ▭ G Overmeyer, *America's First Hamlet* (1957)

Payne-Gaposchkin, Cecilia Helena, née Payne 1900–79
US astronomer
Born in Buckinghamshire, England, she studied natural sciences at Cambridge, before moving to the USA to work under Harlow Shapley at Harvard College Observatory. Her doctoral thesis, *Stellar Atmospheres* (1925), led to her pioneering work on determining the relative abundances of chemical elements in stars and in space. She remained at Harvard for the rest of her life, becoming the first woman professor there (1956). With her husband and colleague Sergei I Gaposchkin, she identified and measured variable stars on photographic plates, an immense programme which resulted in a catalogue of variable stars published in 1938. They later carried out a similar project on variable stars in the Magellanic Clouds in 1971.

Payton, Walter, nicknamed Sweetness 1954–
US footballer
Born in Columbia, Missouri, he played college football for Jackson State before joining the Chicago Bears as a running back in 1975. Between then and his retiral in 1987 he established a National Football League rushing record of 16,726 yards. In one game (1977) he rushed for a record 275 yards. He scored 125 touchdowns between 1975 and 1987. In 1986, the Bears defeated the New England Patriots 46-10 to win the Super Bowl.

Paz, Octavio 1914–98
Mexican poet and Nobel Prize winner
Born in Mexico City, he attended the National University of Mexico and identified with the Republican side in the Spanish Civil War. Diplomat (he was Mexican ambassador to India, 1962–68), essayist and editor, he is best known for his poetry, such as *Piedra de sol* (1957, Eng trans *Sun Stone*, 1963), written in 10 volumes. Other works include a study of Mexican character and culture, *El laberinto de la soledad* (1950, revised edn 1959, Eng trans *The Labyrinth of Solitude*, 1962), *Postdata* (1970, Eng trans *The Other Mexico: Critique of the Pyramid*, 1972), written after the student massacre and other events in 1968, *El arco y la lira* (1956, Eng trans *The Bow and the Lyre*, 1973) and *Vislumbres de la India* (1995, 'Glimpses of India'). He was awarded the Nobel Prize for literature in 1990. ▭ I Ivask, *The Perpetual Present: the poetry and prose of Octavio Paz* (1973)

Paz Estenssoro, Víctor 1907–
Bolivian revolutionary and politician
He was born in Tarija and educated at the University Mayor de St Andres, entering politics in the 1930s. He was the founder in 1941 of the left-wing Movimiento Nacionalista Revolucionario (MNR, National Revolutionary Movement), then went on to become its principal

leader. He was exiled to Argentina (1946–51) but, following the 1952 revolution, he served as President (1952–56), and held office again from 1960 to 1964, when he was ousted by a military coup. He went into exile in Peru, returning to Bolivia (1971) as an adviser to the government of President Hugo Banzer Suárez. He failed to win election in 1979, but in 1985, after no candidate managed to achieve a majority, Congress elected him President. His main achievement in office (1985–90) was to reduce the raging inflation which had been crippling Bolivia's economy.

p'Bitek, Okot 1931–82
Ugandan poet, writing in English

He was born in Gulu, northern Uganda, and attended the Government Training College at Mbarara (1952–54), returning to his home township as a teacher of English and religious knowledge. His first publication was *Lak tar miyo Kinyero wi lobo?* (1953, Eng trans *White Teeth*, 1989), written in the Acoli language. Also a gifted footballer, p'Bitek was a Ugandan international player. He decided to remain in England following a soccer tour and studied law at the University College, Aberystwyth, and social anthropology at Oxford, a discipline he then rejected along with the Christianity of his upbringing. He returned to Uganda for a time in 1962 and began to research folk culture and oral literature. *Song of Lawino* (1966) and its 'response' *Song of Ocol* (1970) were originally written in Acoli but translated by the poet himself. He controversially steered the Ugandan national theatre in the direction of folk arts; he was dismissed from the Cultural Centre in Kampala, and thereafter spent much of the rest of his life working in universities in Zambia, Nigeria and in the USA. He returned to Makerere as Professor of Creative Writing shortly before his death. Other works include collections of Acoli songs and tales, *The Horn of My Love* (1974) and *Hare and Hornbill* (1978), and an important book of essays *Africa's Cultural Revolution* (1973). 📖 G A Heron, *The Poetry of Okot p'Bitek* (1976)

Peabody, Elizabeth Palmer 1804–94
US reformer, abolitionist and educator

Born in Billerica, Massachusetts, she established a school there, but she was not a good businesswoman and the venture collapsed. In 1840 she opened a bookshop in Boston which flourished for several years as a literary centre frequented by such people as Margaret Fuller, who edited *The Dial*, the transcendentalist journal published by Peabody. In 1860 she founded in Boston the first English-speaking kindergarten. This became a showcase for Fredrich Froebel's ideas concerning child nurture and education, concepts that she went to Europe to study further (1867–68). Upon her return, she lectured extensively to establish kindergartens and training schools throughout the USA. She also succeeded in convincing publishers Ernst Steiger and Milton Bradley to produce materials for children.

Peabody, George 1795–1869
US merchant, financier and philanthropist

Born in South Danvers, Massachusetts, now called Peabody, he became a partner in a Baltimore dry-goods store in 1815. He established himself in London in 1837 as a merchant and banker, raising loans for US causes. In his lifetime he gave away a fortune for philanthropic purposes. He fitted out Elisha Kane's Arctic expedition to search for Sir John Franklin, and founded and endowed the Peabody Institutes in Baltimore and Peabody, and the Peabody Museums at Yale and Harvard. He also set up the Peabody Education Fund for the promotion of education in the southern USA and built working men's tenements in London.

Peacock, Sir Alan Turner 1922–
Scottish economist and economic adviser

Educated at Dundee High School and St Andrews University, he began lecturing in economics at St Andrews University (1947–48) and proceeded with a lectureship then readership in public finance at London University (1948–56). He succeeded Alexander Gray as Professor of Economic Science at Edinburgh University (1957–62) and was Professor of Economics at York (1962–78) and Buckingham (1978–80) where he succeeded Lord Beloff as Principal, then as Vice-Chancellor (1980–84). From 1973 to 1976 he was also chief economic adviser to the Department of Trade and Industry. His first work, *The Economics of National Insurance* (1952), concentrated on economic policy, while later works expressed his devotion to market principles, for example in *The Economic Theory of Fiscal Policy* (1976, with G K Shaw) and *The Economic Analysis of Government and Related Themes* (1979). In 1987 he was knighted, and became Research Professor in Public Finance at Heriot-Watt University, Edinburgh.

Peacock, Thomas Love 1785–1866
English novelist and poet

He was born in Weymouth, Dorset, the son of a London merchant, and entered the service of the East India Company in 1819 after producing three satirical romances, *Headlong Hall* (1816), *Melincourt* (1817) and *Nightmare Abbey* (1818). *Crotchet Castle* (1831) concluded this series of satires, and in 1860 *Gryll Grange* appeared. He also published two romances, *Maid Marian* (1822) and *The Misfortunes of Elphin* (1829). The framework of his satirical fictions is always the same—a company of humorists meet in a country house and display the sort of crotchets or prejudices which Peacock, the reasonable man, most disliked: the mechanical sort of political economy, morbid romance, the 'march of science' and transcendental philosophy. The major poets of the Romantic school, Wordsworth, Coleridge, Byron, Shelley (one of Peacock's friends), and Robert Southey, are caricatured along with the Edinburgh Reviewers, who offer the extra target of being Scots. 📖 M van Doren, *Thomas Love Peacock* (1911)

Peake, Mervyn Laurence 1911–68
English writer and artist

Born in south China, where his father was a missionary, he was educated at Tientsin Grammar School, Eltham College and the Royal Academy Schools. While living on Sark (1933–35) and thereafter teaching at the Westminster School of Art, his reputation as an artist grew. His first book was a children's story, *Captain Slaughterboard Drops Anchor* (1939), with his own illustrations. *The Craft of the Lead Pencil* (1946), a book on drawing, was published in the same year as his first novel, *Titus Groan*, the first part of a Gothic fantasy trilogy completed in *Gormenghast* (1950) and *Titus Alone* (1959). Another novel, *Mr Pye*, appeared in 1953, and his only play, *The Wit to Woo*, in 1957. He published two volumes of verse, *Shapes and Sounds* (1941) and *The Glassblowers* (1950), a ballad set during the blitz, and lighter sketches collected posthumously in *A Book of Nonsense* (1972). He illustrated several classics, notably *Treasure Island*, *The Hunting of the Snark* and *The Ancient Mariner*. 📖 John W Batchelor, *Mervyn Peake: A Biographical and Critical Exploration* (1979)

Peale, Anna Claypoole 1791–1878
US artist

She was born into a famous family of US painters and was trained by her father James Peale and uncle Charles Willson Peale, both notable late-18th-century painters. She assisted her father with his commissions and became well known in her own right for her portrait miniatures. She and her younger sister Sarah Peale often shared commissions, Anna executing the miniatures and Sarah the full-scale portrait oils. They became the first women to be elected members of the Pennsylvania Academy (1824).

Peale, Charles Willson 1741–1827
US painter, naturalist and inventor

Born in Queen Annes County, Maryland, the eldest son of a schoolmaster, he travelled to London in 1767 where he studied painting for two years under **Benjamin West**. He became known for his many portraits of the leading figures of the American Revolution, painted in a neo-classical style after the manner of **Jacques Louis David**. His works include the earliest known portrait of George Washington (1772). He is said to have caused a stir when, as a staunch Democrat, he refused to remove his hat in the presence of **George III**. In 1775 he settled in Philadelphia and from 1779 to 1780 was a Democratic member of the Pennsylvania Assembly. He established the first art gallery in the USA when he opened his Portrait Gallery of the Heroes of the Revolution in 1782, and in 1786 he founded the Peale Museum of natural history and technology. He had 17 children, all of whom he named after great artists of the past. Four of them became painters: Raphaelle (1774–1825), Rembrandt (1778–1860), Rubens (1784–1865) and Titian (1799–1881).

Peale, Norman Vincent 1898–1993
US Christian Reformed pastor and writer

Born in Bowersville, Ohio, he was educated at Ohio Wesleyan University and Boston University, ordained as a Methodist Episcopal minister in 1922, and held three pastorates before beginning his long ministry at Marble Collegiate Reformed Church, New York City (1932–84). He established a psychiatric clinic called the American Foundation of Religion and Psychiatry, next door to his church. He wrote the bestseller, *The Power of Positive Thinking* (1952), and was much in demand as a lecturer on public affairs. His other works include *The Tough-Minded Optimist* (1962), *Jesus of Nazareth* (1966), and *Power of the Positive Factor* (1987).

Peale, Sarah Miriam 1800–85
US artist

Born in Philadelphia, the younger sister of **Anna Peale**, she was taught by her artist father James Peale. A famous portrait painter of prominent US families, she painted, among others, the Secretary of State **Daniel Webster**, Senator Thomas Hart Benton and the **Marquis de Lafayette**. Sarah would paint a full portrait while Anna undertook the miniature. She visited her cousin Rembrandt Peale in Baltimore for tuition in oil painting and glazing techniques in 1825 and remained there for 20 years. In 1846 she moved to St Louis where she undertook a series of still-life paintings. She is regarded by many as the first professional woman painter in the USA.

Peano, Giuseppe 1858–1932
Italian mathematician

Born in Cuneo, he was educated at the University of Turin, where he later taught and became Extraordinary Professor of Infinitesimal Calculus (1890) and then full Professor in 1895. He did important work on differential equations and discovered continuous curves passing through every point of a square. He later moved to mathematical logic, and advocated writing mathematics in an entirely formal language, the symbolism he invented becoming the basis of that used by **Bertrand Russell** and **Alfred Whitehead** in their *Principia Mathematica*. He also promoted Interlingua, a universal language based on uninflected Latin. ▥ Hubert C Kennedy, *Giuseppe Peano* (1974)

Pearlstein, Philip 1924–
US painter

Born in Pittsburgh, Pennsylvania, he served in the army (1943–46), then worked as a graphic designer and in 1949 moved to New York. In the 1950s, he produced landscapes in a bold painterly style, but from 1960 turned to making detailed studies of the male and female nude. His work emphasizes the impersonal aspect of the subject, often omitting or 'chopping' the head of his model to concentrate on an unidealized representation of the naked body, as in *Female Model Reclining on Bentwood Love Seat* (1974). ▥ J Perreault, *Philip Pearlstein* (1988)

Pears, Sir Peter Neville Luard 1910–86
English tenor

Born in Farnham, Surrey, he was an organ scholar of Hertford College, Oxford, then studied singing (1933–34) at the Royal College of Music. He toured the USA and Europe with **Benjamin Britten**, and in 1943 joined Sadler's Wells. After the success of *Peter Grimes* (1945) he joined Britten in the English Opera Group, and was co-founder with him, in 1948, of the Aldeburgh Festival. He was noted for his sympathy with and understanding of modern works. ▥ Marion Thorpe (ed), *Peter Pears: A Tribute on His 75th Birthday* (1985)

Pearsall, Phyllis Isobel, *née* Gross 1906–96
English artist, writer and publisher

Educated at Roedean School, she went to France at the age of 14 where she taught English and studied at the Sorbonne. She survived on the money earned by painting portraits and writing for newspapers before returning to England where she established a reputation as a writer and artist. The idea of the *A/Z* (later *A–Z*) was born when Pearsall was lost in London on a selling expedition for her father's map company, and she instigated a rigorous personal regime of 18-hour walks every day in order to research the book which was drawn up by draughtsman James Duncan and published in 1936. As founder and director of The Geographer's A to Z Map Company, she proved a successful businesswoman and well-respected employer, despite poor health suffered later in life as the result of an air crash. She chaired the Geographers' Map Trust from 1987, and published *From Bedsitter to Household name: the personal story of A to Z maps* in 1990.

Pearse, Patrick 1879–1916
Irish writer, educationist and nationalist

Born in Dublin, he was the son of an English monumental sculptor and an Irish mother. A leader of the Gaelic revival, he joined the Gaelic League in 1895, became editor of its journal, and lectured in Irish at University College. In 1908 he founded a bilingual school, St Enda's, at Ranelagh, and later moved to Rath Farnham. In 1915 he joined the Irish Republican Brotherhood. In the 1916 Easter Rising he was Commander-in-Chief of the insurgents, and was proclaimed President of the provisional government. After the revolt was quelled he was arrested, court-martialled and then shot. Despite late 20th-century revisionism, he remains a totem for much Republican thinking in Ireland and an inspiration for the positive role of Irish heritage in education. He wrote poems, short stories and plays in English and Irish. ▥ R D Edwards, *Patrick Pearse: The Triumph of Failure* (1977)

Pearson, Sir Cyril Arthur 1866–1921
English newspaper and periodical proprietor

Born in Wookey, Somerset, and educated at Winchester, he became a journalist and founded, amongst other periodicals, *Pearson's Weekly* in 1890. He became associated with newspapers in 1900, founded the *Daily Express*, and amalgamated the *St James Gazette* with the *Evening Standard*. He became blind, founded St Dunstan's home for blinded soldiers and was president of the National Institution for the Blind.

Pearson, Hesketh 1887–1964
English biographer

He was born in Hawford, Worcestershire, and worked in a shipping office before beginning a successful stage career in 1911. In 1931 he emerged as a writer of popular and racy biographies. Among these are *Gilbert and Sullivan* (1935), *Shaw* (1942), *Conan Doyle* (1943), *Oscar Wilde* (1946), whose *Works* and *Essays* he edited, *Dizzy* (Disraeli, 1951), *Sir Walter Scott* (1955), *Johnson and Boswell* (1958) and *Charles II* (1960).

Pearson, Karl 1857–1936
English mathematician and scientist

Born in London, he turned from the law to mathematics, becoming Professor of Applied Mathematics (1884) and Galton Professor of Eugenics (1911) at University College London. He published *The Grammar of Science* (1892) and works on eugenics, mathematics, and biometrics. He was a founder of modern statistical theory, and his work established statistics as a subject in its own right. Pearson was also motivated by the study of evolution and heredity. In his *Life of Galton* (1914–30) the head of the Eugenics Laboratory applied the methods of his science to the study of its founder. He founded and edited the journal *Biometrika* (1901–36) and wrote on the history of statistics.

Pearson, Lester Bowles 1897–1972
Canadian statesman

He was born in Newtonbrook, Ontario, and educated at Toronto and Oxford universities. He became successively First Secretary at the London office of the Canadian High Commissioner (1935–39), assistant Under-Secretary of State for External Affairs (1941), and ambassador in Washington (1945–46). He was a senior adviser at the Charter Conference of the UN in 1945 and was later leader of Canadian UN delegations. In 1952–53 he was President of the UN General Assembly, and in 1957 was awarded the Nobel Peace Prize. Secretary of State for External Affairs (1948–57), and leader of the Opposition Party from 1958, he became Prime Minister in 1963, retaining power with a minority government in 1965. As Prime Minister he introduced a comprehensive pension plan and socialized medicine, and sought solutions to the growing separatist feeling in Quebec. He resigned as party leader and as Prime Minister in 1968.

Peary, Robert Edwin 1856–1920
US naval commander and explorer

Born in Cresson Springs, Pennsylvania, he graduated from Bowdoin College and served in the navy's civil engineering corps. He made eight Arctic expeditions from 1886, exploring Greenland and the region later called Peary Land. In 1906 he reached 87° 6' N, and on 6 April 1909 attained the North Pole. His claim to be first to reach the North Pole was substantiated when Dr Frederick Cook's own claim was discredited, although some doubt still exists regarding whether he reached the precise 90° position. ▢ J E Weems, *Peary* (1967)

Pease, Francis Gladheim 1881–1938
US astronomer and designer of optical instruments

Born in Cambridge, Massachusetts, he was observer and optician at Yerkes Observatory, Wisconsin (1901–04) and then instrument-maker (1908–13) at the Mount Wilson Observatory, Pasadena, where he designed the 100in telescope, and the 50ft interferometer telescope by means of which he gained direct measurements of star diameters. He was also associated in the design of the 200in Palomar telescope.

Pechstein, Max 1881–1955
German painter and print-maker

Born in Zwickau, he studied in Dresden and joined the avant-garde group Die Brücke in 1906. Going to Berlin in 1908 he helped found the rival Neue Sezession. He developed a colourful style indebted to Henri Matisse and to the Fauvists; he visited the Pacific just before World War I, and whilst at Palau he painted figures in tropical settings reminiscent of Paul Gauguin. He taught at the Berlin Academy from 1923 until he was dismissed by the Nazis in 1933; he was reinstated in 1945.

Peck, (Eldred) Gregory 1916–
US film actor

Born in La Jolla, California, he acted for two years with the Neighbourhood Playhouse in New York City before making his Broadway debut in *Morning Star* (1942), which led to a flood of film offers. He made his cinema debut as a Russian guerrilla in *Days of Glory* (1944) and became one of the first major postwar film stars. Good-looking and soft-spoken, he portrayed men of action and everyday citizens distinguished by their sense of decency in films such as *Spellbound* (1945), *Twelve O'Clock High* (1949) and *The Gunfighter* (1950). He was nominated five times for an Academy Award, winning Best Actor for his role as a liberal Southern lawyer in *To Kill A Mockingbird* (1962). He also produced films, including *The Trial of the Catonsville Nine* (1972), an anti-Vietnam war drama reflecting his own off-screen involvement with liberal causes and support of the Democratic Party. Later films include *The Omen* (1976), *The Boys from Brazil* (1978), *The Old Gringo* (1989) and *Cape Fear* (1991).

Peckinpah, Sam 1925–84
US film director

Born in Fresno, California, he studied drama at Fresno State College and worked as a theatre director, propman, assistant editor and actor before directing extensively for US television. He made his film debut with the western *The Deadly Companions* (1961) and was to prove a master of the genre, revealing both the savagery and the lyricism of the Wild West in such films as *Ride the High Country* (1962), *Major Dundee* (1965) and his masterpiece *The Wild Bunch* (1969). Later films include *Straw Dogs* (1971), *Junior Bonner* (1972) and *The Osterman Weekend* (1983).

Pecquet, Jean 1622–74
French anatomist

Born in Dieppe, he worked at Montpellier University, where in 1647 he was the first to see clearly the thoracic duct. He described his findings in *Experimenta nova anatomica* (1651).

Peden, Alexander c.1626–1686
Scottish Covenanter

Born in Ayrshire, he studied at Glasgow, became a schoolmaster in Tarbolton, and minister at New Luce, Galloway (1660). In 1662 he was ejected from his charge, and subsequently travelled the country preaching at conventicles and hiding in caves. Declared a rebel in 1665, he went to Ireland, but returned in 1673 and was then imprisoned on the Bass Rock until 1678. Several of his statements were regarded as prophecies.

Pedersen, Charles 1904–90
US chemist and Nobel Prize winner

Born in Pusan, Korea, of Japanese–Norwegian extraction, he studied chemical engineering in the USA (University of Dayton, Ohio) and took a master's degree in organic chemistry at the Massachusetts Institute of Technology. Throughout his life he worked for Du Pont de Nemours as a research chemist. The work for which he is best known was the accidental preparation of a cyclic polyether, a molecule shaped rather like a crown, given the name 'crown ether'. Many compounds of this type bind alkali metal ions (sodium, potassium) very strongly, and their discovery initiated the study of guest–host chemistry, and enhanced the understanding of which metal ions transport across membranes in living organisms. He retired in 1969 and shared the 1987 Nobel Prize for chemistry with Donald Cram and Jean-Marie Lehn.

Pedersen, Christiern 1480–1554
Danish theologian and historian

Born probably in Elsinore, he accompanied King Kristian II of Denmark into exile in the Low Countries (1523), and was converted to Protestantism. He made the first translation into Danish of the New Testament (1529). Returning to Denmark as a leader of the Reformation, he worked on the famous 'Kristian III' version of the Bible, which appeared in 1550. He also compiled a Danish–Latin dictionary.

Pedro (Peter), *known as* the Cruel 1334–69
King of Castile and León

He was born in Burgos, and succeeded his father, Alfonso XI, in 1350. Their attempts to assert strong monarchic government aroused resentment among the nobility, who found a leader in Pedro's illegitimate brother, Henry of Trastámara. A revolt (1354) was suppressed and Henry fled to France, but returned in 1366 with French and Aragonese support. With the help of Edward, the Black Prince, Pedro defeated his rival at Nájera (1367) but after Edward's departure from Spain, Pedro was finally routed and killed by Henry at Montiel (1369).

Pedro I 1798–1834
Emperor of Brazil

Born in Queluz, Portugal, the second son of John VI of Portugal, he fled to Brazil with his parents on Napoleon I's invasion (1807), and became Prince Regent of Brazil on his father's return to Portugal (1821). A liberal in outlook, he declared Brazilian independence in 1822 and became emperor, and was crowned as Pedro I in 1826. The new empire did not start smoothly: his autocratic nature, dislike of parliamentary government, and his continued Portuguese connections, annoyed his subjects. In 1831 he abdicated and withdrew to Portugal. He was Pedro IV of Portugal on the death of his father (1826), but abdicated within months in favour of his daughter, Donna Maria da Glória.

Pedro II 1825–91
Emperor of Brazil

Born in Rio de Janeiro, he was the son of Pedro I and succeeded on his father's abdication in 1831, being crowned in 1841. Benevolent, popular, and distinguished by his love of learning and scholarly tastes, he reigned in peace until the 1889 Revolution drove him to Europe. His remains were returned to Brazil in 1920.

Peebles, Phillip James Edwin 1935–
Canadian cosmologist

Born in Winnipeg and educated at the University of Manitoba, he went on to Princeton University, where he has been Professor of Physics since 1965 and Einstein Professor of Science since 1985. In collaboration with Robert Dicke he attempted to detect a cosmic background radiation left over from the early 'primeval fireball' phase of the universe. Observations of such radiation (1966) followed shortly after its original discovery by Arno Penzias and Robert Wilson. Peebles was the first to study the physics of, and the abundances of helium and deuterium in, the early universe (1968). This topic includes the analysis of galactic clusters and the study of the mechanisms of galaxy formation. His recent studies (1988) consider the implications of observed large-scale velocities of galaxies over and above the general expansion of the universe. One of the leading cosmologists of his generation, his books *Physical Cosmology* (1971) and *The Large Scale Structure of the Universe* (1979) are classics in the

field. Other works include *Quantum Mechanics* (1992) and *Principles of Physical Cosmology* (1993). He was elected Fellow of the Royal Society in 1982.

Peel, Lady See Lillie, Beatrice Gladys

Peel, Sir Robert 1788–1850
English statesman and Prime Minister

He was born near Bury, in Lancashire, the son of Sir Robert Peel (1750–1830), from whom he inherited a great fortune. He was educated at Harrow and Christ Church, Oxford, and entered parliament in 1809 as Tory member for Cashel. In 1811 he was appointed Under-Secretary for the colonies, and became Secretary for Ireland (1812–18). Known as 'Orange Peel' he displayed strong anti-Catholic spirit, and was so fiercely attacked by Daniel O'Connell that he challenged him to a duel. From 1818 till 1822 he remained out of office, but was MP for the University of Oxford. In 1819 he was chairman of the Bank Committee, and moved the resolutions which led to the resumption of cash payments. In 1822 he re-entered the Ministry as Home Secretary, working well with George Canning, Foreign Secretary and devoting himself to the currency. However, when Canning formed a Whig-Tory ministry, Peel, along with the Duke of Wellington and others, withdrew from office over Catholic emancipation (1827). Paradoxically, when the death of Canning led to the Wellington–Peel government in 1829, it advocated the relief of the Roman Catholics. As Home Secretary Peel organized the London police force (the 'Peelers' or 'Bobbies'). In 1830 the Wellington–Peel ministry was succeeded by a Whig ministry under Earl Grey, which, in 1832, carried the Reform Bill. Peel opposed parliamentary reform and sought to hamper the new Liberalism. Rejected by Oxford in 1829, but returned for Westbury, he represented Tamworth from 1833 till his death. In November 1834 he accepted office as Prime Minister but was replaced by Lord Melbourne in April 1835. The general election of 1841 was virtually a contest between Free Trade and Protection, and Protection won. The Conservative Party, headed by Peel, were returned to office. The Whigs wanted a fixed but moderate duty on foreign corn, and the Anti-Corn-Law League demanded repeal while Peel carried (1842) a modification of the sliding-scale. Obliged to impose (1842) an income tax of 7d in the pound, to be levied for three years, Peel revised the general tariff, and either abolished or lowered the duties on several very important articles of commerce. He repressed Irish unrest, and broke O'Connell's influence, and in 1845 the Irish unsectarian colleges were founded. But the potato blight in Ireland, and subsequent famine, rendered cheap corn a necessity. Richard Cobden and the League redoubled their exertions. Peel informed his colleagues that the Corn Laws were doomed. Lord Stanley (afterwards Earl of Derby), who replaced Peel, Lord George Bentinck, Benjamin Disraeli and others, formed a 'no-surrender' Tory party, but with the Duke of Wellington, Sir James Graham, the Earl of Aberdeen, William Gladstone and other eminent Conservatives the Laws were repealed. Defeated on an Irish Protection of Life Bill, he retired in June 1846, giving place to a Whig administration under Lord John Russell to which he gave independent but general support. During 1847–48 he was one of the most important props of the government, whose free trade principles he had now accepted. He had a keen interest in sport, literature and the arts. On 29 June 1850, he was thrown from his horse, and died. ▫ Norman Gash, *Sir Robert Peel* (1972)

Peele, George c.1558–1596
English dramatist

He was born in London, and educated at Oxford. By 1581 he had moved to London, where for 17 years he lived a bohemian life as actor, poet and playwright. He was one of those warned to repentance by **Robert Greene** in his *Groatsworth of Wit* (1592). Peele's plays include *The Arraignment of Paris* (1584)—a dramatic pastoral containing ingenious flatteries of Queen **Elizabeth I**, *Polyhymnia* (1590) and *Edward I* (1593), which contained slanders against Queen **Eleanor of Castile**. *The Old Wives' Tale* (1595), probably gave **Milton** the subject for his *Comus*. 📖 P H Cliford, *George Peele* (1913)

Peeters, Clara 1594–c.1657
Flemish artist

She was born in Antwerp, and little is known of her early life, except that she was married in 1639. Between 1608 and 1657 she completed over 32 signed works in several still-life categories, including flower paintings and elaborate 'food' and vessel paintings. Perhaps best known for her highly detailed 'meal' still lifes, she often depicted fish and many reflective surfaces. Four of these paintings are in the Prado, Madrid, and others in Vienna and the USA.

Péguy, Charles Pierre 1873–1914
French nationalist, publisher and neo-Catholic poet

Born in Orleans, he was educated at the École Normale and the Sorbonne, after which he opened a bookshop. In 1900 he founded the *Cahiers de la quinzaine*, in which were first published his own works as well as those of such writers as **Romain Rolland**. Deeply patriotic, he combined sincere Catholicism with socialism and his writings reflect his desire for justice and truth. His most important works include *Le Mystère de la charité de Jeanne d'Arc* (1910, 'The Mystery of Joan of Arc's Charity'), *Victor Marie, Comte Hugo* (1910, 'Victor Hugo'), *L'Argent* (1912, 'Money') and *La Tapisserie de Notre Dame* (1913, 'The Tapestry of Notre Dame'). He was killed in World War I. 📖 R Rolland, *Charles Péguy* (1944)

Pei, I(eoh) M(eng) 1917–
US architect

He was born in Canton, China, and emigrated to the USA in 1935, studying first at the Massachusetts Institute of Technology and later with **Walter Gropius** at Harvard in the mid-1940s. He became a naturalized US citizen in 1954 and founded his own firm in 1955, becoming renowned for Modernist designs that feature elegant abstract shapes and vast interior spaces. His principal projects include Mile High Center in Denver (1955), the 60-storey John Hancock Tower (1973) and the Kennedy Library (1979) in Boston, the glass pyramids at the Louvre in Paris (1988), and the Rock and Roll Hall of Fame in Cleveland, Ohio (1995). A controversial, adventurous designer, he won the 1983 Pritzker Prize for architecture and was awarded the US Medal of Freedom in 1993.

Peierls, Sir Rudolf Ernst 1907–95
British theoretical physicist

Born in Berlin, Germany, and educated there, he studied under **Arnold Sommerfeld** in Munich and **Werner Heisenberg** in Leipzig and became **Wolfgang Pauli**'s assistant in Zurich. Research at Rome, Cambridge and Manchester universities followed, and he was appointed professor at Birmingham University in 1937. In 1963 he moved to Oxford University, where he was Wykeham Professor of Physics, and from 1974 to 1977 was at the University of Washington, Seattle. He studied the theory of solids and analysed electron motion in them, developed the theory of diamagnetism in metals, and in nuclear physics studied the interactions of protons and neutrons. During World War II, Peierls and **Otto Frisch** studied uranium fission and the accompanying neutron emission, publishing a report in 1940 that showed the possibility of producing an atomic bomb. The British Government appointed Peierls to lead a group developing ways of separating uranium isotopes and calculating the efficiency of the chain reaction. The work was moved

to the USA as part of the combined Manhattan Project (1943). He was awarded the Royal Society's Royal (1959) and Copley (1986) medals, and knighted in 1968. He retired from Oxford in 1974 then taught for three years at the University of Washington. Among his publications are *The Laws of Nature* (1955), *Surprises in Theoretical Physics* (1979), *More Surprises in Theoretical Physics* (1991) and the autobiography *Bird of Passage* (1985). He became a British citizen in 1940.

Peirce, Benjamin 1809–80
US mathematician

Born in Salem, Massachusetts, he became professor at Harvard in 1833, astronomer to the American Nautical Almanac in 1849, and was superintendent of the Coast Survey (1867–74). His papers on the discovery of Neptune (1848) and on Saturn's rings (1851–55) and his *Treatise on Analytic Mechanics* (1857) attracted great attention. He also did important work in algebra.

Peirce, Charles Sanders 1839–1914
US philosopher, logician and mathematician

Born in Cambridge, Massachusetts, the son of **Benjamin Peirce**, he graduated from Harvard (1859) and began his career as a scientist, working for the US Coast and Geodetic Survey (1861). He became a lecturer in logic at Johns Hopkins University (1879) but left (1894) to devote the rest of his life in seclusion to the private study of logic and philosophy. In his scientific work, he developed the theory of gravity measurement using pendulums, and conducted gravity experiments in Europe and North America. He also made an early determination of the metre in terms of a wavelength of light. In philosophy, he was a pioneer in the development of modern, formal logic and the logic of relations, but he is best known as the founder of pragmatism, which he later named 'pragmaticism' to distinguish it from the work of **William James**. His theory of meaning helped establish the new field of semiotics, which has become central in linguistics as well as philosophy. His enormous output of papers was collected and published posthumously in eight volumes (1931–58).

Pelagius c.360–c.420AD
British monk and heretic

Born in Great Britain or Ireland, he settled in Rome (c.400AD), where he disputed with **Augustine of Hippo** on the nature of grace and original sin. His view that salvation could be achieved by the exercise of one's basically good moral nature (Pelagianism) was condemned as heretical by the Councils in 416 and 418, and he was then excommunicated and banished from Rome.

Pelé, *pseudonym of* Edson Arantes do Nascimento 1940–
Brazilian footballer

Born in Três Corações, Minas Gerais, he made his international debut at the age of 16, and in 1958 won his first World Cup medal, scoring twice in Brazil's win in the final over Sweden. He won another World Cup medal (1970), and in the intervening two tournaments played in the early matches. For most of his senior career he played for Santos, of which he is now director (1993–), and in November 1969 he achieved the staggering mark of 1,000 goals in first-class football. In 1975 he signed a multimillion dollar contract for New York Cosmos, and led the team to the 1977 North American Soccer League Championship, as well as giving soccer a temporary burst of popularity in the USA. He is considered one of the finest inside-forwards in the history of the game. His publications include *My Life and the Beautiful Game* (1977) and a novel, *The World Cup Murders* (1988).

Pelham, Henry c.1695–1754
English statesman

He took an active part in suppressing the Jacobite Rising of 1715, became Secretary for War in 1724, and was a zealous supporter of Robert Walpole. He took office as Prime Minister in 1743. Notable events during his ministry (reconstructed in 1744 as the 'Broad-bottom administration') were the Austrian Succession War, the Jacobite Rising of 1745, the Financial Bill of 1750, the reform of the calendar, and the Earl of Hardwicke's Marriage Act (1754). His brother was Thomas Pelham-Holles.

Pelham, Henry Pelham-Clinton 1811–64
English politician

The 5th Duke of Newcastle and 12th Earl of Lincoln, he represented South Nottinghamshire in Parliament from 1832 to 1846, when he was ousted for supporting Robert Peel's Free Trade measures. He was a Lord of the Treasury (1834–35), First Commissioner of Woods and Forests (1841–46), and then Irish Secretary. He succeeded to the dukedom in 1851, and returned to office in 1852, being Colonial Secretary in the Aberdeen government. At the Crimean War he was made Secretary of State for War—the first to hold that office. But the sufferings of the British army in the winter of 1854 caused popular discontent, and he resigned. He was Colonial Secretary under Palmerston (1859–64).

Pelham-Holles, Sir Thomas, 1st Duke of Newcastle-under-Lyme 1693–1768
English statesman

He was the brother of Henry Pelham and added the name Holles to his own on succeeding to the estates of his uncle John Holles in 1711. George I created him Earl of Clare (1714) and Duke of Newcastle (1715). A Whig and a supporter of Robert Walpole, he became Secretary of State in 1724, and held the office for 30 years. In 1754 he succeeded his brother Henry as premier, but he retired in 1756. In July 1757 he was again premier, and was compelled to take William Pitt, later Earl of Chatham, into his ministry and to give him the lead in the House of Commons and the supreme direction of the war and of foreign affairs. On the accession of George III, the Earl of Bute superseded Pelham (1762). In the Rockingham ministry (1765), he was for a few months Lord Privy Seal. ⊞ Reed Browning, *The Duke of Newcastle* (1975)

Pelikan, Jiri 1923–
Czechoslovak student politician and media reformer

An underground member of the Communist Party in World War II, he was President of the Czechoslovak Students Union in 1948 and became President of the International Union of Students (1953–63). He then switched to another political appointment as Director of Czechoslovak state television. In the course of the Prague Spring (1968) this brought him into the forefront of the reform movement, for the opening of television had an important impact within Czechoslovakia and abroad. After the Soviet invasion of August 1968, he had to leave the country, much to the detriment of Czech broadcasting for some 20 years.

Pell, John 1610–85
English mathematician and clergyman

Born in Southwick, Sussex, and educated at Cambridge, he was appointed Professor of Mathematics at Amsterdam in 1643 and lecturer at the New College, Breda, in 1646. Employed by Oliver Cromwell, first as a mathematician and later in 1654 as his agent, he went to Switzerland in an attempt to persuade Swiss Protestants to join a Continental Protestant league led by England. In 1661 he became rector at Fobbing in Essex and in 1663 vicar of Laindon. In mathematics, he is remembered chiefly for the equation named after him, and for introducing the division sign ÷ into England.

Pelletier, Pierre Joseph 1788–1842
French chemist

Born in Paris, he qualified as a pharmacist in 1810 and became professor and later assistant director at the School of Pharmacy in Paris, at the same time running a pharmacy and a chemical manufacturing business. His first research was on gum resins and other natural products such as amber and toad venom. He collaborated with Joseph Bienaimé Caventou (1817–21). They investigated the green pigment of leaves, naming it chlorophyll, and won international fame for their investigation of alkaloids. This research marked the beginning of alkaloid chemistry, led to more careful preparation of natural drugs and opened up the possibility of producing them synthetically. When his collaboration with Caventou came to an end, Pelletier continued research on his own, particularly on the alkaloids of opium. In 1823, with Jean Baptiste André Dumas, he proved that alkaloids contain nitrogen in a ring structure, and in 1838, with Philippe Walter, he discovered toluene.

Pelopidas d.364BC
Theban soldier

In 382BC he was driven from Thebes by the oligarchic party, who were supported by the Spartans, and went to Athens. He returned with a few associates in 379, and recovered possession of the citadel. His 'sacred band' of Theban youth largely contributed to Epaminondas's victory at Leuctra (371), which drove the Spartans out of central Greece. In the expedition against Alexander of Pherae (368) he was treacherously taken prisoner, but rescued by Epaminondas the following year. He was then made ambassador to the Persian court. In command of a third expedition against Alexander of Pherae, he marched into Thessaly in 364, and won the Battle of Cynoscephalae, but was himself killed.

Peltier, Jean Charles Athanase 1785–1845
French physicist

Born in Ham, Picardy, he was apprenticed to a clockmaker at the age of 15, and by 1806 had established his own shop in Paris, retiring in 1815. Largely self-taught, he published many of his investigations into phrenology, anatomy, microscopy, meteorology and electricity. A series of experiments led him in 1834 to observe that at the junction of two dissimilar metals, an electric current produced a rise or fall in temperature, depending on the direction of the current flow (Peltier effect). This phenomenon was given new significance in the subsequent work of James Joule and Lord Kelvin on thermodynamics and thermoelectricity.

Pelton, Lester Allen 1829–1918
US inventor and engineer

Born in Vermillion, Ohio, he was a carpenter when he joined the gold rush to California in 1849. He failed to strike it rich but became interested in the water wheels used to drive mining machinery, and devised an improved type of undershot wheel powered by a jet of water striking pairs of hemispherical cups. He tested a prototype at the University of California and was granted a patent in 1880, later selling the rights to the Pelton Water Wheel Company of San Francisco. Pelton wheels are now in use all over the world for high-head hydropower generation, at efficiencies approaching 90 per cent.

Pemberton, Sir Max 1863–1950
English writer

Born in Birmingham and educated at Merchant Taylors' School and Gonville and Caius College, Cambridge, he was editor of *Chums* (1892–93) and of *Cassell's Magazine* (1896–1906). The author of a succession of historical romances including *Impregnable City* (1895), *Queen of the Jesters* (1897), *The Show Girl* (1909), *Captain Black* (1911) and *The*

Mad King Dies (1928), he also wrote revues and plays. He founded the London School of Journalism, and in 1920 became a director of Northcliffe newspapers, two years later publishing a biography of Lord Northcliffe (**Alfred Harmsworth**).

Pen, Jean-Marie Le See **Le Pen, Jean-Marie**

Penck, Albrecht 1858–1945
German geographer and geologist

Born in Leipzig, he was appointed to a professorship of physical geography at Vienna (1885–1906) and at Berlin (1906–26). He examined the sequence of past Ice Ages, providing a basis for later work on the European Pleistocene. In 1894 he produced his classic *Morphology of the Earth's Surface*; he identified six topographic forms and is believed to have introduced the term geomorphology.

Penda c.577–655
King of Mercia

A champion of paganism and hammer of Christian Northumbria, he was certainly in power by 628. He defeated (in alliance with the Welsh king, **Cadwallon**) **Edwin** (St Edwin) of Northumbria at Hatfield Chase (633), and attacked Northumbria again (642), defeating and killing King **Oswald** at Maserfeld (Old Oswestry). He was an Anglo-Saxon war-leader in the old heroic mould, and made inroads on Wessex and East Anglia. However, in another onslaught on Northumbria (655) he was defeated and killed by King Oswiu at the Battle of the Winwaed in Yorkshire.

Penderecki, Krzysztof 1933–
Polish composer

Born in Debica, he studied at the Kraków Conservatory and later taught there and in Essen. He achieved worldwide recognition for two innovative scores of the late 1960s: *Trenofiarom Hiroszimy* for 52 strings (1960, *Threnody to the Victims of Hiroshima*) and *The Passion according to St Luke* (1965). Several oratorios followed, as well as operas, including *Die schwarze Maske* (1986) and other large-scale pieces (1976–78, *Paradise Lost*, 1983–84, *Polish Requiem*), two symphonies, concertos and many others. Recent works include *Flute Concerto* (1992–93) and *Violin Concerto No 2* (1995).

Penfield, Wilder Graves 1891–1976
Canadian neurosurgeon

He was born in Spokane, Washington, USA, and after undergraduate studies at Princeton, went to Oxford as a Rhodes Scholar in 1914, where he studied physiology under **Charles Sherrington**; the outbreak of World War I interrupted his studies. Wounded in the war, he returned to the USA, where he finished his medical education at Johns Hopkins University. Further scientific study in Oxford and Spain prepared him for his experimental neurosurgical work, which he developed in conjunction with surgical practice in New York at the Presbyterian Hospital and the College of Physicians and Surgeons at Columbia University. He moved to a neurosurgical appointment at McGill University in 1928, and was instrumental in founding the world-famous Montreal Neurological Institute of which he became the first director (1934–60). An outstanding practical neurosurgeon, his experimental work on animals and on the exposed brains of conscious human beings assisted in understanding the higher functions of the brain, and the causes of symptoms of brain disease such as epilepsy, and the mechanisms involved in speech. He became a Canadian citizen in 1934. Following his retirement in 1960, he began a successful second career as a novelist and biographer.

P'eng Chen See **Peng Zhen**

Peng Dehuai (P'eng Te-huai) 1899–1974
Chinese communist general

He was born in Hunan. He fought in the Sino-Japanese War (1937–45), became second-in-command to **Zhu De**, and led the Chinese 'volunteer' forces in the Korean war.

Peng Pai (P'eng P'ai) 1896–1929
Chinese rural revolutionary

From a landlord family, he studied in Japan before joining the Chinese Communist Party and organizing rural tenants in his home district of Haifeng in the southern province of Guangdong (Kwangtung). He succeeded in 1923 in establishing a peasants' association, which campaigned for lower rents, led anti-landlord boycotts, and organized welfare activities. When the association was crushed by a local warlord in 1924 he fled to the Guomindang (Kuomintang) base at Guangzhou (Canton), where he became secretary of the Peasants' Bureau and director of the Peasant Movement Training Institute. By 1925 he had helped form the Guangdong Provincial Peasant Association, which claimed 200,000 members. During the Northern Expedition (1926–28) Peng returned again to his home district and organized China's first rural soviet. In the wake of **Chiang Kai-shek's** counterrevolution against the communists, however, Peng's soviet was crushed in 1928. He was captured and executed by the Guomindang.

P'eng Te-huai See **Peng Dehuai**

Peng Zhen (P'eng Chen) 1902–97
Chinese politician

He was born in Quwo County, Shanxi (Shansi) Province. A leading member of the Chinese Communist Party and Mayor of Beijing (Peking) (1951–66), he was the first high-ranking party member to be purged during the Cultural Revolution. Accused by **Mao Zedong** of protecting party intellectuals who had been critical of the policies of his Great Leap Forward, he disappeared from public view in 1966 and was not rehabilitated until 1979, three years after Mao's death. He was reappointed to the party's Central Committee and became known as a hardliner opposed to **Deng Xiaoping's** free market reforms. He retired in 1988 but remained a significant force in politics.

Peniakoff, Vladimir, *nicknamed* Popski 1897–1951
Belgian soldier and author

He was born in Belgium of Russian parentage and educated in England. He joined the British army and from 1940 to 1942 served with the Long Range Desert Group and the Libyan Arab Force. In October 1942, with the sanction of the army, he formed his own force, Popski's Private Army, which carried out spectacular raids behind the German lines. He rose to the rank of lieutenant-colonel and was decorated for bravery by Great Britain, France and Belgium. He wrote *Private Army* (1950).

Penn, William 1644–1718
English Quaker reformer and colonialist, founder of Pennsylvania

He was born in London, the son of Admiral Sir William Penn (1621–70). He was sent down from Christ Church, Oxford, for refusing to conform to the restored Anglican Church, and his father sent him to the Continent, in the hope that the gaiety of French life would change him. He returned a polished man of the world, having served briefly in the Second Dutch War (1665–67). He studied law at Lincoln's Inn for a year, and in 1666 his father dispatched him to look after his estates in Cork. There he attended Quaker meetings, was imprisoned, and returned to England a convinced Quaker. In 1668 he was sent to the Tower for writing *Sandy Foundation Shaken*, which attacked the ordinary doctrines of the Trinity. While in prison he wrote the most popular of his books, *No Cross, No Crown*, and *Innocency with her Open Face*, which contributed to his liberation, obtained with the intervention of his father's friend, the Duke of York (the future James VII and II). In 1670 he was again imprisoned for preaching and in 1671 he was sent to Newgate Prison for six months. He took advantage of the Indulgence for making preaching tours, championing religious tolerance, and visited the Netherlands and Germany for the advancement of Quakerism. Meanwhile, as one of the Quaker trustees of the American province of West Jersey, he had drawn up the settlers' celebrated 'Concessions and Agreements' charter. In 1681 he obtained a grant of territory in North America, called 'Pensilvania' in honour of his father, intending to establish a home for his co-religionists. He sailed with his emigrants for the Delaware in 1682. In November he held his famous interview with the Native Americans on the site of Philadelphia. He planned the city, and for two years governed the colony wisely and tolerantly, within the restrictions of Puritanism. He returned to England (1684–99) to help his persecuted Quaker brethren. His influence with James VII and II and his belief in his good intentions were curiously strong and through his exertions, in 1686 all persons imprisoned on account of their religious opinions (including 1,200 Quakers) were released. After the accession of William III, Penn was accused of treasonable adherence to the deposed king, but was acquitted in 1693. In 1699 he returned to Pennsylvania, where his constitution had proved unworkable, and had to be much altered. He did something to mitigate the evils of slavery, but held black slaves himself. He departed for England in 1701. His last years were embittered by legal disputes and he spent nine months in the Fleet Street debtors' prison (1708). He was twice married, and wrote over 40 works and pamphlets. 🕮 Catherine O Peare, *William Penn: A Biography* (1957)

Penney, William George, Baron 1909–91
English physicist
Born in Sheerness, Kent, he was educated at the universities of London, Wisconsin and Cambridge, became Professor of Mathematics at Imperial College, London, and worked at Los Alamos on the Manhattan atomic bomb project (1944–45). Later he was appointed director of the Atomic Weapons Research Establishment at Aldermaston (1953–59), and chairman of the UK Atomic Energy Authority (1964–67). He was the key figure in the UK's success in producing its own atomic (1952) and hydrogen bombs (1957). Knighted in 1952, he was created a life peer in 1967, and became Rector of Imperial College (1967–73).

Pennington, Michael Vivian Fyfe 1943–
English actor
He has appeared at the Royal Court Theatre, London, the Cambridge Theatre and in the West End, but is one of Great Britain's leading Shakespearean actors, and spent seven years with the Royal Shakespeare Company (1975–81). He joined the National Theatre in 1984, and co-founded and became joint artistic director, with the stage director Michael Bogdanov, of the English Shakespeare Company (1986). He resigned as head of the ESC (1993), following a dispute with the Arts Council over funding. He published *The English Shakespeare Company* (1990) and *Hamlet: a user's guide* (1995).

Penrose, Lionel Sharples 1898–1972
English geneticist
Born in London, he studied psychology at Cambridge and worked in psychiatry in Vienna, developing a strong interest in mental illness. Returning to the UK in 1925, he studied medicine and in the 1930s carried out a major survey into the causes of mental illness, the Colchester Survey. In 1945 he became Galton Professor of Eugenics at London, although he objected strongly to the attempts of 'eugenics' to improve human characteristics through genetics, and changed his title to Professor of Human Genetics. Under his direction (1945–65), the Galton Laboratory became an international centre for human genetics, conducting research projects on Down's syndrome, the mapping of genes on chromosomes, and palm and finger prints.

Penrose, Sir Roger 1931–
English mathematical astronomer
Born in Colchester, Essex, he was educated at University College London, and then obtained a doctorate at Cambridge. Since 1973 he has been Rouse Ball Professor of Mathematics at Oxford. He is known for his work on black holes, showing (jointly with Stephen Hawking) that once collapse of a very massive star at the end of its life has started, the formation of a black hole—a point of zero volume and infinite density—is inevitable. Penrose also put forward the hypothesis of 'cosmic censorship', proposing that there must be an 'event horizon' around a black hole, isolating its physically unlawful behaviour from the rest of the universe. At Oxford Penrose has been working on 'twistor theory' in which the four dimensions of space–time are quantized by imaginary numbers as opposed to real numbers. He received the Einstein Medal in 1990 and was knighted in 1994. His publications include *Shadows of the Mind* (1994).

Penrose, Sir Roland Algernon 1900–84
English painter, connoisseur and art collector
Born in London, he graduated from Queen's College, Cambridge, in 1922, and lived in Paris from 1922 to 1935, when he began to collect Cubist and Surrealist art. In 1936 he organized the International Surrealist Exhibition in London. He founded the Institute of Contemporary Arts, London, in 1947. His friendship with Picasso led to his writing the standard biography (1958) and organizing a major exhibition of his work (Tate Gallery, London, 1960).

Pentreath, Dolly, *married name* **Dolly Jeffery**
1685–1777
English fishwife
Born in Mousehole on Mounts Bay, Cornwall, she was an itinerant fishwife and fortune-teller and is reputed to have been the last person to speak native Cornish.

Penzias, Arno Allan 1933–
US astrophysicist and Nobel Prize winner
Born in Munich, Germany, a refugee with his family from Nazi Germany, he was educated at Columbia University, New York, and joined the Bell Telephone Laboratories in 1961, finally becoming vice-president of research there in 1981. In 1963 he and his colleague Robert Wilson were assigned the task of tracing the radio noise that was interfering with Earth–satellite–Earth communications, eventually discovering the residual relic of the intense heat that was associated with the birth of the universe following the hot Big Bang. This was the cosmic microwave background radiation predicted to exist by George Gamow and Ralph Alpher in 1948. In 1970, with Wilson and K B Jefferts, Penzias discovered the radio spectral line of carbon monoxide; this has since been used as a tracer of galactic gas clouds. Penzias and Wilson were awarded the Nobel Prize for physics in 1978, along with Peter Kapitza. He published *Ideas and Information* in 1989.

Pepin II, the Younger, *known as* **Pepin of Herstal**, *French* **Pépin d'Héristal** d.714
Frankish ruler
He was born in Jupille, near Liège (now in Belgium). He was Mayor of the Palace in Austrasia, to which he added after 687 the similar vice-royalties of Neustria and

Burgundy, and called himself Duke and Prince of the Franks. He was their real ruler during several Merovingian reigns and also the father of **Charles Martel**.

Pepin III, the Short c.715–768
King of the Franks
The illegitimate son of **Charles Martel** and father of **Charlemagne**, he founded the Frankish dynasty of the Carolingians. He was chosen king (751) in place of Childeric III, the last of the Merovingians. When Pope Stephen III was hard pressed by the Longobards, Pepin led an army into Italy (754), compelled the Lombard Aistulf to become his vassal, and laid the foundation of the temporal sovereignty of the popes (756). The rest of his life was spent in wars against Saxons and Saracens.

Pépin d'Héristal See Pepin II, the Younger

Peploe, Samuel John 1871–1935
Scottish artist
Born in Edinburgh, he went to Paris in 1911, as an established painter, and later returned to Edinburgh to remodel his style in accordance with Fauve colouring and Cézannesque analysis of form. His later still-life paintings brought him fame as a colourist, and he became a leading member of the Scottish Colourists in 1930.

Pepusch, Johann Christoph 1667–1752
German composer and musical theorist
Born in Berlin, he was appointed to the Prussian court at the age of 14. Settling in London in 1704, he is best known as the arranger of the music for **John Gay**'s *The Beggar's Opera* (1728) from popular and traditional sources. Pepusch was a prolific composer of music for the theatre and church as well as of instrumental works.

Pepys, Samuel 1633–1703
English diarist and Admiralty official
The son of a London tailor, he was educated at St Paul's School and Trinity Hall and Magdalene College, Cambridge. After the Civil War he lived in poor circumstances with his young wife, Elizabeth St Michel, whom he married in 1655, but after the Restoration, through the patronage of the 1st Earl of **Sandwich**, his father's cousin, he rose rapidly in the naval service and became Secretary to the Admiralty in 1672. He lost his office and was imprisoned on account of his alleged complicity in the Popish Plot (1679), but was reappointed in 1684 and also became president of the Royal Society. At the Revolution (1688) he was again removed from office. The celebrated Diary, which ran from 1 January 1660 to 31 May 1669, is interesting both as the personal record (and confessions) of a man with an abounding love of life, and for the vivid picture it gives of contemporary life, including naval administration and Court intrigue. The highlights are probably the accounts of the three disasters of the decade—the great plague (1665–66), the great fire of London (1666) and the sailing up the Thames by the Dutch fleet (1665–67). The Diary was written in cipher (a kind of shorthand), in which form it remained in Magdalene College until 1825, when it was deciphered and edited. 📖 A Bryant, *Pepys* (3 vols, 1933–38)

Perahia, Murray 1947–
US pianist
He was born in New York, and in 1972 he became the first American to win the Leeds International Piano Competition. He is renowned as an exponent of **Mozart**, having performed and recorded all the piano concertos, directing them from the keyboard. He is closely associated with the Aldeburgh Festival, and became one of its directors. He now lives in London.

Perceval, John de Burgh 1923–
Australian ceramic artist and painter
Born in Bruce Rock, Western Australia, he was a self-taught artist, developing his precocious talent for Surrealist paintings while bed-ridden with poliomyelitis at the age of 12. In 1939 he joined the Australian Army Survey Corps, where he met artists such as **Sidney Nolan**, and the brothers **Arthur** and **Guy Boyd**. After being exhibited in Melbourne, some of his paintings were then reproduced in the avant-garde periodical *Angry Penguins*. After travelling to Europe he returned in 1965 to take up the first creative arts fellowship at the Australian National University, Canberra. A major retrospective of his work was held in 1992 at the National Gallery of Victoria and the Art Gallery of New South Wales.

Perceval, Spencer 1762–1812
English statesman
The son of the Earl of Egremont, he was born in London, educated at Harrow and at Trinity College, Cambridge, and called to the Bar in 1786. An MP from 1796, he was Solicitor-General (1801), Attorney-General (1802), and Chancellor of the Exchequer (1807), before he became Prime Minister (1809–12). An efficient administrator, he had established his Tory government by the time he was shot dead by a bankrupt Liverpool broker, John Bellingham.

Percier, Charles 1764–1838
French architect
He was born in Paris. With his friend and partner, Pierre Fontaine (1762–1853), he was among the first to create buildings in the Empire style. For **Napoleon I** they remodelled the Malmaison, worked on the Rue de Rivoli, the palace of St Cloud, the Louvre and the Tuileries, and in the gardens of the latter erected the Arc du Carrousel in 1807.

Percival, James Gates 1795–1856
US poet
Born in Berlin, Connecticut, he graduated from Yale in 1815, studied botany and medicine, and became Professor of Chemistry at West Point in 1824 and of Geology at Wisconsin in 1854. His poems *Prometheus* and *Clio* appeared between 1822 and 1827, and *The Dream of a Day* in 1843. 📖 F Cogswell, *James Gates Percival and His Friends* (1902)

Percy
A noble north of England family
Their founder, William de Percy (c.1030–1096), arrived with **William the Conqueror**, and received lands in Yorkshire, Lincolnshire, Hampshire and Essex. Richard (c.1170–1244) was one of the barons who extorted Magna Carta. Henry (c.1272–1315) aided **Edward I** in subduing Scotland and was Governor of Galloway. He also received a grant of **Robert Bruce**'s forfeited earldom of Carrick and the wardship of Bamburgh and Scarborough Castles from **Edward II**. In 1309 he purchased the barony of Alnwick, the chief seat of the family ever since. His grandson fought at Crécy; his great-grandson, Henry (1342–1408), 4th Lord Percy of Alnwick, in 1377 was made marshal of England and Earl of Northumberland. The latter's son, **Henry Percy**, was the famous 'Harry Hotspur' whom James, 2nd Earl of Douglas and Mar defeated at Otterburn (1388), and who fell fighting against **Henry IV** at Shrewsbury, where his uncle, Sir Thomas, Earl of Worcester, was captured and soon after executed. His father, who had helped Henry of Lancaster to the throne, was dissatisfied with the king's gratitude, and with his sons plotted the insurrection. He joined Archbishop Scrope's plot, and fell at Bramham Moor (1408), when his honours were forfeited, but they were restored (1414) to his grandson, who became High Constable of England. The title and estates were passed to a brother of **Richard Warwick**, the Kingmaker, but in 1469

Henry, son of the 3rd earl (d.1461), was restored by Edward IV. The 6th earl (once the lover of **Anne Boleyn**) died childless in 1537, and as his brother, Sir Thomas Percy, had been attainted and executed for his share in the Pilgrimage of Grace, the title of Duke of Northumberland was conferred by **Edward VI** upon John Dudley, Earl of Warwick, who in turn was attainted and executed under **Mary I** in 1553. In 1557 Mary granted the earldom to Thomas Percy (1528–72), son of the attainted Sir Thomas. A devoted Catholic, he took part in the Rising of the North, and was beheaded at York. His brother Henry, 8th earl, became involved in **Francis Throckmorton's** conspiracy in favour of **Mary, Queen of Scots**, and was committed to the Tower, where he was found dead in bed (1585). His son, 9th earl, was imprisoned for 15 years in the Tower, and fined £30,000 on a baseless suspicion of being privy to the Gunpowder Plot. His son, 10th earl, was a Parliamentarian. On the death of his son (1670), 11th earl, the male line of the family became extinct. **Charles II** created his third bastard by the Duchess of Cleveland, Earl, and afterwards Duke, of Northumberland, but he died childless in 1716. The 11th earl's daughter, Baroness Percy, married **Charles Seymour**, 6th Duke of Somerset; their son was created Baron Warkworth and Earl of Northumberland in 1749, with remainder to his son-in-law, Sir Hugh Smithson (1715–86), who assumed the name of Percy, and in 1766 was created Duke of Northumberland. 📖 Bertram Wyatt-Brown, *The Literary Percys: Family History, Gender, and the Southern Imagination* (1994)

Percy, Sir Henry, *also known as* **Hotspur** 1364–1403
English nobleman

He was the eldest son of Henry Percy, the earl of Northumberland, and was called 'Hotspur' because of his fiery temper. His father had helped Henry of Lancaster (**Henry IV**) to the English throne but was dissatisfied with the king's lack of gratitude. Both father and son joined **Owen Glendower's** rebellion against Henry IV, and Hotspur was killed in the defeat at Shrewsbury.

Percy, Thomas 1729–1811
English antiquary, poet and churchman

Born in Bridgnorth, and educated at Christ Church, Oxford, he became vicar of Easton Maudit in Northamptonshire (1753) and rector of Wilby (1756), and was later appointed chaplain to **George III**, then dean of Carlisle (1778) and Bishop of Dromore (1782). He published the first English version of a Chinese novel, *Hau Kiou Choaun* (1761, translated from the Portuguese), and also *Miscellaneous Pieces translated from the Chinese* (1762). Prompted by the success of **James Macpherson's** spurious Ossianic translations, he also published, anonymously, *Runic Poetry translated from the Icelandic language* (1763), a group of five poems actually translated from Latin versions. However, his fame rests on his *Reliques of Ancient English Poetry* (1765), largely compiled from a 17th-century manuscript of medieval ballads and other material found in a house in Shifnal, Shropshire, and much 'restored' by him. He later wrote a ballad of his own, *The Hermit of Warkworth* (1771).

Percy, Walker 1916–90
US novelist

Born in Birmingham, Alabama, he studied medicine, intending to make this his career, but had to abandon it when he contracted tuberculosis. His first and best novel, *The Moviegoer* (1961), won a National Book Award. He was a philosophical writer, and his novels are firmly grounded in his social observations as a liberal and unconventional Catholic Southerner, and his unassuming heroes often pass from a pleasant state of alert detachment into a full-blown crisis of alienation and despair. *Love in the Ruins* (1971) was subtitled 'The Adventures of a Bad Catholic at

a Time Near the End of the World'. Other novels include *The Last Gentleman* (1966), *The Second Coming* (1980) and *The Thanatos Syndrome* (1987). He also wrote *Novel-Writing in an Apocalyptic Time* (1984). 📖 L A Lawson and V A Kramer, *Conversations with Walker Percy* (1985)

Perdiccas d.321BC
Macedonian soldier

He was second-in-command to **Alexander the Great**. He was virtually regent of the empire after Alexander's death, but was soon murdered by mutineers from his own army.

Perdita See **Robinson, Mary**

Pereda, José Maria de 1833–1906
Spanish novelist

He was born in Polanco, near Santander, and his novels give a realistic picture of the people and scenery of the region where he was born, and where much of his life was spent. An outstanding example is *Sotileza* (1885, 'Subtlety'). Other novels are *Del tal palo tal astilla* (1880, 'Like Father, Like Son') and, perhaps his finest, *Peñas arriba* (1895, 'Up the Mountain'). He was called 'the modern **Cervantes**'. 📖 R Gullon, *Vida de Pereda* (1944)

Peregrinus, Petrus, *also called* **Peter the Pilgrim** or **Peter de Maricourt** 13th century
French scientist and soldier

Born in Picardy, and a Crusader, he was the first to mark the ends of a round natural magnet and call them poles. He also invented a compass with a graduated scale.

Pereira, Aristedes Maria 1923–
Cape Verde statesman

Born on Boa Vista island, he began his career as a radio telegraphist and progressed to being head of the telecommunications service of Guinea-Bissau. He became politically active and co-founded the African Party for the Independence of Portuguese Guinea and Cape Verde (PAIGC) in 1956. When Cape Verde won its independence in 1975 he became its first President and was re-elected in 1981 and 1986. His careful leadership earned him and his country wide respect. His presidency ended in 1991.

Pereira, Valdir See **Didi**

Perelman, S(ydney) J(oseph) 1904–79
US humorist

He was born in Brooklyn, New York City. Graduating from Brown University in 1925, he contributed to magazines until the publication of *Dawn Ginsbergh's Revenge* in 1929, which had the nation in stitches and secured the author's fame. He went to Hollywood and wrote scripts for, among others, the **Marx Brothers**. From 1931 much of his work was published first in the *New Yorker*. His writing is remarkable for its linguistic dexterity and ingenuity, and several modern sitting ducks sank under his humorous attacks. He is at his best in *Crazy Like a Fox* (1944), *Westward Ha! or, Around the World in 80 Clichés* (1948), *The Swiss Family Perelman* (1950) and *The Road to Miltown, or, Under the Spreading Atrophy* (1957). *The Most of S J Perelman* was published in 1958. 📖 D Herrmann, *S J Perelman: A Life* (1986)

Peres, Shimon 1923–
Israeli statesman and Nobel Prize winner

Born in Wolozyn, Poland, he emigrated with his family to Palestine (1934), and was raised on a kibbutz. He received most of his education in the USA, studying at New York and Harvard universities. In 1948 he became head of naval services in the new state of Israel, and later Director-General of the Defence Ministry (1953–59). In 1959 he was elected to the Knesset. He was Minister of Defence (1974–77), and in 1977 became Chairman of the Labour Party and leader of the Opposition until 1984, when he entered into a unique power-sharing agreement with the leader of the Consolidation Party (Likud), **Yitzhak Shamir**. Under this agreement, Peres was Prime Minister from 1984 to 1986, when Shamir took over. After the inconclusive 1988 general election Peres eventually rejoined Shamir in a new coalition. However the second coalition collapsed in 1990 and a government was formed by Shamir. In 1992 Peres was defeated in the Labour leadership by **Yitzhak Rabin** and Rabin went on to become Prime Minister that year. When Rabin was assassinated in 1995, Peres took over the premiership, but was defeated in elections in May 1996 by **Binyamin Netanyahu**. Shortly afterwards he announced that he would not stand for Prime Minister in the next election or party leader in 1997.

Peretz or Perez, I(saac) L(oeb) 1852–1915
Polish–Jewish writer
He was the first to write fiction about Hasidic culture and the lives of impoverished European Jews, and is known as the father of modern Yiddish literature. In later years he became the leader of the Yiddishist movement, which rejected Zionism and celebrated the culture of the Diaspora and the richness of the Yiddish language. His short-story collections include *Stories and Pictures* (1901) and *Hasidic Tales* (1908). He also wrote plays, poems, and satires.

Perey, Marguerite Catherine 1909–75
French physicist
Born in Villemomble, she was educated in Paris, and from 1929 worked at the Radium Institute under **Marie Curie**. She moved to Strasbourg University, becoming Professor of Nuclear Chemistry in 1949 and director of the Centre for Nuclear Research in 1958. During studies of the radioactive decay of actinium-227, in 1939 she discovered the element francium. She was the first female member of the French Academy of Sciences (1962).

Perez, I L See Peretz, I(saac) L(oeb)

Pérez de Ayala, Ramón 1881–1962
Spanish novelist, poet and critic
He was Born in Oviedo, and first attracted attention with his poetry when *La paz del sendero* ('The Peace of the Path') was published in 1904. A sequel volume appeared in 1916 under the title *El sendero innumerable* ('The Innumerable Path'). As a novelist he combines realism with beauty, best shown in the philosophical *Belarmino y Apolonio* (1921, 'Belamino and Apolonio'). Other novels include the humorous and satirical *Troteras y Danzaderas* (1913, 'Trotters and Dancers'), the anti-Jesuit *A.M.D.G.* (1910), and perhaps his best, *Tigre Juan* (1924) which, with *El Curandero de su honra* (1926, 'The Saviour of his Honour'), was published in English as *Tiger Juan* (1933). Among his works of criticism are *Máscaras* (1917, 'Masks') and *Política y Toros* (1918,'Politics and Bulls'). He was ambassador to London from 1931 to 1936. 📖 F Agustin, *Ramón Pérez de Ayala, su vida e su obras* (1927)

Pérez de Cuéllar, Javier 1920–
Peruvian diplomat
Born in Lima, the son of a businessman who died when Javier was only four, he studied at Lima University and embarked on a career in the Peruvian diplomatic service, representing his country at the first United Nations assembly in 1946 and as Peru's first ambassador to the USSR. He succeeded **Kurt Waldheim** as UN Secretary-General in 1982, his quiet, modest approach contrasting sharply with that of his predecessor. His patience and diplomacy secured notable achievements, particularly in his second term, including a ceasefire in the Iran–Iraq War and the achievement of independence for Namibia. His work enhanced not only his own reputation but that of the UN as well. He was succeeded as Secretary-General in 1992 by **Boutros Boutros-Ghali**.

Perez Esquivel, Adolfo 1931–
Argentine civil rights leader and Nobel Prize winner
Born in Buenos Aires, he studied art and architecture and became a professor of art and a well-known sculptor. He is a devout Catholic and an admirer of Mahatma **Gandhi**, and in 1974 he gave up his career to become head of the Service for Peace and Justice, a church-based network of organizations promoting social justice in Latin America by non-violent means. In this capacity he became a defender of human rights, and he spoke out on behalf of the thousands who disappeared during the Argentine military junta's campaign against political dissidents. He was imprisoned and tortured (1977–78) by the military regime. He was awarded the Nobel Peace Prize in 1980, and he continued to run the Service for Peace and Justice until 1986.

Pérez Galdós, Benito 1843–1920
Spanish novelist
Born in Las Palmas, Canary Islands, he moved to Madrid as a student in 1861, and supported his family by writing. He was a prolific novelist and dramatist, and also wrote journalism, travel diaries, criticism, and memoirs. He divided his novels, which are largely naturalistic in style, into categories in the manner of Honoré de **Balzac**, the principle two being the novels of contemporary Spanish life and the 46-volume historical series he called 'Episodios nacionales'. He was an acute, psychologically percipient observer of life, and has been considered the greatest Spanish novelist after **Cervantes**. His best book is the novel *Fortunata y Jacinta* (1886–78, Eng trans *Fortunata and Jacinta*, 1986). 📖 B J Dendle, *Galdós: the mature thought* (1980)

Pergolesi, Giovanni Battista 1710–36
Italian composer
Born in Jesi, he attended the Conservatorio dei Poveri di Gesò Cristo in Naples, becoming a violinist, and was appointed maestro di cappella (1732) to the Prince at Naples. His comic intermezzo *La serva padrona* (1733, 'The Maid as Mistress') was very popular, and influenced the development of *opera bouffe*. He wrote much church music, and later left Naples for a Capuchin monastery in Pozzuoli, where he composed his *Stabat Mater* (1736).

Peri, Jacopo 1561–1633
Italian composer
Born in Rome, he became attached, as a student, to the **Medici** family in Florence. He was the leading composer in a group of artists who aimed to restore what they believed to be the true principles of Greek tragic declamation. Experimenting in an instrumentally-accompanied declamatory style, Peri wrote *Dafne* (1598) and *Euridice* (1600), with libretti by the poet **Ottavio Rinuccini**, which have been historically accepted as the first genuine operas.

Periander c.625–585BC
Tyrant of Corinth
He succeeded his father **Cypselus**. Under him Corinth's power and position in the Greek world developed further, with great commercial prosperity, and he cultivated extensive links with foreign rulers. He is remembered by later tradition as an example of a repressive tyrant, yet he was also included in the canon of the Seven Wise Men of Greece. The tyranny came to an end soon after his death.

Pericles See panel p1448

Périers, Bonaventure Des See Despériers, Bonaventure

Peri Rossi, Cristina 1941–
Uruguayan writer and journalist

Pericles c.490–429BC
Athenian statesman

Pericles was born into the aristocratic Alcmaeonid family in Athens. He was the son of Xanthippus, who had won the naval victory over the Persians at Mycale in 479BC, and of Agariste, a niece of the Alcmaeonid reformer **Cleisthenes**. He was *choregos* (provider of the chorus) in 472BC, when **Aeschylus's** *Persae* was produced. He came rapidly to the fore as a supporter of the new democracy. He helped prosecute the conservative **Cimon** in 463, who was subsequently ostracized, and with **Ephialtes** in 462/1, he brought in measures limiting the power of the old aristocratic Areopagus. When Ephialtes was murdered, Pericles became the dominant figure in Athenian politics, being elected 15 times to the office of *strategos* (general, but with political functions) between 451 (when he introduced a popular law which restricted citizenship) and his death.

Athens under Pericles followed an expansionist policy, in which the Delian League, founded to keep the defeated Persians away from Greece, was turned into an Athenian empire. Tribute was exacted from the former allies, and attempts to secede were crushed by force (notably Samos in 439). Colonies and other settlements were founded in the Thracian Chersonese (notably Amphipolis, after two failed attempts) and in southern Italy at Thurii (433). According to some accounts (but not **Thucydides**, the principal source), Pericles planned a grand Hellenic confederation to put an end to mutually destructive wars, which was frustrated by Spartan opposition but the Spartan aristocrats brought the scheme to nothing. However, the historicity of this event is doubtful.

Athens and Sparta were almost continuously at war during these years, culminating in the Peloponnesian War which broke out in 431. In 446 there was a peace (the so-called Thirty Years' Peace) in which Sparta recognized much of Athens' imperial ambition. During the respite that followed, Pericles undertook a major building programme which glorified Athens with the Parthenon, the Propylaea, and other buildings on the Acropolis. He was opposed for a time by Thucydides son of Melesias (not to be confused with the historian), who was ostracized in 433, leaving

Pericles virtually unopposed. What opposition there was found its expression at the expense of Pericles' associates, such as Pheidias, the sculptor of the statue of Athena, who was accused of embezzlement and impiety and died in prison.

When war broke out again with Sparta in 431, Pericles advocated a policy of caution on land, allowing the invading Spartans to destroy the fields while the population was concentrated behind the strong city walls and the city's supply lines could be protected by the powerful Athenian navy. Thucydides puts into Pericles' mouth the famous funeral oration commemorating the victims of the first year of fighting. In 430 plague broke out in the city; the Athenians' patience broke and Pericles was removed from office. He was again elected *strategos*, but he died soon afterwards, a victim himself of the plague.

Thucydides the historian said of Athens under Pericles that it was in fact a democracy but was in practice ruled by its first citizen. No other Athenian statesman before or since achieved such a dominant position. He had an imposing visage, as the surviving busts of him (always helmeted) show, and he enjoyed the company of the poets and intellectuals of the day, including **Sophocles**, whose personal friend he was. He divorced his wife, and took as his mistress **Aspasia**, a noted *hetaera* (courtesan).

📖 There is a life by **Plutarch**, which supplements the information in Book I of Thucydides' history. See also J K Davies, *Classical Greece* (Fontana History of the Ancient World, 2nd edn, 1993); A R Burn, *Pericles and Athens* (1970).

Other biographies from Periclean Athens: *playwrights* **Aeschylus, Sophocles, Euripides**; *historians* **Herodotus, Thucydides**; *philosophers* **Anaxagoras, Zeno, Protagoras, Socrates**, *artists and architects* **Ictinus, Myron, Phidias**.

'Famous men have the whole earth as their memorial.'
Attributed to Pericles by Thucydides, *History of the Peloponnesian War*, 2.43 (trans by R Warner).

Her work is among the best experimental fiction written by a Latin-American writer, and tests the limits of genre, language and form. Her main interests lie in shifting literature, society, and gender roles, and both her poetry and her prose employ humour and irony to illustrate the disintegration of out-dated modes of social interaction. Among her awards are the **Benito Pérez Galdós** prize for *La rebelión de los niños* (1976, 'The Children's Rebellion') and the Ciudad de Palma prize for *Linguistica General* (1979). She has lived in exile in Barcelona since 1972.

Perkin, Sir William Henry, Snr 1838–1907
English chemist

Born in Shadwell, London, he enrolled at the Royal College of Chemistry in 1853 to study under **August Hofmann**. At the age of 17 he became Hofmann's personal assistant, but his first major discovery was made in a private laboratory he fitted out in his home. Here, in 1856, he attempted to synthesize quinine, much in demand for the treatment of malaria. He was not successful, but after conducting the same experiment with toluidine, he was able to extract a brilliant purple dye, subsequently named mauveine. With the encouragement of the dyeing firm J Pullar and Son, he built a factory to manufacture mauveine, which was a great commercial success, initiated the modern synthetic dyestuffs industry and introduced a new range of colours into human life. In 1874 Perkin sold his dye works in order to devote himself exclusively to his chemical research, which reached an

important point in 1881 when he observed the magnetic rotatory power of a number of the organic compounds he had made. He held no academic post and conducted his research in his private laboratory, but the Royal Society of Chemistry named its organic chemistry section the Perkin Division. He received many honours both in Great Britain and in the USA, including election to the Royal Society in 1866 and a knighthood in 1906. His three sons all became distinguished chemists.

Perkins, Frances 1882–1965
US social reformer and politician

She was born in Boston, Massachusetts, into a middle-class family, and was educated at Mount Holyoke College, Massachusetts, where a speech by **Florence Kelley** first sparked her interest in feminism. Later, while a teacher, she visited various Chicago settlement houses, in particular Hull House, and grew convinced that the workers' conditions would be improved by practical deeds not political doctrines. Moving to New York, she became secretary of the New York Consumers' League (1910–12), then secretary of the Committee on Safety of the City of New York (1912–17), campaigning with enormous energy on many fronts and helping to secure passage of state legislation that set factory safety standards and minimum wages and limited working hours. In 1918 she became the first woman member of the New York State Industrial Commission (chairman 1926, commissioner 1929). She joined the Democratic Party and for 30 years served as an expert on labour issues. She was appointed US Secretary of Labor (1933–45) by Franklin D Roosevelt and, becoming the first US female Cabinet member, was an influential member of his administration. As an advocate of unemployment compensation, old age insurance and the regulation of working hours and child labour, she helped shape New Deal policies and bring about passage of the Social Security Act and the Fair Labor Standards Act. She resigned in 1945, but served on the Civil Service Commission until 1952.

Perkins, Jacob 1766–1849
US mechanical engineer and inventor

Born in Newburyport, Massachusetts, he was apprenticed at the age of 13 to a goldsmith, making dies for the state coinage, and went on to develop steel plates that could be used in place of copper in the engraving process, enabling highly complex patterns to be used for banknotes and making counterfeiting more difficult. He and his partner moved to England in 1818 and established an engraving factory which in 1840 printed the first penny postage stamps. While in England he became interested in high-pressure steam boilers and experimented with pressures far higher than those considered safe by most engineers. In 1831 he invented an early form of water tube boiler, but it attracted little interest and his experiments had to be abandoned.

Perkins, Maxwell Evarts 1884–1947
US editor, publisher and journalist

Born in New York City, he studied economics at Harvard, worked as a reporter on the *New York Times* (1907–10), then joined Scribner's the publishers, eventually becoming editor-in-chief. Associated with writers like Ernest Hemingway and F Scott Fitzgerald, his greatest achievement was to convert Thomas Wolfe's manuscript of *Look Homeward, Angel* into a US classic. Wolfe made him the prototype for his character 'Foxhall Edwards' in his *You Can't Go Home Again* (1941).

Perlman, Itzhak 1945–
Israeli violinist

He was born in Tel Aviv, the son of Polish immigrants, and moved in 1958 to study at the Juilliard School, New York. He first played on US radio aged 10, at Carnegie Hall in 1963, and in London in 1968. Now one of the most highly acclaimed violinists of his time, he is noted for his brilliant technique and attention to detail, and usually plays 19th- and 20th-century works. He contracted polio at the age of four, and as a result, plays seated.

Permeke, Constant 1886–1951
Belgian painter and sculptor

Born in Antwerp, he studied at Bruges and Ghent, and later settled in Laethem-Saint-Martin, where he became the leader of the modern Belgian Expressionist school. After 1936, he concentrated on sculpture.

Perón family See panel p1450

Perot, H(enry) Ross 1930–
US billionaire and politician

He was born in Texarkana, Texas. In 1962 he founded Electronic Data Systems (EDS), a computer services company, and after selling it to General Motors in 1984, he acquired interests in real estate, gas, and oil. Drawing on his vast fortune to buy media time, he ran for President as an independent in 1992 but was not elected. He later fought US ratification of the North American Free Trade Agreement. In 1996 he again ran for President as a third-party candidate.

Pérouse, Jean, Comte de La See La Pérouse, Jean François de Galaup, Comte de

Perovskaya, Sophie 1854–81
Russian feminist socialist

Born in rural Russia, she was a typical young woman for that period who in the 1860s and 1870s left home in order to study and become politically active. She became a member of the Russian 'Amazons', a network of study groups promoted and supported by Yelizaveta Kovalskaya, which evolved into conspiratorial revolutionary organizations. In 1881 she was publicly hanged, with four men, for assassinating Tsar Alexander II. The entry of women into Russian universities, which had been permitted since 1876, was subsequently forbidden on the basis that a woman had been responsible for the death of the Tsar. This was not re-instated until the 1905 revolution.

Perrault, Charles 1628–1703
French writer

Born in Paris, he studied law, and from 1654 to 1664 worked for his brother, the receiver-general of Paris. In 1663 he became a secretary or assistant to Jean-Baptiste Colbert. His poem, *Le Siècle de Louis le Grand* (1687, 'The Century of Louis XIV'), and Nicolas Boileau's outspoken criticisms of it, opened up the dispute about the relative merits of the ancients and moderns. To the modern cause Perrault contributed his poor *Parallèle des anciens et des modernes* (1688–96, 'Comparison of the Ancients and the Moderns'), and his *Hommes illustres qui ont paru en France pendant ce siècle* (1696–1700, 'Great Men Who Emerged in France this Century'). His *Mémoires* appeared in 1769. All his writings would have been forgotten but for his eight inimitable fairy tales, the *Histoires ou Contes du temps passé* (1697, Eng trans *Perrault's Popular Tales*, 1888), including 'Belle au bois dormant' ('The Sleeping Beauty'), 'Le Petit chaperon rouge' ('Red Riding Hood') and 'Barbe-Bleue' ('Bluebeard'). 🕮 M Soriano, *Les contes de Perrault* (1968)

Perret, Auguste 1874–1954
French architect

Born in Brussels, he spent most of his life in Paris, where he pioneered the use of reinforced concrete in a number of buildings, mainly in the neoclassical style, including the Théâtre des Champs Élysées and the Musée des Travaux Publics. He also designed churches at le Raincy and Montmagny.

Perrin, Jean Baptiste 1870–1942
French physicist and Nobel Prize winner

Born in Lille, Nord-Pas-de-Calais, he was educated at the École Normale Supérieure in Paris and from 1898 to 1940 was on the physical chemistry staff of the University of Paris, as full professor from 1910. In 1940 he escaped to the USA following the invasion of France. His earliest work helped to establish the nature of cathode rays as negatively charged particles, but he is most remembered for his studies of the Brownian movement. He demonstrated that the suspended particles which show Brownian motion essentially obey the gas laws, and used such systems to determine a fairly accurate value for the Avogadro number. His book *Les Atomes* (1913), which described this work, became a classic. He was awarded the Nobel Prize for physics in 1926, was elected a Foreign Member of the Royal Society in 1918, and served as president of the French Academy of Sciences in 1938.

Perronet, Jean Rodolphe 1708–94
French civil engineer

He was born in Suresnes. After training as an architect and working as a civil engineer in French government service, he was appointed the first director of the newly-created École des Ponts et Chaussées (1747). He built a number of impressive masonry arch bridges, including the Pont de Neuilly and the Pont de la Concorde in Paris, setting new standards of aesthetic and engineering

Perón, Juan, Eva and Isabelita
Argentine political and populist leaders

Perón, Juan Domingo 1895–1974
Argentine soldier and statesman

Juan Perón was born in Lobos, in the province of southern Buenos Aires. He joined the army in 1913, and took a leading part in the army revolt of 1943 which toppled the pro-Axis President, Ramón Castillo. He was well-read, a hypnotic public speaker and a close student of **Benito Mussolini**; he developed a broad base of popular support, augmenting his rule with force.

He used his position as Secretary of Labour to gain union support, while using his other position as Under-Secretary of War to cultivate junior officers. He organized the *descamisados*, a civilian paramilitary organization which, like both **Hitler's** Brownshirts and Mussolini's Blackshirts, was drawn from the lower classes. Their affections were secured by his politically astute wife, **Eva Perón**, and when she died in 1952 they greatly mourned her. In 1945, senior army and navy officers, alarmed at Perón's mobilization of the masses, imprisoned Perón, but released him after thousands gathered in the public squares demanding his return.

In 1946 after a populist campaign laced with strong nationalist and anti-American rhetoric, 'El Líder' was elected President and set about building a corporatist state. He reduced the legislature and the judiciary to rubber-stamps, tried to crush all opposition by any means including torture, and sought to modernize and industrialize the economy through large-scale government intervention and by nationalizing foreign-owned enterprises (including the railways). In 1955, with the economy in a shambles and having alienated the church, the military, the middle-class and some of the labour movement, he was deposed by the army and fled to Spain.

But his movement lived on. Failing to crush the Perónists, the military returned the government to civilian rule until 1966 when it again took over to prevent a Perónist party electoral victory. It again failed to destroy the Perónists by force, and again allowed elections, which were won by the Perónist candidate who resigned in favour of 'El Líder'. Perón died a year after his triumphal return in 1973, leaving his office to the vice-president, his third wife, **Isabelita Perón**.

📖 Robert Crossweller, *Perón* (1987); Joseph A Page, *Perón* (1983); Robert J Alexander, *Perón* (1979).

Perón, (Maria) Eva Duarte De, *known as* Evita 1919–52
Argentine popular leader and social reformer

The second wife of **Juan Perón**, Eva Perón was born into a poor family in Los Toldos, Buenos Aires. She was a radio and stage actress before her marriage to Juan Perón in 1945. She played a major part in his successful presidential campaign the following year, and became a powerful political influence and mainstay of the Perón government. Meanwhile she used her position to press for women's suffrage, by founding the Peronista Feminist Party in 1949, and by acquiring control of newspapers and business companies.

As *de facto* Minister of Health and Labour, she gained politcal support for her husband from among the working classes. Idolized by the populace herself, she founded the Eva Perón Foundation for the promotion of social welfare. After her death, support for her husband waned. When he was overthrown in 1955 her body was stolen and kept hidden until the early 1970s; it was repatriated by **Isabelita Perón** after Juan Perón's death in 1974.

Evita Perón's life story was the theme of a popular musical by **Andrew Lloyd-Webber** and **Tim Rice** (1978).

📖 Eva Perón's autobiography was published in English as *My Mission in Life* (1953). See also N Fraser and M Navarro, *Eva Perón* (1980); Julie M Taylor, *Evita Perón: The Myths of a Woman* (1979); John Barnes, *Evita, First Lady: A Biography of Eva Perón* (1978).

Perón, Isabelita, *popular name of* Maria Estela Martínez de Perón, *née* Cartas 1931–
Argentine politician

Maria Cartas was born in La Rioja Province and adopted the name Isabel when she began her career as a dancer. She became the third wife of the deposed President Juan Perón in 1961, and lived with him in Spain until his triumphal return to Argentina as President in 1973, when she was made Vice-President.

She took over the presidency at his death in 1974, but was ousted in a military coup in 1976 and placed under house arrest for five years. On her release in 1981 she settled in Madrid, and in 1988 she returned to Argentina.

---

design, for example, by his realization that if all the spans were built simultaneously the thickness of the interior piers could be greatly reduced.

Perronneau, Jean Baptiste c.1715–1783
French portrait painter

He usually painted in pastels, and became best known for his *Girl with a Kitten* (1745). He travelled widely in Europe so his work lacked unity, but is nevertheless admired for its delicacy.

Perrot, Jules Joseph 1810–94
French dancer, choreographer and ballet-master

Born in Lyons, he started his theatrical career as a child acrobat and pantomimist before studying ballet with master teacher **Auguste Vestris**. He danced at the Paris Opera Ballet (1830–34), partnering **Maria Taglioni**. He met **Carlotta Grisi** while touring Europe in 1836, and became her lover, partner and mentor, and though uncredited, he devised the steps for her solos in *Giselle* (1841). He moved his base to London (1842–48) and choreographed nearly two dozen ballets, the most famous being *Pas de Quatre* (1845). From 1850 he was ballet master and principal dancer in St Petersburg. He was

considered one of the great dancers of the Romantic movement. Afterwards he retired to Brittany with his wife, the Russian ballerina Capitoline Samovskaya.

Perry, (Mary) Antoinette 1888–1946
US actress and director

Born in Denver, Colorado, she had a long career on the stage from 1905 and as a director from 1928. In 1941 she founded the American Theatre Wing. The annual Tony awards of the New York theatre are named after her.

Perry, Fred(erick John) 1909–95
US tennis player

He was born in Stockport, Cheshire, England, the son of a Labour MP. His first sport was table-tennis, at which he was world singles champion in 1929. He only took up lawn tennis when he was 19, and between 1933 and the end of 1936, when he turned professional, he won every major amateur title, including the Wimbledon singles three times, the US singles three times, and the Australian and French championships, and helped to keep the Davis Cup in Great Britain for four years. He was the first man to win all four major titles. As a professional, he moved to the USA, took US citizenship (1938), and pursued a career in coaching, writing and broadcasting.

Perry, Matthew Calbraith 1794–1858
US naval officer

He was born in Newport, Rhode Island, and in 1837 he was appointed commander of the *Fulton*, one of the first naval steamships. He was active in suppression of the slave trade on the African coast in 1843. In the Mexican War (1846–48) he captured several towns and took part in the siege of Veracruz. From 1852 to 1854 he led the naval expedition to Japan, forcing it to open diplomatic negotiations with the USA and grant the first trading rights. He was the brother of **Oliver Hazard Perry**.

Perry, Oliver Hazard 1785–1819
US naval officer

Born in South Kingston, Rhode Island, he entered the navy in 1799 and served in the Mediterranean during the Tripolitan War. In the War of 1812 he defeated a British squadron on Lake Erie (1813), a victory he reported with the famous message, 'We have met the enemy and they are ours'. He died of yellow fever on a mission to Venezuela. He was the brother of **Matthew Calbraith Perry**.

Perry, William James 1927–
US government official

Born in Vandergrift, Pennsylvania, he served in the US army of occupation in postwar Japan from 1946, then studied mathematics at Stanford University and received a PhD in the same subject at Pennsylvania State University. In 1964 he co-founded ESL, Inc, a military electronics company, and he won attention for his success as a defence industry entrepreneur known for his astute management. He served in the defence department during the **Carter** administration (1977–81) and became deputy Secretary of Defense in 1993 in the **Clinton** administration, succeeding Les Aspin as Secretary of Defense in 1994. His tasks as Defense Secretary have included attempts to limit or defuse the nuclear threat in countries such as North Korea and the smaller nations of the former Soviet Union, and to pin down the elusive strategic goals of US forces in Bosnia.

Perse, Saint-John See Saint-John Perse

Perseus c.213–c.165BC
Last King of Macedonia in the Antigonid dynasty

He succeeded his father **Philip V** (179BC), and pursued Philip's policy of consolidating his kingdom after the defeat by Rome, but his success provoked Roman and Greek jealousy. This brought about the Third Macedonian War (171–168), in which Perseus was defeated at Pydna (168) and taken to Italy, where he died in captivity. The monarchy of Macedonia was then abolished.

Pershing, John Joseph, *known as* Black Jack 1860–1948
US soldier

Born in Linn County, Missouri, he was a schoolteacher before he enrolled at West Point in 1880. He later served on frontier duty against the Sioux and Apaches (1886–98), in the Spanish–American War (1898), and during the Moro insurgencies in the Philippines (1903). In 1906 he was promoted from captain to brigadier general by **Theodore Roosevelt** and in 1916 he led a US force into Mexico in an unsuccessful effort to track down **Pancho Villa**. As Commander-in-Chief (1917–18) of the American Expeditionary Force in Europe during World War I, he insisted that US troops should fight as a separate army under their own flag and led them effectively in the final battles of the war. From 1921 to 1924 he was US Chief of Staff. He wrote *My Experiences in the World War* (1931, Pulitzer Prize). ▢ D Smyth, *Pershing* (1986)

Persius, *properly* Aulus Persius Flaccus 34–62AD
Roman satirist

He was born in Volaterrae, Etruria, of a distinguished equestrian family, and was educated in Rome, where he came under Stoic influence. He wrote fastidiously and sparingly, leaving at his death only six admirable satires, the whole not exceeding 650 hexameter lines. These were published by his friend Cornutus after his death. **Dryden** and others have translated them into verse. ▢ E V Marmorale, *Persio* (1956)

Pert, Candace, *née* Beebe 1946–
US pharmacologist

Born in Manhattan, New York, she was educated at Bryn Mawr College and Johns Hopkins University Hospital Medical School, where she stayed as Research Fellow (1974–78) and Research Pharmacologist (1978–82) until her appointment as chief of the section of brain chemistry of the National Institute of Mental Health. Pert realized that synthetic opiates at very small doses must bind to highly selective target receptor sites, and her search for these sites bore fruit in 1973, when she reported the presence of such receptors in specialized areas of the mammalian brain. This suggested the existence of natural opiate-like substances in the brain, later discovered by **Hans Kosterlitz** and **John Hughes**. Her research continues on the chemical characteristics of brain tissue and neural functioning.

Pertinax, Publius Helvius AD126–93
Roman emperor

He was born at Alba Pompeia in Liguria, the son of a freed slave. When the assassins of **Commodus** forced him to become emperor, his accession was hailed with delight by the senate, but his fiscal conservation caused him to be slain by the rebellious praetorian guard three months later.

Pertwee, Jon, *originally* John Devon Roland Pertwee 1919–96
English actor

Born in London, son of playwright Roland Pertwee, he made his name during World War II in the radio series *HMS Waterlogged*, which continued later as *Waterlogged Spa*, and his other radio successes included *Up the Pole* and *The Navy Lark*. His films included *Knock on Wood* (1954, standing in for Danny Kaye in the London scenes), three *Carry On* pictures and *A Funny Thing Happened on the Way to the Forum* (1966). He was best known for his starring roles on television in *Doctor Who* (1970–74) and *Worzel Gummidge* (1979–82), which he recreated in *Worzel Gummidge Down Under* (1987, 1989).

Perugino, *properly* Pietro di Cristoforo Vannucci c.1450–1523
Italian painter

Born in Città della Pieve in Umbria, he established himself in Perugia (hence the nickname). In Rome, where he went about 1483, **Sixtus IV** employed him in painting the Sistine Chapel; his fresco *Christ Giving the Keys to Peter* is the best of those still visible, others being destroyed to make way for **Michelangelo's** *Last Judgement*. In Florence (1486–99) he had **Raphael** for his pupil. In Perugia (1499–1504) he adorned the Hall of the Cambio. After 1500 his art visibly declined. In his second Roman sojourn (1507–12) he also, along with other painters, decorated the Stanze of the Vatican. One of his works there, the Stanza del Incendio, was the only fresco spared when Raphael was commissioned to repaint the walls and ceilings.

Perutz, Max Ferdinand 1914–
British biochemist and Nobel Prize winner

Born in Vienna, Austria, he graduated at the university there, and emigrated to the UK (1936) where he has worked single-mindedly on the structure of haemoglobin at Cambridge ever since. He became director of the Medical Research Council (MRC) Unit for Molecular Biology (1947–62) and since 1962 has been director of the MRC Laboratory for Molecular Biology. In 1951 the presence of the alpha helix was predicted to occur in haemoglobin by Perutz, Francis Crick and Sir Lawrence Bragg, and Perutz later determined the haemoglobin structure to 5.5 angstroms. In further studies he predicted the detailed distribution of amino acids in haemoglobin (1964). He and John Kendrew were awarded the 1962 Nobel Prize for chemistry. Since then, Perutz has studied the effects of genetic variants, the evolutionary development and numerous other aspects of haemoglobin. His publications include *Is Science Necessary?* (1988) and *Protein Structures* (1992). He was elected FRS in 1954 and was appointed to the Order of Merit in 1988.

Peruzzi, BaldassareTommaso 1481–1536
Italian architect

Born in Ancajano near Volterra, he went to Rome (1503), where he designed the Villa Farnesina and the Ossoli Palace, and painted frescoes in the Church of S Maria della Pace in 1516. After a short period as city architect in Siena, he returned to Rome in 1535 and designed the Palazzo Massimo. He was influenced by Donato Bramante and ancient Italian architecture; drawings and designs by him are in the Uffizi Gallery, Florence.

Pessoa, Fernando António Nogueira
1888–1935
Portuguese poet

Born in Lisbon and educated in South Africa, he studied at Lisbon University, worked as a commercial translator and founded the journal *Orfeu*. After 1914, Pessoa created four stylistically distinct 'heteronyms': the Symbolist 'Fernando Pessoa', the pastoral 'Alberto Caeiro', the Futurist 'Álvaro de Campos', and the elegant classicist 'Ricardo Reis'. He also created several partial heteronyms and his/their complete works were published from 1952 (English translation by Jonathan Griffin, 4 vols, 1974). Three volumes of *English Poems* had already appeared in 1921. It has been suggested that, far from being a conscious literary strategy, this heteronymity was a symptom of multiple personality disorder. He remains an important figure in the Modernist movement. ◫ G Monteiro (ed), *The Man Who Never Was* (1982)

Pestalozzi, Johann Heinrich 1746–1827
Swiss educationist

Born in Zurich, he devoted his life to the children of the very poor. Believing, like Jean Jacques Rousseau, in the moralizing virtue of agricultural occupations and rural environment, he set up a residential farm school for his collected waifs and strays on his estate at Neuhof in 1774; but owing to faulty domestic organization it had to be abandoned after a five-year struggle (1780), and he wrote his *Evening Hours of a Hermit* (1780). In 1798 he opened his orphan school at Stanz, but at the end of eight months it had to close. In partnership with others, and under the patronage of the Swiss government, he opened a school of his own at Berthoud. While there he published *How Gertrude Educates her Children* (1801), the recognized exposition of the Pestalozzian method. In 1805 he moved his school to Yverdon, and applied his method in a large secondary school, but his incapacity in practical affairs resulted in the school's closure in 1825. He wrote *Schwanengesang* ('Swan Song'), a last educational prayer, in 1826. ◫ Kate Silber, *Pestalozzi: The Man and His Work* (4th edn, 1976)

Pétain, (Henri) Philippe (Omer) 1856–1951
French soldier and statesman

He was born in Cauchy-à-la-Tour of peasant parents. As a junior officer his confidential report was marked 'If this officer rises above the rank of major it will be a disaster for France', but seniority brought him the military governorship of Paris and appointments on the instructional staff. His defence of Verdun (1916) made him a national hero. As Commander-in-Chief in 1917, his appeasement policies, after the widespread mutinies that followed General Nivelle's disastrous offensive, virtually removed the French army from the war. Minister forWar in 1934, he sponsored the ineffective Maginot Line and when France collapsed in early 1940, he succeeded Paul Reynaud as the head of the government, immediately arranging terms with the Germans. His administration at Vichy involved active collaboration with Germany, particularly through Pierre Laval and Marcel Deat. With the liberation of France (1944) Pétain was brought to trial, his death sentence for treason being commuted to life imprisonment on the Île d'Yeu. He died in captivity in 1951. ◫ Herbert R Lottman, *Pétain, Hero or Traitor: The Untold Story* (1985)

Peter, St, *originally* Symeon or Simon bar Jona ('son of Jonah') 1st century AD
One of the 12 Apostles of Jesus Christ

He came from Bethsaida, but during the public ministry of Jesus Christ had his house at Capernaum. Originally a fisherman, and brother of Andrew, he soon became leader amongst the 12 Apostles, and was regarded by Jesus, who renamed him Cephas or Peter ('rock'), with particular favour and affection. Despite his frailty at the time of the Crucifixion, when he denied Jesus three times, he was entrusted with the 'keys of the Kingdom of Heaven'. He was the spokesman for the others on the day of Pentecost, he was the first to baptize a Gentile convert, and he took a prominent part in the council at Jerusalem. In Antioch he worked in harmony with Paul for a time, but the famous dispute (Galatians 2.11–21), with other causes, led to the termination of Paul's ministry in that city. Peter's missionary activity seems to have extended to Pontus, Cappadocia, Galatia, Asia and Bithynia. That he suffered martyrdom is clear from John 21.18, 19, and is confirmed by ecclesiastical tradition: Eusebius of Caesarea says he was impaled or crucified with his head downward. Tradition from the end of the 2nd century suggests he died in Rome and he is regarded by the Catholic Church as first Bishop of Rome. The first Epistle of Peter is usually accepted as genuine, but not the second. His feast day is 29 June. He was succeeded as Bishop by Linus (d.c.80AD), a son of Caractacus. ◫ J Lowe, *Saint Peter* (1956)

Peter I, *known as* the Great 1672–1725
Tsar and Emperor of Russia

He was born in Moscow, the fourth son of theTsar Alexis I Mikhailovich by his second wife. He was made co-tsar in 1682 jointly with his mentally disabled half-brother Ivan V (1666–96) on the death of their elder brother, Fyodor III, and under the regency of their sister, the Granduchess Sophia (d.1704). He became emperor in 1721. An energetic military enthusiast and contemptuous of political and religious ceremony, in 1689 he had his sister arrested and immured in a convent, and ruled on his own with his brother as a figurehead. In 1689 he married Eudoxia (1669–1731), the pious daughter of a boyar, by whom he had a son in 1690, the tsarevitch Alexis (father of the future Peter II). In 1695 he served as a humble bombardier in war against theTurks, in 1696 he captured the vital sea-port of Azov, and in 1697 he set off on a tour of Europe, travelling incognito in a 'Grand Embassy' whose main official purpose was to secure allies against the Turks. In the course of the 16th-month journey he amassed knowledge of western technology and hired thousands of craftsmen and military personnel to take back to Russia. He returned to Russia in the summer of

1698 to repress a revolt of the *streltsy* (regiments of musketeers), with the help of a Scottish general, Patrick Gordon. Eudoxia, accused of conspiracy, was divorced and sent to a convent. Peter, often brutally and against the wishes of his people, set about the westernization of Russia. In 1700, in alliance with Denmark and **Augustus II, the Strong**, King of Poland and Elector of Saxony, he launched the Great Northern War against Sweden (1700–21). Initially defeated, Peter ordered the church bells in Moscow to be melted down to make new cannons, and by refusing to permit the election of a new patriarch was able to divert ecclesiastical revenues to the war effort. He triumphed over the Swedish army in 1709 at the Battle of Poltava in the Ukraine, and the 1721 Peace of Nystadt saw Sweden cede parts of Finland plus Ingria, Estonia and Latvia. In 1703 Peter had begun the construction of the new city and port of St Petersburg, which was designated as the capital of the empire. In 1712 he married his Lithuanian mistress, Catherine (the future **Catherine I**). In 1718 his son Alexis was imprisoned for suspected treason and died after torture. In 1722 the Act of Succession gave the ruling sovereign liberty to choose his or her successor, and in the following year Peter had Catherine crowned empress. The move was unpopular, but at his death she succeeded him without opposition. Peter had achieved during his reign a kind of cultural revolution that made Russia part of the general European state system for the first time in its history, and established it as a major power. 📖 M S Anderson, *Peter the Great* (1978)

Peter II 1715–30
Tsar of Russia
The grandson of **Peter I**, the Great, and the son of the Tsarevich Alexis (1690–1718), he was born in St Petersburg, and succeeded to the throne in 1727 on the death of his step-grandmother, **Catherine I**. He died of smallpox on the day designated for his wedding. He was succeeded by the Empress **Anna Ivanova**, daughter of Peter the Great's half-brother and co-tsar, Ivan V.

Peter III 1728–62
Tsar of Russia
The grandson of **Peter I**, the Great and the son of Peter's youngest daughter, Anna, and Charles Frederick, Duke of Holstein-Gottorp, he was born in Kiel. In 1742 he was declared heir presumptive to his aunt, the Empress Elizabeth Petrovna (daughter of Peter the Great and **Catherine I**), and in 1745 he married Sophia-Augusta von Anhalt-Zerbst (the future Empress **Catherine II**). A weak and unstable man, and a great admirer of **Frederick II, the Great**, he withdrew Russia's forces from the Seven Years War as soon as he succeeded to the throne (1762), and restored East Prussia to Frederick. This enraged the army and aristocracy, while the Church was annoyed by his fondness for Lutheranism. Peter was deposed (June 1762) by a group of nobles inspired by his wife Catherine and led by her lover, Count Orlov. He was strangled in captivity a few days later, and Catherine was proclaimed empress.

Peter I 1844–1921
King of Serbia
The son of Prince Alexander **Karadjordjević**, he was born in Belgrade. He lived in exile for 45 years after his father's abdication (1858), fought in the French army in the Franco-Prussian War (1870–71), and was elected King of Serbia by the Serbian parliament (1903). A liberal and strong believer in constitutional government, in World War I he accompanied his army into exile in Greece (1916). He returned to Belgrade (1918) and was proclaimed titular King of the Serbs, Croats and Slovenes until his death, although, because of his ill health, his second son, Alexander (later **Alexander I**), was regent.

Peter II 1923–70
King of Yugoslavia
Born in Belgrade, the son of **Alexander I**, he was at school in England when his father was assassinated (1934). His uncle, Prince Paul Karadjordjević (1873–1976), a nephew of **Peter I**, was Regent until 1941 when he was ousted by pro-Allied army officers, who declared King Peter of age, and he assumed sovereignty. The subsequent German attack on Yugoslavia forced the king to go into exile within three weeks. He set up a government in exile in London, but lost his throne when Yugoslavia became a republic (1945). From then on the ex-king lived mainly in California.

Peter of Amiens See **Peter the Hermit**
Peter of Verona See **Peter the Martyr, St**
Peter the Cruel See **Pedro**

Peter the Hermit, *also called* Peter of Amiens
c.1050–c.1115
French monk
Born in Amiens, he served as a soldier, then became a monk. When **Urban II** launched the First Crusade at a council in Clermont in 1096, Peter traversed Europe, generating enthusiasm with vivid and emotive preaching. He rallied an army of 20,000 peasants, and led one section of the crusading army to Asia Minor, where it was defeated by the Turks at Nicaea. He later founded the monastery of Neufmoutier at Liée, Belgium.

Peter the Martyr, St, *also called* Peter of Verona
c.1205–52
Italian preacher, and patron saint of the Inquisition
Born in Verona, he became a Dominican. He was assassinated at Como for the severity with which he carried out his inquisitorial duties. He was canonized in 1253 and his feast day is 29 April.

Peterborough, Charles Mordaunt, 3rd Earl of c.1658–1735
English commander and politician
Between 1674 and 1680 he took part in naval expeditions to the Barbary coast. He was an extreme Whig, and an early intriguer in the overthrow of **James VII and II**. After the Revolution he rose high under the new king who made him Earl of Monmouth, but later he opposed **William III** and his policies and in 1697 was committed to the Tower for three months. In 1705, during the War of the Spanish Succession (1701–14), now as the Earl of Peterborough, he took 4,000 troops to Spain. He defeated a French army, but disagreements with his colleagues, and outbreaks of his violent temper led to his recall to England (March 1707) and the virtual end of his military career.

Peters, Ellis, *pseudonym of* Edith Mary Pargeter
1913–95
English crime writer and novelist
She lived in Shropshire. Always a prolific writer, she wrote a string of quietly successful detective novels under her pseudonym, many featuring Inspector Felse (*Fallen into the Pit*, 1951, was the first of these). Real success, however, came when she was in her sixties when, reading about a historical incident in which the relics of St Winifred were moved to Shrewsbury Abbey, she hit upon the idea of Brother Cadfael, a medieval detective. *A Morbid Taste for Bones: A Mediaeval Whodunnit* (1977, as Ellis Peters) was an instant hit, and a series was born. The Cadfael books are prime examples of the sort of quintessentially English detective fiction where there is no gore and anything too unpleasant is described from a discreet distance. The series was filmed for television starring Sir **Derek Jacobi** in the title role. The period setting, though a strong selling point, is incidental.

Pargeter was awarded the Crime Writers' Association Diamond Dagger award—its highest—in 1993. Also an accomplished translator of Czech-language literature, she won the 1968 Czechoslovak Society for International Relations gold medal and ribbon. Her 21st novel was unfinished at her death.

Peters, Karl 1856–1918
German traveller and administrator

He was born in Neuhaus in Hanover. In 1884 he helped to establish German East Africa as a colony by his negotiations with indigenous chiefs. In the same year he had formed the Gesellschaft für deutsche Kolonisation (German Colonization Society). Without the sanction of Bismarck, he claimed Uganda for Germany and was made Commissioner of Kilimanjaro (1891–93), but his harsh treatment of the local peoples caused his recall. He returned to Africa in 1906 when gold was discovered in the Zambesi district.

Peters, Sir Rudolf Albert 1889–1982
English biochemist

Born in London, he studied at King's College London, and at Cambridge, where he assisted Sir Joseph Barcroft and Frederick Gowland Hopkins. In 1917 he worked with Barcroft at Porton Military Research Establishment on problems of chemical warfare, and graduated in medicine at St Bartholomew's Hospital, London. In 1918 he became a lecturer at Oxford, where he was later appointed Whitley Professor of Biochemistry (1923–54), and began research on thiamine and the vitamin B complex. In 1937 he independently isolated thiamine from yeast and demonstrated its involvement in intermediary metabolism. With Severo Ochoa, he partially resolved the cofactors necessary for this metabolic reaction, and his observations led to the discovery of an effective treatment for victims of the blistering war gas, lewisite. Peters discovered fluoracetate and fluoroleic acid, poisonous components of certain plants, which form part of the Hans Krebs cycle. He also found that fluoride combined organically in bone (1969). Peters was elected Fellow of the Royal Society (1935), received its Royal Medal (1949) and was knighted in 1952.

Peters, Winston Raymond 1946–
New Zealand politician and lawyer

Born in Whananaki (Northland) of Maori and Scots descent, he was educated at Auckland University. He entered politics for the National Party (1979), taking the Hunua seat on disputed return, but was defeated at the 1981 election. He won the seat of Tauranga in 1984 and was Minister of Maori Affairs under Prime Minister Jim Bolger (1935–) in 1990, but was expelled from the Cabinet in 1991 and from the National Party in 1993. He founded the New Zealand First Party which won a strategic role in the 1996 elections and formed a coalition with the National Party; Peters became deputy Prime Minister and took the newly created post of Treasurer.

Petersen, Nis 1897–1943
Danish poet and novelist

Born in South Jutland, the cousin of Kaj Munk, he rebelled against a strict upbringing and became a journalist, casual labourer and vagabond. He became famous for his novel of Rome in the time of Marcus Aurelius, *Sandalmagernes Gade* (1931, Eng trans *The Street of the Sandal-makers*, 1932). His later poetry is highly thought of, and a collection of his verse was published in 1949. His adult life was haunted by alcoholism and spiritual crisis.
📖 J Andersen, *Nis Petersen* (1957)

Peterson, Oscar Emmanuel 1925–
Canadian jazz pianist and composer

He was born in Montreal, the son of immigrants from the West Indies. He studied piano from childhood and developed a phenomenal technique and driving style, comparable with that of Art Tatum, of whom he was an admirer and friend. From 1949 Peterson's work with the touring 'Jazz at the Philharmonic' groups brought him international recognition. A prolific recording artist, he has achieved some of his finest work as the leader of a trio, and has also worked extensively as a soloist. His compositions include *Canadiana Suite* (1963), *Royal Suite* (1981) and *Africa Suite* (1983), written for ballet. A 12-time winner of the Down Beat Award for best jazz pianist of the year, he was made Commandeur, L'Ordre des Arts et des Lettres in 1989.

Peterson, Roger Tory 1908–96
US ornithologist and artist

Born in Jamestown, New York, he studied art and design in New York City, then pursued an interest in ornithology while teaching in Massachusetts. In 1934 he published his *Field Guide to the Birds*, the first in a series of popular guides to the birds of North America and Mexico. The books are illustrated with his own paintings, which are not intended to be perfectly lifelike but instead emphasize the distinguishing features of each species. Although his artistic gift was fairly ordinary, he had a rare ability to systematize natural history and make it comprehensible to a layman, and he became one of the most eminent ornithologists of his time.

Peterson-Berger, Wilhelm 1867–1942
Swedish composer, writer and music critic

He studied at the Stockholm Conservatory (1886–89) and later at Dresden (1889–90). Music critic for *Dagens Nyheter* from 1896 to 1930, he won acclaim for his lyric pieces *Frösöblomster* (1896–1914) and three series of *Svensk lyrik* (1896–1926), settings of poems by Erik Karlfeldt, Verner von Heidenstam and others. They show clearly the influence of Scandinavian folk music and of Edvard Grieg, and were a major contribution to the Swedish national dramas for which he provided his own text. Most popular of these is *Arnljot* (1909), which tells of a warrior found in Snorri Sturluson's *St Olaf's saga*. Of his prolific but uneven output, his Symphony No 3 (1913–15, known as the 'Lappland'), the *Cantata Norrbötten* (1922), *Opera Cantata* (1923) and his Violin Concerto (1928), are among the best-known. His idealistic music criticism, which could be ruthless and personal, antagonized many and hampered his career, but his atmospheric, colourful music greatly influenced Swedish cultural life early in this century.

Pétion, Alexandre Sabès 1770–1818
Haitian revolutionary leader

He was the mulatto son of a wealthy French colonist, and after fighting to liberate Haiti from the English and French, he became president of an independent republic in South Haiti (1807–18). His policy of dividing up plantations and redistributing land led to economic troubles, as subsistence farming replaced lucrative cash crops. From 1811 to 1818 he was at war with Henri Christophe, a freed slave who ruled North Haiti.

Pétion de Villeneuve, Jérôme c.1756–1794
French revolutionary

Born in Chartres, he was elected Deputy to the Third Estate (1789), became a prominent member of the Jacobin Club, and was a great ally of Robespierre. He was one of those who brought back the royal family from Varennes (1791) and advocated the deposition of King Louis XVI. He was elected Mayor of Paris and was the first President of the Convention. A Girondin, he voted at the King's trial for death, but headed the unsuccessful attack on Robespierre. Proscribed on 2 June 1793, he escaped to Caen, and from there, on the failure of the attempt to make armed opposition against the Convention, to the Gironde, where his body and that of François Buzot (1760–94) were later found partly devoured by wolves.

Petipa, Marius 1818–1910
French dancer, ballet-master and choreographer

He was born in Marseilles. After touring France, Spain and the USA as a dancer, he went to St Petersburg in 1847 to join the Imperial Theatre where his father Jean had been a teacher. In 1858 he became the company's second ballet-master, and four years later staged his first ballet, *Pharaoh's Daughter*, setting the style of *ballet à grand spectacle* which was to dominate Russian ballet for the rest of the century. In 1869 he became ballet-master, and in the 34 years until his retirement in 1903 he created 46 original ballets, the most famous being Tchaikovsky's *The Sleeping Beauty* (1890) and *Swan Lake* (1895). 🕮 Vera Krasovskaia, *Marius Petipa and 'The Sleeping Beauty'* (1972)

Petit, Alexis Thérèse 1791–1820
French physicist

Born in Vesoul, Haute-Saône, he became Professor at the Lycée Bonaparte, and enunciated with Pierre Louis Dulong the 'law of Dulong and Petit' that for all elements the product of the specific heat and the atomic weight is the same.

Petit, Roland 1924–
French choreographer and dancer

Born in Paris, he began his studies at the Paris Opera under Serge Lifar at the age of nine, becoming the company's principal dancer (1943–44). Following a short period with the Ballets des Champs-Elysées, he founded his own troupe in 1948, Les Ballets de Paris de Roland Petit. In 1972 he became artistic director of the Ballet National de Marseilles. He created many new ballets including *Le Rossignol et la rose* (1944, 'The Nightingale and the Rose'), a story by Oscar Wilde set to Schumann's music; *Les Forains* (1945, 'The Fairground People') with Jean Cocteau; *Le Jeune Homme et la Mort* (1946, 'Death and the Young Man'), which Cocteau had rehearsed strictly to jazz until the opening night when J S Bach was substituted; *Les Demoiselles de la Nuit* (1948, 'The Young Ladies of the Night'); *Pink Floyd Ballet* (1972); *Nana* (1976) and *Marcel Proust Remembered* (1980). During the 1950s he was very active in the film industry, creating the ballet sequences in the film *Hans Christian Andersen* (1952), danced by his wife, Zizi Jeanmaire, and *Daddy Long Legs* (1954).

Petit de Julleville, Louis 1841–1900
French critic

Born in Paris, he became professor at the École Normale Supérieure and the Sorbonne. He wrote the *Histoire du théâtre en France* ('History of the Theatre in France') and edited a monumental *Histoire de la langue et de la littérature française* ('History of French Language and Literature').

Petöfi, Sándor 1823–49
Hungarian poet

He was born in Kiskörös, and became an actor, soldier, then literary hack, but by 1844 had made his name as a poet, his most popular work being *János vitéz* (1845, 'János the Hero'). His poetry broke completely with the old pedantic style, and, full of national feeling, began a new epoch in Hungarian literature. He also wrote a novel called *A hóhér kötele* (1846, 'The Hangman's Rope'), and translated Shakespeare's *Coriolanus*. In 1848 he threw himself into the revolutionary cause, somewhat to the discomfiture of the gentry leader, Lajos Kossuth, and wrote numerous war songs, before falling in battle at Segesvár, possibly to a Russian bullet. He was ever after regarded as a martyr in the cause of popular nationalism,

and the Petöfi Circle, one of the revolutionary centres in the 1956 Hungarian Uprising, was named after him. 🕮 L Havatny, *Igy élt Petöfi* (5 vols, 1955–57)

Pétomane, Le See Pujol, Joseph

Petrarch, Francesco Petrarca See panel p1456

Petri, Laurentius 1499–1573
Swedish reformer

Born in Örebro, he studied under Martin Luther at Wittenberg, was made a professor at Uppsala, and in 1531 the first Protestant Archbishop of Uppsala. He and his brother Olaus Petri did most to convert Sweden to the Reformed doctrines, and superintended the translation of the New Testament into Swedish (1541).

Petri, Olaus 1493–1552
Swedish reformer and statesman

Born in Örebro, he studied at Wittenberg University from 1516 to 1518, studying with Martin Luther. After his return (1519) from Wittenberg, Gustav I Vasa made him (1531) Chancellor of the kingdom—a post he resigned in 1539 to spend the rest of his life as the first pastor of Stockholm. His works include memoirs, a mystery-play, hymns and controversial tracts. He was the brother of Laurentius Petri.

Petrie, Sir (William Matthew) Flinders 1853–1942
English archaeologist and Egyptologist

Born in Charlton, Kent, he was educated privately. He surveyed Stonehenge (1874–77), but turned from 1881 entirely to Egyptology, beginning by surveying the pyramids and temples of Giza and excavating the mounds of Tanis and Naucratis. The author of over 100 books, and renowned for his energy and spartan tastes, he became the first Edwards Professor of Archaeology at London (1892–1933), and continued excavating in Egypt and Palestine until well into his eighties. 🕮 Margaret S Drower, *Flinders Petrie* (1985)

Petrokov, Nikolai Yakovlevich 1937–
Soviet reform economist

A brilliant graduate of Moscow University, he joined the Communist Party and became deputy director of the Institute of Mathematical Economics in 1965. He joined Mikhail Gorbachev's team of advisers in 1985, and in 1990 was appointed personal assistant. However, in the autumn of that year Petrokov failed to persuade Gorbachev to adopt serious economic reforms, which proved to be part of his undoing.

Petronio, Stephen 1956–
US dancer and choreographer

Born in Nutley, New Jersey, he was studying medicine at college when a chance visit to a dance class changed the course of his life. He trained in contact improvisation with Steve Paxton and also with such leading modern dance experimentalists as Yvonne Rainer and Trisha Brown. He began choreographing while still a member of Brown's company (1979–86). He now heads his own troupe, and has established a reputation as one of the USA's most original younger choreographers.

Petronius Arbiter 1st century AD
Roman satirist writer, author of the Satyricon

He is usually supposed to be the voluptuary Gaius Petronius, whom Tacitus calls 'arbiter elegantiae' at the court of Nero. He was governor of Bithynia for a time. The *Satyricon* ('Tales of Satyrs') is a long satirical romance in prose and verse, of which only parts of the 15th and 16th books, in a fragmentary state, still survive. The work depicts with wit, humour and realism the licentious life in southern Italy of the moneyed class. The favour Petronius enjoyed as Nero's aider and abettor and his entourage in

Petrarch, Francesco Petrarca 1304–74
Italian poet and scholar, one of the earliest and greatest of modern lyric poets

Petrarch was the son of a Florentine notary, who was exiled in 1302 along with **Dante** and settled in Arezzo, where Francesco was born. In 1312 his father went to Avignon, then the seat of the papal court, and there and in Bologna Francesco devoted himself with enthusiasm to the study of the classics. After his father's death Petrarch returned to Avignon (1326). To obtain an income he became a churchman, although perhaps not a priest, and he lived on the small benefices conferred by his many patrons.

It was at this period (1327) that he first saw Laura (possibly Laure de Noves, married in 1325 to Hugo de Sade; she died, the mother of 11 children, in 1348). She inspired him with a passion which has become proverbial for its constancy and purity. Also at this time he began his friendship with the powerful Roman family of the **Colonnas**. As the fame of Petrarch's learning and genius grew, his position became one of unprecedented influence, and the most powerful sovereigns of the day competed for his presence at their courts. He travelled repeatedly in France, Germany and Flanders, searching for manuscripts. In Liège he found two new orations of **Cicero**, in Verona a collection of his letters, and in Florence an unknown portion of **Quintilian**.

Invited by the Senate of Rome on Easter Sunday, 1341, he ascended the Capitol clad in the robes of his friend and admirer, King Robert of Naples, and there, after delivering an oration, he was crowned Poet Laureate. In 1353, after the death of Laura and his friend Cardinal Colonna, he left Avignon and his country house at Vaucluse for ever, disgusted with the corruption of the papal court. His remaining years were passed in various different towns of northern Italy.

📖 Petrarch may be considered as the earliest of the great humanists of the Renaissance. He himself chiefly founded his claim to fame on his epic poem *Africa*, the hero of which is **Scipio Africanus**, and his historical work in prose *De Viris Illustribus*, a series of biographies of classical celebrities. Other Latin works are the eclogues and epistles in verse; and in prose the dialogues *De Contemptu Mundi* (or *Secretum*), the treatises *De Otio Religiosorum* and *De Vita Solitaria*, and his letters—he was in constant correspondence with **Boccaccio**. It is as a poet that his fame has lasted for over five centuries. His title deeds to fame are in his *Canzoniere*, in the Italian sonnets, madrigals, and songs, almost all inspired by his unrequited passion for Laura. The *Opera Omnia* appeared at Basle in 1554. His Italian lyrics were published in 1470, and have since gone through innumerable editions. See also K Foster, *Petrarch* (1987) and T Bergin, *Petrarch* (1970).

> *Continue morimur, ego dum hec scribo, tu dum leges, alii dum audient dumque non audient, ego quoque dum hec leges moriar, tu moreris dum hec scribo, ambo morimur, omnes morimur, semper morimur.*
> 'We are dying continuously: I while I write this, you while you read it, others while they hear or do not hear it. I will be dying as you read this, you will be dying as I write it. We are both dying, we are all dying, we are always dying.' From a letter to Philippe de Cabassoles (c.1360).

every form of sensual indulgence aroused the jealousy of another confidant, Tigellinus, who procured his disgrace and banishment. Ordered to commit suicide, he cut open his veins. 📖 H Rankin, *Petronius the Artist* (1971)

Petrosian, Tigran Vartanovich 1929–84
Russian chess player

He was born in Tbilisi, Georgia. He won the world championship from **Mikhail Botvinnik** in 1963 and made one successful defence, before losing it to **Boris Spassky** in 1969. His awkward, defensive style of chess earned him the nickname, 'Iron Tigran'.

Petrovitch, Aleksis See **Aleksis Petrovitch**

Petrov-Vodkin, Kuzma Sergeyevich 1878–1939
Russian painter

Born in Khvalynsk (Saratov region), he trained initially as an icon painter, and later studied painting in St Petersburg and Moscow, after which he travelled in Africa. He was associated with the Blue Rose Group (whose exhibition in 1907 marked the beginning of the Russian avant-garde movement), but he did not become identified with any particular school. After the 1917 Revolution, his paintings reflected new concerns, as in *The Year 1918 in Petrograd* (1920), and *Workers* (1926). Later he developed a new theory concerning the depiction of space. His importance rests mainly on his influence as a teacher of the first generation of Soviet painters at the Leningrad (now St Petersburg) Art Academy.

Petrus de Alliaco See **Ailly, Pierre d'**

Pettenkofer, Max von 1818–1901
German chemist

Born near Neuberg, he was educated at the University of Munich, worked briefly in the court pharmacy, abandoned an unpromising career as an actor in order to marry, and then studied medical chemistry under **Justus von Liebig** at Giessen. He was Professor of Chemistry at Munich (1847–94) and his greatest achievements lay in the field of hygiene and public health. He emphasized the role of chemistry in nutrition, sanitation and forensic medicine. He established the vital role of protein in diet and showed that diabetics use extra protein and fat. After being asked to report on possible health hazards from a new system of central heating for Maximilian II of Bavaria, he began to study the effects of ventilation systems, clothing, building materials and soils on health. He was responsible for purifying the Munich water supply and for the introduction of its sewage system. He also advocated heating art galleries, pointing out that the varnish on oil paintings became opaque with damp. Pettenkofer's work on hygiene and epidemiology brought him international renown and in 1879 he was appointed director of the world's first Institute of Hygiene.

Petty, Richard 1937–
US motor-racing driver

He was born in Level Cross, North Carolina. During more than three decades in stock-car racing (1958–92), he won 200 National Association for Stock Car Auto Racing (NASCAR) races, almost twice as many as any other driver. His victories included a record of seven Daytona 500 races and seven NASCAR championships.

Petty, Sir William 1623–87
English economist

Born in Romsey, Hampshire, he went to sea, and then studied at a Jesuit college in Caen, and in Utrecht, Amsterdam, Leyden, Paris and Oxford. He taught anatomy at Oxford, and music at Gresham College, London. Appointed physician to the army in Ireland (1652), he executed a fresh survey of the Irish lands forfeited in 1641 and started ironworks, lead mines, sea-fisheries and other industries on estates he bought in south-west Ireland. He was made Surveyor-General of Ireland by **Charles II**. The inventor of a copying machine (1647), and a double-keeled sea boat (1663), he was one of the first members of the Royal Society. In political economy he was a precursor of **Adam Smith**, and wrote a *Treatise on Taxes* (1662) and *Political Arithmetic* (1691), the latter a discussion of the value of comparative statistics. He married Baroness Shelburne, and his sons were successively Lord Shelburne.

Pétursson, Hallgrímur 1614–74
Icelandic devotional poet, pastor and hymn-writer
Born in the north of Iceland, he ran away to Denmark to become a blacksmith's apprentice, but was put to school in Copenhagen by an Icelandic patron, the future Bishop Brynjólfur Sveinsson. In 1627 Pétursson rehabilitated the Icelandic survivors of a Moorish pirate raid on Iceland, whose captives had been sold as slaves and were now in Copenhagen after being ransomed. He married one of them and worked as a labourer in Iceland before becoming pastor of the church at Saurbær (1651). Here he wrote his masterpiece, *Passion Hymns* (1666), a cycle of 50 meditations on the Crucifixion. One of the hymns, *Allt eins og blómstrið eina* ('Just as the one true flower') is still sung at funerals in Iceland. The new cathedral in Reykjavík was named Hallgrímskirkja after him. 📖 M Jónsson, *Hallgrímur Pétursson* (2 vols, 1947)

Peuerbach, Georg von See Purbach, Georg von

Peutinger, Conrad 1465–1547
German scholar and antiquary
A keeper of the archives of Augsburg, he published a series of Roman inscriptions. His *Tabula Teutingeriana*, now in Vienna, is a copy, made in 1264, of an itinerary or a Roman map of the military roads of the 4th century AD.

Pevsner, Antoine 1886–1962
French Constructivist sculptor and painter
Born in Orël, Russia, he studied art in Kiev. He helped to form the Suprematist Group in Moscow with **Kasimir Malevich**, **Vladimir Tatlin** and his brother, **Naum Gabo**. In 1920 he broke away from the Suprematists and issued the *Realist Manifesto* with his brother. This ultimately caused their exile from Russia, and he went to Paris. Several of his completely non-figurative constructions (mainly in copper and bronze) are in the Museum of Modern Art, New York. 📖 Pierre Peissi, *Antoine Pevsner* (1961)

Pevsner, Sir Nikolaus Bernhard 1902–83
British art historian
Born in Leipzig, Germany, he was lecturer in art at Göttingen University until the Nazis came to power in 1933, when he fled to Great Britain and there became an authority on English architecture. From 1934 he investigated British industrial design, and wrote *An Enquiry into Industrial Art in England* (1937). He also wrote *Pioneers of the Modern Movement* (1936), and the very popular *An Outline of European Architecture* (1942), and became art editor of Penguin Books (1949). He was Slade Professor of Fine Art at Cambridge (1949–55). He also produced a series for Penguin Books, *The Buildings of England* (50 vols, 1951–74).

Pezza, Michele See Fra Diavolo

Pfeffer, Wilhelm Friedrich Philipp 1845–1920
German botanist
Born near Kassel, he trained as a pharmacist, became a specialist in plant physiology, and was appointed professor successively at the universities of Bonn, Basle, Tübingen and Leipzig. Noted particularly for his researches on osmotic pressure, he also experimented with dyes on plant cells, and established the structure and nature of vacuoles. He alluded to the importance of transpiration in plant growth, and his work on chloroplasts showed the effects of light intensity and other factors on photosynthesis. His *Handbuch der Pflanzenphysiologie* (1881) was a standard work on plant physiology for many years.

Pfeiffer, Michelle 1958–
US film actress
Born in Santa Ana, California, she began her career in television commercials before making her feature-film debut in *Falling in Love Again* (1980). She appeared in many films before gaining critical recognition for her role in *Scarface* (1983). Her first major commercial success was in *The Witches of Eastwick* (1987), and her delicate performance in *Dangerous Liaisons* (1988) brought her a Best Supporting Actress Academy Award nomination. She has consolidated her success with roles in *The Fabulous Baker Boys* (1989), *The Russia House* (1990), *Frankie and Johnny* (1991), *Batman Returns* (1992) and *The Age of Innocence* (1994). Later films include *Dangerous Minds* (1995) and *One Fine Day* (1996).

Pfeiffer, Richard Friedrich Johannes 1858–1945
German bacteriologist
Born near Posen (Poznan, Poland), he became professor at the universities of Berlin (1894), Königsberg (1899) and Breslau (1901). During the influenza epidemic of 1889–92 he discovered the influenza bacillus, but his most significant discovery was his observation, for the first time, of a complex immune reaction (1894). He injected live cholera vibrios into guinea pigs which had already been immunized, then extracted some of the germs and observed their development. He showed that the same development process occurred *in vitro*, and that the reaction would cease when heated to over 60 degrees Celsius. Pfeiffer published books on hygiene and microbiology.

Pfitzner, Hans Erich 1869–1949
German musician and composer
Born in Moscow, Russia, of German parents, he taught in various German conservatories, and conducted in Berlin, Munich and Strassburg. He composed *Palestrina* (1917) and other operas, choral and orchestral music, and chamber music. A romantic, he refused to follow passing fashions.

Phaedrus, Gaius Julius c.15BC–c.50AD
Translator and adaptor of Aesop's fables into Latin verse
Born in Macedonia, he was taken to Rome at an early age and became the freedman of **Augustus** or **Tiberius**. Under Tiberius he published the first two books of his fables, but his biting allusions to the tyranny of the emperor and his minister Sejanus caused him to be accused and condemned—his punishment is unknown. On the death of Sejanus he published his third book. The fourth and fifth books belong to his last years. In addition to reproducing the fables of **Aesop**, he invented his own and also borrowed from other sources.

Phalaris 6th century BC
Greek tyrant of Acragas (Agrigentum) in Sicily
He greatly embellished the city, and extended his sway over large districts in Sicily. After holding power for 16 years he was overthrown, and allegedly roasted alive in his own invention, the brazen bull. The 148 letters bearing his name were proved by **Richard Bentley** in 1697–99 to be spurious.

Phan Boi Chau 1867–1940
Vietnamese nationalist
Born into a Confucian scholar family, he was in essence a Confucian revolutionary. Together with **Phan Chau Trinh**, he dominated the anti-colonial movement in Vietnam in the early 20th century. In 1905 he went to Japan where, working under the supervision of the exiled Liang Qichao (Liang Ch'i-ch'ao), he wrote a history of Vietnam's

loss of independence to the French, copies of which were then smuggled back to Vietnam. In 1912, now in China, he was involved with other Vietnamese in the establishment of the 'Revival Society' (Quang Phuc Hoi) which sought to bring about a democratic republic in Vietnam. Forces were raised which launched, from South China, poorly-organized attacks on French units (1915). He was arrested in 1925 by French agents in Shanghai and returned to Vietnam. Brought before the Criminal Commission (1925), he was sentenced to life imprisonment. The ensuing widespread public outcry led to his release and he spent the rest of his life in gently guarded retirement at Hue.

Phan Chau Trinh 1872–1926
Vietnamese nationalist
Along with **Phan Boi Chau**, he was a leading figure in the anti-colonial movement in Vietnam in the early 20th century. In contrast to Phan Boi Chau's commitment to a revolutionary monarchism, Phan Chau Trinh advocated Western-style republicanism. Between 1911 and 1925 he was in France, spending some of that time in prison. From France he launched strong attacks on the Vietnamese monarchy. His funeral in 1926 was held in Saigon, provoking unprecedented mass demonstrations and student strikes. This heralded a new phase in the anti-colonial struggle in Vietnam, one that would involve greater popular participation.

Pheidias See Phidias

Phelps, Samuel 1804–78
English actor-manager
Born in Devonport, Devon, his first career was as a reader on the *Globe* and *Sun* newspapers, but by 1826 his interest in acting led him to the stage. By 1837 he was well known, especially for his performance as Shylock. He became manager of Sadler's Wells after the monopoly of patent theatres ended and for 18 years successfully produced all but four of **Shakespeare's** plays, in which he often appeared in both comic and tragic roles.

Phibunsongkhram 1897–1964
Thai military leader and statesman
Born of humble origins, he was educated at the Thai Military Academy and then at the French Artillery School on a government scholarship. In France he met a group of Thai students who were disaffected with the absolute monarchy in Bangkok and became involved in the coup which toppled the absolute regime (24 June 1932). Phibun gained authority in the first constitutional governments, becoming Prime Minister in 1938. During his premiership, he developed close relations with Japan, allowing Japanese forces to cross his country in order to attack the British in Burma and Malaya in 1941. However, when the war turned against Japan, Phibun fell from office (July 1944). He returned as Prime Minister in 1947, this time aligning Thailand closely with the USA. He was overthrown in a Sarit Thanarat coup in September 1957 and died in exile in Japan.

Phidias or Pheidias c.500BC–?
Greek sculptor, one of the major ancient Greek artists
He was born in Athens, and received from **Pericles** a magnificent commission to execute the chief statues with which he proposed to adorn the city, and was superintendent of all public works. He supervised the construction of the Propylaea and the Parthenon, designed the sculpture on the walls, and is thought to have made the gold and ivory *Athena* there, and the *Zeus* at Olympia (both lost) himself. Charged with appropriating gold from the statue and carving his own head on an ornament, he was accused of impiety, and disappeared from Athens. 📖 Hans Schrader, *Phidias* (1924)

Philaret or Filaret, *originally* Vasili Mikhailovich Drozdov 1782–1867
Russian prelate
He became Bishop of Reval in 1817 and Archbishop of Tver in 1819 and Metropolitan, or Archbishop of Moscow, in 1821. He was considered the greatest preacher and the most influential Russian churchman of his day.

Philaretus See Geulincx, Arnold

Philby, Harry St John Bridger 1885–1960
English Arabist and explorer
Born in Ceylon (now Sri Lanka), he was educated at Westminster and Trinity College, Cambridge, joined the Indian Civil Service in 1907 and served in the Punjab. While in charge of the British Political Mission to Central Arabia (1917–18), he crossed Arabia by camel from Uqayr to Jedda, exploring a large area of south-central Arabia and becoming the first European to visit the Nejd. For this he was awarded the Founder's Medal of the Royal Geographical Society in 1920, and he later wrote *The Heart of Arabia* (1922). He retired from the Indian Civil Service in 1925 after quarrelling with British government policy in Arabia, set up business in Jedda in 1926, advised King **Ibn Saud**, and became a Muslim in 1930. In 1931 he made an epic crossing of the Empty Quarter from north to south, shortly after Bertram Thomas made his crossing. From 1932 to 1937 he mapped the Yemen highlands, and in 1937 made a return journey from the Empty Quarter of Saudi Arabia to the Hadhramaut, described in *Sheba's Daughters* (1939). He lived in Arabia until his death.

Philby, Kim, *properly* Harold Adrian Russell Philby 1911–88
British double-agent
He was born in Ambala, India, the son of **Harry St John Philby**. He was educated at Westminster and Trinity College, Cambridge, where, like **Guy Burgess**, **Donald Maclean** and **Anthony Blunt**, he became a communist, and was recruited as a Soviet agent. He was employed by the British Secret Intelligence Service (MI6) and was head of the anti-communist counter-espionage (1944–46). In 1949–51 he was posted in Washington DC as chief liaison officer between MI6 and the CIA, but was asked to resign because of his earlier communist sympathies. He was a journalist in Beirut from 1956 until 1963, when he admitted his espionage and defected to the USSR, where he was granted citizenship and became a colonel in the KGB (Soviet Intelligence Service). In 1968 he published *My Silent War* (1968). His third wife, Eleanor, wrote *Kim Philby: The Spy I Loved* (1968). 📖 Phillip Knightley, *Philby: The Life and Views of the KGB Masterspy* (1988); Rufina Ivanova Pukhova, *I Did It My Way* (1997)

Philidor, François André Danican 1726–95
French composer of operas, and chess master
Born in Dreux, into a family of Scots origin who had served for several generations as court musicians at Versailles, he was destined to a career as composer and arranger. His 1765 adaptation of **Henry Fielding's** *Tom Jones* was the most popular of the 21 operas he wrote, but he also had a career in chess, which brought him greater financial rewards. Unchallenged as the strongest player of his day, he gave public exhibitions in Paris, Holland, Germany and England of his ability to defeat two opponents simultaneously while blindfolded. His *L'Analyze du jeu des échecs* (1749, 'Analysis of the Game of Chess') was the first book to lay down the theoretical and strategical principles of chess, appearing in over 100 editions in 10 languages.

Philip, St 1st century AD
One of the 12 Apostles of Jesus Christ
From Bethsaida, Galilee, he is listed in Mark 3.14 and Acts 1. John's Gospel relates that he led Nathanael to **Jesus** (1.43), was present at the feeding of the 5,000 (6.1)

and brought some Greeks to meet Jesus (12.21). His later career is unknown, but traditions suggest he was martyred on a cross. He is not to be confused with Philip 'the Evangelist' (Acts 6.5 and Acts 8). His feast day is 1 May (West) or 14 November (East).

Philip I 1052–1108
King of France

The son of **Henri I**, he ruled from 1060. Although he increased royal wealth, his reign marked a low point in the prestige of the Capetian monarchy, largely due to his elopement with Bertrada, wife of Fulk of Anjou, a scandal which led to his excommunication. Extreme obesity caused him to allow his son **Louis VI** to administer the kingdom from 1104.

Philip II, *known as* Philip Augustus 1165–1223
First great Capetian King of France

The son of **Louis VII**, he was born in Paris and crowned joint king in 1179. He succeeded his father (1180) and married Isabella of Hainault, the last direct descendant of the Carolingians. He supported the sons of **Henry II** of England against their father. **Richard I** and he set out on the Third Crusade (1190–91), but he soon returned to France, and partitioned Richard's French territories with **John**. Richard's sudden return caused an exhausting war till 1199. Philip supported Richard's (and John's) nephew, Prince **Arthur** against John in France, but was distracted by his quarrel with the pope, who refused to let him divorce and remarry. After Arthur's murder in 1203 he won back English possessions in France. In 1204 he conquered Normandy, Maine, Anjou and Touraine, with part of Poitou, and secured the overlordship of Brittany. The victory of Bouvines (1214) over the Flemish, the English, and the Emperor **Otto IV** established his throne securely. His efficient, centralized government was based on royal officials controlling the feudal nobility, backed by the new university in Paris. Notre Dame remains a lasting monument of his attention to the fortification and layout of Paris. ⌑ Jean Jacques Quesnot de la Chesnée, *Le parallèle de Philippe II et de Louis XIV* (1709)

Philip III, the Bold ('le Hardi') 1245–85
King of France

He was with his father **Louis IX** (St Louis) at his death in Tunis (1270), and succeeded him to the throne. He fought several unlucky campaigns in Spain, the last of which, the attack on Aragon, caused his death from fever.

Philip IV, the Fair ('le Bel') 1268–1314
King of France

Born at Fontainebleau, he succeeded his father, **Philip III, the Bold**, in 1285. By his marriage with Queen Joanna of Navarre he acquired Navarre, Champagne and Brie. He overran Flanders, but was defeated by the Flemings at Courtrai (1302). His struggle with Pope **Boniface VIII** arose from his attempts to tax the French clergy. The pope forbade this (1296) in the Papal Bull *Clericis laicos*, to which Philip replied by prohibiting the export of money or valuables. A temporary reconciliation was ended (1301) by a fresh quarrel, precipitated by Philip's arrest and trial of Bernard Saisset, Bishop of Pamiers. The king's reply to the Papal Bull *Unam Sanctam* was to send his Minister William de Nogaret to seize Boniface, who escaped but died soon afterwards (1303). After the short pontificate of Benedict XI, Philip procured the elevation of the pliant Frenchman, **Clement V** (1305), who came to reside at Avignon, thus beginning the 70 years' 'Babylonish captivity' of the papacy. Coveting the wealth of the Templars, Philip forced the pope to suppress the order (1312) and he appropriated their property. He fostered a strong central adminstration in France, encouraged French unity by summoning the Estates General and appointed capable ministers.

Philip VI, of Valois 1293–1350
First Valois King of France

The son of Charles of Valois, younger brother of **Philip IV, le Bel**, he became king on the death of **Charles IV** (1328). His right was denied by **Edward III** of England, son of Philip IV's daughter, who declared that females, though excluded by the Salic Law, could transmit their rights to their children. Thus began the Hundred Years War with England in 1337. The French fleet was destroyed off Sluys (1340), and in 1346 Edward III landed in Normandy, ravaged to the environs of Paris, and defeated Philip at Crécy, just as the Black Death was about to spread through France. ⌑ Abbé de Choisy, *Histoires de Philippe de Valois et du roi Jean* (1688)

Philip II 382–336BC
King of Macedonia

The father of **Alexander the Great**, he was born in Pella, the youngest son of Amyntas, and made himself king in 359BC. He built up the army, developed the resources of Macedonia, and pursued a policy of expansion and opportunism. He warred with most of Greece, made peace with the Athenians (346BC), but was back at war with them (340) when he besieged Byzantium and Perinthus. In 339 the Amphicytyonic Council declared war against the Locrians of Amphissa, appointing Philip as their Commander-in-Chief. The Athenians formed a league with the Thebans against him, but their forces were decisively defeated at Chaeronea (338), and Philip organized the Greek states in a federal league under him (the League of Corinth). Philip was assassinated before he could invade Persia (Iran) in 336. His son Alexander the Great took over where Philip left off and conquered the Persian Empire. ⌑ W Adams, *Philip II* (1982)

Philip V 238–179BC
King of Macedonia in the Antigonid dynasty

Adopted by Antigonus Doson whom he succeeded in 221BC, he inherited a strong kingdom but, ambitious and active, he came into conflict with the growing power of Rome. He made an alliance with **Hannibal** (215) during the Second Punic War, which resulted in a first (indecisive) conflict with Rome (214–205). Conflict broke out again with Rome, in the Second Macedonian War (200–196). Decisively defeated at Cynoscephalae (197), he had to give up all control of Greece and follow Rome's dictates. He was succeeded by his son **Perseus**.

Philip I, the Handsome 1478–1506
King of Castile

The son of Emperor **Maximilian I** and Mary of Burgundy, he was born at Bruges, and as Archduke of Austria and Duke of Burgundy he was married in 1496 to the Infanta of Spain, **Juana**, daughter of **Ferdinand, the Catholic**, of Aragon and **Isabella of Castile**. Isabella's death (1504) made Juana Queen of Castile, but Ferdinand declared himself her Regent. In 1506 Philip went to claim the throne, but died in the same year, and Juana, who suffered from depression, was confined by her father. Their children were the Holy Roman Emperors **Charles V** and his successor, **Ferdinand I**.

Philip II of Spain and I of Portugal 1527–98
King of Spain and of Portugal

He was born in Valladolid, the only son of Emperor **Charles V**. In 1543 he married the Infanta Mary of Portugal, who died in 1546 giving birth to their son, **Don Carlos**. In 1554 he married **Mary I** (Mary Tudor) of England, but spent only 14 months in that country, where the marriage was not popular. However, it provided him with a potentially useful ally for Spain upon the Continent, and opened the prospect of a union between England and the Spanish Netherlands. In 1555–56 Charles abdicated the sovereignty of Spain, the

Netherlands, and all Spanish dominions in Italy and the New World to Philip (King of Spain from 1556), who remained in Flanders until after his father's death (1558), and returned in 1559 to a Spain suffering serious financial crisis and panicking at the apparent spread of religious heresy. Philip increasingly indentified himself with the Spanish Inquisition, which he saw as useful both for combating heresy and for extending his control over his own dominions. He was involved in war against France and the papacy (1557–59), and against the Turks in the Mediterranean (1560), both wars necessitating a sharp increase in domestic taxation which served only to increase unrest. Mary Tudor died in 1558. Philip failed to secure the hand of her sister and successor, Elizabeth I, married Isabella of France (daughter of Henri II) in 1559 to seal the Valois–Habsburg peace, and in 1570 married as his fourth wife, his cousin Anna, daughter of the Emperor Maximilian II, by whom he had a son, the future Philip III. At home, he faced threats from the Moriscos (converted Muslims) of Granada, who rebelled between 1568 and 1570 and, more seriously, from the Netherlands, in open revolt from 1573. Abroad, Spain contributed to the Holy League against the Ottoman Turks, which, under the command of Philip's half-brother, Don John of Austria, defeated the Ottoman fleet at Lepanto in 1571. In 1575, for the second time in Philip's reign, the Spanish crown was obliged to declare itself bankrupt and in 1576 the discontented and unpaid Spanish troops in the Netherlands ran wild and sacked the city of Antwerp. In 1579 seven United Provinces of the Low Countries won independence, although this was not formally accepted by Spain until the truce of 1609. In 1580 Philip succeeded to the Portuguese throne. The increase in trade-revenue from the New World in the 1580s resulted in a new prosperity and a more confident expansionist policy. Portugal was annexed to Spain in 1580, and attempts to re-conquer the northern Netherlands came close to success. In 1588, the year after Sir Francis Drake's sack of Cadiz, the great Armada was launched against England but was destroyed. The 1590s saw further revolt in Aragon (1591–92), and renewed financial crisis leading in 1596 to a third bankruptcy. Philip died two years later, leaving his empire divided, demoralized and economically depressed. The violence of his campaign against Protestants had destroyed all harmony within his dominions, while constant wars continued to deplete Spain's financial resources. 📖 Geoffrey Parker, *Philip II* (1978)

Philip III 1578–1621
King of Spain
Born in Madrid, he was the son of Philip II (by his fourth marriage), whom he succeeded in 1598. Pious and indolent, he left government to his favourites Lerma and Uceda, and devoted himself to hunting, bullfights and court entertainments. During his reign, agriculture and industry declined, and foreign wars (after 1618) drained the treasury. From 1609 to 1614, 275,000 Moriscos (Muslim converts to Christianity) were expelled from Spain with serious economic and demographic effects. He was succeeded by his son, Philip IV.

Philip IV 1605–65
King of Spain
Born in Valladolid, he was the son and successor in 1621 of Philip III. A discerning patron of the arts (particularly of Velazquez), and a periodically remorseful debauchee, he had no interest in politics and left the administration of government to his favourite (*valido*), the Count-Duke of Olivares. Spain declined as a dominant European power during his reign. France declared open war (1635), in 1640 Portugal regained its independence, and the United Provinces confirmed theirs at the Treaty of Westphalia (1648), while in 1659 the Treaty of the Pyrenees cost Spain her frontier fortresses in Flanders. His daughter, Maria

Theresa (1638–83), was the first wife of Louis XIV of France. He was succeeded by his four-year-old son, Charles II, the last of the Spanish Habsburgs.

Philip V 1683–1746
Duke of Anjou and first Bourbon King of Spain
The grandson of Louis XIV of France, he was born at Versailles, and in 1700 succeeded to the Spanish throne under the will of Charles II. The prospect of a French prince ruling Spain precipitated the War of the Spanish Succession (1701–13), during which French influence was dominant at court. Spain lost Gibraltar and Minorca to the British, the Spanish Netherlands and Naples to Austria, and Sicily to the House of Savoy. Within Spain, the Catalans had been in open revolt since 1705 and Barcelona was not recaptured until 1714. Although vigorous in his youth, Philip became depressed, weary and eccentric, under the domination of his second wife, Isabella Farnese of Parma, and her Italian favourite, Guilio Alberoni, who aimed at gaining territory in Italy for her sons. In 1724 he abdicated in favour of his son, Louis I, but resumed the throne when Louis died the same year. In 1732 Oran was reconquered from the Moors and war with Austria (1733–36) regained Naples and Sicily. At Philip's death, Spain was involved in the War of the Austrian Succession (1740–48).

Philip I, the Arab d.249AD
Roman emperor
Of Arab descent, he came to power (244) by causing the death of Gordian III. He celebrated the 1,000th anniversary of the founding of Rome with a mammoth secular games (248), the last time they were celebrated in Roman history. He also founded the city of Philipopolis. His reign was plagued by usurpations, and he was killed in battle by Decius, who succeeded him.

Philip, Prince See Edinburgh, Duke of
Philip Neri, St See Neri, St Philip

Philip the Bold ('le Hardi') 1342–1404
Duke of Burgundy
Born in Pontoise, the youngest son of John, the Good, King of France, he fought at Poitiers (1356) and shared his father's captivity in England. He was made Duke of Burgundy in 1364, and married Margaret, heiress of Flanders, in 1369. In 1382 he subdued a Flemish rebellion at Roosebeke, and soon gained that country (1384–85). His wise government won the esteem of his new subjects. He encouraged arts, manufactures and commerce, and his territory was one of the best governed in Europe. Following the insanity of his nephew, the French king, Charles VI, he became virtual ruler of France.

Philip the Good 1396–1467
Duke of Burgundy
Born in Dijon, the grandson of Philip, the Bold, he became Duke of Burgundy in 1419. Though he at first recognized Henry V of England as heir to the French Crown, he concluded a separate peace with the French (1435) and created one of the most powerful states in later medieval Europe. He added Brabant, Holland, Zeeland and Luxembourg (1430–43), and his richly extravagant Burgundian court was a model for Europe. He founded the chivalrous Order of the Golden Fleece and Jan van Eyck was one of his court painters. A committed crusader, he maintained a fleet for operations against the Ottoman Turks. 📖 Richard Vaughan, *Philip the Good: The Apogee of Burgundy* (1970)

Philip the Magnanimous 1504–67
Landgrave of Hesse
Born in Marburg, the son of Landgrave William II, he was converted to Lutheranism (1524) and was a major driving force in the Protestant Schmalkaldic League

(1531). He established Hesse as a sovereign state where the Protestant Church was prominent in the provision of state schools and hospitals, and he founded the first Protestant university at Marburg. Despite pressure from radical Anabaptists, Hesse maintained a tolerant religious regime that accommodated pastors of different Protestant persuasions and where no one was executed for religious reasons. Philip developed syphilis (1539) and contracted a bigamous marriage with Margaret van der Saale (1540). This moral ambiguity, and his lengthy imprisonment after the Schmalkaldic War (1547–52), lessened his influence in European affairs.

Philip, properly Metacomet c.1638–76
Native American leader

Born on the lands of the Wampanoag people (now part of Massachusetts and Rhode Island), he was the son of Wampanoag chief Massasoit (d.1661), and in 1662 he succeeded his older brother as chief. Called Philip or King Philip by the English, he led a confederation of tribes against the European settlers in an attempt to stem the erosion of his ancestral domain. King Philip's War (1675–76) raged throughout New England and was characterized by atrocities on both sides. Philip himself was shot after the final battle by one of his own braves, and his wife and nine-year-old son, along with hundreds of his people, were sold into slavery by the victorious colonists. His head was displayed on the fort at Plymouth, Massachusetts, for 25 years.

Philippa of Hainault c.1314–1369
Queen of England

On her marriage to her second cousin Edward III at York (1327), she took Flemish weavers to England, encouraged coal-mining, and made the French poet and historian Jean Froissart her secretary. She is said to have roused the English troops before the defeat of the Scots at Neville's Cross (1346), and to have interceded (1347) with Edward for mercy for the Burgesses of Calais. The Queen's College, Oxford, founded by Philippa's chaplain (1341), was named after her.

Philips, Ambrose c.1674–1749
English poet

Born in Shrewsbury, Shropshire, he was educated at St John's College, Cambridge, where he became a Fellow. He was MP for Armagh, secretary to the Archbishop of Armagh, purse-bearer to the Irish Lord Chancellor, and registrar of the Prerogative Court. A friend of Joseph Addison and Richard Steele, he did hack writing for publisher Jacob Tonson, and gained a reputation by the *Winter-piece* in the *Tatler* and six pastorals in Tonson's *Miscellany* (1709). These were praised in the *Guardian* at Pope's expense, and Pope's jealousy started a bitter feud. Of his plays only *The Distrest Mother* (1712), based on Racine's *Andromaque*, found favour with his contemporaries. ▢ Dr S Johnson, *Lives of the Most Eminent English Poets* (10 vols, 1779–81)

Philips, John 1676–1709
English poet

Born in Bampton, Oxfordshire, he was educated at Winchester and Christ Church, Oxford. He wrote three very popular poems: *The Splendid Shilling* (1701), a Miltonic burlesque; *Blenheim* (1705), a Tory celebration of the Duke of Marlborough's great victory; and *Cyder* (1708), an imitation of Virgil's *Georgics*. He has a monument in Westminster Abbey. ▢ Dr S Johnson, *Lives of the Most Eminent English Poets* (10 vols, 1779–81)

Philips, Katherine, *née* Fowler, *called the* Matchless Orinda 1631–64
English poet

She was born in London, and at 16 married James Philips of Cardigan Priory. She is the first English woman poet to have her work published (it included an address to the Welsh poet Henry Vaughan), and she received a dedication from Jeremy Taylor (*Discourse on the Nature, Offices and Measures of Friendship*, 1659). She translated Pierre Corneille's *Pompée*, which was performed in Dublin in 1663, and the greater part of his *Horace*. Her own poems, surreptitiously printed in 1663, were issued in 1667. She ran a literary salon, described in the *Letter of Orinda to Poliarchus* (1705). She died of smallpox on a visit to London. ▢ P W Souers, *The Matchless Orinda* (1931)

Philipson, Sir Robin (Robert James) 1916–92
Scottish painter

Born in Broughton-in-Furness, he studied at Edinburgh College of Art (1936–40), where he became head of drawing and painting (1960–82). During World War II he served in India and Burma. His first one-man show was at the Scottish Gallery, Edinburgh, 1954. He was president of the Royal Scottish Academy from 1973 to 1983. Like many Scottish artists of his generation, he handled paint freely and colours boldly, but always retained a precise figurative element in his work, which embraced many themes, ranging from cockfights and World War I to rose windows, altars and the female nude.

Phillip, Arthur 1738–1814
English naval commander

Born in London, he trained at Greenwich and joined the navy in 1755. He served in the Mediterranean with George Byng, and was at the taking of Havana. In 1787 he was appointed commander of the 'First fleet' carrying convicts to Australia. He landed on 26 January 1788 (subsequently celebrated as Australia Day), founded his penal colony settlement at Sydney, and explored the Hawkesbury River. He was founder and first Governor of New South Wales. He left in 1792, and was promoted vice-admiral in 1810.

Phillip, John 1817–67
Scottish painter

Born in Aberdeen, he was sent to London to study art. Most of his early subjects were Scottish, but after a visit to Spain (1851) for health reasons, his main successes were with Spanish themes (he was influenced by Velazquez) and earned him the nickname 'Phillip of Spain'.

Phillips, David Graham 1867–1911
US feminist novelist and journalist

Born in Madison, Indiana, he played a part in the 'muckraker' movement of reform-minded journalism in the early 20th century. He also wrote powerfully in several novels in favour of the emancipation of women, notably *The Plum Tree* (1905) and *Susan Lennox: Her Fall and Rise* (1917), and was assassinated by a lunatic who thought his work encouraged female moral depravity. ▢ L Filler, *Voice of Democracy* (1978)

Phillips, Edward 1630–c.1696
English writer

He was the son of Milton's sister Ann, brought up and educated by his uncle, and was the brother of John Phillips. He went to Oxford in 1650, but left the following year without taking a degree. In 1653 he was tutor to the son of John Evelyn, and he is mentioned in Evelyn's *Diary* as 'not at all infected by Milton's principles', yet he not only extolled his uncle in his *Theatrum Poetarum, or a Complete Collection of the Poets* (1675), but wrote a short life of the poet. Among his numerous other works are a complete edition (the first) of the poems of William Drummond of Hawthornden (1656), *New World of English Words* (1658, a philological dictionary) and the *Continuation* of Sir Richard Baker's *Chronicle of the Kings of England* (1665).

Phillips, John 1631–1706
English writer

He was the brother of **Edward Phillips**, and a nephew of **Milton**. He was educated by his uncle, replied to **Claude Salmasius**'s attack on him, and acted as his secretary. His *Satyr against Hypocrites* (1655) was a bitter attack on Puritanism, and *Speculum Crape Gownorum* (1682) criticized High Churchmen.

Phillips, John Bertram 1906–82
English Bible translator, writer and broadcaster

Born in Barnes, London, he was made famous by *Letters to Young Churches* (1947), translations of St Paul's epistles begun in 1941 to encourage his church youth club, and by the complete *New Testament in Modern English* (1958). He wrote a dozen bestsellers, including *Your God is Too Small* (1952), *A Man Called Jesus* (1959) and *Ring of Truth: A Translator's Testimony* (1967). Few were aware of his continuous battle against depression from 1961, until the posthumous publication of his autobiography, *The Price of Success* (1984), and letters to others in similar situations (*The Wounded Healer*, 1984).

Phillips, Mark Anthony Peter 1948–
Former husband of Princess Anne

Born in Tetbury, Gloucestershire, he was educated at Marlborough and Sandhurst, joining the Queen's Dragoon Guards in 1969. In 1973 he married Princess Anne, but separated from her in 1989; they were divorced in 1992. A noted horseman, he was a regular member of the British Equestrian Team (1970–76), and won many team events, including the gold medal at the Olympic Games in Munich (1972). He was coach for the US three day event team (1993–96) and has been consultant for the Gleneagles Mark Phillips Equestrian Centre in Scotland since 1992.

Phillips, Ulrich Bonnell 1877–1934
US historian

Born in La Grange, Georgia, he was a graduate of Georgia University and Columbia, and a pupil of **William Archibald Dunning**. He studied the ante-bellum South rather than its postwar Reconstruction, and won fame for his *American Negro Slavery* (1918), which defended slavery as preferable for black slaves as well as white owners. He also wrote *Life and Labour in the Old South* (1929), *Georgia and States Rights* (1902), *History of Transportation in the Eastern Cotton Belt* (1908) and *The Life of Robert Toombs* (1913).

Phillips, Wendell 1811–84
US abolitionist

Born in Boston, he graduated at Harvard in 1831 and was called to the Bar in 1834. By 1837 he was the chief orator of the antislavery party, closely associated with **William Lloyd Garrison**. He called for defiance of the Fugitive Slave Law and argued that slaves deserved not only their freedom but land, education and civil rights. He also championed the causes of temperance and the rights of women and of Native Americans.

Phillpotts, Dame Bertha Surtees 1877–1932
English Scandinavian scholar and educationist

Born in Bedfordshire, she studied medieval and modern languages at Girton College, Cambridge (1898–1902), and was a research student in Iceland and Denmark from 1903 to 1906. In 1913 she was appointed the first Lady Carlisle Fellow at Somerville College, Oxford, and in 1920 became Principal of Westfield College, London. She was Mistress of Girton (1922–25), and director of Scandinavian Studies at Cambridge from 1926 to 1932. She wrote *The Elder Edda and Ancient Scandinavian Drama* (1920) and *Edda and Saga* (1931). In 1931 she married the astronomer Hugh Frank Newall (1857–1944).

Phillpotts, Eden 1862–1960
English novelist, dramatist and poet

Born in Mount Aboo, India, he studied for the stage in London, but turned to literature instead (1893). He made his name by realistic novels mainly set in Devonshire, such as *Lying Prophets* (1896), *Children of the Mist* (1898) and *Widecombe Fair* (1913), and wrote more than 250 books in all. Of his plays, *The Farmer's Wife* (1917, staged 1924) and *Yellow Sands* (1926), which he wrote with his daughter Adelaide, were perhaps the most successful. He also collaborated with **Arnold Bennett** and **Jerome K Jerome** on plays. ⌨ *From the Angle of 88* (1951)

Philo 2nd century AD
Byzantine scientist

He wrote a treatise on military engineering of which some fragments remain. He was probably the first to record the contraction of air in a globe over water when a candle is burnt in it.

Philo Judaeus c.20BC–c.40AD
Hellenistic Jewish philosopher

He was born in Alexandria, Egypt, where he was a leading member of the Jewish community. A prolific author, his work brought together Greek philosophy and Jewish scripture, and greatly influenced subsequent Greek Christian theologians like **St Clement of Alexandria** and **Origen**. Most of his works consist of commentaries on the Pentateuch, many of which survive in the original Greek. In c.40AD he headed a deputation to the mad Emperor **Caligula** to plead with him on behalf of Jews who refused to worship him, as he records in *De Legatione*. ⌨ Harry A Wolfson, *Philo* (2 vols, rev edn, 1948)

Philopoemen c.253–182BC
Greek soldier and politician

He was born in Megalopolis in Arcadia. As Commander-in-Chief of the Achaean League, he crushed the Spartans at Mantinea (208BC), and sought to unite Greece against the Romans. In his later years he took part in an expedition against Messene, but was captured and poisoned by the Messenians.

Philostratus, Flavius c.170–245AD
Greek Sophist

He studied at Athens, and established himself in Rome, where he wrote an idealized Life of **Apollonius of Tyana**, the bright *Lives of the Sophists*, and the amatory *Epistles*. The *Heroicon* and the *Imagines*, a description of 34 paintings on mythological themes supposedly in a villa near Naples, are now ascribed to his son-in-law, Philostratus the Lemnian, and further *Imagines* to a third and related Philostratus, probably a grandson.

Phipps, Sir William 1651–95
American colonialist

Born in Pemmaquid, Maine, he was successively shepherd, carpenter and trader, and in 1687 he recovered £300,000 from a wrecked Spanish ship off the Bahamas, which gained him a knighthood and the appointment of Provost-Marshal of New England. In 1690 he captured Port Royal (now Annapolis) in Nova Scotia, but he failed in 1691 in a naval attack upon Quebec. In 1692 he became Governor of Massachusetts and, also in that year, when his wife was accused of witchcraft, the force behind the Salem witchcraft trials finally diminished.

Phiz See **Browne, Hablot K (night)**

Phocas 547–610
Byzantine emperor

Thracian by origin, he overthrew his predecessor, Maurice, in 602. Through his monstrous vices, tyranny and incapacity the empire sank into utter anarchy, and he was overthrown (610) by **Heraclius**.

Phocion c.397–318BC
Athenian soldier and politician

Elected general 45 times, he commanded a division of the Athenian fleet at Naxos in 376BC, and helped to conquer Cyprus in 351 for **Artaxerxes III**. In 341 he crushed the Macedonian party in Euboea, and in 340 forced **Philip II** of Macedonia to evacuate the Chersonesus, but advised Athens to make peace with him. The advice was not taken, but the disastrous Battle of Chaeronea in 338 proved its sense. Subsequently, he consistently opposed resistance to Macedonia; on the death of **Alexander the Great** in 323, he attempted to prevent the Athenians from going to war with **Antipater**, Regent in Macedonia. During a brief return to democracy in Athens, he was put to death on a charge of treason.

Phomvihane, Kaysone 1920–92
Laotian statesman

Born in Savannakhet province and educated at Hanoi University, he fought with the anti-French forces in Vietnam after World War II and joined the exiled Free Lao Front (Neo Lao Issara) nationalist movement in Bangkok in 1945. He later joined the communist Pathet Lao, becoming, with North Vietnamese backing, its leader in 1955. He successfully directed guerrilla resistance to the incumbent rightist regime and in 1975 became Prime Minister of the newly formed People's Democratic Republic of Laos and General-Secretary of the Lao People's Revolutionary Party. Initially he attempted to follow a radical socialist programme of industrial nationalization and rural collectivization, but later began a policy of economic and political liberalization. He was generally viewed as a mellowing radical.

Photius c.820–91
Byzantine prelate

Born in Constantinople (Istanbul), Photius was hurried through holy orders and installed as Patriarch of Constantinople, when Ignatius was deposed (858). In 862, however, Pope **Nicholas I** called a council at Rome to declare Photius's election invalid and reinstate Ignatius. Supported by the Emperor Michael, Photius assembled a council at Constantinople (867) which condemned many points of doctrine of the Western Church and ex-communicated Nicholas. Photius was then deposed and reinstated on several occasions, erased the *Filioque* clause from the Creed (879), and was finally exiled to Armenia (886). His main surviving works are *Myriobiblon* or *Bibliotheca*, a summary review of 280 works which Photius had read, and many of which are lost, a lexicon, the *Nomocanon*, a collection of the acts and decrees of the councils and ecclesiastical laws of the emperors, and a collection of letters. His feast day is 6 February (East).

Phryne 4th century BC
Greek courtesan

Born in Thespiae, Boeotia, she became enormously rich through her many lovers. Accused of profaning the Eleusinian mysteries, she was defended by the orator **Hyperides**, who threw off her robe in court, showing her loveliness, and so gained the verdict.

Phyfe, Duncan 1768–1854
US cabinetmaker

Born in Scotland, he emigrated to Albany in the USA in 1784, and after serving an apprenticeship to a local cabinetmaker, moved to New York City in the early 1790s. He started up his own business and by the beginning of the 19th century had become a major exponent of the Directory style which, in turn, was influenced by the British Regency, and was later known as the 'Phyfe style' in appreciation of his influence on the interpretation of new US fashion. His work was characterized by designs that made use of figured mahogany, combined with restrained ornamentation in the form of reeding on legs and uprights, carved foliate details and paw feet. He supplied furniture to a wide variety of wealthy patrons, and when the shop closed in 1847 it marked the end of over 50 years of continuous production. Examples of his work can be found in the Winterthur Museum, Delaware.

Piaf, Edith, *originally* Edith Giovanna Gassion 1915–63
French singer

Born in Paris, she started her career by singing in the streets. Graduating to music hall and cabaret, she became known as Piaf, from the Parisian argot for 'little sparrow', which suited her waif-like appearance. She appeared in stage-plays—**Jean Cocteau** wrote *Le Bel Indifférent* for her—and in films, including **Jean Renoir**'s *French-Cancan*. However, it was for her songs with their undercurrent of sadness and nostalgia, written by herself and songwriters such as **Jacques Prévert**, that she became well known, travelling widely in Europe and the USA. After a severe illness she made a very successful but brief return to the stage in 1961, before recurring ill health led to her death two years later. Among her best-remembered songs are *Le Voyage du pauvre nègre, Mon Légionnaire, Un Monsieur m'a suivi dans la rue, La vie en rose,* and *Non, je ne regrette rien*. She was the daughter of the famous acrobat Jean Gassion. 📖 Simone Berteaut, *Piaf: A Biography* (1972)

Piaget, Jean 1896–1980
Swiss psychologist, a pioneer in the study of child intelligence

Born in Neuchâtel, he studied zoology then turned to psychology and became Professor of Psychology at Geneva University (1929–54), director of the Centre d'Epistémologie génétique and a director of the Institut des Sciences de l'Éducation. He is best known for his research on the development of cognitive functions (perception, intelligence, logic), for his intensive case-study methods of research (using his own children), and for postulating 'stages' of cognitive development. His books include *The Child's Conception of the World* (1926), *The Origin of Intelligence in Children* (1936), and *The Early Growth of Logic in the Child* (1958). 📖 S and C Modgil, *Jean Piaget* (1982)

Piast fl.c.870
Semi-legendary Polish ploughman and dynasty founder

His son Siemowit established the consolidation of Great Poland, culminating in the coronation (1025) of Boleslaw I (the Brave). The Crown passed to Bohemia (1296), and the Piast dynasty ended when Casimir III, the Great (1310–70, king from 1333), was succeeded by his nephew, Louis I of Hungary (1370).

Piatigorsky, Gregor 1903–76
US cellist

Born in Yekaterinoslav, Russia (now Dnipropetrovsk), he gave concerts throughout his home country from the age of nine, and studied at the Moscow Conservatory. Principal Cellist of the Moscow Imperial Opera from 1919 to 1921, he played at the same level in the Warsaw (1921–23) and Berlin (1924–28) Philharmonic Orchestras, before embarking on a solo career. He toured internationally and made his US debut in 1929. His recital partners included **Vladimir Horowitz**, **Artur Schnabel**, **Jascha Heifetz**, and **Rachmaninov**, and many works were composed for him. He became a US citizen in 1942 and was a distinguished teacher at the Curtis Institute, Philadelphia, and subsequently at several universities.

Piazzi, Giuseppe 1746–1826
Italian astronomer

Born in Ponte, northern Italy, he became a Theatine monk (1764), was appointed Professor of Mathematics at Palermo in Sicily in 1780, and founded on behalf of the

Bourbon government two observatories, at Naples and at Palermo. After 22 years of observing at Palermo with a vertical circle made by the English optician Jesse Ramsden, he published a monumental catalogue of 7,646 stars (1813). In the course of his observations he discovered on the night of 1 January 1801 the very first minor planet (or asteroid), which he named Ceres after the tutelary deity of Sicily.

Picabia, Francis 1879–1953
French Dadaist painter

He was born in Paris. He was originally an Impressionist, but took part in every modern movement—Neo-Impressionism, Cubism, Futurism, and finally, with **Marcel Duchamp**, Dadaism, which they introduced to New York in 1915. His anti-art productions, often portraying imaginary machinery in satirical comparisons to the human condition, include *Parade amoureuse* (1917), *Infant Carburettor*, and many of the cover designs for the US anti-art magazine *291*, which he edited.

Picard, (Charles) Émile 1856–1941
French mathematician

Born in Paris, he became professor at the Sorbonne (1886–97) and was elected a member of the French Academy of Sciences in 1889. Noted for his work in complex analysis, and integral and differential equations, he investigated complex functions and wrote the definitive work of his generation on the theory of complex surfaces and integrals. Picard also introduced the method of 'successive approximations', a powerful technique for determining whether solutions to differential equations exist.

Picard, Jean 1620–82
French astronomer

Born in La Flèche, Anjou, in 1645 he became professor in the Collège de France and helped to found the Paris observatory. He made the first accurate measurement of a degree of a meridian and thus arrived at an estimate of the radius of the Earth. He visited **Tycho Brahe's** observatory on the island of Hven, and determined its latitude and longitude.

Picasso, Pablo See panel p1465

Piccard, Auguste Antoine 1884–1962
Swiss physicist

Born in Basle, Switzerland, he became a professor at Brussels in 1922 and held posts at Lausanne, Chicago and Minnesota universities. With his brother **Jean Felix Piccard**, he ascended 16–17km by balloon (1931–32) into the stratosphere. In 1948 he explored the ocean depths off west Africa in a bathyscape constructed from his own design. His son Jacques, together with a US naval officer, Donald Walsh, established a world record by diving more than seven miles in the US bathyscape *Trieste* into the Marianas Trench of the Pacific Ocean in 1960.

Piccard, Jean Felix 1884–1963
US chemist

Born in Basle, Switzerland, he was the twin brother of **Auguste Antoine Piccard**. He took a chemical engineering degree at the Swiss Institute of Technology in 1907, subsequently held a chair at New York, and became Professor Emeritus of Aeronautical Engineering at Minnesota University. His chief interest was in exploration of the stratosphere and he designed and ascended (with his wife) in a balloon from Dearborn, Detroit, in 1934, to a height of 57,579ft (17,550m), collecting valuable data concerning cosmic rays.

Piccaver, Alfred 1884–1958
English tenor

Born in Long Sutton, Lincolnshire, he studied in New York, and made his debut in Prague (1907). He was the leading tenor at Vienna (1910–37), singing **Beethoven**, **Richard Wagner**, **Verdi** and **Puccini** roles, and taught in Vienna from 1955.

Piccinni, Niccola 1728–1800
Italian composer

Born in Bari, he wrote over 100 operas as well as oratorios and church music. In 1766 he was summoned to Paris, and became the representative of the party opposed to **Christoph Gluck**.

Pick, Frank 1878–1941
English administrator and design patron

Born in Spalding, Lincolnshire, he trained as a solicitor and joined the London Underground Electric Railways in 1906 as assistant to the general manager. He was promoted rapidly, becoming vice-chairman of the London passenger transport board (1933–40). It was his vision which transformed London Transport into the model, unified, modern system that it became. A founder-member of the Design and Industries Association, he employed some of the best artistic and design talents available. Among these were the architect Charles Holden, the sculptors **Eric Gill** and **Jacob Epstein**, and graphic artists such as **Edward McKnight Kauffer**.

Pickering, Edward Charles 1846–1919
US astronomer

Born in Boston, he was educated at Harvard, and became Professor of Physics at the Massachusetts Institute of Technology. In 1876 he was appointed Professor of Astronomy and director of the observatory at Harvard, a post he held for 42 years. In 1884 he published the first catalogue of 4,260 visual stellar magnitudes, the *Harvard Photometry*. A revised version containing 45,000 stars was published in 1908. In 1889 he discovered the first spectroscopic binary star. These stars are so close together that they are best distinguished by the **Doppler** movement of their spectral lines. Around 1890 Pickering introduced the colour index. This measures the difference between a star's photographic (blue) and visual (yellow) magnitudes, and is related to the surface temperature of a star. He oversaw the production of the *Henry Draper Catalogue*, which classified 225,000 stars according to their spectra, and was responsible for the *Photographic Map of the Entire Sky* (1903). He was the brother of **William Henry Pickering**.

Pickering, Sir George White 1904–80
English medical scientist

Born in Whalton, Northumberland, he graduated in natural sciences from Pembroke College, Cambridge (1926), and trained in medicine at St Thomas's Hospital, London, qualifying in 1928. He was appointed to the staff of the Medical Research Council (1931) and spent eight years working with Sir **Thomas Lewis** at University College Hospital (UCH) in London. In 1932 he presented results of experiments on headaches and went on to work on hypertension (high blood pressure). He also conducted important experimental work on the mechanism of pain in peptic ulcers. He became a lecturer in cardiovascular pathology at UCH in 1936, Professor of Medicine at St Mary's Hospital Medical School (1939–56) and Regius Professor of Medicine at Oxford (1956–68). He was a key figure in medical education in Great Britain from the 1950s, and published widely on historical and cultural issues. He was knighted in 1957.

Pickering, Ron(ald James) 1930–91
English sports commentator, broadcaster and athletics coach

Born in Hackney, London, he was educated at Stratford Grammar School, Carnegie College, Leeds, and Leicester University. Working as a schoolteacher, he coached

Picasso, Pablo 1881–1973
Spanish painter, the dominating figure of early 20th-century French art and a pioneer of Cubism

Picasso was born in Malaga, Andalusia, the son of an art teacher, José Ruiz Blasco, and Maria Picasso y Lopez, whose maiden name he adopted. At the age of 14 he entered the academy at Barcelona (where his family had moved); there he painted *Barefoot Girl* (1895). After two years he transferred to Madrid for more advanced study. In 1898 he won a gold medal for *Customs of Aragon*, which was exhibited in his native town.

In 1901 he set up in a studio at 13 Rue de Ravignon (now Place Émile-Goudeau), Montmartre. By now he was a master of the traditional forms of art, shown for example in his *Gypsy Girl on the Beach* (1898), and he quickly absorbed the Neo-Impressionist influences of the Paris school of **Toulouse-Lautrec**, **Edgar Degas** and **Édouard Vuillard**, as exemplified in *Longchamp* (1901), *The Blue Room* (1901), and other works. However, he soon began to develop his own idiom.

The blue period (1902–04; referring to colours as well as mood), a series of striking studies of the poor in haunting attitudes of despair and gloom, gave way to the bright, life-affirming pink period (1904–06), in which Picasso achieved for harlequins, acrobats and the incidents of circus life what Degas had done for the ballet. Pink turned to brown in *La Coiffure* (1905–06) and the remarkable portrait of **Gertrude Stein** (1906).

His interest in sculpture and his new enthusiasm for black art are fully reflected in the transitional *Two Nudes* (1906), which heralded his epoch-making break with tradition in *Les Demoiselles d'Avignon* (1906–07), the first full-blown example of analytical Cubism, an attempt to render the three-dimensional on the flat picture surface without resorting to perspective. Nature was no longer to be copied, decorated or idealized, but exploited for creative ends. Its exclusive emphasis on formal, geometrical criteria contrasted sharply with the cult of colour of the Fauvists, to whom he and **Georges Braque** for a time belonged, before the two joined forces in 1909 for their exploration of Cubism through its various phases; analytic, synthetic, hermetic and rococo, in which collage, pieces of wood, wire, newspaper and string became media side by side with paint. The *Ma Jolie* series of pictures, after the music-hall song score which appears in them (1911–14), are examples of the last phase.

Braque broke with Picasso in 1914. From 1917 Picasso, through **Jean Cocteau**, became associated with **Sergei Diaghilev**'s Ballets Russes, designing costumes and sets for *Parade* (1917), *Le Tricorne* (1919), *Pulcinella* (1920), *Le Train bleu* (1924), in both Cubist and neoclassical styles, and thus made the former acceptable to a wider public. The grotesque facial and bodily distortions of the *Three Dancers* (1925) foreshadows the immense canvas of *Guernica* (1937), which expressed in synthetic Cubism Picasso's horror of the bombing of this Basque town during the Civil War, of war in general and compassion and hope for its victims. The canvas was exhibited in the Spanish Pavilion in the Paris World Fair (1937) and Picasso became director of the Prado Gallery, Madrid (1936–39).

During World War II Picasso was mostly in Paris, and after the liberation he joined the Communists. Neither *Guernica* nor his portrait of **Stalin** (1953) commended him to the Party. He designed stage sets for Cocteau and **Roland Petit**, illustrated translations of classical texts, experimented in sculpture, ceramics and lithography, allowed his canvas to be filmed while at work and wrote a play.

Picasso worked in a great variety of media, and was above all an innovator. As well as sculpture and painting, he produced constructions in metal, pottery, drawings, engravings, aquatints and lithographs. A film was made of him at work in his studio. His first wife was Olga Kokhloven, a dancer with Diaghilev's Ballets Russes. After leaving her in 1931 he had a series of mistresses, some of whom modelled for him and one of whom, Jacqueline Roque, married him in 1961.

📖 John Richardson, *A Life of Picasso* (2 vols, 1996); Norman Mailer, *Portrait of Picasso as a Young Man* (1996); T Hilton, *Picasso* (1976); R Penrose, *Picasso: His Life and Work* (1958).

'Art is not the application of a canon of beauty but what the instinct and the brain can conceive beyond any canon. When we love a woman we don't start measuring her limbs.' From an interview in 1935 with Christian Zervos, editor of *Cahiers d'Art*, translated by A H Barr in *Picasso: Fifty Years of his Art* (1946).

---

athletics in his spare time until 1961, when he was appointed national coach to Wales and south-west England by the Amateur Athletic Association. He was a team coach at the 1964 Tokyo Olympics and the 1966 Commonwealth Games in Jamaica. He began television commentaries for the BBC in 1968, covering sports including athletics, skiing and gymnastics. He also presented sports programmes, and documentaries in the *World About Us* series. He was noted for his enthusiasm and wide knowledge, and was also an anti-drugs campaigner.

Pickering, William 1796–1854
English publisher

He was apprenticed to Quaker publishers and booksellers in London (1810), but left in 1820 to set up his own business in Lincoln's Inn Fields. He first published a series of reprints of classical authors in miniature volumes, known as the Diamond Classics (1821–31). Valued for their typographical excellence, they included the first specimen of a diamond Greek typeface. In 1829 he began a long association with Charles Whittingham and the Chiswick Press, and in 1830 began to produced reprints under the Aldine Press imprint. His 1844 reprints of the *Book of Common Prayer* (6 vols, folio) are among the finest known specimens of typography.

Pickering, William Hayward 1910–
US engineer and physicist

Born in Wellington, New Zealand, he emigrated to the USA in 1929, studied physics at the California Institute of Technology in 1936, and in 1944 joined the Jet Propulsion Laboratory there, where he developed the first telemetry system used in US rockets. He was director of the Jet Propulsion Laboratory from 1954 to 1976, and initiated the space exploration programme that launched the first US satellite, *Explorer I*, in 1958. He supervised the Ranger lunar-impact flights in 1964–65, and the Mariner flights to Venus and Mars which provided the first close-up photographs ever taken of the surface of another planet. He was elected to the US National Academy of Sciences in 1962, and was awarded the National Medal of Science in 1976.

Pickering, William Henry 1858–1938
US astronomer

Born in Boston, he was the brother of **Edward Charles Pickering**. In 1919 he discovered Phoebe, the 9th satellite of Saturn. He was in charge of an observation station at Arequipa, Peru and from 1900 was director of a station at Mandeville, Jamaica.

Pickett, George Edward 1825–75
Confederate general in the US Civil War

Born in Richmond, Virginia, he graduated last in his class from West Point in 1846. He is best remembered for leading 'Pickett's charge', an unsuccessful assault on the Union centre at Gettysburg (3 July 1863). Less than one fourth of his 4,300 men survived the disastrous charge, which marked a turning point in the Civil War.

Pickford, Mary, *originally* Gladys Mary Smith
1893–1979
US actress

Born in Toronto, Canada, she first appeared on the stage at the age of five as 'Baby Gladys', and in 1909 made her first film, *The Violin Maker of Cremona*, directed by D W Griffith. Her beauty and her image of unsophisticated charm soon won her the title of 'America's Sweetheart' and she played the innocent heroine in many silent films, including *Rebecca of Sunnybrook Farm* (1917), *Pollyanna* (1920) and *Little Lord Fauntleroy* (1921). She won an Academy Award for her first talkie, *Coquette* (1929), and retired from the screen in 1933. She co-founded United Artists Film Corporation in 1919, the year in which she married Douglas Fairbanks, Snr, her second husband.
📖 Robert Windeler, *Sweetheart* (1974)

Pickup, Ronald Alfred 1940–
English actor

Born in Chester, he trained at RADA and made his London stage debut as Octavius in *Julius Caesar*, at the Royal Court Theatre (1964) and acted in more than 20 plays with the National Theatre Company at the Old Vic (1965–73). His many television roles include Randolph Churchill in *Jennie, Lady Randolph Churchill* (1974), George Orwell in *Orwell on Jura* (1983), Prince Yakimov in *Fortunes of War* (1987), Andrew Powell in *A Time to Dance* (1992), Roger Tundish in *The Riff Raff Element* (1993–94), Daniel Byrne in *The Rector's Wife* (1994) and the title role in *King Henry IV* (1994). His films include *The Day of the Jackal* (1973), *The Thirty-Nine Steps* (1978) and *The Mission* (1986).

Pico Della Mirandola, Giovanni, Comte
1463–94
Italian philosopher and humanist

Born in Mirandola, Ferrara, he studied in Italy and France, and settled later in Florence, where he came under the influence of Marsilio Ficino. In Rome he wrote his *Conclusiones* (1486), offering to dispute his 900 theses on logic, ethics, theology, mathematics and the *Kabbala* against all-comers, but the debate was forbidden by Pope Innocent VIII on the grounds that many of the theses were heretical, and he suffered persecution until Pope Alexander VI finally absolved him in 1493. He wrote various Latin epistles and elegies, a series of florid Italian sonnets, *Heptaplus* (1490, a mystical interpretation of the Genesis creation myth), and some important philosophical works including *De ente et uno* (1492, an attempt to reconcile Platonic and Aristotelian ontological doctrines) and *De hominis dignitate oratio* (1486, on freewill).

Pictet, Marc-Auguste 1752–1825
Swiss physicist

Born in Geneva, he qualified in law (1774), but his true interests lay in the natural sciences. He was appointed to the chair of philosophy at the Geneva Academy in 1786 on the resignation of his mentor, Horace Bénédict de Saussure. His studies in geology, meteorology and astronomy were characteristically wide-ranging. Best known throughout Europe was the *Essai sur le Feu* (1790) recording researches on heat and hygrometry. There he described how radiant heat could be reflected, like light. Pictet's journal, the *Bibliothèque Britannique*, sustained intellectual contact between Great Britain and the rest of Europe during the Napoleonic Wars.

Pictet, Raoul Pierre 1846–1929
Swiss physicist

Born in Geneva, he studied physics and chemistry in Geneva and in Paris (1868–70), returning to Geneva to devote himself to the study of low temperatures in connection with developing refrigeration techniques. He was appointed Professor of Industrial Physics at the University of Geneva in 1879. In 1886 he moved to Berlin to establish an industrial research laboratory and to market his refrigeration inventions. Later he returned to Paris. Working in Geneva in 1877, he liquefied oxygen in bulk by 'cascade' cooling and compression. Louis Paul Cailletet in Paris liquefied oxygen independently at around the same time, but in much smaller quantities.

Pieck, Wilhelm 1876–1960
East German politician

Born near Berlin, the son of a labourer, he initially worked as a carpenter and was active from an early age in socialist politics. In 1915 he helped found the Spartacus League and in 1918 the German Communist Party (KPD), leading the unsuccessful 'Spartacus uprising' in Berlin in 1919. During the Weimar Republic, Pieck was elected as a Communist to the Reichstag in 1928, but was forced into exile in 1933 when Hitler came to power. He fled to Moscow where he became, in 1935, Secretary of the Comintern. In 1945 he returned to Berlin in the wake of the Red Army and founded, in 1946, the dominant Socialist Unity Party (SED). From 1949 he served as President of the German Democratic Republic, the post being abolished on his death.

Pierce, Franklin 1804–69
14th President of the USA

Born in Hillsborough, New Hampshire, he studied law and was admitted to the Bar in 1827. From 1829 to 1833 he was a member of the state legislature, the last two years as Speaker. In 1833 he was elected to Congress as a Jacksonian Democrat, and in 1837 to the US Senate, where he showed himself a loyal member of his party. He resigned in 1842 to practise law in Concord, New Hampshire, and in 1846 he volunteered for the Mexican War, rising to the rank of brigadier-general. Pierce was nominated in 1852 as a compromise candidate for the presidency and was elected by a generous margin over Winfield Scott, the Whig nominee. The events of his administration (1853–57) included the treaty for reciprocity of trade with the British American colonies, the Gadsden purchase from Spain, the expeditions of William Walker to Nicaragua and of others to Cuba, and, especially, the repeal of the Missouri Compromise and the passing of the Kansas-Nebraska Act, which led to bitter debates about the possible expansion of slavery, and contributed to the formation of the Republican Party. The unpopularity of this act led to his enforced retirement from politics, as he was passed for the 1856 Democratic presidential nomination.

Pierce, John Robinson 1910–
US electrical engineer

Born in Des Moines, Iowa, he graduated from the California Institute of Technology (Caltech) and worked in the Bell Telephone Laboratories (1936–71), before returning to Caltech as Professor of Engineering (1971–80). A man of wide scientific interests, he made important discoveries in the fields of microwaves, radar and pulse-code modulation. In collaboration with William Shockley he was one of the first to devise an effective electrostatically-focused electron multiplier, and later with Rudolf Kompfner he developed the travelling-wave tube which is now an essential part of microwave technology. In the 1950s he was one of the first to see the possibilities of satellite communication, taking a leading part in the development work that resulted in the launch of *Echo* in 1960 and *Telstar* in 1962. He has published many books and technical papers as well as works of science fiction.

Piero della Francesca c.1420–1492
Italian painter

Born in Borgo San Sepolcro, he also worked in Urbino, Ferrara, Florence and Rome, but by 1442 he was a town councillor at Borgo. A number of influences can be seen in his work, notably Domenico Veneziano, his teacher, but also Masaccio, Leon Alberti and Paolo Uccello. As a scientist and mathematician he developed a very precise and geometric attitude towards composition, which he wrote about in his treatise *On Perspective in Painting*. He also wrote a treatise on geometry. Complementing this is a subtle use of pale colour and a concern for proportion and scale. Perugino and Luca Signorelli were both pupils of his and through them his influence extends to the entire Italian school. In his own lifetime he was overshadowed by his more fashionable contemporaries, but during the 20th century his work has become the favourite from this period. His major work is a series of frescoes illustrating *The Legend of the Holy Cross* in the choir of San Francesco at Arezzo, painted c.1452–66. Other works include the *Flagellation* (c.1456–57) at Urbino. An unfinished *Nativity* in the National Gallery, London, shows some Flemish influence.

Piero di Cosimo, *properly* Piero di Lorenzo
c.1462–c.1521
Italian painter

He was a pupil of Cosimo Rosselli, whose name he adopted. His later style was influenced by Luca Signorelli and Leonardo da Vinci, and among his best-known works are the mythological scene *The Battle of the Lapiths and Centaurs* (1486, National Gallery, London), *The Death of Procris* (c.1500, National Gallery, London), and *Perseus and Andromeda* (c.1515, Uffizi, Florence).

Pierre, Abbé, *properly* Henri Antoine Groués
1912–
French priest

Born in Lyons, he served with distinction during World War II and became a member of the Resistance movement in 1942. Elected deputy in the constituent assembly after the war, he resigned in 1951 to concentrate on helping the homeless of Paris. Forming a group known as the Companions of Emmaus, he provided, with little monetary assistance, at least a minimum of shelter for hundreds of families and finally secured the aid of the French government in dealing with this problem. He was made an Officer of the French Legion of Honour in 1980.

Pieterse, Zola See Budd, Zola

Pigalle, Jean Baptiste 1714–85
French sculptor

Born in Paris, he became an extremely popular artist in his day, and was patronized by Louis XV and Madame de Pompadour. His works, in a style which reconciled the baroque and the classical traditions, include a statue of Voltaire (1776, Paris) and the tomb of Marshal Maurice, Comte de Saxe in Strasbourg (1753–56). His *Vénus, l'Amour et l'Amitié* (1758) is in the Louvre, Paris.

Piggott, Lester Keith 1935–
English jockey

He was born in Wantage. Appearing aloof and severe, partly due to imperfect hearing and a speech impediment, he was champion jockey in England on 11 occasions. He rode his first winner in 1948, and within two years was 11th on the list of top British jockeys. He frequently came into conflict with the stewards of the Jockey Club, and received various suspensions and fines. From 1955 to 1966 he had an extremely successful partnership

with Noel Murless. He became officially freelance in 1967. At five feet nine inches, Piggott was known as the 'the Long Fellow', and had to diet rigorously to make the weight. In all he rode 30 Classic winners, including nine Derbies. Many of his greatest successes came on horses trained by Vincent O'Brien. When he retired from riding he became a trainer, but he was tried for tax irregularities (1987) and sentenced to three years' imprisonment. He was released on parole after one year, and resumed his career as a trainer. He eventually returned to riding and, after a gap of seven years, won the 2000 Guineas (his 30th Classic victory) at Newmarket in 1992. He is considered the most brilliant jockey since World War II. He retired in 1995. ⌨ Dick Francis, *Lester, the official biography* (1986); James Lawton, *Lester Piggott* (1980)

Pignon, Edouard 1905–93
French painter

Born in Marles-les-Mines, he studied with and was much influenced by the Cubists and by Jacques Villon. Many of his pictures are studies of miners, such as the *Mineur mort* (1952, 'Dead Miner'), and of harvest scenes and peasants.

Pigott, Richard c.1828–1889
Irish journalist and forger

Born in County Meath, he became editor and proprietor of *The Irishman* (1865) and two Fenian or extreme nationalist papers, which he disposed of in 1881 to Charles Stewart Parnell and others. Already suspected by his party, in 1886 he sold to the Irish Loyal and Patriotic Union (an anti-Home Rule organization) papers accusing Parnell of complicity in the Phoenix Park tragedy, on which were based *The Times* articles 'Parnellism and Crime' (1887). Under cross-examination in court, he confessed that he had forged the more important papers. He then fled, and shot himself in Madrid.

Pijper, Willem 1894–1947
Dutch composer

Born in Zeist, he was one of the foremost of modern composers of the Netherlands. He taught at the Amsterdam Conservatory, writing symphonies and other orchestral pieces, and an opera, *Halewijn*.

Pike, Kenneth Lee 1912–
US linguist

Born in Woodstock, Connecticut, he graduated in theology in 1933. He became involved in linguistic studies through the Summer Institute of Linguistics whose purpose is to study previously unwritten languages with the aim of producing translations of the Bible in them. Between 1948 and 1979, he was first Associate Professor, then Professor, of Linguistics at the University of Michigan at Ann Arbor. He developed the system of linguistic analysis known as tagmemics. Among his many books are *Phonetics* (1943), *Phonemics* (1947), *Tone Languages* (1948), and *Language in Relation to a Unified Theory of the Structure of Human Behavior* (1954–60).

Pike, Zebulon Montgomery 1779–1813
US explorer

He was born in Lamberton, New Jersey, the son of an army officer, and became a cadet at the age of 15. As an army lieutenant he led an expedition (1806–07) from St Louis to the Arkansas River and the Rocky Mountains, and he tried but failed to scale the Colorado peak now named after him. He later fought in the War of 1812 and was killed in the successful assault on York (now Toronto).

Pilate, Pontius d.c.36AD
Roman prefect of Judea and Samaria

He presided at the trial of Jesus Christ and ordered his crucifixion. Under his rule there were many uprisings, and Vitellius sent him to Rome to answer to Emperor Tiberius (36) on charges of rapacity and cruelty. Eusebius

of Caesarea says that Pilate committed suicide, others say he was banished to Vienna Allobrogum (Vienne), or beheaded under Nero. Tradition makes him (or his wife) accept Christianity, and associates him with Pilatus in Switzerland. The so-called *Acts of Pilate* are unauthentic.
📖 Adrian Johns, *Pontius Pilate* (1988)

Pilbeam, David Roger 1940–
English physical anthropologist
Born in Brighton, Sussex, he trained at Cambridge and Yale, and became Professor of Social Science at Harvard in 1990 and director of the Peabody Musem there in 1991. A leading student of human and primate evolution, his many publications include *Evolution of Man* (1970) and *The Ascent of Man* (1972) and he was joint editor (with Steve Jones and Robert Martin) of *The Cambridge Encyclopedia of Human Evolution* (1992).

Pilcher, Percy Sinclair 1867–99
English aeronautical pioneer
Born in Bath, to an English father and Scottish mother, he entered the Royal Navy as a cadet in 1880, but resigned in 1887 to take up an apprenticeship with Randolph, Elder and Company, shipbuilders at Govan in Glasgow. He had already become interested in gliding when he was appointed an assistant lecturer at Glasgow University (1891), and after visiting Otto Lilienthal in Germany he completed his first glider, the *Bat*, and made some trial flights on a hill overlooking the Clyde at Cardross. By 1896 he had built his fourth machine, the *Hawk*, in which he made many successful flights, including a record of 250 metres in 1897. Over the next two years he is known to have built a lightweight engine with the intention of fitting it to one of his machines, but in September 1899 the *Hawk* disintegrated in the air, and Pilcher died from his injuries two days later.

Pile, Sir Frederick Alfred 1884–1976
English soldier
In World War I he won the Distinguished Service Order and the Military Cross, and throughout World War II commanded Britain's anti-aircraft defences. In 1945 he was appointed director-general of the Ministry of Works.

Pilger, John Richard 1939–
Australian journalist and documentary filmmaker
Born in Sydney, he was a reporter and sub-editor on the Sydney *Daily Telegraph* and *Sunday Telegraph* (1958–62), before moving to the UK, where he worked first as a sub-editor with Reuters and then as a writer on the *Daily Mirror* (1963–85), making his name as a war correspondent and campaigning journalist. His first television documentaries were for *World in Action* (1970), before his own series, *Pilger* (1974–) and, since 1978, single documentaries, such as *Do You Remember Vietnam?* (1978), *Year Zero – The Silent Death of Cambodia* (1979) and *Death of a Nation* (1994), about the slaughter in East Timor. He won the Journalist of the Year award twice (1967, 1979), the BAFTA Richard Dimbleby award (1991) and an Emmy award (1991).

Pilkington, Sir Alastair, *properly* Sir Lionel Alexander Bethune Pilkington 1920–95
English inventor
Educated at Trinity College, Cambridge, he joined the family firm of glass-makers and in 1952 conceived the idea of float glass as a method of manufacturing plate glass without having to grind it to achieve a satisfactory finish. He led the team which, after seven years' work, successfully introduced the new technique of pouring glass straight from the furnace onto the surface of a bath of molten tin. It floats while cooling, the smooth surface of the tin giving the glass a perfect finish, allied to an extremely uniform thickness and an absence of defects.

Pilnyak, Boris, *pseudonym of* Boris Andreyevich Vogau 1894–1937
Russian writer
He was born in Mozhaisk and educated in Nizhny Novgorod and Moscow. He wrote short stories and novels, including *Golý gok* (1922, Eng trans *The Naked Year*, 1929) and *Volga vplavaet b kaspinskoe more* (1930, Eng trans *The Volga Flows Down to the Caspian Sea*, 1932). His main theme was the effect of the Revolution on the middle classes in Russia, and his work was highly popular in the 1920s. However, despite his efforts to please the ruling hierarchy, as in the anti-US novel *O-Key* (1932), his writing met with disapproval and he was arrested, charged with spying for Japan, and executed. 📖 P Jensen, *Nature as Code: the achievement of Boris Pilnyak* (1979)

Pilon, Germain 1537–90
French sculptor
He was born in Paris. Among his works in a Mannerist style are the statues of Henry II and Catherine de Médicis at St Denis, the *Virgin of the Sorrows* in St Paul de Louis in Paris, the marble *Christ Risen* (Louvre, Paris) and the bronze Cardinal René de Birague in the Louvre. In these, in contrast with his earlier more conventional work, such as *The Three Graces* (1561–63, Louvre), his keen feeling for and observation of nature have produced figures which are both more realistic and more emotional. He also produced skilful medals, especially of the French royal family.

Piłsudski, Józef 1867–1935
Polish soldier and statesman
Born in Zulöw (Wilno), he was sent to Siberia for five years in 1887, and on his return became leader of the Polish Socialist party. After further terms of imprisonment in Warsaw and St Petersburg he escaped to Kraków and began to form a band of troops which fought on Austria's side at the beginning of World War I. In 1917, however, he disbanded his forces and was imprisoned in Magdeburg by the Germans. In 1918 Piłsudski became provisional President of a new Polish republic, and in 1920, now a marshal, he triumphed in a struggle with the Red Army to establish Poland's frontiers. In 1921 he retired owing to a disagreement with the government, but in 1926 he returned to become Minister of War, then premier. Although he resigned his premiership in 1928, he remained the real ruler of the country in his capacity of Minister of War.

Pimen, Patriarch 1910–90
Russian Orthodox patriarch
Ordained a priest in 1932, he spent the later Stalin years in jail. However he was consecrated a bishop in Nikita Khrushchev's time (1957), and in Leonid Brezhnev's time (1971) became the patriarch. He supported Soviet peace initiatives and was a member of the World Peace Committee. In 1988 he met with Mikhail Gorbachev and secured his permission to celebrate the millennium of Christianity in Russia.

Pimentel, George Claude 1922–89
US physical chemist
Born in Rolinda, California, he studied chemistry at the University of California, Los Angeles, advanced to associate professor of chemistry, and from 1959 was Professor of Chemistry at the University of California, Berkeley. Pimentel's best-known work was his development of chemical lasers and the trapping of transient species in solid noble gases. He also devised the rapid-scan infrared spectrometers carried on NASA's Mariner 6 and 7 probes of Mars in 1969. Pimentel was also the editor of a school textbook which was very influential worldwide. Among his many honours were the Priestley Medal

of the American Chemical Society (1989), of which he was president in 1986, and honorary fellowship of the Royal Society of Chemistry (1987).

Pinchbeck, Christopher c.1670–1732
English clockmaker and toymaker
Born in London, he invented the gold-coloured alloy of copper and zinc, 'pinchbeck', for making imitation gold watches.

Pinchbeck, Christopher c.1710–1783
English inventor
Born in London, the son of Christopher Pinchbeck (c.1670–1732), he invented astronomical clocks, automatic pneumatic brakes and patent candle snuffers, among other devices.

Pinchot, Gifford 1865–1946
US conservationist
Born in Simsbury, Connecticut, he graduated from Yale in 1889 and studied at the École Nationale Forestière in France. He was one of the earliest advocates of systematic forest management in the USA, and from 1898 to 1910 he was chief of the Forestry Service. In 1912 he helped found the Progressive Party with Theodore Roosevelt. He also served two terms as Governor of Pennsylvania (1923–27, 1931–35).

Pinckney, Charles Cotesworth 1746–1825
US politician
Born in Charleston, South Carolina, he was sent to England and educated at Oxford. He read law and studied at Caen Military Academy and afterwards settled as a barrister in Charleston. He was George Washington's aide-de-camp at Brandywine and Germantown, and was taken prisoner by the British at the surrender of Charleston (1780). A member of the convention that framed the US Constitution (1787), he introduced the clause forbidding religious tests. In 1804 and 1808 he was Federalist candidate for the presidency.

Pincus, Gregory Goodwin 1903–67
US physiologist
Born in Woodbine, New Jersey, he graduated in science from Cornell University in 1924, undertook postgraduate study at Harvard (1924–27) and then worked at Cambridge and Berlin universities (1927–30). He was a member of the biology faculty at Harvard (1930–38) and of the experimental zoology department at Clark University (1938–45). In 1944 he established the Worcester Foundation for Experimental Research, which became internationally renowned for work on steroid hormones and mammalian reproduction. In 1951 he began work on developing a contraceptive pill, studying with John Rock and Min Chueh Chang the antifertility effect of those steroid hormones which inhibit ovulation in mammals. Synthetic hormones became available in the 1950s and Pincus organized field trials of their antifertility effects in Haiti and Puerto Rico in 1954. The results were successful, and oral contraceptives ('the pill') have since been widely used, despite concern over some side effects. Their success is a pharmaceutical rarity, as synthetic chemical agents do not usually show nearly 100 per cent effectiveness in a specific physiological action, or have such remarkable social effects.

Pindar, *Greek* Pindaros c.518–c.438BC
Greek lyric poet
Born near Thebes, Boeotia, he began his career as a composer of choral odes at 20 with a song of victory still extant (*Pyth.* X, written 498BC). He composed odes for the tyrants of Syracuse and Macedonia, as well as for the free cities of Greece. He wrote hymns to the gods, paeans, dithyrambs, odes for processions, mimic dancing songs, convivial songs, dirges, and odes in praise of princes. Of all these poems only fragments are extant, but his *Epinikia* ('Triumphal Odes') can be read in their entirety. They are divided into four books, celebrating the victories in the Olympian, Pythian, Nemean and Isthmian games. ⌨ C M Bowra, *Pindar* (1964)

Pindar, Peter See Wolcot, John

Pindling, Sir Lynden Oscar 1930–
Bahamanian statesman
Educated in the Bahamas and at London University, he practised as a lawyer before becoming centrally involved in politics, eventually as leader of the Progressive Liberal Party (PLP). He became Prime Minister in 1969 and led his country to full independence, within the Commonwealth, in 1973. The PLP, under Pindling, was re-elected in 1977, 1982 and 1987. He was defeated in the 1992 general election by Hubert Alexander Ingraham.

Pine, Courtney 1964–
English jazz saxophonist
Born in London of Jamaican parents. He became the figurehead of the so-called British jazz boom of the late 1980s with the success of his debut album, *Journey To The Urge Within* (1986), and was the subject of much media attention. His early music reflected his interest in soul, reggae and funk, while other projects have concentrated on a more purely defined jazz idiom, as in *Destiny's Dance (& the Image of Pursuance)* (1988) or *Within the Realms of Our Dreams* (1990). A powerful and charismatic performer, he broadened his range still further by incorporating Hip-Hop DJs in his live act, and on *Modern Day Jazz Stories* (1996).

Pinel, Philippe 1745–1826
French physician and pioneer in psychiatry
Born in Languedoc, he graduated at Toulouse, worked in Montpellier and in 1793 became head of the Bicêtre men's asylum in Paris, later working at the Salpêtrière, Paris. His humanitarian methods, emphasizing the psychological approach, reformed treatments of the insane and are contained within his great *Traité médico-philosophique sur l'aliénation mentale* (1801, 'Medico-Philosophical Treatise on Mental Alienation or Mania').

Pinero, Sir Arthur Wing 1855–1934
English playwright
Born in London, he studied law, but in 1874 made his debut on the stage in Edinburgh, and in 1875 joined the Lyceum company. His first play, *£200 a Year*, appeared in 1877, followed by a series of comedies. In 1893, with *The Second Mrs Tanqueray*, generally reckoned his best, he began a period of realistic tragedies which were received with enthusiastic acclamation and made him the most successful playwright of his day. He was the author of some 50 plays, including *The Squire* (1881), *The Magistrate* (1885), *Dandy Dick* (1887) and *The Profligate* (1889), and later *The Gay Lord Quex* (1899), *His House in Order* (1906) and *Mid-Channel* (1909). ⌨ C Hamilton, *The Social Plays of Arthur Wing Pinero* (4 vols, 1917–22)

Pinkerton, Allan 1819–84
US detective
He was born in Glasgow, Scotland, became a Chartist, and emigrated to the USA in 1842, settling in Dundee, Illinois. He became a detective and deputy-sheriff, and in 1850 founded the Pinkerton National Detective Agency in Chicago. He headed a federal intelligence network for General George B McClellan during the American Civil War, and his agency later took a leading part in breaking up the Molly Maguires (a secret terrorist society) and in policing other labour disputes. ⌨ James D Horan, *The Pinkertons* (1967)

Pink Floyd
English progressive rock band

The band's name is derived from bluesmen Pink Anderson and Floyd Council. It was formed in 1965–66 by poet and singer Syd Barrett (originally Roger Barrett, 1946–), who dictated the nursery-rhyme surrealism of the early album, *Piper at the Gates of Dawn* (1967). After Barrett's departure the music became increasingly sentious and humourless, with guitarist David Gilmour (1944–), bassist and singer Roger Waters (1944–), keyboard player Richard Wright (1945–) and drummer Nick Mason (1945–) experimenting with long-form compositions and technology. *Dark Side of the Moon* (1973), *Wish You Were Here* (1975) and *The Wall* (1979), an elaborate operatic examination of the very pressures that were then driving the group apart, were all huge commercial successes. *The Division Bell* (1994) was well received, while the band's live show continued to grow ever more gargantuan.
📖 N Schaffner, *Saucerful of Secrets* (1991)

Pinkham, Lydia E(stes) 1819–83
US housewife and manufacturer
Born in Lynn, Massachusetts, she trained as a teacher. She espoused various causes such as temperance and abolition, and married Isaac Pinkham in 1843. When he went bankrupt in 1875, she began selling a home remedy made from herbs and roots (and alcohol as preservative) specifically aimed at 'female complaints'. Its phenomenal success resulted in a successful family business and national fame for Pinkham, who corresponded personally with her customers. For many years after her death her 'Vegetable Compound' remained the best-known patent medicine in the USA.

Pinochet Ugarte, Augusto 1915–
Chilean soldier and statesman
He joined the army in 1933 and was a general by 1973. He was an instructor at Chile's senior military school, the Academy of War, from 1954 to 1964, when he became deputy director. He was made Commander-in-Chief of the armed forces in 1973 and in the same year led a coup which ousted, and resulted in the death of, the Marxist President, Salvador Allende. Pinochet took over the presidency, crushing all opposition. Despite widespread opposition to his harsh regime, and an assassination attempt, he announced in 1986 that he was considering remaining in office for another eight years. However a plebiscite in October 1988, asking for support for his continuing in office, produced a decisive 'No'. His presidency ended in March 1990 but he retained his military command. 📖 Genaro Arriagada, *Pinochet: The Politics of Power* (1988)

Pintasilgo, Maria de Lourdes 1930–
Portuguese politician
Born in Abrantes, she became president of Pax Romana, a Catholic student organization, whilst studying chemical engineering. She honed her oratorial skills and developed left-wing and feminist views, and from 1970 to 1974 she chaired the National Committee on the status of women. After the 1974 revolution she was made Minister for Social Affairs, legislating above all on women's rights. She was Ambassador to UNESCO (1976–79), acted as caretaker Prime Minister (1979–80), then was adviser to the president (1981–85). She has also been a member of the World Policy Institute since 1982 and has written widely on international affairs and women's issues.

Pinter, Harold 1930–
English dramatist
Born in London, the son of an East End tailor of Portuguese–Jewish ancestry (da Pinta), he studied for a short time at RADA, then the Central School of Speech and Drama in London. He became a repertory actor and wrote poetry and later plays. His first London production, *The Birthday Party* (1959), was trounced by critics unused to his highly personal dramatic idiom. A superb verbal acrobat, he exposes and utilizes the illogical and inconsequential in everyday talk to induce an atmosphere of menace in *The Birthday Party*, or of claustrophobic isolation in *The Caretaker* (1958, filmed 1963). His television play *The Lover* (1963) won the Italia Prize. Other early plays include *The Collection* (television 1961, stage 1962), *The Dwarfs* (radio 1960, stage 1963), and *The Homecoming* (1965). His filmscripts include *The Servant* (1963) and *The Pumpkin Eaters* (1964). Later plays include *No Man's Land* (1975), and *Betrayal* (1978), the story of an adulterous relationship told in reverse chronological order. He did not produce another full-length play until *Party Time* (1991) which was followed by *Moonlight* (1993). Three short pieces, under the title *Other Voices*, were shown at the National Theatre, London, in 1982, whilst Pinter was associate director there (1973–83). *One for the Road* (1984) and *Mountain Language* (1988), both about 25 minutes in length, and *A New World Order* (1990), deal with explicitly political themes. More recent filmscripts include *The French Lieutenant's Woman* (1981), from the novel by John Fowles, *The Handmaid's Tale* (1987), from the novel by Margaret Atwood, and *The Comfort of Strangers* (1990), from the novel by Ian McEwan. In 1991 he helped launch a campaign against the celebration of Columbus's 'discovery' of America. 📖 Michael Billington, *The Life and Work of Harold Pinter* (1996); G Almansi and S Henderson, *Harold Pinter* (1983)

Pinturicchio, *properly* Bernardino di Betto Vagio 1454–1513
Italian painter
Born in Perugia, he helped Perugino with the frescoes in the Sistine Chapel at Rome, and himself painted frescoes in several Roman churches and in the Vatican Library, as well as in Orvieto, Siena and elsewhere. His delight in brilliant colour and ornamental detail is evident in these lavish decorative schemes.

Pinza, Ezio, *originally* Fortunio Pinza 1892–1957
Italian bass
He was born in Rome and studied at Bologna. His wide range extended from Mozart to Wagner and Verdi, and he sang in all the major opera houses of Europe and beyond, including the Metropolitan Opera in New York (often with Bruno Walter), where he became the most celebrated Don Giovanni of the post-war years. From 1948 he sang in Broadway musicals, most notably in *South Pacific*.

Pinzón, Vicente Yáñez c.1460–c.1524
Spanish explorer and discoverer of Brazil
Born into a wealthy Andalusian family, he commanded the *Nina* in the first expedition of Columbus (1492). In 1499 he sailed on his own account, and in 1500 landed near Pernambuco on the Brazil coast, which he followed north to the Orinoco river. He was made governor of Brazil by Ferdinand, the Catholic and Isabella of Castile.

Piozzi, Hester Lynch, *previous married name* Thrale, *née* Salusbury 1741–1821
Welsh writer
She was born in Bodvel, Caernarvonshire, and in 1763 married Henry Thrale, a prosperous Southwark brewer. Two years later Dr Samuel Johnson conceived an extraordinary affection for her. He lived in her house at Streatham Place for over 16 years, and her husband made him one of his four executors. Henry Thrale died in April 1781, leaving 12 children, and in 1784 she married the Italian musician Gabriel Piozzi. After extensive travels in Europe, the couple returned to England in 1787, to Streatham in 1790. She wrote poems and on hearing of Johnson's death whilst in Italy, published *Anecdotes of the late Dr Johnson* (1786) and *Letters to and from the late Dr Johnson* (1788).

Pipe, Martin 1945–
English racehorse trainer

Born in Somerset, the son of a bookmaker, he was an amateur point-to-point rider before he became a National Hunt trainer. His first winner was Hit Parade at Taunton in May 1975 and he obtained his first training licence in 1977. The principal National Hunt trainer and leading jump trainer from 1988 to 1993, he had his best season overall in 1990–91 with 230 winners and winnings of over £1 million. Scientific training methods account for much of his success, as does his association with the jockey Peter Scudamore, who won a record 211 races in 1988–89. By the end of that season, Pipe had become the first man to train 200 winners on the Flat or over jumps. The Grand National and Irish Grand National are among the races won by horses trained by Pipe.

Piper, John 1903–92
English artist

Born in Epsom, in 1933 he met **Georges Braque**, and experiments in many media, including collage, led to a representational style which grew naturally from his abstract discipline. He designed sets for the theatre, working with **W H Auden** and **Stephen Spender**, and for opera, working with his wife Myfanwy Evans (1911–97) and **Benjamin Britten**, and he collaborated with **John Betjeman** on books. He also made stained glass and painted a series of topographical pictures, such as the watercolours of *Windsor Castle* commissioned by **Elizabeth II** (1941–42), and dramatic pictures of war damage. He designed the stained glass for Coventry Cathedral. His publications include *Brighton Aquatints* (1939), *British Romantic Artists* (1942) and *Buildings and Prospects* (1949).

Piper, Otto 1891–1982
German theologian

Born in Lichte, he studied in Jena, Marburg, Paris and Göttingen, and taught theology at Göttingen and at Münster, before fleeing from the Nazis in 1933 to Great Britain. He taught briefly in Bangor and Swansea, then moved to Princeton, USA, in 1937, where he was Professor of New Testament from 1941. He advocated a 'biblical realism' which neither took Scripture literally nor ignored its teaching, but sought to be true to the writers' intentions. His books include *God in History* (1939), *The Christian Interpretation of Sex* (1941, rewritten as *The Biblical View of Sex and Marriage*, 1960) and *Christian Ethics* (1970).

Pippard, Sir (Alfred) Brian 1920–
English physicist

Born in London, he studied at Cambridge, worked as a scientific officer at the Radar Research and Development Establishment (1941–45), then returned to Cambridge where he became Plummer Professor of Physics (1960–71) and Cavendish Professor of Physics (1971–82). His observations on the electromagnetic response of superconductors at very high frequencies led him to introduce into one of the London electrodynamic equations a new fundamental parameter called 'coherence length'. This new parameter meant that macroscopic superconductor volumes had to be considered when making theoretical descriptions of their electromagnetic properties, and the coherence length of a superconductor became one of its most important descriptive parameters. He was elected Fellow of the Royal Society in 1956 and knighted in 1975. His publications include *Response and Stability* (1985) and *Magnetoresistance* (1989).

Piquet, Nelson, *properly* Nelson Souto Maior 1952–
Brazilian motor-racing driver

Born in Rio de Janeiro, he changed his name so that his parents would not find out about his racing exploits. He was British Formula Three champion in 1978, and

Formula One world champion in 1981, 1983 (both with Brabham), and 1987 (with Williams). He won 20 races from 157 starts between 1978 and 1988.

Pirandello, Luigi 1867–1936
Italian dramatist, novelist and short-story writer, and Nobel Prize winner

Born in Girgenti (Agrigento), Sicily, he studied philology at Rome and Bonn, becoming a lecturer in literature at Rome (1897–1922). After writing powerful and realistic novels and short stories, including *Il Fu Mattia Pascal* (1904, rev edn 1921, Eng trans *The Late Mattia Pascal*, 1923) and *Si Gira* (1916, Eng trans *Shoot!*, 1926), he turned to the theatre and quickly established his own extraordinary genre. Among his plays are *Sei personaggi in cerca d'autore* (1921, Eng trans *Six Characters in Search of an Author*, 1922), *Enrico IV* (1922, Eng trans *Henry IV*, 1922) and *Come Tu Mi Vuoi* (1930, Eng trans *As You Desire Me*, 1931). In 1925 he established a theatre of his own in Rome, the Teatro d'Arte, and his company took his plays all over Europe. Many of his later plays have been filmed. He was awarded the Nobel Prize for literature in 1934. 📖 D Vittorini, *Luigi Pirandello* (1937)

Piranesi, Giambattista or Giovanni Battista 1720–78
Italian copper engraver and architect

Born in Venice, he worked in Rome, producing innumerable etchings of the city both in ancient times and in his own day. His most imaginative work is perhaps the *Carceri d'Invenzione*, a series of engravings of imaginary prisons. 📖 Alpheus H Mayor, *Giovanni Battista Piranesi* (1952)

Pire, (Dominique) Georges 1910–69
Belgian Dominican priest and Nobel Prize winner

Born in Dinant, he lectured in moral philosophy at Louvain (1937–47) and was awarded the Croix de Guerre for resistance work as priest and intelligence officer in World War II. After the war he devoted himself to helping refugees and displaced persons, and was awarded the 1958 Nobel Peace Prize for his scheme of 'European villages', including the 'Anne Frank village' in Germany for elderly refugees and destitute children.

Pirenne, Henri 1862–1935
Belgian historian

He studied medieval history at the universities of Liège, Leipzig and Berlin and also in Paris, and was Professor of Medieval and Belgian History at Ghent (1886–1930). He wrote on the history of the medieval town in *Medieval Cities* (1925) and *Economic and Social History of Medieval Europe* (1936), and of Belgium in *Histoire de Belgique* (7 vols, 1900–32). During World War I he was imprisoned by the Germans (1916–18) for refusing to teach during their occupation of Belgium, and while imprisoned he wrote from memory a *History of Europe* (posthumously published, and unfinished). His other major posthumously published work is *Mahomet et Charlemagne* (1937). He is known as the father of Belgian history and of medieval economic history.

Piron, Alexis 1689–1773
French poet and playwright

Born in Dijon, he began by writing farces for fairground theatres, and eventually graduated to the legitimate stage, writing both tragedies and comedies. His works include the comic opera *Endriaque* (1723) and a variety of plays, of which the extravagant satire *La métromanie* (1738) is the best known. Piron described himself as 'nothing, not even an Academician'. 📖 P Chapònnière, *Piron* (1910)

Pisanello, Antonio, *real name* Antonio Pisano 1395–1455
Italian painter and medallist

Born in Pisa, he was the foremost draughtsman of his day. His drawings are marked by an accurate observation of reality and a naturalism which contrasts with the stylized manner of his great contemporary Gentile da Fabriano. These drawings became models for later Renaissance artists. Pisanello travelled widely and painted frescoes (all since destroyed) in the Doge's Palace at Venice (1415–20) and in the Lateran Basilica in Rome (1431–32). His surviving frescoes include the *Annunciation* (1423–24, Saint Fermo, Verona), and *St George and the Princess of Trebizond* (c.1437–38, S Anastasia, Verona). Other surviving works include numerous precise drawings of costumes, birds, and animals. His most famous picture, however, is the *Vision of Saint Eustace*. He is also known as a portrait medallist, the greatest of his day.

Pisano, Andrea, *also called* Andrea da Pontedera
c.1270–1349
Italian sculptor
Born in Pontedera, he became famous as a worker in bronze and marble, and settled in Florence, where he completed the earliest bronze doors of the Baptistery (1336), and in 1337 succeeded Giotto as chief artist in the Cathedral. In 1347 he became chief artist in the cathedral at Orvieto, working on reliefs and statues.

Pisano, Giovanni c.1250–c.1320
Italian sculptor and architect
He was the son of Nicola Pisano, and worked with him on the pulpit in Siena, on the fountain in Perugia, and then between 1284 and 1286 on a group of impressive, life-size statues for the façade of Siena Cathedral. He also sculpted figures for the entrance to the Baptistery at Pisa (now in the Museo Nazionale), and made a number of free-standing Madonnas, the most famous of which is in the Arena Chapel, Padua. His style is intensely dramatic and expressive, more dynamic than that of his father. He was one of the great sculptors of his day in the Italian Gothic tradition, and his innovation pointed the way to Renaissance sculptural ideals. ⬚ Michael Ayrton, *Giovanni Pisano: Sculptor* (1969)

Pisano, Nicola c.1225–c.1284
Italian sculptor, architect and engineer
Raised in Apulia, his first great work was the sculpted marble panels for the pulpit in the Baptistery in Pisa, finished in 1260, whose powerful dramatic composition carved in high relief is in striking contrast to all earlier pulpit decoration. On a second pulpit, for the cathedral at Siena (1268), and on the Fontana Maggiore in Perugia (1278), he collaborated with his son, Giovanni Pisano. Although working in a traditional Gothic style, Nicola studied Classical sculpture like the Roman sarcophagi he found in the Campo Santo at Pisa, and incorporated their forms into his own work. ⬚ G H and E R Crichton, *Nicola Pisano and the Revival of Sculpture in Italy* (1938)

Piscator, Erwin Friedrich Max 1893–1966
German theatre director
Born in Ulm, he joined the German Communist Party in 1918, and opened his own theatre in Berlin in 1926. A major exponent of German political theatre, he developed a style of agitprop which underlies the later epic theatre. Among his more notable productions was *The Adventures of the Good Soldier Schweik*, adapted by Bertolt Brecht from the novel by Jaroslav Hasek (1927). He was in the Soviet Union from 1933 to 1936, and worked in the USA (1938–51), where he became head of the Dramatic Department of the New School for Social Research, and where his adaptation of *War and Peace* was first produced (1942). In 1951 he decided to settle in West Germany, and from 1962 was director of the Freie Volksbuhne in Berlin, where he produced a number of German plays, including

Rolf Hochhuth's *The Representative* (1963) and Peter Ulrich Weiss's *The Investigation* (1965).

Pisistratus, *Greek* Peisistratos c.600–527BC
Tyrant of Athens
He rose to power during the aristocratic factional quarrels that followed the reforms of Solon. His first two bids for power (c.561 and c.556BC) failed, but eventually he established himself (c.546) with support from other Greek states. He curbed aristocratic faction-fighting, enforced a period of internal peace and stability, favoured the peasantry of Attica, and was remembered as a popular ruler. At his death he transmitted his power to his sons Hippias and Hipparchus.

Pissarro, Camille 1830–1903
French Impressionist artist
Born in St Thomas, West Indies, he went in 1855 to Paris, where he was much influenced by Jean Corot's landscapes. In 1870 he lived in England for a short time, this being the first of several visits. Most of his works were painted in the countryside around Paris, and he lived in Pontoise from 1872 to 1884. In the next year he met Paul Signac and Georges Seurat and for the next five years adopted their Divisionist style. Pissarro was the leader of the original Impressionists, and the only one to exhibit at all eight of the Group exhibitions in Paris (1874–86). He had considerable influence on Cézanne and Paul Gauguin at the beginning of their artistic careers. His famous painting of the *Boulevard Montmartre* by night (1897) is in the National Gallery, London.

Pissarro, Lucien 1863–1944
French painter, designer, wood-engraver and printer
Son of Camille Pissarro, he went to England in 1890, where he founded (1894) the Eragny press, designed types, and painted landscapes in the Divisionist style.

Piston, Walter 1894–1976
US composer
Born in Rockland, Maine, he trained as an artist, and first took a serious interest in music as a student at Harvard. He later studied in Paris under Nadia Boulanger and returned to Harvard as Professor of Music (1944–60). Composing in a modern, neoclassical style that includes elements from jazz and popular music, he also published books on harmony, counterpoint and orchestration.

Pitcairn, Robert c.1745–1770
English sailor
He was a midshipman on board the *Swallow* in July 1767, when he was the first to sight the island later called Pitcairn Island, which was to become the refuge of the *Bounty* mutineers, led by Fletcher Christian.

Pitcairne, Archibald 1652–1713
Scottish physician and satirist
Born in Edinburgh, he practised medicine there before being appointed professor at Leyden (1692). Returning to Edinburgh in 1693, he was notorious as a Jacobite, an Episcopalian and satirist of Presbyterianism. He founded the medical faculty at Edinburgh and his medical writings appeared in 1701 under the title *Dissertationes medicae*.

Pitcher, Molly See McCauley, Mary Ludwig Hays

Pitman, Benjamin 1822–1910
English educationist and pioneer of shorthand in the USA
Born in Trowbridge, Wiltshire, he was sent to the USA in 1852 by his brother, Sir Isaac Pitman, to teach his shorthand system there, and established the Phonographic Institute in Cincinnati in 1853. In 1855 he invented an electrochemical process of relief engraving, and he taught at Cincinnati Art School from 1873.

Pitt, William, *known as* Pitt the Younger 1759–1806
English statesman

William Pitt, the Younger was born in Hayes near Bromley, the second son of the Earl of **Chatham**. He suffered poor health as a child and was educated at home, although by the age of 14 his condition had improved sufficiently for him to go to Pembroke Hall, Cambridge, where he graduated at the age of 17. He was called to the Bar in 1780 but clearly saw his career in the political field. He failed to win a seat at Cambridge on his first attempt but was elected for Appleby in 1781.

Pitt joined the opposition to Lord **Frederick North** and soon made his mark as an orator. At the age of 23 he became Chancellor of the Exchequer and leader of the Commons in the ministry of Lord **Shelburne**, replacing **Charles James Fox**, who then became his bitter rival. When Shelburne resigned in 1783 the king offered Pitt the premiership but he declined, leaving it to **William Bentinck**, 3rd Duke of Portland. However, when Portland's government collapsed in December of the same year, Pitt decided to accept the challenge and, at the age of 24, became Britain's youngest prime minister.

Pitt had clear ideas of what he wished to achieve. He wanted good relations with America, union with Ireland, a reduction in the national debt, reform of parliament, and reorganization of the East India Company. He did not achieve all his aims but, despite his inexperience and fierce opposition from Fox, made considerable progress. He took steps to reduce the national debt, passed the India Act of 1784 to establish dual control of the East India Company, effected a division between the French and

English through the Canada Act of 1791, and achieved union with Ireland in 1800.

In 1801 the king refused to approve his Bill to emancipate the Catholics and Pitt resigned in protest, but within three years he was persuaded to return in the face of a threatened invasion by **Napoleon I**. He formed a coalition with Russia, Austria and Sweden, and the French were defeated at Trafalgar (1805). Pitt was hailed as the saviour of Europe, and his words of reply became immortal: 'England has saved herself by her exertions, and will, I trust, save Europe by her example'. He was dismayed when the coalition he had formed broke up and Napoleon triumphed against the Russians and Austrians at Austerlitz in 1805. He died nearly 10 years before Napoleon's final defeat at Waterloo.

Although Pitt was a popular national figure his private life was comparatively sad and lonely. He had no close friends and did not marry. He died so heavily in debt that the House of Commons raised £40,000 to pay off his creditors.

📖 Robin Reilly, *William Pitt the Younger* (1979); Derek Jarrett, *Pitt the Younger* (1978); J Holland Rose, *William Pitt and National Revival* (1911).

'He was not merely a chip off the old block, but the old block itself.' **Edmund Burke** commenting on Pitt's maiden speech in the House of Commons (26 February 1781).

Pitman, Sir Isaac 1813–97
English educationist and inventor of a shorthand system

He was born in Trowbridge, Wiltshire, the brother of **Benjamin Pitman**. First a clerk, he became a schoolmaster at Barton-on-Humber (1832–36) and at Wotton-under-Edge, where he issued his *Stenographic Sound Hand* (1837). Dismissed from Wotton because he had joined the New (Swedenborgian) Church, he established a Phonetic Institute for teaching shorthand in Bath (1839–43). In 1842 he brought out the *Phonetic Journal*, and in 1845 opened premises in London. 📖 Alfred Baker, *The Life of Sir Isaac Pitman (Inventor of Phonography)* (1913)

Pitman, Jenny (Jennifer Susan), *née* Harvey 1946–
English National Hunt racehorse trainer

Born in Hoby, Leicestershire, she married Richard Pitman in 1965 (separated 1978) and set up her first training stables with him. Since then her horses have won the Midland National, the Massey Fergusson Gold Cup, the Welsh National, the Cheltenham Gold Cup, the Hennessey Gold Cup and the Whitbread Trophy. Corbiere won the Grand National in 1983, while Esha Ness won the abandoned Grand National in 1993 (the race was void because of problems at the start), and Royal Athlete won it in 1995. Burrough Hill Lad won the King George VI Cup, the Hennessey Gold Cup and the Cheltenham Gold Cup in 1984. She has been declared the Piper Heidsieck Trainer of the Year several times (1983–84, 1989–90) and the Golden Spurs Best National Hunt Trainer (1984). She published her autobiography *Glorious Uncertainty* in 1984.

Pitot, Henri 1695–1771
French hydraulic and civil engineer

Born in Aramon, in the Languedoc, he had little formal education but made the acquaintance of the great physicist **René Réaumur**, whose laboratory assistant he became in 1723. He developed a particular interest in hydraulic engineering, was appointed superintendent of the Canal

du Midi and constructed an aqueduct for the water supply of Montpellier. In 1730 he invented the device now known as the 'Pitot tube', by means of which the relative velocity of a fluid past the orifice of the tube may be measured.

Pitt, William or Pitt the Elder See **Chatham, 1st Earl of** (panel)

Pitt, William or Pitt the Younger See panel above

Pittacus of Mitylene c.650–c.570BC
Greek ruler

He was one of the Seven Wise Men of Greece. His experience, according to the ancients, was embodied in 'Know thine opportunity' and other aphorisms.

Pitter, Ruth 1897–1992
English poet

Born in Ilford, Essex, she wrote verse from a very early age and later was encouraged by **Hilaire Belloc**. Her inspiration came mainly from the beauty of natural things and from her Christian faith. In 1936 she won the Hawthornden prize with *A Trophy of Arms*, and in 1955 she was awarded the Queen's Gold Medal for poetry. Other volumes include *First and Second Poems* (1927), *A Mad Lady's Garland* (1934), *Urania* (1951), *The Ermine* (1953), *Still by Choice* (1966) and *End of Drought* (1975). A *Collected Poems* appeared in 1990. 📖 A Russell, *Homage to a Poet* (1969)

Pitt-Rivers, Augustus Henry Lane-Fox 1827–1900
English soldier and archaeologist

He was born in Yorkshire. Educated at Sandhurst, he worked to improve army small arms training and was a promoter of the Hythe school of musketry, ultimately becoming a lieutenant-general (1882). Having in 1880 inherited from his great-uncle, Lord Rivers, Wiltshire estates rich in Romano-British and Saxon remains, he devoted himself to archaeology, evolving a new scientific approach to excavation which became a model for later workers. His collections were presented to Oxford Museum. In 1882 he became the first inspector of ancient monuments.

Pius II, *originally* Eneo Silvio de Piccolomini or Aeneas Silvius 1405–64
Italian pope

Born in Corsignano, Republic of Siena, he was employed on diplomatic missions (1432–35) before taking orders and becoming Bishop of Trieste (1447) and a cardinal (1456). As pope (1458–64), he attempted to organize an armed confederation of Christian princes to resist the Turks, following their victory at Constantinople (Istanbul) in 1453. One of the most eminent humanist scholars of his age, his works are chiefly historical.

Pius IV, *originally* Giovanni Angelo de' Medici
1499–1565
Italian pope

Born in Milan, he became Archbishop of Ragusa in 1547 and a cardinal in 1549, before being elected pope in 1559. He brought to a close the deliberations of the Council of Trent, and issued (1564) the Creed of Pius IV, or Tridentine Creed. He reformed the sacred college of cardinals, and established the Index of Forbidden Books. A notable patron of the arts, he built many public buildings and was patron to Michelangelo.

Pius V, St, *originally* Michele Ghislieri 1504–72
Italian pope

Born in Cesena, he became a bishop in 1556, and a cardinal in 1557. As pope from 1566, he implemented the decrees of the Council of Trent (1545–63), excommunicated Queen Elizabeth I (1570), and inspired the Holy League (1571) against the Turks. The league's campaign culminated in the victory of the Christian fleet under Don John of Austria at the Battle of Lepanto in the Gulf of Corinth (1571). He was canonized in 1712, and his feast day is 30 April. ⌑ F A P de Falloux, *Histoire de St Pie V* (2 vols, 1844)

Pius VI, *originally* Giovanni Angelo Braschi 1717–99
Italian pope

Born in Cesena, Papal States, he became cardinal in 1773 and pope in 1775. To him Rome owes the drainage of the Pontine Marsh, the improvement of the port of Ancona, the completion of St Peter's, the foundation of the New Museum of the Vatican, and the embellishment of the city. In the American Revolution he released the American Catholic clergy from the jurisdiction of the vicar apostolic in England. In the 1780s he went to Vienna, but failed to restrain the reforming Emperor Joseph II from further curtailing papal privileges. Soon after came the French Revolution and the confiscation of Church property in France. The pope launched his thunders in vain, and then the murder of the French agent in Rome (1793) gave the Directory an excuse for the attack. Napoleon I took possession of the Legations, and afterwards the March of Ancona, and extorted (1797) the surrender of these provinces from Pius. The murder of a member of the French embassy in December was avenged by Alexandre Berthier's taking possession of Rome in 1798. Pius was called on to renounce his temporal sovereignty, and on his refusal was seized, carried to Siena, the Certosa, Grenoble and finally Valence, where he died.

Pius VII, *originally* Barnaba Gregorio Chiaramonti
1742–1823
Italian pope

Born in Cesena, Papal States, he became Bishop of Tivoli, and, already a cardinal, succeeded Pius VI in 1800. Rome was now restored to the papal authority and the next year French troops were withdrawn from most of the papal territory. Pius restored order in his states, and in 1801 concluded a concordat with Napoleon I, which the latter altered by autocratic *Articles organiques*. In 1804 Napoleon compelled Pius to come to Paris to consecrate him as emperor. He failed to get any modification of the articles, and soon after his return to Rome the French seized Ancona and entered Rome. This was followed by the annexation (May 1809) of the Papal States to the French Empire. In June the pope excommunicated the robbers of the Holy See, then he was removed to Grenoble, and finally to Fontainebleau, where he was forced to sign a new concordat and sanction the annexation. The fall of Napoleon (1814) allowed him to return to Rome, and the Congress of Vienna restored to him his territory. Brigandage was suppressed, as well as secret societies, while the Jesuits were restored. ⌑ Erasmo Pistolesi, *Vita del sommo pontefice Pio VII* (1824)

Pius IX, *originally* Giovanni Maria Mastai Ferretti, *also called* Pio Nono 1792–1878
Italian pope

Born in Sinigaglia, Papal States, he took deacon's orders (1818), and was made Archbishop of Spoleto (1827), and Bishop of Imola (1832). In 1840 he became a cardinal, and was elected pope on the death of Gregory XVI in 1846. He entered at once on a course of reforms. He granted an amnesty to all political prisoners and exiles, removed most of the disabilities of the Jews, authorized railways, and projected a council of state, and in 1848 published his *Statuto Fondamentale*, a scheme for the temporal government of the Papal States by two chambers, one nominated by the pope, the other (with the power of taxation) elected by the people. At first the new pope was the idol of the populace. But the revolutionary fever of 1848 spread too fast for a reforming pope, and his refusal to make war upon the Austrians finally forfeited the affections of the Romans. In 1848 his first minister, Count Pelegrino Rossi, was murdered, and two days later a mob assembled in the square of the Quirinal. The pope escaped to Gaeta, and a republic was proclaimed in Rome. In 1849 a French expedition was sent to Civita Vecchia; in July General Oudinot took Rome after a siege of 30 days; and henceforward the papal government was re-established. Pius IX proved an unyielding conservative and Ultramontane, closely allied with the Jesuits. The war of the French and Sardinians against Austria in 1859 and the popular vote of 1860 incorporated a great part of papal territory with the Sardinian (Italian) kingdom, but Pius always refused to recognize the fact. He re-established the hierarchy in England, sanctioned a Catholic University in Ireland, and condemned the Queen's Colleges. He concluded a reactionary concordat with Austria. By the bull *Ineffabilis Deus* in 1854 he decreed the Immaculate Conception; his famous encyclical *Quanta Cura* and the *Syllabus of Errors*, appeared in 1864. The Vatican Council (1869–79) proclaimed the infallibility of the pope. For the last 10 years the pope's temporal power had only been maintained by the French garrison, and on its withdrawal in 1870 the soldiers of Victor Emmanuel II entered Rome. For the rest of his days the pope lived a voluntary 'prisoner' within the Vatican. ⌑ Frank J Coppa, *Pope Pius IX* (1979)

Pius X, *originally* Giuseppe Sarto 1835–1914
Italian pope

Born in Riese, near Venice, and ordained in 1858, he became Bishop of Mantua (1884) and cardinal and patriarch of Venice (1893) before being elected pope in 1903. He condemned theological modernism in his encyclical *Pascendi* in 1907, and revolutionary movements, but was a champion of social reforms (especially in the Catholic Action movement). He reformed the liturgy, re-codified canon law, and was canonized in 1954.

Pius XI, *originally* Ambrogio Damiano Achille Ratti
1857–1939
Italian pope

Born in Desio, near Milan, and ordained in 1879, he was a great linguist and scholar, and librarian of the Ambrosian (Milan) and Vatican libraries. He became Cardinal Archbishop of Milan in 1921. As pope from 1922, he signed the Lateran Treaty with Mussolini (1929), which brought into existence the Vatican state, and made concordats with many countries. He also broke new ground by appointing six Chinese bishops, and clarified the basis for Catholic school education.

Pius XII, *originally* Eugenio Pacelli 1876–1958
Italian pope

Born in Rome, he distinguished himself in the papal diplomatic service and as Secretary of State to the Holy See before succeeding Pius XI in 1939. Under his leadership, the Vatican did much humanitarian work during World War II, notably for prisoners of war and refugees. There has been continuing controversy, however, over his attitude to the treatment of the Jews in Nazi Germany, critics arguing that he could have used his influence with Catholic Germany to prevent the massacres, others that any attempt to do so would have proved futile and might possibly have worsened the situation. In the postwar years the plight of the persecuted churchmen in the communist countries, and the fate of Catholicism there, became his personal concern. He was widely respected as a distinguished scholar and as a man of immense moral authority. 📖 J O Smit, *Pope Pius XII* (Eng trans, 1951)

Pixérécourt, René Charles Guilbert de
1773–1844
French dramatist

He was born in Nancy. Known as 'the father of melodrama', he wrote 111 plays. He had initial difficulties, but following the successful comedy *Les Petits Auvergnats* (1797, 'The Little Citizens of the Auvergne'), did not look back. He wrote all sorts of plays, but his Gothic melodramas, such as his dramatization of the *Mysteries of Udolpho* of Mrs Radcliffe (1797), did more than the plays of any other single writer to provide the standard fare of the 19th-century playgoer. A master-craftsman, he ably defended his own procedures. He was, wrote a modern French critic, 'superior to his work'. 📖 M W Disher, *Blood and Thunder* (1949)

Pizarro, Francisco c.1478–1541
Spanish soldier and conqueror of Peru

Born in Trujillo, he served under Gonsalvo di Cordova in Italy, and under Vasco Núñez de Balboa when he discovered the Pacific. In 1526 Pizarro and Diego de Almagro sailed for Peru where they collected information about the Incas. He returned to Spain for authority to undertake the conquest, which he received in 1529. He sailed again from Panama in 1531, Almagro following with reinforcements. The Spaniards began the march inland in May 1532, and in November entered Cajamarca. Pizarro captured the Inca Atahualpa by treachery, and after extorting an enormous ransom, (£3,500,000) put him to death (1533). He then marched to Cuzco, and was founding Lima and other cities on the coast when a Native American insurrection broke out. Both Cuzco and Lima were besieged, and his half-brother Juan Pizarro (1505–36), Governor of Cuzco, was killed, but in spring 1537 Almagro returned from Chile, raised the Siege of Cuzco, and took possession of the city. Pizarro had no intention of allowing his rival to retain Cuzco. Too old to fight himself, he entrusted the command of his forces to his brothers, who defeated Almagro soon afterwards. One of Almagro's followers formed a conspiracy to assassinate Pizarro. The conspirators attacked his house in Lima and murdered him. His brother, Hernando Pizarro, was imprisoned for having beheaded Almagro at Cuzco. 📖 Manuel Ballesteros Gaibrois, *Francisco Pizarro* (1940)

Pizarro, Gonzalo c.1506–1548
Spanish soldier

He accompanied his half-brother Francisco Pizarro in the conquest of Peru, and in 1539 undertook an expedition to the east of Quito, enduring severe hardships. One of his lieutenants, Francisco de Orellana, deserted his starving comrades, discovered the whole course of the River Amazon, and returned to Spain; only 90 out of 350 Spaniards returned with Gonzalo in June 1542. On his half-brother's assassination (1541) Gonzalo retired to Charcas. In 1544 the new viceroy arrived in Peru to enforce the 'New Laws'. The Spaniards, dismayed, entreated Gonzalo to protect their interests. He mustered 400 men, entered Lima in October 1544, and was declared Governor of Peru; the viceroy was defeated and killed (1546). When news of this revolt reached Spain, Pedro de la Gasca, an able ecclesiastic, was sent to Peru as President to restore order. Gonzalo Pizarro defeated a force sent against him, and met Gasca near Cuzco in April 1548. But his forces deserted him, and he gave himself up and was beheaded.

Pizzetti, Ildebrando 1880–1968
Italian composer

Born in Parma, he studied at the Parma Conservatory, and in 1908 became Professor of Harmony and Counterpoint at the Instituto Musicale, Florence. Director there from 1917 to 1924, when he became director of the Giuseppe Verdi Conservatory, Milan, he earned a considerable reputation as an opera composer with *Fedra* (1912) and *Debora e Jaele* (1923). In 1936 he succeeded Ottorino Respighi as Professor of Composition at the Accademia di Sancta Cecilia, Rome. He composed extensively in all forms.

Plaatje, Sol T 1876–1932
South African journalist, politician and literary figure

One of the founders of black nationalism, he first worked as a Post Office messenger and later a magistrates' court interpreter in Kimberley. He was in the town throughout the siege (1899–1900) during the Boer War and kept a lively diary of its events. After the war he founded and edited newspapers, wrote books (including *Native Life in South Africa*), translated Shakespeare into Tswana, his native tongue, and was one of the founders of the South African Native National Congress (1912), later the ANC (African National Congress).

Place, Francis 1771–1854
English radical and reformer

Born in London, a self-educated tailor, he was a champion of radicalism and the right to form trade unions, and contrived the repeal of the anti-union Combination Acts in 1824. He was a leading figure in the agitation which brought about the passing of the Reform Bill in 1832. Drafter of the People's Charter, and a pioneer of birth-control study, he wrote *The Principle of Population* (1822).

Planché, James Robinson 1795–1880
English playwright, antiquary and herald

Born in London, of Huguenot ancestry, he was a prolific writer of burlesque and extravaganzas, such as *Amoroso, King of Little Britain* (1818), *Success; or, a Hit if you like it* (1825) and *High, Low, Jack and the Game* (1833). His best-known work is *The Vampire; or the Bride of the Isles* (1820). He wrote the libretto for Carl Weber's *Oberon*, and other operas. As a heraldic scholar he wrote *History of British Costumes* (1834) and other works. He was appointed Somerset Herald in 1866. 📖 H Granville-Barker, *Exit Planché—enter Gilbert* (1932)

Planck, Max Karl Ernst 1858–1947
German theoretical physicist and Nobel Prize winner

Born in Kiel, Schleswig-Holstein, he studied at Munich University and under **Gustav Kirchhoff** and **Hermann von Helmholtz** at Berlin University, where he succeeded the former in the professorship (1889–1926). His work on the law of thermodynamics and black body radiation led him to abandon classical dynamical principles and formulate the quantum theory (1900), which relied on **Ludwig Boltzmann's** statistical interpretation of the second law of thermodynamics, and assumed energy changes to take place in small discrete instalments or quanta. This successfully accounted for and predicted certain phenomena inexplicable in the classical Newtonian theory. **Albert Einstein's** application of the quantum theory to light (1905) led to the theories of relativity, and in 1913 **Niels Bohr** successfully applied it to the problems of sub-atomic physics. Planck was awarded the Nobel Prize for physics (1918). In 1930 he was elected president of the Kaiser Wilhelm Institute, but resigned in 1937 in protest against the Nazi regime. He was eventually reappointed as president of the renamed Max Planck Institute. ⊞ J L Heilbron, *The Dilemmas of an Upright Man: Max Planck as Spokesman for German Science* (1986)

Planquette, Robert 1850–1903
French composer

Born in Paris, he was educated at the Paris Conservatoire. He composed *Paul Jones* (1889) and other successful light operas.

Plantagenet
Angevin family name

In 1154 they succeeded to the throne of England through **Henry II**. *Plante-geneste* ('Broom') was the nickname of Geoffrey, Count of Anjou, husband of **Matilda**, daughter of **Henry I**. The first to use *Plantaginet* (sic) as his family name was Richard, Duke of York (1460), in laying claim to the crown. But the sovereigns called Plantagenet kings are **Henry II**; **Richard I**; **John**; **Henry III**; **Edward I**, **Edward II** and **Edward III**; **Richard II**; **Henry IV**, **Henry V** and **Henry VI**; **Edward IV** and **Edward V**; and **Richard III**. The legitimate male line ended (1499) with the execution of Edward, Earl of Warwick, grandson of Richard, Duke of York.

Planté, Gaston 1834–89
French physicist

Born in Orthy, he worked in Paris, as a lecture assistant in physics at the Conservatoire des Arts et Métiers (from 1854) and then from 1860 as Professor of Physics at the Association Polytechnique pour le Développement de l'Instruction Populaire. He followed up **Johann Ritter's** discovery of the secondary cell and constructed the first practical lead–acid storage battery or accumulator (1859).

Plante, Lynda La See **La Plante, Lynda**

Platière, Jeanne Manon Roland de la See **Roland de la Platière, Jeanne Manon**

Plantin, Christophe 1514–89
French printer

Born in St Avertin near Tours, he settled as a bookbinder in Antwerp in 1549 and six years later began to print. His *Biblia Polyglotta* (1569–73, 'Polyglot Bible'), his Latin, Hebrew and Dutch Bibles, and his editions of the classics are all famous. His printing-houses in Antwerp, Leyden and Paris were carried on by his sons-in-law. His office in Antwerp, bought by the city in 1876, is now the 'Musée Plantin'.

Plantinga, Alvin 1932–
US philosopher of religion

Born in Ann Arbor, Michigan, he became a professor at Calvin College, Grand Rapids (1963–82) and at the University of Notre Dame, Indiana (1982–). He is concerned with philosophical questions about God, as in *Does God have a Nature?* (1980). In other books, such as *God and Other Minds* (1967), he argues that God's existence is no less probable than our own: it can be supported by the ontological argument (*The Nature of Necessity*, 1974), and belief in His goodness is tenable despite the fact of evil (*God, Freedom and Evil*, 1974).

Plaskett, John Stanley 1865–1941
Canadian astronomer

Born in Woodstock, Ontario, and educated at the University of Toronto, he graduated in mathematics, obtained a PhD (1899) and became assistant in the physics department. He joined the staff of the Dominion Observatory in Ottawa in 1903 in advance of its formal opening (1905) and was responsible for designing and making use of spectroscopes to measure the radial velocities of stars. In 1917 he moved to Victoria, British Columbia, to become head of the new Dominion Astrophysical Observatory which was equipped with a reflector designed by him for stellar spectroscopy. He remained director of this observatory until his retirement in 1935. Among his many discoveries (1922) was a pair of the most massive stars then known, named after him. Plaskett is regarded as the founder of modern astronomy in Canada. His son and collaborator, Harry Hemley Plaskett (1893–1980), himself an outstanding solar spectroscopist, became Savilian Professor of Astronomy at Oxford.

Plateau, Joseph Antoine Ferdinand 1801–83
Belgian physicist

Born in Brussels, he was Professor of Physics at Ghent University from 1835. In his study of optics he damaged his own eyesight by looking into the Sun for 20 seconds in order to find out the effect on the eye. By 1840 he was blind, but he continued his scientific work with the help of others. During the course of his studies on fluids he produced soap films in two- or three-dimensional wire frames, discovered rules governing the geometry of such films, and realized that these are surfaces of minimum area, which stimulated substantial mathematical studies of minimum-area surfaces. He discovered the tiny second drop, named after him, which always follows the main drop of a liquid falling from a surface.

Plater, Alan Frederick 1935–
English dramatist

Born in Jarrow, Tyne and Wear, he trained as an architect, and his writing was first published in *Punch* (1958). Since 1960 he has built up an enormous body of work, reflecting his working-class background, his political beliefs and his interest in jazz. He was a regular writer for the BBC series *Z Cars* (1963–65), and his many television plays include *Ted's Cathedral* (1964), *Close the Coalhouse Door* (1968) and *The Land of Green Ginger* (1974). He is also responsible for the literate and skilled screen translations *The Good Companions* (1980), *Fortunes of War* (1987) and *A Very British Coup* (1988). Equally prolific in other media, he has contributed to *The Guardian*, and written film scripts, such as *The Virgin and the Gypsy* (1969) and *Priest of Love* (1980), and the novels *Misterioso* (1987) and *The Beiderbecke Affair* (1985, from his television series of the same title). He was made Fellow of the Royal Society of Literature (1985) and the Royal Society of Arts (1991), and received a BAFTA Writer's Award in 1989. ⊞ J R Taylor, *The Second Wave* (1971)

Plath, Sylvia 1932–63
US poet

Born in Boston, she was educated at Bradford High School and Smith College, where she suffered from depression and attempted suicide. She won a Fulbright

Plato c.428–c.348BC
Greek philosopher

Plato was born probably in Athens, of a distinguished aristocratic family that claimed descent from the early king Codrus, but little is known of his early life. His works show the profound influence of **Socrates**, who converted Plato to philosophy after early attempts at poetry. Plato gives an account of Socrates' last days in 399BC in three of his dialogues: the *Apology* (not strictly a dialogue, but an account of the trial), the *Crito* (a discussion set in Socrates' prison cell) and the *Phaedo* (describing Socrates' final hours and death). After Socrates' death, he and other disciples took temporary refuge at Megara with the philosopher **Euclides**, and he then travelled widely in Greece, Egypt, southern Italy, where he encountered the Pythagoreans, and Sicily, where he became the friend and teacher of **Dion**, brother-in-law of **Dionysius I** of Syracuse.

Plato returned to Athens (c.387) where he founded the Academy, which was named after the grove of the hero Academus where the school was situated. It became a famous centre for philosophical, mathematical and scientific research, and Plato himself presided over it for the rest of his life. Plato refers in his Epistles to an interest in entering politics; he says that he attempted this on two occasions, in 404 after the defeat of Athens in the Peloponnesian War, and again after the restoration of democracy in 403. He was soon disillusioned with politicians, and formed the conclusion, expounded in the *Republic* and other writings, that the only hope for the Greek cities was to trust in philosopher-kings, who have a knowledge of goodness and are able to lead others to goodness.

He visited Sicily again on the death of Dionysius I in 367, at Dion's request, to teach Dion's nephew **Dionysius II** to become a philosopher-king, but Dionysius mistrusted Dion and had him banished. Plato returned to Athens and, despite a second visit in 361–60, this attempt to put principles into practice was a failure, as Plato himself went to great lengths to explain in his *Epistles*.

Among Plato's pupils were **Aristotle**, who eventually founded the Peripatetic School at the Lyceum in Athens, **Speusippus**, Plato's successor as head of the Academy, and **Theophrastus**.

📖 The corpus of writings attributed to Plato consists of about 30 philosophical dialogues and 13 *Epistles* (Letters), of which the Seventh and Eighth are probably genuine. The Seventh is the most important biographically and philosophically.

The dialogues are conventionally divided into three groups (early, middle and late), although the exact chronology is in some cases uncertain.

The early Socratic dialogues are centred on Socrates, who is usually portrayed as interrogator in a series of questions and answers aimed at examining the validity of assumed ideas about important matters, especially about moral virtues (piety in the *Euthyphro*, courage in the *Laches*, and temperance in *Charmides*), and seeking conclusions about them, even though this may mean that we cannot know the truth.

In the later dialogues, Socrates expresses more positive and systematic views; it is an important question to what extent they are Socrates' views and to what extent Plato's. This group includes the most dramatic and literary of the dialogues—the *Symposium*, *Gorgias*, *Phaedo* and *Republic*—and presents the central Platonic doctrines: the theory of knowledge as recollection, the dualism of the immortal soul and the mortal body, and above all the Theory of Forms (or Ideas) which contrasts the transient, material things of this world with the Ideas that they reflect, which are the true objects of knowledge.

The *Republic*, which opens with the question 'What is justice?', begins like a dialogue but ends up as an exposition by Socrates. It describes a political utopia, ruled by philosopher-kings who have mastered the discipline of dialectic and, unlike the majority, have knowledge of Justice and the Good. The state is formed on a rigid class structure of workers, soldiers and rulers, on the education of the rulers (both men and women), and on communism of property and family. These last precepts have been the subject of much subsequent discussion (and sometimes misrepresentation), and have had a profound effect on later European political thought.

The final group of dialogues is generally less literary in form and represents a critical reappraisal of the metaphysical and logical assumptions of Plato's earlier doctrines. The *Parmenides*, *Theaetetus* and *Sophist* in particular have attracted the interest of contemporary analytical philosophers and contain some of Plato's most original and demanding work. The *Laws*, which represent a revision of Plato's political thinking in the light of experience (eg in Sicily), were published after his death. See also C Rowe, *Plato* (1986), R M Hare, *Plato* (1982) and J Annas, *An Introduction to Plato's Republic* (1981).

> 'Our argument is about no ordinary matter, but about the way we ought to live our lives.' From *Republic*, bk 1, 352d.

Fellowship to Newnham College, Cambridge (1956), where she studied English and married **Ted Hughes**. After teaching in the USA they settled in England (1959), first in London, then Devon, but separated in 1962, a year before Sylvia committed suicide. Writing poetry from early childhood, she published her first volume, *A Winter Ship* (1960), anonymously, but put her name to the second, *The Colossus* (1960). After the birth of her second child she wrote a radio play, *Three Women* (1962), set in a maternity home. Often termed a 'confessional' poet, she was influenced by poets such as **Robert Lowell**. Her late poetry was published posthumously in *Ariel* (1965), *Crossing the Water* (1971) and *Winter Trees* (1972). Her only novel, *The Bell Jar* (1963), was published just before her death, under the pseudonym Victoria Lucas. *Collected Poems*, edited by Hughes, was published in 1982. 📖 A Stevenson, *Bitter Fame* (1989)

Plato See panel above

Plautus, Titus Maccius or Maccus
c.250–184BC
Roman comic dramatist

He was born in Sarsina, Umbria, and it is probable that he went to Rome while still young, and there learned his mastery of the most idiomatic Latin. He found work in connection with the stage, and then started a business in foreign trade. It failed, however, and he returned to Rome in such poverty that he had to work for a baker, turning a handmill. He probably began to write about 224BC. He borrowed his plots to a large extent from the New Attic Comedy, which dealt with social life to the exclusion of politics, and his plays show close familiarity with seafaring life and adventure, and an intimate knowledge of all the details of buying and selling and book-keeping. About 130 plays were attributed to him in the time of **Aulus Gellius**, who believed most of them to be the work of earlier dramatists revised and improved by Plautus. **Marcus Terentius Varro** limited the genuine comedies to 21, and these so-called 'Varronian comedies' are those which are now extant, the *Vidularia* ('The Rucksack Play') being fragmentary. 📖 K McLeish, *Roman Comedy* (1976)

Play, Pierre Guillaume Frédéric Le See Le Play, Pierre Guillaume Frédéric

Player, Gary 1936–
South African golfer

He was born in Johannesburg. Small and slightly built, he nonetheless won three British Opens (1959, 1968, 1974), the US Masters thrice (1961, 1974, 1978), the US Open once (1965), and the US Professional Golfers' Association title twice (1962, 1972). He also won the South African Open 13 times, and the Australian Open seven times. His fitness and skill have remained undiminished. He won both the British and the American Seniors' Championship in 1988. He published *To Be the Best* in 1991. 📖 *Gary Player, World Golfer* (1975)

Playfair, John 1748–1819
Scottish mathematician, physicist and geologist

Born in Benvie, near Dundee, he studied at St Andrews University and in 1785 became joint Professor of Mathematics at Edinburgh, where he produced a successful edition of Euclid's *Elements*, but in 1805 he exchanged his appointment for the chair of natural philosophy. He was a strenuous supporter of James Hutton's uniformitarian theory in geology and travelled widely to make geological observations. His *Illustrations of the Huttonian Theory* (1802) was a landmark in British geological writing. He published his contributions to mathematics in *Elements of Geometry* (1795).

Playfair, Lyon Playfair, 1st Baron 1819–98
Scottish scientist and politician

Born in Chunar, India, he studied medicine at Glasgow and Edinburgh, and under Justus von Liebig at Giessen. He was appointed Professor of Chemistry at the School of Mines in London, and ended his academic career as Professor of Chemistry at Edinburgh. In 1868 he was elected to Parliament, and from 1880 to 1883 he served as deputy speaker in the House of Commons. He was a prominent member of many government committees, for example on public health, the Irish potato famine, and the reform of the Civil Service. He was a member of the committee which organized the Great Exhibition of 1851, and later helped to establish the Royal College of Science and the South Kensington Museum (the latter was renamed the Victoria and Albert Museum and gave up its science collection to create the Science Museum in 1909). One of the first scientists to hold important public positions, he worked throughout his life to promote scientific and technical education, and to encourage industry to make use of scientific advances.

Playfair, Sir Nigel Ross 1874–1934
English actor-manager and producer

He was born in London and after a career as a barrister, he went on the stage. From 1902 to 1918 he was a successful character actor. As manager of the Lyric Theatre, Hammersmith, from 1919, he was responsible for a long series of successful productions, many of which were drawn from 18th-century comedy. One of the most outstanding of these was *The Beggar's Opera*, and others included *The Duenna* and *The Rivals*. He wrote *The Story of the Lyric Theatre, Hammersmith* (1925) and *Hammersmith Hoy* (1930).

Playfair, William Henry 1789–1857
Scottish architect

Born in London, he was brought up in Edinburgh. He designed many of Edinburgh's most prominent buildings, including the National Gallery of Scotland, the Royal Scottish Academy, the National Monument on Calton Hill, Surgeon's Hall and Donaldson's Hospital. He was the nephew of John Playfair.

Playford, Sir Thomas 1896–1981
Australian statesman

Born in Norton Summit, South Australia, he served with the Australian Imperial Forces during World War I at Gallipoli and in France. In 1933 he was elected to the South Australian House of Assembly, entering the ministry in March 1938 and becoming premier of South Australia in November the same year, a position which he was to hold until March 1965. His grandfather, Thomas Playford (1837–1915), was premier of South Australia from 1887 to 1892, and was a senator in the first federal government from 1901 to 1906.

Pleasant, Mary Ellen, *known as* Mammy Pleasant 1814–1904
US entrepreneur

Born into slavery in the American South, she went to California in 1850 with a legacy of several thousand dollars from her deceased husband. She invested this in a boarding house, and attracted influential financiers and politicians into her sphere. Investing in further property, she lent money at exorbitant interest, and became a financial adviser. Her most significant exploit was her successful suing in 1864 of San Francisco streetcar companies for refusing her right to board, on grounds of colour. However, the only explanation San Francisco society could offer for her success as a black woman was that she used black magic. This reputation plagued her and she was implicated in numerous rumours of poisonings and other deaths.

Pleasence, Donald 1919–95
English stage and film actor

Born in Worksop, Nottinghamshire, he made his first appearance in Jersey in 1939, served in the RAF during World War II and returned to the stage in 1946. He worked at various repertory theatres, including Birmingham and the Bristol Old Vic, but scored a huge success as the malevolent tramp Davies in Harold Pinter's *The Caretaker* (1960). After the 1960s, his London stage appearances were rare, but he made many television appearances and was in constant demand for film work, usually as a villain, as in *Dr Crippen* (1962), *Cul-de-Sac* (1966), *You Only Live Twice* (1967), in which he played James Bond's arch-enemy Blofeld, and in the horror film series *Halloween* which started in 1978.

Plekhanov, Georgi Valentinovich 1856–1918
Russian revolutionary and Marxist philosopher

Born in Gundalovka, he joined the Narodnist Populist movement as a student at military school and led the first popular demonstration in St Petersburg (1876). In 1880 he left Russia and in 1883 founded the first Russian Marxist group, the Liberation of Labour Group (which became the Russian Social Democratic Workers' Party in 1898) in Geneva, where he spent the years 1883–1917 in exile. From 1889 to 1904 he was Russian delegate to the Second International. He was a major intellectual influence on Lenin, with whom he edited the journal *Iskra* (1900, 'The Spark'). He argued that Russia would have to go through industrialization and capitalism before arriving at socialism, and in 1903 he supported the Mensheviks against Lenin's Bolsheviks. He returned to Russia in 1917, where he edited a paper. He denounced the October Revolution and after 1917 he moved to Finland. His commentaries on Marxist theory fill 26 volumes, and he is known as the father of Russian Marxism. 📖 Samuel H Baron, *Plekhanov: The Father of Russian Marxism* (1963)

Plessner, Helmuth 1892–1985
German philosopher and social theorist

Born in Wiesbaden, he studied zoology, medicine and philosophy at the universities of Freiburg, Heidelberg and Berlin. He was professor at Cologne (1926–34), then moved to Groningen in Holland to escape the Nazis and became Professor of Sociology there (1934–42). Expelled during the Nazi occupation, he later became Professor of Philosophy there (1946–51), before returning to Germany in 1951. He helped found, with **Max Scheler**, the new discipline of 'philosophical anthropology': humans are distinguished from animals by the 'eccentric position' by which they can distance themselves from their own bodies through self-consciousness and can thus have access to experiences, expressions, language and institutions of a very different order of significance. This philosophy is explained in works like *Die Einheit der Sinne* (1923, 'The Unity of the Senses'), *Die Stufen des Organischen und der Mensch* (1928, 'Man and the Stages of the Organic') and *Lachen und Weinen* (1941, 'Laughter and Weeping'). He also wrote on social philosophy and the origins of Fascism in *Das Schicksal deutschen Geistes im Ausgang seiner bürgerlichen Epoche* (1935, 'The Destiny of the German Spirit at the End of the Bourgeois Epoch') and *Grenzen der Gemeinschaft: Eine Kritik des sozialen Radikalismus* (1972, 'Limits of Society: a Critique of Social Radicalism').

Plethon, Georgios Gemistos c.1355–1450
Greek scholar
Probably a native of Constantinople (Istanbul), he was counsellor in the Peloponnesus to **Manuel II, Palaeologus**, and was sent to the Council of Florence in 1439. Here he did much to spread a taste for **Plato**, and founded the Platonic Academy of Florence.

Pleydell-Bouverie, Katherine 1895–1985
English potter
She studied at the Central School of Arts and Crafts, London, and with **Bernard Leach** at St Ives, Cornwall, in 1924. She established a pottery in Wiltshire, producing domestic wares in stoneware, experimenting with wood and vegetable ash glazes. In 1946 she established an oil-fired kiln in Kilmington Manor near Warminster where her output consisted of a series of unique small works often decorated with vertical ribbing.

Pleyel, Ignaz Joseph 1757–1831
Austrian composer
Born near Vienna, he became kapellmeister of Strasbourg Cathedral in 1783. In 1791 he visited London, in 1795 opened a music shop in Paris and in 1807 added a pianoforte manufactory. His compositions included quartets, concertos and sonatas.

Plimsoll, Samuel, *known as* the sailors' friend
1824–98
English social reformer
He was born in Bristol. In 1854 he started business in the coal trade in London and soon began to interest himself in the dangers affecting the merchant navy. He entered parliament for Derby in 1868, but it was not until he had published *Our Seamen* (1873) and had made a public appeal that the Merchant Shipping Act (1876) was passed. This required every owner to mark upon his ship a circular disc (the 'Plimsoll Mark'), with a horizontal line drawn through its centre, down to which the vessel might be loaded. He retired from parliamentary life in 1880. In 1890 he published *Cattle-ships*, exposing the cruelties and dangers of cattle-shipping.

Pliny, Gaius Plinius Caecilius Secundus, *called* the Younger c.62–c.113AD
Roman writer and orator
He was born in Novum Comum, the nephew and adopted son of **Pliny, the Elder**. He wrote a Greek tragedy in his 14th year, and under **Quintilian's** tuition became one of the most accomplished men of his time. His skill as an orator enabled him at 18 to plead in the Forum, and he served as consul in AD100, in which year he wrote his eulogy to **Trajan**. From 103 to 105 he was propraetor of the Provincia Pontica and, among other offices, was also curator of the Tiber. His second wife, Calpurnia, is fondly referred to in one of his most charming letters for the ways in which she sweetened his rather invalid life. His 10 volumes of letters give an intimate picture of the upper class in the 1st century AD; above all, his correspondence with Trajan clearly shows how the Romans regarded the early Christians and their 'depraved and extravagant superstition'.

Pliny, Gaius Plinius Secundus, *called* the Elder
AD23–79
Roman scholar
He was born at Novum Comum (Como), where his wealthy Italian family had estates. He was educated in Rome, and when aged about 23 entered the army, became colonel of a cavalry regiment, and a comrade of the future Emperor **Titus**, and wrote a treatise on the throwing of missiles from horseback and compiled a history of the Germanic wars. He also made a series of scientific tours in the region between the Rivers Ems, Elbe and Weser, and the sources of the River Danube. Returning to Rome in AD52, he studied law, but withdrew to Como and devoted himself to reading and authorship. Apparently for the guidance of his nephew, he wrote his *Studiosus*, a treatise defining the culture necessary for the orator, and the grammatical work, *Dubius Sermo*. By **Nero** he was appointed procurator in Spain, and through his brother-in-law's death (71) became guardian of his sister's sons, Pliny, the Younger, whom he adopted. **Vespasian** was now emperor, and became a close friend, but he continued to study, and he brought down to his own time the history of Rome by Aufidius Bassus. A model student, amid metropolitan distraction he worked assiduously, and by lifelong application filled the 160 volumes of manuscript which, after using them for his universal encyclopedia in 37 volumes, *Historia Naturalis* (77), he bequeathed to his nephew. In 79 he was in command of the Roman fleet stationed off Misenum when the great eruption of Mount Vesuvius was at its height. Eager to witness the phenomenon as closely as possible, he landed at Stabiae (*Castellamare*), but had not gone far before the stifling vapours rolling down the hill killed him. His *Historia Naturalis* alone of his many writings survives. Under that title the ancients classified everything of natural or non-artificial origin. Pliny adds digressions on human inventions and institutions, devoting two books to a history of fine art, and dedicates the whole to Titus. His second-hand observations show no discrimination between the true and the false, between the marvellous and the probable, and his style is inartistic, often obscure. But he supplies information on an immense variety of subjects about which we would otherwise be ignorant. 📖 H N Wethered, *The Mind of the Ancient World* (1937)

Plisetskaya, Maya Mikhailovna 1925–
Soviet dancer
Born in Moscow, she trained at the Bolshoi school, becoming a principal immediately on joining the company in 1943. Celebrated for her fast technique, she established herself in classical roles such as Odile/Odette in *Swan Lake* (1957) and came to represent the epitome of the Bolshoi style. A performer of charisma both on and off stage, she was able to travel at a time when this was difficult for most Soviet artists. Best known for the role created for her in *Carmen Suite* (1967) by Alberto Alonso, she also danced for **Roland Petit** in *La Rose malade* (1973) and for **Maurice Béjart** in 1979. Film roles, both dancing (1975, *Vernal Floods*) and acting (1972, *Anna Karenina*) punctuated her career. She was the niece of dancers Sulamith and **Asaf Messerer**.

Plutarch, Greek Ploutarchos c.46–c.120AD
Greek historian, biographer and philosopher

Plutarch was born in Chaeroneia in Boeotia, of a wealthy and cultured family. He spent most of his later life there, but before that he studied philosophy in Athens and travelled in Italy and Egypt, building a circle of cultivated friends. He paid more than one visit to Rome, and gave public lectures in philosophy.

His extant writings amount to about a half of his total output, and fall into two categories: the historical works, and those which are grouped under the general head of *Opera Moralia*. To the former belong his *Parallel Lives*, the work by which he is best known. These are biographies of 23 Greek great politicians and soldiers paired with 23 Roman lives that offer points of similarity, followed (in all but four cases) by a short comparison of each pair (regarded by some critics as spurious). The Lives concentrate on the moral character of each subject rather than on the political events of the time, so that a minor incident or anecdote will acquire a greater importance in the narrative than it would in a standard histroy or biography. They are none the less of great literary value for the information they contain, which is often additional to that found in the narrative histories of a particular time.

The others and less known half of his writings—the *Morals*—are a collection of short treatises, 60 or more (although certainly not all from Plutarch's hand), on various subjects, including *Ethics, Politics, History, Health, Facetiae, Love-stories, Philosophy* and *Isis and Osiris*. Some of the essays breathe quite a Christian spirit, although the writer probably never heard of Christianity. The nine books of his *Symposiaca* or Table-talk exhibit him as the most amiable and genial of boon companions; while his dialogue *Gryllus* reveals a remarkable sense of humour.

Though not a profound thinker, Plutarch was a man of rare gifts, and occupies a unique place in literature as the encyclopaedist of antiquity. The translation by Sir **Thomas North** (1579) was the major source for **Shakespeare's** Roman plays.

📖 Donald A Russell, *Plutarch* (1973); C P Jones, *Plutarch and Rome* (1971); Reginald H Barrow, *Plutarch and His Times* (1967).

> 'I am writing biography, not history, and the truth is that the most brilliant exploits often tell us nothing of the virtues or vices of the men who performed them, while on the other hand a chance remark or a joke may reveal far more of a man's character than the mere feat of winning battles in which thousands fall, or of marshalling great armies, or laying siege to cities.' From *Life of Alexander*, ch.1 (trans I Scott-Kilvert).

Plojhar, Josef 1902–81
Czechoslovak politician

A member of the People's Party and an active Catholic priest, he agreed to support the communists in their takeover of power (1948) and to be a member of the new National Front government. He was appointed Minister of Health and remained in his post until 1968 when the reformers removed him. Archbishop Beran banned him from preaching, but his clerical collar gave his government some degree of respectability abroad.

Plomer, William Charles Franklin 1903–73
British writer

Born in Pietersburg, Transvaal, of British parents, and educated at Rugby, England, he was a farmer and trader in South Africa before becoming an author, and also lived for a while in Greece and Japan. With **Roy Campbell** he ran a South African literary review, and in World War II he served at the Admiralty. His works include the novels *Turbott Wolfe* (1926), *Sado* (1931) and *Ali the Lion* (1936), the collections of short stories *I Speak of Africa* (1928) and *Paper Houses* (1929), and *Collected Poems* (1960). He edited the diaries of **Francis Kilvert** and the poems of **Herman Melville**, and wrote the librettos for several of **Benjamin Britten's** operas, including *Gloriana*. He also wrote the autobiographical *Double Lives* (1943). 📖 W Doyle, *William Plomer* (1969)

Plotinus c.205–270AD
Greek philosopher and founder of Neoplatonism

Born probably in Lycopolis, Egypt, of Roman parents, his intellectual background was Greek. He studied in Alexandria (under **Ammonius**), and in Persia (Iran), and settled in Rome (AD244) where he became a popular lecturer, advocating asceticism and the contemplative life, though he seemed to live in some style himself. At the age of 60 he made an unsuccessful attempt to found a 'Platonopolis', a Platonic 'Republic' in Campania, a venture which was halted by the Emperor **Gallienus**. His 54 works, produced between 253 and 270, were edited posthumously by his pupil **Porphyry**, who arranged them into six groups of nine books, or *Enneads*. They established the foundations of Neoplatonism as a philosophical system, combining the doctrines of **Plato** with those of Pythagoras, **Aristotle** and the Stoics. He greatly influenced early Christian theology, and Neoplatonism was the dominant philosophy in Europe for a thousand years, establishing a link between ancient and medieval thought. 📖 John M Rist, *Plotinus: The Road to Reality* (1967)

Plowden, Lady Bridget Hortia, née Richmond 1907–
English educationist

Educated at Downe House, she was the first woman to chair the Central Advisory Council for Education, from 1963 to 1966, and subsequently became chairman of the Independent Broadcasting Authority (1975–80). Her report, *Children and their Primary Schools* (1967), concentrated public attention on the relationship between the primary school and the home and social background of children. It argued that education must be concerned with the whole family and that increased resources were needed for nursery education and for areas starved of new investment—'educational priority areas'. It took child-centred approaches to their logical limits, insisting on the principle of complete individualization of the teaching/learning process. The *Plowden Report* marks a watershed in the development of English primary education She was appointed DBE in 1972.

Plowright, Joan Ann 1929–
English actress and stage director

She was born in Brigg, Lincolnshire, and trained at the Old Vic Theatre School. In 1956 she became a member of the English Stage Company at the Royal Court Theatre, London, where she played opposite **Laurence Olivier**, whom she married in 1961. She played Jean Rice in John Osborne's *The Entertainer* (1957), and Beattie in Arnold Wesker's *Roots* (1959). In 1963 she joined the National Theatre in its first season. A talented classical actress, she is also an accomplished stage director. She has also worked in television and won two Golden Globe awards for Best Supporting Actress (1993) for the film *Enchanted April* and the mini-series *Stalin* (1992). Recent films include *On Promised Land* (1994) and *The Scarlett Letter* (1994).

Poe, Edgar Allan 1809–49
US poet and short-story writer, the pioneer of the modern detective story

Edgar Allan Poe was born in Boston, Massachusetts. After being orphaned in his third year, he was adopted by John Allan (1780–1834), a wealthy and childless merchant in Richmond, Virginia. The family lived in England from 1815 to 1820, where Poe went to school in Stoke Newington. He spent a year at the University of Virginia (1826) but after turning to gambling in an attempt to pay off his debts, he had a quarrel with his patron (Allan) and ran away to Boston.

In 1827 he published his first volume of verse, *Tamerlane and other Poems*, and enlisted in the US army, becoming sergeant-major in 1829. John Allan procured his discharge and, after a year's delay in which Poe published a second volume of verse, *Al Aaraaf* (1829), his admission to West Point Military Academy (1830). The following March he was dismissed for deliberate neglect of duty. Again reliant on his own resources, he went to New York City and brought out a third edition of his *Poems* (1831), which contained 'Israfel', his earliest poem of value, and 'To Helen'.

He then turned to journalism and story-writing, living in Baltimore with his aunt, Mrs Clemm, until 1835. His story 'A MS. found in a Bottle' won a prize in 1833. In 1835 he went to Richmond as assistant editor on the *Southern Literary Messenger* (1835–37), and the following year married his 13-year-old cousin Virginia Clemm. He left Richmond in 1837, returned briefly to New York, where he published *The Narrative of Arthur Gordon Pym*, and established himself in Philadelphia in 1838. There he was co-editor of *Burton's Gentleman's Magazine* (1839–40) for which he wrote the well-known story 'The Fall of the House of Usher', and he published *Tales of the Grotesque and Arabesque* (1839) in 1840. He resigned from *Burton's* in 1840, and went on to edit *Graham's Magazine* (1841–42), in which he published his pioneering detective story 'The

Murders in the Rue Morgue'. He won another short-story competition in 1843 with 'The Gold Bug'.

In 1844 he returned again to New York, where he held various journalistic posts. His poem 'The Raven' appeared first in the New York *Evening Mirror*, then in *The Raven and Other Poems* (both 1845), and won him immediate fame but not fortune.

His wife died in 1847, and in November 1848 he attempted suicide. Recovering from alcohol addiction in 1849, he spent over two months in Richmond, lecturing there and at Norfolk, became engaged to a lady of means, but died after being found in a wretched, delirious condition in Baltimore. The poems 'The Bells' and 'Annabel Lee', the tale 'The Domain of Amheim', and the bizarre philosophical 'prose poem' *Eureka* (1848) were his last works of note.

Weird, wild, fantastic, and dwelling by choice on the horrible, Poe's genius was nevertheless great. His short stories show genuine originality, and his poems, the chief charm of which is exquisite melody, have been admired by **W B Yeats, Hart Crane** and others.

📖 Daniel G Hoffman, *Poe Poe Poe Poe Poe Poe Poe* (1973); W Bittner, *Poe: a biography* (1962); Arthur H Quinn, *Edgar Allan Poe: A Critical Biography* (1941, reprinted 1969).

> 'Once upon a midnight dreary, while I pondered, weak and weary,
> Over many a quaint and curious volume of forgotten lore,
> While I nodded, nearly napping, suddenly there came a tapping,
> As of some one gently rapping, rapping at my chamber door.
> 'Tis some visitor, I muttered, tapping at my chamber door;
> Only this and nothing more.'
> 'The Raven', stanza 1 (1845)

Plücker, Julius 1801–68
German mathematician and physicist

Born in Eberfeld, he became Professor of Mathematics at Bonn University in 1836, and of Physics in 1847. He investigated diamagnetism, originated the idea of spectrum analysis, and in 1859 discovered cathode rays, produced by electrical discharges in gases at low pressures. His mathematical work was concerned with line geometry and algebraic curves.

Plume, Thomas 1630–1704
English theologian

Born in Maldon, Essex, he was educated in Chelmsford and at Christ's College, Cambridge. He was vicar of Greenwich from 1658 and archdeacon of Rochester from 1679. He endowed an observatory and the Plumian chair of astronomy and experimental philosophy at Cambridge, and bequeathed his extensive library to the town of Maldon, where it still exists intact.

Plumer, Herbert Charles Onslow 1857–1932
English soldier and colonial administrator

He served in Sudan (1884) and led the Rhodesian relief force to Mafeking (1900). In World War I he distinguished himself as commander of the 2nd army of the British Expeditionary Force (1915–18), notably at the great attack on Messines, and General Officer Commanding Italian Expeditionary Force (1917–18). He was made a field marshal in 1919, was Governor of Malta (1919–24), and High Commissioner for Palestine (1925–28).

Plunkitt, George Washington 1842–1924
US politician

Tammany leader of the New York Fifteenth Assembly District, Sachem of the Tammany Society and chairman of the Election Committee of Tammany Hall, he was at various times an assemblyman, state senator, police magistrate, county supervisor and alderman. At one time he held four public offices and drew salaries from three of them simultaneously, a fact of which he was inordinately proud. He was immortalized in a series of 'Very Plain Talks on Very Practical Politics', recorded by the journalist William L Riordon, and published under the title *Plunkitt of Tammany Hall* (1905). It was a cheerfully ingenuous defence of machine politics, and has become a minor classic of US political science.

Plutarch See panel p1480

Pobedonostsev, Konstantin Petrovich 1827–1907
Russian jurist and politician

Born in Moscow, he was educated at home and at the Oldenburg School of Law in St Petersburg. Tutor, and later adviser, to **Alexander III** and **Nicholas II**, he became Professor of Civil Law at Moscow in 1858 and, as a member of a judicial commission in 1863, favoured liberal reforms in the law. However, after becoming procurator of the Holy Synod in 1866, he reacted against this, strongly opposing any westernizing changes in Russia and becoming the most influential as well as the most uncompromising champion of the autocracy and of the supremacy of the Russian Orthodox Church. He was eventually forced to resign in 1905 in the midst of the revolution of that year, but he had by that time done considerable damage to 'the progress of normal constitutional change.

Pocahontas, *Native American name* **Matoaka**
1595–1617
Native American princess
Born near the future Jamestown, Virginia, she was the daughter of an American-Indian chief, **Powhatan**. According to the English adventurer **John Smith**, she twice saved his life when he was at the mercy of her tribe, and she helped to maintain peace between the settlers and her people. Cajoled to Jamestown, Virginia (1612), she embraced Christianity, was baptized Rebecca (1613), married an English settler, John Rolfe (1613), and in 1616 went with him to England, where she was received by royalty. Having embarked for Virginia the following year, she died of smallpox off Gravesend. She left one son, and several Virginia families claim descent from her.
📖 Frances Mossiker, *Pocahontas: The Life and the Legend* (1976)

Po Chü-i, See **Bo Juyi**

Podgorny, Nikolai Viktorovich 1903–
Soviet politician
Born in Karklova, Ukraine, the son of a foundry worker, he worked in the sugar industry and in due course held managerial, educational and ministerial posts connected with food. He joined the Communist Party (1930), and after World War II took a leading role in the economic reconstruction of the liberated Ukraine. He held various senior posts (1950–65), becoming a full member of the politburo in 1960. Following the dismissal of **Nikita Khrushchev** (1964), he became Chairman of the Presidium and therefore titular head of state from 1965 until 1977, when he was replaced by **Leonid Brezhnev**.

Poe, Edgar Allan See panel p1481

Poelzig, Hans 1869–1936
German Expressionist architect
Born in Berlin, he joined the Prussian Ministry of Works in 1899, becoming Professor of Architecture at the Academy of Arts in Breslau in 1900 (subsequently director). From 1916 to 1920 he served as city architect of Dresden. The early inventive projects such as the Luban Chemical Works in Posen, Silesia (1911–12), and the monumental Water Tower and Exhibition Hall, also in Posen (1910–11), disseminated his uncompromising Expressionist ideals. Later works include the remodelling of Grosses Schauspielhaus in Berlin (1919), Salzburg Festival Theatre (1920–22), and the conservative and imposing design of the I G Farben Headquarters, Frankfurt (1928–31).

Poggendorff, Johann Christian 1796–1877
German physicist and chemist
Born in Hamburg, he worked as a pharmacy assistant and studied at the University of Berlin, where he became Extraordinary Professor of Chemistry in 1834. He made discoveries in connection with electricity and galvanism, and his inventions included a 'multiplying' galvanometer (1821), a magnetometer (1827), the compensating circuit for determining electromotive force, a thermopile and the mercurial air-pump. While collaborating with **Justus von Liebig** he coined the word 'aldehyde' and the modern chemical notation. He was highly influential as the editor of the journal *Annalen der Physik und Chemie* (1824–74), bringing out 160 volumes during his editorship. He also produced a useful two-volume collection of brief biographies of 8,000 physicists of all countries and periods until 1858, since extended to 18 volumes.

Poggio, Gian Francesco Bracciolini 1380–1459
Italian humanist

Born in Florence, he became a secretary to the Roman curia in 1403. At the Council of Constance (1414–18) he explored the Swiss and Swabian convents for manuscripts and recovered some of Quintilian, Ammianus Marcellinus, Lucretius, Silius Italicus, Vitruvius and others. In 1453 he retired to Florence, and became chancellor and official historian to the republic. His writings include letters, moral essays, a rhetorical Latin *History of Florence*, a series of invectives against his contemporaries, and—his most famous book—the *Liber Facetiarum*, a collection of humorous stories, mainly against monks and secular clergy.

Poggio, Giovanni dal See **Giovanni di Paolo**

Pohl, Frederik 1919–
US science-fiction writer
He was born in Brooklyn, New York City, and in 1938 became a founder-member of a group of left-wing science-fiction writers called the Futurists, which included **Isaac Asimov** among others. He served in the air force in World War II, worked as a literary agent, and edited various science-fiction magazines (1953–69). He describes his own multifarious books as 'cautionary literature', seeing science fiction as a kind of alarm signal. Of his vast output of novels, stories and anthologies, *The Space Merchants* (1953) and *Gladiator-at-Law* (1955), both written with C M Kornbluth, exemplify his social concern and strength as a storyteller. 📖 *The Way the Future Was* (1978)

Poincaré, Jules Henri 1854–1912
French mathematician
Born in Nancy, he studied at the École Polytechnique, and became Professor of Mathematics in Paris in 1881. He created the theory of automorphic functions, non-Euclidean geometry and complex functions, and showed the importance of topological considerations in differential equations. Many of the basic ideas in modern topology—such as triangulation, homology, the Euler–Poincaré formula and the fundamental group—are due to him. In a paper on the three-body problem (1889) he opened up new directions in celestial mechanics, and began the study of dynamical systems in the modern sense. In his last years he published several articles (later collected as books) on the philosophy of science and scientific method, including *Science et méthode* (1909). 📖 Tobias Dantzig, *Henri Poincaré, Critic of Crisis* (1954)

Poincaré, Raymond Nicolas Landry 1860–1934
French statesman
He was born in Bar-le-Duc, the cousin of **Jules Poincaré**. He studied law, becoming a deputy (1887) and senator (1903), holding office as Minister of Public Instruction (1893, 1895), of Finance (1894–95 and 1906), and of Foreign Affairs (1912–13 and 1922–23). Elected Prime Minister (1912–13) and President (1913–20), he sought to play a more directive role than previous incumbents. He had some success at first, especially in foreign affairs, but when **Georges Clemenceau** became Prime Minister in 1917, he found himself sidelined, and was unable to influence decisions at the post-war peace conference. As Prime Minister once again (1922–24) he sought to enforce the terms of the Treaty of Versailles (notably the payment of reparations) against a recalcitrant Germany by occupying the Ruhr (1923–24). Although Germany was thus forced to negotiate, Poincaré had by then been defeated in the 1924 elections, and his successor as Prime Minister, **Édouard Herriot**, bowing to British and US pressure, conceded much of what Poincaré had hoped to achieve. He was brought back to power (1926–29), as Prime Minister and Finance Minister, to deal with a financial crisis; he stabilized the franc, inaugurating a brief period of prosperity before France succumbed to the Great Depression. A member of the Académie Française (1909),

he wrote on both literature and politics, in *Memoirs* (Eng trans 1925), and *How France is Governed* (1913). 📖 Sisley Huddleston, *Poincaré* (1924)

Poindexter, John Marlan 1936–
US naval officer and political adviser
Born in Washington, Indiana, the son of a bank manager, he was educated at the US Naval Academy and California Institute of Technology (Caltech), where he obtained a doctorate in nuclear physics. He became chief of naval operations during the 1970s and was deputy head of naval educational training from 1978 to 1981. In 1981 he joined President Ronald Reagan's National Security Council (NSC), becoming National Security Adviser in 1985. He resigned, together with his assistant, Lieutenant-Colonel Oliver North, in 1986 in the aftermath of the Iran-Contra affair. Poindexter retired from the navy in 1987, and in 1990 was convicted by a Federal court on charges of obstructing and lying to Congress. He was sentenced to six months in prison, but his sentence was overturned by the Federal appeals court in 1991.

Poiret, Paul 1879–1944
French fashion designer
Born in Paris, he worked for Jacques Doucet and Charles Worth before opening his own fashion house in 1904. Influenced by the exotic oriental costumes of the Ballets Russes, which was first in Paris in 1908, his designs of the period featured such garments as turbans and harem pants. A brochure of 1911, illustrated by Georges Lepape under the title *Les Choses de Paul Poiret*, showed a rich and varied collection of an early leader of fashion rather than a designer for the individual client. After World War I he was never able to adapt sufficiently to changed circumstances in order to re-establish his prominence, and he died in poverty.

Poisson, Siméon Denis 1781–1840
French mathematical physicist
Born in Pithiviers, Loiret, he was educated at the École Polytechnique under Pierre Laplace and Joseph de Lagrange, and became the first Professor of Mechanics at the Sorbonne. He published extensively on mathematical physics, and his contributions to potential theory and the transformation of equations in mechanics by means of Poisson brackets have proved of lasting worth. He is also remembered for discovering the 'Poisson distribution', a special case of the binomial distribution in statistics.

Poitier, Sidney 1924–
US actor and director
Born in Miami, Florida, he was raised in the Bahamas and later studied at the American Negro Theater in New York. He appeared on stage in *Lysistrata* (1946) and *Anna Lucasta* (1946–48) before making his film debut in the documentary *From Whence Cometh My Help* (1949). His Hollywood debut followed in *No Way Out* (1950), and he gave strong performances in *Cry, the Beloved Country* (1952), *The Blackboard Jungle* (1955) and *The Defiant Ones* (1958). He won an Academy Award for *Lilies of the Field* (1963). Handsome and unassuming, he brought dignity to the portrayal of noble and intelligent characters in such films as *In the Heat of the Night* (1967) and *Guess Who's Coming to Dinner* (1967). He has also directed a number of comedies, including *Stir Crazy* (1980) and *Ghost Dad* (1990). He returned to acting after a 10-year absence in *Little Nikita* (1988) and *Shoot to Kill* (1988). His autobiography, *This Life*, was published in 1980. Recent television appearances include *Children of the Dust* (1995) and *To Sir With Love II* (1996).

Poitiers, Diane de See Diane de Poitiers

Polanski, Roman 1933–
French–Polish film director, scriptwriter and actor
Born in Paris, France, and brought up in Poland, he was an actor on radio and in the theatre, attended the State Film School in Todź (1954–59), and made a number of short films beginning with the uncompleted *Rower* (1955, *The Bicycle*). His feature-length debut *Nóz w Wodzie* (1962, *Knife in the Water*) brought him international recognition and he has subsequently worked in London, Paris and Los Angeles on films which often explore the nature of evil and personal corruption, including *Repulsion* (1965), *Cul de Sac* (1966) and *Rosemary's Baby* (1968). Later productions include *Chinatown* (1974), controversial interpretations of *Macbeth* (1971) in England and *Tess* (1979) in France, *Frantic* (1988), and *Bitter Moon* (1992). A traumatic life that includes his internment in a German concentration camp, the early death of his mother and the horrifying murder of his pregnant second wife, actress Sharon Tate, has been reflected in his creative work. On stage, he has directed *Lulu* (1974) and *Rigoletto* (1976) and acted in *Amadeus* (1981) and *Metamorphosis* (1988). His candid autobiography, *Roman*, was published in 1984.

Polanyi, John Charles 1929–
Canadian physical chemist and Nobel Prize winner
Born in Berlin, Germany, the son of Michael Polanyi, he grew up and studied in Manchester, worked at the National Research Council in Ottawa and at Princeton University, and joined the chemistry staff at the University of Toronto in 1956, where he was made full professor in 1962. In 1974 he was given the title of University Professor. Polanyi has worked extensively on the infrared light emitted during chemical reactions. Analysis of such radiation gives information about the distribution of energy within molecular species and sheds light on the events which occur during reactions. The technique complements the molecular beam method developed by Dudley Herschbach and Yuan Tseh Lee, who shared the 1986 Nobel Prize for chemistry with Polanyi for these advances. He has also studied how reaction rates depend on the molecular motion of the reactants, and has written articles on science policy and on control of armaments. He was made a Companion of the Order of Canada in 1977, was elected a Fellow of the Royal Society in 1971 (receiving its Royal Medal in 1989) and became an Honorary FRS of Chemistry in 1991.

Polanyi, Karl 1886–1964
US economic historian
Born in Vienna and educated in Budapest, he held the post of foreign editor of the economic journal *Österreichische Volkswirt* throughout the 1920s. He emigrated to England in 1933, lecturing at Oxford and for the Workers' Educational Association, moving in 1940 to Canada, where he was a resident scholar at Bennington College (1940–43) and from where he wrote his first book, *The Great Transformation* (1944; UK: *Origins of our Time: The Great Transformation*, 1945). At the age of 61 he was invited to Columbia University as visiting Professor of Economic History, remaining there beyond his retirement to collaborate on *Trade and Market in the Early Empires* (with Conrad Arensberg and Harry Pearson, 1957). In this publication he contributed the article 'The Economy as Instituted Process', a highly influential paper in the field of economic anthropology which generated debate between substantivists and formalists throughout the 1960s.

Polanyi, Michael 1891–1976
British physical chemist, social scientist and philosopher
Born in Budapest, Hungary, he qualified in medicine at the University of Budapest in 1913, and studied physical chemistry with Georg Bredig at the Technische Hochschule, Karlsruhe. During World War I he was a medical officer in the Austrian army. From 1920 to 1923 he worked at the Kaiser Wilhelm Institute for Fibre Chemistry in Berlin, and then moved to the Institute of

Physical Chemistry under **Fritz Haber**, where he worked on X-ray diffraction by fibres and then began his studies of chemical kinetics, which continued for some 25 years. When **Hitler** rose to power in 1933 Polanyi accepted the chair of physical chemistry at Manchester University. He built up an excellent school of physical chemistry, and was much involved in the development of transition state theory during this time, but his interests were already moving to wider cultural and philosophical matters. He left physical chemistry and was given a personal chair in social studies in 1948. He became Senior Research Fellow of Merton College, Oxford, in 1958. His social and philosophical interests are best indicated by the titles of some of his books: *The Contempt of Freedom* (1940), *Full Employment and Free Trade* (1945), *Science, Faith and Society* (1946), *Personal Knowledge* (1958) and *Knowing and Being* (1969). His writings often met with suspicion and criticism in philosophical circles. He was elected FRS in 1944. 📖 Richard Gelwick, *The Way of Discovery: An Introduction to the Thought of Michael Polanyi* (1977)

Pole, Reginald 1500–58
English Roman Catholic churchman

Born in Stourton Castle, Staffordshire, he studied at Oxford, then in Padua, Italy. He was the son of Sir Richard Pole and Margaret, Countess of Salisbury (1473–1541). He received several Church posts, and gained **Henry VIII**'s favour, but lost it after opposing the king on divorce and left for Italy, where he was made a cardinal by the Pope **Paul III** (1536). In 1549 he was on the point of being elected pope, but on the election of **Julius III** lived quietly until the death of **Edward VI**. In 1554, during the reign of the Catholic Queen **Mary I**, he returned to England as Papal Legate, became one of her most powerful advisers, returned the country to Rome, and became Archbishop of Canterbury in succession to **Thomas Cranmer** (1556). It is alleged that he was responsible for the hardening of Mary's attitude to the Protestants.

Poliakoff, Stephen 1952–
English dramatist

Born in London, he studied at Cambridge, and began writing plays as a teenager. He achieved recognition with the plays *Hitting Town* and *City Sugar* (both 1975), which addressed the plight of the urban young in a Great Britain of concrete shopping arcades and consumerism. Several plays followed on the same theme, but *Breaking the Silence* (1984), set in the aftermath of the Russian Revolution, is his finest work to date. *Coming Into Land* (1987) follows the fortunes of a Polish refugee as she tries to enter Great Britain. Other stage plays include *Strawberry Fields* (1977), *Shout Across the River* (1978) and *Sienna Red* (1992). His television plays include *Caught on a Train* (1980). He made his debut as a film director with *Hidden City* (1987), and both wrote and directed *Close My Eyes* (1991), based on *Hitting Town*. He published *Plays One* in 1991.

Polignac, Auguste Jules Armand Marie, Prince de 1780–1847
French statesman

He was born in Versailles. He was arrested for conspiring against **Napoleon I** (1804), became a peer at the **Bourbon** Restoration, and received the title of prince from the pope in 1820 for being a committed exponent of papal and royal authority. English ambassador in 1823, he became head of the last Bourbon ministry in 1829, which decreed the St Cloud Ordinances that cost **Charles X** his throne (1830). Imprisoned until 1836, he then lived in exile in England, and returned to Paris in 1845.

Politian, *properly* Angelo Ambrogini 1454–94
Italian humanist, scholar and poet

He was born in Montepulciano in Tuscany, and called *Poliziano* (Politian) from the Italian name of his birthplace. At the age of 10 he was sent to Florence, and made incredible progress in the ancient languages. At 17 he began the translation of the *Iliad* into Latin hexameters, and having secured the friendship of the all-powerful **Lorenzo de' Medici** (whose sons he taught) he was soon recognized as the prince of Italian scholars. He was appointed Canon of Florence in 1480, and became Professor of Greek and Latin at Florence (1482–86). Lorenzo's death in 1492 was a serious blow, and he mourned his death in a remarkable Latin elegy. Among his other works were Latin translations of a long series of Greek authors, and an excellent edition of the *Pandects* of **Justinian I**. His *Orfeo* (1480) was the first secular drama in Italian.

Polk, James K (nox) 1795–1849
11th President of the USA

Born in Mecklenburg County, North Carolina, the son of a prosperous farmer, he was admitted to the Bar in 1820. He was elected to Congress as a Democrat in 1825, becoming Speaker of the House in 1835 and advancing **Andrew Jackson**'s legislative aims, including the attack on the Bank of the United States. He served as Governor of Tennessee (1839–41), and in 1844 he gained the Democratic nomination as a compromise candidate and was elected President, defeating the Whig candidate **Henry Clay**, mainly because of his advocacy of the annexation of Texas. Congress voted to annex Texas just before Polk's inauguration in 1845, and when an effort to buy California from Mexico was rebuffed, the President forced hostilities by advancing the US army to the Rio Grande, thus beginning the Mexican War. The capital was taken in 1847, and by the terms of peace the USA acquired California and New Mexico. A strong leader who set himself major objectives and achieved them, Polk succeeded in reducing the tariff, restoring the independent treasury system and settling the Oregon boundary dispute with Great Britain. By the end of his term, however, he was exhausted and in poor health, and he died a few months after leaving office. 📖 E I McCormac, *James K Polk: A Political Biography* (1922)

Polk, Leonidas 1806–64
US soldier

Born in Raleigh, North Carolina, he was a cousin of **James K Polk**. He held a commission in the artillery, but resigned to study divinity and in 1831 received holy orders in the Episcopal church. In 1838 he was consecrated a missionary Bishop of Arkansas, and from 1841 until his death was Bishop of Louisiana, even when at the head of an army corps. In the Civil War (1861–65) he was made major-general by **Jefferson Davis**. At Belmont, in November 1861, he was driven from his camp by **Ulysses S Grant**, but finally forced him to retire. At Shiloh and Corinth he commanded the first Corps; promoted to lieutenant-general, he conducted the retreat from Kentucky. After Chickamauga, where he commanded the right wing, he was relieved of his command; reappointed in December 1863, he opposed **William Sherman**'s march.

Pollaiuolo, Antonio 1429–98
Florentine goldsmith, medallist, metalcaster and painter

He cast sepulchral monuments in St Peter's in Rome for Popes **Sixtus IV** and Innocent VIII. His pictures are distinguished for their life and vigour. He was one of the first painters to study anatomy and apply it to art, and he was skilled in suggesting movement. His brother Piero (1443–96) worked with him.

Pollard, Albert Frederick 1869–1948
English historian

Born in Ryde, Isle of Wight, he graduated at Oxford, and became assistant editor of *The Dictionary of National Biography*. Later he was Professor of Constitutional History at London University (1903–31), founding in 1920 its Institute of Historical Research, and from 1908 to 1936 he was a Fellow of All Souls College, Oxford. Among his many historical works are biographies of *Henry VIII* (1902), *Thomas Cranmer* (1904) and *Wolsey* (1929), *A Short History of the Great War* (1920) and *Factors in American History* (1925). The Historical Association was founded by him in 1906 and he was editor of *History* from 1916 to 1922.

Pollard, Alfred William 1859–1944
English scholar and bibliographer

Born in London and a graduate of Oxford, he was an assistant in the department of printed books at the British Museum (from 1883), and keeper from 1919 to 1924. He was appointed Reader in Bibliography at Cambridge (1915) and Professor of English Bibliography at King's College London (1919–32). He was an authority on **Chaucer** and **Shakespeare**, and his contributions to Shakespearean criticism included his *Shakespeare Folios and Quartos* (1909) and *Shakespeare's Fight with the Pirates* (1917). Important earlier work on Chaucer had produced *A Chaucer Primer* (1893) and his edition of the Globe *Chaucer* (1898). In 1926 was completed the *Short Title Catalogue of Books Printed in England, Scotland and Ireland, 1475–1640*, for which he was largely responsible.

Pollio, Gaius Asinius 76BC–AD4
Roman orator and soldier

In the Civil War against **Pompey** he sided with **Julius Caesar**; in 39BC he commanded in Spain, and, appointed by **Mark Antony** to settle the veterans on the lands assigned them, saved **Virgil**'s property from confiscation. He founded the first public library in Rome, and was the patron of Virgil and **Horace**. Only a few fragments of his writings survive.

Pollitt, Harry 1890–1960
English Communist politician

Born in Droylesden, Lancashire, he entered a cotton mill at the age of 12 and joined the Independent Labour Party at 16. Later he became a boilermaker and was a shop steward by the age of 21. He was Secretary of the National Minority Movement from 1924 to 1929, when he became Secretary of the Communist Party of Great Britain. A stormy demagogue, he frequently clashed with authority, being imprisoned for seditious libel in 1925 and being deported from Belfast in 1933. During the Spanish Civil War he helped to found the British battalion of the International Brigade. In 1956 he resigned the secretaryship of the party and became its chairman. He wrote an autobiography, *Serving My Time* (1940).

Pollock, Sir Frederick 1845–1937
English jurist

Born in London, the son of the jurist Sir William Frederick Pollock (1815–88), he was educated at Eton and Trinity College, Cambridge. He was called to the Bar in 1871, then became a Professor of Jurisprudence at University College, London (1882), and at Oxford (1883). He was Professor of Common Law in the Inns of Court (1884–90) and edited the Law Reports (1895) and the Law Quarterly Review (1885–1919). His publications include *Principles of Contract* (1875), *Digest of the Law of Partnership* (1877), *Law of Torts* (1887), and a *History of English Law before Edward I* (1895, with **Frederic William Maitland**). He corresponded for many years with **Oliver Wendell Holmes**.

Pollock, (Paul) Jackson 1912–56
US artist

Born in Cody, Wyoming, he was trained at the Art Students' League in New York and became the first exponent of tachism or action painting in the USA. His art developed from Surrealism to abstract art and the first drip paintings of 1947. This technique he continued with increasing violence and often on huge canvases, eg *One*, which is 17ft (5.2km) long. Other striking works include *No. 32*, and the black and white *Echo and Blue Poles*. He was killed in a motor accident. ⌨ Francis V O'Connor, *Jackson Pollock* (1967)

Pollock, Robert Graeme 1944–
South African cricketer

He was born in Durban. One of the great batsmen of the 1960s, he was the last South African cricketer to make an impact at international level before that country's exclusion from Test cricket. From 1970 to 1991 South Africa were banned from international sport. In 23 Tests he averaged more than 60.9, a score second only to **Don Bradman**'s. Against Australia at Durban in 1969–70 he made 274, and he shares three record partnerships.

Polo, Marco See panel p1486

Pol Pot, *also known as* Saloth Sar 1925–98
Cambodian politician

He was born in Kompong Thom province. After working on a rubber plantation in his early teens, he joined the anti-French resistance movement under **Ho Chi Minh** during the early 1940s, becoming a member of the Indo-Chinese Communist Party and Cambodian Communist Party in 1946. During the 1960s and early 1970s he led the pro-Chinese Communist Khmer Rouge in guerrilla activity against the Kampuchean governments of Prince Sihanouk and Lieutenant-General Lon Nol, and in 1976, after the overthrow of Lon Nol, became Prime Minister. He proceeded brutally to introduce an extreme Communist regime which resulted in the loss of more than two million lives. The regime was overthrown by Vietnamese troops in January 1979 and Pol Pot took to the resistance struggle once more. Despite announcing his 'official' retirement as the Khmer's military leader in August 1985, he remained an influential and feared figure within the movement. The Khmer Rouge began to splinter in 1996, and in 1997 Pol Pot was arrested by an opposing faction. He died whilst under house arrest.

Polybius c.205–c.123BC
Greek historian

Born in Megalopolis, Arcadia, he was one of the 1,000 noble Achaeans who, after the conquest of Macedonia in 168BC, were sent to Rome and detained as political hostages in honourable captivity. He was the guest of **Lucius Aemilius Paullus** and became the close friend of his son, **Scipio Aemilianus**, who helped him to collect material for his great historical work. In 151 the exiles were permitted to return to Greece, but Polybius rejoined Scipio, followed him in his African campaign, and was present at the destruction of Carthage in 146. The war between the Achaeans and Romans called him back to Greece, and, after the taking of Corinth by Rome (146), he procured favourable terms for the vanquished. In furtherance of his historical labours he travelled to Asia Minor, Egypt, upper Italy, southern France and Spain. His *History*, which shows why all the civilized countries of the world fell under the dominion of Rome, covers the period 221–146. Of 40 books only the first five are preserved complete.

Polycarp, St c.69–c.155AD
Greek Christian and one of the Apostolic Fathers

He was Bishop of Smyrna during the little-known period between the Apostle **John**, who was his teacher in Ephesus, and his own disciple **Irenaeus**. The author of the *Epistle to the Philippians*, he visited Rome to discuss the timing of Easter, and was martyred on his return to Smyrna. His feast day is 23 February.

Polo, Marco 1254–1324
Venetian merchant, traveller and writer

Marco Polo was born of a noble Venetian merchant family. At the time of his birth, his father and uncle were on an expedition to Bokhara and Cathay (China). They were well-received by **Kublai Khan**, who commissioned them as envoys to the pope to seek a hundred learned Europeans for the imperial court. They were unsuccessful in this commission (1269), and started out again in 1271, taking the young Marco with them. They arrived at the court of Kublai Khan in 1275, after travelling across Central Asia and through the Gobi Desert to Tangut and Shangtu. The emperor took special notice of Marco, and sent him as envoy to Yunnan, northern Burma, Karakorum, Cochin-China and southern India.

For three years Marco Polo served as Governor of Yang Chow, and helped to subdue the city of Saianfu. The emperor at first refused to allow the Polos to leave his court, but eventually they sailed to Persia, finally reaching Venice in 1295, and bringing with them the great wealth they had accumulated.

In 1298 he commanded a galley at the Battle of Curzola, and after the Venetians' defeat he was taken prisoner for a year at Genoa. There he wrote an account of his travels, *Divisament dou Monde*, either from memory (dictated to a fellow prisoner) or from notes which he had written for Kublai Khan. This account is one of the most important sources for our knowledge of China and the East before the 19th century. After his release (1298), he returned to Venice, where he spent the rest of his life.

📖 Frances Wood, *Did Marco Polo go to China?* (1995); H H Hart, *Marco Polo, Venetian Adventurer* (1967); Milton Rugoff, *Marco Polo's Adventures in China* (1964).

'I have not told even the half of the things that I have seen.' Comment on being accused of exaggeration in his accounts of China (c.1320). Quoted in R H Poole and P Finch (eds), *Newnes Pictorial Knowledge* (vol 2, 1950).

Polyclitus 5th century BC
Greek sculptor

He was from Samos, and was a contemporary of **Phidias**. A specialist in statues of muscular athletes, he is now best known for the lost bronze *Doryphorus* (Spear Bearer), a fragment of which is in the Uffizi Gallery, Florence. His works were often copied, and he was highly thought of by **Pliny**.

Polycrates d.c.522BC
Tyrant of Samos

He conquered several nearby islands and towns on the Asiatic mainland and was one of the most conspicuous and powerful Greek tyrants of his time. He made an alliance with Amasis II, King of Egypt, but later broke it by giving support to the Persian King **Cambyses II** in his invasion of Egypt. He successfully resisted an attack from Spartans, Corinthians and disaffected Samians, but was later lured to the mainland by Oroetes, a Persian satrap, seized, and crucified.

Polygnotus 5th century BC
Greek painter

Born on the island of Thasos, he was the first to indicate perspective and landscape in his works. His principal works were in Athens, Delphi and Plataea.

Pombal, Sebastião José de Carvalho e Mello, Marquês de 1699–1782
Portuguese statesman

He was born near Coimbra. Appointed Secretary for Foreign Affairs (1750), he showed resourcefulness in re-planning Lisbon after the great earthquake (1755), and the following year was made Prime Minister. He opposed the tyranny of the Church and the intrigues of nobles and Jesuits, and banished the Jesuits in 1759. He established elementary schools, reorganized the army, introduced fresh colonists into the Portuguese settlements and established West India and Brazil companies. The tyranny of the Inquisition was broken. Agriculture, commerce and finance were improved. In 1758 he was made Count of Oeyras, and in 1770 Marquês de Pombal. His power ended on the accession of Maria I (1777).

Pompadour, Jeanne Antoinette Poisson, Marquise de, *known as* Madame de Pompadour 1721–64
French courtier and mistress

Born in Paris, possibly the child of Le Normant de Tournehem, a wealthy *fermier-général*, she was married in 1741 to her nephew, Le Normant d'Étiales. She caught the attention of King **Louis XV**, and was installed at Versailles and ennobled as Marquise de Pompadour. For 20 years she made her own favourites ministers of France and swayed the policy of the state, but Louis XV took the decisions. Her policy and wars were disastrous (the loss of Canada was blamed on her), and the ministry of the Duc de **Choiseul** was the only creditable portion of the reign. With Louis, she founded the École Militaire, the Place Louis XV (Place de la Concorde) and the royal porcelain factory at Sèvres, and was a lavish patron of poets and painters. She retained the king's favour by relieving him of all business and countenancing his debaucheries. Her *Mémoires* (1766) are not genuine. 📖 Nancy Mitford, *Madame de Pompadour* (1964)

Pompey, *originally* Gnaeus Pompeius Magnus, *called* the Great 106–48BC
Roman soldier and politician

At 17 he fought in the Social War against **Marius** and **Cinna**. He supported **Sulla**, and destroyed the remains of the Marian faction in Africa and Sicily. He drove the followers of **Lepidus** out of Italy, extinguished the Marian party in Spain under **Sertorius** (76–71BC), annihilated the remnants of the army of **Spartacus** and was popularly elected consul for the year 70. A member of the aristocratic party, latterly he had been looked upon with suspicion, but he now espoused the people's cause and carried a law restoring the tribunician power to the people. He cleared the Mediterranean Sea of pirates, defeated **Mithridates VI** of Pontus, Tigranes of Armenia, and Antiochus of Syria, subdued the Jews and captured Jerusalem, and entered Rome in triumph for the third time in 61. But now his star began to wane. Distrusted by the aristocracy, and second to **Julius Caesar** in popular favour, the Senate declined to accede to his wish that his acts in Asia should be ratified. He and Caesar, with the plutocrat **Crassus**, formed the all-powerful 'First Triumvirate'. Pompey's acts in Asia were ratified, Caesar's designs were gained and Caesar's daughter, Julia, was married to Pompey. Jealousies arose, Julia died in 54 and Pompey returned to the aristocratic party. Caesar was ordered to lay down his office, which he consented to do if Pompey would do the same. The Senate insisted on unconditional resignation, otherwise he would be declared a public enemy. But crossing the Rubicon, Caesar defied the Senate and its armies. After his final defeat at Pharsalia in 48, Pompey fled to Egypt, where he was murdered. His younger son, Sextus, secured a fleet manned largely by slaves and exiles, and, occupying

Sicily, ravaged the coasts of Italy. But in 36 he was defeated at sea by **Agrippa**, and in 37 slain at Mitylene. ⨶ Peter A L Greenhalgh, *Pompey: The Roman Alexander* (1980)

Pompidou, Georges Jean Raymond 1911–74
French statesman

Born in Montboudif in the Auvergne, and trained as an administrator, he joined **de Gaulle's** staff in 1944. He held similar opinions to de Gaulle, but was more moderate in his views. He held various government posts from 1946, culminating in his appointment as Prime Minister in 1962 (he was elected to the National Assembly in 1967). During the 'Événements' of May 1968 Pompidou played a key role in defusing and resolving the political crisis, but was dismissed by his increasingly jealous patron, de Gaulle, soon after the parliamentary election held in June. However, in 1969, following de Gaulle's resignation, he was comfortably elected President and proceeded to pursue a somewhat more liberal and internationalist policy programme, as reflected in his own more open and gregarious personality. He died in office. The Centre Georges Pompidou (Centre Beaubourg in Paris), the idea of which was conceived by Pompidou himself in 1969, was completed in his memory in 1978. ⨶ Pierre Rouanet, *Pompidou* (1969)

Ponce de León, Ernesto Zedillo See **Zedillo Ponce de León, Ernesto**

Ponce de León, Juan 1460–1521
Spanish explorer

Born in San Servas, he was a court page, served against the Moors and became Governor, first of part of Hispaniola, then (1510–12) of Puerto Rico. On a quest for the fountain of perpetual youth, he discovered Florida in March 1512, and was made Governor. Failing to conquer his new subjects, he retired to Cuba, and died there from a wound inflicted by a poisoned arrow. ⨶ V M Sanz, *Juan Ponce de Léon* (2nd edn, 1985)

Ponce de León, Luis 1527–91
Spanish monk, scholar and poet

He was born in Granada, entered the Augustinian order in 1544, and became Professor of Theology at Salamanca in 1561. From 1572 to 1576 he was imprisoned by the Inquisition for his translation and interpretation of the *Song of Solomon*, but shortly before his death he became general of his order. His poetical remains, published in 1631, comprise translations from **Virgil**, **Horace** and the *Psalms*. His few original poems are lyrical masterpieces.

Poncelet, Jean Victor 1788–1867
French engineer and geometrician

Born in Metz, he was a military engineer, and during **Napoleon I's** Russian campaign, he was taken prisoner by the Russians on the retreat from Moscow. He became Professor of Mechanics at Metz (1825–35) and Paris (1838–48). His *Traité des propriétés projectives des figures* (1822, 'Treatise on the Projective Properties of Figures') gives him an important place in the development of projective geometry.

Ponchielli, Amilcare 1834–86
Italian composer

Born in Paderno Fasolare, near Cremona, he studied for 11 years at Milan Conservatorio, and became musical director at Bergamo Cathedral (1881–86). He wrote several operas, including *La Gioconda* (1876, 'The Joyful Girl'), and a successful ballet, *Le due Gemelle* (1873).

Ponge, Francis 1899–1987
French poet and essayist

He was born in Montpellier. A committed communist from 1936 until after World War II, and perhaps always a dialectical materialist, he began publishing in 1926, but was virtually unknown until the mid-1940s. Of all the many avant-garde poets of France he was the most sheerly phenomenological with regard to language: his project throughout his writings was to make language 'an object of scientific enquiry'. He therefore became one of the heroes of the Structuralist magazine *Tel Quel*, edited by Philippe Sollers, who wrote on him (1963). A cerebral poet, or, rather, prose-poet (he wanted to abolish the distinction), he deliberately eschewed the lyricism of emotion except as an object of enquiry. His most accessible work is the long meditation on soap, *Le Savon* (1967, Eng trans *Soap*, 1969), actually written during World War II when soap was a scarce commodity. His most characteristic work is to be found in the prose-poems of *Proêmes* (1948). He became a grand old man of French literature in his last years.

Poniatowski, Joseph Antony 1762–1813
Polish soldier and patriot

Born in Warsaw, the nephew of **Stanisław II Augustus Poniatowski**, he trained in the Austrian army. In 1789 the Polish Assembly appointed him commander of the army of the south, with which he defeated the Russians (1792). He also commanded under **Tadeusz Kościuszko** (1794). When the Duchy of Warsaw was constituted (1807) he was appointed Minister of War and Commander-in-Chief. In 1809, during the war between Austria and France, he invaded Galicia. Three years later, with a large body of Poles, he joined **Napoleon I** in his invasion of Russia, fighting at Smolensk, at Borodino, and at Leipzig, where he was drowned.

Poniatowski, Stanisław See **Stanisław Poniatowski**

Pons, Jean-Louis 1761–1831
French astronomer

Born in Peyre, near Dauphine, at the age of 28 he became the porter and door-keeper at the Marseilles Observatory, and after tuition he became the *astronome adjoint* in 1813. In 1819 he was appointed as director of the Lucca Observatory in northern Italy, and in 1825 he became director of the Florence Observatory. His main interest was comets, and the 37 comets which he discovered amounted to three-quarters of all the comets discovered between 1801 and 1827.

Pons, Lily (Alice Joséphine) 1898–1976
US soprano

Born in Draguignan, France, she was a fine operatic coloratura. Greatly successful in Paris, London, South America and, especially, at the New York Metropolitan, she also sang in films, and during World War II toured North Africa and the Far East.

Ponselle, (Ponzillo) Rosa 1897–1981
US soprano

Born in Meridan, Connecticut, she began her career in vaudeville. At **Enrico Caruso's** suggestion she appeared as Leonora in *La forza del destino* ('The Force of Destiny') at the New York Metropolitan (1918). She sang in leading French and Italian grand opera roles there until 1937, also appearing at Covent Garden, London (1929–31), and later taught and directed opera in Baltimore.

Pont (de Nemours), Pierre-Samuel Du See **Du Pont (de Nemours), Pierre-Samuel**

Ponte, Giacomo da See **Bassano, Jacopo da**

Ponte, Lorenzo Da See **Da Ponte, Lorenzo**

Pontecorvo, Guido 1907–
British geneticist

Born in Pisa, Italy, where he studied agricultural science, he then supervised cattle breeding in Tuscany. He moved to the Institute of Animal Genetics in Edinburgh in 1938, and from 1941 worked at the University of Glasgow, where he became Professor of Genetics in 1956. From 1968 to 1975 he was a member of the research staff at the Imperial Cancer Research Fund, London. In 1950 he described the parasexual cycle in fungi, which allows genetic analysis of asexual fungi. Soon afterwards he proposed that the gene is the unit of function in genetics, an idea developed by **Seymour Benzer** and others in 1955.

Pontedera, Andrea da See **Pisano, Andrea**

Pontiac c.1720–1769
Native American leader

Born near Maumee River in Ohio, he became chief of the Ottawa. In 1763 he organized a rising against the British garrisons, conducting an extended and ultimately unsuccessful siege of Detroit. Although Pontiac's forces captured several other forts, they were unable to match mounting British reinforcements, and the rebellion faltered by 1764. Pontiac was later murdered by a Native American from Illinois, causing a bitter inter-tribal war.

Pontoppidan, Henrik 1857–1944
Danish novelist and joint Nobel Prize winner

He was born in Fredericia, the son of a pastor, and trained as an engineer before he turned to writing. Among his novels are *Det forjaettede land* (1891–95, Eng trans *Land of Promise*, 1896), the transparently autobiographical *Lykke-Per* (1898–1904, 'Lucky Per'), the story of a young engineer's conflict with his spiritual father, and *De dødes rige* (1912–16, 'The Realm of the Dead'). He shared the 1917 Nobel Prize for literature with his fellow Danish novelist, Karl Gjellerup. ▨ K Ahnlund, *Henrik Pontoppidan* (1956)

Pontormo, Jacopo da 1494–1552
Italian painter

Of the Florentine school, he was influenced by **Leonardo da Vinci** and **Piero di Cosimo** and worked under **Andrea del Sarto**. His works included frescoes, notably of the Passion (1522–25), in the Certosa near Florence. The *Deposition* (c.1525), which forms the altarpiece in a chapel in Sta Felicità, Florence, is probably his masterpiece, and is a prime example of the early Mannerist style. He also painted portraits and the **Medici** villa at Poggio a Caiano was partly decorated by him. His later work shows the influence of **Michelangelo**.

Pontryagin, Lev Semyonovich 1908–88
Russian mathematician

Born in Moscow, he graduated from university there, where he became professor in 1935. One of the leading Russian topologists, he worked on topological groups and their character theory, on duality in algebraic topology, and on differential equations with applications to optimal control. His book *Topological Groups* (translated 1939) is still a standard work. At the end of his life he was an influential member of the Russian mathematical establishment.

Popé c.1630–c.1690
Native American medicine man and revolutionary leader

He is thought to have been born at the Tewa Pueblo (in present-day New Mexico). In 1680 he led Pueblo tribes in a revolt against the Spanish in Santa Fe, New Mexico, killing more than 400 colonists and driving the others out of the region. Under his leadership, the Pueblos obliterated all traces of Catholicism and Spanish culture and restored native customs and religion. His people suffered under his despotic rule, however, and in 1692, two years after Popé's death, the Spanish regained control.

Pope, Alexander 1688–1744
English poet

He was born in London, the son of a linen merchant. The family moved to Binfield in Windsor Forest when Pope was an infant. He was largely self-taught, which left gaps in his knowledge of literature. At the age of three he suffered his first serious illness and at 12 he was crippled by a tubercular infection of the spine which accounted for his stunted growth (4ft 6in/1.37m). He began writing at an early age. 'Ode to Solitude' was completed in the same year as his illness (1700). Reading and writing feverishly, he got to know members of the literati—William Walsh, Henry Cromwell and Sir William Trumball—who acted as mentors, critics and encouragers. He wrote *The Pastorals* while a teenager and they were eventually published by Jacob Tonson in 1709. Metrically adept, they are remembered for his mastery of technique rather than their poetry. He produced his seminal work *An Essay on Criticism* (1711), whose couplets caused a stir. *The Rape of the Lock* (1712) confirmed him as a poetic force. A mock epic, it can be enjoyed throughout as a true epic diminished to contemporary proportions. With *Windsor Forest* (1713) his popularity was further enhanced and he became a favourite in London, where he was now living. **Joseph Addison** and **Jonathan Swift** were among his acquaintances and he became a member of the Scriblerus Club. His persistent ambition was to translate **Homer**, and the first instalment of the *Iliad* appeared in 1715; when completed in 1720 its genius was immediately acknowledged though it bore flimsy resemblance to the original. During this time he also issued his *Works* (1717), a mix of odes, epistles, elegies and a translation of **Chaucer's** *The House of Fame*. He also met and befriended Lady **Mary Wortley Montagu**, a friendship which foundered after they quarrelled in 1723. Pope contemptuously dismissed her in a few lines in his *Imitations of Homer*. With the success of the *Iliad*, Pope was financially secure and was regarded as the senior figure of English letters. He bought a villa in Twickenham and lived there until his death. In 1726 he completed the *Odyssey*, following the failure of his edition of **Shakespeare** (1725) which Lewis Theobald (1688–1744) criticized for its slip-shoddiness and poor scholarship. Pope got his revenge in *The Dunciad* (1728), a mock-heroic satire, published anonymously, whose butt is 'Dulness' in general and, in particular, all the authors whom he wanted to hold up to ridicule. It is not, however, confined to personal animus, and literary vices are likewise exposed and scorned. With Swift, **John Gay**, Lord Oxford, **John Arbuthnot** and **Henry, 1st Viscount Bolingbroke** he arranged the publication of a *Miscellany* (3 vols, 1727–28). Pope's contributions included *An Epistle to Dr Arbuthnot* (published separately in 1735) and *Martinus Scriblerus peri Bathous: or The Art of Sinking in Poetry*, a satirical invective that insulted various poetasters. That and *The Dunciad* prompted a long, tiresome literary feud. In 1733–34 he published his *Essay on Man* and wrote *Moral Essays* (1731–35). His last years were engaged in organizing his correspondence for publication but while this marked a new development in English literature he tinkered too much with the originals and their value as social documents was impaired. Since his death his reputation has waxed, waned and waxed again. His technical brilliance has never been in doubt, but he lacked the surface warmth that endears lesser poets to the reading public. Nor was he an attractive figure, either in manner or physique. Much of this may have been due to inconsistent health, but without his abrasive side English satire would be the poorer, for he was the sharpest and most innovative of its practitioners. ▨ M Mack, *Alexander Pope, a life* (1985)

Pope, John 1822–92
US general

Born in Louisville, Kentucky, he trained at West Point, and served with the engineers in Florida (1842–44) and in the Mexican War (1846–48). He was exploring and surveying in the west until the Civil War (1861–65), when as brigadier-general in 1861 he drove the guerrillas out of Missouri. He commanded the army of the Mississippi (1862) and then that of Virginia, but was defeated at the second Battle of Bull Run (1862). He was transferred to Minnesota, where he kept the Native Americans in check.

Pope, Sir William Jackson 1870–1939
English chemist
Born in London, he studied at Finsbury Technical College and the Central Technical College at South Kensington, where he worked with Henry Armstrong. In 1897 he became head of the chemistry department of the Goldsmiths' Institute and in 1901 he moved to the Municipal School of Technology in Manchester. His final appointment in 1908, at the early age of 38, was to the chair of organic chemistry at Cambridge. He worked on a number of topics, including mustard gas, camphor, organometallic compounds and photographic sensitizers, but is best known for his work on optical activity. In 1899 he reported the synthesis and resolution of enantiomeric nitrogen compounds, and at Cambridge repeated this with sulphur and selenium. For his scientific work he was awarded the freedom and livery at the Goldsmiths' Company in 1919 and served as prime warden (1928–29). He was knighted in 1919.

Pope-Hennessy, Sir John 1913–94
English art historian
Born in London, he was educated at Balliol College, Oxford. He joined the staff of the Victoria and Albert Museum, London, in 1938, and has subsequently held many academic and curatorial posts, including Slade Professor of Fine Art at Oxford (1956–57), and at Cambridge (1964–65). He was director of the Victoria and Albert Museum (1967–73), and of the British Museum (1974–76), before going to New York, where he has been consultative chairman, department of European paintings, at the Metropolitan Museum since 1977. He was a leading authority on Italian renaissance art, and his many books include studies of Sienese painting, Paolo Uccello and Fra Angelico, and a series of definitive volumes on Italian sculpture.

Popham, Sir John c.1531–1607
English lawyer
Born near Bridgwater, Somerset, he became Speaker of the House of Commons in 1580 and Lord Chief Justice in 1592. He presided at the trial of Guy Fawkes.

Popiełuszko, Jerzy (Alfons) 1947–84
Polish priest
Born in Okopy, near Svchowola, Podlasie, he served in several Warsaw parishes after ordination and, inspired by the faith of his compatriot, St Maximilian Kolbe (1894–1941), he became an outspoken supporter of the Solidarity trade union, especially when it was banned in 1981 with the introduction of martial law. His sermons at 'Masses for the Country' regularly held in St Stanisław Kostka Church were widely acclaimed. He resisted official moves to have him silenced, but was kidnapped and murdered by the secret police in October 1984, more than a year after the lifting of martial law. It was probably this tragedy more than any other event that, in a profoundly Catholic country, spelt the eventual demise of the Communist Party. His grave and his church became a place of national pilgrimage.

Popov, Aleksandr Stepanovich 1859–1905
Russian physicist
Born in Bogoslavsky, he studied physics at St Petersburg University, and while still a student worked at the Elektrotekhnik artel (1881), which ran the first Russian small generating plants and arc light installations. He was appointed an instructor at the Russian navy's Torpedo School in Kronstadt (1881), and later professor at the St Petersburg Institute of Electrical Engineering (1905). Independently of Guglielmo Marconi, he is acclaimed in Russia as the inventor of wireless telegraphy (1895). He was the first to use a suspended wire as an aerial.

Popov, Gavril Kharitonovich 1936–
Soviet economist and politician
Of Greek ethnic background, he graduated in economics in Moscow and joined the Communist Party in 1959. He was appointed Dean of the Faculty of Economics in 1971 and, with official backing, proceeded to introduce management studies. He blossomed on Mikhail Gorbachev's accession to power. In 1989 he was elected to the Congress of Deputies and in 1990 became Mayor of Moscow. A fierce critic of the slow pace of change, he left the party in 1990 to survive Gorbachev's downfall in 1991.

Popova, Lyubov Sergeyevna, *née* Eding 1889–1924
Russian painter and stage designer
Born near Moscow, she studied in Paris (1912–13), then returned to Russia where she met Vladimir Tatlin, the founder of Soviet Constructivism. In the year before her death she designed textiles for the First State Textile Print Factory, Moscow, where she was given a memorial exhibition in 1924. Her work was especially important for its exploration of abstract colour values.

Poppaea Sabina d.65AD
Roman society beauty
She divorced her first husband in favour of her lover, Nero's playboy friend, the future Emperor Otho. She then became Nero's mistress, divorcing Otho to marry him in AD62. Her influence over Nero allegedly extended to his having his mother Agrippina, the Younger, and his former wife Octavia put to death, and ordering the philosopher Seneca to commit suicide. Poppaea Sabina shared the then fashionable interest in Judaism, and has been thought by many to have encouraged Nero in his vicious attack on the Christians in the aftermath of the Fire of Rome (64). Tradition relates that she was kicked to death by Nero while pregnant.

Popper, Sir Karl Raimund 1902–94
British philosopher
Born in Vienna, Austria, he studied at the university there and associated with the 'Vienna Circle' of philosophers, though he sharply criticized their logical positivism and their views, for example, on meaning and verification. He left Vienna in 1937 under the threat of German occupation, and taught philosophy at Canterbury University College, New Zealand (1937–45), and then was reader (1945–48) and later professor (1949–69) at the London School of Economics. His major work in scientific methodology, *Die Logik der Forschung* (1934, Eng trans *The Logic of Scientific Discovery*, 1959), stressed the importance of 'falsifiability' as a defining factor of true scientific theories, and contrasted these with 'pseudosciences', like Marxism and psychoanalysis, that would never specify in advance the conditions under which they could be tested and refuted. He extended the critique of Marxism in *The Open Society and its Enemies* (1945), a polemic directed against all philosophical systems with totalitarian political implications, from Plato to Karl Marx. He also attacked more generally the idea that historians and social scientists can discover large-scale laws of historical development with predictive potential and deals with the same theme in *The Poverty of Historicism* (1957). His later works include *Conjectures and Refutations* (1963), *Objective Knowledge* (1972), and *The Self and Its Brain* (1977, with Sir John Eccles). Knighted in 1965, he held the rare distinction of being a Fellow of both the British Academy and the Royal Society.

Pordenone, Il, *properly* Giovanni Antonio Licinio de Sacchis 1483–1539
Italian religious painter

Born in Corticelli near Pordenone, he settled in Venice in 1535, and was summoned by the Duke to Ferrara in 1538. He painted frescoes in the cathedral at Cremona and in Sta Maria da Campagna at Piacenza.

Porphyry c.232–c.305AD
Neoplatonist philosopher

Born of Syrian parents, probably in Tyre, where he spent his boyhood, he studied at Athens and gained a reputation as a polymathic scholar, 'a living library and a walking museum'. He went to Rome (c.263AD) where he became a disciple of Plotinus, and later his biographer and editor. He is probably most important as a popularizer of Plotinus's thought, but his own works include a celebrated treatise *Against the Christians*, of which only fragments remain, commentaries on Plato, Plotinus and Aristotle, *De Abstinentia* (a vegetarian tract), and a moral address to his wife, Marcella. His most influential work was the *Isagoge*, a commentary on Aristotle's *Categories*, which was translated into Latin by Boethius and was widely used in the Middle Ages.

Porpora, Niccola Antonio 1686–1766
Italian composer and teacher of singing

Born in Naples, he established a school for singing, which fostered many famous singers. From 1725 to 1755 he was in Dresden, Venice, London (1734–36) and Vienna (where he taught Haydn), composing operas and teaching. He is mentioned in George Sand's *Consuelo* (1842–44).

Porritt (of Wanganui and of Hampstead), Arthur Espie Porritt, Baron 1900–94
New Zealand diplomat, surgeon and Olympic athlete

He was born in Wanganui and became the first native-born Governor-General of New Zealand (1967–72). Educated at Otago University and at Magdalen College, Oxford, he took part in the Paris Olympics of 1924 as captain of the New Zealand team and won a bronze medal over 100 metres. He was captain in Amsterdam in 1928, and was manager of the New Zealand team in Berlin in 1936. In his professional career, he became a Fellow of the Royal College of Surgeons (1930) and was Surgeon to the Royal Household (1937–45), to George VI (1945–52) and Sergeant-Surgeon to Elizabeth II (1956–67). President of the British Medical Association (1960–61), the Royal College of Surgeons (1960–63) and the Royal Society of Medicine (1966–67), he was made a life peer in 1973. His eldest son is Jonathon Porritt.

Porritt, Sir Jonathon Espie 1950–
English broadcaster, writer and environmentalist

Born in London, the son and heir of Arthur Porritt, he was educated at Eton and Magdalen College, Oxford, where he read modern languages. He was a teacher until 1984, when he became director of Friends of the Earth (FoE). He stood as a candidate for the Ecology Party and later the Green Party in the UK general elections in 1979 and 1983 and European elections in 1979 and 1984, without success. In the late 1980s he became a well-known environmental figure through his work at FoE, publications and regular television appearances. He resigned from FoE in 1990 to concentrate on his freelance career as a writer and broadcaster. His books include *Seeing Green—the Politics of Ecology* (1984) and *The Coming of the Greens* (1988). In 1991 he presented the BBC television series *Where on Earth Are We Going?*, and he later became an adviser to Charles, Prince of Wales, and director of Forum for the Future (1996–).

Porsche, Ferdinand 1875–1951
German car designer

Born in Hafersfdorf, Bohemia, he designed cars for Daimler and Auto Union, but set up his own independent studio in 1931. In 1934 he produced the plans for a revolutionary cheap car with rear engine, to which the Nazis gave the name *Volkswagen* ('People's car') and which they promised to mass-produce for the German workers. After World War II the 'Beetle', as it was known, became a record-breaking German export. He also designed the distinctive sports car that bears his name. 📖 Richard von Frankenberg, *Porsche: The Man and His Cars* (1961)

Porsenan or Porsenna, Lars 6th century BC
Etruscan ruler of Clusium

In Roman tradition he laid siege to Rome after the overthrow (510BC) of Tarquinius Superbus, but was prevented from capturing the city by the heroism of Horatius Cocles defending the bridge across the Tiber. However, this tradition may conceal a temporary occupation of Rome by Porsena.

Porson, Richard 1759–1808
English Classical scholar

Born in East Rushton, Norfolk, the son of the parish clerk, he was precocious as a child and was educated by benefactors at Eton and Trinity College, Cambridge. He was appointed Regius Professor of Greek at Cambridge in 1792. He made his name as a defender of Erasmus Darwin in his brilliant *Letters to Archdeacon Travis* (1788–89) in the *Gentleman's Magazine* on the authenticity of the text of a passage in the First Epistle of St John (verse 7). He edited four plays by Euripides (1797–1801), and contributed hugely to Greek scholarship through his elucidation of idiom and usage and prosody.

Porta, Carlo 1776–1821
Italian poet

Born in Milan, and writing in the Milan dialect, he showed his insight into human character in narrative poems which are satirical and grimly realistic. These include *La Nomina del Capellan* (1819, 'The Selection of the Chaplain') and *Disgrazzi de Giovannin Bongee* (1812, 'The Misadventures of Giovannino Bongeri'). 📖 H Auréas, *Carlo Porta* (1959)

Porta, Giacomo Della 1541–1604
Italian architect

Born in Rome, he was a pupil of Giacomo Vignola, and is best known for the cupola of St Peter's and his work on the Palazzo Farnese, left unfinished by Michelangelo. He was also responsible for some of the fountains of Rome.

Porta, Giovanni Battista Della 1535–1615
Italian natural philosopher

He was born in Naples and was probably self-educated, though few details of his life are known apart from his writings. He wrote on such varied subjects as physiognomy, natural magic, crystallography and the classification of plants, besides several comedies. Most of his original work was in optics and the applications of steam. He was one of the first to study the camera obscura, discovered that the condensation of steam in a closed vessel leaves an empty space (the concept of a vacuum was then unknown), and designed a rudimentary steam-pump. Porta founded a number of scientific academies, and was admitted in 1610 as a member of the Accademia dei Linceị in Rome.

Portal (of Hungerford), Charles Frederick Algernon Portal, 1st Viscount 1893–1971
English air force officer

Born in Hungerford, Berkshire, of an ancient Huguenot family, he joined the Royal Engineers in 1914 and served in the Royal Flying Corps (1915–18). Promoted air vice-marshal in 1937, he was director of organization at the Air Ministry (1937–38). In 1940 (April–October) he was

Commander in Chief of Bomber Command, before becoming Chief of Air Staff (1940–46). He was controller of the Atomic Energy Authority (1946–51) and chairman of the British Aircraft Corporation (1960–68).

Portales, Diego 1793–1837
Chilean politician
A major trader in Valparaiso, he acquired a great interest in national affairs in 1824 when he was awarded the government monopoly on the sale of tobacco, tea and alcoholic beverages in return for servicing a British loan. As Chief Minister (1830–32, 1835–37), he was the key figure in creating a new and stable political system. He imposed the conservative constitution of 1833, which lasted until 1925, and created a centralized state, dominated by the Church and the landed classes. By 1835, he was effectively a dictator, having evolved a government of merchants and powerful landowners, whose tenants (inquilinos) served as an effective military force. He was murdered near Valparaiso by a group of soldiers during the war against General Andrés Santa Cruz's Peru–Bolivian Confederation, which was seen as a direct threat to the country.

Portalis, Jean Étienne Marie 1745–1807
French jurist and politician
He practised law in Paris, was imprisoned during the Revolution, but under Napoleon I was a principal draftsman of the *Code Civil*.

Porteous, John d.1736
Scottish soldier
Born in Edinburgh, he trained as a tailor, but then enlisted in the army. He was appointed to the Edinburgh town guard, which was being trained as a civil militia against the 1715 Jacobite Rising. On 14 April 1736 he was in charge at the execution of Andrew Wilson, a smuggler. There was some stone-throwing, and the guard fired on the mob, wounding 12 persons and killing three (the so-called 'Porteous Riot'). Porteous was tried and condemned to death (20 July), but reprieved by Queen Caroline of Anspach. However, on the night of 7 September a mob snatched Porteous and hanged him. The story is told in Walter Scott's *The Heart of Midlothian*.

Porter, Cole 1891–1964
US composer
Born in Peru, Indiana, he studied law at Harvard before deciding upon a musical career. From his first hit on Broadway in 1929 he created a series of successful musical comedies, including *Anything Goes* (1934) and *DuBarry Was a Lady* (1939), writing both lyrics and music for numerous classics of US popular song, such as 'You Do Something To Me', 'I Get a Kick Out of You', 'You're the Top' and 'Just One of Those Things'. In 1937 he was severely hurt in a riding accident, which left him in permanent pain, but he continued to compose, reaching the height of his success with *Kiss Me Kate* (1948) and *Can-Can* (1953). His style ranges from the unabashed romanticism of 'Night and Day' (1932) to the droll wordplay and doubles entendres of 'Too Darn Hot'.

Porter, David 1780–1843
US naval officer
Born in Boston, he joined the navy in 1798, became captain in 1812, and captured the first British warship taken in the War of 1812. In 1813 he took possession of the Marquesas Islands, but in 1814 his frigate was captured by the British off Valparaiso. He afterwards commanded an expedition against pirates in the West Indies (1823–25). He resigned in 1826, and for a time commanded the Mexican navy. In 1829 the USA appointed him consul-general to the Barbary States, and then Minister at Constantinople (Istanbul).

Porter, David Dixon 1813–91
US naval officer
Born in Chester, Pennsylvania, the son of David Porter, he accompanied his father against the pirates in the West Indies, and in the Mexican navy. In the Civil War, as commander of the federal mortar flotilla, he bombarded the New Orleans forts in April 1862. In September, with the Mississippi squadron, he passed the batteries of Vicksburg, and bombarded the city, and in January 1865 he took Fort Fisher. He was made Admiral of the Navy in 1870. As well as three romances, he wrote *Incidents of the Civil War* (1885) and *History of the Navy During the War of the Rebellion* (1887).

Porter, Eleanor, *née* Hodgman 1868–1920
US novelist
She was born in Littleton, New Hampshire, and studied music at the New England Conservatory. Her first novels included *Cross Currents* (1907) and *Miss Billy* (1911). In 1913 she published *Pollyanna*, the story of an orphaned girl who goes to live with her stern aunt, which was an immediate success and has retained its popularity ever since. A sequel, about the 'glad child', *Pollyanna Grows Up*, was published in 1915, and two volumes of short stories, *The Tangled Threads* and *Across the Years*, appeared posthumously in 1924.

Porter, Eric Richard 1928–95
English actor
Born in London, he made his first appearance in 1945 at the Arts Theatre, Cambridge, and his London debut in 1946. After service in the RAF (1946–47) he toured with Donald Wolfit's company, and joined John Gielgud's company at the Lyric Theatre, Hammersmith (1952–53). He has built up a formidable reputation as an actor in both classical and modern roles at the Old Vic, the Royal Shakespeare Company, and the National Theatre, where he gave a magnificent performance as Big Daddy in Tennessee Williams's *Cat on a Hot Tin Roof* in 1988 and, the following year, as King Lear in Jonathan Miller's dark and brooding revival at the Old Vic. In 1992 he was a hilariously tactless and vain Professor Serebryakov in *Uncle Vanya*. He also made several film and television appearances, notably in the BBC television series, *The Forsyte Saga*.

Porter (of Luddenham), George Porter, Baron 1920–
English physical chemist and Nobel Prize winner
Born in Stainforth, Yorkshire, he studied chemistry at Leeds University, and then entered Cambridge for his PhD. He became Professor of Physical Chemistry at Sheffield University in 1955, in 1963 transferring to the Firth Chair of Chemistry. In 1966 he was appointed Resident Professor and Director of the Royal Institution, where he remained until 1985. His researches have mainly been concerned with gaseous reactions, especially photochemical reactions, and with photochemistry generally. In the late 1940s, Ronald Norrish and Porter developed the technique of flash photolysis, which became important in the study of very rapid gas reactions. With Manfred Eigen, they were awarded the 1967 Nobel Prize for chemistry for this work. In flash photolysis a very brief flash of intense light causes photochemical change, allowing the unstable chemical intermediates produced to be studied through their absorption spectra. Improvements over the past 40 years have enabled species to be studied even if they only survive for the tiniest fraction of a second. Porter has been prominent in refining these techniques and in exploring the range of fast processes which may be studied. In later years he became prominent as a spokesman for science in the UK. He was knighted in 1972, admitted to the Order of Merit in 1989, and made a life peer in 1990.

He was elected Fellow of the Royal Society in 1960, served as its president from 1985 to 1990, and was president of the Chemical Society from 1970 to 1972.

Porter, Katherine Anne Maria Veronica Callista Russell 1890–1980
US writer

Born in Indian Creek, Texas, she was brought up by a grandmother near Kyle, Texas, and after running away and getting married at the age of 16, she divorced at 19. She worked as a reporter and actress, moved to Greenwich Village, New York, and then went to Mexico (1920–22), where she took up Mexican causes. She had started writing at a very early age, but allowed nothing to be published until 1930, with her first collection of stories, *Flowering Judas*. Later, in Paris, she wrote her first novel, *Hacienda* (1934). Back in the USA, three short novels, published as *Pale Horse, Pale Rider* (1939), were a success. *Ship of Fools* (1962), a huge allegorical novel analysing the German state of mind in the 1930s, was almost universally regarded as a failure. A volume of essays, *The Days Before*, appeared in 1952. Her *Collected Short Stories* (1965) won a Pulitzer Prize. □ R B West, *Katherine Anne Porter* (1963)

Porter, Michael c.1947–
US management theorist

Born in Ann Arbor, Michigan, he trained as an economist at Princeton and Harvard Business School. He became a lecturer at Harvard (1973) and subsequently professor (1982). In 1983 he founded Monitor Co Inc, a strategic consulting organization. He was in great demand throughout the 1980s as a lecturer and consultant to many leading US and UK organizations. In 1980 he published *Competitive Analysis* and in 1989 *The Competitive Advantage of Nations and Their Firms*.

Porter, Noah 1811–92
US clergyman

Born in Farmington, Connecticut, he studied at Yale and was a Congregational pastor (1836–46). He was Professor of Moral Philosophy at Yale, and from 1871 to 1886 was president of the college. He was editor-in-chief of *Webster's American Dictionary of the English Language* (1864) and *Webster's International Dictionary of the English Language* (1890). Among his other works are *The Human Intellect* (1868), *Books and Reading* (1870), and *Moral Science* (1885).

Porter, Peter Neville Frederick 1929–
Australian poet and critic

Born in Brisbane, he has lived in England since 1951 and has worked as a bookseller, journalist, clerk and advertising copywriter. His collections include *Once Bitten, Twice Bitten* (1961), a satirical treatment of 1960s Great Britain, *Words Without Music* (1968), *A Porter Folio* (1969), *The Last of England* (1970) and *The Cost of Seriousness* (1978). His *Collected Poems* (1983) confirmed him as a gifted aphorist, and he won the Whitbread award for *The Automatic Oracle* (1987). He has published two volumes of translation from Latin, *Epigrams by Martial* (1971) and *After Martial* (1972), showing an affection for the classics which is evident in his poem 'On First Looking Into Chapman's *Hesiod*' (1975). Later publications include *Possible Worlds* (1989), *The Chair of Babel* (1992) and *Millennial Fables* (1995). □ R Garfit, in *British Poetry since 1960* (1972, eds M Schmidt and G Lindop)

Porter, Rodney Robert 1917–85
English biochemist and Nobel Prize winner

Born in Newton-le-Willows, Lancashire, he studied there and with **Frederick Sanger** in Cambridge (1946–49), then worked at the National Institute for Medical Research (1949–60) and St Mary's Hospital Medical School in London (1960–67), before becoming Professor of Biochemistry at Oxford in 1967. He studied the biochemistry of antibodies, and was the first to propose the bilaterally symmetrical four-chain structure which is the basis of all immunoglobulins. **Gerald Edelman** carried out complementary structural studies on immunoglobulins in the USA, and for this work they were jointly awarded the Nobel Prize for physiology or medicine in 1972. Porter was elected a Fellow of the Royal Society in 1964, and was awarded its Royal (1973) and Copley (1983) medals. In 1985 he was run over and killed while crossing a road. □ S V Perry, *Professor Rodney Porter: a biographical memoir* (1987)

Porter, Dame Shirley, *née* Cohen 1930–
English Conservative politician

Born in London, the daughter of Jack Cohen, the founder of the Tesco supermarket chain, she married a businessman, Sir Leslie Porter, in 1949 and began a career in public life. She was elected to Westminster City Council as a Conservative in 1974, became its leader in 1983, then was Lord Mayor between 1991 and 1992. Her policies were controversial and included the rehousing of poor people outside Westminster and the selling of council houses, which led to a public inquiry over accusations of gerrymandering before the 1990 election. She subsequently appealed against the district auditor's findings in the inquiry.

Portillo, Michael 1953–
English Conservative politician

Born in Bushey, Hertfordshire, and educated at Harrow County School and Peterhouse, Cambridge, he joined the Conservative Research Department in 1976 and was elected Conservative MP for Enfield Southgate in 1984. He became Chief Secretary to the Treasury in 1992 and later served as Secretary of State for Employment (1994) and Secretary of State for Defence (1995–97). With his beliefs in a free market economy he stands to the right of the party and was regarded as a potential future leader, but he lost his seat in the 1997 general election.

Portland, 3rd Duke of See **Bentinck, William Henry Cavendish**

Porto-Riche, Georges de 1849–1930
French dramatist

He was born in Bordeaux. After an early success with *La Chance de Françoise* (1889, 'Françoise's Luck'), he wrote several successful psychological plays which investigated the relationships between men and women in love, including *L'Amoureuse* (1891, 'The Woman in Love'), *Le Vieil homme* (1911, 'The Old Man') and *Le Marchand d'estampes* (1917, 'The Print Seller').

Portsmouth, Louise de Kéroualle or Querouaille, Duchess of 1649–1734
French courtesan, mistress of Charles II of Britain

Born in Brittany, she went to England in 1670 in the train of **Henrietta-Anne**, Duchess of Orléans, **Charles II's** cherished sister, ostensibly as a lady-in-waiting, but secretly charged to influence the king in favour of the French alliance. Charles made her his mistress and ennobled her (1673) and her son, who became Duke of Richmond. Rapacious and haughty, 'Madame Carwell', as she became known, was universally detested.

Posidonius, *nicknamed* the Athlete c.135–c.51 BC
Greek philosopher, scientist and polymath

Born in Apamea, Syria, he studied at Athens as a pupil of **Panaetius**, spent many years on travel and scientific research in Europe and Africa, then settled in Rhodes, where he was head of the Stoic school, and later Rome (86 BC). There he became a friend of **Cicero** and other leading figures of the day. He wrote on a vast range of subjects, including geometry, geography, astronomy, meteorology, history and philosophy, although only fragments of his works survive. He made important contributions to the development of Stoic doctrines, and also

ultimately influenced **Columbus** by his reported remark that a man sailing west from Europe would reach India.
📖 Jurgen Malitz, *Die Historien des Poseidonius* (1983)

Post, Emily, *née* Price 1873–1960
US writer and socialite

Born into a wealthy family in Baltimore, Maryland, she was educated in New York and married in 1892, but divorced after having two children. She then began a career writing novels and society journalism, gradually allowing her interest in correct social behaviour to develop. She found lasting fame with *Etiquette in Society, in Business, in Politics and at Home* (1922), which became better known as *Etiquette: The Blue Book of Social Usage*. By the time of her death it had sold more than a million copies. She also wrote *How to Behave Though a Debutante* (1928) and a book about interior decorating, *The Personality of a House* (1930). In 1946 she founded the Emily Post Institute for the Study of Gracious Living.

Post, Sir Laurens van der See van der Post, Sir Laurens Jan

Post, Wiley 1900–35
US pioneer aviator

Born in Grand Saline, Texas, he toured the country as a mechanic, stunt parachutist and wingwalker in the early 1920s, and learned to fly in 1924. On 23 June 1931 he left Roosevelt Field, New York City, in a Lockheed Vega monoplane, with the Australian Harold Gatty (1903–57) as navigator, to fly around the world in eight days, 15 hours and 51 minutes. (The previous record had been made by the Graf Zeppelin in 21 days.) In 1933 he made the first solo flight round the world, in seven days, 18 hours and 49 minutes. He was killed in an air crash in Alaska.

Postan, Eileen Edna le Poer, *née* Power 1889–1940
English expert on women's historical studies

Born in Altringham, Cheshire, she excelled in her scholastic career at Cambridge, in Paris, and at the London School of Economics. She became fascinated by women's role in economic history, and was appointed Professor of Economic History at LSE. Now recognized as an expert in British women's historical studies, she produced an outstanding series of publications, from *Medieval English Nunneries* (1922) through the *Economic History Review*, which she founded in 1927, to *Medieval Women*, published 35 years after her death.

Potemkin, Grigori Aleksandrovich 1739–91
Russian soldier and politician

Born near Smolensk, of a noble but impoverished Polish family, he entered the Russian Horse Guards in 1755, and attracted the notice of **Catherine the Great** by his good looks. In 1774 he became her lover, and directed Russian policy. They may have secretly married. In charge of the newly acquired lands in the south, he made an able administrator, and constructed a fleet in the Black Sea. In the Second Turkish War (1787–92) he headed the army, and took the credit for Count **Suvorov**'s victories (1791). He gained for Russia the Crimea and the north coast of the Black Sea, and he founded Sebastopol, Nikolaev and Yekaterinoslav (Dnipropetrovsk). 📖 George Soloveytchik, *Potemkin* (1938)

Pothier, Robert Joseph 1699–1772
French jurist and judge

He carried out a close study of **Justinian**'s *Corpus Juris Civilis* with its confused order of texts, and between 1748 and 1752 published the texts rearranged within the titles in logical order. He also added a learned preface about the sources of Roman law and the characteristics of the jurists from whose works excerpts appear in the *Digest*. In 1749 he

became Professor of Law at Orleans and revived that law school. In 1761 he produced a work on the customary law of Orleans, comparing it with other regional customs. This was followed by a series of texts on the specific topics of the law, such as sale, hiring, ownership, possession, etc. The most influential of these has been the *Treatise on Obligations*. Large parts of his works were incorporated almost verbatim in the French Civil Code of 1808.

Potok, Chaim (Herman Harold) 1929–
US novelist

Born and educated in New York City, he studied there at Yeshiva University and the Jewish Theological Seminary. He was ordained as a rabbi in 1954. After teaching in seminaries, he became scholar-in-residence at Har Zion Temple in Philadelphia (1959–63) and, later, special projects editor at the Jewish Publication Society, for whom he wrote a 14-pamphlet series on *Jewish Ethics* (1964–69). His novels explore the problems of Orthodox and Hasidic communities within an aggressively secular society, but they are, if anything, more directly concerned with conflicts *within* Judaism than between Jews and WASPs. His work includes *The Chosen* (1967), and the controversial *My Name Is Asher Lev* (1972), in which the hero abandons his religious calling to become a painter, shocking his community with a work called 'Brooklyn Crucifixion'. Later works include *The Book of Lights* (1982) and *Davita's Harp* (1985), and in 1990 his troubled artist-hero reappeared in *The Gift of Asher Lev*. His *Wanderings* (1978) is a scholarly but personal history of the Jews.

Pott, Percival 1714–88
English surgeon

Born in London, he became assistant and then senior surgeon at St Bartholomew's Hospital, where he introduced many improvements to make surgery more humane. He wrote *Fractures and Dislocations* (1765), in which he described a compound leg fracture suffered by himself, still called 'Pott's fracture', and gave a clinical account of 'Pott's disease' of the spine.

Potter, Beatrix See panel p1494

Potter, Dennis Christopher George 1935–94
English dramatist

He was born in Forest of Dean, Gloucestershire, and was educated at Oxford, working as a journalist and television critic before turning to writing plays. Although he wrote for the stage (*Sufficient Carbohydrate*, 1984), he was primarily a television dramatist. Following *Vote, Vote, Vote for Nigel Barton* (1965), he wrote over 25 television plays and series. *Son of Man* (1969) was the first television screenplay that depicted Christ as a man who struggled as much with his own doubts as with those opposed to his teaching. Other controversial plays include *Brimstone and Treacle* (1978), *The Singing Detective* (1986) and *Blackeyes* (1989). He was also technically innovative: *Pennies from Heaven* (1978) required the actors to mime to popular songs of the 1920s and 30s that intercut the action, and *Blue Remembered Hills* (1979), a memory play, required the adult actors to impersonate children. Later television dramas include *Lipstick On Your Collar* (1993). His novel *Ticket to Ride* (1986) was adapted as the film *Secret Friends* (1992). The undisputed master of the serious television play, he completed two final dramas just before his death, *Karaoke* and *Cold Lazarus*, which were broadcast in 1996.

Potter, Paul 1625–54
Dutch painter and etcher

He was born in Enkhuizen, the son of a painter. His best pictures are small pastoral scenes with animal figures. He also painted large pictures, his life-size *Young Bull* (1647) being especially celebrated.

Potter, (Helen) Beatrix 1866–1943
English author and illustrator of books for children

Beatrix Potter was born in Kensington, London, into a wealthy family. The atmosphere at home was oppressively quiet and Beatrix, supervised by nurses and educated by governesses, grew up a lonely town child longing for the country. She taught herself to draw and paint, and while still quite young did serious natural history studies of fungi with the intention of making a book of watercolours.

She turned to sketching pet animals dressed as human beings in order to amuse younger children. The original version of *The Tale of Peter Rabbit* was enclosed with a letter to her ex-governess's child in 1893 and later published at her own expense, with fuller illustrations, in 1900, as was *The Tailor of Gloucester* (1902). When Frederick Warne took over publication in 1903 she had her first popular success with *The Tale of Squirrel Nutkin* (1903). In an appreciative, if gently satirical, review **Graham Greene** considered *The Roly-Poly Pudding* (1908, later changed to *The Tale of Samuel Whiskers*), to be her masterpiece. Miss Potter was not amused.

In 1913, eight years after she had moved to a farm at Sawrey, near Lake Windermere (where six of her books are set), she married William Heelis, a Lake District solicitor. Thereafter she devoted herself almost entirely to farming and the National Trust (founded in 1895). *Johnny*

Town-Mouse (1918) was her last book in the familiar style. She devised an elaborate cryptic diary whose code was later broken and published as *The Journal of Beatrix Potter 1881–1897* (1966).

Beatrix Potter wrote with great realism and without sentimentality; the animal world she describes is constantly threatened by deceit, physical harm and death. She was the outstanding writer and artist of picture-story books of her time, and her characters have become classics of children's literature. Despite the essential Englishness of her stories, they have been translated into many languages, including Welsh, French, German, Dutch and Japanese.

📖 More has been written about Beatrix Potter than about any other children's writer except **Lewis Carroll**. Her diary was published by L Linder, *The Journal of Beatrix Potter* (1966). See also M Lane, *The Tale of Beatrix Potter* (1946) and *The Magic Years of Beatrix Potter* (1978).

'You may go into the field or down the lane, but don't go into Mr McGregor's garden: your Father had an accident there; he was put in a pie by Mrs McGregor.' From *The Tale of Peter Rabbit.*

Potter, Philip 1921–
Dominican ecumenical leader

He was born in Roseau, Dominica, and after studying law and pastoring a Methodist church in Haiti, he became secretary of the youth department of the World Council of Churches in 1954. Appointed Methodist Missionary Society (London) field secretary for Africa and the West Indies (1960–67) and chairman of the World Student Christian Federation (1960–68), he was promoted director of World Mission and Evangelism (1967–72) and then general secretary (1972–84) of the World Council of Churches. His aim has been described as one of keeping the ecumenical movement theologically faithful and socially credible, and his publications include *Life in All its Fullness* (1981).

Potter, Stephen 1900–69
English writer and radio producer

He joined the BBC in 1938, and was co-author with **Joyce Grenfell** of the *How* series. He wrote a novel, *The Young Man* (1929), and an educational study, *The Muse in Chains* (1937), but made his name with a series of comic books on the art of establishing personal supremacy by demoralizing the opposition: *Gamesmanship* (1947), *Lifemanship* (1950), *One-Upmanship* (1952), *Potter on America* (1956) and *Supermanship* (1958). 📖 Alan Jenkins, *Stephen Potter: Inventor of Gamesmanship* (1980)

Poujade, Pierre 1920–
French political leader

Born in Saint Céré, after serving in World War II, he became a publisher and bookseller there. In 1951 he was elected a member of the Saint Céré municipal council, and in 1954 he organized his Poujadist movement (union for the defence of tradesmen and artisans) as a protest against the French tax system. His party had successes in the 1956 elections to the National Assembly, but disappeared in 1958. **Jean-Marie Le Pen**, leader of the National Front, was first elected as a Poujadist Deputy in 1956. Poujade published his manifesto *J'ai choisi le combat* in 1956.

Poulenc, Francis 1899–1963
French composer

Born in Paris, he studied composition under **Charles Koechlin**, came under the influence of **Erik Satie**, and as a member of Les Six was prominent in the reaction against 'Debussyesque' Impressionism. He wrote chamber music in a cool, limpid style, often for unusual combinations of instruments, and is also known for impressive stage works, especially the ballet *Les Biches* (1923, 'The Little Darlings'), and the operas *Les Mamelles de Tirésias* (1944, 'The Breasts of Tiresias') and *Dialogues des Carmélites* (1953–56, 'The Carmelites' Dialogues'). His cantata *Figure humaine* (1945) has as its theme the occupation of France. Perhaps his major contribution to music is his considerable output of songs, more romantic in outlook than his other compositions, which include *Poèmes de Ronsard* (1924), and *Fêtes galantes* (1943). 📖 Pierre Bernac, *Francis Poulenc: The Man and His Songs* (1977)

Poulet, Sir Amyas See **Paulet, Sir Amyas**

Poulsen, Valdemar 1869–1942
Danish electrical engineer

He was born in Copenhagen. While working for the Copenhagen Telephone Company, he invented the telegraphone, a wire recording device which was a forerunner of the magnetic tape recorder (1898). In 1903 he devised an arc generator for use in wireless telegraphy.

Pound, (Alfred) Dudley Pickman Rogers 1877–1943
English naval commander

He became captain in 1914, commanded with distinction the battleship *Colossus* at the Battle of Jutland (1916), and for the remaining two years of World War I directed operations at the Admiralty. Promoted rear admiral, he was Commander-in-Chief Mediterranean fleet (1936–39), becoming in 1939 Admiral of the Fleet and First Sea Lord.

Pound, Ezra Loomis 1885–1972
US poet, translator and critic

He was born in Hailey, Idaho, and brought up in Wyncote, near Philadelphia. He graduated from Pennsylvania University in 1906, became an instructor in Wabash College in Crawfordsville, Indiana, and after four months left for Europe, travelling widely in Spain, Italy and Provence. He published his first collection of poems,

A Lume Spento (1908, 'With Tapers Quenched'), in Venice. In London he met **Ford Madox Ford**, **James Joyce** and **Wyndham Lewis**, and published *Personae* and *Exultations* in 1909, followed by a book of critical essays, *The Spirit of Romance* (1910). He was co-editor of *Blast* (1914–15), the magazine of the short-lived 'Vorticist' movement, and London editor of the Chicago *Little Review* (1917–19), and in 1920 became Paris correspondent for *The Dial*. From 1924 he made his home in Italy. He became involved with fascist ideas and created resentment by anti-democracy broadcasts in the early stages of World War I. In 1945 he was escorted back to the USA and indicted for treason. The trial did not proceed, however, as he was adjudged insane, and placed in an asylum until 1958 when he returned to Italy. In addition to poetry, he wrote books on literature, music, art and economics, and translated much from Italian, French, Chinese and Japanese. As a poet of the Imagist school at the outset of his career, he was a thoroughgoing experimenter, deploying much curious and often spurious learning in his illustrative imagery and in the development of his themes. **T S Eliot** regarded him as the motivating force behind 'modern' poetry, the poet who created a climate in which English and US poets could understand and appreciate each other. *Homage to Sextus Propertius* (1919) and *Hugh Selwyn Mauberley* (1920) are among his most important early poems. His *Cantos*, a loosely-knit series of poems, appeared first in 1917, continuing in many instalments, via the *Pisan Cantos* (1948) to *Thrones: Cantos 96–109* (1959). His work in the classics and Chinese poetry are discernible in their form. Apart from his life work in poetry, his significant collections are *Translations of Ezra Pound* (1933) and *Literary Essays* (1954). 📖 H Kenner, *The Pound Era* (1971); N Stock, *The Life of Ezra Pound* (1970, revised edition 1982)

Pound, Roscoe 1870–1964
US jurist and botanist

Born in Lincoln, Nebraska, he was educated at Nebraska University and Harvard Law School. His appointments included Commissioner of Appeals of the Supreme Court of Nebraska (1901–03), assistant Professor of Law at Nebraska University (1899–1903), and successively Professor of Law at Northwestern University (1907), Chicago University (1909) and Harvard Law School (1910–37). An able and influential teacher, especially of jurisprudence, he emphasizes the importance of social interests in connection with the law, and his theories have had a universal effect. His many legal writings include *Readings on the History and System of the Common Law* (1904), *Introduction to the Philosophy of Law* (1922), *Law and Morals* (1924), *Criminal Justice in America* (1930) and *Jurisprudence* (5 vols, 1959). An authority also on botany, he was largely responsible for the botanical survey of Nebraska, and on this subject, in collaboration with Dr F E Clements, wrote *Phyto-geography of Nebraska* (1898). A rare lichen is named after him.

Pounds, John 1766–1839
English shoemaker and philanthropist

Born in Portsmouth, he became an unpaid teacher of poor children, and is regarded as the founder of ragged schools.

Poussin, Gaspard See Dughet, Gaspard

Poussin, Nicolas See panel p1496

Powderly, Terence Vincent 1849–1924
US labour leader

Born into an Irish immigrant family in Carbondale, Pennsylvania, he began working on the railroad at the age of 13. After four years' apprenticeship he became a machinist in 1869, joined its union in 1871, became president in 1872, and worked as Pennsylvania organizer for the Industrial Brotherhood. He joined the secret oath-bound Knights of Labor in 1874, and became its Grand Master Workman in 1879 and General Master Workman from 1883 to 1893. He worked to make the Knights a union for all forms of labour, brought it into touch with developing new ideas of labour organization and philosophy such as that of **Henry George**, politicized it, and sought to further labour causes wherever possible. He was critical of the use of strikes, although strongly interested in the development of the boycott from its use in Ireland in the Land War of 1879–82. He saw the Knights mushroom to a million members in 1886, but his ideas and charisma were not matched by administrative skills. The Knights had declined badly by the time Powderly took up a second career in law. He was Commissioner-General of Immigration (1897–1902), and head of the division of information in the Immigration Bureau (1907–21). He wrote *Thirty Years of Labor* (1889) and a posthumously published autobiography, *The Path I Trod* (1940).

Powell, Adam Clayton, Jnr 1908–72
US politician

Born in New Haven, Connecticut, the son of the pastor of the Abyssinian Baptist Church in Harlem, New York City, he earned a doctorate in divinity from Shaw University and succeeded his father as pastor in 1937. With the African-Americans of New York solidly behind him, he served in the US House of Representatives (1945–67, 1969–71). He was the first to use the phrase 'Black Power' (at Howard University in 1966) and he acted as convenor of the first National Conference on Black Power. Known for his insistence on complete equality for African-Americans, he fought against segregation and for fair employment practices. He was stripped of his House seat in 1967 after being charged with the misuse of public funds and other improprieties, but the Supreme Court overturned his expulsion in 1969. He lost his seat in 1970.

Powell, Anthony Dymoke 1905–
English novelist

Born in London, the son of an army officer, he was educated at Eton and Balliol College, Oxford, where he met several other young writers, including **Evelyn Waugh** and **Graham Greene**. He worked in publishing and journalism before World War II, and by 1936 had published four satirical novels, among them *Afternoon Men* (1931), *Venusberg* (1932) and *What's Become of Waring?* (1939). After the war he returned to book-reviewing, wrote a biography of **John Aubrey** (1948), and began the series of novels he called *A Dance to the Music of Time*—12 volumes, beginning with *A Question of Upbringing* (1951), covering 50 years of British upper-middle-class life and attitudes. In this series the light, witty, satirical tone of the pre-war novels developed into an intricate and disciplined interweaving of personal relationships, ironic, humorous, and with extraordinary scope and depth of vision. He has won the James Tait Black Memorial Prize and W H Smith Literary award. Since the completion of the cycle with *Hearing Secret Harmonies* (1975), he has published a four-volume autobiography, *To Keep the Ball Rolling* (1976–82), and two novels, *O, How the Wheel Becomes It!* (1983) and *The Fisher King* (1986), and two volumes of criticism, *Miscellaneous Verdicts* (1990) and *Under Review* (1992). His *Journals 1982–1986* were published in 1995. 📖 B Bergonzi, *Anthony Powell* (1962)

Powell, Bud (Earl) 1924–66
US jazz pianist

He was born in New York City. A jazz virtuoso, he was the most influential bebop stylist on his instrument. Playing from the age of six, he became interested in jazz as a teenager, involving himself with the modern jazz movement in the 1940s with encouragement from **Thelonious Monk**. His mental instability brought periodic visits to mental hospitals, and a concomitant unevenness (and

---

Poussin, Nicolas 1594–1665
French painter, among the greatest exponents of 17th-century Baroque Classicism

Poussin was born in Les Andelys, Normandy. After struggling to make a living in Paris, he earned enough money to visit Rome in 1624, where he received commissions from Cardinal Francesco Barberini (1597–1679, nephew of the reigning pope, **Urban VIII**) and soon became rich and famous. Among the masterpieces dating from this period is *The Adoration of the Golden Calf*, now in the London National Gallery.

In 1640 he was ordered by King **Louis XIII** and Cardinal **Richelieu** to return to France, where he was appointed painter-in-ordinary to the king. However, the types of work he was expected to carry out, principally altarpieces and mural decorations, were unsuited to his abilities and in 1643 he returned to Rome.

He constructed his historical pictures with great deliberation and after much experimentation, even going so far as to make small clay models of his scenes to make sure the lighting was right. From this relentless search for perfection he evolved the prototype for the History Picture, which was considered academically as the highest form of art; painters strove to emulate Poussin's achievements

for the next two centuries. His œuvre also includes biblical subjects, mythological works and, from his later years, landscape.

Among the most admired works of Poussin are *Cephalus and Aurora* (1630, National Gallery, London), *The Inspiration of the Poet* (1636, Louvre, Paris), *The Rape of the Sabine Women* (1636–37, Metropolitan Museum of Art, New York), *Bacchanalian Festival* (1640, National Gallery, London), *The Arcadian Shepherds* (1638–39), and *Landscape with the Burial of Phocion* (1648, Louvre).

📖 Anthony Blunt, *Poussin* (2 vols, 1967–68) and *The Paintings of Nicolas Poussin* (1966); W F Friedlaender, *Nicolas Poussin: A New Approach* (1966).

> 'The grand manner consists of four elements: subject or theme, concept, structure, and style. The first requirement, fundamental to all the others, is that the subject and the narrative be grandiose, such as battles, heroic actions, and religious themes.' Quoted in Giovanni Pietro Bellori, *Lives of the Modern Painters* (1672).

---

ultimate decline) in his creative powers. That instability was exacerbated by narcotics, and the death of his brother, pianist Richie Powell, in a car accident in 1956 which also killed the brilliant trumpeter, Clifford Brown. He moved to Paris from 1959 to 1964, where he led a trio featuring American expatriate drummer Kenny Clarke, another bebop innovator. He died in New York. 📖 A Groves, *The Glass Enclosure* (1993)

Powell, Cecil Frank 1903–69
English physicist and Nobel Prize winner

Born in Tonbridge, Kent, he was educated at Cambridge, where he received his PhD in 1927. Throughout his career he worked at the University of Bristol, as Wills Professor of Physics (1948–63) and subsequently as director of the Wills Physics Laboratory. A former pupil of **Ernest Rutherford** and **Charles Wilson**, Powell used specially developed photographic emulsions to study nuclear interactions and improved the techniques used to analyse nuclear particle tracks. In 1950 he was awarded the Nobel Prize for physics for his development of nuclear emulsions and his part in the discovery of the charged pion, a particle which had been predicted by **Hideki Yukawa** in 1935. In addition to his scientific work he was one of the leaders of the movement to increase the social responsibility of scientists.

Powell, Colin Luther 1937–
US soldier

Born in Harlem, New York City, the son of Jamaican immigrants, he received an elementary education before joining the US army in 1963. He rose through the ranks, winning a Purple Heart and Bronze Star during the Vietnam War, to become the first US commander never to have attended West Point. He served as National Security Adviser (1987–89) to **Ronald Reagan**, and in 1989 he was appointed chairman of the Joint Chiefs of Staff, the youngest man and the first African-American to attain this position. In the prelude to the 1991 Gulf War he was given charge of Operation Desert Shield as supreme commander of all US air and land forces, answering directly to **George Bush**. Although he tended to be eclipsed in media terms during the height of the conflict by his second-in-command, General **Norman Schwarzkopf**, he played a major role in planning the successful US strategy of Operation Desert Storm. He resigned as chairman in 1993. The publication of his bestselling autobiography,

My American Journey (1995), led to widespread speculations about his possible presidential candidacy in 1996, but he declined to run.

Powell, (Elizabeth) Dilys 1901–95
British film critic and writer

She was educated at Bournemouth High School and Somerville College, Oxford, where she met her first husband, Humfry Payne. She married him in 1926 and moved to Greece. Two years later she started work at the *Sunday Times*. Payne died suddenly in Greece in 1936, prompting Powell to write, amongst other works, *The Traveller's Journey is Done* (1943) and *The Villa Ariadne* (1973). She worked as a film critic for the *Sunday Times* (1939–79) and married its literary editor, Leonard Russell, in 1943. She sat on the Board of Governors at the British Film Institute (1948–52), reviewed films on television from 1976, and wrote film reviews for *Punch* (1979–92). Her reviews have been published as *The Golden Screen* (1989) and *The Dilys Powell Film Reader* (1991).

Powell, (John) Enoch 1912–98
English Conservative politician and scholar

Born in Stechford, Birmingham, he was educated at King Edward's School, Birmingham, and Trinity College, Cambridge, becoming Professor of Greek at Sydney University (1937–39). He enlisted in World War II as a private in 1939, was commissioned in 1940 and rose to the rank of brigadier. In 1946 he joined the Conservative Party, and in 1950 entered parliament as MP for Wolverhampton. He held offices including Parliamentary Secretary, Ministry of Housing (1955–57); Financial Secretary to the Treasury from 1957, resigning with **Peter Thorneycroft** over policy differences in 1958; and Minister of Health from 1960, resigning again over the appointment of Sir Alec Douglas-Home (Lord **Home**) as Prime Minister in 1963. His austere brand of intellectualism, his adherence to the principles of high Toryism in economic planning, and his radical views on defence and foreign commitments made him a significant figure within his party. He created more general controversy by his outspoken attitude to non-white immigration and racial integration and alarmed many people with his 1968 'rivers of blood' speech. Because of his opposition to the Common Market, he did not stand for election in 1974, but returned to parliament as an Ulster Unionist from October 1974 until he was defeated in the 1987 general election. He published numerous academic and political works, including *Reflections of a Statesman* (1991). Other titles include *Collected Poems* (1990) and *The Evolution of the Gospel* (1994). ⌐D E Schoen, *Enoch Powell and the Powellites* (1977)

Powell, John Wesley 1834–1902
US geologist
Born in Mount Morris, New York, of English parents, and almost entirely self-educated, he served in the American Civil War. He led daring boat expeditions down the Colorado River through the Grand Canyon (1869), demonstrating that the canyon resulted from the river erosion of rock strata which were being progressively uplifted. From 1874 to 1880 he directed the US Geological and Geographical Survey of Territories, organizing the 'Powell Surveys' to explore and map various parts of the USA. He subsequently became the second director of the combined US Geological Survey (1880–94) and after retirement he continued to work on behalf of the Bureau of Ethnology, which he co-founded in 1884. He undertook extensive work on water supplies in arid regions, and also wrote on crustal movements and human evolution.

Powell, Lewis Franklin, Jnr 1907–98
US jurist
Born in Suffolk, Virginia, he studied at Washington and Lee University and at Harvard and joined a law firm in Richmond, Virginia, in 1932. He served as president of the American Bar Association (1964–65) and was appointed to the Supreme Court by President Richard Nixon, serving as an associate justice from 1972 to 1987. Though he tended to take conservative stands on issues of crime and law enforcement, he cast pivotal votes in favour of affirmative action, the right to abortion, and separation of church and state.

Powell, Michael 1905–90
English film director, scriptwriter and producer
Born in Bekesbourne, near Canterbury, Kent, he became frustrated by the mundane routine of his job in a bank, and began work at the studios of director Rex Ingram, where he learned every technical aspect of the filmmaking process. *Two Crowded Hours* (1931), his directorial debut, was one of two dozen 'quota quickies' he made over six years. More prestigious assignments followed, including *The Edge of the World* (1937), and *The Spy in Black* (1939). He was co-director on *The Thief of Baghdad* (1940) for Alexander Korda, who introduced him to the writer Emeric Pressburger with whom he began a partnership that lasted until 1957. Known as 'The Archers', they collaborated on such films as *The Life and Death of Colonel Blimp* (1943), *Black Narcissus* (1947) and *Red Shoes* (1948), creating a body of work unique in its flamboyant use of colour, expressionism and sensuality. After the partnership ended, Powell made the controversial *Peeping Tom* (1959), which was attacked for its 'bad taste' and 'sadism' but later reclaimed as a masterly commentary on the voyeurism of film, and *The Boy Who Turned Yellow* (1972). Often considered ahead of his time, he lived to see 'The Archers' hailed as one of the most daring and distinctive forces in the history of British cinema. The first volume of his autobiography, *A Life in Movies*, was published in 1986, followed by the posthumous *Million Dollar Movie* in 1992.

Powers, Hiram 1805–73
US sculptor
Born in Woodstock, Vermont, the son of a farmer, he worked as an artist for a waxworks museum in Cincinnati, and in 1835 went to Washington, where he executed busts. In 1837 he went to Florence in Italy, where he lived until his death. There he produced his *Eve*, and in 1843 the still more popular *Greek Slave*, which caused a sensation at the 1851 Exhibition in London. Among his other works were busts of George Washington, John Calhoun, Daniel Webster, and Henry Longfellow.

Powhatan d.1618
Native American chief
The civil but energetic ruler of the Powhatan confederacy of New England tribes, despite considerable provocation he managed to maintain peace with the white settlers in Virginia. His favourite daughter, Pocahontas, was carried off by settlers in 1609, but married a white colonist with her father's consent. Powhatan was succeeded by his more warlike brother, Opechancanough.

Powys, John Cowper 1872–1963
English novelist, poet and essayist
He was born in Shirley, Derbyshire, the son of a vicar; his mother was descended from John Donne and William Cowper, and his brothers T F Powys and Llewelyn Powys were also novelists. He was brought up in the Dorset-Somerset countryside and though he spent much of his later life in the USA, his formative years greatly influenced his work. Educated at Sherborne and Corpus Christi College, Cambridge, he taught and lectured before becoming a prolific author. Of some 50 books, his best known are his novels, particularly *Wolf Solent* (1929); *A Glastonbury Romance* (1932), gargantuan in scale, in which the myths surrounding the ancient abbey have a supernatural effect on the citizens of the town; *Weymouth Sands* (1934); *Maiden Castle* (1936); and *Owen Glendower* (1940). His reputation is the subject of much argument, but his standing is probably that of a cult author, rather than a widely recognized one. ⌐H P Collins, *John Cowper Powys, Old Earthman* (1966)

Poynings, Sir Edward 1459–1521
English soldier and diplomat
He took part in a rebellion against Richard III, escaped to the Continent and joined the Earl of Richmond (Henry VII), with whom he later returned to England. In 1493 he was Governor of Calais, and in 1494 went to Ireland as Deputy-Governor for Prince Henry (Henry VIII). His aim was to anglicize the government of Ireland. This he accomplished by means of the Statutes of Drogheda, known as Poynings' Law, to the effect that all Irish legislature had to be confirmed by the English privy council. This was not repealed until 1782. He was often abroad on diplomatic missions. In 1520 he was present at the Field of the Cloth of Gold, which he had taken an active part in arranging.

Poynter, Sir Edward John 1836–1919
English painter
He was born of Huguenot ancestry in Paris, the son of the architect Ambrose Poynter (1796–1886). He studied (1853–54) in Rome and from 1856 to 1860 in Paris and elsewhere. He made designs for stained glass, and drawings on wood for *Once a Week* and other periodicals, and for Edward Dalziel's projected illustrated Bible. This led to studies in Egyptian art, which resulted in his *Israel in Egypt* (1867). His watercolours are numerous. In 1871 he became Slade Professor at University College London. He was director for art at South Kensington (1876–81) and director of the National Gallery (1894–1905), and in 1896 was made president of the Royal Academy. Among his works are *The Ides of March* (1883), *The Visit of the Queen of Sheba to Solomon* (1891), a portrait of Lillie Langtry and *Nausicaa and her Maidens* (1872–79). In 1869–70 he designed the cartoons for a mosaic of St George in the Houses of Parliament.

Poynting, John Henry 1852–1914
English physicist

Born in Monton, Lancashire, he was educated at the universities of Manchester and Cambridge, becoming Professor of Physics at Birmingham University (1880). He investigated electrical phenomena, the radiation pressure on dust in the solar system, the phase transition between solid and liquid states (1881), osmotic pressure (1896), and determined the constant of gravitation. In 1884 he introduced the Poynting vector, giving a simple expression for the rate of flow of electromagnetic energy. He wrote *On the Mean Density of the Earth* (1893), for which he was awarded the Adams prize at Cambridge, and a *Textbook of Physics* (2 vols, 1899, 1914) with J J Thomson. He was elected Fellow of the Royal Society in 1888, and in 1905 he was awarded the Royal Society's Royal Medal and elected president of the Physical Society.

Pozzo, Andrea 1642–1709
Italian artist

Born in the north of Italy, he became a Jesuit lay brother in 1665. In Rome from 1681, he decorated the church of S Ignazio, the ceiling of which he painted in the illusionstic perspective style known as *sotto in sò*. He was in Vienna from 1702, but his work in the Liechtenstein palace is all that survives. His treatise *Perspectiva Pictorum et Architectorum* (1693–98) had considerable influence on 18th-century artists.

Pozzo di Borgo, Carlo Andrea, Count
1764–1842
Russian diplomat

Born in Alala, Corsica, he practised as an advocate in Ajaccio. In 1790 he joined the party of Paoli, who made him president of the Corsican Council and Secretary of State, but in 1796 was obliged to seek safety from the Bonapartes in London. In 1798 he went to Vienna and effected an alliance of Austria and Russia against France. In 1803 he entered the Russian diplomatic service. Although he resigned again over the Treaty of Tilsit in 1807, he returned in 1812 and worked to unite the enemies of Napoleon I against him, seduced Bernadotte from the Napoleonic cause, and urged the allies to march on Paris. He represented Russia in Paris, at the Congress of Vienna (1814–15) and the Congress of Verona, and was ambassador to London from 1834 to 1839, when he settled in Paris.

Praagh, Dame Peggy Van See Van Praagh, Dame Peggy

Praed, Rosa, *pseudonym* Mrs Campbell Praed
1851–1935
Australian novelist

Born in Bromelton, Logan River, Queensland, she based her romantic novels *An Australian Heroine* (1880) and *The Romance of a Station* (1889) on the privations of her early married life on outback Queensland stations. In 1875 she and her husband moved to London where she became a popular novelist, mixing in literary circles which included Oscar Wilde. During the next 40 years she produced almost as many novels, many with an Australian setting, including *Policy and Passion* (1881) and *The Bond of Wedlock* (1887). The failure of her marriage, and the death of her four children in tragic circumstances, turned her to aspects of spiritualism and she set up house with a 'medium', Nancy Harward (1899–1927), producing a number of occult books.

Prance, Sir Ghillean Tolmie 1937–
English botanist

Born in Brandeston and educated at Oxford, from 1963 to 1988 he held various posts at New York Botanical Garden, including vice-president (1977–81), director of research (1975–81) and senior vice-president (1981–88). In 1988 he became director of the Royal Botanic Gardens at Kew. From numerous expeditions to Amazonia he has published many papers and several books on tropical botany, including *Extinction is Forever* (1977), *Biological Diversification in the Tropics* (1981), *Key Environments: Amazonia* (1985) and *Bark* (1993). He was elected FRS in 1993 and knighted in 1994.

Prandtl, Ludwig 1875–1953
German pioneer of the science of aerodynamics

Born in Freising, Bavaria, he studied mechanical engineering in Munich and gained a PhD in 1900. Although apparently destined for a career in elasticity, while working for the company MAN his interest was redirected to aerodynamics. In this field he made outstanding contributions to boundary layer theory, airship profiles, supersonic flow, wing theory and meteorology. He was director of Technical Physics at the University of Göttingen (1904–53), and director of the Kaiser Wilhelm Institute for Fluid Mechanics (now the Max Planck Institute) from 1925.

Prasad, Rajendra 1884–1963
Indian statesman

Born in Zeradei, Bihar, he left legal practice to become a follower of Mahatma Gandhi. A member of the Working Committee of the All-India Congress in 1922, he was president of the Congress several times between 1934 and 1948. In 1946 he was appointed Minister for Food and Agriculture in the government of India, and president of the Indian Constituent Assembly. He was the first President of the Republic of India from 1950 to 1962. He wrote several books, including *India Divided At the Feet of Mahatma Gandhi* and an autobiography, *Atma Katha* (1958).

Prati, Giovanni 1815–84
Italian lyric and narrative poet

Born near Trento, he became court poet to the House of Savoy, a deputy to the Italian parliament (1862) and a senator (1876). His volumes of lyrics include *Canti lirici* (1843, 'Lyrical Songs'), and *Canti del popolo* (1843, 'Songs of the People'). He enjoyed a popular success with the romantic poem *Edmenegarda* (1841). 📖 P L Mannucci, *Giovanni Prati* (1934)

Pratt, John Henry 1809–71
English clergyman, mathematician and geophysicist

Born in Ghazipur, India, he received an MA at Christ's and Sidney Sussex colleges, Cambridge (1836). He obtained a chaplaincy with the East India Company (1838), became chaplain to the Bishop of Calcutta (1844) and was appointed archdeacon (1850–71). A keen scientist, he postulated the isostasy principle to account for gravity anomalies resulting from nearby mountains, such as those observed by Sir George Everest in his survey of India, suggesting that high mountain ranges have lower density than the underlying crust. From the shape of the Earth he assumed it was essentially fluid, thus the surface topography was due to a number of independent blocks of different densities; the whole crust, having a common depth, would be buoyant relative to a common compensation depth. An opposing theory was put forward by Sir George Airy (1854). Pratt calculated that the Earth was an oblate spheroid, with a shortening of the polar axes of 26.9 miles (43.3 km); it is now known to be 21 km.

Praxiteles 4th century BC
Greek sculptor, one of the greatest Greek artists

He was a citizen of Athens. His works, usually in marble, have almost all perished, though his *Hermes Carrying the Infant Dionysus* was found at Olympia in 1877. Several of his statues are known from Roman copies, for example *Aphrodite of Cnidos* (c.350BC, Vatican Museum, Rome), possibly the first female nude.

Prchlik, Václav 1922–
Czechoslovak general and politician

He joined the forces and the Communist Party at the end of World War II, rose through various official appointments to be political administrator of the army (1955–68), and in 1968 apparently foiled an attempt by some of his colleagues to suppress the reform movement before it began. During 1968 he began a purge of the top security services and prepared to transfer the political responsibility for them from the party to parliament. After the Soviet invasion in August, which he was prepared to resist, he was dismissed, and fear of the secret police returned to Czechoslovakia.

Pré, Jaqueline du See du Pré, Jaqueline

Preda, Marin 1922–
Romanian novelist and story writer
Of peasant origin, he steered a cunning and sometimes funny line between criticism of the Communist regime and appearing to approve of it. He was unpopular with some of his colleagues, especially for serving as a vice-president of the Writers' Union, but is considered to be one of the outstanding writers of his country. His chief work is *Morometii* (1955–67), the first part of which was translated as *The Moromites* (1957). In this book his chief character, Ilie Moromete, is a philosophical peasant who delights in leading everyone up the garden path, and is in certain respects a representation of his creator, who has never seriously sought anyone's approval.

Preece, Sir William Henry 1834–1913
Welsh electrical engineer
Born in Caernarfon, Gwynedd, he was instructed in electrical engineering by Michael Faraday at the Royal Institution of Great Britain, London. After service with several telegraph companies, in 1870 he was attached to the Post Office, of which he became engineer-in-chief and finally consulting engineer. A pioneer of wireless telegraphy and telephony, he also improved the system of railway signalling and introduced the first telephones to Great Britain. He wrote several books, including *Telegraphy* (1876) with J Sivewright and *A Manual of Telephony* (1893) with A J Stubbs. He was knighted in 1899.

Pregl, Fritz 1869–1930
Austrian chemist and Nobel Prize winner
Born in Laibach (Ljubljana, Slovenia), he studied medicine at Graz University and spent most of his working life there, becoming Professor of Medical Chemistry in 1913. Finding that traditional methods of analysis were useless when applied to the minute quantities of biochemical materials that he wished to investigate, he devised new techniques for microanalysis, including a balance which could weigh within an accuracy of 0.001mg. His innovations were fundamental to the development of biochemistry and brought him the Nobel Prize for chemistry in 1923.

Prelog, Vladimir 1906–
Swiss organic chemist and Nobel Prize winner
Born in Sarajevo (now in Bosnia), he was educated at the Prague Institute of Technology and then worked as an industrial chemist before moving to Zagreb University. In 1941, when the Germans invaded Yugoslavia, he taught at the Federal Institute of Technology in Zurich, and was Professor of Chemistry (1950–76). Following his notable work in organic chemistry, and especially in stereochemistry, he shared the Nobel Prize for chemistry in 1975 with Sir John Warcup Cornforth.

Premadasa, Ranasinghe 1924–93
Sri Lankan statesman
Born in a North Colombo slum, a member of the lowly dhobi (laundrymen's) caste, he was educated at St Joseph's College, Colombo. He began his political career attached to the Ceylon Labour Party, forming a temperance group

dedicated to moral uplift, then joined the United National Party (UNP) in 1950 and became deputy Mayor of the Colombo municipal council in 1955. Elected to Sri Lanka's parliament in 1960, he served, successively, as UNP Chief Whip (1965–68, 1970–77), the Minister of Local Government (1968–70) and Leader of the House (1977–78), before becoming Prime Minister, under President Junius Jayawardene, in 1978. During 10 years as prime minister, Premadasa implemented a popular housebuilding and poverty alleviation programme, which provided the basis for his election as President in 1988. He faced mounting civil unrest, both in the Tamil north and Sinhala south, and deteriorating relations with India. He was assassinated by a suicide bomber, thought to have been a member of the Tamil Tigers separatist group.

Preminger, Otto 1906–86
US film director and producer
Born in Vienna, Austria, he studied law at Vienna University, then acted with Max Reinhardt, joined the Theater in der Josefstadt (1928) and became its director (1933). He directed his first film, *Die Grosse Liebe*, in 1932. He emigrated to the USA in 1935, becoming naturalized in 1943. After directing several Broadway productions, including *Libel!* (1935) and *Outward Bound* (1938), he moved to Hollywood, first as an actor then as a director under contract to Twentieth Century Fox, where he specialized in costume dramas and film noir thrillers like *Laura* (1944) and *Where the Sidewalk Ends* (1950). An independent filmmaker from 1952, he boldly tackled controversial themes such as drug addiction in *The Man with the Golden Arm* (1955), rape in *Anatomy of a Murder* (1959), Jewish repatriation in *Exodus* (1960), homosexuality in *Advise and Consent* (1962) and racism in *Hurry Sundown* (1966). Other notable films include *Carmen Jones* (1954), *Bonjour Tristesse* (1959) and *Porgy and Bess* (1959). The stereotype of the old-style autocratic film director, he was also a showman, craftsman and talent-spotter who was prepared to fight antiquated notions of censorship in the Supreme Court. His later theatrical work includes *The Trial* (1953) and *Full Circle* (1973). He also acted in the film *Stalag 17* (1953) and the television series *Batman* (1966), and published an autobiography, *Preminger* (1977). His last film was *The Human Factor* (1979). 📖 Willi Frischauer, *Behind the Scenes of Otto Preminger: An Unauthorised Biography* (1973)

Prem Tinsulanonda 1920–
Thai general and statesman
Educated at the Chulachomklao Royal Military Academy, Bangkok, he began as a sub-lieutenant in 1941 and rose to become Commander-General of the 2nd Army Area in 1974 and assistant Commander-in-Chief of the Royal Thai army in 1977. During the military administration of General Kriangsak Chomanam (1977–80) he served as deputy Minister of the Interior and, from 1979, as Defence Minister, before being appointed Prime Minister in March 1980. Prem formally relinquished his army office and established a series of civilian coalition governments. He withstood coup attempts in 1981 and 1985 and ruled in a cautious, apolitical manner, retaining the confidence of key business and military leaders. Under his stewardship, 'newly industrializing' Thailand achieved rapid annual economic growth rates in excess of 9 per cent. He retired on 'personal grounds' in 1988.

Prendergast, Maurice Brazil 1859–1924
US painter
Born in St John's, Newfoundland, he grew up in Boston and studied art in Paris from 1891 to 1894. He eventually settled in New York City where he became a member of the group of US painters known as the Eight, and he exhibited at the Armory Show in 1913. Much of his work was

influenced by Post-Impressionism, and his lively paintings often depict crowds in the city or at places of leisure, as in *Umbrellas in the Rain* (1899) and *Central Park* (1901).

Prescott, John Leslie 1938–
English Labour politician

Born in Prestatyn, Clwyd, after leaving school he worked as a trainee chef and then served in the merchant navy (1955–63). He continued his education through part-time classes, correspondence tuition and then full-time study at Ruskin College, Oxford and Hull University. He became a full-time officer of the National Union of Seamen (NUS) in 1968 and two years later entered the House of Commons, sponsored by the NUS, as Labour MP for Hull East. Although opposed to Britain's membership of the European Community, in 1975 he was elected to the European parliament and was leader of the Labour Group (1976–79). Never afraid to voice his feelings publicly, he has sometimes been openly critical of his party's leadership and in 1988 unsuccessfully opposed **Roy Hattersley** for the deputy leader's post. A member of the Labour Party's Shadow Cabinet from 1983, he was spokesman for employment, energy and transport and deputy Leader of the Labour Party under **Tony Blair** (1994–97). When Labour won a landslide victory in the 1997 general election, he was appointed deputy Prime Minister and given a joint Environment, Transport and Regions portfolio.

Presley, Elvis Aron   See panel p1501

Pressburger, Emeric (Imre) 1902–88
Hungarian screenwriter

Born in Miskolc and educated at Prague and Stuttgart, he worked as a journalist in Hungary and Germany before entering the film industry. Resident in Great Britain from 1935, he worked on various projects for Sir **Alexander Korda** before writing the thriller *The Spy In Black* (1939) for director **Michael Powell**. Together they formed 'The Archers', one of the most innovative production units in the history of British cinema. As filmmakers they turned from the social realism typical of British cinema of the period, and embraced poetry, fantasy and sensuality. Among their most distinctive films are *The Life And Death Of Colonel Blimp* (1943), *A Matter Of Life And Death* (1946), *Black Narcissus* (1947) and *The Red Shoes* (1948). The partnership was dissolved in 1957. Working alone Pressburger had directed *Twice Upon A Time* (1953) then subsequently wrote a number of short stories and novels, one of which was adapted into the film *Behold A Pale Horse* (1964). He re-united with Powell as the writer of the children's film *The Boy Who Turned Yellow* (1972).

Preston, Margaret Rose 1875–1963
Australian artist and teacher

Born in Port Adelaide, South Australia, she studied at Melbourne, Munich and Paris. She travelled widely in Europe before returning to Sydney in 1919. An enthusiastic traveller, she visited various south Pacific islands, south-east Asia and China in the 1920s, and Africa and India in the late 1950s. She was an active champion of Aboriginal painting, and its influence is clearly seen in her still lifes of Australian flowers and her wood and linocut engravings with their strong design and colours.

Prestwich, Sir Joseph 1812–96
English geologist, hydrologist and prehistorian

Born in Pensbury, Clapham, he was educated in Paris, Reading and at University College London. Until the age of 60 he was a wine merchant in the family business, his business interest aiding rather than restricting his geological studies with frequent trips to France and Belgium as well as around Great Britain. He undertook early studies of the stratigraphy of Coalbrookedale, Shropshire, publishing *The Geology of Coalbrookedale* (1836), and on the

correlation of the English Eocene with that of France. His principal work was on the stratigraphic position of flint implements and human remains in England and France, helping to confirm the antiquity of early man. His work on *The Water-bearing Strata of the Country around London* (1851) was a standard authority. In 1874 he became Professor of Geology at Oxford, where he wrote *Geology, Chemical and Physical, Stratigraphical and Palaeontological* (2 vols, 1886–87). He was knighted in 1896.

Pretorius, Andries Wilhelminus Jacobus
1799–1853
Afrikaner leader

Born in Graaff-Reinet, Cape Colony, he became a prosperous farmer, and was one of the leaders of the Great Trek of 1837 into Natal. After Zulu atrocities, he defeated Dengaan's force of 10,000 at Blood River in 1838. He accepted British rule, but later led another trek across the Vaal River and made war against the British. Eventually (1852) the British recognized the Transvaal Republic (later the South African Republic), the new capital of which, Pretoria, was founded in 1855 and named after him.

Pretorius, Marthinus Wessels 1819–1901
Afrikaner soldier and statesman

He became commandant-general on succeeding his father **Andries Pretorius** in 1853. He was elected President of the South African Republic in 1857, and of the Orange Free State in 1859. Failing in his ambition to unite the two republics, he resigned the presidency of the Orange Free State in 1863. The discovery of gold in Bechuanaland and diamonds in the Vaal River led to difficulties with the *Volksraad*, and he resigned the presidency of the South African Republic in 1871. He fought against the British again in 1877, until the independence of the Republic was recognized in 1881. He lived to see it extinguished in 1901 during the Second Boer War.

Prévert, Jacques 1900–77
French poet and screenwriter

Born in Neuilly-sur-Seine, he was a shop worker who turned to writing after his military service, working for *L'Argus de la Presse* and the publicity agency Damour. A member of the Surrealist movement until he was expelled for irreverence, he first made his name as the author of humorous, anarchic 'song poems' about street life in Paris, collected in *Paroles* (1946, Eng trans in part *Paroles: Selections*, 1958) and *Spectacle* (1951). A writer and performer with the agit-prop theatre group Octobre, he wrote the screenplay for their film *L'Affaire est dans le sac* (1932, 'It's in the Bag') then pursued a career as a screenwriter. With director **Marcel Carné**, he made the films *Quai Des Brumes* (1938, 'Port of Mists') and *Le Jour se lève* (1939, 'Daybreak'), as well as the masterpiece, *Les Enfants du Paradis* (1944, Eng trans 1968). In later years he collaborated with his brother, the director Pierre Prévert (1906–88) on short, animated films for children, and worked extensively for French television (1961–68). 📖 J Queval, *Jacques Prévert* (1955)

Previn, André George 1929–
US conductor and composer

Born in Berlin, he emigrated to the USA in 1938 and was naturalized in 1943. He studied music mainly in California and Paris and became musical director of the Houston Symphony Orchestra (1967–69), of the London Symphony Orchestra (1968–79), of the Pittsburgh Symphony Orchestra (1976–86), of the Royal Philharmonic Orchestra (1985–87), and of the Los Angeles Philharmonic Orchestra (1986–88). Since 1988 he has been a busy freelance conductor and chamber-music pianist. He was appointed conductor laureate of the London Symphony Orchestra in 1992. The composer of musicals, film scores and orchestral works, including a cello concerto (1967) and a guitar concerto (1971), he has achieved

Presley, Elvis Aron 1935–77
US popular singer

Elvis Presley was born in Tupelo, Mississippi. His family were Pentecostalists, and he began singing in his local church choir, then taught himself the rudiments of the guitar. He was 'discovered' in 1953 by Sam Phillips, president of Sun Records, in Memphis, Tennessee, who heard a record Presley had made privately for his mother. Phillips had been searching for a white singer who could sound black, and had a local hit in 1954 with his first single, Arthur 'Big Boy' Crudup's blues 'That's All Right Mama', backed by Bill Monroe's 'Blue Moon of Kentucky'. The combination proved incendiary; Sun sold his contract to RCA in 1955, and by 1956 he was the most popular performer in the USA and, before long, the world.

Presley's unparalleled contribution to popular music sprang from his ability to combine white country and western with black rhythm and blues, the basic formula underpinning rock and roll. This, together with his overtly sexual style, made him controversial: moralists accused him of obscenity; racists attacked him for performing black music. Two years of national service with the US army in West Germany did little to dim his popularity, though he produced few really outstanding records after the album *Elvis is Back* (1960).

The raw energy and sass of his 1950s classics were largely dissipated during the 1960s, when he was re-moulded as a middle-of-the-road popular icon. His appearances were mainly restricted to a succession of mediocre films made at the behest of his domineering manager, 'Colonel' Tom Parker (1909–97), often with dire songs, although he still succeeded in turning out the occasional pop classic amid the accumulated trash. He abandoned live performance altogether for seven years, until a celebrated television special in 1968, which suggested the old flame had not burned out entirely.

In the 1970s he re-emerged as a nightclub performer in Las Vegas, often performing twice a day, six days a week, to audiences of 3,500 thrilled by the energy and showiness of his stage act. During his career he recorded over 450 original songs, as well as many by other artists, and he became the biggest-selling artist in history.

Suffering in his last years from ill health caused by obesity and narcotics, he died suddenly in 1977. His home in Memphis, Graceland, has become a shrine for his fans, while rumours that he is still alive—and endless bizarre stories of alleged sightings of 'The King'—continue to enliven the tabloid news media. If he remains alive, though, it is only in his classic recordings.

♫ Presley's greatest records were singles rather than albums. They include: 'That's All Right Mama' (1954), 'Mystery Train' (1955), 'Heartbreak Hotel' (1956), 'Blue Suede Shoes' (1956), 'Hound Dog' (1956), 'Love Me Tender' (1956), 'All Shook Up' (1957), 'Jailhouse Rock' (1958), 'King Creole' (1958), 'It's Now or Never' (1960), 'His Latest Flame' (1961), 'Return To Sender' (1962), 'Crying in the Chapel' (1965), 'In the Ghetto' (1969), 'Suspicious Minds' (1969) and 'Burning Love' (1972).

📖 Peter Guralnick, *Last Train To Memphis: The Rise of Elvis Presley* (1994); L Cotton, *All Shook Up* (1985); Albert Goldman, *Elvis* (1981); Jerry Hopkins, *Elvis: The Final Years* (1981).

> In his seminal study of American rock music, *Mystery Train* (1975), Greil Marcus sees the gargantuan excess of Presley's comeback as a fulfilment of a communal fantasy: 'The version of the American dream that is Elvis's performance is blown up again and again, to contain more history, more people, more music, more hopes; the air gets thin but the bubble does not burst, nor will it ever. This is America when it has outstripped itself, in all of its extravagance, and its emptiness is Elvis's ultimate throwaway.'

popular success through his work, on television and in the concert hall, bringing classical music to the attention of a wider public. He has written *Music Face to Face* (1971) and *No Minor Chords* (1992). 📖 Martin Bookspan, *André Previn: a biography* (1981)

Previn, Dory, *née* Langdon c.1936–
US singer, lyricist and playwright

Born in Woodbridge, New Jersey, she sang and danced as a child, then studied acting. Her song lyrics interested film and television companies and she collaborated with **André Previn**, to whom she was married from 1959 to 1970. She received Academy Award nominations for some of her film songs, including 'The Faraway Part of Town' (1960), sung by **Judy Garland**. Her own singing emerged on three semi-autobiographical, semi-fictional albums recorded in 1971 and 1972: *Mythical Kings and Iguanas*, *Reflections in a Mud Puddle* and *Mary C. Brown and the Hollywood Sign*. Her verse was collected in *On My Way to Where* (1973), and she has written memoirs concerning her struggle with schizophrenia and various kinds of abuse.

Prévost, Abbé (Antoine François Prévost d'Exiles) 1697–1763
French novelist

Born in Artois, he was educated by the Jesuits. He enlisted in the army at 16, but in 1720, following an unhappy love affair, joined the Benedictines of St Maur, and spent the next seven years in religious duties and in study. Around 1727 he fled France for six years, going first to London, where he started to write *Histoire de Cleveland*, and then to Holland (1729–31). He issued volumes 1–4 of *Mémoires d'un homme de qualité* (Eng trans *Memoirs of a Man of Quality*, 1938) in 1728 and volumes 5–6 in 1731. However, his reputation stands on the eighth volume, *Manon Lescaut* (Eng trans 1738), distinguished by its perfect simplicity, and flowing, natural style. He employed himself in additional novels—*Le Philosophe anglais; ou, Histoire de Monsieur Cleveland, fils naturel de Cromwell* (1731–39, Eng trans *The Life and Adventures of Mr Cleveland*, 1734) and *Le Doyen de Killerine* (1735–40, Eng trans *The Dean of Coleraine*, 1742–43)—and in translations. In London again after another affair he started *Le Pour et contre* (1733–40, 'Arguments For and Against'), a periodical review of life and letters, modelled on the *Spectator*. In France by 1735, he was appointed honorary chaplain to the Prince de Conti. He went on to compile over a hundred volumes more. 📖 H Roddier, *Prévost, l'homme et l'œuvre* (1955)

Prevost, Sir George 1767–1816
British colonial administrator

Born in New York, he entered the British army and served in the West Indies, then became Lieutenant Governor of Nova Scotia in 1808. As Governor-in-Chief of Canada (1811–15), he was known for his conciliatory treatment of French–Canadians. He commanded British troops in the War of 1812, but his career was ruined when he ordered unnecessary retreats at Sackets Harbor, New York (1813), and Plattsburg, New York (1814).

Prey, Hermann 1929–98
German baritone

Born in Berlin, he sang at the Hamburg Opera (1953–60) and (as Wolfram in *Tannhäuser*) made his debut at Bayreuth (1956) and the New York Metropolitan (1960). Equally distinguished as an interpreter of lieder and in stage roles, he specialized in the **Mozart** repertoire and was accomplished in 20th-century German opera from **Alban Berg** to **Hans Henze**. He published his memoirs in 1981.

Prez, Josquin des See **Josquin des Prez**

Price, George 1919–
Belize statesman

Educated in Belize City and the USA, he was elected to the Belize City council in 1947 and in 1950 founded the People's United Party (PUP), a left-of-centre grouping which grew out of a smaller group, the People's Committee, and called for the independence of Belize. Partial self-government was achieved in 1954 and Price became Prime Minister, continuing to lead his country until it achieved full independence in 1981. In 1984 PUP's 30 years of uninterrupted rule ended when the general election was won by the United Democratic Party (UDP), led by **Manuel Esquivel**, but Price unexpectedly returned to power in 1989 and remained there until 1993.

Price, H(enry) H(abberley) 1899–1985
Welsh philosopher

Born in Neath, Glamorgan, he was educated at Oxford, where he was Professor of Logic (1935–59). His first and major work was *Perception* (1932), in which he argued against causal theories of perception; in later works he argued that our conceptual awareness consists of more than just sense data. He also wrote sympathetically on religion, parapsychology and psychic phenomena, and published *Thinking and Experience* (1953), *Belief* (1969) and *Essays in the Philosophy of Religion* (1972).

Price, (Mary Violet) Leontyne 1927–
US soprano

Born in Laurel, Mississippi, she studied at the Juilliard Music School in New York City. She was a notable Bess (1952–54) in **George Gershwin's** *Porgy and Bess*, an impressive **Verdi** singer, and was much associated with **Samuel Barber's** music. In 1961 she made her debut at the Metropolitan Opera in New York, and in 1966 she sang the role of Cleopatra in the original production of Barber's *Anthony and Cleopatra*. She has won many awards including the 1985 National Medal of Arts, and was made Commandeur, L'Ordre des Arts et des Lettres in 1986.

Price, Richard 1723–91
Welsh moral philosopher and Unitarian Minister

Born in Tynton, Glamorgan, he attended a Dissenting Academy in London, and became a preacher at Newington Green and Hackney. He first established his reputation with the *Review of the Principal Questions in Morals* (1758), which was directed principally against **David Hume** in arguing that 'morality is a branch of necessary truth'. He was admitted to the Royal Society in 1765 for his work on probability; his *Obervations on Reversionary Payments* (1771) helped to establish a scientific system for life insurance and pensions; and he wrote *An Appeal to the Public on the subject of the National Debt* (1772), which influenced **William Pitt**, the Younger. He also wrote books on the American Revolution (*Observations on the nature of Civil Liberty, the Principles of Government, and the Justice and Policy of the War with America*, 1776) and the French Revolution (*A Discourse on the Love of our Country*, 1789) which brought him into political prominence, the latter also provoking **Edmund Burke's** *Reflections on the Revolution in France*.

Price, Vincent Leonard 1911–93
US film actor

Born in St Louis, Missouri, he established a career on the English stage and Broadway before entering film in *Service De Luxe* in 1938. Though given mainly minor roles, in the 1940s he appeared in the major films *Laura* (1944) and *Dragonwyck* (1946). Having appeared in low-budget horror movies in the 1950s, in 1960 he was cast by Roger

Corman (1926–) as Roderick Usher in **Edgar Allan Poe's** tale *The Fall of the House of Usher*. Instantly his star rose and he went on to major success in six more collaborations with Corman on Poe's horror tales, for which he is now best remembered. His last film appearance was as the elderly inventor in *Edward Scissorhands* (1991).

Prichard, James Cowles 1786–1848
English physician and ethnologist

Born in Herefordshire, he studied medicine and from 1810 practised in Bristol. In 1813 he published *Researches into the Physical History of Man*, in which he argued for a single human species. In *The Eastern Origin of the Celtic Nations* (1831) he established Celtic as an Indo-European language with close affinity with the Sanskrit, Greek, Latin and Teutonic languages. Besides several medical works, he published an *Analysis of Egyptian Mythology* (1819) and *The Natural History of Man* (1843).

Prichard, Katharine Susannah 1883–1969
Australian writer

Born in Levuka, on Ovalau, where her father was editor of the *Fiji Times*, she began by working on a Melbourne newspaper, and in 1912 went to London as a journalist. Her first novel, *The Pioneers* (1915), won the 'colonial' section of a publisher's competition and was filmed in Australia the following year. Returning to Australia in 1916, she became a founding member of the Australian Communist Party (1920), and her socialist convictions coloured much of her subsequent work, especially her powerful trilogy set in the West Australian goldfields, *The Roaring Nineties* (1946), *Golden Miles* (1948) and *Winged Seeds* (1950). Her last novel, *Subtle Flame* (1967), was a study in the conflicts facing a newspaper editor. She also wrote poems, plays and short stories, and an autobiography, *Child of the Hurricane* (1963). Her son, Ric Prichard Throssell, wrote a biography of her, *Wild Weeds and Wind Flowers* (1975). ⊞ H D Brochmann, *Katharine Susannah Prichard* (1967)

Pride, Charley 1938–
US country singer

Born in Sledge, Mississippi, he is the only black musician to have become a major star in country music, his chosen field after growing up hearing it on the radio. **Chet Atkins** signed him to RCA in 1965, but his debut record was issued without publicity pictures. His singing won immediate favour, and he was able to surmount the colour barrier implicit in country music. He went on to become one of its most successful performers, and only **Elvis Presley** exceeded his record sales for RCA. He parted company with the label in 1986, a victim of changing fashions, but has continued to command a large audience for his work. ⊞ *The Charley Pride Story* (1994)

Pride, Thomas d.1658
English parliamentarian

Born perhaps near Glastonbury, he was a London drayman or brewer, then, at the beginning of the Civil War, became Parliamentary captain, quickly rising to colonel. He commanded a brigade in Scotland, and when the House of Commons sought to effect a settlement with the king he was appointed to expel its Presbyterian Royalist members. In 'Pride's Purge' over 100 were excluded, and the House, reduced to about 80 members, proceeded to bring **Charles I** to justice. Pride sat among his judges, and signed the death warrant. He was present at the battles of Dunbar (1650) and Worcester (1651) but, opposed to **Cromwell** becoming 'king', he played little part in protectorate politics.

Priest, Ivy Maud Baker, *née* Baker 1905–75
US politician

Born in Kimberly, Utah, she served in many offices in the Republican party, including president of Utah Young Republicans (1934–36) and president of the Utah Legislative League (1937–39). She ran unsuccessfully for the Utah State Legislature in 1934 and for Congress in 1950, but in 1952 President **Dwight D Eisenhower** appointed her treasurer of the USA. She was the second woman to hold that post and served for eight years. From 1966 to 1974 she was treasurer for the state of California. In 1968 she placed **Ronald Reagan** in nomination for the Republican party's candidate for US President, the first woman to perform that act. Her autobiography *Green Grows Ivy* was published in 1958.

Priest, Oscar Stanton De See **De Priest, Oscar Stanton**

Priestley, J(ohn) B(oynton) 1894–1984
English novelist, playwright and critic
Born in Bradford, he was educated there and at Trinity Hall, Cambridge. He had already made a reputation by critical writings such as *The English Comic Characters* (1925) and books on **George Meredith** (1926) and **Thomas Love Peacock** (1927) in 'The English Men of Letters' series when the geniality of his novel *The Good Companions* (1929) gained him a wide popularity. It was followed by other novels, though not all of equal merit, including *Angel Pavement* (1930), *Let the People Sing* (1939), *Jenny Villiers* (1947) and *The Magicians* (1954). His reputation as a dramatist was established by *Dangerous Corner* (1932), *Time and the Conways* (1937), and other plays on space-time themes, as well as popular comedies such as *Laburnum Grove* (1933), and his psychological mystery, *An Inspector Calls* (1947). Best known as a writer of novels, Priestley was also master of the essay form. He was an astute, original and controversial commentator on contemporary society—*Journey Down the Rainbow* (1955), written with his archaeologist wife, **Jacquetta Hawkes**, was a jovial indictment of US life. In a serious vein, his collected essays, *Thoughts in the Wilderness* (1957), deal with both present and future social problems. ▣ J Braine, *J. B. Priestley* (1978)

Priestley, Joseph 1733–1804
English clergyman and chemist
Born in Fieldhead, Leeds, he spent four years at a dissenting academy in Daventry and in 1755 became minister at Needham Market, and wrote *The Scripture Doctrine of Remission*. In 1758 he went to Nantwich, and in 1761 became a tutor at Warrington Academy. During visits to London he met **Benjamin Franklin**, who supplied him with books for his *History of Electricity* (1767). In 1767 he became minister of a chapel at Mill Hill, Leeds, where he took up the study of chemistry. In 1774, as literary companion, he accompanied Lord **Shelburne** on a continental tour and also published *Letters to a Philosophical Unbeliever*. But at home he was branded as an atheist in spite of his *Disquisition relating to Matter and Spirit* (1777), affirming our hope of resurrection from revelation. He was elected to the French Academy of Sciences in 1772, to the St Petersburg Academy in 1780, and became minister of a chapel in Birmingham the same year. His *History of Early Opinions Concerning Jesus Christ* (1786) occasioned renewed controversy, and his reply to **Edmund Burke**'s *Reflections on the French Revolution* led a Birmingham mob to break into his house and destroy its contents (1791). He then settled in Hackney, London, and in 1794 moved to the USA, where he was well received. He died in Northumberland, Pennsylvania, believing himself to hold the doctrines of the primitive Christians, and looking for the second coming of **Jesus Christ**. Priestley was a pioneer in the chemistry of gases, and one of the discoverers of oxygen (see **Carl Wilhelm Scheele**). ▣ F W Gibbs, *Joseph Priestley: Adventurer in Science and Champion of Truth* (1965)

Prieto, Indalecio 1883–1962
Spanish socialist leader
He served under the Second Republic, first as Minister of Finance (1931), then as an innovative Minister of Public Works (1931–33). The outstanding parliamentary orator of the Socialist Party, he also led its moderate wing. He was unable to take up the premiership in May 1936 because of the opposition of **Largo Caballero**, the leader of the party's left wing. Such a move may have thwarted the military rising of July 1936 which led to civil war. During the Spanish Civil War, he proved a defeatist Minister of the Navy and Air Force (1936–37) and Minister of Defence (1937–38). He was forced to resign because of his opposition to the Communist Party. After the war, he tried to unite the socialists with the Republicans and even the monarchists in an effort to overthrow the **Franco** regime.

Prigogine, Ilya, Vicomte 1917–
Belgian theoretical chemist and Nobel Prize winner
Born in Moscow, Russia, he moved to Belgium at the age of 12. He was educated at the Free University of Brussels, where he held a chair of chemistry from 1951 to 1987 and became emeritus professor. Since 1967 he has been director of the Ilya Prigogine Center for Statistical Mechanics, Thermodynamics and Complex Systems at the University of Texas, and since 1987 has also been associate director of studies at the École des Hautes Études en Sciences Sociales in France. Following the pioneering work of **Lars Onsager**, Prigogine continued the development of the thermodynamics of irreversible processes and discovered how to treat systems far from equilibrium. His methods are applicable to a wide range of chemical and biological systems. For this work he was awarded the Nobel Prize for chemistry in 1977. He is the author of a number of important books, including *Non-equilibrium Statistical Mechanics* (1962), *Thermodynamic Theory of Structure, Stability and Fluctuations* (1971, with P Glansdorff), and *Order out of Chaos—Man's New Dialogue with Nature* (1984). He holds the Grand Cross of the Order of Leopold II, is a Commander of the French Legion of Honour, and holds the Rumford Medal of the Royal Society.

Primaticcio, Francesco c.1504–1570
Italian painter
Born in Bologna, he went to France in 1531 at the invitation of **Francis I** to help in the decoration of the palace of Fontainebleau. A collection of his drawings is in the Louvre, Paris.

Primo de Rivera (y Orbaneja), Miguel, Marqués de Estella 1870–1930
Spanish general and politician
Born in Jerez de la Frontera, he served in Cuba and the Philippines during the Spanish–American War (1898), and in Morocco (1909–13). Military Governor of Cadiz (1915–19), Valencia (1919–22), and Barcelona (1922–23), he led a military coup d'état in 1923, inaugurating a dictatorship (1923–30). He brought the Moroccan War to an end in 1927, but soon afterwards lost the support of the army, the ruling class, and King **Alfonso XIII**. He resigned in 1930. His son José Antonio (1903–36) founded the Spanish Fascist Party *Falange Española* (1933), and was executed by the Republicans.

Primus, Pearl 1919–
US dancer, choreographer and teacher
Born in Trinidad, West Indies, she moved with her family to New York City at the age of three. She studied medicine and anthropology at Columbia University before making her dance debut in 1941 as a last-minute replacement. Her first solo recital followed two years later, and in 1944 she first appeared with her own group. She continued to present concerts and choreographed on

Broadway, but her real direction lay in dance and anthropological research in Africa. She made her first extended study trip there in 1948, and on subsequent trips was assisted in the preservation of primitive dance forms by her husband, dancer Percival Borde. She took a PhD in educational anthropology at New York University in 1978.

Prince, in full Prince Roger Nelson 1958–
US pop singer and composer

Born in Minneapolis, Minnesota, he was raised in a musical family (he was named after the Prince Roger Trio, a jazz band in which his father was a pianist). He was signed to Warner Brother Records while still in his teens, and released his first album, *For You*, in 1978. Subsequent albums, including *Prince* (1979), *Dirty Mind* (1980) and *Controversy* (1981), attracted increasing controversy with their tendency to mix religious and overtly sexual themes. International success followed the release of *1999* (1982), and the film and album *Purple Rain* (1984) confirmed Prince as one of the USA's most commercially successful artists, comparable only to **Bruce Springsteen** in the 1980s. Other recordings have included *Sign 'O' The Times* (1987), *Lovesexy* (1988), *Diamonds and Pearls* (1991) and *Come* (1994). Feeling that his name had become a commodity that no longer expressed his essence as a person, Prince changed his name in 1993 to an unpronounceable symbol combining the signs for male and female, a move that has led to his being universally referred to in the press as 'the singer formerly known as Prince'. A more recent album is *Emancipation* (1996).

Prince, Hal (Harold Smith) 1928–
US stage director and producer

Born in New York City, he took part in student productions at the University of Pennsylvania, and became a stage manager on Broadway. His first production was *The Pajama Game* (1954), followed by *Damn Yankees* (1955), *West Side Story* (1957), **Stephen Sondheim's** *A Funny Thing Happened on the Way to the Forum* (1963), *Fiddler on the Roof* (1964) and *Cabaret* (1968). He has maintained a long association with Sondheim, producing and directing many of the composer's shows, including *Company* (1970), *Follies* (1971), *A Little Night Music* (1973), *Pacific Overtures* (1976), *Sweeney Todd* (1979) and *Merrily We Roll Along* (1981). He also directed *Evita* (1978), *The Phantom of the Opera* (1986), *Kiss of the Spider Woman* (1990, 1993) and *Showboat* (1993, 1994). He is now one of the most successful producers and directors of stage musicals in the world.

Prince, Henry James 1811–99
English clergyman and eccentric

Born in Bath, he studied medicine but took Anglican orders, and in 1849 at Spaxton, Somerset, he founded what he called the Agapemone ('Abode of Love'), a community of religious visionaries who shared all their property and, it was believed, their womenfolk.

Princip, Gavrilo 1895–1918
Serbian nationalist and revolutionary

Born in Bosnia, he was a member of a secret Serbian terrorist organization known as the 'Black Hand', dedicated to the achievement of independence for the South Slav peoples from the Austro-Hungarian empire. On 28 June 1914, he and a group of young zealots assassinated the archduke **Franz Ferdinand** of Austria and his wife Sophie when they were on a visit to Sarajevo. The murder precipitated World War I, after Austria declared war on Serbia on 28 July. Princip died in an Austrian prison.

Pringle, Sir John 1707–82
Scottish physician and reformer

Born in Roxburgh, he was educated at St Andrews University and at Leyden. He taught philosophy and practised medicine in Edinburgh, then moved to London and later became head of the Army Medical Service and physician to various members of the royal family, including King **George III**. His *Observations on Diseases of the Army* (1752) remains a classic of military hygiene, and established many principles for preventing typhus, dysentery and other common diseases of soldiers and others who live in crowded conditions.

Pringle, Mia Lilly Kellmer 1920–83
Austrian educational psychologist

Born in Vienna, she was educated at King's College and Birkbeck College, London, and taught in primary schools from 1942 to 1945. She was appointed psychologist in the Hertfordshire School Psychology and Child Guidance Service (1945–50), deputy head of the Child Study Centre (1954–63) and lecturer (senior lecturer from 1960) in educational psychology at Birmingham University (1950–63). She was director of the National Children's Bureau from 1963 to 1981. Her publications include *Early Child Care and Education* (1974) and *Psychological Approaches to Child Abuse* (1980).

Pringle, Thomas 1789–1834
Scottish writer

He was born in Blakelaw, Roxburghshire, the son of a farmer. Educated at Kelso Grammar School and at Edinburgh University, he became an archivist in the Register Office in 1811. In 1817 he started the *Edinburgh Monthly Magazine*, later *Blackwood's Magazine*. In 1820 he emigrated to Cape Colony, and for three years was government librarian at Cape Town. He started a Whig paper, but it was suppressed by the Governor. Returning to London in 1826 he became secretary of the Anti-Slavery Society. He wrote *African Sketches* (1834) and published two collections of poems and lyrics, *The Autumnal Collection* (1817) and *Ephemerides* (1828). □ W Hay, *Thomas Pringle* (1912)

Pringsheim, Ernst 1859–1917
German physicist

Born in Breslau (now Wrocław, Poland), he studied at Heidelberg and Breslau universities and under **Hermann von Helmholtz** at Berlin. He received his doctorate in 1882, and in 1905 was appointed Professor of Theoretical Physics at Breslau. Working with **Otto Lummer**, he studied the radiation emitted by hot bodies, and highlighted inconsistencies which arose from the black-body radiation formulae of **Wilhelm Wien** and **Max Planck**, which led Planck to return to the problem and to formulate his quantum theory.

Pringsheim, Nathaniel 1823–94
German botanist

Born in Wziesko, Silesia (now in Poland), he was professor at Jena for a short time, but for the most part worked privately in Berlin. He worked on algae, but also contributed extensively to the study of other cryptogams, including mosses. He was the first scientist to observe and demonstrate sexual reproduction in algae. On observing freshwater and aquatic fungi, he concluded that fertilization consisted of the material union of two reproductive substances. He introduced a uniform terminology for the reproductive structures of the algae, which aided the elucidation of their life cycles.

Printemps, Yvonne 1894–1977
French actress

Born in Ermont, Seine-et-Oise, she made her debut at the Théâtre Cigale, Paris (1908), and appeared regularly in revue and musical comedy until 1916, when she began to work with **Sacha Guitry**, whom she subsequently married. She appeared in London and New York, but did not perform in English until 1934, when she played in **Noël Coward's** *Conversation Piece*. In 1937 she returned to Paris as manager of the Théâtre de la Michodière.

Prior, Matthew 1664–1721
English poet and diplomat

Born in Wimborne, Dorset, the son of a joiner, he was sent to Westminster School under the patronage of Lord Dorset, and from there he went with a scholarship from the Duchess of Somerset to St John's College, Cambridge. He was first employed as secretary to the ambassador to The Hague. In Queen **Anne**'s time he turned Tory, and was instrumental in bringing about the Treaty of Utrecht (1713), for which dubious service he was imprisoned for two years (1715–17) after the queen's death. His Tory friends recouped his fortunes by subscribing handsomely to a folio edition of his works (1719). Prior was a master of neat, colloquial and epigrammatic verse. His first work, a collaboration with Charles Montagu (Lord **Halifax**), was *The Hind and the Panther Transvers' to the story of the Country and the City Mouse* (1687), a witty satire on **Dryden**'s *Hind and the Panther* (1685). His political verse, with the exception of his brilliant burlesque of **Nicolas Boileau**'s *Épître au roi* (c.1669, *An English Ballad on the Taking of Namur*), is now of historical interest only. He is best known as a poet of light occasional verse—mock-lyrics such as *A Better Answer (to Chloe Jealous)*, and more seriously, *Lines Written in the Beginning of Mézeray's History of France*, a favourite with Sir **Walter Scott**. 💷 F Bickley, *Matthew Prior* (1914)

Priscian, (Priscianus Caesariensis) fl.500AD
Latin grammarian

A native of Caesarea, he taught Latin at Constantinople (Istanbul) at the beginning of the 6th century. As well as his 18-volume *Institutiones Grammaticae* ('Grammatical Foundations'), which was highly thought of in the Middle Ages, he wrote six smaller grammatical treatises and two hexameter poems.

Priscillian c.340–85AD
Spanish Bishop of Ávila

He was excommunicated by a synod at Saragossa in AD380, then tolerated, but was ultimately executed—the first case of capital punishment for heresy in the history of the Church. His doctrine, said to have been brought to Spain from Egypt, contained Gnostic and Manichaean elements, and was based on dualism. The Priscillianists were ascetics, eschewed marriage and animal food, and were said to hold strict truth obligatory only among themselves.

Pritchett, V S, *in full* Sir Victor Sawdon Pritchett
1900–97
English writer and critic

He was born in Ipswich, Suffolk, educated at Dulwich College, London, and after working in the leather trade became a newspaper correspondent in France, Morocco and Spain. He published his first novel, *Claire Drummer*, in 1929. His style is witty and idiosyncratic, his themes are satirical, and he was particularly interested in the fanaticism and guilt of the 'puritan', as portrayed with increasing humour in the novels *Nothing Like Leather* (1935), *Dead Man Leading* (1937) and *Mr Beluncle* (1951). Highly regarded as a literary critic, he travelled and lectured widely, especially in the USA. Among his critical works are *The Living Novel* (1946), *Books in General* (1953), and a biography of **Honoré de Balzac** (1973). He also wrote many volumes of short stories, and two autobiographical books, *A Cab at the Door* (1968) and *Midnight Oil* (1973). His *Complete Essays* was published in 1991. He was knighted in 1975 and made Companion of Honour in 1993.

Probus, Marcus Aurelius AD232–82
Roman emperor

Born in Sirmium, in Pannonia, he came to power through a military career, though the details are little known. He became sole emperor in 276, and fought campaigns in Gaul, Germany and Illyricum. A strict disciplinarian, he was murdered by discontented troops near Sirmium.

Probus, Marcus Valerius 1st century AD
Latin grammarian and critic

A native of Berytus (Beirut), he wrote a biography of **Persius**, and prepared annotated editions of classical authors, including Persius, **Horace**, **Terence** and **Lucretius**. The *Institutia Artium*, a grammatical treatise on the parts of speech attributed to Probus, cannot have been written before the 4th century AD. The *Appendix Probi*, a list of misspelt words coupled with the correct spelling which dates from the end of the 3rd century, was found appended to a manuscript of the *Instituta*. It is useful in that it indicates the pronunciation of the colloquial Latin of the time.

Proclus c.410–485AD
Greek Neoplatonist philosopher

Born in Constantinople (Istanbul), of aristocratic parents from Lycia, Asia Minor, he was educated in Lycia, Alexandria and then Athens, where he was a pupil of Syrianus, whom he succeeded to become the last head of **Plato**'s Academy. He was a champion of paganism above Christianity and theurgy above philosophy. His approach, based on **Plotinus**, combined the Roman, Syrian and Alexandrian schools of thought in Greek philosophy into one theological metaphysic. His works were translated into Arabic and Latin, and were influential in the Middle Ages. 💷 Lucas Siorvanes, *Proclus: Neo-Platonic Philosophy and Science* (1996)

Procop or Prokop, Andrew, *also known as* Procopius the Great c.1380–1434
Bohemian Hussite leader

Originally a monk, he became a member of the conservative Utraquist Hussite movement and later the commander of the peasant Taborites. Under him the fearful raids into Silesia, Saxony and Franconia were carried out, and he repeatedly defeated German armies. He headed the internal conflict of the Taborites with the more moderate Calixtines, and was killed at Lipan, near Böhmischbrod.

Procopius c.499–565AD
Byzantine historian

Born in Caesarea, Palestine, he studied law, and accompanied **Belisarius** against the Persians (526), the Vandals in Africa (533), and the Ostrogoths in Italy (536). He was highly honoured by **Justinian I**, and seems to have been appointed prefect of Constantinople (Istanbul) in 562. His principal works are his *Historiae* (on the Persian, Vandal and Gothic wars), *De Aedifiis*, and *Anecdota* or *Historia Arcana*, an attack on the court of Justinian and the Empress **Theodora**. 💷 J A S Evans, *Procopius* (1972)

Procopius the Great See Procop, Andrew

Procter, Adelaide Ann, *pseudonym* Mary Berwick
1825–64
English poet

Born in London, she was the daughter of **Bryan Waller Procter**. In 1851 she became a Roman Catholic. Her *Legends and Lyrics* (1858–60), some of which were written for *Household Words*, won her poetical renown. Her poems include 'The Lost Chord', which was set to music by Sir **Arthur Sullivan**. 💷 J Janku, *Adelaide Ann Procter: ihr Leven und ihre Werke* (1912)

Procter, Bryan Waller, *pseudonym* Barry Cornwall
1787–1874
English poet

Prokofiev, Sergei Sergeyevich 1891–1953
Russian composer

Prokofiev was born in Sontsovka in the Ukraine. He was taught the piano by his mother, and studied with Glière from 1902, by which time he had already composed two operas. He entered the St Petersburg Conservatory in 1904, and remained there for 10 years, studying with **Anatol Liadov** and **Rimsky-Korsakov**, and forming a lifelong friendship with **Nikolai Myaskovsky**. His compositions of this period, including his first two piano concertos and two piano sonatas, caused a furore among teachers and critics.

In 1914 he visited London, where he heard **Stravinsky's** music and met **Sergei Diaghilev**. He returned to St Petersburg and avoided war service by again enrolling at the Conservatory. There he completed his opera *The Gambler*, the third and fourth piano sonatas, the *Classical* symphony (a revival of the musical world of **Haydn**) and the first of two violin concertos. In May 1918 he left Russia, intending to return when political circumstances were more favourable to the performance of new music. In fact, he remained in exile for 18 years. In the USA he enjoyed success as a pianist, especially of his own works, and had *The Love for Three Oranges* staged by **Mary Garden** at the Chicago Opera. In 1920 he moved to Paris, where he completed another opera, *The Fiery Angel* (1927), as well as a second version of *The Gambler* (Brussels, 1929), a fifth piano sonata, a cantata called *We are Seven*, the second, third and fourth symphonies, the fourth and fifth piano concertos, and (for Diaghilev) a ballet entitled *The Prodigal Son*.

All this time Prokofiev kept in touch with musical life in the USSR, to which he continued to feel emotionally and spiritually drawn. He had several premières there and toured regularly from 1927. Finally, in 1936, he settled again in Moscow, unfortunately coinciding with the emergence of 'social realism' as the political doctrine for the arts. His principal musical outlets proved to be ballet (*Romeo and Juliet* and *Cinderella*) and film scores (for **Sergei Eisenstein**, including *Lieutenant Kijé* and *Alexander Nevsky*, which was first written for Hollywood and later recast as a dramatic cantata), as well as the fifth, sixth and seventh symphonies, the sixth to ninth piano sonatas, a fifth piano concerto, and a 'children's piece', *Peter and the Wolf* (1936). In 1941 he began work on the opera generally considered his greatest, *War and Peace*.

From this time the USSR became more and more isolated artistically from the West. Prokofiev made his last visit to western Europe and the USA in 1938; in 1939 he wrote a cantata *Hail to Stalin*, and when the USSR entered World War II in 1941, his health declined progressively because of a heart condition. From 1941 he became estranged from his first wife (who was sent to labour camps from 1948) and lived with Mira Mendelson, who wrote the texts for several late works. In 1948 he was included among those named by the Communist Party Central Committee as composers of music 'marked with formalist perversions' and 'alien to the Soviet people'. His last opera, *The Story of a Real Man*, was judged to be unsuitable by the Union of Composers, and was performed only after **Stalin** died, coincidentally on the same day as Prokofiev—5 March 1953.

  Prokofiev's own reminiscences are collected in *Prokofiev by Prokofiev: A Composer's Memoir* (translated by Guy Daniels, 1979). See also D Gutman, *Prokofiev* (1988); H Robinson, *Sergei Prokofiev* (1984); Victor Seroff, *Prokofiev: A Soviet Tragedy* (1968); I V Nestev, *Prokofiev* (1960). In 1989 a manuscript was discovered that described Prokofiev's 1927 visit to Russia; this was published in an English translation by O Prokofiev and C Palmer, *Soviet Diary 1927 and Other Writings* (1991).

> 'Bach on the wrong notes.' On Stravinsky's music. Quoted in V Seroff, *Sergei Prokofiev* (1968).

He was born in Leeds, Yorkshire, and after studying at Harrow with **Byron** and **Robert Peel** he became a solicitor, went to London and in 1815 began to contribute poetry to the *Literary Gazette*. In 1823 he married Anne Benson Skepper (1799–1888). He had meanwhile published poems and produced a tragedy at Covent Garden, *Mirandola*, whose success was largely due to the acting of **William Charles Macready** and **John Philip Kemble**. He was called to the Bar in 1831, and from 1832 to 1861 was a metropolitan commissioner of lunacy. His works comprise *Dramatic Scenes* (1819), *Marcian Colonna* (1820), *The Flood of Thessaly* (1823) and *English Songs* (1832), besides memoirs of **Edmund Kean** (1835) and **Charles Lamb** (1866). R W Armour, *Barry Cornwall* (1935)

Procter, Dod, *née* Doris M Shaw 1892–1972
English artist and traveller

Born in London, she studied at Elizabeth and Stanhope Forbes's painting school at Newlyn, Cornwall, then attended the Atelier of Colarossi, Paris (1910). In 1912 she married the artist Ernest Procter and with him designed the decoration for the Kokine Palace in Rangoon in 1920. This commission awakened her interest in travel which she continued after her husband's death (1935). She first exhibited at the Royal Academy in 1913 and was elected a member in 1942. Her work has a rounded, sculptural quality which has been attributed to the early influence of Cubism. Her most famous painting, *Morning*, was acclaimed picture of the year in 1927 and was purchased by the *Daily Mail* for the Tate Gallery, London.

Prodicus 5th century
Greek Sophist and teacher

He was born in the Ionian city of Iulis on Ceos, and seems often to have visited Athens on official missions. He became one of the professional, freelance educators who were dubbed 'Sophists' and were caricatured in **Plato's** dialogues. He is supposed to have written works *On Nature*, *On the Nature of Man*, and *Horai*, and to have composed the celebrated story 'The Choice of Herakles'. He was evidently a humanist, with a rationalistic view of religion, and he had special linguistic interests in 'the correctness of names'.

Proesch, Gilbert See **Gilbert and George**

Profumo, John Dennis 1915–
English politician

Educated at Harrow and Oxford, he became a Conservative MP in 1940. He held several government posts before becoming Secretary of State for War in 1960. He resigned three years later during the scandal following his admission that he had earlier deceived the House of Commons about the nature of his relationship with **Christine Keeler**, who was at the time also involved with a Russian diplomat, Captain Yevgeny Ivanov, whose memoirs appeared in 1992. After his resignation, Profumo turned to charitable service for which he was awarded the CBE in 1975. *Scandal*, a film based on an account of his affair with Miss Keeler, appeared in 1989. Anthony Summers and Stephen Dorril, *Honeytrap* (1987)

Prokhorov, Aleksandr Mikhailovich 1916–
Soviet physicist and Nobel Prize winner

Proust, Marcel 1871–1922
French novelist

Marcel Proust was born in Auteuil, Paris. He was a semi-invalid all his life, and was cosseted by his mother. In the 1890s he moved in fashionable circles in Paris, and in 1896 he published a collection of stories and essays called *Les Plaisirs et les jours* (Eng trans *Pleasures and Regrets*, 1948). In 1897 he became involved in the **Dreyfus** affair, in which he supported Alfred Dreyfus. But his mother's death in 1905, when he was 34 years old, caused him to withdraw from society and immure himself in a soundproof apartment, where he gave himself over entirely to introspection. Delving into the self below the levels of superficial consciousness, he set himself the task of transforming into art the realities of experience as known to the inner emotional life.

It is evident from the 13 volumes which make up *À la recherche du temps perdu* ('Remembrance of Times Past'), a series of autobiographical novels, that no detail escaped his observant eye. Influenced by the philosophy of **Henri Bergson**, he subjected experience to searching analysis to divine in it beauties and complexities that escape the superficial response of ordinary intelligence. Proust evolved a mode of communication by image, evocation and analogy for displaying his characters: not as a realist would see them, superficially, from the outside, but in terms of their concealed emotional life, evolving on a plane that has nothing to do with temporal limitations.

📖 *À la recherche* began with *Du côté de chez Swann* (1913, Eng trans *Swann's Way*, 1922) and, after a delay caused by World War I, *À l'ombre des jeunes filles en fleur* (1919, Eng trans *Within a Budding Grove*, 1924), which won the Prix **Goncourt** in 1919. *Le Côté de Guermantes* (1920–21, 2 vols, Eng trans *The Guermantes' Way*, 1925) and

Sodome et Gomorrhe (1922, 3 vols, Eng trans *The Cities of the Plain*, 1927) followed. These achieved an international reputation for Proust and an eager public awaited the posthumously published titles, *La Prisonnière* (1923, Eng trans *The Captive*, 1929), *Albertine disparue* (1925, Eng trans *The Sweet Cheat Gone*, 1930) and *Le Temps retrouvé* (1927, Eng trans *Time Regained*, 1931), each in two volumes. Apart from his masterpieces, there was also posthumous publication of an early novel, *Jean Santeuil* (1952, Eng trans 1955) and a book of critical credo, *Contre Sainte-Beuve* (1954, Eng trans *By Way of Sainte-Beuve*, 1958).

A new English translation of *À la recherche* by D J Enright (1920–) appeared under the title *In Search of Lost Time* in 1992.

📖 R Hayman, *Proust* (1990); André Maurois, *Proust* (Eng trans 1984); G D Painter, *Proust: A Biography* (2 vols, 1959–65).

> *Il vaut mieux rêver sa vie que la vivre, encore que la vivre ce soit encore la rêver.*
> 'It is better to dream your life than to live it, and even though you live it, you will still dream it.' From *Les Plaisirs et les jours.*
>
> *Pour écrire ce livre essentiel, le seul livre vrai, un grand écrivain n'a pas, dans le sens courant, à l'inventer puisqu'il existe déjà en chacun de nous, mais à le traduire.*
> 'To write the essential book, the only true book, a great writer does not need to invent because the book already exists inside each one of us and merely needs translation.' From *Le Temps retrouvé.*

Born in Atherton, Queensland, Australia, of Russian émigré parents, he and his family returned to the USSR after the Russian Revolution, and he graduated from Leningrad (now St Petersburg) University in 1939. He took a junior post at the Lebedev Physical Institute, rising to become deputy director in 1968. In 1952, with his colleague **Nikolai Basov**, he used a beam of molecular ammonia to amplify electromagnetic radiation, and went on to describe a new way in which atomic systems could produce amplification of microwaves. This led to the development of the maser and eventually the laser (the terms stand for Microwave/Light Amplification by Stimulated Emission of Radiation). For this work he won the 1964 Nobel Prize for physics jointly with Basov and **Charles Townes**.

Prokofiev, Sergei Sergeyevich See panel p1506

Prokop, Andrew See **Procop, Andrew**

Prokopovich, Feofan 1681–1736
Russian prelate and politician

He was educated at Kiev Orthodox Academy (where in 1711 he was appointed rector) and in Rome. While he was in St Petersburg, his sermons and theories for church reforms brought him to the notice (1716) of **Peter I, the Great**, who made him his adviser, Bishop of Pskov and in 1724 Archbishop of Novgorod. He was responsible for a new Spiritual Regulation which included setting up a Holy Synod instead of the existing patriarchate (which Peter had kept vacant since 1700). This consisted of 10, and later 12, clerics presided over by a lay procurator, and by and large ensured tsarist control of the Orthodox Church.

Prony, Gaspard François Clair Marie Riche, Baron de 1755–1839
French civil engineer

Born in Chamelet, he studied at the École des Ponts et Chaussées, Paris (1776–80), and three years later became assistant to **Jean Perronet** in Paris, for whom he undertook some analyses of masonry arch bridges. After the French Revolution he occupied several teaching posts until he was appointed inspector general of roads and bridges in 1805. He is most noted for the equations he developed in dealing with the flow of water, and for the Prony brake (1821) which measures the power of an engine under test.

Propertius, Sextus c.48–c.15BC
Roman elegiac poet

Born probably in Asisium (Assisi), Italy, he was educated in Rome and became a poet. He won the favour of **Maecenas**, to whom he dedicated a book of his poems, and of **Augustus**. The central figure of his inspiration was his mistress, Cynthia, to whom he devoted his first book of poems, the only one published during his lifetime.
📖 G Luck, *The Latin Love Elegy* (1969)

Prost, Alain 1955–
French racing driver

Born in St Chamond, he had the talent to become a professional footballer, but opted instead for racing driving, and won his first Grand Prix in 1981. He was world champion four times (1985, 1986, 1989, 1993) and was runner-up four times (1983, 1984, 1988, 1990). In 1987 he surpassed **Jackie Stewart's** record of 27 Grand Prix wins, thus becoming the most successful driver in the history of the sport. He retired in 1994. 📖 Christopher Hilton, *Alain Prost* (1992)

Protagoras c.490–c.420BC
Greek Sophist and teacher

Born in Abdera in north-east Greece, he was a regular visitor to Athens, and was the first and most famous of the 'Sophists' who, for a fee, offered a professional training in public life and in other skills. He became a friend of Pericles and was invited by him to draft a legal code for the new pan-Hellenic colony of Thurii. His many works are lost, except for an agnostic first sentence from *On the Gods*. Much of our information about him comes from Plato's dialogues, one of which was named after him and portrays him memorably (and respectfully). His most famous maxim was 'Man is the measure of all things', which is usually taken to imply a sceptical or relativistic view of human knowledge.

Protogenes 5th century BC
Greek painter
Born in Caunus in Caria, he lived in Rhodes, where he worked steadily through the siege of 305–304BC.

Proudhon, Pierre Joseph 1809–65
French journalist and political theorist
Born in Besançon, he issued *Qu'est-ce que la propriété?* ('What is Property?') in 1840, affirming the bold paradox 'property is theft', because it involves the exploitation of others' labour. In 1842 he was tried for his revolutionary opinions but later acquitted. In 1846 he published his greatest work, *Système des contradictions économiques* (Eng trans *System of Economic Contradictions*, 1888). During the Revolution of 1848 he was elected for the Seine department, and published several newspapers advocating the most advanced theories. Sentenced to three years' imprisonment, in March 1849 he fled to Geneva, but returned to Paris in June and gave himself up. In 1852 he was released, but in 1858 was again condemned to three years' imprisonment when his three-volume *De la justice dans la Révolution et dans l'église* ('On Justice in the Revolution and the Church') was seized; he went to Belgium, and received an amnesty in 1860. A forerunner of Karl Marx, he emphasized liberty, equality and justice.

Proust, Joseph Louis 1754–1826
French analytical chemist
Born in Angers, he studied pharmacy and chemistry in Paris, and spent most of his working life in Spain. In the early 1780s he conducted aerostatic experiments with Pilatre de Rozier and Jacques-Alexandre-César Charles, and in 1784 was one of the first people to make an ascent in a balloon. He was appointed Professor of Chemistry at the Royal Artillery College at Segovia and director of the Royal Laboratories at Madrid (1789–1808), after which he returned to France. Proust made two significant advances in analytical chemistry: he developed the use of hydrogen sulphide as a reagent and he gave the results of his analyses in terms of percentage weights. By means of the percentages he realized that the proportions of the constituents in any chemical compound are always the same regardless of what method is used to prepare it. He announced this discovery, known as the 'law of definite proportions', in 1794. Not all his contemporaries accepted his findings, his principal adversary in a renowned controversy being Claude Louis Berthollet. Although Proust was correct in his observations, the reason why reagents behave in this way did not become clear until John Dalton formulated his atomic theory in 1803.

Proust, Marcel See panel p1507

Prout, Ebenezer 1835–1909
English composer and writer on musical theory
Born in Oundle, Northamptonshire, he edited Handel's *Messiah* (1741), for which he provided additional accompaniments. In 1894 he became Professor of Music at Dublin.

Prout, Father See Mahony, Francis Sylvester

Prout, Margaret Millicent, *née* Fisher 1875–1963
English artist
Born in Chelsea, London, she was the only daughter of the English Impressionist Mark Fisher, with whom she painted during her childhood in England and France. She then studied at the Slade School of Art, London, and taught life classes at Hammersmith School of Art. She developed some interesting techniques, such as washing out pigment and adding body colour and charcoal to great effect. She exhibited at the Royal Society of Painters in Water Colours and the New English Art Club, was elected associate member of the Royal Academy, London, in 1948, and was awarded a medal from the Paris Salon. She was still showing in Academy 42 years after the appearance of her first exhibit.

Prout, Samuel 1783–1852
English watercolourist
Born in Plymouth, he was elected to the Watercolour Society in 1815, and went to Rouen in 1818. His numerous elementary drawing-books were widely influential. He was famed for his picturesque views of buildings and streets, and his work was admired by John Ruskin.

Prout, William 1785–1850
English physician
Born in Horton, Gloucestershire, he studied medicine at Edinburgh University, then settled in London. Taking up physiological chemistry, he furnished his own laboratory and gave a course of chemical lectures (1813). From numerous analyses he deduced the famous 'Prout's hypothesis', that the atomic weights of all the elements are multiples of the atomic weight of hydrogen (1815). He was the first to analyse the constituents of urine and originated several of the revolutionary ideas attributed to Justus von Liebig, for example, that the various excretions (eg urea, uric acid, carbonic acid) are derived from the waste or destruction of tissues which once formed a constituent part of the organism. He also discovered hydrochloric acid in healthy stomach juice (1823), and was the first to divide foodstuffs into carbohydrate, fats and proteins (1827). He was elected FRS in 1819.

Prowse, Philip 1937–
Scottish stage designer and director
Born and brought up in Worcestershire, he studied at the Slade School of Art, London, then worked for a year in the model rooms at Covent Garden, before he began designing ballet. He moved to Glasgow in 1969, and has been based there ever since, designing and directing numerous productions at the Glasgow Citizen's Theatre. His designs vary from severe austerity to extravagant luxury. He also designs and directs for the National Theatre, the Royal Shakespeare Company, and opera. Since 1995 he has been head of the theatre design department at the Slade School of Art.

Prudentius, Marcus Aurelius Clemens AD348–c.410
Latin Christian poet
Born in northern Spain, he practised as a pleader, acted as civil and criminal judge, and afterwards received high office at the imperial court. A Christian all his life, in his later years he wrote religious poetry. His principal poems include *Cathemerinon Liber*, a series of 12 hymns (Eng trans 1845); *Peristephanon*, 14 lyrical poems in honour of martyrs; *Apotheosis*, a defence of the Trinity; *Hamartigeneia*, on the origin of evil; *Psychomachia* (Eng trans *War of the Soul*, 1743); *Contra Symmachum*, against the heathen gods; and *Diptychon*. He is the best-known of the early Christian verse-makers. 📖 T R Glover, *Life and Letters in the 4th Century* (1901)

Prud'hon, Pierre Paul 1758–1823
French painter

Born in Cluny, he trained with engravers in Paris and, having won the Prix de Rome, went to Italy. He did little work there, but returned to Paris to draw and paint in a refined style not in accord with revolutionary Paris. Patronized, however, by the empresses of Napoleon I, he was made court painter, and among his best work is a portait of the empress Joséphine. Many of his paintings had mythological and allegorical subjects and were commissioned for public buildings, such as his celebrated *Crime Pursued by Justice and Vengeance* (1808). He also designed furniture and interiors on classical lines.

Prus, Bolesław, *pseudonym of* Aleksander Głowacki 1847–1912
Polish novelist

He was born in Hrubieszów, and belonged to the period of realism in literature which followed the unsuccessful revolt against Russian domination (1863–64). His novels and short stories are written as social commentaries, mainly about common people, and include *Omyłka* ('The Blunder'), *Lalka* (1887, 'The Doll'), a vivid and sympathetic picture of Warsaw which is considered to be his masterpiece, and *Emancypantki* (1893, 'Emancipated Women'). ◻ S Malkowski, *Boleslaw Prus* (1964)

Pryce, Jonathan 1947–
Welsh actor

Born in Holywell, Clwyd, he trained at RADA and acted in *Comedians* with the Old Vic Company in London and New York, played the title role in *Hamlet* (1980) at the Royal Court Theatre, acted with the Royal Shakespeare Company, appeared in the West End and on Broadway in *Miss Saigon* (1989–91, winning a Tony award) and starred as Fagin in the London Palladium revival of *Oliver!* (1994). On television, he played Gerd Heidemann in *Selling Hitler* (1991) and John Wroe in *Mr Wroe's Virgins* (1993). His films include *The Ploughman's Lunch* (1983), *Consuming Passions* (1987), *Deadly Advice* (1994) and *Carrington* (1995), for which he won a Cannes Film Festival Best Actor award.

Pryde, James Ferrier 1866–1941
Scottish artist, lithographer and poster designer

Born in Edinburgh, he studied at the Royal Scottish Academy Schools, and in Paris at the Académie Julian. With his brother-in-law William Nicholson he set up the Beggarstaff Brothers (c.1894), which profoundly influenced poster design in the 1890s. He also had some experience as an actor, touring Scotland in 1895 with Edward Gordon Craig. He is best known for his large street scenes which have a theatrical quality, and he had a wide circle of artistic friends, among them James McNeill Whistler, Thomas Carlyle and Augustus John, and exhibited internationally.

Prynne, William 1600–69
English pamphleteer

Born in Swanswick, near Bath, he graduated from Oriel College, Oxford, in 1621, and was called to the Bar. In 1633 he published his *Histrio-Mastix: the Players Scourge*, for which, on account of a supposed reflection on the virtue of Queen Henrietta Maria, he was sentenced in 1634 to have his book burnt by the hangman, pay a fine of £5,000, be expelled from Oxford and Lincoln's Inn, lose both ears in the pillory, and suffer life imprisonment. Three years later, for attacking Archbishop Laud and the hierarchy in two more pamphlets, he was branded on both cheeks with *S L* ('seditious libeller'). He was released from prison by a warrant of the House of Commons (1640), acted as Laud's bitter prosecutor (1644), and in 1648 became MP for Newport, Cornwall. However, he opposed the Independents and Charles I's execution, and was 'purged' and imprisoned (1650–52). On Cromwell's death he returned to parliament as a Royalist, and after the Restoration Charles II made him keeper of the Tower

records. He was a great compiler of constitutional history, and his best works were the *Calendar of Parliamentary Writs* and his *Records*.

Pryor, Richard 1940–
US comedian

Born in Peoria, Illinois, he served in the US army before developing an act as a stand-up comic. Performing on television and in nightclubs, he was dubbed the 'black Lenny Bruce'. He made his film debut in *Busy Body* (1967). In the 1970s he developed into one of the USA's most popular live entertainers, offering savagely witty, shockingly profane commentaries on the prejudices and injustices of the world. An award-winning scriptwriter for television, he released a number of bestselling albums and his film career flourished too with roles in *Lady Sings The Blues* (1972), *Silver Streak* (1976) and *Blue Collar* (1978). He suffered from third-degree burns when he set fire to himself whilst freebasing, but recovered and appeared in later films including *Stir Crazy* (1980), *Superman III* (1982) and *Jo Jo Dancer, Your Life is Calling* (1986), which he also directed. Despite suffering from multiple sclerosis, he continues to perform live, and returned to the screen after a long absence in *Lost Highway* (1997). ◻ *Pryor Convictions* (1995)

Prys-Jones, Arthur Glyn 1888–1987
Welsh poet

Born in Denbigh, Clwyd, he was educated at Llandovery College and Jesus College, Oxford. A teacher by profession, he edited the first anthology of Anglo-Welsh poetry, *Welsh Poets* (1917), and published six volumes of his own, including *Poems of Wales* (1923), *Green Places* (1948), *High Heritage* (1969) and *Valedictory Verses* (1978). The doyen of Anglo-Welsh writers, he was president of the Welsh Academy from 1970 until his death.

Przhevalski, Nikolai Mikhailovich 1839–88
Russian traveller

He was born near Smolensk, and from 1867 travelled in Mongolia, Turkestan and Tibet, reaching to within 160 miles (258km) of Lhasa. He explored the upper Hwang Ho, reaching as far as Kiachta. During his travels he amassed a valuable collection of plants and animals, among them a wild camel and a wild horse which now bears his name.

Przybyszewski, Stanisław 1868–1927
Polish novelist, dramatist and critic

Born in Lojewo, he was educated in Germany, and from 1898 lived in Kraków, where he became editor of *Life* and a leader of the new literary 'Young Poland' movement. His work, reflecting his 'naturalist' ideas, includes *Homo Sapiens* (1901), *Matka* (1903) and the drama *Śnieg* (1903, Eng trans *Snow*, 1920). ◻ S Halsztynski, *Stanisław Przybyszewski* (1958)

Psalmanazar, George, *known as* the Formosan c.1679–1763
French literary imposter

Born probably in Languedoc, he was educated by monks and Jesuits, turned into a vagabond at the age of 16, and wandered through France, Germany and the Low Countries. He found an accomplice in Sluys (1703) in one Innes, chaplain to a Scottish regiment, who baptized him 'George Lauder' and took him to London. For Bishop Henry Compton he translated the Church Catechism into the 'Formosan' language, and he dedicated his *Historical and Geographical Description of Formosa* (1704) to him, which found many believers in spite of its patent absurdities. Later he was the alleged importer of a white 'Formosan' enamel, a tutor, a regimental clerk (1715–17), a fan-painter and, lastly, for years a diligent hack-writer. The *Universal*

History was largely of his compiling, as was a popular *Essay on Miracles*. He was esteemed by Dr Johnson as 'the best man he ever knew'.

Ptashne, Mark Steven 1940–
US molecular biologist

Born in Chicago, he was educated at Harvard, where he remained as a lecturer in biochemistry (1968–71), and since 1971 has been professor there. Previous studies of *Escherichia coli* had implied the existence of a repressor protein that turns off specific genes when lactose is absent from the cell. It was shown by Ptashne and others that the lac repressor inhibits genes by binding to a specific nucleotide sequence called the operator, preventing the binding of RNA polymerase to the gene and the transcription of adjacent gene sequences. With lactose present, a breakdown product dislodges repressor from the operator and allows RNA polymerase attachment. The lactose system has been of crucial importance as a model for similar mechanisms in higher organisms. This concept that genes can be specifically activated or deactivated has been essential to our understanding of the normal and abnormal functioning of cells. He was the recipient of the Cancer Research Foundation award in 1990. His publications include *A Genetic Switch* (1986) and *A Genetic Switch II* (1992).

Ptolemy I, Soter c.367–283BC
Egyptian king and soldier

A son of Lagus, he was one of the greatest generals of Alexander the Great, upon whose death he obtained Egypt (323BC). Subject to the Macedonian kings, he occupied the first half of his reign in repelling outside attacks and consolidating his government. In 306BC he was defeated by Demetrius Poliorcetes in a sea-fight off Salamis in Cyprus, but still assumed the royal title (305BC) and defended his territories against Antigonus (Monophthalmos) and Demetrius. In 304BC he defended the Rhodians against Demetrius, and received from him his title Soter ('Saviour' or 'Preserver'). Alexandria, his capital, became the centre of commerce and Greek culture. ⊞ E R Bevan, *The House of Ptolemy: A History of Egypt Under the Ptolemaic Dynasty* (rev edn, 1968)

Ptolemy II, Philadelphus 308–246BC
King of Egypt

He was the son and successor (246BC) of Ptolemy I, Soter, and under him the power of Egypt attained its greatest height. He was generally successful in his external wars, founded the Museum and Library, purchased many valuable manuscripts of Greek literature, and attracted leading Greek intellectuals to his court. The Egyptian history of Manetho was dedicated to him, but the story that he commissioned the Greek translation of the Hebrew scriptures (the Septuagint) is open to doubt. ⊞ E R Bevan, *The House of Ptolemy: A History of Egypt Under the Ptolemaic Dynasty* (rev edn, 1968)

Ptolemy III, Eurgetes c.285–222BC
King of Egypt

The son and successor (283BC) of Ptolemy II, Philadelphus, he extended the limits of the empire in the Aegean and to the south, and for a time won much of Seleucid Asia. At the time of his death Egypt was prosperous and internally stable. ⊞ E R Bevan, *The House of Ptolemy: A History of Egypt Under the Ptolemaic Dynasty* (rev edn, 1968)

Ptolemy IV, Philopator d.205BC
King of Egypt

The son and successor (222BC) of Ptolemy III, Eurgetes, he began his reign by murdering his mother, Berenice. Hostile classical writers portray him as debauched, indolent, and ruled by favourites, and ascribe to him the decline of Ptolemaic power at home and abroad. ⊞ E R Bevan, *The House of Ptolemy: A History of Egypt Under the Ptolemaic Dynasty* (rev edn, 1968)

Ptolemy V, Epiphanes c.210–180BC
King of Egypt

He was the son and successor (205BC) of Ptolemy IV, Philopater. Egypt's decline dates from his reign, and from the internal conflicts that plagued the dynasty for most of the rest of Ptolemaic history. The belated attempt of Cleopatra to revive Ptolemaic power with Roman help ended in failure, and after her, Egypt became a Roman province. ⊞ E R Bevan, *The House of Ptolemy: A History of Egypt Under the Ptolemaic Dynasty* (rev edn, 1968)

Ptolemy VI, Philometor d.145BC
King of Egypt

The son and successor of Ptolemy V, Epiphanes, he acceded to the throne as a child and his mother, Cleopatra, governed the country during his minority. On her death (176BC), power devolved on courtiers who went to war with the Seleucid King, Antiochus IV. As a result, Egypt was invaded in 170BC, and Memphis was attacked. The young Ptolemy was captured, but reinstated as king. However, his brother (later Ptolemy VIII, Euergetes II) had assumed the title of king in Alexandria. The Seleucids attacked Egypt again in 168BC but were forced to withdraw by the Romans. In 164BC Euergetes II expelled Ptolemy VI, who went to Rome and was restored by the Romans to his kingdom, while Euergetes obtained Cyrene as a separate realm. From this time onward, Egypt was under the protection of Rome. ⊞ E R Bevan, *The House of Ptolemy: A History of Egypt Under the Ptolemaic Dynasty* (rev edn, 1968)

Ptolemy VIII, Euergetes II d.116BC
King of Egypt

One of the most unsavoury of the kings of the Ptolemaic Dynasty, he was nicknamed *Physcon* ('Pot-belly') on account of his corpulence, and his cruelty was notorious. He clashed with his brother, Ptolemy VI, Philometor, and in 164BC drove him from Egypt. The intervention of Rome restored Ptolemy VI, and Euergetes II was established as ruler of Cyrene. His reign (170–164, 145–116) was characterized by intrigue and ruthless elimination of rivals. He married his sister, Cleopatra II, the widow of Ptolemy VI, and executed his nephew, Ptolemy Eupator, to have sole right to the throne. In 130BC, Cleopatra II was declared Queen in Egypt after he was forced to flee to Cyprus because of a revolt in Alexandria. As a result he had Memphitis (his son by Cleopatra) murdered. ⊞ E R Bevan, *The House of Ptolemy: A History of Egypt Under the Ptolemaic Dynasty* (rev edn, 1968)

Ptolemy XII Neos Dionysos
1st century BC
King of Egypt

Proclaimed king in 80BC by the Alexandrians, he earned the name *Auletes* ('flute-player') because he performed in public on the instrument. He was eager for the Roman senate's support for his title to the throne of Egypt, and it was only on the appointment of Julius Caesar to the consulship that he was able to purchase this by bribery. Ptolemy's over-taxed subjects forced him into exile (58–55BC) in Rome, where he asked the senate to restore him to his kingdom. Some members of a delegation from Alexandria were sent to Rome to plead their cause, but Ptolemy arranged for them to be intercepted and the majority were put to death. By further bribes, Ptolemy was again placed on the throne through the agency of the pro-consul of Syria. On his return, he executed his eldest daughter, Berenice IV, who had ruled Egypt during her father's exile. After his death in 51, he bequeathed the kingdom in his will to Cleopatra VII and her elder son,

Ptolemy XIII, asking Rome to ensure the succession.
📖 E R Bevan, *The House of Ptolemy: A History of Egypt Under the Ptolemaic Dynasty* (rev edn, 1968)

Ptolemy, Latin Claudius Ptolemaeus c.90–168AD
Egyptian astronomer and geographer

He flourished in Alexandria. His 'great compendium of astronomy' seems to have been denominated by the Greeks *megistē* ('the greatest'), from which the Arab name *Almagest* by which it is generally known was derived. His *Tetrabiblos Syntaxis* is combined with another work called *Karpos* or *Centiloquium*, because it contains a hundred aphorisms—both treat astrological subjects, so have been held by some to be of doubtful authenticity. There is also a treatise on the fixed stars or a species of almanac, the *Geographia* and other works dealing with map-making, the musical scale and chronology. As astronomer and geographer, Ptolemy was the main influence on scientific men down to the 16th–17th centuries, but he seems to have been not so much an independent investigator as a corrector and improver of the work of his predecessors. For example, in astronomy he depended largely on **Hipparchos**. However, as his works form the only remaining authority on ancient astronomy, the system they expound is called the *Ptolemaic System*. The system of **Plato** and **Aristotle**, this was an attempt to reduce the common understanding of the motions of the heavenly bodies to scientific form. The Ptolemaic astronomy, handed on by Byzantines and Arabs, assumed that the Earth is the centre of the universe, and that the heavenly bodies revolve round it. Beyond and in the ether surrounding the Earth's atmosphere were eight concentric spherical shells, to seven of which one heavenly body was attached, the fixed stars occupying the eighth. The apparent irregularity of their motions was explained by a complicated theory of epicycles. As a geographer, Ptolemy is the corrector of a predecessor, Marinus of Tyre. His *Geography* contains a catalogue of places; with latitude and longitude; general descriptions; and details regarding his mode of noting the position of places. He also calculated the size of the Earth, and constructed a map of the world and other maps. His Earth-centred view of the universe dominated cosmological thought until swept aside by **Copernicus** in the 16th century.

Puapua, Tomasi 1938–
Tuvaluan politician

After training at the Fiji School of Medicine and Otago University, New Zealand, he worked as a doctor and gradually moved into the political arena. In 1981 he was elected Prime Minister of Tuvalu, replacing Toaripi Lauti, who had been implicated in an investment scandal. He was re-elected in 1985, but defeated in the general election of 1989 and replaced as premier by Bikenibeu Paeniu. During his period as Prime Minister he was outspoken in his opposition to France's testing of nuclear weapons on Mururoa Atoll, in French Polynesia.

Pucci, Emilio, Marchese di Barsento 1914–92
Italian fashion designer

Born in Naples, he studied social sciences in Italy and the USA, and was a member of Italy's Olympic ski team in 1934. He served in the Italian air force in World War II and in 1965 became a member of the Italian Parliament. He started designing ski clothes in 1947, and in 1950 opened his own couture house, creating casual, elegant, print dresses for women. He became renowned for his use of bold patterns and brilliant colour.

Puccini, Giacomo (Antonio Domenico Michele Secondo Maria) 1858–1924
Italian composer of operas

Born in Lucca, he was an organist and choirmaster there at the age of 19, his first extant compositions being written for use in the Church. Poverty prevented his undertaking regular studies until a grant from Queen Margherita enabled him to attend the Milan Conservatorio (1880). His first opera, *Le Villi* (One-act version 1883, Two-act version 1884, 'The Wilis'), failed to secure a prize in the competition for which it was composed, but impressed Ricordi, the publisher, sufficiently to induce him to commission a second work, *Edgar*, which failed at its first performance in 1889. *Manon Lescaut* (1893) was his first great success, but it was eclipsed by *La Bohème* (1896, 'Bohemian Life'). *Tosca* and *Madama Butterfly* (both 1900) have also remained popular favourites. His last opera, *Turandot*, was left unfinished at his death, and was completed by his friend Franco Alfano (1875–1954). He was, perhaps, the last great representative of the Italian operatic tradition, which absorbed almost all his energies throughout his mature working life.

Pudovkin, Vsevolod Illarionovich 1893–1953
Russian film director and writer

Born in Penza, he joined the State Institute for Cinematography in Moscow and in his first feature, *Mat* (1926, 'Mother'), applied his techniques of cross-cutting and montage to depict the characters' emotions. There followed the silent classics *Konets Sankt-Peterburga* (1927, 'The End of St Petersburg') and *Potomok Chingis-Khan* (1928, 'Storm Over Asia'), and such sound films as *Dezertir* ('Deserter', 1933).

Puffendorf or Pufendorf, Samuel, Freiherr von 1632–94
German writer on jurisprudence

Born near Chemnitz, he studied at Leipzig and at Jena. He was tutor to the sons of the Swedish ambassador at Copenhagen when war broke out between Denmark and Sweden. He was imprisoned, and there thought out his *Elementa Jurisprudentiae Universalis*, (1660, 'Elements of Universal Jurisprudence'), dedicated to the Elector Palatine, who made him Professor of the Law of Nations at Heidelberg (1661). As 'Severinus de Monzambano' he exposed anomalies of the constitution of the Germanic empire in *De Statu Imperii Germanici* (1667, Eng trans *The Present State of Germany*, 1690). In 1670 he became a professor at Lund, and wrote his great *De Jure Naturae et Gentium Libri Octo* (1672, Eng trans *Of the Law and Nature of Nations*, 1703), based upon **Hugo Grotius** with features from **Thomas Hobbes**. Appointed Swedish historiographer to King **Karl XI**, he published a history of Sweden from the wars between **Gustav II Adolf** to the death of Queen **Kristina**. In 1688 the Elector of Brandenburg invited him to Berlin to write the history of **Frederick William**, the Great Elector.

Pugachev, Yemelyan Ivanovich c.1744–1775
Russian Cossack soldier and pretender

He fought in the Seven Years War (1756–63) and in the war against Turkey (1769–74) before retiring to a lawless life in the south of Russia. In 1773 he proclaimed himself to be **Peter III**, the assassinated husband of **Catherine the Great**, and began a reign of organized rebellion in the south. By 1774 his power had spread alarmingly. Catherine finally sent a proper army against him, and in a battle near Tsaritsyn (now Volgograd) he was defeated, captured and conveyed in an iron cage to Moscow, where he was executed.

Puget, Pierre 1622–94
French sculptor, painter and architect

Born in Marseilles, he did most of his architectural work there. He also worked on the ceilings of the Berberini Palace in Rome and the Pitti Palace in Florence. Examples of his sculpture, such as those of Hercules, **Milo of Croton**, **Alexander the Great** and **Diogenes**, may be seen in the Louvre, Paris.

Pugh, Clifton Ernest 1924–90
Australian artist

Born in Richmond, Victoria, he studied at the Art School of the National Gallery of Victoria, Melbourne. He had his first major exhibition in 1957 and became famous with exhibitions at the Whitechapel and Tate Galleries, London, in the early 1960s. His paintings divide into two genres: his love of native Australian wildlife, reflected in his 'bush' paintings, and his perceptive portraits of academics and politicians which won him the Archibald prize in 1965, 1971 and 1972. He has also designed stage sets and illustrated a number of popular books on conservation.

Pugin, August Welby Northmore 1812–52
English architect

Born in London, the son of Auguste Pugin (1762–1832), a French architectural draughtsman, and educated at Christ's Hospital School, he trained in his father's office in London by making drawings for his father's books on Gothic buildings. He was employed by Sir **Charles Barry** to make detailed drawings for the Houses of Parliament (1836–37), for which he designed and modelled a large part of the decorations and sculpture. A convert to Roman Catholicism, he designed several Roman Catholic churches, including the cathedral in Birmingham and St Oswald's in Liverpool. He did much to revive Gothic architecture in England, and his aesthetic theories influenced people as diverse as **John Ruskin** and Sir **Henry Cole**, and provided much of the foundation for the Art and Crafts movement. He published *Contrasts between the Architecture of the 15th and 19th Centuries* (1836), *Chancel Screens* (1851) and *True Principles of Christian Architecture* (1841). 📖 Phoebe Stanton, *Pugin* (1971)

Puig, Manuel 1932–90
Argentine novelist

Born in General Villegas, a gifted writer who wrote in both Spanish and English, he has been called a 'magical realist' for his stylistic diversity and playful imagination. He came to attention with *La traición de Rita Hayworth* (1968, Eng trans *Betrayed by Rita Hayworth*, 1971), which made an ironic contrast of the 'gaucho' myth with a contemporary Argentine culture dominated by Hollywood and television, which Puig loved. *Boquitas pintadas* (1969, Eng trans *Heartbreak Tango*, 1973) was followed by a detective novel, *The Buenos Aires Affair* (1973). His biggest success was *El beso de la mujer araña* (1976, Eng trans *Kiss of the Spider Woman*, 1979). The story of the relationship which develops between two unlikely prisoners, it has been adapted for film and stage. The posthumous *Tropical Night Falling* appeared in 1992.

Pujol, Joseph, *known as* 'Le Pétomane' 1857–1945
French entertainer

Born in Marseilles, he became a music-hall entertainer as a result of his capacity for breaking wind. He appeared in public in Marseilles in 1887, and in 1892 moved to Paris, where his unusual act topped the bill at the Moulin Rouge. In 1895 he opened his own theatre, the Pompadour. Three years later he sued the Moulin Rouge for presenting a female 'Pétomane', but before the case came to court she was exposed as a fraud, having concealed various whistles and bellows in her skirts. He retired from the stage in 1914 when the outbreak of World War I made his speciality act of mock artillery barrages seem inappropriate.

Pułaski, Kazimierz 1748–79
Polish nobleman and soldier

He fought against Russia, and was outlawed at the partition of Poland (1772). In 1777 he went to the USA, and for his conduct at Brandywine was given a brigade of cavalry. In 1778 he organized 'Pułaski's legion', entered Charleston in 1779, and held it until it was relieved. He was mortally wounded at the Siege of Savannah.

Pulci, Luigi 1432–84
Italian poet

Born in Padua, he was a protégé of **Cosimo de' Medici** and wrote *Il Morgante Maggiore* (1481, 'Morgante the Giant'), a burlesque epic with **Roland** as the hero. It is one of the most valuable specimens of the early Tuscan dialect. He also produced a comic novel and several humorous sonnets. 📖 A Gianni, *Pulci uno e due* (1967)

Pulitzer, Joseph 1847–1911
US newspaper proprietor

He was born in Makó, Hungary, of Magyar-Jewish and Austro-German parents, and was educated there before emigrating to join the US army in 1864. Discharged the following year, he went penniless to St Louis, Missouri. There he became a reporter, was elected to the state legislature, and began to acquire and revitalize old newspapers, including the *New York World* (1883) which sealed his success. He endowed the Columbia University School of Journalism, and in his will established annual Pulitzer Prizes for literature, drama, music and journalism, which were first awarded in 1917. 📖 W A Swanberg, *Pulitzer* (1967)

Pullman, George Mortimer 1831–97
US inventor and businessman

He was born in Brocton, New York. A cabinetmaker by trade, he became a contractor in Chicago and a storekeeper in Colorado before designing a 'Pullman' railroad sleeping-car (patented in 1864 and 1865). The Pullman Palace Car Company was formed in 1867, and in 1880 he founded 'Pullman City' for his workers, since absorbed by Chicago.

Pulszky, Ferenc Aurelius 1814–97
Hungarian politician and writer

Born in Eperies, he studied law, travelled, and published (1837) a successful book on England. In 1848 he became **Esterházy's** factotum, but after joining the revolution went to London in 1849 to plead for help, which was never given. He stayed there to become a journalist. When **Lajos Kossuth** went to England, Pulszky became his companion and travelled with him to the USA. He was condemned to death in 1852, but after living in Italy (1852–66) and being imprisoned in Naples as a **Garibaldian**, he was pardoned in 1867 at the time of the Ausgleich. He returned to Hungary, sat in parliament and was Director of Museums.

Pulu See **Tiglath-Pileser III**

Pupin, Michael Idvorsky 1858–1935
US physicist and inventor

Born in Idvor, Austria-Hungary (formerly Yugoslavia), he arrived in the USA in 1874 as a penniless immigrant, graduated at Columbia University in 1883, and subsequently studied under **Hermann von Helmholtz** and **Gustav Kirchhoff** in Germany. He returned to the USA to become Professor of Electromechanics at Columbia (1901–31). His many inventions included a system of multiplex telegraphy using electrical tuning, and the fluoroscope, by which X-rays can be observed and photographed on a fluorescent screen. The 'Pupin inductance coil' made long-distance telephony practical by amplifying the signal at intervals along the line without distortion. His autobiography, *From Immigrant to Inventor* (1923), won the Pulitzer Prize.

Purbach or Peuerbach, Georg von 1423–61
Austrian astronomer and mathematician

Purcell, Henry 1659–95
English composer

Purcell was born in London, the son of Thomas Purcell, a court musician and Chapel Royal chorister. He was himself one of the 'children of the chapel' from about 1669 to 1673, when, his voice having broken, he was apprenticed to the keeper of the king's keyboard and wind instruments, whom he ultimately succeeded in 1683. In the meantime he had followed **Matthew Locke** as 'composer for the king's violins' (1677), and had been appointed organist of Westminster Abbey (1679) and of the Chapel Royal (1682).

It is known that he began to compose when very young, though some early pieces ascribed to him are probably the work of his uncle Henry, also a professional musician. In about 1680 he began writing incidental music to plays by **William Congreve**, **John Dryden**, **Aphra Behn**, and others for performance at the Duke of York's Theatre, and from this time until his early death his output was prolific. Although his harpsichord pieces and his well-known set of trio-sonatas for violins and continuo have retained their popularity, his greatest masterpieces are among his vocal and choral works.

In his official capacity he produced a number of fine 'welcome odes' in celebration of royal birthdays, St Cecilia's Day, and other occasions, also many anthems and services. In 1685 he wrote an anthem, *My Heart is Inditing*, for the coronation of **James II**, and he wrote music for the coronation of **William III** four years later, as well as funeral music for Queen **Mary II** in 1694.

He is credited with six operas, but of these only the first, *Dido and Aeneas*, written to a libretto by **Nathum Tate** in 1689, is opera in the true sense; it is now regarded as the first great English opera. The others, *Dioclesian* (1690; adapted from **Francis Beaumont** and **John Fletcher**), *King Arthur* (1691; John Dryden), *The Fairy Queen* (1692; adapted from *A Midsummer Night's Dream*), *The Tempest*

(1695; **Thomas Shadwell**'s adaptation) and *The Indian Queen* (1695; Dryden and Sir Robert Howard), consist essentially of spoken dialogue between the main characters interspersed with masques and other musical items supplied by nymphs, shepherds, and allegorical figures. Many of the incidental songs, such as 'I Attempt from Love's Sickness' (*The Indian Queen*), are performed as separate pieces.

Purcell was writing at a time when the new Italian influence was first beginning to be felt in England, and his music includes superb examples in both this and the traditional English style, as well as in the French style exemplified by **Jean Baptiste Lully**. John Blow's fine ode on his untimely death, and tributes by other contemporary musicians, show that he was recognized in his own time, as now, as the greatest English composer of the age. His brother Daniel (c.1663–1718) was also a distinguished composer and was for some time organist of Magdalen College, Oxford.

Purcell's fame declined after his death, and did not fully revive until the bicentenary of his death; later English composers, especially **Gustav Holst**, **Ralph Vaughan Williams** and above all **Benjamin Britten**, have done much to rehabilitate him by performance and adaptation of his music.

📖 M Burden, *The Purcell Companion* (1995); A Hutchings, *Purcell* (1982); Franklin B Zimmerman, *Henry Purcell 1659–1695: His Life and Times* (1967).

> 'Music is the exaltation of poetry. Both of them may excel apart, but surely they are most excellent when they are joined, because nothing is then wanting to either of their proportions; for thus they appear like wit and beauty in the same person.' From the Preface to *Dioclesian* (1690).

The teacher of **Regiomontanus**, he became court astrologer to **Frederick III, of Germany**, and Professor of Mathematics and Astronomy at Vienna. In astronomy he was a proponent of **Ptolemy**'s system of the solid spheres, and his extensive observational work resulted in the publication of a table of lunar eclipses in 1459. In mathematics he is thought to have been the first to introduce sines into trigonometry and he compiled a sine table. He is considered to be the first great modern astronomer.

Purcell, Edward Mills 1912–
US physicist and Nobel Prize winner

Born in Taylorville, Illinois, he studied electrical engineering at Purdue University, Illinois, and received his PhD from Harvard, where he became an associate instructor in 1938. In 1949 he was made a full professor and he was Gerhard Gade Professor of Physics from 1960 to 1980. During World War II he worked as a group leader at the Massachusetts Institute of Technology's radiation laboratory. His research has covered nuclear magnetism, radio astronomy, radar, astrophysics and biophysics. Independently of **Felix Bloch**, he developed nuclear magnetic resonance and was able to tune into resonances when nuclei were placed in a magnetic field. He was awarded the 1952 Nobel Prize for physics with Bloch for his work and won the National Medal of Science in 1979.

Purcell, Henry See panel above

Purchas, Samuel 1577–1626
English compiler of travel books

Born in Thaxted, Essex, he studied at St John's College, Cambridge, and became vicar of Eastwood (1604), then rector of St Martin's, Ludgate. He assisted **Richard Hakluyt** in his later years. His own great works were

Purchas his Pilgrimage, or Relations of the World in all Ages (1613) and *Hakluytus Posthumus, or Purchas his Pilgrimes* (1625), based on the papers of Hakluyt and archives of the East India Company. Another work is *Purchas his Pilgrim: Microcosmus, or the History of Man* (1619).

Purkinje or Purkyne, Jan Evangelista
1787–1869
Czech physiologist

Born in Libochowitz, he trained for the priesthood, studied philosophy, and finally graduated in medicine. He rose to become professor at Breslau University and later in Prague. Much of his work centred on cell observations, and in 1837 he outlined the key features of the cell theory, describing nerve cells with their dendrites, nuclei and 'Purkinje cells' in the cerebellar cortex. In 1838 he observed cell division, and in the following year promoted the word 'protoplasm' in the modern sense. He made improvements in histology, and was interested in the peculiarities of the eyes, experimenting on the visual effects of pressure applied to the eyeball. The effect of being able to see the shadows of the retinal blood vessels in one's own eye is now known as 'Purkinje's figure'.

Purkyne, Jan Evangelista See Purkinje, Jan Evangelista

Pusey, E(dward) B(ouverie) 1800–82
English theologian and leader of the 'Oxford Movement'

He was born in Pusey, Berkshire, and his father had assumed the name Pusey when he inherited the Pusey estates. He was educated at Eton and Christ Church, Oxford, was elected a Fellow of Oriel College, Oxford (1823), and whilst living in Germany (1825–27) acquainted himself with German theological teaching. In

Pushkin, Alexander Sergeyevich 1799–1837
Russian poet and writer

Pushkin was born in Moscow into an illustrious family. He attended the Lyceum at Tsarskoe Selo near St Petersburg, where his talent for poetry first emerged. In 1817 he entered government service, but because of his liberalism he was exiled in 1820 to the south. In 1824 he was dismissed and confined to his estate near Pskov, and did not return to Moscow until after the accession of Nicholas I. He married Natalia Goncharova in 1832, whose beauty attracted Baron Georges D'Anthès, a French Royalist in the Russian service. Pushkin challenged him to a duel and was mortally wounded.

Regarded as Russia's greatest poet, he had his first success was the romantic poem *Ruslan and Lyudmilla* (1820), followed by *The Prisoner of the Caucasus* (1822), *Fountain of Bakhchisarai* (1826), *Tzigani* (1827), and his

masterpiece, *Eugene Onegin* (1828), a sophisticated novel in verse that was much imitated but never rivalled. Prolific for one whose life was so short, he also wrote lyric poems, essays, the blank verse historical drama *Boris Godunov* (1825), and, in 1830, the four 'Little Tragedies': 'Mozart and Salieri', 'The Covetous Knight', 'The Stone Guest' and 'The Feast during the Plague'.

📖 W Vickers, *Pushkin* (1970); D Magarshak, *Pushkin: A Biography* (1967); B Tomashevsky, *Alexander Pushkin* (1956–61).

> 'Moscow … what surge that sound can start
> In every Russian's inmost heart!'
> *Eugene Onegin*, ch.7, stanza 36 (trans A Room).

1828 he was ordained deacon and priest, and was appointed Regius Professor of Hebrew at Oxford, a position which he retained until his death. His first work was an essay on the causes of rationalism in recent German theology, which was criticized as being itself rationalistic. His aim was to prevent the spread of Rationalism in England. He joined Cardinal John Newman, and they, with John Keble, became the leaders of the Oxford Movement (1833). Pusey wrote his contributions to the *Tracts*, especially those on Baptism and the Holy Eucharist, and in 1836 commenced the *Oxford Library of the Fathers*, to which his chief contributions were translations of Augustine's Confessions and works of Tertullian. In 1843 Pusey was suspended from preaching in Oxford for two years following his sermon asserting the presence of God in the Holy Eucharist, but at the first opportunity he reiterated his teaching. His numerous writings during this period include a letter on the practice of confession (1850) and *A Letter to the Bishop of London* (1851), a general defence of his position. He also wrote *The Doctrine of the Real Presence* (1856–57), the series of three *Eirenicons* (1865–69), and a pamphlet on *Collegiate and Professorial Teaching*. He spent large sums in helping to provide churches in East London and Leeds, and in founding sisterhoods.
📖 Henry Parry Liddon, *Life of Edward Bouverie Pusey* (4 vols, 1893–97)

Pushkin, Alexander See panel above

Putnam, Frederic Ward 1839–1915
US archaeologist and ethnographer, the founder of archaeology in the USA

Born in Salem, Massachusetts, he trained as a zoologist, turning to archaeology on being appointed curator of the Peabody Museum at Harvard (1875–1909). He was Professor of American Archaeology and Ethnology at Harvard from 1887, and curator of anthropology at the American Museum of Natural History in New York City from 1894. The author of more than 400 articles, he was also an energetic excavator, and was one of the first to study archaeological remains of the native Americans. He directed pioneer field expeditions to the Ohio River Valley, and to New Jersey, the American Southwest, Mexico, and South America. Organizer of the anthropological exhibit at the 1893 Chicago Exposition, he helped found the Field Museum of Natural History in Chicago and the department of anthropology at the University of California at Berkeley (1903). For 25 years he also served as secretary of the American Association for the Advancement of Science.

Putnam, George Palmer 1814–72
US publisher

Born in Brunswick, Maine, he went to London in 1840 and opened a branch bookshop selling US books. In 1848 he returned to the USA and founded a book-publishing business, established in 1866 as the firm of G P Putnam & Sons (now G P Putnam's Sons). In 1853 he founded *Putnam's Monthly Magazine*. He was the great-nephew of Israel Putnam.

Putnam, Hilary 1926–
US philosopher

Born in Chicago, he held teaching positions at Northwestern University and Princeton, and was Professor of the Philosophy of Science at the Massachusetts Institute of Technology (1961–65). Since 1965 he has been Professor of Philosophy at Harvard. Much of his early work was on problems arising out of physics, mathematics and logic, but he has gone on to work creatively in virtually all the main areas of philosophy. He has argued strongly for a conception of philosophy that makes it essential to a responsible view of the real world and our place in it. His main publications are *Philosophical Papers* (3 vols, 1975, 1975, 1979), *Meaning and the Moral Sciences* (1978), *Reason, Truth and History* (1982) and *Renewing Philosophy* (1992).

Putnam, Israel 1718–90
American Revolutionary soldier

Born in Danvers, Massachusetts, he was a farmer before volunteering for military service in the French and Indian War (1755–63). As a captain he helped to repel a French invasion of New York, and was present at the Battle of Lake George (1755). In 1758 he was captured and tortured by Native Americans, and he was about to be burnt alive when a French officer rescued him. In 1764 he helped to relieve Detroit, but was then besieged by Pontiac. In 1775, after Concord, he was given command of the forces of Connecticut and distinguished himself at the Battle of Bunker Hill. He held the command at New York and at Brooklyn Heights (1776), where he was defeated by Viscount Howe. In 1777 he was appointed to the defence of the Highlands of the Hudson. He was a cousin of Rufus Putnam.

Putnam, Rufus 1738–1824
American Revolutionary general

Born in Sutton, Massachusetts, he served against the French from 1757 to 1760, then settled as a farmer and millwright. In the American Revolution (1775–83) he served as an engineer, commanded a regiment, and in 1783 became brigadier-general. In 1788 he founded Marietta, Ohio, and in 1789 he was appointed a judge of the Supreme Court of the Northwest Territory. From 1793 to 1803 he was surveyor-general of the United States. He was a cousin of Israel Putnam

Puttnam, David Terence Puttnam, Baron
1941–
English filmmaker
Born in Southgate, London, he produced his first feature film *S.W.A.L.K* (1969) after a very successful background in advertising and photography. Subsequently he helped encourage new directorial talents with stylish, low-budget features such as *Bugsy Malone* (1976) and *The Duellists* (1977). *Chariots of Fire* (1981), which won four Academy Awards, epitomized the type of intelligent, humanist drama he wanted to make, and its international commercial appeal allowed him to progress to larger scale films such as *Local Hero* (1983), *The Killing Fields* (1984) and *The Mission* (1986). A tireless spokesman and figurehead of the British film industry in the early 1980s, he was chairman and chief executive of Columbia Pictures (1986–88), but his anti-establishment stance led him to return to independent production with *Memphis Belle* (1990) and *Meeting Venus* (1991). During 1992 he helped set up a European Film Studio school in Paris. He was knighted in 1995 and created a peer in 1997.

Puvis de Chavannes, Pierre 1824–98
French decorative, symbolic painter
Born in Lyons, he painted murals of the life of St Geneviève (1898) which may be seen in the Panthéon, Paris, and large allegorical works such as *Work* and *Peace*, on the staircase of the Musée de Picardie, Amiens. He created striking new images with paintings such as *The Poor Fisherman* (1881, Musée d'Orsay, Paris), which influenced younger painters and sculptors, such as Georges Seurat and Aristide Maillol, while his decorative style influenced Paul Gauguin and Odilon Redon.

Puyi (P'u-i), *personal name of* Xuan Tong (Hsuan T'ung) 1906–67
Last Emperor of China and the first Emperor of Manchuguo (Manchukuo, Manchuria)
After the revolution of 1912 the young emperor was given a pension and a summer palace near Beijing (Peking). He became known as Henry P'u-i, but in 1932 he was called from private life to be provincial dictator of the Japanese puppet state of Manchuguo and (from 1934) emperor under the name of Kang De (K'ang Te). He was imprisoned by the Russians (1945–50) and subsequently by the Chinese Communists (1950–59), who undertook his political re-education. After that he lived as a private citizen in Beijing until his death. He wrote *From Emperor to Citizen* (1964). The 1987 film *The Last Emperor* was based on his life.

Puzo, Mario 1920–
US novelist
Born in New York City and educated at Columbia University, he served in the US air force during World War II and worked for 20 years as an administrative assistant in government offices at home and overseas. His first novel was *The Dark Arena* (1955), but his breakthrough came with his novel about the Mafia, *The Godfather* (1969). The epic story of Don Corleone and his extended 'family' of Sicilian immigrants, it became a bestseller, and was filmed by Francis Ford Coppola in 1972 with Marlon Brando playing Corleone. This was followed by *The Last Don* (1996).

Pye, David 1914–93
English woodworker, designer and writer
He trained at the Architectural Association and decided to specialize in wooden buildings. However, World War II led to a shortage of wood for building, so he turned to designing furniture and making carvings. He was Professor of Furniture Design at the Royal College of Art (1964–74) and published, among others, *The Nature of Design* (1964) and *The Nature and Art of Workmanship* (1968).

Pye, Henry James, *known as* Poetical Pye
1745–1813
English poet
Born in London, he studied at Magdalen College, Oxford. He held a commission in the Berkshire militia, became MP for that county in 1784, and succeeded Thomas Warton as Poet Laureate in 1790. In 1792 he was appointed a London police magistrate. His works include *Alfred: an Epic* (1801), with numerous birthday and New-Year odes.

Pye, John David 1932–
English zoologist
Born in Mansfield, Nottingham, he was educated at University College of Wales, Aberystwyth, and Bedford College, London. He taught at King's College London, and from 1977 to 1982 was appointed head of the department of zoology, Queen Mary College, London, then professor (1973–91). His principal research has been in the use of ultrasound, which is used by a wide range of animals as a means of communication and navigation. Much of his work has concerned the echolocation used by bats to obtain food and avoid obstacles while flying, but the applications of his work have raised the possibility of controlling the social behaviour of insects, in particular those which are pests.

Pye, Poetical See Pye, Henry James

Pyle, Howard 1853–1911
US illustrator and writer
He was born in Wilmington, Delaware. In 1876 *Scribners Magazine* accepted some of his sketches while he was still helping in his father's leather business and on the strength of this success he moved to New York City. Returning to Wilmington a few years later, he began to write children's books and a growing reputation for line-and-wash depictions of colonial life led to the opening of his own art school in 1900. His children's publications indulged a liking for medieval lore and legend, and included versions of Robin Hood and King Arthur.

Pym, Barbara Mary Crampton 1913–80
English novelist
Born in Oswestry, Shropshire, she was educated at St Hilda's College, Oxford. For most of her adult life she worked at the International African Institute in London (1958–74). Her fiction is deliberately confined within narrow bounds, characteristically exploring the tragicomic lives of frustrated middle-class spinsters in a delicate, understated fashion. She published three novels in the 1950s, the best of which is *A Glass of Blessings* (1958), then lapsed into obscurity until, partly through the support of Philip Larkin, her *Quartet in Autumn* appeared in 1977. *The Sweet Dove Died* (1979) was the last book published in her lifetime, but four more novels, *A Few Green Leaves* (1980), *An Unsuitable Attachment* (1982), *Crampton Hodnet* (1985) and *An Academic Question* (1986), were published posthumously.

Pym, Francis Leslie Pym, Baron 1922–
English politician
Educated at Eton and Cambridge, he served in World War II and was awarded the Military Cross. A Conservative MP from 1961, he gained political advancement through the whips' office (assistant Whip 1962, deputy Chief Whip 1967, Government Chief Whip 1970) before he was appointed Secretary of State for Northern Ireland (1973–74). He spent two years as Defence Secretary (1979–81), and was appointed Foreign Secretary during the Falklands crisis of 1982. However, his comparatively gloomy assessments of economic prospects did not endear him to the Prime Minister, Margaret Thatcher, and he was dropped from the government following the Conservatives' 1983 landslide election victory. It seemed for a

Pythagoras c.580–c5.00BC
Greek philosopher, mystic and mathematician

Pythagoras was probably born in Samos, although the traditions regarding his life are confused. About 530 he left Samos, perhaps because of enmity to the ruler **Polycrates**, and settled in Croton, a Greek colony in southern Italy, where he attracted followers and established a community with its own rule of life. Its members, and members of other Pythagorean societies that grew up during his lifetime and later, were active in politics and were eventually suppressed. He may later have been exiled to Metapontum, where he died. Pythagoras left no writings, and his whole life is shrouded in myth and legend.

Pythagoreanism was first a way of life rather than a philosophy. Its principal belief was in the immortality and transmigration (ie reincarnation) of the soul, which is imprisoned in the body; and it emphasized moral asceticism and purification and various ritual rules of abstinence (most famously, from beans, although the reason for this is unclear). By leading a pure life, the soul can eventually achieve its release from the body, as in Orphism.

Pythagoras is also associated with mathematical discoveries involving the chief musical intervals, the relations of numbers, the theorem on right-angled triangles which bears his name, and with more fundamental beliefs about the understanding and representation of the world of nature through numbers. The equilateral triangle of 10 dots, the tetracys ('foursome') of the decad, itself became an object of religious veneration, referred to in the Pythagoran oath 'Nay, by him that gave us the *tetracys* which contains the fount and root of ever-flowing nature'.

It is impossible to disentangle Pythagoras's own views from the later accretions of mysticism and neoplatonism, but he had a profound influence on **Plato** and on later philosophers, astronomers and mathematicians.

📖 J S Kirk et al, *The Presocratic Philosophers* (2nd edn, 1983); G E R Lloyd, *Early Greek Science: Thales to Aristotle* (1970).

'There is geometry in the humming of the strings. There is music in the spacings of the spheres.' Quoted in **Aristotle**, *Metaphysics*.

---

time that he might lead an anti-Thatcher faction within the Conservative Party, but support for his 'Centre Forward' group failed to coalesce and he accepted a life peerage in 1987. He published *The Politics of Consent* in 1984.

Pym, John 1584–1643
English politician

Born in Brymore, near Bridgwater, he became a student of the Middle Temple. In 1614 he became an MP for Calne, exchanging that seat in 1625 for Tavistock. He became a member of the Country party, opposing monopolies, papistry, the Spanish match and absolutism with such vigour that he was imprisoned for three months. In 1626 he took a prominent part in the impeachment of the Duke of **Buckingham**. In 1628 he was second only to Sir **John Eliot** in supporting the Petition of Right, but opposed him on tonnage and poundage. In the Long Parliament he named the Earl of **Strafford**, formerly his friend and ally, as the 'principal author and promotor of all those counsels which had exposed the kingdom to so much ruin'. He played the leading part in Strafford's ensuing impeachment, and was also conspicuous in the proceedings against Archbishop **Laud**. He was one of the five members whom **Charles I** attempted to arrest in 1642. When war broke out he remained in London. He died a month after being appointed Lieutenant of the Ordnance. 📖 C E Wade, *John Pym* (1912)

Pynchon, Thomas 1937–
US novelist

He was born in Glen Cove, New York, and educated at Cornell University. *V* (1963), his first novel, is a loose, episodic book, influenced by the Beat generation and by Pynchon's developing use of paranoia as a structural device, centring on a mysterious female principle at work in modern history. Seen by some as wilfully obscure, by others as a swashbuckling experimentalist, he uses sprawling and loquacious language, and fabulous structures in which the normal conventions of the novel have been largely abandoned. Studiously avoiding public forums, he is obsessively studied and mined for autobiographical and more arcane references, of which there is no shortage. Subsequent publications include *The Crying of Lot 49* (1966) and *Gravity's Rainbow* (1973), concerning Tyrone Slothrop, lost in a surreal labyrinth but imbued with the wherewithal—in his reproductive organ—to predict exactly the sites of V-2 explosions in London. *Vineland* (1990) appeared to return to an earlier, more freewheeling and satirical style and received mixed reviews, particularly in Great Britain. *Slow Learner* (1984) collected early stories and included a disarmingly straightforward introduction. He published *Mason & Dixon* in 1997. 📖 T H Schaub, *Pynchon: the voice of ambiguity* (1981)

Pynson, Richard d.1530
French printer

Of Norman birth, he studied at the University of Paris, learned printing in Normandy, and practised his trade in England. In 1497 his edition of **Terence** appeared, the first classic to be printed in London. He became printer to **Henry VIII** (1508), and introduced roman type in England (1509).

Pyrrho or Pyrrhon c.365–270BC
Greek philosopher, and founder of the school of Scepticism

Born in Elis, he travelled in Persia (Iran) and India with **Alexander the Great**, and returned to Elis where he effectively established the philosophical tradition later called Scepticism. Like **Socrates**, he wrote nothing himself but had a great effect on his pupils and contemporaries. His views were reported by his disciple Timon the Sillographer. He taught that we can know nothing of the nature of things, and recommended 'suspending judgement' as an appropriate response which would bring with it 'an imperturbable peace of mind'.

Pyrrhus c.319–272BC
King of Epirus

A general ranking with **Alexander the Great**, his second cousin, he is best-known for his wars against the Romans in Italy. As king (from 307BC) he had early difficulties and lost his throne (302–297) but later emancipated Epirus from Macedonian control when the Tarentines asked for his support against Rome (281). He won battles on the River Siris (280) and at Asculum (279), after which he made the comment which has led to a victory being won at too great costs being called a 'Pyrrhic victory'. He assisted the Sicilian Greeks against the Carthaginians (278) but suffered a setback at Lilybaeum, and relations with his Greek allies broke down. In 275 he resumed his war against the Romans, but was defeated by the consul Curius Dentatus near Beneventum. He was then forced to abandon Italy and return to Epirus, where he engaged in war with **Antigonus II Gonatas**, King of Macedonia, then invaded the Peloponnese, where he failed to capture Sparta and was killed in a street fight in Argos. ◫ Petros Garoufalias, *Pyrrhus, King of Epirus* (1979)

Pythagoras See panel p1516

Pytheas of Marseilles 4th century BC
Greek navigator and geographer

Born in Massalia, he was commissioned to reconnoitre a new trade-route to the tin and amber markets of northern Europe in about 330BC. He sailed past Spain, Gaul and the east coast of Britain, and reached 'Thule', six days' sail to the north, formerly identified as Iceland but more probably northern Norway. His report on his voyage survives only in fragmentary references in later publications by other authors. ◫ C F C Hawkes, *Pytheas: Europe and the Great Explorers* (1977)

Qaboos, Bin Said 1940–
Sultan of Oman

Born in Salalah, the son of Said bin Taimar, he was educated in England and trained at Sandhurst. He disagreed with the medieval views of his father, and after five years under surveillance, overthrew him (1970) in a bloodless coup and assumed the sultanship, the 14th descendant of the ruling dynasty of the Albusaid family. He proceeded to pursue more liberal and expansionist policies, while maintaining an international position of strict non-alignment.

Qaddafi, Muammar See Gaddafi, Muammar

Qi Baishi (Ch'i Pai-shih) 1863–1957
Chinese artist

Born in Xiang Tan, Hunan, into a poor farmer's home, he took up the study of painting at 27. He also mastered calligraphy, poetry and seal-carving. His art is deeply rooted in the folk tradition, with a direct and vivid style. He attempted to assimilate influences from the early Qing (Ch'ing) individualists into his earlier background of folk art, and the innovative style which evolved reflected these influences together with a keen observation of nature. He painted birds, flowers, fruit and landscapes, and many other subjects from daily life previously considered to be inappropriate subjects for art. His spontaneous, calligraphic and even humorous style was unique. Sometimes called China's **Picasso**, he was a prolific and versatile artist whose school became established as the mainstream in contemporary Chinese painting.

Qiu Jin (Ch'iu Chin) 1875–1907
Chinese feminist and revolutionary

She left her family to study in Japan in 1904, where she became actively involved in radical Chinese student associations calling for the overthrow of the Manchu Qing (Ch'ing) dynasty. Returning to China in 1906, she founded a women's journal in which she argued that the liberation of women was an essential prerequisite for a strong China. In 1907 she was implicated in an abortive anti-Manchu uprising and was executed by the Qing authorities.

Quadros, Jânio da Silva 1917–
Brazilian politician

He worked as a teacher and lawyer before being appointed governor of São Paulo in 1955, and served a seven-month term as President in 1961 before resigning and seeking exile. He eventually returned to his country, was rehabilitated, and became Mayor of São Paulo in 1985.

Quant, Mary 1934–
English fashion designer

Born in London, she studied at Goldsmiths College and began fashion design when she opened a small boutique in Chelsea in 1955. Two years later she married one of her partners, Alexander Plunkett Greene. Her clothes became extremely fashionable in the 1960s when the geometric simplicity of her designs, especially the miniskirt, and the originality of her colours, became an essential feature of the 'swinging Britain' era. In the 1970s she extended into cosmetics and textile design. In 1990 she won the British Fashion Council's Hall of Fame award. 📖 *Quant by Quant* (1966)

Quantz, Johann Joachim 1697–1773
German flautist and composer

Born near Göttingen, he spent many years in the service of the King of Saxony, touring extensively in Italy, France and England, and becoming the teacher of **Frederick II, the Great**, and later his court composer. Author of a treatise on flute-playing, he composed some 300 concertos for one or two flutes as well as a great quantity of other flute music.

Quarles, Francis 1592–1644
English religious poet

Born near Romford, Essex, he studied at Christ's College, Cambridge, and at Lincoln's Inn. He was successively cup-bearer to the princess Elizabeth (Queen of Bohemia) when she went to marry Elector **Frederick V** in Germany (1613), secretary to Archbishop **Ussher** (c.1629), and chronologer to the City of London (1639). Because he was a Royalist, his books and manuscripts were destroyed. He wrote abundantly in prose and verse, his *Emblems* (1635) being his best-known work, although *Hieroglyphikes of the Life of Man* (1638) was also popular. Other poetical works include *A Feast of Wormes* (1620), *Argalus and Parthenia* (1629), *Divine Poems* (1630), *The Historie of Samson* (1631) and *Divine Fancies* (1632). His prose includes *Enchyridion* (1640, a book of aphorisms) and *The Profest Royalist* (1645). 📖 J Horder, *Francis Quarles* (1953)

Quarton, *sometimes* Charonton *or* Charrenton, Enguerrand 15th century
French painter

Active in Avignon, he is the best-known late medieval French artist. Documents relating to six of his important paintings survive, one of which (for a Coronation of the Virgin) is among the most comprehensive and interesting documents of early French art, since it includes the views both of the patron and the artist. Quarton's style united French and Italian influences and some have attributed to him the most famous of 15th-century French paintings, the *Pietà* of Villeneuve-lès-Avignon.

Quasimodo, Salvatore 1901–68
Italian poet and Nobel Prize winner

Born in Syracuse, Sicily, he was a student of engineering, then a travelling inspector for the Italian state power board, before taking up a career in literature and music. A Professor of Literature at the Milan Conservatorio, he wrote several volumes of poetry using both Christian and mythological allusions. His works include *Ed è Subito Sera* (1942, 'And Suddenly It Is Evening'), *La Vita non è sogno* (1949, 'Life is Not a Dream') and *La Terra impareggiabile* (1958, 'The Matchless Earth'). A collection of translated works was published as *Selected Poems* (1965). He won the Nobel Prize for literature in 1959. 📖 P Mazzamutto, *Salvatore Quasimodo* (1967)

Quastel, Juda Hirsch 1899–1987
English biochemist

Born in Sheffield, he studied chemistry at Imperial College, London, and worked on bacterial metabolism at Cambridge with **Frederick Gowland Hopkins**. In 1930 he became staff biochemist at Cardiff City Mental Hospital, where he began pioneer studies on biochemical aspects of mental disease. He proceeded on three main, complementary fronts: examining the metabolism of brain tissue; co-ordinating his laboratory research with clinical investigations, and developing tests for schizophrenia; and investigating the neurochemistry of neuroactive chemicals, especially the synthesis of acetylcholine. During World War II he worked at Rothamsted Experimental Station (1940–47) on soil biochemistry, examining the structure and metabolic profiles of different types of soil, developing artificial chemical conditioners and producing a particularly powerful selective herbicide. In 1947 he accepted an invitation to go to Montreal to return to brain chemistry, becoming Professor of Biochemistry at McGill University and deputy director of a biochemical research unit of Montreal General Hospital, where he worked on a wide range of neurochemical problems. In 1964 he moved to the Kinsman Laboratories at Vancouver, working on acid metabolism in the brain.

Quayle, Sir Anthony 1913–89
English actor and director

Born in Ainsdale, Lancashire, he made his first stage appearance in 1931, and joined the Old Vic Company (1932–39). After six years' army service in World War II he joined the Shakespeare Memorial Theatre company at Stratford-upon-Avon as actor and theatre director (1948–56). During his years there he played 20 leading roles, directed 12 plays, and transformed a provincial repertory company into a theatre of international standing, providing much of the groundwork for the creation of the Royal Shakespeare Company (1960). He returned to London, and during the next decade appeared in several contemporary plays now established as classics. In 1982 he founded the Compass Theatre Company, dedicated to touring classical plays to the regions of Great Britain. He also had a successful film career, with roles in major films, including *The Guns of Navarone* (1961) and *Lawrence of Arabia* (1962). He was knighted in 1985.

Quayle, Dan (James Danforth) 1947–
US Republican politician

Born in Indianapolis, Indiana, into a rich and influential newspaper-owning family, he studied political science, then underwent legal training and was admitted to the Indiana Bar in 1974. He was elected to the House of Representatives as a Republican from Indiana in 1977 and to the Senate in 1981. He had little national reputation when, in 1988, he was chosen as the running-mate of **George Bush** in an effort to add youth and good looks to the election campaign. His selection pleased the right wing of the party, which admired his conservative views on defence, fiscal and moral matters, but was elsewhere strongly criticized by those who pointed to his relative lack of experience and his difficulty in managing syntax. During Quayle's vice-presidency (1989–93), his sometimes ill-chosen remarks and actions served as a constant source of material for critical commentators and for comedians. He published *Standing Firm* in 1994. ⌂ Bob Woodward and David S Broder, *The Man Who Would be President: Dan Quayle* (1992)

Queen, Ellery, *pseudonym of* Frederick Dannay 1905–82 and Manfred B Lee 1905–71
US writers of crime fiction

Both born in Brooklyn, New York City, they were cousins. As businessmen they entered a detective-story competition, and won with *The Roman Hat Mystery* (1929). From then on they concentrated on detective fiction, using Ellery Queen both as pseudonym and as the name of their detective. Others of their very popular stories are *The Greek Coffin Mystery* (1932), *The Tragedy of X* (1940) and *Double, Double* (1950). They also wrote under the pseudonym Barnaby Ross, featuring the detective Drury Lane. In 1941 they founded *Ellery Queen's Mystery Magazine*. ⌂ F M Nevins Jnr, *Royal Bloodline: Ellery Queen, Author and Detective* (1974)

Queensberry, Sir John Sholto Douglas, 8th Marquis of 1844–1900
Scottish representative peer, and patron of boxing

In 1867 he supervised the formulation by **John Graham Chambers** of new rules to govern boxing, since known as the 'Queensberry Rules'. In 1895 he was unsuccessfully sued for criminal libel by **Oscar Wilde**, of whose friendship with his son, Lord **Alfred Douglas**, he disapproved, and it was his allegations of homosexuality that led in turn to Wilde's trial and imprisonment.

Queipo de Llano, Gonzalo, Marquis of Queipo de Llano y Sevilla 1875–1951
Spanish soldier

Born in Valladolid, he fought in Cuba and Morocco, and became a major-general in the Republican army. He went over to the rebel side at the beginning of the Spanish Civil War, and his forces captured Seville in 1936. He became Commander-in-Chief of the Southern army. In one of his many propaganda broadcasts from Seville he originated the phrase 'fifth column', using it to describe the rebel supporters inside Madrid, who were expected to add their strength to that of the four columns attacking from the outside. In 1950 he was given the title of marquis.

Queneau, Raymond 1903–76
French novelist, poet and painter

He was born in Le Havre and educated at the Sorbonne. From 1938 he worked on *Encyclopédie de la Pléiade* and became its director for two decades (1955–75). His novels included *Le Chiendent* (1933, Eng trans *The Bark Tree*, 1968), a witty reworking of **Descartes**, the untranslatable, punning verse novel *Chêne et chien* (1937), *Pierrot mon ami* (1942, Eng trans *Pierrot*, 1950) and *Zazie dans le métro* (1959, Eng trans *Zazie*, 1960). Queneau was a founder member of OuLiPo, the hermetic Ouvroir de Littérature Potentielle, a philosophy related to the 'Pataphysical science of imaginary solutions'. His most famous book is the *Exercices de style* (1947, Eng trans *Exercises in Style*, 1958), which gives a multiplicity of versions of exactly the same literary 'opening'. His verse was published in *Cent mille milliards de poèmes* (1961, Eng trans *One Hundred Million Million Poems*, 1983); an English edition of his poetry appeared in 1970. He also wrote as Sally Mara and published 'her' *Œuvres complètes* in 1962. ⌂ R Cobb, *Queneau* (1976)

Quennell, Sir Peter Courtney 1905–93
English biographer

Born in London and educated at Balliol College, Oxford, he became Professor of English at Tokyo in 1930, and wrote *A Superficial Journey through Tokio and Pekin* (1932). The author of several books of verse and a novel, and editor of *The Cornhill Magazine* (1944–51), he is best known for his biographical studies of **Byron** (1935, 1941), **Caroline of Ansbach** (1939), **John Ruskin** (1949), **Shakespeare** (1963), **Pope** (1968) and **Samuel Johnson** (1972), as well as those of James Boswell, Edward Gibbon, Laurence Sterne and John Wilkes in *Four Portraits* (1945), and *Hogarth's Progress* (1955). He edited many volumes of literary studies, and wrote two autobiographical books, *The Marble Foot* (1976) and *The Wanton Chase* (1980). He was knighted in 1992.

Quental, Anthero de 1842–91
Portuguese poet

Born in Ponta Delgada in the Azores, he studied at Lisbon and Coimbra, publishing his first collection of sonnets in 1861 and his *Odes Modernas* in 1865. He then published a pamphlet, *Good Sense and Good Taste*, which exposed the view that poetry depends upon richness and vitality of ideas rather than upon technical skill with words. He lived in Paris and the USA from 1866 to 1871, and on his return to Portugal was a leading socialist until, after a severe nervous illness, he committed suicide. ⌂ J B Carreira, *Anthero de Quental* (1948)

Quentin, Dorothy, *properly* Madeleine Batten
1911–
New Zealand writer
She was a prolific writer of romantic fiction who, in 30 years, wrote an average of two novels a year. From *Brave Enterprise* (1939) to *Goldenhaze* (1969), her 59 books are mainly set in a New Zealand which she portrays as an ideal society in a sub-US utopia. Only occasionally, as in *Lugano Love Story* (1960), does the scene move to England or Europe. Her books were published in London and were written for a large international readership.

Quercia, Jacopo Della c.1367–1438
Italian sculptor
He was born in Quercia Grossa, Siena, and spent some time in Lucca, where one striking example of his work in the Cathedral is the tomb of Ilaria del Carretto with its mixture of Gothic and Renaissance styles (c.1406). In direct contrast are the strongly dramatic reliefs for the doorway of the Church of San Petronio in Bologna which he left unfinished at his death. His *Fonte Gaia* (1419) is in Siena Museum, and between 1417 and 1431 he worked on the Baptistery doors in Siena.

Quesada, Gonzalo Jiménez de c.1497–1579
Spanish conquistador
Born in Córdoba or Granada, he was appointed magistrate at Santa Marta, in present-day Colombia. In 1536 he conquered the rich territory of the Chibchas in the east, naming it New Granada, and its chief town Santa Fé de Bogotá. In 1569, during a later expedition in search of El Dorado, he reached the river Guaviare not far from the point where it meets the Orinoco. His history, *Los tres ratos de Suesca*, is lost.

Quesnay, François 1694–1774
French physician and economist
Born in Mérey, near Paris, he studied medicine in Paris, and rose to become first physician to Louis XV. His fame, however, depends on his essays in political economy. Around him and his friend, M de Gournay, the famous group of the *Économistes* gathered, also known as the Physiocratic school. Quesnay's views were set forth in *Tableaux économiques* ('Economic Tables'). Only a few copies were printed (1758), and these are lost, but Quesnay's principles are well known from his contributions to the *Encyclopédie* and from his *Maximes du gouvernement économique* ('Maxims of Economic Government') and *Le Droit naturel* ('Natural Law'). He was sometimes known as the 'European Confucius'.

Quesnel, Pasquier 1634–1719
French Jansenist theologian
Born in Paris, he studied at the Sorbonne, and in 1662 became director of the Paris Oratory, where he wrote *Réflexions morales sur le Nouveau Testament* (1692, 'Reflections on Morality on the New Testament'). In 1675 he published the works of Leo I, the Great, which, for Gallicanism in the notes, was placed on the *Index*. Having refused to condemn Jansenism in 1684, he fled to Brussels, where his *Réflexions* were published (1687–94). The Jesuits were unceasing in their hostility and Quesnel was flung into prison (1703), but escaped to Amsterdam. His book was condemned in the bull *Unigenitus* (1713).

Quételet, (Lambert) Adolphe Jacques
1796–1874
Belgian statistician and astronomer
Born in Ghent and educated at the Lycée de Ghent, he became Professor of Mathematics at the Brussels Athenaeum (1819) and Professor of Astronomy at the Military School (1836). In his greatest book, *Sur l'homme* (1835, Eng trans *A Treatise on Man and the Development of His Faculties*, 1842), as in *L'Anthropométrie* (1871), he showed the

use that may be made of the theory of probabilities as applied to the 'average man', he advocated the use of statistics to formulate social laws and his views on this aroused considerable controversy. His grasp of the mathematical theory of statistics is thought to have been slight, and his methods unsophisticated.

Quevedo y Villegas, Francisco Gómez de
1580–1645
Spanish writer
He was born in Madrid and his father was secretary to the queen, his mother a lady-in-waiting. He attended the University of Alcalá. The fatal result of a duel drove him in 1611 to the court of the Duke of Ossuna, Viceroy of Sicily, but because Quevedo was involved in Ossuna's fall in 1619, he was put in prison, though allowed to retire to the Sierra Morena. He returned to Madrid in 1623 and was a favourite at the court of Philip IV. His *Política de Dios* (1626, 'Politics of God') was followed in 1628 by *Discorso de todos los diablos, o Infierno enmendado* ('Discourse on the Devil's Death; or, Hell Reformed'). He was one of the most prolific Spanish poets, but except for the *Flores* of Espinosa (1605), the few pieces published in his lifetime were printed without his consent. About a dozen of his short pieces are extant. His first book of prose (1620) was a biography of St Thomas de Villanueva, and his last one of St Paul (1644). Most of his prose is devotional. His picaresque novel, *Historia de la Vida del Buscón Pablos* (1626, Eng trans *The Life and Adventures of Buscon the Witty Spaniard*, 1657), or, as it was called after his death, the *Gran Tacaño*, took its place beside Enrique Moreno Baez's *Guzmán de Alfarache*. His five *Sueños* (Eng trans *Visions*, 1640) were printed in 1627. 📖 O H Green, *Courtly Love in Quevedo* (1952)

Quezon, Manuel Luis 1878–1944
Philippine statesman
Born in Baler, Luzon, he studied at Manila, served with Emilio Aguinaldo during the insurrection of 1898 and in 1905 became Governor of Tayabas. In 1909 he went to Washington as one of the resident Philippine commissioners and began to work for his country's independence. President of the Philippine senate from 1916 to 1935, he was elected first President of the Philippine Commonwealth (1935). He established a highly centralized government verging on one-man rule and displayed great courage during the Japanese onslaught on General Douglas MacArthur's defences in 1941, refusing to evacuate to the USA until appealed to by President Franklin D Roosevelt. He died in Saranac, in the USA. The new capital of the Philippines on the island of Luzon is named after him.

Quiller-Couch, Sir Arthur 1863–1944
English writer
Born in Bodmin, Cornwall, he was educated at Clifton College and Trinity College, Oxford, where he became a lecturer in classics (1886–87). After some years of literary work in London and in Cornwall, where he lived from 1891, he became Professor of English Literature at Cambridge (1912). He edited the *Oxford Book of English Verse* (1900) and other anthologies, and published volumes of essays, criticism, poems and parodies, among them *From a Cornish Window* (1906), *On the Art of Writing* (1916), *Studies in Literature* and *On the Art of Reading* (1920). He is also remembered for a series of humorous novels set in a Cornish background, written under the pseudonym 'Q'. 📖 B Willey, *The Q Tradition* (1946)

Quilter, Roger 1877–1953
English composer
Born in Brighton, Sussex, he studied in Germany and lived entirely by composition, holding no official posts and making few public appearances. His works include

an opera, *Julia* (1936), a radio opera *The Blue Boar*, and the *Children's Overture* (1919), based on nursery tunes. He is best known, however, for his songs, including *Songs of the Sea* (1900), 'Now Sleeps the Crimson Petal' (1904) and 'To Julia' (1906).

Quimby, Harriet 1882–1912
US aviator and journalist
Born in Arroyo Grande, California, she became the first woman to earn her pilot's licence in 1911, eight years after the first flight of the **Wright** Brothers. She was also the first woman to fly across the English Channel on 12 April, 1912, which **Louis Blériot** had done for the first time in 1909.

Quin, James 1693–1766
English actor
Born in London, he was educated in Dublin and made his debut there in 1714. He first found success at Drury Lane, London, when in 1716 the sudden illness of a leading actor led to Quin's being called on to play Bajazet in *Tamerlane*. At Lincoln's Inn Fields (1718–32) and at Covent Garden and Drury Lane (1734–41) he became established as a leading tragic actor. His last years were spent in vain rivalry with **David Garrick**, whose more 'natural' style superseded the declamatory tradition mastered by Quin. He retired in 1751.

Quincey, Thomas De See De Quincey, Thomas

Quincy, Josiah 1772–1864
US politician
Born in Boston, he graduated at Harvard, and was called to the Bar in 1793. He was a leading member of the Federal Party and, elected to Congress in 1804, distinguished himself as an orator. He denounced slavery and, in a remarkable speech, declared that the admission of Louisiana would be a sufficient cause for the dissolution of the union. Disgusted with the triumph of the Democrats and the War of 1812, he declined re-election to Congress. He was a member of the Massachusetts legislature, served as Mayor of Boston from 1823 to 1828, and from 1829 to 1845 was president of Harvard.

Quine, William Van Orman 1908–
US philosopher and logician
Born in Akron, Ohio, he was trained, initially in mathematics, at Oberlin College in Ohio, then at Prague, Oxford and at Harvard under **Alfred Whitehead**, and became Professor of Philosophy at Harvard (1948–78). He was greatly influenced by **Rudolf Carnap**, the 'Vienna Circle' of philosophers and the empiricist tradition generally, but went on to make his own distinctive and original contributions to philosophy. He made many important technical contributions to mathematical logic, but is best known through such philosophical works as *Two Dogmas of Empiricism* (1951), *From a Logical Point of View* (1953), *Word and Object* (1960) and *The Roots of Reference* (1973). In these he challenges the standard, sharp distinctions between analysis and synthetic truths and between science and metaphysics, and presents a systematic philosophy of language of his own which successfully challenged the hitherto dominant linguistic philosophy of **Ludwig Wittgenstein** and **John Langshaw Austin**. More recent publications include *The Logic Sequences* (1990) and *From Stimulus to Science* (1995).

Quinet, Edgar 1803–75
French writer and politician
Born in Bourg, he studied at Strasbourg, Geneva, Paris and Heidelberg. The remarkable introduction to his translation of **Johann Herder**'s *Philosophy of History* (1825) won him the friendship of **Victor Cousin** and **Jules Michelet**. His reputation was established by *Ahasvérus*

(1833), a kind of spiritual imitation of the ancient mysteries. Appointed Professor of Foreign Literature at Lyons in 1839, he began the lectures which formed his *Du génie des religions* (1842, 'On the Genius of Religions'). Recalled to the Collège de France in Paris, he joined Michelet in attacking the Jesuits, and his lectures caused so much excitement that the government suppressed them in 1846. During the 1848 revolution Quinet took his place on the barricades, and in the National Assembly voted with the extreme left. After the coup d'état of 1851 he was exiled. He wrote the historical works *La Révolution religieuse au XIXe siècle* (1857, 'The Religious Revolution of the 19th Century'), *Histoire de mes idées* (1858, 'History of My Ideas'), *Histoire de la campagne de 1815* (1862, 'History of the Campaign of 1815') and *La Révolution* (1865). After the downfall of **Napoleon III** he returned to Paris. He sat in the National Assemblies at Bordeaux and Versailles, and aroused great enthusiasm by his speeches. 📖 A Vales, *Edgar Quinet, sa vie et son œuvre* (1935)

Quinn, Anthony Rudolph Oaxaca 1915–
US actor
Born in Chihuahua, Mexico, he worked at a variety of menial jobs before making his stage debut in *Clean Beds* (1936) and his film debut in *Parole!* (1936). In Hollywood from 1936, he played villains and supporting characters of all nationalities in numerous exotic adventure stories. His versatility and strength as an actor became more apparent in the 1950s when he starred in *La Strada* (1954), received Best Supporting Academy Awards for *Viva Zapata!* (1952) and *Lust for Life* (1956), and was also nominated for *Wild is The Wind* (1957). He received a further nomination for *Zorba the Greek* (1964) and has since played a number of larger-than-life characters in films like *The Secret of Santa Vittoria* (1969) and *The Greek Tycoon* (1978). His stage work includes *A Streetcar Named Desire* (1950) and the musical *Zorba!* (1983–86). He has also directed the film *The Buccaneer* (1958). 📖 *The Original Sin* (1972) and *One Man Tango* (1995)

Quintana, Manuel José 1772–1857
Spanish poet and advocate
He was born in Madrid, where his house was frequented by advanced liberals. Besides his classic work *Vidas de los Españoles célebres* (2 vols, 1807–34, 'Lives of Famous Spaniards'), he published tragedies and poetry written in a classical style, the best of which are his patriotic odes. On the restoration of **Ferdinand VII** he was imprisoned (1814–20), but he recanted, and by 1833 had become tutor to Queen **Isabella**. He was crowned national poet in 1855. 📖 J V Selma, *Idearioo de Manuel José Quintana* (1961)

Quintero, Serafín and Joaquín Álvarez See Álvarez Quintero, Serafín and Joaquín

Quintilian, *properly* Marcus Fabius Quintilianus
c.35–c.100AD
Roman rhetorician
Born in Calagurris (Calahorra), Spain, he studied oratory at Rome, and returned there in 68AD in the train of **Servius Sulpicius Galba**. He became eminent as a pleader, and still more as a state teacher of the oratorical art, his pupils including **Pliny the Younger** and the two great-nephews of **Domitianus**. The emperor named him consul and gave him a pension. His reputation rests on his great work *Institutio Oratoria* ('Education of an Orator'), a complete system of rhetoric in 12 books, remarkable for its sound critical judgements, purity of taste, admirable form and the perfect familiarity it exhibits with the literature of oratory. Quintilian's own style is excellent, though not free from the florid ornament and poetic metaphor characteristic of his age.

Quirk, (Charles) Randolph Quirk, Baron
1920–
British grammarian and writer on language

He was born in Lambfell on the Isle of Man and studied at University College London where, after a period as lecturer and professor at Durham (1954–60), he was appointed Professor of English (1960–81). He has also been director of the Survey of English Usage (1959–81). He has written widely on grammar, most notably in *A Comprehensive Grammar of the English Language* (1985). He was Vice-Chancellor of London University (1981–85) and President of the British Academy (1985–89), and was knighted in 1985 and created a life peer in 1994.

Quiroga, Horacio 1878–1937
Uruguayan story writer and poet

He was born in Salto. His life was a chapter of horrible accidents out of which he drew his inspiration to create a new genre: the mature horror story crossed with the animal fable. His father shot himself (probably), and so did his first wife and two of his children. He himself shot and killed a friend by accident at the turn of the century, and had to flee to Buenos Aires. He was a manic-depressive, subject to strange states of anxiety, tension, agitated depression and hypomania—all of which he tried to relieve through drink. He became a cotton planter in the Chaco region of Argentina, and no writer has evoked this uncanny wilderness with more accuracy. He is not always seen at his best in the English-language collections *Stories of the Jungle* (1922, 1923, 1940). He had the ability to see men in animals, and vice versa, but in his tales morbidity is taken to its last extreme. When he learned that he had cancer he also shot himself. 📖 N Jitrik, *Horacio Quiroga* (1967, in Spanish)

Quiros, Pedro Fernandez de 1565–1615
Portuguese navigator

He was born in Evora. In 1595 he sailed from Peru as chief pilot and master of the *San Geronimo* during the expedition of Don Alvaro de Mendaña y Castro to colonize the Solomon Islands. Mendaña died at Santa Cruz and command of the fleet was assumed by his widow Doña Ysabel Barreto. A second attempt was made in 1605 and Quiros landed on an island he named Austrialia [sic] del Espiritu Santo, believing it to be part of the northern coast of the Great South Land (Australia). Forced to sail on after a mutiny, Quiros abandoned his second-in-command, Luis Vaez de Torres. He returned to Spain in 1607, but died at Panama in 1615 on his way back to Peru to begin another voyage. 📖 Markham (trans & ed), *Voyages of P F de Quiros 1595–1606* (1903)

Quisling, Vidkun (Abraham Lauritz Jonsson)
1887-1945
Norwegian fascist leader

Born in Fyresdal, he embarked on a military career, graduating from military academy in 1911, and went on to serve as a military attaché in Russia and Finland (1918–21) and to work with Fridtjof Nansen as a relief administrator in the USSR (1922–26). Quisling entered politics in 1929 and was Minister of Defence from 1931 to 1932. In 1933 he founded a new party, Nasjonal Samling (National Union), in imitation of the German National Socialist Party. However, the party met with little electoral success and disintegrated after 1936. He then turned to Germany and in 1939 made contact with the Nazi leader, Alfred Rosenberg, and the head of the German navy, Admiral Erich Raeder, as well as with Hitler himself. Following the German invasion of Norway in 1940, Quisling declared himself head of a government but won no support and was forced to step down six days later. It was from this point onward that his name became synonymous with 'traitor'. The German occupation authorities reluctantly allowed Quisling to head a puppet government from 1942 onwards. At the end of World War II he was arrested and put on trial, and executed by firing squad in 1945. 📖 Paul M Hayes, *Quisling: The Career and Political Ideas of Vidkun Quisling, 1887–1945* (1972)

Raab, Julius 1891–1964
Austrian statesman
Born in St Pölten, he became an engineer and was a Christian Socialist member of the Austrian Diet (1927–34), and Federal Minister of Trade and Transport (1938). He retired from politics during the Nazi regime, and in 1945 was one of the founders of the People's Party, chairman of the party (1951–60), Minister of Economic Reconstruction, and in 1953 was elected Chancellor of Austria.

Rabearivelo, Jean-Joseph 1901–37
Malagasy Francophone poet
Although he never perfected his knowledge of French, by a mixture of luck and genius, he managed to construct a poetic French which reflected the heart of Malagasy experience. He made use of popular ballad forms of Madagascar, especially the 'hain-teny' (traditional love poetry), to write hauntingly tropical poems evocative of the excited melancholy which was native to him. He killed himself when French officials, whose relentlessness had already driven him to drugs, refused to allow him to visit France, where he had hoped to study. An English translation of his poetry was published as *24 Poems* (1962).

Rabelais, François See panel p1524

Rabi, Isidor Isaac 1898–1988
US physicist and Nobel Prize winner
Born in Rymanow, Austria, he was a graduate of Cornell and Columbia universities, the latter granting him his doctorate in 1927. He was appointed professor at Columbia in 1937 and remained there until his retirement in 1967. Rabi developed the resonance method for accurately determining the magnetic moments of fundamental particles, which won him the 1944 Nobel Prize for physics. He contributed to the development of radar and the nuclear bomb, and to the development of the laser and the atomic clock. He was one of the founders of the Brookhaven National Laboratory, and as a member of UNESCO, he originated the movement that established CERN (Conseil Européen pour la Recherche Nucléaire) in Geneva. ☐ John S Rigden, *Rabi: American Physicist* (1987)

Rabin, Yitzhak See panel p1525

Rabuka, Sitiveni 1948–
Fijian soldier and politician
He was born in the village of Drekeniwai, north of Sura. After leaving the Queen Victoria School he joined the Fijian army and was trained at Sandhurst in England. After serving with the UN peacekeeping force in Lebanon, he returned to Fiji with the rank of colonel. After the 1987 elections, which resulted in an Indian-dominated coalition government, he staged a coup which removed Prime Minister Kamisese Mara, and set up his own provisional government. The country was declared a republic and in December Prime Minister Mara was reinstated, but Rabuka retained control of the security forces and internal affairs. He became Deputy Prime Minister in 1991, then Prime Minister in 1992.

Rachel, Élisa, *properly* **Élisa Félix** 1821–58
French actress
Born in Mumpf, Switzerland, the daughter of Alsatian-Jewish pedlars, she was taken to Paris about 1830. There she was taught singing and elocution, and made her debut in *La Vendéenne* (1837), with moderate success. In 1838 she appeared as Camille in *Horace* at the Théâtre Français and soon became established as a great classical actress, scoring her greatest triumph as Phèdre in Racine's play.

She achieved further success in *Adrienne Lecouvreur*, written for her by Legouvé and **Eugène Scribe**, and was enthusiastically received on visits to London, Brussels, Berlin and St Petersburg. She died in the USA of tuberculosis.

Rachman, Peter 1919–62
British property developer
Born in Poland of Jewish parents, he survived persecution by the Nazis and a Stalinist labour camp. When **Hitler** invaded Russia in 1941, he was sent to fight alongside the British in the Middle East, and in 1946 he went to Great Britain where he was settled at various refugee camps. After some years working in a factory and as a tailor's assistant, in 1950 he started letting flats to prostitutes at exorbitant rents. As a result, he was rapidly able to indulge his taste for a lavish and expensive lifestyle. He also let rooms and flats to homeless West Indian tenants, and his name gave rise to the term 'Rachmanism', the exploitation of poor tenants by unscrupulous landlords. By 1959 many of his tenants had taken him to the rents tribunal, and he was obliged to sell off his properties. He became involved with **Christine Keeler** and **Mandy Rice-Davies**. After his death neither his creditors nor his family could believe that he had no money, but the supposed 'missing million' was never traced.

Rachmaninov or **Rakhmaninov, Sergei Vasilevich** 1873–1943
Russian composer and pianist
Born in Nizhny Novgorod, he studied at the St Petersburg Conservatory and later in Moscow, where he won the gold medal for composition. A distinguished performer, he travelled all over Europe on concert tours, visiting London in 1899. Having fled from the Russian Revolution, he settled in the USA in 1918. An accomplished composer as well, he wrote operas, orchestral works and songs, but is best known for his piano music, which includes four concertos, the first three of which achieved great popularity. The popular Prelude in C Sharp Minor was so much in demand that even the composer himself grew tired of it. His style, largely devoid of national characteristics, epitomizes the lush romanticism of the later 19th century, which is still apparent in *Rhapsody on a Theme of Paganini* (1934) for piano and orchestra, a work of great craftsmanship which has remained a concert favourite. ☐ S Norris, *Rachmaninov* (1976)

Racine, Jean See panel p1526

Rackham, Arthur 1867–1939
English artist and book illustrator
Born in London, he studied at the Lambeth School of Art. He became a water-colourist and book illustrator, who was well known for his typically Romantic and grotesque pictures in books of fairy tales, including *Peter Pan* (1906) and his own *Arthur Rackham Fairy Book* (1933).

Radcliffe, Ann, *née* **Ward** 1764–1823
English romantic novelist
She was born in London, and in 1789 published the first of her Gothic romances, *The Castles of Athlin and Dunbayne*, followed by *A Sicilian Romance* (1790), *The Romance of the Forest* (1791), *The Mysteries of Udolpho* (1794) and *The Italian* (1797). She travelled widely, and her journal reveals a keen eye for natural scenery and ruins. A sixth romance, *Gaston de Blondeville*, with a metrical tale, 'St Alban's Abbey', and a short *Life*, was published in 1826. Her reputation among her contemporaries was considerable. She was praised by Sir **Walter Scott**, and influenced writers such as **Byron**,

Rabelais, François 1483 or 1494–1553
French monk, physician and satirist

Rabelais was born in or near the town of Chinon in the Loire Valley, where his father was an advocate. Almost nothing is known of his private life. He became a novice of the Franciscan order, and entered the monastery of Fontenay-le-Comte, where he had access to a large library. There he learned Greek, Hebrew and Arabic, studied all the Latin and French authors whose works he could find, and took an interest in medicine, astronomy, botany and mathematics. Eventually he became dissatisfied with the Franciscan attitude to learning, and obtained permission to pass from the Franciscan to the Benedictine order (1524).

He went to Montpellier to study medicine, and in 1532 became a physician in Lyons, then a considerable intellectual centre. There he began the series of books for which he is best known. In 1532 he wrote *Pantagruel*, a sequel to *The Great and Inestimable Chronicles of the Grand and Enormous Giant Gargantua*, which was not by him), in which serious ideas are set forth side by side with satirical comment and irreverent mockery. In 1534 he wrote a new *Gargantua*, which was more serious in tone than *Pantagruel*. Both books were published under the name of Alcofribas Nasier, an anagram of François Rabelais, and were enormously successful, though disapproved of by the Church due to their irreverence.

In 1533 and 1536 he travelled in Italy with Jean du Bellay, Bishop of Paris, who later became a cardinal. There Rabelais spent his time collecting plants and curiosities, and he gave France the melon, artichoke and carnation. He also received permission to go into any Benedictine house which would receive him, and was enabled to hold ecclesiastical offices and to practise medicine. From 1537 (when he took his doctorate) to 1538 he taught in Montpellier.

From 1540 to 1543 he was in the service of the cardinal's brother, Guillaume du Bellay, partly in Turin (where Guillaume was Governor), and partly in France. Guillaume died in 1543, in which year Rabelais was appointed a *maître des requêtes*, or counsel of the Conseil d'État. In 1546 he published his *Tiers Livre* ('Third Book'), this time under his own name. It was again condemned, and he fled to Metz, where he practised medicine. In 1548, Jean du Bellay, now in Rome, sent for Rabelais to be his physician, and Rabelais received a living from him for two years. A *Quart Livre* ('Fourth Book') appeared in part in 1548, and complete in 1552–53; it was again banned by the theologians. A professed fifth book, *L'Isle sonante* (or *L'Île sonnante*), perhaps founded on scraps and notes by Rabelais, appeared in 1562.

The riotous licence of his mirth has made Rabelais as many enemies as his wisdom has made him friends. His work was appreciated by **Montaigne**, and was read widely in Europe in the 16th and 17th centuries; his reputation then went into decline but revived in the 19th century, when he was admired by **Victor Hugo** and **Gustave Flaubert**. His works remain the most astonishing treasury of wit, wisdom, common sense and satire that the world has ever seen.

📖 M A Screech, *Rabelais* (1979); Donald M Frame, *François Rabelais: A Study* (1977); Mikhail Bakhtin, *Rabelais and His World* (Eng trans 1971).

> *Nature n'endure mutations soudaines sans grande violence.*
> 'Nature does not endure sudden changes without great violence.' From *Gargantua*, bk 1, ch.23.

> *Je vais quérir un grand peut-être … Tirez le rideau, la farce est jouée.*
> 'I am going to seek a great perhaps … Bring down the curtain, the farce is played out.' Unauthenticated last words.

Shelley and **Charlotte Brontë**. Her particular brand of writing found many imitators, most of them inferior to herself, and it prompted **Jane Austen**'s satire *Northanger Abbey*. 📖 C F MacIntyre, *Ann Radcliffe in Relation to her Time* (1920)

Radcliffe, Cyril John Radcliffe, Viscount
1899–1978
English lawyer and judge

He was educated at Haileybury and New College, Oxford. From 1941 to 1945 he was director-general of the Ministry of Information, in 1949 was appointed a Lord-of-Appeal-in-Ordinary and a life peer, and in 1962 he was created Viscount. He was chairman of many commissions and committees, notably those on taxation of profits and income, and on the frontier between India and Pakistan. In 1956, as Constitutional Commissioner for Cyprus, he drew up the island's constitution.

Radcliffe, James See Derwentwater, 3rd Earl of

Radcliffe, John 1650–1714
English physician

Born in Wakefield, Yorkshire, he studied at University College, Oxford, and became a Fellow of Lincoln College. In 1684 he moved to London, where he soon became the most popular physician of his time. Despite being a Jacobite, he attended **William III** and Queen **Mary**. In 1713 he was elected MP for Buckingham. He bequeathed the bulk of his large property to the Radcliffe Library, Infirmary and Observatory, all named after him, to University College, Oxford, and St Bartholomew's Hospital in London.

Radcliffe-Brown, Alfred Reginald 1881–1955
English social anthropologist

He was born in Birmingham, and after studying at Cambridge carried out field research in the Andaman Islands (1906–08) and Australia (1910–11), which served as a basis for his later works on *The Andaman Islanders* (1922) and *The Social Organization of Australian Tribes* (1930–31). After moving to South Africa in 1920 he became Professor of Anthropology at Cape Town, but in 1926 returned to Australia to take up the chair in anthropology at Sydney. He was subsequently professor at Chicago and Oxford. Along with **Bronisław Malinowski**, Radcliffe-Brown was the principal architect of modern social anthropology, but despite his early fieldwork his major contribution was more theoretical than ethnographic. Greatly influenced by the sociology of **Émile Durkheim**, he regarded social anthropology as the comparative study of 'primitive' societies, whose aim was to establish generalizations about the forms and functioning of social structures. He also distinguished social anthropology sharply from ethnology, which he saw as a descriptive rather than a theoretical enterprise. His *Structure and Function in Primitive Society* (1952) contains all the essentials of his theoretical programme.

Radde, Gustav Ferdinand Richard 1831–1903
German naturalist, ornithologist and explorer

Rabin, Yitzhak or Itzhak 1922–95

Israeli soldier and statesman, Prime Minister of Israel 1974–77 and 1992–95, and Nobel Prize winner

Yitzhak Rabin was born in Jerusalem and brought up in Tel Aviv. He was the older of two children of Nehemiah Rabin, a Russian-born immigrant to Israel. After studies at Kandoorie Agricultural High School, the outbreak of World War II forced him to abandon plans to go to the University of California to study engineering, and he embarked instead on an army career. During the war he took part in sabotage operations against the Vichy French in Lebanon and Syria. In 1954 he spent a year at Camberley Staff College in England. He fought in the 'War of Independence' (1948–49) and represented the Israeli Defence Forces (IDF, replacing the old Palmach) at the armistice in Rhodes. He rose to become Chief of Staff in 1964, heading the armed forces during the Six-Day War of 1967, in which the territory of Israel increased over threefold. The credit for Israel's success in this war was due as much to Rabin as to the more widely acknowledged Defence Minister, **Moshe Dayan**.

After serving as ambassador to the USA (1968–73) he moved decisively into the political arena, becoming Leader of the Labour Party after the resignation of **Golda Meir** (1974). He resigned this position in 1977 and spent several years on the opposition back benches while Likud was in power under **Menachem Begin**. Appointed Defence Minister under the Likud coalition government (1984–90) of **Yitzhak Shamir** and **Shimon Peres**, in 1985 Rabin withdrew troops from Lebanon, which Israel had invaded three years earlier. However, he earned a name for harshness by his severe and at times uncharacteristically brutal handling of the Palestinian insurgents in the Gaza *intifada* of 1987.

In 1990 Shamir formed a more hard-line government, which fell at the beginning of 1992, having alienated all its friends including the USA. Rabin won back the leadership of the Labour Party and in 1992 was again Prime Minister of a centre-left government that favoured Palestinian self-government. In 1993, after secret talks in Oslo, he signed an accord with the PLO (Palestine Liberation Organization), granting self-rule to the Palestinians of Gaza and Jericho and stipulating a phased withdrawal of Israeli forces. In 1994 he signed a peace treaty with Jordan; the same year he was awarded the Nobel Peace Prize jointly with Shimon Peres and **Yasser Arafat**.

In 1995 he signed a second accord agreeing to further troop withdrawals from the West Bank and further expansion of Palestinian self-rule on the West Bank. These concessions aroused extreme and often violent opposition in Israel, and Rabin was booed and heckled at a number of public occasions. Finally, he was assassinated on 4 November 1995 by a young Israeli extremist while attending a peace rally in Tel Aviv. He was succeeded as Prime Minister by his old rival, Shimon Peres.

📖 Rabin's memoirs were published in English in 1979. See also D Horovitz (ed), *Yitzhak Rabin: Soldier of Peace* (1996); R Slater, *Rabin of Israel* (1993).

> 'I have learned something in the past two and a half months—among other things that you can't rule by force over 1.5 million Palestinians.' Comment in 1988, after the *intifada*; quoted in *Time*, 3 January 1994.

Born in Danzig (Gdansk, Poland), he trained as an apothecary, but later turned to the study of natural history. He travelled widely in the Caucasus and surrounding regions, and became director of a museum he established in Tiflis (Tbilisi). He wrote *Ornis Caucasica* (1884) and many other works. Radde's Warbler and Radde's Accentor are named after him.

Radek, Karl Bernhardovich, *originally* Karl Solbelsohn 1885–1939
Russian politician

He was born of Jewish parentage in Lvov, Ukraine and educated in Kraków and Bern. He developed left-wing views, and became a journalist in Germany and Switzerland. He was active in Petrograd (now St Petersburg) following the Bolshevik Revolution and participated in the unsuccessful German revolution of 1918. Returning to the USSR, he became a leading member of the Communist International, but lost standing with his growing distrust of extremist tactics. He was charged as a supporter of **Trotsky**, and expelled from the party (1927–30). He was readmitted after recanting, but in 1937 he was a victim of one of **Stalin's** show trials, being sentenced to 10 years in prison, where he is believed to have been murdered by fellow-prisoners two years later. In 1988 he was among those posthumously rehabilitated by the Soviet Supreme Court. 📖 Warren Lerner, *Karl Radek* (1970)

Radetzky von Radetz, Joseph, Count 1766–1858
Austrian general

Born in Trebnitz, Bohemia, he fought against the Turks (1788–89) and French (1792–1815). In 1831 he became Commander-in-Chief of the Austrian forces in Italy. Forced from Milan after the famous Cinque Giornate ('five days') of street fighting in March 1848, he took

refuge in the Quadrilateral (a defensive position on the borders of Lombardy and Venetia) before defeating the Piedmontese army at Custozza (25 July 1848). When King Charles Albert (1798–1849) once again invaded Lombardy in 1849, Radetzky's forces routed them at the Battle of Novara (23 March), causing the King of Piedmont to abdicate. It was Radetzky who negotiated with the new king, **Victor Emmanuel II**, at Vignale the following day; contrary to popular tradition, he did not demand the abolition of the new Constitution known as the Statuto. Following the collapse of the Revolutions of 1848–49 Radetzky became Governor-General and military commander of the Kingdom of Lombardy–Venetia until he retired in 1857.

Radhakrishnan, Sir Sarvepalli 1888–1975
Indian philosopher and statesman

Born in Tiruttani, Madras, he was educated at Madras Christian College. He was professor at the universities of Mysore, Calcutta and Oxford, where he became Spalding Professor of Eastern Religions and Ethics in 1936. He also lectured in the USA in 1926 and 1944, and in China in 1944. From 1931 to 1939 he was in Geneva as a member of the Committee of Intellectual Co-operation of the League of Nations. In 1946 he was chief Indian delegate to UNESCO, becoming its chairman in 1949. A member of the Indian Assembly in 1947, he was appointed first Indian ambassador (1949), then Vice-President of India (1952–62) and President (1962–67). He was appointed to the Order of Merit in 1963. He wrote scholarly philosophical works including *Indian Philosophy* (1927), his Hibbert lectures of 1929 published as *An Idealist View of Life* (1932), which is often thought to be his greatest work, and *Eastern Religions and Western Thought* (1939).

Radić, Stjepan 1871–1928
Croatian politician

Racine, Jean 1639–99
French dramatist and poet

Racine was born in La Ferté-Milon, the son of a solicitor. He studied at the college of Beauvais and with the Jansenists at Port Royal. There he developed a faculty for verse-making and a liking for romance that disturbed his teachers. At 19 he went to study philosophy at the Collège d'Harcourt, where he wrote the first of many odes, *La Nymphe de la Seine*, (1660, 'The Nymph of the River Seine') on the marriage of **Louis XIV**, and made the acquaintance of **Jean de la Fontaine**, the critic Jean Chapelain (1595–1674), and other men of letters.

In 1664 his first play, *La Thébaïde ou Les Frères ennemis* (Eng trans *The Fatal Legacy*, 1723), was acted by **Molière**'s company at the Palais Royal. His second, *Alexandre le grand* (1665, Eng trans *Alexander the Great*, 1714), was after its sixth performance played by the rival actors at the Hôtel de Bourgogne, which led to a break with Molière. During the following 10 years Racine produced his greatest works—*Andromaque* (1667, Eng trans *Andromache*, 1675); *Les Plaideurs* (1668, Eng trans *The Litigants*, 1715), satirizing lawyers; *Britannicus* (1669, Eng trans 1714); *Bérénice* (1670, Eng trans *Titus and Berenice*, 1701); *Bajazet* (1672, Eng trans *The Sultaness*, 1717); *Mithridate* (1673, Eng trans *Mithridates*, 1926), produced almost at the moment of his admission to the Academy; *Iphigénie* (1675, Eng trans *Achilles; or, Iphigenia in Aulis*,

1700), a masterpiece of pathos; and *Phèdre* (1677, Eng trans *Phaedre and Hippolytys*, 1756), a marvellous representation of human agony.

When the *troupe du roi* introduced a rival *Phèdre*, by Jacques Pradon, supported by a powerful party, Racine retired from dramatic work, married in June 1677, and settled down to 20 years of domestic happiness. His wife provided him with money, and bore him two sons and five daughters. In 1677, jointly with **Nicolas Boileau**, he was appointed royal historian. In 1689 and 1691 he wrote two plays on Old Testament themes: *Esther* for Madame de **Maintenon**'s schoolgirls at Saint-Cyr, and *Athalie*.

Racine was greatly influenced by Greek drama and adopted its principles as well as taking its subjects (often women). He is regarded, especially in France, as one of the greatest masters of tragic pathos.

📖 Philip Butler, *Racine* (1974); Geoffrey Brereton, *Jean Racine: A Critical Biography* (1973); L Goldman, *Racine* (1973).

> *Ah! je l'ai trop aimé pour ne le point haïr!*
> 'Oh! I loved him too much not to hate him now!'
> From *Andromaque*, act 2, scene 1.

An admirer of the Czech leader, Tomáš Masaryk, Radić and his brother, Antun, founded the Croat People's Peasant Party (HPSS) in 1904. A member of the National Council which represented the South Slavs of the Habsburg monarchy in the months before the creation of the Kingdom of Serbs, Croats and Slovenes (1918), he was deeply suspicious of the motives of **Nicola Pašić** and of the Serbs in general. He was imprisoned in 1919, and on his release (1920) he sought foreign support for an autonomous Croatian republic. He visited Moscow (1924) and affiliated the HPSS with the Communist Peasant International. The Belgrade government accused him of co-operation with Comintern and imprisoned him and the other HPSS leaders until 1925 when, in an apparent volte-face, he accepted the constitution and agreed to co-operate with the Serbian Radical Party. He alternately sat and withdrew from the Belgrade parliament until 1928, when he and his nephew Pavle Radić were shot by a Montenegrin deputy during a parliamentary sitting. His death shortly afterwards brought an end to any semblance of Croat–Serb co-operation and precipitated the establishment of the royal dictatorship.

Radiguet, Raymond 1903–23
French novelist and poet

He was born in Saint-Maur, and, on moving to Paris, became known in literary circles at the age of 16. He became a protégé of **Jean Cocteau** and is best known for two stories, *Le Diable au corps* (1923, 'The Devil in the Flesh') and *Le Bal du Comte d'Orgel* (1924, 'The Count of Orgel's Ball'). Acclaimed as the **'Rimbaud** of the novel', he produced writing as austerely controlled as his personal behaviour was erratic and unpredictable, aggravated by alcoholism and high living. The nature of love is his dominant theme, and his treatment of it in his fiction is comparable to the high moral conception of love in the tragedies of **Racine**. 📖 C R Goesch, *Raymond Radiguet* (1955)

Radin, Paul 1883–1959
US cultural anthropologist

He was born in Łódź, Poland, and emigrated with his family to New York when he was a baby. He studied under **Franz Boas** at Columbia University, with brief spells at the

universities of Munich and Berlin between 1905 and 1907, and returned to the USA to complete his doctorate in 1910. His speciality lay in the fields of religion, mythology, and the ethnography of Native Americans, although he is perhaps best remembered for his collaboration with **Carl Jung** and Karl Kerényi on *The Trickster* (1958). Other major works include *Primitive Man as Philosopher* (1927), *The Method and Theory of Ethnology* (1933) and *Primitive Religion* (1937).

Rae, John 1813–93
Scottish explorer

Born near Stromness, Orkney, he studied medicine at Edinburgh, and in 1833 became doctor to the Hudson Bay Company. In 1846–47 he joined two exploratory expeditions to the Arctic, and in 1848 accompanied **Sir John Richardson** on a **Franklin** search voyage. In 1853–54 he commanded an expedition to King William's Land, and it was on this journey that he met the Inuit who gave him definite news of Franklin's expedition and its probable fate. In 1860 he surveyed a telegraph line to the USA via the Faroes and Iceland, visited Greenland, and in 1864 made a telegraph survey from Winnipeg over the Rockies.

Raeburn, Sir Henry 1756–1823
Scottish portrait painter

Born near Edinburgh, he studied for two years in Rome (1785–87), then returned to Edinburgh and soon attained pre-eminence among Scottish artists, working first in watercolours and later in oils. He was knighted by **George** IV in 1822, and appointed King's Limner for Scotland a few days before his death. His style was to some extent founded on that of Sir **Joshua Reynolds**, to which he brought a positive quality by means of bold brushwork and the use of contrasting colours. He painted the leading members of Edinburgh society and among his sitters were Sir **Walter Scott**, David Hume, James Boswell, John Wilson ('Christopher North'), Lord Melville (**Henry Dundas**), Henry Mackenzie and Lord **Jeffrey**. Among his best-known works is *The Reverend Robert Walker Skating* (1784, National Gallery, Edinburgh).

Raeder, Erich 1876–1960
German naval commander

He joined the navy in 1894 and during World War I was Chief of Staff to Admiral **Franz von Hipper**. In 1928 he was promoted admiral and became Commander-in-Chief of the navy, and rebuilt the fleet, especially submarines and fast cruisers. In 1939 **Hitler** made him a grand admiral, but in 1943 he was relieved of his command for disagreements with Hitler over strategy. At the Nuremberg Trials in 1946 he was sentenced to life imprisonment. He was released in September 1955.

Raemaekers, Louis 1869–1956
Dutch political cartoonist and artist
Born in Roermond, he attained worldwide fame in 1915 by his striking anti-German war cartoons.

Raff, (Joseph) Joachim 1822–82
Swiss composer
Born in Lachen, he taught music at Wiesbaden until 1877, when he was appointed director of the Conservatory at Frankfurt am Main. Among his compositions are the Symphonies 'Lenore' and 'Im Walde' ('In the Forest'), and works for violin and piano. He wrote *Die Wagner-Frage* (1854, 'The Wagner Question') in support of **Richard Wagner**.

Raffles, Sir (Thomas) Stamford 1781–1826
English colonial administrator and oriental scholar
Born off Port Morant, Jamaica, he was appointed to a clerkship in the East India House in 1795, and secretary to an establishment at Penang in 1805. In 1811 he accompanied an expedition against Java, and on its capture, as Lieutenant-Governor, completely reformed the internal administration. In 1816 ill health sent him home to England, where he wrote his *History of Java* (1817). As Lieutenant-Governor of Benkoelen in West Sumatra (1818–23), he formed a settlement at Singapore to counter Dutch influence in the area. This rapidly grew into one of the more important trading centres in the East. He was closely involved in the establishment of the Zoological Society of London in the early 1820s. 🕮 C E Wurtzburg, *Raffles of the Eastern Isles* (1954)

Rafsanjani, Hojatoleslam Ali Akbar Hashemi 1934–
Iranian cleric and politician
Born near Rafsanjan in south-eastern Iran, into an affluent pistachio-farming family, he trained as a mullah from 1950 under Ayatollah **Ruholla Khomeini** at the holy city of Qom. His friendship with Khomeini led him to opposition against Shah **Mohammed Reza Pahlavi** and brief imprisonment in 1963. During the 1970s he became wealthy from involvement in the construction business in Teheran, but continued to keep in close touch with the exiled Khomeini. Following the Islamic Revolution of 1979–80 he became Speaker of the Iranian parliament (Majlis), emerging as an influential and pragmatic power-broker between fundamentalist and technocrat factions within the ruling Islamic Republican Party, and he played a key role in securing an end to the Gulf War (1980–88). In August 1989, soon after the death of Ayatollah Khomeini, Rafsanjani became State President and effective national leader.

Ragaz, Leonhard 1862–1945
Swiss Reformed pastor and social activist
Born in Canton-Graubuenden, and educated at Basle, Jena and Berlin, he was ordained in 1890. He encountered opposition through his profound social concern: during World War I he denounced violence as an evil solution, and he later rejected Fascism, Nazism and Communism. On a visit to the USA he described the status of black people as 'utterly offensive'. In 1921 he resigned his theological chair at Zurich 'to represent Christ in poverty', and

established an educational centre for working people. He regarded social change and religious reform as interdependent.

Raglan, Fitzroy James Henry Somerset, 1st Baron 1788–1855
English field marshal
Born in Badminton, Gloucestershire, he served on the Duke of **Wellington**'s staff in the Peninsular War (1808–12), then fought at Waterloo (1815), losing his sword arm. Thereafter he sat in parliament as MP for Truro and spent many years at the War Office. He was appointed Master-General of the Ordnance and was elevated to the peerage in 1852. In 1854 he headed an ill-prepared expeditionary force against the Russians in the Crimea, in alliance with the French. He won the Battle of Alma, but lack of cohesion among the Allies prevented an effective follow-up. At Balaclava he gave the order that led to the disastrous Charge of the Light Brigade (1854). He won the Battle of Inkerman, but was blamed for the failure of the Commissariat during the terrible winter of 1854–55. He died shortly before the storming of Sebastopol. The raglan overcoat is named after him. 🕮 John Sweetman, *Raglan: From the Peninsular to the Crimea* (1993)

Rahab fl.c.1400BC
Biblical character
She was a prostitute who protected **Joshua**'s spies while they surveyed the defences of Jericho. In return for helping them, she and her family were saved when the city fell to the Israelites. She is probably the Rahab named as the mother of Boaz, and so an ancestor of King **David**. The New Testament also cites her as an example of faith (Hebrews 11.31).

Rahbek, Knud Lyne 1760–1830
Danish poet, critic and editor
Born in Copenhagen, he became Professor of Aesthetics at Copenhagen University, and edited several literary journals, notably *Den Danske Tilskuer* ('The Danish Spectator'). As well as poetry, he wrote many plays, songs and works on drama. 🕮 A E Jensen, *Rahbek og Danske Digtere* (1960)

Rahere d.1144
English churchman
Of Frankish descent, he made a pilgrimage to Rome, where he suffered an attack of malarial fever. During his convalescence he made a vow to found a hospital, and on his return to London he was granted the site at Smithfield by **Henry I**. In 1123 the building of St Bartholomew's Hospital and St Bartholomew's Church was begun. He remained in charge of the hospital until 1137, when he retired to the priory.

Rahner, Karl 1904–84
German Roman Catholic theologian
Born in Freiburg im Breisgau, he joined the Society of Jesus in 1922 and was ordained a priest in 1932. He is probably the most influential Roman Catholic theologian of the 20th century. Much influenced by the doctrines of **Thomas Aquinas**, he began his teaching career in Innsbruck in 1937. There, and later at Munich and Münster, his lectures and writings maintained a dialogue between traditional dogma and contemporary existential questions, based on the principle that grace is already present in human nature. He played a major role as consultant at the Second Vatican Council (1962–66). The substance of his *Theological Investigations* (1961–81) is laid out in *Foundations of Christian Faith* (1978) and *The Practice of Faith* (1985), and his mystical beliefs are reflected in his *Prayers for a Lifetime* (1984) and the autobiographical interviews *I Remember* (1985).

Raikes, Robert 1735–1811
English publisher and philanthropist
He was born in Gloucester. In 1757 he succeeded his father as proprietor of the *Gloucester Journal*. In 1780, disturbed by the misery and ignorance of many children in his native city, he began one of the first Sunday schools for children.

Raimu, *originally* Jules Auguste César Muraire
1883–1946
French actor
Born in Toulon, and an amateur performer as a child, his first professional engagement was at the Casino de Toulon (1899–1900). He worked in mime and as a croupier before moving to Paris, making his film debut in *L'Homme nu* (1912) and appearing on stage in *Monsieur Chasse* (1916). He appeared throughout the 1920s in revues, operettas and comedies before creating the character of César in *Marius* (1929), which he repeated on film (1931). He was able to combine pathos and humour in his truculent portrayals of the dignified French working man. His films include *Fanny* (1932), *Gribouille* (1937, *Heart of Paris*), *Un Carnet de Bal* (1937) and *Les Inconnus dans la maison* (1942, *Strangers in the House*); and he also played with the Comédie Française (1944–45). He died from injuries in a car accident.

Raine, Craig Anthony 1944–
English poet
He was born in Bishop Auckland, County Durham. He was educated at Oxford where he has spent most of his life apart from a short spell as poetry editor at Faber (1981). He is currently Fellow of New College (1991–). His first collection, *The Onion, Memory* (1978), established a characteristic method of attempting to 'see' familiar things in new and unusual ways, which he developed in even greater depth in the 'alien' viewpoint adopted in *A Martian Sends A Postcard Home* (1979). Later collections include *A Journey to Greece* (1979), *Rich* (1984), including a prose memoir of his childhood, 'A Silver Plate', and a collection of essays, *Haydn and the Valve Trumpet* (1990). *1953* (1990) was a version of *Racine's* drama *Andromaque*. Recent works include *History: The Home Movie* (1994).

Rainer, Yvonne 1934–
US experimental dancer, choreographer and filmmaker
Born in San Francisco, she moved to New York City in 1956 and took classes at the Martha Graham School. She returned to California in 1969 where she joined Anna Halprin's experimental summer course, which had a considerable effect on her work. On her return to New York she studied with Merce Cunningham, and enrolled in Robert Dunn's pioneering composition class along with Trisha Brown, Steve Paxton, David Gordon and Lucinda Childs. The radical Judson Dance Theater, for which she was a prolific choreographer, evolved out of these alternative sessions. Her signature piece, *Trio A* (1966, part of the larger work *The Mind is a Muscle*), was designed for performance irrespective of age and level of training. *Continuous Project—Altered Daily* was started in 1970 and *Grand Union Dreams* was made in 1971. She is considered to have had a great influence on post-modern dance. In 1973, she turned from dance to filmmaking.

Rainey, Gertrude Pridgett, *known as* Ma Rainey, *née* Pridgett 1886–1939
US blues singer
Born in Columbus, Georgia, she began her career as a singer with the Rabbit Foot Minstrels. She claimed that she first introduced blues into her act in 1902, after hearing a girl in Missouri sing a song about the man who had deserted her. She won a large following among African-American Southerners and toured with Bessie Smith, who was her protégée. From 1923 to 1928 she made a series of recordings on the Paramount label, which won her an audience in the North. Often called the 'Mother of the Blues', she is considered to be the first of the great black blues singers, with a style of singing that preserves the continuity from early African-American music to jazz. Her best-known songs include 'See See Rider' and 'Slow Driving Moan'.

Rainey, Joseph Hayne 1832–87
US politician
Born in Georgetown, South Carolina, he was a barber by trade. After the Civil War he served in the South Carolina state senate as a Republican. During the Reconstruction he became the first African-American elected to the US House of Representatives (1870–79). As a member of Congress, he campaigned vigorously on behalf of civil rights legislation.

Rainey, Ma See **Rainey, Gertrude Pridgett**

Rainier III, *properly* Rainier Louis Henri Maxence Bertrand de Grimaldi 1923–
Prince of Monaco
Born in Monaco, he served in the French army during World War II and succeeded his grandfather Louis II in 1950. He is the twenty-sixth ruling prince of the House of Grimaldi, which was founded in 1297. In 1956 Rainier married the US film actress Grace Kelly, by whom he has a son, Prince Albert (1958–), the heir to the throne, and two daughters, Princess Caroline (1957–) and Princess Stephanie (1965–). He is the chairman of one of the world's most powerful multinational conglomerates, Monaco Inc. ▣ Anne Edwards, *The Grimaldis of Monaco* (1992)

Rainwater, (Leo) James 1917–86
US physicist and Nobel Prize winner
Born in Council, Idaho, he was educated at the California Institute of Technology (Caltech) and at Columbia University. During World War II he contributed to the Manhattan atomic bomb project. He became Professor of Physics at Columbia University in 1952 and was director of the Nevis Cyclotron Laboratory there from 1951 to 1953 and 1956 to 1961. At the time, there were two theories to describe the atomic nucleus. In one, the nuclear particles were arranged in concentric shells, in the other, the nucleus was described as analogous to a liquid drop. Rainwater produced a collective model combining the two ideas. Together with Aage Bohr and Ben Roy Mottelson, he developed this theory and obtained experimental evidence in its support. The three shared the Nobel Prize for physics in 1975 for this work. Rainwater also worked with Val Fitch on studies of muonic X-rays, and developed an improved theory of high-energy particles scattering.

Rainy, Robert 1826–1906
Scottish theologian
Born in Glasgow, he studied at Glasgow University and at New College in Edinburgh, and, after being minister of the Free Church in Huntly (1851) and the Free High Church in Edinburgh (1854), was from 1862 to 1900 Professor of Church History in the New (Free Church) College in Edinburgh, becoming its principal in 1874. He organized the union in 1900 of the Free and United Presbyterian Churches as the United Free Church of Scotland, and became the first moderator of its general assembly.

Raitt, Bonnie 1949–
US country blues singer and guitarist
Born in Burbank, California, the daughter of the stage singer John Raitt, she worked with Freebo and with Bluesbusters (1969–71) before her eponymous debut album was released. She did not achieve mass appeal, perhaps because her records *Give It Up* (1972) and *Streetlights*

(1974) had a less readily marketed flavour of jazz. However, she attained cult status with blues fans, particularly after her collaboration with **John Lee Hooker** on his album *The Healer* (1989). In the 1990s, however, she had a huge breakthrough in popularity in the USA, winning Grammy awards and receiving invitations to perform in large concerts.

Raiz, Gilles de Laval, Baron See **Retz, Gilles de Laval, Baron**

Rajagopalachari, Chakrovati 1879–1972
Indian political leader and Tamil (and Anglophone) writer
Born in Hosur, he was educated at Central College, Bangalore, and Presidency and Law colleges, Madras, and was called to the Bar in 1900. He practised until 1919 at Salem, then joined the non-co-operation and Satyagraha movements and was elected Congress general-secretary (1921–22). A member of the Congress Working Committee (1922–42, 1946–47, 1951–54), he was Prime Minister of Madras from 1937 to 1939, a member of the interim government (1946–47), Governor of West Bengal (1947–48), acting Governor-General of India (November 1947), and then the first Governor-General of free India (1948–50). Later he was Chief Minister of Madras (1952–54) and founded the Swatantra Party (1959). His chief work in English is his translation of the Tamil version of the great classical text, the *Ramayana*. He also wrote for children.

Rájá Rám Mohán Rái See **Rammohun Roy**

Rajasinha II 1629–87
King of Kandy (Sri Lanka)
He succeeded his father, **Senerat** in 1635, and continued the struggle for Sinhalese independence against the Portuguese, whose language he spoke and wrote fluently. When the Potuguese invaded Kandy (1638), they were defeated by Rajasinha at Gannoruwa. In alliance with the Dutch, the king captured all the island's important towns, but a breach between the allies allowed the Portuguese to recover until war broke out again (1652). In 1655 Colombo fell to a combined force of Dutch and Sinhalese. Rajasinha's government was tyrannical and arbitrary, but he maintained the independence of his people from both the Portuguese and the Dutch.

Rajk, László 1908–49
Hungarian politician
An early convert to communism, he was expelled from Budapest University for his political activities and became a building worker and union organizer. He was party secretary to the Hungarian battalion of the International Brigades during the Spanish Civil War but was eventually imprisoned in France. He returned to Hungary in 1941 to become a secretary to the Communist Party Central Committee, but he was first interned by the Hungarians and then imprisoned by the Germans. He rose rapidly after 1945, becoming a full member of the Central Committee, Minister of the Interior, and then Foreign Minister. In 1949 he was arrested and tried on trumped-up charges during the Stalinist purges and was executed. In 1955 he was posthumously rehabilitated.

Rajneesh, Baghwan Shree, *originally* Rajneesh Chandra Mohan 1931–90
Indian guru
He was born in central India and educated at Saugar University. He became an exponent of yogic spirituality and taught at the Sanskrit college of Raipur, attracting many Westerners to his ashram in Poona during the 1970s. He transferred his base to Oregon, USA, in 1981, but his advocacy of free sexual expression as a form of therapy met with increasing opposition. His popularity declined,

although a nucleus of Western devotees remained loyal up to his death in 1990. 📖 Ian Harris et al, *Contemporary Religions—A World Guide* (1992); Shirley Harrison, *Cults—The Battle for God* (1990)

Rakhmaninov, Sergei Vasilevich See **Rachmaninov, Sergei Vasilevich**

Rákóczi, Francis II 1676–1735
Hungarian nobleman and rebel leader
He was born into a princely family of Hungary and Transylvania, and in 1703 led a Hungarian revolt against Austrian rule. He was hailed as a national hero, but his forces met with severe defeats (1708, 1710), and in 1711 he went into exile rather than accept a peace settlement. His later years were spent as a Carmelite monk.

Rakosi, Matyas 1892–1971
Hungarian politician
He was active in the labour movement as a teenager and served in World War I. He spent most of the war years as a prisoner in Russia and moved further to the left, joining the Hungarian Communist Party on his return home. He was commander of the Red Guard in **Béla Kun**'s Soviet Republic in 1919 and then fled to the USSR where he became the secretary of Communist International. Returning to Hungary in 1924, he was imprisoned (1925–40). On his release he returned to Moscow, and led the Hungarian communist émigrés there. He came back to Budapest in 1945 as their general secretary. He was deeply implicated in the Stalinist purges, and was much criticized after **Stalin**'s death. In 1955 he attempted to reinstate Stalinist practices, thus helping to provoke the 1956 Hungarian Uprising. He was then removed from office and, in 1962, expelled from the party.

Raleigh, Sir Walter See panel p1530

Ramabai, Sarasvati, *also known as* Pandita Ramabai 1858–1922
Indian Christian educator
Born near Mangalore in southern India, the daughter of a Brahmin, she was orphaned in 1874, but survived by reciting Hindu Scriptures, and her skill in Sanskrit earned her the name Pandita ('teacher' or 'mistress of learning'). She went to England for education (1883–86) and to the USA for study and fundraising (1886–89), returning to Bombay to open a boarding school for high-caste child widows. After the famines of 1896–97, she established the Mukti Sadan ('House of Salvation') orphanage and training institute for women and children at Kedgaon, near Poona. She wrote *The High Caste Hindu Woman* (1887) and *Testimony* (1917), translated the Bible into Marathi, and was awarded the Kaiser-i-Hind gold medal in 1919.

Ramakrishna Paramahasa, *originally* Gadadhar Chatterjee 1836–86
Indian mystic
He was born in the Hooghly district of Bengal. A priest at Dakshineswar Kali temple, near Calcutta, he took instruction from several gurus of different schools in his spiritual search, finally coming to believe in self-realization and God-realization, and that all religions were different paths to the same goal. His simple but effective retelling of traditional stories, and his personality, attracted the interest of Calcutta intellectuals, including **Vivekananda**, who became Ramakrishna's spiritual heir. 📖 R R Diwakar, *Paramahansa Sri Ramakrishna* (1956)

Raman, Sir Chandrasekhara Venkata 1888–1970
Indian physicist and Nobel Prize winner
Born in Trichinopoly, Tamil Nadu, he was educated at Madras University, then worked in the Indian Finance Department before becoming Professor of Physics at

Raleigh or Ralegh, Sir Walter 1552–1618
English courtier, navigator and poet

Walter Raleigh was born in Hayes Barton in Devon. He studied briefly at Oxford, but left to volunteer for the Huguenot cause in France. In 1578 he joined a piratical expedition against the Spaniards organized by his half-brother Sir **Humphrey Gilbert**; and in 1580 he went to Ireland, where he brutally suppressed the rising of the **Desmond**s. He became a favourite of Queen **Elizabeth I**, who heaped favours upon him, including estates, the 'farm of wines', and a licence to export woollen broadcloths. However, the story of Raleigh laying his plush cloak over a puddle for the queen to walk on, which is told by **Thomas Fuller**, is probably untrue. In 1585 he was appointed Lord Warden of the Stannaries and Vice-Admiral of Devon and Cornwall. The same year he entered parliament as the member for Devon.

From 1584 to 1589 he sent an expedition to America to take unknown lands in the queen's name, and despatched an abortive settlement to Roanoke Island, North Carolina (1585–86). He later made unsuccessful attempts to colonize Virginia, and introduced tobacco and potatoes into Britain. Eclipsed as court favourite in 1587 by the young 2nd Earl of **Essex**, he went to Ireland and planted his estates in Munster with settlers, and became a close friend of the poet **Edmund Spenser**. On his return to England in 1592 he was committed to the Tower for a secret affair with Bessy Throckmorton, one of the queen's maids of honour, and for more than four years was excluded from the queen's presence; he and Bessy later married.

In 1595, with five ships, he explored the coasts of Trinidad, and sailed up the Orinoco, and in 1596 took part with **Charles Howard** and Essex in the sack of Cadiz. In 1600 he became Governor of Jersey, and in three years did much to promote the island's trade. He took little part in the dark intrigues at the end of Elizabeth's reign, but was arrested on 17 July 1603, and attempted suicide. He defended himself ably at his trial at Winchester, but even so he was condemned to death, and it was only on the scaffold that his sentence was commuted to life imprisonment. In the Tower of London Raleigh spent his time studying and writing, and carrying out chemical experiments.

In 1616 he was released to make an expedition to the Orinoco in search of a goldmine. But the mission was a failure; Raleigh lost his fleet, and his son, and broke his terms by razing a Spanish town. On his return in 1618 the Spanish Minister in London invoked the suspended death-sentence, and he was beheaded at Whitehall.

Raleigh's expedition of 1595 is described in *The Discovery of Guiana*. His *History of the World* (1614), of which the first and only volume reaches the second Roman war with Macedonia, was written in the Tower. During captivity he also wrote *The Prerogative of Parliaments* (1628), *The Cabinet Council* (1658) and *A Discourse of War*. Only fragments of his poetry survive, and some poems formerly attributed to him, such as 'The Lie', are now thought to be not his work. See also Stephen Coote, *The Play of Passion: The Life of Sir Walter Raleigh* (1993); A Sinclair, *Sir Walter Raleigh and the Age of Discovery* (1984); Robert Lacey, *Sir Walter Raleigh* (1974).

> 'What is our life? a play of passion;
> Our mirth the music of division;
> Our mothers' wombs the tiring-houses be
> Where we are dressed for this short comedy.
> Heaven the judicious sharp spectator is,
> That sits and marks still who doth act amiss;
> Our graves that hide us from the searching sun
> Are like drawn curtains when the play is done.
> Thus march we, playing, to our latest rest,
> Only we die in earnest—that's no jest.'
> 'On the Life of Man' (1612).

Calcutta University (1917–33). In 1930 he was awarded the Nobel Prize for physics for his work in demonstrating that the interaction of vibrating molecules with photons passing through altered the spectrum of the scattered light. This 'Raman effect' became an important spectroscopic technique. He also researched the vibration of musical instruments and the physiology of vision. He was the first Indian director of the Indian Institute of Science (1933–48), a founder of the Indian Academy of Sciences (1934), and in 1947 the founding director of the Raman Institute in Mysore. He was knighted in 1929.

Ramana Maharishi 1879–1950
Indian sage

Born in Tirukuli, Madurai district, he became attracted in 1896 to the holy mountain Arunachala, south-west of Madras, following a religious experience, and remained there until his death. Much of the time he lived in caves on the mountain and avoided publicity, but he later allowed devotees to establish an *ashram* at Villupuram, at the foot of the mountain. His philosophy of seeking self-knowledge through integration of the personality in the 'cave of the heart' became known to Westerners through the books of Paul Brunton as well as his own *Collected Works* (1969), *Forty Verses on Reality* (1978) and other anthologies.

Ramanuja 11th–12th century
Tamil Brahmin philosopher

He was born near Madras, South India, and although little is known of his life, he holds an important position in Indian thought. Rejecting Śankara's *advaita* or non-dualistic Vedanta for *Viśishtadvaita* (which held that the soul was united with a personal god rather than absorbed into the Absolute) he prepared the way for the *bhakti* or devotional strain of Hinduism that was taken up by **Madhva**, Nimbarka, Vallabha and **Caitanya**.

Ramanujan, Srinivasa 1887–1920
Indian mathematician

Born in Eroda, Madras, he taught himself mathematics from an elementary textbook written in English. While working as a clerk, he devised over 100 remarkable theorems which he sent to **Godfrey Hardy** at Cambridge. These included results on elliptic integrals, partitions and analytic number theory. Hardy was so impressed that he arranged for him to go to Cambridge in 1914. There Ramanujan published many papers, the most remarkable being an exact formula for the number of ways an integer can be written as a sum of positive integers. He arrived at his results by an uncanny form of intuition, often having no idea of how they could be proved or even what the form of an orthodox proof might be. He was elected FRS and a Fellow of Trinity in 1918. He was one of the most remarkable self-taught prodigies in the history of mathematics.

Ramaphosa, (Matamela) Cyril 1952–
South African trade unionist and politician

Born in Johannesburg, he became chairman of the all-black South African Students' Organization in 1974 and after 11 months' detention (1974–75) became an articled

---

Rambert, Dame Marie, *stage name of* Cyvia Rambam 1888–1982
Polish-born British ballet dancer and teacher

Marie Rambert was born in Warsaw. She was sent to Paris to study medicine, but became involved in artistic circles and began to study eurhythmics. In 1913 she worked on Igor Stravinsky's *Rite of Spring* with Sergei Diaghilev's Ballets Russes. She moved to London and began to dance and teach, marrying playwright Ashley Dukes in 1918. In 1930, 10 years after opening her own dance studio, she formed the Ballet Club, a permanent producing and performing organization which featured dancer Alicia Markova and choreographer Frederick Ashton. She was particularly interested in promoting new ballets, and always encouraged her pupils to produce works; this led inevitably to occasional financial difficulties. Her company (which had become Ballet Rambert

in 1935) had been expanding since the 1940s, but by 1966 was reduced to a small group which concentrated on new works and began to embrace modern dance techniques.

In the mid-1970s the company performed work by Glen Tetley, John Chesworth and Christopher Bruce; it has grown to become one of Great Britain's major touring contemporary dance companies. She exerted a major influence on the development of modern dance and was made a DBE in 1962.

📖 Mary Clarke, *Dancers of Mercury* (1962); Lionel Bradley, *Sixteen Years of Ballet Rambert, 1930–1946* (1946).

---

clerk there and was active in the BPC (Black People's Convention). He graduated from the University of South Africa with a law degree in 1981. He later became general secretary of the National Union of Mineworkers (1982) and led the first legal strike by black mineworkers (1984). He brought the NUM into COSATU (Congress of South African Trade Unions) and was elected Secretary-General of the ANC (1991).

Ramazzini, Bernardini 1633–1714
Italian physician and pioneer of occupational health

Born in Capri, he studied both philosophy and medicine at Parma University. He practised medicine for a while near Rome, and then settled in Modena where he eventually became Professor of Medicine. He moved to Padua in 1700. His major work *De Morbis Artificum Diatriba* (1700, Eng trans *Diseases of Workers*, 1705), was the first systematic treatise on occupational diseases, and includes many shrewd observations about environmental hazards (for instance, exposure to lead by potters and painters). He also made important observations on epidemics in human beings and animals, especially cattle plague.

Rambert, Dame Marie See panel above

Rambouillet, Catherine de Vivonne, Marquise de 1588–1665
French noblewoman

She was born in Rome, the daughter of Jean de Vivonne, Marquis of Pisani. At the age of 12 she was married to the son of the Marquis de Rambouillet, who succeeded to the title in 1611. She disliked the morals and manners of the French court, and for 50 years she gathered together in the famous Hôtel de Rambouillet the talent and wit of the French nobility and literary world, including Condé, François de Malherbe and Pierre Corneille. Although later satirized by Molière for its preciosity, her salon helped to set the standard for correct and elegant language.

Rameau, Jean Philippe 1683–1764
French composer and musical theorist

Born in Dijon, he became an organist, and in 1722 settled in Paris, where he published his *Traité de l'harmonie* (1722, 'Treatise on Harmony'), a work of fundamental importance in the history of musical style. He wrote many operas, notably *Hippolyte et Aricie* (1733) and *Castor et Pollux* (1737), as well as ballets, harpsichord pieces (for which he is best known today), chamber music and vocal music.

Ramée, Pierre de la See Ramus, Petrus

Ramelli, Agostino c.1531–c.1610
Italian military engineer

Born in Ponte Tresa, he trained in the arts of war in the service of the Marquis of Marignano. In about 1570 he was summoned to France by the Duke of Anjou (later

Henry III), and took part in the Siege of La Rochelle in 1572. He was renowned in his lifetime as a military engineer, and achieved lasting fame through the publication in 1588 of his one work, *The Various and Ingenious Machines of Agostino Ramelli*, in which he described and illustrated in great detail almost 200 devices such as water pumps, cranes, grain mills, military bridges and ballistic engines. There is no evidence that he had actually constructed any of the machines, but such collections played a valuable part in the dissemination of ideas.

Rameses II, *known as* Rameses the Great, *also spelt* Ramesses *or* Ramses 1304–1237BC
Egyptian pharaoh

The third king of the 19th dynasty, he was a master of political propaganda, and his reign marked the last zenith of Egyptian imperial power. He claimed to have defeated the Hittites at Kadesh (but failed to capture it), then formed a peace with them, and married a Hittite princess. His reign (c.1292–1237BC) is the most renowned in Egyptian history for temple building: he completed the mortuary temple of his father Seti I at Luxor and the colonnaded hall of the Karnak temple, and built the rock temples of Abu Simbel, dedicating the smaller one to his queen, Nefertari. He is sometimes identified as the Old Testament Pharaoh of the oppression. His mummy was found at Deir-el-Bahari (1881). 📖 K A Kitchen, *Pharaoh Triumphant: The Life and Times of Ramesses II, King of Egypt* (1982)

Rameses III 1198–1167BC
Egyptian pharaoh

He was the second king of the 20th dynasty. He campaigned against the Philistines and other Sea Peoples and repeated the conquest of Ethiopia. He is sometimes identified with the Old Testament Pharaoh of the Exodus. His mummy was found at Bulak (1886).

Ramesses See Rameses

Rammohun Roy or Rájá Rám Mohán Rái 1774–1833
Indian religious reformer

Born in Burdwan, Bengal, of high Brahmin ancestry, he questioned his ancestral faith, and studied Buddhism in Tibet. A revenue collector for some years in Rangpur, in 1811 he acquired wealth on his brother's death. He published various works in Persian, Arabic and Sanskrit, with the aim of eliminating idolatry, and he was influential in the abolition of suttee. He issued an English abridgement of the *Vedanta*, which provided a digest of the Veda. In 1820 he published *The Precepts of Jesus*, accepting the morality preached by Christ, but rejecting his deity and miracles, and he wrote other pamphlets hostile both to Hinduism and to Christian Trinitarianism. In 1828 he began the Brahmo Samaj Association, and in 1830 the

Emperor of Delhi bestowed on him the title of raja. In 1831 he visited England, where he gave useful evidence before the board of control on the condition of India.

Ramón y Cajal, Santiago 1852–1934
Spanish physician, histologist and Nobel Prize winner

Born in Petilla de Aragon, he graduated from Saragossa University in 1873. He joined the Army Medical Service and served in Cuba, where he contracted malaria and was soon discharged through ill health. He returned to Saragossa for further anatomical training and in 1883 began his academic career, as Professor of Anatomy at Valencia (1883–86), then as Professor of Histology at Barcelona (1886–92) and finally as Professor of Histology and Pathological Anatomy at Madrid (1892–1922). His major work was on the microstructure of the nervous system, and revealed how nerve impulses are transmitted to the brain. He made use of the specialized histological staining techniques of **Camillo Golgi**, and the two men shared the 1906 Nobel Prize for physiology or medicine. Ramón y Cajal's many articles and books include *Estudios sobre la degeneración y regeneración del sistema nervioso* (2 vols, 1913–14, Eng trans *The Degeneration and Regeneration of the Nervous System*, 1928). ⌨ Garcia Duran Munoz and Francisco Alonso Buron, *Ramón y Cajal* (1960)

Ramos, Fidel Valdez 1928–
Philippine general and statesman

Born in Manila, he was educated at the National University and at West Point. He served with the US forces in the Korean War (1950–53) and in Vietnam, and was made Chief of Staff of the Philippine army in 1986. At the time **Ferdinand Marcos** had used fraudulent means to claim victory over **Cory Aquino** in the general election. When Aquino challenged Marcos, Ramos supported her, and after she became President, he served as her defence secretary (1988–92). When he succeeded Aquino as President in 1992, he introduced reforms in order to create a free market economy and to help modernize the country's industries.

Ramos, Graciliano 1892–1953
Brazilian novelist

Born in Quebrangulo, Alagoas, the son of a corrupt local judge, he was not a convinced Communist, and was placed in a concentration camp by President **Getúlio Vargas** (1936). His experiences there were published in *Memórias do Cárcere* (1953, 'Memories of Imprisonment') and led to his early death. He wrote psychologically penetrating novels of great power, starting with *Caetés* (1933). It was followed by the acclaimed *São Bernardo* (1934, Eng trans, *Saint Bernard*, 1940), *Angústia* (1936, Eng trans *Anguish*, 1940), which is probably the most lucid and moving study of a sex killer written in the 20th century, and *Vidas sêcas* (1938, Eng trans *Barren Lives*, 1965). Ramos's collected works appeared in Brazil in 1961–62. He wrote the best prose of his generation and is considered by some to be the heir of **Joaquim Machado de Assis**. ⌨ B M Woodbridge, *Graciliano Ramos* (1954)

Ramphal, Sir Shridath Surrendranath, *also known as* Sir Sonny Ramphal 1928–
Guyanan and Commonwealth lawyer and diplomat

After studying law at King's College London, he was called to the Bar in 1951. He returned to the West Indies, and from 1952 held increasingly responsible posts in Guyana and the West Indies before becoming Guyana's Foreign Minister and Attorney-General in 1972, and Justice Minister in 1973. During much of this time he sat in the Guyanan National Assembly. From 1975 to 1989 he was Secretary-General of the Commonwealth.

Rams, Dieter 1932–
German product designer

Born in Wiesbaden, he trained and worked as an architect. He is best known as the chief designer, since 1955, for the Frankfurt electrical appliance manufacturer, Braun AG. In association initially with Hans Gugelot of the Hochschule für Gestaltung ('High School for Design') in Ulm, he transformed the company's product range. His food mixers, record players, radios, shavers, hair driers and clocks are all examples of unadorned modern design. He was made an honorary Royal Designer for Industry in 1968.

Ramsay, Allan c.1685–1758
Scottish poet

Born in Leadhills, Lanarkshire, he was apprenticed to a wigmaker in Edinburgh (1704–09). By 1718 he had become known as a poet, having issued several short humorous satires printed as broadsides, and he had also written (1716–18) two additional cantos to the old Scots poem, *Christ's Kirk on the Green*. He then started a business as a bookseller, and his new circulating library (1725) is thought to have been the first in Great Britain. His works include *Tartana, or the Plaid* (1718), *Poems* (collected edition published by subscription in 1721), *The Monk and the Miller's Wife* (1724), *The Tea-table Miscellany*, a collection of songs (4 vols, 1724–37), and *The Gentle Shepherd, a Pastoral Comedy* (1725), his most popular work. His eldest son was the painter **Allan Ramsay**. ⌨ John Burns Martin, *Allan Ramsay, a Study of His Life and Works* (1931)

Ramsay, Allan 1713–84
Scottish portrait painter

He was born in Edinburgh, the eldest son of the poet **Allan Ramsay**. Trained in Italy, he was a distinguished portrait painter, working first in Edinburgh, but settling in London in 1762. His portrait of *Dr Richard Mead* (1747, Coram Foundation, London) is a fine example of his early period. In 1767, he was appointed portrait painter to **George III** (National Portrait Gallery, London, and work in Royal Collection). In his best works his painting is simple and delicate and he was at his most impressive in his portraits of women, notably that of his wife (National Gallery of Scotland, Edinburgh). He delighted in conversation and was acquainted with many of the writers of his day, including **Samuel Johnson**. He also corresponded with **Jean Jacques Rousseau**, **François Voltaire** and others. He gave up painting in about 1770, to pursue a literary career, writing essays and political pamphlets. ⌨ Alastair Smart, *The Life and Art of Allan Ramsay* (1952)

Ramsay, Sir Bertram Home 1883–1945
Scottish naval officer

Born in London into an old Scottish family, he served as the commander of a destroyer in the Dover Patrol in World War I. He resigned from the navy in 1938, but was recalled on the outbreak of World War II. He served as flag officer in Dover (1939–42) and directed the Dunkirk evacuation of 338,000 Allied troops in May–June 1940. He was deputy to Admiral **Andrew Cunningham** for the North African landings in 1942, and commanded the British naval forces for the Allied invasion of Sicily (1943). Reinstated on the active list as an admiral in 1944, he was Allied Naval Commander-in-Chief for the Normandy landings in 1944. He was killed in an aircraft accident near Paris.

Ramsay, James Andrew Broun See Dalhousie, Marquis of

Ramsay, Sir William 1852–1916
Scottish chemist and Nobel Prize winner

He was born in Glasgow and studied classics at Glasgow University and chemistry at Tübingen. He then became an assistant at Anderson's College, Glasgow and Professor of Chemistry at University College, Bristol (1880–87). He subsequently became professor at University College

London (1887–1913). At Glasgow he studied the alkaloids and at Bristol he worked on the vapour pressure of liquids. In 1894, in conjunction with Lord John Kayleigh, he discovered argon. In 1895 he isolated a light inert gas resembling argon by boiling a mineral called cleivite. Spectroscopic analysis showed that this gas was helium, which Sir **Norman Lockyer** and Edward Frankland had discovered in the spectrum of the Sun nearly 30 years earlier. Working with **Morris William Travers**, Ramsay found the green and yellow lines of krypton, the crimson of neon and the blue lines of xenon in 1898. Further research confirmed the inert nature of these gases and their atomic weights. In 1908 Ramsay obtained radon—discovered by **Frederich Ernst Dorn** in 1900—in sufficient quantities to show that it belonged to the same family as helium and the other inert gases. He was elected FRS in 1888, knighted in 1904 and awarded the Nobel Prize for chemistry in the same year. ▭ William Augustus Tilden, *Sir William Ramsay* (1918)

Ramses See **Rameses**

Ramsey, Arthur Michael, Baron 1904–88
English prelate, Archbishop of Canterbury

Born in Cambridge, the son of a Cambridge academic, he was educated at Repton School (where the headmaster was the man he would succeed as archbishop, Dr **Geoffrey Fisher**), and Magdalene College, Cambridge, where he was president of the Union (1926). He wrote his first book *The Gospel and Catholic Church* in 1936 and was appointed vicar at St Benet's, Cambridge in 1938. He then became Professor of Divinity at Durham and a canon of the cathedral (1940), Regius Professor of Divinity at Cambridge (1950), Bishop of Durham (1952) and Archbishop of York (1956). As Archbishop of Canterbury (1961–74) he worked tirelessly for Church unity, making a historic visit to Pope **Paul VI** in the Vatican in 1966, but was disappointed in his attempts to forge a reconciliation with the Methodist Church. He was an eminent scholar, and published many theological works, notably *The Resurrection of Christ* (1945) and *The Glory of God and the Transfiguration of Christ* (1949). His last book was *Be Still and Know* (1982). He was made a life peer in 1974.

Ramsey, Frank Plumpton 1903–30
English philosopher and mathematician

Born in Cambridge, he read mathematics at Trinity College, and was elected Fellow of King's College when he was 21. In his short life (he died after an operation) he made outstanding contributions to philosophy, logic, mathematics and economics, to an extent which was only properly recognized years after his death. He was much stimulated by his Cambridge contemporaries **Bertrand Russell**, whose programme of reducing mathematics to logic he developed, and **Ludwig Wittgenstein**'s *Tractatus*. He was among the first both to appreciate and criticize, rejecting the idea of ineffable metaphysical truths beyond the limits of language with the famous remark, 'What we can't say we can't say, and we can't whistle it either'. The best of his work is collected in *Philosophical Papers* (edited by D H Mellor, 1990).

Ramsey, Ian Thomas 1915–72
English prelate, theologian and philosopher of religion

Born in Kearsley, near Bolton, he taught at Cambridge from 1941, became Nolloth Professor of the Philosophy of the Christian Religion at Oxford in 1951, and was appointed Bishop of Durham in 1966. He was respected both as a diocesan bishop and for his intellectual contribution to the Church of England's Board for Social Responsibility, to the Doctrine Commission, and to the committee on religious education that produced *The Fourth R* (1970). His enthusiasm for new causes left him relatively little time to develop his philosophical work on

language about God and the understanding of religious experiences as 'disclosure' situations (*Models and Mystery*, 1964, and *Models for Divine Activity*, 1973).

Ramsey, Norman 1915–
US physicist and Nobel Prize winner

Born in Washington DC, he was educated at Columbia University and at Cambridge, and became Associate Professor of Physics at Harvard in 1947. Since 1966 he has been Higgins Professor of Physics there. He was awarded the 1989 Nobel Prize for physics jointly with **Wolfgang Paul** and **Hans Dehmelt** for his development of the 'separated field' method, in which an electromagnetic field applied to a beam of atoms or molecules induces transitions between specific energy states. This allows atomic transitions to be measured with great accuracy, and led to the development of the atomic clock, which now provides international time standards. Ramsey has also contributed to the development of the hydrogen maser. He was awarded the Einstein Medal in 1993.

Ramus, Petrus, *Latin name of* Pierre de la Ramée 1515–72
French humanist

Born in Cuth, near Soissons, he became servant to a rich scholar at the Collège de Navarre, and by studying at night made rapid progress in learning. The dominant philosophy of the day dissatisfied him, and he put higher value on 'reason' than on 'authority'. Graduating at 23, he had great success as lecturer on the Greek and Latin authors, and set out to reform the science of logic. His attempts were greeted by hostility from the Aristotelians, and his *Dialectic* (1543) was fiercely attacked by the scholars of the Sorbonne, Paris, who had it suppressed. But cardinals of Bourbon and Lorraine (**Charles Guise**) had him appointed Principal of the Collège de Presles (1545), and Guise instituted a chair for him at the Collège Royal (1551). He took part in the literary and scholastic disputes of the time, and ultimately became a Protestant. Forced to flee from Paris, he travelled in Germany and Switzerland, but he returned to France (1571) and was killed in the St Bartholomew's Day Massacre (1572). He wrote treatises on arithmetic, geometry and algebra, and was an early adherent of the Copernican system. His theories had considerable influence after his death, and the Ramist system of logic was adopted and taught throughout Europe.

Ramuz, Charles-Ferdinand 1878–1947
Swiss writer

He was born in Cully, near Lausanne, and wrote in French, mainly about life in his native canton of Vaud. His first book, *Le Petit Village* ('The Little Village'), appeared in 1903, and from then on he wrote prolifically. His pure prose style and fine descriptive power won him wide admiration and esteem. His works include *Jean Luc persécuté* (1909, 'Jean Luc Persecuted'), *Beauté sur la terre* (1927, Eng trans *Beauty on Earth*, 1929) and *Besoin de grandeur* (1937, 'Need for Grandeur'). He also wrote the narration for **Stravinsky**'s *A Soldier's Tale*. ▭ G Guisan, *Charles-Ferdinand Ramuz* (1967)

Rancé, Armand Jean le Bouthillier de 1626–1700
French monk, the founder of the Trappists

An accomplished but worldly priest, he became abbot of the Cistercian Abbey of La Trappe in 1662. Affected by the tragic deaths of two of his friends, he underwent a conversion, undertook a reform of his monastery, and finally established what was practically a new religious order, its principles perpetual prayer and austere self-denial. Intellectual work was forbidden, and only manual labour was allowed to the monks. He wrote of his order in *Traité de la sainteté et des devoirs de la vie monastique* (1683, 'Treatise on the Holiness and the Duties of the Monastic Life'), which caused much controversy on the place of study in monastic life.

Randall, James Ryder 1839–1908
US poet

Born in Baltimore, he became a teacher, then a journalist. His lyrics, which in the Civil War gave powerful aid to the Southern cause, include 'Maryland, My Maryland' (1861), 'Stonewall Jackson' and 'There's life in the old land yet'. A posthumous collection called *Poems* was published in 1910.

Randall, Samuel Jackson 1828–90
US politician

Born in Philadelphia, he was a member of the House of Representatives (1863–90). As Speaker (1876–81), he codified the rules of the House and considerably strengthened the Speaker's power.

Randolph, A(sa) Philip 1889–1979
US black labour leader and civil rights activist

He was born in Crescent City, Florida, the son of a clergyman. He was educated locally, and studied economics, philosophy and science at City College, New York. Initially a supporter of the black nationalist Marcus Garvey, Randolph opposed the idea of economic separatism in his own journal, *The Messenger*. In 1925 he organized the Brotherhood of Sleeping Car Porters, the first black union to gain major successes, including recognition by the Pullman Company. In 1941 he organized a march on Washington to demand equal employment opportunities for blacks in the defence industries, and racial desegregation in the armed forces. The march was called off after President Franklin D Roosevelt established the Fair Employment Practices Committee, but the tactic was revived during the civil rights movement of the 1960s, when he organized the March on Washington for Jobs and Freedom (28 August 1963), at which Martin Luther King was the principal speaker.

Randolph, Edmund Jennings 1753–1813
US politician

Born near Williamsburg, Virginia, he studied at the College of William and Mary and trained as a lawyer under his father. His Loyalist family went to England at the outbreak of the Revolution, but he stayed behind and became an aide-de-camp to George Washington. He soon entered Virginia state politics, serving as a delegate to the Continental Congress (1779–82) and the Constitutional Convention (1787), and as Governor of Virginia (1786–88). He was working on a codification of the state laws of Virginia when Washington appointed him Attorney-General (1789). In 1794 he was appointed Secretary of State, but resigned over false charges of bribery (1795) and was practically ruined. He resumed law practice at Richmond, Virginia, and was chief counsel for Aaron Burr at his treason trial.

Randolph, John, *known as* John Randolph of Roanoke 1773–1833
US politician

He was born in Cawsons, Virginia, and in 1799 he entered Congress, where he became distinguished for his wit and eccentricity. He was the Democratic Leader of the House of Representatives, but quarrelled with Thomas Jefferson and opposed the war of 1812; he also opposed the Missouri Compromise and Nullification. From 1825 to 1827 he sat in the Senate, and in 1830 was appointed Minister to Russia. He was a second cousin of Edmund Randolph.

Randolph, Sir Thomas d.1332
Scottish soldier and statesman

He was the nephew of Robert I the Bruce, who created him Earl of Moray. He recaptured Edinburgh Castle from the English (1314), commanded a division at Bannockburn, took Berwick (1318), won a victory at Mitton (1319), reinvaded England (1320, 1327), and was Guardian of the Kingdom from Bruce's death (1329) until his own death at Musselburgh.

Randolph, Thomas 1605–35
English poet and dramatist

Born in Newnham, near Daventry, Northamptonshire, he studied at Trinity College, Cambridge, where he was elected a Fellow, and soon began to write, gaining the friendship of Ben Jonson and leading a boisterous life. He left a number of bright, fanciful poems, and six plays: *Aristippus, or the Jovial Philosopher* (c.1626), *The Muses' Looking-glass* (1630), *Amyntas, or the Impossible Dowry* (1630), *The Conceited Peddler* (1631), *The Jealous Lovers* (1632) and *Hey for Honesty* (1651). 📖 S A and D R Tannenbaum, *Thomas Randolph* (1947)

Ranjit Singh, *known as* the Lion of the Punjab 1780–1839
Sikh ruler

He succeeded his father, a Sikh chief, as ruler of Lahore (1801), and directed all his energies to founding a kingdom which would unite all the Sikh provinces. With the help of an army trained by western soldiers, including generals Ventura and Allard, he became the most powerful ruler in India. He was a firm ally of the British, the boundary between their territories having been amicably fixed at the Sutlej River. In 1813 he procured the Koh-i-noor diamond, as payment for his military support for an Afghan prince. Soon after his death the Sikh state collapsed amid chieftain rivalry. 📖 N K Sinha, *Ranjit Singh* (1933)

Rank, J(oseph) Arthur, Baron 1888–1972
English film magnate

Born in Hull, Humberside, he worked in his father's flour-milling business but developed an interest in films as a means of propagating the Gospel. He became chairman of many film companies, including Gaumont-British and Cinema-Television, and did much to promote the British film industry at a time when Hollywood and the US companies seemed to have gained a monopoly. A staunch and active supporter of the Methodist Church, he was keenly interested in social problems. He was raised to the peerage in 1957. 📖 Michael Wakelin, *J Arthur Rank: The Man Behind the Gong* (1996)

Rank, Otto 1884–1939
Austrian psychoanalyst

Born in Vienna, he was a protégé of Sigmund Freud and asserted, contrary to Freud's teachings, that the fundamental cause of neurosis is the trauma of birth. He was also known for his analysis of the psychological significance of myths.

Ranke, Leopold von 1795–1886
German historian

Born in Wiehe, Thuringia, he studied at Halle and Berlin, and in 1818 became a schoolmaster at Frankfurt an der Oder, but he was determined to study history. His early work was concerned with the Romance and Teutonic peoples in the Reformation period, and he criticized contemporary historians; as a result of this activity, he was appointed Professor of History at Berlin (1825–72). From a study of the archives of Vienna, Venice, Rome and Florence (1827–31), he produced a work on south Europe in the 16th and 17th centuries (1827), books on Serbia and Venice, and a *History of the Popes in the 16th and 17th Centuries* (1834–37, Eng trans 1846). Then he wrote on the German Reformation, and Prussian, French and English history. Other books were on the Seven Years War (1871), the

Revolutionary Wars of 1791 to 1792 (1875), Venetian history (1878), a universal history (1881–88), and the history of Germany and France in the 19th century (1887), as well as biographies of **Albrecht Wallenstein** (1869) and others.

Rankin, Jeannette 1880–1973
US feminist and pacifist

Born near Missoula, Montana, she was educated at the University of Montana and the New York School of Philanthropy, and went on to become a social worker in Seattle (1909), where she involved herself in the women's rights movement. In 1914 she was appointed legislative secretary of the National American Woman Suffrage Association, and in 1916 was elected to the House of Representatives as a Republican, becoming the first woman to serve in Congress. During her two terms there (1917–19, 1941–43) she promoted labour reform health care as well as women's rights, and was instrumental in the adoption of the first bill granting married women independent citizenship. She was the only member of Congress to vote against US participation in both world wars. She continued to campaign for peace and women's issues throughout her career, and worked for the National Council for the Prevention of War from 1928 to 1939. In 1968 at the age of 87 she led the Jeannette Rankin Brigade, a group of 5,000 women who marched on Capitol Hill, Washington, to protest against the Vietnam War. ◫ See biography by Hannah Josephson (1974).

Rankine, William John MacQuorn 1820–72
Scottish engineer and scientist

He was born in Edinburgh, and with **William Kelvin** and **Rudolf Clausius** he shaped the new science of thermodynamics, particularly in its practical dimension by patenting an elaborate air engine with his friend James Robert Napier of the famous Clyde shipbuilding family. Rankine introduced the terms 'actual' (kinetic) and 'potential' energy. Later he proposed an abstract 'science of energetics' which sought to unify physics. In 1855 he was appointed to the chair of engineering at Glasgow. He was elected FRS in 1853, and his works on the steam engine, machinery, shipbuilding and applied mechanics became standard textbooks. He also contributed to the theory of elasticity. In addition he wrote humorous and patriotic *Songs and Fables* (1874). ◫ Hugh Brown Sutherland, *Rankine: His Life and Times* (1973)

Ranković, Aleksander 1909–
Yugoslav politician

He joined the Communist Party in 1928 and was imprisoned during the dictatorship of King **Alexander I**. During World War II he fought with **Tito** and the partisans and in 1945 became director of the secret police, overseeing the ruthless elimination of all opposition to communist rule. He was also Minister of the Interior (1946–53) and Vice-President of Yugoslavia (1963). After bugging Tito's home, he was accused of abusing his authority and was forced to resign (1966).

Ransom, John Crowe 1888–1974
US poet and critic

Born in Pulaski, Tennessee, he graduated from Vanderbilt University in 1909 and was a Rhodes scholar at Christ Church, Oxford. From 1914 he taught English at Vanderbilt, where he gathered a group of students and colleagues including **Allen Tate** and **Robert Penn Warren**, who contributed to the poetry magazine *The Fugitive* (1922–25) and shared an allegiance to the Southern agrarian ideal. Much of Ransom's poetry dates from this period, and his collections *Poems About God* (1919), *Chills and Fever* (1924) and *Two Gentlemen in Bonds* (1927) illustrate his aptitude as a balladist and elegist. His long association with Kenyon College (1937–58), where he was Carnegie Professor of Poetry, led to his founding of the *Kenyon*

Review. His criticism includes *God Without Thunder* (1930) and *The New Criticism* (1941). ◫ T D Young, *Gentleman in a Dustcoat* (1976); T H Parsons, *John Crowe Ransom* (1969)

Ransome, Arthur Mitchell 1884–1967
English journalist and children's writer

Born in Leeds, the son of a history professor, he was educated at Rugby where he was a poor scholar and, by virtue of bad eyesight, inept at games. He worked as an office boy in a publishing house before graduating to ghost-writing, reviewing and writing short stories, meanwhile living a bohemian existence. He became a reporter for the *Daily News* and, in 1919, for the *Manchester Guardian*. He was widely travelled and, having learned Russian in 1913, was sent to cover the Revolution, a welcome relief from his stormy relationship with his first wife. They were divorced in 1924 and he married **Trotsky**'s secretary, Evgenia Shelepin, with whom he fled from Russia, staying for a while in Estonia before settling in the Lake District. He had been a published author for a quarter of a century before the appearance of *Swallows and Amazons* (1930), the first of 12 perennially popular novels featuring two families of adventurous but responsible children, the Blacketts and the Walkers, who spend their school holidays revelling in the open air, free from the cramping attention of adults. Of his numerous other books, *Old Peter's Russian Tales* (1916) is worthy of note. He also wrote *The Autobiography of Arthur Ransome* (1976). ◫ A B Shelley, *Arthur Ransome* (1960)

Ransome, Robert 1753–1830
English maker of agricultural implements

He was born in Wells, Norfolk. In 1789 he founded at Ipswich the great Orwell Works for agricultural implements. His most important patent was for a new kind of ploughshare (1803).

Rantzen, Esther Louise 1940–
English television presenter and producer

Born in Berkhamsted, Hertfordshire, and educated at Somerville College, Oxford, she joined the BBC in 1963, making sound effects for radio drama. Moving into research for *Man Alive* (1965–67), she joined *Braden's Week* (1968–72) as a reporter. From 1973 to 1994 she wrote, produced and presented *That's Life*, a consumer programme combining investigative journalism with a sequence of comical items. She has also campaigned against child abuse and drug addiction in a variety of documentaries such as *Childwatch* (1987). In 1977 she married broadcaster Desmond Wilcox (1931–); their joint publications include *Kill the Chocolate Biscuit* (1981) and *Baby Love* (1985). She is the presenter of her own television chat show, *Esther* (1994–), and in 1996 presented *The Rantzen Report* which looked at real-life stories. In 1988 she received the Richard Dimbleby award for her contributions to factual television.

Rao, P(amulaparti) V(enkata) Narasimha 1921–
Indian politician

A follower of **Indira Gandhi**, he joined the Congress (I) Party shortly after its foundation, and was Minister of the State of Andhra Pradesh (1969–73) and Minister for Foreign Affairs (1980–84) before he became Prime Minister (1991–96). His administration was marked by continuing opposition from the growing Hindu nationalist movement and by secessionist fighting against Indian rule in Kashmir. However, he achieved a pact with China (1993) to reduce the military presence on the border, in an attempt to bring peace to the Himalayas. Following his party's defeat in the 1996 election, he was eventually succeeded by H D Deve Gowda (1933–) and a United Front coalition.

Raoult, François Marie 1830–1901
French physical chemist

Raphael, *properly* Raffaello Santi or Sanzio 1483–1520
Italian painter, one of the greatest artists of the Renaissance

Raphael was born in Urbino, the son of the poet-painter Giovanni Santi (d.1494). He studied from about 1500 at Perugia under **Perugino**. Among his early paintings were the *Mond Crucifixion* (1502–03) and *Assumption of the Virgin* (1504), which clearly show Perugino's influence. In 1505 he went to Siena, where he assisted **Pinturicchio** and took commissions including several Madonnas. He then moved to Florence, where he studied the work of **Michelangelo** and **Leonardo da Vinci**. In Raphael's portraiture especially, da Vinci's influence is visible, and the likeness of *Maddalena Doni* (Florence) is inspired by the *Mona Lisa*. Of special interest is the *St George*, sent by the Duke of Urbino to **Henry VII** of England, while the painter's own likeness and the *Madonnas* of Orléans, of the Palm, of St Petersburg and of Canigiani are attractive in other ways. The Borghese *Entombment* (1507) is an embodiment of all the new principles which Raphael acquired in Florence and of colour such as only he could give.

He became attracted by the style of **Fra Bartolommeo** and, under his influence, he completed the *Madonna del Baldacchino* in Florence. Some of the best work of his Florentine period was now produced: the small *Holy Family*, the *St Catherine*, the *Bridgewater* and *Colonna Madonnas*, the *Virgin and Sleeping Infant*, the large *Cowper Madonna*, the *Belle Jardinière*, and the *Esterhazy Madonna*.

In 1508 he went to Rome at the instigation of his relative **Donato Bramante**, then in high favour with Pope **Julius II**, who had laid the foundation of the new cathedral of St Peter, and who commissioned the redecoration of the papal chambers because he disliked the frescoes of the older masters. Among Raphael's work there was the fresco series *The School of Athens*, centred on **Plato** and **Aristotle**. Raphael divided his time between the labours of the Vatican and easel pictures. The portraits of Julius II and the Virgin of the Popolo were now executed, drawings

were furnished to the copperplate-engraver Marcantonio for the Massacre of the Innocents, and Madonnas and Holy Families were composed.

The use of pupils also enabled Raphael in the three years 1511–14 to finish the *Madonna di Foligno*, the *Isaiah of St Agostino*, the *Galatea of the Farnesina*, the *Sibyls of the Pace*, and the mosaics of the Popolo ordered by Agostino Chigi. He also painted the *Madonna of the Fish* (Madrid) and *Madonna della Sedia* (Florence), while in portraits such as *Altoviti* (Munich) and *Inghirami* (Florence) he rises to the perfect rendering of features and expression which finds its greatest triumph in the *Leo X* (Florence). **Leo X** selected Raphael to succeed Bramante as architect of St Peter's in 1514, and secured from him for the Vatican chambers the frescoes of the Camera dell' Incendio, which all illustrate scenes from the lives of Leonine Popes.

Much of Raphael's attention was meanwhile taken up with the cartoons executed, with help from assistants, for the tapestries of the Sistine Chapel. He went with Leo X to Florence and Bologna, and found there new patrons for whom he executed the *Sistine Madonna*, the *St Cecilia* of Bologna, and the *Ezechiel* of the Pitti, Florence. The labours subsequently completed were immense, including the *Spasimo*, the *Holy Family* and *St Michael*, which the pope sent to the king of France in 1518, the likeness of the vice-queen of Aragon, and the *Violin-player*. In wall-painting he produced, with help, the cycle of the Psyche legend at the Farnesina, the gospel scenes of the Loggie of the Vatican, and the Frescoes of the Hall of Constantine. His last work, the *Transfiguration*, was left unfinished when he died.

📖 James Beck, *Raphael* (1976); J Pope-Hennessy, *Raphael* (1970); Sir Joseph Archer Crowe, *Raphael: His Life and Works* (1882–85).

Born in Fournes, near Lille, he studied in Paris, but financial problems forced him to abandon the course, and from 1853 to 1867 he taught science in various schools, completing his doctorate in 1863. In 1867 he began to teach chemistry at the University of Grenoble, and in 1870 he was promoted to the chair of chemistry, which he occupied until his death. He is remembered for his work on the freezing points and vapour pressures of solutions (1878–92). His findings provided the basis for methods of determining molecular weights. Raoult's law, which states that the vapour pressure of solvent above a solution is proportional to the mole fraction of solvent in the solution, is named after him. He became an honorary Fellow of the Chemical Society in 1898.

Raphael See panel above

Rapp, George 1770–1847
US religious leader, a founder of the Harmony Society

Born in Württemberg, Germany, he was a linen-weaver by trade, and became the leader of a group of separatists. In 1803, to escape persecution, he and his son and some of his followers emigrated to Western Pennsylvania, where they established a settlement named Harmony. After migrating to New Harmony in Indiana (1815), they returned in 1824 to Pennsylvania and founded Economy on the Ohio, 15 miles north-west of Pittsburgh. Looking for the speedy second coming of Christ, the community of Harmonites (or Rappites) sought to amass wealth for the Lord's use, practised rigid economy, self-denial and celibacy, and community of property. Diminished in

number, they owned farms, dairies and vineyards, as well as shares worth millions of dollars. The community came to an end in 1906.

Rask, Rasmus Christian 1787–1832
Danish philologist

Born on the island of Fyn, he mastered some 25 languages and dialects, and is said to have studied twice as many. Along with the works of **Franz Bopp** and **Jacob Grimm**, his *Essay on the Origin of the Ancient Scandinavian or Icelandic Tongue* (1818), in which he demonstrated the affinity of Icelandic to other European languages, opened up the science of comparative philology. He was one of the first to recognize that the Celtic languages are Indo-European, and, developing the work of the Swedish philologist **Johan Ihre**, he anticipated Grimm in formulating the Germanic consonant shift described in what has become known as Grimm's Law. He became Professor of Literary History in 1825, of Oriental Languages in 1828, and of Icelandic in 1831.

Rasmussen, Knud Johan Victor 1879–1933
Danish explorer and ethnologist

Born in Jacobshavn, Greenland, the son of a Danish Inuit mother, he directed several expeditions to Greenland (from 1902) in support of the theory that the Inuit and the North American Indians were both descended from migratory tribes from Asia. In 1910 he established Thule base on Cape York, and crossed from Greenland to the Bering Strait by dog sledge (1921–24) to visit all the Inuit groups along the route. 📖 Nils Aage Jensen, *Knud Rasmussen – manden med slaeden* (1994)

Rasputin, Grigori Efimovich 1871–1916
Russian peasant and self-styled religious 'elder' (starets)

He was born in Pokrovskoye, Tobolsk. A member of the schismatic sect of *Khlysty* (flagellants), he arrived in St Petersburg at a time when mystical religion was fashionable, and obtained an introduction to the royal household. There he quickly gained the confidence of Tsar Nicholas II and the Empress Alexandra, by his apparent ability to control through hypnosis the bleeding of the haemophiliac heir to the throne. However, he soon created a public scandal through his sexual and alcoholic excesses, and achieved notoriety through his political influence in securing the appointment and dismissal of government ministers. He was murdered by a clique of aristocrats, led by Prince Felix Yusupov, a distant relative of the tsar. 📖 Alex De Jonge, *Life and Times of Gregorii Rasputin* (1988)

Rassam, Hormuzd 1826–1910
Turkish Assyriologist

He was born in Mosul, the son of Chaldaean Christians. An English national, he assisted Austen Layard at Nineveh (1845–47, 1849–51), and succeeded him, until 1854, as British agent for Assyrian excavations, including among his achievements the excavation of the palace of Ashurbanipal. After holding political offices at Aden and Muscat, he was sent (1864) to Abyssinia (Ethiopia), where King Kassai Theodore (1816–68) imprisoned him until 1868, when he was released by Sir Robert Napier. From 1876 to 1882 he undertook explorations in Mesopotamia for the British Museum, London, conducting notable excavations at Tell Balawat and Abu Habbah (ancient Sippar). He wrote on his Abyssinian experiences (1869), and did much work for the British Academy.

Rastell, John 1475–1536
English printer, lawyer and dramatist

Born in Coventry, he was called to the Bar, and in 1510 set up his own printing press. Married to the sister of Sir Thomas More, he printed More's *Life of Pico*, a grammar by Thomas Linacre, the only copy of Henry Medwall's play *Fulgens and Lucres*, and many law books. Himself a dramatist, his plays, printed on his own press, include *Nature of the Four Elements* (1519), *Of Gentylness and Nobylyte...* (c.1527) and *Calisto and Meleboea* (c.1527). He was an ingenious deviser of pageants, and presented several of them at court. His attempt to found a settlement in the 'New Found Lands' in 1517 was frustrated by mutiny on his ship. 📖 A W Reed, *Early Tudor Drama* (1926)

Rastell, William 1508–65
English printer and lawyer

He was born in Coventry, the son of John Rastell and nephew of Sir Thomas More. He attended Oxford but left without graduating and worked with his father until 1529, then set up his own printing press. He printed many of More's works, Robert Fabyan's *Chronicle*, Henry Medwall's *Nature* and plays by his brother-in-law, John Heywood, as well as many law books, notably *A Collection of All the Statutes* (1557) and *A Collection of Entrees* (1566). Abandoning printing for law when More fell from favour with the king, he was by 1549 treasurer of Lincoln's Inn. His kinship with More and his marriage to a daughter of More's protégé, John Clement, drove him into exile with the Clements at Louvain. With him went letters and other works written by More in the Tower. These, which he edited and printed, appeared in More's *English Works* (1557). He was exiled again during the reign of Elizabeth I, and died abroad.

Rastrick, John Urpeth 1780–1856
English civil and mechanical engineer

Born in Morpeth, Northumberland, he was articled to his father, an engineer and machinist, at the age of 15. From about 1801 he gained experience with several firms of iron-founders, and from 1815 to 1816 he designed and built the cast-iron bridge over the Wye at Chepstow, Gwent. In 1822 he was engineer of the Stratford and Moreton horse-drawn railway, and in 1826, with George Stephenson, supported the use of steam locomotives on the Liverpool and Manchester railway. He was one of the judges at the Rainhill trials in 1829, and in the same year built a colliery railway in Staffordshire, which he worked with the locomotive *Agenoria*. A similar engine, the *Stourbridge Lion*, was the first to run in North America. His greatest achievement was the construction of the London and Brighton railway, which opened in 1841, and included the 37-span Ouse viaduct and three major tunnels.

Rathbone, Eleanor Florence 1872–1946
English feminist and social reformer

Born in Liverpool, she read classics at Somerville College, Oxford. Later, she made an extensive study of the position of widows under the poor law, and became the leading British advocate for family allowances (*The Disinherited Family*, 1924; *The Case for Family Allowances*, 1940). A leader in the constitutional movement for female suffrage, she was an independent member of Liverpool City Council from 1909, working in the housing campaign between the wars. She was elected as independent MP for the Combined English Universities, fought to gain the franchise for Indian women, and denounced child marriage in India (*Child Marriage: The Indian Minotaur*, 1934). She also attacked appeasement of Hitler in *War Can Be Averted* (1937), advocated intervention in the Spanish Civil War, and denounced Italian aggression in Ethiopia. She was a vigorous worker on behalf of refugees, as a result of which she became a supporter of Zionism.

Rathbone, Harold Stewart 1858–1929
English painter, designer and poet

He founded the Della Robbia Pottery with the sculptor, Conrad Dressler in 1893 in Birkenhead, Merseyside, producing architectural earthenware, relief plaques, vases and bottles, plates, dishes and clock cases. These were decorated with graffito and elaborate modelled relief decoration inspired by Italian majolica. The Italian sculptor, Carlo Manzoni, joined in 1895, and among the many designers were Ford Madox Ford, Robert Anning Bell and Christopher Dresser. The pottery merged with a firm of ecclesiastical sculptors in 1900 and went into liquidation in 1906.

Rathenau, Walther 1867–1922
German electrotechnician and industrialist

Born in Berlin of Jewish parents, he was head of the Allgemeine Elektrizitäts Gesellschaft (AEG), founded in 1883 by his father Emil Rathenau (1838–1915), and took responsibility for German war industries during World War I. As Minister of Reconstruction (1921) and Foreign Minister (1922), his attempts to negotiate a reparations agreement with the victorious Allies, and the fact that he was Jewish, made him extremely unpopular in nationalist circles, and he was murdered by extremists in the summer of 1922. His works include *Die neue Wirtschaft* (1918, 'The New Economy').

Rathke, Martin Heinrich 1793–1860
German biologist

Born in Danzig (Gdansk, Poland), he studied medicine at the universities of Göttingen and Berlin, and returned to Danzig to practise medicine. He became Professor of Physiology at the universities of Dorpat in 1829 and Königsberg in 1835. Deeply interested in embryology and animal development, in 1829 he discovered gill-slits and gill-arches in embryo birds and mammals. 'Rathke's pocket' is the name given to the small pit on the dorsal side of the oral cavity of developing vertebrates. He was also interested in the embryonic development of the sexual organs.

Ratsiraka, Didier 1936–
Malagasy sailor and politician

Born in Vatomandry, and educated and trained for naval service in Madagascar and France, he served in the navy (1963–70) and was military attaché in Paris, with the rank of lieutenant-commander (1970–72). Since independence in 1960 frequent clashes had occurred between the country's two main ethnic groups, the highland Merina and the coastal Cotiers. From independence in 1960 until 1972 the government had favoured the Cotiers but in 1972 the army, representing the Merina, took control. A deteriorating economy and Cotier unrest led to the imposition of martial law in 1975, but this was lifted and, under a new constitution, Ratsiraka, who was a Cotier, was elected President. In 1976 he formed the Advance Guard of the Malagasy Revolution (AREMA) which became the nucleus of a one-party state, based on the National Front for the Defence of the Malagasy Socialist Revolution (FNDR). Although AREMA won overwhelming support in the Assembly elections of 1983 and 1989, discontent continued, particularly among the Merina. He was President until 1993, though he relinquished his executive powers two years previously.

Rattazzi, Urbano 1808–73
Italian statesman

Born in Alessandria, he practised as advocate at Casale, and in 1848 entered the Second Chamber at Turin, becoming Minister of the Interior and later of Justice until after Novara. In 1853 he took the justice portfolio under Camillo Benso, Conte di Cavour but, accused of weakness in suppressing the Mazzinian movement, retired in 1858. In 1859 he was appointed Minister of the Interior, but retired because of the cession of Savoy and Nice (1860). Twice Prime Minister for a few months (1862, 1867), he twice had to resign because of his opposition to Garibaldi.

Rattigan, Sir Terence Mervyn 1911–77
English playwright

He was born in London, educated at Harrow and Oxford, and scored a considerable success with his comedy *French Without Tears* (1936). His work displays not only a wide range of imagination but a deepening psychological knowledge. Best known are *The Winslow Boy* (1946), based on the Archer Shee case, *The Browning Version* (1948), *The Deep Blue Sea* (1952), *Separate Tables* (1954) and *Ross* (1960), a fictional treatment of T E Lawrence. He was responsible for several successful films made from his own and other works.

Rattle, Sir Simon 1955–
English conductor

He was born in Liverpool. He won the Bournemouth International Conducting Competition at the age of 17, and made his London debut at the Royal Albert Hall and Festival Hall in 1976. Assistant conductor of the BBC Scottish Symphony Orchestra (1977–80), he was appointed principal conductor (1980–91) and music director (1991–) of the City of Birmingham Symphony Orchestra. He was principal guest conductor of the Los Angeles Philharmonic Orchestra from 1981 to 1992. In 1991 he launched *Towards the Millennium*, a 10-year retrospective survey of 20th-century music which features a different decade of music every year until 2000. He is also principal conductor of the Orchestra of Enlightenment (1992–). In 1996 he announced that he would leave the City of Birmingham Symphony Orchestra in 1998, on the expiry of his contract. 📖 Nicholas Kenyon, *Simon Rattle: The Making of a Conductor* (1987)

Rau, Johannes 1931–
German politician

Born in Wuppertal, in North Rhine-Westphalia, the son of a Protestant pastor, he began his career as a salesman for a Church publishing company before being attracted to politics as a follower of Gustav Heinemann. He joined the Social Democratic Party (SPD) and was elected to the Diet of his home Land (state), the country's most populous, in 1958. He served as chairman of the SPD's parliamentary group (1967–70), and as Minister of Science and Research in the Land (1970–78) before becoming its Minister-President in 1978. His successful record as Land leader, his moderate political stance, and his optimistic and youthful personality persuaded the SPD to elect him Federal Party deputy chairman in 1982 and Chancellor-Candidate for the 1987 Bundestag election. However, the party was heavily defeated, and since this setback he has concentrated on his work as Land premier.

Rauch, Christian Daniel 1777–1857
German sculptor

Born in Arolsen, he practised sculpture while serving as valet to Frederick-William III of Prussia, and in 1804 went to Rome where he came under the classicizing influence of Antonio Canova and Bertel Thorvaldzen, but his own style was naturalistic. From 1811 to 1815 he carved the recumbent effigy for the tomb of Queen Louisa at Charlottenburg. Other works include statues of Blücher, Dürer, Goethe, Schiller, Kant, and Schleiermacher. His masterpiece was the equestrian statue of Frederick the Great (1851) in Berlin.

Rauschenberg, Robert 1925–
US avant-garde artist

Born in Port Arthur, Texas, of German and Indian descent, he studied art at the Kansas City Art Institute, in Paris, and at Black Mountain College, North Carolina, under Josef Albers from 1948 to 1949. His collages and 'combines' incorporate a variety of junk items (rusty metal, old tyres, stuffed birds, fragments of clothing, etc) splashed with paint. Sometimes categorized as a Pop Artist, his work has strong affinities with Dadaism and with the 'ready-mades' of Marcel Duchamp.

Ravel, Maurice See panel p1539

Ravenscroft, Thomas 1592–1640
English composer and author

He was born possibly in Sussex. He wrote *Pammelia* (1609), *Melismata* (1611) and *The Whole Book of Psalms* (1621). *Pammelia*, a collection of rounds and catches, was the first book of its kind in England. He wrote some well-known tunes, such as 'St Davids' and 'Bangor'.

Ravilious, Eric William 1903–42
English artist, designer and illustrator

He studied at Eastbourne School of Art, London (1919–22) and at the Design School of the Royal College of Art (1922–25), where he was taught by Paul Nash. He designed printed patterns for J Wedgwood & Sons, including many famous designs such as the travel series, coronation mugs and Christmas tableware. Wood-engraving, however, was the centre of his activity, and he was commissioned to illustrate many books including *Twelfth Night* (1932) and *Elm Angel* (1930). During the late 1930s he turned increasingly to watercolour painting and colour lithography. He was appointed official war artist in 1940 and was lost on air patrol off the coast of Iceland.

Ravi Shankar 1920–
Indian musician

Ravel, Maurice 1875–1937
French composer

Ravel was born in Ciboure in the Basque region. He went to the Paris Conservatoire as a piano student in 1889, and later joined **Gabriel Fauré**'s composition class. His first orchestral piece, the overture *Schéhérazade*, had a hostile reception on its first performance in 1899, but he won recognition in the same year with the *Pavane pour une infante défunte* ('Pavane for a Dead Princess'), which is strongly redolent of his Basque background.

He tried four times for the Prix de Rome, and the fourth time he was barred from entering. He himself was indifferent, but the case was seized on by the press as an example of personal prejudice in high quarters. Now at the height of his powers, he wrote a string quartet (1902–03), the exotic and beautiful *Introduction and Allegro* for a group of instruments including harp, and the piano pieces *Sonatine* (1905, 'Little Sonata'), *Miroirs* (1905, 'Mirrors'), *Ma Mère l'Oye* (1908, 'Mother Goose') and *Gaspard de la nuit* (1908, 'Gaspard of the Night'). In 1909 he began the music for the **Diaghilev** ballet *Daphnis et Chloé* ('Daphnis and Chloe'), which was first performed in 1912. His comic opera *L'Heure espagnole* ('The Spanish Hour') was completed in 1907 and produced in 1911.

When World War I broke out he joined the army and for a short time saw active service until he was discharged for health reasons; his *Tombeau de Couperin* (1917, 'The Tomb of Couperin'), a piano suite in 18th-century style which he later orchestrated, was dedicated to friends killed in action. The choreographic poem *La Valse*, epitomizing the spirit of Vienna, was staged in 1920, and the opera *L'Enfant et les sortilèges* ('The Child and His Spells'), written to a libretto by **Colette**, in 1925. To this late period also belong the two piano concertos (1929–31), one for the left hand and written for the pianist Paul Wittgenstein, who had lost his right arm in the war, and *Boléro* (1928), originally intended as a miniature ballet.

He visited England in 1928 and received an honorary doctorate at Oxford University. In 1933 his mental faculties began to fail, and it was found that he had a tumour on the brain. He composed no more but remained fairly active physically, and was able to tour Spain before he died.

His music is scintillating and dynamic; he defied the established rules of harmony with his unresolved sevenths and ninths and other devices, his syncopation and strange sonorities, and he made the piano sound as it had never sounded before. His orchestrations are brilliant, especially in their masterly use of wind instruments and unusual percussion effects, often characteristically French, sometimes with a Spanish flavour. It is interesting that his only work written purely for orchestra is *Rapsodie espagnole* (1907); everything else orchestral is either opera, ballet, or orchestrated piano pieces.

📖 Ravel's own writings, and memoirs by **Jean Cocteau**, Colette and others, are listed in R Nichols, *Ravel* (1977), which is an excellent short biographical study. See also James Burnett, *Ravel, His Life and Times* (1983); Rollo H Myers, *Ravel: Life and Works* (1960); Victor I Seroff, *Maurice Ravel* (1953).

'I've still so much music in my head. I have said nothing. I have so much more to say.' Spoken on his deathbed; quoted in H Jourdan-Morhange, *Ravel et nous* (1945).

He is widely regarded as India's most important musician, both as a virtuoso player of the sitar, and as a teacher and composer. His own early training as a dancer was followed by years of intensive musical study. He set up schools of Indian music, founded the National Orchestra of India, and by the mid-1950s his reputation had spread so widely that he became the first Indian instrumentalist to undertake an international tour. He found himself in demand in the West as a performer and teacher in all areas of music. George Harrison of the **Beatles** was one of his pupils. He has written several film scores, the most notable being for **Satyajit Ray**'s trilogy, *Apu*. 📖 *My Music, My Life* (1968)

Rawlings, Jerry John 1947–
Ghanaian leader

He was born in Accra. He was at the centre of a peaceful coup in 1979, the intentions of which were to root out widespread corruption and promote 'moral reform'. After four months, Rawlings and his supporters returned power to a civilian government under an elected president, Hilla Limann, but Rawlings threatened to take over again if the politicians put their own interests before those of the nation. Despite being forcibly retired from the armed forces and sidelined by the civilian government, his popularity remained high among the lower ranks of the army and the general public, and he returned with his Armed Forces Revolutionary Council to seize power again at the end of 1981. He remained head of government, despite attempts to overthrow him twice in 1983 and again in 1987, imposing an austerity plan to control inflation. After a referendum in 1992 voted for the return of constitutional government, Rawlings was elected president in multi-party elections.

Rawlings, Marjorie 1896–1953
US novelist

Born in Washington DC and educated at the University of Wisconsin, Madison, she worked as a journalist, editor, and syndicated verse writer before devoting herself to full-time creative writing in 1928. She was awarded the O Henry Memorial award in 1933 for her short story 'Gal Young Un'. She published her first novel, *South Moon Under*, in the same year but is best remembered for her Pulitzer Prize-winning novel *The Yearling* (1938, later filmed), which describes a young boy's attachment to his pet fawn. Her autobiographical work *Cross Creek* (1942) heightened her reputation as a 'regionalist' writer. 📖 E Silverthorne, *Marjorie Kinnan Rawlings: Sojourner at Cross Creek* (1988)

Rawlinson, Sir Henry Creswicke 1810–95
English scholar and diplomat

Born in Chadlington, Oxfordshire, he entered military service with the East India Company in 1827. From 1833 to 1839 he helped to reorganize the Persian army, at the same time studying the cuneiform inscriptions and translating the Behistun inscription of **Darius**. He was political agent at Kandahar (1840–42) and Baghdad (1843), and made excavations and collections. A director of the East India Company in 1856, he was British Minister in Persia (1859–60), MP (1858, 1865–68) and a member of the Council of India (1858–59, 1868–95). He wrote books on cuneiform inscriptions and the Russian question, and a *History of Assyria* (1852).

Rawlinson, Henry Seymour, 1st Baron Rawlinson 1864–1925
English soldier

He was the eldest son of Sir **Henry Creswicke Rawlinson**. He served in Burma, Sudan and South Africa. In World War I he commanded the 4th Army at the Somme (1916). In 1918 he broke the Hindenburg line near Amiens. He was Commander-in-Chief in India (1920).

Rawls, John 1921–
US philosopher

Born in Baltimore, Maryland, he studied at Princeton, and taught at Princeton and Cornell, before an appointment as professor at Harvard (1962). His best-known work is *A Theory of Justice* (1962), which has been widely discussed in social and political philosophy and gave this field a new direction and energy. In it he presents a fully elaborated description first of the theoretical principles of his theory of justice, second of its implications in detail for social institutions, and third of its grounding and support in moral psychology. Later works include *Justice as Fairness* (1991) and *Political Liberalism* (1993).

Rawsthorne, Alan 1905–71
English composer

Born in Haslingden, Lancashire, he first studied dentistry, but developed an interest in music at the age of 20 and studied at the Royal Manchester College of Music. From 1932 to 1934 he taught at Dartington Hall, and settled in London in 1935. His works, forthright and polished, include symphonies, *Symphonic Studies* for orchestra (1939), concertos for piano and for violin, and choral and chamber music.

Ray, John 1627–1705
English naturalist

Born in Black Notley, near Braintree, Essex, he was educated at Cambridge, and became a Fellow of Trinity College in 1649, but lost his post in 1662 when he refused to take the oath to the Act of Uniformity after the Restoration. Accompanied and supported by a wealthy former pupil and fellow naturalist, Francis Willoughby, he toured extensively in Europe (1662–66), studying botany and zoology. He originated the basic principles of plant classification into cryptogams, monocotyledons and diocotyledons in his pioneering *Catalogus Plantarum Angliae* (1670) and *Methodus Plantarum Nova* (1682). His major work was *Historia Generalis Plantarum* (3 vols, 1686–1704), and his *Wisdom of God Manifested in the Works of the Creation* (1691) was immensely influential in its time. His zoological work, in which he developed the most natural pre-Linnaean classification of the animal kingdom, has been considered of even greater importance than his botanical achievements. The Ray Society was founded in his memory in 1844, and he was elected FRS in 1667. 📖 Charles E Raven, *John Ray, Naturalist* (2nd edn, 1950)

Ray, Man, *pseudonym of* Emanuel Rabinovitch 1890–1976
US painter, sculptor, photographer and filmmaker

Born in Philadelphia, he studied art in New York, and became a major figure in the development of Modernism, establishing (with Marcel Duchamp and Francis Picabia), the New York Dadaist movement. He experimented with new techniques in painting and photography, moving to Paris, where he became interested in filming. After working with René Clair, he made surrealist films like *Anemic Cinema* with Marcel Duchamp (1924) and *L'Étoile de Mer* (1928, 'Star of the Sea'). During the 1930s he published and exhibited many photographs and 'rayographs' (photographic images made without a camera), and returned to the USA in 1940, teaching photography in Los Angeles. In 1961 he was awarded the gold medal at the Biennale of Photography in Venice. He published his autobiography, *Self Portrait*, in 1963.

Ray, Satyajit 1921–92
Indian film director

Born in Calcutta, he graduated from Santiniketan University, and worked as a commercial artist in an advertising agency while writing screenplays and attempting to finance his first film. With government support he eventually completed *Pather Panchali* (1955, *On the Road*), which was an international success at the Cannes Film Festival. Together with *Aparajito* (1956, *The Unvanquished*) and *Apu Sansar* (1959, *The World of Apu*), it formed the Apu trilogy, an understated, affectionate portrait of social change in rural life. Later, he made documentaries and filmed tales from Indian folklore, such as *Devi* (1960, *The Goddess*), before revealing a strong interest in the complex political issues facing his country, tackling famine in *Ashanti Sanket* (1973, *Distant Thunder*) and business ethics in *Jana-Arnaya* (1975, *The Middle Man*). He has frequently composed the music for his films, and worked in Hindi for the first time with *Shatranj Ke Khilari* (1977, *The Chess Players*). Later features include *Hirok Rajar Deshe* (1980, *The Kingdom of Diamonds*) and *Ghare-Baire* (1984, *The Home and the World*). Poor health temporarily interrupted his career, but he returned to direction with such films as *Ganashatru* (1989, 'An Enemy of the People') and *Agantuk* (1991, 'The Stranger'). He received a special Academy Award in 1992. 📖 Andrew Robinson, *Satyajit Ray: The Inner Eye* (1989)

Rayburn, Sam(uel Taliaferro) 1882–1961
US legislator

Born in Roane County, Tennessee, he grew up on a Texas farm and studied law with the intention of entering politics. He was elected to the House of Representatives as a Democrat from Texas in 1913 and remained in Congress until his death, serving a record 17 years as Speaker of the House (1940–47, 1949–53, 1955–61). Though he did not consider himself an orator, he wielded political influence through a network of personal contacts and was influential in passing Franklin D Roosevelt's New Deal.

Rayleigh, John William Strutt, 3rd Baron 1842–1919
English physicist and Nobel Prize winner

Born near Maldon, Essex, he graduated from Trinity College, Cambridge, as Senior Wrangler and Smith's Prizeman, and was elected a Fellow (1866). He succeeded his father as third baron in 1873, and was appointed Professor of Experimental Physics at Cambridge (1879–84). He was appointed Professor of Natural Philosophy at the Royal Institution (1888–1905), president of the Royal Society (1905–08) and Chancellor of Cambridge University in 1908. Rayleigh researched vibratory motion in both optics and acoustics, and with Sir William Ramsay he discovered argon (1894), for which he was awarded the Nobel Prize for physics in 1904. His research on radiation led to the Rayleigh–Jeans formula, which accurately predicts the long-wavelength radiation emitted by hot bodies. His books included *The Theory of Sound* (1877–78) and *Scientific Papers* (1899–1900). 📖 Bruce Lindsay, *Lord Rayleigh: The Man and His Work* (1970)

Rayleigh, Robert John Strutt, 4th Baron 1875–1947
English physicist

He was born at Terling Place, Essex, the son of John Rayleigh, and became Professor of Physics at the Imperial College of Science from 1908 to 1919. Notable for his work on rock radioactivity, he became a Fellow of the Royal Society in 1905 and a Rumford medallist. His writings include two biographies, one of his father, the other of Sir Joseph John Thomson.

Raymond, Alex (Alexander Gillespie) 1909–56
US strip cartoonist

Born in New Rochelle, New York, he studied at the Grand Central School of Art. In 1933 appeared three new strips he created for King Features Syndicate: *Jungle Jim*, the science-fiction adventurer, *Flash Gordon*, and *Secret Agent X9* (scripted by Dashiell Hammett). In 1946 he created a new daily strip, *Rip Kirby*, whose realism was far removed from the fantasy of Flash Gordon.

Rayner, Claire Berenice 1931–
English writer, broadcaster and journalist

Raised and educated in London, she worked there as a nurse and midwife before becoming the medical correspondent for *Woman's Own* magazine (as Ruth Martin 1966–75, and as Claire Rayner 1975–87). She was also the 'agony aunt' for several national newspapers and on television and radio broadcasting, appearing on the BBC's *Breakfast Time*, TV-am (1985–92) and *Good Morning…with Anne & Nick*. Drawing on her medical knowledge and family experience, she has published over 75 advice books since *Mothers and Midwives* (1962). She also writes fiction, both under her own name and as Sheila Brandon, and contributes to medical journals under the name Ann Lynton.

Rāzī, ar-, *Latin* Rhazes c.865–923/932
Persian physician and alchemist

Born in Baghdad, he wrote many medical works, some of which were translated into Latin and had considerable influence on medical science in the Middle Ages. He successfully distinguished smallpox from measles, and was considered the greatest physician of the Arab world.

Raziya fl.1236–40
First woman ruler of the Delhi Sultanate of the Mamluk ('Slave') dynasty

She was named by her father Iltutmish as his successor since none of her brothers were considered worthy of the throne. This was a highly unusual step and she incurred the hostility of her brothers and the powerful Turkish nobles. In the event, she retained the throne for only four years. Her brief period of rule marked the beginning of a power-struggle between the monarchy and the Turkish chiefs, sometimes called 'the forty' or the *chahalgani*. She defended herself bravely, discarding female apparel and holding court with her face unveiled, as well as hunting and leading the army. Her behaviour, however, was found unacceptable and a powerful group of provincial nobles banded against her. Despite a spirited defence, she was defeated and killed.

Read, Sir Herbert 1893–1968
English art historian, critic and poet

Born at Muscoates Grange, near Kirkbymoorside, North Yorkshire, he was educated in Halifax and at Leeds University. He became assistant keeper at the Victoria and Albert Museum in London (1922–31), Professor of Fine Art at Edinburgh University (1931–33) and editor of the *Burlington Magazine* (1933–39), and he held academic posts at Cambridge, Liverpool, London and Harvard universities. As an art critic he revived interest in the 19th-century Romantic movement, and championed modern art movements in Great Britain. He was interested in industrial design, and his *Art and Industry* (1936) was seminal in the development of this new discipline. He was director of the first major British design consultancy, the Design Research Unit. His poetry included *Naked Warriors* (1919, based on his war experiences) and *Collected Poems*, published in 1946. His other publications include *English Prose Style* (1928), *The Meaning of Art* (1931), *Form in Modern Poetry* (1932), *The Philosophy of Modern Art* (1952) and his autobiography, *The Contrary Experience* (1963).

Reade, Charles 1814–84
English novelist and playwright

He was born at Ipsden House, Oxfordshire, the youngest of 11 children. After five harrowing years at Iffley school, and six under two milder private tutors, in 1831 he gained a scholarship at Magdalen College, Oxford, and in 1835, having taken first-class honours, was duly elected to a lay fellowship. The next year he entered Lincoln's Inn, and in 1843 was called to the Bar, but never practised. He first wrote for the stage in 1850, and went on to produce 40 dramas. Through one of these dramas he formed a

platonic friendship with Mrs Seymour, a warm-hearted actress, who from 1854 until her death (1879) kept house for him. After 1852 he wrote a succession of unsuccessful plays and successful, usually profitable novels. The novels illustrate social injustice and cruelty in one form or another, and his writing is realistic and vivid. They include *Peg Woffington* (1852), *Hard Cash* (1863), *Foul Play* (1869, with Dion Boucicault), *A Terrible Temptation* (1871) and *A Woman-hater* (1877). His masterpiece was his long historical novel of the 15th century, *The Cloister and the Hearth* (1861). 📖 M Elvin, *Charles Reade* (1931)

Reading, Rufus Daniel Isaacs, 1st Marquess of 1860–1935
English lawyer and statesman

Born in London and educated in London, Brussels and Hanover, he entered parliament as Liberal MP for Reading in 1904, and acquired a reputation as an advocate. In 1910 he was appointed Solicitor-General and later Attorney-General; in 1912, he was the first Jew to become a member of the Cabinet. He was appointed Lord Chief Justice in 1913, and during World War I was special envoy to the USA in negotiating financial plans. He was British ambassador in Washington (1918–21), and thereafter Viceroy of India until 1926. Created marquess on his return, he took charge of many business concerns, including the chairmanship of United Newspapers Ltd and the presidency of ICI (Imperial Chemical Industries). In 1931 he was for a short time Foreign Secretary in the national government.

Reagan, Nancy Davis, *originally* Anne Francis Robbins 1923–
First Lady of the USA

Born in New York City and educated at Smith College, Massachusetts, she was an MGM contract player (1949–56), during which time she married Ronald Reagan in 1952. Her husband was US President from 1981 to 1989, and as First Lady she campaigned against substance abuse, winning numerous honours and awards. She was honorary chair of the 'Just Say No' Foundation and the National Federation of Parents for Drug Free Youth. She was thought to have a considerable influence on her husband. Her book of memoirs, *My Turn*, was published in 1989.

Reagan, Ronald Wilson See panel p1542

Reardon, Ray(mond) 1932–
Welsh snooker player

Born in Tredegar, Monmouthshire, he was Welsh amateur champion six times (1950–55), and turned professional in 1968, after careers as a miner and policeman. The first of the great snooker players of the modern era, he was dominant in the 1970s. He was world professional champion six times (1970, 1973–76, 1978), and until 1982 headed the snooker ratings.

Réaumur, René Antoine Ferchault de 1683–1757
French natural philosopher

Born in La Rochelle, he moved to Paris in 1703 and five years later became a member of the Academy of Sciences. In gathering the material required for the monumental *Description des arts et métiers* he acquired a wide knowledge of contemporary science and technology. He developed improved methods for producing iron and steel, and became one of the greatest naturalists of his age, publishing the first serious and comprehensive work of entomology. His thermometer of 1731 used a mixture of alcohol and water instead of mercury, and was calibrated with a scale (the Réaumur scale) 80 degrees between the freezing and boiling points of water.

Rebecca See Rebekah

Reagan, Ronald Wilson 1911–
40th President of the USA, and former film actor

Ronald Reagan was born in Tampico, Illinois, the son of an Irish immigrant shoe salesman who was bankrupted during the Great Depression, and graduated in economics from Eureka College, Illinois. He worked as a sportscaster in Des Moines, Iowa, before being signed as a film actor by Warner Brothers in 1937. He moved to Hollywood and, after making his debut in *Love is in the Air* (1937), starred in 50 films, including *Bedtime for Bonzo* (1951) and *The Killers* (1964). He married the actress **Jane Wyman** in 1940, but they divorced in 1948. During this period Reagan was a liberal Democrat and admirer of **Franklin D Roosevelt**. He became interested in politics when serving as president of the Screen Actors' Guild between 1947 and 1952, and moved increasingly towards Republicanism, particularly following his marriage in 1952 to the affluent actress Nancy Davis (see **Nancy Reagan**), a devout Presbyterian.

During the later 1950s he began promotional work for the General Electric Corporation and became a committed free-enterprise conservative, before officially joining the Republicans in 1962 and delivering a rousing television appeal for the party's 1964 presidential election candidate, **Barry M Goldwater**. In 1966 Reagan was elected Governor of California, having been persuaded to stand by businessmen friends, and remained in the post for eight years. He unsuccessfully contested the Republican presidential nomination in 1968 and 1976, being defeated by **Richard Nixon** and **Gerald R Ford** respectively. In 1980, however, after eventually capturing the party's nomination, he proceeded convincingly to defeat the incumbent **Jimmy Carter**. His campaign stressed the need to reduce taxes, deregulate the economy and build up and modernize the USA's defences to enable the country to negotiate abroad 'from a position of strength'.

He survived an attempted assassination in 1981 and, despite initial serious economic problems between 1981 and 1983, secured re-election by a record margin in 1984. The successful anti-Marxist invasion of Grenada (October 1983), which served to generate a revival in national self-confidence, and his domestic programme of tax cuts and deficit financing, which brought about a rapid economic upturn between 1983 and 1986, were crucial factors behind this victory. During his second term, Reagan, the one-time arch 'hawk', despite advocating a new Strategic Defence ('Star Wars') Initiative of space-based military defence, became a convert to detente, holding four summit meetings with Soviet leader **Mikhail Gorbachev** between 1985 and 1988, and signing a treaty for the scrapping of intermediate nuclear forces.

During 1986–87, however, the President's position was temporarily imperilled by the 'Iran-Contra Affair' concerning illegal arms-for-hostages deals with Iran by senior members of his administration and the laundering of profits intended, equally illegally, to supply the anti-Marxist Contra guerrillas fighting in Nicaragua. As a result of the scandal, White House Chief of Staff **Donald Regan** and his National Security Adviser Rear-Admiral **John Poindexter** were forced to resign, but Reagan escaped unscathed. Described as the 'great communicator' for his accomplished use of modern media, Reagan had a unique, populist rapport with 'mainstream America' and left office an immensely popular figure. However, his policies in Central America and with respect to domestic social programmes were less widely supported, and he left for his successor, **George Bush**, the serious problem of record budget and trade deficits.

📖 H Johnson, *Sleeping Through History: America in The Reagan Years* (1991); J Mayer and D McManus, *Landslide: The Unmaking of The President 1984–88* (1988); G Will, *Reagan's America: Innocents at Home* (1987); P Erickson, *Reagan Speaks: The Making of an American Myth* (1985).

> 'My belief has always been—that wherever in this land any individual's constitutional rigths are being unjustly denied, it is the obligation of the Federal government—at point of bayonet if necessary—to restore that individual's constitutional rights.' Statement at a press conference, 17 May 1983, as recorded by J Simpson in *Simpson's Contemporary Quotations* (1988).

Rebekah or Rebecca fl.c.1860 BC
Biblical character

She was the daughter of **Abraham**'s nephew Bethuel. She married Isaac, and after 20 childless years of marriage Isaac's prayers were answered with the birth of the twins **Esau** and **Jacob**. An oracle foretelling their future rivalry was borne out by Rebekah's favouring Jacob while Isaac favoured Esau. As Isaac's death approached, Rebekah planned Jacob's impersonation of Esau in order to obtain the blessing that belonged by right to the first-born son. When the deception was discovered, she protected Jacob from revenge by sending him away to her brother Laban.

Reber, Grote 1911–
US radio engineer

Born in Wheaton, Illinois, he was an enthusiastic radio 'ham' before studying at the Illinois Institute of Technology. Hearing of **Karl Jansky**'s discovery of weak radio noise originating outside the solar system, he built the first radio telescope in his own backyard (1937), and for several years after its completion was the only radio astronomer in the world. He found that the radio map of the sky was quite different from that produced by conventional telescopes. In 1944 he was the first to detect radio emission from the Andromeda galaxy and from the Sun. He moved his radio telescope from Illinois to Virginia University in 1947, then to Hawaii (1951) and Tasmania (1954).

Rebuck, Gail 1952–
English businesswoman

Born in London, she was educated at the Lycée Français and the University of Sussex. She entered publishing as production assistant at Grisewood & Dempsey (1975–76) and progressed through the editorial ranks at Robert Nicholson Publications to become publisher (1976–78). She joined the Hamlyn Group in 1979 and helped to establish its mass-market paperbacks, before becoming a founding director at Century Publishing (1982–85). When the merger with Century Hutchinson took place in 1985, Rebuck was appointed publisher, and in 1989 when the company was taken over by Random House Inc, she became chairman of the Random House Division. In 1991 she was appointed chairman and chief executive of Random House UK Ltd, taking on the responsibility for the group and its subsidiaries in South Africa, New Zealand and Australia.

Récamier, Jeanne Françoise Julie Adélaïde, *née* Bernard 1777–1849
French socialite

She was born in Lyons, and in 1792 married a rich banker, Jacques Récamier, who was three times her age. Her salon was soon filled with the brightest wits of the day, and when her husband was financially ruined she visited Madame de Staël at Coppet (1806), who featured in her novel *Corinne* (1807), and met Prince August of Prussia. A marriage was arranged, provided Monsieur de Récamier would consent to a divorce. He did consent, but Madame de Récamier refused to desert him in adversity. The most distinguished friend of her later years was Vicomte **René de Chateaubriand**.

Rechinger, Karl Heinz 1906–
Austrian botanist and traveller

Born and educated in Vienna, from 1927 to 1942 he made several collecting trips to the Aegean Islands, resulting in his *Flora Aegaea* (1943) and *Phytogeographia Aegaea* (1951). From 1938 to 1971 he was responsible for the botany department at the Natural History Museum, Vienna, eventually becoming the museum's director (1962–71). His greatest work has been *Flora Iranica* (published from 1963 with over 160 parts to date), the first Flora for many years to cover Iran, mountainous Iraq and Afghanistan.

Recorde, Robert c.1510–1558
English mathematician

Born in Tenby, Pembrokeshire, Wales, he studied at Oxford, and in 1545 studied medicine at Cambridge. He was physician to **Edward VI** and Queen **Mary I** and became the foremost English mathematician of the 16th century, but died in prison after losing a lawsuit brought against him by the Duke of Pembroke. He wrote the first English textbooks, in the form of dialogues, on elementary arithmetic and algebra, including *The Ground of Artes* (1543) and *The Whetstone of Witte* (1557). These became the standard works in Elizabethan England, and introduced the equals sign to mathematics.

Red Cloud, *Sioux name* Mahpiua Luta 1822–1909
Native American leader

Born in north-central Nebraska, he proved his prowess as a warrior and became chief of the Oglala Sioux. He led the resistance to the Bozeman Trail, which crossed Native American lands in Nebraska, Wyoming and Montana. By carrying out raids on soldiers at frontier forts, he and his warriors forced the US government to abandon the trail in 1868. He signed a treaty with the USA in 1869 and thereafter lived at peace with whites, ending his days on a reservation in South Dakota.

Redding, Otis 1941–67
US soul singer

He was born in Dawson, Georgia, and as a high school student in Macon, Georgia, he was so impressed by the success of **Little Richard** that he decided to become a full-time performer. His early work, including 'Shout Bamalama' (1960), was heavily influenced by Richard's frantic jump-blues style. Despite several minor hits he did not gain the widespread acceptance of US rock fans until an appearance at the Monterey pop festival in 1967. He died in a plane crash in December of that year. The posthumously released ballad 'Dock of the Bay' became his first number-one US hit early in 1968. Several of his songs, including 'I've Been Loving You Too Long' (1965), 'Try A Little Tenderness' and 'Mr Pitiful' (1965), are now regarded as soul classics. Although he never achieved a major US pop hit until after his death, he was one of the most influential soul singers of the late 1960s.

Redfield, Robert 1897–1958
US cultural anthropologist

Born in Chicago, he studied biology at Harvard but returned to Chicago to study law. Discontented with law practice and influenced by a trip to Mexico, he was encouraged by his father-in-law, the sociologist **Robert Ezra Park**, to take up anthropology. He went on to conduct field research in an Aztec community near Mexico City, on which he based his monograph *Tepoztlán, a Mexican Village* (1930). During the ensuing years, he continued to carry out field research in Central America, publishing

The Folk Culture of the Yucatán in 1941. He became a leading theorist in the study of peasant societies, introducing the concept of the 'folk-urban continuum', and examining the process of urbanization in terms of an interplay between 'great' and 'little' traditions. His major works include *The Primitive World and Its Transformations* (1953) and *Peasant Society and Culture* (1956). He was Professor of Anthropology at Chicago from 1934 to 1958.

Redford, (Charles) Robert 1937–
US film actor and director

Born in Santa Monica, California, he studied at the American Academy of Dramatic Art and landed small roles in television and on stage before making his film debut in *War Hunt* (1962). The long-running Broadway comedy *Barefoot in the Park* (1963) established him as a leading man, and the film version of the play (1967) brought him his first great success. Tall, blond and athletic, his good looks and image of integrity made him popular in films including *Butch Cassidy and the Sundance Kid* (1969, with **Paul Newman**), *The Candidate* (1972), *The Way We Were* (1973), *The Sting* (1973), *Out of Africa* (1985) and *Indecent Proposal* (1993). Other projects have reflected his interests in the American West, and in ecology and politics. In 1976 he produced and starred in *All The President's Men*. He has directed *Ordinary People* (1980), for which he won an Academy Award, *A River Runs Through It* (1993), *Quiz Show* (1994), and other films.

Redgrave, Sir Michael Scudamore 1908–85
English stage and film actor

Born in Bristol, Avon, the son of actor parents, he was educated at Clifton College, Bristol, and Magdalene College, Cambridge. He taught modern languages at Cranleigh School, before taking up an acting career with Liverpool Repertory Company (1934–36). His sensitive, intellectual approach to acting was most successful in classical roles, including *Hamlet* (Old Vic and Elsinore, 1949–50), *Richard II* (1951) and *Uncle Vanya* (1963). Other plays in which he appeared include *Tiger at the Gates* (1955) and his own adaptation of *The Aspern Papers* (1959). He was equally successful in films, among them **Alfred Hitchcock**'s *The Lady Vanishes* (1938), *The Way to the Stars* (1945), *The Browning Version* (1951), *The Loneliness of the Long Distance Runner* (1962) and *Nicholas and Alexandra* (1971). He was nominated for an Academy Award for *Mourning Becomes Electra* (1947). He was knighted in 1959, and became director of the Yvonne Arnaud Theatre at Guildford in 1962. He married the actress Rachel Kempson (1910–) in 1935, and their three children are all in the acting profession: **Vanessa**, Corin (1939–) and Lynn (1943–).
📖 Richard Findlater, *Michael Redgrave, Actor* (1956)

Redgrave, Steve (Steven Geoffrey) 1962–
English oarsman and sculler

Born in Marlow, Oxfordshire, he has won four successive Olympic gold medals, an unprecedented achievement in world rowing matched by only four other sportsmen in 100 years of Olympic history. Five times world champion, he also won a record three gold medals in the 1986 Commonwealth Games. For Leander he had 10 wins in the Head of the River race (Mortlake to Putney) in a record time of 17 minutes 30.29 seconds. His formidable partnership with Matthew Pinsent (1970–) is characterized by exciting and powerful finishes. Redgrave and Pinsent were world coxless pairs champions in 1991, 1992 and 1994, Olympic champions in 1992 and 1996, and they set a world record time in Lucerne in 1994. Later they won the coxless fours race in the 1997 world championships.

Redgrave, Vanessa 1937–
English actress

She was born in London, the eldest daughter of Sir Michael Redgrave and actress Rachel Kempson (1910–). A student at the Central School of Speech and Drama (1954–57), she made her professional debut at the Frinton Summer Theatre (1957) and her London stage debut opposite her father in *A Touch of the Sun* (1958). She joined the Royal Shakespeare Company in the 1960s. Her first film, *Behind the Mask* (1958), was followed by many others, notably *Morgan, a Suitable Case for Treatment* and *Blow-Up* (both 1966). Active in several media, she has proved herself one of the most distinguished performers of her generation. A stage performer of conviction and integrity, her work in the theatre includes *The Prime of Miss Jean Brodie* (1966), *The Lady from the Sea* (1976–77) and *Orpheus Descending* (1988–89). She received Academy Award nominations for *Morgan, Isadora* (1968), *Mary, Queen of Scots* (1971) and *The Bostonians* (1984), winning a Best Supporting Actress award for *Julia* (1977). On television she won an Emmy for *Playing for Time* (1980). Her later film appearances include *Prick Up Your Ears* (1987), *Howards End* (1992, Academy Award nomination) and *Mission Impossible* (1996). She is also well known for her active support of left-wing and humanitarian causes.

Redi, Francesco 1626–97
Italian physician and poet

Born in Arezzo, he studied at the universities of Florence and Pisa and became physician to the dukes of Tuscany. He carried out a series of experiments to investigate whether organisms appeared through spontaneous generation. In 1668 he compared sets of flasks containing meat, with one covered and the other left open. Maggots appeared only in the uncovered flasks, casting doubt on the spontaneous generation theory. His best-known poem is the dithyrambic celebration of Bacchus and the wines of Tuscany, *Bacco In Toscana* (1685).

Redman, Don (ald Matthew) 1900–64
US saxophonist, arranger and bandleader

Born to a musical family in Piedmont, West Virginia, he was able to play a wide range of wind instruments while still at school, and after studies at music schools, including Boston Conservatory, began to work professionally as a clarinettist, alto saxophonist and arranger. His first achievement was the creation in the mid-1920s of a distinctive style for the Fletcher Henderson Orchestra. Redman's principles of swing-style orchestration, heard in recordings by McKinney's Cotton Pickers and Redman's own band from 1931 to 1940, influenced nearly every important jazz composer of the era and are still respected in big-band music.

Redmond, John Edward 1856–1918
Irish politician

Born in Ballytrent, County Wexford, the son of a Wexford MP, he was called to the Bar at Gray's Inn in 1886, and entered parliament in 1881. A champion of Home Rule, he became chairman of the Nationalist Party in 1900. He declined a seat in H H Asquith's coalition ministry (1915), but supported World War I, deplored the Irish rebellion, and opposed Sinn Féin. 📖 Denis Gwynn, *The Life of John Redmond* (1932)

Redon, Odilon 1840–1916
French painter and lithographer

Born in Bordeaux, he studied in Paris under Jean Léon Gérôme. He made many charcoal drawings and lithographs of imaginative power, including *Les Yeux clos* (1890, 'Closed Eyes', Musée d'Orsay, Paris). After 1900 he painted, mainly in pastel, pictures of flowers and portraits in intense colour. His *Profile of a Woman with a Vase of Flowers* (c.1895–1905) is in the Tate Gallery, London. A distinguished writer, he published his diaries (1867–1915) as *À soi-même* (1922), and his *Letters* in 1923. He is usually

regarded as a forerunner of Surrealism because of the use of dream images in his work, as in *Le Char d'Apollon* (1905–14, 'Apollo's chariot', Musée d'Orsay).

Redondo, Nicolás c.1927–
Spanish trade union leader

He helped to revive the Spanish Socialist Party (PSOE) in the late 1960s and early 1970s. He was arrested 13 times between 1951 and 1973, and in 1971 became the leader of the General Union of Workers (UGT). In 1974 he was effectively offered the PSOE leadership, but he turned it down. He became increasingly critical of the Socialist government, breaking with it in 1988. In the same year he organized Spain's first general strike since 1934.

Redouté, Pierre Joseph 1759–1840
French botanical painter

Born in St Hubert, Belgium, he was patronized by successive French courts from Louis XV to Louis-Philippe. Specializing in roses, he made many prints for china, table mats, wall-pictures, etc. He published *Les Liliacées* (1802–15), a collection of lilies in 500 plates, and *Choix des plus belles fleurs* (1827–37). His finest achievement is generally considered to be *Les Roses* (1817–21).

Redpath, Anne 1895–1965
Scottish painter

Born in Galashiels, Selkirkshire, she studied at Edinburgh Art College, and lived in France from 1919 to 1934, when she returned to live in Hawick. One of the most important modern Scottish artists, her paintings in oil and watercolour, mainly of landscapes and still-lifes, show great richness of colour and vigorous technique, notably *Altar at Chartres* (1964, Prudential Assurance, London). She was elected a member of the Royal Scottish Academy in 1952.

Redpath, James 1833–91
US reformer and journalist

He was born in Berwick-upon-Tweed, Northumberland, England, and emigrated to Michigan in 1850. A fervent abolitionist reporter for Horace Greeley's New York *Tribune*, he covered the Kansas conflict (1854–58), reported on his tour of Southern slavery in *The Roving Editor* (1858), defended John Brown's Harpers Ferry Raid in *The Public Life of Captain John Brown* (1860), published incendiary *Southern Notes for National Circulation* (1860), supported ex-slave migration to Haiti, encouraged Walt Whitman and Louisa M Alcott, and covered General William Tecumseh Sherman's punitive march through Georgia and South Carolina. He was made superintendent of schools in captured Charleston, South Carolina, in 1865. He organized the Redpath Lecture Lyceum Bureau, covered Ku Klux Klan atrocities in Louisiana (1875), the disputed Hayes-Tilden election (1876–77) and the Irish Land War (1880–82), adopting the term 'Boycott' which he publicized with influence on the US labour movement.

Redpath, Jean 1937–
Scottish folk and traditional singer

She was born in Edinburgh and became involved in folk music while studying at the university there. She emigrated to the USA in 1961, where her pure voice and outstanding ability were quickly recognized, particularly in her interpretation of traditional Scots ballads and the songs of Robert Burns. She lectured in music at Wesleyan University for a time. *The Scottish Fiddle* (1985) was an important recording, and she has made a special study of the songs of Burns which she has recorded in two separate projects, one using the controversial musical arrangements written by the US composer Serge Hovey, which extended to seven volumes before his death. She continues to perform on the international circuit.

Redwood, John Alan, *nicknamed* the Vulcan
1951–
English Conservative politician

Educated at Oxford, he was a member of Margaret Thatcher's policy unit (1983–85) before his election as MP for Wokingham in 1987. He entered John Major's Cabinet as Secretary of State for Wales in 1993, but resigned in 1995 and made a vain bid for the leadership. Fiercely Eurosceptic and opposed to the single currency, he entered the Conservative leadership contest following Labour's victory in the 1997 general election.

Reed, Sir Carol 1906–76
English film director

Born in London and educated at King's School, Canterbury, he took to the stage (1924) and acted and produced for Edgar Wallace until 1930. He produced or directed such memorable films as *Kipps* (1941), *The Young Mr Pitt* (1942), *The Way Ahead* (1944), the Allied war documentary *The True Glory* (1945), and *The Fallen Idol* (1948), but is best remembered for his Cannes Film Festival prizewinning version of Graham Greene's novel *The Third Man* (1949), depicting the sinister underworld of postwar partitioned Vienna. *Outcast of the Islands* (1952), based on a Joseph Conrad novel, was another successful literary adaptation, and *Our Man in Havana* (1959) marked a return to his postwar brilliance. He won an Academy Award for *Oliver!* (1968). 📖 Nicholas Wapshott, *The Man Between: A Biography of Carol Reed* (1990)

Reed, John 1887–1920
US radical and war correspondent

Born into a wealthy family in Portland, Oregon, he graduated from Harvard in 1910 and became a journalist. His work reflected his left-wing beliefs, and in 1914 he won national attention for his brilliant reportage on the struggles of Pancho Villa's army in the Mexican Revolution. He also reported from the front in World War I, and in 1917 he went to Petrograd (St Petersburg) to witness the October Revolution, recording his observations in *Ten Days That Shook the World* (1919). After helping to found the Communist Labor Party in the USA, he was indicted for sedition in the Red Scare of 1919–20 and fled to Russia. He died of typhus in Moscow and was buried in the Kremlin.

Reed, Lou, *real name* Louis Firbank 1944–
US rock singer, guitarist and songwriter

Born in Long Island, New York, he initially gained fame as a member of The Velvet Underground, a band which was closely associated with Andy Warhol and his organization, The Factory, and whose importance and influence were not fully realized until after it had disbanded in 1970. The Velvet Underground's albums include *The Velvet Underground & Nico* (1967), *White Light, White Heat* (1968) and *The Velvet Underground* (1969). In 1972 he moved to England to record *Lou Reed* (1972). His 1973 album, *Transformer*, included 'Walk On The Wild Side', a paean to transsexuality which somehow bypassed radio censorship to become the first major hit of his career. Subsequent albums have included *Rock 'n' Roll Animal* (1974), *Street Hassle* (1978), *New Sensations* (1984), *New York* (1989), *Magic and Loss* (1992) and *Set The Twilight Reeling* (1996). He reunited with fellow Velvet Underground founder John Cale (1940–) to create a tribute to Warhol, *Songs for 'Drella* (1990). The band then re-formed for a tour and recording sessions in 1993, but the death of guitarist Sterling Morrison put an end to their activities. He published *Thought and Expression* in 1991. 📖 V Bokris, *Lou Reed* (1994)

Reed, Walter 1851–1902
US army surgeon

Born in Belroi, Virginia, he entered the medical corps in 1875, and was appointed Professor of Bacteriology in the Army Medical College, Washington, in 1893. Investigations carried out by him in 1900 proved that yellow fever was transmitted by mosquitoes, and his researches led to the eventual eradication of the disease from Cuba. 📖 William B Bean, *Walter Reed: A Biography* (1982)

Rees, Lloyd Frederick 1895–1988
Australian artist

He was born in Yeronga, Queensland. Influenced by the pen drawings of Joseph Pennell, he worked in Sydney Ure Smith's studio in Sydney from 1917 and then travelled in Europe for two years. His early drawings, meticulous in draughtsmanship and romantic in style, were etched or lithographed. In 1931 he held his first exhibition in Sydney. He turned to oils, producing mainly landscapes of the south coast of New South Wales, and in 1942 the Art Gallery of New South Wales held a retrospective exhibition of his work, followed by another in 1969. Rees made four more journeys to Europe between 1952 and 1973, and the influence of the Italian landscape lightened the tone of his oils. His later works were more lightly covered almost abstract landscapes, capturing the pearly light of Sydney and of Tasmania, where he spent his last years.

Rees, Sir Martin John 1942–
English astrophysicist

Born in York, he was educated at Cambridge, and became a staff member of the Institute of Theoretical Astronomy there. He returned to Cambridge as Plumian Professor of Astronomy and Experimental Philosophy (1973–91) and director of the Institute of Astronomy (1977–82, 1987–91). Since 1992 he has been Royal Society Research Professor. Rees has made important contributions to the study of stellar systems and 'dark matter', and his best-known work is in the study of active galactic nuclei. He demonstrated that the variations in brightness observed in quasars and active galaxies could be best understood if the nuclei contained gas which is outflowing at almost the speed of light. Observational evidence for this appeared in the 1970s. Rees also showed that the strong radio-emitting regions of some galaxies could be produced by beams of particles moving outwards from the nuclei at almost the speed of light. He was elected FRS in 1979 and became president of the Royal Astronomical Society in 1992, the year in which he was knighted. In 1995 he became Astronomer Royal.

Rees-Mogg, William Rees-Mogg, Baron
1928–
English journalist

Born in Bristol and educated at Charterhouse and Balliol College, Oxford, he joined the *Financial Times* in 1952, as assistant editor. In 1960 he moved to the *Sunday Times* and became deputy editor (1964), then in 1967 he assumed the editorship of *The Times*, a post he held for 14 years. Having been vice-chairman of the BBC and chairman of the Arts Council, he was appointed to head the new Broadcasting Standards Council (1988–93). A recent publication is *The Great Reckoning* (1991). He was made a life peer in 1988.

Reeve, Clara 1729–1807
English novelist

Born in Ipswich, Suffolk, the daughter of the rector of Freston, she translated John Barclay's *Argenis* (1772), and wrote *The Champion of Virtue, a Gothic Story* (1777, renamed *The Old English Baron*), which was avowedly an imitation of Horace Walpole's *The Castle of Otranto*. Her other novels include *The Two Mentors* (1783), *The Exiles* (1788), *Memoirs of Sir Roger de Clarendon* (1793), and *Destination* (1799). She also wrote a critical account of *The Progress of Romance* (1785). 📖 Sir Walter Scott, memoir in *Old English Baron* (1823)

Reeves, Sir Paul Alfred 1932–
New Zealand prelate

He was born in Wellington and educated at Victoria University, Wellington, and Oxford. He returned to New Zealand and in 1979 became Bishop of Auckland. He was Primate and Anglican Archbishop of New Zealand from 1980 until 1985, when he became Governor-General of New Zealand (1985–90). He was the first Anglican Observer at the United Nations (1991–93), and was chairman of the Fijian Constitutional Review Commission (1995–96).

Reeves, William Pember 1857–1932
New Zealand politician, reformer and writer

Born in Lyttelton, Canterbury, he trained in law and journalism, became an MP (1887–96), and as a Cabinet Minister under Ballance and Seddon's government (1891–96) introduced important reforms in industrial legislation. In 1905 he was posted to London as High Commissioner, and was director of the London School of Economics from 1908 until 1919. As a writer, he is best known for his long poem 'A Colonist in his Garden', which was included in his *New Zealand and Other Poems* (1898). His works include *The Passing of the Forest* (1925) and *The Long White Cloud: Ao Tea Roa* (1898, rev edn 1924), which includes many incisive portraits of contemporary figures. ⊞ K Sinclair, *William Pember Reeves: New Zealand Fabian* (1965)

Regan, Donald Thomas 1918–
US politician

Born in Cambridge, Massachusetts, the son of an Irish Catholic railway guard, he studied English and economics at Harvard, where he was a contemporary of John F Kennedy. He switched allegiance from the Democrats to the Republicans in 1940, and during World War II distinguished himself by becoming the youngest ever US Marine line-major. After the war he joined Merrill Lynch as a sales trainee and rose to become its president in 1968, building the company into the USA's largest securities brokerage corporation. Attracted by his strong belief in supply-side free-market economics, President Ronald Reagan appointed him the Secretary of the Treasury in 1981. He proceeded to push through radical tax-cutting legislation, but left a growing budget deficit. He became White House Chief of Staff in January 1985, but was forced to resign two years later as a result of criticisms of his role in the 1985–86 Iran-Contra Affair. He published his controversial memoirs, *For the Record*, in 1988.

Regener, Erich Rudolph Alexander 1881–1955
German physicist

Born in Schleussenau (Bydgoszcz, Poland), and educated at Berlin University, he became Professor of Physics at the Agricultural College in Berlin and from 1920 at the Technische Hochschule in Stuttgart, but was dismissed in 1937 for political reasons. In 1937 a research station for stratospheric physics was built for him at Lake Constance, and this later became the Institute for Stratospheric Physics at Weissenau. He served there as director until his death, and was also reinstated at Stuttgart in 1946. His early work in nuclear physics accurately determined the electric charge, and his main contributions were to cosmic-ray research, in which he instigated the intensity of cosmic rays in the upper atmosphere. In 1933 he demonstrated for the first time that events occurring in stars are a source of cosmic rays.

Reger, Max (Johann Baptist Joseph Maximilian) 1873–1916
German composer

Born in Brand, Bavaria, he taught music at Wiesbaden and Munich, became director of music at Leipzig University (1907), and Professor of Music (1908). He composed piano concertos, choral works and songs, and is best known for his organ works; these include the fantasy on *Ein feste Burg: Phantasie und Fuge über B-A-C-H* and the *Sonata in F Sharp Minor*.

Regiomontanus, *originally* Johannes Müller 1436–76
German mathematician and astronomer

He took his name from his Franconian birthplace, Königsberg (*Mons Regius*), which is now Kaliningrad in Russia. He studied at Vienna and in 1461 accompanied Cardinal Bessarion to Italy to learn Greek. In 1471 he settled in Nuremberg, where he was supported by the patrician Bernhard Walther. The two laboured at the *Alphonsine Tables* and published *Ephemerides 1475–1506* (1473), a work used extensively by Christopher Columbus. Regiomontanus established the study of algebra and trigonometry in Germany and wrote on waterworks, burning-glasses, weights and measures, and the quadrature of the circle. He was summoned to Rome in 1474 by Pope Sixtus IV to help reform the calendar.

Regnard, Jean François 1655–1709
French dramatist

Born in Paris, he inherited a considerable fortune at the age of 20, and travelled widely. In his autobiographical romance, *La Provençale* ('A Woman from Provence'), he tells of his and his mistress's capture and sale as slaves by Algerian corsairs, their bondage in Constantinople (Istanbul) and their ransom. He found his vocation in the success of *Le Divorce*, performed by the Théâtre-Italien in Paris in 1688. Subsequent plays include *Le Joueur* (1696, 'The Gambler'), *Le Retour imprévu* (1700, 'The Unexpected Return') and his masterpiece, *Le Légataire universel* (1708, Eng trans *The Sole Heir*, 1912). ⊞ A Caleme, *Jean François Regnard, sa vie et son œuvre* (1960)

Regnault, Alexandre Georges Henri 1843–71
French painter of mythological, Spanish and Moorish subjects

Born in Paris, the son of Henri Victor Regnault, he won the Prix de Rome in 1866. In 1869 he painted his equestrian portrait of Juan Prim, and in 1870 his *Salome* and *Moorish Execution*. He was killed in the Franco-Prussian War.

Regnault, Henri Victor 1810–78
French chemist and physicist

Born in Aix-la-Chapelle (Aachen, Germany), he studied at the École Polytechnique in Paris from 1829, and later at the École des Mines. He worked with Justus von Liebig at Giessen and received an appointment at Lyons. In 1840 he became Professor of Chemistry at the École Polytechnique and in 1841 Professor of Physics at the Collège de France. In 1847 he published a major treatise on chemistry. In 1854 he was appointed director of the porcelain factory at Sèvres. His early research was in organic chemistry. He carried out extensive studies of aliphatic chloro-compounds, and discovered vinyl chloride and other materials which have become industrially important. He improved the techniques for determining the specific heats of solids and liquids, and devised a method for determining the specific heats of gases. His laboratory at Sèvres was wrecked in the Franco-Prussian War of 1870 and the results of much of his later work were lost. Regnault was admitted to the Legion of Honour in 1850. He received the Rumford (1848) and Copley (1869) medals of the Royal Society, and was made an honorary Fellow of the Chemical Society in 1849.

Régnier, Henri François Joseph de 1864–1936
French Symbolist poet, novelist and critic

Born in Honfleur, he studied law in Paris, and then turned to writing. His *Poèmes anciens et romanesques* (1890, 'Ancient Poems and Romances') revealed him to be a

Symbolist, though later he returned to more traditional verse forms. Poetical works include *La Sandale ailée* (1906, 'The Winged Sandal'), *Vestigia flammae* (1921, 'Traces of the Flame') and *Flamma tenax* (1928, 'The Steadfast Flame'). His novels, which are mainly concerned with France and Italy in the 17th and 18th centuries, include *La Double maîtresse* (1900, 'The Double Mistress') and *Le Bon plaisir* (1902, 'One's Pleasure'). ⌨E Buenzod, *Henri Régnier* (1966)

Régnier, Mathurin 1573–1613
French satirist
Born in Chartres, he took holy orders, and grew up dissipated and idle, then obtained a canonry at Chartres, and enjoyed the favour of **Henri IV**. His entire work hardly exceeds 7,000 lines and includes satires, epistles, elegies, and some odes, songs and epigrams; these place him among the most renowned French poets. The satires give a lively picture of the Paris of his day. ⌨J Vieney, *Mathurin Régnier* (1896)

Rego, Paula 1935–
Portuguese artist
Born in Lisbon, she studied at the Slade School of Art, London, then returned to Portugal where she established a reputation as a narrative artist. She has been influenced by an interest in folk and fairy tales, illustrative art and strip cartoons. Her early work used animals to express human behaviour, but she then turned to human figures, collectively exploring issues such as power, gender stereotypes, sexuality and human emotions. These factors combine to give an eerie feel to her work that draws from Surrealism. She has lived and worked in the UK since 1976.

Regulus or Rule, St 4th century AD
Semi-legendary monk
Tradition holds that he was a monk of Constantinople or Bishop of Patras. In AD347 he is said to have gone to Muckross or Kilrimont (afterwards St Andrews), taking relics of **St Andrew** from the East. William Skene suggested his possible identification with an Irish St Riagail of the 6th century.

Regulus, Marcus Atilius d.c.250BC
Roman general and politician
He was active in the First Punic War. Captured (255BC) and imprisoned for five years by the Carthaginians, he was sent to Rome on parole to petition for peace. Having dissuaded the Senate from agreeing to their terms, he voluntarily returned to Carthage, where he was tortured to death. His heroic death earned him legendary status.

Rehnquist, William 1924–
US jurist
Born in Milwaukee, Wisconsin, he studied political science at Stanford and Harvard and law at the Stanford Law School. After 1952 he practised law in Phoenix, Arizona, and became active in the Republican Party. In 1969 he was appointed head of the Office of Legal Counsel in the Justice Department by President **Richard Nixon**, and in this post supported such controversial measures as pretrial detention and wiretapping. He impressed Nixon who appointed him associate justice of the Supreme Court in 1972. He duly emerged as the Court's most conservative member and in 1986 was appointed Chief Justice. Initially, the new Rehnquist Court differed little from its predecessor, but by 1989 a 'new right' majority had been established by President **Ronald Reagan** and a series of conservative rulings on abortion and capital punishment was framed.

Reibey, Molly (Mary), *née* Haydock 1777–1855
Australian businesswoman and philanthropist

Born in Bury, Lancashire, England, she ran away dressed as a boy after she was orphaned and was sentenced to death for horse-stealing, but when her sex was discovered the sentence was commuted to transportation. On arrival in Sydney in 1792 she became a nursemaid. She married Thomas Reibey, an Irish East India Company employee, in 1794, and helped him and a partner to set up business as ship-owners and merchants. When the two men died in 1811, she took over and expanded the business. By 1816 her property was valued at £20,000 and she was a benefactor of charities and education. The first office of the Bank of New South Wales opened in her home in 1817.

Reich, Ferdinand 1799–1882
German physicist
Born in Bernburg, Sachsen-Anhalt, he was educated at the University of Göttingen and later became professor at the Freiburg School of Mines. Using spectroscopy and working in collaboration with his assistant **Hieronymous Richter**, Reich discovered the metal indium in zincblende in 1863.

Reich, Robert 1946–
US government official
Born in Scranton, Pennsylvania, he graduated from Dartmouth College in 1986 and was awarded a Rhodes scholarship to Oxford; he met fellow scholar and future US President **Bill Clinton** on the ship bound for England. He became a leading neoliberal economic theorist and a lecturer at Harvard (from 1981), and he influenced Democratic policies with books such as *The Next American Frontier* (1983) and *The Work of Nations* (1991). As Secretary of Labor (1993–) in the Clinton administration, he has backed the North American Free Trade Agreement (NAFTA) and called for higher minimum wages and tax incentives to discourage corporate lay-offs. In an increasingly centrist administration he has served as a link to the labour movement and an advocate for the unemployed and underemployed.

Reich, Steve 1936–
US composer
Born in New York, he has been strongly influenced by his training in drumming, his love of the music of **Stravinsky**, and the pulse of jazz and the rhythms of African and Balinese music. He has evolved a style of vigorous tonality, hypnotic contrapuntal patterns, and percussive virtuosity. He has written for a great variety of vocal and instrumental forces and timbres, and has used taped and electronic effects. Recent compositions are *The Cave* (1993) and *City Life* (1995).

Reich, Wilhelm 1897–1957
Austrian psychoanalyst
He was born in Dobrzcynica, Galicia, in the Austro-Hungarian Empire. He became a practising psychoanalyst while still a medical student in Vienna, and became convinced of the necessity of regular orgasms for the mental health of both men and women. Much of his writing reflects this conviction (*The Function of the Orgasm*, 1927, trans 1942). One of his most notorious eccentricities was the invention of the 'orgone accumulator', which purported to collect and transmit massless particles enhancing the user's sexual satisfaction and emotional health. He attempted a synthesis of psychoanalysis with Marxism, arguing that abolition of the bourgeois family would eliminate the Oedipus complex and allow fuller sexual satisfaction in adults. He was expelled from the German Communist Party in 1933 and the International Psychoanalytical Association in 1934, left Germany for Scandinavia in 1933 and emigrated to the USA in 1939. He established an Orgone Institute, but died in prison after being prosecuted for promoting a fraudulent treatment. During the sexual revolution of the 1960s, he became

something of a cult figure in the USA. His other works include *Charackteranalyse* (1933, Eng trans *Character Analysis*, 1945) and *The Sexual Revolution* (1936–45).

Reicha, Antonín 1770–1836
Czech composer, teacher and music theorist
Born in Prague, he was from 1785 flautist with the Electoral Orchestra in Bonn, in which Beethoven also played. After teaching piano in Hamburg (1794–99), he went to Paris in search of operatic success. He failed to achieve this, but had two symphonies performed. From 1801 to 1808 he lived in Vienna, seeing much of his friends Beethoven and Haydn, and taking lessons from Antonio Salieri. Subsequently he lived in Paris, where his pupils included Franz Liszt, Hector Berlioz, César Franck and Charles Gounod. His use of counterpoint and instrumental sonority was highly original, as is seen in his *36 Fugues* (dedicated to Haydn) and his use of timpani chords. His 24 quintets for woodwind have remained popular.

Reichenbach, Georg Friedrich von 1772–1826
German engineer, instrument-maker and inventor
He was born in Durlach, near Karlsruhe, and graduated from the School of Army Engineers in Mannheim. On the initiative of Benjamin Thompson, Count Rumford, he spent the next two years in England studying the latest advances in engineering and scientific instrument-making with such eminent men as James Watt and Jesse Ramsden (1735–1800). Returning to Germany, he designed improved muskets and a rifled cannon for the Bavarian army, and in 1804 established a firm in Munich for the manufacture of precision instruments. These became famous among astronomers and surveyors for their high quality. In his later years he turned to hydraulic engineering and built a pipeline 67 miles (107.8km) long, in the course of which he used 11 hydraulic rams to pump salt water to a height of 1,200 feet (366m).

Reichenbach, Hans 1891–1953
US philosopher of science
Born in Hamburg, Germany, he became Professor of Philosophy at Berlin (1926–33), Istanbul (1933–38) and California, Los Angeles (from 1938). He was an early associate of the Vienna Circle of logical positivists, and with Rudolf Carnap he founded the journal *Erkenntnis* ('Perception') in 1930 (which continued until 1938, then reappeared in 1975 in an English edition in the USA). He made an important technical contribution to probability theory in which two truth tables are replaced by the multivalued concept 'weight', and wrote widely on logic and the philosophical bases of science. He is best known for his *Warscheinlichkeitslehre* (1935, 'Theory of Probability') and *Philosophie der Raum-Zeit-Lehre* (1928, 'Philosophy of Space and Time'). 📖 Wesley C Salmon, *Hans Reichenbach, Logical Empiricist* (1979)

Reichenbach, Karl, Baron von 1788–1869
German natural philosopher and industrialist
He was born in Stuttgart and educated at the University of Tübingen. He was interested in metallurgy, and designed a novel charcoal oven which he used to isolate creosote and paraffin in the 1830s. Around 1844, after studying animal magnetism, he believed that he had discovered a new force which he called 'Od'; this was intermediate between electricity, magnetism, heat and light, and was recognizable only by the nerves of sensitive persons. He expended much energy trying to convert the scientific world to his views, neglecting his businesses and living as a recluse. He also wrote on the geology of Moravia and on meteorites, of which he had a large collection (now in the University of Tübingen).

Reichstein, Tadeus 1897–1996
Swiss chemist and Nobel Prize winner
Born in Włocławek, Poland, he spent his early childhood in Kiev before moving to Zurich (1905), where he trained at the State Technical College (Eidgenössische Technische Hochschule). After an industrial interlude working on coffee chemistry, he returned to the institute as an assistant to Ružička, and was appointed associate professor there in 1937. He then moved to the University of Basle as head of the pharmacology department (from 1938), the organic division (from 1946) and the university's new Organic Institute (from 1960). His early academic work on carbohydrate chemistry led to the first synthesis of vitamin C (1933) independently of Sir Norman Haworth, as well as some sugars. From 1934 he also began synthesizing new steroids and isolating and identifying the life-maintaining natural steroids, of ox adrenal gland. For his outstanding work on the chemistry of the adrenal hormones Reichstein received, with Edward Kendall and Philip Hench, the 1950 Nobel Prize for physiology or medicine. He was elected a Foreign Member of the Royal Society in 1952. He retired from his chair in chemistry at the age of 70, then, aged 75, began a 25-year career in botany and became an expert in the classification of ferns.

Reid, Beryl 1919–96
English comedienne and actress
Born in Hereford, she made her first stage appearance in a concert party at the Floral Hall, Bridlington, in 1936. In the ensuing years she built a reputation as a variety entertainer and soubrette-cum-impressionist. The radio series *Educating Archie* (1952–56) established the comic character of schoolgirl Monica, and her other creations include Midlands teddy girl Marlene. She was a veteran of revues and pantomimes, and made her film debut in *Spare a Copper* (1940). Her long television career includes such series as *The Girl Most Likely* (1957), *Man o' Brass* (1964), *The Hen House* (1964), *Alcock and Gander* (1972), *The Secret Diary of Adrian Mole Aged 13* (1985), and straight roles in *The Rivals* (1970), *Tinker, Tailor, Soldier, Spy* (1982), *Smiley's People* (1983), *The Irish RM* (1983) and *Cracker* (1993). *The Killing of Sister George* (1965) established her as a serious actress and she won a Tony award for its Broadway production (1966), repeating her role on film in 1968. Her other films include *Star!* (1968) and *Entertaining Mr Sloane* (1970). 📖 *So Much Love* (1984)

Reid, Sir Bob (Robert Paul) 1934–
Scottish industrial executive
Born in Cupar, Fife, the son of a butcher, he graduated from St Andrews University in 1956, and joined Shell, for whom he worked in overseas subsidiaries until 1983, when he returned to the UK. He was appointed chairman and chief executive of Shell UK in 1985. In 1988, as chairman of the British Institute of Management, he took a leading role in the reshaping of management education. From 1990 to 1995 he was chairman of British Rail and in 1991 launched 'Future Rail', a 10-year plan to upgrade and improve the rail network. In 1992, however, the government launched proposals for the privatization of some sections of BR, which were eventually implemented in 1996. He is currently chairman of London Electricity (1994–) and Sears (1995–). He was knighted in 1990.

Reid, Sir George Houstoun 1845–1918
Australian politician
Born in Johnstone, Renfrew, Scotland, he emigrated to Melbourne with his parents in 1852. He studied law, and in 1878 became secretary to the Attorney-General of New South Wales. In 1880 he was elected to the Legislative Assembly of NSW, becoming premier of the state from 1894 to 1899. He moved to the first federal parliament in 1901, still representing his old constituency, and became the Leader of the Opposition in the House of Representatives. He was Prime Minister of Australia for a short time in 1904 but was defeated in 1905 and retired

from politics in 1908. In 1909 he was appointed Australia's first High Commissioner to London. At the end of his term in 1916, he took up the seat for Hanover Square in the British House of Commons, which he held until his death.

Reid (of Drem), James Scott Cumberland, Lord 1890–1975
Scottish judge
Born in Drem, East Lothian, he was educated at The Edinburgh Academy, Jesus College, Cambridge, and Edinburgh University. After serving in World War I, he practised at the Scottish Bar, and became Dean of the Faculty of Advocates (1945–48). An MP from 1931 to 1935 and from 1937 to 1948, he was Solicitor-General for Scotland (1936–41) and Lord Advocate (1941–48). He then sat as a Lord-of-Appeal-in-Ordinary (1948–75), and won a reputation for accurate thought, precise reasoning and careful application of principle.

Reid, Robert 1774–1856
Scottish architect
He was born in Edinburgh, but little is known about his education or training. He flourished as government architect to Scotland, becoming Master of Works and Architect to King George IV in 1824. His known career began with the design for new Law Courts in Parliament Square, Edinburgh (1803). Working with fellow architect William Sibbald, he masterminded the northern extension to the Edinburgh New Town. Other major works include the Customs House, Leith (1811), the east wing to Paxton House, Berwickshire (1812) and the United College, St Andrews (1829). His public architecture was influenced by the Adam brothers, but received mixed acclaim from contemporaries.

Reid, Thomas 1710–96
Scottish philosopher
Born in Strachan, Kincardineshire, he was educated at Aberdeen, and became librarian of Marischal College (1733). He was appointed minister of New Machar in Aberdeenshire (1737) and Professor of Philosophy at Aberdeen (1751). He succeeded Adam Smith as Professor of Moral Philosophy at Glasgow (1764–80), and then retired to write. He was leader of the group known as the 'Common Sense' or later the 'Scottish' school, in opposition to the empirical philosophy of David Hume. Reid reasserted the existence of external objects by denying that simple 'ideas' are our primary data. His best-known works are his *Inquiry into the Human Mind on the Principles of Common Sense* (1764), *Essays on the Intellectual Powers of Man* (1785) and *Essays on the Active Powers of Man* (1788).

Reid, Thomas Mayne 1818–83
Irish children's writer
Born in Ballyroney, County Down, he emigrated to New Orleans in 1840, settled as a journalist in Philadelphia (1843), and served in the US army during the Mexican War (1847), in which he was severely wounded. Returning to Great Britain in 1849, he settled down to a literary life in London. His vigorous style and stories of hair's-breadth escapes delighted his readers. Among his books, many of which were popular in translation in Poland and Russia, are *The Rifle Rangers* (1850), *Boy Hunters* (1853), *War Trail* (1857) and *Headless Horseman* (1866). He went back to New York in 1867 and founded the *Onward Magazine*, but returned to England in 1870. 📖 J Steele, *Captain Mayne Reid* (1977)

Reiner, Fritz 1888–1963
US conductor
He was born in Budapest, Hungary, and studied law and music at Budapest University. Between 1909 and 1914 he conducted the city opera. He moved to Dresden where he conducted the opera until he moved to the USA in 1922 to conduct the Cincinatti Symphony Orchestra. Reiner was head of the orchestra and opera departments at the Curtis Institute in Pennsylvania from 1931 to 1941, and Leonard Bernstein was among his students. He was in charge of the Pittsburgh Orchestra (1938–48), conducted at the New York Metropolitan Opera (1949–53), and was musical director of the Chicago Symphony Orchestra (1953–63). His autocratic manner on the rostrum and in rehearsal gave him an awesome reputation, but the music he produced was far from cold and unyielding. He gained a considerable reputation for his interpretations of Richard Wagner, Richard Strauss and Béla Bartók.

Reines, Frederick 1918–98
US physicist and Nobel Prize winner
Born in Paterson, New Jersey, he was educated at the Steven's Institute of Technology in Hoboken, New Jersey, and at New York University. Between 1944 and 1959 he was a group leader at Los Alamos, working on the physics of nuclear explosions. He became head of physics at the Case Institute of Technology, Cleveland, and later Professor of Physics and Dean of Physical Sciences at the University of California at Irvine (from 1966). Together with Clyde Cowan, Jnr, he proved the existence of nature's most elusive particle, the neutrino. Later, Reines became interested in neutrinos arising from astronomical sources and used large underground detectors in his research. For his discovery of the neutrino he was awarded the Nobel Prize for physics jointly with Martin Perl in 1995.

Reinhardt, Ad(olf Frederick) 1913–67
US painter and critic
Born in Buffalo, New York, he studied at the National Academy of Design, New York (1936), and the following year joined the American Abstract Artists, an avant-garde association which promoted hard-edge abstraction. Between 1946 and 1950 he was influenced by oriental art. His final style was typified in about 1960 by five-foot square canvases divided into nine equal squares, each painted black. These expressed for him the essence of art and the ultimate minimal painting. He continued to paint in this style until his death. However, what always emerges from his apparently monochrome canvas, is a cruciform structure, such as *Abstract Painting No.5* (1962, Tate, London).

Reinhardt, Django (Jean Baptiste) 1910–53
Belgian guitarist
One of the first European jazz virtuosi, he was born in Liverchies to a family of Gypsy entertainers. Despite losing the use of two fingers of his left hand in a caravan fire, he developed an outstanding technique. After working as a cabaret player in Paris cafés, he joined violinist Stephane Grapelli in 1934 to form the Quintette du Hot Club de France, which established a distinctive French jazz style. In 1946 he joined the Duke Ellington Orchestra for a US tour, changing from acoustic to electric guitar; although this project was not a success, he became a powerful influence among swing-style guitarists. 📖 C Delauney, *Django Reinhardt* (1961)

Reinhardt, Max, *originally* Max Goldmann 1873–1943
Austrian theatre manager
He was born in Baden, Germany. An innovator in theatre art and technique, his work often involved large-scale productions (for example, *The Miracle*, London 1911, which used over 2,000 actors). He co-founded the Salzburg Festival (1920), where he produced *Everyman* and *Faust* for the festivals of 1920 and subsequent years. He left Germany for the USA in 1933, and opened a theatre workshop in Hollywood.

Reiniger, Lotte 1899–1981
German film animator

Born in Berlin, she studied design at Max Reinhardt's theatre school in 1916. She developed a special technique of silhouette animation and became a leading innovator in that art, utilising her techniques in many films. She made the first ever full-length animated feature film, *Die Abenteuer des Prinzen Achmed* (*The Adventures of Prince Achmed*) in 1926. She lived in England from 1935 until the end of the war, and returned to live there permanently in 1950. She worked for the celebrated animation section of the National Film Board of Canada in the 1970s, and wrote a number of books on animation.

Reisner, George Andrew 1867–1942
US Egyptologist
Born in Indianapolis, he graduated in law from Harvard, and studied Egyptology in Berlin, returning to Harvard, first as assistant Professor (1905–14) and later (1914–42) as Professor of Egyptology. His reputation for meticulous excavation was established early when he was appointed to lead California University's exploration of the burial grounds of Koptos (1899–1905). Subsequently he directed the Egyptian government's survey of the Nubian monuments that were threatened by the construction of the Aswan Dam (1907–09), returning (1916–23) to explore the pyramids of Meroe and Napata. In Lower Egypt, he excavated the Valley Temple and pyramid of Mycerinus at Giza and many private mastaba tombs. The discovery in 1925 of the tomb of Queen Hetepheres, mother of Cheops, was outstanding: it constituted the only major find of jewellery and furniture surviving from the Old Kingdom.

Reith (of Stonehaven), John Charles Walsham Reith, 1st Baron 1889–1971
Scottish engineer and pioneer of broadcasting
Born in Stonehaven, Kincardineshire, and educated at Glasgow Academy and Gresham's School, Holt, he served an engineering apprenticeship and later entered the field of radio communication. The first general manager of the British Broadcasting Corporation in 1922, he was its director-general from 1927 to 1938, before becoming MP for Southampton (1940) and Minister of Works and Buildings (1940–42). He chaired the Commonwealth Telecommunications Board from 1946 to 1950. He wrote the autobiographical *Into the Wind* (1949) and *Wearing Spurs* (1966). He was the architect of public service broadcasting in the UK, and the BBC Reith Lectures on radio were instituted in 1948 in honour of him. ⊞ Ian McIntyre, *The Expense of Glory: A Life of John Reith* (1993)

Reitz, Dana 1948–
US dancer and choreographer
Born in New York City, she spent part of her teenage years in Japan, before studying dance theatre at the University of Michigan at Ann Arbor. Graduating in 1970, she moved to New York to study classical ballet and t'ai chi chu'an, and to study with Merce Cunningham. Briefly a member of Twyla Tharp and Laura Dean's companies, she began choreographing in 1973. Her work is noted for its quiet energy and gestural detail. Although she is best known as a soloist, she has collaborated with other dancers, musicians and lighting designers. She made a significant contribution to Robert Wilson and Philip Glass's opera *Einstein on the Beach* (1976). Mikhail Baryshnikov performed in the premiere of her work, *Unspoken Territory*, in 1995.

Reizenstein, Franz 1911–68
German composer and pianist
Born in Nuremberg, he studied under Paul Hindemith and in 1934 moved to England, where he was a pupil of Ralph Vaughan Williams. Among his compositions are cello, piano and violin concertos, the cantata *Voices of Night*, two radio operas, and chamber and piano music.

Réjane, Gabrielle 1856–1920
French actress
Born in Paris, she was noted for her playing of such parts as the title role in Victorien Sardou's 1893 play *Madame Sans-Gêne*. Equally gifted in both tragic and comic roles, she was regarded in France almost as highly as Sarah Bernhardt, and was also popular in England and the USA.

R.E.M.
US rock band
R.E.M. was formed in 1980 in their home town of Athens, Georgia, by singer Michael Stipe, Peter Buck (guitar), Mike Mills (bass) and Bill Berry (drums). Their early music had a distinct country-rock influence, which persisted from their debut album, *Murmer* (1983), until the late 1980s, when they began to experiment with string sections and layered production. The influence of the denser grunge sound became more overt, notably on *Monster* (1994). Stipe's oblique lyrics and distinctive singing have brought him most attention, but the group has remained a tight-knit unit, and has retained critical credibility while achieving considerable commercial success. Berry survived a brain aneurysm during a world tour in 1995. ⊞ J Greer, *R.E.M.: Behind the Mask* (1993)

Remak, Robert 1815–65
German physician and pioneer in electrotherapy
Born in Posen, Prussia (Poznań, Poland), he studied pathology and embryology as a student of Johannes Müller in Berlin. He remained there to develop a general practice and to pursue a university career, although he was prevented from obtaining a senior teaching post because he was a Jew. He did significant work on the microscopy of the nerves, discerning that nerves are not merely (as they had been viewed for centuries) structureless hollow tubes, but possess a flattened solid structure. A pioneer embryologist, he was one of the first to fully depict cell division, and to hold that all animal cells came from pre-existing cells. He discovered the fibres of Remak (1830), and the nerve cells in the heart known as Remak's ganglia (1844).

Remarque, Erich Maria 1898–1970
US novelist
Born in Osnabrück, Germany, he served in World War I, after which he published his famous war novel, *Im Westen nichts Neues* (1929, Eng trans *All Quiet on the Western Front*, 1929). He lived in Switzerland from 1929 to 1939, and published *Der Weg zurück* (1931, Eng trans *The Road Back*, 1931). In 1939 he emigrated to the USA, and became a naturalized citizen. There he wrote *Flotsam* (English and German language versions, 1941), *Arc de Triomphe* (1946, Eng trans *Arch of Triumph*, 1946), *Der schwarze Obelisk* (1956, Eng trans *The Black Obelisk*, 1957) and *Die Nacht von Lissabon* (1962, Eng trans *The Night in Lisbon*, 1964). ⊞ W K Pfeiler, *War and the German Mind* (1941)

Rembrandt See panel p1551

Remigius, St See Remy, St

Remington, Frederic 1861–1909
US artist
Born in Canton, New York, he studied at Yale and at the Art Students League in New York City, then travelled through the West working as a prospector and cow-puncher and sketching constantly. He is best known for his sculptures and paintings of cowboys, Native Americans, and other Western subjects. In sculptures such as *Bronco Buster* (1895), he sought to convey a sense of motion and to reproduce physical details accurately. He also wrote and illustrated books about the West. ⊞ B M Vorpahl, *Frederic Remington and the West* (1978); H McCracken, *Frederic Remington—Artist of the Old West* (1947).

Rembrandt, *properly* Rembrandt Harmensz van Rijn 1606–69
Dutch painter, the greatest northern European artist of his age

Rembrandt was born in Leiden, the ninth of 10 children of Harmen Gerritsz van Rijn, a prosperous miller, and Neeltgen van Suytbrouck, a baker's daughter. After six years at the Latin School he enrolled at Leyden University, but he moved to Amsterdam, where he worked under Pieter Lastman before returning to his home town and setting up independently. He quickly achieved a high reputation as a portrait painter, and by 1628 had a pupil, Gerard Dou. Rembrandt excelled at group portraits of the burghers of Amsterdam after settling permanently there in 1631.

In 1634 he married Saskia van Ulenburgh, the well-connected daughter of a Leeuwarden burgomaster. Saskia features in a number of paintings of the time, including two versions of *Saskia as Flora* (1634, St Petersburg; c.1635, National Gallery, London). Other works from this period are *Rembrandt's Mother as the Prophetess Hannah* (1631, Rijksmuseum, Amsterdam), *The Anatomy Lesson of Doctor Tulp* (1632, Mauritshuis, The Hague), *The Entombment of Christ* (c.1635, Hunterian Gallery, Glasgow), and *Belshazzar's Feast* (c.1636, National Gallery, London).

Rembrandt lived prosperously while Saskia was alive, and they had a son, Titus, who features in portraits. Saskia died in 1642, and in the same year Rembrandt produced his most famous painting, *The Military Company of Captain Frans Banning Cocq* (better known as 'The Night Watch'), a dramatically lit, dynamically composed group portrait of a local militia band.

In spite of increasing fame, Rembrandt's financial situation declined over the next 25 years, and he narrowly avoided bankruptcy in 1656. From about 1647 he lived with Hendrickje Stoffels, who bore him a daughter, Cornelia. There are about six portraits that have been identified with her, including a fine one in the National Gallery, London (c.1659). In 1660 Titus and Hendrickje formed a company for dealing in art, and they employed Rembrandt, thereby affording him some financial relief. During these years he turned to biblical subjects, including *Christ and the Woman taken in Adultery* (1644, National Gallery, London), *Susanna surprised by the Elders* (c.1647, Gemäldegalerie, Berlin), *Jacob blessing the Sons of Joseph* (c.1656, Cassel), and *The Return of the Prodigal Son* (c.1669, Hermitage, St Petersburg). Also among his greatest achievements were his group portraits, notably the *Staalmeesters* (1662, 'Officials of the Guild of Drapers', Rijksmueum); his individual portraits, including the *Portrait of Jan Six* (1654, Rijksmueum); and a superb series of self-portraits, as well as etchings and ink-and-wash drawings.

Rembrandt virtually reinvented the media he worked in, bringing to them an original technical mastery, a sense of drama created by a subtle use of chiaroscuro, and his own overwhelming sense of humanity. His self-portraits are the first psychological studies in the history of art. His output was enormous: over 600 paintings (including 60 self-portraits), about 300 etchings, and about 2,000 drawings. He has been much forged, and in recent times many works previously attributed to him have been categorized as copies or works of pupils.

📖 M Kitson, *Rembrandt* (3rd edn, 1992); J Rosenberg, *Rembrandt: Life and Work* (1981); K Clark, *An Introduction to Rembrandt* (1978).

Remington, Philo 1816–89
US inventor

Born in Litchfield, New York, he entered his father's small-arms factory, and for 25 years superintended the mechanical department. As president of the company from 1860, he perfected the 'Remington' breech-loading rifle.

Remizov, Aleksei Mikhailovich 1877–1957
Russian writer

He was born in Moscow, and lived in St Petersburg, but left Russia after the Revolution, going first to Berlin and finally settling in Paris. His main works are the novels, *Prud* ('The Pond'), *Chacy* ('The Clock'), *Pyataya yazva* ('Fifth Pestilence') and *Krestovye syostri* ('Sisters of the Cross'). He also wrote legends, plays and short stories. His writing is full of national pride and a deep love of old Russian traditions and folklore, and combines realism, fantasy and humour.

Rémusat, Charles François Marie, Comte de 1797–1875
French writer

He was born in Paris, son of the Comte de Rémusat (1762–1823), who was chamberlain to Napoleon I. As a young man he developed liberal ideas, and took to journalism. He signed the journalists' protest which brought about the July Revolution (1830), was elected deputy for Toulouse, and became Under-Secretary of State for the Interior (1836) and Minister of the Interior (1840). He was exiled after the coup d'état of 1848, and devoted himself to literary and philosophical studies, until in 1871 Thiers called him to the portfolio of Foreign Affairs, which he retained until 1873. Among his writings are *Essais de philosophie* (1842, 'Essays in Philosophy'), *L'Angleterre au XVIIIe siècle* (1856, 'Eighteenth-century England'), *Histoire de la philosophie en Angleterre de Bacon à Locke* (1875, 'History of English Philosophy from Bacon to Locke'), and two philosophical dramas, *Abélard* (1877) and *La Saint Barthélemy* (1878, 'Saint Bartholomew's Day').

Rémusat, Jean Pierre Abel 1788–1832
French physician and Sinologist

Born in Paris, he took his diploma in medicine in 1813, but in 1811 had published an essay on Chinese literature. In 1814 he was made Professor of Chinese in the Collège de France. Among his numerous works are one on the Tartar tongues (1820) and his great *Grammaire chinoise* (1822). He wrote also on Chinese writing (1827), medicine, topography and history, and *Mélanges* (1843). In 1822 he founded the Société Asiatique, and in 1824 became curator of the Oriental department in the Bibliothèque Royale.

Remy or Remigius, St, *known as* the Apostle of the Franks c.438–533
Frankish prelate

He became Bishop of Rheims and, according to Gregory of Tours, he baptized Clovis, King of the Franks, in the Christian faith.

Renan, (Joseph) Ernest 1823–92
French philologist and historian

Born in Tréguier, Brittany, he trained for the Church, but abandoned traditional faith after studying Hebrew and Greek biblical criticism. In 1850 he started work at the Bibliothèque Nationale, and published *Averroès et l'Averroïsme* (1852, 'Averroës and Averroism'), *Histoire générale des langues sémitiques* (1854, 'General History of the Semitic Languages'), and *Études d'histoire religieuse* (1856, 'Studies of Religious History'). His appointment as Professor of Hebrew at the Collège de France in 1861 was not confirmed until 1870 by the clerical party, especially after the appearance of his controversial *La Vie de Jésus*

(1863). It was the first of a series on the history of the origins of Christianity, which included books on the Apostles (1866), St Paul (1869) and Marcus Aurelius (1882). Among his other works were books on Job (1858) and Ecclesiastes (1882), and his *Histoire du peuple d'Israël* (1887–94, Eng trans *History of the People of Israel*, 1888–96).

Renaudot, Théophraste 1586–1653
French physician and journalist
Born in Loudun, he was the founder of the first French newspaper. He settled in Paris in 1624 and was physician to the king. Appointed commissary-general for the poor, he started an information agency for them, which in 1631 became a regular journal, *Gazette de France*. He opened a free medical clinic in 1635, with free dispensaries, and also opened the first pawnshop (1637).

Rendell, Ruth Rendell, Baroness 1932–
English detective-story writer
She was born in London. She worked as a journalist and managing director of a local newspaper before the publication of her first novel, *From Doon with Death* (1964). She has written various detective stories featuring Chief Inspector Wexford (eg *Shake Hands Forever*, 1975), and mystery thrillers (eg *A Judgement in Stone*, 1977). Since 1986, she has also written psychological thrillers such as *King Solomon's Carpet* (1991) under the pen name of Barbara Vine. Recent publications include *Simisola* (1994) and a collection of short stories, *Blood Linen* (1995). Several of her works have been adapted for the cinema and for television. She was created a life peer in 1997.

René I, the Good, *also called* René of Anjou
1409–80
Duke of Anjou, and Count of Provence and Piedmont
He was born in Angers and was Duke of Anjou from 1430, Duke of Bar from 1434 and Count of Provence and Piedmont. Having failed in his efforts (1438–42) to make good his claim to the Crown of Naples, he married his daughter Margaret of Anjou to Henry VI of England (1445), and ultimately devoted himself to Provençal poetry and agriculture at Aix. He is sometimes called the Last of the Troubadours.

René, (France-)Albert 1935–
Seychelles politician
Educated in the Seychelles, Switzerland and at King's College London, he was called to the Bar in 1957. He returned to the Seychelles and took up politics, establishing the Seychelles People's United Party (SPUP), a socialist grouping, in 1964. In 1970 he pressed for full independence for the Seychelles, while his contemporary, James Mancham of the Seychelles Democratic Party (SDP), favoured integration with the UK. Despite their differences the two men agreed to form a coalition; when independence was achieved in 1976, Mancham became President and René Prime Minister. In 1977, while Mancham was abroad, René staged a coup, made himself President and created a one-party state. He subsequently followed a non-nuclear policy of non-alignment and resisted attempts to remove him. He was elected in 1979, and re-elected in 1984, 1989 and 1993.

Renfrew, (Andrew) Colin 1937–
English archaeologist
Born in Stockton-on-Tees, County Durham, he was educated at St John's College, Cambridge. Inspired by the writings of Gordon Childe, his work has ranged widely, and is essentially concerned with the nature of cultural change in early history. The origin, development, and interaction of language, agriculture, urbanism, metallurgy, trade, and social hierarchy are constant themes, pursued in such books as *Before Civilization* (1973) and *Archaeology and Language* (1987). He has excavated in Greece (1964–76) and on Orkney, Scotland (1972–74),

notably at the chambered tomb of Quanterness. Since 1981 he has been Professor of Archaeology at Cambridge, and since 1986 Master of Jesus College, Cambridge. His other major publications include *The Emergence of Civilization* (1972), *Approaches to Social Archaeology* (1986) and *The Cycladic Spirit* (1991). He has also contributed to several pioneering archaeological broadcasts, notably the BBC's *Chronicle* series. He was made a life peer in 1991.

Reni, Guido 1575–1642
Italian painter
Born near Bologna, he studied under Denys Calvaert and Ludovico Carracci, and went to Rome in 1599 and again in 1605. *Aurora and the Hours* (1613) is usually regarded as his masterpiece. After a quarrel with Cardinal Spinola regarding an altarpiece for St Peter's he left Rome and settled in Bologna, where he died. He was a prolific early painter of the classical style, although he was later criticized by John Ruskin for sentimental tendencies. He also produced some vigorous etchings.

Renn, Ludwig, *pseudonym of* Arnold Friedrich von Golssenau 1889–1979
German novelist
He was born in Dresden. One of the greatest chroniclers of World War I, his style in his early and greatest book, *Krieg* (1928, Eng trans *War*, 1929), was influenced by the explorer Sven Hedin. This pungent account has long been overshadowed by Erich Maria Remarque's more facile *All Quiet on the Western Front* (1925). His later work, especially after he turned to communism, is less impressive. ⌑W K Pfeiler, *War and the German Mind* (1941)

Rennenkampf, Pavel Karlovich von 1853–1918
Russian cavalry officer
His family was of Baltic German origin. He commanded a force in the Russo-Japanese War (1904–05). In World War I, he commanded the 1st Army, and defeated the German 8th Army at Insterburg and Gumbinnen (August 1914), but he was decisively defeated by Paul von Hindenberg at Tannenberg a few days later. He was appointed Governor of St Petersburg in 1915, and Commander-in-Chief of the Northern Front in 1916. After the October Revolution he was shot by the Bolsheviks.

Renner, Karl 1870–1950
Austrian statesman
Born in Unter-Tannowitz, Bohemia, he trained as a lawyer, joined the Austrian Social Democrat Party, and became the first Chancellor of the Austrian republic (1918–20). He was imprisoned as a Socialist leader following the brief civil war in 1934, but was Chancellor again in 1945. He wrote political works and a national song. From 1946 until his death he was President of Austria. ⌑ Walter Raucher, *Karl Renner: ein österreichischer Mythos* (1995)

Rennie, George 1791–1866
Scottish engineer
Born in London, he was the eldest son of John Rennie. He was superintendent of the machinery of the Mint, and aided his father in his engineering business. With his brother Sir John Rennie he carried on a considerable business, working on shipbuilding, railways, bridges, harbours, docks, machinery and marine engines. He built the first screw vessel for the Royal Navy, the *Dwarf*.

Rennie, John 1761–1821
Scottish civil engineer
He was born at Phantassie farm, East Linton, East Lothian, and after working as a millwright with Andrew Meikle (1719–1811), he studied at Edinburgh University (1780–83). In 1784 he entered the employment of Messrs Boulton & Watt, and in 1791 set up in London as an engineer and soon became famous as a bridge-builder, constructing bridges at Kelso, Leeds, Musselburgh,

Newton-Stewart, Boston, New Galloway, as well as Southwark and Waterloo bridges, and he planned London Bridge. He built many important canals, drained fens, designed the London Docks, and others at Blackwall, Hull, Liverpool, Dublin, Greenock and Leith, and improved harbours and dockyards at Portsmouth, Chatham, Sheerness and Plymouth, where he constructed the celebrated breakwater (1811–41). 📖 Wallace Reyburn, *Bridge Across the Atlantic: The Story of John Rennie* (1972)

Rennie, Sir John 1794–1874
Scottish engineer

Born in London, he was the second son of **John Rennie** and the brother of **George Rennie**. He completed London Bridge to his father's design in 1831. He was engineer to the Admiralty and wrote on harbours.

Reno, Janet 1938–
US politician and lawyer

Born in Miami, Florida, she was educated at Cornell and Harvard universities and was admitted to the Florida Bar in 1963. After practising for 10 years she was appointed administrative assistant state attorney for the 11th Judiciary Circuit Florida, Miami (1973–76), then state attorney in Florida (1978–93). In 1993 she was nominated and confirmed as the US Attorney-General, the first woman in US history to hold this position.

Renoir, Jean 1894–1979
US film director

Born in Paris, France, son of **Pierre Auguste Renoir**, he won the Croix de Guerre in World War I. He turned from scriptwriting to filmmaking, his version of **Zola**'s *Nana* (1926), *La grande illusion* (1937, *Grand Illusion*), *La Bête humaine* (1939, *The Human Beast*), *La Carrozza d'Oro* (1953, *The Golden Coach*), in Italy, and *Le Déjeuner sur l'herbe* (1959, *Picnic on the Grass*), all of which are among the masterpieces of the cinema. He left France in 1941 for the USA and became a naturalized US citizen. His later films include *Le Caporal épinglé* (1962, *The Elusive Corporal*) and *Le Petit théâtre de Jean Renoir* (1969). 📖 Raymond Durgnat, *Jean Renoir* (1974)

Renoir, Pierre Auguste 1841–1919
French Impressionist artist

Born in Limoges, he began at the age of 13 as a painter on porcelain, and later of fans. He made his first acquaintance with the work of **Antoine Watteau** and **François Boucher**, which was to influence his choice of subject matter as deeply as Impressionism was to influence his style. He entered the studio of **Charles Gleyre** in 1862 and began to paint in the open air about 1864. From 1870 onwards he obtained a number of commissions for portraits. In 1874–79 and in 1882 he exhibited with the Impressionists his important, controversial picture of sunlight filtering through leaves, the *Moulin de la Galette* (in the Louvre), dating from 1876. He visited Italy in 1880 and during the next few years (1884–87) painted a series of *Bathers* in a more cold and classical style influenced by **Jean Ingres** and **Raphael**. He then returned to hot reds, orange and gold to portray nudes in sunlight, a style which he continued to develop until his death, although his hands were crippled by arthritis in later years. His works include *The Umbrellas* (c.1883, National Gallery, London) and *The Judgement of Paris* (c.1914).

Rensch, Bernhard 1900–
German zoologist

Born in Thale, he studied zoology at the University of Halle, and worked at the zoological museums at Berlin and Münster before becoming Professor of Zoology at the University of Münster in 1947. He investigated a wide range of problems in the area of genetics and evolution. He was a strong supporter of the idea that random mutations form the basis of evolutionary change, and investigated kladogenesis, the process whereby animal groups diverge, giving rise to many new species of which only a few survive. He argued that trans-specific evolution, ie that above the species level, was subject to the same selective factors as at the specific level, and also developed the idea that evolution affects development. His many research papers and books were mainly published in German, and his major work did not appear in translation until 1959 as *Evolution above the Species Level*.

Renshaw, Willie (William Charles) 1861–1904
English lawn tennis player

Born in Cheltenham, Gloucestershire, he started playing at Cheltenham School with his twin brother Ernest (1861–99), who also became a champion. Willie won Wimbledon singles champion seven times (1881–86, 1899), and also won the Wimbledon doubles title seven times with Ernest (1880–81, 1884–86, 1888–89).

Rensselaer, Stephen Van See Van Rensselaer, Stephen

Renta, Oscar de la See de la Renta, Oscar

Renwick, James 1790–1863
British–US physicist

Born in Liverpool of Scottish–US parents, he was taken to the USA as a child and graduated from Columbia College (later Columbia University), New York, in 1810. He was appointed professor at Columbia College, and became a recognized authority on every branch of engineering. Among the major projects on which he was consulted was the Morris Canal, for which he devised a system of inclined planes to overcome differences in level without the necessity for the time-consuming passage of flights of locks. The most notable of his scientific works were *Outlines of Natural Philosophy* (1822–23) and *Treatise on the Steam-Engine* (1830). His three sons became well-known engineers, and his second son James was also a famous architect.

Repin, Ilya Yefimovich 1844–1930
Russian painter

Born in Chuguyev, he lived in France from 1873 to 1876. He and his family then joined the Abramtsevo colony, a progressive community near Moscow, which is today considered the cradle of the modern movement in Russian art. Repin is possibly the most famous of the Realist group The Wanderers, which had founded a new artistic code aimed at bringing art to the people. The major representative of naturalism in Russia during the second half of the 19th century, he gained popularity with paintings such as *The Reply of the Cossacks of Zaporoguus to Sultan Mahmoud IV* (1884), which his contemporaries saw as a symbol of the Russian people throwing off their chains, and he also painted portraits of famous contemporaries such as **Modest Mussorgsky** (1881) and **Leo Tolstoy** (1887). Although he prepared the development of Russian painting towards colourism, he did not support the new movements, such as World of Art and the Blue Rose, and his own painting eventually exhausted itself in a stale naturalism. He was appointed Professor of Painting at the St Petersburg Academy (1893–1907), and retired to his estate in Finland after the Revolution of 1917.

Repton, Humphrey 1752–1818
English landscape designer

Born in Bury St Edmunds, Suffolk, the natural successor to **Lancelot 'Capability' Brown**, he completed the change from formal gardens of the early 18th century to the picturesque, and coined the phrase 'landscape gardening'. He drew designs for Uppark in Sussex and Sheringham

Hall in Norfolk, and wrote *Observations on the Theory and Practice of Landscape Gardening* (1803). ⌑ Dorothy Stroud, *Humphrey Repton* (1962)

Resnais, Alain 1922–
French film director

Born in Vannes, France, he began studying at the Institute of Advanced Cinematographic Studies in Paris, where he made a series of prizewinning short documentaries, including *Van Gogh* (1948, Academy Award), *Guernica* (1950) and *Nuit et Brouillard* (1955, *Night and Fog*), a haunting evocation of the horror of Nazi concentration camps. His first feature film, *Hiroshima mon amour* (1959, 'Hiroshima My Love'), intermingles the nightmare war memories of its heroine with her unhappy love for a Japanese soldier against the tragic background of contemporary Hiroshima. His next film, *L'Année dernière à Marienbad* (1961, *Last Year at Marienbad*), illustrates his interest in the merging of past, present and future to the point of ambiguity, being hailed as a Surrealistic and dreamlike masterpiece by some, as a confused and tedious failure by others. Works as diverse as *Je t'aime, Je t'aime* (1967), *Mon Oncle d'Amérique* (1980, 'My American Uncle') and *Mélo* (1985) had similarly mixed receptions, although he enjoyed commercial success with the duo *Smoking* and *No Smoking* in 1993. ⌑ John Ward, *Alain Resnais, or, The Theme of Time* (1968)

Respighi, Ottorino 1879–1936
Italian composer

Born in Bologna, he studied under Max Bruch and Rimsky-Korsakov, and in 1913 became Professor of Composition at the St Cecilia Academy in Rome. His works include nine operas, the symphonic poems *Fontane di Roma* (1916, 'Fountains of Rome'), *Pini di Roma* (1924, 'Pines of Rome'), *Gli uccelli* (1927, 'The Birds') and *Feste Romane* (1928, 'Roman Festivals'), and the ballet *La Boutique fantasque* ('The Fantastic Toyshop'), produced by Sergei Diaghilev in 1919.

Restif or Rétif de la Bretonne, Nicolas Edmé 1734–1806
French writer

He was born in Sacy, Yonne, and as a youth worked for a printer in Auxerre. His many voluminous and licentious novels, notably *Le Pied de Fanchette* (1769, 'Fauchette's Foot') and *Le Paysan perverti* (1775, 'The Corrupted Peasant'), give a vivid picture of 18th-century French life, and entitle him to be considered a forerunner of Realism. His 16-volume work *Monsieur Nicolas* (1794–97, Eng trans 1930) is based loosely on his own life. He also wrote on social reform. ⌑ C R Dawes, *Rétif de la Bretonne* (1946)

Reszke, Edouard de 1856–1917
Polish bass

Born in Warsaw, he was successful throughout Europe in a wide range of parts, and often appeared with his brother Jean de Reszke.

Reszke, Jean de 1850–1925
Polish tenor

Born in Warsaw, he began his career as a baritone and, after his debut as a tenor in 1879, succeeded in most of the leading French and Italian operatic roles, adding Wagnerian parts after 1885. He often appeared with his brother Edouard de Reszke.

Reszke, Joséphine de 1855–91
Polish soprano

Born in Warsaw, she sang at the Paris Opera but withdrew from the stage following her marriage to Baron von Kronenburg. She was the sister of Edouard and Jean de Reszke.

Rethel, Alfred 1816–59
German historical painter and graphic artist

Born in Diepenbend, near Aachen, he decorated the imperial hall of the Römer, Frankfurt am Main. He also executed a series of fantastic designs (1842–44, Dresden) on the theme of Hannibal's crossing of the Alps and decorated the Council House of Aachen with frescoes of the *Life of Charlemagne* (1847–52).

Rétif de la Bretonne, Nicolas Edmé See Restif de la Bretonne, Nicolas Edmé

Retz or Rais or Raiz, Gilles de Laval, Baron 1404–40
French soldier and alleged murderer

Born in Champtoceaux, France, he was a Breton of high rank who fought beside Joan of Arc at Orleans. He became Marshal of France at the age of 25, but soon retired to his estates, where he is alleged to have indulged in satanism and orgies, kidnapping and killing 150 children. He was tried for heresy, and was hanged and burned at Nantes. His story is often connected with that of Bluebeard.

Retz, Jean François Paul de Gondi, Cardinal de 1614–79
French prelate

Born in Montmirail, he studied theology at the Sorbonne. He plotted against Jules Mazarin, and exploited the Frondes (1648) to further his own interests and the power of the Church. He transferred his allegiance from the rebel factions to the Crown, and became a cardinal (1652), but in the same year he was imprisoned on Louis XIV's personal orders. After making peace with Louis in 1662, he received the abbacy of St Denis. He covered his extensive debts by making over to his creditors his entire income apart from 2,000 livres. Retz appears in the letters of Madame de Sévigné. His own distinguished memoirs (1655) throw much light on the Frondes.

Reuchlin, Johann 1455–1522
German humanist and Hebraist

Born in Pforzheim, he studied Greek at Paris, and wrote a Latin dictionary at Basle (1476). In 1481 he began lecturing at Tübingen, and in 1496 moved to Heidelberg, where he became the main promoter of Greek studies in Germany. In 1506 he published the first Hebrew grammar, *Rudimenta Linguae Hebraicae* ('The Rudiments of Hebrew'). From 1510 to 1516 he was involved in controversy with the Dominicans of Cologne over the burning of Jewish books, but in 1519 the Duke of Bavaria appointed him professor at Ingolstadt. He edited various Greek texts, and published a Greek grammar, a series of polemical pamphlets, and a satirical drama (against the Obscurantists), *De Verbo Mirifico* and *De Arte Cabbalistica*.

Reuter, Fritz 1810–74
German humorist

He was born in Stavenhagen, Mecklenburg-Schwerin, and studied law at Rostock and Jena. In 1833 he was condemned to death, together with other Jena students for his criticism of the Fatherland, but his sentence was commuted to 30 years' imprisonment. When he was released in 1840 in a ruined state of health, he tried to resume his legal studies, learned farming, and took up teaching. His rough *Plattdeutsch* (Low German) verse setting of the jokes and merry tales of the countryside, *Läuschen und Rimels* (1853, 'Anecdotes and Rhymes'), became at once a great favourite, and most of his other best works were written in Low German prose. *Ut de Franzosentid* (1860, Eng trans *The Year '13*, 1873), *Ut mine Festungstid* (1862, 'During my Imprisonment') and *Ut mine Stromtid* (1862–64, 'During my Apprenticeship') made him famous throughout Germany. He lived in Eisenach from 1863 until his death. ▢ K Batt, *Fritz Reuter, Leven und Werk* (1967)

Reuter, Paul Julius Reuter, Baron von,
originally Israel Beer Josaphat 1816–99
British journalist
Born in Kassel, Germany, he was the founder of the first newsagency. He changed his name to Reuter in 1844, and in 1849 formed in Aachen an organization for transmitting commercial news by telegraph and pigeon post. In 1851 he fixed his headquarters in London, and gradually his system spread to the remotest regions.

Reuther, Walter Philip 1907–70
US trade-union leader
He was born in Wheeling, West Virginia, and worked for Ford and in the USSR before helping to found the United Auto Workers' (UAW) union in 1935. He organized the automobile workers into what later became the largest union in the world, and fought against communist influence in trade unionism. He was UAW president from 1946 to 1970.

Revans, Reginald William 1907–
English pioneer of action learning
He was born in Portsmouth and educated at University College London, and Cambridge. He was an Olympic athlete in 1928. As deputy chief officer of Essex (1935–45) and as Director of Education in the coal industry (1945–50), he promoted 'action learning', whereby the skills of managing are learned by managers reviewing their own experience with their peers and asking appropriate questions of each other. He was Professor of Industrial Administration at Manchester University (1955–65), and has subsequently worked as a consultant in many overseas countries. Since 1986 he has been Professorial Fellow in Action Learning at Manchester University. In 1995 the Revans Centre for Action Learning and Research at Salford University was named in his honour.

Revelle, Roger 1909–91
US oceanographer and sociologist
Born in Seattle, Washington, he worked mainly at the Scripps Institution of Oceanography at La Jolla (1931–64). On the basis of his geophysical studies of the Pacific Ocean, he contributed to the theory of sea-floor spreading. Between 1964 and 1976 he was Professor of Population Policy at Harvard.

Revels, Hiram Rhoades 1822–1901
US politician and clergyman
Born of free parents in Fayetteville, North Carolina, he was a minister of the African Methodist Episcopal Church who recruited three regiments of black troops during the Civil War and served as chaplain of a black regiment. Elected to the Mississippi state legislature in 1869, he was chosen the following year to complete Jefferson Davis's last term in the Senate, becoming the first African-American senator (1870–71).

Revere, Paul 1735–1818
American patriot
Born in Boston, he became a silversmith and copperplate printer and served as a lieutenant of artillery (1756). He was one of the raiders in the Boston Tea Party (1773), and was at the head of a secret society formed to keep watch on the British. On 18 April 1775, the night before the Battle of Lexington and Concord, he rode from Boston to Lexington and Lincoln, warning the people of Massachusetts that the British were on the move. His ride was celebrated in Henry Wadsworth Longfellow's *The Midnight Ride of Paul Revere*. He designed and printed the

first issue of Continental money. In 1801 he founded the Revere Copper Company at Canton, Massachusetts, for rolling sheet copper.

Rexroth, Kenneth 1905–82
US poet, critic and father figure to the Beat Generation
Born in South Bend, Indiana, he was largely self-educated. He worked as a manual labourer in the 1920s and became a prominent figure in the libertarian movement on the West Coast during the 1930s. He was a conscientious objector during World War II, serving as a hospital orderly in San Francisco; during this time he published his first book of verse, *In What Hour?* (1940). Other volumes include *The Signature of All Things* (1950), the quest-poem *The Dragon and the Unicorn* (1952) and *In Defense of the Earth* (1956). *Collected Shorter Poems* appeared in 1967, and a volume of longer works a year later. The best of his critical writing was published in *The Rexroth Reader* (1972). ▢ M Gibson, *Kenneth Rexroth* (1982)

Reyes, Alfonso 1889–1959
Mexican poet, critic, essayist and diarist
Born in Monterrey, he became a diplomat, and was his country's ambassador to Argentina and Brazil. His poetry was influenced by European poets, especially Mallarmé, on whom he wrote *Mallarmé de nosotros* (1938, 'Mallarmé Between Ourselves'). His *Diario 1911–1930* (1960) provides an understanding of Mexican literature in the period it covers. He spent many years in Spain, and became one of the world's leading authorities on the Golden Age of Spanish literature. *Selected Essays* (1964) is a good introductory selection, while two important books on Mexico, *The Position of America* (1950) and *Mexico in a Nutshell* (1964), have been translated. ▢ B B Aponte, *Alfonso Reyes and Spain* (1972)

Reymont, Władysław Stanisław 1867–1925
Polish novelist and Nobel Prize winner
He was born in Kobiele Wielke, near Radon, and had various occupations as wandering actor, tailor, and novice monk. His first novel, *Ziemia obiecana* (1899, Eng trans *The Promised Land*, 1928), dealt with urban life in the industrial town of Łódź; his masterpiece is a study of rural life, *Chłopi* (1904–09, Eng trans *The Peasants*, 1924–25), a tetralogy which was instrumental in his being awarded the Nobel Prize for literature in 1924. Other books are *Komediantka* (1896, Eng trans *The Comédienne*, 1920), and a historical trilogy, *Rok 1794* (1914–19, 'The Year 1794'). ▢ L Budnecki, *Władysław Stanisław Reymont* (1953)

Reynaud, Paul 1878–1966
French statesman
He was born in Barcelonnette. Originally a barrister, he held many French government posts; he was influenced by De Gaulle's advocacy of armoured warfare and opposed appeasement. He was appointed Prime Minister in 1940 with the intention of instigating a more rigorous war effort but the German onslaught led to his fall. He was replaced by Philippe Pétain, who sought an armistice. Reynaud was imprisoned by the Germans during the war. Afterwards he re-entered politics but without regaining his former influence, and lost his seat in 1962. He was a delegate to the Council of Europe (1949).

Reynolds, Albert 1932–
Irish politician
He was born in Rooskey, County Roscommon. His early career was as an entrepreneur in the entertainment and food-manufacturing industries. He became Fianna Fáil MP for Longford-West Meath (1977) and was appointed Minister for Industry and Commerce (1987–88) and Finance (1988–91). Dismissed after an unsuccessful challenge to Charles Haughey (1991), he nevertheless won the party leadership by a large majority after Haughey's

resignation (1992), and became Prime Minister (1992–94). In 1993 he entered into talks concerning the future of Northern Ireland with British Prime Minister John Major.

Reynolds, Burt 1936–
US actor

Born in Waycross, Georgia, he was a college football star before winning a scholarship to the Hyde Park Playhouse. He made his film debut in *Angel Baby* (1961) and was a regular performer in television series including *Riverboat* (1959–60), *Gunsmoke* (1962–65) and *Dan August* (1970–71). The combination of a starring role in *Deliverance* (1972) and his decision to pose naked for *Cosmopolitan* magazine in 1972 consolidated his position as a top screen star. After the success of *Smokey and the Bandit* (1977) and *Hooper* (1978) he was voted the USA's number-one box-office star. His popularity declined in the 1980s, although he showed ability as a character actor in *Breaking In* (1989). He has also directed such films as *Gator* (1976) and *Sharky's Machine* (1981). He found renewed popularity in the television series *Evening Shade* (1990–94) for which he received an Emmy award. ☐ *My Life* (1994)

Reynolds, Sir Joshua 1723–92
English portrait painter

Born in Plympton Earls, near Plymouth, he settled in Plymouth Dock (now Devonport) in 1747. In Rome (1749–52) he studied Raphael and Michelangelo; while visiting the Vatican he caught a chill, which permanently affected his hearing. He then established himself in London and by 1760 was at the height of his fame. In 1764 he founded the Literary Club of which Dr Johnson, David Garrick, Edmund Burke, Oliver Goldsmith, James Boswell and Richard Sheridan were members. He was one of the earliest members of the Incorporated Society of Artists, and on the establishment of the Royal Academy (1768) was elected its first president. He was knighted in 1769, and in that year he delivered the first of his Discourses to the students of the Academy. In 1784 he became painter to the king, and finished his painting of Sarah Siddons as the *Tragic Muse*, a work which exists in several versions. In 1789 his sight deteriorated, and he gave up painting. Reynolds' reputation rests largely on his portraits. These are notable for their power and expressiveness, and for the beauty of their colouring. His pictures of children have a special tenderness and beauty, as in *The Strawberry Girl, Simplicity*, and many others. His other works include *Commodore Keppel* (1753, National Maritime Museum, London), and *Dr Samuel Johnson* (c.1756, National Portrait Gallery, London). He was buried in St Paul's Cathedral.

Reynolds, Osborne 1842–1912
English engineer

Born in Belfast of a Suffolk family, and a graduate of Cambridge, he became the first Professor of Engineering at Manchester (1868) and a Royal Society gold medallist (1888). Some of his best work was in the field of hydrodynamics, and he greatly improved centrifugal pumps. The 'Reynolds number', a dimensionless ratio characterizing the dynamic state of a fluid, takes its name from him.

Reynolds, Walter d.1327
English prelate

He was made Treasurer by Edward II (1307), Bishop of Worcester (1308), Chancellor (1310), and Archbishop of Canterbury (1314), despite the opposition of the monks. He later declared for Edward III, whom he crowned in 1327.

Rhazes See Rāzī, ar-

Rhee, Syngman 1875–1965
Korean statesman

Born near Kaesong, he was imprisoned from 1897 to 1904 for campaigning for reform and a constitutional monarchy. Soon after his release he went to the USA, where he was influenced by Woodrow Wilson, the apostle of self-determination. In 1910 he returned to Japanese-annexed Korea, and after the unsuccessful rising of 1919 he became President of the exiled Korean provisional government. On Japan's surrender in 1945 he returned to Korea, and in 1948 was elected President of the Republic of South Korea. He opposed the Korean truce of 1953, describing Korea's continued partition as an 'appeasement of the Communists'. Re-elected for a fourth term as President in March 1960, he was obliged to resign in April after large-scale riots and the resignation of his Cabinet, and went into exile. A man of inflexible and often bellicose patriotism, his immense personal authority was derived from a lifetime of resistance and exile. His publications include *Japan Inside Out* (1941). ☐ Q Kim, *The Fall of Syngman Rhee* (1982)

Rheinberger, Joseph 1839–1901
German composer

Born in Vaduz, Liechtenstein, he entered the Munich Conservatory at the age of 12, and remained there for seven years, later becoming a teacher. He became royal professor and kapellmeister. His works include two operas and 18 organ sonatas.

Rheticus, *real name* Georg Joachim von Lauchen 1514–74
German astronomer and mathematician

Born in Feldkirch, Austria, he became Professor of Mathematics at Wittenberg (1537). He is noted for his trigonometrical tables, some of which went to 15 decimal places. For a time he worked with Copernicus, whose *De Revolutionibus Orbium Coelestium* he was instrumental in publishing. His own *Narratio Prima de Libris Revolutionum Copernici* (1540, 'The First Account of the Book on the Revolutions by Nicolaus Copernicus') was the first account of the Copernican theory.

Rhigas, Konstantinos 1760–98
Greek poet

Born in Velestino, he organized the anti-Turkish revolutionary movement in Vienna, but was betrayed and shot. He is mainly remembered as a patriotic hero, and was also the author of many patriotic songs and poems and translated works of European literature into Greek.

Rhine, Joseph Banks 1895–1980
US psychologist, pioneer of parapsychology

Born in Waterloo, Pennsylvania, he studied botany at Chicago, switched to psychology under William McDougall at Duke University, and in 1937 became Professor of Psychology there. He co-founded the Parapsychology Laboratory there (1930), and the Institute of Parapsychology in Durham, New Carolina (1964). His laboratory-devised experiments involving packs of specially designed cards established the phenomenon of extrasensory perception and of telepathy on a statistical basis, since some participants achieved considerably better results than the average chance successes. He wrote *New Frontiers of the Mind* (1937), *Extrasensory Perception* (1940) and *The Reach of the Mind* (1948). ☐ Louisa E Rhine, *Something Hidden* (1983)

Rhodes, Cecil John See panel p1557

Rhodes, Wilfred 1877–1973
English cricketer

Born in Kirkheaton, Yorkshire, he played for Yorkshire and England, and during his career (1898–1930) took a world record 4,187 wickets and scored 39,722 runs. He took 100 wickets in a season 23 times, and performed the double feat of 1,000 runs and 100 wickets 16 times, a

Rhodes, Cecil John 1853–1902
South African statesman

Cecil Rhodes was born in Bishop's Stortford, Hertfordshire, where his father was a vicar. He was sent to Natal because of his ill health, and subsequently made a fortune at the Kimberley diamond diggings, where he succeeded in amalgamating the several diamond companies to form the De Beers Consolidated Mines Company in 1888. (In that year he sent £10,000 to **Charles Stewart Parnell** to forward the cause of Irish Home Rule.) He returned to England, entered Oriel College, Oxford, and although his residence was cut short by ill health, he ultimately took his degree. He entered the Cape House of Assembly as member for Barkly.

In 1884 General **Gordon** asked him to accompany him to Khartoum as secretary; but Rhodes declined, having just taken office in the Cape ministry. In 1890 he became Prime Minister of Cape Colony; but even before this he had become a ruling spirit in the extension of British territory in securing first Bechuanaland (later Botswana) as a protectorate (1884) and later (1889) the charter for the British South Africa Company, of which he was managing director until 1896, and whose territory was later to be known as Rhodesia. His policy was the ultimate

establishment of a federal South African dominion under the British flag.

In 1895 he was made a member of the Privy Council. The following year he was forced to resign the Cape premiership in the aftermath of the **Jameson** Raid. In the same year he succeeded in quelling the Matabele rebellion by personal negotiations with the chiefs. In 1899 he received the award of Doctor of Civil Law at Oxford. He was a conspicuous figure during the war of 1899–1902, when he organized the defences of Kimberley during the siege.

Rhodes left a remarkable will which, besides making great benefactions to Cape Colony, founded scholarships at Oxford for Americans, Germans and members of the British Empire (later Commonwealth).

📖 Robert I Rotberg, *The Founder: Cecil Rhodes and the Pursuit of Power* (1988); Brian Roberts, *Cecil Rhodes: Flawed Colossus* (1987); J G Lockhart and C M Woodhouse, *Rhodes* (1963, also published as *Cecil Rhodes: The Colossus of Southern Africa*).

'So little done, so much to do.' Attributed last words.

---

record in first-class cricket. The oldest man to play Test cricket, he was 52 years and 165 days old when he played for England against the West Indies at Kingston in April 1930.

Rhodes, Zandra 1940–
English fashion designer

She was born in Chatham, Kent, studied textile printing and lithography at Medway College of Art, then won a scholarship to the Royal College of Art. She designed and printed textiles, and with others opened The Fulham Road Clothes Shop, later setting up on her own. She showed her first dress collection in 1969, and is noted for her distinctive exotic designs in floating chiffons and silks. In 1972 she was British Designer of the Year, and won an Emmy award in 1984 for her costumes for the televised production of *Romeo and Juliet on Ice*.

Rhondda, David Alfred Thomas, 1st Viscount
1856–1918
Welsh coal owner, financier and politician

He was born in Ysgyborwen, near Aberdare in Glamorganshire. Educated at Caius College, Cambridge, he was Liberal MP for Merthyr Tydfil from 1888 to 1910. During World War I, he was sent to the USA by **Lloyd George** to negotiate the supply of munitions to Great Britain. His success won him a peerage, and was followed by an equally successful period as Minister of Food (1917–18), during which wartime food rationing was introduced. On his death in 1918 his peerage passed, by special remainder, to his daughter, Viscountess Rhondda (**Margaret Haig Thomas**).

Rhys, Ernest Percival 1859–1946
English editor and writer

Born in London, he grew up in Carmarthen, Wales, and in Newcastle. There he became a mining engineer, but turned to writing, and in 1886 moved to London and became a poet and freelance editor and critic. In 1892 and 1894 he contributed to the collections of poems by the Rhymers' Club, which he had founded with **W B Yeats**. He is best known as editor of the Everyman's Library of classics (983 vols, 1906–46). He wrote two novels and some volumes of verse.

Rhys, Jean, *pseudonym of* Gwen Williams
1894–1979
British novelist

She was born in the West Indies, her father a Welsh doctor, and her mother a Creole. Educated at a convent in Roseau, Dominica, she moved to England in 1910 to train at the Royal Academy of Dramatic Art, but her father's death after only one term obliged her to join a touring theatre company. At the end of World War I she married a Dutch poet, Max Hamer, and went to live on the Continent, spending many years in Paris. There she met writers and artists, including **Ernest Hemingway, James Joyce** and **Ford Madox Ford** (the last-named in particular encouraged her writing). In 1927 she published *The Left Bank and Other Stories*, set mostly in Paris or in the West Indies of her childhood. Four novels followed: *Quartet* (originally published as *Postures*, 1928), *After Leaving Mr Mackenzie* (1930), *Voyage in the Dark* (1934) and *Good Morning Midnight* (1939). Her heroines were women attempting to live without regular financial support. After nearly 30 years she published in 1966 what was to become her best-known novel, *Wide Sargasso Sea*, which was based on the character of Rochester's mad wife in **Charlotte Brontë's** *Jane Eyre*. Further short stories followed in *Tigers are Better Looking* (1968) and *Sleep It Off, Lady* (1976). An autobiography, *Smile Please*, was published posthumously in 1979. 📖 P Wolfe, *Jean Rhys* (1980)

Rhys, Sir John 1840–1915
Welsh philologist

Born in Cardiganshire, he taught in Anglesey until 1865, when he entered Jesus College, Oxford, and continued his studies in France and Germany. From 1871, he was an inspector of schools in Wales, and in 1877 he became the first Professor of Celtic at Oxford, in 1881 a Fellow of Jesus College, Oxford, and in 1895 its principal. He was a distinguished authority on Celtic philology, and author of numerous works, including *Celtic Britain* (1882) and *Celtic Heathendom* (1888).

Riain, Liam P O See Ryan, William Patrick

Ribalta, Francisco de 1550–1628
Spanish painter

Born in Castellón de la Plana, he studied in Rome and settled in Valencia. He was noted as a painter of historical subjects and for his use of chiaroscuro. His works include *The Last Supper* and his *Christ Nailed to the Cross* (1582) in Madrid. His sons, José (1588–1656) and Juan (1597–1628), were also painters.

Ribas, Oscar 1909–
Lusophone Angolan writer

Born in Luanda of mixed parentage, he was blind from 1930. A major figure in African literature, he is the world's leading authority on his own people, the Kimbundu, whose folk beliefs and religion he has studied through his stories, ethnographic writings and poetry.

Ribbentrop, Joachim von 1893–1946
German Nazi politician

Born in Wesel, he became a wine merchant. He joined the National Socialist Party in 1932, and as Hitler's adviser in foreign affairs he was responsible in 1935 for the Anglo-German naval pact. The following year he was appointed ambassador to Great Britain, and then Foreign Minister (1938–45). He was captured by the British in 1945, condemned to death at Nuremberg and executed. 📖 John Weitz, *Hitler's Diplomat: The Life and Times of Joachim von Ribbentrop* (1992)

Ribera, Jusepe de, *called* Lo Spagnoletto ('The Little Spaniard') 1588–1656
Spanish painter and etcher

Born in Játiva, he settled in Naples and became court painter there. He delighted in the horrible, often choosing such subjects as the martyrdom of the saints and painting them with a bold, unsympathetic style. Later works were calmer and more subtle, and include *The Immaculate Conception* and paintings of the Passion.

Ricard, Marthe, *née* Betenfeld 1889–1982
French pilot and spy

Born in Alsace-Lorraine, she qualified as a pilot in 1911, and after her husband died in World War I, undertook secret intelligence work for France. Her seduction of a German baron in Spain enabled her to elicit important naval information, and she was later decorated with the Légion d'Honneur. In World War II she worked for the Resistance, and after her third marriage, as Marthe Ricard, she was elected to the municipal council in Paris. She campaigned successfully to rid the city of its prostitutes, eradicating what she viewed as female exploitation. In later years she appears to have modified her views, tolerating a controlled sex industry as somewhat less exploitative.

Ricardo, David 1772–1823
English political economist

Born in London, he was a Dutch Jew by birth, and converted to Christianity on his marriage to Priscilla Ann Wilkinson, a Quaker, in 1793. In 1799 his interest in political economy was awakened by Adam Smith's *Wealth of Nations*. His pamphlet, *The High Price of Bullion, a Proof of the Depreciation of Banknotes* (1809), was an argument in favour of a metallic basis to currency. In 1817 he published *Principles of Political Economy and Taxation*, a discussion of value, wages, rent, etc. In 1819 he became Radical MP for Portarlington. 📖 J H Hollander, *David Ricardo: A Centenary Estimate* (1910)

Ricardo, Sir Harry Ralph 1885–1974
English mechanical engineer

Born in London, he studied at Trinity College, Cambridge (1903–07), where he designed and built several small petrol engines and began to work on problems of ignition, combustion and detonation. He soon recognized the importance of fuel type in avoiding detonation or 'knocking', and this led to the use of octane numbers to measure the anti-knock properties of petrols. His improved design of the combustion chamber in side-valve engines has been universally adopted, and he has many other important inventions to his credit.

Ricasoli, Bettino, Baron 1809–80
Italian statesman

Born in Florence, he was a leading agriculturalist and for 10 years worked successfully at draining the Tuscan Maremma. In 1859 he opposed the Grand Duke, on whose flight he was made dictator of Tuscany. A strong advocate of the unification of Italy, he supported **Camillo Cavour** in the struggle to join Piedmont with Tuscany. When Cavour died he became premier of Italy (1861–62, 1866–67).

Ricci, Marco 1676–1730
Italian painter

Born in Belluno, he was a pupil of his uncle **Sebastiano Ricci**, and, although based in Venice, travelled extensively. Taken to England by the Earl of Manchester in 1708, he seems to have worked mostly on the design of stage scenery for opera. In 1710 he returned to Venice to take his uncle to England, where they worked together from 1712 to 1716. Little is known of his later career, but he appears to have worked for Sebastiano painting landscape backgrounds for large religious pictures.

Ricci, Matteo 1552–1610
Italian founder of the Jesuit missions in China

Born in Macerata, Papal States, he studied in Rome, was ordained in India (1580), and then went on to China (1582). His mastery of Chinese enabled him to write works which received much commendation from the Chinese literati. He was a successful missionary, although his methods aroused much controversy.

Ricci, Nina 1883–1970
Italian couturier

Born in Turin, Italy, she became a dressmaker's apprentice at the age of 13, was in charge of an atelier by 18 and head designer at 20. In 1932 she opened her own Paris couture house with her jeweller husband Louis. Her son Robert has managed the business since 1945. She became known for a high standard of workmanship that appealed to an elegant and wealthy clientele. She also made trousseaux for young brides-to-be. Her perfume, L'air du Temps, launched in 1948 in a Lalique flacon with a frosted glass stopper, is still highly popular worldwide.

Ricci, Sebastiano 1659–1734
Italian painter

Born in Belluno, he was trained in Venice, where he fully assimilated the work of **Veronese** and developed a decorative style which was to influence **Giovanni Battista Tiepolo**. After extensive travel in Italy he worked for two years (1701–03) in Vienna. In 1712 he travelled to England, via the Netherlands, with his nephew **Marco Ricci**. The only complete work to survive from this time is a *Resurrection* in the apse of Chelsea Hospital chapel. He left England for Venice in 1716 when he failed to gain the commission to decorate the dome of St Paul's (which went to Sir **James Thornhill**).

Riccio, David See Rizzio, David

Rice, Edmund Ignatius 1762–1844
Irish philanthropist

Born at Westcourt, near Callan, County Kilkenny, he became a wealthy provision merchant in Waterford. He retired from business on the death of his wife (1789) and devoted himself to good works, taking religious vows in 1808. He founded a school for poor boys at Waterford in 1803, and many others elsewhere; these were sanctioned by the pope in 1820 as the Institute of the Brothers of the Christian Schools of Ireland. He was superior-general of the order as Brother Ignatius until 1838.

Rice, Elmer, *originally* Elmer Reizenstein 1892–1967
US dramatist

Born in New York, he studied law, then turned to writing plays. His prolific output includes *The Adding Machine* (1923), *Street Scene* (1929), which won a Pulitzer Prize, *The Left Bank* (1931), *Two on an Island* (1940) and *Cue for Passion* (1958). 🕮 *Minority Report* (1963)

Rice, James 1843–82
English novelist
Born in Northampton and educated at Queen's College, Cambridge, he drifted from law into literature, and in 1868 became proprietor and editor of *Once a Week*. From 1872 he wrote novels with Sir **Walter Besant**, beginning with the successful *Ready-Money Mortiboy* (1872). 🕮 J Rice, *The Autobiography of Sir Walter Besant* (1902, ed S S Sprigge)

Rice, Jerry Lee 1962–
US player of American football
Born in Starkville, Mississippi, he has a legendary record of catching touchdown passes. His formidable catching skill was spotted early by his brothers, who threw him bricks as they helped their father, a mason, to build houses. He turned professional in 1985, joined the San Francisco 49ers, and by 1986 led the League with 86 catches. In 1987 he broke the National Football League (NFL) record when he caught 22 touchdown passes in just 12 games. He won many of the 1987 NFL awards. By 1994 he had 139 touchdowns. He helped lead the 49ers to three victories in the Super Bowl (1989, 1990, 1995).

Rice, Sir Tim(othy Miles Bindon) 1944–
English lyricist
Born in Buckinghamshire, he studied law, but abandoned it to join the record company EMI. As a first musical contribution he wrote the lyrics to music by **Andrew Lloyd Webber** for *Joseph and the Amazing Technicolour Dreamcoat* (1968). The partnership went on to produce *Jesus Christ Superstar* (1971), *Evita* (1978) and *Cricket* (1986). Rice has also written *Chess* (1984), to music by Benny Andersson and Björn Ulvaeus; the lyrics for the film musical *Aladdin* (1992) to music by Alan Menken, which earned him the 1993 Best Original Song Oscar for 'A Whole New World'; *Beauty and the Beast* (1994), also with Menken; and *The Lion King* (1994), to music by **Elton John**. In addition to his television appearances and various publications, he has been chairman of the newly formed Foundation for Sport and the Arts since 1991. He was knighted in 1994.

Rice-Davies, Mandy (Marilyn) 1944–
Welsh model and show girl
Born in Wales, the daughter of a police officer, she grew up in the West Midlands, where she worked in a department store before becoming a show girl at Murray's Cabaret Club, London. There she met and befriended **Christine Keeler** and the osteopath **Stephen Ward**, who introduced her to influential London society. She was a witness at Ward's trial, and in reply to a suggestion that Lord Astor denied knowing her, she gave the celebrated retort: 'He would, wouldn't he?'. After the trial she moved to Israel, where she established two night clubs called Mandy. She married twice and published her autobiography. Eventually she returned to live in London.

Rich, Adrienne Cecile 1929–
US poet
Born in Baltimore, Maryland, and educated at Radcliffe College, Cambridge, Massachusetts, she published her first volume of verse, *A Change of World* (1951), while she was still an undergraduate. It foreshadowed her emergence as the most forceful US woman poet since **Elizabeth Bishop** and **Sylvia Plath**. She was Professor of English and Feminist Studies at Stanford from 1986 to 1993. Later collections include *Snapshots of a Daughter-in-Law* (1963) and *The Will to Change* (1971). After her husband's suicide,

Rich began to align herself more directly with the women's movement, and her prose became almost as influential as her verse. Her novels include *Of Woman Born* (1976), *On Lies, Secrets, and Silence* (1979), a collection of prose, and *Blood, Bread, and Poetry* (1986). Later verse appeared as *The Dream of a Common Language* (1978), *A Wild Patience Has Taken Me This Far* (1981) and *Dark Fields of the Republic* (1995). *The Fact of a Doorframe* (1984) collected her poetry from 1950. 🕮 M Díaz-Diocaretz, *The Transforming Power of Language* (1984)

Rich, Barnabe c.1540–1617
English soldier and writer
He was born in Essex, and under the patronage of Sir Christopher Hatton (1540–91) served as a soldier in France, the Low Countries and Ireland. He was the author of exaggerated tales in *The Strange and Wonderful Adventures of Don Simonides* (1581) and *The Adventures of Brusanus, Prince of Hungaria* (1592). His *Apolonius and Silla* (contained in *Riche, his Farewell to the Militarie Profession*, 1581) was used by **Shakespeare** as a source for *Twelfth Night*. He was also a prolific pamphleteer on military matters, and on Ireland.

Richard I, *known as* Cœur de Lion ('the Lion Heart') 1157–99
King of England
He was born in Oxford, the third son of **Henry II** and **Eleanor of Aquitaine**. Of his 10-year reign he spent only a few months in England, and it is doubtful that he spoke English. For the rest of the time he was taking part in the crusades or, induced by his mother, in rebellion with his brothers Henry and Geoffrey against their father Henry II (1173 and 1189), on the second occasion in league with **Philip II** of France. Richard became King of England, Duke of Normandy and Count of Anjou on 5 July 1189. He had already taken the crusader's vow; and in 1190 he and Philip set out to join the Third Crusade. They spent the winter in Sicily, where the throne had recently been seized by the Norman **Tancred**; Tancred made his peace with Richard by giving up to him Richard's sister Johanna, the widowed queen, and her possessions, and by betrothing his daughter to Prince **Arthur**, Richard's nephew and heir. When in 1191 part of Richard's fleet was wrecked off Cyprus, the island's ruler **Isaac I, Comnenus** treated the crews with hostility. Richard sailed back from Rhodes, defeated and deposed Isaac, and give his crown to **Guy of Lusignan**. In Cyprus he married Berengaria of Navarre, and on 8 June landed near Acre, which surrendered. Richard's exploits, including his march to Joppa, two advances on Jerusalem (which he failed to regain), his capture of the fortresses in southern Palestine, and his relief of Joppa, excited the admiration of Christendom. In September he concluded a three years' peace with **Saladin**, and set off alone on the journey home. He was shipwrecked in the Adriatic, and made his way in disguise through the dominions of his enemy, Leopold, Duke of Austria. He was recognized, and was seized and handed over to the Emperor **Henry VI** (1193), who demanded a heavy ransom for his release. Richard's subjects raised the money, and despite his brother John's attempts to prevent him, he returned home in March 1194, after concluding useful political alliances with the empire. John was forgiven, and Richard set off again for France, where he spent the rest of his life campaigning against Philip, mainly on the Norman-French border which he held for the Angevins. The government of England was meanwhile entrusted to the justiciar, **Hubert Walter**. Richard was killed while besieging the castle of Chalus, and was buried at Fontevrault. 🕮 K Norgate, *Richard the Lion Heart* (1924)

Richard II 1367–1400
King of England

Born in Bordeaux, France, the son of **Edward the Black Prince**, he succeeded his grandfather, **Edward III** in 1377 at the age of 10, and the government was entrusted to a council of 12, although for a time his uncle, **John of Gaunt**, gained control. Richard's reign was characterized by a struggle between his own desire to act independently, and the barons' concern to check his power. Richard showed great resolution and courage in facing the Peasants' Revolt of 1381, which had been largely caused by the introduction of the notorious poll tax to pay for war with France and the extravagance of the court (for which **John of Gaunt** was largely held responsible). The men of Kent, led by **Wat Tyler**, ran riot pillaging and killing in London. They met the king at Smithfield (15 June) where, during the negotiations, Tyler was struck down, but Richard declared that he would grant them the concessions they demanded. From this time John of Gaunt exercised less power, and in 1386 he retired to live in the Continent. In 1385 Richard invaded Scotland and burned Edinburgh. Meanwhile his uncle, Thomas of Woodstock, Duke of Gloucester (1355–97), formed a baronial coalition in opposition to him. They impeached several of his friends in the so-called 'Merciless Parliament' of 1388, and had many of them executed. However, on 3 May 1389 Richard promptly declared himself of age, and for eight years he ruled as a moderate constitutional monarch. Later, and especially after his marriage in 1396 to Isabella (1389–1409), daughter of Charles VI of France, he took a more despotic view of the monarchy, and he had a number of his enemies, including Gloucester, **Thomas Arundel** and Thomas de Beauchamp, Earl of Warwick (c.1345–1401), arrested and executed or murdered. In 1398 several lords were banished, including John of Gaunt's son Henry Bolingbroke. The following year John died, and Henry succeeded him as Duke of Lancaster. Richard went over to Ireland in May, and Henry landed on 4 July. Richard hurried back, submitted at Flint (19 August), and was put in the Tower. On 29 September he resigned the Crown, and next day was deposed by parliament in favour of Lancaster, who succeeded as **Henry IV**. Richard was imprisoned in Pontefract Castle, and died there, probably murdered, early in 1400. ⊞ Michael Senior, *The Life and Times of Richard II* (1981)

Richard III 1452–85
King of England

He was born in Fotheringay Castle. After the defeat and death of his father Richard, 3rd Duke of **York**, in 1460, he was sent to Utrecht for safety; he returned to England after his brother Edward had won the Crown as **Edward IV** (1461), and was created Duke of Gloucester. When Edward went into exile in 1470, Richard went with him, and he helped bring about Edward's restoration the following year. He may have been implicated in the murder of Prince Edward, **Henry VI**'s son, after Edward's victory at Tewkesbury, and in the murder of Henry himself in the Tower. In 1472 Richard married Anne, the younger daughter of the Earl of Warwick. This alliance was resented by Richard's brother, the Duke of **Clarence**, who had married the elder sister and did not wish to share Warwick's extensive possessions. Clarence was impeached and put to death in the Tower in 1478. Richard has been suspected of his murder, but the evidence is inconclusive. In 1482 Richard commanded the army that invaded Scotland and captured Berwick. In 1483, while still in Yorkshire, he heard of King Edward's death, and learned that he himself had been designated guardian of his 13-year-old son and heir, **Edward V**. On his way south, the Protector arrested the 2nd Earl **Rivers** and Lord Richard Grey, the uncle and stepbrother of the young king, and rallied the old nobility to his support. He accused Lord Hastings, a leading member of the council, of treason, and had him beheaded. The dowager queen was

induced to give up her other son, the little Duke of York, and he was put into the Tower together with his younger brother, the king. Richard is believed to have had his nephews murdered; but the deed was done so secretly that the country did not know of it until some time later, and there was no proof of Richard's guilt. Parliament sought Richard's accession to the throne, and on 6 July 1483 he was crowned, Rivers and Grey having been executed on 25 June. Richard's principal supporter, Henry Stafford, 2nd Duke of Buckingham, changed sides soon after Richard's coronation and entered into a plot with the friends of Henry Tudor, Earl of Richmond (afterwards **Henry VII**) and chief representative of the House of Lancaster, to achieve Richard's overthrow and proclaim Henry king. The attempted rising collapsed, and Buckingham was executed on 2 November. Henry landed at Milford Haven on 7 August 1485. Richard met him at Bosworth Field on 22 August; he fought with courage but the odds turned decisively against him with the desertion of the Stanleys to Henry, and in the end he lost his kingdom and his life. Richard was a capable ruler, and would probably have been a great king had he come to the throne in more normal circumstances. ⊞ Charles Ross, *Richard III* (1981)

Richard, Sir Cliff, *real name* Harry Roger Webb 1940–
English pop-singer

He was born in Lucknow, India, and taken to England at the age of eight. He began his professional career playing with the Dick Teague Group, and formed his own band, The Shadows (originally called The Drifters), in 1958. Following the success of 'Living Doll' (1959), The Shadows were hailed as Great Britain's answer to US rock. Cliff Richard made a series of family musical films during the 1960s, including *Expresso Bongo* (1960), *The Young Ones* (1961) and *Summer Holiday* (1962). After his conversion to Christianity, his clean-cut image damaged his reputation with rock fans, but he became a British entertainment institution. He was knighted for services to pop music in 1995, and appeared alongside Vera Lynn (1917–) at the VE celebration that year. In 1996 he took to the stage, playing the eponymous hero in *Heathcliff*, the musical based upon **Emily Brontë**'s *Wuthering Heights*. ⊞ S Turner *Cliff Richard* (1993)

Richard de Bury See **Aungerville, Richard**

Richards, Alun 1929–
Welsh novelist, short-story writer and playwright

Born in Pontypridd, Glamorgan, he was educated at the Monmouthshire Training College, Caerleon, and at University College, Swansea. He has published six novels, including *The Elephant You Gave Me* (1963), *A Woman of Experience* (1969) and *Barque Whisper* (1979), and two collections of short stories (*Dai Country*, 1973, and *The Former Miss Merthyr Tydfil*, 1976). For much of his material he drew on his varied experiences working as a probation officer, a sailor and a teacher. Besides editing several short-story anthologies, he has written a book about Welsh rugby, and many plays and adaptations for television, notably *The Onedin Line*. ⊞ Autobiography in *Artists in Wales* (1971, ed M Stephens)

Richards, Audrey 1899–1984
English social anthropologist

Born in London, she spent most of her childhood in India, where her father worked as a lawyer. After returning to Great Britain in 1911, she studied at Newnham College, Cambridge, graduating in 1921. She published her first study of primitive tribal life in 1932 without carrying out any fieldwork, but later undertook first-hand field studies among primitive societies in Rhodesia (now Zimbabwe). She was appointed director of the East African Institute of Social Research in Uganda in 1950. She retired 16 years later and died unmarried.

Richards, Ceri 1903–71
Welsh artist

Born in Dunvant, near Swansea, he studied at Swansea School of Art (1920–24) and at the Royal College of Art, London (1924–27), holding his first one-man show at the Glynn Vivian Art Gallery, Swansea, in 1930. In 1932 he began making collages and constructions which showed the influence of Max Ernst and the Surrealists generally. He joined the London Group in 1937, and taught at Chelsea School of Art (1945–55), at the Slade School of Art (1956–61) and at the Royal College (1961–62). In addition to his paintings, he designed opera sets, stained-glass windows and vestments. He won the Einaudi prize at the Venice Biennale in 1962.

Richards, Dickinson Woodruff 1895–1973
US physician and Nobel Prize winner

Born in Orange, New Jersey, and educated at Yale, he specialized in cardiology, which he taught at Columbia University (1928–61), becoming Professor of Medicine there from 1947. With André Cournand, Richards developed Werner Forssman's technique of cardiac catheterization into an important procedure for studying blood pressure, oxygen tension and a variety of other physiological variables in health and disease. Their work led to better understanding and treatment of shock, and provided the basis for much of modern cardiology. The three men shared the 1956 Nobel Prize for physiology or medicine. Richards was also an eloquent advocate for improved standards of medical care for the elderly and disadvantaged.

Richards, Frank, *pseudonym of* Charles Hamilton
1875–1961
English children's writer, author of the 'Billy Bunter' series

Born in London, he was educated privately and began to write stories for magazines and comics while still a schoolboy. He wrote for boys' papers, particularly *The Gem* (1906–39) and *The Magnet* (1908–40), and produced many well-known school stories in book and play form, including the 'Tom Merry' and 'Billy Bunter' series. His *Autobiography* was published in 1952. ⌨ M Cadogan, *The Man Behind Chums* (1985)

Richards, Sir Gordon 1904–86
English jockey

Born in Oakengates, Shropshire, he was the son of a coalminer. In 34 seasons (1921–54) he was champion jockey 26 times, and rode 4,870 winners. Towards the end of his career, in 1953, he finally rode his first Derby winner, Pinza; he was knighted in the same year. He took up training in 1954 after retirement.

Richards, Henry Brinley 1819–85
Welsh pianist and composer

Born in Carmarthen, Dyfed, he was educated at the Royal Academy of Music, London. An accomplished pianist, he was also a prolific composer of songs, piano pieces and choruses. During a study trip to Paris he befriended Frédéric Chopin. His best-remembered piece is 'God Bless the Prince of Wales'.

Richards, I(vor) A(rmstrong) 1893–1979
English scholar and literary critic, initiator of the so-called 'New Criticism' movement

Born in Sandbach, Cheshire, he studied psychology at Magdalene College, Cambridge. Later professor at Cambridge (1922–29), with C K Ogden he developed the idea of Basic English, and in 1924 published the influential *Principles of Literary Criticism*, followed by *Science and Poetry* (1925) and *Practical Criticism* (1929). In 1939 he left Cambridge to take up a professorship at Harvard (1939–63). There he taught William Empson, became a friend of Robert Lowell, Jnr, and began himself to write poetry, publishing, among other collections, *Goodbye Earth and other poems* (1958), *The Screens* (1960) and *New and Selected Poems* (1978). ⌨ P Schiller, *I A Richards's Theory of Literature* (1969)

Richards, Keith See Rolling Stones, The

Richards, Renée, *originally* Richard Raskind 1934–
US doctor, tennis player and transsexual

Born in New York City, he began a life of academic and athletic accomplishment, and was scouted for baseball by the Yankees and captain of Yale's tennis team. He later became a leading ophthalmologist. As a teenager, he developed a feeling that he was really female; he underwent hormone treatments and transsexual surgery, and was renamed Renée Richards. Her 1983 book, *Second Serve*, details her life, her surgery and her struggles to be accepted in women's tennis.

Richards, Sir Rex Edward 1922–
English chemist and administrator

Born in Colyton, Devon, he studied chemistry at Oxford, and from 1947 to 1964 was a tutor and Fellow of Lincoln College. In 1964 he became Dr Lee's Professor of Physical Chemistry, and in 1969 was appointed Warden of Merton College, a position he held until 1984. Since retiring from Oxford he has been director of the Leverhulme Trust. From the late 1940s he carried out pioneering studies in nuclear magnetic resonance spectroscopy (NMR), and later worked on the applications of NMR to biological problems and the development of the medical technique of magnetic resonance imaging. He became Vice-Chancellor of the University of Oxford (1977–81), then Chancellor of Exeter University (1982–), was elected a Fellow of the Royal Society in 1959, and received its Davy (1976) and Royal (1986) medals. Knighted in 1977, he served as president of the Royal Society of Chemistry in 1992.

Richards, Theodore William 1868–1928
US chemist and Nobel Prize winner

Born in Germantown, Pennsylvania, he was educated at Haverford College and at Harvard, where he was awarded a PhD in 1888. He held the Erving chair of chemistry from 1912 until his death. Over the course of 40 years the atomic weights of 25 elements were determined by Richards and his students. His investigation of the variation of the atomic weight of lead with source proved the existence of isotopes (1914). He also carried out extensive work on various topics in physical chemistry. He was awarded the Nobel Prize for chemistry in 1914 for his work on atomic weights. He also received the Davy Medal of the Royal Society in 1910 and was made a Foreign Member in 1919. He became an Honorary Fellow of the Chemical Society in 1908 and was awarded its Faraday Medal in 1911.

Richards, Viv (Isaac Vivian Alexander) 1952–
Antiguan cricketer

Born in St John's, he has played in the UK for Somerset (1974–86) and Glamorgan (1990–93), and scored a world record in 1976 with 1,710 Test runs. He usually wore a cap and not a helmet, and his orthodox right-handed batting was feared by bowlers for its style of attack from the first ball. His timing, power and range enabled him to score Test cricket's fastest century (off 56 balls) against England in 1986. He was official captain of the West Indies from 1985 to 1991 and holds the West Indies record for the most caps.

Richardson, Dorothy M(iller) 1873–1957
English novelist

She was born in Abingdon, Oxfordshire, and after her mother's suicide in 1895 moved to London and worked as a teacher, clerk, and dentist's assistant. She became a Fabian and had an affair with **H G Wells**, which led to a miscarriage and a near-collapse in 1907. She started her writing career with works about the Quakers and **George Fox** (1914). Her first novel, *Painted Roofs* (1915), began a 12-volume sequence entitled *Pilgrimage*, culminating with *Clear Horizon* (1935) and *Dimple Hill* (1938). She was the first exponent of the 'stream of consciousness' style later made famous by **Virginia Woolf**. 📖 G G Fromm, *Dorothy Richardson* (1977)

Richardson, Henry Hobson 1838–86
US architect
Born in Priestley Plantation, Louisiana, he was educated at Harvard and studied architecture in Paris. He initiated the Romanesque Revival in the USA, leading to a distinctively US style of architecture. He designed a number of churches, especially Trinity Church, Boston (1872), the Allegheny Co Buildings in Pittsburgh, and halls of residence at Harvard, and his range extended to private houses as well as railway stations and wholesale stores.

Richardson, H(enry) H(andel), *pseudonym of* Ethel Florence Lindesay Robertson, *née* Richardson 1870–1946
Australian novelist and short-story writer
She was born in Fitzroy, Melbourne, and after an unhappy childhood in which her father died insane, she travelled widely with her mother and studied music with distinction at the Leipzig Conservatory, graduating with honours in 1892. She married a fellow-student, John George Robertson, and they moved to London, where her first novel, *Maurice Guest*, was published in 1908. Her major work was the trilogy *The Fortunes of Richard Mahoney* (1917–30). A later novel, *The Young Cosima* (1939), a study of the lives of **Franz Liszt**, **Richard Wagner** and Wagner's second wife Cosima von Bülow, reflects her musical interests. She also wrote some short stories, and the autobiographical *Myself when Young* (posthumous, 1948). 📖 V Buckley, *Henry Handel Richardson* (1970); N Palmer, *Henry Handel Richardson: a Study* (1950)

Richardson, Ian William 1934–
Scottish actor
He was born in Edinburgh and trained at the Royal College of Dramatic Art in Glasgow. His many plays with the Royal Shakespeare Company include *A Midsummer Night's Dream* (1962), *The Tempest* (1970) and *Richard III* (1975). His other theatre work includes Broadway appearances in *My Fair Lady* (1976) and *Lolita* (1981). He made his television debut in *As You Like It* (1962) and followed it with appearances in *Tinker, Tailor, Soldier, Spy* (1979), *Porterhouse Blue* (1987), *The Winslow Boy* (1989) and as Francis Urquhart in *House of Cards* (1990), *To Play the King* (1993) and *The Final Cut* (1995). His film appearances include *A Midsummer Night's Dream* (1968), *The Darwin Adventure* (1971), *Brazil* (1985), *The Fourth Protocol* (1987) and *Cry Freedom* (1987).

Richardson, Sir John 1787–1865
Scottish naturalist and explorer
Born in Dumfries, Dumfries and Galloway region, he was a surgeon in the Royal Navy (1807–55), and served in the Arctic expeditions of **Sir William Parry** and **Sir John Franklin** (1819–22, 1825–27), and the Franklin search expedition of 1848–49. He wrote *Fauna Boreali-Americana* (1829–37) and *Ichthyology of the Voyage of HMS Erebus and Terror* (1844–48), and made great contributions to the knowledge of ichthyology of the Indo-Pacific region especially.

Richardson, Lewis Fry 1881–1953
English philosopher and meteorologist

Born in Newcastle upon Tyne, he graduated from Cambridge in 1903 and became superintendent of the Eskdalemuir Observatory (1913). Later he held a teaching post at Westminster Training College (1920–29), and was Principal of Paisley Technical College (1929–40). In the first attempt at weather forecasting, he observed different points in the atmosphere and used fundamental equations to calculate the conditions at these points six hours ahead. The resulting forecast was a failure, but his ideas formed the basis on which more powerful computers now perform numerical weather prediction. His book *Weather Prediction by Numerical Process* (1922) describes his work. Richardson also carried out original research on turbulence, devising the Richardson number of atmospheric turbulence.

Richardson, Sir Owen Willans 1879–1959
English physicist and Nobel Prize winner
Born in Dewsbury, Yorkshire, he was educated at Cambridge, where at the Cavendish Laboratory he began his famous work on thermionics, a term he coined to describe the phenomenon of the emission of electricity from hot bodies. For this work he was awarded the Nobel Prize for physics in 1928. He was appointed Professor of Physics at King's College London, in 1914, and from 1924 to 1944 was Yarrow Research Professor of the Royal Society.

Richardson, Sir Ralph David 1902–83
English actor
Born in Cheltenham, Gloucestershire, he established his reputation with the Birmingham Repertory Company from 1926. He moved to the Old Vic Company (1930), taking many leading parts, including the title roles of **W Somerset Maugham**'s *Sheppey* (1930–32) and **J B Priestley**'s *Johnson over Jordan* (1938) and later leading its postwar revival, as co-director after his service in World War II. He played with the Stratford-on-Avon company (1952), and toured Australia and New Zealand (1955). His many stage appearances included *Home at Seven*, *The White Carnation*, *A Day at the Sea* and, later, *West of Suez* (1971), *The Cherry Orchard* (1978) and *The Understanding* (1982). His films include *Things to Come* (1936), *Anna Karenina* (1948), *The Heiress* (1949), *Dr Zhivago* (1965), *Oh, What a Lovely War* (1969), *A Doll's House* (1973) and *Invitation to the Wedding* (1983). 📖 Gary O'Connor, *Ralph Richardson: An Actor's Life* (1982)

Richardson, Robert Coleman 1937–
US physicist and Nobel Prize winner
Born in Washington DC, he studied at Virginia Polytechnical Institute and State University and at Duke University. After serving in the US army he worked as a research associate at Cornell University (1966–67). There he became assistant Professor of Physics (1968–71), associate Professor (1972–74), then Professor (1975–   ). His research on the changing pressures of superfluids near freezing point and the co-discovery of the isotope helium-3 (3He) led to his being jointly awarded the 1996 Nobel Prize for physics with **David Lee** and **Douglas Osheroff**.

Richardson, Samuel 1689–1761
English novelist
Born in Mackworth, Derbyshire, he was apprenticed to a printer, married his master's daughter, and set up in business for himself in Salisbury Court, London. Although he was represented as the model parent and champion of women, his three daughters seem to have had a repressed upbringing. His first novel, *Pamela* (1740), is 'a series of familiar letters ... published in order to cultivate the Principles of Virtue and Religion', and this was the aim of all his works. In his second novel, *Clarissa, Or the History of a Young Lady* (7 vols, 1748), Richardson depicts the high life, of which he confessed he knew little, but the

Richelieu, Armand Jean Duplessis, Duc de, *known as* Cardinal Richelieu 1585–1642
French prelate and statesman

Richelieu was born into a noble but impoverished family near Chinon, and was consecrated Bishop of Luçon, which was in the family's control, at the age of 22. In 1614 he became adviser to **Marie de Médicis**, regent for her son **Louis XIII**, and in 1616 he rose to be Secretary for War and Foreign Affairs. In 1622 he was made cardinal, in 1624 Minister of State to **Louis XIII**. In this capacity he made an alliance with Great Britain, which he strengthened by the marriage (1625) of the king's sister **Henrietta Maria** with **Charles I**.

One of his principal aims was to destroy the political power of the Huguenots. La Rochelle was starved into submission (1628), and he destroyed Montauban, the last refuge of Huguenot independence. From 1629 he was Chief Minister and effective ruler of France. In 1630 he entered Italy with a large army and reduced Savoy. He sought to reduce the power of the **Habsburgs** by supporting the Protestants of the North and **Gustav II Adolf** of Sweden, to whom he gave large subsidy, and the two treaties of Cherasco (1631) gave France a strategic supremacy. Meanwhile Richelieu successfully overcame a powerful conspiracy launched against him by the queen mother, the House of **Guise** and others. He was made duke, and Governor of Brittany. Further intrigues and attempted rebellions were crushed with merciless severity.

In July 1632 Richelieu seized the Duchy of Lorraine, and in 1635 entered the Thirty Years War by declaring war on Spain. After some initial reverses, he swept the enemy out of Picardy while Bernard of Saxe-Weimar drove them across the Rhine, and in 1638 destroyed the imperial army at Rheinfelden. His policy soon led to the disorganization of the power of Spain, and to the victories of Wolfenbüttel and Kempten over the imperialist forces in Germany, and at length in 1641 in Savoy, as well as to the ascendancy of the French party.

At home the great French nobles continued to plot his downfall, and his safety lay in the king's helplessness without him. The last conspiracy against him was that of Henri Cinq-Mars, whose intrigues with the Duke of Bouillon and the Spanish court were soon revealed to the cardinal by means of a network of espionage which covered the whole of France. Cinq-Mars and De Thou were arrested and executed.

At the cost of high taxation and the suppression of constitutional government, Richelieu had built up the power of the French Crown and achieved for France a dominating position in Europe. Although he put what he thought were the interests of his country before personal ambition, he too often forgot in his methods the laws of morality and humanity.

📖 Richelieu had a considerable literary ambition. His *Mémoires* are still read with interest. Other works include *Instruction du chrétien* (1619) and *Traité de la perfection du chrétien* (1646). He founded the French Academy in 1634. See also William F Church, *Richelieu and Reason of State* (1973); D P O'Connell, *Richelieu* (1968); C V Wedgwood, *Richelieu and the French Monarchy* (1962).

> *Savoir dissimuler est le savoir des rois.*
> 'Knowing how to dissimulate is the knowledge of kings.'
> From *Mirame* (1641).
>
> *Qu'on me donne six lignes écrites de la main de plus honnête homme, j'y trouverai de quoi le faire pendre.*
> 'Give me six lines written by the hand of an honourable man, and I will find in them something to make him hang.'
> Attributed.

---

novel made Richardson famous, and he became acquainted with **Dr Johnson** and **Edward Young** among others. His third novel, *Sir Charles Grandison* (1754), designed to portray the perfect gentleman, turns on the question of divided love. His work influenced writers such as **Jean Jacques Rousseau** and **Denis Diderot**, and the epistolary method was a means to suggest authenticity at a time when mere fiction was frowned upon. 📖 I Watt, *The Rise of the Novel* (1957); A Dobson, *Samuel Richardson* (1902)

Richelieu, Armand Jean Duplessis, Duc de
See panel above

Richepin, Jean 1849–1926
French poet, playwright and novelist
Born in Médéa, Algeria, the son of a doctor, he began studying medicine but turned to literature at the École Normale. He was a sailor and actor before the appearance of his first romance in 1872. In his poetry he focused on the lower levels of society, using bold imagery, and his revolutionary book of poems, *La Chanson des gueux* (1876, 'The Beggars' Song'), led to a fine and his imprisonment due to its coarse language. 📖 A Zevcas, *Les Procès littéraires au XIXième siècle* (1924)

Richet, Charles Robert 1850–1935
French physiologist and Nobel Prize winner
Born and educated in Paris, he was professor there from 1887 to 1927. For his work on the phenomenon of anaphylaxis (a sometimes fatal susceptibility to injected foreign material brought about by a previous introduction of it), he was awarded the 1913 Nobel Prize for physiology or medicine. He also undertook research on serum therapy.

Richier, Germaine 1904–59
French sculptor
Born in Grans, near Arles, she studied at the École des Beaux-Arts, Montpellier, and then studied in Paris under **Émile Bourdelle**. She is best known for her insect-like figures which, with their lacerated, pock-marked skin and metal wires defining their space, express a situation of entrapment or struggle for survival, eg *Storm Man* (1948, Tate, London, cast 1995), *Hurricane Woman* (1949, Tate) and *Diabolo* (1950, Tate, cast 1994). She exhibited widely in Europe and the USA, and in Brazil and Jerusalem. The 1958 Venice Biennale was her fourth and last. Late work includes *Christ on the Cross* (Assy) and her painted *Chess Pieces* (1959).

Richler, Mordecai 1931–
Canadian novelist
Born in Montreal, he grew up in a Jewish working-class neighbourhood and attended Baron Byng high school and Sir George Williams College. He travelled in Europe, but returned to Canada in 1952, working for the Canadian Broadcasting Corporation before moving to England in 1959, since when he has been a professional writer. His first novel, *The Acrobats* (1954), owed much to **Ernest Hemingway** and he subsequently disowned it. In 1955 he published *Son of a Smaller Hero*, about a young man endeavouring to escape the Jewish ghetto and North American society in general. It was the first of several books for which he was accused of anti-Semitism. It was followed by *A Choice of Enemies* (1957), and he achieved a breakthrough with *The Apprenticeship of Duddy Kravitz* (1959), about an endearing shyster. Subsequent novels, such as *The Incomparable Atuk* (1963), *Cocksure* (1968), *St Urbain's Horseman* (1971) and *Solomon Gursky Was Here* (1990), have enhanced his reputation as one of Canada's richest

novelists, a bawdy humorist and vitriolic satirist. He published an autobiography in 1972 entitled *The Street*, and a volume of memoirs, *This Year in Jerusalem*, in 1994. ◻ V Ramraj, *Mordecai Richler* (1983)

Richmond, John 1960–
English fashion designer

Brought up in Rochdale, Greater Manchester, he studied design at Kingston Polytechnic, producing 22 designs for his degree show. When he first made his mark in the fashion world in the 1980s, in partnership with Maria Cornejo, his hallmark was the combination of traditional British materials, such as flannel, gaberdine and pin-stripes, with bikers' leather jackets. The partnership was dissolved in 1986, after which he concentrated on his own label and his shop in Soho. In 1993 he exhibited in Paris for the first time, combining leather and traditional fabrics in new ways.

Richmond, Sir Mark Henry 1931–
British microbiologist

Born in Sydney, Australia, he studied in England at Cambridge, and then became a member of the Medical Research Council scientific staff, taking up a readership in molecular biology at the University of Edinburgh in 1965. In the area of antibiotic resistance, Richmond showed the importance of DNA-mediated resistance to antibiotics, and also demonstrated that resistant organisms often occur in areas of high antibiotic usage, eg in hospitals. In 1968 he took up the chair of bacteriology at the University of Bristol, leaving in 1981 to become Vice-Chancellor and Professor of Molecular Microbiology at the University of Manchester. Since 1981 his main activities have concerned university education and the development of policies concerned with science. From 1990 to 1994 he was chairman of the Science and Engineering Research Council. Active on many national bodies, he was elected FRS in 1980 and knighted in 1986.

Richter, Burton 1931–
US particle physicist and Nobel Prize winner

He was born in New York City, and graduated from the Massachusetts Institute of Technology (MIT), where he received his PhD in 1956. He then joined the high-energy physics laboratory at Stanford University, where he became professor in 1967. He was largely responsible for the Stanford Positron–Electron Accelerating Ring (SPEAR), an accelerator designed to collide positrons and electrons at high energies, and to study the resulting elementary particles. In 1974 he led a team which discovered the J/y hadron, a new heavy elementary particle which supported **Sheldon Glashow**'s hypothesis of charm quarks. Many related particles were subsequently discovered, and stimulated a new look at the theoretical basis of particle physics. He shared the 1976 Nobel Prize for physics with **Samuel Ting**, who had discovered the J/y almost simultaneously. Richter became a strong proponent of the modern trend in particle physics towards building ever-larger particle accelerator rings.

Richter, Charles Francis 1900–85
US seismologist

He was born near Hamilton, Ohio. Educated at Stanford University and the California Institute of Technology (Caltech), he worked at the Carnegie Institute where he met **Beno Gutenberg** and became interested in seismology, before returning in 1936 to the California Institute of Technology. With Gutenberg he devised the Richter scale of earthquake strength (1927–35). In 1937 he returned to Caltech where he spent the rest of his career, as research assistant and Professor of Seismology from 1952. He played a key role in establishing the southern California seismic array and published *Seismicity of the Earth* (1954, with Gutenberg) and *Elementary Seismology* (1958).

Richter, Conrad Michael 1890–1968
US novelist and short-story writer

Born in Pine Grove, Pennsylvania, he moved to New Mexico after working variously as a farm hand, clerk and journalist, and he was profoundly affected by the landscape of the South West. His best-known novel, *The Sea of Grass* (1937), concerns a cattle baron. He then wrote a frontier trilogy, *The Trees* (1940), *The Fields* (1946) and *The Town* (1950), published in collected form as *The Awakening Land* (1966). Other novels include *Always Young and Fair* (1947), *The Light in the Forest* (1953), *The Waters of Kronos* (1960) and *The Mountain on the Desert* (1955). ◻ E Gaston, *Conrad Richter* (1965)

Richter, Hans 1843–1916
Hungarian conductor

Born in Raab, he conducted in Munich, Budapest and Vienna, then gave a series of annual concerts in London (1879–97). In 1893 he became first court kapellmeister at Vienna, and from 1897 to 1911 conducted the Hallé Orchestra. He was an authority on the music of **Richard Wagner**, with whom he was closely associated in the Bayreuth Festival.

Richter, Hieronymous Theodor 1824–98
German chemist

Born in Dresden, he became assistant to **Ferdinand Reich** at the Freiburg School of Mines and its director in 1875. Using spectroscopy and working in collaboration with Reich, Richter discovered the metal indium in zinc blende in 1863.

Richter, Jeremias Benjamin 1762–1807
German chemist

Born in Hirschberg, he spent seven years in the engineering corps of the Prussian army, studied mathematics and philosophy at the University of Königsberg, and after some years as an independent chemical consultant was appointed chemist to the Royal Porcelain Works in Berlin. He believed that all chemical reactions are guided by mathematical laws. He analysed a vast number of compounds to determine the proportions of their reagents by weight and described this new mathematical approach as 'stoichiometry'. Although his results demonstrated that reagents do indeed combine in fixed proportions, he never formulated this observation into a law and it was **Joseph Louis Proust**, working independently in France and Spain, who first proposed the 'law of definite proportions' in 1794. Richter's work was little noticed in his lifetime but its importance became apparent after the atomic theory of **John Dalton** provided the explanatory framework for his hypothesis in 1803.

Richter, Johann Paul Friedrich, *pseudonym* Jean Paul 1763–1825
German novelist and humorist

He was born in Wunsiedel, north Bavaria, and in 1781 was sent to Leipzig to study theology, but he turned to literature. He got into debt, and in 1784 fled to live in poverty with his widowed mother at Hof. From 1787 to 1796 he worked as a tutor, and wrote, among other works, the satirical *Auswahl aus des Teufels Papieren* (1789, 'Extracts from the Devil's Papers'), idylls such as *Dominie Wuz* (1793) and *Quintus Fixlein* (1796, translated by **Thomas Carlyle**, 1827), and the grand romances, *Die unsichtbare Loge* (1793, Eng trans *The Invisible Lodge*, 1883) and *Campanerthal* (1797). The *Invisible Lodge* was his first literary success, and *Hesperus* (1795, Eng trans 1865) made him famous. For a few years he was widely idolized. He married in 1801 and three years later settled at Bayreuth. His later works include the romances *Titan* (1800–03, Eng trans 1862), which he considered his masterpiece, and *Dr. Katzenbergers Badereise* (1809, 'Dr. Katzenberger's Trip to the Spa'), the best of his satirico-humorous writings. He also wrote reflections on literature (*Vorschule der Aesthetik*, improved edition 1812), various patriotic writings (1808–12), and an unfinished *Autobiography* (1826).

Richter, Svyatoslav Teofilovich 1915–97
Russian pianist

Born in Zhitomir, Ukraine, he studied at the Moscow Conservatory (1942–47). He made extensive concert tours, and with a repertoire ranging from **Bach** to 20th-century composers, he was awarded the Stalin prize in 1949, the Order of Lenin in 1965, and the Order of October Revolution in 1991.

Richthofen, Ferdinand Baron von 1833–1905
German geographer and traveller

Born in Karlsruhe, Silesia, he accompanied a Prussian expedition to eastern Asia in 1860, and during the next 12 years travelled in Java, Siam, Burma, California, the Sierra Nevada, and China and Japan (1868–72). After his return (1872) he became president of the Berlin Geographical Society (1873–78), Professor of Geology at Bonn (1875), and Professor of Geography at Leipzig (1883) and at Berlin (1886). His reputation rests upon his great works *China* (1877–1912) and *Aufgaben und Methoden der heutigen Geographie* (1833, 'Tasks and Methods of Present-day Geography').

Richthofen, Manfred, Baron von 1882–1918
German airman

Born in Schweidnitz, he joined the cavalry and then the German air force. During World War I, as commander of the 11th Chasing Squadron ('Richthofen's Flying Circus'), he was noted for his high number (80) of aerial victories. He was shot down behind the British lines.

Rickenbacker, Eddie (Edward Vernon) 1890–1973
US aviator

Born in Columbus, Ohio, his skill as a leading racing-car driver earned him the position of chauffeur to General **Pershing** in World War I. He applied for aviation duties, and in four months of combat flying scored 26 victories, receiving a hero's welcome in the USA and the Congressional Medal of Honor. He returned to motor racing and formed the Rickenbacker Motor Company (1921), and joined Eastern Air Lines in 1934 as a pilot. During World War II he undertook a wide range of assignments in military aviation.

Rickert, Heinrich 1863–1936
German philosopher

Born in Danzig (Gdansk, Poland), he became professor at Freiburg (1894) and Heidelberg (1916). He was a pupil of **Wilhelm Windelband**, and with him a founder of the Baden school of neo-Kantianism, which developed a distinctive theory of historical knowledge and the foundations of the social sciences. Rickert argued for a *Kulturwissenschaft* (science of culture) which could be an objective science of those universal concepts like religion, art and law that emerge from the multiplicity of individual cultures and societies. His views were strongly contrasted to those of **Wilhelm Dilthey** and were a great influence on **Max Weber** and others. His most notable publications are *Die Grenzen der naturwissenschaftlichen Begriffsbildung* (1896–1902, 'The Boundaries of the Scientific Forming of Concepts') and *Kulturwissenschaft und Naturwissenschaft* (1899, 'The Science of Culture').

Rickey, (Wesley) Branch, *nicknamed the* Mahatma 1881–1965
US baseball manager and administrator

Born in Stockdale, Ohio, he had a profound influence on top-class baseball. In 1919, as manager of the St Louis Cardinals, he introduced the 'farm system' whereby major league clubs linked themselves to lower-grade clubs to develop their own young players. This brought his team four world championships and made them the most profitable in baseball. While manager of the Brooklyn Dodgers (1942–50) he signed the first major league black baseball player, **Jackie Robinson**. In 1967 he was posthumously elected to the National Baseball Hall of Fame.

Rickman, Alan 1947–
English actor

Born in London of Irish–Welsh parents, he trained at RADA then worked for various theatre companies in England. He was spotted playing Valmont in *Les Liaisons Dangereuses* on Broadway by a Hollywood scout in 1985 and was hired to play Hans Gruber in the hugely successful action film *Die Hard*. He won a BAFTA Best Supporting Actor award for his Sheriff of Nottingham in *Robin Hood, Prince of Thieves* in 1991. His other films include *Truly, Madly, Deeply* (1991), *Close My Eyes* (1991), *Sense and Sensibility* (1995) and *Michael Collins* (1996). His television work includes *The Barchester Chronicles* (1982) and *Rasputin* (1996), for which he received an Emmy award. In 1996 he directed his first film, *The Winter Guest*.

Rickover, Hyman George 1900–86
US naval engineering officer

Born in Makov, Russia (now in Poland), he was taken to the USA as a child. He graduated from the US Naval Academy in 1922, and in 1929 received a master's degree in electrical engineering from Columbia University. His greatest achievement was leadership of the team that successfully adapted nuclear reactors as a means of ship propulsion, the first vessel so equipped being the USS *Nautilus*, the world's first nuclear submarine, launched in 1954.

Rickword, Edgell 1898–1982
English poet and critic

He was born in Colchester and educated at Oxford. The youngest of the trench poets in World War I, he was influenced originally by **Siegfried Sassoon** but came to find his own voice, which found expression in erotic and satirical lyrics as well as Symbolist poetry. His first published work was *Behind the Eyes* in 1921. Later collected editions of poetry (1947, 1970, 1976) found gradual favour. A socialist from boyhood, he joined the Communist Party in 1934, edited the influential *Left Review*, joined the International Union of Revolutionary Writers and became known for uncompromising Far-Left orthodoxy; he left the communists, however, in the exodus of 1956. ▥ C Hobday, *Edgell Rickword: A Poet at War* (1989)

Ricoeur, Paul 1913–
French philosopher

Born in Valence, Drôme, and educated at the Lycée de Rennes and at the University of Paris, he became professor successively at Strasbourg (1948–56), Paris-Nanterre (1956–70) and Chicago (1970). He was a pupil of **Gabriel Marcel**, and as a prisoner in World War II studied **Karl Jaspers**, **Martin Heidegger** and **Edmund Husserl**. Their influence is evident in his work, and he published commentaries on Husserl—in particular *Husserl: an analysis of his Phenomenology* (1967) and *Entretiens Paul Ricoeur-Gabriel Marcel* (1973, 'Conversations Paul Ricœur–Gabriel Marcel', a dialogue with Marcel). He has been an influential figure in both French and Anglo-US philosophy, engaging critically with various contemporary methodologies across a wide range of problems about the nature of language, interpretation, human action and will, freedom and evil. His other publications include a major work on the will, *Philosophie de la volonté* (3 vols, 1950–60, *Philosophy of the Will*), *Histoire et Vérité* (1955, *History and Truth*), *De l'interprétation: Essai sur Freud* (1965, *Freud and Philosophy*) and *La Métaphore vive* (1975, 'The Living Metaphor').

Riddell, George Allardice Riddell, 1st Baron
1865–1934
Scottish lawyer and newspaper proprietor
Born in Duns, Berwickshire and educated in London, he rose from boy clerk to solicitor. Through one of his clients, the Cardiff *Western Mail*, he became further involved in the newspaper world, at first as legal adviser to the *News of the World*, later as its chairman. He also became chairman of George Newnes, Ltd, and was knighted in 1909. He represented the British press at the Paris peace conference in 1919, and was raised to the peerage the following year.

Riddell, William Renwick 1852–1945
Canadian judge and legal historian
He was educated at Cobourg Collegiate Institute, Victoria University and Syracuse University. He was a judge of the High Court of Ontario from 1906 and of the Supreme Court of Canada from 1917. A prolific writer, he made notable contributions to Canadian history, particularly legal history, such as *The Legal Profession of Upper Canada in its Early Years* (1916) and *The Bar and the Courts of the Province of Upper Canada or Ontario* (1928). In addition, he wrote biographies of early Canadian public men and judges, as well as a large number of papers in legal and historical journals.

Ride, Sally Kristen 1951–
US astronaut, the first US woman in space
Born in Los Angeles, she was educated at Westlake High School, Los Angeles, then enrolled at Stanford University, where she studied physics and English, taking a doctoral degree in physics in 1978. While a student she achieved national ranking as a tennis player, but chose not to take up the sport as a career. In 1978 she was selected as an astronautical candidate by NASA (National Aeronautics and Space Administration), and she became a mission specialist on Space Shuttle flight crews, including a six-day flight of the orbiter Challenger in 1983. In 1987, her final year as an astronaut, she published a report to the NASA on 'Leadership—and America's Future in Space'. Since 1989 she has been Professor of Physics at the University of California, San Diego, and director of the California Space Institute. She co-wrote *To Space and Back* in 1986.

Rideal, Sir Eric Keightley 1890–1974
English physical chemist
Born in Sydenham, Kent, he took the Natural Sciences Tripos at Trinity Hall, Cambridge. Thereafter he studied in Aachen and in Bonn, gaining a doctorate from Bonn in 1912 for a thesis on the electrochemistry of uranium. In 1920 he was appointed H O Jones Lecturer in Physical Chemistry at Cambridge. From 1930 to 1946 he was Professor of Colloid Science at Cambridge, and for three further years Fullerian Professor at the Royal Institution. From 1950 to 1955 he was Professor of Physical Chemistry at King's College London. Rideal's work during World War I aroused his interest in catalysis, and in his spare time he wrote *Catalysis in Theory and Practice* (1919, with Hugh Taylor). In World War II the Colloid Science Laboratory under his direction was much involved in work on explosives, fuels and polymers. He was awarded an MBE in 1918 and knighted in 1951. He was elected a Fellow of the Royal Society in 1930 and awarded its Davy Medal in 1951. He served as president of the Chemical Society from 1950 to 1952 and of the Faraday Society from 1938 to 1945.

Ridge, William Pett 1857–1930
English writer
He was born in Chatham, Kent, educated at the Birkbeck Institution, London, and worked as a civil servant for several years before taking up journalism and writing. A prolific writer of novels, he published over 60 books in all, and is best known as an exponent of cockney humour, in works including *A Clever Wife* (1895) and *Mord Em'ly* (1898).

Ridgeway, John 1938–
English transatlantic oarsman and explorer
Educated at the Nautical College, Pangbourne, he served in the Merchant Navy, before completing his national service with the Royal Engineers. After two years at the Royal Military Academy, Sandhurst, he was commissioned into the Parachute Regiment and served in Canada, Norway, Greece, the Arabian Gulf, Kenya and Malaysia. In 1966 he rowed across the Atlantic Ocean in 92 days from the USA to Eire with Chay Blyth. He then sailed the Atlantic Ocean single-handed to South America, led an expedition along the Amazon River from its source to the sea, and another across the Chilean ice-cap. He participated in the 1977–78 Round the World Race with a team from the School of Adventure run from his home at Ardmore in Scotland.

Ridgway, Matthew B(unker) 1895–1993
US general
Born in Fort Monroe, Virginia, he trained at West Point, then commanded the 82nd Airborne Division in Sicily (1943) and Normandy (1944). He commanded the 18th Airborne Corps in the North West Europe campaign (1944–45) and the US 8th Army in United Nations operations in Korea (1950). He replaced Douglas MacArthur as commander of US and UN forces in Korea and in occupied Japan (1951), and succeeded General Eisenhower as supreme allied commander in Europe (1952–53). He later served as army Chief of Staff (1953), and was awarded the Presidential Medal of Freedom in 1986.

Ridgway, Robert 1850–1929
US ornithologist
Born in Mount Carmel, Illinois, he was curator of birds at the US National Museum, and devised the Ridgway colour system for bird identification. His books include *A History of North American Birds* (1874–84) and *The Birds of Middle and North America* (8 vols, 1901–19).

Riding, Laura, *née* Reichenfeld, *later* Laura Riding Jackson 1901–91
US poet, critic, story writer, novelist and polemicist
The daughter of an Austrian immigrant, she took courses at Cornell University, and married Louis Gottschalk, a history teacher there. Her first collection of poetry, *The Close Chaplet*, was published in England under the imprint of the Hogarth Press, which was run by Leonard and Virginia Woolf. She was the lover (1926–29) and then the literary associate (1929–39) of Robert Graves, with whom she lived in Mallorca, London and Rennes. In 1941 she married Schuyler Jackson, a minor poet and farmer, with whom she wrote an unpublished study of language. Her poetry is unlike any other poetry of the 20th century: based rhythmically on a four-accent line, it seeks to examine the reasons for human existence, and to establish the nature of human obligations. *First Awakenings* (1992), edited by her friend Robert Nye and assistants, adds considerably to the canon. ⬚ Riding's introduction to *Collected Poems* (1938); J P Wexler, *Laura Riding's Pursuit of Truth* (1979)

Ridley, Nicholas c.1500–55
English Protestant churchman
Born near Haltwhistle, Northumberland, he studied at Cambridge, Paris and Louvain (1527–30). His various posts included chaplain to Thomas Cranmer and Henry VIII, Master of Pembroke (1540), Bishop of Rochester (1547) and Bishop of London (1550). He was an outspoken reformer, and helped Cranmer to prepare the Thirty-Nine Articles. On the death of Edward VI he

denounced **Mary I** and **Elizabeth I** as illegitimate, and supported the cause of Lady **Jane Grey**. On Mary I's accession, he was imprisoned and executed.

Ridley (of Liddesdale), Nicholas Ridley, Baron 1929–93
English Conservative politician

He was born in Newcastle upon Tyne, the son of the 3rd Viscount Ridley. He was educated at Eton and Oxford, and embarked on an industrial career; later he turned to politics, winning the safe Conservative seat of Cirencester and Tewkesbury in 1959. He held junior ministerial posts under **Harold Macmillan**, Sir **Alec Douglas-Home** and **Edward Heath** (1962–70), and in 1979 joined the **Thatcher** government, entering the Cabinet in 1983. Regarded as one of Mrs Thatcher's closest allies, he moved from the Department of Environment (1986–89), where he was responsible for introducing the generally unpopular community charge (poll tax), to the Department of Trade and Industry (1988–90). He resigned his office following a controversial magazine article in which he denounced federalist European ideas and German ambitions. He retired from active politics the following year, and he was awarded a life peerage.

Ridolfo, Roberto di, *also called* Roberto Ridolfi 1531–1612
Florentine conspirator

He was born in Florence and went to London on business. In 1570 he organized a Roman Catholic plot, supported by Spain, to marry **Mary, Queen of Scots** to **Thomas Howard**, 4th Duke of Norfolk, and overthrow Queen **Elizabeth I**. The plot, which comprised the murder of Elizabeth and a Spanish invasion of England, was discovered when an emissary was seized. Ridolfo returned to Italy and in 1600 became a Florentine senator.

Rie, Dame Lucie, *née* Gomperz 1902–95
Austrian potter

Born in Vienna, she trained at the Kunstgewerbeschule. In 1938 she and her husband moved to England, where **Bernard Leach** was the dominant force in studio ceramics; he became a lifelong friend. From the end of World War II until 1960 she shared a workshop with **Hans Coper**, producing ceramic jewellery and buttons while continuing her individual work. She pioneered the production of stoneware in an electric kiln, and produced stoneware, tin-glazed earthenware and porcelain pots throughout her working life with a precision and technical control that influenced many leading contemporary potters. Her work bridged the gap between the craft of pottery and the art of sculpture. She was made a DBE in 1991 and a special exhibition was devoted to her work at the New York Metropolitan Museum of Art in 1994.

Riefenstahl, Leni (Helene Bertha Amalie) 1902–
German film director

Born in Berlin, she studied fine art and ballet and was a professional dancer before making her film debut in *Der Heilige Berg* (1926, 'The Holy Mountain'). She appeared in some of the mountaineering films made by Arnold Fanck (1889–1974), who has been credited with training her. In 1931 she formed Riefenstahl Films and made her directorial debut with *Das Blaue Licht* (1932, 'The Blue Light'). She was appointed film adviser to the Nationalist Socialist Party by **Hitler**. Both her *Triumph Des Willens* (1934, 'Triumph of the Will'), a compelling record of the Nuremberg rally, and *Olympische Spiele 1936* (1936, 'Olympiad') were propagandist documentaries of impressive technique. At the end of World War II she was interned by the Allies and held on charges of pro-Nazi activity, although these were subsequently dropped. She never fully went back to her filmmaking, and became a photo-

journalist under the name of Helen Jacobs, covering the 1972 Olympic Games for the *Sunday Times*. She published her autobiography, *The Sieve of Time*, in 1993.

Riegger, Wallingford 1885–1961
US composer

Born in Albany, Georgia, he studied at Cornell University, at the Institute of Musical Art, New York, and in Berlin. He later held posts at Drake University and the Ithaca Conservatory, New York. His works, which show the influence of **Arnold Schoenberg**'s twelve-note technique, received little attention until the performance of his 3rd Symphony in 1948, after which he was increasingly recognized. He wrote extensively for orchestra and for chamber music combinations.

Riel, Louis 1844–85
Canadian politician

He was born in St Boniface, Manitoba. He succeeded his father as a leader of the Métis of mixed Native American and French parentage, who were opposed to the incorporation of the North-West Territories into the Dominion of Canada as well as to the encroachment of white, English-speaking settlers on their lands in Manitoba. He headed the Red River Rebellion in 1869–70, setting up a provisional government with himself as president. The rebellion failed, and he was forced to flee to the USA, but he soon returned to Canada, and in 1873 he was elected to the House of Commons in Ottawa. After his re-election in 1874, a motion was introduced by Mackenzie Bowell demanding his expulsion from the House. He was finally granted an amnesty in 1875 on condition that he agreed to a further five years' exile. He spent this time as a schoolteacher in the USA. In 1884 Riel responded to the pleas of the Métis in Saskatchewan and became involved in a second rebellion. In 1885 he established another rebel government; the rebellion was suppressed, and he was hanged for treason.

Riemann, (Georg Friedrich) Bernhard 1826–66
German mathematician

Born in Breselenz, he studied in Göttingen, where he was appointed Professor of Mathematics in 1859. His first publication (1851) was on the foundations of the theory of functions of a complex variable, including the result now known as the Riemann mapping theorem. In a later paper on Abelian functions (1857), he introduced the idea of 'Riemann surface' to deal with 'multi-valued' algebraic functions; this was to become a key concept in the development of analysis. His famous lecture in 1854, 'On the hypotheses that underlie geometry', first presented his notion of an n-dimensional curved space. These ideas were essential in the formulation of **Albert Einstein**'s theory of general relativity, and have led to the modern theory of differentiable manifolds, which now plays a vital role in theoretical physics. Riemann's name is also associated with the zeta function, which is central to the study of the distribution of prime numbers. The 'Riemann hypothesis' is a famous unsolved problem concerning this function.

Riemenschneider, Tilman (Till) 1460–1531
German sculptor

Born in Osterode, he spent his life after 1483 in Würzburg, where he rose to become burgomaster, but was imprisoned for participating in the Peasants' Revolt of 1525. One of the great carvers of his time, he executed many fine sepulchral monuments and church decorations in the Gothic style. His best work, such as *Ascension of the Virgin* (Creglingen, altarpiece), was in wood, and he also worked in stone, notably on the tombs in Würzburg and Bamberg cathedrals.

Riemerschmid, Richard 1868–1957
German architect and designer

He was born in Munich, and in 1897, after varied experience, he founded *Werkstätten* (craft workshops) there, for which he designed furniture. His early furniture resembled the linear freedom of Art Nouveau without the naturalistic decoration, whereas his designs of 1905 for the Deutsche Werkstätten in Dresden were functional, of simple construction and suitable for mass production. He was a founder-member of the Deutsche Werkbund (1907). His large output over almost 50 years included building, furniture and interiors, glass and ceramics, cutlery, light-fittings and graphics. He was a major influence in 20th-century German design and industry.

Rienzo or Rienzi, Cola di c.1313–1354
Italian patriot

Born in Rome, he tried to persuade Pope Clement VI to return there from Avignon (1343), but failed. In 1347 he incited the citizens to rise against the nobles. The senators were driven out, and at Rienzo's request the Italian states sent deputies to Rome to devise measures for unification and common good, while he was crowned tribune. However, the nobles turned the papal authority against him and he fled to Naples. He returned to Rome in 1354, and tried to re-establish his position, but was killed in a rising against him. Richard Wagner's opera *Rienzi* (1840) was based on his life.

Riesener, Jean Paul 1734–1806
French cabinetmaker

Born in Gladbeck, Münster, Prussia (now in Germany), he worked in Paris from 1754. He became a master of marquetry and ebony work, and favoured by Louis XVI's court, became the best-known cabinetmaker.

Riesz, Frigyes (Frédéric) 1880–1956
Hungarian mathematician

Born in Györ, he studied at the universities of Zurich, Budapest and Göttingen, then returned to Hungary as a lecturer at the University of Szeged. In 1945 he was appointed Professor of Mathematics at the University of Budapest. He worked in functional analysis, integral equations and subharmonic functions, and developed a new approach to the Lebesgue integral. His work was instrumental in allowing the matrix and wave mechanics methods of quantum theory to be identified as equivalent. Riesz's textbook on functional analysis, *Leçons d'analyse fonctionnelle* ('Lessons of Functional Analysis', 1952) written with Bela Szökefalvi-Nagy (1887–1953), is regarded as a classic.

Rietschel, Ernst 1804–61
German sculptor

One of the Dresden school, he executed the Goethe and Schiller Monument at Weimar, the Martin Luther Memorial at Worms, and many other monuments and portrait busts.

Rietveld, Gerrit Thomas 1888–1964
Dutch architect and furniture designer

Born in Utrecht, he started his career as a woodworker, opening his own cabinetmaking workshop in Utrecht in 1911. He studied architecture at evening school, and started to make furniture designed by his teacher P J Klaarhamer. Inspired by these remarkable pieces, Rietveld began to design his own furniture, including the famous 'red-blue' chair of 1918. The exploitation of space and its relation to physical objects were at the core of all Rietveld's work. The architectural equivalent of the chair was the Schröder House in Utrecht (1924), both also exhibiting the rectilinear quality and use of colour associated with the De Stijl movement. He designed many buildings and pieces of furniture, and the culmination of his work is the building housing the Van Gogh Museum, Amsterdam, completed posthumously in 1973.

Rieu, E(mile) V(ictor) 1887–1972
English editor and translator

He was born in London. A classical scholar, he formed the habit of translating aloud to his wife, and it was her interest in *The Odyssey* that encouraged him to start on his own version. It was offered to Allen Lane, the founder of Penguin, and published in 1946. It formed the cornerstone of the new Penguin Classics of which Rieu became editor, and had sold over two million copies by 1964.

Rifkind, Sir Malcolm Leslie 1946–
Scottish Conservative politician

Born in Edinburgh, he was educated at George Watson's College and Edinburgh University, and became a barrister. He was Conservative MP for Edinburgh Pentlands from 1974 to 1997. Despite resigning from the Opposition front bench in protest at the anti-devolution policy of his party, he was appointed Scottish Office Minister (1979–82) and Foreign Office Minister (1982–86). After serving as the youngest-ever Secretary of State for Scotland (1986–90), he became Secretary of State for Transport in 1990, Defence Secretary in 1992 and Foreign Secretary in 1995. He lost his seat in the 1997 election when the Labour Party came to power, and was knighted that year.

Rigas, Velestinlis Pheraios 1757–98
Greek national hero, writer and revolutionary

He was well educated and worked for both the Phanariots in Constantinople (Istanbul) and the Danubian Principalities. He was inspired by the ideals of the Enlightenment and the French Revolution, and translated various French works into vernacular Greek and wrote many revolutionary pamphlets. In Vienna in 1796 he began publishing revolutionary literature, including the *Declaration of the Rights of Man*, and issued a map of the Balkan Peninsula and Asia Minor which anticipated the Greater Greece of the 'Megale Idea' ('Grand Scheme'). He drew up proposals for a Greek constitution and composed the *War Hymn* for which he is now best remembered. He was involved in many conspiracies, and eventually he was arrested by the Austrian government, handed over to the Ottoman authorities and executed.

Rigaud, Hyacinthe 1659–1743
French portrait painter

Born in Perpignan, he settled in Paris in 1681 as a portrait painter to the French court. His portrait of Louis XIV in full robes (1701) is in the Louvre.

Rigg, Dame (Enid) Diana (Elizabeth) 1938–
English actress

She was born in Doncaster, South Yorkshire, and after studying at RADA, made her professional debut in *The Caucasian Chalk Circle* (1957) at the York Festival. She appeared in repertory before joining the Royal Shakespeare Memorial Company (later the RSC) (1959–64). Her long and distinguished stage career includes *Twelfth Night* (1966) for the RSC, *Jumpers* (1972), *Macbeth* (1972) and *The Misanthrope* (1973) at the National Theatre, and such later productions as *Follies* (1987), *All For Love* (1991), *Medea* (1993–94, Tony award) and *Who's Afraid of Virginia Woolf?* (1996–97). On television, she won lasting fame as the leather-clad Emma Peel in *The Avengers* (1965–68). Her other television work includes her own series *Diana* (1973), *In This House of Brede* (1975), *King Lear* (1983), *Bleak House* (1984), and *Mother Love* (1989), for which she received a BAFTA award. Her films include *On Her Majesty's Secret Service* (1969) and *The Hospital* (1971). She was made a DBE in 1994 and has compiled a volume of theatrical anecdotes, *No Turn Unstoned* (1982).

Righi, Augusto 1850–1920
Italian physicist

Born in Bologna, he was educated in his home town, taught physics at Bologna Technical College (1873–80), and left to take up the newly established chair of physics at the University of Palermo. He was Professor of Physics at the University of Padua (1885–89) and later returned to a professorship at Bologna. He invented an induction electrometer (1872) capable of detecting and amplifying small electrostatic charges, formulated mathematical descriptions of vibrational motion, and discovered magnetic hysteresis (1880). He was the first person to generate microwaves, and opened a whole new area of the electromagnetic spectrum to research and subsequent application. His *L'ottica delle oscillazioni elettriche* (1897), which summarized his results, is considered a classic of experimental electromagnetism. By 1900 he had begun to work on X-rays and the **Zeeman** effect. In 1903 he wrote the first paper on wireless telegraphy. He also studied gas under various conditions of pressure and ionization, and worked on improvements to the **Michelson–Morley** experiment from 1918.

Riis, Jacob August   1849–1914
US journalist and social critic

Born in Ribe, Denmark, he emigrated to the USA in 1870, and became a police reporter on the New York *Tribune* (1877–88) and *Sun* (1888–99). He published a horrifying description of immigrant poverty in New York in 1890 which he called *How the Other Half Lives*, and which marked the first use of photographic evidence in social reportage. He supported the reforms of **Theodore Roosevelt** and wrote a study of him; he also published an autobiography, *The Making of an American* (1901). He was active in the movement for small parks and playgrounds, and for the reform of tenement housing and schools.

Riisager, Knudåge   1897–1975
Danish composer

Born in Port Kunda, Russia, he had returned with his parents to Denmark by 1900. He took a degree in political economy at Copenhagen, then went to Paris, where he studied under Paul le Flem and **Albert Roussel**, and was influenced by other French composers. On his return to Denmark he shocked conventional musical circles by his revolutionary compositions and writings. Polytonality, polyrhythm and unique syncopations are predominant in his works, which include the overtures *Erasmus Montanus* and *Klods Hans*, as well as symphonies, ballets (including *Quarrtsiluni*, 1942) and a piano sonata (1931).

Riley, Bridget Louise   1931–
English painter

Born in London, she studied at Goldsmith's College of Art (1949–52) and at the Royal College of Art (1952–55), holding her first one-woman show in London in 1962. A leading Op artist, she manipulates overall flat patterns, originally in black and white but later in colour, using repeated shapes or undulating lines, often creating an illusion of movement, as in *Fall* (1963, Tate Gallery, London) and *Winter Palace* (1981, Rowan Gallery, London). She was the first English painter to win the major painting prize at the Venice Biennale (1968). A visit to Egypt in 1981 resulted in a warmer range of colours, and inspired her decorative scheme for the Royal Liverpool Hospital in 1983. Recent retrospectives of her work have been held at the Hayward Gallery, London (1992) and the Tate (1994). 📖 *Maurice de Sausmarez, Bridget Riley* (1970)

Riley, James Whitcomb   1849–1916
US poet

Born in Greenfield, Indiana, he was dismissed from a newspaper job early in his career after forging a poem attributed to **Edgar Allan Poe**. He made his name from contributing dialect poems to the *Indianapolis Journal*

(1877–85), and went on to publish several volumes of poetry. He was called the 'Hoosier Poet' and is also known for his poems about children, including 'Little Orfant Annie' and 'The Raggedy Man', published under the pseudonym Benjamin F Johnson. 📖 *P Revell, James Whitcomb Riley* (1970)

Rilke, Rainer Maria   1875–1926
Austrian lyric poet

Born in Prague, he left his military academy to study art history in Prague, Munich and Berlin. His early works include *Vom lieben Gott und Anderes* (1900, Eng trans *Stories of God*, 1931) and *Das Stundenbuch* (1905, Eng trans *Poems from the Book of Hours*, 1941), written after two journeys to Russia (1899–1900), where he met **Leo Tolstoy** and was influenced by Russian Pietism. In 1901 he married Klara Westhoff, a pupil of **Auguste Rodin**, whose secretary Rilke became in Paris, publishing *Auguste Rodin* (1903, Eng trans 1919). He also wrote *Neue Gedichte* (1907, 1908, 'New Poems') and *Die Aufzeichnungen des Malte Laurids Brigge* (1910, Eng trans *Journal of My Other Self*, 1930), a key text of existentialism which prefigured such works as **Jean-Paul Sartre**'s *La Nausée*. In 1923 he wrote his two major works, *Die Sonnette an Orpheus* (Eng trans *Sonnets to Orpheus*, 1936) and *Duineser Elegien* (Eng trans *Duino Elegies*, 1939). He is one of the most important figures in modern European literature. 📖 *J F Hendry, The Sacred Threshold* (1983)

Rimbaud, (Jean Nicolas) Arthur   1854–91
French poet

He was born in Charleville, Ardennes, the son of an army captain and his stern disciplinarian wife. After a brilliant academic career at the Collège de Charleville, in 1870 he published his first book of poems and ran away to Paris. He soon returned to Charleville, where he lived as a writer and indulged in a life of leisure, drinking and bawdy conversation. There he published *Le Bateau ivre* (1871, Eng trans *The Drunken Boat*, 1952) which, with its verbal eccentricities, daring imagery and evocative language, is among his most popular works. Soon after its publication in August 1871, **Paul Verlaine** invited him to Paris, where they began a homosexual relationship. In Brussels in July 1873 he threatened to terminate the friendship; Verlaine shot and wounded him, and was imprisoned for attempted murder. From the summer of 1872, when the relationship was at its strongest, date many of his *Les Illuminations* (Eng trans 1971), which most clearly state his poetic doctrine. These prose and verse poems show Rimbaud as a precursor of Symbolism, especially in his use of childhood, dream and mystical images to express dissatisfaction with the material world and a longing for the spiritual. In 1873 he published *Une Saison en enfer* (Eng trans *A Season in Hell*, 1939), a prose volume which symbolized his struggle to break with his past. He was bitterly disappointed at its cool reception by the literary critics, burned all his manuscripts, and at the age of 19 turned his back on literature. For a time he occupied himself travelling in Europe and the East, taking on the role of soldier, trader, explorer and gunrunner. Meanwhile, in 1866, Verlaine published *Les Illuminations* as by the 'late Arthur Rimbaud'. Rimbaud knew of the sensation they caused and the reputation they were making for him, but reacted with indifference. In 1891, troubled by a leg infection, he left Harar and sailed to Marseilles; there his leg was amputated, and he died. 📖 *E Starkie, Rimbaud* (1961)

Rimet, Jules   1871–1956
French football administrator

Born in Theuley, he is sometimes called the 'Father of the World Cup'. He became a lawyer, and dedicated most of his life to FIFA (Fédération Internationale de Football Association), working to establish the World Cup as the main focus for international football. When he joined FIFA as France's representative, there were just 20 members; by 1955, when he left, there were 85. (And by 1990, there were 160.) He played a part in creating the first World Cup in 1930, persuaded FIFA to choose Uruguay as the venue; he also provided the 30.5cm, 3.6kg solid gold statue sculpted by Abel Lafleur, which became known as the Jules Rimet trophy.

Rimington, Dame Stella 1935–
English former director-general of the Secret Service
Born in London, she read English at Edinburgh University, then joined MI5, evidently playing an important part in the F2 branch, which deals with domestic 'subversion'. Towards the end of the 1980s she became director of counter-terrorist activities, and was appointed director-general of MI5 in 1992, the first woman to hold the post, and the first of either sex to be identified publicly. She retired in 1996, and was made a DCB (Dame Commander of the Order of the Bath) the same year.

Rimini, Francesca da See Francesca da Rimini

Rimsky-Korsakov, Nikolai Andreyevich
1844–1908
Russian composer
Born in Tikhvin, Novgorod, he was introduced in 1861 to Mili Balakirev, who became his friend and mentor, and in 1865 to Mussorgsky, who encouraged him to write his 1st Symphony. In 1871 he became a professor at the St Petersburg Conservatory, where he worked hard on his technique. He arranged and reorchestrated much of Mussorgsky's output at this time. In 1887–88 he produced his three great orchestral works, *Capriccio Espagnol, Easter Festival* and *Scheherazade*. He then turned to opera, in which his best known works are *The Snow Maiden* (1882, *Snegurochka*), *Legend of Tsar Saltan* (1900), *The Invisible City of Kitesh* (1906, *Skazaniye o neridimom grade Kitezhe*) and *The Golden Cockerel* (1907, *Zolotoy petushok*), his last work, based on a satire against autocracy by Alexander Pushkin and banned at first from the Russian stage. His music is notable for its vitality and for its range of orchestral colour. Constantly aware of his earlier technical shortcomings, he rewrote almost all his early work. He also edited and arranged the works of other composers, notably Mussorgsky's *Boris Godunov*. Stravinsky was his pupil. His autobiography, *My Musical Life*, was translated into English by Joffe in 1942.

Ringan See Ninian, St

Rinuccini, Ottavio 1562–1621
Italian poet
He wrote *Dafne* (1594), the first Italian melodrama, based on the 3rd-century romance *Daphnis and Chloe* by Longus.
📖 E Li Gotti, *Restauri trecenteschi* (1947)

Ripken, Cal(vin Edwin) 1960–
US baseball player
Born in Havre de Grace, Maryland, the son of a Baltimore Orioles coach, he grew up with the team, questioning players about strategy and taking part in batting practices while still in high school. He was drafted by the Baltimore Orioles in 1981 and became the team's shortstop in 1982. A heavy hitter and skilful fielder, he was named the American League's most valuable player in 1983 and 1991. In 1995 he broke Lou Gehrig's 56-year-old record of 2,130 consecutive games played (1927–39), and amassed 2,632 before sitting one out in September 1998.

Ripley, George 1802–80
US social reformer and literary critic
Born in Greenfield, Massachusetts, he was a graduate of Harvard, and a Unitarian pastor in Boston until 1841. He joined the Transcendental Movement with Bronson Alcott, founded *The Dial* in 1840, and helped Margaret Fuller to edit it. In 1841 he organized and led the idealistic communal experiment at Brook Farm, near Boston, based on the socialist theories of Charles Fourier, but this was declared bankrupt in 1847. He became literary critic for the *New York Tribune* (1849–80). In 1850 he founded *Harper's New Monthly Magazine*, and was joint-editor with Charles Anderson Dana of the *New American Cyclopaedia* (1858–63).

Rippon (of Hexham), Geoffrey Rippon, Baron 1924–97
English Conservative politician
Educated at King's College, Taunton, and Brasenose College, Oxford, he practised as a barrister in his mid-twenties, and became increasingly active in local politics for the Conservative Party. He entered the House of Commons in 1955 and served in the governments of Harold Macmillan, Alec Douglas-Home and Edward Heath. A committed European, he led the UK delegation to the Council of Europe and the Western European Union (WEU) (1967–70). He left the House of Commons in 1987 to concentrate on business interests, and was made a life peer. He was a director of the Maxwell Communications Corporation (1986–92) when its financial dealings were investigated after the death of Robert Maxwell in 1991. In 1994 he became Pro-Chancellor of London University.

Riquet de Bonrepos, Pierre Paul, Baron 1604–80
French canal engineer
Born in Béziers, he became convinced, through his intimate knowledge of the region, of the practicality of a canal linking the Atlantic with the Mediterranean by way of the rivers Garonne and Aude. Eventually, through Jean-Baptiste Colbert, he obtained the support of Louis XIV, and work began in 1666. With a labour force of more than 8,000 he supervised the construction of the Languedoc Canal (also called the Canal du Midi) from Toulouse to Sète, a distance of 156 miles (260km) which required 100 locks, several aqueducts and a short tunnel. He died a few months before the completion of the canal in 1681.

Riskin, Robert 1897–1955
US playwright and screenwriter
He was born in New York City. After serving in the US navy during World War I, he turned to writing. He enjoyed success as a Broadway playwright before moving to Hollywood. From 1931 he was under contract to Columbia, where he worked in collaboration with director Frank Capra on a succession of sparkling popular comedies which often celebrated the idealism of the common man as he triumphed over the cynicism of his corrupt masters. He won an Academy Award for *It Happened One Night* (1934), and received further nominations for *Lady For A Day* (1933), *Mr Deeds Goes To Town* (1936) and *You Can't Take It With You* (1938). He also adapted James Hilton's *Lost Horizon* (1937) for the screen; and as a producer, he formed the Overseas Motion Picture Bureau in 1942. Ill health forced his early retirement, but his body of work was honoured with the Laurel award from the Writer's Guild of America in 1954.

Ristori, Adelaide, *also* Adelaide del Grillo
1822–1906
Italian tragedienne
She was born in Cividale, Friuli, Italy, and rapidly became the leading Italian actress of her day, although her marriage with the Marquis del Grillo (1847) temporarily interrupted her theatrical career. International recognition came in France in 1855, where she was regarded as a rival

to Élisa Rachel, in other European countries, the USA (1866, 1875, 1884–85) and South America. She wrote *Memoirs and Artistic Studies* (trans 1907).

Ritchie, Anne Isabella Thackeray, Lady
1837–1919
English writer
Born in London, she was the daughter of William Makepeace Thackeray. A close companion of her father and well acquainted with his literary and artistic friends, she contributed valuable personal reminiscences to an 1898–99 edition of his works. She also wrote memoirs of their contemporaries, including Tennyson and Ruskin. Her novels include *The Village on the Cliff* (1867), *Old Kensington* (1873) and *Mrs Dymond* (1885).

Ritchie, Sir Neil Methuen 1897–1983
Scottish soldier
Born in Essequibo, British Guiana, the son of a Scottish sugar planter, he was educated at Lancing College, Sussex, and Sandhurst, and was commissioned in the Black Watch in 1915. During World War I he served in Flanders and Mesopotamia and was awarded the DSO and MC for his bravery under fire. He commanded the King's Own Royal Regiment in Palestine (1938), and after the British withdrawal from Dunkirk was promoted major-general with responsibility for rebuilding the 51st (Highland) Division. In North Africa he caught the eye of Sir Claude Auchinleck and was given command of the 8th Army. It was an unhappy appointment for, although he raised the siege of Tobruk, he failed to counter Rommel's offensive in May 1942 and was relieved of his command. Although he was later promoted to the rank of general and given postwar command of the Far East Land Forces, his career never recovered from this setback.

Ritchie-Calder, Baron See Calder, Ritchie

Ritschl, Albrecht 1822–89
German Protestant theologian
Born in Berlin, he became Professor of Theology at Bonn (1851–64), where he had begun teaching in 1846, and at Göttingen (1864–89). His principal work is on the doctrine of justification and reconciliation (1870–74). Other works were on Christian perfection (1874), conscience (1876), pietism (1880–86), theology and metaphysics (1881). The distinguishing feature of the Ritschlian theology is the prominence it gives to the practical and ethical side of Christianity. He was the cousin of the German classical scholar Friedrich Wilhelm Ritschl (1806–76), who founded the Bonn school of classical scholarship. 📖 Otto Ritsch, *Albrecht Ritschls Leben* (2 vols, 1892–96)

Ritson, Joseph 1752–1803
English antiquary
Born in Stockton-on-Tees, Cleveland, he went to London in 1775 and practised as a conveyancer, also finding time to devote to antiquarian studies. He was as noted for his vegetarianism, whimsical spelling and irreverence as for his attacks on literary reputations. His first important work was an onslaught on Thomas Warton's *History of English Poetry* (1782). He assailed (1783) Dr Johnson and George Steevens (1736–1800) for their text of Shakespeare, and Thomas Percy for his *Reliques*, in *Select Collection of English Songs* (1783). In 1792 appeared his *Cursory Criticisms* on Edmund Malone's Shakespeare. He also exposed John Pinkerton's forgeries, in *Select Scottish Ballads* (1784), and the Shakespeare forgeries of Samuel Ireland.

Ritter, Johann Wilhelm 1776–1810
German physicist
Born in Samitz, Silesia (now in Poland), he was trained as an apothecary before studying medicine at the University of Jena. He taught at Jena and at Gotha before becoming a full member of the Bavarian Academy of Sciences in Munich (1804). While working in Jena in 1801 he discovered the ultraviolet rays in the spectrum, although his chief contributions are considered to be in electrochemistry and electrophysiology. He demonstrated in 1800 that galvanic electricity was a manifestation of electricity, made the first dry cell (1802), the first accumulator (1803), and was the first to propose an electrochemical series.

Ritter, Karl 1779–1859
German geographer
Born in Quedlinburg, he became Professor of Geography at Berlin (1829) and director of studies of the Military School. He laid the foundations of modern scientific geography in his most important work, *Die Erdkunde im Verhältniss zur Natur und Geschichte des Menschen* (1817, 'Earth Science in Relation to Nature and the History of Man'), stressing the relation between man and his natural environment. He also wrote a comparative geography (Eng trans 1865).

Rivadavia, Bernardino 1780–1845
Argentine politician
He was born in Buenos Aires and fought in the country's patriot militia which evicted the British in 1807. He supported the independence movement from Spain in 1810 and dominated the first revolutionary triumvirate in 1811. Greatly influenced by the reforms of Charles III of Spain and by the French radicals, and a convinced Benthamite, he initiated a torrent of legislation which decreed the end of the high courts (*audiencia*) and the slave trade, liberalized commerce and standardized the currency. When he returned to Argentina in 1821, after several years in Europe, he became a minister and propounded schemes to encourage immigration, abolished ecclesiastical privileges (*fueros*) and founded the University of Buenos Aires. His land law of 1824 established the system of landholding which is still in force. Elected President in 1826, he was forced to resign in the wake of the inconclusive conflict with Brazil and provincial reaction to his centralist constitution. He was exiled, and died in Paris.

Rivarol, Antoine 1753–1801
French writer
He was born in Bagnols, Languedoc, and went to Paris in 1780. There he adopted the aristocratic form 'Comte de', and worked his way into fashionable society, where he found much material for his sardonic writings. In 1788 he set the whole city laughing at the sarcasms in his *Petit Almanach de nos grands hommes* ('Little Almanac of Our Great Men'). He emigrated in 1792 and, supported by Royalist pensions, wrote pamphlets in Brussels, London, Hamburg and Berlin. 📖 A Le Breton, *Antoine Rivarol* (1896)

Rivera, Diego 1886–1957
Mexican painter
Born in Guanajuato, he won a travel scholarship to study in Madrid and Paris after a successful one-man show. He began a series of murals in public buildings in 1921, depicting the life and history (particularly the popular uprisings) of the Mexican people. From 1930 to 1934 he completed a number of frescoes in the USA, mainly of industrial life. His art is a blend of folk art and revolutionary propaganda, eg *The Agrarian Leader Zapata* (1931, Museum of Modern Art, New York), with overtones of Byzantine and Aztec Symbolism; it was a significant influence on the US realist art of the 1930s, especially Ben Shahn. His mural *Man at the Crossroads* for the Rockefeller Center in New York (1933) was destroyed because it contained an apparent portrait of Lenin, but he painted another version in Mexico City. Works of the 1940s and 1950s expounding his atheism and his views on war and peace likewise created a scandal and were

similarly suppressed. He was married (twice) to **Frida Kahlo**, and on her death he donated her childhood home to Mexico City as a museum. ▢ Florence Arquin, *Diego Rivera* (1971)

Rivera, Miguel See **Primo de Rivera (y Orbanejo), Miguel, Marqués de Estella**

Rivers, Anthony Woodville, 2nd Earl
c.1442–1483
English nobleman

The son of **Richard Woodville 1st Earl**, and brother of **Elizabeth Woodville** (who married **Edward IV** in 1464), he gave his allegiance (1461) to Edward, who made him Captain-General of the forces. He followed Edward into exile (1470), becoming Lieutenant of Calais, and helped him make his triumphant return (1471). He was governor of the Prince of Wales (the future **Edward V**), and translated from French the *Dictes and Sayings of the Philosophers* which **William Caxton** published (1477); it was the first dated book published in England. After King Edward's death, he was executed by **Richard III**.

Rivers, Augustus Pitt- See **Pitt-Rivers, Augustus**

Rivers, Joan, *originally* Joan Alexandra Molinsky
1933–
US comedienne and writer

Born in Larchmont, New York, she appeared in *Seawood* (1959) and other minor plays. When she began work with the Chicago improvisational troupe Second City (1961–62), she developed her prowess as an acid-tongued, stand-up comedienne. Success came with an appearance on *The Tonight Show* in 1965 and she made her Las Vegas debut in 1969. In 1978, she directed the film *Rabbit Test*, and in 1983 recorded the album *What Becomes A Semi-Legend Most*. On television, she hosted her own programmes, *That Show Starring Joan Rivers* (1968) and *The Joan Rivers Show* (1989–), was the regular guest host of *The Tonight Show* (1971–86) and has also hosted *The Late Show* (1986–87) and *Hollywood Squares* (1987–).

Rivers, Richard Woodville, 1st Earl d.1469
English soldier

Esquire to **Henry V**, he fought in France, and on the Lancastrian side in the Wars of the Roses. His daughter Elizabeth married **Edward IV**, causing him to join the Yorkists, and Edward made him Constable of England, Baron Rivers (1448) and Earl Rivers (1466). The favour shown to the Rivers family offended the old nobility, while their avarice aroused popular enmity, and in 1469 Earl Rivers was beheaded at Northampton.

Rix, Brian Norman Roger Rix, Baron
1924–
English actor and manager

Born in Cottingham, Humberside, he made his professional debut in Shakespeare (1942), joined the **Donald Wolfit** Company (1943), appeared with the White Rose Players, Harrogate (1943–44), and served in the RAF (1944–47). He founded his own company, Rix Theatrical Productions, at Ilkley, Yorkshire (1948), forming a second company at the Hippodrome, Margate (1949). He had a great success with the farce *Reluctant Heroes* (1950), which ran at the Whitehall Theatre for four years, and became closely identified with the Whitehall farces which he both appeared in and managed during the 1950s and 1960s. In 1967 he moved to the Garrick Theatre. He has also produced and appeared in several films. In 1980 he left the theatre to work for Mencap, a charity for the mentally handicapped, becoming its chairman in 1988. Also in that year, he returned to the Lyric to star in a revival of *Dry Rot* (1989). Recent publications include his auto-

biography, *Farce About Farce* (1989), and *Life in the Farce Lane* (1995). He was knighted in 1986, and raised to the peerage in 1992.

Rizal, José 1861–96
Filipino patriot and writer

Born in Calamba, Luzon, he studied medicine at Madrid, and on his return to the Philippines published a political novel, *Noli me tangere* (1886, 'Do not touch me'), whose anti-Spanish tone led to his exile. He practised in Hong Kong, where he wrote *El Filibusterismo* (1891), a continuation of his first novel. Returning to the Philippines, he arrived at a time when an anti-Spanish revolt was on the point of breaking out; he was accused of instigating it, and was shot. ▢ A Coates, *Rizal: Philippine Nationalist and Martyr* (1968)

Rizzio or Riccio, David c.1533–1566
Italian courtier and musician

Born in Pancalieri, near Turin, he went to Scotland with the Duke of Savoy's embassy, and entered the service of **Mary, Queen of Scots** in 1561. He quickly became her favourite, and was made her French secretary (1564). He negotiated her marriage with **Darnley** (1565), with whom he was at first on good terms. Soon, however, Darnley suspected that Rizzio and Mary were lovers, and, with **James Douglas, Earl of Morton, William Ruthven** and others, entered into a plot to kill him. Rizzio was brutally murdered in the queen's antechamber at Holyroodhouse, Edinburgh.

Roa Bastos, Augusto 1917–
Paraguayan novelist and poet

Born in Iturbe, Asunción (Paraguay), he was made to fight in the Chaco War against Bolivia at the age of 15. He was exiled to Buenos Aires after supporting the losing side in the 1947 Civil War. He was a man of culture and travelled widely in Europe. His poetry has been somewhat neglected, although the novels *Hijo de hombre* (1959, Eng trans *Son of Man*, 1988) and *Yo el Supremo* (1974, Eng trans *I the Supreme*, 1988) have been widely acclaimed. The first traces the unhappy history of his country by means of episodes related by a narrator, and the second is about the legendary 19th-century dictator of Paraguay, **Dr Francia**. ▢ D W Foster, *Augusto Roa Bastos* (1978); D W Foster, *The Myth of Paraguay in the Fiction of Roa Bastos* (1969)

Roach, Hal, *originally* Harald Eugene Roach
1892–1992
US film producer

He was born in Elmira, New York. After a spell prospecting in Alaska, he entered the film industry as a stuntman and extra (1911). In 1915 he formed a production company to make short silent comedy films featuring **Harold Lloyd**, who played Willie Work and later Lonesome Luke. He became an expert in the mechanics of screen humour and slapstick, helping to foster the careers of Charlie Chase, **Will Rogers** and, most successfully, the partnership of **Stan Laurel** and **Oliver Hardy**. From 1928 he worked with sound, devised the series of 'Our Gang' films and won Academy Awards for *The Music Box* (1932) and *Bored of Education* (1936). His range of full-length productions includes *Bonnie Scotland* (1935), *Way Out West* (1937), *Of Mice and Men* (1939) and *One Million B.C.* (1940), which he co-directed, and the comedy features *Topper* (1937) and *Topper Returns* (1941). During World War II he made a number of propaganda and training films; later he branched into television production. His last film was the compilation *The Crazy World of Laurel and Hardy* (1967). In 1984 he received a Special Academy Award.

Roach, Max(well) 1924–
US jazz drummer and composer

He was born in New Land, North Carolina. His mother was a gospel singer, and his early musical experiences were in church. He studied music formally for a time, and became involved with the evolution of bebop from 1942. He played in the quintets of Dizzy Gillespie and Charlie Parker, and assumed the mantle of the leading bop drummer from Kenny Clarke. From the late 1950s he began to broaden the scope of his music, using free jazz, vocal music, symphony orchestras, percussion ensembles, and elements from rap and hip-hop. He is an eloquent spokesman for Black cultural and political movements, and a respected teacher.

Robards, Jason, Jnr 1922–
US actor

Born in Chicago, the son of Jason Robards (1893–1963), he studied at the American Academy of Dramatic Arts and made his New York stage debut as the back end of a cow in *Jack and the Beanstalk* at the Children's World Theater in 1947. Acclaimed for his performances in *The Iceman Cometh* (1956) and *Long Day's Journey Into Night* (1958), he won a Tony award for *The Disenchanted* (1959) and gained a reputation as one of the USA's finest actors, with a particular affinity for the works of Eugene O'Neill. His many theatrical appearances include *A Thousand Clowns* (1962), *Moon for the Misbegotten* (1973) and *No Man's Land* (1993). He made his film debut in *The Journey* (1959) and developed into a reliable character actor winning Best Supporting Actor Oscars for both *All the President's Men* (1976) and *Julia* (1977). His many television appearances include *Inherit the Wind* (1988) for which he won an Emmy award.

Robbe-Grillet, Alain 1922–
French novelist

Born in Brest, he was educated in Paris, and worked for a time as an agronomist and then in a publishing house. His first novel, *Les Gommes* (1953, Eng trans *The Erasers*, 1964), was controversial, and his subsequent work (*Dans le labyrinthe*, 1959, Eng trans *In the Labyrinth*, 1960, etc), established him as a leader of the *nouveau roman* ('new novel') group. He uses an unorthodox narrative structure and concentrates on a kind of external reality. He has also written film scenarios, eg, *L'Année dernière à Marienbad* (1961, Eng trans in novel form and filmed as *Last Year at Marienbad*, 1962) and essays, *Pour un nouveau roman* (1963, Eng trans *Towards a New Novel*, 1965). Other publications include the novel *Projet pour une révolution à New York* (1970, 'Project for a Revolution in New York'), *La Belle Captive* (written with René Magritte, 1976; adapted as a screenplay, 1983, 'The Beautiful Prisoner'), *Djinn* (1981, Eng trans 1982), *Angélique ou l'enchantement* (1984, 'Angelique; or, The Enchantment') and *Les Dernières jours de Corinthe* (1994, 'The Last Days of Corinth'). 📖 J Fletcher, *Alain Robbe-Grillet* (1983)

Robbia, Luca Della See Della Robbia, Luca

Robbins, Frederick Chapman 1916–
US physiologist, paediatrician and Nobel Prize winner

Born in Auburn, Alabama, he trained at Missouri University and Harvard University Medical School, where he graduated in 1940. He served as intern at the Children's Hospital Medical Centre, Boston (1941–42), and spent four years with the Army Medical Corps before returning to Boston to complete his paediatric training and join the Infectious Diseases Research Laboratory of the Children's Hospital. Robbins, John Enders and Thomas Weller had all worked on improving techniques for cultivating viruses, and they decided to apply their improvements to the cultivation of the poliomyelitis virus. Their success led to quicker and cheaper means of diagnosis, and was also an important step in the development of a polio vaccine. For this work the three scientists were awarded the 1954 Nobel Prize for physiology

or medicine. Robbins was Professor of Paediatrics at Case Western Reserve University, Cleveland, from 1952 until 1980, becoming Professor Emeritus in 1987.

Robbins, Harold, *pseudonym of* Francis Kane 1916–97
US novelist

Born of unknown parentage in the Hell's Kitchen area of Manhattan, New York City, he dropped out of high school at the age of 15, left his foster parents and eventually became an inventory clerk in a grocery store. During the Depression he showed entrepreneurial flair by buying up crops and selling options to canning companies and the canning contracts to wholesale grocers. He was a millionaire by the time he was 20, but speculation in sugar before the outbreak of World War II lost him his fortune. He turned to writing in 1949; drawing on his knowledge of street life, high finance and Hollywood, he produced a series of escapist bestsellers, including *The Dream Merchants* (1949), *A Stone for Danny Fisher* (1952), *The Carpetbaggers* (1961), *Dreams Die First* (1977), *Descent for Xanadu* (1984) and *Tycoon* (1997).

Robbins, Jerome 1918–98
US dancer and choreographer

Born in New York City, he danced with American Ballet Theater for four years and in Broadway musicals, before making his first choreographic pieces *Fancy Free* (1944). He joined New York City Ballet in 1949, dancing principal roles in George Balanchine ballets and choreographing a total of nine ballets in ten years, including *The Cage* (1951) and *The Concert* (1956). During that time he also worked on Broadway in *The King and I* (1951), *Peter Pan* (1954) and *West Side Story* (1957), a unique achievement which combined the commercial theatre with artistic skill. In order to free himself to experiment, he formed the small company 'Ballet: USA', out of which came *Moves*, a ballet without music (1959). Further Broadway successes included *Gypsy* (1959) and *Fiddler on the Roof* (1964). He returned to New York City Ballet in 1969 to make *Dances at a Gathering*. After the death of Balanchine in 1983, he was made joint ballet master-in-chief with Peter Martins, holding that post until 1989. Blending classical ballet with more earthy folk styles, he was one of the USA's most impressive choreographers. Other works include *The Goldberg Variations* (1971), *Watermill* (1972), *Opus 19/The Dreamer* (1979), *Glass Pieces* (1983), *Quiet City* (1986), *A Suite of Dances* (1994) and *2 + 3 Part Inventions* (1994). He won Academy Awards for the 1961 Hollywood version of *West Side Story*.

Robbins (of Clare Market), Lionel Charles Robbins, Baron 1898–1984
English economist

Born in Sipson, Middlesex, he was Professor of Economics at the London School of Economics (1929–61), and directed the economic section of the War Cabinet. He resigned from the LSE to become chairman of the *Financial Times* (1961–70). From 1961 to 1964 he chaired the Robbins Committee on the expansion of higher education in the UK. His best-known work is *An Essay on the Nature and Significance of Economic Science* (1932). He also wrote *The Economic Problem in Peace and War* (1947), *Classical Political Economy* (1952) and *The Evolution of Modern Economic Theory* (1970).

Robbins, Tim(othy Francis) 1958–
US actor and director

Born in West Covina, California, the son of a folk-singer, he was raised in a politically active household and joined the avant-garde acting group Theater For The New City when he was 12. A drama major at UCLA, he was one of the founders of the experimental theatre company the Actors' Gang in 1981. He made his film debut in *No Small Affair* (1984), and worked extensively in mainstream film and television to subsidize the radical theatre work that he often co-wrote. Among his plays are *Slick Slack Griff Graff* (1985) and *Carnage: A Comedy* (1987), about religious fundamentalism. His film career progressed with roles as the dim-witted pitcher in the popular baseball comedy *Bull Durham* (1988), as the disturbed Vietnam veteran in *Jacob's Ladder* (1990) and as the murderous studio boss in the black comedy *The Player* (1992). He directed and acted in the political satire *Bob Roberts* (1992) and also directed *Dead Man Walking* (1995) which won a Best Actress Academy Award for his off-screen partner Susan Sarandon. He has also acted in *The Hudsucker Proxy* (1994) and *The Shawshank Redemption* (1994).

Robens (of Woldingham), Alfred Robens, Baron 1910–
English trade unionist and industrialist
He was born in Manchester, and became a full-time trade union officer of the Union of Distributive and Allied Workers. He was elected to parliament in 1945, and for six months in 1951 was a member of the Cabinet as Minister of Labour and National Service. From 1961 to 1971 he was chairman of the National Coal Board, and then served on the board of several other companies. He was made a life peer in 1961.

Robert I See Bruce, Robert

Robert II 1316–90
King of Scotland and founder of the Stewart dynasty
The son of Walter Stewart and Marjory, only daughter of Robert Bruce, he twice acted as regent (1338–41, 1346–57) during the exile and captivity of David II. On David's death (1371) he became king by right of his descent from his maternal grandfather, Robert Bruce, and founded the royal Stewart dynasty. During his reign the kingdom was largely administered by his sons, but divisions were avoided, both over the succession and in relation to England, despite two English invasions (1384–85). Stewart lands were extended, enabling grants to be made to his legitimate sons and the establishment of a nobility. His complicated matrimonial history, however, was to bring problems for later Stewart kings. The legitimacy of his first marriage to Elizabeth, daughter of Sir Adam Mure of Rowallan, was doubted on the grounds of their consanguinity. His second marriage (1355) was to Euphemia, Countess of Moray, and daughter of Hugh, Earl of Ross. A papal dispensation for the children of the first marriage was granted in 1347, and they were further recognized by an Act of Succession (1373). Robert also had at least eight illegitimate sons. ⌨ Stephen I Boardman, *The Early Stuart Kings: Robert II and Robert III, 1371–1406* (1996)

Robert III c.1340–1406
King of Scotland
The eldest son of Robert II by his first marriage, and originally called John, he was created Earl of Carrick (1368) and took the name Robert on his accession (1390). The issue of guardianship dominated politics since he was a permanent invalid, the result of a kick from a horse. The main contenders were his brother, Robert, Duke of Albany (c.1340–1420), and his elder son, David, Duke of Rothesay (c.1378–1402), who was appointed Lieutenant of Scotland by a general council in 1398. Rothesay's fall (1402), imprisonment and subsequent death at Falkland Castle brought Albany to an unrivalled position of power, which was further increased by the imprisonment in England of many Scots nobles captured at Homildon Hill (1402). Robert, anxious for the safety of his younger son, James (the future James I), sent him to France, but Robert died shortly after news arrived of James's capture by the English.

Robert Curthose c.1054–1134
Duke of Normandy

He was the eldest son of William the Conqueror and Matilda of Flanders. Although his father's successor, he was excluded from government and after an unsuccessful revolt, was exiled to France. On William's death (1087) Robert succeeded to Normandy, while England passed to the second son, William II, Rufus. A protracted struggle between the two brothers gave William control of Normandy and was interrupted by Robert's courageous participation in the First Crusade (1096–1101). In his absence, his younger brother Henry I seized the English throne when Rufus died (1100). In 1106 Henry invaded Normandy and Robert was captured at the Battle of Tinchebrai. He spent the rest of his life a prisoner at Devizes, Bristol and Cardiff, where he died. His only legitimate son, William Clito, was killed in battle (1128).

Robert of Brunne See Mannyng, Robert

Robert of Jumièges fl.1037–52
Norman prelate
Born in Normandy, he was abbot of Jumièges from 1037. He went to England in 1043 with Edward the Confessor, who made him Bishop of London (1044) and Archbishop of Canterbury (1050). He was the head of the anti-English party which in 1051 banished Earl Godwin and his sons. Their return the next year drove him to Normandy. The Witan stripped him of his archbishopric in 1052 and he died about 1055 in Jumièges.

Robert of Melun d.1167
English theologian
He taught in Paris and Melun, and was elected Bishop of Hereford in 1163. He acted as a mediator between Thomas à Becket and Henry II, and ultimately gave his support to Becket.

Roberti, Ercole de' c.1455–1496
Italian painter
He was born in Ferrara. His *Madonna* (Brera Gallery, Milan), and *Pietà* (Walker Art Gallery, Liverpool), are characteristic of his work, which combines the austere precision of Francesco del Cossa and Cosima Tura with the modernistic qualities of Giovanni Bellini and Piero Della Francesca.

Roberts, Sir Charles George Douglas 1860–1943
Canadian writer and naturalist
He was born in Douglas, New Brunswick. A graduate of Fredericton, he became a professor at King's College, Nova Scotia (1885–95), then settled in New York as an editor, joining the Canadian army at the beginning of World War I. He wrote several volumes of outstanding lyric poetry, including *Orion and Other Poems* (1880) and *In Divers Tones* (1887), as well as a history of Canada, *Canada in Flanders* (1918), and nature studies, in which he particularly excelled, including *The Feet of the Furtive* (1912) and *Eyes of the Wilderness* (1933). ⌨ W J Keith, *Sir Charles Roberts* (1969)

Roberts, David 1796–1864
Scottish painter
He was born in Edinburgh and found work as a scene-painter at Drury Lane in London. His pictures of Rouen and Amiens cathedrals, which he exhibited at the Royal Academy, attracted attention. Much of his work was inspired by his extensive travels; notable are *Departure of the Israelites from Egypt* (1829), *Jerusalem* (1845), *Rome* (1855) and *Grand Canal at Venice* (1856).

Roberts, Frederick Sleigh Roberts, 1st Earl 1832–1914
English field marshal

Born in Cawnpore, India, he was educated at Clifton, Eton, Sandhurst and Addiscombe, and entered the Bengal Artillery in 1851. He was active during the Indian Mutiny (1857–58) and won the VC at Khudagani in 1858. He served in the Abyssinian (1868) and Lushai (1871–72) expeditions, and his action in the Second Afghan War of 1878–79 led to the Afghan defeat and his assumption of the government. In 1880 he relieved Kandahar and routed Ayub Khan. From 1885 to 1893 he was Commander-in-Chief in India. Created Lord Roberts of Kandahar and Waterford in 1892, he became field marshal, and Commander-in-Chief in Ireland in 1895. He published *The Rise of Wellington* (1895) and *Forty-One Years in India* (1895). In 1899 he assumed chief command in the Second Boer War, relieved Kimberley and made the great advance to Pretoria; he returned home in 1901 as Commander-in-Chief. Created earl in 1901, he retired in 1904, and died while visiting troops in the field in France.

Roberts, Sir Gilbert 1899–1978
English civil engineer

Born in London and educated at the City and Guilds of London Institute, he assisted Ralph Freeman on the design of the Sydney Harbour Bridge. He then joined Sir William Arrol & Company in Glasgow where he became director and chief engineer, extending the uses of welding and high-tensile steels in bridges and other structures. In 1949 he joined Freeman, Fox & Partners, and after the death of Sir Ralph Freeman, was entrusted with the design of the Forth, Severn, Auckland Harbour, Bosphorus (Turkey) and Humber bridges as well as radio telescopes, goliath cranes and many other steel structures. He was made FRS and was knighted in 1965.

Roberts, John D 1918–
US chemist

Born in Los Angeles, he studied at the University of California, and after working as a postdoctoral Fellow and instructor at Harvard he joined the Massachusetts Institute of Technology (MIT), and became associate professor in 1950. In 1953 he moved to the California Institute of Technology as professor, and later became divisional chairman, provost and Institute professor emeritus (1988). His major contributions have been to physical organic chemistry, particularly reaction mechanisms, and in applying nuclear magnetic resonance spectroscopy to determine the structure of important organic molecules, arguably the single most important development in chemistry since World War II. He is the author, with M C Caserio, of *Basic Principles of Organic Chemistry* (1967). He was awarded the Priestley Medal of the American Chemical Society (1987), the Robert A Welch Award in Chemistry (1990) and the National Medal of Science (1991). A more recent publication is *At the Right Place at the Right Time* (1991).

Roberts, Julia 1967–
US film actress

Born in Smyrna, Georgia, her earliest ambition was to be a veterinary surgeon, but she decided to study acting and at the same time joined a modelling agency. She gained recognition as the town beauty in *Mystic Pizza* (1988), and was nominated for a Best Supporting Actress Academy Award as the diabetic daughter of Sally Field in *Steel Magnolias* (1989). The success of *Pretty Woman* (1990) made her a star and added box-office appeal to *Flatliners* (1990) and *Sleeping With The Enemy* (1991), in which she also appeared. Later films include *The Pelican Brief* (1993), *Something to Talk About* (1995) and *The Conspiracy Theory* (1997).

Roberts, Kate 1891–1985
Welsh novelist and short-story writer

She was born in Rhosgadfan, near Caernarfon, Gwynedd, and educated at the University College of North Wales, Bangor. She then taught Welsh at Ystalyfera (1915–17) and Aberdare (1917–28), and later (with her husband Morris T Williams) bought Gwasg Gee, the publishers of the newspaper *Baner ac Amserau Cymru* (later *Y Faner*), and settled in Denbigh. Sometimes described as 'the Welsh Chekhov', she is generally regarded as the most distinguished prose writer in Welsh in the 20th century. Her work includes *O Gors y Bryniau* (1925, 'From the Swamp of the Hills'), *Traed mewn Cyffion* (1936, Eng trans *Feet in Chains*, 1977) and *Stryd y Glep* (1949, 'Gossip Street'). 📖 B Jones, *Kate Roberts* (1969)

Roberts, Kenneth Lewis 1885–1957
US novelist, essayist and dowsing expert

Born in Kennebunk, Maine, he attended Cornell University, and worked as a journalist (1909–28). He is considered one of the best historical novelists the USA has produced; his work includes *Arundel* (1930), *Rabble in Arms* (1933), *Captain Caution* (1934), *Northwest Passage* (1937) and *Oliver Wiswell* (1940).

Roberts, (Granville) Oral 1918–
US evangelist and faith healer

Born near Ada, Oklahoma, the son of a Pentecostal preacher and a half Cherokee mother, he was ordained at the age of 18 in the Pentecostal Holiness Church. Flamboyant and enterprising, he gained a reputation for faith healing, and won wide support when he founded Oral Roberts University in Tulsa in 1967. By 1978 it had 3,800 students and assets of about $150 million. In 1981 Roberts also opened a medical centre in Tulsa. From 1968 he preached by means of a weekly national television programme, his own radio station and a mass-circulation monthly magazine. His writings include *If You Need Healing, Do These Things* (1947), *The Miracle Book* (1972) and *How to Resist the Devil* (1989).

Roberts, Richard 1789–1864
Welsh mechanical engineer and inventor

Born in Carreghwfa, Montgomeryshire, he was a labourer in a quarry before moving to England, where he worked for John Wilkinson and Henry Maudslay. In 1816 he established his own machine-tool business in Manchester, where he devised a number of improvements to Maudslay's screw-cutting lathe and built one of the first metal-planing machines. His power loom was introduced in 1822, and from 1825 to 1830 he developed the self-acting spinning mule, an improvement on Samuel Crompton's original design of 1779. He was offered a partnership by Thomas Sharp in 1828, and the firm of Sharp, Roberts & Company manufactured his spinning mule as well as railway locomotives, until Sharp's death in 1842. Roberts continued to invent practical machines and other devices, but had little financial success.

Roberts, Richard 1943–
British molecular biologist and Nobel Prize winner

He was born in Derby and educated at the University of Sheffield. In 1969 he moved to the USA and worked at Cold Spring Harbor Laboratory in New York from 1972. Since 1992 he has been research director at New England Biolabs in Beverly, Massachusetts. In 1977 he announced his intriguing discovery that genes contain sections of DNA (now known as 'introns') which carry no genetic information. He shared the 1993 Nobel Prize for physiology or medicine with Phillip Sharp, who had independently come to the same conclusions about the same time.

Roberts, Sir Stephen Henry 1901–71
Australian historian and political writer

Born in Maldon, Victoria, he was educated at Melbourne University, and at London and Paris. He joined the history department of Melbourne University and wrote his first book, *History of Australian Land Settlement* (1923). In 1929 he became Challis Professor of History at Sydney University. His *History of Modern Europe* (1933), *The Problems of Modern France* (1937) and *The House that Hitler Built* (1937) brought him wider attention. In the years before World War II, he became a radio and newspaper commentator. In 1947 he resigned his chair to become Vice-Chancellor of Sydney University, and was Principal from 1955.

Roberts, Tom (Thomas William) 1856–1931
Australian landscape and portrait painter
Born in Dorchester, England, he studied at the Royal Academy after a brief spell in Melbourne. On his return to Australia he formed, in 1886, with **Frederick McCubbin** and friends, the first artists' camp at Box Hill, Victoria. In 1888 he joined **Arthur Streeton** and **Charles Conder** in Heidelberg, Victoria, to form the first indigenous Australian school of painting. Sixty-two of his paintings were exhibited in 1889 in the famous '9 x 5 Impression' exhibition. With Streeton, he camped at Sirius Cove on Sydney harbour from 1891 to 1896, and there produced a sparkling series of harbour and beach scenes which beautifully captured the prevailing light. He was commissioned to paint the official opening of the first Australian federal parliament in Melbourne in 1903, a subject which required over 250 individual portraits. He is most respected for his sensitive paintings of the Australian bush and pioneering life (eg *Bailed Up*, 1895).

Roberts, William Patrick 1895–1980
English artist
Born in Hackney, London, he was educated at St Martin's School of Art and the Slade School of Art. He was associated with the Vorticists, including **Roger Fry** and **Wyndham Lewis**, and the London Group, and was an official war artist in both world wars. He painted figures in everyday situations, in a cylindrical style and with a certain satirical emphasis, eg *The Cinema* (1920, Tate, London) and *Rush Hour* (1971, Private Collection).

Roberts-Austen, Sir William Chandler 1843–1902
English metallurgist
Born in Kennington, London, he went to the Royal School of Mines at the age of 18 and was awarded an associateship in 1865. In 1880 he was appointed professor at the Royal School of Mines, and two years later became chemist and assayer at the Mint. He was a pioneer in the developing field of alloys. In 1901 he produced the first nearly correct iron–carbon equilibrium diagram. The iron–carbide solid solution 'austenite' formed in cooling steel is named after him. He also demonstrated the possibility of diffusion occurring between a sheet of gold and a block of lead and experimented with early versions of the pyrometer. He was elected FRS in 1875, and was knighted in 1899.

Robertson, George Islay Macneill 1946–
Scottish Labour politician
He was born in Port Ellen, Isle of Islay. Educated at St Andrews and Dundee universities, he joined the Scottish Executive of the Labour Party in 1973 and became MP for Hamilton in 1978. He was front bench spokesman for Scottish Affairs, Defence and then Foreign Affairs before becoming the principal Opposition spokesman on European Affairs (1984–93) and joining the Shadow Cabinet as principal spokesman for Scotland (1993–97). While in this position the massacre of 16 schoolchildren and their teacher by a gunman took place in Robertson's home town of Dunblane (1996), the Stone of Scone was returned to Scotland, and the Labour Party attempted to formulate plans for Scottish devolution before their landslide victory in the 1997 general election. He entered **Tony Blair**'s Cabinet as Secretary of State for Defence (1997–). He was appointed to the German Order of Merit in 1991 and voted Parliamentarian of the Year in 1993 for his role during the Maastricht Bill ratification.

Robertson, Sir James Jackson 1893–1970
Scottish educationist
He was educated at Kilmarnock Academy and Hutchesons' Grammar School, Glasgow, and graduated in classics from Glasgow University. He became head teacher of Aberdeen Grammar School (1942–59). An influential member of the Advisory Council on Education in Scotland, he was author of its forward-looking and enlightened report *Secondary Education* (1947), which set a target for educational reform for the next 20 years and is still quoted. He chaired such national bodies as the Schools Broadcasting Council for Scotland.

Robertson, Jeannie 1908–75
Scottish folk-singer
She was born in Aberdeen and virtually unknown beyond the north-east of Scotland until discovered in 1953 by **Hamish Henderson**. Her huge repertoire of classic traditional ballads and other songs, together with her powerful and magnetic singing style, exerted a profound influence on the folk-music revival. Although she lived most of her life in Aberdeen, she belonged to the 'travelling folk', whose music was passed down orally from generation to generation.

Robertson, J(ohn) M(ackinnon) 1856–1933
Scottish scholar, critic, social scientist and politician
Born in Brodick, Isle of Arran, he left school at the age of 13 but continued to educate himself through extensive reading. In 1884 he began working with **Charles Bradlaugh** on the rationalist *National Reformer*, eventually becoming editor himself (1891–93). From 1906 to 1918 he was Liberal MP for Tyneside, and served as Parliamentary Secretary to the Board of Trade (1911–15). A determined apostle of the application of reason to all subjects, he wrote many books, which fall into three categories: religion and freethinking (eg *History of Freethought in the 19th Century*, 1929), literary criticism (eg *The Genuine in Shakespeare*, 1930), and political and social issues (eg *Free Traders before Adam Smith*, 1924). As a humanist and scholar, he often emphasized the need for learning to be lifelong, and while some of his contentions are controversial, such as his argument that many contributed to the work attributed to **Shakespeare**, the power of his intellect and the range of his knowledge have never been disputed. ▢ G A Wells (ed), *J. M. Robertson: liberal, rationalist, scholar* (1987); M Page, *Britain's Unknown Genius: the life work of J. M. Robertson* (1984)

Robertson, T(homas) W(illiam) 1829–71
English dramatist
Born in Newark-on-Trent, Nottinghamshire, the brother of **Madge Kendal**, he went to London in 1848, where he worked as an actor, prompter and stage manager, wrote plays (which at first proved unsuccessful), contributed to newspapers and magazines, and translated French plays. His first notable success as a dramatist was with *David Garrick* (1864), followed by *Society* (1865), and his next comedy, *Ours* (1866), which established his fame. *Caste* (1867), *Play* (1868), *School* (1869), *M.P.* (1870), all performed by the **Bancrofts** at the Prince of Wales Theatre, London, and also *Home* and *Dreams* (both 1869) were all equally successful. ▢ I E Pemberton, *Life and Work of Thomas William Robertson* (1893)

Robertson, Sir William Robert 1860–1933
English field marshal

Robespierre, Maximilien Marie Isidore de 1758–94
French Revolutionary politician

Robespierre was born at Arras, of Irish parentage. He became a successful advocate, and entered the Estates General (National Assembly) in 1789. By aligning himself with the extreme left and speaking virtually every sitting day, he soon became immensely popular with the Paris commune and the extreme republican members of the Jacobin Club. His impartiality and support of democratic principles won him the nickname 'Incorruptible'. In 1792 he resigned his office as public accuser and petitioned for a revolutionary tribunal and a new convention. Elected for Paris to the National Convention, he emerged as leader of the Mountain, strenuously opposed to the Girondins, whom, with the support of **Georges Danton** and **Jean Paul Marat**, he helped to destroy. The murder of Marat the following year resulted in the proscription of the Girondins and Robespierre's election to the Committee of Public Safety. Robespierre and the Jacobins supported **Louis XVI**'s execution, which took place on 21 January 1793.

With real power at his disposal for the first time, he purged the National Assembly of ultra-revolutionaries, introduced strict economic control, and embarked on the establishment of a form of welfare state. However,

Robespierre's growing autocracy coincided with a new era of ascendancy for the French army, resulting from successes such as the Battle of Fleurus in 1794, that served to question the purpose of the Reign of Terror, and the prospect of Robespierre heading a dictatorship finally spurred his enemies into action.

On 27 July 1794, he was denounced in the convention, and a deputy called for his arrest. He was apprehended by the National Guard after being shot in the jaw, and the next day he and 21 of his supporters were guillotined without trial.

📖 David Jordan, *The Revolutionary Career of Maximilien Robespierre* (1985); Gerard Walter, *Robespierre* (2 vols, 1961); J M Thompson, *Robespierre* (2 vols, 1935).

Je ne suis pas ni le courtisan, ni le modérateur, ni le tribun, ni le défenseur du peuple, je suis peuple moi-même.
'I am not a courtesan, not a moderator, not a tribune, and not a defender of the people; I myself am the people.'
From a speech, 1792.

He enlisted as a private in 1877 and rose to be field marshal in 1920. In World War I he was Quarter-Master General (later Chief of General Staff) of the British Expeditionary Force, and became Chief of the Imperial General Staff from 1915 to 1918. He wrote his autobiography, *From Private to Field-Marshal* (1921).

Robeson, Paul (Bustill) 1898–1976
African-American singer and actor

Born in Princeton, New Jersey, he was admitted to the Bar before embarking on a stage career in New York (1921) and Great Britain (1922). Success as an actor was matched by popularity as a singer, and he appeared in works ranging from *Show Boat* to plays by **Eugene O'Neill** and **Shakespeare**. He was known particularly for his portrayal of Othello, a part which he first played in London in 1930 and in which he scored a triumphant success in the USA 10 years later. He gave song recitals, notably of Negro spirituals, throughout the world, and appeared in numerous films. In the 1950s, his left-wing views caused him to leave the USA, and he lived in England from 1958 to 1963, when he retired and returned to the USA. He published his autobiography, *Here I Stand*, in 1958.

Robespierre, Maximilien Marie Isidore de
See panel above

Robey, Sir George, *originally* George Edward Wade 1869–1954
English comedian

Born in Herne Hill, London, he first appeared on the stage in 1891. He made a name for himself in musical shows such as *The Bing Boys* (1916) and later emerged as a **Shakespeare**an actor, playing Falstaff. Dubbed the 'Prime Minister of Mirth', he was famous for his robust, often **Rabelais**ian humour, his bowler hat, long black collarless frockcoat, hooked stick and thickly painted eyebrows. He was knighted in 1954. 📖 James Harding, *George Robey and the Music Hall* (1990)

Robia, Luca Della See Della Robbia, Luca

Robin, Gordon de Quetteville 1921–
Australian geophysicist and glaciologist

He was born and educated in Melbourne, where he read physics. He later moved to the UK, where he became a research student and lecturer at Birmingham University. In 1958 he was appointed director of the Scott Polar

Research Institute, Cambridge (1958–82), and was secretary (1958–70) and president (1970–74) of the International Scientific Committee on Antarctic Research. While working in the Antarctic, Robin obtained the first seismic traverse from the coast to the Antarctic Plateau, and developed a theory of flow and temperature distribution in ice sheets. He was involved in the study of ice sheets using radio echo-sounding techniques, the penetration of ocean waves into pack ice, and the role of ice sheets in global warming.

Robineau, Adelaide Alsop, *née* Alsop 1865–1929
US ceramic designer and decorator

Born in Connecticut, she taught herself china painting from books and taught others in Minnesota. She then moved to New York to study painting under **William Chase**. In 1899 she and her husband Samuel Robineau began editing a successful magazine called *Keramic Studio*. Moving to Syracuse, New York, they built a workshop and kiln, and in 1903 she began working in porcelain, experimenting with different glazes to achieve her distinctive crystalline effects. Her work was exhibited in many international exhibitions and sold in Tiffany & Co, New York. In 1909 she met Edward Gardner Lewis and worked in his pottery at University City, St Louis. During this time she produced some of her finest work, including a scarab vase which took 1,000 hours to make and won the Grand Prize at the Turin International Exhibition.

Robin Hood c.1250–c.1350
Semi-legendary English outlaw

The hero of a group of old English ballads, the gallant and generous outlaw of Sherwood Forest, he is said to have spent his time under the greenwood tree with Little John, Scarlet, Friar Tuck, and his merry men. Unrivalled with bow and quarter-staff, he gave generously to the poor and needy at the expense of proud abbots and rich knights, helping himself to their riches. The 'rymes of Robyn Hood' are named in *Piers Plowman* (c.1377) and the plays of Robin Hood in the *Paston Letters* (1473). Tradition made the outlaw into a political figure, a dispossessed Earl of Huntingdon and other characters, and in Sir **Walter Scott**'s *Ivanhoe* he is a Saxon holding out against the Normans; but there is no evidence that he was anything but the creation of popular imagination, a yeoman counterpart to the knightly King **Arthur**.

Robins, Benjamin 1707–51
English mathematician

Born in Bath, he became a teacher of mathematics in London, published several treatises, conducted experiments on the resisting force of the air to projectiles, studied fortification, and invented the ballistic pendulum. In 1735 he refuted George Berkeley's objections to Isaac Newton's calculus, in a treatise entitled *Newton's Methods of Fluxions*. His *New Principles of Gunnery* appeared in 1742, and inspired Leonhard Euler and Johann Lambert to investigate the subject. He was the father of the art of gunnery.

Robinson, Arthur Howard 1915–
US geographer

Born in Montreal, Canada, he was educated at the universities of Miami and Wisconsin. He taught at Wisconsin (1936–38) and Ohio State (1938–41) universities, followed by a period as chief of the map division at the Office of Strategic Services (1941–46). He was appointed Professor of Geography at Wisconsin (1945–80), becoming Lawrence Martin Professor of Cartography in 1967. He has held various senior government posts and has received numerous awards. He is known internationally through his major cartographic textbooks, notably his *Elements of Cartography*.

Robinson, Brooks 1937–
US baseball player

He was born in Little Rock, Arkansas. A highly proficient batter who hit more than 250 home runs and over 1,300 runs batted in, he was outstanding for the quality of his work in the field, and is universally recognized as the greatest third baseman of all time. He won the Golden Glove in that position for 15 consecutive years from 1960 and was named as the American League's Most Valuable Player (MVP) in 1960 and the Outstanding Player of the 1970 World Series.

Robinson, Edward 1794–1863
US scholar

Born in Southington, Connecticut, he studied in Germany, and became Professor of Theology at Andover (1830–37) and at the Union Theological Seminary, New York (1837–63). In 1838 he explored Palestine and Syria, and wrote *Biblical Researches in Palestine and Adjacent Countries* (1841). He was the founder-editor of *American Biblical Repository* (1831–35), and compiled a *Hebrew and English Lexicon of the Old Testament* and a *Greek and English Lexicon of the New Testament* (both 1836). He became known as the 'father of biblical geography'.

Robinson, Edward G, *originally* Emanuel Goldenberg 1893–1973
US actor

He was born in Bucharest, Romania, and emigrated to the USA with his parents (1903). He studied at the American Academy of Dramatic Arts in New York City and made his stage debut in *Paid in Full* (1913). He appeared on Broadway in *Under Fire* (1915), but his career was interrupted by service in the US navy during World War I. A prolific stage performer, his work includes *Banco* (1922), *Androcles and the Lion* (1925) and *The Racket* (1927). His first appearance in silent films was in *The Bright Shawl* (1923), and it was his vivid portrayal of the vicious gangster Rico in *Little Caesar* (1930) that brought him stardom. He played a succession of hoodlums and gangsters in films including *The Whole Town's Talking* (1935), *The Last Gangster* (1937) and *Key Largo* (1948), roles which his short squat appearance and wry humour made distinctive. His versatility as an actor is seen in his roles as the paranoid captain in *The Sea Wolf* (1941), a dogged insurance investigator in *Double Indemnity* (1944), a hen-pecked husband in *Scarlet Street* (1945) and the patriarch in *All My Sons*

(1948). Off the screen he was a man of culture and a connoisseur of art. He was also a supporter of democratic causes, and his career was jeopardized by the political activities of the McCarthy years. Nevertheless, he enhanced his reputation as a powerful character star on stage in *Middle of the Night* (1956–58) and in films including *The Cincinnati Kid* (1965) and *Soylent Green* (1973). His autobiography, *All My Yesterdays*, was published in 1973, and he received a Special Academy Award in 1972. ⌨ Alan L Gansberg, *Little Caesar: A Biography of Edward G Robinson* (1983)

Robinson, Edwin Arlington 1869–1935
US poet

Born in Head Tide, Maine, he was brought up in Gardiner, Maine, which provided the background for 'Tilbury Town', the fictional New England village of his best poetry. He was educated at Harvard, and went to New York to find work. He made a name with an early collection of poetry, *The Children of the Night* (1897), followed by *Captain Craig* (1902), *The Town down the River* (1910), *The Man against the Sky* and *King Jasper* (1935), his last work. Poems such as 'Miniver Cheevy' and 'Richard Cory' are recognized as American classics. He won Pulitzer Prizes for his *Collected Poems* (1922), *The Man Who Died Twice* (1925) and *Tristram* (1927), one of his modern renditions of Arthurian legends. ⌨ H Hagedorn, *Edwin Arlington Robinson* (1938)

Robinson, George Augustus 1788–1866
Australian social worker

Born probably in London, he trained as a builder and engineer, and showed an interest in community and religious affairs. He emigrated to Australia, arriving in Hobart in 1824, and set up in business. This prospered, and in 1829 he was appointed Protector of Aboriginals by the Lieutenant-Governor of Van Diemen's Land (Tasmania), Sir George Arthur. Robinson spent nearly five years travelling round Van Diemen's Land, persuading the natives to leave their traditional areas. Arthur thought the same policies could be effective on the mainland and in 1839 Robinson left for the settlement of Port Phillip. In 1849 the Port Phillip protectorate was abolished and he left for Europe a wealthy man, later settling in Bath.

Robinson, (William) Heath 1872–1944
English artist, cartoonist and book illustrator

Born in Hornsey Rise, London, he attended the Islington School of Art and the Royal Academy schools in London. The first of many works illustrated by him was *Don Quixote* (1897); others include editions of *Arabian Nights* (1899), *Twelfth Night* (1908) and *Water Babies* (1915). His fame rests mainly on his humorous drawings, in which he satirizes the machine age with depictions of Heath Robinson contraptions of absurd and fantastic design, which are made to perform simple and practical operations, such as laying a table for dinner, or the shuffling and dealing of cards.

Robinson, Henry Crabb 1775–1867
English journalist and diarist

He was articled to a Colchester attorney (1790–95), then travelled in Germany where he met Goethe and Schiller, and studied at Jena University. He joined *The Times* in 1807 as a foreign correspondent, and covered the Peninsular War as a war correspondent (1808–09); in this capacity he was the first of his kind. He worked as a barrister from 1813 to 1828. He corresponded with major literary figures, including Coleridge, Wordsworth, Charles Lamb and William Blake, all of whom feature in his diaries, correspondence and reminiscences. He was one of the founders of London University (1828) and of the Athenaeum Club in London.

Robinson, Henry Peach 1830–1901
English photographer

Born in Ludlow, Shropshire, he opened a studio at Leamington Spa in 1857. He tired of formal portraiture and moved to 'high art photography', creating literary tableaux in the mid-Victorian style, often by combining several separate images of costumed models and painted settings. Although criticized for artificiality, he had considerable influence until the end of the century. He was a founder-member of The Linked Ring (1892), an association of photographers whose aims were artistic rather than technically accurate; this developed into the international Photo-Secession under **Alfred Stieglitz** and others. He wrote *Pictorial Effect in Photography* (1869).

Robinson, Sir Hercules George Robert, 1st Baron Rosmead 1824–97
British colonial administrator

He was born in Westmeath, Ireland, the son of Admiral Hercules Robinson (1789–1864). After being administrator in Ireland during the Potato Famine (1848), he became Governor of Hong Kong (1859), Ceylon (1865), New South Wales (1872), New Zealand (1878) and the Cape Colony (1880), and British High Commissioner for South Africa (1880–89). He negotiated a peace treaty with the Boers in 1881, and was Governor of South Africa in 1895 when he secured the release of prisoners taken in the 'Jameson Raid' into the then South African Republic. Robinson became Baron Rosmead in 1896, and retired from the colonial service the following year. His brother Sir William Cleaver Francis Robinson (1834–97) was, at various times, Governor of Western Australia and of South Australia, and acting Governor of Victoria.

Robinson, Jackie, *properly* John Roosevelt Robinson 1919–72
US baseball player

Born in Cairo, Georgia, he was the first black player to play major league baseball. After World War II he became a star infielder and outfielder for the Brooklyn Dodgers (1947–56). Known for his fierce competitiveness and skill at stealing home plate, he led the Dodgers to six National League pennants and one World Series victory (1955). He was Rookie of the Year in 1947, and in 1949 he was league batting champion and was named Most Valuable Player (MVP). He retired in 1956 with a lifetime batting average of .311, and in 1962 was elected to the National Baseball Hall of Fame. He was largely responsible for the acceptance of black athletes in professional sports, and wrote of the pressures on him in his autobiography *I Never Had It Made* (1972).

Robinson, James Harvey 1863–1936
US historian

Born in Bloomington, Illinois, he taught European history at Pennsylvania (1891–95) and Columbia (1895–1919). He wrote highly acclaimed textbooks, collaborating with **Charles Beard** in *The Development of Modern Europe* (1907), and published *The New History* (1911), in which he called for history to reflect all of human experience, including scientific, environmental, intellectual, cultural and social concerns. His major work was a study of human understanding, *The Mind in the Making* (1921).

Robinson, Jancis 1950–
English wine writer and broadcaster

She was born and brought up in Carlisle. In her writing and broadcasts she seeks to explain the complexities of wine in a practical way to average consumers. In 1984 she was the first journalist to become a member of the Institute of Masters of Wine, and in 1986 she was declared Wine Writer of the Year. She has been the *Financial Times* wine correspondent since 1989, and wrote *The Oxford Companion to Wine* (1994).

Robinson, Joan Violet, *née* Maurice 1903–83
English economist

Born in Camberley, Surrey, and educated at Girton College, Cambridge, she married an economist, Austin Robinson, in 1926. After a brief period in India she taught economics at Cambridge (1931–71) and in 1965 succeeded her husband as professor. She was one of the most influential economic theorists of her time and a leader of the Cambridge school, which developed macroeconomic theories of growth and distribution based on the work of **John Maynard Keynes**. Her books include *The Economics of Imperfect Competition* (1933), *Essay of Marxian Economics* (1942), *The Accumulation of Capital* (1956), *Essays in the Theory of Economic Growth* (1962) and *Economic Heresies* (1971).

Robinson, John c.1576–1625
English clergyman

Born in Sturton-le-Steeple, Nottinghamshire, he studied at Cambridge, held a curacy at Norwich and became a Separatist after refusing to agree with Anglican Anti-Puritan laws passed in 1604. In 1608 he escaped to Leyden, where he established a church in 1609. In 1620, after a memorable sermon, he saw part of his congregation set sail in the *Speedwell* for Plymouth, where they joined the pilgrims of the *Mayflower*.

Robinson, John Arthur Thomas 1919–83
English Anglican prelate and theologian

Born in Canterbury, he was a student and lecturer at Cambridge before his appointment as Bishop of Woolwich (1959–69). In 1963 he published *Honest to God*, which he described as an attempt to explain the Christian faith to modern man. It was highly successful, but it scandalized conservative elements in the Church, and adversely affected his prospects of further ecclesiastical advancement. He also made significant and more orthodox contributions to biblical studies in other publications, including *Jesus and His Coming* (1957), *The Human Face of God* (1973), *Redating the New Testament* (1976) and *The Priority of John* (1985, posthumous).

Robinson, (Esmé Stuart) Lennox 1886–1958
Irish dramatist

He was born in Douglas, County Cork. His first play, *The Clancy Name*, was produced in 1908 at the Abbey Theatre, Dublin, where he was appointed manager in 1910 and then director from 1923 to 1956. Other plays include *The Cross Roads* (1909), *The Dreamers* (1915) and *The White-Headed Boy* (1920). He also compiled volumes of Irish verse, including the Irish *Golden Treasury* (1925), and edited Lady **Gregory**'s *Journals* (1946). His autobiographical works were *Three Homes* (1938) and *Curtain Up* (1941). 📖 F O'Connor, *My Father's Son* (1969)

Robinson, Mary, *née* Darby, *known as* Perdita 1758–1800
English actress, poet and novelist

She was born in Bristol. She played Perdita and other **Shakespearean** roles at Drury Lane (1776–80), and became mistress (1779) to the future **George IV**, who gave her a bond for £20,000 which he never paid. In 1783 she received a pension of £500, but died in poverty. Her prolific output as a writer included *Sappho and Phaon* (1796), *Lyrical Tales* (1800), two plays, and several novels, including the bestselling *Vancenza* (1792). 📖 *Memoirs* (1801), ed J F Molloy (1930); R D Bass, *The Green Dragoon: the lives of Banastre Tarleton and Mary Robinson* (1957); M Steen, *The Lost One* (1937)

Robinson, Mary, *née* Bourke 1944–
Irish Labour politician and President

Born in Ballina, County Mayo, she became Professor of Law at Trinity College, Dublin in 1969. As a member of the Irish Senate (1969–89), she participated in the legal activities of the EC (European Community), and campaigned for the rights of women and of single parents, and for the decriminalization of homosexuality. She was nominated for the presidency in 1990 by the Labour Party, from which she had resigned in 1985 over the Anglo-Irish Agreement, and unexpectedly defeated the Fianna Fáil candidate Brian Lenihan (1930–96). As President, she gained the support of most of the Irish people. In 1993 she led a mission of reconciliation to Belfast, and met the Sinn Féin leader Gerry Adams, and in 1995 she visited Queen Elizabeth II in London. She stepped down in 1997 and became UN High Commissioner for Refugees.

Robinson, Ray (Arthur Napoleon Raymond)
1926–
Trinidad and Tobago politician
Educated in Trinidad and at Oxford, he qualified as a barrister. On his return to the West Indies, he became politically active and on independence in 1967, became deputy leader of the People's National Movement (PNM). In 1984 he formed a left-of-centre coalition which became the National Alliance for Reconstruction (NAR), and which in the 1986 general election swept the PNM from power, making Robinson Prime Minister. In 1991 the NAR were ousted by a rejuvenated PNM under Patrick Manning. When they returned to power under Basdeo Panday in 1995, Robinson served as adviser to the Prime Minister for two years; he was elected President in 1997.

Robinson, Sir Robert
1886–1975
English chemist and Nobel Prize winner
Born in Chesterfield, Derbyshire, he went to the Victoria University at Manchester in 1902 to study chemistry, and on graduation studied the dyestuff brazilin at the research laboratory of William Henry Perkin, Jnr (1860–1929). He took up a chair of organic chemistry in Sydney between 1912 and 1914, when he returned to Great Britain to take up chairs of chemistry at Liverpool and later St Andrews. He continued research on natural products, and also developed many of his ideas on mechanistic organic chemistry. When the chair at Manchester fell vacant in 1922 he moved there. After a brief spell at University College London (1928–30) he became Waynflete Professor of Chemistry at Oxford, where he remained until 1955. During World War II he played an important role in the development of penicillin. He was a close friend of Robert Maxwell and with his support founded a number of learned journals. He served on many government committees, was knighted in 1939, awarded the Order of Merit in 1949, and became president of the Royal Society in 1945. He received the Nobel Prize for chemistry in 1947. 📖 Trevor Lloyd Williams, *Robert Robinson: Chemist Extraordinary* (1990)

Robinson, Sugar Ray, *originally* Walker Smith
1920–89
US boxer
Born in Detroit, he gained the welterweight title in 1946 and won the middleweight championship five times between 1951 (when he knocked out Jake La Motta) and 1958 (when he defeated Carmen Basilio). His skill and speed brought him close to winning the world light-heavyweight championship in 1952 despite a considerable physical disadvantage. He fought 202 professional bouts in his career and lost only 19, most of them when he was over 40. He was a professional boxer for 20 years but bore few, if any, visible signs of the ring. He was very popular in Europe, and travelled in considerable style.

Robinson, William
1838–1935
Irish gardener and horticultural writer
Born in County Down, he received little formal education. He became a garden-boy at Ballykilcaven, County Laois, and from 1861 worked at the Royal Botanic Society's gardens at Regent's Park, London. He published 18 books, including *Gleanings from French Gardens* (1868), *Alpine Flowers for English Gardens* (1870) and *The English Flower Garden* (1883), and founded and edited three horticultural journals: *The Garden* (1872), *Gardening Illustrated* (1879) and *Flora and Sylva* (1903).

Rob Roy, Gaelic for Red Robert, properly Robert MacGregor
1671–1734
Scottish outlaw
He was born in Buchanan, Stirlingshire. As a young man he lived quietly grazing sheep at Balquhidder, but was forced to raise a private army to protect himself from the activities of outlaws. When these followers joined the Jacobite cause in the 1690s, he turned to plundering, and became an outlaw in 1712 when his lands were seized by the Duke of Montrose. Legends about him soon developed around Loch Katrine and Loch Lomond; they told of his hair's-breadth escapes, and of his generosity to the poor, whose wants he supplied at the expense of the rich. Although he enjoyed the patronage of John, 2nd Duke of Argyll, he was arrested in 1727 and sentenced to transportation, but was pardoned. His life was romanticized in Sir Walter Scott's *Rob Roy* (1818). 📖 L R Frewin, *Legends of Rob Roy* (1954)

Robson, Dame Flora McKenzie
1902–84
English actress
Born in South Shields, Tyne and Wear, she made her first professional appearance in 1921 and became famous for her mainly historical roles in plays and films, such as Queen Elizabeth I in *Fire over England* (1931), and Thérèse Raquin in *Guilty* (1944), based on Zola's story. Memorable stage performances included George Bernard Shaw's *Captain Brassbound's Conversion* (1948) and Ibsen's *Ghosts* (1958). She was made a DBE in 1960.

Roburt, Hammer De See DeRoburt, Hammer

Rocard, Michel
1930–
French politician
Born in the Paris suburb of Courbevoie, he was the son of a nuclear physicist who worked on the development of a French atomic bomb. He trained at the École National d'Administration, where he was a classmate of Jacques Chirac. He began his career in 1958 as an inspector of finances, and in 1967 became leader of the radical Unified Socialist Party (PSU), standing as its presidential candidate in 1969 and being elected to the National Assembly in the same year. He joined the Socialist Party (PS) in 1973, emerging as leader of its moderate social democratic wing, and unsuccessfully challenged François Mitterrand for the party's presidential nomination in 1981. After serving as Minister of Planning and Regional Development (1981–83) and as Minister of Agriculture (1983–85) in the ensuing Mitterrand administration, he resigned in 1985 in opposition to the government's expedient introduction of proportional representation. In 1988, however, as part of a strategy termed the 'opening to the centre', Mitterrand appointed him Prime Minister, but replaced him with Mme Edith Cresson in 1991. He became an MEP (Member of the European Parliament) representing the Party of European Socialists in 1994.

Rochambeau, Jean Baptiste Donatien de Vimeur, Comte de
1725–1807
French soldier
Born in Vendôme, he fought at the Siege of Maestricht, and distinguished himself at Minorca in 1756. In 1780 he was sent out with 6,000 men to support the Americans,

and in 1781 provided effective help at Yorktown. On his return to France (1783) he served with the Napoleonic army, and was made a marshal in 1803.

Roche, Mazo de la See de la Roche, Mazo

Rochefoucauld, François See La Rochefoucauld, François, 6th Duc de

Rochester, John Wilmot, 2nd Earl of 1647–80
English courtier and poet
Born in Ditchley, Oxfordshire, he was educated at Burford School and Wadham College, Oxford. He travelled in France and Italy, and then returned to the court of Charles II, where he was a prominent figure. He is said to have been a patron of the actress Elizabeth Barry, and of several poets. He led a life of debauchery, yet wrote letters, satires (particularly 'A Satyr against Mankind', 1675), and bacchanalian and amatory songs and verses. Among the best of his poems are imitations of Horace and Nicolas Boileau, *Verses to Lord Mulgrave*, and *Verses upon Nothing*. 📖 V de Sola Pinto, *Rochester, Portrait of a Restoration Poet* (1935)

Rockefeller, John D (avison) 1839–1937
US oil magnate and philanthropist
Born in Richford, New York, he became clerk in a commission house in 1857 and then worked in a small oil refinery at Cleveland, Ohio. In 1870 he founded the Standard Oil Co with his brother William (1841–1922), and this eventually gave him control of the US oil trade. He gave over $500 million in support of medical research and to universities and Baptist churches, and in 1913 he established the Rockefeller Foundation, avowedly 'to promote the well-being of mankind'. His son, John Davison, Jnr (1874–1960), became chairman of the Rockefeller Institute of Medical Research, and built the Rockefeller Center in New York (1939). He also restored colonial Williamsburg in Virginia. His grandsons included John Davison III (1906–78) who became chairman of the Rockefeller Foundation in 1952, and Nelson Aldrich Rockefeller. 📖 Allan Nevins, *John D Rockefeller: The Heroic Age of American Business* (2 vols, 1940)

Rockefeller, Nelson Aldrich 1908–79
US politician
He was born in Bar Harbor, Maine, the grandson of industrialist John D Rockefeller. After graduating from Dartmouth College in 1930, he worked in the family businesses and philanthropic foundations. Entering politics as a liberal Republican, he served four terms as Governor of New York (1958–73), and during the 1960s he made three unsuccessful attempts to gain his party's presidential nomination. In 1974 he was named Vice-President by Gerald R Ford, and he remained in office until 1977.

Rockingham, Charles Watson-Wentworth, 2nd Marquess of 1730–82
English statesman
He became a leading Whig, but was dismissed from his appointments in 1762, when he opposed the policies of Bute. He became Prime Minister (1765–66, 1782), and died in office. He repealed the Stamp Act, and supported American independence.

Rockne, Knute Kenneth 1888–1931
US coach of American football
Born in Voss, Norway, he was taken to the USA as a child. He graduated from Notre Dame in 1914 and became head football coach there shortly after the end of World War I. He dominated US college football, having markedly changed the emphasis from sheer physical brawn to pace, elusiveness and ball handling. He was famous for his rousing exhortations to players, 1596 and built Notre

Dame into a national collegiate football power, compiling a record of 105 wins, 12 losses and five draws. He died in an air crash.

Rockwell, Norman 1894–1978
US illustrator
Born in New York City, he studied at the Art Students League there and became a magazine illustrator, selling his first cover painting to the *Saturday Evening Post* in 1916. His nostalgic anecdotal scenes of everyday small-town life in the USA appeared on the cover of the *Post* for half a century, and through them he was enshrined in American popular culture. He also created patriotic posters and paintings during World War II, including his *Four Freedoms* series (1943).

Rod, Édouard 1857–1910
Swiss writer
Born in Nyon, Vaud, he studied at Lausanne, Bonn and Berlin, was professor at Geneva, and settled in Paris. Among his 30 novels are *La Chute de Miss Topsy* (1882, 'Miss Topsy's Fall'), *La Course à la mort* (1885, 'The Race to Death'), *Le Sens de la vie* (1889, 'The Sense of Life'), *Le Dernier Refuge* (1896, 'The Last Refuge') and *Les Unis* (1909, 'The United'), all of them being introverted psychological studies. 📖 C Delhorbe, *Édouard Rod* (1938)

Rodbertus, Johann Karl 1805–75
German economist and politician
Born in Greifswald, he studied law at Göttingen and Berlin. He held law appointments under the Prussian government, but in 1836 settled on his estate. In 1848 he entered the Prussian National Assembly; in 1849 he carried the adoption of the Frankfurt constitution. He was an early socialist, and believed that labour was the only source of wealth; he maintained that the socialistic ideal would come to pass gradually (perhaps over five centuries) according to the natural laws of change and progress. The state would then own all land and capital, and superintend the distribution of all products of labour.

Rodchenko, Aleksandr Mikhailovich 1891–1956
Russian painter, designer and photographer
Born in St Petersburg, he studied at the Kazan Art School and met Vladimir Tatlin and the young Russian avant-garde. After the revolution he worked for the People's Commissariat of Enlightenment and taught in Moscow (1918–26). His most original works were abstract spatial constructions and documentary photographs of the new communist society. His painting of a black square (*Black on Black*, 1918) owed much to the Suprematism of Kasimir Malevich's *White on White*.

Roddick, Anita Lucia 1942–
English retail entrepreneur
Born in Brighton, East Sussex, she was educated at Maude Allen School for girls and studied at Newton Park College of Education, Bath. In 1976 she founded the Body Shop with her husband Thomas Gordon Roddick, to sell cosmetics 'stripped of the hype' and made from natural materials. The company has since established many stores in the UK and overseas. She lectures on environmental issues and conducts campaigns with Friends of the Earth, and in 1989 she won the UN environmental award. In 1991, she published her autobiography *Body and Soul* and in 1993 won a libel suit against Channel Four, who had aired a television programme which questioned the Body Shop's social commitment.

Rodenberry, Gene 1921–91
US scriptwriter, producer and director

Rodin, (François) Auguste (René) 1840–1917
French sculptor

Rodin was born in Paris, the son of a clerk. He made three unsuccessful attempts to enter the École des Beaux-Arts, and from 1864 (the year in which he produced his first great work, *L'Homme au nez cassé*, 'The Man with the Broken Nose') until 1875 he worked in Paris and Brussels under the sculptors **Antoine Barye**, and Carrier-Belleuse, and with Van Rasbourg, with whom he collaborated in some of the decorations for the Brussels Bourse.

In 1875 he travelled in Italy, studying the work of **Donatello**, **Michelangelo** and others, and in 1877 made a tour of the French cathedrals (he published *Les Cathédrales de la France* much later, in 1914). The Italian masters and the Gothic cathedrals both influenced Rodin's work considerably, as did his interest in the ancient Greeks, but the greatest influence on him was the current trend of Romanticism. In 1877 he exhibited anonymously at the Paris Salon *L'Âge d'airain* ('The Age of Bronze'), which aroused controversy because of its realism; indeed, the sculptor was accused of taking the cast from a living man. In 1879 he exhibited the more highly developed *Saint Jean Baptiste* ('St John the Baptist').

In 1880 he was commissioned by the government to produce the *Porte de l'enfer* ('The Gate of Hell'), inspired by **Dante**'s *Inferno*, for the Musée des Arts Décoratifs, and during the next 30 years he was primarily engaged on the 186 figures for these bronze doors. It was never completed, but many of his best-known works were originally conceived as part of the design of the doors, among them *Le Baiser* (1898, 'The Kiss') and *Le Penseur* (1904, 'The Thinker'). From 1886 to 1895 he worked on *Les Bourgeois de Calais* ('The Burghers of Calais').

His statues include those of a nude **Victor Hugo** (1897) and **Honoré de Balzac** in a dressing gown (1898), the latter being refused recognition by the Societé des Gens de Lettres who had commissioned it; and among his portrait busts are those of Madame Rodin, **Bastien-Lepage**, **Puvis de Chavannes**, Victor Hugo and **George Bernard Shaw**.

His works are represented in the Musée Rodin, Paris, in the Rodin Museum, Philadelphia, and in the Victoria and Albert Museum, London, where there is a collection of his bronzes which he presented to the British nation in 1914.

📖 Ionel Jianou, *Rodin* (1970); Robert Descharnes and J F Chabrun, *Auguste Rodin* (1967); Albert Edward Elson, *Auguste Rodin: Readings on His Life and Works* (1965).

> Among the artists whom Rodin inspired were the French sculptor **Camille Claudel** and the Welsh artist **Gwen John**, who each became his mistress.

He was born in Texas and was a pilot before turning to writing, going on to work mainly in television. He is best known as the creator of the popular *Star Trek* series.

Roderic d.711
Last Visigothic King of Spain

He was elected on the death of Witiza (710), and died on the Guadalete, near Cape Trafalgar, in battle against the invading Muslims from Tangier, who marched on to Toledo and forced the capitulation of most of Spain.

Rodgers, Jimmie (James Charles) 1897–1933
US country music singer and songwriter

Born in Meridian, Mississippi, he was known as 'The Singing Brakeman' from the railway overalls he wore, and as 'The Blue Yodeller' from his style of singing. He is regarded by many as the father of modern country music, and was its first solo star. He worked on the railway until he contracted tuberculosis in 1924, and by 1927 he was broadcasting on radio in North Carolina. He recorded the historic first country sides for Ralph Peer in 1927, and by 1928 was a well-known name. His music took in aspects of blues, jazz and even Hawaiian music, and his ground-breaking recordings (111 in all) have been immeasurably influential. He died of tuberculosis. 📖 N Porterfield, *Jimmie Rodgers* (1979)

Rodgers, Richard 1902–79
US composer

Born in New York City, he studied at Columbia University, then studied composition at the Institute of Musical Art (now the Juilliard School) in New York City. He collaborated with the lyricist Lorenz Hart in a number of musicals including *The Garrick Gaieties* (1925), *Babes in Arms* (1937, whose songs included 'The Lady is a Tramp'), *The Boys from Syracuse* (1938, which included 'Falling in Love with Love') and *Pal Joey* (1940, which included 'Bewitched, Bothered and Bewildered'). After Hart's death (1943), Rodgers worked on a series of hit musicals with **Oscar Hammerstein II**, notably *Oklahoma!* (1943, Pulitzer Prize), *Carousel* (1945), *South Pacific* (1949, Pulitzer Prize), *The King and I* (1951), *The Flower Drum Song* (1958) and *The Sound of Music* (1959). 📖 David Ewen, *Richard Rodgers* (1957)

Rodgers, William Thomas Rodgers, Baron 1928–
English politician

Born in Liverpool and educated at Oxford, he served as general secretary of the Fabian Society between 1953 and 1960 before being elected a Labour MP for Stockton-on-Tees in 1962. He held a succession of posts in the Labour governments of the 1960s and 1970s, including Transport Secretary between 1976 and 1979. He was a strong supporter of membership of the EC (European Community) and was concerned by the leftward tendency of his party. In 1981 he left the Labour Party to form the Social Democratic Party (SDP) in conjunction with **Roy Jenkins**, **David Owen** and **Shirley Williams** (with whom he formed the 'Gang of Four'). Although he lost his seat in the 1983 election, he continued to play an influential organizational role as SDP vice-president between 1982 and 1987, directing the party's alliance with the Liberals. Despite expressing support for the SDP–Liberal merger of 1987–88, he formally withdrew from party politics in 1987 to become director-general of the Royal Institute of British Architects. He was made a life peer in 1992.

Rodin, Auguste See panel above

Rodney (of Stoke-Rodney), George Brydges Rodney, 1st Baron c.1718–1792
English naval commander

Born in London of an old Somerset family, he joined the navy in 1732, and in 1747 took part in Admiral **Edward Hawke**'s victory against the French off Cape Finisterre. He was Governor of Newfoundland from 1748 to 1752. In 1759 as rear admiral he destroyed the flotilla assembled at Le Havre for the invasion of England. In 1761 he was appointed Commander-in-Chief on the Leeward Islands station, where in 1762 he captured Martinique, St Lucia and Grenada. He became Commander-in-Chief in Jamaica (1771–74), and in the Leeward Islands (1779–82), and captured a Spanish convoy off Cape Finisterre and defeated another squadron off Cape St Vincent (1780). 1781 he captured Dutch islands in the West Indies on which American contraband trade depended. In 1782 he gained a brilliant victory over the French off Dominica.

Rodney, Walter 1942–80
Guyanese historian and politician
Formerly Professor of African History at the University of Dar es Salaam, his deportation from Jamaica (1968) for supposed connections with Black Power provoked a riot. Although debarred from holding the history chair at the University of Guyana, he returned to his homeland and founded the Working People's Alliance, which was antipathetic to the policies of **Forbes Burnham**'s ruling People's National Congress. The author of *How Europe Underdeveloped Africa* (1972), he was killed by a bomb in mysterious circumstances in Guyana.

Rodnina, Irina Konstantinova 1949–
Soviet figure skater
She was born in Moscow. Her first partner on the skating rink was Aleksei Ulanov, with whom she won four world championships. In 1972 she formed a pair with the younger and stronger Aleksandr Zaitsev, who became her husband in 1976. Together they achieved a perfect mark from all the judges at the European championships in 1973, and went on to win the world championship six times. As well as her record 10 world championship wins, she won the Olympic pairs three times and the European championship 11 times, establishing another record. She retired after the 1980 Olympics.

Rodó, José Enrique 1872–1917
Uruguayan essayist
He was born in Montevideo, and spent most of his life there. He became Professor of Literature (from 1898) at the National University, and was the author of *Ariel* (1900, Eng trans 1922), an immensely influential essay pleading for spiritual values to be upheld in the coming age of materialism (represented by Caliban), and he attacked the USA as the materialistic state par excellence. He was the foremost prose writer of the Modernist movement in Latin America. His chief work, however, was his treatise on work and fulfilment, *Los motivos de Proteo* (1914, Eng trans *The Motives of Proteus*, 1928).

Rodoreda, Mercè 1909–83
Catalan writer
She was born in Barcelona and began her career as a writer soon after the proclamation of the Spanish Republic. She published five novels and numerous short stories in literary magazines (1932–37), which established her as a rising star of Catalan literature. When the Catalan language was suppressed, her books were banned and she fled to France where she remained unpublished until the appearance of *Vint-i-dos Contes* (1957, 'Twenty-two Stories'). The stream-of-consciousness novel *La Plaça del Diamant* (1962, 'Diamond Plaza') was followed by *Carrer de les Camèlies* ('Camellia Street'), about war-torn Barcelona in the 1940s and 1950s, and *La Meva Cristina i Altres Contes* (1967, 'My Christina and Other Stories'). She returned to Spain in 1979, after **General Franco**'s death.

Rodrigo, Joaquin 1902–
Spanish composer
Born in Sagunto, near Valencia, he became totally blind at the age of three; in spite of this he learned to play the piano. He went to Paris to study with **Paul Dukas** and on returning to Spain was encouraged by **Manuel de Falla**, who nurtured in him a love of Spanish folk music and rhythms. He won a national competition with an orchestral work, *Cinco Piezas Infantiles* (1925, *Five Pieces from Childhood*), and in 1946 was appointed Professor of Musical History at Madrid University. Much of his music involves the guitar, including his most frequently played work, the *Concierto de Aranjuez* (1939, *Aranjuez Concerto*). He has also written concertos for the violin, the harp and the flute.

Roe, Edward Rayson 1838–88
US clergyman and novelist
Born in New Windsor, New York, he became chaplain in the volunteer service (1862–65), and afterwards pastor of a Presbyterian church in Highland Falls. The Chicago fire of 1871 furnished him with the subject of his first novel, *Barriers Burned Away* (1872), whose success led him to resign his pastorate in 1874. His other moralistic bestsellers included *A Knight of the Nineteenth Century* (1877).

Roe, Sir Edwin Alliot Verdon 1877–1958
English aircraft manufacturer
Born in Patricroft, near Manchester, he went to Canada when only 15 years old to assist in making drawings for a flying machine. After apprenticeship in locomotive engineering and a study of naval engineering at King's College London, he went to sea as a marine engineer (1899–1902). He won the highest award for a competition for model aeroplanes in 1907 and built his first biplane in 1907 at Brooklands, Kent. He was also the first Englishman to design, build and fly his own aircraft. With his brother Humphrey Verdon Roe (1878–1949, husband of Dr **Marie Stopes**), he formed A V Roe & Co in 1910, producing the famous AVRO 504 bomber/trainer type that set a standard for design for many years. He sold out to Armstrong Siddeley in 1928 and formed Saunders–Roe (SARO) to build flying boats at Cowes. AVRO is known for its Lancaster and Vulcan Bombers and SARO for the first jet-propelled flying boat, the SR-A1 and the Princess.

Roebling, John Augustus 1806–69
US civil engineer
Born in Mühlhausen, Prussia (now Mulhause, France), and educated in the Royal Polytechnic Institute in Berlin, he emigrated to the USA in 1831 and began farming with his brother near Pittsburgh. He soon took up work as a canal engineer, where his observation of hemp ropes on inclines led him to develop machinery for the fabrication of superior wire ropes, the first to be made in the USA. At the same time he worked on the design of suspension bridges, completing the first, incorporating his wire ropes, in 1846. He went on to build the pioneer railway suspension bridge at Niagara Falls (1851–55, replaced 1897), and had completed the design for the Brooklyn Bridge in New York when an injury to his foot resulted in tetanus from which he died. His son Washington Augustus (1837–1926), after graduating at Rensselaer Polytechnic Institute, became his assistant and succeeded him as chief engineer of the Brooklyn Bridge project, which he saw through to its completion in 1883.
📖 Hamilton Schuyler, *The Roeblings: A Century of Engineers, Bridge-Builders and Industrialists* (1931)

Roebuck, John 1718–94
English inventor
Born in Sheffield, he studied at Edinburgh, and graduated MD at Leyden. He gave up his practice in Birmingham to resume his research in chemistry, which led to improvements in methods of refining precious metals and in the production of chemicals. In 1759 he founded the Carron ironworks in Stirlingshire, and he later became a friend and patron of **James Watt**.

Roehm, Ernst See **Röhm, Ernst**

Roemer, Olaus 1644–1710
Danish astronomer
Born in Aarhuus, he worked at the Paris Observatory (1672–81) where he discovered that the intervals between successive eclipses of a satellite in Jupiter's shadow were less when Jupiter and the Earth were approaching than when they were receding (1675). He concluded that this was due to the finite velocity of light (which was a new discovery); from the observed intervals and the known

rates of motion of Jupiter and the Earth, he obtained the first estimate of the velocity of light. He also invented the transit instrument, a telescope movable only in the meridian, which greatly increased the accuracy attainable in the determination of both time and right ascension. In 1681 he returned as royal mathematician and University Professor of Astronomy to Copenhagen, where he remained for the rest of his life.

Roethke, Theodore 1908–63
US poet
Born in Saginaw, Michigan, he was the son of a florist and often played in his father's greenhouses, an atmosphere later evoked in the horticultural imagery of his poems. He was educated at the University of Michigan and Harvard, and was Professor of English at Washington University from 1948. It was not until the publication of his fourth collection, *The Waking* (1953, Pulitzer Prize), that he became widely known. His best poems are lyrical and inventive and reveal his grace in handling rhyme and meter. He was an alcoholic who suffered from periodic mental breakdowns, and he often reflected on his madness and despair in his poetry. **Robert Lowell** and others of the 'Confessional' poets were influenced by him. *Words for the Wind* (1958) is a selection from his first four books; the *Collected Poems* appeared posthumously in 1968. ☐ J Parini, *Theodore Roethke: an American romantic* (1979)

Roger I 1031–1101
Norman ruler in Sicily
The brother of **Robert Guiscard**, he helped to conquer Calabria (1060). He supported Sicily against the Saracens, and took Messina (1061). In 1071 the Saracen capital Palermo was captured, and Robert made Roger Count of Sicily and Calabria. After Robert's death (1085), Roger succeeded to his Italian possessions, and became the head of Norman power in southern Europe. He created an efficient centralized government and gave religious freedom to Greek Christians, Jews and Muslims.

Roger II 1095–1154
First Norman King of Sicily
The second son of **Roger I**, he succeeded his elder brother Simon as Count of Sicily (1105). On the death (1127) of the Duke of Apulia, grandson of **Robert Guiscard**, his duchy passed to Roger, who united Sicily and South Italy into a strong Norman kingdom, of which he was crowned king by the antipope Anacletus (1130). He later added Capua (1136), Naples and the Abruzzi (1140) to his kingdom. In 1139 he imprisoned Pope Innocent II, until Innocent recognized him as King of Sicily and Roger acknowledged Innocent's overlordship. Antagonized by the Byzantine Emperor **Manuel I Comnenus**, Roger used his powerful navy to ravage the coasts of Dalmatia and Epirus; he took Corfu and plundered Corinth and Athens (1146). He captured some silk workers, and introduced the silk industry into Sicily. Finally (1147), he won Tripoli, Tunis and Algeria. An intellectual interested in the science of government, he ruled in the manner and with the splendour of an oriental monarch. He set up a Civil Service envied by the rest of Europe, with a new code of law and centralized finances, run by his Arab subjects. His racially and culturally integrated court was a centre of science, philosophy and the arts. He is the subject of an opera by **Symanowski**.

Roger of Taizé, *originally* Roger Louis Schutz-Marsauche 1915–
Swiss founder of the Taizé Community
Brother Roger was born in Provence, France, the son of a Protestant pastor. In 1940 he went to Taizé, a French hamlet between Cluny and Citeaux, to establish a community devoted to reconciliation and peace in Church and society. Since Easter 1949, when the first seven

brothers took their vows, the community has attracted thousands of pilgrims, especially young people drawn by the distinctive worship in the Church of Reconciliation, which was built in 1962. His publications include *The Dynamic of the Provisional* (1965), *Violent for Peace* (1968), and several volumes of extracts from his journal. In 1992 he was awarded the Robert Schuman prize for his participation in the construction of Europe.

Roger of Wendover d.1236
English chronicler
A Benedictine monk at the monastery of St Albans, he revised and extended the abbey chronicle from the creation to the year 1235, under the title *Flores Historiarum* ('Flowers of History'). The section from 1188 to 1235 is believed to be Roger's first-hand account. The chronicle was later extended by **Matthew Paris**.

Rogers, Carl R(ansom) 1902–87
US psychotherapist, the originator of client-centred therapy
Born in Oak Park, Illinois, he took his doctorate in psychology at Columbia University's Teachers College (1931), then worked as director of the child guidance centre in Rochester, New York, and taught at Chicago University (1945–57). His research there on the one-to-one relationship in therapy is the subject of his book *Client-Centred Therapy* (1951). Sometimes known as non-directive therapy, this form of psychotherapy attempts to elicit and resolve a person's problems by verbal means, but explicitly renounces attempts to talk the subject into accepting any doctrinaire interpretation of his or her symptoms, the procedure practised by **Sigmund Freud** and his followers. It led to the proliferation of open therapy sessions and encounter groups in which patients talk out their problems under the supervision of a passive therapist. Rogers was also a notable pioneer in carrying out systematic evaluations of the efficacy of psychotherapy. He was resident Fellow at the Western Behavioral Science Institute (1964–68) and the Centre for Studies of the Person at La Jolla, California (1968–87). His other books include *Psychotherapy and Personality Change* (1954) and *On Becoming a Person* (1961).

Rogers, Claude 1907–79
English artist
Born in London, he was Professor of Fine Art at Reading University (1963–72) and president of the London Group from 1952 to 1965. With **Victor Pasmore** and **William Coldstream** he founded the Euston Road School in 1937.

Rogers, Ginger, *originally* Virginia Katherine McMath 1911–95
US actress and dancer
Born in Independence, Missouri, she began her professional career as a dancer in vaudeville and switched from the stage to film after her successful appearance on Broadway in the **Gershwin** musical *Girl Crazy* in 1930. With her screen partner, **Fred Astaire**, she made a series of Hollywood film musicals, performing elaborate dance routines with exuberant grace. The 10 films they made together, including *Top Hat* (1935), *Follow the Fleet* (1936) and *Swing Time* (1936), were enormously popular with audiences in the Depression. She also played dramatic roles in films such as *Kitty Foyle* (1940, Academy Award). She made her last film appearance in *Harlow* (1965). Her many stage appearances included *Hello Dolly!* (1965) on Broadway, and *Mame* (1969) in London. Her lively kiss-and-tell autobiography, *Ginger: My Story*, was published in 1991.

Rogers, John c.1500–1555
English Protestant reformer

Born near Birmingham, he studied at Cambridge. He was a London rector (1532–34) who was converted to Protestantism in Antwerp, and helped to prepare the new translation called 'Matthew's Bible' (1537). He returned to England in 1548, preached an anti-Catholic sermon at St Paul's Cross in 1553, shortly after the accession of **Mary I**, and was burned as a heretic.

Rogers, Kenny 1938–
US country and pop singer and actor
He was born in Houston, Texas, in a poor housing project, and went on to become one of the most successful artists in modern music. He began his career in jazz bands before joining the New Christy Minstrels, then launched his own band, The First Edition, in a country-pop vein. He went solo in the mid-1970s, and began a sequence of immense hits with the country song 'Lucille'; one, 'The Gambler', was turned into a film, in which Rogers took the leading role. Although aware of his own limitations as a performer, he has been able to forge a remarkable success story, both in his music and his many business ventures. ▢ M Hume, *Gambler, Dreamer, Lover* (1981)

Rogers, Randolph 1825–92
US sculptor
He was born in Waterloo, New York, and studied in Florence and Rome, living in Rome from 1885. His statues include *Ruth* (Metropolitan Museum, New York City) and *Lincoln* (Philadelphia). He is best known for his *Columbus Doors* of the Capitol in Washington DC, and the heroic figure of *Michigan* on the Detroit Monument.

Rogers, Richard George Rogers, Baron 1933–
English architect
Born in Florence, Italy, he studied at the Architectural Association in London, and was a founder-member with **Norman Foster** and their wives of Team 4. Like Foster, he was concerned with advanced technology in architecture and pushed the limits of design through exhaustive research. Two important works have caused widespread praise and controversy: the Beaubourg or Pompidou Centre, Paris (1971–79, with Renzo Piano), a large open interior space clothed in highly coloured services; and Lloyds of London (1979–85), a masterful and dramatic exercise in steel and glass. He also designed the European Court of Human Rights in Strasbourg (opened 1995). Knighted in 1991, he was created a life peer in 1996.

Rogers, Samuel 1763–1855
English poet
Born in Stoke-Newington, London, he became a partner in his father's bank in 1784, and in 1793 became head of the firm. He contributed essays to the *Gentleman's Magazine* in 1781, wrote a comic opera the following year, and in 1786 published *An Ode to Superstition*. *The Pleasures of Memory*, on which his poetical fame is chiefly based, appeared in 1792, followed by *An Epistle to a Friend* (Richard Sharp) (1798), the fragmentary *Voyage of Columbus* (1812), *Jacqueline* (1814, published with **Byron's** *Lara*), and the inimitable *Italy* (1822–28). The last, in blank verse, proved a financial failure, but the loss was recouped by a splendid edition of it and his earlier poems, brought out at a cost of £15,000 (1830–34), with 114 illustrations by **J M W Turner** and **Thomas Stothard**. He was quietly generous to **Thomas Moore**, as well as to some unknown writers, but he had so unkind a tongue that 'melodious Rogers' is better remembered today by a number of ill-natured sayings than by his poetry. ▢ P W Claydon, *Samuel Rogers* (1889)

Rogers, Will, *properly* William Penn Adair Rogers 1879–1935
US actor, rancher and humorist
He was born in Oolagah, Indian Territory (Oklahoma), the son of a rancher. His colourful early life included foreign travels to Buenos Aires and Johannesburg, and

spells as a ranch hand and cow-puncher; the skills he acquired in riding and lariat-throwing gained him employment from 1902 as 'The Cherokee Kid' in a variety of Wild West shows. He also appeared at the St Louis World's Fair (1904) and featured in the musical *The Girl Rangers* (1907). His first Broadway performance was in *The Wall Street Girl* (1912) and he later became a regular attraction at the *Ziegfeld Follies* (1917–18). By this time his act had expanded to include homespun philosophy, wise-cracking and rustic ruminations. He made a number of silent films, including *Laughing Bill Hyde* (1918), *Jubilo* (1919) and *Doubling for Romeo* (1921). The first of his many books, *The Cowboy Philosopher at the Peace Conference*, was published in 1919. He wrote a syndicated column from 1926, wrote for the *Saturday Evening Post*, made frequent radio broadcasts, and came to personify the wisdom of the common man. He returned to Broadway in *Three Cheers* (1928) and made his first sound film, *They Had to See Paris* (1929). The directors of his many subsequent movies allowed him to ad-lib freely. *Will Rogers' Political Follies* (1929) illustrates his homely liberalism and cracker-barrel philosophy, and films like *State Fair* (1933), *Judge Priest* (1934) and *Steamboat Round the Bend* (1935) catapulted him to the top of cinema popularity polls. At the time of his death in a plane crash (with his friend the aviator **Wiley Post**), he was widely regarded as an irreplaceable American folk hero. *The Autobiography of Will Rogers* (1949) was compiled by Donald Day from his writings and sayings. ▢ H Croy, *Our Will Rogers* (1953)

Rogers, William Pierce 1913–
US Republican politician
Born in Norfolk, New York, he was educated at the University of Colgate and Cornell University Law School. He was assistant district attorney in New York under **Thomas Dewey**. In 1957 he became Attorney-General in the Eisenhower government, and in this capacity he played a leading role in drafting the Civil Rights Act of 1957. He was a delegate to the United Nations (1967), and Secretary of State in the **Nixon** administration (1969–73).

Rogers, Woodes c.1679–1732
English navigator
He led a privateering expedition against the Spanish (1708–11) which rescued **Alexander Selkirk** from one of the Juan Fernández Islands, and on his successful return wrote *Voyage Round the World* (1712). As Governor of the Bahamas (1718–21, 1729–32) he suppressed piracy, founded a house of assembly and resisted Spanish attacks.

Roget, Peter Mark 1779–1869
English physician and scholar and creator of 'Roget's Thesaurus'
He was the son of a Huguenot minister and studied medicine, becoming physician to the Manchester Infirmary in 1804. He was secretary of the Royal Society (1827–49) and Fullerian Professor of Physiology at the Royal Institution (1833–36). He wrote *On Animal and Vegetable Physiology* (Bridgewater Treatise, 1834). In his retirement he devoted his time to the conclusion of a linguistic project that he had been planning for some years. This was published as the *Thesaurus of English Words and Phrases* (1852) and made the name of Roget famous. In it English vocabulary is organized not alphabetically as in conventional dictionaries but according to concepts and themes. ▢ Donald Lewis Emblen, *Peter Mark Roget: The Word and the Man* (1970)

Rohan-Guéménée, Louis René Édouard, Prince de 1734–1803
French prelate
He was born in Paris. In 1778 he was appointed a cardinal, and in 1779 Bishop of Strasbourg. He fell prey to **Alessandro di Cagliostro** and the Comtesse de La Motte, who tricked him into believing that Queen **Marie**

Antoinette, who knew nothing of the affair, wished him to stand security for her purchase by instalments of a priceless diamond necklace. The adventurers collected the necklace from the jewellers supposedly to give it to the queen, but left Paris in order to sell the diamonds for their own gain. When the plot was discovered Rohan-Guémenée was arrested, but he was acquitted by the parlement of Paris (1786). He was elected to the Estates General in 1789, but refused to take the oath to the constitution in 1791, retiring to the German part of his diocese.

Rohde, Ruth, *née* Bryan 1885–1954
US diplomat and feminist
Born in Jacksonville, Illinois, she was educated at Monticello Female Academy and Nebraska University. In 1910 she married Reginald Owen, an English army major who was left an invalid after World War I. To support her family she entered politics as a Democrat in Florida, and in 1928 successfully ran for Congress, becoming the first Congresswoman from the South. Defying accusations of ineligibility for Congress because of her marriage to a foreigner, her remarkable victory on feminist grounds resulted in an amendment to the Cable Act. In 1933 she was appointed US Minister to Denmark, the first US diplomatic post ever held by a woman. Returning to the USA in 1936, she helped to draft the United States Charter, and received the Order of Merit from King Frederik IX of Denmark.

Rohlfs, Gerhard 1831–96
German explorer
Born in Vegesack, near Bremen, he studied medicine, and joined the Foreign Legion in Algeria in 1855. While travelling through Morocco (1861–62), he was robbed and left for dead in the Sahara. From 1864 he travelled widely in North Africa, the Sahara and Nigeria, and, commissioned by the German emperor, undertook expeditions to Wadai in 1878, and Abyssinia (Ethiopia) in 1885, before becoming German consul in Zanzibar.

Röhm or Roehm, Ernst 1887–1934
German soldier and Nazi politician
Born in Munich, he became an early supporter of Hitler and played a vital role in fostering good relations between the Nazi Party and the Bavarian authorities up until November 1923. He was the organizer and commander of the SA or stormtroopers ('Brownshirts') during the mid-1920s and from 1931 to 1934; however, his plans to pursue policies independently of the NSDAP (German National Socialist Workers Party) and to increase the SA's power led to his summary execution on Hitler's orders.

Rohmer, Sax, *pseudonym of* Arthur Sarsfield Ward 1886–1959
English writer of mystery stories
He was born in Birmingham and worked in London, first in commerce, then in journalism. He was interested in Egyptian antiquities and found literary fame with his sardonic, oriental 'Fu Manchu', whose sinister and criminal schemes featured in many spine-chilling tales, including *Dr Fu Manchu* (1913), *The Yellow Claw* (1915), *Moon of Madness* (1927) and *Re-enter Fu Manchu* (1957).

Rohrer, Heinrich 1933–
Swiss physicist and Nobel Prize winner
Born in Buchs, he was educated in physics at the Swiss Institute of Technology in Zurich, then moved to the USA to take up a research post at Rutgers University in New Jersey (1961–63). Returning to Zurich in 1963, he joined the IBM Research Laboratory, where he ultimately became manager of the physics department. His work with Gerd Binnig on the scanning tunnelling microscope began in 1978, and by 1981 they had completed the instrument, which won them the 1986 Nobel Prize for

physics (jointly with Ernst Ruska). The operation of the microscope is based on a quantum-mechanical effect, in which an electron tunnels across a narrow gap between two surfaces. The microscope uses a needle with a tip of just one atom positioned above a sample, and with a potential difference applied a tunnelling current flows, allowing the sample to be scanned. The scanning tunnelling microscope is now found in laboratories around the world, and is especially used in the development of small solid-state electronic devices. He became a Fellow of IBM in 1986.

Roh Tae Woo 1932–
South Korean politician
Born in the farming hamlet of Sinyong, in the southeastern region of Kyongsang, he was educated at the Korean Military Academy (1951–55), where he was a classmate of a future president, Chun Doo-Hwan. He fought briefly in the Korean War and was a battalion commander during the Vietnam War. He became commanding general of the Capital Security Command in 1979, in which role he helped General Chun seize power in the coup of 1979–80. He retired from the army in 1981 and successively served, under President Chun, as Minister for National Security and Foreign Affairs (1981–82) and Minister for Home Affairs (from 1982). He was elected Chairman of the ruling Democratic Justice Party in 1985, and in 1987, following serious popular disturbances, drew up a programme of political reform which restored democracy to the country. He was elected President in 1987, and was succeeded by Kim Young Sam in 1992. In 1995 he was arrested on charges of accepting bribes in return for contracts, and apologized to the nation for his wrongdoing.

Rokitansky, Karl, Baron von 1804–78
Austrian pathologist
Born in Königgrätz, he was Professor of Pathological Anatomy at Vienna University (1834–75), and was one of the founders of modern pathological anatomy. He wrote the influential *Handbuch der pathologischen Anatomie* (1842–46, Eng trans *Treatise of Pathological Anatomy*, 1849–52).

Rokossovsky, Konstantin Konstantinovich 1896–1968
Russian soldier
Born in Warsaw of Polish descent, he served in World War I in the tsarist army and joined the Red Guards in 1917. He was imprisoned during the Stalin purges. In World War II he took part in the Battle of Stalingrad 1942–43, and led the Russian race for Berlin. He became Commander-in-Chief of Soviet forces in Poland (1945–49), and in 1949 was appointed Polish Minister of Defence as Stalin's man in Warsaw, a post he was made to resign in 1956 during the anti-Soviet unrest in Poland. In return Władysław Gomułka became premier, with greater control over Polish domestic affairs while supporting Soviet foreign policy. Rokossovsky was a Deputy Minister of Defence of the USSR from 1956 to 1962, apart from a brief period of military command in Transcaucasia.

Roland d.778
Semi-legendary French knight
The hero of the *Chanson de Roland* (11th century, 'The Song of Roland'), and most celebrated of the Paladins of Charlemagne, he is said to have been Charlemagne's nephew, and the ideal of a Christian knight. The only evidence for his historical existence is a passage in Einhard's *Life of Charlemagne*, which refers to Roland as having fallen at Roncesvalles, fighting against the Basques. Matteo Maria Boiardo's *Orlando Innamorato* and Ludovico Ariosto's *Orlando Furioso* depart widely from the old traditions.

Roland de la Platière, Jean Marie 1734–93
French statesman

He was born near Villefranche-sur-Saône, and became a leader of the Gironde, with Brissot de Warville, Pétion de Villeneuve and François Buzot (1760–94). In March 1792 Roland became Minister of the Interior, but he was dismissed three months later. He was recalled after King Louis XVI's removal to the Temple, but became unpopular with the Jacobins when he protested against the September Massacres (1792), and took part in the last struggle of the Girondins. On 31 May 1793 he was arrested, but he escaped and fled to Rouen, where he attempted unsuccessfully to organize insurrection. Madame Roland was imprisoned for five months, and guillotined on 8 November 1793. Two days later Roland committed suicide.

Roland de la Platière, Jeanne Manon, *known as* Madame Roland, *née* Philipon 1754–93
French writer and revolutionary

Born in Paris, the daughter of an engraver, she was educated in a convent and, influenced by the works of writers such as Plutarch and Rousseau, went on to become a woman of letters. She established a salon in Paris in 1791 and became well known for her Republican sympathies. She married Jean Marie de la Platière in 1780, who became Minister for the Interior in 1792; they both belonged to the Girondin Party. Her influential personality caused her to be held responsible for the anti-Parisian policy shared by themselves and their friends, and, despite her husband's earlier resignation, she was arrested in June 1793 and refused the permission to speak in her own defence. Before being sent to the guillotine in November of the same year, she wrote her *Mémoires*, upon which her literary reputation is primarily based. ◻ Gita May, *Madame Roland and the Age of Revolution* (1970)

Rolfe, Frederick William, *styled* Baron Corvo 1860–1913
English novelist and essayist

He was born in London. A convert to Roman Catholicism, he felt his life was shattered by his rejection from the novitiate for the Roman priesthood at the Scots College in Rome, but it prompted his most famous work, *Hadrian VII* (1904), in which a comparable and obviously self-modelled 'spoiled priest' is unexpectedly chosen for the papacy, institutes various reforms and is ultimately martyred. He contributed to the *Yellow Book* in the 1890s with *Stories Toto Told Me* (republished in book form, 1895) and is also remembered for *Chronicles of the House of Borgia* (1901) and the posthumous *The Desire and Pursuit of the Whole*, published in 1934. Other novels are *Don Tarquino* (1905), and the posthumously published *Nicholas Crabbe* (1958) and *Don Renato* (1963). ◻ A J A Symons, *In Quest of Corvo* (1934)

Rolfe, John 1585–1622
English colonist in Virginia

He emigrated from England to Jamestown, Virginia, in 1610 and discovered a method of curing tobacco, which made possible export of the crop and thus helped to establish the colony's lucrative tobacco trade. In 1614 he married Pocahontas, the daughter of a Powhatan chief, and two years later he took her to England. After her death he returned to Virginia and remarried.

Rolland, Romain 1866–1944
French musicologist, writer and Nobel Prize winner

Born in Clamecy, Nièvre, he studied in Paris and at the French School in Rome, and in 1910 became Professor of the History of Music at the Sorbonne, Paris. In the same year he published *Beethoven*, the first of many works which also included biographies of Michelangelo (1906), Handel (1910), Tolstoy (1911) and Mahatma Gandhi (1924). His 10-volume novel cycle *Jean-Christophe*, the hero of which is a musician, was written between 1904 and 1912, and in 1915 he was awarded the Nobel Prize for literature. In World War I he was unpopular for the pacifist and internationalist ideals expressed in *Au dessus de la mêlée* (1915, 'Above the Fray'). He lived in Switzerland until 1938, completing another novel cycle, *L'Âme enchantée* (1922–33, 'The Enchanted Spirit'), a series of plays about the French Revolution, and numerous pieces of music criticism. On his return to France he became a mouthpiece of the opposition to fascism and the Nazis, and his later works contain much political and social writing. ◻ S Zweig, *Romain Rolland* (1929)

Rolle de Hampole, Richard c.1290–1349
English hermit, mystic and poet

Born in Thornton, Yorkshire, he studied at Oxford. At the age of 19 he became a hermit, first at Dalton and then at Hampole, near Doncaster. He wrote lyrics, meditations and religious works in Latin and English, and translated and expounded the Psalms in prose. ◻ F Comper, *The Life of Richard Rolle* (1928)

Rollin, Alexandre August Ledru- See Ledru-Rollin, Alexandre Auguste

Rolling Stones, The
British rock group

The group was formed in 1961 in London, and its original members were Mick Jagger, Keith Richards (1943–), Bill Wyman (1936–), Charlie Watts (1941–) and Brian Jones (1944–69). One of the longest-running and most successful pop groups, they released their first single, a version of Chuck Berry's 'Come On', in 1963. Initially in the shadow of the Beatles, their carefully cultivated rebellious image and greater reliance on black blues and rhythm and blues won them their own following. Although their uninhibited lifestyles often hit the headlines (with Jones dying from drug abuse and Jagger and Richards both convicted of possessing drugs) it was the quality of their compositions and the popularity of their stage act which ensured their continuing success. Controversy continued to surround them, with a murder taking place at their infamous Altamont concert in 1969, and Richards being convicted of possessing heroin in Canada in 1977. Jones was replaced shortly before his death by Mick Taylor, an outstanding blues guitarist, who was replaced in turn by the less subtle Ronnie Wood in 1976, while Bill Wyman was replaced by Darryl Jones. They remain the quintessential rock-and-roll band of the mid-1990s, and have recorded some of the classics of the genre in such singles as 'Jumpin' Jack Flash' (1968) and 'Honky Tonk Women' (1969), and albums including *Beggar's Banquet* (1968), *Let it Bleed* (1969), *Sticky Fingers* (1971) and *Exile on Main Street* (1972). ◻ Peter Goddard, *The Rolling Stones* (1982)

Rollins, Sonny (Theodore Walter) 1930–
US jazz saxophonist and composer

Born in New York, he learned to play the piano, and alto and tenor saxophone while at school. He worked and recorded with major bebop figures such as Charlie Parker, Bud Powell and Miles Davis in the early 1950s, and emerged from the middle of that decade as an important and highly individual voice in the 'hard bop' movement. His classic *Saxophone Colossus* (1956) is a landmark of the form. He is one of the most powerful jazz improvisers (on both tenor and soprano saxophones) to emerge in the post-Parker period, creating a turbulent but lucidly structured thematic style distinct from that of the Coltrane school. His use of calypso themes such as his famous 'St Thomas' and 'Don't Stop The Carnival' reflects his mother's roots in the Virgin Islands. He took on some of the avant garde directions of the 1960s, and experimented with jazz-fusion in the 1970s, but returned to his roots in small-group acoustic jazz in the 1980s, as well as performing extended solo concerts, as captured on *The Solo Album* (1985). *Silver City* released in 1996 comprises mainly recordings made in the 1980s and 1990s. He remains a major figure in jazz music. ▢ C Blancq, *The Journey of a Jazzman* (1983)

Rollo (Hrolf), *known as* the Ganger ('Walker') c.860–c.932
Viking founder of the duchy of Normandy
The son of a Norse earl of Orkney (Rognvald of Möre), he became the leader of a band of mercenary Vikings foraging in France (911). In peace talks with King Charles III he was offered a large tract of land on the lower Seine in return for becoming Charles's vassal. This territory (Northmandy) was the nucleus of the future duchy of Normandy. One of his descendants was William the Conqueror. Rollo (Hrolf) is said to have been such a large man that no horse could carry him, hence his nickname.

Rolls, Charles Stewart 1877–1910
English car manufacturer and aviator
Born in London and educated at Eton and Cambridge, he was the third son of the 1st Baron Llangattock. He experimented from 1895 with the earliest motor cars and in 1902 founded C S Rolls & Co with Claude Johnson (1864–1926). In 1906 he went into partnership with Henry Royce. The same year he crossed the English Channel by balloon, and in 1910 made the first non-stop double crossing by aeroplane. He died in a plane crash shortly afterwards. Rolls-Royce remains the manufacturer of some of the world's most famous motor-car and aircraft engines. ▢ John Rowland, *The Rolls-Royce Men: The Story of Charles Rolls and Henry Royce* (1969)

Rölvaag, Ole Edvart, *originally* Ole Pedersen 1876–1931
US writer
He was born in a small fishing community in northern Norway, and took the name of a cove near his birthplace when he settled in the USA. He was an avid reader from childhood; inspired by his reading of *The Last of the Mohicans* (in Norwegian), which seemed to offer promise of the New World, at the age of 20 he accepted an offer of a ticket from his uncle in South Dakota. His journey and early experiences as an immigrant are described in *Amerika-Breve* (1912,'Letters from America'). Unsuited to the harshness of life as a prairie farmer, however, Rölvaag enrolled in a local school to improve his English, went from there to university and eventually took up a teaching career at St Olaf College, Minnesota. His major work was *Giants in the Earth* (1927), a grimly realistic, tragic story of the personal and psychological costs of pioneer life, published initially in Norwegian as *I De Dage* (1924, 'In Those Days') and *Riket Grundlaegges* (1925,'Founding the Kingdom'). ▢ P Reigstad, *Rölvaag, his life and art* (1972)

Romains, Jules, *pseudonym of* Louis Farigoule 1885–1972
French writer
He was born in Saint-Julien Chapteuil, and after graduating in both science and literature at the École Normale Supérieure in Paris, he taught in various lycées. In 1908 his poems, *La Vie unanime* ('The Unanimous Life'), established his name and, along with his *Manuel de déification* (1910,'A Treatise on Deification'), the Unanimist school. The novels *Mort de quelqu'un* (1910, Eng trans *The Death of a Nobody*, 1914) and *Les Copains* (1913, 'The Friends'), were followed by *Knock, ou le triomphe de la médecine* (1923, Eng trans *Doctor Knock*, 1925), his most successful play. His later poetry includes *Chants des dix années 1914–1924* (1928,'Songs of the Ten Years 1914–24') and *L'Homme blanc* (1937, 'The White Man'). He became president of the International PEN Club (1936–41), and between 1932 and

1946 produced the great cycle *Les Hommes de bonne volonté* (27 vols, partial Eng trans in 18 vols as *Men of Good Will*, 1933–40), covering French life in the early 20th century. He published his autobiographical *Souvenirs et confidences d'un écrivain* ('Memories and Confidences of a Writer') in 1958. ▢ M Berry, *Jules Romains* (1960, in French)

Roman, Johan Helmich 1694–1758
Swedish composer
Born in Stockholm, he twice visited England, where he met Handel, Geminiani and other leading figures in contemporary music. He travelled in France and Italy, and in 1745 was appointed *intendent* of music to the Swedish court. His compositions include symphonies, concerti grossi, trio sonatas, a Swedish mass, vernacular settings of the Psalms, and occasional music, all showing the influence of the Italian style and, less markedly, of Handel and the French and North German schools.

Romano, Guilio See Guilio Romano

Romanov
Family of Russian tsars
The family emigrated from (Slavonic) Prussia to the principality of Moscow. Michael Romanov, head of the family, was elected tsar by the other Russian boyars (1613), and the tsardom became hereditary in his house until 1762, when on the death of the Tsaritsa Elizabeth, the Duke of Holstein-Gottorp, son of Peter I's daughter, succeeded as Peter III. Later tsars were descended from him and his wife, Catherine II, the Great.

Romberg, Sigmund 1887–1951
US composer of operettas
Born in Nagy Kaniza, Hungary, he settled in the USA in 1909, becoming a US citizen. He wrote more than 70 works, of which the most famous are *Blossom Time* (1921), *The Student Prince* (1924), *The Desert Song* (1926) and *The New Moon* (1928).

Romer, Alfred Sherwood 1894–1973
US palaeontologist
Born in White Plains, New York, he studied at Columbia University and became Professor of Vertebrate Palaeontology at Chicago (1923–34), and later Professor of Zoology and director of the Museum of Comparative Zoology at Harvard (1934–65). He was interested in the evolution of early vertebrates and wrote papers on the importance of the development of the amniotic egg and other preadaptations for terrestrial life. This formed the basis of his *The Vertebrate Story* (1959). His *Vertebrate Palaeontology* (1933) and *The Vertebrate Body* (1949) became standard texts on their subjects.

Romero y Galdames, Oscar Arnulfo 1917–80
Salvadorean Roman Catholic prelate and Nobel Prize winner
He was born in Ciudad Barrios. Ordained in 1942, and generally conservative in outlook, he was made bishop in 1970 and (to the dismay of the progressives) archbishop in 1977. Acts of political violence and repression of the poor made his public utterances and actions more outspoken. After thousands had died in a brutal persecution he himself was murdered while preaching, one year after he was nominated for the Nobel Peace Prize by a large number of US and British parliamentarians. Some of his 'Thoughts' appeared in translation (by James Brockman) as *The Church Is All of You* (1984).

Romilly, Sir Samuel 1757–1818
English lawyer and law reformer
He was born in London, the son of a watchmaker of Huguenot descent. He entered Gray's Inn at the age of 21, and worked mainly in Chancery practice. Appointed Solicitor-General in 1806, he entered parliament and endeavoured to mitigate the severity of the criminal law. He

took part in anti-slavery agitation, and opposed the suspension of the Habeas Corpus Act and the spy system. He wrote *Observations on the Criminal Law of England* (1810), *Speeches* (1820), and *Memoirs* (1840). He committed suicide three days after his wife's death. His second son John, Baron Romilly (1802–74), was made Solicitor-General in 1848, Attorney-General in 1850, Master of the Rolls in 1851 and a baron in 1866.

Rommel, Erwin 1891–1944
German soldier

He was born in Heidenheim. He served in World War I and became an instructor at the Dresden Military Academy, where he was an early Nazi sympathizer. He commanded Hitler's headquarters guard, and displayed such skill while leading a panzer division during the invasion of France in 1940 that he was appointed to command the Afrika Corps. His spectacular successes against the attenuated Allied 8th Army earned him the title 'Desert Fox' and the admiration of his opponents. He drove the British back to El-Alamein, but in November 1942 was defeated there by Montgomery and retreated to Tunis. In March 1943 he was withdrawn, a sick man, from North Africa at Mussolini's insistence. Hitler subsequently appointed him commander of the Channel defences in France. Returning home wounded in 1944, he supported the July plot against Hitler's life. After its failure, he committed suicide. 📖 Desmond Young, *Rommel* (1950)

Romney, George 1734–1802
English painter

Born in Dalton-in-Furness, Lancashire, he specialized in portraiture from 1757, and was greatly influenced by Sir Joshua Reynolds and to a lesser extent Thomas Gainsborough. He went to London in 1762. Most of the leading aristocratic and cultural figures of his day sat for him, including Emma, Lady Hamilton. His technique was ostentatiously fluent and elegant. In 1798 he returned to Kendal.

Romulus Augustulus, *properly* Flavius Momyllus Romulus Augustus 5th century
Last Roman emperor of the West

His father Orestes, a Pannonian, established Augustus (the diminutive 'Augustulus' was a nickname) as puppet emperor in AD475–76, retaining all substantial power in his own hands. Orestes failed to conciliate the troops, who had helped him against the previous emperor, Julius Nepos, and was killed. Augustus surrendered immediately to Odoacer, and was dismissed to a villa near Naples with an annual pension of 6,000 pieces of gold.

Ronalds, Sir Francis 1788–1873
English inventor

Born in London, he studied practical electricity, and in 1816 fitted his garden at Hammersmith with an electric telegraph. Although his offer of the invention to the Admiralty was refused, he published a description of it in 1823. He also invented (1845) a system of automatic photographic registration for meteorological instruments. He was made superintendent of the Meteorological Observatory at Kew, London, in 1843.

Ronsard, Pierre de 1524–85
French poet

Born in La Possonnière, he served the Dauphin and the Duc d'Orléans as page, and accompanied James V with his bride, Mary of Lorraine (Guise), to Scotland, and stayed there for three years. Despite the onset of partial deafness, he studied under the humanist Jean Daurat, at first with Jean Antoine de Baïf and later with Joachim du Bellay and Rémy Belleau. His seven years of study produced *Odes* (1550), *Amours* (1552), *Bocage* (1554), *Hymnes* (1555), the conclusion of his *Amours* (1556), and the first

collected edition of his poetry (1560). He subsequently wrote two bitter reflections on the state of France, *Discours des misères de ce temps* (1560–69, 'Discourse on the Wretchedness of these Times') and *Remonstrance au peuple de France* (1563, 'Admonission of the French People'), and in 1572, following the massacre of St Bartholomew, *La Franciade*, an unfinished epic. Charles IX heaped favours on Ronsard, who became the most important poet of 16th-century France, being the chief exemplar of the doctrines of the Pléiade, which aimed at raising the status of French as a literary language. 📖 G Cohen, *Ronsard, sa vie et son œuvre* (1924)

Röntgen or Roentgen, Wilhelm Konrad von 1845–1923
German physicist and Nobel Prize winner

Born in Lennep, Prussia (now Remscheid, Germany), he studied mechanical engineering at Zurich, and after teaching at Strassburg University, he was appointed Professor of Physics successively at the universities of Giessen (1879), Würzburg (1888), where he succeeded Friedrich Kohlrausch, and Munich (1899–1919). At Würzburg in 1895 he discovered the electromagnetic rays which he called X-rays (known also as Röntgen rays), so called because of their unknown properties; for his work on them he was awarded the Rumford Medal in 1896, jointly with Philipp Lenard, and in 1901 the first Nobel Prize for physics. He also achieved important results on the heat conductivity of crystals, the specific heat of gases, and the magnetic effects produced in dielectrics.

Rook, Jean 1931–91
English journalist

Born in Hull, Humberside, she studied English at London University and embarked on a career in local journalism in Yorkshire. She later moved to Fleet Street, first to the *Daily Sketch*, then the *Daily Mail*, and finally the *Daily Express*, where her outspoken and individual viewpoint and her 'common touch' made her the highest-paid of female journalists and earned her the title 'First Lady of Fleet Street'.

Rooke, Sir George 1650–1709
English admiral

Born near Canterbury, he became post captain at the age of 30, and rear admiral in 1689. In 1692 he served with distinction at Cape La Hogue and was knighted. In 1702 he commanded the expedition against Cadiz, and destroyed the French and Spanish at Vigo. With Sir Cloudesley Shovel he captured Gibraltar (1704), and then engaged a much heavier French fleet off Malaga.

Rooney, Mickey, *originally* Joe Yule, Jnr 1920–
US entertainer

Born in Brooklyn, New York City, he appeared on stage as part of his parents' vaudeville act from the age of 15 months. He made his film debut in *Not To Be Trusted* (1926) and, between 1927 and 1934, starred in about 80 Mickey McGuire short films. Small in stature and irrepressibly energetic, he sang, danced and acted, and played the all-American boy Andy Hardy in a series of films from *A Family Affair* (1937) to *Andy Hardy Comes Home* (1958). The USA's most popular film star between 1939 and 1941, he appeared in other films including *Babes in Arms* (1939), *The Human Comedy* (1943) and *National Velvet* (1944). After wartime service in the army, his youthful persona was no longer to the public's taste, but he developed into a prolific and enduring character actor in films including *The Bold and The Brave* (1956), *Requiem for a Heavyweight* (1962) and *The Black Stallion* (1979). He won an Emmy award for a television film *Bill* (1981) and found great success in the stage revue *Sugar Babies* (1979–85), which he still occasionally performs. He also received special Academy

Awards in 1938 and 1983. He has been married eight times and has written two volumes of autobiography, *I. E.* (1965) and *Life is Too Short* (1991).

Roosevelt, (Anna) Eleanor 1884–1962
US humanitarian

She was born in New York City, the niece of Theodore Roosevelt, and in 1905 became the wife of Franklin D Roosevelt. She undertook extensive political activity during her husband's illness from polio, and proved herself an invaluable social adviser when he became President. In 1941 she became assistant director of the Office of Civilian Defense and after her husband's death in 1945 she extended the scope of her activities. She was a delegate to the UN Assembly in 1946, chairman of the UN Human Rights Commission (1947–51) and US representative to the General Assembly (1946–52). She was also chairman of the American UN Association. Her publications include *The Lady of the White House* (1938), *The Moral Basis of Democracy* (1940), *On My Own* (1958), and her autobiography (1962). 📖 Archibald MacLeish, *The Eleanor Roosevelt Story* (1965)

Roosevelt, Franklin D(elano), *also called* FDR
1882–1945
US Democratic statesman and 32nd President of the USA

A distant cousin of Theodore Roosevelt, he was born into a wealthy family in Hyde Park, New York, and educated in Europe and at Harvard and Columbia Law schools. He was admitted to the New York Bar in 1907 and successively served as a state senator (1910–13) and as Assistant Secretary of the Navy (1913–20), before becoming the Democratic nominee for the vice-presidency in 1920. Stricken by polio and paralysed (1921–23), he was none-theless elected Governor of New York (1928–32). He defeated Herbert Hoover in the presidential election of 1932, in which the repeal of prohibition was a decisive issue. At once he was faced with a serious economic crisis, the Great Depression of 1933; he met this by launching his innovative New Deal programme, which involved abandonment of the gold standard, devaluation of the dollar, state intervention in the credit market, agricultural price support, and the passage of a Social Security Act (1935) which provided for unemployment and old age insurance. On the strength of his success in these reforms, Roosevelt was elected by a landslide in 1936 and secured a third term in 1940 and a fourth in 1944. Roosevelt inculcated a new spirit of hope through his skilful and optimistic radio 'fireside chats', and constructed a new rural-urban 'majority coalition' for the Democratic Party. He also served significantly to extend the reach of the 'presidential sector'. During the late 1930s he endeavoured to avoid involvement in a European conflict, but on the outbreak of World War II he modified the USA's neutrality in favour of the Allies (for example, by the Lend-Lease plan); eventually the country was brought fully into the conflict by Japan's attack on Pearl Harbor (December 1941). A conference with Churchill at sea produced the 'Atlantic Charter', a statement of peace aims; and there were other notable meetings with Churchill and Stalin at Teheran (1943) and Yalta (1945). He died three weeks before the Nazi surrender. 📖 Frank Freidel, *Franklin D Roosevelt* (4 vols, 1952–73)

Roosevelt, Theodore, *nicknamed* Teddy
1858–1919
26th President of the USA and Nobel Prize winner

Born in New York City of Dutch and Scottish descent, he studied at Harvard. He became leader of the New York legislature in 1884, and president of the New York police board from 1895 to 1897. He was Assistant Secretary of the Navy when in 1898 he raised and commanded the volunteer cavalry known as the 'Roughriders' in the Spanish-American War, returning to serve as Governor of New York State (1898–1900). Elected Vice-President in 1900, he became President on the assassination of William McKinley (1901), and was re-elected in 1904. During his presidency (1901–09), he strengthened the navy, initiated the construction of the Panama Canal, and introduced a 'Square Deal' policy for enforcing anti-trust laws. His administration acquired the Panama Canal Zone (1903) and began the construction of the Canal, and he received the Nobel Peace Prize in 1906 for his part in the negotiations which ended the Russo-Japanese War. He returned from a great hunting tour in Central Africa in time to take an active part in the elections of 1910, and created a split in the Republican Party, forming a 'progressive' section with his supporters. As Progressive candidate for the presidency in 1912 he was defeated by Woodrow Wilson. After exploring the Rio Duvida, of Teodoro, in Brazil (1914), he campaigned vigorously during World War I in the cause of US intervention. He wrote on US ideals, ranching, hunting and zoology. He was an immensely popular president; the teddy bear is named after him. 📖 William Henry Harbaugh, *The Life and Times of Theodore Roosevelt* (new rev edn, 1975)

Root, Elihu 1845–1937
US jurist, statesman and Nobel Prize winner

Born in Clinton, New York, he became a corporation lawyer in New York City. As Secretary of War (1899–1904), he drafted the Platt Amendment, which protected US interests in Cuba, and established the Army War College (1901). As Secretary of State (1905–09) he improved US relations with Latin America, negotiated the 'Gentleman's Agreement' limiting immigration from Japan, and ended the US–British dispute over fishing rights. He served as president of the Carnegie Endowment for International Peace (1910–25), and in 1912 he was awarded the Nobel Peace Prize for his promotion of international arbitration. He later supported the League of Nations and the development of the World Court.

Rootes, Billy (William Edward) Rootes, 1st Baron 1894–1964
English car manufacturer

Born in Hawkhurst, Kent, he was educated at Cranbrook School, and in 1917, with his brother Reginald, bought up existing car manufacturing firms, among them Humber, Hillman, Sunbeam and Talbot, and quickly established the largest car-distribution business in Great Britain. The purchase of Singer Motors in 1955 marked the high point of their acquisitions. Lord Rootes was chairman of the Rootes Group until his death, and described himself as its engine, while his brother was the steering and the brakes. He received a baronetcy in 1959.

Rootes, (William) Geoffrey Rootes, 2nd Baron 1917–92
English motor-industry executive

Born in Loose, Kent, he was educated at Harrow and Christ Church, Oxford. He joined the family motor vehicle business, founded by his father Billy Rootes and his uncle Reginald, as a trainee in 1937. By then the company controlled the Humber, Hillman, Sunbeam and Talbot firms. After service in World War II he became managing director (1950) of several of the Group's concerns, then became chairman of Rootes (Scotland) where Hillman Imps were manufactured. The Group, however, faced increasing competition from larger firms such as Ford, and by the end of 1964, when the first Lord Rootes died, much of the business had been bought by Chrysler in the USA. The chairmanship passed to Reginald Rootes, with Geoffrey (now the second Lord Rootes) as deputy until 1967, when he became chairman. In that year the Rootes

Group was completely taken over and renamed Chrysler UK. Rootes resigned in 1973 and later took up the chairmanship of Game Conservancy (1975–79).

Roozeboom, Hendrick Willem Bakhuis
1854–1907
Dutch physical chemist
Born in Alkmaar, he became Professor of Chemistry at Amsterdam, where he demonstrated the practical application of **Josiah Gibbs**'s phase rule. With his students, he also investigated the iron–carbon system, which was fundamental to understanding the behaviour of steel. In 1901 he began publication of an extensive work (in German) on the phase rule. After his death his work was completed by some of his students.

Rorem, Ned 1923–
US composer and writer
Born in Richmond, Indiana, he studied at the Juilliard School of Music in New York. He spent most of the 1950s in Paris, where he was much influenced by contemporary French culture. As well as many songs, he has composed three symphonies and much other orchestral music, six operas, numerous concertos, ballets and other music for the theatre, and choral and chamber music. His *Air Music* (1976) won a Pulitzer Prize. His published essays, diaries and literary criticism are written in a candid and elegant style.

Rorschach, Hermann 1884–1922
Swiss psychiatrist and neurologist
Born in Zurich, he studied at the university there, after deciding against a career in art. He devised a diagnostic procedure for mental disorders based upon the patient's interpretation of a series of standardized ink blots (the 'Rorschach test').

Rorty, Richard McKay 1931–
US philosopher
Born in New York City, he studied at Chicago and Yale, and taught at Yale (1955–57), Wellesley College (1958–61) and Princeton (1961–82), before becoming Professor of Humanities at Virginia University (1982–). His *Philosophy and the Mirror of Nature* (1979) constituted a forceful and dramatic attack on the foundationalist, metaphysical aspirations of traditional philosophy. It was hailed by its supporters as the first major text in post-analytical philosophy, and was denounced by its opponents as unscholarly special pleading. He has subsequently attracted a wider readership among those interested in literary criticism, social theory and intellectual history generally, with works such as *Contingency, Irony and Solidarity* (1988) and *Objectivity, Relativism and Truth* (1991).

Rosa, *originally* Carl August Nicolas Rose 1842–89
German impresario and violinist
Born in Hamburg, he became konzertmeister there in 1863, and appeared in London as a soloist in 1866. In 1875 he founded the Carl Rosa Opera Company in London, greatly enhancing the cause of English opera and opera performed in English.

Rosa, Salvator 1615–73
Italian painter and poet
Born near Naples, he worked in Rome, where his rebellious talents as a painter brought him fame. He made powerful enemies with his satires, and withdrew to Florence for nine years. After that he returned to Rome, where he died. He owes his reputation mainly to his wild and savage landscapes, although he also completed a number of etchings. His *Satires* were published in 1719.

Rosas, Juan Manuel de 1793–1877
Argentine dictator
He was born in Buenos Aires, became Commander-in-Chief of the army (1826), and was appointed Governor of Buenos Aires province (1829–32, 1835–52). With a private army he overthrew the regime of **Bernardino Rivadavia** in 1827. His rule was one of terror and bloodshed. In 1849 he secured for Buenos Aires the entire navigation of the rivers Plate, Uruguay and Paraná. This action incurred the hostility of the other river provinces, and Urquiza, Governor of Entre Rios, supported by Brazil, overthrew Rosas at Monte Caseros, near Buenos Aires (1852). He escaped to England, where he lived until his death.
📖 John Lynch, *Argentine Dictator Juan Manuel de Rosas 1829-1852* (1981)

Roscellinus, Johannes c.1050–after 1120
French scholar
Born probably in Compiègne, he studied at Soissons, and defended his principle of Nominalism against attacks by his pupil **Peter Abelard**. In 1092 the council of Soissons condemned his teaching as implicitly involving the negation of the doctrine of the Trinity.

Roscius, *in full* Quintus Roscius Gallus c.134–62BC
Roman comic actor
Born into slavery, he became the greatest comic actor in Rome, and was freed by the dictator **Sulla**, with whom he was on close terms. He gave **Cicero** lessons in elocution, and wrote a treatise on eloquence and acting. When he was sued for 50,000 sesterces, Cicero defended him in his oration, *Pro Q. Roscio Comoedo*.

Roscius, Young See Betty, William Henry West

Roscoe, Sir Henry Enfield 1833–1915
English chemist
Born in London, the grandson of the English historian William Roscoe (1783–1831), he was educated at University College London and the University of Heidelberg where, with **Robert Bunsen**, he carried out research on quantitative photochemistry. In 1857 he was appointed Professor of Chemistry at Owens College, Manchester. He encouraged links with industry and was energetic in promoting lectures on science for the general public. He was Liberal MP for South Manchester from 1885 to 1895 and Vice-Chancellor of London University from 1896 to 1902. In 1865 he isolated vanadium from copper ores in the Cheshire mines. Previously, vanadium had only been found in very small quantities and its properties were imperfectly known. Roscoe showed that it belongs to the same family as phosphorus and arsenic. He was also the author of influential textbooks. He was elected FRS in 1863 and knighted in 1884. He became president of the British Association for the Advancement of Science in 1887, and a privy councillor in 1909.

Rose of Lima, St, *originally* Isabel de Santa Maria de Flores 1586–1617
Peruvian visionary
Born in Lima and known as Rosa from an early age, she lived a life of self-imposed austerity from girlhood, refusing the attentions of young men attracted by her beauty (which she tried to destroy by defacing her smooth skin) and working hard to alleviate her parents' financial hardship. Although they longed for her to marry, Rosa made a vow of lifelong virginity, taking Catherine of Siena as her role model. She joined the Dominican tertiaries in 1606 and retired to a hut in the family garden, where she is said to have experienced many visions and to have worn a crown of thorns. News of her mystical experiences spread, and when earthquakes hit the city Rosa was often credited with the survival of its inhabitants. Despite her reclusive life, she devoted time to the

concerns of others. The first person in the Americas to be canonized a saint, she is the patron saint of all South America, and her feast day is 23 August.

Rose, Sir John 1820–88
Canadian diplomat

Born in Turriff, Aberdeenshire, and educated at Udny Academy and King's College, Aberdeen, he emigrated with his parents to Huntingdon, Lower Canada (Quebec), in 1836, and was called to the Montreal Bar in 1842. He became involved in the operations of Hudson's Bay Company, acquired numerous directorates, and became a close friend and political associate of John Alexander Macdonald. He was drawn into Anglo-American arbitration initially in deciding Oregon-related questions directly arising from his Hudson's Bay brief (1863–69); at the same time he entered into partnership in London with the US financier and future Vice-President, Levi Morton. He played a critical part in improving British–US relations after the Civil War. He later settled in England, but died in Scotland during a stag shoot.

Rose, Pete (Peter Edward) 1941–
US baseball player and manager

Born in Cincinnati, Ohio, he played with the Cincinnati Reds from 1963 to 1978, then went on to Philadelphia and Montreal before returning to the Reds as player–manager in 1984. In September 1985 he broke Ty Cobb's 57-year-old record of career base hits (4,191). By the time he retired from playing in 1986 he had hit 4,256 base hits, an all-time record. He was manager of the Reds from 1987 to 1989, when an investigation into an alleged gambling offence led to his being banned from baseball for life.

Rose, William Cumming 1887–1984
US biochemist

Born in Greenville, South Carolina, he studied at Yale and spent his career at Illinois University. From the 1930s he studied mammalian nutrition, in one series of experiments replacing all protein by amino acids, and finding that not all 20 of them are essential for a given species. In the rat 10 are essential, but in the adult human diet only eight are, as he showed by experiments using student volunteers.

Roseanne, *properly* Roseanne Barr, *previously known as* Roseanne Arnold 1952–
US comedienne

Born into a Jewish family in Salt Lake City, Utah, she became a teenage mother and housewife, and later worked as a cocktail waitress. She moved to Los Angeles in 1985, and became a regular club and television performer before recording and writing *The Roseanne Barr Show* (1987). She subsequently starred in and wrote the popular television show *Roseanne* (1988–). She has also appeared in such films as *She-Devil* (1989), *Even Cowgirls Get the Blues* (1994) and *Smoke* (1995), and has published the books *Roseanne: My Life as a Woman* (1989) and *My Lives* (1994).

Rosebery, Archibald Philip Primrose, 5th Earl of 1847–1929
Scottish statesman

He was born in London and educated at Eton and Christ Church, Oxford. He succeeded his grandfather in 1868. From 1881 to 1883 he was Under-Secretary for the Home Department, and in 1884 became first Commissioner of Works. In 1886 and again from 1892 to 1894, he was Secretary for Foreign Affairs in the Gladstone administration. In 1889–90 and 1892 he was chairman of the London County Council. On Gladstone's retirement he became Liberal Prime Minister (1894). After his government had been defeated at the general election (1895), he remained Leader of the Liberal Opposition until his resignation in 1896. He was a spokesman for imperial

federation and an imperialist during the Boer War. His political stance in 1909–10 was Independent or Conservative. In 1911 he was created Earl of Midlothian. He published books on William Pitt (1891), Robert Peel (1899), Napoleon (1900), the Earl of Chatham (1910), and a collection called *Miscellanies* (2 vols, 1921). In 1878 he married Hannah (1851–90), the only daughter of Baron Meyer de Rothschild. A devoted race-goer, he won the Derby three times (1894, 1895, 1905). ⌨ Robert Rhodes James, *Rosebery* (1963)

Rosecrans, William Starke 1819–98
US soldier

He was born in Kingston, Ohio. At the outbreak of the Civil War (1861–65) he became aide to George McClellan, whom he succeeded, and kept Robert E Lee out of Western Virginia. In 1862 he commanded a division at the Siege of Corinth, and after its capture commanded the army of the Mississippi. In September he defeated Price at Iuka, and in October defended Corinth against Price and Van Dorn. He won battles at Stone River (December 1862 and January 1863) against Braxton Bragg, but at Chickamauga (September 1863) he was defeated although he held Chattanooga. He was superseded by Ulysses S Grant, but in 1864 repelled Price's invasion of Missouri. In 1868–69 he was Minister to Mexico, from 1881 to 1885 a member for California of the US House of Representatives, and from 1885 to 1893 registrar of the US treasury.

Rosegger, Peter, *known until 1894 as* P K (Petri Kettenfeier) 1843–1918
Austrian poet and novelist

He was born near Krieglach, Styria, of peasant parents, and in 1870 published *Zither und Hackbrett* ('Zither and Chopping-board'), a volume of poems in the Styrian dialect. It was followed by autobiographical works such as *Waldheimat* (1897, 'Home in the Woods') and *Mein Himmelreich* (1901, 'My Heavenly Kingdom'), and several novels, including *Die Schriften des Waldschulmeisters* (1875, 'Writings of a Woodland Schoolmaster'), *Der Gottsucher* (1883, 'The Searcher After God') and *Jakob der Letzte* (1888, 'Jacob the Last'), vividly portraying Styria and its people.

Rose-Innes, Sir James 1855–1942
South African judge

Born in Uitenkage, he was educated at the University of the Cape of Good Hope. He became Attorney-General (1890–93, 1900–02), and then Judge President (later Chief Justice) of the Supreme Court of the Transvaal (1902–10), Judge of Appeal (1910–14), and Chief Justice of the Union of South Africa (1914–27). He advocated a liberal policy towards the Bantu and, as head of a strong bench, was probably one of the most influential of all South African judges. His opinions are notable for their clarity and their willingness to rely on both the English and Roman-Dutch traditions. He was also one of the early translators of the works of Johannes Voet.

Rosen, Michael Wayne 1946–
English writer and performer

He was born in Harrow, London. His first collection, *Mind Your Own Business* (1974), appealed to children with its direct and even crude themes. His humorous, quirky collections also include *Wouldn't You Like to Know* (1977), *You Can't Catch Me* (1981), *Quick Let's Get Out of Here* (1983), *Don't Put Mustard in the Custard* (1984) and *We're Going On A Bear Hunt* (1989). Many of his books are illustrated by Quentin Blake. He has received several prizes for his poetry, including the Signal Poetry award (1982) and the Smarties award (1989). He has also hosted and taken part in radio programmes and readings.

Rosenberg, Alfred 1893–1946
German Nazi politician

He was born in Estonia. An avid supporter of National Socialism, he joined the Nazis in 1920, edited their journals, for a time (1933) directed the party's foreign policy, and in 1934 was given control of its cultural and political education policy. In his *The Myth of the 20th Century* (1930) he expounded the extreme Nazi doctrines which he later put into practice in eastern Europe, for which crimes he was sentenced to death at Nuremberg in 1946.

Rosenberg, Isaac 1890–1918
English poet and artist

Born in Bristol, the son of Jewish émigrés from Russia, he was educated at council schools in the East End of London, and was apprenticed as an engraver before studying art at the Slade School of Art. He went to South Africa in 1914 but returned to England the following year, enlisted in the army and was killed in action in France. His first collection, *Night and Day*, appeared in 1912, followed by *Youth* in 1915 and the posthumous *Poems* in 1922, a selection edited by **Gordon Bottomley** and introduced by **Laurence Binyon**. Alhough he was revered by the cognoscenti, his reputation languished until the appearance in 1937 of his *Collected Works* (with a new edition in 1979).

Rosenberg, Julius 1918–53 and Ethel, *née* Greenglass 1915–1953
US Communist spies

Julius Rosenberg joined the Communist Party as a young man and graduated in electrical engineering. He and his wife Ethel were part of a transatlantic spy ring uncovered after the trial of **Klaus Fuchs** in Great Britain. Julius was employed by the US army, and Ethel's brother, David Greenglass, at the nuclear research station at Los Alamos. They were convicted of passing on atomic secrets through an intermediary to the Soviet vice-consul. Greenglass turned witness for the prosecution and saved his life. The Rosenbergs were sentenced to death in 1951 and, despite numerous appeals from many West European countries and three stays of execution, were executed at Sing Sing prison, New York. They were the first US citizens to be executed for espionage. 📖 Alvin H Goldstein, *The Unquiet Death of Julius and Ethel Rosenberg* (1975)

Rosenquist, James Albert 1933–
US painter

Born in Grand Falls, North Dakota, he studied at the Minneapolis School of Art (1948), Minnesota University (1952–54), and the Art Students League (1955). He began as an abstract painter but took to Pop Art in the mid-1960s, painting enlarged pieces of unrelated everyday objects, eg *Horse Blinders* (1969, Ludwig Museum, Cologne). He held an exhibition at the Whitney Museum of American Art in 1972. He is drawn to shiny surfaces and advertising logos, and the superimposition of one image on another in his work is often traced to the inspiration of his early employment as a billboard painter.

Rosenthal, Jack Morris 1931–
English dramatist

Born in Manchester, and educated at Sheffield University, he joined the promotions department of Granada television in 1956 and began his professional writing with over 150 episodes of *Coronation Street* (1961–69). He was also a contributor to the influential satirical programme *That Was The Week That Was* (1963), and created the series *The Lovers!* (1970). His warmly humorous television plays, dramatizing real-life stories, wartime nostalgia and Jewish domestic issues, include *The Evacuees* (1975), *Barmitzvah Boy* (1976), *Spend, Spend, Spend* (1977) and *London's Burning* (1986). He also wrote the film scripts *Lucky Star* (1980) and *Yentl* (1983) in collaboration with

Barbra Streisand, and his stage work includes *Smash!* (1981) and *Our Gracie* (1983). Later television works include *Wide-Eyed and Legless* (1993) and *Moving Story* (1994). He is married to **Maureen Lipman**.

Rosenzweig, Franz 1886–1929
German theologian

Born in Kassel, to a Jewish family, he first studied medicine, then turned to Hegel's political philosophy, but later abandoned this in favour of an existential approach that emphasized the experience and interests of the individual. He was on the point of converting from Judaism to Christianity, but a religious experience in 1913 caused him to reaffirm his Jewishness and devote the rest of his life to the study and practice of Judaism. His major work was *Der Stern der Erlösung* ('The Star of Redemption'), begun while on active service in World War I and published in 1921. From 1922 he suffered progressive paralysis, but still collaborated with **Martin Buber** from 1925 on a new German translation of the Hebrew Bible. After his death his work exercised a profound influence on Jewish religious thought.

Rosmini-Serbati, Antonio 1797–1855
Italian theologian and philosopher

Born in Rovereto in the Italian Tirol, he was ordained in 1821. In 1828 he founded a new institution for the training of teachers and priests called the 'Institute of the Fathers of Charity', which eventually gained papal approval despite hostility from the Jesuits. In 1830 he published *Nuovo saggio sull' origine delle idee* (3 vols, 'The Origin of Ideas'). His next important work was *Il rinnovamento della filosofia in Italia* (1936, 'The Renewal of Philosophy in Italy'). He became an adviser to Pope **Pius IX**, and worked for a federation of the Italian states under the pope as permanent president, embodied in his *La constituzione secondo la giustizia sociale* (1848, 'Constitution according to Social Justice'). But he fell into disfavour and several of his works, including *Delle cinque piaghe della santa Chiesa* (1848, 'The Five Wounds of the Holy Church'), were prohibited in 1849 by the Congregation of the Index. He retired to Stresa to immerse himself in philosophy and devotion.

Rosny, *joint pseudonym of* Henri Boëx 1856–1940 and Séraphin Justin François Boëx 1859–1948
French novelists

They were brothers, born in Brussels. Their extensive output of social novels, naturalistic in character, includes *L'Immolation* (1887, 'The Sacrifice') and *L'Impérieuse bonté* (1905, 'Pressing Kindness'), signed jointly. After 1908, when they ceased to write together, the older Rosny wrote *L'Appel au bonheur* (1919, 'The Appeal to Happiness') and *La Vie amoureuse de Balzac* (1930, 'Balzac's Love Life'), among other works. Titles by his brother include *La Courtisane passionée* (1925, 'The Passionate Prostitute') and *La Pantine* (1929, 'The Puppet'). 📖 M C Poinsou, *Joseph Henri Boëx* (1907)

Ross, Betsy, *née* Griscom 1752–1836
US seamstress

Born in Philadelphia, Pennsylvania, she was married to an Episcopal clergyman in 1773 and ran an upholstering business after his death in 1776. According to tradition she was visited by **George Washington** and other patriots in June 1776 and asked to make a flag for the new nation. The design she suggested, the Stars and Stripes, was voted the national flag by the Continental Congress on 14 June 1777.

Ross, Diana, *professional name of* Diane Earle 1944–
US pop singer and film actress

She was born in Detroit, where she grew up in a poor housing project. Together with Florence Ballard and Mary Wilson, she formed the Primettes, later to become the Supremes. Their classic Tamla Motown hits 'Baby Love' (1964) and 'Stop! In the Name of Love' (1965) were characteristic of their style. The group, which was by then her backing band, went their own way in 1970 and Ross began a solo career, both as singer and actress. She played the role of Billie Holiday in *Lady Sings the Blues* (1972) and later acted in *Mahogany* (1975) and *The Wiz* (1978). *Diana* (1980) and *Swept Away* (1984) are among her most acclaimed solo albums to date. In recent years, Ross has returned to her sanitized version of Holiday's style, having relaunched herself in 1990 as a jazz diva. She published an autobiography, *Secrets of the Sparrow* (1993), and her television work includes the drama *Out of Darkness* (1994). Her lavish live shows remain popular.

Ross, Harold Wallace 1892–1951
US editor

He was born in Aspen, Colorado. After working as a reporter and editing *Stars and Stripes* and other magazines, he founded the *New Yorker* in 1925. The magazine became legendary for its high standard of writing and attention to detail, as well as for its clever one-line cartoons. Known for his irascible temper and keen journalistic instincts, Ross drafted many gifted writers for the staff of the *New Yorker* and served as its editor until his death.

Ross, Sir James Clark 1800–62
Scottish explorer and naval officer

Born in London, the son of a rich merchant, he first went to sea with his uncle, Sir John Ross, at the age of 12, conducting surveys of the White Sea and the Arctic, and assisting in Ross's first attempt to find the Northwest Passage in 1818, and accompanied William Parry on four Arctic expeditions (1819–27). From 1829 to 1833 he was joint leader with his uncle of a private Arctic expedition financed by the distiller, Sir Felix Booth, and in 1831 he located the Magnetic North Pole. After conducting a magnetic survey of the British Isles, he led an expedition to the Antarctic (1839–43) on the *Erebus* and the *Terror*, during which he discovered Victoria Land and the volcano Mt Erebus. He was knighted on his return in 1843, and wrote an account of his travels in *Voyage of Discovery* (1847). He made a last expedition in 1848–49, searching for the ill-fated Franklin expedition in Baffin Bay. Ross Island, the Ross Sea and Ross's Gull are named after him.

Ross, Sir John 1777–1856
Scottish explorer and naval officer

Born at Inch manse in Wigtownshire, he joined the navy at the age of nine and served with distinction in the Napoleonic Wars. From 1812 he conducted surveys in the White Sea and the Arctic, leading an expedition in 1818, including his nephew Sir James Clark Ross and Sir Edward Sabine, in search of the Northwest Passage. He led another such expedition (1829–33) with his nephew, financed by the distilling magnate Sir Felix Booth, during which he discovered and named Boothia Peninsula, King William Land and the Gulf of Boothia. In 1850 he made an unsuccessful attempt to discover the fate of Sir John Franklin. 📖 M J Ross, *Polar Pioneers: John Ross and James Clark Ross* (1994)

Ross, John *Cherokee name* Kooweskoowe *or* Coowescoowe 1790–1866
Native American leader and Cherokee chief

Born near Lookout, Mount Tennessee, the son of a Scottish father and a part-Cherokee mother, he was raised among the Cherokee but was taught by white tutors and attended an academy in Kingston, Tennessee. He served in a Cherokee regiment under General Andrew Jackson in the War of 1812 and fought in the Battle of Horseshoe

Bend (1814) against the Creek Indians. In 1820 the Cherokee adopted a republican form of government, and Ross sought to promote literacy and Christianity among his people in the hope that by establishing institutions parallel to those of the USA, they could win toleration and perhaps even statehood. He helped to found the Cherokee capital at New Echota, Georgia, and to write their constitution (1827), which established the Cherokee nation under the government of an elected chief, a senate, and a house of representatives. As chief of the eastern Cherokee (1828–39), he spent a decade resisting the campaign by the state of Georgia to take over Cherokee ancestral lands. He led a number of delegations to Washington and successfully brought the Cherokee's case before the US Supreme Court, which ruled in their favour in 1832. President Jackson, whom Ross and other Cherokee had served loyally in the Creek War, favoured the policy of 'Indian removal' and refused to enforce the Court's decree, and in 1838 the Cherokee were evicted from Georgia. Unwillingly Ross led his people on the Trail of Tears (1838–39), an 800-mile trek to Indian Territory in Oklahoma, during which 4,000 Cherokee—almost a quarter of the nation—died of exhaustion, hunger, exposure and disease. Among those who perished on the journey was Ross's wife, Quatie. From 1839 until his death, Ross was chief of the eastern and western Cherokee, which were united in one nation in the new territory.

Ross, Mother See Davies, Christian

Ross, Robert Baldwin 1869–1918
Canadian authority on art

The son of the attorney-general of Upper Canada, he was taken to Europe at the age of two after his father's death. He became a literary journalist and art critic, associated with Oscar Wilde (whom he is believed to have drawn into homosexual life) and the Decadents, later writing a study of Aubrey Beardsley, but also associated with their critics, including W E Henley. He acted as Wilde's main psychological support during his imprisonment and subsequent life, and after Wilde's death (1900) worked to pay off the bankruptcy on the Wilde Estate, reclaim its properties and produce a comprehensive edition of Wilde's works (1908). His publication of part of Wilde's long prison letter as *De Profundis* (1905) led to violent persecution from Lord Alfred Douglas.

Ross, Sir Ronald 1857–1932
British physician and Nobel Prize winner, discoverer of the malaria parasite

Born in Almara, Nepal, the son of an army officer, he studied medicine at St Bartholomew's Hospital in London and entered the Indian Medical Service in 1881. Investigating Sir Patrick Manson's belief that malaria is transmitted through mosquito bites, Ross discovered the malaria parasite in the stomachs of mosquitoes that had bitten patients suffering from the disease, and by 1898 had worked out the life cycle of the malaria parasite for birds. He returned to England in 1899 to lecture at the newly founded Liverpool School of Tropical Medicine, was elected FRS in 1901, and knighted in 1911. From 1926 he directed the Ross Institute in London. He was a gifted if eccentric mathematician who also wrote poetry and romances. His award of the 1902 Nobel Prize for physiology or medicine was contested by Giovanni Grassi (1854–1925), an Italian parasitologist who had independently and almost simultaneously worked out the life cycle of the human malaria parasite.

Ross (of Marnock), Willie (William) Ross, Baron 1911–88
Scottish Labour politician

Born in Ayr, the son of a train driver, he was educated at Ayr Academy and Glasgow University and became a schoolteacher before World War II. He entered parliament as MP for Kilmarnock in a by-election in 1946, and represented that constituency until 1979, when he was created a life peer. As the longest-serving Secretary of State for Scotland (1964–70, 1974–76), he was responsible for the creation of the Highlands and Islands Development Board and the Scottish Development Agency.

Rossby, Carl-Gustaf Arvid 1898–1957
US meteorologist

Born in Stockholm, Sweden, he graduated from Stockholm University where he obtained a doctorate in 1925. He joined the Bergen School under Vilhelm F K Bjerknes (1919). In 1926 he went to the USA and became professor at Massachusetts Institute of Technology (MIT, 1931–39) and Chicago University (1941–50), before returning to Stockholm University (1950–57). In 1927 he established in California the first US weather service for airways, which became the model for others. During his years at MIT he was largely responsible for the general acceptance of the Norwegian methods of synoptic analysis in the USA. Rossby played an important role in establishing rigorous training courses for meteorologists both at MIT and Chicago. During World War II he was largely responsible for the varied courses needed for different theatres of war. His theoretical work greatly assisted the programming for numerical weather prediction when computers of sufficient speed became available.

Rosse, William Parsons, 3rd Earl of 1800–67
Irish astronomer and landowner

Born in York, England, he was educated at Trinity College, Dublin, and Oxford, where he graduated in mathematics (1822). With the help only of the workers on his feudal estate of Birr Castle at Birr (then Parsonstown) he constructed on the model of Sir William Herschel's instruments a gigantic metal-mirror telescope, the 'leviathan of Parsonstown'. With this, the largest telescope before the construction of the 100-in reflector in California (1917), he discovered the spiral structure of the nebula Messier 51 near the tail of the Great Bear (1845), the first ever observation of a spiral galaxy. Drawings of this and of many other nebulae, including spirals, were published in Rosse's catalogue of nebulae (1850). His giant mirror is preserved in the Science Museum, London.

Rossellini, Roberto 1906–77
Italian film director

Born in Rome, he entered the film industry as a sound technician and editor before graduating by way of short films to his feature-length directorial debut with *La Nave Bianca* (1941). Immediately after World War II, his trilogy, *Roma Città aperta* (1945, *Rome, Open City*), *Paisà* (1946, *Paisan*) and *Germania, Anno Zero* (1947, *Germany, Year Zero*), helped establish the neorealist movement with their raw, naturalistic depictions of everyday life which combined drama with factual accuracy. His affair with Ingrid Bergman (whom he later married, 1949–57) provoked worldwide condemnation, and the films they made together, such as *Stromboli* (1950) and *Viaggio in Italia* (1953, *Strangers*), were critically undervalued and sometimes banned. This damaged his international standing, but he enjoyed a popular success with *Il Generale della Rovere* (1959, *General della Rovere*) and spent his later years making television documentaries on historical figures, including *Socrates* (1970) and *The Messiah* (1977). One of his daughters by Ingrid Bergman, Isabella Rossellini (1952–), is an actress. 📖 P Brunette, *Roberto Rossellini* (1987)

Rossellino, Antonio 1427–c.1479
Italian sculptor

Born in Florence, he was the youngest brother and pupil of Bernardo Rossellino, and is best known for his terracotta sculptural reliefs of the *Madonna and the Laughing Child* (1465, Victoria and Albert Museum, London), and marble portrait busts, notably that of the Florentine Matteo Palmieri (1468). His style is less austere than his brother's and his preference for suggesting movement is well demonstrated in his most important monument, the marble tomb of the Cardinal of Portugal (1466) in San Miniato al Monte, Florence. His last work, in 1478, was the marble *Madonna della Latte* on the Nori monument in Santa Croce, Florence.

Rossellino, Bernardo 1409–64
Italian architect and sculptor

Born in Florence, he was the brother and teacher of Antonio Rossellino. As an architect he worked under Leon Battista Alberti, executing his designs for the church of S Maria Novella, Florence. His most complete architectural work is the palace and cathedral of Pienza. In 1451 he was appointed architect to Pope Nicholas V and designed, though never built, a new façade for St Peter's in Rome. His sculptural masterpiece is the tomb of the chancellor Leonardo Bruni (1450) in S Croce, Florence, which in its austere classical style is the epitome of Italian Renaissance art.

Rosseter, Philip 1568–1623
English lutenist and composer

Born possibly in London, he was a musician at the court of James VI and I when he published his *Ayres* (1601). His *Lessons for Consort* appeared in 1609, and from that time he was active in court theatricals.

Rossetti, Christina Georgina 1830–94
English poet

Born in London, the sister of Dante Gabriel Rossetti, she was educated at home, and was to have been a governess, but retired through ill health. Her grandfather printed a pamphlet by her before she was in her teens and her earliest lyrics were published in the first issue of *The Germ* (1850) under the pseudonym Ellen Alleyne. *Goblin Market* (1862) was her best-known collection, and *The Prince's Progress* appeared in 1866 and *Sing Song: A Nursery Rhyme Book*, illustrated by Arthur Hughes, in 1872. She was a devout Anglican, and her later works include *A Pageant and Other Poems* (1881), *Time Flies: A Reading Diary* (1895) and *The Face of the Deep: A Devotional Commentary on the Apocalypse* (1892). 📖 E W Thomas, *Christina Georgina Rossetti* (1931)

Rossetti, Dante Gabriel, *properly* Gabriel Charles Dante Rossetti 1828–82
English poet, painter and translator

Born in London, he was the son of Gabriele Rossetti and brother of Christina and William Rossetti. He was educated at King's College School and attended Cary's Art Academy, having shown an early inclination towards poetry and art. With Holman Hunt and John Millais he formed the Pre-Raphaelite Brotherhood. Throughout the 1840s he developed his poetry and painting, completing on canvas *The Girlhood of Mary Virgin* (1849) and *Ecce Ancilla Domini* (1850), both in the Tate Gallery, London. Like his sister Christina, several of his poems, eg 'The Blessed Damozel' and 'My Sister's Sleep', appeared in *The Germ* (1850). He met Elizabeth Siddal (or Siddall) in 1849–50 and tutored her in her painting and writing, encouraging her to model for him. He married her in 1860. He met John Ruskin in 1854 and two years later William Morris, whom he manifestly influenced. In 1861 he published *The Early Italian Poets*, which consisted of translations from 60 poets, such as Dante and Guido Cavalcanti. His wife's

Rossini, Gioacchino Antonio 1792–1868
Italian operatic composer

Rossini was born in Pesaro, the son of a strolling horn-player and a baker's daughter turned singer. He was taught to sing and play at an early age, and in 1806 began to study composition at the Liceo in Bologna, where in 1808 he won the prize for counterpoint with a cantata. Tiring of the stern academic routine, he wrote several small-scale comic operas, among them *La Scala di seta* (1812, 'The Silken Ladder'), whose lively overture has remained popular although the opera itself was a failure.

His first successes were *Tancredi* (1813) and *L'Italiana in Algeri* (1813, 'The Italian Girl in Algiers'). In 1816 his masterpiece, *Il Barbiere di Seviglia* ('The Barber of Seville'), was received in Rome with enthusiasm despite a disastrous opening night. *Otello* (1816) has since been eclipsed by **Verdi**'s masterpiece. In 1817 *La Cenerentola* ('Cinderella') was favourably received in Rome and *La Gazza Ladra* ('The Thieving Magpie') in Milan, and these were followed in Naples by *Armide* (1817), *Mosè in Egitto* (1818, 'Moses in Egypt') and *La Donna del Lago* (1819, 'The Lady of the Lake'). *Semiramide* (1823), the most advanced of his works, had only a lukewarm reception from the Venetians.

In 1821 Rossini had married a beautiful Spanish singer, Isabella Colbran, who performed several of his leading roles, including that of *Semiramide*. They now won fresh laurels in Vienna (where Rossini met **Beethoven**) and in London, and Rossini was invited to become director of the Italian Theatre in Paris. There he adapted several of his works to French taste: *Maometto II* (1820) as *Le Siège de Corinth* (1826, 'The Siege of Corinth'), *Mosè in Egitto* as *Moïse et Pharaon* (1827), and the stage cantata *Il viaggio a Reims* (1825) as *Le Comte Ory* (1828, 'Count Ory'). In 1829 what is arguably his greatest work, *Guillaume Tell* ('William Tell'), written in a nobler style than his Italian operas, was first performed. In 1837 he separated from Isabella, and in 1847 married Olympe Pelissier, who had been nurse to his children.

After 1829 Rossini wrote little music, except for the *Stabat Mater* (1841), the *Petite messe solennelle* (1863, 'Little Solemn Mass') and a number of vocal and piano pieces. In 1836 he retired to Bologna and took charge of the Liceo, whose fortunes he revived. The Revolutionary disturbances in 1847 drove him to Florence in deep depression, but he recovered and returned to Paris in 1855.

With **Donizetti** and **Bellini**, Rossini helped form the 19th-century Italian operatic style which became the inheritance of **Verdi**. Many of his works are still much performed, and the wit and vivacity of the overtures ensures them a place in the concert repertory.

📖 A Kendall, *Gioacchino Rossini, The Reluctant Hero* (1992); R Osborne, *Rossini* (1986); J Harding, *Rossini* (1971); H Weinstock, *Rossini: A Biography* (1968).

'I was born for *opera buffa*, as well Thou knowest. Little skill, a little heart, and that is all. So be Thou blessed and admit me to Paradise.' Manuscript inscription on the score of his 'Petite Messe Solennelle' (1863).

---

death in 1862 from an overdose of laudanum affected him deeply and his work became increasingly morbid. From 1869 he formed a liaison with Jane, the wife of William Morris, and she became his model during his sojourn at Kelmscott Manor (1871–74) and later, notably for *The Daydream* (1880, Victoria and Albert Museum, London). In 1872 he became depressed and attempted suicide. Nevertheless, *Ballads and Sonnets* with the sonnet sequence 'The House of Life' and 'The King's Tragedy' appeared in 1881. At odds with Victorian morality, his work is lush, erotic and medieval, romantic in spirit, and of abiding interest. 📖 C Davies, *Dante Gabriel Rossetti* (1925)

Rossetti, Gabriele 1783–1854
Italian poet and writer

The father of **Christina Rossetti**, **Dante Gabriel Rossetti** and **William Michael Rossetti**, he was the curator of ancient bronzes in the Museum of Bronzes at Naples. He was a member of the provisional government set up by **Joachim Murat** in Rome (1813). After the restoration of **Ferdinand I** to Naples, he joined the Carbonari secret society and greeted the constitution demanded by the patriots in 1820 in a famous ode. On the overthrow of the constitution he went to London (1824), where he became Professor of Italian at the new University of London. Besides writing poetry he was a student of **Dante**, whose *Inferno* he maintained was chiefly political and antipapal. 📖 R D Williams, *The Rossetti Family* (1932)

Rossetti, William Michael 1829–1919
English critic

He was the son of **Gabriele Rossetti** and brother of **Christina** and **Dante Gabriel Rossetti**. He worked as an inland revenue official, but was chiefly a man of letters. He became one of the seven Pre-Raphaelite 'brothers', and edited their manifesto *The Germ* (1850). He was art critic of *The Spectator* from 1850, wrote biographies of **Shelley** and **Keats**, and published editions of **Coleridge**, **Milton**, **William Blake** and **Walt Whitman**. Like all his family he was devoted to the study of **Dante**, whose *Inferno* he translated. He also wrote memoirs of his brother (1895) and his sister (1904).

Rossi, Bruno, *also* Giovanni Battista de Rossi 1905–
US physicist

Born in Venice, Italy, he was educated at the universities of Padua (1923–25) and Bologna (1925–27) and subsequently took up an assistantship in the physics department at the University of Florence (1928–32). In 1932 he was appointed Professor of Physics at the University of Padua, where his early research on cosmic rays showed that these energetic particles can traverse great thicknesses of matter. He also demonstrated that incident primary radiation from space may collide with atoms in the atmosphere to generate cascades of secondary particles, now called 'showers'. This primary radiation he found to be positively charged (in fact cosmic rays consist mainly of protons). In 1939 he moved first to the University of Manchester, and then to the USA, where he continued his work on cosmic rays at the University of Chicago, before becoming Professor of Physics at Cornell University in 1940. Five years later he moved to the Massachusetts Institute of Technology (MIT) where he spent the rest of his working life.

Rossi, Giovanni Battista de See Rossi, Bruno

Rossi, Giovanni Battista de 1822–94
Italian archaeologist

Born in Rome, he is known for his researches on the Christian catacombs of St Callistus there, and has been called the founder of Christian archaeology.

Rossini, Gioacchino Antonio See panel above

Rossiter, Leonard 1926–84
English actor

Born in Liverpool, Merseyside, he was an insurance clerk before turning to the stage, where he made his first appearance in 1954. Hawk-like features, combined with expert timing and energetic attack, allowed him to portray the furtively sinister or the manically comic. His first film appearance in *A Kind of Loving* (1962) was followed by many others, including *Billy Liar* (1963) and *Barry Lyndon* (1975). His notable stage work included *The Resistible Rise of Arturo Ui* (1968–69) and *Banana Box* (1973). The latter was made into a television series, *Rising Damp* (1974–78), where his performance as the leering landlord Mr Rigsby brought widespread popularity. Later television appearances included *The Fall and Rise of Reginald Perrin* (1976–80), and later stage appearances included *Tartuffe* (1976) and *Loot* (1984).

Rossner, Judith Perelman 1935–
US novelist
Born and educated in New York City, she established her interest in women who are trapped within their roles in society in her first book, *To the Precipice* (1966). This was handled with heavier irony in *Nine Months in the Life of an Old Maid* (1969) and in *Any Minute I Can Split* (1972), but had its definitive statement in *Looking for Mr Goodbar* (1975), an unforgiving and ruthless exploration of female sexuality and sexual stereotyping. Later works include *Attachments* (1977) and *August* (1983).

Rosso, Fiorentino, *real name* Giovanni Battista de Jacopo di Gasparre 1494–1540
Italian painter
A leading exponent of Mannerism, he was trained under **Andrea del Sarto**, but his angular, tortured style owes more to **Michelangelo**. Along with other Italian painters of his generation he was invited to France by **Francis I** in 1530. There he was responsible for what was in many ways the fullest flowering of the Mannerist style—the Fontainebleau School. His most famous work is an extraordinary, almost Expressionist *Descent from the Cross* at Volterra.

Rostand, Edmond 1868–1918
French poet and dramatist
He was born in Marseilles. He published *Les Musardises* ('Dawdlings'), a volume of verse, in 1890, but rose to fame with *Cyrano de Bergerac* (1897, Eng trans 1898; also trans by **Anthony Burgess** for the film by Jean Paul Rappeneau, 1992), *L'Aiglon* (1900, Eng trans 1900), *Chantecler* (1910, Eng trans 1910), and other plays in verse which eschewed the prevailing moods of Naturalism and Expressionism in favour of a lighter, more vivacious popular style.
📖 R Gérard, *Edmond Rostand* (1935)

Rostopchin, Fyodor Vasilevich, Graf 1763–1826
Russian soldier, politician and writer
He was born in Livny to a noble family of Tatar descent, and joined the Russian army in 1785. He won influence over the unbalanced Tsar **Paul I** and was for two years his Foreign Minister. As a conservative, he was out of favour in **Alexander I**'s early years, but as a patriot he regained favour in the war against **Napoleon I** as Governor of Moscow. It was he who may have planned, or at least had a share in, the burning of Moscow against Napoleon I in 1812. He wrote historical memoirs and two comedies and other plays, in Russian and French.

Rostow, Walt Whitman 1916–
US economist
Born in New York City and a graduate of Yale, he was a Rhodes Scholar at Oxford (1936–38). After serving with the US army as a major (1942–45), he was assistant chief of the German Austrian Economic Division of the State Department until becoming Harmsworth Professor of History at Oxford and then Professor of American History at Cambridge until 1950. He worked at the Massachusetts Institute of Technology Center for International Studies (1950–60), and became special adviser to Presidents **John F Kennedy** (1961–63) and **Lyndon B Johnson** (1966–69). Since 1969 he has been Professor of Economics and History at Texas University. He has published many books, particularly relating to questions of economic growth, and is best known for his theory that societies pass through five stages of economic growth. His publications include *The Stages of Economic Growth: A Non-Communist Manifesto* (1960), *Politics and the Stages of Growth* (1971), *Rich Countries and Poor Countries* (1987) and *Theories of Economic Growth* (1990).

Rostropovich, Mstislav Leopoldovich 1927–
Russian cellist and conductor
Born in Baku, he was awarded the Lenin prize in 1964, and left the USSR in 1974 with his wife, soprano Galina Vishnevskaya (1926–). He was musical director of the National Symphony Orchestra, Washington (1977–94), and joint artistic director of the Aldeburgh Festival in England. He was deprived of Soviet citizenship in 1978, although it was restored in 1990. **Benjamin Britten** was a close friend and wrote several cello works for him. He became an honorary KBE in 1987.

Roswitha or Roswita See Hrostwitha

Roth, Henry 1906–95
US novelist
He was born in Tysmenica in the Austro-Hungarian Empire, and was taken to the USA as a baby. His childhood is fictionalized in *Call It Sleep* (1934), one of the classics of 20th century US literature. Although 'authentic', it is by no means a sociological documentary, and is marked by a hallucinatory inwardness which is influenced by **James Joyce**. During the Depression Roth worked for the New Deal Works Progress Administration, then worked variously as a teacher, mental hospital assistant, duck farmer and machine toolist. *Shifting Landscape*, a collection of occasional pieces, was published in 1987. He took many years to complete his long-projected second novel, the second volume of which, *Mercy Of A Rude Stream*, appeared in 1994. 📖 *Nature's First Green* (1979)

Roth, Joseph 1894–1939
Austrian novelist, short-story writer and critic
He was born in Brody, Galicia, in the Austro-Hungarian Empire, the son of an Austrian father and a Russian Jewish mother. His father left before he was born, the war disrupted his education, his wife became insane, and he survived by undertaking menial work and taking up journalism until the 1930s; then, exiled in Paris, he became an alcoholic and died destitute. His major themes are not dissimilar to those of **Robert Musil**. His concern for those brought up in the Austro-Hungarian Empire, however, was linked with that of the Jewish diaspora. He was a versatile and prolific writer, but narratively conventional, and he is still underrated, though more of his work has been translated in recent years. Key works include *Hiob: Roman eines einfachen Mannes* (1930, Eng trans *Job: The Story of a Simple Man*, 1931), *Radetzkymarsch* (1932, Eng trans *The Radetzky March*, 1934), *Beichte eines Mörders* (1936, Eng trans *Confessions of a Murderer*, 1938) and *Die Kapuzinergruft* (1938, 'Grave of the Capucins'). 📖 *Juden auf der Wanderschaft* (1926, 'Wandering Jews')

Roth, Philip Milton 1933–
US novelist
Born in Newark, New Jersey, he attended Bucknell University as an undergraduate and received a master's degree from Chicago University, where he also taught (1956–58). His upbringing was Jewish, conventional and lower middle-class, and he did not begin to fight the 'taboos that had filtered down to [him]' until he was in his

late teens. An uncompromising, tough-minded writer, he has frequently irritated rabbis and Jewish organizations with his portrayal of Jews as adept at scheming and compromise; and his discussion of sexual matters has led him into conflict with conservatives, who have sought to restrict access to his books. His first book was *Goodbye Columbus* (1959), a collection of short stories, each obsessed with confrontations between Jews of radically different persuasions and temperaments. There followed two accomplished novels, *Letting Go* (1962) and *When She Was Good* (1967), before publication of his 'masturbation' masterpiece, *Portnoy's Complaint* (1969), made him notorious. The success of the monotone confession of Alexander Portnoy to his psychiatrist lies in the fascination of the narrator's 'voice'. Roth's prolific career has taken many turns as he constantly explores the relationship 'between the written and the unwritten world'. Nathaniel Zuckerman, a writer, is the central presence in the trilogy of novels, *The Ghost Writer* (1979), *Zuckerman Unbound* (1981) and *The Anatomy Lesson* (1983), and its epilogue, *The Prague Orgy* (1985), collected in *Zuckerman Bound* (1985). *The Counterlife* appeared in 1987 and the autobiographical *Patrimony* (which bore the teasing subtitle 'A True Story') in 1991. In 1993 he published the novel *Operation Shylock* and in 1995, *Sabbath's Theater*. He was married to the actress Claire Bloom from 1990 to 1995. Amongst many other awards, he won the 1960 National Book award for fiction and the 1991 National Arts Club Medal of Honor for literature. ◻ *The Facts: A Novelist's Autobiography* (1988)

Rothacker, Erich 1888–1965
German philosopher
Born in Pforzheim, Baden-Württemberg, he was a leading exponent of philosophical anthropology, which seeks to construct a coherent picture of human beings in their biological, cultural and social aspects. He proposed an empirical examination of all human cultures and historical periods on their own terms and in all their authentic particularity and diversity. The human sciences therefore have an essential involvement with the *Weltanschauungen* (worldviews) of their objects. His main works were *Logik und Systematik der Geisteswissenschaften* (1920), *Probleme der Kulturanthropologie* (1948, 'Problems of Cultural Anthropology') and *Philosophische Anthropologie* (1966, 'Philosophical Anthropology').

Rothenstein, Sir John Knewstub Maurice
1901–92
English art historian
Born in London, he was the son of Sir William Rothenstein. He studied at Worcester College, Oxford, and University College London. From 1927 to 1929 he taught in the USA, and was director of Leeds and Sheffield city art galleries between 1932 and 1938, when he was appointed director and keeper of the Tate Gallery; he retired in 1964. His many works on art include *Modern English Painters* (1952–73) and his autobiography (3 vols, 1965, 1966, 1970).

Rothenstein, Sir William 1872–1945
English artist
Born in Bradford, Yorkshire, he studied at the Slade School of Art, London, and in Paris, and won fame as a portrait painter. He was Principal of the Royal College of Art, and was an official war artist in both world wars.

Rothermere, 1st Viscount See Harmsworth, Harold Sydney

Rothko, Mark, *originally* Marcus Rothkovitch
1903–70
US painter
Born in Dvinsk, Latvia, he emigrated with his family to the USA in 1913 and later studied at Yale (1921–23). Largely self-taught as an artist, he had his first one-man show in New York in 1933. During the 1940s he was influenced by Surrealism but by the early 1950s had evolved his own peaceful and meditative form of Abstract Expressionism, staining huge canvases with rectangular blocks of pure colour and later with sombre reds and blacks. Among his works in this style, which was dubbed 'colour field painting', are *Light, Earth, and Blue* (1954) and *The Black and the Red* (1956). In 1958–59 he was commissioned to paint a series of murals for the Four Seasons Restaurant in the Seagram Building, New York, but he withheld them and in 1969 donated a selection of them to the Tate Gallery, London, eg *Black on Maroon*. On the day of their arrival in 1970 a cable from New York announced that he had been found dead in his studio. He had recently completed the decoration of the de Menil Chapel in Houston, Texas.

Röthlisberger, Hans 1923–
Swiss glaciologist
Born in Langnau, near Bern, he studied petrology at the Swiss Federal Institute of Technology (ETH) in Zurich, where in 1954 he described a new method for grain size determinations in sedimentary rocks. He held various appointments at ETH, finally becoming head of the glaciology section of the Laboratory of Hydraulics, Hydrology and Glaciology (1980–87), and made expeditions to Baffin Island in 1950 and 1953, during which he undertook seismic soundings across glaciers. His main contributions lie in glacial hazard assessment, and in englacial and subglacial drainage of meltwater, where he showed that the rate of melting caused by the frictional heat of running water is equivalent to the rate of conduit closure caused by ice overburden pressure. He published *Seismic Exploration in Cold Regions* (1972), and was president of the International Glaciological Society (1984–87).

Rothschild (of Tring), Lionel Walter Rothschild, 2nd Baron 1868–1937
English collector, taxonomist and patron
Born near Peterborough, Cambridgeshire, the son of Nathan Mayer Rothschild, 1st Baron Rothschild, he was educated at Bonn and Cambridge universities, became the sponsor of many collecting expeditions, and donated his private collection at Tring to the National History Museum. Rothschild's collections, and the publications based on them, educated biologists worldwide about species distribution, varieties, transitional forms, population variation and classification.

Rothschild, Mayer Amschel 1744–1812
German financier
Born in Frankfurt am Main, he was named from the 'Red Shield' signboard of his father's house. Trained as a rabbi, he founded a business as a moneylender and became the financial adviser to the Landgrave of Hesse. The house received a heavy commission for transmitting money from the English government to the Duke of Wellington in Spain, paid the British subsidies to Continental princes, and negotiated loans for Denmark between 1804 and 1812. At his death, the founder left five sons, all of whom were made barons of the Austrian Empire in 1822. Anselm Mayer (1773–1855), the eldest son, succeeded as head of the firm in Frankfurt; Solomon (1774–1855) established a branch in Vienna; Nathan Mayer (1777–1836) one in 1798 in London; Charles (1788–1855) one in Naples (discontinued in about 1861); and James (1792–1868) one in Paris. They negotiated many of the great government loans of the 19th century, and Nathan raised the house to be first among the banking houses of the world. He staked his fortunes on the success of Great Britain in her duel with Napoleon, and, receiving the first news of the outcome at Waterloo, sold and bought stock which brought him over £1 million profit. His son Lionel (1808–79) achieved much for the civil and political

emancipation of the Jews in Great Britain. Lionel's son, Nathan (1840–1915), succeeded (1876) to his uncle Anthony's baronetcy (1846), and was made Baron Rothschild in 1885. 📖 Frederick Morton, *The Rothschilds* (1962)

Rothschild, Nathaniel Mayer Victor Rothschild, 3rd Baron 1910–90
English administrator
Born in London, he served in military intelligence from 1939 to 1945, then spent two years with BOAC (British Overseas Airways Corporation). He was chairman of the Agricultural Research Council (1948–58), assistant director of the Department of Zoology at Cambridge and research director/co-ordinator of Shell UK (1950–70). From 1971 to 1974 he was in government service as director-general of the Central Policy Review Staff.

Rotrou, Jean de 1609–50
French playwright
Born in Dreux, he qualified as a lawyer in Paris, and turned to writing plays, as well as becoming one of the five poets who worked the ideas of Cardinal **Richelieu** into dramatic form. His first pieces were in the Spanish romantic style. Next followed a classical period, culminating in three masterpieces, *Saint-Genest* (1646), a tragedy of Christian martyrdobradley henrytm, *Don Bernard de Cabrère* (1648) and *Vénceslas* (1647). He died of the plague. Thirty-five of his plays are still extant. 📖 H Chandon, *La vie de Rotrou* (1884)

Rouault, Georges Henri 1871–1958
French painter and engraver
Born in Paris, he was apprenticed to a stained-glass designer in 1885. He used glowing colours, outlined with black, to achieve a concise depiction of the clowns, prostitutes and biblical characters he chose as his subjects. He studied under **Gustave Moreau**, and in 1898 was made curator of the Moreau Museum, Paris. About 1904 he joined the Fauves (**Henri Matisse**, **André Derain** and others), and in 1910 held his first one-man show. Many of his works were acquired by the art dealer Ambroise Vollard (1865–1939), who commissioned the series of large religious engravings published after Vollard's death as *Miserere* and *Guerre*.

Roubillac or Roubiliac, Louis François
1702/1705–1762
French sculptor
Born in Lyons, he studied at Paris, and in the 1730s settled in London. His rococo statue of **Handel** for Vauxhall Gardens (1738, now in the Victoria and Albert Museum, London) first made him popular. His other most famous statues, also in a lively and informal style, are those of Sir **Isaac Newton** (1755) in Trinity College, Cambridge, of **Shakespeare** (1758, now in the British Museum, London) and another of Handel (1761) in Westminster Abbey, London. Busts include **William Hogarth** (c.1740, National Portrait Gallery, London), **David Garrick** (1758, National Portrait Gallery) and a self portrait (National Portrait Gallery). His first major commission in London was the Argyll monument in Westminster Abbey (1749).

Rouget de Lisle, Claude Joseph 1760–1836
French soldier
Born in Lons-le-Saunier, he wrote the words and music of the French national anthem *La Marseillaise* (originally *Chant de guerre pour l'armée du Rhin*, 'War Song for the Army on the Rhine') when stationed in Strasbourg in 1792 as captain of engineers. Wounded at Quiberon (1795), he left the army, and in 1796 published *Essais en vers et en prose* ('Essays in Prose and Verse'). The *Marseillaise* was made known in Paris by troops from Marseilles. 📖 M Henry-Rosier, *Rouget de Lisle* (1937)

Roumain, Jacques 1907–44
Haitian writer and politician
Born into an élite family, he was a poet, diplomat, essayist, editor and politician (he founded the Haitian Communist Party in 1934). His magazine *Revue Indigène* educated Haitian intellectuals. His best novel is his last: *Gouverneurs de la rosée* (1944, Eng trans *Masters of the Dew*, 1947).

Roumanille, Joseph 1818–91
French writer
Born in Saint-Rémy, Bouches-du-Rhône, he taught at Avignon, where his pupils included **Frédéric Mistral**. In 1847 he published *Li Margarideto*, a book of his own poems, in 1852 a volume of Provençal poems, and later many volumes of verse and prose in the Provençal dialect. With Mistral and others he founded the 'Soci dou Félibrige' for the revival of Provençal literature. 📖 E Ripert, *Joseph Roumainille* (1948)

Rous, Francis 1579–1659
English hymnwriter
Born in Dittisham, Devon, and educated at Oxford, he was a member of the Long Parliament, sat in the Westminster Assembly of Divines, and in 1644 was made Provost of Eton. His writings were collected in 1657. His metrical version of the Psalms (1643) was recommended by the House of Commons to the Westminster Assembly, and is still substantially the Presbyterian psalter.

Rous, (Francis) Peyton 1879–1970
US pathologist and Nobel Prize winner
Born in Baltimore, Maryland, he was educated at Johns Hopkins University and Medical School, and held various posts at the Rockefeller Institute for Medical Research in New York City. From 1909 he began studying a sarcoma in chickens, which he demonstrated to have been caused by a virus. In the 1930s he discovered a rabbit tumour which was also caused by a virus, and found that coal tar and the virus could stimulate each other in making the tumour malignant. This was the first time that a virus was implicated in cancer, and the discovery of many other oncogenic (cancer-causing) viruses from the 1950s made his early work more widely appreciated. He shared with **Charles B Huggins** the 1966 Nobel Prize for physiology or medicine.

Rousseau, Henri Julien Félix 1844–1910
French primitive painter
Born in Laval, he joined the army at the age of about 18, but spent most of his life as a minor tax collector in the Paris toll office, hence his nickname *Le Douanier*. He retired in 1885 and spent his time painting and copying at the Louvre. From 1886 to 1898 he exhibited at the Salon des Indépendants and again from 1901 to 1910. He met **Paul Gauguin**, **Camille Pissarro** and later **Picasso**, but his painting remained unaffected. Despite its denial of conventional perspective and colour, it has a fierce reality more Surrealist than primitive. He produced painstaking portraits, and painted dreams, such as the *Sleeping Gipsy* (1897), and exotic imaginary landscapes with trees and plants, which he had seen in the Jardin des Plantes. 📖 D Vallier, *Henri Rousseau* (1961, Eng trans 1964)

Rousseau, Jean Baptiste 1671–1741
French poet
Born in Paris, he wrote for the theatre, and composed lampoons on the literary frequenters of the Café Laurent; these gave rise to feuds and lawsuits, and eventually a sentence of banishment (1712). Thereafter he lived in Switzerland, Vienna (with Prince **Eugene of Savoy**) and Brussels. He wrote sacred odes and elaborate *cantates*, but is best known for his short vigorous epigrams.

Rousseau, Jean Jacques   See panel p1600

Rousseau, Jean Jacques 1712–78
French political philosopher, educationist and author

Rousseau was born in Geneva, Switzerland. His mother died at his birth, and he had little early family life and no formal education. In 1728 he ran away from Geneva to Italy and Savoy, where he lived with Baronne Louise de Warens (1700–62). He was baptized a Catholic, and after an itinerant existence for a few years eventually became her lover and general factotum (1733–41). In 1741 he was supplanted, and moved to Paris where he began to thrive, making a living from secretarial work and music copying. There he began a lifelong association with an illiterate maidservant at his inn, Thérèse le Vasseur; together they had five children, all of whom he consigned to foundling hospitals, despite his later proclamations about the innocence of childhood. He became acquainted with **Voltaire** and **Denis Diderot**, and contributed articles on music and political economy to the *Encyclopédie*.

In 1750 he made his name with a prize essay, *Discours sur les arts et sciences* (Eng trans *A Discourse on the Arts and Sciences*, 1752), which argued that civilization had corrupted our natural goodness and decreased our freedom; and in 1752 he triumphed with an operetta, *Le Devin du village* (Eng trans *The Cunning Man*, 1766). He was now a celebrity, and in 1754 wrote *Discours sur l'origine et les fondements de l'inégalité parmi les hommes* ('Discourse on the Origin and Foundations of Inequality Among Men'), in which he attacked private property and argued that man's perfect nature was corrupted by society. He travelled restlessly first to Geneva, where he was much influenced by Calvinism, back to Paris and then to Luxembourg in 1757.

In 1762 he published his masterpiece, *Du contrat social* (Eng trans *A Treatise on the Social Contract*, 1764), in which every individual is made to surrender his rights totally to the collective 'general will', which is the sole source of legitimate sovereignty and by definition represents the common good; the aberrant can then, in the sinister phrase, 'be forced to be free' in their own interests. His text, with its slogan 'Liberty, Equality, Fraternity', became the bible of the French Revolution and of progressive movements generally, though the main thesis is vulnerable to totalitarian misrepresentations.

Also in 1762 he published his theory of education in the form of a novel, *Émile, ou de l'éducation* (Eng trans *Emilius and Sophia; or, A New System of Education*, 1762–73), a simple romance of a child reared apart from other children as an experiment. This work greatly influenced educationists such as **Johann Pestalozzi** and **Friedrich Froebel**, but so outraged the political and religious establishment that he had to escape to Switzerland. He moved to England in 1766 at the invitation of **David Hume** and went to live at Wootton Hall near Ashbourne in Derbyshire (1766–67), where he began writing his *Les Confessions* (Eng trans *Confessions*, 1783–90) , a remarkably frank work published posthumously (1782–89).

He became mentally unstable at about this time, quarrelled with his English friends (particularly Hume), developed a persecution complex, and fled back to France in 1767. In Paris from 1770 to 1778 he completed his *Confessions* and other works. He declined further, became seriously insane, and died in Ermenonville. In 1794 his remains were placed alongside those of Voltaire in the Panthéon in Paris.

📖 R D Masters, *The Political Philosophy of Rousseau* (1968); J H Broome, *Rousseau: A Study of His Thought* (1963); D Vallier, *Henri Rousseau* (1961, Eng trans 1964).

> *L'homme est né libre, et partout il est dans les fers.*
> 'Man is born free, yet everywhere he is in chains.'
> From *Du contrat social*, ch.1.

Rousseau, (Pierre Étienne) Théodore 1812–67
French landscape painter

Born in Paris, he began painting directly from nature in the Forest of Fontainebleau in the 1830s and first exhibited in the Salon of 1831, and in 1834 his *Forest of Compiègne* was bought by the Duc d'Orléans. Some 12 years of discouragement followed at the end of which he moved to Barbizon and became leader of the Barbizon school. In 1849 he resumed exhibiting, and was thereafter prominent. He was an exceedingly prolific, if a somewhat variable, painter.

Roussel, Albert 1869–1937
French composer

Born in Tourcoing, he joined the navy and saw service in Indo-China, but at the age of 25 he resigned his commission to study music in Paris with Gigout, joining the Schola Cantorum in 1896 under **Vincent d'Indy**. A journey to India and the Far East gave him an interest in oriental music which, combined with the influence of **Stravinsky**, inspired the choral *Évocations* (1912) and the opera *Padmâvatî*, begun in 1914 and completed after World War I. Service in the war ruined his health, and after his demobilization he largely retired into seclusion, devoting his time entirely to composition. His works include ballets, the best-known of which are *Bacchus et Ariane* (1931) and *Le Festin de l'araignée* (1912, 'The Spider's Feast'), four symphonies and numerous choral and orchestral works. His works are adventurous in harmony and texture, reconciling modern experimental styles with the conservative tradition of his teachers.

Roussel, Ker Xavier 1867–1944
French artist

Born in Lorry-lès-Metz, he was a member of the Nabis, and associated with **Pierre Bonnard, Édouard Vuillard** and **Maurice Denis**. He is best known for his classical subjects portrayed in typical French landscapes, using the Impressionist palette.

Roussel, Raymond 1887–1933
French fabulist

He was born in Paris to a stockbroker father and an eccentrically artistic mother. He wrote verse at a young age and his first novel, *La Doublure*, at the age of 10. His most important work is *Impressions d'Afrique* (1910, Eng trans *Impressions of Africa*, 1965), a surreal fantasy about parts of the continent he had never visited. The book is full of non-sequiturs, quasi-documentary asides and free invention. It made a considerable impact on such US writers as **John Ashbery** and **Harry Mathews**, who named their experimental journal after a later book of Roussel's; *Locus Solus* was published in part in 1918, but only appeared in its entirety in 1963. He was a homosexual and suffered from a heavy addiction to barbiturates, which is reflected in the astonishing pace and rhythmic freedom of his prose. He committed suicide. 📖 M Foucault, *Death and the Labyrinth: The World of Raymond Roussel* (1966)

Routledge, George 1812–88
English publisher

He was born in Brampton, Cumberland, went to London in 1833, and set up in business as a bookseller in 1836 and a publisher in 1843. In 1848 he founded his 'Railway Library' of cheap reprints, and about the same time he took his two brothers-in-law, W H and Frederick Warne, into partnership. In 1947 the firm acquired Kegan Paul, Trench, Trubner and Co Ltd.

Roux, Albert 1935– and Michel André 1941–
French chefs and restaurateurs

After training and working in Paris, the brothers moved to London and opened Le Gavroche in 1967. This restaurant is now run by Albert, while Michel presides at the Waterside Inn at Bray, Berkshire. They are both especially renowned for their patisserie, and in 1993 they were the only two restaurateurs in Great Britain to be awarded three Michelin stars. They appeared together on television in *At Home with the Roux Brothers* (1988), and have jointly written cookery books including *Cookery for Two* (1991) and *Desserts: A Lifelong Passion* (1994).

Roux, (Pierre Paul) Émile 1853–1933
French bacteriologist

Born in Confolens, Charente, he studied at the universities of Clermont-Ferrand and Paris, where he became assistant to Louis Pasteur, and in 1904 succeeded him as director of the Pasteur Institute. With Pasteur he tested the anthrax vaccine, and contributed much of the early work on the rabies vaccine. With Alexandre Yersin he showed that the symptoms of diphtheria are caused by a lethal toxin produced by the diphtheria bacillus; and, following the principles of Emil von Behring and Shibasaburo Kitasato, he tested on patients large quantities of blood serum containing the antitoxin from horses. As a result the mortality rate fell dramatically. He also made important contributions to research into syphilis.

Roux, Wilhelm 1850–1924
German anatomist and physiologist

Born in Jena, he studied medicine at the university there, before spending 10 years (1879–89) at the anatomical institute in Breslau. In 1895 he was appointed head of anatomy at Halle University, where he remained until 1921. A prolific researcher, he accomplished extensive practical and theoretical work on experimental embryology; he sought to understand evolutionary processes at cellular and molecular levels, focusing in particular on experimental embryology and applying the findings of physics and chemistry. On the basis of extensive and often violent embryological experimentation, Roux endorsed the idea that the material of the germ plasm is passed on intact from parent to offspring, thereby pointing to a physical basis for heredity.

Rowbotham, Sheila 1943–
English social historian and feminist

Born in Leeds, she was educated at Oxford and became involved in the women's movement in the late 1960s. An active socialist, she wrote for several socialist papers, and provoked controversy with *Beyond the Fragments: Feminism and the Making of Socialism* (1979, with Segal and Wainwright). Among her most important historical works are *Women, Resistance and Revolution* (1972), *Hidden from History* (1973) and *Woman's Consciousness, Man's World* (1973).

Rowe, Nicholas 1674–1718
English poet and dramatist

Born in Little Barford, Bedfordshire, he was educated at Westminster, London, and called to the Bar, but from 1692 devoted himself to literature. Between 1700 and 1715 he produced eight plays of which three were popular: *Tamerlane* (1702), *The Fair Penitent* (1703) and *The Tragedy of Jane Shore* (1714), followed by *The Tragedy of Lady Jane Grey* (1715). Lothario in *The Fair Penitent* was the prototype of Lovelace in Samuel Richardson's *Clarissa*, and the name is still the eponym for a fashionable rake. Rowe translated Lucan's *Pharsalia*, and his edition of Shakespeare (1709–10) contributed to the popularity of that author. He was under-secretary to the Duke of Queensberry from 1709 to 1711, and in 1715 was appointed Poet Laureate and a surveyor of customs to the port of London. The Prince of Wales made him clerk of his council, and Lord Chancellor

Parker appointed him clerk of presentations in chancery. 📖 Dr Johnson, *Lives of the Most Eminent English Poets* (10 vols, 1779–81)

Rowland, Henry Augustus 1848–1901
US physicist

Born in Honesdale, Pennsylvania, he was educated at the Rensselaer Polytechnic Institute to which he returned as an instructor in physics in 1872. From 1875 to 1901 he was Professor of Physics at the new Johns Hopkins University and he established there a laboratory on the European model. A meticulous experimenter and gifted designer of instruments, he invented the concave diffraction grating used in spectroscopy, discovered the magnetic effect of electric convection, and improved on James Joule's work on the mechanical equivalent of heat. Shortly before his death he invented a multiplex telegraph, which was shown at the Paris Exhibition of 1900.

Rowland, Tiny, *originally* Roland Walter Fuhrhop 1917–98
British financier

Born in India, and educated at Churcher's College, Petersfield, he joined Lonrho (London and Rhodesian Mining and Land Company) in 1961 and became chief executive and managing director. In 1993 he became joint chief executive with the German businessman Dieter Bock, in whose favour Rowland stepped down in 1995. He was chairman of the *Observer* newspaper from 1983 to 1993, when the *Guardian* took over the company. In 1985 he tried unsuccessfully to take over the House of Fraser. The Lonrho empire embraces a variety of interests, including steel-based companies, hotels, currency printing, bedlinen, and gas, tea and beer in Africa.

Rowlandson, Thomas 1756–1827
English caricaturist

Born in London, from the age of 15 he studied art in Paris, where he acquired a taste for high living on the strength of a £7,000 legacy from a French aunt, which he squandered on gambling and tavern life. In 1777 he returned to London to work as a portrait painter, and turned to watercolour caricatures, and book illustrations for authors including Tobias Smollett, Laurence Sterne and Oliver Goldsmith. He also engraved a popular series, *Tour of Dr Syntax in Search of the Picturesque* (1812, with sequels in 1820 and 1821), also *The English Dance of Death* (1815) and *The Dance of Life* (1816). 📖 R Paulson, *Rowlandson: A New Interpretation* (1972)

Rowley, William c.1585–c.1626
English actor and playwright

Little is known about him, except that he collaborated with Thomas Dekker, Thomas Middleton, John Heywood, John Webster, Philip Massinger and John Ford. Four plays published under his name are extant: *A New Wonder, a Woman Never Vext* (1632), *All's Lost by Lust* (c.1620, a tragedy), *A Match at Midnight* (1633), and *A Shoemaker, a Gentleman* (1638). 📖 C W Stock, *William Rowley* (1910)

Rowling, Sir Wallace Edward 1927–95
New Zealand politician

He was born in Motueka, South Island. After graduating from Canterbury University he joined the New Zealand army and served in the education corps before becoming active in the Labour Party. He entered parliament in 1962 and was Finance Minister in the administration of Norman Kirk. When Kirk died in 1974, Rowling succeeded him as Prime Minister until the National Party, under Robert Muldoon, returned to power in 1985. Rowling was then awarded a knighthood after his retiral and became ambassador to the USA (1985–88). From 1990 until his death he was president of the New Zealand Institute of International Affairs.

Rowntree, Joseph 1836–1925
English Quaker industrialist and reformer

Born in York, he was the son of Joseph Rowntree, a Quaker grocer. With his brother, Henry Isaac (d.1883), he became a partner in a cocoa manufactury in York in 1869, and built up welfare organizations for his employees. He was succeeded as chairman by his son Seebohm Rowntree. 📖 Anne Vernon, *A Quaker Business Man: The Life of Joseph Rowntree 1836–1925* (1982)

Rowntree, (Benjamin) Seebohm 1871–1954
English manufacturer and philanthropist

Born in York, the son of Joseph Rowntree, he was educated at the Friends' School in York and Owens College, Manchester. He became chairman of the family chocolate firm (1925–41), and introduced enlightened schemes of worker-participation. He devoted his life to the study of social problems and welfare, and wrote many books, including *Poverty: A Study of Town Life* (1901), *Poverty and Progress* (1941) and *Poverty and the Welfare State* (1951).

Rowse, Alfred Leslie 1903–97
English historian

Born into a poor family in Tregonissey, near St Austell in Cornwall, he won a scholarship to Oxford and in 1925 became a Fellow of All Souls College. He wrote many works on English history including *Tudor Cornwall* (1941), *The Use of History* (1946) and *The England of Elizabeth* (1950). He also wrote poetry (collected as *A Life*, 1981), much of it on Cornwall, and many literary works, including biographies of Shakespeare and Christopher Marlowe, and two volumes of autobiography, *A Cornish Childhood* (1942) and *A Cornishman at Oxford* (1965). Later works include *All Souls in My Time* (1993) and *Historians I Have Known* (1995).

Roy, Rammohun See Rammohun Roy

Royce, Sir (Frederick) Henry 1863–1933
English engineer

Born near Peterborough, Cambridgeshire, he was initially apprenticed to the Great Northern Railway. When he became interested in electricity and motor engineering, he founded the firm of Royce Ltd, mechanical and electrical engineers in Manchester (1884). He made his first car in 1904, and his meeting with Charles Rolls in that year led to the formation in 1906 of Rolls-Royce Ltd, motor-car and aero-engine builders, of Derby and London. He later designed the aero-engines that developed into the Merlin engines for Spitfires and Hurricanes in World War II. 📖 John Rowland, *The Rolls-Royce Men: The Story of Charles Rolls and Henry Royce* (1969)

Royce, Josiah 1855–1916
US philosopher

Born in Grass Valley, California, he trained as an engineer. He later turned to philosophy, studied in Germany and at Johns Hopkins, Baltimore (under Charles Sanders Peirce), and taught at Harvard from 1882. He was greatly influenced by Hegel, and developed a philosophy of idealism emphasizing the importance of the individual in *Religious Aspects of Philosophy* (1885) and *The World and the Individual* (1900–01). He also wrote on mathematical logic, social ethics, psychology and religion.

Royden, (Agnes) Maud 1876–1956
English social worker and preacher

Born in Liverpool, and educated at Lady Margaret Hall, Oxford, she was prominent in the women's suffrage movement. From 1917 to 1920 she was assistant at the City Temple. She later helped to establish the Fellowship Services in Kensington. She published, among other titles, *Woman and the Sovereign State*, *The Church and Woman* and *Modern Sex Ideals*.

Royds, Mabel Alington 1874–1941
English artist and printmaker

Born in Little Barford, Bedfordshire, she studied at the Slade School of Art, London, under Henry Tonks. Influenced by Walter Richard Sickert, whom she met in Paris at the turn of the century, she became an accomplished printmaker, using the medium of woodcuts. From 1911 she taught at Edinburgh College of Art and in 1914 married the printmaker Ernest Stephen Lumsden (1883–1948). She travelled extensively, particularly in India and Tibet. Her works are in many public collections, including the Victoria and Albert Museum and the British Museum.

Royer-Collard, Pierre Paul 1763–1845
French philosopher and politician

Born in Sompuis, Champagne, he became an advocate, and at the outbreak of the French Revolution was elected a member of the municipality of Paris. In 1792 he fled from the Jacobins to his birthplace, and in 1797 served for a few months on the Council of Five Hundred. As Professor of Philosophy in Paris from 1810, he exercised a profound influence on French philosophy, rejecting the purely sensuous system of Étienne de Condillac, and giving special prominence to the principles of the Scottish School of Thomas Reid and Dugald Stewart. Strongly spiritualist as opposed to materialist, he originated the Doctrinaire school of Théodore Jouffroy (1796–1842) and Victor Cousin. He was later president of the Commission of Public Instruction (1815–20), deputy for Marne (1815), and became a member of the Académie Française (1827). He was also president of the Chamber of Representatives (1828), and presented the address of March 1830, which the king refused to hear.

Roy Manabendra Nath, *also called* Narendranath Bhattacharya 1887–1954
Indian political leader

Involved with terrorist groups against British rule, he was sent in 1915 to request aid from the Germans in Batavia. When his mission failed, he fled to San Francisco in 1916, where he changed his name. He went on to Mexico, where he helped to found the Mexican Communist Party, and to Moscow, where he became a member of the Executive Committee of the Comintern, and founded the Communist Party of India in Tashkent (1920). He broke with the Comintern in 1929 but was arrested and imprisoned on his return to India. After independence, he abandoned communism.

Rozanov, Vasili Vasilevich 1856–1919
Russian writer, thinker and critic

Born in Vetluga, Kostroma, he studied history at the University of Moscow, then became a teacher in provincial schools. A study of 'The Grand Inquisitor' chapter of Dostoevsky's *The Brothers Karamazov* was published in 1894 and brought him into prominence. Although a Christian, in his prolific writings he adopted a Nietzschean standpoint in criticizing the contemporary standards in morals, religion, education, and particularly the excessively strict attitude towards sex, which was for him the very soul of man. Much of his work is highly introspective, and his literary reputation is firmly based on the two books of fragments and essays, *Uyedinyonnoe* (1912, Eng trans *Solitaria*, 1927) and *Opavshie listya* (1913, 1915, Eng trans *Fallen Leaves*, 1929).

Rozeanu, Angelica, *née* Adelstein 1921–
Romanian table tennis player

She won 12 world titles between 1950 and 1956, including the singles title a record six times (1950–55), and was a member of the Romanian Corbillon Cup winning team

Rubens, Peter Paul 1577–1640
Flemish painter

Rubens was born in Siegen in Westphalia, the son of a lawyer. He studied from 1587 in Antwerp, and in 1600 went to Italy; in Venice he studied the works of **Titian** and **Veronese**. He next entered the service of Vincenzo Gonzago, Duke of Mantua; and in 1605 was dispatched on a mission to **Philip III** of Spain, thus beginning his career as a diplomat. While in Madrid he executed many portraits, as well as several historical subjects.

On his return from Spain he travelled in Italy, copying celebrated works for the Duke of Mantua. His paintings of this Italian period are much influenced by the Italian Renaissance, and already show the Rubens characteristics of vigorous composition and brilliant colouring. In 1608 he returned home, and, settling in Antwerp, was appointed court painter to the archduke Albert (1609), and soon afterwards married his first wife, Isabella Brant, whom he often portrayed.

Rubens was then approaching his artistic maturity, and his triptych *Descent from the Cross* (1611–14) in Antwerp Cathedral is usually regarded as his masterpiece. By this time he was famous, and pupils and commissions came in a steady stream to the master's studio, from which issued vast numbers of works, witnesses to his extraordinary energy and ability. In 1620 he was invited to France by **Marie de Médicis**, who was then engaged in decorating the Luxembourg Palace in Paris; and he undertook for her 21 large subjects on her life and regency.

In 1628 he was dispatched on a diplomatic mission to **Philip IV** of Spain. In Madrid he made the acquaintance of **Velázquez**, and executed some 40 works, including five portraits of the Spanish monarch. In 1629 he was appointed envoy to **Charles I** of Great Britain, to treat for peace; and, while he conducted a delicate negotiation with tact and success, he painted the *Peace and War* (National Gallery, London) and also made sketches for the *Apotheosis* of **James VI and I** for the banqueting hall at Whitehall, completing the pictures on his return to Antwerp.

His first wife died in 1626, and in 1630 he married Helena Fourment, retiring to his estate at Steen, where he turned to landscape painting. In 1635 he designed the decorations which celebrated the entry of the Cardinal Infant Ferdinand into Antwerp as Governor of the Netherlands; and, having completed *The Crucifixion of St Peter* for the church of St Peter in Cologne, he died in Antwerp.

Rubens was a successful diplomat, a distinguished humanist, a man of wide erudition and culture, and in his own time was outstanding for versatility and for the power, spirit and vivacity of his artistic output.

📖 N Gerson, *Peter Paul Rubens: A Biography of a Giant* (1973); J Fletcher, *Peter Paul Rubens* (1968); C V Wedgwood, *The World of Rubens, 1577–1640* (1967).

(1950–51, 1953, 1955–56). She was made a Master of Sport, and was appointed to the Romanian Olympic Commission. She retired in 1960 and emigrated to Israel.

Rózsa, Miklós Nicholas 1907–95
Hungarian composer

Born in Budapest, he began composing orchestral works from an early age, and graduated from the University of Leipzig in 1931. Working in Paris and later in London, he composed symphonies and ballet music before being commissioned to write his first film score for *Knight Without Armour* (1937). He worked in Hollywood from 1940, where his use of jolting chords and pounding rhythms heightened the emotional impact of psychological melodramas and film noirs such as *Double Indemnity* (1944), *The Lost Weekend* (1945) and *The Killers* (1946). Later, he concentrated on lush accompaniments to historical epics, including *Quo Vadis* (1951) and *El Cid* (1961). His work outside the film industry is equally renowned; it includes a violin concerto (1953) written for **Jascha Heifetz** and a cello concerto (1968) for Janos Starker (1924–). He received Academy Awards for *Spellbound* (1945), *A Double Life* (1947) and *Ben Hur* (1959). His autobiography, *A Double Life*, was published in 1982.

Rubbia, Carlo 1934–
US physicist and Nobel Prize winner

Born in Gorizia, Italy, and educated at Pisa, Rome and Columbia universities, from 1960 he worked at CERN (Conseil Européen pour la Recherche Nucléaire) in Geneva. In 1971 he accepted a chair in physics at Harvard, while continuing his research at CERN. He was head of the team that discovered the W and Z bosons which mediate the weak nuclear force, thus putting the unified theory of electromagnetic and weak forces (the 'electroweak' theory) on a firm experimental footing. For this he shared the 1984 Nobel Prize for physics with **Simon van der Meer**. As director-general of CERN (1989–93), he was the force behind the LEP (an electron–positron collider) and LHC (Large Hadron Collider) projects. He has been senior physicist of CERN since 1993.

Rubbra, Edmund 1901–86
English composer and music critic

Born in Northampton, he took piano lessons from **Cyril Scott**, and in 1919 won a composition scholarship to Reading University. There he studied under Howard Jones and **Gustav Holst**, and won a scholarship to the Royal College of Music, where he was a pupil of **Ralph Vaughan Williams** and Reginald Owen Morris. An interest in the polyphonic music of the 16th and 17th centuries is reflected in his characteristic contrapuntal style of composition, which he uses not only in works such as the 'Spenser Sonnets' (1935), madrigals and masses (1945 and 1949), but also in his larger symphonic pieces, where he is more flexible in his interpretation of polyphonic principles. He wrote 11 symphonies, and chamber, choral and orchestral music, songs and works for various solo instruments. He was senior lecturer in music at Oxford (1947–68), and was made a Fellow of Worcester College in 1963, and Professor of Composition at the Guildhall School of Music (1961–74). 📖 Ralph Scott Grover, *The Music of Edmund Rubbra* (1993)

Rubens, Peter Paul See panel above

Rubik, Ernö 1944–
Hungarian architectural designer and inventor

Born in Budapest, he studied architecture and industrial design at the Technical University in Budapest, and became a teacher at the School of Industrial Design there. He conceived the idea of his 'Rubik cube' puzzle in 1974 and patented it the following year. By 1981 it had become a great international success and millions had been sold, many of them pirated. Although he has produced other puzzles, they have not caught the public imagination in the same way.

Rubin, Gerald Mayer 1950–
US molecular biologist

Born in Boston, he was educated at the Massachusetts Institute of Technology (MIT) and at Cambridge. Subsequently he became Helen Hay Whitney Foundation Fellow at Stanford University School of Medicine in

California (1974–76) and assistant Professor of Biological Chemistry at the Sidney Farber Cancer Institute, Harvard Medical School (1977–80). He then joined the Carnegie Institute of Washington, Baltimore, from 1980 until 1983, when he became John D McArthur Professor of Biological Chemistry at the University of California at Berkeley. He has simultaneously been investigator at the Howard Hughes Medical Institute since 1987. Rubin produced the first transgenic fruit flies, which involved introducing specific genes into the germ line of the fruit fly. This technique provides a powerful tool for studying how specific genes are controlled, as artificially introduced genes can be tracked throughout the development of the fruit fly, and can be mutated in specific ways so that the function of precise DNA sequences can be determined.

Rubinstein, Anton Grigorevich 1829–94
Russian pianist and composer
Born in Vykhvatinets, Moldavia, he studied in Berlin and Vienna, and in 1848 settled in St Petersburg, where he taught music and took a part in founding the conservatory, of which he was director (1862–67, 1887–90). He undertook concert tours in Europe and the USA, gaining widespread acclaim and lasting distinction for his technique and musical sensitivity. His compositions, which include operas, oratorios and piano concertos, have not retained their popularity, apart from some songs and melodious piano pieces. His brother Nikolai (1835–81) founded the Moscow Conservatory. He wrote an autobiography (1890, Eng trans 1891).

Rubinstein, Artur 1887–1982
US pianist
Born in Łódź, Poland, he appeared in Berlin at the age of 12, and after further study with Ignacy Paderewski, began his career as a virtuoso, appearing in Paris and London in 1905 and visiting the USA in 1906. After World War II he lived in the USA, making frequent extensive concert tours. He took US citizenship in 1946, and was made an honorary KBE in 1977. He published his autobiographical *My Young Years* in 1973 and *My Many Years* in 1980. 📖 Harvey Sachs, *Artur Rubinstein: A Life* (1996)

Rubinstein, Helena 1870–1965
US businesswoman
Born in Kraków, Poland, she studied medicine and went to Australia in 1902, taking with her a facial cream made by her mother. When she found that it sold well, she opened a shop in Melbourne and offered advice on cosmetics to customers. She then studied dermatology in greater depth and launched her business in Europe. She opened her Maison de Beauté in London (1908) and Paris (1912), then went to the USA and opened salons there, starting in New York City. In 1917 she began wholesale distribution of the products and after World War II built cosmetics factories all over the world. She created a personal fortune of around $100 million and remained active in the running of Helena Rubinstein Inc into her nineties. In 1953 she established the Helena Rubinstein Foundation. Her autobiography, *My Life for Beauty*, was published in 1965.

Rublev, Andrei fl.1400
Russian painter
Although little is known about his life or works, he is generally regarded as the greatest Russian icon painter. It is known that he became a monk, probably quite late in life, in the monastery of Troitse-Sergiev, and that he was an assistant of the Greek painter Theophanes, with whom he worked on the Kremlin in Moscow from 1405. In 1422 he returned to Troitse-Sergiev, where he is said to have completed his most famous work, the icon of the Old Testament Trinity, represented by three graceful angels.

His style is less dramatic and more lyrical than that of his Byzantine master. He was the subject of a highly acclaimed film portrait by Andrei Tarkovsky (1968).

Rubruck, Wiliam See William of Rubruck

Ruccellai, Giovanni 1475–1525
Italian poet
The nephew of Lorenzo de' Medici, he lived in Rome and took holy orders. His works include the blank verse *Le Api* ('The Bees'), an instructive poem based on book four of Virgil's *Georgics*. He also wrote early Italian tragedies, such as *Rosamunda* (1515) and *Oreste* (1525). 📖 A Marpicati, *Saggi critica* (1934)

Rudbeck, Olof 1630–1702
Swedish physiologist
Born in Västerås, he studied medicine at the University of Uppsala, and familiarized himself with recent work on the lymphatic system. Independently of Jean Pecquet, he discovered the thoracic duct, and there followed a controversial priority dispute involving Pecquet, who had published first, and Thomas Bartholin, the Elder, who had been working separately in Copenhagen on the lymphatic system. Further studies at Leyden were followed by appointment to a medical chair in Uppsala. In later years Rudbeck pursued botanical studies, developing a tradition of which Carolus Linnaeus was the later beneficiary.

Ruddock, Joan Mary 1943–
Welsh anti-nuclear campaigner and politician
She was born in Pontypool and educated in Wales and at Imperial College, London. She worked for Shelter, the national campaign for the homeless, between 1968 and 1973, and was then director of an Oxford housing aid centre. In 1977, she joined the Manpower Services Commission, where she had special responsibilities for the young unemployed, and was chairperson of the Campaign for Nuclear Disarmament (CND) from 1981. When she entered Parliament for Labour in 1987, she almost immediately became a member of the Opposition Front Bench. Her books include *The CND Story* (1983), *CND Scrapbook* (1987) and *Voices for One World* (1988).

Rude, François 1784–1855
French sculptor
Born in Dion, and trained in the classical tradition, he began as a smith, but later became known for his dramatic public monuments in Paris. His most famous works are the relief group *Le Départ* (1836, meaning 'the Departure of the Volunteers', known as the Marseillaise) on the Arc de Triomphe, and the statue of *Marshal Ney* in the Place de l'Observatoire (1853). His *Joan of Arc* (1852) is in the Louvre.

Rudolf I 1218–91
Uncrowned Holy Roman Emperor, founder of the Habsburg dynasty
He was the most powerful prince in Swabia when he was elected King of Germany (1273), although he was never crowned emperor. He attempted to restore the power of the monarchy by resuming lands and rights usurped by the princes since 1245. His victory at Durnkrüt on the Marchfeld (1278) over Ottokar II of Bohemia, who had occupied Austria and Styria, brought him control of these two duchies, which passed to his son Albert I and became the seat of Habsburg power.

Rudolf II d.937
King of Burgundy
He was the son of Rudolf I, whom he succeeded (912), and father of the Empress St Adelaide. He became King of Italy (922), but resigned the throne (926) in return for Provence.

Rudolf II 1552–1612
King of Hungary and of Bohemia, and Holy Roman Emperor

Born in Vienna, he ruled Hungary (1572–1608) and Bohemia (1575–1611) and became Holy Roman Emperor on the death of his father Maximilian II in 1576. Residing for most of his reign in Prague, he made the city a centre for writers, artists and humanist scholars, including the astronomers Tycho Brahe and Johannes Kepler, and mystics such as Giordano Bruno and John Dee. He waged an indecisive and underfinanced war against the Turks (1591–1606). His catholicizing policies provoked opposition among the Bohemian Protestants, who looked to his younger brother, Matthias, for support. He was shy and melancholy, and his mental instability became more pronounced in his later years, during which he was gradually superseded by Matthias. ▫ R J W Evans, *Rudolf II and his World* (1973)

Rudolph, Wilma Glodean 1940–94
US sprinter

Born in Clarksville, Tennessee, the 20th of 22 children, she overcame childhood polio and came to prominence as a teenager as part of an athletics team known as the 'Tennessee Belles'. As a 16-year-old she won a sprint relay bronze medal at Melbourne in the 1956 Olympic Games, and in the 1960 Olympics at Rome she won gold medals in the 100 metres, 200 metres and sprint relay events. Although her 100-metre record time at the Olympics was later invalidated on account of wind assistance, she set a record in the same event the following year. She retired in 1964 and was inducted into the National Women's Hall of Fame in 1994.

Rue, Warren de la See De la Rue, Warren

Rueda, Lope de c.1510–1565
Spanish dramatist

He was born in Seville, and became manager of a group of strolling players. A pioneer of Spanish drama, he wrote comedies in the Italian style, such as *Los engañados* and *Enfensa*. He also wrote short humorous pastoral dialogues, known as *pasos*, a form developed by Cervantes, and 10 burlesques. ▫ D V Otero, *Lope de Rueda* (1960)

Ruether, Rosemary Radford 1936–
US theologian

Born in Minneapolis, she has been Professor of Applied Theology at Garrett-Evangelical Theological Seminary, Evanston, since 1976. She has written extensively on women and theological issues, analysing the effects of male bias in official Church theology and seeking to affirm feminine aspects of religion and the importance of women's experience. Her books include *New Woman/New Earth* (1975), *Mary: The Feminine Face of the Church* (1979), *Sexism and God-Talk* (1983), *The Wrath of Jonah* (1989) and *Gaia and God* (1992).

Ruffini, Giovanni Domenico 1807–81
Italian writer

Born in Genoa, he joined the Young Italy Republican Movement in 1833, and in 1836 was forced to flee to England. He wrote *Lorenzo Benoni: Passages in the Life of an Italian* (1853), *Dr Antonio* (1855), *Vincenzo* (1863), and other novels in English, as well as the libretto for Gaetano Donizetti's *Don Pasquale* (1843). From 1875 he lived in Taggia in the Riviera. ▫ A Linaker, *Giovanni Ruffini* (1882)

Ruggles, Carl 1876–1971
US composer

Born in Marion, Massachusetts, he was the founder of the Winona Symphony Orchestra, Massachusetts (1912), and taught composition at Miami University (1938–43). His radical modernity and use of atonality were not generally liked, and in later years he concentrated on painting. He published few works, the longest of which is the 17-minute orchestral *Sun-treader* (1926–31).

Ruggles-Brise, Sir Evelyn John 1857–1935
English penal reformer

Born in Finchingfield, Essex, he became a civil servant and was appointed chairman of the Prison Commission (1895–1921). He introduced many reforms to humanize penal treatment, including the borstal system, which separated young offenders from adult prisoners, and was brought in under the Children Act of 1908.

Ruïsdael or Ruysdael, Jacob van c.1628–1682
Dutch landscape painter

Born in Haarlem, he was possibly a pupil of his father and uncle Salomon van Ruïsdael (c.1600–1670), a Haarlem landscape painter. He became a member of the Haarlem painters' guild in 1648, and in about 1655 moved to Amsterdam, thereafter travelling in Holland and Germany. One of the greatest landscape and seascape painters of the Dutch school, he excelled in dramatic skies and magnificent cloud effects. He was not highly regarded by his contemporaries, but is now more widely admired. He is represented in the Rijksmuseum, Amsterdam (*The Jewish Cemetery*, *The Windmill at Wijk*), the National Gallery, London (*Holland's Deep* and *Landscape with Ruins*), the Glasgow Art Gallery (*View of Katwijk*), the Louvre (*Le Coup de Soleil*) and elsewhere. He was the teacher of Meindert Hobbema.

Rule, St See Regulus, St

Rulfo, Juan 1918–86
Mexican novelist and short-story writer

He was born in Sayula, Jalisco, and much of his writing is based on his early life in the provinces, where his once-wealthy family lost their fortune in the revolution. His early stories were collected in *El Llano en Llamas* (1953, Eng trans *The Burning Plain*, 1956); his novel *Pedro Páramo* (1955, Eng trans 1959), is considered his most important work, and uses modernist techniques, such as interior monologues, combined with the voices of dead peasants, to construct a panorama of Mexican life in the early part of this century.

Rumford, Benjamin Thompson, Count 1753–1814
US administrator and scientist

Born in Woburn, Massachusetts, he became a major in the 2nd New Hampshire regiment, but fled to England in 1776, possibly for political reasons. In England he experimented with gunpowder and was elected FRS in 1779. In 1784 he entered the service of Bavaria, where his military, legal and agricultural achievements led to his appointment as head of the Bavarian war department. It was here that he observed the immense heat generated by the boring of cannon, from which he deduced the relationship between the work done and the heat generated. He reported these findings to the Royal Society in 1798 in a classic paper of experimental science, *An Experimental Inquiry concerning the Source of Heat Excited by Friction*. He invented the Rumford shadow photometer, designed the so-called Rumford oil lamp, and introduced the concept of the standard candle. He endowed two Rumford medals of the Royal Society, and two of the American Academy. In 1799 he left the Bavarian service, returned to London, and founded the Royal Institution. ▫ Sanborn Brown, *Count Rumford: Physicist Extraordinary* (1962)

Rumsey, James 1743–92
US engineer and inventor

He was born in Cecil County, Maryland. His steamboat, propelled by the ejection of water from the stern, and exhibited on the Potomac River in 1787, was one of the earliest constructed. He died in London while preparing a second version for exhibition on the Thames.

Runcie, Robert Alexander Kennedy Runcie, Baron 1921–
English prelate and Archbishop of Canterbury
He was educated at Oxford and served in the Scots Guards during World War II, for which he was awarded an MC. He was ordained in 1951 and was Bishop of St Albans for 10 years before being consecrated Archbishop of Canterbury (1980–91). His office was marked by a papal visit to Canterbury, the war with Argentina, after which he urged reconciliation rather than triumphalism, continuing controversies over homosexuality and the role of women in the Church, his highly acclaimed chairmanship of the Lambeth conference, and the captivity of his envoy **Terry Waite** in Beirut (1987–91). His successor, **George Carey**, was announced in 1990 and he retired from the post in 1991, the year he was made a life peer. ◫ Jonathan Mantle, *Archbishop: The Life and Times of Robert Runcie* (1991)

Runciman, Alexander 1736–85 and John 1744–68
Scottish painters
The two brothers were born in Edinburgh and worked closely together. John, who seems to have been the more inventive, produced *King Lear in the Storm* (1767), a remarkable painting which anticipates the Romantic movement of the early 19th century. By this time Alexander was one of the major decorative painters in Scotland, and his major work was the decoration of Penicuik House (1772) with scenes from Ossian and the history of Scotland. This work no longer survives, but parts are known from etchings made by the artist.

Runciman, Walter Runciman, 1st Viscount 1870–1949
English politician
He entered the House of Commons as a Liberal in 1899 and held a number of ministerial posts in Liberal and coalition administrations from 1908 to 1939. He is remembered for his mission to Czechoslovakia in 1938 to persuade the government to make concessions to Nazi Germany as part of Great Britain's appeasement strategy.

Rundstedt, Karl Rudolf Gerd von 1875–1953
German soldier
He was born in the Old Mark of Brandenburg. He served in World War I, and in 1938 commanded occupation troops in the Sudetenland, but was 'purged' for his outspokenness about **Hitler**. Recalled in 1939, he directed the *Blitzkrieg* in Poland and France. In 1942 he commanded the Western Front stretching from Holland to the Italian frontier. His last great action was the Ardennes offensive (the 'Battle of the Bulge', 1944). He lost his command for the fourth time and in May 1945 was captured by the Americans in Munich. Proceedings against him for war crimes were dropped on the grounds of ill health, and he was kept prisoner in Great Britain from 1946.

Runeberg, Johan Ludvig 1804–77
Finnish poet
Born in Jakobstaed (Pietarsaari), he wrote in Swedish, and his style was much influenced by his studies of Finnish folk-poetry. He taught at Helsinki (1830–37) and at Porvoo (1837–57). He wrote several volumes of lyric verse, and his major works were *Elgskyttaråe* ('The Elk Shooters', 1832), a Norse epic, *Kung Fjalar* (1844, Eng trans *King Fjalar*, 1904), and his collection of patriotic ballads, *Fänrik Ståls Sägner* (1848–60, 'Tales of Ensign Stål', 2 vols), on the theme of Finland's war of independence (1808–09). It begins with 'Vårt land' ('Our land'), which

has become the Finnish national anthem. He wrote epic poetry, notably *Hanna* (1836) and *Julquällen* (1841, 'Christmas Eve'), and plays, and edited for the Lutheran Church of Finland a Psalm Book which contained some 60 pieces of his own. He is considered the greatest Finnish poet and was a leader of the national-Romantic school. ◫T Wretö, *Johan Ludvig Runeberg* (1980)

Runge, Friedlieb Ferdinand 1795–1867
German dye chemist and pioneer of chromatography
Born near Hamburg, he studied medicine in Berlin, Göttingen and Jena, and then spent three years visiting factories and laboratories throughout Europe. He was appointed to the chair of technical chemistry at Breslau (Wrocław, Poland) in 1828; from 1831 to 1852 he managed a chemical factory at Oranienburg and thereafter worked independently as a chemical consultant. At Oranienburg he isolated phenol (carbolic acid), aniline (cyanol) and other compounds. In 1834 he patented the process for obtaining the dye 'aniline black' from cyanol. He conducted experiments with a process that can now be identified as paper chromatography.

Runge, Philipp Otto 1777–1810
German Romantic painter
Born in Wolgast in what was then Swedish Pomerania, he studied in Copenhagen (1799–1801) then met **Caspar David Friedrich** in Dresden and visited **Goethe** in Weimar. His art, which was intensely mystical, was described by Goethe as 'enough to drive one mad, beautiful and at the same time nonsensical'. His allegorical figures were influenced, not least in their linearity, by **William Blake** and **John Flaxman**.

Runyon, (Alfred) Damon 1884–1946
US writer and journalist
He was born in Manhattan, Kansas. After service in the Spanish–US war (1898) he turned in 1911 to journalism, principally sports reporting and feature writing. His first books were volumes of verse, *Tents of Trouble* (1911) and *Rhymes of the Firing Line* (1912), and it was his racy short stories, written with liberal use of slang and angst, and depicting life in underworld New York and on Broadway, which won him popularity. His collection *Guys and Dolls* (1932) was adapted as a musical revue (1950). Other books include *Take it Easy* (1939), and the play, with Howard Lindsay, *A Slight Case of Murder* (1935). From 1941 he worked as a film producer. ◫T Clark, *The World of Runyon* (1978)

Rupert, Prince, *also called* Rupert of the Rhine 1619–82
English cavalry officer
Born in Prague, he was the third son of the Elector Palatine **Frederick V** and Elizabeth, daughter of **James VI and I** of Scotland and England, and nephew of **Charles I**. He fought against the Imperialists in the Thirty Years War (1618–48) until he was taken prisoner at Vlotho. In 1642 he returned to England and was appointed General of the Horse by Charles I. He served the king with great loyalty and courage and was the ablest Royalist soldier, showing tactical skill and swiftness in cavalry actions, although at times his pursuit was too headlong. Charming but lacking in tact, he was handicapped by royal indecisiveness and obstructionism by courtiers. After his defeat at Naseby and surrender of Bristol (1645), Charles (who in 1644 had created him Duke of Cumberland and Commander-in-Chief), dismissed him. He was acquitted by a court martial and resumed his duties, but surrendered at Oxford to **Thomas Fairfax** (1646). Banished by parliament from England, he took command of the small Royalist fleet (1648) and preyed on English shipping; in 1650 Admiral **Robert Blake** attacked his squadron, burning or sinking most of his vessels. Rupert escaped to the

West Indies, and in 1653 returned to France, where he chiefly lived until the Restoration. Thereafter he served under the Duke of York (the future **James VII and II**) in naval operations against the Dutch, and took part in founding the Hudson's Bay Company (1670). One of the founders of the Royal Society, he experimented with firearms, and produced beautiful mezzotints. ⌸ Patrick Morrah, *Prince Rupert of the Rhine* (1976)

Rüppell, (Wilhelm Peter) Eduard (Simon)
1794–1884
German zoologist and explorer

Born in Frankfurt am Main, he studied natural history at Pavia and Genoa in Italy, and made his first major expedition to the Sudan from 1821 to 1827, and to Abyssinia (Ethiopia) from 1830 to 1834. He published extensive maps and scientific accounts of his travels, including the monumental *Reise in Abyssynien* (1838–40, 'Travels in Abyssinia'). Rüppell's Warbler is named after him.

Rush, Benjamin 1745–1813
American physician and politician

Born in Byberry, Pennsylvania, he studied medicine at Edinburgh and Paris, and became Professor of Chemistry at Philadelphia (1769) and later at Pennsylvania (1791). Elected a member of the Continental Congress, he signed the Declaration of Independence (1776). In 1777 he was appointed surgeon-general, and later physician-general, of the Continental army, but he resigned his post and resumed his professorship in the following year. In 1786 he set up the first free dispensary in the USA. In 1799 he became treasurer of the US Mint.

Rush, Ian 1961–
Welsh footballer

He was born in St Asaph, Wales. After playing one season with Chester, he moved to Liverpool in 1981 and immediately achieved a good scoring rate, with 110 goals in 182 league matches. He won all the major honours in British football and, in addition, a European Cup medal in 1984. In 1986 he joined Juventus, the side which had defeated Liverpool in the European Cup final of 1985, but returned to Liverpool in 1988. He has been a regular member of the Welsh international team since 1980. The record-holder for the most goals in FA Cup finals (two in 1986, two in 1989, one in 1992), he has scored a total of 41 goals in all his Cup appearances and shares the record with **Denis Law** for the most Cup goals in a career.

Rushd, Ibn See **Averroës**

Rushdie, (Ahmed) Salman 1947–
British novelist

He was born in Bombay, India, and his family moved to Pakistan when he was 17. He was educated at the Cathedral School, Bombay, then at Rugby in England where he experienced what he described as 'minor persecutions and racist attacks which felt major at the time'. He emigrated to Great Britain in 1965 and graduated from King's College, Cambridge in 1968. He worked as an actor and an advertising copywriter before becoming a full-time writer. Writing in the tradition of **James Joyce**, **Günter Grass** and the South American 'magic realists', he published his first novel, *Grimus*, in 1975, a muddled fable which sold poorly. With *Midnight's Children* (1981), a tour de force poised at the moment when India achieves independence, he emerged as a major international writer, an inventive and imaginative storyteller. It was awarded the Booker Prize. *Shame* (1983), a trenchant satire and a revisionist history of Pakistan and its leaders, was similarly conceived on a grand scale and was widely acclaimed. In *The Satanic Verses* (1988) he turned his attention towards Islam, in his familiar hyperbolic mode. The book was banned in India in 1988, and in 1989 **Ayatollah Khomeini** of Iran declared it blasphemous and issued a

fatwa, or order of death, against him. Demonstrations followed and copies of the book were burned in Bradford along with effigies of the author, who was forced into hiding under police protection. Despite having to remain in hiding, he has published *Haroun and the Sea of Stories* (1990, Writers' Guild award), a children's book, a book of essays, *Imaginary Homelands* (1991), *East, West* (1994) and *The Moor's Last Sigh* (1995, Whitbread Fiction award). His public appearances are infrequent, and are usually part of a continuing attempt to have the *fatwa* revoked. ⌸ W J Weatherby, *Salman Rushdie* (1990)

Rushton, Willie (William George) 1937–96
English actor, cartoonist and broadcaster

He was born in London and educated at Shrewsbury School, where he developed a talent for acting. He completed his National Service, and did not attend university. His public stage debut was in **Spike Milligan's** *The Bed-sitting Room* at the Marlowe theatre in Canterbury in 1961, the same year he helped to set up the satirical magazine *Private Eye*. He achieved his greatest fame from broadcasting, both in television (*That Was the Week That Was*, 1962–63) and in radio (*I'm Sorry I Haven't A Clue*, 1976–96). He also made a number of cameo film appearances, and wrote several humorous books, including *Willie Rushton's Great Moments of History* (1985). He was less well known for his cartoons, which he contributed to a wide range of periodicals.

Rushworth, John c.1612–1690
English historian

Born at Ackington Park, Warkworth, Northumberland, he studied at Oxford, and settled in London as a barrister. When the Long Parliament met in 1640 he was appointed clerk-assistant to the House of Commons. He represented Berwick (1657–60, 1679, 1681) and was secretary to **Thomas Fairfax** (1645–50), and in 1677 to the Lord Keeper. In 1684 he was imprisoned for debt, and died in captivity. His *Historical Collections of Private Passages of State* (8 vols, 1659–1701), which cover the period 1618 to 1648, are a valuable commentary on the Civil War.

Rusk, (David) Dean 1909–94
US politician

Born in Cherokee County, Georgia, he was educated at Davidson College, North Carolina, and at Oxford, and in 1934 was appointed Associate Professor of Government and Dean of Faculty at Mills College. After service in the army in World War II he held various governmental posts, including that of Special Assistant to the Secretary of War (1946–47), assistant Secretary of State for UN Affairs, deputy Under-Secretary of State and Assistant Secretary for Far Eastern Affairs (1950–51). In 1952 he was appointed president of the Rockefeller Foundation and from 1961 was Secretary of State in the **Kennedy** administration, in which capacity he played a major role in handling the Cuban missile crisis of 1962. He retained the post under the **Johnson** administration, retiring in 1969. He was made an honorary KBE in 1976. ⌸ T J Schoenbaum, *Waging Peace and War: Dean Rusk in the Truman, Kennedy and Johnson Years* (1988)

Ruska, Ernst August Friedrich 1906–88
German electrical engineer and Nobel Prize winner

Born in Heidelberg, he was educated at the technical universities of Munich and Berlin. In 1931 he developed the world's first electron microscope, which he continued to improve in subsequent work. In 1986 he received a half share of the Nobel Prize for physics along with the inventors of the tunnelling electron microscope, **Gerd Binnig** and **Heinrich Rohrer**.

Ruskin, John 1819–1900
English author and art critic

Russell, Bertrand Arthur William Russell, 3rd Earl 1872–1970
English philosopher, mathematician, writer and Nobel Prize winner

Bertrand Russell was a controversial public figure throughout his long and extraordinarily active life. He was born in Trelleck, Gwent; his parents died when he was very young and he was brought up by his grandmother, the widow of Lord John Russell, the Liberal Prime Minister and 1st Earl. He was educated privately and at Trinity College, Cambridge, where he took first-class honours in mathematics and philosophy. He graduated in 1894, was briefly attaché to the British Embassy in Paris, and became a Fellow of Trinity in 1895, shortly after his marriage to Alys Pearsall Smith.

His most original contributions to mathematical logic and philosophy are generally agreed to belong to the period before World War I, as expounded in The Principles of Mathematics (1903), which argues that the whole of mathematics could be derived from logic, and the monumental Principia Mathematica (with Alfred North Whitehead, 1910–13), which worked out this programme in a fully developed formal system and stands as a landmark in the history of logic and mathematics. Russell's famous 'theory of types' and his 'theory of descriptions' belong to this same period.

Ludwig Wittgenstein went to Cambridge to be his student from 1912 to 1913 and began the work that led to the Tractatus Logico-philosophicus (1922), for the English version of which Russell wrote an introduction. He wrote his first genuinely popular work in 1912, The Problems of Philosophy, which can still be read as a brilliantly stimulating introduction to the subject. Politics became his dominant concern during World War I and his active pacifism caused both the loss of his Trinity fellowship (1916), and his imprisonment (1918), during the course of which he wrote his Introduction to Mathematical Philosophy (1919).

He had now to make a living by lecturing and journalism, and became a celebrated controversialist. He visited the USSR, where he met Lenin, Trotsky and Gorky, which sobered his early enthusiasm for Communism and led to the critical Theory and Practice of Bolshevism (1919). He also taught in Beijing (1920–21). In 1921 he married his second wife, Dora Black, and with her founded (in 1927) and ran a progressive school near Petersfield; he set out his educational views in On Education (1926) and Education and the Social Order (1932).

In 1931 he succeeded his elder brother, John, 2nd Earl Russell, as 3rd Earl Russell. His second divorce (1934) and marriage to Patricia Spence (1936) helped to make controversial his book Marriage and Morals (1932); and his lectureship at City College, New York, was terminated in 1940 after complaints that he was an 'enemy of religion and morality', although he later won substantial damages for wrongful dismissal. The rise of Fascism led him to renounce his pacifism in 1939; his fellowship at Trinity was restored in 1944, and he returned to England after World War II to be honoured with an Order of Merit, and to give the first BBC Reith Lecture in 1949. He was awarded the Nobel Prize for literature in 1950.

He had meanwhile continued publishing important philosophical work, mainly on epistemology, in such books as The Analysis of Mind (1921), An Enquiry into Meaning and Truth (1940) and Human Knowledge: Its Scope and Limits (1948), and in 1945 published the bestselling History of Western Philosophy. He also published a stream of popular and provocative works on social, moral and religious questions, some of the more celebrated essays later being collected in Why I am not a Christian (1957).

After 1949 he became increasingly preoccupied with the cause of nuclear disarmament, taking a leading role in CND (Campaign for Nuclear Disarmament) and later the Committee of 100, and engaging in a remarkable correspondence with various world leaders. In 1961 he was again imprisoned, with his fourth and last wife, Edith Finch, for his part in a sit-down demonstration in Whitehall. His last years were spent in North Wales, and he retained to the end his lucidity, independence of mind, and humour. The last major publications were his three volumes of Autobiography (1967–69).

📖 R Monk, Bertrand Russell: The Spirit of Solitude (1996); C Moorehead, Bertrand Russell: A Life (1992); C W Kilminster, Russell (1986); A J Ayer, Russell (1972).

> 'The essential characteristic of philosophy, which makes it a study distinct from science, is criticism. It examines critically the principles employed in science and in daily life; it searches out any inconsistencies there may be in these principles, and it only accepts them when, as the result of a critical inquiry, there is no reason for rejecting them.' From The Problems of Philosophy, ch.14.

He was born in London, where he was tutored privately. In 1836 he went to Christ Church, Oxford, where he won the Newdigate prize for poetry. Shortly after graduating, he met J M W Turner and championed his painting in Modern Painters (1843–60). Along with The Seven Lamps of Architecture (1848) and The Stones of Venice (1851–53), this book established him as the major art and social critic of the day. In 1869 he became the first Slade Professor of Fine Art at Oxford. He settled at Coniston in the Lake District, and published various Slade lectures and Fors Clavigera, a series of papers addressed 'To the Workmen and Labourers of Great Britain' (1871–84). He founded the St George's Guild, a non-profit-making shop in Paddington Street in which members gave a tithe of their fortunes, the John Ruskin School at Camberwell, and the Whitelands College at Chelsea.

Russell, Anna, properly Claudia Anna Russell-Brown 1911–
English singer and musical satirist

Born in London, she studied singing and pursued an orthodox operatic career until she realized the possibilities of satire offered by opera and concert singing. She first appeared as a concert satirist of musical fads in New York in 1948, and has since achieved widespread fame in this medium. Her autobiography is entitled I'm Not Making This Up, You Know.

Russell, Bertrand Arthur William Russell, 3rd Earl See panel above

Russell, Charles Taze, known as Pastor Russell 1852–1916
US religious leader, founder of the Jehovah's Witnesses

Born in Pittsburgh, he was a Congregationalist and became a travelling preacher. In Pittsburgh in 1872 he founded the international Bible Students' Association (Jehovah's Witnesses), a sect with specific views on prophecy and eschatology. He founded the journal The Watchtower in 1879.

Russell, Sir Edward John 1872–1965
English agriculturist

Born in Frampton-on-Severn, Gloucestershire, he studied chemistry at Owens College (later Manchester University) and then undertook a study to improve agriculture and found rural settlements for the unemployed. In 1912 he became the director of the Rothamsted Experimental Station and published his classic Soil

Conditions and Plant Growth. His contributions to the rising status of Rothamsted and of agricultural science were substantial. In his long working life he published some 20 books.

Russell, Francis, 4th Earl of Bedford 1593–1641
English nobleman
He was the son of William, 1st Baron **Russell**. With the help of **Inigo Jones** he developed Covent Garden and built the mansion of Woburn. He also continued the fen drainage scheme initiated by his father and known as the Bedford Level.

Russell, Francis, 5th Duke of Bedford
1765–1802
English nobleman
He was a friend of the Prince of Wales. He built Russell and Tavistock squares in London and employed **Henry Holland** to make additions to Woburn.

Russell, Sir Frederick Stratten 1897–1984
English marine biologist
Born in Doncaster, South Yorkshire, and educated at Cambridge, he joined the Plymouth Laboratory of the Marine Biological Association, of which he was director between 1946 and 1965. He is best known for his work on medusae (*The Medusae of the British Isles*, 2 vols, 1953, 1970), larval fish (*Eggs and planktonic stages of British marine fish*, 1976) and zooplankton communities. By painstaking laboratory rearing, Russell succeeded in solving major taxonomic problems to link the medusa to the polyp phase for many species, and he established the 'Russell cycle' of environmental changes in plankton communities. Russell's work has potential applications in the assessment of changes in water circulation, and possibly climate change, in addition to predictions for commercially important fish populations. He was elected FRS in 1938 and knighted in 1965.

Russell, George William 1857–1951
English horticulturist
Born in Stillington, Yorkshire, he studied at the Metropolitan School of Art in Dublin. After 25 years of research and experiment he succeeded in producing lupins of greatly improved strains and of over 60 different colours.

Russell, George William, pseudonym Æ or A.E.
1867–1935
Irish poet, painter, writer and economist
He was born in Lurgan, County Armagh. In 1877 his family went to Dublin, where at the Metropolitan School of Art he met **W B Yeats**, and, already something of a mystic, through him became interested in theosophy. This led him to give up painting, except as a hobby. Having worked first in a brewery, then as a draper's clerk, he published his first book in 1894, *Homeward: Songs by the Way*, which established him as a recognized figure in the Irish literary renaissance. He was editor of the *Irish Homestead* from 1906 to 1923, when it amalgamated with the *Irish Statesman*, and as editor of the latter from 1923 to 1930 he aimed at a balanced expression of Irish opinion, although he held nationalistic sympathies. His writings include books on economics, *The Candle of Vision* (1918), and on religious philosophy, essays, many volumes of verse, which reflect his mysticism, among them *The Divine Vision* (1903) and *Midsummer Eve* (1928), and a play, *Deirdre* (1907). ▢ D Figgis, *A Study of a Man and a Nation* (1916)

Russell, Sir (Sydney) Gordon 1892–1980
English designer, manufacturer and administrator
He was born in Cricklewood, London. In 1923 he started running his own furniture-making business in Broadway, Worcestershire, with designs in the Cotswold Arts and Crafts tradition. However, under the influence of his younger brother R D (Dick) Russell (1903–81), an architect who later became Professor in charge of Furniture at the Royal College of Art, London (1948–64), Gordon Russell Limited produced some of the finest furniture of the 1930s in a logical modern idiom. In World War II he was chairman of the panel responsible for 'utility' furniture (1943–47), and from 1947 to 1959 was director of the Council of Industrial Design (now the Design Council) during its formative years. He was elected a Royal Designer for Industry in 1940.

Russell, Henry Norris 1877–1957
US astronomer
Born in Pyster Bay, New York, after studies at Princeton and Cambridge, UK, he was appointed Professor of Astronomy in Princeton in 1905 and six years later director of the university observatory there. He developed with **Harlow Shapley** methods for the calculation of the orbits and dimensions of eclipsing binary stars and for the determination of the distances of double stars. He worked on the theory of stellar atmospheres from the analysis of stellar spectra. His most famous achievement was the formulation of the **Hertzsprung–Russell** diagram (1913) correlating the spectral types of stars with their luminosity, which became of fundamental importance to the theory of stellar evolution.

Russell, Herbrand, 11th Duke of Bedford
1858–1940
English nobleman
Born in London, he was the son of Francis Russell, 9th Duke of Bedford (1819–91), and succeeded his brother, the 10th Duke, in 1893. He declined political office, preferring to preside over his landed estates. He established the collections of rare animals at Woburn, which include the Prjevalsky wild horses and the Père David deer. He helped create Whipsnade Zoo and was president of the Zoological Society (1899–1936). His wife, the duchess Mary du Caurroy (1865–1937), kept a model hospital at Woburn from 1898, in which she later worked as a radiographer. She took up flying at the age of 60 and participated in record-breaking flights to India and Africa before being lost off the east coast of England while flying solo (1937).

Russell, Jack (John) 1795–1883
English 'sporting parson'
He was born in Dartmouth, Devon, and educated at Oxford. He was perpetual curate of Swymbridge, near Barnstaple (1832–80), and master of foxhounds. He developed the West Country smooth-haired, short-legged terrier named 'Jack Russell' after him. ▢ Lois Lamplugh, *Parson Jack Russell of Swimbridge* (1994)

Russell, (Ernestine) Jane (Geraldine) 1921–
US actress
Born in Bemidji, Minnesota, the daughter of a former actress, she worked as a chiropodist's receptionist and photographer's model before studying acting with Maria Oupenskaya (1876–1949). Her voluptuous figure brought her fame as the star of *The Outlaw* (1943), a western whose notoriety resulted from the censor's concern over the amount of her cleavage exposed on screen. She subsequently appeared in such films as *The Paleface* (1948) and *Gentlemen Prefer Blondes* (1953). As her film career faded, she appeared in cabaret, endorsed Playtex bras on television, and starred on Broadway in *Company* (1971) and in the television series *Yellow Rose* (1983). Her autobiography, *My Path and Detours*, was published in 1985.

Russell, John, 1st Earl of Bedford c.1486–1555
English courtier
He became a gentleman usher to King **Henry VIII**, was entrusted with several diplomatic missions, and later held many court appointments, including those of

Comptroller of the Household (1537) and Lord Privy Seal (1542). Among the rich possessions which he amassed were the abbeys of Woburn and Tavistock, and the London properties of Covent Garden and Long Acre. He was created earl in 1550 and led the mission to Spain (1554) which escorted King Philip II of Spain to marry Mary I.

Russell, John Robert, 13th Duke of Bedford
1917–
English nobleman

He was estranged from his family at an early age and lived in poor circumstances in a Bloomsbury boarding house until, having been invalided out of the Coldstream Guards (1940), he became in turn house agent, journalist and South African farmer. After succeeding to the title he became famous for his energetic and successful efforts to keep Woburn Abbey for the family by running it commercially as a show place with popular amenities and amusements.

Russell (of Kingston Russell), John Russell, 1st Earl 1792–1878
English statesman

Born in London, the third son of the 6th Duke of Bedford, he studied at the University of Edinburgh, and in 1813 was returned as MP for Tavistock. His strenuous efforts in favour of reform won many seats for the Liberals at the 1830 election. Wellington was driven from office, and in Earl Grey's ministry Russell became paymaster of the forces. He was one of the four members of the government entrusted with the task of framing the first Reform Bill (1832). In 1834 he left office with Lord Melbourne, but with the downfall of Robert Peel in 1835 he became Home (and later Colonial) Secretary and Leader of the Lower House. Immediately after the repeal of the Corn Laws in 1846 Peel was defeated and Russell became Prime Minister, at the head of a Whig administration (1846–52). In Lord Aberdeen's coalition of 1852 he was Foreign Secretary and Leader of the Commons again, but his inopportune Reform Bill (1854), the mismanagement of the Crimean campaign and his bungling of the Vienna conference combined to make him unpopular, and for four years he was out of office. In 1859 he returned as Foreign Secretary, under Lord Palmerston, and in 1861 was created Earl Russell. On Palmerston's death in 1865 he again became Prime Minister but was defeated in June on his attempt to introduce another Reform Bill and resigned.

Russell, John Scott 1808–82
Scottish engineer

Born near Glasgow, he graduated from the University of Glasgow at the age of 17 and moved to Edinburgh, where he taught mathematics and natural philosophy. He inaugurated a scheme to build and operate steam coaches on the roads of Scotland, and in 1834 a service between Glasgow and Paisley began. After only a few months of successful operation, however, an accident involving several fatalities put an end to the project. He invented the 'wave-line system' of shipbuilding, and took a large part in the design and building of Isambard Kingdom Brunel's *Great Eastern* steamship (1858).

Russell, Ken, *in full* Henry Kenneth Alfred Russell
1927–
English film director

Born in Southampton, he worked as a ballet dancer, actor and photographer before making short documentary films. The BBC commissioned him to make musical biographies for *Monitor* (1962–65), as well as *Portrait of a Goon* (1959), *Lotte Lenya Sings Kurt Weill* (1962) and *Isadora, The Biggest Dancer in the World* (1966). He turned to feature films with *French Dressing* (1963) and had international

success with *Women in Love* (1969). His flamboyant style and musically inspired themes continued in *The Music Lovers* (1971) and *Mahler* (1974). Other productions include the films *The Devils* (1971), *Savage Messiah* (1972), *Crimes of Passion* (1984), *The Rainbow* (1989) and *Mindbender* (1995) and on television, *Lady Chatterley* (1993).

Russell, Lillian, *originally* Helen Louise Leonard
1861–1922
US singer and actress

Born in Clinton, Iowa, she was educated at the Sacred Heart Convent in Chicago. She achieved great success in the 1880s and 1890s as a soprano in light opera and burlesque theatre. Her beautiful face, hourglass figure, and flamboyant personal life were among the sources of her fame. She married four times and often appeared in the company of Diamond Jim Brady.

Russell, Morgan 1886–1953
US painter

Born in New York City, he moved to Paris in 1906 and studied briefly with Henri Matisse. In 1912 he and the US painter Stanton McDonald-Wright (1890–1973) developed the theory of Synchromist colour, in which colour was given precedence over descriptive form. One of his best-known works in this genre is *Synchromy in Orange: To Form* (1913–14). From 1920 he reverted to figurative painting. He returned to the USA in 1946.

Russell (of Thornhaugh), William Russell, Baron 1558–1613
English politician

The son of Francis Russell, 2nd Earl of Bedford (1527–85), he studied at Magdalen College, Oxford, and became Governor of Flushing (1587–88) and Lord Deputy of Ireland (1594–97). With experience of lowland drainage methods from his time at Flushing, he initiated reclamation work in the Cambridgeshire fens. He was granted a peerage by James VI and I in 1603.

Russell, Lord William 1639–83
English politician

The third son of William Russell, 5th Earl and 1st Duke of Bedford, he made the Grand Tour, and at the Restoration was elected MP for Tavistock. He took to duelling and had many debts, but was rescued from this lifestyle by his marriage (1669) with Lady Rachel Wriothesley (1636–1723). In 1674 he spoke against the actions of the Cabal, and became an active adherent of the Country Party. He led the attempt to exclude the Duke of York (later James VII and II) from the accession as a popish recusant. He was arrested with Robert Devereux, 2nd Earl of Essex and Algernon Sidney for participation in the Rye House Plot, was found guilty of high treason by a packed jury, and was beheaded.

Russell, William, 12th Duke of Bedford
1888–1953
English nobleman

The son of Herbrand Russell, 11th Duke of Bedford, he acquired a reputation for his collection of parrots and homing budgerigars, and for his adherence to pacifism, Buchmanism and near-fascism which almost landed him in difficulties during World War II. He was killed in a shooting accident.

Russell, Sir William Howard 1821–1907
Irish war correspondent

Born near Tallaght, County Dublin, he was educated at Trinity College, Dublin, then joined *The Times* in 1843. From the Crimea (1854–55) he wrote the famous despatches (published in book form in 1856) about the sufferings of the soldiers during the winter of 1854–55, and in 1858 he witnessed the Indian Mutiny. He established the *Army and Navy Gazette* in 1860; and in 1861 the Civil

War took him to the USA, where his account of the Federal defeat at the first Battle of Bull Run made him unpopular. He accompanied the Austrians during the war with Prussia (1866), and the Prussians during the war with France (1870–71). He visited Egypt and the East (1874) and India (1877) as private secretary to the Prince of Wales (Edward VII), and went with Viscount Wolseley to South Africa in 1879. Among his books are *The Adventures of Dr Brady* (1868), *Hesperothen* (1882) and *A Visit to Chile* (1890).

Russell, Willy (William) 1947–
English playwright
Born in Whiston, Merseyside, he became a teacher after several years of working in industry. He is one of the most frequently performed of contemporary British dramatists, and is best known for the highly successful stage play and film *Educating Rita* (1979). Combining poignant and mildly abrasive social comment with broad, sentimental humour, this is probably his most representative work. The musical *Blood Brothers* (1983) continues the formula in a story of two brothers separated at birth and brought up in different social classes. His popular play *Shirley Valentine* (1986) was made into a film in 1989. Russell is a founder-member and director of Quintet Films and an honorary director of the Liverpool Playhouse.

Rust, Mathias 1968–
West German aviator
He achieved worldwide fame in May 1987 when he piloted a light Cessna 172 turboprop aeroplane from Finland to Moscow, landing in Red Square. His exploit highlighted serious deficiencies in the Soviet air defence system and led to the immediate dismissal of Defence Minister Marshal Sergei Sokolov. Rust was found guilty of malicious hooliganism and sentenced to four years' imprisonment. After serving 14 months in a KGB prison in Lefortovo he was released in August 1988 and flown home to West Germany as a 'goodwill gesture' by the Gorbachev administration.

Rutebeuf c.1230–1286
French epic poet
Born in the Champenois, he lived in Paris and was the author of the semi-liturgical drama *Miracle de Théophile* (c.1260, a prototype of the Faust story), the *Dit de l'herberie* ('The Tale of the Herb Market'), a monologue by a quack doctor, full of comic charlatanesque rhetoric, and also several stories. 📖 L Chédat, *Rutebeuf* (1909)

Ruth 12th century BC
Biblical character
She was a Moabite woman who had married one of the two sons of Elimelech and Naomi. When Naomi's husband and sons had died, she resolved to return to her home-town of Bethlehem. Ruth insisted on accompanying her, believing that the God of Israel would protect them, and she later married a distant relative, the wealthy landowner Boaz. The story in the Book of Ruth can be interpreted as a parable of divine providence and devotion to duty, or as a reaction against teaching that forbids mixed marriages.

Ruth, Babe, *properly* George Herman Ruth
1895–1948
US baseball player
Born in Baltimore, he started his career as a left-handed pitcher with the Boston Red Sox (1914–19). He became famous for his powerful hitting with the New York Yankees (1920–34). In 1920 he scored a then-record of 54 home runs, and in 1927 he hit 60 home runs. In all he played in 10 World Series, and hit 714 home runs, a record that stood for 30 years until it was surpassed by Hank Aaron in 1974. In 1935 he moved to the Boston Braves, and ended his career as coach for the Brooklyn Dodgers

(1938). In 1936 he was elected to the National Baseball Hall of Fame. He is considered the greatest all-rounder in the history of the game.

Rutherford (of Nelson), Ernest Rutherford, 1st Baron See panel p1612

Rutherford, Dame Margaret 1892–1972
English theatre and film actress
Born in London, she made her first stage appearance in 1925 at the Old Vic theatre, London, and her first film in 1936. She gradually gained fame as a character actress and comedienne, with a gallery of eccentrics including Miss Prism in *The Importance of Being Earnest* (stage 1939, film 1952), Madame Arcati in *Blithe Spirit* (stage 1941, film 1945), and Miss Whitchurch in *The Happiest Days of Your Life* (stage 1948, film 1950). She was also an extremely successful Miss Marple in several films based on the novels of Agatha Christie from 1962, appearing with the actor Stringer Davis (1896–1973), whom she had married in 1945. She was created DBE in 1967, and won an Academy Award as Best Supporting Actress for her part in *The V.I.P's* (1963). 📖 Dawn Langley Simmons, *Margaret Rutherford: A Blithe Spirit* (1983)

Rutherford, Mark See White, William Hale

Ruthven, William, 4th Baron Ruthven and 1st Earl of Gowrie c.1541–1584
Scottish nobleman
He was involved in the murder of David Rizzio (1566), and later was the custodian of Mary, Queen of Scots during her captivity at Loch Leven (1567–68). He was created Earl of Gowrie in 1581. In 1582 he kidnapped the boy king, James VI, and took him to Castle Ruthven, near Perth; for this he was first pardoned and then ordered to leave the country. He was later beheaded at Stirling for his part in a conspiracy to take Stirling Castle.

Rutledge, John 1739–1800
US statesman and jurist
Born into the Southern planter aristocracy in Charleston, South Carolina, he was a delegate to the Continental Congress (1774–76, 1782–83) and the Constitutional Convention (1787), where he championed slavery and argued for a strong central government. He later served as President (1776–78) and Governor (1779–82) of South Carolina. From 1789 to 1791 he was an associate justice of the Supreme Court. He was named Chief Justice in 1795, but the Senate rejected the nomination, and he sat for only five months.

Ruysch, Rachel 1664–1750
Dutch artist
Born in Haarlem, she studied with the flower painter Willem von Aelst and in 1693 married the portrait painter Juriaen Poole. The couple were admitted into The Hague Corporation of Painters in 1701, and in 1708 were appointed court painters to the Elector Palatine. Moving to Düsseldorf, they painted exclusively for the Prince until his death in 1716, when they returned to Amsterdam. She is the most celebrated Dutch flower painter of the 18th century.

Ruysdael, Jacob van See Ruïdael, Jacob van

Ruyter, Michiel Adriaanszoon de 1607–76
Dutch naval commander
Born in Flushing, he became a captain in the Dutch navy. In the first Anglo-Dutch War (1652–54) he served with distinction under Cornelis Tromp against Robert Blake and George Monk, and in the second Anglo-Dutch War (1665–67) he defeated Monk in the Four Days' Battle off Dunkirk (1666). In 1667 he sailed up the River Medway, burned some of the English ships, and next sailed up the River Thames, as well as attacking Harwich. In the war

Rutherford (of Nelson), Ernest Rutherford, 1st Baron 1871–1937
New Zealand physicist, the 'Father of nuclear physics', and Nobel Prize winner

Ernest Rutherford was born at Brightwater, near Nelson, South Island. He was the fourth of a farmer's 12 children. He won scholarships to Nelson College and Canterbury College, Christchurch, and his first research projects were on magnetization of iron by high-frequency discharges (1894) and magnetic viscosity (1896).

In 1895 he was admitted to the Cavendish Laboratory and Trinity College, Cambridge, on a scholarship. There he made the first successful wireless transmissions over two miles (3.2km). Under the brilliant direction of **J J Thomson**, Rutherford discovered the three types of uranium radiations. In 1898 he became Professor of Physics at McGill University, Canada, where, with **Frederick Soddy**, he formulated the theory of atomic disintegration to account for the tremendous heat energy radiated by uranium. In 1907 he became professor at Manchester and there established that alpha particles were doubly ionized helium ions by counting the number given off with a counting device, which he jointly invented with the German physicist **Hans Geiger**.

This led to a revolutionary conception of the atom as a miniature universe in which the mass is concentrated in the nucleus surrounded by planetary electrons. Rutherford's assistant, **Niels Bohr**, applied to this the quantum theory (1913), and the concept of the 'Rutherford–Bohr atom' of nuclear physics was born. During World War I, Rutherford did research on submarine detection for the Admiralty. In 1919, in a series of experiments, he discovered that alpha-ray bombardments induced atomic transformation in atmospheric nitrogen,

liberating hydrogen nuclei. The same year he succeeded Thomson to the Cavendish professorship at Cambridge and reorganized the laboratory, the world centre for the study of *The Newer Alchemy* (1937). In 1920 he predicated the existence of the neutron, later discovered by his colleague, **James Chadwick**. He was awarded the Nobel prize for chemistry in 1908 and was president of the Royal Society from 1925 to 1930.

📖 He wrote many memoirs on atomic structure, disintegration and the conduction of electricity and gases, and also *Radioactivity* (1904), *Radioactive Transformations* (1906) and *Radioactive Substances* (1930) and *The Newer Alchemy* (1937). See also David Wilson, *Rutherford, Simple Genius* (1983); M Bunge and W R Shea (eds), *Rutherford and Physics at the Turn of the Century* (1979); **E N da C Andrade**, *Rutherford and the Nature of the Atom* (1964).

> Rutherford, though not conceited, had no doubts about the power of his intellect. Lord Snow (the writer **C P Snow**) wrote of him in *Variety of Men* (1967): 'His estimate of his own powers was realistic, but if it erred at all, it did not err on the modest side.'
>
> During an interview about the dawn of the atomic age, a writer said: 'You are a lucky man, Rutherford, always on the crest of the wave !' Rutherford replied, 'Well, I *made* the wave, didn't I?' And then added quietly, 'At least to some extent.'

with France and England (1672–78) he attacked the French and English fleets in Solebay (28 May 1672), and defeated Prince Rupert and d'Estrées (1673), thus preventing an English invasion. In 1675 he sailed for the Mediterranean to help the Spaniards against the French, but was mortally wounded in a battle off Sicily. 📖 Petrus J Blok, *Life of Admiral de Ruyter* (1933)

Ružička, Leopold Stephen 1887–1976
Swiss chemist and Nobel Prize winner

Born in Vukovar, Croatia, he trained at the Technische Hochschule, Karlsruhe, studying the chemistry of the pyrethrins and other insecticides (1912), and continued this work at the Polytechnic in Zurich (1916). From 1921 he collaborated with a perfume factory on the synthesis of aromatic terpenes (hydrocarbons found in plant oils). After a short stay in Utrecht (1926–29), he returned as Professor of Organic and Inorganic Chemistry to Zurich. He went on to study terpenes in great detail. In the 1930s he discovered their structural relationship to the steroids, which led him to enunciate in 1953 the rule by which these five carbon compounds combine to form steroids. In 1935 he was able to announce the synthesis of the still undiscovered male hormones, testosterone and methyltestosterone. With **Adolf Butenandt**, he was awarded the 1939 Nobel Prize for chemistry.

Ruzzante, *properly* Angelo Beolco 1502–42
Italian dramatist and actor

Born in Padua, he acted under the name of Ruzzante ('The Gossip'). He believed that the artist should shun grand effects in favour of simple truths, and most of his plays were comedies and dramas of rural life. 📖 C Grabler, *Ruzzante* (1953)

Ryan, Desmond 1893–1964
Irish socialist and historian

Born in London, the son of **William Patrick Ryan**, he grew up in the Dublin of the Irish Renaissance, vividly described in his autobiography of youth, *Remembering Sion* (1934). He was educated at **Patrick Pearse's** school, St Enda's, and became Pearse's secretary. He fought in the General Post Office in the Easter Rising (1916), and edited Pearse's account of the school on release from internment, after which he wrote brief studies of Pearse and **James Connolly**. He supported the Anglo-Irish Treaty but left Ireland in disgust at the civil war, and in London wrote novels (*Invisible Army*, 1932, an emotive account of **Michael Collins**, and the hypnotically picaresque *St Eustace and the Albatross*, 1934), and penetrating analyses of **Éamon de Valera** and **John Devoy**, and of the Irish language (*The Sword of Light*, 1938). He returned to Dublin in the 1940s and produced in *The Rising* (1946) the definitive narrative of the Easter Rising, and edited *Devoy's Post Bag* (1948, 1953, consisting of Fenian correspondence) as well as writing a biography of **James Stephens** (*The Fenian Chief*, published in 1957).

Ryan, Elizabeth 1892–1979
US lawn tennis player

Born in Anaheim, California, she won 19 Wimbledon titles (12 doubles and seven mixed doubles), a record which stood from 1934 until 1979, when it was surpassed by **Billie Jean King**. Six of her women's doubles titles were with **Suzanne Lenglen**.

Ryan, Nolan 1947–
US baseball player

Born in Refugio, Texas, he was measured as the fastest baseball pitcher of all time in 1974, his fast ball in that year being recorded at 100.8 mph. He played for the New York Mets (1966–71), California Angels (1972–79), Houston Astros (1980–88) and Texas Rangers (1989–93), retiring from the game in 1993. He holds more than 50 major league all-time records, including most seasons pitched (27), most strikeouts (5,714) and most no-hitters (7).

Ryan, William Patrick, *also known as* **Liam P O Riain**, *and as* **W P O'Ryan** 1867–1942
Irish journalist and historian
Born in Templemore, County Tipperary, he worked in London as a journalist, but returned to Ireland to edit the *Irish Peasant* and other journals (1906–11), only to find his expectations of cultural emancipation blighted by clerical intervention. He expressed his anger in *The Plough and the Cross* (1918) and *The Pope's Green Island* (1912), and also wrote *The Irish Literary Revival* (1894) and *The Irish Labour Movement* (1919). He became assistant editor of the London *Daily Herald*, and later published *Seanchas Filidheachta* (1940) and a study of European contributions to Gaelic scholarship, *Gaelachas i Gléin* (1933).

Rydberg, Johannes Robert 1854–1919
Swedish physicist
Born in Halmstad, he was educated at the University of Lund where he remained throughout his career, becoming professor in 1901. Working on the classification of optical spectra, he developed an empirical formula relating the frequencies of spectral lines, incorporating the constant known by his name, which was later derived by **Niels Bohr** using his quantum theory of the atom.

Rydberg, (Abraham) Viktor 1828–95
Swedish writer and scholar
He was born in Jönköping, and after a hard childhood and early struggles to gain an education he worked as a journalist on the liberal newspaper *Göteborgs Handels-och Sjöfartstidning* (1855–76). He wrote historical novels, including *Fribytaren på Östersjön* (1857, 'Freebooter in the Baltic'), *Den siste atenaren* (1859, 'The Last Athenian') and *Vâpensmeden* (1891, 'The Armourer'), and several volumes of biblical criticism. From 1884 to 1895 he was professor at Stockholm. The leading cultural figure of his day, he also wrote works on philosophy, philology and aesthetics, translated **Goethe**'s *Faust*, and published a mythological study, *Undersökningar i germanisk mytologi* (1886–89). ⊞ K Warburg, *Viktor Rydberg* (1900)

Ryder, Samuel 1859–1936
English businessman
Born in Cheshire, the son of a nurseryman. He built up a prosperous business in St Albans, mainly through selling penny packets of seeds. In 1927 he donated the Ryder Cup, competed for between teams of British (now European) and US professional golfers.

Ryder (of Warsaw and Cavendish), Sue Ryder, Baroness 1923–
English philanthropist
Born in Leeds, she has promoted residential care for the sick and disabled. Educated at Benenden School in Kent, she joined the First Aid Nursing Yeomanry in World War II and worked with the Polish section of the Special Operations Executive in occupied Europe. As a result of her experiences she determined to establish a 'living memorial' to the dead and to refugees and other oppressed people. The Sue Ryder Foundation, which was first established at Cavendish, near Sudbury, Suffolk, in 1953, now links 80 centres worldwide. In some countries projects function under the auspices of the Ryder-Cheshire Foundation, which links her work with that of **Leonard Cheshire**, whom she married in 1959. She has written *And the Morrow Is Theirs* (1975) and the autobiographical *Child of My Love* (1986).

Rykov, Aleksei Ivanovich 1881–1938
Russian revolutionary and government official
Born in Saratov into a poor peasant family, he was educated at Kazan University and soon became involved in social democratic politics, being arrested, imprisoned and exiled several times. He was elected to the Moscow Soviet (1917) and helped to organize the October Revolution in Petrograd (now St Petersburg), becoming People's Commissar for Internal Affairs in the first Soviet government. He held a number of senior government posts (1919–37), and was also a member of the politburo (1919–29). In 1928, together with **Nikolai Bukharin** and Tomsky, he led the 'right opposition' against **Stalin**'s economic policies and had to give up his Party positions. In 1937 he was arrested for alleged anti-Party activities, and was shot the following year. He was rehabilitated during the **Gorbachev** era, with other prominent victims of Stalin's purges.

Rylands, John 1801–88
English textile manufacturer and merchant
He was born in St Helens, Lancashire. In 1899 his widow established the John Rylands Library in Manchester.

Ryle, Gilbert 1900–76
English philosopher
Born in Brighton, Sussex, he studied at Queen's College, Oxford, and became Waynflete Professor of Metaphysical Philosophy at Oxford (1945–68) after service in World War II. He was an influential defender of linguistic or 'ordinary language' philosophy, holding that 'philosophy is the detection of the sources in linguistic idioms of recurrent misconstructions and absurd theories'. He was editor of the journal *Mind* (1947–71) and helped make Oxford a centre of philosophy in the English-speaking world in the postwar years. His first and best-known work is *The Concept of Mind* (1949), which aimed to exorcise 'the ghost in the machine' in a behaviourist analysis directed against traditional Cartesian mind/body dualism. His other works include *Dilemmas* (1954) and *Plato's Progress* (1966). ⊞ Oscar P Wood and George Pitcher, *Ryle* (1971)

Ryle, Sir Martin 1918–84
English physicist, radio astronomer and Nobel Prize winner
Born in Brighton, Sussex, he was educated at Bradfield College, Berkshire, and Christ Church, Oxford, graduating in 1939. For the duration of the war he was involved in important research in the field of radar. At the end of the war he joined the Cavendish Laboratory in Cambridge, where he investigated the emission of radio waves from the Sun and improved the low resolving power of radio telescopes. He then turned to studies of radio waves from the universe and found that the numbers of radio sources increased as their intensities decreased (1955), a result which pointed to an evolving universe starting with a Big Bang. He mapped radio sources by his ingenious method of 'aperture synthesis'. Ryle was one of the most outstanding scientists of his generation. He was awarded a knighthood in 1966, was appointed to the first chair of radio astronomy in Cambridge in 1969, and in 1972 became the first Astronomer Royal to come from the field of radio astronomy. In 1974 he received the Nobel prize for physics with his colleague **Antony Hewish**.

Rymer, Thomas 1641–1713
English critic and historian
Born in Northallerton, Yorkshire, he was the son of a Roundhead hanged in 1664. He studied at Sidney Sussex College, Cambridge, and entered Gray's Inn in 1666. He published translations, critical discussions on poetry, dramas and works on history, and in 1692 was appointed historiographer royal (1692). His principal critical works are *The Tragedies of the Last Age Consider'd* (1678) and *A Short View of Tragedy* (1693), which later earned him scorn for its attacks on **Shakespeare**. He is chiefly remembered as the compiler of the collection of historical materials known as the *Foedera* (20 vols, 1704–35).

Rysbrack, (John) Michael c.1693–1770
Flemish sculptor

He was born possibly in Antwerp, and settled in London in 1720. Among his works in a classical style influenced by the baroque are the monument to Sir **Isaac Newton** in Westminster Abbey (1731), a bronze equestrian statue of **William III** (1735, Bristol), and statues of Queen **Anne** (Blenheim), and **George II** (1735, Greenwich). Busts include **Alexander Pope** (1730, National Portrait Gallery, London), Sir **Robert Walpole** (1738, National Portrait Gallery) and Sir **Hans Sloane** (c.1737, British Museum). His later monument to Admiral **Edward Vernon** (1763) in Westminster Abbey shows the influence of Rococo style.

Ryskind, Morrie 1895–1985

US lyricist and sketch writer

He was born in New York City and educated at Columbia University. He wrote sketches for *The 49ers* (1922) and *Merry Go Round* (1927), and co-wrote *Animal Crackers* (1928) with **George S Kaufman**. Other work with Kaufman included *Of Thee I Sing* (1931), which brought him a Pulitzer Prize for drama in 1932, shared with Kaufman and lyricist **Ira Gershwin**, a collaboration which also produced *Let 'Em Eat Cake* (1933). His other work includes screenplays and a number of less successful musicals.

Ryzhkov, Nikolai Ivanovich 1929–

Soviet politician

Born in the Urals industrial region, he began his working life as a miner before studying engineering at the Urals Polytechnic in Sverdlovsk (now Yekaterinburg). He then worked his way up from welding foreman in a local heavy machine-building plant to head of the giant Uralmash engineering conglomerate, the largest industrial enterprise in the USSR. A member of the Communist Party of the Soviet Union (CPSU) since 1956, in 1975 he went to Moscow to work as first Deputy Minister for Heavy Transport and Machine Building. Four years later, he became first deputy chairman of Gosplan, and in 1982 was inducted into the CPSU secretariat as head of economic affairs by **Yuri Andropov**. He was brought into the politburo by **Mikhail Gorbachev** in April 1985 and made Prime Minister in September, with a special brief to restructure the discredited state planning process. More cautious in his approach to reform than Gorbachev, and considerably less flamboyant than **Boris Yeltsin**, he was viewed as a steadying and stable influence in overcoming the economic and constitutional problems that blighted Gorbachev's reformed USSR. He stepped down as Prime Minister in 1991.

Saadi See **Sádi**

Sa'adia, ben Joseph 882–942
Jewish philosopher, polemicist and scholar
Born in Dilaz in al-Fayyum, he left Egypt (c.905) and after a period in Palestine settled in Babylonia, where he became *gaon* (head) of the rabbinic Academy of Sura in two periods of tenure (928–35, 937–42), which were separated by a brief spell in which he was excommunicated after various personal and political struggles by the head of Babylonian Jewry, David ben Zakkai. He was one of the most important medieval Jewish thinkers and produced a Hebrew-Arabic dictionary, translated much of the Old Testament into Arabic, and wrote treatises on Talmudic law and religious poetry, as well as a major philosophical work, *Kitāb al-amānāt wa al-i'tigādāt* (935, 'The Book of Beliefs and Opinions'), a rationalistic study in theology which became a basic Jewish text.

Saarinen, Eero 1910–61
US architect and furniture designer
Born in Kirkknonummi, Finland, he emigrated at the age of 13 with his father, **Eliel Saarinen**, to the USA. After studying sculpture in Paris and architecture at Yale University he went into partnership with his father in 1937. He designed many public buildings in the USA and Europe, including the Jefferson Memorial Arch in St Louis, the General Motors Technical Centre in Warren, Michigan, the Columbia Broadcasting System HQ in New York City, the US embassies in London and Oslo, the TWA terminal at New York's John F Kennedy Airport and Washington's Dulles International Airport. 📖 Allan Temko, *Eero Saarinen* (1962)

Saarinen, (Gottlieb) Eliel 1873–1950
US architect
He was born in Rantasalmi, Finland. The leading architect of his native country, he designed the Helsinki railway station (1904–14) before emigrating to the USA in 1923, where he designed the buildings for the Cranbrook Academy of Art in Michigan, of which he became president (1932–48). An eloquent opponent of skyscrapers, he formed a partnership with his son, **Eero Saarinen**, and designed the Tabernacle Church of Christ in Columbus, Independence, and the Christ Lutheran Church in Minneapolis. His writings include *The City, Its Growth, Its Decay, Its Future* (1943) and *Search for Form* (1948).

Saavedra Lamas, Carlos 1878–1959
Argentine diplomat, jurist and Nobel Prize winner
Born in Buenos Aires, he graduated from the University of Buenos Aires in 1903 and stayed there to teach political economy and constitutional law. He served as Minister of Foreign Affairs (1932–38) and President of the Assembly of the League of Nations (1936), and after presiding over a conference in 1935 that ended the Chaco war, he was awarded the 1936 Nobel Peace Prize.

Saba, Umberto, *pseudonym of* **Umberto Poli**
1883–1957
Italian Jewish poet
He was born in Trieste. He kept himself apart from Italian literary politics and wrote freely on themes of his choice. The collection to which he added throughout his life, *Canzionieri*, is described as a 'massive lyric autobiography' and 'a type of Odyssey of man in our times'. In this way a series of lyrics developed into an epic, and is one of the most celebrated and loved long poems of recent times. 📖 J Cary, *Three Modern Italian Poets* (1969)

Sabah, Sheikh Jaber al-Ahmad al-Jaber al- 1928–
Kuwaiti politician and Emir of Kuwait
Born in Kuwait City, he was educated at Almubarakiyyah School, Kuwait, and privately. Part of the family that has ruled the country since the 18th century, he was appointed Governor of the Ahmadi and oil areas (1949–59), president of the department of finance and economy (1959), Minister of Finance, Industry and Commerce (1963, 1965), and Prime Minister (1965–67). Proclaimed Crown Prince in 1966, he succeeded his uncle as Emir in 1978. His rule has been marked by the suspension of the legislature in 1976–81 and again in 1986, and the invasion of Kuwait by Iraqi forces led by **Saddam Hussein** in August 1990, after which the country was liberated in February 1991 by an alliance of western and Arab forces. The first elections since the suspension of parliament in 1986 were held in October 1992.

Sabas, St See **Sava, St**

Sabatier, Paul 1854–1941
French chemist and Nobel Prize winner
Born in Carcassonne, after secondary education at the École Normale Supérieure he taught briefly at a lycée in Nîmes and then moved to Paris to work with **Marcellin Berthelot**. He received his doctorate in 1880 and moved to Bordeaux for a year before taking an established post at Toulouse. In 1913 he was among the first scientists to be elected to a chair (one of six) newly created by the Academy of Sciences for provincial members. He made a number of important discoveries in inorganic chemistry, and is best known for his discovery of catalysed hydrogenation of unsaturated organic compounds, such as the conversion of ethene to ethane over reduced nickel. He took little interest in the commercial application of his studies but received the Nobel Prize for chemistry in 1912.

Sabatini, Gabriela 1970–
Argentine tennis player
Born in Buenos Aires, she became at the age of 13 the youngest player to win the Under 18's Orange Bowl. After turning professional in 1985, she failed to fulfil her early promise, and won just one Grand Slam title (the 1990 US Open) and one Olympic silver medal (1988). She also played unsuccessfully in the longest women's Grand Slam match in the quarter-finals of the 1993 French Open. She retired from the Tour in October 1996.

Sabatini, Rafael 1875–1950
British novelist
He was born in Jesi, Italy, of Italian and British parentage. Writing in English, he first made his name as an author of historical romances with *The Tavern Knight* (1904), which he followed after settling in England in 1905 with other tales, including *The Sea Hawk* (1915), *Scaramouche* (1921) and *Captain Blood* (1922). He also wrote historical biographies, and a study of *Torquemada* (1913).

Sábato, Ernesto 1911–
Argentine novelist and essayist
Born in Rojas into an Italian family, he married a woman of Russian–Jewish origin, and has had to defend himself from anti-Semites, Peronists such as Leopoldo Maréchal (1900–70), Nazis and hardline Marxists (Sábato himself was a Communist until 1934). He was a Professor of Theoretical Physics, but was dismissed in 1944 for his criticism of **Perónism**. He claims to be primarily a novelist of the inner life, and his work appeals to introspective readers. His phantasmagoric novels *El túnel* (1950, Eng trans, *The*

Outsider, 1950; *The Tunnel*, 1988), *Sobré héroes y tumbas* (1961, Eng trans, *On Heroes and Tombs*, 1981), and *Abaddón el exterminador* (1974, Eng trans *The Angel of Darkness*, 1991) are complex but readable, and his humane non-fiction, which includes a series of dialogues with **Jorge Luis Borges**, forms a guide to Argentine and Latin-American problems. ▢ H D Oberhelman, *Ernesto Sábato* (1970)

Sabbatai Zebi or Shabbetai Tzevi 1626–76
Turkish Jewish mystic

Born in Smyrna, he declared himself the Messiah in 1648, and gained a large following, with which he travelled in the Middle East. He was arrested in Constantinople (Istanbul) in 1666, and promptly embraced Islam to save his life.

Sabin, Albert Bruce 1906–93
US microbiologist

Born in Bialystok, Russia (now in Poland), he was educated at New York University, and in 1946 was appointed Research Professor of Pediatrics at the University of Cincinnati. After working on developing vaccines against dengue fever and Japanese B encephalitis, he became interested in the polio vaccine and attempted to develop a live attenuated vaccine (as opposed to **Jonas Salk**'s killed vaccine). In 1959, as the result of 4.5 million vaccinations, his vaccine was found to be completely safe; it presented a number of advantages over that of Salk, especially in affording a stronger and longer-lasting immunity and in being capable of oral administration.

Sabin, Florence Rena 1871–1953
US medical researcher

Born in Central City, Colorado, she studied science at Smith College and medicine at Johns Hopkins, where in 1902 she became the first woman member of staff, and in 1917 the first woman professor. She was also the first woman elected to the National Academy of Sciences (1925), and the first woman president of the American Anatomical Society. At the Rockefeller Institute for Medical Research in New York she began studying the aetiology of tuberculosis. Following her retirement in 1938 she became involved in public health legislation in Colorado.

Sabine, Sir Edward 1788–1883
Irish soldier, physicist, astronomer and explorer

Born in Dublin and educated at Marlow and the Royal Military Academy at Woolwich, he was commissioned in the Artillery and served in Gibraltar and Canada. He accompanied his lifelong friend Sir **James Clark Ross** as astronomer on **John Ross**'s expedition to find the North-West Passage in 1818 and on **William Parry**'s Arctic expedition of 1819–20. He conducted important pendulum experiments at Spitzbergen and in tropical Africa to determine the shape of the Earth (1821–23), and devoted the rest of his life to work on terrestrial magnetism. He made the important discovery that there is a correlation between variations in the Earth's magnetism and solar activity, which followed a 10–11 year cycle. He retired from the army in 1877 as a major-general. Sabine's gull is named after him. He was elected FRS (1818) and served for many years as the Royal Society's president (1861–71). He was knighted in 1869. An adroit politician, he was involved in the reforms of the Royal Society in the 1840s and was a leading figure in the British Association for the Advancement of Science. His brother Joseph Sabine (1770–1837), Inspector-General of Taxes, was a noted botanist.

Sabine, Wallace Clement Ware 1868–1919
US physicist

He was born in Richwood, Ohio. After graduating from Ohio State University in 1886, he entered Harvard, where he remained throughout his life, apart from service during World War I; from 1908 he was Dean of the Graduate School of Applied Science which he had initiated. When in 1895 Harvard opened its Fogg Art Museum, the auditorium was found to have extremely poor acoustics. Sabine analysed the problem and made the theatre functional. By 1898 he had devised the Sabine formula (linking reverberation time, total absorptivity and room volume), which he used as a consultant for the new Boston Symphony Hall (1898–1900). The unit of sound absorbing power (the sabin) was named after him.

Sacagawea, *also* Sacajawea c.1786–c.1812
Native American interpreter and guide

Born in western Montana or eastern Idaho, a member of the Snake tribe of the Shoshone, she, known as 'Bird Woman', was captured by the Hidatsas and sold to a Canadian trapper, Toussaint Charbonneau, whom she married (1804). Joining the **Lewis** and Clark Expedition as interpreters and guides, they travelled with the explorers from the Missouri River and guided them over the mountains to the Pacific Ocean. They obtained horses for the explorers from the Shoshone and left the expedition in about 1806, choosing to remain with the Wind River Shoshone tribe in Wyoming.

Sacchi, Andrea c.1599–1661
Italian painter

Born in Netturo near Rome, he became a pupil of **Francesco Albani** and master of **Carlo Maratti** and upheld the classical tradition in Roman painting. An admirer of **Raphael**, his style focuses on spiritual unity and individual emotion, and is represented by the *Vision of St Romuald* and the *Miracle of Saint Gregory*, painted for Pope **Urban VIII**, and by religious works in many Roman churches.

Sacco, Nicola 1891–1927
US anarchist

He was born in Italy, and he and Bartolomeo Vanzetti (1888–1927) emigrated to the USA and settled in Massachusetts, where Sacco worked in a shoe factory and Vanzetti peddled fish, and they became interested in socialism and radical political activities. Arrested and brought to trial for robbing and killing a shoe-factory paymaster (1920), they were found guilty, although the evidence was conflicting and circumstantial. Worldwide protests and appeals for clemency, on the grounds that Sacco and Vanzetti were believed to be victims of prejudice, led to an investigation, which upheld the verdict of the trial. The men were executed in the electric chair (1927). The case remained controversial for many years.

Sacher, Paul 1906–
Swiss conductor

He studied at Basle University and founded the Basle Chamber Orchestra in 1926. He also conducted at Glyndebourne, England (1954–63), and at the Metropolitan Opera in New York. He commissioned many works that are now in the standard repertory, including **Bartók**'s *Divertimento for Strings* (1939) and works by **Berio**, **Henze**, **Hindemith**, **Honegger**, **Strauss**, **Stravinsky** and **Tippett**.

Sacher-Masoch, Leopold von 1836–95
Austrian lawyer and writer

He was born in Lemberg, and wrote many short stories and novels, including *Der Don Juan von Kolomea* (1866), depicting the life of small-town Polish Jews. Sexual pleasure derived from receiving pain, which was a feature of his later works, was termed *masochism* after him.

Sacheverell, Henry c.1674–1724
English political preacher

Born in Marlborough, he went in 1689 to Magdalen College, Oxford, where he shared rooms with **Joseph Addison**, who dedicated to his 'dearest Henry' *An Account of the Greatest English Poets* (1694). He was granted the Staffordshire vicarage of Cannock, and in 1709 delivered two sermons, one at Derby assizes, the other at St Paul's, attacking the Whig government with such rancour that he was impeached (1710) before the House of Lords. He was found guilty and suspended from preaching for three years. The **Godolphin** ministry fell that same summer, and in 1713 Sacheverell was selected by the House of Commons to preach the Restoration sermon. He was presented to the rich rectory of St Andrew's Holborn, where he squabbled with his parishioners, and was suspected of complicity in a Jacobite plot.

Sacheverell, William, *sometimes called* the First Whig 1638–91
English politician

Born in Marlborough, he entered the House of Commons as member for Derbyshire in 1670 and rapidly became one of the leaders of the anti-Court party, which was instrumental in framing the Test Act which overthrew **Charles II**'s 'Cabal' ministry. He was prominent among those later demanding the resignation of **Thomas Leeds**, Lord Danby, and was a keen supporter of the Exclusion Bill. Fined by Judge **George Jeffreys** in 1682 for opposing the King's remodelled charter for Nottingham, and defeated in the 1685 election, he sat in the Convention parliament of 1689 which offered the throne to **William III**. Throughout his career in opposition he was distinguished for his powers of parliamentary oratory.

Sachs, Hans 1494–1576
German poet and dramatist

Born in Nuremberg, he became a shoemaker and from 1511 travelled through Germany, practising his craft and frequenting the schools of the *Meistersinger* ('master singers'), returning to Nuremberg in 1516. His literary career produced more than 6,300 works. He celebrated the Reformation and sang **Martin Luther**'s praises in an allegorical tale called *Die Wittenbergisch Nachtigall* (1523, 'The Nightingale of Wittenberg'), and his 200 poetical leaflets furthered the Protestant cause. His later poetry deals rather with ordinary life and manners. His best works are *Schwänke* ('Merry Tales'), serious tales, allegorical and spiritual songs, and Lenten dramas. He was the basis for the character of the same name in **Richard Wagner**'s opera *Die Meistersinger von Nürnberg* (1886, 'The Master Singers of Nuremberg'). 📖 H von Wendler, *Hans Sachs* (1933)

Sachs, Julius von 1832–97
German botanist

Born in Breslau (Wrocław, Poland), he studied at the University of Prague, became lecturer in botany at an agricultural college near Bonn, and from 1868 held the post of Professor of Botany at Würzburg University. There he carried out important experiments on the influence of light and heat upon plants, and the organic activities of vegetable growth. He established the mineral requirements of plants, observed the conversion of sugar into starch in chloroplasts, and suggested that enzymes are involved in the conversion of oil into starch, starch into sugar, and proteins into soluble nitrogen compounds. His *Lehrbuch der Botanik* (1868) and its English translation *Textbook of Botany* (1875) exerted widespread influence. He is regarded as the founder of modern plant physiology.

Sachs, Nelly Leonie 1891–1970
Swedish poet and playwright and Nobel Prize winner

Born in Berlin of Jewish descent, she first published a book of stories, *Tales and Legends* (1921), and several volumes of lyrical poetry. With the rise of Nazi power she studied Jewish religious and mystical literature, and in 1940 escaped to Sweden through the intercession of the Swedish royal family and **Selma Lagerlöf**. After World War II she wrote plays and poetry on the theme of the anguish of the Jewish people. She was awarded the 1966 Nobel Prize for literature, jointly with the Israeli novelist **Shmuel Yosef Agnon**. 📖 W A Berendon, *Nelly Sachs zu Ehren* (1966)

Sacks, Jonathan 1948–
English rabbi

Born in London and educated at Cambridge, he is a respected Jewish scholar and teacher and was Principal of Jews College, London, before succeeding **Immanuel Jakobovits** as chief rabbi of Great Britain in 1991. His concern for the future of the Jewish faith and tradition in contemporary society is reflected in his published works, which include *Tradition in an Untraditional Age* (1990), *Orthodoxy confronts Modernity* (1991), *Will we have Jewish Grandchildren?* (1994) and *Faith in the Future* (1995).

Sacks, Oliver Wolf 1933–
English neurologist and writer

Born in London, the son of physicians, he graduated from Oxford and studied for his medical degree at Middlesex Hospital. In 1960 he emigrated to the USA, and after further studies at the University of California at Los Angeles, he became, in 1965, Professor of Clinical Neurology at Albert Einstein College of Medicine in New York City, where he also practises neurology. He has written extensively on his experiences with patients, chronicling neurological conditions such as autism, Tourette's syndrome, Amnesia and colour-blindness. His best-known works, *Awakenings* (1973) and *The Man Who Mistook his Wife for a Hat* (1985), are studies of neurological disorders couched in the form of narrative 'clinical tales'. *Awakenings* was adapted as a film with the same title, and by **Harold Pinter** as a play, *A Kind of Alaska* (1982). In 1976 Sacks suffered a serious injury to his leg while mountaineering in Norway, and he wrote an account of the treatment, this time from the patient's point of view, in *A Leg to Stand On* (1984). *Seeing Voices* (1989) is a study of children deprived through deafness of the knowledge of language. Later works include *An Anthropologist on Mars* (1995).

Sackville, Charles, 6th Earl of Dorset
1638–1706
English courtier and poet

He succeeded to the earldom in 1677, having two years before been made Earl of Middlesex. He was returned by East Grinstead to the first parliament of **Charles II**, and became a favourite of the King, notorious for his boisterous and dissipated lifestyle. He served under the Duke of York (later **James VII and II**) at sea, but could not endure his tyranny as king and supported the cause of **William III**. In his later years he was the generous patron of **Matthew Prior**, **William Wycherley** and **John Dryden**. He wrote lyrics (including 'To all you Ladies now at Land') and satirical pieces. 📖 B Harris, *Charles Sackville* (1940)

Sackville, Thomas, 1st Earl of Dorset
1536–1608
English poet and statesman

Born in Buckhurst in Sussex, he studied law at Hart Hall, Oxford, and St John's College, Cambridge, and became a barrister. In 1558 he entered parliament. With **Thomas Norton** he produced the blank-verse tragedy of *Ferrex and Porrex* (later called *Gorboduc*), which was acted (1560–61) before Queen **Elizabeth I**, who was Sackville's second cousin. This work, written after the style of **Seneca**, is claimed to be the first play in blank verse. He also wrote the Induction and *The Complaint of Buckingham* for *A Mirror for Magistrates* (1563), in which the downfall of famous individuals is told in verse. His prodigality brought

Sādāt, (Muhammad) Anwar el- 1918–81
Egyptian soldier, politician and Nobel Prize winner

Anwar el-Sādāt was born into an Egyptian–Sudanese family in the Tala district of Egypt. He joined the army and was commissioned in 1938. Imprisoned in 1942 for contacts with the Germans in World War II, he continued to work for the overthrow of the British-dominated monarchy, and in 1952 was one of the group of officers who carried out the coup deposing King Farouk I. He held various posts under Gamal Abd al-Nasser, being one of the four vice-presidents from 1964 to 1967, and sole vice-president in 1969–70 when the office was revived.

An ardent Egyptian nationalist and Muslim, he was editor of *Al-Jumhuriya* and *Al-Tahrir* in 1955–56, and held strong anti-Communist views. He became President of the United Arab Republic in 1970 after the death of Nasser, at a time when Egypt's main preoccupation was the confrontation with Israel. In March 1973 he temporarily assumed the post of Prime Minister, and proclaimed himself military Governor-General in the Arab–Israeli war that broke out in November of that year.

In 1974 a referendum endorsed his social and economic plan for the future of Egypt. In September 1974 he relinquished the premiership to Dr Hagazy, and from then sought diplomatic settlement of the conflict, meeting the Prime Minister of Israel Menachem Begin in Jerusalem in December 1977 and at Camp David at President Carter's invitation in September 1978. In the same year he and Begin were jointly awarded the Nobel Peace Prize. He was the only Arab leader to sign a peace treaty with Israel, and was fiercely criticized by other Arab statesmen and hardline Muslims. He failed to match his international success with an improvement in Egypt's own struggling economy, and he was suspected of harsh treatment of his political opponents. In 1981 he was assassinated by Muslim extremists while reviewing troops.

⊞ Sādāt's autobiography, *In Search of Identity*, was published in 1978. See also R A Hinnebusch, *Egyptian Politics Under Sādāt* (1988); B K Narayan, *Anwar el-Sādāt: A Man with a Mission* (1977).

'Peace is much more precious than a piece of land.' From a speech, 8 March 1978.

Sackville into disgrace, but he was later restored to political favour. It was he who announced Queen Elizabeth's death sentence to Mary, Queen of Scots in 1586. In 1599 he was made Lord High Treasurer, and in 1604 Earl of Dorset. ⊞ P Bacquet, *Un contemporain de Elisabeth I* (1966)

Sackville-West, V (ictoria Mary), *also called* Vita 1892–1962
English poet and novelist

Born in Knole, Kent, she was educated privately, and started writing novels and plays as a child. In 1913 she married the diplomat Harold Nicolson, and their marriage survived despite Nicolson's homosexuality and her own lesbian affair. Her first published works were a collection of poems, *Poems of West and East* (1917), and a novel, *Heritage* (1919). In her *Orchard and Vineyard* (1921) and her long poem *The Land*, which won the 1927 Hawthornden Prize, she expresses her closeness to the countryside where she lived. Her prose works include the novels *The Edwardians* (1930), *All Passion Spent* (1931) and *No Signposts in the Sea* (1961), an account of her family in *Knole and the Sackvilles* (1947), and studies of Andrew Marvell and Joan of Arc. *Passenger to Teheran* (1926) records her years in Persia with her husband, and she was the model for Virginia Woolf's *Orlando* (1928). She was a passionate gardener at her home at Sissinghurst in Kent (now owned by the National Trust), and wrote a weekly gardening column for the *Observer* for many years. ⊞ M Steven, *Vita Sackville-West: a critical biography* (1973)

Sacrobosco, Johannes de, *English* John of Holywood *or* Halifax fl.mid-13th century
English mathematician

Born probably in Halifax, he is said to have studied at Oxford and taught mathematics at Paris, where he died in 1244 or 1256. He was one of the first to use the astronomical writings of the Arabians, but his elementary knowledge of the Ptolemaic system is demonstrated by the fact that he reproduced mistakes made previously by Alfargani and Albattani. His treatise, *De Sphaera Mundi*, based on Ptolemy's *Almagest* and Arab writings, became the basic text on astronomy of the Middle Ages, and more than 60 editions were printed between 1472 and 1547.

Sādāt, (Muhammad) Anwar el- See panel above

Sade, Donatien Alphonse François, Comte de, *known as* Marquis de Sade 1740–1814
French writer

He was born in Paris, and entered the army as an army officer in the Seven Years War (1756–63). In 1772 he was condemned to death at Aix for his cruelty and for sexual perversion. He made his escape, but was afterwards imprisoned at Vincennes and in the Bastille, Paris, where he wrote works of sexual fantasy and perversion, including *Les 120 Journées de Sodome* (1784, Eng trans *The 120 Days of Sodom*, 1954), *La Philosophie dans le boudoir* (1793, Eng trans *The Bedroom Philosophers*, 1965) and *Les Crimes de l'amour* (1800, Eng trans, in part, as *Quartet*, 1963). He died in a mental asylum at Charenton. 'Sadism', the inflicting of pain for sexual pleasure, is named after him. ⊞ J Lély, *La vie de Sade* (1952–57)

Sādi *or* Saadi *or* Sa'adi, *assumed name of* Sheikh Muslih Addin c.1184–?1292
Persian poet

A descendant of Alī, Muhammad's son-in-law, he studied at Baghdad and travelled widely. Near Jerusalem he was taken prisoner by the Crusaders, but was ransomed by a merchant of Aleppo, who gave him his daughter in marriage. His works comprise 22 different kinds of writings in prose and verse, in Arabic and Persian, of which odes and dirges form the predominant part. The most celebrated writing is the *Gulistan* ('Rose Garden'), a kind of moral work in prose and verse, intermixed with stories, maxims, philosophical sentences, puns, etc. He also wrote the *Bostan* ('Orchard Garden'), written in verse, and the *Pend-Nameh* ('Book of Instructions'). ⊞ H Massé, *Essai sur le poète Sādi* (1919)

Sadler, Flora Munro, *née* McBain 1912–
Scottish astronomer

Born in Aberdeen, she was educated at Aberdeen University. She was a member of the British Expedition which successfully observed the total eclipse of the Sun in Omsk in Siberia (1936). The following year she was appointed to the scientific staff of the Royal Observatory, Greenwich, the first woman scientist to be employed there. Her work in the Observatory's Nautical Almanac Office, where she was Principal Scientific Officer until 1973, involved the production of astronomical and navigational tables and almanacs for the use of astronomers. She represented Great Britain on the International Astronomical Union's Commissions on the Moon and

Astronomical Ephemerides (1948–70), and played an active part in the affairs of the Royal Astronomical Society, becoming its first woman secretary from 1949 to 1954.

Sadler, Sir Michael Ernest 1861–1943
English educational pioneer
He was born in Barnsley, Yorkshire, and educated at Rugby and Trinity College, Oxford. As secretary of the extension lectures sub-committee of the Oxford University examinations delegacy in 1885, he oversaw an enormous expansion in its work, but he realized that much of the value was lost because of the early age at which most students had left school. He was a member of the Bryce Commission on secondary education which reported in 1895, and became director of the office of special inquiries and reports in the Department of Education in the same year. He made his office an effective research bureau and in the process virtually founded the study of comparative education. Resigning in 1903, he became Professor of Education at Manchester University and advised extensively on the organization of secondary education. Vice-Chancellor of Leeds from 1911, he transformed the university from a little-known college to a major institution. As president of a commission on Calcutta University (1917), he produced a notable report which had widespread and long-lasting effects. He was Master of University College, Oxford (1923–34).

Sadoleto, Jacopo 1477–1547
Italian prelate
Born in Modena, he went to Rome in 1502, and took holy orders. Leo X made him Apostolical Secretary, an appointment he retained under Clement VII and Paul III. In 1517 he was made Bishop of Carpentras by Leo, and a cardinal by Paul in 1536. In 1544 he was a legate to Francis I. Sadoleto ranks as one of the great churchmen of his age. He corresponded with many Protestant leaders, and sought to find a basis for reunion.

Saenredam, Pieter Jansz 1597–1665
Dutch painter
Born in Assendelft, he studied painting in Haarlem. He was acquainted with the architect Jacob van Campen and may have been inspired by his architectural drawings to specialize in paintings of church interiors, a subject of which he is an acknowledged master. His paintings convey, in a distinctive high tonality, the subtle effects of light and atmosphere, and, unlike previous architectural paintings, are precisely drawn images of known and identifiable churches.

Safdie, Moshe 1938–
Israeli–Canadian architect
Born in Haifa, Israel, he emigrated to Canada with his family in 1954 and received a degree in architecture from McGill University, later studying with US architect Louis I Kahn. He designed the plan for the international fair Expo '67 (Montreal), which included his famous Habitat, a prefabricated concrete housing project with individual apartment units composed of irregularly stacked and interlocking cubes. He designed similar buildings in Puerto Rico, Israel, and the USA, as well as the National Gallery of Canada (1988, Ottawa) and Quebec City's Musée de la Civilisation (1988). He was director of the urban design programme at Harvard (1978–84), and his works include *Form and Purpose: Is the Emperor Naked?* (1982) and *Beyond Habitat by Twenty Years* (1987).

Sagan, Carl Edward 1934–96
US astronomer
Born in New York City, he studied at Chicago and Berkeley, worked at Harvard then moved to Cornell, becoming Professor of Astronomy and Space Science in 1970. Interested in most aspects of the solar system, he did work on the physics and chemistry of planetary atmospheres and surfaces. He also investigated the origin of life on Earth and the possibility of extraterrestrial life. He was an active member of the imaging team associated with the Voyager mission to the outer planets, and after 1983 gave considerable thought to the concept of the nuclear winter. In the 1960s he worked on the theoretical calculation of the Venus greenhouse effect. Sagan and James Pollack were the first to advocate that temporal changes on Mars were non-biological and were in fact due to wind-blown dust distributed by seasonally changing circulation patterns. Through books and a television programme, *Cosmos*, Sagan did much to interest the general public in this aspect of science. His *Cosmic Connection* (1973) dealt with advances in planetary science; *The Dragons of Eden* (1977, Pulitzer Prize) and *Broca's Brain* (1979) helped to popularize recent advances in evolutionary theory and neurophysiology. He was president of the Planetary Society (1979–96) and was a strong proponent of SETI, the search for extraterrestrial intelligence.

Sagan, Françoise, *pseudonym of* Françoise Quoirez 1935–
French novelist
Born in Cajarc, Lot, she was educated at a convent in Paris and in private schools. At the age of 18 she wrote, in only four weeks, the bestselling *Bonjour tristesse* (1954, Eng trans 1955; filmed 1958), followed by *Un Certain Sourire* (1956, Eng trans *A Certain Smile*, 1956; filmed 1958), both strikingly direct testaments of affluent adolescence, written with the economy of a remarkable literary style. Irony creeps into her third, *Dans un mois, dans un an* (1957, Eng trans *Those Without Shadows*, 1957), and moral consciousness takes over in her later novels, such as *Aimez-vous Brahms...* (1959, Eng trans 1960; filmed 1961 as *Goodbye Again*) and *La Chamade* (1966, Eng trans 1966). A ballet to which she gave the central idea, *Le Rendez-vous manqué* ('The Missed Rendezvous'), enjoyed a temporary succès de scandale in Paris and London in 1958. Her later works have had a mixed critical reception; these include the plays *Château en Suède* (1960, 'Castle in Sweden') and *Un Piano dans l'herbe* (1970, 'A Piano on the Grass'), and the novels *La Femme fardée* (1981, Eng trans *The Painted Lady*, 1983) and *Un Orage immobile* (1983, Eng trans *The Still Storm*, 1984). Her collected works were published in 1993.
📖 G Hourdin, *Le cas de Françoise Sagan* (1958)

Sager, Ruth 1918–
US geneticist
She gained a PhD in genetics from Columbia University in 1948 and worked as a research fellow in several institutions before becoming Professor of Biology at Hunter College (1966–75), then Professor of Cellular Genetics at Harvard (1975–88, Emeritus Professor 1988–). Most of her experimental work used the single-celled algae *Chlamydomonas* which she observed through numerous mutations, and in 1963 provided the clinching evidence that DNA existed in the cytoplasm. She postulated cytoplasmic inheritance (the inheritance of genes contained in the cell body or cytoplasm) in addition to the well-established inheritance of genes in the cell nucleus. She was elected to the National Academy of Sciences in 1977.

Saha, Meghnad 1894–1956
Indian astrophysicist
Born in Dacca (now in Bangladesh), he was educated at Presidency College, Calcutta, and subsequently visited Europe on a travelling scholarship. He taught at Allahabad University and in 1938 was appointed Professor of Physics at Calcutta. He worked on the thermal ionization that occurs in the extremely hot atmospheres of stars and in 1920 demonstrated that elements in stars are ionized in proportion to their temperature, a

result known as 'Saha's equation'. He later turned to nuclear physics and helped in the creation in India of the Saha Institute for its study. ☐ S N Sen (ed), *Professor Meghnad Saha: His Life Work and Philosophy* (1954)

Sahib, Tippoo See Tippoo Sahib

Sahlins, Marshall David 1930–
US cultural anthropologist

Born in Chicago, he was educated at Michigan and Columbia. He became Professor of Anthropology at Michigan in 1964, and has been professor at Chicago University since 1974. He has made major contributions in the field of Oceanic ethnography, cultural evolution, economic anthropology and the analysis of symbolism. In his early work, as in *Evolution and Culture* (1960), he presented a materialist and progressivist view of cultural evolution heavily influenced by the theory of **Leslie White**. In *Culture and Practical Reason* (1976), however, he inverts this perspective, insisting on the autonomy of cultural systems. In economic anthropology, he has been a strong advocate of the substantivist view of **Karl Polanyi**, as in *Stone Age Economics* (1972). His other publications include *The Use and Abuse of Biology* (1977), *Historical Metaphors and Mythical Realities* (1981), on the early history of the Sandwich Islands, *Islands of History* (1985), on the relationship between history and structure in the context of Polynesian ethnography, and *How 'Natives' Think* (1995).

Said Faik 1906–54
Turkish story writer and poet

He was born in the Anatolian town of Adapazari. He wrote in colloquial Turkish of the common people of Istanbul, especially those who lived on the periphery of society. They include, in particular, fishermen, vagabonds and tramps. *A Dot on the Man* (1979) is a selection from his tales. The family house he lived in became a museum after his death.

Sailer, Toni (Anton) 1935–
Austrian alpine skier

Born in Kitzbühel, he became the first man to win all three Olympic skiing titles (downhill, slalom and giant slalom) in 1956. He was the world combined champion in 1956 and 1958, and the world downhill and giant slalom champion in 1958.

Sainsbury (of Drury Lane), Alan John Sainsbury, Baron 1902–98
English retailer

Born in Hornsey, Middlesex, and educated at Haileybury, he joined (1921) the family grocery business founded by his grandparents in 1869. He became chairman (1956–1967), and from 1967 was joint president of J Sainsbury plc with his younger brother, Sir Robert (1906–). His elder son, Baron John Davan Sainsbury of Preston Candover (1927–), has been president of the company since 1992 (chairman 1969–92). Sir Robert's son, Baron David John Sainsbury of Turville (1940–) was deputy chairman in 1992–98.

Saint Amant, Antoine Girard de 1594–1661
French poet

Born in Rouen, he was an early exponent of French burlesque poetry, as in *Rome ridicule* (1649). He also wrote the mock heroic *Albion* (1643), the biblical epic, *Moyse sauvé* (1653, 'Moses Saved'), and an ode, *A la solitude* ('To Solitude'). ☐ J Legmy, *Le poète Saint Amant* (1965)

Saint Denis, Ruth, *originally* Ruth Dennis 1879–1968
US dancer, director, choreographer and teacher

Born in Somerville, New Jersey, she began performing in vaudeville at an early age and became known, first in Europe, for the exotic and colourful eastern dances which

were to characterize her work (*Cobras*, *The Incense* and *Radha* were all made in 1906). She married **Ted Shawn** in 1914 on her return to the USA, and founded the Denishawn school and company with him in Los Angeles in 1915 (later in New York), which was frequented by many Hollywood stars. In 1916 she choreographed the Babylonian dances for **D W Griffith**'s film *Intolerance*. Presenting a fusion of many dance forms, the company toured the USA until 1931, when the couple separated and the company was closed. She danced into her eighties, and published an autobiography, *An Unfinished Life*, in 1939.

Saint-Denys Garneau, Hector de 1912–43
French–Canadian poet and painter

Born in Montreal, he suffered from a heart ailment, and wrote virtually all his poetry between 1935 and 1938. He initiated the modern movement in French–Canadian poetry with his collection *Regards et jeux dans l'espace* (1937, 'Gazes and Games in Space'), in which he made the 'first free and unashamed use of free verse rhythms and techniques'. His *Poésies complètes* appeared in 1949. His cousin was the equally gifted Anne Hébert (1916–), who was also (as a child) an invalid. His *Journal* (1954, Eng trans 1962) is valued highly for its awareness of Canadian problems and for its lucid expression of its author's anguish. ☐ J Glassco (trans), *Complete Poems* (1985); E Kushner, *Saint-Denys-Garneau* (1967)

Sainte-Beuve, Charles Augustin 1804–69
French writer and critic

Born in Boulogne-sur-Mer, he was educated at the Collège Charlemagne in Paris, and then studied medicine (1824–27). Together with the philosopher Théodore Jouffroy (1796–1842), Charles Rémusat, Jean-Jacques Ampère (1800–64) and **Prosper Mérimée**, he was a contributor to the literary and political paper the *Globe*. In 1827 he published a review praising the *Odes et Ballades* of Victor Hugo, and the subsequent friendship with Hugo lasted until Sainte-Beuve's affair with Madame Hugo in 1834. In 1828 he published *Tableau de la poésie française au seizième siècle* ('Survey of 16th Century French Poetry'). After the Revolution of July 1830 he joined the staff of the *National*, the organ of extreme republicanism, and in 1835 he published his only novel, *Volupté* ('Voluptuousness'). He then lectured on the history of Port Royal at Lausanne (1837), and in book form these lectures contain some of his finest work. In 1840 he was appointed keeper of the Mazarin Library, and for the next eight years he wrote mainly for the *Revue des deux mondes*. In 1848 he became Professor of French Literature at Liège, where he gave lectures on *Chateaubriand et son groupe littéraire* (1851, 'Chateaubriand and his Literary Set'). The following year he returned to Paris, where he wrote numerous articles for the *Constitutionnel*, and from 1869 for the *Temps*. In 1854, on his appointment by the emperor as Professor of Latin poetry at the Collège de France, the students refused to listen to his lectures, and he was forced to resign the post. However, he was nominated a senator in 1865, and regained popularity by his spirited speeches in favour of liberty of thought. His many other literary works include *Critiques et portraits littéraires* (1836–39, 'Literary Portraits and Critical Essays'), *Portraits de femmes* (1844, 'Portraits of Women'), and, published posthumously, *M. de Talleyrand* (1870) and *Souvenirs et indiscrétions* (1872, 'Recollections and Indiscretions'). ☐ A Billy, *Sainte-Beuve et son temps* (1952)

Sainte-Claire Deville, Henri Étienne 1818–81
French chemist

Born on St Thomas, West Indies (now part of the Virgin Islands), he studied medicine in Paris and developed an interest in chemistry. From 1845 to 1851 he was Professor of Chemistry at the University of Besançon. In 1851 he returned to Paris as successor to **Antoine Jérôme Balard** at the École Normale Supérieure, and from 1853 he also gave lectures in chemistry at the Sorbonne. He was made an Honorary Fellow of the Chemical Society in 1860. His early work was on turpentine and other natural products, and later he extended his interests to inorganic chemistry. In 1849 he isolated nitrogen pentoxide. He devised a process for the large-scale production of aluminium and developed related processes for the large-scale production of boron, silicon and titanium. He is also remembered for his extensive measurements of the vapour densities of substances at high temperatures, which led to the recognition of reversible thermal dissociation, of great significance for the theory of chemical equilibrium.

Sainte-Marie, Buffy (Beverly) 1941/42–
Native American singer and songwriter

Born of Cree descent in Saskatchewan, Canada, she was raised in Massachusetts by adoptive parents, and after studying music at the University of Massachusetts went to New York City to sing folk music. She had a hit with her antiwar protest song 'Universal Soldier', which was included in her first album *It's My Way* (1964). She vocalized her support of the Native American rights movement with songs such as 'Now That The Buffalo's Gone'; and her song 'Up Where We Belong', the theme tune for the film *An Officer and a Gentleman* (1982), won an Academy Award in 1983. She founded Native Creative to help increase cultural awareness in American children, and writes on North American Indian life for periodicals such as *Thunderbird* and *American Indian Horizons*.

Saint-Évremond, Charles Marguetel de Saint Denis, Seigneur de 1610–1703
French writer and wit

Born in St Denis le Gast, near Coutances, he fought at Rocroi, Freiburg and Nördlingen and was steadily loyal throughout the Fronde, but in 1661 he fled by way of the Netherlands to England on the discovery of his witty and sarcastic letter to Créqui on the Peace of the Pyrenees. He was warmly received by Charles II, and spent much of the rest of his life in London, delighting the world with his wit. His satire, *La Comédie des académistes* (1644, 'The Comedy of the Academy'), is masterly, and his correspondence with Anne Lenclos has great charm.
📖 M Willmotte, *Saint-Évremond, critique littéraire* (1921)

Saint-Exupéry, Antoine de 1900–44
French novelist and airman

Born in Lyons, he became a commercial airline pilot and wartime reconnaissance pilot. His philosophy of 'heroic action' based on the framework of his experiences as a pilot is expressed in his sensitive and imaginative *Courrier sud* (1929, 'Southbound Mail'), *Vol de nuit* (1931, Eng trans *Night Flight*, 1932), *Terre des Hommes* (1939, Eng trans *Wind, Sand and Stars*, 1939) and *Pilote de guerre* (1942, Eng trans *Flight to Arras*, 1942). His most popular work is *Le Petit prince* (1943, Eng trans *The Little Prince*, 1944), a touching allegory about a boy from another planet who befriends a pilot stranded in the desert. Saint-Exupéry was declared missing after a flight in World War II. 📖 C Cate, *Saint-Exupéry, his life and times* (1971)

Saint-Gaudens, Augustus 1848–1907
US sculptor

He was born in Dublin, the son of a French shoemaker, and taken to the USA as a baby. After training as a cameocutter, he studied sculpture in Paris, and later in Rome, where he was influenced by the work of the Italian Renaissance. He returned to the USA in 1873, and became the foremost sculptor of his time. His major works include *Lincoln* (1887) in Lincoln Park, Chicago (replica in Parliament Square, London), *The Puritan* (1887, Deacon

Chapin, in Springfield, Massachusetts), and the **Henry Adams** Memorial in Rock Creek Cemetery, Washington DC.

Saint Germain, Christopher c.1460–1540
English legal writer

He was born in Shilton, Warwickshire and educated at Oxford. He is remembered for the treatise known as *Doctor and Student* (1523), a dialogue between a doctor of divinity and a student of the common law of England, urging that principles of law must sometimes be applied with discretion and reason to temper the otherwise excessive rigidity of the common law. The first significant critical discussion of the common law to be published, it provoked a *Replication of a Serjeant at the Laws of England*, to which he answered with *A Little Treatise Concerning Writs of Subpoena*. He also wrote a *Treatise concerning the Division between the Spirituality and the Temporality* (1532) which argued for the power of parliament to reform the Church.

Saint-Hilaire, Étienne Geoffrey See Geoffrey Saint-Hilaire, Étienne

Saint-Hilaire, Isidore Geoffrey See Geoffrey Saint-Hilaire, Isidore

Saint-Hilaire, Jules Barthélemy See Barthélemy Saint-Hilaire, Jules

Saint John, Henry See Bolingbroke, 1st Viscount

Saint-John Perse, *pseudonym of* Marie René Auguste Alexis Saint-Léger Léger 1887–1975
French poet and diplomat and Nobel Prize winner

Born in St Léger des Feuilles, an island near Guadeloupe, he studied at Bordeaux, and after many adventures in New Guinea and a voyage in a skiff along the China coast, he entered the French foreign ministry in 1904. He became Secretary-General in 1933, was dismissed in 1940 and fled to the USA, where he became an adviser on French affairs to Franklin D Roosevelt. The Vichy government burnt his writings and deprived him of French citizenship, but it was restored in 1945. Symbolism was an influence on his earliest verse, and his blank verse utilizes a vocabulary of rare words. His best known works include the long poem *Anabase* (1924; Eng trans *Anabasis* by T S Eliot, 1930), *Exil* (1942, 'Exile'), *Pluies* (1944, 'Rain'), *Amers* (1957, Eng trans *Seamarks*, 1958) and *Chroniques* (1960, Eng trans 1961). He was awarded the Nobel Prize for literature in 1960. 📖 J Champier, *Saint-John Perse* (1962)

Saint Joseph, John Kenneth Sinclair 1912–94
English aerial photographer and archaeologist

Born in Worcestershire and educated at Selwyn College, Cambridge, he was successively curator, director, and Professor of Aerial Photographic Studies at Cambridge (1948–80). Trained as a geologist, he came to recognize the value of aerial survey in the 1930s through meeting and working with Osbert Crawford. After wartime service in Operational Research at RAF Bomber Command, he became involved in 1948 in developing a unique university department with its own aircraft, pilot, and servicing facilities, establishing a valuable photographic archive. The emphasis was on systematic reconnaissance designed to reveal new sites, and on low level oblique photography of natural landscapes and of archaeological monuments in their landscape setting. The results were published in *The Journal of Roman Studies* (1951–77), the journal *Antiquity* (1964–80), and in a series of books, including *Monastic Sites from the Air* (with David Knowles, 1952), *Medieval England: An Aerial Survey* (with Maurice Beresford, 1958, 1979) and *Roman Britain from the Air* (with Sheppard Frere, 1983).

Saint-Just, Louis Antoine Léon Florelle de
1767–94
French revolutionary

He was born in Decize, studied law, and while in Paris began to write, producing in 1791 a revolutionary essay, *L'Esprit de la Révolution et de la constitution de France*. He was elected to the Convention (1792), where he attracted notice by his fierce tirades against the King, and as a devoted follower of **Robespierre** was sent on missions to the armies of the Rhine and the Moselle. He joined the Committee of Public Safety and began the attacks on **Jacques Hébert** which were to send him to the guillotine with **Georges Danton**. In 1794 he led the attack on the Austrians at Fleurus. In the same year he laid before the Convention a comprehensive report on the police, sponsored the radical Ventôse Laws for redistributing property to the poor, and proposed Robespierre's scheme for institutions in which boys would be brought up by the state from the age of seven. He was guillotined during the Thermidorian Reaction.

Saint Laurent, Louis Stephen 1882–1973
Canadian politician

Born in Compton, Quebec, he became a lawyer and professor of law at Laval University, and in 1941 he entered the Dominion parliament as a Liberal. **Mackenzie King** appointed him Minister of Justice and, unlike other Quebec Liberals, he supported King on conscription in 1944 and was made Secretary of State for External Affairs in 1946. King's own choice as his successor, Saint Laurent became Prime Minister in 1948; he launched a social programme that included the extension of the old-age pension scheme and hospital insurance. He also helped to found the North Atlantic Treaty Organization (NATO). Under his leadership, the Liberals were re-elected in 1949 and 1953, but he was defeated by the Conservatives under **John G Diefenbaker** in 1957.

Saint Laurent, Yves (Henri Donat Mathieu)
1936–
French designer

He was born in Oran, Algeria, and studied in Paris, graduating in modern languages. In 1955, after winning an international design competition, he was employed by **Christian Dior**, whom he succeeded in 1957. In 1962 he opened his own house, and launched the first of his 160 Rive Gauche boutiques in 1966; by selling ready-to-wear clothes, he set a trend which many other designers were to follow. His honours include receiving a Best Fashion Designer Academy Award and being made Chevalier of the French Legion of Honour, both in 1985.

Saint Leger, Anthony 1731/32–89
English soldier and racing enthusiast

He was born in Grangemellan, Ireland, and educated at Eton and Cambridge. As a lieutenant-colonel during the American Revolution, he was with General **James Wolfe** at Quebec. In 1776 he founded the classic St Leger Stakes at Doncaster, British racing's oldest classic.

Saint-Léon, (Charles Victor) Arthur 1821–71
French dancer, choreographer and ballet master

Born in Paris, he studied with his father, a ballet master in Stuttgart, before making his teenage debut dancing and playing the violin in Munich. He later danced and staged ballets all over Europe (1845–51), often with and for his wife, the ballerina **Fanny Cerrito**; they created leading roles in **Jules Perrot**'s *Ondine* (1843) and *La Esmeralda* (1844). He was ballet master with the St Petersburg Imperial Theatre (1859–69) and Paris Opéra (1863–70). The classic *Coppelia*, his last and only surviving ballet, dates from 1870. In this and other works, he was one of the first choreographers to incorporate national and ethnic dances into classical ballet.

Saint Leonards (of Slaugham), Edward Burtenshaw Sugden, Lord 1781–1875
English legal writer and judge

He achieved professional fame with his *Practical Treatise of the Law of Vendors and Purchasers of Estates* (1805) and his *Practical Treatise on Powers* (1808). He became an MP in 1828 and Solicitor-General in 1829, then Lord Chancellor of Ireland (1834, 1841–46) and Lord Chancellor of Great Britain (1852). A learned and industrious judge, he is chiefly remembered for his legal texts which were standard works during most of the 19th century.

Saint-Phalle, Niki de, *real name* (Catherine) Marie-Agnès Fal de Saint-Phalle 1930–
French sculptor and children's writer

She was born in Neuilly-sur-Seine, Paris, in the year her father's banking interests collapsed in New York, and spent her early years with grandparents in the Nièvre. She was educated in the USA and used the name Niki from the age of seven. Considered disruptive and unteachable at school, she eloped at the age of 18 and in 1953 suffered a nervous breakdown, during which she took up painting as a therapy. In 1955 she discovered the work of **Antonio Gaudí** in Barcelona and met **Jean Tinguely** (whom she married in 1971). Her first 'shooting paintings'—assemblages spattered with paint—were produced in 1961, followed in 1963 by a series of figures chronicling the complex role of women in society. Two years later her first unashamedly erotic *Nanas* (French slang for *dames*) were exhibited in Paris and New York. Her well-known *Black Venus* (1967, Whitney Museum, New York) also belongs to this period. Her work is joyous, impudent, transcultural, and often architectural in scale. In 1966 thousands waited in Stockholm to pass between the gigantic polyester thighs of her sprawling earth mother *Hon*. Inside there was a bar, an art gallery and a cinema. Other outdoor commissions followed, in Jerusalem, Paris, New York, Tokyo, and the Nièvre. In 1987 she collaborated on Tinguely's *Cyclops Head*, now a national monument, in the Forest of Fontainebleau. Throughout the 1980s she worked in charge of a team on her glass and ceramic extravaganza in Tuscany, the *Tarot Garden*, while producing gallery pieces such as her transparent linear 'skinnies'. She also writes for children, and in 1986 published *AIDS: You Can't Catch It Holding Hands*, which was distributed free to all schoolchildren in France and was made into a cartoon film. In 1991, on the death of Tinguely, she produced her first kinetic sculpture, *Meta-Tinguely*.

Saint Pierre, Jacques Henri Bernardin de
1737–1814
French writer

He was born in Le Havre, and served for some time in the army engineers, but quarrelled with his superiors and was dismissed. He was greatly influenced by the writings of **Jean Jacques Rousseau**, and travelled to Russia with dreams of founding a utopian state on the shores of the Aral Sea, but returned in dejection to Warsaw. He then joined a government expedition to Madagascar, but abandoned it at the Île de France (Mauritius), where he spent almost three years, resulting in *Voyage à l'Île de France* (1778, 'Journey to the Isle of France'), which gave a distinctly new element to literature in its close portrayal of nature. His *Études de la nature* (3 vols, 1784, 'Studies of Nature') again reflected the influence of Rousseau. A fourth volume (1788) contained the popular *Paul et Virginie* (Eng trans *Paul and Mary*, 1789), a story of love untainted by 'civilization'. It was followed by *Vœux d'un solitaire* (1789, 'A Hermit's Vows'), the novel *La Chaumière indienne* (1791, 'The Indian Cottage'), and *Harmonies de la nature* (1796), a pale repetition of the *Études*. **Napoleon I** heaped favours upon him, and he lived comfortably for the rest of his days.

Saint-Saëns, (Charles) Camille 1835–1921
French composer and music critic

Born in Paris, he entered the Paris Conservatoire in 1848, and was a pupil of Benoist and **Fromental Elié Halévy**. He began his long and prolific career of composition with his prizewinning *Ode à Sainte Cécile* (1852, 'Ode to St Cecilia'), followed shortly afterwards by his 1st Symphony (1853). He was a distinguished pianist, and from 1858 to 1877 won considerable renown as organist of the Madeleine in Paris, also giving recitals in London, Russia and Austria. Although conservative as a composer, he was a founder in 1871 of the Société Nationale de Musique, which was influential in encouraging the performance of works by young contemporary French composers. He wrote four further symphonies, 13 operas, including his best-known, *Samson et Dalila* (1877), four symphonic poems, including *Danse macabre* (1874), five concertos for piano, three for violin and two for cello, *Carnaval des animaux* (1886, 'Carnival of the Animals') for two pianos and or-chestra, church music, including his *Messe solennelle* (1855, 'Solemn Mass'), and chamber music and songs. He was a sound music critic, although in later life he look askance at some of his younger contemporaries. His writings include *Harmonie et mélodie* (1885, 'Harmony and Melody'), *Portraits et souvenirs* (1899, 'Portraits and Souvenirs') and *Au courant de la vie* (1914 'During a Lifetime').

Saintsbury, George Edward Bateman
1845–1933
English literary critic and scholar

Born in Southampton, he was educated at King's College School, London, and Merton College, Oxford. From 1868 to 1876 he was a schoolmaster in Manchester, Guernsey and Elgin, but soon afterwards established himself as one of the most active critics of the day. From 1895 to 1915 he was Professor of English Literature at Edinburgh. He contributed to the major journals (he edited *Macmillan's*) and to encyclopedias. Among his books are histories of literature, both French and English; books on **John Dryden**, the Duke of **Marlborough**, Sir **Walter Scott**, **Matthew Arnold**, **William Thackeray**, the early Renaissance, and minor Caroline poets; histories of criticism (3 vols, 1900–04), English prosody (1906–10), and prose rhythm (1912); and a novel (1912). After his retirement came *The Peace of the Augustans* (1916), *A History of the French Novel* (1917–19), *Notes on a Cellar-book* (1920) and *Scrapbooks* (1922–24).

Saint-Simon, Claude Henri de Rouvroy, Comte de 1760–1825
French social reformer and founder of French socialism

Born in Paris, he served in the American Revolution (1776–83). During the French Revolution he was im-prisoned as an aristocrat, but made a small fortune by speculating in confiscated lands. Lavish expenditure re-duced him to utter poverty and he turned to writing. His first socialist ideas were expressed in *L'Industrie* (1817), followed by *L'Organisateur* (1819), *Du système industriel* (1821), *Catéchisme des industriels* (1823), and his last and most important work, *Nouveau christianisme* (1825). In opposi-tion to the destructive spirit of the Revolution, he sought a positive reorganization of society, with the feudal and military system being superseded by an industrial order and the spiritual direction of society passing from the Church to men of science. He remained poor and would have died of starvation but for the support of friends and family.

Saint Vincent, John Jervis, Earl of 1735–1823
English naval commander

Born in Stone, Staffordshire, he entered the navy in 1749 and distinguished himself in the Quebec expedition of 1759. In 1778 he fought in the action off Brest, and in 1782 captured the *Pégase*. He commanded a successful expedition against the French in the West Indies (1793), and as admiral commanded the Mediterranean fleet in 1795. In 1797 off Cape St Vincent, he defeated the French, Dutch and Spanish fleets who were preparing to invade England. His dispositions led to **Nelson**'s victory at the Battle of the Nile (1798). As commander of the Channel fleet he subdued the spirit of sedition, and was First Lord of the Admiralty (1801–04).

Sakharov, Andrei Dimitriyevich 1921–89
Soviet physicist, dissident and Nobel Prize winner

Born in Moscow, the son of a scientist, he graduated in physics from Moscow State University in 1942 and was awarded a doctorate for work on cosmic rays. He worked under **Igor Tamm** at the Lebdev Institute in Leningrad (now St Petersburg). He took a leading part in the devel-opment of the Soviet hydrogen bomb and in 1953 became the youngest-ever entrant to the Soviet Academy of Sciences. During the early 1960s he became increasingly estranged from the Soviet authorities when he cam-paigned for a nuclear test-ban treaty, peaceful interna-tional co-existence and improved civil rights within the USSR. In 1975 he was awarded the Nobel Peace Prize, and in 1980, during a period of Soviet oppression of dis-sidents, he was sent into internal exile in the 'closed city' of Gorky (now Nizhny Novgorod). Here he undertook a series of hunger strikes in an effort to secure permission for his wife, **Yelena Bonner**, to receive medical treatment overseas. He was eventually released in 1986 under the personal orders of **Mikhail Gorbachev**. He continued to campaign for improved civil rights and in 1989 he was elected to the Congress of the USSR People's Deputies. His non-scientific writing includes *Progress, Co-existence and Intellectual Freedom* (1968) and *Alarm and Hope* (1978). 📖 George Bailey, *The Making of Andrei Sakharov* (1989)

Sakmann, Bert 1942–
German electrophysiologist and Nobel Prize winner

Born in Stuttgart and educated in medicine at Munich University, he is currently director of the department of cell physiology at the Max Planck Institute for Medical Research, Heidelberg (1989–). His work with **Erwin Neher** revolutionized cell physiology with the invention of the 'patch-clamp' recording technique, which made it possible to record the electrical activity of very small areas of membrane, and enabled them to pursue their studies of neural transmission in the central nervous system. Sakmann and Neher's method has stimulated research in many fields, including studies of nerve impulse prop-agation, egg fertilization, the regulation of the heart-beat, and investigations into the mechanisms of disease. In 1991 they shared the Nobel Prize for physiology or medicine.

Sakutaro Hagiwara 1886–1942
Japanese poet

He was the first major Japanese poet to use colloquial language, and he claimed that all new styles stemmed from his *Howling to the Moon* (1978, from the collection *Tsuki ni hoeru*, 1917). He was much influenced by European poetry, but he sought to keep his own work essentially Japanese. Other work translated into English includes *Face at the Bottom of the World* (Eng trans 1969).

Sala, George Augustus Henry 1828–95
English journalist and novelist

Born in London of Italian ancestry, he studied art and drew book illustrations. In 1851 he became a contributor to *Household Words*, and he later contributed to the *Welcome Guest*, *Temple Bar* (which he founded and edited 1860–66), the *Illustrated London News* and *Cornhill*. As a special cor-respondent of the *Daily Telegraph* he was in the USA during the Civil War, in Italy with **Garibaldi**, in France in 1870–71, in Russia in 1876 and in Australia in 1885. He wrote the social satire *Twice Round the Clock* (1859), novels such as *The Strange Adventures of Captain Dangerous* (1863) and *Quite Alone* (1864), many travel books, and the autobiographical *Life and Adventures* (1895).

Salacrou, Armand 1899–1990
French dramatist

He was born in Rouen and brought up in Le Havre. He was first encouraged, as a young socialist on the fringes of the Surrealist and Dada groups, by Tristan Tzara. He made a fortune in advertising, but abandoned this for the theatre. A remarkable stage technician, he wrote all kinds of plays: boulevard farces, spectacle plays, dramas and 'problem plays'. A thoughtful and in no way superficial dramatist, his real concern was the search for true morality in the absence of a universal religious faith. One of his best plays is *L'Inconnue d'Arras*, (1935, 'The Unknown Woman of Arras'). ☐ J Guichardnaud, *Modern French Theatre* (1961)

Saladin, *properly* Salah al-Din al-Ayyubi 1138–93
Sultan of Egypt and Syria, and founder of a dynasty

Born in Takrit on the Tigris, he entered the service of Nureddin, Emir of Syria, and was made Grand Vizier of the Fatimid caliph (1169). In 1171 he made himself sovereign of Egypt, and on Nureddin's death he became Sultan of Egypt and Syria (1175), reduced Mesopotamia, and received the homage of the Seljuk princes of Asia Minor. He fought the Christians and consolidated his dominions. In 1187 he defeated King Guy of Jerusalem and a united Christian army at Hattin near Tiberias, and then captured Jerusalem and almost every fortified place on the Syrian coast. This provoked the Third Crusade. After a two-year siege (1189–91), Acre was captured, while in 1191, Richard I defeated Saladin at Arsuf (1191), took Caesarea and Jaffa, and obtained a three years' treaty. Saladin died in Damascus. His overriding belief in *jihad* (holy war) led him to patronize Muslim religious institutions, and his wise administration left a legacy of citadels, roads and canals. ☐ Stanley Lane-Poole, *Saladin and the Fall of the Kingdom of Jerusalem* (new edn, 1926)

Salam, Abdus 1926–96
Pakistani theoretical physicist and Nobel Prize winner

Born in Jhang, Maghiana, Punjab, and educated at Punjab University and Cambridge, he became Professor of Mathematics at the Government College of Lahore and at Punjab University (1951–54). He lectured at Cambridge (1954–56) and then became Professor of Theoretical Physics at Imperial College of Science and Technology, London (1957–93). His concern for his subject in developing countries led to his setting up the International Centre of Theoretical Physics in Trieste in 1964. In 1979 he was awarded the Nobel Prize for physics, with Steven Weinberg and Sheldon Glashow. Independently each had produced a single unifying theory of both the weak and electromagnetic interactions between elementary particles. The predictions of the 'electroweak' theory were confirmed experimentally in the 1970s and 1980s. He was made an honorary KBE in 1989.

Salan, Raoul 1899–1984
French general

From 1956 he was Commander-in-Chief of the French army in Algeria. In 1958 he played an important part in the crisis that brought Charles de Gaulle back to power, and was appointed by him as delegate of the government in Algeria, with full powers. An opponent of Algerian independence, he was brought back to France in 1959, and retired in 1960. In 1961 he joined in an attempted coup led by General Challe, but when this failed he went underground in Algeria and launched the OAS (*Organisation Armée Secrète*), using terrorist methods in its struggle against de Gaulle's Algerian policy. He was arrested in 1962, condemned to life imprisonment, but was later amnestied.

Salandra, Antonio 1853–1931
Italian politician

Elected a deputy in 1886, Salandra was a right-wing liberal who held various ministerial posts in the Pelloux and Sonnino governments. After 1910, he tried to become the focus for moderate and conservative forces, becoming Prime Minister in 1914. Together with Sidney Sonnino he was responsible for Italy's entry into World War I; he resolved to support France and Great Britain against Italy's former allies, Austria and Germany, believing that such a policy would bring greater territorial gains. He was replaced as Prime Minister in 1916, but formed part of the delegation to the Paris Peace Conference. He refused to form a government in 1922 and made little effort to oppose Mussolini. After the murder of Giacomo Matteotti, Salandra withdrew his support from the Fascists.

Salazar, António de Oliveira 1889–1970
Portuguese dictator

Born near Coimbra, he was educated in a seminary and became a lecturer in economics at Coimbra. He was active in a Catholic lay group and stood as a parliamentary candidate under the First Republic on three occasions. His economic expertise led to his ascendancy under the military dictatorship of General Antonio Carmona (1926–32). During the early 1930s he laid the foundations of the *Estado Novo* (New State) which he would dominate as dictator for over 35 years. The authoritarian and supposedly corporatist Salazarist state was underpinned by the army and the feared security police, the PIDE. His retrogressive economic policies made Portugal the poorest country in Europe, while greatly enhancing the wealth of its opulent oligarchy. His economic failure made Portugal determined not to give up its African colonies, but the revolt of the army led to the downfall of the regime after his death. He relinquished power in 1968 through ill health. ☐ Hugh Kay, *Salazar and Modern Portugal* (1970)

Salchow, (Karl Emil Julius) Ulrich 1877–1949
Swedish figure skater

The first man to win an Olympic gold medal for this sport (1908), he was world champion a record 10 times (1901–11) and nine times European title-holder between 1898 and 1913.

Saleh, Ali Abdullah 1942–
North Yemeni soldier and politician

Born in Bayt al-Ahmar, North Yemen, he became a colonel in the army of the Yemen Arab Republic and took part in the 1974 coup when Colonel Ibrahim al-Hamadi seized power amid rumours that the monarchy was to be restored. Hamadi was assassinated in 1977 and Colonel Hussein al-Ghashmi took over, only to be killed by a South Yemen terrorist bomb in 1978. Against this background of death and violence Saleh became president. Under his leadership, the war with South Yemen was ended and the two countries agreed to eventual re-union. He was re-elected in 1983 and 1988.

Salieri, Antonio 1750–1825
Italian composer

Born in Verona, he worked in Vienna for 50 years. A teacher of Beethoven and Schubert, he became court composer (1774) and hofkapellmeister (1788), writing over 40 operas, an oratorio and masses. A rival of Mozart, he was later alleged to have poisoned him, although there is no substantive evidence of this. ☐ Alexander Wheelock Thayer, *Salieri: Rival of Mozart* (1989)

Salinas (de Gortari), Carlos 1948–
Mexican politician

He was educated in Mexico and the USA, and taught economics at Harvard. He joined the Mexican government in 1971 and became Finance Minister. In 1988 he was elected President of Mexico by a small majority and immediately faced problems of corruption and drug-trafficking. The presidential candidate nominated as his successor, Luis Donaldo Colosio, was murdered in mysterious circumstances shortly before the elections in 1994, and the following year Salinas chose exile in the USA when his brother Raul became implicated in another assassination attempt.

Salinger, J(erome) D(avid) 1919–
US novelist and short-story writer

He was born in New York. His father was a Jewish cheese importer, his mother Scots, and he was brought up 'an affluent big-city boy'. He attended schools in Manhattan, and in 1934 his father enrolled him at Valley Forge Military Academy ('Pencey Prep' of *The Catcher in the Rye*). He left school at the age of 17, took a job as a dancing-partner for wealthy spinsters on a cruise liner, and dabbled in writing, then attended Columbia University, where his performance was said to be below average. His constant ambition was to become a writer, and after service as an infantryman in World War II he progressed from popular magazines to the *New Yorker*. *The Catcher in the Rye* (1951), his first novel (which sells 250,000 copies annually) made him the guru of disaffected youth. Its hero, Holden Caulfield, plays hookey from his Pennsylvania boarding-school and goes to New York, where he tries in vain to lose his virginity. Written in a slick and slangy first-person narrative, disrespectful to adults and authority, it provoked a hostile response from some critics who objected to the forthright language, iconoclasm and élitism. It was succeeded by four works about the Glasses: *Nine Stories* (1953, published in the UK as *For Esmé—With Love and Squalor, and Other Stories*), *Franny and Zooey* (1961), *Raise High the Roof Beam, Carpenters* and *Seymour: an Introduction* (both 1963). Twice married and divorced, Salinger lives in rural reclusion in New Hampshire, apparently still writing and cultivating Zen philosophy. He published a novella *Hapworth 16, 1924* in 1997, his first published work in 34 years; it had originally appeared in the *New Yorker* in 1965. ▣ I Hamilton, *In Search of J D Salinger* (1988)

Salisbury, 1st Earl of See Cecil, Robert

Salisbury, 5th Marquis of See Cecil, Robert Arthur James Gascoyne-

Salisbury, Edward James 1886–1978
English botanist and ecologist

Born in Harpenden, Hertfordshire, and educated at University College London, he was a senior lecturer in botany at East London (now Queen Mary) College (1914–18) before joining the staff of University College (1918–43; Professor of Botany, 1929–43). He researched the quantity of seeds produced by plants, publishing his results in *The Reproductive Capacity of Plants* (1942). From 1943 to 1956 he was director of the Royal Botanic Gardens, Kew. He continued to publish on plant ecology, including two of his best-known books, *Downs and Dunes* (1952) and *Weeds and Aliens* (1961). He had a special gift of synthesizing data from many different fields into a unified whole, and his ability to popularize his subject is seen in his textbooks and in his synthesis of biology, ecology and horticulture, *The Living Garden* (1935). He founded the British Ecological Society in 1917.

Salisbury, John of See John of Salisbury

Salisbury, Richard Anthony, *originally* Richard Anthony Markham 1781–1829
English botanist and horticulturist

Born in Leeds, he was educated at Edinburgh University. He wrote *Prodromus Stirpium* (1796) and *Paradisus Londinensis* (1805–08), and received criticism for unethical professional behaviour and the unwarranted changing of botanical names. His *Genera Plantarum* was edited and published posthumously (1866). He assumed the surname of Salisbury to fulfil the conditions of a bequest.

Salk, Jonas Edward 1914–95
US virologist

Born in New York City, he was educated at New York University, obtaining his MD in 1939. He taught there and at other schools of medicine and public health. In 1963 he became director of the Salk Institute in San Diego, California. Some of his early research was on the influenza virus, and in 1954 he became known worldwide for his work on the 'Salk vaccine' against poliomyelitis. His killed virus vaccine had to overcome initial opposition arising from 1935 when killed and attenuated vaccines given to over 10,000 children proved ineffective and unsafe. However, a trial in 1954 showed that Salk's vaccination was 80–90 per cent effective, and by the end of 1955 over 7 million doses had been administered. Later the vaccine was superseded by the **Sabin** vaccine, which used a live attenuated strain and could be given orally instead of by injection, but in 1996 the US government advisory committee on immunization recommended reinstating the Salk vaccine to prevent the handful of polio cases contracted each year from the Sabin vaccine itself. Salk spent the last years of his life researching the HIV virus. ▣ Richard Carter, *Breakthrough: The Saga of Jonas Salk* (1965)

Salle, St Jean Baptiste Abbé de La See La Salle, St Jean Baptiste Abbé de

Sallé, Marie 1707–56
French dancer

Born in Paris, she was a child performer and the daughter of an acrobat, appearing in London in pantomime and making her Paris debut in 1718. She studied with François Prévost and in 1727 first performed with the Paris Opera in the Lavals' *Les Amours des dieux*. Rival to **Maria Camargo**, the other well-known dancer of the time, she counted **Handel** and **Voltaire** among her acquaintances. She is known to have given remarkable performances in the Lavals' *Castor et Pollux* (1737), in Rameau's *Les Indes galantes* (1735) and in the comedy ballets of **Molière** and **Raymond Lully**. She created some roles of her own, most notably in *Pygmalion* (1733), and Terpsichore in the prologue to Handel's *Il Pastor fido* (1734). She retired in 1739. She is known today as one of the pioneers of the ballet d'action.

Salle, René Robert Cavalier, Sieur de La See La Salle, René Robert Cavalier, Sieur de

Sallinen, Aulis 1935–
Finnish composer

Born in Salmi, he studied at the **Sibelius** Academy with **Aarre Merikanto** and Joonas Kokkonen, and taught there from 1963 to 1976. His works include the operas *The Horseman* (1975), *The Red Line* (1978), *The King Goes Forth to France* (1983) and *Kullervo* (for the new Helsinki opera house), orchestral works including six symphonies, chamber music including five string quartets, concertos, songs and choral music, all in an eclectic adventurous but mainly tonal idiom. He also wrote the score for the film *The Iron Age* (1983).

Sallinen, Tyko Konstantin 1879–1955
Finnish painter

Born in Narmes, after studying art in Helsinki he went to Paris in 1909 and was deeply affected by the works of Kees van Dongen (1877–1968) and the Fauvists. His favourite subjects were landscapes and Finnish peasants, which he painted in a colourful, vividly Expressionist style.

Sallust, Latin Gaius Sallustius Crispus 86–34BC
Roman historian and politician

Born in Amiternum, in the Sabine country, he became tribune in 52BC when he helped to avenge the murder of Clodius upon Milo and his party. In 50BC he was expelled from the senate and joined the cause of Julius Caesar; and in 47BC he was made praetor and restored to senatorial rank. He served in Caesar's African campaign, and was left as Governor of Numidia. His administration was marked by oppression and extortion, and from his gains he laid out famous gardens on the Quirinal and built the mansion which became an imperial residence of Nerva, Vespasian and Aurelian. He was unsuccessfully prosecuted on his return to Rome. In his retirement he wrote his histories, the *Bellum Catilinae*, the *Bellum Iugurthinum* and the *Historiarum Libri Quinque* (78–67BC). Although weak on details, Sallust's work reflects a rigorous historical approach and a concern for causation, and his terse style anticipated that of Publius Tacitus.

Salmasius, Claudius, also called Claude de Saumaise 1588–1653
French scholar

Born in Semur in Burgundy, he studied philosophy at Paris and law at Heidelberg (1606–09), where he professed Protestantism. His chief work, *Plinianae Exercitationes in Solinum*, appeared in 1629; after this he mastered Hebrew, Arabic and Coptic. In 1631 he was called to Leyden to occupy Joseph Scaliger's chair. He is best known for his *Defensio Regio pro Carolo I*, published in 1649 at the request of Charles II, which was answered by Milton in 1651 with his *Pro Populo Anglicano Defensio*.

Salmond, Alex(ander Elliot Anderson) 1955–
Scottish Nationalist politician

Born in Linlithgow, West Lothian, he joined the Scottish National Party at the age of 19, while a student at St Andrews University. He graduated in economics and worked for the Royal Bank of Scotland before winning Banff and Buchan for the SNP in the 1987 general election. He achieved a clear victory in the party's 1990 election of a successor to party leader Gordon Wilson. His hopes for parliamentary advances were not realized in 1992 but in the general election of 1997 the number of SNP MPs returned to Westminster rose from three to six.

Salmond, Sir John William 1862–1924
New Zealand jurist and judge

He was a Professor of Law at Adelaide (1897–1906) and Wellington (1906–07), and then worked in government legal service until 1921, when he was appointed a judge of the Supreme Court of New Zealand. While at Adelaide he published *Jurisprudence* (1902) and *Torts* (1907), the latter still a definitive work.

Salome 1st century AD
Judean princess

She was the granddaughter of Herod the Great and daughter of Herodias by her first husband, Herod Philip, who was the brother of her second husband, Herod Antipas. She is identified by the historian Josephus as the girl in Mark 6.17–28 and Matthew 14.1–12 who danced before Herod Antipas and at her mother's instigation demanded the head of John the Baptist, who had denounced the marriage with Antipas. She is the subject of a play (1894) by Oscar Wilde, which in turn provided the libretto for an opera by Richard Strauss (1905).

Salote 1900–65
Queen of Tonga

Educated in New Zealand, she succeeded her father, King George Tupou II, in 1918. Her prosperous and happy reign saw the reunion, for which she was mainly responsible, of the Tongan Free Church majority with the Wesleyan Church (1924). She is remembered in Great Britain for her colourful and engaging presence during her visit in 1953 for the coronation of Queen Elizabeth II.

Salt, Dame Barbara 1904–75
English diplomat

Educated at Seaford in Sussex and at Munich and Cologne universities, she acted as vice-consul in Tangier during World War II before joining the Foreign Office as a first secretary to the United Nations. She was promoted to counsellor in 1955, and was appointed ambassador to Israel in 1962, but was unable to take up the post because of an illness which resulted in the loss of both her legs. Nevertheless she remained in the Foreign Office and became head of the Special Operations Executive, a post she held from 1967 until her retirement in 1972.

Salt, Sir Titus 1803–76
English manufacturer and philanthropist

Born in Morley near Leeds, he was a wool stapler at Bradford, started wool-spinning in 1834, and was the first to manufacture alpaca fabrics in England. Round his factories in a valley, three miles from Bradford, on the Aire, rose the model village of Saltaire (1853). He was elected Mayor of Bradford in 1848, and served as its Liberal MP from 1859 to 1861. He was created a baronet in 1869.

Salten, Felix, pseudonym of Siegmund Salzmann 1869–1945
Austrian novelist and essayist

He was born in Budapest, Hungary, and became a journalist and art critic at the age of 18. He is known especially for his animal stories, particularly *Bambi* (1929) which, in translation and as a film by Walt Disney (1941), achieved great popularity in the USA and Great Britain. He also wrote *Florian* (1934, Eng trans *Florian: An Emperor's Horse*, 1934) and *Bambis Kinder* (1940, Eng trans *Bambi's Children*, 1940).

Salvator Rosa See Rosa, Salvator

Salviati, Antonio 1816–90
Italian mosaicist

Born in Vicenza, he revived in 1860 the glass factories of Murano and the art of mosaic. His mosaics can be seen in Westminster Abbey and St Paul's Cathedral in London.

Salviati, Cecchino, originally Francesco de' Rossi 1510–63
Italian painter

Born in Florence, he was a pupil of Andrea del Sarto and a close friend of Giorgio Vasari. In about 1530 he travelled to Rome and entered the service of Cardinal Giovanni Salviati, whose name he adopted. He travelled extensively in Italy and executed decorative schemes, painted portraits and designed tapestries in Rome, Venice and Florence. In 1554 he was called to the French court, but returned to Rome the following year. He is regarded as one of the major Italian Mannerist painters, and his work is characterized by strong colour, complex figure arrangements and spatial ambiguity.

Salvius Julianus c.100AD–c.169AD
Roman jurist

In about AD130 he was commissioned by the emperor Hadrian to revise and rearrange the Praetorian Edict, which was thereafter fixed and settled. He later held high offices and was a member of the emperor's *Consilium*. He wrote a *Digesta* in 90 books, which was much quoted in later works and in **Justinian's** *Digest*, commentaries and *Responsa*. He was a distinguished jurist, and represented the apex of Roman legal science.

Samain, Albert Victor 1858–1900
French poet
Born in Lille, he was a clerk in the Prefecture of the Seine. His Symbolist poetry, though not original in subject, was well received in his lifetime. Among his collections of verse are *Au jardin de l'infante* (1893, 'In the Infanta's Garden'), *Aux flancs du vase* (1898, 'On the Sides of the Vase') and *Le Chariot d'or* ('The Chariot of Gold'), published posthumously.

Samaranch, (Juan) Antonio 1920–
Spanish sports administrator and diplomat
He was born into a wealthy commercial family in Barcelona, had connections with the **Franco** family, and was a multi-millionaire by the late 1960s. He entered politics, became Minister of Sport, ambassador to the USSR (1977–80), and president of the International Olympics Committee. In this capacity he added several events to the Games, further increased its professional status and its commercialism, and successfully oversaw the Seoul Olympics of 1988. 🕮 Vyv Simpson and Andrew Jennings, *The Lords of the Rings: Power, Money and Drugs in the Modern Olympics* (1992); David Miller, *The Biography of Juan Antonio Samaranch* (1992)

Samaras, Lucas 1936–
US sculptor
Born in Kastoria in northern Greece, he grew up during World War II and the ensuing Greek civil war. In 1948 he emigrated to the USA with his family, settling in New Jersey and later winning an art scholarship to Rutgers University. He had his first one-man show of pastels and paintings in New York City in 1959, and in the early 1960s he became known as a sculptor influenced by surrealism and pop art. His inventive and often menacing sculptures consist of objects such as boxes and chairs grouped in patterns and transformed by the addition of pointed pins, razor blades, knives, and scissors. He also works with photographs and mirrors to create bizarre abstract self-portraits.

Sambourne, Edward Linley 1844–1910
English cartoonist and illustrator
Born in London, at the age of 16 he was apprenticed to marine engineering works at Greenwich, and later joined the staff of *Punch* as a cartoonist (1867–1910). He illustrated **Charles Kingsley's** *Water Babies*, **Hans Christian Andersen's** *Fairy Tales*, and other books.

Samoilova, Konkordiya Nikolaevna 1876–1921
Russian socialist, political activist, writer and journalist
She was born in Siberia and educated in St Petersburg. She was a political activist and supporter of **Lenin**, and played a variety of roles in the revolutionary movement, including the editorship of *Pravda* from its foundation in 1912 and co-editorship of the women's newspaper *Rabotnitsa*. In 1921 she died of cholera contracted while on a mission for the Soviet government in the Volga Region.

Samoset d.c.1653
Native American leader
He was chief of the Pemaquid band of Abnakis, who lived on Monhegan Island off the coast of present-day Maine. Having learned some English from fishermen in Maine, he spoke welcoming words to the Pilgrims in the Plymouth colony and introduced the colonists to **Squanto** and the chief Massasoit, both of the Wampanoag tribe. In 1625 he sold 12,000 acres of Pemaquid land to **John Brown**, thereby executing the first land transfer between a Native American and an Englishman.

Sampras, Pete 1971–
US tennis player
He was born in Washington DC. Four times winner of the US Open (1990, 1993, 1995–96) and five times winner of Wimbledon (1993–95, 1997–98), at the age of 25 he had won eight Grand Slam championships (US Open, Wimbledon, and Australian Open). He is especially known for his powerful serves.

Sampson, Agnes d.1592
Scottish witch
Born in Haddington, East Lothian, she was a lay-healer, and seems to have practised witchcraft. She was put on trial after being accused as the 'eldest witch of them all'. She confessed under torture to celebrating black Mass in which Satan gave instructions to plot the death of the king and queen. She also claimed to have organized meetings in North Berwick at Hallowe'en, at which 200 people danced in a circle by the sea. She was finally interrogated by **James VI**, and was subsequently executed.

Samson, St c.485–c.565
Welsh religious
Born in south Wales, he was educated and ordained by St Illtud in Glamorgan, became an abbot and was later consecrated bishop. He is said to have evangelized in Cornwall and the Channel Islands, and later went to Brittany, where he established a monastery at Dol which became an episcopal see. His feast day is 28 July.

Samson
Old Testament ruler
He was the last of the 12 judges in the Book of Judges. The biblical account represents him not as a leader but as an individual whose deeds on behalf of Israel made him a popular hero. After a number of encounters with the Philistines he was lured into a trap by Delilah, who cut off his hair to reduce the strength that God had given him. Blinded by the Philistines, he took his revenge once his hair had grown again by bringing down the temple at Gaza. 🕮 Watson Kirkconnell, *That Invincible Samson* (1964)

Samsonov, Aleksandr Vasilevich 1859–1914
Russian general
He commanded a force in the Russo-Japanese War (1904–05). In World War I he commanded the army which invaded East Prussia in August 1914, and was decisively defeated by **Paul von Hindenberg** at the Battle of Tannenberg on 26–31 August. He later committed suicide.

Samuel 11th century BC
Old Testament ruler and Hebrew prophet
The son of Elkanah and his wife Hannah, he was an Ephraimite who was dedicated to the priesthood as a child by a Nazarite vow. 'Samuel' in Hebrew means 'name of God'. After the defeat of Israel and loss of the Ark of the Covenant to the Philistines, he endeavoured to keep the tribal confederation together, moving in a circuit among Israel's shrines. He presided, apparently reluctantly, over **Saul's** election as the first King of Israel, but later criticized Saul for assuming priestly prerogatives and disobeying divine instructions. Samuel finally anointed **David** as Saul's successor, rather than Saul's own son, Jonathan.

Samuel, Herbert Louis Samuel, 1st Viscount 1870–1963
English Liberal politician and philosophical writer
Born into a banking family, he was educated at University College School and Balliol College, Oxford. Entering parliament in 1902, he held various offices, including that of Chancellor of the Duchy of Lancaster (1909), Postmaster-General (1910, 1915), and Home Secretary (1916, 1931–32) and was the High Commissioner for

Palestine (1920–25). His philosophical works include *Practical Ethics* (1935), *Belief and Action* (1937) and *In Search of Reality* (1957).

Samuelson, Paul Anthony 1915–
US economist and journalist and Nobel Prize winner
Born in Gary, Indiana and educated at Chicago and Harvard, he was a professor at the Massachusetts Institute of Technology (1940–85). He wrote *Foundations of Economic Analysis* (1947) and *Economics* (1948), which was considered a classic textbook. He was awarded the Nobel Prize for economics in 1970 for raising the level of scientific analysis in economic theory. He has won several other awards including the 1983 University of Chigaco Alumni Medal and the 1989 Britannica Award.

Samuelsson, Bengt Ingemar 1934–
Swedish biochemist and Nobel Prize winner
Born in Halmstad, he entered the medical school of the University of Lund, where he worked in Sune Bergström's laboratory. In 1958 he moved to the Karolinska Institute in Stockholm, where he graduated in medicine (1961) and was appointed assistant Professor of Medical Chemistry. Samuelsson studied the biosynthesis of prostaglandins, substances which act as chemical messengers, showing that they are produced from an unsaturated fatty acid found in certain foodstuffs. Samuelsson and Bergström also investigated two groups of prostaglandins, one known as the E series, which lowers blood pressure and is used in treating circulatory diseases, and another, the F series, which raises blood pressure, and has been used to induce abortion. Samuelsson became Professor of Medical Chemistry at the Royal Veterinary College in Stockholm (1967–72) and then Professor of Chemistry at the Karolinska. He shared the 1982 Nobel Prize for physiology or medicine with Bergström and Sir John Vane and won the 1990 Abraham White Science Award.

Sanchez, Francisco c.1550–1623
Portuguese or Spanish physician and philosopher
Born probably in Braga, Portugal, he studied medicine in Montpellier and became Professor of Philosophy (1585) and later of Medicine (1612) at Toulouse, France. His main work is a study of philosophical scepticism, *Quod Nihil Scitur* (written in 1576, published in 1581, 'That Nothing is Known'), which is a radical critique of Aristotle and argues that true knowledge is impossible.

Sánchez Coello, Alonso c.1515–1590
Spanish portrait painter
In 1571 he succeeded Anthonis Mor as court painter to Philip II of Spain; his portrait of Philip is in the National Gallery, London. He was a forerunner of the great Spanish portrait painters.

Sanctorius (Santorio Santorio) 1561–1636
Italian physician
Born in Justinopolis, Venetian Republic (Koper, Slovenia), he studied philosophy and medicine at Padua and practised medicine in various places before settling in Venice in 1599. Professor of Theoretical Medicine at Padua from 1611, he is best known for his investigations into metabolism, consisting of an elaborate series of measurements of his own weight, food intake and excretia. He also invented instruments to measure humidity and temperature, a syringe for extracting bladder stones, and other devices. A friend of Galileo, he represents the quantifying spirit in the medicine of his time.

Sand, George See panel p1629

Sandage, Allan Rex 1926–
US astronomer
Born in Iowa City, he studied at Illinois University and California Institute of Technology (Caltech) before joining the Hale Observatories, initially as an assistant to Edwin Powell Hubble. With Thomas Matthews, a junior colleague, he found in 1960 a faint optical object at the same location as the compact radio source 3C 48 and found it to have an unusual spectrum. This was soon shown by Maarten Schmidt to be the result of a huge Doppler red shift, which suggested that the object, now known as a quasar, is receding from the Earth at enormous speed. This is now interpreted to suggest that it is extremely remote and as luminous as hundreds of galaxies. Sandage went on to identify many more quasars and showed that most quasars are not radio emitters. He has won many international awards including the Royal Astronomical Society Eddington Medal (1963) and the Swiss Physical Society Tomalla Gravity Prize.

Sandburg, Carl 1878–1967
US poet
Born in Galesburg, Illinois, of Swedish descent, after trying various jobs, fighting in the Spanish–American war and studying at Lombard College, he became a journalist in Chicago and started to write for *Poetry*. His verse reflects the industrial USA. Among his volumes of poetry are *Chicago Poems* (1915), *Corn Huskers* (1918), *Smoke and Steel* (1920), *Slabs of the Sunburnt West* (1922) and *Good Morning, America* (1928). His *Complete Poems* gained him the Pulitzer Prize in 1950. He published a collection of American folk-songs and ballads in *The American Songbag* (1927). He also wrote an extensive *Life of Abraham Lincoln* (1926–39), which won a Pulitzer Prize. 📖 Gay Wilson Allen, *Carl Sandburg* (1972)

Sandby, Paul 1725–1809
English painter
Born in Nottingham, the brother of Thomas Sandby, he has been called the father of the watercolour school. His career began as a draughtsman, and later, living at Windsor with his brother, he made 76 drawings of Windsor and Eton. His watercolours, outlined with the pen and only finished with colour, took the purely monochrome drawing of the watercolour school one step forward. He was an original member of the Royal Academy.

Sandby, Thomas 1721–98
English artist and architect
The brother of Paul Sandby, he ran an academy at Nottingham with him, and became private secretary and draughtsman to William Augustus, Duke of Cumberland. He was deputy ranger of Windsor Park from 1746, and became the first Professor of Architecture to the Royal Academy (1770). He built Lincoln's Inn Fields (1776) and was joint architect of His Majesty's works with James Adam (1777).

Sandeau, Jules Léonard Sylvian Julien 1811–83
French writer
Born in Aubusson, he went to Paris to study law, but soon devoted himself to literature. He co-wrote *Rose et Blanche* (1831, 'Rose and Blanche') with George Sand. His first independent novel was *Madame de Sommerville* (1834) and his first success was *Marianna* (1840). His books give an accurate picture of the social conflicts of the France of his day, and he was master of the *roman de mœurs*, the social novel. He became keeper of the Mazarin Library in 1853, and librarian at St Cloud in 1859. 📖 M Silver, *Sandeau, l'homme et la vie* (1937)

Sandel, Cora, *pseudonym of* Sara Fabricius 1880–1974
Norwegian author and painter

Sand, George, *pseudonym of* Amandine Aurore Lucie Dupin, Baronne Dudevant 1804–76
French novelist

George Sand was born in Paris, the illegitimate daughter of Marshal de Saxe, who died when she was still a child. She lived mostly with her grandmother, and inherited her property. At the age of 18 she married Casimir, Baron Dudevant, and had two children, but after nine years left him and went to Paris with her children to make her living by literature in the Bohemian society of the period (1831). She scandalized bourgeois society for many years with her unconventional ways and her love affairs.

Her first lover was **Jules Sandeau**, from whose surname she took her pseudonym, and with whom she wrote a novel, *Rose et Blanche* (1831). She was always interested in poets and artists, including **Prosper Mérimée**, **Alfred de Musset**, with whom she travelled in Italy, and **Chopin**, who was her lover for 10 years. Later her attention turned to philosophers and politicians, such as **Félicité de Lamennais**, the socialist Pierre Leroux, and the republican Michel de Bourges. After 1848 she settled down as the quiet 'châtelaine of Nohant', and spent the rest of her life writing and travelling.

📖 Her work can be divided into four periods. When she first went to Paris, her candidly erotic novels, *Indiana* (1832), *Valentine* (1832), *Lélia* (1833) and *Jacques* (1834), emanated the Romantic extravagance of the time, and declared themselves against marriage. In the next period her philosophical and political teachers inspired the socialistic rhapsodies of *Spiridion* (1838, Eng trans 1842), *Consuelo* (1842–44, Eng trans 1846), *La Comtesse de Rudolstadt* (1843–45, Eng trans *The Countess of Rudolstadt*, 1847) and *Le Meunier d'Angibault* (1845, Eng trans *The Miller of Angibault*, 1847). Between the two periods came the fine novel *Mauprat* (1837, Eng trans 1847). Then she began to turn towards the studies of rustic life, *La Mare au diable* (1846, Eng trans *The Haunted Marsh*, 1848), *François le Champi*, (1847–48, Eng trans *Francis the Waif*, 1889) and *La Petite Fadette* (1849, Eng trans *Little Fadette*, 1850) which are considered her best works. The fourth period comprises the miscellaneous works of her last 20 years, some of them, such as *Les Beaux messieurs de Bois-Doré* (1858, Eng trans *The Gallant Lords of Bois-Doré*, 1890), *Le Marquis de Villemer* (1860–61, Eng trans *The Marquis of Villemer*, 1871) and *Mademoiselle la Quintinie* (1863), being of high quality. Her complete works (in over 100 volumes), besides novels and plays, include the autobiographical *Histoire de ma vie* (1855, 'The Story of My Life'), *Elle et lui* (on her relations with de Musset, 1859, Eng trans *He and She*, 1900), and her letters, published after her death.

📖 Renee Winegarten, *The Double Life of George Sand, Woman and Writer* (1978); André Maurois, *Lélia: The Life of George Sand* (1953); M Louise Pailleron, *George Sand* (2 vols, 1938–43).

> *L'art n'est pas une étude de la réalité positive; c'est une recherche de la vérité idéale.*
> 'Art is not a study of positive reality; it is a search for ideal truth.' From *La Mare au diable* (1846).

Born in Oslo and brought up in Tromsø in northern Norway, she lived as a painter in Paris (1906–21) and published her first novel, *Rosina*, in 1922. After this, her writing career continued in earnest with the 'Alberte' trilogy, *Alberte* (1926), *Alberte og Friheten* (1936, 'Alberte and Freedom') and *Bare Alberte* (1939, 'Just Alberte'), in which she describes a woman's experiences of power and powerlessness among middle-class social mores, a theme which runs consistently through all her writing. In the short novel collection *Vårt vanskelige liv* (1960, 'Our Difficult Life') Sandel addresses women's longing for acknowledgement and self-determination, while a further collection, *Barnet som elsket veier* (1973, 'The Child who loved Roads'), reflects her empathy with a child's view of the world. 📖 A H Lervik, *Menneske og miljø i Cora Sandels diktning* (1977)

Sander, August 1876–1964
German photographer
Born in Herdorf, he studied painting in Dresden and opened a studio in Linz in 1902 and another in Cologne. For many years he worked towards a comprehensive photographic documentary study, *Men in the 20th Century*. He published the first part, entitled *Faces of Our Times*, in 1929, but his social realism was discouraged by the Nazi Ministry of Culture after 1934 and he published little more. Much of his large collection of negatives was destroyed in the bombing of Cologne and in a fire at his studio in 1946, but surviving material has provided penetrating portraits of all levels of German life in the early part of the century.

Sanders, Howard Lawrence 1921–
US marine biologist
Born in Newark, New Jersey, he was educated at the universities of British Columbia, Rhode Island and Yale, and worked throughout his career at Woods Hole Oceanographic Institution in Massachusetts. He remained there as Scientist Emeritus following his retirement in 1986. From 1969 to 1980 he simultaneously held posts as adjunct professor at the State University of New York, and as associate professor at Harvard. His early research concerned the fauna of shallow water invertebrates, and led to the discovery of a primitive class of crustacea, the Cephalocarida. He then devoted his attention to fauna living on the deep-sea bed on the north-west Atlantic continental shelf. During the mid-1960s, Sanders and his colleagues began to formulate the 'stability–time' hypothesis to account for the exceptional levels of species diversity of deep-sea benthic communities. During the 1970s he also became a leading expert on oil spills and their environmental consequences.

Sanderson, Robert 1587–1663
English theologian and casuist
Born in Yorkshire, he studied at Lincoln College, Oxford, of which he became a Fellow (1606–19), Reader of Logic (1608) and Sub-Rector (1613–16). Regius Professor of Divinity from 1642 to 1648, he was deprived of his professorship during the Civil War but was reinstated and became Bishop of Lincoln in 1660. He wrote the second preface to the Prayer Book and perhaps the General Thanksgiving, as well as works on casuistry.

Sanderson, Tessa (Theresa Ione) 1956–
English sportswoman and television presenter
Born in Wolverhampton, West Midlands, she first threw the javelin for Great Britain in 1974; together with her great rival **Fatima Whitbread**, she kept the country at the top of the event for the ensuing decade. In a career latterly dogged by injury, she won three Commonwealth gold medals (1978, 1986 and 1990) and one Olympic gold medal at the Los Angeles games in 1984. In 1989 she became a sports newsreader for Sky TV. She has published an autobiography, *My Life in Athletics* (1985).

Sandino, Augusto César 1895–1934
Nicaraguan revolutionary

Born in Niquinohomo (La Victoria), he made the mountains of northern Nicaragua his stronghold and led guerrilla resistance to US occupation forces after 1926. His success in evading the US forces and the Nicaraguan National Guard generated sympathy for his cause, and a great deal of anti-American feeling. After the withdrawal of the US Marines (1933), **Anastasio Somoza** arranged a meeting with him, apparently to discuss peace. This, however, was a ruse and Sandino was murdered on Somoza's orders near Managua. The Nicaraguan revolutionaries of 1979 (later known as the Sandinistas) regarded him as their principal hero.

Sandow, Eugene 1867–1925
US strong-man
He was born in Königsberg, Prussia (now Kaliningrad, Russia), of Russian parents, and made his name as a strong-man at the Chicago World's Fair in 1893. He then became an artist's model and exponent of physical culture, and opened an Institute of Health in St James's Street, London.

Sandracottus See **Chandragupta**

Sands, Bobby (Robert) 1954–81
Irish revolutionary
Born in Belfast, he joined the IRA in 1972, and was sentenced to five years' imprisonment in 1973 for possession of guns. In 1977 he was sentenced to 14 years after the bombing of a furniture factory. On 1 March 1981, while at Long Kesh prison in Northern Ireland, he went on hunger strike in protest against the authorities' refusal to consider himself and his fellow-IRA prisoners as political prisoners. On 9 April he was elected Westminster MP for Fermanagh-South Tyrone in a by-election. He remained on hunger strike for 66 days and died on 5 May, the first of 10 to die in the same year.

Sandwich, Edward Montagu, 1st Earl of 1625–72
English naval commander
In the Civil War he fought on the parliamentary side as a soldier at Marston Moor (1644), sat in parliament (1645–48), shared the command of the fleet with **Robert Blake** from 1653, and fought in the first Anglo-Dutch War. On the restoration of the monarchy (1660), which he supported, he was appointed Admiral of the Narrow Seas. As ambassador to Spain (1666–69) he helped to negotiate King **Charles II**'s marriage, and escorted his bride **Catherine of Braganza** to England. In the Dutch War with France and England (1672–78), he fought in the Battle of Southwold Bay, and was blown up with his flagship, the *Royal James*.

Sandwich, John Montagu, 4th Earl of 1718–92
English politician
As First Lord of the Admiralty from 1748 to 1751 and 1771 to 1782, his ineptness contributed to British failures in the American Revolution. Notoriously corrupt, he was a member of **Francis Dashwood**'s 'Mad monks of Medmenham Abbey', and was involved in the persecution of his former friend, **John Wilkes**. The Sandwich (now Hawaiian) Islands were named after him by Captain **Cook**. The 'sandwich' is reputed to have been invented by him as a snack for eating at the gaming-table. 📖 George Martelli, *Jemmy Twitcher* (1962)

Sandys, Duncan Edwin See **Duncan-Sandys, Baron**

Sanford, Katherine 1915–
US medical researcher
Born and educated in Wellesley, Massachusetts, she received her PhD from Brown University, and then moved to the National Cancer Institute where she spent her entire research career. She worked initially with Dr Virginia

Evans and colleagues, developing tissue-culture techniques and examining ways of promoting cancerous transformations in cultured cells. Her cloning of a mammalian cell (the isolation of a single cell in order that it might propagate itself, producing a colony of identical cells) has become a vital tool for the detailed pathological study of cancer-causing mechanisms.

Sangallo, Antonio Giamberti da, the Younger 1485–1546
Italian architect and engineer
Born in Florence, he was the most notable of a family of architects, the nephew of Giuliano (c.1445–1535) and Antonio the Elder (1455–1535), with whom he studied before departing for Rome about 1503. He began as draughtsman to **Donato Bramante** and **Baldassare Peruzzi**, and from 1516 served as assistant to **Raphael** at St Peter's, becoming chief architect there in 1539. He was a leading architect of the High Renaissance in Rome, designing in a confident manner disapproved of by **Michelangelo**. His works include the Palazzo Palma-Baldassini in Rome (c.1520), and his masterpiece, the Palazzo Farnese, also in Rome (1534–46, completed by Michelangelo). He was also a military engineer, and designed the fortifications around Rome.

Sanger, Frederick 1918–
English biochemist and Nobel Prize winner
Born in Rendcombe, Gloucestershire, he was educated at Cambridge, and in 1951 joined the staff of the Medical Research Council in Cambridge (1951–83). During the 1940s he devised methods of deducing the sequence of amino acids in the chains of the protein hormone insulin. For this he was awarded the Nobel Prize for chemistry in 1958. He then turned to the structure of nucleic acids, working on RNA and DNA; eventually he was able to deduce the full sequence of bases in the DNA of the virus Phi X 174 and mitochondrial DNA. Such methods led to the full base sequence of the **Epstein**–Barr virus by 1984. For this work Sanger shared (with **Walter Gilbert** and **Paul Berg**) the 1980 Nobel Prize for chemistry, thereby becoming the first scientist to win two Nobel Prizes in this field. His other awards include the royal medal of the Royal Society (1969) and the gold medal of the Royal Society of Medicine (1983), and he was appointed to the Order of Merit in 1986.

Sanger, John 1816–89 and George 1825–1911
English showmen
Brothers, they both called themselves 'Lord', and became famous with their travelling circuses throughout Great Britain.

Sanger, Margaret Louise, née Higgins 1883–1966
US social reformer and founder of the birth-control movement
Born in Corning, New York and educated at Claverack College, she became a trained nurse, and married William Sanger in 1902. Appalled by some of her experience as a nurse, she published in 1914 a radical feminist magazine, *The Woman Rebel*, which gave advice on contraception. In 1916 she founded the first American birth-control clinic, in Brooklyn, New York City, for which she was imprisoned. After a world tour, she founded the American Birth Control League in 1921. Divorced in 1920, she married J Noah H Slee in 1922. Her many books include *What Every Mother Should Know* (1917), *Motherhood in Bondage* (1928) and *My Fight for Birth Control* (1931).

Sangster, Robert Edmund 1936–
English racehorse owner and breeder
He founded the Coolmore Stud with Irish breeder John Magnier and trainer Vincent O'Brien, and in 1975 formed a multi-million-pound syndicate of big owners who dealt mostly in stallions. Particular success came from their

importation of Kentucky stallions, notably Alleged, which won the Prix de l'Arc de Triomphe twice, was bought for $175,000 and syndicated for $16 million. Sangster was the leading owner five times before giving way to Sheikh Mohammed Al Maktoum. Sangster bought the 2,500-acre training business at Manton, Wiltshire, in 1986 and had 62 horses in training in 1996.

Sanguinetti, Julio Maria 1936–
Uruguayan politician
A member of the long-established progressive Colorado Party (PC), which had its origins in the civil war of 1836, he was elected to the assembly in 1962, and appointed Minister of Labour and Industry, and Minister of Education and Culture (1969–73). The oppressive regime of Juan Maria Bordaberry (1972–76) was forcibly removed, and military rule imposed before democratic government was restored in 1985. The 1966 constitution was restored with some modifications, and Sanguinetti was elected President. He took office in 1986, leading a government of National Accord until the completion of his term in 1990. He was re-elected in 1994.

Sanjurjo, José 1872–1936
Spanish soldier
As director of the Civil Guard he played an important role in the establishment of the Second Republic in 1931 by refusing to place his forces at the service of the king, Alfonso XIII. Nevertheless, he led an abortive monarchist rising against the new regime in 1932. Sentenced to life imprisonment, he was amnestied by the right-wing government of Alejandro Lerroux in 1934. Popular with the army for his direct and practical approach, he accepted the leadership of the Nationalist rising of July 1936 against the Republic, only to die on 20 July in an air crash.

Śankara c.700–50
Hindu philosopher and theologian
Born in Kalati, Kerala, he was the most famous exponent of *Advaita* (the *Vedanta* school of Hindu philosophy), and is the source of the main currents of modern Hindu thought. His thesis was that Brahma alone has true existence and the goal of the self is to become one with the Divine. This view, familiar to modern Westerners through the teaching of the Ramakrishna Mission, was strongly opposed by Ramanuja and his successors in the *Bhakti* tradition.

Sankara, Thomas 1950–87
Burkina Faso soldier and politician
He joined the army in Ouagadougou in 1969 and attended the French Parachute Training Centre (1971–74), where he began to develop radical political ideas. As a minister in Saye Zerbo's government, he increasingly came to believe in the need for a genuinely popular revolution to expunge the consequences of French colonialism. Leading a coup in 1983, he became Prime Minister and Head of State and introduced a wide range of progressive policies which made him enemies. Despite his great symbolic popularity among young radicals (outside Burkina Faso as much as inside), he was shot during a coup led by his close associate Blaise Compaoré on 15 October 1987.

San Martin, José de 1778–1850
Argentine soldier and politician
Born in Yapeyu, he played a large part in winning independence for Argentina, Chile and Peru. He was an officer in the Spanish army (1789–1812), but aided Buenos Aires in its struggle for independence (1812–14). He raised an army in Argentina (1814–16), which in January 1817 he led across the Andes into Chile, and with Bernardo O'Higgins defeated the Spanish at Chacabuco (1817) and Maipo (1818), thus achieving independence for Chile. In 1821, after creating a Chilean navy with Thomas Cochrane, he entered Lima and declared Peru's independence. He became Protector of Peru but resigned in 1822 after differences with Simón Bolívar, and died in exile in Boulogne. 📖 John C Metford, *San Martin: The Liberator* (1950)

Sanmichele, Michele c.1484–1559
Italian architect and military engineer
Born in San Michele, he was responsible with Jacopo Sansovino for introducing the Roman High Renaissance to the Veneto. Regarded as the true successor of Donato Bramante, and a friend of Giorgio Vasari, he gained a knowledge of classical antiquities through designing forts across the Venetian Empire. Capella Pellegrini, in Verona (1527–57), was his first church, in which a simply detailed domed cylinder rises severely from a more elaborate centralized plan. Palazzo Grimani, Venice (1551–59), is the quintessential Renaissance palace, in which the skeletal structure of columns dissolves the wall plane. He drew on various influences and produced a cohesive architecture which influenced Andrea Palladio and others.

Sannazaro, Jacopo c.1458–1530
Italian poet
He was born in Naples, and sought favour at the court. His *Arcadia* (1485), a pastoral medley of prose and verse which was influenced by Boccaccio, won him considerable fame. He also wrote Latin elegies and religious works. 📖 A Altamure, *Jacopo Sannazaro* (1951)

Sansovino, *properly* Andrea Contucci 1460–1529
Italian sculptor and architect
He was born in Monte San Savino, from which he derived his name, and worked in Florence, Portugal (at the court of John II) and in Rome. Some of his work survives, including, in Florence, the Corbinelli altar at Santo Spirito (c.1486–91) and, at Santa Maria del Popolo in Rome, the tomb of Cardinal Ascanio Sforza (1505–09). A *Virgin and Child with St Anne* (1512, Sant' Agostino) shows a gift for the realistic portrayal of old age. He was also in charge of architecture at Loreto (c.1513–27) and at San Savino.

Sansovino, Jacopo, *originally* Jacopo Tatti 1486–1570
Italian sculptor and architect
Born in Florence, he was a pupil of Sansovino, and took his name. From 1529 he was state architect in Venice, where he did his best work. His most noteworthy works in architecture are the Libreria Vecchia, the Palazzo della Zecca and the Palazzo Corner, and in sculpture the two giants on the steps of the ducal palace.

Santa Anna, Antonio López de 1797–1876
Mexican soldier and statesman
Born in Jalapa, he joined Augustín de Itúrbide in 1821 in the struggle for Mexican independence, but in 1823 overthrew him, and in 1833 became President of Mexico. His reactionary policy resulted in the loss of Texas in 1836; he commanded the Mexican force at the siege and massacre of the Alamo, but was routed by Samuel Houston and imprisoned for eight months. In 1838 he lost a leg in the defence of Vera Cruz against the French. From 1841 to 1844 he was either President or the President's master; he was exiled in 1845 but recalled in 1846 to resume office during the war with the USA, in which he was twice defeated. He was recalled from Jamaica by a revolution in 1853 and appointed President for life, but in 1855 was again overthrown, and went to Cuba. Under Ferdinand Maximilian he intrigued continually and in 1867, after the emperor's death, he tried to effect a landing; he was captured, and sentenced to death, but allowed to retire to New York. He returned to Mexico City in 1874 and died in poverty. 📖 Oakah L Jones, *Santa Anna* (1968)

Santamaria, Bartholomew Augustine 1915–98

Australian social and political writer

He was born in West Brunswick, Victoria. After graduating in law from Melbourne University he became involved with the Catholic Rural Movement and other organizations, becoming president of the Catholic Social Movement in 1943, director of Catholic Action in 1947, and president of the National Civic Council in 1957. A leading force against Communist influence in Australia, and in the establishment of the Democratic Labour Party, he wrote a number of right-wing texts, including *The Price of Freedom* (1964) and *The Defence of Australia* (1970). In 1978 he published a biography of his patron, Archbishop **Daniel Mannix**.

Santander, Francisco de Paula 1792–1840

Colombian general and politician

Born in Rosario de Cúcuta, New Granada, he was a revolutionary who fought for independence from Spain, and he served as Vice-President of Gran Colombia under Simón Bolívar (1821–28) until he was banished for his supposed complicity against Bolívar. In 1830 Gran Colombia was dissolved, and in 1832 Santander returned from exile and refounded the country as New Granada (comprising modern Colombia and Panama). He was President of New Granada (1832–37).

Santayana, George, *originally* Jorge Agustín Nicolás Ruiz de Santayana 1863–1952

Spanish – US philosopher, poet and novelist

Born in Madrid, and educated from 1872 in the USA, he taught at Harvard (from 1889) and was professor there (1907–12), but retained his Spanish citizenship and returned to Europe in 1912. He lived for some time in Oxford, but settled in Rome (1924) and spent his last years as the guest of a convent there. He is widely regarded as a literary philosopher and a fine stylist. His writing career began as a poet with *Sonnets and Other Verses* (1894). He was also a successful novelist with *The Last Puritan* (1935), and a cultivated literary critic, aesthetician and essayist. Philosophy, however, became his main interest, and his principles were eclectic in origin. His general outlook was naturalistic and materialistic, and he was critical of the transcendental claims of religion and of German idealism. He was also a sceptic, maintaining that knowledge of the external world depends on an act of 'animal faith'. But he was at the same time a Platonist in temperament and attitude, and was devoted to the institutions, if not the doctrines, of the Catholic Church. His philosophical works include *The Sense of Beauty* (1896), *The Life of Reason* (1905–06), *Scepticism and Animal Faith* (1923), which is itself an introduction to the comprehensive *Realms of Being* (4 vols, 1927–40), *Platonism and the Spiritual Life* (1927) and *The Last Puritan* (1935). He also wrote an autobiography, *Persons and Places* (3 vols, 1944–53). ▢ W E Arnett, *George Santayana* (1968)

Santer, Jacques 1937–

Luxembourg politician

Born in Wasserbillig, he was educated at the universities of Paris and Strasbourg and at the Institute of Political Studies in Paris. After graduating he became an advocate at the Luxembourg Court of Appeal, but changed to a political career in 1963. As Parti Chrétien-Social member he held several ministerial positions before becoming Prime Minister (1984–95). In 1995 he was elected President of the European Commission. Although he was considered a compromise candidate he proved to be an able and judicious moderator of European politics at a time when the EC was moving towards greater cohesion and integration.

Santillana, Iñigo López de Mendoza, Marqués de 1398–1458

Spanish scholar, soldier and poet

Born in Carrión de los Condes, he led expeditions against the Moors in Spain, but is best known as a patron of the arts. He was created marquis by John II of Castile in 1445 for his services on the field of battle. He was influenced by the poetry of **Dante** and **Petrarch** and introduced their style and methods into Spanish literature. His shorter poems, especially his *serranillas* (pastoral songs), are among his best work, and he was the first Spanish poet to write sonnets. His principal prose work, *Proemio e carta a condestable de Portugal* (1449, 'Proem and Letter to the Constable of Portugal'), is a discourse on the European literature of his day. ▢ J Delgado, *Iñigo de Santillana* (1968)

Santley, Sir Charles 1834–1922

English baritone

Born in Liverpool, he trained in Milan (1855–57), and made his debut in **Haydn**'s *Creation* in 1857. From 1862 he devoted himself to Italian opera, though he became better known for his concert work and performance in oratorio. He was knighted in 1907, and published his *Reminiscences* in 1909.

Santos-Dumont, Alberto 1873–1932

Brazilian aeronaut

Born in São Paolo, he built and flew a cylindrical balloon with a gasoline engine (1898). In 1901 he built an airship in which he made the first flight from St Cloud round the Eiffel Tower and back. In 1903 he built the first airship station at Neuilly, then experimented with heavier-than-air machines, and eventually flew 715 feet (218m) in a machine constructed on the principle of the box-kite. In 1909 he built a light monoplane, a forerunner of the modern light aircraft.

San Yu, U 1919–96

Burmese politician and soldier

He was born in Prome. During World War II, he fought under **U Ne Win** and held a succession of senior army posts following independence. He was a member of the Revolutionary Council which seized power in the March 1962 coup and was appointed Minister of Finance, Minister of Defence, army Chief of Staff and, between 1973 and 1981, Secretary-General of the ruling Burmese Socialist Programme Party (BSPP). Popular within the BSPP and viewed as more pragmatic than Ne Win, San Yu succeeded him as State President in November 1981. With other senior BSPP figures he was forced to resign in July 1988, after popular anti-government demonstrations in Rangoon.

Sapir, Edward 1884–1939

US linguist and anthropologist

Born in Lauenburg, Pomerania (now Poland), he went to the USA with his family in 1889, and studied ethnology and American Indian languages at Columbia University. One of the founders of ethnolinguistics, he is best known for his work on the languages of the North American Indians, particularly his studies of the relationship between language and culture. His conclusions as to the effect that the grammatical structure and vocabulary of a language may have on the way its speakers perceive the world were developed by his pupil **Benjamin Lee Whorf**, and came to be known as the Sapir–Whorf hypothesis. After serving as head of anthropology at the Canadian National Museum (1910–25) and as Professor of Anthropology and Linguistics at Chicago University (1925–31), he became Sterling Professor of Anthropology and Linguistics at Yale (1931–39). His best-known book is *Language* (1921).

Sapper, *pseudonym of* Herman Cyril McNeile
1888–1937
English novelist and short-story writer
Born in Bodmin, Cornwall, McNeile was educated at
Cheltenham and at the Royal Military Academy at
Woolwich. He joined the Royal Engineers as a regular in
1907 and was promoted to Captain on the eve of World
War I; he won the Military Cross and rose to lieutenant-
colonel before his retirement. He is remembered chiefly
for the invention of Captain Hugh 'Bulldog' (originally
'Bull-Dog' Drummond), a laddish sprig of Edwardian
England, introduced in 1920 in an eponymous novel
bearing the tellingly Hannay-ish subtitle *The Adventures of a
Demobilized Officer Who Found Peace Dull*. The best of the
seven Drummond thrillers is *The Female of the Species* (1928,
published in the USA as *Bulldog Drummond Meets ...*, 1943),
in which the hero rescues his wife from kidnap by
Sapper's stock gang of cheap foreign thugs.

Sappho c.610–c.580BC
Greek lyric poet
Born on the island of Lesbos, she went into exile about
596BC from Mytilene to Sicily, but after some years returned to Mytilene. She seems to have been the centre of a
circle of women and girls, probably her pupils. Tradition
represents her as homosexual because of the passionate
love and admiration she expresses in some of her poems
addressed to girls; but she married and had a daughter,
Cleis. Only two of her odes are extant in full, but many
fragments have survived. It is from her that the term
'lesbian' has acquired its meaning and the four-line
sapphic stanza (used in Latin by Catullus and Horace) its
name. 🕮 C M Bowra, *Greek Lyric Poetry* (1961)

Sapru, Tej Bahadur 1875–1949
Indian political leader
He studied law and practised as a lawyer in Allahabad. He
entered politics in 1907 as a moderate, joined Annie
Besant's Home Rule League Movement (1917) and became a member of Lord Reading's Executive Council in
1921, but resigned in 1923 after the conviction and imprisonment of Mahatma Gandhi. At the Round Table
Conference in London (1930), he reiterated the demand
for provincial autonomy with responsibility to the legislature at the centre. He was member of the Privy Council
in 1934 and was in favour of a new constitution under the
Government of India Act in 1935. A Persian and Urdu
scholar and one of the greatest statesmen of the Indian
freedom movement, he was the first President of the
Indian Council of World Affairs (1943), a position which
he held until his death.

Sarah, *also spelt* Sarai 19th century BC
Biblical character in the Old Testament
Sarah, whose name means 'princess' in Hebrew, was the
wife of Abraham and mother of Isaac. She accompanied
Abraham from Ur to Canaan (Genesis 12–23) and pretended to be Abraham's sister before Pharaoh in Egypt
and Abimelech in Gerar, since her beauty and their desire
for her might have endangered Abraham's life. Pharaoh
took her as his wife, and Abraham prospered, but when
the truth was revealed, Pharaoh banished them both.
Long barren, she eventually gave birth to Isaac in her old
age, fulfilling God's promise that she would be the ancestor of nations (Genesis 17.16). She died at the age of 127
in Kiriath-arba. In the New Testament Paul uses the
miracle of the birth of Isaac through God's promise to the
free-born Sarah (rather than the slave-woman Hagar, who
bore Abraham's first son) to explain to the Galatian
Christians that they were freed by the covenant of Christ
and therefore inheritors of the heavenly Jerusalem
(Galatians 4.22–31). Peter cites her as an exemplary wife
who afforded her husband due obedience and respect (1
Peter 3.6).

Sarandon, Susan Abigail, *née* Tomalin 1946–
US film actress
Born in New York City, she studied drama at the Catholic
University in Washington DC, where she met her future
husband, actor Chris Sarandon. She made her film debut
in *Joe* (1970) and worked extensively in television soap
operas and in theatre before graduating to more interesting roles in cinema, including Janet in *The Rocky Horror
Picture Show* (1975). She received a Best Actress Award
nomination for her role in *Atlantic City* (1980), but good
work eluded her until her casting in *The Witches of Eastwick*
(1987) and *Bull Durham* (1988). Increasingly in demand as
a mature woman displaying strong sexuality, her subsequent triumphs include *White Palace* (1990), *Thelma and
Louise* (1991), *Lorenzo's Oil* (1992), *The Client* (1994) and
Dead Man Walking (1995, Academy Award), directed by her
off-screen companion Tim Robbins.

Sarasate, Martin Meliton 1844–1908
Spanish violinist and composer
Born in Pamplona, he studied with distinction at the
Paris Conservatoire, and in 1857 began to give concerts. A
skilled performer in concertos, he was perhaps best at
playing the Spanish dance music he composed himself.
Various works were specially composed for him, including Édouard Lalo's *Symphonie espagnole*, Max Bruch's second
violin concerto and his *Scottish fantasy*, and several pieces
by Camille Saint-Saëns.

Sarazen, Gene, *originally* Eugenio Saraceni 1902–
US golfer
Born in Harrison, New York, he took up golf as a teenager
on his doctor's recommendation to improve a lung condition. He won the Open Championship (1932), the US
Open (1922, 1932) and the US PGA (Professional Golfers'
Association) Championship (1922, 1923, 1932), but it was
his victory in the 1935 Masters (in only its second year)
which helped establish the event worldwide.

Sardanapalus See Ashurbanipal

Sardar See Patel, Vallabhbhai Jhaverbhai

Sardou, Victorien 1831–1908
French dramatist
He was born in Paris. His early works were failures, but
through his marriage to the actress Virginie Brécourt he
became acquainted with the actress Pauline Déjazet
(1799–1875), for whom he wrote successfully *Monsieur
Garat* (1860) and *Les Prés Saint-Gervais* (1860, Eng trans *The
Meadows of Saint-Gervais*, 1871). He rapidly amassed a fortune and became the most successful European play-
wright of his day, also enjoying immense popularity in
the USA. *Nos intimes* (1861, Eng trans *Our Friends*, 1879),
La Famille Benoîton (1865, 'The Benoîton Family'),
Divorçons (1880, 'Let's Get Divorced'), and *Marquise* (1889)
are representative of his work. For Sarah Bernhardt he
wrote *Fédora* (1882, Eng trans 1883) and *La Tosca* (1887,
Eng trans *Tosca*, 1900), among others, and for Sir Henry
Irving *Robespierre* (1899, Eng trans as a novel, 1899) and
Dante (1903, Eng trans 1903). He attempted the higher
historical play in *La Patrie!* (1869, Eng trans *The Mother
Country*, 1915). Today his plays appear over-technical and
over-theatrical, and the plot and characters shallow and
rather obvious. 🕮 J A Hunt, *Sardou and the Sardou Plays*
(1913)

Sargent, John Singer 1856–1925
US painter
Born in Florence, Italy, the son of a US physician, he
studied painting there and in Paris, where he first gained
attention at the Salon with *Madame X* (1884). Most of his
work, such as *Lord Ribblesdale* (1902, National Gallery,
London), was, however, executed in England from 1885,
where he became the most fashionable and elegant

portrait painter of his age. To this period belongs his well-known *Carnation Lily, Lily, Rose* (1885–86, Tate, London). In 1907 he exhibited with the English artists at the Venice Biennale. His early painting shows a French Impressionist influence, but Spanish art had a more lasting effect and *Carmencita* is perhaps the best example of this. Visiting the USA constantly, he worked on portraits and series of decorative paintings for public buildings, such as *The Evolution of Religion* for Boston Library (1889–c.1915). He also painted landscapes, especially in later life, and often in watercolour. He was an official war artist in World War I, producing *Gassed* (1818, Imperial War Museum, London) and other works.

Sargent, Sir (Harold) Malcolm Watts
1895–1967
English conductor
Born in Stamford, Lincolnshire, he originally studied as an organist, first appearing as a conductor when his *Rhapsody on a Windy Day* was performed at a Promenade Concert in 1921. He was conductor of the Royal Choral Society from 1928, of the Liverpool Philharmonic Orchestra (1942–48), and of the BBC Symphony Orchestra (1950–57). From 1948 he directed the London (Henry Wood) Promenade Concerts. His fine conducting of choral music, as well as his sense of occasion and unfailing panache, won him great popularity at home and abroad. ▢ Phyllis Matthewman, *Sir Malcolm Sargent* (1959)

Sargeson, Frank (Norris Frank Davey)
1903–82
New Zealand short-story writer and novelist
Born in Hamilton, he qualified as a lawyer but did not practise, spent two years in Europe (1926–28), and worked briefly in various jobs before taking up freelance journalism. He made his name with collections of short stories such as *Conversations with My Uncle* (1936), *A Man and His Wife* (1940) and *That Summer and Other Stories* (1946), in which he satirized the provincial attitudes of his surroundings. His *Collected Stories, 1935–1963* appeared in 1964 and an expanded edition, as *The Stories of Frank Sargeson*, in 1973. His novels include *Memoirs of a Peon* (1965) and *Joy of the Worm* (1969). On account of his easy use of colloquial idioms and speech patterns, he is regarded as the founder of modern New Zealand writing. He wrote three works of autobiography, *Once is Enough* (1973), *More than Enough* (1975) and *Never Enough!* (1977), collected in one volume as *Sargeson* in 1981. ▢ B Benson, introduction to *The Collected Stories of Frank Sargeson* (1964)

Sargon II d.705BC
King of Assyria
He was probably a son of Tiglath-Pileser III, named partly after Sargon of Akkad. One of the most powerful of Assyrian kings (721–705BC), he consolidated the empire he had inherited in a long series of campaigns to the north, east and west of Assyria. He continued the military campaigns of his predecessor Shalmaneser V in Samaria, from where he conducted a mass deportation of thousands of Israelites, and exercised a hold over Syria and Babylonia and even Cyprus. He was succeeded by his son Sennacherib.

Sargon of Akkad fl.c.2370BC
Mesopotamian ruler
In Mesopotamian tradition, he was brought up by a gardener and became a cup-bearer to the King of Kish. In his inscription he claims that he defeated the King of Uruk and 'built Akkad', and that his territory extended from the Persian Gulf to the Mediterranean. He was long remembered as a powerful ruler and a model for later Near-Eastern conquerors.

Sarin, Madhu 1945–
Indian architect
She studied architecture at the Punjab University, Chandigarh (1962–67), then at the Architectural Association, London (1969–70). After graduating she worked in London as consultant to the UN Economic and Social Commission for Asia and the Pacific, with responsibility for co-ordinating policies on slums. In 1977 she returned to Chandigarh and became consultant to the Indian government, speaking at conferences all over the world. In response to a fuel shortage, she designed an energy-efficient stove that has benefited thousands of people worldwide. She has also developed ferro-cement roofing components for use in areas where traditional timber roofs are unavailable as a result of deforestation. In 1988 she was appointed to the Indian Ministry of Education National Resource Group to work on Education for Women's Equality.

Sarmiento, Domingo Faustino 1811–88
Argentine writer and politician
An outspoken critic of the dictator Juan Manuel de Rosas and the *caudillo* Juan Facundo Quiroga, he spent much of his early life in exile in Chile (1831–36, 1840–45, 1848–51), also travelling to Europe and the USA. He later served as Governor of San Juan (1862–64) before becoming, at a time of great change, his country's first civilian President (1868–74). An especially vigorous promoter of education and immigration, he was also a prolific and forceful writer. With Juan Bautista Alberdi and Bartolomé Mitre, he was one of the most important architects of modern Argentina. *Civilización y Barbarie: La vida de Juan Facundo* (1848, 'Civilization and Barbarism: The Life of Juan Facundo'), better known simply as *Facundo*, is a combination of essay, novel and political treatise on the peoples of Argentina, and was the most important essay of his day.

Sarney (Costa), José 1930–
Brazilian politician
Born in Maranhao state, he became a follower of the UDN (Union Democrática Nacional) Bossa Nova (nationalist) group in the early 1950s and in 1956 was elected to the state assembly. He became ARENA (National Renewal Alliance) Governor of Maranhão in 1965 under Humberto Castelo Branco, and was a prominent senator during the 1970s, leading the Social Democratic Party (PDS) under Figueiredo. He was deputy to Tancredo Neves in the first civilian government for 21 years in 1985, and became President on Neves's sudden death despite public concern over his former military associations. His attempt to retain the executive during the 1987–88 Constituent Congress succeeded, but at enormous political and economic cost. He was succeeded in 1990 by Fernando Collor de Mello, and is now president of the Brazilian senate.

Sarnoff, David 1891–1971
US radio and television pioneer
Born near Minsk, Russia, he emigrated to New York with his family at the age of nine and later studied engineering at the Pratt Institute. A telegraph operator for the Marconi Wireless Co (1912), he picked up distress signals from the sinking ship *Titanic* and stayed at his post for 72 hours to cover the disaster. As general manager (1921), president (1930), and chairman of the board (1947) of the Radio Corporation of America (RCA), he guided the founding of the National Broadcasting Co (NBC), encouraged research and manufacturing of television, and the production of colour television. ▢ Carl Dreher, *Sarnoff: An American Success* (1977)

Saro-Wiwa, Ken 1941–95
Nigerian writer and minority-rights activist
He was born in Bori, Nigeria, and educated at the University of Ibadan. He was a lecturer at the University of Lagos and held government office before devoting

himself to writing and publishing. A prolific writer, he wrote poetry and radio plays, and several novels, beginning with *Sozaboy: A Novel in Rotten English* (1985), as well as the television series *Basi and Company*, which satirized the Nigerians' desire to make fortunes with minimal effort, and some political writing. He supported the Ogoni people against dispossession in the development of Nigeria's oil industry, and founded the Movement for the Survival of Ogoni People to protect their rights. Arrested in 1994 by Nigeria's military government for his part in promoting the cause of Ogoni nationalism, he was hanged the following year despite worldwide protests. ⌨ C E N Nnolim, *Critical Essays* (1992)

Saroyan, William 1908–81
US playwright and novelist
He was born in Fresno, California, and was largely self-educated. He won literary fame with his first work, *The Daring Young Man on the Flying Trapeze* (1934), a volume of short stories; this offered a hallucinatory but strikingly sympathetic view of the USA during the Depression, and was a great critical success. He continued to write unconventional and impressionistic stories, which were published in collections such as the autobiographical *My Name Is Aram* (1940). Idealistic and opposed to commercialism, he refused the Pulitzer Prize awarded in 1940 for his play *The Time of Your Life* (1939). Among his later works are several other plays, novels including *The Human Comedy* (1943), and the memoirs *Places Where I've Done Time* (1975) and *Obituaries* (1979). ⌨ *Short Drive, Sweet Chariot* (1966)

Sarpi, Pietro, Fra Paolo 1552–1623
Italian historian, scientist and theologian
Born in Venice, he entered the Servite Order in 1565, and became vicar-general in 1599. He became the champion of Venice in the dispute with Pope **Paul V** over the immunity of clergy from the jurisdiction of civil tribunals, resisting the intrusion of Rome in the internal affairs of the Republic and opposing the interdict that sought to debar all priests from their functions. He was himself excommunicated and was seriously wounded by assassins. His main preoccupation then became the great *Istoria del Concilio Tridentino* (Eng trans *History of the Council of Trent*), which was published in London in 1619 under the pseudonym Pietro Soave Polano. He studied a wide range of subjects, including oriental languages, mathematics, astronomy, physiology and medicine, and is credited with various later anatomical discoveries concerning the venous valves and the circulation of blood.

Sarrail, Maurice Paul Emmanuel 1856–1929
French soldier
Born in Carcassonne, he led the 3rd army in World War I at the Battle of the Marne (1914), and commanded the Allied forces in the East at Salonica from 1915 to 1917, where he called for the abdication of **Constantine I** of Greece. He was High Commissioner in Syria (1924–25), but was recalled after the bombardment of Damascus during a rising.

Sarraute, Nathalie, *née* Tcherniak 1900–
French writer
She was born in Ivanovno-Voznesenk, Russia. Her parents settled in France when she was a child, and she was educated at the Sorbonne, Paris, graduating in arts and law. She then spent a year at Oxford (1922–23) and studied sociology in Berlin, before establishing a law practice in Paris. Her first book was a collection of sketches on bourgeois life, *Tropismes* (1939, Eng trans *Tropisms*, 1934), in which she rejected traditional plot development and characterization in order to describe a world between the real and the imaginary. She developed this style in later novels, including *Portrait d'un Inconnu* (1948, Eng trans *Portrait of a Man Unknown*, 1958), *Le Planétarium* (1959, Eng

trans 1960), *Entre la vie et la mort* (1968, Eng trans *Between Life and Death*, 1969) and *Ici* (1995, 'Here'). She has also written plays, *Le Silence, suivi du Mensonge* (1967, Eng trans *Silence, and The Lie*, 1969), *Isma* (1970, Eng trans *Izzuma*, 1980) and *Elle est là* (1978, Eng trans *It Is There*, 1980), and essays. ⌨ G R Besser, *Nathalie Sarraute* (1979)

Sars, Michael 1805–69
Norwegian marine biologist
Born in Bergen, he was made Extraordinary Professor of Zoology at Christiania (Oslo) University in 1854. He was one of the founders of marine zoology, and his expeditions included many trips to the northern seas, the Mediterranean, and the Adriatic (1851). His chief interest was in the migration of marine organisms and the life cycles of marine invertebrates, and he demonstrated the previously unrecognized link between larval and adult forms. He was the first to describe the larva of marine molluscs (1837) and starfish (1844). Using a deep-sea dredge he collected many specimens, his most spectacular discovery being the first specimen of a living crinoid, previously believed to have been extinct. He published *On Some Remarkable Forms of Animal Life from the Great Deeps off the Norwegian Coast* (1868).

Sarsfield, Patrick, Earl of Lucan ?1645–1693
Irish soldier
Born in Lucan, County Dublin, he joined the English Life Guards, and in 1685 fought against the Duke of **Monmouth** at Sedgemoor. In 1688 he was defeated at Wincanton, and crossed over to Ireland. Created Earl of Lucan by **James II**, he drove the English out of Sligo, was present at the Boyne (1690) and Aughrim (1691), defended Limerick, and on its capitulation (1691) left Ireland under amnesty and entered the French service in the Irish Brigade. He fought at Steenkirk (1692), and was mortally wounded at Neerwinden.

Sarto, Andrea del, *properly* d'Agnolo 1486–1531
Italian painter
He got his name from his father's trade of tailor. From 1509 to 1514 he was engaged by the Servites in Florence to paint a series of frescoes for their Church of the Annunciation (1509–14), and a second series was next painted for the Recollets. In 1518 he went to Paris on the invitation of **Francis I**. He returned to Italy the next year with a commission to purchase works of art, but squandered the money and dared not return to France. Many of his most celebrated pictures, such as *Madonna of the Harpies* (1517), are in Florence. He was a rapid worker and accurate draughtsman, displaying a refined feeling for harmonies of colour. His pupils included **Jacopo da Pontormo, Fiorentino Rosso** and **Giorgio Vasari**.

Sarton, George Alfred Leon 1884–1956
US historian of science
Born in Ghent, Belgium, he studied at the university there, and emigrated to the USA in 1915. He became a dominant figure in the history of science, founding its principal journal, *Isis*, in 1912, and *Osiris* in 1936. His *Introduction to the History of Science* (3 vols, 1927–48) reaches only to 1400. His many other books and articles largely shaped the subject as a separate discipline. He was supported by the Carnegie Institution and based at Harvard.

Sartre, Jean-Paul 1905–80
French existentialist philosopher, dramatist, novelist and Nobel Prize winner
Born in Paris, he studied at the Sorbonne and taught philosophy at Le Havre, Paris and Berlin (1934–35). He was taken prisoner in World War II (1941), and after his release became a member of the Resistance in Paris. In 1945 he emerged as the most prominent member of the left-wing, left-bank intellectual life of Paris. In 1946, with **Simone de Beauvoir**, he founded and edited the avant-garde monthly *Les Temps modernes* ('Modern Times'). A

disciple of **Martin Heidegger**, he developed his own characteristic existentialist doctrines, which found full expression in his autobiographical novel *La Nausée* (1938, Eng trans *Nausea*, 1949) and other fiction. The Nazi occupation provided the grim background to such plays as *Les Mouches* (1943, Eng trans *The Flies*, 1946), a modern version of the Orestes theme, and *Huis clos* (1944, Eng trans *In Camera*, 1946; also known as *No Exit* and *No Way Out*). *Les Mains sales* (1948, Eng trans *Crime Passionnel*, 1949) movingly portrayed the tragic consequences of a decision to join an extremist party. His atheistic existentialist doctrines are outlined in *L'Existentialisme est un humanisme* (1946, Eng trans *Existentialism and Humanism*, 1948) and are fully worked out in *L'Être et le néant* (1943, Eng trans *Being and Nothingness*, 1956). Other notable works include the trilogy *Les Chemins de la liberté* ('Paths of Freedom'). In 1964 he was awarded the Nobel Prize for literature, but he declined it. In the late 1960s he became closely involved in opposition to US policies in Vietnam, and expressed support for the student rebellions of 1968. He wrote an autobiography, *Les Mots* (1963, Eng trans *The Words*, 1964). 📖 A C Solal, *Sartre* (1988)

Sassetta, originally **Stefano di Giovanni** c.1392–1450
Italian painter
Born in Siena, he was taught painting in the conservative late 14th-century Sienese manner, although he was receptive to contemporary developments of the courtly International Gothic style and the Florentine Early Renaissance. These influences he blended into a highly inventive style, full of narrative interest though never truly concerned with naturalism. His finest work was the altarpiece of St Francis (1437–44), painted for San Francesco, Borgo San Sepolcro, but now dispersed; some of the finest predella panels are in the National Gallery in London.

Sassoon, Siegfried Louvain 1886–1967
English poet and novelist
Born in Brenchley, Kent, he suffered experiences in World War I that made him detest war, and led to their fierce expression in *The Old Huntsman* (1917), *Counter-Attack* (1918) and *Satirical Poems* (1926). A semi-fictitious autobiography, *The Complete Memoirs of George Sherston* (1937), had as its first part *Memoirs of a Fox-Hunting Man* (1928, Hawthornden Prize 1929), and continued in *Memoirs of an Infantry Officer* (1930) and *Sherston's Progress* (1936). *The Old Century* (1938), *The Weald of Youth* (1942) and *Siegfried's Journey 1916–20* (1945) are all autobiographical, and he also wrote a biography of **George Meredith** (1948). His later poems, including those in *Vigils* (1935) and *Sequences* (1956), are predominantly spiritual, and he became a Roman Catholic in 1957. His *Collected Poems* appeared in 1961. 📖 John Keegan, *Biography of Siegfried Sassoon* (1987)

Sassou-Nguesso, Denis 1943–
Congolese soldier and politician
He joined the army and trained in Algeria and France. An active member of the radical Parti Congolais du Travail (PCT), he was appointed Minister of Defence in 1975 and survived the military coup of 18 March 1977 in which President N'Gouabi was assassinated. In 1979, under popular pressure, power was transferred to the PCT and Sassou-Nguesso became President of the Congo later in the year. Since then, he has moved politically towards the centre, rebuilding links with France and establishing more harmonious relations with the USA. He was re-elected in 1984 and is the leader of the Forces Démocratiques Unies.

Sastri, V S Srinivasa, *in full* Valangunian Sankarana-Rayana Srinivasa Sastri 1869–1946
Indian politician

Greatly influenced by **Annie Besant**, C P Ramaswami Aiyar and **Gopal Gokhale**, he was the Secretary of the Madras session of Congress (1908). He took an active part in drawing up the Lucknow Pact between the Congress and Muslim League, which demanded 'responsive government for India', and was opposed to **Mahatma Gandhi's** policy of non-violence and non-co-operation. Elected to the Madras Council in 1913, he became a member of the Imperial Legislative Council in 1915 and of the Council of State in 1921. He was a member of the delegation to South Africa which led to the Cape Town agreement, which committed the South African government to shelving its Class Area Bill to segregate Indians. He also struggled for the cause of Indians living in Kenya and British East Africa and was president of the Servants of India Society for some years. In 1945 he strongly opposed **Muhammad Ali Jinnah's** two-nation theory.

Satie, Erik Alfred Leslie 1866–1925
French composer
Born in Honfleur of French-Scottish parents, he worked as a café composer, and studied under **Vincent d'Indy** and **Albert Roussel**. In his own work — ballads, lyric dramas, whimsical pieces and the ballet *Parade* (1917) — he was in revolt against Wagnerism and orthodoxy in general, and had some influence on **Claude Debussy, Maurice Ravel** and others. 📖 Alan M Gillmor, *Erik Satie* (1988)

Sato Eisaku 1901–75
Japanese politician and Nobel Prize winner
The younger brother of **Kishi Nobusuke**, he was an official in the Ministry of Railways before World War II, and was first elected to the Diet in 1949. Indicted for corruption in 1954, he was released in 1956 as part of a general amnesty celebrating Japan's entry into the UN. During his period as premier (1964–72), relations with South Korea were normalized (1965) and US-held Okinawa was returned to Japan (1972). Although the 1960 security treaty with the USA was automatically extended in 1970, a dispute over Japanese textile exports and President **Richard Nixon's** normalization of relations with China, done without consulting Japan, soured US–Japanese relations during his last years in office. It is widely believed that his three non-nuclear principles (non-manufacture, non-possession and non-introduction into Japan of nuclear weapons) earned him the Nobel Peace Prize in 1974.

Saud, *in full* Saud ibn Abd al-Aziz 1902–69
King of Saudi Arabia
He was the older son of **Abdul Aziz Ibn Saud**, and had been Prime Minister for the last three months of his reign when he succeeded him in 1953. His rule was characterized by inefficiency and corruption, and by financial disorder except for the periods when his brother **Faisal** served as Finance Minister. Eventually his brothers formed a group to press for reform, and a number of airforce officers defected to Egypt, where they were supported by President **Nasser**. In 1964 the Council of Ministers deposed Saud and he agreed to pledge allegiance to his brother Faisal, who replaced him.

Sauer, Carl Ortwin 1889–1975
US geographer
Born in Warrenton, Missouri, he was educated at Northwestern University and at Chicago. He became Professor of Geology and Geography at Michigan (1915–22) and made vital and practical contributions to the improved use of land in Michigan State. He was Professor of Geography at the University of California, Berkeley (1923–54), researching the historical geography of Latin America and the relation between human societies and plants. He had a major impact on the growth of geography in the USA.

Saul 11th century BC
Biblical ruler

A Benjamite, the son of Kish, he was the first king elected by the Israelites; his name means 'asked for'. He conquered the Philistines, Ammonites and Amalekites, but became intensely jealous of **David**, his son-in-law, and was ultimately at feud with the priestly class. At length **Samuel** secretly anointed David king. Saul fell in battle with the Philistines at Mount Gilboa. ▣V Long, *The Reign and Rejection of King Saul* (1989)

Saumaise, Claude de See Salmasius, Claudius

Saumarez, James, 1st Baron de 1757–1836
British naval commander

Born in Guernsey, he served (1774–82) in the navy during the American Revolution , and distinguished himself in the third Dutch War. He fought at L'Orient (1795) and Cape St Vincent (1797), and was second in command at the Battle of the Nile (1798). In 1801, as vice-admiral, he fought his greatest action off Cadiz. He commanded the British Baltic fleet sent to assist the Swedes from 1809 to 1813. He was promoted admiral in 1814, and subsequently commanded at Plymouth (1824–27).

Saunders, Dame Cicely Mary Strode 1918–
English founder of the modern hospice movement

Born in Barnet, Greater London, she was educated at Roedean School and St Anne's College, Oxford, and trained at St Thomas's Hospital Medical School and the Nightingale School of Nursing. As founder (1967), medical director (1967–85) and chairman (1985–) of St Christopher's Hospice, Sydenham, she has promoted the principles of dying with dignity, maintaining that death is not a medical failure but a natural part of living and that its quality can be enhanced by sensitive nursing and effective pain-control. She has received many awards for her pioneering work, including the Templeton Prize (1981) and the BMA Gold Medal (1987). She was made a DBE in 1980 and was awarded the Order of Merit in 1989. She has written and edited a number of books, including *Care of the Dying* (1960), *The Management of Terminal Disease* (1978), *Hospice: The Living Idea* (1981), *Living With Dying* (1983), *St Christopher's in Celebration* (1988), and *Beyond the Horizon* (1990).

Saunders, Deion Sanders 1967–
US player of baseball and American football

He was born in Fort Myers, Florida. Unusually in American sport, he plays both American football and baseball, making him one of the world's richest athletes. He made a record-breaking deal for $13 million when he left Super Bowl champions San Francisco 49ers in 1995 and signed with American football team Dallas Cowboys. He played baseball for the New York Yankees (1988–90); the Atlanta Braves (1991–94); and the Cincinnati Reds (1994–95), whom he left for the San Francisco Giants.

Saunders, Jennifer 1958–
English comedienne and actress

Born in Sleaford, Lincolnshire, she trained at the Central School of Speech and Drama in London, where she met **Dawn French**. They formed a highly successful comedy double-act, starting at the Comedy Store in London. In 1980 they joined the new Comic Strip club and later appeared on television in *The Comic Strip Presents...* films (1982–93), series such as *Girls on Top* (1985–86), which they wrote with Ruby Wax, and their own series, *French and Saunders* (1987–). Away from the partnership, she wrote and starred (with **Joanna Lumley**) in *Absolutely Fabulous* (1992–95), winning an Emmy award for the script and a

BAFTA award for her performance, and took a straight acting role in *Queen of the East* (1995), in the 'Heroes and Villains' series.

Saussure, Ferdinand de 1857–1913
Swiss linguist

Born in Geneva, in 1878 he published his *Mémoire sur le système primitif des voyelles dans les langues indo-européenes*. He was appointed Professor of Indo-European Linguistics and Sanskrit at the University of Geneva in 1901, and also Professor of General Linguistics in 1907. His lectures on general linguistics showed his dissatisfaction with the theoretical foundations of linguistics as then practised, and constituted the first serious attempt to determine the nature of language as the object of which linguistics is the study. He is often described as the founder of modern linguistics. His *Course in General Linguistics* (1916; 5th edn 1955; English translation by Baskin, 1959) was compiled by two of his students after his death, mainly from lecture notes. As well as introducing the important dichotomy of *langue* (the system of language) and *parole* (an individual's actual speech), he pointed out that language can be viewed descriptively (synchronically) or historically (diachronically). His methodology inspired a great deal of the later work done by semiologists and structuralists. ▣ Jonathan Culler, *Ferdinand de Saussure* (rev edn, 1986)

Saussure, Horace Bénédict de 1740–99
Swiss physicist and geologist

Born in Conches, near Geneva, at the age of 22 he became Professor of Physics and Philosophy at Geneva (1762–88), although his first love was botany. He travelled in Germany, Italy and England; he crossed the Alps by several routes and ascended Mont Blanc (1787). *Voyages dans les Alpes* ('Travels in the Alps'), describing his observations on mineralogy, geology, botany and meteorology, was published in several volumes between 1779 and 1796. The mineral saussurite is named after him.

Saussure, Nicolas Théodore de 1767–1845
Swiss botanist

The son of **Horace Bénédict de Saussure**, he accompanied his father on many expeditions, and in 1789 he climbed Monte Rosa and corroborated **Edmé Mariotte's** observations on the weight of air. He began accumulating observations on plant mineral nutrition, and from 1802 he was named Honorary Professor of Mineralogy and Geology at Geneva Academy. He continued his studies of plant physiology, performing a series of fundamental experiments on carbonic acid in plant tissues, the phosphorus content of seeds, the conversion of starch into sugars and the biochemical processes during flower and fruit maturation. His most important publication was *Recherches Chimiques sur la Végétation* (1804, 'Chemical Research on Vegetation'), which established the science of phytochemistry. Saussure also completed pioneering work in the modern fields of ecology and soil science.

Sauvé, Jeanne, née Benoit 1922–
Canadian politician, journalist and broadcaster

Born in Saskatchewan and educated at the universities of Ottawa and Paris, she became National President of the Jeunesse Étudiante Catholique in Montreal (1942–47). She married Maurice Sauvé in 1948. She worked for UNESCO in Paris, and on returning to Canada made her career as a journalist and broadcaster for CBC. In 1972 she became a member of parliament representing Montreal-Ahuntsic and was appointed Secretary of State for Science and Technology. Her successful political career led to her appointment as the first woman Speaker of the House of Commons, and in 1983 she became Governor-General of Canada.

Sava or Sabas, St c.1174–1235/6
Serbian monk, founder of the Serbian Orthodox Church

Born in Rastko Nemanja, the son of Stephen I Nemanja, King of Serbia, he took the name Sava upon entering monastic life on Mount Athos. There, with the help of his father, he founded the Monastery of Hilandar which became a centre for Serbian culture and religious life. Returning to Serbia (c.1208), he became head of the Studenica Monastery and founded a monastery at Žiča. He organized the Serbian Orthodox Church with the aim of countering the influence of the Bogomils and of the Roman Church, and, with the sanction of the Patriarch of Constantinople, he became its first Archbishop in 1219. He made a pilgrimage to the Holy Land and died at Trnovo in north Bulgaria.

Savage, Richard c.1697–1743
English poet
He claimed to be the illegitimate child of Richard Savage, the fourth and last Earl Rivers, and the Countess of Macclesfield, but the story of his noble descent has been discredited. In 1727 he killed a man in a tavern brawl, and narrowly escaped the gallows. He led a dissipated life and the queen's pension (1732) of £50 for a birthday ode was squandered in a week's debauchery. On Queen Caroline's death (1737) Pope tried to help him, but after about a year he went to Bristol, was jailed for debt, and died there. He wrote a comedy, *Love in a Veil* (1718), in the dedication of which he asserted his parentage, and *The Tragedy of Sir Thomas Overbury* (1723), and at least one notable poem, *The Wanderer* (1729). He owes his reputation mainly to Dr Johnson, who wrote a fine short biography of him. 📖 S V Makover, *Richard Savage: a mystery in biography* (1909)

Savarin, (Jean) Anthelme Brillat- See Brillat-Savarin, (Jean) Anthelme

Savart, Félix 1791–1841
French physician and physicist
He was born in Mézières in the Ardennes. During his medical studies at the military hospital at Metz and at the University of Strasbourg, he developed an interest in the physics of sound, presenting several papers on the subject. He succeeded Augustin Jean Fresnel as a member of the Paris Academy (1827), and was appointed Professor of Experimental Physics at the Collège de France in Paris in 1828. He invented 'Savart's wheel' for measuring tonal vibrations, and the 'Savart quartz plate' for studying the polarization of light. With Jean-Baptiste Biot he discovered the law (named after them) defining the intensity of magnetic field produced at a given point near a long straight current-carrying conductor.

Savery, Thomas c.1650–1715
English inventor and military engineer
Born in Shilstone, Devonshire, he patented an invention for rowing vessels by means of paddle-wheels (1696), and in 1698 developed the first practical high-pressure steam engine for pumping water from mines. It was superseded in 1712 by the much improved version designed in partnership with Thomas Newcomen.

Savi, Paolo 1798–1871
Italian naturalist and zoologist
Born in Pisa, he studied physics and natural science there and soon became Professor of Natural History (Zoology from 1840) at Pisa University, and also director of the Pisa Museum. He extended the museum considerably, and became a senator in 1862. His great work, *Ornitologia Italiana*, was published posthumously (1873–76). Savi's Warbler is named after him.

Savigny, Friedrich Karl von 1779–1861
German jurist
Born in Frankfurt am Main of an Alsatian family, he was educated at the universities of Göttingen and Marburg. In 1803 he became a professor of law at Marburg, and

published a treatise on the Roman law of possession that won him European fame. In 1808 he was called to Landshut and in 1810 to Berlin, where he was (1810–42) appointed a member of the commission for revising the code of Prussia. He resigned office in 1848. He rejected the call for a German Civil Code and became the leader of the historical school of jurists, contending that law evolved from the spirit of a people rather than being made for them. His most notable books were his *Roman Law in the Middle Ages* (1815–31), and *System of Roman Law* (1840–49), with its continuation in *Obligations* (1851–53).

Savile, George See Halifax, 1st Marquis of

Savile, Sir Henry 1549–1622
English scholar and courtier
Born in Bradley, near Halifax, and educated at Brasenose College, Oxford, he became a Fellow of Merton College, Oxford, and was later appointed Warden of Merton (1585) and also Provost of Eton (1596). In 1578 he visited the centres of European learning to meet students of astronomy and mathematics. On his return to England he became Latin secretary and tutor in Greek to Queen Elizabeth I, and later he was one of the scholars appointed by King James VI and I to prepare the Authorized Version of the Bible. He translated part of the histories of Tacitus (1591) and the *Cyropaedia* of Xenophon. He also published the first edition of St John Chrysostom (1610–13). He helped Sir Thomas Bodley in the founding of the Bodleian library, and in 1619 he founded the Savilian chairs of mathematics and astronomy at Oxford.

Savile, Sir Jimmy (James Wilson Vincent) 1926–
English broadcaster and charity worker
Born in Leeds, Yorkshire, he became a miner, a ballroom manager with Mecca, then a radio disc-jockey and television presenter, with regular appearances on *Top of the Pops* (1963–). An ebullient figure with an ostentatious lifestyle, he has used his celebrity status to work tirelessly for worthwhile causes, raising over £10 million to construct a National Spinal Injuries Centre at Stoke Mandeville Hospital, acting as a voluntary helper at Leeds Infirmary and Broadmoor Hospital, and running countless fund-raising marathons. On television he has campaigned for car safety and was the host of *Jim'll Fix It* (1975–94), in which he helped to fulfil the special wishes of ordinary people. His books include the autobiographical *As It Happens* and *Love Is An Uphill Thing* (both 1975), and *God'll Fix It* (1978). He was knighted in 1990.

Savimbi, Jonas Malheiro 1934–
Angolan soldier and nationalist
Educated in Angola and at Lausanne University, he moved to Zambia and became a leader of the Popular Union of Angola, being designated Foreign Minister of the Angolan government-in-exile (1962–64). After a period with the Angolan National Liberation Front (FNLA), he broke away to form the National Union for the Total Independence of Angola (UNITA). Unable to agree with the leaders of the People's Movement for the Liberation of Angola (MPLA) and the FNLA, he continued the struggle against the MPLA from bases in the south of Angola, supported by South Africa and the USA. Although he represented democratic and capitalist Angola, these associations made him unpopular in third world politics. However, his negotiations led to a series of meetings designed to end the civil war and remove the Cubans from Angola. Agreement for a ceasefire and democratic elections was finally achieved in Estoril in 1991, but when Savimbi lost the subsequent elections the armed struggle broke out again. A further ceasefire began in 1995 with the confinement of UNITA troops.

Savonarola, Girolamo 1452–98
Italian religious and political reformer

He was born into a noble family in Ferrara, and in 1474 entered the Dominican order at Bologna. After initial failures he was soon acclaimed as a great and inspiring preacher and in 1489 he was called to Florence, where a humanist revival in art and literature was supported by **Lorenzo de' Medici**. Savonarola's preaching pointed to a political revolution as a divinely ordained means of spiritual regeneration. When, after the intervention of **Charles VIII** of France, the Medici were expelled and a republic was established in Florence, Savonarola became its leader. The republic of Florence was to be a Christian commonwealth, of which God was the sole sovereign, and his Gospel the law; many flocked to the public square to fling down their costliest ornaments, which Savonarola's followers made into a huge 'bonfire of vanities'. His claim to the gift of prophecy led to his being cited (1495) to answer a charge of heresy in Rome, and when he failed to appear he was forbidden to preach. He disregarded the order, and was excommunicated in 1497. In the following year the Medici party came back into power. Savonarola was again forbidden to preach. He was tried for false prophecy and was hanged in Rome. His works are mainly sermons, theological treatises, the chief *The Triumph of the Cross*, an apology of orthodox Catholicism, some poems, and a discourse on the government of Florence. ▢ Roberto Ridolfi, *The Life of Girolamo Savonarola* (1959)

Savundra, Emil, *originally* Michael Marion Emil Anecletus Savundranayagam 1923–76
Singalese swindler and fraudster

He was born in Ceylon (Sri Lanka) into a highly respected family. He gave himself the title of 'Doctor', and perpetrated substantial financial swindles in Costa Rica, Goa and Ghana. When he was arrested in Great Britain on charges of forgery in 1954, he had the first of several heart attacks, which may have been more convenient than genuine. He is best known in Great Britain for the failure of his Fire, Auto and Marine Insurance company which left 400,000 British motorists without insurance cover in 1966. In an attempt to defend his actions he made a television appearance on *The Frost Programme* which was later described as 'trial by television'. He was arrested in February 1967 and sentenced to eight years in prison.

Sawchuk, Terry (Terrance Gordon) 1929–70
US ice hockey player

Born in Winnipeg, Canada, he started his career with the Detroit Red Wings in 1950, and later played for the Boston Bruins, Toronto Maple Leafs, Los Angeles Kings, and New York Rangers. He was a renowned goalminder and kept a clean sheet in a record 103 National Hockey League games. He appeared in 971 games (1950–70), a record for a goalminder.

Sax, Adolphe See Sax, Antoine Joseph

Sax, Antoine Joseph, *known as* Adolphe Sax 1814–94
Belgian musician and inventor

He was born in Dinant, the son of a Brussels musical-instrument maker. With his father he invented a valved brass wind-instrument which he called the sax-horn (patented 1845), and also the saxophone, the saxtromba and the sax-tuba. He moved to Paris to promote his inventions, and was an instructor at the Paris Conservatoire, but failed to make his expected fortune despite the encouragement of **Berlioz** and other musicians.

Saxe, Maurice, Comte de, *also called* Marshal de Saxe 1696–1750
Marshal of France

Born in Goslar, the illegitimate son of **Augustus II**, at the age of 12 he ran off to join the army of the Duke of **Marlborough** under Prince **Eugène of Savoy** in Flanders. He fought against the Turks in Hungary, and in 1726, elected Duke of Courland, he maintained himself against the Russians and Poles. In the War of the Polish Succession (1733–38) he opposed his half-brother Augustus III and in 1744, as Marshal of France, he commanded the French army in Flanders. In 1745 he defeated the Duke of **Cumberland** at Fontenoy and retired two years later. His treatise on the art of war, *Mes Rêveries*, was published in 1751. ▢ Jon E M White, *Marshal of France* (1962)

Saxe-Coburg-Gotha, Alfred Ernest Albert, Prince of 1844–1900
British prince

He was born at Windsor Castle, the second son of Queen **Victoria**. He joined the Royal Navy (1858), and became Commander-in-Chief in the Mediterranean (1886–89) and at Devonport (1890–93). He was elected King of Greece (1862), but declined the dignity. He was created Duke of Edinburgh (1866) and in 1874 married the Russian Grand Duchess Marie Alexandrovna (1853–1920), daughter of Tsar **Alexander II** of Russia. In 1893 he succeeded his uncle as reigning Duke of Saxe-Coburg-Gotha.

Saxo Grammaticus, *known as* the Scholar c.1150–c.1220
Danish chronicler

Born on Zealand, he was secretary or clerk to Bishop **Absalon** of Roskilde. He compiled a monumental *Gesta Danorum*, a Latin history of legendary and historical kings of Denmark to 1186 (16 vols, probably written 1185–1216). He is remembered as the first national historian of Denmark.

Saxton, Christopher 1542/44–c.1611
English surveyor and cartographer

Born probably in Sowood, Yorkshire, he is thought to have been educated at Cambridge, and in cartography by John Rudd, vicar of Dewsbury. He was commissioned by Queen **Elizabeth I** to carry out the first survey of all the counties of England and Wales, and worked under the patronage of Thomas Seckford, Master of the Queen's Requests. His atlas (1579) was the first national atlas of any country. He also published a wall map of England and Wales (1583). He is known as 'the father of English cartography'.

Say, Jean Baptiste 1767–1832
French political economist

Born in Lyons, he spent part of his youth in England. On the outbreak of the Revolution he was secretary to the Minister of Finance. From 1794 to 1800 he edited *La Décade*, in which he expounded the views of **Adam Smith**. In 1803 he issued his *Traité d'économie politique* (Eng trans *A treatise on Political Economy*, 1821). He operated a cotton mill from 1807 to 1813, and in 1814 the government sent him to England to study the country's economics. From 1817 he lectured on political economy at the Conservatoire des Arts et Métiers, and in 1831 became professor at the Collège de France. Both as a disciple of Adam Smith and through his own writings, he greatly influenced French economics during the first half of the 19th century.

Say, Thomas 1787–1834
US naturalist and entomologist

Born in Philadelphia, he made expeditions to the Rocky Mountains, Minnesota, Florida, Georgia and Mexico (1818–29), and was the author of *American Entomology* (1824–28). As curator of the American Philosophical Society (1821–27) and professor at Pennsylvania University (1822–28), he went to **Robert Owen's** Utopian settlement at New Harmony, Indiana, in 1824, where he and his wife published his *American Conchology* (1830–34).

Sayce, Archibald Henry 1845–1933
English philologist

Born in Shirehampton near Bristol and educated at Grosvenor College, Bath, and Queen's College, Oxford (where he read classics), he became Professor of Assyriology at Oxford (1891–1919). A member of the Old Testament Revision Company, he wrote on biblical criticism and Assyriology, including an *Assyrian Grammar* (1872), *Principles of Comparative Philology* (1874–75), *The Monuments of the Hittites* (1881), and *The Early History of the Hebrews* (1897).

Sayers, Dorothy L(eigh) 1893–1957
English detective-story writer

Born in Oxford, and educated at the Godolphin School, Salisbury, and Somerville College, Oxford (where she took a first in modern languages), she taught for a year and then worked in an advertising agency until 1931. Beginning with *Whose Body?* (1923) and *Clouds of Witness* (1926), her novels tell the adventures of her hero Lord Peter Wimsey in various accurately observed milieux, such as advertising in *Murder Must Advertise* (1933) or campanology in *The Nine Tailors* (1934). Her other stories included *Strong Poison* (1930), *Gaudy Night* (1935), *Busman's Honeymoon* (1936) and *In the Teeth of the Evidence* (1939). She earned a reputation as a leading Christian apologist with two successful plays, *The Zeal of Thy House* (1937) and *The Devil to Pay* (1939), a series for broadcasting (*The Man Born to be King*, 1943) and a closely reasoned essay (*The Mind of the Maker*, 1941). A translation of **Dante's** *Inferno* appeared in 1949 and of *Purgatorio* in 1955. *Paradiso* was left unfinished at her death, and completed by her biographer Beatrice Reynolds. □ B Reynolds, *Dorothy L. Sayers, Her Life and Soul* (1993)

Sayers, Gale 1943–
US football player

Born in Wichita, Kansas, he was the star running back with the Chicago Bears from 1965 to 1972. The holder of numerous records, he was elected to the sport's Hall of Fame in 1977. He once scored six touchdowns in one game (12 December 1965). After retiring from the sport, he coached and became a computer company executive.

Sayers, James 1912–
British physicist

Born in Ballymena, County Antrim, Northern Ireland, he was a member of the British team associated with the Manhattan Project at Los Alamos in World War II to develop the nuclear bomb. He became Professor of Electron Physics at Birmingham University (1946) and in 1949 received a government award for his work on the cavity magnetron valve, which was of great importance in the development of radar.

Sayers, Peig 1873–1958
Irish Gaelic storyteller

She was born in Dunquin, County Kerry, among purely Irish-speaking neighbours, and lived most of her life on the Great Blasket Island. The disappearance of the Irish language from most of Ireland made her powers of recollection and her hold on traditional narratives deeply respected by scholars. Her prose, as recorded in *Peig* (edited by Máire Ní Chinnéide, 1936) and *Machtnamh Sean-Mná* (1939, translated as *An Old Woman's Reflections*, 1962), is straightforward and clear, with decided authority.

Sayers, Tom 1826–65
English boxer

Born in Pimlico, London, he became a bricklayer before taking up boxing in 1849. He became English heavyweight champion in 1857 despite weighing only 11 stone, which would be normal for a middleweight. Throughout his career he lost only one fight, earning the nickname 'the Napoleon of the Prize Ring'. His last and most famous contest was with the US champion John C Heenan for the first world championship title. The fight lasted 2 hours and 6 minutes, and was declared a draw after 42 rounds.

Sayles, John Thomas 1950–
US screenwriter, novelist, actor and filmmaker

Born in Schenectady, New York, he worked at a number of jobs after his graduation from Williams College, before winning **O Henry** Memorial Awards for the short stories *I-80 Nebraska*, *M.490–M.205* (1975) and *Breed* (1977). His novels *Pride Of The Bimbos* (1975) and *Union Dues* (1979) earned extensive praise for their wit, irony and his ear for dialect. As a screenwriter he brought a knowing humour to such projects as *Piranha* (1978) and *The Howling* (1980). He made his directorial debut with *The Return Of The Secaucus Seven* (1979), an examination of the sense of disillusionment experienced at a reunion of 1960s college radicals, which received an Academy Award nomination for Best Original Screenplay. His most accomplished films include *Lianna* (1982), *Matewan* (1987), *City Of Hope* (1991) and *Passion Fish* (1992), for which he received a further Academy Award nomination. An occasional playwright and actor, he returned to novel writing with *Los Gusanos* (1991), an epic account of Cuban exiles in Miami. In 1996 he wrote and directed the film *Lone Star*.

Scales, Prunella, *originally* Prunella Margaret Rumney Illingworth 1932–
English actress

Born in Sutton Abinger, Surrey, she appeared on Broadway in *The Matchmaker* (1955) and with the company at the Shakespeare Memorial Theatre (1956) before West End successes such as *Hay Fever* (1968) and *Breezeblock Park* (1977). On television, she starred as Kate Starling in *Marriage Lines* (1963–66), Sybil Fawlty in *Fawlty Towers* (1975–79), Miss Elizabeth Mapp in *Mapp & Lucia* (1985–86), Sarah in *After Henry* (1988–92), Elizabeth II in *A Question of Attribution* (1991), Marjorie Richardson in *The Rector's Wife* (1994) and Mrs Tilston in *Searching* (1995). Her films include *A Chorus of Disapproval* (1989), *An Awfully Big Adventure* (1995) and *Stiff Upper Lips* (1997). She is married to the actor **Timothy West**.

Scaliger, Joseph Justus 1540–1609
French scholar

He was born in Agen, the son of **Julius Caesar Scaliger**. After studying at Bordeaux with his father, and in Paris, he acquired a surpassing mastery of the classics and eventually boasted a command of 13 languages, ancient and modern. While in Paris he became a Calvinist (1562) and later visited Italy, England and Scotland, only the last of which seems to have appealed to him, especially through the beauty of its ballads. In 1570 he settled at Valence and for two years studied under the jurist Cujacius. From 1572 to 1574 he was professor at Calvin's College at Geneva. He then spent 20 years in France and there produced works which placed him at the head of European scholars. Among them are his editions of **Gaius Catullus**, **Albius Tibullus**, **Sextus Propertius** and **Eusebius of Caesarea**. By his edition of Manilius and his *Opus De Emendatione Temporum* (1583) he founded modern chronology. From 1593 he held a chair at Leyden and to his inspiration Holland owes her long line of scholars.

His last years were embittered by controversy, especially with the Jesuits, who charged him with atheism and profligacy.

Scaliger, Julius Caesar, *originally probably* Benedetto Bordone 1484–1558
French scholar and physicist

Born in Italy, the son of a sign-painter, he claimed descent from the princely della Scala family of Verona. He also claimed that he was brought up a soldier under his kinsman the Emperor Maximilian I, gaining distinction in the French armies attempting the conquest of Italy. He changed his name to Scaliger, and graduated in medicine at Padua. He became a French citizen in 1528 and settled at Agen, where he produced learned works on Latin grammar and on Theophrastus, Aristotle and Hippocrates. His powers of invective, as in his attack on Erasmus, were considerable.

Scarfe, Gerald 1936–
English cartoonist, caricaturist and animator

Born in London, his first cartoon, drawn as a schoolboy, was published in the comic *Eagle* (1952). He studied art at St Martin's School, London, and freelanced cartoons for the *Daily Sketch* and *Punch*. He then worked for the satirical *Private Eye*, causing controversy with his *Annual* cover of Harold Macmillan. The *Sunday Times* refused to publish his commissioned caricature of Winston Churchill, but his work met with more approval in the US magazines *Life* and *Esquire*. He designed the animated sequences for the film, *Pink Floyd: The Wall* (1982). *Scarfeface* (1993) is a recent publication. 📖 *Scarfe* (1986)

Scargill, Arthur 1938–
English trade union leader

Born in Leeds and educated in Yorkshire, he entered the mining industry at the age of 18 and was soon involved in politics, joining the Young Communist League in 1955, the Co-operative Party in 1963, and the Labour Party in 1966. He was also active in the National Union of Mineworkers (NUM), becoming a Yorkshire branch committee member in 1960 and area president in 1973. He steadily established himself as a powerful speaker and in 1982 became national president. He constantly warned the union of the threat of massive pit closures, and in 1984 led them into a national strike. Its collapse ten months later raised doubts about his leadership tactics, but his predictions of pit closures and job losses proved to be correct. In 1992 he launched a resistance campaign against a new wave of proposed pit closures, and in January 1996 he broke away from the Labour party to form his own Socialist Labour Party. 📖 Michael Crick, *Scargill and the Miners* (1985)

Scarlatti, Alessandro 1659–1725
Italian composer

Born in Palermo, Sicily, he began his musical career in Rome, where in 1679 he produced his first opera, *Gli equivocinel Sembiante*. This gained him the patronage of Queen Kristina of Sweden, whose maestro di cappella he became. A few years later he went to Naples, where he was musical director at the court (1693–1703) and conducted at the Conservatorio. He was the founder of the Neapolitan school of opera, writing nearly 120 works. About 70 of these survive, of which the best known is perhaps *Il Tigrane* (1715). He also wrote 200 masses, 10 oratorios, 500 cantatas, and many motets and madrigals.

Scarlatti, (Giuseppe) Domenico 1685–1757
Italian composer

Born in Naples, the son of Alessandro Scarlatti, he was the founder of the modern piano technique. From 1711 in Rome he was maestro di cappella to the Queen of Poland, for whom he composed several operas, and he also served in Lisbon from 1720 and Madrid from 1729. As choir-master of St Peter's, Rome (1714–19), he wrote much church music. A skilled performer on the harpsichord, he is said to have met Handel in a competition on the instrument; the result was a tie although Handel was judged the better organist. It is as a writer of harpsichord sonatas that Scarlatti is best remembered; he wrote over 550, which had an important effect on the development of the form.

Scarlett, Sir James Yorke 1799–1871
English soldier

The second son of James Scarlett, Baron Abinger (1769–1844), he commanded the 5th Dragoon Guards (1840–53), and in October 1854 led the heavy cavalry in the charge at Balaclava after the disastrous Charge of the Light Brigade (see also Raglan). He subsequently commanded the cavalry in the Crimea, and from 1865 to 1870 commanded at Aldershot.

Scarman, Leslie George Scarman, Baron 1911–
English jurist and law reformer

Born in London and educated at Radley and Brasenose College, Oxford, he was called to the Bar in 1936. He became a High Court judge in 1961 and was the first chairman of the Law Commission (1965) for the reform of English law. He left the Law Commission on appointment to the Court of Appeal (1973) and entered the House of Lords as a Lord-of-Appeal-in-Ordinary (1977–86). His investigation of the cause of the Brixton and Notting Hill riots (1981) resulted in a much discussed report. He was a strong supporter of human rights, and with Lord Devlin pressed for a reassessment of the case of the Guildford Four. His books include *Pattern of Law Reform* (1967) and *English Law: The New Dimension* (1974). He was made a life peer in 1977.

Scarron, Paul 1610–60
French writer

Born in Paris, he became an abbé, and in about 1634 paid an extended visit to Italy. In 1638 he began to suffer from an illness which ultimately left him paralysed. He obtained a prebend in Mans (1643), but giving up all hope of remedy, returned to Paris in 1646 to write for a living. His metrical comedy, *Jodelet, ou le maître valet* (1645, 'Jodelet; or, the Master-Butler'), was a great success, and he followed it with a number of similar works, including the popular *L'Héritier ridicule* (1653, 'The Ridiculous Heir'). An intensely bitter satire directed at Cardinal Mazarin, which he wrote for the Fronde, probably lost him his pensions. The burlesque predominates in most of his writing, but it is as the creator of the realistic novel that he is remembered. *Le Roman comique* (1651–57, Eng trans *The Comical Romance*, 1665) was a reaction against the euphuistic and interminable novels of Madeleine de Scudéry and Honoré d'Urfé, and the work of Alain Lesage, Daniel Defoe, Henry Fielding and Tobias Smollett owes much to him. In 1652 he married Françoise d'Aubigné (later Madame de Maintenon), who brought a hitherto unknown decorum into his household and writings. 📖 E Magne, *Scarron et son milieu* (1923)

Scarry, Richard McClure 1919–94
US illustrator and children's writer

Born in Boston, he was educated at Boston Museum School of Fine Arts, and served in the US army in the Mediterranean and North Africa. His popular children's books, with illustrations that are whimsical, humorous and detailed, teach young children about aspects of daily life. They include *What Do People Do All Day?* (1968) and *Hop Aboard, Here We Go!* (1972).

Scève, Maurice 1510–64
French Renaissance poet

Born in Lyons, he was a leader of the *école lyonnaise*, which paved the way for the Pléiade, a group of poets working with **Pierre de Ronsard**. His most important poem is *Délie, objet de plus haute vertu* (1544, 'Delia, Object of the Highest Virtue'), on the subject of love. Other works include *La Saulsaye* (1547), and a didactic poem on the history of humankind, *Microcosme* (1563). ◫ V C Saulnier, *Maurice Scève* (1948)

Schacht, Hjalmar Horace Greely 1877–1970
German financier

Born of Danish descent in Tinglev, North Schleswig, he was brought up in New York City where his father was a merchant. In 1923 he became president of the Reichsbank, and founded a new currency which ended the inflation of the mark. He resigned in 1929, was called back by the Nazis in 1933, and the following year, as Minister of Economics, succeeded in restoring the German trade balance. He resigned his post in 1937, and in 1939 was dismissed from his office as president of the Reichsbank after disagreeing with **Hitler** over expenditure on rearmament. He was charged with high treason and interned by the Nazis; in 1945 he was acquitted by the Allies at Nuremberg of crimes against humanity, and was finally cleared by the German de-Nazification courts in 1948. In 1952 he advised Dr **Mohammed Mossadeq** on Persia's economic problems, and in 1953 set up his own bank in Düsseldorf.

Schadow, Friedrich Wilhelm von 1788–1862
German artist

Born in Berlin, he was the second of three sons of **Johann Gottfried Schadow**. A painter of the Overbeck school, he joined the Nazarenes in Rome in 1811 and from 1819 was professor at Berlin. He was head of the Düsseldorf Academy (1826–59) and he changed his name to Schadow-Godenhaus.

Schadow, Johann Gottfried 1764–1850
Prussian sculptor

Born in Berlin, he studied in Rome, becoming court sculptor in 1788 and director of the Academy of Arts in Berlin from 1816. He executed many public monuments in a neoclassical style touched with Baroque liveliness, including the *Quadriga of Victory* for the Brandenburg Gate (1793), *Frederick the Great* (Stettin), and *Luther* (Wittenberg).

Schadow, Rudolf 1786–1822
Prussian sculptor

He was born in Berlin, the son of **Johann Gottfried Schadow**, and executed *Spinning Girl* and the *Daughters of Leucippos* at Chatsworth, England.

Schaefer, Vincent Joseph 1906–93
US physicist

Born in Schenectady, New York, he graduated from the Davey Institute of Tree Surgery in 1928, before working in the research laboratories of the General Electric Company, where he became assistant to **Irving Langmuir**. In World War II they worked together on the problem of icing on aeroplane wings, which led to the discovery that dry ice (solid CO_2) introduced into a cold box containing water vapour resulted in a miniature snowstorm. In 1946 he demonstrated for the first time the possibility of artificially inducing rainfall by seeding clouds with dry ice, and his colleague **Bernard Vonnegut** subsequently showed that the same effect could be more conveniently produced by using silver iodide crystals. Schaefer became director of research at the Munitalp Foundation in 1954, and Professor of Physics at the State University of New York, Albany, in 1959. He was a founder of the Atmospherics Research Center (director 1966–76), and co-wrote some 300 scientific papers and books.

Schäfer, Sir Edward Sharpey- See Sharpey-Shäfer, Sir Edward

Schaff, Philip 1819–93
US Presbyterian theologian

Born in Coire, Switzerland, he was *privat-dozent* in Berlin, when in 1844 he was appointed to a chair at the German Reformed seminary at Mercersburg, Pennsylvania. In 1870 he became professor at the Union Seminary, New York. A founder of the American branch of the Evangelical Alliance, he was president of the American Old Testament Revision Committee. Among his works are a *History of the Christian Church* (1883–93) and *The Creeds of Christendom* (1877).

Schall, Johann Adam von 1591–1669
German Jesuit missionary and astronomer

Born in Cologne, he studied the astronomical system of Galileo in Rome. He was sent out to China as a missionary in 1622, and at Peking (Beijing) was entrusted with the reformation of the Chinese calendar and the direction of the mathematical school. The Jesuits obtained permission from the Manchu emperor to build churches (1644), and in 14 years they are said to have made 100,000 converts. Schall, however, was accused of plotting against the next emperor (1664) and died in captivity. A large manuscript collection of his Chinese writings is preserved in the Vatican. He wrote a Latin history of the China Mission (1655).

Schally, Andrew Victor 1926–
US biochemist and Nobel Prize winner

Born in Wilno, Poland (now Vilnius, Lithuania), he fled from Poland in 1939 and studied at the National Institute for Medical Research in London and McGill University in Montreal. He later worked at the Baylor Medical School (1957–62) and Tulane University (from 1962). While studying 'releasing factors' from the brain hypothalamus which stimulate the release of hormones from the pituitary gland, Schally discovered an assay system for this *in vitro* (1955). He also worked on the isolation of corticotrophin-releasing hormone (CRH), which was eventually achieved by W Vale in 1981. Schally shared the 1977 Nobel Prize for physiology or medicine with **Roger Guillemin** and **Rosalyn Yalow**. He also studied the distribution and function of adrenocortical trophic hormone (ACTH), somatostatin and other factors.

Schamyl See Shamil

Schapiro, Meyer 1904–96
US art historian and critic

Born in Siauliai, Lithuania, he emigrated to New York City with his family in 1907 and entered Columbia College in 1920, receiving a PhD in art history in 1929. He taught at Columbia University, New York University, and the New School for Social Research, where he was known for his fiery lectures and for his enthusiasm for art and knowledge in general. Believing that art is inextricably linked to culture, he studied early Christian, medieval, and contemporary art and wrote books including *Modern Art: 19th and 20th Centuries* (2 vols, 1978–79) as well as several essays ('The Nature of Abstract Art', 1937, and 'Leonardo and Freud', 1956).

Scharnhorst, Gerhard Johann David von 1755–1813
German soldier and military reformer

The son of a Hanoverian farmer, he fought in Flanders against the French (1793–95) and directed the training-school for Prussian officers (1801). From 1807 he worked with **August von Gneisenau** to reform the Prussian army after its defeat by **Napoleon I**, introducing the short-service system and restoring morale, so making possible the defeat of Napoleon at Leipzig (1813). He also served as Chief of Staff to **Gebbard von Blücher** and was fatally wounded fighting the French at Lützen.

Scharrer, Berta, née Vogel 1906–95
US endocrinologist

Born and educated in Munich, she married and worked with her fellow student Ernst Scharrer in 1934 until his death in 1965. In 1940 they were able to move to the Western Reserve University in the USA. In 1965, after Ernst's death, she was appointed Professor of Anatomy at the Albert Einstein School of Medicine in New York. Their extensive work on the comparative anatomy and physiology of neurosecretion, the ability of some specialized nerve cells to behave like gland cells of the endocrine system, led to its establishment as an important biological concept. Her work in the 1970s was important in extending and re-fashioning the concept. She was elected a member of the National Academy of Sciences in 1978.

Scharwenka, Xaver 1850–1924
Polish pianist and composer

Born in Samter, near Posen, he started a music school in Berlin (1881), and went to New York (1891), where he directed the Scharwenka Music School until 1898. He composed symphonies, piano concertos and Polish dances.

Schaudinn, Fritz Richard 1871–1906
German zoologist and microbiologist

Born in Röseningken, East Prussia, he studied philology at the University of Berlin, and turned to zoology, and became director of the department of protozoological research at the Institute for Tropical Diseases in Hamburg (1904). Schaudinn demonstrated the nature of tropical dysentery and discovered its cause. With the dermatologist Erich Hoffmann, he discovered the spirochaete which causes syphilis (1905), *Spirochaeta pallida*, now known as *Treponema pallidum*. In other investigations, Schaudinn demonstrated that human hookworm infection is contracted through the skin of the feet. He also researched malaria and made important contributions to zoology.

Schaufuss, Peter 1949–
Danish dancer and director

Born in Copenhagen, he came from a dancing family (his mother and father were both principals with the Royal Danish Ballet). He began his training in 1956 and made his professional debut the same year. In 1964 he moved to Canada to become a soloist with the National Ballet of Canada, with which he danced leading roles in *Don Quixote* and *The Nutcracker*. He returned to Denmark two years later and contributed to the first workshop performance at the Royal Danish Ballet (1969). Independent of spirit, he spent a short time moving from company to company, becoming a principal with London Festival Ballet in 1970 and spending several seasons (1974–77) with New York City Ballet. In 1984 he was appointed artistic director of London Festival Ballet (renamed English National Ballet in 1989), where he has fostered a strong commitment to contemporary ballet as well as the classics. He became artistic director of the Royal Danish Ballet in 1994 but resigned the following year.

Schaukal, Richard 1874–1942
Austrian Symbolist poet

Born in Brünn, he entered the Austrian civil service. Like **Hugo von Hofmannsthal**, he turned away from the decadence of the declining Austrian Empire and wrote *Gedichte* (1893, 'Poems'), *Tage und Träume* (1899, 'Days and Dreams'), *Sehnsucht* (1900, 'Yearning'), and the posthumous collection *Spätlese* (1943, 'Late Harvest').

Schawlow, Arthur Leonard 1921–
US physicist and Nobel Prize winner

Born in Mount Vernon, New York, he studied at Toronto and Columbia (1949–51), where he worked with **Charles Townes**. He moved to Bell Telephone Laboratories (1951–61) and was appointed Professor of Physics at Stanford University (1960–91, now emeritus). Townes and Schawlow collaborated to extend the maser principle to light, thereby establishing the feasibility of the laser, although it was **Theodore Maiman** who constructed the first working ruby laser in 1961. From the early 1970s Schawlow worked on the development of laser spectroscopy. Working with German-born physicist Theodor Hänsch, he was able to make precise measurements of the energy levels the electron can occupy in the hydrogen atom, allowing the value of the **Rydberg** constant, a basic physical quantity, to be determined with unprecedented accuracy. For this work Schawlow shared the 1981 Nobel Prize for physics with **Nicolaas Bloembergen** and **Kai Siegbahn**. In 1991 he won a National Medal of Science.

Schechter, Solomon 1847–1915
Hebrew scholar

He was born in Focsani, Romania. His 1896 excavations in Cairo, Egypt, unearthed 50,000 important manuscripts, including some lost chapters of the Hebrew text of Ecclesiasticus (published as *The Wisdom of Ben Sira*, 1899). He was Professor of Hebrew at the University of London, then served as president (1902–15) of the Jewish Theological Seminary in New York City, which became the foremost centre of Jewish studies in the USA. The leader of US Conservative Judaism, he founded the United Synagogue of America (1913).

Scheel, Walter 1919–
West German statesman

Born and educated in Solingen, he served in the Luftwaffe in World War II. After the war he went into business, joined the Free Democratic Party (FDP), and was elected to the city council of Solingen in 1948, and to the Bundestag in 1953. In 1958 he became vice-chairman of the Free Democrats and guided their policies closer to the SPD, thereby preparing the ground for the coalition of 1969. In 1970 he negotiated treaties with the USSR and Poland, regarded as major advances in east–west relations. From 1969 to 1674 he was Vice-Chancellor and Foreign Minister, and became President (for five years) of the Federal Republic of Germany in 1974 on the resignation of **Gustav Heinemann**.

Scheele, Carl Wilhelm 1742–86
Swedish chemist

He was born in Stralsund (now in Germany) and was apprenticed to an apothecary. In 1775, the year that he was elected to the Stockholm Royal Academy of Sciences, he moved to Köping, where he became the town pharmacist. In the 1760s he began to investigate air and fire, and soon came to doubt the received view that substances contain a vital essence which they lose when they burn. He passed on information about his experiments to **Antoine Lavoisier**, who subsequently discovered the true nature of combustion and named the new flammable gas 'oxigine'. Scheele subsequently discovered a great many other substances, including hydrofluoric acid, chlorine, copper arsenide (known as 'Scheele's green'), hydrogen sulphide, and many important organic acids. In 1781 he distinguished between two very similar minerals, plumbago (graphite) and molybdena, discovering the metal molybdenum in the process. His investigations of plant and animal material were fundamental to the development of organic chemistry. 📖 Georg Urdang, *Pictorial Life History of the Apothecary Chemist Carl Wilhelm Scheele* (2nd edn, 1958)

Scheemakers, Pieter 1691–1781
Flemish sculptor

He was born in Antwerp, and lived for much of his life in London (1735–69), where he was a rival to Rysbrack and executed several monuments and portrait busts, including those of **Shakespeare** (1740), the eminent physician Richard Mead (c.1754) and **John Dryden** (1731) in Westminster Abbey. He was the teacher of **Joseph Nollekens**. His Baroque treatment of the monument to Shakespeare established his reputation. He had a brother Henry, also a sculptor, who died in 1748.

Scheer, Reinhard 1863–1928
German naval commander

Born in Hesse-Nassau, he went to sea as a naval cadet in torpedo craft. As vice-admiral he commanded the 2nd Battle Squadron of the German High Seas fleet at the outset of World War I. He succeeded as Commander-in-Chief in 1916 and was in command at the indecisive Battle of Jutland (1916).

Scheffel, Joseph Viktor von 1826–86
German poet and novelist

Born in Karlsruhe, he studied law at Heidelberg, Munich and Berlin, and in 1852 went to Italy to write. His major book is *Der Trompeter von Säckingen* (1854, 'The Säckingen Trumpeter'), a romantic and humorous tale in verse. Other well-known books are the historical novel *Ekkehard* (1855), and the Lieder and student songs of *Gaudeamus* (1868). 📖 J Proelss, *Scheffels Leben und Dichten* (1887)

Scheffer, Ary 1795–1858
Dutch painter

Born in Dordrecht, of German parentage, he studied mainly in France under **Pierre Guérin**, and became known for his subject pictures and portraits in the romantic style eg *Francesca da Rimini* (1835, Wallace Collection, London). **Pierre Puvis de Chavannes** was his pupil.

Scheidemann, Philipp 1865–1939
German political leader

A leading member of the Social Democratic Party (SPD), he was Minister of Finance and Colonies in the provisional government of 1918, and first Chancellor of the German Republic in 1919. He resigned rather than sign the Treaty of Versailles.

Scheler, Max 1874–1928
German philosopher and social theorist

Born in Munich, he taught at the universities of Jena (1900–06), Munich (1907–10), Cologne (1919–27) and Frankfurt am Main (1928). He developed a distinctive version of **Edmund Husserl's** phenomenology, which emphasized the importance of emotions as well as reason. This is set out in two major works in ethics, *Der Formalismus in der Ethik und die materiale Wertethik* (1913, Eng trans *Formalism in Ethics and Non-Formal Ethics of Values*, 1973) and *Die Sinngesetze des emotionalen Lebens: Wesen und Formen der Sympathie* (1923, Eng trans *The Nature of Sympathy*, 1954). He also wrote influential books on the sociology of knowledge. Later books include *Die Stellung des Menschen im Kosmos* (1928, Eng trans *Man's Place in Nature*, 1961).

Schelling, Friedrich Wilhelm Joseph von 1775–1854
German philosopher

Born in Leonberg, Württemberg, he studied at Tübingen and Leipzig, and taught at Jena (1798–1803, as **Johann Fichte's** successor), Würzburg (1803–08), Munich (until 1820, as secretary of the Royal Academy of Arts), Erlangen (1820–27), Munich again (1827–40), and Berlin (1841–46). His early work, influenced by **Kant** and Fichte, culminated in the *Ideen zur einer Philosophie der Natur* (1797, Eng trans *Idealism and Philosophy of Nature*, 1978), and the *System des transzendentalen Idealismus* (1800, 'System of Transcendental Idealism'), which examined the relation of the self to the objective world and argued that consciousness itself is the only immediate object of knowledge and that only in art can the mind become fully aware of itself. He thus became an important influence on romanticism. His later works include *Philosophische Untersuchungen über das Wesen der menschlichen Freiheit* (1809, *Of Human Freedom*, 1936) and *Die Weltalter* (1811, *The Ages of the World*, 1942).

Schepisi, Fred 1939–
Australian film director

Born in Melbourne, he intended to join the Catholic Church and spent 18 months in a monastery. As a teenager he joined an advertising agency and, by 1966, had bought the company and was making documentaries and commercials. Acquiring a comprehensive knowledge of filmmaking technique, he made a short fictional film *The Party* (1970) and one segment of the multi-part *Libido* (1972). His first major feature, *The Devil's Playground* (1976), reflecting his early experiences with Catholicism, won the Australian Film Institute Award for Best Film, and established him as one of Australia's most promising directors. After *The Chant of Jimmie Blacksmith* (1978), a true story of racism, he moved to the USA where his interest in myth and superstition was seen in *Barbarosa* (1982) and *The Iceman* (1984). He enjoyed an international success with the comedy *Roxanne* (1987), while *Plenty* (1985) and *A Cry in the Dark* (1988) reveal his continuing concern with issues of class and social injustice. Recent, less incisive, films include *The Russia House* (1990), *Mr Baseball* (1992) and *Fierce Creatures* (1996).

Scheutz, Edvard Georg Raphael 1821–81
Swedish engineer

Born in Stockholm, the son of **Pehr Georg Scheutz**, he was educated at the Royal Technological Institute, Stockholm. In 1843 he created the world's first complete difference engine (on which work was begun by his father), and built a second version in 1853. The device mechanized the production of numerical tables, but the limited demand for such machines meant that it could not be marketed successfully

Scheutz, Pehr Georg 1785–1873
Swedish lawyer, publisher, and inventor

Born in Jönköping, he was educated in law at Lund. In the 1830s he read about **Charles Babbage's** difference engine and then designed his own calculating machine, later completed by his son, **Edvard Scheutz**.

Schiaparelli, Elsa 1890–1973
French fashion designer

She was born in Rome, the daughter of a professor of oriental languages. She studied philosophy and lived in the USA for a time, working as a film scriptwriter. In 1920 she and her daughter moved to Paris, where she designed and wore a black sweater knitted with a white bow that gave a *trompe l'œil* effect, which brought her orders from an American store and enabled her to start a business in 1929. Her designs were inventive and sensational, and she was noted for her use of colour, including 'shocking pink', and her original use of traditional fabrics. She featured zippers and buttons, and made outrageous hats. She opened a salon in New York in 1949, and retired in 1954.

Schiaparelli, Giovanni Virginio 1835–1910
Italian astronomer

Born in Savigliano, Piedmont, he graduated at Turin in 1854 and later worked under **Wilhelm Struve** at Pulkova before becoming head of the Brera Observatory, Milan, from 1860. He worked on the relationship between meteors and comets and achieved the first identification of a meteoroid stream with a specific comet, the pair being the Perseids and comet Swift–Tuttle (1862 III). In 1877 Schiaparelli began observations of Mars as a basis for producing a detailed map. He detected linear markings on the surface, which he termed *canali* (ie channels), and noticed that they changed as a function of the Martian season, sometimes splitting into two and sometimes disappearing altogether. In 1882–89 he concluded from observations that Mercury orbited the Sun in such a way that one of its hemispheres always pointed towards the Sun, and he later established the same phenomenon in relation to Venus. ⌑ Francesco Zagar, *Giovanni Schiaparelli nel cinquanteenario della morte* (1960)

Schickard, Wilhelm 1592–1635
German inventor

Born in Herrenberg, and educated at the University of Tübingen, he was a pioneer in the construction of calculating machines. His 'calculating clock' was designed and built in about 1623, but lay forgotten until the discovery of his papers allowed its reconstruction in 1960.

Schickele, René 1883–1940
German Alsatian writer

He was born in Oberehnheim, the son of a German father and a French mother. A journalist by profession, he also wrote poems, plays and novels, including the poetry collections *Weiss und Rot* (1911, 'White and Red') and *Die Leibewache* (1914, 'The Bodyguard'), and the trilogy of Realist novels *Das Erbe am Rhein* (1925–31, 'The Inheritance on the Rhine'). He was a pacifist, and argued in his writings for cultural unity in Europe.

Schiele, Egon 1890–1918
Austrian painter

Born in Tulln, he studied at the Vienna Academy of Art from 1906 to 1909. Much influenced by **Gustav Klimt**, he joined the Wiener Werkstätte, a craft studio which promoted the fashionable Art Nouveau style. He developed a personal form of Expressionism in which figures, often naked and emaciated and drawn with hard outlines, fill the canvas with awkward anguished gestures. In 1912 he was arrested and some of his work was destroyed by the police. He also painted intense and psychologically disturbing portraits.

Schillebeeckx, Edward Cornelis Florentius Alfons 1914–
Belgian Dominican theologian

He was born in Antwerp, and was Professor of Dogmatics and the History of Theology at Nijmegen in the Netherlands from 1958 to 1983. His publications have ranged widely across the whole field of theology, from sacraments (*Christ the Sacrament*, 1963) to the presentation of the gospel in contemporary society (*Jesus in our Western Culture*, 1987). Like **Hans Küng**, he has attracted Vatican investigations for questioning received interpretations of doctrine and Church order, as in *The Church with a Human Face* (1985, replacing *Ministry*, 1981); and *Jesus* (1979), *Christ* (1980), and *Church* (1990). He has also published sermons (*God Among Us*, 1983, and *For the Sake of the Gospel*, 1989), and autobiographical interviews, *God is New Each Moment* (1983).

Schiller, (Johann Christoph) Friedrich (von) 1759–1805
German dramatist, poet and historian

He was born in Marbach on the Neckar. His father was an army surgeon in the service of the Duke of Württemberg. He was educated in Ludwigsburg, and was intended for the Church, but at the age of 13 was obliged to attend the duke's military academy. He studied law instead of theology, but finally qualified as a surgeon (1780) and was posted to a regiment in Stuttgart. Although conforming outwardly to army life he preferred reading and eventually writing *Sturm und Drang* ('Storm and stress') verse

and plays. His first play, the apparently anarchical and revolutionary *Die Räuber* (1781, Eng trans *The Robbers*, 1792), published at his own expense, was an instant success when it reached the stage at Mannheim (1782). Schiller absconded from his regiment to attend the performance and was arrested. In hiding at Bauerbach, he finished the plays, *Fiesko* (1783, Eng trans *Fiesco; or, The Genoese Conspiracy*, 1796) and *Kabale und Liebe* (1783, Eng trans *Cabal and Love*, 1795). For a few months he was dramatist to the Mannheim theatre, and in 1784 he began a theatrical journal, *Die rheinische Thalia*, in which were first printed most of his play *Don Carlos*, many of his best poems, and the stories *Verbrecher aus verlorener Ehre* (1786, Eng trans *The Dishonoured Irreclaimable*, 1826) and *Der Geisterseher* (1787–88, Eng trans *The Ghost-Seer, or Apparitionist*, 1795). In 1785 he was invited to Leipzig, and in Dresden, where **Karl Theodor Körner** was living, he found rest from emotional excitement and financial worries. Here he finished *Don Carlos* (1787), which was written in blank verse, not prose, and was his first mature play. Among the results of his discussions with Körner and his circle are the poems *An die Freude* (c.1788, 'Ode to Joy'), later set to music by **Beethoven** in the last movement of his choral symphony, and *Die Künstler* (1858, 'The Artists'). After two years in Dresden he went to Weimar, where he studied **Kant**, met his future wife, Charlotte von Lengefeld, and began his history of the revolt of Netherlands. In 1788 he was appointed honorary Professor of History at Jena, and married, but his health broke down from overwork. He had been writing a history of the Thirty Years War, the letters on aesthetic education (1795) and the famous *Über naive und sentimentalische Dichtung* (1795–96, Eng trans *On Simple and Sentimental Poetry*, 1884), in which he distinguishes ancient from modern poetry by their different approaches to nature. His short-lived literary magazine, *Die Horen* (1795–97), was followed by the celebrated *Xenien* (1797, 'Epigrams'); these were a collection of satirical epigrams against philistinism and mediocrity in the arts, in which his newly-found friendship with **Goethe** found mutual expression. This inspired the great ballads (1797–98), *Der Taucher* ('The Diver'), *Der Ring des Polykrates* ('The Ring of Polykrates'), *Die Kraniche des Ibykus* ('The Cranes of Ibycus'), the famous *Lied von der Glocke* (completed in 1799, 'Song of the Bell') and, under the influence of **Shakespeare**, the dramatic trilogy *Wallenstein* (1796–99), comprising *Wallensteins Lager, Die Piccolomini* and *Wallensteins Tod*, which is considered the greatest historical drama in the German language. This was followed by *Maria Stuart* (1800, translated by **Stephen Spender**, 1957), a psychological study of the two queens, **Elizabeth I** and **Mary, Queen of Scots**, in which Mary by her death gains a moral victory. He again alters history in *Die Jungfrau von Orleans* (1801, Eng trans *The Maid of Orleans*, 1835), in which **Joan of Arc** dies on the battlefield and is resurrected. *Die Braut von Messina* (1803, Eng trans *The Bride of Messina*, 1837) portrays the relentless feud between two hostile brothers; and the half-legend of *Wilhelm Tell* (1804, Eng trans *William Tell*, 1825) is made by Schiller the basis of a dramatic manifesto for political freedom. ⌑ W Witte, *J C F Schiller* (1949)

Schiller, Karl 1911–94
German economist and politician

A distinguished academic, he was also a member of the Social Democratic Party and from 1949 he became increasingly involved in municipal and national politics. In 1966 he became Economics Minister in the Social Democrat–Christian Democrat coalition, retained the post in the Social Democrat–Free Democrat coalition of 1969–72 and also served as Finance Minister (1971–72) before resigning from the government. He is credited with Germany's economic recovery from the recession of

1966 and with introducing a Keynesian style of economic management in Germany.

Schimper, Andreas Franz Wilhelm 1856–1901
German botanist

The son of Wilhelm Philipp Schimper, he was born in Strasbourg, and was educated there before working first at the botanic garden in Lyons, and then at the University of Würzburg. He visited Florida and the West Indies, where he became interested in plant geography. He also studied epiphytic and carnivorous plants. In 1882 he went to work with Eduard Strasburger in Bonn. He continued to travel widely, visiting South America, Asia and Africa to study the vegetation there. As professor at Basle University (1898–1901), he was noted as a plant geographer, and divided the continents into floral regions. He also proved in 1880 that starch is a source of stored energy for plants. He published *Pflanzengeographie auf physiologischer Grundlage* ('Plant Geography on Physiological Principles') in 1898.

Schimper, Karl Friedrich 1803–67
German naturalist and poet

Born in Mannheim, he studied theology at Heidelberg University, collected plants and studied medicine in the south of France, and taught at Munich University. He is remembered as a pioneer of modern plant morphology. He was notable for his work on phyllotaxis, and in geology for his theory of prehistoric alternating hot and cold periods. Many of his scientific ideas were published as poems; several hundred are known. He experimented with types of mosses, and discussed the arrangement of leaves on plant stems according to geometrical principles. He contributed to F W L Succow's *Flora Mannheimensis*, and to F C L Spenner's *Flora Friburgensis*, and probably originated the modern concepts of ice ages and climatic cycles. He was a cousin of Wilhelm Schimper.

Schimper, Wilhelm Philipp 1808–80
German botanist

Born in Dosenhain, he studied philosophy, philology, theology and mathematics at the University of Strasbourg, where he became director of the Natural History Museum in 1835. He was an authority on mosses and co-authored *Bryologia Europaea* (6 vols, 1836–55). He studied the Triassic flora of the Vosges region, and contributed the volume *Paläophytologie* to Karl von Zittel's *Handbuch der Paläontologie* in 1879. He was a skilled observer, making exceptionally detailed descriptions. He was a cousin of Karl Schimper.

Schinkel, Karl Friedrich 1781–1841
German architect and painter

Born in Neuruppin, Brandenburg, he was state architect of Prussia from 1815 and professor at the Berlin Royal Academy from 1820. He designed numerous military buildings, museums and churches in romantic-classical style and designed boulevards and squares in Berlin. He also attained distinction as a painter and illustrator.

Schirach, Baldur von 1907–74
German Nazi politician

Born in Berlin, he became a member of the National Socialist Party in 1925 and a member of the Reichstag in 1932. In 1933 he founded and organized the Hitler Youth, of which he was leader until his appointment as *gauleiter* of Vienna in 1940. He was captured in Austria in 1945 and found guilty at the Nuremberg Trials of participating in the mass deportation of Jews; he was sentenced to 20 years' imprisonment. He was released from Spandau prison in 1966.

Schlaf, Johannes 1862–1941
German novelist and dramatist

He was born in Querfurt, and studied at Berlin. With Arno Holz he wrote a volume of short stories titled *Papa Hamlet* (1889), the social drama *Die Familie Selicke* (1890, 'The Selicke Family'), *Peter Boies Freite* (1902, 'Peter Boie's Wooing'), and others. 📖 S Bergen, *Johannes Schlaf* (1941)

Schlegel, August Wilhelm von 1767–1845
German scholar

Born in Hanover, the brother of Friedrich von Schlegel, he studied theology at Göttingen, but soon turned to literature. In 1795 he settled in Jena, and in 1796 married a widow, Caroline Böhmer (1763–1809), who separated from him in 1803 and married Friedrich von Schelling. In 1798 he became Professor of Literature and Fine Art at Jena, and founded with his brother the literary journal *Das Athenäum*. In 1801–04 he lectured at Berlin. Most of the next 14 years he spent in the house of Madame de Staël at Coppet, although he lectured on *Dramatic Art and Literature* (English translation 1815) at Vienna in 1808, and was secretary to the Crown Prince of Sweden (1813–14). From 1818 until his death he was Professor of Literature at Bonn. He translated 17 plays of Shakespeare, and also translated works by Dante, Calderón, Cervantes and Luis de Camoëns, and edited the *Bhagavad-Gita* and the *Ramayana*. He is regarded as a pioneer of the German Romantic movement. 📖 Ruth Schirmer, *August Wilhelm Schlegel und Seine Zeit: ein Bonner Leben* (1986)

Schlegel, (Karl Wilhelm) Friedrich von 1772–1829
German man of letters and critic

He was born in Hanover, the brother of August von Schlegel. Educated at Göttingen and Leipzig, in 1798 he eloped with Dorothea (1763–1839), daughter of Moses Mendelssohn and mother of Philipp Veit the religious painter; this experience inspired a notorious romance *Lucinde* (1799). He then joined his brother at Jena, and with him wrote and edited the literary journal *Das Athenäum*, a vehicle of the German Romantic movement. He studied oriental languages at Paris (1802–04), and in 1808 published a pioneering work on Sanskrit and Indo-Germanic linguistics, *Über die Sprache und Weisheit der Indier* ('On the Language and Wisdom of the Indians'). In 1808 he became a Roman Catholic, and joined the Austrian foreign service, drawing up the Austrian proclamations against Napoleon I in 1809. His best-known books are lectures on the *Philosophy of History* (Eng trans 1835) and *History of Literature* (trans 1859). There are also English versions of his *Philosophy of Life* (1847) and *Lectures on Modern History* (1849). 📖 E Behler, *Friedrich von Schlegel* (1966)

Schleicher, August 1821–68
German philologist

Born in Saxe-Meiningen, he became Professor of Slavonic Languages at Prague (1850), and honorary professor at Jena (1857). He compiled the *Comparative Grammar of the Indo-Germanic Languages* (1861–62).

Schleicher, Kurt von 1882–1934
German soldier and politician

Born in Brandenburg, he was on the general staff during World War I. Politically active during Heinrich Brüning's chancellorship, he became Minister of War in Franz von Papen's government of 1932, and succeeded him as Chancellor. His failure to obtain either a parliamentary majority or emergency powers gave Hitler the opportunity to seize power in 1933. Schleicher and his wife were executed by the Nazis in 1934 on a trumped-up charge of treason.

Schleiden, Matthias Jakob 1804–81
German botanist

Born in Hamburg, he studied law at Heidelberg University (1824–27) and established a legal practice in Hamburg, but abandoned the profession soon afterwards and in 1833 began to study natural science at Göttingen University, later transferring to Berlin. At Berlin he worked in the laboratory of the physiologist **Johannes Müller**, producing many publications and gaining a doctorate from the University of Jena (1839), where he became Professor of Botany (1850–62). After a spell in Dresden he was briefly Professor of Anthropology at Dorpat University. He was responsible for furthering the development of cell theory in 1838, using **Robert Brown**'s discovery of the cell nucleus to explain the role of the nucleus in cell formation. The theory is best explained in his botanical textbook, *Grundzüge der wissenschaftlichen Botanik* (1842, 'Essentials of Scientific Botany'), which marks the start of plant cytology.

Schleiermacher, Friedrich Ernst Daniel
1768–1834
German theologian and philosopher
Born in Breslau, Lower Silesia (Wrocław, Poland), he was brought up in the Moravian faith but became intellectually disillusioned with its dogmatism and studied philosophy and theology at the University of Halle. In 1796 he became a clergyman at the Charité, a Berlin hospital, and joined the literary and intellectual circles associated with **Friedrich** and **August von Schlegel** and **Karl Wilhelm von Humboldt**. He became a professor at Halle (1804–06) and Berlin (1810), and had a significant role in the union of the Lutheran and Reformed Churches in Prussia in 1817. His works include *Reden über die Religion* (1799, 'On Religion: Speeches to its Cultured Despisers'), *Monologen* (1800, 'Soliloquies'), a translation of **Plato** (started in collaboration with Schlegel, 1804–10), his major treatise *Der christliche Glaube* (1821–22, 'The Christian Faith'), and an influential life of Jesus, published posthumously. He was involved in German romanticism and the critique of traditional and Kantian religious and moral philosophy. He defends a view of religious liberalism and an understanding of Christianity rooted in historical tradition, and is now regarded by many as the founder of modern Protestant theology.
📖 Martin Redeker, *Friedrich Schleiermacher: Leben und Werk* (1968, Eng Trans 1973)

Schlemmer, Oskar 1888–1943
German painter, sculptor, designer, dancer and theorist
Born in Stuttgart, he was on the faculty of the Bauhaus from 1919 to 1933, where he developed his notions of theatre as a mixture of colour, light, form, space and motion. Using puppet-like human figures as the centrepiece, he called his experimental productions 'architectonic dances'. All were created between 1926 and 1929 except for the best-known *Triadic Ballet* (three versions: 1911, 1916, and 1922). He exerted a considerable, if indirect, impact on the creation and perception of dance in the 20th century.

Schlesinger, Arthur Meier 1888–1965
US historian
Born in Xenia, Ohio, and educated at Columbia University, New York, he taught at Ohio State University (1912–19), the University of Iowa (1919–24) and Harvard (from 1924). While at Harvard he established the Schlesinger Library on the History of Women. His most important work is *New Viewpoints in American History* (1922), in which he emphasized social and cultural history, a new departure in American historiography. He also wrote *The Rise of the City 1878–98* (1933) and *History of American Life* (13 vols, 1928–43).

Schlesinger, Arthur Meier, Jnr 1917–
US historian

Born in Columbus, Ohio, the son of **Arthur Meier Schlesinger**, he was educated at Harvard and Cambridge. He was Professor of History at Harvard (1954–61) before becoming special assistant to President **John F Kennedy** (1961–63). He was Professor of Humanities at the City University of New York from 1966 to 1995, and president of the American Institute of Arts and Letters from 1981 to 1984, then Chancellor (1984–87). His publications include *The Age of Jackson* (1945, Pulitzer Prize 1946), *The Politics of Freedom* (1950), *The Age of Roosevelt* (3 vols, 1957–60), *The Politics of Hope* (1963), *A Thousand Days: John F Kennedy in the White House* (1965, Pulitzer Prize 1966), *The Imperial Presidency* (1973), *The Cycles of American History* (1986) and *The Disuniting of America* (1991).

Schlesinger, John Richard 1926–
English actor and film, stage and opera director
Born in London, he was a student at Oxford where he joined the dramatic society and directed his first short film, *Black Legend* (1948). Thereafter he worked as a small-part actor, making his film debut in *Singlehanded* (1952). At the BBC (1956–61) he directed documentaries for the *Tonight* and *Monitor* series. He directed his first feature film, *A Kind of Loving*, in 1962, followed by *Billy Liar* (1963), *Darling* (1965) and *Far from the Madding Crowd* (1967). He won an Academy Award for his first US film *Midnight Cowboy* (1969). Later films include *Sunday, Bloody Sunday* (1971), *Marathon Man* (1976) and *Madame Sousatzka* (1988). He has also staged opera, including *The Tales of Hoffman* (1980, London), and occasionally directs for television, notably *An Englishman Abroad* (1982), *A Question of Attribution* (1991) and *Cold Comfort Farm* (1995).

Schlick, Moritz 1882–1936
German philosopher
Born in Berlin, he first studied physics at the universities of Heidelberg, Lausanne and Berlin. He taught at Rostock and Kiel, and was Professor of Inductive Sciences at Vienna (1922–36), where he became a leader of the Vienna Circle of logical positivists. He elaborated their central verificationist theory of meaning and extended it to the field of ethics, which he argued was a factual science of the causes of human actions. An early exponent of **Einstein**'s relativity theories, his major works include *Allgemeine Erkenntnislehre* (1918, 'General Theory of Knowledge') and *Fragen der Ethik* (1930, 'Problems of Ethics'). He was murdered by a deranged student on the steps of the university library.

Schlieffen, Alfred, Count von 1833–1913
Prussian soldier
He was born in Berlin. Chief of General Staff (1891–1905), he devised the 'Schlieffen Plan' in 1895 on which German strategy was unsuccessfully based in World War I. In the event of a German war on two fronts, he envisaged a German breakthrough in Belgium and the defeat of France within six weeks by a colossal right-wheel flanking movement through Holland and then southwards, cutting off Paris from the sea, meanwhile holding off any Russian intervention with a smaller army in the east.
📖 Arden Bucholz, *Schlieffen and Prussian War Planning* (1990)

Schliemann, Heinrich 1822–90
German archaeologist, excavator of Mycenae and Troy
Born in Neubuckow, he went into business in Amsterdam (1842–46) and St Petersburg (1846–63), acquiring a considerable fortune and a knowledge of the principal modern and ancient European languages. At the age of 46 he retired to realize his childhood ambition, set out in *Ithaka, der Peloponnes und Troja* (1869, 'Ithaca, the Peloponnese, and Troy'), of finding the site of Homeric Troy by excavating the mound of Hisarlik in Asia Minor. Excavations were begun in 1871–73, and continued in

1879, 1882–83 and 1889–90. Assisted by the professional archaeologist **Wilhelm Dörpfeld**, he discovered nine superimposed city sites, one of which contained a considerable treasure, which was eventually housed in the Ethnological Museum in Berlin (1882). He also excavated the site of Mycenae (1876), and worked in Ithaca (1869 and 1878), at Orchomenos (1874–76, 1880) and at Tiryns (1884). An amateur who consistently kept his own counsel in the face of expert opinion, he was responsible for some of the most spectacular archaeological discoveries of recent times. His obsessional enthusiasm is well conveyed in his autobiography (1891). ⌑ Katerina Von Burgh, *Heinrich Schliemann* (1989)

Schlüter, Poul Holmskov 1929–
Danish politician

After studying at Aarhus and Copenhagen universities, he qualified as a barrister and Supreme Court attorney and was politically active at an early age, becoming leader of the youth movement of the Conservative People's Party (KF) in 1944. He became its national leader in 1951 and in 1952 a member of its Executive Committee. He was elected to parliament (Folketinget) in 1964 and 10 years later became chairman of the KF, and Prime Minister from 1982 to 1993, heading a centre-right coalition which survived the 1987 election but was reconstituted, with support from one of the minor centre parties, Det Radikale Venstre, in 1988. After the election of 1990 the coalition consisted of only two parties: Schlüter's Conservative Party and the Danish Liberal Party, Venstre.

Schmelzer, Johann Heinrich 1623–80
Austrian composer

Born in Scheibbs, he was trained as a musician in the emperor's service and became famous throughout Europe as a violinist. In 1679 he became kapellmeister to **Leopold I**, but the following year died of the plague in Prague, where the court had fled from the great epidemic in Vienna. The first to adapt the tunes of the Viennese street musicians and Tyrolean peasants to the more sophisticated instrumental styles of the court, he is often regarded as the true father of the Viennese waltz.

Schmidt, Bernhard Voldemar 1879–1935
Estonian optical instrument-maker

Born on the island of Naissaar, near Tallin, he studied at the Chalmers Institute in Göteborg, Sweden, and joined the engineering school at Mittweida in Germany (1901), where he established a reputation as an optician and where in 1926 he installed a small observatory. In the same year he joined the staff of the Hamburg Observatory in Bergedorf, where he developed his idea of a coma-free mirror and completed his first 0.5m Schmidt telescope in 1932. His optical system overcame the aberrations produced by spherical mirrors by introducing a specially shaped correcting plate at their centre of curvature. His invention was of great importance to optical astronomy.

Schmidt, Birgit, née Fischer 1962–
German canoeist

Born in Brandenburg, she became a physical education teacher and has won four Olympic gold medals, three for East Germany and one for Germany. Her final Olympic gold medal was achieved in a return to competition after a three-year break while she had her second child. She also has five world championship K1 titles, seven K2 titles and seven K3 titles. Her husband, Jorg Schmidt, is also a world champion canoeist.

Schmidt, Franz 1874–1939
Austrian composer

Born in Pressburg, his teachers included **Anton Bruckner** for composition and Leschetizsky for piano. He played cello in the Vienna Philharmonic Orchestra (1896–1911) and from 1901 to 1937 was a distinguished teacher at various Viennese institutions. He continued the style of Austro-German lavish late-Romanticism in his four symphonies, an oratorio *Das Buch mit sieben Siegeln* (1938), the operas *Notre Dame* (1914, 'Our Lady') and *Fredigundis* (1922), two piano concertos for the left hand alone, chamber and organ music.

Schmidt, Helmut Heinrich Waldemar 1918–
West German statesman

Born in a working-class district of Hamburg, he was a group leader in the **Hitler** Youth organization, and won the Iron Cross for his service in the Wehrmacht in World War II. After the war he studied economics at Hamburg University and in 1947 became the first national chairman of the Socialist Student Leagues. He had joined the Social Democratic Party (SPD) in 1946, and entered the Bundestag in 1953. While senator for domestic affairs in Hamburg in 1962 he won acclaim for his efficient handling of the Elba flood-disaster. From 1967 to 1969 he was SPD 'floor leader' in the Bundestag and from 1969 to 1972 Minister of Defence. While he was Minister of Finance from 1972 to 1974 his financial policy consolidated the Wirtschaffswunder (economic miracle), giving Germany the most stable currency and economic position in the world. In 1974 he succeeded **Willy Brandt** as Chancellor, and described his aim as the 'political unification of Europe in partnership with the United States'. He established himself as an energetic international statesman, urging European co-operation and international economic co-ordination. In 1977 he emerged as the 'hero of Mogadishu' after taking a firm stand against domestic and international terrorism. He was re-elected Chancellor in 1980, but was defeated in parliament in 1982 following the switch of allegiance by the SPD's coalition allies, the Free Democratic Party. He retired from federal politics at the general election of 1983, having encountered growing opposition from the SPD's left wing, who opposed his moderate stance on defence and economic issues. His publications include *Menchen und Mächte* (1987, Eng trans *Men and Powers*, 1989). ⌑ Hélène Miard-Delacroix, *Partenaires de choix? le chancelier Helmut Schmidt et la France, 1974–1982* (1993)

Schmidt, Maarten 1929–
US astronomer

Born in Groningen, the Netherlands, he was educated there and at Leyden, and moved to the USA in 1959 to join the staff of the Hale Observatories. He became Professor of Astronomy in 1964 and director of the Hale Observatories in 1978. He made important contributions to the study of galactic structure and dynamics, and is best known for his astounding results in the study of quasars. He studied the spectrum of an optically identified quasar and discovered that the peculiarities of its spectrum were caused by a massive **Doppler** red shift; it appeared to be receding from the Earth at nearly 16 per cent of the speed of light. Such high velocities are now interpreted to mean that quasars are distant objects, which must be as luminous as hundreds of galaxies in order to be visible on Earth. He also found that the number of quasars increases with distance from Earth, providing evidence for the 'Big Bang' theory for the origin of the universe.

Schmidt, Wilhelm 1868–1954
German priest and ethnologist

Born in Hörde, Westphalia, he joined the Society of the Divine Word Missionary order (SVD) in 1883 and was ordained a priest in 1892. After studying oriental languages at Berlin University (1893–95), he became professor in the St Gabriel Mission Seminary at Mödling, where he remained until 1938. He also taught at Vienna and Fribourg. His interest in ethnology stemmed from the observations of the SVD missionaries, and from the influence of **Fritz Graebner**. He sought to develop and refine Graebner's system of '*Kulturkreise*' or trait clusters, proposing a theory of devolution to counter that of cultural evolution. In 1906 he founded the journal *Anthropos*.

Schmidt-Rottluff, Karl 1884–1976
German painter and print-maker

Born in Rottluff, he began as an architectural student in Dresden and in 1905 was one of the founder members of the avant-garde group of painters known as Die Brücke. He developed a harsh angular style which is well exemplified in his powerful woodcuts. In Berlin from 1911, he shared the current interest in African sculpture. He was appointed to the Prussian Academy in 1931, but was dismissed from it by the Nazis in 1933, and in 1941 was forbidden to paint; he was reinstated after World War II, and taught at the Berlin Academy of Fine Arts.

Schnabel, Artur 1882–1951
Austrian pianist and composer

Born in Lipnik, he studied under Leschetizsky and made his debut at the age of eight. He taught in Berlin, making frequent concert appearances throughout Europe and the USA. When the Nazis came to power, he settled first in Switzerland, and from 1939 in the USA. He was an authoritative player of a small range of German classics—notably **Beethoven**, **Mozart** and **Schubert**, and his compositions include a piano concerto, chamber music and piano works.

Schnabel, Julian 1951–
US painter

Born in New York City, he attracted attention in the 1980s with his expressionistic treatment of some of the grand themes of classical art—the crucifixion, mankind, and nature. He uses thick paint, from which ghostly faces emerge, to convey a mood of loneliness and loss, as in *The Unexpected Death of Blinky Palermo in the Tropics* (1981, Stedelijk Museum, Amsterdam). Influenced by the work of **Antonio Gaudí** in Barcelona, he also applies paint to shards of crockery fixed to plywood, with menacing effect, as in *Humanity Asleep* (1982, Tate, London), a portrait of his friend the Italian painter Francesco Clemente.

Schneider, Vreni 1964–
Swiss skier

Born in Elm, she holds an unprecedented 11 Olympic and world championship medals. She has won 55 races on the World Cup circuit and the overall World Cup title three times. Her Olympic golds came in the slalom and giant slalom in Calgary in 1988, and in the slalom in Lillehammer in 1994, where she also won a silver medal in the combined and a bronze medal in the giant slalom. She retired after winning her third World Cup overall title at Bormio in 1995.

Schneiderman, Rose 1884–1972
US trade unionist, labour leader and social reformer

Born in Poland, she emigrated to the USA when she was eight. She spent most of her childhood in institutions and had to work from the age of 13; in 1904 she was elected to a union executive board, the highest position yet held by a woman in any US labour organization. After 1908 she worked mainly with the Women's Trade Union League. During **Franklin D Roosevelt**'s presidency, she was the only woman in the National Recovery Administration, and was appointed secretary of the New York State Department of Labour (1937–43). She was a dynamic orator, and became one of the most respected activists for improving the conditions of working people. 📖 *All for One* (1967)

Schnittke, Alfred 1934–98
Soviet composer

He was born in Engels near Saratov. His musical studies began in 1946 in Vienna where his father worked for a Soviet German-language paper. In 1948 he moved to Moscow, trained as a choirmaster, and studied composition at the Moscow Conservatory (1953–58), where he taught from 1962 to 1972. His prolific output has attracted more western attention than any Soviet composer since **Dmitri Shostakovich**. It is bold and eclectic, frequently referring to music of the past and to more modern styles such as jazz. Yet, underlying his originality and experimental tendencies, he retains formal, melodic and harmonic characteristics that anchor him in the mainstream of Russian music. His works include four symphonies and other orchestral works, numerous concertos, choral-orchestral works, ballets, film scores, and chamber, vocal and piano works. In 1993 he was awarded the Russian Triumph Prize and the Hamburg Bach Prize.

Schnitzler, Arthur 1862–1931
Austrian dramatist and novelist

Born in Vienna, he practised as a physician there from 1885 before becoming a playwright. His highly psychological and often strongly erotic short plays and novels are set in Vienna and generally underline some social problem. *Anatol* (1893, Eng trans 1911) and *Reigen* (1900, Eng trans *Hands Around*, 1920; better known as *La Ronde*, the title of a 1959 translation) are cycles of one-act plays, each play linked to the next by a single character. Other notable works include *Der grüne Kakadu* (1899, Eng trans *The Green Cockatoo*, 1913), *Der Weg ins Freie* (1908, Eng trans *The Road to the Open*, 1923), *Professor Bernhardi* (1912, Eng trans 1913), on anti-Semitism, and *Flucht in die Finsternis* (1931, Eng trans *Flight into Darkness*, 1931). 📖 B von Brentano, *Arthur Schnitzler* (1965)

Schnorr von Carolsfeld, Baron Julius 1794–1872
German historical and landscape painter

He was born in Leipzig and studied in Vienna. In Rome (1818–25) he became associated with the Nazarene school of **Peter von Cornelius** and **Johann Overbeck**, and helped decorate the Villa Massimo with frescoes. He moved to Munich in 1825 and was made Professor of Historical Painting, painting frescoes of the *Nibelungenlied*, **Charlemagne**, **Barbarossa** and others. In 1828 he painted *The Flight into Egypt* (Kunstmuseum, Düsseldorf). In 1846 he became a professor at Dresden and director of the Dresden Gallery. He painted many frescoes, and in addition designed stained-glass windows for Glasgow Cathedral.

Schoenberg, Arnold Franz Walter See panel p1650

Schoenheimer, Rudolf 1898–1941
US biochemist

Born in Berlin, Germany, he studied and taught in Germany for 10 years before moving to the USA in 1933. At Columbia University, where he worked with the chemist **Harold Clayton Urey**, he used two new isotopes discovered by Urey (deuterium and heavy nitrogen) to trace biochemical pathways. His work soon showed that many materials of the human body which had been regarded as somewhat static have in reality a steady turnover (of, for example depot fats, proteins and even bone). He distinguished the pathways of unsaturated and saturated fatty acids, and showed that the former are not involved in the production of the latter (1937). Schoenheimer also established how the sterol coprostanol and vitamin D in cows milk are produced. The methods he pioneered have since been used with a variety of isotopic tracers for a range of biochemical studies.

Schöffer, Peter c.1425–1502
German printer

Schoenberg, Arnold Franz Walter 1874–1951
Austrian-born composer, conductor and teacher

Schoenberg was born in Vienna. He learned the violin as a boy but was largely self-taught. In his twenties he earned his living by orchestrating operettas and from 1901 to 1903 he was in Berlin as conductor of a cabaret orchestra. The works of his first period were in the most lush vein of post-Wagnerian Romanticism and include the string sextet *Verklärte Nacht* (1899, 'Transfigured Night'), a symphonic poem *Pelleas und Melisande* (1903) and the mammoth choral–orchestral *Gurrelieder* (1900–01; orchestrated by 1911). He was a notable teacher from his Berlin days until his last years, and his two most famous pupils, **Anton von Webern** and **Alban Berg**, joined him in Vienna in 1904.

His search for a new and personal musical style began to show in such works as the first Chamber Symphony (1907) and the second String Quartet (1908), which caused an uproar at their first Vienna performances through their free use of dissonance. His works written before World War I, including *Erwartung* (1909, 'Expectation') and *Pierrot Lunaire* (1912), may be described as Expressionist; extremely chromatic in harmony, with tonality almost obscured, they met with incomprehension and hostility.

During periods of compositional crisis Schoenberg turned to painting, and he exhibited with **Wasily Kandinsky**'s group Der Blaue Reiter. During the war he was twice called up and discharged as physically unfit. From 1915 to 1922 he worked on the text and music for an oratorio, *Die Jacobsleiter*, which remained unfinished. Gradually Schoenberg saw the need to harness his totally free chromatic style, and he logically evolved the discipline known as the 'twelve-note method', dodecaphony, or serialism; its first use was in the Piano Suite Op 25 (1921–23).

Although he never formally taught this method or publicized his theory, it was adopted by Webern and many others. Schoenberg himself used thematic serialism both strictly and freely, and in some later works departed from it entirely, even returning to tonality. In the 1920s he made many tours, conducting his own works, and in 1925 succeeded **Ferruccio Busoni** as director of the composition masterclass at the Berlin Academy of the Arts. There he wrote his third String Quartet, *Variations for Orchestra*, a one-act opera, *Von Heute auf Morgen* ('From One Day to the Next'), a cello concerto and two acts of his greatest stage work, *Moses und Aaron* ('Moses and Aaron', unfinished).

When the Nazis came to power he left Berlin for Paris, where he formally rejoined the Jewish faith, and set sail for the USA (October 1933), never to return to Europe. In America, Schoenberg suffered from bouts of ill health, money troubles, and general misunderstanding and neglect of his work. Yet after settling in Los Angeles (1934) he wrote much fine music, became a popular teacher at the University of California, taught privately, and wrote a number of valuable textbooks on composition. The Violin Concerto (1935–36) and fourth String Quartet are complex twelve-note works, while the Suite for Strings (1934) and a Hebrew setting *Kol Nidre* (1938) are more traditionally tonal.

His isolation in an alien cultural atmosphere and his spiritual agony over the atrocities committed against his race in Europe are felt in such powerful works as the Piano Concerto (1942), *Ode to Napoleon* (1942) and *A Survivor from Warsaw* (1947). Sickness, financial cares and fear of neglect dogged Schoenberg's last years, but interest in his works was already increasing among a younger generation; a few years after his death his stature as a composer and teacher of immense influence was recognized, even if he never attained the popular audience with whom he strove to communicate.

📖 A selection of Schoenberg's letters is available in E Stein (ed), *Arnold Schoenberg Letters* (translated by E Wilkins and E Kaiser, 1964). See also C Dahlhaus, *Schoenberg and the New Music* (translated by D Puffett and A Clayton, 1987); C Rosen, *Schoenberg* (1975); E Wellesz, *Arnold Schoenberg* (translated by W H Kerridge, 1921, reprinted 1971).

> 'The introduction of my method of composing with twelve notes does not facilitate composing; on the contrary, it makes it more difficult.' From *Style and Idea* (1950).

Born in Mainz and educated in Paris, he and his father-in-law **Johann Fust** took over and ran the printing works of **Johannes Gutenberg**. They completed the Gutenberg Bible (1456), and in 1457 they issued the Mainz Psalter, the first work on which the name of the printer and date of publication appears. After the death of Gutenberg and Fust, he claimed to be the inventor of printing.

Schofield, John McAllister 1831–1906
US soldier

Born in Gerry, New York, he graduated from West Point in 1853. In the Civil War he distinguished himself at Franklin (1864) and Wilmington (1865), rising to the rank of major-general. He became Secretary of War (1868–69) and was commanding general of the US army (1888–95).

Scholastica, St c.480–c.543AD
Italian nun

Born in Nursia, she is traditionally the twin sister of St **Benedict of Nursia**, who founded Western monasticism. Her life is known from the *Dialogues* of **Gregory the Great**. She established a convent at Plombariola not far from her brother's headquarters at Monte Cassino, and they met once a year to discuss spiritual matters. She is said to have prolonged their last meeting by invoking a storm through prayer to prevent him leaving; she is said to have died three days later. Her feast day is 10 February, and she is the patron saint of Benedictine nuns.

Scholasticus See **Evagrius**

Scholes, Percy Alfred 1877–1958
English musicologist

Born in Leeds, he graduated from Oxford in 1908. He was a university extension lecturer there and at Manchester, London and Cambridge. He was a music critic of the *Observer* (1920–25) and the first Music Adviser to the BBC. He edited *The Oxford Companion to Music* (1938), and did much to encourage musical appreciation and knowledge. His major works include *The Puritans and Music* (1934) and *The Life of Dr Burney* (1948).

Scholey, Sir Robert 1921–
English steel executive

He was educated at King Edward VII School, Lytham, and Sheffield University, and joined the United Steel Corporation in 1947, holding a variety of posts within the company until it was absorbed into the British Steel Corporation in 1968. He became a director and chief executive of the new company (1973), then deputy chairman (1976–86). As chairman of British Steel from 1986 to 1992, he presided over a period of politically unpopular decisions to streamline the company, taking a hardline economic view of closures and job losses. He was also a director of Eurotunnel from 1987 and a non-executive director of the National Health Service Policy Board

(1989), and has held a number of chairmanships and presidencies of international steel bodies. He was knighted in 1987.

Schomberg, Frederick Hermann, 1st Duke of 1615–90
French soldier

Born in Heidelberg, Germany, of a German father and English mother, he fought in the Thirty Years War (1618–48) for the Netherlands and Sweden. He was captain in the Scottish Guards in the French army (1652–54) and fought at the Battle of the Dunes (1658). He was in Portuguese service from 1660 to 1668, but became a French citizen in 1668 and, though a Protestant, obtained a marshal's baton in 1675. After the revocation of the Edict of Nantes (1685) he retired to Portugal. He commanded under William of Orange (William III) in the English expedition (1688), became a naturalized British citizen and was created Duke of Schomberg (1689), and was Commander-in-Chief in Ireland. He conducted the Battle of the Ulster campaign, and was killed at the Boyne.

Schomburgk, Sir Robert Hermann 1804–65
British traveller and official

Born in Prussia, he surveyed (1831) in the Virgin Islands, where he was a merchant, and was sent by the Royal Geographical Society to explore British Guiana (1831–35). In ascending the Berbice River he discovered the magnificent Victoria Regia lily. He was employed by the government in Guiana from 1841 to 1843 to draw the controversial 'Schomburgk-line' as a provisional boundary with Venezuela and Brazil. From 1848 to 1857 he was British consul in San Domingo, and from 1857 to 1864 consul in Siam (Thailand).

Schön, Martin See Schongauer, Martin

Schönbein, Christian Friedrich 1799–1868
German chemist

Born in Metzingen, Württemberg, he studied pharmacy, worked in two chemical factories and taught at a technical institute at Keilhau. He also taught and travelled in England and France, and was professor at Basle from 1835 until his death. He conducted research in many areas, and is mainly remembered for his discovery of ozone in 1839. In 1845 he treated cotton wool with a mixture of sulphuric acid and nitric acid, washing out the excess acid. The result was nitrocellulose (gun cotton), a highly inflammable fluffy white substance which was soon widely used as an explosive. By treating cotton wool with less nitric acid, Schönbein made collodion, which was to have applications in photography and medicine. He was also one of the pioneers of chromatography.

Schongauer or Schön, Martin 1450–91
German painter and engraver

He was born in Colmar, where his famous *Madonna of the Rose Garden* altarpiece shows Flemish influence, probably that of Rogier van der Weyden. Other religious paintings attributed to Schongauer have not been authenticated, but well over 100 of his engraved plates have survived, including *The Passion, The Wise and Foolish Virgins, Adoration of the Magi*, and other religious subjects.

Schoolcraft, Henry Rowe 1793–1864
US ethnologist

Born in Albany County, New York, he went with Lewis Cass as geologist to Lake Superior in 1820. In 1822 he became Indian agent for the tribes round the lakes, and in 1823 married a wife of Indian blood. In 1832 he commanded an expedition which discovered the sources of the Mississippi (*Narrative*, 1834). While superintendent for the Indians, he negotiated treaties by which the government acquired 16 million acres of territory. In 1845 he

collected the statistics of the Six Nations (*Notes on the Iroquois*, 1848) and later prepared for the government his *Information respecting the Indian Tribes of the United States* (6 vols, 1851–57).

Schoonmaker, Thelma 1945–
US film editor

Raised in Africa, she is one of the leading editors in contemporary US cinema. She met Martin Scorsese at New York University, and has been closely associated with his films since his debut, *Who's That Knocking At My Door?* (1968). She has been influential in helping create his distinctive visual style. She received an Academy Award for her work on *Raging Bull* (1980), and was also nominated for *Goodfellas* in 1990, and for the rock documentary *Woodstock* in 1970. She was married to the director Michael Powell from 1984 until his death in 1990.

Schopenhauer, Arthur 1788–1860
German philosopher

He was born in Danzig (Gdansk, Poland), where his father was a banker and his mother a novelist. The family moved to Hamburg in 1793 and he was reluctantly prepared for a business career. After his father's sudden death in 1805 he embarked on an academic education at Gotha, Weimar, Göttingen (where he studied medicine and natural science), and finally Berlin and Jena (where he completed his dissertation in philosophy in 1813). Throughout his unhappy life he was dark, distrustful, misogynistic and truculent. He reacted strongly against the post-Kantian idealist tradition represented by Hegel, Johann Fichte and Friedrich von Schelling and found his inspiration in the work of Plato, Kant, the ancient Indian philosophy of the *Vedas*, and Goethe (with whom he collaborated on the 'theory of colours'). His major work was *Die Welt als Wille und Vorstellung* (1819, 'The World as Will and Idea'), which included reflections on the theory of knowledge and its implications for the philosophy of nature, aesthetics and ethics. He emphasized the active role of Will as the creative but covert and irrational force in human nature, in a way that was greatly to influence Nietzsche and Freud, and he argued that art represented the sole kind of knowledge that was not subservient to the Will. His work is often characterized as a systematic philosophical pessimism. He took a teaching position in Berlin (1820) and combatively timed his lectures to coincide with those of Hegel, but he failed to attract students, his book was virtually ignored, and he retired to live a bitter and reclusive life in Frankfurt am Main, accompanied for the most part only by his poodle. He continued his work, defiantly elaborating and defending the same basic ideas in such publications as *Über den Willen in der Natur* (1889, 'On the Will in Nature'), *Die Beiden Grundprobleme der Ethik* (1841, 'The Two Main Problems of Ethics') and a second edition of his major work (1844). In the end he achieved success with a collection of diverse essays and aphoristic writings published under the title *Parerga und Paralipomena* (1851); and he subsequently influenced not only philosophical movements, notably existentialism, but also a wide range of figures including Richard Wagner, Leo Tolstoy, Marcel Proust and Thomas Mann. ▣ R Taylor (ed), *The Will to Live: Selected Writings* (1962); A S Zimmern, *Arthur Schopenhauer: His Life and Philosophy* (1932)

Schotz, Benno 1891–1986
Estonian sculptor based in Scotland

Born in Estonia, he went to Darmstadt, Germany, in 1911 to study engineering, although by 1912 he was in Glasgow working in a shipyard; he remained there for nine years. During this time he attended evening classes in sculpture, and became a professional sculptor in 1923. In 1981 he received the title of Queen's Sculptor in Scotland and the freedom of the city of Glasgow. A prolific artist, he was best known for his portrait busts, and also produced important religious works, most notably the *Stations of the Cross* for St Charles Chapel, Glasgow.

Schouten, Willem Corneliszoon c.1580–1625
Dutch mariner, the first man to round Cape Horn
He was born in Hoorn, Holland. In the service of the East India Company, he was the first to traverse Drake Passage in 1615; he discovered Cape Horn in 1616, and named it after his birthplace.

Schouvaloff, Pyotr Andreyevich, Graf See Shuvalov, Pyotr Andreyevich, Graf

Schrader, Paul Joseph 1946–
US filmmaker
Born in Grand Rapids, Michigan, and raised in a strict Calvinist household, he did not see his first film until he was in his late teens, and he soon became a voracious filmgoer and an incisive critic, whose influential writing includes *Transcendental Style In Film: Ozu, Bresson and Dreyer* (1972). He became a student of film at the University of California at Los Angeles (UCLA), and entered the film industry as a screenwriter, collaborating to memorable effect with director Martin Scorsese on a series of films including *Taxi Driver* (1976), *Raging Bull* (1980) and *The Last Temptation Of Christ* (1988). He made his directorial debut with *Blue Collar* (1978), a gritty exposé of union corruption, and has worked as a writer–director on a diverse range of films dominated by a strong visual sensibility and an emotional coldness. His work includes *American Gigolo* (1980), an examination of redemption through love, *Mishima* (1985), a stylized dramatization of the life and work of the Japanese writer Yukio Mishima, and *Light Sleeper* (1992), a convincing portrait of mid-life anxiety and the desire for change.

Schreiber, Lady Charlotte Elizabeth, *née* Bertie 1812–95
Welsh scholar diarist
Born in Uffington, Lincolnshire, she was a daughter of the earl of Lindsey. She became interested in the literature and traditions of Wales after her marriage in 1833 to Sir Josiah John Guest, the ironmaster of Dowlais, Merthyr Tydfil. She was widowed in 1852, and in 1855 married Charles Schreiber, former MP for Cheltenham and Poole. She is best known for her part in translating and editing *The Mabinogion* (1838–49) with the help of Thomas Price, John Jones and others. A lifelong collector, she became an authority on fans and playing cards, and bequeathed her collections to the British Museum. Her famous collection of china was presented to the Victoria and Albert Museum, London.

Schreiner, Olive 1855–1920
South African writer and feminist
Born in Wittebergen Mission Station, Cape of Good Hope, the daughter of a German Methodist missionary and an English mother, she grew up largely self-educated and at the age of 15 became a governess to a Boer family near the Karoo desert. She later lived in England (1881–89), where her novel *The Story of an African Farm* (1883) was published under the pseudonym 'Ralph Iron'. In her later works she was a passionate propagandist for women's rights, pro-Boer loyalty and pacifism. Titles include the allegorical *Dreams* (1891) and *Dream Life and Real Life* (1893), the polemical *Trooper Peter Halket* (1897), a sociological study of *Woman and Labour* (1911), and her last novel *From Man to Man* (1926). In 1894 she married S P Cronwright, who took her name, wrote her biography (1924) and edited her letters (1926). 📖 S C Cronwright-Schreiner, *The Life of Olive Schreiner* (1924)

Schrieffer, John Robert 1931–
US physicist and Nobel Prize winner
Born in Oak Park, Illinois, he studied electrical engineering and physics at the Massachusetts Institute of Technology (MIT) and Illinois University. He worked on super conductivity for his PhD under John Bardeen, and his collaboration with Bardeen and Leon Cooper led to the BCS (Bardeen-Cooper-Schrieffer) theory of superconductivity, for which all three shared the 1972 Nobel Prize for physics. Schrieffer's particular contribution to the theory was the generalization from the properties of a single Cooper electron pair to that of a solid containing many pairs. Following post-doctoral work in Europe and short-term posts in the USA, Schrieffer held professorships at the universities of Pennsylvania (1962), Cornell and California. Since 1992 he has been University Professor at Florida State University. He is the author of *Theory of Superconductivity* (1964), and has also worked on dilute alloy theory, surface physics and ferromagnetism. In 1985 he was awarded the US National Medal of Science.

Schröder, Friedrich Ludwig 1744–1816
German actor, playwright and theatre manager
A leading actor of his day, he was also manager of the Hamburg National Theatre (1771–80, 1785–98) and the Vienna Burgtheater (1780–84). He was responsible for bringing Shakespeare's plays to Germany.

Schrödinger, Erwin 1887–1961
Austrian physicist and Nobel Prize winner
Born in Vienna, he was educated at Vienna University. From 1920 he was professor at Stuttgart (1920), Jena (1920–21), Breslau (1921) and Zurich (1921–27). He succeeded Max Planck as Professor of Physics at the University of Berlin before returning to Austria as professor at Graz University (1936–38). After the *Anschluss*, he fled to Dublin where he worked at the Institute for Advanced Studies (1938–56), then returned to Austria as emeritus professor at Vienna University. Inspired by Louis-Victor de Broglie's proposal of wave-particle duality, Schrödinger originated the science of wave mechanics as part of the quantum theory with his celebrated wave equation. P A M Dirac soon developed a more complete theory of quantum mechanics from their foundations, and for this work Schrödinger and Dirac shared the 1933 Nobel Prize for physics. Schrödinger wrote *What is Life* (1946) and *Science and Man* (1958). 📖 William T Scott, *Erwin Schrödinger: An Introduction to His Writings* (1967)

Schubart, Christian Friedrich Daniel 1739–91
German poet
Born in Obersontheim, Swabia, he wrote satirical and religious poems. He was imprisoned at Hohenasperg (1777–87) by the Duke of Württemberg, whom he had offended in an epigram. He is largely remembered for his influence on Schiller, and as the poet of Schubert's song *Die Forelle* ('The Trout'). 📖 K M Klos, *Christian Schubart* (1908)

Schubert, Franz Peter See panel p1653

Schulenburg, Countess Ehrengard Melusina von der 1667–1743
German noblewoman
The mistress of George I of Great Britain, she was born in Emden and gained her nickname 'the Maypole' because of her lean figure. She was created Duchess of Kendal in 1719. Unattractive and avaricious, she made a fortune by dealing in South Sea stock and selling titles and offices.

Schuller, Gunther Alexander 1925–
US writer, composer and musician
He was born in New York City. He played French horn in symphony orchestras, then turned to jazz, where he made important contributions to the jazz–classical fusion he christened Third Stream music. He made important records, notably *Jazz Abstractions* (1960), and wrote

Schubert, Franz Peter 1797–1828
Austrian composer

Schubert was born in Vienna, the son of a schoolmaster who gave him early instruction in the violin and piano. At the age of 11 he entered the Stadtkonvikt, a choristers' school attached to the court chapel. He played in the orchestra there, and wrote his first symphony (in D) for it (1813). In 1814 he became assistant master at his father's school; he continued to write music, among which were two fine early songs, the beautiful *Gretchen am Spinnrade* ('Gretchen at the Spinning Wheel') from **Goethe's** *Faust*, and the powerful and sinister *Erlkönig*. In 1815 Schubert poured out a flood of over 100 songs, including eight written on a single day, as well as other works.

From 1817 he gave up schoolteaching, to which he was not temperamentally suited, and lived a precarious existence in Vienna, earning a living by giving lessons. His friends at this time included the operatic baritone J Michael Vogl, and amateur artists and poets, of whom the poet Johann Mayrhofer was the closest. With these friends he was to found the new Viennese entertainment, the 'Schubertiads', private and public accompanied recitals of his songs, which made the group of men known throughout Vienna.

In 1818 the first public performance of Schubert's secular music included the overtures written in the style of **Rossini**, whom Schubert greatly admired. In 1818, and again in 1824, he stayed at Zseliz as the tutor of Count **Esterházy's** three daughters; there he heard Hungarian folk and gypsy music. The 'Trout' quintet for piano and strings in A major (named after its set of variations on a theme from his song, *Die Forelle*), was written after a walking tour with Vogl in 1819. Schubert's veneration of **Beethoven** made him visit the coffee house that the older composer frequented, but he was too awestruck ever to approach him, except when Beethoven was sick, when he sent him his compositions—in 1822 a set of variations for a piano duet dedicated to Beethoven, and in 1827 a collection of his songs, which the dying Beethoven greatly admired.

In 1822 he composed the Unfinished Symphony (No 8), and the Wanderer Fantasy for piano (based on a theme from his song, *Der Wanderer*); about this time he began to be troubled by ill health, possibly syphilis. The song cycle *Die schöne Müllerin* ('The Fair Maid of the Mill') and the incidental music to *Rosamunde* were written in 1823, the string quartets in A minor and D minor (including variations on a theme from his song *Der Tod und das*

Mädchen, 'Death and the Maiden') and the octet in F for wind and strings in 1824. In 1825 he sent **Goethe** a number of settings of his poems, but they were returned without acknowledgement.

In the last three years of his life Schubert wrote the *Winterreise* ('Winter Journey') song cycle and a posthumously published group of songs (not a cycle as such), *Schwanengesang* ('Swan Song'), the string quartet in G major, the string quintet in C, piano trios in B flat and E flat, the *moments musicaux* for piano, three piano sonatas, the fantasy in F minor for four hands, and a mass. The symphony in C major, formerly dated to 1828, is now thought to have been written three years earlier. He died on 19 November 1828 and was buried as near as possible to Beethoven's grave; later both composers were exhumed and reburied in the Central Cemetery in Vienna.

Other works include six masses, the unfinished oratorio *Lazarus* (1820), and the operas *Alfonso und Estrella* (1821–22) and *Fierabras* (1823). Schubert's music, even when it is overtly happy, is affected by a deep sadness that becomes almost unbearably poignant in his last works, especially the chamber and instrumental music and the songs. His contribution to the creation of the Lied is alone of monumental proportions, and the romantic pathos of his poor existence and short life contrasts with the beauty and profound originality of his musical achievement.

📖 Documentary material can be found in O E Deutsch, *Schubert: A Documentary Biography* (translated by E Blom, 1946); a standard biography is A Einstein, *Schubert* (Eng trans 1951). See also E N McKay, *Schubert: A Biography* (1996); J Reed, *Schubert* (1987); and J Reed, *Schubert: The Final Years* (1972), which gives a detailed account of the last two years. Schubert's works were catalogued by O E Deutsch (Eng edn, 1951; revised German edn, 1978) and are usually cited from this catalogue with the prefix 'D'.

> 'O Mozart, immortal Mozart, how many, how infinitely many inspiring suggestions of a finer, better life have you left in our souls!' From Schubert's diary, 1816. Quoted in Derek Watson, *Music Quotations* (1991).
>
> 'A review, however favourable, can be ridiculous at the same time if the critic lacks average intelligence, as is not seldom the case.' From a letter, 1825. Ibid.

---

compositions for several key jazz figures. His work as a writer and scholar has been equally influential, notably in his monumental studies *Early Jazz* (1968) and *The Swing Era* (1989), both part of a work-in-progress intended to cover the entire history of jazz.

Schultz, Theodore William 1902–
US economist and Nobel Prize winner

Born in Arlington, South Dakota, and educated at South Dakota State College and the University of Wisconsin, he held professorships at Iowa State College (1930–43) and the University of Chicago (1943–72), and wrote *Transforming Traditional Agriculture* (1964). His work stressed the importance of the human factor in agriculture. He was awarded the Nobel Prize for economics in 1979 (with Sir **Arthur Lewis**). Later works include *The Economics of Being Poor* and *Origins of Increasing Returns* (both 1993).

Schultze, Max Johann Sigismund 1825–74
German zoologist

Born in Frieburg, he studied at the universities of Greifswald and Berlin and taught at the University of Bonn, where he became director of the Anatomical Institute in 1872. He studied the anatomy of a variety of animals and in particular single-cell organisms, which led him to define the structure of the cell (1861) as the basic building block of all living organisms. Among other discoveries, he showed that the retina of birds possesses two different sensory nerve endings, the rods and cones, with which he identified separate functions. He proposed the duplicity theory of vision in 1866, which was a forerunner of modern theories.

Schulz, Bruno 1892–1942
Polish writer

He grew up in the predominantly Jewish town of Drohobycz and taught art at the local school. He published only two books in his lifetime. *Sklepy cynamonowe* (1934, published in the UK as *The Street of Crocodiles*, in the USA as *Cinnamon Shops and Other Stories*, 1963) is a collection of magical transformations and cabbalistic connections, centred on the experience of one Joseph N, a projection

Schumann, Robert Alexander 1810–56
German composer

Schumann was born in Zwickau in Saxony. He studied law at Leipzig and Heidelberg, but was always more interested in music. After hearing **Rossini**'s operas performed in Italy and **Paganini** playing at Frankfurt am Main, he persuaded his parents to allow him to study the piano under the formidable teacher Friedrich Wieck of Leipzig. However Wieck was absent for much of the time organizing concert tours for his highly gifted daughter Clara, and Schumann was left to his own devices. He studied **J S Bach**'s *Well-tempered Clavier*, and wrote reviews and articles, including a significant one heralding the genius of the young **Chopin**. He managed to cripple a finger of his right hand with a finger-strengthening contraption that he had devised (1832), permanently ruining his prospects as a performer.

The deaths of a brother and a sister-in-law and an obsessive fear of insanity drove him to attempt suicide. His first compositions, the Toccata, Paganini studies, and Intermezzi, were published in 1833, and in 1834 he founded the *Neue Zeitschrift für Musik*, of which he was editor for 10 years. His best contributions were collected and translated under the title *Music and Musicians* (1877–80). He was a champion of romanticism, and in 1853 contributed another prescient essay, on the young **Brahms**. In 1834 he founded the so called *Davidsbünder* ('David Club') to fight the artistic philistines in Germany. In his music, he identified in himself two personalities, the impetuous Florestan and the contemplative Eusebius.

In 1835 he met Chopin, **Ignaz Moscheles** and **Mendelssohn**, who had become director of the Leipzig *Gewandhaus*. The F sharp minor Piano Sonata was begun and another in G minor written post-haste for the **Beethoven** commemorations, but not published until 1839. In 1838 Schumann visited Vienna and came across the manuscript of **Schubert**'s C major symphony; Schumann sent it to Mendelssohn, who had it performed. Schumann's attachment to Clara Wieck (the future **Clara Schumann**) was met with disapproval from her father, who took her away on concert tours as much as possible. He did not know that they were secretly engaged, however. Clara dutifully repudiated Schumann, who retaliated by having a brief relationship with the Scottish pianist Robina Laidlaw, to whom he later dedicated his *Fantasiestücke*.

In 1839 the lovers were reconciled and after a long legal wrangle to obtain permission to marry without her father's consent, they married in 1840. Schumann had meanwhile written his first songs, the Fool's Song in *Twelfth Night*, and the Chamisso songs *Frauenliebe und -Leben* ('Woman's Love and Life'). After the marriage, he poured out his heart into a flood of new songs and song cycles, including *Dichterliebe* ('Poet's Love'). Clara now influenced him to turn to orchestral composition, and her efforts were rewarded by the first Symphony in B flat major, which was performed under Mendelssohn's direction at the *Gewandhaus*. This was followed by the A minor Piano Concerto, the Piano Quintet, the choral *Paradise and the Peril*, the scenes from *Faust*, completed in 1848, the 'Spring' Symphony in B flat, and other works.

cont

of Schulz himself. In *Sanatorium pod klepsydra* (1937, Eng trans *Sanatorium Under the Sign of the Hourglass*, 1978), Schulz brings his special vision to bear on wider social and philosophical questions. He was murdered by a Wehrmacht officer during the Nazi occupation of Poland. ▣ E Baur, *Die Prose von Schulz* (1975)

Schulz, Charles M (onroe) 1922–
US strip cartoonist

Born in Minneapolis, Minnesota, he learned cartooning from a correspondence course, and contributed cartoons to the *Saturday Evening Post* (1947). He is best known as the cartoonist of *Peanuts* (from 1950), featuring Charlie Brown (based on Schulz himself), Snoopy and Linus. In 1990 he was made Commandeur, L'Ordre des Arts et des Lettres.

Schumacher, Kurt Ernst Karl 1895–1952
German statesman

Born in Kulm, Prussia, he studied law and political science at the universities of Leipzig and Berlin. From 1930 to 1933 he was a member of the Reichstag and of the executive of the Social Democratic parliamentary group. An outspoken opponent of National Socialism, he spent 10 years from 1933 in Nazi concentration camps, where he showed outstanding courage. He became in 1946 chairman of the Social Democratic Party and of the parliamentary group of the Bundestag in Bonn. He strongly opposed the German government's policy of armed integration with western Europe.

Schumacher, Michael 1969–
German racing driver

Born in Hürth-Hermuhlheim, he made a remarkable debut in the 1991 Belgium Grand Prix when he unexpectedly qualified in seventh place, and he joined the Bennetton team two weeks later. He won the Formula 1 world championship in 1994 and 1995. In 1996 he signed a $26 million contract with Ferrari.

Schuman, Robert 1886–1963
French statesman

Born in Luxembourg, he was a member of the Resistance during World War II. He became Prime Minister in 1947 and 1948, and propounded the 'Schuman plan' (1950) for pooling the coal and steel resources of western Europe. He was elected president of the Strasbourg European Assembly in 1958 and was awarded the Charlemagne Prize. He survived de Gaulle's electoral reforms, being re-elected to the National Assembly in 1958.

Schuman, William Howard 1910–92
US composer

Born in New York City, he studied under **Roy Harris** and at Salzburg, winning in 1943 the first Pulitzer Prize to be awarded to a composer. He became president of the Juilliard School of Music (1945–62) and of the Lincoln Center for the Performing Arts (1962–69) in New York. His work ranges from the lighthearted (such as his opera, *The Mighty Casey*, 1953), to the austere. He composed 10 symphonies, concertos for piano and violin, and several ballets, as well as choral and orchestral works.

Schumann, Clara Josephine, *née* Wieck 1819–96
German pianist and composer

Born in Leipzig, she was the daughter of a Leipzig piano teacher, Friedrich Wieck, who taught her to be a highly skilled concert pianist. She gave her first Gewandhaus concert when only 11 and the following year four of her polonaises were published. She married **Schumann** in 1840, despite her father's opposition, and became his foremost interpreter. She undertook a concert tour of Russia (without him) in 1844. From 1856 she played regularly for the Royal Philharmonic Society in London, promoting her husband's work wherever she went. From 1878 she was principal piano teacher at the Frankfurt am Main Conservatory. Her own compositions include piano music and songs. She was a close friend of **Brahms** during her husband's last illness and after his death.

Schumann, Robert Alexander cont

In 1843 he was appointed professor of the new Leipzig Conservatory. The Schumanns' Russian concert tour, during which Clara played before Nicholas I (1844), inspired him to write five poems on the Kremlin. Increasing symptoms of mental illness prompted the move from Leipzig to Dresden. In 1847 the Symphony in C major was completed and the death of his great friend Mendelssohn prompted him to write a set of reminiscences, first published in 1947.

Revolution broke out in Dresden in 1849 when Prussian troops confronted republican revolutionaries, among them Richard Wagner. The Schumanns fled, but Robert wrote some stirring marches. His mental state allowed him one final productive phase in which he composed piano pieces, many songs and the incidental music to Byron's *Manfred*.

His appointment as musical director at Düsseldorf in 1850 saw a happy interlude and the composition of the *Rhenish* Symphony, but his condition remained unstable and in 1854 he threw himself into the Rhine, only to be rescued by fishermen. He died in an asylum two years later.

🎵 Schumann was primarily a composer for the pianoforte, whose repertory he enriched with works of intense poetry and romanticism. Notable among these are the *Abegg Theme and Variations* (dedicated to his friend Meta Abegg), *Papillons, Davidsbündlertänze, Carnaval, Fantasiestücke, Études symphoniques* ('Symphonic Studies'), *Kinderszenen* ('Scenes from Childhood'), *Kreisleriana, Novelleten, Waldscenen* ('Forest Scenes'), and *Albumblätter* ('Album Leaves'). He also wrote many songs and song cycles, picking up the mantle of Schubert. In addition to the above-mentioned (*Frauenliebe und -Leben* and *Dichterliebe*), the *Liederkreis* (two cycles, on poems by Heinrich Heine and Joseph Eichendorff respectively) is also well known.

📖 Alan Walker (ed), *Robert Schumann: The Man and His Music* (2nd edn, 1974); Joan Chissell, *Schumann* (1967); Robert H Schauffler, *Florestan: The Life and Work of Robert Schumann* (1945).

'I have been composing so much that it really seems quite uncanny at times. I cannot help it, and should like to sing myself to death, like a nightingale.' From a letter to Clara, 1840. Quoted in Derek Watson, *Music Quotations* (1991).

'Schumann is the composer of childhood ... both because he created a children's imaginative world and because children learn some of their first music in his marvellous piano albums.' Igor Stravinsky, in *Themes and Conclusions* (1972). Ibid.

Schumann, Elisabeth 1889–1952
US soprano

Born in Merseburg, Germany, she was engaged by Richard Strauss and sang in his and Mozart's operas all over the world, making her London debut in 1924. Later she concentrated on lieder, especially those of Schubert, Brahms, Hugo Wolf and Richard Strauss. She left Austria in 1936 and in 1938 became a US citizen.

Schumann, Robert Alexander See panel p1654

Schumpeter, Joseph Alois 1883–1950
US economist

Born in Trest, Moravia, he was a professor at the University of Graz, Austrian Minister of Finance (1919–20), and Professor of Economics at Bonn, before emigrating to the USA (1932) and becoming a professor at Harvard. He studied capitalist development, cycles of business growth, and the role of the entrepreneur. His books include *The Theory of Economic Development* (1911), *Business Cycles* (1939), and *Capitalism, Socialism, and Democracy* (1942).

Schur, Issai 1875–1941
Russian mathematician

Born in Mogilev, he taught in Berlin from 1916 to 1935, when as a Jew he was forced to retire, in 1939 escaping to Israel. A pupil of Ferdinand Georg Frobenius, he worked on representation theory and group characters, and established a simple but central result that is still known as Schur's lemma.

Schurz, Carl 1829–1906
US politician and journalist

Born near Cologne, Germany, he joined the revolutionary movement of 1849. In the USA from 1852 he was politician, lecturer, major-general in the Civil War, journalist, senator (1869–75) and Secretary of the Interior (1877–81). He wrote biographies of Henry Clay and Abraham Lincoln, and his own autobiography (1909).

Schuschnigg, Kurt von 1897–1977
Austrian statesman

He was born in Riva, South Tirol. He served with honours in World War I and then practised law. He was elected a Christian Socialist deputy in 1927 and was appointed Minister of Justice (1932) and Minister of Education (1933). After the murder of Engelbert Dollfuss in 1934, he succeeded as Chancellor until March 1938, when Hitler annexed Austria. Imprisoned by the Nazis, he was liberated by US troops in 1945. He was Professor of Political Science at St Louis in the USA (1948–67).

Schuster, Sir Arthur 1851–1934
British physicist

Born in Frankfurt, Germany, of Jewish parents, he studied at the universities of Heidelberg and Cambridge and became Professor of Applied Mathematics (1881) and Professor of Physics (1888) at Owens College, Manchester. He worked principally in spectroscopy and earth magnetism. The Schuster–Smith magnetometer is the standard instrument for measuring the Earth's magnetic field. He was elected FRS in 1879, and was the founder (and the first secretary) of the International Research Council. He was knighted in 1920.

Schutz, Alfred 1899–1959
US social philosopher

Born in Vienna, he became a banker and emigrated to the USA in 1939 to continue his career in New York, where he became professor in the New School of Social Research in 1952. He reacted against the positivism and behaviourism of the Vienna Circle and developed a descriptive sociology in which the sociologist is a factor in any investigation. He influenced, among others, the critical theory of Jürgen Habermas. His main work is *Die sinnhafte Aufbau der sozialen Welt* (1932, Eng trans *The Phenomenology of the Social World*, 1967).

Schütz, Heinrich 1585–1672
German composer

Born in Köstritz, near Gera, he went to Venice in 1609 to study music, becoming a pupil of Giovanni Gabrieli. In 1611 he published a book of five-part madrigals, showing the Italian influence. Returning to Germany in 1613, he was appointed hofkapellmeister in Dresden (1617), where he introduced Italian music and styles, including madrigals, the use of continuo, and instrumentally-accompanied choral compositions, for example his *Psalms of David* (1619, *Psalmen Davids*). He is therefore regarded by many as the founder of the Baroque school of German music. A visit to Italy in 1628 familiarized him with Monteverdi's more recent musical developments, and from 1633 until his return to Dresden in 1641 he travelled between various courts, including those at Copenhagen and Hanover. Creatively he lies between the polyphony of Palestrina and the more elaborate orchestration of Bach and Handel. His compositions include much church music, notably four passion settings and 'The Seven Words on the Cross' (1619, *Sieben Worte Jesu Christi am Kreuz*), a German requiem, and the first German opera, *Dafne*, produced in Torgau in 1627 and now lost.

Schuyler, Philip John 1733–1804
American general and politician
Born in Albany, New York, he was a member of the colonial assembly from 1768 and delegate to the Continental Congress of 1775, which appointed him one of the first four major-generals. George Washington gave him the northern department of New York, and he was preparing to invade Canada when ill health compelled him to resign. Besides acting as commissioner for Indian affairs and making treaties with the Six Nations, he sat in Congress (1777–81), and was state senator for 13 years between 1780 and 1797, US senator 1789–91 and 1797–98, and surveyor-general of the state from 1782. With Alexander Hamilton and John Jay he shared the leadership of the Federal party in New York, and helped to prepare the state's code of laws.

Schwabe, Heinrich Samuel 1789–1875
German apothecary and amateur astronomer
Born in Dessau, for 33 years he made systematic observations of the Sun in a search for a planet revolving within the orbit of Mercury, in the course of which he discovered an approximately 10-year periodicity in the frequency of sunspots. The average period was later fixed at 11 years. Referring to this accidental discovery, Schwabe compared himself with King Saul in the Bible who 'went out to find his father's asses and found a throne'.

Schwann, Theodor 1810–82
German physiologist
Born in Neuss, he was educated in Cologne and studied medicine, graduating in Berlin in 1834. He remained in Berlin for four years as assistant to Johannes Müller, studying digestion, and isolating the enzyme pepsin from the stomach lining. He later showed the role of yeast cells in producing fermentation. Schwann also discovered the 'Schwann cells' which compose the sheath around peripheral nerve axons, and he showed an egg to be a single cell which, once fertilized, evolves into a complex organism. His most renowned work, however, was on cell theory. In a major book of 1839 he contended that the entire plant or animal was comprised of cells, that cells have in some measure a life of their own, but that the life of the cells is also subordinated to that of the whole organism. The cell theory became pivotal to 19th-century biomedicine. In 1838 he emigrated to Belgium, where he became professor at the University of Leuven, and in 1848 at the University of Liège.

Schwartz, Delmore 1913–66
US poet, story writer and critic
Born in Brooklyn, New York City, he was educated at New York University and wrote his first poetry while still a student. Writing lyrics, fiction, drama and criticism, he was associated with the *Partisan Review* group of writers (editor 1943–55), and was editor of *The New Republic* (1955–57). He was a profound ironist, and in 1960 he became one of the youngest winners of the Bollingen prize. His collections of verse include *In Dreams Begin*

Responsibilities (1938), *Shenandoah* (1941), *Vaudeville for a Princess* (1950) and *Summer Knowledge* (1959). His stories are collected in *The World is a Wedding* (1948) and *Successful Love* (1961). Saul Bellow memorably portrayed him in *Humboldt's Gift* (1975). 📖 J Atlas, *Delmore Schwartz: the life of an American poet* (1977)

Schwartz, Melvin 1932–
US physicist
Born in New York City, he was educated at the University of Columbia where he received his PhD in 1958 and later became professor of physics (1963–66). From 1966 he held professorships at Stanford University, but in the early 1980s he left academic research to work in the computer industry until 1991, when he became associate director of High Energy and Nuclear Physics at Brookhaven National Laboratory. He was awarded the 1988 Nobel Prize for physics jointly with Leon Lederman and Jack Steinberger for demonstrating the existence of the muon neutrino (1962). He published *Principles of Electrodynamics* in 1972.

Schwarz, Berthold, *originally* Konstantin Anklitzen fl.1320
German Franciscan monk
Born in Freiburg or Dortmund, he gained the name Schwarz ('black') as a nickname due to his chemical experiments. In about 1320 he is said to have brought gunpowder (or guns) into practical use.

Schwarz, Harvey Fisher 1905–88
US electrical engineer
Born in Edwardsville, Illinois, he studied electrical engineering at Washington University, St Louis, and helped to develop Radiola 44, the first domestic radio receiver to use the newly invented screen-grid valve. As chief engineer of Brunswick Radio Corporation, he was sent to Great Britain in 1932 to design radios and radiograms for manufacture in the UK, and made his home there for the rest of his life although remaining a US citizen. During World War II he and William O'Brien developed a prototype radio-navigation system for ships and aircraft, which was put into operation for the first time during the D-Day landings in the seaborne invasion of Normandy in 1944.

Schwarzenberg, Felix Ludwig Johann Friedrich 1800–52
Austrian statesman
During the Revolution of 1848 he was made Prime Minister, and created a centralized and absolutist imperial state. He sought Russian military aid to suppress the Hungarian rebellion (1849), and demonstrated Austrian superiority over Prussia at the Olmütz Convention (1850). His bold initiatives temporarily restored Habsburg domination of European affairs. 📖 Adolph Schwarzenberg, *Prince Felix zu Schwarzenberg, Prime Minister of Austria 1848–1852* (1946)

Schwarzenberg, Karl Philipp, Prince of 1771–1820
Austrian general and diplomat
He took part in the War of the Second Coalition (1792–1802). He was ambassador to Russia in 1808, and when Austria declared war on France in 1809 he participated in the unsuccessful campaign. After the peace treaty he pursued a diplomatic career until Napoleon I demanded him as general of the Austrian contingent in the invasion of Russia in 1812. When Austria turned on Napoleon, Schwarzenberg was made generalissimo of the allied armies which won the battles of Dresden and Leipzig in 1813. In 1814 he helped to occupy Paris.

Schwarzenegger, Arnold 1947–
US film actor

He was born in Thal, near Graz in Austria. A body-builder and former Mr Universe, he made his film debut in *Hercules Goes to New York* (1969). Small roles followed before more of his personality was seen in *Stay Hungry* (1976) and the documentary *Pumping Iron* (1977). His physical prowess won him roles in such epics as *Conan the Barbarian* (1981) and his stardom was confirmed as the taciturn cyborg in *The Terminator* (1984). His most successful films include *Predator* (1987) and *Total Recall* (1990). Despite attempts to broaden his appeal in comedies like *Twins* (1988) and *Jingle All the Way* (1996), he remains most popular in spectacular big-budget adventure stories like *True Lies* (1994), *Eraser* (1996) and *Batman and Robin* (1997).

Schwarzkopf, Dame Elisabeth 1915–
Austrian – British soprano

Born in Jarotschin, she studied at the Berlin High School for Music, making her debut there in 1938. Later, she sang in the Vienna State Opera (1944–48). She settled in Great Britain in 1948 and joined the Royal Opera, Covent Garden, London (1948–51), at first specializing in coloratura roles (notably as Zerbinetta in Strauss's *Ariadne auf Naxos*) and only later appearing as a lyric soprano. She eschewed modern music, although she sang the first Anne Trulove in Stravinsky's *The Rake's Progress* (1951) and William Walton wrote Cressida for her. She is chiefly celebrated for her performance in the central German repertory, in opera, especially Mozart (the Countess in *Le Nozze di Figaro* and Elvira in *Don Giovanni*), and in lieder, especially Schubert and Hugo Wolf. She was made a DBE in 1992.

Schwarzkopf, H Norman, *known as* Stormin' Norman 1935–
US general

Born in Trenton, New Jersey, into a military family, he became a cadet at the age of 10 and joined the US Army after graduating from West Point. After distinguished service in the Vietnam War and in the 1986 US invasion of Grenada, he became a four-star general in 1988. He was given overall command of the coalition land forces in Operation Desert Shield and Desert Storm following the Iraqi invasion of Kuwait in November 1990, and led the offensive that in just 100 hours brought an end to the Gulf War with minimal casualties among the coalition forces. He retired from the army on his return from the Gulf in 1991 and became an international consultant on modern warfare. He also wrote an autobiography, *It Doesn't Take a Hero* (1992).

Schwarzschild, Karl 1873–1916
German astronomer

Born in Frankfurt am Main, he was the first to predict the existence of black holes. He became interested in astronomy as a schoolboy and had published two papers on binary orbits by the time he was 16. Educated at the universities of Strassburg and Munich, he was appointed director of the Göttingen Observatory (1901) and the Astrophysical Observatory in Potsdam (1909). His lasting contributions are theoretical and were largely made during the last year of his life. In 1916, while serving on the Russian front, he wrote two papers on Einstein's general theory of relativity, giving the first solution to the complex partial differential equations of the theory. He also introduced the idea that when a star contracts under gravity, there will come a point at which the gravitational field is so intense that nothing, not even light, can escape. The radius to which a star of given mass must contract to reach this stage is known as the Schwarzschild radius. Stars that have contracted below this limit are now known as black holes.

Schwatka, Frederick 1849–92
US explorer

Born in Galena, Illinois, he was lieutenant of cavalry on the frontier until 1877, meanwhile being admitted to the Nebraska Bar and taking a medical degree in New York. From 1878 to 1880 he commanded an expedition to the Arctic which discovered the skeletons of several of Sir John Franklin's party, and provided information to supplement the narratives of Sir John Rae and Admiral McClintock, besides taking part in a sledge journey of 3,251 miles (5,234km). In 1883 he explored the course of the Yukon, in 1886 led the *New York Times* Alaskan expedition, and in Alaska, in 1891, opened up 700 miles (1,127km) of new country.

Schweigger, Johann Salomo Christoph
1779–1857
German physicist

Born in Erlangen, he held chairs in chemistry and physics at Nuremberg, Erlangen and Halle. He was one of the inventors of the simple galvonometer, work to which Johann Poggendorff, André Ampère and Amedeo Avogadro also contributed.

Schweinfurth, Georg August 1836–1925
German explorer, botanist and anthropologist

Born in Riga, he studied botany and palaeontology at Heidelberg, Munich and Berlin universities, and from 1864 to 1866 undertook botanical expeditions along the Red Sea and inland along the Nile to Khartoum. He returned in 1869, travelling from Khartoum up the White Nile and through the country of the Dinka, Bongo and Niam-Niam peoples, confirming the existence of the Pygmy Akka. He also discovered the Welle River. His collections were destroyed by fire, but much important detail is recorded in his *Heart of Africa* (2 vols, 1873). From 1873 to 1874 he travelled with Gerhard Rohlfs in the Libyan desert and then settled in Cairo, where he became curator of museums and established a geographical society. In 1889 he moved to Berlin but continued his explorations in Eritrea.

Schweitzer, Albert 1875–1965
Alsatian medical missionary, theologian, musician and philosopher, and Nobel Prize winner

He was born in Kaysersberg, in Alsace, and brought up in Günsbach in the Münster valley, where he attended the local *realgymnasium*, learned the organ under Charles Widor in Paris, and studied theology and philosophy at Strasbourg, Paris and Berlin. In 1896 he resolved to live for science and art until he was 30 and then devote his life to serving humanity. In 1899 he obtained his doctorate on Kant's philosophy of religion, became curate at St Nicholas Church, Strasbourg, in 1902 *privat-dozent* at the university, and in 1903 principal of the theological college. In 1905 he published his authoritative study, *J S Bach, le musicien-poète* (1905, Eng trans by Ernest Newman, 1911), followed in 1906 by a notable essay on organ design. In 1913 he published *Geschichte der Leben-Jesu Forschung*, (Eng trans *The Quest of the Historical Jesus*, 1910), which emphasized the role of Jesus Christ as the herald of God's kingdom at hand and reduced the importance of Christ's ethical teaching. It marked a revolution in New Testament criticism. Several studies of St Paul, including *Geschichte der Paulinischen Forschung* (1911, Eng trans 1912) and *Die Mystik des Apostels Paulus* (1930, Eng trans *The Mysticism of Paul the Apostle*, 1931), were intended as companion volumes. In addition to his internationally recognized work as musicologist, theologian and organist, he began to study medicine (1905), resigned as Principal of the theological college (1906) and, when he had qualified in 1913, went with his new wife to set up a hospital to fight leprosy and sleeping sickness at Lambaréné, a deserted mission station on the Ogowe river in the heart of French Equatorial Africa. Except for his internment by the French (1917–18) as a German and periodic visits to

Europe to raise funds for his mission by giving organ recitals, he made his self-built hospital the centre of his paternalistic service to Africans, in a spirit 'not of benevolence but of atonement'. His newly discovered ethical principle 'reverence for life' was fully worked out in relation to the defects of European civilization in *Verfall und Wiederaufbau der Kultur* (1923, Eng trans *The Decay and Restoration of Civilization*, 1923) and philosophically in *Kultur und Ethik* (1923, Eng trans 1923). He was Hibbert lecturer at Oxford and London (1934) and Gifford lecturer at Edinburgh (1934–35). He was awarded the Nobel Peace Prize in 1952. His other works include *On the Edge of the Primeval Forest* (Eng trans 1922), *More from the Primeval Forest* (Eng trans 1931), *Out of My Life and Thought* (1931, postscript 1949), and *From My African Notebook* (1938). 📖 George Seaver, *Albert Schweitzer, Christian Revolutionary* (1956)

Schwenkfeld, Kaspar von c.1490–1561
German reformer and mystic
Born in Ossig, near Liegnitz, he studied at Cologne and Frankfurt universities. He served at various German courts, and about 1525 became a Protestant, rejecting both Lutheranism and Catholicism and aiming at 'Reformation by the Middle Way'. He was banished and persecuted, but attracted large numbers of disciples. Most of his 90 works were burned by both Protestants and Catholics. Some of his persecuted followers (most numerous in Silesia and Swabia) emigrated to Holland. In 1734, 40 families emigrated to England, and from there to Pennsylvania, where, as Schwenkfeldians, they maintained a distinct existence.

Schwimmer, Rosika 1877–1948
Hungarian feminist and pacifist
Born in Budapest, she was active as a journalist in the Hungarian women's movement, and was a co-founder of a feminist-pacifist group. She became vice-president of the Women's International League for Peace and Freedom, and from 1918 to 1919 was Hungarian Minister to Switzerland. In 1920, in order to escape the country's anti-Semitic leadership, she emigrated to the USA, but was refused citizenship on the grounds of her pacifism. She continued to campaign for peace and before the outbreak of World War II was outspoken in her criticism of growing European Fascism.

Schwinger, Julian 1918–94
US physicist and Nobel Prize winner
One of Harvard's youngest professors, he shared the 1965 Nobel Prize for physics with Richard Feynman and Sin-Itiro Tomonaga. He was one of the founders of quantum electrodynamics. He served as Professor of Physics at the University of California in Los Angeles from 1972 to 1980, and University Professor from 1980 until his death.

Schwitters, Kurt 1887–1948
German artist
Born in Hanover, he studied at the Dresden Academy and painted abstract pictures before joining the Dadaists. His best-known contribution to the anarchic movement was *Merz*, his name for a form of collage made from everyday detritus: broken glass, tram tickets, scraps of paper picked up in the street. From 1920 he slowly built a three-dimensional construction (his '*Merzbau*') which filled his house until it was destroyed in an air raid in 1943. In 1937 he fled from the Nazi regime to Norway, and from there in 1940 to England, where he built but did not complete another *Merzbau* (1947–48).

Sciascia, Leonardo 1921–89
Sicilian novelist
Born in Racalmuto, he was a teacher and politician, and his first published work was *Favole della dittatura* (1950, 'Fables of Dictatorship'). He took Sicily as the focus of his work; his themes embrace its society, past and present, which he saw as exemplifying the political, social and spiritual tensions to be found throughout Europe. *Le parrocchie di Regalpetra* (1956, Eng trans *Salt in the Wound*, 1969) pointed the way ahead for his fiction and subsequent works developed his early themes. *Candido* (1977) was published in English in 1977 and in the 1980s his novels, several of which were re-translated, reached a wider English-speaking audience. These include *Il consiglio d'Egitto* (1963, Eng trans *The Council of Egypt*, 1966) and *A ciascuno il suo* (1968, Eng trans *A Man's Blessing*, US 1968; UK 1969). 📖 G Jackson, *Sciascia: a thematic and structural study* (1981)

Scipio Africanus, Publius Cornelius, *known as* Scipio the Elder 236–183BC
Roman soldier and politician
Hero of the Second Punic War (218–201BC), he brought Spain under Roman control, expelling the Carthaginians led by Hasdrubal. He was elected consul in 205, and in 204 he sailed with 30,000 men to carry on the war in Africa, where his successes forced the Carthaginians to recall Hannibal from Italy. His victory at Zama in 202 ended the war. Scipio was granted the surname Africanus, and held a second consulship in 194. In 190 he and his brother Lucius defeated Antiochus III of Syria in the campaign of Magnesia. However, their leniency towards Antiochus caused the Senate to charge them with receiving bribes. Despite popular support, Scipio retired to his estate in Campania. His daughter was Cornelia, mother of the Gracchi.

Scipio Aemilianus Africanus, Publius Cornelius, *known as* Scipio the Younger 185–129BC
Roman general and politician
He was a son of Lucius Aemilius Paullus who conquered Macedon, but was adopted by his kinsman Publius Scipio, son of Scipio Africanus the Elder. He served in Spain under Lucius Lucullus (151BC), and later his distinction as military tribune in the Third Punic War (149–146) attracted attention. He was elected consul in 147 and, although he did not qualify for the office, was given supreme command. Polybius records Scipio's famous Siege of Carthage, which fell and was sacked by Roman troops in 146. In 134 he held a second consulship and defeated the Numantines in a prolonged siege and with subsequent destruction of their city. He subsequently took a leading role in Roman politics in opposition to his brother-in-law Tiberius Gracchus. He died suddenly in 129, perhaps murdered by an adherent of the Gracchi.

Scofield, (David) Paul 1922–
English actor
Born in Hurstpierpoint, Sussex, he was interested in amateur dramatics as a child, joined the Croydon Repertory School and studied at the London Mask Theatre before making his professional debut in *Desire Under the Elms* (1940). He appeared with various repertory companies before settling in London, where his early successes included *The Seagull* (1949), *Ring Round the Moon* (1950) and *Time Remembered* (1954–55). His range continued to broaden in plays as diverse as *The Power and the Glory* (1956), *Expresso Bongo* (1958) and as Sir Thomas More in *A Man for All Seasons* (1960), which he repeated on Broadway (1962), winning a Tony Award. He made his first film, *That Lady*, in 1955 but has since made only rare film appearances, despite winning an Academy Award for the screen version of *A Man for All Seasons* (1966). He appeared as the King of France in Kenneth Branagh's film of *Henry V* (1989) and as the ghost in *Hamlet* (1990). Associate director of the National Theatre (1970–72), his later stage work includes *Amadeus* (1979), *Othello* (1980),

I'm Not Rappaport (1986), *Heartbreak House* (1992) and *John Gabriel Borkman* (1996). Recent films include *Quiz Show* (1994) and *The Crucible* (1996).

Scogan, John fl.1480–1500
English jester
He performed at the court of **Edward IV**, and his *Jests* are said to have been compiled by **Andrew Boorde**.

Scopas 4th century BC
Greek sculptor
Born on Paros, he moved to Athens and was the founder with **Praxiteles** of the later Attic school. He worked on the sculptures for the temple of Athena at Tegea and on the tomb of Mausolus at Halicarnassus. His work was noted for its depiction of strong emotion, and there are copies of his dancing maenads and Meleager.

Scopes, John Thomas 1900–70
US educator
Born in Salem, Illinois, he became a high-school teacher in Dayton, Tennessee, where he broke a state law by teaching **Charles Darwin**'s theory of evolution and was brought to trial. In the famous Scopes ('Monkey') Trial (1925), he was defended by **Clarence Darrow** in opposition to prosecuting attorney **W(illiam) J(ennings) Bryan** in a struggle between modern science and Christian fundamentalism. He was convicted and fined $100, but his conviction was overturned on a technicality.

Scorel, Jan van 1495–1562
Netherlandish painter
Born in Schoorel, near Alkmaar, he studied painting in Amsterdam and, by 1517, was working in Utrecht. In 1519 he travelled to Germany in order to visit **Albrecht Dürer** at his home in Nuremberg but found him preoccupied with the activities of **Martin Luther**. He went on to Venice where he was much influenced by the work of **Giorgione**. After a pilgrimage to Jerusalem, he returned to Italy in 1521 and in Rome received the patronage of the Utrecht pope **Adrian VI**. During this stay he studied the work of **Michelangelo** and **Raphael**. He returned to Utrecht and stayed there, except for a journey to France in 1540. Much of his work was destroyed by the iconoclasts of the Reformation but his surviving work demonstrates how much he was affected by the art of the south, combing the ideals of the Renaissance with the atmospheric traditions of Netherlandish art. His work had a great influence on subsequent Netherlandish painters.

Scoresby, William 1789–1857
English explorer and scientist
He was born near Whitby, Yorkshire, and as a boy went with his father, a whaling captain, to the Greenland seas. He studied chemistry and natural philosophy at Edinburgh University, and then made several voyages to the whaling grounds which he described in *An Account of The Arctic Regions* (1820), the first scientific accounts of the Arctic seas and lands. In 1822 he surveyed 400 miles (644km) of the east coast of Greenland. He was ordained in 1825 and held various charges at Exeter and Bradford, but continued his scientific investigations, travelling to Australia in 1856 to study terrestrial magnetism. He became involved in the controversy about the fate of the explorer Sir **John Franklin**, and wrote *The Franklin Expedition* (1851). He worked on improving the marine compass, and was elected FRS in 1824.

Scorsese, Martin 1942–
US film director
Born in Queens, New York City, as a student at New York University he made a number of short films, beginning with *What's A Nice Girl Like You Doing in a Place Like This?* (1963). He then worked towards his first feature, *Who's That Knocking at My Door?* (1969) and subsequently lectured, made commercials and served as an editor before returning to direction with *Boxcar Bertha* (1972). His work has sought to illuminate masculine aggression and sexual inequality, frequently questioning traditional US values, and with films such as *Alice Doesn't Live Here Anymore* (1974), *Taxi Driver* (1976) and *Raging Bull* (1980), he established himself as one of the foremost directors of his generation. In 1988 he achieved a long-held ambition to film **Nikos Kazantzakis**' controversial novel *The Last Temptation of Christ*. His subsequent films include *Goodfellas* (1990), *Cape Fear* (1991), *The Age of Innocence* (1993) and *Casino* (1995).

Scot or Scott, Reginald c.1538–1599
English author
He studied at Hart Hall, Oxford, was MP for Shepway (1588–89), and is credited with the introduction of hop-growing into England. His *Perfect Platform of a Hop-garden* (1574) was the first manual on hop culture in the country, and his famous *Discoverie of Witchcraft* (1584) is an exposure of the current fashion for witchcraft. King **James VI and I** ordered it to be burnt.

Scott
Scottish Border family
Originating in Peeblesshire, they possessed Buccleuch in Selkirkshire in 1415, and Branxholm, near Hawick (from 1420). Sir Walter Scott fought for **James II** at Arkinholm against the Douglases (1455), and his descendants acquired Liddesdale, Eskdale, Dalkeith, and other places, with the titles Lord Scott of Buccleuch (1606) and Earl of Buccleuch (1619). They fought at Flodden (1513), and were involved in the rescue of **William Armstrong** ('Kinmont Willie') in 1596. Anna (1651–1732), the daughter of the 2nd Earl, married James, Duke of **Monmouth**, who took the surname Scott and was created Duke of Buccleuch. The Harden branch (represented by Lord Polwarth) separated from the main stem (1346), and from this sprang the Scotts of Raeburn, ancestors of the novelist Sir **Walter Scott**.

Scott, Agnes Neill See Muir, Willa

Scott, Alexander c.1515–1584
Scottish lyric poet
He became musician and organist at the Augustinian priory of Inchmahome in the Firth of Forth in 1548, and had associations with the court of **Mary, Queen of Scots**. He was a canon of Inchaffray in Perthshire in 1565, and in 1567 bought an estate in Fife. He wrote 36 short poems, either courtly love lyrics or poems offering moral advice. A poet of the school of **William Dunbar**, he is considered to be the last of the Scottish 'Makars', poets of the 15th–16th centuries. 📖 A K Scott (ed), *Poems* (1953)

Scott, C(harles) P(restwich) 1846–1932
English newspaper editor
Born in Bath, he was educated at Corpus Christi College, Oxford. At the age of 26 he was appointed editor of the *Manchester Guardian*, which he developed into a serious liberal rival of *The Times*. It was characterized by independent and often controversial editorial policies, such as opposition to the Boer War, and by high literary standards. He was a Liberal MP (1895–1906).

Scott, Cyril Meir 1879–1970
English composer
Born in Oxton, Cheshire, he studied the piano in Frankfurt am Main, later returning there to study composition. His works were heard in London at the turn of the century, and in 1913 he was able to introduce his music to Vienna. His opera *The Alchemist* had its first performance in Essen in 1925. He wrote three symphonies, piano, violin and cello concertos, and numerous choral

and orchestral works; he is best known for his piano pieces and songs. He also wrote poems, and studies of music, homoeopathy and occultism.

Scott, David 1806–49
Scottish historical painter

Born in Edinburgh, he was apprenticed to his father as a line-engraver. He studied at the Trustee's Academy and in 1831 designed his 25 'Illustrations to the *Ancient Mariner*' (1837). He visited Italy in 1832–33, and painted *The Vintager*, now in the National Gallery, London. Many imaginative and historical paintings followed, such as *The Traitor's Gate* and *Ariel and Caliban*. He was the brother of William Bell Scott.

Scott, Douglas 1913–90
English designer

Born in Lambeth, London, he trained as a silversmith at the Central School of Arts and Crafts. His first designs were light fittings for town halls and cinemas; later he moved to the office of Raymond Loewy and worked on household equipment and car bodies. He worked at De Havillands during World War II, and afterwards taught a design course at the Central School, London. His most famous achievement is the Routemaster bus designed for London Transport. He became a Royal Designer for Industry in 1970.

Scott, Doug (las Keith) 1941–
English mountaineer

Born in Nottingham, he has been one of the world's leading climbers since 1965, when he made the first ascent of Tarso Teiroko in the Sahara. He initially concentrated on 'big wall' routes in Yosemite, USA, and elsewhere, but then turned to expeditions to major peaks. He has made several first ascents, including Mt McKinley, the Ogre, Kangchenjunga, Nuptse, Shisha Pangma and Chamlang. In 1975 he and Dougal Haston (1940–77) were among the first Britons to reach the summit of Mt Everest by way of the south-west face, on an expedition led by Chris Bonington. Also with Bonington, Scott made an epic five-day descent of the Ogre, after he had broken both his legs in a fall. He was president of the Alpine Climbing Group (1976–82), is vice-president of the British Mountaineering Council (1993–), and his publications include *Himalayan Climber* (1992).

Scott, Dred c.1795–1858
US slave

Born in Southampton County, Virginia, he made legal and constitutional history as the nominal plaintiff in a test case that sought to obtain his freedom on the ground that he lived in the free state of Illinois—the celebrated Dred Scott Case (1848–57). The Supreme Court ruled against him, but he was soon emancipated, and became a hotel porter in St Louis, Missouri.

Scott, Dukinfield Henry 1854–1934
English botanist

Born in London, he was the son of Sir George Gilbert Scott. He studied at the universities of Oxford and Würzburg, and became assistant Professor of Botany at the Royal College of Science and later keeper of Jodrell Laboratory, Kew (1892), devoting himself to plant anatomy and later to palaeobotany. He collaborated with William Crawford Williamson in a number of brilliant studies of fossil plants, particularly their fruiting bodies, and in 1904 established the class Pteridospermeae. With Williamson he demonstrated the close evolutionary relation between ferns and cycads, which was important to phylogenetic studies. He published several notable textbooks, including *Introduction to Structural Botany* (1894–96) and *Studies in Fossil Botany* (1900).

Scott, Francis George 1880–1958
Scottish composer

Born in Hawick in the Borders, he studied at the universities of Edinburgh and Durham, and in Paris under Roger-Ducasse. From 1925 to 1946 he was a lecturer in music at Jordanhill Training College for Teachers, Glasgow. His *Scottish Lyrics* (5 vols, 1921–39) comprise original settings of songs by William Dunbar, Robert Burns and other poets, most notably of Hugh MacDiarmid; they exemplify Scott's aim of embodying in music the true spirit of Scotland. Primarily a song composer, he also wrote the orchestral suite *The Seven Deadly Sins* (after Dunbar's poem) and other orchestral works.

Scott, Sir George Gilbert 1811–78
English architect

Born in Gawcott, Buckinghamshire, he was inspired by the Cambridge Camden Society and an article of August Pugin (1840–41). He became the leading practical architect in the Gothic revival, and oversaw the building or restoration of many public buildings, ecclesiastical and civil. Examples of his work are the Martyrs Memorial at Oxford (1841), St Nicholas at Hamburg (1844), St George's at Doncaster, the new India office (exceptionally, owing to pressure by Lord Henry Palmerston, in the style of the Italian Renaissance), the Home and Colonial Offices (from 1858), the Albert Memorial (1862–63), St Pancras station and hotel in London (1865), Glasgow University (1865), the chapels of Exeter and St John's Colleges, Oxford, and the Episcopal Cathedral in Edinburgh. In 1868 he was appointed Professor of Architecture at the Royal Academy. The establishment of the Society for Protection of Ancient Buildings (1877) was due to his inspiration. He wrote works on English medieval church architecture. He was buried in Westminster Abbey, London. 🕮 *Personal and Professional Recollections* (1879)

Scott, Sir Giles Gilbert 1880–1960
English architect

Born in London, he was educated at Beaumont College, Old Windsor. He won a competition in 1903 for the design of the Anglican Cathedral in Liverpool (consecrated 1924). Later designs include the new nave at Downside Abbey, the new buildings at Clare College, the new Bodleian Library at Oxford (1936–46) and the new Cambridge University Library (1931–34). He planned the new Waterloo Bridge (1939–45) and was responsible for the rebuilding of the House of Commons after World War II. He was the grandson of Sir George Gilbert Scott.

Scott, James Brown 1866–1943
US international lawyer

Born in Kincardine, Ontario, Canada and educated at Philadelphia and Harvard, he taught law in several universities and was solicitor to the US Department of State (1906–10). He was a delegate to the Second Hague Peace Conference (1907) and an arbitrator in international disputes. He wrote *The Hague Peace Conferences of 1899 and 1907* (1909) and *Law, the State and the International Community* (1939); he edited the *American Journal of International Law* (1907–24) and was president of the American Institute of International Law (1915–40).

Scott, Mackay Hugh Baillie 1865–1945
English architect and designer

Born in Kent, he designed the decoration for the palace of the Grand Duke of Hesse at Darmstadt, which was carried out by the Guild of Handicraft in consultation with Charles Ashbee in 1898. In 1901 he gave up his practice in Douglas and moved to Bedford. His furniture is simple, solid, bold and generally decorated with a degree of Art Nouveau ornamentation. He went on to design numerous houses in Great Britain and Europe before retiring in 1939.

Scott, Michael c.1175–c.1230
Scottish scholar and astrologer

Born probably in Durham, of Border ancestry, he studied at Oxford, Paris and Padua, and was tutor and astrologer at Palermo to **Frederick II** of Germany. He settled at Toledo (1209–20) and translated Arabic versions of **Aristotle's** works and **Averroës's** commentaries. Returning to the Imperial court at Palermo, he rejected an offer of the archbishopric of Cashel (1223). He wrote a learned work on astrology, *Quaestio curiosa de natura solis et lunae* (1622), and his translations of **Aristotle** were seemingly used by St **Albertus Magnus**, and was one of the two familiar to **Dante**. He was known as the 'wondrous wizard' and Dante alludes to him in the *Inferno* in a way which proves that his fame as a magician had already spread over Europe; he is also referred to by Albertus Magnus and Vincent de Beauvais. There is a grave said to be his in Melrose Abbey.

Scott, Michael 1789–1835
Scottish writer

He was born in Cowlairs, Glasgow, and educated at Glasgow University (1801–05), and then went to seek his fortune in Jamaica. He spent a few years in the West Indies and in 1822 settled in Glasgow. His vivid and amusing stories on life in the Caribbean, *Tom Cringle's Log* (1829–33) and *The Cruise of the Midge* (1834–35), first appeared serially in *Blackwood's Magazine*. ◫ Sir G Douglas, *The Blackwood Group* (1897)

Scott, Michael 1907–83
English Anglican missionary and social and political activist

He was educated at King's College, Taunton, and St Paul's College, Grahamstown, and served in a London East End parish and as chaplain in India (1935–39), where he collaborated with the communists. He was invalided out of the RAF in 1941, and served in various missions in South Africa (1943–50). No longer associating with communists, he exposed the atrocities in the Bethal farming area and in the Transvaal, defended the Basutos against wrongful arrest, and brought the case of the dispossessed Herero tribe before the United Nations. As a result, he became persona non grata in the Union and in the Central African Federation. He founded the London Africa Bureau in 1952. In 1958 he suffered a brief period of imprisonment for his part in nuclear-disarmament demonstrations, and he was expelled from Nagaland in 1966. He wrote an autobiography, *A Time to Speak* (1958), and *A Search for Peace and Justice* (1980).

Scott, Paul Mark 1920–78
English novelist

Born in London, he served in the British army (1940–43), and in the Indian army in India and Malaya (1943–46). The first of his 12 novels was *Johnnie Sahib* (1952), and his best-known work is *The Raj Quartet* (*The Jewel in the Crown*, 1966; *The Day of the Scorpion*, 1968; *The Towers of Silence*, 1971; *A Division of Spoils*, 1975). Set in the years 1939–47, the overlapping novels provide a vivid portrait of India during the last years of the Raj; they were adapted for television and brought Scott a late acclaim. *Staying On* (1977), which can be seen as a coda to the *Quartet*, was awarded the Booker Prize. ◫ Hilary Spurling, *Paul Scott* (1991)

Scott, Sir Percy Moreton, 1st Baronet 1853–1924
English naval commander and gunnery expert

Born in London, he entered the navy in 1866 and saw active service in Ashanti (Gold Coast), Egypt, South Africa and China. Retiring in 1909, he returned to active service as gunnery adviser to the British fleet. His methods and inventions transformed naval gunnery, although he had influential opponents. He commanded the anti-aircraft defences of London (1915–18), and foresaw the importance of air power at sea. He wrote *Fifty Years in the Royal Navy* (1919).

Scott, Sir Peter Markham 1909–89
English artist and ornithologist

He was born in London, the son of **Robert Falcon Scott**, was educated at Cambridge, and became an enthusiastic hunter of wildfowl. He went on to the State Academy School at Munich and the Royal Academy of Art Schools in London to study painting, and became a professional artist, holding his first exhibition in 1933. He represented Great Britain in single-handed dinghy sailing at the 1936 Olympic Games, served with distinction with the Royal Navy in World War II, founded the Severn Wild Fowl Trust in 1948, explored in the Canadian Arctic in 1949, and was leader of several ornithological expeditions (Iceland, 1951, 1953; Australasia and the Pacific Ocean, 1956–57). Through television he helped to popularize natural history, and his writings include *Morning Flight* (1935), *Wild Chorus* (1938), *The Battle of the Narrow Seas* (1945) and *Wild Geese and Eskimos* (1951). He also published an autobiography, *The Eye of the Wind* (1961). ◫ Elspeth Huxley, *Peter Scott: Painter and Naturalist* (1993)

Scott, Reginald See **Scot, Reginald**

Scott, Robert Falcon 1868–1912
English explorer

Born near Devonport, Devon, he joined the navy in 1881. In the *Discovery* he commanded the National Antarctic expedition (1901–04) which explored the Ross Sea area, and discovered King Edward VII Land. He was promoted captain in 1904. In 1910 he embarked upon his second expedition in the *Terra Nova*, and with a sledge party which consisted of **Edward Wilson**, **Lawrence Oates**, H R Bowers, Edgar Evans and himself, reached the South Pole on 17 January 1912, only to discover that the Norwegian expedition under **Roald Amundsen** had beaten them by a month. Delayed by blizzards and the sickness of Evans and Oates, who both died, the remaining members of the team eventually perished in the vicinity of One Ton Depot at the end of March, where their bodies and diaries were found by a search party eight months later. Scott was posthumously knighted, and the Scott Polar Research Institute at Cambridge was founded in his memory. He was the father of Sir **Peter Markham Scott**.

Scott, Ronnie, *originally* Ronald Schatt 1927–96
English saxophonist and philosophical humorist

Born in London, he learned his trade, like so many British jazzmen, on the transatlantic liners. He founded his own group in 1953, and his legendary London jazz club in Gerrard Street in 1959 (in Frith Street from 1965). The album title *Never Pat a Burning Dog* (1991) gives a sense of his more philosophical side. The US bassist **Charles Mingus** identified him as the most blues-soaked of the white saxophonists; he remained a distinctive player with a less-than-conventional approach to harmony. John Fordham's biography, *Let's Join Hands and Contact the Living* (1986), immortalizes a famous line delivered to an unresponsive audience.

Scott, Rose 1847–1925
Australian feminist and social reformer

Born in Glendon, near Singleton, New South Wales, she was educated by governesses. After her father's death (1879) she moved to Sydney, where she became a founder of the Women's Literary Society (1889). This developed into the Women's Suffrage League, of which she became secretary in 1891. She lobbied tirelessly for women's suffrage until 1902, when the Women's Suffrage Act was passed in New South Wales. She also campaigned for

Scott, Sir Walter 1771–1832
Scottish novelist and poet

Walter Scott was born in Edinburgh. His father was Walter Scott, a Writer to the Signet, and his mother was Anne Rutherford, a daughter of the Professor of Medicine at Edinburgh University. As a young boy he contracted polio in his right leg, which lamed him for life, and was sent to his grandfather's farm at Sandyknowe in Tweedale to recuperate, thus coming to know the Border country which figures often in his work. He studied at the High School, Edinburgh (1779–83), and at the University, but his real education came from people and from books such as Henry Fielding and Tobias Smollett, Horace Walpole's Castle of Otranto, Edmund Spenser and Ariosto and, above all, Bishop Percy's Reliques (1765) and German ballad poetry. He entered his father's office as a law clerk, did well and rose to become an advocate in 1792.

His first publication consisted of rhymed versions of ballads by Gottfried Bürger in 1796. The following year he was a volunteer in the yeomanry during the Napoleonic Wars, and married Charlotte Charpentier, the daughter of a French émigré, in Carlisle on Christmas Eve. In 1799 he was appointed Sheriff-Depute of Selkirkshire.

The ballad meanwhile absorbed all his literary interest: a translation of Goethe's Göetz von Berlichingen (1799) was followed by his first original ballads, Glenfinlas and The Eve of St John. His earlier 'raids' into the western Borders, especially Liddesdale, to collect ballads led to the publication by James Ballantyne, a printer in Kelso, of Scott's first major work, The Minstrelsy of the Scottish Border (vols 1 and 2, 1802; vol 3, 1803). The Border ballads collected in these volumes had often been edited, or 'improved', by Scott. The Lay of the Last Minstrel (1805), which grew from a ballad he had composed for the third volume of The Minstrelsy, made him the most popular author of the day. The other romances which followed— Marmion (1808) and The Lady of the Lake (1810)—enhanced his fame, but the lukewarm reception of Rokeby (1813), The Lord of the Isles (1815) and Harold the Dauntless (1817) turned his attention away from the ballad form and toward writing novels. Some years later, he admitted in a letter to a friend that he had 'felt the prudence of giving way before the more forcible and powerful genius of Byron'.

In 1811 he bought some land and began to build his country seat, Abbotsford, near Galashiels, in the Borders. Meanwhile, in Edinburgh, the publishing firm which he had set up (although his involvement had not been made public) with James Ballantyne and his brother John following the success of The Minstrelsy, was expanding. However, Scott's and the firm's connections with publisher Archibald Constable and his London agents were to be their undoing: Scott lost all control over the financial side of the extensive publication programme on which he now embarked. He was declared bankrupt, along with Ballantyne's and Constable's, in 1826—in the middle of his great career as a novelist. Only following this bankruptcy did he publicly acknowledge the authorship of his novels, which had been published under the name of 'The Author of Waverley'.

The Waverley novels fall into three groups: first, from Waverley (1814) to The Bride of Lammermoor (1819) and A Legend of Montrose (1819); next, from Ivanhoe (1820) to The Talisman (1825), the year before his bankruptcy; Woodstock (1826) opens the last period, which closes with Castle Dangerous and Count Robert of Paris (1832), in the year of his death. The first period established the historical novel based, in Scott's case, on religious

cont

protective legislation, for juvenile offenders to be tried in special children's courts and for the age of consent for girls to be raised to 16. She remained unmarried, and worked for the International League of Women and was president of the Peace Society from 1907. She remained true to her pacifist views throughout World War I and earned a reputation as a patron of Australian art and literature.

Scott, Sheila, originally Sheila Christine Hopkins
1927–88
English aviator

Born in Worcester, she joined the Royal Naval Section of the Voluntary Aid Detachment, and after World War II spent a year acting under the stage name of Sheila Scott. In 1959 she took her pilot's licence and came fifth in a race from London to Cardiff. She took part in many races and in 1966 she flew 31,000 miles in 33 days and 189 flying hours, the longest solo flight in a single-engined aircraft. Her light-aircraft records include a solo flight from equator to equator over the North Pole (1971). She wrote three books describing her career: I Must Fly (1968), On Top of the World (1973) and Bare Feet in the Sky (1974).

Scott, Terry, originally Owen John Scott 1927–94
English actor

Born in Watford, Hertfordshire, he began his career working with seaside repertory companies and in clubs and pantomime. He and Bill Maynard formed a comedy duo which appeared in a television sit-com, Great Scott It's Maynard (1955), before he appeared in films such as Blue Murder at St Trinian's (1957), I'm All Right, Jack (1959) and seven Carry On films. His string of television successes included Hugh and I (1962–66), Hugh and I Spy (1968), both with Hugh Lloyd, and three different series with June Whitfield: Scott On— (1969–74), Happy Ever After (1974–78) and Terry and June (1979–87).

Scott, Tom 1918–95
Scottish poet

He was born in Partick, Glasgow; as a 'mature student' he graduated from Edinburgh University in the 1950s. With encouragement from T S Eliot he translated poems by François Villon into Scots (Seeven Poems o Maister Francis Villon, 1953). An Ode til New Jerusalem (1956), The Ship and Ither Poems (1963) and the biographic narrative Brand the Builder (1975) established him as a 'maister' in the language. In English, his near epic The Tree (1977) and the angry humanist poem The Dirty Business (1986) were further evidence of his skill as polemicist and poet. The Collected Shorter Poems appeared in 1993.

Scott, Sir Walter See panel above

Scott, Sir William See Stowell, 1st Baron

Scott, William 1913–89
Scottish–Irish painter

Born in Greenock, Strathclyde, Scotland, he studied at Belfast College of Art (1928–31) and at the Royal Academy Schools (1931–35). After World War II he taught at Bath Academy of Art, Corsham (1946–56) and played a leading role in bringing British painting back into the international mainstream. He visited Canada and New York in 1953, meeting Jackson Pollock, Willem de Kooning and other leading Abstract Expressionists. His preferred subject was still life, painted in a simplified, nearly abstract way, eg Frying Pan and Blue Fish (1947). He won first prize in the John Moores Liverpool Exhibition in 1959.

Scott, Sir Walter *cont*

dissension and the clash of English and Scottish, and Highland and Lowland cultures, his aim being to illustrate manners but also to soften animosities. In *Guy Mannering* (1815) and *The Antiquary* (1816) his great humorous characters first appear; these are also found in *Old Mortality* (1816), *Rob Roy* (1817) and *The Heart of Midlothian* (1818).

Scott turned to medieval England in *Ivanhoe*, a novel whose enormous contemporary popularity has sometimes obscured the more lasting appeal of his Scottish novels. With *The Monastery* and *The Abbot* (1820), both set in Scotland, he moved to Reformation times. These and his later works are distinguished by their portraits of queens, kings and princes, such as **James VI and I** in *The Fortunes of Nigel* (1822). The highlights in his last period include *Woodstock* (1826) and *The Fair Maid of Perth* (1828), where again the ballad motif appears.

Scott's shorter verse worked best on a traditional or ballad theme, as in Madge Wildfire's song, 'Proud Maisie', in *The Heart of Midlothian*, and 'Jock o' Hazeldean'. But Highland themes, as in *Pibroch of Donuil Dhu* (1816), equally proved his lyric powers. He was also writing and editing other books, much of which was simply hack work—the editions of **John Dryden** (1808), of **Jonathan Swift** (1814), and the *Life of Napoleon* (9 vols, 1827). However, the *Tales of a Grandfather* (1828–30), a history of Scotland written for his grandson, has a lasting charm, and his three letters 'from Malachi Malagrowther' (1826), are remembered for their patriotic assertion of Scottish interests.

A national figure, Scott helped to supervise the celebration for **George IV**'s visit to Edinburgh in 1822. His last years were plagued by illness, and in 1831–32 he toured the Mediterranean in a government frigate. He died at Abbotsford soon after his return, and was buried in the ruins of Dryburgh Abbey. Publication of a definitive edition of the *Waverley Novels* was begun in 1993 by Edinburgh University Press. The project is scheduled to take 10 years to complete, and the texts will incorporate a mass of textual corrections, and undo the substitution and excisions of Scott's original editors.

📖 W E K Anderson (ed), *The Journal of Sir Walter Scott* (1972); Sir E Johnson, *Sir Walter Scott: the Great Unknown* (2 vols, 1970); J G Lockhart, *Memoirs of the Life of Sir Walter Scott, Bart* (10 vols, 1839).

> J G Lockhart, in his biography of Scott, records an anecdote relating to Scott's tireless dedication to his writing. In June 1814, Lockhart was dining with friends whose house was in George Street, Edinburgh, and after dinner the party retired to the library, which had a window looking north to Castle Street (where Scott had his town residence). After an hour or so, Lockhart noticed that one of the company looked pale, and asked if he felt unwell. 'No,' was the reply, 'I shall be well enough if you will only let me sit where you are, and take my chair; for there is a confounded hand in sight of me here, which has often bothered me before, and now it won't let me fill my glass with a good will. Since we sat down I have been watching it—it fascinates my eye—page after page is finished and thrown on the heap and still it goes on unwearied—and so it will be till candles are brought in, and God knows how long after that. It is the same every night—I can't stand a sight of it when I am not at my books.' 'Some stupid, dogged, engrossing clerk, probably,' said somebody else. 'No,' said the host, 'I well know that hand—'tis Walter Scott's.' This was the hand, Lockhart concludes, that in the evenings of three summer weeks, wrote the last two volumes of *Waverley*.
>
> From *Memoirs of the Life of Sir Walter Scott, Bart* (1839).

Scott, William Bell 1811–90
Scottish painter and poet

Born in Edinburgh, the brother of **David Scott**, while training as an engraver, he also began to write poetry and had verses published for the first time in 1831. He exhibited paintings at the Royal Scottish Academy from 1834. He moved to London in 1837 and, in the following year his first volume of poetry was published. He began exhibiting at the Royal Academy in 1842, and became master of the Government School of Design in Newcastle in 1843. His most notable paintings were of scenes of Northumberland history, which were exhibited in London and Newcastle prior to their installation (1861) at Wallington Hall, Northumberland. He moved back to London in 1864, and in 1875 published *Poems* dedicated to his friends **Dante Gabriel Rossetti**, **William Morris** and **Algernon Charles Swinburne**. His *Autobiographical Notes* were published in 1892.

Scott, Winfield 1786–1866
US general

Born near Petersburg, Virginia, he was admitted to the Bar in 1807, and obtained a commission as artillery captain in 1808. He became a national hero for his part in the War of 1812, rising from lieutenant-colonel to brigadier-general and distinguishing himself at the Battle of Lundy's Lane (1814). After framing the General Regulations and introducing French tactics into the US army, he commanded the war against the seminoles and the Creeks in Florida (1835–37), and helped to settle the disputed boundary line of Maine and New Brunswick (1839). He succeeded to the chief command of the army in 1841. In the Mexican War he took Vera Cruz (26 March 1847), put **Antonio de Santa Anna** to flight and entered the Mexican capital (14 September). Known as 'Old Fuss and Feathers' because of his insistence on military punctilio, he was an unsuccessful Whig candidate for the presidency (1852), and he retained nominal command of the army until October 1861. He was the most notable US military leader in the period between the Revolution and the Civil War.

Scott Brown, Denise 1931–
US architect and urban planner

Born in Nkana, Zambia, she studied at the Architectural Association in London, and at the University of Pennsylvania, where she was assistant professor for five years. Since 1967 she has worked for Venturi, Scott Brown and Associates in Philadelphia, where she introduced a planning division strongly based on the ideas of urban design. She has also designed fabrics, china, glassware, wallpaper, jewellery and furniture. She designed the extension to the National Gallery in London (completed in 1989) and contributed to 25 urban planning schemes, including the master plan for part of Austin, Texas. She was awarded the National Medal of Arts (1992) and the RSA Benjamin Franklin Award (1993). She published *A View from the Campidiglio: Selected Essays 1953–84* (1984, with her husband **Robert Venturi**) and *Urban Concepts* (1990).

Scougall or Scougal, David fl.1654–77
Scottish painter

Little is known about his life, but he was the most important portrait painter in Scotland after the generation of George Jamesone (1588–1644). Many Scottish houses contain portraits attributed to him, although some of these may be by his nephew John Scougall.

Scriabin or Skriabin, Aleksandr Nikolayevich 1872–1915
Russian composer and pianist

Born in Moscow, he studied at the Moscow Conservatory with **Rachmaninov** and **Nikolai Medtner**, and became Professor of Pianoforte (1898–1904). His compositions, which include a piano concerto, three symphonies, two symphonic poems, and 10 sonatas, show an increasing reliance on extramusical factors (even coloured light, as in *Prometheus* of 1910), and the influence of religion and theosophical ideas. His earlier work was influenced by the late romantics, especially **Liszt** and **Chopin**. Among his most widely played works is the *Poem of Ecstasy* (1908).

Scribe, (Augustin) Eugène 1791–1861
French dramatist
He was born in Paris. After 1816 his productions became so popular that he established a 'theatre workshop' in which numerous *collaborateurs* turned out plays under his supervision. The best known are *Un Verre d'eau* (1850, Eng trans *A Glass of Water*, 1851), *Adrienne Lecouvreur* (1848, Eng trans 1883) and *Bataille des dames* (1851, Eng trans *The Ladies' Battle!*, 1851). Scribe also wrote novels and composed the libretti for 60 operas, including *Fra Diavolo* (1842, Eng trans 1857), *Les Huguenots* (1842, Eng trans *The Huguenots*, 1842) and *Le Prophète* (1847, Eng trans *The Prophet*, 1850). 📖 E Legouv̇, *Augustin Scribe* (1874)

Scribner, Charles, *originally* Scrivener 1821–71
US publisher
Born in New York, he graduated from Princeton in 1840, and in 1846 founded with Isaac Baker the New York publishing firm which became Charles Scribner's Sons in 1878. He founded *Scribner's Monthly* (1870–81), which reappeared as *The Century* (1881–1930) after it was bought by the Century Company. His three sons continued the business. 📖 *In the Company of Writers: A Life in Publishing* (1990)

Scripps, Edward Wyllis 1854–1926
US newspaper publisher
Born near Rushville, Illinois, he began his newspaper career with a job on the *Detroit Tribune* in 1872 and joined the staff of the *Detroit Evening News* when it was founded (1873) by his half-brother James Edmund Scripps (1835–1906). With James and another half-brother he founded the *Cleveland Penny Press* in 1878, and two years later they bought papers in St Louis and Cincinnati, thereby creating the first newspaper chain in the USA. To collect and disseminate news by telegraph, Edward joined the partners to establish (1897) the Scripps–McRae Press Association, which became the United Press Association in 1907. In 1902 he founded the Newspaper Enterprise Association to syndicate feature articles, columns and cartoons. His half-sister Ellen Browning (1836–1932), born in London, served on many of the family newspapers. The family interest passed to Robert Paine (1895–1938), Edward's son.

Scroggs, Sir William 1623–83
English judge
Born in Deddington, Oxfordshire, he was Chief Justice of the King's Bench from 1678. He was notorious for cruelty and partiality during the 'Popish Plot' trials (see **Titus Oates**). In 1680 he was impeached and was removed from office on a pension by the king.

Scruggs, Earl See Flatt and Scruggs

Scruton, Kit (Christopher) 1911–90
English engineer
Born in Shipley, Yorkshire, he was a pioneer of wind engineering and industrial aerodynamics. He worked at the National Physical Laboratory and was involved in the 1960s in the testing of long-span bridges, including the Humber and Tamar. He also designed the 'strake', a device to be applied to tall chimneys and similar structures, such as offshore rigs, to prevent vortex-induced oscillations.

Scruton, Roger Vernon 1944–
British political philosopher
He was educated at Jesus College, Cambridge, and was called to the Bar in 1978. He was appointed Professor of Aesthetics at the University of London in 1985 and Professor of Philosophy at Boston University in 1992. He is politically conservative and has defended cultural tradition against aesthetic modernism. He has edited the *Salisbury Review* since 1982, and his publications include *Art and Imagination* (1974, 2nd edn 1982), *The Meaning of Conservatism* (1980) and *Spinoza* (1986).

Scrutton, Sir Thomas Edward 1856–1934
English legal text-writer and judge
Born in London, he was educated at Mill Hill and London University. After an impressive academic career he developed a busy commercial practice and wrote *The Contract of Affreightment as Expressed in Charter-parties and Bills of Lading* (1886). This is still a standard text, while several other of his legal works remain useful. He was made a judge of the King's Bench Division (1910–16) and of the Court of Appeal (1916–34).

Scudamore, Peter 1958–
English National Hunt jockey
Educated at Belmont Abbey School, Hereford, he became stable jockey to David Nicholson in 1978. He was champion jockey for the first time in the 1981–82 season and in 1985 rode his first winner for trainer Martin Pipe. Together they formed a partnership that was to dominate British racing for the next eight years. Although he never won the Grand National or the Gold Cup, he was champion jockey for seven consecutive seasons (1986–93), breaking the season record with 221 wins in 1988–89. In 1993 he retired and turned to training, having ridden a record 1,677 winners. He published his autobiography, *Scu*, in the same year.

Scudder, Samuel Hubbard 1837–1911
US entomologist
Born in Boston, he became an authority on fossil insects, wrote on the Orthoptera and Lepidoptera, and published *Butterflies of the Eastern United States and Canada* (1888–89).

Scudéry, Georges de 1601–67
French writer
He was born in Le Havre, and after a brief military career he wrote a number of plays which achieved some success. In 1637 his *Observations sur le Cid* led to a controversy with **Pierre Corneille**. The brother of **Madeleine de Scudéry**, he later wrote novels and had a small share in his sister's works, which first appeared under his name. 📖 C Clare, *Un Matamore des lettres* (1929)

Scudéry, Madeleine de 1608–1701
French novelist
She was born in Le Havre, the sister of **Georges de Scudéry**. Left an orphan at six, she went to Paris in 1639 and with her brother was accepted into the literary society of Mme de **Rambouillet**'s salon. From 1644 to 1647 she was in Marseilles with her brother. She had begun her literary career with the romance *Ibrahim ou l'illustre Bassa* (1641, Eng trans *Ibrahim; or, The Illustrious Bassa*, 1652), and her most famous work was the 10-volume *Artamène, ou le Grand Cyrus* (1649–59, Eng trans *Artamenes, or the Grand Cyrus*, 1653–55), written with her brother, followed by *Clélie* (10 vols, 1654–60, Eng trans *Clelia*, 1656–61) and *Mathilde d'Anguilon* (1667, 'Mathilda of Aquilar'). They were popular at the court because of their lampooning of public figures. She was satirized by **Molière** in *Les précieuses ridicules* (1659, 'The Conceited Young Ladies'). 📖 C Aragonnès, *Madeleine de Scudéry, Reine du tendre* (1934)

Sculthorpe, Peter Joshua 1929–
Australian composer

Born in Launceston, Tasmania, he studied at the Conservatorium of Melbourne University, and later in Oxford with Egon Wellesz and Edmund Rubbra. Small-scale works, chamber music and the *Irkanda* series (1961) were followed by his four *Sun Music* pieces (1965, new recording 1996). In 1974 the Australian Opera performed his opera *Rites of Passage*, and in 1982 the Australian Broadcasting Corporation commissioned an opera for television, *Quiros*, to mark its 50th anniversary. *Sun Song* (1989), specially written for the Australian group Synergy, employs Aboriginal themes originally noted down by the French explorer Nicolas Baudin in the early 19th century. Other major works include a cello requiem (1979) and a piano concerto (1983). He is a leading figure in promoting Australian music overseas. His work, though not prolific, is much influenced by the Australian landscape and is now a popular feature in the repertoire of Australian orchestras touring abroad. His later works include *Port Arthur: In Memoriam* (1996), which alludes to the Tasmanian massacre of April 1996.

Seaborg, Glen Theodore 1912–
US atomic scientist and Nobel Prize winner

He was born in Ishpeming, Michigan, and educated at the University of California at Los Angeles and at Berkeley, where he became an instructor in chemistry in 1939, professor in 1945 and Chancellor from 1958 to 1961. Following the work of Frederick Soddy, his earliest work was on isotopes, discovering many previously unknown isotopes among the common elements. His principal work was with Enrico Fermi's team, which achieved the first chain reaction in uranium-235 in 1942. It was his laboratory which, in 1945, produced enough plutonium for the first atomic bomb. Seaborg and his team continued research on further transuranic elements and in 1944 synthesized americium and curium. In 1950, by bombarding these with alpha rays, they produced berkelium and californium. They later produced einsteinium, fermium, mendelevium and unnilhexium. In 1951 Seaborg shared the Nobel Prize for chemistry with McMillan. He was Chairman of the US Atomic Energy Commission from 1961 to 1971, then University Professor of Chemistry at Berkeley (1971–). His many publications include *Stemming the Tide* (1987) which focuses upon arms control in the Johnson years.

Seabury, Samuel 1729–96
American clergyman

Born in Groton, Connecticut, he graduated at Yale in 1748, studied medicine at Edinburgh and received orders in the Church of England in 1753. After three years as a missionary, he became rector of Jamaica, Long Island, in 1757 and of Westchester, New York, in 1767. Despite imprisonment for his loyalty to Great Britain which as a royalist army chaplain he maintained through the American Revolution, he was elected first Episcopal Bishop of Connecticut in 1783. The Church of England refused to consecrate him because he could not take the Oath of Allegiance, and three bishops of the Scottish Episcopal Church performed the ceremony at Aberdeen (1784).

Seaga, Edward Philip George 1930–
Jamaican politician

Born in Boston, Massachusetts, to Jamaican parents, he went to school in Kingston, Jamaica, returning to the USA to study at Harvard University. He was on the staff of the University of the West Indies before moving into politics, joining the Jamaica Labour Party (JLP) and becoming its leader in 1974. He entered the House of Representatives in 1962 and served in the administration of Hugh Shearer (1967–72) before becoming Leader of the Opposition. In 1980 he and the JLP had a resounding and surprising win over Michael Manley's People's National Party (PNP), and Seaga became Prime Minister. He called a snap election in 1983 and won all the assembly seats, but in 1989 Manley and the PNP returned to power with a landslide victory.

Seaman, Elizabeth Cochrane, *pseudonym* Nellie Bly 1867–1922
US journalist

Born in Cochran's Mills, Pennsylvania, she adopted her pen name from a popular song when working as a journalist for the *Pittsburgh Dispatch*, and reported on issues of reform and taboo subjects such as divorce. Moving to New York, she worked for Joseph Pulitzer's *World*, writing dramatic exposés of working conditions, women prisoners and other issues. She was given an assignment to travel around the world in less than 80 days, which she achieved in 1889. Her accounts of the expedition, which was undertaken by public transport, became front-page news. She wrote about the experience in *Nelly Bly's Book: Around the World in Seventy-Two Days*.

Seaman, Sir Owen 1861–1936
English writer

He was educated at Shrewsbury and Clare College, Cambridge, became Professor of Literature at Newcastle (1890), and was editor of *Punch* (1906–32). His parodies and verses on society, which include *Paulopostprandials* (1833), *In Cap and Bells* (1889) and *From the Home Front* (1918), achieved popularity.

Searle, Humphrey 1915–82
English composer

Born in Oxford, he studied at the Royal College of Music and in Vienna with Anton von Webern, becoming musical adviser to Sadler's Wells Ballet (1951–57). An exponent of the twelve-note technique, he composed five symphonies, two piano concertos, and a trilogy of works for speaker, chorus and orchestra to words by Edith Sitwell and James Joyce, many other choral–orchestral works and three operas, the last of them *Hamlet* (1968). He wrote *Twentieth Century Counterpoint*, and a study of the music of Franz Liszt (1954).

Searle, John 1932–
US philosopher

Born in Denver, Colorado, he taught at Oxford (1956–59) and since 1959 has been Professor of Philosophy at the University of California at Berkeley. In such works as *Speech Acts* (1969) and *Expression and Meaning* (1979) he expounded a distinctive approach to the study of language and its relation to mind, which has greatly influenced linguists and cognitive scientists as well as philosophers. He also wrote a famous account of the student riots in California, *The Campus War* (1971), and delivered the Reith Lectures on *Minds, Brains, and Science* in 1984. Recent works include *The Rediscovery of the Mind* (1992) and *The Construction of Social Reality* (1995).

Searle, Ronald William Fordham 1920–
English cartoonist, painter and author

He was born in Cambridge, and studied at Cambridge School of Art while working as a solicitor's clerk. He drew his first cartoon for the *Cambridge Daily News* in 1935, and contributed a further 200 before moving on to magazines; these included *Lilliput*, *London Opinion* and *Punch*. In World War II he served in the Royal Engineers painting camouflage; he was taken prisoner of war for over three years, and later published a book of sketches he made in Changi Camp. In 1956 he became staff theatrical caricaturist for *Punch* and in 1961 moved to Paris, where in 1973 he became the first foreign artist to exhibit at the Bibliothèque Nationale. He designed animated films like *Dick Deadeye* (1975), the animated sequences for

Those Magnificent Men in Their Flying Machines (1965), and titles for features based on the St Trinian's schoolgirls, whom he created. His many publications include *Marquis de Sade meets Goody Two-Shoes* (1994). 📖 Russell Davies, *Ronald Searle: A Biography* (1990)

Sebastian, St d.288
Roman Christian
Born in Narbonne, France, of Roman parents, he is said to have been a captain of the Praetorian guard, and a secret Christian. According to tradition, **Diocletian**, hearing that he favoured Christians, ordered his death. But the archers did not quite kill him, and a woman named Irene nursed him back to life. When he criticized the tyrant for his cruelty, Diocletian had him beaten to death with rods. His feast day is 20 January.

Sebastian 1554–78
King of Portugal
The grandson of Emperor **Charles V** and nephew of **Philip II** of Spain, he was born in Lisbon, and succeeded his grandfather John III in 1557. Following the regencies of his grandmother, Catalina (1557–62) and great-uncle, Cardinal Henry (1562–68), he took control of the government at the age of 14. Lost in dreams of conquest and crusading zeal, he launched a futile and costly war against the Moors of North Africa, and fell in the Battle of Alcazar-Qivir, Algeria. His death without an heir opened the way for the union of Portugal with Spain under his uncle, but continuing rumours that he was still alive fuelled Portuguese nationalism and gave rise to a series of four impostors (1584–98). The popular belief that he would come again re-emerged as late as 1807–08 when Portugal was occupied by the French.

Sébastiani, Count François Horace Bastien 1772–1851
French soldier and diplomat
Born near Bastia, Corsica, he became one of **Napoleon I**'s most devoted partisans. He fought at Marengo (1800), was wounded at Austerlitz (1805), twice undertook missions to Turkey (1802–06), commanded an army corps in Spain, and distinguished himself in the Russian campaign (1812) and at Leipzig (1813). He joined Napoleon on his return from Elba, and after 1830 was ambassador at Naples and London. He was made Marshal of France in 1840.

Sebastiano del Piombo, *properly* Sebastiano Luciani c.1485–1547
Italian painter
He was called del Piombo ('of the Seal') from his appointment in 1523 as sealer of briefs to Pope **Clement VII**. He studied under **Giovanni Bellini** and **Giorgione**, and went to Rome about 1510, where he worked in conjunction with **Michelangelo**. In 1519 he painted his masterpiece, the *Raising of Lazarus* (now in the National Gallery, London). He was also an accomplished portrait painter.

Sebillot, Paul 1843–1918
French folklorist
Born in Matignon, Côtes-du-Nord, he abandoned law for painting, and from 1870 to 1883 exhibited in the Salon in Paris. He then held a post in the ministry of public works, and devoted himself to the study of Breton folk tales, on which he published the standard work, *Le Folklore de France* (1907).

Secchi, Angelo 1818–78
Italian astronomer
Born in Reggio Emilia, he joined the Society of Jesus in 1833 and in 1841 was made Professor of Physics and Astronomy at the Jesuit College in Loreto. In 1948 he became Professor of Astronomy at the Roman College of the Society, but he was expelled with all the Jesuits from

Italy in the same year, and spent a brief exile in England and the USA before returning to become director of the Observatory of the Roman College in 1849. He established a new observatory on the roof of the church of Saint Ignatius, which he used particularly for observations of the Sun. At the total solar eclipse of 1860 observed in Spain he succeeded in photographing the prominences and the corona. Using an objective prism, he observed several thousand stellar spectra and divided the stars into three types—white, yellow and red—which corresponded roughly to their temperatures. He thus initiated the field of spectral classification. His beautifully illustrated book on the Sun, *Le Soleil* (1875), became widely known. In addition to his astronomical research, he did much work on the phenomena of terrestrial magnetism and meteorology.

Secombe, Harry Donald 1921–
Welsh singer and entertainer
Born in Swansea, he sang in a choir as a boy. After army service during World War II, he made his stage debut in *Revuedeville* (1947–48) before becoming a regular on the radio show *Variety Bandbox* (1947). He joined **Peter Sellers**, **Spike Milligan** and **Michael Bentine** in the radio *Goon Show* (1951–60). His stage appearances include *Humpty Dumpty* (1959), *Pickwick* (1963), *The Four Musketeers* (1967) and *The Plumber's Progress* (1975). He is a popular singer with many albums to his credit, and his film appearances include *Davy* (1957), *Oliver!* (1968), *Song of Norway* (1970) and *Doctor in Trouble* (1970). More recently he has hosted the religious television series *Highway* (1983–93) and *Sunday Morning with Secombe* (1994). His autobiography, *Arias and Raspberries*, was published in 1989. He was knighted in 1981.

Secord, Laura 1775–1868
Canadian heroine
She was born in Great Barrington, Massachusetts. She became a legendary heroine of the War of 1812 when she walked 20 miles through a dangerous area of wilderness to warn the British military post at Beaver Dam (Ontario) about a surprise attack that was being planned by American troops. Native Americans, joined by the British, then ambushed the Americans and defeated them.

Seddon, Richard John 1845–1906
New Zealand politician
Born in Eccleston, Lancashire, England, he settled in New Zealand in 1866, and entered parliament in 1879. As Prime Minister (1893–1906) he led a Liberal Party government remembered for its social legislation, which included the introduction of old-age pensions (1898), and free secondary education (1903). His administration also saw the normalizing of relations with Australia, troop support to Britain in the Boer War, and annexation of the Cook Islands. As 'King Dick' he dominated New Zealand politics from 1893 until his death in office.

Sedgwick, Adam 1785–1873
English geologist
Born in Dent, Cumbria, he graduated in mathematics from Trinity College, Cambridge (1808) and became Woodwardian Professor of Geology there in 1818. In 1831 he began geological mapping in Wales and introduced the Cambrian system in 1835. He had carried out studies in the Lake District as early as 1822, but it was not until the Cambrian and Silurian systems had been established in Wales and the Welsh Borders that he was fully able to understand its geology. Sedgwick became embroiled in controversy with **Roderick Impey Murchison**; the dispute was finally resolved with the introduction of the Ordovician system by **Charles Lapworth**. His best work was on *British Palaeozoic Fossils* (1854). With Murchison he

studied the Lake District, the Alps and south-west England, where they identified the Devonian system.
📖 Colin Speakman, *Adam Sedgwick: Geologist and Dalesman, 1785–1873* (1982)

Seebeck, Thomas Johann 1770–1831
German physicist

Born in Tallin, Estonia, he went to Germany to study medicine and qualified in 1802, but spent his time thereafter studying physics. His first research (1806) was on the heating and chemical effects of the colours of the solar spectrum, and he also investigated optical polarization in stressed glass (1812). His most significant discovery was that of thermoelectricity, which he called 'thermomagnetism' (1822), which occurs when an electric current is generated through the application of heat to a junction of two metals.

Seebohm, Henry 1832–95
English industrialist and ornithologist

Born in Bradford, Yorkshire, of German extraction, he established an iron and steel foundry in Sheffield, which prospered and provided the financial backing for his ornithological interests. He travelled widely in pursuit of his hobby, and was particularly famed during his lifetime for his journeys to Imperial Russia and Siberia, which he documented in his books *Siberia in Europe* (1880) and *Siberia in Asia* (1884). He wrote *A History of British Birds* (1883–85), which became a classic, and acquired a particular interest in the osteology of birds, from which he began to develop a classification scheme. His *Coloured Figures of Eggs of British Birds* (1896) and *The Birds of Siberia* (1901) were published posthumously.

Seeckt, Hans von 1866–1936
German army officer

He was born in Schleswig, Prussia. After serving with merit as a staff officer in World War I, he acted as military expert to the German delegation at the Treaty of Versailles (1919) before becoming army Chief of Staff in 1920. He failed to act decisively against far-right conspirators in the Kapp Putsch (1920), but in the troubles of 1923–24 emergency powers enabled him to uphold order. Eventually he was forced to resign in 1926. As Chief of Staff he had been a strong advocate of military co-operation with the USSR, not least to undermine Poland. He served in the Reichstag (1930–32, 1934–35), and functioned briefly thereafter as a military adviser in China.

Seefried, Irmgard 1919–88
Austrian soprano

She was born in Köngetried, Germany. She studied in Augsburg and made her debut in 1940 in Aachen as the Priestess in Verdi's *Aïda*. She was famous for her performances with Vienna State Opera from 1943, especially in the operas of Richard Strauss (notably the composer in *Ariadne auf Naxos*) and Mozart, including Fiordiligi in *Così fan tutte*, and Susanna in *Le nozze di Figaro* which she sang at Covent Garden in 1947. She also became a noted lieder singer, and often appeared in concert with her husband, the violinist Wolfgang Schneiderhan.

Seeger, Alan 1888–1916
US poet

Born in New York City and educated at Harvard, he left the USA to settle in Paris. When war was declared in Europe in 1914, he enlisted in the French Foreign Legion and fought courageously up to his death at the Battle of the Somme. His collection, *Poems*, was published later the same year. Although unjustly neglected in favour of the English war poets, Seeger is remembered for the poem, 'I Have A Rendezvous With Death', which is often included in anthologies.

Seeger, Pete 1919–
US folk-singer and songwriter

Born in New York City, he studied sociology at Harvard University before becoming a professional musician in the late 1930s. In 1940, along with Woody Guthrie, he formed the Almanac Singers, whose repertoire of radical songs marked the start of the 'protest' movement in contemporary folk music. A later Seeger group, the Weavers, carried on this tradition. Seeger's unpretentious singing style and homely banjo playing made him a popular solo artist, but his uncompromising political stance caused him to fall foul of the Un-American Activities Committee in the 1950s, and for many years he was shunned by the US media. He remained an activist on issues of ecology, politics, and individual liberties. His best-known songs include 'On Top of Old Smokey', 'Where Have All the Flowers Gone?' and 'Little Boxes', although his name will always be associated with 'We Shall Overcome', which he adapted from a traditional song. He was influential in bringing about the US folk-music revival of the 1960s.

Seferis, George, *pseudonym of* George Seferiades 1900–71
Greek poet and diplomat and Nobel Prize winner

Born in Smyrna in Asia Minor, he moved with his family to Athens in 1914. He studied law in Paris and London, and spent the rest of his life as a diplomat, serving as the Greek ambassador to London (1957–62). His first collection of poetry, *Strophe* ('Turning Point'), published in 1931, was an immediate success. His debt to Modernists such as Ezra Pound and T S Eliot became clear in *Mythistorima* (1935, 'Myth History'), which contained some of the first free-verse poems in modern Greek. His later collections include *Hemerologhia Katastromatos* ('Logbook') *I*, *II* and *III* (1940, 1944 and 1965). He was also a noted translator, and worked on versions of Paul Valéry, W B Yeats, Eliot and Pound. Some of his poems were set to music by Mikis Theodorakis. In 1963 he became the first Greek winner of the Nobel Prize for literature. 📖 K K Katsimbalis, *Vivliografia* (1961)

Sefström, Nils Gabriel 1765–1829
Swedish physician and chemist

Born in Ilsbo, North Helsingland, he qualified as a physician at Uppsala in 1813. He became a lecturer in chemistry at the Royal Military Academy at Carlberg and was later appointed as professor at the Artillery School at Marieberg, while also teaching at the new School of Mines at Falun. Researching both at Falun and in Jöns Jacob Berzelius's laboratory in Stockholm, he discovered vanadium (which is now important industrially) in Swedish iron and in the spoil from an ironworks.

Segal, George 1924–
US sculptor

Born in New York City, he studied at Cooper Union (1941) and the Pratt Institute of Design (1947), finally graduating from New York University in 1950 and Rutgers in 1963. Beginning as a painter, he turned to sculpture in the later 1950s and is best known for his plaster figures, including *Girl in a Doorway* (1969). Cast from life and usually unpainted, they exist as ghostly presences within the realistic environments he assembles for them. Other works include *The Bowery* (1970) and *The Curtain* (1974).

Segar, Elzie Crisler 1894–1938
US strip cartoonist

Born in Chester, Illinois, he took a correspondence course in cartooning and went to Chicago for the daily strip, *Charlie Chaplin's Comic Capers* (1916). His first creation was *Barry the Boob* (1917) for the *Chicago Herald*. In New York he started *Thimble Theater* (1919) for King Features, originally a burlesque on stage melodramas. The cast included heroine Olive Oyl, whose brother Castor encountered a one-eyed sailor named Popeye in January 1929. Popeye moved into **Max Fleischer** animated cartoons from 1933. He also popularized the hamburger, and added *jeep* and *goon* (from his characters Eugene the Jeep and Alice the Goon) to the English language.

Seghers, Hercules Pietersz c.1589–c.1635
Dutch landscape painter and etcher

Born probably in Haarlem, he was a pupil of G van Coninxloo and from 1614 worked in Amsterdam. His dramatic landscapes suggest that he travelled, most likely to Italy via the Alps. His works were highly regarded and influential in his own day, and **Rembrandt** is known to have owned eight of his paintings. A virtuoso etcher, he often used tinted paper to modify lighting effects. In 1678 the Dutch painter Samuel van Hoogstraten (1627–78) published a biography which appears to be a fanciful account of Segher's life.

Segonzac, André Dunoyer de 1884–1974
French painter and engraver

Born in Boussy-Saint-Antoine, he was influenced by **Gustave Courbet** and **Jean Corot**, and produced many delicate watercolour landscapes, etchings and illustrations. His series of engravings of *Beaches* was published in 1935.

Segovia, Andrés 1893–1987
Spanish guitarist

Born in Linares, he was largely self-taught, and quickly gained an international reputation. Influenced by the Spanish nationalist composers, he evolved a revolutionary guitar technique that allowed the performance of a wide range of music, and many composers wrote works for him. In 1981 he was created Marquis of Salobrēna by royal decree. 📖 G Wade, *Maestro Segovia* (1987); *Segovia* (1984)

Segrè, Emilio 1905–89
US physicist and Nobel Prize winner

Born in Rome, Italy, he was educated at Rome University, studying engineering and physics, and obtained his doctorate in 1928. He remained at Rome University working with **Enrico Fermi**, but left Italy under **Mussolini's** regime. He moved to the University of California at Berkeley and worked on the Manhattan atom bomb project during World War II. In 1937 Segrè discovered the first entirely man-made element, technetium, and three years later was involved in the discoveries of astatine and plutonium (1940). In 1955 the research team led by Segrè discovered the anti-proton, the anti-particle of the proton (with identical mass but negative electric charge) which had been predicted by **P A M Dirac**. For this work he shared the 1959 Nobel Prize for physics with **Owen Chamberlain**. 📖 *A Mind Always in Motion: The Autobiography of Emilio Segrè* (1993)

Seguier, William 1771–1843
English artist

Born in London of Huguenot descent, he studied under **George Morland**, but abandoned painting for the art of the restorer and connoisseur, and helped **George IV** to assemble the Royal Collection. When the National Gallery was inaugurated, he became its first Keeper. As superintendent of the British Institution, he was succeeded at his death by his brother John (1785–1856), who was also a painter and his partner in the picture-restoring business.

Séguin, Marc 1786–1875
French mechanical and civil engineer

Born in Annonay, he was taught science informally by his uncle **Joseph Montgolfier**, and maintained an interest throughout his life in problems such as the mechanical equivalent of heat. His principal achievements were in engineering, notably his association with the development of wire-rope suspension bridges from 1825 onwards, and his invention of the multi-tubular (fire-tube) boiler which he patented in 1827. He used this successfully in 1829 on the railway he had built between Lyons and St-Étienne, in a locomotive which employed forced draught from a fan driven by the wheels of the tender. It was also used by **George Stephenson** in his locomotive *Rocket*.

Segundo, Juan Luis 1925–
Uruguayan Jesuit liberation theologian

Born in Montevideo, he studied in Argentina and Europe, and became director of the Pedro Fabbro Institute of socio-religious research in Montevideo. Though critical of the methodology of some liberation theologians in *The Liberation of Theology* (1976), he defended them against Vatican criticisms in *Theology and the Church* (1986). He advocates employing a 'hermeneutical circle', in which questioning of prevailing ideological and theological assumptions that govern the received way of interpreting scripture leads to new understanding. His own multi-volume exposition of liberation theology is *Jesus of Nazareth Yesterday and Today* (5 vols, 1984–88).

Ségur, Sophie Rostopchine, Comtesse de 1799–1874
French writer

She was born in Russia, the daughter of a Russian soldier and statesman, Count **Fyodor Rostopchin**. After her marriage to Comte Eugéne de Ségur she lived in France, where she wrote children's books based on a central character called 'Sophie', such as *Les malheurs de Sophie* (1859, 'The Troubles of Sophie') and *Mémoires d'un Âne* ('Memoirs of a Donkey').

Seiber, Mátyás 1905–60
British composer

Born in Budapest, he studied under **Zoltán Kodály**, and later became a private music teacher (1925) and Professor of Jazz (1928–33) at Hoch's Conservatory in Frankfurt am Main. He settled in Great Britain in 1935 and in 1942 became a tutor at Morley College, London. His compositions include three string quartets, of which the second (1935) is the best-known, other chamber works, piano music and songs, and the cantata *Ulysses* (1946–47) based on **James Joyce's** novel. He gained only belated recognition as a composer, with strong musical affinities to **Béla Bartók** and **Arnold Schoenberg**. He was killed in a motor accident in South Africa.

Seidelman, Susan 1952–
US film director

Born in Abington, Pennsylvania, and educated at Drexel University and the New York University Graduate School of Film and TV, she won a student Oscar for her satirical short film *And You Act Like One, Too* (1976). Her first feature film, the self-financed *Smithereens* (1982), became the first independent US feature to be accepted in the main competition at the Cannes Film Festival. Moving into the mainstream, she directed *Desperately Seeking Susan* (1985), a popular contemporary comedy featuring **Madonna**. Her best work shows a strong visual sensibility and a flair for creating appealing feminist heroines from unlikely characters.

Seidler, Harry 1923–
Australian architect

Born in Vienna, Austria, he studied at the Vasa Institute in Vienna, and later at Harvard where he studied under **Walter Gropius**. He worked in New York, and later with **Oscar Niemeyer** in Brazil, before setting up practice in Sydney in 1948. In 1951 his first design for a private house won the Sulman Medal, and since then Seidler has won many awards for public and private buildings. He has worked in Mexico and Hong Kong, and designed the Australian embassy in Paris. His application of modern building techniques were well demonstrated in his Maori Language Commission Centre and the award-winning Australia Square tower in Sydney. In 1992 he published *Harry Seidler: Four Decades of Architecture*.

Seifert, Jaroslav 1901–86
Czech poet and Nobel Prize winner

He was born in Prague. His first collection, *Město v slzáck* (1921, 'City of Tears'), reflects on the human waste of World War I and urges a working-class revolution. In 1923 he moved to Paris and translated Guillaume Apollinaire, and produced his second collection, *Samá láska* (1923, 'All Love'). He was expelled from the Communist Party in 1929 and joined the Social Democrats. After the Nazi occupation, his patriotism emerged in *Přílba Llíny* (1945, 'A Helmet of Earth'); his most memorable poems are those which evoke the four days in May 1945 when the citizens of Prague rose against the remaining Nazi forces. *Morový sloup* (1977, Eng trans *The Prague Column*, 1979) was published abroad. He was awarded the Nobel Prize for literature in 1984. 📖*Vseck krasy sveta pribehy a vzpominky* (1981)

Selacraig, Alexander See Selkirk, Alexander

Selborne, Roundell Palmer, 1st Earl of 1812–95
English jurist, judge and hymnologist

Born in Mixbury, Oxfordshire, he became Solicitor-General (1861) and Attorney-General (1863–66). His opposition to Gladstone's Irish Church policy delayed his promotion to Lord Chancellor (1872–74, 1880–85). He was an impressive judge, promoted much legislation, and reformed the English court system, merging all the old courts into the Supreme Court of Judicature (1875). He also wrote hymnological and liturgical studies.

Selby, Hubert, Jnr 1928–
US novelist and short-story writer

He was born in Brooklyn, New York. He enlisted in the US Merchant Marines in 1944, but was admitted to hospital two years later with tuberculosis. In all, he spent nearly five years as a patient, subsequently working at a number of jobs until the publication of his controversial bestseller, *Last Exit to Brooklyn* (1964), a set of connected stories. It is a bleak and pitiless account of an urban hell characterized by violence, sexual brutality and drug abuse. Obscenity trials followed the book's publication. His other novels include *The Room* (1971), *The Demon* (1976), and *Requiem for a Dream* (1978). His stories have been collected as *Song of the Silent Snow* (1986). 📖'Hubert Selby issue', *Review of Contemporary Literature* (1981)

Selden, John 1584–1654
English jurist, historian and antiquary

Born near Worthing, Sussex, he studied at Oxford and London. He was an opponent of the divine right of kings, and was twice imprisoned for his views. In 1623 he was elected MP for Lancaster, and in 1628 he helped to draw up the Petition of Right, for which he was committed to the Tower with Sir John Eliot, Baron Holles and others. He entered the Long Parliament (1640) for Oxford University, sat as a lay member in the Westminster Assembly in 1643, and was appointed keeper of the records in the Tower and, in 1644, an Admiralty commissioner. His works include *Duello* (1610, 'Single Combat'), *Titles of Honour* (1614), which is still an authority, *Analecton Anglo-Britannicon* (1615), *De Diis Syriis* (1617) and *History of Tithes* (1618). He also wrote in Latin, books on the Arundel Marbles (1624) and on Hebrew law (1634–50), besides posthumous tracts and treatises, of which the most valuable is his *Table Talk* (1689).

Seles, Monica 1973–
US tennis player

Born in Novi Sad, Yugoslavia, she moved to the USA in 1986. Turning professional at the age of 15, she has won the French Open three times (1990–92), the US Open twice (1991–92) and the Australian Open three times (1991–93). In 1992 she was defeated by Steffi Graf in the Wimbledon singles final. During a tournament in Hamburg in April 1993, she was injured in a knife attack by a member of the crowd and was unable to compete for over two years. After her return she won every match she played until in 1995 she was narrowly beaten by Graf in the US Open final. In 1996 she won the Australian Open and led the US team in winning the Federation Cup. She became a US citizen in 1994.

Seleucus I Nicator ('the Conqueror')
c.358–281BC
Macedonian general, founder of the Seleucid dynasty

After the death of Alexander the Great (323BC) he rose from being Governor of Babylonia (321) to being the ruler of an empire (312) which stretched from Asia Minor to India. He assumed the title of king in 305, and founded a new, more central capital at Antioch in northern Syria (300). He defeated two successive rivals, Antigonus I at Ipsus (301) and Lysimachus at Corupedium (281). Crossing into Europe to claim the throne of Macedonia, he was killed by Ptolemy Ceraunus, the son of Ptolemy I Soter. He was succeeded by his son Antiochus I.

Selfridge, Harry Gordon 1858–1947
British merchant

Born in Ripon, Wisconsin, USA and educated privately, he joined a trading firm in Chicago and brought new ideas and great organizing ability into the business. In 1892 he was made a junior partner. While visiting London in 1906 he bought a site in Oxford Street, which he used to build the large department store which bears his name (opened 1909). He took British nationality in 1937.

Seligman, Charles Gabriel 1873–1940
English anthropologist

Born in London, he studied as a physician and later joined the Cambridge anthropological expedition to the Torres Straits (1898–99); he also carried out field research in New Guinea, Ceylon (Sri Lanka) and the Sudan. His principal works, which were based on this research, include *The Melanesians of British New Guinea* (1910), *The Veddas (Ceylon)* (1911) and *Pagan Tribes of the Nilotic Sudan* (1932), the last of these written jointly with his wife Brenda, who collaborated in all his later research. Throughout the earlier part of his career, he continued with his studies in pathology, until his appointment in 1913 to the first chair of ethnology at London University turned his interests decisively towards anthropology. He pioneered the application of a psychoanalytic approach and had a strong influence on the later work of both Bronisław Malinowski and Sir Edward Evans-Pritchard.

Selim I, the Grim 1467–1520
Ottoman Sultan of Turkey

In 1512 he dethroned his father, Bayezit II, and caused him, his own brothers, and nephews to be put to death. He declared war against Persia in 1514, and took Diyarbakir and Kurdistan. He later conquered Egypt (1517), Syria and the Hejaz and won from the sherif of Mecca the control of the holy cities of Mecca and Medina. He introduced new codes of criminal law, expanded trade, refined the recruitment of janissaries, completed the transfer of government from Edirne to Istanbul, and built a powerful new fleet. He was succeeded by his son, Süleyman the Magnificent.

Selim II 1524–74
Ottoman Sultan of Turkey

The son of **Süleyman the Magnificent**, whom he succeeded in 1566, he proved to be an indolent drunkard, controlled by the women of the harem. The government was run by his able Grand Vizier Mehmed Sokollu. During his reign, a revolt in Yemen was successfully crushed (1569–70) and Cyprus was captured (1571). A naval force under **Don John of Austria** defeated the Turkish fleet at Lepanto (1571), but the victors did not follow up their success, and the Ottomans recaptured Tunisia (1574).

Selim III 1761–1808
Ottoman Sultan of Turkey
Succeeding his uncle in 1789, he pursued the war with Russia. The Austrians joined the Russians, and Belgrade surrendered to them, while the Russians took Bucharest. He came under French influence and attempted westernizing reforms in the areas of finance, provincial administration and land tenure. He also established embassies in the main European capitals. But attempts at reform cost him his throne (1807) and his life.

Selkirk or Selacraig, Alexander 1676–1721
Scottish sailor
Born in Largo, Fife, he is said to have inspired **Daniel Defoe**'s *Robinson Crusoe*. He ran away to sea in 1695, and in 1704 joined the South Sea buccaneers. He quarrelled with his captain, **William Dampier**, and at his own request was put ashore on the uninhabited island of Juan Fernández (1704). Having lived alone there for four years and four months, he was rescued by a physician, Thomas Dover (1660–1742). He returned to Largo in 1712, and at the time of his death was a lieutenant on a man-of-war. 🕮 James Howell, *The Life and Adventures of Alexander Selkirk, the Real Robinson Crusoe* (1836)

Selkirk, Thomas Douglas, 5th Earl of 1771–1820
Scottish colonizer
He settled 800 emigrants from the Scottish Highlands in Prince Edward Island (1803) and in the Red River Valley, Manitoba, although twice evicted by soldiers from the Fort William post of the Northwest Fur Company (1815–16).

Sella, Philippe 1962–
French rugby union player
He was born in Clairac and his home club was Agen. In 1993–94 he succeeded fellow Frenchman **Serge Blanco** as the most capped international player of all time with a record 111 caps. His first cap came at the age of 20 when he had already represented France at school, junior and university levels, and he went on to score 30 international test tries. In the same period (1982–95) he was also France's most capped centre. After his retirement from international tests after the 1995 World Cup, he committed himself to the English rugby club Saracens.

Sellar, Patrick 1780–1851
Scottish lawyer and estate factor
Born in Morayshire, he studied law in Edinburgh. He became notorious during the Highland Clearances, as factor to the 1st Duke of Sutherland, for the brutality with which he evicted the crofting tenant families of Strathnaver in 1814. He was brought to trial by Robert MacKid, the Sheriff Substitute of Sutherland, but was acquitted, and later became a sheep farmer in Morvern.

Sellars, Peter 1958–
US stage director
Born in Pittsburgh, Pennsylvania, he directed several plays while still a student at Harvard. He was director of the Boston Shakespeare Company (1983–84), and director of the American National Theater at the Kennedy Center in Washington (1984–86), where his radical staging of **Sophocles**'*Ajax* divided audiences and critics.

He is internationally recognized as a daringly innovative director of opera, setting his productions in the cultural landscape of the USA in the 20th century. These include **Handel**'s *Orlando* (1981), in which Orlando was made into an astronaut, *The Mikado* (1984), and *The Magic Flute* for Glyndebourne Opera, in which Sarastro was represented as leader of a hippie commune. In 1990 he was appointed director of the Los Angeles Festival and in 1991 directed his first film, *The Cabinet of Dr Ramirez*.

Sellers, Peter 1925–80
English actor and comedian
He was born in Southsea, Hampshire. After a spell as a stand-up comic and impressionist, first with the Entertainments National Services Association, then at the Windmill Theatre in London (1951–59), he moved into radio. His meeting with comedian **Spike Milligan** inspired the *Goon Show*. He made his film debut with *Penny Points to Paradise* (1951), the first of a run of successful British comedy films in the 1950s and 60s. His versatile range of characterizations was demonstrated in films such as *The Ladykillers* (1955), *I'm Alright Jack* (1959) and *Only Two Can Play* (1962). Two films with **Stanley Kubrick** established his international reputation: *Lolita* (1962) and *Dr Strangelove* (1963), in which he played three roles. He is perhaps best remembered as the incompetent French detective Inspector Clouseau in a series of films that began with *The Pink Panther* in 1963. He received an Academy Award nomination for *Being There* (1979). 🕮 Peter Evans, *Mask Behind the Mask* (1969)

Sellon, Priscilla Lydia 1821–76
English religious reformer
In 1849, at Plymouth, she founded the second Anglican sisterhood. Its spiritual director was **E B Pusey**.

Selous, Frederick Courtenay 1851–1917
English explorer and big-game hunter
Born in London, he first visited South Africa in 1871, fought in Matabeleland (1893, 1895), and for 18 years hunted freely between the Transvaal and the Congo, making important ethnological finds and collecting specimens for museums. His extensive travels in south-central Africa helped gain more public knowledge of Rhodesia (Zimbabwe). In 1916 he won the DSO and fell in action in West Africa. The Selous National Park in Tanzania is named after him.

Selwyn, George Augustus 1809–78
English prelate
Born in Hampstead, London, he was educated at Eton and St John's College, Cambridge, where he rowed in the first university boat race (1829), and graduated in 1831. In 1841 he was consecrated the first (and only) Bishop of New Zealand and Melanesia, of whose Church he played a large part in settling the constitution. In 1867 he was appointed Bishop of Lichfield, where on his initiative the first Diocesan Conference, in which the laity were represented, met in 1868. Selwyn College at Cambridge was founded in 1882 in his memory. His son, John Richardson (1844–98), was Bishop of Melanesia (1877), and Master of Selwyn College, Cambridge.

Selwyn-Lloyd, (John) Selwyn (Brooke), Baron 1904–78
English Conservative politician
Born in the Wirral of Anglo-Welsh parentage and educated at Fettes College, Edinburgh, and Cambridge, he studied law and became a barrister in 1930 with a practice in Liverpool. He stood unsuccessfully as Liberal candidate for Macclesfield and in 1931 joined the Conservative Party. In 1936 he entered local government as chairman of the Hoylake Urban District Council. After service in World War II, he entered parliament in 1945 as the Conservative MP for Wirral; he continued to practise law,

becoming a KC in 1947. In 1951 he was appointed Minister of State, and in 1954 became successively Minister of Supply and Minister of Defence. As Foreign Secretary in 1955, he defended Anthony Eden's policy on Suez; he became Chancellor of the Exchequer in 1960, but resigned in Harold Macmillan's purge of 1962. He was Lord Privy Seal and Leader of the House (1963–64) and Speaker of the House of Commons (1971–76). He was created a life peer in 1976.

Selye, Hans Hugo Bruno 1907–82
Canadian physician

Born in Vienna, Austria, he studied medicine in Prague, Paris and Rome, and was assistant in experimental pathology at the German University (1929–31) before emigrating to the USA. After one year as a Research Fellow at Johns Hopkins University, he moved to McGill University in Montreal (1933–45) and then became director of the Institute for Experimental Medicine and Surgery at the University of Montreal in 1945. He is best known for his 'general adaptation syndrome', which he defined as the 'physiological mechanism which raises resistance to damage as such' (1949); this links stress and anxiety, and their biochemical and physiological consequences, to human disorders such as hypertension, nephrosclerosis and rheumatic diseases.

Selznick, David O(liver) 1902–65
US film producer

Born in Pittsburgh, Ohio, he worked for his father Lewis J Selznick (1870–1933) in film distribution and promotion before becoming a producer with the short film *Will He Conquer Dempsey?* (1923). Employment as a story editor and associate producer at MGM and Paramount led to his appointment as vice-president in charge of production at RKO when the studio created such films as *A Bill of Divorcement* (1932) and *King Kong* (1933). He was renowned for masterminding every aspect of a production and for the long detailed memos he sent to colleagues. In 1937 he formed his own production company, which produced *A Star Is Born* (1937) and the screen adaptation of *Gone With the Wind* (1939), for which he received an Academy Award. Other successes included *Rebecca* (1940), *Duel in the Sun* (1946), *The Third Man* (1949) and *A Farewell to Arms* (1957), which starred his second wife, the actress Jennifer Jones (1919–).

Semenov, Nikolai Nikolayevich 1896–1986
Soviet physical chemist and Nobel Prize winner

Born in Saratov, he graduated in 1917 from the university of Petrograd (now St Petersburg). From 1920 he worked at the Physico-Technical Institute there, becoming professor in 1928, and later director. In 1931 he became a full member of the USSR Academy of Sciences. From 1944 he was also professor at Moscow State University. He is best known for his contributions to chemical kinetics, particularly in connection with chain reactions. He investigated explosion limits and many other features of combustion, flames and detonation. Much of his work was parallel to that of Cyril Hinshelwood, with whom he shared the 1956 Nobel Prize for chemistry. Semenov was the author of several influential books, notably *Chemical Kinetics and Chain Reactions* (1934) and *Some Problems of Chemical Kinetics and Reactivity* (1954). He was awarded the Order of Lenin five times, and became a Foreign Member of the Royal Society in 1958.

Semiramis 9th century BC
Semi-legendary Queen of Assyria

She is said to have been coveted by King Ninus of Assyria, who married her and fell under her spell. With him she is supposed to have founded Babylon. According to one story, she was killed by her son Ninyas. The historical basis of the story has been identified with the three years' regency of Sammu-ramat (811–808BC), widow of Shamshi-Adad V, but the details are legendary, and are derived from Ctesias and the Greek historians, with elements of the Astarte myth.

Semmelweis, Ignaz Philipp 1818–65
Hungarian obstetrician

Born in Buda (Budapest), he studied at the University of Pest and in Vienna. From 1845 he worked in the first obstetrical clinic of the Vienna general hospital. He succeeded in reducing the mortality rate by initiating a strict regime of washing hands and instruments in chlorinated lime solution between autopsy work and examining patients. However, there was much opposition to his ideas, and he left Vienna in 1850 for Pest. His later years were clouded by frustration and mental instability, and he died in a mental asylum. His ideas were idiosyncratic, but in the later bacteriological age he came to be seen as a pioneer of antiseptic obstetrics. 📖 G Gortvay and I Zoltán, *Semmelweis élete és munkássága* (1966, Eng trans *Semmelweis: His Life and Work*, 1968)

Semmes, Raphael 1809–77
US naval officer

Born in Charles County, Maryland, he joined the US navy in 1826, and studied law in his free time. He saw active service during the Mexican War, and on the outbreak of the Civil War he commanded the confederate raider *Sumter*, and then the *Alabama*, with which he captured 65 vessels. In 1864 the *Alabama* was sunk in action off Cherbourg by the US cruiser *Kearsarge*, but Semmes escaped. Later he edited a newspaper and practised law in Mobile, and wrote several books on service at sea.

Semper, Gottfried 1803–73
German architect

Born in Hamburg, he abandoned law for architecture and travelled in France, Italy and Greece. In 1834 he was appointed professor at Dresden, but his part in the Revolution of 1848 compelled him to flee to England, where he designed the Victoria and Albert Museum. He eventually settled in Vienna, where the Burgtheater, the imperial palace and two museums, as well as the art gallery and railway station at Dresden, testify to his adaptation of the Italian Renaissance style. 📖 Wolfgang Herrmann, *Gottfried Semper: In Search of Architecture* (1984)

Sempill, Robert c.1530–95
Scottish ballad writer

He spent some time in Paris, but left after the St Bartholomew's Day Massacre in 1572 and lived for most of the rest of his life in Edinburgh. He wrote witty ballads full of coarse vigour, such as *The Legend of a Lymmaris Life* and *Sege of the Castel of Edinburgh*. He was an enemy of Mary, Queen of Scots and wrote satirical Reformation pieces, such as the *Life of the Tulchene Bishop of St Andrews*.

Sempill, Robert c.1595–c.1665
Scottish poet

He was from the hamlet of Beltrees, Renfrewshire. He was a Royalist, and there is evidence that he was employed at court. He revived the methods of the Scottish 'Makars', and wrote vernacular poetry that proved to be popular; he also invented the six-line stanza later called the 'Standard Habbie'. He wrote *Habbie Simson*, *The Blythesome Bridal* and, possibly, *Maggie Lauder*. His father Sir James Sempill (1566–1625) and his son Francis Sempill (c.1616–82) also wrote poetry. 📖 J Paterson (ed), *The Sempill Ballads* (1849)

Sen, Amartya Kumar 1933–
Indian economist

Born in India, he studied at Calcutta University, and was a Fellow of Trinity College, Cambridge from 1957 to 1963. He was successively Professor of Economics at New Delhi University, the London School of Economics, Oxford, and Harvard. He is noted for his work on the nature of poverty and famine. His publications include *Inequality Re-examined* (1992).

Senanayake, Don Stephen 1884–1952
Sri Lankan statesman
He was born in Colombo and worked on his father's rubber estate. He entered the Legislative Council in 1922, founded the co-operative society movement in 1923, and was elected to the State Council in 1931, where he was Minister of Agriculture for 15 years. After independence he became Sri Lanka's first Prime Minister (1947–52), as well as Minister of Defence and External Affairs. He died of a fall from his horse.

Sénancour, Étienne Pivert de 1770–1846
French writer
Born in Paris, he spent nine years in Switzerland as a young man, but returned to his native city about 1798. His fame rests on three books: *Rêveries sur la nature primitive de l'homme* (1799, 'Thoughts on the primitive nature of man'), *Obermann* (1804) and *Libres méditations d'un solitaire inconnu* ('Meditations of a stranger alone'). He was neglected in his day, but was appreciated by **George Sand, Charles Saint-Beuve** and **Matthew Arnold**. The influence of Goethe's *Werther* is reflected in his work.

Sendak, Maurice Bernard 1928–
US illustrator and writer of children's books
Born in Brooklyn, New York City, he was the son of poor Jewish immigrants from Poland. He attended Lafayette High School in New York and worked as a window-dresser. He encountered classic illustrators in a toy store and was subsequently commissioned by a publisher to illustrate *The Wonderful Farm* (1951) by Marcel Aymé. In 1956 came *Kenny's Window*, the first book for which he also wrote the text, and the more controversial *Where the Wild Things Are* (1963), which explored the fantasy world of mischievous Max. This was a great commercial success and won the Carnegie Medal. Other works include *In The Night Kitchen* (1970), *Outside Over There* (1981), *Dear Mili* (1988), *I Saw Esau* (1992) and *We are All in the Dumps with Jack and Guy* (1993).

Senebier, Jean 1742–1809
Swiss botanist, plant physiologist and pastor
Born in Geneva, he was ordained pastor of the Protestant Church, Geneva, in 1765. During a year in Paris he met many scientists and began experiments in plant physiology. He was pastor of Chancy near Geneva (1769–73) and librarian for the Republic of Geneva from 1773. Senebier was the first to demonstrate the basic principle of photosynthesis, his most important papers being *Action de la Lumière sur la Végétation* (1779, 'Action of Sunlight on Vegetation') and *Expériences sur l'Action de la Lumière Solaire dans la Végétation* (1788, 'Experiments on the Action of Sunlight on Vegetation'), and was also the first to establish a precise experimental method.

Seneca, Lucius Annaeus, *called* Seneca the Younger c.4BC–c.65AD
Roman Stoic philosopher, statesman and tragedian
Born in Corduba (Cordoba), Spain, the son of **Marcus Annaeus Seneca**, he began a career in politics and law in Rome in 31AD. However, he was banished to Corsica (41–49) by Emperor **Claudius** on a charge of adultery with Claudius's niece Julia, and there wrote the three treatises *Consolationes*. Recalled to Rome in 49 through the influence of **Agrippina the Younger**, he became tutor to her son, the future Emperor **Nero**. He enjoyed considerable political influence for a while and was made consul by

Nero in 57, but he later withdrew from public life and devoted himself to writing and philosophy. In 65 he was implicated in the conspiracy of Piso and ordered to commit suicide. His writings include *Epistolae morales ad Lucilium* and the *Apocolocyntosis divi Claudii* (literally, 'The Pumpkinification of the Divine Claudius'), a scathing satire. The publication in translation of his *Tenne Tragedies* (1581) was important in the evolution of English Elizabethan drama, which took from them the principal division into five acts. 📖 A L Motto, *Seneca* (1973)

Seneca, Marcus Annaeus, *called* Seneca the Elder c.55BC–c.40AD
Roman rhetorician
He was born in Corduba (Cordoba), Spain, and educated at Rome. In addition to a history of Rome, which is now lost, he wrote for his sons a collection of imaginary court cases, *Oratorum et Rhetorum Sententiae*, *Divisiones*, *Colores Controversiae* (partly lost), and *Suasoriae*, a collection of earlier, rhetorical styles. He was the father of **Lucius Annaeus Seneca** and grandfather of **Lucan**.

Senefelder, Aloys 1771–1834
Bavarian printer and inventor
He was born in Prague and after studying briefly at the University of Ingolstadt became a successful actor and playwright. He invented lithography (c.1796) after accidentally discovering the possibilities of drawing with greasy chalk on wet stone. After various trials in 1806 he opened an establishment in Munich to teach others in the process. He became director of the Royal Printing Office in Munich, and established a school at Offenbach.

Senerat d.1635
King of Kandy (Sri Lanka)
He succeeded to the throne in 1604, having served as Commander-in-Chief of the army in his predecessor's wars with the Portuguese, who controlled the remainder of the island. The early part of his reign was a period of peace and prosperity and enjoyed increased trade with the Portuguese. When Portuguese aggression led to the renewal of hostilities (1629), Senerat destroyed the Portuguese army at Radenwiela (1630). He was unable to capture the Portuguese capital of Colombo and in 1634 a peace settlement was agreed.

Senesh, Hannah 1921–44
Hungarian and Israeli heroine of World War II
Born and educated in Budapest, she emigrated to Palestine in 1939 and studied at Nahalal Agricultural School before working on the Sdot-Yam kibbutz in Caesarea. When news of the extermination of European Jews reached Palestine she volunteered to be parachuted into Yugoslavia as a member of the British Armed Forces to warn the Jews of the danger and to help in the rescue operation. After making her way to the Hungarian border she was captured, tortured, tried and executed. In 1950 her body was re-buried with military honours in Israel. Her diary and poems were published posthumously.

Senghor, Léopold Sédar 1906–
Senegalese statesman and poet
Educated in Dakar and at the Sorbonne in Paris, he taught classics in France from 1935, where he became involved with literary figures and wrote poetry advocating the concept of 'negritude' to glorify African civilization and values. After World War II he sat in the French National Assembly (1946–58) and was a leader of the Senegalese independence movement. After independence in 1960, as leader of the Senegalese Progressive Union (UPS), he became the new nation's first President. In 1976 he reconstituted the UPS as the Senegalese Socialist Party (PS) and gradually the one-party political system which he had created became more pluralist,

although the PS remained the dominant force. Senghor was re-elected several times until his retirement in 1980. His successor was **Abdou Diouf.** ⌂ A Guibert, *Léopold Sédar Senghor* (1961)

Senna, Ayrton 1960–94
Brazilian racing driver

Born in São Paulo, he made his Grand Prix debut in Brazil in 1984 with the Toleman team. He later drove for Lotus (1985–87), McLaren (1988–93) and Williams (1994). He was Formula One world champion in 1988, 1990, and 1991, but lost his title to **Nigel Mansell** in 1992. He was killed after crashing during the San Marino Grand Prix.

Sennacherib d.681BC
King of Assyria

He succeeded his father **Sargon II** in 705BC. He sacked Babylon (689) and besieged Hezekiah unsuccessfully in Jerusalem. He rebuilt Nineveh, and undertook building schemes for the embankment of the Tigris and for canals and water-courses. He was killed by one of his sons, and was succeeded by **Esarhaddon.**

Sennett, Mack, *originally* Michell Sinott 1880–1960
US film producer

Born in Richmond, Quebec, he was a child singing prodigy. Hoping to pursue a career in opera, he also appeared on Broadway and in burlesque (1902–08). He joined Biograph Studios in 1908 and made his first film *Baked in the Altar*, the same year. Under **D W Griffith**, he became a leading man and directed *The Lucky Toothache* (1910). By 1912 he had formed his own company, Keystone Co, in Los Angeles, and set about altering and defining the conventions of US screen comedy. He recruited **Charlie Chaplin**, Fatty Arbuckle and others, and made hundreds of short comedies which established a whole generation of players and a tradition of knockabout slapstick involving the Keystone Komics (1912), the Keystone Kops, and the Sennett Bathing Beauties (1920). His feature films include *Tillie's Punctured Romance* (1914), *The Goodbye Kiss* (1928) and *Way Up Thar* (1935). He went into partial retirement in 1935, and received a Special Academy Award in 1937. An autobiography, *Mack Sennett: King of Comedy*, was published in 1954. ⌂ Gene Fowler, *Father Goose* (1934)

Senusrit See Sesostris

Séquard, Édouard Brown- See Brown-Séquard, Édouard

Sequoyah, *also called* George Guess c.1770–1843
Native American scholar

Born in Tennessee, he was probably the son of an English trader but was raised by his part-Cherokee mother. He invented a Cherokee syllabary of 85 characters in 1826. He taught thousands of Cherokee to read and write and served as a political envoy for his people. His name was given to a genus of giant coniferous trees (*Sequoia*) and to a national park. ⌂ Grant Foreman, *Sequoyah* (1938)

Serao, Matilde 1856–1927
Italian novelist and journalist

Born in Patras, Greece, the daughter of a Greek father and a mother who was a Neapolitan political refugee, she graduated as a teacher in Naples, worked in a telegraph office, and started writing articles for newspapers (1876–78). Her first novel of Neapolitan life was *Cuore Infermo* (1881), after which she joined the Rome newspaper *Capitan Fracassa*. She enjoyed a huge success with her next romantic novel, *Fantasia* (1882), and this was followed by *Conquista di Roma* (1886, 'Conquest of Rome'), *Riccardo Joanna* (1887), *All' Erta Sentinella* (1889) and *Il Paese di Cuccagna* (1891, 'The Land of the Cockayne'). ⌂ A Barti, *Serao* (1965)

Serf, St 6th century
Scottish religious

He founded the church of Culross at a date that cannot be established. He figures in the legend of St **Kentigern** as his teacher. He is also associated with an island on Loch Leven.

Sergei 1876–1944
Russian Orthodox religious leader

Already a bishop by 1901, he survived the Russian Revolution of 1917 and the subsequent suppression of religion. In 1925 he became patriarch by default when Patriarch **Tikhon** died, and in 1927 made a declaration of loyalty to the state which allowed Orthodoxy to continue. During World War II, **Stalin** sought his support in defence of the country and allowed him to call a council in 1943, at which he was formally elected.

Sergeyev-Tsensky, Sergei Nikolayevich 1875–1958
Russian novelist

He was born in Tambov province. From a Dostoevskian passion for morbid characterization, as in *Tundra* (1902, 'The Tundra'), he developed greater simplicity of style and social sense in the massive 10-volume novel sequence, *Preobrazhenye zapiski* (1914–40, 'Transfiguration'), which won him the Stalin Prize in 1942. ⌂ A V Pryenkov, *Sergeyev Tsensky* (1963)

Serkin, Rudolf 1903–91
US pianist

Born in Eger, Hungary, he studied composition with Joseph Marx and **Arnold Schoenberg** in Vienna and made his debut there in 1915. He was closely associated with **Adolf Busch** (whose son-in-law he became) in chamber music. In 1939 he settled in the USA and took US citizenship. He directed the Curtis Institute, Philadelphia, from 1968 to 1976, and founded the Marlboro School of Music (1949) and the Marlboro Music Festival (1950).

Serling, Rod 1924–75
US science-fiction writer and television playwright

He was born in Syracuse, New York. A combat paratrooper during World War II, he attended Antioch College and began writing radio scripts before securing a radio staff job in Cincinnati. He first wrote for television in 1951, and in 1955 won the first of six Emmy awards for his play *Patterns*. Other plays include *Requiem for a Heavyweight* (1956) and *The Comedian* (1957). He created, wrote and hosted the popular anthology series *The Twilight Zone* (1959–64). His scripts reflect his interest in the individual's struggle against social and political pressures, and showed a mastery of the surprise ending; they have been much imitated. He also created *Night Gallery* (1970–73), was the author of over 200 television plays, and wrote the film script *Seven Days in May* (1964).

Serlio, Sebastiano 1475–1554
Italian architect and painter

Born in Bologna, he studied there and in Rome with **Peruzzi.** He moved to Venice in 1527, and in 1540 was called to France by **Francis I**. Especially influential was his treatise on Italian architecture, *Regole generali di architettura* (1537–51, and posthumously 1575), which included plans bequeathed by **Peruzzi.** The treatise was widely consulted, and was later published in English, German and Dutch editions. As master of works at Fontainebleau, his most important work was the Grand Ferrare (1541–48, demolished), where the pioneering use of an enclosed U-plan set the precedent for French town-houses in subsequent years. The quadrangular château at Ancy-le-Franc, Tonnerre (from 1546), was also noteworthy.

Serra, Junípero, *originally* Miguel José Serra, *called* the Apostle of California 1713–84
Spanish missionary

Born on the island of Majorca, he studied at the cathedral school in Palma and entered the Franciscan order in 1730. He became a doctor of theology and lectured at the University of Palma until 1749, when he went to Mexico to proselytize among the South American Indians. He worked at missions in Sierra Gorda and Mexico City, and in 1767 he was sent to California. Known as the 'walking friar', he was determined to follow the Franciscan injunction to travel on foot, despite an ulcerated leg that afflicted him for most of his life. His indifference to hardship and danger and his rigorous self-flagellation were proofs of his piety, and he won many converts. He founded nine missions in upper California, including San Diego (1769), the first European settlement in California, San Francisco de Assisi and San Juan Capistrano (1776), and San Buenaventura (1782). He was an advocate of land rights of converted Native Americans and at times interceded to limit their exploitation by the Spanish; but his missionary work necessarily increased the Spanish military and economic presence in California and eroded Native American cultural autonomy. He was beatified by John Paul II in 1985.

Serra, Richard 1939–
US sculptor

Born in San Francisco, he studied art at Berkeley and Yale, and from 1964 to 1966 studied in Paris and Florence, then settled in New York. In the late 1960s he produced a series of films, and began manufacturing austere minimalist works from sheet steel, iron and lead, barely altering the original form of the metal, for example in *Shovel Plate Prop* (1969, Tate Gallery, London), and *Corner Prop No.7: for Nathalie* (1983, Pompidou Centre, Paris). Many of his works are of huge dimensions: notable are the long arcs of sheet metal which can span city squares and the cubic structures composed of massive metal plates balanced vertically against one another. Public commissions for such works have made him a controversial but highly influential artist. He published *Weight and Measure* in 1992.

Serrano, Francisco, Duke de la Torre 1810–85
Spanish politician

He fought against the Carlists and, nominally a Liberal, was favoured by Isabella II and played a conspicuous part in various ministries. He was banished in 1866, but in 1868 he drove out Isabella and was made regent until the accession of Amadeus I of Savoy (1870). He waged successful war against the Carlists in 1872 and 1874; again regent in 1874, he resigned power into the hands of Alfonso XIII.

Serre, Jean-Pierre 1926–
French mathematician and Nobel Prize winner

He was born in Bages, and studied at the École Normale Supérieure before working at the National Centre for Scientific Research (CNRS) and the University of Nancy. He became professor at the Collège de France in 1956. For his early work in homotopy theory and topology, he was awarded the Fields Medal in 1954. Later he turned to algebraic geometry and other branches of mathematics. A recent publication is *Topics in Galois Theory* (1992).

Sertorius, Quintus 123–72BC
Roman soldier

He was born in Nursia in the Sabine country. He fought with Marius in Gaul (102BC) and supported him against Sulla. In 83 he became praetor and was given Spain as his province. In 80 he led a successful rising of natives and

Roman exiles against Rome, holding out against Sulla's commanders (including Pompey) for eight years until he was murdered by his chief lieutenant.

Servetus, Michael 1511–53
Spanish theologian and physician

Born in Tudela, he studied law in Toulouse, and worked largely in France and Switzerland. In *De Trinitatis Erroribus* (1531) and *Christianismi Restitutio* (1553) he denied the Trinity and the divinity of Jesus. He escaped the Inquisition but was burnt by John Calvin in Geneva for heresy. He lectured on geography and astronomy, practised medicine at Charlien and Vienna (1538–53), and discovered the pulmonary circulation of the blood, prefiguring William Harvey.

Service, Robert William 1874–1958
Canadian poet

Born in Preston, England, he went to Canada, and travelled as a reporter for the *Toronto Star*. He served as an ambulance driver in World War I and wrote popular ballads, most notably 'The Shooting of Dangerous Dan McGrew', which appeared in *Songs of a Sourdough* (1907), and those in *Rhymes of a Rolling Stone* (1912). His characteristic use of alliteration persisted in *Ballads of a Bohemian* (1920), *Rhymes of a Rebel* (1952) and *Carols of a Codger* (1954). He also wrote novels, of which *The House of Fear* (1927) is the most accomplished. 📖 *Harper of Heaven* (1948); *Ploughman of the Moon* (1945)

Servius Sulpicius Galba See **Galba, Servius Sulpicius**

Servius Tullius fl.578–535BC
Semi-legendary sixth King of Rome

He was brought up as a slave in the house of his predecessor, Tarquinius Priscus. Public works and constitutional reform, including a reorganization of the citizen body, have been attributed to him.

Sesostris or **Senusrit**
Egyptian monarch

According to Greek legend, he invaded Libya, Arabia, Thrace and Scythia, subdued Ethiopia, placed a fleet on the Red Sea, and extended his dominion to India. He was possibly Sesostris I (c.1980–1935BC), II (c.1906–1887BC) and III (c.1887–1849BC) compounded into one hero.

Sesshū, Toyo 1420–1506
Japanese painter and priest

Born in Bitchu Province, he was educated as a Zen monk and painter at the Shokokuji in Kyoto, where the teaching of Tensho Shubun (d.c.1445) became the determining factor of his career. From 1467 to 1469 he travelled in Ming China, and his mature style, determined by a clear and solid composition, shows the influence of Chinese painting. Eventually he returned to monastic life. His knowledge of Zen Buddhism and his close communion with nature allowed him to renew the traditional lyricism of Japanese landscapes, while retaining a unique expression which distinguishes him from his contemporaries. His technique of 'pom' shows certain similarities to Jackson Pollock's 'dripping' and related techniques of lyrical abstraction of the 20th century.

Sessions, Roger 1896–1985
US composer

Born in Brooklyn, New York, he studied under Ernest Bloch and from 1925 to 1933 lived in Europe. He later taught in the USA, and held professorships at Berkeley and Princeton. He also taught at the Juilliard School of Music in New York from 1965. His compositions include nine symphonies, a violin concerto, piano and chamber music, the operas *The Trial of Lucullus* (1947, based on a work by **Bertolt Brecht**) and *Montezuma* (1941–63), and a *Rhapsody for Orchestra* (1970).

Seth, Vikram 1952–
Indian poet, novelist and travel writer

He was born in Calcutta and educated at universities in England, the USA and China. His first poetry collection was *Mappings* (1980). A travel book, *From Heaven Lake: Travels Through Sinkiang and Tibet*, appeared in 1983. His first novel, *The Golden Gate* (1986), was written in verse and describes the lives of the contemporary Californian professional classes. His next novel was even more ambitious. At over 1,300 pages, *A Suitable Boy* (1993) is one of the longest single-volume novels in English. Set in post-independence India, it is a love story which encompasses a large number of characters and attempts a comprehensive portrait of Indian social, political and cultural life.

Seton, St Elizabeth Ann, *née* Bayley 1774–1821
US religious, and the first native-born saint of the USA

Born into New York upper-class society, she married at the age of 19 into a wealthy trading family, and in 1797 founded the Society for the Relief of Poor Widows with Small Children. In 1803 she herself was left a widowed mother of five. She was converted to Catholicism from Episcopalianism, took vows, founded a Catholic elementary school in Baltimore, and in 1809 founded the USA's first religious order, the Sisters of Charity. She was beatified by Pope **John XXIII** in 1963, and canonized in 1975.

Seton, Ernest Thompson, *pseudonym of* Ernest Seton Thompson 1860–1946
Canadian writer and nature book illustrator

He was born in South Shields, County Durham, England, and became a naturalized Canadian. He founded the Boy Scouts of America. His books on animals were instructive and popular; the best known are *Biography of a Silver Fox* (1909) and his autobiography, *The Trail of an Artist-Naturalist* (1940).

Settle, Elkanah 1648–1724
English dramatist

Born in Dunstable, Bedfordshire, he went from Oxford to London to make a living by writing. In 1671 he achieved success with a bombastic tragedy *Cambyses*. He is principally remembered for his rivalry with **Dryden**, who attacked him fiercely in the second part of *Absalom and Achitophel*; Settle replied in *Reflections on several of Mr Dryden's Plays* (1687). In 1691 he was made poet of the City of London, and he contributed pageants until 1708. He adapted *A Midsummer Night's Dream* as *The Fairy Queen* in 1692, with music by **Henry Purcell**. He also wrote short comic pieces known as 'drolls', of which only one, *The Siege of Troy* (1707), survives. 📖 F C Brown, *The Life and Work of Elkanah Settle* (1910)

Seurat, Georges Pierre 1859–91
French artist

He was born in Paris and studied at the École des Beaux-Arts. He was an early exponent of Neo-Impressionism, and developed the technique known as Pointillism, in which the whole picture is composed of tiny rectangles of pure colour which merge together when viewed from a distance. The technique was founded on the colour theories of **Eugène Delacroix** and the 'chroma' theory of chemist **Michel Eugène Chevreul**, and the compositions were constructed architecturally according to scientific principles. He completed only seven canvases in this immensely demanding discipline, including *Une Baignade, Asnières* (1883–84, Tate Gallery, London), *Un Dimanche d'été à la Grande-Jatte* (1884–86, 'Sunday Afternoon on the Island of La Grande Jatte', Chicago), *Les Poseuses* (1887–88) and *Le Cirque* (1891). His colour theories influenced **Paul Signac, Camille Pissarro, Degas** and **Renoir**.

Seuss, Dr, *pseudonym of* Theodor Seuss Giesel 1904–91
US children's author and illustrator

Born in Springfield, Massachusetts, he graduated from Dartmouth College, New Hampshire, in 1925, and after graduate study at Oxford, became a freelance cartoonist and illustrator. *And to Think that I Saw it on Mulberry Street* (1937) was the first of his many children's books, which are characterized by their engaging rhymed narratives and their imaginative, almost anarchic illustrations of animal characters that have been described as 'boneless wonders'. Set in a bizarre world that manages to be both crazy and surreal, his immensely popular stories include *The 500 Hats of Bartholomew Cubbins* (1938), *If I Ran the Zoo* (1950) and *Green Eggs and Ham* (1960). His story *How the Grinch Stole Christmas* (1957) was made into an animated television cartoon, and he also wrote the screenplay for the cartoon *Gerald McBoing Boing* (1950), which won an Academy Award. In 1957 he began to write and draw a series of 'Beginner Books', intended to help teach reading, for Random House, starting with *The Cat in the Hat* (1958) and *Yertle the Turtle* (1958). By 1970, 30 million copies had been sold in the USA and Seuss had become synonymous with learning to read. He also wrote a best-selling book for adults, *You're Only Old Once!* (1986). 📖 M Stoffer, *Dr Seuss From Then to Now* (1986)

Severin, Giles Timothy 1940–
English historian, traveller and author

He was educated at Tonbridge School and Keble College, Oxford, where he took a research degree in medieval Asian exploration. He has re-created many voyages following the routes of early explorers and navigators, using vessels reconstructed to the original specifications. They include those of St **Brendan**, the legendary Irish monk, Sinbad whose seven long voyages in an Arab dhow took him from Arabia to China, and the early Greek quests of Jason and Ulysses in a bronze-age ship. His publications include *The China Voyage* (1994).

Severini, Gino 1883–1966
Italian artist

Born in Cortona, he studied in Rome under **Giacomo Balla** from 1900 to 1906, then moved to Paris where he worked as a Pointillist. In 1910 he signed the first Futurist manifesto in 1910, associating with Balla and **Umberto Boccioni**, with whom he exhibited in Paris and London, including *Dynamic Hieroglyphic of the Bal Tabarin* (1912). After 1914 he evolved a personal brand of Cubism and Futurism in which he painted many striking nightclub scenes. In 1921 he reverted to a more representational neoclassical style, which he used in fresco and mosaic work, particularly in private houses and a number of Swiss and Italian churches. After 1940 he adopted a decorative Cubist manner. His many publications include *Du Cubisme au Classicisme* (1921).

Severus, Lucius Septimius AD146–211
Roman emperor

The founder of the Severan dynasty, he was born near Leptis Magna in North Africa. After the murder of **Publius Pertinax** (AD193) he was proclaimed emperor, defeated two rivals (195–197), campaigned in the East, took Byzantium, and defeated the Parthians (197–99). At Rome (202) he entertained magnificently, and distributed extravagant largesse. In 208 he marched to northern Britain to strengthen the frontier. He repaired the fortifications on Hadrian's wall and was busy preparing a campaign into Scotland when he died at Eboracum (York). See also **Alexander Severus**. 📖 Anthony Birley, *Septimius Severus: The African Emperor* (1972)

Sevier, John 1745–1815
US soldier and politician
Born near New Market, Virginia, he grew up on the frontier and became a farmer and land speculator. As a militia leader in Lord Dunmore's War against Native Americans in Tennessee (1773–74), he won a victory over British Loyalists at King's Mountain (1780) and became a hero. He was chosen as Governor of the short-lived state of Franklin (1784–88), was elected to the US House of Representatives (1789–91, 1811–15) and became the first Governor of Tennessee (1796–1801, 1803–09).

Sévigné, Madame de, *née* Marie de Rabutin-Chantal 1626–96
French letter-writer
Born in Paris, she was orphaned at an early age and brought up by an uncle at the Abbaye de Livry, Brittany. She became a member of French court society, and after the marriage of her daughter in 1669 she began a series of letters to her which continued over 25 years and recount the current news and events of the time of **Louis XIV** in great detail and in a natural colloquial style. The letters were published posthumously in 1725. 📖 J Aldis, *Madame de Sévigné* (1907)

Sewall, Samuel 1652–1730
American colonial merchant and jurist
Born in Bishopstoke, England, he travelled to Boston with his parents (who had already lived in New England) in 1661 and graduated from Harvard in 1671. As a justice of the Massachusetts superior court (1692–1728), he condemned 19 people to be executed during the Salem witchcraft trials (1692). Five years later, he publicly confessed the error of his decisions. His writings include an antislavery essay (*The Selling of Joseph*, 1700) and a plea for humane treatment of Native Americans (*A Memorial Relating to the Kennebeck Indians*, 1721). He also kept a diary from 1673 to 1729 (omitting the years 1677 to 1685), which was first published in the late 19th century and is of great historical value for its information on the lives and characters of the New England Puritans.

Seward, Sir Albert Charles 1863–1941
English palaeobotanist
Born in Lancaster, Lancashire, he studied at Cambridge and Manchester, and was later Professor of Botany at Cambridge (1906–36). He is best known for his works on English palaeobotany, *Wealden Flora* (1894–95), *Jurassic Flora* (1900–03), the four-volume *Fossil Plants* (1898–1919), and a panoramic survey, *Plant Life Through the Ages* (1931). He was knighted in 1936.

Seward, Anna, *known as* the Swan of Lichfield 1747–1809
English poet
Born in Eyam Rectory, Derbyshire, she lived from the age of 10 at Lichfield, where her father, himself a poet, became a canon. When he died in 1790, she continued to live on in the bishop's palace, and wrote romantic poetry. Her 'Elegy on Captain Cook' (1780) was commended by Dr **Johnson**. She bequeathed all her poems to Sir **Walter Scott**, who published them in 1810 as *Poetical Works*. 📖 J Pearson, *The Swan of Lichfield* (1956)

Seward, William Henry 1801–72
US politician
Born in Florida, New York, he was admitted to the Bar at Utica in 1822. He was elected to the state senate in 1830 and won the governorship of New York State in 1838. During the 1850s he became a major spokesman for the antislavery movement and a leader of the Republican

Party. His 'irrepressible conflict' speech was thought by many Democrats to be responsible for John Brown's violence at Harpers Ferry Raid. He served as an effective Secretary of State under **Abraham Lincoln**, taking an uncompromising attitude towards French support for Archduke **Ferdinand Maximilian** as Emperor of Mexico, which he saw as a breach of the Monroe Doctrine. Severely injured during the assassination of Lincoln, he recovered to remain Secretary of State in President **Andrew Johnson**'s Cabinet. In 1867 he secured the purchase for $7.2 million of Alaska from Russia (known as 'Seward's folly') by persuading a reluctant Congress of its vast mineral wealth.

Sewell, Anna 1820–78
English novelist
She was born in Great Yarmouth, Norfolk, and was an invalid for most of her life. In her youth she helped edit her mother's novels which were popular at that time. Her only book is *Black Beauty, The Autobiography of a Horse* (1877), a work for children which was written as a plea for the more humane treatment of animals. 📖 M Bayly, *The Life and Letters of Mrs Sewell* (1881)

Sex Pistols
English punk band
The band was a product of the London King's Road punk scene in 1975, a counterblast to rock's perceived effeteness. After hearing Richard Hell and other New York punks, their opportunist manager, Malcolm McLaren, returned to the UK and recruited the sneering Johnny Rotten (originally John Lydon, 1956–) as vocalist (his lack of experience was not seen as a drawback), guitarist Steve Jones (1955–), bassist Glen Matlock (1956–), and drummer Paul Cook (1956–). Matlock was later replaced by the nihilistic Sid Vicious (originally John Simon Ritchie, 1957–79). During its brief existence the band offended many people and it was often banned from appearing at its concert venues. Their only real album was *Never Mind The Bollocks* (1977), but they were hugely influential, and 'Anarchy in the UK' (1976) remains a rock classic. The original band re-formed for an openly money-making tour in 1996. 📖 J Savage, *England's Dreaming* (1991)

Sexton, Anne, *née* Harvey 1928–74
US poet
Born in Newton, Massachusetts, she was a 'confessional' poet in the mould of her teacher, **Robert Lowell**, and her friend, **Sylvia Plath**, with whom she is often associated. She wrote frankly about her personal experiences, including a nervous breakdown. She taught at Boston University (1969–71) and Colgate (1971–72). To *Bedlam and Part Way Back* (1962) was her first collection of poetry. Others include *Live or Die* (1966), *Love Poems* (1969), *Transformations* (1971), *The Book of Folly* (1972), and the posthumously published *The Awful Rowing Towards God* (1975) and *45 Mercy Street* (1976). The *Complete Poems* were published in 1981. She committed suicide. 📖 D W Middlebrook, *Anne Sexton: A Biography* (1990)

Sexton, Thomas 1848–1932
Irish nationalist politician
Born in Ballygannon, County Waterford, he worked as a railway clerk before becoming leader writer on the *Nation*. He was elected MP for Sligo as Home Rule supporter of **Charles Parnell** in 1880, capturing West Belfast for Parnell in 1886. He was defeated there in 1892 after the Parnell split, subsequently being MP for Kerry North from 1892 to 1896. He was Lord Mayor of Dublin in 1888–89. He controlled the leading Home Rule daily newspaper, the *Freeman's Journal*, from 1892 to 1912. Sexton is generally regarded as a parliamentary orator second only to **Gladstone**.

Sextus Empiricus 2nd century
Greek philosopher and physician
He was active at Alexandria and Athens, and is the main source of information for the Sceptical school of philosophy. Little is known of his life, but his surviving writings, *Outlines of Pyrrhonism* and *Against the Dogmatists*, had an emormous influence when they were rediscovered and published in Latin translations in the 1560s.

Seyfert, Carl Keenan 1911–60
US astronomer
Born in Cleveland, Ohio, and educated at Harvard, he worked at the McDonald and Mount Wilson observatories, then became associate Professor of Astronomy and Physics and director of Barnard Observatory, Vanderbilt University (1946–51). From 1951 he was Professor of Astronomy and director of the Arthur J Dyer Observatory. He is famous for his work on a special group of galaxies (named after him) which have very bright bluish star-like nuclei, and spectra containing broad high-excitation emission lines. They are now thought to be the low-luminosity cousins of quasars.

Seymour, Charles, 6th Duke of Somerset 1662–1748
English nobleman
He held high posts under Charles II, William III and Queen Anne, including Master of the Horse (1702). In 1682 he married Elizabeth, daughter of the last Earl of Northumberland and the heiress of the Percies, which brought him extensive estates, including Alnwick Castle, Petworth and Syon House.

Seymour, Edward, 1st Duke of Somerset,
known as Protector Somerset c.1506–1552
English soldier and statesman
The eldest son of Sir John Seymour and brother of Jane Seymour, he was successively created Viscount Beauchamp and 1st Earl of Hertford, and enjoyed high office under his brother-in-law, Henry VIII. As warden of the Scottish marches, he led the invading English army that devastated southern Scotland and Edinburgh in the 'Rough Wooing' of 1543–44, after the Scots rejected a proposed marriage between Prince Edward (the future Edward VI) and the infant Mary, Queen of Scots. At Henry's death in 1547 he was named Protector of England during the minority of Edward VI and was king in all but name. He defeated a Scottish army at Pinkie (1547), and furthered the Reformation with the first *Book of Common Prayer* (1549). Also in 1549 his younger brother Thomas Seymour was executed for attempting to marry Princess Elizabeth (the future Queen Elizabeth I), and soon he himself was indicted for 'over-ambition' and deposed by John Dudley, Earl of Warwick (1549), and eventually executed.

Seymour, Jane See Jane Seymour

Seymour, Lynn 1939–
British dancer
Born in Wainwright, Alberta, Canada, she trained in Vancouver, spending two years at the Royal Ballet School in London, and making her debut in 1956 with the Sadler's Wells branch of the company. She is best known for her passionate interpretations of the choreography of Kenneth MacMillan and Frederick Ashton. MacMillan cast her first in *The Burrow* (1958), and after that she was frequently teamed with Christopher Gable. Her dancing career was a volatile one and had its disappointments, as when she was asked to step down in favour of Margot Fonteyn for MacMillan's première of *Romeo and Juliet* (1965). She was acclaimed, however, in Ashton's *Five Brahms Waltzes in the Manner of Isadora Duncan* and *A Month in the Country* (both 1976). In 1978 she spent an unsuccessful season as director of the Bavarian Opera in Munich. She

returned to the stage as Tatiana in *Onegin* and the mother in Gable's *A Simple Man* (both 1988). While best known as a dancer, she has choreographed several pieces, *Rashomon* (1976) and *Wolfi* (1987) being perhaps the best known. Her book *Lynn* (1984) describes her life as an international ballet dancer.

Seymour (of Sudeley), Thomas Seymour, Baron c.1508–1549
English soldier and politician
Son of Sir John Seymour and younger brother of Edward Seymour, Duke of Somerset, and brother-in-law to Henry VIII through Henry's marriage to Jane Seymour, he became High Admiral of England in 1547, and in the same year married the dowager queen Catherine Parr, widow of Henry VIII. He schemed against his brother to marry Edward VI to Lady Jane Grey. After Catherine Parr's death in 1548 he tried to marry Princess Elizabeth of England, but was executed by his brother for treason.

Seymour, William, 2nd Earl of Hertford and 3rd Duke of Somerset 1588–1660
English soldier
Grandson of Edward Seymour, Earl of Hertford, he fell into disfavour in 1610 by secretly marrying Lady Arabella Stuart (1575–1615), first cousin to King James VI and I. He fled to Paris, but later played a conspicuous part in the Royalist cause (1642–43) during the Civil War, capturing Hereford, Cirencester and Bristol, and defeating Sir William Waller at Lansdown. At the Restoration he took his seat in the House of Lords as the 3rd Duke of Somerset.

Seyss-Inquart, Artur von 1892–1946
Austrian Nazi collaborator
Born in the Sudetenland, he practised as a lawyer in Vienna and saw much of Kurt von Schuschnigg. When the latter became Chancellor in 1938, he took office under him, informing Hitler of every detail in Schuschnigg's life, in the hope of becoming Nazi Chancellor of Austria after the Anschluss. Instead, he was appointed Commissioner for the Netherlands in 1940, where he ruthlessly recruited slave labour. In 1945 he was captured by the Canadians, tried at Nuremberg and executed for war crimes.

Sforza
Italian family
This celebrated family was founded by a peasant of the Romagna called Muzio Attendolo (1369–1424), who became a great *condottiere* or soldier of fortune, and received the name of Sforza ('Stormer'—ie, of cities).

Sforza, Carlo, Count 1873–1952
Italian statesman
He was born in Montignoso. After a successful early career in the diplomatic service both before and after World War I, he became Foreign Minister under Giovanni Giolitti, and in 1921 negotiated the Rapallo Treaty which returned the strategically important port of Fiume to Yugoslavia; this ensured his unpopularity with the rightist extremists and resulted in his demotion to ambassador to France, which post he resigned when Mussolini assumed power the following year. He continued to lead the anti-Fascist opposition in the Senate until 1926, but then emigrated to France. In 1940 he fled the German occupation to live briefly in the UK and then the USA, where he cultivated his involvement in a post-war administration, returning to his homeland after the war as a member of the provisional Government. He served as Foreign Minister again (despite strenuous British opposition) under Alcide de Gasperi, and was a strong advocate of NATO, until ill health forced his resignation in 1951. His writings include *European Dictatorships* (1931) and *Contemporary Italy* (1944).

Sforza, Francesco 1401–66
Duke of Milan

The illegitimate son of Muzio Attendolo Sforza, he was the father of Galeazzo Maria and Ludovico Sforza. He sold his sword to the highest bidder, fighting for or against the pope, Milan, Venice and Florence. When he married the Duke of Milan's daughter in 1450, he became heir to the duchy; and before his death he had extended his power over Ancona, Pesaro, all Lombardy and Genoa.

Sforza, Galeazzo Maria 1444–76
Italian nobleman

He was the son of Francesco Sforza and Duke of Milan from 1466. Though a competent ruler who encouraged agriculture and silk and wool manufacture, he was notoriously debauched and prodigal, and was assassinated.

Sforza, Ludovico, *also known as* the Moor
1452–1508
Duke of Milan and patron of Leonardo da Vinci

The son of Francesco Sforza, he was born near Milan and acted as regent for his nephew Gian Galeazzo (1469–94) from 1476, but expelled him (1481) and gained the dukedom for himself. His usurpation was legitimized on his nephew's death (1494) by Emperor Maximilian I. He made an alliance with Lorenzo de' Medici of Florence, and under his rule Milan underwent extensive civil and military engineering work and became the most glittering court in Europe. He helped to defeat the attempts of Charles VIII of France to secure Naples, but was expelled by Louis XII (1499) and imprisoned in France, where he died.

Shabbetai Tzevi See Sabbatai Zebi

Shackleton, Sir Ernest Henry 1874–1922
Irish explorer

Born in Kilkea, County Kildare, he was apprenticed in the Merchant Navy, and became a junior officer under Commander Robert Scott, on the *Discovery*, in the National Antarctic expedition of 1901–04. In 1908–09, in command of another expedition, he reached a point 97 miles (156.2km) from the South Pole, which was at that time a record. During a further expedition (1914–16), his ship *Endurance* was crushed in the ice. By means of sledges and boats he and his men reached Elephant Island, from where he and five others made a perilous voyage of 800 miles (1,288km) to South Georgia and organized relief for those remaining on Elephant Island. He died in South Georgia while on a fourth Antarctic expedition, begun in 1922. ☐ Roland Huntford, *Shackleton* (1986)

Shadwell, Thomas c.1642–1692
English dramatist

Born at Broomhill House, Brandon, Suffolk, he was educated at Cambridge and at the Middle Temple, London. He achieved success with the first of his 13 comedies, *The Sullen Lovers* (1668). He also wrote three tragedies. Dryden, grossly assailed by him in the *Medal of John Bayes* (1682), heaped ridicule on him in *MacFlecknoe* ('Shadwell never deviates into sense'), and as 'Og' in the second part of *Absalom and Achitopel*. His works exhibit talent and comic force. He succeeded Dryden as Poet Laureate in 1689. ☐ M W Alssid, *Thomas Shadwell* (1967)

Shaffer, Peter Levin 1926–
English dramatist

He was born in Liverpool and studied at Cambridge. His plays are variations on the themes of genius and mediocrity, faith and reason, and the question of whether God, if he exists, is benevolent or not. These ideas form the intellectual core of *The Royal Hunt of the Sun* (1964), *Equus* (1973) and *Amadeus* (1979). His first play was *Five Finger Exercise* (1958), followed by the comedies *The Private Ear* and *The Public Eye* (both 1962). *Yonadab* (1985), a story of incest and envy set in the Jerusalem of 1000BC, was not

well-received, but *Lettice and Lovage* (1987), a comedy, was a success. Other plays include *Black Comedy* (1965), *White Lies* (1967), *The Battle of Shrivings* (1970) and *The Gift of the Gorgon* (1992). ☐ Gene A Plunka, *Peter Shaffer* (1988)

Shaftesbury, Anthony Ashley Cooper, 1st Earl of 1621–83
English politician

Born in Wimborne St Giles, Dorset, he served with the Royalists in the Civil War, and then joined the Parliamentarians, becoming a member of Cromwell's Council of State. He was always suspected of Royalist sympathies, however, and in 1659 he was tried and imprisoned. He was one of 12 commissioners sent to France to invite Charles II home. In 1661 he was created Baron Ashley, and from then until his elevation as the Earl of Shaftesbury in 1672 was Chancellor of the Exchequer. He was subsequently made Lord Chancellor but dismissed by Charles a year later. He was a leading member of the movement to exclude the Roman Catholic Duke of York (James II) from the throne, exploiting for his own purposes the fictitious 'Popish Plot' allegedly uncovered by Titus Oates. He was subsequently tried for treason but acquitted, and moved to Amsterdam, where he died. He was satirized as 'Achitobel' in John Dryden's *Absolom and Achitobel* (1651). Although he was a man of great deviousness, his instincts were basically liberal, as is revealed by his association with John Locke in securing the amendment of the Habeas Corpus Act in 1679. ☐ K H D Haley, *The First Earl of Shaftesbury* (1968)

Shaftesbury, Anthony Ashley Cooper, 3rd Earl of 1671–1713
English philosopher, politician and essayist

He was born in London, and his early education was supervised by John Locke before he attended Winchester College. He was Whig MP for Poole (1698–99). After he succeeded as 3rd Earl in 1699 he regularly attended the House of Lords until ill health forced him to abandon politics for literature (1702). He moved to Naples in 1711 and died there. He wrote essays on a wide range of philosophical and cultural topics, collected under the title *Characteristicks of Men, Manners, Opinions, Times* (3 vols, 1711). He is usually regarded as one of the principal English deists, and he argued (both against orthodox Christianity and against Thomas Hobbes) that we possess a natural 'moral sense' and natural affections directed to the good of the species and in harmony with the larger cosmic order. He was more highly regarded abroad than at home, and Gottfried Leibniz, Voltaire, Diderot and Gotthold Lessing were among those attracted by his work. He was the grandson of the 1st Earl of Shaftesbury. ☐ R L Brett, *The Third Earl of Shaftesbury* (1951)

Shaftesbury, Anthony Ashley Cooper, 7th Earl of 1801–85
English factory reformer and philanthropist

Born in London, and educated at Harrow and Christ Church, Oxford, he entered parliament in 1826. As Lord Ashley, he took over the leadership of the factory reform movement from Michael Sadler in 1832. He also piloted successive factory acts (1847, 1850, 1859) through the House of Commons, achieving the 10-hour day and the provision of lodging-houses for the poor (1851). His Lunacy Act (1845) achieved considerable reform and his Coal Mines Act (1842) prohibited underground employment of women and of children under 13. He was Chairman of the Ragged Schools Union for 40 years, assisted Florence Nightingale in her schemes for army welfare and took an interest in missionary work. Strongly evangelical, he opposed radicalism although he worked with the trade unions for factory reforms. ☐ G F A Best, *Shaftesbury* (1964)

Shagari, Alhaji Shehu Usman Aliyu 1925–
Nigerian politician

Educated in northern Nigeria, he became a schoolmaster before being elected as a member of the Federal Parliament (1954–58). He was Minister of Economic Development (1959–60), Minister of Establishments (1960–62), Minister of Internal Affairs (1962–65) and Minister of Works (1965–66). After the 1966 coup, he was both State Commissioner for Education in Sokoto province and Federal Commissioner for Economic Development and Reconstruction (1968–70), and then Commissioner for Finance (1971–75). He was a member of the Constituent Assembly which drew up the Constitution for the Second Republic, and was the successful presidential candidate for the National Party of Nigeria in 1979. He was President of Nigeria from 1979 until 1983, when he was overthrown in a military coup. He published his collected speeches in 1981, entitled *My Vision of Nigeria.*

Shah, Eddy (Selim Jehane) 1944–
English newspaper magnate and novelist

He was born in Cambridge. He attended several schools, including Gordonstoun in Scotland, then worked as an assistant stage manager in a repertory theatre, and in television. He launched the *Sale and Altrincham Messenger* in 1974, and the *Stockport Messenger* in 1977. He grabbed national attention by confronting the unions over working practices, and arguably laid the foundations of the subsequent revolution in Fleet Street when he defeated a protracted strike over working practices. He launched *Today* in 1986, and was its chairman and chief executive until 1988. He also launched the ill-fated *Post* in 1988, which collapsed after a few months. His novels include *Ring of Red Roses* (1991) and *The Lucy Ghosts* (1992).

Shah Jahan 1592–1666
Mughal emperor

Born in Lahore, he was in open revolt against his father, **Jahangir**, from 1624 until the latter's death in 1627. Disputes with the Sikhs of the Punjab led to defeats of the Mughal troops (1628, 1631), and Kandahar was lost (1653) to the Persians, but the emperor was able to consolidate his power in the Deccan, subjugating Ahmadnagar, Bijapur and Golconda (1636). When he fell ill in 1658, his sons rebelled, and the victor was the third son, **Aurangzeb**, who became effective ruler of the empire, imprisoning Shah Jahan until his death. The Peacock Throne, the Taj Mahal, the Pearl Mosque, the Red Fort in Delhi, and the 98-mile Ravi Canal were among the achievements of his reign. 📖 B P Saksena, *History of Hahjahan of Dihli* (rev edn, 1958)

Shahn, Ben (jamin) 1898–1969
US painter

Born in Kovno (Kaunas), Lithuania, he emigrated with his parents to New York in 1906. Studying painting at night school, he visited the European art centres (1922) and came under the influence of **Georges Rouault**. His didactic pictorial commentaries on contemporary events, such as his 23 satirical gouache paintings on the trial of the Italian anarchists **Nicola Sacco** and Bartolomeo Vanzetti (1932, Museum of Modern Art, New York), and the 15 paintings of Tom Mooney, the Labour leader (1933), earned him the title of 'American **Hogarth**'. In 1933 he worked with **Diego Rivera** on murals for the Rockefeller Center, and later became one of the leading US Realist painters with work such as *Miners' Wives* (1948, Philadelphia). He was the first painter to deliver the Charles Eliot Norton Lectures at Harvard, published as *The Shape of Content* (1958).

Shaka c.1787–1828
Zulu leader, and founder of the Zulu nation

An illegitimate son, he seized power from his half-brother to become clan chief (1816). He organized a permanent army and conquered the Nguni peoples of modern Natal, exterminating many smaller clans, and built up a centralized, militaristic Zulu kingdom covering most of southern Africa. He became increasingly autocratic, to the point of insanity after the death (1827) of his mother Nandi, and was murdered by his half-brothers.

Shakespeare, John c.1530–1601
English glover and wool dealer

Born in Snitterfield, near Stratford, Warwickshire, he was the father of **William Shakespeare**. After apprenticeship to a leathersmith and glove-maker, he set up his own business in Stratford. It prospered and he was soon securely established in his house and workshop in Henley Street. In 1557 he married Mary, daughter of Robert Arden, a gentleman farmer and landowner in the nearby parish of Wilmcote; she inherited good farm land when her father died. In 1559 he was elected burgess, and six years later became an alderman. In 1568 he was made Bailiff (Mayor) of Stratford and a justice of the peace. His wool business failed in 1577, but he managed to retain possession of his house in Henley Street, although his wife's inheritance had to be mortgaged. In 1592 he was rescued by his son William, whose earnings in the London theatre were by then enough to restore the family's position. John Shakespeare never again played an active part in Stratford's civic life, but he received his coat of arms in 1596.

Shakespeare, William See panel p1680

Shakhlin, Boris Anfiyanovich 1932–
Soviet gymnast

Born in Ishin, he was the first man to win 10 individual and three team gold medals at World and Olympic championships. He was Olympic champion by 1956 and European champion by 1958 on the pommel horse, and in the 1960 Rome Olympics he won gold medals as winner in the overall, parallel bars, pommel horse and vault; silver medals for the rings; and a bronze for the horizontal bar. He now shares the male record for six individual gold medals with **Nikolai Andrianov**, and is still remembered for his skills of endurance.

Shalyapin, Fyodor Ivanovich See **Chaliapin, Feodor Ivanovich**

Shamil, *also spelt* Schamyl *or* Shamyl c.1797–1871
Caucasian chief

Born in Gimry, Dagestan, he led the Muslim Dagestan and Chechen peoples in the Caucasus in their 30-year struggle against Russia. He was a Sufi mullah, and strove to end the tribal feuds. A leader in the defence of Gimry against the Russians in 1831, he was chosen in 1834 to be the third iman (political and religious leader) of Dagestan, and continued to secure successes against the Russians. In 1839, and again in 1849, he escaped from the Russian stronghold of Ahulgo to continue preaching a holy war against the infidels. During the Crimean War (1854–56), the Allies supplied him with money and arms, but after peace was signed the Russians compelled the submission of the Caucasus. In 1859 his chief stronghold at Vedeno was taken. He was hunted for several months and, after a desperate resistance, was captured. He was exiled to Kaluga, south of Moscow.

Shamir, Yitzhak, *originally* Yitzhak Jazernicki 1915–
Israeli politician

Born in Poland, he studied law at Warsaw University and, after emigrating to Palestine, at the Hebrew University of Jerusalem. In his twenties he became a founder member of the Stern Gang (Fighters for the Freedom of Israel), the

Shakespeare, William 1564–1616
English playwright, poet and actor, the greatest English dramatist

William Shakespeare was born in Stratford-upon-Avon in Warwickshire, the eldest son of **John Shakespeare**, a glover and wool dealer, and Mary Arden. The traditional date of his birth is 23 April, which is probably influenced by its coincidence with St George's Day and by the fact that Shakespeare is known to have died on that day. He lived for 52 years, partly in Stratford and partly in London. He was most likely educated at Stratford Grammar School; the numerous classical allusions in his plays and poems show a knowledge of the Latin and Greek poets and writers who were studied there, and John Shakespeare's civic status entitled him to have his son educated free of charge.

Shakespeare's life can be divided into three periods. The first was spent wholly in Stratford, and included boyhood and education, early marriage and the birth of his three children. The second period lasted for 25 years from the time when he left Stratford, still a young man, to work in London as an actor and playwright; he divided his time in these years between Stratford and London and continued to own property and take an interest in Stratford. Finally, when he was in his late forties and with ample means, he left London to live entirely in Stratford, where he spent the rest of his life.

During the winter of 1582–83, at the age of 18, he married Anne Hathaway, a farmer's daughter who lived in Shottery, near Stratford. She was 26, and pregnant by him. Less than six months after their wedding, their first child, Susanna, was baptized in Stratford church. Early in 1585, Anne gave birth to twins: Hamnet, their only son (who died young), and Judith, their second daughter. With a wife and three children to maintain, and still dependent on his father, Shakespeare joined one of the London acting companies that had been touring in Stratford; three troupes were playing there from 1583 to 1588.

By 1595 he had written several successful plays in all the forms of drama then popular, although the chronology and order of the early works is still disputed. They include histories, comedies, and the revenge-tragedy *Titus Andronicus*. Between 1592 and 1594, when the theatres were closed by an outbreak of plague, Shakespeare turned to poetry, writing sonnets and two long narrative poems: *Venus and Adonis* (published 18 April 1593) and *The Rape of Lucrece* (published 9 May 1594). Both were dedicated to the 3rd Earl of **Southampton**, who was a patron of the arts, although nothing is known of the nature of Shakespeare's connection with him. In the literary and courtly circles in which they were read, the poems were highly praised for their eloquent treatment of classical subjects.

The 154 extant sonnets were probably written between 1592 and 1598, although they were not published until 1609, and the order in which he wrote them is not known. The poems of the first group are addressed to a young man, and of the second group to the 'Dark lady'; despite many attempts nobody has succeeded in identifying real people in these allusions, and it is doubtful that there is any real autobiographical basis for them. The language in which they treat recurrent themes, love's ecstasy and despair, implacable time, lust and its shames, separation, betrayal, fame and death, echoes that of the plays.

When the theatres reopened in 1594, Shakespeare joined the newly-formed Lord Chamberlain's Men, and was entitled to a share of the profits. The company already had some of the best actors, including **Richard Burbage**, **Edward Alleyn**, and **Will Kempe**, and performed regularly at the court of Queen **Elizabeth I**, notably during the Christmas festivities of 1594–95. Shakespeare's considerable output of six comedies, five histories and one tragedy (*Romeo and Juliet*) between 1594 and 1598 took the London theatre world by storm, and the language and the characters of the plays captured people's imagination and entered their daily conversation.

The income received from these successes enabled Shakespeare to meet the heavy expenses incurred when his father was awarded a grant of arms in October 1596. Henceforth, John Shakespeare was entitled to the style of 'Gentleman', an honour that would descend in due course to his eldest son although, two months earlier, Shakespeare's only son Hamnet had died at the age of 11.

cont

Zionist terrorist group which carried out anti-British attacks on strategic targets and personnel in Palestine. He was arrested by the British (1941) and exiled to Eritrea in 1946, but given asylum in France. He returned to the new State of Israel in 1948 and spent the next 20 years on the fringe of politics, immersing himself in business interests. He entered the Knesset in 1973, becoming its Speaker (1977–80). He was Foreign Minister (1980–83), before taking over the leadership of the right-wing Likud Party from **Menachem Begin**, and becoming Prime Minister (1983). From 1984, he shared power in an uneasy coalition with the Israel Labour Party and its leader, **Shimon Peres**. In 1990 the 'national unity' government collapsed, and in June 1992 Likud was defeated in the general election by the Labour Party, led by **Yitzhak Rabin**.

Shammai c.1st century BC–1st century AD
Jewish scholar and Pharisaic leader

Apparently a native of Jerusalem, he was head of a famous school of Torah scholars, whose interpretation of the Law was often in conflict with the equally famous school led by **Hillel I**. Relatively little is known of Shammai himself, except that his legal judgements were often considered severe and literalistic, compared to Hillel's. Both are often referred to in the Mishnah.

Shankly, Bill (William) 1913–81
Scottish footballer and manager

He won an FA Cup medal with Preston North End and five Scotland caps, and as a postwar manager he found success with Liverpool after unremarkable spells with Carlisle, Grimsby, Workington and Huddersfield. He created a team which was not only highly successful in Great Britain and Europe but encouraged individual expression and communicated great exhilaration to the spectators. With **Jock Stein** and Sir **Matt Busby** he is considered one of the greatest football managers of recent times. He is also remembered for saying: 'Some people think football is a matter of life and death. I don't like that attitude. I can assure them it is much more serious than that' (quoted in the *Sunday Times*, 4 October 1981).

Shannon, Claude Elwood 1916–
US applied mathematician

He was born in Gaylord, Michigan, and educated at Michigan University and at the Massachusetts Institute of Technology (MIT), where he gained a PhD in mathematics. A student of **Vannevar Bush**, he worked on the differential analyser, and in 1938 published a seminal paper (*A Symbolic Analysis of Relay and Switching Circuits*) on the application of symbolic logic to relay circuits. The central concept of his work—that information can be treated like any other quantity and can be manipulated by

Shakespeare, William cont

In 1597 Shakespeare bought and renovated New Place, a large and imposing mansion in Stratford, close by the Guild Chapel and the grammar school and a few minutes' walk from his parents' house. Two years later, the Chamberlain's Men dismantled the Theatre and used much of its material to build a new playhouse, called the Globe, on Bankside, south of the Thames. It was a bold and successful venture. Situated in the heart of London's pleasure-land of gaming-houses, bear-gardens, brothels and theatres, the Globe was both bigger and better equipped than any of its rivals. Its huge stage permitted the rapidity and continuity of action which the dramas of the day demanded and which Shakespeare was able to exploit in the plays he wrote for performance there. The Globe opened with *Henry V*, and its success was followed by *Julius Caesar*, *Twelfth Night*, *Hamlet* and *Othello*.

When James I (**James VII and I**) succeeded to the English throne in 1603, he immediately conferred his own royal patronage on Shakespeare and his fellow sharers. They became the King's Men ('His Majesty's Servants') and were granted a patent. The number of court performances was greatly increased, and the King's Men received twice the pay they had received from Elizabeth. The darker tone of the plays that Shakespeare wrote in the early years of James's reign has led to speculation that it reflected some kind of personal and spiritual crisis. But nothing that is known about him amounts to a feasible explanation of why he wrote a succession of so-called problem plays (or 'dark comedies') and tragedies between 1602 and 1609: *All's Well*, *Measure for Measure*, *King Lear*, *Macbeth*, *Antony and Cleopatra*, *Timon of Athens*, *Coriolanus* and *Troilus and Cressida*.

These plays were great popular successes at the Globe, and were also received with acclaim at court and when performed for wealthy and socially exclusive audiences in private halls and in the lawyers' Inns of Court. In 1608 the King's Men took over Blackfriars Theatre, one of the more comfortable and better equipped 'private' theatres that were enclosed with a roof; they used it for the winter seasons and the Globe in the summer. Shakespeare had bought a share in the Blackfriars Theatre, and began to write plays that could be performed with equal success on two very different stages.

He solved the technical problems with increasing sureness in the so-called 'Last Plays': *Pericles*, *The Winter's Tale*, *Cymbeline* and *The Tempest*, which were the results of his characteristic urge to experiment with and make a distinctive contribution to developments in the art and craft of drama.

Meanwhile, Shakespeare was preparing to return to Stratford, where there was much to demand his attention. His parents were now dead and he took his position as head of the family seriously. In 1607, Susanna had married a respected physician, Dr John Hall, and a daughter, Elizabeth, Shakespeare's first grandchild, was born in 1608. Soon after writing *The Tempest*, he freed himself of his major commitment to the company by bringing forward **John Fletcher** to take over as the King's Men's chief dramatist. The company could stage any of his existing plays whenever the wished, and he was therefore able to spend more time in Stratford. By 1612 he had completed his withdrawal, although he collaborated with Fletcher in at least two plays, *Henry VIII* and *The Two Noble Kinsmen*.

Shakespeare died at his home in Stratford on 23 April 1616. Two days later, he was buried in the church in which he had been christened. The nature of his illness is not known, but the male Shakespeares of his generation were not long-lived. He had made provision in his will to keep the bulk of his estate intact, entailed for the benefit of his descendants; but his direct line of descent ended when his granddaughter died childless in 1670. In 1623 a monument to him was erected in Holy Trinity Church. A few months later, the first collection of his plays, known as the First Folio, was published (see below).

📖 *The Chronology of Shakespeare's Works*

None of the original manuscripts of the plays, either autographs or copies, have survived. Nineteen plays were printed in Quarto editions, although the extent of Shakespeare's own involvement in their publication is not clear. In 1623, seven years after Shakespeare's death, two of his former fellow-actors in the King's company, John Heminges and Henry Condell, collected 36 plays in the so-called First Folio, which forms the basis of the accepted canon. (Later editions were published in 1632, 1664 and 1685.)

cont

---

a machine—had a profound impact on the development of computing. After graduating from MIT, he worked on information theory at the Bell Telephone Laboratories (1941–72). He wrote *The Mathematical Theory of Communications* (1949, with Warren Weaver).

Shao-chi, Liu See **Liu Shaoqi**

Shapiro, Karl Jay 1913–
US poet and critic

Born in Baltimore, Maryland, he was educated at the University of Virginia, Charlottesville, and at Johns Hopkins University, Baltimore. He published his first collection of verse, *Poems*, in 1935, and his first major book, *V-Letter* (1944), was written during military service in World War II. This won him the Pulitzer Prize and was followed by *Essay on Rime* (1945) and *Trial of a Poet* (1947). He turned to freer verse forms and prose poetry, drawing on the unconscious as an inspiration, as in *The Bourgeois Poet* (1964). An influential critic, he was initially concerned with prosody but widened his range considerably with *Beyond Criticism* (1953, rev edn as *A Primer for Poets*, 1965). He rejected the Europeanism of **T S Eliot** and **Ezra Pound** in favour of a robust Americanism, his models being **Walt Whitman**, **William Carlos Williams** and **Randall Jarrell**, on whom he wrote an influential study (1967). He

has written one novel, *Edsel* (1971), a satire on academic life based on his university experiences. 📖 J Reino, *Karl Shapiro* (1981)

Shapley, Harlow 1885–1972
US astronomer

Born in Nashville, Missouri, he studied astronomy at the University of Missouri and at Princeton (1911–14), and was appointed to the staff of the Mount Wilson Observatory in California (1914–21). There he established the distances of globular star clusters and discovered that the centre of the globular cluster system is far removed from the Sun (1918); this result placed the Sun near the edge of the stellar system and not at its centre as had been the accepted view. Although Shapley's findings were widely accepted, a memorable 'Great Debate' on the question took place between Shapley and **Heber Doust Curtis** in 1921. Shortly afterwards Shapley was appointed director of Harvard College Observatory (1921) where he remained until his retirement in 1952. His research includes the discovery of the first two dwarf galaxies, companions to our own galaxy and investigations on the Magellanic Clouds.

Sharaff, Irene 1910–93
US costume designer

Shakespeare, William *cont*

The First Folio omitted *Pericles*, although this had been published in a Quarto edition in 1609, and other texts differ substantially from the Quarto versions; some of the differences may be due to changes arising from experience in performance. Some Quartos (eg of *Henry V*) are known to be corrupt, often representing unauthorized versions concocted from actors' memories. Of other plays attributed to Shakespeare in later years, *Edward III* is thought not to be by him but to have included a contribution from him. At the end of his life he collaborated with John Fletcher in *Henry VIII* and *The Two Noble Kinsmen*, published in a Quarto edition in 1634 with both names on the title-page. A manuscript in the British Museum preserves 147 lines of his contribution to a play called *Sir Thomas More*.

Dates given below are approximate dates of performance; Q precedes a date for a Quarto publication.

Early Plays:
The Two Gentlemen of Verona (1590–91)
Henry VI, Part I (1592)
Henry VI, Part II (1592)
Henry VI, Part III (1592)
Titus Andronicus (1592; Q1594)
The Taming of the Shrew (1593; Q1594)
The Comedy of Errors (1594)
Love's Labour's Lost (1594–95; Q1598)
Romeo and Juliet (1595; Q1597, 1599)
Histories:
Richard III (1592–3; Q1597)
Richard II (1595; Q1597)
King John (1595–96)
Henry IV, Part I (1596–97; Q1598)
Henry IV, Part II (1596–97; Q1600)
Henry V (1598–99; Q1600)
Later comedies:
A Midsummer Night's Dream (1595–96; Q1600)
The Merchant of Venice (1596–97; Q1600)
The Merry Wives of Windsor (1597–98; Q1602)
Much Ado About Nothing (1598; Q1600)
As You Like It (1599–1600)
Twelfth Night (1601)
Troilus and Cressida (1602; Q1609)

Measure for Measure (1603)
All's Well That Ends Well (1604–05)
Roman plays:
Julius Caesar (1599)
Antony and Cleopatra (1606)
Coriolanus (1608)
Later tragedies:
Hamlet (1600–01; Q1603, 1604)
Othello (1603–04; Q1622)
Timon of Athens (1605)
King Lear (1605–06; Q1608)
Macbeth (1606)
Late Plays:
Pericles (1607; Q1609)
The Winter's Tale (1609)
Cymbeline (1610)
The Tempest (1611)
Henry VIII (1613)
Non-dramatic works:
Venus and Adonis (1593)
The Rape of Lucrece (1594)
'The Phoenix and the Turtle' (1601, in a collection by Robert Chester)
Sonnets (1609)
'A Lover's Complaint' (1609, with the sonnets)

📖 The literature on Shakespeare is vast, and the works cited here are intended as general introductions in which more detailed bibliographical information will be found: S Wells, *The Cambridge Companion to Shakespeare Studies* (1986); S Schoenbaum, *Shakespeare's Lives* (1970), *William Shakespeare: A Documentary Life* (rev edn, 1977); O J Campbell and E G Quinn (eds), *A Shakespeare Encyclopaedia* (1966); A L Rowse, *Shakespeare: A Biography* (1963). See also the introductory material to *The Oxford Shakespeare* (1988). Special periodicals include *Shakespeare Quarterly* (from 1950) and *Shakespeare Studies* (annually from 1965).

'Shakespeare—the nearest thing in incarnation to the eye of God.' Remark by actor **Laurence Olivier.** Quoted in 'Sir Laurence Olivier' in *Kenneth Harris Talking To…*

Born in Boston, she studied art in New York and Paris, and began her career as a costume designer with the Civic Repertory Theatre Company in 1929. She became a successful designer in Hollywood, contributing to such famous musicals as *An American In Paris* (1951), *Brigadoon* (1954), *Guys and Dolls* (1955), *West Side Story* (1961) and *Hello Dolly!* (1969). She was nominated for 16 Academy Awards and won five, including *The King and I* (1956) and *Who's Afraid of Virginia Woolf?* (1966).

Sharett, Moshe 1894–1965
Israeli politician

Born in Ukraine, he settled in Palestine in 1906. He served in the Turkish army during World War I, after which he studied at the London School of Economics. Returning to Palestine, he was prominent in the Jewish Agency in the 1930s and 1940s, and was arrested by the British authorities along with other Jewish leaders in 1946. He was Israel's first Foreign Minister, and later Prime Minister (1954–55). From 1960 he headed the executive of the World Zionist Organization and the Jewish Agency.

Sharman, Helen 1963–
English chemist and astronaut

Born in Sheffield, she trained as a chemist at Sheffield University. Her first job was as a research technologist with Mars Confectionery. She joined the Anglo-Soviet Juno mission in May 1991 as the first ever British astronaut, and flew on the *Soyuz TM-12* spacecraft 250 miles above the Earth to the Soviet *Mir* space station, where she worked for a week carrying out scientific and medical tests.

Sharon, Ariel 1928–
Israeli general and politician

Prominent in the War of Independence (1948) and Sinai Campaign (1956), he became a major-general shortly before the Six-Day War of 1967, during which he recaptured the Milta Pass in the Sinai Peninsula. He left the army in 1973 but was recalled to fight in the Yom Kippur War. In the same year he helped to form Likud (a coalition of right-wing parties led by the Herut (Freedom) Party), and was voted into the Knesset. As Defence Minister (1981–83) under **Menachem Begin**, Sharon planned Israel's invasion of Lebanon in 1982. He became a leading member of the right-wing Likud Party and in 1991 chaired the Cabinet Committee to oversee Jewish immigration from the former Soviet Union.

Sharp, Cecil James 1859–1924
English collector of folk songs and dances

He was born in London and practised law in Australia before turning to music and working as an organist. After returning to England (1892) he was principal of the Hampstead Conservatory (1896–1905) and published numerous collections of folk songs and dances. His work is commemorated by the Cecil Sharp House in London, the headquarters of the English Folk Dance (founded by him in 1911), and by song societies. 📖 Stefan Szczelkun, *The Conspiracy of Good Taste: William Morris, Cecil Sharp, Clough Williams-Ellis and the Repression of Working Class Culture in the 20th Century* (1993)

Sharp, Granville 1735–1813
English abolitionist

He was born in Durham. In 1758 he acquired a post in the ordnance department, but resigned in 1776 on account of his sympathy with American independence. He was active in the anti-slavery movement and, while defending a black immigrant named James Sommersett (or Somerset), he won a legal decision that secured the freedom of any slave who set foot on British soil. He worked with **Thomas Clarkson** for the abolition of Negro slavery, and developed a plan for a home for freed slaves in Sierra Leone.

Sharp, James 1613–79
Scottish churchman

Born in Banff, he signed the National Covenant against **Charles I** in 1638. In 1651–52 he was taken as a prisoner to London with some other ministers, and in 1657 he was chosen by the more moderate party in the Church to plead their cause before **Cromwell**. Sent by **George Monk** to Breda, he had several interviews with **Charles II** in exile there (1660). A letter to the Earl of Middleton proves that Sharp was co-operating with Edward Hyde, Earl of **Clarendon** and the English bishops for the re-establishment of Episcopacy in Scotland; and in 1660 he was consecrated Archbishop of St Andrews. As the crafty executor of John Maitland, Duke of **Lauderdale's** policies, he soon became an object of popular detestation and of contempt to his employers. On 3 May 1679, 12 Covenanters, led by **John Balfour** of Kinloch and David Hackston, dragged him from his coach on Magus Muir and murdered him.

Sharp, Sir Percival 1867–1953
Pioneer English educationist

Educated at the Endowed School, Bishop Auckland, and Homerton College, Cambridge, he became head of Bowerham School, Lancashire (1898–1902), Secretary for Education at St Helen's (1905–14) and Director of Education at Newcastle-upon-Tyne (1914–19) and Sheffield (1919–32), and was a member of the Burnham Committee (1919–49). As secretary of the Association of Education Committees (1933–44) his work was formative in relations between local authorities and teachers' associations, and he played a prominent part in the development of English education in the first half of this century.

Sharp, Phillip Allen 1944–
US molecular biologist and Nobel Prize winner

Born in Kentucky, he was educated at Union College in Barbourville, Kentucky and at the University of Illinois. He was a postdoctoral Fellow at the California Institute of Technology (1969–71), held a senior post at Cold Spring Harbor Laboratories, New York (1972–74), and became associate professor at the Massachusetts Institute of Technology (MIT) (1974–79). He was appointed Professor of Biology there in 1979, and also served as director of the MIT Center for Cancer Research (1985–91), becoming head of its biology department in 1991. He was also a co-founder of Biogen, where he has been a director since 1978 and chairman of the scientific board since 1987. Sharp invented the mapping technique used extensively in the analysis of RNA molecules. This led to his discovery in 1977 that genes are split into several sections, separated by stretches of DNA known as 'introns' which appear to carry no genetic information. The discovery has prompted much research on how this phenomenon might be involved in genetic diseases and evolutionary processes. Sharp shared the 1993 Nobel Prize for physiology or medicine with **Richard Roberts**, who had discovered split genes at about the same time.

Sharp, William, *pseudonym* Fiona Macleod
1855–1905
Scottish writer

Born in Paisley, Renfrewshire, he was educated at Glasgow University. After a period in Australia he settled in London (1879), working as a journalist and editor. Throughout his life he travelled widely. He published a collection of poetry, *Earth's Voices*, in 1884. He wrote books on contemporary English, French and German poets, but is chiefly remembered as the author of the remarkable series of Celtic (or neo-Celtic) tales and romances by 'Fiona Macleod', a pseudonym he did not acknowledge. They include *Pharais* (1894), *The Mountain Lovers* (1895), *The Sin-Eater* (1895) and *The Immortal Hour* (1900). 📖 *William Sharp, a Memoir by Mrs Sharp* (1912)

Sharpe, Tom (Thomas Ridley) 1928–
English satirical novelist

He was born in London. After graduating from Cambridge, he served in the Royal Marines and worked as a social worker, teacher and photographer before turning to full-time writing. Among his best novels, which combine farcical comedy and mild sexual titillation with an acute observation of English social manners and well-aimed satire, are *Porterhouse Blue* (1973) and *Blott on the Landscape* (1975). Later novels include *Wilt* (1976) and *Vintage Stuff* (1982).

Sharpey-Schäfer, Sir Edward 1850–1935
English physiologist

Born in Hornsey, he was educated at University College London and was appointed professor there (1883–99) and later at Edinburgh (1899–1933). He gained many distinctions, becoming FRS in 1878 and President of the British Association in 1912, and receiving a knighthood in 1913. His research interests included neurophysiology and in particular the theory of brain localization. He also worked in the emergent discipline of endocrinology, investigating the role of the pancreas in carbohydrate metabolism, and suggesting the existence of a then hypothetical fluid which he named 'insuline'. He was perhaps most widely known for devising the prone-pressure method of artificial respiration, known as the Schäfer method and practised worldwide. He championed the materialist doctrine of life and was a passionate defender of vivisection. He lived most of his later life in North Berwick, Scotland, where he created a famous garden.

Shastri, Lal Bahadur 1904–66
Indian politician

Born in Benares, the son of a legal clerk, he joined **Mahatma Gandhi's** independence movement at 16 and was seven times imprisoned by the British. He excelled as a Congress Party official and politician in the United Provinces and joined Nehru's Cabinet in 1952 as Minister for the Railways, becoming Minister of Transport (1957) and of Commerce (1958) and Home Secretary (1960). Under the Kamaraj plan to invigorate the Congress Party at popular level he resigned with other Cabinet Ministers in 1963; but he was recalled by Nehru in 1964 to be Minister without Portfolio, and he succeeded Nehru as Prime Minister in 1964. He died suddenly of a heart attack while in Tashkent, USSR, for discussions on the India–Pakistan dispute.

Shastri, Ravi (shankar Jayadritha) 1962–
Indian cricketer

Born in Bombay, he is one of international cricket's most respected all-rounders with his familiar slow left-arm bowling and steady right-arm batting. In the 1985 Ranji Trophy against Baroda he scored the fastest double hundred in history (off 123 balls) for Bombay. His innings included 13 sixes, six of which came from one over to equal the record set by Gary Sobers.

Shatalin, Stanislav Sergeyevich 1934–97
Soviet economist

In 1989 he was appointed secretary of the Economics Division of the Academy of Sciences and in 1990 he was made a member of Mikhail Gorbachev's new presidential council. He acquired particular fame in the autumn of 1990 when he proposed a radical economic reform, the '500-days plan', as an alternative to Nikolai Ryzhkov's more conservative plan. Gorbachev promised to amalgamate the two but retreated in the face of conservative opposition.

Shaw, Anna Howard 1847–1919
US suffragist

Born in Newcastle upon Tyne, she emigrated with her family to the USA as a young child (1851). In 1880 she became the first woman to be ordained as a Methodist Protestant preacher and in 1886 she graduated in medicine from Boston University, but decided to work instead for the cause of women's suffrage. An eloquent lecturer, she campaigned widely, and from 1904 to 1915 was president of the National American Woman Suffrage Association. She was head of the Women's Committee of the Council of National Defense during World War I and published her autobiography, *The Story of a Pioneer*, in 1915.

Shaw, Artie, *originally* Arthur Arshawsky 1910–
US bandleader and clarinettist

Born in New York City, he took up writing and numerous music jobs before achieving success as a swing band leader, notably with 'Begin the Beguine' (1938), 'Star Dust' (1940), and 'Moonglow' (1941); he rivalled Benny Goodman as a clarinet soloist. He married eight times, and his wives included the actresses Lana Turner, Ava Gardner, and Evelyn Keyes. He retired from performing in 1955.

Shaw, Fiona, *originally* Fiona Bolton 1958–
Irish actress

Born and brought up in Cork, she took a degree in philosophy and trained at RADA, making her debut in 1982. Recognized early by director Peter Wood, she appeared as Julia in his production of *The Rivals* at the National Theatre (1983). She went on to perform for the Royal Shakespeare Company, with roles including Madame de Volanges in *Les Liaisons Dangereuses* (1985) and Katharina in *The Taming of the Shrew* (1987), and became associated with highly emotional roles, notably the title roles in *Electra* and *Hedda Gabler*. A frequent collaborator with Deborah Warner, she played King Richard in *Richard II* in 1995.

Shaw, George Bernard 1856–1950
Irish dramatist and critic and Nobel Prize winner

He was born in Dublin of Irish Protestant parents. After unhappy years at school and working for a firm of land-agents, he left Ireland to follow his mother and sister to London. There he entered a long period of struggle and poverty, and five novels written between 1879 and 1883 were all rejected. He came under the influence of Henry George, whom he met in 1882, and the works of Karl Marx, and developed a belief in socialism which underlay all his future work. He joined the executive committee of the Fabian Society (1884–1911), for which he edited *Fabian Essays* (1889) and wrote many well-known socialist tracts. As music critic for the new *Star* newspaper (1888–90), and later in his dramatic criticism for Frank Harris's *Saturday Review* (1895–98), he made his first impact on the intellectual and social consciousness of his time. To this period also belong *The Quintessence of Ibsenism* (1891), and *The Perfect Wagnerite* (1898), which represents Wagner's *Ring of the Nibelung* as a social allegory. The rest of Shaw's life, especially after his marriage (1898) to the Irish heiress Charlotte Payne-Townshend, is mainly the history of his plays. His first was *Widowers' Houses*, begun in 1885 in collaboration with his friend William Archer. This was followed by *Mrs Warren's Profession* (1898, on prostitution), *Arms and the Man* (publ 1898) and *Candida* (1897, one of the first in a series of remarkable female portrayals), *Three Plays for Puritans*: *The Devil's Disciple* (publ 1897), *Caesar and Cleopatra* (1901), and *Captain Brassbound's Conversion* (1900). Shaw's long correspondence with the actresses Ellen Terry and Mrs Patrick Campbell also developed during these years, and his reputation was growing in England and abroad. This was reinforced by *Man and Superman* (1902), one of his greatest philosophical comedies, on the theme of the human quest for a purer religious approach to life. Other notable plays from this time are *John Bull's Other Island* (1904), *Major Barbara* (1905), *The Doctor's Dilemma* (1906), and two uniquely Shavian discussion plays, *Getting Married* (1908) and *Misalliance* (1910). These embrace a wide range of subject matter, from politics and statecraft to family life, prostitution and vaccination, and he sometimes fell foul of the censors. In the years before the outbreak of World War I came two of his best-known plays; *Androcles and the Lion* (1912), a 'religious pantomime', and *Pygmalion* (1913), an anti-romantic comedy which was later adapted as a musical play, *My Fair Lady* in 1956 (filmed in 1964). He created wartime controversy and recrimination with his provocative *Common Sense About the War* (1914). After the war followed three of his greatest dramas: *Heartbreak House* (1919), an attempt to analyse in an English Chekhovian social environment the causes of present moral and political discontents; *Back to Methuselah* (1921), five plays in one, and *Saint Joan* (1923), in which Shaw's essentially religious nature, his genius for characterization (above all of saintly yet very human women), and his powers of dramatic argument are most clearly displayed. In 1931 he visited Russia, and the following year made a world tour with his wife. Greater perhaps than any of the plays written during the last years of his life are the two prose works: *The Intelligent Woman's Guide to Socialism and Capitalism* (1928), one of the most lucid introductions to its subjects, and *The Black Girl in Search of God* (1932), a modern *Pilgrim's Progress*. Of the later plays, only *The Apple Cart* (1929) has been regularly staged, although *Too True to Be Good* (1932) and *The Simpleton of the Unexpected Isles* (1934) have many innovative features. Shaw was a passionate advocate of spelling reform, and left money in his will to fund the development of a new writing system on phonetic principles. He was awarded the Nobel Prize for literature in 1925. 📖 The Bodley Head Collected Plays with their Prefaces (7 vols, 1970–74). For Shaw's criticism see *Our Theatres in the Nineties* (3 vols, 1932) and *Shaw's Music* (ed Dan H Laurence, 1981). See also M Holroyd, *George Bernard Shaw* (3 vols, 1989–91)

Shaw, Martin Edward Fallas 1876–1958
English composer and organist

Born in London, he studied under Charles Stanford at the Royal College of Music, composed the ballad opera, *Mr Pepys* (1926), with Clifford Bax, and set T S Eliot's poems to music. He is best known for his songs and as co-editor with his brother, Geoffrey Turton Shaw (1879–1943), of national songbooks, and with Ralph Vaughan Williams of *Songs of Praise* (1925) and the *Oxford Carol Book* (1928). He was organist at St Martin-in-the-Fields (1920–24).

Shaw, Sir (William) Napier 1854–1945
English meteorologist

Born in Birmingham, he studied mathematics and natural science under **James Clerk Maxwell** at Emmanuel College, Cambridge, and with **Hermann von Helmholtz** in Berlin. He was appointed demonstrator (1879), lecturer (1887) and assistant director (1898) at the Cavendish Laboratory. A member of the Meteorological Council from 1879, he became its secretary in 1900. He was appointed director of the Meteorological Office (1905–20), first Professor of Meteorology at Imperial College, London (1920–24) and president of the International Meteorological Committee (1906–21). He completely reorganized the British Weather Service. In a classic paper (with Lempfert) entitled *The Life History of Surface Currents*, he developed the analysis of air currents and showed that discontinuities occurred in the atmosphere. He came close to defining 'fronts', and devised the aerological diagram known as the tephigram, which is still in use. His four-volume work *Manual of Meteorology* (1926–31) stressed the mathematical basis of the subject and gave a complete account of its historical development. He was awarded the Symons Gold Medal in 1910, and the Royal Medal of the Royal Society in 1923, and he was knighted in 1915.

Shaw, Richard Norman 1831–1912

English architect

Born in Edinburgh, he worked with his partner William Eden Nesfield (1835–88) in many styles ranging from Gothic Revival to neo-Baroque, and became an acknowledged leader in the revival of Georgian design, which found expression in the English Domestic Revival. His major buildings include the Old Swan House, Chelsea (1876), New Scotland Yard (1888), the Gaiety Theatre, Aldwych (1902, now demolished), and the Piccadilly Hotel (1905). He also designed the garden suburb at Bedford Park, London. ⌂ Andrew Saint, *Richard Norman Shaw* (1976)

Shawcross, Hartley William Shawcross, Baron 1902–

English jurist

Born in Giessen, Germany, he was educated at Dulwich College. He was called to the Bar at Gray's Inn in 1925 and was senior lecturer in law at Liverpool (1927–34). After service in World War II, he was Attorney-General (1945–51) and President of the Board of Trade (1951) in the Labour government. He established an international legal reputation for himself as chief British prosecutor at the Nuremberg Trials (1945–46), led the investigations of the Lynskey Tribunal (1948) and was prosecutor in the **Klaus Fuchs** atom spy case (1950). Finding the narrow opposition tactics of the Labour Party irksome, he resigned his parliamentary seat in 1958. Knighted in 1945, he was created a life peer in 1959 and published his memoirs, *Life Sentence*, in 1995.

Shawn, Ted (Edwin Myers) 1891–1972

US dancer and director

Born in Kansas City, Missouri, he studied theology and began dancing in order to strengthen his legs after suffering diphtheria. In 1914 he met and married **Ruth Saint Denis** in New York, and in 1915 they founded Denishawn, an influential dance school which was favoured by the Hollywood studios and branched right across the USA with a wide-ranging curriculum of classes from ballet to oriental dance. When the couple separated in 1931, Denishawn broke up and Ted Shawn moved to a farm in Lee, Massachusetts; there he founded his own group, Ted Shawn and His Men Dancers, which toured for several years presenting dance inspired by Native American and Aboriginal work. In June 1941 the farm became the setting for Jacob's Pillow, an annual summer school and festival. His books include *The American Ballet* (1925), *Dance We Must* (1940) and *One Thousand And One Night Stands* (1960).

Shawn, William 1901–92

US journalist and editor

Born in Chicago, he was educated at Michigan University and was the second editor of the *New Yorker* (1952–87), in succession to **Harold Wallace Ross**.

Shays, Daniel c.1747–1825

American Revolutionary captain

He was born probably in Hopkinton, Massachusetts. After service in the American army during the Revolution (1775–83), he returned to farming in Pelham, Massachusetts, but like many of his fellows he found himself subjected to impossible economic demands. In 1786–87 he led a short-lived rural insurrection, known as Shays' Rebellion, against his state's policies on taxes and repayment of debt. It was crushed by state troops, but provided a major impetus to the drafting of the Federal Constitution at the Constitutional Convention of 1787.

Shcharansky, Natan, *originally* Anatoli Borisovich Shcharansky 1948–

Soviet mathematician and dissident

Born in Donetsk, Ukraine, the son of a Jewish filmwriter and journalist, he was a brilliant mathematician who became disillusioned with Soviet society. In 1973 the authorities' rejection of several applications for a visa to emigrate to Israel led him to become more closely involved in the Soviet dissident movement. In 1976 he joined Yuri Orlov's Helsinki Watch Group, a body formed to monitor Soviet human rights violations, and in 1977 he was sentenced to 13 years in a labour colony on charges of spying for the CIA. He was freed from confinement in 1986 as part of an east–west exchange and joined his wife Avital in Israel, where he assumed the name Natan. In 1989 he was nominated as Israeli ambassador to the UN. He published *Fear No Evil* in 1988.

Shchedrin, Rodion Konstantinovich 1932–

Russian composer

He was born in Moscow and, showing promise as a pianist, studied composition with Yuri Shaporin (1887–1966) at the Conservatory (1951–55). He later taught there (1964–69), exerting a strong influence on many younger composers. In 1981 he was made a People's Artist of the USSR. His music uses contemporary ideas and techniques and is frequently included in concerts outside Russia. He has written several ballet scores, including *Carmen* (1968, based on the **Bizet** opera) and *Anna Karenina* (1972). He married the ballerina **Maya Plisetskaya**.

Shcherbitsky, Vladimir Vasilevich 1918–90

Soviet politician

A chemical engineer and wartime soldier, after 1945 he progressed in the Communist Party machine to become a member of the politburo and, by 1972, First Secretary for the Ukraine. He opposed the nationalist movement and suppressed dissidents, thereby forming an obstacle to the progress of perestroika. He was dismissed by **Mikhail Gorbachev** in 1990, shortly before his death.

Sheba, Queen of See **Solomon** (panel)

Sheehy-Skeffington, Francis Joseph Christopher, *originally surnamed* Skeffington 1878–1916

Irish pacifist and feminist

Born in Cavan, the son of a school inspector, he was educated at University College, Dublin. He was the first lay registrar (1902–04) and married Hanna Sheehy, daughter of the Irish Nationalist MP David Sheehy. They combined their names, becoming active socialists and secularists and campaigning for female suffrage and women's rights. He became increasingly drawn to pacifism, edited the *Irish Citizen* from 1912, and contributed to the *Manchester Guardian*, *L'Humanité* and the *Call* (US). On the outbreak of World War I he was sentenced to six months' imprisonment for campaigning against recruiting; after six days' hunger strike, he was released, and continued to campaign in the USA. He opposed the Easter Rising of 1916 and sought to stop the looting, but was arrested and shot in Portobello Barracks.

Sheehy-Skeffington, Hannah, *née* Sheehy
1877–1946
Irish patriot and feminist

Born in Kenturk, County Cork, and educated at the National University of Ireland, she became a teacher and was a founder-member of the Irish Women Graduates' Association (1901). With Margaret Cousins she established the Irish Women's Franchise League (1908) which was in her own words 'an avowedly militant association'. In 1912 she was imprisoned for three months for rioting at Dublin Castle in protest at the exclusion of women from the Home Rule Bill. Her husband was the pacifist Francis Sheehy-Skeffington.

Sheeler, Charles 1883–1965
US painter and photographer

Born in Philadelphia, he studied at the Pennsylvania Academy of the Fine Arts, and during several trips to Europe (1904–09) was much influenced by the Cubist movement, as is evident from the painting he exhibited at the Armory Show in New York (1913). From 1912 he worked as an industrial photographer, recording particularly the skyscrapers of Manhattan, and he collaborated on the film *Mannahatta* with Paul Strand (1920). In 1927 he was commissioned to photograph the building of the Ford Motor installation at River Rouge, Michigan and was widely acclaimed for this. He was staff photographer at the New York Museum of Modern Art (1942–45). His photographic work helped bring about the shift in his painting from Cubism to the direct, clear-cut method known as Precisionism.

Sheen, Fulton John 1895–1979
US Roman Catholic prelate and broadcaster

He was born in El Paso, Illinois, and educated at the Catholic University of America, and at Louvain in Belgium. Ordained in 1919, he returned to the Catholic University to teach philosophy (1926–59) before becoming national director of the Society for the Propagation of the Faith. Meanwhile he had gained a reputation as a broadcaster on the *Catholic Hour*, which was heard worldwide (1930–52), and he acquired an even larger audience with the television programme *Life is Worth Living* (1952–65). He was auxiliary bishop of New York (1951–65) and Bishop of Rochester (1966–69), then retired as titular archbishop. His many writings include *Peace of Soul* (1949), *Those Mysterious Priests* (1974) and *The Electronic Christian* (1979).

Sheene, Barry Stephen Frank 1950–
English motorcycle racer

Born in London, he made his racing debut in 1968, won the British 125cc title in 1970 and was beaten by Spain's Angel Nieto to the world 125cc title in 1971. Despite a bad crash in 1975 at Daytona, which left him with fractures and a pin in his leg, he won the 500cc world championship in 1976 to give Suzuki their first victory. He repeated it in 1977 and was runner-up in 1978. He holds the fastest-ever average speed for a world championship race (217.37kmh/135.07mph). He raced for Yamaha in 1981. After another crash in 1982 at Silverstone he retired to take up a career in broadcasting in Australia.

Sheffield, John, 1st Duke of Buckingham and Normanby 1648–1721
English political leader and poet

He served in both the navy and the army and was Lord Chamberlain to James II (James VII and II) and a cabinet councillor under William III, who in 1694 made him Marquis of Normanby. Queen Anne made him Duke of Buckingham (1703); but for his opposition to Sidney, Earl of Godolphin and John Churchill, Duke of Marlborough he was deprived of the Seal (1705). After 1710, under the Tories, he was Lord Steward and Lord President until the queen's death, when he lost all power and intrigued for the restoration of the Stuarts. Patron of Dryden and friend of Pope, he wrote two tragedies, a metrical *Essay on Satire* (1679), an *Essay on Poetry* (1682), and other works. 📖 J H Wilson, *The Court Wits of the Restoration* (1948)

Sheil, Richard Lalor 1791–1851
Irish dramatist and politician

Born in Drumdowney, Kilkenny, he wrote a series of plays, aided Daniel O'Connell in forming the new Catholic Association (1825), and supported the cause with impassioned speeches. He entered parliament in 1839 under Viscount Melbourne and became Vice-President of the Board of Trade and a privy councillor, the first Catholic to gain that honour. In 1846 he became Master of the Mint.

Shelburne, William Petty, 2nd Earl of
1737–1805
English politician

Born in Dublin, the great-grandson of Sir William Petty, he studied at Christ Church, Oxford. He served in the army, entered parliament, succeeded his father to the earldom in 1761, and in 1763 was appointed President of the Board of Trade and in 1766 Secretary of State in the Earl of Chatham's second administration (1766). When Lord North's ministry fell in 1782 he declined to form a government, but became Secretary of State under Charles, Marquis of Rockingham. When Rockingham died the same year the king offered Shelburne the Treasury. Charles Fox resigned, and Shelburne introduced William Pitt, the Younger, into office as his Chancellor of the Exchequer, but this ministry fell when it was defeated by a coalition of Fox and North (February 1783). A radical, he was a strong advocate of free trade and Roman Catholic emancipation. At Lansdowne House and Bowood, Wiltshire, he collected an impressive gallery of pictures and a fine library.

Sheldon, Gilbert 1598–1677
English prelate

Chaplain to Charles I, he was Warden of All Souls, Oxford (1626–48), but was ejected by the Parliamentarians. At the Restoration in 1660 he was appointed Bishop of London, and in 1663 Archbishop of Canterbury. He built the Sheldonian Theatre in Oxford (1669).

Shelley, Mary Wollstonecraft, *née* Godwin
1797–1851
English writer

She was born in London, the daughter of William Godwin and Mary Wollstonecraft. In 1814 she eloped with Percy Bysshe Shelley, and married him as his second wife in 1816. They lived abroad throughout their married life. Her first and most impressive novel was *Frankenstein, or the Modern Prometheus* (1818), her second *Valperga* (1823). After her husband's death in 1822 she returned from Italy to England with their son in 1823. Her husband's father, in granting her an allowance, insisted on the suppression of the volume of Shelley's *Posthumous Poems* edited by her. *The Last Man* (1826) is a futuristic noble-savage romance of the ruin of human society by pestilence. In *Lodore* (1835) the story is told of Shelley's alienation from his first wife.

Her last novel, *Falkner*, appeared in 1837. Of her occasional pieces of verse the most remarkable is 'The Choice'. Her *Journal of a Six Weeks' Tour* (partly by Shelley) tells of their excursion to Switzerland in 1814, and *Rambles in Germany and Italy* (1844) describes tours of 1840–43. Her *Tales* were published in 1890, and two mythological dramas, *Proserpine* and *Midas*, in 1922. ⌨ E Bigland, *Mary Shelley* (1959)

Shelley, Percy Bysshe 1792–1822
English lyric poet and writer, a leading figure in the Romantic movement

He was born in Field Place, near Horsham in Sussex, and educated at Syon House Academy and Eton. He attended University College, Oxford, but was expelled for his contribution to a pamphlet called *The Necessity of Atheism*. He met and eloped with 16-year-old Harriet Westbrook, causing a further rift with his family that was never repaired. He lived for the next three years in York, in the Lake District where he met **Robert Southey**, in Dublin, and at Lynmouth in Devon where he set up a commune. At this time he wrote *Queen Mab* (1813), but it made little impact. He moved to London, and there fell in love with Mary (see **Mary Shelley**), the 16-year-old daughter of **William Godwin** and **Mary Wollstonecraft**. They eloped in 1814, accompanied by her half-sister, Jane 'Claire' Clairmont, and were married after Harriet drowned herself in 1816. Meanwhile Shelley wrote an unfinished novella, *The Assassins* (1814) and published *Alastor* (1816). His son William was born in 1816, and he spent time with **Byron** at Lake Geneva. In 1818 he published *The Revolt of Islam*, and in the same year finally left England for Italy, where he was to spend the rest of his life. In 1819 came the major part of *Prometheus Unbound*, generally considered his masterpiece. The death of his son William in Rome devastated him and he moved to Tuscany, finally settling in Pisa. For the next few months he experienced a burst of creative energy which resulted in the completion of the fourth part of *Prometheus*, *The Masque of Anarchy* (1819), inspired by the Peterloo massacre, 'The Ode to the West Wind', 'To Liberty' and 'To Naples', 'To A Skylark', 'The Cloud', the intimate *Letter to Maria Gisborne* (1820) and *The Witch of Atlas*. These were followed by a series of prose pieces, *A Philosophical View of Reform* (1820), *Essay on the Devil* (1821), *The Defence of Poetry* (1821) and *Swellfoot the Tyrant* (1820), a burlesque, *Adonais* (1821), an elegy on the death of Keats, and *Epipsychidion* (1821), the fruit of a platonic affair with a beautiful Italian heiress held in a convent. *Hellas* (1822), a verse drama inspired by the Greek war of independence, was his last work. Returning from a visit to Byron and **Leigh Hunt** at Livorno in August 1822, Shelley and his companions were drowned in a sudden squall. His body was cremated at Viareggio and his ashes taken to Rome. ⌨ K N Cameron, *Shelley: The Golden Years* (1974) and *Young Shelley* (1951); R Holmes, *Shelley: The Pursuit* (1974); N I White, *Shelley* (rev edn, 1972).

Shen Gua (Shen Kua) 1031–95
Chinese administrator, engineer and scientist

Born in Hangzhou, he made significant contributions to such diverse fields as astronomy, cartography, medicine, hydraulics and fortification. His first appointment was in 1054 and in the following years he accomplished notable work in land reclamation. As director of the astronomical bureau from 1072, he improved methods of computation and the design of several observational devices; in 1075 he constructed a series of relief maps of China's northern frontier area and designed fortifications as defences against nomadic invaders. He surveyed and improved the Grand Canal over a distance of 150 miles. In 1082, following the defeat of troops under his command, he was forced to resign from his government posts, and spent his last years writing *Brush Talks from Dream Brook*, a remarkable compilation of about 600 observations,

now one of the most important sources of information on early Chinese science and technology.

Shenstone, William 1714–63
English poet

Born near Halesowen, Worcestershire, he studied at Solihull Grammar School and Pembroke College, Oxford. In 1735 he inherited the estate of the Leasowes, and spent most of his income on 'landskip gardening' (a term which he coined) to turn it into a show garden. In 1737 he published his best-known poem, 'The Schoolmistress' (revised in 1742), which was written in imitation of **Edmund Spenser** and foreshadowed **Thomas Gray's** *Elegy*. He published *The Judgement of Hercules* in 1741. His *Pastoral Ballad* (1755) was commended by Gray and Dr Johnson. ⌨ A R Humphreys, *William Shenstone* (1937)

Shepard, Alan Bartlett 1923–98
US astronaut, the first American in space

Born in East Derry, New Hampshire, he graduated from the US Naval Academy in 1944 and served in the Pacific. He won his wings in 1947 and subsequently flew jet aircraft on test and training missions. He was one of the original seven NASA astronauts, and on 5 May 1961, 23 days after **Yuri Gagarin's** historic orbit of the earth, he was launched on 'Freedom 7' on a ballistic sub-orbital trajectory to a height of 116 miles, controlling the whole 15-minute flight manually. He was director of astronaut training at NASA (1965–74), and commanded the Apollo 14 lunar mission in 1971.

Shepard, E(rnest) H(oward) 1879–1976
English artist and cartoonist

He was born in London, the son of an architect. He studied art while still at school, and won a scholarship to the Royal Academy Schools. After service in the Royal Artillery in World War I, he worked for *Punch*, and made his name with illustrations for children's books such as **A A Milne's** *Winnie the Pooh* (1926) and **Kenneth Grahame's** *The Wind in the Willows* (1931).

Shepard, Francis P(arker) 1897–1985
US geological oceanographer

Born in Brookline, Massachusetts, he was educated at Harvard and at the University of Chicago, where he received a PhD in geology in 1922. He then joined the University of Illinois, being promoted to professor in 1939. Around 1930 his interests turned towards the sea, and his study of sea-bed processes led to a part-time appointment at Scripps Institution of Oceanography, La Jolla, California. The award of a grant to Shepard and colleagues in 1936 marked the beginning of Pacific marine geology, and in 1948 he was appointed Professor of Submarine Geology at the Institution. Shepard studied extensively the environmental conditions involved in the formation of ancient marine strata, making comparisons with more recent examples, and distinguishing sedimentation processes in different environments. He published *Submarine Geology* in 1948.

Shepard, Sam, *originally* Samuel Shepard Rogers 1943–
US dramatist and actor

Born in Fort Sheridan, Illinois, he studied agriculture at college for a year, joined a touring company, and then moved to New York City, where he worked in the avant-garde theatre of the 1960s with one-acters. His first plays, *Cowboy* and *The Rock Garden*, were written in 1964 and produced by Theater Genesis in New York, followed by *Dog* and *Rocking Chair* (both 1965) at La Mama. Subsequent works included a rock drama *The Tooth of Crime*, staged at the Royal Court Theatre, London (1974), *The Curse of the Starving Class* (1976), and *Buried Child* (1978), which won the Pulitzer Prize. He was resident playwright for several years at the Magic Theater, San Francisco, and

two of his plays were first staged there, *True West* (1980) and *Fool For Love* (1983). *A Lie of the Mind* (1985) was highly successful in the USA, but *Simpatico* (1993) was less so. Few living US playwrights have such sensitivity for landscape and time as Shepard, and few can produce such economic theatrical intensity. He also appeared in films, and has written screenplays, including *Paris, Texas* (1984). He published a volume of short stories, *Cruising Paradise*, in 1996.
📖 R Mottram, *Inner Landscapes* (1984)

Shephard, Gillian, *née* Watts 1940–
English Conservative politician
Born in Norfolk and educated at Oxford, she began working as an education officer and schools inspector in Norfolk (1963–75). She also became a magistrate, deputy leader of Norfolk County Council, where she was councillor from 1977 to 1989, and health authority chairman, first of west Norfolk and Wisbech (1981–85) and then of Norwich (1985–87). She was elected MP for South West Norfolk in 1987 and rose swiftly to enter the Cabinet in 1992 as Secretary of State for Employment. She was Minister of Agriculture, Fisheries and Food (1993–94) and then Secretary of State for Education and Employment (1994–97) at a time of tense relations between the teaching profession and the government. She retained her seat in 1997 when Labour won the general election.

Sheppard, David Stuart 1929–
English Anglican prelate, and former test cricketer
Born in Reigate, Surrey, he graduated at Cambridge, and worked in London's East End as warden of the Mayflower Family Centre in Canning Town (1957–69). He was Bishop of Woolwich before becoming Bishop of Liverpool (1975–). There his profound social concern, the remarkable rapport in which he and his Roman Catholic counterpart, Derek Worlock, worked together, and perhaps also his past record as former England and Sussex cricket captain, made a lasting impact on the city. In 1991 he became chairman of the Church's Board of Social Responsibility. He has written *Parson's Pitch* (1964), *Built as a City* (1974), *Bias to the Poor* (1983) and, with Worlock, *Better Together* (1988), *With Christ in the Wilderness* (1990) and *With Hope in Our Hearts* (1994).

Sheppard, Dick (Hugh Richard Lawrie)
1880–1937
English Anglican clergyman and pacifist
He was born in Windsor, Berkshire. A popular preacher with modern views on the Christian life and a pioneer of religious broadcasting, he was vicar of London's St Martin-in-the-Fields (1914–27), published *The Human Parson* (1927) and *The Impatience of a Parson* (1927), and became dean of Canterbury (1929–31) and canon of St Paul's Cathedral (1934–37). He was an ardent pacifist and founded the Peace Pledge Union in 1936.

Sheppard, Jack 1702–24
English robber
Born in Stepney, London, he committed the first of many robberies in 1720, and in 1724 was five times caught, and four times escaped. He was eventually hanged at Tyburn in the presence of 200,000 spectators, and became the subject of many plays and ballads, tracts by Daniel Defoe and a novel by William Ainsworth.

Sheppard, Philip MacDonald 1921–76
English ecological geneticist
He was educated at Marlborough College and Worcester College, Oxford, and became Professor of Genetics at Liverpool University in 1963. Sheppard carried out significant work on mimicry and human genetics, and on polymorphism in the land snail. He showed that the banding patterns on snails were highly influential under certain circumstances, and went on to demonstrate the importance of linked complexes of genes ('super-genes')

in insects, and in human characteristics such as the Rhesus blood group system. Sheppard also played a key role in introducing genetical concepts to medicine. He was elected FRS in 1965.

Sher, Antony 1949–
British actor and writer
Born in Cape Town, South Africa, he went to England in 1968 and studied at the Webber–Douglas Academy of Dramatic Art. He appeared in plays at the Royal Court Theatre, including David Hare's *Teeth 'n' Smiles* (1975), and joined the Royal Shakespeare Company (1982). In 1984 he gave a performance of macabre brilliance in the title role of Bill Alexander's production of *Richard III*, a performance given theatrical virtuosity by his use of crutches. In 1992 he played the lead in Terry Hands' RSC production of *Tamburlaine the Great*. A powerful stage presence, he has also appeared occasionally in television drama, notably in *The History Man* (1982). In his book *The Year of the King* (1985), he describes his work on *Richard III*. He illustrated the book himself, as he did his first novel, *Middlepost* (1988). He subsequently wrote a film script, *Changing Step* (1989), two more novels, *The Indoor Boy* (1991) and *Cheap Lives* (1995), and co-authored *Woza Shakespeare!* (1996, with Gregory Doran), which discusses the staging of *Titus Andronicus*.

Sherard, Robert Harborough, *originally* Robert Harborough Kennedy 1861–1943
English biographer, and defender of Oscar Wilde
The great-grandson of Wordsworth, he lived most of his life in France and Corsica, and wrote lives of Zola, Alphonse Daudet and Guy de Maupassant, all of whom he had known, as well as informative memoirs of French life, *Twenty Years of Paris*, *Modern Paris*, *My Friends the French*, and an important exposé, *The White Slaves of England*. He befriended Oscar Wilde in 1883; although deeply shocked by the scandal over Wilde's homosexuality, he stood by him, sometimes passionately, and wrote several books and pamphlets on him. By far the best of these was issued (at first anonymously) two years after Wilde's death: *Oscar Wilde: the Story of an Unhappy Friendship* (1902).

Sheraton, Thomas 1751–1806
English furniture designer and writer
Born in Stockton-on-Tees, Cleveland, he settled in London around 1790, but never had a workshop of his own. Although there is no extant furniture attributable to him, he achieved fame in his lifetime through his elegant neoclassical designs, influenced by Thomas Chippendale and George Hepplewhite. His major work, *The Cabinet-Maker and Upholsterer's Drawing Book*, was published in parts between 1791 and 1794. He was ordained in 1800.

Sherbrooke, Robert Lowe, 1st Viscount
1811–92
English politician
Born in Bingham, Nottinghamshire, he was educated at Winchester and University College, Oxford. Called to the Bar in 1842, he emigrated the same year to Australia, soon built up a lucrative practice, and took a leading part in politics. Having returned to England in 1850, he entered parliament (1852) and took office under the Earl of Aberdeen and Viscount Palmerston. From 1859 to 1864 he was vice-president of the Education Board, and introduced the Revised Code of 1862 with its 'payment by results'. Gladstone appointed him Chancellor of the Exchequer in 1868 and Home Secretary in 1873.

Shere Ali 1825–79
Amir of Afghanistan
He was the younger son of Dost Mohammed, whom he succeeded in 1863. Disagreements with his half-brothers soon arose, which kept Afghanistan in anarchy; he fled to Kandahar, but regained possession of Kabul (1868), with

assistance from the Viceroy of India, Baron John Lawrence. In 1879 his eldest son Yakub Khan rebelled, but was captured and imprisoned. His refusal to receive a British mission (1878) led to war, and after severe fighting, he fled to Turkestan, where he died.

Sheridan, Philip Henry 1831–88
US soldier

Born in Albany, New York, of Irish parentage, he commanded a Federal division at the beginning of the American Civil War (1861–65), and took part in many of the campaigns. In 1864 he was given command of the Army of the Shenandoah, turning the valley into a barren waste, and defeating General Robert E Lee. He had a further victory at Five Forks in 1865, and was active in the final battles which led to Lee's surrender. He never lost a battle. 📖 Richard O'Connor, *Sheridan, the Inevitable* (1953)

Sheridan, Richard Brinsley 1751–1816
Irish dramatist

He was born in Dublin, the grandson of Jonathan Swift's friend, Thomas Sheridan (1687–1738), and the son of Thomas Sheridan (1719–88), author of a *Life of Swift*. His mother, Frances (1724–66), was the author of several plays, and a novel called *Sidney Biddulph*. He was educated at Harrow, and after leaving school, with a schoolfriend wrote a three-act farce called *Jupiter* and tried a verse translation of the *Epistles of Aristoenetus*. In 1773 he married Elizabeth Linley. The couple settled in London to a life that was beyond their means and Sheridan devoted more time to dramatic composition. In 1775 *The Rivals* was successfully produced at Covent Garden, London, and in the same year appeared a poor farce called *St Patrick's Day* and also *The Duenna*. In 1776 Sheridan, with the aid of Thomas Linley and another friend, bought half the patent of Drury Lane Theatre for £35,000 from David Garrick, and in 1778 the remaining share for £45,000. His first production was a purified edition of John Vanbrugh's *Relapse*, under the title of *A Trip to Scarborough*. In 1777 he produced his most famous play, *The School for Scandal*, a satirical comedy of manners. *The Critic* (1779), teeming with sparkling wit, was his last dramatic effort, apart from a less successful tragedy, *Pizarro*. In 1780 he was elected MP for Stafford, and became Under-Secretary for Foreign Affairs (1782) under Charles, Marquis of Rockingham, and afterwards Secretary to the Treasury in the coalition ministry (1783). His parliamentary reputation dated from some great speeches in the impeachment of Warren Hastings. In 1794 he again electrified the House by a magnificent oration in reply to Lord Mornington's denunciation of the French Revolution. He remained the devoted friend and adherent of Charles Fox till Fox's death, and was also the defender and mouthpiece of the Prince Regent. In 1806 he was appointed Receiver of the Duchy of Cornwall, and in 1806 Treasurer to the navy. In 1812 he lost his seat. In 1792 his first wife died, and three years later he married Esther Ogle, daughter of the dean of Winchester, who survived him. The affairs of the theatre had gone badly. The old building had to be closed as unfit to hold large audiences, and a new one, opened in 1794, was burned in 1809. This last calamity put the finishing touch to Sheridan's pecuniary difficulties, which had long been serious. He died in great poverty, but was given a magnificent funeral at Westminster Abbey. 📖 L Gibbs, *Sheridan* (1947)

Sheriff, Lawrence d.1567
London grocer and philanthropist

Born in Rugby, Warwickshire, he was a London grocer by trade. He was the founder of Rugby School in 1567 by his bequest and endowment.

Sherley, Sir Anthony See Shirley, Sir Anthony

Sherlock, Dame Sheila Patricia Violet 1918–
British physician

She trained in medicine at Edinburgh University and was a Beit Research Fellow from 1942 to 1947. After a period at Yale University (1948), she became physician and lecturer in medicine at the Royal Postgraduate Medical School in London (1948–59), then Professor of Medicine at the Royal Free Hospital Medical School, London. She has published extensively on liver function, structure and disease, and has received honorary degrees and fellowships from several universities and medical colleges. She has worked for many medical organizations, including the Royal College of Physicians (Councillor 1964–68, Censor 1970–72, Senior Censor and Vice-President 1976–77). She was created DBE in 1978.

Sherman, Henry Clapp 1875–1955
US biochemist

Born in Ash Grove, Virginia, he trained at Maryland Agricultural College (1893–95) and moved to Columbia University where he became successively Professor of Analytical Chemistry (1905–07), Professor of Organic Analysis (1907–11), Professor of Food Chemistry (1911–24) and Mitchill Professor of Chemistry (from 1924). His principal research was in the field of nutrition and vitamins. He established the human daily requirement of calcium (1931) and B vitamins (1932), and his major study on vitamin A defined a suitable weekly dose (1934), and its storage in the body (1940). Sherman also identified iron-deficiency anaemia, and began investigating cobalt in 1946. He published *Science in Nutrition* in 1943.

Sherman, John 1823–1900
US statesman

He was born in Lancaster, Ohio, the brother of General William Sherman. He was in turn chairman of financial committees in both Houses of Congress. He was largely responsible for the bills dealing with the reconstruction of the seceded states and for the resumption of specie payment in 1879. He was appointed Secretary of the Treasury in 1877 and in 1878 prepared a redemption fund in gold that raised the legal tender notes to par value. In 1881 and 1887 he was again returned to the senate and became its president, and was afterwards chairman of the Foreign Relations Committee, and Secretary of State (1897–98). The Sherman Act (1890; repealed 1893) sanctioned large purchases of silver by the Treasury.

Sherman, Roger 1721–93
American statesman and patriot

Born in Newton, Massachusetts, he lived in Connecticut from 1743. First elected to the State Assembly in 1755, he became a judge of the Superior Court (1766–89) and Mayor of New Haven (1784–93). He was a signatory of the Declaration of Independence, and as a delegate to the Convention of 1787 took a prominent part in the debates on the Constitution.

Sherman, William Tecumseh 1820–91
US soldier

Born in Lancaster, Ohio, the brother of John Sherman, he trained at West Point. At the outbreak of the Civil War (1861–65) he was commissioned as colonel (1861), and at Bull Run was promoted to brigadier-general of volunteers. He was sent to Kentucky, at first under Robert Anderson, but was later deprived of his command. After the Battle of Shiloh (April 1862) he was made major-general. In 1863, promoted to brigadier, he drove General Joseph Johnston out of Jackson, Mississippi; he joined Ulysses S Grant at Chattanooga, and soon after relieved Ambrose Burnside, besieged at Knoxville. In March 1864 he was appointed to the command of the south-west and drove Johnston to Atlanta, which was evacuated on 1 September. He then marched to the sea with 65,000 men, destroying everything in his path and finally capturing the coastal town of Savannah. In February 1865 he reached Columbia. From there he moved on Goldsboro', fighting two battles on the way. On 9 April Lee surrendered, and Johnston made terms with Sherman (which were disapproved of as too lenient by Secretary Edwin Stanton). For four years he commanded the Mississippi division and when Grant became President was made head of the army. In 1884, to make room for Philip Sheridan, he was retired on full pay. ⊞ Lloyd Lewis, *Sherman: Fighting Prophet* (1932)

Sherriff, R(obert) C(edric) 1896–1975
English playwright, novelist and scriptwriter
Born in Hampton Wick, Surrey, he achieved an international reputation with his first play, *Journey's End* (1929), which was based on his experiences in the trenches during World War I. His other plays include *St Helena* (1934), on the last years of the exiled Napoleon, and *The White Carnation* (1953), a ghost story. He also wrote several novels, and film scripts including *The Invisible Man* (1933), *Goodbye Mr Chips* (1939), *The Four Feathers* (1938), *Lady Hamilton* (1941) and *The Dambusters* (1954).

Sherrington, Sir Charles Scott 1857–1952
English physiologist and Nobel Prize winner
Born in London, after studying at Cambridge he became a lecturer in physiology at St Thomas's Hospital and professor-superintendent of the Brown Animal Sanatory Institute. In 1895 he became Professor of Physiology at Liverpool University, and was later appointed Waynflete Professor of Physiology at Oxford (1913–35). His career focused on the structure and function of the nervous system. His analysis of the reflexes is summarized in *The Integrative Action of the Nervous System* (1906), a book which constituted a significant landmark in modern neurophysiology. He described the reciprocal action by which the activity of one set of excited muscles is integrated with another set of inhibited muscles, and coined the word 'synapse' to describe the junction between nerve cells. He also mapped the motor areas of the cerebral cortex of mammals, and produced an influential textbook on experimental physiology, *Mammalian Physiology* (1919). He was president of the Royal Society (1920–25), and shared the 1932 Nobel Prize for physiology or medicine with Lord Adrian. ⊞ Sir John Eccles and W C Gibson, *Sherrington* (1979)

Sher Shah (Sher Khan) c.1486–1545
Afghan ruler
He was able to contest the supremacy of the Mughals in India, defeating Emperor Hamayun at Chausa on the Ganges (1539) and forcing him into exile. A formidable warrior and able administrator, he also built a new city at Delhi and a mausoleum at Sasaram in Bihar. His death in battle and the inefficiency of his successors allowed the Mughals to emerge triumphant.

Sherwood, Mary Martha, *née* Butt 1775–1851
English children's writer
She was born in Stanford, Worcestershire, the daughter of a chaplain to George II. In 1803 she married Henry Sherwood and two years later accompanied him to India, where she remained until 1816. There she adapted Bunyan's *The Pilgrim's Progress* for Indian readers, as *The Indian Pilgrim*. Her 77 works include *Little Henry and his Bearer* (1815), and the long-popular *History of the Fairchild Family* (1818–47). Her books are characterized by religious fervour and moral didacticism, but are always readable and often exciting. ⊞ N G Royde Smith, *The State of Mind of Mary Sherwood* (1946)

Sherwood, Robert E(mmet) 1896–1955
US playwright and author

Born in New Rochelle, New York, he wrote his first play, *Barnum Was Right*, while at Harvard. After service in World War I he became editor of *Life* (1924–28), and a member of the celebrated literary group known as the Algonquin Round Table. He won four Pulitzer Prizes, the first three for drama with *Idiot's Delight* (1936), *Abe Lincoln in Illinois* (1938) and *There Shall Be No Night* (1940). His play about Abraham Lincoln attracted the attention of Eleanor Roosevelt, and through her introduction Sherwood later became President Franklin D Roosevelt's chief speechwriter. He won his last Pulitzer Prize for his autobiographical *Roosevelt and Hopkins* (1949), which drew on his friendship with the President and with Harry L Hopkins. His screenplay, *The Best Years of Our Lives*, won an Academy Award in 1946.

Shetrup Akong Tarap See Akong Tulku Rinpoche

Shevardnadze, Eduard Amvrosevich 1928–
Georgian and Soviet politician
He was born in the Georgian village of Mamati, the son of a teacher. Having studied at the Kutaisi Institute of Education, he joined the Communist Party in 1948, and rose rapidly through the Komsomol youth league to the party apparatus during the 1950s and to the Georgian Ministry of the Interior in 1964. There he gained a reputation as a stern opponent of corruption, and he became Georgian Party Secretary himself in 1972. He introduced imaginative agricultural reforms, and in 1978 was brought into the politburo as a candidate member. Having enjoyed longstanding connections with Mikhail Gorbachev, he was promoted to full politburo status and appointed Foreign Minister in 1985. He rapidly overhauled the Soviet foreign policy machine and, alongside Gorbachev, was responsible for the Soviet contribution to the ending of the Cold War. He was also a powerful influence for political reform inside the USSR and during the winter of 1990–91 constantly warned Gorbachev against the danger of a coup. In 1992 he returned to Georgia, then in the midst of a civil war, and became President (1995) of the newly independent state. He survived an assassination attempt in 1995.

Shevchenko, Taras Grigorevich 1814–61
Ukrainian poet and prose writer
Born a serf in Kirilovka (Kiev), he came to be considered the father of modern Ukrainian literature and the country's foremost 19th-century poet. He showed an early interest in writing and drawing, and was adopted by a literary circle in St Petersburg, who bought his freedom in 1838. His early poems included Romantic ballads, love songs and historical subjects. He became professor at Kiev (1845), and founded an organization for radical social reforms. He was exiled to central Asia for 10 years for working for Ukrainian independence, but was freed in 1857, although kept under surveillance. He is remembered as the creator of a new Ukrainian literary language. ⊞ W K Matthews, *Taras Sevchenko* (1951)

Shidehara Kijuro 1872–1951
Japanese politician
From a wealthy landlord family who had close links (through marriage) with the Mitsubishi financial combine, he was ambassador to the USA and a delegate to the Washington Conference (1921–22) before becoming Foreign Minister in the reforming Kenseikai government (1924–26, 1929–31). He adopted a policy of co-operation with the Western powers toward China and aroused the ire of ultranationalists when he supported the 1930 London Naval Treaty, which placed restrictions on Japan's naval expansion. He served as the second postwar Prime Minister (1945–46) but was defeated in Japan's first postwar election (1946).

Shi Huangdi (Shih Huang-ti) c.259–210BC
Chinese emperor and founder of the Qin (Ch'in) dynasty

The creator of the first unified Chinese empire (221BC), he assumed the title of 'first emperor', and greatly extended and consolidated the empire with the establishment of a centralized administration, the abolition of territorial feudal power, and far-reaching measures for standardization. He ordered a system of road construction and, using convict labour, he linked together earlier fortifications to make the Great Wall (completed in 214BC) to keep out invaders, particularly the Turkish Huns. In 213BC he had all historical documents (except those relating to the Qin and those in the imperial library) burned in order to maintain himself and his successors in power. In 1974, excavation of his tomb yielded several thousand terracotta soldiers and horses which had been buried with him.

Shillaber, Benjamin Penhallow 1814–90
US humorist

He founded and edited *The Carpet Bag* (1851–53) and was the author of *The Life and Sayings of Mrs Partington* (1854), which used a popular invented character as a medium for contemporary comment and satire.

Shinwell, Emmanuel Shinwell, Baron, *known as* Manny Shinwell 1884–1986
English Labour politician

Born in Spitalfields, London, he began work as an errand boy in Glasgow at the age of 12. An early student of public-library and street-corner socialism, he was elected to the Glasgow Trades Council in 1911 and, as one of the 'wild men of Clydeside', served a five months' prison sentence for incitement to riot in 1921. He entered parliament in 1931 and was appointed secretary to the Department of Mines (1924, 1930–31). In 1935 he defeated Ramsay MacDonald at Seaham Harbour, Durham, in one of the most bitterly contested British election battles of modern times. From 1942 he was Chairman of the Labour Party committee which drafted the manifesto 'Let us face the future', on which Labour won the 1945 election. As Minister of Fuel and Power he nationalized the mines (1946), and the following year, when he was said to be a scapegoat for the February fuel crisis, he became Secretary of State for War. From 1950 to 1951 he was Minister of Defence. Shinwell's considerable administrative ability outshone his prickly party-political belligerence and earned him the respect of Churchill and Montgomery. In his later years he mellowed into a backbench 'elder statesman'. He was parliamentary Labour Party chairman 1964–67, was created Companion of Honour in 1965 and was awarded a life peerage in 1970. His autobiographical works include *Conflict without Malice* (1955), *I've Lived through it All* (1973), and *Lead with the Left* (1981). 📖 Peter M Slowe, *Manny Shinwell: An Authorized Biography* (1993)

Shipton, Eric Earle 1907–77
English mountaineer

He gained his early mountaineering experience during five expeditions to the mountains of East and Central Africa, climbing Kamet (25,447 ft) in 1931. He obtained much of his knowledge of the East during his terms as consul-general in Kashgar (1940–42, 1946–48) and Kunming (1949–51). Between 1933 and 1951 he led or was a member of five expeditions to Mount Everest, and he contributed greatly to the successful Hunt–Hillary expedition of 1953. 📖 *That Untravelled World* (1969)

Shipton, Mother, *originally* Ursula Southiel 1488–c.1560
English witch

She was born near Knaresborough, Yorkshire, and married a builder, Tony Shipton, at the age of 24. According to S. Baker, who edited her 'prophecies' (1797), she lived for more than 70 years. A book by Richard Head (1684) tells how she was carried off by the devil and bore him an imp. A small British moth, with wing-markings resembling a witch's face, is named after her.

Shirer, William Lawrence 1904–93
US journalist, broadcaster and author

He was born in Chicago, and after working as a newspaper correspondent in Europe, he joined CBS in 1937 as a war correspondent in Europe. He wrote a column for the New York *Herald Tribune* (1942–48). His major work, *The Rise and Fall of the Third Reich* (1960), won the National Book Award. His other books include *Berlin Diary: The Journal of a Foreign Correspondent, 1934–41* (1941), *The Collapse of the Third Republic* (1969) and *Gandhi: A Memoir* (1979). He also published three volumes of memoirs.

Shirley *or* Sherley, Sir Anthony 1565–c.1635
English adventurer

After serving with the Earl of Essex from 1597, he was granted a knighthood by the King of France; this was without the assent of Queen Elizabeth I, who had him imprisoned until he renounced it. He undertook a voyage to America and Jamaica (1595), which is recorded by Richard Hakluyt. In 1599 he went on a trade mission to Persia, and returned as the shah's envoy in an unsuccessful attempt to form an alliance against the Turks. He wrote an account of this adventure (1613).

Shirley, James 1596–1666
English dramatist

He was born in London and studied at St John's, Oxford, and St Catharine's, Cambridge. He then took orders and was given a living at St Albans. Later, he converted to Catholicism, and taught (1623–24) in the grammar school there, but soon went to London and became a playwright. Francis Beaumont, John Fletcher and Ben Jonson were his models, but he has little of the grand Elizabethan manner. His chief plays include *The Lady of Pleasure* (1635), the most brilliant of his comedies, the tragedy *The Cardinal* (1641), which the author himself described as 'the best of his flock' and *The Traitor* (1631). As a masque writer he is second only to Jonson; his work includes *The Triumph of Peace* (1633) and *The Contention of Ajax and Ulysses* (1659). The suppression of stage plays in 1642 forced him to return to teaching. He died as a result of the Great Fire of London. 📖 A H Mason, *James Shirley* (1915)

Shirreff, Emily Anne Eliza 1814–97
English pioneer of women's education

She was largely self-educated. With her sister, Maria Georgina Gray, she wrote *Thoughts on Self-Culture, Addressed to Women* (1850) and two novels, and she founded the National Union for the Higher Education of Women (1871). She was Mistress of Girton College, Cambridge (1870–97), and published works on kindergartens and the Froebel system.

Shirreff, Patrick 1791–1876
Scottish farmer

Born near Haddington, East Lothian, he was the pioneer of cereal hybridizing, and produced many varieties of wheat and oats.

Shivaji 1627–80
Ruler of the Maratha Empire

Born near Poona, he was the son of Shahaji Bhosle, a Maratha nobleman who had defied the power of the Mughals in Bijapur. When the Bijapur authorities sent a large army against him (1659), he killed their general and ambushed the leaderless army. During the 1660s Maratha power continued to increase and he had himself crowned as raja (1674). He profited from the conflict between the Mughal Emperor **Aurangzeb** and the Afghans to achieve conquests in the south. He was a devotee of Hinduism, but tolerated other religions. The Maratha Empire that he created maintained its independence until 1818.

Shklovsky, Iosif Samuilovich 1916–85
Soviet astronomer
Born in Glukhov, Ukraine, he studied first at the Far-Eastern State University and later at the University of Moscow. He proceeded to study theoretical astrophysics at the State Astronomical Institute in Moscow, was responsible for setting up in 1953 the radio astronomy division of the Astronomical Institute, and designed equipment for the Soviet space programme. Shklovsky's outstanding contributions were in high-energy astrophysics and radio technology. In 1954 he was appointed professor at Moscow State University. He collaborated with **Carl Sagan** on the popular book *Intelligent Life in the Universe* (1966) and was awarded the Lenin Prize in 1959 for his contributions to space research.

Shockley, William Bradford 1910–89
US physicist and Nobel Prize winner
Born in London, the son of two US mining engineers, he was brought up in California, and educated at the California and Massachusetts Institutes of Technology before starting work at the Bell Telephone Laboratories in 1936. During World War II he directed anti-submarine warfare research and he became consultant to the Secretary for War in 1945. Returning to Bell Telephones he collaborated with **John Bardeen** and **Walter Brattain** in trying to produce semiconductor devices to replace thermionic valves, and they invented the point-contact transistor in 1947. A month later Shockley developed the junction transistor (for transfer of current across a resistor). These devices led to the miniaturization of circuits in radio, television and computer equipment. Shockley, Bardeen, and Brattain shared the Nobel Prize for physics in 1956. From 1963 to 1974 Shockley was Professor of Engineering at Stanford.

Shoemaker, Willie (William Lee) 1931–
US jockey
He was born in Fabens, Texas. In 1953 he rode a record 485 winners in a season. In the USA his major successes included four Kentucky Derbies, five Belmont Stakes, and two wins in the famous Preakness event at Baltimore. The first jockey to saddle more than 8,000 winners, he moved to Europe late in his career, proving equally successful there. He was one of the most successful jockeys in the history of racing and retired in 1990 with 8,833 wins.
📖 William Shoemaker and Barney Nagler, *Shoemaker* (1988)

Sholokhov, Mikhail Aleksandrovich 1905–84
Russian novelist, winner of the Nobel Prize for literature
Born in Kruzhilin, he was educated at schools in Moscow, Boguchar and Veshenskaya. From 1920 to 1922 he served in the army, after which he had various occupations: teacher, tax inspector, labourer, playwright and actor. During World War II he was a war correspondent. His literary career began with some 30 short stories written between 1923 and 1927, which demonstrate his rapid development into an original writer. His masterpiece is *Tikhy Don* (4 vols, 1928–40, rev edn 1953, Eng trans in 2 vols: *And Quiet Flows the Don* and *The Don Flows Home to the Sea*, 1934–40). Set in the years 1912–22, it is a monument to the Don Cossacks, offering a broad view of their life in times of peace and during the turbulent years of the civil war and revolution. The characterization is splendid and the dialogue earthy. Since 1928 his authorship of the novel has been questioned, but the evidence to support these reservations is thin. *Podnyataya tselina* (1932–60, Eng trans in 2 vols: *Virgin Soil Upturned* and *Harvest on the Don*,

1935–60) is considered inferior, partly because of his alcoholism, and partly from his toeing of the official line. He won the 1941 Stalin Prize and the 1965 Nobel Prize for literature. 📖 I G Lezhnev, *Mikhail Sholokhov* (1948)

Shore, Jane d.c.1527
English courtesan
She was born in London, and as a young woman married William Shore, a goldsmith. In 1470 she captivated **Edward IV** with her wit and beauty and became his mistress. Her husband abandoned her, but she lived in luxury until Edward's death in 1483. Thereafter she became the mistress of Thomas, Lord Hastings and on his death, it is said, of the Marquis of Dorset. **Richard III** made her do public penance. She forms the subject of a tragedy by **Nicholas Rowe** (1714).

Shore, John, 1st Baron Teignmouth 1751–1834
English colonial administrator
He originated the Bengal *zamindari* system and many of Lord **Charles Cornwallis**'s reforms. He supported **Warren Hastings** during his impeachment (1788–95) and settled the Oude succession. He was first president of the British and Foreign Bible Society, and an Irish peer from 1798.

Shore, Peter David Shore, Baron 1924–
English Labour politician
Educated at Cambridge, he joined the Labour Party in 1948 and headed its research department for five years before becoming MP for Stepney (1964–97). He was parliamentary private secretary to **Harold Wilson**, and held several government posts, including Secretary of State for Economic Affairs (1967–69), for Trade (1974–76) and for the Environment (1976–79). A member of the Fabian Society, he was an unsuccessful candidate in the Labour Party leadership elections of 1983. After holding various Opposition spokesman posts, he became Shadow Leader of the Commons (1984–87). A persistent critic of European economic union, he launched a 'No to Maastricht' campaign in 1992. He published *Leading the Left* in 1993 and was awarded a life peerage in 1997.

Short, Clare 1946–
English Labour politician
Educated at the universities of Keele and Leeds, she joined the Home Office in 1970. She married a former Labour MP, Alexander Ward Lyon (1931–93), in 1981 and became MP for Birmingham Ladywood in 1983. Gradually gaining recognition, she has been an influential member of the National Executive Committee since 1988. She was Opposition front bench spokesperson on employment (1985–88), social security (1989–91), environmental protection (1992–93), women's issues (1993–95), transport (1995–96) and overseas development (1996–97), and then entered **Tony Blair**'s Cabinet as International Development Secretary when Labour came to power in 1997. In 1996 she was reunited with her son, whom she had given up for adoption in 1965.

Short, Sir Frank 1857–1945
English artist
Born in Stourbridge, West Midlands, he was educated in London, and became a teacher and authority on engraving. As head of the Engraving School at the Royal College of Art, London, he interpreted other masters, in particular **J M W Turner**'s *Liber Studiorum*. He was president of the Royal Society of Painter-Etchers and Engravers (1910–39).

Short, Nigel 1965–
English chess player
He became the world's youngest chess grandmaster, and Britain's youngest champion, at the age of 19. In January 1993 he defeated Dutchman Jan Timman to become the

Shostakovich, Dmitri Dmitriyevich 1906–75
Russian composer

Shostakovich was born in St Petersburg. He was taught to play the piano by his mother, and with the support of **Aleksandr Glazunov** entered the Conservatory in 1919. His 1st symphony, performed in Leningrad and Moscow in 1926, attracted worldwide attention. His musical career falls into two broad periods—up to his 5th symphony, which was written in 1938 in response to savage Soviet criticism, and after it. He always attempted to support Soviet principles, and initially wrote mainly for the theatre and films, notably the ballets *The Age of Gold* (1930, *Zolotoy vek*) and *The Bolt* (1931, *Bolt*), and the opera *The Nose* (1927–28, performed 1930, *Nos*).

His music was at first highly successful, but the development of a more conservative attitude on the part of the Soviet government, coinciding with his own development of a more experimental outlook, led to official criticism of *The Nose*, his 2nd ('October') symphony, and the ballet *Bright Stream* (1934–35, *Svetytoly ruchey*). His second opera, *A Lady Macbeth of Mtensk*, (1930–32, *Ledi Makbet Mtsenskovo uyezda*, later revised in 1956 and performed in 1962 as *Katerina Izmaylova*) had to be withdrawn after violent press attacks on its decadence and its failure to observe the principles of 'Soviet realism'. It is said that **Stalin** hated it, and may have been the author of a fierce attack on Shostakovich published in *Pravda*.

He replied with his 5th symphony, described by a critic as 'A Soviet artist's reply to just criticism', which achieved his rehabilitation and remains one of Shostakovich's most popular works. He composed prolifically in all forms, although he avoided stage works until after the death of Stalin. In 1943 he moved to Moscow and was appointed Professor of Composition at the Conservatory. (This position was taken away from him from 1948 to 1960 owing to another artistic purge.) His 7th symphony (1941,

'Leningrad', based on the Siege of Leningrad which Shostakovich himself experienced), and his 8th (1943) and 10th (1953) symphonies have achieved considerable popularity outside Russia; the 10th uses the motif DSCH, based on his own initials. His 11th symphony (1957), for which he was awarded a Lenin prize in 1958, is based on the events of the October Revolution of 1905, the 12th (1961) celebrates the 1917 Revolution, the 13th (1962) includes male-voice settings of **Yevgeni Yevtushenko**, the 14th (1969) consists of 11 vocal movements; his 15th and last symphony (1974) is purely instrumental.

He also wrote two violin concertos, two cello concertos and two piano concertos, many vocal works, 15 string quartets, a piano quintet (which won the Stalin prize in 1940) and two piano trios, and other chamber music, as well as songs. His music for piano includes a set of 24 preludes and fugues in the manner of **J S Bach**.

Shostakovich visited Great Britain twice in 1958 and 1974, and became a close friend of **Benjamin Britten**. His health was weakened after a heart attack in 1969. His son is the conductor and pianist **Maxim Shostakovich**.

📖 Shostakovich recorded his reminiscences in *Testimony: The Memoirs of Dmitri Shostakovich* (1979). See also I MacDonald, *The New Shostakovich* (1990); Christopher Norris (ed), *Shostakovich* (1982); Eric Roseberry, *Shostakovich: His Life and Times* (1982); David A Rabinovich, *Dmitry Shostakovich* (1959, originally published in Russian).

> 'The entire symphony is my protest against death.'
> Shostakovich on his 14th Symphony. Quoted in Norris (ed), *Shostakovich* (1982).

---

first British chess world championship challenger for over 100 years. He was defeated in his challenge against world champion **Gary Kasparov** in 1993.

Shorter, Frank C 1947–
US marathon runner

Born in Munich, Germany, he won the 1972 Olympic title and a silver medal at the 1976 Games. His success helped inspire the running and jogging boom in the USA. He went on to a career as a television sports commentator.

Shorter, Wayne 1933–
US jazz saxophonist, band leader and composer

Born in Newark, New Jersey, he studied music at New York University. His first long association was with the **Art Blakey** Jazz Messengers (1959–63). For the next six years he worked with **Miles Davis** in his first experiments in electric jazz-rock fusion, which set Shorter on his future direction. He co-founded the quintet Weather Report, which performed from 1971 until the mid-1980s. Since then, Shorter has continued in the electric jazz style, playing tenor and soprano saxophones, at the head of small combos. His solo albums include *Supernova* (1970), *Atlantis* (1986) and *The All Seeing Eye* (1994).

Shostakovich, Dmitri See panel above

Shostakovich, Maxim Dmitriyevich 1938–
US conductor and pianist

He was born in Leningrad (now St Petersburg), and trained at the Moscow Conservatory. The son of **Dmitri Shostakovich**, he has conducted and recorded many of his father's works, including the première of the 15th Symphony, and the 2nd Piano Concerto (as soloist, aged 19), which was written for him. He began his conducting career in 1963 as assistant conductor first of the Moscow

Philharmonic, and then of the USSR State Academic Symphony Orchestra. In 1971 he became principal conductor and artistic director of the USSR Radio and TV Symphony Orchestra. Whilst on tour in 1981 he was granted asylum in the USA, where he settled. He was conductor of the New Orleans Symphony Orchestra from 1986 to 1991.

Shovel, Sir Cloudesley 1650–1707
English naval commander

He served against the Dutch and in the Mediterranean, burned four corsair galleys at Tripoli (1676), and commanded a ship at the battle in Bantry Bay (1689). In 1690 he took part in the battle off Beachy Head, and in 1692 he supported Edward Russell at La Hogue, burning 20 enemy ships. With **George Rooke** he took Gibraltar in 1704. In 1705 he was made rear admiral of England and took part with Charles Mordaunt, Earl of **Peterborough** in the capture of Barcelona. On the voyage home his ship struck a rock off the Scilly Isles and sank. He was buried in Westminster Abbey.

Shrapnel, Henry 1761–1842
English soldier

He saw service in many parts of the world, and invented the shrapnel shell. He was made inspector of artillery in 1804.

Shriver, Duward Felix 1934–
US chemist

Born in Glendale, California, and educated at the University of California at Berkeley and the University of Michigan, he is now chairman of the chemistry department (1992–) at Northwestern University, Illinois, where he is a member of the Materials Research Center and the Ipatieff Catalysis Center. His most important work has been in organometallic chemistry, and has stimulated interest in the relationship between organometallic chemistry and heterogeneous catalytic processes, which are of great industrial importance. His book *Manipulation of Air-Sensitive Materials* (1969) is the standard reference work in its field.

Shriver, Pam 1962–
US tennis player

Born in Baltimore, Maryland, she is one of the most prolific Grand Slam title-holders of all time. Between 1981 and 1992 she won 22 Grand Slam titles—21 doubles titles and one mixed title, the 1987 French Open with Emilio Sanchez. Twenty of her doubles titles were won in partnership with **Martina Navratilova**. From 24 April 1983 to 6 July 1985 they were undefeated in 109 matches. She is co-owner of the baseball team Baltimore Orioles.

Shubert, Lee c.1875–1953
US theatrical manager

Born in Shervient, Lithuania, he emigrated to the USA as a child in 1882, when his family settled in Syracuse, New York. After working odd jobs at local theatres, he joined up with his brothers Jacob (1880–1963) and Sam (1876–1905) to organize theatrical touring companies out of Syracuse. Despite the monopoly of the Theatrical Syndicate, they leased their first theatre in New York, the Herald Square Theatre, in 1900, and within a decade they had become such a powerful force in the New York theatre that they held a near-monopoly themselves. From 1905 until his death Lee served as president of the Shubert Theatrical Corporation, which was interested not only in booking and ticket sales, but in the staging of plays. Between them the Shubert brothers produced 520 plays on Broadway, favouring musicals since they had the largest potential for profit. On Lee's death the last of the brothers, Jacob ('J J'), took over the business.

Shula, Don(ald Francis) 1930–
US player and coach of American football

He was born in Grand River, Ohio. He played professional football for the Cleveland Browns, the Baltimore Colts and the Washington Redskins before he became a coach in 1958. By the mid-1980s the teams he had coached in the NFL had amassed 250 victories. His most successful team were the Miami Dolphins, who won 100 games in 10 seasons and made him the first NFL coach with such a record.

Shultz, George Pratt 1920–
US politician

Born in New York City into an affluent financial family, he studied at Princeton and was an artillery officer during World War II. After the war he taught economics at Massachusetts Institute of Technology (1946–57) and Chicago University (1957–68), then served as Secretary of Labour (1969–70), Budget Director (1970–72) and Secretary of the Treasury (1972–74) in the **Nixon** administration. He was subsequently vice-chairman of the giant Bechtel industrial corporation and economic adviser to President **Ronald Reagan** in 1980, before replacing **Alexander Haig** as Secretary of State in 1982. He retained this post for the remainder of the Reagan administration until 1989. A moderate and pragmatic Atlanticist and supporter of arms control, he acted as a counterweight to the hawkish defence secretary **Caspar Weinberger** and helped to improve US–Soviet relations in the period of détente that followed the accession of **Mikhail Gorbachev**. His greatest achievement was the 1987 Intermediate Nuclear Forces (INF) Treaty. As Secretary of State, he also directed a campaign against international terrorism, backing the USA's bombing of Tripoli in 1986. In 1989 he

became Professor of Political Economy at Stanford University. In 1993 he published *Turmoil and Triumph: My Years as Secretary of State*.

Shumway, Norman Edward 1923–
US cardiac surgeon

Born in Kalamazoo, Michigan, he received his MD from Vanderbilt University and his PhD in surgery from Minnesota University. He joined the faculty at the Stanford University School of Medicine in 1958 where he and his team have been active in many aspects of cardiovascular surgery, including cardiac transplantation. Shumway did much of the early experimental work in the field, before heart transplants were attempted in human beings.

Shuster, Joseph 1914–92
US strip cartoonist

Born in Toronto, Canada, he was co-creator with **Jerry Siegel** of one of the world's most popular comic-book heroes, *Superman*.

Shute, Nevil, *pseudonym of* Nevil Shute Norway 1899–1960
English novelist

Born in Ealing, Middlesex, he served in World War I and immediately afterwards began an aeronautical career. He was chief calculator of the Airship Guarantee Company during the construction of the airship R100, in which he flew the Atlantic twice. He founded Airspeed Ltd, aircraft constructors, and became its managing director. He emigrated to Australia after World War II. His novels include *The Pied Piper* (1942), *Most Secret* (1945), *The Chequerboard* (1947), *No Highway* (1948), *A Town Like Alice* (1949), *Round the Bend* (1951), *Requiem for a Wren* (1955), *Beyond the Black Stump* (1956) and *On The Beach* (1957), about an atomic war catastrophe. His success was largely due to his brisk style and his ability to express technical concepts in language that is understandable to ordinary readers.
📖 *Slide Rule* (1954)

Shuvalov or Schouvaloff, Pyotr Andreyevich, Graf 1827–89
Russian politician and diplomat

He served in the Crimean War, became head of the Third Department or secret police in 1866, and proved a dangerous opponent of reform. In 1873, sent on a secret mission to London, he arranged the marriage between the Duke of Edinburgh and the only daughter of Alexander II. In 1878 he was one of the Russian representatives at the Congress of Berlin.

Shvarts, Yevgeni Lvovich 1896–1958
Russian–Jewish playwright, novelist and storyteller

He was born in Kazan. Early acting experience gave him a good knowledge of the theatre. His most important works, which managed to escape the Stalinist censors, include *Ten* (1940) and *The Shadow* and *Drakon* (1943, Eng trans *The Dragon* in *Three Soviet Plays*, 1966). He wrote for puppets and for live casts, and for audiences of both adults and children, and he used the fairy tale as a vehicle for satisfying political extremes, both Nazi and Stalinist. He has been described as the only Soviet playwright of status.

Sibbald, Sir Robert 1641–1722
Scottish physician and naturalist

Born in Edinburgh, he studied there and at the University of Leyden, where he graduated in medicine in 1661. He founded a physic garden in Edinburgh in 1670, in order to grow plants for use by the physicians of the town. This garden formed the nucleus of the present day Royal Botanic Garden. He founded the Royal College of Physicians of Edinburgh, and became the first Professor of Medicine at Edinburgh University in 1685. King

Charles II commissioned him to undertake a survey of the natural history and archaeology of Scotland, his *Scotia Illustrata*, which was published in 1684. The genus *Sibbaldia* is named in his honour. He was knighted in 1682.

Sibelius, Jean Julius Christian 1865–1957
Finnish composer
Born in Hämeenlinna (Tavastehus), he abandoned a legal career to study music. He was a passionate nationalist, and wrote a series of symphonic poems (eg *Kullervo*, 1892; *Swan of Tuonela*, 1893) based on episodes in the Finnish oral epic *Kalevala*. A state grant enabled him to devote himself entirely to composition from 1897, and his seven symphonies, symphonic poems (notably *En Saga*, 1892, revised 1901; *Finlandia*, 1899; *Tapiola*, 1925–26)) and violin concerto have established him as a major 20th-century composer both nationally and internationally.

Sibley, Dame Antoinette 1939–
English dancer
Born in Bromley, Kent, she trained with the Royal Ballet and appeared as a soloist for the first time in 1956 in *Swan Lake*; she played the leading role in place of an indisposed principal, and became famous overnight. A dancer of sensuality and beauty, her roles in Frederick Ashton's *The Dream* (1964) and Kenneth MacMillan's *Manon* (1974) are among her most celebrated, and she formed a famous partnership with Anthony Dowell. A knee injury forced an early retirement in 1976, but she was persuaded by Ashton to dance again five years later to great acclaim. In 1989 she became vice-president of the Royal Academy of Dancing, then president in 1991. She was made DBE in 1996.
📖 Barbara Newman, *Antoinette Sibley* (1988)

Sibley, Henry Hastings 1811–91
US politician
Born in Detroit, he was the first Governor and 'Father of Minnesota'. He put down the Sioux outbreak of 1862.

Sica, Vittorio De See De Sica, Vittorio

Sickert, Walter Richard 1860–1942
British artist
Born in Munich, Germany, of mixed Dutch and Danish parentage, after three years on the English stage (an interest reflected in many pictures of music halls) he studied at the Slade School and under James McNeill Whistler. While working in Paris, he was much influenced by Degas. He had many studios in London, paying regular visits to France, and he used Degas's technique to illustrate London low life. He was a member of the New English Art Club, and about 1910 the Camden Town Group (later the London Group) was formed under his leadership. His famous interior *Ennui* (Tate, London) belongs to this period. Both his painting and his writings on art have had great influence on later English painters. His autobiography *A Free House!* was published in 1947.
📖 Denys Sutton, *Walter Sickert* (1976)

Sickingen, Franz von 1481–1523
German knight
Born in Ebernburg, near Kreuznach, he fought against the Venetians for Emperor Maximilian I (1508). In peace he led the life of a soldier of fortune and amassed considerable wealth. He supported the election of Charles V as Holy Roman Emperor (1519) and fought for him in his French campaign (1521). Ulrich von Hutten, the German humanist, was his constant guest from 1520, and he became a leader of the Lutheran Reformation, declaring a Protestant war against the Archbishop of Trier in 1522. Defeated, he died besieged at his castle of Landstuhl.

Siddiqui, Kalim 1933–96
British muslim leader and spokesman
He was born near Hyderabad, India, and moved with his family to Pakistan after partition in 1947. He went to the UK in 1954 to pursue a career in journalism, and became increasingly involved in Muslim affairs, founding the Muslim Institute in London in 1972. After the Iranian Revolution of 1979, he became more radical, calling for a Muslim Parliament and the publication of a Muslim Manifesto; this cost him the support of some of his less militant co-religionists. He was a strong supporter of the fatwa against Salman Rushdie (1989) and, although he had no formal spiritual authority, he remained a self-styled spokesman for Islam until his death.

Siddons, Sarah, *née* Kemble 1755–1831
English actress
She was born in Brecon, Wales, the eldest child of Roger Kemble, manager of a small travelling theatrical company, of which Sarah was a member from her earliest childhood. In 1773 she married her fellow actor, William Siddons. Her first appearance at Drury Lane in 1775, as Portia, was unremarkable, but her reputation grew so fast in the provinces that in 1782 she returned to Drury Lane, and made her appearance as Isabella in David Garrick's adaptation of Thomas Southerne's *Fatal Marriage*. Her success was immediate, and she soon became the unquestioned queen of the English stage. In 1803 she followed her brother John Philip Kemble to Covent Garden, where she stayed until her farewell appearance as Lady Macbeth in 1812. Thereafter she appeared occasionally, and sometimes gave public readings. Her gifts and her expressive and beautiful face, queenly figure, and rich, flexible voice gave her great distinction as a tragic actress. In comedy, however, she was less successful. 📖 Kathleen Mackenzie, *The Great Sarah: The Life of Mrs Siddons* (1968)

Sidgwick, Henry 1838–1900
English philosopher
Born in Skipton, Yorkshire, he was educated at Rugby School and Cambridge, where he became a Fellow of Trinity College (1859) and Knightbridge Professor of Moral Philosophy (1883). His best-known work, *Methods of Ethics* (1874), contains a sophisticated and distinctive development of the utilitarian theories of John Stuart Mill, combining them with views drawn from Kant. He was a founder and the first president of the Society for Psychical Research (1882). He was also active in promoting higher education for women and was involved in founding (1871) a house for women students which became Newnham College, Cambridge (1880). His wife, Eleanor Balfour (the sister of Arthur James Balfour) became Principal of Newnham (1892–1910). 📖 David G Jones, *Henry Sidgwick: Science and Faith in Victorian England* (1970)

Sidgwick, Nevil Vincent 1873–1951
English chemist
Born in Oxford, he was a student of Augustus Vernon Harcourt at Christ Church, Oxford, where he gained first-class honours in chemistry and classics. After acting as demonstrator in the Christ Church laboratory for a year, he went to work in Wilhelm Ostwald's laboratory in Leipzig and then with Hans von Pechmann at Tübingen. He returned to be a Fellow and Tutor of Lincoln College, a position he held until retirement in 1947. In the university he became reader (from 1924) and professor (from 1935). Up to 1920 he carried out various physico-chemical solution studies involving kinetics, ionic equilibria or phase equilibria. He was greatly stimulated, however, by the nascent electronic theory of valency, and he devoted some of his research to this subject. Sidgwick was appointed CBE in 1935, was elected a Fellow of the Royal Society in 1922 and received its Royal Medal in 1937. He was president of the Faraday Society from 1932 to 1934 and of the Chemical Society from 1935 to 1937.

Sidi Mohammed ben Youssef 1911–61
Sultan and King of Morocco
He was born in Meknès, a scion of the Alouite dynasty, and succeeded his father as sultan in 1927. Exercising both spiritual and temporal power, he supported the nationalist Istaqlal Party and constantly obstructed French hegemony. Tribal hostility to him gave the French the chance to depose him (1953), but he was restored (1955) and when Morocco attained independence (1957) he became King Mohammed V. He died suddenly after a minor operation and was succeeded by his eldest son, Prince Moulay Hassan, who had already emerged as the spokesman of chauvinistic Moroccan youth. His eldest daughter, Princess Lalla Ayesha, repudiated the yasmak and became a leader of the women's emancipation movement.

Sidmouth, Henry Addington, 1st Viscount
1757–1844
English politician
Born in London, he was educated at Winchester and Brasenose College, Oxford. He entered Parliament as MP for Devizes in 1783, and was elected Speaker of the House of Commons (1789–1801). When William Pitt, the Younger, resigned in 1801, he formed the administration which negotiated the Peace of Amiens in 1802. He was created Viscount Sidmouth in 1805 and held several Cabinet posts. As Home Secretary (1812–21) he took severe measures against Luddite rioters and suspended the Habeas Corpus Act; it was in his period of office that the 'Peterloo Massacre' took place in Manchester in 1819, during an open-air meeting in support of parliamentary reform.

Sidney or Sydney, Algernon c.1622–1683
English politician
Born probably in Penshurst, Kent, the grandnephew of Sir Philip Sidney and second son of the second Earl of Leicester, he was wounded during the Civil War at Marston Moor (1644), fighting on the Parliamentary side. He was elected to the Long Parliament in 1645, but retired in 1653 on Cromwell's usurpation of power, and retired to Penshurst (1653–59). After the Restoration he lived on the Continent until 1677, when he returned to England. He was always thought dangerous and unreliable, and in 1683 he was implicated in the Rye House Plot to kill Charles II. He was found guilty on slender evidence, and, with Lord William Russell, beheaded.

Sidney, Sir Henry 1529–86
English administrator
As Lord Deputy of Ireland (1565–71, 1575–78) he crushed Shane O'Neill (c.1530–1567) in Ulster (1566–67), failed to establish English settlers, but organized a system of presidency councils. He served also as president of the council of Wales (1559–86).

Sidney, Sir Philip 1554–86
English poet and patron
Born in Penshurst, Kent, he was the eldest son of Sir Henry Sidney (Lord Deputy of Ireland). He was educated at Shrewsbury School and Christ Church, Oxford, and from 1572 to 1575 he travelled in France, Germany, Austria and Italy, where he spent a year studying history and ethics, and was painted by Veronese. Returning to England, he was knighted in 1582 and appointed Governor of Flushing in 1585. He spent his last year in the Netherlands, where he successfully plotted an attack on the town of Axel; he later led an assault on a Spanish convoy transporting arms to Zutphen, was shot in the thigh and died from the infection. His work, none of which was published in his lifetime, includes *Arcadia* (1590), *Astrophel and Stella* (1591) and *A Defence of Poetry* (1595). He bestowed patronage on a number of poets, as dedications in various works testify, the most notable being that in Edmund Spenser's *The Shepheardes Calendar* in 1579. 📖 M Wilson, *Sir Philip Sidney* (1931)

Sidney, William Philip See De L'Isle, William Philip Sidney, 1st Viscount

Sidonius Apollinaris, Gaius Sollius
c.430–83AD
Gallo-Roman poet and prelate
Born in Lugdunum (Lyons) of a prominent Christian family, he held high civil offices in Rome, and in 472 became Bishop of Clermont-Ferrand in the Auvergne. His letters are modelled on Pliny's. His poems comprise panegyrics on three emperors, and two poems celebrating a marriage. He was canonized as St Sidonius Apollinaris. 📖 C E Stevens, *Sidonius and his Age* (1973)

Siebold, Karl Theodor Ernst von 1804–65
German zoologist
Born in Würzburg, the brother of Philipp Franz von Siebold, he became professor at the University of Munich. He worked on invertebrate research, and studied salamanders, parthenogenesis, and the freshwater fish of central Europe.

Siebold, Philipp Franz von 1796–1866
German physician and botanist
He was born in Würzburg. He became medical officer to the Dutch in Batavia (Djakarta), Java, and was stationed at a Dutch outpost in Nagasaki from 1823 to 1829, when he was expelled for obtaining too much information about Japan. He was largely responsible for the introduction of western medicine into Japan and many Japanese plants into European gardens, and in collaboration with German and Dutch scientists published important works on the flora and fauna of Japan. He was the brother of Karl Siebold.

Sieff (of Brimpton), Israel Moses Sieff, Baron 1889–1972
English businessman
Born in Manchester, he was educated at Manchester Grammar School and Manchester University. A schoolfellow of Simon Marks, each married the other's sister and together they developed the business called Marks and Spencer. He was joint managing director of the company from 1926 to 1967 and succeeded Lord Marks as chairman (1964–1967). His younger son, Marcus Joseph (1913–), who took a life peerage in 1980 as Lord Sieff of Brimpton, was chairman of Marks and Spencer from 1972 to 1984, when he became president of the company. 📖 *Sieff* (1970)

Siegbahn, Kai Mann Börje 1918–
Swedish physicist and Nobel Prize winner
He was born in Lund, the son of Karl Siegbahn, and was educated at Stockholm University, where he was Professor of Physics at the Royal Institute of Technology until 1954, and thereafter professor at Uppsala University (1954–84). In the early 1950s his studies on the energies of electrons emitted from solids exposed to X-rays revealed sharp peaks at energies which were characteristic of the materials. This technique, which became known as ESCA (electron spectroscopy for chemical analysis), offered a delicate but powerful experimental method for studying the energies of electrons around bonded atoms. The method has been extended for use with liquids and gases as well as solids. He shared the 1981 Nobel Prize for physics with Nicolaas Bloembergen and Arthur Schawlow for his work in developing high-resolution electron spectroscopy.

Siegbahn, Karl Manne Georg 1886–1978
Swedish physicist and Nobel Prize winner

Born in Örebro, he was educated at the University of Lund, and became professor there (1920) and at Uppsala University (1923). From 1937 he was professor of the Royal Academy of Sciences and director of the Nobel Institute for Physics at Stockholm University. Improving on the techniques of **Charles Barkla** and **Harry Moseley**, he succeeded in producing X-rays of various wavelengths and penetrating power, the discovery of which reinforced **Aage Niels Bohr's** shell model of the atom. For his development of X-ray spectroscopy, Siegbahn was awarded the Nobel Prize for physics in 1924. In the same year he showed that X-rays could be refracted, like light, by means of a prism.

Siegel, Jerry 1914–96
US strip cartoonist
Born in Cleveland, Ohio, he met **Joseph Shuster** at high school, where they published their own science fiction magazine. After a series of strips for various comic books, they created *Superman* for *Action Comics* in 1938. It became an instant success, leading to huge spin-offs in films and television. The partners had no copyright on the characters in the strip and failed to benefit until the owners (Warner Communications) agreed, after protracted lawsuits, to pay them a comfortable pension in 1975 and restore their credits to the strip.

Siegen, Ludwig von 1609–c.1675
German engraver
Born in Utrecht, of Dutch origin, he became a German military officer, and was thought to have been influenced by **Rembrandt**. In 1642 he invented the mezzotint process, sending a portrait of Landgravine Amelia Elizabeth of Bohemia to the Landgrave with a letter stating that the invention was his. He also disclosed his invention to Prince Rupert in Brussels in 1654. Only a handful of his prints exist.

Sielmann, Heinz 1917–
German naturalist and nature film photographer
Born in Königsberg (now Kaliningrad, Russia), and interested in animal photography from boyhood, he started making films in 1938 and won the German Academy Award for documentary films three years running (1953–55). He evolved techniques enabling him to film the interiors of the lairs of animals and inaccessible types of birds' nests (for example, the woodpecker), which revolutionized the study of animal behaviour.

Siemens, Ernst Werner von 1816–92
German electrical engineer
He was born in Lenthe, Hanover. In 1834 he entered the Prussian artillery, and in 1844 took charge of the artillery workshops in Berlin. He developed the telegraphic system in Prussia, discovered the insulating property of gutta-percha, and devoted himself to making telegraphic and electrical apparatus. In 1847 he established factories for making telegraphy equipment in Berlin and elsewhere (in 1867 the business became known as Siemens Brothers). Besides devising numerous forms of galvanometer and other electrical instruments, he was one of the discoverers of the self-acting dynamo. He determined the electrical resistance of different substances, and the SI Unit was named after him. In 1886 he endowed a technological institute. He was the brother of Sir **William Siemens**, and his son Wilhelm (1855–1919) was one of the pioneers of the incandescent lamp. 📖 Kurt Busse, *Werner von Siemens* (1966)

Siemens, Sir (Charles) William, *originally* Karl Wilhelm Siemens 1823–83
British electrical engineer
He was born in Lenthe, Hanover, Germany. He was educated in Lübeck and Magdeburg, and studied physics, chemistry and mathematics at the University of Göttingen. In 1843 he visited England to introduce a process for electrogilding which he invented with his brother, **Ernst Werner von Siemens**, and in 1844 he patented his differential governor. He became a British citizen in 1859. As manager in England of the firm of Siemens Brothers, he was actively engaged in the construction of telegraphs, designed the steamship *Faraday* for cable-laying, promoted electric lighting, and constructed the Portrush Electric Tramway in Ireland (1883). In 1861 he designed an open-hearth regenerative steel furnace which became the most widely used in the world. Other inventions included a water meter, pyrometer and bathometer. He was elected FRS in 1863. Other appointments included first president of the Society of Telegraph Engineers (1872) and chairman of the Royal Society of Arts (1882). He was knighted in 1883.

Sienkiewicz, Henryk 1846–1916
Polish novelist and Nobel Prize winner
Born near Luków, he studied literature, philology and history at Warsaw University, but left without a degree in 1871. He lived in the USA from 1876 to 1878, and after a hunting expedition in East Africa (1892) wrote the children's story *W pustyni i w puszczy* (1911, Eng trans *In Desert and Wilderness*, 1912). Most of his works, however, are strongly realistic. Many have been translated, among them the trilogy, *Ogniem i mieczem* (1884, Eng trans *With Fire and Sword*, 1890), *Potop* (1886, Eng trans *The Deluge*, 1892) and *Pan Wolodyjowski* (1887–88, Eng trans *Pan Michael*, 1895), and also *Rodzina Polanieckich* (1894, Eng trans *Children of the Soil*, 1895) and *Quo Vadis?* (1896, Eng trans 1896). He was awarded the Nobel Prize for literature in 1905. 📖 M Gardner, *The Novels of Henryk Sienkiewicz* (1926)

Siepi, Cesare 1923–
Italian bass
Born in Milan, he was largely self-taught and worked his way up through the operatic ranks, making his first major appearance in 1945 at Verona in **Verdi's** *Nabucco*. He was noticed by La Scala, Milan, and sang there regularly from 1946. Siepi's smooth rich voice, together with good looks and a fine acting ability, assured his place on the world's stages and he sang often at Covent Garden between 1962 and 1973, and at the New York Metropolitan Opera. Don Giovanni was a favourite role, which he performed on several occasions with **Wilhelm Furtwängler**.

Sierpiński, Wacław 1882–1969
Polish mathematician
He was born in Warsaw, where he studied and was professor from 1919 to 1960. The leader of the Polish school of set theorists and topologists, he was a prolific author, publishing more than 700 research papers on set theory, topology, number theory and logic, and several books. In 1919 he founded the still-important journal *Fundamenta Mathematicae* to publish work in these areas.

Sierra, Gregorio Martínez See **Martínez Sierra, Gregorio**

Sieyès, Emmanuel Joseph, *called* the Abbé Sieyès 1748–1836
French cleric and political theorist
Born in Fréjus, he studied theology. He became canon at Tréguier (1775), then chancellor and vicar-general of Chartres (1788), and as such was sent to the assembly of the clergy of France. His three pamphlets gained him popularity: *Vues sur les moyens d'exécution* (1788, 'Views on the Methods of Execution'), *Essai sur les privilèges* (1788, 'Essay on the Privileged'), and the most famous of all, *Qu'est-ce que le tiers-état?* (1789, 'What is the Third Estate?'). He was elected to the Estates General, and suggested the name National Assembly when it was united into one body. He was a prominent figure in the early years of the French

Revolution, being one of the founders of the Jacobin club. As the Revolution became more extreme, he withdrew from centre stage, and became famous for his reply to the question as to what he had done during the Revolution: 'I survived'. He became one of the Directors, and in 1799 was a leading figure in the Brumaire coup that brought **Napoleon I** to power. He withdrew from public life under the First Empire; he was exiled at the Restoration (1815) and lived in Brussels until 1830, when the July Revolution allowed him to return to Paris.

Sigismund 1368–1437
Holy Roman Emperor

The younger son of Emperor **Charles IV**, he became King of Hungary (1387) as husband of Mary, daughter of Louis I, the Great, after defeating his Angevin rival Charles of Durazzo, King of Naples. He was also King of Bohemia (1419) and of Lombardy (1431). His dominions were continually eroded by Venetians, Angevins and the Turks, who defeated him and his crusading allies at Nicopolis (1396). As Emperor (from 1410) he presided over the Council of Constance, which attempted to end the Hussite Schism. His refusal to provide the safe conduct he had granted **Jan Huss** led to Huss being burned and, in turn, to the Hussites' refusal to recognize him as King of Bohemia, and ultimately to the Hussite wars (1420–33). A year before his death he negotiated a compromise settlement which allowed his return as king in exchange for recognition of the Hussite principles embodied in the *Four Articles of Prague*. 📖 Wilhelm Baum, *Kaiser Sigismund: Hus, Konstanz und Türkenkriege* (1993)

Sigismund III Vasa 1566–1632
King of Poland and of Sweden

Born in Gripsholm, the Catholic son of King **Johan III** of Sweden and nephew of Sigismund II Augustus of Poland, he was elected to the Polish throne in 1587. He was haughty and naïve, and most of his reign was dominated by the chancellor, John Zamoyski, who defeated an attempt by the Archduke Maximilian to invade Poland and obliged the emperor to relinquish all Habsburg claims there (1588–89). In 1592 he succeeded his father as King of Sweden (1592–99), but before his coronation (1594), his uncle, the future **Karl IX**, promoted a convention renouncing Catholicism in Sweden, and after Sigismund's return to Poland, Karl ruled as Regent. In 1598 he was defeated by Karl at Stångebro, and for several years he tried without success to regain the Swedish throne. In 1609 he invaded Russia in pursuit of the Russian Crown, and captured Moscow and Smolensk, causing his son Ladislas to be temporarily elected tsar. He fought in Moldavia against Ottoman forces (1617–21), and lost Livonia and the Prussian ports in a war with **Gustav II Adolf** of Sweden (1621–29). He was succeeded in Poland by his son, Ladislas IV Vasa.

Signac, Paul 1863–1935
French artist

He was born in Paris. He exhibited with the Impressionists in 1884 and was later associated with Henri Edmond Cross (1856–1910) and **Georges Seurat** in the Neo-Impressionist movement. Signac, however, used mosaic-like patches of pure colour, as compared with Seurat's Pointillist dots. He published *D'Eugène Delacroix au Néo-impressionisme*, in which he sought to establish a scientific basis for his Divisionist theories (1899).

Signorelli, Luca c.1441–1523
Italian painter

Born in Cortona, he worked, especially in frescoes, in Loreto, Rome, Florence, Siena, Cortona and Orvieto. Orvieto Cathedral contains his greatest works, the frescoes of *The Preaching of Anti-Christ* and *Last Judgement* (1499–1504), which display his great technical skill in the drawing of male nudes. He was one of the painters summoned by Pope **Julius II** in 1508 to adorn the Vatican, but was dismissed in favour of **Raphael**.

Signoret, Simone, *originally* Simon-Henriette Charlotte Kaminker 1921–85
French actress

Born in Wiesbaden, Germany, and raised by her French parents in France, she left her job as a typist to become a film extra in *Le Prince Charmant* (1942) and soon achieved leading roles. Frequently cast as a prostitute or courtesan, her warmth and sensuality found international favour in such films as *La Ronde* (1950), *Casque d'Or* (1952, 'Golden Marie') and *Les Diaboliques* (1955, *Diabolique*). Her rare appearances in English-language productions included *Room at the Top* (1959, Academy Award) and *Ship of Fools* (1965). Unafraid to show her age, she matured into one of France's most distinguished character actresses, in films including *Le Chat* (1971, 'The Cat') and *Madame Rosa* (1977). Married to actor **Yves Montand** from 1951, she later turned to writing, completing an autobiography, *Nostalgia Isn't What It Used To Be* (1976), and a novel, *Adieu Volodia* (1985).

Sigurðsson, Jón 1811–79
Icelandic scholar and politician

Born in Hrafnseyri in the Westfjords, he was educated at the University of Copenhagen. As archivist of the Royal Norse Archaeological Society (1847–65) he published several editions of Icelandic sagas as well as authoritative works on the history and laws of Iceland. He led the movement to secure political autonomy and freedom of trade from Denmark. He persuaded King **Kristian IX** to restore the ancient Althing (parliament) as a consultative assembly, and sat as MP for the Westfjords from 1845. His independence campaign culminated in 1874 with the granting by Denmark of a constitution allowing limited self-government in domestic affairs. He is known as the father of Iceland's independence, and his birthday (17 June) was chosen as Iceland's National Day.

Sigurdsson, Sverrir See **Sverrir Sigurdsson**

Sigurjónsson, Jóhann 1880–1919
Icelandic dramatist and poet, pioneer of Icelandic theatre

Born in Laxamýri, he studied veterinary science in Copenhagen but turned to literature instead. He wrote simultaneously in Danish and Icelandic in order to gain a wider audience, and became the first Icelandic writer in modern times to achieve international recognition. His most successful plays used Icelandic folk-tale motifs, as in *Fjalla-Eyvindur* (1911, Eng trans *Eyvind of the Mountains*, 1911), which was made into the film *Berg Eyvind och hans hustru* (1917) by the Swedish director **Victor Sjöström**, and *Galdra-Loftur* (1914, Eng trans *The Wish*, 1967). His other plays are *Dr Rung* (1908), *Bónden á Hrauni* (1908, 'The Farmer at Hraun') and *Løgneren* (1917, 'The Liar'), based on a theme from *Njál's Saga*. He also wrote lyric poetry of touching sensitivity. 📖 H Toldberg, *Jóhann Sigurjónsson* (1965)

Sihanouk, Prince Norodom 1922–
Cambodian (Kampuchean) politician

Educated in Vietnam and Paris, he was elected King of Cambodia in 1941. He negotiated the country's independence from France (1949–53), before abdicating (1955) in favour of his father so as to become an elected leader under the new constitution. As Prime Minister and, after his father's death (1960), head of state, he steered a neutral course during the Vietnam War. In 1970 he was deposed in a right-wing military coup led by the US-backed lieutenant-general Lon Nol. Fleeing to Beijing (Peking), he formed a joint resistance front with **Pol Pot**, which successfully overthrew Lon Nol (1975). Prince Sihanouk was reappointed head of state but was ousted (1976) by the communist Khmer Rouge leadership. In 1982, while living in North Korea, he was elected head of a new broad-based Democratic Kampuchea (Cambodia) government-in-exile, which sought to overthrow the Vietnamese-installed puppet régime in Cambodia. After the withdrawal of Vietnamese troops (1989), he was elected king in 1993.

Sikandar Hayat Khan 1892–1942
Indian politician

From a rich landed family, he was educated in Aligarh, and at University College London. In World War I he was appointed an honorary recruiting officer and was granted a commission. During the third of the Afghan Wars he acted as a company commander (1919). He was elected to the Punjab legislative council (1921), and was appointed chairman of Punjab Reforms Committee to work with the Simon Commission. He was knighted in 1933 and was appointed Governor of the Reserve Bank in 1935. Elected Chief Minister of Punjab at the start of World War II, he launched rural reconstruction programmes, extended irrigation facilities, laid new roads, and established and strengthened panchayats. After his death the Punjab was plunged into political turmoil.

Sikorski, Władysław 1881–1943
Polish statesman and soldier

Born in Galicia, he joined the underground movement for Polish freedom from tsarist rule. He served under General Józef Piłsudski (1867–1935) as head of the war department, and after the treaty of Brest-Litovsk was imprisoned by the Austrians. In 1921 he became Commander-in-Chief and in 1922 was elected premier. After Piłsudski's coup d'état (1926) he retired to Paris. He returned to Poland in 1938 and advocated a strong alliance with Great Britain and France, but was refused a command when Poland was invaded. He became Commander-in-Chief of the Free Polish forces and leader in London of the Polish government in exile from June 1940. He signed a treaty with the Soviet Union in 1941 which annulled the Russo-German partition of Poland in 1939, but the discovery of Polish officers' graves at Katyn (1943) destroyed diplomatic relations between the two countries. He was killed in an air crash over Gibraltar. 📖 Roman Wapinski, *Władysław Sikorski* (1978)

Sikorsky, Igor Ivan 1889–1972
US aeronautical engineer

Born in Kiev, Ukraine, he began experimenting with building helicopters in 1909, and turned to aircraft, building and flying the first four-engined aeroplane in 1913. He emigrated to Paris (1918) and to the USA (1919), where he founded the Sikorsky Aero Engineering Corporation (1923), which was later merged into the United Aircraft Corporation. He built several flyingboats, including the *American Clipper*, and in 1939 he built the first successful helicopter, the VS-300. He became a US citizen in 1928. 📖 F J Delear, *Igor Sikorsky: His Three Careers in Aviation* (1969)

Silius Italicus, Tiberius Catius Asconius
AD25–101
Latin poet and politician

He was born in Patavium (Padua) and became a prominent orator in the Roman courts. He was consul in AD68, and then proconsul of Asia (AD77). He lived thereafter in retirement on his rich estates near Naples, and became a patron of literature and the arts. Having contracted an incurable disease, he starved himself to death. He was the author of the longest surviving Latin poem, *Punica*, an epic in 17 books on the 2nd Punic War. Most of our information about him comes from his contemporaries, Pliny the Younger and Martial. 📖 H M Butler, *Post Augustan Poets* (1926)

Sillanpää, Frans Eemil 1888–1964
Finnish novelist and Nobel Prize winner

He was born in Hämeenkyrö, of a peasant family, and the themes of his work reflect his background. His major books are *Hurskas kurjuus* (1919, 'Meek Heritage'), a novel about the Finnish civil war, *Nuorena nukkunut* (1931, Eng trans *The Maid Silja*, 1931), about the collapse of traditional values in Finland, and *Ihmiset suviyössä* (1934, 'People in the Summer Night'). He was the foremost Finnish writer of his time, and received the 1939 Nobel Prize for literature. In old age he became a much loved radio broadcaster. 📖 A Laurila, *F E Sillanpään Romaantaide* (1979)

Sillars, Jim (James) 1937–
Scottish nationalist politician

Born in Ayrshire and educated at Ayr Academy, he was a fireman by profession. He soon rose to prominence in his union, and entered parliament as Labour MP for South Ayrshire in 1970. In 1976 he left the Labour Party to form the Scottish Labour Party, which advocated greater self-government, but lost his seat in 1979. After winding up the party, he joined the Scottish National Party, and in the early 1980s was the leader of the left-wing element in the SNP's internal struggles. He returned to parliament as SNP candidate for Govan in 1988, but lost his seat in the 1992 general election. In 1993 he became assistant to the Secretary-General at the Arab–British Chamber of Commerce.

Silliman, Benjamin 1779–1864
US chemist

Born in Trumbull, Connecticut, he was admitted to the Bar in 1802, and became Professor of Chemistry at Yale and studied chemistry at Philadelphia, Edinburgh and London, specializing in electrolysis. He was founder (1818) and editor of the *American Journal of Science*.

Silliman, Benjamin 1816–85
US chemist

Born in New York City, he was the son of **Benjamin Silliman**. He became professor at Yale, assisted his father in his editorial work and showed that petroleum is a mixture of hydrocarbons, is different in character from vegetable oils, and can be separated by fractional distillation.

Sillitoe, Alan 1928–
English novelist and short-story writer

Born in Nottingham, he left school to work in a bicycle factory at the age of 14, and served as a wireless operator in the RAF (1946–49). He lived in France and Spain (1952–58), and began writing while convalescing from tuberculosis. He achieved a major success with his first novel, *Saturday Night and Sunday Morning* (1958), with its energetic young anti-hero, Arthur Seaton. The film based on the novel, for which he wrote the screenplay (1960), profoundly influenced the British film industry. The stories in *The Loneliness of the Long Distance Runner* (1959) were equally acclaimed. The outsider struggling in a brutal society is a recurring theme in his subsequent and more overtly political novels and stories, and the best of them echo the Midlands setting and gritty realism of his earlier books. They include *Key to the Door* (1962), *The Widower's Son* (1977), *Last Loves* (1991) and *Leonard's war* (1991). He has written plays and screenplays from his novels, several volumes of poems, plays and children's books and published his autobiography, *Life Without Armour*, in 1994. He married the writer Ruth Fainlight (1931–) in 1959.

Sills, Beverly, *originally* Belle Miriam Silverman
1929–
US soprano

Born in Brooklyn, New York, of Russian–Jewish descent, she had a varied and remarkable career as a child star and made her operatic debut in 1947. She later appeared with various US companies, including the New York City Opera (from 1955) and the Metropolitan Opera, as well as performing at Vienna and Buenos Aires (1967), La Scala in Milan (1969), Covent Garden, London, and the Deutsche Oper Berlin (1970). A musical, intelligent and dramatically gifted coloratura, she retired from the stage at the age of 50, to become general director of New York City Opera (1979–89) and chairwoman of Lincoln Center (1994–). She published her autobiography, *Beverly*, in 1987.

Silvers, Phil, *originally* Philip Silver 1912–85
US comic actor

Born in Brownsville, Brooklyn, New York, he made an early professional debut in 1925 as part of the *Gus Edwards Revue* in Philadelphia. He worked in vaudeville and also with the Minsky Burlesque Troupe (1934–39) before his Broadway debut in *Yokel Boy* (1939). After signing a contract with MGM, he appeared in supporting roles in films such as *Tom, Dick and Harry* (1941) and *Cover Girl* (1944). After World War II, he enjoyed notable Broadway hits with *High Button Shoes* (1947) and *Top Banana* (1951), for which he received a Tony Award. The television series *The Phil Silvers Show* (1955–59) earned him three Emmy Awards and established him irrevocably as Sergeant Bilko, 'a Machiavellian clown in uniform', forever pursuing get-rich-quick schemes with fast-talking bravado. He achieved further Broadway success in *Do Re Me* (1960) and *A Funny Thing Happened on the Way to the Forum* (1972, Tony Award). Latterly in poor health, he continued to make guest appearances on television and in increasingly inferior films. His autobiography, *The Laugh Is On Me*, was published in 1973.

Silvester, James Joseph See Sylvester, James Joseph

Silvia 1943–
Queen of Sweden

She was born in Heidelberg as Silvia Renate Sommerlath, the daughter of a West German businessman, Walther Sommerlath, and his Brazilian wife, Alice (*née* Soares de Toledo). She lived for many years in São Paulo, Brazil, where her father represented a Swedish company. In 1971 she was appointed chief hostess in the Organization Committee for the Olympic Games in Munich (1972), where she met Carl Gustaf (**Carl XVI Gustav**), who was then heir to the Swedish throne. They were married (1976) and have three children, Crown Princess Victoria (1977–), Prince Carl Philip (1979–), and Princess Madeleine (1982–).

Sim, Alastair 1900–76
Scottish actor

Born in Edinburgh and destined to follow in the family tailoring business, he was pulled elsewhere by his theatrical interests. He was a lecturer in elocution at Edinburgh University (1925–30) and made his professional stage debut in a London production of *Othello* (1930). Further stage work, including a season with the Old Vic, led to his film debut in *Riverside Murder* (1935). His lugubrious manner, distinctive features and inimitable vocal range made him a valued performer, equally at home in comic or sinister characterizations. His numerous films include *Green for Danger* (1946), *The Happiest Days of Your Life* (1950), *Scrooge* (1951), *Laughter in Paradise* (1951) and *The Belles of St. Trinians* (1954). On stage he enjoyed a long association with playwright James Bridie and appeared in *The Tempest* (1962), *Too True To Be Good* (1965), *The Magistrate* (1969) and *Dandy Dick* (1973) among many others.

Simak, Clifford Donald 1904–88
US science-fiction writer

He was born in Milville, Wisconsin, of an immigrant Czech father and a US mother. During the Depression he entered journalism in Michigan and then joined the Minneapolis *Star*, to which he contributed a weekly science column for the rest of his life. He started publishing science-fiction stories in 1931. His major work was the story sequence *City* (1952), a chronicle in which dogs and robots take over a world abandoned by humans. He also wrote *Way Station* (1962) and *All Flesh is Grass* (1965).

Sima Qian (Ssu-ma Ch'ien) c.145–87BC
Chinese historian

He succeeded his father, Sima Tan (Ssu-ma T'an), in 110BC as Grand Astrologer, but incurred Emperor Wudi's wrath for taking the part of a friend who, in command of a military expedition, had surrendered to the enemy. Sima Qian was imprisoned for three years and castrated, but was gradually restored to favour. He is chiefly remembered for the *Shi Ji*, the first history of China compiled as dynastic histories in which annals of the principal events are supplemented by princely and other biographies and notes on economic and institutional history.

Sima Xiangru (Ssu-ma Hsiang-ju) 179–117BC
Chinese poet

Born in Chengdu, Sichuan (Szechwan) province, he wrote the poem *Zi Xu Fu*, describing and denouncing the pleasures of the hunt, which hold an important place in Chinese literary history. 📖 Y Hervouet, *Un poète de cour sous les han* (1964)

Simenon, Georges Joseph Christian 1903–89
French novelist

He was born in Liège, Belgium, and at the age of 16 began work as a journalist on the *Gazette de Liège*. He moved to Paris in 1922 and became a prolific writer of popular fiction, writing under many pseudonyms. He also wrote more serious psychological novels, much-admired but neglected in favour of almost a hundred short, economical novels featuring Jules Maigret, the dogged pipe-smoking detective, now known the world over, partly through film and television adaptations. The first two in the series were published in 1931: *M. Gallet décède* (Eng trans *The Death of Monsieur Gallet*, 1932) and *Le Pendu de Saint-Pholien* (Eng trans *The Crime of Inspector Maigret*, 1933). In *Les Mémoires de Maigret* (1960, Eng trans *Maigret's Memoirs*, 1963), Maigret is ostensibly the author, describing his childhood and career, and with laboured humour displaying slight resentment at the liberties taken by his creator. Simenon published more than 500 novels and innumerable short stories; he told the *New Yorker*, 'I have no imagination; I take everything from life'. Autobiographical writings include *Quand j'étais vieux* (1970, Eng trans *When I Was Old*, 1971) and *Mémoires intimes* (1981, Eng trans *Intimate Memoirs*, 1984). 📖 B de Fallois, *Georges Simenon* (1961, in French)

Simeon, Charles 1759–1836
English evangelical clergyman

Born in Reading, Berkshire, he became a Fellow of King's College, Cambridge, and was appointed perpetual curate (1783–1836). A renowned preacher, he led the evangelical revival in the Church of England, and helped form the Church Missionary Society (1793).

Simeon Stylites, St AD387–459
Syrian Christian ascetic

Born in Sisan, Cilicia (near modern Aleppo, Syria), he lived for nine years without leaving his monastery cell, then became widely known as a miracle-worker. In c.420AD, he established himself on top of a pillar about 20m high in Telanessa, near Antioch, where he spent the rest of his life preaching to crowds. His many imitators were known as *stylites*. His feast day is 5 January (in western churches) or 1 September (in eastern churches).

Simmel, Georg 1858–1918
German sociologist and philosopher

Born in Berlin, he studied at Berlin University, where he became a lecturer in philosophy and ethics in 1885, and Professor of Sociology in 1900. In 1914 he was appointed to a chair in philosophy at Strasbourg. He was the principal representative of German sociological formalism, which emphasizes the form of a phenomenon rather than its nature or content. He was particularly concerned to encourage the growth of an independent sociology, and to define its boundaries with other disciplines. He also wrote extensively on philosophy, and his books include *Philosophy of Money* (1900, trans 1978), and a collection of essays published as *Georg Simmel: On Women, Sexuality and Love* (1984).

Simmonds, Kennedy Alphonse 1936–
St Christopher-Nevis politician and physician

He studied medicine at the University of the West Indies, worked in hospitals in Jamaica, the Bahamas and the USA, and returned to his native country in 1964 to establish his own practice. He entered politics and in 1965 founded the People's Action Movement (PAM) as a centre-right alternative to the Labour Party. After a series of unsuccessful elections, in 1980 Simmonds and PAM won enough seats in the Assembly to form a coalition government with the Nevis Reformation Party (NRP) and he became Prime Minister. Full independence was achieved in 1983 and his coalition was re-elected in 1984.

Simmons, Jean Merilyn 1929–
English actress

Born in London and educated at the Aida Foster School of Dancing, she made her film debut in *Give Us the Moon* (1944). She quickly rose to the forefront of young English actresses with accomplished performances as Estella in *Great Expectations* (1946) and Ophelia in **Laurence Olivier's** *Hamlet* (1948). She developed into a fine and beautiful actress; she signed a contract with **Howard Hughes** in Hollywood from 1951 but found few roles worthy of her abilities. Her best film work includes *The Actress* (1953), *Elmer Gantry* (1960) and *The Happy Ending* (1969), for which she received an Academy Award nomination. She continues to bring distinction to a range of television work and won an Emmy for *The Thorn Birds* (1983). Her rare stage appearances include *Big Fish, Little Fish* (1964) and *A Little Night Music* (1976). Later film appearances include *How to Make an American Quilt* (1995).

Simms, William Gilmore 1806–70
US novelist

Born in Charleston, West Virginia, he edited the *City Gazette* there and also published poetry, including *Lyrical and other Poems* (1827), *The Vision of Cortes* (1829), *The Tricolour* (1830) and *Atalantis* (1832). *The Yemassee* (1835), perhaps his best book, is a sympathetic account of Native Americans, a subject he returned to in the short stories collected in *The Wigwam and the Cabin* (1845–46) and *The Cassique of Kiawah* (1859). Despite his liberal sympathies, he was an apologist for slavery and the South. 📖 E W Parks, *William Gilmore Simms as Literary Critic* (1962)

Simnel, Lambert c.1477–c.1525
English pretender

The son of a joiner, he bore a resemblance to **Edward IV**, and was carefully coached (1487) by an Oxford priest, Roger Symonds, before being set up in Ireland as, first, the younger son of Edward IV, and then as the Duke of **Clarence's** son, Edward, Earl of Warwick (1475–99). Backed by Margaret of Burgundy, his supposed aunt, Simnel achieved some success in Ireland and was crowned in Dublin as Edward VI (1487), but, landing in

Lancashire with 2,000 German mercenaries, he was defeated at Stoke Field, Nottinghamshire (1487), and subsequently became a royal scullion and falconer.

Simon the Canaanite See **Simon the Zealot, St**

Simon the Zealot, St, *also called* Simon Zelotes and Simon the Canaanite 1st century AD
One of the 12 Apostles of Jesus Christ

Always mentioned among the last in lists of names of the Apostles, he may have belonged to the Jewish nationalist party (the Zealots) some time before 70AD. He is not mentioned in the New Testament although traditions associate him with Edessa as the place of his death. In Western traditions he preached in Egypt before joining St **Jude** in Persia (Iran) where both were martyred. The Feast of St Simon and St Jude is 28 October (in Western Churches) or 21 August (Greek Orthodox).

Simon, Carly 1945–
US composer and singer

Born in New York City, she began her career in 1964, recording with her sister Lucy as the Simon Sisters. She received a Grammy for Best New Artist in 1971, the year of her hit songs 'That's The Way I Always Heard It Should Be' and 'Anticipation'. Her single 'Let the River Run' for the 1988 film *Working Girl* won an Academy Award for best original song in 1989. Among her other singles are 'You're So Vain' and the James Bond film theme, 'Nobody Does It Better'. Her albums include *Carly Simon* (1971), *Anticipation* (1972) and *Letters Never Sent* (1994).

Simon, Claude Henri Eugène 1913–
French novelist and Nobel Prize winner

Born in Tananarive, Madagascar, the son of a cavalry officer who was killed during World War I, he was raised by his mother in Perpignan, France. He was educated at the Collège Stanislas, Paris, and briefly at Oxford and Cambridge universities, and studied painting before serving in the French cavalry. In World War II he joined the Resistance in Perpignan. Some align him with practitioners of the *nouveau roman* but he owes more to **Marcel Proust**, **Joseph Conrad**, **James Joyce** and **William Faulkner** than to his contemporary, **Albert Camus**. The absence of story, time and punctuation is his hallmark, and his style is rich, sensuous and complex. *Le Vent* (1957, Eng trans *The Wind*, 1959) and *La Route des Flandres* (1960, Eng trans *The Flanders Road*, 1962) are his most important novels, both eloquently expressing his innate pessimism. A more recent work is *L'Acacia* (1989, 'The Acacia'). In 1985 he was awarded the Nobel Prize for literature. 📖 R Jean, *La littérature et le réel* (1965)

Simon, Sir Francis Eugene 1893–1956
German physicist

Born in Berlin, he read physics (1912) at Munich University, and after World War I completed his doctorate with **Walther Nernst** on specific heats at low temperatures. By 1927 he was professor at the university in Berlin, and in 1931 was appointed director of the Physical Chemistry Laboratory at Breslau University. With the rise of Nazism he left Germany for Oxford at the invitation of Frederick Lindemann (Lord **Cherwell**). He became Reader in Thermodynamics in 1935 and succeeded Lindemann as Professor of Experimental Philosophy and director of the Clarendon laboratory. He verified experimentally the third law of thermodynamics, and under his guidance Oxford became one of the world's leading centres for the study of low-temperature physics. Involvement in the atomic energy and weapons project (1940–46) earned him a CBE (1946). He was elected FRS in 1941, and knighted in 1954.

Simon, Herbert Alexander 1916–
US economist and Nobel Prize winner

Born in Milwaukee, Wisconsin, he was educated at the University of Chicago. He has written on psychology and computers, as well as economics and political science, and was awarded the Nobel Prize for economics in 1978 for his 'pioneering research into the decision-making process in economic organization'. A university administrator as well as a scholar, he has held professorships at Illinois Institute of Technology (1946–49) and Carnegie-Mellon University (1949–). His publications include *Administrative Behavior* (1947), *Models of Man* (1957), *Human Problem Solving* (1972), *Reason in Human Affairs* (1983) and *Models of My Life* (1991). His other awards include one for lifetime contribution to psychology from the American Psychology Association.

Simon, Sir John 1816–1904
English surgeon and public-health reformer

Born in London, he trained for surgery through an apprenticeship and subsequently lectured in surgery and pathology at King's College Hospital and St Thomas's Hospital, London. He became the first medical officer of health for London (1848), and as chief medical officer to the General Board of Health (from 1855) combined his epidemiological and scientific skills with political sensitivity, to effect sweeping changes in public health practice in Great Britain. He demonstrated the advantages of compulsory smallpox vaccination, and influenced a succession of Parliamentary bills, culminating in the Public Health Act of 1875, which was one of the most comprehensive legislative health packages in the world. His account of *English Sanitary Institutions* (1890) is still a valuable historical source. He was knighted in 1887.

Simon, (Marvin) Neil 1927–
US dramatist

Born in New York City, and educated at New York University, he began by writing jokes for radio and television performers, and achieved a hit with his first comedy, *Come Blow Your Horn* (1961). His stage works include the musical farce *Little Me* (1962), *Barefoot in the Park* (1963), *The Odd Couple* (1965), *The Star-Spangled Girl* (1966) and the musical *Promises, Promises* (1968). *The Gingerbread Lady* (1970), a play about alcoholism, was not as enthusiastically received, but he persevered with serious themes, as in *The Prisoner of Second Avenue* (1972) and *The Sunshine Boys* (1972). Moving from New York to California he made another hit with *California Suite* (1976). *Chapter Two* opened in 1977, and in 1979 his fourth musical, *They're Playing Our Song*, gave him another hit. Later he produced a semi-autobiographical trilogy: *Brighton Beach Memoirs* (1983), *Biloxi Blues* (1985) and *Broadway Bound* (1986). Recent works include *Lost in Yonkers* (1991), which won him a Pulitzer Prize and a Tony Award, *Laughter on the 23rd Floor* (1993) and *London Suite* (1995). He is the only living US playwright to have had a Broadway theatre named after him. 📖 R Johnson, *Neil Simon* (1983)

Simon, Paul 1941–
US singer, songwriter and guitarist

He was born in Newark, New Jersey. One of the USA's finest pop lyricists, he had the most successful album of the early 1970s, as one half of the duo Simon and Garfunkel, with *Bridge Over Troubled Water* (1970). Simon originally worked with Art Garfunkel (1941–) at the age of 15 (when they were known as Tom and Gerry), but he also pursued a solo career under various pseudonyms, before 'The Sound Of Silence' (1965) brought the duo their first major success. In 1968, Simon's songs were used in the soundtrack of the film *The Graduate*, one of the first major films to incorporate rock music in this way. After separating from Garfunkel (1971), Simon returned to a solo career, taking songwriting classes in New York prior to releasing his album *Paul Simon* in 1972. Regular albums followed, the most successful of which were *There Goes Rhymin' Simon* (1973) and *Graceland* (1986), which featured the work of several South African musicians, and generated considerable controversy as well as large sales. A similar attempt to incorporate South American music in *The Rhythm of the Saints* (1990) was less well received. One of his film roles was in **Woody Allen's** *Annie Hall* (1977). 📖 P Humphries, *Paul Simon* (1990)

Simon, Richard 1638–1712
French theologian and biblical critic

Born in Dieppe, he entered the Oratory in 1659, lectured on philosophy, and catalogued the oriental manuscripts in the library of the order at Paris. His criticisms of **Antoine Arnauld** caused great displeasure among the Port-Royalists, and the scandal caused by the liberalism of his *Histoire critique du Vieux Testament* (1678, 'Critical History of the Old Testament'), in which he denied that **Moses** was the author of the Pentateuch, led to his expulsion from the order and retirement to Belleville as curé. In 1682 he resigned his parish and lived in literary retirement. Few writers of his age played a more prominent part in polemics. His *Histoire critique* (Eng trans 1682), suppressed through **Jacques Bossuet's** and the Jansenists' influence, often anticipates the later German rationalists, and is the first work to treat the Bible as a literary product.

Simone, Nina, *professional name of* Eunice Kathleen Waymon 1933–
US singer, pianist and composer

Born in Tryon, North Carolina, she was a gifted child pianist and her home town raised cash for her musical education at the Juilliard School in New York City, although she later claimed that her classical ambitions were frustrated by racist attitudes. She became a nightclub singer in Atlantic City and began writing her own highly charged and often overtly political material in the early 1960s. Her first hit was **George Gershwin's** 'I Loves You, Porgy' in 1959, but later songs such as 'Mississippi Goddam', a response to the race murder of children, were more typical. In the later 1960s Simone left the USA to live in Africa and then Europe. Though her subsequent career has been dogged by personal problems, she has enjoyed continued success, often boosted by use of her material on television commercials. 📖 N Simone and S Cleary, *I Put A Spell On You* (1991)

Simonides of Ceos 556–468BC
Greek lyric poet

Born on the island of Ceos, he travelled widely in the Greek world, and lived for many years in Athens as a guest of the tyrant Hipparchus. He celebrated the heroes and the battles of the Persian Wars in elegies, epigrams, odes and dirges. He won poetical contests 56 times, and his elegy on the heroes who fell at Marathon in 490BC was preferred to that of **Aeschylus**, who had fought in the battle. Many stories and anecdotes about him circulated in antiquity, and he was noted for a fondness for money. A handful of epigrams in the Greek Anthology are all that survive of his work. 📖 B Gentili, *Simonide* (1959)

Simon Magus, *known as* Simon the Magician
1st century AD
New Testament Samaritan sorcerer

According to the New Testament (Acts 8), he became influential in Samaria through his magic. He was converted by the preaching of Philip the Evangelist, and tried to buy the power of the Holy Spirit from **Peter** and **John** (hence the term 'simony'). The apocryphal Acts of Peter (2nd century AD) describe the rivalry between Simon Magus and Simon Peter. Later Christian authors claim that he went to Rome and became the author of heresies.

Simonov, Konstantin Mikhailovich 1915–79
Russian writer

Born in Petrograd (now St Petersburg), he worked as a metal-cutter as a teenager, and studied at evening classes in order to become a journalist. He was a war correspondent in Mongolia (1934–38), and much of his best writing came out of his experiences in World War II, including his novel about the defence of Stalingrad, *Dni i nochi* (1945, Eng trans *Days and Nights*, 1945). He achieved a considerable reputation with his historical poem about Alexander Nevsky, his poems of World War II, and the play *Russkye liudi* (1943, Eng trans *The Russians*, 1944). He was awarded the Stalin Prize three times. ▫ L Lazarev, *Dramaturgiye Konstantin Simonov* (1952)

Simpson, Bill 1931–86
Scottish actor

Born in Dunure, Ayrshire, he worked as an insurance clerk and served in the RAF, before winning a place at drama college in Glasgow. He then spent two years as an announcer with Scottish Television before playing a thief in *Z Cars*. His best-known work was in the title role of A J Cronin's *Dr Finlay's Casebook* (1962–71), in which he played for over 200 episodes. His subsequent television appearances included roles in *Scotch on the Rocks* (1972) and *The Good Companions* (1980).

Simpson, Sir George 1792–1860
Canadian explorer

Born in Scotland, he was administrator (1821–56) of the Hudson's Bay Company, and in 1828 made an overland journey round the world. Simpson's Falls and Cape George Simpson are named after him.

Simpson, Sir George Clarke 1878–1965
English meteorologist

Born in Derby, he became a lecturer at Manchester University (1905). He was Captain Robert Falcon Scott's meteorologist on the Antarctic expedition of 1910. He investigated the causes of lightning and was elected president of the Royal Meteorological Society (1940–42).

Simpson, George Gaylord 1902–84
US palaeontologist

Born in Chicago and educated at the universities of Colorado and Yale, he joined the staff of the American Museum of Natural History in New York City in 1927, and from 1959 to 1970 taught at Harvard. He is considered one of the leading 20th-century palaeontologists, and he proposed a classification of mammals which is now standard. Although mainly concerned with taxonomy, after World War II he devoted himself to demonstrating that the neo-Darwinian ideas of geneticists such as Ernst Mayr and Theodosius Dobzhansky could be reconciled with the palaeontological evidence. He was particularly concerned with the circumstances which gave rise to the evolution of new species. His influential books *Tempo and Mode in Evolution* (1944) and *The Major Features of Evolution* (1953) were concerned with the fusion of palaeontology and evolutionary genetics. Some of his ideas are presented in popular form in *The Meaning of Evolution* (1949).

Simpson, Helen de Guerry 1897–1940
British writer

Born in Sydney, Australia, she began by writing verse, a play, and a collection of fairy stories, and subsequently gained notice for her novel *Boomerang* (1932), which despite its title had little Australian content. Her historical novel *Under Capricorn* (1937), a story of Sydney in the early 1800s, was filmed by Alfred Hitchcock in 1949, and nine further novels followed, including *Saraband for Dead Lovers* (1935) which was also filmed, and three in collaboration with Clemence Dane. Other writings include

historical biographies, *The Spanish Marriage* (1933) and *Henry VIII* (1934), and a study of the English traveller Mary Henrietta Kingsley, *A Woman among Wild Men* (1938).

Simpson, Sir James Young 1811–70
Scottish obstetrician and pioneer of anaesthesia

Born in Bathgate, West Lothian, he went to Edinburgh University at the age of 14, studying arts and medicine, and becoming Professor of Midwifery in 1840. He originated the use of ether as an anaesthetic in childbirth (1847) and, experimenting on himself and his assistants in the search for a better anaesthetic, discovered the required properties in chloroform (November 1847). He championed its use against medical and religious opposition until its use on Queen Victoria at the birth of Prince Leopold II (1853) signalled general acceptance. He founded gynaecology through his rigorous procedures, championed hospital reform, and in 1847 became physician to the Queen in Scotland. He was made a baronet in 1866. ▫ Myrtle Simpson, *Simpson, the Obstetrician: A Biography* (1972)

Simpson, Myrtle Lillias, *née* Emslie 1931–
Scottish Arctic explorer, travel writer, mountaineer and long-distance skier

Born in Aldershot to Scottish parents, she was educated in many different places as her father was an army officer. She spent her early twenties climbing in New Zealand and Peru. In 1957 she married the medical researcher and explorer Dr Hugh Simpson, with whom she travelled Surinam and the Arctic. In 1965, as a member of the Scottish Trans-Greenland Expedition, she became the first woman to ski across the Greenland ice cap. In 1969 she attempted unsuccessfully to ski to the North Pole unsupported, hauling a sledge for 45 days and covering a distance of 90 miles from Ward Hunt Island. She nevertheless reached the most northerly point a woman had ever attained unsupported. She is the author of several books and has chaired the Scottish National Ski Council.

Simpson, O(renthal) J(ames) 1947–
US football player

He was born in San Francisco. He played for the University of Southern California in 1967 and 1968, winning the Heisman Trophy as the outstanding player in the major college conferences in the latter year. Turning professional, he played with the Buffalo Bills (1969–77) and San Francisco 49ers (1978–79). He combined blistering pace with an astute strategical appreciation of the game, and in 1973, playing with the Buffalo Bills, established a record of 2,003 yards gained in rushing. After retiring from football he became a popular commentator and film actor, appearing in *The Towering Inferno* (1974), *Naked Gun* (1988) and *Naked Gun 2½: The Smell of Fear* (1991). After the fatal stabbings of his former wife Nicole Brown Simpson and her friend Ronald Goldman in 1994, Simpson was charged with murder, and his televised trial became a media circus, which ended with his acquittal in 1995. The relatives of the victims brought a successful civil suit against him in 1996, charging him with unlawful death, and were awarded substantial damages, but he lodged an appeal against the decision. ▫ Larry Fox, *The O J Simpson Story: Born to Run* (1974)

Simpson, Robert Wilfred Levick 1921–97
English composer and writer on music

Born in Leamington Spa, Warwickshire, he studied with Herbert Howells and was for almost 30 years a BBC music producer in London, until 1980. His works include 11 symphonies, 15 string quartets, much other chamber music, and concertos for violin, piano, flute and cello. His work is basically tonal, and his orchestration is sure of colour and effect. Among his written work are important studies of

Carl Nielsen and Anton Bruckner: *Carl Nielsen, Symphonist* (1952) and *The Essence of Bruckner* (1966). He also wrote *The Proms and Natural Justice* (1981).

Simpson, Tom 1938–67
English cyclist

He was born in Easington, County Durham. In 1962 he became the first Briton ever to wear the leader's yellow jersey in the Tour de France. Known as 'Major Tom' to the French, he led the race for just one day. During the 1967 Tour de France he died from heart failure while riding the 13th stage, the climb of Mont Ventoux. A postmortem revealed traces of amphetamines in his blood. A memorial stone was built near the spot where he died.

Simpson, Wallis, Duchess of Windsor, *née* Bessie Wallis Warfield 1896–1986
US socialite, wife of Edward, Duke of Windsor

She was born in Blue Ridge Summit, Pennsylvania. She divorced her second husband, Ernest Simpson, in order to marry **Edward VIII**, who abdicated the throne (1936) to marry her (1937). Estranged from the British royal family, they lived in France and the Bahamas and were celebrities in the international social scene. After Edward's death she lived in Paris, virtually a recluse. She published her autobiography, *The Heart Has Its Reasons*, in 1956.

Sims, William Sowden 1858–1936
US naval officer

Born in Port Hope, Ontario, of US parents, he studied at the US Naval Academy, Annapolis, and became a gunnery specialist. He served in China during international action against the Boxer Rebellion (1900) and was a naval attaché in Paris and St Petersburg. He wrote a classic textbook on navigation, and improved US naval gunnery. He took part in Anglo-American action against the U-boat campaign as Commander of US Naval Forces in Europe, devising a convoy system to protect merchant shipping.

Sin, Jaime L 1928–
Philippine cardinal

He was born in New Washington, Aklan, and was ordained in 1954. After a period of missionary work, he served as Domestic Prelate to **Pope John XXIII** and became Archbishop of Jaro in 1972 and of Manila in 1974. He was created a cardinal in 1976. A significant figure in the Liberation Theology movement, he has expressed his concern for justice and human rights in several major works: *Revolution of Love* (1992), *The Church above Political Systems* (1973), *Christian Basis of Human Rights* (1978) and *Slaughter of the Innocents* (1979).

Sinatra, Frank (Francis Albert) 1915–98
US singer and film actor

Born in Hoboken, New Jersey, he started his long and successful career as a recording artist singing with the bands of Harry James and **Tommy Dorsey** on radio, becoming a teen idol. He made his film debut in musicals in 1941, leading to films such as *Anchors Aweigh* (1945) and *On The Town* (1949). His appeal declined, until he won an Academy Award as Best Supporting Actor for his role in *From Here to Eternity* (1953). This led to more film work, notably in *The Man With the Golden Arm* (1955), *Pal Joey* (1957), *The Manchurian Candidate* (1962) and *The Detective* (1968). His revival as an actor led to new singing opportunities, and he produced an impressive series of recordings (1956–65), notably the albums *For Swinging Lovers*, *Come Fly with Me* and *That's Life*. His fine musical phrasing and choice of material made him one of the best-selling recording artists of the 1950s and 1960s as well as a top concert performer into the 1990s. In a highly publicized private life, he was married on four occasions; his wives included **Ava Gardner** and **Mia Farrow**. 📖 Nancy Sinatra, *Frank Sinatra, My Father* (1985)

Sinclair, Sir Clive Marles 1940–
English electronic engineer and inventor

He was educated in Guildford and Reading, and attended St George's College, Weybridge. He worked for three years as a publisher's editor before launching his own electronics research and manufacturing company, Sinclair Radionics Ltd (1958), which developed and successfully marketed a wide range of calculators, miniature television sets and personal computers. He later embarked on the manufacture of a small three-wheeled 'personal transport' vehicle powered by a washing-machine motor and rechargeable batteries. It was widely condemned as unsafe and impractical, and its failure led to a period of retrenchment in Sinclair's business activities. In 1984 he won the Royal Society's Mullard Award. 📖 Rodney Dale, *The Sinclair Story* (1985)

Sinclair, Sir Keith 1922–93
New Zealand poet, biographer and historian

Born in Auckland and educated at Auckland University and the University of London, he won numerous prizes for history, notably the Walter Frewen Lord prize (1951) and the Ernest Scott prize (1958, 1961). He was Professor of History at Auckland University (1963–87) and edited the *New Zealand Journal of History* (1967–87). His books include the standard *A History of New Zealand* (1959, revised 1980 and 1993) and biographies of poet–politician **William Pember Reeves** (1965) and **Walter Nash** (1976). He also edited the *Oxford Illustrated History of New Zealand* (1990) and wrote six collections of verse. 📖 *Halfway Round the Harbour* (1993)

Sinclair, May (Mary Amelia) c.1865–1946
English novelist

Born in Rock Ferry, Cheshire, she was the daughter of a shipping magnate who became an alcoholic when faced with bankruptcy. She was educated at Cheltenham Ladies' College, and became an advocate of women's suffrage. She also took an interest in psychoanalysis, as revealed in some of her 24 novels. They include *The Divine Fire* (1904), *The Creators* (1910), *The Three Sisters* (1914, based on the **Brontë**s) and *The Dark Night* (1924). In *Mary Olivier* (1919), which is partly autobiographical, and *The Life and Death of Harriett Frean* (1922), she adopted the stream-of-consciousness style of writing. She also wrote books on philosophical idealism. 📖 H D Zegge, *May Sinclair* (1976)

Sinclair, Upton Beall 1878–1968
US novelist and social reformer

Born in Baltimore, Maryland, he horrified the world with his exposure of meat-packing conditions in Chicago in his novel *The Jungle* (1906), which resulted in the passing by Congress of a Pure Food and Drug Bill ('I aimed at the public's heart, and by accident I hit it in the stomach'). Later novels such as *Metropolis* (1908), *King Coal* (1917), *Oil!* (1927) and *Boston* (1928) were increasingly influenced by his socialist beliefs. He was for many years prominent in Californian politics and attempted to found a communistic colony in Englewood, New Jersey (1907). He also wrote a monumental 11-volume series about Lanny Budd, starting with *World's End* (1940) and including *Dragon's Teeth* (1942), which won the Pulitzer Prize. He also wrote two autobiographical works (1932, 1962) and *A World to Win* (1946). 📖 L Harris, *Upton Sinclair: American Rebel* (1975)

Sinden, Sir Donald 1923–
English actor

He was born in Plymouth and made his first appearance with the Mobile Entertainments Southern Area in 1941. After performing comedies on tour to the armed forces, he joined the Shakespeare Memorial Theatre company at Stratford-upon-Avon in 1946, and the Old Vic company in 1948. He alternated between classical roles with the Royal Shakespeare Company, such as Malvolio in *Twelfth*

Night (1969, 1970), and lightweight comedy in the West End, and in later years turned to farce. During the 1950s he appeared in films during a five-year period and for several seasons he played an English butler in the television comedy series *Two's Company*. His two volumes of autobiography are *A Touch of the Memoirs* (1982) and *Laughter in the Second Act* (1985). He was knighted in 1997.

Sinding, Christian 1856–1941
Norwegian composer
Born in Königsberg (now Kaliningrad, Russia), he studied in Germany, and wrote two violin concertos, a piano concerto and three symphonies, as well as chamber music and songs. He had two brothers; Otto (1842–1909) was a painter and Stephan (1846–1922) was a sculptor.

Singer, Isaac Bashevis 1904–91
US Yiddish writer and Nobel Prize winner
He was born in Radzymin, Poland, the son of a rabbi and the brother of Esther and **Israel Joshua Singer**. He was educated at the Tachkemoni Rabbinical Seminary in Warsaw (1920–22), and worked for 10 years as a proofreader and translator. He emigrated to the USA in 1935, where he joined his brother working as a journalist for the *Jewish Daily Forward*. A firm believer in storytelling rather than commentary by the author, he set his novels and short stories among the Jews of Poland, Germany and the USA, combining a deep psychological insight with dramatic and visual impact. He was awarded the Nobel Prize for literature in 1978. His novels include *The Family Moskat* (1950), *The Magician of Lublin* (1960), *The Manor* (1967), *The Estate* (1970) and *Enemies: A Love Story* (1972). Among his short stories are *Gimpel the Fool and Other Stories* (1957), *The Séance* (1968), and *A Crown of Feathers* (1973). He also wrote a play, *Schlemiel the First* (1974), and many stories for children. He wrote his autobiography, *In My Father's Court*, in 1966 and his *Collected Stories* were published in 1981.
📖 C Sinclair, *The Brothers Singer* (1987)

Singer, Isaac Merritt 1811–75
US inventor and manufacturer
Born in Pittstown, New York, he patented a rock drill in 1839, a carving machine in 1849 and at Boston in 1852 an improved single-thread, chain-stitch sewing machine. He was sued by **Elias Howe** for infringement of patent for the so-called 'Howe needle', but despite having to pay compensation he established the success of his Singer Manufacturing Company.

Singer, Israel Joshua 1893–1944
US Yiddish writer
Born in Bilgorai, Poland, the brother of Esther and **Isaac Bashevis Singer**, he studied at the Rabbinical Yeshivah School in Warsaw, and after World War I became a journalist in Kiev. He became foreign correspondent in Warsaw for the New York *Jewish Daily Forward*, for which he continued to write after emigrating to the USA in 1933. His novels have been widely translated, and include *Yoshe Kalt* (1933, Eng trans *The Sinner*), *The Brothers Ashkenazi* (1936), *The River Breaks Up* (1938) and *East of Eden* (1939).
📖 C Sinclair, *The Brothers Singer* (1987)

Singh, V(ishwanath) P(ratap) 1931–
Indian statesman
Born in Allahabad, Uttar Pradesh, the son of an influential local raja, he was educated at Poona and Allahabad universities. In 1971 he was elected to the Lok Sabha (federal parliament) as a representative of the Congress (I) Party. During the administrations of **Indira Gandhi** and **Rajiv Gandhi**, he served as Minister of Commerce (1976–77, 1983), Chief Minister of Uttar Pradesh (1980–82), Minister of Finance (1984–86) and Minister of Defence (1986–87), instigating a zealous anti-corruption drive in the Finance and Defence posts. In 1987 he was ousted from the government and Congress (I) when he exposed

the 'Bofors scandal', which involved payments for arms deals to senior officials closely connected with Rajiv Gandhi. Respected for his probity and sense of principle, as head of the broad-based Janata Dal coalition he emerged as the most popular Opposition politician in India. He was elected Prime Minister in 1990, but in November he was defeated on a vote of confidence and succeeded by Chandra Shekar.

Siqueiros, David Alfaro 1896–1974
Mexican mural painter
Born in Chihuahua, he was a revolutionary from youth and fought in **Francisco Madero's** revolution of 1910–11 which overthrew **Porfirio Díaz**. With **Diego Rivera** and **José Orozco**, he launched the review *El Machete* in Mexico City in 1922, and painted the frescoes for the National Preparatory School there. An active trade unionist, he was frequently imprisoned for revolutionary activities. He was expelled from the USA in 1932 after founding the Experimental Workshop in New York City, and during the 1930s he worked in South America. In 1944 he founded the Centre of Realist Art in Mexico City. One of the principal figures in 20th-century Mexican mural painting, he is noted for his experiments in the use of modern synthetic materials. His most celebrated works include *From Porfirio's Dictatorship to the Revolution* (National History Museum), and *March of Humanity* (Hotel de Mexico).

Siraj-ud-Dawlah See **Suraja Dowlah**

Sirani, Elisabetta 1638–65
Italian artist
Born in Bologna, she learned to paint in the workshop of her father Gian Andrea, and by the age of 19 was recognized to have exceptional talent. In 1664 Cosimo, Crown Prince of Tuscany, visited Bologna and after watching her paint a portrait of his uncle, Prince Leopold, he commissioned a Madonna for himself. She also painted the *Baptism of Christ* for the Church of the Certosini at Bologna and executed many highly regarded etchings of biblical subjects before her sudden death, perhaps from poisoning, at the age of 27.

Sirhan, Sirhan c.1943–
US assassin of Senator Robert Kennedy
Born in Palestine, he was a refugee whose family settled in Pasadena, California, in 1956. Sirhan was angered by the pro-Israeli stand taken by Robert Kennedy in his campaign for the Presidential nomination in 1968. On the night of 5 June 1968 he shot Kennedy in the head as the senator passed through the Ambassador Hotel in Los Angeles on his way to a victory press conference. He was found guilty of pre-meditated murder of the first degree and the death penalty was recommended; however, Senator **Edward Kennedy's** plea for leniency led to this sentence being commuted to life imprisonment.

Sisley, Alfred 1839–99
French Impressionist painter and etcher
Born in Paris of English ancestry, he joined **Camille Monet** and **Renoir** in the studio of **Charles Gleyre** and was also influenced by **Camille Corot**. He painted mostly landscapes, particularly in the valleys of the Seine, the Loire and the Thames, and was noted for his subtle treatment of skies. 📖 Raymond Cogniat, *Sisley* (1978)

Sisulu, Walter Max Ulyate 1912–
South African nationalist
He was born in Transkei. After working as a labourer in Johannesburg and then running a real estate agency, he joined the ANC in 1940, becoming Treasurer of the Youth League in 1944. A leader of the Programme of Action in 1949, he was elected Secretary-General of the ANC in the same year. He resigned his post in 1954 because of

banning orders, but continued to work underground. Captured in 1963, he was found guilty of treason, and sentenced to life imprisonment (1964). He was released in 1989 and took responsibility for the party's internal organization after its legalization in 1990, becoming deputy president of the ANC in 1991. His wife Nontsikelelo Albertina (1919–) was also placed under house arrest on several occasions for her ANC activities, and in 1984 was jailed for three years. In 1989 she led a delegation of the United Democratic Front, of which she is president, to the USA and Britain.

Sithole, Reverend Ndabaningi 1920–
Zimbabwean clergyman and politician
He was a prominent member of the National Democratic Party and the Zimbabwe African People's Union (ZAPU) before becoming President of the Zimbabwean African National Union (ZANU) in 1963. With Abel Muzorewa, he was regarded as one of the more moderate advocates of independence based on majority rule and in 1978 was party to an agreement with Prime Minister Ian Smith for an internal constitutional settlement. This was, however, rejected as insufficient by the two nationalist leaders, Robert Mugabe and Joshua Nkomo, and by the United Nations. When an internationally accepted settlement was achieved in 1979, Sithole's power and influence declined. In 1995 he was arrested in connection with an alleged plot to assassinate Mugabe, but many considered this to be a conspiracy to remove Mugabe's competition.

Sitsky, Larry 1934–
Australian composer, pianist and teacher
He was born of Russian parents in Tientsin, northern China, where he made his piano debut at the age of 11. He emigrated to Australia in 1951 and attended the New South Wales Conservatorium of Music until 1955, studying composition with Raymond Hanson, and later studied at Oxford and at the San Francisco Conservatorium, California, under Egon Petri. Returning to Australia, he held various teaching positions before becoming head of composition in 1978. He is a prolific writer in many genres, and his vocal compositions include *Fall of the House of Usher* (1965), *Fiery Tales* (1975), *Lenz* (1970) and *The Golem* (1979), all to libretti by Gwen Harwood. Orchestral and instrumental works include *Concerto for Wind Quintet and Orchestra* (1971), a Concerto for Violin, Orchestra and Female Voices (1971), and *Twenty-two Paths of the Tarot: concerto for piano and orchestra* (1991). His second violin concerto (1978) subtitled *Gurdjieff*, is in seven movements with a cadenza to the fourth movement utilizing Georgei Gurdjieff's 'Law of Four and Three'. Later works include a third violin concerto and *Sphinx: concerto for cello and orchestra* (1993). A specialist in the music of Ferruccio Busoni, Sitsky has published *Busoni and the Piano* (1986) and *Music of the Repressed Russian Avant-Garde* (1993).

Sitter, Willem de 1872–1934
Dutch astronomer and cosmologist
Born in Sneek, Friesland, he studied mathematics at the University of Groningen, but later became an astronomer at Cape Town Observatory. He returned to Groningen working as assistant to Jacobus Kapteyn, was appointed director and Professor of Astronomy at the University of Leyden in 1908, and from 1919 was also director of the observatory there. He studied the distributions and motions of stars, and the satellites of Jupiter. His interest in Einstein's theory of general relativity led to its publicity in Great Britain and other English-speaking countries, with important consequences for cosmology. Einstein had produced a description of a static universe with curved space ('matter with no motion'), but de Sitter demonstrated that an expanding universe of constantly decreasing curvature was another possible solution ('motion with no matter'). Edwin Hubble's discovery of the recession of distant galaxies added great weight to this theory. Later modifications produced a much simpler description known as the Einstein–de Sitter universe.

Sitting Bull, *Indian name* Tatanka Iyotake c.1834–90
Native American warrior, Chief of the Dakota Sioux
Born near Grand River, South Dakota, he was a leader in the Sioux War (1876–77), and led the massacre of General Custer and his men at the Little Big Horn (1876). He escaped to Canada but surrendered in 1881, and was put into the reservation at Standing Rock. He was featured in Buffalo Bill Cody's Wild West Show (1885), and was killed attempting to evade the police in the Ghost Dance uprising (1890). 📖 Stanley Vestal, *Sitting Bull, Champion of the Sioux* (1932)

Sitwell, Dame Edith Louisa 1887–1964
English poet
Born in Scarborough, Yorkshire, she was the sister of Osbert and Sacheverell Sitwell. She had an unhappy childhood until her governess introduced her to music and literature, in particular the poetry of Algernon Charles Swinburne and the Symbolists. She first attracted notice when she edited an anthology of new poetry, *Wheels* (1916–21), and the first volume of her own poetry, *Façade* (1923), with William Walton's music, was given a controversial public reading in London. It was followed by *Bucolic Comedies* (1923), *The Sleeping Beauty* (1924) and *Elegy for Dead Fashion* (1926), the last two written in an elegiac romantic style. The short poems of this romantic period are 'Colonel Fantock', 'Daphne', 'The Strawberry' and 'The Little Ghost who died for Love'. During World War II she denounced human cruelty in *Street Songs* (1942), *Green Song* (1944) and *The Song of the Cold* (1945). Other works include *The English Eccentrics* (1933), *Victoria of England* (1936), *Fanfare of Elizabeth* (1946) and *The Queens and the Hive* (1962). Her autobiography, *Taken Care Of*, was published posthumously in 1965. 📖 V Glendinning, *A Lion among the Unicorns* (1981)

Sitwell, Sir (Francis) Osbert 1892–1969
English writer
Born in London, the brother of Edith and Sacheverell Sitwell, he was educated at Eton. He served in the Brigade of Guards during World War I, and in 1916 was invalided home. This provided him with the opportunity to satirize war and the types of people who prosper ingloriously at home. Many of his satirical poems were collected in *Argonaut and Juggernaut* (1919) and *Out of the Flame* (1923). After the war he narrowed his literary acquaintance to his sister and brother, Ezra Pound, T S Eliot and Wyndham Lewis. The object of the group was the regeneration of arts and letters, and in this pursuit the Sitwells acquired notoriety, Osbert not least by his novel *Before the Bombardment* (1927), which anatomized the grandees of Scarborough and by implication the social orders in general. Neither this nor his other novel, *Miracle on Sinai* (1933), was successful, and his strength was always in short stories, especially those, like the collection *Dumb Animal* (1930), in which his delicacy of observation and natural compassion are more in evidence than his satire. He also wrote travel books, including *Winters of Content* (1932), and is best known for his five-volume autobiographical series, which begins with *Left Hand: Right Hand* (1944). Other collections of essays and stories include *Penny Foolish* (1935), *Sing High, Sing Low* (1944), *Alive-Alive Oh* (1947) and *Pound Wise* (1963). 📖 J Lehman, *A Nest of Tigers* (1968)

Sitwell, Sacheverell 1897–1988
English writer and art critic
Born in Scarborough, North Yorkshire, the younger brother of Edith and Osbert Sitwell, he was educated at Eton, before becoming an officer in a Guards regiment,

enjoying extensive travel abroad. After World War I the brothers toured Spain and Italy. Italy became their second country, resulting in Sacheverell's *Southern Baroque Art* (1924), followed by *The Gothic North* (1929). His *German Baroque Art* (1927) completed his study of European art. A prolific writer, he published poetry, and is best remembered for his mannered but lively travel books and eccentric cultural commentaries, such as *Monks, Nuns and Monasteries* (1965). His reminiscences also attracted some attention. ▢ J Lehmann, *A Nest of Tigers* (1968)

Sixtus
Name assumed by five popes
Sixtus I was beheaded c.125AD; II was martyred in 258; III was pope (432–440) when St **Patrick** began his mission in Ireland.

Sixtus IV, *originally* Francesco della Rovere 1414–84
Italian pope
Born in Cella Ligura, Genoa, he was a famous Franciscan preacher. He became a cardinal in 1467 and pope in 1471. His nepotism led to many abuses, and he is said to have connived at the Pazzi conspiracy against the **Medici** at Florence, which was engineered by his nephew, the future **Julius II**. Although he fostered learning and built the Sistine Chapel and the Sistine Bridge, he compromised the moral authority of the papacy. His alliance with the Venetians in 1482 led to a general Italian war.

Sixtus V, *originally* Felice Peretti 1521–90
Italian pope
He was born in Grottammare, Ancona. A Franciscan preacher, and a professor of theology, he was made a cardinal in 1570. Although he was elected for his apparent feebleness (1585), his rule was characterized by vigorous reform. He repressed licence and disorder, reformed the administration of the law and the disposal of patronage, and secured a surplus for the treasury. His foreign policy sought to maintain the balance of the Catholic powers and to combat Protestantism, and, he extended a measure of liberty to the Jews. He also instigated the building of the Vatican Library at the Lateran Palace.

Sjöström, Victor 1879–1960
Swedish actor and film director
Born in Silbodal, Sweden, and trained as an actor, he joined the expanding film company Svenska Bio (1912). He worked as both actor (often under **Mauritz Stiller**'s direction) and director, his notable successes including *Ingeborg Holm* (1913), *Terje Vigen* (1917, *A Man There Was*, based on **Ibsen**'s poem) and above all *Körkarlen* (1920, *The Phantom Carriage*). His ability to adapt classic Swedish writers, above all **Selma Lagerlöf**, to the screen gave Swedish cinema popular appeal. He later worked in Hollywood (1923–30, using the name Seastrom) and made a **Lon Chaney** film, *He who gets slapped* (1924) and two masterpieces, *The Scarlet Letter* (1926) and *The Wind* (1928), with **Lillian Gish**. As a director he did not adapt well to sound cinema and directed only two films after returning to Sweden. As an actor, however, he created several memorable parts, notably as Knut Borg in Molander's *The Word* (1943) and as Professor Borg in *Wild Strawberries* (1957), an egocentric academically successful old doctor forced to admit his failure in human relationships.

Skalkottas, Nikolaos 1904–49
Greek composer
Born in Chalkis on the Greek island of Euboea, he studied at the Athens Conservatory (1914–20) and was a pupil of **Kurt Weill** and **Arnold Schoenberg** in Berlin. He returned to Greece in 1933 and was a notable and individual exponent of the twelve-note technique. He collected Greek folk music, which he used in his own work. Most of his music was ignored in his lifetime.

Skallagrímsson, Egil (I) c.910–990
Icelandic skaldic poet and warrior
He was born on the farm of Borg in Iceland. His father had emigrated to Iceland from Norway, and Egil became a Viking warrior and court-poet. He fought for King **Athelstan** of England at the Battle of Brunanburh (937), fell out with King **Erik** 'Blood-Axe' **Haraldsson** of Norway, but visited him in York in 948, and escaped execution by composing in Erik's honour a eulogy called the *Höfuðlausn* ('Head Ransom'). In 960 he lost two young sons, and composed the greatest lament in Old Icelandic poetry, *Sonatorrek* ('On the Loss of Sons'). His other major verse-sequence was *Arinbjarnarkvíða* ('The Lay of Arinbjörn'). Egil is the eponymous hero of the Icelandic *Egils saga*, probably written by his descendant, **Snorri Sturluson**, which also contains more than 40 occasional verses ascribed to him. ▢ H Palsson and P Edwards, introduction to *Egil's Saga* (1976)

Skanderbeg, *originally* George Castriota or Kastrioti, *also known as* Iskander Bey c.1403–68
Albanian national hero
The son of a prince of Emathia, he was taken hostage by Turks at the age of seven and brought up as a Muslim. He became a favourite commander of Sultan Murad II. In 1443 he changed sides, renounced Islam, and drove the Turks from Albania, where he valiantly defeated every force sent against him. For 20 years he maintained the independence of Albania with only occasional support from Naples, Venice and the pope. After his death, however, Albanian opposition to the Turks collapsed.

Skeat, Walter William 1835–1912
English philologist
Born in London and educated at King's College School and Christ's College, Cambridge, he became a Fellow in 1860 and in 1878 Professor of Anglo-Saxon. He was founder and first director of the Dialect Society (1873), and he contributed more than any scholar of his time to a sound knowledge of Middle English and English philology generally. He edited several important texts, notably *Piers Plowman* (1867–85). Other works include *A Moeso-Gothic Glossary* (1868), *Etymological English Dictionary* (1879–82), *Principles of English Etymology* (1887–91), *Chaucer* (6 vols, 1894–95), the *Student's Chaucer* (1895), *A Student's Pastime* (1896), *Chaucerian and other Pieces* (1897), *The Chaucer Canon* (1900), *Glossary of Tudor and Stuart Words* (1914), and papers on place names.

Skelton, John c.1460–1529
English satirical poet
Born in Norfolk, he studied at Oxford and Cambridge, and was created 'poet laureate' by both. Later he was tutor to Prince Henry (the future **Henry VIII**), took holy orders in 1498, and became rector of Diss in 1502, but seems to have been suspended in 1511 for having a mistress or wife. He produced translations and elegies in 1489, and became known for his satirical vernacular poetry, including the allegorical poem *The Bowge of Courte*, *Colyn Cloute*, on corruptions of the Church, and *Why come ye nat to Courte*, an invective against **Thomas Wolsey**, for which Skelton had to take sanctuary at Westminster. Other works include *The Boke of Phyllyp Sparowe* and *The Tunnyng of Elynour Rummynge*. ▢ C J Lloyd, *John Skelton* (1938)

Skinner, Burrhus Frederic 1904–90
US psychologist
Born in Susquehanna, Pennsylvania, he was educated first at Hamilton College and then at Harvard, where he taught for many years (1931–36 and 1947–74). He also taught at Minnesota University (1936–45). He was the most consistent and radical proponent of Behaviourism, developing and refining the ideas of **John Broadus Watson**, who advocated the study of behaviour as the

only possible road for a scientific psychology to travel. He invented the 'Skinner Box', a chamber containing mechanisms for an animal to operate and an automatic device for presenting rewards, as a contribution to the study of animal behaviour. In education, his ideas led to the development and proliferation of 'programmed learning', a technique which seeks to direct teaching to the needs of each individual and to reinforce learning by regular and immediate feedback. He has also written fiction, autobiography, and philosophy. His honours include the Distinguished Scientific Contribution award (1958), the Gold Medal of the American Psychological Association (1971) and the National Medal of Science (1968). 📖 Richard I Evans, *Skinner* (1968)

Skinner, James 1778–1841
Indian soldier

Of Eurasian origin, he joined the army at the age of 15, was promoted to lieutenant for gallantry, but was dismissed by General Perron in 1803 because of his mixed origin. Under General Lord Lake, he formed Skinner's Horse, one of the most famous regiments in India. With the fabulous wealth of 30 years' looting, and several wives, he settled down to the life of a rich Mogul in his town house at Delhi and his country seat nearby. Always inclined to scholarship and philanthropy, he wrote books in flawless Persian, with decorations and numerous paintings by local artists, on the princes, castes and tribes of Hindustan. He also built a mosque, a temple, and the Church of St James in Delhi.

Skinner, James Scott, *called* the Strathspey King
1843–1927
Scottish fiddler and composer

He was born in Banchory, Kincardineshire, and as a child learned the rudiments of Scots music and also received classical tuition. At the age of 19 he was able to outplay many leading Scots fiddlers in a national competition, moving the judge to say: 'Gentlemen, we have never before heard the like of this from a beardless boy'. His virtuoso playing continued to impress audiences during his long career as a concert performer both in Great Britain and the USA. Several recordings, made when he was probably past his peak, are available. Of his many compositions, the most popular are 'The Bonnie Lass o' Bon-Accord', 'The Laird o' Drumblair' and 'The Miller o' Hirn'.

Skoblikova, Lidiya Pavlovna 1939–
Soviet speed-skater

She was born in Zlatoust, near Chelyabinsk. The most decorated female Olympian of all time, in 1960 she won the 3,000 metres and 1,500 metres titles at the Olympics, setting a world record for the 1,500 metres which she improved upon in 1964, the year she accomplished a clean sweep of titles over every distance (500m, 1000m, 1500m, 3000m) and claimed four further gold medals. This performance made her the first woman ever to achieve the Olympic 'Grand Slam' and she set three Olympic records in the process: at 500 metres, 1,000 metres and at 1,500 metres. She also won world championship titles in 1963 and 1964.

Skobtsova, Maria 1891–1945
Russian Orthodox nun

Born in Riga, she was the first woman to enrol at the Ecclesiastical Academy, St Petersburg. As a student she identified herself with the Social Revolutionaries, but became disillusioned by Bolshevik excesses and was among those who escaped to France. She began work with the Russian Orthodox Student Christian Movement which administered also to refugees, and in 1932, despite having been divorced twice, became a nun. Unconventional and radical, she worked to feed and house those rejected by society. During World War II she

worked with the Jews in Paris, and in 1943 she was arrested and sent to Ravensbrück concentration camp, where she brought Christian light and hope despite appalling conditions. She was gassed on the eve of Easter in 1945, reportedly going voluntarily 'in order to help her companions to die'.

Skoda, Joseph 1805–81
Austrian physician

Born in Plzeň, Bohemia (now the Czech Republic), he studied first theology and then natural sciences and medicine, receiving his MD from Vienna University in 1831. He worked for almost all of his career at the General Hospital in Vienna, where he was particularly concerned with the use of the stethoscope, which had been invented by René Laënnec, in understanding diseases of the heart and lungs. He worked closely with the pathologist Karl von Rokitansky, and between them they raised the medical school in Vienna to an institution of international standing. Skoda was extremely sceptical about the effectiveness of the remedies routinely used by his contemporaries.

Skorzeny, Otto 1908–75
Austrian soldier

He was born in Vienna. Noted for his commando-style operations during World War II, he was selected by Hitler to kidnap Mussolini from internment in a mountain hotel on the Gran Sasso range, a mission which he achieved in September 1943. In September 1944 he abducted Miklós Horthy, Regent of Hungary, and forcibly prevented him from making a separate peace with Stalin. He failed to capture Tito, but during the Ardennes offensive in December 1944 he carried out widespread sabotage behind Allied lines, for which he was tried as a war criminal but acquitted (1947).

Skram, (Bertha) Amalie, *née* Alver 1847–1905
Norwegian novelist

She was born in Bergen, whose commercial life was the main setting for her work, and after divorcing her first husband in 1878 she worked as a critic and short-story writer. In 1884 she married Erik Skram, a Danish writer, and thereafter wrote a collection of novels in which she explored women's issues, and marriage in particular. Her best-known works include *Constance Ring* (1885, Eng trans 1988), the tetralogy *Hellemyrsfolket* (1887–98, 'The People at Hellemyr'), and *Forraadt* (1892, Eng trans *Betrayed*, 1987). She was divorced from Skram in 1900, and suffered a breakdown in mental health, which ironically reflected the plight she had described in *Professor Hieronimus* (1895, Eng trans 1899) and *På St Jørgen* (1895, 'At St Jørgen's'). 📖 I Engelstad, *Amalie Skram* (1978)

Skriabin, Aleksandr Nikolayevich See Seriabin, Aleksandr Nikolayevich

Skum, Nils Nilsson 1872–1951
Lappish artist

Born into a nomadic Sami family of reindeer hunters, he was the first of his people to draw pictures, using the traditional inspiration of Sami craftwork. His paintings form one of the first comprehensive studies of traditional Sami life.

Sky, Alison 1946–
US architect

She trained at Adelphi and Columbia universities in New York before founding SITE, a group which is renowned for radical ideas and prefers their work to be called 'De-Architecture'. They transform the conventions of society into a form of public art by strengthening the relationship between architecture and art. One of the group's major clients is the discount sales company BEST, which has commissioned several retail outlets, giving SITE widespread publicity. The showrooms have brick façades that peel away at the edges, have holes punched through them, and appear to defy gravity.

Slade, Felix 1790–1868
English antiquary and art collector

Born in Halsteads, Yorkshire, he bequeathed his engravings and Venetian glass to the British Museum, and endowed professorships in art at Oxford and Cambridge. He also founded the Slade School of Art in London.

Slaney, Mary Tereza Decker, *née* Decker 1958–
US athlete

Born in New Jersey, she was acclaimed as the 'Golden girl' of US athletics, and set world records for the mile and the 5,000 metres in 1982. She followed this by winning the gold medals in the 3,000 metres and 1,500 metres at the world championships in Helsinki. Frequently in the news, she spoke out against the USA's boycott of the 1980 Moscow Olympics. She is also remembered for her collision with **Zola Budd** (now Zola Pieterse) in the 3,000 metres at the Los Angeles Olympics in 1984, which put her out of the race.

Slánský, Rudolf 1901–52
Czechoslovak politician

He was born in Moravia. An intellectual, he joined the Communist Party when it was founded in 1921 and, in 1929, became one of **Klement Gottwald's** chief aides in revolutionizing or 'bolshevizing' it. He spent much of World War II in Moscow and in 1944 was flown in to Slovakia to assist the Slovak uprising. As Secretary-General of the Communist Party (1945–51), he masterminded much of what produced and followed the February Revolution in 1948. He was arrested and executed during the Stalinist purges.

Slater, Jim (James Derrick) 1929–
English financier and writer

Born in the Wirral, Cheshire, he was educated at Preston Manor County School. He entered industry as an accountant, later moving into management, becoming director of AEC Ltd in 1959, and deputy sales director of Leyland Motor Group in 1963. In 1964 he and his associates launched Slater Walker Securities, of which he was chairman and managing director, and later chief executive, until his resignation in 1975. After a rapid decline in his fortunes, he turned to writing, beginning with an autobiography, *Return to Go* (1977), followed by a number of books for children, including the *Goldenrod* and *Grasshopper* books, and the *Roger the Robot* series. In 1983 he became chairman of Salar Properties, which deals partly in timeshares for rights to fish Scotland's salmon rivers, and of Parentcare in 1988. His publications include *Modern Television Systems* (1991), *The Zulu Principle* (1992) and *Pep Up Your Wealth* (1994).

Slater, Samuel 1768–1835
US mechanical engineer

Born in Belper, Derbyshire, England, he was apprenticed to Jedediah Strutt, and gained a detailed knowledge of the most advanced textile machinery and its operation. At the time the textile industry in the USA was offering bounties to skilled mechanics from Europe. Despite a British ban on the emigration of textile workers, Slater sailed from England in 1789 in disguise. Blessed with a photographic memory, he was able within a year to build up-to-date spinning machines for a struggling cotton mill in Rhode Island, becoming a partner in the firm of Almy, Brown & Slater, whose prosperity laid the foundation for the success of the US cotton industry.

Sleep, Wayne 1948–
English dancer and choreographer

Born in Plymouth, he studied tap dancing and ballet as a child, joining the Royal Ballet School at the age of 12 and graduating into the company itself in 1966. Promoted to principal dancer in 1973, his small stature, extrovert personality and technical prowess led to leading roles in such ballets as **Frederick Ashton's** *A Month in the Country* (1976) and **Kenneth MacMillan's** *Manon* (1974). He also works on the musical stage, cinema and television, and he appeared as Squirrel Nutkin and one of the Bad Mice in the 1971 film *Tales of Beatrix Potter* (choreography by Ashton) and in the original production of *Cats* (1981). In 1980 he formed his own touring group, Dash, and later adapted his series *The Hot Shoe Show* (1983–84) into a fast-paced, eclectic live revue. He danced in and jointly choreographed the stage show *Bits and Pieces* in 1989 and has published *Variations on Wayne Sleep* (1983).

Slessor, Sir John Cotesworth 1897–1979
British air-marshal

Born in Rhanikhet, India, he was educated at Haileybury. He served in the Royal Flying Corps in World War I and was awarded the MC. He was instructor at the RAF Staff College (1924–25) and at Camberley (1931–34). His part in the Waziristan operations (1936–37) earned him the DSO. During World War II he was Commander-in-Chief of Coastal Command (1943) and of the Mediterranean theatre (1944–45). He was promoted to the rank of marshal in 1940, and to Chief of the Air Staff (1950–52). His unorthodox views on nuclear strategy are expressed in *Strategy for the West* (1954) and *The Great Deterrent* (1957).

Slessor, Kenneth Adolf 1901–71
Australian poet and journalist

Born in Orange, New South Wales, he worked as reporter and columnist on various Sydney and Melbourne newspapers until he joined *Smith's Weekly* in 1927, later becoming editor-in-chief (until 1939). He was an official war correspondent and covered the Battle of Britain and then followed the Australian Imperial Forces through the Near East and North Africa, and on to New Guinea. He contributed many poems to various periodicals; in 1924 he published *Thief of the Moon*, and in 1926 *Earth-Visitors*. *Darlinghurst Nights and Morning Glories* (1933) celebrates 'The Cross', the bohemian district of Sydney. The title poem in his last collection *Five Bells* (1939) was written in memory of a friend who was drowned after falling overboard from a Sydney ferry. His verse was collected in *One Hundred Poems: 1919–1939* (1944, reissued as *Poems*, 1957) and the best of his prose in *Bread and Wine* (1970). He edited *Australian Poetry* (1945) and co-edited the *Penguin Book of Australian Verse* (1958, rev edn 1961). ▢ D Stewart, *A Man of Sydney—An Appreciation of Kenneth Slessor* (1977)

Slessor, Mary 1848–1915
Scottish missionary

Born in Aberdeen, she worked as a mill girl in Dundee from childhood but, conceiving a burning ambition to become a missionary, persuaded the United Presbyterian Church to accept her for teaching in Calabar, Nigeria (1876). There she spent many years of devoted work among the local peoples, who called her 'Great Mother'.

Slevogt, Max 1868–1932
German Impressionist painter and graphic artist

Born in Landshut, Bavaria, he studied in Munich, Paris and Berlin. He later taught at the Berlin Academy, and worked with the Impressionists **Louis Corinth** and **Max Liebermann**. His works include murals of historical scenes at Cladow (1912), Bremen (1927) and Ludwigshafen (1932) and swiftly executed landscapes and portraits. His book illustrations include editions of *Ali Baba and the Forty Thieves* (1903), *The Iliad* (1907), and **Mozart's** *The Magic Flute* (1920).

Slidell, John 1793–1871
US politician and diplomat

Born in New York City, he graduated from Columbia College in 1810 and later settled in New Orleans, where he practised law. He was a diplomat for President James K Polk, was later a US congressman (1843–45) and senator (1853–61), and was influential in the administration of President James Buchanan. In 1861 he withdrew from the US Senate and joined the Confederacy. As Confederate states commissioner, he was arrested on a journey to France and sent with Senator James Mason (1798–1871) to Boston in an incident known as the *Trent Affair*. He was unsuccessful in his efforts to gain France's recognition of the Confederacy.

Slim, William Joseph, 1st Viscount 1891–1970
English soldier

Born in Bristol, the son of an iron merchant, he attended King Edward's School, Birmingham, where he had moved with his family in 1903. During World War I he served in Gallipoli, France and Mesopotamia. In 1943 he became Commander of the 14th 'forgotten' Army in Burma, which he led to victory over the Japanese. In 1945–46 he was Supreme Allied Commander in southeast India. He was Chief of the Imperial General Staff (1948–52), and Governor-General of Australia (1953–60). He wrote *Defeat into Victory* (1956) and his memoirs, *Unofficial History* (1959). 📖 Ronald Lewin, *Slim, the Standard-bearer* (1976)

Slipher, Vesto Melvin 1875–1969
US astronomer

Born in Mulberry, Indiana, he studied at Indiana University before working at the Lowell Observatory, Arizona, where he remained over 50 years, becoming its director in 1926. He obtained the first successful photographs of Mars and demonstrated that methane is present in the atmosphere of Neptune. The research which led to the discovery of the planet Pluto was carried out under his direction. Primarily a spectroscopist, his spectral studies revealed the presence of gaseous interstellar material. By measuring the Doppler shift in light reflected from the edges of planetary discs, he determined the periods of rotation of Uranus, Jupiter, Saturn, Venus and Mars in 1912. In his most important work, he extended this method to the Andromeda nebula, which was not yet perceived as an extragalactic object, and established that it is approaching the Earth at around 300 kilometres per second (1912). His results directed Edwin Hubble to the concept of the expanding universe, in which galaxies are moving apart at relative speeds proportional to their separation.

Sloan, Alfred Pritchard, Jnr 1875–1966
US industrialist and philanthropist

Born in New Haven, Connecticut, he studied electrical engineering at the Massachusetts Institute of Technology (MIT). From 1920 to 1924 he worked with Pierre Du Pont to reorganize and restructure General Motors. He became president in 1924 and chairman of the board from 1937 to 1956. Under his guidance the company became one of the largest industrial corporations in the world. A noted philanthropist, he founded the Alfred P Sloan Foundation in 1937 and the Sloan–Kettering Institute for Cancer Research in 1945. His autobiography, *My Years with General Motors* (1964), is a classic in management literature.

Sloan, John 1871–1951
US artist

Born in Lock Haven, Pennsylvania, he studied at Philadelphia Spring Garden Institute and Pennsylvania Academy of Fine Arts, and worked initially as a commercial artist and newspaper illustrator. Influenced by Robert Henri, he produced a series of etchings based on New York City life and became known as a member of the so called 'Ashcan School'. Throughout his career he continued this individual documentation of life in the metropolis, and his work placed him in the forefront of the US Realist tradition. Notable paintings include *Wake of the Ferry* (1907), *Sunday, Women Drying Their Hair* (1912) and *McSorley's Bar* (1912).

Sloane, Sir Hans 1660–1753
British physician and naturalist

Born in Killyleagh, County Down, he studied in London and in France, and settled in London as a physician. From 1685 to 1686 he was physician to the governor of Jamaica, where he collected a herbarium of 800 species. He was secretary to the Royal Society (1693–1713), physician-general to the army (1716) and first physician to George II. He founded the Chelsea Physic Garden in 1721 and his museum and library formed the core collection of the British Museum. His great work was the *Natural History of Jamaica* (1707–25). 📖 Martin Brown, *Hans Sloane, 1660–1753* (1995)

Slocum, Joshua 1844–c.1910
US mariner

Born in Wilmot Township, Nova Scotia, Canada, he first went to sea as a ship's cook, and in 1869 was captain of a trading vessel off the Californian coast. In 1886 he set off for South America with his second wife and two sons in a converted bark, *Aquidneck*; he was wrecked on a Brazilian sandbar, and from the wreckage built a canoe which took them all back to New York. In 1895 he set out from Boston on the sloop *Spray* for the first solo cruise round the world, arriving back at Newport in 1898, having supported himself by lecturing on the way. In November 1909 he set out once more, but was not heard of again.

Slovo, Joe 1926–95
South African lawyer, nationalist and Communist politician

Born in Obelai, Lithuania, he emigrated in 1935 to South Africa, where he worked as a clerk before volunteering for service in World War II. After joining the South African Communist Party (SACP) in 1942, he qualified as a lawyer and defended many figures in political trials. He married Ruth First, daughter of the SACP Treasurer, and was a founding member of the Congress of Democrats in 1953. Charged in the treason trial of 1961, he escaped in 1963, and worked abroad for the ANC and SACP. In 1985 he became Chief of Staff of the military wing of the ANC, Umkhonto we Sizwe, of which he had been a founding member since 1961, but resigned to become General Secretary (1987–91) and later Chairman of the SACP. He returned to South Africa in 1990 after the legalization of the SACP and was a major figure in the negotiations between the nationalist parties and the government. The first white member of the ANC's National Executive (from 1986), he was appointed Minister of Housing in 1994, and when he died from cancer he was given a state funeral. 📖 *Unfinished Autobiography* by Joe Slovo (1996)

Słowacki, Juliusz 1809–49
Polish poet

Born in Krzemieniec, he settled in Paris in 1831. He belonged to the Romantic school, and dominated the Romantic movement in Polish literature. The influence of Byron, among others, is perceptible in his work, which includes the historical drama *Marja Stuart* (1830, 'Mary Stuart'), the dramatized legend *Balladyna* (1834, Eng trans 1938), *Lilla Weneda* (1840), perhaps the most famous Polish tragedy, and *Mazeppa* (1839, Eng trans 1930). His letters from exile to his mother are regarded as classic models of Polish prose.

Sluter, Claus c.1350–1405
Flemish sculptor

musicians, including **Fletcher Henderson** and **Louis Armstrong**, and these are regarded as classic blues statements. In 1929 she had the leading role in a film, *St Louis Blues*, which was the title of one of her favourite songs. She died from injuries in a car crash. ⌨ Chris Albertson, *Bessie* (1972)

Smith, David Roland 1906–65
US sculptor

He was born in Decatur, Indiana. In 1925 he worked in the Studebaker car factory at South Bend and learned how to cut and shape metal. From 1926 he studied under the Czech abstract artist Jan Matulka at the Art Students' League in New York. His first welded-steel pieces, inspired by magazine photographs of similar work by **Picasso**, date from 1932, and during the rest of the decade he assimilated several avant-garde European styles, including Cubism, Surrealism and Constructivism. His personal idiom developed from c.1940 and during World War II he worked as a welder. His 15 bronze relief plaques, *Medals of Dishonour*, attacked violence and greed. Other works include *Hudson River Landscape* (Whitney Museum, New York City), and *Subi XVIII* and *Subi XIX* (both 1964, Tate Gallery, London).

Smith, Delia 1941–
English cookery writer and broadcaster

She was born in Woking, Surrey, and left school at the age of 16. Her interest in English cuisine led her to read about it in the British Library. She began by writing for the *Daily Mirror* magazine (1969), where her future husband, Michael Wynn Jones, was deputy editor, and for the London *Evening Standard* (1972–85). Her first cookery book, *How to Cheat at Cooking* (1973), achieved wide popularity. She has since sold over five million copies of her books, including those associated with her television broadcasts. She is a committed Christian and writes religious books, including *A Feast for Lent* (1983) and *A Journey into God* (1980).

Smith, Dodie, *pseudonym (until 1935)* C L Anthony 1896–1990
English playwright, novelist and theatre producer

Born in Manchester, she took up acting and a career in business. Her first play, *Autumn Crocus* (1930), was an instant success and enabled her to devote herself entirely to writing. Other plays include *Dear Octopus* (1938), *Letter from Paris* (adapted from *The Reverberator* by **Henry James**, 1952) and *I Capture the Castle* (adapted from her own novel, 1952). Other works include the highly popular children's book *The Hundred and One Dalmatians* (1956). She also published the autobiographical works *Look Back with Love* (1974), *Look Back with Mixed Feelings* (1977), *Look Back with Astonishment* (1979) and *Look Back with Gratitude* (1985).

Smith, E(dward) E(lmer), *nicknamed* Doc 1890–1965
US science-fiction writer

He was born in Sheboygan, Wisconsin. A PhD in food chemistry was the basis of his writing nickname. He was an immensely popular creator of science-fiction space adventure stories in the 'pulp' magazine era before World War II, and is widely regarded as the progenitor of 'space opera'. His books have been consistent bestsellers. Colourful, racy and exciting, they play fast and loose with both probability and literary rectitude. His best-known works are the multi-volume sequences *Skylark* (begun 1928) and *Lensman* (begun 1948). The later *Family d'Alembert* series (begun 1964) appeared posthumously, and was completed by other writers.

Smith, Eli 1801–57
US churchman and missionary

Born in Northford, Connecticut, he became a Congregationalist. He went to Syria in 1926 as a missionary, and founded the American Mission at Urumiah. He translated the Bible into Arabic.

Smith, Sir Francis Pettit 1808–74
English inventor of the screw propellor

He was born in Hythe. In 1836 he took out a patent for the screw propellor, just ahead of **John Ericsson**. Smith built the first successful screw-propelled steamer, the *Archimedes* (1839), which eventually convinced the Admiralty of the superiority of this type of ship, and in 1841–43 he built the first screw warship for the Royal Navy, the *Rattler*. In 1860 he was appointed curator of the Patent Office Museum in London.

Smith, Frederick Edwin See **Birkenhead, 1st Earl of**

Smith, George 1824–1901
English publisher

Born in London, he joined his father's firm of Smith & Elder in 1838, and became head in 1846. He founded the *Cornhill Magazine* in 1860 with **William Thackeray** as editor, and the *Pall Mall Gazette* in 1865. He published the works of George Eliot, the Brownings, Mrs Gaskell, Anthony Trollope, and others. He also published the *Dictionary of National Biography* (63 vols, 1885–1900).

Smith, George 1840–76
English Assyriologist

Born in London, he was a banknote engraver who studied cuneiform inscriptions in the British Museum, and in 1867 he became an assistant there. He helped Sir **Henry Rawlinson** with his edition of *Cuneiform Inscriptions* (1870) and deciphered from **Austen Layard's** tablets in 1872 the *Epic of Gilgamesh*, a pre-biblical flood story. In 1873 he found the missing fragments of the tablet in Nineveh. He made two further expeditions on behalf of the British Museum, and died at Aleppo. He wrote *Assyrian Discoveries* (1875) and the popular *Chaldean Account of Genesis* (1876).

Smith, Gerrit 1797–1874
US reformer and philanthropist

Born in Utica, New York, he was active in diverse reform movements, including Sunday observance, abstinence, vegetarianism, prison reform and women's suffrage. He became a prominent abolitionist in 1835, and supported **John Brown's** anti-slavery campaigns. (1800–59).

Smith, Goldwin 1823–1910
Canadian publicist

Regius Professor of Modern History at Oxford (1858–66), he settled permanently in Canada in 1871 and founded a chair of history at Toronto. He became one of the major figures in Canada First, and in *Canada and the Canadian Question* (1891) he argued for the union of Canada with the USA.

Smith, Hamilton Othanel 1931–
US molecular biologist and Nobel Prize winner

Born in New York City, he graduated from Johns Hopkins Medical School, Maryland, where he was appointed Professor of Microbiology (1973) and Professor of Molecular Biology and Genetics (1981). In the 1970s he obtained enzymes from bacteria which would split genes to give genetically active fragments; these 'restriction enzymes' therefore allowed the possibility of genetic engineering of a new kind. Smith went on to isolate 'type II' enzymes which would split a DNA strand at a specific and predictable site, allowing the nucleotide sequence of DNA to be established. He shared the 1978 Nobel Prize for physiology or medicine with **Werner Arber** and **Daniel Nathans**.

Smith, (Robert) Harvey 1938–
English showjumper

He was born in Yorkshire. After winning several British championships, he represented Great Britain in the 1968 Olympics in Mexico City and the 1972 Olympics in Munich. Horses most closely associated with him include Salvador, O'Malley, Mattie Brown, Farmer's Boy and Harvester. With the increasing popularity of showjumping, Smith soon became a well-liked figure, though typifying the blunt, bluff Yorkshireman. With his wife Sue he runs a training stable for 'rekindling' racehorses for the showjumping arena. He wrote two books, *Show Jumping with Harvey Smith* (1979) and *Bedside Jumping* (1985).

Smith, Henry John Stephen 1826–83
Irish mathematician

Born in Dublin, he was educated at Rugby School and Balliol College, Oxford, of which he was elected a Fellow. In 1860 he became Oxford's Savilian Professor of Geometry. The greatest British authority of his day on the theory of numbers, he wrote an influential report on the subject for the British Association for the Advancement of Science. He was posthumously awarded the prize of the Paris Academy of Sciences for his work on the representation of integers as sums of squares (sharing the prize with Hermann Minkowski). He also wrote on elliptic functions and geometry.

Smith, Horatio or Horace See Smith, James

Smith, Iain Crichton, *Gaelic* Iain Mac A'Ghobhainn 1928–98
Scottish poet and novelist

Born on the island of Lewis, he was educated at the Nicolson Institute, Stornoway, and at Aberdeen University. His career as a writer ran in parallel with teaching in Clydebank, Dumbarton and Oban until 1977. Bilingual in Gaelic and English, his writing is rooted in the native culture but is sensible to the wider audience that English admits. His first collection of poems, *The Long River*, appeared in 1955. Five years later came *Burn is Aran*, stories and poems in Gaelic which were highly praised. The novel *Consider the Lilies* (1968) is undoubtedly the best-known work from his prolific output. Focusing on the plight of an old woman who is evicted from her croft and betrayed by the Church (Smith was no admirer of the Free Church), it is a powerful indictment of the Clearances and the harsh reality of Highland life. *My Last Duchess* (1971) and *An End to Autumn* (1978) are similarly beautiful but bleak, although not without humour. In *Murdo and Other Stories* (1981) there are signs of a writer hell-bent on mischief, the absurd side of his nature triumphing over a tendency towards introspection. In his poetry, however, Calvinism and Lewis fuse to generate love and hate in almost equal measure, producing in the best poems a dramatic grandeur and awesome tension. His *Selected Poems* were published in 1982.

Smith, Ian Douglas 1919–
Rhodesian politician

Born in Selukwe, he was educated at Chaplin High School in Rhodesia and at Rhodes University, South Africa. He was a fighter pilot in World War II and became an MP in 1948. From 1953 he was a member of the United Federal Party, resigning in 1961 to become a member of the Rhodesian Front, which was dedicated to immediate independence for Rhodesia without African majority rule. He replaced Winston Field as Prime Minister in April 1964 and unilaterally declared independence in November 1965. Britain declared his government rebels and, with UN support, applied increasingly severe economic sanctions. His meetings (1966 and 1968) with Harold Wilson, aboard HMS *Tiger* and HMS *Fearless* off Gibraltar failed to resolve the situation, and majority rule

was granted in 1979. Bishop Abel Muzorewa's caretaker government appointed Smith Minister without Portfolio and a member of the Transitional Executive Council of 1978–79 to prepare for the transfer of power. He was elected a member of parliament in the government of Robert Mugabe, but was suspended from parliament in April 1987 because of his connections with South Africa. In May of that year he resigned the leadership of the white opposition party.

Smith, Ian McKenzie 1935–
Scottish painter

Born in Montrose, Angus, he studied at Gray's School of Art, Aberdeen (1953–58), became a teacher in Fife (1960–63), then worked as an education officer for the Council of Industrial Design. He was appointed director of Aberdeen Art Gallery and Museums in 1968, and was one of the first Scottish painters to adopt a style based on American minimal abstraction, whose intention is to evoke a meditative response. His work is characterized by a restrained use of colour and tonal range.

Smith, James 1789–1850
Scottish agricultural engineer and philanthropist

Born in Deanston, Perthshire, and manager of the cotton mills there from 1807, he was the inventor of 'thorough drainage' by means of a subsoil plough.

Smith, James 1775–1839 and Horatio or Horace 1779–1849
English writers

They were brothers, both educated at Chigwell, Essex. James succeeded his father as solicitor to the Board of Ordnance, and Horace made a fortune as a stockbroker. Both wrote for magazines. When in 1812 a prize was advertised for an address to be spoken at the opening of the new Drury Lane Theatre, London, the brothers produced a series of supposed 'Rejected Addresses': James furnished imitations of Wordsworth, Robert Southey and Coleridge, and Horace those of Sir Walter Scott, Byron, M G Lewis and Thomas Moore. James also wrote for Charles Mathews. Horace was the author of the *Tin Trumpet* (1836) and other novels, and a volume of *Poems* (1846), the best known of which is the 'Ode to an Egyptian Mummy'.

Smith, Sir James Edward 1759–1828
English botanist

Born in Norwich, Norfolk, he studied medicine at Edinburgh University and in London. In 1783, aged only 24, he bought the entire natural history collection of Carolus Linnaeus and took it to London. He became a founder-member and first president of the Linnaean Society of London (1788–1828), and wrote many botanical articles, among them *English Botany* (36 vols, 1790–1814), *Flora Britannica* (3 vols, 1800–04), and *English Flora* (4 vols, 1824–28).

Smith, James Moyr 1839–1912
Scottish graphic artist and designer

Born in Glasgow, he trained as an architect, and after working as an ecclesiastical architect in Manchester, he moved to London (1867) to work in the studios of Christopher Dresser, designing furniture, wallpaper, fabrics, ceramics and book plates. Between 1870 and 1897 he worked as an independent designer and became a proponent of the design reform movement in the second half of the 19th century. He edited the magazine *Decoration* from 1881 and became a prolific writer, his works including *Ancient Greek Female Costume* (1882), *Ornamental Interiors Ancient and Modern* (1887), *Studies for Pictures* (1868) and *Album of Decorative Figures* (1882). His work was exhibited at the Royal Academy in the 1870s and 1880s, and his designs formed part of the Minton exhibition at the Exposition Universelle in Paris (1878).

Smith, Jedediah Strong 1799–1831
US fur-trader and explorer

Born in Jericho, New York, he went to St Louis to trade furs, and undertook two major explorations in the Far Southwest of North America between 1823 and 1830, covering more than 16,000 miles (25,760km), first in the Central Rockies and Columbia River areas, trapping and providing intelligence on the activities of the Hudson's Bay Company. He later became the first white man to reach California overland across the Sierra Nevada mountains and Great Basin to the Pacific Ocean. He was killed by Comanches while leading a wagon train to Santa Fe.

Smith, John 1580–1631
English adventurer

Born in Willoughby, Lincolnshire, he fought in France and Hungary, but was captured by the Turks and sold as a slave. He escaped to Russia and in 1607 joined an expedition to colonize Virginia. Saved from a Native American tribe by the chief's daughter **Pocahontas**, his experience in dealing with the tribal people led to his being elected President of the colony (1608–09), but he returned to England in 1609. In 1614 he was sent to New England and explored the coast. His works include *A True Relation of Virginia Since the First Planting of that Colony* (1612), *A Description of New England* (1616) and *The Generall Historie of Virginia, New England, and the Summer Isles* (1624). He also wrote *The True Travels, Adventures, and Observations of Captaine John Smith* (1630).

Smith, John 1724–1814
Scottish bookseller

Born in Strathblane, Stirlingshire, he fought at the Battle of Laffeldt in Flanders (1747) and was wounded in action. In 1751 he founded the firm of John Smith and Son, having already set up three bookshops in Glasgow. He also established the first Circulating Library in Glasgow in 1753 (**Allan Ramsay** having introduced libraries to Scotland in 1725). Smith's Circulating Library was the largest collection in Glasgow for over 70 years. He died at the age of 90, and the bookselling business he had founded was continued by his sons.

Smith, John 1825–1910
Scottish dentist

He was born in Edinburgh, the son of a dentist, whose practice he inherited in 1851. He published a *Handbook of Dental Anatomy and Surgery* in 1864. He was appointed surgeon dentist to the Royal Public Dispensary in 1857–59, and founded the Edinburgh Dental Dispensary in 1860. Largely as a result of his efforts, the Edinburgh Dental Hospital and School was established in 1879, the Dispensary being merged with it. Smith left the running of the school to others, but remained a significant influence on its development. His practice was later shared and ultimately inherited by his son-in-law **William Guy**. He was an enthusiast of the theatre, writing the scripts of several Edinburgh Lyceum pantomimes and successfully adapting Sir **Walter Scott**'s *Waverley* for the stage.

Smith, John 1938–94
Scottish Labour politician

Educated at Dunoon Grammar School and Glasgow University, where he studied law, he was called to the Scottish Bar in 1967 and made a QC in 1983. He distinguished himself as a public speaker at an early age, winning the *Observer* Mace debating competition in 1962. He entered the House of Commons in 1970, representing Lanarkshire North and from 1983 Monklands East. He served in the administrations of **Harold Wilson** and **James Callaghan**, becoming Trade Secretary in 1978. From 1979 he was opposition Front Bench spokesman on Trade, Energy, Employment and Economic Affairs. His career

seemed to be threatened by a heart attack in 1988, but he returned in 1989 as one of Labour's most respected politicians. He succeeded **Neil Kinnock** as Labour Party Leader in 1992, but died suddenly of a further heart attack in 1994.

Smith, John Stafford 1750–1836
English composer and musical scholar

Born in Gloucester, he wrote vocal music and the tune of *The Star-spangled Banner*.

Smith, Joseph 1805–44
US religious leader, regarded as the founder of the Mormons

Born in Sharon, Vermont, he received his first 'call' as a prophet in 1820. In 1823 he claims that an angel told him of a hidden gospel written on golden plates and in 1827 the sacred records were apparently delivered into his hands on a hill near Palmyra, New York. This, the so-called *Book of Mormon* (1830), contains a postulated history of America to the 5th century of the Christian era, supposedly written by a prophet named Mormon. Smith was to be the instrument of the Church's re-establishment, and despite ridicule and hostility, and sometimes open violence, 'the new Church of Jesus Christ of Latter-day Saints' (founded in 1830) rapidly gained converts. In 1831 it established its headquarters at Kirtland, Ohio, and built Zion in Missouri. Hostility became intense, and in 1838 a general uprising took place in Missouri against the Mormons. In 1840 they moved to Illinois, and within three years the Mormons there numbered 20,000. Smith was an advocate of polygamy (calling his wives 'spiritual wives'). Finally he was shot dead by a mob who broke into Carthage jail, where he was under arrest on charges of conspiracy.

Smith, (Ernest) Lester 1904–92
English biochemist

Born in Teddington, Middlesex, he was educated at Chelsea Polytechnic, and in 1928 joined the pharmaceutical firm of Glaxo, later becoming Senior Research Biochemist there. He was responsible for the first commercial production of penicillin in England, and discovered that the biosynthesis of some forms of penicillin could be promoted by adjusting the growth medium. He independently isolated vitamin B_{12} in crystalline form in the same year as **Karl Folkers** in the USA (1948), and went on to separate and characterize the various forms of the vitamin. In 1958 he isolated an antibiotic complex which proved effective against streptococci that had developed resistance to other known antibiotics. He was elected Fellow of the Royal Society in 1957.

Smith, Logan Pearsall 1865–1946
British writer

Born in Millville, New Jersey, USA, and educated at Harvard and Oxford, he settled in England and took British citizenship in 1913. He produced critical editions of various authors, and published *Milton and His Modern Critics* (1941). He is best remembered for his delightful essays, collected in *All Trivia* (1933) and *Reperusals and Re-collections* (1936), and his short stories.

Smith, Dame Maggie (Margaret Natalie) 1934–
English actress

Born in Ilford, Essex, she was a student at the Oxford Playhouse School before making her stage debut with the Oxford University Dramatic Society in a production of *Twelfth Night* (1952) and appearing in New York as one of the *New Faces of '56*. After winning increasing critical esteem for her performances in *The Rehearsal* (1961) and *Mary, Mary* (1963), she joined the National Theatre to play in *Othello* (1963), *Hay Fever* (1966), *The Three Sisters* (1970) and other plays. Her film debut in *Nowhere to Go* (1958) was followed by scene-stealing turns in such films as *The V.I.P.s* (1963) and *The Pumpkin Eater* (1964), but her tour de force was in *The Prime of Miss Jean Brodie* (1969, Academy Award). Recent stage work includes *Virginia* (1980) and *Lettice and Lovage* (1987). Her many film roles show a penchant for eccentric comedy and the portrayal of acidic spinsters, and include award-winning performances in *California Suite* (1978), *A Private Function* (1984, BAFTA Award for Best Actress), *A Room With a View* (1985) and *The Lonely Passion of Judith Hearne* (1987). In 1992 she played the Mother Superior in *Sister Act* and a wizened Wendy in *Hook*, and she returned to the stage as Lady Bracknell in *The Importance of Being Earnest*. The following year she appeared in a television broadcast of *Suddenly Last Summer*. More recent film work includes *The First Wives Club* (1996) and *Washington Square* (1997).

Smith, Margaret Chase, *née* Chase 1897–1995
US Republican politician

Born in Skowhegan, Maine, the daughter of a barber, she worked as a teacher then on a newspaper, marrying its publisher, Clyde Smith, in 1930. He became US Representative in Washington and when he died in 1940 she took over his position, becoming Maine's first congresswoman. Eight years later she became the first woman elected a US senator in her own right and the first woman to be elected to both houses of the US Congress. In 1949 she also became the first woman to read the address to the Senate. Re-elected three times, she served until 1973. During this time, in 1950 she became one of the first Republican senators to speak out against Senator Joseph McCarthy, and in 1964 she campaigned for the office of US President, the first woman to do so since Victoria Woodhull. She wrote the books *Gallant Women* (1968) and *Declaration of Conscience* (1972).

Smith, Maria Ann c.1801–1870
Australian orchardist

In the 1860s she was growing various seedlings on her orchard in Eastwood, near Sydney, and experimented with a hardy French crab-apple from the cooler climate of Tasmania. From this was developed the late-ripening 'Granny Smith' apple which, because of its excellent storing qualities, formed for many years the bulk of Australia's apple exports.

Smith, Sir Matthew Arnold Bracy 1879–1959
English artist

Born in Halifax, Yorkshire, he studied at the Slade School of Art, London. He first went to Paris in 1910, meeting Henri Matisse and the Fauves, who had a dramatic impact on his work as a colourist. He was also associated with Walter Sickert and Sir Jacob Epstein. His best-known work includes *Lilies and Apples on a Dish* (1919, Tate, London), two *Fitzroy Street Nudes* (British Council, 1916), *Winter Landscape, Cornwall* (1920, Swansea) and a portrait of *Augustus John* (1944, National Gallery of Modern Art, Edinburgh). In 1920 he joined the London Group. He lived mainly in France until 1940. In 1950 he exhibited 26 pictures at the Venice Biennale, and in 1953 the Tate Gallery, London, held a retrospective of his work.

Smith, Michael 1932–
Canadian biochemist and Nobel Prize winner

Born in Blackpool, Lancashire, and educated at the University of Manchester, he moved in 1956 to the University of British Columbia, where he became Professor of Biochemistry in 1970, director of the Biotechnology Laboratory in 1987 and Peter Wall Distinguished Professor of Biotechnology in 1994. In 1978 he published his discovery of 'site-specific mutagenesis', a technique which allows scientists to alter the genetic code through mutations induced at specific locations, whereas all previous methods of mutation had produced only random mutations. This new method has allowed the production of a whole new range of proteins with diverse functions. Smith was awarded the 1993 Nobel Prize for chemistry jointly with Kary Mullis. He was elected Fellow of the Royal Society of Canada in 1981 and FRS in 1986.

Smith, Richard 1931–
English painter

Born in Letchworth, Hertfordshire, he spent two years with the RAF in Hong Kong before studying at St Albans School of Art and the Royal College of Art. He became associated with Pop artists such as Peter Blake, but developed his own style based on the aesthetics of glossy advertising rather than its superficial image, eg *Soft Pack* (1963, Hirshhorn Collection, New York). Moving to New York in 1959, he began to develop large three-dimensional and often kite-shaped canvases, typified by *Tailspan* (1965, Tate, London). This technique was developed further in the 1970s when he detached his canvases from their stretchers and suspended with ropes and metal rods, these forming part of the work. In 1966 he won the Scull Prize for a young non-American artist at the Venice Biennale, and exhibited at the Whitechapel Gallery. A second retrospective at the Tate Gallery in 1975 emphasized the serial nature of his work.

Smith, Robyn 1943–
US jockey

She began her thoroughbred riding career in 1969. In 1972 she was the only American jockey of international standing, coming seventh with 98 mounts and 20 per cent of the winnings. She maintained her top US rank from 1972 to 1978. In 1973 she was the first woman jockey to win a stakes race when she rode North Sea to victory in the Paumonok Handicap. She married Fred Astaire in 1980.

Smith, Rodney, *known as* Gipsy Smith 1860–1947
English evangelist

Born of nomadic gypsy parents, near Epping Forest, he was converted at a Primitive Methodist meeting in 1876. Soon afterwards he joined William Booth and became one of the first officers in the newly formed Salvation Army, which he left in 1882 to carry on his evangelism under the auspices of the Free Church, preaching forcefully in the USA, Australia and elsewhere as well as in Great Britain.

Smith, Sir Ross MacPherson 1892–1922
Australian aviator

Born in Semaphore, South Australia, he joined the Australian Imperial Forces and fought at Gallipoli, then transferred to the Australian Flying Corps (1916) and became its most decorated pilot. He flew over Jerusalem, the first pilot to do so, taking T E Lawrence to meet Sharif Nazir. After World War I he flew a Handley-Page bomber from Cairo to Calcutta, a distance of nearly 2,400 miles and a record at that time. In 1919 the Australian government offered £10,000 for the first Australian-crewed plane to fly to Australia from England within 30 days. Ross and his elder brother Keith (1890–1955) flew from London in a Vickers Vimy bi-plane, with two Australian engineers, arriving in Darwin 28 days later, a feat for which both brothers were knighted. Ross was killed in a trial flight of a Vickers Viking amphibian plane, while preparing for a round-the-world flight with his brother.

Smith, Sophia 1796–1870
US philanthropist

Born in Hatfield, Massachusetts, she inherited her brother's fortune. On her pastor's advice she willed this money to be used to found a women's college. Smith College, Northampton, in Massachusetts, was opened in 1875.

Smith, Stevie, *pseudonym of* Florence Margaret Smith 1902–71
English poet and novelist

Born in Hull, Humberside, she moved with her family at the age of three to London, where she attended the North London Collegiate School for Girls before working for the Newnes publishing company. Her first novels, *Novel on Yellow Paper* (1936, an autobiographical monologue in conversational style), *Over the Frontier* (1938) and *The Holiday* (1949), were written on the advice of a publicist reacting to her poetry. Meanwhile her reputation as a humorous poet on serious themes was becoming established with *A Good Time Was Had By All* (1937) and *Not Waving but Drowning* (1957), with loneliness the theme as in much of her work. Her poetic style ranged from the childish and whimsical to the deeply religious. She wrote many reviews and critical articles, and produced a volume of the line-drawings that often accompanied her poems, entitled *Some Are More Human Than Others* (1958). Her *Collected Poems* appeared in 1975. 📖 K Dick, *Ivy and Stevie* (1971)

Smith, Sydney 1771–1845
English clergyman, essayist and wit

Born in Woodford, Essex, he was educated at Winchester and New College, Oxford, of which he became a Fellow. He was ordained (1794) and served at Netheravon, near Amesbury, and Edinburgh. In 1802, with Francis Jeffrey, Francis Horner and Henry Brougham, he started the *Edinburgh Review*. He lived six years in London, where he made his mark as a preacher, a lecturer on moral philosophy at the Royal Institution (1804–06), and an accomplished speaker, but in 1809 he was 'transferred' to the living of Foston in Yorkshire. In 1828 Lord Lyndhurst presented him to a prebend of Bristol, and the next year enabled him to exchange Foston for Combe-Florey rectory, Somerset. In 1831 Earl Charles Grey appointed him a canon of St Paul's. His writings include 65 articles, collected in 1839 from the *Edinburgh Review*, *Peter Plymley's Letters* (1807–08) in favour of Catholic emancipation, *Three Letters on the Ecclesiastical Commission* (1837–39), and other letters and pamphlets on the ballot, US repudiation, the game laws, prison abuses, and other topics. He is chiefly remembered as the creator of 'Mrs Partington'. 📖 H Pearson, *The Smith of Smiths* (1940)

Smith, Sir Sydney Alfred 1883–1969
New Zealand forensic medical expert

Born in Roxburgh, and educated at Victoria College, Wellington, and Edinburgh University, he was medical officer of health for New Zealand, Professor of Forensic Medicine at Cairo and from 1917 principal medico-legal expert for the Egyptian government. He was Regius Professor of Forensic Medicine at Edinburgh (1928–53) and Dean of the medical faculty from 1931, playing a leading part in the medical and ballistic aspects of crime detection, notably in the Merrett (1926) and Ruxton (1936) murder cases, often effectively opposing his brilliant English colleague, Sir Bernard Spilsbury. He wrote a *Text-Book of Forensic Medicine* (1925), edited Taylor's *Principles and Practices of Medical Jurisprudence*, and wrote an autobiography, *Mostly Murder* (1959). His son, Sydney Goodsir Smith, was a poet.

Smith, Sydney Goodsir 1915–75
Scottish poet

Born in Wellington, New Zealand, he moved to Edinburgh in 1928 when his father Sir Sydney Alfred Smith was appointed Regius Professor of Forensic Medicine there. He studied at Edinburgh University and Oriel College, Oxford, and with such works as *Skail Wind* (1941), *The Devil's Waltz* (1946), *Under the Eildon Tree* (1948, a modern love poem), *So Late into the Night* (1952) and *Orpheus and Eurydice* (1955), *Figs and Thistles* (1959), he

established a reputation as the best modern Lallans (lowland Scots) poet after Hugh MacDiarmid. He published a loving description of Edinburgh in *Kynd Kittock's Land* in 1965. His first play, *The Wallace*, was commissioned for the Edinburgh Festival of 1960. He also wrote a comic novel, *Carotid Cornucopius* (1947). His *Collected Poems 1941–75* appeared in 1975. 📖 H MacDiarmid, *Sydney Goodsir Smith* (1963)

Smith, Theobald 1859–1934
US microbiologist and immunologist

Born in Albany, New York, he was the greatest US bacteriologist of his generation. He received his medical degree from the Albany Medical College, and was subsequently associated with several US institutions, including Harvard University (as professor, 1896–1915) and the Rockefeller Institute for Medical Research (1915–29). He studied both animal and human diseases, and first established the role of insects in the spread of disease when he showed that Texas cattle fever is spread by ticks. He distinguished the forms of bacillus causing human and bovine tuberculosis, and laid the scientific foundations for a cholera vaccine. He also improved the production of smallpox vaccine and diphtheria and tetanus antitoxins, and established precise techniques for the bacteriological examination of water, milk and sewage.

Smith, Thomas Southwood 1788–1861
English physician and sanitary reformer

Born in Martock, Somerset, he took charge of a Unitarian chapel in Edinburgh in 1812 while studying medicine. In 1824 he became physician at the London Fever Hospital, publishing in 1830 his *Treatise on Fever*. Jeremy Bentham left him his body for dissection and Smith kept the skeleton fully clothed until it was transferred to University College London.

Smith, Tommie 1944–
US athlete

He was born in Ackworth, Texas. He set world records for both the 220 yards and the 200 metres in 1966 and was a member of the US team which broke the world record for the 4 × 400 metres relay. In the 1968 Olympics in Mexico City he won the gold medal in the 200 metres in a world record time of 19.8 seconds.

Smith, Tommy (Thomas) 1967–
Scottish jazz musician, composer and bandleader

Born in Luton, Bedfordshire, to Scottish parents, he was brought up in Edinburgh and took up the saxophone at the age of 12. A teenage prodigy, he had made television and radio performances with internationally known musicians, as well as two records for Scottish labels, before he was 16. After studies in the USA at Berklee College, Boston, he brought his own quartet, Forward Motion, to play in Europe. In 1986 he became a member of vibraphone player Gary Burton's quintet, taking part in international tours and recording sessions. He soon became established as one of the brightest new jazz stars, playing wind synthesizer as well as saxophone, and leading a variety of groups in jazz and jazz-related settings.

Smith, W Eugene 1918–78
US photojournalist

He was born in Wichita, Kansas, and became a photographer for two local newspapers while still at school. He went to New York City and worked for several magazines before becoming a war correspondent for *Life* magazine in 1942. Severely wounded at Okinawa in 1945, he did not photograph again until 1947, the year of his famous *The Walk to Paradise Garden* (showing two children walking away towards a sunlit forest clearing) which Edward Steichen included in his *Family of Man* exhibition at the Museum of Modern Art in 1955. Smith returned to *Life* and produced a series of eloquent photo-essays (eg

Country Doctor, 1948; _Spanish Village_, 1951) which were to mark him out as one of the most important photojournalists of his time. His last great work was a photographic record of a Japanese fishing village suffering the maiming effect of mercury poisoning from factory pollution: _Minimata: Life Sacred and Profane_ (1973).

Smith, William 1769–1839
English civil engineer and geologist

Born in Churchill, Oxfordshire, he became an assistant to a surveyor in 1787 and he was later appointed engineer to the Somerset Coal Canal (1794–99). His survey work during canal construction introduced him to a variety of rock sequences of different ages and in 1799 he produced a coloured geological map of the country around Bath. From 1799 he was a consultant engineer and surveyor, travelling great distances in the course of his work and later settling in London (1804). He used fossils to aid his identification of strata and to fix their position in the succession. He produced the first geological map of England and 21 coloured geological maps of the English counties (1819–24) assisted by his nephew John Phillips (1800–74). Smith is often regarded as the father of English geology and stratigraphy. ⬜ John Phillips, _Memoirs of William Smith_ (1844)

Smith, Sir William 1813–93
English lexicographer

Born in London, he was educated at University College London. His great work was as editor and part-author of the _Dictionary of Greek and Roman Antiquities_ (1840–42), followed by the _Dictionary of Greek and Roman Biography and Mythology_ (1843–49) and the _Dictionary of Greek and Roman Geography_ (1853–57). He edited Edward Gibbon's _Decline and Fall_ (1854), and also produced a _Dictionary of the Bible_ (1860–63), a _Dictionary of Christian Antiquities_ (1875–80), and a _Dictionary of Christian Biography and Doctrines_ (1877–87). He was editor of _The Quarterly Review_ from 1867 until his death.

Smith, Sir William 1854–1914
Scottish businessman, and founder of the Boys' Brigade

Born near Thurso, Caithness, an active worker in the Free College Church, Glasgow, and a member of the Lanarkshire Volunteers from 1874, he was well embarked on a successful career in commerce when he began his movement for 'the advancement of Christ's Kingdom among Boys' in 1883. Intended to meet a need at a vital stage in their lives, the organization aimed to instil habits of discipline and to provide recreation through camps and other pursuits, and was firmly based on Christian principles. By the year of Queen Victoria's Jubilee (1897) (in which a B B captain was Lord Mayor of London), the movement had spread to every continent.

Smith, William Henry 1792–1865
English newsagent

He entered the newsagent business of his father in the Strand, London, in 1812 and aided by his brother, Henry Edward Smith, expanded it into the largest in Great Britain by making extensive use of railways and fast carts for country deliveries. His son William Henry Smith took over the business and maintained its expansion.

Smith, William Henry 1825–91
English bookseller and politician

Born in London, the son of William Henry Smith, he became his father's partner in a bookselling business in 1846 and later assumed full control. The business steadily expanded, and in 1849 secured the privilege of selling books and newspapers at railway stations. Smith entered parliament in 1868, was Financial Secretary of the Treasury (1874–77), First Lord of the Admiralty (1877–

80), and Secretary for War (1885). In the second Salisbury ministry he was First Lord of the Treasury and Leader of the House of Commons until his death.

Smith, William Robertson 1846–94
Scottish theologian and orientalist

Born in Keig, Aberdeenshire, he studied at Aberdeen, Edinburgh, Bonn and Göttingen, and in 1870 became Professor of Hebrew and Old Testament Exegesis in the Free Church College, Aberdeen. His _Encyclopaedia Britannica_ article 'Bible' (1875) was attacked for heterodoxy; he was exonerated (1880), but he was deprived of his professorship the following year for another article on 'Hebrew Language and Literature'. He later became Lord Almoner's Professor of Arabic at Cambridge (1883), university librarian (1886) and Adams Professor of Arabic (1889), and he was appointed co-editor and chief editor (1887) of the _Encyclopaedia Britannica_. His chief works were _The Old Testament in the Jewish Church_ (1881), _The Prophets of Israel_ (1882) and _The Religion of the Semites_ (1889).

Smith, Sir William Sidney 1764–1840
English naval commander

Born in Westminster, London, he entered the navy in 1777, and in 1780 was promoted to the rank of lieutenant for his bravery at Cape St Vincent. He acted as adviser to the King of Sweden (1790–92), and was decorated—hence his nickname 'the Swedish Knight'. In 1793 he aided Samuel, 1st Viscount Hood to burn the shops and arsenal at Toulon. In 1798 he was sent as plenipotentiary to Constantinople (Istanbul), and in 1799 raised Napoleon's siege of Acre. He aided Ralph Abercromby in Egypt, destroyed the Turkish fleet off Abydos (1807), blockaded the Tagus, and became vice-admiral of the Blue in 1810.

Smith-Dorrian, Sir Horace Lockwood 1858–1930
English general

He was born in Haresfoot, Hertfordshire, and educated at Harrow and Sandhurst. He saw service in the Zulu War, India and Egypt and commanded a battalion at the Battle of Omdurman in 1898. In 1907 he returned to Britain and did much to encourage the creation of the new Territorial forces. During World War I he commanded the British II Corps in France but his military career came to an end in April 1915 when he was relieved of his command for ordering British forces to withdraw after a German gas attack during the Battle of Ypres. He retired from the army in 1923 and died as a result of a motoring accident.

Smithers, Leonard Charles 1861–1907
English publisher

Born in Sheffield, he first practised as a solicitor, and was drawn into publishing through editing Sir Richard Burton's verse translation of Catullus, adding his own prose translation of the remainder with scholarly skill (1894). His high aesthetic standards in production were maintained in Oscar Wilde's _The Ballad of Reading Gaol_ (1898) and the then neglected _Importance of Being Earnest_ and _An Ideal Husband_ (1899), as well as the _Savoy_ (which replaced the _Yellow Book_). He also published most of Aubrey Beardsley's later work, the poems of Ernest Dowson and Arthur Symons, and the first collection of Max Beerbohm's drawings. He was declared bankrupt in 1900 and, after trafficking in piracy and pornography, died destitute.

Smithson, Alison Margaret, _née_ Gill 1928–93
English architect

Born in Sheffield, she set up a private practice with her husband Peter Smithson (1923–) in 1950, and the couple became an internationally renowned team. They are best known for their involvement with the Team X group of the Congress Internationaux d'Architecture Moderne, which attempted to break down the barriers between the arts and the sciences. The Smithsons' work includes the Secondary Modern School in Hunstanton (1950–52) and the 'House of the Future' at the Ideal Homes Exhibition (1956). Their more recent work includes the Economist complex in Westminster, London.

Smithson, James Louis Macie 1765–1829
English chemist
He was born in Paris, the illegitimate son of Sir Hugh Smithson Percy, 1st Duke of Northumberland, and Elizabeth Macie. At first known as Macie, he changed his name in 1801 after the death of his mother. He was educated at Oxford, showing an early aptitude for mineralogy, and he was elected FRS in 1787. Zinc carbonate was later named 'smithsonite' after him. He also proposed an innovative balance for weighing very small quantities. However, he is chiefly remembered for his bequest for the foundation 'at Washington, under the name of the Smithsonian Institution, an Establishment for the increase and diffusion of knowledge among men'. This was established by Act of Congress in 1846.

Smithson, Robert 1938–73
US land artist
Born in Passaic, New Jersey, he studied at the Art Students' League (1955–56) and at the Brooklyn Museum School. He took up Minimal Art in the 1960s, but from c.1966 he began to exhibit his 'Non-Sites'—maps of sites he had visited, together with samples of rocks and soil. He is best known for such earth works as the *Spiral Jetty on the Great Salt Lake, Utah* (1970). He was killed in a plane crash in Texas while engaged in aerial photography of one of his earth works.

Smollett, Tobias George 1721–71
Scottish novelist
Born on the farm of Dalquharn in the Vale of Leven, Dunbartonshire, he was educated at Dumbarton Grammar School and Glasgow University, where he took a degree in medicine. He moved to London in 1740 to find a producer for his tragedy, *The Regicide* (1749) but, failing to do so, sailed as surgeon's mate in the expedition to Carthagena against the Spanish in 1741. Three years later he settled in London, and began to practise as a surgeon, but writing was his real interest. His first novels *Roderick Random* (1748), modelled on Alain Lesage's *Gil Blas* (1715), and *Peregrine Pickle* (1751), describe the adventures in love and war of an unprincipled hero. He translated Cervantes' *Don Quixote* in 1755, but his attempt to imitate him in *Sir Launcelote Greaves* (1762) is less successful. In 1753 he settled in Chelsea, editing the new *Critical Review*, which led to his imprisonment for libel in 1760, and writing his *History of England* (3 vols, 1757–58). After being ordered abroad for his health, he wrote the caustic record *Travels in France and Italy* (1766), followed in 1769 by a coarse satire on public affairs, *The Adventures of an Atom. Humphrey Clinker* (1771), which is more kindly in tone and still a favourite, was written in the form of a series of letters from and to members of a party touring England and 'North Britain'. He spent the last years of his life abroad, and died in Livorno, Italy. 📖 L Melville, *The Life and Letters of Tobias Smollett* (1976)

Smout, T(homas) C(hristopher) 1933–
English economic and social historian of Scotland
Born in Birmingham and educated at Leys School, Cambridge, and Clare College, Cambridge, he became Reader and later Professor in the Department of Economic and Social History at Edinburgh University (1959–79). He published *Scottish Trade On the Eve of the Union* (1963), the hugely popular *A History of the Scottish People 1560–1830* (1969), and *A Century of the Scottish People 1830–1950* (1986). He participated in Michael Flinn's *Scottish Population History from the Seventeenth Century to the 1930s*

(1977), and co-operated with Ian Levitt to write *The State of the Scottish Working Class in 1843* (1979). He also established co-operative research between Scottish, Irish, Scandinavian and other European social and economic historians. He has also written many individual essays, including pioneer work on Scottish sexual history and conservation history. As Professor of Scottish History at St Andrews University (1980–91), he bridged the gap between scholars who treat Scotland as an academic preserve and those more interested in its culture. In 1990 he published, with Sydney Wood, an anthology of social history, *Scottish Voices*. Since 1986 he has been increasingly involved in the conservation movement with the Nature Conservancy Council, and in 1991 he was appointed deputy chairman of Scottish Natural Heritage. He was appointed Historiographer to the Queen in Scotland in 1993.

Smuts, Jan Christian 1870–1950
South African statesman
He was born in Malmesbury, Cape Colony, and educated at Christ's College, Cambridge. In the Boer War he fought with de la Rey. He entered the House of Assembly in 1907 and held several cabinet offices, succeeding Louis Botha as Prime Minister of the Union of South Africa (1919). Entrusted during World War I with operations in German East Africa, he was made a member of the Imperial War Cabinet. As Minister of Justice under J B M Hertzog, his coalition with the Nationalists in 1934 produced the United party, and he became Prime Minister in 1939. During World War II his counsel was sought by the War Cabinet. 📖 F S Crafford, *Jan Smuts: A Biography* (1943)

Smyslov, Vasili Vasilevich 1921–
Soviet chess player
Born in Moscow, he made chess his career after narrowly failing an audition for the Bolshoi Opera in 1950. After drawing a world championship match against Mikhail Botvinnik in 1954, which allowed the holder to retain his title, he beat him in 1957, but lost to him again in the 1958 re-match.

Smyth, Charles Piazzi 1819–1900
British astronomer
Born in Naples, the godson of Giuseppe Piazzi, he was educated at Bedford School and studied practical astronomy at home. After holding the post of chief assistant at the Royal Observatory, Cape of Good Hope, South Africa (1827–37), he succeeded Thomas Henderson as Astronomer Royal for Scotland and Professor of Astronomy at the University of Edinburgh. His most important contribution to astronomy was his expedition to the island of Tenerife (1856), in which he proved the superiority of a mountain site for every type of observation. A successful early photographer, he was the inventor of a flat-fielding lens for cameras (1874).

Smyth, Dame Ethel Mary 1858–1944
English composer
Born in London, she studied at Leipzig. She composed a Mass in D minor, symphonies, choral works, and operas including *The Wreckers* (1906) and *The Boatswain's Mate* (1916). A campaigner for women's suffrage, she composed the battle-song of the Women's Social and Political Union (1911, 'The March of the Women'), and was imprisoned for three months. She was made a DBE in 1922, and wrote the autobiographical *Female Pipings for Eden* (1933) and *What Happened Next* (1940).

Smythe, Pat(ricia Rosemary), married name Koechlin-Smythe 1928–96
English show jumper and writer
Born in Barnes, London, she was a member of the British show jumping team from 1947 to 1964, and won the European championship a record four times on Flanagan

(1957, 1961–63). In 1956 she was the first woman to ride in the Olympic Games, winning a bronze medal in the team event. Her numerous wins include the Queen Elizabeth II Cup on Mr Pollard in 1958. She competed infrequently after her marriage in 1963 to the Swiss lawyer and businessman Sam Koechlin (d.1985), but she continued to write. After *Jump for Joy: Pat Smythe's Story* was published in 1954, she wrote over 20 books, including several for children and her autobiography, *Jumping Life's Fences*, in 1992.

Smythe, Reg, *originally* Reginald Smith 1917–98
English strip cartoonist

Born in Hartlepool, Cleveland, he started as a butcher's errand boy (1931), then became a regular soldier. After World War II he joined the Post Office and freelanced joke cartoons to the *Daily Mirror*, who invited him to contribute a regular joke for their new Northern edition in 1958. This became *Andy Capp*, the adventures of a cocky and idle layabout, more fond of beer than of his wife, Florrie, and representing a stereotype of the British working man. He eventually became the first British strip cartoon to be syndicated worldwide. The strip was adapted as a stage musical and television series starring James Bolam (1987).

Smythson, Robert c.1535–1614
English architect

Trained as a mason, his first recorded work was at Longleat (1568), and his first major work was Wollaton Hall, Nottingham (1580–88), a lavish palace richly modelled and detailed. He developed a new vertical plan with the great hall set transversely, which revolutionized the spatial possibilities of contemporary buildings. Hardwick Hall, Derbyshire (1591–97), provides the quintessential Elizabethan house of state, combining a magnificent suite of state rooms, a grand processional route and the large distinctive windows. Other buildings attributed to Smythson include Worksop Manor, Balborough and Bolsover Little Castle.

Snead, Sam (Samuel Jackson) 1912–
US golfer

He was born in Ashwood, Virginia. Of the Majors, he won the Open championship once (1946), the Masters three times (1949, 1952, 1954) and the Professional Golfers' Association championship three times (1942, 1949, 1951). His success was achieved despite problems with his putting, which he cured by using the 'sidewinder' putting technique—the player holds the putter to the side rather than in front of the body. He holds the record number of US Tour victories (84), the last of which came at the age of 52 years 10 months, making him the oldest winner on Tour. 📖 Sam Snead and G Mendoza, *Slammin' Sam* (1986)

Snell, George Davis 1903–96
US geneticist and Nobel Prize winner

Born in Bradford, Massachusetts, he graduated from Dartmouth College in 1926, worked at Harvard University, and was awarded a fellowship at the University of Texas, where he demonstrated for the first time that X-rays can induce mutations in mammals. In 1933 he became assistant professor at Washington University, and in 1935 he joined the Jackson Laboratory in Bar Harbor, Maine. In the late 1930s he studied the genes responsible for rejection of tissue transplants in mice, later named the major histocompatibility complex (MHC). Snell, Jean Dausset and Baruj Benacerraf shared the 1980 Nobel Prize for physiology or medicine. His publications include *Search for a Rational Ethic* (1988).

Snell, Peter 1938–
New Zealand athlete

Born in Opunake, Taranaki, he was a surprise winner of the Olympic 800 metres in 1960, and then went on to win gold medals in both the 800 and 1,500 metres in the 1964 Olympics. He also achieved the Commonwealth Games double in 1962 and set world records at 800 metres and one mile (twice). In 1962 he broke the world mile record at Wanganui, New Zealand, on an outdated all-grass track, to become his country's first athlete to run a mile in less than four minutes.

Snell, Willebrod van Roijen, *Latin* Snellius 1580–1626
Dutch mathematician

Born in Leyden, he was Professor of Mathematics at the University of Leyden (1613) and discovered the law of refraction known as Snell's law, which relates the angles of incidence and refraction of a ray of light passing between two media of different refractive index. He extensively developed the use of triangulation in surveying.

Snow, C(harles) P(ercy), 1st Baron 1905–80
English novelist and physicist

Born in Leicester, he was educated at Alderman Newton's School, then studied science at Leicester University College, and Christ's College, Cambridge, and became a Fellow of Christ's College (1930–50) and a tutor there (1935–45). He was chief of scientific personnel for the Ministry of Labour during World War II, and a Civil Service commissioner from 1945 to 1960. His major sequence of novels began with *Strangers and Brothers* (1940), which gave its name to the series as a whole, and features the character Lewis Eliot, through whose eyes the dilemmas of the age are focused. It was followed after the war by *The Light and the Dark* (1947) and *Time of Hope* (1949). *The Masters* (1951) stages the conflict aroused by the election of a new master in a Cambridge college. *The New Men* (1954) poses the dilemma faced by scientists in the development of nuclear fission. Other books include *Corridors of Power* (1964) and *The Sleep of Reason* (1968). Several have been adapted for theatre and television. Though the chief characters of his cycle are rather supine, being manipulated to exhibit the expressed problems, mostly of power and prestige, his work shows a keen appreciation of moral issues in a science-dominated age. His controversial *Two Cultures* (Rede Lecture, 1959) discussed the dichotomy between science and literature and his belief in closer contact between them. Created a life peer in 1964, he was made Parliamentary Secretary at the Ministry of Technology (1964–66) and Lord Rector of St Andrews University (1961–64). In 1950 he married the novelist, Pamela Hansford Johnson. 📖 J Thale, *C P Snow* (1964)

Snow, John 1813–58
English anaesthetist and epidemiologist

Born in York, he was a young general practitioner when cholera first struck Great Britain in 1831–32, and his experience then convinced him that the disease was spread through contaminated water. After 1836 he practised in London, where he carried out brilliant epidemiological investigations during the cholera outbreaks of 1848 and 1854, tracing one local outbreak to a well in Soho, into which raw sewage was seeping. His additional work concentrated on the river Thames, into which many of London's sewers drained and from which much of London's domestic water was obtained. Snow was also a pioneer anaesthetist. He completed important experimental work on ether and chloroform, devised equipment to administer anaesthetics, and in 1853 administered chloroform to Queen Victoria, during the birth of Prince Leopold.

Snowdon, Antony Charles Robert Armstrong-Jones, 1st Earl of 1930–

English photographer

Born in London and educated at Eton and Cambridge, he started as a photographic assistant in the studios of Baron (Nahum). He was married to HRH Princess Margaret (1960–78), and was created Earl of Snowdon in 1961. He became a freelance photojournalist in 1951 and an artistic adviser to many publications, designing the aviary of London Zoo in 1965. A *Vogue* photographer since 1954, his informal portraits of the famous have often captured unusual facets of character, especially those taken during stage performances. Recently, he has sympathetically recorded the plight of the handicapped and disabled, both old and young, and has produced documentaries for television on similar themes. He was the presenter of the television series Snowdon on Camera (1981) and was awarded the Royal Photographic Society Silver Progress Medal in 1985. His publications include *Stills 1983–1987* (1987) and *Public Appearances 1987–1991* (1991). 📖 Helen Cathcart, *Lord Snowdon* (1968)

Snyder, Gary 1930–

US poet

Born in San Francisco, he was educated at the University of California. Originally associated with the Beat poets and portrayed as 'Japhy Ryder' in Jack Kerouac's *The Dharma Bums* (1958), he showed great concern for the natural world and the values of simple living and hard physical work, earning his living as a lumberjack and forestry warden. He spent eight years in Japan studying Zen Buddhism (1958–66), and his writing is influenced by an interest in Asian religious practices and literary traditions, as is evident in *Myths and Texts* (1960), *The Back Country* (1968), and the Whitmanesque *Axe Handles* (1984). *Turtle Island* (1974) was awarded a Pulitzer Prize. *Earth House Hold* (1969) was a founding text of the ecology movement. 📖 B Almon, *Gary Snyder* (1979)

Snyder, Solomon Halbert 1938–

US psychiatrist and pharmacologist

Born in Washington, he studied medicine at Georgetown University (1962), and then worked at the National Institute of Medical Health in Bethesda, Maryland (1963–65), and Johns Hopkins Hospital in Baltimore (1965–68). He held a number of professorships at Johns Hopkins Medical School, and in 1980 became Distinguished Service Professor in Neuroscience, Psychiatry and Pharmacology there. From the mid-1960s Snyder investigated the biochemistry of nervous tissue, studying neurotransmitter substances and the ornithine decarboxylase enzyme, which is possibly involved in regulating RNA synthesis. His other major interest is in the effects of opiates and psychotropic drugs on the brain and the naturally occurring brain hormones, enkephalins and endorphins. In 1973 he successfully demonstrated the presence of opiate receptors in nervous tissue, and he has studied many neurologically important compounds. More recently he has studied ion transport across membranes and the calcium-regulated enzyme nitric oxide synthase which synthesizes nitric oxide (1990).

Snyders, Frans 1579–1657

Flemish painter

Born in Antwerp, a pupil of Pieter Brueghel the Younger, he specialized in still life and animals, often assisting Rubens and other painters in hunting scenes. He was court painter to the Governor of the Low Countries.

S O See Davies, Stephen Owen

Soames, (Arthur) Christopher John, Baron Soames 1920–87

English Conservative politician

Educated at Eton and Sandhurst, he was commissioned in the Coldstream Guards and during World War II served in the Middle East, Italy and France. In 1947 he married Mary, daughter of Sir Winston Churchill, and embarked on a political career, entering the House of Commons in 1950. He held junior ministerial posts under Churchill and Sir Anthony Eden before becoming War Secretary in 1958 in Harold Macmillan's administration and then Agriculture Minister (1960–64). He was ambassador to France (1968–72) and a member of the European Commission (1973–77). He was made a life peer in 1978 and, with the return of the Conservatives under Margaret Thatcher in 1979, was made Lord President and Leader of the House of Lords. He will be best remembered for period as Governor of Rhodesia (1979–80), in which he oversaw its transition to the independent state of Zimbabwe.

Soane, Sir John 1753–1837

English architect

Born near Reading, Berkshire, he studied architecture under George Dance (the Younger) and was assistant to Henry Holland. He then won the travelling scholarship of the Royal Academy and spent 1777–80 in Italy, developing a restrained neoclassical style of his own. He designed the Bank of England (1788–1833, now destroyed), Dulwich College Art Gallery (1811–14), and his own house in Lincoln's Inn Fields, London, which he bequeathed to the nation as the Sir John Soane Museum. He was professor at the Royal Academy from 1806. 📖 John Summerson, *Sir John Soane* (1952)

Soares, Mário Alberto Nobre Lopes 1924–

Portuguese politician

Born in Lisbon and educated at Lisbon University and in the Faculty of Law at the Sorbonne, Paris, he was politically active in the democratic socialist movement from his early twenties and was imprisoned for his activities on several occasions. In 1968 he was deported by António Salazar to São Tome, returning to Europe in 1970 and living in exile in Paris until 1974, when he returned to co-found the Social Democratic Party (PSD). In the same year he was elected to the Assembly and was soon brought into the government. He was Prime Minister (1976–78, 1983–85), and in 1986 was elected Portugal's first civilian President for 60 years.

Sobers, Gary, properly Sir Garfield St Auburn Sobers 1936–

West Indian cricketer

He was born in Bridgetown, Barbados. In 93 Test matches for the West Indies (captain 1965–74), he scored more than 8,000 runs (including 26 centuries), and took 235 wickets and 110 catches. A cricketing phenomenon, he could deliver three kinds of bowling (fast, medium and slow spin) and bat with tireless brilliance and power. He held the world record for the highest Test innings (365 not out, made at Kingston, Jamaica, in 1958), until Brian Lara made 375 against England in 1994. In county cricket he played for Nottinghamshire (captain 1968–74), and achieved the remarkable feat of scoring a maximum of 36 runs (six sixes) off one over against Glamorgan at Swansea in 1968. This feat has since been equalled by Ravi Shastri in the 1984–85 season. He was knighted on his retirement from cricket in 1975. 📖 Gordon Bell, *Sir Garfield Sobers* (1978)

Sobrero, Ascanio 1812–88

Italian chemist

Born in Casale, Montferrato, he studied medicine at Turin, and organic chemistry at Paris and with Justus von Liebig at Giessen. From 1844 he taught at Turin, being appointed to the chair in 1847. In 1844 or 1845 he created nitroglycerine, of which he described the explosive properties and investigated the effects as a drug.

Sobukwe, Robert 1924–77
South African nationalist leader

Educated at mission schools and Fort Hare College, he was president of the Students' Representative Council in 1949 and a member of the ANC Youth League. He was dismissed from his teaching post in 1952 because of his participation in the defiance campaign, and taught for the next seven years at Fort Hare College. He helped found the Pan-African Congress (PAC) in 1959 and was elected its president. He was banned in 1960 and imprisoned until 1969.

Socinus, Faustus, *Latin name of* Fausto Paulo Sozini 1539–1604
Italian religious reformer

Born in Siena, the nephew of Laelius Socinus, and co-founder with his uncle of Socinianism, he studied theology at Basle, where he developed his uncle's anti-Trinitarian doctrines, arguing that Martin Luther and John Calvin had not gone far enough and that human reason alone was the only solid basis of Protestantism. Later he became secretary to Duke Orsini in Florence (1563–75). In 1578, on the publication of his *De Jesu Christo Servatore*, he narrowly escaped assassination, and moved to Poland, where he became leader of an anti-Trinitarian branch of the Reformed Church in Kraków. At the synod of Bresz in 1588 he argued against all the chief Christian dogmas, including the divinity of Christ, original sin, and justification by faith. He was denounced by the Inquisition in 1590 and his possessions were confiscated. Destitute, he sought refuge in the village of Luclawice, where he died.

Socinus, Laelius, *also called* Lelio Francesco Maria Sozini 1525–62
Italian Protestant reformer

He was born in Siena and studied law. Turning to biblical research, he settled in Zurich in 1548, and then travelled widely, meeting leading Protestant Reformers including John Calvin and Philip Melanchthon. He developed an anti-Trinitarian doctrine that sought to reconcile Christianity with humanism, which profoundly influenced his nephew, Faustus Socinus.

Socrates 469–399BC
Greek philosopher

He was born in Athens, the son of a stonemason (which he also became). In middle age he married Xanthippe, by whom he had three sons. He fought bravely as a hoplite in the Peloponnesian War, opposed the collective sentence on the generals convicted after Arginusae (406), and refused to co-operate with the Thirty Tyrants. He is represented as ugly, snub-nosed and with a paunch. He wrote nothing, founded no school and had no formal disciples, but along with Plato and Aristotle is one of the three great figures in ancient philosophy. His pivotal influence was such that all earlier Greek philosophy is classified as 'pre-Socratic', and he was responsible for the shift of philosophical interest from speculations about the natural world and cosmology to ethics and conceptual analysis. He was caricatured by Aristophanes in *The Clouds*, in which he is associated with the Sophists, whom in fact he opposed, and was adulated by Xenophon. The principal sources for his life are the dialogues of Plato, especially the *Apology*, *Crito* and *Phaedo*, which describe Socrates' trial, last days and death; in later dialogues he makes Socrates the mouthpiece for what were undoubtedly his own opinions. He held aloof from politics, guided by his 'voice' which impelled him to philosophy and to the examination of conventional morality. The 'Socratic method' was to ask for definitions of familiar concepts such as justice, courage and piety, to elicit contradictions in the responses of his interlocutors, and thus to demonstrate their ignorance, which he

claimed to share. This unpopular activity no doubt contributed to the demands for his conviction for 'impiety' and 'corrupting the youth', and he was tried at the age of 70. He rejected the option of merely paying a fine, declined a later opportunity to escape from prison, and was sentenced to die by drinking hemlock. ☐ W K C Guthrie, *Socrates* (1971)

Soddy, Frederick 1877–1965
English radio chemist and Nobel Prize winner

Born in Eastbourne, Sussex, he studied at the University College of Wales, Aberystwyth and at Oxford. In 1900, after two years research at Oxford, he was appointed demonstrator in chemistry at McGill University, Montreal, where he and Ernest Rutherford studied radioactivity. Working in London and Glasgow, he demonstrated that radium produces helium when it decays, and that uranium decays into radium. His principal achievement was the discovery of isotopes, which was of fundamental importance to all physics and chemistry. In 1914 he was appointed to the chair at Aberdeen, where he was employed on chemical research connected with World War I. Moving to Oxford in 1919 as Dr Lee's Professor of Chemistry (1919–1936), Soddy reorganized the laboratory facilities and the teaching syllabus. In 1921 he was awarded the Nobel Prize for chemistry. After his retirement he wrote on ethics, politics and economics, urging fellow scientists to restrict their research to areas which had peaceful applications. ☐ George B Kauffman, *Frederick Soddy* (1986)

Söderberg, Hjalmar 1869–1941
Swedish novelist and playwright

Born in Stockholm, he wrote several collections of witty short stories, such as *Historietter* (1898, Eng trans *Selected Short Stories*, 1935), and novels of upper-middle-class life in Stockholm, including *Förvillelser* (1895, 'Aberrations'), *Martin Bircks ungdom* (1901, Eng trans *Martin Birck's Youth*, 1930) and *Doktor Glas* (1905, Eng trans 1963). His plays included *Gertrud* (1905). In the last period of his life, he turned from fiction to religious scholarship, obsessively researching the historicity of the New Testament. He is often called 'the Anatole France of Sweden'. ☐ B Bergman, *Hjalmar Söderberg* (1951)

Söderblom, Nathan 1866–1931
Swedish churchman and Nobel Prize winner

Born in Trönö, near Söderhamn, he was educated at Uppsala, ordained in 1893, and became Lutheran minister of the Swedish Church in Paris, then Professor of History of Religion at Uppsala (1901) and Leipzig (1912). In 1914 he was appointed Archbishop of Uppsala and primate of the Swedish Lutheran Church. A leader in the ecumenical movement, he wrote several works on comparative religion and was the principal promoter of the Life and Work movement. He was awarded the Nobel Peace Prize in 1930. ☐ P Katz, *Nathan Söderblom: A Prophet of Christian Unity* (1949)

Södergran, Edith 1892–1923
Finno-Swedish Expressionist poet

The daughter of a peasant who worked in Alfred Nobel's factory, she moved with her family to the Karelia peninsula, where the landscape and the people had a profound effect on her. After an unhappy love affair, she published *Dikter* (1916, 'Poems'). This was followed by *Septemberlyran* (1918, 'September Lyre'), *Rosenaltaret* (1919, 'The Rose Altar') and the ironically titled *Fremtidens skugga* (1920, 'The Shadow of the Future'), each of which attested to a growing sense of the poet as a prophetic, almost magical figure. She still exerts considerable influence on younger Swedish poets, who value her passionate imagery and a robust metre that occasionally suggests the works of **Emily Dickinson**. ▥ G S Schoolfield, *Edith Södergran* (1984); L de Freyes, *Edith Södergran* (1970)

Söderström, Elisabeth Anna 1927–
Swedish soprano
Born in Stockholm, she studied at the Stockholm Opera School, and was engaged by the Royal Opera (1950). She made her debut at Glyndebourne in 1957, at the Metropolitan Opera Company in 1959 and at Covent Garden, London in 1960, and subsequently sang in all the leading international opera houses, touring extensively in Europe, the USA and the USSR. Her roles range from Nero in **Monteverdi's** *Poppea*, to roles in **Mozart**, **Tchaikovsky**, **Strauss**, **Debussy**, **Janáček** and **Benjamin Britten**. In 1959 she sang all three leading female roles in *Der Rosenkavalier*. She has published two autobiographical works, *I min tonart* (1978) and *Sjung ut, Elisabeth* (1986).

Sodoma, Il, *sobriquet of* Giovanni Antonio Bazzi 1477–1549
Italian religious and historical painter
Born in Vercelli, a Lombard, he painted frescoes in Monte Oliveto Maggiore near Siena before being called to the Vatican in 1508, where he started painting the fresco of *The Marriage of Alexander and Roxane* in the Villa Farnese, but was later superseded by **Raphael**. His masterpieces date from his second Siena period and include *Christ at the Column*, *St Sebastian* and *Ecstasy of St Catherine*.

Soeharto, Thojib N J See Suharto, Thojib N J

Soekarno, Ahmed See Sukarno, Ahmed

Soffici, Ardengo 1879–1964
Italian poet and painter
Born in Rignano, he was in Paris in the decade before World War I, where he met **Max Jacob**, **Guillaume Apollinaire** and **Picasso**. He returned to Italy to broadcast his new ideas in the review *Leonardo*, and became a ferocious adherent of the Futurism of **Emilio Marinetti**. He embraced fascism with enthusiasm, and survived to take a part in later literary-political activity. Among his writings are *Giornale di bordo* (1915), *Estetica futurista* (1920) and *Diario di Borghi* (1933).

Soglo, Nicéphore 1934–
Benin politician
Born in Lomé, Togo, and educated at the University of Paris-Sorbonne, he became Inspector General of Finances at the Benin Finance Ministry and a Governor of the International Monetary Fund. As leader of the Benin Renaissance Party, he was Prime Minister of a transitional national executive council in 1990–91 after a civilian coup, and President of Benin in a coalition government from 1991 to October 1996.

Sokolow, Anna 1912–
US dancer, choreographer and teacher
Born in Hartford, Connecticut, she studied at the School of American Ballet and Metropolitan Opera Ballet School, and became one of **Martha Graham's** original dancers (1930–39). She took up choreography in 1934, founded her own troupe and, in 1939, the first modern dance company in Mexico, called La Paloma Azul. She retired from the stage in 1954, but continued to teach and choreograph dances for her own and other companies, for stage, television and film. As a choreographer, she is an uncompromising social critic. She has also conducted pioneering collaborations with experimental jazz composers.

Solario, Antonio, *nicknamed* Lo Zingaro ('the Gypsy') c.1382–1455
Neapolitan painter
Born in Civita in the Abruzzi, originally a blacksmith, he painted frescoes in the Benedictine monastery at Naples.

Sole, David Michael Barclay 1962–
Scottish rugby player
Born in Aylesbury, Buckinghamshire, he was educated at Glenalmond and Exeter University. He played club rugby there before returning to Scotland to join Edinburgh Academicals. He was first selected for his country in 1986, and succeeded Finlay Calder (1957–) as captain in 1990, leading the team to the Grand Slam in that year, and to the semi-final of the World Cup in 1991. Relatively short for a prop forward, he compensated with a combination of strength and expert technique. He played three times for the British Lions in 1989. With over 20 appearances as captain, he is the most capped player in that role. He retired in 1992.

Soleri, Paolo 1919–
Italian–US architect and urban planner
Born in Turin, Italy, he gained a doctorate in architecture at the Torina Politècnico, then emigrated to the USA in 1947 and studied with **Frank Lloyd Wright**. A visionary architectural designer, he has planned compact housing communities (*arcologies*, from *architecture* and *ecology*), which are characterized by geometric forms and are designed to preserve the environment and conserve energy. Working in Arizona, where he established the Cosanti Foundation, he constructed his first experimental city (Arcosanti) in the 1970s.

Solis y Ribadeneyra, Antonio de 1610–86
Spanish writer
He was private secretary to **Philip IV** and historiographer of the Indies. He wrote poems and dramas, and *Historia de la Conquista de México* (1684). ▥ L Arocene, *Antonio de Solis y Ribadeneyra* (1963)

Sologub, Fyodor, *pseudonym of* Fyodor Kuzmich Teternikov 1863–1927
Russian novelist
He was born in St Petersburg, and worked as a schoolmaster for 25 years before concentrating on writing. His best-known book is *Myelki byes* (1907, Eng trans *The Little Demon*, 1916). He also wrote a trilogy of symbolic novels, *Tvorimaya legenda* (1908–12, Eng trans *The Created Legend*, 1916), and many short stories, fables, fairytales and poems. ▥ S Rubinovitz, *Sologub's Literary Children* (1980)

Solomon See panel p1724

Solomon, *professional name of* Solomon Cutner 1902–88
English pianist
Born in London, he played with great success as a child, then retired for further study. Later, he re-established his reputation as a performer of the works of **Mozart**, **Beethoven**, **Brahms** and modern composers, notably **Arthur Bliss**. In 1955 he suffered a stroke which cut short his career.

Solomon, Solomon Joseph 1860–1927
English portrait and mural painter
He was born in London. He served in World War I and initiated the use of camouflage in the British army.

Solomos, Dionysios 1798–1857
Greek poet
He was born on the island of Zakynthos, where his father was a rich nobleman and tobacco grower. He studied at the university in Cremona and tutored in Italian at the University of Padua from 1815. He wrote his first poetry there in Italian, and returned to Zakynthos in 1818. He was embraced by the Society of Friends, a secret organization supporting Greek independence and a popular uprising against the Turks, and thereafter wrote all his

Solomon c.962–922BC
King of Israel

The reign of Solomon, who was the second son of **David** and **Bathsheba**, is described in 1 Kings 1–11 and 2 Chronicles 1–10. It is characterized by expansion in trade and political contacts, by an elaborate building programme, and by the centralization of authority in the Crown. His predecessor David had subdued the neighbouring Aramaeans, and the major kingdoms of the Near East were all in a relatively weak state, especially Egypt under the last kings of Tanis, and Assyria under the ineffectual Tiglath-Pileser II. Solomon strengthened his army more as a warning than as an intention, and was free for most of his reign from the need to undertake extensive military campaigns. He built up a corps of chariots and founded chariot cities (1 Kings 10.26), of which those at Gezer, Megiddo and Hazor have been excavated.

Solomon developed trade links with Phoenicia, Egypt, South Arabia, and in the north in Syria and Cilicia. He married Pharaoh's daughter, and developed relations with Hiram of Tyre. The principal building in Jerusalem was the Temple and royal palace, both described in detail in 1 Kings. To finance this programme, Solomon reorganized the administrative districts of Israel, reducing the old tribal loyalties and increasing revenues to the Crown. He also subjugated the Canaanite population, drafting many of them into his workforces.

Apart from his building, Solomon is famous especially for his wisdom, as shown in the story of the two prostitutes (1 Kings 3.16–28); as a legendary wise man several books were later attributed to him, including the Song of Solomon, the Wisdom of Solomon, Proverbs, and some of the Psalms. There was also a Book of the Acts of Solomon (1 Kings 11.41), but nothing further is known of it. In later Jewish and Muslim literature he was believed to control the spirits of the invisible world.

The heavy burden of taxation entailed by the luxury of the court bred the discontent that led in the reign of Solomon's son Rehoboam to the disruption of the kingdom; and the king's alliance with heathen courts and his idolatrous queens and concubines provoked the discontent of the Prophetic Party.

Among Solomon's contacts in the Arabian world was the queen of a country called Sheba, a country that makes its first appearance in history in this connection. The Queen of Sheba was the ruler of the Sabeans, a people who seem to have occupied a part of SW Arabia (modern Yemen), though they are placed by some in N Arabia.

She journeyed to Jerusalem to test the wisdom of Solomon and exchange extravagant gifts, such as spices, gold and jewels, although this may imply a trade pact. The story, as told in 1 Kings 10 and 2 Chronicles 9, describes the splendour of Solomon's court and extols his great wisdom, thus emphasizing the growing importance of Jerusalem and depicting the sagacious and diplomatic nature of international relations in the ancient Near East.

The story of the Queen of Sheba and Solomon can also be read in the Qur'an. According to later, Ethiopian tradition, the couple married and their son founded the royal dynasty of Ethiopia.

📖 Eugene H Maly, *World of Solomon and David* (1966).

'And when the queen of Sheba heard of the fame of Solomon concerning the name of the Lord, she came to prove him with hard questions.' 1 Kings 10.1.

poems in Greek. In 1823 he published *Hymnus is tis Eleftherian* (Eng trans *Hymn to Liberty*, 1957), a series of 158 quatrains personifying liberty as rising from the bones of all Greek heroes who had died in her defence; it was set to music by Mazaro in 1863, and became the national anthem of Greece. Described by **Goethe** as 'the **Byron** of the East', he is perhaps most famous for the hymn on the death of Byron, which he wrote in 1824. He moved to Corfu in 1828, and lived there until his death.

Solon c.638–559BC
Athenian lawgiver

He was born into an aristocratic Athenian family, and was elected archon in 594BC, in a time of economic distress, and was appointed to reform the constitution. He set free all people who had been enslaved for debt (by the so-called Seisachtheia), reformed the currency, admitted a fourth class (Thetes) to the citizenship, and set up a *Boulé* (council) of 400. He sought a compromise between democracy and oligarchy, and repealed the more stringent laws of Draco except those relating to murder. He wrote elegiac and iambic poetry, some of which survives, as a vehicle for his political and social observations; in particular he praised the concept of *Eunomia* (good Order), which he sought in his reforms. He is said to have travelled for 10 years after the completion of his work (although an alleged meeting with **Croesus** of Lydia is probably unhistorical). He died soon after his kinsman **Pisistratus** seized power.

Soloviev, Vladimir Sergeyevich 1853–1900
Russian philosopher, theologian and poet

Born in Moscow, the son of the historian Sergei Mikhailovich Soloviev, he proposed a universal Christianity which would unite the Catholic and Orthodox churches, and attempted a synthesis of religious philosophy with science. His main works were *The Crisis of Western Philosophy* (1875), *The Philosophical Principles of Integral Knowledge* (1877), *Russia and the Universal Church* (1889) and *The Justification of the Good* (1898).

Solow, Robert Merton 1924–
US economist and Nobel Prize winner

Born in Brooklyn, New York City, and educated at Harvard, he has been a professor at the Massachusetts Institute of Technology since 1949. He was awarded the 1987 Nobel Prize for economics for his 'study of the factors which permit production growth and increased welfare'. His publications include *The Labor Market as a Social Institution* (1990).

Solti, Sir Georg *originally* György Stern 1912–97
British conductor

Born in Budapest, Hungary, he appeared as a pianist at the age of 12, and entered the Franz Liszt Academy of Music, studying with Béla Bartók, Ernst von Dohnanyi and Zoltán Kodály. He assisted Bruno Walter and Arturo Toscanini at Salzburg (1935–37) and made a notable conducting debut at the Budapest Opera with *Le nozze di Figaro* (1938, 'The Marriage of Figaro'). Anti-Semitic pressure forced him to leave in 1939 for Switzerland, where he achieved success as a pianist and conductor. Postwar appointments included musical directorships of the Munich Opera (1946–52), Frankfurt am Main (1952–61) and Covent Garden (1961–71). Later, he conducted the Chicago Symphony Orchestra (1969–91), with which he toured extensively, and the London Philharmonic Orchestra (1979–83). He made a pioneering recording of Richard Wagner's *Ring of the Nibelung* for the Decca company, and conducted it at Salzburg and Bayreuth (1983). He was appointed artistic director of the Salzburg Easter Festival (1992–93). He took British nationality in 1972 and was the recipient of many international honours, including KBE (1971) and Commandeur dans l'Ordre des Arts et des Lettres in 1995. ⌂P Robinson, *Solti* (1979)

Solvay, Ernest 1838–1922
Belgian industrial chemist
Born in Rebecq-Rognon, he worked in his father's salt-purifying business and then helped to manage his uncle's gas works. He noticed that ammonia, carbon dioxide and salt in solution react to form sodium bicarbonate which can easily be converted into the soda ash required by glass, soap and porcelain manufacturers. He built the first sizeable plant with his brother Alfred at Couillet, near Charleroi, in 1865, and used the wealth generated by his process to found institutes of physics, chemistry and sociology.

Solzhenitsyn, Aleksandr Isayevich 1918–
Russian writer and Nobel Prize winner
Born in Kislovodsk, he was brought up in Rostov where he graduated in mathematics and physics in 1941. After distinguished service with the Red Army in World War II, he was imprisoned (1945–53) for unfavourable comment on Stalin's conduct of the war. Rehabilitated in 1956, his first novel, *Odin den' Ivana Denisovicha*, (1962, Eng trans *One Day in the Life of Ivan Denisovich*, 1963), set in a prison camp, was acclaimed both in Nikita Khrushchev's Russia and the West, but his denunciation in 1967 of the strict censorship in Russia led to the banning of his later novels, *Rakovy Korpus* (1968, Eng trans, 2 vols, *The Cancer Ward*, 1968–69) and *V Kruge pervom* (1968, Eng trans *The First Circle*, 1968). He was expelled from the Soviet Writers' Union in 1969, and was awarded the Nobel Prize for literature in 1970. *Arkhipelag Gulag* (3 vols, 1973–76, Eng trans *The Gulag Archipelago 1918–56*, 1974–78), a factual account of the Stalinist terror, was first published in the West between 1973 and 1975. In 1974 he was deported to West Germany; he later settled in the USA, and in 1994 returned to Russia. His memoirs, *Bodalsya telyonok s dubom* (1975), were published in translation in 1980 as *The Oak and the Calf*, and *Kak Nam Obustroit' Rossiyu?* (Eng trans *Rebuilding Russia*, 1991) in 1990. He won the Russian State Literature prize the same year. ⌂M Scammell, *Alexander Solzhenitsyn* (1984)

Somare, Michael Thomas 1936–
Papua New Guinea politician
Educated at Sogeri Secondary School, he was a teacher (1956–62) and a journalist (1966–68) before founding the pro-independence Pangu Pati (PP, Papua New Guinea Party) in 1967. He was elected to the House of Assembly a year later and in 1972 became Chief Minister. After independence in 1975 he was Prime Minister, heading a coalition government. He was forced to resign in 1980 in the wake of a government corruption scandal, but returned as Prime Minister (1982–85). In 1988 he stepped down as PP leader and became Foreign Minister in the government of Rabbie Namaliu until 1994.

Somers, Sir George 1554–1610
English colonist
A founder of the South Virginia company, he was commander (1610) of a fleet of settlers which was shipwrecked on the Bermudas (originally known as the Somers Islands), and claimed the islands for the British Crown.

Somers (of Evesham), John Somers, 1st Baron 1651–1716
English Whig statesman
Born in Worcester, he was called to the Bar in 1676. Associated with the 'country party', he was one of the counsel for the Seven Bishops (1688) and helped draft the Declaration of Rights. After the Revolution he held several posts until in 1697 he became Lord Chancellor and Baron Somers of Evesham. He was William III's most trusted minister, and was the object of frequent attacks, which resulted in his being deprived of the Seal (1700), and an impeachment by the Commons, rejected by the Lords (1701). He was President of the Privy Council under Queen Anne (1708–14). The *Somers Tracts* (1748), state papers from his library, were re-edited by Sir Walter Scott (1809–15).

Somerset, 6th Duke of See Seymour, Charles

Somerset, Edward See Worcester, 6th Earl and 2nd Marquis of

Somerville, Edith (Anna Oenone) 1858–1949
Irish novelist
She was born in Corfu, the daughter of an army officer, and was taken as a baby to the family home of Drishane in Skibbereen, County Cork. Educated at Alexandra College, Dublin, she studied painting in London, Düsseldorf and Paris, and became a magazine illustrator. In 1886 she met her cousin, Violet Martin (pseudonym 'Martin Ross') with whom she began a lasting literary partnership as 'Somerville and Ross'. They are known chiefly for a series of novels caricaturing the Irish. Beginning with *An Irish Cousin* (1889), they completed 14 works together, including *The Real Charlotte* (1894) and *Some Experiences of an Irish R.M.* (1899), the success of which led to two sequels, *Further Experiences…* (1908) and *In Mr Knox's Country* (1915). After Violet's death in 1915, Edith continued to write as 'Somerville and Ross', producing *Irish Memoirs* (1917) and *The Big House at Inver* (1925). A forceful character, she became the first woman Master of Foxhounds in 1903, and was Master of the West Carberry pack from 1912 to 1919. She was also a founder-member of the Irish Academy of Letters (1933). ⌂V Powell, *The Irish Cousins* (1970)

Somerville, Sir James Fownes 1882–1949
English naval commander
As a specialist in radio communications he served in the Dardanelles (1915), and in the Grand Fleet (1915–18). In 1939 he was invalided home from the West Indies with suspected tuberculosis, and was recalled to the active list in 1940. As vice-admiral in the Mediterranean, he sank the French ships at Oran (1940), shelled Genoa (1941), helped in the sinking of the *Bismarck* (1941), took part in the Malta convoy battle (1941), and after the entry of the Japanese into the war, became Commander-in-Chief of the British fleet in the Indian Ocean. In 1945 he was promoted to Admiral of the Fleet.

Somerville, Mary, née Fairfax 1780–1872
Scottish mathematician and astronomer
Born in Jedburgh, she was inspired by the works of Euclid and studied algebra and classics, despite strong disapproval from her family. From 1816 she lived in London, where she moved in intellectual and scientific circles and corresponded with foreign scientists. In 1826 she presented a paper on *The Magnetic Properties of the Violet Rays in the Solar Spectrum* to the Royal Society. In 1831 she published *The Mechanism of the Heavens*, her account for the general reader of Pierre Simon Laplace's *Mécanique Céleste*. This had great success and she wrote several further expository works on physics, physical geography and microscopic science. She supported the emancipation and education of women, and Somerville College (1879) at Oxford is named after her.

Somerville, Mary 1897–1963
Scottish educationist and broadcasting executive
Born in New Zealand, she was brought up in Gullane, East Lothian, Scotland, and educated at Somerville College, Oxford, where she met John Reith (later Lord Reith). Seeing radio as a powerful educational tool, she

asked Reith to employ her on a trial basis at the British Broadcasting Company (later Corporation) in 1925. By 1929 she was responsible for all broadcasting to schools. In 1947 she was made Assistant Controller, Talks, with a wider remit, and rose to Controller, Talks in 1950, the first woman to hold the post of Controller in the BBC.

Somes, Joseph 1787–1845
English shipowner

He was born in Stepney, London. In 1816 he took over the family company, and by the 1830s it had become the largest in England. He brought ships from the defunct East India Company for the new Australasian trade, chartering vessels to the government for the transport of convicts, troops and stores. By 1842 he was the largest private shipowner in the world, with 40 ships registered at Lloyd's, and was one of the group that in 1834 had revived *Lloyd's Register of Shipping*. Somes invested in colonial companies, particularly the New Zealand Company of which he became governor in 1840, and entered the British parliament in 1844, transferring nominal ownership of his ships to his nephews in order to escape disqualification as a government contractor.

Sommerfeld, Arnold 1868–1951
German physicist

Born in Königsberg, Prussia (now Kaliningrad, Russia), he was educated at the University of Königsberg and appointed as professor at the universities of Clausthal (1897), Aachen (1900) and Munich (1906). With Felix Klein he developed the theory of the gyroscope. He researched into wave spreading in wireless telegraphy, and generalized the quantization rules developed by Niels Bohr so that Bohr's quantum model of the atom could be applied to multi-electron atoms. He also evolved a theory of the electron in the metallic state.

Somoza (García), Anastasio 1896–1956
Nicaraguan dictator

Born in San Marcos, Nicaragua, the son of a wealthy coffee planter, he was educated there and in the USA. As Chief of the National Guard, he established himself in supreme power in the early 1930s. With army backing, he deposed President Juan Bautista Sacasa and replaced him in 1937. Exiling most of his political opponents and amassing a huge personal fortune, he retained power until his assassination. His sons, Luis Somoza Debayle (1923–67) and Anastasio Somoza Debayle (1925–80), continued dynastic control of Nicaragua until the 1979 revolution.

Sondheim, Stephen Joshua 1930–
US composer and lyricist

Born in New York City, he saw little of his wealthy parents but was taken under the wing of Oscar Hammerstein II, who taught him to write lyrics. He wrote incidental music for *Girls of Summer* (1956) before providing the lyrics for Leonard Bernstein's *West Side Story* (1957). The first shows for which he (somewhat unusually) wrote both the music and the lyrics were *A Funny Thing Happened on the Way to the Forum* (1962) and *Anyone Can Whistle* (1964). *Company* (1970, Tony Award), about married life in New York, was followed by *Follies* (1971, Tony award) and *A Little Night Music* (1973, Tony award), *Pacific Overtures* (1976), *Sweeney Todd, The Demon Barber of Fleet Street* (1979, Tony award), *Merrily We Roll Along* (1981), *Sunday in the Park with George* (1984, Pulitzer Prize), *Into the Woods* (1986), *Assassins* (1991) and *Passion* (1994). His complex and eclectic musicals are regarded as classics of the genre, the more extraordinary for having been produced in an era when the US musical is generally seen as being in decline. He departed from musicals in 1995 with the comedy thriller *The Doctor Is Out* which he co-wrote with George Furth.

Song Jiaoren (Sung Chiao-jen) 1882–1913
Chinese revolutionary and champion of parliamentary government

He was one of the leading members of Sun Yat-sen's revolutionary anti-Manchu organization, the Tongmenghui (T'ungmenghui, Alliance League), before 1911, helping to set up a branch in central China. On the establishment of a republic in 1912, the Tongmenghui was transformed into a political party, the Guomindang (Kuomintang, Nationalist Party). Song became its principal spokesman in the elections of 1912, carrying out a vigorous western-style electioneering campaign which called for a figure-head presidency, a responsible cabinet system and local autonomy. The Guomindang won the elections and Song was widely tipped to become Prime Minister. His programme, however, was a direct challenge to the hegemonic ambitions of the President, Yuan Shikai, and he was assassinated at Shanghai railway station by Yuan's henchmen.

Song Meiling See Chiang Kai-shek

Song Qingling (Soong Ch'ing-ling) 1892–1981
Chinese politician

The daughter of Charles Jones Soong, she married Sun Yat-sen in 1916. She played an increasingly active political role after his death (1925) and became associated with the left wing of the Guomindang (Kuomintang). She was elected to the Central Executive Committee of the Guomindang (1926) and was a member of the left-wing Guomindang government established at Wuhan in 1927 in opposition to her brother-in-law Chiang Kai-shek. After the collapse of the Wuhan government, she spent two years in Moscow (1927–29). During the 1930s she was a prominent member of the China League for Civil Rights. She returned to China from Hong Kong during the Japanese war in 1937. In 1950 she was one of the three non-communist vice-chairmen of the new Chinese Communist Republic, and between 1976 and 1978 served as acting head of state. 📖 Emily Hahn, *The Soong Sisters* (1941)

Sonnino, (Giorgio) Sidney Sonnino, Baron 1847–1922
Italian diplomat and politician

Born in Pisa of an English mother, he entered parliament in 1880 and occupied various ministerial posts, including Treasury Minister (1894–96). He was twice Prime Minister (1906, 1909–10), and as Foreign Minister was responsible with Antonio Salandra for bringing Italy into World War I on the side of the Allies. He remained Foreign Minister throughout the war and was part of the Italian delegation to the postwar conference in Paris.

Son of Sam See Berkowitz, David

Sontag, Susan 1933–
US writer and critic

Born in New York City, she attended the University of Chicago and Harvard. Although she emerged first as an experimental fiction writer, as author of *The Benefactor* (1963) and *Death Kit* (1967), her main impact has been as a critic. Her influential books include *Against Interpretation* (1966), *Styles of Radical Will* (1969), *On Photography* (1976) and *Illness as Metaphor* (1978), a study of the mythology of cancer (Sontag was later a sufferer herself), which she revised as *AIDS and its Metaphors* (1989) to take account of AIDS. She has made four films, *Duet for Cannibals* (1964), *Brother Carl* (1971), *Promised Lands* (1974), and *Unguided Tour* (1983). More recently she published another novel, *The Volcano Lover* (1992) and a play, *Alice in Bed* (1993). She was formerly married to the Freudian intellectual Philip Rieff.

Sophocles c.496–405BC
Athenian tragedian, one of the great figures of Greek drama

Sophocles was the son of Sophilus, a wealthy arms manufacturer of Colonus near Athens. In 480BC he led the chorus which sang the hymn celebrating the Greek naval victory over the Persians at the Battle of Salamis. He won his first dramatic victory at the Great Dionysia in 468, defeating **Aeschylus** apparently at his first attempt. He was twice elected *strategos* (general), once with **Pericles** in 440 (when they had to put down the revolt of Samos), and was appointed one of the commissioners to investigate the failure of the expedition to Sicily in 413. He was a personal friend of the historian **Herodotus**, and of the poet Ion of Chios; a conversation between Sophocles and Ion appears in Athenaeus (book 13, section 603). Unlike Aeschylus and **Euripides**, Sophocles is said to have declined invitations to live at royal courts. He left two sons, one by each of his two wives.

Aristotle regarded Sophocles as an innovator, for adding a third actor to the usual two, increasing the chorus from 12 to 15, and for giving each play in a trilogy its own theme and plot. The principal characteristics of his dramatic style concern the conflict of the individual and the state (most notably in *Antigone* and *Oedipus Tyrannus*), the action of individuals as showing their heroic stature, and the relation between an individual's character and behaviour. A generally good person, like Oedipus, can have a tragic end because of a defect in character (in this case, pride). Use of dialogue and dramatic irony are important elements in Sophocles' art. The problem of burial is prominent in both *Ajax* and *Antigone*; in the first as an Olympian directive that hatred should not pursue a noble adversary beyond the grave; in the second as a clash between sisterly compassion for a dead brother and the obligations to the state demanded by Creon.

The play generally regarded as Sophocles' greatest is *Oedipus Tyrannus*, in which the apparently innocent Oedipus is gradually revealed as the murderer of his father and the husband of his mother, and suffers the fate imposed by his own sentence. Aristotle based his aesthetic theory of drama in the *Poetica* on this play, and from it **Sigmund Freud** derived the name and function of the 'Oedipus complex'. In contrast to Aeschylean tragedy, where the plot is essentially static and the hero is virtually doomed from the beginning, the plot in Sophocles develops.

📖 Sophocles is said to have written 130 plays (of which seven were spurious), and won the dramatic prize on 24 occasions with 96 plays. Seven of the tragedies have survived: *Ajax* (date uncertain), *Antigone* (441), *Oedipus Tyrannus* (c.429), *Trachiniai* (c.429, 'Women of Trachis'), *Electra* (between 418 and 410), *Philoctetes* (409), *Oedipus Coloneus* (produced 401, after his death). In addition, a papyrus discovered in modern times contains a large fragment of a satyr-play *Ichneutai* ('Trackers'). See also R P Winnington-Ingram, *Sophocles* (1980); H D F Kitto, *Sophocles: Dramatist and Philosopher* (1958); C M Brown, *Sophocles's Imagination* (1944).

'There are many marvellous things, and nothing more so than man.' From *Antigone*, l.333.

Soong, Charles Jones d.1927
Chinese merchant and Methodist missionary

Born on Hainan Island, he went to the USA in 1880, where he became a convert to Christianity and was educated at Vanderbilt University. He returned to Shanghai, founded the first YMCA there and set up as Bible publisher and salesman. He was the father of Song Qingling, Song Meiling (b.1897, see **Chiang Kai-shek**) and T V Soong.

Soong, T V (Tse-Ven) (Tzu-Wen Sung or Ziwen Song) 1894–1971
Chinese financier and politician

Born in Shanghai, the son of **Charles Jones Soong**, he studied at Harvard and Columbia universities. His sister Song Qingling married Sun Yat-sen, and consequently he too became closely associated with the Guomindang (Kuomintang). A second sister, Song Meiling (b.1897), married **Chiang Kai-shek** in 1927. T V Soong provided the financial stability which made possible the 1926 Northern Expedition that reunited China under the Nationalists. He was Finance Minister of the Nationalist government at Guangzhou (Canton) (1925–27) and at Nanjing (Nanking) (1928–33), and was Foreign Minister from 1942 to 1945. He westernized Chinese finances, standardized the Chinese currency, and founded the Bank of China (1936). When the Nationalist government was overthrown in 1949, he went to the USA.

Soong Ch'ing-ling See Song Qingling

Soper, Donald Oliver Soper, Baron 1903–98
English Methodist minister

He was born in Wandsworth, London. Widely known for his open-air preaching at London's Tower Hill, he was superintendent of the West London Mission (1936–78), and wrote many books on Christianity and social questions, particularly on international issues from the pacifist angle. He was president of the Methodist Conference in 1953, and was created a life peer in 1965. His publications include *Calling for Action* (1984). 📖 Douglas Thompson, *Donald Soper: A Biography* (1971)

Sophia 1630–1714
Electress of Hanover

The youngest daughter of **Frederick V**, Elector Palatine, and **Elizabeth**, Queen of Bohemia, she was born in The Hague. In 1658 she married Ernest Augustus, Duke of Brunswick-Lüneburg, afterwards (1692) Elector of Hanover. She was the mother of **George I**. 📖 Maria Kroll, *Sophie, Electress of Hanover* (1973)

Sophia Alekseyevna 1657–1704
Regent of Russia

She was born in Moscow, the daughter of Tsar **Alexis I Mikhailovich** and his first wife Maria Miloslavskaya. After the death of her brother, Tsar Fyodor III (1682), she opposed the accession of her half-brother Peter and took advantage of a popular uprising in Moscow to press the candidature of her mentally deficient brother Ivan. A compromise was reached and both Ivan and Peter were proclaimed joint tsars, with Sophia as regent. Supported by her adviser and lover Prince Vasili V Gallitzin (or Golitsyn), she became the de facto ruler of Russia. During her regency a treaty of permanent peace was signed with Poland and treaties were also signed with Sweden and Denmark (1684) and with China (1689). However, unsuccessful campaigns against the Turks in the Crimea (1687, 1689) did much to discredit the regent and she was removed from power by nobles in 1689. She spent the rest of her life in a convent in Moscow.

Sophocles See panel above

Sophonisba d.c.204BC
Carthaginian noblewoman

The daughter of a Carthaginian general, during the Second Punic War (218–202BC) she married Syphax, King of Numidia, and urged him to join the Carthaginian side. In 203BC he was defeated by a Roman army led by Rome's Numidian ally Masinissa, who took Sophonisba captive and married her. The Romans, fearful of Sophonisba's influence on him, objected to the marriage and Masinissa complied, but, according to Livy, sent her poison to prevent her being sent as a captive to Rome. Corneille, Voltaire and Vittorio Alfieri have written tragedies based on this story.

Sopwith, Sir Thomas Octave Murdoch
1888–1989
English aircraft designer and sportsman
Born in London, he won the Baron de Forest Prize in 1910 for flying across the English Channel. In 1912 he founded the Sopwith Aviation Company at Kingston-on-Thames, London, where he designed and built many of the aircraft used in World War I, including the Pup and the Camel. He was chairman of the Society of British Aircraft Constructors (1925–27) and chairman (later president) of the Hawker Siddeley Group (1935, 1963). A keen yachtsman, he competed for the America's Cup in 1934. He was knighted in 1953. ▢ Robert Sopwith, *Thomas Sopwith, Surveyor: An Exercise in Self-Help* (1994)

Sorabji, Cornelia 1866–1954
Indian lawyer
Educated as the first female student at Decca College, Poona, she came first in her year and was awarded a British university scholarship, but this was refused on account of her sex. Eventually some friends arranged for her to attend Somerville College, Oxford, in 1888. Continuing her law studies at Lincoln's Inn, she became the first woman to sit the Bachelor of Civil Law examination (1893), although women were not admitted to the English Bar for 30 more years. She returned to India and took up the cause of women in purdah who were wards of court, becoming their legal adviser in Assam, Orissa and Bihar in 1904. In 1923 she moved to Calcutta and practised as a barrister. Her publications include *India Calling* (1934) and *India Recalled* (1936).

Sorabji, Kaikhosru Shapurji, *originally* Leon Dudley 1892–1988
British composer, pianist, and polemical essayist
Born in Chingford, Essex, of Parsee and Spanish–Sicilian descent, he was largely self-taught. His compositional style combines technical complexity with contrapuntal ingenuity, lavishness of texture and epic form. These qualities are exemplified in his *Opus Clavicembalisticum* (1930, premiered by him in Glasgow), a work lasting four hours, in three parts with 12 subdivisions. In 1936 Sorabji discouraged performance of his music, relenting only in 1975. In addition to piano music he wrote concertos, organ works, choral music and songs. His witty and outspoken critical writings were collected in *Around Music* (1932) and *Mi Contra Fa: The Immoralisings of a Machiavellian Musician* (1947).

Soraya, *properly* Princess Soraya Esfandiari Bakhtiari 1932–
Queen of Persia
Born in Isfahan of Persian and German parents, she was educated at Isfahan, and later in England and Switzerland. She became Queen of Persia (Iran) on her marriage to Muhammad Reza Pahlavi (1951). The marriage was dissolved in 1958.

Sorbon, Robert de 1201–74
French churchman
Born in Sorbon, near Rethels, he was educated in Rheims and Paris. He was the confessor of Louis IX and founded the college of the Sorbonne in Paris (c.1257).

Sorby, Henry Clifton 1826–1908
English geologist and metallurgist

Born in Woodbourne, Sheffield, he inherited a modest fortune which allowed him to devote his time to science. He was the first to study rocks in thin sections under the microscope, in order to determine their structure and origin. He also adapted the technique for the study of metals and other materials. In 1858 he published *On the Microscopical Structure of Crystals*, which marks a prominent landmark in petrology. He also wrote on biology, architecture and Egyptian hieroglyphics.

Sorel, Agnès, *known as* Dame de Beauté
c.1422–1450
French mistress of Charles VII of France
She was born in Fromenteau, Touraine. She was in the employment of Isabel of Lorraine, who was related by marriage to Charles, and was the king's mistress from 1444 until her death. Sorel was the first to be publicly acknowledged as the 'official' mistress of the king, a position of some significance during the *ancien régime*. A beautiful woman beloved by Charles, she exerted considerable influence over him and, was given an estate at Beauté-sur-Marne, hence her nickname. Soon after the birth of her fourth child, she died of dysentery, but the atmosphere of intrigue that had developed at the court resulted in her death being attributed to poison. The dauphin (later Louis XI) was suspected, probably by scandal-mongers trying to discredit him before the king.

Sorel, Georges 1847–1922
French social philosopher
Born in Cherbourg, Manche, he studied engineering and worked in the government department of bridges and roads (1870–92). He resigned his post to devote himself to the study of philosophy and social theory, and in particular the works of Nietzsche, Marx and Henri Bergson. His best-known work is *Réflexions sur la violence* (1908, 'Reflections on Violence'), in which he argued that political opposition must resort to violence and that socialism would only be achieved by confrontation and revolution. His work was read by political leaders as diverse as Lenin and Mussolini.

Sørensen, Søren Peter Lauritz 1868–1939
Danish chemist
Born in Havrebjerg, he was educated in Copenhagen, where he later became director of the Carlsberg Research Laboratory. In 1923, after several years research in enzyme activity, he devised the pH scale for measuring acidity.

Sorley, Charles Hamilton 1895–1915
Scottish poet
Born in Aberdeen, he was educated at King's College Choir School, and in 1908 he won a scholarship to Marlborough College. There, impressed by the rolling Wiltshire countryside, he started to write poetry. In 1914, prior to taking up his place at University College, Cambridge, he visited Germany, and found himself with divided loyalties when war broke out. One of the first to enlist, he believed in the war as a necessary evil, as his poems show. In 1915 he went with his battalion to France, where he was killed by a sniper at the Battle of Loos. *Marlborough and Other Poems* was published posthumously by his family in 1916. Sorley left fewer than 40 complete poems, the best of which are unsentimental and direct. *The Collected Poems of Charles Hamilton Sorley* were edited in 1985.

Sorokin, Pitirim A(leksandrovich) 1889–1968
US sociologist
Born in Turia, Russia, he went to the USA in 1923. After a career as factory hand, journalist and tutor, he became Professor of Sociology (1919–22) in Petrograd (now St Petersburg), specializing in the social structure of rural communities. Banished by the Soviet government in 1922, he became professor at Minnesota (1924–30) and

later at Harvard (1930–64), where he founded the department of sociology in 1930. He developed a theory which divided socio-cultural systems into 'sensate' and 'ideational' types. His works include *Sociology of Revolution* (1925), *Crisis of our Age* (1941), *Russia and the United States* (1944) and *Fads and Foibles of Modern Sociology* (1956).

Sorolla y Bastida, Joaquin 1863–1923
Spanish painter
Born in Valencia, he became one of the leading Spanish Impressionists, known especially for his sunlight effects, as in *Swimmers* and *Beaching the Boat* (Metropolitan, New York).

Sorsa, (Taisto) Kalevi 1930–
Finnish politician
Born in Keuruu and educated at what is now the University of Tampere, he worked in publishing and with the UN in the Ministry of Education. In 1969 he became Secretary-General of the Social Democratic Party and went on to become its president in 1975. He was elected to the Eduskunta in 1970, and served two terms as Foreign Minister between 1977 and 1987. When in 1987 the SDP formed a government with their main rivals, the conservative National Coalition Party, he became deputy Prime Minister.

Sosigenes fl.c.40BC
Alexandrian astronomer
He was adviser to Julius Caesar in his reform of the calendar, introducing the leap year with an extra day every four years. This system remained in force in the West until the Gregorian reform of 1582.

Sotheby, John 1740–1807
English auctioneer and antiquary
He was the nephew of Samuel Baker (d.1778) who in 1744 founded at York Street, Covent Garden, London, the first sale room in Great Britain devoted exclusively to books, manuscripts and prints. He became a director of the firm (1780–1800) which became known as Leigh and Sotheby. In 1803 it was transferred to the Strand. The business was continued by his nephew, Samuel (1771–1842), and great-nephew, Samuel Leigh (1806–61), an authority on cataloguing and early printing.

Soto, Hernando or Fernando de c.1500–1542
Spanish explorer in America
He was born into the nobility in Jerez de los Caballeros, Spain, but his family's fortunes were in decline, and he sailed to Central America in 1519. After helping Francisco Pizarro conquer the Incas in Peru, he was appointed Governor of Cuba and Florida (1536). In 1539 he set out to explore Florida, a region then known only vaguely. Following illusory tales of gold and often clashing with Native American people, he and his soldiers travelled through much of present-day Georgia, North and South Carolina, Tennessee, Alabama, and Oklahoma. They became the first Europeans (1541) to see the Mississippi River, and when de Soto died of a fever his body was sunk in the river to prevent its being desecrated by Native Americans.

Sottsass, Ettore, Jnr 1917–
Italian architect and designer
Born in Innsbruck, Austria, he studied architecture in Turin, graduating in 1939. After serving in World War II and a short period in an architectural practice, he moved to Milan and set up his own design office in 1946, becoming involved in the reconstruction of northern Italian towns. As an industrial designer he is associated from 1958 with the firm of Olivetti for which he designed several typewriters and other office equipment. He departed from mainstream design in the 1970s, becoming a leader in the Memphis group (formed 1981).

Soufflot, Jacques Germain 1709–80
French architect
Born in Irancy, he trained in Italy (1731–38) and became the leading French exponent of neoclassicism. He designed the Panthéon and the École de Droit in Paris, the Hôtel Dieu in Lyons, and the cathedral in Rennes.

Soult, Nicolas Jean de Dieu 1769–1851
French general
Born in Saint-Amans-la-Bastide, Tarn, he was made general of division (April 1799) by André Masséna, who owed him much of the credit for his Swiss and Italian campaigns. In 1804 Soult was appointed a Marshal of France by Napoleon I. He led the right wing in the campaign that closed at Austerlitz, and fought in the Prussian and Russian campaigns (1806–07). In Spain he pursued the retreating British and, though repulsed at La Coruña, forced them to evacuate the country. He then conquered Portugal, governing it until the arrival of the Duke of Wellington at Coimbra forced him to retreat to Galicia. In 1809–10, as Commander-in-Chief in Spain, he overran Andalusia, but was defeated by William Beresford at Albuera (1811). After the advance of the British on Madrid, Soult, vexed at the obstinacy of Joseph Bonaparte and the rejection of his plans, demanded his recall; but Napoleon, after Vitoria, sent him back to Spain. He neutralized the strategy of Wellington, but was defeated at Orthez and Toulouse. He turned a Royalist after Napoleon's abdication, but joined him again on his return from Elba and was made Chief of Staff. After Waterloo he rallied the wreck of the army at Laon, but agreed with Lazare Carnot as to the uselessness of further resistance. He was banished until 1819, when he was gradually restored to all his honours. 📖 Pater Hayman, *Soult: Napoleon's Much Maligned Marshal* (1990)

Souness, Graeme James 1953–
Scottish footballer and manager
Born in Edinburgh, he joined Liverpool in 1978 after spells with Tottenham Hotspur and Middlesbrough, and brought the club league championships and European Cups. He played for Italian club Sampdoria (1984–86), then returned home to become player-manager of Rangers, transforming the Scottish game by buying leading English internationalists. He succeeded Kenny Dalglish as manager of Liverpool in 1991, and resigned in 1994. He published an autobiography, *No Half Measures*, in 1985. In 1996 he became manager of Southampton.

Souphanouvong, Prince 1902–95
Laotian statesman
A half-brother of Prince Souvanna Phouma, he was educated in Paris, where he studied engineering. On returning to Laos (1938) he became active in the nationalist movement, and in 1950 he founded the Chinese-backed Communist Pathet Lao (Land of the Lao), to fight first against French rule and then, from 1954, against the ruling Lao Issara and rightist forces. His pro-Vietnamese, Communist ties led to his imprisonment (1959–60). During the civil war in Laos in the 1960s, he and the Pathet Lao escaped to the hills. In 1974 he became chairman of a coalition National Political Consultative Council and, following the declaration of a socialist republic (1975), he became President of the Lao People's Democratic Republic, retaining this largely ceremonial position until he retired in 1986. He was a moderating influence within the ruling Lao People's Revolutionary Party.

Sousa, John Philip 1854–1932
US composer and bandmaster
Born in Washington DC, he gained experience as a conductor of theatre orchestras, and in 1880 he became conductor of the United States Marine Band. His own band,

formed twelve years later, won an international reputation. He composed more than 100 popular marches, notably 'Semper Fidelis' (1988) and 'The Stars and Stripes Forever' (1987). He also composed 10 comic operas, the most successful of which was *El Capitán* (1896). He is known as the inventor of the sousaphone, a large brass wind instrument resembling the tuba.

Soutar, William 1898–1943
Scottish poet

Born in Perth, he was educated at Perth Academy. He was conscripted into the Royal Navy (1916–19), and contracted a form of spondylitis which confined him to bed for the last 13 years of his life. After demobilization he studied medicine and then English at Edinburgh, returning to Perth in 1923. As an undergraduate he published his first volume of verse anonymously, as *Gleanings by an Undergraduate* (1923), followed by *Conflict* (1931). In 1933 he published his first volume of verse in Scots, *Seeds in the Wind*, for children. This was followed by his *Poems in Scots* (1935) and *Riddles in Scots* (1937), which gave him a permanent place in the Scottish literary revival. The best examples of his work in English are *In the Time of Tyrants* (1939) and the collection *The Expectant Silence* (1944). His remarkable *Diaries of a Dying Man* were published in 1954, and his *Collected Poems* appeared in 1948. 🕮 A Scott, *Still Life* (1958)

South, Robert 1634–1716
English High Church theologian and preacher

Born in Hackney, London, he was educated at Westminster and Christ Church, Oxford. He was for a time in sympathy with Presbyterianism, but in 1658 he received orders secretly and in 1660 was appointed public orator of Oxford. His sermons, which are full of mockery of the Puritans, delighted the restored royalists. He became domestic chaplain to Edward, 1st Earl Clarendon, prebendary of Westminster (1663), canon of Christ Church (1670) and rector at Islip (1678), but his outspokenness prevented further preferment. He acquiesced in the Glorious Revolution of 1688, but strongly opposed the scheme of Comprehension. He published *Sermons on Several Occasions* (new edition 1878).

Southall, Ivan Francis 1921–
Australian author

Born in Canterbury, Victoria, he has written prolifically for children, including the escapist adventure series featuring airman Simon Black which began with *Meet Simon Black* (1950). His later books, which concentrate on more contemporary youth concerns, have won many awards, including *Ash Road* (1966), *The Long Night Watch* (1986) and *Let the Balloon Go* (1968, filmed in 1975). His World War II experiences, for which he received the DFC, led him to write a history of 461 Squadron, Royal Australian Air Force, *They Shall not Pass Unseen* (1956), and biographies of air hero Keith Truscott and aviation pioneer Lawrence Hargrave. *Bread and Honey* (1970) is about a teenage boy's relationship with a younger girl; *Josh* (1971) won the Carnegie Medal. Later works include *What About Tomorrow?* (1976), *King of the Sticks* (1979), which is set in 19th-century Australia, and *The Mysterious World of Marcus Leadbeater* (1990).

Southampton, Henry Wriothesley, 3rd Earl of 1573–1624
English soldier

The son of Henry Wriothesley, the 2nd Earl, he was born in Cowdray, Sussex. He was a patron of poets, particularly of Shakespeare, who dedicated to him his *Venus and Adonis* (1593) and *The Rape of Lucrece* (1594) and, according to some scholars, addressed the sonnets to him. He accompanied Robert, 2nd Earl of Essex, to Cadiz (1596) and the Azores (1597), incurred Queen Elizabeth I's wrath

by marrying the cousin of Essex, and took part in his rebellion. He revived *Richard II* in order to arouse anti-monarchic feeling, and was sentenced to death, but was released by James VI and I and restored to his peerage (1603). He aided the expedition to Virginia (1605) and was a member of a number of trading companies. He was imprisoned in 1621 on charges of intrigue, and died while in charge of the English volunteer contingent helping the Dutch against Spain. 🕮 A L Rowse, *Shakespeare's Southampton* (1965)

Southampton, Sir Thomas Wriothesley, 1st Earl of 1505–50
English statesman

He held various state offices under Thomas Cromwell, with whom he participated in the iconoclastic measures associated with the Dissolution. He came to favour with Henry VIII on the fall of Cromwell, having opposed the now discredited marriage to Anne of Cleves. Lord Chancellor from 1544 to 1547, he won a reputation for brutality, especially towards reformers. He was made an earl on the accession of Edward VI, but was soon afterwards deprived of the Great Seal for dereliction of duty.

Southcott, Joanna c.1750–1814
English religious fanatic

A farmer's daughter in Devon, she declared herself about 1792 to be the woman of Revelations, Chapter 12, declaring the imminent arrival of Christ. She came to London on the invitation of William Sharp the engraver (1749–1824), and published *A Warning* (1803) and *The Book of Wonders* (1813–14). Her announcement that she was to give birth on 19 October 1814 to a second Prince of Peace was received by her followers with devout reverence. But she fell into a coma and died of a brain tumour in December 1814. Some followers, who believed that she would rise again, still existed at the beginning of the 20th century. 🕮 J Duncan M Derrett, *Prophecy in the Cotswolds, 1803–1947: Joanna Southcott and Spiritual Reform* (1994)

Southerne, Thomas 1660–1746
Irish dramatist

He was born in Oxmantown, County Dublin. From Trinity College, Dublin, he passed to the Middle Temple, London, and in 1682 began his career with a compliment to the Duke of York (later James VII and II) in *The Loyal Brother*. Dryden wrote the prologue and epilogue, and Southerne finished Dryden's *Cleomenes* (1692). He served a short time under the Duke of Berwick and, at his request, wrote the *Spartan Dame*. His best-known plays are *The Fatal Marriage* (1694) and *Oroonoko* (before 1696), based on Aphra Behn. 🕮 J W Dodds, *Thomas Southerne, Dramatist* (1933)

Southey, Robert 1774–1843
English poet and writer

Born in Bristol, he was sent to Westminster School, but he was expelled in 1792 for his Jacobin sympathies and for denouncing whipping in the school magazine, and went on to Balliol College, Oxford. He met Coleridge in Bristol in 1794 and they wrote a topical drama together, *The Fall of Robespierre* (1794); Southey published a volume of *Poems* (1795) and an epic poem, *Joan of Arc* (1795). Also in 1795 he married Edith Fricker (d.1838), whose elder sister Sara married Coleridge. He made two trips to Lisbon (1795 and 1800) and then, after studying law, settled in Keswick. He had only £160 a year from a friend on which to live, until the government gave him a similar amount in 1807, by which time Southey's political views had mellowed. He had joined the Tory *Quarterly Review* in 1809 and remained a contributor under William Gifford and John Lockhart. He became Poet Laureate in 1813. Many of his short poems are well-known, such as 'Holly Tree' and 'After Blenheim'. His other works include biographies of

Nelson (1813), *Wesley* (1820) and *Bunyan* (1830), *A Vision of Judgment* (1821), *Naval History* (1833–40), and *The Doctor* (1834–47), a miscellany, which includes the nursery classic *The Three Bears*. He also published a *Journal of a Tour of Scotland in 1819* (1929). 📖 J Simmons, *Robert Southey* (1945)

Southwell, Robert 1561–95
English poet and Jesuit

Born in Horsham, Norfolk, he was educated at Douai and Rome, and became a Jesuit in 1578. He was appointed prefect of the English College, was ordained priest in 1584, and two years later went to England as a missionary and became chaplain to the Countess of Arundel, in whose service he wrote his *Consolation for Catholics* and most of his poems. In 1592 he was betrayed for supporting persecuted Catholics, and was tortured and thrown into the Tower, eventually suffering death at Tyburn for high treason. He was beatified in 1929. His longest poem is *Saint Peter's Complaint*, and his most famous is *The Burning Babe*. 📖 Christopher Devlin, *The Life of Robert Southwell* (2nd edn, 1967)

Southwood, Sir (Thomas) Richard (Edmund) 1931–
English zoologist and ecologist

Educated at the University of London (1949–55), he later became director of Imperial College Field Station at Silwood Park (1967–69) and Professor of Zoology and Applied Entomology (1969–79). He then moved to Oxford, where he became Linacre Professor of Zoology (1979–93) and Vice-Chancellor (1989–93). Since 1993 he has been Pro-Vice Chancellor there. He wrote *Land and Water Bugs of the British Isles* (1959, with D Leston), a volume which married scientific rigour with a popular approach, and has investigated the relation between insects and plants. He was Chairman of the Royal Commission on Environmental Pollution (1981–86) and Chairman of the Anglo-Scandinavian Committee for the Surface Water Acidification Programme, and became Chairman of the National Radiological Protection Board in 1985. He was elected Fellow of the Royal Society in 1977, and served as its vice-president (1982–84). He was knighted in 1984.

Soutine, Chaim 1893–1943
French artist

Born in Smilovich, Lithuania, he studied at Vilno and moved to Paris in 1913. He is best known for his paintings of carcases, his series of *Choirboys* (1927) and the magnificent psychological study, *The Old Actress* (1924, Moltzau collection, Norway). After his death, his vivid colours and passionate handling of paint gained him recognition as one of the foremost Expressionist painters.

Souza, Madame de, *née* Adelaïde Marie Emilie Filleul 1761–1836
French novelist

She was born in the Norman château of Longpré, and married the Comte de Flahaut. At the outbreak of the French Revolution (1789) she found refuge in Germany and England, and there learned of her husband's execution at Arras. She turned to writing, and in 1794 published her first book, *Adèle de Sénange* (1794). In 1802 she married the Marquis de Souza-Botelho (1758–1825), Portuguese minister in Paris. Later novels include *Émilie et Alphonse* (1799) and *Charles et Marie* (1801).

Sowerby, Leo 1895–1968
US composer and organist

Born in Grand Rapids, Michigan, he studied in Chicago and Rome, and became a teacher at the American Conservatory of Music in Chicago (1925–62). His music, which includes a wide range of symphonies, concertos and choral works, employs a traditional European style in

works often evocative of US scenes, such as *Prairie* (1929), an orchestral symphonic poem, and the suite *From the Northland*.

Soyer, Alexis 1809–58
French chef

Born in Meaux, he was destined for the Church, but fled to London in 1830, and became chef in the Reform Club (1837–50). He went to Ireland during the famine (1847), and in 1855 tried to reform the food supply system in the Crimea, by introducing the 'Soyer stove'. He was the most famous cook of his time, and wrote, among other works, *Culinary Campaign in the Crimea* (1857).

Soyinka, Wole, *in full* Akinwande Oluwole Soyinka 1934–
Nigerian dramatist, poet, novelist and Nobel Prize winner

Born in Western Nigeria, he was educated in Abeokuta and Ibadan before moving to England to do research at Leeds University and study the contemporary theatre. He became a play-reader for the Royal Court Theatre, London, and it was there that his first play, *The Invention*, was performed in 1955. He returned to Ibadan in 1959, and productions of *The Swamp Dwellers*, and a contrasting joyously ribald comedy *The Lion and the Jewel*, immediately established him in the forefront of Nigerian literature. He founded the Masks amateur theatre company (1960), and the professional Orisun Repertory (1964), companies which played an important part in his development of a new Nigerian drama, written in English but using the words, music, dance and pantomime of the traditional festivals. From 1967 to 1969 he was a political prisoner, and he later became Professor of Comparative Literature at the Ife University (1976–85), and Professor of Africana Studies and Theatre at Cornell University (1988–92). His writing is concerned with the tension between old and new in modern Africa, and includes his first novel, *The Interpreters* (1964), the poetic collection *A Shuttle in the Crypt* (1972), and the mostly prose 'prison notes', *The Man Died* (1973). His play *The Beautification of Area Boy* (1995) was banned by the Nigerian government but received its world premiere at the West Yorkshire Playhouse at the same time as its publication. He was awarded the Nobel Prize for Literature in 1986.

Sozini, Fausto Paulo See Socinus, Faustus

Sozini, Lelio Francesco Maria See Socinus, Laelius

Spaak, Paul Henri 1899–1972
Belgian statesman

He was born in Brussels, where he began to practise law in 1922. A socialist deputy for Brussels in 1932, he rose to become in 1938 the first socialist premier of Belgium, but resigned the following year. He was Foreign Minister with the government-in-exile in London during World War II, and in 1946 was elected President of the first General Assembly of the United Nations. He was Prime Minister again in 1946 and from 1947 to 1949. As president of the consultative assembly of the Council of Europe (1949–51) he was in the forefront of the movement for European unity, and as Foreign Minister (1954–57), instrumental in helping to set up the EEC. He was Secretary-General of NATO (1957–61), and Foreign Minister again from 1961 until his resignation from parliament in 1966. 📖 J H Huizinga, *Mr Europe, a Political Biography of Paul Henri Spaak* (1961)

Spaatz, Carl Andrews 1891–1974
US general and airman

Born in Boyertown, Pennsylvania, he was educated at West Point. During World War I he served with the newly created US army air force and shot down three German aircraft. Subsequently a committed supporter of air power as an integral part of modern warfare, he put his theories into practice in World War II when he commanded the 8th US Air Force in the strategic bombing campaign against Germany. In 1945 he was in charge of the operation which dropped atomic bombs on the Japanese cities of Hiroshima and Nagasaki.

Spallanzani, Lazaro 1729–99
Italian biologist and naturalist

Born in Scandiano in Modena, he studied law at Bologna and became a priest, and later rose to become Professor of Mathematics and Physics at Reggio University (1757), moving to Modena in 1763 and to the chair of natural history at the University of Pavia in 1769. He is remembered for his skills in experimental physiology, where he pursued wide-ranging and fruitful experimentation. Deeply interested in reproduction, he set about disproving the long-established theory of spontaneous generation, showing in 1765 that broth, boiled thoroughly and hermetically sealed, remained sterile. He argued that gastric juice constituted the key digestive agent, was the first to observe blood passing from arteries to veins in a warm-blooded animal, and was successful in artificially inseminated amphibians, silkworms and a spaniel.

Spark, Dame Muriel Sarah, *née* Camberg 1918–
Scottish novelist, short-story writer, biographer and poet

Born in Edinburgh, the daughter of a Jewish engineer, she was educated there at James Gillespie's School for Girls (the model for Marcia Blaine School in *The Prime of Miss Jean Brodie*) where she was 'the school's Poet and Dreamer', and Heriot-Watt College. She was married in 1938 and spent some years in Central Africa. When the marriage failed, she returned to Britain in 1944 and worked in the Political Intelligence Department of the Foreign Office; she remained in London after the war to become general secretary of the Poetry Society and editor of *Poetry Review* (1947–49). In 1951 she won a short-story competition with *The Seraph and the Zambesi*. Three years later she was converted to Roman Catholicism, an event reflected in much of her later writing. Since the early 1960s she has lived mainly in New York and Italy. She is pre-eminently a novelist and short-story writer. *The Comforters* (1957) was hailed by Evelyn Waugh as 'brilliantly original and fascinating' and her reputation grew steadily with the publication of *Memento Mori* (1959), *The Ballad of Peckham Rye* (1960), and *The Bachelors* (1961). She achieved public success with her sixth novel, *The Prime of Miss Jean Brodie* (1961), an eerie portrait of a schoolteacher with advanced ideas and her influence over her select band of pupils on the eve of war in Europe. In a newspaper interview in 1990, she maintained that the book was 'more progressive than I realized'. Later works include *The Girls of Slender Means* (1963), set in a Kensington hostel, *The Mandelbaum Gate* (1965), a much longer novel set in Jerusalem, *The Abbess of Crewe* (1974), an allegorical fantasy set in an abbey and satirizing the Watergate scandal, *Loitering with Intent* (1981), *The Only Problem* (1984), echoing the book of Job, and *A Far Cry from Kensington* (1988), a comic but sinister portrayal of London in the 1950s. Her stories were collected in 1967 and 1985, and the first volume of her autobiography, *Curriculum Vitae*, was published in 1992. She has also published a book for children, *The French Window and the Small Telephone* (1993), and has also written critical works on the Brontës, Wordsworth, and others. She was created DBE in 1993.
📖 A Bold, *Muriel Spark* (1990)

Sparks, Jared 1789–1866
US historian and biographer

Born in Willington, Connecticut, he was a tutor at Harvard and, for a while, a Unitarian minister at Baltimore, and chaplain to Congress (1821). He edited the *North American Review* (1823–29) and in 1832 began his *Library of American Biography*. At Harvard, he was McLean Professor of History (1839–49) and president (1849–53). He wrote, among other works, biographies of John Ledyard (1828) and Gouverneur Morris (1832), and edited works of George Washington (1834–37) and Benjamin Franklin (1836–40).

Spartacus d.71BC
Roman gladiator and rebel

Born in Thrace, he was a shepherd who became a robber, but was captured and sold to a trainer of gladiators at Capua. In 73BC he escaped and built an army of c.90,000 slaves and the dispossessed, with whom he defeated several Roman armies and devastated much of southern Italy. He was defeated by Marcus Licinius Crassus near the river Silarus in 71, and executed by crucifixion with his followers. The remnants of his army were annihilated by Pompey on his return from Spain.

Spassky, Boris Vasilevich 1937–
Russian chess player

He was born in Leningrad (now St Petersburg). He won the world championship from Tigran Petrosian in 1969, but lost, in his first defence, to Bobby Fischer in Reykjavík, Iceland, in 1972.

Speaight, Robert William 1904–76
English actor and author

He was the son of the architect Frederick William Speaight (1869–1942). He played most of the major Shakespearean roles for the Old Vic from 1930, and played Becket in T S Eliot's *Murder in the Cathedral* at the Canterbury Festival (1935). He wrote many biographies including *Hilaire Belloc* (1956), edited Belloc's correspondence (1958) and published works on drama.

Spears, Laurinda 1951–
US architect

She trained at Brown University, Rhode Island, and Columbia University, New York, and is principal and co-founder of the Arquitectonica International Corporation. The company, which employs over 80 architects, planners, designers and other related professions, designed over 60 buildings with a combined value of over $500 million in its first 12 years. Its hallmark was the incorporation of a giant rectangular void into the buildings. Their buildings include the Banco de Credito Corporate headquarters in Peru (1989) and the North Blade Justice Centre. The firm has received many awards, including the Virginia Chapter Award (1989) for the Centre of Innovative Technology in Fairfax, Virginia.

Spedding, Frank Harold 1902–84
US nuclear scientist

Born in Hamilton, Ontario, he studied chemical engineering at the University of Michigan and took his doctorate at the University of California at Berkeley. He spent his working life at Iowa State University at Ames. In 1942 he was co-opted into the Manhattan Project at the University of Chicago to develop the first atomic bomb. He and his co-workers produced six tons of uranium in the form of large pellets ('Spedding's eggs') which were dropped into matching holes in the graphite core. The pile became critical on 2 December 1942 in the first man-made nuclear chain reaction. After World War II, Spedding looked for cheaper ways of separating the lanthanides and developed the ion-exchange chromatograph. He used the same technique to separate the actinides, heavy metals of atomic weights of 89–103 with properties similar to the lanthanides.

Spee, Count Maximilian von 1861–1914
German naval commander

Born in Copenhagen, he joined the Imperial German Navy in 1878. In 1908 he became Chief of Staff of the North Sea Command. At the outbreak of World War I in 1914 he was in command of a commerce-raiding force in the Pacific Ocean. Off Coronel, Chile, he encountered an inferior British squadron and sank HMS *Good Hope* and *Monmouth*. He attempted an attack on British coaling and wireless stations in the Falklands, but six German ships were sunk by the British squadron under **Frederick Sturdee**. Von Spee and two of his sons went down with his flagship.

Speed, John 1542–1629
English antiquary and cartographer

Born in Cheshire, he worked for most of his life in London as a tailor. Through his historical learning he met Sir **Fulke Greville** and Sir Henry Spelman, and he published his 54 *Maps of England and Wales* (1608–10), incorporated into *The Theatre of Great Britain* and *History of Great Britain* (both 1611).

Speer, Albert 1905–81
German architect and Nazi government official

He joined the National Socialist Party in 1931 and undertook architectural commissions for the party, becoming **Hitler**'s chief architect in 1934. From 1941 to 1945 he was a member of the Reichstag, representing Berlin, and in 1942 was made Minister of Armaments; his talent for organization resulted in greatly improved industrial performance. Always more concerned with technology and administration than Nazi ideology, he openly opposed Hitler in the final months of the war, and was the only Nazi leader at the Nuremberg trials to admit responsibility for the regime's actions. He was sentenced to 20 years' imprisonment in Spandau fortress, and after his release in 1966 published *Inside the Third Reich* (1970) and *Spandau: The Secret Diaries* (1976). 📖 William Hamsher, *Albert Speer—Victim of Nuremberg?* (1970)

Speidel, Hans 1897–1984
German soldier

Born in Metzingen, Württemberg, he served in World War I and in 1939 was a senior staff officer. From 1940 to 1942 he was Chief of Staff to the German commander in occupied France. In July 1944, while Chief of Staff to **Rommel**, he was imprisoned after the failed plot to assassinate **Hitler**. In 1951 he became military adviser to the West German government. His NATO appointment as Commander-in-Chief of land forces, Central Europe (1957–63), aroused widespread controversy. He became President of the Institution of Science and Politics in 1964. He wrote 'Invasion 1944' as a contribution to *The Destiny of Rommel and the Reich* (1949), and the autobiography *Out of Our Times* (1977).

Speight, Johnny 1920–98
English comic screenwriter

Born in London, he worked as a milkman, insurance salesman and member of a jazz band, and after World War II began writing for such comic stars as **Frankie Howerd**, Arthur Haynes and **Morecambe and Wise**. He made his mark on television with the play *The Compartment* (1962), and the creation of the loud-mouthed, working-class bigot Alf Garnett in the controversial assault on sacred cows like religion and royalty, *Till Death Do Us Part* (1964–74). The series earned him Screenwriters' Guild Awards in 1966, 1967 and 1968, and the character was revived in another series *In Sickness and In Health* (1985–86). His other television work includes *Spooner's Patch* (1979–82) and *The Nineteenth Hole* (1989). Among his publications are *It Stands to Reason* (1973), *The Thoughts of Chairman Alf* (1973), and his autobiography, *For Richer, For Poorer* (1991).

Speke, John Hanning 1827–64
English explorer

Born in Jordans, Ilminster, Somerset, he served with the Indian army in the Punjab. In 1854 he joined **Richard Francis Burton** in a hazardous expedition to Somaliland and in 1857 the Royal Geographical Society sent them out to search for the equatorial lakes of Africa. Speke, while travelling alone, discovered the Victoria Nyanza and saw in it the headwaters of the Nile. In 1860 he returned with **James Grant**, explored the lake, and tracked the Nile flowing out of it. He was about to defend the identification against Burton's doubts at the British Association meeting at Bath, when he accidentally shot himself while partridge-shooting. 📖 Alexander Maitland, *Speke* (1971)

Spemann, Hans 1869–1941
German zoologist and Nobel Prize winner

Born in Stuttgart, he was educated there and in Heidelberg, and became professor at Rostock University (1908–14), director of the Kaiser Wilhelm Institute of Biology in Berlin (1914–19) and professor at Freiburg University (1919–35). An experimental embryologist, he discovered the 'organizer function' of certain tissues during development, showing that the fate of embryonic cells is not programmed at an early stage but rather by the tissues with which they are in contact. He wrote *Embryonic Development and Induction* (1938) and won the Nobel Prize for physiology or medicine in 1935.

Spence, Sir Basil Urwin 1907–76
Scottish architect

Born in India of Scots parents and educated at George Watson's College, Edinburgh, and London and Edinburgh Schools of Architecture, he assisted Sir **Edwin Lutyens** with the drawings of the Viceregal Buildings in Delhi. He was twice mentioned in dispatches during World War II. In the postwar years, he gradually emerged as the leading British architect, with his fresh approach to new university buildings and conversions at Queen's College, Cambridge, Southampton, Sussex, and other universities; his pavilions for the Festival of Britain (1951); the British Embassy in Rome; and his prizewinning designs for housing estates at Sunbury-on-Thames (1951). His best-known work is his prize design for the new Coventry Cathedral (1951) which boldly merged new and traditional structural methods. He was Professor of Architecture at Leeds (1955–56) and at the Royal Academy from 1961. 📖 Brian Edwards, *Basil Spence, 1907–1976* (1995)

Spence, Catherine Helen 1825–1910
Australian writer and feminist

Born near Melrose, Scotland, she emigrated to Australia in 1839. She published the first novel of Australian life written by a woman (*Clara Morrison*, 1854) and wrote five more novels, the last one (*Handfasted*, 1984) not published until after her death. A concern with social problems led her to make lecture tours of Great Britain and the USA. She pressed for proportional representation in *A Plea for Pure Democracy* (1861), and wrote Australia's first social studies textbook, *The Laws We Live Under* (1880). In 1897 she stood for the Federal Convention, becoming Australia's first woman candidate. *Catherine Helen Spence: an Autobiography* was completed after her death by her companion Jeanne Young in 1910. 📖 J Young, *Catherine Helen Spence: a Study and an Appreciation* (1937)

Spence, Joseph 1699–1768
English writer

He was educated at New College, Oxford, where he became Professor of Poetry (1727), and is remembered for his *Essay on Pope's Odyssey* (1727) and his anecdotes of **Pope** and other celebrities.

Spence, (James) Lewis Thomas Chalmers
1874–1955
Scottish poet and anthropologist
Born in Broughty Ferry, Dundee, he studied dentistry at Edinburgh, but turned to writing and in 1899 became a sub-editor on *The Scotsman* newspaper, and subsequently *The British Weekly* (1906–09). He became an authority on the folklore and mythology of central and South America and elsewhere, writing numerous books including *Mythologies of Mexico and Peru* (1907), *Dictionary of Mythology* (1913), *Encyclopaedia of Occultism* (1920), and *The Magic Arts in Celtic Britain* (1945). As a poet he was a pioneer of the use of archaic Scots language, in such collections as *The Phoenix* (1924) and *Weirds and Vanities* (1927). An ardent nationalist, he was one of the founder members of the National Party of Scotland in 1928, and the first nationalist to contest a parliamentary seat.

Spence, Peter 1806–83
Scottish industrial chemist
Born in Brechin (now in Cumbria), he worked in a grocery in Perth and then in a gasworks in Dundee, meanwhile reading all the scientific books he could find. One of the first to realize that valuable chemicals could be retrieved from the waste products of gas manufacture, he set up a plant at Burgh in Cumberland (Cumbria), where he concentrated on the production of copperas (ferrous sulphate) and particularly on alum (potassium aluminium sulphate), which had many industrial uses. In 1845 he took out a patent for a process which made the manufacture of alum much cheaper, although it brought serious health hazards in the form of noxious fumes. A few years later he moved the plant to Pendleton, near Manchester, where it grew to be the largest alum manufactory in the world.

Spence, William Guthrie 1846–1926
Australian trade unionist and politician
Born in the UK, he emigrated with his family to Australia in 1852, had no formal education and was working by the age of 13. His beliefs stemmed from his experiences, his eclectic reading and his Nonconformist background. Secretary of the Amalgamated Miners Association (1882–91), and foundation president of the Amalgamated Shearers Union (1886–93), his activities contributed to the maritime strike of 1890 and the shearers' strike of 1891, both of which ended in defeat for the workers. In 1894 he founded the Australian Workers Union, becoming secretary (1894–98) and president (1898–1917). A member of the New South Wales assembly (1898–1901), he entered federal politics in 1901, but although he was made Postmaster-General (1914–15), his major contribution to the Australian labour movement lay in his leadership and organization of rural unionism. Forced out of the union and the Australian Labor Party for supporting conscription in 1916–17, he sat as a Nationalist until defeated in 1919.

Spencer
English noble family
It was founded by the Honourable John Spencer, younger son of the 3rd Earl of Sunderland, and Anne, daughter of the great Duke of Marlborough (his brother became 3rd duke). His only son, John (1734–83), was created Earl Spencer in 1765.

Spencer, Sir (Walter) Baldwin 1860–1929
Australian anthropologist and biologist
Born in Stretford, Greater Manchester, England, he graduated in natural sciences from Exeter College, Oxford in 1884, in 1886 was elected to a fellowship at Lincoln College, and a year later was made foundation Professor of Biology at Melbourne University. In 1894 he joined Horn's expedition to Central Australia, where he collaborated with Francis Gillen in anthropological

studies which resulted in a number of invaluable published works, including *Native Tribes of Central Australia* (1889) and *Northern Tribes of Central Australia* (1904). In 1912 Spencer was appointed Chief Protector of the Aboriginals, and he was knighted in 1916.

Spencer, Herbert 1820–1903
English revolutionary philosopher
Born in Derby, he had a varied career as a railway engineer, teacher, journalist and sub-editor of *The Economist* (1848–53) before becoming a full-time writer. His particular interest was in evolutionary theory, which he expounded in *Principles of Psychology* in 1855, four years before Charles Darwin's *The Origin of Species*. Spencer regarded Darwin's work as welcome scientific evidence for his own a priori speculations and a special application of them. He also applied his evolutionary theories to ethics and sociology. An advocate of Social Darwinism, he coined the phrase 'survival of the fittest'. His major work was the nine-volume *System of Synthetic Philosophy*, which brought together metaphysics, ethics, biology, psychology and sociology; it was announced in 1860, and was published between 1862 and 1893. He viewed philosophy itself as the science of the sciences, distinguished by its generality and unifying function. His other works include *Social Statics* (1851), *Education* (1861), *The Man Versus the State* (1884) and *Autobiography* (1904). 📖 J Y D Peel, *Herbert Spencer: The Evolution of a Sociologist* (1971)

Spencer, Sir Stanley 1891–1959
English painter
Born in Cookham, Berkshire, he studied at the Slade School of Art, London, where he learned the linear drawing style which informs most of his work. Never part of any of the main movements in 20th-century British art, he remained an eccentric figure, tackling unfashionable religious subjects in his precise and distinctive style. These he transposed into his own local context at Cookham, especially in *The Resurrection* (1922–27). He was an official war artist in World War II when he painted a series of panels depicting shipbuilding on the Clyde. His best-known work is his decorative scheme of murals of army life for the Sandham Memorial Chapel, Burghclere (1926–32). His brother Gilbert (1892–1976) was also an artist. 📖 Kenneth Pople, *Stanley Spencer: A Biography* (1991)

Spencer Jones, Sir Harold See Jones, Sir Harold Spencer

Spender, Dale 1943–
Australian feminist writer and teacher
Born in Newcastle, New South Wales, she studied at the universities of Sydney and London before working as a series editor for Penguin Australia's Women's Library. The co-originator of the first international database on women, *Women's International Knowledge: Encyclopedia and Data*, she worked as a lecturer and taught Women's Studies courses on the politics of knowledge and the intellectual aspects of sexism. As well as being the Australian representative for a number of international academic journals, she sat on the management committee of the Australian Society of Authors, and has edited several anthologies of literature, as well as the journal *Women's Studies International Forum*. Her feminist books include *Man Made Language* (1981), *Invisible Women* (1982) and *There's Always Been A Women's Movement this Century* (1983).

Spender, Sir Stephen 1909–95
English poet and critic
Born in London, he was educated at University College, Oxford. One of the 'modern poets' of the 1930s, he was left-wing in outlook and essentially a liberal in thought. From 1939 to 1941 he was co-editor, with Cyril Connolly, of *Horizon*, and from 1953 to 1967 was co-editor of *Encounter*,

and was Professor of English at University College London (1970–77). He translated **Schiller**, Ernst Toller, **Rainer Maria Rilke** and **Federico García Lorca**, among others, besides writing much literary criticism. From his beginnings in 1930 with the novella *Twenty Poems* to *Engaged in Writing* (1957), he relived his experiences in the Spanish Civil War and World War II in *Poems from Spain* (1939), *Runes and Visions* (1941), *Poems of Dedication* (1941) and *The Edge of Darkness* (1949). Critical evaluations include *The Destructive Element* (1936), *Life and the Poet* (1942), *The Creative Element* (1944), and his first autobiography, *World within World* (1951). His later work includes *The Year of the Young Rebels* (1969), *The Thirties and After* (1978) and *Chinese Journal* (with David Hockney, 1982). *Collected Poems 1930–85* was published in 1985, and his *Journals* (1939–83) in 1987. In 1991, he compiled the volume *Character Studies*, with proceeds from sales going to AIDS patients. His acclaimed volume of poetry, *Dolphins*, was published in 1994. ⌨ H David, *Stephen Spender* (1993)

Spengler, Oswald 1880–1936
German philosopher of history

Born in Blankenburg, Harz, he studied at Halle, Munich and Berlin, and taught mathematics in Hamburg (1908) before devoting himself entirely to the compilation of the morbidly prophetic *Untergang des Abendlandes* (2 vols, 1918–22, Eng trans *The Decline of the West*, 1926–29), which argues, by analogy, that all civilizations or cultures are subject to the same cycle of growth and decay in accordance with predetermined 'historical destiny'. The soul of Western civilization is dead. The age of soulless expansionist Caesarism is upon us. It is better for Western man, therefore, to be engineer rather than poet, soldier rather than artist, politician rather than philosopher. Unlike **Arnold Joseph Toynbee**, whom he influenced, he was concerned with the present and future rather than with the origins of civilizations. Despite a certain amount of affinity between his political ideas and Nazi dogma, Spengler both criticized and was criticized by the National Socialist Party. Another work attempted to compare Prussianism with socialism (1920).

Spens, Sir Will(iam) 1882–1962
Scottish educational administrator

Born in Glasgow and educated at Rugby and King's College, Cambridge, where he studied both science and theology, he was Master of Corpus Christi College, Cambridge, from 1927 to 1952. He was chairman of the Consultative Committee on Education from 1934 and produced the report on *Secondary Education (Grammar Schools and Technical High Schools)* in 1938, which recommended the raising of the school-leaving age to 15 and a widening of the provision of secondary education. It embodied the best thinking of the interwar period and paved the way for the *Norwood Report* (1943) and the Education Act of 1944.

Spenser, Edmund c.1552–1599
English poet

He was born in London, the son of a gentleman tradesman. He was educated at Merchant Taylors' School and Pembroke Hall, Cambridge. His early writings, partly written at Cambridge, include translations of the *Visions* of **Petrarch** and some sonnets of **Joachim du Bellay**. Shortly after leaving Cambridge (1576) he obtained a place in Robert Dudley, Earl of **Leicester**'s household and this led to a friendship with Sir **Philip Sidney** and the Areopagus, a society of wits. His first original work, *The Shepheard's Calender* (1579), dedicated to Sidney, heralded the age of Elizabethan poetry and no doubt assisted in his career as a courtier. In 1580 he was appointed secretary to Lord Grey de Wilton, Lord Deputy in Ireland, and was rewarded for his involvement in crushing the Trim rebellion with Kilcolman Castle in Cork. He settled there

(1586), hoping to find leisure to write his *Faerie Queene* and other courtly works; these were written with an eye to the court no less than as a brilliant presentation of the art and thought of the Renaissance. In 1589 he visited London with Sir **Walter Raleigh**, who had seen the first three books of *The Faerie Queene* at Kilcolman and now carried him off to lay them at the feet of Queen **Elizabeth I**. Published in 1590, they were an immediate success, but a previous misdemeanour, the attack in *Mother Hubberd's Tale* on the proposed match between Elizabeth and the Duc d'Alençon, was not forgotten and the poet returned to Ireland in 1591 a disappointed man. He later published his wry reflections on his visit in *Colin Clout's Come Home Again* (1595). *Complaints*, published in 1591, contains, beside his early work, the brilliantly coloured but enigmatic *Muiopotmos, Mother Hubberd's Tale*, to which was now added a bitter satire on court favour, *The Early Tears of the Muses*, which lamented the lack of patronage; and his pastoral elegy for Sir Philip Sidney which is so frigid as to put their friendship in question. In 1594 he married Elizabeth Boyle and celebrated his courtship in the sonnet sequence *Amoretti* and his wedding in the supreme marriage poem *Epithalamion*. He revisited London in 1596 with three more books of *The Faerie Queene*, which were published along with the *Four Hymns*. In the same year, he wrote *Prothalamion*, and his prose *View of the Present State of Ireland*. Kilcolman Castle was burned in the 1598 Irish rising, but the Spensers escaped to Cork and from there to safety in London. ⌨ A C Judson, *The Life of Spenser* (1945)

Speransky, Count Mikhail 1772–1839
Russian politician and reformer

He became Tsar **Alexander I**'s adviser and in 1809 produced a plan for the reorganization of the Russian structure of government on the Napoleonic model, but was dismissed when **Napoleon I** invaded Russia (1812). Under **Nicholas I** he regained power and was responsible for the trial and conviction of the Decembrist conspirators of 1825. He also prepared major works on Russian law.

Speranza See **Wilde, Lady Jane Francesca**

Sperry, Elmer Ambrose 1860–1930
US inventor and electrical engineer

He was born in Cortland, New York. His chief invention was the gyroscopic compass (1911) and stabilizers for ships and aeroplanes. He also devised a new type of dynamo, an electrolytic process for obtaining pure caustic soda from salt, and a high-intensity arc searchlight (1918). He founded several companies for the manufacture of these inventions. ⌨ Thomas Parke Hughes, *Elmer Sperry: Inventor and Engineer* (1971)

Sperry, Roger Wolcott 1913–94
US neuroscientist and Nobel Prize winner

Born in Hartford, Connecticut, he studied zoology at Chicago University, then worked at Harvard and the Yerkes Laboratory of Primate Biology (1941–46). He taught at Chicago University (1946–52), and was Hixon Professor of Psychobiology at the California Institute of Technology (Caltech) from 1954 to 1984. He first made his name in the field of developmental neurobiology, in which his experiments helped to establish the means by which nerve cells come to be connected in particular ways in the central nervous system. In the 1950s and 1960s he pioneered the behavioural investigation of 'split-brain' animals and humans, establishing that each hemisphere possessed specific higher functions, the left side controlling verbal activity and processes such as writing, reasoning etc; whereas the right side is more responsive to music, face and voice recognition etc. These conclusions led him into the philosophy of the mind. He shared the Nobel Prize for physiology or medicine in 1981 with **David Hubel** and **Torsten Wiesel**.

Spielberg, Steven 1946–
US filmmaker

Steven Spielberg was born in Cincinnati, Ohio, the eldest of four children of an electrical engineer. His academic achievement was modest both at school and at California State College, where he studied English. He enjoyed filmmaking from an early age, and became one of the youngest television directors at Universal on projects that included *Night Gallery* (1969). A highly praised television film, *Duel* (1971), brought him the opportunity to direct for the cinema, and he followed this with a picaresque comic drama, *Sugarland Express* (1974). Since then, a succession of hits has made him the most commercially successful director ever, and by the age of 49 he had directed 15 films.

His films have explored primeval fears, as in *Jaws* (1975), or expressed childlike wonder at the marvels of this world and beyond, as in *Close Encounters of the Third Kind* (1977) and *E.T.* (1982). Other films include *Raiders of the Lost Ark* (1981), *Poltergeist* (1983), *Indiana Jones and the Temple of Doom* (1984) and *Gremlins* (1984). Later he concentrated on grand literary adaptations such as *The Color Purple* (1985) and *Empire of the Sun* (1987) and on the continuing adventures of his dare-devil hero Indiana Jones.

In 1984 he founded his own production company, Amblin Entertainment, which was responsible for *Gremlins*

(1984), *Back to the Future* (1985), *Who Framed Roger Rabbit* (1988), *Empire of the Sun* (1988), *Hook* (1991), *Jurassic Park* (1993) and *Casper* (1995). He also suffered disappointments, notably *Young Sherlock Holmes* (1985). In 1986 he was awarded the Directors Guild of America Fellowship. Despite his commercial success, he did not win an Academy Award until 1994, when he was voted Best Director for *Schindler's List* (1993), which was based on Thomas Keneally's true story about a self-seeking German industrialist who was transformed into a hero by employing Jews in his factory during World War II; produced in black and white, it had the characteristics of documentary, in marked contrast to the brilliance and excitement of his other films.

Spielberg has been twice married; his second wife since 1989 is the actress Kate Capshaw.

📖 Andrew Yule, *Steven Spielberg: father to the man* (1996); John Baxter, *Steven Spielberg: The Unauthorised Biography* (1996).

> 'The most expensive habit in the world today is celluloid not heroin and I need a fix every two years.' Quoted in *OM*, December 1984.

Speusippus c.407–339BC
Greek philosopher

He lived in Athens and was Plato's nephew and his successor as head of the Academy in 348BC. He produced a large body of work, but only a few fragments survive. He was admired by Aristotle.

Spielberg, Steven See panel above

Spillane, Mickey, *properly* Frank Morrison Spillane 1918–
US mystery and detective novelist

He was born in Brooklyn, New York City. He wrote for pulp magazines to pay for his education. The author of almost 30 books, Spillane is a leading exponent of the sensational school of detective fiction. His first book, *I, the Jury* (1947), introduced Mike Hammer, a womanizing, hard-drinking, hard-fighting, private investigator who punches his way with enormous relish through several books, including *Vengeance is Mine!* (1950) and *The Body Lovers* (1967). Spillane treats sex pruriently, and women as well as men become the objects of Hammer's insatiable sadism and violence. The novels have inspired many films and a television series. 📖 B Docherty, *American Crime Fiction* (1988)

Spilsbury, Sir Bernard Henry 1877–1947
British pathologist

Born in Leamington, Warwickshire, he studied physiology at Oxford, then entered the medical school of St Mary's Hospital, Paddington, and specialized in what was then the new science of forensic pathology. He made his name at the trial of Hawley Harvey Crippen (1910), and was appointed pathologist to the Home Office. As an expert witness for the Crown, he was involved in many notable murder trials, such as those of Mahon (1924), Thorne (1925) and Rouse (1931). His last important case was the murder of de Antiquis (1947).

Spinello Aretino c.1330–1410
Italian painter

Born in Arezzo, he spent most of his life there or in Florence. His principal frescoes were done for S Miniato, Florence, for the *campo santo* in Pisa and for the municipal

buildings of Siena. He tended to borrow stock scenes from the Florentine and Sienese masters, and his neat realism reveals some of the Gothic style.

Spingarn, Joel Elias 1875–1939
US critic, author, and social reformer

Born in New York City, he received a PhD from Columbia College in 1895 and taught comparative literature there until 1911, when he became an independent scholar. He is remembered chiefly for his work with the National Association for the Advancement of Colored People (NAACP), which he helped to found in 1901 and headed as president (from 1930). The Spingarn Medal, established in 1914, is awarded every year to an African-American who has reached high achievement in his or her field. He was also a founder of the publishing company Harcourt, Brace and Co (1919).

Spink, Ian 1947–
Australian dancer, choreographer and director

Born in Melbourne, he trained in classical ballet, and joined the Australian Ballet in 1969. In 1974 he went to perform with the Dance Company of New South Wales (now Sydney Dance Company). Moving to England in 1977 he formed the Ian Spink Group, and it was in partnership with Siobhan Davies and Richard Alston in Second Stride (founded 1982) that he achieved his first success there, becoming sole artistic director in 1987. Up-beat and theatrical, his work is both innovative and popular, and includes *Further and Further...*, *Bosendorfer Waltzes*, *Weighing the Heart* (1987) and *Four Marys* (1992).

Spinka, Matthew 1890–1972
US church historian

Born in Stitary, Czechoslovakia, he graduated from the University of Chicago and the Faculty of Protestant Theology, Prague. He taught church history at Central Theological Seminary, Dayton, Ohio and Chicago University before taking up an appointment as professor at Hartford Theological Seminary in 1943. He specialized in Central and Eastern European subjects, and edited the distinguished *Church History* journal (1932–49). His numerous books include *The Church and the Russian Revolution*

(1927), *Christianity Confronts Communism* (1936), *John Amos Comenius* (1943), *Nicholas Berdyaev* (1950) and *John Hus* (1968).

Spinola, Ambrogio, Marquis of Los Balbases
1539–1630
Genoese soldier
In 1602 he raised and maintained 9,000 troops at his own expense and fought against Maurice, Count of Nassau in the Spanish Netherlands. He was one of the plenipotentiaries at The Hague Conference which made the 12-year truce in 1609. In the early stages of the Thirty Years War he served the Habsburg cause by subduing the Lower Palatinate. He was recalled to the Netherlands to fight once more against Maurice of Nassau who, however, died of a fever while attempting to relieve Breda, which fell to Spinola in 1625. The event was commemorated in a famous painting by Velázquez.

Spínola, António Sebastião Ribeiro de
1910–96
Portuguese general and politician
Born into a wealthy landed family, he fought on the side of General Franco during the Spanish Civil War and was sent to Nazi Germany for training. A teetotaller and non-smoker, Spínola's trade-marks were his monocle, riding crop and African cane. As Governor-General of Guinea-Bissau (1968–73), he endeavoured to halt the independence movement through a combination of welfare and community projects (designed to win over the local population) and the latest counter-insurgency methods. Although he believed the war could not be won by military means, he returned to Portugal a war hero. When António Salazar fell in April 1974, the conservative Spínola became President as a compromise candidate. He proved a limited and naïve politician. Moreover, he clashed gravely with the Armed Forces Movement (MFA) over the granting of independence (July 1974) to Angola, Mozambique and Guinea. The ensuing power struggle led to his resignation in September 1974, and after attempting an unsuccessful coup the following March, he fled into exile. He returned in 1976 and was restored to his former rank of general.

Spinoza, Benedict de, *Hebrew* Baruch 1632–77
Dutch philosopher and theologian
He was born in Amsterdam into a Jewish émigré family that had fled from Portugal to escape Catholic persecution. His deep interest in the new astronomy and his radical ideas in theology and the philosophy of Descartes led to his expulsion from the Jewish community for heresy in 1656 and his persecution by Calvinists. He became the leader of a small philosophical circle and made a living grinding and polishing lenses, moving in 1660 to Rijnsburg near Leyden, where he wrote his 'Short Treatise on God, Man and His Well-Being' (c.1662), the *Tractatus de Intellectus Emendatione* (1662, 'Treatise on the Correction of the Understanding') and most of his geometrical version of Descartes's *Principia Philosophiae* (1663, the only book published in his lifetime with his name on the title page). He moved in 1663 to Voorburg near The Hague and in 1670 to The Hague itself. The *Tractatus Theologico-Politicus* was published anonymously in 1670 and aroused great interest but was banned in 1674 for its controversial views on the Bible and Christian theology. In 1673 he refused the chair of philosophy at Heidelberg University, in order to protect his independence. He advocated a strictly historical approach to the interpretation of biblical sources and argued that complete freedom of philosophical and scientific speculation was consistent with what was important in the Bible, that is the moral and practical doctrines and not the factual beliefs assumed or expressed. He had sent Gottfried Leibniz his tract on optics in 1671, and Leibniz came to The Hague to visit him in

1676. But Spinoza was by then in an advanced stage of consumption, aggravated by the glass-dust in his lungs, and he died the following year in Amsterdam, leaving no heir and few possessions. His major work was the *Ethics*, which was published posthumously in 1677. As the Latin title suggests (*Ethica Ordine Geometrico Demonstrata*), this was a complete deductive metaphysical system, intended to be a proof of what is good for human beings derived with mathematical certainty from axioms, theorems and definitions. He rejects the Cartesian dualism of mind and matter in favour of a pantheistic God who is identified with the ultimate substance of the world—infinite, logically necessary and absolute—and has mind and matter as two of his attributes. Spinoza's work was first condemned as atheistical and subversive, but his reputation was restored by literary critics such as Gotthold Lessing, Goethe and Coleridge and later by professional philosophers, and he is now regarded, along with Descartes and Leibniz, as one of the great Rationalist thinkers of the 17th century. 📖 Roger Scruton, *Spinoza* (1986)

Spitteler, Karl Friedrich Georg 1845–1924
Swiss poet and novelist and Nobel Prize winner
Born in Liestal, Basle, he studied law and theology at Basle, Zurich and Heidelberg, was a tutor in Russia and a teacher and journalist in Switzerland, and retired to Lucerne in 1892. *Der Olympische Frühling* (1900–03, 'The Olympic Spring') is a mythological epic, but perhaps his most mature work is *Prometheus der Dulder* (1924, 'Prometheus the Sufferer'). As well as poetry he wrote tales, which include *Konrad der Leutnant* ('Conrad the Lieutenant'), essays, including *Lachende Wahrheiten*, ('Laughing Truths'), and reminiscences. He was awarded the Nobel Prize for literature in 1919. 📖 J Frankel, *Karl Friedrich Spitteler* (1945)

Spitz, Mark (Andrew) 1950–
US swimmer
Born in Modesto, California, he earned worldwide fame at the 1972 Olympics by winning seven gold medals, achieving a world record time in each event. He also won two golds in the 1968 Games, and set a total of 26 world records between 1967 and 1972. He turned professional in 1972.

Spitzer, Lyman, Jnr 1914–97
US astrophysicist
Born in Toledo, Ohio, he was educated at Yale and Princeton, where he was Professor of Astronomy from 1947 to 1982. His interest in energy generation in stars led to his early attempt to achieve controlled thermonuclear fusion. In 1951, with Walter Baade, he suggested that the class of galaxies known as S0 were formed when spiral galaxies collided. With Martin Schwarzschild (1912–97), he postulated in 1956 the existence of giant molecular clouds in interstellar space long before they were observed. In 1958 Spitzer studied the tidal shock that occurs between cluster stars and the galactic disc; he summarized many of his ideas in *Dynamical Evolution of Globular Clusters* (1987). In 1991 he was awarded the Franklin Medal by the American Philosophical Department.

Spock, Dr Benjamin McLane 1903–98
US paediatrician
He was born in New Haven, Connecticut, and studied at both Yale (where he became a star oarsman and rowed in the 1924 Olympics) and Columbia. He qualified as a doctor, having trained in both paediatrics and psychiatry, and started a practice in Manhattan in 1933. He transformed the attitudes of the postwar generation to parenthood with his seminal book *The Common Sense Book of Baby and Child Care* (1946), which has sold more than 30 million copies. In the 1960s he was an outspoken opponent of the Vietnam War, and was in turn accused of having been responsible for raising a weak and permissive generation

of pacifists. In 1968 he was convicted on a charge of helping young men to evade the draft, but appealed successfully and published *Dr Spock on Vietnam*. He continued his political interest with *Decent and Indecent: Our Personal Political Behaviour* (1970), and helped to form the People's Party, running for the US presidency in 1972 and the vice-presidency in 1976. Later works include *A Better World for Our Children* (1994). 📖 Lynn Z Bloom, *Doctor Spock: Biography of a Conservative Radical* (1972)

Spode, Josiah 1754–1827
English potter

Born in Stoke-on-Trent, Staffordshire, he learned his trade in his father's workshops, and in 1770 founded a firm which manufactured pottery, porcelain and stoneware. In 1800 he began to use bone as well as feldspar in the paste, which resulted in porcelain of a special transparency and beauty. He did much to popularize the willow pattern and became the foremost china manufacturer of his time. He was appointed potter to **George III** in 1806. After merging in 1833 with William Taylor Copeland, the firm also made numerous white imitation marble (*Parian*) figures.

Spoerli, Heinz 1941–
Swiss dancer, choreographer and ballet director

Born in Basle, he studied locally and at the School of American Ballet and the London Dance Centre before joining Basle Ballet (1960–63), Cologne Ballet (1963–66), Royal Winnipeg Ballet (1966–67), Les Grands Ballets Canadiens (1967–71) and Geneva Ballet (1971–73). He assumed directorship of Basle Ballet in 1973, gradually turning what was strictly a provincial ballet company attached to the state opera into one of the most impressive of Europe's smaller dance ensembles. He is a prolific choreographer for companies throughout the Continent, working in both modern dance and classical ballet.

Spohr, Ludwig 1784–1859
German composer, violinist and conductor

Born in Brunswick, he was kapellmeister at the court of Hesse-Kassel from 1822 to 1857. He was principally a composer for the violin, for which he wrote 17 concertos, and he also composed operas, oratorios and symphonies.

Spontini, Gasparo Luigi Pacifico 1774–1851
Italian composer

Born near Ancona, he was intended, like his brothers, for the priesthood, but determined to follow a musical career. He studied at Naples, where he began to compose. In 1803 he settled in Paris, and his operas *La Vestale* (1807, 'The Vestal Virgin') and *Ferdinand Cortez* (1809) were greeted with enthusiasm. He was conductor at the Berlin Court Opera from 1820 to 1842, and caused much hostility by favouring Italian works at the expense of the newer works in German, despite his own *Agnes von Hohenstaufen* (1829).

Spooner, William Archibald 1844–1930
English clergyman and educationist, after whom the spoonerism is named

He was Dean (1876–89) and Warden (1903–24) of New College, Oxford. His name is associated with his own nervous tendency to transpose initial letters or half-syllables, as in 'a half-warmed fish' for 'a half-formed wish'. Many spoonerisms, such as 'You must leave Oxford by the next town drain' are probably apocryphal. 📖 Sir William Hayter, *Spooner: A Biography* (1977)

Spotted Tail, Sioux name Sinte-galeshka c.1823–81
Native American leader

Born in the Sioux nation near Fort Laramie, Wyoming, he became chief of the Brulé and an advocate of compromise and accommodation with white society. He restrained his followers from war when settlers invaded the Black Hills in the 1870s, and he helped to persuade his nephew **Crazy Horse** to surrender to the army in 1877. He was assassinated on the Rosebud Reservation by another Sioux, Crow Dog.

Spottiswoode, Alicia Anne, married name Lady John Scott 1810–1900
Scottish poet and songwriter

Born in Westruther, Berwickshire, she was a collector of traditional songs and wrote 69 of her own, often reworking original material, as with her most famous compositions, 'Annie Laurie' and 'Durisdeer'. A friend of Charles Kirkpatrick Sharpe, in 1836 she married Lord John Scott, a brother of the 5th Duke of Buccleuch.

Spottiswoode, William 1825–83
English mathematician and physicist

Born in London, he was educated at Harrow and in mathematics at Balliol College, Oxford, and in 1846 succeeded his father as head of the printing house of Eyre and Spottiswoode. Spottiswoode did original work on the polarization of light and electrical discharge in rarefied gases, using an early form of transformer. He wrote a series of original memoirs on the contact of curves and surfaces, and the first elementary mathematical treatise on determinants (1851). He was elected Fellow of the Royal Society in 1871 and was its president from 1878.

Sprague, Frank Julian 1857–1934
US electrical engineer and inventor

Born in Milford, Connecticut, he graduated from the US Naval Academy in Annapolis, Maryland in 1878 and served in the US navy until 1883, after which he worked for a year under **Thomas Edison** before setting up the Sprague Electric Railway & Motor Company. He developed a new type of motor for street railways (trams), which was first used in 1887 in Richmond, Virginia. By 1890 this had become so successful that his company was absorbed by the Edison General Electric Company. He turned to the manufacture of electric lifts, and as a result of his experience with them perfected in 1895 a system of control for multiple-unit trains, which he later developed into an automatic train control system. He has been called the father of electric railway traction.

Sprengel, Christian Konrad 1750–1816
German amateur botanist

Born in Brandenburg, he became rector of Spandau, where he discovered the part played in the pollination of plants by nectaries and insects. He suggested that flowers had adapted specifically to allow for insect pollination, studied the phenomenon of dichogamy, the floral process which favours cross-pollination by preventing self-pollination. His work influenced many contemporary entomologists.

Sprengel, Hermann Johann Philipp 1834–1906
British chemist, physicist and inventor

He was born in Schillerslage, Germany, and educated at the universities of Göttingen and Heidelberg. In 1859 he moved to England, later becoming a British citizen. He carried out research at Oxford and in the laboratories of several institutions in London. He mechanized the pump devised by **Heinrich Geissler** in 1858, making its action much swifter and more efficient, and enabling its use in the investigation of radiation and in other applications. He also developed the pyknometer, a U-shaped vessel for determining the density and expansion of liquids, and researched and wrote extensively on high explosives. He was elected FRS in 1878.

Sprenger, Jacob 15th century
German theologian

A Dominican, and Professor of Theology in Cologne, he compiled with Henricus Institor the famous *Malleus Maleficarum* (1489), which first formulated the doctrine of witchcraft, and formed a textbook of procedure for witch trials. They were appointed inquisitors by Innocent VIII in 1484.

Spring, Dick (Richard) 1950–
Irish Labour politician

Born in Tralee and educated at Trinity College and King's Inns, Dublin, he worked as a lawyer before entering parliament as Labour MP for Kerry North in 1981. In 1982 he became Leader of the Labour Party and was appointed deputy Prime Minister, a post he held until 1987. As John Bruton's deputy and Foreign Minister, he was instrumental in arranging the peace talks with Irish republican groups which led to the ceasefire of 1994. He has also played rugby union football for Ireland.

Spring, Howard 1889–1965
Welsh novelist

Born in Cardiff, he became a newspaper reporter and literary critic, and established himself as a writer with his bestselling *Oh Absalom* (1938, renamed *My Son, My Son*). His novels usually contain a poor hero who rises dramatically to prosperity; they include *Fame is the Spur* (1940), *Dunkerleys* (1946), *These Lovers Fled Away* (1955) and *Time and the Hour* (1957), and three autobiographical works (1939, 1942 and 1946).

Springfield, Dusty, *professional name of* Mary O'Brien 1939–
English pop singer

Born in Hampstead, London, she left the Lana Sisters to form The Springfields (1961), together with her brother Tom and Mike Hurst. Her first solo single was 'I Only Want To Be With You' (1964), followed by 'You Don't Have To Say You Love Me' (1966) and 'Son of a Preacher Man' (1968), all of which were big hits. She performed little in the 1970s, but achieved renewed popularity with the theme song to the film *Scandal* (1989, based on the events connected with Christine Keeler in the 1960s) and subsequent collaborations with The Pet Shop Boys.

Springsteen, Bruce 1949–
US rock singer and guitarist

He was born in Freehold, New Jersey. From the release of his first album, *Greetings From Asbury Park, NJ* (1973), he was hailed by critics as the new Bob Dylan. He quickly developed a strong cult following, although it was not until the release of *Born To Run* (1975) that he met with major commercial success. His live performances were also highly acclaimed. Later albums included *Darkness On The Edge Of Town* (1978), *The River* (1980), *Nebraska* (1982), *Born In The USA* (1984)—both Ronald Reagan and Walter F Mondale used the lyrics in their Presidential campaigns in 1984—*Tunnel Of Love* (1987) and *Human Touch* (1992). By the mid-1980s he was the world's most popular white rock star, and succeeded in combining his celebrity status with a populist style. He has more recently returned to form with the stark acoustic set *The Ghost of Tom Joad* (1995).
📖 Dave Marsh, *Glory Days* (1990)

Spruance, Raymond Ames 1885–1969
US naval officer

Born in Baltimore, Maryland, he was educated at the US Naval Academy, Annapolis, and became a specialist in gunnery. He commanded the USS *Mississippi* in 1938, and led Task Force 16 at the decisive Battle of Midway (June 1942). He played an important part in the planning and execution of large-scale amphibious operations supported by carrier-borne and shore-based aircraft (1942–45), notably as Commander of the Fifth Fleet (1944–45). He was US ambassador to the Philippines (1952–55).

Spruce, Richard 1817–93
English botanist

Born near Malton, Yorkshire, he became a schoolmaster, first at Haxby, then at St Peter's Collegiate School, York, and as a recreation studied botany, collecting bryophytes and other plants from the North Yorkshire Moors. In 1844 he decided to make botany his career. After making collections in the Pyrenees, he was sent by Sir William Jackson Hooker to South America in 1849, and he spent the following 15 years exploring the Amazon, Orinoco, the Andes and Ecuador. He brought back thousands of plant specimens, maps of three previously unexplored rivers, and vocabularies of 21 Amazonian tribes. His most famous publication was *Notes of a Botanist in the Amazon*, edited by Wallace (2 vols, 1908).

Spry, Constance 1886–1960
English flower arranger and cookery writer

Born in Derby, she was educated in Ireland and, returning to England during World War I, became a welfare worker in London's East End. She began to work with flowers in the 1920s, opening flower shops and becoming chairman of the Constance Spry Flower School. She excelled in organization, and was adviser to the Ministry of Works on flower decoration for the coronation of Elizabeth II. She became joint Principal, with Rosemary Hume, of the Cordon Bleu Cookery School in London and of the 'finishing school' at Winkfield in Berkshire. She wrote *The Constance Spry Cookbook* (1956) with Rosemary Hume, and wrote many books on flower arranging, including *How to do the Flowers*, *Simple Flowers* and *Favourite Flowers*.

Spurgeon, Charles Haddon 1834–92
English Baptist preacher

Born in Kelvedon, Essex, he became pastor of the New Park Street Chapel, London, in 1854. The Metropolitan Tabernacle, seating 6,000, was erected for him in 1859–61 and provided him with a pulpit until his death (it burned down in 1898). In 1887 he withdrew from the Baptist Union because no action was taken against those charged with fundamental errors. Apart from 50 volumes of sermons, he wrote collections of pithy sayings in *John Ploughman's Talk* (1869) and many other works.

Spurr, Josiah Edward 1870–1950
US geologist

Born in Gloucester, Massachusetts, he was mining engineer to the Sultan of Turkey (1901), geologist in the US Geological Survey (1902) and Professor of Geology at Rollins College (1930–32). His work enabled the age of the Tertiary period to be estimated at 45 to 60 million years ago. His exploration in Alaska in 1896 and 1898 was commemorated by the naming of Mt Spurr. He also undertook major research on lunar topography and geology, and wrote *Geology Applied to Mining* (1904) and *Geology Applied to Selenology* (1944–49).

Spyri, Johanna 1827–1901
Swiss writer

She was born near Zurich, the daughter of a doctor. She wrote to raise money for refugees of the Franco-Prussian War. *Heidi* (1880) is her best-known work; she also wrote other children's stories set in the Swiss Alps.

Squanto, *also called* Tisquantum d.1622
Native American interpreter

He was born into the Pawtuxet group near Plymouth, Massachusetts. An interpreter for the Wampanoag chief, Massasoit, he became known as a friend of the Pilgrims, teaching them how to plant corn and where to fish. He was taken from New England by English fishermen to be sold as a slave in Spain, but escaped to England, and made his way back to America (1619). Because the Pawtuxets had been wiped out by disease, he joined the Wampanoags, whom he helped to conclude a peace treaty with the Pilgrims.

Squarcione, Francesco 1394–1474
Italian painter

Credited as the founder of the so-called Paduan school, which was characterized by Classical influences and a harsh approach to perspective, he was the teacher of many more famous painters, eg Andrea Mantegna. He painted panels and frescoes for the church of S Francesco in Padua, and was also a tailor and art dealer.

Squier, Ephraim George 1821–88
US archaeologist

He was born in Bethlehem, New Hampshire. While a newspaper editor in Ohio in the 1840s, with the help of the physician Edwin Hamilton Davis, he surveyed and analysed the Native American burial mounds and earthworks of the Mississippi Valley, publishing the results in the earliest classic of North American archaeology, *Ancient Monuments of the Mississippi Valley* (1848). A second survey, of the mounds of western New York State, was published the following year. Squier then became a diplomat, first in Nicaragua (from 1849), and later (from 1863) in Peru. His experiences of travel and exploration are recounted in two popular books, *Nicaragua* (1852) and *Peru* (1877).

Squire, Sir John Collings 1884–1958
English writer

Born in Plymouth, and educated at St John's College, Cambridge, he was literary editor of *The New Statesman* (1913–17), then acting editor (from 1917) and founder editor of *The London Mercury* (1919–34). His work consists of light verse and parody, as in *Steps to Parnassus* (1913) and *Tricks of the Trade* (1917). In anthologies he favoured minor poets. His writings also include criticisms and short stories. His *Collected Poems*, edited by John Betjeman, appeared in 1959.

Srî-Kantha See Bhavabhûti

Ssu-ma Ch'ien See Sima Qian

Ssu-ma Hsiang-ju See Sima Xiangru

Staal, Marguerite Jeanne, Baronne de 1684–1750
French writer of memoirs

She was born in Paris, the daughter of a poor Parisian painter, Cordier, whose name she dropped for that of her mother, Delaunay. Her devotion to the interests of her employer, the Duchess of Maine, brought her two years in the Bastille, where she had a love affair with the Chevalier de Menil. In 1735 she married the Baron Staal. Her *Mémoires* (1755, Eng trans 1892) describe the world of the regency with intellect, observation and a subtle irony, and are written in a clear and individual style. Her *Œuvres complètes* ('Complete Works') appeared in 1821.

Stabler, Harold 1872–1945
English designer and craftsman

Trained as a woodworker, he studied metalwork at Keswick School of Art, and taught there before moving to London in the early 1900s, and joining the staff at the Sir John Cass Technical Institute. He was an instructor at the Royal College of Art from 1912 to 1926 and served on the first council of the Design and Industrial Association in 1915. With his wife, Phoebe Stabler, he designed and produced ceramic figures and groups, decorative and architectural details, enamels and jewellery. He became a partner in the Poole pottery firm of Carter & Co in 1921, changing the name to Carter, Stabler & Adams when he acted as the firm's artistic consultant.

Stack, Lee d.1924
British soldier

He was Sirdar (British Commander-in-Chief of the Egyptian Army) in 1924, at a time when a combination of the first Wafdist government in Egypt and the first Labour government in Britain led to a measure of British sympathy for Egyptian nationalist aspirations. However, when Saad Zaghlul went to London for negotiations his demands were well beyond what the British government was prepared to concede. The result of this failure was increased hostility to the British in Egypt, especially to the position of the Sirdar, and Stack was murdered in Cairo in late 1924. The British subsequently presented a strong ultimatum to Egypt which, together with accusations that certain Wafdists were implicated in political murder, was enough to bring down the Wafdist government.

Stacpoole, Henry de Vere 1863–1951
Irish physician and writer

Born in Kingstown (Dun Laoghaire), Ireland, he was educated at Malvern College and St George's and St Mary's hospitals in London, and made several voyages as a ship's doctor. He was the author of over 50 popular novels, including *The Blue Lagoon* (1909), *The Pearl Fishers* (1915) and *Green Coral* (1935). He wrote two volumes of autobiography, *Men* (1942) and *Mice* (1945).

Staël, Madame de, *pseudonym of* Anne Louise Germaine Necker, Baroness of Staël-Holstein 1766–1817
French writer

She was born in Paris, the only child of the financier and statesman, Jacques Necker. In her girlhood she attended her mother's salon and turned to writing romantic comedies, tragedies, novels, essays and the celebrated *Lettres sur Rousseau* (1789). In 1786 she married Baron Eric Magnus of Staël-Holstein (1742–1802), the bankrupt Swedish ambassador in Paris. She bore him three children, but the marriage was unhappy and she had many affairs. Her brilliant Parisian salon became the centre of political discussion, but with the Revolution she had to leave for Coppet, by Lake Geneva, in 1792. By 1795 she had returned to Paris, where her husband had re-established himself as ambassador. She prepared for a political role by her *Réflexions sur la paix intérieur* (1795, 'Reflections on Civil Peace'), but was advised to return to Coppet. Her *Influence des passions* appeared in 1796. She published her famous *Littérature et ses rapports avec les institutions sociales* (Eng trans *The Influence of Literature upon Society*, 1812) in 1800, followed by the novel *Delphine* (Eng trans 1903) in 1802. She had returned to Paris but Napoleon I made her unwelcome. In December 1803, now a widow, she set out with her children for Germany, where she dazzled the Weimar court and met the German writers Schiller, Goethe and August von Schlegel. In 1805 she returned to Coppet and wrote *Corinne* (1807, Eng trans 1807), a romance which brought her fame throughout Europe. She visited Germany at the end of 1807, and her famous work *De l'Allemagne* (Eng trans *Germany*, 1813) was finished in 1810 and partly printed, when the whole impression was seized and destroyed, and she herself was exiled. She escaped secretly to Berne, and from there made her way to St Petersburg, Stockholm and (1813) London, where admiration reached its climax on the publication of *De l'Allemagne*. It revealed Germany to the French and made Romanticism—she was the first to use the word—acceptable to the Latin peoples. Louis XVIII welcomed her to Paris in 1814, but the return of Napoleon drove her away, and she spent the winter in Italy with Albert de Rocca, an Italian officer in the French service, whom she had married secretly in 1816. She returned to Paris, where she died. Her surviving son and daughter published her unfinished *Considérations sur la Révolution française* (1818, Eng trans *Considerations on the Principal Events of the French Revolution*, 1818)—considered her masterpiece by the great French literary critic **Charles Sainte-Beuve**—the *Dix années d'exil* (1821, Eng trans *Ten Years' Exile*, 1821), and her complete works (1820–21).

Staël, Nicolas de 1914–55
French painter

Born in St Petersburg, Russia, he studied in Brussels, travelled in Spain and Italy, and worked in Paris. His paintings were at first abstract, and he made inspired use of rectangular patches of colour, for example in *Marathon* (1948, Tate, London), which is suggestive of a head under attack. His later pictures were more representational, as with his *Football Players*, and included landscapes, such as *The Roofs* (1952, Pompidou Centre) and his vivid *Agrigente* (1954, private collection), which preceded his suicide.

Stafford, Jean 1915–79
US short-story writer and novelist

She was born in Covina, California, and educated at Colorado University, where she won a travelling scholarship to Heidelberg, Germany, in 1936. On her return to the USA, she met and married **Robert Lowell** against his family's wishes in 1940. She worked on the *Southern Review* and taught at Flushing College. *Boston Adventure*, her first novel, was published in 1944 to great acclaim, and *The Mountain Lion*, her second, appeared in 1947. However her stormy marriage to Lowell collapsed, and she was admitted to psycho-alcoholic clinics; the couple divorced in 1948. She published *The Catherine Wheel* in 1952, and during the 1960s she taught, and published short stories, children's books and a series of interviews with the mother of **Lee Harvey Oswald**, *A Mother in History* (1966). One of the USA's most admired short-story writers, she won a Pulitzer Prize for her *Collected Stories* (1969).

Stafford-Clark, Max 1941–
English stage director

Born in Cambridge, he began his career in 1966 as associate director of the Traverse Theatre, Edinburgh, and was artistic director there in 1968–70. He became director of the Traverse Theatre Workshop Company (1970–74), after which he co-founded the Joint Stock Theatre Company. He became artistic director of the English Stage Company at the Royal Court Theatre, London, from 1981 until 1993, when he relinquished the post to **Stephen Daldry**, becoming associate director. The same year he became artistic director of the Out of Joint Theatre Company. He published *Letters to George* in 1989.

Stagnelius, Erik Johan 1793–1823
Swedish Romantic poet

The son of the Bishop of Kalmar, after graduating at Uppsala he became an unsalaried civil servant in Stockholm. He led a solitary life, and suffered from ill health. His works were collected and published (1824–26) after his death. His considerable output, all written within a decade, comprises epics, such as *Vladimirden store* (1817, 'Vladimir the Great'), plays including *Martyrerna* ('The Martyrs') and *Bacchanterna* (1822, 'The Bacchanalians'), and lyric poetry, much of it found in *Liljan i Saron* (1821, 'Lilies of Sharon'). He was constantly torn between idealism and erotic sensualism, and was influenced by his reading of **Plato**, **Friedrich Schelling**, theosophy, gnosticism and Romantic contemporaries. He contrasts dream and reality in a series of poems that include *Endymion*, *Narcissus* and *Till Natten* ('Ode to Night'). In other poems themes from nature symbolize the soul's longing for heaven, as in *Floden* ('The River') and *Flyttfåglarna* ('Migrant Birds'). He employs a variety of verse forms with great skill. Little known in his lifetime,

he became the most influential of Swedish Romantics on succeeding generations. 📖 D Andreae, *Erik Stagnelius* (1919)

Stahl, Georg Ernst 1660–1734
German chemist

Born in Ansbach, he became Professor of Medicine (1694) at Halle and personal physician (1714) to the King of Prussia. He expounded the phlogiston theory of combustion and fermentation and the theory of animism. His theories remained dominant for over a century.

Stahlberg, Kaarlo Juho 1865–1952
Finnish politician

Having established his reputation as Professor of Law at Helsinki University and as a judge and a member of the Finnish Diet, in 1919 he drafted Finland's constitution and served as the republic's first president (1919–25). He was kidnapped by members of a pro-Fascist movement in 1930, and was narrowly defeated in the elections of 1931 and 1937.

Stainer, Sir John 1840–1901
English composer

Born in London, he became organist of Magdalen College, Oxford (1860) and of St Paul's (1872), and Oxford Professor of Music (1889). He wrote cantatas and church music, notably *The Crucifixion* (1887).

Stair, James Dalrymple, 1st Viscount 1619–95
Scottish jurist

He studied at Glasgow University, served in the Covenanting army, and, as Regent in Philosophy, taught at Glasgow (1641–47). After joining the Bar (1648), he was recommended by General **George Monk** to **Cromwell** in 1659 for the office of a Lord of Session, and he advised Monk to call a free parliament (1660). He was created a Nova Scotia baronet in 1664, and in 1671 he was made president of the Court of Session and member of the Privy Council. When the Duke of York (later **James VII and II**) came to govern at Edinburgh in 1679 he retired to the country, and worked on his famous *Institutions of the Law of Scotland*, still one of the most authoritative works on Scots law. Devoted to the cause of Covenanters, he became involved in a fierce dispute with Viscount **Dundee**, and fled in 1682 to Holland. He returned with **William III**, was restored to the presidency, and soon after was created Viscount Stair (1690). He also published reports of court decisions and works on physics and religion. The marriage in 1669 of his daughter Janet inspired Sir **Walter Scott's** *The Bride of Lammermoor* (1819).

Stair, Sir John Dalrymple, 1st Earl of 1648–1707
Scottish judge and politician

The son of James Dalrymple, Viscount **Stair**, he studied law, and was knighted in 1667. He came into violent collision with Viscount **Dundee**, and was imprisoned and heavily fined, but early in 1686 became King's Advocate, and in 1688 Lord Justice-Clerk. Under **William III** he was Lord Advocate, and as Secretary of State from 1691 he had the chief management of Scottish affairs. He was held responsible for the massacre of Glencoe (1692), and resigned in 1695. He took an active part in the debates and intrigues that led to the Treaty of Union.

Stalin, Joseph See panel 1742

Stallone, Sylvester 1946–
US film actor

He was born in New York City, the son of Italian immigrants. After a series of minor parts, he appeared in **Woody Allen's** comedy *Bananas* (1971). Inspired by watching **Muhammad Ali** fight in 1975, he wrote a screenplay about a boxer and made it a condition of selling the script that he would play the lead role. The success of *Rocky*

Stalin, Joseph, *originally* Iosif Vissarionovich Dzhugashvili 1879–1953
Soviet revolutionary and leader

Stalin was born near Tiflis (now Tblisi) in Georgia, the son of a shoemaker. He was educated for the priesthood at the Theological Seminary, but was expelled, probably for propagating Marxism. He joined the Bolshevik underground, was arrested and transported to Siberia, but escaped in 1904. The ensuing years witnessed his closer identification with revolutionary Marxism, his many escapes from captivity, his growing intimacy with **Lenin** and **Nikolai Bukharin**, his early disparagement of **Trotsky**, and his co-option, in 1912, to the illicit Bolshevik Central Committee.

With the 1917 Revolution and the forcible replacement of the **Kerensky** government by Lenin and his supporters, Stalin was appointed commissar for nationalities and a member of the politburo, although his activities throughout the counter-revolution and the war with Poland were confined to organizing a Red 'terror' in Tsaritsin (later Stalingrad, and now Volgograd). With his appointment as General Secretary to the Central Committee in 1922, Stalin stealthily began to build up the power that would ensure his control of the situation after Lenin's death. When this occurred in 1924, he took over the reins, successfully testing his overriding authority in 1928 by engineering Trotsky's downfall.

Stalin's reorganization of the USSR's resources, with its successive five-year plans, suffered many industrial setbacks and encountered consistently stubborn resistance in the field of agriculture, where the *kulaks*, or peasant proprietors, steadfastly refused to accept the principle of collectivization. The measures taken by the dictator to 'discipline' those who opposed his will involved the death by execution or famine of up to 10 million peasants (1932–33). The blood bath which eliminated the Old Bolsheviks and the alleged right-wing intelligentsia was followed by a drastic purge of some thousands of the officer corps, who were accused of pro-German sympathies.

Red Army forces and material went to the support of the Spanish Communist government in 1936, although Stalin was careful not to commit himself too deeply. After the Munich crisis, Franco-British negotiations for Russian support in the event of war were drawn out to the point at which Stalin signed a non-aggression pact with **Hitler**, allowing him time to prepare for the German invasion he regarded as inevitable. In 1941 the success of the Nazis' initial thrust into Russia was partly due to the disposal of the Red Army on the frontiers, ready to invade rather than repel invasion. Eventually, the German invasion was defeated by a war of attrition, with the harsh Russian winter contributing to the enormous numbers of casualties.

Sustained by many millions of pounds' worth of war material furnished by Great Britain and the USA, the Red Army obediently responded to Stalin's call to defend Mother Russia, although the dictator lost no time in demanding a 'Second Front' in Europe to relieve the strain on his unnumbered forces. Quick to exploit the unwarranted Anglo-American fear that Russia might withdraw from the alliance, Stalin easily outwitted the allied leaders at the conferences at Teheran (1943), Yalta (1945) and Potsdam (1945), which left him in political control of most of Eastern Europe.

While Stalin consolidated his gains, an 'iron curtain' cut off Soviet Russia and her satellites from the outside world. At the same time the *Khozyain* ('boss') inaugurated a ruthless 'cold war' against all non-Communist countries, which included the blockade of Berlin. At home his ruthless purge of all opposition continued, and his fierce anti-Semitism resulted in 1952 in the execution of a number of Jews for alleged Zionist conspiracy.

Stalin was twice married and had three children: two sons and a daughter, Svetlana Alliluyeva (1926–). He died in mysterious circumstances; the official cause was said to be a brain haemorrhage.

Stalin's 'cult of personality' and the brutal purges of his rule were denounced after his death by **Nikita Khrushchev**. In 1961, by a vote of the Party Congress, Stalin's embalmed body was removed from the Mausoleum of Lenin and buried in an ordinary grave near the Kremlin. Stalinism was more in favour under **Leonid Brezhnev**, but later **Mikhail Gorbachev** praised his wartime leadership and agreed that the strategy of collectivization was substantially correct, but admitted that Stalin had committed 'unforgivable crimes' and had seriously distorted the Soviet political system. In 1988 Stalin's official biographer, Dmitri Volkognov, went further, castigating the September 1939 'friendship pact' with Nazi Germany, his resort to bloody purges and his reliance on incompetent advisers, and suggesting that the once revered leader may have been insane. Many of the opponents of Stalin who were found guilty in the 1930s show trials have since been posthumously rehabilitated.

📖 R C Tucker, *Stalin in Power* (1990); A de Jonge, *Stalin and the Shaping of the Soviet Union* (1986).

> 'The State is an instrument in the hand of the ruling class, used to break the resistance of the adversaries of that class.' From *Foundations of Leninism* (1924).

(1976) catapulted him to stardom, giving him starring roles in the film's three sequels and leading to the role of John Rambo in *First Blood* (1982) and its two sequels. Later films include *Cliffhanger* (1992), *The Specialist* (1994) and *Daylight* (1996).

Stamboliski, Alexander 1879–1923
Bulgarian politician

A staunch republican, in 1906 he took over the leading role in the Bulgarian Agrarian National Union (BANU). During World War I, he was imprisoned by the pro-German **Ferdinand I** for his outspoken support of the Allies. In 1918 he led a march on Sofia and forced the king to abdicate, briefly declaring a republic. After the 1919 elections, he became Prime Minister and represented defeated Bulgaria at the Paris Peace Conference. He established an authoritarian regime, organizing the anti-communist Orange Guard, undermining the position of the urban middle class and introducing a programme of radical reform designed to turn Bulgaria into a model agricultural state. In foreign policy, he sought to improve Bulgaria's international position, joining the League of Nations and attempting to mend relations with Yugoslavia. In 1923 he was overthrown in a military coup and was tortured and decapitated by members of VMRO (Internal Macedonian Revolutionary Organization).

Stamitz, Carl Philipp 1745–1801
German composer and violinist

Born in Mannheim, he studied under his father, **Johann Stamitz**, and became a travelling instrumentalist in Paris, London, St Petersburg, Prague and Nuremberg. He wrote over 50 symphonies, 30 sinfonie concertantes, and concertos for various instruments. His brother, Anton Johann Baptista (c.1754–1809), was also a musician.

Stamitz, Johann 1717–57
Bohemian violinist and composer

Born in Deutschbrod (now Havlickuv Brod, Czechoslovakia), he first attracted attention at the coronation celebrations for Karl VII in Prague (1742). Engaged by the Mannheim court, he became a highly salaried court musician and concert master, and established the style of composition later known as the Mannheim school. His compositions include 74 symphonies, concertos for various instruments, chamber music and a mass. He developed the sonata form, introduced sharp contrasts into symphonic movements and wrote fine concerto music. His two sons were **Carl Philipp Stamitz** and Anton Johann Baptista Stamitz (c.1754–1809).

Stamp, Sir Lawrence Dudley 1898–1966
English geographer
Born in London, he was educated at King's College London. He undertook fieldwork in Burma and became Professor of Geology and Geography at Rangoon in 1923. He became Reader (1926) and Professor of Geography (1945–58) at the London School of Economics. He founded and worked on the British Land Utilization Survey until after World War II, and both during and after the war he was adviser to the government on many land-related topics.

Standish, Myles c.1584–1656
English soldier and colonist
Born probably in Ormskirk, Lancashire, he served in the Netherlands, and in 1620 was hired by the Pilgrim Fathers to accompany them on the *Mayflower*. He was appointed military captain of the settlement at Plymouth, supervised the defences, and negotiated with the Native Americans. In 1625 he went to London to negotiate ownership of their land. He became treasurer of Massachusetts (1644–49), and in 1631 was one of the founders of Duxbury, Massachusetts. **Henry Wadsworth Longfellow** and **James Russell Lowell** wrote about his exploits against the Native Americans. 📖 G V C Young, *Pilgrim Myles Standish: First Manx American* (1984)

Stanford, Sir Charles Villiers 1852–1924
Irish composer
Born in Dublin, he studied at Cambridge, Leipzig and Berlin, and became organist at Trinity College (1872–93), and a professor at the Royal College of Music (1882). As Cambridge Professor of Music (1887), he taught generations of young British composers. Among his works are choral settings of **Tennyson**'s *Revenge* (1886) and *Voyage of Maeldune* (1889); the oratorios *The Three Holy Children* (1885) and *Eden* (1891); the operas *The Veiled Prophet of Khorassan* (1881), *Savonarola, The Canterbury Pilgrims* (1884), *Shamus O'Brien* (1896), *Much Ado About Nothing* (1901) and *The Critic* (1916); and church music, notably his church service in B flat (1879, revised 1910).

Stanford, (Amasa) Leland 1824–93
US philanthropist and politician
Born in Watervliet, New York, he settled in San Francisco in 1856, became president of the Central Pacific Company, and was Governor of California (1861–63) and a US senator from 1885. In memory of their only son, he and his wife founded and endowed Leland Stanford Junior University (Stanford University) at Palo Alto (1891).

Stanhope, Charles Stanhope, 3rd Earl Stanhope 1753–1816
English scientist and politician
Born in London, the grandson of James, 1st Earl Stanhope, and educated at Eton and Geneva, he married Lady Hester Pitt, sister of **William Pitt, the Younger** in 1774 and became an MP in 1780. He broke with Pitt over the French Revolution, and advocated peace with **Napoleon I**. As a scientist he invented a microscope lens that bears his

name, two calculating machines, the first hand-operated iron printing press, and a process of stereotyping adopted in 1805 by the Clarendon Press in Oxford. He also experimented with electricity, and wrote *Principles of Electricity* (1779).

Stanhope, Lady Hester Lucy 1776–1839
English traveller
The eldest daughter of **Charles Stanhope**, she went in 1803 to live with her uncle, the statesman **William Pitt**, the Younger, and on his death (1806) received a pension of £1,200 from the king. Bored without the excitement of public life, she left England in 1810, travelled in the Levant, went to Jerusalem, camped with Bedouins in Palmyra, and in 1814 settled on Mount Lebanon. She adopted oriental manners, and was regarded by the local people as a kind of prophetess. Her last years were poverty-stricken on account of her reckless generosity.

Stanhope, James Stanhope, 1st Earl 1673–1721
English soldier and politician
After a distinguished career in the field under the Duke of **Marlborough** in the War of the Spanish Succession (1701–14), he became leader of the Whig opposition in 1711. He helped to suppress the Jacobite Rising of 1715, and became Chief Minister to **George I** in 1717.

Stanhope, Philip Dormer See **Chesterfield, 4th Earl of**

Stanhope, Philip Henry Stanhope, 5th Earl 1805–75
English historian
Born in Walmer, Kent, he studied at Oxford, entered parliament in 1830, was instrumental in passing the Copyright Act (1842), and was Foreign Under-Secretary under Sir **Robert Peel** (1834–35) and Secretary to the Indian Board of Control (1845–46). He was known as Lord Mahon until he succeeded to the earldom. His principal work was *A History of England 1713–83* (1836–54). He helped to secure the appointment of the Historical MSS Commission and the foundation of the National Portrait Gallery.

Stanier, Roger Yate 1916–
Canadian microbiologist
Born in Victoria, British Columbia, he was educated at the University of British Columbia before moving to the USA, studying at the University of California at Los Angeles and at the University of Stanford, where he worked with **Cornelis Van Niel**. He worked at Cambridge in 1945, and became professor at Berkeley (1947–71), and later at the Pasteur Institute. Stanier's principal research was in bacterial amino acid metabolism. He also made major contributions to coloured pigments and carotenoid pigments. Elected Fellow of the Royal Society in 1978, his many honours include the Carlsberg Medal.

Stanier, Sir William Arthur 1876–1965
English mechanical engineer
Born in Swindon, Wiltshire, where his father was stores superintendent at the Great Western Railway's works, he began as an apprentice there in 1892 and became chief mechanical engineer of the London, Midland & Scottish Railway (1932–42). He produced many successful locomotive designs, including the 4-6-2 'Coronation' class in 1937, at first streamlined and later in conventional form with distinctive tapered boilers.

Stanislavsky, *professional name of* Konstantin Sergeyevich Alekseyev 1863–1938
Russian actor, theatre director and teacher
Born in Moscow, he co-founded the Moscow Society of Art and Literature (1888) and in 1898 he helped to found the Moscow Arts Theatre, which became an influential

Stanton, Elizabeth Cady, *née* Cady 1815–1902
US social reformer who launched the suffrage movement in the USA

Elizabeth Cady was born in Johnstown, New York. While studying law under her Congressman father, she determined to readdress the inequality that she discovered in women's legal, political, and industrial rights, and in divorce law. In 1840 she married the lawyer and abolitionist Henry Brewster Stanton, insisting on dropping the word 'obey' from the marriage vows. She accompanied him to the international slavery convention in London, where she encountered, with much indignation, a ruling that women delegates were excluded from the floor.

In 1848, with **Lucretia Mott**, she organized the first women's rights convention at Seneca Falls, New York, which launched the women's suffrage movement and accepted the set of resolutions for the improvement of the status of women which Stanton had drawn up. Woman suffrage was included, although Mott allegedly did not agree. Stanton teamed up with **Susan B Anthony** in 1850, producing the feminist magazine *Revolution* (1868–70), and founding the National Woman Suffrage Movement in 1869. Stanton was President of the National Woman

Suffrage Association (called from 1890 the National American Woman Suffrage Association) from 1869 to 1892.

With Mott and **Matilda Joslyn Gage** she compiled three out of the six volumes of the *History of Woman Suffrage* (1881–86). She also wrote her autobiography *Eighty Years and More 1815–1897* (1898). Stanton's daughter was the suffragette **Harriot Stanton Blatch**.

📖 Elisabeth Griffith, *In Her Own Right: The Life of Elizabeth Cady Stanton* (1984); Lois W Banner, *Elizabeth Cady Stanton: A Radical for Women's Rights* (1980).

> 'We hold these truths to be self-evident: that all men and women are created equal; that they are endowed by their Creator with certain inalienable rights; that among these are life, liberty, and the pursuit of happiness.' The 'Declaration of Sentiments', Seneca Falls Women's Rights Convention, 19–20 July, 1848, modelled on the American Declaration of Independence.

company. He gave up acting because of illness, but his teaching and his system of actor-training were major contributions to 20th-century theatre. The 'Method' style derived from his teaching is characterized by improvisation, spontaneity, and an emphasis on psychological realism, and has been widely practised, especially in the USA.

Stanisław I Leszczyński, *English* Stanislas or Stanislaus 1677–1766
King of Poland

Born in Lemberg, he had the support of **Karl XII** of Sweden and defeated **Augustus II, the Strong** to become king in 1704. However after Karl's defeat at the Battle of Poltava in 1709, Stanisław was driven out by **Peter I, the Great** to make room for Augustus again. His daughter Maria married **Louis XV** of France in 1725, a union which facilitated his re-election as King of Poland on Augustus's death in 1733. After losing the War of the Polish Succession, he formally abdicated in 1736, receiving the duchies of Lorraine and Bar. He died of burns in an accident in Lunéville.

Stanisław Poniatowski, *English* Stanislas or Stanislaus 1677–1762
Polish administrator and soldier

He was the father of **Stanisław II Augustus Poniatowski**, the last King of Poland. He joined **Karl XII** of Sweden in supporting **Stanisław I Leszczyński** and later under Augustus II and III was appointed to several administrative posts in Lithuania and Poland.

Stanisław II Augustus Poniatowski, *English* Stanislas or Stanislaus 1732–98
Last King of Poland

The son of **Stanisław Poniatowski**, he became the lover of the empress, **Catherine the Great**, and, largely through her influence, he was elected king (1764–95). **Frederick II, the Great**, who had gained the consent of Austria to a partition of Poland, made a similar proposal to Russia, and the first partition of Poland was effected (1772). Although he set up a new constitution (1791), the intrigues of discontented nobles led to further Russian and Prussian intervention, and a second fruitless resistance was followed (1793) by a second partition. The Poles became desperate, a general rising took place (1794), the Prussians were driven out, and the Russians were several times routed. When Austria became involved, **Kościuszko** was defeated, Warsaw was taken, the remainder of Poland

was annexed by Russia, Prussia and Austria, and the Polish monarchy came to an end. Stanisław resigned his Crown (1795) and died in St Petersburg.

Stanley, Edward Geoffrey Smith See **Derby, 14th Earl of**

Stanley, Francis Edgar 1849–1918
US inventor and manufacturer

Born in Kingfield, Maine, he and his twin brother, Freelan O (1849–1940), are best known for their invention of the steam-powered Stanley Steamer automobile. Their Stanley Motor Carriage Co (1902–17) manufactured the cars, one of which broke the world record for fastest mile in a steam car (28.2 sec). They also invented processes for the manufacture of photographic dry plates and the mass production of violins and wrote and lectured widely on many topics.

Stanley, Sir Henry Morton, *originally* John Rowlands 1841–1904
British–US explorer and journalist

He was born in Denbigh, Wales. In 1859 he went as cabin boy to New Orleans, where he was adopted by a merchant named Stanley. He served in the Confederate army and US navy, contributed to several journals, and in 1867 joined the *New York Herald*, accompanying Lord **Napier's** Abyssinian expedition in 1868. In October 1869 he received from **James Gordon Bennett** the laconic instruction, 'Find **Livingstone**'; on his way he visited Egypt for the opening of the Suez Canal, and travelled through Palestine, Turkey, Persia and India. On 10 November 1871 he 'found' Livingstone at Ujiji in Tanganyika, and the two explored Lake Tanganyika. In 1872 he returned alone and published *How I found Livingstone*. In 1874 he returned to Africa, determined the shape of Lake Tanganyika, passed down the Lualaba to Nyangwé, and traced the Congo to the sea. Having published *Through the Dark Continent* (1878), in 1879 he again went out to found, under the auspices of the Belgian king, the Congo Free State, having been refused help in England. He took part in the Congo Congress in Berlin (1884–85). In March 1886 he undertook an expedition for the relief of **Emin Pasha**, in the course of which he discovered Lake Edward and Mount Ruwenzori (1888–89). In 1890 he married the artist, Dorothy Tennant. He was naturalized as a British subject in 1892, and sat as a Unionist for Lambeth (1895–1900). 📖 Frank Hird, *H M Stanley: The Authorized Life* (1935)

Stanley, John 1713–86
English composer

Born in London, he was blind from the age of two as the result of an accident. He became organist at All Hallows, Bread Street, at the age of 11, and later he held posts at St Andrew's, Holborn, and at the Inner Temple. His compositions, which include oratorios (*Zimri* and *The Fall of Egypt*), cantatas, organ voluntaries, concerti grossi and instrumental sonatas, have won increasing recognition, and today he is held in high esteem.

Stanley, Wendell Meredith 1904–71
US biochemist and Nobel Prize winner

Born in Ridgeville, Indiana, he was educated at Illinois University, where he received his PhD in 1929. He was a Research Fellow in Munich (1930–31) and in 1931 joined the Rockefeller Institute for Medical Research, Princeton, before holding a series of professorships at the University of California from 1940. He was appointed director of the Virus Laboratory at the University of California at Berkeley in 1948. He isolated the tobacco mosaic virus (1935) using the salt fractionation techniques of John Howard Northrop, and showed it to contain protein and nucleic acid (1936). He went on to characterize the physical and chemical properties of the virus, and determined the protein amino acid sequence (1960). Stanley also isolated other plant viruses, compared virus variants using immunological techniques and independently noted that viruses can cause cancer (1949). He shared the 1946 Nobel Prize for chemistry with Northrop and James Sumner.

Stanley, William 1858–1916
US electrical engineer

He was born in Brooklyn, New York. After working for Hiram Maxim, he set up on his own and invented the transformer (1885). His work also included a long-range transmission system for alternating current.

Stansgate, William Wedgwood Benn, 1st Viscount 1877–1960
English politician

He was a Liberal MP from 1906 until 1927, when he joined the Labour Party; he was elected MP for North Aberdeen the next year. From 1929 to 1931 he was Secretary for India and in 1945–46 Secretary for Air. He won the DSO and DFC in World War I, served in the RAF in World War II, and was created a viscount in 1941. He was the father of Tony Benn.

Stanton, Edwin McMasters 1814–69
US lawyer and politician

Born in Steubenville, Ohio, he rose to legal prominence when he successfully opposed the plan for bridging the Ohio River at Wheeling on the grounds of interference with navigation. He was appointed US Attorney General by President James Buchanan (1860), then became Secretary of War under Abraham Lincoln (1862), continuing in that post under Andrew Johnson. Outspoken and abrasive, he alienated Johnson by taking sides against him on the issue of Reconstruction and was suspended by the President (1867) but was reinstated by the Senate. When Johnson's impeachment failed, Stanton resigned (1868). He was nominated to the Supreme Court by President Ulysses S Grant (1869), but died four days after his confirmation.

Stanton, Elizabeth Cady See panel p1744

Stanwyck, Barbara, *originally* Ruby Stevens 1907–90
US actress

Born in Brooklyn, New York City, she worked from the age of 13. She became a dancer, appearing in the *Ziegfeld Follies of 1923*, and made her dramatic stage debut in *The Noose* (1926). Her first film was *Broadway Nights* (1927). Established as a major star in the 1930s, she is best remembered in roles as gutsy, pioneering women in westerns such as *Annie Oakley* (1935) and *Union Pacific* (1939), or as sultry femmes fatales, as in *Double Indemnity* (1944). A durable leading lady, she was frequently seen as strong-willed women, often struggling to escape from the wrong side of the tracks, although her range also extended to melodramas such as *Stella Dallas* (1937) and deft comic performances as in *Lady Eve* (1941) and *Ball of Fire* (1941). Active in radio and television, she enjoyed a long-running series *The Big Valley* (1965–69). She received a Special Academy Award in 1982.

Stapleton, Maureen 1925–
US actress

Born in Troy, New York, she made her Broadway debut in *The Playboy of the Western World* (1946). She won a Tony award for her role as Serafina in *The Rose Tattoo* (1951) which began a long association with the works of Tennessee Williams. Her numerous appearances on the stage include *Orpheus Descending* (1957), *Toys in the Attic* (1960), *The Gingerbread Lady* (1971, Tony) and *The Little Foxes* (1981). She received a Best Supporting Actress Academy Award nomination for her film debut in *Lonelyhearts* (1958) and subsequent nominations for *Airport* (1969) and *Interiors* (1978) before winning for *Reds* (1981). She won an Emmy for *Among the Paths to Eden* (1967) and subsequent nominations for *Queen of the Stardust Ballroom* (1975), *The Gathering* (1977) and *Miss Rose White* (1992).

Stapleton, Ruth, *née* Carter 1929–83
US evangelist and faith healer

Born in Plains, Georgia, she was the younger sister of President Jimmy Carter, and is said to have been influential in his conversion to Christianity. Unlike many of her fellow Southern Baptists, she co-operated with other Christians, including Roman Catholics, and she used her graduate training in psychology in a remarkable ministry which stressed the necessity for inner healing ('communicating love to the negative, repressed aspects in a human being'). In the 1976 presidential campaign she addressed the National Press Club, Washington DC, largely on her brother's behalf; it was said to be the first time that it heard a woman preacher.

Starčević, Ante 1823–96
Croatian nationalist

At first a follower of Ljudevit Gaj and the Illyrian Movement, in 1861 with Eugen Kvaternik he founded the Croatian Party of Right. An extreme nationalist, he advocated the creation of an independent Croatia which would include not only Croats but also Slovenes and Serbs, whom he considered to be of Croatian nationality. During the anti-Croat regime of Ban Khuen-Héderváry, membership of his party grew to dominate Croatian political life in the 1880s.

Stark, Dame Freya Madeline 1893–1993
English writer and traveller

Born in Paris, France, she spent her childhood in England and Italy, before attending Bedford College, London University. She was a nurse on the Italian front during World War I, and afterwards studied Arabic at the School of Oriental and African Studies in London, and was invited to Baghdad by the Prime Minister. There she worked on the *Baghdad Times*, and mapped the Valley of the Assassins in Luristan, described in *Valley of the Assassins* (1934). During World War II she worked for the Ministry of Information in Aden and Cairo, and was personal assistant to Lady Wavell, describing her experiences in *West is East* (1945). She travelled extensively, financed by her writings, in Europe, Asia and the Middle East, and produced more than 30 travel books, including *The Southern*

Gates of Arabia (1938), *Traveller's Prelude* (1950), *Beyond Euphrates* (1951), *The Coast of Incense* (1953), *Ionia: A Quest* (1954), *The Lycian Shore* (1956), and *The Journey's Echo* (1963).

Stark, Harold Raynsford 1880–1972
US naval officer

Born in Wilkes-Barre, Pennsylvania, he was educated at the US Naval Academy, Annapolis, and served in a destroyer flotilla (1914–15). He was chief of the Bureau of Ordnance (1934–37). Chief of Naval Operations from 1939 to 1942, he was relieved after the bombing of Pearl Harbor (December 1942) and became commander US Naval Forces Europe (1942–43) with headquarters in London, where he contributed to the success of Allied Operations in the European theatre.

Stark, Johannes 1874–1957
German physicist and Nobel Prize winner

Born in Schickenhof, he was educated at Munich and held numerous teaching posts before being appointed to chairs at the universities of Aachen (1909), Greifswald (1917) and Würzburg (1920). He was awarded the Nobel Prize for physics in 1919. He later joined the Nazi Party and was rewarded with appointment to several prominent posts, but he did not hold these posts for long because of his quarrelsome nature and internal political struggles, and he retired in 1936. He discovered the 'Stark effect' concerning the splitting of spectrum lines by subjecting the light source to a strong electrostatic field, and also the **Doppler** effect in 'canal rays'. He argued that these phenomena reinforced **Albert Einstein's** theory of special relativity and **Max Planck's** quantum theory.

Stark, John 1728–1822
American Revolutionary soldier

Born in Londonderry, New Hampshire, he saw service in the French and Indian War (1754–59). In the American Revolution (1775–83) he served at Bunker Hill (1775), and won a victory at Bennington (1777). He was a member of the court martial which condemned **John André**.

Starkie, Enid Mary 1897–1970
Irish critic of French literature

Born in Killiney, County Dublin, the daughter of the classicist W J M Starkie and sister of the Hispanicist and gypsy-lover, Walter Starkie (author of *Raggle-Taggle*, *Spanish Raggle-Taggle*, and *Scholars and Gypsies*), she was educated at Alexandra College, Dublin, Somerville College, Oxford, and the Sorbonne, where she wrote a doctoral thesis on **Emile Verhaeren**. She taught modern languages at Exeter and Oxford, wrote perceptively on **Baudelaire** (1933) and **André Gide** (1954), played a major part in establishing the poetic reputation of **Arthur Rimbaud** (1938), and crowned her work by two outstanding volumes on **Gustave Flaubert** (1967, 1971). In 1951 she campaigned successfully for the Professor of Poetry at Oxford to be a poet rather than a critic; as a result **C S Lewis** was defeated and **Cecil Day-Lewis** elected. She portrayed her early life in *A Lady's Child* (1941).

Starley, James 1831–81
English inventor

Born in Albourne, Sussex, he worked in a factory in Coventry manufacturing sewing-machines and bicycles. He invented and manufactured a new, improved sewing-machine, the 'Coventry' tricycle and the 'Ariel' geared bicycle in 1871.

Starling, Ernest Henry 1866–1927
English physiologist

Born in London, he qualified in medicine in 1889 from Guy's Hospital, where he was then appointed lecturer in physiology. He moved to chairs at University College (1899–1927) and with Sir **William Bayliss** began a series of experiments on the nervous control of the viscera, in the course of which they discovered the pancreatic secretion secretin (1902), coining the word 'hormone' to describe it. He did much to elucidate the physiology of the circulation and the mechanisms of cardiac activity, still known today as 'Starling's law of the heart', and his work on capillary function gave rise to 'Starling's equilibrium'. He chaired the Royal Society's Food Committee and wrote many influential texts, including *Principles of Human Physiology* (1912).

Starr, Ringo See Beatles, The

Stassen, Harold Edward 1907–
US politician

Born in West St Paul, Minnesota, he studied law at the University of Minnesota, and became at 31 the youngest governor in Minnesota's history. He served in the navy in World War II, failed in 1948 and 1952 to secure the Republican presidential nomination, and became administrator of foreign aid under General **Eisenhower**. He represented the USA at the London disarmament conference in 1957, but resigned in 1958 as a result of disagreements with **John Foster Dulles**. He wrote *Where I Stand* (1947) and co-wrote *Eisenhower: turning the world toward peace* (1991).

Statius, Publius Papinius c.45–96AD
Roman poet

Born in Naples, he won a poetry prize in Naples, and went to Rome, where he flourished as a court poet and an improviser in the favour of **Domitian** until AD94, when he retired to Naples. His major work was the *Thebaïs*, an epic in 12 books on the struggle between the Theban brothers Eteocles and Polyneices. Of another epic, the *Achilleïs*, only a fragment remains; it was interrupted by the poet's death. His *Silvae*, or occasional verses, have freshness and vigour. He was admired by later poets, notably **Dante** and **Pope**. 🕮 H E Butler, *Post Augustan Poetry* (1909)

Staudinger, Hermann 1881–1965
German chemist and Nobel Prize winner

Born in Worms, he studied chemistry at the University of Halle and the Technical University at Darmstadt. He obtained his doctorate at Halle in 1903 for a study of malonic esters. He then became assistant to Johannes Thiele in Strassburg where he discovered keten. On being appointed assistant professor in the Technical University at Karlsruhe he began research on the structure of rubber, and in 1910 found a new and simpler way to synthesize isoprene, the basic unit of rubber. In 1912 he succeeded **Richard Willstätter** at the Federal Institute of Technology in Zurich, where he worked on the synthesis of natural products. During the 1930s he undertook the study of complex biological macromolecules and in the 1940s he turned to molecular biology. He was awarded the Nobel Prize for chemistry in 1953 for his discoveries in the field of macromolecular chemistry. A research institute was established for Staudinger at the University of Freiburg in the 1940s and he remained there until his retirement in 1956.

Stauffenberg, Count Claus von 1907–44
German soldier

He was born in Bavaria. He was a colonel on the General Staff, and initially a supporter of **Hitler**, but he became alienated by Nazi brutality. He planted a bomb in the unsuccessful attempt to assassinate Hitler at his headquarters at Rastenburg on 20 July 1944. He was shot in the evening of the same day.

Stauning, Thorvald 1873–1942
Danish politician

He became a member of the Folketinget (1906), and was leader of the Danish Social Democratic Party (1910) and Scandinavia's first Social Democratic Minister (1916).

After the general election of 1924, he became premier of Denmark's first Social Democratic government. He was the longest-serving Danish premier of the 20th century (1924–26, 1929–42), and one of the achievements of his administration was the social reform bill of 1933 based on the principle of the needy citizen's right to public support. In the general election of 1935, fought by the Social Democrats under the slogan 'Stauning or Chaos', the party's popularity reached its peak when 46 per cent of the electorate voted for it. His programme was interrupted with the German occupation of Denmark (1940), but he continued as premier of a national coalition government until his death. His funeral became a manifestation of popular and national solidarity.

Staunton, Howard 1810–74
English Shakespearean scholar, actor and chess player

He studied at Oxford, then took up journalism in London. He was world chess champion (1843–51), and his published works include *The Chess-player's Handbook* (1847), and a critical edition of **Shakespeare**'s works.

Stavisky, Serge Alexandre c.1886–1934
French swindler

Born in Kiev, Ukraine, he moved to Paris in 1900, and floated fraudulent companies, liquidating the debts of one by the profits of its successor. In 1933, he was discovered to be handling bonds to the value of more than 500 million francs on behalf of the municipal pawnshop in Bayonne. Stavisky fled to Chamonix and probably committed suicide, but in the meantime the affair had revealed widespread corruption in the Government and ultimately caused the downfall of two ministries. Stavisky was found guilty during a trial that ended in 1936 with the conviction of nine others. He became a French citizen in 1914.

St Clair, Arthur 1736–1818
American Revolutionary soldier

Born in Thurso, Scotland, he served in the British army in the American Colonies and Canada until 1762, when he resigned his commission and became a farmer and fur trader in Pennsylvania. He joined the Continental Army at the outset of the Revolution in 1775, and by the time he served under **George Washington** in New Jersey, he had risen to the rank of brigadier-general. When Fort Ticonderoga fell while under his command (1777), he was criticized but exonerated of blame in a court-martial. A member of the Continental Congress (1785–87, president 1787) and Governor of the Northwest Territory (1787–1802), he resigned from the army after being defeated in battle by Native American forces near Fort Wayne, Indiana (1791). When he tried to prevent Ohio from achieving statehood, he was removed from his governorship by President **Thomas Jefferson** (1802), and he died in poverty in Pennsylvania.

Stead, Christina Ellen 1902–83
Australian novelist

She was born in Rockdale, Sydney, the daughter of David George Stead, a leading English naturalist and writer. She trained as a teacher, but in 1928 left Australia for Europe, where she lived in London and Paris, working as a secretary in a Paris bank (1930–35). She went to live in Spain but left at the outbreak of war and settled in the USA, becoming a senior writer for MGM in Hollywood (1943). Her first novel to gain recognition was *Seven Poor Men of Sydney* (1934), notable for its interweaving of dissimilar but casually connected lives. *House of All Nations* (1938) took a critical look at the world of big finance, and her autobiographical novel, *The Man Who Loved Children* (1940), described suffocating family life under an egotistical father. Many of her short stories appeared in the *New Yorker*. She left the USA in 1947 and settled in

England, but finally returned to her homeland in 1974, in which year she was the first winner of the **Patrick White** Literary Award. Her later novels of suburban US and European life, such as *Miss Herbert (The Suburban Wife)* (1976) were less successful. *I'm Dying Laughing*, a novel begun in the 1940s and ridiculing US Hollywood radicals, was published posthumously in 1986. 📖 R G Geering, *Christina Stead* (1969)

Stead, Tim 1952–
English wood sculptor and furniture maker

Born in Helsby, Cheshire, he trained as a sculptor in Cheshire, in Nottingham and at Glasgow School of Art. One of his earliest projects was the interior of the Café Gandolfi in Glasgow, where he created a distinctive wooden sculptured effect. He has received many public and private commissions, has exhibited regularly and has work in many public and private collections.

Stead, William Thomas 1849–1912
English journalist and reformer

Born in Embleton, Alnwick, Northumberland, he was editor of the Darlington *Northern Echo* (1871–80), and assistant editor (1880–83) and editor (1883–90) of the *Pall Mall*. He drew attention to the practice of purchasing child prostitutes by openly committing the offence himself and writing an article about it (*The Maiden Tribute of Modern Babylon*), for which he was imprisoned for three months; it led to the Criminal Amendment Act of 1885. He founded the *Review of Reviews* (1890), crusaded for peace and spiritualism, and was the author of *If Christ Came to Chicago* (1893) and *The Americanization of the World* (1902). He was drowned in the *Titanic* disaster.

Stearn, William Thomas 1911–
English botanist, bibliographer and horticulturist

Born in Cambridge, he was librarian of the Royal Horticultural Society (1933–41, 1946–52). From 1952 to 1976 he was a botanist at the British Museum (Natural History), London. He is the world's foremost authority on **Carolus Linnaeus**, with an encyclopedic knowledge of his life and works. His immense output includes the books *Botanical Latin* (1966) and *Gardener's Dictionary of Plant Names* (1972). His botanical researches have ranged widely, including studies of *Symphytum*, *Vinca*, *Epimedium* and the onion genus *Allium*. He has also published many papers on the history and bibliography of botany. A recent publication is *Flower Artists of Kew* (1990).

Stebbins, Emma 1815–82
US painter and sculptor

She was born in New York City, where her amateur portraits of family and friends won her election as an associate of the National Academy of Design. Her sculptures, which are displayed in some prominent public places, include a bronze of the US educationist and politician **Horace Mann**, in front of the State House in Boston, and *The Angel of the Waters* for the Bethesda Fountain in Central Park, New York City.

Stebbins, George Ledyard 1906–
US botanist

Born in Lawrence, New York, he studied biology at Harvard University and spent his career at the University of California at Berkeley (1937–50) and Davis (1950–73), where he established the department of genetics. He was the first to apply modern ideas of evolution to botany, as expounded in his *Variation and Evolution in Plants* (1950). From the 1940s he used artificially induced polyploidy (the condition of having more than twice the basic number of chromosomes) to create fertile hybrids, a technique of value both in taxonomy and in plant breeding. His other books include *Processes of Organic*

Evolution (1966), *Flowering Plants: Evolution Above the Species Level* (1974) and *Darwin to DNA* (1982).

Stedman, Edmund Clarence 1833–1908
US poet, critic and financier
Born in Hartford, Connecticut, he studied at Yale, was war correspondent of the *New York World* (1861–63), and then became a New York stockbroker and banker. He published *Poems* (1860), *Victorian Poets* (1875), *Edgar Allan Poe* (1880), *Poets of America* (1886), *Nature of Poetry* (1892), *Victorian Anthology* (1896), and other works. He also co-edited a *Library of American Literature*, issued in 11 volumes between 1888 and 1890, which may have influenced early modernist writers.

Steed, Henry Wickham 1871–1956
English journalist and author
Born in Long Melford, Suffolk, he was educated at Sudbury Grammar School, and the universities of Jena, Berlin and Paris. He joined *The Times* as foreign correspondent in 1896, becoming first foreign editor (1914–19) and then editor (1919–22). He was proprietor and editor of the *Review of Reviews* from 1923 to 1930. He published a number of books on European history and affairs, and broadcast for the BBC on the Overseas Service (1937–47).

Steel, David Martin Scott Steel, Baron 1938–
Scottish politician, last leader of the Liberal Party
Born in Kirkcaldy, Fife, he became a journalist and broadcaster, and was the youngest MP when first elected in 1965. His constituency was first Roxburgh, Selkirk and Peebles (1965–83), then Ettrick and Lauderdale (1983–97). He sponsored a controversial Bill to reform the laws on abortion (1966–67) and was active in the Anti-Apartheid Movement before succeeding Jeremy Thorpe as leader of the Liberal Party in 1976. He led his party into an electoral pact with Labour (1977–78) and subsequently an alliance with the Social Democratic Party (SDP) (1981–88), but despite Steel's undoubted popularity, they won only 23 seats. After the 1987 general election he called for a merger of the Liberals and SDP; this took place in 1989 under the leadership of Paddy Ashdown as Steel declined to seek the leadership. He became president of Liberal International (1994–96). He published his autobiography, *Against Goliath: David Steel's Story*, in 1989, and was awarded a knighthood in 1990 and a life peerage in 1997. ◻ Peter Bartram, *David Steel: His Life and Politics* (1981)

Steel, Dawn 1946–97
US film executive and producer
Born in New York City, she studied at the NYU School of Commerce, then worked as a sports reporter and merchandise editor for *Penthouse* magazine. In 1978 she moved to Los Angeles and worked for Paramount Pictures, where she was instrumental in the making of such successful films as *Flashdance* (1983), *Top Gun* (1986) and *Fatal Attraction* (1987). In 1987 she was appointed president of Columbia Pictures, holding the post for two and a half years. Her films as an independent producer include *Cool Runnings* (1993). She published her autobiography, *They Can Kill You But They Can't Eat You*, in 1993.

Steele, Sir Richard 1672–1729
Irish essayist, dramatist and politician
Born in Dublin, he was educated at Charterhouse, where Joseph Addison was a contemporary, and Merton College, Oxford, after which he entered the army as a cadet in the Life Guards. His first venture in periodical literature, *The Tatler*, ran from 1709 to 1711, and concentrated on social and moral essays, with occasional articles on literature. With Addison he also founded *The Spectator* (1711–12) and *The Guardian* (1743). He briefly entered parliament (1713), but was expelled for supporting the Hanoverian cause. On the succession of George I he

was awarded with the appointment of supervisor of Drury Lane Theatre, and a knighthood followed. Financial troubles caused him to retire to Wales (1722). His letters to his wife ('dearest Prue') attest the sincerity of his sermons on married love. ◻ R P Bond, *The Tatler* (1972)

Steele, Tommy, *originally* Thomas Hicks 1936–
English actor, singer and director
Born in London, he achieved considerable success as a pop singer in the 1950s and 1960s, after making his stage debut in variety at the Empire Theatre, Sunderland (1956), and his London variety debut at the Dominion Theatre (1957). He played Tony Lumpkin in Oliver Goldsmith's *She Stoops to Conquer*, at the Old Vic (1960). He continued to appear in musicals during the 1960s, most notably in *Half a Sixpence* (1963–64), had a one-man show in London (1979), and starred in and directed a stage adaptation of *Singin' In The Rain* at the London Palladium (1983). In 1992 he starred in and directed *Some Like It Hot*.

Steell, Sir John 1804–91
Scottish sculptor
He was born in Aberdeen, and studied art in Edinburgh and Rome. Most of his chief works, in marble or bronze, are in Edinburgh, including a prancing equestrian statue of the Duke of Wellington (1852), *Alexander Taming Bucephalus* (1882–83) at the City Chambers, Sir Walter Scott (1846) on the Scott Memorial, and Prince Albert (1876) on the Albert Memorial.

Steen, Jan 1626–79
Dutch painter
Born in Leyden, he was a pupil of Adriaan van Ostade and Jan van Goyen. He joined the Leyden guild of painters in 1648 and next year went to The Hague until 1654, afterwards following his father's trade as a brewer in Delft. He spent his last years as an innkeeper in Leyden. A versatile artist, he painted a wide range of religious, historical and mythological subjects, adapting the techniques of other artists such as Frans Hals to his own style. His best works are genre pictures of social and domestic scenes depicting the everyday life of ordinary folk with rare insight and subtle humour. He also painted some fine portraits, and a well-known self-portrait playing the lute (Lugano).

Steensen, Niels See Steno, Nicolaus

Steenstrup, Johannes Iapetus Smith 1813–97
Danish zoologist
Born in Vang, Norway, and educated in Aalborg and at the University of Copenhagen, from 1846 to 1873 he was Professor of Zoology and director of the Zoology Museum at Copenhagen. He is best known for his pioneering studies on cephalopods, and also worked on marine invertebrates and achieved fame for his demonstration of an alternation of sexual and asexual generations in certain animals. He was a founder of scientific archaeology through his work on the animal and plant remains in Danish peat bogs, recognizing significant climatic changes in prehistoric times. He also wrote on the distribution and extinction of the great auk.

Steenwijk, Hendrik van c.1550–1603
Dutch painter of architectural interiors
He was born in Holland, and worked in Flanders and Germany, settling in Frankfurt in 1579. His *Cathedral at Aachen* is one of the earliest paintings of the genre. His son Hendrik (1580–1649), also a painter, came to London on Van Dyck's advice in 1629.

Steer, Philip Wilson 1860–1942
English painter
Born in Birkenhead, he studied in Paris, and began as an exponent of Impressionism, to which he added a traditionally English touch. A founder of the New English

Art Club, he taught at the Slade. He excelled, too, as a figure painter, as shown in the Pitti *Self-Portrait,The Music Room* (Tate Gallery, London), and the *Portrait of Mrs Hammersley*, painted in the style of Thomas Gainsborough.

Stefan, Josef 1835–93
Austrian physicist

Born near Klagenfurt, he became Professor of Physics at Vienna University in 1863 after seven years of school-teaching. In 1866 he was appointed director of the Institute for Experimental Physics founded in Vienna by Christian Doppler in 1850. In 1879 he proposed Stefan's law (or the Stefan–Boltzmann law), that the amount of energy radiated from a black body is proportional to the absolute temperature, and he used this law to make the first satisfactory estimate of the Sun's surface temperature. He also designed a diathermometer to measure heat conduction, and worked on the kinetic theory of heat and on the relationship between surface tension and evaporation (1886).

Stefanik, Milan Rastislav 1880–1919
French hero of the Slovak National Movement

Born in Slovakia and educated in Prague, he moved to Paris in 1904 and became a French citizen in 1910. An astronomer and civil servant, he volunteered for the French air force in 1914 and was appointed general in 1918. He also worked with Jan Masaryk and Eduard Beneš as a representative of the Slovaks. As a spokesman at the Versailles peace conference in 1919, his words carried great weight with the French and with his own Slovaks. In 1919 he was killed in an air crash while travelling back to Slovakia.

Stefánsson, Davið 1895–1964
Icelandic poet

Born in Fagriskógur, Eyjafjörður, he was educated in Akureyri and Reykjavík, and worked as a librarian in Akureyri (1925–52). He became the most popular Romantic poet of his time with a series of volumes of lyrical poetry, starting with *Svartar fjaðrir* (1919, 'Black Feathers') and including *Kveðjur* (1924, 'Greetings'), *Í byggðum* (1933, 'In Human Habitations') and *Að norðran* (1936,'From the North'). He also wrote a historical novel, *Sólon Íslandus* (2 vols, 1940), and a successful play, *Gullna Hliðið* (1941,'The Golden Gate'). ⌨ E Heage, introduction to *The Golden Gate* (1967)

Stefánsson, Jón 1881–1962
Icelandic landscape painter

Born in Sauðárkrókur in the north of Iceland, he was one of the three founders, with Ásgrímur Jónsson and Jóhannes Kjarval, of modern art in Iceland. He went to Copenhagen to study engineering in 1900, but in 1903 decided to devote himself to art. He went to Paris in 1908 and studied under Henri Matisse. A man of strong temperament, he painted landscapes on a grand scale, exploiting colour with extraordinary luminosity.

Stefánsson, Vilhjalmur 1879–1962
Canadian explorer

Born of immigrant Icelandic parents in Arnes, Manitoba, he studied anthropology and archaeology before travelling to the Arctic to live among the Inuit (1906–07). Between 1908 and 1912 he conducted further studies among the Mackenzie and Copper Inuit. From 1913 to 1918 he led the Canadian Arctic expedition to map the Beaufort Sea, the last such expedition to be carried out without the support of radio or aircraft. Later he became a consultant on the use of Arctic resources. He wrote several popular books, including *My Life with the Eskimo* (1913) and *The Friendly Arctic* (1921).

Steffens, (Joseph) Lincoln 1866–1936
US journalist

Born in San Francisco, he studied at French and German universities as well as graduating from the University of California. He worked on the New York *Evening Post* (1892–98) and *Commercial Advertiser* (1898–1902). As managing editor of *McClure's Magazine* (1902–06), he contributed to an article on city corruption in St Louis, which led to a series later republished as *The Shame of the Cities* (1904). The articles were distinguished by careful research, and an insistence that public apathy was much to blame. He then wrote an analysis of corruption and reform on state level (*The Struggle for Self-Government*, 1906), and became the associate editor of the *American* and *Everybody's* magazines (1906–11). He visited post-Revolutionary Russia in 1919 and popularized his famous comment 'I have seen the future and it works'. His *Autobiography* (2 vols, 1931) is ironic and somewhat disillusioned, but is informative about his times.

Steichen, Edward Jean 1879–1973
US photographer

Born in Luxembourg, he was taken as a child to the USA, where he grew up in Michigan. He studied art in Milwaukee (1894–98) and worked as a painter and photographer in Europe until 1914. A member of The Linked Ring in England, he was noted for his nude studies. In 1902 he helped Alfred Stieglitz to found the American Photo-Secession Group, and through their gallery in New York City exercised considerable influence in establishing photography as an acceptable art form. In World War I he commanded the photographic division of the US army, and in the 1920s moved into New Realism, achieving success with fashion photography. He was head of US Naval Film Services during World War II and director of photography at the New York Museum of Modern Art (1945–1962), organizing the well-known exhibition *The Family of Man* in 1955.

Stein, Sir (Mark) Aurel 1862–1943
British archaeologist and explorer

Born in Budapest, Hungary, he held educational and archaeological posts under the Indian government, from 1900 to 1930 conducting a series of expeditions in Chinese Turkestan and Central Asia tracing the ancient caravan routes between China and the West. His discoveries included the Cave of a Thousand Buddhas near Tan Huang, walled up since the 11th century. Later superintendent of the Indian Archaeological Survey (1910–29), he died at Kabul when about to begin an exploration of Afghanistan.

Stein, Charlotte von, *née* von Schardt 1742–1827
German writer

She was a lady-in-waiting at the Weimar court, and in 1764 married Friedrich von Stein, the Duke of Saxe–Weimar's Master of the Horse. In 1775, she met Goethe, who fell in love with her. Their friendship was broken suddenly (1788), but was renewed before her death. She was the inspiration for many of his love poems and plays. She herself wrote dramas such as *Rino* (1776), a play about Goethe, and *Dido* (1792, published 1867), a prose tragedy lamenting the end of their affair.

Stein, Edith, *known as* Sister Teresa Benedicta of the Cross 1891–1942
German Carmelite philosopher

Born in Breslau to a Jewish family, she was converted to Catholicism in 1922 and began interpreting the phenomenology she had learned under Edmund Husserl from a Thomistic point of view. She completed her project when she entered the Carmelite convent in Cologne in 1934, and for safety she transferred to the house in Echt, Holland, in 1938, where she wrote a phenomenological study of St John of the Cross. She was executed in Auschwitz concentration camp, together with priests and nuns with Jewish connections who had been rounded up as a result of Church criticism of Nazi anti-Semitism. She was beatified in 1987.

Stein, Gertrude 1874–1946
US writer

She was born in Allegheny, Pennsylvania, and spent her early years in Vienna, Paris and San Francisco. She then studied psychology at Radcliffe College under William James, and medicine at Johns Hopkins University. She then settled in Paris, where she was absorbed into the world of experimental art and letters and came into contact with writers and artists including **Picasso** and **Matisse**. From 1907 she shared an apartment with a close friend from San Francisco, Alice B Toklas. Stein sometimes attempted to apply the theories of abstract painting to her own writing, which led to a magnified reputation for obscurity and meaningless repetition. However, her first book, *Three Lives* (1908), reveals a sensitive ear for speech rhythms, and by far the larger part of her work is immediately comprehensible. The prose of *Tender Buttons* (1914) is repetitive, canonic and extremely musical. *The Making of Americans* (1925) is a vast, virtually unreadable family saga, but she took a more ironic stance in the playfully titled *The Autobiography of Alice B. Toklas* (1933) and *Everybody's Autobiography* (1937). *Four Saints in Three Acts* (1934) and *The Mother Of Us All* (1947) were operas with music by **Virgil Thomson**. She stayed in Germany in the village of Chloz during World War II, and afterwards wrote *Wars I Have Seen* (1945) and the novel, *Brewsie and Willie* (1946), about the liberation by US soldiers. 📖 J Hobhouse, *Everybody Who Was Anybody: a biography of Gertrude Stein* (1975)

Stein, Heinrich Friedrich Carl, Baron von 1757–1831
Prussian politician and German nationalist

Born in Nassau, he entered the service of Prussia in 1780, and became president of the Westphalian chambers (1796). During his tenure as Secretary for Trade (1804–07) he abolished the last relics of serfdom, created peasant proprietors, extirpated monopolies and hindrances to free trade, promoted municipal government, and supported **Gerhard von Scharnhorst** in his schemes of army reform. **Napoleon I** demanded his dismissal and he withdrew (1808) to Austria, but not before issuing his *Political Testament*. In 1812 he went to St Petersburg and built up the coalition against Napoleon. He liberalized the Prussian state, but at the same time fostered the myth of German destiny and aggressive nationalism, not least by founding the *Monumenta Germaniae Historica* in 1815.

Stein, Jock (John) 1922–85
Scottish footballer and manager

He was born in Burnbank, Lanarkshire. He became a great Scottish football manager after an undistinguished playing career, managing first the unfashionable Fife club Dunfermline Athletic, which he led to victory in the Scottish Cup. A short successful spell with Hibernian followed and in 1965 he took over Glasgow Celtic, for whom he had previously played. In the next 13 years Celtic won nine championships in a row, the League Cup on five consecutive occasions and several Scottish Cups. They also won the European Cup in 1967 and were finalists in 1970. Stein left Celtic in 1978 for a brief period as manager of Leeds United, but returned to Scotland to become national manager. Under him the Scottish side qualified for the World Cup Finals in Spain in 1982. He died at an international against Wales at Cardiff as his side was about to qualify for a World Cup play-off.

Stein, William Howard 1911–80
US biochemist and Nobel Prize winner

Born in New York City, he studied at Harvard and Columbia universities, and joined the staff of the Rockefeller Institute, where he became Professor of Biochemistry in 1954. With **Stanford Moore**, he developed a column chromatographic method for the identification and quantification of amino acid mixtures in proteins and physiological tissues. They automated the analysis of the base sequence of RNA (1958), and studied a novel protease from streptococcus, showing that its molecular structure differed from that of the plant protease papain. This was the first example of the phenomenon called convergent evolution, whereby two enzymes of similar function arise by different evolutionary paths. Stein, Moore and **Christian Anfinsen** shared the Nobel Prize for chemistry in 1972.

Steinarr, Steinn, *pseudonym of* Aðalsteinn Kristmundsson 1908–58
Icelandic poet

Born in Nauteyrarhreppur, north Iceland, he moved to Reykjavík and joined the Communist Party as a young man. He wrote poetry of great sensibility which became progressively more abstract and metaphysical. A pioneer of Modernist poetry in Iceland, he wrote *Rauður loginn brann* (1934, 'The Red Flame Burned'), *Spor í sandi* (1940, 'Tracks in the Sand'), *Ferð án fyrirheits* (1942, 'Journey without Promise') and his final masterpiece, *Tíminn og vatnið* (1948, 'Time and Water').

Steinbeck, John Ernest 1902–68
US novelist and Nobel Prize winner

Born in Salinas, California, he studied marine biology at Stanford University and worked as an agricultural labourer and semi-skilled technician, while writing steadily. *Tortilla Flat* (1935), his first novel of repute, is a faithful picture of the shifting *paisanos* of California, foreshadowing the solidarity which characterizes his major work, *The Grapes of Wrath* (1939), a study of the poor in the face of disaster and threatened disintegration. His journalistic grasp of significant detail and pictorial essence make this book a powerful plea for consideration of human values and common justice. It led to much-needed reform, and won the 1940 Pulitzer Prize. His other works include *In Dubious Battle* (1935), *Of Mice and Men* (1937), *The Moon is Down* (1942), *The Pearl* (1947), *Burning Bright* (1950), *East of Eden* (1952) and *Winter of our Discontent* (1961), as well as the light-hearted and humorous *Cannery Row* (1945) and *The Short Reign of Pippin IV* (1957). He won the Nobel Prize for literature in 1962, a testament to his currently undervalued liberal humanism and generous solidarities. 📖 Jay Parini, *John Steinbeck: A Biography* (1994); E Steinbeck and R Wallsten (eds), *John Steinbeck: A Life in Letters* (1975)

Steinberg, Saul 1914–
US artist

He was born in Rîmnicu-Sarat, Romania, settled in the USA in 1942, was naturalized and joined the US navy in 1943. Soon after the end of World War II, he became a nationally known graphic artist and cartoonist. His witty and satirical drawings, which are filled with unexpected ideas and images and often include bizarre figures speaking forms of fantastic words, have appeared regularly in the *New Yorker* magazine.

Steinberger, Jack 1921–
US physicist

Born in Bad Kissingen, Germany, he moved to the USA in 1935, and was educated at the University of Chicago. He held professorships at Columbia University from 1950 to 1972, and from 1968 to 1986 was a staff member at CERN, the European centre for nuclear research in Geneva, where he was a director from 1969 to 1972. He proved the existence of a neutral pion by observations of its decay at the Berkeley synchroton, measured the spin and parity of the charged pion, and established the existence of two distinct neutrino types. Steinberger was later involved in research at CERN, and was awarded the 1988 Nobel Prize for physics jointly with **Leon Lederman** and **Melvin Schwartz**. Since 1986 he has been Professor of Physics at the Scuola Normale Superiore, Pisa.

Steinem, Gloria 1934–
US feminist and writer
Born in Toledo, Ohio, she studied at Smith College in Northampton, Massachusetts. She became a journalist and emerged as a leading figure in the women's movement in the 1960s and early 1970s. A co-founder of Women's Action Alliance (1970) and the National Women's Political Caucus (1971), she was also founding editor of *Ms Magazine* (1972), which brought women's issues to the fore. Her published works include *Outrageous Acts and Everyday Rebellions* (1983), *Marilyn* (1986), a story of media manipulation and *Revolution from Within: A Book of Self-Esteem* (1992).

Steiner, George 1929–
US critic and scholar
Born in Paris of Austrian–Jewish parents, he was educated at Chicago, Harvard, and Balliol College, Oxford. He taught at Princeton (1956–60) and Cambridge (1961–), and became Professor of English and Comparative Literature at the University of Geneva (1974–94). He was then Weidenfeld Professor of Comparative Literature and Fellow of St Anne's College, Oxford (1994–95). He sees literature as a part of a broader social and cultural context, and has made penetrating and controversial studies in the role and nature of language and the influences on it. His publications include *The Death of Tragedy* (1960), *Language and Silence* (1967), *After Babel* (1975), regarded as his most important work, *Antigones* (1984) and *Real Presences* (1989).

Steiner, Jakob 1796–1863
German–Swiss geometer
Born in Utzensdorf, Switzerland, he became professor at Berlin University in 1834, and pioneered 'synthetic' geometry, particularly the properties of geometrical constructions, ranges and curves. He also published many ingenious proofs (not all rigorous) of the obvious but elusive proposition that the circle encloses the greatest area of all curves of a given length.

Steiner, Max(imilian Raoul Walter) 1888–1971
US film composer
Born in Vienna, he was a student at the Imperial Academy there, and developed into a child prodigy, his first operetta *The Beautiful Greek Girl* being performed in 1902. He was a conductor of musical comedies in London, Paris and Berlin, and in 1914 was invited by **Florenz Ziegfeld** to New York, where he worked for a number of impresarios in the Broadway theatre. In Hollywood, he conducted music for a film of *Rio Rita* (1929), and was subsequently offered a permanent position at RKO, where he was able to establish the power of music to enhance dramatic mood, seen most notably in *King Kong* (1933). At **Warner** Brothers from 1936, he contributed many vivid and full-blooded scores to some of the most enduring screen classics, among them *Gone With the Wind* (1939), *Casablanca* (1942) and *The Treasure of the Sierra Madre* (1948). He was nominated on 26 occasions for an Academy Award, winning for *The Informer* (1935), *Now Voyager* (1942) and *Since You Went Away* (1945).

Steiner, Rudolf 1861–1925
Austrian social philosopher, the founder of anthroposophy
Born in Kraljevic, Croatia, he studied science and mathematics, and edited **Goethe**'s scientific papers in Weimar (1889–96). He was temporarily influenced by **Annie Besant** and the Theosophists, and went on to found his own Anthroposophical Society in 1912 and establish his first Goetheanum, or 'school of spiritual science' in Dornach, Switzerland. His aim was to integrate the psychological and practical aspects of life into an educational, ecological and therapeutic basis for spiritual and physical development, and restore the capacity for spiritual perception, dulled by the material preoccupations of the modern world. His first school was founded for the children of the Waldorf Astoria factory workers in 1919, the first of many hundreds of Waldorf or Steiner schools now operating. His system of anthroposophy has been influential in the realms of music, art, medicine and farming, and his work also inspired curative education as exemplified by the Camphill homes, schools and villages in Britain. Writers too have been influenced by aspects of it, including **Andrei Bely** and Arturo Onofri. His principal publications were *The Philosophy of Freedom* (1894, also translated as *The Philosophy of Spiritual Activity*), *Occult Science: an Outline* (1913) and *Story of my Life* (1924). ⌨ *Knowledge of the Higher Worlds* (1923)

Steinitz, Wilhelm 1836–1900
Czech chess player
He was born in Prague and moved to Vienna to complete studies in mathematics which he funded by playing chess for stakes. From 1862 he settled in London for 20 years as a chess professional, supplementing his income as chess editor of *The Field*. After moving to New York he won decisively in the 1886 match organized to decide the first official world championship. He defended his title three times successfully before losing it in 1894 to **Emanuel Lasker**. He died impoverished in a New York mental asylum.

Steinmetz, Charles Proteus, *originally* **Karl August Rudolf** 1865–1923
US electrical engineer
Born in Breslau, Germany, and educated at the Technical High School, Berlin, he was forced to leave Germany in 1888 for socialist activities and emigrated to the USA in 1889. He was consulting engineer to General Electric from 1893 and a professor at Union College, Schenectady, from 1902. One of his earliest achievements was to work out in complete detail, using complex numbers, the mathematical theory of alternating currents. He discovered magnetic hysteresis, a simple notation for calculating alternating current circuits, and lightning arresters for high-power transmission lines.

Steinway, Heinrich Engelhard, *originally* Steinweg 1797–1871
US piano-maker
Born in Wolfshagen, Germany, he fought in the Prussian army at the Battle of Waterloo (1815) and in 1836 established a piano factory in Brunswick. In 1850 he moved with his family to the USA and established a business in New York, where he introduced many innovations into the instrument, such as a cast-iron frame.

Stella, Frank Philip 1936–
US painter
Born in Malden, Massachusetts, he studied at Phillips Academy and Princeton (1954–58). His earliest minimal paintings, symmetrical patterns of black stripes, date from 1959. Using house-painters' techniques to avoid any trace of artistic brushwork, he creates a totally impersonal effect, which has made a significant impression on younger artists such as **Donald Judd**.

Stella, Joseph, *originally* **Giuseppe Stella** 1877–1946
US painter
Born in Muro Lucano, near Naples, Italy, he emigrated to New York City in 1896 and returned to Europe in 1909. In Italy he painted in an Impressionist style, then visited Paris in 1911. He returned to New York in 1913 and painted

the first American Futurist pictures, swirling compositions in the manner of **Gino Severini**, and interpretations of NewYork scenery, eg *Brooklyn Bridge* (c.1919).

Steller, *originally* **Stöhler, Georg Wilhelm** 1709–46
German naturalist and explorer
Born in Windsheim, near Nuremberg, he studied theology at Wittenburg, but changed to medicine and botany, and joined the Academy of Sciences at St Petersburg. Seconded to the second Kamchatka expedition led by **Vitus Bering** (1737–44), he travelled across Russia to the east, explored Siberia and Kamchatka, and met Bering in Okhotsk. They sailed on the *St Peter* and *St Paul* via the Aleutian Islands to Alaska, landed on Kayak Island, and returned via Bering Island where they were shipwrecked and where Bering died. There Steller wrote his most famous work, *De Bestiis Marinis* (published posthumously in 1751, 'On Marine Animals'). He died on the journey back to St Petersburg. Steller's sea-cow (now extinct), Steller's sea lion and Steller's eider are named after him.

Stendhal, *pseudonym of* **Henri Marie Beyle**
1783–1842
French novelist
He was born in Grenoble, where he was educated at the École Centrale, and wrote for the theatre. A cousin offered him a post in the Ministry of War, and from 1800 he followed **Napoleon I**'s campaigns in Italy, Germany, Russia and Austria. Between wars he spent his time in Paris drawing-rooms and theatres. When Napoleon fell he retired to Italy, adopted his pseudonym, and began to write books on Italian painting and on **Haydn** and **Mozart**, as well as copious journalism. After the 1830 revolution he was appointed consul at Trieste and Civitavecchia, but his health deteriorated and he returned to Paris. His recognized masterpieces, *Le Rouge et le noir* (Eng trans *Red and Black*, 1900; better known as *Scarlet and Black*, the title of a 1938 translation), and *La Chartreuse de Parme* (Eng trans *The Charterhouse of Parma*, 1895), were published in 1830 and 1839 respectively. The first follows the rise and decline of Julien Sorel, a provincial youth in the France of the Restoration, and the second recounts the fortunes of Fabrice del Dongo at an insignificant Italian court during the same period. These are remarkable and original works, and were admired by **Honoré de Balzac**, although neither received great understanding during Stendhal's lifetime. His autobiographical volumes include *Souvenirs d'égotisme* (1892, Eng trans *Memoirs of an Egotist*, 1949). 📖 Wallace Fowlie, *Stendhal* (1969)

Stenmark, Ingemar 1956–
Swedish champion skier
Born in Tärnaby, he began competing at the age of eight when he won a regional Donald Duck trophy. His international fame began in 1974–75 when he won the slalom and was second overall in the World Cup. He subsequently won the World Cup three years in succession (1976–78) and went on to become the most successful competitor in slalom and grand slalom ever recorded. He was World Master in 1978 and 1982 and won the Olympic gold medal at Lake Placid in 1980. He was the first man to win three consecutive slalom titles (1980–82). Between 1974 and 1989 he won a record 86 World Cup races. He retired in 1989.

Steno, Nicolaus, *also known as* **Niels Stensen** or **Steensen** 1638–86
Danish physician, naturalist and theologian
Born a Protestant in Copenhagen, he was converted to Catholicism and settled in Florence. He was appointed personal physician to the grand duke of Tuscany in 1666 and Royal Anatomist at Copenhagen in 1672. He became a priest in 1675, and gave up science on being appointed Vicar-Apostolic to North Germany and Scandinavia. He

discovered Steno's duct of the parotid gland, and investigated the function of the ovaries. He also worked in crystallography (establishing Steno's law on crystal structure) and in geology and palaeontology, sketching what are perhaps the earliest geological sections. 📖 Harald Moe, *Nicolaus Steno: An Illustrated Biography* (1994)

Stepanova, Varvara Fyodorovna 1894–1958
Russian painter and avant-garde textile designer
Born in Lithuania, she trained at the Kazan Art School in western Russia, and at the Stroganov School, Moscow. She taught at the Fine Art Studio of the Academy of Social Education from 1921 and in the textile department of the Vkhutemas (1924–25). A proponent of Russian Constructivism, she and Alexei Gan and her husband **Aleksandr Rodchenko** founded the First Working Group of Constructivists in 1921. She was involved in the journals *LEF* (1923–25) and *Novyi* (1927–28), and produced her own futurist books, working with the poet **Vladimir Mayakovsky** in the 1930s and 1940s.

Stephansson, Stephan G, *originally* **Stefán Guðmundarson** 1853–1927
Canadian poet
Born in Kirkjuhóll, Skagafjörður, Iceland, he emigrated with his family to North America in 1873, and worked as a railroad labourer and farmhand in Wisconsin before settling as a farmer in Markerville, Alberta in 1889. There he raised a large family, took a prominent part in local affairs, and composed several volumes of poetry in Icelandic, including *Úti á víðavangi* (1894, 'Out in the Open'), *Á ferð og flugi* (1900, 'En route'), and his major work, *Andvökur* (6 vols, 1909–38, 'Wakeful Nights'). A lifelong socialist, he expressed his horror of war in a controversial volume, *Vígslóði* (1920, 'The War Trail'). He is recognized as one of the best Icelandic poets, and his works give a vivid picture of landscapes and conditions in western Canada. 📖 S Nordal, *Stephan Stephansson* (1959)

Stephen, St 1st century AD
New Testament figure and the first Christian martyr
All we know about him is from Acts 6–7. He was possibly a Hellenistic Jew, and was appointed by the Apostles to manage the finances and alms of the early Church. He was tried by the Sanhedrin for blasphemy and stoned to death. His feast day is 26 December (in the West) and 27 December (in the East). 📖 Marcel Simon, *St Stephen and the Hellenists in the Primitive Church* (1958)

Stephen I c.977–1038
First King of Hungary
Baptized by St **Adalbert** of Prague, he married Gisela, sister of Emperor Henry II, and succeeded to his father's dukedom in 997. He united Pannonia and Dacia, which were inhabited by semi-independent Magyar chiefs, and was crowned king (1000) with the title of 'Apostolic King' bestowed by Pope **Sylvester II**. During a peaceful reign he organized a standing army, suppressed paganism, reformed the Church and endowed abbeys, and he laid the foundations of many institutions surviving to this day. He was canonized in 1083, and his feast day is 16 August. He is the patron saint of Hungary.

Stephen c.1097–1154
King of England
He was the grandson of **William the Conqueror**. In 1114 he was sent to the court of his uncle, **Henry I** of England, who gave him Mortain in Normandy, and he acquired Boulogne by his marriage to Matilda, daughter of the Count of Boulogne. Stephen swore fealty to Henry's heir, his daughter **Matilda** (or the Empress Maud), widow of the Emperor **Henry V**, but on Henry's death (1135), Stephen took the crown himself. Although personally courageous and decisive, he was too genial to provide strong leadership. King **David I** of Scotland supported

Matilda in two invasions, while Stephen antagonized Robert, Earl of Gloucester, an illegitimate son of Henry I, and also Bishop Roger of Salisbury. The ensuing civil war brought devastation to parts of the country, though the extent of the anarchy has often been exaggerated. In 1141 Matilda imprisoned Stephen and was acknowledged queen; but her harshness and greed soon harmed her cause. London rose against her and in November 1141 Stephen regained his liberty and his crown. In 1148 Matilda finally left England, but her son Henry of Anjou (**Henry II**) succeeded Stephen, his own son, Eustace, having died (1153). 📖 R H C Davis, *King Stephen* (1967)

Stephen, Sir Leslie 1832–1904
English scholar and critic

Born in London, he was the brother of Sir James Fitzjames Stephen and grandson of the abolitionist James Stephen, and father of **Virginia Woolf** and **Vanessa Bell**. Brought up in a Christian circle known as the 'Clapham Sect', he was educated at Eton, King's College London and Trinity Hall, Cambridge. He was ordained and became a Fellow of Trinity Hall (1864), but he left the church in 1870 and became an agnostic. He published his reasons in *Essays on Free Thinking and Plain Speaking* (1873) and *An Agnostic's Apology* (1893). He helped to found the *Pall Mall Gazette*, and was editor of the *Cornhill Magazine* (1871–82). He launched the *English Men of Letters* series with a biography of **Dr Johnson** (1878), and in 1876 he published *The History of English Thought in the Eighteenth Century* (1876), which is generally regarded as his most important work. He also wrote *The Science of Ethics* (1882), and *The Utilitarians* (3 vols, 1900), and was the first editor of the *Dictionary of National Biography* (1882–91), from 1890 jointly with Sir **Sidney Lee**. A noted athlete and mountaineer, he published a collection of mountaineering sketches in *Playground of Europe* (1871). 📖 Noel G Annan, *Leslie Stephen: His Thought and Character in Relation to His Time* (1952)

Stephen, Sir Ninian Martin 1923–
Australian jurist and statesman

Born in Nettlebed in Berkshire, England, he was educated in Edinburgh and went to Australia aged 16. He served with the Australian Imperial Forces in the Pacific, studied law at Melbourne University and became a QC in 1966. He was a justice of the High Court of Australia from 1972 until his appointment as Governor-General of Australia (1982–89). As Australia's first ambassador on the environment he represented Australia at many conferences. In 1991 he also chaired peace talks for South Africa. In 1993 he was a member of a UN Tribunal on war crimes in the former Yugoslavia and in 1994 was elevated to the Order of the Garter to fill the vacancy created by the death of Sir **Paul Hasluck**.

Stephen Dushan c.1308–1355
King and Emperor of Serbia

The last of the Nemanjic family, he deposed his father (1331) to become king, and was crowned Emperor of the Serbs and Greeks (1346). He extended Serbian rule into Macedonia, Bulgaria and Albania. He produced a centralized administration based largely on Byzantine institutions and issued a legal code (1349–54). He achieved great popularity during the 19th century Serbian national revival.

Stephens, Alexander Hamilton 1812–83
US politician

Born near Crawfordsville, Georgia, he was admitted to the Bar in 1834 and sat in Congress (1843–59). He advocated the annexation of Texas in 1838, defended the Kansas-Nebraska Act in 1854, and opposed secession at first, but in 1861 became Confederate Vice-President. He sat in Congress again (1874–83), was elected Governor of Georgia (1882), and wrote *War between the States* (1867–70).

Stephens, James 1882–1950
Irish poet

Born in Dublin and sent to an orphanage as a child, he found work as a solicitor's clerk. His first published work was a volume of poems, *Insurrections* (1909), followed by his first novel, *The Charwoman's Daughter* (1912). A prose fantasy, *The Crock of Gold* (1912), made him famous, and he became a full-time writer. His later volumes were *Songs from the Clay* (1914), *The Demi-Gods* (1914), *Reincarnation* (1917) and *Deirdre* (1923). He moved to London in 1924. His *Collected Poems* was first published in 1926, and revised in 1954. 📖 H Pyle, *James Stephens, writings and an account of his life* (1968)

Stephens, James Kenneth 1825–1901
Irish nationalist

Born in Kilkenny, he was a civil engineer on the railways, and became an active agent of the Young Ireland Party. Wounded during the rising at Ballingarry (1848), he hid for three months in the mountains, and then escaped to France. In 1853 he journeyed round Ireland, and founded the Irish Republican Brotherhood (Fenians) in 1858, of which he became the leader. He started the *Irish People* newspaper (1863) to urge armed rebellion, visited the USA on fund-raising missions, and was arrested in Dublin in 1865, but escaped within a fortnight. He found his way to New York, was deposed by the Fenians and was allowed to return to Ireland in 1886.

Stephens, John Lloyd 1805–52
US archaeologist and traveller

Born in Shrewsbury, New Jersey, and trained as a lawyer, he travelled extensively in the Levant, the Balkans, and central Europe before embarking with the architect and artist Frederick Catherwood (1799–1856) on an extended exploration of Mesoamerica in 1839–42. Their work founded the field of Maya archaeology, and rediscovered the cities of Copan, Quirigua, Palenque, Uxmal and Chichen Itza, then unknown except to the local people. It was published as *Incidents of Travel in Central America, Chiapas and Yucatan* (1841) and *Incidents of Travel in Yucatan* (1843), and with **Ephraim Squier's** surveys of the Mississippi Valley, established American archaeology as a discipline in its own right.

Stephens, Joseph Rayner 1805–79
Scottish social reformer

Born in Edinburgh, he was expelled from his Methodist ministry in 1834 for supporting church disestablishment. He made himself a name as a factory reformer, opened three independent chapels at Ashton-under-Lyne, and took an active part in the anti-poor-law demonstrations (1836–37) and the Chartist movement, of which, however, he refused actual membership. He was imprisoned for his struggle for the Ten Hours Act (1847).

Stephens, Meic 1938–
Welsh poet and editor

Born in Treforest, near Pontypridd, Glamorgan, he was educated at the universities of Wales and Rennes. He founded *Poetry Wales* in 1965, and his poetry collections include *Exiles All* (1973). A noted editor, he compiled and edited *The Oxford Companion to the Literature of Wales* in both Welsh and English (1986), edited the second edition of the *Oxford Illustrated Literary Guide to Great Britain and Ireland* (1992), and is co-editor of the *Writers of Wales* series (1970–), which comprises 80 volumes. He was literature director of the Welsh Arts Council from 1967 to 1990.

Stephenson, Elsie 1916–67
English nurse educator

Born in County Durham, she trained as a nurse at the West Suffolk General Hospital and qualified in midwifery at Queen Charlotte's Hospital, London, in 1938. After service in the Red Cross during World War II, she was awarded a fellowship to study advanced public health administration at Toronto University (1946). She then undertook missions to Germany, Singapore, and elsewhere. As Nursing Officer for Newcastle-Upon-Tyne in 1950, she helped to produce the influential Jameson Report 'An Inquiry into Health Visiting' (1956). She was also a member of the World Health Organization (WHO) Advisory Panel of the Expert Committee on Nursing.

Stephenson, George 1781–1848
English railway engineer

Born in Wylam, near Newcastle, he became a fireman in a colliery, while undergoing a rudimentary education at night school. In 1815 he invented, at the same time as Humphry Davy, a colliery safety lamp, the 'Geordie', for which he received a public testimonial of £1,000. In 1812 he had become engine-wright at Killingworth Colliery, and there in 1814 he constructed his first locomotive, *Blucher*. This was slow and unreliable on the inadequate wooden colliery tram roads, and Stephenson's reputation stemmed from his success in improving both locomotives and rails. In 1821 he was appointed engineer for the construction of the Stockton & Darlington mineral railway (opened September 1825), and in 1826 for the Liverpool & Manchester Railway which, after considerable difficulties, was opened in September 1830. The previous October had seen the memorable contest of engines at Rainhill, resulting in the triumph of Stephenson's *Rocket* at 30 mph (48.3kph). Thereafter he was engineer on the North Midland, Manchester & Leeds and Birmingham & Derby Railways, and many other railways in England; he was also consulted about proposed lines in Belgium and Spain. ⌑ Hunter Davies, *George Stephenson* (1977)

Stephenson, Robert 1803–59
English mechanical and structural engineer

He was born in Willington Quay, Northumberland, the son of **George Stephenson**. He was apprenticed to a coalviewer at Killingworth, and in 1822 went for six months to Edinburgh University. In 1823 he assisted his father in surveying the Stockton to Darlington Railway and, after three years in Colombia, he returned to manage his father's locomotive engine-works in Newcastle upon Tyne. He attained independent fame by his Britannia Tubular Bridge (1850), those at Conway (1848) and Montreal (1859), the High Level Bridge at Newcastle upon Tyne (1849), the Royal Border Bridge at Berwick (1850), and others. He was an MP for many years from 1847 and was buried in Westminster Abbey, London. ⌑ R M Robbins, *George and Robert Stephenson* (1966)

Stepinac, Aloysius 1898–1960
Yugoslav prelate and cardinal, primate of Hungary

Born in Krasić near Zagreb, he was imprisoned by **Tito** (1946–51) for alleged wartime collaboration. His health failed, and he was later released, but lived the remainder of his life under house arrest.

Stepnyak, *nom de guerre of* Sergei Mikhailovich Kravchinsky 1852–95
Russian revolutionary

His name means 'Son of the Steppe'. He was an artillery officer who was arrested and then kept under surveillance for revolutionary activities. He left Russia and settled in Geneva (1876), and later in London (1885). He was believed to be the assassin of General Mesentzieff, head of the St Petersburg police (1878). He was run over by a train in a London suburb. Among his works were *La Russia*

Sotteranea (1881, Eng trans *Underground Russia*, 1883), studies of the Nihilist movement, *Russia under the Tsars* (trans 1885), and the novel *The Career of a Nihilist* (1889)

Steptoe, Patrick Christopher 1913–88
English gynaecologist and reproduction biologist, pioneer of in vitro fertilization

Born in Witney, Oxfordshire, he was educated in London at King's College and St George's Hospital Medical School. After military service, he specialized in obstetrics and gynaecology, becoming senior obstetrician and gynaecologist at the Oldham Hospitals in 1951. In 1980 he became medical director of the Bourn Hall Clinic in Cambridgeshire. He had long been interested in laparoscopy (a technique of viewing the abdominal cavity through a small incision in the umbilicus) and in problems of fertility. He met **Robert Edwards** in 1968, and together they worked on the problem of *in vitro* fertilization of human embryos, which 10 years later resulted in the birth of a baby after *in vitro* fertilization and implantation in her mother's uterus.

Sterling, John 1806–44
Scottish man of letters

Born at Kames Castle on the island of Bute, he was educated at Glasgow University and Trinity College, Cambridge. He turned to writing, and bought the literary magazine *The Athenaeum*, which he edited. He published numerous essays and long poems, and a novel, *Arthur Coningsby* (1833). He is best known as the subject of **Thomas Carlyle's** *Life of John Sterling* (1851).

Stern, Daniel See Agoult, Marie de Flavigny, Comtesse d'

Stern, Isaac 1920–
US violinist

Born in Kreminiecz, USSR, he was taken to the USA as a child. He studied at the San Francisco Conservatory (1928–31) and made his recital debut in 1935 and his concert debut with the San Francisco Symphony Orchestra in 1936. He played subsequently as soloist and in chamber music throughout the world. The recipient of numerous awards, such as being made a Commander of the French Légion d'Honneur (1989), he is regarded as one of the world's foremost violinists.

Stern, Otto 1888–1969
US physicist and Nobel Prize winner

Born in Sohrau, Germany, and educated at Breslau University, where he obtained his doctorate in 1912, he held posts at the universities of Zurich, Frankfurt and Rostock before becoming Professor of Physical Chemistry at the University of Hamburg (1923–33). With the rise of the Nazis he moved to the USA, where he became Research Professor of Physics at the Carnegie Institute of Technology in Pittsburgh (1933–45). In collaboration with Walther Gerlach in 1920–21, he projected a beam of silver atoms through a non-uniform magnetic field and produced two distinct beams, thus proving the quantum theory prediction that an atom's magnetic moment can only be oriented in two fixed directions relative to an external magnetic field. For this work he was awarded the Nobel Prize for physics in 1943. He also determined the magnetic moment of the proton.

Stern, Robert A M 1939–
US architect

Born in New York City, he was educated at Columbia University, New York and at Yale. He became a well-known author and teacher before starting his own practice, and believes in design as a process of cultural assimilation, architecture being a communicative art. A designer principally of private houses and apartments, such as Chilmark, Martha's Vineyard, Massachusetts

(1979–83), he is known also for the Norman Rockwell Museum, Stockbridge, Massachusetts (1987–92) and for hotels for Euro-Disney in Marne-la Vallée, France. He has been a Fellow of the American Institute of Architects since 1984, and his publications include *The Anglo-American Suburb* (1981).

Sternberg, Josef Von See Von Sternberg, Josef

Sterne, Laurence 1713–68
Irish novelist

He was born in Clonmel, County Tipperary, the son of an impoverished infantry ensign, and was educated at Halifax Grammar School in Yorkshire, and Jesus College, Cambridge. He was ordained in 1738, and was appointed to the living of Sutton-on-the-Forest and made a prebendary of York, where, in 1759, the first two volumes of *The Life and Opinions of Tristram Shandy* were published. These were well received, and further volumes appeared from 1761 to 1767. His health was now failing and he lived mostly in France and Italy. *A Sentimental Journey through France and Italy* appeared in 1768, shortly before he died in London of pleurisy. His novels display great mastery, and he developed the form of the novel as a channel for the utterance of the writer's own sentiments. His *Letters from Yorick to Eliza* (1775–79) contain his correspondence with a young married woman to whom he was devoted. 💻W C Cross, *Life and Times of Laurence Sterne* (1909–25)

Sternhold, Thomas 1500–49
English psalmist

Born near Blakeney, Gloucestershire, or in Hampshire, he was joint author with John Hopkins of the English version of psalms formerly attached to the Prayer Book. The first edition (undated) contains only 19 psalms, the second (1549), 37. A third edition, by Whitchurch (1551), contains seven more by Hopkins. The complete book of psalms, which appeared in 1562, formed for nearly two centuries almost the whole hymnody of the Church of England and was known as the 'Old Version' after the rival version of Nahum Tate and Nicholas Brady appeared in 1696. Forty psalms bore the name of Sternhold. He was Groom of the Robes to both Henry VIII and Edward VI.

Steuben, Frederic William Augustus Steuben, Baron 1730–94
American Revolutionary soldier

He was born in Magdeburg, Germany. In 1762 he was on the staff of Frederick II, the Great. While in Paris in 1777 he was induced by Benjamin Franklin to go to America. There Congress and George Washington appointed him inspector-general, and he prepared a manual of tactics for the army, remodelled its organization, and improved its discipline. He became a naturalized US citizen in 1783, and Congress in 1790 voted him an annuity of 2,400 dollars and land near Utica, New York. From 1778 to 1789 he published *Regulations for the Order and Discipline of the Troops of the United States.*

Stevens, Alfred 1818–75
English painter and sculptor

Born in Blandford, Dorset, he studied in Italy, and became assistant to Bertel Thorvaldsen in Rome and teacher of architectural design at Somerset House, London (1845–47). During the next 10 years he decorated and designed household furniture, fireplaces and porcelain. From 1856 he worked in St Paul's Cathedral in London on the Wellington Monument (which was completed after his death by John Tweed) and the mosaics under the dome. He also designed the lions at the British Museum.

Stevens, John 1749–1838
US engineer and inventor

Born in New York City, he studied law at King's College (now Columbia University) but never practised. After some years' service in the Revolutionary Army, he saw John Fitch's steamboat on the Delaware River (1787) and resolved to improve on the design. In 1803 he patented a multi-tubular boiler and used it in his first steamboat, the *Little Juliana*, which was propelled by twin Archimedean screws driven through gears by a high-pressure steam engine. The high pressure gave trouble and he had to revert to paddle-wheels which could be driven by low-pressure engines, as used in the *Juliana* (1811) which became the world's first steam ferry. In this and other enterprises he was assisted by his son Robert Livingston Stevens.

Stevens, Nettie Maria 1861–1912
US biologist

Born in Cavendish, Vermont, she studied physiology at Stanford University, received a PhD from Bryn Mawr College, Pennsylvania (1903), and was later appointed to research posts there. Stevens was one of the first to explain the principle that sex is determined by particular chromosomes. She also studied sex determination in various plants and insects, demonstrating unusually large numbers of chromosomes in certain insects and the paired nature of chromosomes in mosquitoes and flies.

Stevens, Robert Livingston 1787–1856
US engineer and inventor

Born in Hoboken, New Jersey, son of the inventor John Stevens, he began at an early age to assist his father in the design and construction of steamboats, experimenting with various improvements to the hulls and engines in pursuit of speed, strength and efficiency. In 1830 he became president and chief engineer of the Camden & Amboy Railroad and Transportation Company. He invented the cow-catcher and the hook-headed railroad spike, and was the first to burn anthracite coal in a locomotive engine. He spent many years on the design of an armour-plated warship but it was still unfinished at the time of his death.

Stevens, Siaka Probin 1905–89
Sierra Leone politician

He was born in Tolubu of mixed Christian and Muslim parentage; which helped him to understand both religions. He was a member of the Sierra Leone police force for seven years, and later a railwayman and miner, founding the Mineworkers Union in 1943. After a period of study at Ruskin College, Oxford in 1945, he helped found the Sierra Leone People's Party (APC) in 1951. The APC won the 1967 general election but the result was disputed by the army and Stevens withdrew from the premiership. In 1968 an army revolt brought him back and in 1971 he became Sierra Leone's first President. He established a one-party state and remained in power until his retirement at the age of 80.

Stevens, Stanley Smith 1906–73
US experimental psychologist

Born in Ogden, Utah, he was educated at Harvard (gaining a PhD in 1933) and taught there from 1932 until his death. He made important contributions to the relatively new science of psychophysics. He made a number of contributions to our understanding of the sense of hearing, and devised general theories and experimental techniques for the study of the 'scaling' of sensory qualities (eg, loudness, brightness, pain). He also edited a major work of reference, *The Handbook of Experimental Psychology* (1951).

Stevens, Thaddeus 1792–1868
US politician

Born in Danville, Vermont, he practised law at Gettysburg, Pennsylvania, from 1816 and became a dominant member of the House of Representatives (1849–53, 1859–68). An opponent of slavery and a firm believer in equality, he was a leader of Radical Republicans during Reconstruction, arguing that President **Andrew Johnson**'s policies were too moderate and that the South should be seen as a 'conquered province'. He proposed the Fourteenth and Fifteenth Amendments and sponsored Reconstruction measures which used military rule to guarantee black suffrage in the South. He also introduced the resolution to impeach Johnson in 1868.

Stevens, Wallace 1879–1955
US poet

Born in Reading, Pennsylvania, he was educated first at private schools, and later at schools attached to Lutheran churches and Reading Boys' High School. He enrolled at Harvard (1897–1900) and afterwards moved to New York, where he started out in journalism. He entered New York Law School in 1901 and at the age of 28 began working for various law firms, then joined an insurance company in Hartford, Connecticut. He wrote poetry in his spare time, and his first collection, *Harmonium*, was not published until 1923. Most of his early work, both poems and short stories, was published in *The Harvard Advocate*. Later works include *Ideas of Order* (1936), *The Man With the Blue Guitar* (1937), *Parts of a World* (1942), *Transport to Summer* (1947) and *The Auroras of Autumn* (1950). *Collected Poems* was published in 1954. ◻ G Lensing, *Wallace Stevens: a poet's growth* (1986)

Stevenson, Adlai Ewing 1900–65
US Democratic politician and lawyer

Born in Los Angeles, he was the grandson of another A E Stevenson (1835–1914) who was Vice-President of the USA under **Grover Cleveland** (1893–97). He studied at Princeton, spent two years editing a family newspaper and then took up law practice in Chicago. From 1943 he took part in several European missions for the State Department and from 1945 served on US delegations to the foundation conferences of the United Nations Organization. In 1948 he was elected Governor of Illinois, where his administration was exceptional for efficiency and lack of corruption. He stood against General **Eisenhower** as Democratic presidential candidate in 1952 and 1956, but each time his urbane and intellectual campaign speeches, published under the titles *Call to Greatness* (1954) and *What I Think* (1956), had more appeal abroad than at home. He was US ambassador to the UN (1962–65). ◻ Bert Cochran, *Adlai Stevenson: Patrician Among the Politicians* (1969)

Stevenson, Juliet Anne Virginia 1956–
English actress

Born into an army family in Kelvedon, Essex, she joined the Royal Shakespeare Company in 1978, and the following year was made an RSC associate artist. Her many leading roles there include Titania and Hippolyta in *A Midsummer Night's Dream* (1981), Isabella in *Measure for Measure* (1983), Rosalind in *As You Like It*, Cressida in *Troilus and Cressida* and Madame de Tourvel in *Les Liaisons Dangereuses* (1985). At the Royal National Theatre, she has played the title role in *Hedda Gabler* (1989), and at the Royal Court and the West End she appeared in *Death and the Maiden* (1990, 1991). She has also appeared in films, including *Truly, Madly, Deeply* (1991), *The Trial* (1993) and *The Secret Rapture* (1994).

Stevenson, Robert 1772–1850
Scottish engineer

Born in Glasgow, he lost his father in infancy, and in 1798 his mother married Thomas Smith, first engineer of the Northern Lighthouse Board. Stevenson took to engineering, and in 1796 succeeded his stepfather. During his 47 years' tenure of office he planned or constructed 23 Scottish lighthouses, most notably that on the Bell Rock off Arbroath, employing the catoptric system of illumination, and his own invention of intermittent or flashing lights. He also acted as a consulting engineer for roads, bridges, harbours, canals and railways.

Stevenson, Robert Louis Balfour 1850–94
Scottish writer

He was born in Edinburgh, the grandson of **Robert Stevenson** and son of Thomas Stevenson, engineer to the Board of Northern Lighthouses. His childhood was afflicted by constant illness, and he suffered throughout his life from a chronic bronchial condition which may have been tuberculosis. He studied engineering briefly at Edinburgh University (1867), but transferred to law, becoming an advocate in 1875. He never practised, however, and his true inclination was for writing. His first major works, *Inland Voyage* (1878) and *Travels with a Donkey in the Cévennes* (1879), describe travels in Belgium and northern France undertaken to improve his health. It was in France that he met Fanny Osbourne, *née* Vandegrift (1840–1914), an American woman separated from her husband. He followed her to America and they married in 1880 after her divorce, returning to Europe with her son **Lloyd Osbourne**. Initially dependent on his father, Stevenson began to make a living by writing for journals and magazines, especially *Cornhill Magazine*. The romantic adventure story *Treasure Island* brought him fame in 1883 and was followed by *Kidnapped* (1886), *Catriona* (1893) and *The Master of Ballantrae* (1889). *The Strange Case of Dr Jekyll and Mr Hyde* (1886) illustrates Stevenson's metaphysical interest in evil. Also written about this time were *The Black Arrow* (1888), the unfinished *Weir of Hermiston* (published posthumously in 1896) and *St Ives*, which was completed by Sir **Arthur Quiller Couch** in 1897. Stevenson's work as an essayist is seen at its best in *Virginibus Puerisque* (1881) and *Familiar Studies of Men and Books* (1882). *A Child's Garden of Verses* (1885) is a recollection of childhood in verse. Vernacular poems such as *A London Sabbath Morn* subtly describe the Calvinism he had renounced but which always intrigued him. In 1888 Stevenson set off with his family for the South Seas, famously visiting a leper colony and settling in Samoa, where with his wife and stepson he spent the last five years of his life on his estate of Vailima, which gives its name to the series of letters written to his friend Sidney Calvin. With his stepson he wrote *The Wrong Box* (1889), *The Wrecker* (1892) and *The Ebb-Tide* (1894). ◻ F McLynn, *Robert Louis Stevenson: a Biography* (1993); J C Furnas, *Voyage to Windward* (1950)

Stevenson, Ronald 1928–
Scottish composer, pianist and writer on music

Born in Blackburn, Lancashire, of Scottish parents, he studied at the Royal Manchester College of Music. Amongst his works are the 80-minute *Passacaglia on DSCH* for piano (1960–62), a piano concerto 'The Continents' (1972), a violin concerto (1979), choral settings, many songs ranging from settings of Scots to Japanese haiku, and his transcriptions from a broad range of music. He promotes music as world-language, seeking in his works to embrace a large spectrum of international culture. He has composed for mentally handicapped children and played in geriatric homes. An eminent contrapuntist, he is also a master of keyboard technique and a distinguished melodist. He has written *Western Music: An Introduction* (1971), and many articles on music, and is an authority on **Ferruccio Busoni**.

Stevenson, Teofilo 1952–

Cuban amateur boxer

Jamaican-born, he grew up in Cuba. His outstanding achievement of three Olympic heavyweight titles could not be extended because of Cuba's political boycotts of events. His stinging left jab and powerful right won him his first Olympic title in Munich in 1972, and he won two more gold medals (Montreal 1976 and Moscow 1980). He rejected numerous offers to turn professional and in 1986 won the world amateur championship at the age of 34.

Stevenson, William d.1575

English scholar

He entered Christ's College, Cambridge, in 1546, and became a Fellow, and is known to have staged plays there. He was probably the author of the earliest surviving English comedy, *Gammer Gurton's Needle* (1553), which is sometimes attributed to John Still or John Bridges. 💻 F P Wilson, *English Drama, 1485–1585* (1969)

Stevin, Simon 1548–1620

Flemish mathematician and engineer

Born in Bruges, he held offices under Prince Maurice of Orange, wrote on fortification and book-keeping and invented a system of sluices and a carriage propelled by sails. He was responsible for introducing the use of decimals, which he had advocated in his book *De Thiende* (1585). He advocated rational experimentation in the new sciences, wrote important works on statics, and developed the law of the inclined plane.

Steward, Julian Haynes 1902–72

US cultural anthropologist

Born in Washington DC, he studied at Cornell and the University of California, and subsequently taught at Michigan, Utah and California. In 1935 he joined the Bureau of American Ethnology, becoming director of the Institute of Social Anthropology at the Smithsonian Institution in 1943. In 1946 he was appointed professor at Columbia, and from 1956 to 1972 was Research Professor in Anthropology at Illinois. He developed the method of cultural ecology which seeks regularities in the relation between environment, technology, social organization and culture. His views are set out in his *Theory of Culture Change* (1955) and *Evolution and Ecology* (1977). He also edited the encyclopedic *Handbook of South American Indians* (6 vols, 1946–50; index, 1959), the major reference work on the subject.

Stewart or Stuart

Scottish noble family

The royal line of the (Stuart) sovereigns of Scotland, and later of Great Britain and Ireland, from Robert II of Scotland (1371) to Queen Anne (1714) is descended from this family. The original family was descended from a Breton immigrant, Alan Fitzflaald (d.c.1114), who received the lands of Oswestry in Shropshire from Henry I. His elder son was William Fitzalan (c.1105-60).

Stewart, Alexander, Earl of Buchan, *also called* the Wolf of Badenoch c.1343–c.1405

Scottish nobleman

The fourth son of Robert II by Elizabeth Mure, and overlord of Badenoch, he received the earldom on his marriage (1382). He earned his nickname from his continued attacks on the bishopric of Moray, for which he was excommunicated.

Stewart, Alexander Turney 1803–76

US merchant

Born near Belfast, Northern Ireland, he acquired great wealth in the USA in the retail-store business. A noted philanthropist, he founded Garden City, Long Island, as a model middle-class township. His body was stolen in 1878, and restored to his widow three years later on payment of $20,000 through a lawyer.

Stewart, Andy (Andrew) 1933–94

Scottish comedian and singer

Born in Glasgow, he entered show business as an impressionist, appearing in revue on the Edinburgh Festival Fringe singing 'Ye Canna Shove Yer Granny Off a Bus'. He presented the television pop music show *Dance Party Roof* (1958) and went on to appear regularly in BBC Scotland's *White Heather Club* (from 1960), and nationally in the annual Hogmanay TV special, singing his own composition, 'A Scottish Soldier'. His own series, *The Andy Stewart Show*, followed (1963), and his radio shows included the series *17 Sauchie Street* and *Scotch Corner* (1952).

Stewart, Prince Charles Edward See Stuart, Prince Charles Edward (panel)

Stewart, Douglas Alexander 1913–85

Australian writer

Born in Eltham, Taranaki, New Zealand and educated at the Victoria University College, he became editor (1940–61) of the 'Red Page' in the *Bulletin* magazine, and was then literary editor for the Australian publishers Angus & Robertson. His early books of lyric verse, *Green Lions* (1936) and *The White Cry* (1939), evoke his homeland. His first Australian verse was in *The Dosser in Springtime* (1946) in which he began to use ballad form, later put to dramatic effect in *Glencoe* (1947), a sequence on the Scottish massacre. He also wrote the classic radio drama *Fire in the Snow* (1939) on Captain Scott's ill-fated Antarctic expedition. Later titles include *Back of Beyond* (1954) and *The Birdsville Track* (1955), on the life of the Australian interior. *Selected Poems* was published in 1963 (rev edn 1973) and *Collected Poems 1936-1967* in 1967. He edited a number of anthologies and two collections of bush ballads (1955–57), and his biographies include *Norman Lindsay, a Personal Memoir* (1975) and *A Man of Sydney, an Appreciation of Kenneth Slessor* (1977). 💻 *Springtime in Taranaki* (1983); J McAuley, in *The Literature of Australia* (1964, ed G Dalton)

Stewart, Dugald 1753–1828

Scottish philosopher

Born and educated in Edinburgh, where his father was professor of mathematics, he also studied at Glasgow under Thomas Reid. He succeeded his father as professor (1775), then was Professor of Moral Philosophy at Edinburgh (1785–1810) in succession to Adam Ferguson. He was much influenced by Reid's 'Common Sense' philosophy and himself became the leader of the Scottish School. He was not a highly original thinker but a great teacher and lecturer, of whom a pupil said 'without derogation from his writings it may be said that his disciples were among his best works'. He was a prolific author, his principal work being *Elements of the Philosophy of the Human Mind* (3 vols, 1792, 1814, 1827). He also wrote *Outlines of Moral Philosophy* (1793) and *Philosophical Essays* (1810). A remarkably large monument on Calton Hill, Edinburgh, attests to his fame at the time of his death.

Stewart, Frances Teresa, Duchess of Richmond and Lennox, *known as* La Belle Stewart 1647–1702

Scottish noblewoman

The daughter of the 6th Duke of Lennox, she was brought up in France until 1663, when she was appointed maid of honour to Charles II's queen, Catherine of Braganza. She is thought to have become one of Charles's mistresses, and posed as the effigy of Britannia on the coinage. In 1667 she secretly married the 3rd Duke of Richmond, but was soon restored to the king's favour.

Stewart, Jackie (John Young) 1939–
Scottish racing driver

Born in Dunbartonshire, he won the Dutch, German and US Grand Prix in 1986. He had been third in the world championships in 1965, his first season of Grand Prix racing, and he won the world title in 1969, 1971 and 1973. He retired at the end of the 1973 season. Since 1989 he has been chairman of the Paul Stewart racing team. ▢ *Faster!* (1972)

Stewart, James See Moray, James Stewart, 1st Earl of

Stewart, Prince James Francis Edward See Stuart, Prince James Francis Edward

Stewart, James Maitland 1908–97
US film actor

Born in Indiana, Pennsylvania, he studied architecture at Princeton University, before his work with a summer stock company prompted him to turn to acting, first on Broadway and later in Hollywood (from 1935). Tall, gangly, and with a distinctive drawl, he was at first cast as naive idealists with integrity in films such as *You Can't Take It With You* (1938), *Mr. Smith Goes to Washington* (1939) and *Destry Rides Again* (1939). After distinguished service in World War II, he returned as the quintessential small-town man in *It's A Wonderful Life* (1946), and starred in the title role of *The Glenn Miller Story* (1953), before developing a more mature image as tough and resourceful heroes in westerns and in thrillers such as *Rear Window* (1954), *Vertigo* (1958) and *Anatomy of a Murder* (1959). Nominated five times for the Academy Award, he won a Best Actor award for *The Philadelphia Story* (1940), and received an honorary award in 1984. His later work included *Fool's Parade* (1971) and *Right of Way* (television, 1983). He published *Jimmy Stewart and His Poems* in 1989. ▢ Howard Thompson, *James Stewart* (1974)

Stewart, James Stuart 1896–1990
Scottish preacher and devotional writer

Born in Dundee, he was a Church of Scotland parish minister before becoming Professor of New Testament at New College, Edinburgh (1947–66), and moderator of the General Assembly of the Church of Scotland (1963–64). He was joint editor of the 1928 English translation of Friedrich Schleiermacher's *The Christian Faith*, wrote popular books on Jesus, Paul, and the art of preaching, lectured widely in Great Britain and overseas, and published several volumes of sermons, including *The Gates of New Life* (1937), *River of Life* (1972) and *King for Ever* (1974).

Stewart, J (ohn) I (nnes) M (ackintosh),
pseudonym Michael Innes 1906–94
Scottish novelist and critic

Born in Edinburgh, he was educated at Edinburgh Academy and Oriel College, Oxford, then subsequently lectured at Leeds University, the University of Adelaide and Queen's University, Belfast. He was also reader in English Literature at Oxford (1969–73). A prolific writer, he is best known for his 'Pattullo' sequence, set in the world of Oxford academics. His novels *A Use of Riches* (1957) and *The Last Tresilians* (1963) are generally regarded as his most important works. He also wrote works on Rudyard Kipling, Thomas Hardy, James Joyce and Joseph Conrad under his own name. As Michael Innes, he has written some notable thrillers, including *Hamlet, Revenge!* (1937), *Lament for a Makar* (1938), *What Happened at Hazelwood?* (1946) and *The Journeying Boy* (1949). His autobiography, *Myself and Michael Innes*, was published in 1987.

Stewart, (Robert) Michael Maitland
Stewart, Baron 1906–90
English Labour politician

Born in London, he was educated at Christ's Hospital and St John's College, Oxford. A schoolmaster before World War II, he stood unsuccessfully for parliament in 1931 and 1935. MP for Fulham from 1945, he had a varied ministerial career. He was Secretary of State for War (1947–51), then for Education and Science (1964–65), and came to the fore as Foreign Minister (1965–66), as Minister for Economic Affairs (1966–67) and as first Secretary of State from 1966. He replaced George Alfred Brown on the latter's resignation in 1968 and was Foreign Secretary (1968–70). He was the leader of the British Labour delegation to the European Parliament (1975–76), and remained an MP until 1979 when he was made a life peer.

Stewart, Ralph Randles 1890–1993
US botanist

Born in West Hebron, New York, he studied botany at Columbia University, where he was later awarded a doctorate to study the flora of western Tibet. He became the foremost authority on the botany of Pakistan and the western Himalayas, and his teaching inspired many students. During 1960–81 he worked as a research associate at the University of Michigan Herbarium, Ann Arbor, and published two important works on the flora of Pakistan: *An Annotated Catalogue of the Vascular Plants of West Pakistan and Kashmir* (1972), and *History and Exploration of Plants in Pakistan and Adjoining Areas* (1982).

Stibitz, George Robert 1904–95
US mathematician and computer scientist

Born in Dayton, Ohio, he attended Denison University and Cornell University, where he was awarded a doctorate in mathematical physics. By 1937 he was working at Bell Telephone Laboratories, where he utilized telephone relays to build a binary adder. In 1939 Bell Laboratories supported Stibitz in constructing a sophisticated complex number calculator, the Model I. Though reliable and easy to use, it was not programmable and did not have a memory. Stibitz later designed program-controlled calculators, but these were soon to be outmoded by the electronic digital computer. He was elected a member of the National Academy of Engineering in 1981.

Stickley, Gustav 1858–1942
US designer and metalworker

Born in Osceola, Pennsylvania, he began his career as a stonemason, but soon turned to chair-making in Pennsylvania as an apprentice to his uncle. In 1898 he met Charles Francis Voysey on a journey through Europe and on his return he formed the Gustav Stickley Company in Eastwood, Syracuse, New York, where he produced solid furniture that was influenced by Art Nouveau. He was influenced by the Arts and Crafts movement and, in particular, William Morris and John Ruskin; subsequently his sturdy oak work became known as 'Mission Furniture'. He set up an office in New York in 1905, but went bankrupt in 1915.

Stieglitz, Alfred 1864–1946
US photographer

Born in Hoboken, New Jersey, he studied engineering and photography in Berlin, and travelled extensively in Europe before returning to New York in 1890. With Edward Steichen he founded the American Photo-Secession Group in 1902, the counterpart of Great Britain's Linked Ring. He consistently influenced the development of creative photography as an art form through his magazine *Camera Work* (1903–17) and his gallery of modern art in New York. From 1910 he was an advocate of 'straight' photography, which was dedicated to precision and clarity of image, especially in his studies of New York architecture (1910–16). He also executed portraits and studies of clouds (*Equivalents*, 1922–31). ▢ Dorothy Norman, *Alfred Stieglitz: An American Seer* (1973)

Stiernhielm, Georg, *originally* Georg Olofsson
1598–1672
Swedish poet and linguist
Born in Vika, he was known as the father of Swedish poetry. He was made a peer with the name of Stiernhielm in 1631, and held various government appointments, including Councillor of War (1663) and director of the College of Antiquities (1667). He was the first Swedish poet to write in hexameters, in *Hercules* (1658), an epic allegorical poem. He helped to reform and purify the Swedish language by studying Old Norse literature and incorporating the old vocabulary into modern Swedish.
📖 B Swartling, *Georg Stiernhielm* (1909)

Stifter, Adalbert 1805–68
Austrian novelist and painter
Born in Oberplan, Bohemia, he studied in Vienna, and as private tutor to various aristocratic families had several unhappy love affairs. Deeply disturbed by the Revolution of 1848, he settled in Linz and became an official in the Ministry of Education. Unhappiness and illness led him to commit suicide. His humanism and his love of traditional values pervade the short stories in *Der Condor* (1840, Eng trans *The Condor*, 1946), *Der Nachsommer* (1857, 'The Indian Summer') and *Witiko* (1865–67), a heroic tale set in 12th-century Bohemia. His other stories were collected as *Studien* (1844–50, augmented 1855) and *Bunte Steine* (1853, Eng trans *Rock Crystal*, 1945). He was also a considerable painter of city views. 📖 A Blackett, *Adalbert Stifter, a critical study* (1948)

Stigand d.1072
English prelate
Chaplain to King Knut Sveinsson, he was Chief Adviser to Knut's widow Emma. He was appointed chaplain by Edward, the Confessor, and then Bishop of Elmham (1044), Bishop of Winchester (1047), and, uncanonically, Archbishop of Canterbury (1052). On the death of Harold II (whom, possibly, he had crowned), he supported Edgar the Ætheling. He was therefore deprived of Canterbury and Winchester (1070) by William the Conqueror, whom he had helped to crown, and he died a prisoner at Winchester.

Stigler, George Joseph 1911–91
US economist and Nobel Prize winner
Born in Renton, Washington, he was educated at Chicago, and held professorships at Minnesota (1944–46), Brown (1946–47), Columbia (1947–57) and Chicago (1958–91) universities. His books include *Production and Distribution Theories* (1941), *The Theory of Price* (1946), *The Citizen and the State* (1975) and *The Economist as Preacher* (1983). He was awarded the Nobel Prize for economics in 1982 for his work on market forces and regulatory legislation.

Stilicho, Flavius c.365–408AD
Roman soldier
Born a Vandal, he married Serena, niece of the Emperor Theodosius I. In AD394 he put Flavius Honorius on the throne of the Western Roman Empire, and ruled through him. On the death of Theodosius (394), Alaric I of the Visigoths invaded Greece and Italy, but was defeated by Stilicho at Pollentia (402) and Verona (403). Stilicho's proposed alliance with Alaric against the Vandals, Alans and Suevi was interpreted as treachery and he was murdered at the command of Honorius.

Still, Clyfford 1904–80
US painter and printmaker
Born in Grandin, North Dakota, he studied art at Spokane University, graduating in 1933. By about 1940 he had evolved a personal style, rejecting European ideas and employing the currently fashionable organic forms of Biomorphism. He taught at the California School of Fine Arts, San Francisco, from 1946 to 1950.

Still, William Grant 1895–1978
US composer
Born in Woodville, Mississippi, he worked as an arranger of popular music and played in theatre and night-club orchestras while studying under Varèse. His music shows the influence of this work and of ethnic and European styles. It includes five operas, four symphonies, one of which is a study of the modern African-American, three ballets, chamber and choral music and orchestral pieces.

Stiller, Mauritz 1883–1928
Swedish film director
Born in Helsinki, Finland, of Finnish–Russian extraction, he settled in Sweden in 1909. In 1912 he began directing films for Svenska Bio. A leading figure of the Swedish silent cinema, along with Victor Sjöström, he learned to combine his instinctive narrative technique with a dramatic force which proved right for the new medium. Of the 45 films he made in Sweden, *Herr Arnes pengar* (1919, *Sir Arne's Treasure*), *Gunnar Hedes saga* (1922, *Gunnar Hede's Saga*) and *Gösta Berlings saga* (1924, *The Story of Gösta Berling*) showed skill in producing cinematically the imaginative world of Selma Lagerlöf. His versatility is shown in *Erotikon* (1920), a sophisticated comedy about sexual rivalry which greatly influenced the comedies of Ernst Lubitsch. Stiller discovered Greta Garbo (some called him her Svengali) and took her to Hollywood in 1925. Being autocratic and demanding complete control as director, he encountered difficulty there and completed only two films, including *Hotel Imperial* (1926) with Pola Negri.

Stilling, Jung See Jung, Johann Heinrich

Stilwell, Joseph Warren, *nicknamed* Vinegar Joe
1883–1946
US soldier
Born in Palatka, Florida, he graduated at West Point in 1904. He was military attaché to the US Embassy in Peking from 1932 to 1939. In 1941 he became US military representative in China and in 1942 commander of the 5th and 6th Chinese Armies in Burma. He was also Chief of Staff to Chiang Kai-shek, for whom he planned the Ledo road (later known as the Stilwell road). In the Burma counter-offensive in 1943 he was commanding general of the US Forces in China, Burma and India, but he was recalled in 1944.

Stimson, Henry Lewis 1867–1950
US politician
Born in New York City, he studied law at Yale and Harvard, and joined the New York Bar in 1891. He became US attorney for the New York Southern district in 1906. Defeated as Republican candidate for New York governor (1910), he was made Secretary of War under President William Taft (1911–13), and became Herbert Hoover's Secretary of State (1929–33). He produced the 'Stimson Doctrine' denouncing Japanese aggression in Manchuria. Recalled by President Franklin D Roosevelt as Secretary of War (1940–45), his influence was decisive in leading President Harry S Truman to use the atomic bomb against Japan. His books include his memoirs, *On Active Service in Peace and War* (1946).

Stirling, Sir Archibald David 1915–90
Scottish soldier and creator of the SAS
Educated at Ampleforth College, Yorkshire, and at Cambridge, he joined the Scots Guards at the outbreak of World War II, and later transferred to 3 Commando Group for service in the Middle East. While convalescing from an injury he formulated the idea of a small 'army within an army' to make swift and secret raids deep behind enemy lines. The result was the SAS (Special Air Service Regiment), which quickly won a high reputation

for its success in destroying aircraft and fuel dumps in German-held territory. In 1943 he was taken prisoner in Tunisia and was held in Colditz prison camp. On his release he left the army to settle in East Africa, and later moved to Hong Kong.

Stirling, James, *known as* the Venetian 1692–1770
Scottish mathematician

Born in Garden, Stirlingshire, he studied at Glasgow and Oxford (1711–16), but left without graduating. His first book, on **Isaac Newton's** classification of cubic curves, was published in Oxford in 1717. He visited Venice at about this time, returned to Scotland in 1724, and then went on to London, where he taught mathematics. From 1735 he was superintendent of the lead mines at Leadhills, Lanarkshire, and corresponded with **Colin Maclaurin**. His principal mathematical work was *Methodus differentialis* (1730), in which he made important advances in the theory of infinite series and finite differences, and gave an approximate formula for the factorial function, which is still in use and named after him.

Stirling, James 1926–92
Scottish architect and town planner

Born in Glasgow, he worked as an architect in private practice from 1956 until his death. His early designs in Britain include the Engineering Building at Leicester University (1959–63), the History Faculty Building at Cambridge University (1964), and the Florey Building at Queen's College, Oxford (1966). His designs in Europe include the Neue Staatsgalerie in Stuttgart (1980–84), with its much-imitated twisting curved glass entrance wall, and the Braun industrial complex in Melsungen (1992). His later work includes the Clore Gallery, an extension built on to the Tate Gallery, London, to house the Turner collection (1987). He also produced a controversial design for the redevelopment of the site at No 1 Poultry in the City of London.

Stirling, Patrick 1820–95
Scottish mechanical engineer

Born in Kilmarnock, Ayrshire, the son of the Rev **Robert Stirling**, he became the most eminent of a family of locomotive engineers that included his brother James (1835–1917), his son Matthew (1856–1931) and his cousin Archibald Sturrock (1816–1909). He was apprenticed to his uncle James (1800–76), who was manager of the Dundee Foundry which built steamers and locomotives, then gained experience in several engineering works before being appointed (1853) locomotive superintendent of the Glasgow & South Western Railway. He moved to the Great Northern Railway in Doncaster in 1866 and succeeded his cousin as chief locomotive superintendent. It was there in 1870 that he developed his famous 8ft (2.4m) diameter driving wheel 4-2-2 'Stirling Single', which became a legend for its speed and power. One of these is preserved in the National Railway Museum in York.

Stirling, Robert 1790–1878
Scottish clergyman and inventor

Born in Cloag, Perthshire, and educated for the ministry at the universities of Glasgow and Edinburgh, he was ordained in the Church of Scotland in 1816, and was minister of Galston, Ayrshire (1837–78). In the same year he patented a hot-air engine operating on what became known as the Stirling cycle, in which the working fluid (air) is heated at one end of the cylinder by an external source of heat. In 1843 a steam engine was modified to work as a Stirling engine, developing some 40 horsepower. In spite of their greater efficiency, hot-air engines were superseded by the internal combustion engine and

the electric motor, although some development work has been undertaken recently because of their non-polluting characteristics.

Stirling, William Alexander, 1st Earl of
c.1567–1640
Scottish poet and courtier

Born in Alva, Clackmannanshire, he tutored young noblemen, and in 1613 he was attached to the household of Prince Charles (later **Charles I**). He had already published a collection of songs and madrigals in *Aurora* (1604); in 1614 he published part one of his huge poem *Doomesday*, (part two, 1637). He received in 1621 the grant of 'Nova Scotia', a vast tract in North America soon rendered valueless by French expansion. In 1631 he became sole printer of the King James version of the Psalms. From 1626 until his death he was Secretary of State for Scotland. He was created Viscount (1630), Earl of Stirling (1633) and Earl of Dovan (1639), but he died insolvent in London. His tragedies include *Darius* (1603), *Croesus* (1604), *The Alexandrean Tragedy* (1605) and *Julius Caesar* (1607). 🕮 T H McGrail, *Sir William Alexander Stirling* (1940)

Stivell, Alan, *originally* Alan Cochevelou 1943–
French harpist

He was born in Brittany, the son of a harp maker, and took up the instrument at the age of nine. He adopted the name Stivell, meaning 'source' or 'spring' in Breton, when he began to perform professionally. He formed a group with Breton guitarist Dan Ar Bras in 1967, and later pursued a solo career. He was a major influence in the growing folk-rock movement of the late 1960s and early 1970s, when his incorporation of rock elements alongside the music of Brittany and the other Celtic traditions enjoyed great popularity.

Stobaeus, Johannes fl.500AD
Greek anthologist

He was born in Stobi in Macedonia. About AD500 he compiled an anthology from 500 Greek poets and prosewriters which has preserved fragments from many lost works.

Stock, Alfred 1876–1946
German chemist

He became famous for his work on the boron hydrides (boranes), in 1912 discovering diborane, and subsequently pioneering the synthesis and isolation of many 'higher' boranes. He worked in Karlsruhe (1926–36) and in 1926 he found that the reaction of diborane with ammonia yielded the compound borazine, which is known as 'inorganic benzene' due to some of its chemical and physical properties. Stock is also famous for his development of high-vacuum apparatus for handling chemical samples—indispensable for his work on the highly air-sensitive boranes.

Stockhausen, Karlheinz 1928–
German composer, regarded as a leader of the avant-garde

Born in Mödrath, he was educated at Cologne and Bonn universities, and studied under **Frank Martin** and Olivier **Messiaen**. He joined the Musique Concrète group in Paris, and experimented with compositions based on electronic sounds. In Cologne, he helped to found the electronic music studio (1953), and was appointed Professor of Composition at the Hochschule für Musik (1971). He has written orchestral, choral and instrumental works, including some which combine electronic and normal sonorities, such as *Kontakte* (1958–60, 'Contact'), and parts of a large operatic cycle, *Licht* (1977– ,'Light'). His *Helicopter Quartet* was premiered in 1995 by the National Symphony Orchestra in Washington.

Stockton, 1st Earl of See Macmillan, Sir Harold

Stockton, Frank R (Francis Richard)

1834–1902

US humorist and engraver

Born in Philadelphia, he abandoned a career in medicine in favour of becoming a wood engraver. He then became assistant editor of *St Nicholas Magazine*, and first attracted notice by his stories for children. He is best known as author of *Rudder Grange* (1879). Later works include *The Lady, or the Tiger?* (1884), a teasing fairy tale still left unresolved in a sequel, *Mrs Cliff's Yacht* (1896), and *The Girl at Cobhurst* (1898). 📖 M J Griffin, *Frank R Stockton: A Critical Biography* (1939)

Stoddard, Richard Henry 1825–1903

US poet and critic

Born in Hingham, Massachusetts, he wrote literary reviews for New York periodicals from 1860. His poems include *Songs in Summer* (1857), *The Book of the East* (1867) and *Lion's Cub* (1891). *Under the Evening Lamp* (1893) and *Recollections* (1903) contain literary studies. His wife, Elizabeth Drew (1823–1902), was a novelist and poet.

Stoddard, Solomon 1643–1729

American Congregational theologian and pastor

Born in Boston, he graduated from Harvard (where he was the first librarian, 1667–74) and ministered at nearby Northampton (1672–1729), where he was succeeded by his grandson, **Jonathan Edwards** (1703–58). He helped prepare the controversial Half-Way Covenant, and urged the admission to full church membership of those who, without having undergone conversion, showed signs of godliness. A significant figure in the development of American Protestantism, he wrote *The Safety of Appearing* (1687), *The Doctrine of Instituted Churches* (1700), *An Appeal to the Learned* (1709) and *A Guide to Christ* (1714).

Stoker, Bram (Abraham) 1847–1912

Irish writer

Born in Dublin, he was educated at Trinity College studying law and science. He entered the Civil Service, but turned to literature, and joined Henry Irving in running the Lyceum Theatre in London from 1878 to 1905. The following year he published *Personal Reminiscences of Henry Irving*. He is best remembered for the classic vampire story *Dracula* (1897), and wrote a number of other novels dealing with futuristic and occult themes, including *The Jewel of the Seven Stars* (1903), *The Lady of the Shroud* (1909) and *The Lair of the White Worm* (1911). 📖 Daniel Farson, *The Man Who Wrote Dracula* (1975)

Stoker, Richard 1938–

English composer and writer

He was born in Castleford, Yorkshire, and trained at the Royal Academy of Music (RAM) under **Lennox Berkeley**, and in Paris under **Nadia Boulanger**, before teaching composition at the RAM (1962–87). He composes mainly chamber and orchestral music in a serial style which is always tonal. His many works include the cantata *Ecce Homo* (1965, 'Behold the Man'), the opera *Johnson Preserv'd* (1967), a Piano Concerto (1977) and the *Chinese Canticle* (1996). He was editor of *Composer Magazine* (1969–80) and has published his autobiography, *Open Window—Open Door* (1985) and the novels *Tanglewood* (1990) and *Diva* (1992).

Stokes, Sir George Gabriel 1819–1903

Irish mathematician and physicist

Born in Skreen, Sligo, he graduated from Pembroke College, Cambridge, in 1841 and in 1849 became Lucasian Professor of Mathematics. From 1887 to 1892 he was Conservative MP for Cambridge University. He used spectroscopy to determine the chemical compositions of the Sun and stars, published a valuable paper on diffraction (1849), identified X-rays as electromagnetic waves produced by sudden obstruction of cathode rays, and formulated Stokes's law relating to the force opposing a small sphere in its passage through a viscous fluid. He is also remembered for his derivation of Stokes's theorem, which is used in vector calculus. He was made a baronet in 1889. 📖 David B Wilson, *Kelvin & Stokes: A Comparative Study in Victorian Physics* (1987)

Stokowski, Leopold (Antonin Stanisław Bolesławawicz) 1882–1977

US conductor

Born in London, England, of Polish origin, he became a US citizen in 1915 and developed an international reputation as a conductor with the orchestras of Philadelphia (1912–36), New York (1946–50) and Houston (1955–60). He is also known for his orchestral transcriptions of **J S Bach**, and for his work in films, especially Walt Disney's *Fantasia* (1940). In 1962 he founded the American Symphony Orchestra in New York City.

Stolypin, Pyotr Arkadevich 1862–1911

Russian statesman

He was born in Dresden. After service in the Ministry of the Interior (from 1884) he became Governor of Saratov province (1903–06), where he put down peasant uprisings and helped to suppress the revolutionary upheavals of 1905. As Prime Minister (1906–11) he introduced a series of agrarian reforms, which had only limited success. In 1907 he suspended the Second Duma (national assembly), and arbitrarily limited the franchise. He was assassinated in Kiev.

Stommel, Hank (Henry Melson) 1920–92

US physical oceanographer

Born in Wilmington, Delaware, he studied physics at Yale, and subsequently moved to Woods Hole Oceanographic Institution to work in physical oceanography (1944–60), becoming Professor of Oceanography at Harvard (1960–62) and at the Massachusetts Institute of Technology (1963–78). Stommel's research covered physical oceanography in both theory and experimental work. He investigated the intensification of oceanic currents caused by the **Coriolis** force, and mapped the thermocline (the base of the warmer surface waters). He found vertical oscillation in the thermocline as it changed depth seasonally, and was one of the first to investigate ocean circulation at great depths.

Stone, Edward Durell 1902–78

US architect

Born in Fayetteville, Arkansas, he founded his own architectural firm in New York City in 1936 and taught design and architecture at New York University (1935–40) and Yale (1946–51). His design (1937, with Philip Goodwin) for the Museum of Modern Art in New York City typifies the functional approach of the International style. Other notable buildings he designed are the US Embassy in New Delhi (1954), the American Pavilion at the Brussels World's Fair (1958), and the Kennedy Center for the Performing Arts in Washington, DC (opened 1971).

Stone, Harlan Fiske 1872–1946

US lawyer and judge

Born in Chesterfield, New Hampshire, he was educated at Amherst College and Columbia University. He practised law in New York and served as Dean of the Columbia Law School (1910–23) before being made Federal Attorney-General (1924–25). Appointed an associate justice of the US Supreme Court in 1925, he became Chief Justice in 1941. He upheld the view that in matters of constitutionality, except where questions of individual liberty were involved, courts should defer to legislatures. He also developed the constitutional test for regulation of inter-state commerce. Many of his early minority opinions supporting the New Deal were later upheld by a majority of the court.

Stone, Irving, *originally* Irving Tennenbaum
1903–89
US novelist and playwright

He was born in San Francisco, and took his stepfather's name when his parents were divorced and his mother remarried. He studied political science at the University of California at Berkeley, and worked as a saxophonist in a dance band. *Lust for Life* (1934), based on the life of Van Gogh, became a bestseller. Other works include *Love Is Eternal* (1954, about Abraham Lincoln's wife), *The Agony and the Ecstasy* (1961), a fictional life of Michelangelo, *Passions of the Mind* (1971, about Sigmund Freud), *The Origin* (1980, about Charles Darwin), and *Depths of Glory* (1985, about Camille Pissarro).

Stone, Isidor Feinstein 1907–89
US radical journalist

Born in Philadelphia into a Jewish family, he studied at Pennsylvania University, then joined the liberal reformist *New York Post* (1933–38) and the weekly *New York Nation* (1938–46). He was hostile to the Cold War, and took positions that were often unpopular, opposing American involvement in Korea and later in Vietnam, and criticizing the rise of militarism in Israel, a country he basically supported. He founded *I F Stone's Weekly*, which he ran with his wife Esther until 1971. He also wrote longer essays in *The New York Review of Books* and elsewhere. His last book was on the trial and death of Socrates.

Stone, Lucy 1818–93
US feminist

Born in West Brookfield, Massachusetts, she studied at Oberlin College and soon started giving lectures on abolitionism and women's suffrage, calling the first national Women's Rights Convention at Worcester, Massachusetts, in 1850. In 1855 she married a fellow-radical, Henry Brown Blackwell, and with his agreement retained her maiden name as a symbol of equality. She helped to establish the American Woman Suffrage Association (1869) and founded the *Women's Journal* (1870), which she co-edited with her husband, and which was later edited by their daughter, Alice Stone Blackwell (1857–1950).

Stone, Nicholas, the Elder 1586–1647
English mason and architect

Master mason to James VI and I and Charles I, he carried out designs of Inigo Jones and completed the tombs of Sir Thomas Bodley in Oxford and John Donne in St Paul's Cathedral. His sons, Nicholas, John and Henry, were also sculptors.

Stone, Oliver 1946–
US film director and screenwriter

He was born in New York City and in 1967 saw active service in Vietnam which made a deep impression on him. He made his directorial debut in 1973 with the Canadian horror film *Seizure*. He won an Academy Award for the screenplay of *Midnight Express* (1978); his other scripts include *Conan the Barbarian* (1982), *Scarface* (1982) and *Year of the Dragon* (1985). He won Academy Awards as best director for *Platoon* (1986) and *Born on the 4th of July* (1989), both dealing with the Vietnam War. Later films include *The Doors* (1991), a biography of rock star Jim Morrison; *JFK* (1991), an examination of the Kennedy assassination; and *Natural Born Killers* (1994), a controversial story of mass murder.

Stone, Sir (John) Richard Nicholas 1913–91
English economist and Nobel Prize winner

Born in London, he studied economics at Cambridge under John Maynard Keynes, and then spent three years in the City and the war years (1939–45) as a government economist. He became director of the Department of Applied Economics at Cambridge (1945–55) and was then appointed Professor of Economics (1955–80). He was awarded the 1984 Nobel Prize for economics, for his development of the complex models on which worldwide standardized national income reports are based. His books include *Mathematical Models for the Economy* (1970).

Stone, Sharon 1958–
US actress

Born in Meadville, Pennsylvania, she was a beauty queen and model before making her film debut in *Stardust Memories* (1980). Over the next 10 years she pursued a career in minor film and television roles before appearing in the box office hit *Total Recall* (1990). Her flamboyant performance in the erotic thriller *Basic Instinct* (1992) raised her to the status of sex symbol and she consolidated her stardom in *Sliver* (1993), *The Specialist* (1994), and other films. An ambitious performer and outspoken celebrity, she strove to extend her range, playing a death-row inmate in *Last Dance* (1995) and earning a Best Actress Academy Award nomination as a drug-addicted showgirl in *Casino* (1995).

Stonehouse, John Thompson 1925–88
English politician

Born in Southampton and educated at the London School of Economics, he served in the Royal Air Force (1944–47). He became active in the co-operative movement, working in Uganda and London (1952–57), and was then elected to the House of Commons, representing Wednesbury, Staffordshire, from 1957 and Walsall North, from 1974. He was appointed Minister of Technology (1967–68) and Minister of Posts and Telecommunications (1968–70). In 1974 he disappeared in Miami, Florida, and was feared drowned, but he reappeared in Australia, amid stories in the popular press of personal and financial problems. He was extradited to Britain in 1975 to face charges of fraud and embezzlement, and in 1976 he was imprisoned, being released for good behaviour in 1979. He became a (not wholly welcome) member of the Social Democratic Party (SDP) in 1982.

Stoney, George Johnstone 1826–1911
Irish physicist

Born in Oakley Park, King's County, and educated at Trinity College, Dublin, he became Professor of Natural Philosophy at Queen's College, Galway (1852), and was elected FRS in 1861. He calculated an approximate value for the charge on the electron (1874), a term he himself introduced, and made important contributions to the theory of gases and spectroscopy.

Stopes, Marie Charlotte Carmichael
1880–1958
British birth-control pioneer and palaeobotanist

Born in Edinburgh, she studied at University College London, and at Munich University, and in 1904 became the first female science lecturer at Manchester University, specializing in fossil plants and coalmining. In 1907 she lectured at Tokyo University, and with Professor Sakurai wrote a book on the *Plays of Old Japan, The Nō* (1913). In 1916, the annulment of her first marriage (to R R Gates) turned her attention to the marital unhappiness caused by ignorance about sex and contraception, and she began a crusade to disseminate information about these subjects. In 1918 her book, *Married Love*, caused a storm and was banned in the USA. That year she married the aircraft manufacturer Humphrey Verdon Roe (see Edwin Roe), with whom she opened the first British birth control clinic, in Holloway, London (1921). Her 70 books include

Wise Parenthood (1918), *Contraception: Its Theory, History and Practice* (1923), *Sex and the Young* (1926), *Sex and Religion* (1929), and a play, *Our Ostriches* (1923). 📖 Ruth Hall, *Marie Stopes: A Biography* (1977)

Stoppard, Miriam, *née* Stern 1937–
English physician, writer and broadcaster

Born in Newcastle upon Tyne, she trained as a doctor at the Royal Free Hospital School of Medicine in London and at King's College Medical School in Durham, specializing in dermatology. After working in various hospitals, she became a research director for a pharmaceutical company before entering television. She made her debut in *Don't Ask Me* (1974–78), and appeared in *Where There's Life* (1981), *So You Want to Stop Smoking?* (1981–82), *Baby & Co* (1984–87) and *Miriam Stoppard's Health and Beauty Show* (1988–　). Her publications include *Miriam Stoppard's Book of Babycare* (1977), *Miriam Stoppard's Health and Beauty Book* (1988) and *The Breast Book* (1996), and she contributes to medical journals and women's magazines. From 1972 to 1992 she was married to the playwright **Tom Stoppard**.

Stoppard, Sir Tom, *originally* Thomas Straussler 1937–
British dramatist

Born in Zlin, Czechoslovakia, he went to England in 1946 from India, his mother having married a British army officer after being widowed in Singapore during World War II. After attending schools in Nottingham and Yorkshire, Stoppard became a journalist in Bristol. He then went to London, where he worked as a freelance journalist and theatre critic and wrote radio plays including *The Dissolution of Dominic Boot* (1964). He made his name with *Rosencrantz and Guildenstern are Dead* (premiered in 1966 at the Edinburgh Festival, staged at the National Theatre, London, in 1967, filmed in 1990). Built around the two 'attendant lords' in **Shakespeare**'s *Hamlet*, the play hilariously examines the meaninglessness of life and questions the possibility of free will. His aim is a 'perfect marriage between the play of ideas and farce': *Jumpers* (1972) is a farcical satire of logical positivism, and *Travesties* (1974) has **James Joyce**, **Lenin** and the Dadaist painter **Tristan Tzara** working together on an amateur production of **Oscar Wilde**'s *The Importance of Being Earnest*. His other plays include *Professional Foul* (1977, written for television and inspired by Amnesty International's Prisoner of Conscience Year), *The Real Thing* (1982), *Arcadia* (1993) and *Indian Ink* (1995). In 1977 he collaborated with **André Previn** on a 'play for actors and orchestra', *Every Good Boy Deserves Favour*. He has also written a novel, *Lord Malquist and Mr Moon* (1966), short stories, screenplays and film scripts, including *The Russia House* (1990) and *Billy Bathgate* (1991). He was knighted in 1997.

Storace, Anna Selina 1766–1817
English singer and actress

She was born in London, of Italian descent. She sang in Florence and at La Scala, Milan, and in London. She was the original Susanna in **Mozart**'s *Nozze di Figaro*, in Vienna (1786) and partnered **John Braham** in a series of concerts in Europe. She was the sister of the composer Stephen Storace (1763–96).

Storey, David Malcolm 1933–
English dramatist and novelist

He was born in Wakefield, Yorkshire. An art student and professional Rugby League player, he made a hit with his novel, *This Sporting Life* (1960). His later novels include *Pasmore* (1972), *Saville* (1976, Booker Prize) and *Present Times* (1984). His first play, *The Restoration of Arnold Middleton*, was staged at the Royal Court Theatre, London, in 1966. *In Celebration* (1969) was followed by *The Contractor* (1969), and *Home* (1970), a piece for four elderly characters who, it transpires, are the inmates of an asylum. *The Changing Room*

(1971) deals with a rugby football team. Subsequent plays include *Cromwell* and *The Farm* (both 1973), *Life Class* (1974), based on his experiences as an art student, *Sisters* (1978), *Early Days* (1980), *The March on Russia* (1989) and *Stages* (1992). He published a collection of poems, *Storey's Lives*, in 1992. 📖 J R Taylor, *David Storey* (1974)

Storm, Theodor Woldsen 1817–88
German poet and story writer

Born in Husum, Schleswig-Holstein, he practised law there until 1853, then became a magistrate and judge (1864–80), and had a wide circle of literary acquaintants and correspondents. His early writings are lyric poems, culminating in the cycle *Tiefe Schatten* (1865, 'Deep Shadows'), but he is remembered for his tales, such as *Der Schimmelreiter* (1888, Eng trans *The Rider on the White Horse*, 1917), characterized by a vivid, often eerie descriptive power. 📖 G Storm, *Theodor Storm* (1912)

Størmer, Fredrik Carl Mülertz 1874–1957
Norwegian mathematician and geophysicist

Born in Skien, and educated at Christiania (now Oslo), he became professor there in 1903. He carried out research on cosmic rays and discovered the 'forbidden' directions lying within the Størmer cone. He gave his name to the unit of momentum at which a particle can circle around the equator.

Storni, Alfonsina 1892–1938
Argentine feminist and poet

Born in Sala Capriasca, Switzerland, she started work young as an actress with a travelling theatrical company, and in 1911 moved to Buenos Aires, Argentina, where she became a teacher and journalist. Her poetry is largely concerned with love and sexual passion. Her books include *La inquietud del rosal* (1916, 'The Solicitude of the Rosebush'), *El dulce daño* (1918, 'Sweet Injury'), *Languidez* (1921, 'Languor'), *Ocre* (1925, 'Ochre') and *Mascarillo y trébol* (1938). She committed suicide on discovering that she was suffering from cancer. An edition of her verse appeared in 1961.

Storr, Paul 1771–1844
English goldsmith

He began his career in partnership with William Frisbee in 1792, establishing his firm in Soho, London, in 1807. He produced much domestic silver and monumental work from the designs of the sculptor **John Flaxman** for the Royal Collection at Windsor Castle.

Storrier, Timothy Austin 1949–
Australian figurative and landscape artist

Born in Sydney, he studied at the National Art School there, and made working trips to central Australia, including Ayers Rock (1973) and Lake Eyre (1976), producing a series of vivid paintings. His delicate colours unite the harsh desert environment with symbolic or domestic *trompe l'œil* objects, blending Classical and Romantic styles. He won the Sulman prize in 1968, and again in 1984 with *The Burn*. His travels to Egypt in that year resulted in his 'Ticket to Egypt' exhibitions at the State Art Galleries of New South Wales and Western Australia (1986). His Sydney exhibition in 1989 included the powerful *Burning of the Gifts* which shows his continuing preoccupation with fire.

Story, John c.1510–1571
English jurist

The first Regius Professor of Civil Law at Oxford (1544), he opposed the Act of Uniformity (1548) and went into exile at Louvain. He returned during Queen **Mary I**'s reign to become a persecutor of Protestants, and Proctor at **Thomas Cranmer**'s trial (1555). Pardoned by Queen **Elizabeth I**, he soon fell foul of the authorities again and fled to Spain but was kidnapped and executed at Tyburn.

Story, Joseph 1779–1845
US jurist
Born in Marblehead, Massachusetts, he graduated from Harvard in 1798, and was admitted to the Bar in 1801. Elected to the state legislature in 1805, he became a leader of the Jeffersonian Republican (later called the Democratic) Party. In 1808 he entered Congress, from 1811 to 1845 was a justice of the Supreme Court, and was also Professor of Law at Harvard from 1829. His numerous works include *Commentaries on the Constitution of the US* (1833), *The Conflict of Laws* (1834) and *Equity Jurisprudence* (1835–36). All were influential in the creation of US law.

Story, William Wetmore 1819–95
US poet and sculptor
Born in Salem, Massachusetts, the son of Joseph Story, he practised law in Boston, but in 1856 settled in Rome and devoted himself to poetry and sculpture, becoming well-known for his sculpture *Cleopatra*. His writings include *Poems* (1847, 1856, 1886), *Roba di Roma* (1862), *Castle of St Angelo* (1877), *He and She* (1883), *Fiametta* (1885), *Excursions* (1891) and *A Poet's Portfolio* (1894). 📖 H James, *William Wetmore Story and His Friends* (1903)

Stoss or Stozz, Veit 1447–1533
German woodcarver and sculptor
He was born probably in Nuremberg. Except for a period in 1486 when he worked in the Church of St Sebald there, he was in Kraców, Poland, from 1477 to 1496, where he carved the high altar of the Marjacki Church. He returned to Nuremberg, and for the next 30 years worked in various churches there, including St Lorenz's, where his *Annunciation* can be seen. Despite the great size of many of his works, they all show great delicacy of form.

Stothard, Thomas 1755–1834
English painter and engraver
Born in London, he produced a series of designs for the *Town and Country Magazine*, followed by illustrations for Bell's *Poets* and the *Novelist's Library*. His earliest pictures exhibited at the Royal Academy, London, were *The Holy Family* and *Ajax Defending the Body of Patroclus*. Some 3,000 of his designs were engraved, including those to John Boydell's edition of *Shakespeare* (9 vols, 1792–1801), and *The Pilgrim's Progress*. His paintings *Canterbury Pilgrims* and *Flitch of Bacon* are well known by engravings. He was librarian of the Royal Academy (1814–34).

Stott, John Robert Walmsley 1921–
English Anglican clergyman and writer
Born in London, he graduated from Cambridge, and had a remarkable ministry at All Souls', Langham Place (in the heart of London's West End) as curate and then rector (1945–75). Widely acknowledged as a leading spokesman for Anglican Evangelicals, he has also had an effective ministry worldwide as a conference speaker, especially among students, and was a royal chaplain from 1959 to 1991. He was director of the London Institute for Contemporary Christianity (1982–86) and subsequently became its president. Since 1991 he has been Extra Chaplain. His many books include *Basic Christianity* (1958), *Fundamentalism and Evangelism* (1959), *Our Guilty Silence* (1967), *Christian Counter-Culture* (1978), *Issues facing Christians Today* (1984), *The Cross of Christ* (1986), *The Message of Romans* (1994) and *The Message of Timothy and Titus* (1996).

Stout, George Frederick 1860–1944
English philosopher and psychologist
Born in South Shields, Durham, he studied at St John's College, Cambridge, and taught at Cambridge (G E Moore and Bertrand Russell were among his students), Aberdeen, and Oxford, and became Professor of Logic and Metaphysics at St Andrews (1903–36). He was editor of the journal *Mind* from 1891 to 1920. He made important contributions to psychology and the philosophy of mind

in his publications *Analytic Psychology* (1896), *Manual of Psychology* (1899) and *Mind and Matter* (1931), and his theories were later to receive experimental development in the work of the Gestalt school of psychology.

Stout, Rex Todhunter 1886–1975
US detective-story writer
He was born in Noblesville, Indiana. Before becoming a writer he invented a school banking system that was installed in 400 cities throughout the USA. His great creation is Nero Wolfe, the phenomenally fat private-eye who with the help of his confidential assistant, Archie Goodwin, got to the bottom of numerous mysteries, among them *The League of Frightened Men* (1935), *Black Orchids* (1942) and *A Family Affair* (1975). 📖 J McAleer, *Rex Stout: a biography* (1977)

Stow, David 1793–1864
Scottish educationist and pioneer of co-education
Born in Paisley, Strathclyde, he founded Glasgow Normal School, and advocated the mixing of the sexes and the abolition of prizes and corporal punishment in schools.

Stow, John 1525–1605
English chronicler
Born in London, he became a tailor in Cornhill, before devoting himself to antiquarian pursuits from about 1560. He became one of the best-known Elizabethan antiquaries. His principal works, which, for his time, are accurate and business-like, are his *Summary of English Chronicles* (1565), *Annals, or a General Chronicle of England* (1580) and the *Survey of London and Westminster* (1598), an account of their history, antiquities, and government for six centuries. He also assisted in a second edition of Raphael Holinshed's *Chronicles* (1585–87) and other editions of earlier writers.

Stow, (Julian) Randolph 1935–
Australian novelist, poet and librettist
He was born in Geraldton, Western Australia, worked as an anthropologist in Australia and Papua New Guinea, and subsequently taught at the universities of Adelaide, Leeds (UK) and Western Australia. His first novel was *A Haunted Land* (1956), followed by *The Bystander* (1957), and *Tourmaline* (1963), an Australian version of T S Eliot's *The Waste Land*. In 1968 and 1969, while living in England, Stow wrote libretti for two music-theatre works by the composer Peter Maxwell Davies: *Eight Songs for a Mad King* and *Miss Donnithorne's Maggot*. Other novels include *The Merry-Go-Round in the Sea* (1965), *Visitants* (1979), and *The Suburbs of Hell* (1984). He also wrote a children's book, *Midnite* (1967), and a collection of verse, *A Counterfeit Silence* (1969). 📖 R Willbanks, *Randolph Stow* (1978)

Stowe, Harriet (Elizabeth) Beecher, *née* Beecher 1811–96
US novelist
Born in Litchfield, Connecticut, the daughter of Lyman Beecher, she was brought up with puritanical strictness and joined her sister Catherine Beecher at the Connecticut Female Seminary at Hartford in 1824. In 1836 she married the Rev Calvin Ellis Stowe, a theological professor at Lane Seminary, with whom she settled at Brunswick, Maine in 1850. She contributed sketches of southern life to *Western Monthly Magazine*, and won a short-story competition with *A New England Sketch* (1834). She became famous for her *Uncle Tom's Cabin* (1852), prompted by the passing of the Fugitive Slave Law, which immediately focused anti-slavery sentiment in the North. Her second anti-slavery novel, *Dred: A Tale of the Dismal Swamp* (1856), had a record sale in Great Britain, largely thanks to a review by George Eliot, but she lost popularity in Great Britain with *Lady Byron Vindicated* (1870), although the charges of incest with his half-sister made against Byron in the book were later proven. She wrote a

host of other books, fiction, biography and children's books. Her best works are those which deal with New England life, such as *The Minister's Wooing* (1859) and *Old Town Folks* (1869). ◫ F Wilson, *Crusader in Crinoline* (1941)

Stowell, Sir William Scott, 1st Baron
1745–1836
English judge
Born in Heworth, County Durham, he was educated at Corpus Christi College, Oxford, later becoming a college tutor (1765–77). He became a close friend of Dr Johnson, and was one of the executor's of Johnson's will. In 1780, Stowell was called to the Bar, and in 1788, was made a judge and Privy Councillor. He was greatly respected both as an ecclesiastical and admiralty judge, and was a distinguished authority on the law of nations. He was MP for Oxford (1801–21) when he was made Baron Stowell.

Stozz, Veit See Stoss, Veit

Strabo c.60BC–c.21AD
Greek geographer and Stoic
Born in Amasia, Pontus, of Greek descent on his mother's side, he apparently spent his life in travel and study. He was at Corinth in 29BC, he explored the Nile in 24BC and seems to have settled at Rome after AD14. Of his great historical work, *Historical Studies* (47 vols), only a few fragments survive, but his *Geographica* (17 vols) has survived almost complete, and is of great value for his extensive observations and copious references to his predecessors, Eratosthenes, Polybius, Aristotle and Thucydides. His name means 'squint-eyed'.

Strachan, Douglas 1875–1950
Scottish artist
Born in Aberdeen, he became political cartoonist for the *Manchester Chronicle* (1895–97) then a portrait painter in London, but he found his true medium in stained-glass work. His first great opportunity was the window group which Great Britain contributed to the Palace of Peace at The Hague. He designed the windows for the shrine of the Scottish National War Memorial. Other examples of his work may be seen in King's College Chapel, Aberdeen, the University Chapel, Glasgow, and the Church of St Thomas, Winchelsea. As an artist he did not identify with any movement. His work glows with rich colour schemes, and his subjects are treated with originality and imagination.

Strachan, John 1778–1867
Canadian bishop
Prominent in the Family Compact, he sought to maintain the ascendancy of the Anglican Church against the challenge of the Methodists (whom he accused of being American in origin and loyalty). As president of the Board of Education, his policy of keeping education under the clergy's control caused resentment throughout Upper Canada. In 1839 he became first Bishop of Toronto and opposed the Reformers over such issues as the secularization of King's College (1849) and the Clergy Reserves (1854).

Strachey, Christopher 1916–75
English computer programmer and theorist
Born in Hampstead, London, he studied mathematics and natural sciences at Cambridge, and then worked on radar. While teaching after World War II at Harrow he did programming work on Alan Turing's ACE computer at the National Physical Laboratory, and on the Manchester University Mark I. In 1952 he was appointed adviser to the National Research Development Corporation (NRDC), which placed him at the heart of the developing British computer industry. His ideas influenced the design of several British computers, and he made significant contributions in the areas of time-sharing, whereby several users could share one computer, and in denotational semantics, which sought to understand the meaning of computer languages in a mathematical way. He was one of the foremost computer architects and logicians of his day.

Strachey, (Evelyn) John St Loe 1901–63
English Labour politician
Born in Guildford, Surrey, and educated at Eton and Magdalen College, Oxford, he was Labour MP from 1929 until 1931, when he resigned from the Labour Party and gave his support to extremist political organizations. He served in the RAF during World War II and in 1945 became Labour Under-Secretary for Air. His controversial period as Minister of Food (1946–50) included the food crisis (1947), the unpopular prolongation of rationing, and the abortive Tanganyika ground-nuts and Gambia egg schemes (1947–49). As Secretary of State for War (1950–51) he had to contend with the Korean war and the communist insurrection in Malaya.

Strachey, (Giles) Lytton 1880–1932
English biographer
Born in London, the son of an Indian civil engineer and soldier, he was educated at Liverpool University, where he read history, and Trinity College, Cambridge. He was a book reviewer for the *Spectator* (1904–14), became a member of the Bloomsbury Group of writers and artists, and began his writing career as a critic with *Landmarks in French Literature* (1912), which shows clearly his affinities with Charles-Augustin Sainte-Beuve and his francophile sympathies. He was a conscientious objector during World War I. *Eminent Victorians* (1918) was a literary bombshell constituting, as it did, a vigorous, impertinent challenge to Victorian self-assurance. Its irony, mordant wit, and the ruthless pinpointing of foible that was his method of evoking character, transformed the genre. His later works include *Queen Victoria* (1921), *Elizabeth and Essex: A Tragic History* (1928) and *Characters and Commentaries* (1933). ◫ M Holroyd, *Lytton Strachey* (2 vols, 1967–68)

Stradella, Alessandro c.1642–1682
Italian composer
He was born in Nepi, near Viterbo. His oratorio *San Giovanni Battista* (1675) influenced Henry Purcell and as well as dramatic oratorios he wrote operas and instrumental works of the concerto grosso type. It is said that he eloped from Venice to Turin with the mistress of one of the Contarini, who sent assassins to murder him. He was wounded, but recovered. Others say that his would-be murderers found him conducting one of his oratorios, and, touched by the music, allowed him to escape. He was eventually murdered in Genoa. His story has been the subject of operas, and F Marion Crawford used it for his novel *Stradella* (1909).

Stradivari or Stradivarius, Antonio c.1644–1737
Italian violin maker
Born in Cremona, he was a pupil of Niccolo Amati. He experimented with the design of string instruments and perfected the Cremona type of violin, assisted by his sons Francesco (1671–1743) and Omobono (1679–1742). It is believed that he made over 1,000 violins, violas and violoncellos, of which around 650 still exist.

Strafford, Thomas Wentworth, 1st Earl of
1593–1641
English politician
Born in London of a Yorkshire family with royal connections, he was knighted in 1611, and in 1614 became MP for Yorkshire. He was originally an opponent of Charles I but in 1628 became a Royalist. In 1632 he was appointed Lord Deputy of Ireland, where he imposed firm rule, his aim being to make Charles 'the most absolute prince in Christendom'. In 1639 he became the King's principal

adviser, and in this capacity was made Earl of Strafford and Lord Lieutenant of Ireland (1640). When he failed to suppress the rebellion in Scotland which had broken out as a result of Charles's policies towards the Scottish kirk (Bishops' Wars, 1639–40), he and Archbishop Laud were impeached by John Pym, leader of the Puritans in the Long Parliament, and despite a famous defence Strafford was executed on Tower Hill, abandoned by the King. ⌑ C V Wedgwood, *Thomas Wentworth, First Earl of Strafford, 1593–1641: A Revaluation* (1961)

Strand, Mark 1934–
US poet and translator

He was born in Summerside, Prince Edward Island, Canada, and moved to the USA at the age of four. His spare verses are clearly mainly inspired from his reading of Samuel Beckett. In his ambitious long poem 'The Untelling', he has, characteristically, written, 'Although I have tried to return, I have always/ended here, where I am now'. He was the US Poet Laureate in 1990–91. ⌑ *Selected Poems* (1980); D Kirby, *Mark Strand and the Poet's Place in Contemporary Culture* (1990)

Strand, Paul 1890–1976
US photographer

Born in New York City, he studied under Lewis W Hine. He became a commercial photographer in 1912 and followed Alfred Stieglitz in his commitment to 'straight' photography of precision and clarity in both landscape and close-up detail. He collaborated with Charles Sheeler in the documentary film *Mannahatta* (1920), and in 1933 was appointed chief of photography and cinematography in the government Secretariat of Education in Mexico. After visiting Sergei Eisenstein in the USSR in 1935 he returned to New York and made documentary films on social issues, both independently and for the US government, until 1942. The best-known include *The Plow That Broke the Plains* (1936). His later work concentrated on still photography, in which he recorded life in many different parts of the world.

Strang, William 1859–1921
Scottish painter and etcher

Born in Dumbarton, Strathclyde, he studied in London at the Slade School of Art from 1875 where he was taught and greatly influenced by Alphonse Legros. A prolific printmaker, he made over 750 etchings, drypoints, mezzotints, aquatints and woodcuts. Many consider his portraits to be his greatest achievement, and his sitters included Rudyard Kipling and Thomas Hardy. He illustrated several books, among them *Paradise Lost*, *Don Quixote*, *The Pilgrim's Progress* and *The Ancient Mariner*. He won several awards at international exhibitions and in later years turned more to painting. He was an elected Royal Academician and was a member of the Royal Society of Painters, Etchers and Engravers.

Strange, Sir Robert, *originally* Robert Strang 1721–92
Scottish line-engraver

He was born in Kirkwall. He fought on the Jacobite side at Prestonpans, Falkirk and Culloden, and in 1747 married a Jacobite, Isabella Lumisden. He studied in Paris and settled in London (1750). He had a European reputation as a historical line-engraver, in opposition to the stippling of his rival, Francesco Bartolozzi. His works include portraits of royalty and engravings of paintings by artists such as Titian and Van Dyck.

Strasberg, Lee, *originally* Israel Strassberg 1901–82
US theatre director, actor and teacher

Born in Budzanow, Austria, he emigrated to the USA in 1909 and became a professional actor in 1925. He gained a reputation with the Theatre Guild of New York and helped to form the Group Theatre in New York (1931), with which he evolved a technique which became known everywhere as 'the Method' or 'method acting'. His teaching style owed much to the Russian director, Stanislavsky, whose book, *An Actor Prepares*, dealt with the psychology of interpretation in acting. He began directing but his time was increasingly taken up by the training of actors. As director of the Actors Studio in New York (1949–82), he taught Marlon Brando, James Dean, Paul Newman, and others. In 1969 he established the Lee Strasberg Institute of Theatre.

Strasburger, Eduard Adolf 1844–1912
German botanist

Born in Warsaw, Poland, he studied botany in Paris, Bonn and Jena and spent his career at the universities of Jena (1869–80) and Bonn (1880–1912). He studied the alternation of generations in plants, the embryo sac found in gymnosperms and angiosperms, and double fertilization in angiosperms. In his book *Cell Formation and Cell Division* (1875) and its later editions he laid down the basic principles of cytology, the study of cells, for which he made Bonn the world's leading centre. His work did much to show that mitosis (normal somatic cell division) in plants is a process essentially similar to that described for animal cells. He observed nuclear fusion in the ovules of gymnosperms and angiosperms, and remarked on the formation of the polar nucleus in their egg-cells. Strasburger's *Textbook of Botany for Universities*, written with other botanists under his guidance, is a classic, much used and widely translated in over 30 editions from 1894 onwards. In its updated form, it is still in print.

Strasser, Valentine c.1965–
Sierra Leone soldier and politician

He was born in Freetown and educated at Sierra Leone Grammar School and the Gbenguema Military School. As an army officer he was promoted to the rank of captain and was a member of the military junta which overthrew the government of President Momoh in 1992. As the chairman of the National Provisional Ruling Council (1992–96) he was virtual dictator of Sierra Leone, and failed to prevent the civil war which devastated the country. In 1996 he was overthrown by his deputy Julius Maada Bio, and went to England to study law.

Stratford (de Redcliffe), Stratford Canning, 1st Viscount 1786–1880
English diplomat

Born in London and educated at Eton and King's College, Cambridge, he became précis writer to his cousin George Canning at the Foreign Office in 1807. In 1808 he was First Secretary to the Constantinople (Istanbul) embassy and in 1810 minister plenipotentiary. In 1812 he negotiated the treaty of Bucharest between Russia and Turkey. He was then Minister in Switzerland (1814–17), Commissioner at the Vienna Congress of 1815 and Minister to the USA (1819–23). As ambassador at Constantinople several times between 1825 and 1858 he built up influence which gained him the name of the 'Great Elchi'. He persuaded the Turkish government to make reforms and worked for Greek independence. Despite his influence he was unable to prevent the outbreak of the Crimean War (1854–56).

Strathcona (of Mount Royal and of Glencoe), Donald Alexander Smith, 1st Baron 1820–1914
Canadian statesman

Born in Forres, Scotland, he emigrated to Canada and progressed from clerk (1838) to governor (1889) of the Hudson's Bay Company. Chief promoter of the Canadian Pacific Railway (completed 1885), he was appointed Canadian High Commissioner for London in 1896, and a peer in 1897.

Strato or Straton of Lampsacus d.c.269BC
Greek philosopher
He succeeded **Theophrastus** as the third head of the Peripatetic School (from c.287 to 269BC) which **Aristotle** founded. His writings are lost, but he seems to have worked mainly to revise Aristotle's physical doctrines. He had an original theory about the void; its distribution explaining differences in the weights of objects. He also denied any role to teleological, and hence theological, explanations in nature, which led naturally to the position **David Hume** called 'Stratonician atheism'—the universe is ultimate, self-sustaining and needs no further external or divine explanation to account for it.

Stratton, Charles Sherwood, *also called* General Tom Thumb 1838–83
US midget showman
Born in Bridgeport, Connecticut, he stopped growing at six months of age and stayed 63cm (25in) until his teens, eventually reaching 101cm (40in). He was exhibited by the circus impresario, **P T Barnum** from the age of five, and toured the USA and Europe. In 1863 he married another midget, Lavinia Warren (1841–1919).

Straus, Oskar 1870–1954
French composer
Born in Vienna, he became a naturalized French citizen in 1939. A pupil of **Max Bruch**, he is best known for his many operettas and comic operas, such as *Ein Walzertraum* (1907, 'A Waltz Dream') and *Der Tapfere Soldat* (1908, 'The Chocolate Soldier', from **George Bernard Shaw**'s *Arms and the Man*).

Strauss, David Friedrich 1808–74
German theologian
Born in Ludwigsburg, Württemberg, he studied for the Church at Tübingen, where he also lectured on philosophy in the university as a disciple of **Hegel**. In his *Leben Jesu* (1835, Eng trans *The Life of Jesus Critically Examined* by George Eliot, 1846) he sought to prove the gospel history to be a collection of myths, and to detect a nucleus of historical truth free from every trace of supernaturalism. The book marks an epoch in New Testament criticism and raised a storm of controversy. Strauss, dismissed from his post at Tübingen, in 1839 was called to be Professor of Dogmatics and Church History at Zurich, but the appointment provoked such opposition that it had to be dropped. His second great work, *Die christliche Glaubenslehre* was a review of Christian dogma (1840–41). A new *Life of Jesus, composed for the German People* (1864, Eng trans 1865), attempts to reconstruct a positive life of **Jesus Christ**. In *Der alte und der neue Glaube* (1872, 'The Old Faith and the New') Strauss endeavoured to prove that Christianity as a system of religious belief is dead, and that a new faith must be built up out of art and the scientific knowledge of nature. He also wrote several biographies, notably that of **Ulrich von Hutten** (Eng trans 1874), and lectures on **Voltaire** (1870). He separated from his wife, the opera singer Agnese Schebest (1813–70).

Strauss, Franz-Josef 1915–88
West German politician
Born and educated in Munich, the son of a butcher, he served in the German Army during World War II and in 1945 joined the Christian Democratic Union (CDU)'s Bavarian-based sister party, the Christian Social Union (CSU), being elected to the Bundestag (federal parliament) in 1949. He became leader of the CSU in 1961 and held a succession of ministerial posts. His career was seriously blighted when, for security purposes, he authorized a raid on the offices of the journal *Der Spiegel*, leading to his sacking as Minister of Defence in 1962. During the 1970s he vigorously opposed the Ostpolitik initiative of the **Brandt** and **Schmidt** administrations.

In 1980 he sought election as Federal Chancellor for the CDU and CSU alliance, but was heavily defeated. Nevertheless, from 1978 he had success as the State premier of Bavaria, using this base to wield significant influence within the Bundesrat (federal upper house) and, from 1982, in the coalition government headed by Chancellor **Helmut Kohl**.

Strauss, Johann, the Elder, *also known as* Johann Strauss I 1804–49
Austrian violinist, conductor, and composer
Born in Vienna, he founded the Viennese Waltz tradition with composer Joseph Lanner (in whose quartet he played), a development from **Schubert**. He toured extensively in Europe with his own orchestra, played during Queen **Victoria**'s coronation celebrations (1838) and composed several marches, including the *Radetzky March* (1848) in honour of the general. He also composed many waltzes including the *Lorelei* and the *Donaulieder*, but was eclipsed by his son, **Johann Strauss, the Younger**.
📖 Heinrich E Jacob, Johann Strauss, *Father and Son* (1939)

Strauss, Johann, the Younger, *also known as* Johann Strauss II 1825–99
Austrian violinist, conductor, and composer
Born in Vienna, he was the son of **Johann Strauss, the Elder**. He studied law, but turned to music and toured with his own orchestra, performing in London in 1869 and visiting the USA in 1872. He composed over 400 waltzes, notably *The Blue Danube* (1867, *An der Schönen blauen Donau*) and *Tales from the Vienna Woods* (1868, *Geschichten aus dem Wienerwald*), as well as polkas, marches, several operettas, including *Die Fledermaus* (1874, 'The Bat'), and the concert piece *Perpetuum Mobile*. His brothers Josef (1827–70) and Eduard (1835–1916) were conductors, and Josef also composed waltzes.

Strauss, Levi c.1829–1902
US clothing manufacturer
Born in Germany, he emigrated to the USA and lived in New York City before sailing around Cape Horn to California during the gold rush in 1850. He intended to become a prospector but found a greater source of income when he began to sell trousers made of tent canvas to miners. He settled in San Francisco and founded Levi Strauss & Co to manufacture the trousers, which the miners called 'Levi's'. Ordering denim from New York, he dyed the fabric blue for uniformity and reinforced the pocket corners with copper rivets, creating what became the standard work trousers throughout the West of the 1860s and probably the most popular trousers in the world today.

Strauss, Richard See panel p1768

Stravinsky, Igor Fyodorovich See panel p1769

Straw, Jack (John Whitaker) 1946–
English Labour politician
Born in Buckhurst Hill, Essex, he won a scholarship to attend Brentwood school before reading law at Leeds University, where from 1969 to 1971 he was president of the National Union of Students and displayed an early belief in law, order and stability, and a deep hatred of violence which would fuel his later toughness on crime. Elected to the Islington borough council (1971–78), he was called to the Bar in 1972, and while practising as a lawyer, became a deputy leader of the Inner London Education Authority (1973–74). On Labour's return to power in 1974, he became adviser to **Barbara Castle**, who was Secretary of State for Social Services; then in 1976 he moved to be adviser to the Environment Secretary. After a couple of years with Granada Television, he became MP for Blackburn (1979–). He joined the Shadow Cabinet in

Strauss, Richard 1864–1949
German composer

Richard Strauss was born in Munich, the son of Franz Strauss, first horn player in the court opera. He began to compose at the age of six, and his first publications date from 1875. In 1882 he entered Munich University, but began musical studies in Berlin the following year, and shortly afterwards became assistant conductor to **Hans von Bülow** at Meiningen. There he was converted from the school of **Brahms**, under whose influence his early compositions had been written, to that of **Wagner** and **Liszt**, composing his first symphonic poems and succeeding von Bülow at Meiningen in 1885. In 1894 he married the soprano Pauline de Ahna, for whom he wrote many of his songs.

After a period (1886–89) as assistant conductor at the Munich opera he moved to Weimar, and was invited by Wagner's wife Cosima to conduct at Bayreuth in 1891. His symphonic poems include *Don Juan* (1889), *Tod und Verklärung* (1889, 'Death and Transfiguration'), *Till Eulenspiegels lustige Streiche* (1895, 'Till Eulenspiegel's Merry Pranks'), *Also sprach Zarathustra*, (1895–96, 'Thus Spake Zarathustra'), *Don Quixote* (1897) and *Ein Heldenleben* (1898, 'A Hero's Life').

The first of his operas, *Guntram*, was produced at Weimar in 1894 and in the same year he became conductor of the Berlin Philharmonic Orchestra. His operas *Salome* (1905), based on a German translation of **Oscar Wilde**'s play, and *Elektra* (1909), the first of his collaborations with the dramatic poet **Hugo von Hofmannsthal**, caused sensations by their erotic treatment of biblical and classical subjects. With Hofmannsthal he went on to compose the popular *Der Rosenkavalier* (1911) and *Ariadne auf Naxos* (1912, revised 1916).

His work with **Stefan Zweig** on *Die schweigsame Frau* (1935, 'The Silent Woman') led him into difficulties with the Nazi government, which had previously appointed him president of the Reichsmusikkammer. He resigned the post, but his commanding position at the head of German musical life protected him from serious political reprisal. Indeed, he went on to produce three operas with Josef Gregor, *Friedenstag* (1938, 'Day of Peace'), *Daphne* (1938) and *Die Liebe der Danae* (1938–40, 'The Love of Danae'). After the completion of his last opera, *Capriccio* (to a libretto by Clemens Krauss, 1942), he turned to instrumental work and song: in 1943 he wrote *Metamorphosen*, an extended piece for 23 strings inspired by the wartime destruction of German cities, and finally a series of small-scale concerto and orchestral works and the valedictory *Vier letzte Lieder* (1948, 'Four Last Songs').

📖 Strauss's own reminiscences are to be found in *Recollections and Reflections* (Eng trans, 1953). See also M Kennedy, *Richard Strauss* (rev edn, 1995); Willi Schuh, *Richard Strauss: A Chronicle of the Early Years, 1864–1898* (vol 1, 1982); Alan Jefferson, *The Life of Richard Strauss* (1973); Ernst Krause, *Richard Strauss: The Man and His Work* (1964); Norman Del Mar, *Richard Strauss: A Critical Commentary on His Life and Works* (3 vols, 1962–72).

At the end of April 1945 American troops occupied Garmisch. When they were about to enter his house the old man of 81 confronted them, saying in English, 'I am Richard Strauss, the composer of the Rosenkavalier!' At that they left the house. From Ernst Krause, *Richard Strauss* (1964).

1987 as principal Opposition spokesman on education (1987–92), on the environment (1992–94) and on home affairs (1994–97), and was appointed Home Secretary by **Tony Blair** when Labour came to power in 1997.

Strawson, Sir Peter Frederick 1919–
English philosopher

Born in London, he was educated at Christ's College, Finchley, and St John's College, Oxford. He taught at Oxford as a Fellow of University College from 1948, and was Waynflete Professor of Metaphysical Philosophy from 1968. He was also a Fellow of Magdalen College, Oxford (1968–87). His early work dealt particularly with the links between logic and language, in the general tradition of 'Oxford' linguistic or 'ordinary language' philosophy, as for example in his *Introduction to Logical Theory* (1952). He went on to extend and integrate this with metaphysical studies of the structure of human thought about the world, as in *Individuals: an Essay in Descriptive Metaphysics* (1959) and *The Bounds of Sense* (1966). Later publications include *Scepticism and Naturalism* (1985) and *Analysis and Metaphysics* (1992).

Streep, Meryl (Mary Louise) 1949–
US actress

Born in Summit, New Jersey, she graduated from Vassar College and Yale Drama School before making her New York stage debut in *The Playboy of Seville* (1969). She appeared in summer stock, off-Broadway and in *Trelawney of the Wells* (1975). Her film debut in *Julia* (1977), *The Deerhunter* (1978) and *Kramer vs. Kramer* (1979, Academy Award) established her as a first-rank star. She has consistently expanded her range, showing sensitivity and a facility with accents in a series of acclaimed characterizations in films like *The French Lieutenant's Woman* (1981), *Sophie's Choice* (1982), for which she won a second Academy Award, *Silkwood* (1983), *Out of Africa* (1985), *Ironweed* (1987), *A Cry in the Dark* (1988) *Postcards From the Edge* (1990), *The House of the Spirits* (1994) and *Before and After* (1996).

Street, George Edmund 1824–81
English architect

Born in Woodford, Essex, he was assistant to Sir **George Gilbert Scott**, and started his own practice in 1849. From his practice, and influence, emerged major figures like **William Morris**, **Philip Webb** and **Norman Shaw**. He restored Christ Church in Dublin, and designed neo-Gothic buildings, including the London Law Courts and scores of churches. His publications include *Brick and Marble in the Middle Ages* (1855), *The Architecture of North Italy* (1855), and *Some Account of Gothic Architecture in Spain* (1865).

Street, Lady Jessie Mary Grey 1889–1970
Australian feminist and writer

Born in Ranchi province of Chota Nagpur, north-east India, she was educated at private schools in England and at Sydney University. She became an early activist for the League of Nations, and in 1920 secretary to the National Council of Women, and later president of the Feminist Club. In 1929 she became founding president of the United Associations of Women, an umbrella group for the New South Wales feminist movement. She stood as Labor candidate in the federal election of 1943 and again in 1946, and in that year was the only woman delegate to the San Francisco conference which marked the beginnings of the United Nations Organization.

Streeter, Alison 1964–
English swimmer

Born in Surrey, she took up swimming to help her asthma but has since clocked up more English Channel crossings than any other female in the world. In 1988 she broke the world record, previously held by a man, for the fastest

Stravinsky, Igor Fyodorovich 1882–1971
Russian-born US composer

Stravinsky was born in Oranienbaum, near St Petersburg, the son of a musician at the Imperial Opera. He studied law but became increasingly interested in musical composition, which he studied with **Rimsky-Korsakov**, whose influence can be heard in the early Symphony in E flat (1907). **Sergei Diaghilev** heard Stravinsky's music and invited him to write a ballet on the legend of *The Firebird* (1910); his enchanting music was an instant success. A second ballet, *Petrushka* (1911), consolidated his international reputation, as did *The Rite of Spring* (1913), although there was a riot at its première.

The **Hans Andersen** opera, *The Nightingale* (1914), was followed by the wartime 'shoe-string' entertainments, *Renard* (1917) and *The Soldier's Tale* (1918), which aptly illustrate Stravinsky's adaptability. Essentially an experimenter, he then plunged headlong into neoclassicism. The ballets *Pulcinella* (1920), based on music by **Giovanni Pergolesi**, *Apollo Musagetes* (1928), *The Card Game* (1937), *Orpheus* (1948) and the austere *Agon* (1957), using **Schoenberg**'s twelve-note system, exemplify this trend, as do the opera-oratorio *Oedipus Rex* (1927), based on a **Jean Cocteau** version and translated into Latin for greater dignity, and the magnificent choral *Symphony of Psalms* (1930) 'composed to the glory of God'.

Stravinsky settled in France in 1934 and finally in the USA, as an American citizen, in 1945. Other characteristic and outstanding works include the *Symphonies of Wind Instruments*, dedicated to **Claude Debussy** (1921); the *Symphony in C major* (1940); the opera *The Rake's Progress* (1951) for which **W H Auden** helped to write the libretto; and the serial-music *In Memoriam Dylan Thomas* (1954), for voice, string quartet and four trombones, *The Flood* (1962), a musical play, *Elegy for J.F.K.* (1964), for voice and clarinets, *Variations* (1965) for orchestra in memory of **Aldous Huxley**, and *Requiem Canticles* (1966), for voice and orchestra.

He was Charles Eliot Norton Professor of Poetry at Harvard in 1939, and in 1954 was awarded the gold medal of the Royal Philharmonic Society.

📖 Stravinsky's autobiography, up to 1936, is *Chronicles of My Life*. His extensive discussions with the musician Robert Craft are recorded in R Craft, *Conversations with Igor Stravinsky* (1959), and his letters in *Selected Correspondence* (1982–85). See also P Griffiths, *Stravinsky* (1992); R Craft, *Stravinsky* (1986); F Routh, *Stravinsky* (1975).

'My music is best understood by children and animals.'
Quoted in *The Observer*, 1961.

See also quotes under **Prokofiev** and **Schumann**.

---

crossing from Scotland to Ireland, and she also set world records for the fastest swims around the Isle of Wight and around Jersey. She is the only person ever to succeed in swimming up the Thames and has raised over £80,000 for charity through the sponsorship of her swims. In 1995 she swam the Channel five times, making her the overall record-holder for cross-Channel swims.

Streeton, Sir Arthur Ernest 1867–1943
Australian landscape painter

Born in Mount Duneed, Victoria, he studied at the National Gallery School in Melbourne and in 1886 joined **Frederick McCubbin** and **Tom Roberts** at their artists' camp at Box Hill, Victoria. In 1888, with Roberts and **Charles Conder**, he helped establish the Heidelberg school of painting named after their camp near there. The next year Streeton contributed 40 paintings to Australia's first impressionist exhibition, '9 x 5 Impressions' in Melbourne. Purchases by the Art Gallery of New South Wales in 1890 of his *Still Glides the Stream* and by the National Gallery of Victoria in 1896 of *The Purple Noon's Transparent Might* confirmed Streeton's national reputation. In 1898 he went to London and exhibited at the Royal Academy in 1900. He visited Europe and his Italian pictures evoked **J M W Turner**'s use of light. Streeton also worked in France as an official war artist from 1914. He returned to Melbourne in 1924, where from 1929 he wrote art criticism for a local newspaper.

Street-Porter, Janet 1944–
English television producer and presenter

Born in London, she studied architecture for a year, then worked as a journalist for various newspapers. She presented evening television shows, such as *Saturday Night People* (1978–80). She then turned to production, and her 1980s current affairs programme *Network 7* won her a BAFTA award for originality. In 1988 she became the BBC's first commissioning editor for youth programmes, responsible for shows such as *Rough Guide to Europe* and *Rapido*, then was promoted to head of youth and entertainment in 1991 and made the series *The Look* (1992) and *The Vampyr* (1992). Becoming head of independent production for BBC TV's entertainment group early in 1994, she left to become managing director of the new national cable television channel, Live TV, but resigned suddenly in 1995.

Streicher, Julius 1885–1946
German journalist and politician

Born in Fleinhausen, he was associated with **Hitler** in the early days of the National Socialist Party, taking part in the 1923 putsch. A ruthless persecutor of the Jews, he incited anti-Semitism through the newspaper *Der Stürmer*, which he founded and edited, and copies of which were widely displayed in prominent red boxes throughout the Reich. He was hanged at Nuremberg as a war criminal.

Streisand, Barbra, *originally* Barbara Joan Rosen 1942–
US actress, director and bestselling singer

Born in Brooklyn, New York, she was spotted in an amateur talent contest as a teenager. Her New York debut in *Another Evening with Harry Stones* (1961) was followed by Broadway successes in *I Can Get It For You Wholesale* (1963) and *Funny Girl* (1964). Her 1965 television special, *My Name is Barbra*, won five Emmy awards and she has been the recipient of numerous Grammy awards, including three as best female vocalist (1964, 1965, 1978). She repeated the success of *Funny Girl* in a film version (1968), earning an Academy Award for her first film appearance. She followed it with *Hello Dolly!* (1969), *The Way We Were* (1973), *A Star Is Born* (1976), which she produced, and *Nuts* (1987). She has won numerous awards as a top-selling recording artist—her albums include *Emotion* (1984), *Til I Loved You* (1989) and *Back to Broadway* (1993)—and film actress, and diversified further in 1983 as the producer, director and co-writer of *Yentl*, in which she also acted and sang. She later acted in and directed *Prince of Tides* (1990) and *The Mirror Has Two Faces* (1996). In 1994 she ended a 27-year break from the mainstream concert stage with performances in Las Vegas and London. 📖 J Kimball, *Barbra* (1992)

Stresemann, Gustav 1878–1929
German politician and Nobel Prize winner

Strindberg, (Johan) August 1849–1912
Swedish dramatist and novelist, regarded as Sweden's greatest modern writer

Strindberg was born in Stockholm. After failing to complete his studies at Uppsala University, he returned to Stockholm and worked as a private tutor, actor, journalist and librarian while attempting to begin his career as an author. His personal life was turbulent, and included three unsuccessful marriages and periods of severe persecution mania. He had a propensity for involvement in cultural and personal feuds and lived abroad for long periods, mainly in France and Italy.

His first major play was *Mäster Olof* (1872, Eng trans 1915), a historical drama—a genre to which he was to return prolifically in the years around 1900 with, for instance, *Gustav Vasa* and *Erik XIV* (both 1899). His breakthrough came with a satirical novel about the art circles of Stockholm, *Röda rummet* (1879, Eng trans *The Red Room*, 1913), which created an uproar, and is regarded as marking the arrival of both the modern realistic novel in Sweden and that of the naturalist movement. His later naturalist novel *Hemsöborna* (1887, *The People of Hemsö*, 1959), his sunniest work, has become a popular classic.

Two collections of short stories, *Giftas I* and *II* (1884–86, Eng trans *Getting Married*, 1913), put forward his ideas on marriage, women and emancipation. A small incident in the first volume led to his trial on a charge of blasphemy, of which he was acquitted. He then published a bitter autobiography, *Tjänstekvinnans son* (1886, *The Son of a Servant*, 1913), followed by *Le Plaidoyer d'un fou* (1888, Eng trans *A Madman's Defense*).

The battle between the sexes is at the centre of the three major plays that follow, in which he combines naturalistic techniques with psychological analysis: *Fadren* (1887, Eng trans *The Father*, 1899), *Fröken Julie* (1888, Eng trans *Miss Julie*, 1918), and *Fordringsägare* (1889, Eng trans *The Creditors*, 1914). In the 1890s he experimented with the occult and pseudo-science, suffered a spiritual crisis verging on madness, and underwent a conversion influenced by the work of the 18th-century mystic, **Emmanuel Swedenborg**. All of this is described in his autobiography, *Inferno* (1898, Eng trans 1912), and is given dramatic expression in the trilogy *Till Damaskus* (1898–1904, *To Damascus*, 1913).

From 1907 Strindberg helped to run the Intima Theatre in Stockholm, for which he wrote several 'chamber plays'; the most fantastic of these is *Spöksonaten* (1907, Eng trans *The Ghost Sonata*, 1916). His efforts to find a dramatic means of expressing inner reality in these and later plays, like *Drömspelet* (1902, Eng trans *A Dream Play*, 1929), mark him as a forerunner of Expressionism and a major influence on modern theatre.

M Meyer, *Strindberg: a biography* (1985); E Sprigge, *The Strange Life of Strindberg* (1949, reprinted 1972).

'[Happiness] consumes itself like fire. It cannot burn eternally but must die. This foreboding of the end destroys my happiness at its very peak.' The husband in *A Dream Play*.

'Strindberg, Strindberg, Strindberg, the greatest of them all…Barrie sits mumbling as he silvers his little model stars and gilds his little model suns, while Strindberg shakes flame from the living planets and the fixed stars. Ibsen can sit serenely in his Doll's House, while Strindberg is battling with his heaven and his hell.' **Sean O'Casey** in *The Letters of Sean O'Casey, 1910–1954* (ed D Kranse, vol 1 1975, vol 2 1980).

He was born in Berlin. Entering the Reichstag in 1907 as a National Liberal, he rose to become leader of that party, and after World War I founded and led its successor, the German People's Party. He was Chancellor of the new German (Weimar) Republic for a few months in 1923, when, and as Minister of Foreign Affairs (1923–29), he pursued a policy of conciliation, and in 1925 negotiated the Locarno Pact of mutual security with **Aristide Briand** and **Austen Chamberlain**. He secured the entry of Germany into the League of Nations in 1926, and shared with Briand the 1926 Nobel Peace Prize for that year. Henry A Turner, *Stresemann and the Politics of the Weimar* (1963)

Streuvels, Stijn, *pseudonym of* Frank Lateur
1871–1969
Flemish novelist

He was born in Heule, and began his professional career as the baker for his village, but after 15 years took to writing, depicting the Flemish peasantry 'with the plastic power of a **Brueghel**' according to one critic. One of his novels, *Langs de wegen* (1902), was translated at the behest of **Ford Madox Ford**, as *Old Jan* (1936). The Belgian novelist Willem Elsschot (1882–1960) also admired him, and under his real name of Alfons de Ridder wrote a book on him (1908). Streuvels' greatest novel is the haunting and hallucinatory *Het leven en de dood in den ast* (1926). A Denedts, *Stijn Streuvels* (1955)

Strijdom or Strydom, Johannes Gerhardus
1893–1958
South African statesman

Born in Willowmore, Cape Province, he was educated at Stellenbosch and Pretoria, and after a start as a farmer, took up law practice in the Transvaal. Elected MP for Waterberg in 1929 he became leader of the extremists in the National Party. His two main political ends were establishing the policy of apartheid and the setting up of an Afrikaner Republic outside the Commonwealth. He succeeded **Daniel F Malan** as Prime Minister of South Africa from 1954 until shortly before his death.

Strindberg, August See panel above

Stringfellow, John 1799–1883
English inventor

Born in Attercliffe, Yorkshire, he was apprenticed to a lacemaker and some years later set up a workshop in Chard to serve the lace industry there. With the assistance of William Henson he built a steam-powered model aeroplane with a 20-foot (6.1m) wing span. They tested it during the summer of 1847, but it proved incapable of sustained flight, and the disappointed Henson left for the USA. Stringfellow built a smaller model, tested it indoors in a disused lace factory, and in 1848 showed that it was capable of climbing flight under its own power. In subsequent tests in London it flew distances of up to 120 feet (36.6m). Some 20 years later he built a model triplane which, however, was never flown. Its engine was particularly remarkable, developing more than one horsepower with a combined weight of engine and boiler of only 13lb (5.9kg).

Strode, William 1602–45
English poet and clergyman

He was born in Plympton, Devon, and educated at Christ Church, Oxford, where he became canon and public orator. He is best known for his elegies and lyric verse, which were rediscovered by Bertram Dobell in 1907, and for his tragi-comedy, *The Floating Island*, performed by the students of Christ Church before **Charles I** in 1636.

Stroessner, Alfredo 1912–
Paraguayan dictator

Born in Encarnación, the son of a German immigrant, he took up military training at Asunción then joined the army, was commissioned in 1932 and rose to become Commander-in-Chief in 1951. In conformity with Paraguay's long history of military governments, operating through the right-wing Colorado party, he became President in a coup d'état in 1954 which deposed Federico Chávez. He was re-elected on seven occasions, despite his record concerning civil rights. One faction with the Colorado Party favoured his continuation in office while another wanted him to retire in 1988. He chose to stay, but in February 1989 he was ousted in a coup led by General Andrés Rodríguez (1923–97), and went into exile in Brazil. 📖 Paul H Hill, *Paraguay Under Stroessner* (1980)

Stroheim, Erich von, *originally* Erich Oswald Stroheim 1885–1957
Austrian film director and actor
Born in Vienna, Austria, he was an officer in the Austrian cavalry (1902–09), then emigrated to the USA and made his film debut with small parts in **D W Griffith's** classics *Birth of a Nation* (1915) and *Intolerance* (1916), in which he was also an assistant to the director. His first success as a film director was with *Blind Husbands* (1919), followed by *The Devil's Passkey* (1920), *Foolish Wives* (1922) and *Greed* (1923). His career was punctuated with furious rows with producers about his extravagance and arrogance, but he had box-office hits with *The Merry Widow* (1925) and *The Wedding March* (1928). In the 1930s he moved to France and starred as a sadistic Prussian officer in **Jean Renoir's** *La Grande Illusion* (1937). He returned to Hollywood for *Sunset Boulevard* (1950, Academy Award nomination).

Stromeyer, Friedrich 1776–1835
German chemist
Born in Göttingen, he was educated there and in Paris. He taught at Göttingen from 1802, becoming Professor of Chemistry in 1810. He was one of the first teachers to insist that his students had opportunities for practical work and **Leopold Gmelin** and **Robert Bunsen** were among his pupils. He was also the inspector of apothecaries for Hanover. He was a noted mineralogist and in 1817 he discovered the presence of cadmium in a sample of zinc carbonate.

Strömgren, Bengt 1908–87
Danish astronomer
Born in Götelorge, he studied astronomy under his father's tuition at the University of Copenhagen, and atomic physics and quantum theory under **Niels Bohr** in the nearby Institute of Theoretical Physics. In 1936 Strömgren joined the second **Otto Struve** at Yerkes Observatory in the USA in work on stellar atmospheres and interstellar gas. His most outstanding work in this field concerns the physics of ionized gas clouds surrounding hot stars. In 1940 he succeeded his father as director of the Copenhagen Observatory, but after World War II returned to the USA as director of Yerkes Observatory and professor at the Princeton Institute for Advanced Studies. In 1967 he returned to Denmark, and became concerned with problems of stellar composition and its correlation with ages of stars. He was awarded many international honours, including the gold medal of the Royal Astronomical Society (1962), and he acted both as general secretary and as president of the International Astronomical Union.

Strong, Augustus Hopkins 1836–1921
US Baptist pastor and educator
He was born in Rochester, New York. He graduated from Yale, and after theological studies held pastorates in Massachusetts and Ohio. He was then appointed Professor of Systematic Theology and president of Rochester Theological Seminary (1872–1912). Trying to

find middle ground between his conservatism and 19th-century German theology, he tended towards the former, as seen in his works, which include *Systematic Theology* (3 vols, 1886), *Philosophy and Religion* (1888) and *The Great Poets and Their Theology* (1897).

Strong, L(eonard) A(lfred) G(eorge) 1896–1958
English novelist and poet
Born in Plymouth, Devon, and educated at Brighton College and Wadham College, Oxford, he worked as a school teacher until he established a reputation as a lyric poet with *Dublin Days* (1921), *The Lowery Road* (1923), and other volumes. He also wrote novels, including the macabre *Dewer Rides* (1929), set on Dartmoor, and *Deliverance* (1955). His collection of short stories, *Travellers*, won the James Tait Black Memorial Prize in 1945. 📖 *Green Memory* (1961)

Strong, Sir Roy Colin 1935–
English art historian and museum director
Born in London and educated at Queen Mary College, London, and at the Warburg Institute, London, he became assistant keeper at the National Portrait Gallery, London, in 1959, then its director in 1967. He was also director of the Victoria and Albert Museum, London (1974–87) and has published books on art, literature and gardens, most recently *The Tudor and Stuart Monarchy* (2 vols, 1995) and *The Roy Strong Diaries 1967–87* (1997). He was knighted in 1982.

Strossmayer, Josip Juraj 1815–1905
Croatian politician, prelate and man of letters
As leader of the Croatian National Party, he defended Croatian interests by pursuing a course of compromise and tactical opportunism towards Vienna. A passionate believer in South Slav unity, he developed the Illyrism of **Ljudevit Gaj** and is considered the intellectual founder of Croatian Yugoslavism.

Stroud, William 1860–1938
English physicist and inventor
He was born in Bristol. From 1885 to 1909 he was Cavendish Professor of Physics at Leeds, where began his long association with **Archibald Barr**, with whom he invented range finders and founded Barr Stroud Ltd (1931), a firm of scientific instrument makers.

Strozzi, Filippo, the Elder 1428–91
Florentine banker
He was banished by the **Medici** to Sicily but returned to Florence in 1466, where he began building the famous Palazzo Strozzi in 1489.

Strozzi, Piero 1510–58
Italian soldier
The son of Filippo Strozzi, the Younger (1489–1538), he fought the **Medici**, escaped to France and was made a Marshal of France by **Henri II** in 1556 after campaigns in Italy. He found out the weaknesses of the defences of Calais before its capture by Francis, 2nd Duke of **Guise** in 1558, and was killed at the Siege of Thionville.

Strube, Sidney 1891–1956
English cartoonist
Born in London, he was apprenticed as a designer of overmantels, and learned cartooning from the **John Hassall** School, selling his first to *The Conservative and Unionist* (1909). After supplying a weekly cartoon to *Throne and Country*, he joined the *Daily Express* as staff cartoonist (1910–46). Among his many characters, the most popular was his 'Little Man'.

Struther, Jan, *pseudonym of* Joyce Anstruther Placzek, *née* Anstruther 1901–53
English writer

Stuart or Stewart, Prince Charles Edward, *known as* the Young Pretender and Bonnie Prince Charlie 1720–88
Claimant to the throne of England and Scotland

Charles Edward Stuart was the elder son of **James Francis Stuart**, the Old Pretender, and grandson of **James VII and II**. He was born and educated in Rome, where he became the centre of Jacobite hopes. In 1744 he went to France to head the projected invasion of England, but was delayed in France for over a year by storms and the threat of the British fleet. In July 1745 he landed with seven followers at Eriskay in the Hebrides, and on 19 August he raised his father's standard in Glenfinnan.

The clansmen flocked to his support. Edinburgh surrendered, but the castle held out; and Charles kept court at Holyroodhouse, the palace of his ancestors. His army won a victory over Sir **John Cope** at Prestonpans (21 September), and on 1 November he left for London at the head of 6,500 men. He took Carlisle and advanced as far as Derby. Londoners became alarmed, with the cream of the British army engaged on the Continent. However, Charles was persuaded against his will to turn back because of lack of support in England, and although he won a further victory against the government forces at Falkirk on 17 January 1746, he suffered a crushing defeat at the hands of the Duke of **Cumberland**'s troops at Culloden Moor on 16 April.

The rising was ruthlessly suppressed, and Charles was hunted in the highlands and islands for five months with a price of £30,000 on his head, but no one betrayed him. He was helped by **Flora Macdonald** when, disguised as her maid 'Betty Burke', he crossed to Portree in June 1746. He landed in Brittany on 29 September, and was given hospitality at the French court until the Peace of Aix-la-Chapelle (1748) required his expulsion from France.

He made two or three secret visits to London between 1750 and 1760, even declaring himself a Protestant. He assumed the title of Charles III of Great Britain and retired to Florence, where he married in 1772 Louisa, Countess of **Albany**, but the marriage was later dissolved. He had a daughter, Charlotte (1753–89), by his mistress Clementina Walkinshaw, whom he created Duchess of Albany. He died in Rome and was buried at Frascati, later at St Peter's.

📖 Margaret Forster, *The Rash Adventurer* (1973); David Daiches, *Charles Edward Stuart* (1973); John Prebble, *Culloden* (1961).

She was born in London and in 1948 married Adolf Kurt Placzek. Her most successful creation was 'Mrs Miniver', whose activities, first narrated in articles in *The Times*, became the subject of one of the most popular films of World War II.

Struve, Otto 1897–1963
US astronomer

Born in Kharkov, Ukraine, Russia, the grandson of Otto Wilhelm Struve, he was educated at the University of Kharkov, but in 1919 left Russia after the defeat of the anti-revolutionary forces. He was offered a post at the Yerkes Observatory in 1921, where in 1932 he was appointed director. In 1939 he founded the McDonald Observatory of the University of Texas and was director of the Leuschner Observatory at the University of California from 1950. He was also the first director of the National Radio Astronomy Observatory (1959–62), and held an appointment at the Princeton Institute for Advanced Studies. Struve performed an immense volume of observational work on stars of various types, on the interstellar medium and on gaseous nebulae. He was awarded the gold medal of the Royal Astronomical Society in 1944, and was president of the International Astronomical Union from 1952 to 1955.

Struve, Otto Wilhelm 1819–1905
Russian astronomer

Born in Dorpat (now Tartu), the son of **Wilhelm Struve**, director of Dorpat Observatory, he went to the University of Dorpat, where he studied under his father and became assistant at the Pulkova Observatory on his father's appointment as its director in 1839. He remained on the staff of the Pulkova Observatory for the rest of his working life, first as assistant (1839–45), then as assistant director (1845–62) and as director in succession to his father (1862–89). Continuing his father's research on double stars, he discovered 500 new pairs. His own most important studies were his determination of the constant of precession and of the solar motion through space (1841), for which he was awarded the gold medal of the Royal Astronomical Society in 1850. He took part in international projects such as the transits of Venus (1874), for which he organized 31 expeditions within and beyond the Russian empire. The Struve dynasty of astronomers

included Otto's sons, (Karl) Hermann (1854–1920), who also received the gold medal of the Royal Astronomical Society (1903) and became director of the Königsberg (1895–1904) and the Berlin-Babelsberg (1904–20) observatories, and (Gustav Wilhelm) Ludwig (1858–1920), director of Kharkov Observatory (1897–1919) and father of the second **Otto Struve**.

Struve, Pyotr Bernhardovich 1870–1944
Russian political economist

He was born in Perm. As a leading Marxist he wrote *Critical Observations on the Problem of Russia's Economic Development* (1894), which was attacked by **Lenin** for its 'revisionism'. He edited several political magazines with Liberal tendencies, was professor at the St Petersburg Polytechnic (1907–17) and was closely connected with the 'White' movement in South Russia after the Revolution. After 1925 he lived in exile in Belgrade and Paris, where he died during the Nazi occupation. His principal work is *Economy and Price* (1913–16). He was the grandson of **Wilhelm Struve**.

Struve, (Friedrich Georg) Wilhelm 1793–1864
Russian astronomer

Born in Altona, near Hamburg, Germany, he studied at the University of Dorpat (now Tartu) in Estonia (then part of the Russian empire) and he was later appointed Professor of Mathematics and Astronomy there (1816–39), also becoming director of Dorpat Observatory in 1818. At Dorpat he carried out a major programme of double star observations, published in a fundamental catalogue of 3,112 double stars entitled *Micrometria Mensurae* (1837). In 1837 he also measured the parallax of the star Vega. In 1835 he was summoned by the Russian Emperor **Nicholas I** to superintend the building and equipping of a new observatory at Pulkova, near St Petersburg. Struve's astronomical research at Pulkova included work on the structure of the Milky Way (1847). He also supervised a huge geodetic survey, completed in 1860, extending from the Baltic Sea to the Caucasus Mountains along an arc of meridian through Dorpat. In 1862 he handed over the directorship of Pulkova to his son and assistant, **Otto Wilhelm Struve**. He was awarded the gold medal of the Royal Astronomical Society in 1827 for his early work on double stars.

Strydom, Johannes Gerhardus See **Strijdom, Johannes Gerhardus**

Stuart See also **Stewart**

Stuart, Prince Charles Edward
See panel p1772

Stuart or **Stewart, Prince James Francis Edward**, *known as* **the Old Pretender** 1688–1766
Claimant to the throne of Great Britain
The only son of **James VII and II** and his second wife, **Mary of Modena**, he was born at St James's Palace, London. Six months later, he was taken by his fugitive mother to St Germain, where, on his father's death (1701), he was proclaimed his successor as **James III**. His attempt to land in Scotland (1708) failed and he returned to France to serve with the French in the Low Countries, distinguishing himself at Malplaquet (1709). He refused to renounce his Catholicism in order to be declared heir to Queen **Anne**. During John Erskine, Earl of **Mar**'s Jacobite rebellion, he landed at Peterhead (1715), but left six weeks later. Unable to return to France, he spent most of the rest of his life in Rome. In 1719 he had married Princess Clementina Sobieski (1702–35), who bore him two sons before retiring to a nunnery (1724).

Stuart, Gilbert Charles 1755–1828
US painter
Born in North Kingstown, Rhode Island, he travelled to Edinburgh (1772) but soon returned to America and began to paint portraits at Newport. In 1775 he went to London, where he studied under **Benjamin West** and became a fashionable portrait painter in the manner of Sir **Joshua Reynolds**. In 1792 he again returned to the USA, and painted portraits of **Thomas Jefferson**, **James Madison**, **John Adams** and 124 of **George Washington**, including that which appears on the one dollar bill, and the so-called *Athenaeum* head (Museum of Fine Art, Boston). With **John Singleton Copley** he was regarded as a pioneer of classical American portraiture.

Stuart, Henry Benedict Maria Clement, Duke of York 1725–1807
Scottish cardinal
Born in Rome, he was the brother of Prince **Charles Edward Stuart** and the last of the Stuarts. After the failure of the 1745 Rising he became a cardinal and priest, and in 1761 Bishop of Frascati. He enjoyed, through the favour of the French court, the revenues of two rich abbeys, as well as a Spanish pension. The French Revolution stripped him of his fortune, and he had to take refuge in Venice for three years. In 1800, **George III** granted him a pension of £4,000. The crown jewels, carried off by **James VII and II**, were bequeathed by him to **George IV**, then Prince of Wales.

Stuart, James Ewell Brown, *known as* **Jeb Stuart** 1833–64
US Confederate soldier
Born in Patrick Country, Virginia, he graduated from West Point in 1854 and served in the US cavalry in Texas and Kansas, resigning his commission at the outbreak of the Civil War in 1861. He became a valued intelligence officer in the Confederate army, and the Confederacy's best-known cavalry commander, scouting Union forces of General **George McClellan** and performing brilliantly in Pennsylvania, at Fredericksburg and Chancellorsville, and in the Wilderness Campaign. He was criticized at the Battle of Gettysburg, however, for arriving too late because he was off on a raid. He was mortally wounded at Yellow Tavern.

Stuart, John McDouall 1815–66
Australian explorer
Born in Dysart, Fife, Scotland, he was educated at the Scottish Naval and Military Academy, Edinburgh. As a draughtsman, he accompanied Captain Charles Sturt (1795–1869) on an expedition to central Australia (1844–45). Between 1855 and 1862 he made six expeditions to the interior and reached the 'inland sea', Lake Eyre. He made three attempts to cross Australia from south to north, and on the first reached the geographical centre and discovered the Finke River and the MacDonnell Ranges. On his third attempt he left Adelaide in October 1861 and reached the northern coast in July 1862. Mount Stuart is named after him.

Stubbes or **Stubbe, John** c.1541–1591
English Puritan pamphleteer
He was born in Norfolk. The author of an answer to Cardinal **William Allen**'s *Defence of the English Catholics*, he also wrote *The Discoverie of a Gaping Gulf* (1579), against the marriage of **Elizabeth I** to the Duke of Anjou, for which he and his printer had their right hands struck off. His kinsman Philip Stubbes (d.1593) was also a Puritan pamphleteer, and wrote *Anatomie of Abuses* (1583), a vehement denunciation of the luxury of the times.

Stubbs, George 1724–1806
English painter and etcher
Born in Liverpool, he became the most famous and original animal painter of his time. He was almost entirely self-taught. He specialized in horses, of which he had a thorough anatomical knowledge (he studied anatomy in York and in 1766 published his *Anatomy of the Horse*, for which he engraved his own plates), but also painted portraits, conversation pieces and rural scenes such as *Reapers* (1785, Tate Gallery, London). His pictures of racehorses are distinguished from other animal paintings by masterly composition, as in *Whistlejacket* (1762, National Gallery, London), and a feeling for atmosphere, as in *Hambletonian* (1800, Mountstewart, Northern Ireland). He often painted wild animals, especially horses frightened by lions, and experimented with enamel, as in *A Lion Devouring a Horse* (1769, Tate). Around 1775 he met **Josiah Wedgwood**, whose Etruria kilns provided the plaques for the enamelled works. 📖 Judy Egerton, *George Stubbs, Anatomist and Animal Painter* (1976)

Stubbs, William 1825–1901
English churchman and historian
Born in Knaresborough, Yorkshire, he studied at Christ Church, Oxford, and became a Fellow of Trinity, vicar of Navestock, Essex (1850), diocesan inspector of schools (1860), Regius Professor of Modern History at Oxford (1866), rector of Cholderton, Wiltshire (1875), a canon of St Paul's (1879), Bishop of Chester (1884) and then of Oxford (1889). Among his works are *Registrum Sacrum Anglicanum*, on the Episcopal succession in England (1858), the monumental three-volume *Constitutional History of England*, down to 1485 (1874–78), and *The Early Plantagenets* (1876). He also began a collection of *British Councils and Ecclesiastical Documents* (1869–78).

Stuckenberg, Viggo 1863–1905
Danish poet
Born in Copenhagen, he was an important figure in the lyrical revival of the 1890s. His works include *Fagre Ord* (1895) and *Flyvende Sommer* (1898).

Studdy, George Edward 1878–1948
English cartoonist
Born in Devon, he tried both engineering and stock-broking before creating the comic strips *Professor Helpemon* and *Bob the Navvy* for *Big Budget* (1903). Graduating to the glossy weekly, *Sketch*, he executed several semi-animated cartoon films for Gaumont, *Studdy's War Studies* (1915). After World War I he began specializing in dog cartoons, from which his Bonzo the Dog character emerged. In

1924 he produced the first fully animated cartoon film series made in England (*Bonzo*: 26 films). He drew a *Bonzo* strip for *Titbits* (1926), and a daily and Sunday strip for US syndication by King Features.

Stukeley, William, *known as* the Arch-Druid
1687–1765
British antiquary

Born in Holbeach, Lincolnshire, and educated at Cambridge, he helped to found the Society of Antiquaries (1718). He took orders in 1729, and in 1747 became a London rector. His 20 works (1720–26) include records of his valuable and objective fieldwork at Stonehenge and Avebury, but are marred by his later speculations relating them to the Druids. His account of his travels round Great Britain was published in *Itinerarium Curiosum* (1724).

Sturdee, Sir Frederick Charles Doveton, 1st Baronet 1859–1925
English naval commander

He joined the navy in 1871. As rear admiral in 1908, he commanded the *Invincible* in the action which wiped out the German squadron under Graf von Spee off the Falkland Islands in 1914. Thereafter he served with the Grand Fleet, including the Battle of Jutland (1916). In 1921 he was promoted Admiral of the Fleet (1921).

Sture, Sten, the Elder c.1440–1503
Swedish regent

On the death of his uncle, King Karl VIII Knutsson (1470), who had opposed the Kalmar Union and attempts to keep all the Scandinavian realms under one (Danish) monarch, he proclaimed himself regent. He strengthened his position by defeating his opponents in the Swedish Council and the Danish King Kristian I at Brunkeberg (1471), and ruled for 27 years. In 1497 King Hans of Denmark and Norway resumed the struggle successfully and Sten relinquished power, although he served as Hans's court master. In 1501 the Swedes rebelled against the Danes and Sten became regent again until his death. Older Swedish histories depicted him as a selfless patriot fighting for Sweden's independence, but more recent studies present him as a ruthless opportunist with a driving personal ambition.

Sturge, Joseph 1794–1859
English Quaker philanthropist and reformer

Born in Elberton, Gloucestershire, he was a prosperous grain merchant in Birmingham. He became a prominent campaigner against slavery in the British West Indies, which he helped to abolish in 1837. In 1841 he toured the US slave states with John Greenleaf Whittier, and later campaigned for the repeal of the Corn Laws, the extension of adult suffrage, and Chartism.

Sturgeon, William 1783–1850
English scientist

Born in Whittington, North Lancashire, he became a shoemaker's apprentice, and in 1825 constructed the first practical electromagnet. This was followed by the first moving-coil galvanometer (1836) and various electromagnetic machines. His *Annals of Electricity* (1836) was the first journal of its kind in Britain.

Sturges, Preston, *originally* Edmund Preston Biden 1898–1959
US screenwriter, film director and inventor

Born in Chicago, and educated in the USA and Europe, he enlisted in the Air Corps in 1917 and later worked in the cosmetics industry, inventing a 'kiss-proof' lipstick, before making his mark as a dramatist (from 1927). He later moved to Hollywood and wrote screenplays such as *The Power and the Glory* (1933) and *The Good Fairy* (1935). A director from 1940, he enjoyed a brief run of successes with inventive, freewheeling comedies that combined wit, slapstick and social concerns. His notable films include *The Lady Eve* (1941), *Sullivan's Travels* (1941) and *Hail, the Conquering Hero* (1944). Commercial success eluded him thereafter and he spent his last ten years in Paris, directing one final film *Les Carnets du Major Thompson* (1955, US title *The French They Are a Funny Race*, UK title *The Diary of Major Thompson*). He received an Academy Award for the script of *The Great McGinty* (1940) and a posthumous Laurel award for achievement in 1974 from the Writer's Guild of America.

Sturluson, Snorri 1179–1241
Icelandic chieftain and historian

He was born in Hvammur in western Iceland and fostered at Oddi by the powerful Jón Loptsson. He acquired the estates of Borg (where the saga hero Egill Skallagrímsson had lived) and Reykholt. He was Lawspeaker of the Althing for 15 years from 1215 and became deeply involved in the turbulent politics of Iceland in the period which led to its loss of independence, first as an ally of King Haakon IV Haakonsson of Norway and then as his opponent. He was assassinated at Reykholt by one of the king's followers. He wrote two of the most important works of Icelandic literature, the *Prose Edda*, from which much of our knowledge of the Old Norse religion and myth derives, and *Heimskringla*, a history of the early kings of Norway.

Sturm, (Jacques) Charles François 1803–55
French mathematician

Born in Geneva, Switzerland, he taught in Paris, was elected to the Académie Française (1836), and became Professor of Mathematics at the École Polytechnique (1838). He discovered the theorem named after him concerning the location of the roots of a polynomial equation. He also did important work on linear differential equations. In 1826 he measured the velocity of sound in water by means of a bell submerged in Lake Geneva.

Sturm, Johannes 1507–89
German educationist

Born in Schleiden, near Aix-la-Chapelle, he was educated at the Liège school of the Brethren of the Common Life and at Louvain University. He went to Paris in 1530 and lectured on Cicero. He favoured the Reformation, and in 1536 was invited by Strasbourg to reorganize the education of the town. He took a prominent part both in religion and politics, siding with Huldreich Zwingli against Martin Luther, and he was sent on missions to France, England and Denmark. Through his efforts, Strasbourg became a great educational centre. In 1538 a gymnasium was established, with Sturm as its rector, and in 1564 an academy, the two together supplying a complete course of instruction. In 1581 he was driven from Strasbourg by Lutheran intolerance, but was eventually permitted to return.

Sturtevant, Alfred Henry 1891–1970
US geneticist

Born in Jacksonville, Illinois, he studied genetics under Thomas Hunt Morgan at Columbia University, and from 1928 spent his career at the California Institute of Technology, as Professor of Genetics (1928–47) and Professor of Biology (1947–62). As an undergraduate he drew up the first chromosome map of the fruit-fly *Drosophila* in 1911, based on Morgan's suggestion that genes which are far apart on the same chromosome are more likely to be separated by the mechanism of recombination or 'crossing-over'. Later, as part of Morgan's 'fly room' group, he provided the mathematical background for genetic mapping experiments on *Drosophila*. Together with Morgan, Hermann Müller and C B Bridges, he established the basis for the chromosomal theory of heredity in *The Mechanism of Mendelian Inheritance* (1915). He also wrote *A History of Genetics* (1965).

Stuyvesant, Peter 1592–1672
Dutch colonialist

Born in Scherpenzeel, he joined the Dutch West India Company, became Governor of Curaçao, losing a leg in the attack on St Martin (1644), then directed the colony of New Netherland (1647–64). A vigorous but arbitrary ruler, a rigid Sabbatarian and an opponent of political and religious freedom, he nevertheless did much for the commercial prosperity of New Amsterdam (later New York City) until his reluctant surrender to the English (1664).

Styron, William 1925–
US novelist

Born in Newport News, Virginia, he graduated from Duke University in Durham, North Carolina in 1947. His first novel, *Lie Down in Darkness*, appeared in 1951. *Set This House on Fire* (1960) portrayed Americans in Europe after the war and was hugely successful in France. Unafraid of controversial topics, he has tackled racism in *The Confessions of Nat Turner* (1967), and the fate of Holocaust survivors in *Sophie's Choice* (1979). Subsequent works include *This Quiet Dust* (1982), *Darkness Visible: A Memoir of Madness* (1990), which chronicled his struggle with clinical depression, and *A Tidewater Morning* (1993). In 1987 he became a member of the American Academy of Arts and Letters.

Suárez, Adolfo 1932–
Spanish politician

A high-ranking Francoist bureaucrat who owed much to his good looks, great charm and single-minded ambition, he was appointed Prime Minister in 1976. He carried out a swift transition from the Franco dictatorship to democracy, the elections of 1977 proving a personal triumph. Backed by the newly established centrist party, the UCD, he undertook the creation of the new democratic state. Having embodied consensual change in the Constitution of 1978, after the 1979 elections economic and regional problems, divisions within both the government and UCD, as well as his own secretiveness and authoritarian style led to his resignation (1981). The following year he founded the CDS (Democratic and Social Centre Party), which has won little support.

Suárez, Francisco de 1548–1617
Spanish philosopher and theologian

Born in Granada, he entered the Society of Jesus (1564), was ordained (1572), taught theology at Segovia, Valladolid, Rome, Alcalá, Salamanca and Coimbra, and is considered by many to be the greatest scholastic philosopher after Aquinas. His *Disputationes Metaphysicae* was a very influential text in Catholic, and some Protestant, universities in the 17th and 18th centuries, and both Descartes and Leibniz studied it closely. He also wrote important studies in political theory, the *Tractatus de Legibus ac Deo Legislatore* (1612) which foreshadows the modern doctrine of international law, and the *Defensio Fidei Catholicae et Apostolicae adversus Anglicanae Sectae Errores* (1613) condemning the divine-right theories of kingship of James VI and I.

Subbotin, Mikhail Fyodorovich 1893–1966
Russian astronomer and mathematician

Born in Ostrolenka, Lomzhinsk Province (now in Poland), he graduated from Warsaw and Rostov-on-Don universities. He then worked in the State Astrophysical Institute (1922–30), before moving to Leningrad (now St Petersburg) University where he became director of the Leningrad Astronomical Institute in 1942. He is best known for his work on celestial mechanics and theoretical astronomy.

Suchet, David 1946–
English actor

Born in London, he trained at The London Academy of Music and Dramatic Art and acted extensively with the Royal Shakespeare Company (1973–79), playing the roles of the Fool in *Lear* (UK 1974, US 1975), Shylock in *The Merchant of Venice* (1978) and Angelo in *Measure for Measure* (1979), among others. He appeared on television as Edward Teller in *Oppenheimer* (1980), the title role in *Blott on the Landscape* (1985) and Inspector Japp in *Thirteen at Dinner* (1985), before playing the Belgian detective Hercules Poirot in *Agatha Christie's Poirot* (1989–97) and Adolf Verloc in *The Secret Agent* (1992). He was in the films *The Falcon and the Snowman* (1984), *Greystoke: The Legend of Tarzan, Lord of the Apes* (1984), *Harry and the Hendersons* (1987) and *A World Apart* (1988).

Suchet, Louis Gabriel, Duc d'Albufera da Valencia 1770–1826
French general

Born in Lyons, he fought in Italy and Egypt and was made a general. He checked an Austrian invasion of the south of France (1800), took part in the campaigns against Austria (1805) and Prussia (1806), and, as generalissimo of the French army in Aragon, reduced the province to submission, defeating Admiral Robert Blake outside Saragossa and again at Belchite. He captured Tortosa in 1811, in 1812 he destroyed Blake's army at Sagunto, and by his capture of Valencia earned the title of Duc d'Albufera da Valencia. He was created a peer of France by Louis XVIII, but joined Napoleon I on his return from Elba. Deprived of his peerage after Waterloo (1815), he did not return to court until 1819.

Suckling, Sir John 1609–42
English poet and dramatist

He was born in Whitton, Middlesex and educated at Trinity College, Cambridge. He lived at court in London, but involvement in political intrigue led him to flee the country, and he died (it is said by his own hand) in Paris. His plays include *Aglaura* (1637), and his major lyrics are included in the posthumously published *Fragmenta Aurea* (1646). It contains what is probably his most famous work, 'Why So Pale and Wan, Fond Lover?' He is credited by John Aubrey with having invented 'the game of Cribbidge' [sic].

Sucksdorff, Arne E 1917–
Swedish film director

Born in Stockholm, he made a series of prominent nature films which although poetic, even magical, at times, emphasize the cruel and dramatic aspects of animal life. An acknowledged master of Swedish nature cinematography in the 1940s, among his best documentaries are *Människor i stad* (1947, *Rhythm of a City*) about Stockholm, *En kluven värld* (1948, *A Divided World*) and *Indisk by* (1951, *Indian Village*). His feature films include stories with exotic settings, for instance *En djungelsaga* (1957, *A Jungle Story*) and *Mitt hem är Copacabana* (1965, *Home in Copacabana*, filmed in Rio de Janeiro's slum district), but the best of them remains *Det stora äventyret* (1953, *The Great Adventure*), a touching story of two Swedish boys learning by experience that animals (here a baby otter) must remain in their natural habitat.

Sucre, Antonio José de 1793–1830
South American soldier, statesman and revolutionary

Born in Cumana, Venezuela, he was Símon Bolívar's lieutenant and first President (1826) of Bolivia, which he freed from Spanish rule by the victory of Aya Cucho (1824). He resigned after a rebellion in 1828. He fought for

Colombia, winning the Battle of Giron (1829) and was assassinated on his way home from the Colombian Congress at Bogotá, of which he had been president. Sucre, the judicial capital of Bolivia, is named after him. 📖 Guillermo Sherwell, *Antonio José de Sucre, Hero and Martyr of American Independence* (1924)

Sudermann, Hermann 1857–1928
German dramatist and novelist

Born in Matzicken, East Prussia, he worked for a chemist before studying at the University of Königsberg. He worked as a journalist, then wrote a succession of skilful, if superficial, realist plays, *Die Ehre* (1889, 'Honour'), *Sodoms Ende* (1891, 'The Fall of Sodom'), *Heimat* (1893, Eng trans *Magda*, 1896), and others. His novels were equally successful, and include *Frau Sorge* (1887, Eng trans *Dame Care*, 1891), *Der Katzensteg* (1890, Eng trans *Regine*, 1894) and *Es war* (1894, Eng trans *The Undying Past*, 1906). 📖 I Leux, *Hermann Sudermann* (1931)

Su Dongpo (Su Tung-p'o), *pseudonym of* Su Shi (Su Shih) 1036–1101
Chinese painter, calligrapher, poet, philosopher and politician

He was born in Mei-shan, now in Sichuan (Szechwan) province, into a family of peasant origins, which had only recently moved into the mandarinate. Su Dongpo's father as well as his own son were literati, collectively known as 'the three Su'. Su Dongpo is almost unanimously referred to as one of the most prominent men of his time, a 'universal genius'. Excelling in all branches of the arts, he epitomized the cultural ideal of 11th-century Chinese humanism, and was briefly Prime Minister before being exiled for holding views too aesthetically-oriented and humanistic to serve the needs of the pragmatic Sung dynasty. Much of Chinese aesthetics derives from his writings and from his formulation of *wen ren hua* (literati painting). Su Dongpo believed that the painter must spiritually identify with the object of his painting: 'To paint the bamboo, it is necessary to have it entirely within yourself.' 📖 Lin Yutang, *The Gay Genius* (1947)

Sue, (Marie Joseph) Eugène 1804–57
French novelist

He was born in Paris, and served as a surgeon in Spain (1823) and at Navarino Bay (1827). He wrote a large number of Byronic novels, many of which were dramatized, idealizing the poor to the point of melodramatic absurdity, but they were nevertheless highly successful at the time. They had a profound influence on **Victor Hugo**, whose *Les Misérables* has much in common with Sue's *Les Mystères de Paris* (1843). Other novels include *Le Juif errant* (1845, 'The Wandering Jew'), *Les Sept péchés capitaux* (1849, 'The Seven Deadly Sins') and *Les Mystères du peuple* (1849, 'Mysteries of the People'), which was condemned as immoral and seditious. A republican deputy, he was driven into exile in 1851. 📖 E de Mirecourt, *Eugène Sue* (1855)

Suess, Eduard 1831–1914
Austrian geologist

Born in London, England, he was the son of a German wool merchant of Jewish extraction. His parents moved to Prague (1843) and then to Vienna (1845) where, after a spell as an assistant in the geological department of the Royal Natural History Museum (1851–57), he rose to great eminence at the university (1857–1901), becoming assistant Professor and Professor of Geology. The greater part of his life was devoted to the study of the evolution of the features of the Earth's surface, particularly the problem of mountain building. He also focused attention on the volcanic islands and associated deep-sea trenches in the Pacific Ocean. His theory that there had once been a great supercontinent made up of the present southern continents was a forerunner of modern theories of continental drift. His four-volume book *Das Antlitz der Erde*

(1885–1909, Eng trans *The Face of the Earth*, 1904–25) was his most important contribution, ranking alongside Sir **Charles Lyell**'s *Principles of Geology* and **Charles Darwin**'s *Origin of Species*. A man of varied interests and enthusiasms, he was a Radical politician, an economist, an educationist and a geographer, and sat in the Austrian Lower House.

Suetonius, *in full* Gaius Suetonius Tranquillus c.69–c.140AD
Roman biographer and antiquary

He was for a time a member of the Imperial service (119–c.122AD) and secretary to the Emperor **Hadrian**. His best-known work is his *Lives of the Caesars* (from **Julius Caesar** to **Domitian**). There survive also short biographies of **Virgil** and other Roman poets. The *De Vita Caesarum* (Eng trans *The Twelve Caesars* by **Robert Graves**, 1957) is an important historical source (though not always dependable without corroboration) and benefit from his access to the Imperial archives and his contact with eye-witnesses. His style is brisk and straightforward, but he evidently enjoyed the numerous scandalous anecdotes he recorded. 📖 Andrew Wallace-Hadrill, *Suetonius: The Scholar and his Caesars* (1983)

Sueur, Eustache Le See **Le Sueur, Eustache**

Sueur, Hubert Le See **Le Sueur, Hubert**

Suffolk, 1st Duke of See **Brandon, Charles**

Suffren de Saint Tropez, Pierre André de 1729–88
French naval commander

He was born in Saint Canat, and served six years in Malta amongst the Knights Hospitallers. He was captured in Admiral **Boscawen**'s destruction of the Toulon fleet (1759), took part in the bombardment of Sallee (1765), was in Malta for four years, and returned to France in 1772. In 1781 he was in command of a French squadron for service in the Indian Ocean, and captured Trincomalee. Returning to Paris in 1784, he was received as one of France's greatest admirals.

Sugar, Alan Michael 1947–
English entrepreneur

Born in London, he was educated at Brooke House School, London. He founded AMSTRAD (the name is a contraction of Alan M Sugar Trading) in 1968. The company expanded rapidly during the personal-computer boom of the 1980s, but ran into problems with the slump at the end of that decade, losing, at one stage, £1 million per week. As a result, Sugar bought the company back into his own private ownership. He has been chairman of Tottenham Hotspur football club since 1991.

Suger c.1081–1151
French prelate and politician

Born near Paris, he was educated at the abbey of St Denis. As abbot of St Denis from 1122, he reformed the abbey and rebuilt its church in the first example of the Gothic style. **Louis VI** and **Louis VII** both employed him on diplomatic missions, and during Louis VII's absence on the Second Crusade, Suger served as regent, displaying particular skills in financial administration. His *Life of Louis VI* is valuable for its contemporary view of the time.

Suggia, Guilhermina 1888–1950
Portuguese cellist

Born in Oporto, she became a member of the Oporto City Orchestra at the age of 12. Aided by a royal grant, she subsequently studied at Leipzig and under **Pablo Casals**, whom she married in 1906. After extensive concert tours she settled in England in 1914, last appearing in public at the 1949 Edinburgh Festival.

Süleyman the Magnificent 1494–1566
Ottoman emperor, one of the greatest of the Ottoman sultans

Süleyman succeeded his father **Selim I** in 1520 at a time when the empire was strong both on land and at sea. He himself was an experienced soldier and administrator, and was known to his own people as *Kanuni*, the 'Lawgiver'. He instituted a programme of internal reforms, aimed at securing higher standards of justice and administration and ensuring freedom of religion throughout the empire. He was an energetic patron of the arts, and literature as well as architecture and the visual arts flourished in Istanbul during his rule.

He extended the bounds of his empire both to the east and west, capturing Belgrade in 1521 and Rhodes (from the Knights of St John) in 1522, and defeating the Hungarians in 1526. His advance to the west was finally checked in 1529 at the gates of Vienna, which he failed to take after a hard siege. In the east, he won territory from the Persians, made territorial gains in North Africa as far as Morocco, and took Aden on the Red Sea. Under **Barbarossa** the Ottoman fleet was able to establish naval supremacy in the eastern Mediterranean and Aegean while also challenging the Portuguese in the east. They twice failed to capture Malta, but annexed Cyprus in 1570.

Constant campaigning led Süleyman to withdraw increasingly from the active direction of government at home, a tendency which under his successors greatly weakened the empire in the long term. Nevertheless during his reign Ottoman power abroad and Ottoman institutions and culture at home reached the peak of their achievement.

📖 N Itzkowitz, *Ottoman Empire and Islamic Tradition* (1972); H Inalcik, *The Ottoman Empire: The Classical Age 1300–1600* (1973); Robert Merriman, *Suleiman the Magnificent, 1520–66* (1944).

Suharto or Soeharto, Thojib N J 1921–
Indonesian soldier and statesman

Born in Kemusu Argamulja, Java, he was educated for service in the Dutch colonial army. In 1943 he was given command of the Japanese-sponsored Indonesian army and in 1965 he became Indonesia's army Chief of Staff. He became a major political figure when the policies of President **Sukarno** led to a threat of civil war in 1965 and 1966, and assumed executive power in 1967, ordering the mass arrest and internment of alleged Communists. He became President in 1968, thereafter being re-elected to office every five years. Although 10 political parties contested the parliamentary elections of 1971, all criticism of the government was banned. Suharto's virtual dictatorship saw an improvement in Indonesia's relations with her neighbours in South-East Asia and the republic's return to membership of the United Nations. By 1970 the currency had stabilized and both the agricultural yield and the output of oil had increased. In 1988 Suharto was re-elected and he instituted a New Order policy to revolutionize the country's economy. However, his period in office was threatened by Islamic fundamentalist extremists and by the long-running civil war in East Timor, and he was driven from power in 1998.

Suk, Joseph 1875–1935
Czech composer and violinist

Born in Křechaovice, he studied in Prague under **Antonín Dvořák**, whose daughter he married. He carried on his teacher's Romantic tradition through his violin *Fantaisie* (1903), the symphonic poem *Prague* (1904) and particularly his Second Symphony, *Asrael* (1905–06), in which he mourned the deaths of Dvořák and of his wife. He was for 40 years a member of the Czech Quartet and in 1922 became Professor of Composition at the Prague Conservatory.

Sukarno or Soekarno, Ahmed, *known as* Bung Karno 1902–70
Indonesian statesman

Born in Surabaya, Eastern Java, he was early identified with the movement for independence, forming the Partai National Indonesia in 1927. Imprisoned and exiled by the Dutch in Bandung (1929–31), he was freed by the Japanese (1942) and became the first President of the Indonesian Republic in 1945. His popularity with the people was gradually eroded as Indonesia suffered increasing internal chaos and poverty, while he and his government laid themselves open to charges of corruption. His protestations of political 'neutralism' were offset by his increasingly virulent anti-Western foreign policy. The abortive Communist coup of 1965 led to student riots and Congress criticism of Sukarno's alleged part in it, and the army eventually took over. Sukarno's absolute powers were gradually weakened until finally in 1967 General **Thojib Suharto** took complete control. He retired in 1968.
📖 John Hughes, *Sukarno: An Autobiography, as told to Cindy Adams* (1965)

Süleyman or Sulaiman II 1642–91
Ottoman sultan

The son of Ibrahim I, he was born in Constantinople (Istanbul), and in 1687 succeeded his deposed brother **Mehmet IV** after 46 years of confinement. He was defeated by the Austrians (1688), but from 1689 his Grand Vizier, **Mustafa Köprülü**, drove the Austrians out of Bulgaria, Serbia and Transylvania, and retook Belgrade. Köprülü also introduced numerous liberal reforms, but was killed in battle (1691).

Süleyman the Magnificent See panel above

Sulh, Taqi al-Din al- 1909–88
Lebanese Sunni politician

He was a fervent campaigner on behalf of the Arab peoples against any form of foreign interference in their affairs. Initially focusing on the way in which the Ottoman Turks had kept the Arab peoples in subjection, he turned his attentions to the French and British. A moderate who aimed at reconciliation between Christians and Muslims in Lebanon, Taqi al-Din, together with his brother Kazim, maintained that, although the Lebanese people were part of the great Arab nation, the regional peculiarities of Lebanon made the country's independence an essential concomitant of its peaceful development. Politically active throughout his life, he played a prominent role in the late 1960s and early 1970s, and was Prime Minister (1973–74).

Sulla, Lucius Cornelius, *also called* Felix ('Lucky') 138–78BC
Roman politician and dictator

His bitter feud with **Marius** began in Africa in 107BC during the Jugurthine War, when he induced the Mauretanian King Bocchus to surrender **Jugurtha**. In 88 he chose to lead his army against the state rather than surrender to Marius his command of the war against Mithridates. He defeated **Mithridates VI**, and on returning to Rome (83) civil war broke out again when he used his forces to defeat the Marians and secure his own (illegal) position. Appointed dictator in 82, he set about reforming the state, and enacted a number of measures to boost the authority of the Senate and reform the criminal courts. The cold-blooded ruthlessness of his dictatorship and the proscriptions were long remembered by later generations of Romans. He retired in 79.

Sullivan, Anne Mansfield See Macy, Anne Mansfield Sullivan

Sullivan, Sir Arthur Seymour 1842–1900
English composer

He was born in London, and studied music under William Sterndale Bennett and at the Leipzig Gewandhaus. Together with his friend George Grove he discovered the lost *Rosamunde* music by Schubert. He was organist and choirmaster of St Michael's, London, from 1861 to 1872, and became first Principal of the National Training College (1871), later the Royal College of Music. His association with the theatre, begun with his music to John Morton's *Box and Cox* (libretto by F C Burnand), was consolidated by his 18-year partnership with W S Gilbert, which produced the 14 comic 'Savoy' operas from 1871, including *HMS Pinafore* (1878), *The Pirates of Penzance* (1880), *Iolanthe* (1882), *The Mikado* (1885), *The Yeomen of the Guard* (1888) and *The Gondoliers* (1889). Sullivan also composed a *Te Deum* (1872), an opera, *Ivanhoe* (1891), cantatas, ballads and hymn-tunes. His best-known songs include 'Orpheus with his Lute', 'The Lost Chord', and the tune for the hymn 'Onward Christian Soldiers'. He was buried in St Paul's Cathedral.

Sullivan, Ed (ward Vincent) 1902–74
US newspaper columnist and broadcaster

Born in New York City, he became a reporter with the Port Chester *Daily Item* (1918–19), and worked as a sports writer and columnist for a variety of publications before becoming a syndicated Broadway gossip columnist based at the New York *Daily News* (1932–74). He was master of ceremonies for such theatrical events as the *Harvest Moon Ball* (1936–52) before moving into radio with *Ed Sullivan Entertains* (1942). Nationwide popularity followed as the host of the television variety show *Toast of the Town*, which was later renamed *The Ed Sullivan Show* and ran from 1948 to 1971. He also wrote books and screenplays, including the film *Big Town Czar* (1938).

Sullivan, Harry Stack 1892–1949
US psychiatrist and educator

He was born in Norwich, New York. His 'interpersonal theory' states that personality, social and cultural environment play an important role in personality development and in the mental health of an individual. A founder and president of the William Alanson White Foundation (1934–43) and the Washington School of Psychiatry (1936–47), he contributed to the understanding and treatment of schizophrenia.

Sullivan, Jim (James) 1903–77
Welsh rugby player

Born in Cardiff, he played rugby union for Cardiff before joining Wigan rugby league club in 1921. He kicked a world record 2,859 goals, including a record 22 in one game (against Flimby & Fothergill, 1925). He was player-coach of Wigan (1932–46), and later became coach to Rochdale Hornets and St Helens.

Sullivan, John 1740–95
American Revolutionary soldier and statesman

He was born in Somersworth, New Hampshire. A member of the Continental Congress, in the American Revolution (1775–83) he served as a major-general in the Siege of Boston (1775–76) and Staten Island (1777). He failed at the Siege of Newport (1778), and in 1779 fought against the Six Nations and won the Battle of Elmira, New York. He resigned his commission in 1779 and became Attorney-General of New Hampshire (1782–86), and later President of the state.

Sullivan, Louis Henry 1856–1924
US architect

Born in Boston, he studied at Massachusetts Institute of Technology and at the influential Paris atelier of Joseph Auguste-Emile Vaudremer (1829–1914), and won the New Exposition building contract (1886) with Dankmar Adler. He was one of the first to design skyscrapers, such as the Wainwright building in St Louis (1890–91) and the Carson store in Chicago (1899–1904). His experimental, functional skeleton constructions of skyscrapers and office blocks, particularly the Gage building and Stock Exchange, Chicago (with Adler), earned him the title 'Father of Modernism' and greatly influenced Frank Lloyd Wright and others. 📖 Hugh Morrison, *Louis Sullivan: Prophet of Modern Architecture* (1935)

Sully, Maximilien de Béthune, Duc de, *also known as* Baron de Rosny 1560–1641
French financier

The second son of the Huguenot Baron de Rosny, he was born in the château of Rosny near Mantes. He accompanied Henri of Navarre (the future Henri IV) in his flight from the French court (1576), took an active part in the war, and helped to decide the victory of Coutras (1587). At Ivry he captured the standard of Mayenne. He approved of the Henri's conversion to Roman Catholicism in 1572, but refused himself to become a Roman Catholic, and throughout the reign remained a trusted counsellor. His first task was the restoration of the economy after 30 years of civil war. Before his time the whole administration was an organized system of pillage; he made a tour through the provinces, examined the accounts, reduced exemptions from taxation and amassed 110 million livres' revenue in the Bastille. The arsenals and fleet were put into good order. He was instrumental in arranging Henri's marriage to Marie de Médicis (1600). In 1606 he was created Duc de Sully. After Henri's assassination (1610) he had to resign, but was presented by Marie de Médicis with 300,000 livres, and retired to his estates, Rosny and Villebon. 📖 David Buisseret, *Sully and the Growth of Centralized Government in France* (1968)

Sully, Thomas 1783–1872
US painter

Born in Horncastle, Lincolnshire, England, the son of actors, he and his family emigrated to Charleston, South Carolina, in 1792. After European travels he settled in Philadelphia in 1810. With a style influenced by Gilbert Stuart in the USA and Benjamin West and Sir Thomas Lawrence in England, he painted elegant, exquisitely coloured portraits and historical paintings. Subjects of his nearly 2,000 portraits include the Marquis de Lafayette, Thomas Jefferson, James Madison, Andrew Jackson, and Queen Victoria; his more than 500 historical works include *Washington Crossing the Delaware* (1818, Museum of Fine Arts, Boston).

Sully-Prudhomme, *pseudonym of* René François Armand Prudhomme 1839–1907
French poet and Nobel Prize winner

Born in Paris, he studied science and developed an interest in philosophy which underlies most of his poetical works. He became one of the best known of the Parnassian poets. His early *Stances et poèmes* (1865, 'Stanzas and Poems') was praised by Charles-Augustin Sainte-Beuve. Subsequent volumes include *Les Épreuves* (1866, 'Proofs'), *Croquis italiens* (1872, 'Sketches of Italy'), *Impressions de la guerre* (1872, 'Impressions of War'), *Les Destins* (1872, 'Destinies'), *La Révolte des fleurs* (1874, 'The Flowers' Revolution'), and the didactic poems *La Justice* (1878, 'Justice') and *Le Bonheur* (1888, 'Happiness'). Other works are a metrical translation of book one of Lucretius (new edn 1886) and his *Œuvres complètes* ('Complete

Works') which appeared between 1883 and 1908. He was awarded the first Nobel Prize for literature in 1901.
📖 P Flottes, *Sully-Prudhomme* (1930)

Sultan-Galiev, Mivza Said 1892–?1939
Tatar intellectual and politician
He joined the Bolsheviks in 1917 in his native Kazan and soon had an official post. Stalin welcomed him on to the commissariat of nationalities in 1920 as one of the few non-Russians and then had him arrested in 1923 for his dissident Islamic views. Freed, he continued to attempt to synthesize Islam and communism, preaching communism as a means of liberating his fellow non-Russian Muslims. He was rearrested in 1929 and disappeared. His name has been much revered among Muslims ever since.

Summers, (Alphonsus Joseph-Mary Augustus) Montague 1880–1948
English priest and writer
He wrote brilliantly on the theatre and drama of the Restoration and on other literary subjects, but his most important works are two major reference books on witchcraft, *The History of Witchcraft and Demonology* (1926) and *The Geography of Witchcraft* (1927).

Summerskill, Edith Clara Summerskill, Baroness 1901–80
English doctor and politician
Born in London and educated at King's College London, she shared a medical practice with her husband in London. She worked with the Socialist Medical Association, and became a member of Middlesex County Council (1934). From 1938 to 1955 she was Labour MP for Fulham West, continuing an unremitting fight for women's welfare on all issues, and often rousing great hostility. She became Under-Secretary to the Ministry of Food (1949), and was Chairman of the Labour Party (1954–55). She was created a life peeress in 1961.

Summerson, Sir John Newenham 1904–92
English architectural historian
Born in Darlington, near Durham, he became interested in architecture after a childhood visit to Riber Castle, Matlock, and was one of the first to make it a scholarly subject. His first teaching appointment was at Edinburgh College of Art (1929–30), and his many other posts include lecturer at the Architectural Association (1950–67), and professorships at Oxford (1958–59) and Cambridge (1966–67). Based at Sir John Soane's Museum where he was curator from 1945 to 1984, his many publications include *Georgian London* (1946), *Architecture in Britain 1530–1830* (1953) and the collection of essays *The Unromantic Castle* (1990). He was awarded the Royal Institute of British Architects Gold Medal for Architecture in 1976.

Sumner, Charles 1811–74
US politician
Born in Boston, he graduated at Harvard, was admitted to the Bar in 1834 and also studied jurisprudence in Europe (1837–40). He took little interest in politics until the threatened extensions of slavery over newly acquired territory. In 1848 he joined with others to form the Free Soil Party. Nominated for Congress, he was defeated by the Whig candidate but in 1851 was elected to the US Senate by the combined Free Soil and Democratic votes of the Massachusetts legislature, a post he held for life. Alone in the Senate as the uncompromising opponent of slavery, in 1856 he was struck on the head in the Senate chamber, by Preston S Brooks, a South Carolina member of Congress, and was incapacitated for nearly four years. The secession of the southern states left the Republican Party in full control of both houses of Congress and in 1861 Sumner was elected chairman of the Senate committee on foreign affairs. He supported the Reconstruction policies of the Radical Republicans, favoured the impeachment of President **Andrew Johnson**, and opposed President **Ulysses S Grant**'s project for the acquisition of San Domingo. His criticisms of Grant's administration created a rift with leading Republican politicians, which was deepened by his support of **Horace Greeley** as candidate for the presidency in 1872.

Sumner, James Batcheller 1887–1955
US biochemist and Nobel Prize winner
Born in Canton, Massachusetts, and educated at Harvard, he became assistant Professor (from 1914) and then Professor of Biochemistry (1929–55) at Cornell University, and director of the Laboratory of Enzyme Chemistry (1947–55). In 1926 he was first to crystallize an enzyme (urease), demonstrated its protein nature, and determined its kinetic and chemical properties. He raised and purified antibodies to urease (1933–34), and purified plant antibody-like globulins in 1938, thereby establishing a firm basis for the serological investigation of proteins. He also purified enzymes important for carrying out oxidative processes in the body and investigated the function of their non-protein components. He shared the 1946 Nobel Prize for chemistry with **John Northrop** and **Wendell Stanley**.

Sumner, John Andrew Hamilton, Viscount 1859–1934
English judge
Born in Manchester, he was educated at Manchester Grammar School and Balliol College, Oxford. He built up an extensive commercial Bar practice, frequently appearing in opposition to Sir **Thomas Scrutton**, and became a judge in 1909, a Lord Justice of Appeal in 1912, and a Lord-of-Appeal-in-Ordinary in 1913. With a sound grasp of legal principles, he was eloquent in his judgements, and greatly respected. He wrote many entries, particularly those of lawyers, for the *Dictionary of National Biography*.

Sumter, Thomas 1734–1832
American Revolutionary soldier
He was born near Charlottesville, Virginia. In the American Revolution (1775–83) he opposed the British under Sir **Banastre Tarleton** in South Carolina. He was defeated at Fishing Creek but gained a victory at Blackstock Hill (1780). He became a member of the US House of Representatives, and the US Senate from 1801 to 1810. Fort Sumter was named after him.

Sunderland, Charles Spencer, 3rd Earl of 1675–1722
English statesman
He became Secretary of State in 1706 and under **George I** rose to be all-powerful, but was forced to resign in 1721 through public indignation at his part in the South Sea Bubble. His grandson, John (1734–83), was created 1st Earl Spencer in 1765.

Sunderland, Robert Spencer, 2nd Earl of 1641–1702
English statesman
Born in Paris, France, he was the son of Henry Spencer, 3rd Baron Spencer, and father of Charles Spencer, 3rd Earl of Sunderland. He was made Secretary of State to Charles II in 1679 and negotiated a secret treaty whereby England would become subservient to France and, in return, Charles would receive an annual pension. The treaty was annulled and Sunderland drew the King's attention to a possible union with Spain. Although he was dismissed as Secretary of State in 1681 for voting to exclude James (**James VII and II**) from the succession, he was reinstated in 1683 and became chief minister under James (1685) and a Catholic (1688). On **William III**'s accession he

fled to Europe, but after renouncing his Catholicism he was allowed to return in 1691, and was Lord Chancellor for a brief period in 1697.

Sung Chiao-jen See **Song Jiaoren**

Sun Yat-sen (Sun Yixian) or Sun Zhongshan (Sun Chung-shan) 1866–1925
Chinese revolutionary politician

He was born in Zuiheng near Guangzhou (Canton), the son of a Christian farmer. He was brought up by his elder brother in Hawaii, and graduated in medicine at Hong Kong (1892), practising at Macao and Guangzhou. He visited Honolulu (1894) and founded his first political organization there, the Xing Zhong Hui (Revive China Society). After his first abortive uprising against the Manchus in Guangzhou in 1895, he lived in Japan, the USA and Great Britain, studying Western politics and canvassing the support of the Chinese in these countries. While in London in 1896, he was kidnapped and imprisoned in the Chinese legation and was saved from certain death by the intervention of Sir James Cantlie, the surgeon, his former tutor, to whom he smuggled out a letter and who enlisted the help of the British Foreign Office to get him released. After 10 unsuccessful uprisings, engineered by Sun from abroad, he was victorious in the revolution of 1911. In February 1912 China was proclaimed a republic with Sun as its provisional President, but he ceded to the Northern General **Yuan Shikai**, who had forced the emperor's abdication. Yuan sought to make himself dictator and Sun, opposing him from the south, was defeated and found himself again in exile. In 1916 Sun married **Song Qingling**, daughter of **Charles Jones Soong**, and Sun's former secretary. In 1923 he was back in Guangzhou and elected President of the Southern Republic. With help from the Russians, Sun reorganized the Guomindang (Kuomintang) and established the Whampoa Military Academy under **Chiang Kai-shek**, who three years after Sun's death achieved the unification of China under a government inspired by Sun's *Three Principles of the People* (1927)—nationalism, democracy and social reform. During a conciliatory conference with other Chinese political leaders he died of cancer in Beijing (Peking). Acknowledged by all political factions as the father of the Chinese Republic, he was re-interred in a mausoleum built in his honour in Nanjing (Nanking) in 1928. Sun was essentially empirical in his political teachings and rejected the communist dogma of the class war.

Sun Zhongshan See **Sun Yat-sen**

Suomi, Verner 1915–
US meteorologist and space scientist

Born in Evaleth, Minnesota, of Scandinavian parents, he went to Chicago University to work on instrument development under **Carl-Gustaf Rossby**. In 1948 he went to Wisconsin University and received a PhD for work on boundary layer processes. His greatest achievement was to design the 'spin-scan' camera for geostationary meteorological satellites. This instrument scans about a quarter of the Earth's surface continuously from one position in space and enables meteorological features to be monitored. Suomi also designed a small radio altimeter which was extensively used in the Global Atmospheric Research Program (1974). In the early 1970s he played a large part in the formation of the Man–Computer Interactive Data System to deal with various types of meteorological data.

Supervielle, Jules 1884–1960
French writer

Born in Montevideo, Uruguay, of French parents, he was educated in Paris, then returned to Uruguay, moving back to Paris eventually in 1945. He wrote many volumes of poems, including the notable *Poèmes de la France malheureuse* (1939–41, 'Poems of Unfortunate France'). He also wrote novels and tales such as *L'Enfant de la haute mer* (1931, 'The Child from the High Seas') and *L'Arche de Noê* (1938, 'Noah's Ark'), plays such as *La Belle au bois* (1932, 'Beauty in the Woods') and *Shéhérazade* (1949), and the libretto for *Bolivar*, an opera with music by **Darius Milhaud** (1950). ▢ J A Hiddleton, *L'univers de Supervielle* (1965)

Suppé, Franz von 1819–95
Austrian composer

Born in Spalato, Dalmatia, he was originally intended for a medical career, but after his father's death he moved to Vienna and took up music. He conducted for the Josephstadt (1841) and Leopoldstadt theatres (1865–95), and began to compose. His works include operettas, songs and masses, and his *Leichte Kavallerie* (1866, 'Light Cavalry') and *Poet and Peasant* (1846) overtures are still firm favourites.

Suraja Dowlah or Siraj-ud-Dawlah c.1732–1757
Nawab of Bengal

He came into conflict wih the British over their fortification of Calcutta, and marched on the city in 1756. Having captured Fort William, he confined his 146 prisoners in the military prison, the Black Hole (300 sq ft). The following morning there were 23 survivors. The British, under **Robert Clive**, joined forces with Suraja Dowlah's general, Mir Jafar, and defeated him at the Battle of Plassey in 1757. He fled to Murshidabad, but was captured and executed.

Surman, John Douglas 1944–
English jazz saxophonist and composer

Born in Tavistock, Devon, he is one of the leading figures in European jazz. He played with **Mike Westbrook** while still at school from 1958, and remained a part of his band for a decade, winning an award as best soloist at the prestigious Montreux Festival in 1968. He formed his first group as leader that year, and was involved in various collaborations in the early 1970s, in a fiercely improvised, experimental jazz mode. At the same time, the English folk themes and multi-layered soundscapes of *Westering Home* (1972) signalled the development of what became the dominant thread in his later music, often featuring his evocative baritone saxophone and bass clarinet against a synthesized accompaniment.

Surrey, Henry Howard, Earl of c.1517–1547
English courtier and poet

The eldest son of **Thomas Howard**, 3rd Duke of Norfolk (1473–1554), he was born in Hunsdon, Hertfordshire. He accompanied **Henry VIII** to France in 1532, and served in Scotland, France, and Flanders. He made enemies in high places, however, and in 1547 was charged with high treason, found guilty and executed. He is best remembered for his love poetry, in which he pioneered the use of blank verse and the Elizabethan sonnet form. Most of his work was first published in 1557, and collected in 1815–16. ▢ E Casady, *Henry Howard, Earl of Surrey* (1938)

Surtees, John 1934–
English racing driver and motorcyclist

Born in Westerham, Kent, he became the only man to win world titles on two and four wheels. He won the 350cc motor cycling world title in 1958–60, and the 500cc title in 1956, and 1958–60 (all on an MV Augusta). He then turned to car racing, and won the 1964 world title driving a Ferrari. He later became a racing-car manufacturer. His publications include *John Surtees—World Champion* (1991).

Surtees, Robert 1779–1834
English antiquary and topographer

Born in Durham, he studied at Christ Church, Oxford, and the Middle Temple, and in 1802 inherited Mainsforth near Bishop Auckland. Here he compiled his *History of the County of Durham* (1816–23). To Sir Walter Scott's *Minstrelsy of the Scottish Border* he contributed two 'ancient' ballads he himself had made—*Barthram's Dirge* and *The Death of Featherstonhaugh*. The Surtees Society was founded in 1834 in his honour to publish unedited manuscripts relating chiefly to the northern counties of England.

Surtees, Robert Smith 1803–64
English journalist and novelist

Born in Durham, where he was educated, he practised as a lawyer and later became a Justice of the Peace and High Sheriff of Durham County. He founded the *New Sporting Magazine* in 1831 where he introduced John Jorrocks, a sporting Cockney, whose adventures were later contained in *Jorrocks's Jaunts and Jollities* (1838, illustrated by H K Browne) and in *Hillingdon Hall* (1845). Their influence on Dickens's *Pickwick Papers* is conspicuous. His other great character, Mr Soapy Sponge, appears in *Mr Sponge's Sporting Tour* (1853, illustrated by John Leech), by which time he was combining his passion for sport with his literary work. ▢ F Watson, *Robert Smith Surtees, a critical study* (1933)

Susann, Jacqueline ?1926–1974
US novelist

She was born in Philadelphia, and had a moderately successful career as an actress before she turned to writing. Her first novel, *Valley of the Dolls* (1968), became an immediate bestseller, and *The Love Machine*, published the following year, enjoyed the same success. She made no literary claims for her work, but aimed to provide her readers with an escape from their daily lives into the more sensational world of show business.

Susanti, Susi 1971–
Indonesian badminton player

Born in Malaysia, she plays for the club Jaya Raya. In 1992 she won the women's singles at the Olympics, and in 1994 she won her record-breaking fourth consecutive world Grand Prix title, as well as the Indonesian, Malaysian, Thailand, Japanese and Chinese Taipei Opens, the World Cup, the Uber Cup final, and the All-England championship. She has won the All-England championship four times, and her victory in 1994 took just 28 minutes.

Suslov, Mikhail Andreyevich 1902–82
Soviet politician

Born in Shakhovskoye, he joined the Communist Party of the Soviet Union in 1921, and was a member of the Central Committee from 1941 until his death. Throughout his long political career he showed himself to be an ideologist very much of the Stalinist school. A graduate of the Moscow Institute of Economics and the Plekhanov Economic Institute, he became a ruthless and strongly doctrinaire administrator. Among other posts, he was the editor of *Pravda* (1949–50). He was first appointed to the Presidium (politburo) in 1952, then permanently from 1955. Suslov differed greatly from Nikita Khrushchev both in temperament (Suslov was introverted and aloof) and in political outlook (he disagreed with Khruschev's 'de-Stalinization', liberalizing measures in literature and the arts, economic reforms and foreign policy), and was instrumental in unseating Khrushchev in 1964. ▢ Serge Petroff, *The Red Eminence: A Biography of Mikhail A Suslov* (1988)

Su Song (Su Sung) 1020–1101
Chinese astronomer and inventor

Born in Fujian (Fukien) Province, he was ordered by the emperor in 1086 to construct an armillary clock far more elaborate than that of Yi Xing almost four centuries previously. The task was of such complexity that he enlisted a team of 10 advisers, and built a full-scale working model in wood which was carefully tested before the metal parts were cast. In 1094 he completed a detailed monograph describing the construction and operation of the clock, from which it is known that it was housed in a tower some 33 feet (10m) in height, was driven by a water wheel some 10 feet (3.3m) in diameter, and was probably accurate to within 100 seconds a day, a much better performance than its European counterparts.

Sutcliffe, Frank Meadow 1853–1941
English photographer

Born near Whitby, Yorkshire, he made studies, from 1880, of the vanishing world of English farmhands and fishermen in Yorkshire, which brought him many awards from international exhibitions between 1881 and 1905. From the late 1890s he used the new lightweight Kodak cameras to capture spontaneous moments rather than formal poses. He retired in 1923. Reviving interest in Victoriana led to the publication of a fully illustrated account of his work in 1974.

Sutcliffe, Peter, *known as* the Yorkshire Ripper 1946–
English murderer

Born in Bingley, near Bradford, Sutcliffe was a lorry-driver. He murdered 13 women over five years in northern England and the Midlands until captured in January 1981, and while his identity was unknown was dubbed the 'Yorkshire Ripper'. Several of his victims were prostitutes, and most were killed in the same way—their heads were beaten with a hammer and they were stabbed with a screwdriver. Sutcliffe, who was married to a schoolteacher, was interviewed by the police several times during the Ripper inquiry, but was released on each occasion. He was finally caught as police conducted a routine check on a prostitute and her client (Sutcliffe). He was found guilty of 13 murders and seven attempted murders in 1981 and was given a life sentence on each account.

Sutcliffe, Reginald Cockroft 1904–91
Welsh meteorologist

Born in Wrexham, Wales, he studied mathematics at Leeds University, joined the Meteorological Office in 1928, and worked in Malta in collaboration with Tor Bergeron (1928–32). He later became director of research at the Meteorological Office (1953), and in 1965 was appointed Professor of Meteorology at Reading University. He was made president of the World Meteorological Organisation Commission for Aerology (1957–61) and of the Royal Meteorological Society (1955–56). His greatest contribution to meteorology was in the theory of development, which he tackled in a systematic three-dimensional way. His most famous paper, *A Contribution to the Theory of Development* (1947), used pressure (instead of height) as a vertical co-ordinate, an innovation which was subsequently widely adopted and which led to practical advances in weather forecasting. Sutcliffe also introduced barotropic and baroclinic numerical weather prediction models into the Meteorological Office forecasting routine. He was the recipient of the International Meteorological Organisation prize (1963) and Symons Gold Medal (1955).

Sutherland, Earl W(ilbur), Jnr 1915–74
US biochemist and Nobel Prize winner

Born in Burlingame, Kansas, he studied medicine at the Washington University School of Medicine in St Louis, and became associate professor in the biochemistry department of Washington University. In 1953 he became director of the pharmacology department of the Western Reserve University in Cleveland. His research concerned the conversion of glycogen (the energy store in liver and muscle) into glucose, and the stimulation of this process.

He showed that a molecule known as cyclic-AMP activates the glycogen–glucose transformation, and proposed that two hormones initiate the entire process by inducing the production of c-AMP. Sutherland had discovered a new principle—the 'second messenger' theory of hormonal action. In 1963 he became Professor of Physiology at Vanderbilt University. For his work on c-AMP as a second messenger he was awarded the 1971 Nobel Prize for physiology or medicine.

Sutherland, Graham Vivian 1903–80
English artist
Born in London, he studied at Goldsmith's College School of Art, and worked mainly as an etcher until 1930. During the next 10 years he made his reputation as a painter of Romantic, mainly abstract landscapes, with superb, if arbitrary, colouring. From 1941 to 1945 he was an official war artist. In 1946 he was commissioned to paint a *Crucifixion* for St Matthew's Church, Northampton, and after that he produced several memorable portraits, including W Somerset Maugham (1949) and a controversial portrait of Sir Winston Churchill (1954) which was destroyed on the instructions of Lady Churchill. He also designed ceramics, posters and textiles: his large tapestry, *Christ in Glory*, was hung in the new Coventry Cathedral in 1962. 📖 Francesco Arcangeli, *Graham Sutherland* (1973)

Sutherland, Dame Joan 1926–
Australian soprano
Born in Sydney, she made her debut there as Dido in Henry Purcell's *Dido and Aeneas* (1947). She went to London in 1951, and joined the Royal Opera, Covent Garden, London (1952–88). She gained international fame in 1959 with her roles in Donizetti's *Lucia di Lammermoor* ('The Bride of Lammermoor') and Handel's *Samson*. Singing regularly in opera houses and concert halls all over the world, she returned to Australia for a tour with her own company in 1965. She retired from the opera stage in October 1990 in a performance at the Sydney Opera House of Meyerbeer's *Les Huguenots*, and now lives in Switzerland. She was appointed to the Order of Merit in 1991. In 1954 she married Richard Bonynge (1930–), who became her principal conductor and with whom she co-wrote her autobiography, *The Joan Sutherland Album* (1986). He later became musical director of the Australian Opera Company (1976–85). 📖 Edward Greenfield, *Joan Sutherland* (1973)

Sutherland, Margaret Ada 1897–1984
Australian composer
Born in Adelaide, South Australia, she studied at the Melbourne Conservatorium of Music and at the age of 19 appeared as piano soloist with the New South Wales State Orchestra under Henri Verbrugghen. She went in 1923 to study in Vienna and London, returning to Australia in 1925, where for many years she was active in music administration and promotional work. Recognition came late, but her Violin Concerto (1954) was warmly received and her opera, *The Young Kabbarli*, based on the life of Daisy Bates, was performed in 1965. She wrote a great deal of chamber music, and set a number of song cycles, including one by Australian poet Judith Wright.

Sutherland, Robert Garioch See Garioch, Robert

Sutherland, Struan Keith 1936–
Australian toxicologist
He was born in Sydney. After graduating from Melbourne University and serving as a surgeon with the Royal Australian Navy (1962–65), he joined Commonwealth Serum Laboratories in 1966. In 1980 he produced the first effective antivenin for the widespread Funnel-

Web Spider, one of Australia's many deadly creatures. He developed venom detection kits which are now distributed to all hospitals, and developed the pressure/immobilization treatment for victims of bites, which has saved many lives worldwide. Now Associate Professor of Pharmacology at Melbourne University (1994–) and director of the Australian Venom Research Unit, he has written standard reference works on toxins and also presented the television series *Holiday Hazards* (1978–84).

Sutro, Alfred 1863–1933
English dramatist
He was born in London. After giving up a successful business, he translated Maurice Maeterlinck, and from 1900 wrote a series of successful plays—*The Foolish Virgins* (1904), *The Walls of Jericho* (1906), *John Glayde's Honour* (1907), *The Perplexed Husband* (1913), and others.

Sutter, John Augustus, *originally* Johann August Suter 1803–80
US pioneer
Born in Kandern, Germany to Swiss parents, he was granted land by the Mexican provincial governor of California and established a settlement at New Helvetia (now Sacramento). When an employee discovered gold on the property, the Gold Rush was begun (1849). Sutter's land was overrun with prospectors, and he became bankrupt and moved to Pennsylvania.

Suttner, Bertha Félicie Sophie, Freifrau von, *née* Kinsky 1843–1914
Czech (Austro-Hungarian) novelist and Nobel Prize winner
She was born in Prague, of Bohemian descent, the daughter of an imperial general, and married Baron Arthur von Suttner (1850–1902), a novelist and engineer, in 1876. In 1891 she founded an Austrian pacifist organization called the Austrian Society of Peace. He pacifist journal, *Die Waffen nieder*, later published in book form (1889, Eng trans *Lay Down Your Arms, the Autobiography of Martha von Tilling*, 1892), shocked her readers by its pacifism and was translated into many European languages. She wrote many other books on pacifism and from 1876 to 1896 corresponded with Alfred Nobel on the subject, which persuaded him to add provision for a peace award to the endowment in his will. She herself was awarded the Nobel Peace Prize in 1905. 📖 E Key, *Florence Nightingale und Bertha von Suttner* (1919)

Su Tung-p'o See Su Dongpu

Suvorov, Aleksandr Vasilevich, Count 1729–1800
Russian soldier
Born in Moscow, he fought in the Seven Years War (1756–63), and in Poland and Turkey, then aided the Austrians against the French in Italy (1799), and won several victories. Directed to join other Russian forces in Switzerland, he found them already defeated, and was forced into a winter retreat across the mountains to Austria.

Suyin, Han See Han Suyin

Suzman, Helen, *née* Gavronsky 1917–
South African liberal politician
She was born in Germiston, in the Transvaal, the daughter of a Lithuanian immigrant. After graduating in economics and statistics from Witwatersrand University, she married Dr Moses Suzman at 20 and then lectured part time at Witwatersrand (1944–52). Deeply concerned about the apartheid system erected by the National Party under Daniel Malan, she joined the Opposition United Party, later the Progressive and then the Democratic Party, and was elected to parliament in 1953. She gradually gained the respect of the black community, including the ANC leader Nelson Mandela and, as a member of the

South African Institute of Race Relations, was a fierce opponent of apartheid. In 1978 she received the UN Human Rights award. She retired from parliament, after 36 uninterrupted years, in 1989.

Suzman, Janet 1939–
British actress

She was born in Johannesburg, South Africa, the niece of the anti-apartheid campaigner Helen Suzman. Moving to England to complete her studies, she made her acting debut in *Billy Liar* at Ipswich in 1962. That year she joined the newly formed Royal Shakespeare Company and subsequently played roles such as Portia in *The Merchant of Venice* (1965), Ophelia in *Hamlet* (1965) and Cleopatra in *Antony and Cleopatra* (1973). In the West End, she played the title role in *Hedda Gabler* (1977). As well as classical roles on television, she has played Florence Nightingale in *Miss Nightingale*, Edwina Mountbatten in *Mountbatten— The Last Viceroy* (1984) and Margaret, Duchess of Chester, in *The Secret Agent* (1992). Her films include *The Draughtsman's Contract* (1982), *Nuns on the Run* (1990) and *Leon the Pig Farmer* (1992). From 1969 to 1986 she was married to the director Trevor Nunn.

Suzuki, Zenko 1911–
Japanese politician

Born in Yamada, Honshu island, he trained at the Japanese agriculture ministry's Academy of Fisheries during the 1930s. In 1947 he was elected to the Lower House of the Diet as a Socialist Party Deputy, but moved to the Liberal Party in 1949 and then, on its formation in 1955, to the conservative Liberal Democratic Party (LDP). During the 1960s and 1970s he held a succession of ministerial and party posts, including Post and Telecommunications (1960–64), Chief Cabinet Secretary (1964–65), Health and Welfare (1965–68) and Agriculture, Forestry and Fisheries (1976–80). Following the death of his patron, Masayoshi Ohira, he succeeded to the dual positions of LDP President and Prime Minister in 1980. His premiership was marred by factional strife within the LDP, deteriorating relations with the USA and opposition to his defence policy. He stepped down in 1982, but remained an influential LDP faction leader.

Svedberg, Theodor 1884–1971
Swedish physical chemist and Nobel Prize winner

Born in Fleräng, near Valbo, he went to the University of Uppsala in 1904 to study chemistry and was associated with that university for the next 45 years. From 1912 to 1949 he was Professor of Physical Chemistry. Although beyond retiring age, he was director of the Gustaf Werner Institute of Nuclear Chemistry from 1949 to 1967. His early work was on colloid chemistry and he also investigated radioactivity. In the 1920s, however, his interest in colloids led him to develop the ultracentrifuge as a means of following optically the sedimentation of particles too small to be seen in the ultramicroscope. His measurements of the molecular weights of proteins were particularly important, and for his work on the ultracentrifuge he received the 1926 Nobel Prize for chemistry. During World War II he developed a synthetic rubber, Sweden's supplies of natural rubber being cut off by the blockade. Svedberg's work at the Werner Institute involved the applications of a cyclotron in medicine, in radiation physics and in radiochemistry. He was made an Honorary Fellow of the Chemical Society in 1923 and elected a Foreign Member of the Royal Society in 1944.

Svein I Haraldsson, 'Fork-Beard' d.1014
King of Denmark and of England

He was the son of Harald Gormsson (Blue-Tooth), but rebelled against his father and deposed him (c.986). He made several campaigns against England (from 994), each bribed away by King Ethelred, the Unready. In 1013 with his son Knut Sveinsson (Canute), he forced King Ethelred to flee to Normandy. Svein took up the Crown, but died five weeks later (February 1014).

Svein II Ulfsson, *sometimes known as* Estridsson d.1074
King of Denmark

The son of a regent of Denmark, Earl Ulf, and nephew of Knut Sveinsson (Canute), he was appointed regent of Denmark (1045) by King Magnus I Olafsson of Norway (and Denmark), and acclaimed king himself when Magnus died (1047). Harald III Sigurdsson (Hardraade), King of Norway, claimed Denmark, starting a war of attrition against Svein. Peace was made (1064) and Harald accepted Svein's right to the throne of Denmark. In 1069, after the conquest of England by William the Conqueror, Svein's army captured York, but he made peace with William (1070) and withdrew. Svein was a major informant for the historian Adam of Bremen.

Sveinsson, Ásmundur 1893–1982
Icelandic sculptor

He was born in the west of Iceland, and studied for many years in Stockholm and Paris, then visited Greece and Italy, returning to Iceland in 1930. His works, in stone, cement, metal or wood, were initially inspired by the monumental Icelandic Sagas and folk-tales, but became increasingly abstract and Expressionist. The spherical workshop he built for himself in Reykjavík is now a museum devoted to his work.

Svendsen, Johan Severin 1840–1911
Norwegian composer

Born in Christiania (now Oslo), he travelled extensively, then became court kapellmeister at Copenhagen (1883). He wrote two symphonies and a violin concerto. His best-known work is *Carnaval à Paris* (1879, 'Carnival in Paris').

Svensson, Jon Stefán 1857–1944
Icelandic writer and churchman

Born in Möðruvellir, and educated in France, he became a Jesuit scholar and taught at a Catholic school in Denmark. During convalescence in Holland from a severe illness (1911–12) he began to write a series of children's books about a boy called Nonni growing up in the north of Iceland. Originally written in German, the *Nonni* books have been translated into many languages, and made Svensson a bestselling author. ▣ H Hannesson, *Nonni Attægur* (1937)

Sverdrup, Harald Ulrik 1888–1957
Norwegian oceanographer and geophysicist

Born in Christiania (now Oslo), he went to university to study science, and in 1911 became assistant to Vilhelm F K Bjerknes, following him to Leipzig to work on atmospheric circulation (1913–18). Later he made atmospheric, oceanographic, magnetic and ethnographic observations on Roald Amundsen's *Maud* expedition to the North Pole. In 1922 he worked at the Carnegie Institute on magnetism and Arctic tidal dynamics, and in 1926 he succeeded Bjerknes as Professor of Geophysics at Bergen University. In 1931 he took a research position at the Christian Michelsens Institute in Bergen, and in 1935 moved to California to become director of Scripps Institution of Oceanography. He returned to Oslo in 1948 as director of the Norwegian Polar Institute and in 1949 became Professor of Geophysics at the University of Oslo, later Dean, and then Vice-Chancellor. A unit of volume transport and the Sverdrup Islands in Arctic Canada are named after him.

Sverdrup, Otto 1855–1930
Norwegian explorer

He went on numerous expeditions to Greenland and the North Pole. As well as searching for lost Russian explorers and an Italian airship crew, he discovered many previously unknown islands.

Sverrir Sigurdsson c.1150–1202
King of Norway

Brought up in the Faroe Islands, he claimed to be the illegitimate son of Sigurd Haraldsson, 'the Mouth' (d.1155). Often called the 'the Usurper', he emerged from obscurity in 1179 to lay claim to the throne from **Magnus V Erlingsson**, whom he finally defeated and killed in 1184, becoming king in that year. He turned out to be one of Norway's greatest kings, strengthening the Crown against both Church and nobles with the support of the freeholding farmers. He commissioned one of the first Icelandic Sagas; a biography of himself, *Sverris saga*, written during his lifetime by his friend, Karl Jónsson, abbot of the monastery of Thingeyrar in Iceland.

Svevo, Italo, *pseudonym of* Ettore Schmitz
1861–1928
Italian novelist

He was born in Trieste, of German–Jewish descent, educated primarily in Bavaria, and wrote in Italian. While working as a correspondence clerk in a Trieste bank, he wrote and published privately his first novel, *Una Vita* (1892, Eng trans, *A Life*, 1963), about a man who feels ill at ease in the commercial world. It was followed in 1898 by *Senilità* (Eng trans *As a Man Grows Older*, 1932). Both novels failed, largely through Svevo's ineptitude as a publisher, and he gave up writing to concentrate on business. However, in 1906 he met **James Joyce**, then teaching English in Trieste, who bolstered his confidence and promoted *La coscienza di Zeno* (Eng trans *The Confessions of Zeno*, 1930). Svevo won recognition in France and the rest of Europe, but died soon afterwards in a car accident. His other novels are *La novella del buon vecchio e della bella fanciulla* (1929, Eng trans *The Nice Old Man and the Pretty Girl*, 1930), and *Il vecchione* (1967, Eng trans *The Grand Old Man*, 1968), which was incomplete on his death. V S Pritchett described him as 'the first of the psychological novelists to be beatified by a spirit of humility'. 📖 P N Furbank, *Italo Svevo, man and writer* (1966)

Svoboda, Ludvík 1895–1979
Czechoslovak soldier and politician

He was born near Bratislava (now in Slovakia). After escaping from Czechoslovakia in 1939 he became commanding general of the Czechoslovak army corps attached to the Red Army in 1943, and helped to liberate Košice, Brno and Prague in 1944 to 1945. In 1948 he joined the Communist Party and was Minister of Defence until 1950. He was mistrusted by the Stalinists but **Nikita Khruschev** supported him and, in 1968, he succeeded the discredited **Antonín Novotný** as President. He supported the abortive reforms of **Alexander Dubček** and, after the hostile Soviet intervention in 1968, he travelled to Moscow to seek relaxation of the repressive measures imposed on the Czechoslovaks. He remained in office until 1975, when failing health forced his retirement.

Swainson, William 1789–1855
English naturalist and bird illustrator

Born in Hoylake, Cheshire, he obtained a post in the army commissariat in Malta and Sicily (1807–15), where he amassed a large collection of zoological specimens. He travelled in Brazil (1817–18), and in London learned the new technique of lithography, with which he produced *Zoological Illustration* (3 vols, 1820–23), *Naturalist's Guide* (1822) and *Exotic Conchology* (1822). In 1825 he moved to Hampshire as a full-time artist and author. He contributed 11 volumes to **Dionysius Lardner**'s *Cabinet Cyclopaedia* (1830–44) and three volumes to Jardine's *Naturalist's Library* (1833–45). He emigrated to New Zealand in 1840. Swainson's Thrush is named after him.

Swallow, John Crossley 1923–94
English physical oceanographer and geophysicist

Born near Huddersfield, Yorkshire, he studied physics at Cambridge, where he later joined the department of geodesy and geophysics. He spent four years at sea conducting seismic refraction experiments, and then worked at the National Institute of Oceanography, concentrating on physical oceanography. He developed a method for measuring deep currents in the ocean using neutrally buoyant floats, which can be tracked acoustically. This led to co-operative work with **Hank Stommel**, revealing the deep western boundary current in the North Atlantic (1957) and the presence of strong eddies in mid-ocean (1960). He took part in many oceanographic cruises in the North Atlantic and Mediterranean, observing the wintertime formation of deep water, the Somali current, and the equatorial circulation in the Indian Ocean. He was elected FRS in 1968.

Swammerdam, Jan 1637–80
Dutch naturalist

Born in Amsterdam, he studied medicine at the University of Leyden but never practised, instead concentrating on the microscopical observation of a great range of biological material, described in his great *Biblia Naturae* (1737–38). He studied the life cycles of a dozen insect types, and classified the insects on the basis of the type of metamorphosis they undergo during their life cycles, the method which is still in general use. Among his many observations was the presence of the butterfly's wing within the pupa, and he correctly surmised that on hatching the wings are expanded by blood pressure. He was first to describe valves in the lymph vessels and the ovarian follicles in mammals. He published *Historia Insectorum Generalis* in 1669.

Swan, Sir Joseph Wilson 1828–1914
English chemist, inventor and industrialist

He was born near Sunderland, and after leaving school at 13 was apprenticed to a druggist, then in 1846 joined a pharmaceutical business in Newcastle. In 1856 he took out a patent for improving the wet-plate collodion photographic process and the following year invented high-speed bromide paper. The patent was bought by **George Eastman**, founder of Kodak, and helped to make photography cheaper and thus widely popular. By 1848 Swan was experimenting with carbonized paper filaments for electric lamps, but it was not until 1879 that he gave his first successful demonstration of a bulb. Within four years he was manufacturing 10,000 lamp bulbs a week, and in 1883, he amalgamated his business with **Thomas Alva Edison**, who had been granted a British patent in 1879, to form the Edison & Swan Electric Light Company. In searching for a better filament for his bulbs, Swan discovered the process that **Chardonnet** later adapted to make rayon. It was further developed by **Charles Cross** and **Edward Bevan** who, in conjunction with Courtaulds, laid the foundations of the synthetic textile industry. Swan also made significant improvements to lead-plate batteries. He was elected FRS in 1874, knighted in 1904, and received many other honours. 📖 Kenneth R Swan, *Sir Joseph Swan and the Invention of the Incandescent Electric Lamp* (1948)

Swanborough, Stella Isaacs, Baroness, *née* Charnaud 1894–1971
English pioneer of social services and WRVS founder

Born in Constantinople (Istanbul), she returned to England with her family before World War I. In 1931 she married Rufus Isaacs, 1st Marquess of **Reading**, and the following year began her volunteer work. She was invited by the Home Secretary in 1938 to form a women's organization to help with air-raid precautions. By the outbreak of World War II the Women's Voluntary Service for

Civil Defence was able to assist with the evacuation of women and children, and with setting up canteens and services for troops. The organization continued after the war, when 'for Civil Defence' was dropped from the title. (When 'Royal' was added in 1966, it became widely known as the WRVS.) The WVS pioneered community service in the form of 'meals on wheels' and 'home helps'. She was made a life peer in 1958, and was one of the first women to take her seat in the House of Lords.

Swann, Donald 1923–94
Welsh composer and lyricist
Born in Llanelli of an Anglo-Russian family, he was educated at Westminster School and Christ Church, Oxford. He began his writing career by contributing music to revues such as *Penny Plain* (1951), *Airs on a Shoestring* (1953), and *Pay the Piper* (1954). His long collaboration with Michael Flanders began in 1956, when he wrote the music, and Flanders the words and dialogue, for *At the Drop of a Hat*, followed by *At the Drop of Another Hat* in 1965. Their partnership ended in 1967 and after 1970 he became a frequent broadcaster on musical and other matters, and wrote a musical fable for Christmas, three books of new carols, and his autobiography, *Swann's Way* (1991).

Swanson, Gloria, *originally* Gloria May Josephine Svensson 1897–1983
US actress
Born in Chicago, after studying as a singer she entered the film industry as an extra and bit part player (1915). She became one of Mack Sennett's bathing beauties before an association with director Cecil B De Mille brought her leading roles as chic sophisticates in the front line of the battle of the sexes. Her many silent features include *Male and Female* (1919), *The Affairs of Anatol* (1921) and *Manhandled* (1924). Despite the extravagances of the unfinished *Queen Kelly* (1928) she survived the arrival of sound, receiving Academy Award nominations for *Sadie Thompson* (1928) and *The Trespasser* (1929). However, her film career gradually dwindled away despite a sensational comeback in *Sunset Boulevard* (1950). Never relinquishing her glamorous star status she continued to appear on stage and television. Married six times, she published her autobiography, *Swanson on Swanson*, in 1980.

Swedenborg, Emanuel, *originally* Swedberg 1688–1772
Swedish mystic, theologian and scientist
He was born in Stockholm, the son of a professor of theology at Uppsala. The family name was Swedberg, but was changed to Swedenborg when they were ennobled in 1719. He studied at Uppsala, travelled widely in Europe, was interested particularly in technology and engineering, and returned to Sweden to be assessor at the Royal Board of Mines (1716–47). He wrote prolifically on technical and mathematical topics—the differential calculus, astronomy, docks, sluices and navigation, followed by a long treatise, *Opera Philosophica et Mineralia* (1734, 'Philosophical and Logical Works'), a mixture of metallurgy and metaphysical speculation on the creation of the world, and huge works on anatomy and physiology entitled *Oeconomia Regni Animalis* (1740–41, 'The Economy of the Animal Kingdom') and *Regnum Animale* (1744–45, 2 vols, 'The Animal Kingdom'). In 1743–44 he had a religious crisis, recorded in his *Journal of Dreams*, which he interpreted as a direct vision of the spiritual world and which led him to resign his scientific post (1747) to expound his experiences and the mystical doctrines he based on them. He produced some 30 volumes of religious revelations in Latin, the best-known being *Arcana Coelestia* (8 vols, 1749–56, 'Heavenly Arcana'), *De Coelo et eius Mirabilibus et de Inferno* (1758, 'On Heaven and Its Wonders

and on Hell') and *Vera Christiana Religio* (1771, 'The Christian Religion'). His followers organized a society in London known as the Church of the New Jerusalem (1787), which proliferated many further branches throughout the world (Swedenborgianism). He influenced William Blake and other writers, including the French Symbolists. 📖 Signe Toksvig, *Emanuel Swedenborg, Scientist and Mystic* (1948)

Sweelinck, Jan Pieterszoon 1562–1621
Dutch composer, organist and harpsichordist
Born in Deventer or Amsterdam, he studied in Venice and composed mainly church music and organ works, developing the fugue. He founded the distinctive North German school of organists which later included Diderik Buxtehude and J S Bach.

Sweet, Henry 1845–1912
English philologist
Born in London, he became Reader in Phonetics at Oxford. He was a pioneer of Anglo-Saxon philological studies and his works include Old and Middle English texts, primers, and dictionaries, a historical English grammar, *A History of English Sounds* (1874), an *Anglo-Saxon Reader* (1867), *A New English Grammar* (1892) and *A History of Language* (1900). He constructed a 'Romaic' phonetic alphabet, and *The Practical Study of Languages* (1899) advocated 'the living philology', ie teaching the spoken language utilizing the new science of phonetics. Professor Higgins of George Bernard Shaw's *Pygmalion* was based on him.

Swettenham, Sir Frank Athelstane 1850–1946
English colonial administrator
He was born in Belper, Derbyshire. He was British Resident in Selangor (1882) and Perak (1889–95), and later Resident-General in the Federated Malay States (1896–1901). He was Governor and Commander-in-Chief of the Straits Settlement from 1901 to 1904 and became an authority on Malay language and history, writing a number of books on the subject.

Swift, Graham 1949–
English novelist and short-story writer
He was born in London and educated at Cambridge and York universities. His writing is frequently preoccupied with history, memory, guilt and the natural world. His first novels, *The Sweet Shop Owner* (1980) and *Shuttlecock* (1981), were critically well received, and international acclaim arrived on publication of his third, the hugely successful *Waterland* (1983), which was shortlisted for the Booker Prize. Partly a social and natural history, partly a fictitious history of his family as remembered and imagined by Tom Crick, a teacher, this work is considered by some as one of the most important novels of its time. In 1996 Swift won the Booker Prize and the James Tait Black Memorial Prize with *Last Orders*, the story of four friends of a deceased London butcher trying to honour his dying wish to have his ashes scattered at sea. Other books include *Out of This World* (1988), which looks at the relationship between a father and daughter, and *Ever After* (1992), which records the life of Bill Unwin, a meditative academic.

Swift, Jonathan 1667–1745
Anglo-Irish satirist and clergyman
He was born in Dublin, of English parents. He was educated at Kilkenny Grammar School and Trinity College, Dublin, where he obtained his degree only by 'special grace' in 1685. Family connections helped him become secretary to the diplomat, Sir William Temple, then resident at Moor Park, Farnham. He supported his patron on the side of the Ancients in the 'Querelle des Anciens et des Modernes' which had spread to Great Britain from

France. His contribution was the mock-epic *Battle of the Books*, published along with the much more powerful satire on religious dissension, *A Tale of a Tub*, in 1704. At Moor Park he first met Esther Johnson (1681–1728), then a child of eight, who from then on as pupil and lover or friend was to play an important role in his life and to survive for posterity in Swift's verse tributes and the *Journal to Stella* (1710–13), but it is uncertain if he ever married her. When Swift was presented to the living of Laracor near Dublin, 'Stella' accompanied him. In 1708, during a visit to London, he met Esther Vanhomrigh (1690–1723), who insisted, to her own detriment, on being near him in Ireland. She is the Vanessa of Swift's clever poem *Cadenus and Vanessa* (1726), a tribute to her but also a manoeuvre of disengagement. His visits to London were largely political, but he also visited the great in literary and aristocratic circles. Having been introduced to politics by Temple, he supported the Whigs, but his interest in the Church steered him towards the Tory party. The friendship of **Robert Harley** assisted the change which was resolved in 1710 when Harley returned to power. His *History of the Four Last Years of the Queen* [**Anne**] (1758) described the ferment of intrigue and pamphleteering during that period. The chief aims of the Tory Party were to secure the Establishment and end the war with France. The latter was powerfully aided by Swift's *On the Conduct of the Allies* (1713), one of the greatest pieces of pamphleteering. The death of Queen Anne (1714) disappointed all the hopes of Swift and his friends of the Scriblerus Club, founded in 1713. Swift accepted his 'exile' to the Deanery of St Patrick's Cathedral, Dublin, and from then on, except for two visits in 1726 and 1727, correspondence alone kept him in touch with London. Despite his loathing for Ireland he threw himself into a strenuous campaign for Irish liberties, denied by the Whig government. The *Drapier's Letters* (1724) is the most famous of these activities, which were concerned with England's restrictions on Irish trade, particularly the exclusion of Irish wool and cattle. This campaign, and his charitable efforts for Dublin's poor, greatly enhanced his reputation. On his first visit to London after the fall of the Tory ministry in 1714 he published the world-famous satire *Gulliver's Travels* (1726). In 1729 he published his ironical *A Modest Proposal*. His light verse now ranged from *The Grand Question Debated* (1729) to the *Verses on His Own Death* (1731), which, with its mixture of pathos and humour, ranks with the great satirical poems in the lighter manner. He himself considered his *On Poetry; a Rhapsody* (1733), his best verse satire. The ironical *Directions to Servants* and *A Complete Collection of Genteel and Ingenious Conversation* followed in 1731. The satire in the first part of *Gulliver's Travels* is directed at political parties and religious dissension. The second part introduces deepening misanthropy, culminating in the king's description of mankind as 'the most pernicious race of little odious vermin that Nature ever suffered to crawl upon the surface of the earth'. The third part, a satire on inventors, is fun though less plausible. The last part, in the country of the Houyhnhnms, a race of horses governed only by reason, is a savage attack on humanity which points to the author's final mental collapse (now thought to have been brought on by Ménière's disease). Politics apart, Swift's influence, like that of the Scriblerus Club generally and **Alexander Pope** in particular, was directed powerfully against the vogue of deistic science and modern invention and in favour of orthodoxy and good manners. 📖 I Ehrenpreis, *Jonathan Swift: the man, his works, the age* (2 vols, 1962–67)

Swinburne, Algernon Charles 1837–1909

English poet and critic

Born in London, he was educated partly in France and in England at Eton and Balliol College, Oxford, but left without taking a degree. He travelled on the Continent, where he came under the spell of **Victor Hugo**, visited **Walter Savage Landor** in Florence (1864), and on his return became associated with **Dante Gabriel Rossetti** and **William Morris**. After a breakdown due to heavy drinking and other excesses, he submitted to the care of his friend **Theodore Watts-Dunton**, in whose house he continued to live in semi-seclusion for the rest of his life. His first success was with *Atalanta in Calydon* (1865), a drama in the Greek form but modern in its spirit of revolt against religious acquiescence in the will of Heaven. However, it was the first of the series of *Poems and Ballads* (1866) which took the public by storm, although the uninhibited tone of certain passages affronted English puritanism. The second and third series (1878, 1889) were less successful. Meanwhile he found scope for his detestation of kings and priests in the struggle for Italian liberty. *Songs before Sunrise* (1871) best expresses his fervent republicanism. A trilogy on **Mary, Queen of Scots** was completed in 1881, and the following year *Tristram of Lyonesse*, an Arthurian romance in rhymed couplets, achieved a real success. Intense and passionate, it must be considered among the best of Victorian dealings with the medieval cycle. His novel *Love's Cross Currents* (1877), published under the pseudonym Mrs H Manners, is a curiosity, but his critical works, above all his work on **Shakespeare** and his contemporaries, are stimulating. His *Essays and Studies* (1875) and *Studies in Prose and Poetry* (1894) are his chief contribution to criticism. 📖 G Lafourcade, *Algernon Swinburne* (1932)

Swinburne, Sir James Swinburne, 9th Baronet 1858–1958

Scottish scientist and electrical engineer

Born in Inverness, he was apprenticed in a locomotive factory in Manchester, and in 1885 began work in Rookes Crompton's electrical engineering firm, where he invented the 'hedgehog' transformer (used in early wireless sets). In 1899 he set up as a consultant in London. He was a pioneer in the plastics industry and is known as 'the father of British plastics'. His research on phenolic resins resulted in a process for producing synthetic resin, but his patent for this was anticipated by one day, by the Belgian chemist **Leo Baekeland**, working in the USA. Almost 20 years later he came to an agreement with Baekeland, and they merged their UK interests to form Bakelite Ltd in 1926. He was elected FRS in 1906.

Swinhoe, Robert 1836–77

English naturalist

Born in Calcutta, India, he went to Hong Kong in 1854, and was posted to Amoy in 1855. He was on the naval expedition that captured Peking and negotiated the Treaty of Tiensin (1860). He was British consul in Formosa (1861–66), Amoy (1866–69) and Ningpo (1871–75). He compiled the first checklist of Chinese birds (1871). Swinhoe's Pheasant, Swinhoe's Petrel and Swinhoe's Snipe are named after him.

Swinton, Alan Archibald Campbell 1863–1930

Scottish electrical engineer and inventor

Born in Edinburgh, he was educated there and in France, and in 1882 began an engineering apprenticeship in the Newcastle works of **William George Armstrong**, for whom he devised a new method of insulating electric cables on board ship by sheathing them in lead. In 1887 he moved to London and began to practise as a consulting engineer, specializing in the installation of electric lighting. At the same time he continued to act as consultant to Armstrongs, and later became a director of Crompton & Company, and the Parsons Marine Steam Turbine Company. Having been interested in photography since childhood, he was one of the first to explore the medical applications of radiography. He published the first X-ray photograph taken in Britain in *Nature* (23 January 1896), and was soon in demand as a consultant radiographer. In a letter to *Nature* (18 June 1908) he outlined the principles of an electronic system of television, which he called 'distant electric vision', by means of cathode rays—essentially the system in use today. He was elected FRS in 1915.

Swinton, Sir Ernest Dunlop, *pseudonym* Ole Luk-Oie 1868–1951
British soldier, writer and inventor
He was born in Bangalore, India. One of the originators of armoured fighting vehicles, he was the first to call them 'tanks'. Under his pseudonym Ole Luk-Oie he wrote *The Green Curve* (1909), *A Year Ago* (1916), and translations. He became Professor of Military History at Oxford (1925–39).

Swithin or Swithun, St d.862
English ecclesiastic
He was adviser to Egbert and was made Bishop of Winchester (852) by Ethelwulf. When the monks exhumed his body in 971 to bury it in the rebuilt cathedral, the removal, which was to have taken place on 15 July, is said to have been delayed by violent rain. The belief therefore arose that if it rains on 15 July it will rain for 40 days more.

Sydenham, Thomas, *known as* the English Hippocrates 1624–89
English physician
Born in Wynford Eagle, Dorset, he served in the Parliamentary army during the Civil War, and in 1647 went to Oxford, where he studied medicine at Wadham College, and was elected Fellow of All Souls College. From 1655 he practised in London. A great friend of such empiricists as Robert Boyle and John Locke, he urged doctors to become close observers at the bedside, where they would learn to distinguish specific diseases, and through trial and error, to find specific remedies. He was much impressed with the capacity of Jesuit's bark (the active principle of which is quinine) to cure intermittent fever (malaria), and believed that other such specific treatments might be found. He wrote *Observationes Medicae* (1667) and a treatise on gout (1683), a disease from which he suffered, distinguished the symptoms of venereal disease (1675), recognized hysteria as a distinct disorder and gave his name to the mild convulsions of children, 'Sydenham's chorea' (St Vitus's dance), and to the medicinal use of liquid opium, 'Sydenham's laudanum'. He remained in London except when the plague was at its peak (1665), and was a keen student of epidemic diseases, which he believed were caused by atmospheric properties (he called it the 'epidemic constitution'). By the time of his death, his reputation was growing and his vivid works, with their astute descriptions of diseases, were often reprinted and translated throughout the 18th century. 📖 G G Meynell, *Materials for a Biography of Dr Thomas Sydenham (1624–1689)* (1988)

Sydney, Algernon See Sidney, Algernon

Sydow, Max Carl Adolf von 1929–
Swedish actor
Born in Lund, he studied at the Royal Academy in Stockholm and made his film debut in *Bara en Mor* (1949). A member of various theatrical companies, he began a long association with director Ingmar Bergman at the Municipal Theatre of Malmö. On film their many collaborations include *Det Sjunde Inseglet* (1957, *The Seventh Seal*), *Sasom in en Spegel* (1961, *Through A Glass Darkly*) and *Skammen* (1968, *The Shame*). He made his US film debut as Jesus Christ in *The Greatest Story Ever Told* (1965) and has spent many years as a character actor of international standing in films like *Hawaii* (1966), *The Exorcist* (1973), *Hannah and*

Her Sisters (1986) and *Pelle, the Conqueror* (1988). He has also continued to appear on stage, making his Broadway debut in *The Night of the Tribades* (1977) and performing at the Old Vic in *The Tempest* (1988). In 1988 he made his debut as a film director with *Katinka*.

Syers, Madge (Florence Madeline), *née* Cave 1882–1917
English ice-skater
Born in Surrey, she was a pioneer in her sport. In 1902 she took the bold step of entering the world championships, as there was no real rule preventing women from doing so, and she finished second, much to the horror of the establishment. Women were afterwards barred from that event, but Syers went on to win two British championships from her male competitors (1903–04). A women's world championship event was introduced in 1906, which she won in its inaugural year and in 1907. She also won a gold medal at the 1908 Olympics, and a bronze medal in the pairs, skating with her husband Edgar.

Sykes, Eric 1923–
English comedy writer and performer
He was born in Oldham, near Manchester, and his wartime service in the RAF allowed him to perform in forces shows. He became a joke writer and progressed to full scripts, writing for such radio shows as *Variety Bandbox* (1947) and *Educating Archie* (1950–54) and rising to become Britain's highest-paid scriptwriter. He starred in his own BBC television series *Sykes* (1960–65, 1971–79). His stage performances include *Large As Life* (1960), *Hatful of Sykes* (1979) and *Cinderella* (1981–82). He also appeared in films such as *Heavens Above!* (1963), *Those Magnificent Men in Their Flying Machines* (1964), *Monte Carlo or Bust!* (1969), *Theatre of Blood* (1973) and *Absolute Beginners* (1986). Almost totally deaf, he has written, directed and acted in the short, wordless comedies *The Plank* (1967) and *Rhubarb* (1970). Other television programmes include *Curry and Chips* (1969), *Mr H Is Late* (1988) and *The Nineteenth Hole* (from 1989).

Sylvester II, *originally* Gerbert of Aurillac c.940–1003
French pope
Born in Aurillac, he became abbot of Bobbio (982) and Archbishop of Ravenna (988), and as pope (from 999) upheld the primacy of Rome against the separatist tendencies of the French Church. His erudition in chemistry, mathematics and philosophy led people to suspect him of being in league with the devil. He is said to have introduced Arabic numerals and to have invented clocks. 📖 Harriet Lattin, *The Peasant Boy Who Became Pope* (1958)

Sylvester or Silvester, James Joseph 1814–97
English mathematician
Born in London, he studied at St John's College, Cambridge and became Second Wrangler in 1837. He was professor at University College London (1837), and the University of Virginia (1841–45). Returning to London, he worked as an actuary, and was called to the Bar in 1850. He re-entered academic life as Professor of Mathematics at Woolwich (1855–70) and later at Johns Hopkins University, Baltimore (1877–83), where he established the first international journal of mathematics in the US. Finally he became Savilian Professor at Oxford (1883–94), where he helped to found the algebraic theory of invariants, which became a powerful tool in resolving physical problems. He also made important contributions to number theory.

Sylvius, Franciscus, *also called* Franz de la Boë or François du Bois 1614–72
German physician
Born in Hanau, Prussia, he became Professor of Medicine at Leyden (1658). The first to treat saliva, the

pancreatic and other body juices chemically, he also described the relationship between the tubercle and phthisis, and founded the iatro-chemical school; this held that chemical action formed the basis of all life and disease.

Syme, Sir Ronald 1903–89
New Zealand historian
He studied classics at Oriel College, Oxford, and was a Fellow of Trinity College, Oxford, from 1929 to 1949, when he became Oxford's Camden Professor of Ancient History. He had served in British Embassies in Belgrade and Ankara during World War I and was made Professor of Classical Philology at Istanbul University (1942–45). He wrote an account of *The Roman Revolution* (1939), in which he ruthlessly subjected politics in Rome after Caesar's murder to objective analysis, deflating such figures as Cicero and Augustus and making an effective case for Mark Antony, whose alliance with Cleopatra he saw as more pragmatic than erotic. His other publications include *Tacitus* (1958), and *Sallust* (1964).

Symington, William 1763–1831
Scottish engineer and inventor
Born in Leadhills, Lanarkshire, he became a mechanic at the Wanlockhead mines. In 1787 he patented an engine for road locomotion and, in 1788, he constructed for Patrick Miller (1731–1815) a similar engine on a boat 25 feet (7.6m) long, fitted with twin hulls and paddle-wheels, which was launched on Dalswinton Loch. In 1802 he completed at Grangemouth the *Charlotte Dundas*, one of the first practical steamboats ever built. It was intended as a tug, but vested interests prevented its use, asserting that the wash would injure the sides of the Forth and Clyde Canal.

Symonds, Henry Herbert 1885–1958
English educationist and classical scholar
He was a leading figure in the establishment of the Youth Hostel movement and the National Parks. After a distinguished career at Oxford, as a teacher at Rugby School, and as headmaster of Liverpool Institute, he retired early to devote his energies to the service of the countryside and its protection from vandalism. He was instrumental in opening the first Youth Hostels in Great Britain (in North Wales 1931) and served as treasurer, later Vice-President, of the Friends of the Lake District, and as drafting secretary of the standing committee on National Parks. His book *Walking in the Lakes District* (1933) became one of the classic guides. He also wrote *Afforestation in the Lake District* (1937).

Symonds, John Addington 1840–93
English writer
Born in Bristol, he was educated at Balliol College, Oxford, where he won the Newdigate Prize for poetry, and was elected a Fellow of Magdalen College in 1862. His *Introduction to the Study of Dante* (1872) was followed by *Studies of the Greek Poets* (1873–76), his great *Renaissance in Italy* (6 vols, 1875–86), and *Shakespeare's Predecessors in the English Drama* (1884). He also wrote sketches of travel in Italy and elsewhere, monographs on Shelley, Sir Philip Sidney and Ben Jonson, and translated the *Sonnets of Michelangelo and Campanella* (1878) and Benvenuto Cellini's autobiography. He suffered from tuberculosis, and spent much of his life in Italy and Switzerland, for health reasons. His last works were a *Life of Michelangelo* (1892), some verse, and an account of his residence in Davos, Switzerland (1892). ⬚ P Grosskurth, *Symonds* (1964)

Symons, A(lphonse) J(ames) A(lbert) 1900–41
English bibliophile and biographer
He was born in London. His greatest success was *The Quest for Corvo* (1934), an extraordinary biography of the writer and novelist Frederick Rolfe, Baron Corvo. He was active in founding the First Edition Club and the Wine and Food Society, and worked for years on a bibliography of 1890s writers. He published brief lives of the explorers H M Stanley and Emin Pasha and also wrote some brilliant impressionistic chapters of a biography of Oscar Wilde which, like many other projects, he left uncompleted. His brother Julian Symons is a novelist and biographer.

Symons, Arthur William 1865–1945
Welsh critic and poet
Born of Cornish stock in Wales, he received little formal education. He did much to familiarize the British with the literature of France and Italy, especially the work of the French Symbolists. He translated Gabriele d'Annunzio (1902) and Baudelaire (1925). He wrote several volumes of lyrics, and critical works, notably *The Symbolist Movement in Literature* (1899) and *The Romantic Movement in English Poetry* (1909). ⬚ R Lhombreaud, *Arthur Symons* (1963)

Symons, George James 1838–1900
English climatologist
Born in Pimlico, London, he showed an early fascination with the weather, making observations whilst at school and becoming a reporter for the *Registrar-General* in 1857. He was particularly interested in rainfall and established a network of voluntary observers in 1860. This became the British Rainfall Organization and under Symons's enthusiasm the number of observers increased rapidly to reach over 3,500 by 1899. In 1863 he founded a circular which later became *Symons' Monthly Meteorological Magazine*. He was interested in instruments and invented the brontometer for recording the sequence of phenomena in thunderstorms, as well as organizing a comparison of thermometer screens which resulted in the Stevenson screen being accepted as the world standard. He compiled a catalogue of over 60,000 meteorological books and his comprehensive collection was bequeathed to the Royal Meteorological Society, for which he had served as secretary and president. He was a member of many scientific committees including the Royal Society Krakatoa Committee, and was elected FRS in 1878. On his death the Royal Meteorological Society opened a memorial fund and the biennial gold medal provided from the proceeds is the society's highest award.

Symons, Julian Gustave 1912–94
English crimewriter and biographer
He was born in London, the brother of the bibliophile and biographer A J A Symons. His first novel, *The Immaterial Murder Case* (1945), was followed by almost 30 novels and volumes of short stories. His *Bloody Murder*, a history of the genre from the detective story to the crime novel, first appeared in 1972 and has been updated several times. It is an indispensable guide to crime fiction.

Synge, (Edmund) J(ohn) M(illington) 1871–1909
Irish dramatist
Born near Dublin, he attended Trinity College, Dublin, and studied music in Germany. He then spent several years in Paris on literary pursuits until, on the advice of W B Yeats, he settled among the people of the Aran Islands (1899–1902), who provided the material for his plays *In the Shadow of the Glen* (1903), *Riders to the Sea* (1904), *The Well of the Saints* (1905), and his humorous masterpiece *The Playboy of the Western World* (1907), which was followed by *The Tinker's Wedding* (1909). He published *Poems and Translations* (1909), and completed his last play, *Deirdre of the Sorrows* (published posthumously in 1910), while dying from Hodgkin's Disease. He had a profound influence on the next generation of Irish playwrights and was a director of the Abbey Theatre, Dublin, from 1904. ⬚ H H Green and E M Stephens, *J. M. Synge* (1959)

Synge, Richard Laurence Millington 1914–
English biochemist and Nobel Prize winner

Born in Chester, Cheshire, he trained at Cambridge, and joined the Wool Industry Research Association in Leeds (1941–43), where he collaborated with **A J P Martin** on the development of partition chromatography and the mixture separation technique (1941), which revolutionized analytical chemistry. They also investigated mild protein hydrolysis and developed methods for the analysis of aldehydes and hydroxyacids. They shared the Nobel Prize for chemistry in 1952 for their work. In 1944 Synge demonstrated the use of powdered cellulose for separating amino acids, and in 1948 he moved to the Rowett Research Institute, Aberdeen, where he showed the relation between the molecular weight of proteins and their dialysability. Around this time he partially determined the structure of the peptide antibiotic gramicidin. From 1967 he worked at the Food Research Institute in Norwich. He was elected FRS in 1950.

Szasz, Thomas Stephen 1920–
US psychiatrist

Born in Budapest, Hungary, he went to the USA in 1938 and received his MD from Cincinnati University in 1944. Since 1956 he has been Professor of Psychiatry at Syracuse University, New York (emeritus since 1990). He has written many books, most of which argue that all disease must be physical, that consequently the idea of 'mental disease' is a myth and that contemporary psychiatrists are often the agents of repression. His brand of individualism interprets all behaviour as purposeful and intentional, and he argues that people should be allowed to do what they wish as long as they do not break the law, and that all psychiatric therapy should be contractual. A recent publication is *Cruel Compassion* (1994).

Szechenyi, Istvan, Count 1791–1860
Hungarian landowner, soldier, innovator and reformer

He was responsible for establishing the Hungarian Academy of Sciences, which from 1825 onwards contributed a cultural core and a broadening social base to aristocratic protests against **Habsburg** rule. He was also behind the building of Adam Clark's famous Chain Bridge across the Danube joining the political weight of Buda to the commercial weight of Pest to form a new capital. He eventually despaired both of the aristocracy and of the new nationalists and committed suicide.

Szell, George 1897–1970
US conductor and pianist

Born in Budapest, Hungary, he was educated at the Vienna State Academy, and made his debut as a conductor in Berlin (1914), later conducting many of the world's major orchestras. He settled in the USA in 1939 and in 1946 was appointed musical director and conductor of the Cleveland Symphony Orchestra, a post he held for the rest of his life.

Szent-Györgyi, Albert von Nagyrapolt 1893–1986
US biochemist and Nobel Prize winner

Born in Budapest, Hungary, he lectured at the universities of Groningen, where he discovered hexuronic acid (vitamin C) in the adrenal cortex, and at Cambridge. He became professor at Szeged University (1931–45), where he crystallized vitamin C, and in consequence, vitamin B_2 (riboflavin). He was later appointed professor at the University of Budapest (1945–47), director of the Institute of Muscle Research at Woods Hole, Massachusetts (1947–75), and scientific director of the National Foundation for Cancer Research, Massachusetts (1975). He also discovered the reducing system involved in the **Krebs** cycle (1935), and made important contributions towards understanding muscular contraction, glycerinated fibres, allowing study of a physiologically active

biochemical system (1948), and muscle relaxation (1953). He was awarded the Nobel Prize for physiology or medicine in 1937. ⌑ R W Moss, *Free Radical: Albert Szent-Györgyi and the Battle Over Vitamin C* (1987)

Szeryng, Henryk 1918–88
Mexican violinist

Born in Warsaw, Poland, he was educated there, and in Berlin. He then studied composition with **Nadia Boulanger** in Paris (1934–39), and during World War II worked as an interpreter for the Polish government in exile while giving concerts for the Allied troops. In 1941 he went to Latin America to help find homes for Polish refugees and settled, along with them, in Mexico. He wrote several violin and chamber music works, and taught internationally. He took Mexican citizenship in 1946, and was Mexican cultural ambassador from 1960.

Szewinska, Irena *née* Kirszenstein 1946–
Polish athlete

Born in Leningrad (now St Petersburg), Russia, her career spanned five Olympic Games from 1964 to 1980. In the first of these she won a gold medal in the sprint relay. At Mexico (1968), she won gold in the 200 metres. At the Montreal Games of 1976, she won the 400 metres in a world record time of 49.28 seconds. She appeared in her fifth Olympics at Moscow in 1980.

Szilard, Leo 1898–1964
US physicist

Born in Budapest, Hungary, he studied electrical engineering there, and physics in Berlin, working with **Max von Laue**. In 1933 he fled from Nazi Germany to England, and in 1938 emigrated to the USA, where he began work on nuclear physics at Columbia University. In 1934 he had taken a patent on nuclear fission as an energy source, and on hearing of **Otto Hahn** and **Lise Meitner's** fission of uranium (1938), he immediately approached **Albert Einstein** in order to write together to warn President **Franklin D Roosevelt** of the possibility of creating an atomic bomb. Together with **Enrico Fermi**, Szilard organized work on the first fission reactor, which operated in Chicago in 1942. He was a central figure in the Manhattan Project leading to the atomic bomb, and after World War II he researched into molecular biology in experimental work on bacterial mutations and theoretical work on ageing and memory. ⌑ Arnulf K and Louise A Esterer, *Prophet of the Atomic Age: Leo Szilard* (1972)

Szold, Henrietta 1860–1945
US Zionist leader

Born in Baltimore, Maryland, she became a teacher, established some of the earliest evening classes for Jewish immigrants, and co-founded the Jewish Publication Society of America, for which she edited the Jewish Yearbook (1892–1916). She became an ardent champion of Zionism (a movement aimed at securing national privileges and territory in Palestine for the Jews), working to establish peace between Arabs and Jews and a binationalist state. In 1912 she founded the women's organization Hadassah, and was its president until 1926. In 1930 she went to live in Palestine, and in 1927 became the first woman to be elected to the World Zionist Organization. When the Nazis rose to power (1933) she founded Youth Aliyah, in order that Jewish children could escape the Holocaust.

Szymanowski, Karol 1883–1937
Polish composer

Born in Tymoszowska, Ukraine, of Polish parents, he became director of the State Conservatory in Warsaw in 1926. Widely considered Poland's most distinguished composer since **Frédéric Chopin**, his works include operas, incidental music, symphonies, concertos, chamber music, piano music and many songs.

Tabari, at-, *in full* Abu Ja'far
Muhammad ibn Jarir at-Tabari
839–923
Arab historian
Born in Amol, Persia, he travelled throughout the Middle East collecting scholarly material, and wrote a major commentary on the Koran and a history of the world from creation until the early 10th century, which provided a basis for later historical and religious studies.

Tabei, Junko, *née* Ishibashi
1939–
Japanese mountaineer
Born in Miharu Machi, she founded the Japanese Ladies Climbing Club in 1969, and made the second ascent of Annapurna III by a new route the following year. In 1975 she became the first woman to climb Mount Everest as part of an all-female expedition organized by herself and Eiko Hisano. Though injured in an avalanche midway through the climb, she refused to call off the expedition, and reached the summit by the South Col route, a feat described at the time as '99 percent impossible'. The expedition was followed by ascents of Shisha Pangma (1981), Peak Communism (1985) and Aconcagua (1987). She has now climbed the highest summits on five continents, and is a major force in Japanese mountaineering. She is a trustee of the Himalayan Adventure Trust and encourages the conservation of mountain environments.

Tache, Edward See **Teach, Edward**

Tacitus, *in full* Publius or Gaius Cornelius Tacitus
c.55–120AD
Roman historian
Born perhaps in Narbonese Gaul, he studied rhetoric in Rome, rose to eminence as a pleader at the Roman Bar, and in 77AD married the daughter of **Agricola**, the conqueror of Britain. By 88 he was already praetor and a member of one of the priestly colleges. He was an eye witness to **Domitian's** reign of terror, and under **Nerva** he became a consul (97). He established a great reputation as an orator, and 11 of **Pliny's** letters were addressed to him. The earliest surviving work generally attributed to him was the *Dialogus de oratoribus*. His major works are the 12-volume *Historiae* ('Histories'), of which only the first four books survive whole, and *Annales* ('Annals'), of which only eight of the probable 18 books have survived. ▣ *The Annals of Imperial Rome* (Eng trans M Grant, 1956)

Taddeo di Bartoli c.1362–c.1422
Italian painter of the Sienese school
Most of his early work was executed in Pisa, where he was responsible for the frescoes of Paradise and Hell in the Cathedral and paintings in the Palazzo Publico. He was also active in Siena, San Gimignano, Perugia and Volterra. His conservative, but agreeable, style was dependent upon **Simone Martini** and **Ambrogio Lorenzetti**. *The Descent of the Holy Ghost* in the church of San Agostino at Perugia is his masterpiece, but he was usually more successful in his smaller pictures.

Tadema, Sir Lawrence Alma- See
Alma-Tadema, Sir Lawrence

Taeuber-Arp, Sophie, *née* Taeuber 1889–1943
Swiss painter and designer
Born in Davos, she studied applied arts in Munich and Hamburg. From 1914 she worked in Zurich, and in 1915 she met **Jean Arp**, whom she married in 1922. In 1918 they drew up the Dada Manifesto and she modelled *Dada Head* (Pompidou Centre, Paris). One of the most talented of the Constructivist artists, she is best known for her distinctive

rhythmic paintings for the Café l'Aubette (1928) at Strasbourg, on which she collaborated with Arp and **Theo van Doesburg**. From 1941 to 1943 she lived with Arp at Grasse, where other refugee artists included **Sonia Delaunay** and Alberto Magnelli. She died on a secret visit to Zurich, as the result of an accident with a leaking gas stove.

Taft, Robert Alfonso 1889–1953
US lawyer and Republican politician
The son of President **William Howard Taft**, he was born in Cincinnati, Ohio and studied law at Yale and Harvard. In 1917 he became counsellor to the American Food Administration in Europe under **Herbert Hoover**. Elected senator in 1938, he co-sponsored the Taft–Hartley Act (1947) directed against the power of the trade unions and the 'closed shop'. A prominent isolationist, he failed three times (1940, 1948, 1952) to secure Republican nomination for the presidency.

Taft, William Howard 1857–1930
27th President of the USA
Born in Cincinnati, Ohio, the son of President **Ulysses S Grant's** Secretary of War and Attorney-General, he studied at Yale and qualified as a lawyer in Cincinnati. He took part in Ohio state politics, and in 1890 became Solicitor-General for the USA. In 1900 he was made president of the Philippine Commission, and in 1901 first civil Governor of the islands. From 1904 to 1908 he was Secretary of War for the USA, and in 1906 provisional Governor of Cuba. From 1909 to 1913 he was President of the USA, continuing the antitrust policies of his predecessor, **Theodore Roosevelt**, and securing a free-trade agreement with Canada, but his conservatism alienated the progressive wing of the Republican Party, and he was defeated by **Woodrow Wilson** for a second term. From 1913 he was Professor of Law at Yale and from 1921 Chief Justice of the US Supreme Court. As such he made a number of useful reforms to the judiciary and proved himself a sound judge. His son was **Robert A Taft**. ▣ Henry Fowles Pringle, *The Life and Times of William Howard Taft* (2 vols, 1939)

Tagliacozzi or **Taliacotius, Gasparo** 1546–99
Italian surgeon
He was born in Bologna, and as professor there of surgery and of anatomy, he developed a technique for repairing injured noses by transplanting skin from the arm.

Taglioni, Maria 1804–84
Italian dancer
Born in Stockholm, she was the daughter of an Italian ballet master Filippo Taglioni and a Swedish mother. Though she had an unpromising build, she danced with grace and individuality, and after some initial setbacks achieved success with her creation of *La Sylphide* in 1832. She married the Comte de Voisins in 1832, and ended her career teaching deportment to the British royal children. Her brother Paul (1808–84) and his daughter Marie Paul (1833–91) were also famous dancers.

Tagore, Rabindranath 1861–1941
Indian poet and philosopher and Nobel Prize winner
Born in Calcutta, he studied law in England (1878–80) and for 17 years managed his family estates at Shileida, where he collected the legends and tales he later used in his work. In 1901 he founded, near Bolpur, the Santiniketan, a communal school aiming to blend Eastern and Western philosophical and educational systems, which became Visva-Bharati University. He was openly critical of Mahatma **Gandhi's** non-co-operation as well as of the

Government attitude in Bengal. His first book was a volume of poetry, *A Poet's Tale* (1878), followed by a novel, *Karuna*, and a drama, *The Tragedy of Rudachandra*. His major works include *Binodini* (1902, Eng trans 1964), the first modern novel by an Indian writer; *The Crescent Moon* (1913), poems about childhood; *Gitanjali* (1912, Eng trans *Song Offerings*, 1912), a volume of spiritual verse; and his best-known play, *Chitra* (1914). He also wrote *My Reminiscences* (1917) and *My Boyhood Days* (1940). He received the Nobel Prize for literature in 1913, the first Asian to do so, and was knighted in 1915—an honour which he resigned in 1919 as a protest against British policy in the Punjab. ▢ K R Kripklami, *Rabindranath Tagore* (1962)

Tah-gah-jute See **Logan, James**

Tai Ai-lien See **Dai, Ailian**

Tailleferre, Germaine, *originally* Germaine Taillefesse 1892–1983
French composer
Born in Parc-St-Maur, near Paris, she studied at the Paris Conservatoire, taking lessons from **Maurice Ravel**. She became the only female member and longest surviving representative of the group known as Les Six with **Georges Auric, Louis Durey, Arthur Honegger, Darius Milhaud** and **Francis Poulenc**, an informal grouping of young, like-minded French composers who performed together for a few years from 1917. Her works include *Concertino* for harp and orchestra (1926) and *Chansons françaises* (1930). In 1974 she published an autobiography, *Mémoires à l'emporte pièce*.

Taine, Hippolyte Adolphe 1828–93
French critic, historian and philosopher
Born in Vouziers, Ardennes, he studied for a year in Paris before becoming an author. He made a reputation by his critical analysis of **La Fontaine**'s *Fables* (1853), followed by the *Voyage aux eaux des Pyrénées* (1855). His positivism was strongly expressed in *Les Philosophes français du dix-neuvième siècle* (1857), *Philosophie de l'art* (1881) and *De l'intelligence* (1870). His greatest work, *Les Origines de la France contemporaine* (1875–94), constitutes a strong attack made on the men and the motives of the Revolution. He also wrote *Derniers essais* (1895), *Carnets de voyage* (1897) and *Notes sur l'Angleterre* (1871).

Tait, Archibald Campbell 1811–82
Scottish Anglican prelate, and Archbishop of Canterbury
Born in Edinburgh, he was brought up as a Presbyterian, and educated at Edinburgh Academy, Glasgow University and Balliol College, Oxford, where he became a Fellow. He entered the Church of England in 1836, and became an opponent of the Oxford Movement, protesting in 1841 against **John Henry Newman**'s *Tract 90*. He succeeded Dr **Thomas Arnold** as headmaster of Rugby (1842), became dean of Carlisle in 1849, and in 1856 Bishop of London. He condemned Bishop **Colenso**'s critical views on the accuracy of the Bible, but intervened on his side against attempts to have him deposed. In 1869 he was appointed Archbishop of Canterbury (the first Scotsman to hold the post), and helped to lull the strife caused by Irish disestablishment, but was less successful in dealing with resentments over the Public Worship and Regulation Act (1874) and the Burials Act (1880). He improved the organization of the church in the colonies, and presided over the 1878 Lambeth Conference. His books included *The Dangers and Safeguards of Modern Theology* (1861) and *Harmony of Revelation and the Sciences* (1864). His biography was published in 1891 by his son-in-law, the future Archbishop of Canterbury, **Randall Thomas Davidson**.

Tait, Peter Guthrie 1831–1901
Scottish mathematician

Born in Dalkeith, Lothian, he was educated at the universities of Edinburgh and Cambridge, where he graduated as Senior Wrangler in 1852. He became Professor of Mathematics at Belfast University (from 1854) and Professor of Natural Philosophy at Edinburgh University (1860–1901). He wrote on quaternions, thermodynamics and the kinetic theory of gases, and collaborated with Lord **Kelvin** on a *Treatise on natural philosophy* (1867), the standard work on the natural sciences in English for a generation. His study of vortices and smoke rings led to early work on the topology of knots. He studied the dynamics of the flight of a golf-ball and discovered the importance of 'underspin'.

Tait, Thomas Smith 1882–1952
Scottish architect
Born in Paisley, Renfrewshire, he trained in Glasgow, becoming an assistant with Sir John James Burnet (1857–1938) in 1903, studying simultaneously under Eugène Bourdon at the Glasgow School of Art. After studying on the Continent, he moved to the firm's London office in 1905 and in 1914 he travelled to New York for a year's work with the modernist Donn Barber. He designed Adelaide House (1921–24), the *Daily Telegraph* office in London (1927) and St Andrew's House, Edinburgh (1934), and won the competition for the Hawkhead Infectious Diseases Hospital in Paisley (1932). He was controlling designer of the Glasgow Empire Exhibition of 1938 and was the most prominent Scots architect of the interwar period.

Tait, William 1792–1864
Scottish publisher
He was the founder of *Tait's Edinburgh Magazine* (1832–64), a literary and radical political monthly, to which **Thomas De Quincey, John Stuart Mill, Richard Cobden** and **Richard Bright** contributed.

Takamine, Jokichi 1834–1922
US chemist
Born in Takaoka, Japan, he studied chemical engineering in Tokyo and Glasgow, and in 1887 opened his own factory, the first to make superphosphate fertilizer in Japan. In 1890 he moved to the USA and set up an industrial biochemical laboratory there. He worked for some time in the laboratory of **John Abel**. In 1898 he published *Testing diastatic substances*, in which he described the iodine test for following the activity of saliva or other fluids in hydrolysing starch to maltose and glucose. He later published (1901) the first description of adrenaline isolated in crystalline form. It was realized that adrenaline, an intravenous injection of which produces an enormous rise in blood pressure, was the first hormone to be isolated in pure form from a natural source.

Takei, Kei 1939–
Japanese post-modern dancer and choreographer
Born in Tokyo, she studied there and then travelled on a scholarship to the Juilliard School of Music, New York, where **Anna Sokolow** taught her dance. In 1969 she formed her own company, Moving Earth, and began her major work, *Light*, which has so far twenty-five parts lasting at least an hour each. Fifteen sections of this harsh depiction of survival, which starts with the Vietnam War and includes both primitive and contemporary images, were shown in a single performance in 1981.

Takemitsu, Toru 1930–96
Japanese composer
Born in Tokyo, he was self-taught and became one of the most significant composers in Japan. In 1951 he founded a workshop aimed at encouraging composers to combine traditional Japanese melodies and new techniques. Between 1975 and 1983 he lectured extensively in the USA, and in 1984 was composer in residence at the

Aldeburgh Festival, England. His aim as a composer was always to 'achieve a sound as intense as silence' and his music is subtle, even mystic. His output is huge and the titles of his work often suggest their mood: *Far Away* (1973), *Undisturbed Rest* (1952–59), *A Flock descends into the Pentagonal Garden* (1977). He also composed the music for several films, including *Woman of the Dunes* (1964). 📖 Noriko Ohtake, *Creative Sources for the Music of Toru Takemitsu* (1993)

Takeshita, Noboru 1924–
Japanese statesman

He was born in Kakeyamachi, in western Japan, the son of an affluent sake brewer. He trained as a kamikaze pilot during World War II. After university and a brief career as a schoolteacher, he was elected to the House of Representatives as a Liberal Democratic Party (LDP) deputy in 1958, rising to become Chief Cabinet Secretary (1971–72) to Prime Minister Sato Eisaku and Minister of Finance (1982–86) under Prime Minister Nakasone. Formerly a member of the powerful Tanaka faction, he founded his own faction, the largest within the party, in 1987, and three months later was elected LDP President and Prime Minister. Although regarded as a cautious, consensual politician, he pushed through important tax reforms. His administration was undermined by the uncovering of the Recruit-Cosmos insider share dealing scandal, which, though dating back to 1986, forced the resignation of senior government ministers, including, eventually, Takeshita himself, in 1989.

Takhtajan, Armen Leonovich 1910–
Armenian botanist

Born in Šuša, Nagorno Karabakh, from 1932 to 1943 he held various posts at Tbilisi, Georgia, and Yerevan Museum and Yerevan University, Armenia, where he studied the evolution and phylogeny of flowering plants. In 1943 he joined the palaeobotanical section of the Institute of Botany of the Academy of Sciences of the Armenian SSR, Yerevan, but later (1954–84) worked at the Botanical Institute of the Academy of Sciences of the USSR in Leningrad (St Petersburg), where he was director of the Department of Floristics, Systematics and Evolution of Higher Plants (1977–84). He has published several versions of a new system of flowering plant classification, the most definitive being *Sistema Magnoliophytov* (1987). Other major works include *Flowering Plants: Origin and Dispersal* (1966) and *Floristic Regions of the World* (1978), a unique synthesis of current thinking on world plant geography.

Tal, Mikhail Nekhemevich 1936–92
Russian chess player

He was born in Riga, Latvia. In 1960 he defeated Mikhail Botvinnik to become the youngest grandmaster to hold the world title until then. His withering stares over the board were held by opponents as attempts at hypnotism, but it is more likely that they succumbed to his unusually inventive style of attack. Major kidney problems terminated his reign at the top, but he remained an active tournament player and chess journalist until his death.

Talbert, Bruce James 1838–81
Scottish designer

Educated at Dundee High School, he became a prolific and influential designer specializing in Gothic-style furniture. Originally apprenticed to a woodcarver, he later trained as an architect. He moved from Glasgow to Manchester and Coventry, working for various firms before settling in London where he published his *Gothic Forms Applied to Furniture and Decoration for Domestic Purposes* in 1867. By 1873 he was working for Villons. Apart from furniture, he designed metalwork, wallpapers, tapestries and carpets.

Talbot
English noble family

They are descended from Richard de Talbot, named in the *Domesday Book*, and from Gilbert (d.1346), the first baron. The Earl of Shrewsbury and Talbot is the premier earl of England and Ireland, and hereditary Lord High Steward of Ireland. The Lords Talbot de Malahide represent a family in Ireland which settled there in 1167.

Talbot, Charles, 12th Earl and Duke of Shrewsbury 1660–1718
English politician

He served under Charles II and James VII and II, but gave money to William of Orange (William III) and did much to bring about the Revolution of 1688. Twice Secretary of State (1689, 1694), he withdrew from public affairs in 1700. In 1710 he helped to bring about the fall of the Whigs and was made Lord Chamberlain. At the crisis on the death of Queen Anne (1714), as Treasurer and Lord Justice he helped secure the peaceful succession of the Hanoverians. He was created Duke of Shrewsbury in 1694, but the dukedom died with him.

Talbot, George, 6th Earl of Shrewsbury
c.1528–1590
English soldier

He took part in the 'Rough Wooing' of Scotland (1543–44) by Edward Seymour, 1st Duke of Somerset. From 1569 to 1584 he was entrusted by Queen Elizabeth I with the custody of Mary, Queen of Scots, at Tutbury, Chatsworth and Sheffield Castle. He was the fourth husband of Elizabeth Hardwick (1518–1608), familiarly known as 'Bess of Hardwick', widow of Sir William Cavendish of Chatsworth.

Talbot, Sir John, 1st Earl Shrewsbury
c.1390–1453
English soldier

A distinguished soldier in France during Henry VI's reign, he was successful in many engagements until he was finally checked at Orleans by Joan of Arc (1429), and taken prisoner at Patay (1429), remaining a captive until 1431. He had further successes in France, and was made Marshal of France. He was Lord-Lieutenant of Ireland twice (1414–19, 1445). Created Earl of Salop (1422), Earl of Shrewsbury (1442) and Earl of Waterford (1455), he was killed at Castillon, after taking Bordeaux.

Talbot, Mary Anne, *known as* the British Amazon
1778–1808
English soldier

She served as a drummer boy in Flanders (1792–93) and as a cabin boy in the navy (1793–96). She later became a maidservant in London, and her story was published in *The Life and Surprising Adventures of Mary Anne Talbot* (1809).

Talbot, William Henry Fox 1800–77
English physicist and pioneer of photography

Born in Melbury Abbas, Dorset, he was educated at Harrow and Trinity College, Cambridge. In 1838 he invented 'photogenic drawing', a system of making photographic prints on silver chloride paper, in the same year as the invention of the daguerrotype by Louis Daguerre. In 1841 he patented the calotype, the first process for photographic negatives from which prints could be made, and was awarded the Rumford Medal of the Royal Society in 1842. He also discovered a method of making instantaneous photographs, using electric spark illumination (the first use of flash photography), in 1851. His *Pencil of Nature* (1844) was one of the first photographically illustrated books to be published. He also wrote works on astronomy and mathematics, and helped to decipher the cuneiform inscriptions at Ninevah. He became an MP in 1833. A 16th-century converted barn at the gates of Lacock Abbey in Wiltshire, where Fox Talbot lived from

1833 onwards, is now a museum of his work and equipment run by the National Trust. 📖 A J P Arnold, *Talbot: Pioneer of Photography and Man of Science* (1977)

Talese, Gay 1932–
US journalist

Born in Ocean City, New Jersey, he became a reporter for the *New York Times* (1955–65), and wrote his first non-fiction 'short stories' for *Esquire* magazine, beginning in 1963. **Tom Wolfe**, generally regarded as the pioneer of 'new journalism' has recognized Talese as its true inventor. His new style reached maturity in his bestselling non-fiction novels, *The Kingdom and the Power* (1969) about the *New York Times*, and *Honor Thy Father* (1971), about the Mafia. He has been described as 'a reporter who can write and a writer who can report'. Later works include *Thy Neighbor's Wife* (1980) and *Unto the Sons* (1992).

Taliacotius, Gasparo See Tagliacozzi, Gasparo

Taliesin fl.c.550
Welsh bard

He is considered (with the mythical Merlin) one of the two great founders of the Welsh poetic tradition. He is named in the *Saxon Genealogies* appended to the *Historia Britonum* of **Nennius**, but later mythical material became attached to his legend. Although a mass of poetry, much of it of later date, has been ascribed to him, there are only eight heroic poems in the 13th-century *Book of Taliesin* thought to be written by him. 📖 J Morris Jones, *Taliesin* (1918)

Tallchief, Maria, *originally* Betty Marie Tallchief
1925–
US ballet dancer

Born in Fairfax, Oklahoma, of a Scots-Irish mother and Osage father, she studied dance with **Bronislava Nijinska**, and with **George Balanchine** (to whom she was later married, 1946–52) at the School of American Ballet, New York. She danced with the Ballet Russe de Monte Carlo (1942–47) then joined the New York City Ballet and became the principal dancer, appearing in *Swan Lake*, *Firebird* and others. She danced for the American Ballet Theater (1960–63) and returned to the New York City Ballet in 1963 until her retirement in 1965. She founded the Chicago City Ballet in 1979.

Tallemant des Réaux, Gédéon c.1619–1700
French man of letters

He was born in La Rochelle, and married his cousin, Élisabeth Rambouillet, whose fortune enabled him to devote himself to letters and society. His famous *Historiettes* (written 1657–59, published 1834–40), 376 in number, are illustrative anecdotes on the leading Parisiennes of the time rather than biographies.

Talleyrand(-Périgord), Charles Maurice de, Prince of Benevento 1754–1838
French politician

He was born in Paris, son of the Comte Talleyrand de Périgord (1734–88). He was educated for the Church and cultivated the character of a rake and a cynical wit. Abbot of St Denis (1775) and agent-général to the French clergy (1780), he was nominated Bishop of Autun by **Louis XVI** (1788), elected to the Estates General (1789), and was one of the members of the Assembly selected to draw up the Declaration of Rights. He took a cynical delight in attacking the clergy to which he still nominally belonged, and proposed confiscating the landed property of the Church. In 1790 he was elected President of the Assembly. In 1791 he consecrated two new bishops, declaring at the same time his attachment to the Holy See, but, ex-communicated, he gave up his clerical career. Early in 1792 he was sent to London, but failed to conciliate **William Pitt**, the Younger; in December he was placed on the list of émigrés. He remained in exile, until January 1794, when the Alien Act drove him to the USA. After the fall of **Robespierre** he returned to Paris (1796), attached himself to the Comte de **Barras**, and was made Foreign Minister under the Directory (1797). He recognized the genius of **Napoleon I** and established friendly relations with him. He was greatly instrumental in consolidating the power of Napoleon as consul for life (1802) and as emperor (1804). For a time he was in disgrace for his willingness to sell his services towards a treaty between Great Britain and the USA. Under the Consulate he was restored to his post, was privy to the kidnapping and murder (1804) of the Duc d'**Enghien**, and disrupted the European coalition against France initiated by Great Britain (1805). He shared responsibility with Napoleon for the organization (1806) of the Confederation of the Rhine. After being created Prince of Benevento (1806), he withdrew from the ministry. He was opposed to the invasion of Russia and on this basis deserted Napoleon in 1814. As far back as Tilsit (1807) he seems to have been in communication with Great Britain. At Erfurt (1808), he had revealed state secrets to Russia and he had mortally offended Napoleon, after the disasters in Spain, by making, with **Fouché**, tentative arrangements for the succession. He led the anti-Napoleonic faction, and through him communications were opened with the allies and the **Bourbons**. He dictated to the Senate the terms of Napoleon's deposition, and became Minister of Foreign Affairs under **Louis XVIII**. He negotiated the treaties by which the allies left France in possession of the boundaries of 1792, and at the Congress of Vienna (1814–15) he established France's right to be heard. After the second Restoration, he became Prime Minister for a short time, but he was now neither popular nor influential. He was **Louis Philippe**'s chief adviser at the July Revolution, for which he was partly responsible, went to London as ambassador and reconciled the British ministry and court to France. He retired into private life in 1834. 📖 Jack F Bernard, *Talleyrand* (1973)

Tallien, Jean Lambert 1767–1820
French revolutionary

Born in Paris, during the Revolution he made himself famous by his Jacobin broadsheets, *L'Ami des citoyens* (1791). He was conspicuous in the attack on the Tuileries and in the September massacres, was elected to the Convention (1792), and played a part in the downfall of the Girondins. On his mission to Bordeaux (1793) during the Terror he quenched all opposition with the guillotine. He was recalled to Paris, and in 1794 was chosen President of the Convention; but **Robespierre** hated him, and Tallien, conspiring with the Comte de **Barras** and **Joseph Fouché**, led the successful attack of 9th Thermidor which brought about his eventual downfall. He helped to suppress the Revolutionary Tribunal and the Jacobin Club, and drew up the accusations against **Jean Baptiste Carrier**, Le Bon and other Terrorists. He was a member of the Council of Five Hundred under the Directory (1795–99) and accompanied **Napoleon I** to Egypt. 📖 Marie-Hélène Bourquin-Simonin, *Monsieur et Madame Tallien* (1987)

Tallis, Thomas c.1505–1585
English composer

He was born in London. In 1575 **Elizabeth I** granted him, with **William Byrd**, a monopoly for printing music and music paper in England. He is considered 'the father of English cathedral music', and one of the most distinguished contrapuntists of the English school, and an adaptation of his plainsong responses, and his setting of the Canticles in D minor, are still in use. He wrote much church music, including a motet in 40 parts, *Spem in alium*.

Talma, François Joseph 1763–1826
French tragedian

Born in Paris, he made his debut in 1787. Actors had previously worn clothing in the style of their own time and country, but Talma made a point of accuracy in costume. He achieved his greatest success in 1789 as **Charles IX** in a play by **André Chénier**.

Tamara, Queen, also called Thamar c.1160–1212
Queen of Georgia

She became co-ruler with her father King George III in 1178 and succeeded to his throne when he died six years later. Tamara kept an eye on her nobles by insisting on their compulsory attendance at court and by accompanying them on their hunting trips. Occasionally she would lead them in battle with her soldiers shouting 'King Tamara'. One such battle involved the defeat in 1205 of a vast Turkish army under the Sultan of Rum at Basiani. By the time of her death her empire was at the peak of its power and included parts of Russia, Persia, Armenia and Turkey, but her children proved too weak to rule and it was ultimately destroyed by the Mongols. Georgia's national poet, Shota Rustaveli, was reputedly in love with Tamara. His *The Knight in Panther's Skin* is an epic poem about a mythological heroine in a world where men and women are equal.

Tamayo, Rufino 1899–1991
Mexican artist

He was born at Oaxaca, studied at the Academy of San Carlos in Mexico City (1917–21), and became interested in traditional Mexican sculpture as a curator at the National Museum of Anthropology (1921–26). He moved to New York in 1936, spent 10 years in Paris (1954–64), then lived and worked primarily in Mexico. His own style combines pre-Columbian art with the art of modern Europe. Among his works are the painting *Women of Tehuantepec* (1939, Albright-Knox Art Gallery, Buffalo), and the murals *Birth of Nationality* and *Mexico Today* (1952–53) for the National Palace of Fine Arts in Mexico.

Tambo, Oliver 1917–93
South African politician

Born in Bizana, Transkei, the son of a peasant farmer, at the age of 16 he travelled to Johannesburg to attend a school set up by the Community for the Resurrection, where he came under the influence of Father **Trevor Huddleston**. After graduating at Fort Hare University he began a teacher's diploma course but was expelled for organizing a student protest and in 1944 joined the African National Congress (ANC), being appointed vice-president of its youth league. As his thoughts turned to the church, he asked Trevor Huddleston to help him join the priesthood, but before he was accepted as a candidate, in 1956, he was imprisoned. He was released the following year. ANC deputy president from 1958, when it was banned in 1960 he left South Africa and went to London to set up an external wing. With the continued imprisonment, until 1990, of **Nelson Mandela**, he became acting ANC president in 1967, president in 1977 and national chairman from 1991, and travelled extensively promoting its cause.

Tamm, Igor Yevgenevich 1895–1971
Soviet physicist and Nobel Prize winner

Born in Vladivostock, he was educated at the universities of Edinburgh and Moscow, and taught at Moscow State University (1924–34) before moving to the Physics Institute of the Academy. Together with **Ilya Frank** he developed a theory to describe the 'Cherenkov effect' discovered by **Pavel Cherenkov**. They demonstrated that this radiation is due to a particle moving through a medium faster than the speed of light in the medium, and related the type of radiation observed to the particle mass and velocity. Tamm shared the 1958 Nobel Prize for physics with Cherenkov and Frank for this work. The effect has been utilized in highly sensitive particle detectors.

Tam'si, Tchicaya U 1931–88
Congolese poet, novelist and playwright

Born in Npili, Moyen Congo (Congolese Republic), he was educated in French Lycées in Orleans and Paris from the age of 15, after his father was elected a deputy to the French National Assembly, and lived in Paris for most of the rest of his life. He published several volumes of Surrealist poetry, notably *Le Mauvais Sang* (1955, 'Bad Blood'), *Le Ventre* (1964, 'The Stomach') and *Feu de Brousse* (1964, 'Bush Fire'). His best-known poems are in *Epitomé* (1962), which records the events surrounding the imprisonment and murder of **Patrice Lumumba**. Poems translated into English by Gerald Moore appeared as *Selected Poems* (1970).

Tanaka, Kakuei 1918–1993
Japanese statesman

He was born into a bankrupted rural family in Futuda village, in western Japan. After training as a civil engineer and establishing a successful building contracting business, he was elected to Japan's House of Representatives in 1947. He rose swiftly within the dominant Liberal Democratic Party (LDP), becoming Minister of Finance (1962–65), Party Secretary-General (1965–67) and Minister of International Trade and Industry (1971–72), before serving as LDP President and Prime Minister (1972–74). He was arrested in 1976, while he was Prime Minister, on charges of accepting bribes from the Lockheed Corporation while in office, and eventually in 1983 was found guilty and sentenced to four years' imprisonment. He had resigned from the LDP in 1976, becoming an independent deputy, but remained an influential, behind-the-scenes, faction leader. His appeal against the 1983 verdict was rejected by the High Court in 1987, but a further appeal was lodged. He died still fighting his appeals.

Tancred 1078–1112
Norman crusader

He went on the First Crusade (1096–99) with his uncle **Bohemond I**, and distinguished himself in many sieges. He established the great principality of Galilee (1099), but soon went to Antioch where he ruled as regent. He is the hero of *Gerusalemme liberata* by **Tasso** (1593) and was the grandson of **Robert Guiscard**. 📖 Robert Lawrence Nicholson, *Tancred* (1940)

Tandy, Jessica 1907–94
US actress

She was born in London and became a naturalized US citizen in 1954. She made her London debut in 1929, and on Broadway the following year. Establishing herself as a major stage star, she starred opposite **John Gielgud** in *Hamlet* (1934) and as Blanche Du Bois in *A Streetcar Named Desire* (1947). She appeared in a number of plays on Broadway with her second husband, Hume Cronyn (1911–), including *A Delicate Balance* (1966), *The Gin Game* (1977) and *Foxfire* (1982). She acted in many films, and won an Academy Award for her title role in *Driving Miss Daisy* (1989).

Taney, Roger Brooke 1777–1864
US jurist

Born in Calvert County, Maryland, he was educated at Dickinson College, Pennsylvania. He was admitted to the Bar in 1799 and elected to the Maryland Senate in 1816. In 1824 he changed his allegiance from the Federalist to the Democratic Party, and gave his support to **Andrew Jackson**, who in 1831 made him Attorney-General, and in 1833 Secretary of the Treasury. In the latter post he was instrumental in persuading Jackson to destroy the Bank of the United States. The Senate, after rejecting his appointment as Chief Justice of the Supreme Court in 1835, confirmed it in 1836. His early decisions were strongly in favour of state sovereignty, but his most famous decision was in the **Dred Scott** case (1857), when he ruled that African-Americans were not citizens and thus could not either sue in federal court or claim rights under the Constitution; he also declared that Congress did not have the authority to ban slavery in the territories, and so branded the Missouri Compromise unconstitutional. Intended to put an end to antislavery agitation, this unjust and ill-considered ruling instead precipitated the Civil War.

Taneyev, Sergei Ivanovich 1856–1915
Russian composer and pianist
Born in Vladimir, he studied at the Moscow Conservatory and was a pupil of **Tchaikovsky**, becoming a director at the Conservatory (1885–89). He wrote music of all kinds, including two cantatas, *John of Damascus* and *After the Reading of a Psalm*, and six symphonies. He was well known as a teacher, and his pupils included **Aleksandr Scriabin** and **Rachmaninov**.

Tanfucio, Neri See Fucini, Renato

Tange, Kenzo 1913–
Japanese architect
He was born and educated in Tokyo. His early buildings such as the Hiroshima Peace Centre (1949–55) owe a debt to tradition and **Le Corbusier**. His later works, such as the Shizoka Press and Broadcasting Centre (1966–67), provide incompleteness, flexibility and ability for change. He also designed the dramatic National Gymnasium for the 1964 Olympic Games, and the theme pavilion for the 1970 Osaka Exposition. Professor of Architecture at Tokyo University (1946–74), he has published several influential works, including *A Plan for Tokyo* (1960). *Toward a Structural Reorganization* (1960) expresses his later structuralist or metabolist approach. Since 1989 he has been president of the Japanese Architectural Association.

Tanguy, Yves 1900–55
US artist
Born in Paris, France, he was mainly self-taught, and began to paint in 1922, joining the Surrealists in 1926. In 1930 he travelled to Africa, and went to the USA in 1939, becoming a US citizen in 1948. All his pictures are at the same time Surrealist and nonfigurative, being peopled with numerous small objects or organisms, whose meaning and identity are unknown, suggesting the landscape of another planet.

Tang Yin (T'ang Yin), *also known as* Tang Liujiu
1470–1523
Chinese painter and poet
Born in the Suzhou region of Jiangsu (Kiangsu) province, he passed the exams for the local government with distinction and found many benefactors, among them various masters of the Wu school of painting. At 28 he went to Beijing (Peking), but a scandal forced him to return home. In order to survive, he started painting in a popular and decorative style for the burghers of Suzhou: portraits, pretty women, erotica. His work presents a refinement of expression rare among the professionals and a technical know-how seldom achieved by the amateurs. He is counted among the Four Great Masters of the **Ming** dynasty.

Tanizaki Junichiro 1886–1965
Japanese novelist and playwright
He was born and educated in Tokyo, where he studied Japanese literature at the Imperial University. After the earthquake of 1923, he removed to Kyoto-Osaka, which was to be the setting of his lengthy novel, *Sasameyuki*

(1943–48, Eng trans *The Makioka Sisters*, 1957), a notable example of descriptive realism. From his first work onwards, Tanizaki was concerned with the transformative power of the imagination; *Shisei* (1910, 'Tattoo') is a story about a girl whose personality is changed by bodily decoration. His story *Tade kuu mushi* (1929, Eng trans *Some Prefer Nettles*, 1955) underlined his cultural nationalism. *Bushuko hiwa* (1935) and *Yoshino kuzu* (1937) appeared together in English translation in 1982 as *The Secret History of the Lord of Musashi* and *Arrowroot* respectively. Other novels include *The Key* (1960) and *Diary of a Mad Old Man* (1962). He wrote a number of plays, literary essays and translations. 🕮 *Setsugoan yawa* (published posthumously, 1968); G B Petersen, *The Moon in the Water* (1979)

Tannhäuser, Der c.1210–c.1270
German poet and Minnesinger
He was probably from Bavaria. He was court poet to the ruler of Austria, and is thought (because of what he says in his poetry) to have travelled a great deal, including taking part in one of the crusades. He broke away from the rigid conventions of previous Minnesang, using humour, irony and even parody, as well as great sensuality in erotic passages. Several of his songs survive with melodies. His name was linked with a legendary German knight in a popular 16th-century ballad. It tells of a man who seeks forgiveness for a life of pleasure but, being refused absolution by the pope, returns to his former ways. The story was the basis for the opera by **Richard Wagner** (1845), and of **Algernon Charles Swinburne's** poem 'Laus Veneris' (1866).

Tansley, Sir Arthur George 1871–1955
English botanist
Born in London and educated at Cambridge, he later lectured at University College London (1893–1906), and then at Cambridge from 1906 to 1923. Sherardian Professor at Oxford (1927–37), he founded the precursor (1904) of the Ecological Society (1914), and was founder-editor of the journal *New Phytologist* (1902). A pioneer British plant ecologist, he published *Practical Plant Ecology* (1923) and *The British Isles and their Vegetation* (1939), and contributed to anatomical and morphological botany as well as physiology. He was president of the British Ecological Society in 1913, chairman of the Nature Conservancy Council from 1949 to 1953, and was awarded a knighthood in 1950.

Tantia Topee, *real name* Ramchandra Pandurangez
d.1859
Indian soldier and rebel
Born in Gwalior, he was **Nana Sahib's** lieutenant in the Indian Mutiny (1857–58). He took part in the massacre of the British at Cawnpore (July 1857). With the Rani of Jhansi he occupied Gwalior and then held the field after his chief had fled. After marching through central India and Khandesh in an attempt to raise up the Marathas in revolt he was betrayed, captured and executed.

Tàpies, Antoni 1923–
Spanish painter
He was born in Barcelona, and studied law there. A self-taught painter, he became a member of the Dau al Set (Die with the Seven) group of avant-garde artists and writers opposed to the **Franco** dictatorship. Inspired by Surrealism, he made collages from everyday rubbish—rags, bits of string, torn canvas—splashed with paint and graffiti, as in *Upside-down Hat* (1967, Pompidou Centre, Paris). In 1957 he was a founder of the El Paso group, which championed Informalism. His first one-man show, in Barcelona (1951), was followed right through to the 1990s by numerous international exhibitions and prizes, such as the Venice Biennale in 1958 and the Barcelona Gold Medal in 1992. His most recent exhibitions include

San Francisco (1991), Vienna (1986), Peking (1989), Prague, Lisbon and Mexico (1991), and Dallas and New York (1992). At the 1993 Venice Biennale he shared the Leone d'Oro prize for best artist with **Richard Hamilton**. In 1984 he was instrumental in setting up the Tàpies Foundation, a permanent collection of his work, in Barcelona. 📖 *Memòria personal* (1978)

Tarantino, Quentin 1963–
US director and screenwriter

He was born in Knoxville, Tennessee, to a half-Irish, half-Cherokee mother and a father of Italian descent who was absent for most of his upbringing. He spent much of his childhood at the movies, before working in a video store and training as an actor (he appears in his own films). With the help of actor **Harvey Keitel**, one of his many scripts was made into Tarantino's debut film as director, *Reservoir Dogs* (1993). In 1994 his second film, *Pulp Fiction*, won the Palme d'Or at the Cannes Film Festival. Characterized by brutality, violent escapism, and an intentional absence of morality, both films exist at the point where cruelty meets humour, bringing Tarantino cult status despite his many critics. He was one of the directors of the film *Four Rooms* in 1995. He is also the original author of the story of **Oliver Stone**'s *Natural Born Killers* (1994).

Tarantula, Black See **Acker, Kathy**

Tarap, Shetrup Akong See **Akong Tulku Rinpoche**

Tarbell, Ida M(inerva) 1857–1944
US reform journalist

Born in Erie County, Pennsylvania, she was educated at Allegheny College, and became associate editor of *The Chautauquan* (1883–91). She then studied in Paris at the Sorbonne (1891–94) and joined *McClure's Magazine* (1894–1906). Her explosive denunciation of **John D Rockefeller**'s fortune-building methods, *History of the Standard Oil Company* (published in book form in 1904), established women in the new 'muckraking' journalism. She also wrote biographies of **Napoleon**, **Madame Roland** and **Abraham Lincoln**. She joined **Lincoln Steffens** and other *McClure's* writers in running the *American* magazine (1906–15), campaigning against corruption and big business interests. Her feminist writing includes *The Business of Being a Woman* (1912) and *The Ways of Women* (1915), and her history, *The Nationalizing of Business* (1936), was a standard work on American post-Civil War economic growth for 20 years. Her last book was an autobiography, *All in the Day's Work* (1939).

Tardieu, André 1876–1945
French politician

A well-known journalist before 1914, he was a deputy (1914–24, 1926–36), High Commissioner in the USA (1917–18), and one of **Georges Clemenceau**'s chief advisers during the negotiation of the peace treaties following World War I. A number of ministerial appointments and his terms as Prime Minister (1929–30, 1932) made him the dominant figure throughout the 1928–32 parliament. During that time, he practised what he called a 'prosperity policy', providing government assistance for the modernization of agriculture and industry, and putting through measures to abolish fees in state secondary schools and to improve social insurance. The victory of the left in the 1932 elections put him in opposition, but after the crisis of February 1934 he was brought back to office in the Doumergue cabinet with the task of producing proposals for constitutional reform. When it became evident that they were not going to be adopted, he left active politics to defend his plans for a stronger executive power in books and articles.

Tareq Aziz 1936–
Iraqi Ba'ath politician

Born in Mosul and educated at Baghdad University, he worked as a journalist, first with *Al-Jumhuriyah* and then with *Al-Jamahiir*, becoming editor of the latter in 1963. Following a period in Syria with the Ba'ath press he returned to Iraq and was elected to the Revolutionary Command Council General Affairs Bureau in 1972. Appointed Foreign Affairs Minister in 1983, he became deputy Prime Minister in 1991. Following Iraq's invasion of Kuwait in 1990 and the war which followed, he emerged as Iraq's principal spokesman and apologist for President **Saddam Hussein**.

Tarkenton, Fran(cis Asbury) 1940–
US footballer

Born in Richmond, Virginia, he played for the Minnesota Vikings and New York Giants (1961–78), and gained 47,003 yards by passing, a National Football League record. He later became a sports commentator and management consultant.

Tarkington, (Newton) Booth 1869–1946
US writer

He was born in Indianapolis. and studied at Purdue and Princeton universities. Many of his novels are set in Indiana, but he is best known as the author of *Monsieur Beaucaire* (1900) and the 'Penrod' books—*Penrod* (1914) and *Seventeen* (1916). His other works include a trilogy, *Growth* (1927), including *The Magnificent Ambersons* (1918), which won the Pulitzer Prize and was made into a successful film by **Orson Welles**; *Alice Adams* (1921, Pulitzer Prize); and a book of reminiscences, *The World does Move* (1928). 📖 A D Dickinson, *Booth Tarkington* (1926)

Tarkovsky, Andrei Arsenevich 1932–86
Russian filmmaker

Born in Moscow, he studied Oriental languages, and worked as a geological prospector in Siberia before studying at the State Film School and directing the short film *Segodnya Otpuska Nye Budyet* (1959, *There Will Be No Leave Today*). His modest body of work gained him critical recognition as one of the cinema's true poets with a distinctive, slow-moving style that incorporated elliptical imagery and lengthy, enigmatic and often impenetrable subject material. He examined youth in *Ivanovo Detstvo* (1962, *Ivan's Childhood*) and *Zerkalo* (1947, *Mirror*) whilst offering bleak visions of the future in *Solaris* (1972) and *Stalker* (1979). He was latterly in exile in Paris, and his final film *Offret* (1986, *The Sacrifice*) featured a man willing to relinquish his own life and possessions to prevent a forthcoming apocalypse, and was characteristic of his concern for the future and his advocacy of peace.

Tarleton, Sir Banastre 1754–1833
English soldier

Born in Liverpool, he served under Sir **Henry Clinton** and **Charles Cornwallis** in the American Revolution (1775–83). He defeated Colonel Abraham Buford at Waxham Creek (1780) and **Horatio Gates** at Camden, but was beaten by General Morgan at Cowpens. He held Gloucester until it capitulated (1782), and then returned to England. He was MP for Liverpool (1790–1806, 1807–12).

Tarleton or Tarlton, Richard d.1588
English comedian

He was introduced to Queen **Elizabeth I** through the Earl of **Leicester** and became immensely popular as one of the Queen's Players (1583), specializing in the dramatic jigs popular at the time. *Tarleton's Jests* (c.1592–c.1611), in three parts, have been ascribed to him.

Tarquinius Priscus, *in full* Lucius Tarquinius Priscus reigned 616–578BC
Traditionally the fifth King of Rome

Of Etruscan origin, he is said to have modified the constitution, and to have begun the Servian agger and the Circus Maximus.

Tarquinius Superbus, *in full* Lucius Tarquinius Superbus reigned 534–510BC
Traditionally the seventh and last King of Rome

According to Roman tradition, his cruelty and the rape of Lucretia by his son Sextus provoked an uprising of the Roman people under Lucius Junius Brutus, his expulsion from Rome, and the establishment of the Republic. He is then said to have tried to re-establish himself in Rome with the help of Lars Porsena of Clusium, but died in exile.

Tarski, Alfred 1902–83
US logician and mathematician

Born and educated in Warsaw, Poland, he became professor there (1925–39), then moved to the USA to work at the University of California at Berkeley (1942–68). He made contributions to many branches of pure mathematics and mathematical logic, including the Banach–Tarski paradox, which seemingly allows any set to be broken up and reassembled into a set of twice the size. He is best remembered, however, for his definition of 'truth' in formal logical languages, as presented in his monograph *Der Wahrheitsbegriff in den Formalisierten Sprachen* (1933, 'The Concept of Truth in Formalized Languages').

Tartaglia Niccolò, *originally* Niccolò Fontana c.1500–57
Italian mathematician

Born in Brescia, he became a teacher of mathematics in several Italian universities, and settled in Florence in 1524. He was one of the first scholars to derive a general solution for cubic equations. He disclosed this result to Girolamo Cardano who fought Tartaglia for priority in the discovery, although the credit for the first solution of a cubic should probably go to Scipione da Ferro, an Italian mathematician of the previous generation. Tartaglia also published an early work on the theory of projectiles, and translated Euclid's *Elements*.

Tartini, Giuseppe 1692–1770
Italian composer and violinist

Born in Pirano, Istria, he was originally intended for the church and the law. Abandoning these for music, he lived in Venice, Ancona and Prague, returning to Padua by 1728. He is highly thought of as a violinist, a composer and a writer on music, and his best-known work is the *Trillo del Diavolo* (c.1735, 'The Devil's Trill').

Tasman, Abel Janszoon 1603–c.1659
Dutch navigator

He was born in Lutjegast, near Groningen. In 1642 he discovered Tasmania—named Van Diemen's Land until 1855—and New Zealand, and in 1643 Tonga and Fiji, having been dispatched in quest of the 'Great South Land' by Antony Van Diemen (1593–1645), Governor-General of Batavia. He made a second voyage (1644) to the Gulf of Carpentaria and the north-west coast of Australia. ⌨ Andrew Sharp, *The Voyages of Abel Janszoon Tasman* (1968)

Tassie, James 1735–99
Scottish modeller and engraver

Born in Pollokshaws, Glasgow, he was apprenticed to a stonemason, and studied art at Foulis Academy, Glasgow. In 1763 he went to Dublin, where he developed a special white enamel composition for making portrait medallions. In 1766 he moved to London where he used his paste to make reproductions of the most famous gems. He also executed many cameo portraits of his contemporaries, and the plaster reproductions of the Portland Vase.

Tasso, Bernardo 1493–1569
Italian poet

Born in Venice of an illustrious family of Bergamo, he suffered poverty and exile owing to the outlawry by Charles V (1547) of his patron, the Duke of Salerno, and took service with the Duke of Mantua. His romantic epic *Amadigi di Gaula* (1560), an epic on Amadis of Gaul, is a melodious imitation of Ludovico Ariosto's style, but exaggerated in sentiment. He began another epic, *Iloridante*, which was finished by his son Torquato Tasso (1587), and wrote numerous lyrics (1560). ⌨ E Williamson, *Bernardo Tasso* (1951)

Tasso, Torquato 1544–95
Italian poet

The son of Bernardo Tasso, he was born in Sorrento. He was sent (1560) to study law and philosophy at Padua, where he published his first work, a romantic poem, *Rinaldo* (1562, Eng trans 1792). At the court of Duke Alphonso II d'Este of Ferrara, he began his major work, the epic poem, *Gerusalemme Liberata* (1580, Eng trans *Godfrey of Bouillon: The Recovery of Jerusalem*, 1600), a story of the First Crusade, which he completed in 1575. He later rewrote it in response to criticisms, as *Gerusalemme Conquistata* (1593, 'Jerusalem Conquered'). For the court theatre he wrote the pastoral play, *Aminta* (1573, Eng trans 1591). In 1579 he was confined at Ferrara by order of the duke as insane, not, as is often alleged, for his love for the Princess Leonora, a story on which Lord Byron based his *Lament of Tasso*. In his seven years' confinement he wrote many verses and philosophical dialogues, and when he was freed in 1586 on the intercession of Prince Vincenzo Gonzaga, he followed his new patron to Mantua, where he wrote his only tragedy, *Il Re Torrismondo* (1586, 'King Torrismondo'). Summoned to Rome by Pope Clement VIII to be crowned on the Capitol as Poet Laureate, he took ill on arrival and died. ⌨ A Solerti, *Vita di Tasso* (3 vols, 1895)

Tata, Jamsetji Nasarwanji 1839–1904
Indian industrialist

Born in Gujarat, he built cotton mills at Nagpur (1877) and at Cooria near Bombay. He did much to promote scientific education in Indian schools. His son, Sir Dorabji (1859–1932), developed the Indian iron-ore industry, applied hydro-electricity to the Cooria cotton mills and founded a commercial airline.

Tate, (John Orley) Allen 1899–1979
US poet

Born in Winchester, Kentucky, he studied at Vanderbilt University, where he fell in with the group of poets led by John Crowe Ransom and known as 'the Fugitives'. He was editor (1944–46) of the influential *Sewanee Review* (1944–45) and taught at several universities, including Princeton (1939–42) and Minnesota (1952–68). A metaphysical poet in thrall to T S Eliot, he often wrote of the desire to answer disblief with faith, and in 1950 he converted to Catholicism. His collections of verse include *Mr Pope and Other Poems* (1928), *The Mediterranean and Other Poems* (1936), *Winter Sea* (1945) and *Collected Poems 1919–76* (1977). Among his other writings are biographies of Stonewall Jackson and Jefferson Davis and critical works such as *On the Limits of Poetry* (1948), which made him one of the leading exponents of New Criticism. He won the Bollingen prize in 1956. He was married to the novelist Caroline Gordon for 35 years. ⌨ G Hemphill, *Allen Tate* (1964)

Tate, Sir Henry 1819–99
English sugar magnate, art patron and philanthopist

Born in Chorley, Lancashire, he patented a method for cutting sugar cubes in 1872 and attained great wealth as a Liverpool sugar refiner. He founded the University

Library at Liverpool and gave the British nation the Tate Gallery, Millbank, London, which was opened in 1897, and contained his own valuable private collection.

Tate, Nahum 1652–1715
Irish poet and dramatist

Born in Dublin, he studied at Trinity College there, and saw his first play staged in London in 1678. With Dr Johnson's approval, he wrote a number of 'improved' versions of **Shakespeare**'s tragedies, substituting happy endings to suit the popular taste. With **John Dryden**'s help he wrote a second part to the poet's *Absalom and Achitophel* (1682) and with **Nicholas Brady** compiled a metrical version of the Psalms. 'While Shepherds watched their Flocks by Night' is attributed to him, and he wrote the libretto of **Henry Purcell**'s *Dido and Aeneas* (1689). He succeeded **Thomas Shadwell** as Poet Laureate in 1692. His best-known work is *Panacea or a Poem on Tea* (1700). ▢ H F S Thomas, *The Life and Times of Nahum Tate* (1934)

Tati, Jacques, *pseudonym of* Jacques Tatischeff 1908–82
French actor, author and film producer

Born in Le Pecq, Paris, he was a skilled rugby player in his youth and began his career in music-hall with a wordless act in which he mimicked various sporting activities, an entertainment he continued in short films like *Oscar, champion de tennis* (1934). His first feature film as a director and performer was *Jour de fête* (1949, *The Big Day*). With *Les Vacances de Monsieur Hulot* (1951, *Monsieur Hulot's Holiday*) and *Mon Oncle* (1958, *My Uncle*) he perfected his best-known character of the pipe-smoking, lugubrious Hulot, forever beset by physical mishaps and confrontations with modern technology. Although he was a graceful pantomimist, inventive visual humorist and exacting perfectionist, his later films such as *Playtime* (1968) and *Traffic* (1981) were less successful. ▢ Penelope Gilliatt, *Jacques Tati* (1976)

Tatian 2nd century AD
Syrian Christian thinker

He became a pupil of the martyr **Justin** at Rome and was converted to Christianity by him. After Justin's death in c.165AD he was estranged from the Catholic Church and returned to Syria (c.172) where he established, or was at least closely associated with, an ascetic religious community of Encratites, which fostered a heretical combination of Christianity and Stoicism. Only two of his many writings survive: the *Oratio ad Graecos* ('Speech to the Greeks'), a denunciation of the intellectualism of Greek culture and the corruption of its moral and religious values, and the *Diatessaron* (literally 'Out of Four'), a patchwork version of the four Gospels arranged as a continuous narrative, which in its Syriac version was used as a text in the Syrian Church for centuries.

Tatlin, Vladimir Yevgrafovich 1885–1953
Russian painter and designer

Born in Moscow, he studied there in 1910, and exhibited with avant-garde artists such as **Natalia Goncharova** and **Mikhail Larionov**, before going to visit Berlin and Paris (where he met **Picasso** in 1913). He founded Russian Constructivism, a movement at first approved by the Soviet authorities, and he was commissioned to design the gigantic *Monument to the Third International*; the model was exhibited in 1920, but the monument itself was never built.

Tattersall, Richard 1724–95
English auctioneer

He was born in Hurstwood, Lancashire. In London he entered the Duke of Kingston's service, became an auctioneer, and in 1776 set up auction rooms at Hyde Park Corner, which became a celebrated mart of thoroughbred horses and a great racing centre. They were transferred to Knightsbridge in 1867.

Tatum, Art(hur) 1910–56
US jazz pianist

Born in Toledo, Ohio, and largely self-taught, he became jazz music's first supreme keyboard virtuoso. Although near-blind from birth, he was a professional musician from his teens. Moving to New York in 1932, he made solo recordings and club appearances which have hardly been equalled for technique, drive and improvisational ability. The most influential of the swing-style pianists, Tatum continued to work in the idiom until his death, most effective as a soloist or leading a piano-bass-guitar trio. ▢ James Lester, *Too Marvelous for Words: The Life and Genius of Art Tatum* (1994)

Tatum, Edward Lawrie 1909–75
US biochemist and Nobel Prize winner

Born in Boulder, Colorado, he studied at the University of Wisconsin, and taught at Stanford University (1937–45, 1948–57), Yale (1945–48) and Rockefeller University, New York (1957–75). With **George Beadle** he demonstrated the role of genes in biochemical processes by growing bread mould spores on a variety of nutritional media. They suggested that each spore had one or more blocks in the metabolic pathway for particular nutrients, which led to the 'one gene, one enzyme' hypothesis, that a single gene codes for the synthesis of one protein. At Yale, Tatum collaborated with **Joshua Lederberg** to show that bacteria reproduce by the sexual process of conjugation. All three shared the 1958 Nobel Prize for physiology or medicine.

Taube, Henry 1915–
US inorganic chemist and Nobel Prize winner

Born in Neudorf, Saskatchewan, Canada, he studied at Saskatchewan University and received his doctorate at the University of California at Berkeley. In 1942 he became a US citizen and subsequently taught at Cornell and Chicago. He was appointed Professor of Chemistry at Stanford in 1962. Using radioisotopes as tracers, he devised new methods for studying the transfer of electrons during inorganic chemical reactions in solution. In 1969 Taube and **Carol Creutz** synthesized a mixed valence cation, a new type of positively charged ion consisting of two atoms of ruthenium each bonded to five molecules of ammonia and separated by a pyrazine ring. They and their colleagues used it to investigate oxidation–reduction reactions in living tissue. Taube was awarded the Nobel Prize for chemistry in 1983.

Tauber, Richard 1892–1948
British tenor

Born in Linz, Austria, he established himself as one of Germany's leading tenors, particularly in **Mozart**ian opera. From 1925 he increasingly appeared in light opera, notably **Franz Lehár**'s *Land of Smiles*, which he took to London in 1931. This won him great popularity, reinforced by his part in his own *Old Chelsea* (1943), and appearances in several films. He appeared at Covent Garden, London, in 1938, and became a British citizen in 1940.

Taufa'ahau, (Tupouto Tungi) Tupou IV 1918–
King of Tonga

The eldest son of Queen **Salote**, Tupou III, he was educated at Newington College and Sydney University. He served successively as Minister for Education (1943) and Minister for Health (1944–49), before becoming Prime Minister under his mother (1949). On succeeding to the throne on his mother's death (1965) he assumed the designation King Taufa'ahau Tupou IV, sharing power with his brother, Prince Fatafehi Tu'ipelehake, who became Prime Minister. King Taufa'ahau, while negotiating the country's independence within the Commonwealth (1970), remains the strongest supporter of the Western powers in the Pacific region.

Taussig, Helen Brooke 1898–1986
US paediatrician

Born in Cambridge, Massachusetts, she received her MD from Johns Hopkins University in 1927 and later became the first woman to become a full professor there. Her work on the pathophysiology of congenital heart disease was done partly in association with the cardiac surgeon **Alfred Blalock**, and between them they pioneered the 'blue baby' operations which heralded the beginnings of modern cardiac surgery. The babies were blue because of a variety of congenital anomalies which meant that much blood was passing directly from the right chamber of the heart to the left without being oxygenated in the lungs. Taussig was actively involved in the diagnosis and after-care of the young patients on whom Blalock operated, and their joint efforts helped create a new specialty of paediatric cardiac surgery.

Tavener, John Kenneth 1944–
English composer

Born and educated in London, where he studied under **Lennox Berkeley**, he was first recognized as a composer with the cantata *The Whale* (1966), based on the story of Jonah. His mature work has been dominated by his conversion to the Greek Orthodox Church (1976) and the bulk of his output has been vocal music of liturgical character, including *Ultimos ritos* (1972, 'Last Rites') for soloists, chorus, and orchestra, and a sacred opera, *Therese* (1979). His more recent works include *The Protecting Veil* (1987) for cello and strings, and *The Repentant Thief* (1990) for clarinet, percussion, and strings.

Taverner, John c.1490–1545
English composer and organist

Born in Boston, Lincolnshire, he was organist there and at Christ Church, Oxford, and composed notable motets and masses. Accused of heresy, he was imprisoned by Cardinal **Wolsey**, but released, 'being but a musitian'.

Taverner, Richard c.1505–75
English writer

He was patronized by Cardinal **Wolsey** and **Thomas Cromwell**, for whom he compiled Taverner's Bible (1539), a revision of *Matthew's Bible* by **John Rogers** (1537). On Cromwell's fall he was sent to the Tower of London, but was soon released, and found favour with **Henry VIII**.

Tavernier, Bertrand 1941–
French film director

Born in Lyons, he was a film enthusiast from an early age. After briefly studying law, he became a writer and critic for publications like *Positif* before working as an assistant to director Jean-Pierre Melville. Following a decade as a freelance press agent and scriptwriter, he made his directorial debut with *L'Horloger de Saint-Paul* (1973, *The Watchmaker of St Paul*). Telling well-rounded narratives with quiet professionalism, his eclectic body of work includes such period dramas as *Dimanche à la campagne* (1984, *Sunday in the Country*) and *La Passion Béatrice* (1988), the science-fiction thriller *La Mort en direct* (1979, *Deathwatch*), the chamber work *Daddy nostalgie* (1990, *These Foolish Things*) and edgy police stories like *L.627* (1992). He has also examined the folly and legacy of World War I in *La Vie et rien d'autre* (1989, *Life And Nothing But*) and *Capitaine Conan* (1996). His documentaries include *La Question* (1978) and *La Guerre sans nom* (1991, *The Undeclared War*) on the Algerian War.

Tavernier, Jean Baptiste, Baron d'Aubonne 1605–89
French traveller

He was born in Paris, the son of a Protestant engraver from Antwerp, and became a dealer in precious stones. His first journey to the East (1631–33) was by way of Constantinople (Istanbul) to Persia, and from there by Aleppo and Malta to Italy. He made a second journey (1638–43), across Syria to Ispaham, Agra and Golconda, and a third (1643–49), through Ispahan, much of Hindustan, Batavia and Bantam, then to Holland by the Cape. He travelled to many districts of Persia and India (1651–55, 1657–62, 1663–68). Louis XIV gave him 'letters of nobility' in 1669, and the following year he bought the barony of Aubonne, near Geneva. In 1684 he started for Berlin to advise **Frederick William**, Elector of Brandenburg, on his projects for eastern trade. In 1689 he went to Russia, and died in Moscow. His *Six Voyages* was published in 1676, and the complementary *Recueil* in 1679.

Tawney, R(ichard) H(enry) 1880–1962
English economic historian

Born in Calcutta, he was educated at Rugby School and Balliol College, Oxford, of which he was elected a Fellow in 1918. During World War I, he was severely wounded during the Battle of the Somme (1916). After a period of social work in the East End of London, he became tutor, executive (1905–47) and president (1928–44) of the Workers' Educational Association. He was Professor of Economic History at London (1931–49), and wrote studies in English economic history, particularly of the Tudor and Stuart periods, of which the best known are *The Acquisitive Society* (1926), *Religion and the Rise of Capitalism* (1926), *Equality* (1931) and *Business and Politics under James I* (1958). 🕮 Anthony Wright, *R H Tawney* (1987)

Tayama Katai 1872–1930
Japanese writer

He was born into a wealthy, upper middle-class family, and sent to England to study. He is credited with inventing the *watakushi shosetsu* (I-novel), the most extreme product of Japanese naturalism, the dominant literary movement in the first half of the 20th century, in which realism is achieved by concentrating solely upon the internal workings of the narrator's mind. In *Futon* (1907), his best and best-known work, nothing very much happens, except for the narrator losing his girlfriend; it is, instead, a long, intricately described account of his feelings and states of mind. *Inaka Kyoshi* (1909, 'The Country Teacher') is constructed along similar lines.

Taylor, A(lan) J(ohn) P(ercivale) 1906–90
English historian

Born in Lancashire, he attended Bootham School, York, and studied at Oriel College, Oxford. He was lecturer in modern history at Manchester University, Fellow of Magdalen College, Oxford (1938–76), and lecturer in international history at Oxford (1953–63). As a diplomatic historian, he established his authority in modern European history by studies of the **Habsburg** monarchy, and of **Bismarck**, and in the first lectures ever given on British television (on the Russian Revolution). His major work was *The Struggle for Mastery in Europe 1848–1918* (1954). Other works include *The Trouble Makers* (1957), which examines critics of British foreign policy from 1792 to 1939, *The Origins of the Second World War* (1961), and *English History 1914–1945* (1965). He inspired many students, was a friend and biographer of Lord **Beaverbrook**, and wrote many essays and an autobiography, *A Personal History* (1983). In 1991 *Letters to Eva 1969–83* was published posthumously, a collection of love-letters to his third wife.

Taylor, (Winifred) Ann, *née* Walker 1947–
British Labour politician

Born in Motherwell, Scotland, and educated at Bradford and Sheffield universities, she worked as an Open University tutor before entering parliament as MP for

Bolton West (1974–83), then returning in 1987 for Dewsbury, West Yorkshire. She was appointed deputy education spokesperson to **Neil Kinnock** (1979), and became Shadow Housing Minister (1981–83). In 1990 she made Shadow Minister for Environmental Protection, the first Cabinet-level portfolio dealing with the environment. Shadow Leader of the House of Commons (1994–97), she was appointed Leader of the Commons in 1997 when Labour came to power after their landslide win in the general election. Her publications include *Choosing Our Future – Practical Politics for the Environment* (1992).

Taylor, (James) Bayard 1825–78
US travel-writer and poet

He was born in Chester county, Pennsylvania, and was apprenticed to a printer. He wrote a volume of poems (1844), visited Europe, published *Views Afoot* (1846), and obtained a post on the *New York Tribune*. As its correspondent he made extensive travels in California and Mexico, up the Nile, in Asia Minor and Syria, and to India, China and Japan, which he recorded in a great number of travel books which he later published. In 1862–63 he was secretary of legation in St Petersburg and in 1878 he became ambassador in Berlin, where he died. 📖 R C Bently, *Bayard Taylor, laureate of the Gilded Age* (1936)

Taylor, Brook 1685–1731
English mathematician

Born in Edmonton, Canada, he studied at St John's College, Cambridge, and in 1715 published his *Methodus incrementorum*, containing the theorem on power series expansions which bears his name. He also wrote on the mechanics of the vibrating string and on the mathematics of the theory of perspective.

Taylor, Cecil Percival 1933–
US avant-garde pianist and composer

He was born in New York City, to a musical family. Given piano lessons from the age of five, he went on to study at the New York College of Music and the New England Conservatory, Boston. His interest in jazz and black culture was awakened in his early twenties, and in 1956 he made his first important quartet recordings which displayed startling divergencies from the established approach to jazz language and harmony. The controversy surrounding **Ornette Coleman's** music in the late 1950s obscured the importance of Taylor's own pioneering experiments to some extent, and his refusal to compromise his artistic direction led to a difficult decade in which he was given little paid work, but made a number of key recordings. His style of dense, powerful extended free improvisation is not destined for mass appeal, but his work found increasing acceptance during the 1970s and 1980s, particularly in Europe, where a festival of his music became the monumental 11-CD box set *In Berlin '88*.

Taylor, Edward c.1645–1729
American colonial poet

Born in Coventry, England, he emigrated to America in 1668 and settled in the Massachusetts Bay Colony. He graduated from Harvard in 1671 and became a physician and Puritan minister, marrying twice and fathering 13 children. He wrote religious verse in the metaphysical style, exploring the relationship of man to God. His work was not published until 1939, but he is now recognized as one of the finest colonial American poets. 📖 N S Grabo, *Edward Taylor* (1962)

Taylor, Elizabeth, *née* Coles 1912–75
English novelist

Born in Reading, Berkshire, she was educated locally at the Abbey School, worked as a governess and librarian, and married John Taylor, the director of a sweet factory,

when she was 24. She wrote her first novel, *At Mrs Lippincote's* (1945), while her husband was in the RAF. This was followed by such novels as *Palladian* (1946), *A Game of Hide-and-Seek* (1951), *Angel* (1957), *The Wedding Group* (1968), *Mrs Palfrey at the Claremont* (1971) and *Blaming*, published posthumously in 1976. Her hallmark is quiet, shrewd observation of middle-class life in the south-east of England, reminiscent of **Jane Austen**. Her stories, collected in four volumes (1954–72), are no less admired than her novels. 📖 R Liddell, *Ivy and Elizabeth* (1966)

Taylor, Elizabeth Rosemond 1932–
US film actress

She was born in London, England, of US parents, and moved with her family to Los Angeles (1939), where she made her screen debut at the age of ten, in *There's One Born Every Minute* (1942). As a child star she made a number of films including two 'Lassie' stories (1943, 1946), *National Velvet* (1944), and *Little Women* (1949). She was first seen as an adult in *The Father of the Bride* (1950), and her career continued through the 1950s with films including *Raintree County* (1957), *Cat on a Hot Tin Roof* (1958) and *Suddenly Last Summer* (1959), for all of which she received Academy Award nominations. She was notable also for her many marriages, her first husband being Nick Hilton (m.1950), her second the actor Michael Wilding (m.1952), her third the producer **Mike Todd** (m.1957), who was killed in an air crash the following year. She then married Eddie Fisher (1959), divorcing him in 1964. In 1960 she won her first Academy Award for *Butterfield 8*. The making of the spectacular epic *Cleopatra* (1962) provided the background to her well-publicized romance with her co-star **Richard Burton** whom she married for the first time in 1964. She made several films with Burton, including *Who's Afraid of Virginia Woolf?* (1966, Academy Award). Divorced from and remarried to Richard Burton, she was divorced from him again (1976), and married the US Senator John Warner (1978), from whom she separated in 1981. Her other films include *Reflections in a Golden Eye* (1967), *A Little Night Music* (1976) and *The Mirror Crack'd* (1981). She made her stage debut in New York with *The Little Foxes* (1981). After treatment for alcohol addiction, she resumed acting, mostly in television with *Malice in Wonderland* (1985), *Poker Alice* (1986), and other films. She married Larry Fortensky in 1991 but filed for divorce in 1996.

Taylor, E(rnest) A(rchibald) 1874–1951
Scottish furniture and stained-glass designer, and painter

He was born in Greenock, Renfrewshire, and trained as a draughtsman in a shipyard before studying at Glasgow School of Art in the 1890s. Influenced by **Charles Rennie Mackintosh** he joined the firm of Wylie & Lochhead, the Glasgow cabinetmakers, in 1900. He designed a drawing-room for their Pavilion at the 1901 Glasgow International Exhibition. When he exhibited at Turin in 1902 alongside his fellow Glasgow School artists, he won a diploma and medal. He married the artist **Jessie King** and moved to Manchester in 1908. From 1911 to 1914 he taught, along with his wife, at the Shealing Atelier of Fine Art in Paris.

Taylor, Frederick W(inslow) 1856–1915
US engineer

Born in Germantown, Pennsylvania, he studied at night while being employed at the Midvale steelworks in Philadelphia (1878–90), and obtained a degree in engineering from the Stevens Institute of Technology in 1883. He became chief engineer in 1889, having invented several devices and modified processes to increase efficiency, and then turned his attention to the part played by the workers themselves, introducing time-and-motion study as an aid to efficient management, known as 'Taylorisation'. From 1893 he worked as an independent consultant in what he called 'scientific management', and applied its principles successfully to both small and large-scale businesses. He published *Shop Management* (1903) and *Principles of Scientific Management* (1911). 📖 Frank Barkley Copley, *Frederick W Taylor: Father of Scientific Management* (2 vols, 1923)

Taylor, Sir Geoffrey Ingram 1886–1975
English physicist and applied mathematician

Born in London, he was educated at Cambridge, where he stayed for the rest of his career. He was appointed Reader in Dynamic Meteorology in 1911, and became Yarrow Research Professor of Physics (1923–52). He was an original researcher in a wide range of studies, particularly on turbulent motion in fluids which he applied to meteorology and oceanography, in aerodynamics and even to Jupiter's Great Red Spot. He proposed in 1934 the important idea of dislocation in crystals, a form of atomic misarrangement which enables the crystal to deform at a stress less than that of a perfect crystal. He was knighted in 1944 and awarded the Order of Merit in 1969.

Taylor, Sir Henry 1800–86
English poet

Born in Bishop-Middleham, Durham, he was an administrator in the colonial office (1824–72). He wrote four tragedies, *Isaac Comnenus* (1827), *Philip van Artefelde* (1834), *Edwin the Fair* (1842) and *St Clement's Eve* (1862). A romantic comedy, *The Virgin Widow* (1850), was later retitled *A Sicilian Summer*. In 1845 he published a volume of lyrical poetry, and in 1847 *The Eve of the Conquest*. His prose includes *The Statesman* (1836) and an *Autobiography* (1885). 📖 J B Bilderbeck, *Sir Henry Taylor and his Drama of Philip van Artevelde* (1877)

Taylor, Jeremy 1613–67
English theologian

Born in Cambridge, he studied at Caius College, Cambridge, and became a Fellow of All Souls College, Oxford (1636), chaplain to Archbishop **Laud**, and in 1638 Rector of Uppingham. During the Civil War Taylor was imprisoned several times. In 1658 he got a lectureship at Lisburn, and at the Restoration the bishopric of Down and Connor. He also became Vice-Chancellor of Dublin University and a member of the Irish Privy Council. His many works, including *The Liberty of Prophesying* (1646), the *52 Sermons* (1651–53), and *Ductor Dubitantium* (1660) are considered some of the most eloquent sacred writings in the English language. They were published as collected works in 1820–22 (revised 1847–54).

Taylor, John, known as the Water-poet 1580–1653
English poet and pamphleteer

Born in Gloucester, he became a Thames waterman, but was pressed into the navy, and served at the Siege of Cadiz (1625). At the outbreak of the Civil War (1642) he kept a public house in Oxford, but he gave it up for another in London, and there wrote his own doggerel poems, full of natural humour and low wit. The chief event of his life was his journey on foot from London to Edinburgh (1618), described in his *Penniless Pilgrimage* (1618); similar books were his *Travels in Germanie* (1617) and *The Praise of Hempseed* (1618), a story of a voyage in a brown paper boat from London to Queensborough. 📖 W Thorp, *John Taylor* (1922)

Taylor, John Edward 1791–1844
English journalist

Born in Ilminster, Somerset, he was the founder in 1821 of the liberal newspaper, the *Manchester Guardian*.

Taylor, John Henry 1871–1963
English golfer

Born in Northam, Devon, he was the first Englishman to win the British Open championship (1894, 1895, 1900, 1909, 1913). He also won the French Open twice, and the German Open once. He was a founder and first president of the PGA (British Professional Golfers' Association).

Taylor, Joseph Hooton Jnr 1941–
US astronomer and physicist, and Nobel Prize winner

Born in Philadelphia, he was educated at Harvard, and held various posts at the University of Massachusetts before becoming Professor of Physics at Princeton University in 1980. During a systematic search for pulsars, the rapidly rotating dense stars which appear to emit regular pulses of radio waves, he made the first discovery of an exotic 'binary pulsar', a pulsar in orbit of another dense neutron star. For this work he shared with **Russell Hulse** the 1993 Nobel Prize for physics. Taylor's later observations have lent support to the general relativity prediction that this system of very massive compact objects will create 'gravitational waves', leaking energy from the system and causing the objects to continually move closer together.

Taylor, Nathaniel William 1786–1858
US theologian

Born in New Milford, Connecticut, he was ordained as a Congregational minister in 1812, and in 1822 he became Professor of Theology at Yale. His 'New Haven theology', long assailed as heretical, was a softening of the traditional **Calvin**ism of New England, maintained the doctrine of natural ability, and denied total depravity; sin is a voluntary action of the sinner, but there is, derived from **Adam**, a bias to sin, which is not itself sinful.

Taylor, Sir Patrick Gordon 1896–1966
Australian pioneer aviator

Born in Mosman, New South Wales, he served with the Royal Flying Corps during World War I, and received the Military Cross. He worked on developing aviation instruments after the war, and was associated with Sir **Charles Kingsford Smith** and **Charles Ulm** in many of their pioneering flights, including a single-engined flight from Australia to the USA (1934). In 1935, over the Tasman Sea with Kingsford Smith in his *Southern Cross*, one engine cut out and oil pressure was lost on another. Taylor spent the rest of the flight clambering across the wings every half-hour, transferring oil from the dead engine into the ailing one; for this he was awarded the George Cross. He created a number of aviation firsts and worked with RAF Transport Command during World War II.

Taylor, Paul Belville 1930–
US modern-dance choreographer

Born in Pittsburgh, Pennsylvania, he studied painting at college and trained as a swimmer. He first studied dancing with **Merce Cunningham** (1953–54) and **Martha Graham** (1958–62). He began choreographing in 1956 and has developed an original, ebullient, lyrical style. Often using classical music to contemporary effect, he creates movement which, whether plumbing depths or reaching to the heavens, is one of earthly life. Although he is not an experimentalist, his dances nevertheless have a creativity and wit which put him among the top US choreographers. Work includes *Three Epitaphs* (1956), *Aureole* (1962), *Big Bertha* (1971), *Esplanade* (1975), *Arden Court* (1981), *Speaking in Tongues* (1989), *Company B* (1991) and *Spindrift* (1993). His autobiography, *Private Domain*, was published in 1987.

Taylor, Peter Hillsman 1917–94
US short-story writer, novelist and playwright

He was born in Trenton, Tennessee, and educated in Nashville, Memphis, and at Kenyon College, Ohio. Concerned with the smaller crises and conflicts of upper middle-class life in the Southern states of the USA, primarily Tennessee, his fiction often focused on the manners and mores of a vanishing society and the intrusion of truths too terrible to find welcome in its narrow gentility. Representative stories are 'The Scoutmaster', 'The Old Forest', 'The Death of a Kinsman' and 'A Long Fourth'. *The Collected Stories of Peter Taylor* was published in 1969. Later works include his novels *A Summons to Memphis* (1987), for which he won a Pulitzer Prize, and *In the Tennessee Country* (1994).

Taylor (of Gosforth), Peter Murray Taylor, Baron 1930–97
English jurist

Born in Newcastle upon Tyne, he was educated there and at Pembroke College, Cambridge. He was called to the Bar in 1954 and became a QC in 1967. He became chairman of the Bar Council in 1979, the year he was the prosecuting counsel when Jeremy Thorpe, the former Leader of the Liberal party, was tried for conspiracy to murder. Though Thorpe was acquitted, Taylor's masterful handling of the case was noteworthy. The following year he was made a High Court judge and was promoted to the Court of Appeal in 1988. As chairman of the inquiry into the 1989 Hillsborough football disaster, he produced a report calling for stadiums to be all-seated, a recommendation which was soon implemented throughout the UK. He succeeded Lord Lane as Lord Chief Justice of England in 1992, acknowledging the need to reform the legal system and restore public confidence, and retired in 1996.

Taylor, Richard Edward 1929–
Canadian physicist and Nobel Prize winner

Born in Medicine Hat, Alberta, and educated at the University of Alberta in Edmonton and Stanford University, he held posts at the Linear Accelerator Laboratory at Orsay, the Lawrence Berkeley Laboratory and the Stanford Linear Accelerator Center (SLAC), California, where he became professor (1968–), and associate director (1982–86). In the 1960s, Taylor led a group of physicists at SLAC who investigated the structure of the nucleons (protons and neutrons) by scattering high-energy electrons from nuclear targets. These experiments established the constituents of nucleons, now known as quarks, as real entities by determining some of their properties. For this work he shared the 1990 Nobel Prize for physics with Jerome Friedman and Henry Kendall. In 1992 he became Distinguished Professor at the University of Alberta.

Taylor, Rowland d.1555
English Protestant

Born in Rothbury, Northumberland, he was a chaplain to Thomas Cranmer in 1540. He became rector of Hadleigh (1544), Archdeacon of Exeter (1551), and a canon of Rochester, spoke in favour of Lady Jane Grey, and under Mary I was imprisoned as a heretic, then burned near Hadleigh.

Taylor, Tom 1817–80
Scottish dramatist and editor

He was born in Sunderland, north east England, and studied at Glasgow University, and Trinity College, Cambridge, where he was elected a Fellow. Professor of English for two years at University College London, and called to the Bar in 1845, he was secretary to the Board of Health (1850–72), and then to the Local Government Act Office. From 1846 he wrote or adapted over a hundred pieces for the stage, among them *Still Waters Run Deep* (1855), *Our American Cousin*, (1858) and *The Ticket of Leave Man* (1863). He edited the autobiographies of Benjamin Haydon and Charles Robert Leslie, completed the latter's *Life and Times of Reynolds*, translated *Ballads and Songs of Brittany* (1865), and in 1874 became editor of *Punch*. He was

The Times art critic, and appeared as a witness for John Ruskin in the libel action brought against him by James McNeill Whistler in 1878.

Taylor, William 1765–1836
English writer

Born in Norwich, he was the son of a Unitarian merchant and entered his father's counting-house in 1779. He travelled extensively on the Continent, and introduced the works of Lessing and Goethe to English readers, mainly through criticisms and translations, collected in his *Historic Survey of German Poetry* (1828–30).

Taylor, William Howson 1876–1935
English potter

He studied at Birmingham School of Art where his father was principal. In 1898 he established the Ruskin Pottery in West Smethwick in an old malthouse. Normally using local clay, he developed a white body containing china clay and calcined flint. He was influenced by the Sung and Ming periods in Chinese pottery, and an admirer of John Ruskin, who allowed his name to be used at the pottery. Taylor's interest in glazes developed into the production of soufflé ware, lustre ware and, the most notable, high-fired ware which he produced at a loss and had to subsidize. He carefully guarded the secret of his glazes and destroyed all his notes and materials shortly before he died.

Taylor, Zachary 1784–1850
12th President of the USA

Born in Montebello, Virginia, he entered the army in 1808. In 1812 he held Fort Harrison on the Wabash against Indians, and in 1832 fought with Black Hawk. In 1836, now colonel, he was ordered to Florida, and in 1837 defeated the Seminoles at Okeechobee Swamp, becoming brigadier-general. In 1840 he was placed in command of the army in the southwest. When Texas was annexed in 1845 he gathered 4,000 regulars, marched to the Rio Grande, and erected Fort Brown opposite Matamoros. In September he captured Monterey. After seven weeks' vain waiting for reinforcements the march was resumed. Victoria was occupied, but the line of communication was too long for the small force, and President James K Polk's Democratic administration, fearing his growing fame, crippled him by witholding reinforcements. Taylor was falling back to Monterey when his regulars were taken from him to form part of a new expedition under General Winfield Scott. Santa Anna, the Mexican general, overtook his 5,000 volunteers near the pass of Buena Vista, but Taylor, on 22 February 1847, won a major victory against the 21,000-strong Mexican force, inflicting heavy losses. Emerging from the war a hero, he was given the Whig presidential nomination, and in 1849 he became President. The main issues of his presidency were the status of the new territories and the extension of slavery there, but he died only 16 months after taking office. He was succeeded by Millard Fillmore.

Tazieff, Haroun 1914–98
French vulcanologist and mountaineer

Born in Warsaw, Poland, he studied in Russia, France and Belgium, firstly agricultural engineering and then geology. After various short-term posts in the Belgian Congo, he became assistant Professor of Mining Geology in Brussels (1950). In 1967 he was made head of research at the National Centre for Scientific Research (CNRS), Paris, and subsequently director (1971–81). He became the first French Secretary of State for the Prevention of Natural and Technological Disasters (1974–86) and was also Mayor of Mirmande (1977–89). He has investigated many of the world's volcanoes, both active and inactive, and from 1958 to 1974 made 26 expeditions to Nyiragongo, Democratic

Tchaikovsky, Pyotr Ilyich 1840–93
Russian composer

Tchaikovsky was born in Kamsko-Votkinsk in the Ural Mountains, the son of a government inspector of mines. His early musical talents were encouraged, but when the family moved to St Petersburg he entered the school of jurisprudence and started his working life as a minor civil servant. In 1862 he enrolled at the recently opened Conservatory, but after three years he was engaged by his previous orchestration teacher, Nicholas Rubinstein, to teach harmony at his new Conservatory in Moscow, which opened in 1866. His operas and 2nd ('Little Russian') Symphony (1872) brought him into the public eye, and in 1875 his Piano Concerto in B flat minor had its première in Moscow.

He married a pupil, Antonina Ivanovna Milyukova, despite his homosexual tendencies, but left her a month after the wedding in a state of nervous collapse (1877). After recuperation abroad he resigned from the Conservatory and retired to the country to devote himself entirely to composition. He made occasional trips abroad and in 1893 was made an honorary Doctor of Music of Cambridge University.

At about the time of his marriage, Tchaikovsky received the moral and financial support of Nadezhda von Meck, the widow of a wealthy engineer; although they never met, they corresponded regularly until 1890. Her support enabled him to devote himself entirely to composition.

Soon after his return to Russia from England in 1893, and after the first performance of his 6th ('Pathétique') symphony, he died in St Petersburg. He was said to have died of cholera from drinking unboiled water (perhaps deliberately), but more recent research (by Alexandra Orlova), published in 1979, suggests that he may have committed suicide through swallowing poison, at the behest of a 'court of honour', following his alleged relationship with a young male aristocrat.

Though acquainted with **Mili Balakirev**, **Rimsky-Korsakov** and other members of the group of late 19th-century composers known as The Five, he was not in sympathy with their avowedly nationalistic aspirations and their use of folk material, and was himself regarded by them as cosmopolitan and not genuinely Russian. The melodiousness, colourful orchestration, and deeply expressive content of his music brought him then and now an enthusiastic following exceeding that of any other Russian composer.

Tchaikovsky's introspective and melancholy nature is reflected in some of his symphonies and orchestral pieces, but much less in his ballet music, Swan Lake (1877), The Sleeping Beauty (1890) and The Nutcracker (1892), which have formed the core of the classical repertory. Other works include six symphonies, of which the last three are the best-known, two piano concertos (a third was left uncompleted), a violin concerto, a number of tone poems including Romeo and Juliet (1870, dedicated to Balakirev) and Italian Capriccio, songs and piano pieces. He also wrote chamber music, including a piano trio and three string quartets. Of his 11 operas, Eugene Onegin (1879) and The Queen of Spades (1890) are still regularly performed, and Mazeppa (1884) occasionally.

📖 Documentary evidence is given in D Brown, Tchaikovsky Remembered (1993). The standard biography is D Brown, Tchaikovsky: A Biographical and Critical Study (3 vols, 1978–91); for a shorter account, see E Garden, Tchaikovsky (1973).

> 'On my word of honour, I have never felt such self-satisfaction, such pride, such happiness, as in the knowledge that I have created a good thing.' On the completion of his 6th Symphony; from a letter to P Jurgenson, August 1893.

Republic of Congo. He wrote around 20 books on volcanoes and world tectonics including *Forecasting Volcanic Events* (1983) and *Surl'Etna* (1984).

Tchaikovsky, Pyotr Ilyich See panel above

Tcherepnin, Nikolai Nikolayevich 1873–1945
Russian composer

Born in St Petersburg, he gave up a legal career to study under **Rimsky-Korsakov**, first appearing as a pianist. In 1901 he became conductor of the Belaiev Concerts and took charge of opera at the Maryinsky Theatre. From 1908 to 1914 he worked with **Sergei Diaghilev**, conducting ballet and opera throughout Europe, and in 1914 he went to Petrograd (now St Petersburg), leaving there four years later to become director of the Tiflis (now Tbilisi) Conservatory. He settled in Paris in 1921. His works include operas, ballets, symphonies, and other orchestral music, and piano pieces. His son, Alexander Nikolayevich (1899–1977), was a conductor, pianist and composer of four symphonies, concertos, sonatas, and other works.

Teach or Tache or Thatch, Edward, known as Blackbeard d.1718
English pirate

Born in Bristol, he was employed as privateer against the Spanish during the War of the Spanish Succession (1701–13) and later turned to piracy, attacking Spanish and French vessels in the West Indies from his ship, *Queen Anne's Revenge*, a 40-gun warship. He formed an alliance with the Governor of North Carolina and the State Collector of Taxes, giving them a percentage of the spoils in exchange for their protection. He would blockade harbours for several days, seizing all the shipping going in and out, and tyrannized the planters of the Carolina coast. On 22 November 1718 he was shot dead and decapitated by Lieutenant Robert Maynard.

Teague, Walter Dorwin 1883–1960
US designer and writer on design

Born in Decatur, Indiana, he moved to New York in 1903 and trained at the Art Students' League, and after varied experience in design established his own industrial design consultancy in 1926. Among his most important clients were Kodak, Ford, National Cash Register and Texaco, for which he created a corporate identity, designing petrol stations, equipment and graphics. From the mid-1940s his office became closely associated with the design, especially of the interiors, of Boeing airliners. He was a first president of the American Society of Industrial Designers which he, **Henry Dreyfuss** and **Raymond Loewy** founded in 1944. His book *Design This Day* (1940) was a comprehensive vindication of modern design in the context of universal aesthetic criteria.

Teasdale, Sara, née Trevor 1884–1933
US poet

Born in St Louis, Missouri, and educated at the Mary Institute and Hosmer Hall, in 1918 she was the first person to receive a Pulitzer Prize for poetry, for her collection *Love Songs* (1917). She initially earned a reputation as a writer of 'feminine' love poetry. However, much of her poetry is in fact based on her own sheltered early life and unhappy marriage, and expresses the conflicting needs for independence and freedom, love and security. She wrote nine collections of poetry, two of which were published after her death, a suspected suicide. ⌨ C B Schoen, *Sara Teasdale* (1986)

Tebaldi, Renata 1922–
Italian soprano

Born in Pesaro, she studied at Parma Conservatorio, made her debut at Rovigo in 1944, and was invited by Toscanini to appear at the re-opening of La Scala, Milan, (1946). She has appeared in the UK, France, Spain, South America and at the Metropolitan, New York, and San Francisco and made many recordings.

Tebaldus See Theobald

Tebbit, Norman Beresford Tebbit, Baron 1931–
English Conservative politician

Born in Enfield, Middlesex, the son of a shop manager, he left grammar school at 16 and began his career as a journalist. After national service in the RAF he became an airline pilot and was later to head the British Airline Pilots' Association (BALPA). He was elected to parliament in 1970, representing Epping, and later Chingford, and became noted for his radical, 'New Right', convictions. Already an influential backroom strategist and junior minister, he was brought into the Cabinet of Margaret Thatcher as Employment Secretary in 1981 and Trade and Industry Secretary in 1983. Noted for his robust invective and anti-union stance, he came to personify a new type of 'Thatcherite' conservativism. His career, however, was partially checked by the injuries he and, in particular, his wife Margaret sustained as victims of the 1984 IRA bombing of the Grand Hotel, Brighton. He was appointed Chancellor of the Duchy of Lancaster and Conservative Party Chairman in 1985 and helped mastermind the 1987 general election victory. However, soon afterwards, his relations with Mrs Thatcher cooled and he retired to the backbenches. In 1992 he decided not to contest his seat in the general election and was made a life peer. He published his autobiography, *Upwardly Mobile*, in 1988, followed by *Unfinished Business* in 1991. In 1995 he started writing for *The Sun* newspaper.

Tecumseh 1768–1813
Shawnee chief

Born in Old Piqua, Ohio, he became chief of the Shawnees. He joined his brother, 'The Prophet', in a rising against the whites, suppressed at Tippecanoe by William Henry Harrison (1811). He passed into English service, and commanded the Indian allies in the war of 1812–13 as brigadier-general. He died fighting at the Thames River in Canada. ⌨ Glenn Tucker, *Tecumseh: Vision of Glory* (1956)

Tedder (of Glenguin), Arthur William Tedder, 1st Baron 1890–1967
Scottish marshal of the RAF

He was born at Glenguin, Stirlingshire. He served in the Colonial Service and Royal Flying Corps during World War I. At the outbreak of World War II he was director-general of research and development at the Air Ministry. From 1940 he organized the Middle East Air Force, later becoming deputy Supreme Commander under General Eisenhower. He was made marshal of the RAF (1945), created a baron in 1946, and in 1950 became Chancellor of the University of Cambridge and also a governor of the BBC. He wrote *Air Power in the War* (1948) and an autobiography, *With Prejudice* (1966).

Tegnér, Elaias 1782–1846
Swedish poet and churchman

Born in Kyrkerud, Värmland, he was educated at Lund, and was appointed lecturer there in 1802. His stirring *Krigssång för Landtvärnet* (1808, 'War-song for the Militia of

Scania') made his name as a poet, and *Svea* (1811) made him famous. He was appointed Professor of Greek at Lund (1812–26), and Bishop of Växjö (1824). His best-known works include *Sång till Solen* (1817, 'Song to the Sun'), *Epilog vid magisterpromotionen i Lund 1820* (1820, 'Degree Day at Lund'), his religious idyll *Nattvardsbarn* (1820, 'The Communion Children'), *Axel*, a narrative romance of the days of King Karl XII (1822), and his masterpiece, *Frithjofs Saga* (1825). He also had a keen interest in education. ⌨ A Werin, *Elaias Tegnér* (1934)

Teilhard de Chardin, Pierre 1881–1955
French Jesuit theologian, palaeontologist and philosopher

Born at the castle of Sarcenat, the son of an Auvergne landowner, he lectured in pure science at the Jesuit College in Cairo, and was ordained as a priest in 1911. He was a stretcher bearer during World War I, and subsequently became Professor of Geology (1918) at the Institut Catholique in Paris. He directed the 1929 excavations at the Choukoutien Peking Man site in China, and later worked in central Asia, Ethiopia, Java and Somalia, but his anthropological researches did not conform to Jesuit orthodoxy and he was forbidden by his religious superiors to teach and publish. Nevertheless, his work in Cenozoic geology and palaeontology became known and he was awarded academic distinctions, including the Legion of Honour (1946). From 1951 he lived in the USA and worked at the Wenner-Gren Foundation for Anthropological Research in New York. Posthumously published, his philosophical speculations employ the concept of 'involution' to explain why *Homo sapiens* seems to be the only species which, in spreading over the globe, has resisted intense division into further species. This leads on to transcendental speculations, which allow him original, if theologically unorthodox, proofs for the existence of God. This work, *La Phénomène humain* (written 1938–40, published 1955, Eng trans *The Phenomenon of Man*), is based on his scientific thinking and argues that humanity is a continuous process of evolution towards a perfect spiritual state; it is complementary to *Le Milieu divin* (1957). ⌨ Robert Speaight, *The Life of Teilhard de Chardin* (1967)

Teisserenc de Bort, Léon Philippe 1855–1913
French physicist and meteorologist

Born in Paris, he joined the Central Meteorological Bureau in Paris (1878), where he was in charge from 1880 to 1892. He demonstrated that weather depended greatly on the barometric pressure at certain centres of action, notably the Azores high and the Iceland low. In 1894 he helped to produce an international cloud atlas, and founded the observatory at Paris (1889) primarily for the study of the upper air using kites and hydrogen-filled balloons carrying instruments for measuring pressure, temperature and humidity. He discovered that the temperature of the atmosphere does not continue to fall with height, but becomes constant at a certain height (the tropopause). He thus identified and named the stratosphere. He also showed that the height of the tropopause varies with latitude, being much higher in the tropics. He was awarded the Symons gold medal of the Royal Meteorological Society (1908).

Teixeira, Pedro c.1575–1640
Portuguese soldier

In 1614 he fought against the French in Brazil. He helped to found Pará in 1615, of which he was governor (1620, 1640). He led an expedition up the Amazon (1637–39) and across the mountains to Quito, returning by the same route.

Te Kanawa, Dame Kiri Janette 1944–
New Zealand soprano

Born in Gisborne, Auckland, she won many prizes and awards in New Zealand and Australia before going to London, where she made her debut with the Royal Opera Company in 1970. She has since taken a wide range of leading roles at all the major opera houses and concert halls, and in 1981 sang at the wedding of **Charles** and **Diana**, Prince and Princess of Wales. In 1988 she made the first of her regular appearances in the ABCs' *Opera in the Outback* concerts, and in 1990 she performed at the opening of the new Aotea Centre, Auckland. She was made a DBE in 1982 and appointed to the Order of Merit in 1995. She published *Land of the Long White Cloud* in 1989. 📖 David Fingleton, *Kiri Te Kanawa: A Biography* (1983)

Tekawitha, Kateri c.1656–80
Native American Catholic convert

She was born in the Mohawk village of Ossernenon (now Auriesville, New York). Her mother was a Christian Algonquin who had been brought up among the French but had been captured by the Iroquois and married to a Mohawk chief. Smallpox at the age of four left Kateri orphaned and nearly blind. On conversion to Christianity in 1676, she was rejected by her people and fled nearly 200 miles to the Indian Christian village of Sault St Louis, near Montreal. She received her first communion at Christmas 1677 and took a private vow of chastity in 1679. She was credited with many miracles, and beatified in 1980.

Teleki, Pál, Count 1879–1941
Hungarian statesman

He was born in Budapest, where he became Professor of Geography at the university in 1919. Combining politics with an academic career, he was also in that year appointed Foreign Minister and, from 1920 to 1921, premier. Founder of the Christian National League and chief of Hungary's Boy Scouts, he was Minister of Education in 1938 and again premier (1939–41). He was fully aware of the German threat to his country, but all measures to avert it, including a pact with Yugoslavia, were unavailing through lack of support. When Germany marched against Yugoslavia through Hungary, he took his own life.

Telemann, Georg Philipp 1681–1767
German composer

Born in Magdeburg, he taught himself music by learning to play a wide range of instruments (including the violin, recorder and zither, and later the shawm, oboe, flute and bass trombone) and studying the scores of the masters. He held several posts as kapellmeister, notably at Frankfurt am Main (1712–21), and was musical director of the Johanneum at Hamburg from 1721 until his death. A prolific composer, he wrote church music, 46 passions, over 40 operas, oratorios, many songs, and much instrumental music. Ranked in his lifetime above his friend **J S Bach**, he was admired by **Handel**, but his popularity waned from his death until the 1930s. Though his grasp of the techniques of all forms of musical composition was always recognized, critics regarded him as unoriginal and condemned his works as lacking in depth and sincerity; but through his study of and admiration for the French composers, notably **Jean Baptiste Lully**, a new grace and richness was introduced into German music. Much of the liveliness in his work sprang from his sense of humour and from an interest in folk music. He wrote three autobiographies, the last of which was published in 1739.

Telford, Thomas 1757–1834
Scottish civil engineer

Born in Westerkirk, Langholm, he was apprenticed to a stonemason at the age of 14. In 1780 he went to Edinburgh, and in 1782 to London. He found work at Portsmouth dockyard in 1784 and in 1787 became surveyor of public works for Shropshire. His reputation was enhanced by his masonry arch bridge over the Severn at Montford (1790–92) and even more by the spectacular Pont-Cysyllte aqueduct and other works on the Ellesmere Canal (1793–1805). In 1801 he was commissioned by the government to report on the public works required for Scotland and he constructed the Caledonian Canal (1803–23), more than 1,000 miles (1,609km) of road, and 1,200 bridges, besides churches, manses, harbours, etc. Other works by him included the road from London to Holyhead, with the remarkable 579ft (174m) span wrought-iron Menai Suspension Bridge (1819–26), and the St Katherine's Docks (1824–28) in London. He was also responsible for draining large tracts of the Fen country. 📖 R M Pearce, *Thomas Telford* (1973)

Tell, William 15th century
Semi-legendary Swiss patriot

He was from Bürglen in Uri, and his name first occurs in a chronicle of 1470. A famous crossbow marksman, he reputedly saved his native district from Austrian oppression. Johannes von Müller (1752–1809), in his *History of Switzerland* (1786), records how Tell was compelled by the tyrannical Austrian governor, Hermann Gessler, to shoot an apple off his own son's head. Later, Tell killed the tyrant, and so initiated the movement which secured the independence of Switzerland. Similar tales are found in the folklore of many countries, and Tell may be pure legend.

Teller, Edward 1908–
US physicist

Born in Budapest, Hungary, he graduated in chemical engineering at Karlsruhe, studied theoretical physics at the universities of Munich and Göttingen, and under **Niels Bohr** at Copenhagen. He left Germany in 1933, lectured in London and Washington (1935) and contributed profoundly to the modern explanation of solar energy. He worked on the Manhattan atomic bomb project (1941–46), and joined **Robert Oppenheimer**'s theoretical study group at Berkeley, California, where he was director of the new nuclear laboratories at Livermore (1958–60). From 1963 to 1966 he was chairman of the department of applied science at California University, then University Professor (1971–75). He repudiated any moral implications of his work, stating that, but for Oppenheimer's moral qualms, the USA might have had hydrogen bombs in 1947. After Russia's first atomic test (1949) he was one of the architects of President **Harry S Truman**'s crash programme to build and test (1952) the world's first hydrogen bomb. Since 1975 he has been Senior Research Fellow at the Hoover Institution. A recent publication is *Conversations on the Dark Secrets of Physics* (1991). 📖 Stanley A Blumberg and Gwinn Owens, *Energy and Conflict: The Life and Times of Edward Teller* (1976)

Temin, Howard Martin 1934–94
US virologist and Nobel Prize winner

Born in Philadelphia, he studied with **Renato Dulbecco** at the California Institute of Technology (Caltech). From 1969 he held various professorships at the University of Wisconsin. Temin formulated the 'provirus' hypothesis, that the genetic material of an invading virus is copied into the host cell DNA. In 1970 he isolated the enzyme reverse transcriptase (independently of **David Baltimore**), which enables new DNA to be inserted into the host cell. Viruses which contain this enzyme are retroviruses. Reverse transcriptase is used to make copies of specific genes, clones, and is widely used for genetic engineering. Temin shared the 1975 Nobel Prize for physiology or medicine with Dulbecco and Baltimore.

Temminck, Coenraad Jacob 1778–1858
Dutch ornithologist

Born in Amsterdam, at the age of 17 he became an auctioneer with the Dutch East India company, and used this contact to collect exotic birds and animals. In 1800 he turned his attention full-time to the study of natural history and became an accomplished taxidermist. His *Catalogue Systématique du Cabinet d'Ornithologie et de la Collection de Quadrumanes* (1807) and *Histoire Naturelle Générale des Pigeons et des Gallinacées* (3 vols, 1813–15) established him as one of the leading European ornithologists. In 1820 he became the first director of the Dutch National Museum of Natural History at Leyden. His *Manuel d'Ornithologie* (1815–40) remained for many years the standard text on European birds.

Temple, Frederick 1821–1902
English prelate and Archbishop of Canterbury
Born in Santa Maura in the Ionian islands, and educated at Balliol College, Oxford, of which he became a mathematics lecturer and Fellow, he was Principal of Kneller Hall Training College (1858–69), and headmaster of Rugby (1857–69). He wrote the first of the allegedly heterodox *Essays and Reviews* (1860), which almost prevented his appointment to the bishopric of Exeter in 1869, and supported the disestablishment of the Irish Church. In 1885 he became Bishop of London and in 1897 Archbishop of Canterbury. He was responsible, with Archbishop Maclagen of York, for the 'Lambeth Opinions' (1889) which attempted to solve some ritual controversies.

Temple, Shirley, *married name* Shirley Temple Black 1928–
US child film actress
Born in Santa Monica, California, she was a precociously talented baby and appeared in a series of short films from the age of three-and-a-half, graduating to full stardom with a leading role in *Little Miss Marker* (1934). An unspoilt personality who sang, danced and did impressions, she captivated Depression-era audiences, becoming the world's favourite golden-haired moppet in films like *Curly Top* (1935) and *Dimples* (1936). Her appeal faded, however, and when attempts at an adult comeback floundered, she retired from the screen. Involved with Republican party politics as Mrs Shirley Temple Black, she was appointed the USA's representative to the United Nations General Assembly in 1969 and served as ambassador to Ghana (1974–76), White House chief of protocol (1976–1977) and ambassador to Czechoslovakia (1989–92). She received an honorary Academy Award in 1934. Her autobiography, *Child Star*, was published in 1988. 📖 Anne Edwards, *Shirley Temple: American Princess* (1988)

Temple, Sir William 1628–99
English diplomat and essay writer
He was born in London, and studied at Emmanuel College, Cambridge. A diplomat from 1655, he became ambassador at The Hague and negotiated the Triple Alliance (1668) against France. In 1677 he helped arrange the marriage of the Prince of Orange (**William III**) to the Princess **Mary**, daughter of James, Duke of York (later **James VII and II**). After the Revolution he declined a political post in order to devote himself to literature. Among his works are *Miscellanea* (1679, 1692) and the famous essay 'Upon the Ancient and Modern Learning'. His essay style was a major influence on 18th-century writers, including **Jonathan Swift**, who was his secretary, and who published his letters (1700–03). 📖 C Marburg, *Sir William Temple* (1929)

Temple, William 1881–1944
English prelate and Archbishop of Canterbury
Born in Exeter, the son of **Frederick Temple**, he was educated at Oxford, where he became a Fellow of Queen's College (1904–10). He took orders in 1908, was head-

master of Repton School (1910–14) and became a canon of Westminster in 1919. He then became successively Bishop of Manchester (1921–29), Archbishop of York (1929–42) and Archbishop of Canterbury (1942–44). He was an outspoken advocate of social reform, combining humanity with great administrative ability in a crusade against usury, slums, dishonesty, and the aberrations of the profit motive. His leadership was also seen in his chairmanship of the Doctrinal Commission of the Church of England and in his work for the Ecumenical Movement of Christian Union. His publications include *Church and Nation* (1915), *Christianity and the State* (1928) and *Christianity and the Social Order* (1942). 📖 F A Iremonger, *William Temple, Archbishop of Canterbury: His Life and Letters* (1948)

Temple, William See **Bull, Phil**

Templer, Sir Gerald 1898–1979
English soldier
Educated at Wellington College and Sandhurst, he served in World War I. In World War II he became Commander of the 6th Armoured Division. He was Vice-Chief of the Imperial General Staff (1948–50), and Chief of the Imperial General Staff (1955–58). As High Commissioner and Commander-in-Chief Malaya (1952–54) he frustrated the Communist guerrillas' offensive. In 1965 he succeeded Field Marshal Lord **Alexander of Tunis** as Constable of the Tower of London.

Templewood, 1st Viscount See **Hoare, Sir Samuel John Gurney**

ten Boom, Corrie 1892–1983
Dutch evangelist and author
Born in the Netherlands, she worked as a watchmaker in her father's shop in Haarlem, and started clubs for teenage girls. The family's wartime role in helping 700 Jews escape the Germans led to their imprisonment in 1944. On unexpected release from Ravensbruck concentration camp in 1945, she carried out plans made with her sister Betsie (who did not survive) to establish a home for rehabilitating concentration camp victims in Holland and a home for refugees in Darmstadt, Germany. The royalties on her many books, such as *The Hiding Place* (1971, filmed 1973), *Tramp for the Lord* (1974) and *In My Father's House* (1976), were used to support Christian missionaries.

Tencin, Claudine Alexandrine Guérin de 1681–1749
French writer and courtesan
Born in Grenoble, she entered a convent at the age of 16, but in 1714 moved to Paris, where her wit and beauty attracted a crowd of lovers, among them the regent **Philippe d'Orléans** and Cardinal **Dubois**. She had much political influence, enriched herself, and facilitated the rise to power of her brother, Cardinal Pierre Guérin de Tencin (1680–1758). However, her influence waned after the deaths of the regent and the cardinal in 1723. In 1726 she was imprisoned for a short time in the Bastille, after one of her lovers had shot himself in her house. Her later life was more decorous, and her salon became one of the most popular in Paris. The writer **Bernard le Fontenelle** was one of her lovers, and the mathematician **Jean d'Alembert** was one of her children. Her romances include *Mémoires du Comte de Comminges* (1735, 'Memoirs of the Count of Comminges'), *Le Siège de Calais* (1739, 'The Siege of Calais') and *Les Malheurs de l'amour* (1747, 'Misfortunes of Love').

Tendulkar, Sachin Ramesh 1973–
Indian cricketer
Born in Bombay, he was recognized as a prodigious batting talent while still at school, and at the age of 15 made a century for Bombay in his debut first-class match. He

made seven Test centuries before he was 21, making him the only batsman ever to have done this. He quickly became India's number-one batsman and one of India's most public figures, although he is a very private man. He joined Yorkshire as their first overseas cricketer in 1992, and despite a slow start in one-day matches, his flamboyant style has guaranteed an astonishing performance.

Teniers, David, the Elder 1582–1649
Flemish genre painter
Born in Antwerp, he generally painted homely tavern scenes, rustic games, weddings and so on. His *Temptation of St Anthony* is well-known.

Teniers, David, the Younger 1610–90
Flemish genre painter
The son of **David Teniers**, the Elder, he quickly gained distinction, becoming court painter in Brussels (from 1647) to Archduke Leopold Wilhelm of Austria, Governor of the Austrian Netherlands, and curator of his art collection. His 700 pictures possess to a superlative degree the qualities that mark his father's work.

Tennant, Charles 1768–1838
Scottish chemist and industrialist
Born in Ochiltree, Ayrshire, he attended the parish school and was then apprenticed to a silk weaver. He studied bleaching and set up his own bleachfields at Darnley, near Paisley. At that time, traditional methods of bleaching were being replaced by chlorine, a method introduced in France by **Claude Louis Berthollet**. The chlorine was used in solution and was difficult to handle. In 1799 Tennant took out a patent for a dry bleaching powder made from chlorine and solid slaked lime, an innovation that was probably the invention of one of his partners **Charles Macintosh**. The powder could be conveniently transported to the expanding textile industry and the chlorine was easily regenerated when required by treating the powder with acid. The St Rollox works, which Tennant established in 1800, grew to be the largest chemical works in the world. Tennant was one of the first men to make a fortune out of the heavy chemical industry.

Tennant, Smithson 1761–1815
English chemist
Born in Selby, Yorkshire, he was educated at Edinburgh University, where he was a pupil of **Joseph Black**, and at Cambridge, where he became an early supporter of **Antoine Lavoisier**. He analysed lime from many parts of Great Britain and showed that some limes contain magnesium compounds and that these are injurious to plant life. In 1797 he demonstrated that diamond is a form of carbon by burning the diamond and showing that it produced the same amount of 'fixed air' (carbon dioxide) as an equal weight of charcoal. In 1800 he entered into partnership with a former fellow student, **William Hyde Wollaston**, to produce platinum equipment for chemical research and industry. In the course of their research they each discovered two new elements, Tennant describing iridium and osmium. He was elected FRS in 1785. In 1814 he was appointed to the chair of chemistry at Cambridge; he was killed the following year in a riding accident.

Tenniel, Sir John 1820–1914
English cartoonist and illustrator
Born in London, he was a self-trained artist, and was selected in 1845 to paint one of the frescoes (Dryden's 'St Cecilia') in the Houses of Parliament. He was on the staff of *Punch* for 50 years (1851–1901), succeeding **John Leech** as chief cartoonist in 1864. His most celebrated cartoon was 'Dropping the Pilot' (1890), referring to **Bismarck**'s dismissal. His main claim to fame, however, are his delicate illustrations for **Lewis Carroll**'s *Alice's Adventures in Wonderland* (1865) and *Through the Looking Glass* (published

in December 1871, dated 1872). He also illustrated *Aesop's Fables* (1848), **Thomas Moore**'s *Lalla Rookh* (1861), and **Richard Barham**'s *Ingoldsby Legends* (1864), amongst others. 📖 Rodney K Engen, *Sir Robert Tenniel: Alice's White Knight* (1991)

Tennyson, Alfred, Lord See panel p1808

Tenzing Norgay, *known as* Sherpa Tenzing 1914–86
Nepalese mountaineer
Born in Tsa-chu, near Makalu, he made his first climb as a porter with a British expedition to Everest in 1935. In the years following he climbed many of the Himalayan peaks and on two later attempts on the ascent of Everest he reached 23,000ft in 1938 and 28,215ft in 1952. In 1953 on Colonel **John Hunt**'s expedition, he, with **Edmund Hillary**, succeeded in reaching the summit of Everest, and for this triumph he was awarded the George Medal. In 1954 he studied at a mountaineering school in Switzerland, and on his return to Darjeeling, was appointed head of the Institute of Mountaineering. He also became president of the Sherpa Association.

Terborch or Terburg, Gerard, the Younger c.1617–1681
Dutch painter
Born in Zwolle, he studied with his father. He was precociously talented, and his earliest dated drawing (now in the Rijksmuseum, Amsterdam) is from 1625. He visited England (1635), Italy (1640) and Germany, where he painted *The Peace Congress of Münster* (1648, National Gallery, London). He also visited **Velázquez** in Spain. From 1654 to his death he lived at Deventer, where he became burgomaster. He worked mostly on a small scale, producing genre pictures and fashionable portraits.

Terbrugghen, Hendrik 1588–1629
Dutch painter
Born in Deventer, he studied under **Abraham Bloemaert**, later settling in Utrecht. He went to Italy from 1604 to 1616, where he came under the influence of **Caravaggio**. Like the latter he excelled in chiaroscuro effects and in the faithful representation of physiognomical details and drapery. His *Jacob and Laban* (1627) is in the National Gallery, London.

Terence, *properly* Publius Terentius Afer c.195–159BC
Roman comic dramatist
Born in Carthage, he became the slave of the Roman senator P Terentius Lucanus, who brought him to Rome, educated him, and freed him. His first play was the *Andria* (166BC, 'The Girl from Andros'). Its success introduced Terence to the most refined society of Rome, and gained him the patronage of Laelius and **Scipio Aemilianus**, the Younger. After spending some years in Rome he went to Greece. Six of his comedies are still extant: *Andria* (166BC), *Hecyra* (165BC, 'Mother-in-Law'), *Heauton Timoroumenos* (163BC, 'Self-Tormentor'), *Eunuchus* (161BC), *Phormio* (161BC), and *Adelphi* (160BC, 'Brothers'). They are Greek in origin and scene, and four of them are directly based on **Menander**. Many of his conventions and plot constructions were later used by **Molière**, **Richard Brinsley Sheridan**, and other European dramatists. 📖 J Strauss, *Terence and Menander* (1955)

Teresa or Theresa of Ávila, St, *also called* Santa Teresa de Jesus 1515–82
Spanish mystic, writer and first woman Doctor of the Church
Born in Ávila, she entered a Carmelite convent there in 1533. She became well known for her asceticism and sanctity. To re-establish the ancient Carmelite rule, she founded the first of her 16 religious houses in 1562, and in 1568 helped St **John of the Cross** found the first

Tennyson, Alfred, 1st Baron Tennyson 1809–92
English poet

Tennyson was born in Lincolnshire, the fourth son of the rector of Somersby. His elder brothers, Frederick and Charles, also wrote poetry. He was educated at Louth Grammar School, and in 1827 went to Trinity College, Cambridge, where he became a member of an ardent group of young men that included his friend Arthur Hallam (1811–33). In 1829 he won a prize with the blank-verse poem 'Timbuctoo', but his other early ventures in verse, *Poems Chiefly Lyrical* (1830) and *Poems* (1833), were slighted by the critics of the day as being too senti-mental; the critics also failed to recognize a great poet in the first version of 'The Lady of Shallott', 'Oenone', 'The Lotus-eaters' and other poems in the 1833 volume. Nine years of revising these poems and adding fresh material resulted in the volume of *Poems* of 1842, which estab-lished Tennyson's fame.

A greater achievement was the completion of the ele-giac poem *In Memoriam* (1850), begun on the sudden death of Hallam abroad in 1833. Also in 1850 he suc-ceeded **William Wordsworth** as Poet Laureate and mar-ried Emily Sarah Sellwood. In 1853 he settled in a house on the Isle of Wight, Farringford, where he wrote 'The Charge of the Light Brigade', and in 1868 built Aldworth in Sussex as a summer home. He was flattered by the homage of the entire nation from Queen **Victoria** down-wards, such was his popularity. He undertook short tours with his wife, but rarely left his Victorian England.

After 1850 he devoted himself to the fashionable verse novelette: *Maud: a Monodrama* (1855), *Enoch Arden* (1864), and *Locksley Hall Sixty Years After* (1886). From 1859 to 1885 he published *Idylls of the King* (1859), a se-quence of poems based on Arthurian legend that were extremely popular, but now seem somewhat compro-mised by the imposition of Victorian morality on the old chivalric matter.

In the 1870s he wrote a number of plays, of which *Becket*, produced by Sir **Henry Irving** in 1893, was the most successful. He continued to write poetry, and his last poem was a 16-line lyric written in 1889 while crossing from Lymington to the Isle of Wight, *Crossing the Bar*.

📖 Hallam Tennyson, *Alfred Lord Tennyson, A Memoir* (1897); T R Lousbury, *The Life and Times of Alfred Lord Tennyson, 1809–1850* (1862). For a modern assessment, see R B Martin, *Tennyson: The Unquiet Heart* (1980) and C Ricks, *Tennyson* (1972).

By Tennyson:
Ring out the want, the care, the sin,
The faithless coldness of the times;
Ring out, ring out my mournful rhymes,
But ring the fuller minstrel in.
From *In Memoriam A.H.H.* (1850), canto 106.

She came to the village church,
And sat by a pillar alone;
An angel watching an urn
Wept over her, carved in stone;
And once, but once, she lifted her eyes,
And suddenly, sweetly, strangely blush'd
To find they were met by my own.'
From *Maud* (1855), part 1, section 8.

Smile and we smile, the lords of many lands;
Frown and we smile, the lords of our own hands;
For man is man and master of his fate.
From *Idylls of the King*, 'The Marriage of Geraint' (1859), lines 353–355.

About Tennyson:
'He could not think up to the height of his own towering style.' **G K Chesterton**.

'His genius was lyrical.' **W H Auden**.

'The great master of metric as well as of melancholia.' **T S Eliot**.

---

community of reformed Carmelite friars. The most famous of her works are her autobiography, *Libro de la vida* (1562, 'The Way of Perfection'), *Libro de las fundaciones* (1610, 'The Book of Foundations'), which describes the jour-neys she made and the convents she founded or reformed, and *Las moradas* (1577, Eng trans *The Interior Castle*, 1852). The most endearing feature of her writing is her dis-tinctive prose style, which effectively captures the rhythm and intimacy of the spoken language, showing a dis-regard for conventional syntax and frequently losing its train of thought in mid-sentence. She was canonized in 1622, and her feast day is 15 October. 📖 E A Peers, *The Complete Works of Saint Teresa of Jesus* (1982); H Hatzfeld, *Estudios literarios sobre mística española* (1968)

Teresa of Calcutta, Mother   See panel p1809

Tereshkova, Valentina Vladimirovna 1937–

Russian astronaut

Born in Maslennikovo, she was the first woman to fly in space. She worked in a textile factory and qualified as a sports parachutist, before training as a cosmonaut (1962). She was the solo crew member in the three-day *Vostok 6* flight which was launched from the Tyuratam Space Station in the USSR on 16 June 1963. She was made a Hero of the Soviet Union, and became a member of the Central Committee of the Soviet Communist Party in 1971. Since 1992 she has chaired the Russian Association of Inter-national Co-operation.

Terkel, Studs (Louis) 1912–

US writer and oral historian

Born in New York City, he studied law at the University of Chicago. He acted in radio soap operas, worked as a disc jockey, a radio commentator and a television host, and has travelled worldwide conducting interviews with the famous and the anonymous. Described by J K Galbraith as 'a national resource', he has published *Giants of Jazz* (1957), *Division Street: America* (1967), *Hard Times* (1970), which recalls the Depression, *Working* (1974), *American Dreams: Lost and Found* (1980), and *The Good War: An Oral History of World War Two* (1984, Pulitzer Prize), and *Coming of Age* (1995). He also published an autobiography, *Talking to Myself* (1977). 📖 Tony Parker, *Studs Terkel: A Life in Words* (1997)

Terman, Lewis Madison 1877–1956

US psychologist, pioneer of intelligence tests

He was born in Johnson County, Indiana. At Stanford University he developed an English version of the **Binet**–Simon intelligence test and introduced Terman Group Intelligence Tests into the US army in 1920. He pioneered the use of the term IQ (Intelligence Quotient) in his *The Measurement of Intelligence* (1916) and launched the five-volume *Genetic Studies of Genius* (1926–59). 📖 May V Sea-goe, *Terman and the Gifted* (1975)

Terry, Daniel c.1780–1829

English actor and playwright

Teresa of Calcutta, Mother, *originally* Agnes Gonxha Bojaxhiu 1910–97
Roman Catholic nun and missionary, and Nobel Prize winner

Mother Teresa was born in Yugoslavia of Albanian parents and lived in Skopje, Macedonia, as a child. She went to India in 1928, where she joined the Irish order of Sisters of Loretto and taught at a convent school in Calcutta, taking her final vows in 1937. She became principal of the school, but in 1948 felt called to help the poor and left the convent to work alone in the slums. She undertook a week-long course in basic nursing in Patna in the Indian state of Bihar.

She was gradually joined in the slums by other nuns, and she opened her House for the Dying in 1952. Her sisterhood, the Order of the Missionaries of Charity, was founded in 1950, and became a pontifical congregation (answering directly to the pope) in 1956. The congregation now has 2,000 sisters and 200 branch houses in several countries. In 1957 she started work with lepers and

established a leper colony called Shanti Nagar ('Town of Peace') near Asansol in West Bengal.

She was awarded the Pope John XXIII Peace Prize in 1971 and the Nobel Peace Prize in 1979.

📖 Christopher Hitchens, *The Missionary Position: The Ideology of Mother Teresa* (1995, a critical view); Vanora Leigh, *Mother Teresa* (1986); Desmond Doig, *Mother Theresa: Her People and Her Work* (1976); Georges Gorree and Jean Barbier, *For the Love of God: Mother Teresa of Calcutta* (1974, trans by Paula Speakman).

'The biggest disease today is not leprosy or tuberculosis, but rather the feeling of being unwanted.' Quoted in *The Observer*, 3 October 1971.

He was born in Bath, and after an architectural apprenticeship he joined a theatrical company in Sheffield, probably in 1805, making his London debut in 1812. He played in many dramatizations of Sir Walter Scott's novels, and became an intimate friend of Scott. He also played the major Shakespearean roles, and in plays by Richard Brinsley Sheridan and others at Covent Garden and Drury Lane, London.

Terry, Dame (Alice) Ellen 1848–1928
English actress

Born in Coventry, she was the daughter of a provincial actor and the sister of Fred Terry. She appeared on the stage at the age of eight as Mammilius in *The Winter's Tale* at the Prince's Theatre, London. From 1862 she played in Bristol and after a brief marriage to the painter, G F Watts (1864), and a second retirement from the stage (1868–74) during which her two children by E W Godwin, Edith and Edward Gordon Craig, were born, she established herself as the leading Shakespearean actress in London, dominating the English and US theatre (1878–1902) in partnership with Henry Irving. In 1903 she entered theatre management without Irving and toured and lectured widely. J M Barrie and George Bernard Shaw wrote parts especially for her, such as Lady Cicely Waynflete in *Captain Brassbound's Conversion* (1905). She married Charles Kelly (Wardell) in 1876 and in 1907 the US actor, James Carew. She received the DBE in 1925.

Terry, Fred 1863–1933
English actor

He was born in London, and was the brother of Ellen Terry. He played in the companies of Herbert Beerbohm Tree, Johnston Forbes-Robertson and Henry Irving, and established a reputation as a romantic actor as Sir Percy Blakeney in *The Scarlet Pimpernel* (1905). His sisters, Kate (1844–1924), Marion and Florence were also actresses, as was his wife Julia Neilson.

Terry-Thomas, *originally* Thomas Terry Hoar-Stevens 1911–90
English actor

Born in Finchley, London, he was initially a buyer for a grocery firm, but drifted into showbusiness, appearing in cabaret, on radio and making his film debut as an extra in such productions as *It's Love Again* (1936) and *Rythmn in the Air* (1936). After wartime service in the Royal Signal Corps, he worked as a stand-up comic in West End revues and television before returning to the cinema as upper-crust rogues and silly asses in comedies like *Private's Progress* (1956), *Carlton Browne of the FO* (1958) and *I'm All Right Jack* (1959). Gap-toothed and bowler-hatted, he became a favourite in Hollywood as a caricature of the

Englishman in the 1960s with prominent roles in films like *Bachelor Flat* (1961) and *How to Murder Your Wife* (1965). He retired in 1980 and, stricken with Parkinson's disease, his final decade was beset with poor health and financial hardship.

Tertullian, *in full* Quintus Septimus Florens Tertullianus c.160–c.220AD
North African Christian theologian

Born in Carthage, he was brought up there as a pagan, then went to Rome, where he was converted to Christianity (c.196AD). His opposition to worldliness in the Church culminated in his becoming a leader of the Montanist sect in c.207, and his writings show increasing hostility to the Church. The first to produce major Christian works in Latin, he had a great influence on the development of ecclesiastical language, and also wrote against heathens, Jews and heretics. His style is vivid, vigorous and concise, and in places shows great eloquence. 📖 Timothy D Barnes, *Tertullian: A Historical and Literary Study* (1971)

Terzaghi, Karl 1883–1963
US civil engineer

Born in Prague, and educated at the Technische Hochschule in Graz, he held professorships at Istanbul, Massachusetts Institute of Technology, Vienna and Harvard, becoming a naturalized US citizen in 1943. Through his teaching and research he established the subject of soil mechanics, the behaviour of soil under stress, as an independent scientific discipline, enabling engineers to design foundations, cuttings and earth dams, for example, on an analytical rather than an empirical basis.

Tesla, Nikola 1856–1943
US physicist and electrical engineer

Born in Smiljan, Croatia, he studied at the universities of Graz, Prague and Paris, emigrating to the USA in 1884. He left the Edison Works at Menlo Park after quarrelling with Thomas Edison and concentrated on his own inventions. Among his many projects, he improved dynamos, and electric motors, invented the high-frequency Tesla coil and an air-core transformer. Firmly in favour of an alternating current electricity supply, by 1888 he had obtained patents on an AC system and in 1893 again demonstrated the feasibility of AC by lighting the 1893 Chicago World Columbian Exposition. He produced a quality of artificial lightning never since equalled, predicted wireless communication two years before Guglielmo Marconi developed it, and experimented with a wireless communication system using the Earth as the conducting medium. ▢ Inez Hunt and Wanetta W Draper, *Lightning in his Hand: The Life Story of Nikola Tesla* (1964)

Tessin, Carl-Gustaf, Count 1695–1770
Swedish statesman, writer and art collector
Son of Nicodemus Tessin, the Younger, he led the anti-Russian Hat party which hoped to regain territory lost to Russia during Karl XII's reign. He was elected leader of the Nobility Estate when the Hats gained a majority in 1738, and was responsible for the unsuccessful war against Russia in 1741. He gained the favour of King Adolf Fredrik and Queen Louisa Ulrika and in 1746 was appointed Head of Chancellory and governor to the future King Gustav III, but his disapproval of their attempts to increase royal power caused him to retire from politics to write his memoirs (31 volumes, mostly in French), fables and didactic letters in the style of Fénelon to the Crown Prince. His art collection, including works by François Boucher and Dutch and Flemish 17th-century masters, forms the basis of the present National Museum and Royal Library in Stockholm.

Tessin, Nicodemus the Elder 1615–81
Swedish architect
Born in Stralsund, Germany, he moved to Stockholm in 1636, where he entered the service of the Lord Chancellor, Axel Oxenstjerna, whose handsome castle Tidö, Västerås, he completed in 1645. He was then appointed royal architect in 1646, drawing up plans in the Renaissance style for several Norrland towns in the late 1640s, and was city architect in Stockholm from 1661. Then, supported by Queen Kristina, he studied in Italy, France and Holland (1651–53), after which his structures show clear Italian (mainly Roman) influence, the furnishings reflect French styles and the gardens reveal the spirit of André Lenôtre. Among his many commissions on returning to Sweden were the *Wrangelska palatset* (1652–64), which now houses the Supreme Court in Stockholm; Kalmar Cathedral (started 1660); the Caroline Mausoleum in Riddarholm Church (1671); and the Bank of Sweden in Stockholm (1676). Most notable of all is the Palace of Drottningholm on Mälaren, the residence of the present monarch, commissioned by Queen Hedvig Eleonara in 1662 and completed some 20 years later by Tessin's son, Nicodemus the Younger.

Tessin, Nicodemus the Younger 1654–1728
Swedish architect
Born in Nyköping, the son of Nicodemus the Elder, he finished his education with long periods in Rome (1673–78) and Paris (1678–80). Under the protection of Queen Kristina, living in Rome since her abdication, he studied ancient and Baroque culture and was highly appreciative of Gian Lorenzo Bernini and Carlo Fontana. His genius lay in his ability to borrow from Baroque and French models and create a harmonious, uniquely northern, edifice. He was appointed royal architect in 1676 and succeeded his father as Stockholm city architect in 1682. He completed Drottningholm Palace and added the royal church (1690–99). Other notable structures include Steninge Castle (1694–98) and his own Tessin Palace (1696–1700), now the Governor's Palace. He planned gardens for royal palaces, including Ulriksdal and Karlberg in the manner of André Lenôtre. He designed ecclesiastical buildings such as Trinity Church, Karlskrona (1697–1747), and Fredrik's Church, Karlshamn (1720–58), and renovated others, notably Västerås Cathedral spire. He also did important work on Amelienborg Castle, Copenhagen (1697), the Louvre (1704–06) and the Apollo Temple, Versailles. His greatest achievement was the Royal Palace, Stockholm. When fire destroyed the old *Tre kronor* castle in 1697 he had designs ready for a royal stately home with an Italian type façade and French interior design but was held up for many years because of severe shortage of money and

manpower caused by Karl XII's disastrous wars. Building started again shortly before Tessin's death and was completed by his son, Carl-Gustaf Tessin.

Tetley, Glen 1926–
US ballet dancer and choreographer
Born in Cleveland, Ohio, he gave up medical studies to become a dancer and trained with Hanya Holm (1946–51). During a period performing on Broadway and with Martha Graham (1957–59), he shifted towards ballet, dancing with both American Ballet Theater and as an original member of the Joffrey Ballet (1956). Working with Netherlands Dance Theatre during the 1960s, guest choreographing for Ballet Rambert, and a two-year contract with Stuttgart Ballet (1973–75) after John Cranko's sudden death, have given him a stronger hold and reputation in Europe than he enjoys in the USA. In 1986 he was commissioned by the National Ballet of Canada to choreograph *Alice*, a popular version of the Lewis Carroll tale. He subsequently became artistic director there. His ballets include *Pierrot lunaire* (1962), *Voluntaries* (1973), *The Tempest* (1979), *La Ronde* (1987) and *Oracle* (1994).

Tetrazzini, Luisa 1871–1940
Italian soprano
Born in Florence, she made her debut there in 1895 in Giacomo Meyerbeer's *L'Africaine* ('The African Woman'). Appearing mostly in Italian opera of the older school, she had her most notable success with *Lucia di Lammermoor* ('The Bride of Lammermoor'). She sang in London and in the USA, becoming a member of the Chicago Opera Company (1913–14). In 1921 she published *My Life of Song*.

Tetzel, Johann c.1465–1519
German monk
Born in Pirna, Saxony, he entered the Dominican Order in 1489, and was appointed in 1516 to sell indulgences in return for contributions to the building fund of St Peter's in Rome. This he did with great ostentation, which provoked the 95 Wittenberg Theses of Martin Luther. In reply he published 122 counter-theses (written for him by Conrad Wimpina), but was rebuked by the papal delegate for his literary extravagance.

Tewfik Pasha, Mohammed 1852–92
Khedive of Egypt
He was the eldest son of Ismail Pasha and succeeded on his abdication in 1879. The chief events of his reign were Arabi's insurrection (1882), the British intervention, the war with the Mahdi Muhammad Ahmed (1884–85), the pacification of the Sudan frontiers, and the improvement of Egypt under British administration. He was succeeded by his son Abbas Hilmi Pasha.

Tey, Josephine, *pseudonym of* Elizabeth Mackintosh, *who also wrote as* Gordon Daviot 1897–1952
Scottish crime and mystery writer
She grew up in Inverness and trained as a physical education teacher. Her main invention, police inspector Alan Grant, tended to prefer cerebral rather than physical exercise. In *The Daughter of Time* (1952), she re-opens the file on Richard III's alleged murder of the little princes in the Tower of London; Grant conducts this masterpiece of retrospective investigation from his hospital bed. Grant was introduced in Tey's first novel, *The Man in the Queue* (1929, published in the USA as *Killer in the Crowd*, 1954), for which she used the Daviot pseudonym. *Miss Pym Disposes* (1946) and *The Franchise Affair* (1948) were non-Grant mysteries, as was the popular *Brat Farrar* (1949, published in the USA as *Come and Kill Me*, 1951). She wrote plays, including *Queen of Scots* (1934) and *Leith Sands* (1946), and an impressive biography of John Graham of Claverhouse, Viscount Dundee (1937). ▢ S Roy, *Josephine Tey* (1980)

Thackeray, Anne Isabella See Ritchie, Anne Isabella Thackeray, Lady

Thackeray, William Makepeace 1811–63
English novelist

He was born in Calcutta, India, where his father was in the service of the East India Company. His father died (1816) and his mother remarried, so Thackeray was sent home. He went to Charterhouse (1822) and Trinity College, Cambridge (1829), but left without taking a degree. His first venture in print was a parody of Tennyson's prize poem *Timbuctoo*. After spending much of his inheritance in travelling abroad, he decided to try journalism, though art equally attracted him. A four-year stay in Paris as an art student came to a close through lack of funds in 1836. He married Isabella Shawe (1836), but financial worry, due to the bankruptcy of his stepfather, finally made him decide to earn a living in journalism, and he returned to London where their first daughter, Anne Thackeray Ritchie, was born. He contributed regularly to *The Times*, the *New Monthly* and *Fraser's Magazine*. He also had problems at home. The birth of his third daughter, Harriett Marian (later the first wife of Leslie Stephen), permanently affected Mrs Thackeray's mind, the home was broken up and the children sent to their grandmother in Paris. His first publications, starting with *The Paris Sketchbook* (1840), and written under a number of pseudonyms (Wagstaff, Titmarsh, Fitz-Boodle, Yellowplush, Snob, etc) were a comparative failure although they included *The Yellowplush Papers*, *The Great Hoggarty Diamond* and *The Luck of Barry Lyndon*, all contributed to *Fraser's Magazine* (1841–44). His work on *Punch* from 1842 exploited the view of society as seen by the butler ('Jeames' Diary') and the great theme of English snobbery, and attracted attention. The great novels that were to follow—*Vanity Fair* (1847–48), *Pendennis* (1848), *Henry Esmond* (3 vols, 1852) and *The Newcomes* (1853–55), all, with the exception of *Henry Esmond*, monthly serials, established his fame. *Vanity Fair* is the first novel to give a view of London society with its mingling of rich parvenus and decadent upper class, through both of which the social climber, Becky Sharp, threads her way. The great historical novel, *Henry Esmond*, shows Thackeray's consuming love of the 18th century. Its sequel, *The Virginians* (1857–59), is not considered a success. *The Newcomes* shows a young love at the mercy of scheming relatives and mean-spirited rival suitors. Thackeray retired from *Punch* in 1854 and became the editor of the *Cornhill Magazine*, where much of his later work appeared—ballads and novels, now largely unreadable. He also undertook lecturing tours at home and in the USA, the fruit of which, apart from *The Virginians*, was *The English Humorists of the 18th century* (1853) and *The Four Georges* (1860). ▣ G N Ray, *William Makepeace Thackeray* (2 vols, 1955–68)

Thaddeus, St See Judas, St

Thais 4th century BC
Greek courtesan

She was born in Athens. Famous for her wit and beauty, she was, according to a doubtful legend, the mistress of Alexander the Great, whom she induced to burn down Persepolis. She had several children by Ptolemy Lagos.

Thalben-Ball, Sir George Thomas 1896–1987
British organist and composer

Born in Sydney, Australia, and educated privately, he attended the Royal Academy of Music, London, and studied composition under Frank Bridge, Sir Charles Stanford, Charles Wood and Sir Hubert Parry. He became assistant organist at the Temple Church, London (1919), and was appointed organist in 1923, a position he held for 58 years. From the early 1920s Thalben-Ball was synonymous with the Temple Church both in radio broadcasts and on HMV records. He also made regular appearances

in the Henry Wood Promenade Concerts for the BBC, as music adviser and consultant from 1941. The composer of much organ and choral music, he was organ professor and examiner at the Royal College of Music, and curator-organist at the Royal Albert Hall, London, in addition to many other professional positions. He toured abroad, and visited Australia in 1951 as guest of the Commonwealth Jubilee celebrations.

Thalberg, Irving G(rant) 1899–1936
US film executive

Born in New York City, he was a clerk in his grandfather's department store before embarking on a secretarial career that brought him employment at Universal Studios, as private secretary to Carl Laemmle. He rose swiftly in the company to become general manager and later played a key role in the formation of MGM. As head of production, he was renowned for a meticulous attention to detail and an obsessive devotion to his work. Among the films he helped put into production were *Grand Hotel* (1932), *Mutiny on the Bounty* (1935) and *Camille* (1936). He was married to the actress Norma Shearer (1900–83). He is said to have inspired the character of Monroe Stahr in *The Last Tycoon* by F Scott Fitzgerald. The Academy Awards still bestow an award in his name to honour consistent excellence in the field of film production.

Thalberg, Sigismond 1812–71
German or Austrian pianist

Born in Geneva, Switzerland, he studied music in Vienna under Johann Hummel, and from 1830 made extensive tours in Europe and North America, settling near Naples in 1858. His compositions comprise fantasias and variations, a piano concerto and operas.

Thales c.620–c.555 BC
Greek natural philosopher, astronomer and geometer

He came from Miletus on mainland Ionia, Asia Minor, as did his intellectual successors Anaximander and Anaximines. He is traditionally the founder of Greek, and therefore European, philosophy, and is important for having proposed the first natural cosmology, identifying water as the original substance and (literally) the basis of the universe. He seems to have had wide-ranging practical and intellectual interests, with a reputation as a politician, engineer, geometer and astronomer. He is supposed to have visited Egypt and developed his interest in land-surveying and astronomical techniques there, to have predicted accurately a solar eclipse in 585 BC, and to have proposed a federation of the Ionian cities of the Aegean. He was included in the traditional canon of 'Seven Wise Men', and attracted various apocryphal anecdotes, for example as the original absent-minded professor who would fall into a well while watching the stars. He left no writings, except possibly a nautical star-guide.

Thamar, Queen See Tamara, Queen

Thant, U 1909–74
Burmese diplomat

Born in Pantanaw, he became a schoolmaster under Thakin Nu, the future Prime Minister, whom he later succeeded as headmaster of Pantanaw National High School. He became a civil servant when Burma became independent in 1948 and became Burma's UN representative in 1957. As Secretary-General of the UN (1962–71) after the death of Dag Hammarskjöld, he played a major diplomatic role during the Cuban Missile Crisis. He also formulated a plan to end the Congolese Civil War (1962) and mobilized a UN peace-keeping force in Cyprus (1964). He died in New York City. The return of his body to Burma provoked major anti-government demonstrations. ▣ Ramses Nassif, *U Thant in New York, 1961–1971* (1988)

Thatcher, Margaret Hilda Thatcher, Baroness, *née* Roberts 1925–
English Conservative politician, the first woman to be Prime Minister of Great Britain (1979–90)

Margaret Thatcher was born in Grantham, the daughter of Alderman Alfred Roberts, a grocer and lay Methodist minister. She was educated at Grantham High School and at Somerville College, Oxford, where she read chemistry. She stood unsuccessfully as a Conservative candidate for Dartford in 1950 and 1951; and in 1951 she married a wealthy businessman, Denis Thatcher. She went on to read law and was called to the Bar in Lincoln's Inn in 1954.

In 1959 she was elected MP for Finchley, and from 1961 to 1964 was joint Parliamentary Secretary to the Ministry of Pensions and National Insurance. She joined the Shadow Cabinet in 1967. As Secretary of State for Education and Science (1970–74) she made herself widely unpopular by abolishing free milk for schoolchildren over the age of eight. From 1974 to 1975 she was joint Shadow Chancellor, and in 1975 was elected Leader of the Conservative Party, defeating **Edward Heath** to become the first woman party leader in British politics.

The Conservative Party was elected to government in May 1979 with a majority of 43 and devoted its energies to combating inflation, achieved at the cost of high unemployment (which doubled from 1979 to 1980) and reduced manufacturing output. None the less, she was re-elected with a majority of 144 in June 1983, her personal popularity having been greatly boosted by the recapture of the Falkland Islands from Argentina the previous year, and by the disarray in the opposition parties. In 1983 she was also elected FRS.

In their second term under her leadership, the Conservatives moved towards a more right-wing position, placing considerable emphasis on the market economy and the shedding of public sector commitments through an extensive privatization programme, including British Telecom, British Airways and Rolls Royce. Major legislation to reduce the power of the unions followed: union leaders were to ballot members on strike action, unions were to be responsible for the actions of their members, and sympathy strikes and the closed shop were banned. A miners' strike that began in the early part of 1984 lasted for 12 months without success, because the government had foreseen it and taken extensive precautionary measures.

Her unpopularity was seen in several incidents. In October 1984, an IRA bomb exploded at the Conservative Party Conference in Brighton, and she narrowly escaped being killed. The following year, the University of Oxford decided by a vote of Congregation not to award her a proposed Honorary Degree, as a protest against the effects of Thatcherism on further education. Although she brushed aside this rebuff, it clearly hurt her and damaged her esteem; the honour was refused again in 1987. Her reputation for intransigent authoritarianism was strengthened by the dramatic resignation in 1986 of **Michael Heseltine**, then Defence Minister, over the European-supported plan to rescue Westland Helicopters; the real issue was Cabinet responsibility.

Despite these difficulties, and the persistence of high unemployment, Thatcher was returned for a third term in the 1987 general election with a majority of 102. After 10
cont

Tharp, Twyla 1941–
US dancer and choreographer

Born in Portland, Indiana, she gained a degree in art history from Barnard College. She studied with **Martha Graham** and **Merce Cunningham**, and danced with the **Paul Taylor** Dance Company (1963–65) before founding her own small troupe in 1965. She became known for her ability to create modern dance with a popular appeal without losing either integrity or depth, and her early work was both structural and sombre. But from *Eight Jelly Rolls* (1971, set to the jazz piano music of **Jelly Roll Morton**), she introduced a humorous, flippant note which charmed audiences. *Coupe*, a piece made to music by the Beach Boys (see **Brian Wilson**) for the Joffrey Ballet in 1973, was a notable success, as was *Push Comes to Shove* (1976), the first dance made by a US choreographer for the Russian star **Mikhail Baryshnikov**, then at the American Ballet Theater, of which Tharp was artistic associate choreographer from 1988 to 1991. Subsequent works include *Sue's Leg* (1976), *Bach Partita* (1984), *The Rules of the Game* (1990), *Cutting Up* (1992, for Baryshnikov) and *Jump Start* (1995). She has also choreographed for Broadway (*When We Were Very Young*, 1980, and *The Catherine Wheel*, with music by David Byrne, 1983) and for films such as *Hair* (1979), *White Nights* (1985) and *I'll Do Anything* (1994). 📖 *Push Comes To Shove: An Autobiography* (1992)

Tharpe, Sister Rosetta, *née* Rubin 1915–73
US gospel and blues singer

Born in Cotton Plant, Arkansas, she sang and accompanied herself on electric guitar, switching without discomfort between sacred songs and very earthy blues material. With the important exception of **Mahalia Jackson**, she has been the most successful female gospel performer ever, with wartime hits like 'Didn't It Rain' (1944). Her appearance at the Newport Jazz Festival in 1968, like Jackson's 10 years earlier, was sensational and revived her career. She recorded doggedly through her last years,

despite losing a leg due to a thrombosis which also impaired her speech. She died in Philadelphia on the eve of a recording session.

Thatch, Edward See **Teach, Edward**

Thatcher, Margaret Hilda, Baroness See panel above

Thayer, James Bradley 1831–1902
US jurist

Born in Haverhill, Massachusetts, he was educated at Harvard, where he became a distinguished teacher of law. He wrote an important *Preliminary Treatise on Evidence at the Common Law* (1898) and many other texts.

Theaetetus c.414–c.369BC
Greek mathematician

He was an associate of **Plato** at the Academy, whose work was later used by **Euclid** in Books X and XIII of the *Elements*. Plato named after him the dialogue *Theaetetus*, which was devoted to the nature of knowledge.

Theed, William 1804–91
English sculptor

He was born in Trentham, Staffordshire, the son of the sculptor William Theed (1764–1817), whose best known work is *Hercules Taming the Thracian Horses* (1816, Royal Mews, London), and studied under **Bertel Thorvaldsen** in Rome, and in London at the Royal Academy schools. His works include the *Africa* group on the Albert Memorial, London, and the bronze relief of Tudor events, in the House of Lords (1853–56). His particular skill was the handling of historical costume. His bust of Prince **Albert** (1862) is at Osborne House, Isle of Wight.

Theiler, Max 1899–1972
US bacteriologist and Nobel Prize winner

Born in Pretoria, South Africa, he settled in the USA in 1922, and worked at the Harvard Medical School (1922–30) and the Rockefeller Institute, New York City

Thatcher, Margaret Hilda Thatcher, Baroness *cont*

years in office she had established a personal political philosophy identified as Thatcherism and based on individualism, the operation of market forces, and minimum intervention by (and support from) the state in people's lives, all forced through with a resolution that overrode objections from her critics and doubts among her supporters. In 1988 she became Britain's longest serving Prime Minister of the century.

On the international stage, her friendship with **Ronald Reagan** survived the Americans' invasion of the British dependency of Grenada in 1983, and in 1986 she allowed him to use British air bases to launch a reprisal attack on Libya, a move which caused storms of public protest. In the Soviet Union, where she had been dubbed the Iron Lady back in 1976 for her denunciation of Communism, she now won the admiration of **Mikhail Gorbachev** for her resoluteness.

From 1989 the tide of events turned decisively against her. The introduction of the community charge (popularly called the poll tax) was widely unpopular and led to public demonstrations. The same year, her resistance to the growing influence of other EC member states over the British economy and to their plans for economic union led to the resignation of Chancellor **Nigel Lawson** (after hostile statements by Sir Alan Walters, her economic adviser, who also subsequently resigned) and of Foreign Secretary **Geoffrey Howe** in 1990. Howe's resignation speech in the Commons was a bitter attack on the Prime Minister,

which effectively sealed her fate. Her leadership was challenged, and in November 1990, after a challenge in the first round of voting by Michael Heseltine, now returned from the political wilderness, she resigned as leader and was succeeded by **John Major**.

In 1992 she declined to stand again for parliament in the general election, and she was created a life peer. She turned instead to extra-parliamentary activities, launching the Thatcher Foundation to promote free enterprise and democracy thoughout the world, particularly in Eastern Europe.

📖 Margaret Thatcher's memoirs have been published in two volumes: *The Downing Street Years 1979–90* (1993), and *The Path to Power* (1995), which deals with her earlier years. See also H Young, *The Iron Lady* (1989) and K Harris, *Thatcher* (1988).

> 'No woman in my time will be Prime Minister. ... Anyway, I would not want to be Prime Minister.' On her appointment in 1969 as Junior Education Minister; quoted in *The Sunday Telegraph*, 26 October.
>
> 'It is exciting to have a real crisis on your hands, when you have spent half your political life dealing with humdrum issues like the environment.' Of the Falklands conflict, in a speech to the Scottish Conservative Party Conference, 14 May 1982.

(1930–64), and was later professor at Yale Medical School (1964–67). He was awarded the 1951 Nobel Prize for physiology or medicine for his work in connection with yellow fever, for which he discovered the vaccine 17-D in 1939.

Themistocles c.523–c.458BC
Athenian politician and naval strategist

He persuaded the Athenians to develop Piraeus as a port (493BC) and use their rich silver deposits to expand their fleet (483). The fleet won a naval victory over the Persians, led by **Xerxes**, at Salamis (480), and laid the foundations of the Athenian maritime empire. The pro-Spartan faction in Athens plotted his downfall after he had persuaded the city to raise the height of its walls (c.470) and he was ostracized and fled to Asia. **Artaxerxes I** of Persia received him with great favour and made him Governor of Magnesia on the Maeander.

Thénard, Louis Jacques 1777–1857
French organic chemist and politician

Born in La Louptière, the son of a peasant farmer, he went to Paris in search of an education and attended lectures by **Antoine François Fourcroy** and by **Nicolas-Louis Vauquelin**, who gave him a home in return for his services as a bottle-washer. In 1798 he was appointed demonstrator at the École Polytechnique; he later succeeded Vauquelin in the chair at the Collège de France (1804), became Dean of the Faculty of Sciences of Paris (1821) and was Chancellor of the University of France (1845–1852). He was a prominent member of many public bodies, particularly those concerned with the application of science to industry, and received many honours culminating in a peerage in 1832. He also served two terms in the Chamber of Deputies. Thénard made many important discoveries in organic chemistry and prepared a wide range of esters. He investigated cobalt and its compounds, and from alumina and copper arsenate prepared a stable brilliant blue pigment (Thénard's blue) which was used in porcelain manufacture to replace the expensive pigments made from lapis lazuli. Between 1808 and 1811 he collaborated with **Joseph Louis Gay-Lussac** to study potassium and

they discovered boron (1808). In 1818 Thénard announced the discovery of hydrogen peroxide, perhaps his greatest achievement. His observation that finely divided metals acted on hydrogen peroxide to produce heat and hydrogen without themselves being affected, together with knowledge of **Johann Döbereiner**'s work on platinum, led him to the study of surface catalysis. He was also the author of an influential textbook, *Traité élémentaire de chimie* (4 vols, 1813–16, 'Elementary Treatise on Chemistry'), which went through six editions and was much translated.

Theobald or Tebaldus d.1161
English ecclesiastic

Born near Bec, Normandy, France, he became a monk at Bec, then abbot (1137) and in 1138 became Archbishop of Canterbury. He crowned King **Stephen** in Canterbury, and after the latter's death refused to regard Stephen's son as his successor and eventually crowned **Henry II** (1154). He advanced his archdeacon, **Thomas à Becket**, to the chancellorship in 1155, introduced the study of civil law into England and resisted all attempts by the monasteries to throw off episcopal jurisdiction.

Theocritus c.310–250BC
Greek pastoral poet

Born probably in Syracuse, Sicily, he was brought up on the island of Cos, but lived for a time at the court of **Ptolemy II, Philadelphus**, in Alexandria, returning later to Cos. The authenticity of some of his 30 extant bucolic poems has been disputed. He wrote a series of poems dealing with heroic legend, especially that of Heracles, and his famous 15th Idyll, *Syracusii* ('The Ladies of Syracuse'), is said to be copied from Sophron. His short pastoral poems, representing a single scene, came to be called Idylls (*eidullia*). **Virgil** imitates him in his *Eclogues*, and **Tennyson** was influenced by him, as were the pastoral poets of the Renaissance. 📖 A S F Gow, *Theocritus* (1952)

Theodora c.500–548
Byzantine empress

The wife of **Justinian I**, she was the daughter of a circus bear-tamer. An actress, she married Justinian in 525 and was empress from 527. As his most trusted counsellor she had enormous influence over government, and probably saved the throne during the Nika riots (532). She was very charitable, especially to women. There is a famous mosaic portrait of her in the Church of San Vitale, Ravenna. ▢ Charles Diehl, *Theodora: Empress of Byzantium* (1972)

Theodorakis, Mikis 1925–
Greek composer

Born in Khios, he studied at the Paris Conservatoire. His first ballet *Antigone* was produced in 1959 at Covent Garden, London. On his return to Greece (1961), he became highly critical of the Greek musical and artistic establishment. When the right-wing government took power in 1967, he was imprisoned and his music banned, but after worldwide appeals he was released (1970). Often inspired by the history, traditions, and folk tunes of Greece, his prolific musical output includes oratorios, ballets, song cycles, and music for film scores, the best known of which is *Zorba the Greek* (1965). He published an autobiography in 1986.

Theodore I, of Corsica, *originally* Baron Theodor von Neuhof *or* Neuhoff 1686–1756
German adventurer

He was born, the son of a Westphalian noble, in Metz, France. He served in the French army and the Swedish diplomatic service, became chargé d'affaires to Emperor Charles VI (1685–1740) and, in 1736, led a Corsican rising against the Genoese, supported by the Turks and the Bey of Tunis. He was elected king, solemnly crowned and raised money by selling knighthoods. He left after seven months to procure foreign aid, but his attempts to return in 1738 and in 1743 were frustrated. He settled in London in 1749, was imprisoned for debt but was set free by a subscription raised by **Horace Walpole**.

Theodore of Canterbury, St, *also called* Theodore of Tarsus c.602–90
Greek prelate

Born in Tarsus, Cilicia, of Greek parents, he was consecrated Archbishop of Canterbury by Pope Vitalian in 668. In Canterbury he established a Greek school, and organized the administrative system of the English Church. His feast day is 19 September.

Theodore of Mopsuestia c.350–428AD
Greek theologian

Born in Antioch of Greek parents, he studied with St **John Chrysostom** under the Greek Sophist Libarines. He became first a monk, then a deacon there, and in AD392 Bishop of Mopsuestia in Cilicia. The teacher of **Nestorius**, he was, perhaps, the real founder of Nestorianism. Already suspected of leaning towards the Pelagians, when the Nestorian controversy broke out, he was attacked over his polemical writings, which were condemned by **Justinian I** (544). The fifth Ecumenical Council (553) confirmed the condemnation. He wrote commentaries on almost all the books of Scripture.

Theodoret c.393–458AD
Greek theologian and historian

Born in Antioch of Greek parents, he entered a monastery, and in AD423 became Bishop of Cyrrhus, in Syria. As a leading representative of the school of Antioch he became deeply involved in the **Nestorian** and **Eutychian** controversies, and was deposed, in his absence, by the 'Robber Council' of Ephesus in 449. He was restored by the general Council of Chalcedon in 451. His works consist of commentaries on Canticles, the Prophets, Psalms and St Paul's Epistles, and religious histories, orations and nearly 200 letters.

Theodoric *or* Theoderic the Great, *known in Germany as* Dietrich von Bern c.455–526AD
King of the Ostrogoths

He founded the Ostrogothic monarchy. He became king (AD475) and was later permitted by Emperor **Zeno** to take Italy from **Odoacer** (493). His reign secured for Italy tranquillity and prosperity. The Goths and the Romans remained distinct but harmonious nations, and Catholics and Jews enjoyed full liberty and protection, although Theodoric was an Arian. His official letters show his great energy and enlightened zeal for his subjects' welfare. The judicial murders of **Boethius** and Symmachus, and acts of oppression against the Catholic Church, occurred during his last three years. To the Germans he is Dietrich von Bern, and one of the great heroes of legend, figuring in the *Nibelungenlied* ('Song of the Nibelungs'). ▢ Thomas Hodgkin, *Theodoric the Goth* (1900)

Theodoric I d.451AD
King of the Visigoths

The son of **Alaric I**, he was elected king in AD418. He betrayed the Romans (c.421) and joined the Vandals. In 435 he attacked the Romans in Gaul and besieged Narbonne. He was forced to retreat to Toulouse, where he defeated a Roman army (439). On the invasion of **Attila** (451), he joined the Romans under **Aëtius**, and at Troyes commanded the right wing. He drove back the Huns under Attila but was killed.

Theodoric II d.466AD
King of the Visigoths

The son of **Theodoric I**, he rebelled against and assassinated his brother and predecessor Thorismund, taking the throne in AD453. His initial policy was to spread Gothic dominion in Spain and Gaul through the Roman alliance, and he supported Eparchius Avitus's imperial bid (455). On Eparchius's abdication (456), he broke his friendship with Rome and besieged Arles, but was forced by Emperor Majorian to make peace. In 462 he made another attempt in Gaul, but was defeated near Orleans (464). He was murdered by his brother Euric, who succeeded him.

Theodorus of Samos 6th century BC
Greek sculptor

He is said to have developed sculptural hollow-casting for large figures in bronze, and to have invented several kinds of tools for use in casting, in a realistic style.

Theodosius I, the Great c.347–395AD
Roman emperor

The son of Theodosius the Elder (d.367AD), he was born in Cauca in north-west Spain. He was appointed by **Gratian** as his co-emperor in the East (379). He campaigned against the Goths, but allowed them to settle within the Roman Empire (382). He secured peace with the Persian Sassanids by partitioning Armenia (c.386). When the usurper **Magnus Maximus** expelled **Valentinian II** from Italy (387), Theodosius marched west and defeated and killed him at Aquileia (388). He was a devout Christian, and St **Ambrose** had great influence over him. When Theodosius massacred the rebellious citizens of Thessalonika, Ambrose excommunicated him for eight months until he had done public penance. In 392 Valentinian II was murdered, and in 394 Theodosius marched against the Franks and their puppet emperor Eugenius. He defeated Eugenius, and for the remaining four months of his life ruled as sole Roman emperor. In 381 he affirmed the Nicene Creed, pursued heretics and pagans, and in 391 ordered the closing of all temples and banned all forms of pagan cult. ▢ Noel Q King, *The Emperor Theodosius and the Establishment of Christianity* (1960)

Theognis fl.544–541BC
Greek elegiac poet
A Dorian noble of Megara on the Isthmus of Corinth, he was driven from Megara during the confusion which followed the overthrow of the tyrant Theagenes, and visited Euboea and Sicily. Under his name survive 1,389 elegiac verses, social, political and gnomic, but perhaps only some of them are his. ◫ C M Bowra, *Early Greek Elegists* (1938)

Theophanes the Greek c.1370–c.1405
Russian–Byzantine painter
He was born probably in Greece, but active mainly in Russia. His early works in Constantinople (Istanbul) and the Crimea are lost, but his extant frescoes in the Church of Our Saviour of the Transfiguration at Novgorod (from 1378) are some of the finest examples of Russian medieval art, fusing Byzantine and Russian influences and inspiring a new generation of artists around Novgorod. He painted from memory with rapid brush strokes in an impressionistic style. He was also famous as a book illustrator (manuscripts in Moscow), and for his icons in Moscow (1395–1405).

Theophano c.955–991
Byzantine princess and Holy Roman Empress
The daughter of the Byzantine Emperor Romanus II, she married King **Otto II** in 972 in Rome as a symbol of the union of the Eastern and Western Empires. He ruled as Holy Roman Emperor, with Theophano as Empress, from 973 until his death in 983. She took an active role in politics and with her mother-in-law **Adelaide** secured the throne for her son **Otto III** on his father's death, ruling as co-regent from 983 to 991. She dealt successfully with enemies at home and abroad during his minority, including Henry the Wrangler and Boleslav II of Bohemia, and secured Lotharingia for the empire. Her influence is visible in many of his later policies, especially his ambitions for the empire.

Theophilus d.412AD
Egyptian patriarch
He became Patriarch of Alexandria (AD385). He destroyed the pagan temple of Serapis, drove out the Origenist monks of Nitria and defended his actions before a synod at Constantinople (Istanbul) called by the Emperor **Arcadius** and St **John Chrysostom**. He made peace with the monks but used his influence with Arcadius's wife, the Empress Eudoxia, to have St John banished to Armenia.

Theophrastus c.372–c.286BC
Greek philosopher
Born in Eresus, Lesbos, he studied at Athens under **Plato** and became the close friend of **Aristotle**. He became head of the Peripatetic School (Lyceum) after Aristotle's death (322BC) and is responsible for preserving many of Aristotle's works. Most of his own prolific output is lost, but surviving work includes important treatises on plants (representative of his interest in natural science), reconstructed fragments of his history of the Presocratic philosophers, and the more literary volume of *Characters*, containing 30 deft sketches of different moral types, which has been widely translated and imitated. ◫ William W Fortenbaugh (ed), *Theophrastus of Eresus: Sources for his Life, Writings, Thought and Influence* (1992)

Theorell, (Axel) Hugo Teodor 1903–82
Swedish biochemist and Nobel Prize winner
Born in Linköping, he studied medicine at the Karolinska Institute, Stockholm, and became a lecturer (1930–32) and assistant professor at Uppsala University (1932–36), and director of the Nobel Institute of Biochemistry at Stockholm (1937–70). He crystallized myoglobin (the oxygen storage protein of muscle) and determined its molecular weight (1932). In Berlin in 1934 he separated the yellow coenzyme (flavine mononucleotide) from the protein and examined its properties. On his return to Uppsala he purified diphtheria antitoxin (1937), and went on to introduce fluorescence spectrometry. He was awarded the 1955 Nobel Prize for physiology or medicine, and was elected a Foreign Member of the Royal Society in 1959.

Theramenes fl.411–403BC
Athenian statesman
He made himself unpopular by a policy of compromise between oligarchy and democracy, and while a member of the government of the Thirty Tyrants incurred the hatred of the most notorious of them all, **Critias**, who had him put to death in the traditional way by giving him hemlock to drink.

Theresa of Ávila, St See Teresa of Ávila, St

Theresa of Calcutta, Mother See Teresa of Calcutta, Mother (panel)

Thérèse of Lisieux, St, *originally* Marie Françoise Thérèse Martin, *also called* The Little Flower *and* St Theresa of the Child Jesus 1873–97
French nun and virgin saint
Born in Alençon, she was an intensely religious child. At the age of 15 she entered the Carmelite convent of Lisieux in Normandy, where she remained until her death from tuberculosis nine years later. She wrote an account of her childhood and later life which was edited and published posthumously as *Histoire d'une âme* (1898, 'Story of a Soul'). Showing how the most ordinary person can attain sainthood by following her 'little way' of simple, childlike, trusting Christianity, the book immediately gained great popularity. She was canonized in 1925, and in 1947 associated with **Joan of Arc** as patron saint of France. Her feast day is 1 October.

Theroux, Paul Edward 1941–
US writer
Born in Medford, Massachusetts, he has led a footloose life that is reflected in his literary output. *Waldo* (1969), his first novel, was followed by fictions based on three years spent in Africa. He subsequently taught at Singapore University (1968–71), a sojourn that resulted in a collection of short stories, *Sinning with Annie* (1976), and a novel, *Saint Jack* (1973, filmed 1979). Other novels, for example *The Family Arsenal* (1976) and *The London Embassy* (1982), have been based in London where he lives part of the year. His novels are urbane and paradoxical, sometimes bleak and frequently funny. *Millroy the Magician* (1993) was a quantum step, concentrating themes and ideas that have surfaced throughout his career. His extended rail journeys are recounted in *The Great Railway Bazaar: By Train Through Asia* (1975) and *The Old Patagonian Express: By Train Through the Americas* (1979), in which Theroux emerges as an intelligent but misanthropic observer. Other works include *Mosquito Coast* (1981, James Tait Black Memorial Prize, filmed 1987), *The Kingdom by the Sea* (1983) and *My Other Life* (1996).

Thesiger, Frederick John Napier See Chelmsford, 1st Viscount

Thesiger, Sir Wilfred Patrick 1910–
English explorer
He was born in Addis Ababa, Abyssinia (now Ethiopia), where his father was British Minister in charge of the Legation. Educated at Eton and Oxford, where he got a blue for boxing, he attended the coronation of **Haile Selassie** in 1930, and in 1933 returned to Abyssinia to hunt with the Danakil tribes, exploring the Sultanate of Aussa. In 1935 he joined the Sudan Political Service and while on leave travelled by camel across the Sahara to the Tibesti

Mountains. He was seconded to the Sudan Defence Force at the outbreak of World War II, and later served in Abyssinia, Syria and with the SAS in North Africa. From 1945 to 1950 he explored the Empty Quarter of southern Arabia and the borderlands of Oman with Bedu companions, which he described in *Arabian Sands* (1959). From 1951 to 1958 he lived with the Marsh Arabs of Iraq and published *The Marsh Arabs* in 1964. He first travelled in East Africa in 1961, and returned to live with tribal peoples there from 1968 onwards, occasionally returning to London. His travels also include the Zagros Mountains of Iran, the Hindu Kush and Karakoram Mountains, Pakistan, Afghanistan and Northern India, the Atlas Mountains of Morocco, and Yemen. His autobiography, *The Life of My Choice*, was published in 1987, followed by *My Kenya Days* in 1994. He was knighted in 1995.

Thespis 6th century BC
Greek poet, the reputed founder of Greek drama

He came from Icaria, and is said to have won the first prize for tragedy at a festival in Athens in c.534BC. According to **Aristotle**, he used single actors to deliver speeches, in addition to the traditional chorus, the first to do so. 🕮 A W Pichard-Cambridge, *Thespis* (1962)

Thiard, Pontus de See Tyard, Pontus de

Thibaud, Jacques 1880–1953
French violinist

Born in Bordeaux, he studied at the Paris Conservatoire and, as well as his solo performances, played with **Alfred Cortot** and **Pablo Casals**. He was particularly renowned for his interpretations of **Mozart, Beethoven** and **Debussy**. He died in an air crash.

Thielicke, Helmut 1908–86
German Lutheran theologian and preacher

Born in Barmen, he was dismissed from his post at Heidelburg for criticizing the Nazis, and in 1944 contributed to a draft declaration on Church–State relations for a revolutionary government to follow a successful plot against **Hitler**. He was appointed Professor of Theology at Hamburg after World War II, becoming Dean of Theology (1954) and University Rector (1960), retiring in 1974. A prolific author, best-known perhaps for *The Waiting Father* (1960) and other volumes of sermons, he published substantial studies in theology and ethics, including *The Evangelical Faith* (1974–82), *Theological Ethics* (1951–64, abridged Eng trans 1966–69), *The Ethics of Sex* (1964) and *Living with Death* (1983), though these appeared in English much later than his devotional works.

Thiers, (Louis) Adolphe 1797–1877
French statesman and historian

Born in Marseilles, he studied law at Aix-en-Provence, where he made the acquaintance of François Mignet (1796–1884) and cultivated literature. In Paris from 1821 he became a journalist, attacking the administration. He was elected Deputy for Aix, was appointed secretary-general to the Minister of Finance, and became one of the most formidable of parliamentary speakers. He held many posts in the government of **Louis Philippe**, and was twice Prime Minister (1836, 1839). He supported **Napoleon III** in 1848, but was arrested and banished in the coup d'état of 1851. He was allowed, however, to return the next year. After the collapse of the Empire during the Franco-Prussian War, he became head of the provisional government, suppressed the Paris Commune, and was elected first President of the Third Republic in August 1870. He negotiated peace with Prussia, and did much to ensure France's economic recovery. Defeated by a coalition of monarchists, he resigned in 1873. His most ambitious literary work was the 20-volume *L'histoire du consulat et*

de l'empire (1845–62, 'History of the Consulate and the Empire'). 🕮 Charles H Pomaret, *Monsieur Thiers et son temps* (1948)

Thierry, Baron Charles Philip Hippolytus de See de Thierry, Baron Charles Philip Hippolytus

Thieu, Nguyen Van See Nguyen Van Thieu

Thin, James 1823–1915
Scottish bookseller

Apprenticed in Edinburgh at the age of 11, he spent five years learning the trade. After a period in which he considered entering the Church, he was persuaded to remain in bookselling and opened his own shop on South Bridge, Edinburgh, in 1848. The business slowly expanded until, some years later, it could claim to be 'the largest retail bookselling establishment' in the city. A keen Church official, he was also a well-known hymnologist, with a collection of more than 2,500 hymnbooks. Since his death the firm has remained within the family.

Thirkell, Angela Margaret, *née* Mackail 1891–1961
English novelist

Born in London, she was the daughter of the classical scholar John William Mackail (1859–1945), granddaughter of Sir **Edward Burne-Jones**, and cousin of **Rudyard Kipling**. She wrote more than 30 novels set in 'Barsetshire', dealing with the descendants of characters from **Anthony Trollope's** 'Barsetshire' novels, including *Coronation Summer* (1937), *Growing Up* (1943) and *The Duke's Daughter* (1951). Her son was the novelist Colin MacInnes (1914–79). 🕮 M Strickland, *Angela Thirkell* (1972)

Thistlewood, Arthur 1770–1820
English conspirator

Born in Tupholme, Lincolnshire, he served in the army. Full of revolutionary ideas from his time in the USA and France, he organized a mutiny at Spa Fields (1816) and in 1820 the Cato Street Conspiracy to murder Viscount **Castlereagh** and other ministers who were dining with Lord Harrowby. The conspirators were arrested and Thistlewood, with four others, was convicted of high treason and was hanged and then publicly decapitated.

Thom, Alexander 1894–1985
Scottish engineer and archaeo-astronomer

Educated at Glasgow University, he worked in various engineering firms then returned to Glasgow as a lecturer (1922–39). He was Professor of Engineering Science at Oxford from 1945 to 1961. From 1934 he was engaged on a detailed study of all the stone circles in the British Isles and Brittany, and after his retirement published two major works, *Megalithic Sites in Britain* (1967) and *Megalithic Lunar Observatories* (1971). He brought his engineering skills of mathematics and surveying to bear on the analysis of the data he had collected, and he claimed to have discovered two basic units, the 'megalithic yard' and the 'megalithic inch', which had been used in the setting out of most, if not all of the circles. His conclusions have not been universally accepted, but his meticulous surveys are of lasting value in themselves.

Thom, René Frédéric 1923–
French mathematician

Born in Montbéliard, he studied at the École Normale Supérieure, and worked at the universities of Grenoble and Strasbourg, where he became professor. From 1964 he worked at the Institut des Hautes Études Scientifiques. In 1958 he was awarded the Fields Medal (the mathematical equivalent of the Nobel Prize). His work has been in algebraic topology, where he helped to create the powerful theory known as cobordism theory, and on the singularity theory of differentiable manifolds, but he is best known for his book *Stabilité structurelle et morphogenèse* (1972, 'Structural Stability and Morphogenesis') which introduced 'catastrophe theory'. This has been applied to widely differing situations such as the development of the embryo, social interactions between human beings or animals, and physical phenomena such as breaking waves, and has attracted much publicity as well as some controversy.

Thomas, St 1st century AD
One of the 12 Apostles of Jesus Christ

He is most prominent in **John**'s Gospel where he is also called Didymus (the Twin), and where he is portrayed as doubting the Resurrection until he touches the wounds of the risen **Jesus Christ** (John 20). Early church traditions describe him subsequently as a missionary to the Parthians or a martyr in India. Many later apocryphal works bear his name, such as the Gospel, Acts, and Apocalypse of Thomas. He is the patron saint of Portugal, and his feast day is 21 December. 📖 F A D'Cruz, *St Thomas the Apostle in India* (1929)

Thomas fl.12th century
Anglo-Norman poet

He was author of the earliest extant text (c.1155–1170) of the legend of Tristan and Iseult, a fragment of 3,144 lines covering the final episodes including the death of the lovers. Though he has greater pretensions to a literary style, he lacks the impressive primitive simplicity of Béroul, author of the slightly later and fuller of the two early versions, both of which appear to be based on an earlier poem now lost. He is sometimes confused with **Thomas the Rhymer**. 📖 M D Legge, *Anglo Norman Literature* (1963)

Thomas à Becket See **Becket, Thomas (à)**

Thomas à Kempis See **Kempis, Thomas à**

Thomas Aquinas, St See **Aquinas, St Thomas**

Thomas of Hereford, St See **Cantelupe, St Thomas de**

Thomas the Rhymer, *also called* Thomas Rymour of Erceldoune *and* Thomas Learmont c.1220–c.1297
Scottish seer and poet

He lived at Erceldoune (Earlston, Berwickshire), and in 1286 is said to have predicted the death of **Alexander III** and the Battle of Bannockburn, thus becoming known as 'True Thomas'. **Boece** calls him Thomas Learmont. Legend relates that he was carried off to Elfland, and after three years allowed to revisit the Earth, but ultimately returned to his mistress, the fairy queen. In a charter of Petrus de Haga de Bemersyde (c.1260–1270) the Rhymer appears as a witness; and in another of 1294 Thomas of Erceldoune, 'son and heir of Thomas Rymour of Erceldoune', conveys lands to the hospice of Soutra. The Rhymer's 'prophecies' were collected and published in 1603. Sir **Walter Scott** believed him to be the author of the poem of *Sir Tristrem*, which was founded on a 12th-century French poem by another **Thomas**. 📖 H M Flasdieck, *Tom der Reimer* (1934)

Thomas, (Charles Louis) Ambroise 1811–96
French composer

Born in Metz, he studied at the Paris Conservatoire (1828–32), where he became Professor of Composition (1852) and then director (1871). He wrote many light operas, of which *Mignon* (1866) is the best known, for the Opéra Comique and the Grand Opéra. He also wrote a great number of cantatas, part-songs and choral pieces.

Thomas, (Walter) Brandon 1849/56–1914
English actor and playwright

Born in Liverpool, he worked in amateur dramatics before making his professional debut as a comedy actor in 1879. He wrote a number of successful light plays, one of which, *Charley's Aunt* (1892), has remained highly popular.

Thomas, (Martha) Carey 1857–1935
US feminist and educationist

Born in Baltimore, Maryland, into a Quaker family, she was educated privately and at Cornell University. She wanted to take a PhD at the newly founded Johns Hopkins University, but was allowed to attend only if she concealed herself behind a screen. Eventually the Swiss allowed her to take her PhD at Zurich (1882), and on her return she helped to establish Bryn Mawr College for girls in Philadelphia, being appointed its first Dean. She was also Professor of English at Bryn Mawr, and later president (1894–1922). An ardent suffragist, she was the first president of the National College Women's Equal Suffrage League in 1908, and later an active member of the National American Woman Suffrage Association. She also established summer schools for women working in industry (1921) and campaigned for women's right to vote. She wrote *The Higher Education of Women* (1900).

Thomas, Dafydd Elis 1946–
Welsh nationalist leader

He was born in Carmarthen, Wales. After an early career as a lecturer, writer and broadcaster, and as a self-proclaimed Marxist, in 1983 he was elected Plaid Cymru MP for Meirionnydd Nant Conway, and continued to lead the party until resigning in 1991 over growing criticism that he was moving to the right and ignoring the interests of traditional Welsh nationalists.

Thomas, D(onald) M(itchell) 1935–
English poet and novelist

Born in Cornwall, he was educated in Australia and at New College, Oxford. He learned Russian while on National Service, and has published numerous translations. His early poems, which range across science fiction, erotica, and evocations of his native Cornwall, were represented in *Selected Poems* (1983). His later poems became more autobiographical, such as *The Puberty Tree: New and Selected Poems* (1992). His first two novels, *The Flute Player* (1979) and *Birthstone* (1980), have been overshadowed by the powerful, semi-fantastic meditation on Freudian psychology, *The White Hotel* (1981). His other fiction includes the five 'improvisations' on Cold War themes which comprise the *Russian Nights* sequence (1983–89), *Flying in to Love* (1992) and *Pictures at an Exhibition* (1993). 📖 *Memories and Hallucinations* (1988)

Thomas, (Edward) Donnall 1920–
US physician and haematologist, and Nobel Prize winner

Born in Mart, Texas, he studied chemistry and chemical engineering at the University of Texas at Austin, then studied medicine at the Harvard Medical School. After posts at the Massachusetts Institute of Technology and the Brigham Hospital, Boston, he joined the Mary Imogene Bassett Hospital in Cooperstown, where he worked on bone marrow transplantation in dogs and in humans. Problems such as graft rejection and 'graft-versus-host' disease were overcome in dogs when bone marrow was transplanted between members of the same litter. In 1963 Thomas became professor at the Washington University School of Medicine, Seattle, where he used tissue-typing techniques and drugs which suppress the immune system to enable bone marrow transplants in the treatment of leukaemia, aplastic anaemia and certain genetic diseases. He joined the Fred Hutchinson Cancer Research Center in 1975, and shared the 1990 Nobel Prize for physiology or medicine with **Joseph Edward Murray**.

Thomas, Dylan Marlais 1914–53
Welsh poet

Born in Swansea, he was the son of a schoolmaster. He worked for a time as a reporter on the *South Wales Evening Post* and established himself with the publication of *Eighteen Poems* in 1934, in which year he moved to London, later settling permanently back in Wales at Laugharne (1949). In 1937 he married Caitlin Macnamara and published *Twenty-Five Poems*. His other works include *The Map of Love* (1939), *Portrait of the Artist as a Young Dog* (1940), *The World I Breathe* (1940), *Deaths and Entrances* (1946) and a scenario, *The Doctor and the Devils*. His *Collected Poems, 1934–52*, were published in 1952. From 1944 he worked intermittently on a radio 'play for voices' about a Welsh seaside village and in its first form it was called *Quite Early One Morning*. Thomas expanded it into *Under Milk Wood*, taking part in a reading of it in New York just before his death, from chronic alcohol abuse, while on a lecture tour of the USA. It was published in 1954. Until then his work had been praised by critics, among them **Edith Sitwell**, for his striking rhythms, his original imagery and his technical ingenuities, but he could in no sense be called a popular writer. *Under Milk Wood* was immediately comprehensible, funny and fresh, with moments of lyric tenderness. It had a second success as a stage play and inspired a jazz suite by **Stan Tracey** (1965). In 1955 an unfinished novel, *Adventures in the Skin Trade*, was published; also *A Prospect of the Sea*, a collection of stories and essays. 📖 C Fitzgibbon, *Dylan Thomas* (1965)

Thomas, (Philip) Edward, *pseudonym of* Edward Eastaway 1878–1917
British poet and nature writer

Born in London of Welsh parents, he was educated at St Paul's School and Lincoln College, Oxford. He became a writer of reviews, critical studies, biographies and topographical works. Not until 1914, encouraged by **Robert Frost**, did he realize his potential as a poet, and he wrote most of his poetry during active service in World War I. *Six Poems* was published in 1916, but he died in action at Arras (April 1917) before the publication of *Poems* (1917), under his pseudonym. His poetry was rooted in the English tradition of nature poetry, but broke with the Georgian tradition in its lack of rhetoric and formality and in its emphasis on the austerity of Nature and solitariness of man. He also wrote a novel, *The Happy-Go-Lucky Morgans* (1913), and several books about the English countryside. 📖 W Cooke, *Edward Thomas, a critical biography* (1930)

Thomas, George Henry 1816–70
US general

Born in Southampton County, Virginia, he trained at West Point. In the Civil War (1861–65) he joined the Federal army in 1861, and in January 1862 won the Battle of Mill Springs. Major-general in command of the centre of William S Rosencrans's army, he saved the Battle of Stones River, and at Chickamauga again made victory a barren one for the Confederates (September 1863). In October 1863 he was given the command of the Army of the Cumberland, and in November captured Mission Ridge. In 1864 he commanded the centre in General **William Sherman**'s advance on Atlanta, was sent to oppose **John B Hood** in Tennessee in December and won the Battle of Nashville. He afterwards commanded the military division of the Pacific.

Thomas, Hugh Owen 1833–91
Welsh orthopaedic surgeon

Born on the island of Anglesey, he studied medicine at University College London, at Edinburgh University, and in Paris, and practised surgery in Liverpool. He pioneered orthopaedic surgery, constructing many appliances which are still used, especially Thomas's splints for the hip and the knee.

Thomas, James Henry 1874–1949
Welsh Labour politician

He was born in Newport, Monmouthshire. An enthusiastic trade unionist, he was elected MP for Derby in 1910. As assistant secretary of the Amalgamated Society of Railway Servants he helped to organize the strike of 1911, and the merger of smaller unions in 1913 to form the National Union of Railwaymen, of which he ultimately became general secretary (1917). He led the successful railway strike of 1919. When Labour came to power in 1924 he was appointed Colonial Secretary, and in **Ramsay MacDonald**'s 1929 Cabinet he was Lord Privy Seal, subsequently becoming Dominions Secretary (1930–35). His adherence to the 1931 National government aroused the hostility of his former Labour colleagues, and the ensuing bitterness clouded the last few years of his political career, which came to an untimely end when, as Colonial Secretary (1935–36), he was found guilty by a judicial tribunal of divulging Budget secrets. He wrote *My Story* (1937).

Thomas, Margaret Haig, Viscountess Rhondda 1883–1958
Welsh feminist

Born in London, she studied, briefly, at Somerville College, Oxford, before the time when women were allowed to graduate, and became a suffragette. On the death of her father (David Alfred Thomas, 1st Viscount **Rhondda**) in 1918 she attempted to take her seat in the House of Lords as Viscountess Rhondda, but was kept out after legal proceedings. She founded *Time and Tide*, a weekly journal of politics and literature, in 1920, and personally ran it from 1926. It was largely liberal rightwing, publishing material which was boycotted elsewhere, such as **George Orwell**'s exposé of Stalinist repression in Republican Spain. She was one of the survivors of the *Lusitania* in 1915.

Thomas, Norman Mattoon 1884–1968
US socialist leader

Born in Marion, Ohio, and educated at Bucknell University and Princeton, he worked in social settlements, studied theology and was ordained a Presbyterian minister, becoming pastor of East Harlem Church in New York City (1911–31). Horrified by the poverty he encountered, he became imbued with the Social Gospel, and became a pacifist and socialist. He founded and edited *The World Tomorrow* (1918–21), helped found the American Civil Liberties Union in 1920, worked as associate editor on the *Nation* weekly (1921–22), and was co-director of the League for Industrial Democracy (1922–37). He was unsuccessful socialist candidate for Governor of New York (1924) and, repeatedly, for the US presidency (1928, 1932, 1936, 1940, 1944, 1948), his best showing being in 1932. He became leader of the Socialist Party of America on the death of **Eugene V Debs** in 1926. His many books included *Is Conscience a Crime?* (1927), *As I See It* (1932), *A Socialist's Faith* (1951) and *The Prerequisites for Peace* (1959).

Thomas, R(onald) S(tuart) 1913–
Welsh poet and priest

Born in Cardiff, and educated at the University College of North Wales, Bangor, he trained for the church at St Michael's College, Llandaff. He was ordained priest in 1937, becoming rector of Manafon (1942–54) and vicar of Eglwysach (1954–67) and of St Hywyn, Aberdaron (1967–78). He became noticed outside Wales with the publication of *Song at the Year's Turning* (1955). His later volumes include *Poetry for Supper* (1958), *The Bread of Truth*

(1963), *Laboratories of the Spirit* (1976) and *Between Here and Now* (1981). He also wrote *Later Poems, 1972–1982* (1983), *Experimenting with an Amen* (1986), *Counterpoint* (1990) and *No Truth with the Furies* (1995). He published an autobiography, *Neb*, in 1985. ◻ R George Thomas, *R. S. Thomas* (1964)

Thomas, Sidney Gilchrist 1850–85
English metallurgist
Born in Canonbury, North London, and educated at Dulwich College, he intended to study medicine, but after the death of his father in 1867 he became a police-court clerk. However, he attended evening classes in chemistry at the Birkbeck Institution and studied metallurgy at the Royal School of Mines. In 1878 he announced that, with the help of his cousin **Percy Gilchrist** and Edward Martin, he had discovered how to remove phosphorus from steel by using dolomite for the furnace lining, together with an addition of lime to produce a basic slag that allowed the removal of both phosphorus and sulphur. This method was described as the 'basic **Bessemer** process' in Great Britain, but was always known as the 'Thomas process' on the Continent. Within a few years, the same principles were applied to the Siemens open-hearth furnace. Ascetic, a pacifist and philanthropist, Thomas died from a lung complaint (probably tuberculosis).

Thomas, Silken See Fitzgerald, Thomas, 10th Earl of Kildare

Thomason, George c.1602–1666
English bookseller and publisher
He was apprenticed to a bookseller in London at the age of 15. He made a complete and valuable collection of tracts and pamphlets printed in England during the years of the Civil War and the Restoration. These were given to the British Museum by **George III** in 1762.

Thompson, Benjamin See Rumford, Benjamin Thompson, Count

Thompson, Daley (Frances Morgan) 1958–
English athlete
Born in London, he became a specialist in the decathlon and won the gold medal at the Olympic Games of 1980 and 1984. He was victorious in the 1983 World Championships, but at Seoul in 1988 was affected by injury and came fourth. He broke the world record four times between 1980 and 1984. He retired in 1992.

Thompson, Sir D'Arcy Wentworth 1860–1948
Scottish zoologist and classical scholar
Born in Edinburgh and educated at Trinity College, Cambridge, he was Professor of Biology at Dundee University (1884–1917) and at St Andrews University (from 1917). The ideas for which he is remembered are contained in his *On Growth and Form* (1917), a book noted both for its biological content and literary style. He interpreted the forms of organs and biological structures based on the physical forces acting upon them during development, and was also able to demonstrate mathematically that the superficial differences between related animals could be accounted for by differential growth rates. His *Glossary of Greek Birds* (1895) and *Glossary of Greek Fishes* (1945) derive from his classical interests. He was knighted in 1937.

Thompson, David 1770–1857
Canadian fur-trader and explorer
He was born in England, and educated at the Grey Coat School, Westminster. Apprenticed to the Hudson's Bay Company, he spent 13 years working as a fur-trader, before becoming surveyor under Philip Turner, mapping the Saskatchewan, Hayes, Nelson and Churchill rivers and a route to Lake Athabasca. In 1797 he joined the North West Company, travelling 4,000 miles (6,440km) from Lake Superior to Lake Winnipeg and across the Rockies to settle on the Columbia River (1807), subsequently surveying its entire course and opening many trading posts. He settled in Montreal in 1812 after travelling 50,000 miles (80,500km) and drew his impressive map of western Canada. He took part in the US–Canada Boundary Commission of 1816. He was married to a half-Indian woman, with whom he had 16 children. He campaigned against alcohol abuse among the Native Americans.

Thompson, Dorothy 1894–1961
US writer and feminist
Born in Lancaster, New York, she was educated at the Lewis Institute of Chicago and Syracuse University. She began her career as a foreign correspondent in Europe, and gained recognition in 1921 when she interviewed Empress Zita of Austria after Zita's husband **Charles**, the last of the **Habsburg** emperors, had unsuccessfully attempted to regain the throne of Hungary. While working for the *New York Evening News* in Berlin, she met the novelist **Sinclair Lewis**, married him in London in 1928 and returned to the USA for a time (divorced 1942). She reported on the rise of Nazism in Europe in the 1930s, and became the first foreign correspondent to be expelled by **Hitler** (1934). She began writing a popular newspaper column for the *New York Herald Tribune* in 1936, and continued her anti-fascist writings, speeches and broadcasts, for which she is perhaps best remembered. She also wrote for the *Ladies Home Journal* for 20 years. Her books include *New Russia* (1928), *I Saw Hitler!* (1932) and *The Courage to Be Happy* (1957).

Thompson, Edith d.1923
English murderess
She was tried in 1922, with her accomplice Frederick Bywaters, for stabbing her husband. The trial at the Old Bailey caused a sensation; the couple were found guilty, and in spite of many petitions for reprieve were executed.

Thompson, Emma 1959–
English actress
Born in London and educated at Cambridge, she began her career with the Cambridge Footlights and appeared in the musical *Me and My Girl* (1985–86) before asserting her dramatic capabilities in **John Byrne's** television series *Tutti Frutti* (1987). She married **Kenneth Branagh** in 1989 (separated 1995), and appeared opposite him on stage in *Look Back in Anger* (1989) and in such films as *Henry V* (1989), *Peter's Friends* (1992) and *Much Ado About Nothing* (1993). Her other films include *The Tall Guy* (1988), *Howards End* (1992), for which she received the Academy Award for Best Actress, *The Remains of the Day* (1993, Academy Award nomination), *In the Name of the Father* (1993, Best Supporting Actress nomination) and *Carrington* (1995), based on the life of the artist **Dora Carrington**. In 1996 she received an Academy Award for her adaptation of **Jane Austen's** *Sense and Sensibility*, in which she starred as Elinor Dashwood. She subsequently appeared in *The Winter Guest* (1996).

Thompson, Flora Jane, *née* Timms 1876–1947
English writer
Born in Juniper Hill, Oxfordshire, she left school at the age of 14 to work in the local post office, married young and with her postmaster husband lived in Bournemouth, Liphook and Dartmouth, writing mass-market fiction to help support her increasing family. During her sixties she published the semi-autobiographical trilogy *Lark Rise* (1939), *Over to Candleford* (1941) and *Candleford Green* (1943, combined as *Lark Rise to Candleford*, 1945). It is a

remarkable feat of observation and memory, showing the erosion of rural society before modern industrialism. 📖 M Lane, *Flora Thompson* (1976)

Thompson, Francis 1859–1907
English poet

Born in Preston, Lancashire, he was brought up in the Catholic faith and studied for the priesthood at Ushaw College. He then turned to medicine at Owens College, Manchester, but failed to graduate, and moved to London, where he became an opium addict. From this he was rescued by Wilfrid and Alice Meynell, to whom he had sent some poems for the magazine *Merry England*. His health was restored and he wrote several poems in the 1890s, including the well-known *Hound of Heaven*, describing God's pursuit of the human soul. His works include *Poems* (1893), *Sister Songs* (1895, written for the Meynell girls) and *New Poems* (1897). His notable *Essay on Shelley* (1909) appeared posthumously, as did his *Life of St Ignatius Loyola* (1909). His poems, mainly religious in theme, are rich in imagery and poetic vision. 📖 E Meynell, *Francis Thompson* (1913)

Thompson, Hunter S(tockton) 1939–
US journalist

Born in Louisville, Kentucky, he is an adherent of the 'new journalism', and eschews objectivity. He was the first reporter to infiltrate the Hell's Angels and he rode with them for a year, which led to his being savagely beaten up and to *Hell's Angels: A Strange and Terrible Saga* (1966). The acme of the anti-establishment, he styled his unique brand of journalism 'Gonzo' and produced a stream of outspoken, outrageous books, including *Fear and Loathing in Las Vegas* (1972), *Fear and Loathing on the Campaign Trail* (1972), *The Great Shark Hunt* (1972), *Generation of Swine* (1988), *Songs of the Damned* (1990) and *Better Than Sex* (1993). Much of his work appeared originally in magazines, particularly *Scanlan's*, *Rolling Stone* and the *National Observer*, and since 1985 he has contributed a weekly column to the *San Francisco Examiner*.

Thompson, John Taliaferro 1860–1940
US soldier and inventor

Born in Newport, Kentucky, he graduated in 1882 at the Military Academy in West Point, New York. In 1920 he invented the 'Thompson' submachine-gun, known as the 'Tommy' gun, which was a .45 calibre gun weighing 10lb (4.54kg). It was first used for military purposes by the US Marines in Nicaragua in 1925.

Thompson, John Vaughan 1779–1847
English zoologist

He studied marine zoology, distinguishing himself by his discoveries, especially that crustaceans pass through a series of metamorphoses when young, and that barnacles are crustaceans and not molluscs.

Thompson, Richard 1949–
English singer and songwriter

He was born in London, and is widely regarded as one of the major songwriters of his era, as well as a compelling artist. He came to attention as a founder-member of the important folk-rock group Fairport Convention in the late 1960s, then spent a decade from 1972 working with his then wife, singer Linda Thompson. He has performed solo or led his own bands since, mixing folk and rock influences to good effect. He has maintained a generally low-key presence on a music scene in which he is held in some veneration, both for his guitar playing and his masterly songwriting. Although his work has a comic side, it characteristically explores the darker, more serious aspects of life. 📖 P Humphries, *Richard Thompson: A Strange Affair* (1996)

Thompson, William 1785–1833
Irish economic theorist and feminist

Born in Rosscarbery, County Cork, he inherited extensive landed wealth, which led him to study economic problems. He adopted the co-operatist ideas of **Robert Owen**, and his awareness of wealth as the product of labour later influenced **Karl Marx** and **James Connolly**. His *An Enquiry into the Principles of the Distribution of Wealth Most Conducive to Human Happiness* (1824) demanded the reapportionment of wealth and denounced unearned income and private property. He followed it with a manifesto calling for sexual equality in *Appeal of One Half of the Human Race, Women, against the Pretentions of the Other Half, Men, to Retain them in Political, and thence in Civil and Domestic, Slavery* (1825). On his death he left most of his estate to aid the poor, but his will was set aside after years of litigation.

Thomsen, Christian Jörgensen 1788–1865
Danish archaeologist and numismatist

Born in Copenhagen, he collected coins, antiquities and paintings from an early age, but continued to work part-time for the family firm until his 50s. In 1816 he was appointed secretary of the Royal Commission for the Preservation of Antiquities, charged with organizing its pre-Roman collections for display in the new National Museum in Copenhagen. On the basis of the material used in making weapons and tools, he classified the specimens into three groups representing chronologically successive ages of Stone, Bronze and Iron. He expounded this Three Age System vigorously to the public when the museum opened in 1819 and eventually described it in print in his *Ledetraad til Nordisk Oldkyndighed* (1836, Eng trans *A Guide to Northern Antiquities*, 1848). The scheme was reinforced in the writings of **Jens Jacob Worsaae**, one of Thomsen's pupils, and became widely influential, establishing the basis for the subsequent development of Old World prehistory.

Thomson, Alexander, *also known as* Greek Thomson 1817–75
Scottish architect

Born in Balfour, Stirlingshire, the seventeenth of 20 children, he spent all his professional life in Glasgow. He was apprenticed to the architect John Baird Snr (1836), and worked in partnership from 1857 to 1871 with his brother George Thomson. As he moved away from the restrictions of orthodox Classicism to experiment with new techniques and materials, his prolific output included tenement blocks and terraces (Moray Place, 1857–59; Great Western Terrace, 1869) and churches (Caledonian Road Church, 1856; St Vincent Street Church, 1857–59) as well as offices and warehouses. He became president of the Glasgow Institute of Architects in 1871, and published statements on the theoretical basis of his work. 📖 Ronald McFadzean, *The Life and Work of Alexander Thomson* (1979)

Thomson, D(avid) C(ouper) 1861–1954
Scottish newspaper proprietor

He was born in Dundee. At the age of 23 he left the family shipping firm to take charge of the newly-acquired Dundee newspaper concern, which he owned and managed until his death. Its principal publications were the *Dundee Courier and Advertiser*, the *Sunday Post*, the *Scots Magazine* (founded in 1739) and *The People's Friend*, but it was known outside Scotland particularly for its many popular children's comics, such as the *Beano* and *Dandy*. Well-known for his concern for local interests, he was a deputy lieutenant for the City of Dundee for 54 years, and a governor of the university college of Dundee for 62 years. He always resisted unionization in his company.

Thomson, Derick, *Gaelic* Ruaraidh MacThómais
1921–
Scottish poet
Born in Stornoway, Isle of Lewis, he was educated at the Nicolson Institute in Stornoway, and at the universities of Aberdeen, Cambridge and North Wales before serving in the RAF during World War II. He taught at the universities of Edinburgh, Aberdeen and Glasgow, where he was Professor of Celtic (1963–91). In 1952 he founded, and remains the editor of, the Gaelic language quarterly *Gairm*, and helped set up the Gaelic Books Council in 1968. He has written important critical works on Gaelic poetry, notably *An Introduction to Gaelic Poetry* (1974, rev edn 1989), compiled a *New English–Gaelic Dictionary* (1981), and edited *The Companion to Gaelic Scotland* (1983). Much of his own poetry is collected, in both Gaelic and his own English versions, in *Creachadh na Clàrsaich* (1982, *Plundering the Harp—Collected Poems 1940–1980*). Later collections include *Smeur an doch ais* (1992, 'The Bramble of Hope') and *Meall Garbh* (1995, 'The Rugged Mountain'). He became a Fellow of the British Academy in 1992.

Thomson, Elihu 1853–1937
US inventor
Born in Manchester, England, he emigrated with his family to the USA when he was a child and was educated in Philadelphia, where he was a chemistry teacher until he decided on a career as an inventor. He became one of the pioneers of the electrical manufacturing industry in the USA, co-operating in 700 patented electrical inventions, which included the three-phase alternating-current generator and arc lighting. With Edwin J Houston, he founded the Thomson–Houston Electric Company (1883), which merged with Thomas Edison's firm in 1892 to form the General Electric Company. He declined the presidency of the Massachusetts Institute of Technology in 1919, but agreed to be acting president from 1921 to 1923. ◻ W Bernard Carlson, *Innovation as a Social Process: Elihu Thomson and the Rise of General Electric, 1870–1900*

Thomson, Sir George Paget 1892–1975
English physicist and Nobel Prize winner
The son of J J Thomson, he was born and educated in Cambridge, where he became a Fellow of Trinity College. He served in the Royal Flying Corps during World War I, was Professor of Physics at Aberdeen University (1922–30) and Imperial College, London (1930–52), and became Master of Corpus Christi at Cambridge (1952–62). In 1927 Thomson and Alexander Reid were the first to notice that a beam of electrons could produce circular interference fringes, firm evidence for Louis-Victor de Broglie's theory that moving particles have wave-like properties. In 1937 Thomson shared the Nobel Prize for physics with Clinton J L Davisson for the discovery of electron diffraction by crystals. During World War II, Thomson advised the government on the making of a superbomb, and after the war supported the peaceful exploitation of nuclear power. He was scientific adviser to the UN Security Council (1946–47) and for his contributions to electrical science he was awarded the Faraday Medal by the Institution of Electrical Engineers (1960). He was elected FRS in 1930, and knighted in 1943.

Thomson, Greek See Thomson, Alexander

Thomson, James 1700–48
Scottish poet
Born in Ednam, Roxburghshire, he was educated at Jedburgh School and studied at Edinburgh University for the ministry, but he abandoned his studies to seek his fortune as a writer in London. He published *Winter* (1726), *Summer* (1727), *Spring*, (1728) and *Autumn*, which appeared with the other three under the collective title *The Seasons* (1730). Substantially revised in 1744, it became a source

book for much later bird poetry, and an influence on Wordsworth, J M W Turner and others. His tragedies include *Sophonisba* (1729), *Agamemnon* (1738), *Edward and Eleonora* (1739), *Tancred and Sigismunda* (1745) and *Coriolanus* (1748). The poem *Liberty* (1735–36) was inspired by the Grand Tour which he undertook as a tutor in 1731, and was dedicated to the Prince of Wales, who awarded him a pension. 'Britannia' (1729), which criticized Sir Robert Walpole's foreign policy, secured him further patronage and the sinecure of Surveyor-General of the Leeward Isles (1744). *Alfred, a Masque* (1740) contains the song 'Rule Britannia', also claimed by David Mallet. The Spenserian *The Castle of Indolence* (1748) appeared a few weeks before his death. ◻ J Grant, *James Thomson* (1957)

Thomson, James 1822–92
Scottish engineer
Born in Belfast, Northern Ireland, he graduated from Glasgow University in mathematics and philosophy. He was Professor of Civil Engineering at Queen's College, Belfast (1857) and Glasgow (1873–89). He also wrote papers on elastic fatigue, under-currents and trade winds. He carried out important researches in fluid dynamics, inventing or improving several types of water-wheels, pumps and turbines. Over a long period he studied the effect of pressure on the freezing point of water, and its influence on the plastic behaviour of ice and the movement of glaciers. He was elected FRS in 1877, and was the elder brother of Lord Kelvin.

Thomson, James, *occasional pseudonym* B V
1834–82
Scottish poet
Born in Port Glasgow, he was educated in the Royal Caledonian Asylum orphanage, and trained as an army schoolmaster at the Royal Military Asylum, Chelsea, but was dismissed from army service for alcoholism (1862). He was a friend of Charles Bradlaugh, editor and owner of the *National Reformer*, and between 1862 and 1875 he contributed many sombre poems to the paper, including *The City of Dreadful Night* (1874), his greatest work. He became a lawyer's clerk in 1862, went into business (1864–69), worked in the USA as a mining agent (1872–73), was war correspondent in Spain with the Carlists (1873), and from 1875 depended largely on the income from his contributions to a tobacconists' trade monthly. Ill health and depression drove him to narcotics and stimulants. *The City of Dreadful Night and other Poems* (1880) was followed by *Vàne's Story* (1881), *Essays and Phantasies* (1881), *A Voice from the Nile* (1884), *Shelley, a Poem* (1885) and *Biographical and Critical Studies* (1896). His pseudonym B V, Bysshe Vanolis, was partly from Shelley's second name, partly from an anagram of Novalis. ◻ T Leonard, *James B.V. Thomson* (1993); I Waller, *James Thomson (BV)* (1950)

Thomson, John 1837–1921
Scottish photographer, traveller and writer
Born and educated in Edinburgh, he travelled in the Far East from 1862 to 1872, then settled in London, where he operated studios from 1881 to c.1910. A highly sensitive and subtle photographic artist, he was also a witty and readable writer, and produced many accounts of his journeys, one of the finest being *Foochow and the River Min* (1873). Described as one of the first great photojournalists, he is best known for *Illustrations of China and its People* (1873–74) and *Street Life in London* (1878, with journalist and activist Adolph Smith Headingly). He was innovative both technically and in terms of his methods of integrating photographs and text for the purposes of social documentation. Although in some ways the quintessential Victorian traveller, he was unusual for the humility of his attitude to his work. In 1875 he wrote: 'The camera should be a power in this age of instruction for the instruction of the age'.

Thomson, Sir J(oseph) J(ohn), *also called* JJ
1856–1940
*English physicist, discoverer of the electron and Nobel
Prize winner*
He was born in Cheetham Hill near Manchester, the son
of a Scottish bookseller. He went to Owen's College,
Manchester, at the age of 14 with the intention of be-
coming a railway engineer, but a scholarship took him to
Trinity College, Cambridge, where he graduated Second
Wrangler. In 1884 he was elected FRS and succeeded Lord
Rayleigh as Cavendish Professor of Experimental Physics, and in 1919 he was himself succeeded by his brilliant student, Ernest Rutherford. Thomson's early theoretical work was concerned with the extension of James
Clerk Maxwell's electromagnetic theories. This led to the
study of gaseous conductors of electricity and in particular the nature of cathode rays. Using Wilhelm Röntgen's
discovery of X-Rays (1895), he showed that cathode rays
were rapidly-moving particles, and by measuring their
speed and specific charge, the latter by two independent
methods, he deduced that these 'corpuscles' (electrons)
must be nearly 2,000 times smaller in mass than the lightest known atomic particle, the hydrogen ion. This, the
greatest revolution in physics since Sir Isaac Newton,
was inaugurated by his lecture to the Royal Institution
(1897) and published in the *Philosophical Magazine*. Thomson successfully studied the nature of positive rays
(1911), and this work was crowned by the discovery of
isotopes, which he demonstrated could be separated by
deflecting positive rays in electric and magnetic fields
—mass spectrometry. During World War I he was engaged in admiralty research and helped to found the
Department of Scientific and Industrial Research. He
made the Cavendish Laboratory the greatest research institution in the world. Although simplicity of apparatus
was carried to 'string and sealing wax' extremes, seven of
his research assistants subsequently won the Nobel Prize,
including Niels Bohr and Ernest Rutherford. He was
awarded the Nobel Prize for physics (1906), was knighted
in 1908, and was the first scientist to become Master of
Trinity College (1918–40). In 1936 he published *Recollections and Reflections*. He was one of the pioneers of nuclear physics. ☐G P Thomson, *J J Thomson and the Cavendish Laboratory in his Day* (1964)

Thomson, Joseph 1858–95
Scottish explorer
Born near Thornhill, Dumfriesshire, he studied geology
at Edinburgh University and then joined the Royal
Geographical Society East-Central African expedition
(1878–79), taking charge on the death of the leader. He
was the first European to reach Lake Nyasa (Malawi) from
the north and went on to Lake Tanganyika which he described in *To the Central African Lakes and Back* (1881). In
1882 he was invited by the Royal Geographical Society to
find a route through the Masai country from the coast via
Mount Kilimanjaro to Lake Victoria. This took him
across the Nijiri Desert through the Great Rift Valley, and
led to his discovery of Lake Baringo and Mount Elgon.
His careful notes greatly added to the geographical
knowledge of East Africa. He later explored Sokoto in
north-west Nigeria (1885) and the Upper Congo (1890),
and also travelled in the Atlas Mountains of Morocco.

Thomson, Robert William 1822–73
Scottish engineer and inventor
Born in Stonehaven, Grampian, he was intended for the
Church but, rebelling against classical studies, spent
some time as a workshop apprentice while educating
himself in mathematics and other practical subjects. In
1845 he patented a vulcanized rubber pneumatic tyre
which was successfully tested in London but was thought
to be too expensive for general use. It had been quite
forgotten by the time John Boyd Dunlop re-invented the

pneumatic tyre in 1888. Thomson patented the principle
of the fountain pen in 1849, and while working as a sugar
plantation engineer in Java he designed the first mobile
steam crane. He also patented (1867) a steam traction engine, with hinged segmental driving wheels supporting
the weight of the vehicle on rubber pads, which proved
very successful in moving the heaviest loads over poor
roads.

Thomson (of Fleet), Roy Herbert Thomson, 1st Baron 1894–1976
British newspaper and television magnate
He was born in Toronto, Canada, the son of a Scottish
barber, and was educated at Jarvis Collegiate, Toronto.
Successively a clerk, salesman, farmer, stenographer and
bookkeeper, he gained a commission in the Canadian
militia during World War I. He set up his own commercial
transmitter at North Bay (1931) in an area of poor reception, founding what later became the NBC network. He
started more radio stations, acquired 28 Canadian and six
US newspapers, which he turned over to his son in 1953,
and settled in Edinburgh on acquiring his first British
paper, *The Scotsman*, and associated publications. In 1957 he
obtained a licence for commercial television in Scotland
and in 1959 became one of Britain's leading newspaper
proprietors with the acquisition of the Kemsley newspapers, which included the *Sunday Times*. In 1966 he acquired *The Times*. Both these papers were bought by
Rupert Murdoch in 1981.

Thomson, Virgil 1896–1989
US composer and critic
Born in Kansas City, Missouri, he was educated at
Harvard and Paris. He set some of the writings of
Gertrude Stein to music, and wrote operas, *Four Saints in
Three Acts* (1934), first performed by a black cast, and *The
Mother of Us All* (1947), besides symphonies, ballets,
choral, chamber and film music. His work was notable for
its simplicity of style. He was music critic of the *New York
Herald Tribune* from 1940 to 1954. His autobiography *Virgil
Thomson by Virgil Thomson* was published in 1966 and his
Selected Letters were published shortly before his death.

Thomson, William See Kelvin, William Thomson, 1st Baron

Thomson, Sir (Charles) Wyville 1830–82
Scottish oceanographer
Born in Linlithgow, Lothian region, he studied at
Edinburgh University, but poor health caused him to
leave the university in 1850. He was lecturer in botany at
the University of Aberdeen (1850–51), Professor of
Natural History at Queen's College, Cork (1853),
Professor of Geology and Professor of Zoology and
Botany, both at Belfast (1853–68), and finally Professor of
Natural History at the University of Edinburgh from
1870. His book *Depths of the Sea* (1877) was the first general
textbook on oceanography, and he also investigated the
mechanisms of evolution, deep-sea temperatures, the
Gulf Stream and the continuity of chalk out to sea. He was
director of the civilian staff aboard the HMS *Challenger*
expedition (1872–76), and on its return was appointed
director of the Challenger Expedition Commission,
overseeing the analysis and reports of the results of the
expedition. *Voyage of the 'Challenger'—the Atlantic* (2 vols)
was published in 1877. The Wyville Thomson Ridge was
named after him, since he had predicted its existence
from water temperature measurements. He was knighted
in 1876.

Thonet, Michael 1796–1871
German furniture manufacturer
Born in Boppard-am-Rhein and trained as a cabinetmaker, he established a workshop in Boppard (1819) and
first gained prominence for his techniques, developed in

the 1830s, of laminating wood veneers with glue to construct a form of bentwood furniture. Having moved to Vienna in 1842 he developed the method of steaming and bending solid beech components for making a wide range of furniture, some of which was mass-produced on an enormous scale. The company passed to his sons as Gebrüder Thonet in 1853, while he retained effective control until his death. The firm built several factories in areas of beech forest in various parts of what are now the Czech Republic and Hungary, and developed into a very substantial furniture-making enterprise. It has adapted readily to technological and design developments, having been a leader in the use of tubular steel and plastics while maintaining its use of laminated veneers.

't Hooft, Gerard 1947–
Dutch physicist
He was educated at Utrecht University, where he was later appointed professor. His work has been concerned with gauge theories of particle physics, which describe the interactions between fundamental particles. Whilst a research student, 't Hooft found a way of making the infinite force predicted by **Steven Weinberg** and **Abdus Salam** both finite and calculable, leading to the universal acceptance of the electroweak theory. He has also shown that recent developments predict the existence of a heavy magnetic monopole (so far undiscovered), and has contributed to the theories of quantum gravity.

Thorarensen, Bjarni Vigfússon 1786–1841
Icelandic Romantic poet and jurist
Born in Brautarholt and brought up at Hlíðarendi, he went to Copenhagen University at the age of 15 to study law. After government service in Denmark, he was appointed a deputy justice in Reykjavík (1811), and justice of the Supreme Court (1817). In 1833 he became Governor of North and East Iceland. As a lyric poet he celebrated Icelandic nature and nationalism, using the metres of classical heroic poetry. One of his poems, *Eldgamla Ísafold* ('Ancient Iceland'), was regarded as an unofficial national anthem, set to the music of *God Save the Queen*. 🕮 Ð Gíslason, *Bjarni Thorarensen* (1932)

Thorarinsson, Sigurdur 1912–83
Icelandic geologist and glaciologist
After field studies in Swedish Lapland (1933), Iceland (1934), and on the Vatnjökull glacier expedition (1936–38), he obtained a degree and his doctorate for his work on the dating of volcanic ash layers. In 1945 he settled in Iceland where he worked as a geologist for the National Research Council and then joined the Museum of Natural History (1947–69). From 1969 he was Professor of Geography and Geology at the University of Iceland. He was the first to use the dating of ash layers to study the eruption history of volcanoes, the first to analyse catastrophic glacier outburst floods, and worked on glacier shrinkage. He made the first determination of glacier mass balance, and also pioneered nature conservation in Iceland.

Thorbecke, Johan Rudolf 1798–1872
Dutch politician
He studied at Amsterdam, Leyden and several German universities, and in 1825 was appointed Professor of History at Ghent University. In 1831 he moved to Leyden University. In the 1830s he became a Liberal, and from 1840 sat in parliament. In 1844 he (with eight others) produced a proposal for a new constitution. In 1848 King William II panicked at riots in other European capitals and made Thorbecke chairman of a constitutional committee; the resulting constitution was a classic liberal document and the foundation of modern democratic politics in the Netherlands. Thorbecke led three governments (1849–53, 1862–66, 1871–72), during which most of

the crucial bills were passed concerning free trade, the abolition of slavery, centralized government, the separation of Church and State, and the construction of the transport infrastructure.

Thorburn, Archibald 1860–1935
Scottish bird artist
Born in Lasswade, near Edinburgh, he studied at St John's Wood School of Art, London. His first paintings were hung in the Royal Academy when he was 20. He painted the majority of the plates of the monumental *Coloured Figures of the Birds of the British Isles* (1885–97). He also published *British Birds* (4 vols, 1915–16) and *British Mammals* (1920), and his paintings were used for T A Coward's *The Birds of the British Isles and their Eggs* (1920) and the popular *Observer's Book of British Birds* (1937). More than 100 of his paintings have been reproduced as prints.

Thoreau, Henry David 1817–62
US essayist and poet
Born in Concord, Massachusetts, he graduated from Harvard in 1837, became a teacher in Concord, and lectured. He gave up teaching, and in about 1839 began his walks and studies of nature which became his main occupation. In 1839 he made the voyage described in his *Week on the Concord and Merrimack Rivers* (1849). In 1845 he built himself a shanty in the woods by Walden Pond, near Concord, where he wrote much of the *Week*, his essay on **Thomas Carlyle**, and the classic, *Walden, or Life in the Woods* (1854). The remainder of his writings were published after his death. He then had various jobs, lecturing now and then, and writing for magazines, and his 1850 trip to Canada produced *A Yankee in Canada* (1866). He kept a daily journal (from 1835) of his walks and observations, from whose 30 volumes were published *Early Spring in Massachusetts* (1881), *Summer* (1884) and *Winter* (1887). Other publications are *Excursions in Field and Forest*, with a memoir by his friend **Ralph Waldo Emerson** (1863), *Cape Cod* (1865), *Familiar Letters* (1894) and *Poems of Nature* (1896), and a celebrated essay, *Civil Disobedience* (1849), provoked by his opposition to the Mexican War. 🕮 R D Richardson Jnr, *Thoreau: a life of the mind* (1986)

Thorez, Maurice 1900–64
French politician
Having worked briefly as a coalminer, he joined the Communist Party in 1920. He was made General-Secretary in 1930, when the earlier generation of leaders fell foul of **Stalin**, and remained in undisputed command of a highly disciplined party until his death. He was one of the creators of the Popular Front, thus bringing the party out of the political wilderness. He survived the difficult period of the German–Soviet Pact (1939–41) by deserting from the French Army into which he had been conscripted, and fleeing to the USSR. He was amnestied, and returned to France in 1944, becoming deputy Prime Minister in the Cabinet of the socialist Paul Ramadier (1946–47). After the exclusion of the party from office he led it through its most Stalinist period, adopting a position of unwavering support for the USSR on all questions until 1956, when he refused to accept **Nikita Khrushchev's** denunciation of Stalin.

Thorfinn, *properly* Thorfinnur Karesefni fl.1000
Icelandic explorer
Around 1000AD he led an expedition of colonists from Greenland, which sailed along the north-east coasts of North America, which had previously been discovered and explored by **Leif the Lucky**. He attempted to found a Norse colony in an area called 'Vínland' (Wineland), somewhere to the south of Newfoundland. The venture was abandoned after three years because of hostility from

the native inhabitants. The story is told in two Icelandic sagas, *Eiriks saga rauða* ('Saga of Eric') and *Grænlendinga saga* ('Tale of the Greenlanders').

Thorkelin, pseudonym of Grímur Jónsson 1752–1829
Icelandic scholar and antiquary

Educated at the university in Copenhagen, he became professor there, and in 1791 was appointed keeper of the secret Danish archives. The first editor of the Anglo-Saxon epic *Beowulf*, he found the manuscript of it in the British Museum in London and made two transcripts. His original edition was destroyed during the British bombardment of Copenhagen in 1807, but he set to work again and published it in 1815 as *De danorum rebus gestis … poema Danicum, dialecto Anglo-saxonica*. He also encouraged John Jamieson in the production of his *Etymological Dictionary of the Scottish Language*.

Thorláksson, Guðbrandur 1542–1627
Icelandic prelate and scholar

Born at Staðarbakki, Miðfjörður, the son of a Catholic priest and his mistress, he studied theology at Copenhagen University, and became a versatile humanist scholar. Appointed Bishop of Hólar, in north Iceland, in 1570, he was responsible for the translation and production of the first complete Bible in Icelandic (*Guðbrandarbiblía*, 1584) at the printing press there. This Bible completed the process of the Reformation in Iceland, and stabilized the classical Icelandic language as effectively as the *Authorized Version* of the English Bible (1611). He wrote and published a host of other works, including a hymnbook (1589), an anthology of poetry (1612), and the best map of Iceland hitherto produced.

Thorláksson, Thórarinn B 1867–1924
Icelandic landscape painter

Born on the farm of Undirfell, he is the founder of modern art in Iceland. The son of the pastor at Undirfell, he worked as a bookbinder in Reykjavík and became the first Icelander to receive a state grant for studies abroad. He spent nine years in Copenhagen, where he turned to painting at the late age of 30. He held a one-man show of his landscape paintings in Reykjavík in 1900 (the first private one-man exhibition in Iceland), where he displayed his most famous painting, *Thingvellir*. In 1902 he returned to Iceland permanently, but remained an amateur all his life, only painting in his spare time.

Thorndike, Edward Lee 1874–1949
US psychologist

Born in Williamsburg, Massachusetts, he studied at Wesleyan University and then at Harvard. As professor at Teachers College, Columbia (1904–40), he formulated important theories in educational psychology and in the psychology of animal learning. He devised intelligence tests and stressed the effect of chance associations in educational processes. His works include *The Principles of Teaching* (1905), *Psychology of Learning* (1914), and *The Measurement of Intelligence* (1926). ▭ Geraldine M Joncich, *The Sane Positivist: A Biography of Edward Lee Thorndike* (1968)

Thorndike, Dame (Agnes) Sybil 1882–1976
English actress

She was born in Gainsborough, Lincolnshire, and although she trained as a pianist she decided to enter the theatre, making her first appearance with Greet's Pastoral Players in *The Merry Wives of Windsor* (1904). After four years touring the USA in Shakespearean repertory, she returned to England and became a prominent member of Annie Horniman's Repertory Company in Manchester, and also worked in London at the Old Vic (1914–19). She eventually played a great variety of male and female roles, including the title role in the first English performance of George Bernard Shaw's *Saint Joan* (1924). During World

War II, she was a notable member of the Old Vic Company, playing at the New Theatre, London. She was created DBE in 1931. With her husband, Sir Lewis Casson, she wrote a biography of Lilian Baylis.

Thorneycroft (of Dunston), (George Edward) Peter Thorneycroft, Baron 1909–
English Conservative politician

He was educated at Eton and the Royal Marine Artillery, Woolwich, served as a regular artillery officer (1930–33), left the army to become a barrister, and entered parliament in 1938. President of the Board of Trade from 1951 to 1957, he was appointed Chancellor of the Exchequer in 1957, but, disagreeing with government financial policy, resigned after a year in office. Successively Minister of Aviation (1960–62), Minister of Defence (1962–64), and Secretary of State for Defence (1964), he lost his parliamentary seat in the 1966 election. In 1967 he was created a life peer. He was chairman of the Conservative Party from 1975 to 1981.

Thornhill, Sir James 1675–1734
English painter

Born in Melcombe Regis, Dorset, he was apprenticed to Thomas Highmore and studied the work of Antonio Vernio and Louis Laguerre. He executed Baroque paintings for the dome of St Paul's (c.1710–1717), the hall at Blenheim Palace, and his masterpiece, the Painted Hall at Greenwich Hospital (1707–c.1727). He painted occasional portraits, including those of Isaac Newton (1710, Trinity College, Cambridge), Richard Steele, the robber Jack Sheppard and a self-portrait. He founded a drawing school, and William Hogarth, who eloped with his daughter, was one of his pupils. He was knighted by George I (1720), becoming History Painter to the King (1728), who commissioned him to paint the ceiling of the Queen's Bedroom at Hampton Court for the future George II and Caroline of Ansbach. From 1722 he was MP for Melcombe Regis. He was the first native-born painter to succeed as a full-time decorative artist in the face of foreign competition.

Thornton, William 1759–1828
US architect

Born on the island of Tortola in the West Indies (now part of the British Virgin Islands), he studied medicine in Scotland, then emigrated to the USA in 1787. Though he was untrained in architecture, he won the competition to design the US Capitol in Washington DC (1792). His plans were later altered, but the façade and central area are much as he conceived them.

Thornycroft, Sir (William) Hamo 1850–1925
English sculptor

He was born in London, where he studied the Greek sculptures in the British Museum, and trained at the Royal Academy Schools, winning the Gold Medal there in 1875. His style reflects the Realism of the late 19th century, tempered with classicism. He made his name with *Warrior Bearing a Wounded Youth* (1876), followed by *Artemis* (1880, Macclesfield Town Hall), *The Mower* (1884, Walker Art Gallery, Liverpool), and *The Sower* (1886, Kew Gardens). Statues include John Bright in Rochdale (1892), and Oliver Cromwell in Westminster (1899), Dean Colet (1900, St Paul's School for Boys, London), King Alfred (1904, Winchester) and W E Gladstone (1905, The Aldwych, London). His grandfather, John Francis (1780–1861), his mother, Mary (1814–95), and his father, Thomas (1815–85), were all sculptors. Mary is known for her work at Osborne House, Isle of Wight, for example *A Hunter* (1859), and Thomas sculpted the famous *Boudicaa* beside Westminster Bridge (1856–70) and Commerce on the

Albert Memorial in London, as well as many other public statues. Hamo's brother, Sir John Isaac (1843–1928), was a naval architect and engineer.

Thoroddsen, Jón, originally Jón Thórðarson
1818–68
Icelandic novelist and poet
Born in Reykhólar, he studied law at Copenhagen, and wrote drinking songs in the style of Carl Bellmann. He was an avid reader of Sir Walter Scott, and used him as a model for his first novel, *Piltur og stúlka* (1850, 'Boy and Girl'). It was the earliest novel produced in Iceland, and he is regarded as the father of the modern Icelandic novel. In 1850 he returned to Iceland and was appointed a district magistrate on the island of Flatey. In addition to a sheaf of lyrics, he wrote an unfinished sequel to his first novel, *Maður og kona* ('Man and Woman'), published posthumously in 1876. 📖 S J Ðorsteinsson, *Thoroddsen og skaldsogur hans* (1943)

Thorpe, Sir (Thomas) Edward 1845–1925
English chemist, physicist and historian of science
Born near Manchester, he was educated at Owens College, Manchester, where he spent some time as Sir Henry Roscoe's assistant, and at the University of Heidelberg under Robert Bunsen and also at Bonn. He was appointed to the chair of chemistry, first at Anderson's College, Glasgow (1870), then at the Yorkshire College of Science at Leeds (1874) and the Royal College of Science, London (1885). In 1894 he became Government Chemist—the first such appointment—and he returned to the Royal College of Science from 1909 to 1912. He discovered several new compounds of chromium, sulphur and phosphorus, including phosphorus pentafluoride, which demonstrated that phosphorus could have a valence of five. He also carried out determinations of atomic weights that were more accurate than any others of the time. He travelled to the West Indies and other places to view four eclipses of the Sun, and in collaboration with Sir Arthur Rücker made a magnetic survey of the British Isles. Thorpe is also remembered for his work in the history of science, particularly his biography of Joseph Priestley. He was elected FRS in 1876, made a Companion of the Bath in 1900 and knighted in 1909.

Thorpe, (John) Jeremy 1929–
English Liberal politician
Educated at Eton and Trinity College, Oxford (where he was president of the Union), he was called to the Bar in 1954. Thorpe, whose father and grandfather were both Conservative MPs, was Liberal MP for North Devon from 1959 to 1979. He was elected leader of the Liberal Party in 1967 but resigned the leadership in 1976 following allegations concerning a previous homosexual relationship with Norman Scott. In 1979, shortly after losing his seat in the general election, he was acquitted at the Central Criminal Court on charges of conspiracy and incitement to murder Mr Scott. 📖 Lewis Chester, *Jeremy Thorpe: A Secret Life* (1979)

Thorpe, William Homan 1902–86
English zoologist
Born in Hastings, Sussex, he studied agriculture at Cambridge, where he developed an interest in agricultural entomology, and investigated the biological control of insect parasites in California (1927–29). He was research entomologist at Farnham Royal Parasite Laboratory of the Imperial Bureau of Entomology (1929–32), became a lecturer in entomology at Cambridge in 1932, and was instrumental in setting up an animal behaviour sub-department at Madingley. In 1966 Cambridge's first chair of ethology was created for him. He had a strong interest in conservation, and was one of the founders of ethology, publishing the influential *Learning and Instinct in Animals* in 1956. His research was mainly concerned with bird song, and he demonstrated that song results from the integration of innate and learned components of sound patterning. He was elected FRS in 1951.

Thorpe Davie, Cedric 1913–83
Scottish composer
Born in London of Scottish parents, he studied at the Royal Scottish Academy in Glasgow, the Royal Academy, the Royal College, and with Zoltán Kodály. He became Professor of Composition at the Scottish National Academy of Music in 1936. His early compositions include a string quartet, a sonatina for cello and piano, and the *Dirge for Cuthullin* for chorus and orchestra (1935). His Symphony in C appeared in 1945, and he wrote the music for Tyrone Guthrie's acclaimed production of Sir David Lyndsay's *Ane Satyre of the Thrie Estaitis* at the 1948 Edinburgh Festival. He also wrote many film scores and music for theatre productions and schools. Master of music at St Andrews University in 1945, he founded its music department in 1947, becoming reader (1956) and then professor (1973–78).

Thorson, Gunnar Axel 1906–71
Danish marine ecologist
Born in Copenhagen, he was educated at Copenhagen University, and subsequently led an expedition to east Greenland, studying the reproductive ecology of Arctic marine invertebrates. He was later appointed to the staff of the Copenhagen University Zoological Museum (1934) and founded his own private laboratory, from which stemmed the research that led to his classic and highly influential monograph *Reproduction and larval development of Danish marine bottom invertebrates* (1946). He was elected to the Royal Danish Academy of Sciences in 1955, and was later formally appointed director of the Helsingør Marine Laboratory. Thorson's geographic categorization of benthic marine invertebrate development is now formalized in the literature as 'Thorson's rule'. A second important contribution was his concept of 'parallel marine bottom communities', a hypothesis that similar biotopes at differing latitudes supported ecologically comparable systems, although he acknowledged that the theory could not be extended to include tropical communities.

Thorvaldsen, Bertel 1770–1844
Danish sculptor
He was born probably in Copenhagen, and was the son of an Icelandic woodcarver. He studied in Copenhagen, and from 1797 lived for the most part in Rome. One of the major figures of the neoclassical movement, he created statues of *Jason* (1802–03, Thorvaldsen Museum, Copenhagen), *Vénus*, *Psyche*, and others. Among his most celebrated works are *Triumphal Entry of Alexander into Babylon*, *Christ and the Twelve Apostles* (Church of Our Lady, Copenhagen), the reliefs *Night and Morning*, the *Dying Lion* at Lucerne and the Cambridge statue of Lord Byron (1829, Trinity College). He also executed the tomb of Pius VII at St Peter's, Rome (1824–31).

Thothmes See Tuthmosis IV

Thrale See Piozzi, Hester Lynch

Thrasybulus d.388BC
Athenian naval commander
A strenuous supporter of the democracy, in 411BC he helped to overthrow the Four Hundred, and was responsible for the recall of Alcibiades. In that year he defeated the Spartans in naval battles at Cynossema, and at Cyzicus in 410. In 404 he was banished by the Thirty Tyrants, but restored the democracy in 403 by seizing

Piraeus. He conquered Lesbos and defended Rhodes, but was slain at Aspendus. **Cornelius Nepos** wrote his biography.

Throckmorton, Francis 1554–84
English conspirator

Son of the courtier John Throckmorton (d.1445), he was apprehended in the act of writing in code to **Mary, Queen of Scots**, in an unsuccessful attempt to overthrow **Elizabeth I**, confessed under torture and was executed at Tyburn.

Throckmorton, Sir Nicholas 1515–71
English diplomat

He fought bravely at Pinkie (1547), was ambassador to France, where he was imprisoned for siding with the Huguenots, and several times ambassador to Scotland (1561–67). In 1569 he was imprisoned in the Tower of London for promoting the scheme for marrying **Mary, Queen of Scots**, to the Duke of Norfolk, but was soon released. His daughter, Elizabeth, married Sir **Walter Raleigh**. Francis Throckmorton was his nephew.

Thubron, Colin Gerald Dryden 1939–
English novelist and travel writer

He was born in London, a descendant of **John Dryden**. He abandoned a career in publishing in order to travel, mainly in Asia and northern Africa, and the vivid accounts of his journeys have made him one of the most highly respected of travel writers. His best-known titles include *Among the Russians* (1983) and *Behind the Wall* (1987), an intriguing insight into modern China, in which personal day-to-day lives are set against the political and economic context. Among his novels are *A Cruel Madness* (1984), a study of instability, *Falling* (1989), a poignant story of love and loss, *Turning Back the Sun* (1991) and *Distance* (1996).

Thucydides c.460–c.400BC
Greek historian

Born near Athens, he suffered in the Athenian plague (c.430BC) but recovered. In the Peloponnesian war he commanded an Athenian squadron of ships at Thasos (424), but after losing the colony of Amphipolis to the Spartans (424BC) he was condemned as a traitor, and retired to his Thracian estates. He lived in exile for 20 years (possibly visiting Sicily), and wrote his eight-volume *De Bello Peloponnesiaco* ('History of the Peloponnesian War'). He probably returned to Athens in 404. According to tradition he was assassinated. His account of the war ends in 411, but the *Hellenica* of **Xenophon** was written to continue Thucydides' narrative to the end of the war in 404.
📖 *The Peloponnesian War* (Eng trans Rex Warner, 1954)

Thumb, General Tom See Stratton, Charles Sherwood

Thunberg, Carl Peter 1743–1828
Swedish botanical explorer

Born in Jönköping, he was taught botany by **Carolus Linnaeus** at Uppsala University, and collected plants for him. After graduation in 1770 he travelled as a ship's surgeon to South Africa, Java and Japan, collecting and describing 3,000 plants, many new to science. From 1778 he taught botany at Uppsala, and in 1784 became professor. His Japanese discoveries were published as *Flora Japonica* (1784), and those from South Africa as *Prodromus Plantarum Capensium* (1794–1800) and *Flora Capensis* (1807–23, with Joseph August Schultes). He also wrote and published monographs on *Protea*, *Ixia*, *Oxalis* and *Gladiolus*.

Thurber, James Grover 1894–1961
US humorist and cartoonist

Born in Columbus, Ohio, he attended schools in Columbus and went to Ohio State University. In the early 1920s he reported for various papers in the USA and Europe but in 1927 **E B White** introduced him to **Harold Ross**, editor of the *New Yorker*, and he was instantly appointed its managing editor. Unsuited to the job, he drifted into writing, but before leaving the staff altogether, he contributed regularly, humorous essays at first, then sketches. His drawings first appeared in *Is Sex Necessary?* (1929) which he co-authored with White. His books include *The Owl in the Attic and Other Perplexities* (1931), *The Seal in the Bedroom and Other Predicaments* (1932), *The Middle-Aged Man on the Flying Trapeze* (1935), *Men Women and Dogs* (1943), *The Wonderful O* (1957) and his fragmentary autobiography, *My Life and Hard Times* (1933). He was also a dramatist and appeared as himself in a brief run of *A Thurber Carnival* in 1960. He also wrote a number of short stories, of which *The Secret Life of Walter Mitty*, filmed with **Danny Kaye** (1946), is best known. *The Years With Ross* (1959) is an anecdotal memoir of his experience of the unpredictable *New Yorker* editor. 📖 B Bernstein, *James Thurber, a biography* (1975)

Thurmond, (James) Strom 1902–
US politician

Born in Edgefield, South Carolina, he became a lawyer and judge and fought in the US army in World War II. He was Governor of South Carolina (1947–51), and his opposition to civil rights legislation led him to run for President as the Dixiecrat candidate in 1948. A conservative and a militarist, he has served in the Senate since 1954; he changed his affiliation from Democratic to Republican in 1964. From 1981 to 1987 he was president pro tempore of the Senate, a position he resumed in 1995.

Thurstan d.1140
Norman prelate

Born in Bayeux, he was secretary to **Henry I**, and was made Archbishop of York in 1114. As Archbishop, he struggled for primacy with Canterbury. On the invasion of King **David I** of Scotland (1137), he first persuaded him to accept a truce, and then collected forces at York and beat him at the Battle of the Standard (1138). A member of the Cluniac Order, he did much to help the growth of monasticism in the North and was concerned in the foundation of Fountains Abbey (1132).

Thurstone, L(ouis) L(eon) 1887–1955
US psychologist

He was born in Chicago. After studies at Cornell University, he gained his PhD in engineering at Chicago University in 1917, by which time he was teaching at the Carnegie Institute of Technology (1915–23). He was the author of the trade tests used by the US army for the occupational classification of conscripts during World War I. He was later Professor of Psychology at Chicago University (1927–52) and then research professor and director of the Psychometric Laboratory at North Carolina University (1952–55). His academic work was devoted to the theory and practice of intelligence testing and the development of statistical techniques (especially multiple-factor analysis) to analyze the results. His battery of tests designed to measure the 'Primary Mental Abilities' have enjoyed wide application, especially in the USA. His books include *The Vectors of Mind* (1935) and *Multiple-Factor Analysis* (1947).

Thutmose or Tuthmosis I fl.1493–1482BC
King of Egypt

He is believed to have come to the throne through marriage to Amhose, the sister of King Amenhotep I. He waged war in Nubia, where he extended Egyptian control into Kush beyond the Third Cataract, and in Syria, where he campaigned as far as the Euphrates. He constructed the fourth and fifth pylons (monumental gateways) at the Temple of Amun in Karnak, and erected a pair of granite obelisks, one of which still stands. His burial in the Valley of the Kings established a pattern for royal internments which was followed for the next 400 years.

Tibbett, Lawrence Mervil, *originally* Lawrence Mervil Tibbet 1896–1960
US baritone

He was born in Bakersfield, California, the son of a local sheriff who was shot dead by a wanted bandit. He joined the US navy during World War I, and on returning to civilian life made a living singing at weddings and funerals. Persuaded not to waste his good voice, he took lessons and in 1923 joined the New York Metropolitan Opera. For more than 25 years he performed all the leading baritone roles, most notably Scarpia in *Tosca*, Rigoletto, Amonasro in *Aida*, and Porgy. He also appeared in the world premières of several operas, including Louis Gruenberg's *Emperor Jones*. His Covent Garden debut was in 1937 as Scarpia. He enjoyed singing popular ballads and often included 'low-brow' music in his concerts.

Tiberius, *in full* Tiberius Julius Caesar Augustus, *originally* Tiberius Claudius Nero 42BC–AD37
2nd Emperor of Rome

He was the son of Tiberius Claudius Nero and of Livia. His father died when Tiberius was nine, and he succeeded his stepfather the Emperor Augustus in AD14. Almost the whole of his first 20 years of adulthood were spent on campaign in Spain, Armenia, Gaul, Pannonia and Germany; he returned to Rome after crushing the Dalmatian revolt (9BC). Tiberius was compelled (12BC) to divorce his wife, Vipsania Agrippina, in order to marry Julia, Agrippa's widow and the profligate daughter of Augustus. He retired to Rhodes (6BC) where he devoted himself to study and astrology. Before his return (AD2) Julia was banished to Pandataria (2BC), and the deaths of the young princes Lucius and Gaius led Augustus to adopt Tiberius (AD4) as imperial heir. He spent the next seven years in active service in north Germany, suppressing insurrections in Pannonia and Dalmatia, and taking vengeance upon the Germans who had annihilated the army of Varus in AD9. Along with Germanicus Caesar he made two marches into the heart of Germany (AD9–10), returning to enjoy a triumph (AD12). Tiberius succeeded Augustus in AD14, but despite his eminent qualities and many services, his loyalty to Augustus and his devotion to the public good, he was not suited to the role of emperor. His rule began well, but was gradually eroded by suspicion and insecurity, which resulted in a growing number of treason trials and executions. He relied increasingly on the services of his friend the praetorian prefect Sejanus. In AD26 he left Rome for Campania, and retired to the island of Capreae (Capri). Sejanus in the meantime assumed effective control in Rome until at last Tiberius became suspicious of his intentions and executed him (AD31). His reign was blighted by internal conflicts: the murder of Agrippa Postumus (AD14), the mysterious death in the East of his heir, the popular Germanicus Caesar (AD19), the alleged poisoning of Tiberius's own son Drusus by Sejanus (AD23), the banishment of Agrippina (the Elder) and the death of her young sons Nero and Drusus (AD31, AD33). These events all but obliterated the memory of much good government earlier in his reign and he died unmourned. 🕮 Robin Seager, *Tiberius* (1972).

Tibullus, Albius c.54–19BC
Roman elegiac poet

Believed to have been born in Gabii, he became friends with the poet-statesman, M Valerius Messala, and joined his staff. In 30BC Augustus commissioned Tibullus to crush a revolt in Aquitania, and although he served with distinction in the campaign, he never liked life as a soldier as much as he enjoyed Roman society. His gentle elegiac love poems to his mistresses persuaded Quintilian to place Tibullus at the head of Roman elegiac poets.

Tickell, Thomas 1686–1740
English poet

Born at Bridekirk, Carlisle, he was a Fellow of Queen's College, Oxford (1710–26). His complimentary verses on *Rosamond* (1709) gained him the favour of Joseph Addison, who, on becoming Secretary of State (1717), made him his Under-Secretary. From 1725 he was Secretary to the Lords Justices of Ireland. He was skilful in occasional poetry, and was favourably reviewed in the *Spectator*, to which he also contributed. His translation of Book One of the *Iliad* appeared in 1715, about the same time as Pope's. Pope professed to believe it the work of Addison, designed to eclipse his own version, and wrote the famous satire on Atticus; but though Addison corrected it, the translation was certainly by Tickell. His poems include *Kensington Gardens*, *Colin and Lucy*, and the elegy prefixed to his edition of Addison's works (1721). 🕮 R E Tickell, *Thomas Tickell and 18th Century Poetry* (1931)

Ticknor, George 1791–1871
US writer

He was born in Boston, Massachusetts, and gave up his legal practice in order to study and travel in Europe, recounted in his interesting *Letters and Journals* (1876). He was Professor of French, Spanish and of Belles Lettres at Harvard (1819–35) and then spent three more years in Europe, collecting materials for his great *History of Spanish Literature* (1849).

Ticknor, William Davis 1810–64
US publisher

He was born in Lebanon, New Hampshire. He became a publisher in Boston in 1832, at first with John Allen, and then with James T Fields (1817–81). As Ticknor & Fields they published the *Atlantic Monthly* and the *North American Review*, and their office was frequented by Ralph Waldo Emerson, Henry Wadsworth Longfellow, Nathaniel Hawthorne, Oliver Wendell Holmes, James Russell Lowell and John Greenleaf Whittier. He was one of the first Americans to remunerate foreign authors, and a cousin of George Ticknor.

Tieck, (Johann) Ludwig 1773–1853
German Romantic writer and critic

He was born in Berlin, and was educated at Halle, Göttingen and Erlangen universities (1792–94). As a writer, he lived in Berlin, Dresden and near Frankfurt an der Oder. He produced a number of clever *Märchendramen* (dramatized versions of folk-tales), such as *Der gestiefelte Kater* (1797, 'Puss in Boots') and *Ritter Blaubart* (1797, 'Blue Beard'). He followed up this first success by the satire *Anti-Faust, oder Geschichte eines dummen Teufels* (1801, 'Anti-Faust, or the Story of a Dim Devil'), the horror story *Der Runenberg* (1804, 'The Rune Mountain'), and *Phantasus* (1812–17), a collection of traditional lore in story and drama. Besides supervising the completion of August von Schlegel's translation of Shakespeare, he edited the doubtful plays and wrote a series of essays (*Shakespeares Vorschule*, 1823–29, 'Shakespeare's Preparatory School'). He translated *Don Quixote* in 1799–1804. He is notable as a dramatic and literary critic for his *Dramaturgische Blätter* (2nd edition 1852, 'Dramaturgical Pages') and *Kritische Schriften* (1848, 'Critical Writings'). 🕮 E H Zeydel, *Ludwig Tieck, the German Romanticist* (1935)

Tiepolo, Giovanni Battista, *originally* Giambattista Chiepoletto 1696–1770
Italian decorative painter

He was born in Venice, and was educated by an unknown artist named Lazzarini. His work is to be found in palaces and churches throughout Europe. Early examples include the Labia Palace at Venice and frescoes at Udine, Milan and Bergamo. His *Perseus and Andromeda* (c.1730) for the Palazzo Archinto, Milan, destroyed in 1943, survives as a study in the Frick Collection, New York. In 1750 he began his most important decorative scheme, in the Archbishop's Palace at Würzburg. *An Allegory with Venus and Time* (National Gallery, London), part of a ceiling in the Contarini Palace, Venice, also belongs to this period (1750s). In 1761 **Charles III** of Spain called him to Madrid to work in the new Royal Palace. The work, however, was still incomplete at his death. Tiepolo's compositions are full of movement and energy, as for example in *Antony and Cleopatra* at the Labia Palace, creating a sense of awe by the use of dramatically exaggerated foreshortening and subtle chiaroscuro. He was a superb draughtsman, and his influence on **Francisco Goya** and on all subsequent decorative painting was enormous. The Courtauld Institute in London owns a rich collection of his work, including *Allegory of the Power of Eloquence* (c.1725), *St Aloysius Gonzaga in Glory* (c.1726), *The Adoration of the Magi* (c.1726), *The Martyrdom of St Agatha* (c.1734) and a series of religious paintings of 1767.

Tiffany, Charles Lewis 1812–1902
US goldsmith and jeweller

Born in Killingly, Connecticut, he began dealing in fancy goods in New York in 1837, and later founded Tiffany and Co. By 1883 he had become so successful that he was one of the largest manufacturers of silverware in the USA. His work reflected current tastes with an accent on the traditional and historical. He held official appointments to 23 royal patrons, including the Tsar of Russia, Queen **Victoria** and the Shah of Persia. He maintained a consistently high standard of workmanship throughout his entire output, whether household wares or special commissions. Latterly, he marketed some of the Art Nouveau lamps made by his son, **Louis Comfort Tiffany**.

Tiffany, Louis Comfort 1848–1933
US glassmaker and interior decorator

Born in New York City, the son of **Charles Lewis Tiffany**, he began studying painting and became interested in the decorative arts in 1878. He established a firm of interior decorators which became one of the most popular in New York by the early 1880s and in 1882 he decorated some rooms in the White House. He became better known, however, for his work in glass, and in 1892 he acquired glass furnaces at Cirona, New York. The first year's production went to museums, but the following year the first lamps were made available to the public, and by 1896 the first Favrile Glass (handmade) was offered for sale. Apart from stained glass, furniture, fabrics, wallpaper and lamps, he produced goblets and glasses in the Art Nouveau style.

Tiglath-Pileser III *also known as* Pulu
8th century BC
King of Assyria

A great empire-builder, he ruled from 745 to 727BC, and conquered the cities of north Syria and Phoenicia, including Damascus and Babylon.

Tikhon 1865–1925
Patriarch of the Russian Orthodox Church

He was the first to have to face up to the new Communist regime. A bishop by 1898, he had few crises to face until he became patriarch in 1918. His first approach was to condemn the new Soviet state, but before his death he called on the faithful to show it political loyalty. Neither policy was to prove successful, and his *de facto* successor, **Sergei**, faced the same problem.

Tikhonov, Alexandr 1947–
Soviet biathlete

A supreme competitor, he holds the Olympic record for winning a gold medal in the biathlon relay on four successive occasions. The combination of skiing and shooting was introduced for men in 1960. But it was alpine skiing that captured the public's imagination, leaving biathlon to the super-fit élite. Surpassing rowing as the most demanding Olympic sport, the combination of skiing and shooting—even over short distances—requires ultimate fitness. Tikhonov also won an Olympic silver medal in the 20km in 1968.

Tikhonov, Nikolai Aleksandrovich 1905–97
Soviet politician

He began his career as an assistant locomotive driver, before training in the late 1920s at the Dnepropetrovsk Metallurgical Institute, where he met **Leonid Brezhnev**, then a Communist Party (CPSU) organizer. Tikhonov worked for two decades in the ferrous metallurgy industry, before being appointed deputy Minister for the Iron and Steel Industry (1955–57), deputy Chairman of Gosplan (1963–65) and deputy Chairman of the Council of Ministers (1965–80). He was inducted into the CPSU politburo as a full member by party leader Brezhnev in 1979 and appointed Prime Minister in 1980, a post which he held until 1985. He was a cautious, centralist Brezhnevite, whose period as state premier was characterized by progressive economic stagnation.

Tilak, Bal Gangadhar 1856–1920
Indian nationalist, scholar, and philosopher

He was born in Ratnagiri. After teaching mathematics, he was owner and editor of two weekly newspapers. A militant member of the 'extremist' wing within the Indian National Congress (and a member of the famous 'Lal, Pal and Bal' trio), he was twice imprisoned by the British for his nationalist activities. He helped to found the Home Rule League in 1914.

Tilden, Bill, *properly* William Tatem Tilden II
1893–1953
US tennis player

Born in Philadelphia, he was Wimbledon singles champion three times (1920, 1921, 1930), and doubles champion in 1927. He was also six times US singles champion, and four times doubles champion in the 1920s. In 1931 he turned professional, and went on circuit for 20 years—one of the first players to do so. He was publisher and editor of *Racquet Magazine* and wrote several books on tennis, including *The Art of Lawn Tennis* (1920) and *The Phantom Drive* (1924), as well as a novel, *Glory's Net*.

Tilden, Samuel Jones 1814–86
US politician

Born in New Lebanon, New York, he was admitted to the Bar and secured a large railway practice. By 1868 he had become leader of the Democrats in the state, and he attacked and destroyed the Tweed Ring, bringing a civil suit against **William Marcy Tweed** to recover the money he had stolen in graft. In 1874 he was elected Governor of New York on a reform ticket. As the Democratic candidate for President in 1876, he won more popular votes than the Republican contender, **Rutherford B Hayes**. Disputes over electoral votes in several states were brought before a Republican-dominated congressional committee, which awarded all the contested votes to Hayes, making him the victor by one electoral vote. Tilden returned to his career as a lawyer and on his death left much of his fortune to found a free library in New York City.

Tilden, Sir William Augustus 1842–1926
English organic chemist

Born in London, he was apprenticed to a pharmacist and studied for a year at the Royal College of Chemistry before becoming a demonstrator at the Pharmaceutical Society (1863–72). For the following eight years he taught chemistry at Clifton College, Bristol, moving to the chair of chemistry at Mason College and then succeeding Edward Thorpe at the Royal College of Science in 1894. He showed that there is only one compound of nitric oxide and chlorine, nitrosyl chloride, and that it is a valuable reagent for investigating the terpenes. He also discovered that if the hydrocarbon isoprene was prepared from terpenes, it separated out into fragments with properties identical to natural rubber. He also discovered that specific heats alter with temperature, decreasing as temperatures fall and increasing as they rise, with the extent of the shift varying inversely as the atomic weight of the element. This discovery has proved very important in many branches of industry. Tilden was elected FRS in 1880, and knighted in 1909.

Tillett, Benjamin 1860–1943
English trade-union leader

He was born in Bristol. He worked as brickmaker, bootmaker, sailor and Labour MP (1917–24, 1929–31). He was notable as organizer of the Dockers' Union in London and leader of the great dockers' strike in 1889, and of the London transport workers' strike (1911). He was expelled from Hamburg and from Antwerp (1896) for supporting dock strikes.

Tilley, Vesta, *stage name of* Matilda Alice, Lady de Frece, *née* Powles 1864–1952
English comedienne

Born in Worcester, she first appeared as The Great Little Tilley, aged four, in Nottingham, and did her first male impersonation the following year. She adopted the name of Vesta Tilley and became, through her charm, vivacity and attention to sartorial detail, the most celebrated of all male impersonators. Of the many popular songs sung by her, 'Burlington Bertie', 'Following in Father's Footsteps', 'Sweetheart May' and 'Jolly Good Luck to the Girl who loves a Soldier' are the best known. She wrote *Recollections of Vesta Tilley* (1934). 📖 Sara Maitland, *Vesta Tilley* (1986)

Tillich, Paul Johannes 1886–1965
US Protestant theologian and philosopher

Born in Starzeddel, Brandenburg, Germany, he became a Lutheran pastor (1912) and served as military chaplain in the German army in World War I, a traumatic experience which led him to take an active political interest in social reconstruction. He taught at Berlin (1919–24) and held professorships in theology at Marburg (1924–25), Dresden (1925–28) and Leipzig (1928–29), and in philosophy at Frankfurt (1929–33). He was an early critic of Hitler and the Nazis and in 1933 was barred from German universities, the first non-Jewish academic 'to be so honoured', as he put it. He emigrated to the USA, and taught at the Union Theological Seminary in New York (1933–55), Harvard Divinity School (1955–62) and Chicago Divinity School (1962–65), becoming a naturalized US citizen in 1940. In his main work, *Systematic Theology* (3 vols, 1951–63), he explains faith as a matter of 'ultimate concern' with a reality transcending finite existence rather than a belief in a personal God, and this has led to oversimplified accusations of atheism or crypto-atheism. His influence on the development of theology in this century has been very substantial, and his popular works like *The Courage to Be* (1952) and *Dynamics of Faith* (1957) have reached very large general readerships.

Tillotson, John 1630–94
English prelate

Born in Sowerby, Yorkshire, he studied at Clare Hall, Cambridge, becoming a Fellow in 1651. Although siding with the Presbyterians at the Savoy conference, he submitted to the Act of Uniformity (1662) and received preferment, becoming dean of Canterbury in 1672 and Archbishop in 1691. He advocated the Zwinglian doctrine of the eucharist. According to Archbishop Gilbert Burnet 'he was not only the best preacher of the age, but seemed to have brought preaching to perfection'. In 1664 he married a niece of Oliver Cromwell.

Tilly, Johann Tserklaes, Count von 1559–1632
Bavarian soldier

Born at the castle of Tilly in Brabant and brought up by the Jesuits, he fought in Hungary against the Turks, and was appointed in 1610 by Duke Maximilian of Bavaria to reorganize his army. Given the command of the Catholic League's army at the outbreak of the Thirty Years War, he separated the armies of Mansfeld and of the Margrave of Baden, beat the latter at Wimpfen (1622), and expelled Christian of Brunswick from the Palatinate, defeating him in two battles. Created a Count of the Empire, he defeated King Kristian IV of Denmark at Lutter (1626), and with Albrecht von Wallenstein compelled him to sign the Treaty of Lübeck (1629). The next year he succeeded Wallenstein as Commander-in-Chief of the imperial forces, and stormed Magdeburg (1631). Gustav II Adolph, at Breitenfeld, drove him to retreat behind the Lech, and forced the passage of the river, after a desperate conflict in which Tilly was fatally wounded.

Timoleon d.c.337 BC
Greek statesman and General of Corinth

He overthrew the tyranny of his brother Timophanes, and retired from public life. But when Dionysius the Younger and others tried to establish themselves in Syracuse, he returned. He manoeuvred Dionysius into abdication and fought the Carthaginians, who were supporting the other tyrants, defeating them at the Crimessus in 341 BC. He then promptly retired again, having taken measures to stabilize the economy of Greek Sicily.

Timon of Athens, *nicknamed* the Misanthrope of Athens 5th century BC
Athenian nobleman

He was a contemporary of Socrates. According to the comic writers who attacked him, he was disgusted with humankind on account of the ingratitude of his early friends, and lived a life of almost total seclusion. Lucian made him the subject of a dialogue. Shakespeare's play *Timon of Athens* is based on the story, as told in William Painter's *Palace of Pleasure*.

Timon of Phlius c.325–c.235 BC
Greek philosopher and poet

Born in the northern Peloponnese, he was Pyrrho's leading disciple and his biographer, and an enthusiastic exponent of the theories of Scepticism. After a period as an itinerant lecturer he retired to Athens where he was a leading member of the local intelligentsia and a versatile author. He wrote satyr-plays, comedies, tragedies, epic poems and a famous series of *Silloi*, satirical mock-heroic poems which parody and insult most earlier Greek philosophers, who are seen as doctrinaire, pretentious and generally aberrant predecessors of the Pyrrhonian enlightenment. Only brief fragments of his work have survived.

Timoshenko, Semyon Konstantinovich 1895–1970
Russian general

He was born in Bessarabia of peasant stock. In 1915 he was conscripted into the tsarist army, but in the Revolution (1917) he took part in the defence of Tsaritsin. In 1940 he smashed Finnish resistance during the Russo-Finnish

War, then commanded in the Ukraine, but failed to stop the German advance (1942). From 1940 to 1941 he served as People's Commissar of Defence, and commanded the Byelo russian district from 1956 until his retirement in 1960. ⌨ R M Portugalskii, *Marshal S K Timoshenko: zhizu i deiatelnost* (1994)

Timoshenko, Stepan (Stephen) Prokofyevich 1878–1972
US civil engineer
Born in the Ukraine and educated at the two technical institutes in St Petersburg, he worked for a time as a railway engineer, then in 1906 began lecturing at Kiev University. Dismissed for his pro-Jewish views in 1911, he nevertheless remained in Russia until 1920 when he fled to Yugoslavia and thence to the USA in 1922. In 1936 he joined the staff of Stanford University in California where he taught engineering mechanics and strength of materials. In 1946 he received the James Watt Gold Medal of the (British) Institution of Mechanical Engineers, and in 1959 he was elected a member of the Soviet Academy of Sciences.

Timothy fl.c.50AD
Early Christian missionary
The son of a Greek father and Jewish mother, he was a native of Lystra. He probably became a Christian during St Paul's first missionary journey, later becoming one of the apostle's protégés. His special mission was to encourage the persecuted churches of Thessalonica and Asia Minor. Though described as being affectionate but fearful, Paul praises his loyalty. Tradition holds that he became Bishop of Ephesus, where he is said to have been martyred under Domitian. His feast days are 22 January (Greek Orthodox) or 24 January (Roman).

Timur, *also called* Timur Lenk, *Turkish for* Timur the Lame, *English* Tamerlane *or* Tamburlaine 1336–1405
Tatar conqueror
Born in Kesh, near Samarkand, he proclaimed himself Mongol Khan in 1370. In a series of devastating wars (in which he sustained the wounds which gave him his nickname) he subdued nearly all Persia from 1392 to 1396, Georgia, and the Tatar Empire, and conquered all the states between the River Indus and the lower Ganges, with his army of nomadic Turks and Mongols. He won Damascus and Syria from the Mamluk sovereigns of Egypt, then defeated the Turks at Ankara (1402), taking Sultan Bayezit I prisoner. He died while marching to conquer China. Although he was always a peripatetic ruler, his capital, Samarkand, was filled with splendid architectural monuments, covered with brightly coloured mosaics.

Tinbergen, Jan 1903–94
Dutch economist and Nobel prize winner
He was born in The Hague, the brother of the Nobel Prize winning ethologist Nikolaas Tinbergen. Educated at Leyden, he taught economics at the Erasmus University in Rotterdam (1933–73). He analysed the Depression in the USA in *Business Cycles in the USA 1919–32* (1939), and was economic adviser to the League of Nations (1936–38). After World War II he directed the Netherlands Central Planning Bureau (1945–55). His publications include *Econometrics* (1941), *Economic Policy: Principles and Design* (1956), and *Shaping the World Economy* (1962). He shared the first Nobel Prize for economics in 1969 with Ragnar Frisch.

Tinbergen, Nikolaas 1907–88
Dutch ethologist and Nobel Prize winner
He was born in The Hague, the brother of the Nobel prize-winning economist Jan Tinbergen. He studied zoology at the university of Leyden, and taught at Oxford (1949–74). With Konrad Lorenz he is considered to be the co-founder of ethology, the study of animal behaviour in relation to the environment to which it is adapted. His best-known studies were on the three-spined stickleback and the herring gull, animals which perform many stereotyped or instinctive behaviour patterns. Much of his work was centred around aspects of social behaviour, elucidating the evolutionary derivation of many of these behaviours through comparative studies. His books include his classic *The Study of Instinct* (1951), *The Herring Gull's World* (1953), *Social Behaviour in Animals* (1953) and *The Animal in its World* (2 vols, 1972–73). In 1973 he published a controversial book *Autistic Children* (with his wife Lies), in which he proposed a behavioural causation for autism. He shared the 1973 Nobel Prize for physiology or medicine with Lorenz and Karl von Frisch.

Tindal, Matthew 1655–1733
English deist
Born in Beer-Ferris rectory, in south Devon, he was elected a Fellow of All Souls College, Oxford. A Roman Catholic under James VII and II, he reverted to Protestantism of a somewhat freethinking type, and wrote *An Essay of Obedience to the Supreme Powers* (1693), and *Rights of the Christian Church asserted against the Romish and all other Priests* (1706). The latter raised a storm of opposition but even a prosecution failed to prevent a fourth edition in 1709. In 1730 Tindal published his *Christianity as Old as the Creation*, which was soon known as 'the deist's Bible', whose aim was to eliminate the supernatural element from religion, and to prove that its morality is its only claim to the reverence of mankind. Answers were issued by Daniel Waterland (1683–1740), William Conybeare (1787–1857), and others.

Tindale, William See Tyndale, William

Tindemans, Leo 1922–
Belgian politician
He studied economics and social sciences at Antwerp, Ghent and Louvain universities. In 1958 he became secretary to the Christian People's Party (CVP), entering parliament for Antwerp in 1961. From 1968 he regularly held cabinet posts, and led the government from 1974 to 1978. In 1979 he became chairman of the CVP, and he is particularly known for his role in the European Community. Since 1992 he has been president of the Group of the European People's Party and in 1993 was the first holder of the Jacques Delors chair in Maastricht.

Ting, Samuel Chao Chung 1936–
US physicist and Nobel Prize winner
Born in Ann Arbor, Michigan, where his father was studying, he was raised in China and educated there and in Taiwan, and at Michigan University (1956–62). He worked in elementary particle physics at CERN (Conseil Européen pour la Recherche Nucléaire) in Geneva and at Columbia University. Later he led a research group at DESY, the German synchrotron project in Hamburg, and from 1967 worked at the Massachusetts Institute of Technology (MIT). In 1974 he was head of a team at the Brookhaven National Laboratory which directed protons onto a beryllium target, and a new product particle was observed and named the J particle. At the same time, and independently, Burton Richter made the same discovery and named the particle γ. It is now named the J/γ particle and for its discovery Ting and Richter shared the 1976 Nobel Prize for physics. In the 1980s and 1990s, Ting led a project at CERN where the standard model of particle interactions was precisely tested.

Ting Ling See Ding Ling

Tinguely, Jean 1925–91
Swiss sculptor

He was born in Fribourg, and studied at the Basle Kunstgewerbeschule from 1941 to 1945. A pioneer of Kinetic Art, he worked in Paris from 1953 onwards, exhibiting his 'meta-mechanical' works. These moving metal constructions, or 'junk mobiles', sometimes powered by small motors, often strike bottles or metal pans, and even make abstract drawings, for example *Monstranz* (1960, New York City) and *Baluba* (1961–62, Pompidou Centre, Paris). From about 1960 he began programming them to destroy themselves, as in *Hommage à New York* (Metropolitan Museum of Art, New York City). At the 1967 Expo in Montreal he erected his machines on the roof of the French Pavilion. There is a large mobile by him in Basle Railway Station, and his *Fasnachts-Brunnen* (1977) is also in the town there.

Tino di Camaino c.1285–1337
Italian sculptor

Born in Siena, he probably trained in Pisa under **Giovanni Pisano**, and was certainly working there in 1311. In 1315 he succeeded Giovanni as master of works at Pisa Cathedral, and was commissioned to make the tomb of Emperor **Henry VII**. He then held an equivalent position at Siena Cathedral, and later worked in Florence, where his sepulchral monuments included that of Bishop Orso in Florence Cathedral. Around 1324 he entered the service of the Angevin rulers in Naples, and worked there on architectural projects as well as sculpture. His dignified, monumental style was influential in both the north and south of Italy.

Tinsley, Pauline 1928–
English soprano

Born in Wigan, Lancashire, she studied singing in Manchester, at the Opera School, London, and with **Eva Turner**. She has sung a wide variety of roles, such Elektra, Turandot, the Dyer's Wife, Lady Macbeth, Kostelnicka, Brünnhilde, Santuzza, and Lady Billows. Her career has taken her all over Great Britain and the USA, to La Scala Milan, Hamburg, Amsterdam and elsewhere in Europe.

Tintoretto, *properly* **Jacopo Robusti** 1518–94
Italian painter

He was born probably in Venice, the son of a silk dyer or *tintore* (hence his nickname of 'Little Dyer'), but little is known of his life. He is supposed to have studied under **Titian**, but only for a short time. He claims to have set up independently, practically untaught, by 1539, but it is likely that he had some supervision. Except for visits to Mantua (1580, 1590–93), he lived all his life in Venice. Tintoretto pioneered the way from the classical to the Baroque, evident in his early work, such as *The Miracle of the Slave* (1548), in which he consciously set out to combine Titian's colours with **Michelangelo's** sculptural draughtsmanship. After 1556 he began to develop his mature style. *The Last Judgement, The Golden Calf* (both c.1560) and *The Marriage of Cana* (1561) were followed by two masterpieces of perspective and lighting effects *The Finding* and *The Removal of the Body of St Mark* (both c.1562). Other notable late works are *The Origin of the Milky Way* (after 1570), the *Paradiso* (1588), famous for its colossal size, *Entombment*, and his last version of *The Last Supper* (1592–94). Three of his seven children also became painters, including Marietta (1560–90), known as La Tintoretta. 📖 Eric Newton, *Tintoretto* (1952)

Tinworth, George 1843–1913
English terracotta artist

Born in London, he entered the Royal Academy schools in 1864, and in 1867 obtained an appointment in the Doulton Art Pottery. The works which made him famous were mainly terracotta panels with groups of figures in high relief illustrating scenes from sacred history.

Tiolkovsky, Konstantin Eduardovich
1857–1935
Russian engineer

He was born in the district of Ryazan. Scarlet fever at the age of 10 led to permanent deafness and limited his schooling and subsequent career. In 1892 he became a teacher in Kaluga, a position he retained until 1920. He built the first wind tunnel in Russia in 1891, designed large airships, and in 1903 published his first scientific paper on spaceflight. He continued to research designs of rocket-propelled aircraft and spacecraft, and, in 1924, presented conceptual studies for manned orbital craft capable of re-entry into the earth's atmosphere. His outstanding work on the fundamental physics and engineering of space vehicles was recognized by the Soviet authorities, and he is known as 'the father of Astronautics'. All his works were translated into English by NASA in 1965.

Tippett, Sir Michael Kemp 1905–98
English composer

Born in London, he studied at the Royal College of Music and from 1940 to 1951 was director of Music at Morley College. He first attracted attention with his chamber music and Concerto for Double String Orchestra (1939), but his oratorio, *A Child of our Time* (1941), reflecting the political and spiritual problems of the 1930s and 1940s, won him wide recognition. A convinced pacifist, he went to prison for three months as a conscientious objector during World War II. He had considerable success with the operas *The Midsummer Marriage* (1952) and *King Priam* (1958). His other works include symphonies, a piano concerto (1957), the operas *The Knot Garden* (1966–70) and *The Ice Break* (1976), piano sonatas and an oratorio *The Vision of St Augustine* (1963–65). Later compositions include *String Quartet No 5* (1991), *The Rose Lake* (1993) and *Caliban's Song* (1995). He was created CBE in 1959, was knighted in 1966 and was awarded the Order of Merit in 1983. He wrote *Moving into Aquarius* (collected writings, rev edn 1974), his memoirs, *Those Twentieth Century Blues* (1991), and *Tippett on Music* (1995). 📖 Meirion Bowen, *Michael Tippett* (1981)

Tippoo Sahib or Tipú Sultán c.1749–99
Sultan of Mysore

The son of **Haidar Ali**, he completely routed Bailey (1780, 1782) and Braithwaite (1782) during his father's wars with the British. In 1782 he succeeded his father as Sultan of Mysore. An able general and administrator, he was cruel to enemies and lacked his father's wisdom. He captured and killed most of the garrison of Bednur (1783), but after the conclusion of peace between France and Great Britain he agreed to a treaty (1784) confirming the status quo. He sent ambassadors to France (1787) to stir up a war with Great Britain, and, failing in this, in 1789 he invaded the protected state of Travancore. In the ensuing war (1790–92) the British, under Stuart and **Cornwallis**, were aided by the Marathas and the Nizam, and Tippoo was defeated (1792), and had to cede half his kingdom. He then sent another embassy to the French. After recommencing hostilities in 1799, he was killed during the siege of Seringapatam by General George Harris (1746–1829).

Tiradentes, *originally* **Joaquim José da Silva Xavier** 1748–92
Brazilian revolutionary

Born in Pombal (now Tiradentes), Brazil, he worked for a time as a dentist, thus earning his nickname Tiradentes (tooth-puller). He led the first conspiracy against Portuguese rule in 1789, but before he and his comrades could put their plans into action, they were betrayed, arrested and then hanged and quartered in Rio de Janeiro. Tiradentes is now considered a Brazilian national hero.

Tiro, Marcus Tullius 1st century AD

Roman freedman, inventor of the Tironian shorthand system

He was a friend and assistant of Cicero, and devised a system to take down dictation and record speeches. He was the author of a lost *Life of Cicero* and editor of some of Cicero's letters. His shorthand system was taught in Roman schools, and was in widespread use for several centuries.

Tirpitz, Alfred Friedrich von 1849–1930

German admiral

Born in Küstrin, Brandenburg, he joined the Prussian navy in 1865. He commanded the Asiatic squadron (1896–97), and as Secretary of State for the Imperial German Navy (1897–1916), he raised a fleet to challenge British supremacy of the seas, and acted as its commander (1914–16). He advocated unrestricted submarine warfare, and resigned when this policy was, initially, opposed in government circles (to be implemented later, on 1 February 1917). He later sat in the Reichstag (1924–28). ▢ Jonathan Steinberg, *Yesterday's Deterrent: Tirpitz and the Birth of the German Battle Fleet* (1965)

Tirso de Molina, *pseudonym of* Gabriel Téllez c.1571–1648

Spanish playwright

He was born in Madrid, and was prior of the monastery of Soria. Lacking his great contemporary Lope de Vega's lyrical gifts, he wrote *Comedias* (5 vols, 1627–36), partly Interludes, and *Autos Sacramentales* (originally about 300). He excelled in the portrayal of character, particularly of spirited women, and in his treatment of the Don Juan legend in his masterpiece, *El burlador de Sevilla* (1634, Eng trans *The Trickster of Seville*, 1959). ▢ Ivy L McClelland, *Tirso de Molina* (1948)

Tischendorf, (Lobegott Friedrich) Konstantin von 1815–74

German biblical scholar

Born in Lengenfeld in Saxony, in 1839 he became a lecturer, and in 1845 a professor at Leipzig. His search for manuscripts of the New Testament resulted in the discovery of the 4th-century Sinaitic Codex at the monastery of St Catherine on Mount Sinai and he described his journeys in *Reise in den Orient* (1846) and *Aus dem Heiligen Lande* (1862). Among his works are the editions of the Sinaitic (1862) and many other manuscripts, the *Editio VIII* of the New Testament (1864–72), an edition of the Septuagint, and the *Monumenta Sacra Inedita* (1846–71). *When were our Gospels Written?* was translated in 1866.

Tiselius, Arne Wilhelm Kaurin 1902–71

Swedish chemist and Nobel Prize winner

Born in Stockholm, he trained and worked at the University of Uppsala, where he became assistant professor in 1930 and was later appointed Professor of Biochemistry (1938–68). He developed an accurate method for determining diffusion constants of proteins, important for analysing ultracentrifuge sedimentation data (1934). He introduced protein analysis by moving boundary electrophoresis (1930–37) which became the best criterion of protein purity. He isolated bushy stunt and cucumber mosaic viruses (1938–39) and invented preparative electrophoresis (1943), electrokinetic filtration (1947) and other analytical techniques. From 1944 he developed methods for the chromatographic separation and identification of amino acids, sugars and other molecules. He worked with Frederick Sanger on the chemistry of insulin (1947) and with Richard Synge on chromatographic analysis (1950). Tiselius became vice-president (1947–60) and president (1960–64) of the Nobel Foundation and was awarded the Nobel Prize for chemistry in 1948. He was elected a Foreign Member of the Royal Society in 1957.

Tiso, Jozef 1887–1947

Slovak priest and politician

Like many other Slovak priests he was attracted to politics by Catholic and ethnic feelings against the Czechs in the united state established in 1918. In 1938 he succeeded Andrei Hlinka as leader of the Populist Party and began talks with Konrad Henlein, the Sudeten leader, whose objective was to enable Hitler to destroy Czechoslovakia. Following the Munich Agreement, ably assisted by Ferdinand Durcansky, he conspired with Hitler and in 1939 obeyed the order to declare Slovakia independent, leaving Czechs to Hitler's mercy in the Bohemian Protectorate. As President of the new Slovakia he eventually, in 1944, invited the Germans in to suppress the patriotic Slovak uprising. In 1947 he was tried and executed in Bratislava. The Slovak–Czech relationship had been little improved by his efforts.

Tisquantum See Squanto

Tissandier, Gaston 1835–99

French aviation pioneer

In 1883, with his brother Albert, he invented a navigable balloon, propelled by electricity.

Tissaphernes d.395BC

Persian satrap in Asia Minor

He was notorious for his duplicity in the conflicts between Athens and Sparta. Deprived of a province in favour of Cyrus, the Younger, brother of Artaxerxes II, he denounced him to Artaxerxes, for whom he fought and won the Battle of Cunaxa (401). He then murdered the leaders of the Greeks, including Cyrus, and harassed Xenophon and the 10,000 Greek mercenaries who had fought in the battle. Satrap from 413, he was himself defeated by Agesilaus in the war with Sparta, and murdered for the murder of Cyrus on the orders of Artaxerxes.

Tissot, James Joseph Jacques 1836–1902

French painter

Born in Nantes, he studied in Paris, where he was influenced by Degas, and after the fall of the Commune took refuge in London in 1871–82, where he did caricatures for *Vanity Fair*, and painted fashionable social occasions, such as *The Ball on Shipboard* (1874, Tate Gallery, London). He was, however, isolated from society when he became involved with a divorcée, returning to Paris when she died in 1882. In London his views of the River Thames earned him the title 'the Watteau of Wapping'. Travelling to Palestine in 1886, he produced a series of 300 watercolours of the life of Christ, but his portraits of Victorian life remain his best known work. ▢ Henri Zerner et al, *James Joseph Jacques Tissot, 1836-1902* (1968)

Titchener, Edward Bradford 1867–1927

US psychologist

Born in Chichester, England, he studied at Oxford and Leipzig before going to the USA in 1892 to Cornell University. A follower of Wilhelm Wundt, under whose influence he had come in Leipzig, he became the great exponent of experimental psychology in the USA, founding the Society of Experimental Psychologists in 1904. He wrote many scholarly works on the subject, including *Experimental Psychology* (4 vols, 1901–05), *Psychology of Feeling and Attention* (1908) and *Experimental Psychology of the Thought Processes* (1909).

Titian See panel p1833

Titmus, Fred(erick John) 1932–

English cricketer

Titian, *properly* Tiziano Vecellio c.1488–1576
Venetian painter, one of the greatest artists of the Renaissance

Titian was born in Pieve di Cadore in the Friulian Alps. He lived from the age of 10 with an uncle in Venice and studied under the mosaicists there, becoming a pupil of **Giovanni Bellini** and **Giorgione**. Bellini's influence is apparent in such early works as *Bishop Pesaro before St Peter* (c.1505). Titian assisted Giorgione with the paintings for the Fondaco dei Tedeschi (1508) and completed many of the works left unfinished at his death, for example *Noli me tangere* (c.1510) and the *Sleeping Venus* (c.1510), which was to serve as a model for Titian's more naturalistic *Venus of Urbino* (1538).

Giorgione continued to be the chief influence on Titian's work. The first works definitely attributable to Titian alone are the three frescoes of scenes in the life of St Anthony at Padua (1511), the pastoral setting of *The Three Ages of Man* (c.1515) and the masterly fusion of romantic realism and classical idealism achieved in his *Sacred and Profane Love* (c.1515). After 1516 restrained postures and colouring give way to dynamic compositions in which bright colours are contrasted, and the classical intellectual approach gives way to sensuous, full-blooded treatment. *Assumption of the Virgin* (1516–18), *Madonna of the Pesaro Family* (1519–26), both in the Frari, Venice, and *St Peter Martyr* (destroyed in 1867) exemplify the beginnings of Titian's own revolutionary style.

For the Duke of Ferrara he painted three great mythological subjects, *Feast of Venus* (c.1515–18), *Bacchanal* (c.1518) and the richly coloured exuberant masterpiece *Bacchus and Ariadne* (1523). In sharp contrast is the finely modelled historical picture, *Presentation of the Virgin* (1534–38). In 1530 he met the Emperor **Charles V**, of whom he painted many portraits, including the striking equestrian *Charles V at the Battle of Mühlberg* (1548), and also the portraits of many notables assembled for the Augsburg peace conference, and was ennobled.

To this period also belongs *Ecce Homo* (1543), and portraits of the Farnese family including Pope **Paul III** and his nephews (1545–46), painted on Titian's first visit to Rome. The impact of the art collections there is reflected in a new sculptural treatment of the *Danae* (1545). For **Philip II** of Spain he executed a remarkable series of mythological scenes, to which belong *Diana and Actaeon* (1559) and *Diana and Callisto* (1559) and *Perseus and Andromeda* (c.1556). To the poignant religious and mythological subjects of his last years belong *The Fall of Man* (c.1570), *The Entombment* (1565), *Christ Crowned with Thorns* (c.1570), *Madonna Suckling the Child* (1570–76), *Lucrezia and Tarquinius* (c.1570) and the unfinished *Pietà* (1573–76).

Titian was ceremoniously buried in the church of S Maria dei Frari, Venice. He revolutionized techniques in oil, and has been described as the founder of modern painting. His influence on later artists, including **Tintoretto**, **Rubens**, **Velázquez**, **Nicolas Poussin**, **Anthony Van Dyck** and **Antoine Watteau**, was profound.

□ C Hope, *Titian* (1980); H E Wethey, *The Paintings of Titian* (2 vols, 1969–71).

'Nobody cares much at heart about Titian; only there is a strange undercurrent of everlasting murmur about his name, which means the deep consent of all great men that he is greater than they.' **John Ruskin**, in *The Two Paths*, lecture 2 (1859).

He was born in London. Although primarily an off-spin bowler who took 153 wickets in 53 Tests, he also scored 1,449 Test runs. In a long career, he first played for Middlesex in 1949. His last appearance was in 1981. He took 2,830 wickets, all in first-class matches, taking 100 wickets in a season on no fewer than 16 occasions.

Tito, *originally* Josip Broz, *also called* Marshal Tito
1892–1980
Yugoslav leader

He was born near Klanjec, in Croatia. In World War I he served with the Austro-Hungarian Army, and, taken prisoner by the Russians, he adopted Communism and took part in the 1917 Revolution. In 1928 he was imprisoned in Yugoslavia for conspiring against the regime. In mid-1941 he organized partisan forces against the Axis conquerors of his country. He contrived to discredit utterly the rival partisan leader, **Draza Mihailovich**, in Anglo-American eyes and win support in arms and material solely for himself. In 1943 Tito established a provisional government at liberated Jajce in Bosnia, and following the expulsion of the remaining Axis forces, a new Yugoslav Federal Republic was declared in 1945. Effectively one-party politics followed, establishing the dominance of the Communist Party, with Tito serving as Prime Minister and, from 1953, as President. In 1948 the new Federal Republic broke with the Cominform (Communist Information Bureau) as a result of growing policy differences, **Stalin** viewing the successful system of decentralized profit-sharing workers' councils introduced by Tito as dangerously 'revisionist'. Thereafter, Tito became a leader of the non-aligned movement, pursuing a policy of 'positive neutralism'. He was made President-for-Life in 1974 and proceeded to establish a unique system of collective, rotating leadership within the country during his later years. □ Phyllis Auty, *Tito* (1970)

Titterton, Sir Ernest William 1916–90
English atomic physicist

Born in Tamworth, Staffordshire, and educated at Birmingham University, he was a research officer for the Admiralty during World War II, before becoming in 1943 a member of the British mission to the USA to participate in the Manhattan Project to develop the atomic bomb. He held a senior role at the first atomic test in 1945, and was adviser on instrumentation at the Bikini Atoll tests in 1946, before returning to Los Alamos, New Mexico, as head of the electronics division until 1947. He then worked at the Atomic Energy Research Establishment at Harwell until 1950 when he became Professor of Nuclear Physics at the Australian National University, Canberra. He was involved in the British nuclear tests at Maralinga, South Australia, until 1957, and subsequently held various research and advisory appointments in the field of nuclear energy. He was knighted in 1970.

Titus 1st century AD
Greek Christian

He was a companion of the Apostle **Paul**. He remained uncircumcized, an important factor in the Church's acceptance of Gentiles. Ecclesiastical tradition makes Titus 'Bishop' of Crete.

Titus, Flavius Sabinus Vespasianus AD39–81
Roman emperor

The eldest son of **Vespasian**, on his father's accession to the throne (AD69) he ended the Jewish war and captured Jerusalem (70). He had a liaison with **Berenice**, sister of **Herod Agrippa II**, and she accompanied him to Rome. There, however, the liaison between the son of the emperor and a Jewess was disapproved of, and he dismissed her. When he assumed power in 79, he put a stop to treason trials, and heavily punished informers. Handsome, cultivated and universally popular in Rome, he completed the Colosseum, built baths, and lavished his generosity upon the sufferers from the eruption of Vesuvius (79), the three days' fire at Rome, and the pestilence. He died suddenly, but the suspicion that he had been poisoned by his brother and successor, **Domitian**, was probably unfounded. ▢ B W Henderson, *Five Roman Emperors* (1927)

Tizard, Dame Catherine Anne 1931–
New Zealand politician

Born in Auckland, she was a tutor in zoology at the University of Auckland for 20 years (1963–83), and a member of Auckland City Council from 1971 to 1983, in which year she was elected the first Labour Mayor of Auckland. She resigned in 1990 on her appointment as New Zealand's first woman Governor-General, a position she held until 1996. She has been active in most areas of public life, especially health, child care, education, the environment and the arts. During her term as Mayor, Auckland's Aotea Centre for the Performing Arts was completed, and she was appointed DBE in 1984. She was married to the Rt Hon Bob Tizard PC (1924–), former deputy Prime Minister of New Zealand; their daughter Judith NgaireTizard (1956–) was elected Labour MP for Panmure (1990–96).

Tizard, Sir HenryThomas 1885–1959
English chemist and administrator

Born in Gillingham, Kent, he studied chemistry at Magdalen College, Oxford, and worked with **Walther Hermann Nernst** in Berlin (1908–09). Returning to Oxford, he was soon appointed Fellow and Tutor of Oriel College, but within a few years his career was interrupted by World War I, and from 1918 to 1919 he was assistant controller of experiments and research for the RAF. He returned to Oxford and became Reader in Thermodynamics, but soon left to become assistant secretary of the department of scientific and industrial research, of which he became permanent secretary in 1927. From 1929 to 1942 he was Rector of Imperial College and from 1942 to 1946 he was president of Magdalen College, Oxford. He then became chairman of the Defence Policy Research Committee and of the Advisory Council on Scientific Policy, from which he retired in 1952. His personal scientific work included some electrochemistry before 1914 and important work on aircraft fuels carried out with David Pye around 1920, which led ultimately to the system of octane rating, which expresses the anti-knocking characteristics of a fuel. In the 1930s and 1940s he was increasingly involved as an adviser to the British Government in the scientific aspects of air defence, particularly in connection with radar. He was chairman of the Aeronautical Research Committee from 1933 to 1943 and led a scientific mission to the USA in 1940. His influence probably made the difference between victory and defeat in the Battle of Britain in 1940. He received many military honours and was elected FRS in 1926.

Tobias, Phillip Vallentine 1925–
South African anatomist and physical anthropologist

Born in Durban, he studied at Witwatersrand University where he has remained nearly all his life, becoming a lecturer in anatomy in 1951 and Professor of Anatomy and Human Biology in 1959. Since 1966 he has been director of the Palaeoanthropological Research Unit, and Honorary Professorial Research Fellow since 1993. He has worked on cytogenetics and human genetics, the human biology of the living peoples of Africa, and palaeoanthropology. He has studied and described hominid fossils in many parts of Africa, and with **Louis Leakey** and J R Napier he described and named the species *Homo habilis*. His many publications include *Australopithecus (Zinjanthropus) boisei* (1967), *The Brain in Hominid Evolution* (1971) and a two-volume work on *Homo habilis* (1991).

Tobin, James 1918–
US economist and Nobel Prize winner

Born in Champaign, Illinois, he was educated at Harvard and, following wartime service in the US navy, went on to teach there. He became a professor at Yale (1955–88) and in 1981 he won the Nobel Prize for economics, primarily for his portfolio selection theory of investment. Recent publications include *Full Employment and Growth* (1996) and *Money Credit and Capital* (1997).

Tocqueville, Alexis Charles Henri Maurice Clérel de 1805–59
French historian and political scientist

Born in Verneuil, he was called to the Bar in 1825 and became assistant-magistrate at Versailles. In 1831 he went to the USA to report on the prison system, and on his return published a penetrating political study, *De la démocratie en Amérique* (1835, 'Democracy in America'), that made his name in Europe. He paid his first visit to England in 1833 and kept an extensive diary of his *Journeys to England and Ireland*. He became a member of the Chamber of Deputies (1839), and in 1849 was Vice-President of the Assembly, and briefly Minister of Foreign Affairs. After **Napoleon III**'s coup d'état he retired to his estate, where he wrote the first volume of *L'Ancien Régime et la Révolution* (1856, 'The Old Regime and the Revolution'), but he died before another volume could be completed. ▢ J P Mayer, *Alexis de Tocqueville: A Biographical Essay in Political Science* (rev edn, 1960)

Todd (of Trumpington), Alexander Robertus Todd, Baron 1907–97
Scottish chemist and Nobel Prize winner

Born in Glasgow, he studied at the University of Glasgow and obtained his first doctorate at Frankfurt on the chemistry of bile acids in 1931. He was awarded an 1851 Exhibition Senior Studentship and worked with **Robert Robinson** at Oxford for a second doctorate on the chemistry of natural pigments (1933). He spent two years in the medical chemistry department in Edinburgh, working on the chemistry of vitamin B, and then moved to the Lister Institute of Preventive Medicine in London. He held the chair of organic chemistry at Manchester from 1938 to 1944. His final post was as professor at Cambridge, where he remained until his retirement in 1971. All his research concerned the chemistry of natural products. However, the work for which he was awarded the Nobel Prize for chemistry in 1957 concerned the structure and synthesis of nucleotides, which was a necessary preliminary to **Francis Crick** and **James Watson**'s proposal of the double helix as the structure of DNA. Todd was elected to the Royal Society in 1942 and was later its president (1975–80). He was knighted in 1954 and was awarded the Order of Merit and made a Life Peer in 1977. He was also the first Chancellor of Strathclyde University (1965–91), where he was a Fellow (1990–96). A man of strong personality, he was known affectionately at Cambridge as Todd Almighty, later Lord Todd Almighty. As a trustee of various charities and as a member of many government committees, he played a substantial part in promoting scientific activity both in Great Britain and abroad. ▢ *A Time to Remember: The Autobiography of a Chemist* (1983)

Todd, Sir (Reginald Stephen) Garfield 1908–92
Rhodesian politician

Born in New Zealand, he was educated there and in South Africa. Having gone to Southern Rhodesia in 1934 as a missionary, he was elected to the Legislative Assembly (1946) and then to the leadership of the United Rhodesia Party (1953) which made him Prime Minister of Southern Rhodesia. He was removed from the leadership by an internal putsch because of his liberalism and he helped form the overtly liberal Central African Party in

1959. After the party's failure in 1962, he returned to farming but remained the spokesman for white liberalism in the country, as a result of which he was restricted by the Rhodesian Front (RF) government under Ian Smith (1965–66, 1972–76). A close friend and ally of Joshua Nkomo, he supported the latter in the 1980 elections.

Todd, Mike (Michael), *originally* Avrom Hirsh Goldbogen 1909–58
US showman

Born in Minneapolis, Minnesota, the son of a poor rabbi, he started life as a fairground attendant at the age of nine, but was already making his first fortune at 14 in sales promotion. In 1927 he went to Hollywood as a sound-proofing expert, staged a real 'Flame Dance' spectacle at the Chicago World Fair (1933), which was later followed by plays, musical comedies and films, including a jazz version of Gilbert and Sullivan, *The Hot Mikado* (1939), and an up-to-date *Hamlet* (1945). He perfected the three-dimensional film with Lowell Thomas and sponsored the 'TODD-AO' wide-screen process, by which his best film, Jules Verne's *Around the World in 80 Days* (1956), was made and presented, winning him an Academy Award. He married his third wife, the film actress Elizabeth Taylor, in 1957. He was killed in an air crash over New Mexico the following year.

Todd, Ron (ald) 1927–
English trade union leader

He was born in Walthamstow, London, the son of a market trader. After serving in the Far East with the Royal Marine commandos, he joined the Ford Motor Company in 1954 as a line-worker and became a member of the country's largest trade union, the TGWU (Transport and General Workers' Union). He rose steadily from shop steward up to district officer, regional secretary and then national organizer, before becoming general secretary (1985–92). A hardworking, skilled and trusted negotiator with a direct oratorical style, Todd won the Union's leadership with strong left-wing support. Although he was viewed as a staunch supporter of the then Labour Party leader Neil Kinnock, on many economic and social issues his Union's and his own personal commitment to unilateral nuclear disarmament led to strains in the TGWU–Labour relationship.

Todd, Sweeney late 18th century
English alleged murderer

Known as the 'Demon Barber of Fleet Street', he supposedly carried out his murders in 1780s London. It has never been proved that he did in fact exist, although his story is well-known. Using a revolving floor which had a barber's chair on each side of it, he is claimed to have swung unsuspecting clients into his cellar via the trap and then cut their throats. Their bodies were carried through a series of underground passages to a nearby bakery. There, Mrs Lovett is said to have used human flesh in her meat pies. The name of Sweeney Todd, also nicknamed 'Old Cut 'Em Up', first appeared in a story, *The String of Pearls*, which was serialized in 1846 in a penny newspaper, *The People's Periodical and Family Library*. This substantiates the notion that Todd was never more than fiction, but it has been argued that his character was based on real murderers. Sawney Bean, a Scottish cannibal, may have been the source of the London tale, as may a French murderer who operated in Paris in 1800.

Todi, Jacopone da c.1230–1306
Italian religious poet

Born in Todi, Spoleto, he practised as an advocate, was converted to an ascetic life in 1268 and became a Franciscan lay brother in 1278. He was imprisoned (1298–1303) for satirizing Pope Boniface VIII. The authorship of the *Stabat Mater* and other Latin hymns is attributed to

him, and he also wrote *laudi spirituale* ('spiritual praises'), which became important in the development of Italian drama.

Todt, Fritz 1891–1942
German engineer

Born in Pforzheim, he was Hitler's inspector of German roads (1933) and was responsible for the construction of the Reichsautobahnen (the motorway system). The 'Todt Organization' was also responsible for the construction of the Siegfried Line (1937). Nazi Minister for Armaments (1940), and Minister for Fuel and Power (1941), he was killed in an air crash.

Togliatti, Palmiro 1893–1964
Italian politician

A member of the Italian Socialist Party in 1914, he was one of the founders of the Italian Communist Party (PCI) in 1921. Forced to flee Italy by the Fascists in 1926, he organized the activities of the party from abroad and was part of the Comintern secretariat in charge of Communists fighting in the Spanish Civil War. He returned to Italy in 1944 and played a key part in the coalition governments that controlled Italy until 1947. Until his death (while visiting Nikita Khrushchev in Yalta), he was Party Secretary, presiding over the PCI's development from a relatively small group of militants into the largest Communist organization in the West.

Togo, *later* Count Heihachiro Togo 1848–1934
Japanese naval commander

He was born in Kagoshima, which was bombarded by British warships in 1863. He was educated at the Naval Academy, Etajima, and in the nautical training ship HMS *Worcester* at Greenhithe, England (1871). He served against China (1894) and was Commander-in-Chief during the Russian war (1904–05). He bombarded Port Arthur, and defeated the Russian fleet at Tsushima in 1905. He was awarded the British Order of Merit (1906), and created count (1907).

Tojo, Hideki 1885–1948
Japanese soldier

Born in Tokyo, in 1919 he was appointed military attaché in Germany. He served with the Kwantung army in Manchuria as Chief of the Secret Police and Chief of Staff from 1937 to 1940. He became Minister of War (1940–41) and from 1941 he was premier and dictator of Japan, resigning in 1944. Arrested, he attempted and failed to commit suicide. He was sentenced to death in 1948. 📖 Courtney Browne, *Tojo: The Last Banzai* (1967)

Tokugawa
Dynasty of 15 Japanese shoguns

They were the effective rulers of Japan for two and a half centuries. Ieyasu (d.1616) became an ally of the warlord Nobunaga whose policy of unification he supported, but later a power struggle resulted in civil war. Ieyasu won and was appointed shogun (generalissimo) by the emperor (1603). He remained in practice the national leader of Japan until his death. His grandson, Iemitsu (shogun 1623–51), passed the three Expulsion decrees (1633–39); aimed at the suppression of Christianity, they effectively closed Japan to foreign trade. Yoshimune (1716–45) drew up the Code of One Hundred Articles, embodying the Tokugawa legal reforms. Thereafter the shogunate lost much of its vigour although it did not finally come to an end until 1867 with the resignation of Hitotsubashi Keiki, the 15th shogun.

Tolbukhin, Fyodor Ivanovich 1885–1949
Russian marshal

Born in the Caucasus region, he joined the army after leaving school and saw service as a captain during World War I. Following the Russian Revolution in 1917 he was sent to the newly formed Frunze Military Academy and was one of the senior officers responsible for modernizing the Red Army. During World War II he commanded Soviet forces in the war against Germany in the Crimea and, later, in the Ukraine. In 1944 he was appointed chairman of the Allied Control Commission in Bulgaria and until he retired in 1947 he was Marshal of the Soviet Union's Southern Group of armies.

Tolkien, J(ohn) R(onald) R(euel) 1892–1973
British philologist and writer

Born in Bloemfontein, South Africa, he was educated at King Edward VI School, Birmingham, and at Merton College, Oxford, and became Professor of Anglo-Saxon there (1925–45), and of English Language and Literature (1945–59). His scholarly publications include an edition of *Sir Gawain and the Green Knight* (1925), and studies on Chaucer (1934) and *Beowulf* (1937). His interest in language and saga and his fascination for the land of Faerie prompted him to write tales of a world of his own invention peopled by strange beings with their own carefully constructed language and mythology. These include *The Hobbit* (1937), a fascinating tale of the perilous journey of Bilbo Baggins to recover treasure from the sly dragon Smaug, and the more complex sequel, *The Lord of the Rings* (3 vols, 1954–55), in which Bilbo's nephew, Frodo, sets out to destroy a powerful but dangerous ring in Mordor, the land of darkness and evil. Later works include *The Adventure of Tom Bombadil* (1962), *Smith of Wootton Major* (1967) and *The Silmarillion* (posthumous, 1977). ⌂ C R Stimpson, *J. R. R. Tolkien* (1970)

Tollens, Hendrik 1780–1856
Dutch poet

Born in Rotterdam, he was author of the Dutch national hymn (until the 20th century), *Wien Neerlandsch Bloed*. He also wrote comedies, a tragedy, romances and ballads. ⌂ G D J Schotch, *Tollens e zijn tid* (1860)

Tolman, Edward C(hace) 1886–1959
US psychologist

Born in West Newton, Massachusetts, he was educated at the Massachusetts Institute of Technology (MIT), Harvard and Yale. After a short spell of teaching at Northwestern University, he taught at the University of California at Berkeley (1918–54). With his first book, *Purposive Behavior in Animals and Men* (1932), he broke with the prevailing Behaviourist tradition, and attempted to introduce explanatory ideas into animal psychology which were widely dismissed as 'mentalistic'. He argued the need to postulate purpose ('goals'), as well as spatial representations ('cognitive maps') in the minds of animals in order fully to explain their behaviour. It was not sufficient, he believed, to rely entirely on passive associations as the basis for all learning. His ideas are now more acceptable in academic psychology, largely as a result of the realization that machines (for example guided missiles) can behave as if they have goals, and also because there is clear evidence that brain damage can cause selective disorders in such capacities as planning and spatial orientation, without affecting simple learning abilities.

Tolstoy, Count Aleksei Konstantinovich 1817–75
Russian dramatist, lyrical poet and novelist

He was born in St Petersburg, and was distantly related to Leo Tolstoy. He was a prominent court figure and travelled often to western Europe. He wrote a historical trilogy in verse (1867, Eng trans *The Death of Ivan the Terrible*, 1869), *Tsar Fyodor Ioannovich* (1868, Eng trans 1874) and *Tsar Boris* (1870), but only the first work was staged in his lifetime. His other works include nonsense verse and a historical novel, *Prince Serebrenni* (1863, Eng trans 1874). ⌂ M Dalton, *Alexey Konstantinovich Tolstoy* (1972)

Tolstoy, Count Aleksei Nikolayevich 1882–1945
Russian writer

He was born in Nikolayevsk, Samara, a distant relation of Leo Tolstoy. He joined the White Army after the 1917 Revolution, which he portrayed vividly in the novel *Khozhdenie po mukam* (1920, Eng trans *Darkness and Dawn*, 1935), and was an émigré in Paris (1919–23), but returned to Russia as an established writer. His other novels include *Khromoi barin* (1912, Eng trans *The Lame Prince*, 1912). ⌂ Y Krestinsky, *Alexey Nicolayevich Tolstoy* (1960)

Tolstoy, Count Leo Nikolayevich See panel p1837

Tomba, Alberto, *nicknamed* La Bomba 1966–
Italian alpine skier

Born in Bologna, he became the superstar of skiing, characteristically winning from seemingly impossible positions. He regularly attracted thousands of chanting Italian fans to watch his phenomenal final runs. In his determination to win he could make costly mistakes but always seemed able to make up the time. His many victories include being world champion (1996), Olympic champion (1988, 1992) and World Cup champion (1995). The last-mentioned was all the more remarkable as he competed in only half the disciplines, having been stopped from skiing the downhill by his concerned mother.

Tombalbaye, N'Garta, *originally* François Tombalbaye 1918–75
Chadian politician

He was a teacher before becoming a trade union organizer. He then helped to organize the Rassemblement Démocratique Africaine (RDA) in Chad in 1947 and was elected to the territorial assembly (1953). He rose to be Prime Minister in 1959 and then President on Chad's independence in 1962. He remained in this position until the military coup of 1975, during which he was killed.

Tombaugh, Clyde William 1906–
US astronomer

He was born in Streator, Illinois. Too poor to attend college, he built his own telescope, and in 1929 became an assistant at the Lowell Observatory. In 1933 he won a scholarship to the University of Kansas and received an MA in 1936. Percival Lowell had predicted the existence of an outermost planet, which he had named Planet X, from his estimates of the perturbation of the orbits of Uranus and Neptune. Tombaugh joined the search team that was run by Vesto Melvin Slipher, who was director of Lowell Observatory from 1926. Tombaugh devised the blink comparator which enabled him to detect if anything had moved in the sky between the taking of two celestial photographs, a few days apart. In 1930, he discovered Pluto in the constellation of Gemini. It was too faint to be the expected Planet X, and he spent another eight years looking, without success. In 1946 he became astronomer at the Aberdeen Ballistics Laboratories in New Mexico and was later appointed astronomer (1955–59), associate professor (1961–65) and professor (1965–73, now emeritus) at New Mexico University.

Tomkins, Thomas 1572–1656
English composer and organist

Born in St David's, Dyfed, Wales, where his father was organist, he studied under William Byrd. In his early twenties he became organist of Worcester Cathedral, where he spent most of his life. In 1621 he was appointed one of the organists of the Chapel Royal, and composed music for the coronation of Charles I five years later. His compositions include a great amount of church music, madrigals, part-songs and instrumental works. He had four brothers who were all accomplished musicians.

Tolstoy, Count Leo Nikolayevich 1828–1910
Russian writer, aesthetic philosopher, moralist and mystic

Tolstoy was born on the family estate of Yasnaya Polyana in Tula province, and was educated privately. He read law and oriental languages at Kazan University, but returned to his estate, which he inherited in 1847, without graduating. According to his own account, the young Tolstoy led a dissolute life in town and played the gentleman farmer. Finally, in 1851, he accompanied his elder brother Nikolai to the Caucasus, where he joined an artillery regiment and there began his literary career. His first published work, *Istoria vcherashchnevo dnya* (1851, 'An Account of Yesterday'), was followed by the remarkable autobiographical trilogy *Detstvo* (1852, 'Childhood'), *Otrochestvo* (1854, 'Boyhood') and *Yunost* (1856, 'Youth').

He received a commission at the outbreak of the Crimean War (1854), and commanded a battery during the defence of Sebastopol (1854–55). The horrors of war inspired *Tales of Army Life* and *Sevastopolskiye rasskazy* (1855–56, Eng trans *Sebastopol*, 1887), sketches which show the influence of **Stendhal**; afterwards he left the army, was welcomed into the literary circle in St Petersburg (1856), and travelled abroad. In 1862 he married Sophie Andreyevna Behrs and settled into domestic life, raising a family of 13 children.

He settled on his Volga estate, devoting himself to the duties of a progressive landlord and to writing his greatest work, *Voinya i mir* (1863–69, Eng trans *War and Peace*, 1866). This is both an epic and a domestic tale, a depiction of Russia's struggle, defeat and victory over **Napoleon I**, set against the fortunes of two notable families, the Rostovs and the Bolkonskis. The proud, shy, duty-conscious Prince Andrew and the direct, friendly, pleasure-loving but introspective, morally questing Pierre reflect the dualism in Tolstoy's own character. On his vivid description of military life Tolstoy mounts his conception of history, which demotes great men to mere creatures of circumstance and ascribes victory in battle to the confused chance events which make up the unpredictable fortunes of war. In Pierre's association with freemasonry, Tolstoy expressed his criticism of the established autocratic order.

His second great work, *Anna Karenina* (1874–76), in which the passion felt by a married woman for a young army officer has tragic consequences for her, stems from Tolstoy's personal crisis between the claims of the creative novelist and the propagation of his own ethical code. This conflict found further expression in *Ispoved'* (1884, Eng trans *A Confession*, 1885) and the dialectical pamphlets and stories such as *Smert' Ivana Ilicha* (1886, Eng trans

The Death of Ivan Ilyitch, 1887), *Kreutserova sonata* (1889, Eng trans *The Kreutzer Sonata*, 1890) and *V chom moya vera?* (1884, Eng trans *My Religion*, 1885). Christianity is purged of its mysticism and transformed into a severe asceticism based on the doctrine of non-resistance to evil. Other works in this vein, *Tsarstvo Bozhye vnutri vas* (2 vols, 1893–94, Eng trans *The Kingdom of God is within You*, 1894), *Khosyain i rabotnik* (1894, Eng trans *Master and Man*, 1895), the play *Plody prosveshcheniya* (1889, Eng trans *The Fruits of Enlightenment*, 1891) and *Voskreseniye* (1899, Eng trans *Resurrection*, 1899), were considered so unorthodox that the Holy Synod excommunicated him (1901).

In *Chto takoye iskusstvo?* (1898, Eng trans *What is Art?*, 1898) Tolstoy argued that only simple works, such as the parables of the Bible, constitute great art. Everything sophisticated, stylized and detailed, such as his own great novels, he condemned as worthless. Eventually he gave up his material possessions to his wife, who refused to participate in his asceticism, and lived as a peasant under her roof. Domestic quarrels made him leave home secretly one October night, accompanied only by his youngest daughter Alexandra and his personal physician, to seek refuge elsewhere. He died of pneumonia in a siding at Astapovo railway station, refusing to the last to see his waiting wife.

Yasnaya Polyana became a place of pilgrimage for those who subscribed to his ethical doctrines. **Mahatma Gandhi**, who had corresponded with him, adopted the doctrine of non-resistance. But Tolstoy is best known as the consummate master of the psychological novel. Many of his works were illustrated by **Boris Pasternak**'s father, Leonid.

📖 A N Wilson, *Tolstoy: A Biography* (1988); I Berlin, *The Hedgehog and the Fox: An Essay on Tolstoy's View of History* (1953); A Maude, *The Life of Tolstoy* (1910).

> 'In historical events great men—so-called—are but labels serving to give a name to the event, and like labels they have the least possible connection with the event itself.' From the opening of Book 3 of *War and Peace* (translated by Rosemary Edmonds).
>
> 'All happy families are alike but an unhappy family is unhappy after its own fashion.' The opening sentence of *Anna Karenina* (translated by Rosemary Edmonds).

Tomlin, Lily (Mary Jean) 1939–
US comedy actress

Born in Detroit, Michigan, she was a pre-med student at Detroit's Wayne State University, before dropping out to pursue a career performing in local cabaret and later moving to New York. Modestly active in all areas of showbusiness, she had her big break as part of television's *Laugh-In* (1960–72). She received an Academy Award nomination for a dramatic role in her film debut *Nashville* (1975) and her subsequent, often infrequent, film appearances include *The Late Show* (1977), *Nine To Five* (1980), *All Of Me* (1984) and *Short Cuts* (1993). Also a television performer and recording artist, her acute sense of observation was seen to its best advantage in the one-woman stage shows *Appearing Nitely* (1977) and *The Search For Signs Of Intelligent Life In The Universe* (1985–86).

Tomlinson, H(enry) M(ajor) 1873–1958
English writer

He was born in London, and worked in a shipping office in the docklands before becoming a journalist. His love of the sea is reflected in books like *The Sea and the Jungle*

(1912), *Tidemarks* (1924) and other travel books, as well as novels such as *Waiting for Daylight* (1922) and his two best-known works, *Gallions Reach* (1927) and *All Our Yesterdays* (1930), an anti-war novel about World War I. He also wrote several other novels, the autobiographical reminiscences in *A Mingled Yarn* (1953), and a biography of **Norman Douglas** (1931).

Tomonaga, Sin-Itiro 1906–79
Japanese physicist and Nobel Prize winner

Born in Kyoto, he was educated at Kyoto Imperial University where he was a classmate of **Hideki Yukawa**. After graduating (1929) Tomonaga joined Yoshio Nishina at Riken, the Institute for Physical and Chemical Research in Tokyo (1932), and during the next five years published papers on positron creation and annihilation, and one on high-energy neutrino–neutron scattering. In 1937 he moved to Leipzig in Germany to work with **Werner Heisenberg** on a model of the nucleus, returning to Riken in 1939. His most important work was a relativistic quantum description of the interaction between a photon and an electron, producing the theory of 'quantum electrodynamics' for which he shared the 1965 Nobel Prize for physics with **Richard Feynman** and **Julian Schwinger**. He was president of the Science Council of Japan (1951) and of Tokyo University (1956).

Tompion, Thomas 1639–1713
English clockmaker

Born possibly in Northill, Bedfordshire, he reputedly began his career as a furrier, but in 1664 was apprenticed to a London clockmaker and by 1704 was a master clockmaker. In 1675, under the supervision of **Robert Hooke**, he made one of the first English watches equipped with a balance spring; this was subsequently gifted to **Charles II**. In 1676 he was appointed clockmaker for the newly opened Royal Observatory. Continuing to develop watch and clockmaking techniques, he patented the cylinder escapement in 1695 (with Edward Barlow), and branched out into barometers and sundials. He was buried in Westminster Abbey, London, and was known as 'the father of English watchmaking'.

Tone, (Theobald) Wolfe 1763–98
Irish nationalist

Born in Dublin, he studied there at Trinity College, and was called to the Bar in 1789, but soon turned to politics. In 1791 he published a pamphlet, *An Argument on Behalf of the Catholics of Ireland*, and helped to found the Society of United Irishmen. In 1792 he became secretary of the Catholic Committee, which worked for the United Catholic Relief Act of 1793. In 1795 he left Ireland to avoid a charge of treason, and went (via the USA) to Paris (1796). He induced the Republican government to invade Ireland under General Lazare Hoche, but the expedition never reached Ireland. In September 1798 he embarked in a small French squadron, which after a fierce fight in Lough Swilly was captured. Tone was taken to Dublin, tried, and condemned to be hanged as a traitor, but cut his throat in prison. ⌨ Henry Boylan, *Theobald Wolfe Tone* (1981)

Tonegawa, Susumu 1939–
Japanese molecular biologist and Nobel Prize winner

Born in Nagoya, he studied chemistry at the University of Kyoto, then joined the department of biology at the University of San Diego. In 1971 he accepted an appointment at the Institute for Immunology in Basle, Switzerland. Tonegawa applied the restriction enzyme and recombinant DNA techniques to resolve the origins of antibody diversity, showing that in the formation of antibody-manufacturing cells the genes undergo changes, allowing them to produce a new wide range of antibodies. His work also provided details of the mechanism by which the genes are changed. In 1981 he returned to the USA as Professor of Biology at the Massachusetts Institute of Technology (MIT), where he has applied the techniques of molecular biology to another aspect of the immune system—the action of the T-lymphocytes. Since 1988 he has also been Howard Hughes Medical Institute Investigator. He was awarded the 1987 Nobel Prize for physiology or medicine.

Tong, Xuan See **Puyi (P'u-i)**

Tonks, Henry 1862–1937
English artist

Born in Solihull, after becoming a Fellow of the Royal College of Surgeons (1888) he gave up medicine for art. He studied under Frederick Brown, becoming his assistant at the Slade School of Art, joined the New English Art Club (1895), and was associated with **Walter Sickert** and **Philip Wilson Steer**. From 1918 to 1930 he was Slade Professor of Fine Art. He bequeathed a collection of his drawings to the Slade School.

Tonti, Lorenzo 1620–90
French banker

He was born in Naples. He proposed the tontine or latest-survivor system of life insurance.

Tooke, John Horne, *originally* **John Horne** 1736–1812
English radical politician

Born in Westminster, London, the son of a poulterer called Horne, he was educated at Eton and Cambridge. He entered the Middle Temple but, to please his father, left to become vicar of New Brentford. Travelling as a tutor, he met **John Wilkes** in Paris. While unsuccessfully trying to obtain a Commons seat, he founded the Constitutional Society which supported the American colonists and parliamentary reform (1771). He then fell out with Wilkes, and carried on an angry correspondence with him in the *Public Advertiser* (1771). In 1773 he went back to study law, and received the patronage of the rich William Tooke of Purley, who greatly admired his spirited opposition to an enclosure bill. Horne added Tooke's surname to his own in 1782, and while in prison for supporting the American rebels he wrote *The Diversions of Purley* (1786), a medley of etymology, grammar and politics. He was tried for high treason in 1794, but acquitted. He was eventually elected MP for Old Sarum in 1801.

Tooker, George Clair 1920–
US painter

Born in Brooklyn, New York City, he was of English, Dutch, Spanish and French descent. His mother was Cuban, and the theme of mixed race runs through his work, as in his *Windows* series (1955–87). He studied at Harvard and at the Art Students League in New York, where he had his first solo exhibition in 1951. His style is surreal, observing with suppressed anger the soullessness and **Kafka**esque bureaucracy of urban life, as in *Government Bureau* (1956, Museum of Modern Art, New York), *Sleepers* (1959, MOMA) and *The Waiting Room* (1959, Smithsonian Institute, Washington). A later work, *The Embrace of Peace* (1988), shows his ability to express pleasure as well as pain.

Toomer, Jean, *originally* **Nathan Eugene Toomer** 1894–1967
US writer of verse and poetic fiction

Raised in Washington DC, where his grandfather had been an influential black politician, he showed no particular academic aptitude and became a physical training instructor. His one major book was *Cane* (1923), an uncategorizable anthology of prose and verse segments which offers a haunting collage of black life in the USA. Toomer refused to align himself with the quasi-nationalism of the 'Harlem Renaissance'. His instincts were metaphysical, as can be seen from the long poem 'Blue Meridian', a passionate vision of a racially and socially harmonized America. In 1924 he went to study with **Georgei Gurdjieff** at Fontainebleau, and later founded Gurdjieff centres in the USA. He largely stopped writing after the 1940s, and *Cane* stands out as his only substantial achievement. A collection of his writings, *The Wayward and the Seeking* (1980), was edited by Darwin Turner, and his *Collected Poems* appeared as late as 1988. ⌨ N Y McKay, *Jean Toomer, Artist: A Study of his Literary Life and Work* (1984)

Toorop, Charley 1891–1955
Dutch painter

Born at Katwijk, near Leiden, to an English mother and the painter **Jan Toorop**, she spent most of her life in the artists' village of Bergen, near Alkmaar. She was a talented violinist destined for a concert career, but about 1914 she began to paint, and by the 1930s and 1940s had become a celebrated Social Realist painter. She was inspired by the grim expressiveness of **Van Gogh** and by the strength of the Cubist style. Many of her pictures are in close-up, showing the influence of German and Russian films, as in *Cheese Market in Alkmaar* (1933, Stedelijk Museum, Amsterdam), *Clown in Ruins* (1941, Otterlo) and *Three Generations* (1941–50, Rotterdam). Her self portraits mercilessly record the ageing process.

Toorop, Jan 1858–1928
Dutch painter
Born in Poerworedjo, Java, of Indonesian descent, he spent his early years on the island of Banka, south-east of Sumatra, before studying in Amsterdam and Brussels. After a long stay in England, where he met James McNeill Whistler and William Morris, he married an English woman, Annie Hall, in 1886, and in 1891 their daughter Charley Toorop was born. At this time he was painting Impressionist portraits, including a triple portrait of the Hall sisters entitled *Trio Fleuri* (1885–86, The Hague). He also painted in a Divisionist (Pointilliste) style until 1908, as in *In the Dunes* (1903, Otterlo), but from the 1890s, under the influence of the Rosicrucians, he turned increasingly to Symbolism. Later work includes *The Three Brides* (1893, Otterlo), *Charley at the Window* (1898, The Hague) and *Pablo Casals* (1904, Rotterdam).

Topelius, Zacharias Sakari 1818–98
Finnish novelist and scholar
Born in Unsikaarlepyy, Russian Finland, he studied at Helsinki, and became editor of the newspaper *Helsingfors Tidningar* (1842–78). He was appointed Professor of Finnish History at Helsinki (1854–78) and Rector (1875–78). He wrote in Swedish, and is regarded as the father of the Finnish historical novel, for his stories of life in the 17th and 18th centuries, published as *Fältskärns berättelser* (1853–67, Eng trans *The Surgeon's Stories*, 1883–84). He also published five volumes of lyrical poetry and wrote some plays. 📖 V Vasenius, *Zacharias Topelius* (6 vols, 1912–56)

Toplady, Augustus Montague 1740–78
English clergyman and hymnwriter
Born in Farnham, Surrey, he was educated at Westminster and Trinity College, Dublin. In 1768 he became vicar of Broad Hembury, Devon, and in 1775 preacher in a chapel near Leicester Fields, London. A strenuous defender of Calvinism, he was a bitter controversialist. He wrote the well-known hymn, 'Rock of Ages' (1775). In 1759 he published *Poems on Sacred Subjects. Psalms and Hymns* (1776), a collection, contained only a few of his own verses.

Topolski, Feliks 1907–89
British painter, draughtsman and illustrator
Born in Poland, he studied at Warsaw, and in Italy and Paris, and went to England in 1935. From 1940 to 1945 he was an official war artist, and he was naturalized in 1947. His lively and sensitive drawings, depicting everyday life, appeared in books and periodicals, and he also designed for the theatre. His publications include *Topolski's Chronicle* (1953–79, 1982–89), a draughtsman's record of life in various countries, *Face to Face* (1964), *Shem, Ham and Japheth Inc.* (1971) and *Topolski's Panoramas* (1981). His large paintings include the mural *The Coronation of Elizabeth II*, which is housed in Buckingham Palace.

Torga, Miguel, *pseudonym of* Alfredo Rocha 1907–90
Portuguese poet, dramatist, novelist, essayist and diarist
He was for many years a doctor in Coimbra, and one of Portugal's most widely read and prolific writers, with several Nobel Prize nominations. He wrote poems and essays, published in his diary from 1941, but his most popular book was *Bichos* (1940, Eng trans *Farruscio the Blackbird*, 1951), the first of a series of animal–human fables. His writing, like the novel *Vindima* (1945), is pessimistic and his poetry is atheistic.

Tormé, Mel(vin Howard) 1925–
US jazz and popular singer, songwriter, arranger and novelist
Born in Chicago, he studied piano and drums as a youngster, and cut his professional teeth touring with Chico Marx in 1943, then led his own pop group, The Mel-Tones. He worked as an arranger after leaving the army in 1946, and began to build his reputation as a sophisticated singer of both jazz and pop music. His soft, slightly husky voice earned him the unwelcome nickname of 'The Velvet Fog', but his impeccable control of phrasing, pitch and expression are much admired by musicians. He has recorded classic albums with arranger Marty Paitch throughout his career, and has worked regularly with pianist George Shearing from the early 1980s. He has written hundreds of songs, as well as novels and books on music, including an autobiography, and a biography of drummer Buddy Rich, and has also both acted and produced for television. 📖 *It Wasn't All Velvet* (1988)

Torquemada, Tomás de 1420–98
Spanish Dominican monk, and the first Inquisitor-General of Spain
Born in Valladolid, he entered the Dominican Order, was later appointed prior of the Convent of Santa Cruz in Segovia, and at about the same time was chosen to be a confessor of Isabella of Castile and Ferdinand, the Catholic (1474). In 1482 he was appointed as one of the seven new inquisitors to continue the work of the recently founded (1480) Inquisition. In 1483 he was chosen to head it as Inquisitor-General, and played a key role in forcing through the introduction of the new Inquisition in the realms of the Crown of Aragon. No evidence exists for attributing to Torquemada the evidently anti-Semitic philosophy of the early Inquisition, or responsibility for its excesses, but it is unquestionable that he was a major force behind the expulsion of the Jews from Spain in 1492, as well as being responsible for around 2,000 burnings. 📖 Thomas Hope, *Torquemada* (1939)

Torrance, Sam 1953–
Scottish golfer
Born in Largs, Ayrshire, he turned professional in 1970, and has been Scottish professional champion four times. He was a regular tournament winner throughout the early 1980s, winning titles such as the Australian PGA (1980), the Spanish Open (1982) and the Benson and Hedges International (1984). The greatest moment of his career, however, came in 1985, when he sank the putt which won the Ryder Cup for Britain and Europe. Latterly, with his career suffering due to bad putting, he took to using an extraordinary 48-inch putter. His father Bob is a leading authority on golf.

Torrance, Thomas Forsyth 1913–
Scottish theologian
Born of missionary parents in Chengtu, Szechwan, western China, he was Professor of Dogmatics at New College, Edinburgh (1952–79), Moderator of the Church of Scotland General Assembly (1976–77), and winner of the Templeton prize (1978). Drawing on the Greek Fathers and Karl Barth, he holds that while much recent theology mirrors an outdated model of detached and objective scientific investigation, post-Einsteinian science is open-ended, responding to the reality it encounters. Theology, therefore, should abandon its preconceptions and do the same, both in relation to science and in the quest for an acceptable ecumenical theology. His views have been expounded in many books including *Theological Science* (1969), *Theology in Reconciliation* (1975), *Divine and Contingent Order* (1981), *The Trinitarian Faith* (1988), *Divine Meaning* (1995) and *Scottish Theology* (1996).

Torrens, Sir Robert Richard 1814–86

Australian legal reformer

A Collector of Customs (1841) and Colonial Treasurer and Registrar General of South Australia (1852), he became an official member of the Legislative Council. Leading a movement for reform of titles to land, he sponsored the Real Property Act of 1857 which introduced the Torrens system, whereby title to land was secured by registration. He became first Registrar-General under the new system, which was widely adopted in Australia, New Zealand and in some states of the USA.

Torres, Luis Vaez de fl.1605–13

Spanish navigator

Though regarded as Spanish, he may have been born in Brittany. He was a military man by training and was in charge of landing parties to quell native opposition. He commanded one of three ships under **Pedro Fernandez de Quiros**. After parting from de Quiros, Torres sailed westward through the strait that now bears his name, between New Guinea and Australia, and sighted the tip of Cape York on the mainland of Australia, which he took to be another island. ⬚ Kelly, *Austrialia del Espiritu Santo* (1966)

Torrey, John 1796–1873

US botanist

Born in New York City, he qualified in medicine before teaching physical sciences at the West Point Military Academy. He joined the US army as assistant surgeon in 1824. He was Professor of Chemistry at West Point, and at Cornell University, before becoming Chief Assayer at the US Assay Office in New York (1854–1873). Throughout his life, his main interest was botany. He founded the New York Lyceum of Natural History, and became Emeritus Professor of Botany and Chemistry at Columbia College in 1856. He prepared several floras for North America and his collection of over 50,000 plant species formed the basis for the herbarium of the New York Botanical Gardens. The genus *Torreya* in the yew family is named after him, as well as the Torrey Botanical Club. His publications include *A Flora of the Northern and Middle Sections of the United States* (1824), *A Flora of North America* (1838–43) and *Flora of the State of New York* (1843).

Torricelli, Evangelista 1608–47

Italian physicist and mathematician

Born probably in Faenza, in 1627 he went to Rome, where he devoted himself to mathematical studies. His *Trattato del Moto* (1641) led **Galileo** to invite him to become his literary assistant, and on Galileo's death he was appointed mathematician to the grand-duke and Galileo's successor as professor to the Florentine Academy. He discovered that, because of atmospheric pressure, water will not rise above 33 feet in a suction pump. To him are owed the fundamental principles of hydromechanics, and in a letter to Ricci (1644) he gave the first description of a mercury barometer or 'torricellian tube'. He greatly improved both telescopes and microscopes, and published a large number of mathematical papers.

Torrigiano, Pietro c.1472–1522

Italian sculptor

He was born in Florence, but was forced to leave the city after he had broken the nose of his fellow-pupil **Michelangelo** in a quarrel. After working in Bologna, Siena, Rome and in the Netherlands, he went to England, where he introduced Italian Renaissance art. He executed the tombs of **Margaret Beaufort** in Westminster Abbey, London, and of her son **Henry VII** and his queen, Elizabeth of York. He later settled in Spain (c.1520), and died in the prisons of the Inquisition.

Torrijos Herrera, Omar 1929–81

Panamanian military ruler

He came to power in a military coup in 1968 and was virtual dictator of Panama until his death, instituting social and economic reforms and suppressing political opposition. Fiercely nationalistic, he denounced US control of the Panama Canal, and in 1977 he concluded the treaty that provided for the transfer of the canal to Panamanian sovereignty.

Torrington, 1st Viscount See **Byng, George**

Tortelier, Paul 1914–90

French cellist, conductor and composer

Born in Paris, he trained at the Conservatoire, and in 1931 made his debut there. His solo career began with the Concertgebouw, Amsterdam (1946), and with Sir **Thomas Beecham** in London (1947), and he subsequently toured worldwide. A leading soloist, he was also a distinguished teacher (his master-classes were televised), and a composer of cello music and of the international anthem *The Great Flag* for the United Nations Organization. His son Yan Pascal (1947–) is a conductor and violinist.

Torvill, Jayne 1957–

English ice-skater

Born in Nottingham, she started skating at the age of 10, and met **Christopher Dean** in 1975. The pair were six times British champions, World ice-dance champions (1981–84), and won the Olympic and European ice-dance titles in 1984. They received a record 136 perfect 'sixes' (the highest award a judge can give in ice-skating). Their highly acclaimed performances included an interpretation of the music from **Ravel's** *Bolero* and the musical *Barnum*. After retiring from competitive skating in 1984, she continued performing professionally with her partner in their own ice-show. In 1994 they returned to competitive ice-dancing, gaining the British and European titles, and winning the bronze medal in the Winter Olympics.

Toscanini, Arturo 1867–1957

Italian conductor

Born in Parma, he won a scholarship to the Conservatorio there at the age of nine. In 1886, while playing the cello in Rio de Janeiro, he was suddenly called upon to replace the unpopular conductor during a performance of *Aida*, which he transformed into a success. He later conducted at La Scala, Milan (1898–1908), the Metropolitan Opera House, New York (1908–15), the New York Philharmonic Orchestra (1926–36), and at the Bayreuth (1930–31) and Salzburg (1934–37) festivals. He founded and became music director of the National Broadcasting Company Symphony Orchestra of America (1937–53). Always faithful to every detail of the musical score, he was possibly the most authoritarian, yet modest, conductor of his time.

Tosti, Sir Francesco Paolo 1846–1916

British composer

Born in Ortona, Abruzzi, Italy, he became a naturalized British subject in 1906. The composer of many popular drawing-room songs, including *Good-bye* and *Mattinata*, he taught the British royal family, and was knighted in 1908.

Tottel, Richard d.1594

English printer

He worked in London and from his shop at the Star in Hand inn at Temple Bar, Fleet Street, published **Thomas More's** *Dialogue of Comfort against Tribulacion* (1553), **John Lydgate's** *The Falls of Princes* (1554), and the Earl of **Surrey's** translations of parts of the *Aeneid*. He also compiled an anthology of contemporary Elizabethan poetry, *Songes and Sonettes* (1557), containing the chief works of Surrey and

Sir **Thomas Wyatt**, which came to be known as *Tottel's Miscellany*. He was an original member of the Stationer's Company, founded in 1557.

Toulouse-Lautrec(-Monfa or Montfa), Henri (Marie Raymond) de 1864–1901
French painter and lithographer

He was born into a wealthy aristocratic family in Albi. The first child of first cousins, he had increasingly severe physical problems, skeletal deformities and dwarfism which were almost certainly hereditary, and several of his cousins (also born to first cousins, his father's sister and his mother's brother) suffered even more extreme forms of the same genetic mishap. He showed early promise as an artist, and from 1882 he studied under **Léon Bonnat** in Paris and in 1884 settled in Montmartre, the area which his paintings and posters were to make famous. His early paintings were mainly of sporting subjects. He was later influenced by his contact with the Impressionists and Post-Impressionists, notably by **Degas**, but whereas Degas painted the world of ballet from a ballet-lover's theatrical point of view, Lautrec's studies of the cabaret stars, the prostitutes, the barmaids, the clowns and actors of Montmartre reveal an unfailing interest in the human being behind the purely professional function as in *The Two Friends* (1894, Tate Gallery, London), *Jane Avril dansant* (c.1892) and *La Clownesse Cha-u-Kao* (1895, the Musée d'Orsay, Paris). He disliked models, preferring to concentrate on the human form caught in a characteristic, often intimate posture by his superb draughtsmanship regardless of chiaroscuro and background effects, as for example in *Le Lit* and *La Toilette* (1892 and 1896, Musée d'Orsay) and *Tête-à-tête supper* (c.1899, Courtauld Institute, London). His revolutionary poster designs influenced by Japanese woodcuts which flatten and simplify the subject matter demonstrate his gift for caricature, as in the posters of the music-hall star Aristide Bruant (1892) and **Yvette Guilbert** (1894). No one has portrayed so effectively the clientèle of these establishments as Toulouse-Lautrec in *Monsieur Boileau at the Café* (1892), *The Bar* (1898) and the *Moulin Rouge* paintings (1894). His works also depict fashionable society, as in *At the Races* (1899), and he executed remarkable portraits of his mother (1887), of **Van Gogh** in pastel (1887, Amsterdam) and a drawing of **Oscar Wilde** (1895). In 1895 he visited London, in 1896 Spain and in 1897 Holland. He was a heavy drinker and probably also suffered from syphilis, and his alcoholism brought on a complete breakdown, forcing him to go into a sanatorium; he recovered to resume his hectic life until his death from a paralytic stroke. Over 600 of his works are in the Musée Lautrec in Albi. 📖 Julia Frey, *Toulouse-Lautrec: a life* (1994); Gerstle Mack, *Toulouse-Lautrec* (1938)

Tour, Frances de la See de la Tour, Frances

Tour, Georges de la See La Tour, Georges de

Tour, Maurice Quentin de la See La Tour, Maurice Quentin de

Tour d'Auvergne, Théophile Malo Corret de la See La Tour d'Auvergne, Théophile Malo Corret de

Touré, Ahmed Sékou 1922–84
Guinean politician

Educated in Quran schools and at Conakry (1936–40), he turned to trade union activity and attended the Confédération Générale des Travailleurs (CGT) Congress in Paris in 1947, after which he was imprisoned for a brief period. He was a founder member of the Rassemblement Démocratique Africaine (RDA) in 1946 and became its secretary-general in 1952, as well as secretary-general of the local CGT branch. He was a member of the Territorial Assembly from 1953, Mayor of Conakry in 1955 and then Deputy in the French National Assembly in 1956. In 1958 he organized an overwhelming 'non' vote to General de Gaulle's referendum on self-government within a French Community. Guinea was granted its independence at once, the French removing as much of their possessions as possible. He was President (1958–84), and retained his uncompromisingly radical views of domestic and foreign politics. He survived several attempts, supported by outside powers, to overthrow him. Soon after his death, the military did take control.

Touré, Kwam See Carmichael, Stokely

Tournefort, Joseph Pitton de 1656–1708
French botanist

Born in Aix-en-Provence, he travelled in Greece and Turkey with the artist **Claude Aubriet**, and became professor at the Jardin des Plantes in Paris (1688–1708). His definitions of the genera of plants were of fundamental importance to **Carolus Linnaeus**, who rejected his general classification in favour of one based on the number of the sexual parts of the flower.

Tourneur, Cyril c.1575–1626
English dramatist

Little is known of his life. In 1600 he published a satirical poem, *Transformed Metamorphosis* (discovered in 1872), and in 1609 a *Funeral Poem* on the English soldier, Sir Francis Vere (1560–1609). He also wrote an *Elegy* (1613) on Prince Henry. His fame rests on two plays, *The Revenger's Tragedy* (printed in 1607), which some critics believe was written by **Thomas Middleton** or **John Webster**, and the inferior *The Atheist's Tragedy*, printed in 1611. 📖 P B Murray, *A Study of Cyril Tourneur* (1964)

Tournier, Paul 1898–1986
Swiss physician and writer

Born in Geneva, he spent his whole professional life as a general practitioner in private practice there. He discovered religious faith through contact with the Oxford Group in 1932, and thereafter emphasized the need to treat his patients as whole human beings. His books, many bestsellers, include *A Doctor's Casebook in the Light of the Bible* (1954) and *Learning to Grow Old* (1972).

Tourtel, Mary 1874–1948
English writer and illustrator

Born in Canterbury, Kent, and educated at Canterbury Art School, she began her career in the 1890s and found lasting fame with her Rupert the Bear cartoon strip in the *Daily Express* (1920–35), after which time Rupert was carried on by Alfred Bestall (to 1965) and others. About 50 Rupert books were published, containing many adventures involving the hero and his friends Bill Badger, Algy Pug and Podgy Pig, and there have also been Rupert annuals and television adaptations of the stories.

Tourville, Anne Hilarion de Cotentin, Comte de 1642–1701
French naval commander

Born in the Château Tourville, near Coutances, he inflicted a disastrous defeat on the English and Dutch off Beachy Head (1690). In 1692, **Louis XIV** having resolved to invade England on behalf of **James VII and II**, Tourville sailed from Brest and defeated the English and Dutch, under Admiral Edward Russell, off Cape La Hogue. In 1693 he defeated an Anglo-Dutch fleet off Cape St Vincent, and also defeated Admiral **Rooke** in the Bay of Lagos, capturing or destroying a large part of the Smyrna fleet. A Marshal of France (1693), Tourville inflicted enormous damage on English shipping (1694).

Toussaint Louverture, originally François Dominique Toussaint 1746–1803
Haitian revolutionary leader

Born a slave in Saint Domingue (Haiti since 1804), but freed in 1777, he joined the insurgents in 1791, and by 1797 was effective ruler of the former colony. He drove out British and Spanish expeditions, restored order, and aimed at independence, but **Napoleon I** sent a new expedition to Saint Domingue and proclaimed the re-establishment of slavery. Toussaint was arrested and died in prison. His surname ('the opening') comes from his bravery in once making a breach in enemy ranks.

Tout, Thomas Frederick 1855–1929
English historian

Born in London and educated at St Olave's School, Southwark, and Balliol College, Oxford, he became a professor at Manchester (1890–1925). He wrote *Chapters in the Administrative History of Mediaeval England* (1920–33), drawing on Public Record Office household and wardrobe accounts not used in previous research, so becoming the leading authority on English medieval history.

Tovey, Sir Donald Francis 1873–1940
English pianist, composer and writer on music

Born in Eton College, Windsor, Berkshire, he studied under Walter Parratt there and **Hubert Parry** at Balliol College, Oxford. He made his professional debut as a pianist in 1900, but his reputation was greater in continental Europe than in Great Britain, where his musical scholarship annoyed the critics. In 1914 he became Professor of Music at Edinburgh, where he built up the Reid Symphony Orchestra. He composed an opera, *The Bride of Dionysus* (1907–08), a symphony, a piano concerto (1903), a cello concerto (1937, for **Pablo Casals**) and chamber music; but his fame rests largely on his writings, remarkable for great musical perception and learning: *Companion to the Art of Fugue* (1931), *Essays on Musical Analysis* (1935–39), and his articles on music in the *Encyclopaedia Britannica*. He edited **Beethoven**'s sonatas, and edited and completed **J S Bach**'s *Art of Fugue*.

Tovey, John Cronyn Tovey, 1st Baron 1885–1971
English naval commander

He distinguished himself as a destroyer captain in World War I, notably at the Battle of Jutland (1916). As Commander-in-Chief of the Home fleet (1941–43) he was responsible for the operations leading to the sinking of the German battleship *Bismarck*. He became Admiral of the Fleet in 1943.

Tower, John 1925–91
US politician

Born in Houston, Texas, the son of an itinerant Methodist minister, he served with the navy during World War II and afterwards undertook political science research at Georgetown University, Texas, and the London School of Economics. Originally a Democrat, he switched parties during the later 1950s and became, in 1961, the first Republican to be elected senator for Texas. Specializing in defence matters, he established himself as an influential figure in the senate, becoming chairman of the Armed Services Committee in 1981. He retired from the senate in 1983 and became a paid consultant to influential arms industry contractors, and also chaired the 1986–87 Tower Commission which investigated the role of the National Security Council in the 'Irangate' scandal. In 1989 he was chosen by President **George Bush** as Defense Secretary, but his nomination was rejected by the senate after voiced concern about his defence industry connections and previous alcohol problems. His memoirs, *Consequences*, were published in 1991. He died in a plane crash.

Towne, Francis c.1739–1816
English painter

Born probably in London, he was little known as a landscapist until the 20th century, when his gift for painting simple but graphic watercolours was recognized. Works done in Italy, which he visited in 1780, are now in the British Museum.

Townes, Charles Hard 1915–
US physicist and Nobel Prize winner

Born in Greenville, South Carolina, he was educated at Furman University, then at Duke University and the California Institute of Technology (Caltech), where he completed his PhD in 1939. During World War II he worked at the Bell Telephone Laboratories, designing radar bombing systems and navigational devices and making the first studies of the microwave spectra of gases. In 1948 he joined Columbia University where he investigated the electrical and magnetic interaction between molecules and nuclei. In need of an intense source of microwaves to extend these investigations, in 1951 he passed a weak beam of microwaves through excited ammonia gas triggering the ammonia molecules to emit their own intense, coherent microwave radiation. Thus he produced the first operational maser (Microwave Amplification by Stimulated Emission of Radiation), the forerunner of the laser. For his work on the maser–laser principles, Townes was joint winner of the Nobel Prize for physics with **Nikolai Basov** and **Aleksandr Prokhorov** in 1964. He was appointed to professorships at the Massachusetts Institute of Technology (MIT, 1961–67) and the University of California at Berkeley (1967–86), and has been active in developing microwave and infrared astronomy techniques. He was made an Officer of the French Legion of Honour in 1990. 📖 Making Waves (1995)

Townsend, Francis Everett 1867–1960
US reformer

Born in Fairbury, Illinois, he studied medicine and became a doctor in South Dakota and California. In 1933 he proposed a federally administered old-age pension plan, which he believed would stimulate the economy and end the Depression. The Townsend Plan was repeatedly defeated in Congress, but its popularity helped bring about the passage of the Social Security Act (1935).

Townsend, Sir John Sealy Edward 1868–1957
Irish physicist

Born in Galway, he graduated from Trinity College, Dublin, in 1890. After teaching mathematics in Ireland he went to Trinity College, Cambridge (1895), as one of J J Thomson's first research students at the Cavendish Laboratory. He became Wykeham Professor of Physics at Oxford in 1900. By 1897 he had determined the elementary electrical charge, and his main area of research continued to be the kinetics of ions and electrons in gases. After 1908 he concentrated on the study of the properties of electron clouds, investigating the electron's mean free path, which later had implications for quantum theory. He was knighted in 1941.

Townshend (of Rainham), Charles Townshend, 2nd Viscount, *nicknamed* Turnip Townshend 1674–1738
English statesman

Born in Raynham Hall, Norfolk, he was educated at Eton and King's College, Cambridge. In 1687 he succeeded his father, Sir Horatio, who, though a Presbyterian, had zealously supported the Restoration. Charles entered public life as a Tory, but soon, as a disciple of Lord **Somers**, co-operated with the Whigs. He was one of the commissioners for the Union with Scotland (1707) and was joint-plenipotentiary with the Duke of **Marlborough** at The Hague. Dismissed in 1712 on the formation of the **Harley** ministry, on the succession of **George I**,

Townshend became Secretary of State. With **James Stanhope**, he formed a Whig ministry, which had **Robert Walpole**, his brother-in-law, for Chancellor of the Exchequer and which passed the Septennial Act (1716). He was Lord Lieutenant of Ireland (1717) and became President of the Council and Secretary for the Northern Department. He became Secretary of State in 1721, but retired in 1730, after which he became interested in agricultural improvement, proposing the use of turnips to improve crop rotation, and thus acquiring his nickname.

Townshend, Charles 1725–67
English politician
Grandson of Charles, 2nd Viscount **Townshend**, he entered the House of Commons in 1747, and became First Lord of Trade and the Plantations in 1763. In the **Chatham** ministry of 1766 he became Chancellor of the Exchequer, and asserted British authority over the American colonies by imposing swingeing taxes, especially on tea, that ultimately provoked the American Revolution (1775–83). He was about to form a ministry when he died. A brilliant speaker, he was able to intoxicate the House of Commons by his witty irrelevancies, as in his famous 'champagne speech' (1767).

Townshend, Sir Charles Vere Ferrers
1861–1924
English general
He joined the Indian army and held Chitral Fort for 46 days (1895). During World War I he was appointed major-general in 1915 and took part in the Mesopotamian campaign. In conjunction with naval forces up the Tigris, he took Amara and then Nasiriya on the Euphrates, but was defeated at Ctesiphon and retreated to Kut, where he held out for a month before surrendering (1916). After the war, he was Independent Conservative MP from 1920. He was the great-grandson of George, 4th Viscount **Townshend**, whose *Military Life* he wrote in 1901.

Townshend, George Townshend, 4th Viscount and 1st Marquess 1724–1807
English general
The brother of **Charles Townshend** (1725–67), he fought at Culloden (1746), but retired after differences with William, Duke of **Cumberland**, in part, by a very unflattering caricature of Cumberland drawn by Townshend. He was brigadier-general under **James Wolfe** at Quebec (1759), and after Wolfe's death assumed the command. As Lord Lieutenant of Ireland (1767–72) his measures to break the power of the 'undertakers', the landowners and proprietors who effectively controlled the country, brought him great unpopularity, and he was recalled for dissipation. He was created marquess in 1786.

Townshend, Pete(r) 1945–
English rock musician and writer
He was born in Chiswick, London, to a saxophonist father and a mother who was a singer. He began playing in Dixieland jazz bands, but quickly switched to rock. The Detours, a band with singer (and later actor) Roger Daltrey and John Entwistle (bass), metamorphosed into The Who with the addition of Keith Moon (d.1978) on drums. Their power pop was initially associated with the Mod movement, but grew increasingly ambitious in rock operas like *Tommy* (filmed 1975) and *Quadrophenia* (filmed 1979), a trait also evident in some of his later solo projects, which he pursued even before the band broke up in 1982. He launched a publishing venture, Eel Pie, in the 1970s, and later joined Faber and Faber as a consulting editor. A reformed addict, he has been a vigorous anti-drug campaigner. He took part in a first-ever live performance of *Quadrophenia* in Hyde Park, London, in 1996. 📖 G Giuliano, *Behind Blue Eyes* (1996)

Toynbee, Arnold 1852–83
English economic historian and social reformer
Born in London, he lectured in economic history at Balliol College, Oxford, and to numerous workers' adult education classes, and undertook social work in the East End of London with **Samuel Barnett**. He is best known as the coiner of the phrase and author of *The Industrial Revolution in England* (1884). Toynbee Hall, a university settlement in Whitechapel, London, was founded in his memory in 1885. His brother, Paget (1855–1932), was a biographer and authority on the works of **Dante**.

Toynbee, Arnold Joseph 1889–1975
English historian
Born in London, the nephew of **Arnold Toynbee**, he was educated at Winchester and Balliol College, Oxford, where he became a Fellow. He married a daughter of **Gilbert Murray** (1913), served in the Foreign Office in both World Wars and attended the Paris peace conferences (1919, 1946). He was Koraes Professor of Modern Greek and Byzantine history at London (1919–24) and director and research professor of the Royal Institute of International Affairs, London (1925–55). His major work was *History of the World* (10 vols,1934–54), echoes of which reverberated through his controversial BBC Reith Lectures, *The World and the West* (1952). His numerous other works include *Greek Historical Thought* (1924) and *War and Civilization* (1951). One of his sons, (Theodore) Philip (1916–81), was a well-known novelist and journalist. 📖 William H McNeill, *Arnold J Toynbee: A Life* (1989)

Toyotomi, Hideyoshi See Hideyoshi Toyotomi

Tracey, Stan (ley William) 1926–
British jazz pianist, bandleader and composer
Born in London, he was largely self-taught. After working with dance orchestras such as the Roy Fox and Ted Heath Bands as well as with modern jazz groups in the 1950s, he was house pianist from 1960–67 at Ronnie Scott's Club, Soho, accompanying many leading contemporary touring musicians. He developed a distinctive, angular, percussive keyboard style, rooted in **Thelonius Monk** and Duke Ellington, but with his own distinctive flavour. Since the mid-1960s he has led a succession of bands from quartets to 16-piece orchestras, has toured abroad and has written jazz suites such as *Under Milk Wood* (1965) and *Genesis* (1987). He recorded for the Blue Note label in the 1990s. In 1992 he was voted best pianist of the year at the British Jazz Awards and best composer/arranger in 1995. He was made a Fellow of the City of Leeds College of Music in 1993. His son, drummer Clark Tracey (1961–), is also an important jazz musician.

Tracy, David 1939–
US theologian
Born in Yonkers, New York, he earned his doctorate at the Gregorian University in Rome and became Professor of Theology at Chicago University Divinity School. He has explored questions of hermeneutics: the problems of theological communication in a modern pluralistic society, in which addressing the Church, the academic world and society in general is a difficult task requiring imagination and sensitivity. Drawing on the thought of **Paul Tillich, Bernard Lonergan, Hans-Georg Gadamer** and others, he develops these themes in *Blessed Rage for Order* (1975), *The Analogical Imagination* (1980) and *Plurality and Ambiguity* (1986).

Tracy, Spencer Bonadventure 1900–67
US film actor
Born in Milwaukee, Wisconsin, he attended the Northwestern Military Academy, Ripon College, and the American Academy of Dramatic Arts. He made his Broadway debut in *A Royal Fandango* (1923) and his feature

film debut in *Up the River* (1930). Initially typecast as a tough guy and gangster, his acting skills and reliability eventually brought him more demanding roles, earning him a reputation as one of the screen's finest performers. Nominated nine times for an Academy Award, he won it for his performances in *Captains Courageous* (1937) and *Boy's Town* (1938). Other notable films include *Dr Jekyll and Mr Hyde* (1941), *Bad Day at Black Rock* (1955) and *Judgement at Nuremberg* (1961). A long personal and professional association with **Katharine Hepburn** resulted in a series of comedies, including *Woman of the Year* (1942) and *Pat and Mike* (1952) as well as his final performance in *Guess Who's Coming to Dinner* (1967).

Tradescant, John, the Elder 1570–c.1638
English naturalist, gardener and traveller
Born probably in Suffolk, he became head gardener to the Earls of Salisbury and later to King **Charles I**. He travelled to Arctic Russia in 1618 and in 1620 to Algeria, and later established a physic garden and the first museum open to the public, the Museum Tradescantianum, in Lambeth, London. He and his son, **John Tradescant**, the Younger, introduced many plants into English gardens including the genus *Tradescantia*, named after him.

Tradescant, John, the Younger 1608–62
English gardener
Born in Meopham, Kent, he went out to Virginia to collect plants and shells (1637) and succeeded his father, **John Tradescant**, the Elder, as head gardener to King **Charles I** in 1638. He bequeathed the celebrated Musaeum Tradescantianum in Lambeth to **Elias Ashmole**, and it became the basis for the Ashmolean Museum in Oxford.

Traherne, Thomas c.1636–1674
English poet
Born in Hereford, he studied at Brasenose College, Oxford, and became rector of Credenhill (1657) and chaplain (1667) to the Lord Keeper of the Great Seal, Sir Orlando Bridgeman. He wrote the anti-Catholic *Roman Forgeries* (1673) and *Christian Ethicks* (1675). His major work, *Centuries of Meditations* in prose, and many of his poems, were found in a notebook on a London bookstall in 1896, the former being first published in 1908, and the latter, as *Poetical Works*, in 1903. *Poems of Felicity* was published in 1910. 🕮 K W Salter, *Thomas Traherne* (1964)

Trajan, originally Marcus Ulpius Trajanus
c.53–117AD
Roman emperor
Born near Seville, he was adopted by **Nerva** as his colleague and successor (AD97), and became sole ruler in 98. From 101 Trajan campaigned against the Dacians, and Dacia eventually became a Roman province (106). In 113 Trajan left Italy to campaign in the east, mainly against the Parthians. He made Armenia and Mesopotamia into Roman provinces, and captured the Parthian capital, Ctesiphon (115). Meanwhile uprisings took place in the rest of the empire and he set sail for Italy, but died at Selinus in Cilicia. His reign saw the Roman Empire at its greatest extent, and the internal administration was excellent. Informers were severely punished and dishonest governors of provinces prosecuted. The empire was covered in all directions by new military routes, canals, bridges and harbours were constructed, new towns built, the Pontine Marshes partially drained, and the magnificent Forum Trajani erected. He also founded the library known as the Bibliotheca Ulpia. He enjoyed great popularity in his lifetime and his reputation remained high after death, though under him the empire showed signs of economic breakdown. 🕮 Lino Rossi, *Trajan's Column and the Dacian Wars* (1971)

Tranströmer, Tomas 1931–
Swedish poet and psychologist
Born in Stockholm, he graduated there in 1956, since when he has worked as a psychologist, including a spell at Roxtuna institution for young offenders. His first collection of poems, *17 dikter* (1954, '17 Poems'), characterized by a visionary reality, aroused attention and he has since become a leading poet of the postwar era. His 10 collections of poems have been translated into English either in part or in full by Robin Fulton in *Three Swedish Poets* (1970), *Selected Poems* (1974) and *Collected Poems* (1987). 🕮 K Espmark, *Resans Formler* (1983)

Tranter, Nigel 1909–
Scottish novelist and historian
Born in Glasgow and educated at George Heriot's School in Edinburgh, he trained as an accountant before becoming a full-time writer in 1936. A prolific writer, he has produced well over a hundred books. His best known novels are those on historical themes, most notably the trilogy on the life of **Robert the Bruce**, *The Steps to the Empty Throne* (1969), *The Path of the Hero King* (1970) and *The Price of the King's Peace* (1971). His non-fiction works include significant studies of Scottish castles and fortified houses. In *Nigel Tranter's Scotland* (1981) he gave an account of his lifelong fascination with rural Scotland's history, heritage, and public affairs. Recent publications include the non-fiction work *Footbridge to Enchantment* (1992) and the novel *A Rage of Regrets* (1994).

Traquair, Phoebe Anna 1852–1936
Irish embroiderer, illustrator and enameller
Born in Dublin and educated at Dublin School of Art, in 1873 she married Ramsay Traquair, the head of the Natural History Museum in Edinburgh. She was one of the most renowned enamellers of her period and her work featured regularly in *Studio* magazine. Much of her later work was of a religious nature and throughout her career she carried out various commissions, including work for Sir **Robert Lorimer**, St Mary's Cathedral, Edinburgh, and many other churches and public buildings in Scotland, where her murals can still be seen. She was awarded medals at the International Exhibitions in Paris, St Louis and London. She remarried in 1887, her full name becoming Phoebe Anna Traquair Reid.

Traube, Ludwig 1818–76
German pathologist
Born in Ratibor, he was educated at the universities of Breslau and Berlin. He became professor at the Berlin Friedrich-Wilhelm Institute (1853) and at Berlin University (1872). He developed the study of experimental pathology in Germany, using animal experimentation, with his most important work concerning the pathology of fever, and the effects of various drugs upon muscular and nervous activity. He explored the effects of digitalis and other drugs in the management of heart disease and described the rhythmic variations in the tone of the vasoconstrictor centre (now known as the Traube–Hering waves). He was the brother of **Moritz Traube**.

Traube, Moritz 1826–94
German wine merchant and chemist
Born in Ratibor, Silesia (now part of Poland), he studied chemistry in Berlin and Giessen, and was encouraged by **Justus von Liebig** and by his elder brother **Ludwig Traube** to pursue the study of fermentation. In 1849 he took over the family wine business in Ratibor, transferred it to Breslau (now Wrocław, Poland) in 1866, and ran it until 1886. Both in Ratibor and in Breslau he carried out research in his private laboratory, mainly on fermentation. He showed that an 'unorganized ferment' (later called an enzyme) produced by yeast was responsible for fermentation. He studied and classified various enzymes. He also showed that protein was not the source of muscle energy, contrary to the views of Liebig.

Traubel, Helen 1899–1972
US soprano

Born in St Louis, Missouri, she made her debut in 1923. She first sang at the New York Metropolitan in 1937, and was the leading **Wagner**ian soprano there after **Kirsten Flagstad**'s departure (1941). She resigned after a dispute over her nightclub appearances (1953). She also worked in film and television, and wrote detective novels.

Traven, B, *pseudonym of* Berick Traven Torsvan, *originally* Albert Otto Max Feige, *second pseudonym* Ret Marut c.1890–1969
German novelist

He was born probably in Swiebodzin, a Polish town now in Germany. His first stories emerged in Germany in 1925 as *Die Baumwollpflücker* (Eng trans *The Cottonpickers*, 1956) and it is thought he was active as a Communist there at the end of World War I. *Das Totenschiff* (1932, Eng trans *The Death Ship*, 1934), an anti-capitalist tale of a seaman caught up in a plan by shipowners to sink the *Yorikke* and cash in on the insurance, was highly popular. In the mid-1920s he went to Mexico and there wrote, in German, 12 novels and short stories, the most famous being *Der Schatz der Sierra Madre* (1927, Eng trans *The Treasure of the Sierre Madre*, 1934, filmed by **John Huston** in 1947). In later years he appeared in public under the name of his supposed 'translator', Hal Croves. ▢ W Wyatt, *The Man who was Traven* (1980)

Travers, Ben (jamin) 1886–1980
English dramatist and novelist

Born in Hendon, London, he was educated at Charterhouse, served in the RAF in both World Wars and was awarded the Air Force Cross (1920). A master of light farce, he wrote to suit the highly individual comic talents of Ralph Lynn, **Robertson Hare** and Tom Walls in such pieces as *A Cuckoo in the Nest* (1925), *Rookery Nook* (1926), *Thark* (1927) and *Plunder* (1928), which played in the Aldwych Theatre, London, for many years. His last work was a comedy, *The Bed Before Yesterday* (1976).

Travers, Morris William 1872–1961
English chemist

He was born in London and educated at the universities of London and Nancy, France. He was a demonstrator (1894–98) and later assistant professor (1898–1903) at University College London, before moving to the chair at University College, Bristol. From 1906 to 1911 he did much to establish the Indian Institute of Science at Bangalore, of which he became director, and during World War I he was put in charge of Duroglass Ltd at Walthamstow, London. He was later president of the Society of Glass Technology. He worked as a consultant chemical engineer, returning to Bristol from 1927 to 1939. During World War II he was a consultant on explosives to the Ministry of Supply. At University College he helped Sir **William Ramsay** to determine the properties of argon and helium. They found helium in meteorites while heating the meteorites in search of new gases. In 1898 Travers discovered krypton, a month later neon and a month after that xenon. In 1920 he began work on high-temperature furnaces and fuel technology, and in 1927 he established a research group at Bristol to work on organic gases at high temperatures. He also wrote a biography of Ramsay (1956) and arranged 24 volumes of his papers. Travers was elected FRS in 1904.

Travis, William Barret 1809–36
Texas revolutionary

Born near Red Banks, South Carolina, he attended a military academy in his home state but was expelled for inciting a revolt among the students. He studied law privately and settled in Texas in 1831, where he became a leader of the 'War Party' of Anglo-Texans who wanted to fight for independence from Mexico. He was in command of Texas troops defending the Alamo, and when **Santa Anna**'s Mexican forces stormed the fort (6 March 1836), he and all his men were killed.

Travolta, John 1954–
US actor

Born in Englewood, New Jersey, he was active in show-business from an early age before making his Broadway debut in *Over Here!* (1975) and his film debut in *The Devil's Rain* (1975). His role as the slow-witted Vinnie Barbarino in the television series *Welcome Back, Kotter* (1976–77) gained him national attention and he received a Best Actor Academy Award nomination for *Saturday Night Fever* (1977). Boyishly handsome, he had his popularity confirmed by the success of the film *Grease* (1978). Subsequent films include *Blow Out* (1981), *Staying Alive* (1983) and *Look Who's Talking* (1989). After a period out of the limelight, he made a welcome comeback as the portly hit-man in *Pulp Fiction* (1994) and starred in a string of hit films including *Get Shorty* (1995), *Broken Arrow* (1996) and *Phenomenon* (1996).

Tredgold, Thomas 1788–1829
English engineer and cabinetmaker

Born in Brandon, Durham, he became a carpenter and studied building construction and science in London. His *Elementary Principles of Carpentry* (1820) was the first serious manual on the subject. He also wrote manuals on cast iron (1821), *The Steam Engine* (1827), and other works.

Tree, Sir Herbert (Draper) Beerbohm 1853–1917
English actor-manager

He was born in London, and was the half-brother of Sir **Max Beerbohm**. Following a commercial education in Germany, he became an actor and scored his first success as Spalding in *The Private Secretary* (1884). He took over the Haymarket Theatre (1887) and, with the box-office success of *Trilby* (1894), he built His Majesty's Theatre (1897), where he rivalled **Henry Irving**'s Shakespearean productions at the Lyceum. He founded the Royal Academy of Dramatic Art (RADA) in 1904, where one of his major successes was the first production of **George Bernard Shaw**'s *Pygmalion* (1914). A great character actor, he excelled in roles such as Svengali, Falstaff, Hamlet, Fagin, Shylock, Malvolio and Micawber. His wife, (Helen) Maud Holt (1864–1937), whom he married in 1883, was also an accomplished actress, and directed His Majesty's Theatre from 1902; she is best remembered for the film *The Private Life of Henry VIII* (1932). ▢ Max Beerbohm, *Herbert Beerbohm Tree* (1920)

Treitschke, Heinrich von 1834–96
German historian

Born in Dresden, he studied at Bonn, Leipzig, Tübingen and Heidelberg, and became a professor at Freiburg (1863), Kiel (1866), Heidelberg (1867) and Berlin (1874). He succeeded **Leopold von Ranke** in 1886 as Prussian historiographer. He was member of the Reichstag from 1871 to 1888. His chief work, *History of Germany in the Nineteenth Century* (1879–94, Eng trans 1915–18), is of literary and historical value, and has been compared with Lord **Macaulay**'s *History of England*. He believed in a powerful Germany with a powerful empire, and in the necessity of war to achieve and maintain this.

Trelawny, Edward John 1792–1881
English author and adventurer

Born of a famous Cornish family, he joined the navy at the age of 11 but deserted, and lived a life of adventure in the East. A friend of **Shelley**, he was the author of the autobiographical *Adventures of a Younger Son* (1831) and of *Records of Shelley, Byron and the Author* (1858).

Trelawny, Sir Jonathan 1650–1721
English prelate
He became Bishop of Bristol (1685), Exeter (1688) and Winchester (1707). Though intensely loyal to the Crown, he was one of the Seven Bishops who petitioned against James VII and II's Declaration of Indulgence (1688) and were tried for libel. He is the hero of R S Hawker's ballad, 'And shall Trelawny die?'

Trench, Richard Chenevix 1807–86
Irish prelate, philologist and poet
Born in Dublin and educated at Harrow and Trinity College, Cambridge, he became curate in 1841 to Samuel Wilberforce, and during 1835–46 published six volumes of poetry. In 1845 he became rector of Itchenstoke and in 1847 Professor of Theology at King's College London. In 1856 he became dean of Westminster and from 1864 to 1884 he was Archbishop of Dublin. He was buried in Westminster Abbey, London. In philology he popularized the scientific study of words, and the *New English Dictionary*, later the *Oxford English Dictionary*, was begun at his suggestion. His principal works were *Notes on the Parables of our Lord* (1841), *Notes on the Miracles of our Lord* (1846), and *The Study of Words* (1851).

Trenchard (of Wolfeton), Hugh Montague Trenchard, 1st Viscount 1873–1956
English marshal of the RAF
He entered the forces in 1893, serving on the North-West Frontier, in South Africa, and with the West African Frontier Force. He became Assistant Commandant, Central Flying School (1913–14), the first general officer commanding the Royal Flying Corps (RFC) in the field, and helped to found the Royal Air Force (1918). Chief of the Air Staff between 1919 and 1929, he was appointed Marshal of the RAF (1927). Subsequently Commissioner of the Metropolitan Police (1931–35), he carried out a number of far-reaching reforms, including the establishment of the Police College at Hendon. He became a peer in 1930. ⌨ H R Allen, *The Legacy of Lord Trenchard* (1972)

Trenck, Franz, Freiherr von der 1711–49
Austrian adventurer
He was born in Reggio, Calabria, Italy, where his father was an Austrian general, and at the age of 16 joined the army. In the Austrian War of Succession (1740–48) he raised (1741) at his own cost a body of Pandours, who were even more distinguished for cruelty than for daring. In 1742, he attacked and destroyed Cham, in the Palatinate, and in 1745 he offered to capture Frederick II, the Great, and managed to seize the king's tent and much booty. He was suspected, however, of treachery, and imprisoned. He escaped, but was recaptured and sentenced to life imprisonment on the Spielberg at Brünn, where he poisoned himself.

Trendall, (Arthur) Dale 1909–95
New Zealand art historian and archaeologist
Born in Auckland, he was educated at King's College there, and at the University of Otago and Trinity College, Cambridge. He studied at the British Schools of Athens and Rome in the early 1930s and from that time embarked upon his life's work to research, classify and publish on the ceramic works of the early Greek settlers in southern Italy. His scholarly studies, in about 20 volumes, were supplemented by a handbook for general readers on the red-figure pottery of the region, and culminated in the three-volume *Red-Figured Vases of Apulia* (1978), tracing the history of the genre from 440BC. He was deputy Vice-Chancellor of Australian National University, Canberra (1958–64), and in 1969 became the first resident Fellow of La Trobe University in Victoria. Among his many honours was the Britannica award for humanities (1973). He is regarded as one of the great classical archaeologists of the 20th century and the leading international authority on South Italian Greek pottery and vase painting.

Trésaguet, Pierre Marie Jérôme 1716–96
French civil engineer
Born in Nevers into a family of engineers, he made his career in the Corps des Ponts et Chaussées, Paris, becoming Inspector-General in 1775. He is best known for the improved method of road construction he introduced, involving the use of carefully placed stones in the base layer with progressively smaller sizes towards the surface. He also emphasized the importance of good drainage and regular maintenance. His system was generally adopted in France and elsewhere in Europe, and in Great Britain it was followed by Thomas Telford and developed by John Loudon McAdam.

Tressell, Robert, *pseudonym of* Robert Noonan 1870–1911
Irish novelist
He was born into a middle-class Dublin family. Having emigrated to South Africa, he settled in England after his wife's death. There he became involved in left-wing politics and worked as a housepainter, both activities feeding into the novel for which he is remembered, *The Ragged Trousered Philanthropists*, a lively attack on the moral turpitude and corruption at the heart of the Edwardian social system. Publishers were understandably wary of this 1,700-page manuscript, and at one point Tressell consigned it to the fire, but on his death he left it in the care of his daughter. It was eventually published in an abridged version in 1914, and in full in 1955. It has become a classic of the Labour movement.

Trethowan, Sir (James) Ian (Raley) 1922–90
English journalist, broadcaster and administrator
Born in High Wycombe, Buckinghamshire, and educated at Christ's Hospital, he left school at the age of 16 to take a shorthand and typing course and became an office boy at the *Daily Sketch*. Moving to Yorkshire, he became a reporter on the *Yorkshire Post*, and returned there after World War II (during which he served in the Fleet Air Arm) as its political correspondent. He moved to ITN as a newscaster in 1956. Successful and respected, in 1961 he moved to the BBC as their main political commentator. In 1968 he was appointed by the BBC chairman, Lord Hill, to become managing director of radio, when the former Home, Light and Third programmes subsequently became Radio 1, 2, 3 and 4. In 1976 he went back to television as managing director, then served as director general from 1977 until his retirement in 1982.

Treurnicht, Andries Petrus 1921–93
South African politician
Born in Piketberg, he studied theology at the universities of Cape Town and Stellenbosch and practised as a minister in the Dutch Reformed Church from 1946 until he was elected as a National Party representative in 1971. Elected Transvaal provincial leader in 1978, he held several Cabinet posts under P W Botha, gaining a reputation as an unreconstructed supporter of apartheid. He opposed even Botha's partial liberalization of the regime and was forced to leave the party with 15 colleagues in 1982. He formed a new party, the Conservative Party of South Africa, which pressed for a return to traditional apartheid values and effective partitioning of the country. The party gained seats and votes, especially from among the less well-off Afrikaners, over the next decade and took over from the moderate Progressive Federal Party as the official opposition within parliament.

Trevelyan, Sir George Otto Trevelyan, 2nd Baronet 1838–1928
English politician

The son of Sir Charles Edward Trevelyan (1807–86) and Hannah Moore, the sister of Lord Macaulay, he was born in Rothley Temple, Leicestershire, and educated at Harrow and Trinity College, Cambridge. He entered parliament in 1865 as a Liberal and became a Lord of the Admiralty (1868–70), Parliamentary Secretary to the Admiralty (1880–82), Chief Secretary for Ireland (1882–84) and Secretary for Scotland (1886, 1892–95). He wrote a number of historical works, among them a life of his uncle, Lord Macaulay (1876–1908), a life of Charles James Foxe (1880), and the *American Revolution* (1909).

Trevelyan, G(eorge) M(acaulay) 1876–1962
English historian

Born in Welcombe, Warwickshire, the son of Sir George Otto Trevelyan, he was educated at Harrow and Trinity College, Cambridge, of which he was elected Master (1940–51). He served in World War I and was Regius Professor of Modern History at Cambridge (1927–40). He is best known for his *English Social History* (1944), a companion volume to his *History of England* (1926). Other works include studies of Garibaldi (1907, 1909, 1911) and John Bright (1913), *British History in the Nineteenth Century* (1922), and several volumes of lectures and essays, including an autobiography (1949). 📖 J H Plumb, *Trevelyan* (1951)

Treves, Sir Frederick 1853–1923
English surgeon

Born in Dorchester, Dorset, he was educated in London, and became professor at the Royal College of Surgeons. He was a founder of the British Red Cross Society and made improvements in operations for appendicitis. Joseph Carey Merrick (1862–90), a sufferer from neurofibromatosis, and known as 'Elephant Man', was one of his patients, as was King Edward VII, on whom Treves operated for appendicitis in 1902.

Trevet, Nicholas See Trivet, Nicholas

Trevino, Lee Buck, *nicknamed* Supermex 1939–
US golfer

Born in Dallas, Texas, he gained his nickname from his Mexican origins. He won six Majors—the US Open twice (1968, 1971), the Open twice (1971, 1972) and the US Professional Golfers' Association twice (1974, 1984)—but is the only man to hold the Open titles of America, Britain and Canada simultaneously. More than his victories, it was his ability to combine wisecracks with excellent golf that made him one of the game's most popular players. In 1975, while playing in the Western Open, he had a remarkable escape from death after being struck by lightning. Since turning 50 he has concentrated on the Seniors Tour.

Trevithick, Richard 1771–1833
English engineer and inventor

He was born in Illogan, Redruth, Cornwall, and was educated locally. He became a mining engineer, and devoted his life to the improvement of the steam engine. Unlike James Watt, he favoured higher steam pressures which gave greater power from smaller cylinders. From 1796 to 1801 he invented a steam carriage, which ran between Camborne and Tuckingmill, and which in 1803 was run from Leather Lane to Paddington via Oxford Street. From 1800 to 1815 he built several steam road carriages, the first steam railway locomotives and a large number of stationary steam engines. He later went to Peru and Costa Rica (1816–27), where his engines were introduced into the silver mines. 📖 H W Dickinson and Arthur Titley, *Richard Trevithick: The Engineer and the Man* (1934)

Trevor, William, *properly* William Trevor Cox 1928–
Irish short-story writer, novelist and playwright

Born in Mitchelstown, County Cork, and educated at St Columba's College and Trinity College, Dublin, he taught history and art, sculpted and wrote advertising copy before devoting himself to literature. His first book was a novel, *A Standard of Behaviour* (1958), but though he has published 10 subsequently, including *Mrs Eckdorff in O'Neill's Hotel* (1969), *The Children of Dynmouth* (1976) and *Nights at the Alexandra* (1987), he is by inclination a short-story writer. He has lived in England for much of his life, but Ireland is the source of his inspiration. His superlative tales have been collected as *The Day We Got Drunk on Cake* (1967), *The Ballroom of Romance* (1972), *Angels at the Ritz* (1975), *The News from Ireland* (1986) and *Family Sins* (1990). *The Stories of William Trevor* appeared in 1983. More recent works include *Felicia's Journey* (1994), which won Trevor the Whitbread Book of the Year award, and *After Rain and other stories* (1996). He has also written a number of plays and screenplays. 📖 G Schirmer, *William Trevor* (1990)

Trevor-Roper, Hugh Redwald, Baron Dacre of Glanton 1914–
English historian and controversialist

Born in Glanton, Northumberland, he was educated at Charterhouse and Christ Church, Oxford, and, having written a somewhat derisive biography of Archbishop Laud, won international fame for his vivid reconstruction of *The Last Days of Hitler* (1947). He was Regius Professor of Modern History at Oxford (1957–80), and wrote on a wide range of topics, including medieval Christendom, European witch-hunting, the Kennedy assassination, the Kim Philby affair, the Scottish Enlightenment, and British devolution, and edited the Goebbels diaries (1978). He also received a great deal of publicity when he asserted the authenticity of diaries purporting to be those of Hitler, later proved to be fraudulent. He was Master of Peterhouse College, Cambridge (1980–1987), then made Honorary Fellow in 1987. A recent publication is *From Counter-Reformation to Glorious Revolution* (1992).

Triduana, St 4th century AD
British Christian religious

She is said to have come to Scotland with St Regulus and lived at Rescobie in Angus. According to legend, she was troubled by the attentions of the local king and learning of his admiration for her eyes, she plucked them out and sent them to him. She retired to Restalrig, where there is a well once famous as a cure for eye diseases. Her feast day is 8 October.

Trilling, Lionel 1905–75
US literary critic

Born in New York City, he was educated at Columbia University, where he became Professor of English in 1948. A trenchant and influential writer, he held that culture was central to the human experience, and that art and literature cannot exist in a vacuum. In the tradition of Matthew Arnold, on whom he wrote a standard book (1939), his interests were wide-ranging and his many publications include *The Liberal Imagination* (1950), *The Opposing Self* (1955), *Beyond Culture* (1965) and *Sincerity and Authenticity* (1972). His only novel, *The Middle of the Journey*, was published in 1947. 📖 M Krupnick, *Lionel Trilling and the Fate of Cultural Criticism* (1986)

Trinder, Tommy (Thomas Edward) 1909–89
English comedian and actor

Born in Streatham, London, he first went on stage at the age of 12 going on to gain experience in small-town variety shows. A jaunty, cheerful performer, he was a master of ad lib and the quick retort, and happily performed without a script. His first big opportunity came in 1939 when he was invited to join the *Band Waggon* show at the London Palladium, and he went on to become well known, both as a stand-up comic in such revues as *Happy and Glorious* and *Best Bib and Tucker*, and as a leading man in films like *Sailors Three* (1940), *The Bells Go Down* (1943) and *Champagne Charlie* (1944). The self-confessed 'Mr Woolworth of show-business' whose famous catchphrase was 'You lucky people', he worked tirelessly during World War II, travelling to Italy, the Middle East and the Far East to entertain the troops. After the war he compered the ITV show *Sunday Night at the London Palladium* (1954–58). He continued to perform until his late seventies. A football enthusiast, he was chairman of Fulham Football Club (1955–76).

Trinh, Phan Chau See Phan Chau Trinh

Trintignant, Jean-Louis 1930–
French actor
Born in Port-St Esprit, he abandoned his legal studies to become an actor, making his Paris stage debut in *A Chacun selon sa faim* (1951). His first major role in *Responsabilité limitée* (1954) led to his film debut in the short *Peachinef* (1955), and his subsequent appearance in Roger Vadim's *Et Dieu créa la femme* (1956, *And God Created Woman*), which made a household name of **Brigitte Bardot**, also brought Trintignant popular attention. His pale-skinned impassivity and sensitive eyes have lent themselves to the portrayal of romantic vulnerability and the illumination of the interior life of the psychologically disturbed. His career includes the comedy *Le Cœur battant* (1960, *The French Game*), the internationally successful romance *Un homme et une femme* (1966, *A Man and a Woman*) and a variety of work for Europe's most distinguished directors including *Les Biches* (1968, 'The Does'), *Z* (1968), *Ma nuit chez Maud* (1969, *My Night at Maud's*) and *Il Conformista* (1970, *The Conformist*). *Under Fire* (1983) marked a rare venture into English-language productions. He has also directed *Une Journée bien remplie* (1972, 'A Well-Filled Day') and *Le Maître nageur* (1979, *The Lifeguard*). Later films include *Merci la vie* (1991), *Trois Couleurs: Rouge* (1994, *Three Colours: Red*) and *Fiesta* (1995).

Trippe, Juan Terry 1899–1981
US airline founder
Born in Seabright, New Jersey, he graduated from Yale in 1922, interrupting his studies to fly with the navy as a night bomber pilot. The following year he organized Long Island Airways, then Colonial Air Transport and founded Pan American Airways in 1927. Other airlines were absorbed into the company, including Compania Mexicana de Aviacion and Grace Airways, from which a subsidiary, PANAGRA, existed until 1965. The company offered the first scheduled round-the-world air service in 1947. In 1955 Trippe placed the first US order for jet transports.

Tristram, Henry Baker 1822–1906
English clergyman, naturalist and traveller
Born in Eglingham, near Alnwick, Northumberland, he was educated at Lincoln College, Oxford, and became an Anglican clergyman, but tuberculosis forced him to go abroad, to Algeria. He wrote *The Great Sahara* (1860), but his main interest was in the flora and fauna of Palestine, where he made several long journeys, and he was the author of the first ornithological surveys of the region, including *The Land of Israel* (1865), *Natural History of the Bible* (1867), *The Flora and Fauna of Palestine* (1884) and *The Land of Moab* (1873). Tristram's Warbler and Tristram's Serin are named after him.

Trivet or Trevet, Nicholas fl.1300
English chronicler
A Dominican friar, he wrote *Annales Sex Regum Angliae*, covering the period from 1136 to 1307, as well as other historical works.

Trog, Walter, *originally* Ernest Fawkes 1924–
British cartoonist and musician
Born in Ontario, Canada, he went to England in 1931 and studied art at Camberwell. He did camouflage work during World War II and joined the *Daily Mail* as staff cartoonist in 1945, creating *Rufus* (later *Flook*), a daily strip for children (1949). The strip developed into satirical comment under many scriptwriters, including Sir **Compton Mackenzie** and eventually Trog himself. Trog (the pen name comes from the Troglodytes, his jazzband for which he played clarinet) expanded into political cartooning in the *Spectator* (1959), then the *Daily Mail* (1968), and colour covers for *Punch* (1971).

Troisi, Massimo 1953–94
Italian filmmaker
Born in Naples, he made his stage debut in 1969 and was a well-known theatre actor before finding national fame as part of the comedy group La Smorfia. He made his film debut in the comedy *Ricomincio Da Tre* (1981, *Beginning With Three*) and soon became a guarantee of box-office success in feisty farces examining modern relationships. Films in which he starred and directed include *Scusate Il Ritardo* (1983, *Sorry, I'm Late*) and *Pensavo Fosse Amore...Invece Era Un Calesse* (1991). He worked sparingly for other directors but won the Venice Film Festival Best Actor prize for his performance in *Che Ora E?* (1989, *What Time Is It?*). Suffering with a heart that had been weakened by rheumatic fever as a child, he died 12 hours after completing *Il Postino* (1994, 'The Postman') in which his tender, poignant performance as a humble, lovestruck postman secured him a posthumous Academy Award nomination and a level of international recognition that had been denied to him during his lifetime.

Trollope, Anthony 1815–82
English novelist
He was born in London, educated (unhappily) at Harrow and Winchester, and with his family moved to Belgium where his father, an unsuccessful lawyer and barrister, died. His mother, **Frances Trollope**, a woman of enviable energy, maintained the family by her prolific writing. He became a junior clerk in the General Post Office in London (1834) and was transferred to Ireland (1841). He left the Civil Service (1867), an important but idiosyncratic official whose achievements included the introduction in Great Britain of the pillar box for letters. A year later he stood unsuccessfully for parliament. His first novels, *The Macdermots of Ballycloran* (1847) and *The Kellys and the O'Kellys* (1848), were not successful, but with *The Warden* (1855), the first of the Barchester novels, came an inkling of his genius. It is the story of the struggle over Harding's Hospital, and introduced into English fiction some of its most durable and memorable characters—Mr Harding, who recurs throughout the Barchester series, Archdeacon Grantly, and Bishop Proudie who with his redoubtable wife dominates *Barchester Towers* (1857). The rest of the series are: *Doctor Thorne* (1858), *Framley Parsonage* (1861), *The Small House at Allington* (1864) and *The Last Chronicle of Barset* (1867). Interconnected by character and unified by their West Country setting in the imaginary town of Barset, the novels are distinguished by their quiet comedy, slow pace and piquant detail. The series format appealed to Trollope's industry and he embarked on a second, more ambitious sequence—known collectively as the 'Palliser' novels, after Plantagenet Palliser, who features in each—with the publication in 1864 of *Can You Forgive Her?*. Its sequel was *Phineas Finn* (1869), and others in the series are *The Eustace Diamonds* (1873), *Phineas Redux* (1876), *The Prime Minister* (1876), and *The Duke's Children* (1880). Several of his books were serialized in the *St Paul's Magazine* which he edited (1867–70). Regarding himself more of a craftsman than an artist, Trollope began work every morning at 5.30 and generally completed his

literary work before he dressed for breakfast. His output was consequently prodigious and comprises 47 novels, travel books, biographies of **Thackeray**, **Cicero** and Lord **Palmerston**, plays, short stories and literary sketches. Other novels worthy of note include *The Three Clerks* (1857), *The Bertrams* (1859), *Orley Farm* (1862), *The Vicar of Bullhampton* (1870), *The Way We Live Now* (1875) and *Doctor Wortle's School* (1881). His *Autobiography* (1883) is an antidote to more romantic accounts of the literary life. 📖 A O J Cockshut, *Anthony Trollope* (1955)

Trollope, Frances, née Milton 1780–1863
English novelist

Born in Stapleton, Avon, she was the mother of **Anthony Trollope**. In 1809 she married Thomas Anthony Trollope (1774–1835), a failed barrister and Fellow of New College, Oxford. In 1827 her husband fell into dire financial difficulties, which were not relieved by moving to the USA. During her three years there she amassed the material for her *Domestic Manners of the Americans* (1832), a critical and witty book much resented in the USA. Widowed in 1835, she travelled widely on the Continent, writing articles and fiction, and eventually settled in Florence (1843). Her most successful novels were *The Vicar of Wrexhill* (1837) and *The Widow Barnaby* (1839), with its sequel *The Widow Married* (1840). In all she wrote 115 volumes, now mostly forgotten. 📖 U Pope-Hennessy, *Three English Women in America* (1929)

Tromp, Cornelis Maartenzoon 1629–91
Dutch naval commander

He was the son of **Maarten Tromp**. He shared the glory of **Michiel de Ruyter**'s Four Days' Battle (1666) off Dunkirk, and won fame in the battles against the combined English and French fleets (7 and 14 June 1673). On a visit to England in 1675 he was created baron by **Charles II** and was appointed Lieutenant-Governor of the United Provinces (1676).

Tromp, Maarten Harpertszoon 1598–1653
Dutch admiral

Born in Briel, he defeated a superior Spanish fleet off Gravelines in 1639, and the same year won the Battle of the Downs. Knighted by **Louis XIII** of France (1640) and by **Charles I** of England (1642), he then fought the French pirates based on Dunkirk, and his encounter with **Robert Blake** in 1652 started the Anglo-Dutch Wars. Victorious off Dover, he was defeated by a superior English fleet off Portland, and finally off Terheijde, near Scheveningen, where he was killed in an engagement with **George Monk**. His son was **Cornelis Tromp**. 📖 M G de Boer, *Tromp en de Duinkerkers* (1949)

Trotsky, Leon, *alias of* Lev Davidovich Bronstein 1879–1940
Russian revolutionary

He was born in Yanovka, Ukraine, and educated in Odessa. At the age of 19 he was arrested as a Marxist and was sent to Siberia. He escaped in 1902, joined **Lenin** in London, and in the abortive 1905 revolution became President of the St Petersburg Soviet. After escaping from a further exile period in Siberia, he became a revolutionary journalist among Russian émigrés in the West. He returned to Russia in 1917, joined the Bolshevik Party and with **Lenin** played a major role in the October Revolution. As Commissar for Foreign Affairs he conducted negotiations with the Germans for the peace treaty of Brest-Litovsk (1918). In the Russian Civil War, as Commissar for War, he created the Red Army of 5 million men from a nucleus of 7,000 men. On Lenin's death in 1924 Trotsky's influence began to decline. **Stalin**, who opposed his theory of 'permanent revolution', ousted him from the politburo, and he was exiled to Central Asia (1927), and then was expelled from the USSR (1929). He

continued to agitate and intrigue as an exile in several countries. In 1937, having been sentenced to death in his absence by a Soviet court, he found asylum in Mexico City. There he was assassinated with an ice pick in 1940 by Ramon del Rio (alias Jacques Mornard). Ruthless, energetic, a superb orator and messianic visionary, Trotsky inspired as much confidence in Lenin as he awakened mistrust in Stalin. In his later years he was the focus of those Communists, Soviet and otherwise, who opposed the endless opportunism of Stalin. He was the revolutionary 'pur sang', a writer of power, wit and venom, an advocate of permanent revolution and, in contrast to Stalin's 'socialism in one country', world revolution. His publications include *History of the Russian Revolution* (1932) *The Revolution Betrayed* (1937), *Stalin* (1948) and *Diary in Exile* (translated 1959), and remain influential in western Marxist circles. In January 1989, as part of the policy of glasnost under **Mikhail Gorbachev**, it was revealed that Trotsky was murdered by the Soviet secret police. Trotsky's son, Sergei Sedov, who was shot dead in Moscow in 1937, was rehabilitated by the Soviet Supreme Court in 1988. 📖 Robert D Warth, *Leon Trotsky* (1977)

Trotta, Margarethe Von See Von Trotta, Margarethe

Trotula 11th century
Italian obstetrician and early medical practitioner

She is thought to have lectured on childbirth at the University of Salerno in the 11th century, and is generally regarded as one of the earliest medical practitioners. Some historians attribute to her a treatise on gynaecology in a 15th-century manuscript originally written in the 11th or 12th century in Salerno, which was an important medical teaching centre at the time.

Troughton, Edward 1753–1835
English instrument-maker

Born in Corney, Cumberland, he was apprenticed to his eldest brother, John, and set up in business with him in London as makers of measuring and surveying instruments. In 1778 John made a copy of Jesse Ramsden's dividing engine and he and his brother began to produce precisely graduated sextants and a variety of other navigational and astronomical instruments. One of Edward's most important innovations was his equatorial mounting for astronomical telescopes, which rapidly became the standard mounting for all large instruments. He also devised the compensated mercurial pendulum whose period is not affected by changes of temperature.

Troyton, Constant 1810–65
French landscape and animal painter

Born in Sèvres, he was a member of the Barbizon Group. Many of his paintings are in the Louvre, Paris, and two are in the Wallace Collection, London.

Trübner, Nicholas 1817–88
German publisher

Born in Heidelberg, he went to London in 1843, started up his business in 1852 and developed a business connection in the USA. An Oriental scholar, he published a series of Oriental texts as well as works for the Early English Text Society. The business was merged in 1889 to become Kegan Paul, Trench, Trübner & Co.

Trudeau, Garry, *in full* Garretson Beekman Trudeau 1948–
US cartoonist

Born in New York City, he was a student at Yale in 1968 when he drew a comic strip featuring irreverent political and social satire, syndicated as *Doonesbury* in 1970. Unlike many cartoonists, Trudeau has not allowed his characters to become trapped in the era in which the strip was conceived but instead has shown them reacting to the contemporary world, in the process addressing social issues such as drug use and homelessness and firing salvos at intolerance and political hypocrisy. He won the Pulitzer Prize for editorial cartooning in 1975, and he has published many *Doonesbury* collections in book form.

Trudeau, Pierre Elliott 1919–
Canadian statesman

Born in Montreal, he was called to the Quebec Bar in 1943. One of the founders in 1950 of *Cité Libre*, a magazine opposed to the policies of **Maurice Duplessis**, then premier of Quebec, he began to practise law in Montreal in 1951. He urged the reform of the educational and electoral systems and the separation of Church and State in Quebec and in 1956 was active in the short-lived *Rassemblement*, a group of left-wing opponents of Duplessis. From 1961 to 1965 he was Associate Professor of Law at the University of Montreal and in 1965, having rejected the New Democratic Party for the Liberal Party, was elected to the House of Commons. In 1966 he was appointed Parliamentary Secretary to the Prime Minister and in 1967, as Minister of Justice and Attorney-General, he opposed the separation of Quebec from the rest of Canada. In 1968 he succeeded **Lester Pearson** as federal leader of the Liberal Party and Prime Minister. He then called a general election at which his party secured an overall majority. His government was defeated in 1979, but returned to power in 1980. He retired from active politics in 1984 and published his memoirs in 1993.

Trueblood, (David) Elton 1900–
US Quaker scholar

Born in Pleasantville, Iowa, he had a comprehensive education, including a Harvard PhD, before teaching philosophy at various institutions, notably at Earlham College (1946–54). He retained his link there as professor-at-large after his appointment in 1954 as chief of religious information at the United States Information Agency. His books include *The Yoke of Christ* (1958), *The Company of the Committed* (1961), *The People Called Quakers* (1966), and *The Validity of the Christian Mission* (1972).

Trueman, Freddy (Frederick Sewards) 1931–
English cricketer

Born in Stainton, South Yorkshire, and educated at Maltby Secondary School, he became an apprentice bricklayer before developing into the first genuine fast bowler in postwar English cricket. A Yorkshire player for 19 years (1949–68), he played in 67 Tests between 1952 and 1965 and took a record 307 wickets, three times taking 10 wickets in a match. In his first-class career he took 2,304 wickets and made three centuries. He has worked as a cricket writer and commentator since he retired. 📖 *Ball of Fire* (1976)

Truffaut, François 1932–84
French film critic and director

He was born in Paris. His early life as an unhappy child, reform school pupil and army deserter later formed elements of his more autobiographical works. His career as a film critic from 1953 led to his 'auteur' concept of film-making. His first film as director was the short *Une Visite* (1955). A founding father of the French *Nouvelle Vague* (New Wave), he made his feature debut with *Les Quatre cents coups* (1959, *The 400 Blows*), a haunting study of deprived childhood that gained him an international reputation. His diverse work includes most of the popular genres, with films like *Jules et Jim* (1962), *Farenheit 451* (1966), *La Mariée était en Noir* (1967, *The Bride Wore Black*), *La Nuit américaine* (1973, *Day for Night*), for which he received an Academy Award, and *Le Dernier métro* (1980, *The Last Metro*). He acted in his own films and in *Close Encounters of the Third Kind* (1977). His many writings included an autobiography, *Les Films de ma vie* (1975).

Truman, Harry S 1884–1972
33rd President of the USA

He was born in Lamar, Missouri, and educated in Independence, Missouri. After World War I, in which he served as an artillery captain on the Western Front, he returned to his farm and later went into partnership in a men's clothing store which failed. In 1922 he became judge for the Eastern District of Jackson County in Missouri, and in 1926 presiding judge, a post he held until 1934 when Missouri elected him as a Democrat to the US Senate. He was elected Vice-President in 1944 and became President in April 1945 on the death of President **Franklin D Roosevelt**. He was re-elected in 1948 in a surprise victory over **Thomas E Dewey**. During his presidency he took many historically important decisions, including dropping the first atom bombs on Hiroshima and Nagasaki; pushing through Congress a huge postwar loan to Great Britain (the **Marshall** Plan); making a major change in US policy towards the USSR, the Truman Doctrine of Communist containment and support for free peoples resisting subjugation; organizing the Berlin Airlift (1948–49); establishing NATO (1949); sending US troops on behalf of the UN to withstand the communist invasion of South Korea (1950). He also established the CIA. In the USA he introduced a liberal programme or 'Fair Deal' of economic reform. He did not stand for re-election in 1952 and retired to Independence. Later became a strong critic of the **Eisenhower** Republican administration. 📖 Alfred Steinberg, *The Man from Missouri* (1962)

Trumbull, John 1756–1843
American historical painter

Born in Lebanon, Connecticut, the son of **Jonathan Trumbull**, after service in the American Revolution, between 1780 and 1785 he made three visits to London to study art under **Benjamin West**, and began a series of celebrated war paintings including *The Battle of Bunker's Hill*, and a number of portraits of **George Washington**. He was later ambassador to London (1794–1804), and in 1817 painted four large historical pictures for the Rotunda of the Capitol in Washington DC. The Trumbull Gallery at Yale was built to accommodate his collection of paintings (1832).

Trumbull, Jonathan 1710–85
American patriot

Born in Lebanon, Connecticut, he became judge, Deputy-Governor, and Governor of the state, and took a prominent part in the American Revolution. 'Brother Jonathan', the personification of the USA, was once thought, wrongly, to refer to him. His son was **John Trumbull**.

Trumpler, Robert Julius 1886–1956
US astronomer

Born in Zurich, Switzerland, he was educated at the university there and at the University of Göttingen, Germany (1911). He worked with the Swiss geodetic survey before moving to the USA, where he served on the staff of the Allegheny Observatory (1915–19) and Lick Observatory (1919–38). From 1938 until his retirement in 1951 he was professor at the University of California at Berkeley. At Lick Observatory he studied the dimensions and brightnesses of open star clusters in the Milky Way and explained the disproportionate faintness of the more distant ones as the effect of absorption of light in interstellar space (1930). This important discovery led to a reassessment of the distance scale of our galaxy. He also demonstrated that the light of distant clusters is reddened as well as dimmed, an effect caused by small grains of dust in the spiral arms of the galaxy. Trumpler was elected to the US National Academy of Sciences in 1932.

Truth, Sojourner, *originally* Isabella Van Wagener
c.1797–1883
US abolitionist

Born a slave in Ulster County, New York, she worked for several years for a variety of owners, but eventually gained her freedom and settled in New York, taking her surname from her previous master and becoming an ardent evangelist. In 1843 she felt called to change her name, and to fight against slavery and for women's suffrage. Preaching widely across the USA, she drew large crowds with her infectious style of speaking. In 1850 she produced a biography, *The Narrative of Sojourner Truth*, which she had dictated to Olive Gilbert. She was appointed counsellor to the freedmen of Washington by Abraham Lincoln, and continued to promote Negro rights, including educational opportunities, until her retirement in 1875.

Tryon, Sir George 1832–93
English naval commander

Born in Bulwick Park, Northamptonshire, he became a midshipman in the Crimean War (1854–55). He was second-in-command of HMS *Warrior*, the first British ironclad (1861), and director of transports to the British expedition against Emperor Theodore of Abyssinia (1867). He became Commander-in-Chief in the Mediterranean in 1891. He died when his flagship, the ironclad *Victoria*, sank in collision with the *Camperdown* off Tripoli. Most of the crew perished with him.

Tsai Lun See Zai Lun

Ts'ai Yüan-p'ei See Cai Yuanpei

Ts'ao Yü See Cao Yu

Tsendenbal, Yumjaagiyn 1916–90
Mongolian dictator

He was born in Davst, Uvs province, into a poor herdsman family. Despite being largely self-educated in his early years, he won admission to the Irkutsk Institute of Finance and Economics, and worked as a teacher at the School of Finance in Ulan Bator. A year later, he joined the only permitted political party, the Mongolian People's Revolutionary Party, and rose rapidly. From 1941 to 1945, he served as deputy Commander-in-Chief and chief of the army's political directorate, and was rewarded with the Order of Lenin in 1944 for organizing aid to Russian troops in World War II. In 1945 he was appointed deputy Prime Minister in the dictatorship of Marshal Horloogiyn Choybalsan, and assumed the premiership on Choybalsan's death in 1952. In 1974, he resigned the premiership to be elected chairman of the People's Great Hural (national assembly), and in 1981 readopted the title of General Secretary. Under his autocratic leadership, dissenting ministers and other leading party figures were removed from office. In 1984, while on a visit to Moscow, he was stripped of office and replaced by premier Jambyn Batmunh. After briefly returning to his homeland in 1984, Tsendenbal went back to Moscow, but in 1988 was denounced for allowing his country to suffer political and economic stagnation and was expelled from the Communist Party. He died while still in exile in Moscow.

Tsensky, Sergei Nikolayevich Sergeyev- See Sergeyev-Tensky, Sergei Nikolayevich

Tshombe, Moise Kapenda 1919–69
Congolese politician

Educated in mission schools, he was a businessman who helped to found the Confederation des Associations Tribales du Katanga in 1957. When Belgium granted the Congo independence in 1960, he declared the copper-rich province of Katanga independent and became its President. On the request of Patrice Lumumba, UN troops were called in to reintegrate the province and Tshombe was forced into exile in 1963, returning in 1964.

Forced into exile again after Sese Seke Mobutu's 1966 coup, Tshombe was kidnapped in 1967 and taken to Algeria, where he died in custody.

Tsiolkovsky, Konstantin Eduardovich
1857–1935
Russian astrophysicist and rocket pioneer

Born in the village of Izheskaye in the Spassk district, he was largely self-educated in science. Unaware of the work of James Clerk Maxwell, in 1881 he independently developed the kinetic theory of gases. By 1895 his published papers had suggested the possibility of space flight, three years later stressing the necessity for liquid fuel rocket engines. In 1903 he published his seminal work, *Exploration of Cosmic Space by means of Reaction Devices*, which established his reputation as 'the father of space flight theory'. From 1911 he developed the basic theory of rocketry, and also multi-stage rocket technology (1929). He continued to publish scientific papers, and also gave his ideas on space travel wider circulation by writing a number of works of science fiction. Towards the end of his life the Soviet government became interested in space flight and his work began to be recognized.

Tsiranana, Philibert 1912–
Madagascan politician

Educated in Madagascar and France, he organized the Social Democratic Party, on whose ticket he was elected a member of the Representative Assembly in 1956, as well as the French National Assembly in 1957. He was deputy President of Madagascar in 1958 and President in the following year. He remained in the post until he was overthrown in a military coup in 1972.

Tso Ch'iu Ming See Zuo Qiu Ming

Tswett *or* Tsvett, Mikhail Semyonovich
1872–1919
Russian organic chemist

He was born in Asti, Italy, and studied at Geneva and Kazan before being appointed as assistant at Warsaw University in 1903. From 1908 to 1917 he taught botany and microbiology at Warsaw Technical University, which moved to Nizhny Novgorod during World War I. In 1917 he was appointed Professor of Botany and director of the botanical gardens at Yuryev (Tartu) University, which was transferred to Voronezh in 1918. As a student he investigated chlorophyll and by 1900 established that it contains at least two green pigments. However, traditional methods of organic analysis proved too destructive for delicate organic materials, and he began to look for a method of separating substances physically in an unchanged state. His method, which he named 'chromatography', did not attract much interest until the 1930s. Since then it has developed into a number of highly specialized and widely used techniques which are employed when complex mixtures have to be separated or substances purified.

Tubin, Eduard 1905–82
Swedish composer

Born in Kallaste, Estonia, he went to Hungary while still a teenager to study composition with Zoltán Kodály. When he returned to Estonia, he spent the years 1931 to 1944 conducting a provincial orchestra in Tartu. On moving to Sweden, where he took citizenship in 1961, he devoted his time to composition. He was working on his 11th Symphony when he died in Stockholm. His best work can be found in his symphonies, which are expansive, melodic works, not in the most modern of idioms, but which stimulate and attract the ear. His *Estonian Dance Suite* deserves popularity in the concert hall. He also wrote concertos for many instruments, including the balalaika and the double bass.

Tubman, Harriet c.1820–1913
US abolitionist

Born in Dorchester County, Maryland, she escaped from slavery there (1849), and from then until the Civil War she was active on the slave escape route, a number of safe-houses called the 'Underground Railroad', making a number of dangerous trips into the South and leading over 300 people to freedom. Famous among abolitionists, she counselled **John Brown** before his attempt to launch the Harpers Ferry slave insurrection (1859). During the Civil War she was a Northern spy and scout, but was denied a federal pension until 1897.

Tubman, William V S 1895–1971
Liberian politician

Educated in a methodist seminary, he was a teacher, lawyer and Methodist preacher. He was elected for the True Whig Party, which protected the interests of the Americo-Liberian élite, and became a member of the Liberian Senate in 1922. In 1937 he was appointed deputy President of the Supreme Court and, in 1944, was chosen as President of Liberia, a post he retained until his death.

Tuchman, Barbara W(ertheim) 1912–89
US historian

Born in New York City, she graduated from Radcliffe in 1933 and worked as a freelance journalist, travelling to Spain as a correspondent for the *Nation* in 1937. Later she became an independent scholar, writing histories praised for their narrative force and illuminating detail. Her best-known book is *The Guns of August* (1962, Pulitzer Prize), an account of the events that led to the outbreak of World War I. *The Proud Tower*, covering the period from 1890 to 1914, was published in 1966. Other works include *Stilwell and the American Experience in China* (1971, Pulitzer Prize), *A Distant Mirror* (1978), and *The March of Folly* (1984).

Tucker, Sophie, *professional name of* Sonia Kalish, *originally* Sophie Abuza 1884–1966
US singer and vaudeville entertainer

Born in Russia, she made her debut in New York as a blackface comedienne and retained strong blues and jazz elements in her singing style. This style won her the title 'the last of the red hot mamas'. Like **Ethel Waters**, she made a significant contribution to perceptions of women in entertainment, and remained close to black composers like **Eubie Blake** and Shelton Brooks, who wrote her theme song 'Some of These Days', the title of which she gave to her autobiography (1945).

Tuckwell, Barry Emmanuel 1931–
Australian conductor and player of the French horn

Born in Melbourne, Victoria, he studied at the Sydney Conservatorium, and played French horn with the Sydney Symphony Orchestra from 1947 to 1950, before going to Great Britain to play with the Hallé (1951–53) and other British orchestras. In 1955 he became principal horn with the London Symphony Orchestra, a position he held for 13 years. As principal and as soloist, he featured on most of the LSO's recordings in this period. Since then he has appeared as a horn soloist and also with his own wind quintet. He was Professor of Horn at the Royal Academy of Music in London (1963–74), and has written two books on the subject. He has conducted many international orchestras such as the Tasmanian Symphony Orchestra (1979–83) and the Maryland Symphony Orchestra (1983–), of which he is also musical director. He became guest conductor of Northern Sinfonia in 1993.

Tudjman, Franjo 1922–
Croatian politician and historian

He served in the partisan army led by Marshal **Tito** and in 1945 became the youngest general in the Yugoslav federal army. In 1972 he was imprisoned during the purge of the Croatian nationalist movement and in 1981 was again sentenced to three years' imprisonment in the first major political trial since Tito's death. A Professor of Modern History at the Faculty of Political Science at Zagreb, he became chairman of the History of the Workers' Movement of Croatia. Following the elections in 1990, as leader of the right-wing Croatian Democratic Union, he became President of Croatia. He declared the Republic of Croatia's independence from the Yugoslav federation (1992), but the republic soon found itself engaged in a brutal war against the Yugoslav federal army. While international recognition of the independence of the Republic of Croatia followed in 1991 and 1992, over a third of the republic still remained beyond the reach of Tudjman's government in Zagreb. He was re-elected as President of Croatia in 1992 and 1997.

Tudor, Antony, *originally* William Cook 1908–87
English dancer, choreographer and teacher

Born in London, he worked at Smithfield meat market there while studying dance with **Marie Rambert** (1928). In 1930 she made him stage manager/secretary of her Ballet Club, which gave him the financial security to perform and train with the Rambert company where he made several key pieces. His first was *Cross Garter'd* in 1931, followed by the celebrated *Lilac Garden* in 1936 and the moody *Dark Elegies* in 1937. That same year he and a number of other Rambert members formed their own group, Dance Theatre, known from 1938 to 1940 as London Ballet. **Agnes De Mille** persuaded Tudor and his friend Harold Laing to move to New York City, where Tudor was position staff choreographer with Ballet Theater (now American Ballet Theater) for 10 years. *Pillar of Fire* (1942) and a one-act *Romeo and Juliet* (1943) were among his ABT successes. The years following were spent primarily in teaching, as director of the Metropolitan Opera Ballet School and tutoring at the Juilliard School of Music, New York, though he was a seasonal guest choreographer with both ABT and the Royal Swedish Ballet. He made *Echoing of Trumpets* in 1963 and *Shadowplay* in 1967, and in 1974 he returned to ABT to create *The Leaves are Fading* (1975) and *The Tiller in the Fields* (1978). Though his output of major work was comparatively small, he is generally considered to be one of the great contemporary choreographers.

Tu Fu See Du Fu

Tuke, Samuel 1784–1857
English psychiatric reformer

Born in York, he acquired in his childhood an intense interest in the York Retreat, the psychiatric hospital founded by his family. He wanted to study medicine but obeyed the family's wishes and entered the family business, though the Retreat, and psychiatric matters more generally, remained his primary concern. His *Description of the Retreat* (1813) contains a classic account of the principles of 'moral therapy', which was the basis of the therapeutic milieu there. He was the grandson of **William Tuke**.

Tuke, William 1732–1822
English Quaker philanthropist

A tea and coffee merchant in York, he founded a home for the mentally sick (the York Retreat) in 1796, the first of its kind in England. Contemporaneously with **Philippe Pinel** in France, he pioneered new methods of treatment and care of the insane.

Tukhachevsky, Mikhail Nikolayevich 1893–1937
Russian soldier and politician

Born near Slednevo, he served as an officer in the Tsarist Army in World War I, but became a member of the Communist Party in 1918. He commanded Bolshevik forces against the Poles under **Władysław Sikorski** and **Józef Piłsudski** in the Russo-Polish War (1920), against the

White Russians (1919–20) and during the Kulak uprising of 1921. From 1926 he was Chief of Staff of the Red Army, which he was influential in transforming from a peasant army into a modern, mechanized force. Appointed to the Military Soviet in 1934, he was created Marshal of the Soviet Union in 1935. However, his vigour and independence made him suspect to Stalin, and in 1937 he was executed, an early victim of the great purge which decimated the Red Army's officer corps.

Tulasne, Louis René 1815–85 and Charles 1816–84
French mycologists
Born in Azay-le-Rideau, they carried out important researches on the structure and development of fungi, and wrote *Selecta Fungorum Carpologia* (1861–65), which is notable for its many fine illustrations. Their work was the first exact study of the smut and rust fungi, and they followed this with a long series of papers on different fungi, especially underground species. They also studied the development of the ergot fungus on rye (1853), spore formation and germination in *Puccinia*, *Ustilago* and others, and the sexual organs of *Peronospora*.

Tull, Jethro 1674–1741
English agriculturist
He was born in Basildon, Berkshire, and educated at St John's College, Oxford. The inventor of a seed drill (1701), he introduced new farming methods in his native county, his chief innovation being the planting of seeds in rows. He wrote *The Horse-Hoing Husbandry* (1733). 🕮 G E Fussell, *Jethro Tull: His Influence on Mechanized Agriculture* (1973)

Tullus Hostilius d.642BC
Third of the legendary kings of Rome
He succeeded Numa Pompilius in c.673BC. He destroyed Alba, and removed the inhabitants to Rome; the other wars credited to him may be unhistorical.

Tulsīdās 1532–1623
Indian Hindi devotional poet
Born in Eastern India, he was traditionally believed to have lived for 120 years, the time allotted to a sinless human being. He wrote more than a dozen works, his best-known being *Rāmacaritamānas* ('The Holy Lake of Rāma's Deeds'), a popular Eastern Hindi version of the *Rāmāyana* epic, which he began in 1574. His *bhakti* or devotional approach, concern for moral conduct, and idea of salvation through Rama incarnated as absolute knowledge and love, suggest a Nestorian Christian influence on his work. 🕮 W D P Will, *The Holy Lake of the Acts of Ram* (1953)

Tung Chee-hwa 1937–
Chinese businessman and politician
He was born into a wealthy family in Shanghai and moved with them to Hong Kong in 1950, following the Cultural Revolution of 1949. He was educated at Liverpool University in England, then went to the USA, returning to Hong Kong in 1985 to take over Orient Overseas, the shipping line established by his father, C Y Tung. That year the shipping empire was on the verge of collapse, but the Chinese government assisted in paying its debts. In 1991 Tung joined Governor Chris Patten's Executive Council, but on becoming a member of the Preparatory Committee (the Chinese body preparing for the transfer of sovereignty) felt conflicting interests and resigned (1995). In 1996 his leadership qualities, international connections, charisma and conservatism contributed to him being chosen as the first chief executive of the Special Administrative Region of Hong Kong, taking effect on Great Britain's handing over of power in Hong Kong to China on 1 July 1997.

Tunnicliffe, Charles Frederick 1901–79
English bird artist

Born in Langley, Macclesfield, he studied at Macclesfield School of Art and won a scholarship to the Royal College of Art, London. He illustrated Henry Williamson's *Tarka the Otter* (1927) and *Salar the Salmon* (1935) with his own wood-engravings, provided innumerable illustrations for the Royal Society for the Protection of Birds, and published six books of his own, including *Shorelands Summer Diary* (1952), *My Country Book* (1945) and *Bird Portraiture* (1945).

Tunström, Göran 1937–
Swedish writer
He was born in Sunne, Värmland, and his father, a clergyman, died when he was 12. His first work, *Inringning* ('Encircling'), appeared in 1958, and he has since published poems, plays, travel books (he and his wife, the painter Lena Cronquist, are intrepid travellers) and several long novels. His novels have inventive plots, borne by vivid, eccentric characters, but recurring themes are lost childhood, father-and-son relationships and a search for identity. He also looks at human responsibility and betrayal in both provincial and international settings. His popular novels include the prize-winning *Juloratoriet* (1982, 'The Christmas Oratorio') and *Tjuven* (1986, 'The Thief').

Tupolev, Andrei Nikolayevich 1888–1972
Russian aeronautical engineer
Born in Moscow, the son of a lawyer, he was educated at Moscow Higher Technical School, and was already working in a Moscow aircraft factory before the revolution. He was a founder of the Central Institute of Aerodynamics and Hydrodynamics (originally the Aerodynamic Aircraft Design Bureau) in Moscow, and became its first assistant director (1918–35). In the 1920s and 1930s he designed several bombers of world class, and even when imprisoned on false accusations of treason in 1937 he continued designing and was therefore released in 1943. In 1955 he built the first Soviet civil jet, the Tu-104, and in 1968 he completed the first test flight of a supersonic passenger aircraft, the Tu-144.

Tupper, Martin Farquhar 1810–89
English writer
He was born in Marylebone, London, and studied at Charterhouse and at Christ Church, Oxford. He was called to the Bar (1835), but soon turned to writing. Of his 40 works, only *Proverbial Philosophy* (1838–67), a series of moralizing reflections in free verse, achieved wide popularity.

Tura, Cosima c.1430–1495
Italian artist
Born in Ferrara, he was the leader, with Francesco del Cossa, of the Ferrarese school. He studied under Francesco Squarcione at Padua, and his metallic, tortured forms and unusual colours give a strange power to his pictures, which include the *Pietà* in the Louvre, Paris, and the *S. Jerome* in the National Gallery, London.

Turbervile, George c.1540–c.1610
English poet
He was born in Whitchurch, Dorset, and was educated at Winchester and New College, Oxford. He was secretary to the political agent Sir Thomas Randolph (1523–90). He wrote epigrams, songs, sonnets, *The Booke of Falconrie* (1575), *The Noble Art of Venerie* (1576), and translated Ovid, the Italian poets and others. He was a pioneer in the use of blank verse.

Turenne, Henri de la Tour d'Auvergne, Vicomte de 1611–75
French soldier

Born in Sedan, he was the second son of the Duc de Bouillon and Elizabeth of Nassau, **William I, the Silent's** daughter. Brought up in the Reformed faith, he fought first in the Dutch War of Independence (1625–30) under his uncle, Prince **Maurice of Nassau**, and in 1630 received a commission from Cardinal **Richelieu**. In the Thirty Years War (1618–48) he fought with distinction for the armies of the Protestant alliance, and in 1641 became supreme commander. He captured Breisach (1638) and Turin (1640), and for the conquest of Roussillon from the Spaniards in 1642 was made a Marshal of France (1644). In the civil wars of the Fronde, Turenne at first joined the *frondeurs*, but then switched sides and saved the government of **Mazarin** and the young King **Louis XIV** by his campaigning (1652–53). In the Franco–Spanish War he conquered much of the Spanish Netherlands, and defeated the **Prince de Condé**, who had deserted to the *frondeurs*, at the Battle of the Dunes (1658). In 1660 he was created Marshal-General of France. He won lasting fame for his campaigns in the United Provinces during the Dutch War (1672–75), but advancing along the Rhine was killed at Sasbach. ⊞ Max Weygard, *Turenne: Marshal of France* (1930)

Turgenev, Ivan Sergeyevich 1818–83
Russian novelist

He was born in the province of Oryel, and after graduating from St Petersburg University went to Berlin to study philosophy, where he mingled with the radical thinkers of the day and became firm friends with **Aleksandr Herzen**. He returned to Russia in 1841 to enter the Civil Service, but in 1843 abandoned this to take up literature. His tyrannical mother strongly disapproved and his infatuation for the singer **Paulina Viardot** also displeased her. She stopped his allowance and until her death in 1850, when he came into his inheritance, he had to support himself by his writings. In 1850 he wrote his finest and best-known play, *A Month in the Country* (published 1869, staged 1872). *Zapiski okhotnika* (1852, Eng trans *A Sportsman's Sketches*), sympathetic studies of the peasant life, made his reputation, but were perceived by the government as an attack on serfdom. A notice praising **Nikolai Gogol** on his death in 1852 resulted in a two years' banishment to his country estates. After his exile he spent much time in Europe, writing several faithful descriptions of Russian liberalism. In his greatest novel, *Ottsy i dety* (1862, Eng trans *Fathers and Sons*, 1867), he portrayed the new generation, with its faith in science and lack of respect for tradition and authority. But the hero, Bazarov, pleased neither the revolutionaries who thought the portrait a libel nor the reactionaries who thought it a glorification of iconoclasm. Turgenev's popularity slumped in Russia but rose abroad, particularly in Great Britain, where the book was recognized as a major contribution to literature. Successive novels were *Dym* (1867, Eng trans *Smoke*, 1868) and *Nov'* (1877, Eng trans *Virgin Soil*, 1877). He also returned to the short story, producing powerful pieces like *Stepnoy Korol' Lir* (1870, Eng trans *A Lear of the Steppes*, 1874) and tales of the supernatural to which his increasing melancholy drew him. ⊞ L Schapiro, *Turgenev, his life and times* (1978)

Turgot d.1115
Anglo-Saxon monk

Born in Durham, where he became an archdeacon, he helped to found the new cathedral. He was Bishop of St Andrews (1109–15), and confessor to St **Margaret**, of whose biography he was the probable author.

Turgot, Anne Robert Jacques 1727–81
French economist and politician

Born in Paris of Norman ancestry, he was destined for the church but became a lawyer. Appointed intendant of Limoges in 1761, he introduced many reforms, including

the abolition of compulsory labour on roads and bridges. Soon after the accession of **Louis XVI** (1774) he was appointed Comptroller-General of Finance and at once he began to introduce wide reforms. He reduced expenditure and increased public revenue without imposing new taxes, established free trade in grain within France and removed the fiscal barriers between the provinces. He abolished the exclusive privileges of trade corporations and sought to break down the immunity from taxation enjoyed by the privileged classes, who pressed for his dismissal. Turgot was removed from office after only 20 months. He then occupied himself with literature and science until his death. His chief work, *Reflexions sur la formation et la distribution des richesses* (1766, Eng trans *Reflections on the Formation and Distribution of Wealth*), was the best outcome of the Physiocratic school (founded by **François Quesnay**) and largely anticipated **Adam Smith**.

Turina, Joaquín 1882–1949
Spanish composer and pianist

Born in Seville, he was encouraged by the organist of Seville Cathedral, and at 15 made his first appearance as a pianist. By the time he went to Madrid, in 1902, and came under the influence of **Manuel de Falla** and the Spanish Nationalist composers, he had a large number of compositions to his credit, including his first opera, *Margot* (1914). In 1905 he went to Paris to study at the Schola Cantorum, and became an important figure in French musical circles. Returning to Madrid in 1914, he was very active as composer, pianist and critic until the Spanish Civil War, in which he was a supporter of General **Franco**, curtailed his work. He wrote four operas, orchestral and chamber works and piano pieces, the best of which combine strong Andalusian colour and idiom with traditional forms.

Turing, Alan Mathison 1912–54
English mathematician

Born in London, he read mathematics at King's College, Cambridge and also studied at the Institute for Advanced Study in Princeton. In 1936 Turing made an outstanding contribution to the development of computer science, outlining a theoretical 'universal' machine (later called a Turing machine) and giving a precise mathematical characterization of the concept of computability. In World War II he worked in cryphography and on Colossus (a forerunner of the modern computer), before joining the National Physical Laboratory (1945). Here Turing put into practice his theoretical ideas on computing, with his brilliant design for the Automatic Computing Engine (ACE). In 1948 he accepted a post at Manchester University, where he made contributions to the programming of the Manchester Mark I computer, researched some complicated theories in plant morphogenesis and explored the problem of machine intelligence. He committed suicide after being prosecuted for homosexuality. ⊞ Andrew Hodges, *Alan Turing: The Enigma* (1983)

Turischeva, Lyudmila Ivanovna 1952–
Soviet gymnast

Born in Grozny, she began gymnastics in 1965, was a member of the Soviet team by the following year, and went on to win all four of the world's major titles: the world championship, Olympic, World Cup and European. She won the world title in 1970 and the European title in Minsk in 1971. She won the combined gold at the Munich Olympics (1972), although she did not win any individual golds, but in 1973 at the European championships she took gold in every discipline, winning the world championship title again the following year and the World Cup in 1975. She later became coach to the Soviet team.

Turnbull, Colin 1924–94
US anthropologist

Born in Harrow, England, he studied at Oxford, then carried out fieldwork first in India (1949–51) and later among the Mbuti pygmies of the Ituri Forest, Zaire (now Democratic Republic of Congo) He worked at the American Museum of Natural History in New York City (1959–69), and was appointed professor at George Washington University in 1976. He wrote many books on social change and relationships in Africa, including *The Forest People* (1961), *Tradition and Change in African Tribal Life* (1966) and *The Human Cycle* (1983).

Turnbull, William 1922–
Scottish artist

Born in Dundee, he studied at the Slade School of Art, London (1946–48), and lived in Paris from 1948 to 1950. He held his first one-man show at the Hanover Gallery, London, in 1950, and taught at the Central School of Arts and Crafts in London from 1952 to 1972. At the Venice Biennale he exhibited in the category New Aspects of British Sculpture. His sculptures are typically upright forms of roughly human height, standing directly on the floor—in the 1950s he favoured organic forms and titles like *Totemic Figure*, but since the 1960s he has preferred purely abstract, geometrical shapes, and painted steel. Work in the Tate Gallery, London, includes *Game* (1948), *Head* (1954) and *5x1* (1966). His work of the 1970s became more concerned with ritual and mystery, and he had a retrospective at the Tate in 1973.

Turner, Ethel S(ibyl) 1872–1958
Australian novelist and children's author

She was born in Doncaster, Yorkshire, England. Her father, Bennett George Burwell, died before she was two, and for her writing she took her stepfather's surname. She moved to Australia at the age of eight, and with her sister Lilian started *Iris*, a magazine for schoolgirls, for which Ethel wrote the children's page, later doing the same for the *Illustrated Sydney News* and the *Bulletin*, under the name 'Dame Durden'. Her first book, *Seven Little Australians* (1894), is now a classic of Australian literature. It has been in print ever since publication, was filmed as early as 1939 and has been adapted for British and Australian television and as a stage musical. A sequel, *The Family at Misrule*, came out in 1895 and there followed a steady stream of juvenile books, short stories and verse. She was the mother of Adrian Curlewis, and her daughter Jean Curlewis (1899–1930) collaborated with her on such books as *The Sunshine Family: a Book of Nonsense for Girls and Boys* (1923).

Turner, Dame Eva 1892–1990
English opera singer

Born in Oldham, Lancashire, she studied at the Royal Academy of Music and made her debut in the Carl Rosa Comany chorus in 1916. During the 1920s she played many leading parts, including Puccini's *Turandot* in 1926, a role for which she became famous. She travelled throughout Europe, pioneering the acceptance of the idea of a British prima donna, and made her US debut with the Chicago Opera in 1928. She retired from the stage in 1948 to devote herself to teaching, both privately and as visiting Professor of Voice at the University of Oklahoma (1949–59), and Professor of Singing at the Royal Academy of Music (1959–66). Gwyneth Jones was among her pupils.

Turner, Frederick Jackson 1861–1932
US historian

Born in Portage, Wisconsin, he studied at Johns Hopkins and returned to Wisconsin University in 1885, becoming a professor in 1892. In 1893 when the American Historical Association met at Chicago World's Fair, he delivered his paper on 'The Significance of the Frontier in American

History', asserting that American democracy derived from its frontier experience and not from its European inheritance. He expanded this theme in *Rise of the New West* (1906) and *The Frontier in American History* (1920), and also wrote *The Significance of Sections in American History* (1932, Pulitzer Prize). He was professor at Harvard from 1910 to 1924.

Turner, John Napier 1929–
Canadian politician

Born in Richmond, England, he went to Canada with his family in 1932. After studying at the University of British Columbia he won a Rhodes Scholarship and read political science and jurisprudence at Oxford. He then practised law in Britain and was called to the English Bar, and later the Bars of Quebec and Ontario, being made a QC in 1968. He entered the Canadian House of Commons in 1962 and was a junior minister in Lester Pearson's government and later Attorney-General and Finance Minister under Pierre Trudeau. When Trudeau retired in 1984, Turner succeeded him as leader of the Liberal Party and Prime Minister. He lost the general election later the same year and became leader of the opposition. He resigned the leadership of his party in 1990.

Turner, J(oseph) M(allord) W(illiam) See panel p1856

Turner, Kathleen 1954–
US film actress

Born in Springfield, Missouri, she studied at the Central School of Speech and Drama in London, then returned to New York and was eventually cast in a television soap opera (1978–80). Her feature film debut was as the conniving wife in the contemporary film noir *Body Heat* (1981). Despite her beauty, she has managed to avoid stereotyping and has appeared in a variety of roles. Her stardom was consolidated with the popular comedy romance *Romancing The Stone* (1984), and its sequel, *Jewel Of The Nile* (1985). Other films include *Crimes Of Passion* (1984), *Prizzi's Honor* (1985), and *Peggy Sue Got Married* (1986, Best Actress Academy Award). She later provided Jessica Rabbit's husky tones in *Who Framed Roger Rabbit?* (1988) and appeared in such films as *V I Warshawski* (1991), *Serial Mom* (1994) and *Moonlight and Valentino* (1996). Her stage work includes *Cat on a Hot Tin Roof* (1989) and *Indiscretions* (1996).

Turner, Lana, *originally* Julia Jean Mildred Frances Turner 1920–95
US film actress

Born in Wallace, Idaho, legend has it that as a teenager she was spotted sipping soda at a drugstore on Sunset Boulevard and asked if she would like to be in the movies. She duly appeared as an extra in *A Star Is Born* (1937) and was signed by MGM and promoted as 'the sweatergirl'. She appeared opposite Clark Gable in *Honky Tonk* (1941), and later notable films included *The Postman Always Rings Twice* (1946), with John Garfield, and *The Bad And The Beautiful* (1952). Later, she appeared on stage in a succession of glossy melodramas such as *Peyton Place* (1957) and *Imitation Of Life* (1959) and also in such television series as *The Survivors* (1969) and the soap opera *Falcon Crest* (1982–83). Her stormy private life, notably the murder of her lover by her daughter, Cheryl Crane, and her seven marriages brought her some notoriety, and in 1982 she published an autobiography *Lana: The Lady, The Legend, The Truth*.

Turner, Nat 1800–31
US slave insurrectionary

Born in Southampton County, Virginia, he learned to read, and in 1831 made plans for a slave uprising. Leading a force of eight, he succeeded in killing 51 whites but

---

Turner, J(oseph) M(allord) W(illiam) 1775–1851
English painter, one of the great masters of landscape art and of watercolour

Turner was born in London. At the age of 14 he entered the Royal Academy in the following year he was already exhibiting. At 18 he began touring England and Wales in search of material and made architectural drawings in the cathedral cities. For three years in the mid-1790s he joined forces with **Thomas Girtin**, the latter drawing the outlines and Turner washing in the colour; between them they raised the art of watercolour to new heights of delicacy and charm.

From 1796, strongly influenced by **Richard Wilson** and **Claude**, he took up oils. In 1802 he visited the Louvre collections, now enriched by **Napoleon I**'s booty, and was greatly attracted by **Titian** and **Nicolas Poussin**. More and more he became preoccupied with the delicate rendering of shifting gradations of light on such diverse forms as waves, shipwrecks, fantastic architecture and towering mountain ranges, conveying a generalized mood or impression of a scene, sometimes accentuated by a theatrically arbitrary choice of vivid colour. Examples of his work from this period are *The Shipwreck* (1805), *Frosty Morning* (1813) and *Crossing the Brook* (1815). He also worked on engravings, the series *Liber Studiorum* (1807–19), which

remained uncompleted and failed because he underpaid the engravers.

He visited Italy several times between 1819 and 1840; and there he completed the famous pictures of Venice, *The Fighting Téméraire* (1839) and *Rain, Steam and Speed* (1844), both in the National Gallery, London.

Turner led a secretive private life; he never married and when not staying with his patron Lord Egremont at Petworth, he lived in London taverns. He died in a temporary lodging at Chelsea under the assumed name of Booth. He bequeathed 300 of his paintings and 20,000 watercolours and drawings to the nation. Turner's revolution in art foreshadowed Impressionism and found a timely champion in **John Ruskin**, whose *Modern Painters* (vol 1, 1843) helped to turn the critical tide in Turner's favour.

📖 M Butlin and E Joll, *The Paintings of J M W Turner* (revised edn, 2 vols, 1984).

'This is the end of Art. I am glad I have had my day.'
Attributed, on first seeing a daguerrotype; quoted in J G Links *Canaletto and his Patrons* (1977).

---

as many as 100 slaves were killed and the revolt quickly collapsed. Captured after six weeks in hiding, he was brought to trial and hanged at Jerusalem, Virginia.

Turner, Ted (Robert Edward) 1938–
US entrepreneur and television broadcasting executive

He was born in Cincinnati, Ohio, educated at Brown University, and on inheriting a failing billboard advertising business in Georgia when his father committed suicide, he built it into a communications empire. He established the first 'superstation', WTBS, in Atlanta in the mid-1970s, transmitting programs by satellite to cable networks around the country. In 1980 he created the Cable News Network (CNN), the first 24-hour news station. He bought the movie company MGM in 1985, and three years later he established a movie channel on television. In 1996 Time Warner Inc merged with the Turner Broadcasting System (TBS) to create the world's largest media company, with Turner becoming its vice-chairman and keeping control of TBS. He owns the Atlanta Braves baseball team and the Atlanta Hawks basketball team; also a yachtsman, he won the America's Cup race in 1977. He has been married to **Jane Fonda** since 1991. 📖 Hank Whittemore, *CNN: The Inside Story* (1990)

Turner, Tina, *professional name of* Annie Mae Bullock 1938–
US pop singer and film actress

She was born in Nutbush, Tennessee. She met Ike Turner in a nightclub in St Louis, Missouri, joined his Revue, and then married him in 1958. Though the relationship was allegedly abusive, they were noted stage performers, and made hits like 'River Deep, Mountain High' (1966), a classic example of producer Phil Spector's 'wall of sound' and one of the greatest pop records ever made, and 'Nutbush City Limits' (1973), before divorcing in 1978. She appeared in **Pete Townshend**'s *Tommy* (1974), and he produced her *Acid Queen* album (1975). Her career declined for a time, but her success in the film *Mad Max Beyond the Thunderdome* (1984) and the albums *Private Dancer* (1984), *Foreign Affair* (1989) and *Wildest Dreams* (1996) propelled her to huge stardom, and her powerful voice and overtly sexual stage act was still filling stadiums in the mid-1990s. 📖 C Welch, *The Tina Turner Experience* (1994)

Turner, Sir Tomkyns Hilgrove c.1766–1843
English soldier

He fought at Aboukir Bay and Alexandria, and brought to Great Britain from French custody the Rosetta stone (1801–02).

Turner, Victor Witter 1920–83
Scottish social anthropologist

Born in Glasgow, he read literature at London University, but after war service studied anthropology under **Max Gluckman** at Manchester. He taught at Manchester (1949–63) before moving to the USA where he was Professor of Anthropology at Cornell (1963–68), and Professor of Social Thought at Chicago (1968–77) and at Virginia (1977–83). He carried out fieldwork among the Ndembu of Northern Rhodesia (now Zambia) from 1950 to 1954, which resulted in the classic monograph *Schism and Continuity in an African Society* (1957). In his later work he moved to the analysis of symbolism, as in *The Forest of Symbols* (1967), *The Drums of Affliction* (1968), *The Ritual Process* (1969) and *Dramas, Fields and Metaphors* (1972).

Turner, W(alter) J(ames Redfern) 1884–1946
British poet and music critic

Born in Melbourne, Australia, he left Australia in 1907 and served in World War I, during which his first and best-known collection of verse, *The Hunter and Other Poems* (1916), was published. After World War I he was sometime literary editor of the *Daily Herald*, drama critic of the *London Mercury* and music critic of the *New Statesman*, and he became literary editor of the *Spectator* in 1942. His other books of verse, mainly on the metaphysical concept of love, include *Marigold* (1926), *Pursuit of Psyche* (1931) and *Fossils of a Future Time* (1946). He wrote nearly 20 plays, though only two were both published and performed. An accomplished amateur musician, he wrote a number of studies on composers, including *Beethoven: the Search for Reality* (1927) and *Mozart: the Man and His Work* (1937). He will perhaps be best remembered as the creator and general editor of the Collins' series 'Britain in Pictures' (1941–46). 📖 W McKenna, *W J Turner: Poet and Music Critic* (1990)

Turner, William c.1510–1568
English clergyman, physician and naturalist

Born in Morpeth, Northumberland, he became a Fellow of Pembroke Hall, Cambridge, and travelled extensively abroad, studying medicine and botany in Italy. He became the author of the first original English works on plants, including *Libellus de re Herbaria Novus* (1538), the

---

Tutu, Desmond Mpilo 1931–
South African Anglican prelate and Nobel Prize winner

Desmond Tutu was born in Klerksdorp in the Transvaal, the son of a primary school headmaster. He studied theology at the University of South Africa and King's College London. After working as a schoolteacher for about four years he attended theological college and became an Anglican parish priest (1961). He rose rapidly to become Bishop of Lesotho (1976–78), Secretary-General of the South African Council of Churches (1978–85), the first black Bishop of Johannesburg (1985–86) and Archbishop of Cape Town (1986–96).

A fierce opponent of apartheid, he repeatedly risked imprisonment for his advocacy of punitive international sanctions against South Africa, although he deplored the use of violence. He was awarded the Nobel Prize for peace in 1984, was appointed Chancellor of the University of the Western Cape in Cape Town in 1988, and has chaired the Truth and Reconciliation Commission since 1995.

📖 He has published *Crying in the Wilderness* (1982), *Hope and Suffering* (1983), *The Words of Desmond Tutu* (1989) and *The Rainbow People of God* (1994).

> 'I am not interested in picking up crumbs of compassion thrown from the table of someone who considers himself to be my master. I want the full menu of rights.' On NBC News, 9 January 1985.

---

first book in which localities for native British plants were recorded, and *Names of Herbes* (1548). His major work is *A New Herball*, published in three instalments (1551–62), which demonstrated Turner's independence of thought and observation. He was dean of Wells (1550–53), left England during the reign of Mary I, but was restored to Wells in 1560. He named many plants, including goats-beard and hawkweed. The basis he laid for 'a system of nature' was developed by John Ray in the following century. He is known as the 'father of British botany'.

Turner-Warwick, Dame Margaret Elizabeth Harvey, *née* Moore 1924–
English physician

Born in London, she studied medicine at Lady Margaret Hall, Oxford, and University College Hospital, London, then worked at University College Hospital and the Brompton Hospital in London. She became a consultant physician at the Elizabeth Garrett Anderson Hospital (1962–67) and at the Brompton and London Chest Hospitals (1967–72), concurrently serving as senior lecturer at the Institute of Diseases of the Chest. Appointed Professor of Thoracic Medicine at the Cardiothoracic Institute, University of London, in 1972, she became Emeritus Professor on her retirement in 1987. From 1989 to 1992 she became the first woman President of the Royal College of Physicians of London. She was created DBE in 1991.

Turpin, Dick (Richard) 1705–39
English robber

He was born in Hempstead, Essex, and was, successively or simultaneously, butcher's apprentice, smuggler, cattle-thief, housebreaker, highwayman and horse-thief. He entered into partnership with Tom King, whom he shot dead by accident, and was hanged at York, for the murder of an Epping keeper. His famous ride to York on his mare Black Bess, recounted in Harrison Ainsworth's *Rookwood* (1824), is now thought to have been done by John Nevison, who in 1676 is said to have robbed a sailor at Gadshill at 4am, and to have established an alibi by reaching York at 7.45pm. 📖 Derek Barlow, *Dick Turpin and the Gregory Gang* (1973)

Tussaud, Marie, *née* Grosholtz, *known as* Madame Tussaud 1761–1850
Swiss modeller in wax

Born in Strasbourg, she was apprenticed to her uncle, Dr Philippe Curtius, in Paris and inherited his wax museums after his death in 1794. After the Revolution, she attended the guillotine to take death masks from the severed heads. After a short imprisonment, she married a French soldier, François Tussaud, but separated from him in 1800 and went to England with her younger son. She toured Great Britain with her life-size portrait waxworks, a gallery of heroes and rogues, and in 1835 set up a permanent exhibition in Baker Street, London, which was moved to Marylebone Road in 1884. The exhibition still contains some of her handiwork, notably Marie Antoinette, Napoleon, Sir Walter Scott, and Burke and Hare in the Chamber of Horrors, the last two having been joined by a succession of notable murderers, including John Christie and his kitchen sink. 📖 Leonard Cottrell, *Madame Tussaud* (1951)

Thutmose or Tuthmosis III, *also called* Thothmes and Tuthmose d.1426BC
Egyptian pharaoh of the 18th dynasty

The son of Thutmose II and father of Amenhotep II, he reigned jointly at first with his aunt and stepmother, Queen Hatshepsut from c.1501BC, and by himself from 1479 to 1447. He invaded Syria, extended his territories to Carchemish on the Euphrates and made several invasions into Asia. He built the great temple of Amen at Karnak, restored those at Memphis, Heliopolis and Abydos, and erected obelisks, including Cleopatra's Needle, taken to London (1878) by Sir Erasmus Wilson.

Thutmose or Tuthmosis IV fl.1400–1390BC
Egyptian pharaoh of the 18th dynasty

He was the son of Amenhotep II and father of Amenhotep III. He fought campaigns in Syria and Nubia.

Tut'ankhamun d.c.1340BC
Egyptian pharaoh of the 18th dynasty

The son-in-law of Akhenaten, he became king at the age of 12 and died at 18. His magnificent tomb at Thebes was discovered in 1922 by Lord Carnarvon and Howard Carter. 📖 Thomas Hoving, *Tutankhamun: The Untold Story* (1978)

Tuthmosis See Thutmose

Tutu, Desmond Mpilo See panel above

Tutuola, Amos 1920–97
Nigerian novelist

Born in Abeokuta, he was educated at a Salvation Army school, and later taught at Lagos High School. *The Palm-Wine Drinkard* (1952), his most popular book, written in a musical pidgin, deals with its hero's adventures among the 'Deads'—the spirits of the departed. A more recent publication is *Pauper, Brawler and Slanderer* (1987). 📖 G Collins, *Amos Tutuola* (1969)

Twain, Mark See panel p1858

Tweed, William Marcy, *nicknamed* Boss Tweed 1823–78
US criminal and politician

Twain, Mark, *pseudonym of* Samuel Langhorne Clemens 1835–1910
US writer and journalist

Mark Twain was born in Florida, Missouri. He was first a printer (1847–55), and later a Mississippi river-boat pilot (1857–61). In his first writing he adopted his pen-name from a well-known call of the man sounding the river in shallow places ('mark twain' meaning 'by the mark two fathoms').

In 1861 he went to Carson City, Nevada, as secretary to his brother, who was in the service of the governor, and while there made an unnnsuccessful attempt at gold-mining. For two years he edited the Virginia City *Territorial Enterprise* and in 1864 moved to San Francisco as a reporter. His first success was *The Celebrated Jumping Frog of Calaveras County* (1865), which was published as a book with other sketches in 1867. In 1867 he visited France, Italy and Palestine, gathering material for his *Innocents Abroad* (1869), which established his reputation as a humorist. After his return he was for a time editor of a newspaper in Buffalo, where he married the wealthy Olivia Landon.

Later he moved to Hartford, Connecticut, and joined a publishing firm which failed, but largely recouped his losses by lecturing and writing. *Roughing It* (1872) is a humorous account of his Nevada experiences, while *The Gilded Age* (1873), written with Charles Dudley Warner, a novel which was later dramatized, exposes the readjustment period after the Civil War. He visited England for a lecture tour in 1872, and as a result wrote *The Prince and the Pauper* (1882) and *A Connecticut Yankee in King Arthur's Court* (1889).

His two greatest masterpieces, *Tom Sawyer* (1876) and *Huckleberry Finn* (1884), are drawn from his own boyhood experiences, and give vivid accounts of life on the Mississippi frontier; other Twain favourites include *A Tramp Abroad* (1880). In 1883 he published *Life on the Mississippi*, an autobiographical account of his days as a riverboat pilot, which includes a famous attack on the influence of Walter Scott.

From the 1890s to the end of his life, Twain was affected by financial problems, which were aggravated by his unsuccessful business ventures. He tried to recover his fortunes by undertaking lecture tours in New Zealand, Australia, India and South Africa; but his difficulties intensified with the death of his wife (1904) and two of his daughters. His writing from these years has a more sombre tone, notably in *The Man that Corrupted Hadleyburg* (1900) and *The Mysterious Stranger* (published posthumously in 1916).

In these last years he dictated his autobiography to his secretary A B Paine, and it was published in different versions.

📖 F G Robinson, *The Cambridge Companion to Mark Twain* (1995); E Emerson, *The Authentic Twain, A Biography of Clemens* (1984); J Kaplan, *Mark Twain, A Biography* (1966).

'Travel is fatal to prejudice.'
The Innocents Abroad, Conclusion.

'Persons attempting to find a motive in this narrative will be prosecuted; persons attempting to find a moral in it will be banished; persons attempting to find a plot in it will be shot.' *The Adventures of Huckleberry Finn*, Notice.

Born in New York City, he trained as a chairmaker, became an alderman (1852–53), sat in Congress (1853–55), and was repeatedly in the state senate. One of the most notorious political bosses of the Tammany Society, he was made commissioner of public works for the city in 1870, and, as head of the 'Tweed Ring', controlled its finances. His gigantic frauds exposed in 1871, he was convicted, and, after escaping to Cuba and Spain (1875–76), died in a New York jail while suits were pending against him for recovery of $6 million.

Twiggy, *originally* Leslie Hornby, *married name* Twiggy Lawson 1949–
English model

Born in London, she began her modelling career in 1966, and quickly shot to fame as a fashion model in newspapers and magazines worldwide, including French and British *Elle* and American *Vogue*. Her adolescent gaucheness was emphasized by the girlish 1960s mini dresses, pale tights and loon pants she modelled and her short hair epitomized the boyish look in vogue at the time. Known as the 'Face of 1966', she became the symbol of the decade. She later proved she could sing, dance and act, and appeared in the films *The Boyfriend* (1971) and *The Blues Brothers* (1980)

Twombly, Cy 1928–
US painter

Born in Lexington, Virginia, he studied at the Boston Museum of Fine Arts School (1948–49), at the Art Students' League (1950–51) and at Black Mountain College (1951–52), going on to settle in Rome in 1957. His gestural or 'doodle' technique derives from Surrealist belief in the expressive power of automatic writing to tap the unconscious. In 1995 the Cy Twombly Gallery opened in Houston, Texas.

Twort, Frederick William 1877–1950
English bacteriologist

Born in Camberley, Surrey, he studied medicine in London, and became Professor of Bacteriology there in 1919. He was the last Superintendent of the Brown Institution of the University of London. Twort studied Jöhne's disease and methods of the culture of acid-fast organisms, and extracted an 'essential substance' (later shown to be of the vitamin K group) from dead tubercle bacilli. In the early part of this century he discovered a 'transmissible lytic agent', now known as the bacteriophage, which is a virus for attacking certain bacteria. In many ways the discovery of the invasion of bacteria by viruses formed the beginnings of molecular biology.
📖 Anthony Twort, *In Focus, Out of Step: A Biography of Frederick William Twort 1877-1950* (1993)

Tyard or Thiard, Pontus de 1521–1605
French poet

Born in Bissy-sur-Fleys, Saône-et-Loire, he belonged to the group of Lyons poets who took Petrarch for their master. Influenced, however, by the work of Pierre de Ronsard, his verse bridges the gap between the Petrarchan style and that of the Pléiade poets. Volumes of poetry include *Erreurs amoureuses* (1549–55, 'Mistakes in Love'), *Le Livre des vers lyriques* (1555, 'Book of Lyrical Verses') and *Œuvres poétiques* (1573, 'Poetic Works'). He was Bishop of Châlon-sur-Saône (1578–94) and wrote both theological and philosophical works, such as *Discours philosophiques* (1587). 📖 K M Hall, *Pontus de Tyard and his Discours philosophiques* (1963)

Tye, Christopher c.1505–c.1572
English musician

Born in Westminster, London, he received his MusD from Cambridge and Oxford in 1548. He was musical instructor to Edward VI, and under Elizabeth I was organist to the Chapel Royal, when he wrote some notable church music.

Tyler, Anne 1941–
US novelist and short-story writer

She was born in Minneapolis, Minnesota, and raised in Raleigh, North Carolina. She graduated at 19 from Duke University, and later became a Russian bibliographer and assistant to the librarian, McGill University Law Library. Writing mainly of life in Baltimore or in Southern small towns, and concerned with the themes of loneliness, isolation and human interactions, she has had a productive career since her debut in 1964 with *If Morning Ever Comes*. Other significant titles include *Morgan's Passing* (1980), *Dinner at the Homesick Restaurant* (1982), *The Accidental Tourist* (1985, filmed 1988), *Breathing Lessons* (1988, Pulitzer Prize) and *Ladder of Years* (1995). 📖 A Petty, *Understanding Anne Tyler* (1990)

Tyler, John 1790–1862
10th President of the USA

Born in Charles City County, Virginia, he was admitted to the Bar in 1809, and having sat in the state legislature (1811–16) he entered Congress. In 1825 he was elected Governor of Virginia, and in 1826 US Senator. He resented the despotic methods by which Andrew Jackson overthrew the United States Bank, supported Henry Clay's motion to censure the President and in 1836 resigned his seat. In 1840 he was elected Vice-President. President Harrison died in 1841, a month after his inauguration, and Tyler became President. His administration (1841–45) was marked by the Ashburton Treaty and the annexation of Texas (1845). Failing to capture his party's nomination in 1844, he retired to his Virginia plantation the following year. On the outbreak of the Civil War he adhered to the Confederate cause, and he was a member of the Confederate Congress until his death.

Tyler, Wat d.1381
English rebel, leader of the Peasants' Revolt

He was probably a tiler from Essex, chosen by a mob of peasants to be their spokesman after taking Rochester Castle (1381). Under him they moved to Canterbury, Blackheath and London. At a conference with Richard II at Smithfield, London, demanding an end to serfdom and greater freedom of labour, blows were exchanged and Tyler was wounded by William Walworth, Mayor of London. Walworth had him dragged out from St Bartholomew's Hospital and beheaded.

Tylor, Sir Edward Burnett 1832–1917
English anthropologist

Born in Camberwell, London, he attended a Quaker school until the age of 16, when, barred from attending university by his faith, he became a clerk in his father's business. Going to the USA in 1855 due to bad health, he travelled with Henry Christy to Mexico and published *Ahahuac*, an account of his journey, in 1861. His first major anthropological study, *Researches into the Early History of Mankind and the Development of Civilization*, appeared in 1865, and in 1871 he published his monumental *Primitive Culture* (2 vols). In this work he sought to show that human culture, above all in its religious aspect, is governed by definite laws of evolutionary development, such that the beliefs and practices of primitive nations may be taken to represent earlier stages in the progress of mankind. After the appearance of Charles Darwin's *The Descent of Man* (1871), he was drawn to the view that cultural variation may be due to racial differences in mental endowment, as reflected in his general introductory work *Anthropology* (1881). Though he never

obtained a university degree, he became one of the leading professional anthropologists of his time, and he is widely regarded as the founder of the systematic study of human culture. He was keeper of the University Museum at Oxford (1883–84), Reader in Anthropology (1884), and from 1896 to 1909 the first Professor of Anthropology at Oxford. 📖 R R Marett, *Tylor* (1936)

Tynan, Katharine 1861–1931
Irish poet and novelist

Born in Clondalkin, County Dublin, she was a friend of Parnell, the Meynells and the Rossettis and a leading author of the Celtic literary revival. Her journalism established her reputation, but she also wrote some 18 volumes of verse, over a hundred novels, including *Oh! What a Plague is Love* (1896), *She Walks in Beauty* (1899) and *The House in the Forest* (1928), and around 40 other books, including five autobiographical works, the last of which was *Memoires* (1924). Her *Collected Poems* appeared in 1930. 📖 M G Rose, *Katharine Tynan* (1974)

Tynan, Kenneth Peacock 1927–80
English theatre critic

He was born in Birmingham. While reading English at Magdalen College, Oxford, where he was regarded as something of a juvenile prodigy, he became deeply involved in the theatre, and his first book, *He that plays the King* (1950) was a brilliant and provocative personal view of the current theatre scene. He became drama critic for several publications, notably the *Observer* (1954–63), where he was one of the first to champion John Osborne and the other new playwrights of the time. He abandoned drama criticism to become literary manager of the National Theatre, London, (1963–69) under Sir Laurence Olivier, and he was an important influence on the image and direction of that company. He also worked as an editor in films and television. A vigorous opponent of censorship, he later achieved some notoriety with his revue *Oh, Calcutta!* (1969) which featured much nudity, and by being the first to use the word 'fuck' on British television. He was a powerful force in British theatre, and his collected reviews were published as *Curtains* (1961) and *Tynan Right and Left* (1967). 📖 Kathleen Tynan, *The Life of Kenneth Tynan* (1987)

Tyndale or Tindale or Hutchins, William c.1494–1536
English translator of the Bible

Born probably in Slymbridge in Gloucestershire, he was educated at Magdalen Hall, Oxford (1510–15), he became a chaplain and tutor, sympathetic to humanist learning. In 1523 he went to London to seek support for his project to translate the Scriptures into the vernacular. Bishop Cuthbert Tunstall having refused his support, Tyndale then went to Hamburg (1524), to Wittenberg, where he visited Martin Luther, and to Cologne (1525), where he began printing his English New Testament in the same year. This had not proceeded beyond the gospels of Matthew and Mark when the intrigues of Johann Cochlaeus forced Tyndale to flee to Worms, where Peter Schoeffer printed for him 3,000 New Testaments in small octavo. The translation owed much to Luther and Desiderius Erasmus, much to his own scholarship and literary skill. Tunstall and William Warham denounced the book and hundreds of copies were burned. In 1527 he moved to Marburg to the protection of Philip the Magnanimous, and in 1529 he was shipwrecked on the way to Hamburg, where he met Miles Coverdale. In 1531 he went to Antwerp and there probably (though ostensibly at Marburg) was published his *Pentateuch* (1530–31) where the marginal glosses, almost all original, contain violent attacks on the pope and the bishops. His version of *Jonah*, with a prologue was printed in 1531. An unauthorized revision of Tyndale's New Testament was made at Antwerp in August 1534, and in November Tyndale issued there his own revised version. One copy of his works was struck off on vellum for presentation to **Anne Boleyn**, under whose favour, apparently, a reprint of Tyndale's revised New Testament was printed in 1536 by T Godfray, the first volume of Holy Scripture printed in England. Tyndale revised his Testament in 1535, this time without the marginal notes. The emissaries of **Henry VIII** had often tried to get hold of him and in 1535 he was betrayed by Henry Philips, a Roman Catholic zealot, arrested in Antwerp, accused of heresy, imprisoned in the Castle of Vilvorde, tried there (1536), and on 6 October strangled and burned. His other original works were *The Parable of the Wicked Mammon* (1528), *The Obedience of a Christian Man*, his most elaborate book (1528), and *Practyse of Prelates* (1530). His *Works* were published in 1573.

Tyndall, John 1820–93
Irish physicist
Born in Leighlin-Bridge, County Carlow, and largely self-educated, he was employed on the ordnance survey and as a railway engineer, before studying physics in England and at Marburg University in Germany under **Robert Bunsen**. He became professor at the Royal Institution in 1854. In 1856 he and **T H Huxley** visited the Alps and collaborated in *The Glaciers of the Alps* (1860), when he made the first ascent of the Weisshorn. In 1859 he began his researches into radiant heat and the acoustic properties of the atmosphere. In the course of his study of light beams, he discovered in 1869 the Tyndall effect (the scattering of light by particles in solution, which makes the light beam visible when viewed from the side). His suggestion that the blue colour of the sky is due to the greater scattering of blue light by particles of atmospheric dust and water vapour was confirmed by Lord **Rayleigh**. Tyndall died from accidental poisoning with chloral. 📖 A S Eve and C H Creasey, *The Life and Work of John Tyndall* (1945)

Typhoid Mary, *real name* Mary Mallon c.1870–1938
US cook and typhoid carrier
She was the first carrier of typhoid identified in the USA, and though she herself was immune to the disease, she was discovered to have caused 51 cases and 3 deaths. Isolated in a New York hospital from 1907 to 1910, she was released after promising not to take a job that involved handling food. After typhoid broke out at two hospitals where she was employed as a cook, she was recaptured and isolated for the rest of her life.

Tyrconnel, Richard Talbot, 1st Earl of 1630–91
Irish political leader
He went to London at the Restoration of **Charles II** and soon gained the favour of the royal family. **James VII and II** created him Earl of Tyrconnel, with command of the troops in Ireland, and in 1687 appointed him Lord Deputy of Ireland. The Revolution of 1688–89 thwarted his plans to undo the Protestant ascendancy in Ireland and he tried in vain to intrigue with **William III**. After the Battle of the Boyne (1690) he retired to France until 1691, when he returned as Lord Lieutenant. He was made titular duke (1689) by the deposed James II.

Tyrone, 2nd Earl of See O'Neill, Hugh

Tyrtaeus fl.c.685–668BC
Greek elegiac poet
He was born probably in Sparta, and his war songs inspired the Spartans during the second Messenian War (650–630BC). 📖 C M Bowra, *Early Greek Elegists* (1938)

Tyson, Edward 1651–1708
English physician
Born in Bristol, he was educated at Magdalen Hall, Oxford. He set up in practice in London, being appointed physician to Bridewell and Bethlehem hospitals, while continuing to pursue anatomical experiments and dissections, and publishing papers in the *Philosophical Transactions* of the Royal Society of London. Tyson saw comparative anatomy as the discipline that would reveal the underlying structural unity of nature, the 'great chain of being', and in 1690 published a monograph on the anatomy of the porpoise, which he believed, transitional in morphological terms between fish and land creatures. He also published anatomical accounts of the lumpfish, rattlesnake and shark, and is remembered for his 1699 work on what he called the 'orang-outang' (in reality a chimpanzee brought back from Malaya). He viewed this primate as intermediate between humans and the apes, and his work helped spark a fierce and continuing debate about the relationship of humans to other primates.

Tyson, Mike (Michael Gerald) 1966–
US boxer
Born in New York City, he turned professional in 1985, and 15 of his first 25 opponents were knocked out in the first round. He beat Trevor Berbick (1952–) for the World Boxing Council (WBC) version of the world heavyweight title in 1986, to become the youngest heavyweight champion (20 years and 145 days), and added the World Boxing Association title in 1987, when he beat James Smith (1954–). In August 1987, he beat Tony Tucker (1958–) to become undisputed world champion, a title he held until February 1990, when he was defeated by James 'Buster' Douglas. In 1992 he was sentenced to six years in jail for charges including rape, served three, and was released in 1995, to remain on probation until 1999. In 1996 he beat **Frank Bruno** to reclaim the WBC title which he then gave up later in the year.

Tytler, James, *known as* 'Balloon' Tytler 1745–1804
Scottish journalist, scientist and balloonist
Born in Fearn, Angus, he was a surgeon's apprentice in Forfar and a student at Edinburgh University. He sailed to Greenland on a whaling ship, before embarking on the first of many ill-fated literary ventures, *The Gentleman and Lady's Magazine*, which lasted 13 issues. He made one of his greatest contributions as editor of the second edition of the *Encyclopaedia Britannica* and worked on it for about seven years, expanding it from three to 10 volumes, much of it written by himself. In 1783 he constructed a balloon, in which he took off on 27 August 1784; he reached a height of 350 feet (107m) and became 'the first person in Great Britain to have navigated the air'. In later life he fell into debt and due to a handbill he printed (1792) that was proclaimed seditious, fled to the USA where he later drowned, intoxicated, in Salem, Massachusetts.

Tyus, Wyomia 1945–
US track and field athlete
Born in Griffin, Georgia, she was a sprinter in high school and college, winning the 1962 Girls' AAU (American Athletic Union) championships in the 100 yard dash, 50 yard dash and the 75 yard dash. At the 1964 Olympics, she won a gold medal in the 100 metres and a silver in the 4 × 100 metre relay. In the 1968 Olympics she won a second gold in the 100 metres, becoming the first athlete to win two consecutive gold medals in that event. She won another gold medal in the 4 × 100 metre relay. She is a founding member of the Women's Sports Foundation, which serves to promote women in all sports. She was elected to the National Track and Field Hall of Fame in 1980 and became a member of the International Women's Sports Hall of Fame in 1981.

Tyutchev, Fyodor Ivanovich 1803–73
Russian lyric poet

Born in Ovstug, Oryol, he spent 20 years abroad in the diplomatic service and then worked in the censorship department. His first collection of poems appeared in 1854 and was received with enthusiasm. A metaphysical romantic, he reached full recognition with the advent of Symbolism. The tragic love poems of his later period are outstanding in Russian literature. 📖 D D Yazykov, *Fyodor Ivanovich Tyutchev* (1904)

Tzara, Tristan 1896–1963
Romanian poet

He was born in Bucharest, but lived in Zurich during and shortly after World War I, and in Paris from 1920. One of the founders of Dadaism, together with **Hans Arp**, Hugo Ball and others, the products of his involvement with the movement include the then revolutionary *Vingt-cinq Poèmes* (1918, '25 Poems') and *Sept Manifestes Dada* (1924, 'Seven Dadaist Manifestos'). After the movement moved its headquarters to Paris in 1920, he contributed to the Dadaist journal *Litterature*, was an active participant in the movement's 'happenings' and was responsible for some splendidly splenetic assaults on the bourgeois order. He became a card-carrying Surrealist in 1929, producing *L'homme Approximatif* ('The Approximate Man') in 1930, but never recaptured the anarchic vitality of his early years.

Tzetzes, Johannes c.1120–1183
Byzantine writer

Born in Constantinople (Istanbul), he wrote commentaries and treatises on grammar, and *Iliaca* as well as *Biblos Istorike*, or *Chiliades*, a review of Greek literature and learning, a collection (in worthless verse) of over 600 stories.

Tz'u Hsi See **Cixi**
Tzu-Wen Sung See **Soong, T V**

Uccello, Paolo c.1396–1475
Florentine painter

Born in Pratovecchio, near Florence, he belonged to the Early Renaissance period, and was primarily concerned with developing the new science of perspective in painting, as in *The Flood* (c.1450, Sta Maria Novella, Florence). He was originally apprenticed to **Lorenzo Ghiberti** but is more closely associated with the circle of **Donatello**. During his lifetime he became unfashionable with patrons and was forgotten until the 20th century when Abstract artists found their own concerns anticipated in his richly patterned compositions. Uccello's style is most evident in the three large-scale panels of the *Battle of San Romano* (1454–57, London, Paris and Florence) executed as decorations for the Palazzo Medici. *The Rout of San Romano* panel, now in the National Gallery, London, is a highly decorative arrangement of diagonal lances, with receding ranks of cavalry depicted in clearly defined space. He also painted in a romantic style, as in *St George and the Dragon* (c.1460, National Gallery, London) and *The Hunt in the Forest* (1468, Ashmolean, Oxford), where the horizontal arrangement draws the viewer's eye to a receding central point.

Udall or Uvedale, John 1560–92
English Puritan clergyman

Educated at Cambridge, he was one of the authors of the underground, anti-clerical *Martin Marprelate* tracts (1588–89). He was arrested in 1590 and sentenced to death, but pardoned. He also wrote a Hebrew grammar (1593) and several volumes of sermons.

Udall or Uvedale, Nicholas 1504–56
English dramatist

Born in Hampshire, he was educated at Winchester and Corpus Christi College, Oxford, and became headmaster of Eton c.1534. He published a selection from **Terence**, *Flowers of Latin Speaking*, for his pupils, who soon learned of his predilection for corporal punishment. His dismissal in 1541 for indecent offences did not affect his standing at the court. **Edward VI** appointed him prebendary of Windsor, and despite his great enthusiasm for the Reformation, he survived the reign of Queen **Mary I** without disfavour. He translated **Erasmus**, selections from the Great Bible and Latin commentaries on the latter, but is chiefly remembered as the author of the comedy *Ralph Roister Doister*, written c.1553 but not published until 1567. Inspired by his favourite classical writers, **Plautus** and **Terence**, it influenced later English writers of comedies. 🕮 C M Saxby, in *Representative English Dramatists* (1903)

Udet, Ernst 1896–1941
German airman

Born in Frankfurt, he was a leading German air ace in World War I, and from 1935 worked in the German air ministry. A *Luftwaffe* quartermaster-general in World War II, he committed suicide by an air crash, having fallen foul of the Gestapo. The authorities described his death as an accident while testing a new air weapon. **Carl Zuckmayer's** play, *The Devil's General*, is based on his life.

Udine, Giovanni da 1487–1564
Italian painter, decorative artist and architect

Born in Udine, he joined the workshop of **Raphael** in Rome and became a specialist in a style of decoration called 'Grotesque' which was influenced by the graceful ornamental schemes, employing fantastic animals, medallions, foliage and similar elements, which were being discovered in the excavations of ancient Rome. He later

moved back to Udine and, by 1552, was in charge of all public building there. His decorative style rapidly spread throughout Europe and was especially popular during the neoclassical period of the 18th century.

Uemura, Naomi 1942–84
Japanese explorer and mountaineer

Born in Tajima region, he studied agriculture at Meiji University, Tokyo, where he started climbing. After solo ascents of Mont Blanc, Kilimanjaro, Aconcagua and Mt McKinley, he reached the summit of Everest with Teruo Matsura in 1970, and so became the first person to reach the highest peak on five continents. From 1977 to 1978 he spent a year living with Inuit people in the Canadian Arctic, travelling by dog sled up the coast of Greenland, and from Greenland to Alaska. He made a solo dog-sled journey from Ellesmere Island to the North Pole, arriving on 1 May 1978, and was then airlifted to his base to undertake a north–south traverse of Greenland using 16 dogs. He left Kap Morris on 12 May 1978 and arrived after 1,600 miles (2,576km) at Narssarssuaq on 22 August 1978. In the winter of 1981 he led the Japanese attempt to climb Mt Everest . However, his planned solo-crossing of Antarctica with an ascent of Mt Vinson was frustrated by the outbreak of the Falklands War (1982). In February 1984 he completed the first winter ascent of the West Buttress Route of Mt McKinley and is presumed to have died during the descent, though his body has not been found.

Ugolino della Gherardesca, Count d.1289
Ghibelline Count of Donoratico

By intriguing with Pisa's enemies, first with the **Guelfs**, then with the Florentines, and through treachery in the city itself, Ugolino came to power in 1284. A tyrant, he was overthrown in 1289, and he and his relations starved to death in the tower in which they were confined. The grisly episode is recalled in **Dante's** *Inferno*.

Uhland, Johann Ludwig 1787–1862
German lyric poet

He was born in Tübingen, where he studied law. He published poems from an early age and gradually added to his *Gedichte* (1815, 'Poems'), which contain such popular songs as 'Der gute Kamerad' ('The Good Comrade'). The leader of the Swabian school, he also wrote a number of admirable literary essays. He was a Liberal deputy for Tübingen at the assemblies of Württemberg (1819) and Frankfurt (1848). 🕮 G Schwarz, *Johann Uhland* (1964)

Uhle, Max 1856–1944
German archaeologist

Trained as a philologist, he later transferred his allegiance to archaeology, becoming interested in Peru while a curator at Dresden Museum. From 1892 he undertook field research for the universities of Pennsylvania and California, excavating on the Peruvian coast at Pachacamac and on Mochica and Chimu sites. He later extended his work into the highlands and to Bolivia, Ecuador, and Chile, making also a notable contribution to North American archaeology with his excavations of the Emeryville shell-mound in San Franciso Bay. The rigour of his approach, influenced by the work of **Flinders Petrie** in Egypt, emphasized stratigraphic excavation and the ordering of finds in their correct evolutionary sequence as a means of establishing chronology. His pioneering work in Peru and Bolivia revolutionized the archaeology of South America.

Uhlenbeck, George Eugene 1900–88
US physicist

Born in Batavia (Jakarta), Indonesia, he studied at the University of Leyden and from 1927 worked at the University of Michigan, where he was appointed Professor of Theoretical Physics in 1939. To explain the results of the **Stern**–Gerlach experiment which showed that a beam of particles passing through a magnetic field are deflected in different directions, Uhlenbeck and his fellow student **Samuel Goudsmit** proposed that electrons in atoms can have intrinsic spin angular momentum as well as orbital angular momentum. **Paul Dirac**'s theory of relativistic quantum mechanics later showed that spin is an intrinsic property of electrons.

Ulanova, Galina Sergeyevna 1910–98
Russian ballerina

Born in St Petersburg, she studied there at the Petrograd State Ballet and made her debut in *Les Sylphides* at the Kirov Theatre in 1928. She joined the Bolshoi Ballet in 1944 and became the leading ballerina of the Soviet Union, winning the **Stalin** Prize four times and the **Lenin** Prize in 1957. She visited London in 1956 with the Bolshoi Ballet, when she gave a memorable perfomance in *Giselle*, perhaps her most famous role. She has appeared in several films made by the Moscow State Ballet Company. She retired in 1961, but continued to teach at the Bolshoi. ⌨ B Lvov-Anokhin, *Galina Ulanova* (1984)

Ulbricht, Walter 1893–1973
East German Communist politician

He was born in Leipzig. In 1928, after some years in Russia, he became Communist deputy for Potsdam. He left Germany when **Hitler** achieved power in 1933. He went first to Paris and was in Spain during the civil war, but spent the greater part of his exile in Russia. As Marshal **Georgi Zhukov**'s political adviser and head of the German Communist Party, he returned in 1945, and by 1950 had become deputy premier of the German Democratic Republic. The same year he was made Secretary-General of the party, and was largely responsible for the 'sovietization' of East Germany. He survived a workers' uprising in 1953 and went on to establish his position. He is remembered chiefly for building the Berlin Wall in 1961. He retired in 1971. ⌨ Carola Stern, *Ulbricht: A Political Biography* (1965)

Ulfilas or Wulfila c.311–383AD
Cappadocian prelate

Born among the Goths north of the Danube, he was consecrated a missionary bishop to the Visigoths by **Eusebius of Nicomedia** in AD341. After seven years' work, he was forced to migrate with his converts across the Danube. For over 30 years he worked in Lower Moesia. He attended the Council of Constantinople in 360 in the interest of the Arian party, and again in 383, only to die a few days after his arrival. He translated the Bible into a Germanic language from Greek.

Ullman, Tracey 1959–
English singer, comedienne and actress

Born in Buckinghamshire, she went to stage school in London and had parts in the musicals *Elvis* and *Grease!* before breaking through as a comic in *Three of a Kind* (1981). Her singing career, consisting largely of cover versions, includes 'Breakaway', 'Move Over Darling', and 'They Don't Know' (Labour Party leader **Neil Kinnock** appeared in the video). She returned to acting and received mixed critical fortunes in Great Britain, but after moving to the USA she began the *Tracey Ullman Show* (1987–), which has achieved five Grammy awards.

Ullmann, Liv Johanne 1939–
Norwegian actress

Born in Tokyo, Japan, she studied acting at the Webber-Douglas School in London before beginning her career with a repertory company in Stavanger, Norway. She made her film debut in *Fjols til Fjells* (1957, *Fools in the Mountains*) but her screen image was largely defined through a long professional and personal association with the Swedish director **Ingmar Bergman** in which she laid bare the inner turmoil of women experiencing various emotional and sexual crises. Their films together include *Persona* (1966), *Viskningar och Rop* (1972, *Cries and Whispers*), *Ansikte mot Ansikte* (1975, *Face to Face*) and *Hostsonaten* (1978, *Autumn Sonata*). Her work for other filmmakers has been less challenging, particularly in English-language productions like *Lost Horizon* (1973). She made her Broadway debut in *A Doll's House* (1975), and regular theatre appearances include *I Remember Mama* (1979) and *Old Times* (1985, London). She has worked extensively for the charity UNICEF and written two autobiographical works: *Changing* (1977) and *Choices* (1984). Her films as director include *Sofie* (1992) and *Enskilda Samtal* (1996).

Ulm, Charles Thomas Philippe 1898–1934
Australian pioneer aviator

Born in Melbourne, Victoria, he fought with the Australian Imperial Forces at Gallipoli in 1915 and later qualified as a pilot. In 1927 he joined **Charles Kingsford Smith** in a record-breaking round-Australia flight, and in 1928 he was co-pilot with Kingsford Smith on the first flight across the Pacific Ocean and on the first trans-Tasman Sea flight. In 1929 they made a 13-day flight from Australia to England, a record Ulm lowered to seven days in his Avro Ten *Faith in Australia* (1933). With Kingsford Smith he formed the first Australian National Airways in 1929, and in 1934 Ulm carried the first airmail deliveries between Australia and New Zealand and, later, New Guinea. While investigating the possibilities of regular airmail flights across the Pacific, he set out from California with two companions in his new twin-engine *Stella Australis*, but the plane vanished without trace over the Hawaiian islands.

Ulpianus, Domitius c.170AD–AD228
Roman jurist

Born in Tyre, he held judicial offices under **Lucius Septimius Severus** and **Caracalla** and, on the accession of **Alexander Severus** (AD222), became his principal adviser and a praetorian prefect. He was murdered by his own soldiers. The last of the great classical jurists, he was a voluminous writer. In **Justinian**'s *Digest* there are 2,462 excerpts from Ulpianus; the originals are almost wholly lost.

Ulrika Eleonora 1688–1741
Queen of Sweden

The younger sister of **Karl XII**, she was born in Stockholm, married to Prince Frederick of Hesse (1715), and was elected queen in 1718 after her brother's death. A new constitution, however, inaugurated the so-called Era of Liberty (1718–71), and saw the abolition of royal absolutism, giving power to the Riksdag (parliament). Ulrika was so displeased that she abdicated (1720) in favour of her husband, who ascended the throne as **Fredrik I**.

Ulugh-Beg 1394–1449
Tatar prince and astronomer

A grandson of **Timur** who drew learned men to Samarkand, he founded an observatory there in 1420, and between 1420 and 1437 prepared new planetary tables and a new star catalogue, the latter being the first since that of **Ptolemy**. Positions were given with precision; this was the first time that latitude and longitude were measured to minutes of arc and not just degrees. His instruments must have been excellent. He was ruler of Turkestan from 1447. He also wrote poetry and history. After a brief reign, he was defeated and slain by a rebellious son.

Umar See **Omar**

Umar Pasha See **Omar Pasha**

Umberto I 1844–1900
King of Italy

Born in Turin, the son and successor of **Victor Emmanuel II**, he distinguished himself at the Battle of Custozza (1866). In 1868 he married his cousin Margherita of Savoy and in 1878 succeeded his father. He is often portrayed as a model constitutional monarch who, despite his conservative sympathies and considerable pressure from reactionary politicians, rarely interfered in parliamentary affairs. In reality, he was content to block ministerial appointments and to use the royal prerogative, especially in matters concerning the army or foreign affairs. Despite a genuine concern for his subjects, manifest particularly at times of natural disaster, there were attempts on his life (1878, 1897), before he was finally assassinated by an anarchist.

Umberto II 1904–83
King of Italy

Made de facto regent (Lieutenant-General of the Realm) by his father, **Victor Emmanuel III** in 1944, he ascended the throne on the latter's abdication (1946), at a time when the monarchy had become widely unpopular. In a referendum later the same year Italians voted in favour of a republic and Umberto was forced to leave Italy, setting up residence in Portugal as the self-styled Count Di Sarre.

Unamuno, Miguel de 1864–1936
Spanish philosopher and writer

Born in Bilbao, of Basque parents, he was educated at the Instituto Vizcaino of Bilbao and the University of Madrid, and was Professor of Greek at Salamanca from 1892. He wrote mystic philosophy, historical studies, essays, books on travel, and austere poetry. Among his most important works are *Vida de Don Quijote y Sancho* (1905, Eng trans *The Life of Don Quixote and Sancho*, 1927), his novel *Niebla* (1914, Eng trans *Mist*, 1928), *Del sentimiento trágico de la vida* (1913, Eng trans *The Tragic Sense of Life in Men and in Peoples*, 1926) and a volume of religious poetry, *El Cristo de Velázquez* (1920, Eng trans *The Christ of Velázquez*, 1951). He was exiled as a Republican to the island of Fuerteventura (1924–30), and reinstated at Salamanca on the founding of the republic (1931). Always a rebel and an individualist though with the deepest faith in and interest of his country at heart, he was soon at variance with the socialist regime. The Civil War for him was a nationalist struggle and he denounced foreign interference. 📖 A Barea, *Miguel de Unamuno* (1952)

Uncas c.1588–c.1683
Native American leader, first chief of the Mohegans

Born into the Pequot people (in present-day Connecticut), he was frustrated in his efforts to become chief, and after leading an unsuccessful rebellion was forced into exile. With his followers he formed the Mohegans, siding with the British in the Pequot Wars (1638), and he later fought a series of wars with the Narragansett (1643–47). In 1675 he was required to leave his sons with the English as a pledge of his neutrality in King Philip's War.

Underhill, Evelyn 1875–1941
English poet and mystic

Born in Wolverhampton, she was educated at King's College London and in 1921 became lecturer on the philosophy of religion at Manchester College, Oxford. A friend and disciple of Baron Friedrich von Hügel (1852–1925), she found her way intellectually from agnosticism to Christianity, and wrote numerous books on mysticism, including *The Life of the Spirit* (1922), volumes of verse, and four novels. Her *Mysticism* (1911) became a standard work.

Underwood, Rory 1963–
English rugby union player

Born in Middlesbrough, he holds England's record as most-capped player, and most-capped wing, with 85 caps from 1985 to 1996. His 49 tries in 85 matches is also a record. As a British Lion he toured Australia in 1989 and New Zealand in 1993, although his service in the RAF sometimes restricted his availability. At club level he has represented Middlesbrough, Durham and Leicester, and he was recruited by **Rob Andrew** for Newcastle in 1995. His brother Tony (1969–) plays for Leicester; they played together for England in 1992–95 and in New Zealand with the Lions in 1993.

Undset, Sigrid 1882–1949
Norwegian novelist and Nobel Prize winner

She was born in Kalundborg, Denmark, the daughter of a noted Norwegian archaeologist. From 1899 she worked in an office, and the problems facing young contemporary women helped to form the basis of her early novels, including *Jenny* (1911). Her masterpiece, *Kristin Lavransdatter* (3 vols, 1920–22), which tells a graphic story of love and religion in 14th-century Norway, was followed by *Olav Audunssön* (4 vols, 1925–27), and *Den trofaste hustru* (1936, Eng trans *The Faithful Spouse*, 1937). She became a Roman Catholic in 1924, after which her work deepened in religious intensity. She was awarded the Nobel Prize for literature in 1928. During World War II she was exiled in the USA, an outspoken opponent of Nazism. 📖 M Brunsdale, *Sigrid Undset* (1988)

Ungaretti, Giuseppe 1888–1970
Italian poet

Born in Alexandria, Egypt, he first visited Italy when he was 26, then fought in the Italian army in World War I. From 1912 to 1914 he studied in Paris where he met **Guillaume Apollinaire**, becoming Professor of Italian Literature at São Paulo, Brazil (1936–42), and at Rome (1942–58). The author of 'hermetic' poems characterized by their symbolism, compressed imagery and modern verse structure, he had his first collection, *Il porto sepolto* ('The Buried Harbour'), published in 1916 with a preface by **Mussolini**. Among his collections is *Vita d'un uomo* (7 vols, 1942–61, 'Life of a Man'), which includes *Il dolore* (1947,'Grief'). 📖 P Piccioni, *Vita di un poeta* (1970)

Ungaro, Emanuel Maffeolti 1933–
French fashion designer

He was born in Aix-en-Provence, of Italian parents. Originally he trained to join the family tailoring business, but went instead to Paris in 1955, worked for a small tailoring firm, and later joined **Cristóbal Balenciaga**. In 1965 he opened his own house, with Sonia Knapp designing his fabrics. Initially featuring rigid lines, his styles later softened. In 1968 he produced his first ready-to-wear lines.

Unitas, Johnny Constantine 1933–
US footballer

Born in Pittsburgh, Pennsylvania, he was one of the game's first television heroes. A quarter-back, he signed for the Baltimore Colts in 1956. Two years later he led them to a championship victory against the New York Giants in overtime. The game was broadcast live in the USA and helped American football to its big television breakthrough. In 1973, at the age of 40, he joined the San Diego Chargers but was injured after only three games and retired. He then set up his own restaurant in Baltimore.

Universalis, Doctor See **Albertus Magnus, St**

Unna, Percy 1878–1950
Scottish environmental philanthropist
Born in London, a civil engineer by profession, he became president of the Scottish Mountaineering Club in the mid-1930s. One of the first to appreciate the unique quality of Scottish mountain scenery, he compiled what are known as 'Unna's Rules'. These were guidelines for the conservation of the Scottish mountains, following the National Trust for Scotland's purchase of important mountain properties, such as Glencoe. His rules remain a touchstone for the management of access and the protection of 'wilderness quality' in the uplands. He was a generous anonymous donator to the National Trust, and his bequests still provide for land management and purchase.

Unruh, Fritz von 1885–1970
German playwright and novelist
He was born in Koblenz, and served in World War I as a cavalry officer, but resigned in 1912 to turn to writing. He was an ardent pacifist, and the ideal of a new humanity underlies all his Expressionist works, particularly the novel *Opfergang* (1916, Eng trans *The Way of Sacrifice*, 1928), and the two parts of an unfinished dramatic trilogy, *Ein Geschlecht* (1916, 'A Species') and *Platz* (1920, 'Place'). He left Germany in 1932 and went to the USA, where he wrote several works, including *Der nie Verlor* (1948, Eng trans *The End is not Yet*, 1948) and *Die jüngste Nacht* (1948, 'The Youngest Night'). He returned to Germany in 1952.
📖 A Kronacher, *Fritz von Unruh* (1946)

Unser, Al 1939–
US Indycar driver
Born in Albuquerque, New Mexico, he is the first in a long line of Indycar Unsers. He has won Indianapolis 500 four times — 1970, 1971, 1978 and 1987. He was three times Indycar champion (1970, 1983 and 1985), was International Race of Champions (IROC) champion in 1978 and won the 24-hour Daytona race in 1985. His brother, Bobby Unser (1934–), was twice Indycar champion (1968 and 1974) and IROC champion in 1975, and his son, Al Unser Jnr (1962–), was Indycar champion in 1990 and 1994 and IROC champion in 1986 and 1988, and won Daytona in 1986 and 1987 and the Marlboro Challenge in 1989.

Unsöld, Albrecht Otto Johannes 1905–
German astrophysicist
Born in Bolheim, Württemberg, he was educated at the universities of Tübingen and Munich, where he studied theoretical physics under Arnold Sommerfeld. He was appointed lecturer at the University of Hamburg (1930–32), and in 1932 he became Professor of Theoretical Physics and director of the observatory at the University of Kiel, where he established a flourishing school of theoretical astrophysics. He is currently emeritus professor there. His main research has been on the physics of stellar atmospheres, discovering the hydrogen convection zone (1931) which explains heat transport in the Sun's outer layers, and his *Physik der Sternatmosphären* (1938, 'Physics of Stellar Atmospheres') is a classic on the subject. Unsöld was awarded the gold medal of the Royal Astronomical Society in 1957.

Unsworth, Barry (Foster) 1930–
English novelist
Born in Durham, he was the first of his family not to work in the coalmines. Educated at Stockton Grammar School and Manchester University, he travelled widely and held a variety of teaching posts, including some time at the University of Istanbul. His first novel, *The Partnership* (1966), was followed by four more before *Pascali's Island* (1980), which was shortlisted for the Booker Prize, and later filmed. His books often reflect on historical themes, and are set in locations which mirror his own wanderings, notably Turkey, Greece, and Italy, the setting for *Stone Virgin* (1985). His major work is the novel *Sacred Hunger* (1992), an epic account of the 18th-century Atlantic slave trade, for which he was jointly awarded the Booker Prize, with Michael Ondaatje. Later novels include *Morality Play* (1995) and *After Hannibal* (1996).

Unverdorben, Otto 1806–73
German chemist
Born in Dahme, near Potsdam, he studied for a year at the Pharmaceutical Institute at Erfurt and later entered the family manufacturing business at Dahme. He experimented with the destructive distillation of organic substances, including resins, shellacs and animal oils. He discovered guaiacol by the destructive distillation of wood, and also aniline (which he termed 'crystalline') by the dry distillation of indigo. Aniline, which was later found to be a primary aromatic amine, became important to the German dye industry.

Unwin, Sir Stanley 1884–1968
English publisher
Educated at Abbotsholme School, Staffordshire, he studied the book-trade in Germany, and became chairman of the firm of George Allen and Unwin, founded in 1914. An international figure in publishing, he was president of the Publishers Association of Great Britain (1933–35) and president of the International Publishers Association (1936–38, 1946–54). His books include *The Truth about Publishing* (1926; rev edn 1960), *Publishing in Peace and War* (1944) and his autobiography, *The Truth about a Publisher* (1960).

Updike, John Hoyer 1932–
US novelist, poet and critic
Born in Shillington, Pennsylvania, he studied at Harvard and the Ruskin School of Drawing and Fine Art in Oxford, England (1954–55). He then worked for the *New Yorker* (1955–57), the beginning of a long and fruitful relationship with the magazine to which he has contributed short stories, poems and book reviews. His status as one of the world's major writers is due largely to his fiction. Sophisticated, linguistically supple, fluent and inventive, his beat is middle-class USA, his concerns those that have dominated the 20th century: sex, marriage, adultery, divorce, religion, materialism. Among his best-known books are *The Centaur* (1963), the Rabbit series—*Rabbit, Run* (1960), *Rabbit Redux* (1971), *Rabbit is Rich* (1981) and *Rabbit at Rest* (1990, Pulitzer Prize)—chronicling the life of a car salesman, *Couples* (1968), *The Coup* (1978) and *The Witches of Eastwick* (1984). More recent works include *Roger's Version* (1986) and *In the Beauty of the Lilies* (1996). *Self-Consciousness*, a memoir, was published in 1989 and his *Collected Poems 1953–1993* were published in 1993. 📖 R Detweiler, *John Updike* (1972, rev edn 1984)

Upfield, Arthur W(illiam) 1888–1964
Australian writer of detective fiction
Brought up in Hampshire, England, and trained as a surveyor and land agent, he emigrated to Australia in 1911, returning to live in England for only a short time after military service in World War I. His first novel, *The House of Cain*, appeared in 1928, but he gained recognition with *The Barrakee Mystery* (1929, published in the USA as *The Lure of the Bush*, 1965) which introduced the character Inspector Napoleon Bonaparte, a half-Aboriginal. He wrote 29 Bonaparte mysteries; an unfinished 30th was completed and published posthumously. The novels, which document a significant sea-change in Australian attitudes to Aboriginal and mixed-race people, include *Death of a Swagman* (1945), *An Author Bites the Dust* (1948), and *Bony and the Black Virgin* (1959). 📖 J Hawke, *Follow My Dust! A Biography of Arthur Upfield* (1957)

Urabi Pasha 1839–1911
Egyptian soldier and nationalist leader

An officer in the Egyptian army, he fought in the Egyptian–Ethiopian War (1875–79) and took part in the officers' revolt that deposed the Khedive, Ismail Pasha, in 1879. He was the leader of a rebellion against the new Khedive, Tewfik Pasha, in 1881 (the Urabi Revolt), which led to the establishment of a nationalist government, in which he was War Minister. The British intervened to protect their interests in the Suez Canal, and he was defeated at Tel el-Kebir in 1882. Sentenced to death, he was exiled to Ceylon (Sri Lanka) instead and was pardoned in 1901.

Urbain, Georges 1872–1938
French chemist

He was born in Paris and educated at the École de Physique et de Chimie in Paris, where Pierre Curie was on the staff, and at the University of Paris. He was Professor of Analytical Chemistry at the Sorbonne from 1906 to 1928, when he became director of the Institut de Chimie de Paris. Between 1895 and 1912 he performed more than 200,000 fractional crystallizations in which he separated the elements samarium, europium, gadolinium, terbium, dysprosium and holmium. In 1907 he discovered lutetium in ytterbium, previously thought to have been in a pure form, and in 1922 isolated hafnium at the same time as George Charles von Hevesy and Dirk Coster working in Copenhagen. Urbain lent samples of the rare earths to Marie Curie who was investigating the radioactive properties of all the known elements. In parallel with his work on the rare earths, he also wrote on isomorphism and phosphorescence.

Urban II, *originally* Odo of Lagery c.1035–1099
French pope

Born in Châtillon-sur-Marne, he became a monk at Cluny, and was made Cardinal Bishop of Ostia in 1078. As pope (1088–99), he introduced ecclesiastical reforms, drove foreign armies from Italy, and launched the First Crusade (1095).

Urban IV, *originally* Jacques Pantaléon c.1200–64
French pope

Born in Troyes, he was Bishop of Verdun (1253) and Patriarch of Jerusalem (1255). He instituted the feast of Corpus Christi (1264).

Urban V, *originally* Guillaume de Grimoard c.1310–70
French pope

Born in Grisac, he was abbot of St Victor at Marseilles, and was elected pope at Avignon (1362). He made a determined attempt to move the papacy to Rome (1367–70), but had to return to Avignon a few months before his death.

Urban VIII, *originally* Maffeo Barberini 1568–1644
Italian pope

Born in Florence, he was Papal Legate in France (1601), and became a cardinal (1606). Becoming pope in 1623, he supported Cardinal Richelieu's policy against the Habsburgs in the Thirty Years War, and carried out much ecclesiastical reform. A great scholar and supporter of the arts, he issued several condemnations of heresy, which included the writings of Galileo and Cornelius Otto Jansen.

Urban, Sylvanus See Cave, Edward

Ure Smith, Sydney George 1887–1949
Australian artist, editor and publisher

Born in Stoke Newington, London, he went to Australia as an infant in 1888, and was educated in Melbourne and at Sydney Grammar School. He attended Julian Ashton's Art School in Sydney, and his etchings appeared in a number of volumes including *The Charm of Sydney* (1918) and *Old Colonial Byways* (1928). He organized the Australian art exhibition held at Burlington House, London, in 1923, published the seminal journal *Art in Australia* from 1916 to 1939, and edited books on Hilder, Arthur Streeton, Blamire Young and others. He founded his own publishing house in 1939 and was active in promoting the contemporary arts in Australia through a variety of periodicals and books.

Urey, Harold Clayton 1893–1981
US chemist and Nobel Prize winner

Born in Walkerton, Indiana, he taught in rural schools and then studied at Montana State University and the University of California at Berkeley. In 1923–24 he worked with Niels Bohr in Copenhagen. From 1924 to 1929 he was an associate in chemistry at Johns Hopkins University and from 1929 to 1945 he was on the chemistry faculty of Columbia University, New York (as full professor from 1934). He worked at the chemistry department and Institute for Nuclear Studies of the University of Chicago from 1945 to 1958, and thereafter continued to be scientifically active in retirement for many years at the University of California at La Jolla. Urey's earliest research was on atomic and molecular spectra and structure, but he is chiefly remembered for his discovery in 1932 of heavy hydrogen (deuterium), together with Ferdinand Brickwedde and George Murphy. Subsequently he made many studies of the separation of isotopes and isotopic exchange reactions. During World War II he was prominent in the attempts to separate uranium-235 for the atomic bomb as part of the Manhattan Project. He later advocated an international ban on nuclear weapons. After 1945 his research interests moved to geochemistry and cosmochemistry, and he wrote *The Planets* (1952) and *Some Cosmochemical Problems* (1961). He was awarded the Nobel Prize for chemistry in 1934. He received the Davy Medal of the Royal Society in 1940 and became a Foreign Member in 1947. He was made an Honorary Fellow of the Chemical Society in 1945, and also received the Priestley Medal of the American Chemical Society. 📖 Alvin and Virginia Silverstein, *Harold Urey* (1971)

Urfé, Honoré d' 1568–1625
French writer

Born in Marseilles, he fought in the religious wars of France and later settled in Savoy. He was the author of the pastoral romance, *Astrée* (1610–27, 'Astrea'), which is regarded as the first French novel. He was killed at Villefranche-sur-Mer during the war between Savoy and Genoa.

Uris, Leon M(arcus) 1924–
US writer

Born in Baltimore, Maryland, he dropped out of high school and joined the Marine Corps, taking part in battles in the Pacific. *Battle Cry* (1956) uses the experience to telling effect. *Exodus* (1958) remains the book by which he is best known. Depicting the early years of the state of Israel, it was made into a highly successful film. *QBVII* (1970) concerns a libel trial over a former Nazi war criminal. Subsequent works include *Trinity* (1976), *The Haj* (1984) and *Redemption* (1995).

Urquhart, David 1805–77
Scottish diplomat

Born in Cromarty, he served in the Greek navy during the Greek War of Independence and received his first diplomatic appointment in 1831 when he went to Constantinople (Istanbul) with Sir Stratford de Redcliffe. His anti-Russian policy caused his recall from Turkey in 1837 and he was MP for Stafford from 1847 to 1852. A strong opponent of Lord **Palmerston**'s policy, he believed Turkey was capable of dealing with Russia without European intervention. He founded the *Free Press*, afterwards called the *Diplomatic Review*, in which these views were expressed. He retired in 1864. Among his many writings were *The Pillars of Hercules* (1850), in which he suggested the introduction of Turkish baths into Great Britain, and *The Lebanon* (1860).

Urquhart, Fred 1912–95
Scottish short-story writer and novelist

Born in Edinburgh, he grew up in Fife, Perth and Wigtown, leaving school at 15 and then working as bookseller's assistant and labourer. He later became a publisher's reader, and literary editor of *Tribune*. His first novel, *Time Will Knit* (1938) was followed by *The Ferret Was Abraham's Daughter* (1949), *Jezebel's Dust* (1951) and *Palace of Green Days* (1979, the first of a projected series). He published 11 collections of his short stories, many initially broadcast by the BBC, and edited nine anthologies of short stories. His greatest achievement was his ability to convey narrative plots through the eyes of female characters, initially in the Scotland of his childhood and adolescence and later using ghost stories, historical fiction and other forms. ⌑ C Affleck, 'Fred Urquhart', in *Dictionary of Literary Biography*, Vol 139 (1994)

Urquhart, Sir Thomas c.1611–60
Scottish writer

Born in Cromarty, he studied at King's College, Aberdeen, and travelled in France, Spain and Italy. On his return he took up arms against the Covenanting party in the north but was defeated and forced to flee to England, where he joined the court and was knighted in 1641. The same year he published his *Epigrams: Divine and Moral*. Returning north in 1642 he produced his *Trissotetras; or a most exquisite Table for Resolving Triangles, etc* (1645), a study of trigonometry based on **John Napier**'s invention of logarithms. In 1649 his library was seized and sold. He again took up arms in the royal cause, and was present at the Battle of Worcester (1651), where he lost most of his manuscripts. In London, through **Cromwell**'s influence, he was allowed considerable liberty, and in 1652 he published his *Pantochronochanon*, which traces the Urquhart family back to Adam, and *Ekskubalauron* (better known as *The Discoverie of a most Exquisite Jewel*), in praise of the Scots nation. Other works include a brilliant translation of **Rabelais** (books 1 and 2, 1653, book 3 published posthumously). He is said to have died abroad, in a fit of mirth on hearing of the Restoration. ⌑ J Willcock, *Sir Thomas Urquhart of Cromartie* (1895)

Ursula, St 4th century AD
Semi-legendary saint

She is especially honoured in Cologne, where she is said to have been killed with her 11,000 virgins by a horde of Huns on her journey home from a pilgrimage to Rome. She became the patron saint of many educational institutes, particularly the teaching order of the Ursulines. Her feast day is 21 October.

Usher, James See Ussher, James

Usigli, Rodolfo 1905–
Mexican dramatist, poet and theatre director

He was born in Mexico City of an Italian father and a Polish mother. He was always highly critical of the Mexican government, and not all his plays have been published or performed. The most original of his many plays is the Pirandellian *El gesticulador* (1937, 'The Gesticulator'), a masterful satirical analysis of Mexico's proneness to lying and the creation of false myths: a mad retired professor impersonates a revolutionary, and dies at the hands of his assassin. Other plays include *Corona de Sombra* (1943, Eng trans *Crown of Shadows*, 1946). ⌑ E Anderson-Imbert, *Spanish-American Literature: A History* (1963)

Ussher or Usher, James 1581–1656
Irish prelate

Born in Dublin, he was a scholar (1594) and Fellow (1599–1605) of Trinity College, Dublin. In 1605, he drew up the Articles of Doctrine for the Irish Protestant Church. In 1620 he was made Bishop of Meath, in 1623 Privy Councillor for Ireland, and in 1625 Archbishop of Armagh, in succession to his uncle Henry Ussher (c.1550–1631). He went to England (1640), and for about eight years was preacher at Lincoln's Inn. He was constant in his loyalty to the throne, yet was treated with favour by **Cromwell**. Distinguished not only by his learning but also by his charity and good temper, he was **Calvin**istic in theology and moderate in his ideas of Church government. Of his numerous writings, the best known is the *Annales Veteris et Novi Testamenti* (1650–54), which fixed the Creation precisely at 4004BC.

Ussing, Hans Henrikson 1911–
Danish biophysicist

He studied physiology at the University of Copenhagen in 1934. His professor, **August Krogh**, led him to study permeability problems using 'heavy water', water containing the deuterium isotope of hydrogen. After World War II he returned to the zoophysiology department to study active and passive transport mechanisms across biological membranes. His experiments utilized frog skin mounted in a specially constructed apparatus, known as an Ussing chamber, which provided information about transport processes across the skin. In 1951 Ussing proposed a cyclical carrier mechanism of permeability which was used during the following decade to demonstrate the active transport of sodium ions. The fundamental properties of biological tissues that Ussing discovered have been important in some areas of medicine, such as absorption, diffusion and secretion in tissues like the gut and kidneys. In Copenhagen he was Research Professor and head of the isotope division of the department of zoophysiology (1951–60), and head of the Institute of Biological Chemistry (1960–80), where he continues as Emeritus Research Professor.

Ustinov, Dmitri Fyodorovich 1908–84
Soviet politician and marshal

Born into a working-class family, he acquired a technical eduation in his twenties, and by 1938 was manager of an arms factory in Leningrad (now St Petersburg). In 1941 he was appointed as People's Commissar for Armaments; from then until 1976, when he became Minister of Defence, his primary function was to develop the arms industry. He gave it a civilian element and secured it an unfair share of the Soviet budget. He also helped find it an outlet by supporting the invasion of Afghanistan in 1979. His death removed from the ministry and the politburo a fierce opponent of **Mikhail Gorbachev**'s campaign to reduce expenditure on the military.

Ustinov, Sir Peter Alexander 1921–
British actor and playwright

He was born in London, the son of White Russian parents, and first appeared on the stage in 1938. He had established himself as an accomplished artist both in revues and legitimate drama by 1942, when four years' army service interrupted his career. As an actor in films such as *Spartacus* (1960) and *Death on the Nile* (1978), a film writer and producer, and a satirical comedian in broadcasting, he has continued to gain in reputation. A prolific playwright, his works are marked by a serious approach to human problems often presented with an acute sense of comedy. The most successful of his plays are *The Love of*

Four Colonels (1951) and *Romanoff and Juliet* (1956). Among his other plays are *Photo Finish* (1962), *The Unknown Soldier and his Wife* (1967) and *Overheard* (1981). His other works include an autobiography, *Dear Me* (1977), the two novellas collected as *The Disinformer* (1989), and *The Old Man and Mr Smith* (1990). His articles for *The European* newspaper have been collected in *Ustinov at Large* (1991) and *Still at Large* (1993, 1995). He has won many awards, and from 1992 until 1996, was president of the World Federalist Movement. A recent film appearance was in *Stiff Upper Lips* (1997). ⊞ Tony Thomas, *Ustinov in Focus* (1971)

Utamaro, Kitigawa 1753–1806
Japanese painter and engraver
Born and trained in Edo (Tokyo), he specialized in portraits of court ladies, in which the gracefulness of face, figure and flowing robes was depicted with precise close-up detail. He also painted flowers, birds and fish, and used the technique of the *ukiyo-e* ('pictures of the floating world') school.

'Uthman c.575–656
Third caliph
He was elected in succession to Umar, in preference to 'Ali (644). He established a commission of scholars who collected the revelations of **Muhammad** to produce the definitive version of the Qur'an. However, his administration was badly organized, and disagreements concerning the division of the gains made in the Muslim conquests gave rise to increasing social tensions, culminating in a revolt in which he was killed.

Uticensis See Cato, Marcus Porcius, the Younger

Utrillo, Maurice 1883–1955
French painter
Born in Montmartre, Paris, he was the illegitimate son of the painter **Suzanne Valadon**. Adopted by the Spanish writer Miguel Utrillo, he began to paint at Montmagny in 1902, but it was the streets of Paris, particularly old Montmartre, and village scenes which were to provide him with most of his subjects. Despite acute alcoholism and drug addiction, and consequent sojourns in various nursing-homes, his productivity was astonishing, and by 1925 he was famous. His 'White Period' paintings of about 1908–14 are much sought after for their subtle colouring and sensitive feeling for atmosphere. He signed his work 'Maurice Utrillo V', which incorporated the initial of his mother's family name. ⊞ Peter Depolnay, *Enfant Terrible: The Life and World of Maurice Utrillo* (1960)

Uttley, Alison 1884–1976
English writer of children's stories
Born on a farm in Derbyshire, she was widowed in 1930 and turned to writing to support herself and her young son. *The Country Child* (1931) was followed by a flood of books, mainly for children, which revealed her great love for and knowledge of the countryside and country lore. Many of her books were in the **Beatrix Potter** tradition, featuring much-loved characters such as Little Grey Rabbit and Sam Pig. ⊞ E Saintsbury, *The World of Alison Uttley* (1980)

Utzon, Jørn 1918–
Danish architect
Born in Copenhagen, he was educated at the Royal Danish Academy. His buildings include the Sydney Opera House, Bank Melhi (Teheran), the Kuwait House of Parliament, Bagsvæ Church (Copenhagen) and Paustian's House of Furniture (Copenhagen). In 1966 he won the competition for the design of the Zurich Schauspielhaus. He was awarded the Bund Deutscher Architekten's Ehrenplachette (1965), the gold medal of the Royal Institute of British Architects (1978), the Alvar Aalto Medal (1982), the Fritz Schumacher Prize (1988) and the Wolf Prize (1992, jointly).

Uvedale See Udall

Vadasz, Christine 1946–
Australian architect

Born in Hungary, she trained at the University of Adelaide, South Australia. She is the director of Christine Vadasz Architects, Byron Bay, New South Wales, which she founded in 1974. Her practice embodies her sensitive and creative approach to the environment and tends to shy away from overt commerciality. Her innovative designs for the Australian Tourist Board have won her repeat commissions and spread her reputation far afield. In 1984 she won the President of the Royal Australian Institute of Architects award for her development of a Regional Approach to architecture, and in 1987 she won the Duncan's Award for Design Excellence in Timber for Bedarra Bay Resort, North Queensland. Since 1985 she has taught at Sydney University.

Vafiadis, Markos 1906–92
Greek politician

Like many other Greeks driven from Anatolia in 1923, he found work in the Greek tobacco industry. He joined the Communist Party of Greece in 1928 and was frequently imprisoned during the 1930s for his communist activities. In 1941 he escaped from the island where he was being held and went to Macedonia where he became Captain of the ELAS 10th Division operating there. During the Greek Civil War (1944–49), he led the Democratic Army of Greece, organized communist bases in the villages and was one of those responsible for the abduction and forced enrolment in the army of many Greek youths and girls. Often at variance with the Party leadership, he fled to Albania in 1949 after a clumsy attempt on his life. He was expelled from the Party the following year and was condemned for never having been 'a real communist'.

Valadon, Suzanne 1869–1938
French painter

The mother of **Maurice Utrillo**, she became an artist's model after an accident ended her career as an acrobat, modelling for **Renoir** and others. With the encouragement of **Toulouse-Lautrec**, **Degas** and **Cézanne**, she took up painting herself and excelled in her realistic treatment of nudes, portraits and figure studies, her work having some affinity with that of Degas.

Valbert, G See **Cherbuliez, Charles Victor**

Valdes, Peter See **Waldo, Peter**

Valdivia, Pedro de c.1510–1559
Spanish soldier

Born near La Serena, Estremadura, he went to Venezuela (c.1534) and then to Peru, where he became **Francisco Pizarro's** lieutenant. He won renown at Las Salinas (1538), and was in real command of the expedition to Chile. He founded Santiago (1541) and other cities, including Concepción (1550) and Valdivia (1552). In 1559, while attempting to relieve Tucapel which was besieged by the Araucanians, he was captured and killed by them. 📖 R B Cunninghame Graham, *Pedro de Valdivia: Conqueror of Chile* (1926)

Valentine, St d.c.269AD
Roman Christian priest

He is said to have been executed during the persecutions under Claudius II, the Goth, but claims have been made for another St Valentine, supposedly Bishop of Turni, taken 60 miles to Rome for martyrdom. Neither Valentine is associated with romance, hardly surprisingly. The custom of sending love letters on his feast day, 14 February, originated in the later Middle Ages, when it was thought the birds' mating season started then.

Valentinian I AD321–75
Roman emperor

Born in Cibalis, Pannonia, the son of an army officer, he rose rapidly in rank under **Constantius** and **Julian**, and on the death of Emperor Jovian (AD331–64) was chosen by the army as his successor in 364. He resigned the East to his brother Valens, and he himself governed the West with watchful care, especially strengthening the Rhine fortification, until his death.

Valentinian II AD371–92
Roman emperor

The second son of **Valentinian I**, he ruled (from AD375) Italy, Illyricum and Africa with his half-brother **Gratian**. During his minority Empress Justina administered the government. About three years after her death Valentinian was murdered, probably by Arbogastes, Commander-in-Chief of his army.

Valentinian III c.419–455
Roman emperor

Great-nephew of **Valentinian II**, and son of Constantius III, he was given the Western Empire by Theodosius II, Emperor of the East, in AD425. Initially, his mother Placidia was the dominant influence, and after 433 the Commander-in-Chief **Aetius**. He lost control of Africa to the Vandal **Gaiseric** in 442. He stabbed Aetius to death (454), but the next year was himself slain by two of Aetius's bodyguards.

Valentino, *originally* Valentino Garavani 1933–
Italian fashion designer

Born in Rome, he studied fashion in Milan and Paris, then worked for Dessès and **Guy Laroche** in Paris. He opened his own house in Rome in 1959, achieving worldwide recognition with his 1962 show in Florence.

Valentino, Rudolph See panel p1870

Valera, Don Juan 1824–1905
Spanish novelist and critic

Born in Cabra, Córdoba, he held diplomatic posts in Europe and the USA, and was a deputy, Minister of Commerce, Minister of Public Instruction and a councillor of state senator. His literary studies *Estudios críticos* (1864), and his essays *Cuentos y Diálogos* (1882) made his reputation but his fame rests on his romances, such as *Pepita Jiménez* (1874, Eng trans 1891), *Las ilusiones del Doctor Faustino* (1876, 'The Illusions of Dr Faustus'), *El comendador Mendoza* (1877, Eng trans *Commander Mendoza*, 1893) and *La buena fama* (1895, 'The Good Reputation'). He was also a noted translator of **Goethe's** *Faust* and other classics. 📖 A Z Romera, *Don Valera y Alcalá Galiano* (1966)

Valerian, Publius Licinius c.193–260AD
Roman emperor

He was proclaimed Emperor by the legions in Rhaetia after the murder of Gallus (AD253), and assumed as colleague his eldest son, **Gallienus**. Throughout his reign trouble hovered on every frontier of the empire. Marching against the Persians, he was completely defeated at Edessa (260). He was seized by King Shapur, and died in captivity, reportedly then being stuffed and displayed as a trophy in a Persian temple.

Valéry, (Ambroise) Paul (Toussaint Jules) 1871–1945
French poet and writer

Valentino, Rudolph, *originally* Rodolpho Alphonso Guglielmi di Valentina d'Antonguolla 1895–1926
Italian-born US film actor, a great screen idol of the 1920s

Rudolph Valentino was born in Castellaneta in southern Italy. He was the son of an army vet, and studied agriculture for a time, but emigrated to the USA in 1913 and first appeared on the stage as a dancer. He moved to Hollywood and after a number of parts as an extra, made his first proper significant appearances as villains in *Out of Luck* (1919) and *Once To Every Woman* (1920). His first starring role was as Julio in *The Four Horsemen of the Apocalypse* (1921), in which his dark flashing eyes and erotic movements caused a sensation.

Subsequent performances in *The Sheikh* (1921), *Blood and Sand* (1922), *The Young Rajah* (1922), *Monsieur Beaucaire* (1924), *The Eagle* (1925) and *The Son of the Sheikh* (1926) established him as the leading 'screen lover' of the 1920s.

His private life became dominated by a stormy second marriage to the actress Natacha Rambova. He died suddenly in New York of peritonitis at the height of his fame, and his funeral was the occasion of wide public mourning. Besides good looks and athletic bearing, he had considerable dramatic gifts. He also wrote a book of poems, called *Daydreams* (1923).

A Walker, *Rudolph Valentino* (1976); Irving Shulman, *Valentino* (1967); Robert Oberfirst, *Rudolph Valentino: The Man Behind the Myth* (1962).

Born in Sète, he settled in Paris in 1892, and after publishing verse in the style of **Stéphane Mallarmé**, he spent the next 20 years involved with mathematics and philosophical speculations. His new poetry was influenced by Symbolism, and he wrote *La Jeune parque* (1917, 'The Young Fate'), followed by the collection *Charmes ou poèmes* (1922), containing 'Le Cimetière marin' (Eng trans *The Graveyard by the Sea*, 1946). His prose works include *Soirée avec M. Teste* (1895, Eng trans *An Evening with Mr Teste*, 1925), and several aesthetic studies, such as the dialogue *Eupalinos ou l'architecte* (1924, Eng trans *Eupalinos; or, the Architect*, 1932), and *L'Âme et la danse* (1924, Eng trans *Dance and the Soul*, 1951). A late, short play entitled *Le Solitaire* ('The Solitary Man'), foreshadows **Samuel Beckett.** F Scarfe, *The Art of Paul Valéry* (1954)

Valette, Jean Parisot de la 1494–1568
French Knight of St John

Born in Toulouse, he became Grand Master in 1557. He successfully defended Malta against the Turks (18 May–8 September, 1565), and founded the city of Valletta there (1566).

Valla, Laurentius c.1405–1457
Italian humanist

Born in Rome, he taught classics at Pavia, Milan and Naples. He was expelled from Rome for attacking the temporal power in his *De Donatione Constantini Magni* (1440, Eng trans *On the Donation of Constantine*, 1922), was prosecuted by the Inquisition in Naples, but in 1448 was again in Rome as apostolic secretary to Pope Nicholas V. His Latin versions of **Xenophon**, **Herodotus** and **Thucydides** were admirable, and he greatly advanced New Testament criticism by his comparison of the Vulgate with the Greek original. His *De Elegantia Latinae Linguae* (1471, 'Elegances of the Latin Language') was long used as a textbook.

Valle-Inclán, Ramón María del 1869–1936
Spanish novelist, dramatist and poet

Born in Puebla de Caramiñal, he studied law before settling in Madrid. Among his works are four *Sonatas* on the seasons (1902–07), written in fine prose in the form of novels, a graphic but erroneous history *La guerra carlista* (1908, 'The Carlist War'), and the masterly *Águila de blasón* (1907, 'The Eagle of Honour') and *Romance de Lobos* (1908, Eng trans *Wolves! Wolves!*, 1957), set against a vivid medieval backdrop. Many of his novels and plays are collected in *Esperpentos*, and among several comedies is his *Cara de Plata* (1923, 'Silver Face'). A Zacharias, *Ramón del Valle-Inclán, an appraisal* (1968)

Vallejo, César Abraham 1892–1938
Peruvian poet, novelist and playwright

Born in Santiago de Chuco into a poor family of mixed descent, he took a law degree, studied medicine in Lima, and held various jobs, including teaching posts. After his political imprisonment (1920–21), he moved to Europe, living mainly in France and Spain until his death. He published only two books of poems during his lifetime; *Los heraldos negros* (1919, 'The Dark Messengers') and *Trilce* (1922, Eng trans *Trilce*, 1973). Both *Poemas humanos* (1939) and *España, aparta de mé este cáliz* (1940, Eng trans *Spain, Take Thou this Cup from Me*) were posthumous, and are included in *The Complete Posthumous Poems* (1978). He also wrote some novels and non-fiction, but his reputation rests on his poetry. English selections are *Neruda and Vallejo: Selected Poems* (1971) and *Selected Poems* (1976). A *Poesia completa* appeared in Spanish in 1978.

Vallière, Louise Françoise, Duchesse de la
See **La Vallière, Louise Françoise, Duchesse de**

Vallotton, Felix 1865–1925
French painter

Born in Lausanne, Switzerland, he studied at the Academy Julian with **Toulouse-Lautrec** and Charles Maurin. Early in his career he assiduously copied the old masters in the Louvre and made engravings in the manner of **Jean François Millet**, **Rembrandt** and others. He was a member of the Nabis symbolist movement, and one of the principal collaborators in *Le Revue Blanche* between 1894 and 1901. His most notable works were wood engravings which were immensely popular and brought him immediate success. He is regarded as a forerunner of the generation of artist engravers which included such names as **Wassily Kandinsky**, **Edvard Munch** and **Aubrey Beardsley**. His main themes of portraits, landscapes and scenes of modern life were much admired throughout his life and his striking images were later transferred to his oil painting.

Valois, Dame Ninette de, *stage-name of* Edris Stannus 1898–
Irish ballerina

Born in Blessington, County Wicklow, she studied under **Cecchetti** and made her stage debut in 1914, in the pantomime at the Lyceum Theatre. She subsequently appeared with the Beecham Opera Company and at Covent Garden. After a European tour with **Sergei Diaghilev** (1923–25), she partnered **Anton Dolin** in England, and became director of ballet at the Abbey Theatre, Dublin. She was a founding member (1931) of the Camargo Society and the Vic-Wells Ballet (later Sadler's Wells Ballet and the Royal Ballet). She was artistic director of the Royal Ballet until 1963 and was regarded as a pioneer of British ballet. Her rarely performed choreographic works include *The Rake's Progress* (1935), *Checkmate* (1937) and *Don Quixote*. She organized the National Ballet School of Turkey (1947) and was created DBE in 1951. She wrote *Invitation to the Ballet* (1937) and the autobiographical *Come Dance with Me* (1957) and *Step by Step*

(1977). In 1974 she became the first woman to win the Erasmus Prize Foundation award, and was appointed to the Order of Merit in 1992.

Vámbéry, Arminius, *properly* Ármín 1832–1913
Hungarian traveller and philologist

Born in Duna-Szerdahely, he was apprenticed at the age of 12 to a ladies' dressmaker and later became a teacher. He travelled to Constantinople (Istanbul), where he taught French in the house of a minister, and in 1858 issued a German–Turkish dictionary. Having travelled between 1862 and 1864 in the disguise of a dervish through the deserts of the Oxus to Khiva and Samarkand, he wrote *Travels and Adventures in Central Asia* (1864). Professor of Oriental Languages in Budapest till 1905, he published works on Turkish and other Altaic languages, the ethnography of the Turks, and the origin of the Magyars.

Van Allen, James Alfred 1914–
US physicist

Born in Mount Pleasant, Iowa, he graduated from Iowa Wesleyan College in 1935 before becoming professor of physics and head of the physics department at the State University of Iowa (1951–85), where he is now Regent Distinguished Professor. During World War II he developed the radio proximity fuse, which guided explosive projectiles towards their targets and then detonated them. This work gained Van Allen expertise in the miniaturization of electronics, which he utilized in experiments carried out after the war into the properties of the Earth's upper atmosphere, particularly the measurement of cosmic-ray intensity at high altitudes. He was involved in the launching of the USA's first satellite, *Explorer I* (1958), which was carrying his cosmic-ray detector. Such detectors later revealed the startling result that above a certain altitude there was much more high-energy radiation than previously expected, and satellite observations showed that the Earth's magnetic field traps high-speed charged particles in two zones known as the Van Allen belts. Van Allen, who has received numerous scientific awards, has been a member of several committees concerned with space exploration. He was awarded the US National Medal of Science in 1987.

Van Andel, Tjeerd Hendrik 1923–
US marine geologist and geological archaeologist

Born in Rotterdam, the Netherlands, he was educated at the University of Groningen, and became a sedimentologist with Shell Oil Company (1950–56). He later became Professor of Geology at the School of Oceanography of Oregon State University (1968–76), and was appointed Wayne Loel Professor of Geology at Stanford University in 1976. Van Andel has been involved in tectonic ocean mapping, deep-sea drilling, mineral resource assessment and palaeo-oceanography. He has published extensively on sediments of the continents and oceans, the origin and nature of the continental shelf, and the geology and geophysics of the mid-ocean ridges. He was a member of the first scientific expedition to view and map the Mid-Atlantic Ridge from a deep-sea submersible (1974).

Vanbrugh, Dame Irene 1872–1949
English actress

Born in Exeter, she was trained by Sarah Thorne and made her first appearance at Margate as Phoebe in *As You Like It* (1888). She married Dion Boucicault, the Younger (1901), and acted with Beerbohm Tree, George Alexander, Robertson Hare and Frohman (1860–1915), winning a reputation as an interpreter of Arthur Wing Pinero and J M Barrie heroines. She was created DBE in 1941. She was the sister of Violet Augusta Mary Vanbrugh.

Vanbrugh, Sir John 1664–1726
English playwright and baroque architect

Born in London, the son of a tradesman and grandson of a Protestant refugee merchant from Ghent, he was educated in France, commissioned into Lord Huntingdon's regiment and suffered imprisonment in the Bastille, Paris, as a suspected spy (1690–1702). A staunch Whig, he became a leading spirit in society life and scored a success with his first comedy, *The Relapse* (1696), followed, again with success, by *The Provok'd Wife* (1697). *The Confederacy* (1705) was put on in the Haymarket, London, where William Congreve and Vanbrugh became theatre managers. *The Provok'd Husband* was left unfinished, and was completed by Colley Cibber (1728). A natural playwright of the uninhibited Restoration comedy of manners period, he also achieved success as architect of Castle Howard (1702) and in 1705 was commissioned to design Blenheim Palace at Woodstock. The immense baroque structure aroused the ridicule of Jonathan Swift and Pope, and the Duchess of Marlborough disliked the plans and was so appalled at its enormous cost that she long refused to pay Vanbrugh. He was made comptroller of royal works in 1714, and was Clarencieux king-of-arms (1705–25). 🕮 L Whistler, *Sir John Vanbrugh* (1938)

Vanbrugh, Violet Augusta Mary 1867–1942
English actress

Born in Exeter, she first appeared in burlesque in 1886 and two years later played Ophelia at Margate, where she had been trained by Sarah Thorne. She joined the Kendals for their US tour and on her return played Ann Boleyn in Henry Irving's production of *Henry VIII*, also understudying Ellen Terry. She married the actor-manager Arthur Bourchier in 1894, and her elegance and ability contributed to his success. She was the sister of Irene Vanbrugh.

Van Buren, Abigail, *pseudonym of* Pauline Friedman Phillips 1918–
US advice columnist

She was born in Sioux City, Iowa. In 1956 she began to write an advice column for readers of the *San Francisco Chronicle*, and her 'Dear Abby' column, which varies from sentiment and sympathy to wisecracking rebukes, has been nationally syndicated for four decades. Her identical twin sister writes an advice column under the pen name Ann Landers.

Van Buren, Martin 1782–1862
8th President of the USA

Born in Kinderhook, New York, he was called to the Bar in 1803, became a lawyer, state Attorney-General (1816–19), senator (1821), Governor of New York (1828), Secretary of State (1829–31) and Vice-President (1833–37). He was a supporter of Andrew Jackson and a member of the group which evolved into the Democratic Party. His presidency (1837–41) was darkened by the financial panic of 1837 and, in response to this, he introduced the Independent Treasury system. This crisis overshadowed his term in office and he was overwhelmingly defeated for re-election by the Whig Party in 1840. In 1848 he ran unsuccessfully for President as the candidate of the Free-Soil Party, which opposed the spread of slavery. 🕮 Edward M Shepard, *Martin Van Buren* (1892)

Vance, Cyrus R(oberts) 1917–
US lawyer and politician

Born in Clarksburg, West Virginia, he served in the navy before practising law, then held a number of government posts, and served as Secretary of State under President Carter. He resigned in 1980 over the handling of the crisis when US diplomats were being held hostage in Iran. In 1991 he was appointed UN special envoy in Yugoslavia, and the following year became co-chairman with Lord Owen of the Yugoslavia Peace Conference (1992–93). He was made an honorary KBE in 1994.

van Ceulen, Ludolph See **Ceulen, Ludolph van**

van Cleve, Joos See **Cleve, Joos van**

Vancouver, George 1757–98
English navigator and explorer
Born in King's Lynn, Norfolk, he sailed with Captain James Cook on his second and third voyages (1772–75 and 1776–79). Promoted captain (1794), he did survey work in Australia, and New Zealand, and extensive detailed charting along the west coast of North America, sailing round Vancouver Island in 1795. ▭ George Godwin, *Vancouver: A Life* (1930)

Van Damm, Sheila 1922–87
English motor-racing driver and theatre owner
She first drove in a rally in 1950, as a publicity stunt to advertise the Windmill Theatre, which belonged to her father. She achieved a run of success in the ladies' sections, and won the Ladies' European Touring Championships in 1954. She was also occupied with her father's theatre, which she inherited from him in 1960. She turned to full-time management but was forced to close it down in 1964, and retired to Sussex. She published her autobiography *No Excuses* in 1957.

Van de Graaff, Robert J (emison) 1901–67
US physicist
He was born in Tuscaloosa, Alabama. An engineering graduate of the University of Alabama (1923), he continued his studies at the Sorbonne, Paris (1924) where Marie Curie's lectures inspired him to study physics. At Princeton in 1929 he constructed the first working model of an improved type of electrostatic generator (later to be known as the Van de Graaff generator). The charge was carried to a hollow metal sphere by means of an insulated fabric belt, allowing potentials of over a million volts to be achieved. At the Massachusetts Institute of Technology (MIT), Van de Graaff adapted his generator for use as a particle accelerator, and this 'Van de Graaff accelerator' became a major research tool of atomic and nuclear physicists. The generator was also employed to produce high-energy X-rays, useful in the treatment of cancer. During World War II he was the Director of the MIT High Voltage Radiographic Project which developed X-ray sources for the examination of the interior structure of heavy ordnance. He was a co-founder of the High Voltage Engineering Corporation which manufactured particle accelerators, and resigned from MIT in 1960 to devote his time to the corporation.

van de Hulst, Hendrik Christoffell See **Hulst, Hendrik Christoffell van de**

Van de Kamp, Peter 1901–
US astronomer
Born in Kampen in the Netherlands, he studied at Utrecht University and in 1923 emigrated to the USA, where he worked at the Lick Observatory in California and Virginia University. He became director of the Sproul Observatory in 1937 and Professor of Astronomy at Swarthmore College, Pennsylvania, and research professor after his retirement in 1972. His best-known work began in the 1960s with his deduction that some stars, other than the Sun, possess planets; by 1988 further evidence led many astronomers to believe that Van de Kamp's view is correct.

Vandenberg, Arthur Hendrick 1884–1951
US Republican politician
Born in Grand Rapids, Michigan, he studied at the university there and was elected to the Senate (1928). An isolationist before World War II, he strongly supported the formation of UNO, and was delegate to the San Francisco conference and to the UN Assembly from 1946.

Vanderbilt, Cornelius 1794–1877
US financier
Born on Staten Island, New York, he bought a boat at the age of 16 and ferried passengers and goods between Staten Island and New York City. By 40 he had become the owner of steamers running to Boston and up the Hudson. In 1849, during the Gold Rush, he established a route by Lake Nicaragua to California, and during the Crimean War a line of steamships to Havre. In 1862 he sold his ships and entered on a great career of railroad financing, gradually obtaining a controlling interest in a large number of railways. He gave a large sum of money to found Vanderbilt University at Nashville, Tennessee. William Henry Vanderbilt (1821–85), his eldest son, greatly extended the Vanderbilt system of railways. Another son, Cornelius Vanderbilt (1843–99), was also very wealthy. ▭ Wayne Andrews, *The Vanderbilt Legend: The Story of the Vanderbilt Family: 1794–1940* (1941)

Vanderbilt-Cooper, Gloria 1924–
US artist, actress, model and fashion designer
Born in New York, she was the subject of a sensational custody trial at the age of 10 between her mother, Gloria Morgan Vanderbilt, and her millionaire aunt Harry (Gertrude) Payne Whitney. Her aunt gained custody until Gloria was 14, at which age Gloria's estate was valued at some $4 million. In 1955 she made her professional acting debut in *The Time of Your Life* on Broadway, and also that year published the first of her six books, *Love Poems*. The winner of several design awards, she designs stationery, fabrics, clothing, household accessories and gave her name to the Vanderbilt perfume and jeans.

Van der Goes, Hugo See **Goes, Hugo van der**

van der Meer, Simon 1925–
Dutch physicist and engineer and Nobel Prize winner
Born in The Hague and educated at the Technical University, Delft, he worked at the Philips research laboratories in Eindhoven (1952–55) before becoming senior engineer (1956–90) for CERN (Conseil Européen pour la Recherche Nucléaire) in Geneva. He developed a method known as 'stochastic cooling' to produce a higher intensity beam of anti-protons in accelerators than had been produced before. This technology made possible the experiments which led to the discovery of the field particles W and Z, which transfer the weak nuclear interaction. Van der Meer shared the 1984 Nobel Prize for physics with Carlo Rubbia for their separate contributions to this discovery.

van der Post, Sir Laurens Jan 1906–96
South African soldier, explorer, writer and philosopher
He served with distinction in World War II in Ethiopia, the Western Desert, Syria and the Far East, where he was captured by the Japanese. On his release he joined Louis Mountbatten's staff in Java. He went on to work for the British government on a variety of missions in Africa, and with the Kalahari Bushmen of southern Africa. A sensitive writer of lyrical insight, his books include *The Lost World of the Kalahari* (1958), *The Seed and the Sower* (1963, filmed as *Merry Christmas, Mr Lawrence*, 1983), *The Hunter and the Whale* (1967), *A Far Off Place* (1974), *Yet Being Someone Other* (1982) and *The Voice of the Thunder* (1993). He was knighted in 1981. ▭ F Carpenter, *Laurens van der Post* (1969)

van der Waals, Johannes Diderik See **Waals, Johannes Diderik van der**

van der Weyden, Rogier See **Weyden, Rogier van der**

Van de Velde, Henri See **Velde, Henri Clemens van de**

Van Doren, Carl Clinton 1885–1950
US critic and biographer

Born in Hope, Illinois, he was the brother of **Mark Albert Van Doren**. He studied at the state university and at Columbia, where he lectured in English literature (1911–30). He was literary editor of the *Nation* (1919–22), of the *Century Magazine* (1922–25) and of the *Cambridge History of American Literature* (1917–21). He was also a distinguished biographer of **Thomas Love Peacock** (1911), **James Branch Cabell** (1925), **Jonathan Swift** (1930), **Sinclair Lewis** (1933) and **Benjamin Franklin** (1938, Pulitzer Prize, 1939). He edited Franklin's *Letters and Papers* (1947), and his critical studies include *The American Novel* (1921) and, with his brother, *American and British Literature since 1890* (1925). He also wrote *The Ninth Wave* (1926), a novel, and his autobiography, *Three Worlds* (1936).

Van Doren, Mark Albert 1894–1972
US poet and critic

The brother of **Carl Clinton Van Doren**, he was born in Hope, Illinois. He studied at the state university and at Columbia, where he taught from 1920 and became Professor of English in 1942. He served in the army during World War I, followed his brother to the editorship of the *Nation* (1924–28) and was awarded the Pulitzer Prize (1940) for his *Collected Poems* (1939). Later volumes include *The Mayfield Deer* (1941), *The Country Year* (1946), *New Poems* (1948) and *Spring Birth* (1953). He collaborated with Carl in *American and British Literature since 1890* (1925), edited the *Oxford Book of American Prose*, wrote critical studies of **Henry Thoreau** (1916), **Dryden** (1920), **Shakespeare** (1939) and **Nathaniel Hawthorne** (1949), and the novels *Transients* (1935) and *Windless Cabins* (1940). Further collections of poetry were published in 1963, 1964 and 1967.

Van Dyck or Vandyke, Sir Anthony 1599–1641
Flemish painter

Born in Antwerp, he studied painting under Hendrick van Balen (1575–1632) and **Rubens**. In 1618 he was admitted a master of the guild of St Luke at Antwerp and in 1620 was commissioned to paint the Lady Arundel, wife of Thomas Howard, 2nd Earl of Arundel. Records show that on this visit to England (1620–21) he also executed a full-length portrait of **James VI and I** at Windsor. He was in Italy from 1621. At Genoa he painted a number of portraits and some religious subjects for the pope, but in this field he did not rival his Italian contemporaries. By 1627 he was back in Antwerp. His fine draughtsmanship is apparent in the heads he etched for his *Iconographia* (1641). At The Hague he painted the Prince of Orange (later **William III**) and his family. In 1632 he returned to London, and was knighted by **Charles I**, who made him a painter-in-ordinary. Back in Holland on leave (1634–35), he painted Ferdinand of Austria and *The Deposition*. His flair for, and psychological accuracy in, rendering the character of his sitters, always with a hint of flattery and in the most favourable settings, greatly influenced the British school of portraiture in the next century and imparted to posterity a thoroughly romantic glimpse of the Stuart monarchy. Among the best of these portraits are the large group of Charles I, Queen **Henrietta Maria** and the two royal children, the equestrian portrait of the king, the three aspects of the king (1637) to serve as a model for **Gian Lorenzo Bernini**'s sculpture (all at Windsor) and the magnificent *Le Roi à la chasse*. His scheme for decorating the banqueting hall in Whitehall with scenes from the history of the Order of the Garter was turned down and he failed to obtain the commission for the decoration of the gallery of the Louvre, which went to **Nicolas Poussin**. He is regarded as one of the great masters of portraiture of the 17th century.

Van Dyke, Dick 1925–
US actor and entertainer

Born in West Plains, Missouri, he became a radio announcer in the US air force during World War II. He later toured as part of the nightclub act The Merry Mutes and as half of 'Eric and Van'. Moving into television, he acted as master of ceremonies on such programmes as *The Morning Show* (1955), *The Cartoon Show* (1956) and *Flair* (1960). His Broadway debut in *The Boys Against the Girls* (1959) was followed by *Bye, Bye Birdie* (1960–61) a role which won him a Tony Award and which he repeated on film (1963). His television series *The Dick Van Dyke Show* (1961–66) won him Emmy awards in 1962, 1964 and 1965. His subsequent films include *Mary Poppins* (1964) and *Chitty Chitty Bang Bang* (1968). After conquering alcoholism, he displayed his dramatic ability on film in *The Morning After* (1974) and *The Runner Stumbles* (1979). Subsequent television series have included *The Van Dyke Show* (1988), *The Carol Burnett Show* (1991) and *Diagnosis Murder* (1993).

Van Dyke, Henry 1852–1933
US clergyman and writer

Born in Germantown, Pennsylvania, he studied theology at Princeton and Berlin and was a prominent pastor of the Brick Presbyterian Church, New York (1883–99). He was Professor of English Literature at Princeton (1899–1923) and, under **Woodrow Wilson**, US Minister to the Netherlands (1913–16). He was awarded the Legion of Honour for his services as naval chaplain in World War I. His many writings include poems, essays and short stories, mostly on religious themes, such as the Christmas tale *The Story of the other Wise Man* (1896), *The Ruling Passion* (1901), *The Blue Flower* (1902), *The Unknown Quantity* (1912) and *Collected Poems* (1911). His brother Paul (1859–1933) was Professor of History at Princeton (1898–1928).

Vane, Sir Henry 1613–62
English politician

Born in Hadlow, Kent, he became a staunch Republican. In 1635 he sailed for New England. He was an unpopular Governor of Massachusetts and in 1637 he returned to England. In 1640 he entered the House of Commons, representing Hull. He played a major part in securing the execution of the Earl of **Strafford**, and between 1643 and 1653 was in effect the civilian head of the Parliamentary government. He was himself executed after the Restoration. 📖 Violet Roe, *Sir Henry Vane the Younger* (1970)

Vane, Sir John Robert 1927–
English pharmacologist and Nobel Prize winner

Born in Tardebigg, Worcestershire, he studied at Birmingham and Oxford before taking up pharmacology appointments at Yale (1953–55) and the Institute of Basic Medical Sciences, Royal College of Surgeons, London (1955–73), where he was appointed professor in 1966. He subsequently moved to the Wellcome Research Laboratories, Kent (1973–85). Working on adrenergic receptors of the nervous system and the role of the lung in drug uptake and metabolism, he devised a bioassay for the detection (1967) and characterization of labile and bioactive arachidonic acid (essential fatty acid) metabolites. He investigated the chemistry of prostaglandins and discovered a type which inhibits blood clots, as well as illuminating the operation of aspirin in treating pain. For this work he shared with **Sune Bergström** and **Bengt Samuelsson** the 1982 Nobel Prize for physiology or medicine. Vane was elected Fellow of the Royal Society in 1974, served as its vice-president (1985–87) and was awarded its Royal Medal (1989). In 1986 he became Professor of Pharmacology and Medicine at the New York Medical College and director of the William Harvey Research Institute, becoming its chairman in 1990. He was knighted in 1984.

Van Gogh, Vincent Willem 1853–90
Dutch Post-Impressionist painter, one of the pioneers of Expressionism

Van Gogh was born in Groot-Zundert, the son of a Lutheran pastor. At 16 he became an assistant (1869–76) with an international firm of art dealers in their shops in The Hague, London and Paris. An unrequited love affair with an English schoolmistress accentuated his inferiority complex and religious passion. He became an assistant master at Ramsgate and Isleworth (1876) and there trained unsuccessfully to become a Methodist preacher. In 1878 he became an evangelist for a religious society at the Belgian coalmining centre of Le Borinage (1878–80), where, first as a resident, later as an itinerant preacher, he practised the Christian virtues with great zeal and gave away his possessions; he also slept on the floor of a derelict hut.

In April 1881 he at last set off for Brussels to study art, but another unfortunate love affair, this time with a cousin, threw him off balance and he eventually settled in The Hague, where he lived with his model Christien or 'Sien', a prostitute. She appears in the drawing *Sorrow* (1882) and *Sien Posing* (1883). In his father's new parish at Nuenen he painted his dark, haunting, domestic scene of peasant poverty, *The Potato Eaters* (1885, Van Gogh Museum, Amsterdam), his first masterpiece, and *Boots* (1887, Museum of Art, Baltimore). His devoted brother Theo, now an art dealer, made it possible for him to continue his studies in Paris (1886–88) under Cormon, and there he met **Paul Gauguin**, **Henri Toulouse-Lautrec**, **Georges Seurat** and the art-collector Tanguy, who is the subject, surrounded by Japanese woodcuts, of one of Van Gogh's remarkable portraits (1887–88).

These new influences brightened his palette and on Lautrec's advice he left Paris to seek the intense colours of the Provençal landscape at Arles, the subject of many of his best works. There also he painted *Sunflowers* (1888),

The Bridge (1888) and *The Chair and the Pipe* (1888, Tate Gallery, London) and invited Gauguin to found a community of artists. Gauguin's stay with him ended in a tragic quarrel in which Van Gogh, in remorse for having threatened the other with a razor, cut off part of his own ear. Placed in an asylum at St Rémy (1889–90), there he painted the grounds, the *Ravine* (1889, with increasingly frantic brushstrokes), the keeper and the physician.

In 1890 he went to live at Auvers-sur-Oise near Paris, under the supervision of a physician, Dr Paul Gachet, himself an amateur painter and engraver, whom Van Gogh painted. That year an exhaustive article appeared by A Aurier which at last brought Van Gogh some recognition. But on 27 July 1890, Van Gogh shot himself at the scene of his last painting, the foreboding *Cornfields with Flight of Birds*, and died two days later. Theo, deeply shocked at the news, followed his brother to the grave within six months.

Van Gogh's output included over 800 paintings and 700 drawings, including portraits, self-portraits, still lifes and landscapes. He used colour primarily for its emotive appeal, and profoundly influenced the Fauves and other experimenters of 20th-century art. His letters were published in English in 1958.

📖 M McQuillan, *Van Gogh* (1989); Griselda Pollock and Fred Orton, *Vincent Van Gogh: Artist of His Time* (1978); Meyer Schapiro, *Van Gogh* (1950).

'I cannot help it that my paintings do not sell. The time will come when people will see that they are worth more than the price of the paint.' Letter to his brother Theo, 24 October 1888.

Van Gogh, Vincent See panel above

Van Goyen, Jan Josephszoon See **Goyen, Jan Josephszoon van**

Vanier, Jean 1928–
French–Canadian founder of L'Arche community
Born in Switzerland, the son of a Canadian diplomat, he pursued a naval career before feeling a call to work for peace. In 1950 he went to live and study in a Christian community outside Paris and later taught philosophy at the University of Toronto. An encounter with mentally handicapped people during a return visit to France led to his founding the first L'Arche community in Trosly, France, in 1964. These ecumenical communities for the handicapped and their helpers have since spread to many countries in Europe, North America and Australia. They are founded on Vanier's profound love for the disadvantaged in society and his strong belief that, while the Church has a ministry to the poor and the handicapped, it also needs the gifts that they alone can bring. His philosophy is expounded in his books *Community and Growth* (1979) and *Man and Woman He Made Them* (1985). 📖 Bill Clarke, *Enough Room for Joy* (1974); Kathryn Spink, *Jean Vanier and L'Arche*

Vanini, Lucilio 1584–1619
Italian philosopher
Born in Taurisano, he studied at Naples and Padua, and took orders. His enthusiasm for the new learning and science of the Renaissance, and perhaps his personality too, soon brought him into conflict with the Church. He moved around, teaching in France, the Low Countries and Switzerland, then fleeing in 1614 to England where he was imprisoned. Finally he was arrested again in Toulouse, had his tongue cut out, and was strangled and

burned as a heretic. His books *Amphytheatrum aeternae providentiae* (1615) and *De admirandis naturae reginae deaeque mortalium arcanis* (1616) discuss a form of extreme, materialistic pantheism, if not technically atheism.

Vanloo, Charles André 1705–65
French painter
Born in Nice, he studied in Rome and settled as a portrait painter in Paris, also executing some sculpture. He was made chief painter to **Louis XV** and director of the Academy in Paris (1763). His colourful, majestic style gave rise to a new French verb 'vanlooter'. He painted portraits of many of his notable contemporaries, and some large genre paintings. **Jean Baptiste Vanloo** was his brother.

Vanloo, Jean Baptiste 1684–1745
French painter
Born in Aix-en-Provence of Flemish parentage, he became a fashionable portrait painter in Paris, and was appointed Professor of Painting in 1735. In 1737 he visited England, where he painted the actor **Colley Cibber** and Sir **Robert Walpole**. He was the brother of **Charles André Vanloo**.

Van Loon, Hendrik Willem 1882–1944
US popular historian
Born in Rotterdam, he emigrated to the USA in 1903 as a journalist and history teacher. In 1922 he published the bestselling, illustrated *Story of Mankind*, and from then onwards produced a number of popular histories.

Van Meegeren, Han See **Meegeren, Han van**

Van Niel, Cornelis Bernardus Kees 1898–
Dutch microbiologist

Born in Haarlem, he studied chemistry at the Technological University in Delft, and in 1929 accepted a position at the Hopkins Marine Station of Stanford University. He made major contributions to the study of photosynthesis in bacteria, showing that sulphur bacteria use hydrogen sulphide and other reduced sulphur compounds as their hydrogen donor, which explains their dependence on these reduced compounds and their inability to produce oxygen. He was also able to delineate the light and dark reactions in *Athiorhodaceae*.

Van Praagh, Dame Peggy (Margaret) 1910–90
English ballet dancer, teacher and producer
Born in London, she acquired impressive technical skills as a child (she could perform 100 *fouettés* on pointes), training with Margaret Craske, and joining the Ballet Rambert in 1933. She created many roles with that company, chiefly in works by **Antony Tudor**: *Jardin aux Lilas* (1936, 'Lilac Garden') and *Dark Elegies* (1937). She moved to Tudor's newly-formed London Ballet in 1938 and introduced the idea of lunchtime performances during the Blitz. In 1941 she joined the Sadler's Wells Ballet as a dancer and teacher, and worked as producer and assistant director with **Ninette de Valois** at the Sadler's Wells Theatre Ballet until 1956. She produced many ballets for BBC television and for international companies, and in 1960 became artistic director for the Borovansky Ballet in Australia. She was founding artistic director for the Australian Ballet (1962–79) and a member of its council and guest teacher until 1982. She was created DBE in 1970.

Van Rensselaer, Stephen 1765–1839
American soldier and politician
Born in New York City, he was a leader of the Federalists in his state, and served in Congress (1823–29). In the War of 1812 he held command on the northern frontier and briefly captured Queenston Heights. He was a member of the US House of Representatives (1822–29). He promoted the construction of the Erie and Champlain canals and founded the Rensselaer Technical Institute (1826).

Vansittart (of Denham), Robert Gilbert Vansittart, Baron 1881–1957
English diplomat
Educated at Eton, he joined the diplomatic service in 1902 and served successively in Paris, Teheran, Cairo and Stockholm. He was Private Secretary to Lord **Curzon** (1920–24) and Permanent Under-Secretary (1930–38) at the Foreign Office. He visited Germany in 1936, talked with **Hitler** and became the uncompromising opponent of Nazi Germany, warning that Britain should arm to meet the German menace. In 1938 his disagreement with **Neville Chamberlain**'s policy of appeasement meant that he was replaced by Sir Alexander Cadogan (1884–1968) and moved to the relatively unimportant post of chief diplomatic adviser to the government. He retired in 1941. After the war he continued to expose Communist methods. His Germanophobic doctrine gave rise to the term for extreme anti-Germanism, 'Vansittartism'.

van't Hoff See Hoff, Jacobus Henricus van't

van Veen, Otto See Veen, Otto van

Van Vleck, John Hasbrouck 1899–1980
US physicist and Nobel Prize winner
Born in Middletown, Connecticut, he studied at Wisconsin and Harvard and took up posts at the universities of Minnesota, Wisconsin and finally Harvard (1934–69). He largely founded the modern theory of magnetism, by applying **Paul Dirac**'s theory of quantum mechanics to the magnetic properties of atoms. In the late 1920s and early 1930s his research in dielectric and magnetic susceptibilities culminated in his classic text, *The Theory of Electric and Magnetic Susceptibilities* (1932). He elucidated chemical bonding in crystals and studied the electric fields experienced by the electrons of an ion or atom due to its neighbours. These fields significantly affect the optical, magnetic and electrical properties of the material. During World War II he contributed to the exploitation of radar, showing that atmospheric water and oxygen molecules could cause troublesome absorption. In 1977 his pioneering research was recognized with the joint award of the Nobel Prize for physics, with **Philip Anderson** and Sir **Nevill Mott**.

Varda, Agnès 1928–
French film writer and director
Born in Brussels, Belgium, she was educated at the Sorbonne in Paris and while studying art history at the École du Louvre, she took evening classes in photography and decided to make a career of it. She made her directorial debut with *La Pointe courte* (1954), a film often cited as an early influence on the *nouvelle vague* (New Wave). Her work favoured the documentary in such films as *Salut les Cubains* (1963, *Salute to Cuba*), but she also co-wrote the feature *Ultimo Tango A Parigi* (1972, *Last Tango in Paris*). Other films include *Lion's Love* (1969), *Sans Toit ni Loi* (1985, *Vagabonde*) and the autobiographical *Jacquot de Nantes* (1990) and *Les cent et une nuits* (1994). Her marriage to the director Jacques Demy lasted from 1962 until his death in 1990, and she published her autobiography *Varda par Agnès* in 1994.

Vardon, Harry 1870–1937
British golfer
He was born in Grouville, Jersey. He won the British Open championship six times, in 1896, 1898, 1899, 1903, 1911 and 1914. He also won the US Open in 1900, the German Open in 1911, and the *News of the World* Tournament in 1912. He turned professional in 1903, and is remembered for the fluency of his swing, and his overlapping grip which is still known as the 'Vardon grip'.
📖 Audrey Howell, *Harry Vardon, the Revealing Story of a Champion Golfer* (1991)

Varèse, Edgar 1885–1965
US composer
Born in Paris of Italo-French parentage, he studied under **Albert Roussel**, **Vincent d'Indy** and **Charles Widor** in Paris, and later under **Ferruccio Busoni**. Until World War I, he worked to bring music to the French people. He settled in New York in 1915, where he founded the New Symphony Orchestra (1919) to promote the cause of modern music. In 1921 he founded the international Composers' Guild, a leading organization of progressive musicians. Almost entirely orchestral, his work often uses unconventional percussion instruments, and its abstract nature is reflected in titles like *Hyperprism* (1923) and *Ionisation* (1931).

Vargas, Getúlio (Dorneles) 1883–1954
Brazilian statesman
Born in São Borja, after serving in the army and training as a lawyer, he was elected a federal deputy in 1923. He was Minister of Finance under Washington Luís Pereira de Souza and headed the Liberal Alliance ticket for the presidency in 1930. Defeated in the polls, he won the support of significant military force to govern with the army from 1930 to 1945. A man who stood aloof from party politics, he sought a conciliação ('conciliation') based upon support from the army, major industrial groups in São Paulo and Minas Gerais to achieve a more centralized state. Ousted in 1945 by the army, he returned as constitutional President in 1951. Four years later, in the face of mounting opposition from the right wing, he committed suicide. He created two political parties, the PSD (Partido Social Democrático) and PTB (Partido

Trabalhista Brasileiro), but his political heirs were **Leonel Brizola** and **João Goulart**. ⬛ John W F Dulles, *Vargas of Brazil: A Political Biography* (1967)

Vargas Llosa, Mario See Llosa, Mario Vargas

Varley, John 1778–1842
English watercolourist

Born in Hackney, London, he studied under Dr Thomas Monro (1759–1833). He himself was a highly successful teacher, and was a founder-member of the Watercolour Society. A friend of **William Blake**, he was also interested in astrology and wrote on perspective. His brothers, Cornelius (1781–1873) and William Fleetwood (1785–1856), were also watercolourists.

Varmus, Harold Elliot 1939–
US molecular biologist and Nobel Prize winner

Born in Oceanside, New York, he was educated at Harvard and Columbia University, New York. He has held various posts at the University of California Medical Centre, San Francisco, where since 1979 he has been Professor of Microbiology and Immunology, simultaneously holding the posts of Professor of Biochemistry and Biophysics and American Cancer Society Professor of Molecular Virology. In 1989 he was awarded the Nobel Prize for physiology or medicine (jointly with **Michael Bishop**) for his contribution to the discovery of onco-genes, normal cellular genes which control cellular growth. If their production is altered in some way the faulty protein gives rise to cancer in the cell, and the discovery of these genes has been of vital importance in understanding cancer mechanisms. Since 1993 Varmus has been director of the National Institutes of Health in Bethesda, Maryland.

Varotnikov, Vitali Ivanovich 1926–
Soviet politician

He began work as a fitter in 1942, joined the Communist Party in 1947, and started to climb the bureaucratic and political ladder in his native Voronezh and Kubyshev. In 1975 he was brought to Moscow to become deputy Chairman of the Russian Ministerial Council, but quickly clashed with **Leonid Brezhnev** and was sent to Cuba as ambassador in 1979. **Yuri Andropov** brought him back as full Chairman in 1938, and **Mikhail Gorbachev** then made him Chairman of the Presidium of the Supreme Soviet in 1988. Not quite able, however, to accept full-blooded reform, he was dropped in 1990.

Varro, Marcus Terentius 116–27 BC
Roman scholar and writer

He was born in Reate, and studied at Athens. Politically opposed to **Julius Caesar**, he fought under **Pompey** in the Civil War and was legate in Spain. He was pardoned by Caesar, who appointed him librarian, but under the second triumvirate **Mark Antony** plundered his villa, burned his books, and placed his name on the list of the proscribed. **Augustus** later restored his property. His prose writings embraced oratory, history, jurisprudence, grammar, philosophy, geography and husbandry. The chief were *Saturae Menippeae* ('Menippean Satires'), *Antiquitates Rerum Humanarum et Divinarum* ('Antiquities in Matters Human and Divine'), *De Lingua Latina* ('On the Latin Language') and *De Re Rusticae* ('Country Affairs'). His *Disciplinarum Libri IX* was an encyclopaedia of the liberal arts. *Imagines*, or *Hebdomades*, was a series of 700 Greek and Roman biographies. ⬛ J Collart, *Varron grammairien latin* (1954)

Varro, Publius Terentius c.82–37 BC
Roman poet

He was called Atacinus, from his birth in the valley of the Atax in Narbonensian Gaul. He wrote satires and an epic poem on **Julius Caesar**'s Gallic Wars, called *Bellum Sequanicum*. His *Argonautica* was an adaptation of **Apollonius Rhodius**, and his erotic elegies pleased **Propertius**.

Varthema, Ludovico de c.1465–c.1510
Italian traveller and writer

Born in Bologna, he was the first European and Christian recorded to have entered, and left alive, the Islamic City of Mecca. He made a six-year journey through Arabia, Persia (Iran), India and on across the Pacific Ocean to the Spice Islands (1502–07). He published an account of his travels in *Itinerario de Lodovico de Várthema Bolognese* (1510, Eng trans *Travels of Ludovico de Várthema*, 1863).

Varus, Publius Quintilius d.9 AD
Roman official

As Governor of Syria he suppressed the revolt of Judea (4BC, also known as the War of Varus), and in AD9 was sent by **Augustus** to command in Germany. There **Arminius** destroyed three Roman legions (the 'Varian Disaster'), and Varus killed himself.

Vasarely, Viktor 1908–97
French painter

Born in Pecs, Hungary, he began as a medical student in Budapest before studying art (1928–29) at the Mühely Academy (the 'Budapest Bauhaus') under **László Moholy-Nagy**. He moved to Paris in 1930, and from c.1947 painted abstract pictures, using repeated geometrical shapes ('cinétisme') which looked forward to the Op Art of the 1960s, as in *Supernovae* (1959–61, Tate Gallery, London) and *Our IV* (1953–64, Pompidou Centre, Paris). He also experimented with Kinetic Art. Exhibiting widely from the late 1940s, he won many prizes, including the Guggenheim Prize in New York (1964) and the Tokyo Biennale (1967). He had two museums in Provence dedicated to him in the 1970s, and one in Pecs.

Vasari, Giorgio 1511–74
Italian artist and art historian

Born in Arezzo, he studied under **Michelangelo**, and lived mostly in Florence and Rome. He was a greater architect than painter, but he is best known for his *Vite de' più eccellenti Pittori, Scultori, e Architettori* (1550, 'Lives of the Most Excellent Painters, Sculptors and Architects'), a book of biographies and art criticism.

Vasco de Gama See Gama, Vasco da

Vasconcelos, Caroline Michaelis de 1851–1925
Portuguese scholar and writer

Born in Berlin, she studied and wrote on romance, philology and literature. An honorary professor of Hamburg University, she lived, after her marriage in 1876, in Oporto, where she did much scholarly research on the Portuguese language, its literature, and especially its folk literature. Most noteworthy is her edition of the late 13th or early 14th century *Cancioneiro da Ajuda*. Other writings include *Notas Vicentinas* (1912), an edition of the poetry of Francisco Sá de Miranda, (1485–1558) and essays, studies and correspondence with other Portuguese scholars.

Vassilou, Georgios Vassos 1931–
Cypriot politician and businessman

Born in Famagusta and educated at the universities of Geneva, Vienna and Budapest, he embarked upon a highly successful business career, eventually becoming a self-made millionaire. Despite a lively interest in politics, he did not align himself with any of the established parties and in 1988, believing that a fresh approach to the divisions in Cyprus was needed, stood as an independent candidate for the presidency and, with Communist Party support, won it. As President, Vassilou has worked consistently towards the reunification of the island, but he was defeated in 1993 elections by Glafkos Clerides of the Democratic Rally (DISY) Party. Since then he has been leader of the Free Democrats Movement in Cyprus.

Vattell, Emmerich de 1714–67
Swiss jurist
Born in Couret, Neuchâtel, he entered the diplomatic service of Saxony, and was Saxon representative at Bern (1746–64). His *Droits des gens* (1758, 'The Law of Nations') systematized the doctrines of Hugo Grotius, Samuel Puffendorf and Christian von Wolff, and modernized the whole law of nations, becoming recognized as a classic work.

Vauban, Sébastien le Prestre de 1633–1707
French military engineer
Born in Saint Léger, he enlisted under the 4th Prince de Condé, and served Spain with him. Taken prisoner in 1653, he was persuaded by Jules Mazarin to enter the French King's service, and by 1658 he was chief engineer under Viconte de Turenne. He introduced the effective method of approach by parallels at the Siege of Maestricht (1673), invented the socket bayonet (1687) and at the Siege of Philippsburg (1688) introduced his ricochet-batteries. In 1703 he became Marshal of France. After the Peace of Ryswick in 1697 he studied the faults in the government of France. His *Dîme royale* (1707), in which he discussed the problem of taxation, was condemned and prohibited, and within a few weeks the disappointed Vauban was dead. ◫P Lazard, *Vauban 1633–1707* (1934)

Vaucanson, Jacques de 1709–82
French engineer and inventor
He was born in Grenoble, and went to Paris to study mechanics. He became adept at constructing automata such as a duck which swam, quacked, flapped its wings and swallowed its food, and for this delicate work designed special lathes, drills and other tools. Appointed an inspector of silk factories in 1741, he devised various improvements to the machines for weaving and dressing the silk, and in 1745 succeeded in making the first fully automatic loom, controlled through a system of perforated cards. It was cumbersome and not wholly reliable, however, and it was not until the turn of the century when it was further improved by Joseph Jacquard, that it came into widespread use.

Vaugelas, Claude Favre de 1585–1650
French grammarian
Born in Meximieux, he was a member of the literary circle of the Marquise de Rambouillet. He was the author of *Remarques sur la langue française* (1647, 'Remarks on the French Language'), which helped to standardize the language, and was also a founder of the Académie Française.

Vaughan, Henry 1622–95
Welsh religious poet
Born in Newton-by-Usk, Breconshire, he was called the self-styled 'Silurist' as a native of south Wales, the land of the ancient tribe of Silures. He entered Jesus College, Oxford, in 1638, and in 1646 published *Poems, with the tenth Satyre of Juvenal Englished*. He took his MD, and practised as a physician first in Brecon and then in Newton-by-Usk. In 1650 he printed his *Silex Scintillans* ('Sparkling Flint'), a volume of mystical and religious poems, and the collection *Olor Iscanus* was published by his twin brother, without authority, in 1651. He also wrote prose (eg *The Mount of Olives*, 1652) and *Thalia Rediviva: the Pastimes and Diversions of a Country Muse* (1678), a collection of elegies, translations and religious pieces, published (1678) without authority by a friend. ◫ R A Dunn, *The Mystical Poetry of Henry Vaughan* (1962)

Vaughan, Herbert (Alfred) 1832–1903
English Roman Catholic prelate and cardinal
Born in Gloucester, he was educated at Stonyhurst and at Rome, entered the priesthood in 1854, and in 1872 was consecrated Bishop of Salford. In 1892 he succeeded Cardinal Henry Manning as Archbishop of Westminster, and the following year was raised to the cardinalate. He was founder of St Joseph's College for foreign missions at Mill Hill, and proprietor of the *Tablet* and the *Dublin Review*. He was responsible for the building of Westminster Cathedral.

Vaughan, Dame Janet 1899–1993
English haematologist and radiobiologist
She was educated at home, then studied physiology at Somerville College, Oxford, and clinical studies at University College Hospital in London. Becoming assistant pathologist there, she developed an interest in the new treatment of a then fatal disease, pernicious anaemia, with a diet including raw liver extract. After studies in the USA with George Minot, who was to be joint winner of the Nobel Prize in 1934 for the discovery, she returned to London to work on blood and bone, and published *The Anaemias* (1934). She helped to establish transfusion depots in London during World War II, and in 1945 went to Belsen with Dr Charles Dent and Dr Rosalind Pitt-Rivers to assess the value of concentrated protein solutions in treating starvation. She also led a successful research group working on the effect of radioactive isotopes on bone formation and metabolism. She was created a DBE in 1957 and elected a Fellow of the Royal Society in 1979.

Vaughan, Sir John 1603–74
Welsh lawyer, judge and politician
Born in Trawscoed, near Aberystwyth, Cardiganshire, he was educated at Christ Church, Oxford, and the Inner Temple. He was an MP from 1640 but withdrew into private life after the execution of Charles I. A Royalist, he was elected to parliament again in April 1661. When he was appointed Chief Justice of the Court of Common Pleas in 1668, he received at the same time a knighthood. Vaughan's ruling that juries could return verdicts against the direction of the judge without being fined was an important legal decision.

Vaughan, Keith 1912–77
English artist
Born in Selsey Bill, West Sussex, he was associated with the younger romantic artists influenced by Graham Sutherland. He executed a large mural in the Festival of Britain Dome of Discovery in 1951. He illustrated several books.

Vaughan, Sarah Lois 1924–90
US jazz singer and pianist
Born in Newark, New Jersey, as a child she sang gospel in church, and spent ten years studying the organ. Winning a talent competition in 1942 at the Apollo Theatre, Harlem, she came to the attention of singer Billy Eckstine, and through him of Earl Hines, who promptly hired her as a singer and pianist. In 1944 she made her first recording with 'I'll Wait and Pray', and launched on a solo career the following year. By the early 1950s she was internationally acclaimed. She acquired the nickname Sassy, and recorded classic jazz sides with trumpeter Clifford Brown and others at that time, but devoted increasing attention to a more commercial style, with lush orchestral backing, which dominated her work in the 1960s. She possessed an operatic vocal range and a consummate mastery of vibrato, intonation, phrasing and expression once described as 'instrumental stunt flying', which does little justice to the artistry involved. She worked with small jazz ensembles again in the 1970s, utilising her advanced harmonic knowledge, and continued to command a huge audience throughout her final decade. ◫L Gourse, *Sassy* (1993)

Vaughan Williams, Ralph 1872–1958
English composer

Born in Down Ampney, Gloucestershire, he studied under **Charles Stanford** at the Royal College of Music, under **Max Bruch** in Berlin and under **Maurice Ravel** in Paris. In touch from the start with the English choral tradition, he had his first success with the choral *Sea Symphony* (1910), set to words by **Walt Whitman**, in which traditional choral styles were married to a vigorously contemporary outlook. Under the influence of **Gustav Holst** he became a leader in the English folk-song movement, adding this tradition to the styles of Tudor church music, of **Charles Parry** and the teaching of Ravel that influenced his own work. He was director of the Leith Hill Festival from 1905. Between the *London Symphony* (1914) and the *Pastoral Symphony* (1922) came a large number of works in all forms, including the ballad opera *Hugh the Drover* (1911–14). The ballet *Job* (1930) was notable for its concern with the moral issues of contemporary life, and it was followed by seven further symphonies, the opera *The Pilgrim's Progress* (1948–49) and numerous choral works. His versatility was demonstrated by his ability to provide music of equal quality for the stage (1909, **Aristophanes'** *The Wasps*), and for films such as *49th Parallel* (1940–41) and *Scott of the Antarctic* (1947–48). He published *National Music* (1934) and *Beethoven's Choral Symphony and Other Papers*, and in 1935 was appointed to the Order of Merit.

Vauquelin, Nicolas-Louis 1763–1829
French chemist

Born in Saint-André-d'Hébertot, Normandy, he was an assistant to pharmacists in Rouen and in Paris where he met **Antoine François Fourcroy**, becoming his assistant around 1784. This was the beginning of a lifelong friendship and scientific collaboration. Among the posts Vauquelin held during the turbulent years of the French Revolution were those of Inspector of Mines, Professor of Assaying at the School of Mines, and official assayer of the precious metals of Paris. From 1804 to 1809 he held the chair of applied chemistry at the Museum of Natural History and from 1811 to 1822 he was Professor of Chemistry at the faculty of medicine of the University of Paris. He is chiefly remembered for the analyses of organic substances that he carried out with Fourcroy and for the discovery of chromium. He also found a new compound, beryllia (beryllium aluminium silicate), but the metal—later named 'beryllium'—was not isolated until 1828 when **Friedrich Wöhler** and Antoine Bussy both prepared it. He was the first to isolate an amino acid, asparagine, which he obtained from asparagus.

Vavilov, Nikolai Ivanovich 1887–1943
Russian botanist and plant geneticist

Born in Moscow, he trained there and at the John Innes Horticultural Institute at Merton, Surrey. In 1920 he was appointed director of the All Union Institute of Plant Industry. From his worldwide travels he gathered the world's largest collection of seeds, and built up a collection of 40,000 species and varieties of wheat. In 1923 he established a network of 115 experimental stations across the USSR to sow the collection over the widest possible range. He published extensively on the centres of origin of crop plants, formulating the principle of diversity which postulates that, geographically, the centre of greatest diversity represents the origin of a cultivated plant. His international reputation was challenged by the politico-scientific theories of **Trofim Lysenko**, who denounced him at a genetics conference (1937) and gradually usurped his position. Arrested in 1940, he died of starvation in a Siberian labour camp. He was the brother of the physicist Sergei Vavilov (1891–1951). 📖 Semen Reznik, *Doroga na eshafot* (1983)

Vazov, Ivan 1850–1921
Bulgarian national poet

Born in Sopot, he wrote a collection of poems and songs under the title *Pod igoto* (1894, Eng trans *Under the Yoke*, 1896), and other novels. He was twice exiled from his native land for his nationalist sympathies, but became Minister of Education in 1897. 📖 N S Derjavin, *Ivan Vazov* (1950)

Veblen, Thorstein (Bunde) 1857–1929
US economist and social critic

Born into a Norwegian immigrant family in Manitowoc County, Wisconsin, he grew up in an isolated farming community in Minnesota and studied at Carleton College and Johns Hopkins University before receiving a PhD in philosophy from Yale. Unable to find a university post, he returned home and spent several unhappy years farming, finally gaining a fellowship at Cornell that became the first in a series of academic appointments, frequent changes being necessitated by his unstable temperament and tumultuous personal life. His emotional distance from the mainstream of US culture perhaps made possible the unorthodox analysis of US social and economic institutions in his major work, *The Theory of the Leisure Class* (1899). In it he held that feudal social divisions continued into modern times, with the lower classes labouring to support the leisure class, and he coined the term *conspicuous consumption* to describe the pointless acquisitiveness through which the leisure class declares its privileges. The book became a classic text of US economics, and with his other writings it helped shape the terms of debate in his discipline.

Vedder, Elihu 1836–1923
US painter and illustrator

Born in New York City, he studied in Paris and in Italy, settling in Rome in 1866. He executed *Minerva* and other murals in the Library of Congress, Washington, and illustrated the *Rubáiyát of Omar Khayyám*.

Veen, Otto van, *Latin* Octavius Vaenius c.1556–1634
Dutch painter

Born in Leyden, he settled first in Brussels, and later in Antwerp, where **Rubens** was his pupil. The name van Veen is also sometimes given to the Haarlem painter, Martin van Heemskerk (1498–1574), whose *Ecce Homo* and *Holy Family* are at Haarlem.

Vega, Garcilaso de la See Garcilaso de la Vega

Vega, Lope de, *in full* Lope Félix de Vega Carpio 1562–1635
Spanish dramatist and poet

Born in Madrid, he was a student and graduate of Alcalá. He served in the Portuguese campaign of 1580, and in the Spanish Armada (1588). He became secretary to the Duke of Alva, Marquis of Malpica, and Marquis of Sarria. He took orders in 1614 and became an officer of the Inquisition. His first notable work was the poem *Angelica* (1602) written at sea in 1588, but it was as a ballad writer that he made his mark. The more remarkable of his miscellaneous works are the *Rimas* (1604); *Peregrino en su Patria* (1604, Eng trans *The Pilgrim of Casteele*, 1621), a romance; *Pastores de Belén* (1612), a religious pastoral; *Filomena* (1621) and *Circe* (1624), miscellanies in the style of **Cervantes**; *Corona Trágica* (1627, 'Tragic Crown'), an epic on **Mary, Queen of Scots**; and *Rimas de Tomé de Burguillos* (1634), a collection of lighter verse. He wrote about 2,000 historical and contemporary plays and dramas. Included in the 480 or 500 that have survived are *Noche de San Juan* ('The Night of St John'), the *Maestro de Danzar*, and *Azero de Madrid*, the source of **Molière's** *Le Médecin malgré lui*. 📖 F C Hayes, *Lope de Vega Carpio* (1967)

Velázquez or Velásquez, Diego de Silva y 1599–1660
Spanish painter who is among the greatest of the 17th century

Velázquez was born in Seville. In 1613 he became the pupil of the painter and art historian **Francisco Pacheco**, whose daughter he married in 1618 and who, in his *Art of Painting* (1639), provides an account of the young Velázquez.

In 1618 Velázquez set up his own studio. His early works were *bodegónes*, characteristically Spanish domestic genre pieces, of which *Old Woman Cooking Eggs* (1618, National Galleries of Scotland) is a typical example. In 1622 he tried his luck at court in Madrid and persuaded the poet **Luis de Góngora y Argote** to sit for him. The following year he achieved lifelong court patronage with his equestrian portrait (now lost) of **Philip IV**, who then had all other portraits of himself withdrawn. The other court artists accused Velázquez of being incapable of painting anything but heads. The king accordingly ordered a competition on a historical subject, which Velázquez won with his *Expulsion of the Moriscos by Philip III* (now also lost).

In 1628 **Rubens** visited Madrid and befriended him. His advice and the palace collection of Italian art encouraged Velásquez's visit to Italy (1629–31). His sombre, austere, naturalistic style was transformed into the lightly modelled, more colourful styles of **Titian** and **Tintoretto**, as is apparent in his *Forge of Vulcan* (c.1630) and *Joseph's Coat* (1630) and in the new type of portrait which Velázquez improvised, of the king (c.1634) or his brother, or son, in hunting costume with dog and landscape. One of the most striking of his many portraits of his royal master is full length (c.1632, National Gallery, London).

The only surviving historical painting is his Baroque *Surrender of Breda* (c.1634). There are also many portraits of the royal children, particularly *Infante Baltasar Carlos on Horseback* (1635–36), the *Infanta Margarita* (1653–54, 1656, 1659) and the *Infanta Maria Theresa* (1652–53), and of the court dwarfs (1644,1655) and jester, nicknamed *Don Juan de Austria* (1652–59). In 1650 he was again in Rome to obtain art treasures for the king and there painted the portrait of Pope **Innocent X** and the two impressionistic *Views from Villa Medici*.

On his return he captured the pathetic facial expression of the new queen, the young Maria Anne of Austria, in his best feminine full-length portrait (1652). But he is best remembered for his three late masterpieces, *Las Meniñas* (1656, 'Maids of Honour'), in which the Infanta Margarita, her dwarf and attendants and the artist himself with easel are grouped around a canvas in a large palace room, hung with paintings, *Las Hilanderas* (c.1657, 'The Tapestry Weavers'), and the famous *Venus and Cupid*, known as the 'Rokeby Venus' (c.1658), one of the few nudes in Spanish painting. Velázquez was apppointed usher to the king's chamber (1627), superintendent of works (1643), palace chamberlain (1652) and was made a knight of the Order of Santiago (1658), the highest court award.

His painting is distinguished for its unflattering realism, in which nothing is imaginatively embellished or otherwise falsified, a remarkable achievement for a court painter. **Goya** carried on his tradition a century later and **James McNeill Whistler**, **Édouard Manet** and the French Impressionists acknowledged his influence.

📖 Xavier De Salas, *Velázquez* (1974); D Brown, *The World of Velázquez* (1969); José Lopez-Rey, *Velázquez' Work and World* (1968).

Vegetius, *properly* Flavius Vegetius Renatus
4th century AD
Roman military writer

He served under the emperor **Theodosius I, the Great**, and after AD375 he wrote the *Epitome Institutionum Rei Militaris*. It describes classic legionary operations, mainly extracted from other authors, and during the Middle Ages was a great authority on warfare. 📖 T R Phillips, *A Collection of Military Classics* (1941)

Veil, Simone, *née* Jacob 1927–
French politician and lawyer

Born in Nice, she and her Jewish family were imprisoned in the Nazi concentration camps Auschwitz and Bergen–Belsen (1944). She studied law at the Institute d'Études Politiques in Paris then joined the Ministry of Justice in 1957. An expert on the law particularly concerning prisoners, women and children, she became Minister of Health (1974–76), then of Health and Social Security (1976–79) in the **Giscard d'Estaing** administration. She won the controversial legalization of abortion in 1974 and made contraception more easily available. In 1979 she became a Member of the European Parliament, becoming the first president (1979–82). An MEP until 1993, she received numerous honorary degrees, medals and foreign decorations for her work.

Veit, Philipp 1793–1877
German painter

Born in Berlin, he was the son of Dorothea Schlegel (1763–1839) and grandson of **Moses Mendelssohn**. A Catholic convert, he settled in Rome in 1815 and became conspicuous among the young German painters who sought to infuse into modern art a medieval earnestness. He became director of the Art Institute at Frankfurt am Main in 1830.

Velázquez or Velásquez, Diego de Silva y
See panel above

Velazquez de Cuellar, Diego 1465–1524
Spanish soldier and colonialist

He accompanied **Columbus** to Hispaniola in 1494, and in 1511 conquered Cuba, of which he became Governor from 1511 to 1524, and founded Havana. He sent out various expeditions of conquest, including in 1519 the Mexican expedition of **Hernán Cortés**.

Velde, Henri Clemens van de 1863–1957
Belgian architect, designer and teacher

He was born in Antwerp. One of the originators of the Art Nouveau style, he started as a painter before pioneering the modern functional style of architecture. A disciple of **William Morris** and **John Ruskin** in the Arts and Crafts Movement, he founded (with his pupil **Walter Gropius**) the Deutscher Werkbund movement in 1906 in Germany, and was a director of the Weimar School of Arts and Crafts from which the Bauhaus sprang. His designs ranged beyond architecture to graphics, furniture, ceramics, metalwork and textiles. His works included the Werkbund Theatre in Cologne, the Museum Kröller-Muller in Otterloo, the university library in Ghent, and the Belgian pavilions at the international exhibitions in Paris (1937), and New York (1939). His publications include *Vöm neuen Stil* (1907), *Les Formules d'une esthétique moderne* (1925) and *Le nouveau style* (1929). 📖 Klaus Weber, *Henry van de Velde: das buchkunstlerische Werk* (1994)

Velde, Willem van de, the Elder c.1611–1693
Dutch marine painter

Born in Leyden, he went to England in 1657 and painted large pictures of sea battles in indian ink and black paint for **Charles II** and **James VII and II**.

Velde, Willem van de, the Younger 1633–1707
Dutch painter
Born in Leyden, the son of Willem van de Velde, the Elder, like his father he was almost exclusively a marine painter. With him he worked in England for Charles II, which accounts for the large number of his works in English collections. He specialized in depicting naval encounters.

Vendôme, Louis Joseph, Duc de 1654–1712
French soldier
Born in Paris, he served under Vicomte de Turenne in Germany and Alsace, in the Low Countries under the Duc de Luxembourg, and in Italy under Catinat. He captured Barcelona (1697), and enjoyed five years of self-indulgence before superseding the Duc de Villeroi in Italy in the War of the Spanish Succession (1701–14). He fought Prince Eugène (of Savoy) at Luzzara (1702), and Cassano (1705), finally defeating the Austrians in 1706. That summer he was recalled to supersede Villeroi in the Low Countries, but the defeat at Oudenarde by the Duke of Marlborough (July 1708) cost him his command. In 1710 he was sent to Spain to aid Philip V, whom he returned to Madrid, defeating the English at Brihuega, and next day the Austrians at Villaviciosa. After a month of gluttony, even by his standards, he died at Vinaroz in Castellón de la Plana. ◻ Jean-Paul Desprat, *Les bâtards d'Henri IV: l'épopée des Vendômes, 1594–1727* (1994)

Vening Meinesz, Felix Andries 1887–1966
Dutch geophysicist
Born in Rotterdam, he graduated in civil engineering from Delft Technical University in 1910. His first appointment was with the Netherlands State Committee to undertake a gravity survey of the Netherlands. He later investigated means of measuring gravity at sea. Working on a naval submarine to avoid wave turbulence during a cruise to Indonesia in 1923, he achieved marine gravity determination to an accuracy comparable with land measurements. In other long submarine voyages which followed, he aimed to determine the Earth's shape, but also discovered that Airy isostasy prevails over the oceans, and that a belt of negative isostatic anomalies exists parallel to trenches, where he calculated an elastic crustal thickness of 35 kilometres. His speculative thoughts on mantle convection, downbuckling and crustal shear failure showed great insights into Earth processes, which with his book *The Earth's Crust and Mantle* (1964) were preludes to modern theories of plate tectonics, although he did not believe that continental drift had occurred during recent geological times. He was Professor of Geophysics at the Rijksuniversiteit, Utrecht (1937–66), where the geophysical laboratory is named after him.

Venizelos, Eleutherios 1864–1936
Greek statesman
Born near Chania, Crete, he studied law in Athens, led the Liberal Party in the Cretan chamber of deputies and took a prominent part in the Cretan rising against the Turks in 1896. When Prince George (George I of Greece) became Governor of Crete, Venizelos first served under him as Minister of Justice, then opposed him from the mountains at Therisso with guerrilla warfare. In 1909 he was invited to Athens, became Prime Minister (1910–15), restored law and order but excluded the Cretan deputies from the new parliament and promoted the Balkan League against Turkey (1912) and Bulgaria (1913), so extending the Greek kingdom. His sympathies with France and Britain at the outbreak of World War I clashed with those of King Constantine I and caused Venizelos to establish a provisional rival government at Salonika and in 1917 forced the king's abdication. He secured further territories from Turkey at the Versailles Peace Conference, but his prestige began to wane with his failure to colonize Turkish Asia Minor and he was heavily defeated in the general elections (1920) which brought the royalists and King Constantine back to power. He was Prime Minister again (1924, 1928–32, 1933). In 1935 he came out of retirement to support another Cretan revolt staged by his sympathizers, but it failed and he fled eventually to Paris, where he died.

Venn, John 1834–1923
English logician
Born near Hull, Humberside, he became a Fellow of Caius College, Cambridge (1857), developed George Boole's symbolic logic, and in his *Logic of chance* (1866), the frequency theory of probability. He is best known for 'Venn diagrams', pictorially representing the relations between sets, though similar diagrams had been used by Gottfried Leibniz and Leonhard Euler.

Ventris, Michael George Francis 1922–56
English linguist
He was born in Wheathampstead and was an architect by profession. As a teenager he became interested in the undeciphered Minoan scripts found on tablets excavated, under Sir Arthur Evans, at palace sites in Crete. These were apparently palace records and inventories. The earlier Linear A tablets had been found exclusively in Crete. Linear B tablets, of the late Minoan period, had appeared only at Knossos, but were beginning to turn up at Mycenaean sites in mainland Greece. His analysis proved that the language of Linear B was an early form of Greek. He was killed in a road accident shortly before the publication of his joint work with John Chadwick (1920–98), *Documents in Mycenaean Greek*.

Venturi, Giovanni Battista 1746–1822
Italian physicist
Born in Bibiano, near Reggio, he was ordained priest at the age of 23, in 1773 became Professor of Geometry and Philosophy at the University of Modena, and later was appointed professor at Pavia. In addition to work on sound and colours, he published geological studies and kept in close touch with the work of Daniel Bernoulli and Leonhard Euler in fluid mechanics. He is remembered for his work on hydraulics (published 1797), particularly for the effect named after him (the decrease in the pressure of a fluid in a pipe where the diameter has been reduced by a gradual taper) which he first investigated in 1791. The Venturi flow meter, based on this phenomenon, was invented by the US engineer Clemens Herschel (1842–1930).

Venturi, Robert Charles 1925–
US architect
Born in Philadelphia, he studied architecture at Princeton University, and in the 1950s he worked for the firms of modernist architects Eero Saarinen and Louis Kahn and was a Fellow (1954–56) of the American Academy in Rome. By the 1960s he was in reaction against the International Style, and began to create eclectic and playful designs that incorporated historical references and ornamentation for its own sake. He became a major figure in post-modernism and helped to establish the tenets of the movement with his 1966 book, *Complexity and Contradiction in Architecture*. With Stephen Izenour and his wife Denise Scott Brown he wrote the influential *Learning from Las Vegas* (1972), which praised the vitality of neon-lit, roadside Las Vegas architecture. His designs include the Vanna Venturi House in Philadelphia (1962), the Brant-Johnson House in Vail, Colorado (1976), and the Sainsbury Wing of the National Gallery in London (opened 1991).

Verdaguer, Jacint 1845–1902
Catalan poet

Verdi, Giuseppe Fortunino Francesco 1813–1901
Italian composer

Verdi was of humble rural origin, the son of a local inn-keeper. He was born in Roncole, near Busseto, and much of his early musical education came from Provesi, organist of Busseto Cathedral. Subsidized by locals who admired his talent, he was sent to Milan, but was rejected by the Conservatory because he was over age and was judged to be a poor pianist. Instead he studied profitably under Lavigna, *maestro al cembalo* at La Scala. On returning home he failed in his ambition to succeed Provesi as cathedral organist, but was given a grant by the Philharmonic Society. Three years later he married the daughter of his friend and patron Barezzi, but both she and their two children died in the space of three years (1838–40).

Verdi's first opera, *Oberto, conte di San Bonifacio*, was produced at La Scala in 1839, but it was with *Nabucco* (1842) that he achieved his first major success. In 1847 *I Masnadieri* ('The Robbers', based on Schiller's drama) was performed in London, with **Jenny Lind** in the cast. Of his other works up to 1850, only *Macbeth* (1847) and *Luisa Miller* (1849) are now regularly performed. *Rigoletto* (1851), *Il Trovatore* (1853) and *La Traviata* (1853) then established his position as the leading Italian operatic composer of the day, and this was confirmed by *Simon Boccanegra* (1857) and *Un Ballo in Maschera* (1859, 'A Masked Ball'). In all these works Verdi faced the opposition of the censors, especially when plots recalled current events; in the political climate of 19th-century Italy this was a constant difficulty. His next three works were all written for performance outside Italy: *La Forza del Destino* (1862, 'The Force of Destiny', for St Petersburg), *Don Carlos* (1867, for Paris) and *Aïda* (1871, commissioned for the new opera house in Cairo, built in celebration of the Suez Canal).

Apart from the *Requiem* (1873), written in commemoration of **Alessandro Manzoni**, there was a 16-year break in output until, in his old age, inspired by his literary collaborator **Arrigo Boito**, Verdi produced his two final masterpieces, *Otello* (1887) and *Falstaff* (1893, his only comic opera apart from an early work). Both had their premières at La Scala, so ending nearly 20 years of feud with that theatre. Apart from completing the *Quattro Pezzi Sacri* (1888–97, 'Four Sacred Pieces'), Verdi wrote no more

before his death. Although his reputation was worldwide he remained at heart a country man, preferring above all to cultivate his property at Busseto in the intervals between composition. He formed a long association with the former operatic soprano Giuseppina Strepponi, and married her in 1859.

Recurring themes in Verdi's compositions include the relationship of father and daughter (eg *Rigoletto*, *Simon Boccanegra* and *La Forza del Destino*) and of mother and son (*Il Trovatore*) and the conflict of political power and human love (notably in *Don Carlos* and *Otello*). He wrote two great tragic operas based on Shakespeare (*Macbeth* and *Otello*), and long contemplated the subject of King Lear but did not realize it. His life coincided with the emergence of Italy as a nation, and he was himself an ardent nationalist, especially in his younger days; some of his choruses were freely construed by patriots as being anti-Austrian, and their performance often led to demonstrations. He himself took little active part in politics, and soon resigned his deputyship in the first Italian parliament (1860), although later in life he became a senator.

Verdi's music is characterized by intimate tenderness as well as by moments of rousing splendour. Though rich and greatly esteemed, Verdi led a simple life, and took almost as much pride in his estate management and in the founding of a home for aged musicians in Milan as in his creative work. He died in a Milan hotel in 1901. His funeral was accompanied by national mourning, and as his coffin passed by, the crowd spontaneously sang 'Va, pensiero', the chorus of exiled Hebrews in *Nabucco*.

📖 Verdi's letters have been published in English versions in *The Letters of Giuseppe Verdi* (ed C Osborne, 1971). See also J Budden, *Verdi* (rev edn, 1993) and *The Operas of Verdi* (rev edn, 3 vols, 1992); Mary Jane Phillips-Matz, *Verdi: A Biography* (1993); Paul Hume, *Verdi* (1977); Carlo Gatti, *Verdi: The Man and his Music* (1955).

> 'Verdi… has bursts of marvellous passion. His passion is brutal, it is true, but it is better to be impassioned in this way that not at all. His music is at times exasperating, but is never boring.' **Georges Bizet**, in a letter to his mother (1859). Quoted in Derek Watson, *Music Quotations* (1991).

Born in Folgarolas, he became a priest with a vast popular following. He wrote *L'Atlántida* (1877) and *Lo Canigó* (1886), two epic poems of great beauty, and on the first of these **Manuel de Falla** based his choral work *Atlántida*. Verdaguer's *Idilis y Cants Místichs* (1870, 'Mystical Idylls and Songs'), also set to music, have become part of the music of the Catalan Church.

Verdi, Giuseppe Fortunino Francesco
See panel above

Verdross, Alfred 1890–1980
Austrian judge and jurist

A member of the Permanent Court of Arbitration at The Hague and the International Law Commission, he was also a judge of the European Court of Human Rights (1958–77), and president of the Institute of International Law. He wrote *Die Verfassung des Völkerrechtsgemeinschaft* (1926), *Völkerrecht* (1937), and other works in international law.

Verdy, Violette, *originally* Nelly Guillerm 1933–
French dancer and ballet director

Born in Pont-L'Abbé-Lambour, she made her debut with Ballets des Champs-Élysées in 1945, and subsequently appeared in films and theatre as an actress and dancer.

She joined **Roland Petit's** Ballets de Paris in 1950, later freelancing with several companies including London Festival Ballet (1954), American Ballet Theater (1957) and New York City Ballet (1958–77). She is popular on both sides of the Atlantic, with her charming, lively stage personality. She was artistic director of Paris Opera Ballet (1977–80) and an associate of Boston Ballet.

Vere, Aubrey Thomas de See De Vere, Aubrey Thomas

Vere, Edward de, 17th Earl of Oxford
1550–1604

English court poet

A cousin of Sir Francis Vere (c.1569–1609) and Sir Horace Vere (1565–1635), he was an Italianate Englishman, both violent and a spendthrift, but one of the foremost Elizabethan courtier-poets. Of his lyrics, published in various collections, 'What cunning can expresse' is perhaps the best known.

Verendrye, Pierre Gaultier de Varennes, Sieur de la 1685–1749
French explorer

Born in Three Rivers, Quebec, Canada, he served with the French army, and after being wounded at Malplaquet, returned to Canada to become a trader, making his base at Nipigon on Lake Superior. Fired by Native American tales, he and his three sons travelled over much of unexplored Canada, discovering Rainy Lake, the Lake of the Woods and Lake Winnipeg. On later expeditions he reached the Mandan country south of the Assiniboine River, upper Missouri, Manitoba and Dakota. One of his sons also traced the Saskatchewan River to its junction.

Vereshchagin, Vasili 1842–1904
Russian painter of battles and executions
Born in Tcherepovets in Novgorod, he joined the navy in 1859, but studied art under **Jean Léon Gérôme** in Paris. He travelled widely as a war correspondent and portrayed what he saw in gruesomely realistic pictures of plunder, mutilated corpses and executions, with **Leo Tolstoy**'s aim of fostering revulsion against war. He was blown up off Port Arthur in the Russo-Japanese War (1904–05).

Verga, Giovanni 1840–1922
Italian novelist
He was born in Catania, Sicily, and wrote numerous violent short stories describing the hopeless, miserable life of the Sicilian peasantry, including *La vita dei campi* (1880, Eng trans *Under the Shadow of Etna*, 1896) and *Cavalleria rusticana* (1884, Eng trans *Cavalliera Rusticana and Other Tales of Sicilian Life*, 1893), which was made into an opera by **Pietro Mascagni**. The same Zolaesque theme prevails in his novels, *I Malavoglia* (1881, Eng trans *The House by the Medlar Tree*, 1890), *Mastro Don Gesualdo* (1888, Eng trans *Master Don Gesualdo*, 1893), and others. **D H Lawrence** translated several of his works, including his *Novelle rusticane* (1882, Eng trans *Little Novels of Sicily*, 1925). 📖 L Russo, *Giovanni Verga* (1947)

Vergil See Virgil (panel)

Vergil, Polydore, *also called* De Castello
c.1470–c.1555
English historian
Born in Urbino, Italy, he was educated at Bologna and Padua. He was sent by Pope **Alexander VI** to England in 1501 as deputy-collector of Peter's pence (a tax or tribute paid to the pope), was ordained and became a clergyman at Church Langton, Leicestershire, in 1503. In 1507 he became a prebendary of Lincoln, in 1508 archdeacon of Wells, and in 1513 a prebendary of St Paul's, having been naturalized in 1510. His works include *Proverbiorum Libellus* (1498), *De Inventoribus Rerum* (1499), the publication of the first genuine edition of **Gildas** (1515), the treatise *De Prodigiis* (1526), and his great *Historiae Anglicae Libri XXVI*, which appeared in Basle in 1534. He returned to Italy in about 1550.

Vergniaud, Pierre Victurnien 1753–93
French politician
He was born in Limoges and was sent to the National Assembly in 1791, where his eloquence made him the leader of the Girondins. In the Convention he voted for the king's death, and as President announced the result. When the Girondins clashed with the rival revolutionary faction, known as the Mountain and composed mainly of Parisians who had borne the brunt of the Revolution and wanted to retain power by dictatorial means, Vergniaud and his party were arrested and guillotined on 31 October 1793.

Verhaeren, Emile 1855–1916
Belgian poet
Born in St Armand near Termonde, he studied law, but turned to literature, writing in French. His poetry hovers between powerful sensuality, as in *Les Flamandes* (1883, 'The Flemish Women'), and the harrowing despair of *Les*

Débâcles (1888)—affirmation of the life force and revulsion at modern industrial conditions. His chief work is possibly *La Multiple Splendeur* (1906). He died in a train accident. 📖 M Sadleir, *Things Past* (1944)

Verlaine, Paul 1844–96
French poet
He was born in Metz. He was educated at the Lycée Condorcet and entered the Civil Service. Already an aspiring poet, he mixed with the leading Parnassian poets and writers in the cafés and salons. Answering their battle cry 'Art for art's sake', against the formless sentimentalizing of the Romantic school, he gained recognition by contributing articles and poems to their avant-garde literary magazines, especially the short-lived *Le Parnasse contemporain*. The youthful morbidity of his first volume of poems, *Poèmes saturniens* (1866, 'Saturnine Poems'), was criticized by **Charles Sainte-Beuve** as trying vainly to outdo **Baudelaire**. The evocation of the 18th century, provided the backdrop to his second work, *Fêtes galantes* (1869, Eng trans *Gallant Parties*, 1917), considered by many his finest poetical achievement. His love for 16-year-old Mathilde Mauté, whom he eventually married, was expressed in *La Bonne chanson* (1870, 'The Pretty Song'). During the Franco-Prussian War (1870) Verlaine did guard duty in Paris and then served as press officer for the Communards. The birth of a son could not resolve his marital difficulties and he escaped (1872) to Flanders, Belgium and England, engaging in a homosexual affair with the fledgling poet **Arthur Rimbaud**, ten years his junior. Their friendship ended in Brussels in 1873, when Verlaine, drunk and desolate at Rimbaud's intention to leave him, shot him in the wrist. His overpowering remorse made it psychologically impossible for Rimbaud to leave, so he staged an incident in the street and had Verlaine arrested, unaware that the police, searching for a motive, would suspect immorality. Verlaine was convicted and sentenced to two years' hard labour, and his past associations with the Communards disqualified him from any intercession by the French ambassador. *Romances sans paroles* (1874, Eng trans *Romances Without Words*, 1921) were written in Mons prison, where he studied **Shakespeare** in the original, and after his wife had left him, he turned Catholic (1874). He unsuccessfully attempted to enter a monastery on release, taught French at Stickney, Lincolnshire, and St Aloysius' College, Bournemouth (1875), where he completed his second masterpiece *Sagesse* (1881, 'Wisdom'), full of the spirit of penitence and self-confession that appeared again in *Parallèlement* (1889, 'In Parallel'). In 1877 he returned to France to teach English at the Collège de Notre Dame at Rethel. There he adopted a favourite pupil, Lucien Létinois, for whom he acquired a farm at Coulommes and whose death of typhus (1883) occasioned *Amour* (1888, 'Love'). *Poètes maudits* (1884, 'Accursed Poets'), comprising critical studies, were followed by the short stories *Louis Leclerc* and *Le Poteau* (1886, 'The Stake'), sacred and profane verse *Liturgies intimes* (1892, 'Intimate Liturgies') and *Élégies* (1893). Verlaine is the master of a poetry which sacrificed all for sound, in which commonplace expressions take on a magic freshness. He lived during his last years in Parisian garret poverty, relieved by frequent spells in hospitals and finally by a grand lecture tour in Belgium, the Netherlands and England (1893), the last sponsored in part by **William Rothenstein**, who drew several portraits of him. 📖 C Morire, *Paul Verlaine, poète maudit* (1947)

Vermeer, Jan 1632–75
Dutch painter
Born in Delft, he inherited his father's art-dealing business and painted purely for pleasure, though he may have studied under **Carel Fabritius**. His work shows some Neapolitan influence as well as that of the genre painting of **Pieter de Hooch**. In 1653 he was admitted master

painter to the guild of St Luke, which he served as headman (1662–63, 1670–71). He gained some recognition in Holland in his lifetime and his work was sought by collectors, but he made little effort to sell his paintings. After his death his baker held two pictures for outstanding bills which his wife, declared bankrupt, could not retrieve. His importance was only established in the late 19th century. Apart from a few portraits, *The Allegory of Faith*, *The Procuress* (1656, Dresden), *Christ in the House of Martha and Mary* and two views of Delft, he confined himself to painting small, detailed domestic interiors of his own house, spiced with an art dealer's furnishings and trappings, every scene perfectly arranged so that everything, material or human, should obtain equal prominence and meticulous attention. Fewer than 40 of his paintings are known, including the *Allegory of Painting* (c.1665, Vienna), *Woman reading a Letter* (c.1662, Amsterdam), *Girl with a Pearl Earring* (The Hague), *Woman with a Water Jug* (c.1658–60, New York) and *View of Delft* (c.1660, The Hague). These paintings are notable for their use of perspective and treatment of the various tones of daylight. During World War II, forged Vermeers were produced by **Han van Meegeren**, who for some time deceived the experts.

Vermuyden, Sir Cornelius c.1595–c.1683
English drainage engineer
Born in the Netherlands, on the island of Tholen, Zeeland, he went to Great Britain on a commission to repair the breach of the Thames at Dagenham (1621). Thereafter he succeeded in draining the 122,000 hectares (301,000 acres) of the Bedford Level (1634–52).

Vernadsky, Vladimir Ivanovich 1863–1945
Russian mineralogist, geochemist and biogeochemist
Born in St Petersburg, he also studied there before being appointed curator of the university's mineral collection in 1886. In 1888 he worked with **Henri Le Chatelier** in Paris, returned to Russia in 1890 to take up a research post at Moscow University, and became Professor of Mineralogy there in 1898. In 1914 he was appointed director of the geological and mineralogical museum of the Academy of Sciences in St Petersburg, and founded the Ukrainian Academy of Sciences. Vernadsky conducted important research on rock-forming silicates, and on crystal form. Later in life he studied the chemical composition of plants and animals. He introduced the term 'biosphere' in 1926, and as a result of his biogeochemical studies concluded that all of the main gases in the atmosphere of the Earth were generated by living organisms.

Verne, Jules 1828–1905
French novelist
He was born in Nantes, studied law, and from 1848 wrote opera libretti until the publication in 1863 of his novel *Cinq semaines en ballon* (Eng trans *Five Weeks in a Balloon*, 1870). In it he struck a new vein of fiction—exaggerating and often anticipating the possibilities of science and describing adventures carried out by means of scientific inventions in exotic places, like submarines and space travel. He greatly influenced the early science fiction of **H G Wells**. His best-known books, all of which have been translated, are *Voyage au centre de la terre* (1864, Eng trans *A Journey to the Centre of the Earth*, 1872), *De la Terre à la lune* (1865, Eng trans *From the Earth to the Moon*, 1873), *Vingt mille lieues sous les mers* (1869, Eng trans *Twenty Thousand Leagues Under the Sea*, 1873) and *Le Tour du monde en quatre-vingts jours* (1873, Eng trans *Around the World in Eighty Days*, 1874). Film versions of the last two achieved an astonishing amount of popularity. 📖 M L Allotte de la Frye, *Jules Verne* (1955)

Vernet, Antoine Charles Horace, *known as* Carle 1758–1835
French historical and animal painter

Born in Bordeaux, the son of **Claude Joseph Vernet**, he went to Italy where he decided to become a monk. Back in Paris, however, he took to painting horses again as well as the vast battle pieces of Marengo and Austerlitz (now at Versailles), for which **Napoleon I** awarded him the Legion of Honour, and *The Race* (Louvre), which earned him the Order of St Michael from **Louis XVIII**.

Vernet, Claude Joseph 1714–89
French landscape and marine painter
He was born in Avignon, the father of **Antoine Charles Vernet**. A voyage to Rome gave him a fascination for the sea and he became primarily known for his seascapes and the paintings in the Louvre of France's 16 chief seaports, commissioned by the king.

Vernet, (Émile Jean) Horace 1789–1863
French battle painter
Born in Paris, the son of **Antoine Vernet**, and grandson of the marine painter **Claude Joseph Vernet**, he became one of the great French military and sporting painters, and decorated the vast Constantine room at Versailles with battle scenes from Valmy, Wagram, Bouvines and *Napoleon at Friedland*. Pictures include *The Dog of the Regiment Wounded* (1819) and *The Wounded Trumpeter* (1819), both in the Wallace Collection, London, and a portrait of **Napoleon I** in the National Gallery, London. His *Painter's Studio* depicts him as he loved to be, surrounded by groups of people, boxing, playing instruments and leading horses.

Vernier, Pierre 1584–1638
French scientific instrument maker
Born in Ornans, near Besançon, he spent most of his life serving the King of Spain in the Low Countries. In 1631 he invented the famous auxiliary scale, named after him, to facilitate the accurate reading of a subdivision of an ordinary scale.

Vernon, Edward, *also called* Old Grog 1684–1757
English naval commander
He entered the navy in 1700, was a captain at 21 and a rear admiral at 24, and became an MP (1727–41). In 1739, at the outbreak of the War of Jenkins' Ear, his capture of Portobello from the Spanish made him a national hero. During the Jacobite rebellion of 1745 his position in the Channel successfully kept the standby Gallic reinforcements in their ports. He was nicknamed 'Old Grog', from his grogram coat, and in 1740 when he ordered the dilution of the navy rum ration with water, it became known as 'grog'.

Vernon, Robert 1774–1849
English horse-breeder
A Member of Parliament (1754–90), he was a founder of the Jockey Club, and established horse-training at Newmarket. In 1847 he gave the Vernon Gallery to the nation. He is regarded as the 'father of the Turf'.

Vernon Harcourt, William Venables 1789–1871
English chemist and clergyman
Born in Sudbury, Derbyshire, he was educated at Oxford. At his first parish, he set up his own chemical laboratory. He worked on the effect of heat on inorganic compounds, and on methods of making achromatic lenses, and in 1824 was elected Fellow of the Royal Society. His principal importance, however, lay in the encouragement he gave to others. He became the first President of the Yorkshire Philosophical Society and helped to establish the British Association for the Advancement of Science, which was founded on the idea that it should be open to everyone interested in science. Harcourt was elected its president in 1839.

Veronese, *pseudonym of* Paolo Caliari c.1528–1588
Venetian painter

Born in Verona, from where he took his name, he was, along with **Titian** and **Tintoretto**, one of the greatest decorative artists of the 16th-century Venetian school. He trained as a stone-cutter and worked in Verona and Mambra, but under the influence of Titian settled in Venice (1553). All his works are bravura displays of technical virtuosity which concentrate on rich costumes set off against sumptuous architectural frameworks. His first frescoes in the Doge's Palace and the Library of Saint Mark's in Venice were admired by the older Titian. In 1573, however, he was called upon by the authorities to explain his rendering of the *The Marriage Feast at Cana* (1562–63, Louvre, Paris) as an opulent party in which dwarves, among other unlikely participators, are introduced into the scene. The religious foundations of Venice provided Veronese with most of his commissions. His major paintings include *The Adoration of the Magi* (1573, National Gallery, London), and the *Feast in the House of Levi* (1573, Venice), which brought him before the Inquisition for trivializing religious subjects. Other works include *The Triumph of Venice* on the ceiling of the Ducal Palace in Venice (c.1535).

Veronica, St 1st century AD
Semi-legendary saint
It is said that she met **Jesus Christ** and offered him her veil to wipe sweat from his brow, when the divine features were miraculously imprinted upon the cloth. The veil is said to have been preserved in Rome from about 700, and was exhibited in St Peter's in 1933. Veronica may simply be a corruption of *vera icon*, 'the true image' of Christ.

Verrazano, Giovanni da c.1480–1527
Italian navigator and explorer
Born in Greve, Italy, he entered the service of **Francis I** of France, and led an expedition to North America in 1524, exploring the coast from Cape Fear northward probably as far as Cape Breton and becoming the first European to enter New York Bay. He later made voyages to Brazil and the West Indies, and is thought to have been captured and eaten by cannibals in the Lesser Antilles.

Verres, Gaius d.43BC
Roman politician
A supporter of **Sulla** and **Dolabella**, he was the notoriously corrupt Governor of Sicily (73–70BC). **Cicero** successfully prosecuted him before the Senate, but he escaped to Massilia (Marseilles), where his wealth attracted his proscription and death under **Mark Anthony**.

Verrier, Urbain Jean Joseph Le See **Leverrier, Urbain Jean Joseph**

Verrio, Antonio c.1640–1707
Italian decorative painter
Born in Lecce, he was established in Paris, when he was persuaded (c.1671) by **Charles II** to go to London and to decorate Windsor Castle (1678–88). He succeeded Sir **Peter Lely** as court painter in 1684, and decorated the walls of Chatsworth and Burghley, where the Heaven Room is his masterpiece. He started work for **William III** at Hampton Court in 1699, executing the ceilings of the King's Great Bedchamber and Little Bedchamber and the King's Staircase. He also decorated rooms for Queen Anne. He died at Hampton Court. His equestrian portrait of Charles II is in the Chelsea Hospital, London.

Verrocchio, Andrea del, *properly* Andrea del Cione c.1435–c.1488
Italian artist
He was born in Florence and is best known as the master of **Leonardo da Vinci**. Although much of his work as goldsmith and sculptor has not survived, his bronze *David* (c.1476, Bargello, Florence) is a milestone in the treatment of the standing male figure by Renaissance

artists. With that of **Donatello** it is one of a trio which culminates in the genius of **Michelangelo**'s nude version. The equestrian monument to **Bartolommeo Colleoni** (1481–88) in Venice shows Verrochio to be as capable of monumental public work of this kind as Donatello. Very little of his painting remains, but his *Baptism* (c.1470, Uffizi, Florence) is a good indicator of his naturalism, ability to create the illusion of space, and superb draughtmanship. According to **Giorgio Vasari**, the head of one of the angels is by da Vinci. ▢ Maud Cruttwell, *Verrocchio* (1904)

Verwoerd, Hendrik Freusch 1901–66
South African politician
He was born in Amsterdam, the Netherlands. He was educated at Stellenbosch where he became Professor of Applied Psychology (1927) and Sociology (1933–37), and edited the nationalist *Die Transvaler* (1938–48). He opposed South Africa's entry into World War II. Exponent of the strict racial segregation policy of apartheid, Verwoerd became Vice-Chairman of the National Party of the Transvaal in 1946, was elected senator in 1948 and Minister of Native Affairs in 1950. He was elected national leader in 1958 by the Nationalist Party parliamentary caucus and as 6th Prime Minister of South Africa he dedicated himself to the founding of a South African republic. After strong opposition to his policy of apartheid and an attempt on his life in 1960, South Africa broke from the commonwealth on becoming a republic in 1962, after which Verwoerd pursued a strict apartheid policy. He was assassinated in 1966 in the House of Assembly in Cape Town. ▢ Alexander Hepple, *Verwoerd* (1967)

Very, Edward Wilson 1847–1910
US ordnance expert and inventor
He served in the US navy from 1867 to 1885, became an admiral, and in 1877 invented chemical flares ('Very lights') for signalling at night.

Very, Jones 1813–80
US mystic and poet
He was born in Salem, Massachusetts, educated at the Harvard Divinity School, and lived quietly in Salem with his sisters, writing sonnets and prose pieces of intense religious inspiration. These were published in *Essays and Poems* (1839). He was briefly committed to a lunatic asylum; his friend **Ralph Waldo Emerson** defended him. ▢ E Gittleman, *Jones Very, the effective years, 1833–40* (1967)

Vesaas, Tarjei 1897–1970
Norwegian novelist and lyric poet
He was born in Vinje and began writing in 1923. His first novel was *Die svarte hestane* (1928, 'The Black Horses'). His mature style emerged in *Kimen* (1940, Eng trans *The Seed*, 1964). A writer of symbolic and allegorical works, he was the most important novelist using *Landsmål* ('country language', later known as *Nynorsk*, 'New Norwegian') after World War II. His best-known books are *Fuglane* (1957, Eng trans *The Birds*, 1968) and *Is-slottet* (1963, 'The Ice Castle'). His autobiography, *Båten om kvelden* ('Boat in the Evening'), was published in 1968. ▢ R Skrede, *Tarjei Vesaas* (1964)

Vesalius, Andreas 1514–64
Belgian anatomist, one of the first dissectors of human cadavers
Born in Brussels, he studied in Paris, Louvain and Padua, where he took his degree. He was appointed Professor of Surgery at Padua University. In 1538 he published his six anatomical tables, still largely Galenist, and in 1541 he edited Galen's works. Comprehensive anatomizing enabled him to point out many errors in the traditional medical teachings derived from Galen. For instance, Vesalius insisted he could find no passage for blood

through the ventricles of the heart, as Galen had assumed. His greatest work, the *De Humani Corporis Fabrica* (1543, 'On the Structure of the Human Body'), was enriched by magnificent illustrations. With both its excellent descriptions and drawings of bones and the nervous system, the book set a completely new level of clarity and accuracy in anatomy. Many structures are described and drawn in it for the first time, eg the thalamus. Perhaps upset by criticism, Vesalius left Padua to become court physician to the emperor **Charles V** and his son **Philip II** of Spain. He died on the way back from a pilgrimage to Jerusalem. ⌑ C D O'Malley, *Andreas Vesalius of Brussels, 1514–1564* (1964)

Vesey, Denmark c.1767–1822
US insurrectionist
Born probably in St Thomas, West Indies, he was brought to Charleston, South Carolina, as a slave in 1783, and he bought his freedom in 1800 after winning a street lottery. A prosperous carpenter and preacher, he denounced slavery as a violation of Christianity, and in 1822 he and 10 slaves were arrested and charged with plotting an uprising against whites. Thousands of blacks were rumoured to have been involved, and though Vesey protested his innocence, he was hanged. The affair led to the passage of more stringent slave codes in many Southern states.

Vespasian, Titus Flavius Vespasianus AD9–79
Roman emperor
Founder of the Flavian dynasty, he was born near Reate. In the reign of **Claudius** he commanded a legion in Germany and in Britain, was consul (AD51), and then proconsul of Africa (c.63). In 67 **Nero** sent him to subdue the Jews. When the struggle began between **Otho** and **Vitellius** he was proclaimed imperator by the legions in the East and on the death of Vitellius was appointed emperor. Leaving the war in Judea to his son **Titus**, he reached Rome in 70, and soon restored the government and finances to order. Bluff and popular, but astute and hard-working, he adopted a simple lifestyle. He embarked on an ambitious building programme in Rome, began the Colosseum, and extended and consolidated Roman conquests in Britain and Germany. ⌑ L P Homo, *Vespasien, l'empereur du bon sens* (1949)

Vespucci, Amerigo 1451–1512
Spanish explorer after whom the continent of America was named
Born in Florence, Italy, he was a contractor in Seville from 1495 to 1498 and provisioned one (or possibly two) of the expeditions of **Christopher Columbus**. Although not a navigator or pilot himself, in 1499 he promoted an expedition to the New World commanded by Alonso de Hojeda and sailed there in his own ship, in which he explored the coast of Venezuela. In 1505 he was naturalized in Spain, and in 1508 was appointed pilot-major of Spain. His name (Latinized as 'Americus') was somewhat fortuitously given to the American continents by the young German cartographer **Martin Waldseemüller** after the publication at St Diè in Lorraine of a distorted account of his travels, based on forged versions of his letters, *Quattuor Americi navigationes* (Eng trans *Four Voyages*, 1507). ⌑ F J Pohl, *Amerigo Vespucci, Pilot Major* (1944)

Vestris, Auguste (Marie Jean Augustin)
1760–1842
French dancer and teacher
Born in Paris, the illegitimate son of Gaetano Vestris (1729–1808), he made his debut at the age of 12, going on to join the Paris Opera. Physically not typical of dancers of the time, his technique and energy led him to become the most well-known dancer in Europe. The French Revolution drove him to London for five years, but he returned in 1793 to continue dancing in Paris until 1816. He then became famous as a teacher, his pupils including

Auguste Bournonville, Maria Taglioni and Charles-Louis Didelot. He is recorded as having danced in his father's ballet *Endymion* (1773), **Jean-Georges Noverre's** *Les petits riens* (1778) and Maximilien Gardel's ballets.

Vestris, Lucia Elizabeth, *known as* Madame Vestris, *née* Bartolozzi 1797–1856
English actress
Born in London, she married at 16 the dancer Armand Vestris (1787–1825), a member of an originally Florentine family of distinguished chefs, actors and ballet dancers. In 1815 they separated and she went on the stage in Paris. She appeared at Drury Lane, London, in 1820, became famous in *The Haunted Tower*, was even more popular as Phoebe in *Paul Pry*, and in light comedy and burlesque was equally successful. In 1830 she took over the Olympic Theatre and in 1838 she married **Charles James Mathews**. She afterwards managed Covent Garden and the Lyceum, and was responsible for many improvements in stage scenery, effects and costumes.

Vian, Boris 1920–59
French playwright, novelist and poet
Born in Ville d'Avray, he was a Bohemian, and dabbled in many things—acting, jazz, engineering, anarchism, pornography—but excelled in fiction. He was a tragi-comic writer, and won a cult following for such novels as *L'Écume des jours* (1947, Eng trans *Froth on the Daydream*, 1967) and *L'Arrache-cœur* (1953, Eng trans *Heartsnatcher*, 1968). ⌑ D Noakes, *Boris Vian* (1964)

Vian, Sir Philip 1894–1968
English naval commander
He was educated at the Royal Naval College, Dartmouth. In 1940, as captain of a destroyer flotilla in HMS *Cossack*, he penetrated Norwegian territorial waters to rescue 300 British from the German supply ship *Altmark*. His flotilla later played a leading role in his final destruction of the German battleship *Bismarck* (1941). As commander of the 15th Cruiser Squadron in the Mediterranean fleet he distinguished himself in the hazardous convoy operations for the relief of Malta (1941–42). He took part in the assault landings in Sicily and Italy (1943), and Normandy (1944), and later commanded an aircraft carrier group in the Far East. He was Fifth Sea Lord (1946), and later Admiral of the Fleet.

Viardot, Pauline, *née* Paulina García 1821–1910
Spanish mezzo-soprano
Born in Paris, the daughter of **Manuel García**, she was tutored in piano by **Franz Liszt**, in compostion by Rejcha, and in singing by her mother, and made her London debut in 1839. She married Louis Viardot in 1840; their children included both the contralto Louise Viardot (1841–1918) and the violinist and composer Paul Viardot (1857–1941). Paulina, a composer of operettas and songs as well as a singer, had a long and highly influential career. Her sister was **Marie Malibran**.

Viau, Théophile de 1590–1626
French poet
Born in Clairac, he wrote the tragedy *Pyramé et Thisbé* (1621) and love poetry distinguished by its naturalness. He was condemned to the stake (1623) for the impiety and obscenity of the poems he contributed to *Le Parnasse satyrique*, but his sentence was commuted to exile for life. ⌑ F Lachèvre, *Le procès de Théophile de Viau* (1909)

Viaud, Louis Marie Julien, *pseudonym* Pierre Loti
1850–1923
French naval officer and novelist
Born in Rochefort, he entered the navy in 1869 and served in the East, then retired as captain in 1910, but was recalled to service in World War I. His voyages provided the scenes for most of his writings and his pseudonym 'Loti'

('Flower of the Pacific'). *Aziyadé* (1879), his first novel, described life on the Bosphorus. It was followed by the highly successful *Rarahu* (1880, published in 1882 as *Le Mariage de Loti*), a semi-autobiographical story of the love of an Englishman for a Tahitian woman. However, the best known of his novels is *Pêcheur d'Islande* (1886), a descriptive study of Breton fisher life in Icelandic waters. Other works include *Le Roman d'un Spahi* (1881), *Madame Chrysanthème* (1887) and *Vers Ispahan* (1904).

Vicat, Louis Joseph 1786–1861
French civil engineer

Born in Nevers, he studied at the École des Ponts et Chaussées, and then worked on various road and canal projects. In 1812 he was sent to build a bridge at Souillac on the Dordogne River, notorious for its severe floods. Searching for a way to build a stronger bridge, after many trials he succeeded in producing a hydraulic lime that would set hard even under water, as **John Smeaton** had done equally fortuitously some 60 years earlier. For 20 years Vicat pursued his research into the manufacture and properties of mortar, hydraulic lime and concrete, publishing his results in a series of papers. With **Joseph Aspdin**, who invented 'Portland cement' in England in 1824, he gave architects and engineers an extremely useful and versatile new building material, concrete.

Vicente, Gil c.1470–c.1537
Portuguese dramatist

Born in Lisbon, he wrote 44 plays, 16 in Portuguese, 11 in Spanish and 17 using both languages. His early plays were religious, but gradually social criticism was added. His farces *Inês Pereira*, *Juiz da Beira* and the three *Autos das barcas* (*Inferno*, *Purgatório* and *Glória*, collective Eng trans *The Ship of Hell*, 1929) are his best. Considered to be the 'father of Portuguese drama', he displays great psychological insight, superb lyricism and a predominantly comical spirit. 📖 L Keats, *The Court Theatre of Gil Vicente* (1962)

Vickers, Jon(athan Stewart) 1926–
Canadian tenor

Born in Prince Albert, he sang in a local church choir for a time, before managing a Woolworths store and working with the Hudson Bay Company. Whenever he sang informally, his voice was noticed and he was persuaded to try for a scholarship to the Royal Conservatory of Music in Toronto. He won it, and by 1952 had made his debut in Toronto as the Duke in *Rigoletto*. Worldwide success followed—Covent Garden (1957), Bayreuth (1958), Vienna (1959) and the New York Metropolitan Opera (1960). He has played most of the great tenor roles, most notably Tristan and Peter Grimes.

Vickrey, William Spencer 1914–96
Canadian economist and Nobel Prize winner

Born in Victoria, British Columbia, he studied at Yale, Columbia and Chicago universities. He worked as a Fellow of the Center for Advanced Study of Behavioural Science at Stanford University (1967–68), but spent most of his career at the University of Columbia, where he was McVickar Professor of Political Economics (1950–59, 1971–81; Professor Emeritus, 1981–96). His work focused on applying economic theory to practical problems such as the auctioning of government bonds and the application of fares on the New York subway. His practical approach to economics was similar to that of **James Mirrlees**, with whom he was awarded the 1996 Nobel Prize for economics. His publications include *Agenda for Progressive Taxation* (1949, 1971) and *Metastatics and Macroeconomics* (1964).

Vicky, pseudonym of Victor Weisz 1913–66
British political cartoonist

Born in Berlin, of Hungarian-Jewish extraction, he emigrated to the UK in 1935. He worked with the *News Chronicle*, the *Daily Mirror*, the *New Statesman* and the *Evening Standard*, and became a talented left-wing political cartoonist. He published collections of his work, including *Vicky's World* (1959), and *Home and Abroad* (1964).

Vico, Giambattista (Giovanni Battista) 1668–1744
Italian historical philosopher

Born in Naples, he lived there for most of his life, apart from a period when he was tutor to the Rocca family at the castle of Vatolla, south of Salerno (1686–95). Devoted to literature, history and philosophy, he became Professor of Rhetoric at Naples (1699). His published work was extremely wide-ranging, but his major work is the *Scienza Nuova* (1725, 'The New Science') which presents an original, and often strikingly modern, view of the methods and presuppositions of historical enquiry. He explains the fundamental distinctions between scientific and historical explanation, rejects the idea of single, fixed, human nature invariant over time, and argues that the recurring cyclical developments of history can only be understood by a study of the changing expressions of human nature through language, myth and culture. It is now recognized as a landmark in European intellectual history. His other works include the *Autobiography* (published 1818), *De nostri temporis studiorum ratione* (1709, 'On method in contemporary fields of study'), *De antiquissima Italorum sapientia* (1710, 'On the ancient wisdom of the Italians'), and two volumes jointly titled *On Universal Law* (1720–22). 📖 Leon Pompa, *Vico: A Study of the New Science* (1974)

Victor Emmanuel I 1759–1824
King of Sardinia

The son of Victor Amadeus III (1726–96), he became king in 1802 on the abdication of his brother, Charles Emmanuel IV (1751–1819), and until 1814 lived at Cagliari in Sardinia, as his mainland possessions were in the hands of the French as a result of the war of 1793–96. After the Vienna Settlement (which awarded Genoa and the Ligurian coastal land to the Kingdom of Sardinia), he returned to Turin, where he fiercely rejected any legacy of French rule and appointed only those conservative aristocrats who had supported him in exile to high office. Discontent grew, especially among those of his subjects who had supported the Napoleonic regime; it culminated in the liberal insurrection led by Annibale di Santarosa in 1821. Faced with mutiny, Victor Emmanuel abdicated in the same year in favour of his brother Charles Felix, appointing the young Charles Albert as regent until the latter's return from Modena.

Victor Emmanuel II 1820–78
King of Sardinia and first King of Italy

Born in Turin, he was the son of Charles Albert of Sardinia, who abdicated in his favour in 1849. He saw peace concluded between Sardinia and Austria (1849). Perhaps the most important act of his reign was the appointment (1852) of the Conte di **Cavour** as his Chief Minister. In 1855 Sardinia joined the allies against Russia and in 1857 diplomatic relations were broken off with Austria. He managed to defeat the Austrians at Montebello, Magenta and Solferino (1859); by the Treaty of Villafranca, Lombardy was ceded to Sardinia and in 1860 Modena, Parma, the Romagna and Tuscany were peacefully annexed to Sardinia. Sicily and Naples were added by **Garibaldi**, while Savoy and Nice were ceded to France. The papal territories were saved from annexation only by the presence of a French occupation force. In 1861 he was proclaimed King of Italy. In the Austro-Prussian War (1866), he allied with Prussia, and added Venetia to his kingdom. After the withdrawal of the French garrison he

Victoria, *in full* Alexandrina Victoria 1819–1901
Queen of the United Kingdom of Great Britain and Ireland, and (from 1876) Empress of India

Victoria was born in Kensington Palace, London, the only child of Edward, Duke of Kent, fourth son of **George III**, and Victoria Maria Louisa of Saxe-Coburg, sister of **Leopold I** of Belgium. Her father died when she was still a baby, and her mother passed into the political ambit of Sir John Conroy, who saw her as a future regent. Victoria became queen at the age of 18 on the death of her uncle, **William IV**, in 1837, and was crowned at Westminster on 28 June 1838.

Victoria quickly developed a grasp of constitutional principles and of the extent of her own prerogative, in which she had been so carefully instructed in the many letters she received from her uncle Leopold; he remained her constant correspondent. As a girl she had been almost constantly in the company of older people, instilling in her a precocious maturity and firmness of will that were now rapidly demonstrated. In particular, she excluded Conroy from court and avoided the influence of her mother. In her early formative years, Lord **Melbourne** was both her Prime Minister and her trusted friend and mentor. During the rest of her reign she was generally well disposed to the more conservative Melbourne and **Disraeli**, and less so to the more radical **Peel**, **Palmerston** and **Gladstone**.

When Melbourne's government fell in 1839, she invited Peel to form a government, but exercised her prerogative by setting aside the precedent which required her to dismiss the current ladies of the bedchamber. As a result, Peel resigned and the Melbourne administration was prolonged until 1841, greatly to the queen's satisfaction.

On reaching marriageable age the queen decided on Prince **Albert** of Saxe-Coburg and Gotha, with whom she was genuinely in love, and they were married in 1840 despite some public resistance to the choice of a 'pauper prince'. The marriage was happy and harmonious, and Albert's morals were uncharacteristically beyond reproach. Four sons and five daughters were born: of these the first, Victoria, the Princess Royal, married **Frederick III** of Germany, and Albert Edward afterwards became king as **Edward VII**. Their other children also formed important dynastic links by their marriages.

Victoria was strongly influenced by Albert, and worked closely with him; after his death in 1861 the stricken queen went into seclusion, which caused her temporary unpopularity. However Disraeli, as Prime Minister from 1864, rekindled her interest in the Empire, and repaid her confidence and affection by consolidating and extending her influence, acquiring for Great Britain a controlling interest in the Suez Canal, by having Victoria proclaimed Empress of India (1876), and by annexing the Transvaal in 1877. These events, and the celebratory golden (1887) and diamond (1897) jubilees, restored her again to her subjects' favour.

Her experience, shrewdness and innate political flair brought powerful influence to bear on the conduct of foreign affairs, as did the response to the country's policy made by her many relatives in the European royal houses. In the long term, the queen's judgement of men and events was rarely to be faulted. The royal couple visited the Scottish Highlands frequently, and Balmoral Castle was rebuilt to Albert's design. Victoria continued to grieve for Albert until her death. She died at Osborne House on the Isle of Wight, and was buried at Windsor.

⌨ Victoria's *Letters*, despite a long-winded style, attest to her industry and dedication. She published *Leaves from the Journal of our Life in the Highlands* (1869) and *More Leaves* (1884). See also C Hibbert, *Queen Victoria in her Letters and Journals* (1985) and J Richardson, *Victoria and Albert* (1977).

'We are not interested in the possibilities of defeat; they do not exist.' Comment during 'Black Week' in the Boer War (1899).

'We are not amused.' Attributed, though not documented.

'He speaks to Me as if I were a public meeting.' Said of Gladstone. Quoted in G W E Russell, *Collections and Recollections* (1898).

---

entered Rome in 1870, where he reigned as a strictly constitutional monarch. ⌨ Denis Mack Smith, *Victor Emmanuel, Cavour, and the Risorgimento* (1971)

Victor Emmanuel III 1869–1947
King of Italy
The son of **Umberto I**, he was born in Naples. He became king in 1900 and generally ruled as a constitutional monarch with **Giovanni Giolitti** as premier, but defied parliamentary majorities in bringing Italy into World War I on the side of the Allies (1915), and when he offered **Mussolini** the premiership (1922). The latter reduced the king to a constitutional façade, conferring on him (1936) the title of Emperor of Abyssinia. The king, however, supported the dictator until the latter's fall (1944). Victor Emmanuel then retired from public life, leaving his son **Umberto II** as Lieutenant-General of the Realm, abdicated (1946) and died in exile in Egypt.

Victoria, Queen See panel above

Victoria, Tomás Luis de, *also called* Tommaso Ludovica da Vittoria 1548–1611
Spanish composer
Born in Avila, he was sent as a priest to Rome by **Philip II** to study music. At Loyola's Collegium Germanicum he was appointed chaplain in 1566 and in 1571 choirmaster. In 1576 he became chaplain to the widowed Empress Maria, sister of Philip, returning with her to Madrid in 1583 to the convent of the Descalzas Reales, where he remained as choirmaster until his death. A devout man, he wrote

only religious music and was often compared with his contemporary **Palestrina**, although his music is more individualistic. Among his 180 works are the *Officium Hebdonadae Sanctae* (1585), books of motets and masses, and his last work, the masterly Requiem Mass, composed at the death of the Empress Maria in 1603 and published in 1605.

Vida, Marco Girolamo, *known as* the Christian Virgil c.1480–1566
Italian Latin poet
Born in Cremona, he was made Bishop of Alba in 1532. He wrote Latin orations and dialogues, a religious epic, *Christias* (1535), *De Arte Poetica* (1537, 'On the Art of Poetry'), and poems on silk culture and chess (1527). ⌨ M P de Cesare, *Vida's Christiad and the Vergilian Epic* (1964)

Vidal, Gore (Eugene Luther, Jnr) 1925–
US novelist, essayist and polemicist
Born at the United States Military Academy in West Point, New York, where his father was an aeronautics instructor, he spent much of his childhood in Washington under the influence of his scholarly, witty and blind grandfather, Senator Thomas Gore. He was educated at Phillips Exeter Academy, but was a mediocre student and in 1943 joined the United States Army Reserve Corps. This gave him the material for his first novel, *Williwaw* (1946), published to some acclaim when he was just 19. However his second novel, *In a Yellow Wood* (1947), was slated and subsequent early novels also had a lukewarm reception.

After a period as a television commentator he returned to the novel in 1964 with *Julian*, his first major book, which purports to be the emperor Julian's autobiographical memoir and journal, followed by a trilogy of books dealing with affairs of state— *Washington, DC* (1967), *Burr* (1973) and *1876* (1976). His liking for camp extravagance reached its apotheosis in the 'apocalyptic' *Myra Breckenridge* (1968) and *Myron* (1974), 'Myra's comeback'. Since then his historical fiction has been dominant. Even *Creation* (1981), his tour de force, was overshadowed by *Lincoln* (1984), an engrossing, meticulously researched, insightful portrait of the USA's 16th President. In *Empire* (1987), his fascination with power (he ran for Congress in 1960) was again to the fore, and also in 1987 he published *Armageddon: Essays 1983–1987*, 'random pieces' that reflect his ambivalent obsession with what he has called, with characteristic hauteur,'the land of the dull and the home of the literal'. He published his memoirs, *Palimpsest*, in 1995. 📖 Robert F Kiernan, *Gore Vidal* (1982)

Vidal de la Blache, Paul 1845–1918
French geographer

Born in Pézenas, Hérault, and educated at the École Normale Supérieure in Paris, he taught at the University of Nancy (1872–77) and the École Normale Supérieure. He became the first Professor of Geography at the Sorbonne (1898–1918) and is regarded as the founder of modern French geography. He advocated a regional geography based on the intensive study of small physically defined regions such as the 'pays' of France. He formulated the concept of possibilism. His expanding influence on French academic geography became known as 'la tradition vidalienne'. He was founder-editor of the journal *Annales de géographie* (1891–1918, 'Annals of Geography').

Vidocq, Eugène François 1775–1857
French criminal

Born in Arras, France, he was known as 'the detective'. The son of an Arras baker, whose till he often robbed, he worked as an acrobat, then served in the army till disabled by a wound. In 1796 he was sentenced for forgery to eight years in the galleys. Escaping, he joined a band of highwaymen, whom he betrayed to the authorities. In 1808 he offered his services as an informer and in 1812 a 'Brigade de Sûreté' was organized, with Vidocq as its chief. It became famous for its efficiency, but suspicions grew that Vidocq himself carried out many of the burglaries that he showed such skill in detecting, and in 1825 he was superseded. His *Mémoires* (1828) are untrustworthy.

Vidor, King Wallis 1894–1982
US film director

Born in Galveston, Texas, he was a cinema projectionist and freelance newsreel cameraman before making his debut as the director of the documentary *Hurricane in Galveston* (1913). In Hollywood (from 1915), he worked as a writer and extra before directing a series of short films on juvenile crime, and a feature, *The Turn of the Road* (1919). A successful mounting of *Peg o' My Heart* (1922) brought him a long-term contract with MGM. Showing an interest in social issues and the everyday struggles of the average American, his many films included *The Big Parade* (1925), *The Crowd* (1928) and *Our Daily Bread* (1934). His range of work also included westerns, melodramas and historical epics like his final feature *Solomon and Sheba* (1959). His autobiography, *A Tree is a Tree*, was published in 1953. He also acted in *Love and Money* (1982). Nominated five times for an Academy Award, he received an honorary award in 1979.

Viebig, Clara, *pseudonym of* Clara Viebig Cohn
1860–1952
German novelist

She was born in Trier, and the menacing landscape of her native Eifel provided the background for much of her fiction. She began as a follower of Zola, and her best-known novel, telling the story of the life of a servant girl, is *Das tägliche Brot* (1900, Eng trans *Our Daily Bread*, 1908). It was followed in 1904 by *Das schlafende Heer* (Eng trans *The Sleeping Army*, 1929), which depicts Polish peasants under the Germans. Her work is now neglected. 📖 C Scheuffler, *Clara Viebig* (1926)

Vieira, Antonio de 1608–97
Portuguese Jesuit missionary

Born in Lisbon, he grew up in Brazil, where he attended the Jesuit College and became a missionary. He returned to Portugal after the restoration of independence (1640), was appointed court preacher (1641–52) to King John IV and became influential. In 1653 he returned to Brazil as Superior of Jesuit missions, but in defending the local Indians he became unpopular with the colonists. Eventually, after years of conflict, Vieira and his fellow Jesuits were expelled from the Amazon and sent back to Lisbon in 1661. There he was put under house arrest and imprisoned by the Inquisition (1663–68). He subsequently went to Rome where he was well received, and in 1681 was able to return with the Jesuits to Brazil. Of his writings, his sermons are noteworthy and his letters give a clear picture of his time.

Vieira, Joao Bernardo 1939–
Guinea-Bissau statesman

Born in Bissau, he joined the African Party for the Independence of Portuguese Guinea and Cape Verde (PAIGC) in 1960, and in 1964 became a member of the political bureau during the war for independence from Portugal. After independence had been achieved in 1974 he served in the government of Luiz Cabral, but in 1980 led the coup which deposed him, becoming Chairman of the Council of Revolution and head of state. In 1984 constitutional changes combined the roles of head of state and head of goverment, making Vieira Executive President.

Viélé-Griffin, Francis 1864–1937
French Symbolist poet

The son of a US general, he was born in Norfolk, Virginia. He made his home in Touraine, France, and became a pre-eminent Symbolist and leading exponent of *vers libre* (free verse). His poems collected under the titles *Cueille d'avril* (1886, 'April Harvest'), *Poèmes et Poésies* (1895, 'Poems and Verses'), *Sapho* (1911) and *La Sagesse d'Ulysse* (1925, 'The Wisdom of Ulysses') are of high lyrical quality and embody a serene outlook on life. 📖 J de Cours, *Francis Viélé-Griffin* (1970)

Vieuxtemps, Henri 1820–81
Belgian violinist and composer

Born in Verviers, he made his debut at the age of eight, and was taken on European tours by his father. He composed six violin concertos, and taught at the St Petersburg and Brussels Conservatories.

Vigée Lebrun, (Marie) Élisabeth Louise, *née* Vigée 1755–1842
French painter

She was born in Paris, the daughter of a painter, and her great beauty and the charm of her painting speedily made her work fashionable. Her portrait of Marie Antoinette (1779, Vienna) led to a lasting friendship with the queen and she painted numerous portraits of the royal family. Her portrait of *Madame Perregaux* (1789) is in the Wallace Collection, London. She left Paris for Italy at the outbreak of the Revolution, and after a triumphal progress through Europe (including Vienna and St Petersburg), arrived in London in 1802. There she painted portraits of the Prince of Wales (later George IV), Lord Byron, and others before returning to Paris in 1805. One of her most admired paintings was *The Artist and her Daughter* (1786, Louvre, Paris). Her *Memoires* were begun in 1835, and tell how she worked in her studio even when in labour.

Vigfússon, Guðbrandur 1827–89
Icelandic scholar and philologist
Born in western Iceland, he studied and lived in Copenhagen (1849–64), and then in London and Oxford. He completed and edited the monumental *Icelandic–English Dictionary* (1874) originally undertaken by Richard Cleasby, and edited and translated (with Frederick York Powell) almost the entire body of Old Icelandic poetry (*Corpus poeticum boreale*, 2 vols, 1883), and a major anthology of early prose (*Origines Islandicae*, 2 vols, 1905). He was appointed Reader in Scandinavian Language and Literature at Oxford in 1884.

Vigneaud, Vincent du 1901–78
US biochemist and Nobel Prize winner
Born in Chicago, he was made head of the George Washington School of Medicine (1932–38) and then professor and departmental head at Cornell University Medical College (1938–67). A prolific scientist, Vigneaud published on a diversity of topics, particularly related to the identification of amino acids and the resolution of their forms. From the early 1930s he studied the chemistry, dietary requirements and metabolic pathways of the sulphur amino acids, and similarly resolved the interrelated roles of the compounds which act as donors of methyl groups in intermediary metabolism. He synthesized thiamine (1942), penicillin and the two neurohypophysial peptide hormones, oxytocin and vasopressin (1953–54). For this last achievement he was awarded the 1955 Nobel Prize for chemistry.

Vignola, Giacomo Barozzi da 1507–73
Italian architect
Born in Vignola, he studied in Bologna and became the leading Mannerist architect of his day in Rome. He designed the Villa di Papa Giulio for Pope Julius III and the church of the Il Gesu in Rome, which with its cruciform plan and side chapels had a great influence on French and Italian church architecture. His other works included the Palazzo Farnese in Piacenza.

Vignoles, Charles Blacker 1793–1875
Irish civil engineer
Born in Woodbrook, County Wexford, he served in the British Army before starting work for Sir John Rennie as a railway civil engineer. He was involved with George Stephenson on the Liverpool to Manchester Railway, built the first railway in Ireland in 1832, and surveyed or built many others at home and abroad over the next 30 years. In 1841 he was appointed the first Professor of Civil Engineering at University College London. From 1848 to 1855 he was engaged on his greatest work, the construction of the four-span Nicholas suspension bridge over the Dnieper river at Kiev, at the time the longest in the world.

Vigny, Alfred Victor, Comte de 1797–1863
French writer
He was born in Loches, Indre-et-Loire, and served in the Royal Guards (1814–28), retiring with a captaincy. His experiences provided the material for *Servitude et grandeur militaires* (1835, Eng trans *Military Servitude and Grandeur*, 1919), a candid commentary on the boredom and frustration induced by peace-time soldiering. He had already published some verse anonymously, and *Poèmes antiques et modernes* (1826, 'Ancient and Modern Poems', expanded edition 1829), which depicts Moses as the hopelessly overburdened servant of God. He married an Englishwoman, Lydia Bunbury, in 1828, but his life was marred by domestic unhappiness, and a failed attempt to enter parliament (1848–49). Much of his work reflects his disappointment and pessimism, particularly the romantic drama *Chatterton* (1835, Eng trans 1847), written for his love, the actress Marie Dorval, and *Stello* (1832) and *Daphné* (1912, posthumous), which describe the tragic fates of the young poets, Thomas Chatterton, Gilbert and André Chénier. Other notable works include the historical novel *Cinq-Mars* (1826, Eng trans *Cinq-Mars; or, a Conspiracy under Louis XIII*, 1847), the plays *Le More de Venise* (1829, based on Shakespeare's *Othello*) and *La Maréchale d'Ancre* (1831, 'The Wife of the Marshal of Ancre'), and his *Journal* (1867). ⌨ A Whitridge, *Alfred de Vigny* (1933)

Vigo, Jean 1905–34
French filmmaker
Born in Paris, he studied ethics, sociology and psychology at the Sorbonne before his fascination with the camera led him to work as an assistant at Franco-Film. He made his debut with the iconoclastic documentary *À propos de Nice* (1930, 'About Nice'). This was followed by the short film *Taris* (1931) and *Zéro de Conduite* (1933, *Zero for Conduct*) which captured the anarchic spirit of rebellious youth. *L'Atalante* (1934) tested the boundaries of film technique, utilising arresting pyrotechnics to embellish a lyrical love story. Perennially in poor health, he died from leukemia shortly after the film's release.

Villa, Pancho (Francisco), originally Doroteo Arangol 1877–1923
Mexican revolutionary
Born near San Juan del Río, Durango, the son of a field labourer, he had various modest occupations before the Mexican Revolution made him famous as a military commander. In a fierce struggle for control of the revolution, he and Emiliano Zapata were defeated (1915) by Venustiano Carranza, with whom Villa had earlier allied himself against the dictatorship of General Victoriano Huerta. Both Villa and Zapata withdrew to strongholds in north and central Mexico and continued to carry on guerrilla warfare. In 1916 Villa was responsible for the shooting of a number of US citizens in the town of Santa Isabel, as well as an attack on the city of Columbus, New Mexico, which precipitated the sending of a US punitive force by President Woodrow Wilson. He eventually made peace with the government (1920) but was murdered in Parral.

Villa-Lobos, Heitor 1887–1959
Brazilian composer and conductor
Born in Rio de Janeiro, his first published composition was *Salon Waltz* (1908), and a set of *Country Songs* (1910) shows his interest in Brazilian folk music and folklore. He made an expedition up the Amazon to study folk music in 1915, after which he composed 12 symphonies, 16 string quartets, five operas and a number of large-scale symphonic poems on Brazilian subjects, also writing the music for several ballets. A meeting with Darius Milhaud in 1918 aroused his interest in modern music and led him to spend several years in Paris, where his music was first heard in 1923. He composed several *Chôros*, in popular Brazilian styles, following these with the series of suites *Bachianas Brasileiras* (1930), in which he treats Brazilian-style melodies in the manner of J S Bach. In 1932 he became director of musical education for Brazil and in 1945 founded the Brazilian Academy of Music. ⌨ Vasco Mariz, *Heitor Villa-Lobos: Brazilian Composer* (1963)

Villard de Honnecourt fl.1225–35
French master mason and craftsman
He worked in north-west France, and is best known for his sketchbook of plans, drawings, details and texts held in the Bibliothèque Nationale, Paris, which served to disseminate the Gothic style and illustrate the operation of a masonic lodge. It is probable that he was the master

mason of Cambrai Cathedral (no longer extant). He travelled widely and was evidently familiar with the cathedrals of Rheims, Chartres and Laon.

Villars, Claude Louis Hector, Duc de 1653–1734
French soldier
He was born in Moulins. He fought in the Third Dutch War (1672–78), and in the War of the Spanish Succession (1701–14). He became Marshal of France, and was commissioned to put down the Camisards (1704). He defended the north-eastern frontier against the Duke of Marlborough, and in 1708 he defeated the attempts of Prince Eugène to penetrate into France. In 1709 he was sent to oppose Marlborough in the north, but at Malplaquet was severely wounded. In 1711 he headed the last army France could raise, and with it fell upon the British and Dutch at Denain (July 1712). He then defeated Prince Eugène and signed the Peace of Rastatt (1714). He became principal adviser on military affairs and on foreign policy and was a strong opponent of the financial measures of the Scottish financier John Law. He fought admirably again in his 80s in the war of 1732–34 in Italy. He died in Turin.

Villehardouin, Geoffroi de c.1160–1213
French nobleman and historian
Born in the castle of Villehardouin in Aube, he participated in the Fourth Crusade (1199–1207) as one of its leaders. His *Conquête de Constantinople* ('Conquest of Constantinople')—he was present at the capture—describing the events from 1198 to 1207, is one of the first examples of French prose.

Villella, Edward (Joseph) 1936–
US ballet dancer
Born in Long Island, New York, he joined the New York City Ballet in 1957 and danced in many works by George Balanchine, including *A Midsummer Night's Dream* (1962) and *Tarantella* (1964), which displayed his speed and high jumps, while Jerome Robbins' *Watermill* (1972) showed his contemplative control. He was also successful in Robbins' *Afternoon of a Faun* (1953) and Balanchine's *The Prodigal Son* (1965). He was artistic director of the Eglevsky Ballet Company (1979–84) and of Ballet Oklahoma (1983–86), and founding artistic director of the Miami City Ballet (1985–).

Villemin, Jean-Antoine 1827–92
French physician and experimentalist
Born in Prey (Vosges), he studied medicine in Strasbourg and Paris, where he received his MD in 1853. A modest man, he continued medical practice in Paris, but in addition operated a private laboratory where he worked assiduously in his spare time. Among his most fundamental observations was the discovery, in the 1860s, that material taken from the lung of a person with tuberculosis would, when inoculated into an animal, produce tuberculosis in the animal. This work pointed towards a specific infective agent, which Robert Koch discovered in 1882.

Villeneuve, Pierre Charles Jean Baptiste Sylvestre de 1763–1806
French naval commander
Born in Valensoles, he commanded the rear division of the French navy at the Battle of the Nile (1798), saving his vessel and four others. In 1805 he took command of the fleet designed to invade England, but was defeated by Lord Nelson off Cape Trafalgar. He was taken prisoner but released in 1806. On his way to report to Napoleon I in Paris, he committed suicide.

Villiers, Barbara, Countess of Castlemaine and Duchess of Cleveland 1640–1709
English mistress of Charles II
Born in London, the daughter of the 2nd Viscount Grandison, she was a noted society hostess. In 1659 she married Roger Palmer, who was created Earl of Castlemaine as a consolation when she became the mistress of Charles II. Notorious for her amours, she became a Roman Catholic (1663) and trafficked in the sale of offices, and in 1670 was created Duchess of Cleveland. Supplanted in the King's favours by the Duchess of Portland in 1673, she moved to Paris, where in 1705 she bigamously became married to Robert 'Beau' Fielding (the marriage was annulled in 1707). She had seven children, five of whom were acknowledged by King Charles as his.

Villiers, Charles Pelham 1802–98
English politician and reformer
The younger brother of George, 4th Earl of Clarendon, he was educated at Haileybury and St John's College, Cambridge, and was called to the Bar in 1827. He was a Free Trader MP for Wolverhampton from 1835, and continued as its member for over 60 years, latterly as a Liberal Unionist, becoming the 'Father of the House of Commons'. He made his first motion in favour of Free Trade in 1838, moving a resolution against the Corn Laws each year until they were repealed in 1846. From 1859 to 1866 he sat with cabinet rank as president of the Poor Law board.

Villiers, George See Buckingham, George Villiers, 2nd Duke of

Villiers de l'Isle Adam, Auguste, Comte de 1838–89
French writer, pioneer of the Symbolist movement
He was born in St Brieuc, Brittany, and claimed descent from the Knights of Malta. He dedicated his *Premières Poésies* (1856–58, 'First Poetic Works') to the Comte de Vigny, but developed into a considerable stylist in prose. His well-known short stories, *Contes cruels* (1883, 'Cruel Stories') and *Nouveaux contes cruels* (1888, 'New Cruel Stories'), are after the manner of Edgar Allan Poe. Hegelian idealism and Wagnerian Romanticism inspire his highly didactic novels and plays. The former include *Isis* (1862) on the Ideal and *L'Eve future* (1886, 'Eve of the Future'), a satire on the materialism of modern science. The latter include his masterpiece, *Axël* (1885). A pronounced Catholic aristocrat, he lived for a while with the monks of Solesmes. 📖 H Chapoutout, *Villiers de l'Isle Adam* (1908)

Villon, François, *originally* François de Montcorbier or de Logos 1431–after 1463
French poet
Born in Paris, he took the surname of his guardian, Guillaume de Villon, who enabled him to study at university, to graduate (1449) and to become MA (1452). In 1455 he had to flee from Paris after fatally wounding a priest in a street brawl, and he joined a criminal organization, the Brotherhood of the Coquille, which had its own secret jargon in which Villon was to write some of his ballades. He served several jail sentences and in 1463 his death sentence was commuted to banishment in January 1463. He left Paris and nothing further is known of him. The first printed edition of his works was published in 1489. The *Petit Testament* comprises 40 octosyllabic octaves, the *Grand Testament* comprises 172, bridged by 16 ballades and other verse forms. Six of the Coquille jargon ballades have been definitely attributed to him. Collections of his work in translation were published in 1968, 1971, 1973 and 1977. 📖 P Champion, *François Villon* (1913, in French)

Villon, Jacques, *real name* Gaston Duchamp 1875–1963
French painter

Born in Damville, the half-brother of **Marcel Duchamp** and **Raymond Duchamp-Villon**, he went to Paris in 1894 to study art, met **Toulouse-Lautrec**, and exhibited at the Salon d'Automne from 1904. He took up Cubism (c.1911) and exhibited with **Fernand Léger** and others working in that style. He was represented in the Armory Show in New York City in 1913, but did not win international fame until after World War II.

Vincent, St d.304AD
Spanish religious
Born in Saragossa, he became a deacon, according to St **Augustine**. Under **Diocletian's** persecutions, he was imprisoned and tortured at Valencia, where he died. His feast day is 22 January.

Vincent de Beauvais, *Latin name* Vincentius Bellovacensius c.1190–1264
French Dominican and encyclopaedist
He gathered together, under the patronage of **Louis IX**, the entire knowledge of the middle ages in his *Speculum Majus* ('Great Mirror'). This was in three parts: *Naturale* ('Natural') and *Doctrinale et Historiale* (1473, 'Doctrinal and Historical'), to which *Speculum Morale* ('Moral Mirror') was added anonymously. ⌑ Astrik Ladislas Gabriel, *Vinzenz von Beauvais: ein mittelalterlicher Erzieher* (1967)

Vincent de Paul, St c.1581–1660
French priest and philanthropist
Born in Pouy, Gascony, and educated by Franciscans in Dax, he was ordained in 1600. He was captured by corsairs (1605) and sold into slavery in Tunis. He persuaded his master, a Savoyard, to return to the Christian faith, and escaped to France (1607). He became almoner to **Henri IV's** queen, forming associations for helping the sick, and in 1619 was made Almoner-General of the galleys. In 1625 he founded the Congregation of Priests of the Missions (called 'Lazarists' from their priory of St Lazare in Paris) and in 1634, the Foundling Hospital and the Sisterhood of Charity. He was canonized in 1737, and his feast day is 27 September. ⌑ Henry Daniel-Rops, *Monsieur Vincent: The Story of St Vincent de Paul* (1961)

Vincentius Bellovacensius See Vincent de Beauvais

Vinci, Leonardo de See Leonardo da Vinci (panel)

Vine, Barbara See Rendell, Ruth

Vine, Frederick J(ohn) 1939–88
English geophysicist
Educated at St John's College, Cambridge, he became associate professor at the department of geological and geophysical sciences at Princeton University (1967–70), then Professor of Environmental Science (1974–88) at the University of East Anglia. He undertook important work with **Drummond Matthews** in the interpretation of marine magnetic anomalies and their use in confirmation of the sea-floor spreading hypothesis. He also studied palaeomagnetism, plate tectonics and energy resources.

Viner, Charles 1678–1756
English legal scholar
Born in Salisbury, he studied law at Oxford but never qualified and never practised. However, he produced a massive *Abridgment* of the law of England in 23 volumes (1741–56). He left most of his considerable estate to Oxford University to enable it to found the Vinerian Scholarships and the Vinerian chair of English law, first held by Sir **William Blackstone**.

Vinje, Aasmund, *originally* Aasmund Olavson 1816–70
Norwegian poet and critic

Born in Vinje, he was a leader of the movement to establish the 'country language' called *Landsmål* (later known as *Nynorsk*, 'New Norwegian'), and produced a weekly journal, *Dølen* (1858–66). He wrote a book of travel reminiscences on Norway (1861), and visited England in 1862, publishing a critical *Norseman's View of Britain and the British* in English in 1863. His poetic works include *En Ballade om Kongen* (1853), his epic cycle *Storegut* (1866) and *Blandkorn* (1867).

Vinogradsky, Boris See Delfont (of Stepney), Bernard Delfont, Baron

Vinson, Frederick Moore 1890–1953
US jurist
Born in Louisa, Kentucky, he began his career practising law in his home town and later served as a Democratic representative from Kentucky in the US Congress (1923–29, 1931–38). After sitting on the US Court of Appeals (1938–43) and serving briefly as Secretary of the Treasury (1945–46), he was appointed Chief Justice of the Supreme Court by President **Harry S Truman** in 1946 and remained on the Court until his death. As Chief Justice he advocated civil rights and favoured a liberal construction of the Constitution.

Viollet-Le-Duc, Eugène Emmanuel 1814–79
French architect and archaeologist
Born in Paris, he studied in France and Italy, and in 1840 he became director of the restoration of the Sainte Chapelle in Paris. From then on, he was the great restorer of ancient buildings in France, including the cathedrals of Notre Dame in Paris, Amiens, Laon, and the Château de Pierrefonds. He served as engineer in the defence of Paris, and was an advanced republican politician. His best-known work was his great *Dictionnaire raisoné de l'architecture française du XIe au XVIe siècle* (1854–86, 'Reasoned Dictionary of French Architecture from the XIth to the XVIth Century').

Viotti, Giovanni Battista 1753–1824
Italian violinist and composer
Born in Fontanetto, he lived mostly in Paris, where he was director of the Italian Opera. He was one of the leading violinists of his day, and his works include many violin concertos, and compositions for piano and for strings. From 1792 he was a wine merchant in London.

Virchow, Rudolf 1821–1902
German pathologist and politician
Born in Schivelbein, Pomerania, he studied medicine in Berlin, and then rose to become Professor of Pathological Anatomy at Würzburg University (1849–56), quickly proving himself a skilful pathologist. In 1845 he recognized leukaemia, and proceeded to study animal parasites, inflammation, thrombosis and embolism. In 1856 he returned to Berlin as Professor of Pathological Anatomy. Adopting **Theodor Schwann** and **Matthias Schleiden's** cell theory, Virchow argued that disease originated in cells, or at least was the response of cells to abnormal circumstances. His suggestions led to much fertile work, and founded modern pathology. His *Cellularpathologie* (1858) established that tumours and all other morbid structures contained cells derived from previous cells. He remained lastingly politically active, sitting as a liberal member of the Reichstag (1880–93), and working in public health in Berlin to improve water and sewage purification. ⌑ E H Ackernecht, *Rudolf Virchow: Doctor, Statesman, Anthropologist* (1953)

Virgil See panel p1892

Virtanen, Artturi Ilmari 1895–1973
Finnish biochemist and Nobel Prize winner

Virgil or Vergil, *full name* Publius Vergilius Maro 70–19BC
Roman poet, one of the greatest of antiquity

Virgil is said to have had a wealthy father of humble origins, and a well-connected mother. He was born in Andes near Mantua in Cisalpine Gaul, and was educated at Cremona and Milan, and at 16 went to Rome to study rhetoric and philosophy. After the Battle of Philippi in 42BC his family estate seems to have been confiscated to provide land for the veterans of **Mark Antony** and Octavian (Emperor **Augustus**), but he went to Rome and was recompensed. He soon became one of the endowed court poets who received the patronage of **Gaius Cilnius Maecenas**, and in 37 his *Eclogues*, 10 pastorals modelled on those of **Theocritus**, were received with great enthusiasm. The same year, Virgil travelled with **Horace** to Brundisium, as recorded by Horace (*Satires* bk 1 no. 5).

Soon afterwards Virgil, now well off from Maecenas's patronage, left Rome and moved to Campania, where he had a villa at Naples and a country house near Nola. In 30 he published the *Georgics*, or *Art of Husbandry*, in four books, dealing with tillage and pasturage, the vine and olive, horses, cattle, and bees; they confirmed his position as the foremost poet of the age. The remaining 11 years of his life were devoted to a larger task, undertaken at the request of Emperor Augustus, the composition of a great national epic based on the story of Aeneas the Trojan, legendary founder of the Roman nation and of the Julian family. The epic covered the hero's life from the fall of Troy to his arrival in Italy, his wars and alliances with the native Italian races, and his final establishment in his new kingdom.

By 19BC the *Aeneid* was nearly completed, and Virgil left Italy to travel in Greece and Asia, but he fell ill at Megara in central Greece, and died at Brundisium on his way home. At his own wish he was buried in Naples, on the road to Pozzuoli; his tomb was worshipped as a sacred place for many hundreds of years.

The supremacy of Virgil in Latin poetry was immediate and almost unquestioned; his works were established classics even in his lifetime, and soon after his death they had become the textbooks of western Europe; commentaries and scholarly discussions were written by **Aelius Donatus**, **Ambrosius Macrobius**, Servius and others who also recorded facts about his life. By the 3rd century AD his poems ranked as sacred books, and were regularly used for purposes of divination; a favourite passage was Dido's curse on Aeneas in Book 4. The early Christian writers saw him as almost one of themselves, and there is a story by an anonymous 13th-century French poet that St **Paul** wept over Virgil's tomb at Naples. His work has been translated and admired by generations of poets, including **John Dryden** and Alfred, Lord **Tennyson**.

📖 J Griffin, *Virgil* (1986); F Klinger, *Vergil* (1967); W A Camps, *An Introduction to Virgil's Aeneid* (1961).

Arma virumque cano, Troiae qui primus ab oris
Italiam fato profugus Laviniaque venit
litora, multum ille et terris iactatus et alto
vi superum, saevae memorem Iunonis ob iram.
'I sing of warfare and a man at war.
From the sea-coast of Troy in early days
He came to Italy by destiny,
To our Lavinian western shore,
A fugitive, this captain, buffeted
Cruelly on land as on the sea
By blows from powers of the air—behind them
Baleful Juno in her sleepless rage.'
The opening of Book 1 of the *Aeneid* (translated by Robert Fitzgerald).

Omnia vincit Amor: et nos cedamus Amori.
'Love conquers all things: let us yield to Love.'
Eclogues 10, l.69.

Born in Helsinki, he was educated at the university there and eventually became Professor of Biochemistry, first at the Finland Institute of Technology (1931–39) and then at the University of Helsinki (1939–48). He studied the bacterial metabolism of sugars to form succinate and lactate, and observed the processes by which the root nodules of leguminous plants release nitrogous substances. He also investigated the ways in which nitrogen is absorbed by legume root nodules and converted into other substances inside the plant (1938). For these discoveries he was awarded the Nobel Prize for chemistry (1945). Virtanen also worked on the nutritional requirements of plants, and the plant biosynthesis of carotene and vitamin A. He isolated and characterized haemoglobin and other pigments from legume nodules, and showed that silage can be preserved by dilute hydrochloric acid.

Vischer, Peter 1455–1529
German sculptor

Born in Nuremberg, he worked mainly in bronze, and was responsible for the *King Arthur* statue on the tomb of the Emperor **Maximilian I** at Innsbruck, the tomb of Archbishop Ernst at Magdeburg and the basic structure of that of St Sebald in Nuremberg.

Visconti, Gian Galeazzo 1351–1402
Milanese statesman

He succeeded his father, Galeazzo II, as joint ruler (1378–85) with his uncle Bernabo, whom he put to death (1385). As duke (1385) he made himself master of the northern half of Italy bringing many independent cities into one state, arranged marriage alliances with England, France, Austria and Bavaria, and was a great patron of the arts.

Visconti, Giovanni 1290–1354
Italian prelate

Born probably in Milan, he was Archbishop and Lord of Milan from 1349, and brought Genoa and Bologna under his jurisdiction.

Visconti, Lodovico Tullio Gioacchino
1791–1853
Italian architect

He was the son of archaeologist Ennio Quirino Visconti (1751–1818). From 1799 he worked in Paris; he built the mausoleum of **Napoleon I** and was responsible for the scheme joining the Louvre and the Tuileries. His nephew, Pietro Ercole (1802–80), was commissioner of antiquities at Rome and curator of the Vatican art collections.

Visconti, Luchino, *real name* Count Don Luchino Visconti Di Morone 1906–76
Italian stage and film director

Born in Milan, an early interest in music and the theatre led him to stage designing and the production of opera (notably his stagings at La Scala for **Maria Callas**), and ballet. A short spell as assistant to **Jean Renoir** turned his attention to the cinema. His first film as director, *Ossessione* (1942, 'Obsession'), took Italy by storm, in spite of trouble from the Fascist censors. In that film, and in *La Terra Trema* (1947, *The Earth Trembles*) and *Rocco e i sui Fratelli* (1960, *Rocco and His Brothers*), he showed the strict realism, formal beauty and concern with social problems which are the hallmarks of all his films. These include *Il Gattopardo* (1963, *The Leopard*), *La Caduta degli Dei* (1969, *The Damned*) and *Morte a Venezia* (1971, *Death in Venice*).

Visser 't Hooft, Willem Adolf 1900–85
Dutch ecumenist
Born in Haarlem, he graduated in theology at Leyden and served young people's organizations until his appointment in 1938 as general secretary of what was to become the World Council of Churches, a post he held until his retirement in 1966. In that role he proved himself one of the foremost ecumenical statesmen of his generation. He insisted that the younger churches be regarded as equal partners in the common Christian task. A versatile scholar who spoke several languages fluently, he wrote many books, among which were *None Other Gods* (1937), *The Struggle of the Dutch Church* (1946), and his *Memoirs* (1973).

Vitellius, Aulus AD15–69
Roman emperor
A favourite of **Tiberius**, **Caligula**, **Claudius** and **Nero**, he was proconsul in Africa (c.61AD) and was appointed by **Galba** to the command of the legions on the Lower Rhine (68). He was proclaimed emperor at Colonia Agrippinensis (Cologne) in 69, and ended the reign of **Otho**. Many of his soldiers deserted when **Vespasian** was proclaimed emperor in Alexandria. Vitellius was defeated in two battles, dragged through the streets of Rome, and murdered. The only positive aspect of his rule was his initiation of free speech.

Vito, Danny De See De Vito, Danny

Vitrac, Roger 1899–1952
French playwright and Surrealist poet
He was associated with Tristan Tzara in the founding of the Dada movement, and with **Antonin Artaud** in that of the Théâtre **Alfred Jarry**. His play *Victor ou les enfants au pouvoir* (1928, 'Victor, or Children in Power'), which was revived in 1962 by **Jean Anouilh**, is a bitter Surrealist parody of superficial bedroom farce, depicting monstrous children, and one of the most effective and playable examples of the many assaults made on the emptiness of bourgeois society. Other plays include *Les Mystères de l'amour* (1927, Eng trans *Mysteries of Love*, in *Modern French Theatre*, 1964).

Vitruvius Pollio, Marcus 1st century AD
Roman architect and military engineer
A northern Italian in the service of **Augustus**, he wrote *De Architectura* (before AD27, 'On Architecture'), which is the only Roman treatise on architecture still extant.

Vittoria, Tommaso Ludovica da See Victoria, Tomás Luis de

Vittorini, Elio 1908–66
Sicilian novelist, critic and translator
Born in Syracuse, he educated himself despite great obstacles, and became founder-editor of *Il Politecnico* (1945–47) and *Il Menabò* (1959–66), and translated modern US writers like **Edgar Allan Poe**, **John Steinbeck** and **William Faulkner**. *Conversazione in Sicilia* (1941, Eng trans *Conversation in Sicily*, 1949) is his metaphorical masterpiece. He was one of Italy's most influential authors, and he supported many younger writers. 📖 S Pautasso, *Elio Vittorini* (1967)

Vittorino da Feltre c.1378–1446
Italian educationist
He was born in Feltre, and in 1423 was summoned to Mantua as tutor to the children of the Marchese Gonzaga. He founded a school for both rich and poor children there (La Giocosa), in which he applied his own methods of instruction.

Vitus, St early 4th century AD
Sicilian Christian
Born in Sicily, he was converted by his nurse Crescentia and her husband Modestus, with whom he was martyred under **Diocletian**. He was invoked against sudden death, hydrophobia and chorea (or St Vitus' Dance), and is sometimes regarded as the patron of comedians and actors. His feast day is 15 June.

Vivaldi, Antonio Lucio 1678–1741
Italian violinist and composer
Born in Venice, he was ordained in 1703, but gave up officiating, and was attached to the Conservatorio of the Ospedale della Pietà in Venice (1703–40). The 12 concertos of *L'Estro Armonico* (1712, 'Harmonic Inspiration') gave him a European reputation, and *The Four Seasons* (1725, *Le quattro stagioni*), an early example of programme music, was very popular. The composer of many operas, sacred music and over 450 concertos, he consolidated and developed the solo concerto, but was forgotten after his death. **J S Bach** transcribed many of his concertos for the keyboard and from the 19th century they were increasingly played. He was known as the 'Red Priest' because of his red hair.

Vivarini, Antonio 15th century
Venetian painter
Born possibly in Murano, Venice, he first worked in partnership with his brother-in-law Giovanni d'Alemagna and later with his brother **Bartolommeo Vivarini**. His paintings, often of Madonnas and saints, were modelled first on **Gentile da Fabriano** and then on **Andrea Mantegna** and **Giovanni Bellini**.

Vivarini, Bartolommeo 15th century
Venetian painter
The brother of **Antonio Vivarini**, he worked under the same influences, but his painting is representative of a step forward towards the Renaissance style.

Vivarini, Luigi or Alvise c.1446–c.1505
Italian painter
The son of **Antonio Vivarini**, he was possibly a pupil of both his father and uncle. Influenced by Antonello da Messina and Giovanni Bellini, his works include portrait busts and altarpieces, especially a *Madonna and Six Saints* (1480) in the Academy, Venice.

Vivekananda, originally Narendranath Dutt or Datta 1863–1902
Hindu missionary
He was born in Calcutta and became the chief disciple of **Ramakrishna Paramahasa**. A highly-educated representative of Vedanta as the universal religion at the Chicago Parliament of Religions (1893), he was a persuasive exponent of Hinduism in the West, and he proclaimed a reformed Hinduism with a social conscience in India. His organization of the now worldwide Ramakrishna Mission owed much to the methods of Christian missionaries. His *Collected Works* were published between 1919 and 1922.

Vives, Juan Luis, also known as Ludovicus 1492–1540
Spanish philosopher and humanist
Born in Valencia, he studied in Paris, France, and went on to become Professor of Humanities at Louvain (1519). He dedicated his edition of **Augustine of Hippo**'s *De Civitate Dei* (412–427 'The City of God') to **Henry VIII**, who summoned him to England in 1523 as tutor to Princess Mary (**Mary I**). But he was imprisoned in 1527 for opposing Henry's divorce from **Catherine of Aragon** and after 1528 lived mostly in Bruges, Belgium. His other writings include a treatise on education, *De Disciplinis libri XX* (1531,

'Twenty Books on Disciplines') and a major three-volume work on psychology and scientific method, *De anima et Vita* (1538, 'Three Books on the Soul and on Life').

Viviani, René 1862–1925
French statesman

He was born in Sidi-bel-Abbès, Algeria. He was Prime Minister at the outbreak of World War I and in order to demonstrate France's peaceful intentions withdrew French forces from the German frontier. He was Minister of Justice (1915) and French representative at the League of Nations (1920).

Vivin, Louis 1861–1936
French Primitive painter

Born in Hadol, he was a post office employee until he retired in 1922. He painted mainly still lifes and views of Paris and its parks. His naïve and charmingly coloured pictures are meticulous in every detail.

Vladimir I, Saint, *called* the Great c.956–1015
First Christian sovereign of Russia

Born in Kiev, the son of Svyatoslav, Grand Prince of Kiev (d.972), he became Prince of Novgorod (970), and seized Kiev from his brother (980) after his father's death, becoming ruler of Russia. Fierce and ambitious, he consolidated the Russian realm from the Baltic to the Ukraine, extending its dominions into Lithuania, Galicia and Livonia, with Kiev as his capital. He made a pact with the Byzantine Emperor Basil II (c.987), marrying his sister and accepting Christianity, which he forced on many of his people. He encouraged education and reformed legal institutions. He died on an expedition against one of his sons. His feast day is 15 July. ⌨Vladimir Volkoff, *Vladimir the Russian Viking* (1984)

Vladimir II, Monomakh 1053–1125
Ruler of Russia

The great-grandson of Vladimir I, he became by popular demand Grand Prince of Kiev (1113), thus founding the Monomakhovichi dynasty. A popular, powerful, enlightened and peaceful ruler, he colonized, built new towns, especially Vladimir, dethroned unruly princes and introduced laws against usury. He left careful instructions to his son and cousin in the manuals *Puchenie* and *Poslanie*.

Vlaminck, Maurice de 1876–1958
French artist

Born in Paris, he was largely self-taught, and for a time was a racing cyclist. In about 1900, he began to work with André Derain. At this time he was much influenced by Van Gogh, and by 1905 was one of the leaders of the Fauves, using typically brilliant colour, as in *The Red Trees* (1906, Pompidou Centre, Paris). From 1908 to 1914, however, he painted more realist landscapes under the influence of Cézanne. His palette was more sombre after 1915, and his style more romantic, though still full of zest. After World War I he lived mainly in the country as a farmer, and this may have given him his consistent sensitivity to the nuances of landscape and atmosphere. He was also a talented violinist, wrote several books, including *Communications* (1921), and was a pioneer collector of African art.

Vlamingh, Willem Hesselsz de fl.1690s
Dutch navigator

Born probably on the island of Vlieland, north-east Holland, he was master of the *Geelvincke*, a vessel of the Dutch East India Company which had left Holland in 1696 to search for a Dutch ship missing off the west coast of Australia. He retrieved a pewter plate, known as the Dirck Hartog Plate, inscribed by that mariner in 1616 and recording probably the earliest contact by Europeans with the Australian continent. Vlamingh left another plate in its place, describing his visit, and also discovered and named the Swan River, which became in 1829 the site of the first settlement on the west coast of Australia.

Vleck, John Hasbrouck van See Van Vleck, John Hasbrouck

Vodkin, Kuzma Sergeyevich Petrov- See Petrov-Vodkin, Kuzma Sergeyevich

Vodnik, Valentin 1758–1819
Slovene poet and teacher

He was born in Zgornja Šiška near Ljubljana. By his writings he helped to revive Slovene nationalism. He wrote poetry, educational and school books in the language of the peasantry, and this became established as the literary language of Yugoslavia. ⌨ F Levstik, *Valentin Vodnik* (1935)

Voelcker, Augustus 1822–84
German agricultural chemist and writer

Born in Frankfurt am Main, he studied at Göttingen and Utrecht. Later, he worked in Edinburgh for the Highland and Agricultural Society of Scotland (1847–49), was appointed Professor of Agriculture at the Royal Agricultural College, Cirencester (1849), and in 1857 became consulting chemist to the Royal Agricultural Society of England. His work on farm feeding-stuffs, on soil research and on artificial manures greatly advanced agricultural chemistry.

Vogel, Hans-Jochen 1926–
German politician

Born in Göttingen into a Catholic family and educated as a lawyer at Munich University, he became Social Democratic Party (SPD) Land (state) chairman in Bavaria in 1972 and was elected, in the same year, Mayor of Munich. He was Minister of Housing and Town Planning (1972–74), and served in the Schmidt Cabinet as Justice Minister (1975–81), before being sent to West Berlin to serve as mayor and to 'clean up' and overhaul the unpopular local party machine. An efficient, if somewhat colourless, party centrist, Vogel was Bundestag Leader of the Opposition from 1983 to 1991 when his party was again defeated by the Christian Democrats under Chancellor Kohl. He did not put himself forward as Chancellor-Candidate in January 1987, but in June replaced Willy Brandt as SPD Chairman, a position he held until 1991. His younger brother, Bernhard, has been Christian Democrat Minister-President of Rhineland-Palatinate since 1976.

Vogel, Hermann Carl 1841–1907
German astronomer

Born in Leipzig and educated at the university there, he was appointed assistant at the Leipzig Observatory, where Johann Karl Friedrich Zöllner stimulated his interest in astrophysics and in 1870 recommended him to a position at a newly founded private observatory at Bothkamp, near Kiel. Vogel made some pioneering studies of the spectra of the major planets which established his reputation as an astrophysicist. Introducing photographic methods into stellar spectroscopy, he was the first to achieve sufficient accuracy to measure radial velocities of stars. In 1889 he discovered the binary nature of Algol from such measurements, thereby opening up the important field of spectroscopic double stars. In 1882 he was appointed director of the Potsdam Astrophysical Observatory, which became under his guidance one of the world's leading centres of astrophysics. He continued in office until his death, though in his later years he became a recluse whose chief interest was to play the organ installed in his official residence at the observatory.

Vogel, Hermann Wilhelm 1834–98
German chemist

Born in Dobrilugk, Brandenburg, he taught at Berlin, and invented the orthochromatic photographic plate (1873). He also studied spectroscopic photography, and designed a photometer.

Vogel, Sir Julius 1835–99
New Zealand statesman
Born in London, he emigrated to Australia where he founded a newspaper, moving to New Zealand in 1861. He was elected Colonial Treasurer there in 1869. He established a government public trust office (1872), improved immigration facilities and planned the introduction of trunk railways, borrowing £10 million for his public works programme. He formed a government in 1872 and was premier (1873–75). He resigned in 1875 to devote himself to business, but was again treasurer during the economic crisis in 1884.

Vogel, Vladimir 1896–1984
Russian composer
Born in Moscow, he studied there and under **Ferruccio Busoni** in Berlin. He composed orchestral works, and chamber music as well as secular oratorios, including *Wàgadu Destroyed* (1935) with saxophone accompaniment.

Vogler, Abt Georg Joseph 1749–1814
German composer
Born in Würzburg, he was ordained priest at Rome in 1773, and made Knight of the Golden Spur and chamberlain to the pope. At Mannheim he established his first school of music (1775), and his second was in Stockholm (c.1786). After years of success in London and Europe as a player on his 'orchestrion' (a modified organ), he settled as kapellmeister at Darmstadt (1807), and opened his third school, where his pupils included **Carl Weber** and **Giacomo Meyerbeer**. His compositions and his theories of music are now forgotten, but his name survives in **Robert Browning**'s poem, 'Abt Vogler'.

Vogt, Peter 1932–
US microbiologist
He was educated at the University of Tübingen and moved to the USA as an assistant Professor of Pathology (1962–66) at the University of Colorado and later became Professor of Microbiology (1969–71) at the University of Washington. He was Hastings Distinguished Professor of Microbiology at the University of Southern California from 1978 to 1980, and has been Chairman of the Microbiology Department there since 1980. A major field of interest for Vogt has been the relationship between oncogenes and retroviruses. Oncogenes are normal cellular genes which can be activated in a variety of ways to become carcinogenic, and Vogt showed that there are basically two ways by which they can be activated by retroviruses. The gene sequence may be altered so that it codes for protein with abnormal function, or it can be brought under the control of powerful viral enhancers or promoters to overproduce a normal gene product. In either case the involvement of retroviruses is clearly of vital importance in certain carcinogenic processes.

Voiture, Vincent 1598–1648
French poet and letter-writer
Born in Amiens, he was an original member of the Académie Française, and enjoyed the favour of Gaston d'Orléans, Cardinal **Richelieu**, Cardinal **Mazarin** and **Louis XIII**. His sonnets, such as 'L'Amour d'Uranie avec Philis', and *vers de société* were popular with the members of the Marquise de **Rambouillet**'s literary salon, but were not published until 1650. His elegant letters, first published in 1654, provide a picture of his age and social milieu. 📖 C A Sainte-Beuve, in *Causeries de lundi* (1867)

Volcker, Paul Adolph 1927–
US economist
Born in Cape May, New Jersey, he graduated from Princeton and Harvard and worked for Chase Manhattan Bank, becoming known for his skilful analysis of international monetary systems. After serving as Under-Secretary in the Treasury (1969–1974) and President of the New York Federal Reserve Bank (1975–79), he was head of the Federal Reserve System from 1979 to 1987, and during President **Ronald Reagan**'s first term he controlled inflation by shrinking money supplies and raising interest rates. High unemployment and a stagnant economy made this policy unpopular, however, and during the second term he favoured increased monetary growth. Since he returned to private life in 1987, he has served as a consultant on mergers and acquisitions.

Volstead, Andrew Joseph 1860–1947
US Republican politician
Born in Goodhue County, Minnesota, he practised law and entered Congress as a Republican in 1903. He was the author of the Farmers' Co-operative Marketing Act, but is best known for the Prohibition Act of 1919, named after him, which forbade the manufacture and sale of intoxicant liquors. This Act, passed over President **Woodrow Wilson**'s veto, was intended to placate the influential temperance movement, which argued that alcohol contributed to crime and poverty, and to divert grain to food production in the wake of World War I. In fact, it proved impossible to enforce effectively and did little other than to create enormous profits for bootleggers and speakeasies, and to provide material for countless Hollywood gangster films. It was repealed in 1933.

Volta, Alessandro Giuseppe Anastasio, Count 1745–1827
Italian physicist and inventor
Born in Como, he was appointed Professor of Physics at the university there (1775) and at Pavia (1778). In 1795 he became Rector of Pavia University; he was dismissed in 1799 for political reasons and later reinstated by the French. He invented the electrophorus (1775, the precursor of the induction machine), the condenser (1778), the candle flame collector of atmospheric electricity (1787) and the electrochemical battery, or 'voltaic pile' (1800), which was the first source of continuous or current electricity. It was inspired by a controversy he had with **Luigi Galvani** concerning the nature of animal electricity. He also invented an 'inflammable air' (hydrogen) electric pistol (1777). **Antoine Lavoisier** followed Volta's suggestion that the mixtures of air and hydrogen should be sparked over mercury (and not water), and identified the resultant to be water (1782). His name is given to the SI unit of electrical potential difference, the volt. 📖 Bern Dobner, *Alessandro Volta and the Electric Battery* (1964)

Voltaire See panel p1896

Volterra, Daniele da, *originally* Ricciarelli
c.1509–1566
Italian artist
Born in Volterra, he was trained by the Sienese painter Il Sodoma, then moved to Rome, where he became the friend and pupil of **Michelangelo**. In 1541 he painted the *Descent from the Cross* in the Trinità dei Monti in Rome. His last work was a bronze bust of Michelangelo (Louvre, Paris), for which he used Michelangelo's death mask.

Volterra, Vito 1860–1940
Italian mathematician
Born in Ancona, he was professor at the universities of Pisa, Turin and Rome. In 1931 he was dismissed from his chair at Rome for refusing to support the Fascist government, and he spent most of the rest of his life abroad. He worked on integral equations, in which his idea of studying spaces of functions proved exceptionally fertile. He also worked on mathematical physics and the

Voltaire, *pseudonym of* François Marie Arouet 1694–1778
French writer and historian, the embodiment of the 18th-century enlightenment

Voltaire was born in Paris, where his father, François Arouet, was a notary in the *chambre des comptes*. He was educated by Jesuits and studied law, but disliked this and turned instead to writing. He soon acquired notoriety as the author of a satire on his successful rival in the poetic competition for an Academy prize. In 1716, on suspicion of satirizing the regent, the Duc d'Orléans, he was banished for several months from Paris, and in 1717–18, a savage attack accusing the regent of all manner of crimes resulted in 11 months' imprisonment in the Bastille. There he rewrote his tragedy *Œdipe*, began a poem on **Henri IV** and assumed the name Voltaire. *Œdipe* was performed in 1718, and was triumphantly successful.

The authorities refused to sanction the publication of 'Henri IV', because it championed Protestantism and religious toleration, so Voltaire had it printed secretly in Rouen (1723) and smuggled into Paris, as 'La Ligue, ou Henri le Grand'. He was now famous and a favourite at court. He got into a quarrel with the Chevalier de Rohan-Chabot and circulated caustic epigrams about him; in the end he was once more thrown into the Bastille, and was freed only on condition that he would leave for England. There he remained for four years (1726–29), became acquainted with **Alexander Pope** and his circle, and familiarized himself with English literature. He was strongly attracted to **John Locke**'s philosophy, and he mastered the elements of **Isaac Newton**'s astronomical physics.

Back in France, he laid the foundation of his great wealth by purchasing shares in a government lottery and by speculating in the corn trade, ultimately increased by the profits from large army contracts. He formed an intimacy with Madame du **Châtelet-Lomont**, and went to live with her at her husband's château of Cirey in Champagne (1734). Here he wrote dramas and poetry, several philosophical works, and scientific treatises. His correspondence (1740–50) testifies to a love affair with his niece, the widowed Madame Denis. His *Princesse de Navarre*, performed on the occasion of the Dauphin's marriage (February 1745), pleased **Louis XV** by its clever adulation; this and the patronage of Madame de **Pompadour** secured Voltaire appointments as official royal historian and gentleman-in-ordinary to the king.

In 1750 Voltaire went to Berlin at the invitation of **Frederick II, the Great**; he was appointed king's chamberlain with a pension of 20,000 francs and board in one of the royal palaces. There he caused offence with his satirical criticisms of **Pierre de Maupertuis** in *Micromégas*, and in March 1753 Frederick and Voltaire parted, never to meet again. He settled in 1755 near Geneva and after 1758 at Ferney, four miles away. There he wrote his satirical short story *Candide*, his best-known work.

In 1762 Voltaire published the first of his anti-religious writings which were to include didactic tragedies, biased histories, pamphlets and the *Dictionnaire philosophique* (1764). He became involved in the affair surrounding the judicial murder (1762) of **Jean Calas**, who had been falsely accused of killing one of his sons to keep him from becoming a Catholic. Voltaire was successful in establishing his innocence and in rescuing members of the Calas family from further punishment. This and similar efforts on behalf of victims of French fanaticism, for whom he provided a refuge at Ferney, won widespread admiration.

In 1778, in his eighty-fourth year, he was welcomed back in Paris to stage his last tragedy, *Irène*. The excitement of this brought on illness and his death. After the Revolution, which his works and ideas helped to foster, his remains were reinterred in the Panthéon in Paris.

📖 **Principal works**

Dramas: *Œdipe* ('Oedipus'); *Mahomet* (1741, Eng trans *Mohamet the Imposter*, 1744) and *Mérope* (1743, Eng trans 1744); *Princesse de Navarre* (1745); *Irène* (1778).

Poetry: *La Ligue ou Henri le Grand* (Eng trans *Henriade*, dedicated to Queen **Caroline of Ansbach** during his English visit, 1732); *Poème sur le désastre de Lisbonne* (1756, 'Poem on the Lisbon Earthquake')

Philosophical tales: *Lettres écrites de Londres sur les Anglais* (1734, Eng trans *Letters Concerning the English Nation*, 1734); *Zadig* (1748, Eng trans *Zadig and Other Stories*, 1971); *Candide* (Eng trans *Candid*, 1759).

Historical and philosophical works: *Traité de métaphysique* (1748, 'Treatise on Metaphysics'); *Siècle de Louis Quatorze* (1751, Eng trans *The Age of Louis XIV*, 1752) and *Les Mœurs et l'esprit des nations* (1756, rev 1761–63, Eng trans *The General History and State of Europe*, 1756); *Dictionnaire philosophique portatif* (1764, Eng trans *The Philosophical Dictionary for the Pocket*, 1765)

Scientific works: *Eléments de la philosophie de Newton* (1738, Eng trans *The Elements of Newton's Philosophy*, 1738).

📖 P Gay, *Voltaire's Politics: The Poet as Realist* (1988); N Mitford, *Voltaire in Love* (1957); S G Tallentyre, *Voltaire* (1903).

Il faut cultiver notre jardin.
'We must cultivate our garden.'
From *Candide*, ch.30.

Le superflu, chose très nécessaire.
'The superfluous, a very necessary thing.'
From *Le Mondain*, l.22. (1736)

mathematics of population change in biology, where he put forward the Lotka–Volterra equations, a pair of differential equations that describe a simple predator–prey population model.

von Braun, Wernher See **Braun, Wernher von**

Vondel, Joost van den 1587–1679
Dutch poet and dramatist

Born in Cologne of Dutch immigrant parents, he became a prosperous hosier in Amsterdam and devoted his leisure to writing satirical verse, himself turning from Anabaptism through Armenianism to Roman Catholicism. Having acquired a wide knowledge of the classics, he turned to Sophoclean drama and produced *Jephtha* (1659) and *Lucifer* (1654), a masterpiece of lyrical religious drama. He greatly influenced the German poetical revival after the Thirty Years War (1618–48).
📖 A J Barouq, *Joost van den Vondel* (1925)

von Euler, Ulf Svante See **Euler, Ulf Svante von**

Von Guerard, Eugene (Eugen John Joseph)
1811–1901
Australian landscape artist

Born in Vienna, Austria, where his father was court painter to King **Francis I**, he studied in Düsseldorf and Naples before arriving in Geelong, Victoria, in 1852 to join the gold rush. He painted and worked in the goldfields around Ballarat, Victoria, before going to Melbourne in 1854. In 1855 he travelled extensively in Tasmania and South Australia and was a member of two expeditions to north Victoria and the Australian alps, which resulted in a number of mature landscapes. A painting from a later visit to New South Wales was accepted by the Royal Academy in 1865, and an album of Von Guerard's lithographs, *Australian Landscapes*, was published in 1867. He was an influential teacher at the National Gallery of Victoria's School of Art from 1870 until 1882.

Vo Nguyen Giap 1912–
Vietnamese military leader

Born in Quang Binh Province, he studied law at Hanoi University, and joined the Vietnamese Communist party. He led the Viet Minh army in revolt against the French, leading to the decisive defeat of their garrison at Dien Bien Phu in 1954. As Vice-Premier and Defence Minister of North Vietnam, he masterminded the military strategy that forced the US forces to leave South Vietnam (1973) and led to the reunification of Vietnam in 1975. He was a member of the Politburo from 1976 to 1982. He wrote *People's War, People's Army* (1961), which became a textbook for revolutionaries, and *Military Art of People's War* (1970).

Von Klitzing, Klaus 1943–
German physicist and Nobel Prize winner

Born in Schroda, he was educated at the Technical University in Munich and at Würzburg University, where he received his doctorate in 1972. He was appointed professor at Munich University in 1980, and in 1985 became director of the **Max Planck** Institute, Stuttgart. In 1977 he presented a paper on two-dimensional electronic behaviour in which the quantum Hall effect was clearly implied, but von Klitzing only appreciated what had occurred in 1980, causing a major revision of the theory of electric conduction in strong magnetic fields. For this work he was awarded the 1985 Nobel Prize for physics.

Vonnegut, Bernard 1914–
US physicist

Born in Indianapolis, Indiana, and educated at the Massachusetts Institute of Technology (MIT), he worked under **Vincent Schaefer** at the General Electric Company (1945–52) then at the A D Little Company until 1967, when he became Professor of Atmospheric Science at New York State University. In 1947 he improved a method for artificially inducing rainfall, by using silver iodide as a cloud-seeding agent.

Vonnegut, Kurt, Jnr 1922–
US novelist

Born in Indianapolis, Indiana, he was educated at Cornell and Chicago universities and at the Carnegie Institute, Pittsburgh, then served in the US army infantry (1942–55) and was given the Purple Heart. During the 1960s he emerged as one of the USA's most influential, potent and provocative writers, a ribald commentator of the horrors of the century: holocaustic wars, the desperate state of the environment, and the dehumanization of the individual in a society dominated by science and technology. *Player Piano* (1952) was his first novel and there were another three before *Slaughterhouse-Five* (1969), in which the two main characters—the author himself and the protagonist, Billy Pilgrim—see beneath the tragic realities of human history but make no attempt to effect change. The central event of the novel is the destruction of Dresden during World War II which the author witnessed as a prisoner-of-war. Later novels, including *Breakfast of Champions* (1973), *Deadeye Dick* (1982) and *Hocus Pocus* (1990), continued to satirize human folly in its various manifestations. He published a collection of essays and speeches in 1991, entitled *Fates Worse Than Death*. 📖 J Lundquist, *Kurt Vonnegut* (1977)

Von Neumann, John (Johann) 1903–57
US mathematician

Born in Budapest, Hungary, he was educated in Berlin and Budapest, and taught at Berlin (1927–29), Hamburg (1929–30), and Princeton (1930–33) before becoming a member of the Institute for Advanced Study at Princeton (1933). In 1943 he worked on the Manhattan Project (atomic bomb) at Los Alamos, and in 1954 joined the US Atomic Energy Commission. His best-known mathematical work was on the theory of linear operators, but he also gave a new axiomatization of set theory and formulated a precise description of quantum theory (1932). He designed some of the earliest computers, and his novel *The Theory of Games and Economic Behavior* (1944) contained a theory applicable both to games of chance and to games of pure skill, such as chess. These ideas have since become important in mathematical economics and operational research. He went on to invent the idea of self-replicating machines and cellular automata.

Von Sternberg, Josef, *originally* Jonas Sternberg 1894–1969
Austrian film director

Born in Vienna, he worked in silent films in Hollywood in the 1920s as scriptwriter, cameraman, and director, but went to Germany to make his most famous film *Der blaue Engel* (1910, 'The Blue Angel') with **Marlene Dietrich**. This was followed by six more Hollywood features in which she starred, the last being *The Devil is a Woman* (1935).

von Sydow, Max Carl Adolf See Sydow, Max Carl Adolf von

Von Trotta, Margarethe 1942–
German film actress and director

Born in Berlin, she studied acting in Munich before making a number of critically acclaimed stage and television appearances such as *Baal* (1969), her first collaboration with future husband Volker Schlöndorff (1939–). She also appeared in films like *Der Plötzliche Reichtum der Armen Leute von Kombach* (1971, *The Sudden Fortune of the Poor People of Kombach*), which she also co-wrote. Working as a scriptwriter on most of Schlöndorff's projects, she wrote and co-directed *Die Verlorene Ehre der Katharina Blum* (1975, *The Lost Honour of Katharina Blum*). She solely directed *Das Zweite Erwachen der Christa Klages* (1977, *The Second Awakening of Christa Klages*), which signalled her interest in the social position of women. Later films include *Schwestern Oder Die Balance des Glücks* (1981, *Sisters, or the Balance of Happiness*), a biographical film about Rosa Luxemburg (1986), *L'Africana* (1990, *The Return*) and *I lungo silencio* (1992). She returned to Germany for *Das Versprechen* (1994, 'The Promise').

von Wolff, Christian See Wolff, Christian von

von Wright, Georg Henrik See Wright, Georg Henrik von

Voragine, Jacobus de 1230–98
Italian prelate and hagiologist

Born in Viareggio near Genoa, he entered the Dominican Order. He became Archbishop of Genoa in 1292. The author of the *Golden Legend*, a collection of lives of the saints, translated by **William Caxton** (1483), he is also said to have produced the first Italian translation of the Bible.

Voronoff, Serge 1866–1951
Russian physiologist

Born in Voronezh, he was educated in Paris and became director of experimental surgery at the Collège de France. Later working in Switzerland, he developed a theory connecting gland secretions with senility. Pioneering endocrinological surgery, Voronoff specialized in grafting animal glands (especially monkey glands) into the ageing human body, with a view to restoring potency and ensuring long life.

Voroshilov, Kliment Yefremovich 1881–1969
Soviet politician

He was born near Dnepropetrovsk in the Ukraine. A Bolshevik from 1903, his political activities led to his exile to Siberia. His military role in World War I and the 1917 Revolution led to rapid promotion within the Party. Appointed Marshal of the Soviet Union in 1935, from 1925 to 1940 he was Commissar for Defence and so mainly responsible for the modernization of the Red Army and its success in defeating Hitler's invasion of 1941. He was President of the Soviet Union from Stalin's death (1953) to 1960. ⌨ V A Akshinskii, *Kliment Efremovich Voroshilov: biograficheskii ocherk* (1976)

Vörösmarty, Michael 1800–55
Hungarian poet and dramatist

Born in Szekesfehervar, he became an advocate and, after Lajos Kossuth's revolution, a member of the National Assembly (1848). He wrote the national song, *Szozat* (1840, 'The Call'), lyric and epic poetry and 11 plays, of which the fairy drama *Csongor es Tünde* (1831, 'Csongor and Tünde') is his masterpiece. He also translated Shakespearean tragedies. ⌨ D Toth, *Michael Vörösmarty* (1957)

Vorster, John, *originally* Balthazar Johannes Vorster 1915–83
South African politician

Born in Jamestown and educated at Stellenbosch University, he became a lawyer and was a leader of the extreme Afrikaner nationalist group, Ossewa Brandwag, in World War II. He was accepted into the National Party, becoming MP for Nigel in 1953. In Hendrik Verwoerd's government he was from 1961 Minister of Justice, being responsible for several controversial measures. After the assassination of Verwoerd in September 1966 he was elected Prime Minister. Under him apartheid remained the official policy. In 1978, after the 'information scandal' involving large-scale misappropriation of government funds, he resigned for health reasons and was elected State President. The following year he resigned this position after an investigation by the Erasmus commission found him jointly responsible. ⌨ John D'Oliviera, *Vorster: The Man* (1977)

Vortigern fl.425–c.450AD
British ruler

He is reported by Gildas, Bede and Nennius to have invited the Saxons, led by Hengist and Horsa, into Britain to help him against the Picts, and to have married Hengist's daughter, Rowena.

Vos, Cornelis de 1585–1651
Flemish painter

Born in Antwerp, he chiefly painted portraits, and religious and mythological pieces. He worked occasionally for Rubens. His brother, Paul (1590–1678), painted animals and hunting scenes.

Voss, Johann Heinrich 1751–1826
German poet and philologist

He was born in Sommersdorf in Mecklenburg, and studied at Göttingen. In 1778 he went from editing the *Musenalmanach* at Wandsbeck to be schoolmaster at Otterndorf. Here he translated the *Odyssey*. In 1782 he became rector of a school at Eutin, and in 1789 he issued his translation of Virgil's *Georgics*. In 1802 he settled in Jena, and in 1805 was appointed professor at Heidelberg, where he translated Horace, Hesiod, Theocritus, Bion, Moschus, Albius Tibullus and Sextus Propertius. Other translations were of Aristophanes and (with the help of his two sons) Shakespeare. *Luise* (1795), an idyll, is his best original poem, although his lyric poems were popular in his own day. ⌨ W Herbst, *Johann Heinrich Voss* (1872–76)

Vouet, Simon 1590–1649
French painter

Born in Paris, after 14 years in Italy he returned to France, where his religious and allegorical paintings and decorations in the Baroque style became very popular. A contemporary of Nicolas Poussin, who criticized him but was not a serious rival during his lifetime, he taught Charles Le Brun and Eustache Le Sueur.

Voysey, Charles Francis Annesley 1857–1941
English architect and designer

Born in London, he was the son of the theologian Charles Voysey (1828–1912). A disciple of John Ruskin and William Morris, he designed traditional country houses influenced by the Arts and Crafts Movement, with accentuated gables, chimney stacks, buttresses and long sloping roofs. He was also an important designer of wallpaper, textiles, furniture and metalwork.

Vranitzky, Franz 1937–
Austrian politician

Educated at what is now the University of Commerce, Vienna, he embarked on a career in banking and in 1970 became adviser on economic and financial policy to the Minister of Finance. After holding senior appointments in the banking world he became Minister of Finance himself in 1984 and two years later succeeded Fred Sinowatz as Federal Chancellor. He resigned in 1997.

Vrchlicky, Jaroslav, *pseudonym of* Emil Frída 1853–1912
Czech poet and translator

Born in Laun, he was a pupil of Victor Hugo, who inspired the *Fragments of the Epic of Humanity*. His best ballads, *Legenda o sv. Prokopu* (1879, 'Legend of St Procopius') and *Zlomky epopeje* (1886, 'Peasant Ballads'), are on nationalistic and patriotic themes. His early lyric poetry on love and the pleasures of life gave way to reflections upon suffering and misfortune. He translated the classics of European poetry and in 1893 he was appointed Professor of European Literature at Prague. ⌨ V Ticly, *Jaroslav Vrchlicky* (1951)

Vreeland, Diana, *née* Dalziel c.1903–89
US fashion editor

Born in Paris, she moved to New York when she was eight. Her first column, 'Why Don't You…?', was for *Harper's Bazaar*, and she became fashion editor there from 1939 to 1962. Her startling memos to staff became legendary and she was parodied as the flamboyant fashion editor who tells staff to 'Think pink!' in the 1956 film *Funny Face*. She had an admirable visual eye and furthered the careers of many models, photographers and designers. After being managing editor of American *Vogue* (1962–71) she became special consultant to the Costume Institute of the Metropolitan Museum of New York. She was awarded the French Order of Merit in 1970 and the French Legion of Honour in 1976.

Vries, Hugo Marie de 1848–1935
Dutch botanist and geneticist

Born in Haarlem, he studied at the universities of Leyden, Heidelberg and Würzburg, and became Professor of Botany at Amsterdam University (1878–1918). From 1890 he studied heredity and variation in plants, significantly developing Mendelian genetics and evolutionary theory. His major work was *Die Mutationstheorie* (1901–03, 'The Mutation Theory'). He described and correctly interpreted the phenomenon of plasmolysis, where the cytoplasm in plant cells shrinks away from the walls, and introduced methods for studying plant cells which have become standard techniques.

Vries, Peter De See De Vries Peter

Vuillard, (Jean) Édouard 1868–1940

French artist

Born in Cuiseaux, he shared a studio with **Pierre Bonnard**, and was strongly influenced by **Paul Gauguin** and by the vogue for Japanese painting. Although his outlook was limited and mainly devoted to flower pieces and to simple and intimate interiors, these are painted with an exquisite sense of light and colour. He also produced murals for public buildings, such as the Théâtre des Champs-Elysees and Palais de Chaillot.

Vygotsky, Lev Semyonovich 1896–1934

Soviet psychologist

Born in Orsha, he studied various social sciences at Moscow University, then turned to psychology and from 1924 until his death worked at the Institute of Psychology in Moscow. His theories of cognitive development, especially his view of the relationship between language and thinking, have strongly influenced both Marxist and Western psychology. His best-known work, *Thought and Language* (1934), was briefly suppressed as being against Stalinist-approved psychology. He was open to intuition, had an undogmatic approach to experimental methodology, and moved easily between the pure and applied fields. He always emphasized the role of the cultural and social factors in the development of cognition. *Thought and Language* is now a classic text in university courses in psycholinguistics.

Vyse, Charles 1882–1971

English potter and sculptor

Born in Staffordshire into a family of potters, he trained as a modeller at the Hanley School of Art, obtaining a sculpture scholarship to the Royal College of Art where he also worked from 1905 to 1910. After working in the Staffordshire Potteries, he established a workshop with his wife in Cheyne Row, Chelsea, where they created stylized figures and groups realistically modelled and coloured. He exhibited his work regularly and experimented with wood-ash glazes and early Chinese glaze effects. In the early 1930s he specialized in skilfully drawn brushwork decoration on more simple forms. The workshop was damaged by air raids in 1940 and they moved from London. He became modelling and pottery instructor at the Farnham School of Art.

Vyshinsky, Andrei Yanuarevich 1883–1954

Soviet jurist and politician

Born of Polish origin in Odessa, he studied law at Moscow University but was debarred from a lectureship on account of his Menshevik revolutionary activities until 1921, when he left the Red Army. He became Professor of Criminal Law and simultaneously Attorney-General (1923–25) and was Rector of Moscow University (1925–28). He was notoriously the public prosecutor at the Metropolitan-Vickers trial (1933) and the subsequent state trials (1936–38) which removed **Stalin**'s rivals, Bukharin, **Karl Radek, Grigori Zinoviev, Lev Kamenev** and Sokolnikov. He was promoted deputy Foreign Minister under **Vyacheslav Molotov** (1940) and was permanent Soviet delegate to the United Nations (1945–49, 1953–54), succeeding Molotov as Foreign Minister in 1949 until the death of Stalin (1953). He was the brilliant advocate of the disruptive Stalin–Molotov foreign policies, the author of many textbooks on Soviet Law and the recipient of the Order of Lenin and the Stalin Prize in 1947.

Waage, Peter 1833–1900
Norwegian chemist

Born near Flekkefjord, he went to the University of Christiania (Oslo) in 1854 to study medicine, but soon changed to science. After working with **Robert Bunsen** at Heidelberg (1859–60), he returned to Christiania as lecturer in chemistry and succeeded Adolf Strecker as Professor of Chemistry in 1866. Waage is chiefly remembered for his work with **Cato Maximilian Guldberg**, his brother-in-law, which established the law of mass action governing the influence of reactant concentrations on rates of reaction (1864). He later turned to practical problems relating to nutrition and public health, and he also engaged in social and religious work.

Waals, Johannes Diderik van der 1837–1923
Dutch physicist and Nobel Prize winner

Born in Leyden, he went to the university there, graduating in 1865. After teaching physics at Deventer and The Hague, he studied again at Leyden. He convincingly accounted for many phenomena concerning vapours and liquids by postulating the existence of intermolecular forces and a finite molecular volume. He derived a new equation of state (the van der Waals equation) which agreed much more closely with experimental data and led to a Nobel Prize for physics (1910). The weak attractions between molecules (van der Waals forces) were named in his honour. As Professor of Physics at Amsterdam University (1877–1907) he gained distinction as a teacher and as an advocate of the chemical thermodynamics of **Josiah Gibbs**. 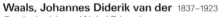 A Y Kipnis, *Van der Waals and Molecular Science* (1996)

Wace, Robert c.1115–c.1183
Anglo-Norman poet

Born in Jersey, he studied in Paris, and was a canon of Bayeux (1160–70). He wrote several verse lives of the saints, but his main work was *Roman de Brut* (1155), a Norman–French version of Geoffrey of Monmouth's *Historia Regum Britanniae*, used by **Layamon** and **Robert Mannyng**. He also wrote the *Roman de Rou* (Rollo), an epic of the exploits of the Dukes of Normandy. M Pela, *Influence de Brut de Wace* (1931)

Wacha Dinshaw Edulji 1844–1936
Indian politician

A member of the Bombay Legislative Council and the Imperial Legislative Council, he worked in close association with **Dadhabai Naoroji** and Ferozshah Mehta for the peaceful development of his country through social reform, education and through participation in politics. A founder-member of the Congress, he was its President in 1901. He criticized the British government's economic and financial policies and freely expressed his nation's viewpoint before the Welby Commission in London.

Wackenroder, Wilhelm Heinrich 1773–98
German writer

He was born in Berlin and studied at Erlangen (1793) and Göttingen (1793–94) universities, later working as a civil servant. He was an early exponent of Romanticism and a close friend of **Johann Tieck**, with whom he collaborated in *Herzensergiessungen eines kunstliebenden Klosterbruders* (1797, 'Outpourings from the Heart of an Art-loving Monk') and *Phantasien über die Kunst* (1799, 'Fantasies about Art'). E Gulzow, *Wackenroder* (1930)

Wadati, Kiyoo 1902–
Japanese seismologist

He studied at Tokyo Imperial University before entering the Central Meteorological Observatory (now the Japan Meteorological Agency). His most important contributions have been to advances in the detection of deep earthquakes. Similar deep, inclined seismic zones were being located by **Victor Benioff** and later it was proved that these Wadati–Benioff zones show the motion of downgoing oceanic crust. Also interested in Antarctic research, Wadati carried out fieldwork at the Showa base (1973–74).

Waddington, Conrad Hal 1905–75
English embryologist and geneticist

Born in Evesham, Hereford and Worcester, he studied geology at Cambridge before turning to embryology. From 1947 to 1970 he was Professor of Animal Genetics at Edinburgh University. He studied the effects of chemical messengers in inducing embryonic cells to form particular tissues during development, and was especially concerned with the ways in which both genes and environmental influences control the development of embryos. His *Organisers and Genes* (1940) covers Mendelian genetics and experimental embryology, and he also wrote a standard textbook of embryology, *Principles of Embryology* (1956). Interested in the popularization of science and in forging links between science and the arts, his more popular books include *The Ethical Animal* (1960) and *Biology for the Modern World* (1962).

Waddington, David Charles Waddington, Baron 1929–
English politician

After studying at Oxford, where he was president of the Conservative Association, he qualified and practised as a barrister but soon sought election to the House of Commons. Following three unsuccessful attempts he became MP for Nelson and Colne in 1968, and subsequently represented the Clitheroe and Ribble Valley constituencies. After a number of junior posts under **Margaret Thatcher** he was made government Chief Whip in 1987 and in 1989, when **Douglas Hurd** became Foreign Secretary, succeeded him as Home Secretary. A right-winger within his party, Waddington became one of the very few Home Secretaries openly to have supported the return of capital punishment. He was Leader of the House of Lords from 1990 until his resignation from parliament in 1992. He was made a life peer in 1990 and in 1992 became Governor and Commander-in-Chief of Bermuda.

Wade, Benjamin Franklin 1800–78
US politician

Born on a farm near Springfield, Massachusetts, he moved to Ohio in 1821 and was admitted to the Bar six years later. As a senator from Ohio (1851–69) and a leader of the Radical Republicans, he advocated harsh punishment for the Confederacy after the US Civil War. In 1864 he was joint author of the Wade–Davis Manifesto demanding congressional rather than executive control of Reconstruction.

Wade, Sir Thomas Francis 1818–95
English diplomat and scholar

Born in London, after a short career as a soldier, including active service in China, he became a member of the diplomatic corps in China and was the British ambassador in Peking (Beijing) from 1871–83. In 1888 he was appointed the first Professor of Chinese at Cambridge, holding this post until 1895. Among his works is the

Peking Syllabary (1859), in which the Wade system of romanization is employed. This transliteration system was later modified by Wade's successor at Cambridge, Herbert Giles.

Wadsworth, Edward 1889–1949
English artist
Born in Yorkshire, he studied engineering in Munich, attended the Slade School in 1910, and was associated with Wyndham Lewis, Roger Fry, Unit One and the London Group. He is known for his still lifes and seascapes with marine objects, painted in tempera with dream-like clarity and precision.

Waerden, Bartel Leendert van der 1903–
Dutch mathematician
Born in Amsterdam, he was professor at the universities of Groningen (1928–31), Leipzig (1931–45), Johns Hopkins (1947–48), Amsterdam (1948–51) and Zurich (1951–62). He worked in algebra, algebraic geometry and mathematical physics, and published books on the history of science and mathematics, for example *Science awakening* (1954). His classic textbook *Moderne Algebra* (1931) was influential in publicizing the new algebra developed by David Hilbert, Emil Artin, Emmy Noether and others, and his book on the application of group theory to quantum mechanics (1932) showed its relevance to physics. He also wrote a series of 20 papers on algebraic geometry devoted to showing the power and rigour of the new algebraic methods.

Wagenfeld, Wilhelm 1900–
German designer
Born in Bremen, he studied, and later taught, at the Bauhaus, and has remained faithful to its principles. His designs are simple, unadorned and functional. The best known are those for mass-produced glass, and for Rosenthal ceramics. He has taught during a great deal of his career, thus extending his influence as a designer.

Wager, Lawrence Rickard 1904–65
English geologist, petrologist and explorer
Born in Batley, Yorkshire, he was educated at Cambridge, and was later appointed as a lecturer at the University of Reading (1929–43). He took part in a series of major scientific expeditions, several of which were to East Greenland (1930–53), where he mapped the geography of the area and carried out his classical study of the local petrology and geochemistry. After World War II, he resumed his geological career as Professor of Geology at Durham University (1944–50) and then at Oxford from 1950. He was elected Fellow of the Royal Society in 1946. His important research on igneous and metamorphic petrology included notable studies of crystal nucleation, and the origin and nature of rock structures in Scotland. In 1955 he helped to establish the Oxford radiometric age determination laboratory.

Wagner, Otto 1841–1918
Austrian architect and teacher
He was Professor at the Vienna Academy (1894–1912), where his pupils included Josef Hoffmann and Joseph Olbrich. His most influential work was produced at the end of his career, such as Karlsplatz Station (1898–99) and Am Steinhof Church (1905–07), both flourishes of Art Nouveau tempered by traditional construction. In the main hall of K K Portsparkasse (savings bank) in Vienna (1904–06), he created what is universally regarded as the first example of modern architecture in the 20th century. His aims were to create an architecture appropriate to the age, out of a synthesis of historical models, modern materials and technology able to function practically and symbolically. He is considered to be the founder of the Modern movement.

Wagner, Richard See panel p1902

Wagner, Robert Ferdinand 1877–1953
US politician
Born in Hesse, Nassau, Germany, he emigrated to the USA with his family in 1885 and settled in New York City. He was a Democratic senator from New York (1927–49) and one of President Franklin Roosevelt's most trusted allies in Congress. He helped to win passage of many important pieces of New Deal legislation, including the National Labor Relations Act of 1935, known as the Wagner Act, which guarantees the right of labour to bargain collectively.

Wagner, Robert John, Jnr 1930–
US actor
Born in Detroit, Michigan, he attended Black-Foxe Military Institute and decided to become an actor, winning a long-term contract with 20th Century Fox. After a small role in *The Happy Years* (1950) he took charming juvenile leads in a succession of war, western and adventure films like *The Silver Whip* (1953), *Prince Valiant* (1954) and *The True Story of Jesse James* (1957). He was cast against type as a killer in *A Kiss Before Dying* (1956) and also played comedy in *The Pink Panther* (1963). However, his greatest popularity has been on television where his boyish romantic appeal, suave manner and light humour were seen as a jewel thief in *It Takes A Thief* (1965–69), an ex-con man in *Switch* (1975–77) and a jet-set detective in *Hart to Hart* (1979–84). He was married to actress Natalie Wood from 1957 to 1962 and again from 1972 until her death in 1981.

Wagner, Siegfried 1869–1930
German conductor and composer musician
Born near Lucerne, the son of Richard Wagner, he was trained as an architect but later became a conductor and composer of operas and other music. He was director of the Bayreuth Festspielhaus from 1909, and in 1915 he married Winifred Williams (1897–1980), who directed the Bayreuth Festivals until 1944.

Wagner, Wieland 1917–66
German opera-house director
He was born in Bayreuth, the son of Siegfried Wagner. He took over the directorship of the Festspielhaus at his father's death and revolutionized the production of the operas, stressing their universality as opposed to their purely German significance.

Wagner-Jauregg or Wagner von Jauregg, Julius 1857–1940
Austrian neurologist, psychiatrist and Nobel Prize winner
Born in Wels and educated in Vienna, he was appointed professor at Graz (1889) and Vienna (1893). Although his chairs were in psychiatry, he remained more interested in general medical aspects of psychiatric disorders, such as the relationship between cretinism and goitre. He won the 1927 Nobel Prize for physiology or medicine for his discovery in 1917 of a treatment for general paralysis (a late stage of syphilis) by infection with malaria. This was based on an older observation that patients with a variety of serious mental disorders occasionally improved after they had suffered from a bout of febrile illness. However, this 'fever therapy' was hardly ideal, and it was abandoned when antibiotics and other better treatments became available.

Wagoner, Dan 1932–
US modern dancer and choreographer
Born in Springfield, West Virginia, he earned a degree in pharmacy, and started dancing for fun. By his mid-twenties, however, he was dancing full time, studying dance at Connecticut College and then with Martha

Wagner, (Wilhelm) Richard 1813–83

German composer, one of a small number of composers who profoundly affected the course of musical history

Wagner was born in Leipzig and educated at Dresden and at the Leipzig Thomasschule. He wrote a Symphony in C in 1832, and his first completed opera was *Die Feen* ('The Fairies'), written in the style of **Carl Maria von Weber's** *Oberon*. It was not, however, performed during his lifetime. His next work, *Das Liebesverbot* ('Forbidden Love', based on **Shakespeare's** *Measure for Measure*), was produced in 1836 at Magdeburg, where Wagner had been appointed music director two years earlier. There he met Minna Planer, a member of the company, who became his wife in 1836.

The Magdeburg opera soon went bankrupt, as did the theatre at Königsberg, where Wagner found his next post. After a period as assistant conductor at Riga (1837–39), he resolved to try his luck in Paris with his partly-finished opera based on **Bulwer Lytton's** romance *Rienzi*. There, in spite of **Giacomo Meyerbeer's** help, he barely made a living by journalism and by undertaking hack operatic arrangements. He left Paris in 1842 with *Rienzi*, which had finished in a debtors' prison, still unperformed, but now accepted for presentation at Dresden, where it scored a resounding success.

Der fliegende Holländer (1843, 'The Flying Dutchman') was also successful, and Wagner was shortly afterwards appointed kapellmeister at Dresden. There he conducted performances of Beethoven's 9th Symphony and other works that became legendary. *Tannhäuser* was produced there in 1845. At this point Wagner began work on the theme that was to develop into the *Ring* cycle. He began with the poem for *Siegfrieds Tod* ('The Death of Siegfried', the future *Götterdämmerung*, 'Twilight of the Gods'), which he completed in 1848. *Lohengrin* was finished in 1848, but by this time Wagner was deeply implicated in the revolutionary movement and barely escaped arrest by fleeing

from Saxony. Aided financially by **Franz Liszt** at Weimar, he went first to Paris and later to Zurich. *Lohengrin* was eventually produced at Weimar by Liszt in 1850.

During his exile Wagner again made a living by writing, and he completed the poem of the *Ring* cycle in 1852; the following year he began to write the music for *Das Rheingold* ('The Rhinegold'), followed by *Die Walküre* (1856, 'The Valkyrie') and Acts 1 and 2 of *Siegfried* (1857). This was interrupted (1857–59) by work on *Tristan und Isolde*, which was based on the old German version of the legend by **Gottfried von Strassburg**, and is often claimed to have been inspired by Wagner's current love affair with Mathilde, wife of his friend and patron Otto Wesendonk. Once again he sought to gain favour in Paris, and eventually **Napoleon III** called for a command performance of *Tannhäuser*, but the opera failed there. In 1861 he was allowed to return to Germany, but he still had a hard battle for recognition. *Tristan* was accepted at Vienna but abandoned as impracticable before it could be performed, and, now aged 50, pursued by creditors and vilified by critics, the composer was on the point of giving up in despair when the tide dramatically turned.

The eccentric young King of Bavaria, **Ludwig II**, impressed by the pageantry of *Lohengrin*, read Wagner's *Ring* poem with its pessimistic preface. He summoned Wagner to his court, and lavished hospitality on him. *Tristan* was staged with brilliant success at Munich in 1865, but Wagner's extravagance, political meddling, and preferential treatment aroused so much hostility that he was obliged to withdraw temporarily to the villa of Tribschen at Lucerne in Switzerland. Cosima, wife of the musical director **Hans von Bülow** and daughter of Liszt, had been having an affair with Wagner since 1863, and now left her husband and joined him; she eventually

cont

Graham in New York (1957). From 1958 to 1962 he performed with her company and with the **Merce Cunningham** Dance Company. He joined **Paul Taylor's** company in 1962, creating many roles there in pieces like *Aureole* (1962) and *Orbs*. In 1969 he formed the small group, Dan Wagoner and Dancers, and has been making work for them since. With the retirement of **Robert Cohan** he was appointed artistic director of London Contemporary Dance Company (1988–90). His works include *Taxi Dances* (1974), *Seven Tears* (1979), *Spiked Sonata* (1981), *An Occasion for Some Revolutionary Gestures* (1985, for Ballet Rambert) and *Fleet as a Bird* (1985). *George's House* (1985), set in and outside the poet George Montgomery's New Hampshire home, was made for video.

Wain, John Barrington 1925–94

English critic and novelist

Born in Stoke-on-Trent, Staffordshire, he studied at, and was elected Fellow of, St John's College, Oxford, and lectured in English literature at Reading University (1947–55) before turning freelance author. His first four novels, *Hurry on Down* (1953), *Living in the Present* (1955), *The Contenders* (1958) and *Travelling Woman* (1959), tilt at postwar British, particularly London, social values as viewed by a provincial. His debunking vigour and humour has affinities with that of **Kingsley Amis**. He has also written poetry such as *Weep Before God* (1961), *Feng* (1975) and *Open Country* (1987), and his *Poems 1949–1979* appeared in 1980. His other work includes plays and critical studies, and he also edited literary magazines. His later novels include *The Young Visitors* (1965), *The Pardoner's Tale* (1978), *Young Shoulders* (1982), *Where The Rivers Meet* (1988), *Comedies* (1990), and the children's book *Lizzie's Floating Shop* (1981).

He also wrote a biography of **Samuel Johnson** (1974). He was Professor of Poetry at Oxford (1973–88). 📖 *Sprightly Running* (1962) .

Wainewright, Thomas Griffiths 1794–1847

English art critic, painter, forger and alleged poisoner

Born in Chiswick, London, he wrote art criticisms and miscellaneous articles for periodicals under various pseudonyms, including 'Janus Weathercock'. He married, committed forgery (1822, 1824), and almost certainly poisoned with strychnine his half-sister-in-law (1830), probably also his uncle (1828), mother-in-law (1830) and possibly others. The half-sister-in-law had been fraudulently insured for £16,000, but two actions to enforce payment failed, and Wainewright was sentenced to life transportation for his forgery. In Van Diemen's Land (Tasmania) he painted portraits, ate opium, and died in Hobart Hospital. He was the subject of several literary works, and was the 'Varney' of **Bulwer Lytton's** *Lucretia* (1846) and the 'Slinkton' of **Dickens's** *Hunted Down* (1860). His *Essays and Criticisms* were edited, with a memoir, by William Carew Hazlitt (1880).

Wainwright, Jonathan Mayhew 1883–1953

US soldier

He was born in Walla-Walla, Washington. In World War II he commanded the epic retreat in the Bataan peninsula after General **MacArthur's** departure in 1942 during the Philippines campaign. Taken prisoner by the Japanese he was released in 1945 and awarded the Congressional Medal of Honour.

Wainwright, Louden, III 1946–

US singer and songwriter

Wagner, (Wilhelm) Richard cont

married him in 1870 after being divorced, Wagner's wife Minna having died in 1866. A son, Siegfried, was born to Wagner and Cosima in 1869.

In Switzerland Wagner finished *Die Meistersinger* ('The Mastersingers'), his only non-tragic drama, which scored a success in 1868. However his greatest ambition, a complete performance of the *Ring*, was as yet unfulfilled. Productions in Munich of *Das Rheingold* in 1869 and *Die Walküre* in 1870 were against Wagner's wishes, as he dreamed of an ideal theatre of his own. Determined to fulfil his wish, he set about raising funds himself, and on a fraction of the required total plus a large amount of credit he started the now famous theatre at Bayreuth, which opened in 1876 with a first complete programme of the *Ring* cycle. By 1874 Wagner and Cosima had moved to their new home, at Bayreuth, Wahnfried, and he had completed work on *Götterdämmerung*, the final part of the *Ring* cycle. *Parsifal*, his last opera, was staged in 1882. The following year, he died in Venice from a heart attack.

Wagner reformed the whole structure of opera. He wrote all his texts himself, after painstaking research, completing the poem for each work before embarking on the music. He was influenced by the work of Weber and Meyerbeer (although in the end he professed to despise him), as well as Liszt and Hector Berlioz. His great objective was the integration of music and drama, and he took the norms of tonality to their extreme in *Tristan*. Of great importance was his development of the *leitmotiv*, and in the *Ring* (in particular) he constructed a network of musical ideas that forms the musical and psychological basis of his drama. His music is often (especially in *Tristan*) deeply erotic.

Wagner's music, life and writings are apt to arouse extremes of adulation and hostility, but seldom in-difference. In his own time, he was set up with Liszt as the hero of the Romantic faction in opposition to the followers of **Johannes Brahms** and **Robert Schumann**, and for many years clashes between the rival partisans were to afflict concert-promoters and conductors all over Europe.

📖 More has been written about (and by) Wagner than perhaps any other figure in the history of European culture. He was a prolific writer of letters and prose, and many editions and translations have appeared. His autobiography is *My Life* (new edn, 1983). See also B Magee, *Aspects of Wagner* (rev edn, 1988); D Cooke, *I Saw the World End, A Study of Wagner's Ring* (incomplete on Cooke's death, 1979); C von Westernhagen, *Wagner: A Biography* (translated by M Whitall, with an extensive bibliography, 1978); R Gutman, *Richard Wagner: The Man, his Mind and his Music* (1968); E Newman, *Wagner Nights* (1949) and *The Life of Richard Wagner* (1933–47).

'Weakness you never shield,
strength alone you guard;
the rage of humans
in rough actions,
murder, pillage
are your achievements,
while mine is only to retain
that one thing holy and sublime.
Wherever peace
is found in conflict;
wherever change
gives to valour
a more gentle aspect
there I listen for its voice.'
Fricka (to Wotan) in lines originally intended for Act 2 of *Die Walküre*, but later cut (translated by Andrew Porter).

Born in Chapel Hill, North Carolina, he was friendly with actress **Liza Minnelli**, as teenagers at the same boarding school. He has studied acting and performed as an actor and presenter, on both stage and screen, but is best known as an idiosyncratic singer and songwriter with a distinctive view of the world, reflected in songs which are unusually witty and literate. His sardonic, satirical, sometimes provocatively controversial and often self-mockingly neurotic songs first began to appear on record in 1969, and he has recorded and performed regularly ever since. He settled in London, where he then reached a new audience with his topical songs on the comedian Jasper Carrott's popular television show from the late 1980s.

Waismann, Friedrich 1896–1959
Austrian philosopher

Born in Vienna, he became a prominent member of the Vienna Circle, together with **Rudolf Carnap** and **Moritz Schlick**, but modified the doctrines of logical positivism. He later taught at Cambridge and at Oxford. He argued that most empirical concepts have an 'open texture', which means that we cannot completely foresee all the possible conditions in which they might properly be used, and that even empirical statements cannot therefore be strictly verified by observation. His main philosophical works include *The Principles of Linguistic Philosophy* (1965) and *How I See Philosophy* (1968).

Waite, Morrison Remick 1816–88
US jurist

Born in Lyme, Connecticut, the son of the state's Chief Justice, he graduated from Yale in 1837 and practised law in Ohio. He won public attention as counsel for the USA in the international arbitration of the *Alabama* claims in 1871–72, and he was appointed Chief Justice of the Supreme Court by President **Ulysses S Grant** in 1874, serving on the Court until his death. He wrote opinions in a series of decisions interpreting the amendments to the Constitution adopted after the Civil War, notably the 14th amendment, under which he held that businesses 'clothed with a public interest' were subject to regulation by the states.

Waite, Terry (Terence Hardy) 1939–
English religious adviser

He was born in Cheshire, and educated at the Church Army College, London and, privately, in the USA. He was appointed lay training adviser to the Bishop of Bristol (1964–68) and the Archbishop of Uganda, Rwanda and Burundi (1968–71), consultant with the Roman Catholic Church (1972–79) and adviser on Anglican Communion affairs to **Robert Runcie**, who was then Archbishop of Canterbury, in 1980. A man of great diplomatic skills, he undertook many overseas assignments and in 1987, while making inquiries in Beirut about European hostages, disappeared. Worldwide efforts to secure his release and that of his fellow hostages finally succeeded in 1991. He subsequently published an account of his experiences in the book *Taken on Trust* (1993). 📖 Trevor Barnes, *Terry Waite: A Man with a Mission* (1991)

Waits, Tom 1949–
US singer, songwriter, musician and actor

Born in Pomona, California, he picked up on the beatnik literary ethos of the 1950s in his early music, and has been an idiosyncratic chronicler of the by-ways of American urban low life. He began singing in 1969, drawing on a cross-section of musical influences which began to achieve a synthesis by the mid-1970s, culminating in *Heartattack and Vine* (1980). His next album, entitled *Swordfishtrombones* (1983), signalled a more surreal departure, drawing on the radical instrumental and sound effects which permeate his subsequent work. His recordings became increasingly sporadic from the late 1980s, as he devoted more time to work on film, both as a composer and an actor, but he remains a cult figure.

Waitz, Georg 1813–86
German historian

Born in Flensburg, he was professor at Göttingen (1849–75), where he formed the Göttingen historical school. Editor of (1875–86) and contributor to the *Monumenta Germaniae Historica*, he wrote the great *Deutsche Verfassungsgeschichte* (1844–78) and works on Schleswig-Holstein and Ulfilas.

Waitz, Grete 1953–
Norwegian athlete

She was born in Oslo. Rising to prominence in 1975, when she set a world record at 3,000 metres (9:34.2, and later, in 1977, 8:46.6), for more than a decade she rivalled Ingrid Kristiansen as the world's greatest female distance runner. She has set a unique four world best times for the marathon. In 1979, in the New York marathon—a race she won eight times—she became the first woman to run it in under two and a half hours. By 1983 she had brought her time down to 2:25.29. As winner of the marathon at the inaugural world championships in 1983, she became the first ever official world champion at any event.

Wajda, Andrzej 1926–
Polish film director

Born in Suwalki, Poland, he was a member of the Polish Resistance in World War II, and later studied art at the Kraków Academy of Fine Arts, and in the Łódź film school. His first feature film, *Pokolenie* (1954, *A Generation*), dealt with the effects of the war on disillusioned Polish youth. The results of war, the hollowness of the idea of military heroism, and the predicament of individuals caught up in political events were themes to which he was continually to return in such films as *Kanal* (1956), *Ashes and Diamonds* (1957), *Lotna* (1959) and *Landscape after the Battle* (1970). In *Everything for Sale* (1968) he used the making of a film as the framework of the story, a device he also used in the two films for which he is now best known outside Poland, *Człowiek z marmaru* (1977, *Man of Marble*) and *Człowiek z Żelaza* (1981, *Man of Iron*). His other films include romantic comedies, epics, and literary adaptations such as *The Wedding* (1972) and *Shadow Line* (1976). Also active in the theatre and television, he was resident in France during the 1980s but returned to Poland as managing director of the Teatr Powszechny (1989–90) and subsequently entered politics, serving as Senator (1989–91). His recent films include *Korczak* (1990), *Nastazja* (1994), *Wielki Tydzien* (1995, 'The Great Week') and *Miss Nobody* (1996). He has published an autobiography, *My Life in Film* (1989).

Wakefield, Edward Gibbon 1796–1862
English colonial politician

Born in London, he was sentenced for abduction in 1827, and wrote in prison *A Letter from Sydney* (1829). This outlined his theory of systematic colonization by the sale of Crown lands at a price sufficient to oblige intending purchasers to work for wages while amassing capital. The intention was to re-create English society as a basis for future self-government, attracting landowners by ensuring a supply of respectable labour (rather than convicts), both male and female, and assisting labourers to emigrate from the proceeds of the land sales. He influenced the South Australian Association (which founded South Australia in 1836) and, as secretary (1838) to Lord Durham, the Durham Report on Canada. He formed (1837) the New Zealand Association and sent a shipload

of colonists there (1839) to force the British government to recognize it as a colony. He emigrated to New Zealand in 1853.

Wakefield Master, The 15th century
English playwright

Nothing whatsoever is known about the person or persons responsible for the Wakefield cycle (also known as the Towneley Cycle) of Miracle plays, written for performance by the townsfolk at their annual pageants. There are 32 plays in all, but six of them, the *First* and *Second Shepherds' Pageants* and four others, are by the same author, known as the Wakefield Master. Rich in humour, in colour and in their use of West Yorkshire dialect, and written in a characteristic nine-line stanza form, they are the best-crafted of all the surviving English Miracle plays. 🕮 A C Cauley (ed), *Everyman and the Medieval Miracle Plays* (1956)

Wakeley or Wakley, Thomas 1795–1862
English surgeon

Born in Membury, Devon, he studied surgery in London and practised there from 1818. He was the founder and first editor of the *The Lancet* (1823); through this weekly medical paper he denounced abuses in medical practice and made exposures which led to the Adulteration of Food and Drink Act (1860). He was MP for Finsbury (1835–52), and coroner from 1839, procuring reforms for coroners' courts.

Waksman, Selman Abraham 1888–1973
US biochemist and Nobel Prize winner

Born in Priluka, Ukraine, he moved to the USA in 1910 and became a US citizen in 1915, graduating in the same year at Rutgers University, where he spent most of his research life, becoming Professor of Microbiology (1930). From 1915 he worked on the microbial breakdown of organic substances in the soil, work which led to a new classification of microbes (1922) and methods for their scientific cultivation (1932). From 1939 he searched for antibiotics of medical importance and discovered the anti-cancer drug actinomycin in 1941, the first anti-tuberculosis drug streptomycin (1944) and several other anti-bacterial agents. For these important discoveries he was awarded the Nobel Prize for physiology or medicine in 1952. He also worked extensively on marine bacteria and the enzyme alginase, and his works include *Enzymes* (1926), *Principles of Soil Microbiology* (1938) and the autobiographical *My Life with the Microbes* (1954).

Walburga, St, *also spelt* Walpurgis or Walpurga
c.710–c.779
English religious

Born in Wessex, she joined St Boniface on his mission to Germany, and became abbess of Heidenheim. Her relics were transferred (c.870) to Eichstätt. Walpurgis Night (30 April) arose from the confusion between the day of the transfer of her remains (the night of 1 May), and popular superstitions regarding the flight of witches on that night. She was the sister of St Willibald. Her feast day is 25 February.

Walcott, Derek Alton 1930–
West Indian poet, dramatist and Nobel Prize winner

Born in St Lucia, he was educated there and at Kingston, Jamaica, to both of which he subsequently returned as a teacher. His first poems were published in Trinidad in 1948, followed by *Epitaph for the Young: XII Cantos* (1949). He founded the Trinidad Theatre Workshop in 1959, and has written and staged numerous plays such as *Dream on Monday Mountain* (1970) and *The Joker of Seville* (1978). His early volumes of poetry include *In A Green Night* (1962), *Castaway* (1965), and *The Gulf* (1969); examples of his later works are *The Fortunate Traveller* and *Omeros* (both 1981). His *Collected Poems* was published in 1986, and he was awarded the Nobel Prize for Literature in 1992. A more recent work is *Odyssey* (1993). He has been visiting Professor of English at Boston University since 1985. □ R D Hamner, *Derek Walcott* (1981)

Wald, George 1906–
US biochemist and Nobel Prize winner
Born in New York City, he studied zoology at New York University and at Columbia University, and worked under Otto Warburg in Berlin. Subsequently he worked at Harvard (1932–77), where he was appointed Professor of Biology (1948–77). He established in 1935 that visual purple, the retinal pigment of the eye, is converted by light to a yellow compound which slowly changes to a colourless compound (vitamin A). His subsequent work was directed mainly towards elucidating the details of this process, and in 1956 he made the key discovery that one isomer of vitamin A combines with the protein opsin to form visual purple (rhodopsin). He discovered a similar system using vitamin A_2 in fish, the visual mechanism common to the eyes of all known animals, and also established the nutritional relationship between vitamin A, night blindness and vitamin-deficient retinopathy. For these discoveries he shared the 1967 Nobel Prize for physiology or medicine with Ragnar Granit and Haldan Hartline.

Waldegrave, William Arthur 1946–
English Conservative politician
He was born at Chewton Mendip, Bath, Somerset, and educated at Eton, Oxford and Harvard, returning to Oxford as a Fellow of All Souls College (1977–86). Following various jobs in the civil service, he became MP for Bristol West (1979–97) and was a Minister in the environment, planning and housing departments before becoming a Foreign Office Minister (1988–90). He went on to be Secretary of State for Health (1990–92), Chancellor of the Duchy of Lancaster (1992–94), Minister of Agriculture (1994–95), and Chief Secretary to the Treasury from 1995 until the general election of 1997. In 1995 he was brought to public attention by the *Scott Report* on the Arms-to-Iraq affair for his role, as a Minister in the Foreign Office, in the governments' failure to inform parliament of the relaxation of guidelines relating to the sale of non-lethal equipment to Iraq.

Waldeyer-Hartz, Wilhelm 1839–1921
German histologist and anatomist
Born in Hehlen and educated in Göttingen, Greifswald and Berlin, he became professor at several universities, including Breslau, Strasbourg and Berlin. He established his reputation with histological studies of cancers, which he classified according to their embryological cells of origin. His other work included studies of the spinal cord, the anatomy of the ape's brain and the embryological development of the tonsils, and a synopsis of surgical anatomy. He coined 'neuron' and 'chromosome'.

Waldheim, Kurt 1918–
Austrian statesman
Born near Vienna, he served on the Russian front during World War II, but was wounded and then discharged (1942). On his return he studied in Vienna, and entered the Austrian Foreign Service in 1945, worked at the Paris embassy (1948–51) and was then head of the personnel department at the Foreign Ministry (1951–55). He was Minister and subsequently ambassador to Canada (1955–60) and Director-General of Political Affairs at the Ministry (1960–64). From that year he was permanent representative at the UN, with a break (1968–70) to take the post of Foreign Minister. In 1971 he fought unsuccessfully the Austrian presidential election, and in 1972 succeeded U Thant as Secretary-General of the UN, a post he held until 1981. In 1986 he sought the Austrian presidency again and this time was successful but his

victory was marred by allegations that, as a Nazi intelligence officer in World War II, he had some involvement in the transportation of Jews to death camps. As a result, Waldheim was defeated in elections in 1992. A US Justice Department report in 1994 confirmed that Waldheim had served as an officer in the German army and had been involved in atrocities against Jews, civilians and Allied soldiers during World War II. □ Richard Bassett, *Waldheim and Austria* (1989)

Waldo or Valdes, Peter fl.1175
French religious leader
Born in Lyons, he became a preacher in Lyons in 1170 and practised voluntary poverty. He was eventually excommunicated and banished from Lyons in 1184 with his followers, who because of their vow of poverty were known as 'The Holy Paupers'. They became known as the Waldenses.

Waldock, Sir Claud Humphrey Meredith 1904–81
English judge and jurist
Born in Colombo, Ceylon (now Sri Lanka), he was educated at Uppingham and Brasenose College, Oxford. He was Professor of International Law at Oxford (1947–72), a member of the European Commission on Human Rights (1954–61, president, 1955–61), and a judge of the European Court of Human Rights (1966–74, president 1971–74). Also a judge of the International Court of Justice (1973–81, president 1979–81), he acted as consultant on many issues of international law, wrote *The Regulation of the Use of Force by Individual States* (1952) and edited Brierley's *Law of Nations* (1963).

Waldseemüller, Martin c.1480–c.1521
German cartographer
He was born in Radolfzell. At St Dié he made use of an account of the travels of Amerigo Vespucci to publish (1507) the map and globe on which the new world was first said to have been called America.

Waldstein, Albrecht Wenzel Eusebius von
See **Wallenstein, Albrecht Wenzel Eusebius von**

Waldteufel, Emile 1837–1915
French composer
Born in Strasbourg, he studied at the Paris Conservatoire and was appointed pianist to the Empress Eugénie, wife of Napoleon III, in 1865. A prolific composer of dance music, several of his waltzes, notably *The Skaters* (1882, *Les Patineurs*) and *Estudiantina* (1883), remain popular.

Wales, Prince of See **Charles, Prince of Wales**

Wales, Princess of See **Diana, Princess of Wales**

Walesa, Lech 1943–
Polish trade unionist and politician, and Nobel prize winner
He was born in Popowo into a once affluent, but by then ruined, agricultural family. Following a technical education, he worked as an electrician at the Lenin Shipyard at Gdansk (1966–76) and became a trade union organizer, chairing the shipyard's strike committee in 1970. In 1980 he founded the Solidarność (Solidarity) 'free trade union'. Solidarność organized a series of strikes which, led by Walesa, a charismatic and devout Catholic, drew widespread public support and forced substantial political and economic concessions from the Polish government during 1980–81. However, in December 1981 Solidarność was outlawed and Walesa arrested, following the imposition of martial law by General Wojciech Jaruzelski. Walesa was released in November 1982 and was awarded the Nobel Peace Prize in 1983 and granted a personal audience with Pope John Paul II when he visited Poland

during the same year. After leading a further series of crippling strikes during 1988, he negotiated a historic agreement with the Jaruzelski government in 1989, under whose terms Solidarność was re-legalized, and a new, semi-pluralist 'socialist democracy' established. He became President following true elections in 1990, a position he retained until 1995 when he lost to Aleksander Kwasniewski (1954–).

Walewska, Marie 1789–1817
Polish countess
She was the mistress of Napoleon I, and their son became Count Walewski.

Walewski, Alexandre Florian Joseph Colonna, Count 1810–68
French diplomat
The illegitimate son of Napoleon I, he held various appointments, including that of ambassador to Great Britain (1851), Foreign Minister (1855–60) and Minister of State (1860–63).

Walker, Alice Malsenior 1944–
US writer
Born in Eatonville, Georgia, and educated at Spelman College, Atlanta, and Sarah Lawrence College, she later worked in voter registration campaigns before becoming a teacher and a lecturer. Her essay *In Search of Our Mother's Gardens* (1983) is an important rediscovery of a Black female literary and cultural tradition. An accomplished poet, she is, however, better known for her novels, of which *The Color Purple* (1982) is her third and most popular. The winner of the 1983 Pulitzer Prize for fiction and later made into a successful film, it tells in letters the story of two sisters in the cruel, segregated world of the Deep South between the wars. It was preceded by *The Third Life of Grange Copeland* (1970) and *Meridian* (1976). Later works include *The Temple of My Familiar* (1989) and *Warrior Marks* (1993). 📖 *Living By the Word* (1989)

Walker, David 1785–1830
US abolitionist
Born in Wilmington, North Carolina, the son of a free black mother and a slave father, he settled in Boston in the 1820s and became active in the abolitionist movement. In 1829 he published his *Appeal to the Colored Citizens of the World,* a denunciation of slavery in which he urges slaves to overthrow the system. It created outrage in the South, and many states passed laws banning such 'seditious' material. A year later he was found dead under mysterious circumstances.

Walker, Dame Ethel 1861–1951
Scottish painter and sculptor
Born in Edinburgh, she lived in London from 1870, where she was educated privately. She attended Putney Art School, the School of Art at Westminster, and then the Slade School of Art (1892–94) in London. Thereafter she moved between London, where she was a familiar figure in Chelsea, and Yorkshire, where she painted notable seascapes. Her early work was influenced by the New English Art Club and Walter R Sickert, but she gradually developed a more individual style which owed something to her study of Impressionism, particularly after World War I. She is best known for her portraits (often of young girls), flower paintings, and seascapes, and for more visionary canvases like *Nausicaa* (1920) or *The Zone of Love* (1931–33). She was created DBE in 1943.

Walker, George 1618–90
Irish clergyman
Born of English parents in County Tyrone, he studied at Glasgow University, and became rector of Lissan, County Derry (1669), and Donaghmore near Dungannon (1674). In 1688 he raised a regiment at Dungannon to help garrison Londonderry for its successful resistance to the 105-day siege (1689) by James VII and II's forces, and became joint governor. For this he received the thanks of William III and the House of Commons, degrees from Oxford and Cambridge, and was nominated Bishop of Derry. He was killed at the Battle of the Boyne and is commemorated by the Walker Monument (1828) in Londonderry. He wrote *A True Account of the Siege of Londonderry* (1689).

Walker, Sir James 1863–1935
Scottish physical chemist
Born in Dundee, he began his career in the flax and jute industry, but left to study science at Edinburgh University. After graduating in 1885, from 1887 to 1889 he worked with Johann Baeyer at Munich and then with Wilhelm Ostwald at Leipzig. He returned to Edinburgh as an assistant, but went on to University College London, to work with Sir William Ramsay, in 1892. From 1894 to 1908 he was Professor of Chemistry at University College, Dundee, and he was then professor at Edinburgh until his retirement in 1928. His research was mainly on the physical chemistry of aqueous solutions. He carried out a pioneering study in 1895 of the kinetics and mechanism of the conversion of ammonium cyanate into urea, a topic to which he subsequently reverted many times. His *Introduction to Physical Chemistry* (1899) was influential in shaping chemical education. During World War I he organized the manufacture of TNT (trinitrotoluene) in Edinburgh. Walker was elected a Fellow of the Royal Society (1900) and received its Davy Medal (1923). He was knighted in 1921, and from 1921 to 1923 he was president of the Chemical Society.

Walker, Jimmy, *in full* James John Walker 1881–1946
US politician
Born in New York City, he began his career as a lawyer and songwriter who was elected Democratic Mayor of New York City in 1925. He was popular for his charm and ready wit as well as for his practical achievements, including improvements in sanitation, the subways, and the hospital system. In 1932 he resigned and went to Europe to avoid the outcome of an investigation into fraud and corruption in his administration.

Walker, John 1732–1807
English lexicographer
Born in Colney Hatch, he was by turns actor, schoolmaster and peripatetic teacher of elocution (from 1771). He compiled a *Rhyming Dictionary* (1775), still in print as the *Rhyming Dictionary of the English Language*, and a *Critical Pronouncing Dictionary* (1791).

Walker, John c.1781–1859
English inventor
He was born in Stockton-on-Tees, Cleveland. A chemist, he made the first friction matches in 1827, which he called 'Congreves' (alluding to William Congreve's rocket). These were later named 'lucifers' and 'matches' by others.

Walker, Kath See Oodgeroo, Noonuccal Moongalba

Walker, Mary Edwards 1832–1919
US physician
She was educated at Syracuse Medical College and then joined her husband Albert Miller in a practice in New York State. She campaigned for rational dress for women, revised marriage and divorce laws and women's rights and often wore male evening dress for her lectures. During the American Civil War she volunteered for army service, becoming the US army's first female surgeon, and was the only woman to receive the Congressional Medal of Honour.

Walker, Peter Edward 1932–
English Conservative politician

As a young man he was sufficiently successful in the City of London to have the wealth to pursue a political career. He was chairman of the Young Conservatives (1958–60) and represented Worcester, where he farms, in the House of Commons from 1961. He held ministerial posts under Edward Heath and in Margaret Thatcher's government was Agriculture Secretary (1979–83), Energy Secretary (1983–87) and Secretary of State for Wales (1987–90). Regarded as a Conservative 'liberal', he was noted for his 'coded criticisms' of some of the extreme aspects of Mrs Thatcher's policies. He retired from full-time politics in 1992 and became the chairman of the Urban Regeneration Agency, which was conceived by Michael Heseltine. His publications include *Staying Power* (1991).

Walker, William 1824–60
US buccaneer and adventurer

Born in Nashville, Tennessee, he studied medicine, which he practised in the USA, at Edinburgh in Scotland and Heidelberg, Germany, as well as law and journalism. In 1853 he landed with a force in the Mexican state of Lower California, and the following year declared it, with the neighbouring Sonora, an independent republic, but was soon forced to withdraw to US territory. In 1855 he invaded Nicaragua, took Granada, and was elected President. His government, recognized in 1856 by the USA, restored slavery. He published *The War in Nicaragua* (1860). Twice expelled (1857) from Nicaragua, he entered Honduras in 1860, taking Trujillo, but was apprehended by the captain of a British sloop-of-war and given up to the Honduran authorities, who had him shot.

Wall, Max, *originally* Maxwell George Lorimer
1908–90
English actor and comedian

Born in London, he made his first stage appearance when he was 14, playing Jack in *Mother Goose* with a travelling pantomime company in the West Country. He made his first London appearance in 1925, as a dancer in *The London Revue*. He subsequently appeared in variety, revue, pantomime and radio. The radio programme, *Our Shed* (1946), which started as part of the wartime show *Hoop-La!* (1944–45), helped to make him a star. Wall gradually perfected a laconic comedy routine, and was considered by many to be one of the most accomplished British comics of his time. In 1966 he appeared as Père Ubu in Alfred Jarry's *Ubu Roi*. Subsequently, he specialized in the plays of Samuel Beckett. He appeared in a notable one-man show, *Aspects of Max Wall*, in 1974. On television, he acted in the comedy series *Born and Bred* (1978, 1980), *Crossroads* and *Coronation Street*.

Wallace, Alfred Russel 1823–1913
English zoo-geographer and pioneer of the theory of natural selection

Born in Usk, Monmouthshire, he worked as a surveyor and teacher in Leicester, then travelled and collected (1848–52) in the Amazon basin. Then with Henry Walter Bates he explored the Malay Archipelago (1854–62), and observed the significant demarcation, now known as Wallace's Line, between the areas supporting Asian and Australasian faunas. While in Malaysia, he conceived the idea of the 'survival of the fittest' as the key to evolution. In 1855 he published his *Essay on the Law that has Regulated the Introduction of New Species*, and his memoir, sent to Charles Darwin in 1858 from the Moluccas, formed an important part of the Linnaean Society meeting which first promulgated the theory of evolution by means of natural selection, and hastening the publication, of Darwin's *The Origin of Species*, a work amplified by Wallace's *Contributions to the Theory of Natural Selection* (1870) and *Darwinism* (1889). In his great *Geographical Distribution of*

Animals (1876), *Island Life* (1880), and earlier work, Wallace contributed much to the scientific foundations of zoo-geography. Other works include *Travels on the Amazon and Rio Negro* (1853), *The Malay Archipelago* (1869), *The Wonderful Century* (1898), *Man's Place in the Universe* (1903), *My Life, an Autobiography* (1905) and *The World of Life* (1910). In 1862 Wallace returned to England, bringing with him the first live Birds of Paradise to be seen in Europe. He was an outspoken advocate of socialism, pacifism, women's rights and other causes, and encapsulated his views in *Social Environment and Moral Progress* (1913). 📖 Harry Clements, *Alfred Russel Wallace* (1983)

Wallace, Dewitt 1889–1981
US publisher

Born in St Paul, Minnesota, the son of the dean (later president) of Macalester Presbyterian College, he dropped out from the University of California, and took various odd jobs while building up a collection of articles he had condensed in order to improve his mind. In 1921 he married a Canadian-born social worker, Lila Bell Acheson (1889–1984), and in 1922 they launched *The Reader's Digest* as a pocket-sized mail-order magazine with 1,500 subscribers. It became the largest-circulation magazine in the world, with its headquarters at Pleasantville, near New York. A British edition was launched in 1938, followed by several foreign-language editions. In 1972 both he and his wife were awarded a Presidential Medal of Freedom, and in 1973, at the age of 83, they both officially retired.

Wallace, (Richard Horatio) Edgar 1875–1932
English writer

He was found abandoned in Greenwich when nine days old and brought up by a Billingsgate fish-porter. He served in the army in South Africa, where he later became a journalist (1899), and in 1905 he published his first success, the adventure story *The Four Just Men*. Another early series in a different vein was set in West Africa and included *Sanders of the River* (1911) and *Bones* (1915). From then on he wrote prolifically—his output numbering over 170 novels and plays—and he is best remembered for his crime novels, such as *The Clue of the Twisted Candle* (1916) and *The Ringer* (1926). He became a scriptwriter in Hollywood, where he died while working on the screenplay of *King Kong* (1933). He published his autobiography, *People*, in 1926.

Wallace, George Corley 1919–98
US politician

Born in Clio, Alabama, he served as a flight engineer in World War II and practised law in Alabama before becoming involved in state Democratic politics. He served four terms as Governor of Alabama (1963–67, 1971–79, 1983–87), earning notoriety in the early 1960s by seeking to block desegregation in the Alabama public schools. He ran for President as a member of the American Independent Party in 1968, capitalizing on white backlash to garner more votes than expected for a third-party candidate, and in 1972 he was shot and paralyzed in an assassination attempt while campaigning for the Democratic presidential nomination. His final term as governor was marked by a renunciation of his earlier racism and an effort to win support from African-American voters.

Wallace, Henry 1836–1916
US agriculturist and writer

Born near West Newton, Pennsylvania, he trained for the church but turned to farming and agricultural journalism, founding in 1895 the successful periodical *Wallace's Farmer*. His son was Henry Cantwell Wallace.

Wallace, Henry Agard 1888–1965
US agriculturist and politician

Born in Adair County, Iowa, the son of **Henry Cantwell Wallace**, he edited *Wallace's Farmer* from 1933 until 1940 and served as Secretary of Agriculture (1933–41) under **Franklin D Roosevelt**, whose New Deal policies he supported. As Vice-President under Roosevelt from 1941 to 1945, he served as Chairman of the Board of Economic Warfare. He failed to obtain renomination as Vice-President in 1944 but he became Secretary of Commerce (1945–46). He unsuccessfully stood for President in 1948.

Wallace, Henry Cantwell 1866–1924
US agriculturist

He was born in Rock Island, Illinois. He helped his father, **Henry Wallace**, to found *Wallace's Farmer* (1895), which he edited from 1916. For a long time secretary of the Corn Belt Meat Producers' Association, he was appointed US Secretary of Agriculture in 1921.

Wallace, Lew(is) 1827–1905
US writer and soldier

He was born in Brookville, Indiana, and served in the Mexican War (1846–48) and with distinction as a major-general in the Federal army in the American Civil War (1861–65). Governor of New Mexico (1878–81) and Minister to Turkey (1881–85), he was author of several novels, including the remarkably successful religious novel *Ben Hur* (1880), which has twice formed the subject of spectacular films. He also wrote an *Autobiography* (1906). 📖 I McKee, 'Ben-Hur' Wallace (1947)

Wallace, Sir Richard 1818–90
English art collector and philanthropist

Born in London, the illegitimate son of the 3rd Marquis of Hertford, he was an MP from 1873 to 1885. In 1842 he inherited from his father a large collection of paintings and objets d'art later bequeathed (1897) by his widow to the British nation. These now comprise the Wallace Collection, housed in Hertford House, London, once his residence. During the Siege of Paris (1870–71) he equipped ambulances and founded a British hospital there.

Wallace, (William) Vincent 1813–65
Irish composer of operas

Born in Waterford, he emigrated to Australia and is well-known for the first of his operas, *Maritana* (1845), and for *Lurline* (1860).

Wallace, Sir William, *also spelt* Walays or Wallensis c.1274–1305
Scottish patriot

He was the chief champion of Scotland's independence, born probably near Paisley. **Blind Harry** associates his early years with Dundee and Ayrshire at the start of the War of Independence, though this is uncertain. Wallace burnt Lanark and defeated **Edward I**'s army at Stirling Bridge. The English were expelled from Scotland and the north of England was raided. In retaliation Edward invaded Scotland in 1298, meeting Wallace at Falkirk, where the Scots were this time defeated. Wallace eventually escaped to France in 1299 where he tried to enlist support. He returned in 1303, but in 1305 was arrested near Glasgow by Sir **John Menteith**, sheriff of Dumbarton. Taken to London he was condemned and hanged, drawn and quartered. His quarters were sent to Newcastle, Berwick, Stirling and Perth.

Wallace, William 1860–1940
Scottish composer

Born in Greenock, Strathclyde, he trained in medicine, but from 1889 devoted himself to music. He was the first British composer to experiment with symphonic poems, of which he wrote six. His other works include a symphony and songs.

Wallach, Otto 1847–1931
German chemist and Nobel Prize winner

Born in Königsberg, Prussia (now Kaliningrad, Russia), he went to the University of Göttingen in 1867 and worked there for his doctorate with Hans Hübner on the positional isomerism of toluene compounds. He moved to Bonn as assistant to **August Kekule von Stradonitz** (1870) and remained there for 19 years. From 1889 until his retirement in 1915 he worked as director of the Chemical Institute in Göttingen. Throughout his life he studied the composition of essential oils obtained from plants and from these oils he isolated many compounds belonging to a class he called terpenes. He was awarded the Nobel Prize for chemistry in 1910. In addition to being a distinguished chemist, he was also a serious art collector.

Wallas, Graham 1858–1932
English political psychologist

Born in Monkwearmouth, Sunderland, he was educated at Shrewsbury and Corpus Christi College, Oxford. He became a lecturer at the London School of Economics, and was an early member of the Fabian Society (1886–1904). He became Professor of Political Science at the University of London (1914–23). He was also involved in local authority politics as a Socialist councillor on London County Council (1904–07). His influential teaching and writings in social psychology, including *Human Nature in Politics* (1908) and *The Great Society* (1914), emphasized the role of irrational forces which determine public opinion and political attitudes.

Wallenberg, André Oscar 1816–86
Swedish financier and politician

He was the founder of a Swedish banking dynasty. After serving as a naval officer (1837–51) and captaining (1846–47) the *Linköping*, Sweden's first propeller-driven ship, he was a businessman in Sundsvall (1851–55) and in 1856 founded Stockholm's Enskilda Bank which pioneered modern Swedish banking methods.

Wallenberg, Knut Agathon 1853–1938
Swedish financier and politician

The son of **André Oscar Wallenberg**, he succeeded his father as managing director of Stockholm's Enskilda Bank. Under his direction the bank took a leading part in Sweden's finance. He was active in founding the Banque du Pays du Nord in Paris (1911), the British Bank of Northern Countries in London (1912), and in the same year was largely instrumental in founding Stockholm's Chamber of Commerce. He was the Conservative Leader of the Upper House of Parliament from 1906 to 1919 and served as Foreign Secretary (1914–17) in **Dag Hammarskjöld**'s wartime ministry. One of Sweden's richest men and greatest benefactors, he founded the Wallenberg Foundation in 1917, which gives donations for the furtherance of science, culture and education.

Wallenberg, Marcus 1899–1982
Swedish financier

The son of **Marcus Laurentius Wallenberg**, he was managing director of Stockholm's Enskilda Bank (1946–58) and of Skandinaviska Enskilda Banken (1972–76). He was active in the reconstruction of several large companies after the **Kreuger** crash in 1932, and in World War II he helped Swedish trade links with the West. He played an important part in setting up Scandinavian Airline Systems, and until his death held prominent positions in large Swedish and international concerns. He was an excellent yachtsman and tennis player, and was the first Swedish tennis player on the centre court at Wimbledon.

Wallenberg, Marcus Laurentius 1864–1943
Swedish financier

The son of **André Oscar Wallenberg** and half brother of **Knut Agathon Wallenberg**, he was managing director of Stockholm's Enskilda Bank (1911–20) and was active in founding or restructuring several concerns, including AB Papyrus and AB Diesels Motorer (later Atlas Copco), and ASEA. With Sam Eyde he also founded Norsk Hydro in 1905.

Wallenberg, Raoul b.1912
Swedish diplomat

He was the nephew of **Marcus Laurentius Wallenberg**. He took a science degree at Ann Arbor, Michigan, in 1935 and then worked at a bank in Haifa, Palestine, where he met Jewish refugees from Nazi Germany. In 1936 he entered partnership with a Hungarian Jew, running an import and export firm, which after 1939 involved business trips to Germany, Hungary and Nazi-occupied France. **Hitler**'s occupation of Hungary in 1944 put its 700,000 Jewish population at immediate risk and the American War Refugee Board and the Swedish government sent Wallenberg to Budapest to initiate a rescue plan. He designed a Swedish protection passport (Schutz-pass) and arranged 'Swedish houses' offering Jews refuge. Through bribery, threats, blackmail or sheer strength of conviction and at great personal risk he saved up to 100,000 Jews. When Soviet troops occupied Hungary in 1945 he was taken to Soviet Headquarters and never returned. On insistent Swedish requests Soviet authorities produced a document signed by Smoltsov, head of Ljubyanka prison hospital, stating that Wallenberg died of a heart attack in July 1947, but testimony of ex-prisoners suggested that he was still alive in the 1950s, and he was rumoured to be still in prison in the 1970s. Wallenberg was made an honorary citizen of the USA (1981), of Canada (1985) and of Israel (1986). A tree in the Avenue of the Righteous in Jerusalem was planted to honour his memory.

Wallenstein or Waldstein, Albrecht Wenzel Eusebius von, Duke of Friedland and of Mecklenburg, Prince of Sagan 1583–1634
Austrian soldier

He was born in Hermanice in Bohemia, the son of a Czech nobleman, and educated by Jesuits. He married a Bohemian widow, whose vast estates he inherited in 1614. In 1617 he commanded a force which he supplied to Archduke Ferdinand (later **Ferdinand II**) for use against Venice. At the outset of the Thirty Years War (1618–48) he helped to crush the Bohemian revolt (1618–20) under **Frederick V**, thereafter acquiring numerous confiscated estates, and consolidating them into Friedland, of which he became Duke in 1623. He was appointed Commander-in-Chief (1625) of all the Imperial forces, and at Dessau Bridge (1626) defeated the army of Count Mansfeld. Establishing the peace in Hungary by a truce imposed on the combined forces of Mansfeld and Bethlen Gabor, he subdued (1627) Silesia, acquiring the dukedom of Sagan, joined Count von **Tilly** against **Kristian IV**, was invested (1628) with the duchies of Mecklenburg, but encountered resistance in garrisoning the Hanse towns, notably at his unsuccessful Siege (1628) of Stalsund, consequently failing to remove the threat of Protestant invasion by sea. This materialized in 1630, following Ferdinand II's Edict of Restitution, when **Gustav II Adolf** of Sweden and his forces invaded northern Germany. The Catholic princes, aroused by Wallenstein's ambition, forced Ferdinand to dismiss him (1630) and appoint Tilly Commander-in-Chief. After Tilly's death, Wallenstein was reinstated. His new army, repulsing the attempt by the Swedish forces to storm his entrenched camp near Nuremberg, prevented the Swedish king from advancing on Ferdinand in Vienna. He was defeated in 1632 by Gustav Adolf at Lützen, where Gustav himself was fatally wounded. In the interests of a united Germany with himself as its supreme authority, Wallenstein now intrigued with

Protestants and Catholics. Finally, his enemies persuaded the emperor to depose him again and denounce him. Threatened in Pilsen by Piccolomini and others, he went to Eger, hoping for support from Bernhard, Duke of Weimar. He was assassinated there by Irish and Scottish officers in his retinue. The Wallenstein trilogy by **Schiller** is based on Wallenstein's career. ◫ Golo Mann, *Wallenstein: Sein Leben erzählt* (4th edn, 1971, Eng trans *Wallenstein: His Life Narrated*, 1976)

Waller, Augustus Volney 1816–70
English physiologist

Born near Faversham, Kent, he studied medicine in Paris, before setting up in general practice in Kensington. Elected FRS in 1851, he devoted himself to full-time research for five years, working in Bonn, and later at the Jardin des Plantes in Paris, before being appointed Professor of Physiology at Queen's College, Birmingham. A fine microscopist, he is remembered for his patient anatomical investigations of the nervous system, discovering the Wallerian degeneration of nerve fibres. He also conducted innovative investigations of the autonomic nervous system, particularly analysing the dilation of the iris under light stimuli.

Waller, Edmund 1606–87
English poet and politician

Born in Coleshill near Amersham, a cousin of **John Hampden**, he was returned MP for Ilchester in 1624, Chipping Wycombe in 1625 and Amersham in 1627. In 1631 he married a London heiress, who died in 1634, and from about 1635 to 1638 he unsuccessfully courted Lady Dorothy Sidney, eldest daughter of the Earl of Leicester, whom he commemorated in verse as 'Sacharissa'. He was returned to the Long Parliament in 1640, and in 1643 was involved in a conspiracy ('Waller's Plot') against parliament on behalf of **Charles I**, arrested, and expelled from the House. He avoided execution by abject confession and the payment of a £10,000 fine, and was banished. He lived mostly in France, entertaining impoverished exiles in Paris, his own banishment being revoked in 1651. His collected poems, reviving the heroic couplet and including 'Go, lovely Rose', had been published in 1645 and were followed by *A Panegyric to my Lord Protector* (1655) and *To the King upon his Majesty's Happy Return* (1660), addressed to **Cromwell** and **Charles II** respectively. ◫ W L Chernaik, *The Poetry of Limitation* (1968)

Waller, Fats (Thomas Wright) 1904–43
US jazz pianist, composer and entertainer

He was born in New York, the son of a Baptist preacher who encouraged him to play the organ for services as a child. A professional musician at 15, he gained experience as a theatre organist, movie-house pianist and in clubs. Influenced by 'stride' pianist **James P Johnson**, who coached him, Waller began his recording career in 1922 and the first records by 'Fats Waller and his Rhythm', featuring his novelty singing, were made in 1934. Waller wrote many jazz standards, such as 'Honeysuckle Rose' (c.1928), 'Ain't Misbehavin'"(1929) and 'Keepin' Out of Mischief Now' (1932).

Waller, Sir William c.1597–1688
English soldier

A member of the Long Parliament (1640–59), he fought in 1643 in the West Country, at Oxford and Newbury in 1644, and at Taunton in February 1645. He suggested reforms on which the New Model Army was to be based, but in April 1645 was removed from command by the Self-Denying Ordinance. By June 1647 he was levying troops against the army. He was imprisoned from 1648 to 1651 for Royalist sympathies, and in 1659 he plotted for a

Royalist rising and was again imprisoned. In 1660 he became a member of the Convention Parliament, but was unrewarded at the Restoration.

Wallich, Nathaniel 1786–1854
Danish botanist

Born in Copenhagen, he became surgeon to the colony at Serampore, India, in 1807. In 1815 he was appointed Superintendent of the Calcutta Botanical Garden, and so began a very active, distinguished botanical career. In 1820 he began to publish the *Flora Indica* written by the Scottish botanist William Roxburgh (1751–1815), with much additional matter written by himself. He collected many plants on expeditions to Nepal (1820), western India (1825), and Burma (Myanma) (1826–27). Between 1830 and 1832 he published his most important work, *Plantae Asiaticae Rariores* (3 vols).

Wallis, Alfred 1855–1942
English painter

Born in Devonport, Plymouth, he never attended school, becoming a fisherman, scrap merchant and ice-cream vendor in St Ives, Cornwall. He did not begin to paint until the age of 70, 'for company' after the death of his wife. He then painted compulsively—on box lids, pots, the tablecloth or the walls—with ship's paint, in a simplified *naïf* style. His subject was the sea and shipping of his youth, painted from memory with an intuitive sense of colour and pattern which exerted enormous influence over the St Ives group when they 'discovered' him in 1928. He was eventually taken to a Penzance workhouse where, with the support of **Ben Nicholson** and others, he continued to paint until he died. His work found its way into many major collections in Great Britain and the USA.

Wallis, Sir Barnes Neville 1887–1979
English aeronautical engineer and inventor

Born in Derbyshire, he won a scholarship to Christ's Hospital, London, then trained as a marine engineer at Cowes. He joined the Vickers Company in 1911, and subsequently designed for them the airship R100 which made its maiden flight in 1929 and successfully crossed the Atlantic. From 1923 he was chief designer of structures at Vickers Aviation, Weybridge, where he designed the Wellesley and Wellington bombers with their revolutionary geodetic fuselage structure, and the 'bouncing bombs' used by the British to destroy the Möhne and Eder dams in Germany during World War II. He then became chief of aeronautical research and development for the British Aircraft Corporation at Weybridge (1945–71). In the early 1950s he was responsible for the design of the first variable-geometry (swing-wing) aircraft, the experimental Swallow. The same design principle was later incorporated in the Panavia Tornado adopted by many of the world's air forces. He was elected FRS in 1945, and knighted in 1968. 📖 J E Morpurgo, *Barnes Wallis* (1972)

Wallis, John 1616–1703
English mathematician

Born in Ashford, Kent, he graduated at Cambridge, and took holy orders, but in 1649 became Savilian Professor of Geometry at Oxford. Besides the *Arithmetica Infinitorum* (1656), in which he offered a remarkable method for finding areas under curves in terms of infinite sums (soon replaced by the more rigorous calculus), he wrote on the binomial theorem and gave an infinite product for pi (π). He also wrote on proportion, mechanics, grammar, logic, theology, and the teaching of the deaf and dumb. Wallis was also an expert on deciphering, and edited the work of some of the Greek mathematicians. He was one of the founders of the Royal Society. 📖 Joseph F Scott, *The Mathematical Work of John Wallis (1616–1703)*

Wallis, Samuel 1728–95
English explorer and naval officer

From 1766 to 1768 he made a circumnavigation of the globe, and discovered Tahiti and the Wallis Islands.

Walpole, Horace, 4th Earl of Orford 1717–97
English writer

Born in London, the son of Sir **Robert Walpole**, he was educated at Eton and at King's College, Cambridge, then undertook the Grand Tour, with the poet **Thomas Gray**. Returning to England in 1741, he became MP for Callington, Cornwall, and interested himself in cases like the **John Byng** trial of 1757. He exchanged his Cornish seat in 1754 for the family borough of Castle Rising, which he vacated in 1757 for the other family borough of King's Lynn. In 1747 he purchased, near Twickenham, the former coachman's cottage which he gradually 'gothicized' (1753–76) into the stuccoed and battlemented pseudo-castle of Strawberry Hill, which helped to reverse the fashion for classical and Italianate design. He also established a private press on which some of his own works as well as **Lucan**'s *Pharsalia*, and Gray's *Progress of Poesy* and *The Bard*, were printed. He wrote essays and verse, and is at his best in such satires as the *Letter from Xo Ho to his friend Lien Chi at Pekin* (1757). His *Castle of Otranto* (1764) set the fashion for supernatural romance. However, his literary reputation rests chiefly upon his letters, which deal, in the most vivacious way, with party politics, foreign affairs, art, literature and gossip. His firsthand accounts in them of such events as the Jacobite trials after the 1745 Rising and the **Gordon** Riots are invaluable. 📖 A Dobson, *Horace Walpole, a memoir* (1893)

Walpole, Sir Hugh Seymour 1884–1941
English novelist

Born in Auckland, New Zealand, the son of Rev G H S Walpole who later became Bishop of Edinburgh, he was educated in England at King's School, Canterbury, and graduated from Emmanuel College, Cambridge, in 1906. He was intended for the Church but became a schoolmaster at a boys' prep school, then an author. Widely read in English literature, he wrote prolifically. His books, which were enormously popular during his lifetime, display a straightforward, flowing style, great descriptive power, and a genius for evoking atmosphere which he unfortunately overworked at times, and which sometimes made his work open to parody. His many novels include *Mr Perrin and Mr Traill* (1911), based on his experience as a schoolteacher, *Fortitude* (1913), *The Dark Forest* (1916), *The Secret City* (1919, James Tait Black Memorial Prize), *The Cathedral* (1922), which owes much to **Anthony Trollope**, one of Walpole's favourite authors, and *The Herries Chronicle* (1930–33). 📖 R Hart-Davis, *Hugh Walpole* (1952)

Walpole, Sir Robert, Earl of Orford See panel p1911

Walpurgis, St See Walburga, St

Walschaerts, Égide 1820–1901
Belgian mechanical engineer

Born in Malines, he studied at Liège and in 1842 entered the state railway workshops. He invented the famous 'Walschaerts valve gear' in 1844 but could not patent it under his own name in Belgium because of the rules of the state railways. He did, however, patent it in other countries, and it was quickly recognized as a considerable advance on **George Stephenson**'s valve gear and became very widely adopted on railway locomotives throughout the world. He invented several other improvements to steam engines, and was awarded a gold medal at the Paris Exposition of 1878.

Walsingham, Sir Francis c.1530–1590
English statesman

Walpole, Sir Robert, 1st Earl of Orford 1676–1745
English Whig politician, the first Prime Minister of Great Britain

Robert Walpole was born in Houghton in Norfolk, and educated at Eton and King's College, Cambridge. He was destined for the Church, and entered politics largely by accident when his two elder brothers died, leaving him the family estate and sufficient wealth to follow a political career. He entered the House of Commons in 1701 as the Whig member for Castle Rising, Norfolk, and in 1702 for King's Lynn. He was a formidable speaker and quickly rose in the ranks of his party during Queen **Anne**'s reign, appointed Secretary for War in 1708 and Treasurer of the Navy in 1710. During the Tory government that followed the Whig collapse in 1710, he was sent to the Tower for alleged corruption (1712), but was recalled by the new king, **George I**, who had succeeded in 1714, and made a Privy Councillor and Chancellor of the Exchequer (1715).

George I could not speak English and gave up attending the proceedings of parliament, thereby leaving Walpole considerable freedom and discretion as leader of the government. Gradually Walpole established his supremacy, chairing, on the king's behalf, a small group of Ministers which was the forerunner of the present-day

Cabinet. As a result, he came to be seen as England's first Prime Minister, although he himself rejected the title. He was knighted in 1725 and created Earl of Orford in 1742.

Walpole's foreign policy was based on a determination to maintain peace, and he resigned when this failed on the outbreak of the so-called War of Jenkins' Ear with Spain. He enjoyed good relations with the Prince of Wales, who became **George II**, and with his wife, Queen **Caroline** and, in addition to his earldom, Walpole was presented with No 10 Downing Street, which was to become the permanent London home of all future prime ministers.

📖 H T Dickinson, *Walpole and the Whig Supremacy* (1973); J H Plumb, *Sir Robert Walpole* (1956–61).

'Madam, there are fifty thousand men slain this year in Europe, and not one an Englishman.' To Queen Caroline, on the reasons for not joining the War of the Austrian Succession. Quoted in John Hervey, *Memoirs 1734–43* (vol 1, 1848).

Born in Chislehurst, Kent, he was sent on an embassy to France in 1570–73 by **William Cecil**, Baron Burghley. He was then appointed one of the principal secretaries of state to **Elizabeth I**, sworn on to the Privy Council, and knighted. In 1578 he was sent on an embassy to the Netherlands, in 1581 to France, and in 1583 to Scotland. He contrived an effective system of espionage at home and abroad, enabling him to reveal the **Babington** Plot, which implicated **Mary, Queen of Scots** in treason, and to obtain, in 1587, details of some of the plans for the Spanish Armada. He was one of the commissioners to try Mary at Fotheringay. He favoured the Puritan party, and in his later years devoted himself to religious meditation. Elizabeth acknowledged his genius and important services, but kept him poor and without honours, and he died in poverty and debt. 📖 Conyers Read, *Mr Secretary Walsingham* (1924)

Walsingham, Thomas d.c.1422
English chronicler and monk
He was associated chiefly with St Albans abbey but for a time was prior of Wymondham. An authority on English history from 1377 until 1422, he compiled *Historia Anglicana, 1272–1422* (1863–64) and other works.

Waltari, Mika Toimi 1908–79
Finnish novelist
Born in Helsinki, he studied theology and philosophy at the university there. He was the best-known of the pre-war 'Torch-bearers' circle of writers on urban themes, contributing the novel *Suuri illusioni* (1928, 'The Great Illusion'). After the war he turned to historical novels, as in *Sinuhe, egyptiläinen* (1945, Eng trans *The Egyptian*, 1949), *Mikael Hakim* (1949, Eng trans *The Wanderer*, 1951) and *Turms, kuolematen* (1955, Eng trans *The Etruscan*, 1957). He also wrote detective stories and plays, many of them pseudonymously. 📖 S Musikka, *Mika Waltari juhlakirje* (1968)

Walter, Bruno, *originally* Bruno Walter Schlesinger 1876–1962
US conductor
Born in Berlin, Germany, he conducted at Cologne while still in his teens. He worked with **Mahler** in Hamburg and Vienna, directed the Munich Opera (1913–22), and became chief conductor of the Berlin Philharmonic Orchestra (1919). Leaving Nazi Germany in 1933 he went to France, taking French citizenship in 1938, then settled

in the USA, where he took US citizenship and became chief conductor of the New York Philharmonic Orchestra (1951). An exponent of the German Romantic tradition, he was noted particularly for his interpretations of **Haydn**, **Mozart** and **Mahler**.

Walter, Hubert c.1140–1205
English churchman and statesman
He became a judge (1185), dean of York and Bishop of Salisbury (1189), and accompanied **Richard I** on the Third Crusade (1190–93). Appointed Archbishop of Canterbury in 1193, he helped to raise the ransom to secure Richard's release from captivity, and to contain the rebellion of the King's brother, **John**. He was made Justiciar of England (1193–98), and was responsible for all the business of government. On John's accession (1199) he became Chancellor.

Walter, John 1739–1812
English printer and newspaper publisher
Born in London, he bought the patent for printing from logotypes (1782) and in 1784 acquired a printing office in Blackfriars, London. In 1785 he founded a scandal sheet, *The Daily Universal Register*, which in 1788 was renamed *The Times*.

Walter, John 1776–1847
English newspaperman
The son of **John Walter** (1739–1812), he became manager and editor of *The Times* in 1803 and under him the newspaper attained great status. He obtained news, especially from abroad, often more rapidly transmitted than official reports and from sources independent of them. In 1814 he adopted for the printing of *The Times* the double-cylinder steam-driven press invented by **Friedrich König**.

Walter, John 1819–94
English newspaper proprietor
Born in London, the son of **John Walter** (1776–1847), he was a barrister by profession. He became proprietor of *The Times* in 1847 and in 1866 introduced the important cylindrical Walter press, in which, for the first time, curved stereotyped plates and reels of newsprint were used. His son Arthur Fraser (1846–1910), was proprietor until 1908, but the fortunes of *The Times* were impaired by the publication in 1887 of articles on **Charles Stewart Parnell** by **Richard Pigott**, and the controlling interest was acquired by **Alfred Harmsworth** in 1908.

Walter, Lucy, *also known as* **Mrs Barlow** 1630–58
English mistress of the future Charles II
She was born probably in Dyfed, Wales, and met the future king in the Channel Islands when he was fleeing England in 1644 during the Civil War. She bore him a son, James, Duke of **Monmouth**.

Walters, Sir Alan (Arthur) 1926–
British economist
After studying at Leicester University and Oxford, he lectured widely in Britain and the USA from 1958, and returned to Oxford as a visiting professor between 1982 and 1984. He then acted as economic adviser to the World Bank until 1986. As an apostle of the strict policies of monetary control that proved so appealing to **Margaret Thatcher**, he subsequently became her special adviser, and his influence eventually brought about the resignation of Chancellor of the Exchequer **Nigel Lawson** in 1989. Walters, adorned with a knighthood in 1983, resumed his academic career in the USA where he was Professor of Economics at Johns Hopkins University, Maryland, until 1991. His works include *Money in Boom and Slump* (1970), *Britain's Economic Renaissance* (1986) and *Sterling in Danger* (1990).

Walters, Julie 1950–
English actress
Born in Birmingham, she trained as a nurse before studying at the Manchester Polytechnic School of Theatre and working at the Liverpool Everyman Theatre. The role of the indomitable, working-class hairdresser in *Educating Rita* (1980) established her reputation and she received an Oscar nomination when she repeated it in the 1983 film version. A skilled mimic, comedienne and versatile character actress, she has appeared on stage in *Macbeth* (1985), *Frankie and Johnny in the Clair de Lune* (1989) and *The Rose Tattoo* (1991). On television, she has performed comedy with **Victoria Wood** in series such as *Wood and Walters* (1981–82), *Victoria Wood—As Seen on TV* (1984–87) and *Victoria Wood* (1989), and drama in the **Alan Bleasdale**-scripted series *Boys from the Blackstuff* (1982), *G.B.H.* (1991) and *Jake's Progress* (1995). Her films include *Personal Services* (1986), *Buster* (1988) and *Stepping Out* (1991). She is also the author of *Babytalk* (1990), a frank and funny account of motherhood.

Walther von der Vogelweide c.1170–c.1230
Austro-German lyric poet
Born probably in Tirol, little is known of his early life, but he was active in Vienna towards the end of the century, and emerges in palace rolls throughout southern Germany during the next 25 years; his last known poem is from the late 1220s. He wrote love poetry—the highly formalized *Minnesang*—largely influenced by French models, but he also pioneered verse as a vehicle for social and political commentary. Much of it is frankly propagandistic, written to serve a courtly patron's interests, but it is marked by a self-assurance that is strikingly 'modern'. The most powerful of these patrons was the Emperor **Frederick II**, from whom Walther gained a grant of land near Würzburg in 1212. The most reliable editions of his work are *Die Gedichte* (1965, 'The Poems'), edited by Lachmann and Kuhn, and the two-volume *Die Lieder* (1967, 1974, 'The Songs'), edited by Friedrich Laurer. The first English translation was by Edwin Zeydel and Bayard Q Morgan in 1952. 📖 G F Jones, *Walther von der Vogelweide* (1968)

Walton, Brian c.1600–1661
English clergyman
Born in Seymour, Yorkshire, he studied at Cambridge, and held curacies in London and Essex. Sequestered in 1641, he went to Oxford, and then in London devoted himself to the editing of the *London Polyglott Bible* (6 vols,

1653–57), aided by **James Ussher**, John Lightfoot (1602–75), Edward Pococke (1604–91) and other scholars. He was made Bishop of Chester in 1660. Nine languages are used in the *Polyglott*—Hebrew, Chaldee, Samaritan, Syriac, Arabic, Persian, Ethiopic, Greek and Latin. Other works were an *Introductio* to oriental languages (1654) and *Considerator Considered* (1659), a defence of the *Polyglott*.

Walton, Cecile 1891–1956
Scottish artist and illustrator
Born in Glasgow, the daughter of the painter Edward Arthur Walton (1860–1922), she studied in Paris, Florence and Edinburgh. Although she illustrated many books, it was as a painter in oils that she attained her major achievements. She married the artist Eric H M Robertson in 1914 and with him became a leading figure in the Edinburgh Group of artists that flourished from 1912 to 1921. In the late 1920s she turned to theatre decor and a few years later joined the BBC as organizer of the Scottish Children's Hour. She retired to Kirkcudbright in 1948 where she took up painting again. She was the first woman painter to receive the Royal Scottish Academy's prestigious Guthrie award.

Walton, E(rnest) T(homas) S(inton) 1903–95
Irish physicist and Nobel Prize winner
Born in Dungarvan, Waterford, he studied at Trinity College, Dublin, and in 1927 went to the Cavendish Laboratory, Cambridge, where he studied under **Ernest Rutherford**. He later became Professor of Natural and Experimental Philosophy at Trinity College, Dublin (1947–74). With Sir **John Cockcroft**, he produced the first artificial disintegration of a nucleus by bombarding lithium with protons in the first successful use of a particle accelerator. By studying the energies of the alpha particles produced they were able to verify **Albert Einstein**'s theory of mass–energy equivalence, and were awarded the 1951 Nobel Prize for physics in recognition of this work. In 1952 he was appointed chairman of the School of Cosmic Physics and the Dublin Institute for Advanced Studies.

Walton, George 1867–1933
Scottish designer
Born in Glasgow, he studied at Glasgow School of Art, set up in practice, and obtained the first of a number of commissions to design for the Cranston tearooms in conjunction with **Charles Rennie Mackintosh**. Their styles were similar, though later work by Walton was clearly influenced by **Charles Francis Annesley Voysey**, who was a close friend. His work extended to architecture, furniture, glass and textiles.

Walton, Izaak 1593–1683
English writer
He was born in Stafford, the son of an alehouse-keeper. In 1621 he settled as an ironmonger in London, where he became friends with **John Donne**. In 1626 he married a great-grandniece of **Thomas Cranmer**, and in 1647 Ann Ken, a half-sister of the hymn writer **Thomas Ken**. He spent most of his time 'in the families of the eminent clergymen of England'. His later years were spent in Winchester. His most celebrated work is his *The Compleat Angler, or the Contemplative Man's Recreation*, which first appeared in 1653. His description of fishes, English rivers, and of rods and lines is interspersed with scraps of dialogue, moral reflections, old verses, songs and sayings, and idyllic glimpses of country life. The anonymous *Arte of Angling* (1577), discovered in 1957, has been found to be one of his chief sources. Equally exquisite are his biographies—of John Donne (1640), Sir Thomas Wotton (1651), **Richard Hooker** (1665), Richard Herbert (1670) and George Sanderson (1678). 📖 J Bevan, *Izaak Walton* (1987)

Walton, Sir William Turner 1902–83
English composer

Born in Oldham, Lancashire, he was a cathedral chorister at Christ Church, Oxford, before going to university in 1918. The same year, he wrote his first major work, a piano quartet, which was performed at the Salzburg festival of contemporary music in 1923. His *Façade* (1923), originally accompanied by declamatory verses by Edith Sitwell, subsequently reappeared as a pair of suites and as ballet music. Scored for an unusual instrumental combination containing saxophone and varied percussion, it caricatures conventional song and dance forms. *Belshazzar's Feast* (1931), a biblical cantata with libretto by Osbert Sitwell, is a powerful work in which instrumentation for an augmented orchestra is contrasted with moving un-accompanied choral passages. His ballet music for *The Wise Virgins* (1940), based on pieces by J S Bach, contains a concert favourite in his orchestral arrangement of the aria *Sheep May Safely Graze*. During World War II he began composing incidental music for films and showed great flair for building up tension and atmosphere, as in Laurence Olivier's *Henry V* (1944), *Hamlet* (1948) and *Richard III* (1955). Later works include the opera *Troilus and Cressida* (1954), a cello concerto (1956), a second symphony and a song cycle, *Anon in Love* (1960), *A Song for the Lord Mayor's Table* (1962), and a comic opera, *The Bear* (1967). ▢ S Walton, *William Walton* (1988)

Wanamaker, Sam 1919–93
US actor and director

Born in Chicago, he worked with summer stock companies there as an actor and director (1936–39), and made his New York stage debut in 1942. After serving in World War II he returned to acting in New York (1946). He made his London debut in Clifford Odets' *Winter Journey* (1952), which he also directed, and remained based in England, directing and acting in several plays. He was appointed director of the New Shakespeare Theatre, Liverpool (1957), and he joined the Shakespeare Memorial Theatre company at Stratford-upon-Avon (1959). He continued to direct on both sides of the Atlantic Ocean, but concentrated latterly upon his ambition to build a replica of Shakespeare's Globe Theatre near its original site on London's Bankside. He founded the Globe Theatre Trust in 1970 and opened a temporary tent theatre in 1972. The Bear Garden Museum, founded by Wanamaker and displaying exhibits from Shakespeare's era, is nearby. The reconstructed Globe theatre opened in 1996 with a production of *Two Gentlemen of Verona*, three years after his death.

Wand, John William Charles 1885–1977
English Anglican churchman and scholar

Born in Grantham, Lincolnshire, he was appointed dean of Oriel College, Oxford, in 1925, and went to Australia as Archbishop of Brisbane in 1934. He returned to Great Britain in 1943 to be Bishop of Bath and Wells, and was Bishop of London from 1945 to 1955. Remembered by students for his many books on church history, he became an even more prolific author in his long retirement, writing numerous popular books commending Christian faith, editing the *Church Quarterly Review*, writing a weekly devotional column for the *Church Times*, and publishing a brief autobiography, *Changeful Page* (1965).

Wang, An 1920–90
US physicist and computer company executive

Born in Shanghai, he graduated in science from Jiao Tong University in Shanghai (1940), and in 1945 emigrated to the USA, where he studied applied physics at Harvard. Possessing technological genius and entrepreneurial ability, he invented magnetic core memories for computers, and in 1951 founded Wang Laboratories in Boston, Massachusetts, which, through the success of Wang's electronic calculator, went on to become a leading manufacturer of minicomputers. However, in the 1980s personal computers and workstations ate into his business, and in 1992 the company filed for bankruptcy. A leading philanthropist in Boston, he was inducted into the National Inventors Hall of Fame in 1988. ▢ *Lessons: an autobiography* (1986)

Wang Ching-wei See Wang Jingwei

Wang Jing (Wang Ching) d.83AD
Chinese civil engineer

He was descended from a family that had gained engineering distinction in Korea, and in the service of the Emperor Ming Di was ordered to reconstruct the 500 mile (800km) Bian Canal which had been extensively damaged by floods on the Yellow River. He erected large dykes at the junction of the canal and the Yellow River, restored the canal's existing flash locks and increased their number to a total of about 200. The work on the Bian Canal was completed in AD70, and eight years later he began to rebuild the Peony Dam, a project that was still incomplete at the time of his death.

Wang Jingwei (Wang Ching-wei) 1883–1944
Chinese politician

An associate of Sun Yat-sen, he studied in Japan, where he joined Sun's revolutionary party, and from 1917 became his personal assistant. In 1927 he was appointed head of the new Guomindang (Kuomintang) government at Wuhan, and in 1932 became the party's president, with his main rival for control of the Guomindang, Chiang Kai-shek, in charge of the military. In 1938, after the outbreak of war with Japan, Wang offered to co-operate with the Japanese, and in 1940 he became head of a puppet regime ruling the occupied areas.

Wang Junxia (Wang Chün-hsia) 1973–
Chinese athlete

Born in Jiaohe City, Jilin (Kirin) Province, she stunned the world in 1993 by creating three new world records at 3,000, 5,000 and 10,000 metres. The staggering 42 seconds she knocked off the 10,000 metres record to run it in 29 minutes, 31.78 seconds at China's National Games sparked accusations that the Chinese athletes had used performance-enhancing drugs. Chinese officials credited the hard endurance-training methods of national coach Ma Junren (Ma Chün-jen) and his tonic of turtle blood and caterpillar-fungus. Later, Wang accused Ma of abuse and led 16 athletes in a walk-out in December 1995 after she claimed that he had kept three Mercedes cars that she and her teammates had won in the 1993 world championships in Stuttgart.

Wang Meng 1934–
Chinese novelist

Born in Beijing (Peking), the son of a philosophy professor, he joined the Communist youth league in 1949 as a schoolboy, and published three novels, *Long Live Youth* (1953), *The Young New-comer in the Organization Department* (1956) and *Ausha 3322* (1995, 'Assassination 3322'). He was denounced as a Rightist in the 'Anti-Rightist Campaign' of 1958, and forced to work as a manual labourer for 20 years in the remote provinces. He was then allowed to return to Beijing, and re-emerged with *Young Forever* (1979). Since then he has held various party posts, and published collections of short stories like *A Night in the City* (1980) and *Andante Cantabile* (1981). After the fall of the Gang of Four he was rehabilitated and became Minister of Culture.

Wang Wei 699–759
Chinese poet and painter of the Tang dynasty

He was an ardent Buddhist. Only a few examples of his work, mainly landscapes, survive. He linked painting with poetry in nature and mood, and may have pioneered monochrome ink painting.

Wankel, Felix 1902–88
German mechanical engineer

Born in Luhran, he was employed in various engineering works before opening his own research establishment in 1930. While carrying out work for several German motor manufacturers he devoted himself to the development of an alternative configuration to the conventional piston-and-cylinder internal-combustion engine. After many trials he produced a successful prototype engine in 1956, with a curved equilateral triangular rotor in a fat figure-of-eight shaped chamber. A few types of motor car have used the Wankel engine, but continuing problems with the sealing of the rotor have prevented its large-scale adoption.

Warbeck, Perkin c.1474–1499
Flemish impostor

Pretender to the English throne, he was born in Tournai. He appeared in 1490 claiming to be Richard, Duke of York, the younger of the two sons of **Edward IV** murdered in the Tower. The Irish and the French, under **Charles VIII**, supported him, and in July 1495 he landed in Kent. In Scotland, **James IV** married him to a daughter of the Earl of Huntly. In 1498 he attempted to besiege Exeter, but ran away to the sanctuary at Beaulieu in Hampshire, surrendered, and was imprisoned. Charged with attempting to escape, he was thrown into the Tower, and executed.

Warburg, Otto Heinrich 1883–1970
German biochemist and Nobel Prize winner

Born in Freiburg, Baden, he was educated at the universities of Berlin and Heidelberg, and won the *Pour le Mérite* (the German equivalent of the Victoria Cross) during World War I. He worked at the Kaiser Wilhelm (later **Max Planck**) Institute in Berlin from 1913, becoming director there in 1953. He was the first to discover the important role of iron, in association with oxidase enzymes, in nearly all cells. In 1926 he demonstrated that oxygen uptake by yeast is inhibited by carbon monoxide and determined that carboxyhaemoglobin is a haem protein. He also discovered the role of riboflavin in the oxidation of glucose compounds by a yeast preparation, and showed the efficiency with which the green alga *Chlorella* produces oxygen from the absorption of red light (1923). The gas manometer developed by Warburg in 1926 was crucial to the discoveries of **Hans Krebs** and others, and continued in use until replaced by the oxygen electrode around 1970. Warburg also engaged in cancer research. He was awarded the 1931 Nobel Prize for physiology or medicine, and in 1944 was offered a second Nobel Prize which, as a Jew, he was prevented from accepting by **Hitler**.
📖 Hans Krebs, *Otto Warburg: Cell Physiologist, Biochemist and Eccentric* (1981)

Warburton, Peter Egerton 1813–89
Australian soldier and explorer

Born in Cheshire, England, he served in the Indian Army for 24 years and then settled in Australia in 1853, where he was a police commissioner until 1867. After earlier journeys to explore the South Australian Salt Lakes, he became in 1873 the first person to cross Australia from the south coast to central Australia via Alice Springs and across the worst of the desert country, to the De Grey River on the west coast.

Ward, Artemus See Browne, Charles Farrar

Ward, Dame Barbara Mary See Jackson (of Lodsworth), Baroness

Ward, David 1922–83
Scottish operatic bass singer

Born in Dumbarton, he studied at the Royal College of Music and with Hans Hotter in Munich, making his debut with Sadler's Wells Opera in 1953, and joining the Royal Opera, Covent Garden, in 1960. He was successful in a variety of roles, from heroic to buffo, most notably as Wotan and Boris Godunov in productions with Scottish Opera. He was made CBE in 1972, and later emigrated to New Zealand.

Ward, Frank Kingdon- See Kingdon-Ward, Frank

Ward, Dame Geneviève 1838–1922
US prima donna and actress

Born in New York City, she was a great singer in her youth and became a great tragedienne. She was still acting at 83. She was created DBE in 1921. She wrote *Both Sides of the Curtain* (1918) with Richard Whiteing.

Ward, Mrs Humphry See Ward, Mary Augusta

Ward, James 1769–1859
English painter

Born in the City of London, he worked as a cider bottler before becoming apprenticed to the English engraver and miniaturist John Raphael Smith (1750–1812). He exhibited at the Royal Academy in 1792 and two years later was appointed painter and engraver to **George IV**. He was commissioned principally to paint animals, but he is best known for his 'sublime' Romantic picture, the huge *Gordale Scar* (c.1812–14, Tate, London), in which great cliffs, topped by storm clouds, tower above tiny figures of cattle.

Ward, James 1843–1925
English psychologist and philosopher

He was born in Hull, Humberside, and studied for the Congregationalist ministry at Spring Hill College in Birmingham, but abandoned his religious beliefs and studied moral sciences at Trinity College, Cambridge, where he became a Fellow in 1875. He published articles on psychology in the ninth and subsequent editions of the *Encyclopaedia Britannica* (from 1886) that were influential in establishing the subject as a proper science in England, and was Professor of Mental Philosophy and Logic at Cambridge (1897–1925). He published in book form two volumes of Gifford Lectures: *Naturalism and Agnosticism* (1899) and *The Realm of Ends* (1911), *Psychological Principles* (1918) and *A Study of Kant* (1922).

Ward, Sir Joseph George 1856–1930
New Zealand statesman

Born in Melbourne, he entered parliament in 1887 and held many prominent posts, including Minister of Public Health (the first in the world). He was Liberal Prime Minister from 1906 to 1912 and 1928 to 1930. With **William Ferguson Massey** he represented New Zealand at the Paris Peace Conference (1919).

Ward, Sir Leslie 1851–1922
English caricaturist and portrait painter

He earned fame as the caricaturist 'Spy' in *Vanity Fair* (1873–1909) and also signed some of his work 'Drawl' (L Ward backwards). He was knighted in 1918, and wrote *Forty Years of 'Spy'* (1915).

Ward, Mary 1585–1645
English religious reformer

The founder of a Catholic society for women, modelled on the Society of Jesus in 1609, she and her devotees founded schools and taught in them, giving up the cloistered existence and the habit of nuns. Although their work was not questioned, these innovations were, and

Pope **Urban VIII** at last called her to Rome and suppressed her society in 1630. She was allowed to return to England in 1639. Her institute was fully restored, with papal permission, in 1877 and became the model for modern Catholic women's institutes.

Ward, Mary Augusta, *known as* Mrs Humphry Ward, *née* Arnold 1851–1920
English novelist
She was born in Hobart, Tasmania, the granddaughter of **Thomas Arnold**, and niece of **Matthew Arnold**. Her family returned to Great Britain (1856), and after attending private boarding schools she joined them in Oxford in 1867. In 1872 she married Thomas Humphry Ward (1845–1926), a Fellow and tutor of Brasenose College, Oxford, and she became secretary to Somerville College, Oxford (1879), before moving to London in 1881, where she wrote for various periodicals. A children's story, *Milly and Olly* (1881), *Miss Bretherton* (1884), a slight novel, and a translation (1885) of **Henri Amiel's** *Journal intime* preceded her greatest success, the bestselling spiritual romance *Robert Elsmere* (1888), which inspired the philanthropist Passmore Edwards to found the Tavistock Square settlement for the London poor in 1897. Her later novels, all on social or religious issues, include *Marcella* (1894), *Sir George Tressady* (1896) and *The Case of Richard Meynell* (1911). She was both an enthusiastic social worker and an anti-suffragette, becoming first president of the Anti-Suffrage League in 1908. She published *A Writer's Recollections* in 1918. ⌑ E M Smith, *Mrs Humphry Ward* (1980)

Ward, Nathaniel 1579–1652
English lawyer and clergyman
Born in Haverhill, Suffolk, he studied law at Emmanuel College, Cambridge, and entered the ministry in 1619, but was dismissed for nonconformity in 1633. In 1634 he went to Massachusetts Bay, where he was pastor of Agawam (Ipswich) for a brief period, and in 1638 was appointed to help to frame the first legal code in New England (enacted 1641). He returned to England in 1645, and wrote a satirical book of political and religious reflections, *The Simple Cobler of Aggawam in America* (1647).

Ward, Nathaniel Bagshaw 1791–1868
English physician and botanist
Born in London, he was involved with the administration of the Chelsea Physic Garden, where he worked on methods of plant cultivation. He invented the 'Wardian case' which enabled live plants to be transported successfully on long voyages, and also their cultivation in Victorian drawing rooms. Among the many plants which owe their establishment to the Wardian case, the most significant is the tea plant, which **Robert Fortune** successfully brought from China to India. He published *On the Growth of Plants in Closely Glazed Cases* (1842), and *Aspects of Nature* (1864).

Ward, Seth 1617–89
English astronomer and clergyman
Born in Hertfordshire, he was educated at Cambridge. He was Savilian Professor of Astronomy at Oxford from 1649 to 1660, propounded (1653) a theory of planetary motion, and took part in **John Wallis** in the latter's controversy with **Thomas Hobbes**. He was Bishop of Exeter from 1662 to 1667, when he became Bishop of Salisbury.

Ward, Stephen 1913–63
English painter and osteopath
He was a London osteopath who was at the centre of the Profumo scandal in 1963. He introduced **Christine Keeler** to **John Profumo** and provided information that disproved Profumo's denial of involvement made in the House of Commons. He became the establishment scapegoat for the whole affair and was tried on charges of living on immoral earnings. He committed suicide before

a verdict was reached. He was also an accomplished painter and included members of the royal family among his subjects.

Wardlaw, Henry d.1440
Scottish prelate
He studied and lived for some years in France, and later became tutor to King **James I** of Scotland. In 1403 he became Bishop of St Andrews, and played a prominent part in the foundation (1411) of St Andrews University, the first university in Scotland, of which he was the first Chancellor. He also restored St Andrews Cathedral.

Warham, William c.1450–1532
English lawyer and prelate
Born near Basingstoke, Hampshire, he took orders, but practised law, and became an advocate in the Court of Arches. His diplomatic services to **Henry VII** obtained him rapid preferment—Master of the Rolls (1494), Lord Chancellor (1501), Bishop of London (1503) and Archbishop of Canterbury (1503). In 1515 he had to resign the great seal to **Thomas Wolsey**. He was a sympathizer of the New Learning and its proponents, but did not desire fundamental reform, though he reluctantly agreed to recognize the king's supremacy.

Warhol, Andy, *originally* Andrew Warhola 1926–87
US pop artist and filmmaker
Born in Pittsburgh, Pennsylvania, of Czech parents, he worked as a commercial designer before becoming in 1961 a pioneer of Pop Art with colourful reproductions of familiar everyday objects (eg *100 Soup Cans* and *Green Coca-Cola Bottles*, 1962) and magazine illustrations directly reproduced by silk-screen. His first films (eg *Sleep*, 1963) endeavoured to eliminate the individuality of the filmmaker by use of a fixed camera viewpoint without sound. In later sound production from his Greenwich Village 'film factory' his avant-garde style employed continual violent changes of visual and aural perspective within long single scenes, typified by *Chelsea Girls* (1967). After 1968, when he was shot and wounded by one of his starlets, his films were controlled by his former assistant and cameraman with much more commercial exploitation of Warhol's cult reputation—*Flesh* (1968), *Trash* (1969), *Frankenstein* (1973) and *Dracula* (1974). In the 1970s Warhol turned to portrait painting, still attempting to suppress artistic individuality by painting in series, as in the 10 Mao portraits of 1972.

Warlock, Peter, *pseudonym of* Philip Arnold Heseltine 1894–1930
English musicologist and composer
Born in London, he met **Frederick Delius** in 1910 and in 1916, Bernard van Dieren, both of whom had a great musical influence on him. His friendship with **D H Lawrence** is also reflected in his music. He founded *The Sackbut*, a spirited musical periodical, in 1920. His works include the song cycle *The Curlew* (1920–22), *Serenade* (1923) dedicated to Delius, the orchestral suite *Capriol* (1926), many songs, often in the Elizabethan manner, and choral works. He edited much Elizabethan and Jacobean music, wrote *Frederick Delius* (1923, under his original name) and *The English Ayre* (1926).

Warmerdam, Cornelius, *known as* Dutch 1915–
US pole-vaulter
Born in Long Beach, California, he was the first man to break the 15ft (4.57m) landmark (1941). Seven times the world record holder, he set a new standard in the sport. Using a bamboo pole, he set records during World War II that were not bettered until the next decade. His career-best indoor vault of 4.78 m, set in 1943, was not beaten for more than 14 years. The development of more flexible

glass-fibre poles since the 1950s have led to dramatic improvements in vaulting records, but in his own time his achievements were exceptional.

Warming, (Johannes) Eugenius Bülow
1841–1924
Danish botanist
Born in the North Frisian island of Manö, he studied botany in Munich and became professor at the universities of Stockholm (1882–85) and Copenhagen (1885–1911). He wrote important works on systematic botany (1879) and plant ecology (*Plantesamfund*, 1895), and was regarded as a founder of the latter. His work demonstrated that groups of species could form a well-defined unity, such as a meadow ecosystem. He produced two excellent textbooks, *Haandbog i den Systematiske Botanik* (1879) and *Den Almindelige Botanik* (1880). Between 1863 and 1866 he travelled in Brazil, making the most detailed and thorough study of a tropical area then produced.

Warne, Shane Keith, *nicknamed* Hollywood
1969–
Australian cricketer
Born in Ferntree Gully, Victoria, he bowled the 'ball of the century' in the 1993 Ashes series against Mike Gatting at Old Trafford. The ball pitched outside the leg-stump, only to pass the outside edge of his bat and hit his off-stump. In an era dominated by fast bowling, Warne's performance has proved there is still a place for spin bowlers. He is now recognized as not only the leading spinner of his day, but among the greatest the world has ever known.

Warner, Charles Dudley 1829–1900
US writer
Born in Plainfield, Massachusetts, he practised law in Chicago until 1869, then settled as an editor in Hartford. In 1884 he became co-editor of *Harper's Magazine*, in which his papers on the South, Mexico and the Great West appeared. He published several books of essays, and in 1873 he co-wrote *The Gilded Age* with Mark Twain. He also wrote literary criticism, most significantly *The Relation of Literature to Life* (1896). 📖 A Fields, *Charles Dudley Warner* (1902)

Warner, Deborah 1959–
English theatre director
Born in Oxford, she was educated at Sidcot School, Avon, and St Clare's College, Oxford, then at the Central School of Speech and Drama. She founded the Kick Theatre Company in 1980, and was its artistic director (1980–86), before becoming resident director at the Royal Shakespeare Company (1987–89) and associate director of the Royal National Theatre in 1989. She repeated the success of the Kick Theatre's productions of Bertolt Brecht's *The Good Person of Szechwan* (1980) and Shakespeare's *King Lear* (1985) at the National Theatre in 1989 and 1990, and won the *Evening Standard* and Laurence Olivier awards for direction in 1988 for her acclaimed *Electra*, which was revived in 1992. She also won an Olivier award for her production of Ibsen's *Hedda Gabler* at the Abbey Theatre in Dublin in 1991. Her controversial production of Beckett's *Footfalls* (1994) was followed by a version of Shakespeare's *Richard II* in which Fiona Shaw played the monarch as a gender-free figure wrapped in bandages, which aimed at the consideration of monarchy aside from personality.

Warner, Jack Leonard, *originally* Jack Leonard Eichelbaum 1892–1978
US film producer
Born in Canada, in London, Ontario, he was the youngest son of a large and impoverished immigrant family. A boy soprano and inveterate performer, he embarked upon a showbusiness career, later joining his brothers Harry, Albert and Samuel in the exhibition and distribution of motion pictures in Pennsylvania. Building a nationwide company, they moved into production with *Perils of the Plains* (1910) and built a studio of their own in Los Angeles (1919). Warners were the first to introduce sound, in *Don Juan* (1926) and *The Jazz Singer* (1927). The sensational popularity of the latter made Warner Brothers into a major studio, specializing in gangster films, musicals and historical biographies, and home to such stars as Bette Davis, James Cagney and Humphrey Bogart. As a tough head of production, Warner supervised such films as *Yankee Doodle Dandy* (1942), *Auntie Mame* (1958), *My Fair Lady* (1964) and *Camelot* (1967) but eventually sold his interest and the name to the Canadian company Seven Arts. He wrote two autobiographies: *My First Hundred Years in Hollywood* (1965) and *Jack of all Trades* (1975).

Warner, Marina Sarah 1946–
English literary critic and writer
Born in London and educated at St Mary's Convent, Ascot, and Lady Margaret Hall, Oxford, she was the Paul Getty Scholar at the Getty Centre for the History of Art and the Humanities (1987–88) and the Tinbergen Professor at Erasmus University, Rotterdam (1990–91). She was Young Writer of the Year in 1969, and winner of the Fawcett prize in 1986 and of the Commonwealth Writers' prize (Eurasia) in 1989. In 1994 she delivered the Reith Lectures, a series entitled 'Six Myths of Our Time', which has since been published as *Managing Monsters* (1994). Other publications include *Alone of all her Sex: The Myth and Culture of the Virgin Mary* (1976), *Monuments and Maidens* (1985) and *Mermaids in the Basement* (1993).

Warner, Rex 1905–86
English writer
Born in Birmingham, he studied classics at Wadham College, Oxford and was a specialist in classical literature, and taught before turning to writing. *The Wild Goose Chase* (1937), *The Professor* (1938) and *The Aerodrome* (1941) established his reputation as a writer concerned with the problems of the individual involved with authority. He is pre-eminently a novelist of ideas, and his distinction lies in the original, imaginative handling of conflicting ideologies. *Men of Stones* (1949) explores the nature of totalitarianism, but it and *Why was I Killed?* (1944) are less successful than his other works. He was perhaps best known for his later historical novels such as *The Young Caesar* (1958), *Imperial Caesar* (1960) and *Pericles the Athenian* (1963). He was a poet of sensuous quality (*Poems*, 1931, and *Poems and Contradictions*, 1945), and also a translator of Greek classics.

Warner, Susan Bogert, *pseudonym* Elizabeth Wetherell 1819–85
US novelist
She was born in New York, and had a huge success with *The Wide, Wide World* (1851), followed by *Queechy* (1852) and other sentimental and emotional tales. She collaborated in many books with her sister Anna Bartlett Warner (1827–1915) who, as 'Amy Lothrop', wrote popular stories such as *Stories of Vinegar Hill* (6 vols, 1892) and was the author of children's hymns like 'Jesus Loves Me, This I Know' and 'Jesus bids us Shine'.

Warner, Sylvia Townsend 1893–1978
English novelist
She was born in Harrow, London, studied music, and was one of the four editors of the 10-volume *Tudor Church Music* (1923–29). She published seven novels, four volumes of poetry, essays, and eight volumes of short stories, many of which had previously appeared in the *New Yorker*. A gifted writer, she produced works which range widely in theme, locale and period, defying any literary strait-jacketing.

Significant titles are *Lolly Willowes* (1926), *Mr Fortune's Maggot* (1927), *Summer Will Show* (1936), *After the Death of Don Juan* (1938) and *The Corner That Held Them* (1948). 📖 W Mulford, *Sylvia Townsend Warner* (1988)

Warner, William c.1558–1609
English poet
Born in London, he was educated at Oxford. He practised as an attorney, wrote *Pan his Syrinx Pipe* (1585), translated **Plautus** (*Menaechmi*, 1595), and gained a high contemporary reputation with his *Albion's England* (1586–1606), a long metrical history in 14-syllable verse.

Warner, William Lloyd 1898–1970
US anthropologist
Born in Redlands, California, he studied at the University of California, and became Professor of Anthropology, Sociology and Human Development at the University of Chicago in 1935. From 1959 to 1970 he was Professor of Social Research at the University of Michigan. He is noted for his studies of Australian Aboriginal social and kinship organization, and for pioneering the field of urban anthropology. His major works include *A Black Civilization* (1937) and *Social Class in America* (1960).

Warnock, (Helen) Mary Warnock, Baroness, *née* Wilson 1924–
English philosopher and educationist
She was born in Winchester and studied at Oxford, where she became a fellow in philosophy at St Hugh's College (1949–66, 1976–84). She was headmistress of Oxford High School (1968–72) and Mistress of Girton College, Cambridge (1985–91), and has contributed to or chaired important committees of inquiry into special education (1974–78), environmental pollution (1979–84), animal experiments (1979–85), human fertilization (1982–84), higher education (1984) and teaching standards (1990). Her publications include *Education: A Way Forward* (1979), *A Question of Life* (1985) and *Teacher Teach Thyself* (The Dimbleby Lecture, 1985). She was awarded a life peerage in 1985.

Warr, 3rd or 12th Baron De la See De la Warr, 3rd or 12th Baron

Warren, Sir Charles 1840–1927
Welsh soldier and archaeologist
Born in Bangor, Gwynedd, he entered the Royal Engineers in 1857. He played a conspicuous part during the late 19th century as a commander of British forces in South Africa, where he helped to delimit Griqualand West, and served also elsewhere. He is, however, chiefly remembered for his work connected with the archaeological exploration of Palestine, especially Jerusalem, and for his writings arising from it: *Underground Jerusalem* (1876), *Temple and Tomb* (1880) and *Jerusalem* (1884). He also wrote on ancient weights and measures.

Warren, Earl 1891–1974
US politician and jurist
Born in Los Angeles and educated at the University of California, he practised law in California and was then admitted to the Bar. An active Republican, he became Governor of California (1943–53) and made an unsuccessful run for the vice-presidency in 1948. He became Chief of Justice of the US Supreme Court in 1953. The Warren Court (1953–69) was active and influential, notably in the areas of civil rights and individual liberties. It was responsible for the landmark decision in *Brown v Board of Education of Topeka* (1954), which outlawed school segregation, and for *Miranda v Arizona* (1966), which ruled that criminal suspects be informed of their rights before being questioned by the police. Warren was chairman of the federal commission (the Warren Commission, 1963–64) that investigated the assassination of President **John F Kennedy** and found that the killing was not part of a domestic or foreign conspiracy. 📖 Leo Katcher, *Earl Warren* (1967)

Warren, Mercy Otis 1728–1814
US writer
Born in Barnstable, Massachusetts, she married James Warren, a leader in state politics, in 1754. She was a patriot and a friend of the leaders of the American Revolution, and she wrote two satirical plays against the Tories, *The Adulateur* (1773) and *The Group* (1775). She published a three-volume history of the Revolution in 1805.

Warren, Robert Penn 1905–89
US novelist and poet
Born in Guthrie, Kentucky, he was educated at Vanderbilt, Berkeley and Yale universities, and was a Rhodes scholar at Oxford. Professor of English at Louisiana (1934–42) and Minnesota (1942–50), he was Professor of Drama (1951–56) and of English (1962–73) at Yale. He established an international reputation with his Pulitzer Prize-winning political novel about the governor of a Southern state, *All the King's Men* (1946, filmed 1949), in which the demagogue Willie Stark closely resembles Governor **Huey Long**. Other works include *John Brown, the Making of a Martyr* (1929), *Night Rider* (1939), *The Cave* (1959), *Wilderness* (1961), the story of a Jew in the Civil War, and *Meet Me in the Green Glen* (1971). He also published some volumes of short stories, and verse including *Promises* (1957, Pulitzer Prize), *Selected Poems, Old and New, 1923–66* (1966), *Or Else* (1974) and *Rumour Verified* (1981). 📖 K Snipes, *Robert Penn Warren* (1983)

Warton, Joseph 1722–1800
English literary critic
Born in Dunsfold, Surrey, the brother of **Thomas Warton**, he was educated at Winchester and Oriel College, Oxford, became rector of Winslade (1748), then returned to Winchester as a schoolmaster (1755), later becoming its head (1766–93). His poetic *Odes* (1746) marked a reaction against **Pope**. However, he is best known for his Classical translations and critical works, which gained him a high reputation. They include an edition of **Virgil** (1753) and *Essay on Pope* (2 vols, 1757 and 1782), with its distinction between the poetry of reason and the poetry of fancy. An edition of **Dryden** was completed by his son (1811). 📖 Joan H Pittock, *The Ascendancy of Taste: The Achievement of Joseph and Thomas Warton* (1973)

Warton, Thomas 1728–90
English critic and poet
Born in Basingstoke, the brother of **Joseph Warton**, he was educated at Winchester and Trinity College, Oxford. In 1751 he became a Fellow of Trinity College, and in 1757 Professor of Poetry. His *Observations on Spencer's Faerie Queene* (1754) established his reputation, but he is best remembered for his *History of English Poetry* (1774–81). In 1785 he became Poet Laureate and Camden Professor of History. His miscellaneous writings included burlesque poetry and prose, genial satires on Oxford, an edition of **Theocritus** (1770), and *Inquiry into the Authenticity of the Rowley Poems*. 📖 Joan H Pittock, *The Ascendancy of Taste: The Achievement of Joseph and Thomas Warton* (1973)

Warwick, Dionne, *also spelt* Warwicke 1940–
US soul and pop singer
Born in East Orange, New Jersey, to a musical family which includes Cissy and **Whitney Houston**, she was discovered by songwriters Burt Bacharach and Hal David, who wrote 'Anyone Who Had a Heart', 'Walk on By' (1964), 'I Say A Little Prayer' (1967) and 'Do You Know the Way to San Jose' (1968) for her, among other songs. She was less successful after splitting from Bacharach and David, but had a number-one hit with The Spinners on

'Then Came You' (1974). She had added the final 'e' to her name for extra class, but dropped it again in the mid-1970s.

Warwick, John Dudley, Duke of Northumberland and Earl of 1502–53
English soldier and statesman
Son of Edmund Dudley, he was deputy governor of Calais, and served under Edward Seymour, Duke of Somerset, in his Scottish campaigns. Created Earl of Warwick in 1546, he was appointed joint regent for Edward VI and High Chamberlain of England in 1547. As virtual ruler of England he was created Duke of Northumberland in 1551 and brought about the downfall and eventual execution of Somerset (1550–52). He married his fourth son, Lord Guildford, to Lady Jane Grey, and proclaimed her Queen on the death of Edward VI in 1553, but was executed on the accession of Mary I.

Warwick, Richard Neville, Earl of, *known as* the Kingmaker 1428–71
English soldier and statesman
He married as a boy the daughter of the Earl of Warwick and so at 21 succeeded to the earldom. He acquired the earldom of Salisbury in his own right when his father died in 1460. Consequently he had so much land and wealth that during the Wars of the Roses he held the balance between the Yorkist and Lancastrian factions. He first supported the Yorkists and established the son of Richard, Duke of York, as Edward IV, supplanting Henry VI. But Edward resented Warwick as the 'power behind the throne' and forced him into exile in France. In 1460 he returned to England, now supporting the Lancastrian cause; he compelled Edward to leave the country so that he could reinstate Henry VI. Edward soon returned, however, and routed Warwick's forces at Barnet in March 1471. The 'kingmaker' was killed in the battle. ▭ Paul Murray Kendall, *Warwick the Kingmaker* (1957)

Warwick, Robert Rich, 2nd Earl of 1587–1658
English colonialist
He played a large role in the early history of the American colonies, and managed New England, Bermudas and Providence companies. In 1628 he got the patent of the Massachusetts Bay colony and in 1635 founded the settlement of Saybrook, Connecticut. A Puritan, he fought for the Parliamentary side as Admiral of the Fleet (1642–49) during the English Civil War. In 1643 he was nominated head of a commission for the government of the colonies, and was instrumental in the incorporation of Providence Plantations (now Rhode Island) in 1644. Warwick on Rhode Island was named after him by Samuel Gorton.

Washburn, Sherwood Larned 1911–
US biological anthropologist
Born in Cambridge, Massachusetts, and educated at Harvard, he later taught at Columbia (1939–47), Chicago (1947–58) and the University of California at Berkeley (1958–79). He is a leading authority on primate and human evolution, and has stressed the importance of field studies of primate behaviour for modelling the behaviour of extinct hominid forms. He has edited *Social Life of Early Man* (1962) and numerous other publications.

Washington, Booker T(aliaferro) 1856–1915
African-American educationist
He was born a slave in Franklin Country, Virginia, and educated at Hampton Institute before becoming a teacher, writer and speaker on Negro problems. In 1881 he was appointed principal of the newly opened Tuskegee Institute, Alabama, and built it into a major centre of African-American education. The foremost black leader in the late 19th century, he encouraged blacks to focus on economic equality rather than fight for social or political equality. He was strongly criticized by William Du Bois, and his policies were repudiated by the 20th-century civil rights movement. He is the author of *Up from Slavery* in 1901, which, with its less well-known predecessor *The Story of My Life and Work* (1900, as *An Autobiography*, 1901), is one of the classic American life-stories, recalling in vivid detail the hardships and racial hatreds of the South.

Washington, Denzel 1954–
US film actor
Born in Mount Vernon, New York, he studied acting with the American Conservatory Theater in San Francisco, then returned to New York, and worked with the Shakespeare in the Park ensemble and in a number of off-Broadway productions. His notable work includes *A Soldier's Play* (1981) and *When the Chickens Come Home to Roost* (1983). He made his film debut in *Carbon Copy* (1981) and had a starring role in the popular television series *St Elsewhere* (1982–88). He played Steve Biko in *Cry Freedom* (1987) and won a Best Supporting Actor Academy Award for *Glory* (1989). His subsequent films include *Malcolm X* (1992), *Much Ado About Nothing* (1993), *Philadelphia* (1993), *Courage Under Fire* (1996) and *The Preacher's Wife* (1996).

Washington, Dinah, *pseudonym of* Ruth Jones 1924–63
US jazz and rhythm-and-blues singer
She was born in Tuscaloosa, Alabama, and was apprenticed to the Sara Martin gospel singers, but made a gradual (though never complete) switch to jazz, joining the Lionel Hampton band in 1943 and shortly thereafter making her first recordings as leader. Commercial success gave her considerable artistic freedom and she divided her activities between lucrative rhythm and blues sessions and more taxing improvisation sessions with the likes of trumpeter Clifford Brown. Plagued by alcoholism, she died aged just 38.

Washington, George See panel p1919

Wasserman, August Paul von 1866–1925
German bacteriologist
Born in Bamberg, he studied medicine at Erlangen, Vienna, Munich and Strassburg, where he graduated in 1888, and worked on bacteriology and chemotherapy at the Robert Koch Institute in Berlin from 1890. In 1906 he discovered and gave his name to a blood-serum test for syphilis. An infected person will produce syphilis antibodies in the blood, and in the 'Wasserman' test these will react with known antigens to form a chemical complex. The test is still widely used in diagnosis.

Wasserman, Jakob 1873–1934
German novelist
He was born in Fürth, Bavaria, and after working in a factory at the age of 17, did a year of military service, which he hated as he was a pacifist and a Jew. He later lived in Vienna and in Syria. His impressive novel *Die Juden von Zirndorf* (1897, Eng trans *The Jews of Zirndorf*, 1933) was followed by a succession of novels, culminating in the trilogy completed just before his death: *Der Fall Maurizius* (1928, Eng trans *The Maurizius Case*, 1930), *Etzel Andergast* (1931, Eng trans 1932) and *Joseph Kerkhovens dritte Existenz* (1934, Eng trans *Joseph Kerkhoven's Third Existence*, 1934). He also wrote short stories, biographical studies of Columbus and Henry Morton Stanley, and an autobiography (1921). ▭ J C Blankenagel, *Writings of Jakob Wasserman* (1942)

Waterhouse, Alfred 1830–1905
English architect
Born in Liverpool, he was a leader of the Gothic Revival and designed Manchester town hall and assize courts. He made designs for several Cambridge colleges and Owens College, Manchester. He was the designer of the Natural

Washington, George 1732–99
1st President of the USA

George Washington was born in Bridges Creek, Westmoreland County, Virginia, of immigrant English stock from Northamptonshire, and was the great-grandson of John Washington, who had acquired wealth and position in Virginia. George's father, Augustine, died while his son was still a boy, leaving a large family and inadequate means. George seems to have been a healthy, sober-minded boy, and the story of his honest admission to cutting down a cherry tree with a hatchet is probably the invention of his biographer, Mason Weems.

Augustine had married twice, and produced six children by his second marriage. In 1747 George went to Mount Vernon to live with his eldest half-brother Lawrence, who had received most of the Washington property. Here he had access to books, and came to know the Fairfaxes, the family of his brother's wife. He showed a talent for surveying, and in 1748 Lord Fairfax employed him to survey his property. Surveying alternated for a while with hunting; he learned, too, the use of arms, and studied the art of war. He accompanied Lawrence, who was dying of consumption, to Barbados (1751), and on his death the next year was left guardian of Lawrence's only daughter and heir to his estates in the event of her death without issue.

In 1752, on the deaths of Lawrence's wife and daughter, George inherited the Mount Vernon estate. In the same year, Governor **Robert Dinwiddie** of Virginia appointed him to the staff of the local militia, and instructed him to warn off the French, who were encroaching on British interests in the Ohio Valley (1753). Washington made a long and hazardous journey to deliver the message, which the French ignored. The following year, promoted to the rank of lieutenant-colonel, he drove them out of Fort Duquesne, but was himself later besieged and forced to surrender.

When the British general **Edward Braddock** arrived in Virginia, Washington joined his service with the rank of colonel. In 1755 Braddock was killed at Fort Duquesne; Washington saved the remnant of the British army and was put at the head of the Virginia forces (1756). In 1759 he married a rich young widow, Martha Custis (1732–1802), and the combined estates of Mount Vernon and his new wife made him one of the richest men in the country. He kept open house, entertained liberally, led the hunting, and farmed successfully.

Washington also entered politics and represented his county in the House of Burgesses. When he showed an interest in the growing dispute of the colonies with the British Crown, he was chosen to represent Virginia in the first (1774) and second (1775) Continental Congresses, and took an active part in them. He was neither orator nor writer, but in plain common sense and in the management of affairs he excelled. As the one American soldier of national reputation, he was the inevitable choice as Commander-in-Chief of the colonial army (1775).

Washington set about an ambitious programme of recruitment and training, and under his leadership a half-armed body of men managed to coop up in Boston a well-equipped British army and to force their evacuation (1776); the retreat from Concord and the slaughter at Bunker Hill were largely due to the incompetence of the English commander. The only able English commander was **Charles Cornwallis**, and he was hampered by the stupidity of his superior. Following reverses in the New York area, Washington made a remarkable retreat through New Jersey, inflicting notable defeats on the enemy at Trenton and Princeton (1777). He suffered reverses at Brandywine and Germantown but held his army together through the winter of 1777–78 at Valley Forge, near Philadelphia.

France entered the war on the American side in 1778, and with the assistance of the Comte de **Rochambeau**, Washington forced the defeat and surrender of Cornwallis at Yorktown in 1781, which virtually ended the War of Independence. Washington resigned his commission in 1783 and retired to Mount Vernon, where he sought to secure a strong government by constitutional means. In 1787 he presided over the convention of delegates from 12 states at Philadelphia which formulated the constitution; and the government under this constitution began in 1789 with Washington as first chief-magistrate or president. The new administration was a strong consolidated government; parties were formed, led by Washington's two most trusted advisers, **Thomas Jefferson** and **Alexander Hamilton**, whom he appointed as his Secretary of State and Treasury Secretary respectively.

In 1793 Washington was elected to a second term, but by this time considerable differences had developed between Jefferson's Democratic Republicans and Hamilton's Federalists. Washington tended to favour the Federalists; in the face of fierce personal attacks from the Republicans he retired from the presidency in 1797. He died at Mount Vernon on 14 December 1799. The federal capital of the USA, in the planning of which he was associated, was named after him.

📖 J Alden, *George Washington: A Biography* (1984); M L Weems, *The Life and Memorable Actions of George Washington* (10th edn, 1962).

'The time is now near at hand which must probably determine whether Americans are to be freemen or slaves. … The fate of unborn millions will now depend, under God, on the courage and conduct of this army. Our cruel and unrelenting enemy leaves us only the choice of brave resistance or abject submission. We have, therefore, to resolve to conquer or die.' From Washington's general orders to his army, July 1776. Quoted in J C Fitzpatrick, *Writings of George Washington* (vol 5, 1932).

History Museum in London's South Kensington (1873–81). His use of terracotta and brick for scholastic institutions gave rise to the term 'redbrick' for new universities and colleges.

Waterhouse, John William 1847–1917
English painter

He was born in Rome and painted classical stories, under the influence of the Pre-Raphaelites. Among his pictures are *Ulysses and the Sirens* (1892), *The Lady of Shalott* (1888, Tate Gallery, London), and *Hylas and the Nymphs* (1897, Royal Academy, London).

Waterhouse, Keith Spencer 1929–
English novelist, dramatist, humorist and journalist

Born in Leeds, he first came to critical and popular attention with *Billy Liar* (1959), a whimsical novel about a working-class dreamer. The following year it became the basis of a successful play, on which he collaborated with **Willis Hall**. Waterhouse has since written various humorous novels, the best of which are *Jubb* (1963), *Office Life* (1978) and *Maggie Muggins, or Spring in Earl's Court* (1981). His plays, with Hall, include *Saturday, Sunday, Monday* (1973) and *Filumena* (1977), both adapted from **Eduardo de Filippo**, and, by himself, *Jeffrey Bernard Is Unwell* (1989). Recent works include *Unsweet Charity* (1992), a novel, *City Lights* (1994) and *Streets Ahead* (1995).

Waters, Ethel, *née* Howard 1896–1977
US jazz singer and actress

Born in Chester, Pennsylvania, she made her first recordings in 1921, when she was backed by the Fletcher Henderson orchestra, and then later worked with Duke Ellington, Benny Goodman and others. From the late 1930s she turned to acting, notably in *Cabin in the Sky* (1943). Growing up in the North gave her a less secure blues feel than either Bessie Smith or Ma Rainey (Gertrude Rainey) and she was much influenced by white vaudevilleans. However, her vocal improvisations made a considerable impact on Ella Fitzgerald. Her autobiography, *His Eye is on the Sparrow* (1951), is a powerfully moving narrative documenting her religious faith.

Waters, Muddy, *real name* McKinley Morganfield
1915–83
US blues singer, composer and guitarist

Born in Rolling Fork, Mississippi. He learned to play the harmonica as a child, and the guitar in his teens. He was first recorded in a classic Delta blues style in 1941 by Alan Lomax, the folk music researcher for the American Library of Congress (see entry on John Avery Lomax), but moved to Chicago in 1943, and became the crucial figure in the development of the electric urban blues style. He recorded his first solo single 'I Can't Be Satisfied' in 1948, and gained his first national success with 'Rollin' Stone' (1950). In that same year he put together a band consisting of Little Walter, Otis Spann and Jimmy Rogers which was to have a profound influence not only on other blues musicians, but also on the white rhythm-and-blues artists of the mid-1960s. The band's best-known singles include 'I've Got My Mojo Working' (1957) and 'Hoochie Coochie Man' (1954). His earthy, rough-hewn vocals and electrifying guitar work won him a large white audience from the late 1950s, but his 1960s and early 1970s recordings varied in quality. *Hard Again* (1977) and *I'm Ready* (1978) signalled a late resurgence in his music.

Waterston, John James 1811–83
Scottish natural philosopher and engineer

Born in Edinburgh, he studied at the University of Edinburgh. Following an engineering apprenticeship he practised as a surveyor in London (1832) and taught navigation and gunnery in Bombay from 1839, only returning to Scotland permanently in 1857. He wrote on astronomy, solar radiation, chemistry, the physiology of the central nervous system, sound and a novel kinetic theory of gases and liquids. His famous speculative memoir of 1845 postulated the basic kinetic theory of gases, but when submitted to the Royal Society it was dismissed by the referees. Although reproduced in 1892 by Lord Rayleigh, many of the key ideas had by then been published by Rudolf Clausius and James Clerk Maxwell.

Watkins, Carleton E 1829–1916
US photojournalist

He was born in Oneonta, New York, and moved to California during the Gold Rush. He learned photography in San Francisco, particularly the use of the wideview camera, and won recognition for his scenic views of such wilderness regions of North America as Yosemite (1861–67), which won him the gold medal at the Paris Exhibition of 1868, the Columbia River and Alaska. He re-photographed scenes after losing his negatives to creditors in the 1870s, but the majority were again lost in the San Francisco earthquake of 1906.

Watkins, Dudley D(exter) 1907–69
English strip cartoonist and illustrator

Born in Manchester, he was acclaimed as a schoolboy genius for his painting of the Nottingham Historical Pageant at the age of 10. He studied at Nottingham School of Art, and joined the window display department of Boots the Chemist, contributing his first cartoon to the staff magazine in 1923. Joining Dundee publisher D C

Thomson's art department, he created *Oor Wullie* and *The Broons* strips for the *Sunday Post* (1936), then *Desperate Dan* for the *Dandy* (1937), *Lord Snooty* for the *Beano* (1938), and many more. He created classic picture serials, such as *Treasure Island*, later reprinted as books (1948). Highly religious, he contributed strips to *Young Warrior* (1960) without charge. He was the first D C Thomson artist allowed to sign his name.

Watkins, Margaret, *originally* Meta Gladys Watkins 1884–1969
Canadian photographer

Born in Hamilton, Ontario, to Scottish parents, she studied at the Clarence White School of Photography in New York City, where she taught from 1917. She was an influential colleague and teacher of photographers such as Laura Gilpin, Paul Outerbridge and Doris Ulmann. In about 1916 she opened her own photographic studio in New York, specializing in advertising work. Her still lifes include *Kitchen Sink* and *Domestic Symphony* (both 1919) and were forerunners of the formalist images of the *Neue Sachlichkeit* (new objectivity). Her work was exhibited widely in the USA. In 1926 she was resident vice-president of the Pictorial Photographers of America. Returning to Europe in 1928, she visited her mother's three elderly sisters in Glasgow and remained there to look after them. She lived a reclusive life until her death, but her work has since been re-exhibited and its importance recognized.

Watkins, Vernon Phillips 1906–67
Welsh poet

Born in Maesteg, Glamorgan, he was educated at Magdalene College, Cambridge. For much of his life he lived at Pennard, Gower, and the shoreline there often provided illustrative material for his poetry. He published eight collections of verse during his lifetime, including *Ballad of Mari Lwyd* (1941), *Death Bell* (1954) and *Affinities* (1962). Regarded as one of the greatest Welsh poets in English, as well as one of the most unusual, he was long overshadowed by his friend Dylan Thomas. A posthumous volume, *Fidelities* (1968), was followed by *The Collected Poems* (1986). 📖 L Norris, *Vernon Watkins* (1970)

Watson, Doc (Arthel) 1923–
US country–folk singer and guitarist

Born in Deep Gap, North Carolina, he played pop and country in local clubs in the 1950s, before an invitation to play at Gerde's Folk City club in New York in 1960 brought him to a new audience in the folk movement of the time. His music was a potent compound of old time mountain music, country, folk, blues and bluegrass, and both his flat-picking and finger-picking guitar styles have been hugely influential. He worked with his son, Merle Watson, until the latter's tragic death in a tractor accident on their farm in 1985. He went into semi-retirement, but has continued both to perform and record, including a late excursion into rockabilly in *Docabilly* (1995).

Watson, James Dewey 1928–
US biologist and Nobel Prize winner

Born in Chicago, he studied zoology at the University of Chicago, and as a postgraduate at Indiana University he studied under Hermann Müller and Salvador Luria. He spent the period 1951–53 at the Cavendish Laboratory in Cambridge, UK, and from 1955 taught at Harvard, where he became Professor of Biology in 1961. He was director of the Cold Spring Harbor Laboratory in New York (1968–94), then president (1994–), and he has also served as director of the National Center for Human Genome Research (1989–92). While in Cambridge in 1951, Watson worked with Francis Crick on the structure of DNA, the biological molecule contained in cells which carries the genetic information. They published their model of a two-stranded helical molecule in 1953, showing each strand consists of a series of the nucleotide bases wound around a common centre, with the strands linked together by hydrogen bonds. For this work, Watson was awarded the 1962 Nobel Prize for physiology or medicine jointly with Crick and **Maurice Wilkins**. Since the mid-1980s, he has been an active supporter of the Human Genome Initiative, which aims to locate all genes in the human body and determine their DNA sequences. He wrote a personal account of the discovery of the DNA structure in *The Double Helix* (1968), and the textbooks *The Molecular Biology of the Gene* (1965) and *Recombinant DNA* (1984). ▤David E Newton, *James Watson and Francis Crick: Discovery of the Double Helix and Beyond* (1992)

Watson, John Broadus 1878–1958
US psychologist
He was born in Greenville, South Carolina. As professor at Johns Hopkins University (1908–20) he was a leading exponent of Behaviourism, holding that a scientific psychology could only study what was directly observable, ie behaviour. His most important work is *Behavior—An Introduction to Comparative Psychology* (1914). He later resigned from Johns Hopkins and became an advertising executive.

Watson, Richard 1737–1816
English theologian and scientist
Born in Heversham, Cumbria, he was educated at Trinity College, Cambridge, where he later became Professor of Chemistry (1764) and Regius Professor of Divinity (1771). He became Bishop of Llandaff in 1782. He published a famous *Apology for Christianity* (1796) in reply to **Tom Paine**. He spent much time on agriculture at his estate on Windermere, and introduced the larch to that district.

Watson, Thomas c.1557–1592
English lyric poet
Born in London, he was educated at Oxford, and studied law in London. Coming to **Christopher Marlowe**'s help in a street fight, he killed a man in 1589. He is best known for English sonnets such as *Hecatompathia or Passionate Century of Love* (1582) and *The Tears of Fancie* (1593), and his sonnets were probably studied by **Shakespeare**. He also translated classics into Latin and English, including **Sophocles, Torquato Tasso**, and Italian madrigals.

Watson, Thomas Edward 1856–1922
US Populist politician and racist demagogue
Born in Columbia County, Georgia, he was admitted to the Bar and became a member of the Georgia House of Representatives (1882–83). He left the Democrats, entrenched in Georgia as the party of rising capitalism, and won election as US congressman for the Populists (1891–93). As Congressman he won the first appropriation for free rural delivery of mails. He was Populist candidate for President in 1904, but the party had been shattered by **William Jennings Bryan**'s defeats and Watson, formerly an advocate of working co-operation with black voters, became a ferocious supporter of segregation, increasingly employing the rhetoric of racial hatred. He also became obsessively anti-Catholic and anti-Semitic. He ultimately won election to the US Senate (1921) and died in office, having violently opposed US involvement in World War I, for which his magazines were banned from the US mail.

Watson, Thomas John 1914–
US businessman and diplomat
Born in Dayton, Ohio, the son of the head of IBM, he joined the company in 1937, served with the US air force from 1940 to 1945 as a lieutenant-colonel, and rejoined IBM in 1946. He succeeded his father as president in 1952, became chairman in 1961 and chief executive officer from 1972 to 1979. He served as US ambassador to the USSR from 1979 to 1981.

Watson, Tom (Thomas Sturges) 1949–
US golfer
He was born in Kansas City, Missouri. Through the mid-1970s and early 1980s Watson, with **Jack Nicklaus**, dominated world golf, winning the US Open, two Masters tournaments and five British Opens. He was the US Player of the Year on six occasions and in 1993 captained the US Ryder Cup team to victory.

Watson, Sir William 1715–87
English scientist
Born in London, he became an apothecary and was one of the earliest experimenters on electricity. He improved the Leyden jar (the first form of capacitor or condenser) and was the first to investigate the passage of electricity through a rarefied gas. In botany, he did much to introduce the Linnaean system to Great Britain. He was elected Fellow of the Royal Society (1841), and awarded the Royal Society's Copley Medal (1745). In 1757 he became a licentiate of the Royal College of Physicians, and was chiefly interested in epidemic children's diseases. He was knighted in 1786.

Watson, Sir (John) William 1858–1935
English poet
He was born in Burley-in-Wharfedale, Yorkshire, and first attracted notice with both *Wordsworth's Grave* (1890), and *Lachrymae musarum* (1892), which contained a eulogy on **Tennyson**, his primary influence. He was a prolific Victorian writer, and his works include *The Father of the Forest* (1895), *For England* (1903), *The Superhuman Antagonists* (1919) and *Poems, Brief and New* (1925). His poem 'April, April, Laugh thy Girlish Laughter' appears in several anthologies, but his other work is largely forgotten.

Watson-Watt, Sir Robert Alexander 1892–1973
Scottish physicist
Born in Brechin, Angus, he was educated at Dundee University and the University of St Andrews, and worked in the meteorological office, the Department of Scientific and Industrial Research and the National Physical Laboratory before becoming scientific adviser to the Air Ministry in 1940. By 1935 he had perfected a shortwave radio wave system called 'RAdio Detection And Ranging', or radar, that was able to locate aeroplanes. He was elected FRS in 1941, and knighted for his role in the development and introduction of radar in 1942. In 1958 he published *Three Steps to Victory*. ▤ John Rowland, *The Radar Man: The Story of Sir Robert Watson-Watt* (1963)

Watt, James 1736–1819
Scottish engineer and inventor
He was born in Greenock, Strathclyde, and was educated by his mother, then at the local grammar school. He was mathematical instrument maker to the University of Glasgow from 1757 to 1763. He was also employed on surveys for the Forth and Clyde Canal (1767), and worked on the improvement of harbours and the deepening of the Forth and Clyde Rivers. In 1763–64 a model of **Thomas Newcomen**'s steam engine was sent to his workshop for repair. He easily put it into order, and seeing the defects in the working of the machine, hit upon the expedient of the separate condenser. This was probably the greatest single improvement ever made to the reciprocating steam engine, enabling its efficiency to be increased to about three times that of the old atmospheric engines. He entered into a partnership with **Matthew Boulton** in 1774, and (under a patent of 1769) the manufacture of the new engine was commenced at the Soho Engineering Works, near Birmingham. Watt's soon superseded Newcomen's machine as a pumping engine, and between 1781 and 1785 he obtained patents for the sun-and-planet motion, the expansion principle, the double-

acting engine, the parallel motion, a smokeless furnace, and the governor. He described a steam locomotive in one of his patents (1784), but discouraged **William Murdock** from further experiments with steam locomotion. In 1785 he was elected FRS. The modern scientific unit of power, the watt, is named after him, and horsepower, the original unit of power, was first experimentally determined and used by him in 1783. His son, James (1769–1848), a marine engineer, fitted the engine to the first English steamer to leave port (1817), the *Caledonia*. 📖 H W Dickinson, *James Watt, Craftsman and Engineer* (1936)

Watteau, (Jean) Antoine 1684–1721
French painter

Born in Valenciennes, he ran away to Paris in 1702 and worked as a scene painter at the Opera and as a copyist. After 1712 his early canvases were mostly military scenes, but it was the mythological *Embarquement pour l'îsle de Cythère* which won him membership of the Academy (1717). While staying at the castle of Montmorency he painted his *Fêtes galantes*, quasi-pastoral idylls in court dress which became fashionable in high society. A lifelong sufferer from tuberculosis, he visited London in 1720 to consult the celebrated Dr Richard Mead (1673–1754), but his health was rapidly deteriorating. On his return he painted his last great work, depicting the interior of the shop of his art-dealer friend Gersaint, drawn from nature and intended as a signboard, but in fact the most classical and most perfectly composed of his paintings. Essentially aristocratic in conception, Watteau's paintings fell into disfavour at the Revolution, and it was not until the end of the 19th century that they regained popularity. He is now regarded as a forerunner of the Impressionists in his handling of colour and study of nature. He influenced and was imitated by many later artists, most notably **Jean Honoré Fragonard** and **François Boucher**.

Watts, George Frederick 1817–1904
English painter

Born in London, he formed his style after the Venetian masters and first attracted notice by his cartoon of *Caractacus* (1843) in the competition for murals for the new Houses of Parliament. He became known for his penetrating portraits of notabilities, 150 of which he presented to the National Portrait Gallery in 1904. These represent his best work, but in his lifetime his moral and allegorical pieces enjoyed enormous popularity, and monochrome reproductions of *Paolo and Francesca*, *Sir Galahad*, *Love Triumphant*, *Hope* and so on adorned the walls of countless late Victorian middle-class homes. He also executed some sculpture, including *Physical Energy* (Kensington Gardens). In 1864 he married **Ellen Terry**, but parted from her within a year.

Watts, Isaac 1674–1748
English hymnwriter

Born in Southampton, he succeeded an Independent minister in Mark Lane, London, in 1702 and became eminent as a preacher. His hymns and psalms are contained in *Horae Lyricae* (1706), *Hymns and Spiritual Songs* (1707–09) and *Psalms of David Imitated* (1719), and include 'Jesus shall reign where'er the sun', 'When I survey the wondrous cross', and 'O God, our help in ages past'.

Watts-Dunton, (Walter) Theodore 1832–1914
English poet and critic

Born in St Ives, Cambridgeshire, he practised law for a time, but in London he became the centre of a remarkable literary and artistic company, and a friend of **Dante Gabriel Rossetti**, **William Morris**, **Algernon Charles Swinburne**, **Philip Marston** and afterwards **Tennyson**. He was a prolific early contributor to the *Athenaeum* literary review (1876–98) and others. *The Coming of Love* (1897) was

a selection of his poems, and in 1898 appeared his novel of gypsy life, *Aylwin*. *Old Familiar Faces* (1915) contains recollections from the *Athenaeum*. At his home in Putney he looked after Swinburne for the last 30 years of the poet's life.

Wauchope, Sir Arthur Grenfell 1874–1947
Scottish soldier and administrator

Born in Edinburgh, he was commissioned into the 2nd Black Watch in 1896. He served in the Boer War and was badly wounded at the Battle of Magersfontein. During World War I he served in France and Mesopotamia. In 1923 he was promoted major-general and commanded the garrison in Northern Ireland. He was a successful British High Commissioner in Palestine (1931–38), and managed to maintain a neutral course between opposing Jewish and Arab interests. His health suffered during the Arab Revolt of 1936, and he retired, apart from service in World War II as titular colonel of the Black Watch.

Waugh, Alec (Alexander Raban) 1898–1981
English novelist and travel writer

Born in London, the brother of **Evelyn Waugh**, he was educated at Sherborne, but was involved in a homosexual scandal there and left in 1915 to become a cadet in the Inns of Court Officers Training Corps at Sandhurst in Berkshire. He spent two years in training before being posted to a machine-gun unit in France, just in time for Passchendaele. In seven and a half weeks he wrote his first book, the autobiographical *Loom of Youth* (1917), in which he expressed the bitterness and love he felt for his school. It was an immediate success, but it was tainted with notoriety and has overshadowed worthy successors: *Wheels within Wheels* (1933), *Where the Clock Chimes Twice* (1952), and various travel books, the most popular being *Island in the Sun* (1956). He wrote several autobiographical volumes including *The Early Years of Alec Waugh* (1962), *My Brother Evelyn and Other Portraits* (1967) and *The Best Wine Last* (1978).

Waugh, Auberon Alexander 1939–
English journalist and novelist

He was born in Pixton Park, Dulverton, Somerset, the eldest son of **Evelyn Waugh**. He did his National Service in the Royal Horse Guards and was sent to Cyprus where he accidentally shot himself, losing a lung, his spleen, several ribs and a finger; he denied speculation that he had been fired on by his own troops. Completing his education at Oxford, he got a job on the *Daily Telegraph* in 1960, the same year he published his first novel, *The Foxglove Saga*. Four more novels followed. He has contributed to most national papers, such as the *Daily Telegraph* (1990–) and the *Sunday Telegraph* (1996–), and to the *New Statesman*, the *Spectator* and *Private Eye* (1970–86), and since 1986 has been editor of the *Literary Review*. A recent publication is *Way of the World* (1994). 📖 *Will This Do?* (1991)

Waugh, Evelyn Arthur St John 1903–66
English writer

He was born in Hampstead, London, the younger brother of **Alec Waugh**. He was educated at Lancing and Hertford College, Oxford, where he read modern history but with little application. He became a schoolmaster (1925–27), and attempted suicide. The experience gave him the material for *Decline and Fall* (1928), his first and immoderately successful novel which had been preceded only by *PRB; an essay on the Pre-Raphaelite Brotherhood* (privately printed in 1926) and a biography of **Dante Gabriel Rossetti** published earlier in 1928. The novel made him the talk of the town for, its comic genius apart, it was obviously a roman à clef. After a brief and unsuccessful marriage, he spent a few years travelling. He contributed variously to newspapers, particularly the *Daily Mail*, published the social satire *Vile Bodies* (1930) and two travel books, *Labels* (1930) and *Remote People* (1931). In 1930 he became a Roman Catholic, an event which he regarded as the most important in his life. Between 1932 and 1937 he visited British Guiana (Guyana), Brazil, Morocco and Abyssinia (Ethiopia), and he cruised in the Mediterranean. After he married Laura Herbert (1937) he settled at Piers Court, Stinchcombe, Gloucestershire, and published *Scoop* (1938), a newspaper farce in which the wrong correspondent is sent to cover the civil war in the African Republic of Ishmaelia. Further travels to Hungary and Mexico followed before the outbreak of World War II, which Waugh spent in a variety of postings as a junior officer. During the war he published four books, including *Put Out More Flags* (1942) and *Brideshead Revisited* (1945), a nostalgic, highly-wrought evocation of halcyon days at Oxford. This period also inspired 'The Sword of Honour' trilogy—*Men at Arms* (1952), *Officers and Gentlemen* (1955) and *Unconditional Surrender* (1961)—in which he described, in parallel to his own experience, the significance to men and women of the ordeal of crisis of civilization which received its climax in World War II. Other books published during this period include *The Loved One* (1947), *Helena* (1950) and *The Ordeal of Gilbert Pinfold* (1957), a painfully personal but fictionalized account of a middle-aged writer's mental collapse. In 1964 he published *A Little Learning*, intended as the first of several volumes of an autobiography he never completed. He was revered as a wit and a stylist and one of the 20th century's greatest comic novelists. *The Diaries of Evelyn Waugh* were published in 1976; his *Letters*, edited by Mark Amory, in 1980. He was the father of **Auberon Waugh**. ▢ Malcolm Bradbury, *Evelyn Waugh* (1964)

Wavell, Archibald Percival Wavell, 1st Earl
1883–1950
English soldier
Born in Winchester, and trained at Sandhurst, he served in the Second Boer War (1899–1902) and on the Indian frontier (1908). He was wounded in 1916 and lost the sight of one eye. He became Chief of Staff to Viscount **Allenby** in Palestine, and from 1938 to 1941 he was Commander-in-Chief of British forces in the Middle East. He conquered Abyssinia, but was defeated by **Rommel** in North Africa. He became Commander-in-Chief in 1941 and Supreme Commander of Allied forces in Southwest Pacific (1942). From 1943 to 1947, during the difficult years which preceded the transfer of power, he was Viceroy in India. He became field marshal and viscount (1943), earl (1947), Constable of the Tower (1948) and Lord Lieutenant of London (1949). He published an anthology of poetry, *Other Men's Flowers* (1944), and wrote a book on *Generals and Generalship* (1941). ▢ John Connell, *Wavell: Soldier and Scholar* (1964)

Waverley, John Anderson, 1st Viscount
1882–1958
Scottish politician
Born in Eskbank, Midlothian, and educated at Edinburgh and Leipzig, he entered the colonial office in 1905. He became chairman of the Board of Inland Revenue (1919–22), and Permanent Under-Secretary at the Home Office from 1922 until his appointment as Governor of Bengal in 1932. He was Home Secretary and Minister of Home Security from 1939 to 1940 (the Anderson air-raid shelter being named after him), became Lord President of the Council in 1940, and Chancellor of the Exchequer in 1943, when he introduced the pay-as-you-earn system of income-tax collection devised by his predecessor Sir **Kingsley Wood**.

Wayne, Anthony, *known as* Mad Anthony 1745–96
American Revolutionary soldier

He was born in Easttown (Waynesboro), Pennsylvania. In Canada he covered the retreat of the provincial forces at Three Rivers. He commanded at Ticonderoga until 1777, when he joined **Washington** in New Jersey. He fought bravely at Brandywine in 1777, led the attack at Germantown, captured supplies for the army at Valley Forge, carried Stony Point, and saved the Marquis de **Lafayette** in Virginia (1781). In 1793 he led an expedition against the Native Americans.

Wayne, John, *originally* Marion Michael Morrison
1907–79
US film actor
Born in Winterset, Iowa, he had a succession of small parts in low-budget films and serials which eventually led to stardom as the Ringo Kid in *Stagecoach* (1939). Known as 'Duke', he went on to make over 80 films in the next 40 years, typically starring in westerns as a tough but warm-hearted gunfighter or lawman, or in war films. He gave notable performances in, among others, *Red River* (1948), *The Searchers* (1956), *True Grit* (1969, Academy Award) and *The Shootist* (1976), his final film and one of his best. ▢ Maurice Zolotow, *Shooting Star: A Biography of John Wayne* (1974)

Waynflete, William of See **William of Waynflete**

Weatherall, Sir David John 1933–
English molecular geneticist
Educated at the universities of Liverpool and Oxford, he became a researcher at the Johns Hopkins Medical School, Baltimore (1960–62, 1963–65) and was later appointed Professor of Haematology (1971–74). He later became Nuffield Professor of Clinical Medicine at the University of Oxford (1974–92), where he has been Regius Professor of Medicine since 1992. Weatherall has worked for many years on the thalassaemias, a group of inherited anaemias which exhibit perturbation of the gene regulation. The clinical outcome is greatly influenced by the detailed knowledge of the causative lesion, by early detection of the problem and by the ability to predict the outcome of a pregnancy. He was elected Fellow of the Royal Society in 1977, knighted in 1987, and received the Royal Medal (1989) and the Buchanan Medal (1994) of the Royal Society.

Weatherill, (Bruce) Bernard Weatherill, Baron 1920–
British politician
After service in World War II, he became managing director of his family's chain of menswear shops, and entered parliament as a Conservative MP in 1964. He served as an Opposition Whip, then as a Treasury Minister, before being appointed deputy Speaker (1979), becoming Speaker (1983–92) on the retirement of George Thomas, a position he relinquished to **Betty Boothroyd**. He was made a life peer in 1992.

Weaver, Sigourney (Susan Alexandra) 1949–
US film and stage actress
Born in New York City, the daughter of an actress and the former president of NBC (National Broadcasting Company), she read English at Stanford University and studied drama at Yale. Entering the acting profession in off-Broadway plays, she was an understudy to **Ingrid Bergman** in *The Constant Wife* (1974) then made her film debut with a tiny role in *Annie Hall* (1977). She achieved major success with her portrayal of Ripley in the *Alien* trilogy (1979, 1986 and 1992). She gave equally powerful performances in *Gorillas In The Mist* (1988) and *Death And The Maiden* (1994), and revealed a flair for comedy in *Ghostbusters* (1984) and *Working Girl* (1988). Her frequent

stage appearances include *Old Times* (1981), *Hurlyburly* (1984) and *The Merchant Of Venice* (1986). In 1997, she returned to the character of Ripley in *Alien Resurrection*.

Webb, Sir Aston 1849–1930
English architect
Born in London, he designed the eastern façade of Buckingham Palace, the Admiralty Arch, Imperial College of Science, and many other London buildings.

Webb, (Martha) Beatrice, *née* Potter 1858–1943
English social reformer, social historian and economist
She was born in Gloucester, and largely self-educated. Following a failed relationship with the Liberal politician Joseph Chamberlain, she undertook social work in London and wrote the book *The Co-operative Movement in Great Britain* (1891). She began to research labour unions and working-class economic conditions, which led to her meeting (1890) Sidney Webb, later Baron Passfield. They married in 1892, forming a partnership that was dedicated to Fabian Socialist values and to a radical approach to social reform. Together they established the London School of Economics and Political Science (1895) and became highly influential in society. Their joint publications include *Decay of Capitalist Civilisation* (1923) and *Soviet Communism: A New Civilization?* (1935), written after a visit to the USSR, and she also wrote *Factory Acts* (1901).

Webb, Harri 1920–
Welsh poet
Born in Swansea, he was educated at Magdalen College, Oxford. He has published two collections of verse, *The Green Desert* (1969) and *A Crown for Branwen* (1974), and two collections of Welsh songs and ballads, *Rampage and Revel* (1967) and *Poems and Points* (1983), and has written numerous scripts for television. His work is ingrained with a strong nationalism and a biting wit. A prolific journalist, public speaker and pamphleteer, he has been active since 1959 on behalf of Plaid Cymru, the Welsh Nationalist party, mainly in the industrial valleys of south-east Wales.

Webb, Mary Gladys, *née* Meredith 1881–1927
English writer
She was born in Keighton, near the Wrekin, and after her marriage (1912), lived mostly in Shropshire, market-gardening and novel-writing. *Precious Bane* (1924) won her belated fame as a novelist of Shropshire country life. Her other works include the novels *The Golden Arrow* (1916), *Gone to Earth* (1917, filmed by Michael Powell and Emeric Pressburger in 1950), *The House in Dormer Forest* (1920), *Seven for a Secret* (1922) and the unfinished *Armour Wherein He Trusted* (1929), the nature essays in *The Spring of Joy* (1917), and poems. ⬚ G M Coles, *The Flower of Light* (1978)

Webb, Matthew 1848–83
English swimmer
Born in Dawley, Shropshire, he was the first man to swim the English Channel. He trained as a seaman and became a master mariner, before becoming a professional swimmer in 1875. In August, 1875, he swam from Dover to Calais in 21¾ hours. He was drowned attempting to swim the Niagara rapids.

Webb, Philip 1831–1915
English architect and designer
He was born in Oxford, and after his training he joined the practice of George Edmund Street (1852) where he met William Morris, who joined Street briefly in 1856. Thus began a long association, Webb becoming a central figure in the Arts and Crafts Movement and its offshoots. He designed furniture, metalwork and stained glass for Morris's firm, as well as animals and birds for textiles, at which Morris himself was not proficient. In architectural practice on his own from 1858, he designed several important houses such as the Red House, Bexley, for William and Jane Morris (1859), Clouds in Wiltshire (1881–86) and Standen, East Grinstead (1891).

Webb, Sidney James, Baron Passfield
1859–1947
English social reformer, social historian and economist
He was born in London, the son of an accountant, and in 1885 graduated LLB at London University. He was largely instrumental in establishing the London School of Economics and Political Science (1895), where he was a Professor of Public Administration (1912–27). An active member of the Labour Party, he entered parliament in 1922 and held several administerial posts between 1924–31. He was also a founder of the Fabian Society (1884). He married Beatrice Potter (see Beatrice Webb) in 1892, and they worked together for social reform. ⬚ M A Hamilton, *Sidney and Beatrice Webb* (1933)

Webber, Andrew Lloyd See Lloyd-Webber, Andrew Lloyd Webber, Baron

Weber, Carl Maria Friedrich von 1786–1826
German composer and pianist
Born near Lübeck, he began to compose early, encouraged by his family. His second opera, *Das Waldmädchen* (1800), was produced at Freiberg before he was 14, and was afterwards remodelled as *Silvana*. He became conductor of the opera at Breslau (Wrocław, Poland) in 1804, but ran into debt, was charged with embezzlement, and ordered to leave the country in 1910. In 1813 he settled in Prague as opera kapellmeister, and was invited by the King of Saxony to direct the German opera at Dresden (c.1816). As founder of German romantic opera, notably *Der Freischütz* (1821, 'The Freeshooter') and *Euryanthe* (1823) and *Oberon* (1826), he was the forerunner of Richard Wagner. He also wrote several orchestral works, piano, chamber, and church music, and many songs.

Weber, Ernst Heinrich 1795–1878
German physiologist
He was born in Wittenberg, the brother of Wilhelm Weber, and studied at the University of Wittenberg and later at Leipzig University. He was appointed to the chair of human anatomy (1818), and then the chair of physiology (1840). He undertook extensive comparative embryological and palaeontological studies, especially on the middle ear of mammals. He also demonstrated that the digestive juices are the specific products of glands, thereby opening up major new fields of physiological and chemical research. In the study of sensory functions, especially skin sensitivity, he probed what was later to be called the sensory 'threshold'. He devised a method of determining and quantifying the sensitivity of the skin, enunciated in 1834, and gave his name to the Weber–Fechner law of the increase of stimuli.

Weber, Max 1864–1920
German sociologist
Born in Erfurt, he was educated at the universities of Heidelberg, Berlin and Göttingen and taught law at Berlin from 1892, political economy at Freiburg from 1894, and economics at Heidelberg from 1897. He accepted a chair of sociology in Vienna in 1918, and in 1919 he took over the chair of sociology at Munich. Regarded as one of the founders of sociology, Weber is best known for his work *Die protestantische Ethik und der Geist des Kapitalismus* (1904, Eng trans *The Protestant Ethic and the Spirit of Capitalism*, 1930). ⬚ Arthur Mitzman, *The Iron Cage* (1970)

Weber, Max 1881–1961
US painter

Born in Bailystok, Russia, he emigrated to the USA with his family in 1891 and studied art in New York (1898–1900), then under **Henri Matisse** in Paris, and became one of the pioneer Abstractionist painters in New York. He later abandoned this extreme form for a distorted naturalism. His works include *Chinese Restaurant* (1915), *The Two Musicians* (1917), *Tranquillity* (1928), *Latest News* (c.1940) and *Three Literary Gentlemen* (1945). His writings include *Cubist Poems* (1914), *Essays on Art* (1916) and *Primitives* (1926).

Weber, Wilhelm Eduard 1804–91
German scientist

Born in Wittenberg, he studied physics at Hake University, then at Göttingen, where he became Professor of Physics (1831–37). He then became professor at Leipzig (from 1843), and worked with **Carl Friedrich Gauss** in his researches on electricity and magnetism. He was the inventor of the electrodynamometer, the first to apply the mirror and scale method of reading deflections, and the author, with his brother **Ernst Weber**, of a notable treatise on waves.

Webern, Anton Friedrich Wilhelm von 1883–1945
Austrian composer

Born in Vienna, he was one of **Arnold Schoenberg**'s first musical disciples and made wide use of twelve-note technique, which led to hostile demonstrations when his works were first performed. They include a symphony, three cantatas, *Four Pieces for Violin and Pianoforte* (1910), *Five Pieces for Orchestra* (1911–13), a concerto for nine instruments and songs, including several settings of **Stefan George**'s poems (1908–1909). His work has had great influence on many later composers. The Nazis banned his music, so he worked as a proofreader during World War II, then was accidentally shot dead by a US soldier near Salzburg.

Webster, Ben (jamin Francis) 1909–73
US jazz saxophonist

Born in Kansas City, Missouri, he began his professional career as a pianist, before turning to saxophone in the early 1930s. He quickly established himself as a leading instrumentalist of the swing era, and worked in many of the leading bands of the period, including those of Benny Moten and Andy Kirk in Kansas City, and **Fletcher Henderson** in New York. His **Coleman Hawkins**-influenced style blossomed in the music of **Duke Ellington**, notably in his second tenure with the band (1940–43). He became a soloist much in demand after leaving the band, and a mainstay of the famous Jazz At The Philharmonic touring packages. He settled in Copenhagen in 1964, and toured frequently in Europe.

Webster, Daniel 1782–1852
US lawyer and politician

Born in Salisbury, New Hampshire, he was called to the Bar in 1805 and served in the US House of Representatives (1813–17). Settling in Boston as an advocate in 1816, he distinguished himself in the Dartmouth College case, and became famous as an orator by his speech on the bicentenary of the landing of the Pilgrim Fathers. He returned to Congress in 1823 as a Massachusetts Representative and in 1827 was trasferred to the Senate. Having previously favoured free trade, he defended the new protective tariff in 1828. His career was marked by a reverence for established institutions and for the principle of nationality. When the Whig Party triumphed in 1840, he was called into Benjamin Harrison's Cabinet as Secretary of State (1841–43). Under President **John Tyler** he negotiated the Webster–Ashburton Treaty (1842) with Great Britain, but resigned in 1843. In 1844 he refused his party's nomination for President and supported **Henry**

Clay. He opposed the Mexican War. In 1850 he voiced his abhorrence of slavery, and unwilling to break up the Union to abolish it, supported compromise measures. Under President **Millard Fillmore**, he was recalled as Secretary of State (1850–52) to settle differences with England. One of the greatest US orators, his speeches were published in 1851.

Webster, John c.1580–c.1625
English dramatist

He is supposed to have been at one time clerk of St Andrews, Holborn, London. In *Lady Jane* and *The Two Harpies* (both lost) he was the collaborator of **Thomas Dekker, Michael Drayton, Henry Chettle** and others, and in 1604 he made some additions to *The Malcontent* of **John Marston**. His other collaborations with Dekker include the *Famous History of Sir Thomas Wyat*, *Westward Hoe* and *Northward Hoe* (all 1607). He is best known, however, for his two tragedies, *The White Devil* (1612) and *The Duchess of Malfi* (1623). *Appius and Virginia* (first published 1654) may be **Thomas Heywood**'s (or partly so). The tragedy, *A Late Murder of the Son upon the Mother* (1624), unpublished and lost, although licensed, was written by **John Ford** and Webster. He was not popular in his own day, and his stature was first recognized by **Charles Lamb**. 🕮 G M Lagarde, *John Webster* (1968)

Webster, Margaret 1905–72
English actress and director

Born in New York, where her actor parents were performing, she was a child actress from 1917, and made her adult debut in the chorus of a classical Greek drama in 1924. Having established her acting career in London, she went back to New York in 1936, where she began to concentrate more on directing. She had a major success directing **Paul Robeson** in *Othello* on Broadway (1943), and three years later co-founded the influential American Repertory Company with **Cheryl Crawford** and **Eva Le Gallienne**. She toured Shakespeare in the USA, and later became the first woman to direct an opera at the Metropolitan Opera House in New York.

Webster, Noah 1758–1843
US lexicographer

Born in West Hartford, Connecticut, he graduated from Yale and, after a spell as a teacher, was admitted to the Bar in 1781. He soon, however, resumed teaching, and published the first part of *A Grammatical Institute of the English Language* (1783; later known as 'Webster's Spelling Book'), which became very popular. He later published *A Compendious Dictionary of the English Language* (1806), an English grammar (1807) and the great *American Dictionary of the English Language* (2 vols, 1828), now *Webster's New International Dictionary of the English Language*. He was a fervent nationalist, and his efforts to standardize US spelling and grammar were informed by his vision of the USA as a nation distinct from Britain by historical destiny. 🕮 Harry R Warfel, *Noah Webster, Schoolmaster to America* (1936)

Webster, Tom (Gilbert Thomas) 1890–1962
English sports cartoonist and animator

Born in Bilston, West Midlands, he won a newspaper cartoon contest (1904), while working as a railway booking clerk. His first sports cartoon was published in *Athletic News*, prompting him to join the art staff of the *Birmingham Sports Argus* where he evolved a unique style of cartoons in a free-ranging strip format with commentary. In 1919 he joined the *Daily Mail*, drawing animated cartoons of several sporting characters, like *Tishy the Racehorse*, and painted the *Cavalcade of Sport* mural on the *Queen Mary* liner (1936). He is considered the greatest sports cartoonist of all time.

Weddell, James 1787–1834
English navigator

Born in Ostend, Belgium, on his principal voyage (1822–23) he penetrated to 74° 15' South by 34° 17' West in Antarctica. Weddell Sea and Weddell Quadrant there are named after him, as is a type of seal which he found.

Wedderburn, Joseph Henry MacLagan
1882–1948
US mathematician

Born in Forfar, Tayside, he graduated in mathematics at Edinburgh University in 1903, visited Leipzig, Berlin and Chicago, and returned to Edinburgh as a lecturer (1905–09). In 1909 he moved to Princeton, New Jersey, but he returned to fight in the British army during World War I. After the war he settled at Princeton University until his retirement in 1945. His work on algebra included two fundamental theorems known by his name, one on the classification of semi-simple algebras, and the other on finite division rings.

Weddington, Sarah Ragle 1946–
US lawyer

Born in Abilene, Texas, after entering the Bar there, in Washington, DC and in District Court, she practised law in Austin, Texas. In 1973 she made her name by successfully arguing the abortion/privacy case *Roe v Wade* before the US Supreme Court, a landmark case that resulted in the legalization of abortion. In 1992 she wrote *A Question of Choice*.

Wedekind, Frank 1864–1918
German dramatist

Born in Hanover, the son of a doctor and an actress, he grew up in Switzerland, but returned to Germany, where he was an actor and cabaret singer as well as a writer. He won fame with *Erdgeist* (1895, Eng trans *Earth Spirit*, 1914), *Frühlings Erwachen* (1891, first performed 1906, Eng trans *The Awakening of Spring*, 1909, better known as *Spring Awakening*, the title of the 1980 translation), *Die Büchse der Pandora* (1903, first performed 1918, Eng trans *Pandora's Box*, 1918), and other unconventional tragedies, which foreshadowed the emergence of the Expressionist movement both in their themes and performance styles. He was imprisoned in 1899 after publishing satirical poems in *Simplicissimus* in Munich. His work is highly individual, but also seems a forerunner of the Theatre of the Absurd. 🕮 S Gittelman, *Frank Wedekind* (1969)

Wedgwood, Josiah 1730–95
English potter

Born in Burslem, Staffordshire, he worked in the family pottery business, became a partner in a Staffordshire firm in 1754, and patented a cream-coloured ware (Queen's ware) in 1763. He emulated antique models, producing the unglazed blue Jasper ware with its raised designs in white and the black basalt ware, and, in 1769, he opened a new factory near Hanley, which he called 'Etruria'. His products, and their imitation, were named after him (Wedgwood ware). From 1775 he employed John Flaxman as designer. 🕮 Anthony Burton, *Josiah Wedgwood* (1976)

Wedgwood, Dame (Cicely) Veronica 1910–97
English historian

Born in Stocksfield, Northumberland, she studied at Lady Margaret Hall, Oxford, and specialized in 17th-century history. Her publications include biographies of *Strafford* (1935), *Oliver Cromwell* (1939), *William the Silent* (1944, James Tait Black Memorial Prize) and *Montrose* (1955), and *The Thirty Years' War* (1938), *The King's Peace* (1955), *The King's War* (1958) and *The Trial of Charles I* (1964). A more recent work is the collection of essays, *History and Hope* (1987). She was created DBE in 1968 and appointed to the Order of Merit in 1969.

Weeks, Willy (Wilford Frank) 1929–
US glaciologist and geophysicist

Born in Champaign, Illinois, he studied geology at the University of Illinois and geochemistry at the University of Chicago. His active service at the Cambridge Research Center, Boston, enabled him to study sea ice along the Labrador coast, marking the start of a long-term interest in this topic. He later transferred to the Cold Regions Research and Engineering Laboratory in Hanover, New Hampshire (1962–86), and since 1986 has been professor at the Geophysical Institute of the University of Alaska, Fairbanks, and chief scientist of the Alaska Synthetic Aperture Radar Facility. He has taken part in numerous field studies near both Poles, and made extensive studies of many aspects of ice and snow.

Weelkes, Thomas c.1575–1623
English madrigal composer

Born possibly in Elsted, Sussex, he was the organist at Winchester College (1597) and Chichester Cathedral (1602), also gaining his BMus at New College, Oxford that year. A friend of **Thomas Morley**, he contributed to the *Triumphes of Oriana* (1601).

Weems, Mason Locke, *known as* Parson Weems
1759–1825
US clergyman and author

Born in Anne Arundel County, Maryland, he became an itinerant evangelist and bookseller whose laudatory fictionalized biography of **George Washington** (first published in 1800) was popular for decades. The 1806 edition contains the apocryphal story of Washington's chopping down his father's cherry tree.

Weenix, Jan 1640–1719
Dutch painter

He was born in Amsterdam, the son and pupil of **Jan Baptist Weenix**. He was known for hunting scenes, animal subjects and still-life paintings featuring dead gamebirds, hares, and other creatures.

Weenix, Jan Baptist 1621–60
Dutch painter

He specialized in landscapes and seaport subjects and also large hunting still lifes.

Wegener, Alfred Lothar 1880–1930
German meteorologist and geophysicist

Born in Berlin and educated at the universities of Heidelberg, Innsbruck and Berlin, he first worked as an astronomer, then joined his brother Kurt at the Prussian Aeronautical Observatory in Tegel. In 1906 he joined a Danish expedition to north-east Greenland and learned the techniques of polar travel while making meteorological observations. On his return he became a lecturer in astronomy and meteorology at the University of Marburg. His second expedition to Greenland (1912) was almost wrecked by calving of the ice. After World War I he joined the German Marine Observatory in Hamburg and was also Professor of Meteorology in Graz, Austria (1924). *Die Entstehung der Kontinente und Ozeane* ('The Origin of Continents and Oceans') was first published in 1915, based on his observations that the continents may once have been joined into one supercontinent (Pangaea), which later broke up, the fragments drifting apart to form the continents as they are today. Wegner provided historical, geological, geomorphological, climatic and palaeontological evidence, but at that time no logical mechanism was known by which continents could drift and the hypothesis remained controversial until the 1960s, when the structure of oceans became understood. He died in Greenland during his fourth expedition there. 🕮 Christine Reinke-Kunze, *Alfred Wegener: Polarforscher und Entdecker der Kontinentaldrift* (1994)

Weidenreich, Franz 1873–1948
German anatomist and anthropologist

He was born in Edenkoben, and studied medicine at the universities of Munich, Kiel, Berlin and Strassburg. He taught anatomy at the universities of Strassburg (1903–18) and Heidelberg (1919–24), and was Professor of Anthropology at Frankfurt University from 1928 to 1933. In 1934 he left Nazi Germany and worked for seven years in China (1935–41) at the Peking Union Medical College, collaborating with Pierre Teilhard de Chardin on fossil remains of Peking Man. From 1941 to 1948 he worked at the American Museum of Natural History in New York City. His early work was concerned with blood, bone, teeth and connective tissue. Later studies of hominid fossil remains led him to espouse an orthogenetic view of human evolution, which he summarized in *Apes, Giants and Man* (1946).

Weidman, Charles 1901–75
US dancer, choreographer and teacher
Born in Lincoln, Nebraska, he was trained at the Denishawn school, later joining the company and remaining there for eight years. In partnership with Doris Humphrey, he formed a company in 1928, developing his work as a choreographer. After the company was disbanded in 1945, he founded a school and his own eponymous company. His choreography at this time included *A Home Divided* (1945), *The War Between Men and Women* (1954) and *Is Sex Necessary?* (1959). He moved to New York City Opera and continued teaching, his pupils including José Limón and Bob Fosse.

Weierstrass, Karl Theodor Wilhelm 1815–97
German mathematician
Born in Ostenfelde and educated at the universities of Bonn and Münster, he became professor at Berlin University in 1856. He became famous for his lectures, in which he gave a systematic account of analysis with previously unknown rigour, basing complex function theory on power series in contrast to the approach of Augustin-Louis Cauchy and Bernhard Riemann. He made important advances in the theory of elliptic and Abelian functions, constructed the first accepted example of a continuous but nowhere-differentiable function, and showed that every continuous function could be uniformly approximated by polynomials. Many of his most profound ideas grew out of his attempts to present a completely systematic, self-contained account of contemporary mathematics.

Weigel, Helene 1900–71
German actress-manager
Born in Austria, she began her acting career in Frankfurt but went to Berlin (1923) and met Bertolt Brecht, whom she married (1929). She accompanied him in his exile from Germany (1933–48). On their return to East Berlin (1948), she and Brecht co-founded and ran the Berliner Ensemble, regarded as one of the great world theatre companies. She became a leading exponent of Brecht's work, particularly in *The Mother (Die Mutter)* and *Mother Courage and her Children (Mutter Courage und ihre Kinder)*. She took control of the Berliner Ensemble after Brecht's death in 1956, and was instrumental in furthering his influence internationally.

Weil, André 1906–
French mathematician
Born in Paris, he studied at the University of Paris, and spent two years in India and some time in Strasbourg (1933–40), the USA (1941–42, 1947–58) and Brazil (1945–47), before settling at Princeton University in 1958. He has worked in number theory, algebraic geometry and topological group theory, was one of the founders of the Bourbaki group, and has written on the history of mathematics. Weil did much to extend the theory of algebraic geometry to varieties of any dimension, and to

define them over fields of arbitrary characteristics. The brother of Simone Weil, he has been one of the most brilliant mathematicians of the century.

Weil, Simone 1909–43
French philosopher and mystic
Born in Paris into a Jewish intellectual family, she had a brilliant academic career there, both at school and at university. She subsequently taught philosophy in schools (1931–38), worked for an anarchist trade union and in a factory, shared her wages with the unemployed, and lived in poverty. She fought against General Franco in the Spanish Civil War and then moved to England, where she died of anorexia. In her profound theological thinking she concluded that God, who certainly existed and exists, withdrew himself from the universe after creating it; man is obliged to withdraw himself likewise, from material considerations, and thus return to God. She is seen at her best in her notebooks, *Cahiers* (1951–56, Eng trans *Notebooks*, 1956), and in *Seventy Letters* (1965). Other influential books include *L'Attente de Dieu* (1949, Eng trans *Waiting for God*, 1959) and *L'Enracinement* (1949–50, Eng trans *The Need for Roots*, 1955). Weil's prose style is important because in it she increasingly and successfully strove to make herself clear to her reader, eschewing all pretension. She has been accused of over-paradoxicality, but she commands wide respect for her ruthless sincerity and lucidity. 📖 M M Davy, *Simone Weil* (1966); R Rees, *Simone Weil* (1965)

Weill, Kurt 1900–50
US composer
Born in Dessau, Germany, he studied under Engelbert Humperdinck and Ferruccio Busoni, and early works included chamber music, two symphonies (1921, 1933) and some stage works. He achieved fame with *Die Dreigroschenoper*, Bertolt Brecht's modernization of John Gay's *Beggar's Opera*, in 1928. Other works of that time included *Aufstieg und Fall der Stadt Mahagonny* (1927–29, 'Rise and Fall of the City of Mahogany'), *Die sieben Todsünden* (1933, 'Seven Deadly Sins'), both with Brecht, *Die Bürgschaft* (1932) and *Der Silbersee* (1933). A refugee from the Nazis, he settled in the USA in 1934, becoming a US citizen in 1943. In all his works Weill was influenced by jazz idioms, and his later songs, operas and musical comedies, many of which contain elements of social criticism, are amongst the most impressive written for the American stage. They include *Lady in the Dark* (1940), *Street Scene* (1946) and *Lost in the Stars* (1949).

Weimar, Marguerite Joséphine See George, Mlle

Weinberg, Robert Allan 1942–
US biochemist
Born in Pittsburgh, Pennsylvania, he studied at the Massachusetts Institute of Technology (MIT), held a series of fellowships in the USA and Europe, and from 1973 to 1982 worked in the Department of Biology and Center for Cancer Research at MIT, where he is currently Professor of Biochemistry. Since 1984 he has also been a member of the Whitehead Institute for Biomedical Research in Cambridge, Massachusetts. Weinberg studies the causes of cancer, and discovered the tumour suppressor gene Rb1, whose loss is associated with a rare childhood cancer in which tumours develop in the retina. Although the retina cancer is rare, there is increasing evidence that loss or inactivation of tumour suppressor genes also plays a part in many common cancers.

Weinberg, Steven 1933–
US physicist and Nobel Prize winner
Born in New York City, he was educated at Cornell and Princeton universities and held appointments at the universities of Columbia and Berkeley, the Massachusetts

Institute of Technology (MIT) and Harvard before becoming Josey Regental Professor of Science at the University of Texas in 1982. In 1967 he unified the electromagnetic and weak nuclear forces and predicted a new interaction due to 'neutral currents', whereby a chargeless particle is exchanged giving rise to a force between particles. This was duly observed in 1973, giving strong support to the theory (now called the Weinberg-Salam theory). As the work was independently developed by Weinberg and **Abdus Salam**, and subsequently extended by **Sheldon Glashow**, all three shared the 1979 Nobel Prize for physics. The combined theory has recently been precisely tested by experiments at the European nuclear research centre, CERN (Conseil Européen pour la Recherche Nucléaire), in Geneva. *The Quantum Theory of Fields* is a recent publication (vol 1, 1995; vol 2, 1996).

Weinberger, Caspar Willard 1917–
US politician

Born in San Francisco, after military service (1941–45) he trained and worked as a lawyer, before entering politics as a member of the California state legislature in 1952. He served as Finance Director (1968–69) in the California administration of **Ronald Reagan** and then moved to Washington, to work first as Director of the Office of Management and Budget (1972–73) and then as Secretary of Health, Education and Welfare (1973–75) in the **Nixon** and **Ford** administrations. Following a period in private industry, he was appointed Defense Secretary by President Ronald Reagan with the brief to oversee a major military build-up. This he successfully did, developing such high-profile projects as the strategic defence initiative, though there was Congressional criticism of the budgetary consequences and of Pentagon inefficiency. A 'hawk' with respect to East-West issues, Weinberger opposed the rapprochement with the USSR during the final years of the Reagan administration and resigned in 1987. He was later, in 1988, awarded an honorary knighthood (KBE) by the British monarch for 'service to British interests', most notably during the Falklands War (May–June 1982). He published *Fighting For Peace* in 1990, and has been chairman of *Forbes Magazine* since 1993.

Weinberger, Jaromir 1896–1967
Czech composer

Born in Prague, he studied under **Max Reger**. He was Professor of Composition at the Ithaca Conservatory, New York (1922–26) and finally settled in the USA in 1939. The composer of theatre music and orchestral works, he also wrote four operas, the most famous of which is *Švanda Dudák* (1927, 'Schwanda the Bagpiper').

Weingartner, (Paul) Felix 1863–1942
Austrian conductor and composer

Born in Zara, Dalmatia, of Austrian parents, he studied under **Franz Liszt**, succeeded **Mahler** as conductor of the Vienna Court Opera (1908), and later toured extensively in Great Britain and the USA. His works include operas, symphonies, and *Über das Dirigieren* (1895, 'On Conducting'). He also wrote the autobiographical work *Lebenserinnerungen* (1923, Eng trans *Buffets and Rewards*, 1937).

Weinstock (of Bowden), Arnold Weinstock, Baron 1924–
English industrial executive

Born in London, he gained a degree in statistics from the University of London. He worked at the Admiralty from 1939 to 1945, was engaged in finance and property development (1947–54) and then entered the radio and allied industries. He joined GEC in 1961, becoming managing director from 1963 to 1996, during which time he greatly developed the power and influence of the company through a series of take-overs.

Weir, Dame Gillian Constance 1941–
New Zealand organist and harpsichordist

Born in Martinborough, Wellington, she studied at the Royal College of Music, London, where she won an international organ competition in 1964. In 1965 she made her international debut as a concert organist at the Royal Festival Hall, London, and was concerto soloist at the opening night of the 1965 Proms. She has appeared with leading orchestras under **Claudio Abbado**, Raymond Leppard, Sir **Charles Mackerras** and others, and at all major music festivals and concert halls. She had her own BBC Television series, *The King of Instruments*, and is a regular writer, commentator and adjudicator, as well as a consultant on organ design.

Weir, Judith 1954–
Scottish lecturer and composer

Born in Cambridge of Scottish parents, she was taught by **John Tavener**, Robin Holloway and Olivier **Messiaen**. She was educated at King's College, Cambridge, and was Cramb Fellow at Glasgow University (1979–82) and Composer-in-Residence at the Royal Scottish Academy of Music (1988–91). She had notable success with her operas *The Black Spider* (1984), *A Night at the Chinese Opera* (Kent Opera, 1987) and *The Vanishing Bridegroom* (Scottish Opera, 1990). Other vocal works include *The Consolations of Scholarship* (1985), *Lovers, Learners and Libations* (1987), *Missa del Cid* (1988) and *HEAVEN ABLAZE* (1989), with two pianos and eight dancers. Her instrumental works include keyboard music, a string quartet (1990), and *Sederunt Principes* (1987, for chamber orchestra), amongst others.

Weir, Peter Lindsay 1944–
Australian film director

Born in Sydney and educated at Sydney University, he joined a local television station (1967) and began directing short films with *Count Vim's Last Exercise* (1967). Early films *Michael* (1970) and *Homesdale* (1971) both won the Australian Film Institute Grand Prix. His feature film debut, *The Cars That Ate Paris* (1974), and the dreamlike ghost story *Picnic at Hanging Rock* (1975), established his reputation. *The Last Wave* (1977) illustrated his fascination with the clash between ancient and modern cultures. Since then he has looked increasingly to international projects, bringing his imaginative flair, sensitivity, and an atmosphere of mystery to such films as *The Year of Living Dangerously* (1982), *Witness* (1985), *Dead Poets Society* (1989) and *Fearless* (1993).

Weismann, August Friedrich Leopold 1834–1914
German biologist

Born in Frankfurt am Main, he studied medicine at Göttingen University, became Professor of Zoology at the medical school of the University of Freiburg in 1867 and subsequently at a new Institute of Zoology there. He investigated the development of the two-winged flies, the Diptera, describing the neuro-humoral organ which bears his name, the Weismann ring. His early work on the development of the Hydrozoa led him to develop his germ-plasm theory, deducing that the information required for the development and final form of an organism must be contained within the germ cells, the egg and sperm, and be transmitted unchanged from generation to generation. He also noted that some form of reduction division must occur if the genetic material were not to double on each generation. His theories were developed in a series of essays, translated as *Essays upon Heredity and Kindred Biological Problems* (1889–92). His *Vorträge über Descendenztheorie* (1902, 'Lectures on Evolutionary Theory') was an important contribution to the subject. ▯E Gaupp, *August Weismann, sein Leben und sein Werk* (1917)

Weiss, Peter Ulrich 1916–82

German dramatist, painter, filmmaker and novelist

He was born in Berlin. Known initially as a graphic artist and filmmaker, he fled Nazi Germany and settled in Sweden in 1939. He became famous with his first play, *Die Verfolgung und Ermordung Jean Paul Marats, dargestellt durch die Schanspielgruppe des Hospizes zu Charenton unter Anleitung des Herrn de Sade* (1964, Eng trans *The Persecution and Assassination of Jean-Paul Marat as Performed by the Inmates of the Asylum of Charenton under the direction of the Marquis de Sade*, 1965), known more simply as *Marat/Sade*. His next play, *Die Ermittlung* (1965, Eng trans *The Investigation*, 1966), was a documentary based on transcripts of the Auschwitz trials. *Gesang vom Lusitanischen Popanz* (1967, Eng trans *The Song of the Lusitanian Bogey*, 1970) was a more cogent attack on the capitalist system. Among his other works are *Diskurs über Viet Nam* (1967, Eng trans *Vietnam Discourse*, 1970) and *Trotski im Exil* (1970, Eng trans *Trotsky in Exile*, 1971). He also wrote the autobiographical novels *Abschied von den Eltern* (1961, Eng trans *The Leavetaking*, 1962) and *Fluchtpunkt* (1962, Eng trans *Vanishing Point*, 1966).

Weiss, Robin (Robert Anthony) 1940–

English molecular biologist

He was educated at University College London, and became a lecturer in embryology there from 1963 to 1970. He joined the staff of the Imperial Cancer Research Fund Laboratories in London (1972–80), from 1980 to 1989 was director of the Institute of Cancer Research, and since 1990 has been head of the institute's Chester Beatty Laboratories. Weiss has made important studies of the link between retroviruses and cancer, and of the HIV virus, particularly the mechanisms by which the virus enters the mammalian cell.

Weissman, N Charles 1931–

Swiss molecular biologist

Born in Budapest, Hungary, he was educated at Zurich University, where he became assistant to Paul Karrer (1960–61). In 1963 he moved to the New York University School of Medicine, becoming assistant Professor of Biochemistry. He returned to Switzerland as Professor Extraordinarius in Molecular Biology at the University of Zurich (1967–70), where he became director of the Institute of Molecular Biology (1967–). He was also president of the Roche Research Foundation (1971–77). Weissman identified the DNA sequences which are recognized by RNA polymerase to give correct high-level expression of genes, and more recently has concentrated on the structure, function and cloning of the insulin genes, subsequently used in the treatment of diabetes.

Weissmuller, Johnny (Peter John), originally Jonas Weismuller 1903–84

US swimmer and actor

Born in Freidorf, Romania, he emigrated with his family to the USA in 1908. He was the first man to swim 100 metres in under one minute, and 440 yards (402m) in less than five minutes. Undefeated from 1921 to 1928, he won a total of five Olympic gold medals. After turning professional in 1932 he modelled swimwear. His physique, swimming prowess and popularity won him the film role of Tarzan in 19 films (1932–48). He is credited with inventing the King of the Jungle's celebrated yodelling signature tune. 📖 *Water, World and Weissmuller* (1967)

Weizmann, Chaim Azriel 1874–1952

Russian chemist and Zionist leader and first President of Israel

Born in Motol, of humble Jewish parentage, he began his scientific education at the gymnasium in Pinsk and later moved to Darmstadt (1893–94) and Berlin (1895–98). He obtained his doctorate from the University of Fribourg, Switzerland, and then moved to the University of Geneva, where he produced a number of commercially profitable patents on dyestuffs. By this time he was already an important figure in the Zionist movement. In 1904 he moved to Manchester to work with William Henry Perkin, Jnr (1860–1929), partly because he felt that Great Britain would do more to establish a Jewish national homeland in Palestine. He continued his work on dyestuffs and commenced a series of studies of fermentation. In 1912 he found a bacterium *Clostridium acetobutylium* which would convert carbohydrate into acetone. This process was of great importance in World War I as acetone is used in large quantities to plasticize the propellant cordite. Partly out of gratitude for the development of the acetone process, the government agreed to the Balfour Declaration promising British help in establishing a Jewish homeland. This conflicted with promises given by T E Lawrence to the Arabs. The Daniel Sieff (later Weizmann) Institute of Science in Rehovot was founded in 1934 and Weizmann continued his research there on industrial chemistry. In 1948 he became the first President of Israel and his scientific work ceased. 📖 Harold M Blumberg, *Weizmann, His Life and Times* (1975)

Weizsäcker, Carl Friedrich Weizsäcker, Freiherr von 1912–

German physicist

Born in Kiel and educated at the universities of Berlin, Göttingen and Leipzig, he was appointed associate professor at the University of Strasbourg before becoming Professor of Philosophy at Hamburg. Independently of Hans Bethe, he proposed that the source of energy in stars is chain nuclear fusion reactions (1938) and described the 'carbon cycle' sequence of reactions involved. In a development of Pierre Laplace's work, he also suggested a possible mechanism for the formation of the planets.

Weizsäcker, Richard, Freiherr von 1920–

West German politician

Born in Stuttgart, the son of a baron-diplomat who was tried at Nuremberg, he was educated at Berlin, Oxford, Grenoble and Göttingen universities, studying history and law. During World War II he served in the Wehrmacht and after the war he worked as a professional lawyer and was active in the German Protestant Church, becoming president of its congress (1964–70). A member of the conservative Christian Democratic Union (CDU) from 1954, he served as a deputy in the Bundestag from 1969, as CDU deputy chairman (1972–79) and, from 1981, as a successful Mayor of West Berlin, before being elected federal President in May 1984. A cultured, centrist Christian Democrat, he has been a popular president, making his mark with a well received speech to the Bundestag in May 1985, on the 40th anniversary of the end of World War II, in which he urged Germans never to forget the lessons of the Nazi era. He was re-elected in May 1989. Weizsacker finally stepped down as President in 1994, after the maximum 10 years, amidst enthusiastic tributes from all sides.

Welch, Raquel, originally Raquel Tejada 1940–

US actress

Born in Chicago, as a child she studied ballet and began entering beauty contests as a teenager. A model, waitress and television weather girl before making her film debut in *A House is Not a Home* (1964), she was launched as a curvaceous sex symbol after her scantily-clad appearance in *One Million Years B.C.* (1966). Rarely challenged by later roles, she did evince some comic ability in *The Three Musketeers* (1973), for which she received a Best Actress Golden Globe Award. A nightclub entertainer and best-selling author of health and beauty books and videos, she has also found some success on stage, notably in the

---

Wellington, Arthur Wellesley, 1st Duke of, *known as* the Iron Duke 1769–1852
Irish-born soldier and statesman

Arthur Wesley (Wellesley after 1798) was born in Dublin, the son of an Irish peer, the 1st Earl of Mornington. He studied at Chelsea, Eton and Brussels, and at a military school at Angers. In 1787 he was appointed to an ensign's commission in the 73rd Foot, and after service in other regiments was promoted to the rank of captain. He also served as aide-de-camp to two lord-lieutenants of Ireland and was member for Trim in the Irish Parliament (1790–95). He proposed marriage to Lady Katherine ('Kitty') Pakenham, but was refused because of his lack of means. His brother **Richard Wellesley** now bought him command of the 33rd Foot, and he campaigned with it in Holland in 1794.

In 1797 his regiment was sent to India, where his brother arrived as Governor-General within a year. He was dispatched to deal with **Tippoo Sahib** of Mysore and, as brigade commander under General George Harris (1746–1829), did admirable work throughout the Seringapatam expedition and as subsequent administrator of the conquered territory. His campaigns against Holkar and Scindia resulted in the capture of Poona (1803), the breaking of Maratha power at Ahmednagar and Assaye, and final victory at Argaum. On his return home he was knighted (1805), and in 1806 he succeeded in marrying Kitty Pakenham, who bore him two sons. He was elected MP for Rye (1806–09), and appointed Irish Secretary in 1807. He was released from his parliamentary duties to

accompany the Copenhagen expedition the same year, and defeated the Danes at Sjaelland.

In 1808 he was sent to help the Portuguese against the French in the Peninsular War; there he defeated **Andoche Junot** at Roliça, and won a victory at Vimeiro. He resumed his parliamentary post; but **John Moore**'s retreat on La Coruña sent him back, in 1809, to assume chief command in the Peninsula. Talavera (July 1809) was nearly a blunder, but it was quickly retrieved, and Wellesley was elevated to the peerage (as Viscount Wellington) after his victory. Salamanca (July 1812) was a decisive victory and, although there were minor setbacks, ultimately the French were driven out of Spain and brought to submission at Toulouse in 1814. Created Duke of Wellington and heaped with honours, after the first Treaty of Paris he was appointed ambassador to **Louis XVIII**, the newly restored King of France.

He remained in Paris until the Congress of Vienna, where for a brief period he served as Viscount **Castlereagh**'s replacement. On learning of **Napoleon I**'s escape from Elba, Wellington hastened from the Congress to take command of the scratch force (which he called 'an infamous army') mustered to oppose him. After the defeat of **Blücher** and his supporting forces at Ligny, Wellington took up opposition on the well-reconnoitred field of Waterloo, where the French were routed on 18 June 1815.

cont

Broadway musical *Woman of the Year* (1982). Active in television drama, she returned to the cinema for the first time since 1977 in *Naked Gun 33⅓: The Final Insult* (1994) and made her British stage debut in *The Millionairess* (1996).

Welch, Robert 1929–
English silversmith and product designer
Born in Hereford, he trained at Birmingham School of Art and afterwards at the Royal College of Art, London. In 1955 he began his long association with the stainless-steel manufacturer J & J Wiggin, for which he designed cutlery, tea sets, etc under the name 'Old Hall'. In the same year he established a workshop in Chipping Campden. His work has included jewellery, ceramics, glass, lighting and ironmongery. He has bridged successfully the gap between the making of single pieces of fine craftsmanship and industrial production. He was made a Royal Designer for Industry in 1965. Retrospectives of his work were held at the Cheltenham, Manchester and Birmingham art galleries between 1995 and 1996.

Weld, Theodore Dwight 1803–95
US abolitionist
Born in Hampton, Connecticut, he underwent a religious conversion at a revival meeting and was an itinerant preacher before beginning formal religious training. He brought many followers with him when he entered Lane Theological Seminary in Cincinnati, Ohio, and when he was dismissed in 1834 for advocating the immediate emancipation of the slaves, he led most of the student body to Oberlin College. He drafted many of the leaders of the abolitionist movement from among his pupils and won numerous converts with his revival-style preaching against slavery. His influential antislavery writings helped inspire **Harriet Beecher Stowe**'s *Uncle Tom's Cabin*.

Weldon, Fay, *originally* Franklin Birkinshaw 1931–
English novelist, television screenplay writer and polemicist
Born in Alvechurch, Worcestershire, she was brought up in New Zealand but returned to England as a child and attended St Andrews University. She became a successful advertising copywriter (credited with creating the slogan

'Go to work on an Egg') before publishing her first novel, *The Fat Woman's Joke* (1967). Her recurring themes include the nature of women's sexuality and experience in a patriarchal world. Her novels include *The Life and Loves of a She-Devil* (1983), in which an ugly and rejected heroine seeks retribution, *Puffball* (1980), which looks at pregnancy and womanhood, and *The Cloning of Joanna May* (1989, televised 1992), which considers genetic engineering. More recent works include *Life Force* (1992), *Wicked Women* (1995) and *Worst Fears* (1996). ⊞ O Kenyon, *Women Novelists Today* (1988)

Welensky, Sir Roy 1907–91
Rhodesian politician

Born in Salisbury, Southern Rhodesia, he was educated in local schools and then started work on the railways at the age of 14. He became leader of the Railway Workers' Union in Northern Rhodesia in 1933, by which time he had also been heavyweight boxing champion (1926–28). Elected to the Northern Rhodesia Legco in 1938, he founded the Northern Rhodesia Labour Party in 1941 and was appointed director of Manpower by the Governor. He became Chairman of the unofficial opposition in 1946. A strong supporter of the proposed Federation of Rhodesia and Nyasaland, he was elected to its first parliament. Welensky was appointed Minister of Transport and Development in 1953, to which he soon added the portfolios of Communications and Posts. He succeeded Sir **Godfrey Huggins** (Lord Malvern) as Prime Minister in 1956, which post he held until the Federation's break-up at the end of 1963. Although considered a champion of white rule, he was strongly opposed to Southern Rhodesia's UDI (Unilateral Declaration of Independence) and tried, unsuccessfully, to return to politics as an opponent of **Ian Smith**. He retired to a smallholding near Salisbury (Harare). ⊞ Don Taylor, *The Rhodesian: The Life of Sir Roy Welensky* (1955)

Weller, Thomas Huckle 1915–
US virologist and Nobel Prize winner

Wellington, Arthur Wellesley, 1st Duke of *cont*

Following this he was appointed Commander-in-Chief during the occupation of France (1815–18).

The Duke was rewarded with the Hampshire estate of Stratfield Saye, and in 1818 he returned to politics, joining the **Liverpool** administration as Master-General of the Ordnance. In 1826 Wellington was made Constable of the Tower, and in 1827 Commander-in-Chief, an office in which he was confirmed for life in 1842. He had represented Great Britain at the Congress of Aix-la-Chapelle (1818) and the Congress of Verona (1822), and in 1826 was sent to Russia by **George Canning** to negotiate binding Britain, France and Russia to impose recognition of Greek autonomy on Turkey; the Duke disapproved of Canning's foreign policy so strongly that he resigned, but with Canning's death in 1827 and the collapse of the nebulous **Goderich** administration, he became Prime Minister. In 1829 he materially assisted in **Robert Peel**'s reorganization of the Metropolitan Police. In general, Wellington's political policy was to refrain from weakening established authority and to avoid foreign entanglements, since Britain did not now possess an army adequate to enforce her will.

His reluctance to oppose the Test and Corporation Acts cost him the allegiance of **William Huskisson** and the Liberals, while his support of Catholic emancipation led to a bloodless duel with the Earl of Winchilsea. His non-intervention in the East after Navarino offended the majority of his party, while his opposition to the indiscriminate enlargement of the franchise brought widespread unpopularity, and broken windows at his London home Apsley House on the anniversary of Waterloo.

In the political crisis of 1834 Wellington again formed a government, and in Peel's temporary absence abroad he acted for all the secretaries of state. He was chosen Chancellor of the University of Oxford in 1834, and with Peel's return to power in 1841 joined his Cabinet, but without portfolio. He retired from public life in 1846. He was appointed Lord High Constable of England, and in 1848 organized the military in London against the Chartists. He was buried in St Paul's Cathedral.

📖 Elizabeth Longford, *Wellington: The Pillar of State* (1972) and *Wellington: The Years of the Sword* (1969); Michael Glover, *Wellington as Military Commander* (1968).

Wellington is thought to have been called 'Iron Duke' after putting up iron shutters at Apsley House when attacked by mobs in 1828. The title is also associated with the harsh discipline he imposed on his regiments.

C'est ici qu'a été gagné la bataille de Waterloo.
'The battle of Waterloo was won on the playing fields of Eton.' Attributed, and probably apocryphal. Quoted in Count Charles de Montalembert, *De l'Avenir politique de l'Angleterre* (1856), ch.10.

'Publish and be damned.' Attributed; said to have been his reply to a threat of blackmail.

Born in Ann Arbor, Michigan, he studied medical zoology at Michigan University, graduating in 1936, then went to Harvard University Medical School, where he conducted research under **John Enders**, who was working on methods for the cultivation of animal cells. After graduating in 1940, Weller was appointed to the staff of the Children's Hospital in Boston, and in 1942 joined the US Army Medical Corps. During World War II he conducted research into tropical diseases, and after the war Enders invited Weller and **Frederick Robbins** to join him at the newly created Infectious Diseases Research Laboratory at the Boston Children's Hospital. Weller and his colleagues developed new techniques for cultivating the poliomyelitis virus which made it possible for other workers to develop the polio vaccine. For this achievement Weller, Enders and Robbins shared the 1954 Nobel Prize for physiology or medicine. Weller also isolated the causative agent of chickenpox, shingles and German measles, and discovered a new viral aetiology of congenital damage, a virus he named 'cytomegalovirus'. In 1954 he was named Strong Professor and head of the department of tropical public health at Harvard, a post he held until his retirement in 1985.

Welles, (George) Orson 1915–85
US film director and actor

Born in Kenosha, Wisconsin, he appeared at the Gate Theatre, Dublin (1931), returned to America, became a radio producer (1934), and founded the Mercury Theatre (1937). His 1938 radio production of **H G Wells**'s *War of the Worlds* was so realistic that it caused panic in the USA. He wrote, produced, directed and acted in *Citizen Kane* (1941), a revolutionary landmark in cinema technique, and produced and directed a screen version of **Booth Tarkington**'s *The Magnificent Ambersons* (1942), a masterly evocation of a vanished way of American life. His later work, giving ample rein to his unpredictable talents, although never equalling his two masterpieces, includes his individual film versions of *Macbeth* (1948), *Othello* (1951), **Franz Kafka**'s *The Trial* (1962) and *Chimes at Midnight* (1965, based on **Shakespeare**'s Falstaff character). As an actor, the most notable of his varied and memorable stage and film performances was as Harry Lime in *The Third Man* (1949). 📖 Simon Callow, *Orson Welles: The Road to Xanadu* (1995)

Wellesley, Richard Colley Wellesley, 1st Marquis 1760–1842
Irish administrator

Born in County Meath, the brother of the 1st Duke of **Wellington**, he was returned to Westminster in 1784. He supported **William Pitt**'s foreign policy and **William Wilberforce**'s efforts to abolish the slave trade, and in 1786 became a Lord of the Treasury. In 1797 he was raised to the English peerage as Baron Wellesley and made Governor-General of India. Under his administration (1797–1805) British rule became supreme in India. The influence of France was extinguished with the disarming of its forces in Hyderabad, the power of the princes much reduced by the crushing in 1799 of **Tippoo Sahib** (at Seringapatam by General George Harris), and in 1803 of the Marathas. The revenue of the East India Company was more than doubled. In 1805 Wellesley returned to England and in 1809 went as ambassador to Madrid. On his return he was made Foreign Minister (1809–12), and later Lord Lieutenant of Ireland (1821, 1833).

Wellesz, Egon Joseph 1885–1974
Austrian composer and musicologist

Born in Vienna, he studied under **Arnold Schoenberg** and subsequently became Professor of Musical History at Vienna (1930–38), specializing in Byzantine, Renaissance and modern music. Exiled from Austria by the Nazis, he became a research Fellow at Oxford in 1938, and was lecturer in music there from 1944 to 1948. His works include five operas, nine symphonies, and choral and chamber music.

Wellington, Arthur Wellesley, 1st Duke of
See panel p1930

Wells, Allan 1952–
Scottish athlete

Born in Edinburgh, the most successful Scottish sprinter since **Eric Liddell**, he was initially more noteworthy as a long-jumper, achieving his first Scottish title when he won the under-15 championship in that event. It was not until 1976 that he concentrated on sprinting. Two years later he won Commonwealth gold in the 100 metres, and silver in the 200 metres. In the Moscow Olympics of 1980 he became the oldest-ever winner of the 100 metres, but was beaten into second place in the 200 metres, despite setting a new British record of 20.21 seconds. He won both sprint titles in the 1982 Commonwealth Games, uniquely sharing the gold medal in the 200 metres with Mike McFarlane of England. A forthright, single-minded figure, he was much helped in his success by his wife Margot, a PE teacher and fitness coach.

Wells, H(erbert) G(eorge) 1866–1946
English novelist, short-story writer and popular historian

Born in Bromley, Kent, he became a draper's apprentice, then a pupil teacher at the Midhurst Grammar School, from where he won a scholarship to the Normal School of Science, South Kensington, and studied biology under **T H Huxley**. He obtained a BSc in 1890 and then lectured until the success of his short stories allowed him to concentrate full-time on writing. Idealistic, impatient and dynamic, he threw himself into contemporary issues— free love, Fabianism, progressive education, scientific theory, 'world government' (he was an early agitator for a League of Nations) and human rights. His private life was no less restless than his public—he was married twice and had numerous affairs, notably with 'new' women, including Elizabeth von Arnim and **Rebecca West**. He achieved fame as a novelist with *The Time Machine* (1895), an allegory set in the year 802701 describing a two-tier society. It pioneered English science fiction, and was followed by significant contributions to the genre, such as *The Invisible Man* (1897), *The War of the Worlds* (1898), *The First Men in the Moon* (1901) and *Men Like Gods* (1923). He also wrote some of the best-known English comic novels— *Love and Mr Lewisham* (1900), *Kipps* (1905) and *The History of Mr Polly* (1910). *Mr Britling Sees It Through* (1916) and *The World of William Clissold* (1926) are lesser books but autobiographically illuminating. His other works include *The Outline of History* (1920), which enjoyed a vast circulation, *The Shape of Things to Come* (1933), a plea to confront fascism before it was too late, and the despairing *Mind at the End of its Tether* (1945). *Experiment in Autobiography* (1934) includes a striking self-portrait and studies of friends and contemporaries. 📖 P Parrinder, *H.G. Wells* (1976)

Wells, John Campbell 1936–98
English actor, dramatist, humorist and director

Born in Ashford, Kent, he read French and German at Oxford, and taught both languages at Eton (1961–63), while contributing material for revues at the Edinburgh Festival. He was a co-editor of the satirical magazine *Private Eye* (1964–67), and continued writing for the magazine throughout his life, most notably the supposed diary of Mrs Wilson, **Harold Wilson**'s wife, and the Dear Bill letters, the supposed correspondence of Denis Thatcher, husband of **Margaret Thatcher**. He wrote a number of plays for the theatre, starting with *Listen to the Knocking Bird* in 1965. *Mrs Wilson's Diary* (1968) was followed by *Anyone for Denis* (1981), in which Wells played the title role. (As an actor he made his London debut in the farce *An Italian Straw Hat*, in 1961.) He was also highly regarded as a translator of plays and opera from French and German. He directed a revival of *The Mikado* in 1989. His publications include *Rude Words* (1991) and *Princess Carabou: her true story* (1994).

Wells, Kitty, *née* Muriel Deason Wright 1919–
US country-and-western singer

Born in Nashville, Tennessee, she sang in gospel choirs as a child before performing on radio in the early 1930s and in the 1950s. She became a regular on *The Grand Ole Opry* country music show in Nashville, and was the first woman to have a number-one country hit with her signature song, 'It Wasn't God Who Made Honky Tonk Angels' in 1952. She was named to the Country Music Hall of Fame in 1976.

Wells-Barnett, Ida, *née* Wells 1862–1931
African-American journalist and activist

Born in Holly Springs, Mississippi, to slave parents, she became a teacher then turned to journalism, writing under the pseudonym Iola for black-owned newspapers. In 1895 she married Ferdinand Lee Barnett, the editor of the *Chicago Conservator*. She was an active campaigner against lynching and chronicled crimes in a pamphlet entitled *Southern Horrors* (1892). She was also one of two women who signed a call for the formation of the NAACP (National Association for the Advancement of Colored People) and, on her own, founded the first black woman suffrage organization, entitled the Alpha Suffrage Club of Chicago.

Welty, Eudora 1909–
US novelist and short-story writer

She was born in Jackson, Mississippi, and educated at the Mississippi State College for Women, the University of Wisconsin and the Columbia University School of Advertizing in New York. A publicity agent with the Works Progress Administration in Mississippi, she travelled extensively in the state, and took numerous photographs, which were later published as *One Time, One Place: Mississippi in the Depression: A Snapshot Album* (1971). During World War II she was on the staff of the *New York Review of Books*. She started writing short stories with 'Death of a Travelling Salesman' (1936), and published several collections from 1941 to 1954. She has also written five novels, mostly drawn from Mississippi life: *The Robber Bridegroom* (1942), *Delta Wedding* (1946), *The Ponder Heart* (1954), *Losing Battles* (1970) and *The Optimist's Daughter* (1972). *The Collected Stories of Eudora Welty* was published in 1980. Among her many accolades, she has received two Guggenheim Fellowships, three **O Henry** Awards, the Pulitzer Prize and the National Medal for Literature. Her autobiography, *One Writer's Beginnings*, was published in 1984 and her collected book reviews were published in *A Writer's Eye* and *Monuments to Interruption* (both 1994). 📖 E Evans, *Eudora Welty* (1980)

Wenceslas or Wenceslaus, St, *also called* Good King Wenceslas c.907–929
Bohemian Prince-Duke, and patron saint of Bohemia

Born in Stochov, he was raised as a Christian by his grandmother. When he came of age (c.924) he was free of his pagan mother's protectorate and could encourage German missionaries to come to Bohemia. He put his duchy under the protection of **Henry, the Fowler** of Germany, and was murdered by his pagan brother Boleslaw. He was regarded as a symbol of Czech nationalism. His feast day is 28 September.

Wenders, Wim 1945–
German film director

Born in Düsseldorf, he studied medicine and philosophy, then attended Munich's Cinema and Television College (1967–70), where he made his first short film, *Schauplätze* (1967). A writer for *Filmkritik* and *Die Süddeutsche Zeitung* (1968–72), he made his feature debut with *Summer in the City* (1970). Concerned with the influence of American culture on postwar German society, his work deals with isolation and alienation, often involving journeys in search of enlightenment. These themes are especially evident in *Alice in den Stadten* (1974, *Alice in the Cities*) and

Der Stand den Dinge (1982, *The State of Things*). He has been frequently honoured by the Cannes Film Festival, winning the International Critics Award for *Im Lauf der Zeit* (1976, *Kings of the Road*), the Golden Palm for *Paris, Texas* (1984) and Best Director for *Der Himmel über Berlin* (1987, *Wings of Desire*). Recent films include *Until the End of the World* (1991), *In Weiter Ferne, So Nah!* (1993, *Faraway, So Close*) and *The End of Violence* (1997). He also co-directed the Michelangelo Antonioni film *Al di la Nuvole* (1995, *Beyond the Clouds*).

Wenner-Gren, Axel Leonard 1881–1961
Swedish financier, industrialist and philanthropist
To exploit an improved vacuum cleaner he founded AB Electrolux in 1919, which he owned until 1956. Through Electrolux he also launched the Platen-Munter refrigerator. He owned Svenska Cellulosa AB from 1934 to 1941 and had interests in AB Bofors, but from 1930 onwards spent most of his time abroad, where his large-scale projects included a holiday resort in the Bahamas, a telephone company in Mexico and, in 1956, a huge development complex in British Columbia comprising electrical plants, mining and forestry. His Swedish interests were united in Fulcrum AB, which went into liquidation in 1975. During his lifetime and in his will he donated vast sums to institutions for scientific research, the best known of which are the Wenner-Gren Institut for experimental biology (1937, part of Stockholm University), the Wenner-Gren Foundation for anthropological research, established in New York in 1941, and above all the Wenner-Gren Center, an international scientific research centre set up in Stockholm in 1962.

Wen Tong (Wen T'ung), *also called* Wen Huzhou (Wen Hu-chou) d.1079
Chinese painter
He was born in Huzhou, in Zhejiang (Chekiang) Province, where he became a magistrate. He was the first great master of bamboo painting. A representative of the last of the five categories of Song painting, the Spontaneous Style (characterized by an intuitive response to nature in combination with brush discipline and mastery of pictorial composition), he owes his place in Chinese art largely to the fact that he was the teacher and close friend of Su Dongpo.

Wentworth, Charles Watson See Rockingham, Charles, Marquis of

Wentworth, Thomas See Strafford, 1st Earl of

Wentworth, William Charles 1793–1872
Australian politician
He was born at sea (his mother being a transported convict). He took part, in 1813, in the first crossing of the Blue Mountains, and in 1816 returned to England to study law. When called to the Bar in 1822, he had already published his classic *Statistical Historical and Political Description of the Colony of New South Wales* (1819). A staunch protagonist of self-government, which he made the policy of his newspaper, *The Australian* (established 1824), he demanded an elected legislature, taxation by consent and trial by jury. He entered the Legislative Council in 1843, was chairman of the committee that drafted the New South Wales constitution, and as a wealthy landowner and defender of squatter interests proposed a lower house elected on a property-owning franchise and an upper house of colonial peers, derisively called the 'bunyip aristocracy' by his opponents who deleted this provision. He accompanied the constitution to London where it was passed in the House of Commons in 1855. He played a leading role in the foundation of Sydney University, and in establishing a state primary education system.

Wenzel, Hanni 1956–
Liechtenstein alpine skier
Born in Staubirnen, Germany, she won the gold medal in the slalom and giant slalom, and the silver in the downhill at the 1980 Olympics. Her total of four Olympic gold medals is a record for any skier. She was combined world champion and overall World Cup winner in 1980.

Werfel, Franz 1890–1945
Austrian writer
Born in Prague, he went to Hamburg to find work when he was young, and after fighting in World War I became a pacifist, for which he was arrested. He began writing in 1916 and lived in Vienna until 1938, then moved to France, whence he fled the Nazi occupation in 1940 to the USA. He was associated with the Expressionist movement, and his early poems and plays betray that influence, but he is best known for his novels, among them *Das Lied von Bernadette* (1941, 'The Song of Bernadette'). 📖 L Zahn, *Franz Werfel* (1966)

Wergeland, (Jacobine) Camilla See Collett, (Jacobine) Camilla

Wergeland, Hendrik Arnold, *known as* Norway's Lord Byron 1808–45
Norwegian poet and patriot
The brother of the novelist Camilla Collett, he championed the cause of Norwegian nationalism in literature. A prolific lyrical poet and playwright, his chief work was a philosophical verse drama, *Skabelsen, mennesket og messias* (1830, 'Creation, Man and Messiah'). His last work, *Den engelske Lods* (1844, 'The English Pilot'), celebrated the liberation of the human mind. 📖 H Beyer, *Hendrik Wergeland* (1964)

Werner, Abraham Gottlob 1749–1817
German geologist
Born in Wehrau, Silesia (now in Poland), he was one of the first to frame a classification of rocks and gave his name to the Wernerian (or Neptunian) theory of deposition. The controversy between the Neptunists and Plutonists became one of the great geological debates of the late 18th century. In essence Werner advocated that crystalline igneous rocks were formed by direct precipitation from sea water, as part of his overall system of strata from the crystalline 'primitive rocks' succeeded by the 'transition rocks', resting on highly inclined strata, the flat-lying and well-stratified 'floetz rocks' and finally the poorly stratified alluvial series. The Plutonists, led by James Hutton, were able to demonstrate the intrusive nature of such rocks. Werner was one of the great geological teachers of his time and many scholars, including Goethe and Leopold von Buch, travelled to Freiburg to study under him.

Werner, Alfred 1866–1919
Swiss inorganic chemist and Nobel Prize winner
He was born in Mulhouse, France, and studied at the Polytechnical School in Zurich, returning to France (1891–92) to work with Claude Louis Berthelot at the Collège de France. He was appointed assistant professor at Zurich in 1893 and full professor from 1895 to 1915. He was the first person to demonstrate that isomerism applies to inorganic as well as to organic chemistry. His views, at first regarded with hostility, gradually won acceptance and were confirmed later by X-ray diffraction. They revolutionized inorganic chemistry and opened up many new areas of research. He was awarded the Nobel Prize for chemistry in 1913.

Werner, Alice 1859–1935
English linguist specializing in African languages

The Wesleys
English Christian evangelists

Wesley, Susanna, *née* Annesley 1669–1742
English mother of 19 children, among them the founders of Methodism

Susanna Annesley was one of three survivors of the 24 children of Samuel Annesley, a dissenting London minister. In 1688 she married Samuel Wesley, rector of Epworth, Lincolnshire (1697–1735). She had become an Anglican at the age of 13 but never lost her Puritan heritage of serious devotion to spiritual and practical responsibilities.

She kept a spiritual journal, read widely in theology, ran a disciplined and obedient household, and gave her children six hours' instruction a day in reading and writing from age five. **John Wesley**, her fifteenth child (out of 19) and second surviving son, was prepared for Confirmation when he was eight. She was always concerned for his spiritual welfare, and he, in his turn, felt able in his early ministry to consult her on theological questions. **Charles Wesley**, another son, is best remembered as the author of over 5,500 hymns.

When Susanna's husband was away, she supplemented what she considered the curate's meagre spiritual offerings by holding informal kitchen meetings on Sunday evenings. They were intended for family and servants but attracted audiences of over 200.

> It is said that when Susanna wanted peace to pray in her busy household, she simply put her apron over her head so that the children knew she could not be disturbed.

Wesley, John 1703–91
English evangelist and founder of Methodism

John Wesley was born in Epworth, Linconshire, where his father was rector. He studied at Oxford, was ordained deacon in 1725 and priest in 1728, and in 1726 became a Fellow of Lincoln and a lecturer in Greek. He was much influenced by the spiritual writings of **William Law**, and became the leader of a small dedicated group which had gathered round his brother **Charles Wesley**, nicknamed the Holy Club and the Oxford Methodists, a name later adopted by John for the adherents of the great evangelical movement which developed from it. They were joined in 1730 by James Hervey and **George Whitefield**.

When their father died (1735), John and Charles went on a missionary journey to Georgia, but they aroused the hostility of the colonists and returned to England (1738). John had been influenced by Moravians on the voyage out, and now he met Peter Böhler, and attended society meetings. At one of these, held in Aldersgate Street, during the reading of **Martin Luther**'s preface to the Epistle to the Romans, he experienced an assurance of salvation which convinced him that he must bring the same assurance to others. But his unwonted zeal alarmed and angered most of the parish clergy, who closed their pulpits against him; this intolerance, Whitefield's example, and the needs of the masses drove him into the open air at Bristol (1739).

cont

She was born in Trieste, Italy, and her father took his seven children to the Americas and to New Zealand, where Alice published some juvenile verse, before they settled in Kent, England. From 1893 Alice was in Nyasaland (now Malawi) and Natal studying the languages, but on the outbreak of the South African Wars she returned to London where she became Professor of Zulu Languages at King's College. From 1911 she studied Swahili in East Africa, and she wrote a translation of *The Life of Job*, before taking up a research fellowship at Cambridge. In 1917 she became inaugural lecturer at the School of Oriental Studies in London, from which she retired in 1930. Of her many publications, the best-known is probably *Myths and Legends of the Bantu* (1935).

Werner, (Friedrich Ludwig) Zacharias
1768–1823
German Romantic dramatist

He was born in Königsberg, Prussia (now Kaliningrad, Russia). His chief works are *Die Söhne des Thals* (1803, 'The Sons of the Valley'), *Das Kreuz an der Ostsee* (1804, 'The Cross on the Baltic Sea') and *Martin Luther* (1806). He subsequently recanted his praise of **Martin Luther**, after converting to Catholicism. He was ordained a priest in Vienna, and became a fashionable preacher. His earlier dramas remained his most significant work, and place him among the leading dramatists of the Romantic movement. 📖 P Hankhamen, *Zacharias Werner* (1970)

Wernicke, Carl 1848–1905
German neurologist and psychiatrist

Born in Tarnowitz, Upper Silesia (now in Poland), he qualified in medicine at the University of Breslau (Wrocław, Poland), and in 1874 published *Der Aphasische Symtomencomplex* ('The Aphasic Syndrome'). The form of aphasia, loss of speech, which he described was marked by a severe defect in the understanding of speech, and it became known as sensory aphasia. This was in contrast to the motor aphasia proposed by **Paul Broca**, which involved loss or defect in the expression of speech. From postmortem studies on his patients' brains, Wernicke showed that his type of aphasia was typically localized in the left temporal lobe, now known as 'Wernicke's area'. He established a clinic in Berlin specializing in diseases of the nervous system, where he worked until 1885 when he returned to Breslau (Associate Professor of Neurology and Psychiatry 1885–90, Professor 1890–1904). In 1904 he moved to Halle as professor, but he died as a result of an accident the following year.

Wertheimer, Max 1880–1943
German psychologist and philosopher

Born in Prague, after studying there and in Berlin and Würzburg, he conducted experiments in perception (1912) with **Kurt Koffka** and **Wolfgang Köhler** which led to the founding of the Gestalt school of psychology. He was professor at Berlin and Frankfurt, but left Germany for the USA in 1933 at the Nazi assumption of power, and taught at the New School for Social Research in New York City (1933–43).

Wertmuller, Lina, *originally* Arcangela Felice Assunta Wertmuller von Elgg 1928–
Italian film director

Born in Rome, she was a rebellious child but became a teacher, then soon turned her attention to the theatre. She spent 10 years as an actress, writer and director, but eventually moved into film through her friendship with **Marcello Mastroianni**, who introduced her to **Federico Fellini**. Her best-known film as a director is *Pasqualino Sette Bellezze* (1976, *Seven Beauties*), set in a Nazi concentration camp, which brought her the distinction of being the first woman director to be nominated for an Academy Award. Her other films include *Saturday, Sunday and Monday* (1990) and *Io Speriamo Che Me La Cavo* (1993, 'Me, Let's Hope I Make It').

Wesker, Arnold 1932–
English dramatist

The Wesleys cont

John founded the first Methodist chapel in Bristol, and in London he bought the ruinous Foundry in Moorfields, which he used to preach in and as his headquarters. Methodist anniversaries have sometimes been reckoned from this event. During his itineraries, 10,000 to 30,000 people would wait patiently for hours to hear him. He gave his strength to working-class neighbourhoods, and most of his converts were colliers, miners, foundrymen, weavers, and day-labourers in towns.

He travelled 250,000 miles and preached 40,000 sermons. Yet he achieved an enormous amount of literary work, and produced grammars, extracts from the classics, histories, abridged biographies, collections of psalms, hymns and tunes, his own sermons and journals, and founded the *Methodist Magazine* (1778). His works were so popular that he made £30,000, which he distributed in charity during his life. He founded charitable institutions at Newcastle and London, and Kingswood School in Bristol.

Wesley broke with the Moravians in 1745. He was determined to remain loyal to the Church of England and urged his followers to do the same; although he ordained one of his assistants (**Francis Asbury**) for work in the USA, he always regarded Methodism as a movement within the Church and it remained so during his lifetime. In 1751 he married the widow Mary Vazeille, who deserted him in 1776. His journeys and spiritual odyssey were recorded in his *Journal*.

📖 Robert Tuttle, *John Wesley: His Life and Work* (1978); C E Vulliamy, *John Wesley* (3rd edition, 1954); J S Simon, *The Life of John Wesley* (1921–34).

'I look upon all the world as my parish.'
From his journal entry, 11 June 1739.

Wesley, Charles 1707–88
English hymnwriter, evangelist and founder of Methodism

Charles Wesley, like his brother **John Wesley**, was born in Epworth, Lincolnshire. He studied at Christ Church, Oxford, where he experienced spiritual renewal which led him in 1729 to form a small group of fellow students, nicknamed the 'Holy Club' or the 'Oxford Methodists', later joined by John.

Ordained in 1735, he accompanied John to Georgia as secretary to Governor **James Oglethorpe**, but found the mission field exhausting and returned to England in 1736. After another spiritual experience in 1738, when he found himself 'at peace with God', he became an evangelist and wrote over 5,500 hymns. These became an important and effective way of conveying the gospel message, and include 'Jesu, Lover of My Soul', 'Hark, the Herald Angels Sing', 'Love Divine, All Loves Excelling' and 'Christ the Lord is Ris'n Today'.

📖 Frederick C Gill, *Charles Wesley* (1964); Frank Baker, *Charles Wesley's Verse* (1964) and *Charles Wesley as Revealed in His Letters* (1948).

'Long my imprisoned spirit lay
Fast bound in sin and nature's night;
Thine eye diffused a quickening ray—
I woke, the dungeon flamed with light,
My chains fell off, my heart was free,
I rose, went forth, and followed thee.'
From the hymn 'And Can it Be' (1738).

He was born in London's East End, of Jewish immigrant parents, and left school at 14. His family background and attempts to earn a living are important ingredients of such plays as the Kahn family trilogy, *Chicken Soup with Barley*, *Roots* and *I'm talking about Jerusalem* (1958–60). *Roots* is an eloquent manifesto of Wesker's socialism: an aesthetic recipe for all which he attempted to put into practice by taking art to the workers through his Centre-42 (1961–70), which was situated in an old locomotive shed in Camden Town, London, and which was heavily involved with the trade union movement. Other plays include *Chips with Everything* (1962), *The Four Seasons* (1965) and *Their Very Own and Golden City* (1966), *The Old Ones* (1972) and *Love Letters on Blue Paper* (1978), originally written for television in 1976. He also wrote the essay collection *Fears of Fragmentation* (1970) and *Words—as Definitions of Experience* (1976). A one-woman play, *Annie Wobbler* (1984), was well received, and his plays were collected in five volumes in 1989–90, but so far his reputation rests firmly on his earliest works. Recent works include the plays *Wild Spring* (1992) and *Tokyo* (1994), the autobiography *As Much As I Dare* (1994) and *The King's Daughters* (1993), a collection of short stories. 📖 J R Taylor, *Anger and After* (1962)

Wesley, Charles See panel above

Wesley, John See panel p1934

Wesley, Mary, *pseudonym of* Mary Aline Siepmann, *née* Farmar 1912–
English novelist

She was born in Englefield Green, Berkshire. She wrote two children's books, *Speaking Terms* and *The Sixth Seal* (both 1969), before publishing her first adult novel, *Jumping the Queue*, in 1983, at the age of 70. Since then she has produced a succession of books dealing with middle-class mores, each written with ironic, detached amusement and taking an unblinkered though compassionate look at sexual values. One of the best known is *The Camomile Lawn* (1984), which considers sexual and emotional relationships in the turmoil of World War II. It was made into a television series in 1991. Recent publications include *An Imaginative Experience* (1994) and *Part of the Furniture* (1997).

Wesley, Samuel 1766–1837
English organist and composer

Born in Bristol, he was an early enthusiast of **J S Bach**. Though a Roman Catholic (to the displeasure of his father, **Charles Wesley**), he wrote also for the Anglican liturgy, leaving a number of fine motets and anthems, including *In Exitu Israel*. One of the most distinguished organists of his day, he had an illegitimate son, Samuel Sebastian (1810–76), who was also a noted organist.

Wesley, Susanna See panel p1934

Wessel, Horst 1907–30
German National Socialist

He was born in Bielefeld. He was the composer of the Nazi anthem 'Die Fahne Hoch', known as the Horst Wessel song.

Wesselmann, Tom 1931–
US painter

Born in Cincinnati, Ohio, he studied psychology at Cincinnati University before taking art courses. In 1961 he moved to New York, abandoning the Abstract Expressionist style and turning instead to Pop Art. Most of his paintings depict overtly erotic female nudes in contemporary all-American environnments. These works form the series known as *The Great American Nude*.

Wesson, Daniel Baird 1825–1906
US gunsmith

He was born in Worcester, Massachusetts. With Horace Smith (1808–93) he devised a new type of repeating mechanism for small-arms (1854), and founded the firm of Smith & Wesson at Springfield, Massachusetts, in 1857.

West, Benjamin 1738–1820
British painter

Born in Springfield, Pennsylvania, USA, he showed early promise as a portraitist and was sent on a sponsored visit to Italy, and on his return was induced to settle in London in 1763. George III was his patron for 40 years. The representation of modern instead of classical costume in his best-known picture, *The Death of General Wolfe* (1771), was an innovation in English historical painting.

West, Fred(erick) 1942–95 and Rosemary 1953–
English alleged murderers

Frederick was a builder by trade. He married Rosemary as his second wife in 1972. They had seven children. In 1994 the remains of their daughter Heather, who had not been seen since 1987, were found underneath the floor of their home in Gloucester. The remains of eight more bodies of young women and girls were discovered there, and three at other sites, some of which had been buried in the 1970s. Fred hanged himself on 1 January 1995 before reaching trial and the murder charges against him were dropped; but Rosemary was found guilty of murdering 10 young women, including one of her daughters, and sentenced to life imprisonment.

West, Mae 1893–1980
US vaudeville performer and film actress

Born in Brooklyn, New York City, she made her debut on Broadway in 1911, exploiting her voluptuousness in roles of sultry sexual innuendo. Noted for her wit, she wrote many of the plays she starred in, such as *Sex* (1926) and *Diamond Lil* (1928), which was later filmed as *She Done Him Wrong* with Cary Grant (1933). Her other films include *I'm No Angel* (1933), *Klondyke Annie* (1934) and *My Little Chickadee* (1940). She returned to the screen in 1970 in *Myra Breckenridge*. The 'Mae West', an inflatable life-jacket, is affectionately named after her. □ George Eells, *Mae West* (1984)

West, Morris Langlo 1916–
Australian novelist and playwright

Born in St Kilda, Victoria, he trained for the priesthood but left before taking vows. After war service he published his first novel, *Moon in My Pocket* (1945, under the pseudonym 'Julian Morris'), which dealt with the conflicts facing a Catholic novitiate. In 1955 he left Australia for Italy, where his fourth novel, *Children of the Sun* (1957), a tale of Neapolitan slum urchins, attracted attention. *The Devil's Advocate* (1959, James Tait Black Memorial Prize, filmed 1977) became an international bestseller, and his subsequent books have been eagerly awaited. They include prize-winning novels such as *The Shoes of the Fisherman* (1963), *Summer of the Red Wolf* (1971), *The Clowns of God* (1981) and *The Ringmaster* (1991). Later works include *The Lovers* (1993), *Vanishing Point* (1996) and *A View From the Ridge* (1996). He has dramatized several of his works, and refuses to write his memoirs, declaring that his large body of writing is a 'serial autobiography'.

West, Nathanael, *pseudonym of* Nathan Wallenstein Weinstein 1903–40
US novelist

He was born in New York City, and after attending Brown University, Rhode Island, he lived in Paris for a few years, where he wrote *The Dream Life of Balso Snell* (1931), self-consciously avant-garde but illuminating in his preoccupation with the hollowness of contemporary life. On his return to New York he mismanaged a hotel and was associate editor with William Carlos Williams of the magazine *Contact*. *Miss Lonelyhearts*, the story of a newspaper agony columnist who becomes more involved with his correspondents than is good for him, appeared in 1933. There are parallels in West's own life, but he renounced journalism and went to Hollywood in 1935 to write scripts for a minor studio, using this experience for *The Day of the Locust* (1939), his surreal masterpiece. His only other novel, *A Cool Million*, was published in 1934. A black humorist and biting satirist, he was killed, along with his wife, Eileen McKenney, when he ignored a traffic signal. □ J Martin, *Nathanael West: the art of his life* (1970)

West, Dame Rebecca, *pseudonym of* Cecily Isabel Andrews, *née* Fairfield 1892–1983
Irish novelist and critic

She was born in County Kerry and moved to Edinburgh with her family when her father, a journalist, left her mother. She was educated at George Watson's Ladies College, and trained for the stage in London, where she adopted (1912) the pseudonym Rebecca West, the heroine of Ibsen's *Rosmersholm* which she had once played, and who is characterized by a passionate will. She was involved with the suffragettes from an early age, joined the staff of the *Freewoman* (1911) and became a political writer on the *Clarion*, a socialist newspaper (1912). Her love affair with H G Wells began in 1913 and lasted for 10 turbulent years during which time they had a son. Her first published book was a critical study of Henry James (1916). Her second, a novel, *The Return of the Soldier* (1918), describes the homecoming of a shell-shocked soldier. After the final break with Wells she went to the USA where she lectured and formed a long association with the *New York Herald Tribune*. In 1930 she married Henry Maxwell Andrews, a banker, and they lived in Buckinghamshire until his death in 1968. She published eight novels including *The Judge* (1922), *Harriet Hume* (1929), *The Thinking Reed* (1936) and the largely autobiographical *The Fountain Overflows* (1957). Her last (unfinished) novel was *Cousin Rosamund* (1988). In the mid-1930s she made several trips to the Balkans to gather material for a travel book, but her interest deepened and resulted in her masterful analysis of Yugoslav politics and history *Black Lamb and Grey Falcon* (2 vols, 1941). It is generally considered her magnum opus. During World War II she supervised BBC broadcasts to Yugoslavia, and she attended the Nuremberg War Crimes Trials (1945–46). From this and other cases came *The Meaning of Treason* (1949) and *A Train of Powder* (1955). Witty, incisive and combative, she was described by George Bernard Shaw as handling a pen 'as brilliantly as ever I could and much more savagely'. □ V Glendinning, *Rebecca West* (1987)

West, Rosemary See West, Fred
West, Thomas See De la Warr, 3rd or 12th Baron

West, Timothy 1934–
English actor

Born in Bradford, West Yorkshire, the son of actor Lockwood West, he started as an assistant stage manager at Wimbledon Theatre (1956) and went on to appear in many West End and Royal Shakespeare Company productions. His many television roles include Mortimer in *Edward II* (1970), Horatio Bottomley in *The Edwardians* (1973), the title role in *Edward the Seventh* (1975), Bounderby in *Hard Times* (1977), Wolsey in *Henry VIII* (1979), Winston Churchill in *Churchill and the Generals* (1979) and *The Last Bastion*, Bradley Hardacre in *Brass* (1983, 1990), Derek Blore in *Blore, MP* (1989), Thomas Beecham in *Beecham* (1990), DCI Jimmy McKinnes in *Framed* (1992) and Lord Reith in *Reith to the Nation* (1993). A later stage appearance was as Falstaff in the English Touring Company's production of Shakespeare's *Henry IV*, parts I and II (1996–97). He is married to Prunella Scales.

Westbrook, Mike (Michael John David)
1936–
English jazz composer, bandleader and pianist
Born in High Wycombe, Buckinghamshire. He turned to
music after studying painting. He concentrated on writing extended pieces specifically for his own ensembles,
ranging from trios to big bands. His work, along with
that of Graham Collier and Mike Gibbs, extended the
possibilities of compositional form in a jazz context. His
major suites have included *The Cortege* (1982), *On Duke's
Birthday* (1984), and *London Bridge is Broken Down* (1987), as
well as settings of Arthur Rimbaud, Federico García
Lorca, William Blake and the Beatles. His operas include
Quichotte (1989), *Coming Through Slaughter* (1994) and *Good
Friday 1663* (1995). Recent compositions include *Stage Set*
(1996) and the film score for *Camera Makes Whoopee* (1996).
He works extensively in partnership with his wife Kate
Westbrook (*née* Bernard, 1937–), who is also a visual
artist, as well as writing and performing on voice, tenor
horn, and piccolo.

Westermarck, Edvard Alexander 1862–1939
Finnish social philosopher
Born and educated in Helsinki, he became lecturer in
sociology there, and Professor of Sociology in London
(1907–30). His *History of Human Marriage* (3 vols, 1922) was
an attack on the theory of primitive promiscuity. He also
wrote on the evolution of ethics, in *The Origin and
Development of Moral Ideas* (1906–08) and *Christianity and
Morals* (1939). Having travelled widely in Morocco, he
published several accounts of its peoples, including
Ritual and Belief in Morocco (2 vols, 1926) and *Marriage
Ceremonies in Morocco* (1914).

Westinghouse, George 1846–1914
US engineer
Born in Central Bridge, New York, he ran away from
school to fight for the North in the American Civil War,
then served for a short time in the US navy, returning in
1865 to work in his father's farm machinery workshop.
The same year he took out the first of his more than 400
patents, for a railway steam locomotive. His most important invention was the air-brake system he patented in
1869, which became known as the 'Westinghouse air
brake'. This allowed the brakes on all the coaches of a train
to be applied simultaneously by the engine driver, and
greatly increased the speed at which trains could safely
travel. He later became a pioneer in the use of alternating
current for distributing electric power, founding the
Westinghouse Electrical Company in 1886, and attracting
Nikola Tesla to work with him. In 1895 he successfully
harnessed the power of the Niagara Falls to generate
sufficient electricity for the town of Buffalo, 22 miles
(35.4km) away. ⊞ H Gordon Garbedian, *George Westinghouse: A Fabulous Inventor* (1943)

Westmoreland, William Childs 1914–
US soldier
Born in Spartanburg County, South Carolina, he grad-
uated from West Point in 1936 and saw action in North
Africa and Europe during World War II. After fighting in
the Korean War, he was appointed superintendent of West
Point (1960–63). As the senior military commander of
US forces in Vietnam (1964–68), General Westmoreland
favoured the strategy of escalating US involvement in the
Vietnam War. After the Tet Offensive he was replaced as
commander, and he returned to the USA where he served
as army Chief of Staff (1968–72).

Weston, Edward 1886–1958
US photographer
Born in Highland Park, Illinois, he established his own
studio in Glendale, California, (c.1910), moving to Mexico
in 1923. He rebelled against the prevalent 'soft-focus' style

and became recognized as a modernist, emphasizing sharp
images and precise definition in landscapes, portraits and
still life. In 1932 he joined Ansel Adams and others in
forming the 'straight photography' purists' Group f/64, in
California. His close-up studies of inanimate objects such
as shells and vegetables exemplified his vision of detailed
form and the richness of his control of tone. He produced
notable landscapes of the Mohave Desert and in 1937, with
the first-ever award of a Guggenheim Fellowship to a
photographer, travelled widely throughout the western
states of the USA. He followed this with a long tour of the
southern and eastern States to illustrate an edition of Walt
Whitman's *Leaves of Grass*.

Weston, Frank 1871–1924
English Anglican Bishop of Zanzibar
Born in south London, he graduated from Oxford, and
after ordination in 1894 served London curacies before
going to East Africa under the Anglo-Catholic Universities' Mission to Central Africa in 1898. Ten years later
he was made Bishop of Zanzibar. A man of great dedication and not a few prejudices, he spoke out against a
scheme to unite East Africa's Protestant denominations
(though not against reunion in principle), and he disliked
theological liberalism. He wrote several books, notably
The One Christ (1907).

Westwood, Vivienne 1941–
English fashion designer
Born in London, she was a primary-school teacher in
early adulthood, then turned her attention to clothes
design on meeting Malcolm McLaren, manager of the
Sex Pistols. They established a shop in London and became known as the leading creators of punk clothing.
Their designs, using rubber, leather and bondage gear,
were influenced by the paraphernalia of pornography.
Since her split from McLaren in 1983, she has become
accepted by the mainstream, and was Designer of the Year
in 1990 and 1991. She was Professor of Fashion at the
Vienna Academy of Applied Arts (1989–91). Hers is a
peculiarly English genius, a contradictory combination
of reverence and iconoclasm, which is nonetheless
greatly esteemed in international fashion.

Wet, Christiaan Rudolf de 1854–1922
Boer soldier and politician
A celebrated big game hunter, he gave distinguished service in the First Boer War in the Transvaal (1880–81), and
in the Second Boer War (1899–1902). He wrote a book on
the war, and in 1907 he became Minister of Agriculture of
the Orange River Colony. In 1914 he joined the Afrikaner
insurrection, but was captured in the field. Sentenced to
six years' imprisonment, he was released in 1915.

Wetherell, Elizabeth See Warner, Susan Bogert

Wette, Wilhelm Martin Leberecht de See De Wette, Wilhelm Martin Leberecht

Weyden, Rogier van der, *real name* Rogier de la Pasture 1400–64
Flemish painter
After the death of Jan van Eyck in 1441, he was the most
important Early Netherlandish painter. Very little is
known of his life and even his identity has been disputed.
Between 1435 and 1449 he was in Brussels where he was
appointed painter to the city. It is likely that he visited
Italy, since there are distinct Italian influences evident
in his work. Patronized by the Burgundian court, his
famous *Last Judgement* was painted for Chancellor Rolin.
Akin to that of other members of the Early Netherlandish
school in its meticulous attention to detail and technical
expertise in describing texture, Weyden's work is distinguished by its ability to convey drama and emotion.

Weygand, Maxime 1867–1965
French soldier

He was born in Brussels. As Chief of Staff to **Ferdinand Foch** (1914–23), he served in World War I. He later became High Commissioner in Syria (1923–24), Chief of Staff (1930), and Commander-in-Chief of the army (1931). Retired in 1935, he was recalled and sent to command in Syria in 1939. In May 1940 he replaced **Maurice Gamelin** as Commander-in-Chief, but was too late to do much more than recommend an armistice. The Vichy Government sent him as its delegate to North Africa, but he was recalled and imprisoned in Germany until the end of World War II. In 1948 he was brought before the High Court for his role in 1940, but the case was dropped, and he retired into obscurity.

Weyl, Hermann 1885–1955
German mathematician

Born in Elmshorn, he studied at the University of Göttingen under **David Hilbert**, and became professor at the universities of Zurich (1913), and Göttingen (1930). He moved to Princeton University in 1933. He gave the first rigorous account of the **Riemann** surfaces, and wrote on the mathematical foundations of relativity and quantum mechanics, and subsequently on the representation theory of **Lie** groups. He originated the gauge theory of particle interactions in his concepts of measurement, wrote on the philosophy of mathematics, on the spectral theory of integral operators, and on algebraic number theory. His book *Symmetry* (1952) is an elegant and largely non-technical account for the general reader of the relation between group theory and symmetry in pattern and design.

Weyman, Stanley John 1855–1928
English novelist

Born in Ludlow, Shropshire, he was educated at Christ Church, Oxford, and taught history, then turned to law (1877–91). He began writing short stories for magazine publication, and published a novel, *The House of the Wolf* (1888–89), but his success as a popular historical novelist dates from *A Gentleman of France* (1893), set in the time of Henri of Navarre (**Henri IV**), and admired by **Robert Louis Stevenson**. He wrote several more in a similar vein, including *Under the Red Robe* (1894), *The Red Cockade* (1895), *Count Hannibal* (1901) and *Chippinge* (1906). Many were successfully dramatized.

Wharton, Edith Newbold, *née* Jones c.1861–1937
US novelist and short-story writer

Born in New York, into a wealthy and aristocratic family, she was educated at home and in Europe. In 1885 she married Edward Wharton, a friend of the family, and they travelled widely, before settling in Paris in 1907. Her husband, however, was mentally unbalanced and they were divorced in 1913. *The Greater Inclination* (1899), her first collection of short stories, was followed by a novella, *The Touchstone* (1900), but it was *The House of Mirth* (1905), a tragedy about a beautiful and sensitive girl who is destroyed by the very society her upbringing has designed her to meet, that established her as a major novelist. Many other works followed, almost 50 in all, including travel books and volumes of verse, but she is known principally as a novelist of manners, a keen observer of society, witty and satirical. Her most uncharacteristic novel is *Ethan Frome* (1911), which deals partly with her unhappy marriage. Important later works are *The Age of Innocence* (1920), *The Mother's Recompense* (1925), *The Children* (1928) and *Hudson River Bracketed* (1929). Socially gregarious, she formed a durable friendship with **Henry James** who did much to encourage and influence her work, and a voluminous correspondence with, among others, the art historian **Bernard Berenson**. Her approach to her work is discussed in *The Writing of Fiction* (1925). *A Backwards Glance* (1934) is her revealing autobiography. 📖 L Auchincloss, *Edith Wharton* (1961)

Wheatley, Phillis c.1753–1785
African-American poet

Born in Africa, possibly Senegal, she was shipped to the slave market in Boston, Massachusetts, as a child (1761), and sold as a maidservant to the family of a Boston tailor, who educated her with the rest of his family. She studied Latin and Greek, and started writing poetry in English at the age of 13. She published *Poems on Various Subjects, Religious and Moral* (1783) and visited England that year, to huge popular interest, although some doubted her poems' authenticity. A *Collected Works* appeared in 1988. 📖 W H Robinson, *Critical Essays on Phillis Wheatley* (1982)

Wheaton, Henry 1785–1848
US jurist

Born in Providence, Rhode Island, he edited (1812–15) the *National Advocate* in New York, where for four years he was a justice of the Marine Court and from 1816 to 1827 reporter for the Supreme Court. From 1827 to 1835 he was chargé d'affaires at Copenhagen, and from 1835 to 1846 Minister at Berlin. His most important work was *Elements of International Law* (1836, with many later editions).

Wheatstone, Sir Charles 1802–75
English physicist

He was born in Gloucester, and first became known as a result of his work in acoustics. He invented the concertina in 1829, and in 1834 was appointed Professor of Experimental Physics at King's College London, a position he held for the rest of his life, in spite of his unwillingness to lecture. In 1837 he and Sir **William Cooke** took out a patent for an electric telegraph, and in conjunction with the new London & Birmingham Railway Company installed a demonstration telegraph line about a mile (1.6km) long. With the needs of the rapidly expanding railways providing the impetus and the finance, by 1852 more than 4,000 miles (6,436km) of telegraph line were in operation throughout Britain. Wheatstone built the first printing telegraph in 1841, and in 1845 devised a single-needle instrument. In 1838, in a paper to the Royal Society (of which he had become a Fellow in 1836), he explained the principle of the stereoscope (later improved by **David Brewster**). He also invented a sound magnifier for which he introduced the term 'microphone'. 'Wheatstone's bridge', a device for the comparison of electrical resistances, was brought to notice (though not invented) by him. He was knighted in 1868. 📖 Brian Bowers, *Sir Charles Wheatstone FRS, 1802–1875* (1975)

Wheeler, Barbara Grumbach 1945–
US theologian and educationist

Born in Oakland, California, and educated in Albany, New York, she graduated from Barnard College in 1967 and has pursued an academic career specializing in the evaluation of educational programmes in theology. She has been president of Auburn Theological Seminary since 1980 and director of its Center for the Study of Theological Education since 1991.

Wheeler, David John 1927–
English computer scientist and programmer

Educated at Trinity College, Cambridge, he joined **Maurice Wilkes's** EDSAC (Electronic Delay Storage Automatic Calculator) team in establishing the world's first computing service. The pioneering work of Wilkes, Wheeler and Gill was later published in an influential book, *The Preparation of Programs for an Electronic Digital Computer* (1951), which detailed the economy and elegance of the EDSAC programming. Wheeler worked in the

USA at the University of Illinois between 1951 and 1953, before returning to Cambridge as Professor of Computer Science (1978–94). He was elected FRS in 1981.

Wheeler, John Archibald 1911–
US theoretical physicist

Born in Jacksonville, Florida, he was educated at Johns Hopkins University, where he received his PhD in 1933, and spent the following two years in Copenhagen. He was appointed professor at Princeton (1947) and later at the University of Texas (1976–86). Wheeler worked with Niels Bohr on the theory of nuclear fission, and on the hydrogen bomb project. He also contributed to the search for a unified field theory, and studied with Richard Feynman the concept of action at a distance.

Wheeler, Sir (Robert Eric) Mortimer
1890–1976
English archaeologist

Born in Glasgow, and educated at Bradford and London, he became director of the National Museum of Wales (1920), and keeper of the London Museum (1926–44). He carried out notable excavations in Great Britain at Verulamium (St Albans) and Maiden Castle, and from 1944 to 1947 was director-general of archaeology in India, and worked to particular effect at Mohenjo-daro and Harappa. He then became Professor of the Archaeology of the Roman Provinces at the newly founded Institute of Archaeology in London (1948–55). Knighted in 1952, he was well known for spirited popular accounts of his subject, in books and on television. His works include *Archaeology from the Earth* (1954), and the autobiographical *Still Digging* (1955). ▣ Ronald W Clark, *Sir Mortimer Wheeler* (1960)

Wheldon, Sir Huw 1916–86
Welsh broadcaster

He was the son of Sir Wyn Wheldon, permanent secretary for education. Partly educated in Germany, he joined the army in 1939 and was awarded the MC in 1944. He joined the BBC in 1952 and was responsible for the seminal arts programme *Monitor* (1957–64) where the cultural life of the land was reviewed with passion and enthusiasm. He became head of documentaries and music programmes in 1963, controller of programmes for BBC Television in 1965, and the Corporation's managing director (1968–75). Afterwards he returned to active programme-making as the co-writer and presenter of *Royal Heritage* (1977) before serving as the president of the Royal Television Society (1979–85).

Whewell, William 1794–1866
English scholar

Born in Lancaster, the son of a joiner, he became a Fellow of Trinity College, Cambridge. He was Professor of Mineralogy at Cambridge (1828–38), and of Moral Theology (1838–55). In 1841 he became Master of Trinity, and in 1855, Vice-Chancellor of Cambridge. His works include *History of the Inductive Sciences* (1837), *Elements of Morality* (1855), and other writings on the tides, electricity and magnetism, besides translations of Goethe's *Hermann and Dorothea*, Hugo Grotius's *Rights of Peace and War* and Plato.

Whichcote, Benjamin 1609–83
English philosopher and theologian

Born in Stoke, Shropshire, he was a student at Cambridge, became a Fellow of Emmanuel College in 1633, was ordained and appointed Sunday Afternoon Lecturer in Trinity Church (1636–56) where he lectured to large audiences each week. He became Provost of King's College in 1644 but lost the post at the Restoration in 1660 by order of Charles II. He published nothing in his lifetime but is regarded as the spiritual founder of the Cambridge Platonists. The posthumous selections from his sermons (1698) and aphorisms (1703) emphasize the moral rather than the doctrinal certainties in religion, and express the general belief that religion must harmonize with reason since God himself endowed human beings with reason and reveals himself principally through the mind.

Whicker, Alan Donald 1925–
English broadcaster and journalist

Born in Cairo, he was commissioned in the Devonshire Regiment during World War II, and served with the Army Film and Photo Unit. Thereafter, he was a war correspondent, reporting on the Inchon landings in Korea before joining the BBC (1957–68) where he worked on the *Tonight* programme (1957–65) and began his *Whicker's World* documentary series in 1958. Television's most travelled man, he has broadcast on the rich and famous, as well as the exotic and extraordinary aspects of everyday lives in all parts of the world. His many series include *Whicker Down Under* (1961), *Whicker Within a Woman's World* (1972), *Whicker's World Aboard the Orient Express* (1982) and *Living With Waltzing Matilda* (1987–88). He has received numerous awards including the Royal Television Society Silver Medal (1968) and the Richard Dimbleby award (1977). Later works for television include *Whicker's Miss World* (1993) and *Whicker's World Aboard the Real Orient Express* (1994). His books include *Some Rise By Sin* (1949), the autobiography *Within Whicker's World* (1982), and *Whicker's World Down Under* (1988).

Whillans, Don(ald Desbrow) 1933–85
English mountaineer

Born in Salford, he started climbing as a teenager and became one of the best-known figures in British mountaineering. His partnership with Joe Brown led to many higher-standard routes being put up on rock faces in the Peak District and North Wales. Whillans also climbed extensively in Scotland and the Alps, where he put up several new routes with Brown and Chris Bonington, among others. From 1960 he concentrated on big expeditions, including the first ascent of the Central Tower of Paine in Patagonia (1962) and of the south face of Annapurna in the Himalayas (1970). He was also popular as a speaker and lecturer.

Whipple, Fred Lawrence 1906–
US astronomer

Born in Red Oak, Iowa, he studied at California University and became Professor of Astronomy at Harvard in 1945. An expert on the solar system (his *Earth, Moon and Planets* published in 1941 is a standard work), he is known especially for his work on comets. He was also the first to define the term micrometeorite and used the rate of decay of meteors as an indicator of the temperature profile of the atmosphere. Whipple (with Fletcher Watson) was responsible for Harvard's two-station meteor programme. He was the prime mover behind the production and use of the Baker Super-Schmidt meteor cameras. He was also a pioneer in the use of these cameras to observe the decay of satellite orbits, and from this obtained measurements of atmospheric density. His meteoroid bumper shield was used to dissipate the energy of impacting dust particles on the Giotto mission to Halley's comet, which confirmed his 'dirty snowball' model. In 1967 he wrote a keynote paper on the origin and evolution of dust in the solar system and his other publications include *The Mystery of Comets* (1985).

Whipple, George Hoyt 1878–1976
US pathologist and Nobel Prize winner

Born in Ashland, New Hampshire, he graduated with a BA from Yale University in 1900, and received a medical degree from Johns Hopkins University in 1905. He worked as an assistant in pathology at Johns Hopkins, then in 1914 was appointed director of the Hooper Foundation for Medical Research at the University of California, and in 1921 Professor of Pathology and Dean of Medicine at University of Rochester in New York. His research there laid the groundwork for **George Minot** and **William Murphy**'s successful treatment of pernicious anaemia with liver (1926), until then a fatal disease, and the three men shared the 1934 Nobel Prize for physiology or medicine.

Whistler, James (Abbott) McNeill 1834–1903
US artist

Born in Lowell, Massachusetts, he spent five years of his boyhood in St Petersburg (Leningrad), where his father, an engineer, was engaged on a railway project for the tsar. After briefly returning home he left the USA, never to return, and went to study art in Paris. His teacher, **Charles Gleyre**, had little influence on his subsequent work, but he was deeply impressed by **Gustave Courbet** and later by the newly-discovered **Katsushika Hokusai**, and he exhibited at the *Salon des réfusés*. London subsequently became the centre of his activities, and he became celebrated as a portraitist. **John Ruskin**'s vitriolic criticism of his contributions to the Grosvenor Gallery exhibition of 1877 (Ruskin accused him of 'flinging a pot of paint in the public's face') provoked the famous lawsuit in which Whistler was awarded a farthing damages. His feelings on the subject are embodied in his *Gentle Art of Making Enemies* (1890). A recalcitrant rebel at a time when the sentimental Victorian subject picture was still *de rigueur*, Whistler conceived his paintings, even the portraits, as experiments in colour harmony and tonal effect; the famous portrait of his mother (1871–72), now in the Louvre, was originally exhibited at the Royal Academy as *An Arrangement in Grey and Black*, and evening scenes such as the well-known *Old Battersea Bridge* (1872–75, Tate Gallery, London) were called 'nocturnes'. If there was little emphasis on draughtsmanship in his painting technique, the reverse is true of his etchings, especially his 'Thames' set, which succeed in imparting beauty to some of the more unpromising parts of the London riverside.

Whistler, Rex John 1905–44
English artist

He studied at the Slade School of Art, London, and excelled in the rendering of 18th-century life, ornament and architecture, particularly in book illustration (eg an edition of *Gulliver's Travels* in 1930), murals (eg in the Tate Gallery, London), and designs for the theatre and ballet.

Whiston, William 1667–1752
English clergyman and mathematician

Born in Norton rectory, Leicestershire, he became a Fellow of Clare College, Cambridge (1693), chaplain to the Bishop of Norwich (1696), and rector of Lowestoft (1698). His *Theory of the Earth* (1696) attracted attention, and in 1703 he became Lucasian professor at Cambridge, in succession to Sir **Isaac Newton**. He was expelled from the university in 1710 for Arianism, and then wrote *Primitive Christianity revived* (1711–12). He spent the remainder of his life in London, engaged in one controversy after another, and joined the Baptists in 1747. His translation of **Josephus** was his best-known work. He also published his whimsical memoirs (1749–50).

Whitaker, Joseph 1820–95
English bookseller and publisher

Born in London, he started the *Educational Register*, *Whitaker's Clergyman's Diary*, *The Bookseller* in 1858, and in 1868 *Whitaker's Almanac*.

Whitaker, Pernell, nicknamed Sweet Pea 1964–
US boxer

Born in Norfolk, Virginia, he is reckoned to be the world's best pound-for-pound fighter (ie if all boxers were the same height and size, he would be the champion). Of his 37 contests he won 35, lost one and drew one. His outstanding technique made him a star of the 1984 Olympics where he won the lightweight gold medal. He has won titles at a range of weights: lightweight, light-welter, welter, and light-middle.

Whitbread, Fatima, originally Fatima Vedad 1961–
English javelin thrower

Abandoned by her parents as a baby and brought up in a children's home in east London, she was adopted by her physical education teacher and trainer, former British international javelin thrower **Margaret Whitbread**. Traditionally considered too short at 1.36 metres to excel at the javelin, Whitbread secured an Olympic bronze in 1984 and in 1985 became the first woman to throw a javelin over 76 metres. She set a world record of over 77 metres the following year (the record is now held by Petra Felke at nearly 80 metres). She took the world championship title in Rome in 1987 and the Olympic silver medal in 1988.

Whitbread, Samuel 1758–1815
English politician

The son of Samuel Whitbread (1720–96), founder of the famous brewing firm, he attended Eton and Oxford, and in 1790 entered Parliament. The intimate friend of **Charles Fox**, under **Pitt**, the Younger, he was Leader of the Opposition, and in 1805 headed the attack on **Henry Dundas** (Viscount Melville).

White, Andrew Dickson 1832–1918
US educationist and diplomat

Born in Homer, New York, he was a scholar of history and English literature, and as a New York state senator from 1863, he was active in educational reform and lobbied to create a state university. He founded Cornell University (Ithaca, New York) with the philanthropist **Ezra Cornell** and served as its first president (1868–85), instituting the system of elective studies and giving modern languages equal status with classics. He also served as US Minister to Russia (1892–94) and ambassador to Germany (1897–1902).

White, Canvass 1790–1834
US civil engineer

Born in Whitesboro, New York, he became an assistant in 1816 to **Benjamin Wright**, chief engineer of New York's Erie Canal. He was later one of the project's leading engineers, working on it until 1824. He was sent to England from 1817 to 1818 to study the latest methods of canal and lock construction, and on his return surveyed an improved route for the canal in several places. He also made a type of cement equal in quality to the much more expensive imported cements, patenting his discovery in 1820. Later he worked on other canals, and reported on the best way of meeting the future water supply needs of New York City.

White, Edward Douglass 1845–1921
US jurist

Born in Lafourche Parish, Louisiana, he fought in the Confederate army, was captured and paroled, and became a lawyer in New Orleans. He served in the Louisiana state senate and on the state Supreme Court as well as in the US Senate (1891–94). As associate justice of the Supreme Court from 1894, he formulated the 'White doctrine' declaring that territories under US sovereignty did not receive all the constitutional protections extended to the states. As Chief Justice of the Supreme Court (1910–21) he presided over antitrust cases against Standard Oil and other companies, and he asserted that the Sherman Antitrust Act does not outlaw all restraints on competition, but only 'unreasonable' ones.

White, Ellen Gould, *née* Harmon 1827–1915
US Seventh-day Adventist leader
Born in Gorham, Maine, she was converted to Adventism in 1842 through the preaching of **William Miller**. In 1846 she married an Adventist minister, James White. She was said to have experienced during her lifetime 'two thousand visions and prophetic dreams'. With the official establishment of the Seventh-day Adventist Church in 1863, she became leader and her pronouncements were regarded as the 'spirit of prophecy'. Through more than 60 works she still dominates the denomination. *Steps to Christ* has gone through numerous editions and sold more than 20 million copies.

White, E(lwyn) B(rooks) 1899–1985
US essayist, children's novelist, poet and parodist
Born in Mount Vernon, New York, in Westchester County, he graduated from Cornell University then began his long association with the *New Yorker* in 1925, and did as much to make its name as it did his. His reputation rests on his three bestselling novels for children (*Stuart Little*, 1945; *Charlotte's Web*, 1952; and *The Trumpet of the Swan*, 1970); the essays he wrote in the column 'One Man's Meat'; his collaboration with **James Thurber** on *Is Sex Necessary? Or Why You Feel The Way You Do* (1929); *The Elements of Style* (1959); a long article entitled 'Here Is New York'; and a peerless parody of **Ernest Hemingway** entitled 'Across the Street and into the Grill'. Inclined towards rusticity, he spent much time in Maine fretting over livestock, retiring to a boathouse to sculpt his pieces. He was married to Katharine Angell, the first fiction editor of the *New Yorker*.

White, Gilbert 1720–93
English naturalist and clergyman
Born in Selborne, Hampshire, he was educated at Oriel College, Oxford (1739–43), where he became a Fellow. He took holy orders in 1747, became junior proctor (1752), and obtained the sinecure college living of Moreton Pinkney, Northamptonshire (1758). His fame is based upon his *Natural History and Antiquities of Selborne* (1789), a natural history of a parish comprising the journal for a whole year and resulting from a series of letters written by White. In its original form, dealing only with the natural history of Selborne, the journal was completed in 1769 but the inclusion of additional letters on antiquarian and parish subjects delayed its publication for almost 20 years. It is still read for its acute observation on the habits and lives of a wide range of birds, mammals and insects. White's thrush is named after him. ◫ R M Lockley, *Gilbert White* (1976)

White, Joseph, *originally* José Maria Blanco 1775–1841
British theological writer
He was born in Seville, Spain, of an Irish Catholic father and an Andalusian mother. Ordained a priest in 1800, he lost his faith in 1810 and went to London, where he edited a monthly Spanish patriotic paper (1810–14). He then received an English pension of £250, was tutor to Lord Holland's son (1815–16), and was admitted to Anglican orders. He was tutor in Archbishop Whately's family in Dublin (1832–35), but fled to Liverpool on adopting unitarian views. He contributed to the *Quarterly* and *Westminster*, edited the short-lived *London Review*, wrote *Letters from Spain* (1822), *Evidence against Catholicism* (1825), and one notable sonnet, 'Night and Death'.

White, Kenneth 1936–
Scottish poet, essayist and travel writer

Born in Glasgow, he studied at Glasgow University, graduating with a double first in French and German. It could be said that he has made a career as an exile, first by spending many years travelling in Europe, the USA and elsewhere, and latterly as an academic in France, where he now holds the chair of 20th-century literature at the Sorbonne, Paris. He is highly acclaimed in France, both as a poet and as a thinker, his ruminative verse and Zen-influenced philosophy finding like minds. He has received some of France's most prestigious literary awards, including the Prix Medicis Etranger and the Grand Prix du Rayonnement. Early publications include *The Cold Wind of Dawn* (1966) and *The Most Difficult Area* (1968). He has found a new generation of Scots more receptive to him, and recent publications, largely reprinting material unavailable in English, include *The Bird Path: Collected Longer Poems* (1989), *Travels in a Drifting Dawn* (1989), *Handbook for the Diamond Country: Collected Shorter Poems 1960–1990* (1990) and *The Blue Road* (1990).

White, Leslie Alvin 1900–75
US cultural anthropologist
He was born in Salida, Colorado, and studied at Columbia University, the New School for Social Research, New York City, and the University of Chicago. He taught at Michigan from 1932 to 1975 (professor from 1943), and carried out many field trips among the Pueblo peoples between 1926 and 1957. He is principally known for his theory of cultural evolution, propounded in *The Science of Culture* (1949) and *The Evolution of Culture* (1959) and several other works, in which he argued that culture in general tends to advance as technological efficiency in harnessing and using environmental energy sources increases.

White, Marco Pierre 1961–
English chef and restaurateur
Born in Leeds, the son of an English father and Italian mother, he left school and home when he was 16 years old and worked as a kitchen porter at the Hotel St George in Harrogate, before going on to the Box Tree at Ilkley and then to London. There, his passionate enthusiasm persuaded **Albert Roux** to give him a job at Le Gavroche when he walked in off the street. Roux was his mentor and guide, but he has also worked for and learned from **Nico Ladenis** and **Raymond Blanc**. Albert Roux provided backing to help him open his own restaurant, Harveys, in 1987, and White was awarded three Michelin stars between 1988 and 1995, becoming the youngest and first British chef to do so. In 1992 he opened The Canteen Resaurant in Chelsea Harbour (a partnership with **Michael Caine**), followed by several others. He opened Quo Vadis in 1996, a restaurant noted for its interior designed by **Damien Hirst**. His publications include *Canteen Cuisine* (1995).

White, Minor 1908–76
US photographer and editor
Born in Minneapolis, Minnesota, he worked for the US government Works Progress Administration from 1937. From 1945 he was greatly influenced by **Edward Weston** and **Alfred Stieglitz**, developing both the realism of the photographic sequence and the abstraction of the 'equivalent', the visual metaphor in which he continued Stieglitz's symbolism of natural formations. In 1946 he moved to San Francisco and worked with **Ansel Adams**, whom he followed as director of the department of photography in the California School of Fine Art (1947–52). White was a prolific and influential writer, founding and editing the periodicals *Aperture* (1952) and *Image* (1953–57). He was Professor of Creative Photography at the Massachusetts Institute of Technology (1965–76).

White, Patrick Victor Martindale 1912–90
Australian novelist and Nobel Prize winner

Born in London, into an old Australian pastoralist family, he was educated at Cheltenham College and then worked in Australia for two years before going to King's College, Cambridge. After war service in the RAF he wrote *Happy Valley* (1939), *The Living and the Dead* (1941) and *The Aunt's Story* (1946), and then bought a farm near Sydney and settled in Australia. He achieved international success with *The Tree of Man* (1954). In this symbolic novel about a small community in the Australian bush, he attempts to portray every aspect of human life and to find the secret that makes it bearable. In 1957 he published *Voss*, an allegorical account, in religious terms, of a gruelling attempt to cross the Australian continent. This was followed by *Riders in the Chariot* (1961), *The Solid Mandala* (1966), *The Eye of the Storm* (1973) and *The Twyborn Affair* (1979). He also published short stories, *The Burnt Ones* (1964) and *The Cockatoos* (1974), and plays, including *Four Plays* (1965) and *Signal Driver* (1981). His own 'self-portrait', *Flaws in the Glass* (1981), describes the background to his supposedly 'ungracious' receipt of the Nobel Prize for literature in 1973. With the proceeds of the prize he established the Patrick White Literary Award, which makes an annual grant to an older Australian writer whose work has not received appropriate critical or financial recognition. 📖 D Marr, *Patrick White: a biography* (1991)

White, Paul Dudley 1886–1973
US cardiologist
The son of a physician who practised in Roxburg, Massachusetts, he was an undergraduate and medical student at Harvard, and for many years on the staff of its famous affiliated hospital, the Massachusetts General Hospital. He studied in 1913–14 with Sir Thomas Lewis in London and returned to the USA fired with enthusiasm over the value of the electrocardiogram in the diagnosis of heart disease. He acquired an international reputation with the publication of his textbook, *Heart disease* (1931), which went through several editions. He treated President Eisenhower when he had a heart attack, and Eisenhower's recovery did much to foster public awareness that heart disease need not be crippling. White emphasized the value of diet, exercise and weight control in the prevention of cardiovascular disease.

White, Pearl Fay 1889–1938
US film actress
Born in Green Ridge, Missouri, she began her film career in 1910, and as the heroine of *The Perils of Pauline* (1914), *The Exploits of Elaine* (1914–15), and others, made an enormous reputation as the exponent *par excellence* of the type of serial film popularly called 'cliff-hanger'. She retired in 1924, and went to live in France.

White, Richard Grant 1821–85
US Shakespearean scholar
Born in New York City, he studied medicine and law before becoming a journalist. His Shakespearean studies included criticisms on John Payne Collier's folio MS emendations (*Shakespeare's Scholar*, 1854) and two editions (1857–65, 1883) of the *Works*. His other publications included *Words and their Uses* (1870), *Everyday English* (1881), and *England Without and Within* (1881). His son was the architect Stanford White.

White, Stanford 1853–1906
US architect
Born in New York City, he learned architecture under H H Richardson and afterwards lived in Paris with the family of sculptor Augustus Sant-Gaudens. In 1879 he and two close friends formed the architectural firm of McKim, Mead & White, which was to design some of the most important buildings in US architectural history. A man of prodigious creative energy and eclectic tastes, White was often responsible for the interior design and decoration

of their buildings. He used a Renaissance style in his two surviving works in New York, the Washington Arch and the Century Club. He designed the old Madison Square Garden in 1889, commissioning for the cupola a statue of Diana that shocked New York with its nudity, and building for himself in the tower a notorious private apartment that he used for his satyr-like amusements. He was finally shot and killed there by a jealous husband.

White, T(erence) H(anbury) 1906–64
English novelist
Born in Bombay, India, he was educated at Cheltenham College and Queens' College, Cambridge. Until 1936 he was a master at Stowe and later lived in a gamekeeper's cottage near the school. Always a keen sportsman, he was an ardent falconer and fisherman, and his knowledge and love of nature are imbued in his work. He wrote more than 25 books, but he is best known for his interpretation of the Arthurian legend, a tetralogy known collectively as *The Once and Future King* (1958), the first part of which, *The Sword in the Stone* (1937), is a children's classic. A fifth volume, found among his papers, was published as *The Book of Merlyn* (1977). *Mistress Masham's Repose* (1947) is another notable children's book. His adult works include *The Goshawk* (1951), set at the onset of World War II, a chronicle of the taming and training of one of Germany's noblest birds of prey, *The Master* (1957), a science-fiction parable, and *The Book of Beasts* (1954), translated from a 12th-century Latin bestiary. 📖 S T Warner, *T. H. White* (1967)

White, William Allen, *known as* the Sage of Emporia 1868–1944
US editor and writer
Born in Emporia, Kansas, he was proprietor and editor of the Emporia *Daily* and *Weekly Gazette* in 1895. He gained national fame in the presidential election of 1896 by his ferocious anti-Populist editorial 'What's the Matter with Kansas?', much used by the Republican (McKinley) campaign, but he later lent support to the growing Progressive movement, backing New York Governor and then President Theodore Roosevelt. He published short stories of mordant social criticism, *Stratagems and Spoils* (1901), and a novel in the same vein, *A Certain Rich Man* (1909). He later wrote about national politicians of his time in *Masks in a Pageant* (1928), and an ironic life of Calvin Coolidge, *A Puritan in Babylon* (1933). He won a Pulitzer Prize for his editorials in 1923.

White, William Hale, *pseudonym* Mark Rutherford 1831–1913
English novelist and journalist
He was born in Bedford, Bedfordshire. Having abandoned his training as an independent religious minister, he worked briefly in the offices of the *Westminster Review*, where he met George Eliot, before entering the Civil Service. He continued writing journalism, becoming London correspondent of *The Scotsman*, and during the 1850s began to publish novels and works of philosophy. All take a high moral tone and are somewhat humourless, even depressing, although the novels are atmospherically strong. The best are *The Autobiography of Mark Rutherford, Dissenting Minister* (1881) and *Mark Rutherford's Deliverance* (1885), recounting White's spiritual journey.

Whitefield, George 1714–70
English evangelist, one of the founders of Methodism
Born in the Bell Inn, Gloucester, he went to Pembroke College, Oxford, as a servitor at 18. The Wesleys had already laid the foundations of Methodism at Oxford, and Whitefield became an enthusiastic evangelist. He took deacon's orders in 1736, and preached his first sermon in the Crypt Church, Gloucester. In 1738 he followed John Wesley to Georgia and was appointed minister at

Savannah. He returned to England in 1739 to be admitted to priest's orders. He was actively opposed by his fellow churchmen, but when the parish pulpits were denied him he preached in the open air, the first time with great effect, on Kingswood Hill, near Bristol. He returned to Georgia and made extensive preaching tours and, about 1741, differences on predestination led to his separation as a rigid Calvinist from John Wesley as an Arminian. His supporters built him a chapel in Bristol and the Moorfields 'Tabernacle' in London. Many of his adherents followed the Countess of Huntingdon in Wales and formed Calvinistic Methodists, so she appointed him her chaplain, and built and endowed many chapels for him. He made seven evangelistic visits to America, and spent the rest of his life in preaching tours through England, Scotland (1741) and Wales. He compiled a hymn book in 1753. He set out for America for the last time in 1769, and died near Boston. ▥ Arnold A Dallimore, *George Whitefield: The Life and Times of the Great Evangelist of the Eighteenth Century Revival* (1970)

Whitehead, Alfred North 1861–1947
English mathematician and Idealist philosopher

Born in London, he was educated at Sherborne and Trinity College, Cambridge, where he was senior lecturer in mathematics until 1911. He became Professor of Applied Mathematics at Imperial College, London (1914–24), and Professor of Philosophy at Harvard (1924–37). Extending the Booleian symbolic logic in a highly original *Treatise on Universal Algebra* (1898), he contributed a remarkable memoir to the Royal Society, *Mathematical Concepts of the Material World* (1905). Profoundly influenced by Giuseppe Peano, he collaborated with his former pupil at Trinity, Bertrand Russell, in the *Principia Mathematica* (1910–13), the greatest single contribution to logic since Aristotle. In his Edinburgh Gifford Lectures, 'Process and Reality' (1929), he attempted a metaphysics comprising psychological as well as physical experience, with events as the ultimate components of reality. Other more popular works include *Adventures of Ideas* (1933) and *Modes of Thought* (1938). He was awarded the first James Scott Prize of the Royal Society of Edinburgh (1922). ▥ Victor Lowe, *Alfred North Whitehead, The Man and His Works* (1985)

Whitehead, Charles 1804–62
English poet and novelist

He was born in London, and devoted himself to writing after publishing *The Solitary*, a reflective poem, in 1831. His *Autobiography of Jack Ketch* (1834) was quite humorous, but when Chapman & Hall asked him for a popular book in instalments he declined, recommending the young Dickens, who thus began the *Pickwick Papers*. Whitehead went on to write the novel *Richard Savage* (1842), which earned the praise of Dickens and Dante Gabriel Rossetti. He went to Melbourne in 1857, but died from alcoholism, leaving unfinished the *Spanish Marriage*, a drama. ▥ M Bell, *A Forgotten Genius* (1884)

Whitehead, Gillian 1941–
New Zealand composer and teacher

She was born of Maori descent in Whangarei. After studying at Auckland University and at Victoria University in Wellington, she moved to Sydney University in 1964 to study composition under Peter Sculthorpe, and in 1965 to London to study with Peter Maxwell Davies. She is conscious of her Maori heritage, and the themes of cultural misinterpretation recur in her work; the text of her *Babel* (1969–70) contains almost 50 languages from all major linguistic groups. She has set texts from New Zealand writers Fleur Adcock and Janet Frame as well as traditional Maori texts and medieval lyrics.

Whitehead, Paul 1710–74
English satirist and poet

Born in Holborn, London, he was apprenticed to a mercer, and later married a short-lived retarded woman with a fortune of £10,000. He spent some years in Fleet prison for the non-payment of a sum for which he had stood security. He became active in politics, was one of the infamous 'monks' of Medmenham Abbey, and became deputy treasurer of the Chamber. Among his satires are *State Dunces* (1733), inscribed to Pope, and *Manners* (1739), for which Robert Dodsley the publisher was brought before the House of Lords. His *Collected Works* appeared in 1777.

Whitehead, Robert 1823–1905
English inventor

Born in Bolton-le-Moors, Lancashire, he trained as an engineer in Manchester and settled (1856) in Fiume, Croatia, where he invented the first self-propelling torpedo (1866).

Whitehead, William 1715–85
English poet and dramatist

Born in Cambridge, he was educated at Winchester and Clare Hall, Cambridge, and became a Fellow in 1742. He travelled as tutor to Lord Jersey's son, became in 1755 Secretary of the Order of the Bath, and in 1757 was appointed Poet Laureate. He defended his acceptance against hostile criticism in *A Charge to the Poets* (1762). He wrote tragedies—*The Roman Father* (1750), in imitation of Pierre Corneille's *Horace*, and *Creusa* (1754)—and also a comedy, *School for Lovers* (1762). His *Plays and Poems* were collected in 1774, with *Complete Poems* following in 1788.

Whitelaw, Billie 1932–
English actress

Born in Coventry, West Midlands, she made her London debut in Georges Feydeau's *Hotel Paradiso* (1956), and joined the National Theatre (1964), appearing in Samuel Beckett's one-act *Play*. She joined the Royal Shakespeare Company (1971) and returned to Beckett in 1973 to play Mouth in *Not I*. Other noted Beckett interpretations include *Footfalls* at the Royal Court (1976), and a revival of *Happy Days* at the Royal Court (1979). She has played many other modern roles on stage, and appeared on television (*Firm Friends*, 1992–94) and in several films, including *The Omen* (1976), *The Water Babies* (1979) and *The Krays* (1990). Her autobiography *Billie Whitelaw—Who He?* was published in 1995.

Whitelaw, Willie (William Stephen Ian) Whitelaw, 1st Viscount 1918–
Scottish Conservative politician

Born in Nairn, he was educated at Winchester and Cambridge, served in the Scots Guards during and after the war, and first became a Conservative MP in 1955. Secretary of State for Northern Ireland (1972–73) and for Employment (1973–74), he was Home Secretary for four years before being made a viscount in 1983 and was Leader of the Lords until 1988. He was made a Companion of Honour in 1974. During the 1975 Conservative leadership contest his loyalty to Edward Heath, which persuaded him not to stand directly against him in the first ballot, is thought to have allowed Margaret Thatcher to win in the second ballot. As her deputy, however, he displayed the same loyalty and was one of her firmest, although sometimes privately critical, allies, being one of her closest advisers in the Falklands War and general election campaigns. He published *The Whitelaw Memoirs* in 1989.

Whiteley, Brett 1939–92
Australian artist

Born in Paddington, Sydney, he studied in Sydney until a scholarship enabled him to go to Italy. He was represented in the 1961 Whitechapel Gallery exhibition and won the international prize at the second Paris Biennale of the same year. His work was then purchased by both the Tate Gallery and the Victoria and Albert Museum in London. He worked in New York from 1967 to 1969, and continued to travel and exhibit abroad regularly, painting in an Abstract Expressionist style. He won the prestigious Archibald Prize in 1976 and again in 1978, the Sulman Prize (1976, 1978) and the Wynne Prize (1977, 1978). His colours are typically ochres, creamy whites, and reddish browns, recalling the hot Australian landscape, with a hint of eroticism, violence and death. He was also an animal painter.

Whiteman, Paul 1891–1967
US bandleader

He was born in Denver, Colorado. He became famous in the 1920s as a pioneer of 'sweet style', as opposed to the traditional 'classical' style jazz. His band employed such brilliant exponents of true jazz as the trumpeter **Bix Beiderbecke**, and Whiteman became popularly regarded as the 'inventor' of jazz itself rather than of a deviation from true jazz style. He was responsible for **George Gershwin's** experiments in 'symphonic' jazz, commissioning the *Rhapsody in Blue* for a concert in New York in 1924.

Whiteread, Rachel 1963–
English sculptor

Born in London, she trained at Brighton Polytechnic and the Slade School, and won a scholarship to Berlin (1992–93), during which time she visited concentration camps and war sites. She takes casts from objects bearing traces of human existence, such as bathtubs, old mattresses, shelves, mortuary slabs, and even whole rooms, capturing the space in and around them, and transforming them into ghostly icons. Thus, the inside of a hot water bottle becomes *Torso* (1991). She also moulds in rubber, as with *White Sloping Bed* (1991) and *Orange Bath* (1996). In 1993–94 she became the most talked-about sculptor for decades when, sponsored by Tarmac Structural Repairs, she cast an entire disused house in East London. Concreted over, it stood like a necropolis until it was bulldozed by the local authority. *House*, together with *Room* (1993), and her exhibitions in Eindhoven, Sydney, Venice and Paris, made her her clear favourite and the winner of the 1993 Turner Prize. Since 1994 she has also worked using resin (*Table and Chair*), her tribute to the influence of **Bruce Nauman**. In 1996–97 her retrospective, *Shedding Life*, was seen at the Tate Gallery, Liverpool, and in November 1996 her cast of a library, with rubber and fibreglass pages bolted on to the outside, was unveiled as the *Holocaust Memorial* in the Judenplatz, Vienna.

Whitfield, June Rosemary 1925–
English comic actress

Born in Streatham, London, she graduated from RADA and worked in revues, musicals and pantomimes as a foil to some of the top comedians in showbusiness before enjoying her own success in the long-running radio series *Take It From Here* (1953–60) as Eth Glum. She has been an indispensable part of television light entertainment in such series as *Fast and Loose* (1954), *Faces of Jim* (1962–63) and *Beggar My Neighbour* (1966–67). A long professional association with **Terry Scott** resulted in the series *Scott on ...* (1969–73), *Happy Ever After* (1974) and *Terry and June* (1979–87). Her film appearances include *Carry on Nurse* (1959), *The Spy With the Cold Nose* (1965), *Bless This House* (1973), *Carry on Columbus* (1992) and *Jude* (1996); stage appearances include *An Ideal Husband* (1987) and *Babes in the Wood* (1990). She has recently revived her television career by appearing in **Jennifer Saunders's** popular comedy series, *Absolutely Fabulous* (1993–96), and the drama *Family Money* (1997). In 1994 she was given the Lifetime Achievement award at the British Comedy Awards.

Whitgift, John c.1530–1604
English prelate

Born in Grimsby, Lincolnshire, he was elected Fellow of Peterhouse, Cambridge in 1555, took orders in 1560, and rose to be Regius Professor of Divinity at Cambridge (1567), dean of Lincoln (1571), Bishop of Worcester (1577), Archbishop of Canterbury (1583) and Privy Councillor (1586). He attended Queen **Elizabeth I** on her death-bed, and crowned **James VI and I**. Although personally biased towards Calvinism, he vindicated the Anglican position against the Puritans and enforced the policy of uniformity in the Church of England. He was the founder of Whitgift School in Croydon, Surrey. 📖 V J K Brook, *Whitgift and the English Church* (1957)

Whiting, John 1917–63
English playwright

He was born in Salisbury, and studied at RADA, London (1935–37). After serving in the Royal Artillery in World War II he resumed his acting career before emerging as a dramatist. *Saint's Day* (1951) gained recognition for his talent although it was not a popular success. It was followed by *A Penny for a Song* (1951, a comedy), and *Marching Song* (1954), in which the main character has to choose between standing trial as a scapegoat for his country's failure or committing suicide. Other works include a dramatization of **Aldous Huxley's** *The Devils of Loudon* for the Royal Shakespeare Company (1961), and the pieces in *Collected Plays* (1969).

Whitlam, (Edward) Gough 1916–
Australian statesman

Educated at the University of Sydney, after war service in the RAAF he became a barrister. He entered politics in 1952 and led the Australian Labor Party (1967–77), forming the first Labor government since 1949. His administration (1972–75) was notable for its radicalism, ending conscription and withdrawing Australian troops from the Vietnam War, recognizing Communist China, relaxing the restrictions on non-white immigrants, abolishing university fees and creating Medibank (the state-funded healthcare system). He was controversially dismissed by the Governor-General **John Kerr** in 1975, after the Senate had blocked his money bills; Labor lost the subsequent election. Whitlam retired from politics in 1977, going on to become Australian ambassador to UNESCO in Paris (1983–86) and a member of its executive board (1985–89). His publications include *The Whitlam Government* (1985).

Whitley, John Henry 1866–1935
English politician

Born in Halifax, Yorkshire, and educated at Clifton and London University, he was Liberal MP for Halifax (1900–28) and Speaker (1921–28) during the difficult period which culminated in the General Strike. He presided over the committee that proposed (1917) Whitley Councils for joint consultation between employers and employees.

Whitman, Walt See panel p1945

Whitney, Anne 1821–1915
US sculptor

She was born in Watertown, Massachusetts. Her early works, created in Boston, reflect her interest in social justice. Following the American Civil War, she travelled and studied extensively in Europe and continued sculpting well into her eighties. At the age of 72, she anonymously entered a competition to create a memorial to US statesman **Charles Sumner**. Her sculpture won but the honour was withdrawn when it was discovered that she was a woman. At least 100 of her works have been catalogued and are owned by such institutions as the Smithsonian and the National Collection of Fine Arts.

Whitman, Walt(er) 1819–92
US poet

Walt Whitman was born in West Hills, Long Island, New York, the son of a radical, free-thinking carpenter. He was brought up in Brooklyn from the age of four, and worked first as an office boy (in a lawyer's, a doctor's and finally a printer's office). He then became an itinerant teacher in country schools. He returned to printing, wrote an earnest temperance novel, *Franklin Evans or, The Inebriate* (1842), and in 1846 became editor of the *Brooklyn Eagle*, a Democratic paper. This and his other numerous press engagements were only of short duration.

In 1848 he travelled with his brothers to New Orleans, where he worked briefly on the New Orleans *Crescent*, before returning to Brooklyn as a journalist (1848–54). He seemed unable to find free expression for his emotions until he hit upon the curious, irregular, recitative measures of *Leaves of Grass* (1855). Originally a small, 12-poem folio of 95 pages published anonymously with the author's portrait in work clothes enigmatically facing the title page, it grew in the eight succeeding editions (until 1891–92) to nearly 440 pages. The untitled poem which introduced the first edition was later called 'Song of Myself' (1881). **Ralph Waldo Emerson**, in a letter to Whitman, praised the first collection as 'the most extraordinary piece of wit and wisdom that America yet has contributed'. The 1860 edition added the 'Calamus' sequence of 45 poems, which is considered by many to be a poetic indication of Whitman's apparent homosexuality. *Leaves of Grass*, along with his prose work *Specimen Days and Collect* (1882–83), constitutes Whitman's main life-work as a writer.

In 1862 Whitman was summoned to tend his brother who had been wounded at Fredericksburg in the Civil War, and he subsequently became a volunteer nurse in the Washington hospitals of the Northern and Southern armies. The exertion, exposure, and strain of those few years left him a shattered and prematurely aged man. In 1865 he received a government clerkship, but was dismissed by Secretary **Harlan** as the author of 'an indecent book' (*Leaves of Grass*); however he almost immediately obtained a similar post. In 1873 he suffered a paralytic

stroke and left Washington for Camden, New Jersey, where he spent the remainder of his life. He would have fallen into absolute poverty but for the help of trans-Atlantic admirers and, later, several wealthy American citizens who liberally provided for his simple wants. The poetry in his last collection of poems and prose, *Good-Bye, My Fancy* (1891), was reprinted in the final edition of *Leaves of Grass*.

Whitman set himself the task of uplifting into the sphere of poetry the whole of modern life and man, including in his verse subjects which, at that time, were considered taboo, and making frequent use of colloquial language. Many of his poems for *Leaves of Grass* are now considered American classics, such as the sequence *Drum Taps* (1865) and its follow-up *Sequel to Drum Taps* (1865–66), which contains the elegies 'When Lilacs Last in the Courtyard Bloom'd' and 'O Captain! My Captain!' written in memory of the assassinated US President **Abraham Lincoln**.

📖 P Zweig, *Walt Whitman: The Making of the Poet* (1984); G W Allen, *The Solitary Singer: A Critical Biography of Walt Whitman* (1955, rev edn 1967); *Memoranda During the War* (autobiographical narrative, 1875, reprinted in *Specimen Days and Collect*, 1882–83).

> 'I believe a leaf of grass is no less than the journey-work of the stars,
> And the pismire is equally perfect, and a grain of sand, and the egg of the wren,
> And the tree toad is a chef-d'œuvre for the highest,
> And the running blackberry would adorn the parlours of heaven,
> And the narrowest hinge in my hand puts to scorn all machinery,
> And the cow crunching with depress'd head surpasses any statue,
> And a mouse is miracle enough to stagger sextillions of infidels.'
> 'Song of Myself' (part 31, written 1855).

Whitney, Eli 1765–1825
US inventor

Born in Westborough, Massachusetts, he was educated at Yale and went to Georgia as a teacher. Finding a patron in Mrs Nathaniel Greene, the widow of a general, he stayed on her plantation, read law and set to work to invent a cotton-gin for separating cotton fibre from the seeds. His machine was stolen, and lawsuits in defence of his rights took up all his profits and the $50,000 voted him by the state of South Carolina. In 1798 he got a government contract for the manufacture of firearms, and he subsequently made a fortune in this business.

Whitney, Gertrude Vanderbilt, *née* Vanderbilt 1875–1942
US sculptor and patron of the arts

She was born into a wealthy family in New York City and married Harry Payne Whitney (1872–1930), a financier, in 1896. She trained at the Art Students League of New York and in Paris, where she was inspired by the work of **Auguste Rodin**. During World War I she established a hospital and worked as a nurse, which became the inspiration for the two panels *Victory Arch* (1918–20) and *The Washington Heights War Memorial* (1921), both in New York City. Other works include the *Aztec Fountain* (1912) and *Titanic Memorial* (1914–31), symbolizing the words in Revelation 20.13: 'The sea gave up its dead'. In 1930 Whitney donated her collection of 500 works of 20th-

century art, and bought 100 more, to found the Whitney Museum of Modern Art in Greenwich Village, which opened in 1931.

Whitney, Josiah Dwight 1819–96
US geologist

Born in Northampton, Massachusetts, he graduated at Yale and in 1840 joined the New Hampshire Survey. He worked in Michigan from 1847 to 1849, and in the Lake Superior region with **James Hall**. Following his studies of mining problems in Illinois, he published *Mineral Wealth of the United States* (1854). He was appointed professor at Iowa University in 1855, State Geologist of California in 1860 and professor at Harvard in 1865. He produced important work on the *Auriferous Gravels of the Sierra Nevada* (1879–80), in which he recognized that the gold deposits were not marine deposits as had been supposed, but were the products of erosion and deposition of pre-existing gold-bearing mineral veins. He also wrote on the *Climate Changes of Later Geological Time* (1880, 1882). Mount Whitney in southern California is named in his honour.

Whitney, William Dwight 1827–94
US philologist

Brother of **Josiah Dwight Whitney**, he studied at Williams and Yale, and in Germany prepared an edition of the *Atharva Veda Sanhita* (1856). In 1854 he became Professor of Sanskrit at Yale, and in 1870 also of Comparative Philology. He was an office-bearer of the American Oriental Society, edited numerous Sanskrit texts, and contributed to the great Sanskrit dictionary of Otto von Böhtlingk and Roth (1855–75). He waged war with **Max Müller** on fundamental questions of the science of language. Among his works were *Language and the Study of Language* (1867), *Material and Form in Language* (1872), *Life and Growth of Language* (1876), *Essentials of English Grammar* (1877) and *Mixture in Language* (1881). He was the editor of the 1864 edition of *Webster's Dictionary* and editor-in-chief of the *Century Dictionary and Cyclopedia* (1889–91).

Whittier, John Greenleaf 1807–92
US Quaker poet and abolitionist
Born near Haverhill, Massachusetts, he was largely self-educated. In 1829 he entered journalism, and in 1831 published *Legends of New England*, a collection of poems and stories. In 1840 he settled at Amesbury, a village near his birthplace, and devoted himself to the cause of emancipation. His later works include the collection *In War Time* (1864), which contains the well-known ballad 'Barbara Frietchie', and *At Sundown* (1892). ☐ E Wagenknecht, *John Greenleaf Whittier* (1967)

Whittington, Dick (Richard) c.1358–1423
English merchant and philanthropist
He was the youngest son of Sir William Whittington of Pauntley, Gloucestershire. As a young man he was apprenticed to a prosperous London merchant, and by 1392 he was a member of the Mercers' Company, and in 1393 an alderman and sheriff. In 1397 he took over as Mayor of London at the previous incumbent's death, and was Mayor again three times in 1398, 1406, and 1419. He became an MP in 1416. He traded with and loaned money to **Henry IV** and **Henry V.** A generous benefactor, he built a library at Greyfriars, and left his fortune to a trust which provided for the building of a library at Guildhall, the rebuilding of Newgate Prison, and the foundation of a college and almshouse (now at East Grinstead). The legend of his cat is an accepted part of English folklore, dating from the early 17th century.

Whittle, Sir Frank 1907–96
English aeronautical engineer and inventor
Born in Coventry, Warwickshire, he joined the RAF as an apprentice (1923), and studied at the RAF College, Cranwell, and at Cambridge (1934–37). He conceived the idea of trying to develop a replacement for the conventional internal combustion aero engine, and began research into jet propulsion before 1930, while still a student. After a long fight against official inertia his engine was first flown successfully in a Gloster aircraft in May 1941, about two years after the world's first flights of both turbo-jet and rocket-powered aircraft had taken place in Germany. He was elected FRS in 1947, and knighted in 1948 on his retirement from the RAF. He then acted as consultant and technical adviser to a number of British firms, and in 1977 was elected a member of the faculty of the US Naval Academy at Annapolis, Maryland. ☐ John Golley, *Whittle: The True Story* (1987)

Whitworth, Sir Joseph 1803–87
English engineer and inventor
He was born in Stockport, near Manchester, and exhibited many tools and machines at the Great Exhibition of 1851 in London. In 1859 he invented a gun of compressed steel, with a spiral polygonal bore. He founded Whitworth scholarships for encouraging engineering science, and was responsible for the standard screw-thread named after him.

Whorf, Benjamin Lee 1897–1941
US linguist
Born in Winthrop, Massachusetts, he was a chemical engineer and fire prevention officer by profession and studied linguistics and Native American languages in his spare time. Influenced by **Edward Sapir's** teaching at

Yale University (1931–32), he developed Sapir's insights into the influence of language on people's perception of the world into what became known as the Sapir–Whorf hypothesis. He illustrated his theory in particular with comparisons between the grammar and vocabulary of what he called 'standard average European' on the one hand and the language of the Hopi on the other.

Whymper, Edward 1840–1911
English wood-engraver and mountaineer
Born in London, he was trained as an artist in wood, but became more famous for his mountaineering. In 1860–69 he conquered several hitherto unscaled peaks of the Alps, including the Matterhorn. In 1867 and 1872 he made many geological discoveries in North Greenland. His travels in the Andes (including ascents of Chimborazo) took place in 1879–80. He illustrated his books *Scrambles amongst the Alps* (1871, 1893) and *Travels Amongst the Great Andes* (1892).

Whyte-Melville, George John 1821–78
Scottish novelist and authority on field sports
Born in Mount-Melville, St Andrews, and educated at Eton, he became a captain in the Coldstream Guards and served in the Crimean War, commanding a regiment of Turkish cavalry irregulars. For the rest of his life he devoted himself to field sports, and wrote numerous novels involving fox-hunting and steeplechasing, for example *Digby Grand* (1853) and *Tilbury Nogo* (1861). He also wrote serious historical novels, including *Market Harborough* (1861), *The Gladiators* (1863) and *The Queen's Maries* (1862), on **Mary, Queen of Scots**, and published *Songs and Verse* in 1869. He was killed in a hunting accident.

Wicliffe, John See Wycliffe, John

Widgery, John Passmore, Lord 1911–81
English judge
Born in South Molton, Devon, he was educated at Queen's College, Taunton. He qualified as a solicitor and was called to the Bar in 1947. He became a judge in 1961, a Lord Justice of Appeal in 1968 and Lord Chief Justice of England (1971–80). He was responsible for overseeing the restructuring of the English courts recommended by a Royal commission, and was also chairman of an enquiry into a clash between the army and demonstrators in Londonderry in 1972.

Widor, Charles Marie 1845–1937
French composer
Born in Lyons, he was organist of St Sulpice, Paris, becoming Professor of Organ and Composition at the Paris Conservatoire in 1891 and Secretary of the Académie des Beaux-Arts from 1914 until his death. He composed 10 symphonies for the organ, as well as a ballet, chamber music and other orchestral works. He wrote *La Technique de l'orchestre moderne* (1904).

Wiechert, Ernst 1887–1950
German writer
He was born in Kleinort, East Prussia, and wrote novels dealing with psychological problems such as postwar readjustment. Early titles include *Der Wald* (1922, 'The Forest'), *Der Totenwolf* (1924, 'The Wolf of Death') and *Der silberne Wagen* (1928, 'The Silver Wagon'). *Das einfache Leben* (1939, Eng trans *The Simple Life*, 1954), is probably his masterpiece. *Wälder und Menschen* (1936, 'Forests and Men') is autobiographical, as is *Der Totenwald* (1946, Eng trans *The Forest of the Dead*, 1947), which describes his six months' confinement in Buchenwald concentration camp. ☐ H Ebling, *Ernst Wiechert* (1947)

Wieland, Christoph Martin 1733–1813
German writer

Born near Biberach, he was invited (1752) by **Johann Georg Bodmer** to Zurich, where he wrote *Der geprüfte Abraham* (1753, 'The Testing of Abraham'). As well as making the first German translation of **Shakespeare** (22 plays, 1762–66), he wrote the romances *Agathon* (1766–67, Eng trans 1773) and *Don Silvio von Rosalva* (1764, Eng trans 1785), *Die Grazien* (1768, Eng trans *The Graces*, 1823) and other tales, and the didactic poem *Musarion* (1768). In Weimar, he was the friend of **Goethe** and **Johann Herder**, and produced his best-known work, the heroic poem *Oberon* (1780, Eng trans 1798). 📖 D M von Abbe, *Christoph Wieland* (1961)

Wieland, Heinrich Otto 1877–1957
German chemist and Nobel Prize winner

Born in Pforzheim, he studied chemistry at the universities of Munich, Berlin and Stuttgart and received a PhD from the University of Munich (1901), where he subsequently became lecturer and, in 1909, associate professor. Four years later he was appointed professor at Munich Technical University. During World War I, while on leave of absence, he worked on chemical weapons at the Kaiser Wilhelm Institute. After the war he returned to Munich until 1921, when he moved to the University of Freiburg for three years. He returned to the University of Munich in 1924 as chairman, a position he held until his retirement in 1950. He made many contributions to the development of organic chemistry. His initial studies involved nitrogen compounds and he also made extensive investigations of oxidation reactions. However, he is most famous for his studies of the bile acids (substances stored in the bladder which aid the digestion of lipids). It was for this work that he received the Nobel Prize for chemistry in 1927. He subsequently studied the chemistry of a number of naturally occurring substances, including butterfly pigments.

Wien, Wilhelm Carl Werner Otto Fritz Franz 1864–1928
German physicist and Nobel Prize winner

Born in Gaffken in East Prussia, he attended the universities of Göttingen, Berlin (where he studied under **Hermann von Helmholtz**) and Heidelberg. He became Helmholtz's assistant in 1890, and was appointed to professorships at the universities of Aachen (1896), Giessen (1899), Würzburg (1899) and finally Munich (1920). His chief contribution was on black-body radiation, in which he advanced the work of **Ludwig Boltzmann** (1884), to show that the wavelength at which maximum energy is radiated is inversely proportional to the absolute temperature of the body (1893). He cleared the way for **Max Planck** to resolve the observed distribution of all frequencies with the quantum theory (1900), and in 1911 was awarded the Nobel Prize for physics for his work on black-body radiation. His subsequent research covered hydrodynamics, X-rays and cathode rays.

Wiener, Norbert 1894–1964
US mathematician

Born in Columbia, Missouri, he studied zoology at Harvard and philosophy at Cornell University, and in Europe studied with **Bertrand Russell** at the universities of Cambridge and Göttingen. He was later appointed Professor of Mathematics at the Massachusetts Institute of Technology (1932–60), where he worked on stochastic processes and harmonic analysis, inventing the concepts later called the Wiener integral and Wiener measure. During World War II he studied mathematical communication theory applied to predictors and guided missiles, and his study of feedback in the handling of information by electronic devices led him to compare this with analogous mental processes in animals in *Cybernetics, or control*

and communication in the animal and the machine (1948) and other works. 📖 Pesi R Masani, *Norbert Wiener, 1894–1964* (1989)

Wieniawski, Henri 1835–80
Polish composer of violin music

Born in Lublin, he was solo violinist to Tsar **Alexander II** for 12 years, and taught at the Brussels Conservatory. His brother, Joseph (1837–1912), a pianist, taught in the Moscow Conservatory, and was a conductor at Warsaw (1871–77).

Wiertz, Anton Joseph 1806–65
Belgian painter

Born in Dinant, in 1836 he settled in Liège and in 1848 in Brussels. His original aim was to combine the excellences of **Michelangelo** and **Rubens**, but around 1848–50 he began to paint speculative and mystical pieces, dreams, visions, and the products of a morbid imagination. In 1850 the state built him a studio which later became the Musée Wiertz.

Wiesel, Elie(zer) 1928–
US writer and Nobel Prize winner

Born in Sighet, Romania, he was a teenager during World War II and was imprisoned in both Auschwitz and Buchenwald, where his parents and a sister perished. After the war he became a journalist and a US citizen (1963). His first novel, *Night* (1958), is an autobiographical account of the horrors of the death camps, and in his subsequent novels, stories, and plays he continued his effort to memorialize the Holocaust. In 1986 he was awarded the Nobel Peace Prize.

Wiesel, Torsten Nils 1924–
Swedish neurophysiologist and Nobel Prize winner

Born in Uppsala, he studied medicine at the Karolinska Institute in Stockholm, and then went to the USA, working initially at Johns Hopkins Medical School in ophthalmology, and then at Harvard Medical School, where he became Professor of Physiology (1967–68), Professor of Neurobiology (1968–74), and Robert Winthrop Professor of Neurobiology (1974–83). Together with **David Hubel** he studied the way in which the brain processes visual information, and they demonstrated that there is a hierarchical processing pathway, of increasingly sophisticated analysis of visual information by nerve cells from the retina to the cerebral cortex. In 1981 Wiesel and Hubel shared the Nobel Prize for physiology or medicine with **Roger Sperry**. He joined Rockefeller University as head of the laboratory of neurobiology in 1983, becoming president in 1992.

Wiggin, Kate Douglas, *née* Smith 1856–1953
US novelist

Born in Philadelphia, she moved to San Francisco to organize the first free kindergarten school in the West (1878). She wrote novels for both adults and children, but was more successful with the latter. *Rebecca of Sunnybrook Farm* (1903) is probably her best-known book, although the *Penelope* exploits, which were adult semi-novels, *The Birds' Christmas Carol* (1888) and *Mother Carey's Chickens* (1911), were all firm favourites. 📖 *My Garden of Memory* (1923)

Wigglesworth, Michael 1631–1705
American poet and clergyman

Born in Yorkshire, England, he was taken to Massachusetts Bay colony at the age of seven, and educated at Harvard. He was married to Mary Reyner (1655), to Martha Mudge (1679), and to Sybil Sparhawk Avery (1691), and eight children resulted. Fellow and tutor at Harvard from 1652 to 1654, and again from 1697 to 1705, he was ordained to the ministry of the Puritan Church in Malden c.1656. His epic poem, the first American epic,'Day of Doom' (1662), takes a lengthy and somewhat pessimistic view of the Day of Judgement. He wrote a shorter poem intended for edification in 1669: 'Meat out of the Eater or Meditations Concerning the Necessity, End and Usefulness of Afflictions Unto God's Children'. His *Diary* was published in 1951. ▣ R Crowder, *No Featherbed to Heaven* (1962)

Wigglesworth, Sir Vincent Brian 1899–1994
English biologist

Born in Kirkham, Lancashire, he was educated at Cambridge and St Thomas's Hospital, and became Reader in Entomology at the universities of London (1936–44) and Cambridge (1945–52), where he was subsequently appointed Quick Professor of Biology (1952–66). He was also director of the Agricultural Research Council Unit of Insect Physiology (1943–67). In a series of studies of insect metamorphosis, Wigglesworth demonstrated the production and the sources of hormones which selectively activate different genetic components of insects. He also succeeded in artificially inducing such changes by manipulating the associated hormone levels. This work led to a much greater understanding of insect physiology and their interactions with the environment. Wigglesworth was elected FRS in 1939, and knighted in 1964. His published works include *Insect Physiology* (1934) and *Insect Hormones* (1970).

Wightman, Hazel Hotchkiss 1886–1974
US tennis player

Born in Healdsburg, California, she began tournament play in 1902 and introduced more active play for women, employing volley and net play for the first time. She also challenged the restrictive women's dress of the day. She won the national triple of the singles, the doubles and the mixed doubles in 1909, 1910 and 1911. In 1919 she promoted international competitions for women, and in the 1920s began teaching. A donated vase to the United States Lawn Tennis Association became known as the 'Hazel Hotchkiss Wightman Trophy'. She is often referred to as the 'Queen Mother of Tennis', and published *Better Tennis* in 1933.

Wigman, Mary, *originally* Marie Wiegmann
1886–1973
German dancer, choreographer and teacher

Born in Hanover, she studied eurhythmics with the Swiss composer Émile Jaques-Dalcroze (1865–1951) and assisted Rudolf von Laban during World War I. She subsequently made her name as a soloist, but her ensemble dances were landmarks in the German Expressionist style. She opened a school in Dresden in 1920, branches of which grew thoughout Germany and, through her star pupil Hanya Holm, in the USA; the Nazis later closed the German schools. The most famous German dancer of her era, she exerted a great influence on European modern dance. She retired from the stage in 1942, but continued to choreograph and opened another school in West Berlin in 1949. ▣ Walter Sorell, *The Mary Wigman Book: Her Writings* (1976)

Wigmore, John Henry 1863–1943
US jurist

Born in San Francisco, he was educated at Harvard. He taught law in Tokyo (1889–93) and at Northwestern University in Evanston, Illinois (1893–1943), where he proved an innovative teacher. He wrote extensively, his major work being *Treatise on Evidence* (1909; 3rd edition, 10 vols, 1940), a work of great scholarship. Other important works include *The Principles* (in the last edition *The Science of Judicial Proof*) and the series which he edited, such as the Modern Legal Philosophy series (1911–22), the Modern Criminal Science series (1911–17), the Continental

Legal History series (1912–28) and the Evolution of Law series (1915–18).

Wigner, Eugene Paul 1902–95
US theoretical physicist and Nobel Prize winner

He was born in Budapest, Hungary, and educated at Berlin, where he was awarded a degree in chemical engineering (1924) and a doctorate in engineering (1925). He moved to the USA in 1930, and apart from two years at the University of Wisconsin (1936–38) he worked at Princeton University throughout his academic career, becoming Thomas D Jones Professor of Theoretical Physics in 1938. Wigner made a number of important contributions to nuclear physics and quantum theory. In 1927 he introduced the idea of parity conservation in nuclear interactions, and in the 1930s, demonstrated that the strong nuclear force has very short range. He is especially known for the Breit–Wigner formula (devised with US physicist Gregory Breit, 1899–1981) which describes resonant nuclear reactions, and the Wigner theorem concerning the conservation of the angular momentum of electron spin. His name is also given to the most important class of mirror nuclides (Wigner nuclides). Wigner's calculations were used by Enrico Fermi in building the first nuclear reactor in Chicago (1942), and he received the Fermi award in 1958, the Atom for Peace award in 1959, and the Nobel Prize for physics in 1963 for his work in furthering quantum mechanics and nuclear physics.

Wilberforce, Samuel 1805–73
English prelate

The third son of William Wilberforce, he was born in Clapham, London. In 1826 he graduated from Oriel College, Oxford, and was ordained in 1828. In 1830 he became rector of Brightstone, Isle of Wight, in 1840 rector of Alverstoke, canon of Winchester and chaplain to Albert, the Prince Consort, and in 1845 Dean of Westminster and Bishop of Oxford. He took part in the controversies of the Renn Hampden, Gorham, *Essay and Reviews*, and John Colenso cases. Instrumental in reviving Convocation (1852), he instituted Cuddesdon Theological College (1854). The charm of his many-sided personality and his social and oratorical gifts earned him the nickname of 'Soapy Sam'. He edited *Letters and Journals of Henry Martyn* (1837), wrote with his brother, Robert, the life of his father (1838), and himself wrote *Agathos* (1839), *Rocky Island* (1840) and *History of the Protestant Episcopal Church in America* (1844). Bishop of Winchester from 1869, he was killed by a fall from his horse. Of his two younger sons, Ernest Roland (1840–1908) became first Bishop of Newcastle (1882) and Bishop of Chichester (1895), and Albert Basil Orme (1841–1916) became archdeacon of Westminster (1900), chaplain to the Speaker, and an eloquent advocate of temperance.

Wilberforce, William See panel p1949

Wilbur, Richard 1921–
US poet

He grew up in New York City and was educated at Harvard, joining the faculty around the time his first major collection, *The Beautiful Changes* (1947), was published. It was followed by *Ceremony and Other Poems* (1950) and *Things of This World* (1956), a hybridization of William Carlos Williams's and Marianne Moore's objectivism with the English Metaphysicals. He published the plain-spoken *Poems* in 1957 and that year began teaching at Wesleyan University. Two years earlier, he had published an acclaimed translation of Molière and in 1957 Leonard Bernstein invited him to contribute songs to his operetta *Candide*. A collection, *The Mind Reader*, and a prose collection, *Responses* (both 1976), reawakened flagging interest in his work.

Wilberforce, William 1759–1833
English philanthropist and reformer

William Wilberforce was born in Hull, the son of a wealthy merchant, and educated at St John's College, Cambridge. In 1780 he was elected MP for Hull, and in 1784 for Yorkshire, and he became a close friend of **William Pitt**, the Younger, while remaining independent of any party. In 1784–85, during a tour on the Continent, he was converted to evangelical Christianity, and in 1787 he founded an association for the reformation of manners.

In 1788, supported by **Thomas Clarkson** and the Quakers, he began a 19-year campaign for the abolition of the slave trade in the British West Indies, which he finally achieved in 1807. He next sought to secure the abolition of the slave trade abroad and the total abolition of slavery itself; but declining health compelled him in 1825 to retire

from parliament. He died one month before the Slavery Abolition Act was passed.

Wilberforce was for long a central figure in the 'Clapham sect' of Evangelicals. He published *A Practical View of Christianity* in 1797, helped to found the *Christian Observer* (1801), and promoted many schemes for the welfare of the community. He was buried in Westminster Abbey.

📖 Garth Lean, *God's Politician: William Wilberforce's Struggle* (1980); Robin Furneaux, *William Wilberforce* (1974); Oliver Warner, *William Wilberforce and His Times* (1962); Robert Isaac Wilberforce and Samuel Wilberforce, *The Life of William Wilberforce* (5 vols, 1838).

Wilbye, John 1574–1638
English composer of madrigals

Born in Diss, Norfolk, he was a household musician at Hengrave Hall (1593–1628), and then at Colchester. His madrigals are marked by sensitive beauty and fine workmanship. 📖 David Brown, *John Wilbye* (1974)

Wilcke, Johan Carl 1732–96
Swedish physicist

Born in Wismar, Germany, his family moved to Sweden in 1739 and he went to Uppsala University to study theology in 1750, but concentrated instead on physics and mathematics. From 1759 he lectured on experimental physics at the Royal Swedish Academy in Stockholm. A painstaking evaluation of existing data culminated in his comprehensive map of the Earth's magnetic inclination (1768). Wilcke is remembered above all for his experimental work into the nature of heat. In 1772 he measured the heat required to melt snow at its freezing point (the latent heat of fusion); and in 1781 he drew up a list of specific heats for different substances. Wilcke began these experiments on specific heats independently of **Joseph Black**.

Wilcox, Ella Wheeler 1850–1919
US journalist and verse writer

Born in Johnstown Center, Wisconsin, she had completed a novel before she was 10, and later wrote at least two poems a day. The first of her many volumes of verse was *Drops of Water* (1872), and the most successful was *Poems of Passion* (1883). She also wrote a great deal of fiction, and contributed essays to many periodicals. Her *Story of a Literary Career* (1905) and *The World and I* (1918) were autobiographical.

Wilde, Lady Jane Francesca, *known as* Speranza, *née* Elgee 1826–96
Irish poet and hostess

Born in Dublin, she was an ardent nationalist, and contributed poetry and prose to the *Nation* from 1845 under the pen name 'Speranza'. In 1851 she married Sir **William Wilde**; their son was **Oscar Wilde**. Her salon was the most famous in Dublin. After her husband's death she moved to London, and published several works on folklore, including *Ancient Legends of Ireland* (1887) and *Ancient Cures* (1891).

Wilde, Oscar Fingal O'Flahertie Wills See
panel p1950

Wilde, Sir William Robert Wills 1815–76
Irish oculist, aurist and topographer

Born in Castlerea, County Roscommon, he studied at London, Berlin and Vienna, and returning to Dublin, served as medical commissioner on the Irish Census (1841 and 1851), publishing a major medical report, *The*

Epidemics of Ireland (1851). He also wrote on ocular and aural surgery, pioneered the operation for mastoiditis, invented an ophthalmoscope and founded St Mark's Ophthalmic Hospital. His topographical works include *The Beauties of the Boyne and the Blackwater* (1849), which established him as the leading authority on the Boyne valley, and *Lough Corrib, with Notes on Lough Mask* (1867). He published a major catalogue of the holdings of the Royal Irish Academy, and was apparently fluent in Gaelic. He married (1851) Jane Francesca Elgee (**Wilde**), famous as the Young Ireland poet 'Speranza' of the Dublin *Nation*, but his own politics seem to have been Tory Home Rule. He was named Queen **Victoria**'s Irish oculist in ordinary and also attended King **Oskar I** of Sweden.

Wildenbruch, Ernst von 1845–1909
German Romantic novelist, poet and dramatist

He was born in Beirut, and served in the army and Foreign Office. He wrote a number of short epic poems, but is best known as a playwright. His strongly expressed patriotism made him the national dramatist of Prussia during the empire of the **Hohenzollern**, to whom he was related. He also wrote short stories. 📖 H M Elster, *Ernst von Wildenbruch* (1934)

Wilder, Billy, *originally* Samuel Wilder 1906–
US filmmaker

Born in Sucha, Austria, he studied law at Vienna University, then worked as a journalist and crime reporter, before making his film debut in Germany as the co-writer of *Menschen am Sonntag* (1929, *People on Sunday*). In Paris he co-directed *Mauvaise Graine* (1933) before moving to Hollywood and embarking on a fruitful collaboration with writer Charles Brackett. Their scripts include *Ninotchka* (1939) and *Ball of Fire* (1941). A US citizen from 1934, he made his directorial debut in the USA with *The Major and the Minor* (1942), then began a distinguished career as the creator of incisive dramas, acerbic comedies and bittersweet romances, winning multiple Academy Awards for *The Lost Weekend* (1945), *Sunset Boulevard* (1950, staged in 1993 by **Andrew Lloyd Webber**) and *The Apartment* (1960). His many popular successes include *Double Indemnity* (1944), *The Seven Year Itch* (1955) and *Some Like It Hot* (1959). He made seven films with actor **Jack Lemmon**, including his final one *Buddy, Buddy* (1981) and worked with writer I A L Diamond from 1957. He was awarded the National Medal of Arts in 1993.

Wilder, Laura Ingalls 1867–1957
US children's writer

Born in Pepin, Wisconsin, she was a farm woman all her life, and it was not until she was in her sixties, when her daughter suggested that she write down her childhood memories, that her evocative 'Little House' series began to appear. *Little House in the Big Woods* (1932) achieved

Wilde, Oscar Fingal O'Flahertie Wills 1854–1900
Irish playwright, novelist, essayist, poet and wit

Oscar Wilde was born in Dublin. His father was Sir **William Wilde**; his mother Lady **Jane Francesca Wilde**. From the age of 9 to 16 he went to Portora Royal School in Enniskillen, which **Samuel Beckett** later attended. He went on to Trinity College, Dublin (1871–74), and to Magdalen College, Oxford (1874–78), where he was dandified, sexually ambiguous, sympathetic towards the Pre-Raphaelites, and contemptuous of conventional morality. He was also an accomplished Classicist, and won the Newdigate prize at Oxford in 1878 for the poem 'Ravenna', which his biographer, **Richard Ellmann**, described as 'a clever hodgepodge of personal reminiscence, topographical description, political and literary history'.

Wilde's first collection of poetry was published in 1881, the year in which he was ridiculed in **Gilbert** and **Sullivan**'s *Patience* as an adherent of the cult of 'Art for Art's sake'. The next year he embarked on a lecture tour of the USA where, when asked if he had anything to declare he allegedly replied, 'Only my genius'. The tour, wrote Ellmann, 'was an advertisement of courage and grace, along with ineptitude and self-advertisement', and Wilde boasted to **James McNeill Whistler**, 'I have already civilized America'.

He married Constance Lloyd, the daughter of an Irish barrister, in 1884 and had two sons for whom he wrote the classic children's fairy stories *The Happy Prince and Other Tales* (1888). His only novel, *The Picture of Dorian Gray* (1891), was modelled on his presumed lover, the poet John Gray, and was originally published to a scandalized reception in *Lippincott's Magazine* (1890). More fairy stories appeared in 1891 in *A House of Pomegranates*. In this year he also published *Lord Arthur Savile's Crime and Other Stories*, and a second play, *The Duchess of Padua*, an uninspired verse tragedy.

Over the next five years he built his dramatic reputation, first with *Lady Windermere's Fan* (1892), followed by A

Woman of No Importance (1893), *An Ideal Husband* (1895) and his masterpiece, *The Importance of Being Earnest* (1895). *Salomé*, originally written in French (1893), was refused a production licence in England as it featured biblical characters, but appeared in 1894 in an English translation by Lord **Alfred Douglas**.

By now Wilde's homosexuality was commonly known, and the 8th Marquis of **Queensberry**, father of Lord Alfred, left a card at Wilde's club addressed 'To Oscar Wilde posing as a Somdomite' (*sic*). Wilde took it that he meant 'ponce and Sodomite' and sued for libel. He lost the case, and was himself prosecuted and imprisoned (1895) for homosexuality. In 1905 his bitter reproach to Lord Alfred was published in part as *De Profundis*. Released in 1897, he went to France under the alias Sebastian Melmoth, the name of his favourite martyr linked with the hero of *Melmoth the Wanderer*, the novel written by his great-uncle, **Charles Maturin**. *The Ballad of Reading Gaol* was published in 1898. He also wrote literary essays, and *The Soul of Man Under Socialism* (1891), a riposte to **George Bernard Shaw**. His last years were spent wandering and idling on the Continent, and he died in Paris.

📖 D Coakley, *Oscar Wilde: The Importance of Being Irish* (1994); Richard Ellmann, *Oscar Wilde* (1987); Rupert Hart-Davis (ed), *The Letters of Oscar Wilde* (1962) and *More Letters of Oscar Wilde* (1985).

'Modern journalism justifies its own existence by the great Darwinian principle of the survival of the vulgarest.' From 'The Critic as Artist' in *Intentions* (1891).

'I hope you have not been leading a double life, pretending to be wicked and being really good all the time. That would be hypocrisy.' Said by Cecily in Act 2, *The Importance of Being Earnest* (1895).

instant popularity in the USA and was followed by the sequels *Farmer Boy* (1933), *Little House on the Prairie* (1935), *By the Shores of Lake Silver* (1939), *Little Town on the Prairie* (1941) and *Those Happy Golden Years* (1943). A television series in the 1950s assured their success in Great Britain.

Wilder, Thornton Niven 1897–1975
US writer and playwright

Born in Madison, Wisconsin, he was educated at Yale and served in both wars, becoming a lieutenant-colonel in 1944. He started his career as a teacher of English at Lawrenceville Academy (1921–28) and the University of Chicago (1930–37). His first novel, *The Cabala*, appeared in 1926. Set in contemporary Rome, it established the cool atmosphere of sophistication and detached irony that was to permeate all his books. These include *The Bridge of San Luis Rey* (1927), a bestseller and winner of the Pulitzer Prize, *The Woman of Andros* (1930), *Heaven's My Destination* (1935) and *The Ides of March* (1948). His first plays—*The Trumpet Shall Sound* (1926), *The Angel That Troubled the Waters* (1928) and *The Long Christmas Dinner* (1931)—were literary rather than dramatic, but in 1938 he produced *Our Town*, a successful play that evokes without scenery or costumes a universal flavour of provincial life. This was followed in 1942 by *The Skin of Our Teeth*, an amusing yet profound fable of humanity's struggle to survive. Both these plays were awarded the Pulitzer Prize. His later plays include *The Matchmaker* (1954), *A Life in the Sun* (1955), *The Eighth Day* (1967), *Theophilus North* (1974) and, in 1964, the musical *Hello Dolly!*, based on *The Matchmaker*. 📖 R Burbank, *Thornton Wilder* (1978)

Wildgans, Anton 1881–1932
Austrian poet and dramatist

Born in Vienna, he trained as a lawyer, but in 1912 gave up his practice to concentrate on literature. His plays include *Dies Irae* (1918, 'Day of Anger') and the biblical tragedy *Kain* (1920). The epic poem *Kirbisch* appeared in 1927, and he published some collections of verse. He was twice director of the Vienna Burgtheater, in 1921–22 and 1930–31.

Wilding, Alison 1948–
English sculptor

Born in Blackburn, Lancashire, she trained at Ravensbourne College of Art and Design in Bromley, Kent, and in 1971 went to the Royal College of Art. Since the mid-1970s she has evolved her own quietly authoritative abstract style using a variety of materials, including brass, steel, acrylic, beeswax, fossils and pigments, often with an outer structure enveloping an inner mysterious core, as in *Red Skies* (1991) and *Fugue* (1992). Exhibitions such as *Immersion* (Tate Gallery, London, and Liverpool) and *Exposure* (Halifax) brought her a Turner Prize nomination in 1992. Recent work includes her stainless steel *Echo* for the Angel Row Art Gallery in Nottingham (1995).

Wilenski, Reginald Howard 1887–1975
English art critic and art historian

He was born in London, and his analysis of the aims and achievements of modern artists, *The Modern Movement in Art* (1927), has had considerable influence.

Wiley, Harvey Washington 1844–1930
US food chemist

Born near Kent, Indiana, he served in the American Civil War and qualified in medicine at Indiana Medical College in 1871. He was Professor of Chemistry at Purdue (1874–83) when he became chief of the chemical division of the US Department of Agriculture, where he did major work on the analysis of foods. However, his main interest was in improving purity and reducing food adulteration, and despite many obstacles his efforts led to the Pure Food and Drug Act of 1906. Conflicts over its enforcement led to his resignation in 1912, but he continued as an active propagandist on food purity until his death. His works include *Not by Bread Alone* (1915).

Wilfrid or Wilfrith, St 634–709
English prelate
Born in Northumbria, he trained at Lindisfarne. He upheld the replacement of Celtic by Roman religious practices at the Synod of Whitby (664), and was made Bishop of Ripon and Bishop of York (c.665). When Archbishop Theodore divided Northumbria into four sees in 678, Wilfrid appealed to Rome, the first British churchman to do so. Pope Agatho decided in his favour, but King Ecgfrid imprisoned him. He escaped to Sussex, but was allowed to return by the new king, Aldfrith, in 686. ▣ Ann Orbach, *Wilfrid and the Church of England* (1981)

Wilhelm I 1797–1888
Seventh King of Prussia and first German emperor
The second son of **Frederick William III**, he was born in Berlin. In 1814 he entered Paris with the allies. During the king's absence in Russia he directed Prussian military affairs. In 1829 he married Princess Augusta of Saxe-Weimar and became heir presumptive (1840). During the Revolution of 1848 his attitude towards the people made him very unpopular. He was obliged to leave Prussia for London, but he returned to subdue disaffection in Baden (1849). He was appointed regent (1858) for his ailing brother, **Frederick William IV**, and when he succeeded in 1861, he made plain his intention of consolidating the throne and strengthening the army. A few months after his accession he narrowly escaped assassination. Despite parliamentary disapproval, Prince **Bismarck** was placed at the head of the ministry, with Albrecht von Roon (1803–79) as War Minister. In 1864 Prussia and Austria defeated Denmark and in 1866 Prussia defeated Austria in the struggle for supremacy over the German states. In 1870 France and Prussia went to war; France was defeated. In 1871 Wilhelm was proclaimed German emperor. An Austro-German alliance of 1871 was strengthened (1873) by the adhesion of the tsar. The rapid rise of socialism in Germany led to severe repressive measures, and in 1878 two attempts were made on the emperor's life by socialists, and another in 1883. Though jealous of his royal prerogatives, he was unassuming in character.

Wilhelm II 1859–1941
German emperor and King of Prussia
He was born in Berlin, the eldest son of Prince Frederick, later **Frederick II, the Great** and of Victoria, the daughter of Great Britain's Queen **Victoria**. He received a strict military and academic education at the Kassel gymnasium and the University of Bonn, taking part in military exercises despite a deformed left arm. A military enthusiast, he had a deep conviction of the divine right of the **Hohenzollerns**, and was intelligent if somewhat temperamental. Emperor of Germany and King of Prussia from 1888 until 1918, he quarrelled with and dismissed (1890) **Bismarck**, who disapproved of his efforts to capture working-class support and who had forbidden any minister to see Wilhelm except in his presence. A long spell of personal rule followed, but in 1908 he suffered a nervous breakdown which greatly lessened his influence on policy-making in the last 10 years of his reign.

Wilhelm's speeches revolved around German imperialism. In 1896 he sent a telegram to President **Kruger** of South Africa congratulating him on the suppression of the **Jameson** raid. His anti-British attitude at the start of the Boer War was replaced by serious, if clumsy, endeavours at Anglo-German reconciliation. However, he also backed Admiral **von Tirpitz**'s plans for a large German navy to match the British, and as an ally of Turkey, he encouraged German economic penetration of the Middle East. He supported immoderate demands on Serbia after the assassination of the Archduke **Franz Ferdinand** at Sarajevo (1914), but made strenuous efforts to avoid the world war he saw as imminent. Political power passed from him to the generals, and during World War I he became a mere figurehead, contrary to the popular image of him as the great warlord. The defeat of Germany forced him to abdicate (9 November 1918) and flee the country. He and his family settled first at Amerongen, then at Doorn near Arnheim, where he wrote his *Memoirs 1878–1918* (translated 1922), and ignored the Nazi *'Liberation'* (1940) of the Netherlands. He also wrote *My Early Life* (1926). In 1881 he married Princess Augusta Victoria of Schleswig-Holstein, by whom he had six sons and one daughter, and after her death in 1921, he married Princess Hermine of Reuss.

Wilhelm, Crown Prince of Germany and Prussia 1882–1951
German soldier
After serving as an army field commander during World War I, he sought exile in the Netherlands in November 1918 and renounced his claims to the German and Prussian thrones the following month. He returned to Germany (1923) and despite identifying with monarchist groups and, for a time, with the Nazi Party, he played a limited role in political life.

Wilhelmina Helena Pauline Maria of Orange-Nassau 1880–1962
Queen of the Netherlands
Born in The Hague, she succeeded her father William III in 1890 at a very early age and until 1898 her mother, Queen Emma, acted as regent. Queen Wilhelmina fully upheld the principles of constitutional monarchy, especially winning the admiration of her people during World War II. Though compelled to seek refuge in Great Britain, she steadfastly encouraged Dutch resistance to the German occupation. In 1948, in view of the length of her reign, she abdicated in favour of her daughter **Juliana** and assumed the title of Princess of the Netherlands. She wrote *Lonely but not Alone* (1960), which revealed her profound religious sentiments. ▣ Philip Paneth, *Queen Wilhelmina, Mother of the Netherlands* (1943)

Wilkes, Charles 1798–1877
US naval officer
Born in New York, he joined the US navy in 1818 and studied hydrography. He explored the South Pacific islands and the Antarctic continent, including the stretch that bears his name (1839–40). During the Civil War he intercepted the British mail-steamer *Trent* off Cuba, and took off two Confederate commissioners accredited to France, thereby creating a risk of war with Great Britain (1861). As acting rear admiral he commanded a squadron against commerce raiders in the West Indies. He was court-martialled for disobedience in 1866, and retired.

Wilkes, John 1727–97
English politician
Born in Clerkenwell, London, he was the son of a distiller. A member of the Hell-fire Club which indulged in orgies at Medmenham Abbey, the home of **Sir Francis Dashwood**, he entered parliament in 1757 and became fiercely critical of **George III**'s Chief Minister, Lord **Bute**.

He established a weekly newspaper *The North Briton*, in which he alleged that ministers were putting lies into the King's mouth. Acquitted of a libel charge, on the ground of parliamentary privilege, he fought a duel after readings from his *Essay on Women* in the House of Lords were claimed to be obscene. Wilkes took refuge in France and when he returned to England in 1768 he was imprisoned for 22 months and not allowed to resume his seat in parliament. However, he was elected Sheriff of Middlesex in 1771, Lord Mayor of London in 1774, and returned to parliament. Despite his apparently outrageous private behaviour, he became a symbol of free speech with the epitaph, which he composed himself, 'a friend of liberty'. 📖 H W Bleakley, *Life of John Wilkes* (1917)

Wilkes, Maurice Vincent 1913–
English computer scientist
Born in Dudley, West Midlands, he was educated at Cambridge, where he was a Mathematical Tripos Wrangler at St John's College. He conducted research in physics at the Cavendish Laboratory, and directed the Mathematical (later Computer) Laboratory at Cambridge (1946–80), where he became known for his pioneering work with the EDSAC (Electronic Delay Storage Automatic Calculator), intended to provide a useful and reliable computing service. This service, the first in the world, was available by early 1950. Besides important software advances, Wilkes's work also included fundamental work on processor controls (microprogramming). Developments at the laboratory continued into the late 1950s, when a new computer, EDSAC II, was designed and built. After 1980 Wilkes became a computer engineer for the Digital Equipment Corporation until 1986. He was elected FRS in 1956, and published *Memoirs of a Computer Pioneer* in 1985, followed by *Computing Perspectives* in 1995. Since 1990 he has been consultant on research strategy with the Olivetti Research Directorate.

Wilkie, Sir David 1785–1841
Scottish painter
Born in Cults manse in Fife, he was sent to study at the Trustees' Academy in Edinburgh in 1799, and returning home in 1804 painted his *Pitlessie Fair*. The great success of *The Village Politicians* (1806) caused him to settle in London. In 1817 he visited Sir **Walter Scott** at Abbotsford and painted the family group now in the Scottish National Gallery, Edinburgh. His fame mainly rests on his genre pictures in the Dutch style, such as the *Card Players*, *Village Festival* (1811), *Reading the Will* (1811), *The Penny Wedding* (1818) and others. Later he changed his style, sought to emulate the depth and richness of colouring of the old masters, and chose more elevated historical subjects, like *John Knox Preaching before the Lords of Congregation* (1832, Tate Gallery, London). He also painted portraits, and was successful as an etcher. In 1823 he was appointed King's Limner in Scotland, and in 1830 painter-in-ordinary to King **William IV**. 📖 H A D Miles and D B Brown, *Sir David Wilkie of Scotland* (1987)

Wilkins, Sir George Hubert 1888–1958
Australian explorer
He was born in Mt Bryan East, and first went to the Arctic in 1913. In 1919 he flew from England to Australia, then spent from 1921 to 1922 in the Antarctic. After his return he collected material in Central Australia on behalf of the British Museum, London. In 1926 he returned to the Arctic, and in 1928 was knighted for a pioneer flight from Alaska to Spitsbergen, over polar ice. In 1931 he undertook a further expedition, this time with the submarine *Nautilus*, but an attempt to reach the North Pole under the ice was unsuccessful. In 1928 he pioneered flying in the Antarctic. After his death his ashes were scattered over the North Pole. He wrote *Flying the Arctic* (1928), *Undiscovered Australia* (1928) and *Under the North Pole* (1931).

Wilkins, John 1614–72
English churchman and scientist
Born near Daventry, Northamptonshire, he was a graduate of Magdalen Hall, Oxford. He became a domestic chaplain but studied mathematics and mechanics, and was one of the founders of the Royal Society. In the Civil War he sided with parliament, and was appointed Warden of Wadham. Although appointed Master of Trinity College, Cambridge in 1659, he was dispossessed at the Restoration. He soon recovered court favour, however, and became a preacher at Gray's Inn, rector of St Lawrence Jewry, dean of Ripon and Bishop of Chester (1668). Amongst his works are *Discovery of a World in the Moon* (1628), in which Wilkins discusses the possibility of communication by a flying-machine with the moon and its supposed inhabitants, *Discourse concerning a New Planet* (1640), which argues that the earth is one of the planets, and *Mercury, or the Secret and Swift Messenger*, which shows how a man may communicate with a friend at any distance.

Wilkins, Maurice Hugh Frederick 1916–
British physicist and Nobel Prize winner
Born in New Zealand, and educated at King Edward's School, Birmingham, and St John's College, Cambridge, he did research on uranium isotope separation at the University of California in 1944. He joined the Medical Research Council's Biophysics Research Unit at King's College London in 1946, becoming director 1970–72 and professor of biophysics (1970–81), now emeritus. **Francis Crick** and **James Watson** deduced their double helix model of DNA from Wilkins and **Rosalind Franklin's** X-ray data of DNA fibres, and Crick, Watson and Wilkins were awarded the 1962 Nobel Prize for physiology or medicine for this work.

Wilkins, Roy 1901–81
US social reformer and civil rights leader
Born in St Louis, Missouri, he graduated from the University of Minnesota in 1923 and for eight years edited the *Kansas City Call*, the leading African-American newspaper of the day. He joined the National Association for the Advancement of Colored People (NAACP) in 1931 and rose to become its executive director (1965–77). He called for the advancement of racial equality through legislative and judicial means, and he was a major force behind school desegregation and the 1964 Civil Rights Act.

Wilkinson, Ellen Cicely 1891–1947
English feminist and Labour politician
Born in Manchester, she was an early member of the Independent Labour Party and an active campaigner for women's suffrage. In 1920 she joined the Communist Party, but had left it by 1924, when she became Labour MP for Middlesbrough East. Losing this seat in 1931, she re-entered parliament in 1935 as MP for Jarrow. In 1940 she became Parliamentary Secretary to the Ministry of Home Security, and in 1945 Minister of Education, the first woman to hold such an appointment.

Wilkinson, Sir Geoffrey 1921–96
English chemist and Nobel Prize winner
He was born in Springside, near Manchester, and studied at Imperial College, London. During World War II he worked on the Canadian branch of the atomic bomb project with the National Research Council of Canada. He then moved to the Lawrence Radiation Laboratory of the University of California at Berkeley and was appointed assistant professor at Harvard (1951). From 1955 to 1988 he was Professor of Inorganic Chemistry at Imperial College then Senior Research Fellow (1988–). His early research was on the chemistry of the transition elements. While at Harvard he studied ferrocene and

discovered that it had a type of structure entirely new to chemistry. This led to new lines of research in organic, inorganic and theoretical chemistry, and to the development of new catalysts used in the production of plastics and low-lead fuels. They are also employed in pharmaceuticals, for example L-dopa, used to treat Parkinson's disease. Wilkinson co-authored (with F A Cotton) a pioneering textbook, *Advanced Inorganic Chemistry* (1962), was elected FRS in 1965 and knighted in 1976. In 1973 he shared the Nobel Prize for chemistry with **Ernst Fischer**, who had worked independently in Germany on organometallic sandwich compounds.

Wilkinson, James Hardy 1919–86
English mathematician and computer scientist
He was educated at Cambridge, where during World War II he worked at the Mathematical Laboratory. In 1946 he joined the Mathematical Division of the National Physical Laboratory (NPL) and produced programs for the several versions of **Alan Turing**'s ACE computer, resulting in some of the earliest floating-point programs. Before he left the NPL in 1980, Wilkinson also published work on rounding errors in algebraic processes. In 1977 he became Professor of Computer Science at Stanford University.

Wilkinson, John 1728–1808
English ironmaster and inventor
He was born in Clifton, Cumberland (now Cumbria), and by 1770 was master of three furnaces. His most important achievement was the invention in 1774 of a cannon-boring machine considerably more accurate than any in use up to that time. He saw that it could be used also to bore more accurate cylinders for steam engines such as those of **Matthew Boulton** and **James Watt**, and supplied them with several hundred cylinders over the next two decades. Wilkinson in turn installed a Watt engine in 1776 as a blowing engine at one of his furnaces, the first Watt engine to be used other than for pumping. He was one of the principal promoters of the iron bridge at Coalbrookdale, built by **Abraham Darby** in 1779.

Willaert, Adrian c.1490–1562
Flemish composer
Born probably in Bruges, he is thought to have studied in Paris, changing from law to music, and to have first gone to Italy, into the service of the D'Este family, in 1515. He was appointed maestro di cappella at St Mark's, Venice, in 1527, and during his 35 years there Venice became the centre of Italian and, indeed, western European music. He gained a great reputation as a composer and teacher, and among his pupils were Zarlino, Ciprian de Rore (who briefly succeeded him at St Mark's) and **Andrea Gabrieli**. He composed works in most of the contemporary genres of sacred music, and also secular chansons and madrigals.

Willard, Emma, *née* Hart 1787–1870
US educationist, a pioneer of higher education for women
Born in Berlin, Connecticut, and educated at Berlin Academy (1802–03), she married Dr John Willard (d.1825) in 1809. From her husband's nephew, who was studying at Middlebury College, she learned about the subjects studied there, such as geometry and philosophy, which were never taught to women. In 1814 she opened Middlebury Female Seminary, offering an unprecedented range of subjects, in order to prepare women for college. Unsuccessful in gaining funding for her school, she moved to Troy, New York, where she received financial help. The school developed fast, and she wrote several highly-regarded history textbooks. Her campaign for equal educational opportunities for women paved the way for coeducation.

Willard, Frances Elizabeth Caroline 1839–98
US temperance campaigner
Born in Churchville, New York, she studied at the Northwestern Female College, Evanston, Illinois, and became Professor of Aesthetics there. In 1874 she became secretary of the Women's Christian Temperance Union, and edited the Chicago *Daily Post*. She helped to found the international Council of Women.

Willenbrandt, Mabel Walker, *née* Walker
1896–1963
US lawyer and government official
Born in Woodsdale, Kansas, she studied law at the University of Southern California, set up a private practice, and was appointed as a non-salaried public defender with special responsibility for women's cases. During World War I she was appointed head of the Legal Advisory Board, the largest draft board in Los Angeles, and after the war was recommended for the post of Assistant Attorney-General of the United States (1921). She was the second woman to hold that post, and the first to hold it for an extended term, during which she became involved in tax, prison and prohibition activities. She resigned in 1928 to return to private practice.

Willett, William 1856–1915
English builder
Born in Farnham, he is chiefly remembered for his campaign of 'daylight saving'. A Bill to introduce daylight saving time was promoted in parliament in 1908, but opposition was strong and the measure was not adopted until a year after his death.

William I (of England) See William the Conqueror (panel p1955)

William II, Rufus c.1056–1100
King of England
He was the second surviving son of **William the Conqueror**, whom he succeeded in 1087. The Norman nobles in England rebelled against him in favour of his eldest brother Robert, Duke of Normandy, but Rufus suppressed the rebellion with the support of the English people after making false promises of a relaxation of the forest laws and of fiscal burdens. He misused ecclesiastical benefices to raise money, until 1093, when he appointed **Anselm** as Archbishop of Canterbury, though he later quarrelled with Anselm over the liberties of the Church. Rufus warred with Robert in Normandy, but peace was made (1091), and in 1096 the duchy was mortgaged to him. In 1098 he conquered Maine, but failed to hold the whole of it. **Malcolm III**, Canmore, King of Scotland, invaded Northumberland (1093), and was killed at Alnwick. Rufus invaded Wales three times. He was killed by an arrow while hunting in the New Forest, but whether this was deliberate has never been established. He was largely responsible for the Norman Conquest of the north of England. 📖 Edward A Freeman, *The Reign of William Rufus and the Accession of Henry the First* (2 vols, 1882)

William III, *also called* William of Orange 1650–1702
Stadtholder of the United Provinces of the Netherlands, and King of Great Britain and Ireland
Born in The Hague, he was the posthumous son of **William II** of Orange and Mary (1631–60), eldest daughter of **Charles I** of Great Britain. Following the assassination of the Grand Pensionary **Jan De Witt** he was chosen Stadtholder of the Netherlands in 1672 and appointed to command the army. An inexperienced soldier, he defied all odds and, by opening the dykes to flood the countryside, was able to halt the advance of the French army and negotiate favourable peace terms at Nijmegen in 1678, concentrating thereafter on defeating French ambition in Europe. Great Britain, who had been an ally of France, was forced out of the war following a highly successful propaganda campaign linking the French alliance with

British fears of Catholicism and arbitrary government. In 1677, in an attempt to retrieve the situation, **Charles II** agreed to a marriage between William and **Mary**, eldest daughter of James, Duke of York (**James VII and II**). When James became King of Scotland and England (1685), his policy of Catholicization provided William with the opportunity for invading his father-in-law's kingdoms in the name of his wife. He landed at Torbay on 5 November 1688, following an invitation from seven British notables (the Immortal Seven), ostensibly to protect the Protestant religion and traditional parliamentary liberties, but was more concerned to mobilize British resources in money and manpower for the continental war-effort. James then fled to France, and William and Mary were crowned in February 1689. The successive defeats of James's supporters at Killiecrankie (July 1689) and on the Boyne (1690) and the surrender of Limerick (1691) effectively ended Jacobite resistance, and William turned his attention to the Continental war, which was ended indecisively at the Peace of Ryswick (1697). Never popular in Great Britain, William found his position materially weakened by the death of Mary in 1694. His reign nevertheless brought stability at home after a period of considerable political unrest, and the financing of the war led directly to the establishment of a system of National Debt and to the founding of the Bank of England (1694). He transferred control of the standing army to parliament (1698) and introduced greater freedom of the press (1695). He died after a fall when his horse stumbled over a molehill, and was succeeded by Mary's sister, Queen **Anne**. 📖 Stephen B Baxter, *William III* (1966)

William IV, *known as* the Sailor King 1765–1837
King of Great Britain
The third son of **George III**, he was born at Buckingham Palace, London. He joined the navy (1779), and in 1789 he was created Duke of Clarence. He was formally promoted through the successive ranks to Admiral of the Fleet (1811), and in 1827–28 he held the revived office of Lord High Admiral. From 1790 to 1811 he lived with the actress **Dorothy Jordan**, who bore him 10 children but in 1818 he married Adelaide (1792–1849), eldest daughter of the Duke of Saxe-Meiningen. Their two daughters died in infancy. By the Duke of York's death (1827) the Duke of Clarence became heir presumptive to the throne, to which he succeeded at the death of his eldest brother, **George IV** in 1830. A Whig up to his accession, he turned Tory, and did much to obstruct the passing of the first Reform Act (1832) but then accepted a succession of liberal reforms. He was succeeded by his niece, **Victoria**. 📖 Philip Zeigler, *King William IV* (1971)

William I, the Silent 1533–84
Prince of Orange
He became the first of the hereditary stadtholders of the United Provinces of the Netherlands in 1572. He joined the aristocratic protest to the oppressive and anti-heretic policies of **Philip II** of Spain, and eventually organized an army against the Duke of **Alva**, Philip's regent in the Netherlands. After initial reverses, he began the recovery of the coastal towns with the help of the Sea-Beggars, and became the leader of the northern provinces, united in the Union of Utrecht (1579) in revolt against Spain in the Eighty Years War. He was a complex character: idealistic but a realist, tolerant, subtle and devious. His *Apologie* (1580) was a vindication of his aims and actions. He was assassinated in Delft by a Spanish agent. His nickname comes from his ability to keep secret **Henri II** of France's scheme to massacre all the Protestants of France and the Netherlands, confided to him when he was a French hostage (1559). 📖 C V Wedgwood, *William the Silent* (1944)

William II 1626–50
Stadtholder of the United Provinces of the Netherlands

Born in The Hague, he was the son of Stadtholder Frederick Henry (1625–47). Anglo-Dutch diplomacy established what would prove a fateful marital linkage of the houses of Orange and Stuart by William's marriage (1641) to Mary, daughter of **Charles I**. Fat, dissolute and lazy, William followed his father in office in 1647. Dutch independence was recognized at the end of the Thirty Years War in the Peace of Westphalia (1648), but William supported the French in their war with Spain in the hope of conquering part of the Spanish Netherlands. He arrested his leading opponents in Holland and then besieged Amsterdam, winning an advantageous compromise, but died of smallpox soon after. His posthumous son was the future **William III** of Great Britain and Ireland.

William IV, *originally* Charles Henry Fris 1711–51
Stadtholder and Captain-General of the United Provinces of the Netherlands
Born in Leeuwarden, of a cadet branch of the House of Orange (Nassau-Dietz), he was named Friesland stadtholder in succession to his father, John William Friso (1711). He was chosen as stadtholder of the other provinces at various intervals, all these posts having been untenanted since the death of **William III** (1702). His appointments were not completed until 1747 when Holland, Zeeland and Utrecht bowed to popular pressure in the riots after the French invasion. His offices were then declared hereditary in male and female lines. Hardworking and intelligent, he attempted reform, but failed to solve the most pressing of his problems.

William V 1748–1806
Stadtholder and Captain-General of the Netherlands
Born in The Hague, he was the son of **William IV**, whom he succeeded in 1751, though regents governed until 1766. He abandoned the old alliance of Orange and Great Britain, leaning instead towards an alliance with Prussia, especially after his marriage to Wilhelmina, sister of the future **Frederick William II**. During the American Revolution (1775–83), Great Britain declared war on the Netherlands because of its financial and moral support for the American rebels, however it was the pro-French Patriots who pressed for reforms and led him to leave The Hague in order to live outside what was now the hostile province of Holland. Prussian armed intervention restored him in 1787. French revolutionary armies invaded the Netherlands (1794) and he fled to England (1795), supporting English occupation of the Dutch provinces. After that he lost heart, allowed his followers to accept office in the Batavian Republic, the French client state which had been formed in his absence, and retired (1802) to his hereditary Nassau lands in Germany.

William I 1143–1214
King of Scotland
He was the grandson of **David I**, and brother of **Malcolm IV**, whom he succeeded in 1165. His epithet, 'the Lion', was not contemporary. He continued the consolidation of Scotland as a feudal kingdom and defended it from the Angevin kings of England, but was forced to pay **Henry II** explicit homage for Scotland and his other lands (1174). This Treaty of Falaise was revoked by **Richard I** (1189) with the Quitclaim of Canterbury in return for payment of 10,000 marks. He enjoyed a reputation for personal piety and was buried in the abbey church at Arbroath, which he had founded in 1178. 📖 G W S Barrow, *The Acts of William I* (1971)

William of Auvergne, *also known as* William of Paris and Guillaume d'Auvergne c.1180–1249
French philosopher and theologian
Born in Aurillac, Aquitaine, he became Professor of Theology in the University of Paris (1225), and was Bishop of Paris (1228–49), when he defended the mendicant orders and introduced various clerical reforms. His

William the Conqueror, *also called* William the Bastard 1027–87
King of England as William I from 1066

William was born in Falaise, the bastard son of Robert, Duke of Normandy, and a tanner's daughter called Arlette. On his father's death in 1035 he was accepted as duke by the nobles, but his youth was passed in difficulty and danger. In 1047 the lords of the western part of the duchy rebelled; **Henri I** of France came to his help, and the rebels were defeated at Val-ès-dunes.

In 1051 he visited his cousin, **Edward the Confessor**, King of England, and may well have received the promise of the English succession. He married Matilda, daughter of Baldwin V, Count of Flanders, in 1053. In the next 10 years William repulsed two French invasions, and in 1063 conquered Maine. It is probable that in 1064 Harold Godwinsson (later **Harold II**) was at his court, and swore to help him to gain the English crown on Edward's death. When, however, Edward died in 1066, Harold himself became king.

William laid his claim to the English throne before the pope and western Christendom. The pope approved his claim, and William invaded England on 28 September, immediately taking the towns of Pevensey and Hastings. At the Battle of Hastings (or Senlac) on 14 October 1066, Harold was defeated and killed, and William was crowned King of England in Westminster Abbey on Christmas Day. The west and north of England were subdued in 1068; the following year the north rebelled, and William devastated the country between York and Durham. English government under William assumed a more feudal aspect, the old national assembly becoming a council of the king's tenants-in-chief, and all title to land was derived from his grant.

In 1086 he ordered the compilation of the Domesday Book, which contains details of the land settlement. The church was also reformed and feudalized. William's rule was successful despite several revolts which occurred even after 1069. In 1070 there was a rebellion in the Fen Country, and under the leadership of **Hereward the Wake**, the rebels for some time held out in the Isle of Ely. English exiles were sheltered by the Scottish king, **Malcolm III Canmore**, who occasionally plundered the northern shires; but William in 1072 compelled Malcolm to do him homage at Abernethy. In 1073 he was forced to reconquer Maine.

William made a successful expedition into South Wales. In 1079 his eldest son, Robert, rebelled against him in Normandy, but they were reconciled. Having entered on a war with **Philip I** of France in 1087, William burned Mantes. As he rode through the burning town his horse stumbled, and he received an injury, of which he died at Rouen on 9 September; he was buried in the abbey he had founded at Caen. He left Normandy to his son Robert, and England to his other surviving son, **William II**.

📖 E A Freeman, *The History of the Norman Conquest* (1974); Frank Barlow, *William I and the Norman Conquest* (1965); David C Douglas, *William The Conqueror* (1964).

'By the splendour of God I have taken possession of my realm; the earth of England is in my two hands.' Attributed remark on falling over shortly after landing at Pevensey.

---

most important work is the monumental *Magisterium divinale* (1223–40, 'The Divine Teaching') and his main achievement was the attempted integration of classical Greek and Arabic philosophy with Christian theology.

William of Auxerre c.1140–1231
French theologian and philosopher

Born in Auxerre, he became a master of theology and was for many years an administrator at the University of Paris. In 1230 he was sent as French envoy to Pope **Gregory IX** to advise on dissension in the university and he pleaded the cause of the students against King **Louis IX**. Gregory appointed him (1231) to a council which was to censor the works of **Aristotle** in the university curriculum to ensure their conformity with the Christian faith, but William was opposed to suppression and died before the council's work was far advanced. His main publication is the *Summa aurea in quatuor libros sententiarum* ('Golden Compendium on the Four Books of Sentences'), a commentary on early and medieval Christian thought, tending to emphasize the value of philosophy and rational analysis as a tool for Christian theology.

William of Jumièges d.c.1090
Norman Benedictine monk

He compiled a history of the Dukes of Normandy from Rollo to 1071, of value for the story of the Norman Conquest.

William of Malmesbury c.1090–c.1143
English chronicler and monk

Born probably near Malmesbury, Wiltshire, he became a Benedictine monk in the monastery at Malmesbury, and eventually librarian and precentor. He took part in the council at Winchester against King **Stephen** in 1141. His *Gesta Pontificum* is an ecclesiastical history of the bishops and chief monasteries of England to 1123. The *Gesta Regum Anglorum* provides a lively history of the kings of England from the Saxon invasion to 1126, and the *Historia*

Novella brings down the narrative to 1142. Other works are an account of the church at Glastonbury and Lives of St **Dunstan** and St **Wulfstan**. 📖 Rodney M Thomson, *William of Malmesbury* (1987)

William of Newburgh c.1135–c.1200
English chronicler

Perhaps a native of Bridlington, he was a monk of Newburgh Priory (Coxwold). His *Historia Rerum Anglicarum* is one of the most important sources for the reign of **Henry II**.

William of Norwich, St c.1132–44
English Christian

Apparently the first of the Christian boys alleged to have been ritually crucified by Jews (see **Hugh of Avalon**). The *Life and Miracles of St William of Norwich* is a story from a 12th-century manuscript of a boy whose mutilated body was found in a wood outside Norwich in 1144, and (much later) was rumoured to have been murdered by Jews. His feast day is 26 March.

William of Orange See **William III**

William of Paris See **William of Auvergne**

William of Rubruck, *also called* Willem van Ruysbroeck, *Latin* Wilhelmus Rubruquis
fl.13th century
French traveller

Born probably in Rubrouck, near St Omer, he entered the Franciscan order, and was sent on a religious mission in 1253 by **Louis IX** to visit the son of the Mongol prince, Batŭ Khan, a supposed Christian. Friar William travelled across the Black Sea and the Crimea to the Volga. At Sartak his father sent him to the Mongol Emperor, Mangŭ Khan, whom he reached about 10 days' journey south of Karakorum in Mongolia. He stayed there until 1254, and then returned to the Volga by way of the

Caucasus, Armenia, Persia (Iran) and Asia Minor, arriving at Tripoli in 1255. He was still living in 1293, when **Marco Polo** was returning from the East.

William of Tyre c.1130–85
Syrian churchman and historian

Born probably in Italy, he became archdeacon of Tyre in 1167, and Archbishop in 1175. He was tutor in 1170 to Baldwin I, son of King Amalric of Jerusalem, and in 1179 was one of the six bishops representing the Latin Church of the East at the Lateran Council. His *Historia Rerum in Partibus Transmarinis Gestarum* deals with the affairs of the East from 1095 to 1184. ⊞ P W Edbury, *William of Tyre: Historian of the Latin East* (1988)

William of Waynflete 1395–1486
English prelate

Educated probably at New College, Oxford, he became provost of Eton in 1443, Bishop of Winchester in 1447, and in 1448 founded Magdalen College, Oxford. Involved in the negotiations which ended **Jack Cade's** 1450 rebellion, he played an important role, as a Lancastrian, advising **Henry VI** in the Wars of the Roses. He was Lord Chancellor (1456–60).

William of Wykeham or Wickham 1324–1404
English churchman and statesman

Born in Wickham, Hampshire, perhaps the son of a serf, he rose in the service of **Edward III** to become Keeper of the Privy Seal (1363), Bishop of Winchester (1367), and twice Chancellor of England (1367–71, 1389–91). He founded New College, Oxford, and Winchester College. Wykeham was not an ardent theologian; he founded his colleges 'first for the glory of God and the promotion of divine service, and secondarily for scholarship'. He has been called the 'father of the public school system', and he established (though he did not invent) perpendicular architecture.

William the Conqueror See panel p1955

Williams, Bernard Arthur Owen 1929–
English philosopher

Educated at Chigwell School, Essex, and Balliol College, Oxford, he taught in London and Oxford, before being appointed Professor of Philosophy at Bedford College, London (1964–67). He became Professor of Philosophy at Cambridge (1967), and Provost of King's College, Cambridge (1979). He has held many visiting positions at universities in the USA, Australia and Africa, and in 1987 emigrated to become Professor of Philosophy in the University of California, Berkeley, as a much-publicized addition to the 'brain-drain'. He returned to the UK to become Professor of Philosophy at Oxford (1990–96). His philosophical work has been wide-ranging, but there have been particularly influential contributions to moral philosophy, in works such as *Morality: an introduction to Ethics* (1972), *Utilitarianism* (with J J C Smart, 1973), *Moral Luck* (1981), *Ethics and the Limits of Philosophy* (1985) and *Shame and Necessity* (1993). He chaired the Committee on Obscenity and Film Censorship which produced the Williams Report in 1979. He was married (1955–74) to the politician **Shirley Williams** and was elected Fellow of the Royal Society of Arts in 1993.

Williams, Betty 1943–
Irish peace activist and Nobel Prize winner

Born in Belfast, a Roman Catholic, she founded with **Mairead Corrigan-Maguire** the Northern Ireland Peace Movement (the 'Peace People') in 1976. They shared the 1976 Nobel Peace Prize.

Williams, Cicely Delphine 1893–1992
British pioneer in maternal and child health

Born in Kew Park, Jamaica, into a plantation-owning family, she attended Somerville College, Oxford, then qualified as a doctor at King's College Hospital (1923). She joined the Colonial Medical Service in the Gold Coast in 1929, where nutrition and mother and child care became her primary concern. This led to her vivid description in the *Lancet* (1935) of the condition kwashiorkor (a disease in newly weaned children caused by protein deficiency). She was in Singapore in 1942 when the Japanese invaded; imprisoned in Changi, she survived being held in cages with the dead and the dying. She later became the first head of Mother and Child Health (1948–52) in the World Health Organization, Geneva, and lectured in more than 70 countries, promoting breast-feeding and combined preventative and curative medicine.

Williams, Edward, pseudonym Iolo Morganwg 1747–1826
Welsh poet and antiquary

Born in Llancarfan, Glamorgan, he worked there as a stonemason, and became a poet in Welsh and English. He had links with 18th-century Radicalism, mingling its ideas with Romantic exaltation of the Welsh past, and established neo-Druidic cults and celebrations in Wales. He published collected poems purportedly by the 14th-century poet Dafydd ap Gwilym, which in fact were his own work, and co-edited *The Myvyrian Archaeology* (3 vols, 1801–07). A vast corpus of cultural material from the Welsh past in varying degrees of authenticity was published posthumously. A brilliant forger whose deceptions far outlived his own time, he prolonged, revived and reinvigorated ancient and modern Welsh culture. ⊞ G J Williams, *Iolo Morganwg* (1963)

Williams, (George) Emlyn 1905–87
Welsh playwright and actor

Born in Mostyn, Clwyd, the son of a steelworks foreman, he won a scholarship to Oxford, where he entered Christ Church. In 1927, attracted by the stage, he joined J B Fagan's repertory company. His successes as a dramatist began with *A Murder has been Arranged* (1930) and included the terrifying psychological thriller, *Night Must Fall* (1935), and *The Corn is Green* (1936). He appeared in productions of many of his own plays, featured in several films, and gave acclaimed readings from the works of **Charles Dickens**. He wrote the autobiographical *George* (1961) and *Emlyn* (1973), as well as *Beyond Belief* (1967), and a novel, *Headlong* (1980).

Williams, Eric 1911–81
Trinidadian statesman and historian

He was Prime Minister of Trinidad and Tobago for 30 years. In 1956 he founded the PNM (People's National Movement) and, as Chief Minister, took Trinidad into the Federation of the West Indies (1958), insisting on a powerful centralized government. When that failed to materialize, Williams took Trinidad out of the union and obtained independence (1962) with the slogan 'Discipline, Production and Tolerance'. His popularity soared until 1970, when an economic downturn and his increasing authoritarianism led to Black Power violence. He committed suicide in 1981.

Williams, Esther Jane 1923–
US swimmer and film actress

Born in Inglewood, near Los Angeles, California, she became a record-breaking swimmer, was selected for the cancelled 1940 Olympics, and entered the fringes of showbusiness as part of a San Francisco Aquacade in 1940. Seen by a Hollywood talent scout, she signed with MGM and made her film debut in *Andy Hardy's Double Life* in 1942. Beginning with *Bathing Beauty* (1944) she specialized in films designed to showcase her aquatic abilities.

A top box-office attraction, she appeared in several films including *Neptune's Daughter* (1949), *Dangerous When Wet* (1953), *Jupiter's Darling* (1955), *The Unguarded Moment* (1956) and *The Big Show* (1961). She later designed a range of swimwear, promoted swimming pools, and worked as a sports commentator. More recently, she hosted *That's Entertainment 111* (1994), a nostalgic celebration of MGM's past.

Williams, Francis c.1700–c.1770
Jamaican poet
He was born of free negro parents and sent to an English grammar school and Cambridge by the Duke of Montagu, who wanted to discover whether a negro, properly educated, could become 'as capable of literature as a white person'. On return to Jamaica he opened a school in Spanish Town, teaching reading, writing, Latin and mathematics. Of his verse only one ode, in elegant Latin, survives. Addressed to George Haldane on his appointment as Governor of Jamaica (1759), it voices conflicting feelings of pride in his British nurture and humility as a black person, but pleads that there is no colour distinction in virtue or learning ('honesto nullus inest animo, nullus in arte color'). 📖 E Long, *The History of Jamaica* (1774)

Williams, Sir Frederic Calland 1911–77
English electrical engineer
Born in Romily, Cheshire, he studied engineering at Manchester University and Oxford. During World War II he was recognized as a world authority on radar. He became Professor of Electrical Engineering at Manchester in 1946 and is chiefly known for his development of the Williams tube, the first successful electrostatic random access memory for the digital computer. This enabled him, together with his collaborator Tom Kilburn, to operate the world's first stored-program computer in June 1948. Williams was elected FRS in 1950, and was knighted in 1976.

Williams, Fred(erick Ronald) 1927–82
Australian landscape painter and etcher
Born in Richmond, Victoria, in the early 1950s he studied in London at the Chelsea and Central Schools of Art. Although he painted distinguished portraits, his considerable reputation lies in his landscapes, where his personal vision, use of colour and sense of scale brought him recognition as the most significant painter of the Australian landscape since Sir Arthur Streeton, acknowledged when their work was shown together at an exhibition held at the National Gallery of Victoria in 1970. An international reputation was secured by his 1977 exhibition *Landscapes of a Continent* at the Museum of Modern Art, New York. He won the Wynne Prize in 1966 and again in 1976.

Williams, Sir George 1821–1905
English social reformer
Born in Dulverton, Somerset, he became a wealthy draper. He made a hobby of temperance work, lay preaching, and teaching in ragged schools. In 1844 he founded the Young Men's Christian Assocation (YMCA).

Williams, (Hiram) Hank 1923–53
US country singer and songwriter
He was born in Mount Olive, Alabama. Inspired by Jimmie Rodgers and Roy Acuff, he won a talent contest in 1937, and had his own local radio show. The war interrupted his career, but he signed to the Acuff-Rose publishing agency as a songwriter in 1946, and had his first big hit in 1949 with 'Lovesick Blues'. Despite continuing problems with alcohol, drugs and failing health, he became country music's biggest star, and wrote and sang some of the genre's greatest songs, including 'Cold, Cold Heart', 'Hey, Good Lookin' and 'I'm So Lonesome

I Could Cry'. He died of alcohol-related heart disease while travelling to a New Year's Day show in Ohio. His son, Hank Williams, Jnr (1949–), also became a leading country singer. 📖 C Escott, *Hank Williams* (1994)

Williams, Harold 1893–1976
Australian baritone
Born in Woollahra, New South Wales, he studied at the Royal Academy of Music. In 1919 he made his recital debut at Wigmore Hall, London, and made his name the following year at a concert under Sir Henry Wood. In the same year he began his long recording career, and soon became a regular member of the English National Opera. In 1929 he returned to Australia, touring in a series of recitals. He was in demand for oratorios, especially in works by Handel, Mendelssohn and Elgar, and was one of the original 16 distinguished soloists for whom Vaughan Williams composed his *Serenade to Music* (1938). In 1938 he toured for the Australian Broadcasting Corporation, but returned to London in 1946. In 1952, he became Professor of Singing at the New South Wales Conservatorium of Music, and made occasional appearances with the Australian National Opera.

Williams, John 1796–1839
English missionary, the martyr of Erromango
Born in Tottenham, London, he was sent in 1817 by the London Missionary Society to the Society Islands, where he worked in Raïatéa with great success. In 1823 he went to Raratonga, christianized the whole Hervey group, and during the next four years visited many of the South Sea islands, including Samoa. In 1834 he returned to England, superintended the printing of his Raratongan New Testament, and raised £4,000 to equip a missionary ship. In 1838 he visited many of his stations, and sailed for the New Hebrides, where he was killed and eaten by the natives of Erromango. He published his *Narrative of Missionary Enterprises* in 1837.

Williams, John Christopher 1941–
Australian classical guitarist
Born in Melbourne, Victoria. He received his training at the Accademia Musicale Chigiana di Siena, Italy, and at the Royal College of Music, London. He became a leading international figure on classical guitar, and has been responsible for commissioning a great deal of contemporary compositions for the instrument. He tours widely, giving solo recitals and performing in chamber groups and as soloist with international orchestras, and his extensive repertoire is well represented on records. He has also performed in rock (notably with the group Sky from 1979–84, and its successors, John Williams and Friends and Attacca), jazz and folk contexts, and has taken a number of recordings into the pop charts.

Williams, J(ohn) P(eter) R(hys) 1949–
Welsh rugby player
Born in Ogmore, Mid Glamorgan, he was a talented all-round athlete and won the Wimbledon Junior tennis championships, before studying medicine. He joined the London Welsh rugby team, won 55 caps and was a star of the highly successful British Lions tour to New Zealand in 1971 and to South Africa in 1974. He subsequently became an orthopaedic surgeon and has been a consultant at the Princess of Wales Hospital in Bridgend, Wales, since 1986. 📖 *JPR: an autobiography* (1979)

Williams, Johnny (John) 1932–
US composer of film music
Born in Floral Park on Long Island, New York, he trained at the Juilliard School of Music and began his career as a jazz pianist. In the late 1950s he started composing for television, turning to film in the 1960s. He began his long professional association with Steven Spielberg in 1974,

and his work includes the Oscar-winning orchestrations of *Fiddler on the Roof* (1971), *Jaws* (1975), *Star Wars* (1977) and *E.T.* (1982).

Williams, Kenneth 1926–88
English actor and comedian

Born in London, he made his London debut as Slightly in *Peter Pan* in 1952, and two years later played the Dauphin in a revival of George Bernard Shaw's *St Joan* in the West End. He later starred in comedies and in such revues as *Share My Lettuce* (1957), *Pieces of Eight* (1959), and *One Over the Eight* (1961). He became well known in such radio series as *Round the Horne*, and *Stop Messing About*, in which his affected style of speech and rich, punctilious enunciation, made him instantly recognizable. He made several films, appearing regularly in the *Carry On* series of comedies.

Williams, Mary Lou 1910–81
US jazz pianist, arranger and composer

Born in Atlanta, Georgia, and brought up in Pittsburgh, she interrupted her high school studies to become a touring show pianist. Her first important period as a performer and arranger was during the 1930s with the Kansas City-based Andy Kirk and his Clouds of Joy. Her outstanding qualities as an arranger brought her work from Duke Ellington (for whom she arranged the well-known *Trumpets No End*), Earl Hines and Benny Goodman, among others. She later embraced the bebop style as well as writing several sacred works, such as 'Mary Lou's Mass' (1970). Her *Waltz Boogie* (1946) was one of the first jazz pieces in 3/4 time.

Williams, Michael 1935–
English actor

Born in Manchester, he made his West End debut as Bernard Fuller in *Celebration* (1961) and has had a long career with the Royal Shakespeare Company, where his roles have included Guildenstern in *Hamlet* (1965), Petruchio in *The Taming of the Shrew* (1967), the Fool in *King Lear* (1968, 1976–77), Troilus in *Troilus and Cressida* (1968–69) and the title role in *Henry V* (1971). On television, he has played Mike in *A Fine Romance* (1980–82), N V Standish in *Double First* (1988), Billy Balsam in *September Song* (1993–95) and Barry Masefield in *Conjugal Rites* (1993–94). He is married to the actress Dame Judi Dench .

Williams, Raymond 1921–88
Welsh critic and novelist

Born in Pandy, Gwent, the son of a railway signalman, he was educated at King Henry VIII Grammar School, Abergavenny and Cambridge. He wrote *Culture and Society* (1958) which required socialists to seek inspiration figures like Edmund Burke, Robert Southey, and Thomas Carlyle. He opened up questions of mass readership and cultural and ethical values in *The Long Revolution* (1966). He was made a Fellow of Jesus College, Cambridge, in 1961, and was Professor of Drama there from 1974 to 1983. He was active in New Left intellectual movements, producing the *May Day Manifesto* (1968), but his novels *Border Country* (1960), *Second Generation* (1964), *The Volunteers* (1978), *The Fight for Manod* (1979), and *Loyalties* (1985) underline the significance of Welsh consciousness for him, and he was later identified with Welsh nationalism. Of his many major works in socio-literary criticism, *The Country and the City* (1973) was possibly the most inspirational.

Williams, Robin 1951–
US film actor

Born in Chicago, Illinois, he was a student of acting at the Juillard School in New York, and later settled in California, developing into a nimble-witted stand-up comic with a restless, inventive mind and a gift for improvisation. Roles in the television series *Happy Days* and *Mork and Mindy* (1978–82) brought national popularity,

and he made his big screen debut in *Popeye* (1980). His cinema career struggled until he received Best Actor Academy Award nominations for *Good Morning Vietnam* (1987), *Dead Poets Society* (1989) and *The Fisher King* (1991). Films like *Mrs Doubtfire* (1993) and *The Birdcage* (1996) have confirmed his status as one of the cinema's current kings of comedy and he has shown his dramatic abilities in *Seize the Day* (1986), *Awakenings* (1990) and *Good Will Hunting* (1997), for which he won an Academy Award. He still performs as a stand-up comic and has been active on behalf of the homeless with Comic Relief.

Williams, Robley Cook 1908–
US biophysicist

Born in Santa Rosa, California, he studied physics at Cornell University and became assistant Professor of Astronomy (1935–45) and Professor of Physics (1945–50) at the University of Michigan. In 1944 Williams used his background in astronomy to examine the size and shape of viruses, enhancing the structure of the virus so as to make it cast a shadow. Specially treated, viruses could be made to cast measurable shadows, and this technique of metal-shadowing became widely used for the electron-microscopic examination of biological materials. This work diverted Williams towards biological problems and he moved to the University of California at Berkeley as Professor of Biophysics (1950–59), Professor of Virology (1959–64) and Professor of Molecular Biology (1964–76). He has greatly increased knowledge of virus structure.

Williams, Roger c.1604–83
American colonist and clergyman

Born in London, he was educated at Charterhouse and Pembroke College, Cambridge. He took Anglican orders, became an extreme Puritan and emigrated in 1630 to the Massachusetts Bay colony. He refused to participate in the Church in Boston, believing it had not separated from the English Church, and moved to Salem where, after challenging the authority of the Puritan magistrates over matters of personal conscience, he was persecuted and eventually banished. He took refuge with the Native Americans, then purchased land from them on which he founded the city of Providence in 1636, establishing the first Baptist church in the USA in 1639. His colony of Rhode Island was a model of democracy and religious freedom. He went to England in 1643 and 1651 to procure a charter for it and served as its president (1654–57). He published a *Key into the Language of America* (1643), *The Bloudy Tenent of Persecution for Cause of Conscience* (1644) and *The Bloudy Tenent yet more bloudy by Mr Cotton's Endeavour to wash it White in the Blood of the Lamb* (1652). ▣C Covey, *The Gentle Radical* (1966)

Williams, Shirley Vivien Teresa Brittain
Williams, Baroness 1930–
English politician

The daughter of Vera Brittain, she studied at Oxford and became a journalist. She first became a Labour MP in 1964, holding ministerial posts in Education and Science (1967–69) and the Home Office (1969–70) before being appointed Secretary of State for Prices and Consumer Protection (1974–76), then for Education and Science (1976–79). She was a co-founder of the Social Democratic Party (SDP) in 1981 and became the party's first elected MP later that year. She became president of the SDP the following year, but lost her seat in the 1983 General Election. In 1988 she joined the new, merged Social and Liberal Democratic Party (SLDP). In the same year she married, for the second time. Her first husband (1955–74) was Bernard Williams, Professor of Moral Philosophy at Oxford and her second husband, Richard Neustadt, Professor of Politics at Harvard (1988–). After her second marriage she moved to the USA and also became Professor of Politics at Harvard, but remains involved in

British politics. She was awarded a life peerage in 1993 and published her autobiography, *Snakes and Ladders*, in 1996.

Williams, Tennessee, *originally* Thomas Lanier
1911–83
US playwright

Born in Columbus, Mississippi, the son of a travelling salesman, he had an itinerant college education, finally receiving a degree from the University of Iowa in 1938. He worked at various menial jobs, among them poet-waiter at a Greenwich Village restaurant, and cinema usher. Recognition of his literary skill came in 1940, when he received a Rockefeller Fellowship for his first play, *Battle of Angels*. In 1943 he signed a six-month contract with MGM, later cancelled when he submitted a script that became *The Glass Menagerie*. This play, which in 1945 earned him the New York Drama Critics' Circle Award, introduced him as an important US playwright. He was awarded the Pulitzer Prize in 1948 for *A Streetcar Named Desire*, and again in 1955 for *Cat on a Hot Tin Roof*. He continued with *Suddenly Last Summer* (1958), *Sweet Bird of Youth* (1959) and *The Night of the Iguana* (1961). He won the Gold Medal for Literature in 1969 from both the American Academy of Arts and Letters and the National Institute of Arts and Letters. In addition to his plays, he published the poetry collections *The Summer Belvedere* (1944) and *Winter of Cities* (1956), and short stories, including *It Happened the Day the Sun Rose* (1982). He wrote one novel, *The Roman Spring of Mrs Stone* (1950), and the scripts for several films, including *Baby Doll* (1956). *Where I Live: Selected Essays* (1978) is autobiographical. ⬚D Spoto, *The Kindness of Strangers* (1985)

Williams, Waldo 1904–71
Welsh poet

Born in Haverfordwest, Dyfed, he was educated at Narberth Grammar School and University College, Aberystwyth. Considered by many to be the most original poet in the Welsh language, he was deeply influenced by the Romantic poets, and his work is concerned with universal brotherhood and the human relationship with the natural world. A committed pacifist, he supported civil disobedience as advocated by Henry Thoreau and Mahatma Gandhi. In 1950 he withheld his income tax in response to the Korean War. He spent six weeks in prison for non-payment of tax in 1960, and served a second sentence in 1961. ⬚B G Owens, *Gwaithacu Waldo Williams* (1972)

Williams, William Carlos 1883–1963
US poet, novelist and cultural historian

Born in Rutherford, Connecticut, with French, Jewish, Basque and British antecedents, he was educated in Switzerland and Paris, then took his MD at the University of Pennsylvania, Philadelphia. There he met both Ezra Pound and Hilda Doolittle ('HD'), both of whom had a considerable impact on his developing interest in poetry. His early volumes, such as *Poems* (1909, published privately), *The Tempers* (1913) and *Sour grapes* (1921), steered him towards the simple free-verse idiom, with its focus on immediate physical detail, which would characterize his work. He reached creative maturity with *Spring and All* (1923) and his ironic *The Great American Novel* (1923). *In the American Grain* (1925) was a brilliant study of American myths, providing a critical counterbalance to prevailing Puritan explanations of American culture. In 1937 he published *White Mule* (1937), the first in a trilogy of novels completed by *In the Money* (1940) and *The Build-Up* (1952). He is best known for his poetic masterpiece, *Paterson*, a vast synoptic study of a (real) American town, begun in 1946. Williams's objectivist credo 'No ideas but in things' became a major tenet of Modernist writing. He continued to published a variety of works, such as *The Collected Later*

Poems (1950, rev edn 1963) and *The Collected Earlier Poems* (1951), and won the Pulitzer Prize for *Pictures from Breughel* (1962). His *Autobiography* appeared in 1951. ⬚C F Terrell, *Williams: Man and Poet* (1983)

Williamson, David Keith 1942–
Australian playwright

Born in Melbourne, Victoria, he graduated in mechanical engineering from Monash University, Melbourne, but turned to writing plays and scripts for films and television. His first works to receive recognition were *The Removalists* (1971) and *Don's Party* (1973). Other successes include *The Club* (1977) and *The Perfectionist* (1982). He portrays many aspects of Australian life, often leaning on the male-oriented Australian 'yuppie' class of businessmen, as in *Sons of Cain* (1985). Some of his stage works have subsequently been filmed, and he has also written other film scripts, including those for *Gallipoli* (1981), *Phar Lap* (1983) and *Money and Friends* (1992).

Williamson, Henry 1895–1977
English writer

He was born in Bedfordshire, and after service in World War I became a journalist, but turned to farming in Norfolk and eventually settled in a cottage on Exmoor. He wrote several semi-autobiographical novels, including his long series *A Chronicle of Ancient Sunlight* (1951–69) on the life story of the hero, Phillip Maddison. He is best known, however, for his classic nature stories, starting with *The Peregrine's Saga* (1923) and *The Old Stag* (1926). He achieved enduring fame with *Tarka the Otter* (1927, Hawthornden Prize) and *Salar the Salmon* (1935). His trenchant anti-war novel *A Patriot's Progress* (1930) was much admired, but his support for Sir Oswald Mosley and Hitler greatly damaged his reputation. He wrote two autobiographical works, *The Wet Flanders Plain* (1929) and *A Clear Water Stream* (1958), and a biography of his friend T E Lawrence (1941). ⬚H F West, *The Dreamer of Devon* (1932)

Williamson, James Cassius 1845–1913
Australian theatrical producer

Born in Mercer, Pennsylvania, USA, he made his stage debut at the age of 16, and was an established actor in New York by 1870. He toured Australia (1874) at the invitation of actor-manager George Coppin, and later visited Europe and London. He returned to Australia in 1879 with his actress wife Maggie Moore (1851–1926), who often starred with him, for example playing Sir Joseph Porter and Buttercup in *HMS Pinafore*, until they divorced in 1899. Williamson leased the Melbourne Theatre Royal and with two partners, went into management, establishing the theatrical organization popularly known as 'The Firm', which was to dominate Australasian theatre for four decades. He supported tours by overseas artists, but concentrated on established, long-running successes such as the Savoy operas, for which he held the Australian rights, rather than the contemporary theatre of the day.

Williamson, Malcolm Benjamin Graham Christopher 1931–
Australian composer

Born in Sydney, he studied under Eugène Goossens and Elizabeth Lutyens, and went to England in 1953. He began his career as a soloist with orchestras in London, Vienna, Haifa, Sydney and Melbourne, and now lives in England, performing as a pianist and organist, lecturing and composing. His operas include *Our Man in Havana* (1963), *The Violins of Saint-Jacques* (1966) and *The Red Sea* (1972). He has written for television and films, including *The Happy Prince* (1965) and *Julius Caesar Jones* (1966), and composed ballets, orchestral works, vocal, choral and piano music, and 'cassations', often involving the audience. He was made Master of the Queen's Music in 1975, and was president of the Royal Philharmonic Orchestra (1977–82).

Williamson, William Crawford 1816–95
English botanist, surgeon, zoologist and palaeontologist
Born in Scarborough, Yorkshire, he trained in medicine and became curator of the Museum of the Manchester Natural History Society (1835–38). He was later appointed the first Professor of Natural History and Geology (later of Botany) at Owens College, Manchester (1851–92). He was the first to investigate thoroughly the plant remains (coal balls) in coal. At the time, however, the full significance of his work in fossil botany was not appreciated and, after 41 years of teaching at Owens College (later Manchester University) he was refused a pension. He is regarded as the founder of modern palaeobotany. He made several contributions to *Fossil Flora of Great Britain* (1831–37).

Williams Pantycelyn, William 1717–91
Welsh hymn writer, poet, translator and prose writer
Born in Cefn-coed in Carmarthenshire, he took his name from the town of Pantycelyn, where his mother took him to live in 1742. He devoted his life to itinerant preaching on behalf of the Methodist movement, and was ultimately regarded as one of the leaders of Welsh Methodism. The most important hymn-writer of Wales, he created an extraordinary achievement in the 5,500-line poem *Golwg ar Deyrnas Crist* (1756, rev edn 1764, 'A View of Christ's Kingdom'). *Bywyd a Marwolaeth Theomemphus* (1764, 'The Life and Death of Theomemphus'), another long poem, is a dramatic work unprecedented in Welsh or any other poetry. He produced over 90 volumes by the time of his death, and seriously deserves attention outside his native land as a poet and thinker of the first rank. 📖 S Lewis, *Williams Pantycelyn* (1927); *Anglo-Welsh Review*, 15, 35 (1965)

Willibald 700–86
Anglo-Saxon churchman and missionary
Born in Wessex, he made a pilgrimage to Palestine, and settled as a monk in Monte Cassino (730–40). He was sent by Pope **Gregory III** to Germany to help his kinsman St **Boniface**, who made him the first Bishop of Eichstätt. His *Hodoeporicon* is an account of his pilgrimage to Palestine. He was the brother of St **Walburga**, and his feast day is 11 July.

Willibrord, St 658–739
English monk
Born in Northumbria, he trained in Ripon Abbey. After working in Ireland, he and 11 others left for the Netherlands as missionaries in 690. Responsible for converting much of the Netherlands to Christianity, the Merovingian and Carolingian Frankish kings legitimized his work in Friesland, which they welcomed as a stabilizing political influence in their interests. Willibrord visited Rome c.692 and 695, and was made Archbishop of the Frisians, based in Utrecht, in 694. In 700 he founded the monastery of Echternach in Luxembourg. His feast day is 7 November.

Willis, Bruce 1955–
US actor
Born in Penn's Grove, New Jersey, he worked as a security guard and played in a blues band before studying drama at Montclair State College and making his off-Broadway debut in *Heaven and Earth* (1977). Other stage appearances include *Bayside Boys* (1981) and *Fool For Love* (1984). An extra in films including *The First Deadly Sin* (1980) and *The Verdict* (1982), he became a star as the wisecracking David Addison in the television series *Moonlighting* (1985–89) for which he received an Emmy award. *Die Hard* (1988) established him as a movie star and he has pursued an erratic career, alternating action-man roles with more sensitive character parts in films like *Mortal Thoughts* (1991), *Pulp Fiction* (1994) and *Nobody's Fool* (1994). His

other films include *Die Hard With A Vengeance* (1995), *Twelve Monkeys* (1995) and *The Day Of The Jackal* (1997). He has been married to actress Demi Moore (1962–) since 1987.

Willis, Nathaniel Parker 1806–67
US editor and writer
Born in Portland, Maine, he published several volumes of poetry, founded the *American Monthly Magazine* in Boston (1829) and in 1831 visited Europe, and contributed to the *New York Mirror* his *Pencillings by the Way*. Appointed attaché to the US legation in Paris, he visited Greece and Turkey, and returned to England in 1837. He contributed to the London *New Monthly* his *Inklings of Adventure* (collected 1836), and published *Letters from under a Bridge* (1840). In 1844 he edited the *Daily Mirror*, revisited Europe, and published *Dashes at Life with a Free Pencil* (1845). Returning to New York in 1846, he established the *Home Journal*. His sister, Sara Payson Willis, 'Fanny Fern' (1811–72), was a popular writer. 📖 C P Aulzer, *Nathaniel Willis* (1969)

Willis, Norman David 1933–
English trade union leader
Educated at Ashford County Grammar School and Ruskin and Oriel colleges, Oxford, he worked for two years for the Transport and General Workers' Union (TGWU) before national service (1951–53). He returned to the TGWU as personal assistant to the General-Secretary (1959–70) and National Secretary for Research and Education (1970–74), before being appointed assistant General-Secretary of the Trades Union Congress (TUC) in 1974. He succeeded **Len Murray** as General-Secretary (1984–93). As a moderate, his measured approach to industrial relations frequently provoked a hostile reaction from leftist union leaders.

Willis, Thomas 1621–73
English physician, one of the founders of the Royal Society
Born in Great Bedwyn, Wiltshire, he studied classics and then medicine at Oxford, graduating MB in 1646. He briefly served in the Royalist army in the Civil War. He was one of the small group of natural philosophers including **Robert Boyle** who met in Oxford in 1648–49 and who in 1662 were to become founder members of the Royal Society of London. He became Sedleian Professor of Natural Philosophy at Oxford (1660–75), but his fame and wealth derived from a fashionable medical practice in London. His *Cerebri Anatomie, cui accessit Nervorum descriptio et usus* (1664, 'Anatomy of the Brain, with a Description of the Nerves and their Function') was the principal study of brain anatomy of its time. In it he offered new delineations of the cranial nerves and described cerebral circulation, discovering the ring of vessels now called the 'circle of Willis'. He was also a pioneer of the clinical and pathological analysis of diabetes, and was the first to recognize that spasm of the bronchial muscles was the essential characteristic of asthma.

Williston, Samuel 1861–1963
US jurist
Born in Cambridge, Massachusetts, he was educated at Harvard. He taught there from 1890 to 1938, then became an Emeritus Professor until his death. His major work was *Treatise on Contracts* (1920), and he was regarded as the most distinguished US scholar of his time on contract law. Mainly responsible for the American Law Institute's *Restatement of Contracts*, he was the draftsman of uniform legislation on sales, bills of lading and stock certificates which led up to the Uniform Commercial Code.

Willkie, Wendell 1892–1944
US politician
Born in Elwood, Indiana, he became first a lawyer and later an industrialist. Having removed his support from the Democrat to the Republican cause in 1940, he was nominated as presidential candidate by the party and

narrowly defeated in the election of that year. In 1941–42 he travelled the world representing the President. An opponent of Isolationism, he was leader of the left-wing element in his party.

Willoughby, Sir Hugh d.c.1554
English explorer

In 1553 he was appointed commander of an expedition which was fitted out by the merchants of London 'for the discovery of regions, dominions, islands, and places unknown'. On 10 May he sailed from Deptford with three vessels, one commanded by Richard Chancellor. They crossed the North Sea, and sighted the coast of Norway, but in September Chancellor's ship parted from the company in a storm. The two others reached Russian Lapland. Willoughby hoped to spend the winter there, but died of scurvy, with his 62 companions. The following year Russian fishermen found the ships and the commander's journal (published by Hakluyt Society, 1903).

Wills, Bob (James Robert) 1905–75
US country fiddler, the creator of Western swing

He was born in Kosse, Texas. His father and grandfather were both fiddlers, and after initial reluctance, he took up the instrument. He worked at various jobs before making music his career around 1930, and began to evolve the music which would become his legacy, and would later be dubbed Western swing. He brought together traditional country music with jazz swing rhythms and instruments (horns, drums), and forged an infectious hybrid which remains influential today. Despite initial hostility to the country establishment, songs like 'San Antonio Rose' and 'Time Changes Everything' became country standards. 🕮 C Townsend, *San Antonio Rose* (1976)

Wills, William Gorman 1828–91
Irish playwright and poet

Born in Kilkenny County, he studied at Trinity College, Dublin, and became a successful portrait painter. As a playwright he had a huge success with *Man o'Airlie* (1866), followed by *Charles I* (1872), *Jane Shore* (1876), *Olivia* (1878) and *Claudian* (1885), as well as a version of *Faust* (1885). He also wrote novels, but considered verse a higher literary form. He published a long poem *Melchior* (1885), and his ballads include 'I'll sing thee Songs of Araby'.

Wills, William John 1834–61
Australian surveyor and explorer

He was born in Totnes, Devon, England, and trained in medicine. He arrived in Victoria in 1852 as a surveyor and joined the staff of Melbourne's new observatory. In 1860 he became second-in-command of Robert O'Hara Burke's ill-fated expedition to cross the continent of Australia from south to north. They set off from Melbourne and reached the tidal marshes of the Flinders River at the edge of the Gulf of Carpentaria, but then ran out of food, ate their camels, and continued on foot. Wills and Burke survived to reach their supply depot at Cooper's Creek seven hours after the support party had left and died of starvation in terrible conditions at the end of June 1861; only John King survived the expedition.

Wills Moody, Helen Newington, *née* Wills
1905–98
US tennis player

Born in Centreville, California, she dominated women's tennis from the retirement of Suzanne Lenglen in 1926 until the outbreak of World War II, winning eight singles finals at Wimbledon and seven US championships. She also won gold medals in the women's singles and doubles at the 1924 Olympics. While she was married (1929–37) she added her husband's name to her own. Her great

rivalry with Helen Jacobs (1908–97) drove her to continue to play during the 1938 Wimbledon final, despite being severely handicapped by injury. She retired in 1939.

Willstätter, Richard 1872–1942
German organic chemist and Nobel Prize winner

Born in Karlsruhe, he studied at Munich and became professor at Zurich, Berlin and finally Munich in 1917. His research included alkaloids and their derivatives, and the work on plant pigments for which in 1915 he was awarded the Nobel Prize for chemistry. In 1925 he resigned his professorship at Munich, and in 1939 left Germany for Switzerland.

Willumsen, Jens Ferdinand 1863–1958
Danish painter and sculptor

He was born in Copenhagen. His best-known painting, *After the Storm* (1905), is in the Oslo National Gallery. As a sculptor his finest work is the *Great Relief*, in coloured marbles and bronze. He bequeathed his works and his art collection to establish a Willumsen museum in Frederikssund.

Wilmore, Michael See **Mac Liammóir, Mícheál**

Wilson, Alexander 1766–1813
US ornithologist

Born in Paisley, Renfrewshire, Scotland, he worked as a weaver from the age of 13, wrote nature poetry and verses about life in the weaving sheds, and published *Poems* (1790) and *Watty and Meg* (1792). He was prosecuted for a libellous poem against the mill-owners, which he denied writing, but was jailed for 18 months. In 1794 he emigrated to the USA, and became a schoolteacher in rural schools in New Jersey and Philadelphia. Encouraged by a neighbour, the naturalist William Bartram (son of John Bartram), he decided to devote himself to ornithology. He made several journeys across the USA, collecting species and drawing them, and wrote a poetic account of his first journey, an excursion on foot to Niagara Falls, in *The Foresters, A Poem* (1805). In 1806 he was employed on the US edition of *Rees's Cyclopaedia*, and prevailed on the publisher to undertake an illustrated *American Ornithology* (7 vols, 1808–14); the 8th and 9th volumes were completed after his death. Wilson's Storm-Petrel and Wilson's Phalarope were named in his honour. He is regarded as the 'father' of American ornithology.

Wilson, A(ndrew) N(orman) 1950–
English novelist, biographer, critic and journalist

Born in Stone, Staffordshire, he was educated at Rugby and Oxford. Since publishing his first novel, *The Sweets of Pimlico* (1977), he has maintained a prolific output. Many of his earlier novels were comedies of manners, but works such as *The Healing Art* (1980) and *Wise Virgin* (1982) deal with specific moral issues. Later works include *A Bottle in the Smoke* (1989), *The Vicar of Sorrows* (1993) and *A Watch in the Dark* (1996). His biographies include *Sir Walter Scott* (1980), *Milton* (1983), *Tolstoy* (1987), the controversial *Jesus* (1992) and *The Rise and Fall of the House of Windsor* (1993). He has frequently given the public impression of being a High Church Conservative, and can be a harsh literary and ethical commentator. He became literary editor of the *Evening Standard* in 1990.

Wilson, Sir Angus Frank Johnstone 1913–91
English writer

Born in Bexhill, Sussex, the son of an English father and a South African mother, he was educated at Westminster School and Merton College, Oxford. He joined the staff of the British Museum library in London in 1937. He began writing in 1946 and rapidly established a reputation with his brilliant collection of short stories, *The Wrong Set* (1949), satirizing the more aimless sections of pre-war middle-class society. *Such Darling Dodos* (1950), *For Whom the Cloche Tolls* (1953) and *A Bit off the Map* (1957) added to his prestige, and in 1955 he gave up his office of deputy-superintendent of the British Museum reading room to devote himself solely to writing. The novels *Hemlock and After* (1952) and *Anglo-Saxon Attitudes* (1956) were both bestsellers, and his later novels, including *The Old Men in the Zoo* (1961), *Late Call* (1965) and *No Laughing Matter* (1967), an ambitious family chronicle of the egocentric Matthews family spanning the 20th century, also received critical acclaim. His later novels include *As If By Magic* (1973) and *Setting the World on Fire* (1980). He also wrote one play, *The Mulberry Bush* (1955). He was Professor of English Literature at the University of East Anglia from 1966 to 1978. 📖 J L Halio, *Angus Wilson* (1964)

Wilson, August 1945–
US playwright

Born in Pittsburgh into a black working-class family, he dropped out of high school, but began to write poetry in his twenties, then turned to drama. His powerful, richly colloquial plays draw on jazz, the blues and African-American idiom and folk culture for their inspiration. In the 1980s he began an ambitious cycle chronicling the lives of African-Americans in the 20th century, with each play focusing on a different decade. He has been lionized as an original by some critics, and rejected by others, and has twice been awarded the Pulitzer Prize for drama, for *Fences* in 1987 and *The Piano Lesson* in 1990. His other works include *Ma Rainey's Black Bottom* (1984), *Joe Turner's Come and Gone* (1986), *Two Trains Running* (1992) and *Seven Guitars* (1995).

Wilson, Brian 1942–
US pop and rock musician and composer

He was born in Hawthorne, California, and was the creative force behind The Beach Boys, the most successful American group of the 1960s. Their early surf hits gave way to more ambitious projects from *Pet Sounds* (1966) onwards, the most famous of which, the fabled *Smile* album, was never made in its projected form. Wilson gave up most performing and retreated to the studio in the wake of a nervous breakdown in 1964, which marked the beginning of a long history of mental disturbance. His involvement in the band and in music became increasingly sporadic, but he returned with a solo album, *Love and Mercy*, in 1988. A second album was shelved amid a lengthy court case involving his cousin, Mike Love, over ownership of lyrics. He sang on Van Dyke Parks's *Orange Crate Art* (1995), and also on the soundtrack to a documentary film about him, *I Just Wasn't Made For These Times* (1995). 📖 T White, *The Nearest Faraway Place* (1994)

Wilson, Charles Thomson Rees 1869–1959
Scottish pioneer of atomic and nuclear physics, and Nobel Prize winner

He was born in Glencorse, near Edinburgh. Educated at Manchester and at Cambridge, where he later became Professor of Natural Philosophy (1925–34), he was noted for his study of atmospheric electricity, one by-product of which was the successful protection from lightning of Britain's wartime barrage balloons. His greatest achievement was to devise the 'cloud chamber' method of marking the track of alpha-particles and electrons. The movement and interaction of atoms could thus be followed and photographed. The principle was also used by Donald Glaser to develop the 'bubble chamber'. In 1927 he shared with Arthur Compton the Nobel Prize for physics, and in 1937 he received the Copley Medal of the Royal Society.

Wilson, David 1938–
Scottish chef and restaurateur

Born in Bishopbriggs, near Glasgow, he developed his interest in eating and cooking while living in Glasgow. In 1966 he left his job as a marketing manager to work for £16 a week in a Huntingdonshire inn, following this with experience in France. In 1972 he and his wife, Patricia, took over the Peat Inn, then a pub in the tiny village of Peat Inn, Fife. Despite its rural location the restaurant gained national and then international recognition, gaining a Michelin rosette in 1987 for its innovative cooking and remarkable wine list.

Wilson, Edmund 1895–1972
US literary critic, social commentator and novelist

Born in Red Bank, New Jersey, he was educated at Princeton and became a journalist with *Vanity Fair*, editor of the *New Republic* (1926–31), and chief book reviewer for the *New Yorker*. A lively, waspish critic of other writers, his own fiction, of which *Memoirs of Hecate Country* (1946) is the most notable example, is largely forgotten. However, few critics have caused such a stir as he, and he was more listened to than most. *Axel's Castle* (1931), a study of Symbolist literature, is a landmark, but *To a Finland Station* (1940), an account of the origins of the Bolshevik Revolution, and *The Wound and the Bow* (1941), a study of the relation between psychic malaise and creativity, are no less significant. In *Patriotic Gore: Studies in the Literature of the Civil War* (1962) he surveyed in detail the writers of the period. Over a wide-ranging oeuvre and argumentative life he published on many subjects and in a variety of forms, encompassing plays, articles, correspondence (see his correspondence with Vladimir Nabokov) and, in *The Scrolls from the Dead Sea* (1955), for which he learned Hebrew, a contentious but illuminating guide to a complex subject. Various memoirs detailing his life have appeared. He married four times, the third marriage being to the novelist Mary McCarthy, whose own turbulent career he defended even after their relationship had foundered. 📖 D Castronovo, *Edmund Wilson* (1984)

Wilson, Edmund Beecher 1856–1939
US zoologist and embryologist

Born in Geneva, Illinois, he studied at Yale and Johns Hopkins universities, and after several teaching posts became Da Costa Professor of Zoology at Columbia University in New York. His research was concerned with cell lineage and the formation of tissues from precursor cells, emphasizing the significance of cells as the building blocks of life. His major contribution was to show the importance of the chromosomes, particularly the sex chromosomes, in heredity and cell structure. His *The Cell in Development and Inheritance* (1896, 1925) was instrumental in the synthesis of cytology and Mendelian genetics. He is considered to be one of the founders of modern genetics.

Wilson, Edward Adrian 1872–1912
English physician, naturalist and explorer

Born in Cheltenham, Gloucestershire, he first went to the Antarctic with Robert Scott in the *Discovery* (1900–04). On his return to England he did research on grouse diseases and made illustrations for books on birds and mammals. In 1910 he returned to the Antarctic on the *Terra Nova* as chief of the expedition's scientific staff. One of the party of five that reached the South Pole just after the Norwegian Roald Amundsen, he died with the others on the return journey.

Wilson, Edward Osborne 1929–
US biologist

Born in Birmingham, Alabama, he studied there and at Harvard, where since 1956 he has been Baird Professor of Science and curator of entomology at the Museum of Comparative Zoology. He has been a major figure in the development of sociobiology, the investigation into the biological basis of social behaviour. His early researches into the social behaviour, communication and evolution of ants resulted in the publication of *The Insect Societies* (1971), in which he outlines his belief that the same evolutionary forces have shaped the behaviours of insects and other animals including human beings. His book *Sociobiology: the New Synthesis* (1975) was acclaimed for its detailed compilation and analysis of social behaviour in a wide range of animals, and it included his controversial claim that the genes control a range of human behaviours, including aggression, homosexuality, altruism and differences between the sexes. His books include *On Human Nature* (1978), *The Ants* (1990, with B Hölldobler), both of which won Pulitzer Prizes, and *The Diversity of Life* (1992). He received the Audubon Medal in 1995 for his contributions to conservation and environmental protection.

Wilson, Sir (William James) Erasmus 1809–84
English surgeon and antiquary

Born in London, he studied at the city's St Bartholomew's Hospital, and became best known as a specialist on skin diseases. He published *Anatomist's Vademecum*, *Book of Diseases of the Skin* (1842), *Report on Leprosy* and *Egypt of the Past*. A generous patron of Egyptian research, he financed the transportation of the obelisk known as Cleopatra's Needle to London in 1878 at a cost of £10,000.

Wilson, Ernest Henry 1876–1930
English plant collector, botanist and prolific writer

Born in Chipping Campden, Gloucestershire, he was apprenticed to nurseries, recommended to the curator of Birmingham Botanic Garden at 16, and then studied at Birmingham Technical School and at Kew. He was recommended to Veitch's Nurseries as a plant collector, and left on an expedition to central China in 1899, and again in 1903. In 1906 he joined the Arnold Arboretum and made further expeditions to China (1906–11), Japan (1914, 1917–19) and Australia, New Zealand, India and Africa (1919–21). He discovered over 3,000 new species and introduced more than 1,000 to cultivation. His last post was as keeper of the Arnold Arboretum (1917–30). His published works included *A Naturalist in Western China* (1913), *Cherries (Prunus) of Japan* (1916), *Conifers and Taxads of Japan* (1916), *Lilies of Eastern Asia* (1925), *The Vegetation of Korea* (1918–20) and *Plant Hunting* (1927).

Wilson, George Washington 1823–93
Scottish photographer and publisher

Born near Banff, the son of a farmer, he was apprenticed as a carpenter before training as a painter in Edinburgh and London, thereafter working as a miniaturist. He went to Aberdeen in 1850, where he first worked as a photographer, opening his own photographic portrait studio in 1855; by the 1880s he was probably the world's largest publisher of photographic views and lantern slides, operating a photographic 'factory', which utilized considerable division of labour in the production process. The firm's catalogue included material bought in from all over the world; views were produced in all the formats fashionable at the time, including lantern slides and postcards, and numerous illustrated topographical books were published between 1856 and 1871. Wilson's artistic training is evident in the composition of many of his picturesque landscapes, although much of his output and that of the firm was unexceptional.

Wilson, (Robert) Gordon 1938–
Scottish Nationalist politician

Born in Glasgow and educated at Douglas High School, Lanarkshire, and Edinburgh University, he qualified as a solicitor. National Secretary of the Scottish National Party (SNP) from 1963 to 1971, he initiated sweeping organizational reforms which modernized the party. He also masterminded important policy developments, in

particular exploiting the benefits to the SNP of North Sea Oil. These laid the basis for the party's electoral gains in the 1970s. MP for Dundee West (1970–87), he was the party's leading parliamentary spokesman. As National Convenor of the SNP (1979–90) he represented the more traditional wing of the party in the conflict with left-wing elements, but eventually succeeded in reconciling the different factions. He was vice-president of the SNP from 1992 to 1997.

Wilson (of Rievaulx), Sir (James) Harold Wilson, Baron 1916–95
English Labour politician

Born in Huddersfield, he was educated there, in Cheshire and at Oxford, where he became a lecturer in economics in 1937. In 1943–44 he was director of economics and statistics at the Ministry of Fuel and Power. Becoming MP for Ormskirk in 1945, he was then appointed Parliamentary Secretary to the Ministry of Works. In 1947 he became successively Secretary for Overseas Trade and President of the Board of Trade until his resignation on the tide of Bevanism in April 1951. In 1951 and 1955 he was re-elected MP for Huyton, the division he had represented since 1950. The youngest Cabinet Minister since William Pitt, the Younger, after 1956, when he headed the voting for the Labour Shadow Cabinet, he became the principal Opposition Spokesman on Economic Affairs. An able and hard-hitting debater, in 1963 he succeeded Hugh Gaitskell as leader of the Labour Party, becoming Prime Minister in 1964 with a precariously small majority and being re-elected in 1966 with comfortably large support. His government's economic plans were badly affected at home by the balance of payments crisis, leading to severe restrictive measures. Abroad he was faced with the Rhodesian problem (increasingly severe economic sanctions being applied), continued intransigence from de Gaulle over Great Britain's proposed entry into the Common Market, and the important question of Britain's new status in world politics as a lesser power. His party lost power in the 1970 general election and he became Leader of the Opposition, but then he led them back into government in 1974, resigning as Labour leader two years later. He was knighted in 1976 and created a life peer in 1983. Although he cultivated a homely, man-of-the-people public image he was noted for his skill as a debater, and is considered to have been one of the shrewdest political operators of the 20th century. His *Memoirs* were published in 1986.

Wilson, Harriet c.1807–c.1870
US writer

Born in Fredericksburg, Virginia, she was the author of the first book by a black American woman—*Our Nig (Sketches from the Life of a Free Black)* (1859). Written in the style of the sentimental 19th-century novel, it tells the story of a mixed marriage. When the book's authorship was first discovered, oversimplistic parallels were drawn between Wilson's own life and the story she told. Since the book's reprinting in 1983 Wilson has been given the credit due for her stylistic intelligence and the cool way in which she handles the power struggles at play in a nominally Christian family.

Wilson, Harriette, née Dubochet 1786–1855
English courtesan

She was born in Mayfair, London, of French descent. Her long career as a genteel courtesan began at the age of 15 with the Earl of Craven, and subsequent paramours included the Duke of Argyll, the Duke of Wellington and the Marquis of Worcester. All these figured in her lively but libellous *Memoirs*, brought out in parts from 1825 to the accompaniment of a barrage of suggestive advance publicity aimed at blackmail of the victims, most of whom echoed the celebrated outburst of Wellington on the occasion—'Publish and be damned!'

Wilson, Henry, *originally* Jeremiah James Colbath
1812–75
US politician
Born in Farmington, New Hampshire, he changed his name when he came of age, worked as a shoemaker, became prominent as an Abolitionist in the 1930s, after his first exposure to slavery in Virginia, and was elected to the Massachusetts legislature and state senate. He was an active leader of the Free-Soilers, assisted in forming the new Republican Party, sat in the US Senate (1855–73), and then became Vice-President of the USA (1873–75) under Ulysses S Grant. He wrote *Rise and Fall of the Slave Power in America* (1872–75).

Wilson, Sir Henry Hughes 1864–1922
Irish field marshal
He was born in Edgeworthstown, County Longford, and served in Burma (1884–87) and South Africa (1899–1901). As director of Military Operations at the War Office (1910–14), he elaborated plans for the rapid support of France in the event of war with Germany. By the end of World War I, he was Chief of the Imperial General Staff. Promoted field marshal and created a baronet (1919), he resigned from the army in 1922, and became an MP. His implacable opposition to the leaders of Sinn Féin led to his assassination on the doorstep of his London home.

Wilson, Henry Maitland Wilson, 1st Baron
1881–1964
English soldier
He fought in South Africa and in World War I, and by 1937 he was General Officer Commanding 2nd Division, Aldershot. On the outbreak of World War II he was appointed General Officer Commanding-in-Chief, Egypt, and after leading successfully the initial British advance in Libya and capturing Bardia, Tobruk and Benghazi, he was given command of the short and ill-fated Greek campaign. In 1943 he was appointed Commander-in-Chief Middle East, and in 1944 he became Supreme Allied Commander in what had become the relatively subordinate Mediterranean theatre. He headed the British Joint Staff Mission in Washington (1945–47) and in 1955 became Constable of the Tower.

Wilson, Horace Hayman 1786–1860
English Orientalist
Born in London, in 1808 he went to India as assistant surgeon, and became assistant to John Leyden (1775–1811) in Calcutta. He was Boden Professor of Sanskrit at Oxford (1832–60), and librarian at East India House (1836–60). His *Sanskrit–English Dictionary* (1819) and Sanskrit grammar (1841), together with his other works, helped to lay the foundations of Indian philology in Europe.

Wilson, Jack See Wovoka

Wilson, James 1742–98
American political ideologist
Born in Carskerdo, Scotland, he studied successively at St Andrews, Glasgow and Edinburgh (1757–65), then moved to Philadelphia where he became an active philosophico-legal publicist in the cause of American devolution. Elected to the Continental Congress in 1775 and again in 1782–83 and 1785–86, he supported independence, advocated stronger US central government, and favoured the creation of new states. As delegate to the Constitutional Congress of 1787, he played a major part in drafting the final document with James Madison. His influence gained almost immediate ratification of the

Constitution of Pennsylvania in 1790, the first major state to do so. He was Associate Justice of the US Supreme Court (1789–98), and was the first Professor of Law at Pennsylvania University (from 1790).

Wilson, James 1805–60
Scottish economist
Born in Hawick, Roxburghshire, he settled in business in London, became an authority on the Corn Laws and the currency, and founded *The Economist* (1843). He entered parliament as a Liberal in 1847, and became Financial Secretary to the Treasury and Vice-President of the Board of Trade. He went to India to be Financier and Member of the Council of India, and established paper currency there.

Wilson, John, *pseudonym* Christopher North
1785–1854
Scottish critic and essayist
Born in Paisley, Renfrewshire, he studied at Glasgow University and Magdalen College, Oxford, where he won the Newdigate Prize for poetry. He bought an estate in 1807 at Elleray, Westmoreland (now Cumbria), and became acquainted with the Lake District circle of poets (Wordsworth, Coleridge, Thomas De Quincey, Robert Southey). There he wrote three long poems, *The Isle of Palms* (1812), *The Magic Mirror* (1812, addressed to Sir Walter Scott) and *The City of the Plague* (1816). Having lost his estate through an uncle's mismanagement, Wilson settled in Edinburgh as an advocate in 1815. In 1817 he joined John Gibson Lockhart and James Hogg in launching *Blackwood's Magazine*. Despite lacking any qualification for the post, he was appointed Professor of Moral Philosophy at Edinburgh (1820–51). As contributing editor of *Blackwood's* he wrote several notable series under his pseudonym, such as *Noctes Ambrosianae* (1822–35), and a series of rural short stories, *Lights and Shadows of Scottish Life* (1822). He also published two novels, *The Trials of Margaret Lyndsay* (1823) and *The Foresters* (1825). His *Works* (1855–58) were edited by his son-in-law, James Frederick Ferrier. ⌨ E Swan, *Christopher North* (1934)

Wilson, John Dover 1881–1969
English Shakespearean scholar
Born in London and educated at Cambridge, he spent some years as teacher, lecturer and HM inspector of adult education, then became Professor of Education at King's College London (1924–35), and of Rhetoric and English Literature at Edinburgh (1935–45). He is best known for his Shakespearean studies, particularly on the problems in *Hamlet*. From 1921 till 1966 he was editor of the New Shakespeare series. His works include *Life in Shakespeare's England* (1911), *The Essential Shakespeare* (1932), *The Fortunes of Falstaff* (1943), *What Happens in Hamlet* (1935) and *Shakespeare's Sonnets—An Introduction for Historians and Others* (1963).

Wilson, Kenneth Geddes 1936–
US theoretical physicist and Nobel Prize winner
Born in Waltham, Massachusetts, he was educated at Harvard and the California Institute of Technology (Caltech), where he received his PhD in 1961. He worked at Harvard and at CERN (Conseil Européen pour la Recherche Nucléaire), in Geneva (1962–63). In 1963 he moved to Cornell University where he became professor of physics in 1971, later holding the same position at the Ohio State University (1988–). He applied ingenious mathematical methods to the understanding of the magnetic properties of atoms, and later used similar methods in the study of phase changes between liquids and gases, and in alloys. He proposed that the properties of a system of large numbers of interacting atoms could be predicted from observations of individual atoms, and his technique is used in many differing fields of study. For

this work he was awarded the Nobel Prize for physics in 1982. More recently, he has applied his technique to the strong nuclear force that binds quarks in the nucleus.

Wilson, Richard 1714–82
Welsh landscape painter

Born in Penegoes rectory, Powys, he gave up portrait painting for landscape after a visit to Italy (1749–56) and anticipated **Thomas Gainsborough** and **John Constable** in forsaking strait-laced Classicism for a lyrical freedom of style. In London in 1760 he exhibited his *Niobe*. Also famous was his *View of Rome from the Villa Madama*. In 1776 he became Librarian to the Royal Academy.

Wilson, Richard, *originally* Ian Colquhoun Wilson 1936–
Scottish actor and director

Born in Greenock, Renfrewshire, he worked as a research scientist before training at RADA. His many television comedy roles include Jeremy Parsons in *A Sharp Intake of Breath* (1978–80), Dr Gordon Thorpe in *Only When I Laugh* (1979–81), Richard Lipton in *Hot Metal* (1988), Eddie Clockerty in *Tutti Frutti* (1987) and Victor Meldrew in *One Foot in the Grave* (1990–). He was also in the television dramas *The Woman He Loved* (1988), *Selling Hitler* (1991), *The Life and Times of Henry Pratt* (1992) and *Under the Hammer* (1994), and has appeared in films such as *A Passage to India* (1984) and *Whoops Apocalypse* (1986). In the theatre, he has worked extensively as an actor and director.

Wilson, Robert 1941–
US epic theatre-maker, director and designer

He was born in Waco, Texas, and trained as a painter in Texas, Paris and New York, developing a sense of visual impact that became evident in his subsequent career as the USA's most flamboyant post-modern creator of theatrical spectacle. In contrast with the traditional language of theatre, he mixes a combination of movement, contemporary music by composers like **Philip Glass** and David Byrne, and exciting imagery, often in very long performances (some have reached 12 hours). His set designs have been exhibited in major museums. His work includes *The Life and Times of Sigmund Freud* (1969), *The Life and Times of Joseph Stalin* (1973), *A Letter for Queen Victoria* (1974), *Death, Destruction and Detroit* (1979), *Great Day in the Morning* (1983), and *The CIVIL WarS* (conceived 1984), one of the most ambitious theatrical events ever proposed and still to be mounted in full. He has collaborated with **Tom Waits**, most notably on the pop operas *The Black Rider* (1990) and *Alice* (1992).

Wilson, Robert Woodrow 1936–
US physicist and Nobel Prize winner

Born in Houston, Texas, he was educated at Rice University and the California Institute of Technology (Caltech). He then joined Bell Laboratories in New Jersey and became head of the radiophysics research department in 1976. There he collaborated with **Arno Allan Penzias** in using a large radio telescope designed for communication with satellites; they detected in 1964 a radio noise background which came from all directions with an energy distribution corresponding to that of a black body at a temperature of 3.5 K. **Robert Dicke** and **Phillip Peebles** suggested that this radiation is the residual radiation from the Big Bang at the universe's creation, which has cooled to 3.5 K by the expansion of the universe. Such a cosmic background radiation had been predicted to exist by **George Gamow, Ralph Alpher, Hans Bethe** and Robert Herman in 1948. Wilson and Penzias (jointly with **Peter Kapitza**) shared the 1978 Nobel Prize for physics for their work, which can reasonably be claimed to be of the most important contributions to cosmology in the 20th century. In 1970 he continued his

collaboration with Penzias and they discovered (with K B Jefferts) the 2.6mm wavelength radiation from interstellar carbon monoxide.

Wilson, Roy (ston Warner) 1900–65
English strip cartoonist

Born in Kettering, Northamptonshire, he studied at Nottingham School of Art and was then apprenticed as a furniture designer (1915). In 1920 he started working on strips for Amalgamated Press children's comics. From 1930 he went solo on *Steve and Stumpy* (*Butterfly*) and many more, notably *George the Jolly Gee-Gee* (*Radio Fun*, 1938) and *Chimpo's Circus* (*Happy Days*, 1938), which was a varidesigned front page in full colour. He designed many painted annual covers and frontispieces and, from 1955, many personality strips, such as *Jerry Lewis*, *Harry Secombe* and *Morecambe and Wise*.

Wilson, Scottie 1888–1972
Scottish artist

Born in Glasgow, he could neither read nor write, and worked as a street vendor in Glasgow, London and Toronto. He discovered his interest in drawing at the age of 40, and began producing highly imaginary paintings and drawings, particularly of fish, birds and trees. His unique naive/surreal style caught the attention of many collectors, including **Pablo Picasso**, and he exhibited widely in both joint and solo exhibitions. He was commissioned to design coffee, dinner and tea ware in 1965 for Royal Worcester. His work can be seen in the Tate Gallery, London, the Scottish National Gallery of Modern Art, Edinburgh, the Museum of Modern Art, New York, and the National Gallery of Canada, Ottawa.

Wilson, Simon 1945–
Scottish jewellery designer

The founding partner of Butler & Wilson jewellery, he was born in Glasgow and started his career in 1968 with his partner Nicky Butler by selling antique, art nouveau and art deco jewellery from a stand in the Antiquarius Antique Market in London. He designed the Regent Street Christmas lights (1979–80), and in the 1980s he began selling his own design pieces, establishing a new international trend for non-precious fantasy jewellery. This move was supported by a national advertising campaign featuring celebrities such as Jerry Hall (1956–), **Catherine Deneuve** and **Faye Dunaway**. As well as his own shops he has shops within prestigious stores in London, Los Angeles and Glasgow.

Wilson, Teddy (Theodore Shaw) 1912–86
US pianist, bandleader and arranger

One of the most influential stylists of the swing era of the late 1930s, he was born in Austin, Texas, and studied music briefly at Talladega College, Alabama. As a teenager he worked in Chicago with major artists **Louis Armstrong** and clarinettist Jimmy Noone, among others. With his move to New York in 1933 to join the **Benny Carter** Orchestra his career as a pianist and arranger was firmly established. When he joined the **Benny Goodman** Trio in 1935 he was one of the first black musicians to appear with whites. He led many studio groups accompanying the singer **Billie Holiday** and these recordings show his elegant, graceful style at its best.

Wilson, Thomas Brendan 1927–
Scottish composer

Born in Trinidad, Colorado, he was taken to Scotland at an early age. He studied with Ernest Bullock and Frederick Rimmer at Glasgow University, and later taught there, becoming a professor in 1977. His works, which have won an international hearing, embrace all forms and almost every medium: opera (including *The Confessions of a Justified Sinner*, 1976), orchestral (including symphonies and two BBC commissions, *Touchstone*, 1967, and *Introit*, 1982), choral-orchestral, a piano concerto (1985), ballet, a large range of chamber works (including four string quartets), brass-band pieces, piano and other solo instrumental works, and vocal music.

Wilson, (John) Tuzo 1908–93
Canadian geophysicist
Born in Ottawa, he read physics and geology at the University of Toronto, studied under **Harold Jeffreys** at Cambridge, then went on to Princeton University, where he received a PhD in geology in 1936. In 1946 he was appointed professor at the University of Toronto. He was a promoter of **Harry Hess's** 1960 theory of sea-floor spreading, and his ideas about permanent hotspots in the Earth's mantle (1963), oceanic transform faults (1965) and mountain building (1966) were major steps towards plate tectonic theory. He became director-general of the Ontario Science Centre and co-authored *Physics and Geology* (1959), one of the first geophysical textbooks. The Wilson Range in Antarctica and the Wilson ocean cycle are named after him. He was elected FRS in 1968.

Wilson, (Thomas) Woodrow 1856–1924
28th President of the USA, and Nobel Prize winner
Born in Staunton, Virginia, he studied at Princeton and Johns Hopkins University. He then practised law at Atlanta, lectured at Bryn Mawr and Princeton, became president of Princeton in 1902, and Governor of New Jersey in 1911. In 1912 and 1916, as Democratic candidate, he was elected President of the United States. Wilson's administration, ending in tragic failure and physical breakdown, is memorable for the prohibition and women's suffrage amendments to the Constitution, trouble with Mexico, US participation in World War I, his part in the peace conference, his 'fourteen points' plan for peace, which led to the Armistice, his championship of the League of Nations, and the Senate's rejection of the Treaty of Versailles which led to his breakdown. He wrote a *History of the American People* (1902) and other works, and was awarded the 1919 Nobel Peace Prize. 📖 Arthur C Walworth *Woodrow Wilson* (3rd edn, 1978)

Winchilsea, Anne Finch, Countess of, née Kingsmill 1661–1720
English poet
Born in Sidmonton near Southampton, she was the daughter of Sir William Kingsmill. In 1684 she married Heneage Finch, Earl of Winchilsea (from 1712). Her longest poem, a Pindaric ode called *The Spleen*, was printed in 1701, and her *Miscellany Poems* in 1713. She was a friend of **Pope**, **Jonathan Swift** and **John Gay**, and her nature poems were admired by **Wordsworth** in his *Lyrical Ballads*. 📖 K M Rogers, in S Gilbert and S Gubar, *Shakespeare's Sisters* (1979)

Winckelmann, Johann Joachim 1717–68
German archaeologist
Born in Stendal, in Prussian Saxony, he studied the history of art, published a treatise on the imitation of the antique (1754), and was librarian to a cardinal in Rome (1755). In 1758 he examined the remains of Herculaneum, Pompeii, and Paestum, and went to Florence. He wrote a treatise on ancient architecture (1762), the epoch-making *Geschichte der Kunst des Altertums* (1764, 'History of the Art of Antiquity'), and *Monumenti Antichi Inediti* (1766). In 1763 he was made superintendent of Roman antiquities. He was murdered in Trieste.

Windaus, Adolf Otto Reinhold 1876–1959
German chemist and Nobel Prize winner
Born in Berlin, he commenced medical studies at the University of Berlin in 1895, but both there and subsequently at the University of Freiburg he became increasingly interested in chemistry. He abandoned medicine and wrote a doctoral thesis on the cardiac poisons of digitalis in 1899. Following a year of military service he returned to Freiburg where he became lecturer and later professor. In 1913 he was appointed Professor of Medical Chemistry at the University of Innsbruck, but two years later he moved to the University of Göttingen where he remained for the rest of his professional life. His most important research was on the structure of cholesterol. In the 1920s he turned to a study of vitamin D, which is structurally related to cholesterol. For his work on cholesterol and vitamins he was awarded the Nobel Prize for chemistry in 1928. During the 1930s he continued to study the structure of natural products, including vitamin B, and colchicine (a drug used in cancer chemotherapy). In 1938 he ceased his research and he retired in 1944.

Windelband, Wilhelm 1848–1915
German philosopher
Born in Potsdam and educated at Jena, Berlin and Göttingen, he became professor at Zurich, Freiburg, Strasbourg and Heidelberg. He was the leading figure in the Baden school of neo-Kantianism, and tried to relate the historical sciences to the natural and mathematical sciences, which had always been taken to represent the archetypes of knowledge, and to show how philosophy stood in a quite separate relationship to all the different sciences and disciplines. Among his publications are *Praeludien: Aufsätze und Reden zur Einführung in die Philosophie* (2 vols, 1884) and *Lehrbuch der Geschichte der Philosophie* (1892, Eng trans *History of Philosophy*, 1893).

Winfield, Sir Percy Henry 1878–1953
English jurist
Born in Stoke Ferry, Norfolk, he was educated at King's Lynn Grammar School and St John's College, Cambridge. He became Rouse Ball Professor of English Law at Cambridge (1928–43), and is principally remembered as a scholar in the law of torts, notably for his perceptive *Province of the Law of Tort* (1931) and *Textbook of the Law of Tort* (1937) which remains a leading textbook. Among his other, scholarly works is *Chief Sources of English Legal History* (1925).

Winfrey, Oprah Gail 1954–
US actress and talk-show host
Born in Kosciusko, Mississippi, she was a bright child with a talent for public oratory and was a contestant in the Miss Black America Pageant in 1971, before securing a job co-hosting the evening news on WTVF–TV in Nashville, Tennessee. She then became the co-host of *Baltimore is Talking* (1977–84) and hosted *A.M. Chicago* in 1984. The following year saw the programme re-titled *The Oprah Winfrey Show* (1985–). Her film debut in *The Color Purple* (1985) resulted in an Academy Award nomination and she has appeared in such television dramas as *The Women of Brewster Place* (1990), produced through her company Harpo Productions. She won Emmy Awards in 1987, 1991 and 1992 for Best Daytime Talk Show Host, and is also the first woman to own and produce her own talk show and the first African-American to own a large television studio. She was inducted into the National Women's Hall of Fame in 1994.

Wingate, Orde Charles 1903–44
English soldier, leader of the Chindits
He served with the Sudan Defence Force from 1928 to 1933 in Palestine and Transjordan. In the Burma theatre in 1942, realizing that the only answer to penetration was counter-penetration, he obtained sanction to organize the Chindits—specially trained jungle-fighters. Supplied by air, they thrust far behind the enemy lines, gravely disrupting the entire supply system. He was killed in a plane crash in Burma. 📖 Christopher Sykes, *Orde Wingate, a Biography* (1959)

Wingti, Paias 1951–
Papua New Guinea statesman
Educated at Port Moresby University, he joined the Pangu Pati (Papua New Guinea Party) and served as Minister of Transport and then Planning under Prime Minister **Michael Somare** during the later 1970s and early 1980s. He eventually became deputy Prime Minister, but resigned in 1985 to form the breakaway People's Democratic Movement (PDM). In November 1985 he became Prime Minister at the head of a five-party coalition. He championed Melanesian interests in both the South Pacific Forum and the newly formed Spearhead Group, which also included Vanuatu and the Solomon Islands. However, with opposition mounting to his economic strategy and leadership style, he was defeated on a 'no confidence' motion in 1988, but re-elected for 1992–94.

Winifred, St 7th century
Semi-legendary Welsh saint
A noble British maiden, she was beheaded by Prince Caradog for refusing his attentions. According to legend, her head rolled down a hill, and where it stopped a spring gushed forth—famous still as a place of pilgrimage, Holywell in Clwyd. Her head was replaced by St Beuno. Her feast day is 3 November.

Wink, Walter 1935–
US theologian
Born in Texas, he was educated at Southern Methodist University, Dallas, and ordained in 1961. Pastoral work in New York and Texas was followed by teaching appointments at Union and Hartford seminaries. Since 1976 he has been Professor of Biblical Interpretation at Auburn Theological Seminary, New York. A New Testament scholar, he has written widely on the Pauline concept of principalities and powers in the three volumes: *Naming the Powers* (1984), *Unmasking the Powers* (1986) and *Engaging the Powers* (1992). While rejecting the myth of redemptive violence, his study of conflict, in South Africa and elsewhere, has made him an advocate of the active, non-violent response to conflict.

Winkelried, Arnold von d.1386
Swiss patriot
The legendary Knight of Unterwalden, his suicidal heroism at the Battle of Sempach (1386), enabled the Swiss to break the Austrian position. The well-armed Austrians were slaughtered, and the Swiss gained a decisive victory.

Winkler, Clemens Alexander 1838–1904
German chemist
He was born in Freiburg, the son of a man who managed a plant for extracting cobalt. He studied at the School of Mines in Freiburg, and held various industrial posts. He was appointed Professor of Analytical and Technical Chemistry at the School of Mines in 1873, retiring in 1902. He designed a gas burette, later known by his name, and prepared sulphuric acid for the dye industry, making use of the well-known properties of platinum as a catalyst. In 1885, while analysing argyrodite (a newly discovered silver sulphide from the Freiburg mines), he discovered that silver and sulphur accounted for only 93 per cent of the compound and suspected the existence of a new element. The following year he isolated germanium, a silvery grey metalloid, which had all the properties which **Dmitri Mendeleyev** had predicted for the missing element at number 32 in the periodic table. The discovery demonstrated the predictive powers of the periodic table and helped to make it more generally accepted. Winkler was a respected teacher and wrote several useful books on analytical chemistry.

Winkler, Hans-Günther 1926–
German showjumper
Born in Wuppertal-Barmen, Westphalia, he is the only man to have won five Olympic gold medals at showjumping (the team golds in 1956, 1960, 1964 and 1972, and the individual title on Halla in 1956). He had previously won the individual world title on the same horse in 1954 and 1955. He made his German international debut in Spain in 1952, and later became team captain.

Winnemucca, Sarah 1844–91
Native American activist and educationist
Born of Northern Paiute descent near the Humboldt River, western Nevada, she was used as an interpreter during the Snake War (1866) because she knew English. In 1872 the Paiutes were relocated to the Malheur reservation in Oregon, where she assisted reservation agent Samuel Parrish with his agricultural programmes and was an interpreter and teacher. His replacement refused to pay the Paiute for their agricultural labour and this led to the Bannock War. She was again used as an interpreter and peacemaker, but the Paiute were forced to another reservation. She wrote *Life Among the Paiutes: Their Wrongs and Claims*. She established a school for Native American children, and in 1994 she was inducted into the National Women's Hall of Fame.

Winslow, Edward 1595–1655
English colonialist
Born in Droitwich, Worcestershire, he sailed in the *Mayflower* in 1620 and from 1624 was Assistant Governor or Governor of the Plymouth colony, which he described and defended in *Good Newes from New England* (1624), *Hypocrisie Unmasked* (1646) and *New England's Salamander* (1647). Sent by **Cromwell** against the West Indies, he died at sea. His son, Josiah (1629–80), was Assistant Governor (1657–73) and then Governor of the Plymouth colony.

Winsor, Justin 1831–97
US librarian and historian
Born in Boston, he studied at Harvard and Heidelberg, and was librarian at Boston (1868–77), then at Harvard. He published bibliographical and other works, including *Memorial History of Boston* (1880–81), *Narrative History of America* (1884–90) and a biography of **Christopher Columbus** (1891).

Wint, Peter de 1784–1849
English watercolourist
He was born, of Dutch descent, in Stone, Staffordshire. His fame rests on his watercolour illustrations of English landscape, architecture, and country life. Among them are *The Cricketers*, *The Hay Harvest*, *Nottingham*, *Richmond Hill* and *Cows in Water*. Many of his works are in Lincoln Art Gallery. His watercolours are well represented in the Victoria and Albert Museum, London, which also owns the oils *A Cornfield* and *A Woody Landscape*.

Winter, Jan Willem de 1750–1812
Dutch naval commander
Born on the island of Texel, he was defeated by **Adam Duncan** at Camperdown in 1797. He was ambassador to France (1798–1802).

Winterhalter, Franz Xaver 1805–73
German painter and lithographer
He made a successful portrait of Grand Duke Leopold of Baden and was appointed his court painter. In 1834 he went to Paris, with Queen Marie Amélie as his patron. One of his many royal sitters was Queen **Victoria**, and he became the fashionable artist of the day. Some of his works are at Versailles, and he is represented in the British royal collection.

Winters, (Arthur) Yvor 1900–68
US critic and poet

Born in Chicago, he was educated there, and at Colorado and Stanford universities, and in 1949 was appointed Professor of English at Stanford. A versifier whose *Collected Poems* were published in 1960, winning the Bollingen prize, he is remembered primarily as a quirky, irascible critic, opposed to the Expressionists and with a sharp eye for detail. Significant books are *In Defence of Reason* (1947), *The Function of Criticism* (1957) and *Uncollected Essays and Reviews* (1976). ⊞ T Comito, *In Defense of Winters* (1986)

Winthrop, John 1588–1649
English colonialist
Born in Groton, Suffolk, he was appointed Governor of Massachusetts colony in 1629. He was periodically re-elected, and probably had more influence than anyone else in forming the political institutions of the northern states of America. The first part of his *Journal* was published in 1790, and the whole in 1825–26. ⊞ Edmund S Morgan, *The Puritan Dilemma* (1958)

Winthrop, John 1606–76
English colonialist
Born in Groton, Suffolk, son of **John Winthrop** (1588–1649), he emigrated to America in 1631, landing in Boston, and became a magistrate in Massachusetts. In 1635 he went to Connecticut, and he founded New London in 1646. In 1657 he was elected Governor of Connecticut, and, except for one year, held that post until his death. He obtained from **Charles II** a charter uniting the colonies of Connecticut and New Haven, and was named first Governor under it.

Winthrop, John, *known as* Fitz-John 1639–1707
Anglo-American soldier and colonial administrator
Born in Ipswich, Massachusetts, he was the son of **John Winthrop** (1606–76). He served under **George Monk** in the Parliamentary army (1660), and settled in Connecticut in 1663. He was a commander against the Dutch, the Native Americans and the French. He was agent in London for Connecticut (1693–97), and Governor of the colony from 1698.

Winthrop, Robert Charles 1809–94
US orator and politician
Born in Boston, a descendant of the colonialist **John Winthrop** (1588–1649), he was admitted to the Bar in 1831 and was in the state legislature (1834–40), then in Congress as Speaker (1847–49). From 1850 to 1851 he was senator from Massachusetts.

Winthrop, Theodore 1828–61
US military writer
Born in New Haven, Connecticut, a descendant of **John Winthrop** (1588–1649), he studied at Yale and was admitted to the Bar (1855). While volunteering in the Civil War (1861–65), fell in battle at Great Bethel. His novels, all published posthumously, include *Cecil Dreeme* (1861), *John Brent* (1861) and *Edwin Brothertoft* (1862).

Wirén, Dag I 1905–86
Swedish composer
Born in Noraberg, he was influenced by **Igor Stravinsky** and **Prokofiev**. At first a neoclassicist, in his Third Symphony (1943–44) he adopted instead a 'metamorphosis technique' by which whole works were created from small units. His large output includes five symphonies, five string quartets, a variety of large-scale orchestral works, film and theatre music, and even 'Waltz for Elsewhere' ('Annorstädes vals'), the (unsuccessful) Swedish entry for the 1965 Eurovision Song Contest. His most popular work remains the *Serenade for Strings* (1937), the last movement of which formed the title music for the BBC2 television series *Monitor*.

Wisdom, Norman 1915–
English comedian
Born in London, he made his stage debut in 1946. In 1948 he appeared in variety at the London Casino, thereafter appearing regularly at the London Palladium. His earliest film success was as a slapstick comedian in *Trouble in Store* (1953). *Man of the Moment* (1955), *Just My Luck* (1958), *There was a Crooked Man* (1960), *On the Beat* (1962), *A Stitch in Time* (1963), *Sandwich Man* (1966), and *What's Good for The Goose* (1969) followed. On television, he played the role of a cancer patient in the play *Going Gently* (1981), but he is best known on the small screen for series such as *Norman* (1970), *Nobody is Norman Wisdom* (1973) and *A Little Bit of Wisdom* (1974–76). Popular as a comic in the USA too, he made a film there, *The Night They Raided Minsky's*, in 1968. His book *Don't Laugh at Me: An Autobiography*, was published in 1992.

Wise, Ernie See **Morecambe and Wise**

Wise, Thomas James 1859–1937
English bibliophile and literary forger
Born in Gravesend, he began collecting books in his youth and built up a library of rare editions of the English poets and other works. These included a collection of pamphlets and MSS, especially of the 19th-century Romantics and the literary wing of the Pre-Raphaelite movement. In 1934 certain pamphlets which he had sold to dealers and others for high prices were alleged to be fakes and a sensational literary scandal ensued which was only checked by his death. His collection (the Ashley Library) was sold to the British Museum.

Wiseman, Nicholas Patrick Stephen 1802–65
English prelate and cardinal
Born in Seville, Spain, of an Irish family, he was brought up at Waterford and Ushaw, entered the English College in Rome, was ordained in 1825, and became Rector of the College from 1828 to 1840. He established the *Dublin Review* (1836), and in 1840 was named coadjutor vicar-apostolic and president of St Mary's College at Oscott. In 1847 he was transferred to the London district. In 1850 he was appointed the first Archbishop of Westminster and a cardinal, arousing religious indignation which resulted in the Ecclesiastical Titles Assumption Act; in response he published his conciliatory *Appeal to the Reason and Good Feeling of the English People* (1850). One of his best known works was a novel *Fabiola* (1854).

Wishart, George c.1513–1546
Scottish reformer
He was born in Pitarrow, Kincardineshire. As a schoolmaster in Montrose (1538), he incurred a charge of heresy for teaching the Greek New Testament, and he then went to Cambridge, where he met the reformer **Hugh Latimer**. The next few years he spent on the Continent, and in 1543 accompanied a commission sent to Scotland by **Henry VIII** to negotiate a marriage contract between his infant son, Prince Edward (the future **Edward VI**) and **Mary, Queen of Scots**. He preached the Lutheran doctrine of justification in several places, but, at the insistence of Cardinal **David Beaton**, he was arrested in 1546, and burned at St Andrews on 1 March. **John Knox** was first inspired by Wishart. ⊞ James William Baird, *Thunder Over Scotland: The Life of George Wishart, Scottish Reformer, 1513–1546* (1982)

Wister, Owen 1860–1938
US writer
Born in Philadelphia, he took a music degree at Harvard and intended to be a composer, but won fame with his novel of cowboy life in Wyoming, *The Virginian* (1902), and other books, including *Lin McLean* (1898) and *Lady Baltimore* (1906). ⊞ D Payne, *Owen Wister: Chronicler of the West, gentleman of the East* (1985)

Wither, George 1588–1667
English poet and pamphleteer

Born in Bentworth, Hampshire, he studied at Magdalen College, Oxford (1604–06), and entered Lincoln's Inn in 1615. For his *Abuses Stript and Whipt* (1613) he was sent to prison where he wrote a book of five pastorals, *The Shepherd's Hunting* (1615), followed by a love elegy, *Fidelia* (1617). After his release, there appeared in 1621 the satirical *Wither's Motto*, which landed him in jail again. His main poem is *Fair Virtue, or the Mistress of Philarete* (1622), which was followed by *Hymns and Songs of the Church* (1623), *Psalms of David translated* (1631), *Emblems* (1634) and *Hallelujah* (1641). He was a Puritan, and Cromwell made him major-general in Surrey and master of the Statute Office. At the Restoration (1660) he lost his position and property, and, on suspicion of having written the *Vox Vulgi*, a satire on the parliament of 1661, was imprisoned, but released in 1663. His poetry fell into almost complete oblivion, but the praises of Robert Southey, Sir Samuel Egerton Brydges, Henry Hallam, and Charles Lamb in particular revived interest in his work. 🕮 C S Hansby, *The Literary Career of George Wither* (1969)

Withering, William 1741–99
English physician

Born in Wellington, Shropshire, he was educated at Edinburgh University, and practised medicine at the County Infirmary in Stafford, and later in Birmingham, where he became chief physician in the General Hospital. In 1776 he published a British Flora, *Botanical Arrangement of all the Vegetables Naturally Growing in Great Britain*. After becoming acquainted with Joseph Priestley, he began studying chemistry and mineralogy as well as botany, and in 1785 he published *An Account of the Foxglove*, introducing digitalis, extracted from that plant, as a drug for cardiac disease. He was the first to see the connection between dropsy and heart disease. Following his involvement in riots after the French Revolution, he fled from Birmingham, and concentrated on writing a third volume of the *Botanical Arrangement* (1792), dealing mainly with fungi and other cryptogamic plants.

Witherspoon, John 1723–94
American clergyman and theologian

Born in Gifford, Lothian, Scotland, he was minister at Beith and then Paisley, and in 1768 emigrated to America to become president of the College of New Jersey (now Princeton University) from 1768 to 1794. He taught several future leaders in American public life, including President James Madison, whose co authorship of *The Federalist* papers bore the influence of his teacher's Calvinist social and political thought. He was a representative of New Jersey to the Continental Congress (1776–82), and helped frame the American Declaration of Independence (1776). His writings include *Ecclesiastic Characteristics* (1753), against the Moderates; *Serious Enquiry into the Nature and Effects of the Stage* (1757); and two on *Justification* (1756) and *Regeneration* (1764).

Witt, Jan de 1625–72
Dutch statesman

Born in Dort, the son of Jacob de Witt, a vehement opponent of William II, Prince of Orange, he was one of the deputies sent by the States of Holland in 1652 to Zeeland to dissuade that province from adopting an Orange policy. In 1653 he was made Grand Pensionary. The Orange Party, during the war between England and Holland, strove to increase the power of the young prince (afterwards William III); the republican (or oligarchic) Party, made up of the nobles and the wealthier burgesses, with de Witt at their head, sought to abolish the office of stadtholder. In 1654, on the conclusion of the war, a secret article in the treaty drawn up between de Witt and Cromwell deprived the House of Orange of all state

offices. After the restoration of Charles II, de Witt favoured France, especially during the two years' renewal of hostilities with England (1665–67).

Witt, Katerina 1965–
German figure skater

Born in Karl-Marx-Stadt, she became East German champion in 1982, and won the first of six successive European titles in 1983. She was world champion (1984–85, 1987–88), and Olympic champion in 1984 and 1988.

Wittgenstein, Ludwig Josef Johann See panel p1970

Wittig, Georg 1897–1987
German chemist and Nobel Prize winner

Born in Berlin, he went to the University of Tübingen in 1916, but soon left to serve in World War I. In 1920 he recommended the study of chemistry for a degree at the University of Marburg where he later joined the staff. He was appointed associate professor at the Technical University of Brunswick (1932) and five years later moved to the University of Freiburg. In 1944 he was made professor at the University of Tübingen and in 1956 he went to Heidelberg. His early work on the solution chemistry of radicals and carbanions established him as a chemist of great skill, but he is most famous for a serendipitous discovery that some ylides (organometallic compounds containing both positive and negative charges) react smoothly with aldehydes and ketones with the creation of an olefinic double bond. This procedure has been of enormous value in the laboratory synthesis of numerous important compounds, including vitamin A, vitamin D, steroids and prostaglandin precursors. For this work he shared the 1979 Nobel Prize for chemistry with Herbert Brown. He continued publishing until the age of 90.

Witz, Konrad c.1400–1444/47
German painter

Born in Rottweil, Swabia, he joined the Basle guild of painters in 1434 and spent most of his life in what is now Switzerland. His extremely realistic style suggests that he was aware of the work of his contemporary Jan van Eyck. The only signed and dated painting of his which survives is a late work, *Christ Walking on the Water* (1444). This particular work is remarkable not only for its quality and attention to detail but also because it is set on Lake Geneva—the earliest known recognizable landscape in European art.

Władysław IV, *English* Ladislas 1595–1648
King of Poland

The son of Sigismund III Vasa of Sweden, he was born in Kraków, and proved popular after his father's haughtiness. His reign (1632–48) was peaceful, since Poland remained neutral during the Thirty Years War. He crushed the Cossack rebellions (1637–38), initiating 10 years of peace in the Ukraine. Although he planned to gain the Swedish throne and to drive the Turks from the Balkans, he failed, given Poland's decentralizing nobility, diverse religions and aggressive neighbours.

Wöckel, Bärbel, *née* Eckert 1955–
German athlete

She was born in Leipzig and studied education before making a mark in her athletics career by winning European Junior gold medals and setting records for 200 metres and 100 metres hurdles in 1973. In 1974 she gained a gold relay medal in the European championships and finished seventh in the 100 metres. She won gold medals at the 1976 and 1980 Olympics for the 200 metres and sprint relay. She then went on to win a silver medal for 100 metres and a gold for 200 metres at the 1982 European championships. She also shared in a total of four East German world relay records.

Wittgenstein, Ludwig Josef Johann 1889–1951
Austrian-born British philosopher, one of the 20th century's most influential figures in British philosophy

Wittgenstein was born in Vienna, the youngest of eight children in a wealthy and cultivated family; his father was an industrialist. He was educated at home until the age of 14, then at an Austrian school for three years. He developed a strong interest in machinery, and went on to study mechanical engineering at Berlin (1906–08) and at Manchester (1908–11), where he undertook research on aeronautics and designed a jet-reaction propeller. There his reading of **Bertrand Russell**'s *The Principles of Mathematics* (1903) turned his attention to mathematics; in 1911 he abandoned his engineering research and moved to Cambridge to study mathematical logic under Russell (1912–13). He studied with enormous intensity and Russell said admiringly that he 'soon knew all that I had to teach'.

Wittgenstein served in World War I as an artillery officer in the Austrian army and was taken prisoner on the Italian front in 1918. Throughout the war he had continued to work on problems in logic, carrying his notebooks round with him in his rucksack, and in the POW camp near Monte Cassino he completed his first work, the only one published in his lifetime, and sent it to Russell in England. It was eventually published in 1921 under the title *Logisch-philosophische Abhandlung* (and then in 1922, with a parallel German–English text and an introduction from Russell, as *Tractatus Logico-Philosophicus*). This was a novel, rather startling work, consisting of a series of numbered, aphoristic remarks centred on the nature and limits of language. Meaningful language, he conceived, must consist in 'atomic propositions' that are pictures of the facts of which the world is composed. On this criterion we must discard as literally meaningless much of our conventional discourse, including judgements of value, and many of the claims of speculative philosophy. And since the limits of language are also the limits of thought he reaches the portentous conclusion that 'what we cannot speak about we must be silent about'.

This scheme for a logically foolproof language, a perfect instrument for meaningful assertion, appeared to represent a kind of terminus and Wittgenstein now turned away from philosophy to find another vocation. He gave away the money he had inherited and lived a simple ascetic life, working as an elementary schoolteacher in Austrian country districts (1920–26), a gardener's assistant in a monastery, and an amateur architect and builder commissioned by one of his sisters. In the late 1920s he was sought out by various philosophers who had found inspiration in the *Tractatus*, particularly **Moritz Schlick** and the logical positivists of the Vienna Circle. He revived his philosophical interests and returned to Cambridge in 1929, first as Research Fellow of Trinity College and then as Professor of Philosophy, a post to which he was

appointed in 1939 but which he could not take up until 1945, at the end of World War II, during which he had served as a medical orderly. After two years, he resigned, and went to live in Ireland for a time.

He became a naturalized British subject in 1938. At Cambridge his philosophy began to take a quite new direction; he attracted a group of devoted pupils and through his lectures and the circulation of his students' notes he came to exert a powerful influence on philosophy throughout the English-speaking world. The work of this second period of his philosophical career is best summarized in the posthumous *Philosophical Investigations* (1953), a discursive and often enigmatic work which rejects most of the assumptions and conclusions of the *Tractatus*.

In the *Investigations* Wittgenstein no longer tries to reduce language to a perfect logical model, but rather points to the variety, open-endedness and subtlety of everyday language and explores the actual communicative and social functions of different modes of speech or 'language games'. Language is seen essentially as a toolkit. Philosophy then becomes a therapeutic technique of 'assembling reminders' of usage, which reveal the source of many philosophical paradoxes in the misunderstanding of ordinary language and the obsessive search for unity or simplicity where none exists. Instead of expecting each concept to have a single, defining essence we should rather look for a range of overlapping 'family resemblances'.

Wittgenstein visited a friend in the USA, returning to England in 1949, where he spent the last two years of his life living with friends in Oxford and Cambridge. He died of cancer in Cambridge in 1951; since then there has been a continuous stream of posthumously edited publications from his prolific notebooks and manuscripts, including *Remarks on the Foundations of Mathematics* (1956), *The Blue and Brown Books* (1958), *Philosophische Bemerkungen* (1964) and *On Certainty* (1969).

📖 Norman Malcolm, *Ludwig Wittgenstein: A Memoir* (2nd edition, 1984); Anthony Kenny, *Wittgenstein* (1973); K T Fann, *Ludwig Wittgenstein: The Man and His Philosophy* (1967).

> *Die Welt ist alles, was der Fall ist.*
> 'The world is all that is the case.'
> *Tractatus Logico-Philosophicus.*
>
> *Die Grenzen meiner Sprache bedeuten die Grenzen meiner Welt.*
> 'The limits of my language mean the limits of my world.'
> *Tractatus Logico-Philosophicus.*

Wodehouse, Sir P(elham) G(renville)
1881–1975
English novelist

Born in Guildford, Surrey, he became a US citizen in 1955. He was educated at Dulwich College, London, and worked for the Hong Kong and Shanghai Bank for two years before beginning to earn a living as a journalist and story writer. In the USA before World War I, he sold a serial to the *Saturday Evening Post* and for a quarter of a century almost all his books appeared first in that magazine. He made his name with *Piccadilly Jim* (1917), but World War II blighted his reputation. Captured by the Germans at Le Touquet, he was interned then released but not allowed to leave Germany. Foolishly he agreed to make broadcasts for the Germans and though they were harmless he was branded as a traitor. Eventually his name

was cleared but he made the USA his home. His copious oeuvre includes over 100 books, but he is best known as the creator of Bertie Wooster and his legendary valet, Jeeves. Of his many felicitous titles, *Right Ho, Jeeves* (1934), *Quick Service* (1940) and *The Mating Season* (1949) stand out. Wodehouse summed up his attitude to writing thus: 'I believe there are two ways of writing novels. One is mine, making a sort of musical comedy without music and ignoring real life altogether; the other is going deep down into life and not caring a damn'. 📖 R Usborne, *Wodehouse at Work* (1961)

Woffington, Peg (Margaret) 1720–60
Irish actress

Born in Dublin, she began her acting career on the Dublin stage at the age of 17, and moved to London, where she made her debut at Covent Garden as Sylvia in

The Recruiting Officer (1740). Her beauty and vivacity brought her many lovers, including **David Garrick**. She was famous for her breeches parts, particularly as Sir Harry Wildair in *The Constant Couple*. She played at Drury Lane until 1746, then Covent Garden, before returning in triumph to Dublin (1750–54). In 1756 she stabbed another actress, **George Anne Bellamy**, and in 1757 was taken ill on stage, never to return. Her last days were devoted to charitable works, endowing alms houses in Teddington. She was the subject of **Charles Reade's** first novel, *Peg Woffington* (1853).

Wogan, Terry (Michael Terence) 1938–
Irish broadcaster and writer

Born in Limerick, he joined Radio Telefis Éireann (1963) as an announcer, and from 1965 hosted various BBC radio programmes, including *Late Night Extra* (1967–69) and *The Terry Wogan Show* (1969–72). Resident in England from 1969, he became popular as the presenter of BBC Radio 2's *Breakfast Show* (1972–84, 1994–). Active on television in many capacities, he presented the game show *Blankety Blank* (1977–81), *You Must Be Joking* (1981) and the annual charity telethon *Children in Need*. He began a regular chat show in 1982 which later became a thrice-weekly fixture (1985–92). In 1977 he enjoyed success in the pop charts with *The Floral Dance*, and he has written several books including *Banjaxed* (1979), *The Day Job* (1981), *Wogan on Wogan* (1987) and *Wogan's Ireland* (1988).

Wöhler, Friedrich 1800–82
German chemist

Born in Eschersheim, he was educated at the universities of Marburg and Heidelberg, and qualified as a doctor of medicine in 1823, but he never practised. He taught chemistry at industrial schools in Berlin (1825–31) and Kassel (1831–36), and became Professor of Chemistry at Göttingen in 1836, remaining there until his death. However, one of the formative experiences of his life was the year he spent with **Jöns Jacob Berzelius** in Stockholm and this led to a lifelong friendship. His friendship with **Justus von Liebig** was equally important to him, and from their common interest in cyanates came Wöhler's most famous discovery. In 1828 he attempted to prepare ammonium cyanate from silver cyanate and ammonium chloride, but instead obtained urea. Equally important was his preparation of aluminium in 1827. The Danish scientist **Hans Oersted** claimed to have extracted the metal from alumina in 1825, but it is doubtful whether the metal he obtained was pure aluminium. Wöhler used a different procedure and the product (still extant) is essentially pure metal. For this work he was honoured by **Napoleon III**, but there are still arguments, mainly nationalistic, about priority. From 1840 onwards he undertook numerous administrative and government duties, and his research output diminished. He was an inspiring teacher and maintained a keen interest in chemistry well into his old age. He was responsible for the translation of the influential annual reports prepared by Berzelius, occasionally moderating the latter's strident language.

Wohlgemuth, Michael See **Wolgemut, Michael**

Wolcot, John, *pseudonym* Peter Pindar 1738–1819
English satirist

Born in Dodbrooke, Devon, he studied medicine for seven years in London, took his MD at Aberdeen (1767) and, going to Jamaica, became physician-general of the island. He returned to England to take holy orders, but soon started a medical practice at Truro. There he discovered the talents of the young painter **John Opie**, and he went with him in 1780 to London, to devote himself to writing audacious satires in verse. His 60 or 70 witty and fluent poetical pamphlets (1778–1818) include *The Lousiad*, *The Apple-dumplings and a King*, *Whitbread's Brewery visited*

by their Majesties, *Bozzy and Piozzi* and *Lyrical Odes* on the Royal Academy exhibitions. 📖 T Girton, *Drama with Two Aunts* (1959)

Wolf, Christa 1929–
German novelist

She was born in Landsberg, and educated at both Leipzig and Jena universities. Many of her books received only limited circulation in East Germany, but the most important of them, *The Quest for Christa T* (1976), was published in English translation and her novel/essay *Kassandra: Erzahlung* (1983) appeared in English in 1985. Her work examines the fate of personality in totalitarian situations: as yet the *Mosakuer Novelle* are untranslated.

Wolf, Emil 1922–
US optical physicist

Born in Prague, Czechoslovakia, he moved to the UK in 1940 and was educated at the University of Bristol. His first research was into the characteristics of high-performance optical systems, and subsequently he worked on optical coherence in Edinburgh, Manchester and Rochester (USA). He was appointed to a full professorship at the University of Rochester in 1961, and became Professor of Physics there and Professor of Optics at the nearby Institute of Optics in 1978. His work on coherence theory paved the way for the later development of quantum optics, and his reformulation of coherence theory in 1982 led to the remarkable prediction that the spectrum of a radiation field may change as it propagates—a prediction which contradicted assumptions held to in every branch of physics, but which was almost immediately confirmed experimentally. Wolf was co-author with **Max Born** of *Principles of Optics* (1959). In 1977 he was Frederick Ives medallist of the Optical Society of America, and he served as the society's president from 1978 to 1981.

Wolf, Hugo 1860–1903
Austrian composer

Born in Windischgraz, Styria, he studied without satisfaction at the Vienna Conservatory, then earned a meagre living by teaching and conducting. From 1884 to 1888 he was music critic of the *Wiener Salonblatt*, disparaging **Brahms** and praising **Richard Wagner**. His best compositions came after 1888 and include the Mörike set of 53 songs (1888), settings of poems by **Goethe** (1888–89), the *Italienisches Leiderbuch* ('Italian Songbook') of Heyse and **Emanuel von Geibel** (1889–90), and three sonnets of Michelangelo (1897). He also wrote an opera, *Der Corregidor* (1895, 'The Mayor'), and other works. He was at his best in his treatment of short lyrical poems, giving many of them a new significance by the sensitive commentary of his settings. In 1897 he became insane, and was confined from 1898 in the asylum at Steinhof, near Vienna, where he died.

Wolf, Maximilian Franz Joseph Cornelius 1863–1932
German astronomer

He was born in Heidelberg, and after completing his mathematical studies at the University of Heidelberg (1888) followed by two years at Stockholm University, set up a private observatory in which he undertook searches for asteroids using photographic methods. On being appointed Professor of Astronomy at the University of Heidelberg (1893) he established a well-equipped observatory on the Königstuhl which became famous for the high quality of its photographs of star clusters, bright and dark nebulae, and star clouds of the Milky Way. The 'Wolf diagram', a useful and widely used method of discovering interstellar dust by star counting, owes its name to him.

Wolfe, Charles 1791–1823
Irish poet and clergyman

Born in Blackhall, County Kildare, he was educated at Winchester, and Trinity College, Dublin. He took holy orders in 1817 and became curate of Ballyclog, County Tyrone, and Donoughmore, County Down (1818). He is remembered for his poem *The Burial of Sir John Moore* after Corunna, which appeared anonymously in 1817 and at once caught the admiration of the public.

Wolfe, Humbert 1885–1940
English poet and critic

Born in Milan, Italy, he entered the Civil Service in 1908, becoming in 1938 deputy Secretary to the Ministry of Labour. He published *London Sonnets* (1919), *Lampoons* (1925), *Requiem* (1927), and several other collections of verse, all marked by deep feeling. His critical writings included *Notes on English Verse Satire* (1929) and studies of Tennyson, Robert Herrick, Shelley and George Moore.

Wolfe, James 1727–59
English general

Born in Kent, he was the eldest son of General Edward Wolfe (1685–1759). In 1745–46 he served against the Scottish Jacobites at Falkirk and Culloden. In 1758, as colonel, Pitt, the Elder, Chatham gave him the command of a brigade in the expedition against Cape Breton under General Jeffrey Amherst, and he was mainly responsible for the capture of Louisburg (1758). Pitt gave Wolfe command of the expedition for the capture of Quebec, and, as major-general and commanding 9,000 men, Wolfe landed below Quebec in June 1759. The attack on Montcalm's strong position foiled Wolfe until on 13 September he reached the Plains of Abraham by scaling the cliffs at a poorly guarded point. After a short struggle Quebec capitulated, and its fall decided the fate of Canada. Wolfe died in the hour of victory.

Wolfe, Thomas Clayton 1900–38
US novelist

He was born in Asheville, North Carolina. His father, an alcoholic, was a skilled stonecutter who sculpted tombstones for a living, and his mother left in 1906 to run a boarding-house. He was educated at North Carolina and Harvard universities. After an abortive start as a playwright, in 1925 he embarked on a turbulent affair with Mrs Aline Bernstein, a maternal figure who did much to encourage his writing, particularly his first novel *Look Homeward, Angel* (1929), which was patently autobiographical. The massive, shapeless manuscript of *Of Time and the River* (1935), its sequel, was honed into shape by Max Perkins, his editor at Scribner's. Both these novels feature Eugene Gant, Wolfe's alter ego. *The Web and the Rock* (1939) and *You Can't Go Home Again* (1940) were published posthumously. Prolix, careless, bombastic and over-ambitious, he nevertheless wrote vividly of people and places. Some assert that his best work is to be found in the stories in *From Death to Morning* (1935). His *Letters* were published in 1956. 📖 C H Holman, *Thomas Wolfe* (1960)

Wolfe, Tom (Thomas Kennerly) 1931–
US journalist, pop-critic and novelist

Born in Richmond, Virginia, he graduated from Washington and Lee University and received his doctorate in American Studies from Yale University. Later he worked as a reporter for the *Springfield Union*, *The Washington Post* and the *New York Herald Tribune*. He was a proponent of 'New Journalism', and his style is distinctive, clever and narcissistic. A fashion leader and follower, he has written a number of books with eye-catching titles: *The Electric Kool-Aid Acid Test* (1968), about Ken Kesey and the Merry Pranksters, *Radical Chic & Mau-Mauing the Flak Catchers* (1970) and *The Kandy-Kolored Tangerine-Flake Streamline Baby* (1965). Much of his work previously

appeared in periodicals like *The Rolling Stone*, as did his first novel, *The Bonfire of the Vanities* (1988), which was a bestseller. His second novel is *A Man in Full* (1998).

Wolfed, George C 1954–
US playwright and director

Born in Frankfort, Kentucky, he graduated from Pomona College in California and studied dramatic writing at New York University. His debut as a writer for the New York theatre came with a failed musical in 1985, but he soon followed it with *The Colored Museum* (1986), a successful satire on African-American stereotypes. He wrote the book for *Jelly's Last Jam* (1991), a hit Broadway musical about jazz musician Jelly Roll Morton, and he was director of the show. He won an Obie award as best director for his own play, *Spunk* (1990), and a Tony award in the same category for his staging of *Angels in America* (1993). In 1993 he took over as director of the New York Shakespeare Festival, filling the void left after the death of Joseph Papp, and he has revitalized the Joseph Papp Public Theater, giving more opportunities to minority actors and playwrights and demonstrating in his choices of casting and direction the keenness of his theatrical instincts.

Wolfenden, John Frederick Wolfenden, Baron 1906–85
English educationist and governmental adviser on social questions

Born in Halifax, Yorkshire, he was Fellow and tutor in philosophy at Magdalen College, Oxford (1929–34), headmaster of Uppingham (1934–44) and Shrewsbury (1944–50), and Vice-Chancellor of Reading University from 1950. He is best known as the chairman of the royal commission on homosexuality and prostitution, (the Wolfenden Report, 1959) which called for the legalization of private homosexual acts between consenting adults aged 21 and over. This recommendation became law under the Sexual Offences Act of 1967. He was also chairman of another royal commission (1960) on sport. He was made a life peer in 1974.

Wolff or Wolf, Christian von 1679–1754
German philosopher

Born in Breslau, Silesia, he studied at the universities of Breslau, Jena and Leipzig and was a pupil of Gottfried Leibniz, on whose recommendation he was appointed Professor of Mathematics at the University of Halle (1707). He was banished (1723), following a theological dispute with the Pietists, became professor at Marburg (1723–40), was recalled by Frederick II, the Great to Halle (1740) to become Professor of the Law of Nations, and also became Chancellor of the university (1743). He was made Baron of the Empire by the Elector of Bavaria. Wolff published widely in philosophy, theology, mathematics and the natural sciences, but his main intellectual achievement was to systematize and popularize the philosophy of Leibniz, in works such as *Philosophia prima sive ontologia* (1729). His work gave rationalism a further great impulse in the German tradition, and he is usually regarded as the German spokesman of the Enlightenment in the 18th century.

Wolff-Bekker, Elizabeth, *originally* Betje Dekker 1739–1804
Dutch writer

She was born in Flushing. In 1759 she married a parson 30 years older than herself, and until his death in 1777 studied literature, wrote amusing verse, and indulged her admiration for Jean Jacques Rousseau. Then she set up house with Agatha Deken, with whom she wrote epistolary novels in the style of Samuel Richardson. Her best book is *Willem Leevend* (1784–85). In 1788 Wolff-Bekker, who sometimes used the pseudonym 'Sylvania', had to go into exile in France with her friend Deken; when 10 years

later they could return, they were forced to do hack translations. They died within a few weeks of each other.
📖 H C M Ghijsen, *Boeket voor Betje en Aagje* (1954)

Wolf-Ferrari, Ermanno 1876–1948
Italian composer

Born in Venice, he was sent to Rome to study painting, but turned to music and became a pupil of **Joseph Rheinberger** in Munich (1893–95). In 1899 he returned to Venice, where his first opera, *Cenerentola* (1900) was unsuccessfully produced the following year. His later operas, however, were equally successful in both Italy and Germany. From 1902 to 1912 he was director of the Liceo Benedetto Marcello, in Venice. He composed choral and chamber works, and music for organ and piano as well as the operas, notably *Il Segreto di Susanna* (1909, 'Susanna's Secret'), *I gioielli della Madonna* (1911, 'The Jewels of the Madonna') and *I quattro rusteghi* (1906, 'The School for Fathers').

Wolfit, Sir Donald 1902–68
English actor-manager

Born in Newark, Nottinghamshire, he began his stage career in 1920, and made his first London appearance in *The Wandering Jew* (1924). Forming his own company (1937), he played **Shakespeare** in the provinces, and during World War II he instituted the first London season of 'Lunchtime Shakespeare' during the Battle of Britain. Known especially for his portrayal of Shakespearean heroes and of **Ben Jonson's** Volpone, he also appeared in several films and on television. His autobiography, *First Interval*, appeared in 1954, and he was knighted in 1957.
📖 Ronald Harwood, *Sir Donald Wolfit CBE: His Life in the Unfashionable Theatre* (1983)

Wolfram von Eschenbach c.1170–c.1220
German poet

Born near Anspach, Bavaria, he lived some time at the court of the Count of Thuringia. His epic *Parzival* (Eng trans 1894), with the history of the Grail as its main theme, is one of the most notable poems of the Middle Ages. From it Wagner derived the libretto of his opera *Parsifal*. He also wrote *Die Lyrik*, seven love songs, a short epic, *Willehalm*, and two fragments called *Titurel*. 📖 M F Riley, *Medieval German Love Lyrics* (1969)

Wolfson, Sir Isaac 1897–1991
Scottish businessman and philanthropist

Born and educated in Glasgow, he left school early and became a travelling salesman. He joined Great Universal Stores in 1932 and became managing director in 1934, and later Honorary Life President. In 1955 he set up the Wolfson Foundation, for the advancement of health, education and youth activities in the UK and the Commonwealth. He also founded Wolfson College, Oxford, in 1966. In 1973, University College, Cambridge, was renamed Wolfson College after a grant from the foundation. He was active in Jewish causes. His son, Leonard (1927–   ), is now a life peer.

Wolgemut or Wohlgemuth, Michael 1435–1519
German painter and engraver

Born in Nuremberg, he was the teacher of **Albrecht Dürer**, who painted a portrait of him. His altarpieces show some Flemish influence.

Wollaston, William Hyde 1766–1828
English chemist

Born in East Dereham, Norfolk, into a family of scientists and physicians, he graduated in medicine at Cambridge in 1793 and was awarded a fellowship at Caius College. He practised in London until 1800, when he entered into a partnership with **Smithson Tennant** to produce platinum. By 1805 Wollaston, who was always the more active partner, had evolved a successful technique. He built up a lucrative business making platinum boilers, wire and other apparatus, keeping the process secret until just before his death, when he described it in a lecture to the Royal Society. He also conducted experiments in many areas including physiology, pathology, pharmacology and botany. In the course of studying crystallography he made improvements to the goniometer, an instrument designed by **René Haüy** for measuring the angles between crystal faces. He wrote extensively on atomic theory, sometimes opposing and sometimes modifying the new and epoch-making theories of **John Dalton**. Wollaston added to Dalton's advances by being one of the first scientists to realize that the arrangement of atoms in a molecule must be three-dimensional, and he also came close to formulating the 'law of definite proportions' which is credited to **Joseph Louis Proust**. He was elected FRS in 1793. He died in London, leaving some of his considerable wealth to the Royal Society and the Geological Society of London to promote scientific research. The mineral wollastonite, one of the three forms of calcium silicate, was named in his honour.

Wollstonecraft, Mary, *later* Mary Godwin 1759–97
Anglo-Irish feminist and writer

Born in London, she obtained work with a publisher (1788) as a translator and became acquainted with a group of political writers and reformers known as the English Jacobins, among whom was her future husband **William Godwin**. In 1790 she wrote *Vindication of the Rights of Man* (a response to **Edmund Burke's** *Reflections on the Revolution in France*), and in 1792 produced her controversial *Vindication of the Rights of Woman*, which advocated equality of the sexes and equal opportunities in education. In Paris in 1792 to collect material for her *View of the French Revolution* (vol 1, 1794), she met a US timber-merchant, Captain Gilbert Imlay, by whom she had a daughter, Fanny, who committed suicide in 1816. Deserted by him, Mary herself tried to commit suicide. In 1797 she married Godwin, and gave birth to a daughter, Mary (the future **Mary Wollstonecraft Shelley**), but died soon afterwards.
📖 Claire Tomalin, *The Life and Death of Mary Wollstonecraft* (1974)

Wolseley, Garnet Joseph, Viscount 1833–1913
British field marshal

He was born in Golden Bridge House, County Dublin. Entering the army in 1852, he served in the Burmese War (1852–53), the Crimean War (where he lost an eye), the Indian Uprising (1857–59), and the Chinese War (1860). In 1870 he put down the Red River rebellion under **Louis Riel** and commanded in the Ashanti War (1873–74). After several senior posts in India, Cyprus, South Africa, and Egypt, he was Commander-in-Chief of the expedition to Egypt in 1882, and was made general in the same year. He commanded the Sudan expedition in 1884 that arrived too late to save General **Gordon** at Khartoum. From 1890 to 1895 he was Commander-in-Chief of the entire army when he carried out several reforms and mobilized forces for the Boer War (1899–1902). Besides his *Story of a Soldier's Life* (1903–04), he wrote *Narrative of the War with China in 1860* (1862), the *Soldier's Pocket Book*, *Field Manoeuvres* (1872), a novel (*Marley Castle*, 1877), a biography of the Duke of **Marlborough** (2 vols, 1894), *The Decline and Fall of Napoleon* (1895), and several essays. 📖 Joseph H Lehmann, *The Model Major-General: A Biography of Field Marshal Lord Wolseley* (1964)

Wolsey, Thomas c.1475–1530
English cardinal and politician

He was born in Ipswich, the son of a prosperous butcher and grazier. He studied at Magdalen College, Oxford, and became a Fellow then master in the seminary attached to the foundation. Having been ordained in 1498, he was given the living at Lymington in Somerset;

influence later brought him the post of secretary and domestic chaplain to the Archbishop of Canterbury. With the primate's death in 1502 Wolsey was endowed with the chaplaincy of Calais, where his ability brought him to the notice of **Henry VII**. Appointed a chaplain to the king (1507), he cultivated the favour of Bishop Fox, the Lord Privy Seal, and that of the treasurer of the royal household, Sir Thomas Lovel. His skill and ability brought him the lucrative deanery of Lincoln. With the accession of **Henry VIII**, Wolsey strove to render himself indispensable. His progress was steady and his growing need for money was only matched by his increasing arrogance. In 1513 Wolsey accompanied Henry to France. His conduct of the negotiations between Henry and **Francis I** brought him the bishopric of Lincoln, the archbishopric of York (1514) and a cardinalate (1515), and the promise of Gallic support for further claims to preferment. In the same year, he was made Lord Chancellor and awarded by Henry the administration of the see of Bath and Wells and the temporalities of the wealthy abbey of St Alban's. Wolsey even hazarded a breach of the statute of praemunire by accepting the appointment of papal legate from **Leo X**. Deep in the king's confidence, he had attained a position more powerful than that enjoyed by any minister of the Crown since **Thomas (à) Becket**. As the controller of England's foreign policy he lent support to France and Germany alternately, entering into a secret alliance with the Emperor **Charles V** against Francis I, always seeking to improve England's position, but this policy ultimately proved unsuccessful. His aim in England was absolute monarchy with himself behind the throne. He established Cardinal's College (Christ Church) at Oxford and a grammar school at Ipswich. Wolsey's downfall originated in his prevarication and evasiveness over the question of Henry's divorce from **Catherine of Aragon**, which provoked the king's anger and aroused the enmity of the **Anne Boleyn** faction and of many other enemies outraged by the cardinal's haughtiness, his parvenu display, and his punishing fiscal exactions. His outmoded assertion of the ecclesiastical right to dominate secular policy was unacceptable to the powerful aristocracy of the counting-house bred by the new spirit of mercantilism. Prosecuted under the statute of praemunire in 1529, the cardinal had to surrender the Great Seal and retire to Winchester. Impeachment by the House of Lords was followed by the forfeiture of all his property to the Crown. Arrested again on a charge of high treason, he died while journeying from his York diocese to London. 🕮 A F Pollard, *Wolsey* (1929)

Wonder, Stevie, *real name* **Steveland Judkins**
1950–
US soul, pop and rock singer and instrumentalist

Born in Saginaw, Michigan, he adopted his mother's maiden name of Morris. A premature baby, he was blinded permanently by receiving too much oxygen in the incubator. He played the harmonica from an early age and was signed to Motown Records in 1961. His first album *Little Stevie Wonder: The 12-Year-Old Genius* (released when he was actually 13) was an immediate success. Most of his early recordings followed the orthodox Motown sound, but 'Where I'm Coming From' (1971) moved towards progressive rock. In 1971 he also renegotiated his recording contract to gain full artistic control over his work, the first Motown artist to do so. During the 1970s he became one of the most proficient users of synthesizer technology and developed musically to the point where he was widely regarded as one of the most important popular composers of the era. His music ranged from the up-tempo rock of 'Superstition' and the social commentary of 'Living In The City' to the simple balladry of 'I Just Called To Say I Love You'. One of America's best-loved entertainers, he also led the campaign to make

Martin Luther King's birthday a national holiday. His most important albums have included *Talking Book* (1972), *Innervisions* (1973), *Songs In The Key Of Life* (1976), and *Hotter Than July* (1980). Later albums include *Characters* (1987) and *Jungle Fever* (1991).

Wood, Christopher 1901–30
English artist

Born in Knowsley, he wandered over most of Europe between 1920 and 1924 and painted in various styles, but it is his landscapes of Cornwall and Brittany that are most characteristic. They are simple and apparently child-like, but show great sensitivity to colour, light, and atmosphere.

Wood, Edward Frederick Lindley See **Halifax, 1st Earl of**

Wood, Grant 1892–1942
US artist

Born on a farm in Anamosa, Iowa, he studied at the Art Institute of Chicago and served in the camouflage division of the army in World War I, returning to Iowa after the war to teach art in Cedar Rapids. In 1928 he went to Munich to execute a commission for a stained-glass window and was deeply impressed by the 15th-century Flemish and German primitive art he saw there. Under its influence he began to paint the life of the rural Midwest in an expressive and sharply detailed style. He is best known for stark portraits such as *American Gothic* (1930) and *Daughters of the Revolution* (1932).

Wood, Haydn 1882–1959
English composer and violinist

Born in Slaithwaite, Yorkshire, he studied at the Royal College of Music and worked for a time in music halls with his wife, Dorothy Court, for whom he wrote a large number of ballads. Of these, the best known is 'Roses of Picardy' (1916). Concentrating on more serious composition, he wrote prolifically for orchestra, brass band, chamber music groups and voices.

Wood, Mrs Henry, *née* **Ellen Price** 1814–87
English novelist

Born in Worcester, the daughter of a manufacturer, she suffered a spinal disease which confined her to bed or a sofa for most of her life. She married Henry Wood and lived in France for 20 years, but returned to England with him in 1860 and settled in Norwood. After his death in 1866 she settled in London, and wrote for magazines. Her second published novel, *East Lynne* (1861), had an immense success. She never rose above the commonplace in her many novels, but showed some power in the analysis of character in her anonymous *Johnny Ludlow* stories (1874–80). In 1867 she bought the monthly *Argosy*, which she edited, and her novels went on appearing in it long after her death. 🕮 William E Lee, *Mrs Henry Wood in Worcester and Malvern* (1992)

Wood, Sir Henry Joseph 1869–1944
English conductor

Born in London, he founded with Robert Newman the Promenade Concerts, which he conducted annually from 1895 until his death. As 'Paul Klenovsky' he arranged J S Bach's Organ Toccata and Fugue in D minor as an orchestral work. He composed operettas and an oratorio, *Saint Dorothea* (1889), but his international reputation was gained as conductor of the Queen's Hall symphony and promenade concerts. He was knighted in 1911. In 1938 he published *My Life of Music*. 🕮 Reginald Pound, *Sir Henry Wood: A Biography* (1969)

Wood, John, the Elder, *known as* **Wood of Bath**
c.1705–1754
English architect

He was responsible for many of the best-known streets and buildings of Bath, such as the North and South Parades, Queen Square, the Circus, Prior Park and other houses. His son John the Younger (d.1782) designed the Royal Crescent and the Assembly Rooms.

Wood, John 1930–
English actor

Born in Derby, he studied at Jesus College, Oxford, and joined the Old Vic in 1954. He made his West End debut in Tennessee Williams's *Camino Real* (1957). During the following decade, he worked extensively in good quality television drama; and on stage in New York, he played Guildenstern in Tom Stoppard's *Rosencrantz and Guildenstern Are Dead* (1967). Returning to Great Britain, he won great acclaim for his performance as Richard Rowan in James Joyce's *Exiles* at the Mermaid Theatre in London (1970), and joined the Royal Shakespeare Company (RSC) at Stratford-upon-Avon (1971), where he established himself as a classical actor of the front rank. He emerged as one of the leading interpreters of Stoppard's work with a stunning performance in the central role of *Travesties* (1974). For the National Theatre he played the title role in *Richard III* (1979) and at the RSC he gave a towering performance as Prospero in *The Tempest* (1988), and in the title role of *King Lear* (1990). He has had film roles in *The Madness of King George* (1994) and Ian McKellen's *Richard III* (1996).

Wood, Sir Kingsley 1881–1943
English politician

Born in London, he was trained as a solicitor and entered parliament in 1918 as Conservative MP for Woolwich West. He was knighted in 1919, and after holding several junior ministerial offices became Postmaster-General (1931–35), Minister of Health (1935–38), Secretary of State for Air (1938–40), and Chancellor of the Exchequer (1940–43), in which capacity he devised the pay-as-you-earn income tax system.

Wood, Natalie, *originally* Natasha Gurdin 1938–81
US film actress

Born in San Francisco, she began her many film appearances aged five in the wartime melodrama *Happy Land* (1943). In 1955 she appeared in the highly influential *Rebel Without a Cause* (1955), earning an Academy Best Supporting Actress nomination, and was also in the popular western, *The Searchers* (1956). *Marjorie Morningstar* (1958) saw her graduate to stardom, followed by *Splendor In The Grass* (1961), *West Side Story* (1961) and *Love With The Proper Stranger* (1963). Her career slowed during the 1970s, and in 1981 she drowned mysteriously with a high blood-alcohol level after being reported missing from her yacht. She was married to actor Robert Wagner from 1957 to 1962, and again from 1972 until her death.

Wood, Robert Williams 1868–1955
US physicist

He was born in Concord, Massachusetts, and educated at Harvard, Chicago and Berlin, becoming Professor of Experimental Physics at Johns Hopkins University (1901–38). He carried out research on optics, atomic and molecular radiation and sound waves, one of his most notable researches being the study of resonance radiation, which led to the optical pumping developed by Alfred Kastler. Wood also pioneered the production of phase gratings and zone-plate lenses, anticipating the much later science of 'diffractive optics'.

Wood, Victoria 1953–
English comedienne and writer

Born in Prestwich, Lancashire, she studied drama at Birmingham University and began singing her own comic songs on local radio and television while still a student. After winning the television talent show *New Faces*

(1975), she gained a regular singing spot on *That's Life* (1976). Her first play, *Talent* (1978), was adapted for television (1979) and won her the Pye award for Most Promising New Writer. Her television series include *Wood and Walters* (with Julie Walters, 1981–82), *Victoria Wood—As Seen on Television* (1984–87), *An Audience With Victoria Wood* (1988, British Academy award), *Victoria Wood* (1989) and *Victoria Wood's All Day Breakfast* (1992). Her frequent stage tours include *Funny Turns* (1982), *Lucky Bag* (1984) and *Victoria Wood* (1987). She has also published several books, including *Up To You, Porky* (1985), *Barmy* (1987) and *Mens Sana in Thingummy Doodah* (1990).

Wood, Willie 1938–
Scottish bowls player

Born in Gifford, East Lothian, he made his debut for his country in 1966, and won a bronze at the Commonwealth Games in 1974. Partnered by Alex McIntosh, he won a silver in the pairs in 1978, then won individual gold in 1982. He was a member of the Scotland team which won the world championship in 1984, as well as being runner-up in the singles. A dispute over professionalism saw him barred from competing in the Edinburgh Commonwealth Games of 1986, but four years later, having been reinstated, he again won a gold medal, this time in the fours, at the Auckland Games. A cheery, modest man, he still lives in his home village, where he works as a car mechanic.

Woodcock, George 1904–79
English trade union leader

Born in Bamber Bridge, Lancashire, he was educated at the local elementary school and, under trade union auspices, at Ruskin College and New College, Oxford, where he obtained first class honours in philosophy and politics. He was a civil servant (1934–36) before joining the research and economic department of the Trades Union Congress (TUC). He became assistant General Secretary (1947–60) and General Secretary (1960–69). A man of great intelligence, he was sometimes seen as vain and arrogant, but did much to enhance the reputation of the TUC. He sat on several royal commissions, including the Donovan Commission on Trade Unions and Employers' Associations (1965–68). After retiring from the TUC he was Chairman of the Commission on Industrial Relations (1969–71).

Woodhull, Victoria, *née* Claflin 1838–1927
US reformer

Born in Homer, Ohio, she was one of a large family which earned a living by giving fortune-telling and medicine shows and performed a spiritualist act with her sister, Tennessee (1846–1923). From 1853 to 1864 she was married to Dr Canning Woodhull, but on her divorce returned to the family business. In 1868 she went with Tennessee to New York where they persuaded the rich Cornelius Vanderbilt to set them up as stockbrokers. At this time they became involved with a socialist group called Pantarchy, and began to advocate its principles of free love, and equal rights and legal prostitution. In 1870 they established the magazine *Woodhull and Claflin's Weekly* (1870–76), outlining these views. A vigorous speaker, Victoria won support from the leaders of the women's suffrage movement, and thus became the first woman nominated for the presidency. In 1877 she moved to London, with Tennessee, where she continued to lecture and write. Her publications include *Stirpiculture, or the Scientific Propagation of the Human Race* (1888) and *The Human Body the Temple of God* (1890, with Tennessee).

Woods, Tiger, *real name* Eldrick Woods 1976–
US golfer

Born in Cypress, California, he was the first man to win both the US junior amateur and US amateur titles. The nickname 'Tiger' is a tribute to a Vietnam colleague of his father. He retained the amateur title for a record three years in a row, and his outstanding amateur career included both Walker Cup (1995) and Eisenhower (1994) appearances. Having turned professional in August 1996, he won twice in seven starts and became the first player to record five top-ten finishes in a row on the US Tour. In 1997 he became the youngest, as well as the first black winner of the US Masters. A superstar in the making, his racial origins (US black father and Thai mother) are exploited to the full by a nation hungry for a new Jack Nicklaus.

Woodsworth, James Shaver 1874–1942
Canadian reformer and political leader
Born in Islington, Ontario, to a Methodist home mission family, after education in Canada and England he was ordained a Methodist minister in 1900. He resigned his ministry as a protest against the Church's support for World War I. Well-informed on the problems of the prairie farmers, he was a founder and president of the Commercial Co-Operative Federation. In 1926 he and A A Heaps were able to take advantage of the government's tiny majority, and pushed through the Old Age Pensions Act in 1927. Winning his last election in 1940, Woodsworth was the one MP who voted against Canada's involvement in World War II, and his speech of conscience was heard in respectful silence.

Woodville, Elizabeth c.1437–1492
Queen of England
The eldest daughter of Sir Richard Woodville, 1st Earl Rivers, she married Sir John Grey, who was killed at St Albans (1461). In 1464 she was married privately to Edward IV, and was crowned in 1465. When Edward fled to Flanders (1470), she sought sanctuary in Westminster. The rise to wealth and power of her numerous family contributed to the animosity within the Yorkist dynasty. In 1483 her sons, Edward V and Richard, Duke of York, were murdered (the Princes in the Tower). After the accession of Henry VII (1485) her rights as dowager queen were restored, but soon she had to retire to the Abbey of Bermondsey, where she died. Her eldest daughter, Elizabeth of York (1465–1503), married Henry in 1486.

Woodville, Richard See Rivers, 1st Earl

Woodward, Sir Arthur Smith 1864–1944
English geologist
Born in Macclesfield, Cheshire, and educated at the University of Manchester, he was appointed as assistant (1881–92), assistant keeper (1892–1901) and keeper of geology (1901–24) at the Natural History section of the British Museum. He did notable work on fossil fish, which developed from his initial brief of cataloguing the museum's fossil fish collection. From 1885 to 1923 he made 30 expeditions abroad, in his vacation time and largely at his own expense, visiting museums, meeting palaeontologists and making collections throughout Europe, the USA, the Middle East and South America. One of Britain's most prolific geologists, he produced some 650 publications, including the four volumes of his *Catalogue of Fossil Fishes in the British Museum (Natural History)* (1889, 1891, 1895, 1901) and *Outlines of Vertebrate Palaeontology* (1898). In spite of this, Woodward is chiefly remembered for his part in the controversy over the Piltdown Man. The amateur geologist Charles Dawson gave him the cranial fragments found at Piltdown from 1908 to 1912 for identification. Together with parts of a jawbone unearthed later, these were accepted by many anthropologists as the 'missing link' in Charles Darwin's theory of evolution, and as such one of the greatest discoveries of the age. Following scientific tests, the skull

was denounced as a fake in 1953; Woodward's firm belief that the remains were human was the main reason the hoax succeeded. He was knighted in 1924.

Woodward, Comer Vann 1908–
US historian
Born in Vanndale, Arkansas, he graduated from Emory University, Georgia, and studied at Columbia University and at the University of North Carolina. He taught at Johns Hopkins (1946–61) and Yale (1961–77). He reflected the agrarian philosophy prominent among interwar white Southern intellectuals, notably that of his friend Robert Penn Warren. He wrote *Tom Watson, Agrarian Rebel* (1938), his major work *Origins of the New South 1877–1913* (1951), its spin-off *Reunion and Reaction: The Compromise of 1877 and the End of Reconstruction* (1951), and several essays later collected in *The Burden of Southern History* (1961). His best-known later work is his edition of the diary of Mary Boykin Chesnut, *Mary Chesnut's Civil War* (1982). Other works include *The Future of the Past* (1990) and *The Old World's New World* (1991). In 1990 he won the gold medal of history.

Woodward, Edward (Albert Arthur) 1930–
English actor
Born in Croydon, Surrey, he trained at RADA and made his West End debut in *Where There's a Will* (1954), also appearing in the 1955 film version. His other films include *Becket* (1963), *Young Winston* (1971), *The Wicker Man* (1973), 'Breaker' Morant (1980) and *Champions* (1983). He starred on television in the title role of *Callan* (1967–73), as Robert McCall in *The Equalizer* (1985–90) and as Nev in *Common as Muck* (1994), and is the presenter of the crime-reconstruction drama series *In Suspicious Circumstances* (1992–). He is married to the actress Michele Dotrice.

Woodward, Joanne 1930–
US film and television actress
Born in Thomasville, Georgia, she appeared on Broadway and in numerous television dramas before Twentieth Century-Fox cast her in a minor western, *Count Three And Pray* (1955). She then won a Best Actress Academy Award for her performance as a schizophrenic in *The Three Faces of Eve* (1957), followed by notable performances in *No Down Payment* (1957), *The Long Hot Summer* (1958) and *The Stripper* (1963). Her career floundered in the 1960s, but she was acclaimed again in *Rachel, Rachel* (1968), directed by her husband Paul Newman, and later in *Mr and Mrs Bridge* (1990) and as the mother of Tom Hanks in *Philadelphia* (1993). Her recent work has been mainly on stage and in television-movie drama.

Woodward, Robert Burns 1917–79
US chemist and Nobel Prize winner
Born in Boston, he had a formal chemical education at Massachusetts Institute of Technology which resulted in a PhD by the age of 20. He then moved to Harvard (1937) and by 1944 had become associate professor, working on the chemistry of the antimalarial drug quinine and the new wonder drug penicillin. For the next 20 years he executed the syntheses of an array of biological compounds. His feel for the art and architecture of constructing complex molecules was astounding. At the same time he became famous for his lectures. He was awarded the Nobel Prize for chemistry in 1965 for the totality of his work in the art of synthetic chemistry, structure determination and theoretical analysis. Woodward and the Swiss chemist Albert Eschenmoser set out to synthesize vitamin B_{12} in a collaborative venture. The work took over 10 years and was completed in 1976. In the course of this synthesis Woodward conceived the idea that molecular orbitals could affect the products obtained in cyclization reactions and he invited a young Harvard theoretician Roald Hoffmann to collaborate. This led

eventually to the Woodward–Hoffmann rules for the conservation of orbital symmetry. Unfortunately Woodward had died from a heart attack before the award of a Nobel Prize for chemistry for this work. He received almost every honour and award possible for an organic chemist and the pharmaceutical company Ciba–Geigy established the Woodward Research Institute for him in Basle. Many think of Woodward as the greatest synthetic organic chemist of all time.

Wooldridge, Sydney William 1900–63
English geographer

Born in Hornsey, North London, he was educated at King's College London. After various teaching appointments at London University, he became Professor of Geography at Birkbeck College there (1944). He moved after about three years to take up the chair of geography at King's College, where he remained until his death. His original research was in geology but he played a leading role in the establishment of geomorphology within British geography. He was an adviser to postwar governments on Greater London, new towns, and on the use of sands and gravel.

Woolf, Arthur 1766–1837
English mechanical engineer

Born in Camborne, Cornwall, he served an apprenticeship as a carpenter then turned to engineering, and in 1786 helped Jonathan Hornblower to repair a compound steam engine he had installed in a London brewery. After the expiry of James Watt's patent in 1800, Woolf patented a compound engine and boiler in 1803, but it was several years before he evolved a satisfactory design. He eventually abandoned the principle of compounding and concentrated on perfecting the high-pressure Cornish engines of Richard Trevithick, in which he was particularly successful.

Woolf, Leonard Sidney 1880–1969
English publisher and writer

Born in London, he was educated at St Paul's School and Trinity College, Cambridge. He worked in the Ceylon Civil Service (1904–11), and his early novels, such as *The Village and the Jungle* (1913), have Ceylon as a background. In 1916 he joined the Fabian Society and in 1917 along with his wife Virginia Woolf he founded the Hogarth Press; the two became the centre of the so-called 'Bloomsbury Group'. His works include *Socialism and Co-operation* (1921), *After the Deluge* (1931, 1939) and *Principia Politica* (1953). He published his autobiography in five volumes, *Sowing* (1960), *Growing* (1961), *Beginning Again* (1964), *Downhill all the Way* (1967), and *The Journey not the Arrival Matters* (1969).

Woolf, Virginia   See panel p1978

Woollcott, Alexander Humphreys 1887–1943
US critic and writer

He was born in Phalanx, New Jersey, and was educated at Hamilton and Columbia universities. He became theatre critic of *The New York Times* (1914–22) and other newspapers, and contributed to the *New Yorker*. He also undertook radio broadcasts in America (*Town Crier*, 1929–42) and in the UK (1929–42), and appeared on stage as Sheridan Whiteside, a character based on himself, in *The Man who Came to Dinner* (1940).

Woollett, William 1735–85
English line-engraver

He was born in Maidstone, Kent. His first important plate, from Richard Wilson's *Niobe*, was published by John Boydell in 1761. In 1775 he was appointed engraver to George III.

Woolley, Sir (Charles) Leonard 1880–1960
English archaeologist

Born in London, he was educated at New College, Oxford, and became assistant keeper of the Ashmolean Museum, Oxford (1905–07). He carried out excavations at Carchemish (1912–14), Al'Ubaid, and Tell el-Amarna, and subsequently directed the important excavations (1922–34) at Ur in Mesopotamia, which in 1926 uncovered gold and lapis lazuli in the royal tombs. He was knighted in 1935, and from 1943 to 1946 was archaeological adviser to the War Office. He wrote several popular accounts of his work, notably *Digging up the Past* (1930). ▫M E L Mallowan, *Sir Leonard Woolley, Expedition* (1960)

Woolley, Sir Richard van der Riet 1906–86
English astronomer

Born in Weymouth, Dorset, he studied at the University of Cape Town before returning to England and entering Cambridge (1925–28) to study mathematics. He was appointed chief assistant at the Royal Observatory, Greenwich (1933–37), returning to Cambridge as John Couch Adams Astronomer (1937–39). In 1939 he was appointed Government Astronomer and Director of the Commonwealth Observatory in Canberra, Australia. During World War II he worked on the optical design of military instruments, but at the same time he established the observatory as an important institution for observations of the southern skies. At Greenwich and Canberra he was mainly concerned with solar and stellar atmospheres, publishing *Eclipses of the Sun and Moon* and *The Outer Layers of a Star*. In 1956 Woolley, as 11th Astronomer Royal, succeeded Sir Harold Jones with charge of the Royal Greenwich Observatory at Herstmonceux in Sussex, where he supervised the completion of the Isaac Newton telescope. He was involved in two further major telescopic projects; the Anglo-Australian 3.8 metre telescope and the United Kingdom 1.2 metre Schmidt telescope, both sited in New South Wales, Australia. In 1971, Woolley, who had received a knighthood on becoming Astronomer Royal, was appointed director of the South African Astronomical Observatory (1972–76).

Woolman, John 1720–72
American Quaker preacher and reformer

Born in Rancocas, New Jersey, he was a tailor by trade. He became a Quaker in 1843 and campaigned against slavery, and published several religious works. His *Journal* (1774) was a favourite book of Charles Lamb. He died in York on a visit to England.

Woolner, Thomas 1826–92
English poet and sculptor

He was born in Hadleigh, Suffolk, and studied at the Royal Academy, London, from 1842. As a conspicuous member of the Pre-Raphaelite Brotherhood he contributed poems to *The Germ*, which with others were published in a volume as *My Beautiful Lady* (1863). From 1852 to 1854 he was in Australia digging for gold. He was a prolific artist and produced statues or portrait busts of most of his famous contemporaries, notably Tennyson (1857, marble) in Westminster Abbey, London. He was Professor of Sculpture at the Academy (1877–79). Other works include Prince Albert (1864, Oxford University Museum), William Gladstone (1866, Ashmolean Museum, Oxford), and William Whewell (1873, Cambridge, Trinity). His late work, *The Housemaid* (1892, The Salter's Company, London) is truly modern in its realism.

Woolton, Frederick James Marquis, 1st Earl of 1883–1964
English politician and businessman

Born in Liverpool, he attended Manchester Grammar School and Manchester University, and then taught mathematics at Burnley Grammar School. During a spell as warden of Liverpool University Settlement, in the dock area, he ran the David Lewis Club and this brought

Woolf, (Adeline) Virginia, *née* Stephen 1882–1941
English novelist, critic and essayist

Virginia Woolf was born in London, the daughter of Sir **Leslie Stephen**. She was close to her sister, **Vanessa Bell**, and was from an early age the family story-teller. She was taught at home, by her parents and governesses, and received an uneven education. In 1891 she started the *Hyde Park Gate News* which was read by grown-ups and appeared weekly until 1895, and which included her first efforts at fiction.

Her father died in 1904 and the family moved to Bloomsbury where they formed the nucleus of the Bloomsbury Group; this comprised—among others— **John Maynard Keynes**, **E M Forster**, **Roger Fry**, **Duncan Grant** and **Lytton Strachey**: philosophers, writers and artists. A year later she became a reviewer for the *Times Literary Supplement*, an association that lasted until just before her death. She married **Leonard Woolf** in 1912 and her first novel, *The Voyage Out*, was published in 1915. It was favourably received and although it was a realistic novel there were hints of the lyricism which would later become her hallmark. However, her health was already poor and she suffered recurring depressions; she had attempted suicide in 1913. In 1917 she and Leonard formed the Hogarth Press, partly for therapeutic reasons. Its first publication was *Two Stories* (1917), one by each of the founders. They went on to publish works by other modern writers, including **Katherine Mansfield** and **T S Eliot**.

Woolf's second novel, *Night and Day*, appeared in 1919. Again its mode is realistic, focusing on Katherine Hilberry, whose activities in a literary milieu are counterpointed with those of her friend Mary who is involved in the women's movement. Some critics still think it her best work. *Jacob's Room* followed in 1922 and marked a turning point in her fiction, showing her experimenting with narrative and language. It was well-received and made her a celebrity. In 1923 she published the essay 'Mr Bennett and Mrs Brown' in the *Nation and Athenaeum*. An attack on the 'Georgian novelists' **Arnold Bennett**, **John Galsworthy** and **H G Wells**, it can be read as her own aesthetic manifesto.

Regarded as a major figure in the Modernist movement, she continued to make a significant contribution to the development of the novel. In six years she published the three novels that have made her one of the century's great writers: *Mrs Dalloway* (1925), *To the Lighthouse* (1927) and *The Waves* (1931), noted for their impressionistic, stream-of-consciousness style. Her most commercially successful novel *Orlando* (1928), which describes the fantastic life of an aristocratic poet as he travels through four centuries, changing sex on the way, was dedicated to her intimate friend, **Vita Sackville-West**.

Her work took its toll on her health, and although she wrote prolifically she was beset by deep depressions and debilitating headaches. Throughout the 1930s she worked on the novel *The Years*, which was published in 1937. A year later *Three Guineas*, provisionally entitled 'Professions for Women' was published. This was intended as a sequel to *A Room of One's Own* (1929), a long essay which is still regarded as a feminist classic, and in which Woolf stated that 'A woman must have money and a room of her own if she is to write fiction.' Her last novel, the experimental *Between the Acts* was published posthumously in 1941, after she had forced a large stone into her pocket and drowned herself in the River Ouse, near her home at Rodmell in Sussex. She is, with **James Joyce** (whose novel *Ulysses* the Hogarth Press declined to publish), regarded as one of the great modern innovators of the novel in English.

📖 Woolf's letters and memoirs have been collected as *Letters* (6 vols, 1975–80, eds N Nicolson and J Trantmann) and *Diaries* (5 vols, 1977–84, eds A Olivier Bell and A McNeillie). See also Hermione Lee, *Virginia Woolf* (1996); Phyllis Rose, *Woman of Letters: A Life of Virginia Woolf* (1978); Quentin Bell, *Virginia Woolf* (1972).

'Life is not a series of gig lamps symmetrically arranged; life is a luminous halo, a semi-transparent envelope surrounding us from the beginning of consciousness to the end.'
From 'Modern Fiction' in *The Common Reader* (1925).

---

him to the attention of Lewis, the managing director of the Manchester store, who took him into the business. He rose rapidly in Lewis's, where he revolutionized the merchandizing side, and became chairman in 1935. He was made a baron in 1939. At the beginning of the war, he went to the Ministry of Supply, but made his name at the Ministry of Food, where from 1940 he had the responsibility of seeing that the entire nation was well-nourished. In 1946 he became chairman of the Conservative Party, and is credited with much of the success in rebuilding the party's reorganization which led it to victory in 1951. He published his memoirs in 1959.

Woolworth, Frank Winfield 1852–1919
US businessman

He was born in Rodman, Jefferson County, New York. In 1873, after several years as a farm worker, he became a shop assistant. His employers backed his scheme to open a store in Utica for five-cent goods only (1879). This failed, but later the same year a second store, in Lancaster, Pennsylvania, selling ten-cent goods as well, was successful. In partnership with his employers, his brother, and cousin, from 1905 he began building a large chain of similar stores, and by the time he died the F W Woolworth company controlled over a thousand stores from their headquarters in the Woolworth building in New York. Woolworth's stores reached Great Britain in 1910, but their main development outside the USA was after the death of the founder.

Woosnam, Ian Harold 1958–
Welsh golfer

Born in St Martins, Shropshire, of Welsh parents, he is a small man but a powerful hitter, his strength deriving from the agricultural work to which he devoted himself before turning professional in 1976. He had a six-year wait for his first European Tour win, the Swiss Open, but by the mid-1980s he was regularly placed in the top 10. In 1987 he won five tournaments, and led Wales to the World Cup. He has been a regular member of Europe's Ryder Cup team since 1983. Although he remains one of the most formidable golfers in the world, he has so far only won two 'majors', the US Masters in 1991 and the British Masters in 1994.

Wootton of Abinger, Barbara Frances
Wootton, Baroness 1897–1988
English social scientist

Born in Cambridge, she studied and lectured (1920–22) in economics at Girton College, Cambridge, and was Director of Studies (1927–44) and Professor in Social Studies (1948–52) at London. A frequent royal commissioner and London magistrate, she is best known for *Testament for Social Science* (1950), an attempt to assimilate the social to the natural sciences. She also wrote *Social Science and Pathology* (1959).

Worcester, Edward Somerset, 6th Earl and 2nd Marquis of 1601–67
English aristocrat and inventor of a steam water-pump

Born probably in London, he sided with King **Charles I** in the Civil War. He was made General of South Wales in 1642, was created Earl of Glamorgan in 1644, and was sent to Ireland to raise troops for the king in 1645. His mission failed, and he was imprisoned. In 1646 he succeeded his father, and in 1648 went into exile in France. He returned to England (1652) and was sent to the Tower of London, but in 1654 was freed and at the Restoration he recovered a portion of his vast estates. His *Century of Inventions* (written 1655, printed 1663) gives a brief account of a hundred inventions: he was especially interested in the calculating machine and the steam engine.

Worcester, Joseph Emerson 1784–1865
US lexicographer
Born in Bedford, New Hampshire, he taught at Salem, Massachusetts, and then became an author, compiling a number of gazetteers, manuals of geography and history. He edited *Johnson's English Dictionary, with Walker's Pronouncing Dictionary* (1828), abridged **John Webster** (1829) without permission, and printed his own *Comprehensive English Dictionary* (1830), a *Critical Dictionary* (1846), and the great illustrated quarto *Dictionary of the English Language* (1860).

Worcester, Sir Thomas Percy, Earl of
1344–1403
English soldier
He fought in France, accompanied **Geoffrey Chaucer** on a diplomatic mission to Flanders in 1377, was made an admiral by **Richard II** and commanded in several expeditions, notably those of **John of Gaunt** to Spain (1386) and of the Earl of Arundel to La Rochelle (1388). He was created an earl in 1397. Having joined the rebellion of Northumberland (**Henry 'Hotspur' Percy**) in 1403, he was captured at Shrewsbury and executed. He was the son of Sir Henry, 3rd Baron **Percy**.

Worde, Wynkyn de d.c.1535
English printer
He was born in Alsace. A pupil of **William Caxton**, he succeeded to his stock-in-trade in Westminster in 1491. In 1500 he moved to Fleet Street. He made great improvements in printing and typecutting, including the use of italic, and printed hundreds of books. 📖 James Moran, *Wynkyn de Worde, Father of Fleet Street* (2nd rev edn, 1976)

Wordsworth, Dorothy 1771–1855
English writer
Born in Cockermouth, Cumberland, the only sister of **William Wordsworth**, she was his constant companion, accompanying him on tours to Scotland, the Isle of Man and abroad. Her *Journals* show that her keen observation and sensibility provided a good deal of poetic imagery for both her brother and his friend **Coleridge**—more than that, they regarded her as the embodiment of that joy in Nature which it was their object to depict. In 1829 she suffered a breakdown from which she never fully recovered. Her *Recollections of a Tour made in Scotland AD 1803* (1874) is a classic. 📖 E de Selincourt, *Dorothy Wordsworth* (1933)

Wordsworth, William 1770–1850
English poet
He was born in Cockermouth, Cumberland, and was orphaned at an early age. He was sent to Hawkshead in the Lake District for board and education and this was one of the formative periods of his life, followed by St John's College, Cambridge (1787–91), where he was exposed to agnostic and revolutionary ideas. A walking tour through France and Switzerland in 1790 showed him France still optimistic from the Revolution, before disillusionment had set in. Two immature poems belong to this period— *An Evening Walk* and *Descriptive Sketches*, both published in 1793. Leaving Cambridge without a profession, he stayed

for a little over a year at Blois. There he had an affair with Annette Vallon, which produced an illegitimate daughter, Ann Caroline, and is reflected in *Vaudracour and Julia* (c.1804, published 1820). He returned to England when war with France was declared, but the depressing poem *Guilt and Sorrow*, from this period, shows that he was still passionate about social justice. For a time he fell under the spell of **William Godwin**'s philosophic anarchism, but the unreadable *Borderers* shows that by 1795 he was turning his back both on the Revolution and on Godwinism. With the help of his sister **Dorothy** and **Coleridge**, who had renounced his revolutionary ardour somewhat earlier, he discovered his true vocation, that of the poet exploring the lives of common people living in contact with divine nature and untouched by the rebellious spirit of the times. The Wordsworths and Coleridge settled in Somerset (1797), and from this close association resulted *Lyrical Ballads* (1798), the first manifesto of the new poetry, which opened with Coleridge's 'Ancient Mariner' and concluded with Wordsworth's 'Tintern Abbey'. This alliance ended when the Wordsworths moved to Grasmere after a visit to Germany with Coleridge, and Wordsworth married Mary Hutchinson (1802). He was set on his proper task and, modestly provided for by a legacy of £900, he embarked upon a long spell of routine work and relative happiness broken only by family misfortunes—the death of his sailor brother John (1805), which may have inspired the 'Ode to Duty', and Dorothy's mental breakdown. Meanwhile **Napoleon I**'s ambitions had completely destroyed the poet's revolutionary sympathies, as the patriotic sonnets sent to the *Morning Post* at about the time of the Peace of Amiens (1802–03) and after show. Apart from the sonnets, this was his most inspired period. The additions to the third edition of *Lyrical Ballads* (1801) contained the grave pastoral *Michael*, *Ruth* and four of the exquisite *Lucy* poems. The first of his tours in Scotland (1803), recorded perfectly by Dorothy, yielded some fine poems, including *The Solitary Reaper*. The great poem he was now contemplating—*The Recluse*—was never finished, but *The Prelude*, the record of the poet's mind, was read to Coleridge in 1805. It remained unpublished until after his death, when it appeared with all the tamperings of a lifetime but substantially in its 1805 form, which fortunately has survived. Two volumes of poems appeared in 1807, the product of five years of intense activity. The ode 'Intimations of Immortality' is only the loftiest of a number of masterpieces, including the patriotic sonnets, the 'Affliction of Margaret', the 'Memorials of a Tour in Scotland', the 'Ode to Duty', and many others. He had now reached the peak of his poetic form and the remainder of his work, including *The Excursion* (1814), the *Ecclesiastical Sonnets* and the *Memorials* of his various tours, do not reflect his genius. He succeeded **Robert Southey** as Poet Laureate in 1843. 📖 M Moorman, *The Life of William Wordsworth* (1957–65)

Wordsworth, William Brocklesby 1908–88
English composer
Born in London, he studied under Sir **Donald Tovey**, and achieved prominence when his Second Symphony won the first award in the Edinburgh International Festival Competition in 1950. He composed symphonies, a piano concerto, songs and chamber music. He was a descendant of the clergyman Christopher Wordsworth (1774–1846).

Worlock, Derek John Harford 1920–96
English Roman Catholic prelate
Born in London, he was educated at St Edmund's College, Ware, and was ordained as a priest in 1944. He was private secretary to the Archbishop of Westminster (1945–64), then became a rector in London (1964–65). He was Bishop of Portsmouth (1965–76) and also served on a number of ecclesiastical councils before becoming Archbishop of Liverpool in 1976. He wrote a number of

religious books, including two in collaboration with the Anglican Bishop of Liverpool, **David Sheppard**, *Better Together* (1988) and *With Christ in the Wilderness* (1990). His other works include *Turn and Turn Again* (1971), *Give me your Hand* (1977) and *Bread Upon the Water* (1991).

Wörner, Manfred 1934–94
German politician

Born in Stuttgart, he was the son of an affluent textile retailer. He studied law at the Universities of Heidelberg, Paris and Munich, then joined the conservative Christian Democratic Union (CDU) and was elected in 1965 to the Bundestag (federal parliament). Establishing himself as a specialist in strategic issues, he was appointed Defence Minister in 1982 by Chancellor **Helmut Kohl** and then oversaw the controversial deployment of American Cruise and Pershing-II nuclear missiles in West Germany, an extension of military service from 15 to 18 months to compensate for a declining birthrate, and, in 1984, the dismissal of General Gunter Kiessling, for alleged, though subsequently disproven, homosexual contacts. Wörner succeeded Lord **Carrington** as Secretary-General of NATO in 1988. Despite being diagnosed with cancer in 1992, he worked until his death to negotiate peace between Bosnia and Herzegovina.

Worrall, Denis John 1935–
South African politician

Born in Benoni, he was educated at Cape Town and Cornell universities, where he subsequently taught political science. He held a succession of academic posts during the 1960s and 1970s and also worked as a journalist before being elected a National Party (NP) senator in 1974 and MP in 1977. He was appointed to the key post of ambassador to the United Kingdom in 1984 by President **P W Botha**, but on his return to South Africa in 1987 resigned from the NP and unsuccessfully contested the general election of that year as an independent. In 1988 he established the Independent Party (IP), and in 1989 the IP merged with other white opposition parties to form the reformist Democratic Party (DP), which advocated dismantlement of the apartheid system and universal adult suffrage. A co-leader of the DP, he was elected to parliament from 1989 to 1994.

Worsaae, Jens Jacob Asmussen 1821–85
Danish antiquary and archaeologist

Born in Vejle, he was assistant to **Christian Jörgensen Thomsen** at the National Museum in Copenhagen (1838–43), inspector of monuments (1847), and director from 1865. In 1842–54 he made repeated visits to Europe and the rest of Scandinavia on archaeological expeditions, and pioneered palaeobotany with his study of vegetation changes in peat-bogs. His major published work was *Danmarks Oldtid* (1843, Eng trans *The Primeval Antiquities of Denmark*, 1849), and he also wrote *The Danes and Norwegians in England* (1852). He was Minister of Education from 1874 to 1875.

Worth, Charles Frederick 1825–95
English fashion designer

Born in Bourn, Lincolnshire, he went to Paris in 1846, and achieved such success as a fashion designer that he gained the patronage of the Empress **Eugénie**. His establishment in the Rue de la Paix became the centre of the fashion world.

Worth, Irene 1916–
US actress

Born in Nebraska, she spent some years as a teacher, before making her professional debut with a US touring company in 1942, appearing on Broadway a year later. In 1944 she moved to London, where she spent much of the next 30 years. Equally at home on both sides of the Atlantic Ocean, she created the role of Celia Coplestone

in **T S Eliot's** *The Cocktail Party* at the Edinburgh Festival (1949), joined the Old Vic (1951) and appeared in the inaugural season at Stratford, Ontario (1953). She later played the title role in **Schiller's** *Mary Stuart* in New York (1957), and joined the Royal Shakespeare Company at Stratford-upon-Avon (1960). Since then she has given memorable performances in most of the major leading roles. Her role in *Lost in Yonkers* in New York (1991) won her a Tony award and she went on to star in the 1993 film version. In 1989 she received an Obie award for outstanding achievement in the theatre.

Wotton, Sir Henry 1568–1639
English traveller, diplomat, scholar and poet

Born in Boughton Malherbe, Kent, he was educated at Winchester and Oxford, then spent the next seven years in Bavaria, Austria, Italy, Switzerland and France. On his return he became the confidant of Robert Devereux, 2nd Earl of **Essex**. Following Essex's downfall (1601), Wotton went to France, then to Italy, and was sent by Ferdinand, Duke of Florence, on a secret mission to **James VI** of Scotland. James later knighted him and sent him as ambassador to Venice (1604), then to the German princes and Emperor **Ferdinand II**. He returned to England a poor man in 1624, was made Provost of Eton, and took orders. His tracts, letters, and so on were collected as *Reliquiae Wottonianae* (1651, prefixed by **Izaak Walton's** *Life of Wotton*). One of his few poems is 'The Character of a Happy Life'. It was Wotton who described an ambassador as an honest man sent abroad to lie for the good of his country.

Wouk, Herman 1915–
US novelist

Born in New York City, the son of Jewish immigrants, he attended Columbia University and wrote radio scripts. He served in the US navy in the South Pacific in World War II, the experience of which he drew on for his classic war novel, *The Caine Mutiny* (1951). It won the Pulitzer Prize and became a successful play and film. Later books— *Marjorie Morningstar* (1955) and *Youngblood Hawke* (1962)— sold well but did not critically eclipse his earlier success. Other books include *The Winds of War* (1971) and *War and Remembrance* (1975), which became popular television serials in 1983 and 1989 respectively.

Wouters, Rik 1882–1916
Belgian painter

Born in Mechlin, he came under the influence of **Cézanne** and was the leading exponent of Fauvism in Belgium. He was also a sculptor, and his work is known for its vibrance, but his talent was not allowed to develop, as he died young during World War I.

Wouwerman, Philips 1619–68
Dutch painter

He was born in Haarlem and is believed to have been a pupil of **Frans Hals**. His pictures are mostly small landscapes of battles and hunting scenes, with lots of energetic figures, and his cavalry skirmishes, with a white horse generally in the foreground, were specially characteristic and popular. He had two brothers, also painters, Peter (1623–82) and Jan (1629–66), who chose similar subjects.

Wovoka, *also known as* Jack Wilson c.1858–1932
Native American religious leader

Born into the Paiute tribe near Walter Lake, Nevada, he was the son of a religious mystic, and at the age of 14, after the death of his father, he went to live and work on the ranch of a local white family. He had a religious vision in late 1888 that prompted him to found the messianic Ghost Dance religion. He promised that if Native Americans lived peacefully and performed the Ghost Dance ritual, whites would disappear, the buffalo would return, and the dead would rise. He won followers among many tribes, especially the Sioux, but after the massacre at Wounded Knee, South Dakota (1890), when many were killed wearing 'ghost shirts' from which they expected supernatural protection, the movement came to an end.

Wrangel, Ferdinand Petrovich, Baron von
1794–1870
Russian vice-admiral and explorer
Born in Livonia, he made extensive explorations in Arctic waters and on Siberian coasts, and made valuable surveys and observations. Wrangel Island, which he almost reached in 1821 (it was sighted by Sir Henry Kellett in 1849), was named after him by a US whaler. He helped to found the Russian Geographical Society, and published *Polar Expedition* (Eng trans 1840).

Wray, Fay 1907–
US actress
Born near Cardston, Alberta, in Canada, and raised in Los Angeles, she made an early film debut in *Blind Husbands* (1919) and appeared in many small roles before starring in *The Wedding March* (1928). After *King Kong* (1933), she specialized in distressed damsels screaming for help. Her stage work includes *Nikki* (1931) and *Golden Wings* (1941). She retired from the screen in 1942 but returned for a handful of matronly character parts before finally appearing in *Dragstrip Riot* (1958). She later wrote plays and acted on television in *Gideon's Trumpet* (1980). Her autobiography, *On The Other Hand*, was published in 1989.

Wren, Sir Christopher 1632–1723
English architect
Born in East Knoyle, Wiltshire, he was the son of Dr Christopher Wren, dean of Windsor. He was educated at Westminster and Wadham College, Oxford, became a Fellow of All Souls, distinguished himself in physics and mathematics, and helped to perfect the barometer. In 1657 he became Professor of Astronomy at Gresham College in London, but in 1661 returned to Oxford as Savilian Professor of Astronomy. Before leaving London, Wren had, with **Robert Boyle**, **John Wilkins** and others, laid the foundation of the Royal Society. In 1663 he was engaged by the dean and chapter of St Paul's to make a survey of the cathedral with a view to repairs. The first work built from a design by Wren was the chapel at Pembroke College, Cambridge (1663), and from 1663–66 he designed the Sheldonian Theatre at Oxford and the library of Trinity College, Cambridge. The Great Fire of London (1666) presented him with a unique opportunity to redesign the whole city, embracing wide streets and magnificent quays, but his scheme was never implemented. In 1669 he was appointed Surveyor-General and was chosen architect for the new St Paul's (1675–1710) and for more than 50 other churches in place of those destroyed by the fire. He also designed the Royal Exchange Greenwich Observatory, the Ashmolean Museum at Oxford, additions to Hampton Court, Buckingham House, Marlborough House, and the western towers and north transept of Westminster Abbey. In 1684 he was appointed comptroller of the works at Windsor Castle, and in 1698 Surveyor-General of Westminster Abbey. He was buried in St Paul's, where his monument reads *Si monumentum requiris, circumspice* ('If you seek a monument, look around you'). ▢ J N Summerson, *Sir Christopher Wren* (1953)

Wren, P(ercival) C(hristopher) 1885–1941
English novelist
Born in Devon, he was successively a teacher, journalist, explorer and soldier in the French Foreign Legion, which provided him with the background for *Beau Geste* (1924), the first of his romantic adventure novels. The book spawned a thousand sequels, among them his own *Beau Sabreur* (1926), and *Beau Ideal* (1928). Among his many

other adventure novels are *Valiant Dust* (1932) and *The Uniform of Glory* (1941). None was able to emulate the success of *Beau Geste*.

Wright, Sir Almroth Edward 1861–1947
English bacteriologist
Born in Yorkshire, and educated in Dublin, Leipzig, Strassburg, Marburg and Sydney, he was subsequently appointed to an army medical school, where he developed a vaccine against typhoid fever. He later became Professor of Experimental Pathology at St Mary's Hospital, London, in 1902. Known principally for his work on the parasitic diseases, and for his research on the protective power of blood against bacteria, he was an important influence on the work of his student Sir **Alexander Fleming**. He was knighted in 1906.

Wright, Benjamin 1770–1842
US civil engineer
Born in Wethersfield, Connecticut, he was trained as a lawyer and surveyor by his uncle, and became chief engineer on the construction between 1817 and 1825 of the Erie Canal, the first major engineering project in the USA, with a total length of 363 miles (580km). He went on to build the original St Lawrence Ship Canal and the Chesapeake and Ohio Canal between 1825 and 1831, then turned to railway engineering and was appointed chief engineer of the New York and Erie Railroad. His son Benjamin Hall Wright also became a civil engineer, and after his father's death completed several of the schemes on which he had been working.

Wright, Billy (William Ambrose) 1924–94
English footballer
He was born in Ironbridge, Shropshire. An industrious wing-half, latterly a central defender, he was the first player to win more than 100 caps for England (105, 90 as captain). His only senior club was Wolverhampton Wanderers, with whom he won one FA Cup medal and three League championships. He went into football managership with Arsenal, and later became a television sports executive.

Wright, Frances or Fanny, *also known as* Frances Darusmont 1795–1852
US reformer and abolitionist
Born in Dundee, Scotland, the heiress to a large fortune, she emigrated to the USA in 1818 and toured widely, publishing *Views of Society and Manners in America* in 1821. In the company of the reformer **Marie Joseph Lafayette** she founded a short-lived community for freed slaves at Nashoba in Western Tennessee. Settling in New York in 1829, she published with **Robert Dale Owen** a socialist journal, *Free Enquirer*. One of the early suffragettes, she campaigned vigorously against religion and for the emancipation of women.

Wright, Frank Lloyd 1867–1959
US architect
Born in Richland Center, Wisconsin, he studied civil engineering at Wisconsin University, but the collapse of a newly built wing of the Wisconsin State Capitol made him turn to architecture with a determination to apply engineering principles to architecture. After setting up in practice in Chicago, he became known for low-built prairie-style bungalows like Chicago's Robie House, but soon launched into more daring and controversial designs that exploited modern technology and cubist spatial concepts. He designed his own home, Taliesin, at Spring Green, Wisconsin (1911), and another home and school, Taliesin West, near Phoenix in Arizona (1938). His best-known public buildings include the earthquake-proof Imperial Hotel in Tokyo (1916–20), the 'Falling Water' weekend retreat at Mill Run, near Pittsburgh in Pennsylvania (1936), the Johnson Wax office block in

Racine, Wisconsin (1936), Florida Southern College (1940), and the Guggenheim Museum of Art in New York (1959), in which the exhibits line the walls of a continuous spiral ramp. He was an innovator in the field of open planning, also designed furniture and textiles and is considered one of the outstanding architects of the 20th century. He wrote an *Autobiography* (1932) and numerous other works. 🕮 Robert C Twombly, *Frank Lloyd Wright: His Life and His Architecture* (1979)

Wright, Georg Henrik von 1916–
Finnish philosopher and logician

Born in Helsinki, he associated with the Vienna Circle of logical positivists and worked closely with **Wittgenstein** in Cambridge (1948–51). He was Professor of Philosophy at Helsinki (1946–61) and held many visiting positions in US universities. He has made particular contributions to philosophical logic and to ethics in works such as *The Logical Problem of Induction* (1941), *Form and Content in Logic* (1941), *The Varieties of Goodness* (1971), *Norm and Action* (1971) and *Freedom and Determination* (1980).

Wright, John 1906–91
South African puppetmaster

Born in South Africa and trained at the School of Applied Art in Cape Town, he was ambitious to be a puppetmaster from an early age, and developed great skill in puppet design and woodcarving, often inspired by African culture. He moved to London and led a touring company from 1947 to 1954. In 1961, with his second wife Lyndie, he founded the Little Angel Theatre in Islington. His productions, with their classical scores and literary scripts, were so highly acclaimed that in 1985 he was invited to play in China, where puppetry is a major art form, and where he was welcomed as a great master of his art.

Wright, Joseph, nicknamed Wright of Derby 1734–97
English genre and portrait painter

He spent his whole life in his native town, except for a few years spent in London, Bath, and Italy. His fireside portrait groups often show unusual light effects. His industrial works include the depiction of experiments made by candlelight (eg *Experiment with the Air Pump*, 1768, London).

Wright, Joseph 1855–1930
English philologist

Born in Bradford, he worked in a wool mill as a boy, but became Professor of Comparative Philology at Oxford, editor of the *Dialect Dictionary*, and the author of many philological works.

Wright, Judith Arundel 1915–
Australian poet

Born in Armidale, New South Wales, she was brought up on a sheep farm, and educated at Sydney University. She travelled in Great Britain and Europe before returning to Sydney (1938–39) to concentrate on her writing. *The Moving Image* (1946) was her first collection, since when she has been an industrious poet, critic, anthologist, editor, and short-story writer. Her main volumes of poetry are *Woman to Man* (1949), *The Gateway* (1953), *The Two Fires* (1955), *Birds* (1962), *City Sunrise* (1964), *The Other Half* (1966), *Alive* (1973) and *Fourth Quarter and Other Poems* (1976). Her *Collected Poems 1942–1970* and *Collected Poems 1942–1987* were published in 1971 and 1994 respectively. *The Cry for the Dead* (1981) is about the impact of European immigration on the Aboriginals, and a collection of essays on Aboriginal culture, *Born of the Conquerors*, was published in 1991. She edited the Oxford anthology, *A Book of Australian Verse*, in 1956 and has written on Charles Harpur (1813–68) and **Henry Lawson**. In 1993 she became

the first Australian to receive the Queen's Medal for poetry. 🕮 A K Thompson, *Critical Essays on Judith Wright* (1968)

Wright, Mark Robinson 1854–1944
English educationist

He taught at High Grade School, Gateshead, before becoming principal of the Day Training College, Newcastle-upon-Tyne (1890). In 1894 he was appointed Professor of Normal Education at Durham University—the first to be appointed to a university chair of education in England—and Professor of Education from 1899 to 1920. He was founder editor of the *Training College Record*, later the *British Journal of Educational Psychology*, and instituted school journeys for teachers in training.

Wright, Orville 1871–1948 and Wilbur 1867–1912
US aviation pioneers

Orville was born in Dayton, Ohio, and Wilbur was born near Millville, Indiana. They operated a bicycle shop together and were self-taught inventors, becoming the first to fly in a heavier-than-air machine (17 December 1903), at Kitty Hawk, North Carolina. Encouraged by this, they patented their flying machine and formed an aircraft production company (1909). In 1915 Orville sold his interests in the business in order to devote himself to research. 🕮 F C Kelly, *The Wright Brothers* (1943)

Wright, Patience Lovell, née Lovell 1725–86
American sculptor

She was born in Bordentown, New Jersey, to a fanatical Quaker farmer. At the age of 20 she ran away to Philadelphia, and in 1748 married Joseph Wright. She began to model figures in clay and her portrait busts were an immediate success. She travelled to England in 1772 and settled in the West End of London near to **George III's** palace. She became known as 'The Promethean Modeller' and was eventually asked by the king to model his portrait. However, she proceeded to berate him for his policies towards the New World, remarks that resulted in her departure for Paris after the start of the Revolution. In Paris she modelled a portrait of **Benjamin Franklin**. She hoped to return to America and had arranged with **George Washington** to model his portrait but died, after a fall, in England.

Wright, Peter 1916–95
English intelligence officer

Born in Chesterfield, Derbyshire, he entered farming before joining the Admiralty's Research Laboratory during World War II. While working for MI5 (counter-intelligence) from 1955, he specialized in the invention of espionage devices and the detection of Soviet 'moles'. He retired from MI5 in 1976, bought a sheep ranch in Tasmania and wrote his autobiography, *Spycatcher* (1987). In it, he alleged that Sir Roger Hollis, the former director-general of MI5, had been a Soviet double-agent, the so-called 'Fifth Man', and that elements within MI5 had tried to overthrow the **Wilson** government during the mid-1960s. Attempts by the **Thatcher** government to suppress both the publication and the distribution of the book were unsuccessful.

Wright, (Philip) Quincy 1890–1970
US international lawyer

He was born in Medford, Massachusetts, and educated at Lombard College and the University of Illinois. A professor at Chicago, he was an adviser to the US State Department and the Nuremburg Tribunal (1945). He wrote *The Enforcement of International Law through Municipal Law in the U.S.* (1916), *The Causes of War and the Conditions of Peace* (1935), *A Study of War* (1942), *Problems of Stability and Progress in International Relations* (1954), *The Study of International Relations* (1955) and *The Role of International Law in the Prevention of War* (1961).

Wright, Richard Nathaniel 1908–60
US novelist, short-story writer and critic

Born on a plantation in Mississippi, the grandson of slaves, he was abandoned in an orphanage aged five, received a poor education, and was subjected to ill-treatment by his relatives and religious fanaticism. During the Depression he left the South and became a journalist, as well as joining the progressive Writers' Project. *Uncle Tom's Children*, a volume of short stories, appeared in 1938. By this time Wright had been manipulated by the Communist Party, consequently becoming a pessimistic humanist. A naturalist and later in Paris an existentialist who was acquainted with Jean-Paul Sartre, he wrote *Native Son* (1940), a novel about an African-American youth who murders a white woman and is sent to the electric chair. This became a central—albeit problematic—work in the development of a black literary sensibility. *Native Son* was followed by *Black Boy* (1945), a harrowing autobiographical novel, and the novel *The Outsider* (1953). ▢ A Gayle Jnr, *Richard Wright: Ordeal of a Native Son* (1980)

Wright (of Durley), Robert Alderson, Lord
1869–1964
English judge

Born in South Shields, Tyne and Wear, he was educated at Trinity College, Cambridge. A pupil of Thomas Scrutton, he developed a large practice in commercial cases and was appointed a judge in 1925. In 1932 he was promoted direct to be a Lord of Appeal, and fulfilled this role until 1947, excepting a period as Master of the Rolls (1935–37). He delivered notable judgements in many important cases and has been highly regarded as thoughtful and forward-looking. He helped to develop the concept of the duty on an employer to provide a safe system of working for his employees, and was also willing to allow the House of Lords to overrule its own previous judgements, a development not formally achieved until 1966. A liberal approach in constitutional cases was a distinguishing feature of his judicial career.

Wright, Sewall 1889–1988
US geneticist

Born in Melrose, Massachusetts, he was educated at Lombard College, the University of Illinois and Harvard. Following studies of breeding methods to improve livestock quality, he developed a mathematical description of evolution. He showed that within small isolated populations, certain genetic features may be lost if the few individuals possessing the genes do not pass the genes on to the next generation. This 'Sewall Wright effect' allows evolution to occur without the involvement of natural selection.

Wriothesley, Thomas See Southampton, 1st Earl of

Wu, Chien-Shiung 1912–97
US physicist

Born in Shanghai, China, she studied at the National Centre University in China, and from 1936 in the USA, at the University of California at Berkeley. From 1946 she was on the staff of Columbia University, New York, where she was appointed professor in 1957. In 1956 Wu and her colleagues tested Tsung-Dao Lee and Chen Ning Yang's hypothesis that parity is not conserved in weak decays, and they observed the emission of electrons preferentially in one direction, thus proving that parity was not conserved. This was later explained by the V–A theory of weak interactions proposed by Richard Feynman and Murray Gell-Mann.

Wu Cheng'en (Wu Ch'eng-en) 16th century
Chinese writer

Born in Shanyang, Huaian (now Jiangsu (Kiangsu) province), he was the author of the novel *Xiyouzhi* (1593, Eng trans *Monkey*, 1942), based on the pilgrimage of Xuan Zang. ▢ C T Hsia, *The Classic Chinese Novels* (1968)

Wulfila See Ulfilas

Wulfstan, St c.1009–1095
Anglo-Saxon prelate

Born in Long Itchington, near Warwick, he was educated at the Abbey of Peterborough. He became a monk, subsequently prior, at Worcester, and was appointed Bishop of Worcester in 1062. At the Norman Conquest of 1066 he made submission to William the Conqueror, and was the only Englishman left in his see. Later he supported William II, Rufus. He preached at Bristol against the slave trade practised by merchants there, putting an end to it. He helped to compile the *Domesday Book*, and may have written part of the *Anglo-Saxon Chronicle*. He was canonized in 1203, and his feast day is 19 January.

Wulfstan d.1023
Anglo-Saxon prelate and writer

He was Bishop of London (996–1002), Archbishop of York from 1002, and also Bishop of Worcester (1003–16). He was the author of homilies in the vernacular, including a celebrated address to the English, *Sermo Lupi ad Anglos*. ▢ K Jost, *Wulfstan Studien* (1950)

Wunderlich, Carl August 1815–77
German physician

He was born in Sulz-on-Neckar. Professor of Medicine at Leipzig, he was the first to introduce temperature charts into hospitals, contending that fever is a symptom and not a disease. His clinical thermometer was a foot (about 30cm) in length and took 20 minutes to register the temperature.

Wundt, Wilhelm Max 1832–1920
German physiologist and psychologist, founder of experimental psychology

Born in Neckarau, Baden, he studied at the University of Heidelberg and under Johannes Müller. In 1858 he became Wilhelm von Helmholtz's assistant at Heidelberg, and in 1875 became Professor of Physiology at Leipzig. He made studies of the nervous system and the senses, relations of physiology and psychology, logic and other subjects, seeking to understand the consciousness by means of its experiences. He published *Vorlesungen über die Menschen und Thierseele* (1863, 'Lectures on the Mind of Humans and Animals'), a book on ethics (1886), *Grundriss der Psychologie* (1896, 'Outlines of Psychology'), and *Völkerpsychologie* (10 vols, 1900–20, 'Ethnic Psychology').

Wurtz, Charles Adolph 1817–84
French chemist

Born in Strasburg, he studied medicine there, but worked with Justus von Liebig in Giessen on the chemistry of hypophosphorous acid. In 1844 he went to Paris and became assistant to Jean Baptiste André Dumas, whom he later succeeded as professor in the École de Médecine, and in 1857 he became professor at the Sorbonne. He was one of the founders of what later became the French Chemistry Society. Apart from his work on phosphorus acids, he is best known for his synthetic route to the larger alkanes and for the discovery of glycol (1,2-ethanediol). He wrote a number of successful textbooks.

Wu Zhao (Wu Chao) 625–705
Chinese concubine and empress

She was concubine to the emperors Tai Zong (T'ai Tsung) and Gao Zong (Kao Tsung) and rose to become the only female sovereign in the history of China, appointing herself empress after Gao Zong's death. She is said to have been responsible for the conquest of Korea (655–675). Subsequently she manipulated power by passing control of the empire between her sons Zhong Zong (Chung Tsung) and Rui Zong (Jui Tsung), although she eventually reclaimed the throne in 690.

Wyatt, James, *nicknamed* Wyatt the Destroyer
1746–1813
English architect

Born in Staffordshire, he was a contemporary of the Adam brothers and made his name with his neoclassical design for the London Pantheon (1772). In 1796 he succeeded Sir William Chambers as surveyor to the Board of Works, and carried out restorations at the medieval cathedrals of Durham, Hereford, Lichfield and Salisbury. His uncritical enthusiasm for rebuilding earned him his nickname. He is best known for the extravagant Gothic Revival country house he built for WilliamThomas Beckford at Fonthill Abbey in Wiltshire. One son, Matthew Cotes Wyatt (1777–1862), was a sculptor, and another, Benjamin Dean Wyatt (1775–1850), designed the Drury LaneTheatre (1811).

Wyatt, Sir Thomas 1503–42
English poet and courtier

Born in Allington, Kent, he studied at St John's College, Cambridge. He published nothing in his lifetime, but has served as an exemplar for English love poets. His best work is his lyrics and sonnets, and he was regarded as the most important of all the English poets who imitated—and then added to—Italian models. The best-known collection of his work was edited by Kenneth Muir (1949, rev edn 1963), who also wrote Wyatt's biography in *Life and Letters* (1963).

Wyatt, Sir Thomas, the Younger c.1520–1554
English soldier

Son of the poet Sir Thomas Wyatt, he fought at the Siege of Landrecies (1544), and continued in service on the Continent till 1550. In 1554, with Lady Jane Grey's father, he led the Kentish men to Southwark and, failing to capture Ludgate, was taken prisoner and executed.

Wycherley, William c.1640–1716
English dramatist

Born in Clive, near Shrewsbury, he was sent to France as a youth, left Queen's College, Oxford, without a degree, and entered the Middle Temple. His *Love in a Wood, or St James's Park*, a brisk comedy based on Charles Sedley's *Mulberry Garden*, was acted and well-received in 1671. The Duke of Buckingham gave him a commission in a regiment, Charles II made him a present of £500, and he served for a short time in the fleet. *The Gentleman Dancing-master* (1672), a clever farcical comedy of intrigue, was followed by *The Country Wife* (1675), Wycherley's coarsest but strongest play, and *The Plain Dealer* (1677), both based on plays by Molière. A little after 1679 Wycherley married the young widowed Countess of Drogheda. She died a few years later, leaving him all her fortune, a bequest which involved him in a lawsuit whereby he was reduced to poverty and cast into the Fleet prison for some years. James VII and II, having seen a representation of *The Plain Dealer*, paid his debts and gave him a pension of £200 a year. At 64 Wycherley made the acquaintance of Pope, then a youth of 16, to whom he entrusted the revision of a number of his verses, the result being a quarrel. Wycherley's money troubles continued to the end of his life. In literary brilliance William Congreve infinitely outshines him, but Wycherley is a far more dexterous playwright. ⌑ R A Zimbando, *Wycherley's Drama* (1965)

Wyckoff, Ralph Walter Graystone 1897–
US biophysicist

Born in Geneva, New York, he studied at Cornell University, gaining a PhD in chemistry. He worked as a physical chemist in the geophysics laboratory of the Carnegie Institute (1919–27) before moving to the subdivision of biophysics at the Rockefeller Institute (1927–38). After a spell in commercial laboratories he moved to the University of Michigan (1943–45) and then to the National Institute of Health until 1959, when he was appointed Professor of Physics and Microbiology at the University of Arizona (1959–81). Whilst at the Rockefeller, Wyckoff developed new techniques to help produce pure viruses, from which effective vaccines could be developed. In 1944, whilst working in epidemiology, he collaborated with Robley Williams in developing the metal shadowing method for providing three-dimensional imaging of viruses in the electron microscope, which has since been widely used. His other achievements include several studies of molecular structure, and investigations of how radiation affects cell structure.

Wycliffe, John, *also spelt* Wycliff, Wyclif, Wicliffe or Wiclif c.1329–1384
English religious reformer

He was born near Richmond, Yorkshire. He distinguished himself at Oxford, where he taught philosophy, was Master of Balliol College (1360), then assumed the college living of Fillingham, which he exchanged in 1368 for Ludgershall, Buckinghamshire. He became rector of Lutterworth (1374), and was sent (doubtless as a recognized opponent of papal intrusion) to Bruges to discuss ecclesiastical abuses with ambassadors from the pope. His strenuous activity gained him support among the nobles and the London citizenry. In 1376 he wrote *De Dominio Divino*, expounding the doctrine that all authority is founded in grace and that wicked rulers (whether secular or ecclesiastical) thereby forfeited their right to rule. His maintenance of a right in the secular power to control the clergy was offensive to the bishops, who summoned him before the archbishop in St Paul's in 1377. Pope Gregory XI banned him, and urged that he be imprisoned and made to answer before the archbishop and the pope. When at last proceedings were undertaken, at Lambeth in 1378, the prosecution had little effect upon Wycliffe's position. The whole fabric of the Church was in the same year shaken by the Great Schism and the election of an antipope. Wycliffe now began to attack the constitution of the Church, and declared it would be better without pope or prelates. He denied the priestly power of absolution, and the whole system of enforced confession, penances, and indulgence, and asserted the right of every man to examine the Bible for himself. He began to write in English instead of Latin, and by issuing popular tracts became a leading English prose writer. He organized a body of itinerant preachers, his 'poor priests', who spread his doctrines widely through the country, and began the first English translation of the Bible. His 1380 attack on the central dogma of transubstantiation was more dangerous. A convocation of doctors at Oxford condemned his theses. Archbishop Courtenay convoked a council (1382) and condemned Wycliffite opinions. His followers were arrested, and all compelled to recant, but for some unknown reason he himself was not judged. He withdrew from Oxford to Lutterworth, where he continued his incessant literary activity. His work in the next two years, uncompromising in tone, is prodigious and consistently powerful. The characteristic of his teaching was its insistence on inward religion in opposition to the formalism of the time. He attacked the established practices of the Church only so far as he thought they had degenerated into mere mechanical uses. The influence of his teaching was widespread in England, and, though persecution suppressed it, continued up to the Reformation. His supporters came to be derisively known as 'Lollards' (from a Dutch word meaning 'mumblers'). Jan Huss was avowedly his disciple, and there were Lollards or Wycliffites in Ayrshire down to the Reformation. Forty-five articles extracted from his writings were condemned as heretical by the Council of Constance (1414), which ordered his bones to be dug up and burned and cast into the River Swift—a sentence executed in 1428. 📖 H B Workman, *John Wyclif: A Study of the English Medieval Church* (2 vols, 1926)

Wyeth, Andrew Newell 1917–
US painter
Born in Chadds Ford, Pennsylvania, he studied under his father, the book illustrator N C Wyeth (1882–1945). His soberly realistic photographic pictures, usually executed with tempera and watercolour rather than oils, often focus on landscapes, as in *April Wind* (1952, Hartford, Connecticut), using off-centre compositions in order to give a sense of haunting unease, as in *Christina's World* (1948, Museum of Modern Art, New York City), perhaps the most famous US picture of the century.

Wykeham, William of See William of Wykeham

Wyler, William 1902–81
US film director
Born in Mülhausen, Germany (now Mulhouse, France), he was invited to the USA by his cousin Carl Laemmle, the head of Universal Pictures. He emigrated in 1922, and began in the publicity department there, graduated to assistant director and directed his first film, *Crook Buster*, in 1925. Over the next five years he made many westerns before undertaking more prestigious productions, usually involving star actors and noted literary sources. He became renowned for his obsessively meticulous approach to composition, performance and narrative structure, and his many films include *These Three* (1936), *Wuthering Heights* (1939), *The Little Foxes* (1941), *The Collector* (1965) and *Funny Girl* (1968). He served as a major in the US Army Air Corps (1942–45) and helped form the Committee to defend the First Amendment in 1947. He received Academy Awards for *Mrs. Miniver* (1942), *The Best Years of Our Lives* (1946) and *Ben Hur* (1959). He retired in 1972. 📖 Axel Madsen, *William Wyler* (1973)

Wylie, Elinor Hoyt, *née* Hoyt 1885–1928
US writer
She was born in Somerville, New Jersey. Her first volume of poetry, *Nets to Catch the Wind*, which won the Julia Elsworth Ford Prize in 1921, was followed by several more collections and by four highly individual novels, *Jennifer Lorn* (1923), *The Venetian Glass Nephew* (1925), *The Orphan Angel* (1927), about **Shelley**, and *Mr Hodge and Mr Hazard* (1928). The fiction is as fantastic and artificial as the poetry is terse, direct and positive. 📖 T A Gray, *Elinor Wylie* (1969)

Wyllie, George 1921–
Scottish sculptor
Born in Glasgow, he attended Bellahouston Academy and Allan Glen's School, Glasgow, and worked as an engineer until 1948 and then as a customs and excise officer until 1976, when he became a full-time artist. Using a wide variety of materials and techniques, from welded metal to mixed media in the creation of his 'scul?ture', he has developed a reputation as an artist with a common touch, shown in the full-scale *Straw Locomotive* (1987). Suspended from the Finnieston crane on the River Clyde, and eventually set alight, this made a dramatically visual comment on the decline of Glasgow's heavy industry. Other major works include his *Paper Boat*, a full-scale sea-going boat, modelled like a paper one and launched on the Clyde in 1989. It was then taken to London and, in 1990, to New York. Wyllie was awarded an honorary doctorate by Strathclyde University in 1990.

Wyman, Bill See Rolling Stones, The

Wyman, Jane, *originally* Sarah Jane Fulks 1914–
US actress
Born in St Joseph, Missouri, she was a child actress, and made her first breakthrough as a radio singer. It was not until her performance in the film *The Lost Weekend* (1945) that she was recognized as a serious actress of real talent. She was nominated for an Academy Award for *The Yearling* (1946), and won one for *Johnny Belinda* (1948), in which she played a deaf mute. She acted in many films, and starred in the television soap opera *Falcon Crest* in the 1980s. She was married to **Ronald Reagan** from 1940 to 1948.

Wyndham, Sir Charles, *originally* Charles Culverwell 1837–1919
English actor-manager
Born in Liverpool, he trained as a doctor before his first appearance on the stage in New York City in 1861. He left the stage temporarily to enlist in the Federal army as a surgeon during the Civil War, but returned to it in 1864. His London debut followed in 1866. Among his most successful roles were those of Charles Surface and David Garrick. In 1899 he built and managed Wyndham's Theatre, which opened with another successful revival of *David Garrick*.

Wyndham, John, *pseudonym of* John Wyndham Parkes Lucas Beynon Harris 1903–69
English science-fiction writer
He was born in Knowle, Warwickshire. As a child he was fascinated by the stories of **H G Wells**, and in the late 1920s began to write science-fiction tales for popular magazines, showing a much greater regard for literary style and moral and philosophical values than was common in this field. In 1951 he published his first novel, *The Day of the Triffids*, which describes the fortunes of the blinded survivors of a thermo-nuclear explosion who are threatened by the triffids, intelligent vegetable beings hostile to man. Here, as in his later novels, he is less concerned with the inventive, imaginative aspect of the 'logical fantasies' than with what happens to man's behaviour and moral values when faced with unforeseen and uncontrollable situations. His other novels are: *The Kraken Wakes* (1953, in the USA, *Out of the Deeps*), *The Chrysalids* (1955, in the USA, *Rebirth*), *The Midwych Cuckoos* (1957), *The Trouble With Lichen* (1960) and *Chocky* (1968). *Consider Her Ways* (1961) and *Seeds of Time* (1969) are collections of short stories.

Wynette, Tammy, *professional name of* Virginia Wynette Pugh 1942–
US country singer
She was born in Tupelo, Mississippi, and raised in Alabama. Nashville producer Billy Sherrill was instrumental in shaping her career. She married four times, the second of which was to singer **George Jones** in 1969. Their string of hit duets continued beyond their divorce in 1975, and the troubled marriage is often said to have added fuel to her most famous solo hits, 'D-I-V-O-R-C-E' (1970) and 'Stand By Your Man' (1971). Less earthy than **Loretta Lynn**, she has remained constant to her style, but had a surprise pop hit in 1992 with 'Justified and Ancient', a collaboration with the British techno-pop group KLF. In 1995, she and Jones released *One*, their first new album together since the late 1970s. 📖 *Stand By Your Man* (1980)

Wynkyn de Worde See Worde, Wynkyn de

Wynne-Edwards, Vero Copner 1906–97
English zoologist
Born in Leeds, he was educated at the University of Oxford and the Marine Biology Laboratory in Plymouth (1927–29), and taught at Bristol University (1929–30) and at McGill University, Montreal (1930–46). In Canada he researched avian biology on Baffin Island, in the Yukon Territory and at the Mackenzie River. He returned to Great Britain in 1946 and became Regius Professor of

Natural History at Aberdeen University (1946–74), where he was also Vice-Principal (1972–74). In 1962 he published *Animal Dispersion in Relation to Social Behaviour*, in which he argued that animal dispersal had evolved in order to control population density. He suggested that individuals of a species can reduce their birth rates so as to benefit the species as a whole, and proposed that groups which exhibited such unselfish behaviour would be at an advantage in competition with populations whose members bred without regard to population pressure. These ideas aroused considerable controversy, but were nevertheless instrumental in stimulating advances in sociobiology and behavioural ecology. He wrote *Evolution through Group Selection* in 1986. He served on the Red Deer Commission as vice-chairman (1959–68) and the Royal Commission on Environmental Pollution (1970–74), and was elected FRS in 1970.

Wyntoun, Andrew of c.1350–c.1420
Scottish chronicler
He was a canon regular of St Andrews, and in about 1395 became prior of the monastery of St Serf on Loch Leven. He wrote *The Orygynale Cronykil of Scotland*, written in rhyming couplets and especially valuable as a specimen of old Scots. It covers the period from the creation until 1406, and the first five of its nine books give a valuable, though fragmentary, outline of the geography and history of ancient and medieval Scotland.

Wyon
English family of seal-engravers
The founder of the dynasty was Thomas Wyon (1767–1830), who was appointed in Birmingham as general die-engraver, then moved to London and became chief engraver of the seals from 1816. His sons were Thomas Wyon, the Younger (1792–1817) and Benjamin Wyon (1802–58). Thomas, the Younger, became chief engraver at the royal mint at the age of 23, and is credited with designing the new silver coinage in 1816, the Waterloo medal and the prize medals for the Society of Arts. In 1831 Benjamin became chief engraver of seals to William IV, for whom he designed the great seal and a number of medals. Benjamin's son Joseph Shepherd Wyon (1836–73) studied at the Royal Academy, London succeeded his father as chief engraver of seals (1858), and designed many medals and the great seal of Canada. William Wyon (1795–1851) was the nephew of Thomas, the Elder. Born in Birmingham, he won the Society of Arts gold medal in 1813, moved to London and became chief engraver to the royal mint in 1828. He designed much of the new British and colonial coinage of George III and George IV. William's son Leonard Charles Wyon (1826–91) succeeded him as chief engraver in 1851 and designed contemporary coinage and military medals, including the Indian, South African and Albert medals.

Wyse, Henry Taylor 1870–1951
Scottish artist, potter, designer and author
Born in Glasgow, he studied at both Dundee and Glasgow Schools of Art, and in Paris at the Académie Julian and Académie Colarossi. He later lectured at Moray House Training College, Edinburgh, and established the Holyrood Pottery (c.1918), producing a range of wares with coloured leadless glazes. He exhibited regularly at the Royal Scottish Academy and the Royal Glasgow Institute and published many books, including *Modern Methods of Art Instruction* (1909) and *Memory and Imaginative Drawing* (1923). The Holyrood Pottery closed in 1927.

Wyspiański, Stanisław 1869–1907
Polish poet and painter
He was born in Kraków. A leader of the Polish Neo-Romantics, he executed window designs for the cathedral and the Franciscan Church at Kraków, as well as portraits and genre pictures. The loss of an arm meant he had to abandon art, so he took up poetry and drama, becoming considered as the father of modern Polish theatre. His plays, such as *Klatwa* (1899, 'The Malediction') and *Wesele* (1901, 'The Wedding') used themes from mythology and Polish history. 📖 S Kolbuszenski, *Stanisław Wyspianski* (1962)

Wyss, Johann Rudolf 1781–1830
Swiss writer
He was born in Bern. Professor of Philosophy at Bern from 1805, he was the author of the Swiss national anthem, 'Rufst du mein Vaterland' ('Call You My Fatherland'), and collected Swiss folk-tales. He is best known for his connection with *Der schweizerische Robinson* (4 vols, 1812–27, Eng trans *The Swiss Family Robinson*, 1814–28), which he completed and edited for his father, Johann David Wyss (1743–1818).

Wyszyński, Stefan 1901–81
Polish prelate and cardinal
Born in Zuzela, near Warsaw, he was educated at Włocławek seminary and Lublin Catholic University. He was professor at the Higher Seminary, Włocławek (1930–39), and founded the Catholic Workers university there (1935). During World War II he was associated with the resistance movement during the German occupation of Poland. In 1945 he became rector of Włocławek seminary, in 1946 Bishop of Lublin and in 1949 Archbishop of Warsaw and Gniezno and primate of Poland. He was made a cardinal in 1952. In 1953, following his indictment of the Communist campaign against the Church, he was suspended from his ecclesiastical functions and imprisoned. Freed after the 'bloodless revolution' of 1956, he agreed to a reconciliation between Church and State under the 'liberalizing' Gomułka regime, but relations became increasingly strained, culminating in the 1966 celebrations of 1,000 years of Christianity in Poland. A further attempt at co-existence was made after widespread strikes in 1970, but uneasiness remained. 📖 Peter K Raina, *Stefan: Kardynal Wyszyński Prymas Polski* (1988)

Wyther, George See Wither

Xanthippe 5th century BC
Wife of Socrates
The traditional description of her as a quarrelsome and shrewish wife made her name proverbial.

Xavier, St Francis See **Francis Xavier, St**

Xenakis, Iannis 1922–
French composer
Born of Greek parentage in Brala, Romania, he studied engineering in Athens and worked as an architect for Le Corbusier in Paris, then turned to

musical composition (1954) with *Metastasis* for orchestra. He developed a highly complex style which incorporated mathematical concepts of chance and probability (so-called *stochastic music*), as well as electronic techniques, in mainly instrumental and orchestral works. In 1991 he was made an Officer of the French Légion d'Honneur and Commander, L'Ordre des Arts et des Lettres.

Xenocrates c.395–314BC
Greek philosopher and scientist
Born in Chalcedon on the Bosphorus, he was a pupil of Plato and in 339BC succeeded **Speusippus** as head of the Academy which Plato had founded. He is recorded as travelling with **Aristotle** after Plato's death in 348BC to do research under the patronage of Hermeias, tyrant of Atarneus in north-west Asia Minor, and as joining some Athenian embassies on foreign diplomatic missions. He wrote prolifically on natural science, astronomy and philosophy, but only fragments of this output survive. He generally systematized and continued the Platonic tradition but seems to have had a particular devotion to threefold categories, perhaps reflecting a Pythagorean influence: philosophy is subdivided into logic, ethics and physics; reality is divided into the objects of sensation, belief and knowledge; he distinguished gods, men and demons; he also probably originated the classical distinction between mind, body and soul.

Xenophanes c.570–c.480BC
Greek philosopher, poet and religious thinker
Born in Colophon, Ionia, Asia Minor, where he probably lived until the Persian conquest of the region (546BC), he seems then to have lived a wandering life round the Mediterranean, perhaps settling in Sicily for a while and visiting Elea in southern Italy. He wrote poetry, fragments of which survive, and seems to have been an independent and original thinker, though later traditions tried to claim him as a member either of the Ionian or the Eleatic school. He attacked the anthropomorphism of popular religion and **Homeric** mythology (pointing out that each race credits the gods with their own physical characteristics, and that animals would do the same), posited by way of reaction a single deity who somehow energizes the world ('without toil he shakes all things by the thought of his mind'), and made some bold speculations about the successive inundations of the Earth based on the observation of fossils. His rather bizarre astronomical theories suggested that a new Sun rises each day and that there is a different Moon for each region or zone of the flat Earth, all the heavenly bodies having been created from clouds which were set on fire.

Xenophon c.435–c.354BC
Greek historian, essayist and soldier
He was born in Attica, the son of Gryllus, an Athenian knight, and disciple of **Socrates**. He was a skilled soldier and inspirational leader of his armies, and saw action in several campaigns, including the 401BC campaign with 10,000 Greek mercenaries under the Persian prince,

Cyrus, the Younger, before returning to Scillus, near Olympia. He went there in 391 with his wife Philesia and his two sons, Gryllus and Diodorus, and spent the next 20 years of his life there, writing his books and indulging in the pursuits of a country gentleman. But the break-up of Spartan ascendancy after the Battle of Leuctra (371) drove him from his retreat, when Elis reclaimed Scyllus. The Athenians, who had now joined the Spartans against Thebes, repealed the sentence of banishment against him, but he settled and died in Corinth. His writings give the impression of having been written with great singleness of purpose, modesty and love of truth. They may be distributed into four groups: (1) historical—the *Hellenica* (Eng trans *History of My Times*, 1966, the history of Greece for 49 years serving as a continuation of Thucydides), *Anabasis* (Eng trans *The March Upcountry*, 1947, the story of the expedition with Cyrus) and *Encomium of Agesilaus*; (2) technical and didactic—*De Praefectura Equestri* (on horsemanship), the *Hipparchicus* ('guide for a cavalry commander') and the *Cynegeticus* ('guide to hunting'); (3) politico-philosophical—*RespublicaLacedaemoniorum*('The Spartan Constitution'), *Cyropaedia* ('the education of Cyrus', rather a historical romance) and *The Revenues* (on Athenian finance); (4) ethico-philosophical—*Memorabilia Socratis* (sketches and dialogues illustrating the life and character of his master), *Symposium* (Eng trans 1970), *Oeconomicus* (Eng trans 1970), *Hieron* and *Apologia* (Eng trans *Socrates' Defence Before the Jury*, 1965). The *Respublica Atheniensium*, an anonymous work written about 415BC, is now known not to be by Xenophon. Xenophon's style and language are unaffected, simple and clear, without any attempt at ornamentation. 📖 F Delebrecque, *Essai sur la vie de Xenophon* (1957)

Xerxes I c.520–465BC
King of Persia
He succeeded his father, **Darius I** in 486BC. He subdued the rebellious Egyptians, then (484) marched on Greece with a vast army drawn from all parts of the empire, and a fleet furnished by the Phoenicians. A bridge consisting of a double line of boats was built across the Hellespont, and a canal cut through Mount Athos. His immense force reached Thermopylae, but was defeated by **Leonidas** (480). Xerxes then destroyed Athens, but was defeated in the naval battle of Salamis (480). He withdrew to the Hellespont, but his hopes of conquest died with the fall of his general, Mardonius, at Plataea (479). He then withdrew to Persia (Iran), where he added monuments to his capital at Persepolis. Xerxes, possibly the Ahasuerus of Ezra 4.6 and Esther 1–10, was later murdered by Artabanus. 📖 Peter Green, *Xerxes at Salamis* (1970)

X-et See **Erixson, Sven**

Xia Gui (Hsia Kuei) fl.1180–1230
Chinese artist
A pupil of Li Tang, he worked for the Song (Sung) dynasty court, and executed delicate, almost impressionistic landscapes.

Ximenes or **Jimenez de Cisneros, Francisco**
1436–1517
Spanish prelate and statesman
Born in Castile, he was educated at Alcala, Salamanca and Rome. Ordained in Rome, his papal nomination was refused by the Archbishop of Toledo and he was imprisoned for six years. On his release, he joined a Franciscan monastery, but soon became confessor to

Queen **Isabella of Castile.** Three years later he replaced the Archbishop of Toledo who had once incarcerated him, and on Isabella's death, and in the absence of her husband, **Ferdinand,** the Catholic, wielded great influence over the country's affairs. He introduced centralized monarchical authority and beneficial fiscal reforms, but was obsessed with persecuting the Moors. When Ferdinand died in 1516, Ximenes became regent but died travelling to meet his new emperor, **Charles V.** He was a generous patron of religion and learning and founded, out of his own private income, the University of Alcala de Henares. His writings include the scholarly Complutensian Polyglot Bible.

Xuan Zang (Hsüan Tsang) 602–64
Chinese Buddhist traveller

Born in Henan (Honan), he became a Buddhist monk in 620 and made a pilgrimage through China and India, travelling 40,000 miles in 16 years. His books graphically describe the Buddhist world of his time, and his travels form the basis for **Wu Cheng'en's** book *Monkey.*

Xu Beihong (Hsü Pei-hung) 1895–1953
Chinese artist

Born in Jiting Qiao, Yixing county, Jiangsu (Kiangsu) province, he was the son of a self-taught painter. Poverty and flooding caused father and son to take up the wandering life, painting and drawing. They returned to their own province when Xu was 17; he became an art teacher. He later attended art lectures at Minzhi University, and in 1917 went to Tokyo to study fine arts. On his return to Beijing (Peking) he became known for his own vigorous style of painting, and he was engaged as a tutor at the Beijing University for the Society of Painting Technique. From 1919 to 1927 he studied abroad, in Paris, Belgium, Italy and Switzerland, mastering the western style of drawing and oils, depicting especially figures, nudes, horses and portraits. He was professor in the art department of the Central University in Nanjing (Nanking) (1928–46) and president of the Art College of Beijing (1946–53). His home in Beijing has been turned into a museum of his works.

Yahya Khan, Agha Muhammad 1917–80
Pakistani soldier

Born in Chakwal town, in Jhelum district, he was the son of a Pathan police superintendent. He was educated at Punjab University and the Indian Military Academy, Dehra Dun, and fought with the British 8th Army during World War II and afterwards rose to become Chief of the Army General Staff (1957–62). He supported General **Ayub Khan**'s successful coup in 1958, became army Commander-in-Chief in 1966 and, in 1969, with popular unrest mounting, replaced Ayub Khan as military ruler. In 1980 he sanctioned the nation's first national elections based on universal suffrage, but his mishandling of the Bangladesh separatist issue led to civil war and the dismemberment of the republic in 1971. After defeat by India in the Bangladesh war, Yahya Khan resigned and was sentenced to five years' house arrest.

Yale, Elihu 1649–1721
English colonial administrator and benefactor

He was born in Boston, Massachusetts, of English parents. They returned to Great Britain in 1652, and he was educated in London. In 1672 he went to India in the service of the East India Company, becoming Governor of Madras in 1687. He lived in England from 1699, and donated money to a collegiate school established (1701) at Saybrook, Connecticut. The school later moved to New Haven, and in 1718 it took the name of Yale College in his honour. In 1887 the much-expanded institution became Yale University, the third oldest in the USA.

Yale, Linus 1821–68
US inventor and manufacturer

He was born in Salisbury, New York, and set up business as a locksmith in Shelburne Falls, Massachusetts. He invented various types of locks, including the small cylinder 'Yale locks', by which his name is known.

Yalow, Rosalyn, née Sussman 1921–
US biophysicist and Nobel Prize winner

Born in New York City, she was the first woman to graduate in physics from Hunter College, New York (1941). She studied further at the College of Engineering of the University of Illinois in 1945, taught physics at Hunter College until 1950, in 1947 becoming consultant to the Radioisotope Unit at the Bronx Veterans Administration (VA) Hospital. From 1950 she collaborated with Solomon Bersonto to research diabetes, in the process developing 'radioimmunoassay' (RIA), an ultrasensitive method of measuring concentrations of substances in the body. They suggested that in adult diabetics antibodies which inactivate injected insulin are formed. In 1977, for her work on RIA, Yalow shared the Nobel Prize for physiology or medicine with **Roger Guillemin** and **Andrew Schally**. Since 1969 she has been chief of the Radioimmunoassay Reference Laboratory and since 1973 director of the Solomon A Berson Research Laboratory of the VA Medical Centre. She was awarded the National Medal of Science in 1988.

Yamagata Aritomo 1838–1922
Japanese soldier and statesman

Born in Hagi, he was made commanding officer of the Kiheitai in 1863. He went on to become Vice-Minister of War (1871) and then Army Minister (1878), emphasizing loyalty to the Meiji Emperor. As Chief of Staff, he motivated the 1882 Imperial Rescript to Soldiers and Sailors and 1890 Imperial Rescript on Education. He was Home Minister (1883–89) and was Japan's first Prime Minister

(1889–91 and 1898–1900). His modernization of the military system led to Japanese victories in the Sino-Japanese War (1894–95) and Russo-Japanese War (1904–05), for which he was made Prince, or *Koshaku*, and the emergence of Japan as a significant force in world politics. From 1903 he alternated with Ito Hirobumi as president of the Privy Council until the latter's death (1909), when he became the dominant senior statesman. His interference in the marriage of the crown prince in 1921 led to his public censure and he died in disgrace the following year. 📖 Roger F Hackett, *Yamagata Aritomo in the Rise of Modern Japan, 1838–1922* (1971)

Yamamoto Isoroku, originally surnamed Takano 1884–1943
Japanese naval officer

Educated at the Naval Academy, Etajima, he was wounded in the Battle of Tsushima in the Russo-Japanese war (1904–05). He studied at Harvard (1917–19), served as a language officer (1919–21), and became naval attaché in Washington (1926–28). He became chief of the aviation department of the Japanese navy in 1935, and Vice-Navy Minister from 1936 to 1939. He was opposed to the Japanese entry into World War II. As admiral (1940) and Commander-in-Chief Combined Fleet (1939–43) he planned and directed the attack on Pearl Harbor in December 1941. His forces were defeated at the Battle of Midway (June 1942), and he was killed when his plane was shot down over the Solomon Islands.

Yamamoto, Yohji 1943–
Japanese fashion designer

He was born in Tokyo, studied law at Kaio University, then helped his mother with her dress shop. He started his own company in 1972 and his first collection was produced in 1976 in Tokyo. After some time in Paris he opened a new headquarters in London in 1987. He designs loose, functional clothes for men and women, which conceal rather than emphasize the body.

Yamani, Sheikh Ahmed Zaki 1930–
Saudi Arabian politician

Born in Cairo, Egypt, and educated at Cairo, New York and Harvard, he was a lawyer before entering politics. Yamani was Minister of Petroleum and Mineral Resources (1962–86), and an important and 'moderate' member of the Organization of Petroleum-Exporting Countries (OPEC). In 1986, he founded the Centre for Global Energy Studies.

Yamashita Tomoyuki 1885–1946
Japanese soldier

He commanded a division in China in 1939, and in 1942 commanded the forces which overran Singapore, and then took over the Philippines campaign, capturing Bataan and Corregidor. Still in charge when General **Douglas MacArthur** turned the tables in 1944–45, he was captured and hanged in Manila for atrocities perpetrated by his troops.

Yamashita, Yashiro 1957–
Japanese judo fighter

Born in Kyushu, he won nine consecutive Japanese titles (1977–85), the Olympic open class gold medal (1984), and four world titles (1979, 1981, 1983 at over 95kg, and 1981, open class). He retired in 1985 after 203 consecutive bouts without defeat from 1977. Since 1992 he has managed the Japanese national judo team.

Yeats, W(illiam) B(utler) 1865–1939
Irish poet and winner of the Nobel Prize for literature

W B Yeats was born in Sandymount, a Dublin suburb. His father was the artist John Butler Yeats (1839–1922). His mother came from Sligo, a wild and naturally beautiful county where Yeats spent much time as a child. When he was two the family moved to London, where he later attended the Godolphin School, Hammersmith (1871–81). In 1881 the family returned to Ireland and lived in Howth, near Dublin where Yeats attended the High School.

In 1884 he enrolled in the Metropolitan School of Art in Dublin, and his first lyrics were published in *The Dublin University Review* (1885). He was preoccupied with mysticism and the occult, and helped to found the Dublin Hermetic Society in 1885. He also pursued his interest in Irish mythology, the source from which so much of his poetry springs. In 1886 his first volume of verse, *Mosada: A Dramatic Poem*, was published.

He returned to London the following year with his family and contributed to anthologies of Irish poets and edited *Fairy and Folk Tales of the Irish Peasantry* (1888). He began to have poems accepted by English magazines, two American newspapers appointed him literary correspondent, and his circle of friends widened to include **William Morris**, **George Bernard Shaw**, **Oscar Wilde** and others. In 1889 he met and fell in love with the ardent Irish nationalist **Maud Gonne**, an event which he described as 'the troubling of my life'. Despite repeated offers from him (until 1903), she refused to marry him. Also in 1889 he published *The Wanderings of Oisin and Other Poems*, which was well reviewed and established him as a literary figure. However, he became increasingly homesick and returned to Ireland in 1891.

A year later he published *John Sherman* and *Dhoya* (1892), two stories on Celtic themes suggested by his father, and the play *The Countess Kathleen* (1892), a Celtic drama rich in imagery and inspired by Maud Gonne. He also became a founder-member of the Irish Literary Society. In 1893 he published *The Celtic Twilight*, a collection of stories and legends, whose title haunted him until his death and stalks his reputation with its connotation of romantic vagueness.

His drama *The Land of Heart's Desire* (1894), which tells of a young woman spirited away by a fairy child, began regular production in London in 1894. Meanwhile, Yeats met Olivia Shakespear, with whom he had an affair, and worked on his collected *Poems* (1895), which elevated him to the ranks of the major poets.

In 1896 he met Lady **Gregory**, the mistress of an estate at Coole in Galway, where he set and composed many of his finest poems. With her encouragement, he helped to found the Irish Literary Theatre in 1899, promoting playwrights such as **J M Synge** and contributing his own plays for performance (eg his most successful play, *Cathleen ni Houlihan* (1902), a propaganda play with Maud Gonne in the title role, which it is thought may have sparked the Easter Rising of 1916). This theatre became the Irish National Theatre, which opened the Abbey Theatre in Dublin in 1904, and Yeats remained actively involved in its promotion for the next decade.

cont

Yameogo, Maurice 1921–
Burkina Faso politician

Educated in Upper Volta (Burkina Faso), he was a civil servant and trade unionist before turning to politics and being elected to the Territorial Assembly in 1946. He was Vice-President of the Upper Volta section of the Confédération Français du Travailleurs Chrétiens and was active within the Rassemblement Démocratique Africaine (RDA). Founder of the Mouvement Démocratique Voltaique, he was Minister of Agriculture (1957–58), Minister of the Interior (1958) and President (1958–66), before being toppled by a military coup led by Lieutenant-Colonel Sangoule Lamizana (1966). He was imprisoned until 1970, when he went into exile in the Ivory Coast.

Yanaev, Gennady Ivanovich 1937–
Soviet lawyer and politician

Born near Gorky (now Nizhny Novgorod), he made his career in the Communist Party of the Soviet Union as a Komsomol official and union apparatchik. That he had some genuine popularity was proved in 1989, when he was elected by the unions to the congress of deputies. In 1990 his promotion was unbelievably fast: chairman of the trade unions, a politburo member, and Soviet Vice-President. In all these positions he attempted to steer a middle course between reform and reaction, but in 1991 opted for reaction. His leadership of the attempted coup was so disastrous as to suggest that neither his heart nor his mind was in it. He was arrested with the others from the 'junta'.

Yang, Chen Ning 1922–
US physicist and Nobel Prize winner

Born in Hofei, China, he was educated in Kuming, before gaining a scholarship to Chicago University in 1945 to work under **Edward Teller**. He became professor at the Institute for Advanced Studies, Princeton (1955–65), and from 1965 was director of the Institute for Theoretical Physics at New York State University, Stony Brook. In 1956 with **Tsung-Dao Lee** he concluded that the quantum property known as parity was unlikely to be conserved in weak interactions, confirmed later that year by a group of physicists headed by **Chien-Shiung Wu**. For this prediction, Lee and Yang were awarded the 1957 Nobel Prize for physics, and the **Einstein** Commemorative Award from Yeshiva University in the same year. Yang was later awarded the 1986 National Medal of Science.

Yang Shangkun (Yang Shang-k'un) 1907–98
Chinese politician

The son of a wealthy Sichuan (Szechwan) province landlord, he joined the Chinese Communist Party (CCP) in 1926 and studied in Moscow (1927–30). He took part in the Long March (1934–35) and the Liberation War (1937–49), and became an alternate member of the CCP's secretariat in 1956, but during the Cultural Revolution (1966–69) was purged for alleged 'revisionism'. He was subsequently rehabilitated in 1978 and in 1982 inducted into the CCP's politburo and military affairs commission. A year later he became a vice-chairman of the State Central Military Commission and in 1988 was elected State President, a position he held until 1993. He was viewed as a trusted supporter of **Deng Xiaoping**, and had strong personal ties with senior military leaders.

Yanofsky, Charles 1925–
US geneticist

Born in New York City, he studied at New York's City College and at Yale, and since 1961 has been Professor of Biology at Stanford University, working on gene mutations. He has shown that the sequence of bases in the genetic material DNA acts by determining the order of the amino acids which make up proteins, including the enzymes which control biochemical processes. In 1967 he showed how the amino acid sequence of certain proteins

---

Yeats, W(illiam) B(utler) *cont*

In 1903, after learning that Maud Gonne had married John MacBride, Yeats went to America. (MacBride was executed in the aftermath of the 1916 Rising, and Yeats remembered him and others in his famous poem, 'Easter 1916'.)

The Collected Works in Prose and Verse in eight volumes were published in 1906, and he worked on *The Player Queen* for the actress Mrs Patrick Campbell, premiered at the Abbey Theatre in 1919. His last attempt to write poetic drama using legends as a source appeared in *The Green Helmet and Other Poems* (1910) and in 1914 he published *Responsibilities*, which marked a tightening and simplifying of his poetic style.

In 1917 he married Georgie Hyde-Lees. Together they shared an interest in psychical research which, along with Georgie's 'automatic writing', influenced later work, including *The Wild Swans at Coole* (1919) and the prose *A Vision* (1925). *Michael Robartes and the Dancer* (1921) pre-empted the outbreak of the civil war and it was seven years before he published his next collection of poems.

During the intervening years he was engaged in playwriting, politics (he became a member of the Irish senate in 1922, on the foundation of the Irish Free State), and in 1923 was awarded the Nobel Prize for literature.

In 1928 he moved to Rapallo in Italy and in that year published *The Tower*, a dark vision of the future exquisitely expressed which, with the powerful collection *The Winding Stair* (1933), is generally regarded as his best poetic work. His controversially idiosyncratic anthology, *The Oxford Book of Modern Verse 1892–1935*, appeared in 1936.

Yeats was very much a grand literary and public figure, although his reputation was slightly tainted by his flirtation with fascism. He moved to Cap Martin, Alpes Maritimes, in 1938, where he died. His body was returned to Ireland in 1948 and buried in County Sligo. A titan of 20th-century literature, he wrote various volumes of autobiography which are collected in *Autobiographies* (1955).

📖 R F Foster, *W B Yeats: A Life—The Apprentice Mage* (vol1, 1997); J Kelly *The Collected Letters of W B Yeats* (vol 1, *1865–95*, 1986; vol 2, *1896–1900*, 1997; vol 3, *1901–04*, 1994); A N Jeffares, *W B Yeats: A New Biography* (1988); Richard Ellmann, *The Identity of Yeats* (1953, 2nd edn 1964) and *The Man and the Masks* (1949, reissued 1987); J B Hone, *W B Yeats 1865–1939* (rev edn, 1952).

> We know their dream; enough
> To know they dreamed and are dead;
> And what if excess of love
> Bewildered them till they died?
> I write it out in a verse—
> MacDonagh and MacBride
> And Connolly and Pearse
> Now and in time to be,
> Wherever green is worn,
> Are changed, changed utterly:
> A terrible beauty is born.
> ('Easter 1916', composed September 25, 1916)

---

corresponds to the genetic map of the gene, and he went on to describe how the production of the amino acid tryptophan is controlled by a process called attenuation (1977).

Yarmouth, Sophia von Walmoden, Countess of d.1765

German noblewoman

Already known to King George II in Hanover, she was taken to England as his mistress after Queen Caroline's death (1737), and was created a countess (1740).

Yates, Dornford, *pseudonym of* Cecil William Mercer 1885–1960

English novelist

He was born in London, educated at Harrow and Oxford, and was called to the Bar, before achieving great popularity with two entertaining series of novels, one of international adventure, including such titles as *Blind Corner* (1927), and one of primarily humorous banter, about the character Berry Pleydell and his rich, indolent circle, for instance *Berry and Co* (1920). A prolific author, he was a nephew of Anthony Hope, whose work may well have been an influence on his. 📖 A J Smithers, *Dornford Yates: a biography* (1985)

Yeager, Chuck (Charles Elwood) 1923–

US test pilot

Born in Myra, West Virginia, he was the first man to break the sound barrier. Enlisting in the air force in 1941, he graduated as a fighter pilot in 1943, and during combat missions he gained 12 victories. On 14 October 1947 he flew the Bell X-1 rocket research aircraft to a level speed of more than 670mph, thus 'breaking the sound barrier', and in the Bell X-1A he flew at more than twice the speed of sound (1953). He was commander of the US Air Force Aerospace Research Pilot School and commanded the 4th Fighter Bomber Wing.

Yeames, William Frederick 1835–1918

British historical and subject painter

Born in Taganrog, Russia, he studied in London, Florence and Rome. His best-known work is *When Did You Last See Your Father?*

Yeats, Jack B (John Butler) 1870–1957

Irish strip cartoonist and impressionist painter

Born in London, he was the son of the artist John Butler Yeats (1839–1922) and brother of W B Yeats. Educated in County Sligo, his first drawing was published in 1888. He sketched horses for *Paddock Life* magazine (1891), then drew joke cartoons for *Cassell's Saturday Journal*, among others (1892). In 1894 he created the first cartoon strip version of Sherlock Holmes, *Chubblock Homes*, for *Comic Cuts*, then many strips featuring horses (*Signor McCoy*, 1897) and show business. He wrote and illustrated children's books beginning with *James Flaunty* (1901), and drew many further strips until 1918, when he concentrated on painting, playwriting and writing.

Yeats, W B See panel p1990

Yeltsin, Boris Nikolayevich 1931–

Russian statesman

Born in Sverdlovsk (now Yekaterinburg) and educated at the same Urals Polytechnic as Nikolai Ryzhkov, he began his career in the construction industry. He joined the Communist Party of the Soviet Union (CPSU) in 1961 and was appointed First Secretary of the Sverdlovsk region in 1976. He was inducted into the CPSU's central committee (CC) in 1985 by Mikhail Gorbachev and briefly worked under the new Secretary for the Economy, Ryzhkov, before being appointed Moscow Party chief in 1985, replacing the disgraced Viktor Grishin. Yeltsin, a blunt-talking, hands-on reformer, rapidly set about renovating the corrupt 'Moscow machine' and was elected a candidate member of the CPSU politburo in 1986; in 1987, at a CC plenum, after he had bluntly criticized party conservatives for sabotaging political and economic reform (*perestroika*), he was downgraded to a lowly administrative post. No longer in the politburo, he returned to public attention in 1989 by being elected to the new Congress of USSR People's Deputies. In 1990 he was elected President of the Russian Federation. He played a high-profile part in the resistance against the failed attempt to depose Gorbachev as President. In 1996 he was re-elected in the first post-Soviet presidential elections; throughout his presidency he suffered recurring bouts of ill health, and underwent heart bypass surgery in the year of his re-election.

Yentob, Alan 1947–
English broadcaster and administrator

He was born in Manchester, the son of a Sephardic Jewish immigrant. He studied at the universities of Grenoble and Leeds, and worked at Bush House for the BBC World Service. He moved to television as an assistant director in arts, began making programmes, and became head of music and arts in 1985. In 1988 he became Controller of BBC2, in 1993 Controller of BBC1, and in 1997 Director of Television. He has been instrumental in re-evaluating the role of the BBC in the 1990s.

Yerkes, Charles Tyson 1837–1905
US railway financier

Born in Philadelphia, he made and lost several fortunes, and in 1899 was forced to sell out in Chicago after allegations of political chicanery. In London in 1900 he headed the consortium that built the London Underground. In 1892 he had presented the Yerkes Observatory to the University of Chicago.

Yersin, Alexandre Émile John 1863–1943
French bacteriologist

Born in Rougemont, Switzerland, and educated at the universities of Lausanne, Marburg and Paris, he performed research at the Pasteur Institute in Paris, working along with Émile Roux on diphtheria antitoxin. In Hong Kong in 1894 he discovered the plague bacillus at the same time as Shibasaburo Kitasato. He developed a serum against it, and founded two Pasteur Institutes in Indo-China, where he also introduced the rubber tree.

Yesenin, Sergei Aleksandrovich 1895–1925
Russian peasant poet

Born in the Ryazan district to a peasant family, he became well known when he began to associate with the Surikov circle of peasant-proletarian poets in Moscow. In his remarkable first collection, *Radunitsa* (1915, 'Memorial Service'), there had been nothing antipathetic to Bolshevism, but his second, *Goluben* (1918), and some subsequent ones, tried—fatally to their integrity—to come to terms with it. His greatest poetry was written after he had rejected Bolshevism, and had become an alcoholic and hooligan, wandering about Russia and elsewhere in a haze of riotous living which became legendary. In 1922 he married the dancer Isadora Duncan, with whom he was unable to exchange a word, as she knew no Russian and he knew no English. In his later collections such as *Moskva kabatskaya* (1924, 'Moscow Tavern') and *Rus sovetskaya* (1925, 'Soviet Russia'), his poetry took on new dimensions in its expression of his regrets for the death of his hopes for himself and for Russia. He hanged himself after writing a suicide note in his own blood. The Communists suppressed his work for many years after his death, but in the 1960s it was revived, with great success.
📖 F de Graff, *Sergei Esenin: A Biographical Sketch* (1966)

Yevonde, Madame, *also known as* Philonie Yevonde and Edith Plummer, *née* Yevonde Cumbers 1893–1975
English photographer

Born in London, she was educated privately and then at the Sorbonne in 1910. On her return to London she became a photographer's apprentice (1911–14) to Lallie Charles, the best-known female portraitist of the time. She set up her own photographic studio and after 1918 became a successful society and advertising photographer. She is noted for her early and effective use of colour and her costumed 'Goddesses' series of debutantes (1935). A major retrospective of her work was shown at the Royal Photographic Society of Great Britain in 1973. She is sometimes referred to as Edith Plummer, an incorrect appellation which arose due to a researcher's error.

Yevtushenko, Yevgeni Aleksandrovich 1933–
Russian poet

Born in Zima, Siberia, he moved to Moscow with his mother in 1944. His work attracted no great attention until the publication of *Trety Sneg* (1955, 'Third Snow'), *Shosse Entuziastov* (1956, 'Highway of the Enthusiasts') and *Obeshchaniye* (1957, 'The Promise') made him a spokesman for the young post-Stalin generation. His long poem *Stantsya Zima* ('Zima Junction') prompted criticism, as did *Babi Yar* (1962), which attacked anti-Semitism in Russia as well as Nazi Germany. Travel abroad inspired poems such as those published in *Vzmakh ruki* (1962, 'A Wave of the Hand'). In 1963 he published his *Avtobiografiya* (Eng trans *A Precocious Autobiography*, 1963). He publicly supported Aleksandr Solzhenitsyn on his arrest in 1974. His later work includes *Love Poems* (1977), *Ivanovskiye sitsy* (1976, Eng trans *Ivan the Terrible and Ivan the Fool*, 1979) and the novel *Yagodnye mesta* (1982, Eng trans *Wild Berries*, 1984). Shostakovich set five of his poems to music, including *Babi Yar*, as his Thirteenth Symphony. In 1995 he published an anthology of 20th-century Russian poetry entitled *Strofy veka* ('The Verses of the Century').

Yilmaz, Mesut 1947–
Turkish politician

Born in Istanbul, he was educated at the Faculty of Political Studies in Ankara, and in London and Germany. A businessman, he was elected deputy for Rize in 1983 and was Minister for Culture and Tourism (1986–87) and Foreign Affairs (1987–90). Prime Minister from June to November 1991, he took over the leadership of the Motherland Party (ANAP) from Yildirim Akbulut and was again Prime Minister in a coalition government with the True Path Party led by Tansu Çiller in 1996, until the coalition broke down.

Yi Xing (I Hsing) 682–727
Chinese inventor

He established a reputation as a holy man and became a Buddhist monk as well as having an influential role in the Chinese court where he assumed the role of seer. He devised a new calendar which was adopted in 724, and wrote several mathematical and astronomical treatises, which led him to experiment with new devices and instruments. His masterpiece was a water-driven celestial sphere, thought to be the first regulated by an escapement, the first to use concentric gears and shafts as part of the mechanism, and the first Chinese clock to strike the hours and half-hours. Sadly, it was in use for only a short time, the bronze and iron parts corroding rapidly, after which it was consigned to a museum.

Yoakam, Dwight 1956–
US country singer

Born in Pikeville, Kentucky, he studied drama in Ohio, and has acted both in stage plays and films. He took a proselytizing stance against the mundanity of early 1980s country music, and was established as a leading figure in the so-called 'new traditionalist' or 'new country' movement with the release of his debut album, *Guitars, Cadillacs, Etc, Etc* (1986), and its successor, *Hillbilly Deluxe* (1987). Both were defiant champions of the driving, hard-edged honky tonk sound which had disappeared from the sanitized Nashville scene. He backed up his music with a powerful stage act and great personal charisma, and has remained loyal to his quest in a succession of albums, including *This Time* (1992) and *Gone* (1995).

Yonai, Mitsumasa 1880–1948
Japanese naval officer and politician
Born of Samurai descent, he was educated at the Naval Academy, Etajima, then served in Russia (1915–17). He was commander of the Imperial fleet from 1936 to 1937. Navy Minister from 1937 to 1939 and from 1944 to 1945, he was briefly Prime Minister in 1940.

Yonge, Charles Maurice 1899–1986
English zoologist and marine biologist
Born in Wakefield, West Yorkshire, he studied history at Oxford and zoology at Edinburgh University, and carried out research in various other marine laboratories, where he studied the feeding behaviour and nutritional physiology of the oyster. He was leader of the Great Barrier Reef Expedition in 1928 which studied all aspects of the ecology and physiology of marine organisms. Yonge researched the role of the symbiotic zooanthellae, and edited the six volumes on the expedition's work. He was Professor of Zoology at Bristol (1933–44) then Glasgow (1944–70), and on retiral continued his research at Edinburgh. His major interest was in the bivalve molluscs, investigating their digestion, filter feeding, structure and function of the mantle cavity. He was elected FRS in 1946. His public services included membership of the Fisheries Advisory Committee (1936–56) and the Colonial Fisheries Advisory Committee (1949–60, chairman from 1955).

Yonge, Charlotte Mary 1823–1901
English novelist
Born in Otterbourne, Hampshire, she achieved great popular success with *The Heir of Redclyffe* (1853) and its successors, publishing some 120 volumes of fiction, High Church in tone. Part of the profits of her *Heir of Redclyffe* was devoted to fitting out the missionary schooner *Southern Cross* for Bishop **George Selwyn**, and the profits of the *Daisy Chain* (£2,000) she gave to build a missionary college in New Zealand. She also published historical works, a book on *Christian Names* (1863), a *Life of Bishop Patterson* (1873), and a sketch of *Hannah More* (1888). She edited the girls' magazine *Monthly Packet* from 1851 to 1890.
📖 Barbara Dennis, *Charlotte Yonge (1823–1901)* (1992)

York, Duke of
Royal British title
It is conferred upon the second son of the reigning British monarch. **Edward III**'s son, Edmund of Langley, founded the House of York that fought the Wars of the Roses. **Charles II**'s brother **James VII and II** bore the title until his accession (1685). **George I** conferred it on his brother Ernest Augustus, and **George III** on his second son, Frederick Augustus. **George V** bore the title until created Prince of Wales (1901), as did **George VI** prior to his accession on the abdication of **Edward VIII**.

York, Prince Andrew, Duke of, *in full* Andrew Albert Christian Edward 1960–
British prince
The second son of Queen **Elizabeth II**, and Prince Philip, Duke of **Edinburgh**, he was educated at Gordonstoun School, Scotland, Lakefield College, Ontario, and the Royal Naval College, Dartmouth. He was commissioned in the Royal Navy, qualifying as a helicopter pilot and serving in the Falklands War (1982). In 1986 he married Sarah Margaret Ferguson (see Duchess of **York**) and was

made Duke of York. They have two children: Princess Beatrice (1988–) and Princess Eugenie (1990–). They were divorced in 1996.

York, Richard, 3rd Duke of 1411–60
English nobleman, and claimant to the English throne
The father of **Edward IV, Richard III**, and George, Duke of **Clarence**, he loyally served the weak-minded **Henry VI** in Ireland and France, and was appointed Protector during his illnesses (1454–56), but was always in conflict with the king's wife, **Margaret of Anjou**, and her Lancastrian forces. In 1460 he marched on Westminster and claimed the Crown, was promised the succession and appointed Protector again, but was killed in a rising by Lancastrian forces at Wakefield.

York, Sarah, Duchess of, *nicknamed* **Fergie**, *née* Sarah Margaret Ferguson 1959–
British member of the Royal Family
She was born in London, the second daughter of Major Ronald Ferguson of the Life Guards, and was brought up at Sunninghill in Berkshire. Her parents were divorced and her mother later married an Argentinian polo-player. After a brief career in publishing, Sarah married Prince Andrew, Duke of **York**, in 1986. They had two daughters, Beatrice (1988–) and Eugenie (1990–). They were separated in 1992 amid intense press publicity about the marriage, and were divorced in 1996. Since then she has written books for children and her autobiography, *My Story* (1996), and has gained celebrity status in the USA.

York, Alvin Cullum, *known as* **Sergeant York** 1887–1964
US soldier
Born in Fentress County, Tennessee, he worked as a blacksmith and underwent a religious conversion at a revival meeting, which prompted him to apply for conscientious objector status in World War I. His petition was denied, and he was inducted into the army and sent to France, where he killed 25 Germans and captured 132 prisoners almost single-handedly at the Battle of the Argonne (1918). He was awarded the Congressional Medal of Honour and the Croix de Guerre and became the most popular US hero of World War I.

York, Susannah, *originally* **Susannah Yolande-Fletcher** 1941–
English actress
Born in London, she was brought up in Scotland and studied at RADA in London. She worked in repertory theatre and pantomime before becoming one of the quintessential faces of the 1960s, making her film debut in *Tunes of Glory* (1960). She followed this with more than 50 pictures, including *There Was a Crooked Man* (1960), *The Greengage Summer* (1961), *Tom Jones* (1963), *A Man for All Seasons* (1968), *The Killing of Sister George* (1968), *They Shoot Horses, Don't They?* (1969), *Oh! What a Lovely War* (1969) and *Just Ask for Diamond* (1988). She played the eponymous hero's mother in the *Superman* films of the 1980s, and has also written screenplays and children's stories. On television, she played Helen Dereham in *We'll Meet Again* (1982), Mrs Cratchit in *A Christmas Carol* (1984) and Rachel Ware in *Trainer* (1991–92). Her stage appearances include the title role in *Hedda Gabler* in New York (1981).

Yorke, Philip, 1st Earl of Hardwicke See Hardwicke, Philip Yorke, 1st Earl of

Yorkshire Ripper See Sutcliffe, Peter

Yoshida Shigeru 1878–1967
Japanese statesman
Born in Tokyo and educated at Tokyo Imperial University, he served as a diplomat in several capitals. He was Vice-Foreign Minister (1928–30), ambassador to Italy

(1930–32) and, after the army had blocked his appointment as Foreign Minister, ambassador in London (1936–38). As a fervent advocate of Japanese surrender, he was imprisoned (June 1945) for this view in the closing stages of World War II. He was released (September 1945) under the US occupation and was appointed Foreign Minister. After **Ichiro Hatoyama**'s removal by the US authorities from public office, he stepped into his shoes as leader of the Liberal Party. As Prime Minister (1946–47, 1949–54), he was instrumental in the socio-economic development of postwar Japan and in fostering relations with the West. In 1954, Hatoyama (who had been rehabilitated in 1951) forced him out of office and, when the Liberal Democratic Party was formed (1955), with Hatoyama as its leader, Yoshida withdrew from politics.

Yoshihito 1879–1926
Emperor of Japan
Born in Tokyo, the only son of Emperor **Mutsuhito**, he was proclaimed crown prince in 1889 and succeeded his father on the imperial throne in 1912. His 14-year reign saw the emergence of Japan as a great world power. Unlike his father, however, he took little part in active politics, for his mental health deteriorated (1921). In the last five years of his life, Crown Prince **Hirohito** was regent. Japanese custom accorded Yoshihito the posthumous courtesy title, Taisho Tenno.

Youlou, Abbe Fulbert 1917–72
Congo politician
Educated in Catholic seminaries and ordained a priest in 1946, he became Mayor of Brazzaville in 1957 and formed a moderate party to oppose the local socialists. He was elected to the territorial assembly in 1957 and was, in turn, Minister of Agriculture (1957–58), Prime Minister (1958–59) and President of the Congo Republic (1959–63), before being forced into exile in Spain as the result of popular opposition within the country.

Young, Andrew Jackson, Jnr 1932–
US clergyman, politician and civil rights leader
Born in New Orleans, he was educated at Howard University and Hartford Theological Seminary. Ordained a minister in 1955, he became a leading figure in the civil rights movement. He served as executive director of the Southern Christian Leadership Conference (1964–70) and in 1972 was elected to the US House of Representatives as a Democrat from Georgia. He represented the USA in the United Nations (1977–79) and later became Mayor of Atlanta (1982–89).

Young, Andrew John 1885–1971
Scottish poet and clergyman
Born in Elgin, Moray, and educated at the Royal High School, Edinburgh, and at New College, Edinburgh, he became a United Free Church minister in Temple, Midlothian, in 1912. During World War I he was attached to the YMCA in France. After the war he took charge of the English Presbyterian Church at Hove, Sussex. Later he joined the Anglican Church and became vicar of Stoneygate, Sussex (1941–59). His early verse—*Songs of Night* (1910), *Boaz and Ruth* (1920) and *Thirty-One Poems* (1922)—revealed an almost mystical belief in the sanctity of nature and the part it plays in Christian faith, later confirmed by *Winter Harvest* (1933), and *Collected Poems* (1936). He also wrote an account of the poetry, folklore and natural history of the British Isles in *The Poets and the Landscape* (4 vols, 1962).

Young, Arthur 1741–1820
English agriculturist and writer
Born in London, he spent most of his life on a small rented farm in Bradfield, Suffolk, where he carried out agricultural experiments. In 1793 he became secretary to the Board of Agriculture. He was one of the first to elevate agriculture to a science. His writings include *A Tour through the Southern Counties* (1768), *A Tour through the North of England* (1771), *The Farmer's Tour through the East of England* (1770–71), *Tour in Ireland* (1780), and 'Agricultural Surveys' of eight English counties, besides many papers in *The Annals of Agriculture*, which he helped to found and edited (1784–1809).

Young, Brigham 1801–77
US Mormon leader
Born in Whitingham, Vermont, he became a carpenter, painter and glazier in Mendon, New York. He first saw the *Book of Mormon* in 1830, and in 1832, converted by a brother of **Joseph Smith**, was baptized and began to preach near Mendon. He was made an elder in Kirtland, Ohio, and preached in Canada (1832–33). In 1835 he was appointed to the Quorum of the Twelve Apostles of the Mormon church, directed the settlement at Nauvoo, Illinois, and in 1844 succeeded Joseph Smith as president. When the Mormons were driven from Nauvoo, he led them to Utah (1847) where they founded Salt Lake City. In 1850 President **Fillmore** appointed Brigham Young Governor of Utah Territory, but the Mormon practice of polygamy caused growing concern, and in 1857 a new governor was sent with a force of US troops under **Albert Sidney Johnston** to suppress it. Young encouraged agriculture and manufacture, made roads and bridges, and carried through a contract for 100 miles of the Union Pacific Railroad. He died leaving $2,500,000 to 17 wives and 56 children. 📖 Leonard J Arrington, *Brigham Young: American Moses* (1985)

Young, Charles Mayne 1777–1856
English tragedian
Born in London, the son of a rascally and brutal surgeon, he was driven from home with his mother and two brothers. He worked for a while as a clerk before making his debut at Liverpool in 1798. In 1807 he appeared in London as Hamlet. He was a most original actor, considered to be second only to **Edmund Kean**, and retired with a fortune of £60,000 in 1832. In 1805 he had married a young actress, Julia Anne Grimani (1785–1806). Their son, Julian Charles Young (1806–73), was rector of Southwick in Sussex (1844–50) and then of Ilmington, Worcestershire. He published extracts from his journal in his entertaining *Memoir of Charles Mayne Young* (1871), and his *Last Leaves* was published posthumously (1875).

Young, Chic (Murat Bernard) 1901–73
US strip cartoonist
Born in Chicago, he studied art at the Chicago Institute and joined Newspaper Enterprise Association, creating his first strip, *Affairs of Jane*, in 1920. Pretty girls dominated his career: *Beautiful Bab* (1922), *Dumb Dora* (1925) and *Blondie* (1930), which became King Features' most widely syndicated strip, with the millionaire's daughter, Blondie Boopadoop, developing into a suburban housewife and mother of two. Twenty-eight films were based on the strip, as well as radio and television series.

Young, Cy, properly Denton True Young 1867–1955
US baseball pitcher
Born in Gilmore, Ohio, he recorded a total of 511 victories between 1890 and 1911, a record that remains unequalled. He is commemorated by the annual Cy Young award to the most successful pitcher in the US major leagues. In 1904 he pitched the first 'perfect game' in baseball, ie one in which no opposing batter reached first base either on a hit or on a walk.

Young (of Graffham), David Ivor Young, Baron 1932–
English Conservative politician and businessman

Educated at Christ's College, Finchley, and University College London, where he took a law degree, he qualified as a solicitor and became an executive with the large clothing and household goods company, Great Universal Stores (GUS), from 1956 to 1961. He continued to pursue a successful industrial career until his talents were recognized by Sir **Keith Joseph** and **Margaret Thatcher**, who persuaded him to become director of the Centre for Policy Studies, a right-wing 'think tank' (1979–82). He was Chairman of the Manpower Services Commission (MSC) (1981–84), then made a life peer and brought into the Thatcher Cabinet, initially as Minister without Portfolio, and then, from 1985, as Employment Secretary. He supplanted **Norman Tebbit** as Thatcher's closest adviser during the 1987 general election campaign but gradually lost influence. In 1989 he moved out of the political centre and returned to commerce. He was chairman of the International Council of Jewish Social and Welfare Services (1981–84) and since 1993 has been chairman of the Central Council for Jewish Community Services. He published *The Enterprise Years* in 1990.

Young, Douglas 1913–73
Scottish poet, scholar and dramatist

Born in Tayport, Fife, he spent his early childhood in India, and was educated at Merchiston Castle School, Edinburgh, St Andrews University, where he read classics, and New College, Oxford. He was a lecturer in Greek at Aberdeen until 1941. Joining the Scottish National Party, he was jailed for refusing war service except in an independent Scotland's army. His attitude split the Scottish National Party, of which he was controversially elected chairman in 1942. Following the war, he became a Labour parliamentary candidate. After teaching at University College, Dundee, and at St Andrews University, he was appointed Professor of Classics at McMaster University in Canada, and in 1970 Professor of Greek at the University of North Carolina. His three collections of verse are *Auntran Blads* (1943), *A Braird o' Thristles* (1947) and *Selected Poems* (1950). He is best known for *The Puddocks* (1957) and *The Burdies* (1959), translations into Lallans of **Aristophanes**' plays.

Young, Edward 1683–1765
English poet

Born in Upham rectory, near Winchester, he was educated at Winchester, and New College and Corpus Christi College, Oxford, and in 1708 he received a law fellowship of All Souls, Oxford. His first poetic work appeared in 1712, an *Epistle* to George Granville on being created Lord Lansdowne. In 1719 he produced a tragedy, *Busiris*, at Drury Lane; his second tragedy, *The Revenge*, was produced in 1721, and his third and last, *The Brothers*, in 1753. His satires, *The Love of Fame, the Universal Passion* (1725–28), brought financial reward as well as fame, and for *The Instalment* (1726), a poem addressed to Sir **Robert Walpole**, he received a pension of £200. In 1724 Young took orders, in 1727 he was appointed a royal chaplain and in 1730 he became rector of Welwyn. *The Complaint, or Night Thoughts on Life, Death and Immortality* (1742–45), usually known as *Night Thoughts*, and occasioned by his wife's death and other sorrows, has many lines which have passed into proverbial use. ▢ H C Shelby, *The Life and Letters of Edward Young* (1912)

Young, Francis Brett 1884–1954
English novelist

Born in Halesowen, Worcestershire, he became a physician, and spent a period as a ship's doctor, but achieved celebrity as the author of *Portrait of Clare* (1927), which won the James Tait Black Memorial Prize. From then on he wrote a succession of novels of leisurely charm, characterized by a deep love of his native country. Noteworthy titles are *My Brother Jonathan* (1928), *Far Forest* (1936), *A*

Man about the House (1942) and *Portrait of a Village* (1951). He also wrote short stories and poetry, including *Poems 1916–1918* (1919) and *The Island* (1944), a history of England told in historically appropriate verse forms.

Young, George Malcolm 1882–1959
English historical essayist

Born in Greenhithe, Kent, he won scholarships to St Paul's School and Balliol College, Oxford, winning a brief fellowship at All Souls College and tutorship at St John's College. He became secretary of the future University Grants Committee. He was joint secretary of the new Ministry of Reconstruction (1917), and accompanied **Arthur Henderson** of the War Cabinet on his journey to post-revolutionary Russia. Leaving the Civil Service in disillusionment, he published his first book, a biography of **Edward Gibbon** in 1932, and then edited the comprehensive *Early Victorian England* (2 vols, 1934), afterwards enlarging his own final essay into *Victorian England: Portrait of an Age* (1936). His *Charles I and Cromwell* (1935) was followed by a volume of essays and reviews entitled *Daylight and Champaign* (1937), with its sequels *Today and Yesterday* (1948) and *Last Essays* (1950).

Young, James 1822–83
Scottish industrialist

He was born in Glasgow, worked as a joiner with his father, and studied chemistry part-time at Anderson's College where he met **Lyon Playfair** and **David Livingstone**, both to be lifelong friends. He became assistant to his teacher **Thomas Graham** in 1832 and moved with him to University College London in 1837. He then turned to industry, working with **James Muspratt** at Newton-le-Willows and **Charles Tennant** in Manchester. In 1848 he set up a small oil refinery at Alfreton, Derbyshire, to exploit an oil seepage in a disused coal mine. Two years later he joined with Edward William Binney and Edward Meldrum to manufacture naphtha and lubricating oils from oil shale. Their plant at Bathgate, West Lothian, began producing paraffin oil and solid paraffin in 1856, following Young's discovery that low-temperature distillation of shale yields the maximum amount of these products. He was appointed president of Anderson's College in 1868, where he founded a chair of technical chemistry. He also helped to finance Livingstone's second and third expeditions, and after Livingstone's death paid for his servants to return to Great Britain. He was elected to the Royal Society of Edinburgh in 1873.

Young, Lester Willis, *known as* Prez 1909–59
US tenor saxophonist and occasional clarinettist

Born in Woodville, Mississippi, he first played alto saxophone in a family band, but changed to tenor saxophone in 1927 and worked with a succession of bands in the Mid-West, including Walter Page's Blue Devils and Eddie Barefield's Band. He joined the newly-formed **Count Basie** Orchestra in 1934 for a spell, rejoining it in 1936. The band's rise to national prominence in the late 1930s brought Young recognition as an innovative soloist, whose light tone and easy articulation marked a break from the baroque swing-style saxophone and inspired such modernists as **Charlie Parker** and Dexter Gordon. Around this time, Young accompanied singer **Billie Holiday** on several important recording sessions. After 1940, Young led small bands and freelanced, rejoining Basie in 1943 for a year. During the 1950s, his dependence on alcohol became marked, and his later performances diminished in creative power.

Young (of Dartington), Michael Young, Baron 1915–
British educationist, and a pioneer in the field of consumer protection

Trained as a sociologist and barrister, he was chairman and later president of the Consumers' Association (1965–), whose journal *Which?* introduced a new openness in the expression of consumer opinion. He also played a leading role in the development of 'distance learning' in the Third World and, via the National Extension College, within Great Britain. His publications include *The Rise of the Meritocracy* (1958), *Distance Teaching for the Third World* (1980), *Revolution from Within* (1983), *Your Head in Mine* (1994), a collection of poems, and *A Good Death* (1996, with L Cullen). He was created a life peer in 1978.

Young, Neil 1945–
Canadian singer and songwriter

Born in Toronto, he moved to Los Angeles, where he co-founded the influential country-rock group Buffalo Springfield, and later was part of a 'supergroup' with Dave Crosby, Stephen Stills and Graham Nash. His albums *After The Gold Rush* (1970) and *Harvest* (1972) were bestsellers, but he turned away from their commercial country-rock vein on denser, darker records in the rest of the decade. His distinctive guitar style influenced the punk and grunge movements (he recorded with Seattle band Pearl Jam in 1995), but he has continually shifted stylistic ground, taking in country, rhythm and blues, early rock and roll, and even electronic music, with varying degrees of irony. Unlike many of his contemporaries, he has retained his credibility with both critics and audiences into the mid-1990s. 📖 D Downing, *A Dreamer of Pictures* (1994)

Young, Sheila 1950–
US speed-skater and cyclist

Born in Birmingham, Michigan, she won her first two speed-skating titles, the US national outdoor competition and the North American outdoor championship, in 1970. In 1971 she defended both titles, and won the Amateur Bicycle League of America women's national sprint title. In 1976 she became the first American to win three gold medals at the Winter Olympics: gold in the 500 metres, silver in the 1,500 metres and bronze in the 1,000-metre speed-skating events. She was a founding member of the Women's Sports Foundation and has served on numerous boards, including the US Cycling Federation and the Special Olympics International. She was the US Olympic Committee's Sportswoman of the Year in 1981 and is in the International Women's Sports Hall of Fame.

Young, Thomas 1587–1655
Scottish Puritan theologian

Born in Perthshire, he studied at St Andrews, was John Milton's tutor until 1622, and afterwards held charges at Hamburg and in Essex. He was the chief author in 1641 of an anti-episcopal pamphlet, *Answer*, by 'Smectymnuus', a reply to Bishop Joseph Hall's Episcopacy. The name of the 'author' is compounded of the initials of Stephen Marshall, Edmund Calamy, Thomas Young, Matthew Newcomen and William Spurstow.

Young, Thomas 1773–1829
English physicist, physician and Egyptologist

Born in Milverton, Somerset, he studied medicine at the universities of London, Edinburgh, Göttingen and Cambridge, and became a physician in London in 1800, but devoted himself to scientific research. In 1801 he was appointed Professor of Natural Philosophy at the Royal Institution, was later appointed physician to St George's Hospital (1811), and held several public offices related to science and navigation. He was elected Fellow of the Royal Society (1794), and was involved in the Royal Society's affairs as Foreign Secretary and Member of Council. He became best known in the 19th century for his wave theory of light, and combined the wave theory of

Christiaan Huygens and Isaac Newton's theory of colours to explain the interference phenomenon produced by ruled gratings, thin plates, and the colours of the rainbow. He also did valuable work in insurance, haemodynamics and Egyptology, and made a fundamental contribution to the deciphering of the inscriptions on the Rosetta Stone. 📖 Alexander Wood, *Thomas Young, Natural Philosopher, 1773–1829* (1954)

Young, Whitney Moore, Jnr 1921–71
US civil rights leader

Born in Lincoln Ridge, Kentucky, he began his career as a social worker and university professor. As executive director of the National Urban League (1961–71), he sought to improve education, housing, and job opportunities for African-Americans in the inner city. In 1963 he developed a 'domestic Marshall Plan', much of which was incorporated into antipoverty legislation under President Lyndon B Johnson.

Younger (of Leckie), Sir George Younger, 1st Viscount 1851–1929
Scottish Conservative politician

Born in Alloa and educated at Edinburgh Academy and Edinburgh University, he left college at the age of 17 on his father's death to run the family brewery. Active in local government in Clackmannanshire, he was president of the Scottish Conservative and Unionist Association in 1904. MP for Ayr Burghs (1906–22), he was Chairman of the (British) Conservative Party organization (1916–23), and helped to run the 'Coupon' general election of 1918, ensuring the return of many Conservatives. In 1922 he was central in breaking up the Lloyd George coalition government and replacing it with the Conservative governments of Andrew Bonar Law and Stanley Baldwin. He was Treasurer of the Conservative Party (1923–29), and was created a peer in 1923. In the tradition of his uncle, William McEwan, he combined a career as a politician with that of a successful brewer.

Younger (of Prestwick), George Kenneth Hotson Younger, Baron 1931–
Scottish Conservative politician

Born in Winchester into a family with deep roots in Scottish Conservatism, and educated at Oxford, he became manager and director of the family brewing business. In 1963 he withdrew as candidate in the West Perth by-election to make way for the Prime Minister, Sir Alec Douglas-Home (later Baron Home of the Hirsel). He was MP for Ayr from 1964 to 1992. Scottish Conservative Whip (1965–67) and Chairman of the Scottish Conservative Party (1974–75), he was Junior Minister at the Scottish Office (1970–74), then Secretary of State for Scotland (1979–86). In this post he built up the Scottish Development Agency and attracted high-technology industry to Scotland to balance the collapse of traditional manufacturing sectors. He was Defence Secretary from 1986 to 1989 and since 1991 has been chairman of the Bank of Scotland Group. He was made a life peer in 1992.

Younghusband, Dame Eileen Louise 1902–81
English social work pioneer

Born in London, she studied at the London School of Economics, where she taught from 1929 to 1957. During World War II she worked for the National Association of Girls' Clubs, directed courses for the British Council for Social Welfare, and set up one of the first Citizens Advice Bureaux. Later she compiled reports on social work training and social work (1947, 1951) and was principal adviser to the National Institute for Social Work Training (1961–67). From this unrivalled perspective she wrote a history of *Social Work in Britain, 1950–75* (1978).

Younghusband, Sir Francis Edward 1863–1942
British explorer

Born in Murree, India, he explored Manchuria in 1886 and on the way back discovered the route from Kashgar into India via the Mustagh Pass. In 1902 he went on the expedition which opened up Tibet to the western world. A British resident in Kashmir (1906–09), he wrote much on India and Central Asia. He was deeply religious and founded the World Congress of Faiths in 1936. ▱ G Seaver, *Francis Younghusband* (1952)

Yourcenar, Marguerite, *pseudonym of* **Marguerite de Crayencour** 1903–87
French novelist and poet

Born in Brussels, Belgium, and educated at home in a wealthy and cultured household, she read Greek authors at the age of eight, and her first poems were privately printed in her teens. Her novels, many of them historical reconstructions, include *Les Mémoires d'Hadrien* (1941, Eng trans *Memoirs of Hadrian*, 1954) and *L'œuvre au noir* (1968, Eng trans *The Abyss*, 1976). She also wrote the long prose poem *Feux* (1939, Eng trans *Fires*, 1981) and an autobiography, *Souvenirs pieux* (1977, 'Pious Memories'). She emigrated to the USA in 1939, but was later given French citizenship by presidential decree, and in 1980 became the first woman writer to be elected to the Académie Française. ▱ Josayne Savigneau, *Marguerite Yourcenar: Inventing a Life* (1993)

Youville, St Marie Marguerite d', *née* **Dufrost de Lajemmerais** 1701–71
Canadian founder of the Sisters of Charity

She was born in Varennes, Quebec, and married François-Madeleine d'Youville in 1722. Widowed in 1730 after an unhappy marriage, she cleared her husband's debts and supported her two surviving sons by running a small shop. With three companions, and against much initial opposition from both family and local citizens, she founded the Sisters of Charity (Grey Nuns) in Montreal in 1737 to care for the poor. In due course her work was recognized and she was asked to restore the derelict Hôpital Général, which she did in 1749 and again after a fire in 1765. She was beatified in 1959 and canonized in 1990.

Youssef, Sidi Mohammed ben See **Sidi Mohammed ben Youssef**

Yrigoyen, Hipólito See **Irigoyen, Hipólito**

Ysaye, Eugene 1858–1931
Belgian violinist

Born in Brussels, he toured extensively in Europe and in the USA. First teacher of the violin at the Brussels Conservatory (1886–98), he composed violin concertos, sonatas, and chamber music. He was widely considered one of the most skilful performers of his time.

Yuan Shikai (Yüan Shih-k'ai) 1859–1916
Chinese politician and soldier

He was born in Henan (Honan) province. He served in the army and became imperial adviser, but remained neutral during the Boxer Rising (1898–1900), so that his army survived intact and he won the gratitude of the foreign powers. On the death of his patron, the Empress Dowager Cixi (1908), he was removed from influence, but recalled after the successful Chinese Revolution of 1911. He became the first President of the Republic (1912–16), Sun Yat-sen standing down for him, but lost support by procuring the murder of the parliamentary leader of the Guomindang (Kuomintang) and making war on them. He accepted Japan's Twenty-One Demands, and proclaimed himself Emperor (1915), but was forced to abdicate. The humiliation may have hastened his death.

Yukawa, Hideki, *originally* **Hideki Ogawi** 1907–81
Japanese physicist and Nobel Prize winner

Born in Tokyo, he was educated at Kyoto Imperial University and after graduating in 1929, he was appointed lecturer there. In 1933 he became a lecturer at Osaka Imperial University and received his doctorate there in 1938. The following year he returned to Kyoto as Professor of Theoretical Physics (1939–50) and he later became director of the Kyoto Research Institute for Fundamental Physics (1953–70). In 1935 he suggested that a strong short-range attractive interaction between neutrons and protons would overcome the electrical repulsion between protons. The existence of the intermediate particles which propagate the interaction was confirmed by Cecil Powell's discovery in 1947 of the p-meson or pion. Yukawa also predicted the capture of atomic electrons by the nucleus, which was soon observed. For his work on quantum theory and nuclear physics, he was awarded the Nobel Prize for physics in 1949, the first Japanese to be so honoured.

Yusuf bin Hassan, *also called* **Jeronimo Chingulia** fl.1526–31
Last Sheik of the Malindi dynasty of Mombasa

He was educated by the Portuguese in Goa, India, and was baptized a Christian as Dom Jeronimo Chingulia. Following his succession (1526) he took up arms (1531) against Portuguese domination. He was driven out of Mombasa (Kenya) and Portuguese rule was established.

Zaccaria, St Antonio Maria
1502–39
Italian religious
Born in Cremona, he studied medicine at the University of Padua until 1524. Ordained a priest in 1528, he founded the Barnabite preaching order (1530), and the Angelicals of St Paul order for women (1535). He was canonized in 1897, and his feast day is 5 July.

Zachariadis, Nikos 1903–73
Greek political leader
The son of a tobacco worker, he was one of the many Greeks who were forced to leave Anatolia in 1923 after the Graeco-Turkish War and who became Communists. He was Secretary-General of the Communist Party of Greece (KKE) from 1931 to 1941. Imprisoned during World War II in Dachau concentration camp, he lived to return home in 1945 to direct Communist opposition to the British-backed Greek government and resumed his post as Secretary-General of the KKE. Believing that the Communists would achieve their victory in the towns, he quickly came into conflict with **Markos Vafiadis**, who was based in the country, and succeeded Vafiadis as commander of the Democratic Army in 1949.

Zacharias, St d.752
Greek pope
Born in Calabria, Italy, of Greek parents, he was pope from 741 to 752, and recognized **Pepin III, the Short** as King of the Franks (752). His feast day is 15 March.

Zacharias, Basileios See **Zaharoff, Sir Basil**

Zadkiel, *pseudonym of* Richard James Morrison
1794–1874
English astrologer
After service in the Royal Navy (1806–29) he started a bestselling astrological almanac in 1831, *Zadkiel's Almanac*.

Zadkine, Ossip 1890–1967
French sculptor
He was born in Smolensk, Russia, studied in Sunderland and at the London Polytechnic, and settled in Paris in 1909. There, he developed an individual style, making effective use of the play of light on concave surfaces, as in *The Three Musicians* (1926), *Orpheus* (1948, carved from a treetrunk), and the war memorial in Rotterdam, entitled *The Destroyed City* (1952). There is a museum of his work in his studio in Paris.

Zaghlul, Saad c.1857–1927
Egyptian politician
He was born in Cairo. As a co-founder in 1918 of the nationalist Wafd Party, he was arrested by the British, but with the granting of limited independence in 1924 he was made Prime Minister for a brief term before being forced to resign, although he remained a strong background influence until his death.

Zaharias, Babe (Mildred Ella), *née* Didrikson
1914–56
US golfer and athlete
She was born in Port Arthur, Texas. She was in the All-American basketball team (1930–32), then turned to athletics and won two gold medals (javelin and 80m sprint) at the 1932 Olympics in Los Angeles. She also broke the world record in the high jump, but was disqualified for using the new Western Roll technique. Excelling also in swimming, tennis and rifle-shooting, she turned to golf in 1934, and after being briefly banned as an amateur for an unauthorized endorsement, she won the US National

Women's Amateur Championship in 1946 and the British Ladies' Amateur Championship in 1947. In 1948 she turned professional and and went on to win the US Women's Open three times (1948, 1950, 1954). She married George Zaharias in 1938.

Zaharoff, Sir Basil, *originally* Basileios Zacharias 1850–1936
French armaments magnate and financier
Born in Anatolia, Turkey, of Greek parents, he was educated in Istanbul and England. He entered the munitions industry in the 1880s and became a shadowy but influential figure in international politics and finance, amassing a huge fortune in arms deals, oil, shipping and banking. He became a French citizen in 1913, and was knighted by the British in 1918 for his services to the allies in World War I. He donated large sums of money to universities and other institutions. 📖 Anthony Allfrey, *Man of Arms: The Life and Legend of Sir Basil Zaharoff* (1989)

Zahir Shah, King Mohammed 1914–
King of Afghanistan
Educated in Kabul and Paris, he was Assistant Minister for National Defence and Education Minister before succeeding to the throne in 1933 after the assassination of his father Nadir Shah. His reign was characterized by a concern to preserve neutrality and promote gradual modernization. He became a constitutional monarch in 1964, but, in 1973, while in Italy receiving medical treatment, was overthrown in a republican coup led by his cousin, General Daud Khan, following a three-year famine. Since then he has lived in exile in Rome and remains a popular symbol of national unity for moderate Afghan opposition groups. He was stripped of his citizenship in 1978 after a Communist take-over, but it was later restored in 1991.

Zai Lun (Tsai Lun) c.50–118AD
Chinese inventor
According to Han history, he was a eunuch at the Han court. He invented (AD105) paper made from tree bark and rags.

Zakharov, Rostislav 1907–84
Russian dancer, choreographer, ballet director and teacher
Born in Astrakhan, he graduated from ballet school in the mid-1920s, and joined both the Kharkov and Kirov Ballets as a soloist and choreographer while continuing to study (until 1932) at the Leningrad (now St Petersburg) Theatre Institute. He was accepted into the Kirov Theatre, where he choreographed *The Fountain of Bakhchisaray*, a milestone in Soviet ballet because of the depth with which its characters were delineated. He was associated with the Bolshoi Ballet from 1936 until the mid-1950s, variously as artistic director, choreographer and tutor.

Zamenhof, Lazarus Ludwig 1859–1917
Polish oculist and philologist
He was born in Bialystok. He invented Esperanto ('One who hopes') as an international language to promote world peace. In 1893, a formal organization was established and annual conferences were held from 1905. Zamenhof translated many well-known works into Esperanto, such as the plays of **Shakespeare, Molière** and **Goethe**, and his *Fundamento de Esperanto* (Eng trans *Basis of Esperanto*, 1979) was published in 1905. 📖 Marjorie Boulton, *Zamenhof, Creator of Esperanto* (1960)

Zamyatin, Yevgeni Ivanovich 1884–1937
Russian writer

He was born in Lebedyan, Tambov Province, and his first published work was *Uyezdnoye* (1913, 'A Provincial Tale'). In 1914 he wrote a novella, *Na kulichkakh* ('At the World's End'), satirizing the life of army officers in a remote garrison town, and was tried but ultimately acquitted of 'maligning the officer corps'. A naval architect by training, he spent 18 months in Glasgow and the north of England during World War I, designing and supervising the building of ice-breakers for Russia. He returned to Russia, to St Petersburg, in 1917 and participated in various co-operative literary projects, but **Trotsky** branded him 'an internal émigré' and he was repeatedly attacked as 'a bourgeois intellectual'. Zamyatin refused to tailor his art to political dogma, and in 1920 wrote *My* (Eng trans *We*, 1924), a dystopian fantasy prophesying **Stalinism** and the failure of the Revolution to be revolutionary. Its influence on **Aldous Huxley**'s *Brave New World* (1932) is striking and it was read by **George Orwell** before he wrote *Nineteen Eighty-four* (1949). His best stories are contained in *The Dragon*, first published in English in 1966. With **Maxim Gorky**'s help he was allowed to leave Russia in 1931 and he settled for exile in Paris, where he died. ⊞ A Shore, *The Life and Works of Yevgeny Zamyatin* (1968)

Zanardelli, Giuseppe 1826–1903
Italian politician
He took part in the anti-Austrian uprisings in his native Brescia during the Revolutions of 1848–49 and supported the Piedmontese invasion of Lombardy in 1859. In 1860 he was elected to the new Italian parliament. Following the electoral victories of the left in 1876, he held a number of ministerial posts until finally becoming Prime Minister in 1901. A left-wing liberal, he was violently anticlerical and a supporter of divorce. He was also responsible for the reform of the penal code. As Prime Minister, he was particularly concerned with improving the economic conditions of the Mezzogiorno.

Zangi, *in full* 'Imad al-Din Zangi 1084–1146
Syrian ruler
The son of Aksundur (d.1094), a Turk in the service of the **Seljuks**, he was appointed Governor of Mosul by Sultan Mahmud II (1126). He created an independent principality in northern Syria, incorporating Aleppo, Hamah and Hims. The capture of Edessa from the Franks (1144) earned him the title *al-malik al-mansur* ('victorious king') from the 'Abbasid caliph and was the direct cause of the Second Crusade. He was murdered by a servant before he could fulfil his greatest goal, the capture of Damascus, and was succeeded by his son, Nur al-Din.

Zangwill, Israel 1864–1926
English writer
Born in London, he went to school in Plymouth and Bristol but was mainly self-taught, and graduated with honours at London University. After teaching, he became a journalist and was editor of the comic journal *Ariel*, in which he published the witty tales collected as *The Bachelors' Club* (1891) and *The Old Maids' Club* (1892). A leading Zionist, he wrote poems, plays and essays, and became widely known for his novels on Jewish themes, including *Children of the Ghetto* (1892) and *Ghetto Tragedies* (1894). Other works are *The Master* (1895), *Without Prejudice* (essays, 1896) and the plays *The Revolted Daughter* (1901), *The Melting Pot* (1908) and *We Moderns* (1925).

Zanuck, Darryl F(rancis) 1902–79
US film producer
Born in Wahoo, Nebraska, he became a script writer for Warner Brothers (1924) and co-founder of Twentieth-Century Pictures (1933), becoming vice-president of that company and, after its merger with Fox Films (1935), of Twentieth-Century Fox Films Corporation. Among his many successful films are *The Jazz Singer* (1927, the first

'talkie'), *Little Caesar* (1930), *The Grapes of Wrath* (1940), *How Green was my Valley?* (1941), *The Robe* (1953), *The Longest Day* (1962), *Those Magnificent Men and Their Flying Machines* (1965), and *The Sound of Music* (1965). He retired in 1971. ⊞ Leo Guild, *Zanuck, Hollywood's Last Tycoon* (1970)

Zapata, Emiliano 1879–1919
Mexican revolutionary
Born in Anencuilio, Morelos, the son of a mestizo peasant, he became a sharecropper and local peasant leader. After the onset of the Mexican Revolution, he occupied estates by force and mounted a programme for the return of land to the Indians in the areas he controlled. He initially supported **Francisco Madero**, and with a small force of men was largely responsible for toppling the dictatorship of **Porfirio Daz**. Along with **Pancho Villa**, he subsequently fought the **Carranza** government. Meanwhile, he continued to implement agrarian reforms in the southern area under his control, creating impartial commissions responsible for land distribution and setting up the Rural Loan Bank. He was eventually lured to his death at the Chinameca hacienda in Morelos.

Zapolya, Stephen d.1499
Hungarian soldier
He gained renown as a military leader under **Matthias I Hunyadi** by his defeat of the Turks and his conquest of Austria, of which he was made Governor (1485). He was the father of John Zapolya, King of Hungary from 1526.

Zapotocky, Antonin 1884–1957
Czechoslovak trade unionist and politician
A stonemason from Kladno, he was active in the socialist youth movement from 1900 and in the Socialist Party from 1907. In 1920 he was a major organizer of an unsuccessful general strike, and in 1921 helped found the Communist Party. Imprisoned during World War II, he emerged in 1945 to become the president of the revolutionary trade-union organization that played a key role in seizing power in 1948. He was appointed Prime Minister and succeeded to the presidency when **Klement Gottwald** died unexpectedly in 1953. His responsibility for the purges was probably less than Gottwald's, but despite the moderation of old age, he lost much of the opportunity to make amends.

Zappa, Frank (Francis Vincent) 1940–93
US rock guitarist, singer and composer
He was born in Baltimore into a family of Sicilian Greek origin, who moved to the west coast in 1949. He began his career as a drummer, then turned to guitar as his principal instrument. Zappa was a multifarious and highly unpredictable talent in rock music, and explored musical areas well beyond the genre's normal boundaries. He established his reputation as a major iconoclast with his group The Mothers of Invention from 1966, and continued to build a vast experimental musical edifice throughout his life, ranging from catchy pop to avant-garde composition, much of which was issued on his own record labels. Rykodisc undertook a massive reissue programme of his work in 1995. ⊞ N Slaven, *Electric Don Quixote* (1996)

Zaradusht See **Zoroaster**

Zarathustra See **Zoroaster**

Zaslavskaya, Tatyana Ivanova 1927–
Soviet economist and sociologist
She was born in Kiev and educated at Moscow University. In 1983 she wrote the 'Novosibirsk Memorandum', a criticism of the Soviet economic system which was one of the factors behind the change of policies in Russia in the late 1980s. She was a member of the Communist Party (1954–90), and has been a full member of the Russian (formerly Soviet) Academy of Sciences since 1981. She

was president of the Soviet Sociological Association of the USSR (1989-91), personal adviser to President **Mikhail Gorbachev** on economic and social matters and, as an academic, is developing the new discipline, economic sociology. Her publications include *The Second Socialist Revolution* (1991).

Zatopek, Emil 1922–
Czech athlete and middle-distance runner

He was born in Moravia, Czechoslovakia (Czech Republic). After many successes in Czechoslovak track events, he won the gold medal for the 10,000 metres at the 1948 Olympics in London. For the next six years, despite an astonishingly laboured style, he proved himself to be the greatest long-distance runner of his time, breaking 13 world records. In the 1952 Olympics in Helsinki he achieved a remarkable golden treble: he retained his gold medal in the 10,000 metres, and also won the 5,000 metres and the marathon. His wife and fellow athlete Dana Zatopkova also won an Olympic gold medal (for the javelin) in 1952.

Zavattini, Cesare 1902–89
Italian author and screenwriter

He was born in Luzzara Emilia. A student and journalist in Milan, he turned his hand to fiction with such novels as *Parliamo Tanto Di Me* (1931, 'Let's Talk a While About Me') before writing his first screenplay for *Daro Un Milione* (1935, 'I'll Give a Million'). His long association with director **Vittorio De Sica** began with *Teresa Venerdi* (1941). Together, they became central architects of the Italian neo-realist school of filmmaking that flourished in the immediate postwar period. His best-known screenplays were for the films *Sciuscia* (1946, 'Shoeshine'), *Ladri Di Biciclette* (1948, 'Bicycle Thieves'), *Umberto D* (1952) and *La Ciociara* (1961, 'Two Women'). He wrote his last film for De Sica, *Una Breve Vacanza* ('A Brief Vacation'), in 1973, and made his directorial debut with the surreal *La Verità-a-a-a-a-a* (1982, 'The Truth').

Zedillo Ponce de León, Ernesto 1951–
Mexican politician

Born in Mexico City, he studied at the National Polytechnic Institute and earned a PhD in economics at Yale (1981). He went to work for the Banco de Mexico and helped to devise a successful programme to manage Mexico's enormous foreign debt. A member of the Institutional Revolutionary Party (PRI), he served as Budget and Planning Minister under President Salinas from 1988, promoting the free trade agreement with the USA and Canada, and as Education Minister from 1992. In 1993 he resigned to manage the campaign of Luis Donaldo Colosio, Salinas's hand-picked successor, but with the assassination of Colosio in March 1994, Zedillo was chosen as the new candidate. Taking office as President of Mexico later that year, he promptly triggered an economic crisis by devaluing the peso. But he also proved unexpectedly sympathetic to democratic reforms, and he has overhauled the corrupt justice system, made the electoral process fairer and signed a peace pact (1996) with the Zapatista rebels.

Zeeland, Paul van 1893–1973
Belgian statesman

He studied law and political science at Louvain University, where he held a chair from 1928 to 1963. He first became a Cabinet Minister (as a Minister without Portfolio) in 1934, and in 1935–37 was Prime Minister and Minister of Foreign Affairs. Having spent World War II in England, he again became Minister of Foreign Affairs (1949–54), and was intensively involved in the moves towards European union during those years.

Zeeman, Sir (Erik) Christopher 1923–
English mathematician

Educated at Christ's Hospital and Cambridge, he was Professor of Mathematics at Warwick University (1964–88) and Principal of Hertford College, Oxford (1988–95). Early work developing topology and catastrophe theory produced many applications to physics, social sciences, and economics. He was knighted in 1991.

Zeeman, Pieter 1865–1943
Dutch physicist and Nobel Prize winner

Born in Zonnemaire, Zeeland, he was educated under **Hendrik Lorentz** at the University of Leyden, where he received his doctorate in 1893. He became a lecturer at Leyden in 1897, and in 1900 was appointed Professor of Physics at Amsterdam University. In 1896 he studied light sources in a magnetic field and deduced that the resultant broadening of spectral emission lines was due to the splitting of spectrum lines into two or three components. This phenomenon became known as the Zeeman effect. Zeeman also investigated the absorption and motion of electricity in fluids, magnetic fields on the solar surface, the **Doppler** effect and the effect of nuclear magnetic moments on spectral lines. In 1902 he shared with Lorentz the Nobel Prize for physics for the discovery and explanation of the Zeeman effect, and he was awarded the Rumford Medal of the Royal Society in 1922.

Zeffirelli, Franco 1923–
Italian stage, opera and film director

Born and educated in Florence, he began his career as an actor and theatre-set and costume designer (1945–51). His first opera production, *La Cenerentola* (1953) at La Scala, Milan, was followed by a brilliant series of productions in Italy and abroad, culminating in *Lucia di Lammermoor*, *Cavelleria Rusticana* and *I Pagliacci* at Covent Garden, London (1959) and an outstanding *Falstaff* at the New York Metropolitan Opera House (1964). His stage productions include *Romeo and Juliet* at the Old Vic, London (1960), universally acclaimed for its originality, modern relevance and realistic setting in a recognizable Verona, and *Who's Afraid of Virginia Woolf?* (Paris 1964, Milan 1965). He has also filmed lively and spectacular versions of *The Taming of the Shrew* (1966) and *Romeo and Juliet* (1968), and, in 1977, *Jesus of Nazareth* for television. He also produced film versions of the operas *La Traviata* (1983) and *Otello* (1986). Recent films include *Hamlet* (1990) and *Jane Eyre* (1996). Turning to politics, he was elected as member of the right-wing Forza Italia in 1994.

Zeiss, Carl 1816–88
German optician and industrialist

Born in Weimar, in 1846 he established the factory at Jena which became noted for the production of lenses, microscopes, field glasses, etc. His business was organized on a system whereby the workers had a share in the profits.

Zeldovich, Yakov Borisovich 1914–87
Soviet astrophysicist

Born in Minsk, he graduated from the University of Leningrad in 1931 and moved to the Soviet Academy of Sciences. In the late 1930s he concentrated on nuclear physics and uranium fission, and later he investigated the oxidation of nitrogen during an explosion, flame propagation and gas dynamics. In the 1950s he turned to cosmology, and studied the initial hydrogen-to-helium ratio and isotropy in the early universe. He also predicted the existence of black holes associated with X-ray-emitting binary stars. In 1972 he discovered how the energy carried by microwave background radiation increases as it passes through the intergalactic medium, an effect which has important cosmological applications and which can be used to estimate the Hubble constant, which measures the rate at which the universe expands.

Zemeckis, Robert 1952–
US film director

Born in Chicago, Illinois, he studied film at the University of Southern California and won a Best Student Film Oscar with *Field Of Honor* (c.1973). He became an editor of television news and commercials, and his talent was spotted by **Steven Spielberg**, who was executive producer on Zemeckis's directorial debut, *I Wanna Hold Your Hand* (1978). He followed this with the brash comedy *Used Cars* (1980) and the sweeping high adventure *Romancing The Stone* (1984). His later films *Back To The Future* (1985), its two sequels, and *Who Framed Roger Rabbit* (1988) showed him to be a master of popular entertainment. He won a Best Director Academy Award for *Forrest Gump* (1994) and subsequently directed *Contact* (1997).

Zemlinsky, Alexander von 1871–1942
Austrian composer and conductor

Born in Vienna of Jewish Polish parents, he became the friend, mentor and brother-in-law of **Arnold Schoenberg**. He was kapellmeister in Vienna (1906–11), opera conductor of the Deutsches Landestheater in Prague (1911–27) and conductor of the Kroll Opera in Berlin (1927–32). His works, in post-Romantic style, include seven complete and six incomplete operas, orchestral works including his *Lyric Symphony* (1923, settings of **Rabindranath Tagore**), and chamber music including four string quartets, choral works and songs. In 1938 he emigrated to the USA, where he died.

Zeno c.440–491AD
Byzantine emperor

An Isaurian noble, he married (AD466) Ariadne, daughter of Leo I, and became sole ruler (474) on the death of their son, Leo II. He tried to achieve a reconciliation between the orthodox and monophysite churches of the east, but his doctrinal compromise, the *Henotikon*, merely antagonized both parties and caused a schism with the Roman Church.

Zeno of Citium c.334–c.265BC
Greek philosopher, the founder of Stoicism

He was born in Citium, Cyprus, went to Athens as a young man (c.315BC) and attended **Plato**'s Academy and other schools there. He then set up his own school (c.300) in the *Stoa poikile* ('painted porch'), which gave the Stoics their name. He had a formative role in the development of Stoicism as a distinctive and coherent philosophy. None of his many treatises survive, but his main contribution seems to have been in the area of ethics, which was in any case always central to the Stoic system. He supposedly committed suicide.

Zeno of Elea c.490–c.420BC
Greek philosopher and mathematician

He was a native of Elea, a Greek colony in southern Italy, where he lived all or most of his life, and was a disciple of Parmenides of Elea. In defence of his monistic philosophy against the Pythagoreans he devised his famous paradoxes which purported to show the impossibility of motion and of spatial division, by showing that space and time could be neither continuous nor discrete. The paradoxes are: 'Achilles and the Tortoise', 'The Flying Arrow', 'The Stadium' and 'The Moving Rows'. **Aristotle** attempted a refutation but they were revived as raising serious philosophical issues by **Lewis Carroll** and by **Bertrand Russell**.

Zeno of Sidon 1st century BC
Greek philosopher

Born in Sidon, Phoenicia, he was head of the Epicurean School at Athens and a contemporary of **Cicero**.

Zenobia 3rd century AD
Queen of Palmyra

Probably of Arab descent, she married the Bedouin Odaenathus, lord of the city, who was recognized by **Gallienus** as governor of the East (AD264). On her husband's murder (c.267) she conquered Egypt (269) and much of Asia Minor (270), declaring her son the eastern emperor. **Aurelian** defeated her in battle, besieged Palmyra, and captured her in 272, taking her to Rome. She blamed the war on her secretary, **Longinus**; he was beheaded and Palmyra destroyed. Zenobia married a Roman senator, and was presented with large possessions near Tivoli, where, with her two sons, she passed the rest of her life in comfort and splendour. Strikingly beautiful, she governed with prudence, justice, and liberality.

Zephaniah 7th century BC
Old Testament prophet

He made his prophecies during the reign of King Josiah of Judah. His account of a coming Day of Wrath inspired the medieval Latin hymn *Dies Irae*.

Zeppelin, Count Ferdinand von 1838–1917
German army officer

Born in Constance, Baden, he served in the American Civil War (1861–65) in the Union Army, and in the Franco-Prussian War (1870–71). From 1897 to 1900 he constructed his first airship (a dirigible balloon of rigid type) named a 'zeppelin', which first flew on 2 July 1900. Zeppelin set up a works for their construction at Friedrichshafen. ⬚Thomas E Guttery, *An Illustrated Life of Count Ferdinand von Zeppelin 1838–1917* (1973)

Zermelo, Ernst Friedrich Ferdinand 1871–1953
German mathematician

Born in Berlin, he studied mathematics, physics and philosophy at the universities of Berlin, Halle and Freiburg, and was professor at the universities of Göttingen (1905–10) and Zurich (1910–16). From 1926 to 1935 he was an honorary professor at Freiburg im Breisgau. Although he worked in physics and the calculus of variations among other subjects, he is now best remembered for his work in set theory. Following **Georg Cantor**'s pioneering work, Zermelo gave the first obvious description of set theory in 1908 which, though later modified to avoid the paradoxes discovered by **Bertrand Russell** and others, remains one of the standard methods of elucidating the theory. He also first revealed the importance of choice being self-evident, when he proved in 1904 that any set could be well-ordered, a key result in many mathematical applications of set theory.

Zernike, Frits 1888–1966
Dutch physicist and Nobel Prize winner

Born in Amsterdam, he was educated at Amsterdam University and became Professor of Physics at the University of Groningen (1910–58). He developed (from 1935) the phase-contrast technique for the microscopic examination of transparent—frequently biological—objects. For this work he was awarded the Nobel Prize for physics in 1953. He also invented the 'coherent background' technique to detect phase variations in interference and diffraction patterns, and made important pioneering contributions to the understanding of optical coherence.

Zeromski, Stefan 1864–1925
Polish novelist

He was born in Strawczyn, and worked as a tutor and a librarian. His early poems were published under the pseudonym 'Zych', to avoid political censorship. He wrote *Ludzie Bezdomni* (1900, 'The Homeless'), *Popioły* (1904, Eng trans *Ashes*, 1928), an epic tale of life during the Napoleonic Wars, *Wierna rzeka* (1912, Eng trans *The Faithful River*, 1943), about the 1883 national uprising, *Walka z*

Szatanem (trilogy, 1916–18, 'The Fight with Satan'), and other books, pessimistic, patriotic, and lyrical in tone. 📖 J Kadziak, *Stefan Zeromski* (1964)

Zetkin, Clara, *née* Eissner 1857–1933
German Communist leader

Born in Wiederau, she studied at Leipzig Teacher's College for Women, becoming a socialist and feminist. She was a member of the Social Democratic Party from 1881 to 1917, when she helped to found the radical Independent Social Democratic Party (the Spartacus League). She also edited a socialist magazine for women, *Die Gleichheit* ('Equality') from 1892 to 1917. Also a founder of the German Communist Party (1919), she was a strong supporter of the Russian Revolution and a friend of Lenin, and spent several years in the USSR.

Zetterling, Mai 1925–94
Swedish actress and director

Born in Vasteras, Sweden, she made both her stage and screen debuts at the age of 16, and went on to become a highly successful actress. Her first major role was in the influential Swedish film *Hets* (1944; USA *Torment*, UK *Frenzy*). She played in many British and US films, before turning her attention to directing with her debut film, the award-winning documentary *The War Game* (1963), which she co-wrote with her husband David Hughes. She directed a number of feature films in Sweden and also wrote novels.

Zeuss, Johann Kaspar 1806–56
German philologist

Born in Vogtendorf in Bavaria, he became a professor of history, and was the founder of Celtic philology. His *Grammatica Celtica* (1853; 2nd edn by Ebel, 1868–71) has been called one of the great philological achievements of the century. He also wrote a number of historical works.

Zeuxis 5th century BC
Greek painter

Born in Heraclea, Italy, he excelled in the representation of natural objects. According to legend his painting of a bunch of grapes was so realistic that birds tried to eat the fruit.

Zhao Ziyang (Chao Tzu-yang) 1918–
Chinese statesman

The son of a wealthy Henan (Honan) province landlord, he joined the Communist Youth League in 1932 and worked underground as a Chinese Communist Party (CCP) official during the Liberation War (1937–49). He then rose to prominence implementing land reform in Guangdong (Kwangtung) (1951–62), becoming the province's CCP First Secretary in 1964. As a supporter of the reforms of Liu Shaoqi, he was dismissed during the 1966–69 Cultural Revolution, paraded through Guangzhou (Canton) in a dunce's cap and sent to Nei Menggu (Inner Mongolia). However, enjoying the support of Zhou Enlai, he was rehabilitated in 1973 and appointed the Party First Secretary of China's largest province, Sichuan (Szechwan), in 1975. Here he introduced radical and successful market-orientated rural reforms, which attracted the eye of Deng Xiaoping, leading to his induction into the CCP politburo as a full member in 1979 and his appointment as Prime Minister a year later. As premier he oversaw the implementation of a radical new 'market socialist' and 'open door' economic programme, and in 1987 replaced the disgraced Hu Yaobang as CCP General-Secretary, relinquishing his position as premier. However, in 1989, like his predecessor, he was controversially dismissed for his allegedly over-liberal handling of student pro-democracy demonstrations in Beijing (Peking), and placed under house arrest for five months.

Zhivkov, Todor 1911–98
Bulgarian statesman

Born and educated in Sofia, he became a printer and joined the (illegal) Communist Party in 1932. He fought with the Bulgarian Resistance in 1943 and took part in the Sofia coup d'état that overthrew the pro-German regime in 1944. He became First Secretary of the Bulgarian Communist Party in 1954, Prime Minister in 1962 and, as Chairman of the Council of State in 1971, became effectively the President of the People's Republic. His period in office was characterized by loyalty to the USSR and conservatism in policy-making, which led to economic problems in the 1980s. He was ousted in 1989 by the reformist Petar Mladenov in a committee-room coup and, with his health failing, was subsequently expelled from the BCP and placed under house arrest, pending trial on charges of nepotism, corruption, and the dictatorial abuse of power. In 1992 his seven-year prison sentence was commuted to detention under house arrest.

Zhou Enlai (Chou En-lai) 1898–1975
Chinese statesman

Born into a declining mandarin gentry family in Jiangsu (Kiangsu) province near Shanghai, he was educated at an American missionary college in Tianjin (Tientsin) and studied up to degree level in Japan (1917–18) and Paris (1920–24), where he became a founder member of the overseas branch of the Chinese Communist Party (CCP). He married Deng Yingchao (Teng Ying-ch'ao) (b.1903) in 1924 and was an adherent to the Moscow line of urban-based revolution in China, organizing communist cells in Shanghai and an abortive uprising in Nanchang in 1927. He served as head of the political department of the Whampoa Military Academy in Canton. In 1935, at the Zunyi conference, Zhou supported the election of Mao Zedong as CCP leader and remained a loyal ally during the next 40 years. Between 1937 and 1946 he served as a liaison officer between the CCP and Chiang Kai-shek's Nationalist government. In 1949 he became Prime Minister, an office he held until his death, also serving as Foreign Minister between 1949 and 1958. Zhou, standing intermediate between the opposing camps of Liu Shaoqi and Mao Zedong, served as a moderating influence, restoring orderly progress after the Great Leap Forward (1958–60) and the Cultural Revolution (1966–69). He was the architect of the 'Four Modernizations' programme in 1975 and played a key role in foreign affairs. He sought to foster Third World unity at the Bandung Conference of 1955, averted an outright border confrontation with the USSR by negotiation with Aleksei Kosygin in 1969 and was the principal advocate of détente with the USA during the early 1970s. 📖 Kai-yu Hsu, *Chou En-lai: China's Gray Eminence* (1968)

Zhu Da (Chu Ta), *also called* Ba Da Shan Ren (Pa Ta Shan Jen) 1626–1705
Chinese painter of the Chan (Zen) School

Born in Nanchang, Jiangxi (Kiangsi), a relation of the Ming Royal House, he retired to a monastery and may have pretended madness in order to survive the purges of the Manchu conquerors. The bravura and individualism of his ink paintings of flowers, birds, fish and landscapes appealed to the Japanese, and his style has become synonymous with Zen painting in Japan. Mocking every rule of classical tradition, his witty and expressive individualism has been influential up to the present day in both Japan and China.

Zhu De (Chu Te or Teh) 1886–1976
Chinese soldier and politician

The son of a wealthy Sichuan (Szechwan) province landlord, he joined the Sun Yat-sen Revolution (1911) and was a brigadier-general in 1916, but became addicted to opium. Cured in 1922, he took part in the Nanchang

Army Revolt (1927), from which he formed the Chinese Red Army. He was elected Commander-in-Chief of the Fourth Army and led it in the famous Long March (1934–36). Working closely with **Mao Zedong**, Zhu devised the successful tactic of mobile guerrilla warfare, leading the Communist military forces during the Second Sino-Japanese War (1937–45). He became Supreme Commander of the renamed People's Liberation Army, which expelled the Nationalists from mainland China during the civil war of 1946–49. He was made a marshal in 1955 and served as head of state and chairman of the Standing Committee of the National People's Congress (1975–76).

Zhukov, Georgi Konstantinovich 1896–1974
Soviet general

He was born of peasant parents in Strelkovka, Kaluga region. In 1918 he joined the Red Army. An expert in armoured warfare, he commanded the Soviet tanks in Outer Mongolia in 1939, and in 1941, as general, became Army Chief of Staff. In December 1941 he raised the Siege of Moscow, and in February 1943 his counter-offensive was successful at Stalingrad (Volgograd). In command of the First Byelo-Russian Army in 1944–45, he captured Warsaw and conquered Berlin. On 8 May 1945, on behalf of the Soviet high command, he accepted the German surrender. After the war he became Commander-in-Chief of the Russian zone of Germany, in 1955 became Minister of Defence, and in 1957 supported **Nikita Khrushchev** against the **Malenkov**–**Molotov** faction. He was dismissed by Khrushchev in 1957, and in 1958 was attacked for his 'revisionist' policy and for his alleged 'political mistakes' in the administration of the forces. 📖 Otto Chaney, *Zhukov* (1971)

Zia, (Begum) Khaleda 1945–
Bangladeshi politician

She was educated at Surendranath College, Dinajpur, and married General **Ziaur Rahman** in 1960. After his assassination in 1981, she became leader of the Bangladesh Nationalist Party (BNP) in 1982. In 1990, when President **Hossain Mohammad Ershad** was forced to resign, elections were called. The BNP's main contestant was the Awami League led by Sheikh Hasina Wajed, but the League only gained 30 per cent of the seats and from 1991 to 1996 Khaleda Zia served as the first woman Prime Minister of Bangladesh. In 1996 she relinquished power to a caretaker government and was defeated by Sheikh Hasina in the general election.

Zia ul-Haq, Mohammed 1924–88
Pakistani soldier and politician

He was born in Jalandhar, into a strict, middle-class Punjabi-Muslim family. He fought in Burma, Malaya and Indonesia during World War II, before becoming an officer in the Pakistan army in 1947. He became army chief of staff in 1976, and led the military coup against **Zulfikar Ali Bhutto** in July 1977, becoming the chief martial law administrator and, in September 1978, President. He proceeded to introduce a new policy of Islamization and a freer-market economic programme. Zia's opposition to the Soviet invasion of Afghanistan in December 1979 drew support from the USA, and from 1981, he began to engineer a gradual return to civilian government. He lifted martial law in December 1985, but was killed in a dubious accident three years later. 📖 Sahid Javed Burki, *Pakistan Under the Military: Eleven Years of Zia Ul-Haq* (1991)

Ziaur Rahman 1935–81
Bangladeshi soldier and politician

He played an important part in the civil war and the eventual emergence of the state of Bangladesh. He was appointed Chief of the Army Staff after the assassination of the ruling Sheikh **Mujibur Rahman** in 1975 and became

the dominant figure within the military. President of Bangladesh from 1977 until his death, he led a government which was military in character, even after the election of 1978 confirmed his popularity, and he survived several attempted coups. He was eventually assassinated in Dhaka.

Ziegfeld, Florenz 1869–1932
US theatre manager

Born in Chicago, the son of the president of Chicago Musical College, he devised and perfected the US revue spectacle, based on the *Folies Bergères*. His *Follies of 1907* was the first of an annual series that continued until 1931 and made his name synonymous with extravagant theatrical production. The *Follies* featured a chorus line of some of the most beautiful women in the USA, all personally chosen by Ziegfeld, whose aim was to 'glorify the American girl'. He also supervised the choice of music (frequently by eminent composers such as **Irving Berlin** and **Jerome Kern**), costumes and stage effects, and directed the production of each number. The result was a popularization of revue, and new standards of artistry and production. The *Follies* also helped the careers of such stars as Eddie Cantor, **Fanny Brice** and **W C Fields**. His wide range of other musical productions included *The Red Feather*, *Kid Boots*, *Sally* (1920), *Show Boat* (1927) and the US production of *Bitter Sweet*. 📖 Charles Higham, *Ziegfeld* (1972)

Ziegler, Karl 1898–1973
German chemist and Nobel Prize winner

Born in Helsa (Oberhessen), he taught at Marburg from 1920, at Heidelberg from 1936, and in 1943 was appointed director of the **Max Planck** Carbon Research Institute at Mulheim. With **Giulio Natta** he was awarded the Nobel Prize for chemistry in 1963 for research on long-chain polymers leading to new developments in industrial materials.

Zimbalist, Efrem 1889–1985
US violinist and composer

Born in Rostov, Russia, he settled in the USA in 1914 and became a US citizen. He became director of the Curtis Institute of Music in Philadelphia (1941–68), and composed for both violin and orchestra.

Zimisces, John c.924–976
Byzantine emperor

He was a successful general who intrigued the Empress Theodora to murder her husband Nicephorus II Phocas (969), but after seizing the throne in the same year he was forced by the Church to repudiate her. He won a major victory over the Bulgars (971) and went on to reconquer much of Syria and Palestine from the Muslims.

Zimmermann, Arthur 1864–1940
German politician

Born in East Prussia, after diplomatic service in China he directed from 1904 the eastern division of the German foreign office and was Foreign Secretary (1916–17). In January 1917 he sent the famous 'Zimmermann telegram' to the German minister in Mexico with the terms of an alliance between Mexico and Germany, by which Mexico was to attack the United States with German and Japanese assistance in return for the US states of New Mexico, Texas and Arizona. This telegram finally brought the hesitant US government into the war against Germany.

Zinder, Norton David 1928–
US geneticist

Born in New York City, he studied at Columbia University, with **Joshua Lederberg** at Wisconsin University, and became Professor of Genetics at Rockefeller University in 1964. In 1951, studies using mutants of the bacterium *Salmonella* led him to describe the process of bacterial transduction, which occurs when a bacterial gene is transmitted from one bacterium to another by means of a viral phage particle. It led to an explanation for the spread of drug resistance in bacteria, and offered a mechanism of inserting specific genes into a host cell bacterium. Recently, Zinder has been chairman of the Program Advisory Committee for the Human Genome Project in the USA.

Zinkernagel, Rolf 1944–
Swiss immunologist and Nobel Prize winner

He was born in Basle and after graduating from the university there he went as a visiting Fellow to the John Curtin School of Medical Research, Australian National University, Canberra. There in 1973 he collaborated with Peter Doherty on research into the human immune system that led to their jointly being awarded the 1996 Nobel Prize for Physiology or Medicine. From 1979 he was with the department of pathology at the University of Zurich, and since 1992 he has been head of the Institute of Experimental Immunology there. His many awards include the 1983 Paul Ehrlich prize.

Zinnemann, Fred 1907–97
Austrian film director

Born in Vienna, he studied law before enrolling at the École Technique De Photographie Et Cinématographie in Paris. An assistant cameraman on films such as *La Marche Des Machines* (1927) and *Menschen am Sonntag* (1929, *People on Sunday*), he moved to Hollywood in 1929. Working at MGM's short film department, he graduated to directing features. Often concerned with conflicts of conscience and the moral dilemmas of reluctant heroes, his films include *The Search* (1948), *High Noon* (1952), *The Nun's Story* (1959) and *Julia* (1977). He received Best Director Academy Awards for *From Here To Eternity* (1953) and *A Man For All Seasons* (1966). He received further Academy Awards for the short film *That Mothers Might Live* (1938) and the documentary *Benjy* (1951). His last film was *Five Days One Summer* (1982). 📖 *An Autobiography* (1992)

Zinoviev, Grigori Yvseyevich 1883–1936
Russian politician

Born in Yelisavetgrad, Ukraine, he was from 1917 to 1926 a leading member of the Soviet government. A letter allegedly written by him to the British Communist Party in 1924 was used in the election campaign to defeat Ramsay MacDonald's first Labour government. In 1927 Zinoviev suffered expulsion, and in 1936 death, having been charged with conspiring with Trotsky and Lev Kamenev to murder Sergei Kirov and Stalin. In 1988 he was posthumously rehabilitated, his 1936 'show trial' sentence having been annulled by the Soviet Supreme Court.

Zinsser, Hans 1878–1940
US bacteriologist and immunologist

Born in New York City, of German extraction, he was educated at Columbia University and its College of Physicians and Surgeons. His interest in science led him into bacteriology and immunology, which he taught at Columbia and Stanford universities, before going to Harvard in 1923. He worked on many scientific problems, including allergy, the measurement of virus size and the cause of rheumatic fever, but is principally remembered for clarifying the rickettsial disease typhus, differentiating epidemic and endemic forms (the endemic form is still known as Brill–Zinsser's disease). He brilliantly described these researches in his popular book *Rats, Lice and History* (1935), and his *Textbook of Bacteriology* (1910) and *Infection and Resistance* (1914) became classics. A highly cultured man, he wrote poetry and essays, and left an evocative autobiography, *As I Remember Him* (1940).

Zinzendorf, Nicolaus Ludwig, Graf von 1700–60
German religious leader

Born in Dresden, he studied at Wittenburg, and held a government post at Dresden. He invited the persecuted Hussite refugees from Moravia to his Lusatin estates in Saxony, where he founded for them the colony of Herrnhut ('the Lord's keeping'). His zeal led to troubles with the government, and from 1736 to 1748 he was exiled. He visited England, and in 1741 went to America. During his exile from Saxony he was ordained at Tübingen, and became Bishop of the Moravian Brethren. He died at Herrnhut, having written over 100 books. His emphasis on feeling in religion influenced German theology. 📖 John R Weinlick, *Count Zinzendorf* (1956)

Zittel, Karl Alfred von 1839–1904
German palaeontologist

He was born in Bahlingen, Baden, and educated at Heidelberg and Paris. He commenced his geological research in Dalmatia during a spell as a voluntary assistant with the Geological Survey of Austria. In 1862 he became an assistant at the Mineralogical Museum in Vienna where he undertook some teaching. The following year he was appointed professor at Kahlsrune. From 1880 he held professorships at Munich, and in 1890 he became keeper of the State Geological Collections. During his career he also served as president of the Bavarian Academy. A distinguished authority on his subjects and their history, he was a pioneer of evolutionary palaeontology and was widely recognized as the leading teacher of palaeontology in the 19th century. His five-volume *Handbuch der Paläontologie* (1876–93, 'Handbook of Paleontology') was arguably his greatest service to science, and it remains one of the most comprehensive and trustworthy of palaeontological reference works. His important textbook *Grundzüge der Paläontologie* first appeared in 1895, with an English translation *Textbook of Palaeontology* produced in 1900. It was later revised by Arthur Smith Woodward (1925).

Zoë 980–1050
Empress of the Eastern Roman Empire

She was the daughter of the Byzantine Emperor Constantine VIII. In 1028 she married Romanus III, but had him murdered in 1034 and made her paramour emperor as Michael IV. When his successor Michael V was deposed (1042) she became joint empress with her sister Theodora, and married her third husband, Constantine IX.

Zoffany, John 1733–1810
British portrait painter

Born in Frankfurt am Main, Germany, he settled in London in 1758 after studying art in Rome. Securing royal patronage, he painted many portraits and conversation pieces. He was a founder member of the Royal Academy in 1768. He travelled to Italy (1772–79), and later was a portraitist in India (1783–90).

Zog I, *originally* Ahmed Bey Zogu 1895–1961
King of the Albanians

Born in central Albania, the son of a highland tribal chieftain, he was educated in Constantinople (Istanbul). He became head of the clan at the age of 12, growing up in an atmosphere of tribal feuds, and in 1912, when Albania declared her independence, Zog took a blood oath to defend it. As the outstanding nationalist leader, he formed a republican government (1922) and was its premier, President and Commander-in-Chief, proclaiming himself king in 1928. When Albania was annexed by the Italians (1939), he went to Great Britain, and in 1946 took up residence in Egypt, moving to France in 1955. In 1938 he married Geraldine Apponyi (1915–), and their

Zola, Émile 1840–1902
French novelist

Zola was born in Paris, the son of an Italian engineer. He entered the publishing house of Hachette as a clerk, and soon became an active journalist. His first short stories were published as *Contes à Ninon* (1864, 'Stories for Ninon'), and other collections followed. In the later years of the Empire he formed a sort of informal society along with **Gustave Flaubert, Alphonse Daudet, Edmond** and **Jules de Goncourt**, and **Ivan Turgenev**, out of which grew the Naturalist school of novel. His first major novel, *Thérèse Raquin* (1867), a powerful picture of remorse, belongs to this school. Later he began the series of novels called *Les Rougon-Macquart*, a collection of some 20 volumes, all connected by the appearance of the same or different members of the family. These include *Nana* (188), *Germinal* (1885), *La Terre* (1887, 'Earth') and *La Bête humaine* (1890, 'The Beast in Man').

In order to describe the human condition effectively, Zola mastered the technical details of most professions, occupations and crafts, as well as the history of recent events in France: this is seen for example in *L'Œuvre* (art and literature), *La Terre* (the peasantry), *Germinal* (mining), *La Bête humaine* (railways), *Le Rêve* (church ritual), and other works listed below.

In 1898 Zola espoused the cause of **Alfred Dreyfus**, indicting the military authorities in his pamphlet *J'accuse* ('I accuse'). He was sentenced to prison, but escaped for a year to England and was welcomed back a hero. He died in Paris, accidentally suffocated by charcoal fumes.

📖 **Principal Works**
Short stories: *Contes à Ninon* (1964, 'Stories for Ninon'), *Nouveaux Contes à Ninon* (1874, 'New Stories for Ninon'), *Le Capitaine Burle, Naïs Micoulin, Attaque de Moulin* (1880, 'Attack on the Mill').

Novels: *Thérèse Raquin* (1867); *La Fortune des Rougon* (1871, 'The Fortunes of the Rougons'); *La Curée* (1872, 'The Rush for the Spoils') and *Son Excellence Eugène Rougon* (1876, 'His Excellency Eugene Rougon'), deal with the society of the later days of the Second Empire; *Le Ventre de Paris* (1873, 'The Underbelly of Paris') deals with the lowest strata of the Parisian population; *Nana* (1880) is devoted to the cult of lewdness. *L'Œuvre* (1886, 'The Masterpiece') deals with art and literature; *La Terre* (1887, 'Earth') is a repulsive study of the French peasant, and *Germinal* (1885) of the miner; *La Bête Humaine* (1890, 'The Beast in Man') contains minute information on the working of railways; *Le Rêve* (1888, 'The Dream') displays a remarkable acquaintance with the details of church ritual; *L'Argent* (1891, 'Money') exploits financial crashes; and *La Débâcle* (1892, 'The Downfall') recounts the great disaster of 1870. *Le Docteur Pascal* (1893, 'Doctor Pascal') is a sort of summing-up. *Fécondité* (1899, 'Fruitfulness'), *Travail* (1901, 'Work') and *Vérité* (1903, 'Truth') form part of 'Les Quatre Évangiles' ('The Four Gospels').

📖 P Walker, *Zola* (1985); F W J Hemmings, *The Life and Times of Zola* (1977); A Wilson, *Émile Zola: An Introductory Study of His Novels* (1952).

'A dead reign… a strange epoch of folly and shame.' Comment on the France of the Second Empire. Quoted in Joanna Richardson, *La Vie Parisienne* (1971).

---

son, Leka (1939–), was proclaimed king in exile on his father's death. 📖 Bernd Jurgen Fischer, *King Zog and the Struggle for Stability in Albania* (1984)

Zohr, Ibn See **Avenzoar**

Zola, Émile See panel above

Zondek, Bernhard 1891–1967
Israeli gynaecologist and endocrinologist

Born in Wronke, Germany, he trained in medicine at the University of Berlin, where he later worked in the Department of Obstetrics and Gynaecology (director, 1929–33). He left Nazi Germany in 1933 to become Professor of Obstetrics and Gynaecology at the Hebrew University, Jerusalem (1934–61). His research interests were predominantly in reproductive endocrinology. In collaboration with Selmar Aschheim he developed the first reliable pregnancy test in 1928, and they later discovered that the production of hormones from the anterior pituitary gland stimulated other endocrine glands, such as the ovary, to release their hormones. This work provided important evidence of control mechanisms in reproduction, and has had widespread significance in attitudes to fertility, infertility, contraception and abortion.

Zorach, William 1887–1966
US sculptor

Born in Eurburg, Lithuania, he emigrated to the USA with his parents and studied at the Cleveland School of Art and the National Academy of Design. He began his career as a painter influenced by the Cubists and Fauvists, whose work he saw during a year in Paris (1910–11). Returning to the USA in 1912 and settling in New York City, he exhibited paintings in the Armory Show. By the 1920s his work had become more conservative, and he turned to sculpting traditional forms in wood and stone.

His simple, monumental sculptures include *Spirit of Dance* (1932, Radio City Music Hall, New York) and *Benjamin Franklin* (1937, Post Office Building, Washington, DC).

Zorn, Anders Leonhard 1860–1920
Swedish etcher, sculptor and painter

He was born in Utmeland, near Mora, and his bronze statue of **Gustav I Vasa** is in Mora. His paintings deal mainly with Swedish peasant life. He achieved European fame as an etcher, with studies of **Paul Verlaine, Marcel Proust, Auguste Rodin** and others, and a series of nudes.

Zoroaster, *Greek form of* Zarathustra, *modern form* Zaradusht, *originally* Spitama c.630–c.553BC
Persian religious leader and prophet, the founder or reformer of Zoroastrianism

Born probably in Rhages, Persia (Iran), he appears as a historical person only in the earliest portion of the *Avesta*, the sacred book of Zoroastrianism. As the centre of a group of chieftains, one of whom was King Vshtâspa, he carried on a political, military, and theological struggle for the defence or wider establishment of a holy agricultural state against Turanian and Vedic aggressors. He apparently had visions of Ahura Mazda, which led him to preach against polytheism. The keynote of his system is that the world and history demonstrate the struggle between Ormuzd and Ahriman (the creator or good spirit, and the evil principle, the devil), in which at the end good will triumph. 📖 E Herzfeld, *Zoroaster and His World* (1947)

Zorrilla y Moral, José 1817–93
Spanish poet and dramatist

Born in Valladolid, he studied law there and at Toledo, and became a prolific poet. In 1889 he was chosen as the national poet and received a state pension. He wrote many poems and plays based on national legends and history, such as *Cantos del trovador* (1841), his first collection of poems. The play *Don Juan Tenorio* (1844), in which Don

Juan is presented as a popular hero saved from hell by the pure love of a woman, is performed annually on All Saints' Day in Spanish-speaking countries. ⌑ A Cortes, *José Zorrilla y Moral, su vita y sus obras* (1947)

Zschokke, Johann Heinrich Daniel 1771–1848
Swiss writer

Born in Magdeburg, Germany, he became a strolling playwright, then a student at Frankfurt, where he also lectured and adapted plays, and finally opened a boarding-school at Reichenau in the Grisons. In 1799 he settled in Aarau, where he became a member of the Great Council. His books include histories of Bavaria and Switzerland, and a long series of tales, including *Der Creole* (1830, Eng trans *The Creole*, 1846), *Jonathan Frock* (1840, Eng trans 1844) and *Meister Jordan* (1845, Eng trans *Labour Stands on Golden Feet*, 1852). The most popular of his works was the *Stunden der Andacht* (1809–16, Eng trans *Hours of Meditation*, 1843), a Sunday periodical, expounding rationalism with eloquence and zeal. His collected writings fill 35 volumes (1851–54). ⌑ P Scheffel, *Heinrich Zschokke* (1949)

Zsigmondy, Richard Adolf 1865–1929
Austrian chemist and Nobel Prize winner

He was born in Vienna and attended the university there, moving to Munich to take his doctorate. He worked briefly in Berlin on the chemistry of glass, studying the colloidal inclusions which give glass its colour and opacity. After teaching in Graz for five years he was employed by the Schott Glass Manufacturing Company in Jena (1897–1900), where he invented Jena milk glass. From 1900 to 1907 he worked independently in his own laboratory and as a result of his discoveries was appointed Professor of Inorganic Chemistry at Göttingen (1900–29). He made colloidal solutions, particularly gold sols, his life's study, and invented the ultramicroscope. This microscope, developed in conjunction with the Zeiss Company of Jena, led to great advances in colloidal chemistry, although it has now been replaced by the electron microscope and ultracentrifuge. Zsigmondy's later work was on silica and soap gels which he investigated by another new technique, ultrafiltration, in which the substances to be separated are drawn through a membrane by a decrease in pressure. In 1925 he became the first person to be awarded a Nobel Prize for colloidal chemistry.

Zuccaro, Taddeo 1529–66 and Federigo 1543–1609
Italian painters

Taddeo was born in S Angelo in Vado, near Urbino. He did much work for the Farnese family, examples of which may be seen in the Farnese residences at Rome and Caparrola. His younger brother Federigo travelled widely, painting portraits of Elizabeth I, Mary, Queen of Scots and others, but devoted most of his time to decorating frescoes in Florence, Venice, the Escorial and elsewhere. Federigo founded the Academy of St Luke in Rome (1595).

Zucchi, Antonio Pietro 1726–95
Italian painter

He was taken to England around 1766 by the Adam brothers, for whom he executed decorative work at Kenwood, Harewood House, Osterley Park and elsewhere. Also working for the brothers was Angelica Kauffmann, whom he married in 1781.

Zuckerman (of Burnham Thorpe), Solly Zuckerman, Baron 1904–93
British zoologist

Born in Cape Town, South Africa, he taught at Oxford from 1932, and during World War II investigated the biological effects of bomb blasts. He became Professor of Anatomy at Birmingham (1946–68) and secretary of the Zoological Society of London in 1955. He was chief scientific adviser to the British government from 1964 to 1971, and wrote official reports on aspects of farming, natural resources, medicine and nuclear policy. The results of his research on baboons at London Zoo were published in two influential books, *The Social Life of Monkeys and Apes* (1932) and *Functional Affinities of Man, Monkeys and Apes* (1933). The first primatologist to consider that such studies could provide insights into the origins and behaviour of humans, he proposed that sex was the original social bond. Knighted in 1956, he was awarded a life peerage in 1971, and published his autobiography, *From Apes to Warlords*, in 1978.

Zuckmayer, Carl 1896–1977
German dramatist

Born in Nackenheim, Rhineland, he lived in Austria, but after its annexation in 1939 went to the USA. He lived in Switzerland from 1946. His best-known plays are *Der Hauptmann von Köpenick* (1931, 'The Captain of Köpenick') and *Des Teufels General* (1942–45, 'The Devil's General'), both filmed. His work also includes the plays *Das kalte Licht* (1955, 'The Cold Light') and *Die Uhr schlägt eins* (1961, 'The Clock Strikes One'), a novel and some poetry. He published an autobiography *Als wärs ein Stück von mir* ('As If It Was a Part of Me') in 1966. ⌑ P Meinherz, *Carl Zuckmayer* (1960)

Zukerman, Pinchas 1948–
Israeli violinist, violist, and conductor

Born in Tel Aviv, Israel, he was a child prodigy, studying first in his native city and then in New York City, where he became the protégé of Isaac Stern. He made his debut with the New York Philharmonic in 1969 and is noted as an interpreter of chamber music for violin and viola. He has served as director of the St Paul Chamber Orchestra (1980–87) and principal guest conductor of the Dallas Symphony Orchestra (1993–).

Zukofsky, Louis 1904–78
US poet

Born in New York City, he was associated with the Objectivist school, and his poetry was first published in *An Objectivists Anthology* (1932), edited by himself. *First Half of 'A'* appeared in 1940 and for the next 38 years he worked on it, completing it in the year of his death. Its main themes are the inter-relationship of literature and music, aesthetics, history and philosophy. ⌑ B Ahearn, *Louis Zukofsky's 'A': an introduction* (1980)

Zukor, Adolph 1873–1976
US film executive

Born in Hungary, he emigrated to America in 1889. His success as a fur trader enabled him to invest in nickelodeons and build a small distribution network. Recognizing the potential of celebrity in attracting audiences to the cinema, he founded the Famous Players Company and was instrumental in establishing the star system. Among those he helped promote were Mary Pickford, Rudolph Valentino and Gloria Swanson. In 1916 he became president of the Famous Players-Lasky Corporation which became Paramount Pictures in 1927. A canny businessman, he helped expand the company's cinema ownership and develop their overseas business interests. Chairman of the board from 1935, he was still chairman emeritus at the time of his death. He received a special Academy Award in March 1949 as 'the man who has been called the father of the feature film in America'. ⌑ *The Public Is Never Wrong* (1945)

Zuloaga, Ignacio 1870–1945
Spanish painter

Born in Eibar, he studied in Rome and Paris and won recognition abroad and at home as a reviver of the national tradition in Spanish painting. He painted bullfighters, gypsies, beggars and other Spanish subjects.

Zúñiga, Alonso de Ercilla y See Zúñiga, Alonso de

Zuo Qiu Ming (Tso Ch'iu Ming) c.6th century BC
Chinese writer

He is mentioned by **Confucius** in his *Analects*, and wrote the *Zuo Zhuan*, a commentary on the *Chun Qiu*, one of the five classics. Scholars also ascribe to him the *Guo Yu*, and these two works comprise the most important historical sources of the period. The simplicity of his style served as a model to later writers.

Zurbarán, Francisco 1598–1662
Spanish religious painter

Born in Fuente de Cantos in Andalusia, he spent most of his life in Seville, where he was appointed city painter, and court painter to **Philip IV** in 1638. He also specialized in religious themes, particularly saints' lives. In Madrid he painted mythological and historical subjects. He came to be called 'the Spanish **Caravaggio**'.

Zurbriggen, Pirmin 1963–
Swiss skier

Born in Saas Almagell, he dominated the slopes in all disciplines in the 1980s, winning a record number of victories in the downhill. He won 39 World Cup victories and only **Marc Girardelli** has beaten his four overall world champion titles. In the 1988 Calgary Winter Olympic Games he won a gold in the downhill and a bronze in the giant slalom, but it was in the World Cup of 1987 that he had his finest hour: he won two gold medals (giant slalom and super G) and two silver medals (downhill and combined) within five days at Crans-Montana.

Zuse, Konrad 1910–95
German computer pioneer

Born in Berlin, he was educated at the Berlin Institute of Technology before joining the Henschel Aircraft Company in 1935. In the following year, he began building a calculating machine in his spare time, a task which occupied him until 1945. He built a number of prototypes, the most historic machine being the Z3, which had a small memory (capable of storing only 64 22-bit numbers), but was fast enough to multiply two rows of digits in only three to five seconds. It was the first operational general-purpose program-controlled calculator. Zuse built up his own firm, Zuse KG, until it was bought out by another firm in the 1960s, and he became honorary professor at Göttingen University in 1966.

Zvereva, Natasha 1971–
Belarus tennis player

Born in Minsk, she holds one of the greatest doubles records of modern times. From the French Open in 1992 to the Championships at Wimbledon in 1993, she and her partner Gigi Fernandez were undefeated in doubles matches at any Grand Slam tournament. The run included a bronze medal at the 1992 Olympics with her team-mate from the Commonwealth of Independent States, Leila Meskhi. Zvereva was also one of four players who appeared before the largest audience that attended a ladies' tennis match: on 21 November 1992, 18,257 spectators went to Madison Square Gardens, New York City, for the Virginia Slims Championships singles semifinals and doubles final session.

Zweig, Arnold 1887–1968
German novelist and critic

He was born in Gross-Glogau, Silesia, into a Jewish family, and began as a fine ironist, impressing with the stories in *Novellen um Claudia* (1917, Eng trans *Claudia*, 1930). During the years of the Third Reich he was forced to live in Palestine, but he returned to East Germany, where he was honoured. His later works are capable, but generally cruder, dedicated to communism and Zionism. However, *Das Beil von Wandsbeck* (1947, Eng trans before German publication as *The Axe of Wandsbeck*, 1946) is an outstanding novel of the Third Reich, and *Der Streit um den Sergeanten Grischa* (1927, Eng trans *The Case of Sergeant Grischa*, 1927), the unforgettable story of a Russian sergeant who falls victim to the bureaucracy of the Prussian war machine, is among the best realist novels of the century. 📖 G Salamon, *Arnold Zweig* (1975)

Zweig, George 1937–
US physicist

Born in Moscow, he was educated at the University of Michigan and the California Institute of Technology (Caltech), and then worked at the CERN (Conseil Européen pour la Recherche Nucléaire) in Geneva (1963–64), before returning to Caltech, where he became professor in 1967. Independently of **Murray Gell-Mann** he developed the theory of quarks as the fundamental physical building blocks. They suggested that three types exist, although there are now believed to be six types of quark.

Zweig, Stefan 1881–1942
British writer

Born in Vienna, of Jewish parentage, he studied in Austria, France and Germany, and settled in Salzburg in 1913. He was first known as poet and translator of **Ben Jonson**, then as biographer of **Honoré de Balzac**, **Dickens**, and **Marie Antoinette**. He also wrote short stories such as *Kaleidoskop* (1934, Eng trans *Kaleidoscope*, 1934) and novels, including *Der Zwang* (1927, Eng trans *Passion and Pain*, 1924) and *Ungeduld des Herzens* (1939, Eng trans *Beware of Pity*, 1939), all notable for their deep psychological insights. From 1934 to 1940 he lived in London, and he took British nationality. He later went to the USA and Brazil, where he committed suicide. His autobiographical *Die Welt von Gestern* (Eng trans *The World of Yesterday*, 1943) was published posthumously in 1943. 📖 A Barrie, *Stefan Zweig* (1969); B Jarnés, *Stefan Zweig* (1942)

Zwemer, Samuel Marinus 1867–1952
US missionary to Islamic countries

He was born in Vriesland, Michigan, and from 1890 worked under the auspices of the independent Arabian Mission which he had founded with two colleagues. His work in Basrah, Bahrain and Muscat was adopted by the mission board of the (Dutch) Reformed Church in the USA in 1894. As a scholar, preacher and evangelist he worked to spread Christianity in Islamic countries and to arouse interest in missions in the USA and Europe, writing numerous popular books and founding (in 1911) and editing *The Moslem World*. He was Professor of Christian Missions at Princeton (1929–37). His early missionary career is recalled in *The Golden Milestone* (1938).

Zwicky, Fritz 1898–1974
US-Swiss astronomer and physicist

Born in Varna, Bulgaria, he was educated at the Federal Institute of Technology at Zurich, graduating with a PhD in physics in 1922. In 1925 he went on a fellowship to California Institute of Technology (Caltech), where he remained all his life, becoming successively Professor of Theoretical Physics (1927–42) and Professor of Astrophysics until his retirement in 1968. His fruitful and wide-ranging research included work on cosmic rays and rocket design as well as many branches of astronomy. He was one of the first to recognize the power of the recently invented Schmidt telescope as a means of exploring the universe on a large scale, and from 1936 onwards used the 18in (45.7cm) Schmidt telescope on Mount Palomar to produce his catalogue of clusters of galaxies. He was the author of an original book on that subject, *Morphological Cosmology* (1957) and the discoverer of compact galaxies (1963), objects of exceptionally high surface brightness which are hence intrinsically very luminous. He was awarded the gold medal of the Royal Astronomical Society for his cosmological research in 1973.

Zwilich, Ellen Taaffe, *née* Taaffe 1939–
US violinist, lecturer and composer

Born in Miami, Florida, she received her doctorate from the Juilliard School of Music in 1975, the first woman to do so. Since then she has gone from strength to strength, seeing many of her compositions performed internationally. She was the first woman to receive the Pulitzer Prize for music.

Zwingli, Huldreich or Ulrich, *Latin* Ulricus Zuinglius 1484–1531
Swiss reformer

Born in Wildhaus, St Gall, he studied at Bern, Vienna and Basle, and was ordained in 1506. He taught himself Greek, and twice went as field-chaplain with the Glarus mercenaries to war in Italy, and took part in the battles of Novara (1513) and Marignano (1515). Transferred in 1516 to Einsiedeln, whose Black Virgin was a great resort of pilgrims, he made no secret of his contempt for such superstition. He was elected preacher at the Grossmünster in Zurich (1518), and roused the council not to admit within the city gates Bernhardin Samson, a seller of indulgences. He preached the gospel boldly, and stopped Zurich joining (1521) the other cantons in their alliance with France. The Bishop of Constance sent his vicar-general (1523), but he could not stop the city adopting the Reformed doctrines as set forth in Zwingli's 67 theses. A second disputation followed (1523), with the result that images and the mass were swept away. On Easter Sunday 1525 he dispensed the sacrament in both kinds, and the Reformation spread widely over Switzerland. Zwingli first made public his views on the Lord's Supper in 1524. At Marburg in 1529 he conferred with other Protestant leaders, and there disagreed with **Martin Luther** over the Eucharist, a dispute which eventually split the Protestant Church. He rejected every form of local or corporeal presence, whether by transubstantiation or consubstantiation. The progress of the Reformation aroused bitter hatred in the Forest Cantons, five of them formed an alliance (1528), Zurich declared war (1529) on account of the burning alive of a Protestant pastor seized on neutral territory, and in October 1531, the Forest Cantons

made a sudden dash on Zurich with 8,000 men, to be met at Cappel by 2,000, including Zwingli. The men of Zurich were completely defeated, with Zwingli among the dead. Zwingli preached the Reformed doctrines as early as 1516, the year before the appearance of Luther's theses. He regarded original sin as a moral disease rather than as punishable sin or guilt. He maintained the salvation of unbaptized infants, and he believed in the salvation of such virtuous heathens as **Socrates, Plato** and **Pindar**. On predestination he was as Calvinistic as **John Calvin**. With less fire and power than Luther, he was the most open-minded and liberal of the Reformers. Zwingli's *Opera* fill four folios (1545). The chief is the *Commentarius de vera et falsa religione* (1525); the rest are mainly occupied with the exposition of scripture and controversies on the Eucharist, and other subjects. 📖 G R Potter, *Zwingli* (1976)

Zworykin, Vladimir Kosma 1889–1982
US physicist

Born in Mourom, Russia, he graduated in electrical engineering from Petrograd Institute of Technology (1912), and studied under **Paul Langevin** in Paris. He settled in the USA because of the Russian Revolution (1919), studied at the University of Pittsburgh, and from 1929 pursued a career with the Radio Corporation of America (RCA), rising to director of electronic research (1946) and vice-president and technical consultant. He is chiefly remembered for applying the cathode-ray tube to television, a development which he patented in 1928. Although electronic scanning based on **Ferdinand Braun**'s cathode-ray tube had already been proposed by others before Zworykin, the technology had not been available to make it a reality. By 1938 Zworykin had developed the first practical television camera, which he called the 'iconoscope'. He made other important contributions to electronic optics with his scientific team at RCA, including the electron microscope (1939) and multipliers in scintillation counters for measuring radioactivity.

Zyuganov, Gennady Adreyevich 1944–
Russian Communist politician

Born in Mymrino Village, Orel Region, he was educated at the Orel Pedagogical Institute and then worked as a teacher. In 1967 his interest in trade union legislation took him into politics, first as a local organizer for the Communist Party and in 1983 as head of propaganda in Moscow. In 1989 he joined the Politburo and became secretary of the Communist Party of the Russian Federation in 1992. Elected to the State Duma in 1993 he emerged as the main Communist leader in parliament. Although he lost to **Boris Yeltsin** in the 1996 presidential election he continued to attract large numbers of traditional voters who regretted the passing of Communism in Russia.